LAROUSSE

ENGLISH
DICTIONARY

ISBN 2-03-406009-1 (hardcover edition)
ISBN 2-03-406013-X (paperback edition)
Larousse, Paris

Distributeur exclusif au Canada : Les Éditions Françaises Inc., Boucherville, Québec

ISBN 2-03-420290-2
Diffusion/Sales : Larousse Kingfisher Chambers Inc., New York

Library of Congress Catalog Card Number
96-076674

LAROUSSE

ENGLISH DICTIONARY

LAROUSSE

Produced by
LAROUSSE

General Editor
FAYE CARNEY

Senior Editor
MICHAEL MAYOR

Editors

RUTH BLACKMORE   SHAY DOLAN   GAVIN WILLIAMS
                        KATHLEEN MICHAM

with

MARTYN BACK   SCOTT FORBES   CHRISTINE PARIS
STEPHANIE BILLECKE   MELBOURNE FRASER   ELAINE POLLARD
GEOFFREY BREMNER   DAVID HALLWORTH   CAMMY RICHELLI
CALLUM BRINES   RUTH HILLMORE   JANE ROGOYSKA
HELEN BRUCE   NICHOLAS JONES   MARTHA ROSS
MARGARET JULL COSTA   VICTORIA KELLER   ELIZABETH SALTER
HAZEL CURTIES   IRENE LAKHANI   ROBERT SHORE
STEVE CURTIS   COLIN·MCINTOSH   TAMSIN SIMMILL
PAUL DUFFY   SARA MONTGOMERY   SUSAN STEINBERG

Phonetics
DR FREDERIKA HOLMES
ANNE SMITH

Copy Preparation
MARIE-PIERRE DEGOULET

Publishing Administration
SOPHIE JAQUET

Data Management
GABINO ALONSO   MARION PEPIN
SOPHIE JAQUET
ROSE ROCIOLA

PREFACE

The LAROUSSE ENGLISH DICTIONARY is an entirely new reference work, written for people around the world who are not just learning English but using it in their everyday lives. For our users, English is a communication tool to be used during work or leisure – for studying, talking or writing to business contacts, reading newspaper articles or fiction, or attending conferences.

This is the first dictionary to recognize that non-native speakers who deal with English in their daily lives need access to a sophisticated range of practical and up-to-date vocabulary, including terms from business, politics, science and technology, literature, and journalism.

Recognizing the importance of understanding the culture of a country, the word list also includes a wide range of cultural terms and encyclopedic entries for people and places. Key cultural and historical information is presented in easy-to-read boxed notes.

A special feature of the dictionary are the sense markers, which have two uses: they guide the user quickly to a particular meaning, and they give a summary of the typical contexts a word or sense is used in.

An international team of editors in the USA, Britain, and Australia has worked on the dictionary to ensure authentic coverage of World English. Thousands of example sentences have been included, collected from international sources and carefully selected to reflect the practical and linguistic needs of the non-native speaker.

Together these features offer the user of the LAROUSSE ENGLISH DICTIONARY the best of both worlds: access to a wide range of vocabulary, combined with the user-friendly presentation of a learner's dictionary.

USING THIS DICTIONARY

encyclopedic information on places

Netherlands [ˈneðəʳləndz]: **the Netherlands** a country in western Europe, on the North Sea between Belgium and Germany. SIZE: 34,000 sq kms. POPULATION: 15,200,000 (*Dutch*). CAPITAL: Amsterdam. ADMINISTRATIVE CAPITAL. The Hague. LANGUAGE: Dutch. CURRENCY: guilder.

information on usage — NOTE: The name *the Netherlands* is used only in official contexts; otherwise the country is called *Holland*.

guide words show typical usage of word and help to identify meanings

neutral [ˈnjuːtrəl] ◊ *adj* -1. [country, person, position] that does not support any person, political cause, country etc in an argument or war □ *neutral territory/waters.* □ *Switzerland remained neutral throughout both World Wars.* -2. [expression, voice, word] that does not show what somebody is feeling. -3. [clothing, shade] pale gray or pale brown. -4. ELECTRICITY [wire] that has no electrical charge. ◊ *n* AUTO the position of the gears of a car in which no power can pass from the engine to the wheels □ *Leave the car in neutral.*

news [njuːz] *n* -1. information about recent events □ *a piece* OR *bit of news* □ *Have you heard the news about Mary?* □ *I have some good/bad news for you.* □ *News is coming in of riots in LA.* ■ **that's news to me** a phrase used to say one did not know something and is a little annoyed at not being told it sooner. ■ **to break the news to sb** to tell sb some bad news. -2. RADIO & TV **the news** a program on the radio or television that reports recent important events □ *I heard about the earthquake on the news.* □ *His arrest made the 6 o'clock news.* □ *a news broadcast/report* ■ **to be in the news** to be mentioned a lot in newspapers, on television etc.

example sentences illustrate frequent usages

set phrases identified by a special symbol

International Phonetic Alphabet (IPA)

Newton [ˈnjuːtn], **Sir Isaac** (1642–1727) a British scientist, astronomer, and mathematician who discovered the law of gravity.

encyclopedic information on people

🐚 NEW YEAR
In the USA, Australia, and Britain people have parties on New Year's Eve (December 31) to "see in" the New Year. When the clocks strike midnight, everyone wishes each other "Happy New Year" and hugs or kisses each other. A traditional song, *Auld Lang Syne*, is often sung. The next day, New Year's Day (January 1), is a public holiday in the USA, Australia, and Britain.

cultural information

NFL (*abbr of* **National Football League**) *n* the organization in charge of professional football in the USA.

NG *n abbr of* **National Guard**.

NGO (*abbr of* **non-governmental organization**) *n* an organization that is not financed by a government.

NH *abbr of* **New Hampshire**.

NHL (*abbr of* **National Hockey League**) *n* a league of US and Canadian professional hockey teams.

in-depth coverage of abbreviations

nibble ['nɪbl] ◊ *vt* to take small bites from <a piece of food> □ *She was nibbling an apple.* ◊ *vi* [animal, person]: *The squirrel was nibbling at* OR *on a nut.*
♦ **nibbles** *npl* small things to eat with one's fingers at a party, e.g. nuts or potato chips.

parts of speech identified by a special symbol

clear entry structure

Nielsen Ratings ['niːlsən-] *npl* **the Nielsen Ratings** in the USA, a set of statistics that show how many people watch the most popular television programs.

encyclopedic information

night depository [US -dɪ'pɒzətɔːɪɪ, GB -'pɒzɪtəɪ] *n* a hole in the outside wall of a bank where customers can leave money and checks after the bank is closed.

night safe *n* GB = **night depository**.

balanced coverage of American and British English

Nikkei ['nɪkeɪ] *n* **the Nikkei (index** OR **average)** the average of the current price of the shares of 225 Japanese companies sold on the Tokyo Stock Exchange.

coverage of business vocabulary

nip [nɪp] (*pt & pp* **nipped**, *cont* **nipping**) ◊ *n* **-1.** [by an animal] a small painful pinch or bite □ *The dog gave me a playful nip on the leg.* **-2.** [of liquid] a small amount of alcoholic drink □ *a nip of brandy*. **-3.** *phrase* **there's a nip in the air** it's slightly cold. ◊ *vt* **-1.** to catch <sthg> between two sharp points or edges □ *I nipped my finger in the door.* **-2.** to bite <sb/sthg> without much damage □ *The dog nipped me on the ankle.* ◊ *vi* GB to go somewhere quickly and for a short time (informal use) □ *I'm just nipping into town/out to the post office.*

different forms of headword shown

meanings clearly numbered

example sentences help to identify meanings

clear register labels (informal, slang, literary, disapproving etc)

nitty-gritty [,nɪtɪ'grɪtɪ] *n* **to get down to the nitty-gritty** to start talking or thinking about the most basic and important aspects of a problem.

word explained in its most frequent context

ABBREVIATIONS AND LABELS
USED IN THIS DICTIONARY

abbr	**abbreviation** □ She has an *MBA*. □ He works for *NATO*.
adj	**adjective** □ You're a *lucky* man. □ Don't be *afraid*.
adv	**adverb** □ He laughed *loudly*. □ It's *really* sad. □ *Frankly*, I hated it.
AUS	**Australian English**
aux vb	**auxiliary verb** □ He *didn't* come. □ *Do* you mind?
comp	**a noun used in front of another noun** □ He's a *football* coach. □ She wore a *cotton* dress.
compar	**irregular comparative form** □ It's *cozier* over here. □ Take this one, it's *better*.
conj	**conjunction** □ I'll call *when* I get there. □ I'd like coffee *and* cake.
cont	**continuous form of a verb** □ The sun is *setting*. □ I'm *getting* better.
det	**determiner** □ That's *my* desk. □ Try *this* size.
excl	**exclamation** □ *Ouch*, that hurt! □ *Goodness*, you've grown tall!
fus	see *vt fus* below
GB	**British English**
infin	**infinitive form of a verb** □ I want to *help*. □ It can *wait*.
modal vb	**modal verb** □ I *can't* believe it. □ *Must* we go?
n	**noun** □ There's something wrong with the *computer*.
npl	**noun that is always plural** □ Where are my *glasses*?
num	**number** □ It cost *eight* dollars. □ She's only *five*.
phrase	a set phrase that has its own meaning □ *There's a nip in the air.*
pl	**irregular plural form** □ They have three *children*.
pp	**irregular past participle of a verb** □ I haven't *spoken* to him.
predet	**predeterminer** □ *It costs half the price.*
prefix	**a word added to the beginning of a word** □ a *mid*-air collision.
prep	**preposition** □ Come *for* lunch. □ She's head *of* sales.
pron	**pronoun** □ *You* must meet *them*. □ *Those* are *mine*.
pt	**irregular past tense of a verb** □ I *spoke* to her recently.
sb	**somebody.** This abbreviation can be replaced by any human noun in a sentence: ***to give sb a ride*** → I gave *John* a ride home.
SCOT	**Scottish English**
sep	see *vt sep* below
sthg	**something.** This abbreviation can be replaced by any non-human noun in a sentence: ***to take part in sthg*** → Twenty runners took part in *the race*.

suffix	**a word added to the end of a word** □ sugar-*free* chewing gum.
superl	**irregular superlative form** □ That's the *funniest* thing I've heard!
US	**American English**
™	**trademark**. This symbol is shown at words considered to be trademarks. However if the symbol has been added or omitted in the dictionary, this should not be regarded as affecting the legal status of the trademark.
vb	**verb**. This abbreviation is used in pronunciations where the stress of a word changes according to its part of speech.
vi	**intransitive verb** □ She *paused* before answering. □ The plane *took off*.
v impers	**impersonal verb** □ *It's snowing.* □ *It appears* that I was wrong.
vt	**transitive verb** □ *Eat* your dinner. □ He *handed* me the note. □ The dog was *run over* by a truck.
vt fus	**a two- or three-part verb that is never split** □ Jane *took to* him at once. □ I don't know how you *put up with* it.
vt sep	**a two- or three-part verb that can be split by its object** □ Thanks for *helping* me out. □ He *let* me *in on* the secret.

SYMBOLS USED IN THIS DICTIONARY

◊ introduces a new part of speech in an entry, e.g. **share** ◊ *n* ... ◊ *vt* ...

◆ introduces a compound or plural form of the headword with its own meaning and part of speech, e.g. ◆ **premises** *npl*, ◆ **on account of** *prep*, ◆ **in short** *adv*, ◆ **take off** *vi*

□ introduces an illustrative example showing how the headword is used in a real context, e.g. **shot** *n* -1. ... □ *Several shots rang out.*

■ introduces a set phrase or idiom with its own meaning, e.g. **shape** *n* ... ■ **to lick or knock sb into shape**

ᵛ marks a word or meaning that belongs to very informal English

▼ marks a word or meaning that belongs to vulgar English or could give offense.

PHONETICS

Vowels

[ɪ] pit, big, rid
[e] pet, bend
[æ] pat, bag, mad
[ʌ] cut, rubber
[ɒ] coffee, log
[ʊ] put, full
[ə] suppose, the
[iː] bean, weed
[ɑː] father, calm
[ɔː] lawn, ball
[uː] loop, loose
[ɜː] furry

Diphthongs

[eɪ] bay, late, great
[aɪ] buy, light, aisle
[ɔɪ] boy , royal
[oʊ] no, road, blow
[aʊ] now, shout, town
[ɪə] hearing, serious
[eə] hairy, carer
[ʊə] tourist, purest, insurance

Semi-vowels

[j] you, spaniel
[ᴶ] new, figure
[w] wet, twin

Consonants

[p] pop, people
[b] bottle, bib
[t] train, tip
[d] dog, did
[k] come, kitchen
[g] rag, great
[tʃ] chain, wretched
[dʒ] jazz, bridge
[f] find, physical, rough
[v] vine, livid
[θ] think, fifth
[ð] this, with
[s] soon, peace
[z] zip, his, houses
[ʃ] sheep, machine
[ʒ] usual, measure
[h] how, perhaps
[m] metal, comb
[n] night, dinner
[ŋ] sung, parking
[l] little, help
[r] right, carry
[ʳ] card, fear
[x] loch, Bach

The system of phonetic transcription used in this dictionary emphasizes the features that American and British English have in common. Separate phonetics for British and American pronunciation are only given where the differences between the two systems are not systematic or predictable, and are important enough to cause possible confusion.

The symbol [^{r}] is used for the [r] sound after a vowel in words such as *car*, *tower*, and *purpose*. It is usually pronounced by Americans but not by Southern British speakers.

The symbol [^{j}] is used for the [j] sound in words such as *duke*, *new*, and *pursue*. It is pronounced by most British speakers but not by most Americans.

The symbol [ˈ] shows that the following syllable carries primary stress. The symbol [ˌ] shows that the syllable that follows carries secondary stress.

A phonetic transcription has been given, where appropriate, after every headword that is spelled as one word. For compound headwords that are spelled hyphenated or are made up of two or more separate words, phonetics are given for any element that does not appear elsewhere in the dictionary in its own right.

ENGLISH IRREGULAR VERBS

Infinitive	Past Tense	Past Participle
arise	arose	arisen
awake	awoke	awoken
be	was, were	been
bear	bore	borne
beat	beat	beaten
befall	befell	befallen
begin	began	begun
behold	beheld	beheld
bend	bent	bent
beseech	besought	besought
	/beseeched	/beseeched
beset	beset	beset
bet	bet	bet
	/betted	/betted
bid	bid	bid
	/bade	/bidden
bind	bound	bound
bite	bit	bitten
bleed	bled	bled
blow	blew	blown
break	broke	broken
breed	bred	bred
bring	brought	brought
build	built	built
burn	burned	burned
	/burnt	/burnt
burst	burst	burst
buy	bought	bought
can	could	–
cast	cast	cast
catch	caught	caught
choose	chose	chosen
cling	clung	clung
come	came	come
cost	cost	cost
creep	crept	crept
cut	cut	cut
deal	dealt	dealt
dig	dug	dug
dive	dived	dived
	/US *also* dove	
do	did	done
draw	drew	drawn
dream	dreamed	dreamed
	/dreamt	/dreamt
drink	drank	drunk
drive	drove	driven

XIII

Infinitive	Past Tense	Past Participle
dwell	dwelt /dwelled	dwelt /dwelled
eat	ate	eaten
fall	fell	fallen
feed	fed	fed
feel	felt	felt
fight	fought	fought
find	found	found
fit	fitted /US also fit	fit
flee	fled	fled
fling	flung	flung
fly	flew	flown
forget	forgot	forgotten
forsake	forsook	forsaken
freeze	froze	frozen
get	got	US gotten/GB got
give	gave	given
go	went	gone
grind	ground	ground
grow	grew	grown
hang	hung /hanged	hung /hanged
have	had	had
hear	heard	heard
hide	hid	hidden
hit	hit	hit
hold	held	held
hurt	hurt	hurt
keep	kept	kept
kneel	knelt /kneeled	knelt /kneeled
know	knew	known
lay	laid	laid
lead	led	led
lean	leaned /leant	leaned /leant
leap	leapt /leaped	leapt /leaped
learn	learned /learnt	learned /learnt
leave	left	left
lend	lent	lent
let	let	let
lie	lied /lay	lied /lain
light	lit /lighted	lit /lighted
lose	lost	lost
make	made	made

Infinitive	Past Tense	Past Participle
may	might	–
mean	meant	meant
meet	met	met
mow	mowed	mowed /mown
pay	paid	paid
put	put	put
quit	quit /GB *also* quitted	quit /GB *also* quitted
read	read	read
rend	rent	rent
rid	rid	rid
ride	rode	ridden
ring	rang	rung
rise	rose	risen
run	ran	run
saw	sawed	US sawed/GB sawn
say	said	said
see	saw	seen
seek	sought	sought
sell	sold	sold
send	sent	sent
set	set	set
shake	shook	shaken
shall	should	–
shear	sheared	sheared /shorn
shed	shed	shed
shine	shone	shone
shoot	shot	shot
show	showed	shown /showed
shrink	shrank	shrunk
shut	shut	shut
sing	sang	sung
sink	sank	sunk
sit	sat	sat
slay	slew	slain
sleep	slept	slept
slide	slid	slid
sling	slung	slung
slit	slit	slit
smell	smelled /GB *also* smelt	smelled /GB *also* smelt
sneek	sneaked /US *also* snuck	sneaked /US *also* snuck
sow	sowed	sown /sowed
speak	spoke	spoken
speed	sped /speeded	sped /speeded

Infinitive	Past Tense	Past Participle
spell	US spelled	US spelled
	/GB spelt	/GB spelt
spend	spent	spent
spill	spilled	spilled
	/GB *also* spilt	/GB *also* spilt
spin	span/spun	span
spit	US spit	US spit
	/GB spat	/GB spat
split	split	split
spoil	spoiled	spoiled
	/GB *also* spoilt	/GB *also* spoilt
spread	spread	spread
spring	sprang	sprung
stand	stood	stood
steal	stole	stolen
stick	stuck	stuck
sting	stung	stung
stink	stank	stunk
	/stunk	
stride	strode	stridden
strike	struck	struck
strive	strove	striven
swear	swore	sworn
sweep	swept	swept
swell	swelled	swollen
		/swelled
swim	swam	swum
swing	swung	swung
take	took	taken
teach	taught	taught
tear	tore	torn
tell	told	told
think	thought	thought
throw	threw	thrown
thrust	thrust	thrust
tread	trod	trodden
wake	woke	woken
	/waked	/waked
wear	wore	worn
weave	wove	woven
	/weaved	/weaved
wed	wedded	wedded
		/wed
weep	wept	wept
will	would	–
win	won	won
wind	wound	wound
wring	wrung	wrung
write	wrote	written

0... - 9...

000 [ˌtrɪplˈoʊ] the telephone number used to call the emergency services in Australia □ *a 000 call.*

0055 number [ˌdʌbloʊdʌblˈfaɪv-] *n* in Australia, a telephone number starting with the code 0055 that is used to call information and entertainment services.

0800 number [ˌoʊeɪtˈhʌndrəd-] *n* in Britain, a telephone number starting with the code 0800 that one can dial without paying. They are usually provided by businesses and government agencies to give information.

0898 number [ˌoʊeɪtˈnaɪneɪt-] *n* in Britain, a telephone number starting with the code 0898 that is used to call information and entertainment services.

1040 [ˌtenˈfɔːrti] *n* US the name of the tax return that most Americans fill out.

1066 [ˌtensɪkstɪˈsɪks] the year when Harold, King of England, was defeated by the Normans under William the Conqueror at the Battle of Hastings. It is a date that every English person is supposed to know.

12 [twelv] *n* in Britain, a classification that means that a movie or video can be seen only by children aged 12 or over.

15 [ˌfɪfˈtiːn] *n* in Britain, a classification that means that a movie or video can be seen only by people aged 15 or over.

1776 [ˌsevəntiːnsevəntɪˈsɪks] the year that the Declaration of Independence was signed in the USA. It is a date that every American is supposed to know.

1788 [ˌsevəntiːneɪtɪˈeɪt] the year that the first British convicts landed in Australia. It is a date that every Australian is supposed to know.

18 [ˌeɪˈtiːn] *n* in Britain, a classification that means that a movie or video can be seen only by people aged 18 or over.

18-wheeler [-ˈwiːlər] *n* US a very large truck with eighteen wheels.

1-800 number [ˌwʌneɪtˈhʌndrəd-] *n* in the USA and Australia, a telephone number starting with the code 1-800 that one can dial without paying. They are usually provided by businesses and government agencies to give information.

20/20 [ˌtwentɪˈtwentɪ] *adj* **20/20 vision** the ability to see perfectly without the aid of glasses or contact lenses.

2.1 [ˌtuːˈwʌn] *n* in Britain and Australia, the upper level of the second-highest class of university degree.

2.2 [ˌtuːˈtuː] *n* in Britain and Australia, the lower level of the second-highest class of university degree.

2×4 [ˌtuːbaɪˈfɔːr] *n* a piece of wood, two inches thick and four inches wide, that is the standard size used by builders and carpenters in the USA □ *Could you pass me that 2×4?* □ *a piece of 2×4.*

3.2 beer [ˌθriːtuː-] *n* beer that contains 3.2 percent alcohol. In the USA it used to be sold to people who were too young to buy other alcoholic drinks.

35mm [ˌθɜːrtɪfaɪvˈmɪləmiːtər] *n* the size of film most widely used in cameras, both for taking photographs and for making movies □ *35 mm film.*

3-D [ˌθriːˈdiː] ◇ *adj* [picture, movie] *see* **three-dimensional.** ◇ *n*: *If you put these glasses on you can see it in 3-D.*

4×2 [ˌfɔːrˈbaɪtuː] *n* a piece of wood, two inches thick and four inches wide, that is the standard size used by builders and carpenters in the UK □ *a piece of 4×2.*

4×4 [ˌfɔːrbaɪˈfɔːr] *n*: *see* **four-wheel drive.**

45 [ˌfɔːrtɪˈfaɪv] *n* a record that is played at 45 rpm and usually has only one song on each side.

.45 [ˌfɔːrtɪˈfaɪv] *n* a pistol that was widely used in the 19th century in the USA.

4-F [ˌfɔːrˈef] ◇ *n* a classification made by the US armed forces to show that a person is unfit for military service □ *I got a 4-F.* ◇ *adj*: *He was declared 4-F.*

4H [ˌfɔːrˈeɪtʃ] *n* a program set up by the US Department of Agriculture to teach young people in country areas useful skills in farming and running a home □ *a 4H club.*

4WD *see* **four-wheel drive.**

78 [ˌsevəntɪˈeɪt] *n* an old type of record that is played at 78 rpm.

800 number [eɪtˈhʌndrəd-] *n* US = **1-800 number.**

900 number [naɪnˈhʌndrəd-] *n* in the USA, a telephone number starting with the code 900 that is used to call entertainment services.

911 [ˌnaɪnwʌnˈwʌn] the telephone number used to call the emergency services in the USA □ *a 911 call.*

999 [ˌnaɪnnaɪnˈnaɪn] the telephone number used to call the emergency services in Britain □ *a 999 call.*

A - Z

a¹ [eɪ] (pl **a's**), **A** [eɪ] (pl **A's**) n the first letter of the English alphabet. ■ **from A to B** from one place to another □ *the fastest way from A to B.* ■ **from A to Z** including every part of something □ *He knows the job from A to Z.* ◆ **A** n **-1.** EDUCATION the highest grade for a piece of work □ *I got an A for my math.* **-2.** MUSIC one of the notes in Western music.

a² [*stressed* eɪ, *unstressed* ə] (before vowel or silent "h" **an**) det **-1.** used when one mentions something for the first time □ *My brother has started a new job.* **-2.** used when one does not want to describe a particular person or thing □ *An old man came up to me.* □ *I heard a noise.* **-3.** used when making general comments □ *A bicycle has two wheels.* **-4.** used for jobs or hobbies □ *He's a lawyer.* □ *She's a good tennis player.* **-5.** used instead of the number "one" □ *I saw them a month ago.* □ *A pint of milk, please.* **-6.** used in fractions □ *They got here (a) half an hour ago.* **-7.** used in words for large numbers □ *The firm made a million dollars last year.* **-8.** used after number words to show prices, proportions etc □ *50 miles an hour* □ *He charges $12 an hour.* □ *The meal cost $25 a person.* □ *We visit them twice a month.* **-9. a Mr Mudd phoned** somebody called Mr Mudd, who I do not know, phoned. **-10. a Van Gogh** a painting by Van Gogh. **-11. I'd like a coffee** I'd like a cup of coffee. ■ **an excellent wine** an excellent type of wine.

a. *abbr of* **acre.**

A-1 [ˌeɪˈwʌn] adj excellent (informal use).

A4 [ˌeɪˈfɔːʳ] n GB a standard paper size (210 x 297 mm) □ *A4 paper.*

AA n **-1.** (abbr of **Alcoholics Anonymous**) an organization for alcoholics who are trying to stop drinking. **-2.** (abbr of **Automobile Association**) **the AA** a British organization for car owners that helps its members when their cars break down. **-3.** (abbr of **Associate in** OR **of Arts**) a US college degree.

AAA [*sense 1* ˌtrɪplˈeɪ, *sense 2* ˌθriːˈeɪz] n **-1.** (abbr of **American Automobile Association**) a US organization for car owners that helps its members when their cars break down. **-2.** (abbr of **Amateur Athletics Association**) **the AAA** a British organization that organizes sports events for athletes.

a.a.e. abbr of **according to age and experience** □ *Salary £14K–£20K, a.a.e.*

AAUP (abbr of **American Association of University Professors**) n **the AAUP** a US labor union for university professors.

AB ◇ n US abbr of **Bachelor of Arts.** ◇ abbr of **Alberta.**

ABA (abbr of **Australian Broadcasting Authority**) n **the ABA** the organization that controls television companies in Australia.

aback [əˈbæk] adv **to be taken aback** to be surprised, especially by something unpleasant □ *He was a little taken aback when I told him I was leaving.*

abacus [ˈæbəkəs] (pl **abacuses** OR **abaci** [-saɪ]) n a frame with rows of sliding beads in it that are used for counting.

abandon [əˈbændən] ◇ vt **-1.** [building, car, child] to leave <a person, place, or thing> with no intention of returning □ *They abandoned the empty van at the side of the road.* □ *The dog had been abandoned by its owners.* **-2.** [project, search, attempt] to stop <an activity, event> etc before it is finished □ *The police abandoned their hunt for the murder weapon.* □ *The game had to be abandoned because of bad weather.* **-3.** [plan, idea] to stop believing that <sthg> is worth doing, likely to happen etc □ *They abandoned all hope of ever seeing him again.* ◇ n **with abandon** in an uncontrolled way □ *Sue danced around the room with wild abandon.*

abandoned [əˈbændənd] adj [building, vehicle] that is no longer used or wanted □ *They staged the performance in an old abandoned farmhouse.*

abashed [əˈbæʃt] adj **to be abashed** [person] to be embarrassed and ashamed □ *He looked genuinely abashed.*

abate [əˈbeɪt] vi [storm, noise, fear] to become less intense.

abattoir [ˈæbətwɑːʳ] n a building where animals are killed for food.

abbess [US ˈæbəs, GB -es] n the nun in charge of a convent.

abbey [ˈæbɪ] n a large church with buildings attached to it where monks or nuns live □ *Westminster Abbey.*

abbot [ˈæbət] n the monk in charge of an abbey.

abbreviate [əˈbriːvɪeɪt] vt to shorten <a word or phrase> □ *Information technology is often abbreviated to IT.*

abbreviation [əˌbriːvɪˈeɪʃn] n the shortened form of a word or phrase □ *IMF is the abbreviation of* OR *for the International Monetary Fund.*

ABC n **-1.** (abbr of **American Broadcasting Company**) one of the main TV companies in the USA. **-2.** (abbr of **Australian Broadcasting**

Company) the Australian state-owned radio and television company. -3. GB = **ABCs**.

ABCs [ˌeɪbiːˈsiːz] US *npl*, **ABC** GB *n* -1. the alphabet □ *The children are learning their ABCs.* -2. **the ABCs of sthg** the most basic information about sthg □ *the ABCs of banking.*

abdicate [ˈæbdɪkeɪt] ◇ *vi* to give up the position of king or queen. ◇ *vt* [responsibility, duty] to no longer accept <sthg>.

abdication [ˌæbdɪˈkeɪʃn] *n*: *see* **abdicate** □ *the abdication of Edward VIII* □ *That would be a complete abdication of our responsibilities.*

abdomen [ˈæbdəmən] *n* the part at the front of one's body between one's chest and hips.

abdominal [æbˈdɒmənl] *adj* [pain, muscles] *see* **abdomen** □ *pain in the abdominal region.*

abduct [əbˈdʌkt] *vt* to take <sb> away, using force or deceit □ *The child was abducted on his way to school.*

abduction [æbˈdʌkʃn] *n* [of a person] *see* **abduct**.

Abel [ˈeɪbl] → **Cain**.

aberration [ˌæbəˈreɪʃn] *n* a change from one's normal behavior or way of thinking □ *The defense insisted that his violent behavior was due to a mental aberration.*

abet [əˈbet] (*pt* & *pp* **abetted**, *cont* **abetting**) *vt* → **aid**.

abeyance [əˈbeɪəns] *n* **to be in abeyance** [law, regulation] not to be in use (formal use).

abhor [əbˈhɔːr] (*pt* & *pp* **abhorred**, *cont* **abhorring**) *vt* [cruelty, violence] to hate <sthg> very much (formal use).

abhorrent [əbˈhɒrənt] *adj* [behavior, attitude] that one finds very unpleasant and completely unacceptable (formal use) □ *Such opinions are utterly abhorrent to me.*

abide [əˈbaɪd] *vt* **I can't abide her/it etc** I dislike her/it etc very much.
♦ **abide by** *vt fus* **to abide by sthg** to accept and obey the law, a rule, decision etc whether one agrees with it or not □ *They agreed to abide by the terms of the treaty.*

abiding [əˈbaɪdɪŋ] *adj* [feeling, interest, memory] that lasts a long time and does not change □ *my abiding passion for Greece.*

ability [əˈbɪlətɪ] (*pl* **abilities**) *n* the power, knowledge, or skill that makes it possible for somebody to do something □ *He has great musical ability.* □ *There is no doubt about her abilities as a team leader.* ■ **to have the ability to do sthg** to be able to do sthg special or unusual □ *Harry has an amazing ability to interrupt just at the wrong moment!* ■ **to do sthg to the best of one's ability** to do sthg as well as one can □ *I'll do it to the best of my ability, but I can't guarantee the result.*

abject [ˈæbdʒekt] *adj* -1. **abject poverty/misery** very great poverty/misery □ *I felt an abject failure.* -2. [person, apology] without self-respect □ *She left him, abject and begging for forgiveness.*

ablaze [əˈbleɪz] *adj* -1. **to be ablaze** [building] to be burning strongly. -2. **to be ablaze with sthg** [building, sky] to be brightly lit by sthg □ *The palace windows were ablaze with light.*

able [ˈeɪbl] *adj* -1. **to be able to do sthg** to have the skill, power, time etc to do sthg □ *If I sit at the back I won't be able to hear the speaker.* □ *Will you be able to come to the meeting?* -2. [person] who is good at an activity, especially their job □ *He's a very able politician.*

able-bodied [-ˈbɒdɪd] *adj* [person] who is physically healthy □ *All able-bodied men were required to join the army.*

ablutions [əˈbluːʃnz] *npl* the act of washing oneself (formal or humorous use).

ably [ˈeɪblɪ] *adv* [assisted, supported] skillfully □ *Mr Jones was ably assisted by a team of local volunteers.*

ABM *n abbr of* **antiballistic missile**.

abnormal [æbˈnɔːrml] *adj* [person, behavior] that is different from what is normal, in a way that seems unpleasant, worrying, or strange □ *The patient's breathing was abnormal.* □ *He had an abnormal interest in death.*

abnormality [ˌæbnɔːrˈmælətɪ] (*pl* **abnormalities**) *n* something abnormal □ *The test will detect any abnormalities in the blood cells.*

abnormally [æbˈnɔːrməlɪ] *adv* **abnormally low/ high** low/high to a degree that seems abnormal □ *abnormally high levels of radiation.*

aboard [əˈbɔːrd] ◇ *adv* onto a ship, plane, bus etc □ *The last passenger came aboard.* ■ **all aboard!** an expression used to tell passengers that it is time to get on a ship, train, bus etc. ◇ *prep* on or into <a ship, plane, bus> etc □ *The terrorists aboard the 747 have released two hostages.*

abode [əˈboʊd] *n* the place where one lives (formal or humorous use) □ *Welcome to my humble abode.* ■ **of no fixed abode** [person] who has no permanent address (legal use).

abolish [əˈbɒlɪʃ] *vt* [law, activity, system] to end <sthg> officially □ *The Government had to abolish the new tax because it was so unpopular.*

abolition [ˌæbəˈlɪʃn] *n* [of a law, activity] *see* **abolish** □ *the abolition of slavery.*

abominable [əˈbɒmɪnəbl] *adj* [conditions, weather, behavior] very bad □ *The service at that restaurant is abominable!*

abominably [əˈbɒmɪnəblɪ] *adv* very badly □ *The prisoners were treated abominably.*

aboriginal [ˌæbəˈrɪdʒnəl] ◇ *n* = **aborigine**. ◇ *adj*: *aboriginal peoples/art.*

Aboriginal Australian *n* = **Aborigine**.

aborigine [ˌæbəˈrɪdʒənɪ] *n* a person who belongs to the race that was living in a country before anybody else arrived there.
♦ **Aborigine** *n* a person who belongs to the race that was living in Australia before Europeans arrived there.

👻 ABORIGINES
There have been Aborigines in Australia for at least 60,000 years. Today there are about 260,000 of them (1.5% of the total population), living mainly in the Northern Territory, Western Australia, and Queensland. About two-thirds of Aborigines now live in towns and cities, and the rest live a more traditional way of life in the outback. Re-

cently Aborigines have been able to claim back the land they were living on before European settlers arrived.

abort [ə'bɔːᵗt] ◇ *vt* -1. MEDICINE to remove <a fetus> from its mother's womb before it is ready to be born, so that it dies □ *The doctors decided to abort the pregnancy.* -2. [launch, mission] to end <an activity> before it is finished because it is difficult or dangerous □ *Takeoff was aborted due to rocket failure.* -3. COMPUTING to stop <a program> before it has finished running. ◇ *vi* [woman] to give birth to a baby too soon during the pregnancy so that it dies □ *She aborted when she was four months pregnant.*

abortion [ə'bɔːᵗʃn] *n* a medical operation in which a fetus is removed from its mother's womb, so that it dies □ *She went abroad to have an abortion.*

abortive [ə'bɔːᵗtɪv] *adj* [attempt, effort, plan] that is not successful □ *The money-making scheme proved abortive.* □ *our abortive attempts to win favor with the locals.*

abound [ə'baʊnd] *vi* -1. [rumors, jobs, examples] to be present in large numbers or amounts □ *a city where opportunities abound.* -2. **to abound with** OR **in sthg** to have plenty of sthg □ *The area abounds in natural resources.*

about [ə'baʊt] ◇ *adv* -1. **about five years/$100** a little more or a little less than five years/ $100 (used with numbers or amounts) □ *I'll see you at about five o'clock.* -2. **to lie/sit about** to lie/sit in no special place, usually not doing anything important □ *The people stood about in groups chatting.* ■ **to run/jump about** to run/jump in different directions, sometimes in an uncontrolled way □ *The book fell on his foot, causing him to hop about in pain.* -3. **to be about** to be somewhere near and possible to find, use, catch etc □ *Are there any teachers about?* □ *There's a lot of flu about.* -4. phrase **to be about to do sthg** to be going to do sthg very soon □ *She's just about to leave.* ◇ *prep* -1. **a book about Paris** a book that has Paris as its subject □ *What was the movie about?* □ *He's always worrying about his health.* -2. **we must do something about it** we must take action to make the situation better □ *So what are you going to do about those people waiting outside?* -3. **to be about a place** to be somewhere in a place □ *"Where's Sue?" — "She's about the house somewhere."* □ *His clothes were lying scattered about the room.* -4. phrases **there is something strange about him** there is something strange in his character or appearance □ *There's something odd about this whole business.* □ *What I like about her is her frankness.* ■ **what** OR **how about sthg?** a phrase used to introduce a topic or to make a suggestion □ *OK, it's a nice car, but what about the cost?* □ *How about a drink?*

about-face US, **about-turn** GB *n* -1. MILITARY a movement in which a soldier or group of soldiers turns to face the opposite direction. -2. a change to the opposite attitude or course of action □ *The Administration has done another about-face on tax increases.*

above [ə'bʌv] ◇ *adv* -1. **the sky above** the sky over one's head □ *He lives in the apartment above.* -2. **the items above** the items that have been mentioned before in a letter, report etc (formal use) □ *See above for details of prices.* -3. **aged five and above** aged five or more. ◇ *prep* -1. **above the door** directly over the door □ *The apartment above mine is empty.* -2. **the person above me** the person who is higher than me in rank or status □ *She has a manager above her who supervises her work.* -3. **to be above suspicion/criticism** to be considered too good or important to deserve any suspicion/criticism. ■ **to be above cheating/stealing** to be too good, honest, or proud to take part in cheating/stealing □ *Are you arguing about money again? I thought you were above all that!*

◆ **above all** *adv* a phrase used to introduce the most important thing of all □ *Above all, I want to succeed.* □ *Be pleasant and friendly, but above all be polite.*

aboveboard [ə'bʌvbɔːᵗd] *adj* **to be aboveboard** [business, agreement] to be honest and not involved in anything secret or illegal □ *He assured us that the deal was all open and aboveboard.*

abracadabra [,æbrəkə'dæbrə] *excl* a word spoken by a magician performing a magic trick that is supposed to make the magic happen.

Abraham ['eɪbrəhæm] in the Bible, the ancestor of the Hebrews.

abrasion [ə'breɪʒn] *n* an injury caused by scraping one's skin accidentally (formal use).

abrasive [ə'breɪsɪv] *adj* -1. [substance, pad, cloth] that is used to make surfaces clean and smooth by rubbing or scratching them. -2. [person, manner] rude and unkind.

abreast [ə'brest] *adv* [walk, ride] beside each other □ *The children were cycling three abreast.*

◆ **abreast of** *prep* **to keep abreast of sthg** [of a situation, subject] to know the most recent facts about sthg because of what one reads, hears etc □ *I like to keep abreast of the latest developments in software.*

abridged [ə'brɪdʒd] *adj* [play, book, version] that has been made shorter by having some parts taken out □ *The novel was abridged for radio by E. M. Nelson.*

abroad [ə'brɔːd] *adv* in or to another country □ *He's gone abroad for the summer.* □ *She's lived abroad for several years now.*

abrupt [ə'brʌpt] *adj* -1. [change, movement] that is sudden and unexpected □ *The party came to an abrupt end.* -2. [person, tone of voice] that is rude and unfriendly □ *There was no need to be so abrupt with her!*

abruptly [ə'brʌptlɪ] *adv* [change, behave etc] *see* **abrupt** □ *The play finished rather abruptly.* □ *"That's enough," she said abruptly.*

ABS brake *n* a type of brake used on some cars that helps to prevent skidding by stopping the wheels from becoming fixed in a particular position.

abscess ['æbses] *n* a painful swelling on one's body that is full of pus.

abscond [əb'skɒnd] *vi* -1. to go away secretly from the place where one works, usually after stealing something □ *He absconded with the takings.* -2. to escape from a place where one is being kept for legal reasons □ *Another prisoner has absconded.*

abseil ['æbseɪl] *vi* GB to go down a cliff, steep slope etc by sliding down a rope and pushing against the slope with one's feet.

absence ['æbsəns] *n* [of a person, thing] *see* **absent** □ *He returned after three months' absence.* ■ **in sb's absence** while sb is absent □ *I'm responsible for managing the office in Sara's absence.* ■ **in the absence of sthg** [of information, evidence] because sthg is not available or does not exist □ *In the absence of accurate statistics, we'll have to make a rough guess.*

absent ['æbsənt] *adj* -1. [worker, student, parent] who is not at work, school, home etc when they are supposed to be there; [thing] that should be a part of something but is missing □ *Any employee absent from work through illness must notify the office.* □ *What was absent from her voice was any feeling of warmth.* ■ **to be absent without leave** MILITARY to be away from one's camp or regiment without permission. -2. [expression, person] that shows a lack of attention □ *"Oh, it's you," she said, looking up from her book with an absent smile.*

absentee [,æbsən'tiː] *n* a person who is absent, especially from work.

absenteeism [,æbsən'tiːɪzm] *n* being away from work or school, especially regularly and without a good reason □ *the problem of absenteeism at work.*

absent-minded [-'maɪndəd] *adj* [person] who often loses or forgets things because they are thinking about something else □ *Ken looked like the typical absent-minded professor.*

absolute ['æbsəluːt] *adj* -1. a word used to show that one feels very strongly about something □ *That's absolute nonsense!* -2. [dedication, secrecy, terror] very great □ *The work demands absolute concentration.* -3. [ruler, power] that is not limited in any way □ *As a director, I require absolute control over the entire creative process.*

absolutely ['æbsəluːtlɪ] ◇ *adv* -1. a word used to show that one feels very strongly about something □ *I absolutely refuse to sell those shares.* □ *You're absolutely right!* -2. to the greatest possible extent □ *I trusted him absolutely.* ◇ *excl* a word used to express complete agreement □ *"Don't you agree?" — "Oh, absolutely!"*

absolute majority *n* a result in an election in which one political party wins more than half of all the votes.

absolution [,æbsə'luːʃn] *n* forgiveness of one's sins by a priest (formal use).

absolve [əb'zɒlv] *vt* to say officially that <sb> is not responsible for a crime, error etc □ *The*

committee's findings completely absolved them of all blame.

absorb [əb'sɔːʰb] *vt* -1. [water, oil] to take in and hold <a liquid> □ *a material capable of absorbing many times its weight in water* □ *The drug is rapidly absorbed into the bloodstream.* -2. [impact, noise] to reduce the effect of sthg unpleasant. -3. [details, instructions] to understand and remember <information> □ *It was too much to absorb all at once.* -4. **to be absorbed in sthg** to give sthg all of one's attention or interest □ *He was utterly absorbed in his reading.*

absorbent [əb'sɔːʰbənt] *adj* [substance, cloth] that can absorb liquids □ *The crystals are highly absorbent.*

absorbing [əb'sɔːʰbɪŋ] *adj* [story, account] very interesting □ *I found the play very absorbing.*

absorption [əb'sɔːʰpʃn] *n*: *see* **absorb**.

abstain [əb'steɪn] *vi* -1. to deliberately avoid something pleasant because it is bad for one's health or morally wrong □ *Patients should abstain from alcohol while taking antibiotics.* -2. to deliberately not vote in an election, ballot etc □ *Ten members voted for the proposal and three abstained.*

abstemious [əb'stiːmjəs] *adj* [person] who does not eat or drink very much (formal use).

abstention [əb'stenʃn] *n* a vote that is deliberately not used by somebody in an election, ballot etc □ *There were three abstentions.*

abstinence ['æbstənəns] *n* [from alcohol, sex, smoking] *see* **abstain** □ *a period of abstinence.*

abstract [*adj* & *n* 'æbstrækt, *vb* æb'strækt] ◇ *adj* -1. [art, painting] that consists of shapes and colors that do not represent objects or people. -2. [thinking, argument] that is concerned with ideas rather than real examples of things □ *This is all rather abstract, isn't it — have you any more definite plans?* ◇ *n* [of an article, speech] a written summary.

abstracted [æb'stræktəd] *adj* [person] who does not notice what is happening because they are thinking of something else □ *He seemed abstracted, and did not appear to hear me.*

abstraction [æb'strækʃn] *n* -1. [of a person, somebody's manner] *see* **abstracted**. -2. [in one's thinking] an idea that is concerned with something general and not with a particular person, situation etc □ *a tendency to think in abstractions.*

abstruse [æb'struːs] *adj* [comment, idea, theory] that is difficult to understand □ *I found his arguments abstruse, to say the least.*

absurd [əb'sɜːʰd] *adj* [idea, situation, decision] that is so strange and different from what is normal or expected that it is hard to believe or take seriously □ *How absurd!* □ *I feel/look absurd in this outfit.*

absurdity [əb'sɜːʰdətɪ] (*pl* **absurdities**) *n* an absurd idea or thing □ *The legal system is full of such absurdities.* □ *You can imagine the absurdity of the situation.*

absurdly [əb'sɜːʰdlɪ] *adv* a word used to express how extreme and unreasonable something is □ *absurdly high prices.*

ABTA ['æbtə] (*abbr of* **Association of British Travel Agents**) *n* an organization that pays money to customers of travel agents if the travel agency goes bankrupt.

Abu Dhabi [US ,ɑːbuː'dɑːbɪ, GB ,æbʊ-] the largest state and capital of the United Arab Emirates, in eastern Arabia. SIZE: 74,000 sq kms. POPULATION: 670,000.

abundance [ə'bʌndəns] *n* an amount of something that is more than one needs □ *an abundance of raw materials.*

◆ **in abundance** *adv* in large amounts □ *There was food in abundance.*

abundant [ə'bʌndənt] *adj* that is more than enough □ *There is an abundant supply of food.*

abundantly [ə'bʌndəntlɪ] *adv* **-1. abundantly clear/obvious** very clear/obvious □ *It was abundantly obvious that Jenny wasn't in the slightest bit interested.* **-2.** [exist, grow] in large amounts □ *Wild asparagus is found abundantly in this area.*

abuse [*n* ə'bjuːs, *vb* ə'bjuːz] ◇ *n* **-1.** [in words] offensive words that somebody uses in order to insult another person □ *They shouted abuse at the police.* □ *a term of abuse.* **-2.** [of a child] cruel or harmful treatment, especially of somebody young or helpless □ *victims of sexual abuse* □ *The abuse went on for years.* **-3.** [of drugs, power] the excessive or unreasonable use of something □ *Such positions are open to abuse.* □ *alcohol abuse.*
◇ *vt* **-1.** [person in authority] to make insulting remarks to <sb> □ *Murray was sent off for abusing the referee.* **-2.** [child, wife] to treat <sb> badly, cruelly, or violently □ *He was abused as a child.* **-3.** [authority, privilege] to use <power> in an excessive or unreasonable way □ *He has abused the system/our trust.*

abuser [ə'bjuːzə^r] *n* a person who abuses somebody or something □ *a clinic for alcohol abusers.*

abusive [ə'bjuːsɪv] *adj* [person, behavior, language] that is offensive and insulting □ *There's no need to be abusive!*

abut [ə'bʌt] (*pt* & *pp* **abutted**, *cont* **abutting**) *vi* **to abut onto sthg** [onto a building, piece of land] to be next to one end of sthg (formal use).

abysmal [ə'bɪzml] *adj* [standard, performance, failure] very bad □ *What abysmal weather!*

abysmally [ə'bɪzməlɪ] *adv* **-1.** [perform, fail] very badly □ *I tried to convince them but I failed abysmally.* **-2. abysmally low/small** very low/small □ *an abysmally slow growth rate.*

abyss [ə'bɪs] *n* (literary use) **-1.** a very deep hole. **-2.** a very dangerous situation.

a/c -1. *abbr of* **account. -2.** *abbr of* **air-conditioning.**

AC *n* **-1.** *abbr of* **athletics club. -2.** *abbr of* **alternating current.**
NOTE: Compare **DC**.

academic [,ækə'demɪk] ◇ *adj* **-1.** [job, qualification, life] that is connected with the field of education, especially at college or university □ *Her academic results are excellent.* **-2.** [pupil, student] who is good at studying, especially in subjects that involve thinking and writing rather than practical work □ *The course stresses academic rather than practical skills.* **-3.** [question, outcome] that has no importance in relation to a real situation □ *From that moment on, the result was purely academic.*
◇ *n* [at college, university] someone who teaches or does research □ *Scott went on to become an academic.*

academically [,ækə'demɪklɪ] *adv* from an educational point of view □ *He is very talented academically, but not good at sports.*

academic year *n* the period of the year when classes take place at college or university.

academy [ə'kædəmɪ] (*pl* **academies**) *n* **-1.** a school or college, usually specializing in one subject □ *a naval/military academy.* **-2.** a society whose aim is to promote science or art □ *the Royal Academy.*

ACAS ['eɪkæs] (*abbr of* **Advisory Conciliation and Arbitration Service**) *n* a British organization that tries to solve disputes between management and unions.

accede [æk'siːd] *vi* (formal use) **-1. to accede to sthg** [to a request, demand] to agree to sthg □ *He finally acceded to their demands.* **-2. to accede to the throne** to become king or queen.

accelerate [ək'seləreɪt] ◇ *vi* **-1.** AUTO [vehicle] to go faster; [driver] to make a vehicle go faster □ *The truck accelerated away.* **-2.** [change, growth, pace] to increase in speed □ *The fall in sales has accelerated over the summer.* ◇ *vt* [change, growth, pace] to make <sthg> happen faster than expected or than before □ *The success of the advertising campaign has accelerated demand.*

acceleration [ək,selə'reɪʃn] *n* **-1.** [of change, growth, pace] *see* **accelerate. -2.** AUTO [of a vehicle] the time it takes for a car, motorcycle etc to reach a high speed □ *This model has good/poor acceleration.*

accelerator [ək'seləreɪtə^r] *n* the pedal in a car, on a motorcycle etc that the driver presses to make the vehicle go faster.

accelerator card *n* an electronic device that can be added to a computer to make it work faster.

accelerator pedal *n* = **accelerator.**

accent ['æksent] *n* **-1.** [of speaker] a way of pronouncing words that may show which region, country, or social class somebody comes from □ *He spoke with a foreign/a Southern accent.* **-2.** [in writing] a mark, usually above a letter, that shows how it should be pronounced □ *There's an accent on the "o" in "matón".* **-3. the accent is on sthg** particular importance is given to sthg □ *The accent here is on teamwork.*

accentuate [æk'sentʃueɪt] *vt* [feature, aspect] to make <sthg> more obvious □ *The thin dress only accentuated her frailness.*

accept [ək'sept] *vt* **-1.** [gift, prize, invitation] to agree to take <sthg that is offered> □ *I was unable to accept their offer of a free trip.* ■ **please accept our apologies/our thanks** an expression used to apologize/to thank somebody (formal use). **-2.** [suggestion, proposal, piece of advice] to say that one agrees with <what somebody says>, and will do what they say □ *The government accepted the recommendations of the committee.* **-3.** [excuse, explanation, account] to say that one finds <sthg> reasonable □ *I can't accept that argument.* □ *It is generally accepted that this chemical can cause cancer.* **-4.** [situation, fact] to decide that one cannot change or improve <sthg> □ *They refused to accept the appalling working conditions.* **-5. to accept responsibility/the blame for sthg** to say that one is responsible/to blame for sthg □ *The company must accept full responsibility for what has happened.* **-6.** [candidate, new member] to say that <sb> can join an institution or organization □ *She's been accepted by Harvard.* **-7.** [newcomer, foreigner] to treat <sb> as if they belong to one's family, group etc □ *It took a long time before she felt accepted by her team-mates.* **-8.** [currency, cash] to take <sthg> as payment □ *We accept all major credit cards.* **-9.** [coin, diskette, data] to be able to work when <sthg> is put in it □ *This machine only accepts quarters.*

acceptable [ək'septəbl] *adj* **-1.** [behavior, dress, situation] that can be tolerated, especially because it is not believed to be morally wrong □ *It is no longer socially acceptable to drink and drive.* **-2.** [plan, piece of work, candidate] that is good enough □ *As a temporary measure it's perfectly acceptable.* □ *We eventually found a solution that was acceptable to everyone.*

acceptably [ək'septəblɪ] *adv* **-1.** [behave, dress] *see* **acceptable** □ *It's possible to eat acceptably without spending a fortune.* **-2. acceptably high/low** high/low enough.

acceptance [ək'septəns] *n* **-1.** [by an institution] an offer of membership, a place etc made by an institution or organization such as a club or university to an applicant or candidate □ *a letter of acceptance.* **-2.** [of a prize, proposal, situation] *see* **accept** □ *an acceptance speech.* **-3. to gain** OR **win acceptance** [idea, method] to be believed or supported by an increasing number of people □ *Vegetarianism has gradually gained acceptance among the middle classes.*

accepted [ək'septəd] *adj* [idea, fact] that is believed by most people to be correct □ *It's now accepted that too much sun ages the skin.*

access ['ækses] ◇ *n* **-1.** [to a building] a way of getting into a place □ *The kitchen gives access to the garage.* ■ **to gain access to a place** to manage to enter a place □ *Thieves had gained access to the house through an upstairs window.* ■ **'disabled access'** a sign indicating a special way into a place designed for people in wheelchairs. **-2.** [to information, a person] the opportunity to use something or contact somebody □ *He has access to the children at weekends.* □ *Access to these files is restricted.* ◇ *vt* COMPUTING [data, files] to get <information> from a computer's memory □ *How do I access the master file?*

accessibility [ək,sesə'bɪlətɪ] *n*: *see* **accessible.**

accessible [ək'sesəbl] *adj* **-1.** [place] that is possible to reach □ *The village is only accessible by boat.* **-2.** [price, product] that many people can

afford □ *Computers are now accessible to everyone.* **-3.** [book, report] that is easy to understand □ *Modern music is becoming more accessible to the man in the street.*

accession [æk'seʃn] *n* [of a king, queen] *see* **accede.**

accessory [ək'sesərɪ] (*pl* **accessories**) *n* **-1.** [for a machine] an extra part that is not essential □ *car accessories.* **-2.** LAW a person who helps a criminal before or after a crime, e.g. by helping to plan it, but is not present when the crime is committed □ *an accessory to murder.*

◆ **accessories** *npl* things, e.g. belts, handbags, or jewelry, that are worn or carried with particular clothes.

access road *n* CONSTRUCTION a road that leads to a building site, housing project etc.

access time *n* the time it takes to access a piece of information that is stored in a computer.

accident ['æksədənt] *n* **-1.** an unexpected event that often causes damage or injury □ *Many accidents in the home involve electricity.* □ *He was killed in a road/riding accident.* □ *a minor/serious accident* □ *accident insurance.* ■ **to have an accident** to damage something or injure oneself without meaning to; [in a car] to crash □ *He had an accident at work.* **-2. it was an accident** it was not done deliberately □ *I didn't mean to break it, it was an accident!*

◆ **by accident** *adv* [meet, discover] without being planned or expected in advance □ *I found out the answer completely by accident.*

accidental [,æksə'dentl] *adj* **-1.** [death, injury] that happens as a result of an accident, e.g. a car accident. **-2.** [meeting, discovery] that happens by accident □ *It was totally accidental that they were both wearing the same dress.* □ *accidental breakages.*

accidentally [,æksə'dentlɪ] *adv* [happen, meet, discover] *see* **accidental** □ *I accidentally knocked over the bottle.*

accident-prone *adj* [person] who often has accidents □ *He's very accident-prone.*

acclaim [ə'kleɪm] ◇ *n* strong praise □ *Her new book had received great critical acclaim.* ◇ *vt* [writer, book, play] to praise <sb/sthg> very much □ *a widely-acclaimed author.*

acclamation [,æklə'meɪʃn] *n* loud approval of somebody or something.

acclimate [ə'klaɪmət] *vt* & *vi* US − **acclimatize.**

acclimatize [ə'klaɪmətaɪz] ◇ *vt* **to acclimatize oneself, to become acclimatized** to get used to a new climate, new surroundings, or new customs. ◇ *vi: You'll soon acclimatize to the heat.*

accolade ['ækəleɪd] *n* public praise and approval □ *This award is the highest accolade the acting profession gives to its members.*

accommodate [ə'kɒmədeɪt] *vt* **-1.** [apartment, car] to have enough room for <sb/sthg> □ *The car will accommodate up to five people.* **-2.** [institution] to provide a place to live for <sb> □ *The council has a duty to accommodate homeless families.* **-3.** [person] to help <sb> by giving them what they need or have asked for □ *The management refused to accommodate the union's requests.*

accommodating [ə'kɒmədeɪtɪŋ] *adj* [person] willing to help □ *The staff at the hotel were very accommodating.*

accommodation [ə,kɒmə'deɪʃn] *n* -1. [in a hotel] a place to live or sleep □ *overnight/furnished/hotel accommodation.* -2. BUSINESS a place to work □ *office accommodation.*

◆ **accommodations** *npl* US food, services, and seats or rooms provided for a guest in a hotel, or a passenger on a ship, plane, or train (formal use).

accompaniment [ə'kʌmpənɪmənt] *n* -1. music played on an instrument as a support while somebody sings or plays the main instrument □ *a piano/guitar accompaniment.* -2. **an accompaniment to sthg** something that goes with sthg and makes it look better or taste better □ *The puree is an excellent accompaniment to roast lamb.*

accompanist [ə'kʌmpənəst] *n* a person who plays a musical accompaniment.

accompany [ə'kʌmpənɪ] (*pt* & *pp* **accompanied**) *vt* -1. to go somewhere with <sb> □ *I accompanied her to the station.* -2. **to be accompanied by sthg** to happen at the same time or be in the same place as sthg □ *The letter was accompanied by an invoice.* -3. MUSIC to play an accompaniment for <a singer or musician> □ *He accompanied her on the guitar.*

accomplice [ə'kʌmpləs] *n* a person who helps somebody else to do something illegal.

accomplish [ə'kʌmplɪʃ] *vt* [task, aim] to complete <sthg> successfully □ *I haven't accomplished much this morning.*

accomplished [ə'kʌmplɪʃt] *adj* [cook, sailor, musician] who is very good at doing a particular job or hobby.

accomplishment [ə'kʌmplɪʃmənt] *n* -1. [of a task, aim] *see* **accomplish**. -2. something that has been successfully done by somebody and that they can be proud of □ *That's quite an accomplishment.*

◆ **accomplishments** *npl* the special skills or talents that a person has □ *one of her many accomplishments.*

accord [ə'kɔːrd] *n* a formal agreement □ *The two countries have reached an accord.* □ *a peace accord.*

◆ **in accord** *adj* **to be in accord with sb/sthg** to agree with sb/sthg.

◆ **of one's own accord** *adv* [go, resign, say something] without being forced or persuaded □ *She left the firm entirely of her own accord.*

accordance [ə'kɔːrdns] ◆ **in accordance with** *prep* following what is stated by <a law, custom, one's instructions> etc □ *Our staff were acting in accordance with standard procedure.*

according [ə'kɔːrdɪŋ] ◆ **according to** *prep* -1. as stated by <a person, report, text> etc □ *According to witnesses, the plane caught fire before crashing.* ■ **to go according to plan** [event, visit] to happen the way that has been planned □ *Everything went according to plan,*

and the party was a success. -2. depending on <age, ability, preference> etc □ *Prices vary according to how long the job will take.* □ *'Salary according to age and experience.'*

accordingly [ə'kɔːrdɪŋlɪ] *adv* -1. [act, behave] in a way that is suitable, considering what has already been said or done □ *I was a good worker and I expected to be paid accordingly.* -2. **accordingly,...** as a result □ *The rains failed to come. Accordingly, many crops died from lack of water.*

accordion [ə'kɔːrdjən] *n* a musical instrument shaped like a box with keys and buttons that is played by squeezing the sides together to make the air inside produce a note.

accordionist [ə'kɔːrdjənəst] *n* a musician who plays the accordion.

accost [ə'kɒst] *vt* to approach <sb who one does not know> and speak to them, sometimes to threaten them (formal use) □ *I was accosted in the street by a tramp.*

account [ə'kaunt] *n* -1. [at a bank] an arrangement to keep money in a bank; the money kept by somebody at a bank □ *a bank account.* □ *I have an account with Eurocity Bank.* □ *It's time we opened a business account.* □ *an account name/number.* -2. [at a store] an arrangement with a store or company for paying for something later □ *Charge it to my account.* □ *I bought it on account.* □ *an account customer.* -3. a customer who does a lot of business with a company □ *Jonathan looks after the Skyways account.* -4. [of an event] a report, description, or explanation □ *She gave her account of the accident to the police.* -5. *phrases* **to call sb to account** to make sb explain why they have done something wrong □ *Despite his mistakes, he was never called to account.* ■ **to give a good account of oneself** to do something well that makes people praise or respect one □ *She gave a good account of herself in the interview.* ■ **to take account of sthg, to take sthg into account** to think carefully about sthg before making a final decision or judgment □ *We have to take into account the fact that he's been under a lot of pressure lately.* ■ **to be of no account** not to be important □ *He is a person of little account.*

◆ **accounts** *npl* a record of money spent and received by a business; the department in a company that deals with this □ *His elder brother keeps the company's accounts.* □ *the accounts department.*

◆ **by all accounts** *adv* according to what everybody says or writes □ *He was, by all accounts, a formidable man.*

◆ **on account of** *prep* because of <sthg> □ *The delivery was late on account of the airline strike.* □ *Don't stay at home just on my account.*

◆ **on no account** *adv* a phrase used to emphasize that something must not happen □ *On no account should you talk to anybody else about this.*

◆ **account for** *vt fus* -1. **to account for sthg** [for one's behavior, a mistake] to explain <sthg that is wrong or unexpected> □ *How do you account for this discrepancy in the figures?* -2. **to**

account for sthg [for a part of sthg] to be a particular amount or part of sthg □ *Direct sales account for 40% of the company's profits.*

accountability [ə,kauntə'bɪlətɪ] *n*: *see* **accountable** □ *There were calls for greater police accountability.*

accountable [ə'kauntəbl] *adj* -1. **to be accountable for sthg** to be responsible for sthg □ *The company cannot be held accountable for damage to clients' property.* -2. **to be accountable to sb** to have to be able to explain one's actions to sb □ *Congress must be fully accountable to the public.*

accountancy [ə'kauntənsɪ] *n* = **accounting**.

accountant [ə'kauntənt] *n* a person whose job is to keep or check accounts, or give financial advice.

account executive *n* a person whose job is to handle the business done with the customers of their company.

accounting [ə'kauntɪŋ] *n* the profession of an accountant □ *an accounting firm/method.*

accouterments [ə'ku:trmənts] US, **accoutrements** [ə'ku:trəmənts] GB *npl* the equipment somebody has with them for travel, sport etc (formal or humorous use).

accredited [ə'kredətəd] *adj* [authority, ambassador, representative] officially accepted □ *Being an accredited journalist allows me to go almost anywhere I want.*

accrue [ə'kru:] *vi* [money, interest] to increase in amount gradually □ *advantages accruing to property owners* □ *accrued interest/income.*

accumulate [ə'kju:mjəleɪt] ◇ *vt* [money, facts, possessions] to collect a large amount of <sthg> over a period of time □ *Over the years he accumulated a collection of fine paintings.* ◇ *vi* [money, substance] to grow in amount over a period of time □ *You have to clean the engine regularly to prevent dirt from accumulating.*

accumulation [ə,kju:mjə'leɪʃn] *n* -1. [of dirt, knowledge, chemicals] a group or amount of things that has grown bigger over a period of time □ *a large accumulation of capital.* -2. [of money, facts, possessions] *see* **accumulate** □ *Their gradual accumulation of smaller companies is viewed with suspicion.*

accuracy ['ækjərəsɪ] *n*: *see* **accurate** □ *The accuracy of his spelling leaves a lot to be desired.* □ *The missile hits its target with 98% accuracy.*

accurate ['ækjərət] *adj* -1. [information, description, report] that is correct because the details are very close to the truth □ *The costumes worn by the actors are historically accurate.* □ *These figures are as accurate as it is possible to be.* -2. [piece of equipment, worker] that produces correct results □ *an accurate typist.*

accurately ['ækjərətlɪ] *adv* [report, describe, type] *see* **accurate** □ *Please quote accurately from your sources.*

accusation [,ækjə'zeɪʃn] *n* -1. a statement that accuses somebody of doing something bad or wrong □ *The mayor resigned amid accusations of corruption.* -2. LAW a formal charge

that officially accuses somebody of a crime □ *They brought an accusation of criminal negligence against the firm.* -3. a feeling that somebody has done something bad or wrong □ *There was a note of accusation in her voice.*

accuse [ə'kju:z] *vt* -1. to say that <sb> has done something bad □ *Are you accusing me of lying?* □ *Several countries were accused of breaking the arms embargo.* -2. LAW to state officially that <sb> has committed a crime □ *Hicks was accused of murder.*

accused [ə'kju:zd] (*pl* **accused**) *n* **the accused** the person in a trial who has been charged with a crime □ *The accused pleads guilty.*

accuser [ə'kju:zər] *n* **one's accuser** the person who accuses one of having done something.

accusing [ə'kju:zɪŋ] *adj* [look, voice] that suggests that somebody has done something wrong □ *He pointed an accusing finger at her.*

accusingly [ə'kju:zɪŋlɪ] *adv* [look, speak] *see* **accusing** □ *"I thought you were on a diet," she said accusingly.*

accustomed [ə'kʌstəmd] *adj* **to be accustomed to sthg** to be used to sthg □ *I'm not accustomed to rich food.* □ *You'll soon get accustomed to driving on the left.*

ace [eɪs] ◇ *n* -1. CARDS the playing card with only one symbol on it that has either the lowest or the highest value □ *the ace of spades.* -2. SPORT a serve in tennis, handball etc that one's opponent cannot reach. -3. *phrase* **to be** OR **come within an ace of sthg** to come very close to sthg □ *They came within an ace of bankruptcy/of being caught.* ◇ *adj* [marksman, athlete] very good.

acerbic [ə'sɜ:bɪk] *adj* [person, remark, wit] unkind and critical.

acetate ['æsəteɪt] *n* -1. a chemical made from acetic acid. -2. a smooth synthetic material used for making curtains, clothes etc.

acetic acid [ə,si:tɪk-] *n* the acid in vinegar. FORMULA: CH_3COOH.

acetone ['æsətoun] *n* a clear liquid, used in solvents, nail polish remover etc, that catches fire very easily. FORMULA: CH_3.

acetylene [ə'setəli:n] *n* a colorless gas that burns brightly and is used in lamps, welding equipment etc. FORMULA: C_2.

ache [eɪk] ◇ *n* a continuous dull pain in a part of one's body □ *aches and pains.* ◇ *vi* -1. [head, back, tooth] to hurt in a dull continuous way □ *My feet were aching after my long walk.* -2. **to be aching to do sthg** to want to do sthg very much □ *She was aching to tell them.*

achieve [ə'tʃi:v] *vt* [aim, goal, effect] to succeed in doing or getting <sthg useful or desirable> □ *In the last two years we have achieved far greater profitability.* □ *I don't feel we've achieved much this morning.*

achievement [ə'tʃi:vmənt] *n* -1. something successful one has done that needs a lot of effort or skill □ *Winning three championships in a row is a magnificent achievement.* □ *Finishing a book gives you a real sense of achievement.* -2. [of a goal, ambition] *see* **achieve**.

Achilles' heel [ə,kılɪːz-] *n* a weakness in the character of a person.

Achilles' tendon *n* the tendon at the back of one's leg above one's heel.

acid ['æsɪd] ◇ *adj* **-1.** [liquid, soil] = **acidic.** **-2.** [fruit, drink] that tastes sour and sharp like lemons □ *It tastes slightly acid.* **-3.** [person, remark] that is unkind, unpleasant, and critical □ *an acid tone of voice.* ◇ *n* SCIENCE a chemical that can combine with other substances and can dissolve things that it touches. It makes litmus paper turn red. □ *sulphuric acid* □ *The acid had leaked out of the batteries.*
NOTE: Compare **alkali.**

acidic [ə'sɪdɪk] *adj* [liquid, soil] that contains an acid or has a pH value of less than 7.
NOTE: Compare **alkaline.**

acidity [ə'sɪdətɪ] *n*: see **acid** □ *the acidity of her comments* □ *high acidity levels.*

acid rain *n* rain containing acid from industrial pollution that can damage the environment.

acid test *n* **the acid test** the best way of proving whether something works or is true □ *The acid test of the new policy will come at the next elections.*

acknowledge [ək'nɒlɪdʒ] *vt* **-1. to acknowledge (that)...** to accept that a particular situation exists or is true □ *While acknowledging (that) mistakes had been made, he continued to defend his policy.* □ *She still refuses to acknowledge her guilt.* **-2.** [contribution, role, achievement] to say officially that somebody has done <sthg valuable or important>. ■ **to be acknowledged as sthg** to be thought by most people to be sthg good or admirable □ *The new senator is acknowledged as one of the country's most talented politicians.* **-3.** [message, letter] to confirm that one has received <sthg> □ *Sign here to acknowledge receipt of this document.* **-4.** [person] to show that one has seen or recognized <sb> □ *She acknowledged him with a shy smile.*

acknowledgement, acknowledgment [ək'nɒlɪdʒmənt] *n* **-1.** [of a fact, person, message] see **acknowledge** □ *in acknowledgment of your letter of June 14* □ *a letter of acknowledgment.* **-2.** [of a letter] a confirmation, usually written, that something has been received □ *Did we receive an acknowledgment for that package we sent?*

◆ **acknowledgments** *npl* the short piece of writing, usually at the beginning of a book, that thanks people who have helped the author.

ACLU (*abbr of* **American Civil Liberties Union**) *n* **the ACLU** a US organization that protects people's rights.

acme ['ækmɪ] *n* [of perfection, one's career] the highest point of something (formal use).

acne ['æknɪ] *n* a skin condition, common among adolescents, that consists of pimples on the face and neck □ *a young boy suffering from terrible acne.*

acorn ['eɪkɔːrn] *n* the nut of the oak tree, half enclosed in a wooden shell.

acoustic [ə'kuːstɪk] *adj* [effect, feature] that is concerned with sound, or the acoustics of a place.

◆ **acoustics** *npl* the way that the shape, size, and wall coverings of a room, theater etc affect how music and speech sound to the audience □ *The acoustics are very good in here.*

acoustic guitar *n* a guitar that is not electric.

acquaint [ə'kweɪnt] *vt* **-1.** (formal use) **to acquaint sb with sthg** [with information, rules] to tell sb sthg □ *Let me acquaint you with the details of the case.* ■ **to be acquainted with sthg** to know sthg or know about it □ *Are you fully acquainted with the facts of this case?* **-2. to be acquainted with sb** to know sb slightly but not well □ *The party was a good opportunity for everyone to get better acquainted.*

acquaintance [ə'kweɪntns] *n* **-1.** a person one knows slightly but not well □ *An acquaintance of mine told me.* **-2. to make sb's acquaintance** to meet sb for the first time (formal use) □ *I'm pleased to make your acquaintance.*

acquiesce [,ækwɪ'es] *vi* to agree to somebody else's demands, terms etc, often unwillingly (formal use) □ *The government will never acquiesce to the terrorists' demands.*

acquire [ə'kwaɪər] *vt* **-1.** [property, company, information] to buy or get <sthg valuable> □ *They have recently acquired shares in the company.* **-2.** [habit, reputation, skill] to gradually begin to have or develop <sthg> □ *The word has acquired a new meaning in recent years.*

acquired taste [ə'kwaɪərd-] *n* something one does not like at first, but may begin to like after trying it several times □ *Oysters are an acquired taste.*

acquisition [,ækwə'zɪʃn] *n* **-1.** something, e.g. a piece of clothing or furniture, that one has acquired □ *The museum's latest acquisition has caused a public outcry.* **-2.** [of knowledge, property, a skill] see **acquire** □ *The company has grown through the acquisition of smaller businesses.*

acquisitive [ə'kwɪzətɪv] *adj* [person] who always wants to get more possessions (disapproving use).

acquit [ə'kwɪt] (*pt* & *pp* **acquitted,** *cont* **acquitting**) *vt* **-1.** LAW to state officially that <sb> is not guilty of a crime they have been accused of □ *He was acquitted of the murder.* **-2. to acquit oneself well/badly** to perform well/badly in a particular situation (formal use).

acquittal [ə'kwɪtl] *n* LAW [of a person] see **acquit.**

acre ['eɪkər] *n* a unit (4,047 square meters) for measuring land □ *a ranch of 300 acres* OR *a 300-acre ranch.*

acreage ['eɪkərɪdʒ] *n* the area of a piece of land, measured in acres.

acrid ['ækrɪd] *adj* [smell, smoke] that makes one's eyes or nose sting; [taste] that is bitter and strong □ *Firefighters were overcome by the acrid fumes.* □ *The leaves had an acrid taste.*

acrimonious [,ækrɪ'moʊnjəs] *adj* [dispute, debate] see **acrimony** □ *They had an acrimonious discussion about money.*

acrimony [US 'ækrəmoʊnɪ, GB -rəmənɪ] *n* anger

and bitterness □ *Their meetings always ended in acrimony.*

acrobat ['ækrəbæt] *n* a person who performs gymnastic acts, usually in a circus.

acrobatic [,ækrə'bætɪk] *adj* [movement, display] that involves difficult gymnastic acts, e.g. somersaults.

◆ **acrobatics** *npl* acrobatic movements □ *an impressive display of acrobatics.*

acronym ['ækrənɪm] *n* a word made from the first letters of the words in a name, title etc, such as *AIDS* or *NATO*.

across [ə'krɒs] ◇ *adv* **-1. to walk across** to walk from one side of a street, room etc to the other □ *She ran across to speak to me.* **-2. to be** OR **measure 40 feet across** to measure 40 feet from one side to the other □ *The lake here is over a mile across.* **-3. 21 across** the word in a crossword written from left to right and with the number 21.
◇ *prep* **-1. to go across the sea** to go from one side of the sea to the other □ *The dog came running across the road toward me.* ■ **to lie across a bed** to lie on a bed, usually sideways, partly covering it □ *He leant across the table to me.* **-2. to live across the street** to live on the other side of the street □ *He stared at me from across the room.*

◆ **across from** *prep* on the other side of the road, room etc from <sb/sthg> □ *The bank is just across from the garage.*

across-the-board *adj* [increase, reduction] that affects everything or everybody in an industry, company, sector etc □ *an across-the-board rise in salaries.*

◆ **across the board** *adv*: *The salary cut will be applied across the board.*

acrylic [ə'krɪlɪk] *n* a synthetic material that looks like cotton or wool □ *an acrylic sweater.*

acrylic (paint) *n* a synthetic paint used by artists.

act [ækt] ◇ *n* **-1.** something that somebody has done □ *an act of war/treason/violence.* ■ **to catch sb in the act** to discover sb doing something bad, illegal etc. **-2.** LAW a law made by a government □ *the Single European Act.* **-3.** THEATER & MUSIC one of the main sections of a play, opera, or ballet □ *a three-act play.* **-4.** THEATER, TV, & RADIO a short performance by an entertainer; a person, group, or animal giving this performance □ *There's a comedy act on after the singer.* **-5. it's all (just) an act** a phrase used to say that somebody's behavior does not show their real feelings □ *She seems very calm, but it's all just an act.* ■ **to put on an act** to pretend to be, do, or feel something □ *He's not really angry, he's just putting on an act.* **-6.** phrases **to get in on the act** to join in or take advantage of something that other people are already doing □ *Other companies are now trying to get in on the act.* ■ **to get one's act together** to begin to behave in a more organized and effective way (informal use) □ *It's time you got your act together and found a job.*
◇ *vi* **-1.** [organization, government, police] to do something that has a particular purpose □

We have to act quickly to help these people. **-2.** [person] to behave in a particular way □ *You've been acting strangely toward me all evening.* □ *I'd been acting like a fool.* □ *She acts as if she's already got the job.* **-3.** THEATER, CINEMA, & TV [actor, actress] to perform in a play or movie, or on television □ *She's been acting professionally since she left school.* **-4.** [person] to pretend to have a particular quality □ *He acts dumb, but he's really a sharp businessman.* **-5.** [chemical, drug] to start to have an effect □ *It acts faster than any other painkiller.* **-6. to act as sthg** [as somebody's agent, guide, lawyer] to work as sthg for somebody; [as a device] to be used as sthg; [as a deterrent, barrier, incentive] to have the effect of being sthg □ *I had to act as interpreter.* □ *The reduction in interest rates should act as a stimulus to the economy.* ■ **to act for** OR **on behalf of sb** [agent, lawyer] to work for sb and deal with a particular matter for them □ *lawyers acting for Mrs Turner.*
◇ *vt* to play <a role> in a play or movie. ■ **to act the fool/innocent etc** to pretend to be more foolish/innocent etc than one really is.

◆ **act on** *vt fus* **-1. to act on sthg** to obey or follow sthg □ *Woods claimed he was acting on instructions from his superiors.* **-2. to act on sb/sthg** to have an effect on sb/sthg □ *The drug acts on the nervous system.*

◆ **act out** *vt sep* **-1. to act sthg out** [fantasy, desire] to express one's feelings or ideas in one's behavior. **-2. to act sthg out** [event, story, scene] to show sthg that has happened by acting, sometimes without words.

◆ **act up** *vi* (informal use) [car, machine] not to work as it should; [child, dog] to behave badly □ *The car's acting up again!*

ACT *abbr of* **Australian Capital Territory**.

acting ['æktɪŋ] ◇ *adj* **acting manager/head etc** the person who is in the position of manager/head etc until a permanent replacement is found □ *Richard has been appointed acting director while Sarah is away.* ◇ *n* **-1.** [in plays, movies] the profession of performing in plays or movies □ *I've decided to go into acting.* **-2.** [of an actor] the quality of an actor's performance □ *His acting is superb.*

action ['ækʃn] *n* **-1.** something that has to be done, usually to solve a problem or difficulty □ *It's time for action.* ■ **to take action** to do something to deal with a problem □ *We must take immediate action if we want to avoid further losses.* □ *The police decided to take no further action and dropped the charge.* ■ **to put sthg into action** [idea, plan] to begin to use sthg or let it work □ *It'll be several months before we can put this plan into action.* ■ **in action** [person, machine] working or performing □ *They're an impressive team: you should see them in action.* ■ **out of action** [person] unable to carry out one's normal activities, usually because of injury; [machine, car] not working because it is damaged □ *I've been out of action for six weeks with a broken leg.* □ *The computer is out of action again.* **-2. one's actions** what one has done on a particular occasion □ *She defended her actions as being entirely justifiable.* **-3.** MILITARY fighting □ *He was killed in action.*

-4. LAW a charge made against somebody in court □ *He brought a libel action against the newspaper.* **-5.** [in a play, book, movie] the events that happen in a book, play etc □ *Most of the action takes place in the last half hour.* **-6.** [of light, a chemical, drug] the effect that something has on something else □ *The caves are formed by the action of water on the rock.* **-7. the action** the most important and exciting events connected with an activity □ *I want to be where the action is!*

action group *n* a group of people formed to persuade politicians to accept or reject a particular proposal or policy.

action replay *n* GB TV a slow replay of part of a sports event.

activate ['æktɪveɪt] *vt* [alarm, missile] to make <an electric or electronic device> start working □ *This button here activates the whole system.*

active ['æktɪv] *adj* **-1.** [person] who is always doing things or moving about □ *She's very active for her age.* **-2. to be active** [animal] to be awake and doing things □ *Bats are active at night.* **-3.** [member, campaigner] who does something to support an organization or a cause □ *The club has 200 active members.* □ *He was active in persuading countries to ban the tests.* **-4.** [encouragement, support] that is done, given etc with energy and enthusiasm □ *We will take active steps to recruit new members.* **-5.** [volcano] that can still erupt; [bomb] that can still explode. **-6. an active ingredient** the substance in a medicine, cleaning product etc that produces a chemical effect.

actively ['æktɪvlɪ] *adv* [encourage, support, consider] *see* **active** □ *The entire workforce was actively involved in the discussions.*

active service *n* military service in a war that involves fighting □ *He was killed while on active service.*

activist ['æktəvəst] *n* a person who is directly involved in political action, e.g. campaigning □ *a political activist.*

activity [æk'tɪvətɪ] (*pl* **activities**) *n* **-1.** [in a place] a situation in which a lot of things are happening □ *There has been very little activity on the stock market today.* **-2.** [by a person] something that somebody does in their spare time for enjoyment □ *He lists his leisure activities as chess and skiing.* □ *an activity leader.*

◆ **activities** *npl* things that people do, usually of a political or illegal kind □ *their involvement in terrorist activities.*

act of God *n* a natural event, e.g. a flood, storm, or earthquake, that cannot be prevented or predicted.

actor ['æktər] *n* a person who acts in plays, movies, or on television.

actress ['æktrəs] *n* a woman who acts in plays or movies, or on television.

ACTU (*abbr of* **Australian Council of Trade Unions**) *n* **the ACTU** the national association of Australian labor unions.

actual ['æktʃʊəl] *adj* **-1.** [size, time, price] that is real, rather than supposed, intended, claimed etc □ *The actual cost was $1,000 more than we had estimated.* □ *I can't remember her actual words.* **-2.** a word used to emphasize the most important part of what is being said □ *The whole trip takes three hours, but the actual flight itself only lasts fifty minutes.*

◆ **in actual fact** *adv* a phrase used to introduce information that says the opposite of what has just been said □ *I thought I'd hate Madrid, but in actual fact I loved it.*

actuality [,æktʃʊ'ælətɪ] ◆ **in actuality** *adv* = **in fact**.

actually ['æktʃʊəlɪ] *adv* **-1.** a word used to say that something is true, that it has happened in real life, and is not a mistake □ *Yes, but did you actually see him take the money?* □ *I didn't actually mean to hurt him.* **-2. actually,...** a word used to draw attention to what one is saying, especially because it is a new idea or because one has just remembered it □ *Actually, on second thought, I'll do it myself.* □ *Oh, actually, I'll be away next week.* **-3. actually,...** a word used to make what one is saying sound more polite, e.g. when one is correcting somebody □ *"I don't suppose you've ever been there."* — *"I have, actually."*

actuary ['æktjʊərɪ] (*pl* **actuaries**) *n* a person whose job is to calculate how much insurance companies should charge their clients.

actuate ['æktjʊeɪt] *vt* to make <a device, mechanism> etc start working (technical use).

Act-Up ['æktʌp] *n* an organization that aims to protect the rights of people with AIDS.

acuity [ə'kjuːətɪ] *n* the ability to see, hear, or understand small details and differences (formal use).

acumen [US ə'kjuːmən, GB 'ækjʊmən] *n* the ability to make good judgments □ *business/political acumen.*

acupuncture ['ækjəpʌŋktʃər] *n* a medical treatment, first used in China, that involves sticking needles into parts of a person's body.

acute [ə'kjuːt] *adj* **-1.** [embarrassment, pain, danger] that is very great; [illness, situation] that becomes dangerous very quickly □ *There's an acute shortage of housing.* □ *By this time the crisis had become acute.* □ *acute appendicitis.* **-2.** [person] who understands things quickly and well □ *He has an acute understanding of the way the media works.* **-3.** [sight, hearing, sense of smell] that can notice slight details and differences □ *Audrey had exceptionally acute powers of observation.* **-4.** LINGUISTICS **e acute** a letter e with an acute accent. **-5. an acute angle** MATH an angle that is less than 90°.

acute accent *n* a symbol (´) in the form of a short line going upward from left to right, placed above a letter.

acutely [ə'kjuːtlɪ] *adv* **-1. to be acutely embarrassing/unhappy etc** to be very embarrassing/unhappy etc □ *I'm acutely conscious of the gaps in my knowledge.* **-2.** [judge, observe, remark] *see* **acute.**

ad [æd] *n* = **advertisement** (informal use).

AD ◇ (*abbr of* **Anno Domini**) since the birth of

Jesus Christ, according to the modern Western calendar (used with dates) □ *in the year 121 AD.* ◇ *n abbr of* **Alzheimer's disease.**
NOTE: Compare **BC.**

adage ['ædɪdʒ] *n* an old wise saying or proverb.

Adam ['ædəm] in the Bible, the first man created by God. He lived with Eve in the Garden of Eden.

Adam, Robert (1728–1792) a British architect and designer. A neoclassical style of architecture is named after him.

adamant ['ædəmənt] *adj* **to be adamant** to refuse to change one's mind or to be persuaded about something □ *He's adamant about it/ adamant that you didn't tell him.*

Adams ['ædəmz], **John** (1735–1826) US President from 1796 to 1800.

Adams, John Quincy (1767–1848) US President from 1825 to 1829. He helped to write the Monroe Doctrine, and campaigned against slavery.

Adam's apple *n* the lump at the front of a man's neck that moves up and down during swallowing.

adapt [ə'dæpt] ◇ *vt* -1. [method, device, system] to change <sthg> so that it is more suitable for a particular purpose □ *The design of the office can be adapted to suit the needs of staff.* -2. CINEMA & TV [book, play] to change <a piece of writing> to make it suitable for television or movies □ *The play was adapted for television by Frank Nooness.* ◇ *vi* to change one's attitude or behavior in order to deal with a new situation □ *She found it hard to adapt to life in a big city.*

adaptability [ə,dæptə'bɪlətɪ] *n* the ability to adapt □ *The job requires a certain degree of adaptability.*

adaptable [ə'dæptəbl] *adj* [person] who is able to change their way of thinking or doing something in order to deal with new situations or places □ *You need to be very adaptable in this business.*

adaptation [,ædæp'teɪʃn] *n* -1. [of a book] a movie or play that has been adapted from a novel □ *the film adaptation of "Gone with the Wind".* -2. [of a method, device, system] *see* **adapt.**

adapter, adaptor [ə'dæptər] *n* ELECTRICITY -1. [for several appliances] a special plug that makes it possible to connect several electrical appliances to a single socket. -2. [for one appliance] a special plug that makes it possible to use an electrical appliance when its plug does not match the socket □ *a travel adapter.*

ADC *n* -1. *abbr of* **aide-de-camp.** -2. (*abbr of* **Aid to Dependent Children**) a state benefit paid to poor families with dependent children in the USA. -3. (*abbr of* **analog-digital converter**) a device that converts an analog electrical signal into a digital form so that it can be processed by a digital system.

add [æd] *vt* -1. to put <sthg> with something else in order to increase its size, amount, or effect □ *Add a drop more wine.* □ *A 10% service charge will be added to the bill.* □ *The arched windows added a certain charm to the building.* -2. MATH to put <numbers> together to make a total □ *Add those two columns together to get the grand total.* □ *Add 4 and 9* OR *4 to 9.* -3. [when speaking] to say <sthg else> after another comment, remark etc □ *I have nothing to add.* □ *"You could always take out a loan," she added.*

◆ **add in** *vt sep* **to add sthg in** to include sthg as part of a total □ *Once you've added in the cost of materials, it works out quite expensive.*

◆ **add on** *vt sep* **to add sthg on** to attach sthg to something else in order to increase its size, amount, or effect □ *We've just added on a new extension to the house.*

◆ **add to** *vt fus* **to add to sthg** to make sthg worse □ *Buying a car would only add to our financial worries.*

◆ **add up** ◇ *vt sep* MATH = **add** □ *He added up the column of figures.* ◇ *vi* **it doesn't add up** it doesn't seem logical (informal use) □ *She told the police she'd never met the man before, but it just didn't add up.*

◆ **add up to** *vt fus* **to add up to sthg** [set of events or circumstances] to mean sthg when considered together □ *All this adds up to an economic crisis of major proportions.*

added ['ædəd] *adj* **an added advantage/bonus** an extra advantage/bonus □ *An added attraction of the property is its large parking lot.*

addendum [ə'dendəm] (*pl* **addenda** [-'dendə]) *n* a section added at the end of a book or document.

adder ['ædər] *n* a small poisonous snake with a black zigzag pattern along its back that is found in Europe and Asia.

addict ['ædɪkt] *n* a person who is addicted to something, especially drugs □ *a heroin/cocaine addict* □ *an exercise/a T.V. addict.*

addicted [ə'dɪktəd] *adj* -1. **to be addicted to sthg** to be unable to stop taking sthg that is bad for one's health, especially drugs □ *She was addicted to heroin.* -2. **to be addicted to sthg** to have a strong need to do or have sthg because one likes it so much □ *I could easily become addicted to these chocolates!*

addiction [ə'dɪkʃn] *n* the state of being addicted to something, especially drugs □ *He developed an addiction to morphine/gambling.* □ *the problem of alcohol addiction.*

addictive [ə'dɪktɪv] *adj* [drug, activity, food] that is easy to become addicted to □ *Heroin is a highly addictive substance.* □ *These chocolates are very addictive!*

addition [ə'dɪʃn] *n* -1. MATH the process of adding numbers together □ *The children are taught simple addition.* -2. the act of adding or including something □ *We are pleased to announce the addition of two new titles to our list.* -3. a person or thing that is added to something □ *Ford has a new addition to its range.* □ *She's been a welcome addition to the team.* ■ **a new addition to the family** a new baby.

◆ **in addition** *adv* a phrase used to add more information to something that has already been mentioned □ *In addition, we'll give you a 10% discount.*

✦ **in addition to** *prep* as well as <sb/sthg> □ *In addition to discounts, they offer free travel to the airport.*

additional [ə'dɪʃənl] *adj* [information, cost, person] extra □ *This service is provided at no additional charge.*

additive ['ædətɪv] *n* a substance that is added to food, drink etc in order to give it color or flavor.

addled ['ædld] *adj* **to be addled** [person, brain] to be confused.

add-on ◇ *n* COMPUTING a piece of equipment that is added to a computer to make it work better or faster. ◇ *adj*: *an add-on hard disk/modem.*

address [*n* US 'ædres, GB ə'dres, *vb* ə'dres] ◇ *n* -1. the number, name of the street, and name of the town that describe where a building is, often used to say where somebody can be contacted □ *You can send it to my Paris address.* □ *a business/mailing address* □ *Write your name and address below.* -2. a formal speech □ *After the meal there was an address by the chairman.*

◇ *vt* -1. **to be addressed to sb** [package, envelope, postcard] to have the name and address of sb written on it □ *It's addressed to you.* □ *This letter's been wrongly addressed.* -2. [meeting, conference] to give a formal speech to <a group of people> □ *She stood up and addressed the audience.* -3. **to address sb as sthg** to use sthg as a name or title when speaking or writing to sb □ *The ambassador should be addressed as "Your Excellency".* -4. **to address a comment/remark etc to sb** to make a comment/remark etc to sb directly □ *Please address your complaints to the manager.* -5. **to address a difficulty/problem etc** to give one's attention to a difficulty/problem etc in order to solve it □ *First, we must address the issue of rising unemployment.* -6. **to address oneself to sthg** to give one's attention to sthg □ *She addressed herself to the immediate problem of finding a place to live.*

address book *n* a book in which one writes people's names, addresses, and phone numbers.

addressee [,ædre'siː] *n* the person that a letter or package is addressed to.

Adelaide ['ædəleɪd] the state capital of South Australia. POPULATION: 1,023,700.

adenoids ['ædənɔɪdz] *npl* the soft tissue at the back of the nose that can become infected and swollen, especially in children.

adept [ə'dept] *adj* [person] who is very skillful □ *She's an adept public performer.* □ *He's very adept at dealing with the press.*

adequacy ['ædɪkwəsɪ] *n: see* **adequate** □ *Critics questioned the adequacy of the existing measures.*

adequate ['ædɪkwət] *adj* -1. [amount, quantity] that is large enough □ *We have adequate supplies of food and medicine.* -2. [person, system, method] that is good enough for a particular

purpose □ *The accommodation was barely adequate.* □ *My salary should be adequate for our needs.* □ *He couldn't give an adequate explanation.* □ *I don't really need a new coat, this one's perfectly adequate.*

adequately ['ædɪkwətlɪ] *adv: see* **adequate** □ *I don't feel adequately prepared.* □ *The problem has not been adequately dealt with.*

adhere [əd'hɪeʳ] ✦ **adhere to** *vt fus* -1. **to adhere to sthg** [to a principle, belief, decision] to act in a way that shows one agrees with or accepts sthg □ *The committee still adheres to the view that offenders should be severely punished.* □ *They have not adhered strictly to the terms of the treaty.* -2. **to adhere to sthg** [to a surface, material] to stick to sthg □ *The glue will not adhere to rough surfaces.*

adherence [əd'hɪərəns] *n* [to a rule, decision, principle] *see* **adhere** □ *Members pledge strict adherence to the code of professional conduct.*

adhesive [əd'hiːsɪv] ◇ *adj* [label, bandage] that is able to stick to another surface □ *This glue has remarkable adhesive properties.* ◇ *n* a substance, e.g. glue, that is used to stick things together.

adhesive tape *n* tape that is sticky on one side and is used for sticking things together.

ad hoc [æd'hɒk] *adj* [committee, arrangement] that only exists when it is needed for a specific purpose and is not permanent □ *The board meets on an ad hoc basis.*

ad infinitum [,ædɪnfɪ'naɪtəm] *adv* [continue, repeat] endlessly □ *and so on ad infinitum.*

Adirondacks [,ædə'rɒndæks]: **the Adirondacks** an area of mountains in New York State, known for its scenery and sports facilities.

adjacent [ə'dʒeɪsnt] *adj* [room, building] that is next to something else □ *The house is adjacent to the police station.*

adjective ['ædʒɪktɪv] *n* a word that describes a person, animal, place, or thing. In the sentences "He's a nice man." and "You'll get fat!" "nice" and "fat" are adjectives.

adjoin [ə'dʒɔɪn] *vt* [room, garden] to be next to and joined to <sthg> □ *The kitchen adjoins the dining room.*

adjoining [ə'dʒɔɪnɪŋ] ◇ *adj* [building, garden, desk] that is next to and joined to something else □ *We had adjoining rooms.* □ *Their office is in the adjoining building.* ◇ *prep* next to <sthg> □ *in the room adjoining mine.*

adjourn [ə'dʒɜːʳn] ◇ *vt* to stop <a meeting, trial> etc for a short time □ *The conference was adjourned until 3 o'clock.* ◇ *vi* -1. [committee, meeting] to stop for a short time □ *The court adjourned for lunch.* -2. to go somewhere, usually to relax after an activity (humorous use) □ *Shall we adjourn to the bar?*

adjournment [ə'dʒɜːʳnmənt] *n* [of a meeting, trial] *see* **adjourn** □ *The judge called for an adjournment.*

Adjt *abbr of* **adjutant.**

adjudge [ə'dʒʌdʒ] *vt* **to be adjudged to be sthg** to be considered to be sthg (formal use) □ *The campaign was adjudged a success.*

adjudicate [ə'dʒuːdɪkeɪt] ◇ *vt* [match, contest,

claim] to act as an official judge of <sthg>. ◇ *vi*: *An industrial tribunal will adjudicate on the case.* □ *I was often asked to adjudicate at local flower shows.*

adjudication [ə,dʒuːdɪ'keɪʃn] *n*: *see* **adjudicate** □ *Adjudication will take place one week after the closing date for entries.*

adjunct ['ædʒʌŋkt] *n* **an adjunct to sthg** a thing that is added to sthg more important and is not an essential part of it □ *He considered his car a necessary adjunct to his life.*

adjust [ə'dʒʌst] ◇ *vt* [machine, brake] to make small changes to the position or setting of <sthg> in order to make it work better; [amount, plan] to make small changes to <sthg> in order to make it suitable for new conditions □ *You'll get better reception if you adjust the antenna.* □ *'Adjust your speed now'* □ *figures adjusted for inflation* □ *The government has adjusted prices upward.* ◇ *vi* to get used to a new situation □ *It took me a long time to adjust to the climate.*

adjustable [ə'dʒʌstəbl] *adj* [machine, timer, chair] that can be adjusted □ *Seats and headrests are fully adjustable.*

adjustable wrench US, **adjustable spanner** GB *n* a wrench that can be adjusted to fit nuts of different sizes.

adjustment [ə'dʒʌstmənt] *n* **-1.** [to a plan, speed, machine] a slight change □ *I've made a few minor adjustments to OR in the schedule.* **-2.** [by a person] the process of changing one's attitude in order to deal with a new situation □ *a period of adjustment* □ *those soldiers failing to make the adjustment from military to civilian life.*

adjutant ['ædʒʊtənt] *n* an officer in the army who is an administrative assistant to a superior officer.

ad-lib [,æd'lɪb] (*pt* & *pp* **ad-libbed**, *cont* **ad-libbing**) *vi* to invent part of a speech, play etc while one is saying it □ *She forgot her lines and had to ad-lib.*

♦ **ad lib** ◇ *n* a joke, remark etc that has not been prepared before one makes it. ◇ *adv* [speak, perform] without preparation.

admin ['ædmɪn] *n* GB the work involved in the organization and running of a business, institution etc, especially the paperwork (informal use) □ *I've been doing admin all morning.* □ *an admin assistant.*

administer [əd'mɪnɪstə^r] *vt* **-1.** BUSINESS to organize and run <a company, institution> etc □ *a fund administered by trustees.* **-2.** LAW to give <justice, a punishment> etc to somebody. **-3.** MEDICINE to give <medicine, a drug> etc to somebody (formal use).

administration [əd,mɪnɪ'streɪʃn] *n* **-1.** [of a company, of justice] *see* **administer** □ *the trustees responsible for the administration of the pension fund.* **-2.** the group of people who organize and run a company, institution etc; the work involved in this □ *We're currently having talks with the administration.* □ *office administration* □ *an administration and finance manager.*

♦ **Administration** *n* **the Administration** the government of a particular US president □ *under the Bush Administration.*

administrative [əd'mɪnɪstrətɪv] *adj* [job, work, staff] that is connected with the administration of a company, institution etc □ *an administrative secretary.*

administrator [əd'mɪnɪstreɪtə^r] *n* a person whose job is to administer a business, institution etc □ *public administrators.*

admirable ['ædmərəbl] *adj* [work, quality, effort] that deserves to be admired □ *He showed an admirable lack of self-interest.* □ *Helen's concern is admirable.*

admirably ['ædmərəblɪ] *adv* [behave, manage] *see* **admirable** □ *I think you've handled it all admirably.*

admiral ['ædmrəl] *n* an officer who holds the highest rank in the navy.

Admiralty ['ædmrəltɪ] *n* **the Admiralty** the government department in Britain that is responsible for the navy.

admiration [,ædmə'reɪʃn] *n* a feeling of respect and approval □ *I'm full of admiration for the work you do.* □ *They watched, speechless with admiration.* ·

admire [əd'maɪə^r] *vt* **-1.** [person, skill, quality] to respect and approve of <sb/sthg> □ *I admire his determination.* □ *I really admire her for not giving up.* **-2.** [painting, house, car] to look at <sthg> with pleasure and approval □ *I was just admiring the view/your new shoes.* □ *Stop admiring yourself in that mirror!*

admirer [əd'maɪərə^r] *n* **-1.** a person who is sexually attracted to somebody □ *one of her many secret admirers.* **-2.** a person who likes and approves of somebody or something □ *I'm a great admirer of her work.*

admiring [əd'maɪrɪŋ] *adj* [look, glance] that expresses pleasure and approval □ *He shot her an admiring glance.*

admiringly [əd'maɪrɪŋlɪ] *adv* [look, glance] *see* **admiring** □ *He gazed at her admiringly.*

admissible [əd'mɪsəbl] *adj* LAW **admissible evidence** evidence that is allowed to be considered during a trial.

admission [əd'mɪʃn] *n* **-1.** [to a place] permission to enter a place □ *'No admission to minors'.* **-2.** [to an organization] permission to join an organization □ *the admission of Turkey to the EU* □ *university admissions.* **-3.** [as money] the cost of entrance to a park, exhibition etc □ *How much is the admission charge?* □ *'Admission free.'* **-4.** [of a crime, mistake] *see* **admit** *an admission of guilt.* ■ **by his/her etc own admission** as he/she etc admits □ *By his own admission, he's not an easy person to work with.*

admit [əd'mɪt] (*pt* & *pp* **admitted**, *cont* **admitting**) *vt* **-1. to admit (that)...** to say or agree that something is true, usually unwillingly □ *I admit (that) I was wrong to lose my temper.* □ *He admitted his mistake.* □ *It's not ideal, I must admit.* **-2. to be admitted** to be allowed to enter a place □ *Ticket-holders only are admitted to the gallery.* ■ **'Admits one/two'** a phrase used on tickets to say that one/two people can enter a club, museum etc with that ticket. ■

to be admitted to the hospital US OR **to hospital** GB to be taken to a hospital and kept in for treatment □ *She was admitted to the hospital with multiple head injuries.* **-3. to admit sb to sthg** [to a group, organization; university] to allow sb to join sthg □ *when Spain was admitted to the EU.*

◆ **admit to** *vt fus* **to admit to sthg** to say or agree that one has done sthg wrong or embarrassing □ *He admitted to the theft.* □ *Nobody would admit to leaking the story to the press.*

admittance [əd'mɪtəns] *n* permission to enter a place □ *'No admittance.'* ■ **to gain admittance to sthg** [to a place, organization] to succeed in getting into sthg (formal use).

admittedly [əd'mɪtədlɪ] *adv* a word used to show that one accepts the truth of something, even if it makes one's argument weaker □ *Admittedly, economics is not his strong point, but he's a good organizer.*

admixture [əd'mɪkstʃər] *n* something that is added to something else (formal use).

admonish [əd'mɒnɪʃ] *vt* to tell <sb> firmly that they have done something wrong (formal use) □ *They were admonished for not having acted more promptly.*

ad nauseam [ˌæd'nɔːzɪæm] *adv* [talk, discuss] for a long time and in a way that becomes annoying □ *He went on ad nauseam about his vacation.*

ado [ə'duː] *n* **without further** OR **more ado** without any more delay □ *Now, without further ado, let me welcome our guest speaker tonight.*

adolescence [ˌædə'lesns] *n* the period of somebody's life during which they develop from a child into an adult □ *in early/late adolescence* □ *Adolescence can be a time of great confusion.*

adolescent [ˌædə'lesnt] ◇ *adj* **-1.** [person] who is developing from a child into an adult. **-2.** [behavior, remark] that is not what one expects from an adult person (disapproving use). ◇ *n* a young person who is no longer a child but not yet an adult.

Adonis [ə'dəʊnəs] *n* a handsome young man.

adopt [ə'dɒpt] *vt* **-1.** [child] to become the legal parent of <a child that is born to other parents> □ *They've adopted a little boy.* **-2.** [method, stance] to decide to use <sthg> as a way of dealing with somebody or something □ *They are adopting a tougher approach toward tax-evaders.* **-3.** [suggestion, proposal] to accept and start acting in agreement with <sthg> □ *The committee adopted the report's recommendations.*

adopted [ə'dɒptəd] *adj* [child] who has been adopted □ *He's/She's adopted.*

adoption [ə'dɒpʃn] *n*: see **adopt** □ *She had to give the child up for adoption.* □ *his country of adoption* □ *The number of adoptions is growing.* □ *Scott argued for the adoption of tougher laws.*

adoptive [ə'dɒptɪv] *adj* who is related to somebody by adoption □ *They are my adoptive parents.*

adorable [ə'dɔːrəbl] *adj* [person, animal] a word used to describe somebody or something

that one thinks is very attractive and lovable □ *That little boy of yours is just adorable!*

adoration [ˌædə'reɪʃn] *n* a feeling of great love and admiration.

adore [ə'dɔːr] *vt* **-1.** to love <sb> very much □ *He adores his mother.* **-2.** to like <sthg> very much □ *I just adore chocolates, don't you?*

adoring [ə'dɔːrɪŋ] *adj* [look, smile] that expresses strong feelings of love and admiration □ *all his adoring fans.*

adorn [ə'dɔːrn] *vt* [person, room, building] to make <sb/sthg> more attractive with jewelry, decorations etc □ *The church was adorned with pine and holly branches.*

adornment [ə'dɔːrnmənt] *n* an object that adorns a person, room, building etc □ *the colorful adornments of baroque architecture.*

ADP (*abbr of* **automatic data processing**) *n* the processing of large quantities of data by computer.

adrenalin [ə'drenəlɪn] *n* a hormone produced in a person's body when they are angry, afraid, or nervous that causes them to react more quickly than normal □ *I could feel the adrenalin pumping through me.*

Adriatic [ˌeɪdrɪ'ætɪk]: **the Adriatic (Sea)** the northeastern part of the Mediterranean Sea, between Italy and the Balkan countries.

adrift [ə'drɪft] ◇ *adj* **to be adrift** [boat] to be floating on the water and moved by the waves, current etc. ■ **to go adrift** [plan] to fail. ◇ *adv*: *The dinghy had been cut adrift.*

adroit [ə'drɔɪt] *adj* [person, answer] that is skillful, especially with words □ *It was an adroit move on her part.* □ *an adroit politician.*

ADT (*abbr of* **Atlantic Daylight Time**) *n* the local time used in summer in eastern Canada and parts of the West Indies.

adulation [ˌædʒə'leɪʃn] *n* a large amount of praise that is given to somebody by a lot of people, often when there is no reason for it. □ *The attitude of the fans bordered on adulation.*

adult [ə'dʌlt, 'ædʌlt] ◇ *adj* **-1.** [person, animal] that is physically mature □ *adult birds* □ *the adult male.* **-2.** [behavior, approach] that is what one expects from an adult person □ *Luckily they've been very adult about the whole thing.* **-3.** [movie, magazine] that is suitable for adults only, usually because of its sexual content □ *adult entertainment* □ *an adult bookshop.* ◇ *n* a physically mature person. □ *Try to behave like an adult* □ *'Adults only.'*

adult education *n* education for people who are no longer at school or college but who wish to continue studying, usually at evening classes.

adulterate [ə'dʌltəreɪt] *vt* to make <food or drink> weaker or less pure by adding a substance of lower quality □ *The wine had been adulterated with water.*

adulterer [ə'dʌltərər] *n* a person who commits adultery.

adultery [ə'dʌltərɪ] *n* sex between a married person and somebody who is not their husband or wife □ *He was accused of committing adultery on several occasions.*

adulthood ['ædʌlthʊd] *n* the period of somebody's life during which they are an adult □ *By the time they reach adulthood, the world will be a very different place.*

advance [US əd'væns, GB -'vɑːns] ◇ *n* -1. [of money] a sum of money lent or paid as part of a later payment □ *The bank gave me an advance of $500.* □ *They gave me an advance on my salary.* -2. [by an army] a movement forward □ *The rebels are planning an advance on the capital.* -3. [in a technique, subject] an improvement □ *There have been significant advances in transplant surgery.* -4. [at an auction] an increase in the price of an item being sold at an auction □ *Any advance on $200?* ◇ *comp* **an advance payment/warning** a payment/warning that happens before the usual or expected time □ *Advance reservations are advisable.* ◇ *vt* -1. **to advance sb's cause/interests** to help sb's cause/interests □ *Such acts of terrorism will do little to advance their cause.* -2. [date, event] to move <sthg> to an earlier time □ *The time of the meeting has been advanced by half an hour.* -3. **to advance sb a sum of money** to pay a sum of money to sb as part of a later payment □ *The bank advanced her $500.* ◇ *vi* -1. [enemy, troops] to move forward □ *The rebel army advanced on the capital.* -2. to make progress □ *Laser technology is advancing rapidly.*

◆ **advances** *npl* **to make advances to sb** to try to start a sexual or friendly relationship with sb □ *I discovered he had been making advances to my wife.*

◆ **in advance** *adv* before a particular event or time □ *It's advisable to reserve in advance.* □ *Let us know well in advance if you need a hotel.*

◆ **in advance of** *prep* -1. more modern and better than <sb/sthg else> □ *The design of this computer is far in advance of any of its rivals.* -2. before <an event or time> □ *They started selling tickets well in advance of the concert.*

advanced [US əd'vænst, GB -'vɑːnst] *adj* -1. [country, system] that has been developed and improved over a long period of time □ *France is technologically very advanced.* -2. [child, student, class] that has a high level of knowledge or ability □ *Toby is very advanced for his age.* -3. **to be at an advanced stage** to be nearly completed □ *Discussions are already at an advanced stage.*

advancement [US əd'vænsmənt, GB -'vɑːns-] *n* -1. [in somebody's career] promotion □ *All he's interested in is his own personal advancement.* -2. [of peace, a cause] progress □ *the advancement of science.*

advantage [US əd'væntɪdʒ, GB -'vɑːnt-] *n* -1. something that helps to put one in a better position □ *Knowledge of French would be an advantage.* □ *Working for a large company is a definite advantage.* -2. one of the good things about something □ *The advantage of this model is that it is low on energy consumption.* □ *Being foreign has its advantages.* ■ **to be to sb's advantage** to make sb more likely to succeed, be chosen etc □ *Your experience of working overseas can only be to your advantage.* ■ **to**

take advantage of sthg [of a situation, opportunity] to use sthg because it is helpful and available □ *I might take advantage of the cheap fares to go and visit my brother.* ■ **to take advantage of sb** to treat sb unfairly in order to improve one's own position □ *He's taking advantage of her good nature.* □ *I just felt I'd been taken advantage of.* -3. TENNIS the point scored after deuce.

advantageous [ˌædvən'teɪdʒəs] *adj* that helps to put one in a better position □ *We're now in a very advantageous position.* □ *These rates are particularly advantageous to first-time buyers.*

advent ['ædvent] *n* **the advent of sb/sthg** the time when sb/sthg first appears or becomes important (formal use) □ *the advent of war.*

◆ **Advent** *n* in the Christian calendar, the period of four weeks before Christmas.

Advent calendar *n* a large card showing a Christmas scene with little doors on it. One door is opened on each day of Advent, showing a picture behind it.

adventure [əd'ventʃər] *n* an exciting, interesting, and possibly dangerous experience □ *Tell us all about your adventures in China.* □ *He set off in search of adventure.* □ *What an adventure!*

adventure holiday *n* GB an organized vacation during which one can take part in various sports activities.

adventure playground *n* GB a small area of land where children can play on wooden or metal structures and equipment, e.g. tires and ropes.

adventurer [əd'ventʃərər] *n* -1. a person who likes adventure □ *She's quite an adventurer.* -2. a person who tries to get money or power by dishonest methods.

adventurous [əd'ventʃərəs] *adj* -1. [person] who is willing to take risks or try new experiences □ *They weren't very adventurous in their choice of music.* -2. [life, trip] exciting and dangerous □ *We had an adventurous few days.*

adverb ['ædvɜːrb] *n* a word that adds information to a verb, an adjective, another adverb, or a sentence, e.g. the word "quickly" in the sentence "He ran quickly."

adversary ['ædvərseri] (*pl* **adversaries**) *n* an opponent □ *Batman's old adversary, the Joker.*

adverse ['ædvɜːrs] *adj* -1. [comment, opinion, publicity] that is critical of somebody or something □ *Adverse publicity has badly affected sales.* -2. [circumstances, effects] that make it difficult to do something □ *The game was canceled due to adverse weather conditions.*

adversely ['ædvɜːrsli] *adv* **to be adversely affected** to be affected in a way that is harmful □ *The stock market was adversely affected by the allegations.*

adversity [əd'vɜːrsəti] *n* a situation that is difficult to deal with □ *They struggled on in the face of adversity.*

advert ['ædvɜːrt] *n* GB = **advertisement**.

advertise ['ædvərtaɪz] ◇ *vt* [product, property, job] to tell the public about <sthg> in a newspaper, on TV, radio, posters etc in order to make them interested in it □ *Where* *did you see the job advertised?* ◊ *vi* **-1.** *They advertised in all the local papers.* **-2. to advertise for sb/sthg** to try to get sb/sthg that one needs by placing an advertisement in a newspaper, magazine etc □ *They're advertising for a systems analyst.*

advertisement [US ‚ædvər'taɪzmənt, GB əd'vɜːtɪsmənt] *n* **-1.** a notice in a newspaper, a broadcast on TV etc that advertises something such as a product or service □ *Over a hundred people replied to the advertisement.* □ *I put an advertisement in the local paper.* **-2.** a person or thing that shows the advantages of something and is likely to persuade other people that it is a good thing □ *She's a great advertisement for the benefits of regular exercise.*

advertiser ['ædvər'taɪzər] *n* a person or company that pays for an advertisement to appear in a newspaper, on TV etc.

advertising ['ædvər'taɪzɪŋ] *n* the business of advertising products, services etc □ *She works in advertising.* □ *television/radio advertising.*

advertising agency *n* a business that plans, designs, and manages advertising for other companies.

advertising campaign *n* a number of advertisements, events etc that are organized over a period of time in order to advertise a product, service etc.

advice [əd'vaɪs] *n* something that one suggests to somebody as the best thing to do in a particular situation □ *She came to me for advice.* □ *Let me give you a piece of advice.* □ *I took* OR *followed your advice and complained.* □ *My advice to you is this...*

advice column *n* a section in a newspaper or magazine where readers are given advice about their emotional, financial, or health problems.

advice note *n* GB a note to a customer that gives information about goods that have been sent but not yet delivered.

advisability [əd‚vaɪzə'bɪlətɪ] *n: see* **advisable** □ *I question the advisability of making such a commitment.*

advisable [əd'vaɪzəbl] *adj* **to be advisable** to be a sensible thing to do □ *It's always advisable to book in advance.* □ *I hardly think that's advisable under the circumstances.*

advise [əd'vaɪz] ◊ *vt* **-1. to advise sb to do sthg** to tell sb what one thinks is the best way to act in a particular situation □ *I advised her to say nothing.* □ *I'd advise you to stay where you are.* ∎ **to advise sb against sthg** to suggest to sb that sthg is not a good idea □ *I'd advise you against another visit.* □ *He advised me against taking legal action.* **-2. to advise sb on sthg** to give professional and expert advice to sb about sthg □ *She advises the senator on all social policy matters.* **-3. to advise sb of sthg** to tell sb about sthg (formal use) □ *Please advise us of any amendments.*

◊ *vi* **-1. to advise against sthg** to suggest that sthg is not a good idea □ *I'd advise against going to meet him.* □ *I wanted to go but Helen advised against it.* **-2. to advise on sthg** to give

professional and expert advice about sthg □ *She advises on social policy.*

advisedly [əd'vaɪzədlɪ] *adv* deliberately □ *It's revolutionary — and I use the word advisedly.*

advisor US, **adviser** GB [əd'vaɪzər] *n* a person whose job is to give advice on a particular subject □ *a legal advisor.*

advisory [əd'vaɪzərɪ] *adj* [committee, organization] that gives advice □ *She was employed in an advisory capacity* OR *role.*

advocacy ['ædvəkəsɪ] *n* [of an idea, course of action] *see* **advocate** □ *her advocacy of reform.*

advocate [*n* 'ædvəkət, *vb* 'ædvəkeɪt] ◊ *n* **-1.** a person who supports and argues strongly for an idea or course of action □ *Green is a strong advocate of education reform.* **-2.** LAW a lawyer who speaks in court to represent somebody. ◊ *vt* to support and argue strongly for <sthg> □ *They advocate a complete overhaul of the system.* □ *The report advocates reducing defense spending.*

advt. *abbr of* **advertisement.**

AEA *n abbr of* **Atomic Energy Authority.**

AEC *n abbr of* **Atomic Energy Commission.**

AEEU (*abbr of* **Amalgamated Engineering and Electrical Union**) *n* **the AEEU** a large British labor union.

Aegean [ɪ'dʒiːən]: **the Aegean (Sea)** the eastern part of the Mediterranean, between Greece and Turkey.

aegis ['iːdʒɪs] ◆ **under the aegis of** *prep* with the support or help of <sb/sthg> □ *The conference was organized under the aegis of the university.*

aeon ['iːən] *n* GB = **eon.**

aerial ['eərɪəl] ◊ *adj* [combat, cable car] that happens or is situated in the air or above the ground; [photograph] that is taken from the air □ *an aerial shot of the factory.* ◊ *n* a device made of wire rods that is connected to a television or radio to help it receive signals □ *The aerial broke off in a car wash.* □ *They're putting a new aerial on the roof.*

aerobatics [‚eərə'bætɪks] *npl* skillful and difficult movements performed by an airplane to entertain people □ *an aerobatics display.*

aerobics [eə'roubɪks] *n* a form of very active exercise that is usually done in a class and accompanied by music.

aerodrome ['eərədroum] *n* an area of land, usually smaller than an airport, where aircraft can take off and land.

aerodynamic [‚eəroudaɪ'næmɪk] *adj* [car, train] that has been designed with a smooth shape to make it go faster or use less fuel □ *It has a new aerodynamic design.*

◆ **aerodynamics** ◊ *n* the study of how objects move through the air. ◊ *npl* [of a car, train] the aerodynamic qualities of a vehicle.

aerogramme ['eərəgræm] *n* an airmail letter written on a special sheet of paper which is folded and does not need an envelope or a stamp.

aeronautics [‚eərə'nɔːtɪks] *n* the study of flight and the design and construction of aircraft.

aeroplane ['eərəpleɪn] *n* GB = **airplane**.

aerosol ['eərəsɒl] *n* a container, usually a can, in which a substance such as paint, polish, or deodorant is kept under pressure and is forced out in the form of a fine spray when a button is pressed □ *an aerosol spray.*

aerospace ['eərouspeɪs] *n* **the aerospace indus-try** the design and construction of rockets, space vehicles etc.

aesthete [US 'esθiːt, GB 'iːs-] *n* a person who appreciates beauty in art and considers it to be very important.

aesthetic [US es'θetɪk, GB iːs-] *adj* [sense, appeal] that is connected with appreciating beauty.

aesthetically [US es'θetɪklɪ, GB iːs-] *adv* **aes-thetically pleasing** that is pleasing to look at.

aesthetics [US es'θetɪks, GB iːs-] *n* the study of beauty, especially in works of art.

afar [ə'fɑːʳ] *adv* **from afar** from a distance □ *People came from afar to witness the spectacle.*

AFB *n* US *abbr of* **Air Force Base**.

AFDC (*abbr of* **Aid to Families with Dependent Children**) *n* a US government program that pays money to poor families who have children under the age of 16.

affable ['æfəbl] *adj* [person] who is friendly, re-laxed, and easy to talk to □ *He seemed fairly affable.*

affair [ə'feəʳ] *n* -1. an event or series of events that has already been mentioned, or that has a particular quality □ *The whole affair was over in about ten minutes.* □ *The party was a riot-ous affair.* -2. [in politics] an important public event □ *the Contra affair.* -3. **one's own affair** something that concerns only oneself □ *How they spend the money is their own affair.* -4. [between two people] a secret sexual relation-ship between two people who are not mar-ried to each other □ *He's having an affair with his wife's best friend.*
 ◆ **affairs** *npl* -1. personal or private matters, especially connected with finance □ *I wish he wouldn't interfere in my affairs.* □ *She felt it was time to put her affairs in order.* -2. all the infor-mation and activities connected with a par-ticular subject □ *She's an expert on African af-fairs.* □ *our religious affairs correspondent* □ *af-fairs of state.*

affect [ə'fekt] *vt* -1. [person, place, thing] to cause <sb/sth> to change □ *How will these measures affect those already receiving welfare?* □ *the areas affected by the hurricane* □ *The dis-ease affects the joints of the feet and hands.* -2. [person] to make <sb> have strong feel-ings of pity, sadness etc □ *They were deeply affected by what they saw.* -3. [attitude, manner] to pretend to have <a particular feeling or way of behaving> (formal use) □ *He affected a southern accent.* □ *She affected indifference to the outcome.*

affectation [,æfek'teɪʃn] *n* an insincere and un-natural way of behaving □ *His eccentric clothes are just an affectation.*

affected [ə'fektəd] *adj* [person, behavior, accent] that is insincere and unnatural, and aimed at impressing other people □ *His voice always sounds so affected.*

affection [ə'fekʃn] *n* a feeling of great liking for somebody or something □ *Dad never showed her much affection.* □ *a sign of affection.*

affectionate [ə'fekʃnət] *adj* [person, manner, kiss] that shows affection □ *They're not very affectionate towards each other, are they?* □ *af-fectionate terms such as "darling" or "dear".*

affectionately [ə'fekʃnətlɪ] *adv* [smile, kiss] *see* **affectionate** □ *the Loch Ness monster, affection-ately known as "Nessie".* □ *Yours affectionately.*

affidavit [,æfə'deɪvɪt] *n* a written statement that one signs to say that it is true, and that may then be used as evidence in a court of law □ *a sworn affidavit.*

affiliate [*vb* ə'fɪlɪeɪt, *n* ə'fɪlɪət] ◇ *vt* **to be affiliat-ed to** OR **with sthg** [with a group, organization, company] to be attached to sthg larger □ *They are affiliated with the electrical workers' labor un-ion.* ◇ *n* a person, organization, or company that is affiliated to a larger organization □ *an affiliate member/organization.*

affiliation [ə,fɪlɪ'eɪʃn] *n*: *see* **affiliate** □ *They have no particular affiliation with any political party.*
 ◆ **affiliations** *npl* the things that one supports or has connections with □ *What are his politi-cal affiliations?*

affinity [ə'fɪnətɪ] (*pl* **affinities**) *n* -1. a feeling one has when one feels close to or able to understand somebody else because their ideas, qualities etc are similar to one's own □ *I felt a close affinity for* OR *with them.* □ *There was a deep affinity between them.* □ *She felt a natural affinity with the work.* -2. a close simi-larity or relationship □ *His work has certain af-finities with Rembrandt's early paintings.*

affirm [ə'fɜːrm] *vt* -1. [innocence, truth] to state that <sthg> is definitely true □ *The federal government affirmed that it would not cut welfare payments.* -2. to say that one supports <a be-lief, policy> etc □ *The council affirmed the right of the refugees to seek asylum.*

affirmation [,æfər'meɪʃn] *n*: *see* **affirm** □ *Follow-ing his affirmation that taxes would remain at their present level...* □ *Turner's previous affirma-tions have turned out to be untrue.*

affirmative [ə'fɜːrmətɪv] ◇ *n* **to answer in the affirmative** to say "yes". ◇ *adj*: *an affirmative answer/reply.*

affirmative action *n* the practice of giving jobs, university places etc to a particular group of people because they have been treated unfairly before.

affix [ə'fɪks] *vt* [stamp, label] to stick or attach <sthg> to something else (formal use) □ *'Affix stamp here.'*

afflict [ə'flɪkt] *vt* to cause <sb> great mental or physical suffering. ■ **to be afflicted with sthg** [with a disease, disability] to suffer from sthg.

affliction [ə'flɪkʃn] *n* something that causes mental or physical suffering, e.g. a disease (formal use) □ *the various afflictions associated with old age.*

affluence ['æfluəns] *n*: *see* **affluent** □ *For many years, they lived in comparative affluence.*

affluent ['æfluənt] *adj* [person] who has a lot of money and possessions □ *the affluent society.*

afford [ə'fɔːʳd] *vt* -1. **I/you/we etc can afford sthg** I/you/we etc have enough money to pay for or buy sthg □ *We can't afford a new car at the moment.* □ *How can they afford to eat out so often?* -2. **I/we etc cannot afford to do it** I/we etc must not do it because it will have harmful effects □ *The company simply cannot afford any adverse publicity.* □ *Can we afford to lose him?* ■ **I/you/we etc can't afford the time** I/you/we etc don't have enough time to do something □ *I'd love to come but I can't afford the time.* -3. to provide somebody with <protection, comfort> etc (formal use) □ *The tower affords a panoramic view of the city.*

affordable [ə'fɔːʳdəbl] *adj* [goods, prices] that one can easily afford □ *Quality clothes at affordable prices.*

afforestation [US ə,fɔːrə'steɪʃn, GB -,fɒrɪ-] *n* the process of planting large numbers of trees in a particular area.

affront [ə'frʌnt] ◇ *n* an action or remark that offends somebody □ *It was an affront to her pride.* ◇ *vt* **to feel affronted** to be offended □ *He was deeply affronted by the remark.*

Afghan ['æfgæn] *adj* & *n*: *see* **Afghanistan.**

Afghan hound *n* a tall thin dog with a long silky coat.

Afghani [æf'gænɪ] *adj* & *n*: *see* **Afghanistan.**

Afghanistan [US æf'gænəstæn, GB -staːn] a mountainous country in central Asia. SIZE: 650,000 sq kms. POPULATION: 16,600,000 (*Afghans, Afghanis*). CAPITAL: Kabul. LANGUAGE: Pashtu, Dari. CURRENCY: afghani.

afield [ə'fiːld] *adv* **far afield** far away □ *Visitors came from as far afield as Japan.*

AFL (*abbr of* **Australian Football League**) *n* **the AFL** the group of teams that play Australian Rules football.

AFL-CIO (*abbr of* **American Federation of Labor and Congress of Industrial Organizations**) *n* **the AFL-CIO** an association of US labor unions.

afloat [ə'fləut] *adj* -1. **to be afloat** [person] to be sailing in a boat or ship □ *We were afloat for two weeks.* -2. **to stay** OR **keep afloat** [person] to float on the surface of water; [business, company] to be able to continue to operate at a time of financial problems □ *The company just about managed to remain afloat by closing down one of its factories.*

afoot [ə'fut] *adj* **to be afoot** to be happening or being planned, especially in a secret way □ *There are plans afoot to bring in a team of outside consultants.*

aforementioned [ə,fɔːʳ'menʃnd], **aforesaid** [ə'fɔːʳsed] *adj* that has been mentioned earlier (formal use) □ *the aforementioned persons.*

AFP (*abbr of* **Australian Federal Police**) *n* **the AFP** the national police force of Australia.

afraid [ə'freɪd] *adj* -1. **to be afraid** to feel fear because one thinks that somebody or something is unpleasant, dangerous etc and might harm one □ *Don't be afraid, it won't hurt you.* □ *I'm afraid of heights.* □ *She's afraid of* walking home in the dark. □ *He was afraid to tell anyone about it.* -2. **to be afraid that...** to be worried that something unpleasant might happen, or might already have happened □ *I was afraid (that) they'd got lost.* □ *He was afraid of offending her.* □ *Don't be afraid to ask if you need anything.* -3. *phrases* **I'm afraid...** a polite phrase used when apologizing or disagreeing □ *I'm afraid I can't help you.* □ *I'm afraid (that) there's been a slight change of plan.* □ *I don't see the point of it, I'm afraid.* ■ **I'm afraid so** unfortunately yes □ *"Is he badly hurt?"* — *"I'm afraid so."* ■ **I'm afraid not** unfortunately no □ *"Can I see her now?"* — *"I'm afraid not."*

afresh [ə'freʃ] *adv* **to start afresh** to start doing something again, e.g. a piece of work, with the intention of doing things differently □ *Sometimes the best thing to do is just throw everything away and start afresh.*

Africa ['æfrɪkə] the second-largest continent, situated between the Atlantic Ocean and the Indian Ocean.

African ['æfrɪkən] *n* & *adj*: *see* **Africa.**

African American *n* a black American.

African violet *n* a plant, originally from Africa, that has purple, white, or pink flowers and rough leaves.

Afrikaans [,æfrɪ'kaːns] *n* a language, related to Dutch, that is spoken in South Africa.

Afrikaner [,æfrɪ'kaːnəʳ] *n* a white South African whose ancestors were Dutch.

Afro-Caribbean [,æfrəukærə'biːən] ◇ *n* a black person from the West Indies. ◇ *adj*: *Afro-Caribbean music/fashion.*

aft [US æft, GB aːft] *adv* at or toward the back of a ship, plane etc □ *'Lavatories aft.'*

AFT (*abbr of* **American Federation of Teachers**) *n* **the AFT** a US labor union for teachers.

after [US 'æftr, GB 'aːftə] ◇ *prep* -1. **after lunch/dinner** in the time following lunch/dinner □ *She got a job in London after leaving school.* ■ **after two weeks** at the end of two weeks. ■ **twenty after two/twelve** US twenty minutes past two/twelve o'clock. -2. **Y comes after X** Y follows X in position or order □ *She smoked one cigarette after another.* □ *Type the letters, put them into envelopes, and after that leave them in my in-tray.* -3. **to call after sb** to shout toward sb who is moving away □ *"Come back!" she called after him.* ■ **to clean up after sb/sthg** to clean up the dirt or damage created by sb/sthg □ *I'm fed up with tidying up after you lot!* ■ **shut the door after you** shut the door when you go out. ■ **after you!** used when one wants to be polite and allow somebody to do something first □ *She held the door open and said, "After you!"* -4. **after what you said** because of what you said □ *After what he did, I'll never speak to him again!* -5. **after everything I've done for you** in spite of everything that I have done for you □ *After all my hard work we still didn't get the contract.* -6. **to be after sb/sthg** to be looking for sb/sthg or trying to get sb/sthg □ *"Can I help you, sir?"* — *"Yes, I'm after a blue shirt."* □ *He's only after her money.* -7. **to be named after sb/sthg** to be called sthg because it is the name of sb/sthg else ◻ *They called their daughter Rose after her grandmother.* **-8. day after day** used to indicate that something is repeated every day ◻ *Night after night he lay awake, worrying.* **-9.** ART **a painting after Velázquez** a painting in the style of Velázquez.

◇ *adv* = **afterward** ◻ *He was badly hurt and died soon after.*

◇ *conj* used to introduce the event that happens first ◻ *After he left college he moved to Santa Fe.* ◻ *She waited until after the guests had gone home to tell us the news.*

◆ **after all** *adv* **-1.** although this did not seem likely before ◻ *I didn't believe her at first, but she was right after all.* **-2.** used to try to persuade somebody that one's opinion is correct, or to point out a reason that one thinks they have ignored ◻ *Don't get upset: after all, it's only a game.*

afterbirth [US 'æftrbɜːrθ, GB 'ɑːftəbɜːθ] *n* the term used to refer to the placenta and umbilical cord when they come out of a woman's womb just after her baby has been born.

aftercare [US 'æftrker, GB 'ɑːftəkeə] *n* GB the care or help that is officially offered to somebody after they come out of an institution such as a prison or hospital.

aftereffects [US 'æftərɪfekts, GB 'ɑːftər-] *npl* the unpleasant effects that result from something such as an accident, disaster, or medical treatment ◻ *She was still suffering from the aftereffects of her illness.*

afterlife [US 'æftrlaɪf, GB 'ɑːftə-] (*pl* **afterlives** [-laɪvz]) *n* in some religions, the life that one is believed to have after one dies.

aftermath [US 'æftrmæθ, GB 'ɑːftə-] *n* the period or situation that follows an event such as a war, storm, or disaster ◻ *In the immediate aftermath of the civil war many families were separated.*

afternoon [US ˌæftr'nuːn, GB ˌɑːftə-] *n* the part of the day between noon and about six o'clock ◻ *I often go for a walk in the afternoon.* ◻ *an afternoon flight.*

◆ **afternoons** *adv* [work, sleep] during the afternoon.

after-sales service *n* the service, e.g. repairs or advice, offered by a company to a customer after they have bought a product such as a car, computer, or washing machine.

aftershave [US 'æftrʃeɪv, GB 'ɑːftə-] *n* a liquid with a pleasant smell that men put on their face after shaving.

aftershock [US 'æftrʃɒk, GB 'ɑːftə-] *n* any of a series of small earthquakes that happens after the main part of an earthquake.

aftersun lotion [US 'æftrsʌn-, GB 'ɑːftə-] *n* a cream used on one's skin to help prevent it from peeling and feeling hot after one has been in the sun.

aftertaste [US 'æftrteɪst, GB 'ɑːftə-] *n* the taste that remains in one's mouth after eating or drinking something ◻ *It has a bitter aftertaste.*

afterthought [US 'æftrθɔːt, GB 'ɑːftə-] *n* an idea that comes into one's mind after one has already said or done something and that was not part of one's original thoughts ◻ *It had been added almost as an afterthought.*

afterward [US 'æftrwrd, GB 'ɑːftəwəd], **afterwards** [US 'æftrwrdz, GB 'ɑːftəwədz] *adv* a word used to say what happens after a particular event or time ◻ *Afterward we all went home.* ◻ *Are you doing anything afterward?*

again [ə'gen] *adv* **-1. say/do that again** say/do that one more time ◻ *We enjoyed the play so much we decided to see it again.* **-2. to be back home again** to be back at home in the same way as before ◻ *He's been very ill, but now he's well again.* **-3.** used to introduce another example or argument similar to the last one ◻ *If we look at the next graph, again we see signs of falling sales.* **-4.** used at the end of questions to ask for information to be repeated ◻ *Where do you live again?* **-5. as much again** the same amount that has already been mentioned.

◆ **again and again** *adv* many times ◻ *I've told him again and again, but he doesn't listen.*

against [ə'genst] ◇ *prep* **-1. to argue against sthg** to argue that it is not a good idea to do sthg ◻ *I'm not against the idea, in principle.* ■ **to advise sb against sthg** to advise sb not to do sthg ◻ *I warned him against buying it.* **-2. to fight/play against sb** to try to beat sb in a fight/game. ■ **the battle against rising crime** the battle to stop crime from getting worse. **-3. to lean against sthg** to lean so that one is touching or pressing on sthg ◻ *The heel of my shoe has been rubbing against my foot.* **-4. to do sthg against sb's wishes/instructions** not to follow sb's wishes/instructions ◻ *She was held against her will.* **-5. to be against the rules/regulations** not to be permitted by the rules/regulations ◻ *That's against the law!* **-6. to be against sb's interests** to be likely to harm sb's interests ◻ *They were accused of plotting against the state.* ◻ *The evidence against the accused couple is very strong.* **-7. to go against the wind** to go in the opposite direction to the wind ◻ *I had to swim against the tide to get back to shore.* **-8. insurance against loss/damage** insurance to protect oneself from loss/damage ◻ *You will need to be vaccinated against malaria.* **-9.** used to make a contrast or comparison. ■ **a tree stood out against the sky** a tree could be seen on a background of sky. ■ **the pound fell against the dollar** the value of the pound fell in comparison with the dollar.

◇ *adv* not in agreement with something ◻ *There were 240 votes in favor and 23 against.*

◆ **as against** *prep* used to compare or contrast two things ◻ *The company made a profit of $1m last year, as against a loss of $2m the year before.*

age [eɪdʒ] (*cont* **aging** OR **ageing**) ◇ *n* **-1.** the length of time that a person or animal has lived or a thing has existed ◻ *She's twenty years of age.* ◻ *He's about my age.* ◻ *She started playing the violin at the age of four* OR *at age four.* ◻ *Whiskey improves with age.* ■ **act your age!** stop behaving like a child! ■ **to be of age** to have reached an age when one is considered to be an adult, usually 18. ■ **to be under age** to be too young to be legally allowed to do something, e.g. buy alcohol or have sex. ■ **to come of age** to reach the age when one is considered to be an adult, usually 18. -2. the state of being old □ *He was bent with age.* □ *The documents were yellow with age.* -3. a particular period of one's life □ *The retirement age is 65.* □ *He's at* OR *of an age now where he's quite capable of making his own decisions.* -4. a period of time in history □ *the Age of Reason* □ *the computer age.* -5. **an age** a long time (informal use) □ *It took her an absolute age to do the work.*

◇ *vt* to make <sb> look older □ *The strain of the job had aged him considerably.*

◇ *vi* to look older □ *It was sad to see how much he had aged.*

◆ **ages** *npl* a long time (informal use) □ *That was ages ago.* □ *I haven't seen her for ages.* □ *It took ages to get here.*

🍃 AGE

The minimum age for voting in a US, British, or Australian election is 18. In most states of the USA the minimum age for drinking or buying alcohol is 21, while in Britain and Australia it is 18. The minimum age for driving a car in most states of the USA is 16, and in Britain and Australia it is 17. In the USA the retirement age is 65, while in Britain and Australia it is 65 for men and 60 for women.

---

aged [*adj sense 1* eɪdʒd, *adj sense 2 & npl* 'eɪdʒɪd] ◇ *adj* -1. **to be aged 10/20 etc** to be 10/20 etc years old □ *The children were aged between 8 and 15.* -2. **an aged parent** a very old parent □ *her aged father.* ◇ *npl* **the aged** people who are very old.

age group *n* all the people of a similar age, or whose ages are between two particular points □ *the 20 to 30 age group* □ *The game is suitable for all age groups.*

ageing ['eɪdʒɪŋ] *adj & n* = aging.

ageless ['eɪdʒləs] *adj* (literary use) [person, beauty] that never seems to grow old; [building, work of art] that never looks old-fashioned □ *Her writing has an ageless charm.*

agency ['eɪdʒənsɪ] (*pl* **agencies**) *n* -1. a business that provides a particular service for a company or person □ *I found my apartment through an agency.* □ *They run an employment agency.* □ *agency fees.* -2. an administrative organization, often run by a government □ *The operation is being coordinated by the various aid agencies.*

agenda [ə'dʒendə] (*pl* **agendas**) *n* a list of things to be discussed at a meeting □ *What's on the agenda today?* □ *The subject of possible takeovers is high on the agenda.*

agent ['eɪdʒənt] *n* -1. BUSINESS a person whose job is to provide a particular service as a representative of an organization □ *He's an agent for a large insurance company.* -2. ARTS a person who is paid by an actor, musician,

writer etc to find them work □ *a theatrical/literary agent* □ *You'll have to speak to my agent.* -3. CHEMISTRY a substance or chemical that has a particular effect on something else □ *a bleaching agent.* -4. = **secret agent.**

age-old *adj* [tradition, custom] that has existed for a very long time □ *The conflict was rooted in age-old prejudices.*

aggravate ['ægrəveɪt] *vt* -1. to make <a situation, problem, illness> etc worse □ *The speech only served to aggravate tensions within the community.* -2. to annoy <sb> very much □ *Stop aggravating her!*

aggravating ['ægrəveɪtɪŋ] *adj* [person, problem, behavior] that one thinks is very annoying □ *You can be so aggravating sometimes!*

aggregate ['ægrɪgət] ◇ *adj* [turnover, output, earnings] representing the total of several amounts added together □ *They have an aggregate income of $50,000 a month.* ◇ *n* -1. the total of several amounts added together □ *an aggregate of 20 years.* -2. the materials, e.g. sand and stone, that are added to cement to make concrete.

aggression [ə'greʃn] *n* -1. aggressive feelings □ *Signs of aggression in young adult males...* -2. aggressive behavior against a person or country □ *The invasion was condemned as an act of aggression.*

aggressive [ə'gresɪv] *adj* -1. [person] who seems ready to attack or fight other people without any reason; [tone, manner] that is angry and threatening □ *He becomes extremely aggressive when he's had too much to drink.* -2. [salesperson, competitor] who is forceful and determined to succeed; [plan] that is forceful and intended to be successful □ *an aggressive advertising campaign.*

aggressively [ə'gresɪvlɪ] *adv* [behave, speak, stare]. *see* **aggressive.**

aggressor [ə'gresər] *n* a person or country that attacks another person or country first.

aggrieved [ə'griːvd] *adj* **to feel aggrieved** to feel very upset and hurt because one thinks that one has been treated unfairly □ *I was aggrieved to learn they had gone ahead without notifying me.*

aghast [US ə'gæst, GB -'gɑːst] *adj* **to be aghast** to be filled suddenly with shock and surprise when one is told something or discovers something □ *She was aghast at the news.*

agile [US 'ædʒl, GB 'ædʒaɪl] *adj* -1. [person, animal] that is able to move quickly and easily □ *She's still very agile for her age.* -2. **an agile mind** a mind that is quick and intelligent.

agility [ə'dʒɪlətɪ] *n*: see **agile** □ *She climbed up onto the chair with remarkable agility.*

aging ['eɪdʒɪŋ] ◇ *adj* [population, machinery] that is growing older and is therefore considered less effective □ *a tired and aging leader.* ◇ *n* [of a person, population] the process of growing old □ *the aging process.*

agitate ['ædʒɪteɪt] ◇ *vt* -1. to make <sb> feel agitated. -2. to shake or stir <a liquid, mixture> etc. ◇ *vi* **to agitate for/against sthg** to argue for/against sthg, often by protesting in public, in order to change a particular situation.

agitated ['ædʒɪteɪtəd] *adj* [person] who cannot keep still, relax, or concentrate because they are worried and nervous □ *He got very agitated.*

agitation [ˌædʒɪ'teɪʃn] *n* a feeling of being agitated.

agitator ['ædʒɪteɪtər] *n* a person who campaigns in public for or against a particular cause or change.

AGM *n* GB *abbr of* **annual general meeting**.

agnostic [æg'nɒstɪk] ◇ *n* a person who believes it is impossible to say whether or not there is definitely a God. ◇ *adj*: *an agnostic upbringing.*

ago [ə'gəʊ] *prep* **five minutes ago** five minutes before now □ *I started working here two years ago.* □ *He died a long time ago.* □ *Not long ago the operation would have been impossible.*

agog [ə'gɒg] *adj* **to be agog** to be very curious and excited about something □ *I was all agog to see her new fiancé.*

agonize, -ise ['ægənaɪz] *vi* to spend a long time thinking and worrying about something □ *I agonized over* OR *about the decision for days.* □ *Don't agonize, just DO it!*

agonized ['ægənaɪzd] *adj* [face, scream] that shows that one is in agony □ *an agonized expression.*

agonizing ['ægənaɪzɪŋ] *adj* -1. [pain, wait] that causes agony. -2. [decision, choice] that is very difficult.

agonizingly ['ægənaɪzɪŋlɪ] *adv* **agonizingly slow** extremely slow □ *The wait was agonizingly long.*

agony ['ægənɪ] (*pl* **agonies**) *n* very great physical or mental suffering □ *She screamed out in agony.* □ *Later I experienced all the agonies of regret.*

agony aunt *n* a woman who gives advice about personal problems in newspapers or magazines or on the radio.

agony column *n* a section in a newspaper or magazine where readers are given advice about their personal problems.

agoraphobia [ˌægərə'fəʊbjə] *n* the fear of open spaces.

agree [ə'griː] ◇ *vi* -1. to have the same opinion as somebody else □ *"I think we should accept the offer." — "I agree."* □ *I agree with you about the new assistant. She's terrific.* ■ **I couldn't agree more** I agree completely. -2. to say yes to something □ *The lawyer tried everything to get him to sign but he wouldn't agree.* □ *They've finally agreed to our proposal.* -3. [figures, stories] to be the same □ *We did the same calculation but our results didn't agree.* -4. GRAMMAR to show a relationship with another word in a sentence by having a particular form, e.g. a feminine or plural ending □ *In French the adjective and the noun must agree* OR *the adjective must agree with the noun.* ◇ *vt* -1. [price, date, course of action] to decide <sthg> with somebody else □ *We still have to agree terms with our partners.* □ *The UN has*

agreed that sanctions must be imposed. -2. **to agree to do sthg** to say that one will do sthg □ *Management has agreed to meet with the unions.* -3. **to agree (that)...** to admit that something is true □ *I agree that it's not an easy task.*

◆ **agree on** *vt fus* **to agree on sthg** [on a price, date, course of action] to agree sthg □ *They can't agree on how best to market the product.*

◆ **agree with** *vt fus* -1. **to agree with sthg** [with a plan, opinion] to approve of sthg □ *I don't agree with his decision/with what he said.* -2. **it doesn't agree with me** it makes me feel unwell □ *I ate something that didn't agree with me.*

agreeable [ə'griːəbl] *adj* -1. [place, weather, experience] pleasant. -2. **to be agreeable** [person] to agree to an idea or suggestion □ *If he's agreeable, I'll let you know.* -3. **to be agreeable to sb** [suggestion, idea] to be acceptable to sb □ *I trust these terms are agreeable to you.*

agreeably [ə'griːəblɪ] *adv*: *see* **agreeable** □ *I was agreeably surprised by the results of the survey.*

agreed [ə'griːd] ◇ *adj* **to be agreed** to have the same opinion about something □ *Are we all agreed on the next step to take?* □ *We're agreed then that we'll meet again next month.* ◇ *adv* -1. a word used to show that one agrees with somebody or something □ *"So, I'll tell them no." — "Agreed."* -2. a word used before an argument or claim to weaken its force □ *Agreed it's not the cheapest product, but it's very reliable.*

agreement [ə'griːmənt] *n* -1. a situation in which everyone has the same opinion □ *After two days of discussion, the delegates finally reached an agreement.* □ *There was complete agreement among the board about how to proceed.* □ *The talks produced no agreement on any of the main issues.* ■ **to be in agreement with sthg** [with a decision, plan, idea] to think that sthg is a good idea. ■ **to be in agreement with sb** to have the same opinion as sb □ *I'm entirely in agreement with you on that point.* -2. the act of saying yes □ *We have to get their agreement before we go ahead with the plan.* -3. LAW & POLITICS a formal contract □ *The two countries signed an agreement on nuclear arms.* -4. GRAMMAR a form of a word that shows its grammatical relationship with another word in a sentence □ *In English, there is no agreement between the adjective and the noun.*

agricultural [ˌægrɪ'kʌltʃrəl] *adj* [land, machinery] *see* **agriculture** □ *Agricultural workers account for 20% of the workforce.*

agriculture ['ægrɪkʌltʃər] *n* the practice of growing crops and raising animals for food □ *The country's agriculture is suffering as a result.* □ *the Department of/Minister for Agriculture.*

aground [ə'graʊnd] *adv* **to run aground** [ship, boat] to become stuck in the shallow part of a sea, river, or lake □ *The tanker ran aground and began to leak oil.*

ah [ɑː] *excl* a sound that shows one is surprised, pleased, in pain etc □ *Ah, here it is!*

aha [ɑː'hɑː] *excl* a sound made to show that one has understood something or has made a discovery □ *Aha, so that's what you've been doing all this time!*

ahead [ə'hed] *adv* **-1.** in front □ *The road ahead was blocked by a van.* ■ **right** OR **straight ahead** directly in front □ *The bank is straight ahead.* **-2.** forward □ *The demonstrators charged ahead.* ■ **to go on ahead** to set out for a place so that one gets there before somebody else □ *I went on ahead to buy the tickets.* □ *You go on ahead. I'll catch up with you later.* ■ **to be sent on ahead** to be sent somewhere before other people or things □ *My luggage has been sent on ahead.* **-3.** in a stronger position than somebody else in a competition, election etc □ *The Republicans are ahead in the polls by 6%.* **-4.** in a better position than expected □ *We're well ahead on our sales figures for this month.* **-5. to lie ahead** to lie in the future □ *The recession means some difficult months ahead.* □ *I haven't thought that far ahead yet.* □ *She likes to plan ahead.*

◆ **ahead of** *prep* **-1.** in front of <sb> □ *There were three people ahead of him in the line.* **-2.** in a better position than <a competitor, target, classmate> etc □ *The Democrats are currently ten points ahead of the Republicans.* □ *They're miles ahead of their closest rivals.* **-3.** before <sb/sthg>; earlier than <sb/sthg> □ *Negotiations began well ahead of the summit meeting.* □ *Paris is one hour ahead of London.*

ahoy [ə'hɔɪ] *excl* a word used by sailors as a greeting. ■ **ship ahoy!** a phrase used to say that there is a ship approaching.

AI *n* **-1.** *abbr of* **Amnesty International. -2.** *abbr of* **artificial intelligence. -3.** *abbr of* **artificial insemination.**

aid [eɪd] ◇ *n* **-1. with/without the aid of sb/sthg** with/without the help of sb/sthg □ *He succeeded with/without the aid of government grants.* ■ **to come/go to sb's aid** to come/go to help sb who is in difficulty □ *Rescue teams went to the aid of the injured climber.* **-2.** [for a task] a device, piece of equipment etc that makes it easier to do something □ *a teaching/learning aid* □ *an invaluable aid to understanding.* **-3.** [to a country] money, food etc given to help another country □ *The USA has pledged billions of dollars in economic aid.* □ *foreign aid* □ *an aid package/organization.*

◇ *vt* **-1.** [person] to help <sb> to do something □ *The police, aided by local volunteers, soon found the missing child.* **-2.** [country] to provide money, food etc for <another country, organization> etc. **-3.** LAW **to aid and abet sb** to help sb to do something illegal.

◆ **in aid of** *prep* intended to raise money for <a cause or charity> □ *a concert in aid of famine relief.*

AID *n* **-1.** (*abbr of* **artificial insemination by donor**) = **DI. -2.** (*abbr of* **Agency for International Development**) **the AID** a US government department that gives money to developing countries.

aide [eɪd] *n* a person whose job is to help somebody important, e.g. a general or member of a government.

aide-de-camp [ˌeɪddə'kæmp] (*pl* **aides-de-camp** [ˌeɪd-]) *n* an officer in the army or navy who helps an officer of higher rank.

AIDS, Aids [eɪdz] (*abbr of* **acquired immune deficiency syndrome**) *n* a serious, usually fatal, disease caused by a virus that destroys the body's immune system □ *an AIDS patient* □ *the AIDS epidemic.*

aid worker *n* a person who works for an organization that provides food, shelter, or medical aid, especially to the Third World.

AIH *n abbr of* **artificial insemination by husband.**

ailing ['eɪlɪŋ] *adj* **-1.** [person] who is ill and not getting better □ *her ailing husband.* **-2.** [economy, company] that is having problems and is not successful enough □ *The news will be a boost for the ailing aircraft industry.*

ailment ['eɪlmənt] *n* an illness that is not usually serious □ *colds and other minor ailments.*

aim [eɪm] ◇ *n* **-1.** a plan that a person, organization etc hopes to carry out □ *Our aim is to expand next year.* □ *They had taken on extra staff with the aim of increasing output.* **-2. sb's aim** sb's skill at pointing a weapon or object correctly at something and hitting it □ *My aim isn't very good.* ■ **to take aim** to prepare to use a weapon or throw an object by holding it in the correct position and checking the direction □ *Joe took aim and fired.*

◇ *vt* **-1. to aim sthg at sb/sthg** [gun, camera] to point sthg at sb/sthg □ *The rifle was aimed at his head.* **-2. to be aimed at doing sthg** [plan, action] to be designed to make sthg happen □ *These measures are aimed at curbing inflation.* **-3. to be aimed at sb** [criticism, campaign] to be intended to be noticed by sb □ *These comments were aimed mainly at new recruits.*

◇ *vi* **-1.** to point a gun, camera etc at somebody or something □ *He aimed at the target, then fired.* **-2. to aim at** OR **for sthg** [at success, improvement] to hope to get or achieve sthg □ *You may not get to college, but it's something to aim for.* ■ **to aim to do sthg** to intend to do sthg □ *We're aiming to finish before the end of the week.*

aimless ['eɪmləs] *adj* [person, life, activity] without a purpose.

aimlessly ['eɪmləslɪ] *adv* [wander, look] *see* **aimless** □ *I wandered aimlessly through the store.*

ain't [eɪnt] (informal use) = **am not, are not, is not, have not, has not.**

air [eə^r] ◇ *n* **-1.** the mixture of gases that surround the Earth and that people breathe □ *I went out for a breath of fresh air.* □ *There was a nasty smell in the air.* **-2. the air** the space between the ground and the sky □ *The dog suddenly leapt into the air.* □ *The ball flew through the air.* **-3. by air** [go, travel] by plane □ *This time I went by air.* **-4.** [of a person, place, thing] a general appearance or quality □ *He has an air of mystery about him.* **-5.** MUSIC a tune (literary use). **-6.** RADIO & TV **to be on (the) air** to be broadcasting □ *We're on the air in ten minutes.* ■ **to go off (the) air** to stop broadcasting □ *They went off the air at midnight.* **-7.** *phrases* **to be in the air** [feeling] to be present but not discussed. ■ **to be up in the air** [decision, project] to be uncertain and not yet decided □ *Our plans for the summer are still up in the air.* ■ **to clear the air** to end a misunderstanding by speaking honestly □ *Tomorrow's meeting should help to clear the air.*

◇ *vt* **-1.** [washing, sheets] to remove any dampness or smells from <clothes or bedding> by putting it in a warm or dry place, or on a washing line □ *Make sure you air those shirts before you iron them.* **-2.** [bedroom, living room] to let fresh air into <a room> □ *I opened the windows to air the office.* **-3.** [thoughts, criticism] to express <one's opinions or feelings> about something □ *Would you care to air your views on the subject?* **-4.** [show, interview] to broadcast <a program> on the radio or television □ *The debate will be aired next week.*

◇ *vi* [washing, sheets] to become dry or fresh.

◆ **airs** *npl* **airs and graces** unnatural behavior that is intended to make one seem more important than one really is. ■ **to give oneself airs, to put on airs** to behave as if one is more important than one really is.

airbag ['eə'bæg] *n* a safety device in cars consisting of a bag that inflates in front of the driver or a passenger immediately after an accident to prevent them from being hurt when they are thrown forward.

airbase ['eə'beɪs] *n* a military airfield where military personnel live.

airbed ['eə'bed] *n* GB = **air mattress**.

airborne ['eə'bɔː'n] *adj* **-1.** [troops, regiment] that is trained to fight on the ground after landing from the air in enemy territory; [attack] that comes from the air. **-2. to be airborne** [plane, helicopter] to be flying in the air □ *We needed the whole runway to get airborne.*

airbrake ['eə'breɪk] *n* a brake that works by using compressed air and is found in trains, buses, trucks etc.

airbus ['eə'bʌs] *n* an airplane used for carrying large numbers of passengers on short flights.

air-conditioned [-kən'dɪʃnd] *adj* [room, building, car] that is kept cool and dry by air-conditioning.

air-conditioning [-kən'dɪʃnɪŋ] *n* a system of keeping the air in buildings and vehicles cool and dry □ *I'm lucky: my office has air-conditioning.* □ *an air-conditioning system.*

aircraft [US 'eə'kræft, GB 'eəkrɑːft] (*pl* **aircraft**) *n* any vehicle that can fly, e.g. a helicopter, glider, or airplane □ *20 different types of aircraft* □ *an aircraft manufacturer.*

aircraft carrier *n* a warship with a long flat deck that is used by aircraft for takeoff and landing.

air cushion *n* an inflatable cushion, usually made of plastic or rubber.

air fare *n* the cost of traveling to a place by plane.

airfield ['eə'fiːld] *n* an area where planes take off, land, and are kept in special buildings.

air force *n* the part of the armed forces

trained to defend and attack from the air □ *the US Air Force* □ *an air force base.*

Air Force One *n* the name of the aircraft used by the US president.

air freight *n* goods that are carried as cargo in an airplane.

air freshener [-freʃnə'] *n* a product that is used to make the air of a room, car etc smell pleasant.

airgun ['eə'gʌn] *n* a gun that uses compressed air to fire special bullets.

air hostess *n* GB a woman whose job is to take care of passengers on a plane.

airily ['eərəlɪ] *adv* [talk, promise] *see* **airy** □ *"Oh, I'll think of something," she replied airily.*

airing ['eərɪŋ] *n* **to give sthg an airing** [sheets, washing] to air sthg; [opinion, grievance, criticism] to discuss sthg with other people.

airing cupboard *n* GB a warm closet used for storing bedding, towels etc and for drying damp clothes.

airlane ['eə'leɪn] *n* a route through the air used by aircraft.

airless ['eə'ləs] *adj* [room, place] that does not have enough fresh air □ *a hot, airless day.*

airletter ['eə'letə'] *n* GB a sheet of thin paper that is already stamped for posting as a letter and that is folded and sent by airmail.

airlift ['eə'lɪft] ◇ *n* an operation in which people, troops, food etc are moved somewhere by air, especially when it is not possible to move them by land. ◇ *vt* to move <people, troops, food> etc in an airlift □ *The civilians were airlifted to safety.*

airline ['eə'laɪn] *n* a company that carries passengers and goods by air in airplanes □ *America's biggest airline* □ *an airline company.*

airliner ['eə'laɪnə'] *n* a large airplane used for carrying passengers.

airlock ['eə'lɒk] *n* **-1.** [in a tube, pipe] a bubble of air that prevents liquids from flowing through something. **-2.** [in a spacecraft, submarine] an airtight room or compartment situated between two places that have different air pressures.

airmail ['eə'meɪl] *n* the system of sending letters and parcels by air □ *'By airmail'* □ *an airmail letter.*

NOTE: Compare **surface mail**.

airman ['eə'mən] (*pl* **airmen** [-mən]) *n* **-1.** a man who serves in the air force. **-2.** a rank in the US Air Force.

air mattress *n* an inflatable mattress that is used as a bed or for lying on in the water.

Air Miles™ *npl* a system used by some British airlines, credit card organizations etc that gives vouchers to customers that can be exchanged for free flights.

airplane ['eə'pleɪn] *n* US a vehicle for traveling in the air that has wings and at least one engine.

airplay ['eə'pleɪ] *n* the number of times a record is played on the radio □ *Their latest record has had a lot of airplay.*

airpocket ['eə'pɒkət] *n* a current of air that

flows downward, causing an aircraft to lose height suddenly.

airport ['eəʳpɔːʳt] *n* a place where aircraft take off and land, with buildings in which passengers wait for their flights □ *airport security.*

air quality *n* the amount of pollution that is in the air at a particular time.

air raid *n* an attack by aircraft in which bombs are dropped.

air-raid shelter *n* a building used to protect people from bombs during an air raid.

air rifle *n* a rifle that uses compressed air to fire special bullets.

airship ['eəʳʃɪp] *n* an aircraft without wings that consists of a large long balloon with a compartment below it to carry passengers.

airsick ['eəʳsɪk] *adj* **to be airsick** to feel sick because of the movement of an aircraft.

airspace ['eəʳspeɪs] *n* the area of sky above a country that is considered to belong to that country □ *The plane had unwittingly entered Russian airspace.*

airspeed ['eəʳspiːd] *n* the speed at which an aircraft travels through the air.

air steward *n* a man whose job is to take care of passengers on a plane.

air strike *n* a military attack with bombs from aircraft.

airstrip ['eəʳstrɪp] *n* a long area of land used by aircraft for takeoff and landing.

air terminal *n* a building at an airport where passengers check in and wait before a flight.

air ticket *n* a ticket for traveling by plane.

airtight ['eəʳtaɪt] *adj* **-1.** [container, compartment] that does not allow air in or out □ *Store in an airtight container.* **-2.** [theory, argument] that does not contain any errors.

airtime ['eəʳtaɪm] *n* the time given to a program, item of news etc on the radio or TV □ *The trial got a lot of airtime.*

air-to-air *adj* **an air-to-air missile** a missile that is used by one aircraft against another.

air-traffic control *n* the work involved in checking the movement of aircraft in the air and telling pilots which routes to take; the people who carry out this work □ *Air-traffic control has notified us about possible delays.*

air-traffic controller *n* a person who works in air-traffic control.

air travel *n* travel by airplane.

airwaves ['eəʳweɪvz] *npl* **-1. on** OR **over the airwaves** broadcast on television or radio □ *The news came over the airwaves.* **-2.** radio waves used in broadcasting.

airy ['eərɪ] (*compar* **airier**, *superl* **airiest**) *adj* **-1.** [room, building] that gives a feeling of space and fresh air □ *Our new offices are light and airy.* **-2.** [attitude, smile] that shows one is not very serious about something □ *He gave an airy wave to the crowd.*

aisle [aɪl] *n* a passage between rows of seats in a church, airplane, theater etc or between rows of shelves in a store. ■ **an aisle seat** a seat next to the aisle in a bus, airplane etc.

ajar [ə'dʒɑːʳ] *adj* **to be ajar** [door] to be slightly open □ *Leave the door ajar.*

AK *abbr of* **Alaska.**

aka *abbr of* **also known as** □ *Marian Morrison, aka John Wayne.*

akin [ə'kɪn] *adj* **akin to sthg** similar to sthg □ *Pulling out would be akin to admitting defeat.*

AL *abbr of* **Alabama.**

Alabama [ˌælə'bæmə] a state in the southeastern USA where the civil rights movement began. ABBREVIATION: AL. SIZE: 131,333 sq kms. POPULATION: 4,040,587 (*Alabamans*). CAPITAL: Montgomery.

alabaster [US ˌælə'bæstr, GB -'bɑːstə] *n* a white stone used for making ornaments □ *an alabaster statue.*

à la carte [US ˌɑːlə'kɑːrt, GB ˌælə'kɑːt] ◇ *adj* **an à la carte menu** a menu that lists a separate price for each dish. ◇ *adv* [eat, dine] by choosing dishes from the à la carte menu. NOTE: Compare **table d'hôte.**

alacrity [ə'lækrətɪ] *n* eagerness (formal use) □ *He replied with alacrity.*

Aladdin [ə'lædɪn] a character in an Arabian folk story who finds a magic lamp in a cave full of treasure. When he rubs the lamp a genie appears and offers to make his wishes come true.

Alamo ['æləmoʊ]: **the Alamo** a fort in Texas that was attacked by a large Mexican force in 1836. The courage of Davy Crockett and his men, who died defending it, inspired other Texans to fight for independence from Mexico.

à la mode [US ˌɑːlə'moʊd, GB ˌælə-] *adj* US [dessert] served with ice cream □ *apple pie à la mode.*

alarm [ə'lɑːʳm] ◇ *n* **-1.** [feeling] a feeling of fear or worry □ *They viewed the proposals with some alarm.* **-2.** [object] a device, e.g. a bell or flashing light, that gives a warning of something or draws attention to something □ *They set off the smoke/car alarm by mistake.* ■ **to raise** OR **sound the alarm** to tell everybody that there is a particular danger □ *The alarm was raised by a night watchman.* **-3.** = **alarm clock.** ◇ *vt* to cause <sb> to feel alarm □ *They were alarmed by his wild appearance.*

alarm call *n* a telephone call made to a hotel guest in the morning to wake them up □ *I'd like an alarm call for seven.*

alarm clock *n* a clock that can be set to wake somebody up at a particular time.

alarmed [ə'lɑːʳmd] *adj* **-1.** [person] who is feeling alarm □ *I was alarmed at the lack of safety precautions.* **-2.** [vehicle, safe] that is fitted with an alarm.

alarming [ə'lɑːʳmɪŋ] *adj* [situation, problem, increase] that causes alarm □ *The floodwaters are reported to be rising at an alarming rate.*

alarmingly [ə'lɑːʳmɪŋlɪ] *adv* [increase, speak] *see* **alarming** □ *Levels of pollution are alarmingly high/have risen alarmingly.*

alarmist [ə'lɑːʳməst] *adj* [person] who causes unnecessary alarm in other people □ *There* *were alarmist reports of an escaped puma prowling the area.*

alas [ə'læs] *excl* a word used to express one's regret (formal use) □ *This is, alas, the end.*

Alaska [ə'læskə] the largest state in the USA in the far northwest of North America. ABBREVIATION: AK. SIZE: 1,530,000 sq kms. POPULATION: 550,043 (*Alaskans*). CAPITAL: Juneau.

Albania [æl'beɪnjə] a country in southeastern Europe. It was a Communist state from 1946 to 1991. SIZE: 29,000 sq kms. POPULATION: 3,300,000 (*Albanians*). CAPITAL: Tirana. LANGUAGE: Albanian. CURRENCY: lek.

albatross ['ælbətrɒs] (*pl* **albatross** OR **albatrosses**) *n* a large white seabird that can fly long distances.

albeit [ɔːl'biːɪt] *conj* although; even though (formal use) □ *He was, albeit briefly, a captain in the army.*

Albert ['ælbət], **Prince** (1819–1861) the husband of Queen Victoria. He became the Queen's chief adviser.

Alberta [æl'bɜːtə] a province in western Canada. ABBREVIATION: AB. SIZE: 661,000 sq kms. POPULATION: 2,545,553 (*Albertans*). CAPITAL: Edmonton.

Albert Hall: the Albert Hall a large concert hall in London, named after Prince Albert.

albino [US æl'baɪnoʊ, GB -'biːnoʊ] (*pl* **albinos**) *n* a person or animal that has a medical condition that gives them white skin, white hair, and pink eyes □ *an albino rabbit.*

album ['ælbəm] *n* -1. (for stamps, photos) a book with blank pages used for keeping and displaying particular things □ *a photo album.* -2. MUSIC a collection of songs or pieces of music, usually recorded on two sides of a record or cassette, each side lasting about 25 minutes □ *the band's latest album.*

albumen [US æl'bjuːmən, GB 'ælbjʊmɪn] *n* the colorless part of a raw egg (technical use).

alchemy ['ælkəmɪ] *n* a type of chemistry, practiced in the Middle Ages, that tried to find ways of turning all metals into gold.

alcohol ['ælkəhɒl] *n* -1. the colorless liquid in beer, wine, and spirits that makes people drunk and is used as a solvent. -2. drinks containing alcohol □ *I never touch alcohol.* □ *alcohol abuse.*

alcoholic [ˌælkə'hɒlɪk] ◇ *adj* -1. that contains alcohol □ *sales of alcoholic drink.* -2. that is caused by alcohol □ *an alcoholic stupor.* ◇ *n* a person who is addicted to alcohol.

alcoholism ['ælkəhɒlɪzm] *n* the condition of being addicted to alcohol.

alcove ['ælkoʊv] *n* the part of a room formed when one section of a wall is built further back than the rest.

alder ['ɔːldər] *n* a tree that grows in Northern regions and has cones and leaves with pointed edges.

alderman ['ɔːldərmən] (*pl* **aldermen** [-mən]) *n* in the USA, Canada, and Australia, a person who is a local government official.

ale [eɪl] *n* a name given to several types of beer.

alert [ə'lɜːrt] ◇ *adj* -1. (person) who is careful to notice things, especially possible dangers □ *They are trained to be alert at all times.* -2. (person) who can think and understand things clearly □ *She may be old, but she's still very alert.* -3. **to be alert to sthg** (to a danger, difficulty, problem) to be aware of sthg □ *He was alert to the risks involved.*
◇ *n* a warning of danger □ *a security alert.* ■ **to be on the alert** to pay full attention and be ready to act, usually after a warning of danger, attack etc □ *Passengers have been told to be on the alert for pickpockets.* □ *Troops have been put on the alert.*
◇ *vt* to warn <sb> about something □ *The campaign is designed to alert schoolchildren to the dangers of drugs.*

A level (*abbr of* **Advanced level**) *n* a school examination taken at the age of 18 in England and Wales. Students usually take three or four A levels in different subjects. They are necessary to get accepted for university.

Alexander technique [US ˌælɪg'zændr-, GB ˌælɪg'zɑːndə-] *n* **the Alexander technique** a technique for changing the way one sits, stands etc that aims to reduce stress and improve one's health.

Alexander the Great (356–323 BC) King of Macedonia from 336 to 323 BC. He created a large empire by conquering Greece, Egypt, and large areas of central and western Asia.

Alexandria [US ˌælɪg'zændrɪə, GB -'zɑːndrɪə] a city and the main port in Egypt, on the Mediterranean. It was an important cultural center of the ancient world. POPULATION: 2,719,000.

alfalfa [æl'fælfə] *n* a plant that is grown for animal food and for its shoots that can be eaten as a vegetable.

alfresco [æl'freskoʊ] ◇ *adj* (meal) that is eaten outside in the open air. ◇ *adv* (eat) *We picnicked alfresco in the garden.*

algae ['ældʒiː] *npl* plants with no stems or leaves that grow in or near water, e.g. seaweed.

Algarve [US ɑː'gɑːrvə, GB æl'gɑːv]: **the Algarve** a region of southern Portugal that is a popular tourist area.

algebra ['ældʒəbrə] *n* a type of math that uses letters and symbols to represent numbers.

Algeria [æl'dʒɪərɪə] a country in northwest Africa, consisting mostly of desert. In the 1950s and 1960s a war of independence was fought against France. SIZE: 2,380,000 sq kms. POPULATION: 27,300,000 (*Algerians*). CAPITAL: Algiers. LANGUAGE: Arabic. CURRENCY: dinar.

Algonquin [æl'gɒŋkwɪn] (*pl* **Algonquin**) *n* a member of a Native American people who used to live in eastern Canada; the language of this people.

algorithm ['ælgərɪðm] *n* a list of instructions, e.g. in a computer program, used to solve a problem, do calculations etc.

alias ['eɪlɪəs] (*pl* **aliases**) ◇ *adv* also called □ *Stein and Janovich, alias Smith and Jones.* ◇ *n* a false name, often used by somebody who is involved in illegal activities □ *She assumed several aliases throughout her criminal career.*

alibi ['ælɪbaɪ] *n* a person, fact, or piece of evidence that proves that somebody who has been accused of a crime was somewhere else when the crime was committed □ *He's got the perfect alibi.*

Alice Springs [,ælɪs'sprɪŋz] a town in central Australia and a popular tourist resort. POPULATION: 23,600.

alien ['eɪljən] ◇ *adj* -1. [society, culture] that is foreign □ *These people come from an alien culture.* -2. [creature, being] that comes from outer space □ *an alien life form.* -3. [practice, behavior] that is unfamiliar □ *Such beliefs are totally alien to our way of thinking.* ◇ *n* -1. a creature from outer space □ *aliens from Mars.* -2. LAW a foreigner □ *All aliens must register with the local authorities.*

alienate ['eɪljəneɪt] *vt* -1. to make <sb> less sympathetic to one's point of view, opinion etc □ *This policy will alienate voters.* -2. **to be alienated from sthg** [from society, one's surroundings] to feel separate from sthg and not involved with it □ *He felt alienated from the other children there.*

alienation [,eɪljə'neɪʃn] *n: see* **alienate** □ *a growing feeling of alienation.*

alight [ə'laɪt] (*pt & pp* **alighted**) ◇ *adj* **to be alight** [fuel, candle] to be burning □ *Soon the whole building was alight.* ■ **to set sthg alight** to make sthg start burning □ *The car was set alight by vandals.* ◇ *vi* (formal use) -1. [bird, insect] to land □ *The butterfly alighted on a leaf.* -2. [passenger] to get off a bus, train etc □ *'Passengers for Heathrow please alight here.'*

align [ə'laɪn] *vt* -1. to put <two parts, edges> etc into the correct position in relation to each other, especially in a parallel position □ *Align the columns with the top of the page.* □ *You'll have to have the wheels aligned.* -2. **to align oneself with sb** to declare one's support for sb □ *They have aligned themselves with the party rebels.*

alignment [ə'laɪnmənt] *n* -1. the position of something in relation to something else. ■ **in/out of alignment** correctly/not correctly aligned. -2. the act of joining a group of people or countries that share the same political aim □ *the alignment of Canada with the rest of the G7 countries* □ *a military alignment.*

alike [ə'laɪk] ◇ *adj* **to be alike** [people, things] to be similar in appearance, behavior etc □ *She and I are very alike.* ◇ *adv* -1. in a similar way □ *Everybody is treated alike.* -2. **young and old alike** both young people and old people □ *The pay cuts affect blue- and white-collar workers alike.*

alimentary canal [,ælɪmentrɪ-] *n* the passage leading from the mouth to the anus through which food passes.

alimony [US 'æləmouni, GB -məni] *n* the money that a court orders a person to pay to their husband or wife after a divorce or legal separation.

A-line *adj* [skirt, dress] that is wider at the bottom than at the top.

alive [ə'laɪv] *adj* -1. **to be alive** [person, animal] to be living; [practice, tradition] to exist; [person] to be full of energy □ *Is he still alive?* □ *They were buried alive in the rubble.* □ *It is important to keep the custom alive.* □ *She had never felt so alive.* ■ **to come alive** [story, description] to become interesting and hold one's attention; [person, place] to become lively □ *The main character never really comes alive.* □ *The resort comes alive in summer.* -2. **to be alive to sthg** [to a problem, situation] to be aware of sthg □ *They are alive to the threat posed by cheap imports.* -3. **to be alive with sthg** [with people, animals] to be full of sthg □ *The whole town was alive with rumor and speculation.*

alkali ['ælkəlaɪ] (*pl* **alkalis** OR **alkalies**) *n* a substance, e.g. soda or ammonia, that neutralizes an acid.

NOTE: Compare **acid**.

alkaline ['ælkəlaɪn] *adj* [chemical, solution] that contains an alkali or has a pH value of more than 7.

NOTE: Compare **acidic**.

all [ɔːl] ◇ *det & predet* -1. **all the trains were late** every one of the trains was late □ *I've read all her books.* □ *All three men died in the crash.* □ *You have to consider all aspects of the problem.* ■ **for children of all ages** for children of every possible age. -2. **I've done all the work** I've done the whole of the work □ *He ate all his dinner.* ■ **she slept all night** she slept for the whole of the night □ *I've known them all my life.*

◇ *pron* -1. **they all smoke, all of them smoke** every one of them smokes □ *You can't all come!* □ *They all got home safely in the end.* -2. **I can't eat it all** OR **all of it** I can't eat the whole amount of it. ■ **take it all** OR **all of it** take everything. ■ **he gave his all** he tried as hard as he possibly could. -3. **all (that) I need is some sleep** the only thing that I need is some sleep □ *You're all I've got.*

◇ *adv* -1. **dressed all in black** dressed completely in black. ■ **all alone** completely alone. ■ **I forgot all about it** I forgot it totally. -2. SPORT **fifteen all** each team or player has scored fifteen goals, points etc □ *The match ended in a one-all draw.* -3. **all the better/quicker** even better/quicker than before □ *Her honesty made me respect her all the more.*

◆ **all but** *adv* **I all but gave up** I almost gave up.

◆ **all in all** *adv* when everything is considered □ *All in all, we've had a pretty good day.*

◆ **all of** *adv* **it's all of two meters tall** it's two meters tall, which is surprisingly tall (used with numbers or amounts) □ *There must have been all of 10,000 people there.*

◆ **all over** *prep & adv* everywhere □ *I've been looking all over for you.*

◆ **all that** *adv* **she's not all that pretty** OR **not as pretty as all that** she is not especially pretty (used after negatives) □ *To be perfectly honest, I never knew her all that well.*

◆ **all told** *adv* in total, when everybody or everything has been counted □ *There were two Americans, four Britons, and three Canadians — nine all told.*

Allah ['ælə] *n* the Muslim name for God.

all-American *adj* [person] who has the qualities that are considered typical or admirable in Americans, such as fitness, wealth, and a strong sense of patriotism □ *He's an all-American guy.*

all-around US, **all-round** GB *adj* -1. [athlete, worker] who has many different skills, abilities etc □ *The job calls for someone with good all-around skills.* -2. [education] general; [increase, improvement] in all areas.

allay [ə'leɪ] *vt* [fear, anger, doubt] to cause <a feeling> to be less strong (formal use) □ *The statement failed to allay public fears of higher interest rates.*

all clear *n* -1. **the all clear** a signal that is given when a dangerous situation, e.g. an air raid, has ended. -2. **to get the all clear** to get permission to proceed with a plan, project etc □ *We haven't been given the all clear from our head office yet.*

allegation [,ælə'geɪʃn] *n* a statement made, without proof, that somebody has done something wrong or illegal □ *A number of allegations have been made about the director.*

allege [ə'ledʒ] *vt* **to allege that...** to say officially that something is true or exists without proving it □ *They allege that no money ever changed hands.* □ *Horner is alleged to have bribed a witness.*

alleged [ə'ledʒd] *adj* [fact, atrocity, misconduct] that is not certain because there is no proof of it □ *The alleged crime took place last May.*

allegedly [ə'ledʒədlɪ] *adv* a word used to show that one is reporting information that has not yet been proved to be true □ *He was allegedly involved in an arms deal.*

allegiance [ə'liːdʒəns] *n* [to a country, king, religion] support for and loyalty to somebody or something □ *All children had to pledge allegiance to the flag.*

allegorical [,ælə'gɒrɪkl] *adj* [story, scene, work] that uses allegory.

allegory [US 'æləgɔːrɪ, GB -gərɪ] (*pl* **allegories**) *n* a story, scene, picture etc in which the characters, events, or images are used to represent something else in order to give people a particular message; the style of writing, painting etc that uses this technique □ *The painting can be seen as an allegory of love.*

alleluia [,ælɪ'luːjə] *excl* = **hallelujah.**

allergic [ə'lɜːrdʒɪk] *adj* [reaction, rash] that is caused by an allergy. ■ **to be allergic to sthg** to have an allergy to sthg □ *I'm allergic to dust/cats.*

allergy ['ælədʒɪ] (*pl* **allergies**) *n* a medical condition that causes somebody to become ill because they are sensitive to particular animals, foods etc □ *a dust/food allergy* □ *I have an allergy to cats/milk.*

alleviate [ə'liːvɪeɪt] *vt* [pain, suffering, poverty] to make <an unpleasant feeling or situation> less serious and easier to deal with (formal use) □ *This lotion should alleviate some of the swelling.*

alley(way) ['ælɪ(weɪ)] *n* a narrow passage between two buildings.

alliance [ə'laɪəns] *n* -1. an agreement between people, countries, political parties etc that share the same beliefs, aims etc; the people, countries etc that sign this agreement □ *They have entered into an alliance with the Christian Democrats.* □ *the Western alliance.* -2. the act of forming an alliance □ *In alliance with other charities, we hope to raise one million dollars.*

allied ['ælaɪd] *adj* -1. [powers, troops] that are united by a political agreement □ *Allied troops entered Germany.* -2. [subjects, matters] that are related, usually because they are similar □ *shipbuilding and other allied industries.*

alligator ['ælɪgeɪtər] (*pl* **alligator** OR **alligators**) *n* a large reptile similar to a crocodile that lives in the USA and China. It is found on land and in rivers and lakes.

all-important *adj* [decision, meeting, letter] very important.

all-in *adj* GB [price, cost] including all charges. ◆ **all in** ◇ *adv* GB *The deal will cost $350, all in.* ◇ *adj* **to feel all in** to feel very tired.

all-inclusive *adj* with everything included □ *an all-inclusive package tour to Hawaii.*

all-in-one *n* a single piece of clothing that covers all of one's body, used especially for sports.

all-in wrestling *n* a type of professional wrestling that has very few agreed rules.

alliteration [ə,lɪtə'reɪʃn] *n* the deliberate repetition of the same sound or letter in a piece of speech or writing to produce a particular effect.

all-night *adj* [party, vigil, session] that lasts all night; [store, cinema] that is open all night.

allocate ['æləkeɪt] *vt* -1. **to allocate sthg to sb/sthg** [money, time, resources] to give sthg to sb/sthg for a particular purpose □ *Ten percent of the budget is allocated to research.* □ *Each speaker has been allocated 30 minutes.* -2. [task, responsibility] to give <a job> to a particular person, department etc □ *Which projects have you been allocated?*

allocation [,ælə'keɪʃn] *n* -1. [for something or somebody] the amount of money, resources, tickets etc allocated for somebody or something □ *We've only been given a small allocation of seats this year.* -2. [of money, responsibility] *see* **allocate** □ *Allocation of resources is always a difficult business.*

All-ordinaries *npl* **the All-ordinaries index** a guide to the changes in share prices, based on an average of top companies on the Australian Stock Exchange.

allot [ə'lɒt] (*pt* & *pp* **allotted**, *cont* **allotting**) *vt* to give a share of <the available money, resources, time> etc to somebody or something for a particular purpose □ *The funds allotted to the project are barely adequate.* □ *It is essential to complete the work in the allotted time.* □ *You are allotted one hour per question.*

allotment [ə'lɒtmənt] *n* -1. the amount of money, resources, time etc allotted □ *How big is your allotment of the budget?* -2. GB a part of an area of land in a town or city that is rented by somebody for growing vegetables, flowers etc.

all-out *adj* [effort, war, strike] that is aggressive and determined and uses all available resources □ *Rebels launched an all-out attack on government forces.*

◆ **all out** *adv* **to go all out** to make the greatest possible effort □ *We're going all out to get that contract.*

allow [ə'laʊ] *vt* -1. to let <sthg> happen without trying to stop it; to let <a person, animal> etc enter a particular place □ *They don't allow smoking/talking.* □ *Children are not allowed in the bar area.* ■ **to allow sb to do sthg** to let sb do sthg without trying to stop them □ *We are not allowed to make personal phone calls from the office.* □ *Allow the wine to stand at room temperature.* ■ **allow me** a phrase used when one offers to do something for somebody else □ *Allow me to open the door for you.* ■ **allow me to introduce myself** a formal phrase that one says before one introduces oneself. -2. [money, time] to make <a particular amount of sthg> available for a particular purpose □ *Allow 28 days for delivery.* □ *I've allowed three weeks for this job.* -3. **to allow sb sthg** to let sb have sthg □ *We're allowed a ten-minute break every hour.* -4. [application, claim] to accept <sthg> as being legal, correct, or proper □ *The referee refused to allow the goal.* □ *The legal procedure allows no appeal.* -5. **to allow (that)...** to admit that something is true □ *I'll allow that he's only partly to blame.*

◆ **allow for** *vt fus* **to allow for sthg** [for changes, delays, increases] to take sthg that might happen into consideration when planning something □ *We must allow for price increases.* □ *That's $25,000, allowing for inflation.*

allowable [ə'laʊəbl] *adj* [behavior, practice] acceptable.

allowance [ə'laʊəns] *n* -1. [for spending] money given to somebody to help them pay for something they need, e.g. clothes, travel etc □ *a cost-of-living allowance* □ *His parents give him a monthly allowance of $100.* -2. [for baggage] the amount of a particular thing that one is allowed to have □ *Your duty-free allowance is 200 cigarettes.* -3. GB FINANCE an amount of money one can earn without paying tax on it. -4. *phrases* **to make allowances for sb** to excuse sb's bad behavior because of their special circumstances, problems etc □ *You'll have to make allowances for him — he's had a hard time.* ■ **to make allowances for sthg** to allow for sthg □ *You have to make allowances for inflation.*

alloy ['ælɔɪ] *n* a metal made from two or more different metals.

all-powerful *adj* [leader, organization] that has complete control.

all right ◇ *adv* -1. [behave, work] in a way that is good enough □ *The fax is working all right again now.* □ *We're doing all right at the moment.* □ *The interview went all right.* -2. yes (informal use) □ *"Will you come to the meeting?"* — *"All right."* -3. a word used to emphasize that something is true □ *It's a challenge all right!* -4. a word used to check that somebody has understood something □ *So, you put the paper in here, all right?* -5. a word used to attract somebody's attention □ *All right, everyone, if we could get down to business.*

◇ *adj* -1. [person, animal] that is not ill, upset, or in danger □ *I hope she's all right.* -2. [object, movie, person] that one thinks is good enough □ *"How was the interview?"* — *"All right, I suppose."* -3. that one thinks is acceptable □ *Is it all right if I make a phone call?* -4. *phrase* **it's/that's all right** a phrase used as a reply to thanks or an apology □ *"Sorry I wasn't there to meet you."* — *"That's all right."* □ *"Thanks for everything."* — *"That's all right."*

all-round *adj* GB = **all-around**.

all-rounder [-'raʊndəʳ] *n* GB a person who has many different skills, abilities etc.

all-time *adj* **an all-time low/best etc** a level that is lower/better etc than ever before □ *The stock market is at an all-time high.* □ *Gibson beat his all-time record.*

allude [ə'luːd] *vi* **to allude to sb/sthg** to talk about sb/sthg in an indirect way □ *What exactly are you alluding to?*

allure [ə'lʊəʳ] *n* [of money, a person, place] an attractive or exciting quality □ *the allure of the Greek islands.*

alluring [ə'lʊərɪŋ] *adj* [person, place] that is very attractive □ *She has an alluring smile.*

allusion [ə'luːʒn] *n* a reference to somebody or something that is made in an indirect way □ *He made no allusion to the recent controversy over his appointment.*

ally [*n* 'ælaɪ, *vb* ə'laɪ] (*pl* **allies**, *pt* & *pp* **allied**) ◇ *n* -1. MILITARY & POLITICS a country that has an agreement with another country to help and support it, e.g. during a war □ *a military ally.* -2. a person who helps and supports somebody else, especially when they face opposition □ *Chalmers is relying on her allies on the board to back her up.* ◇ *vt* **to ally oneself with sb/sthg** [with a country, organization] to support sb/sthg, especially when they face opposition □ *They have allied themselves with the government.*

◆ **Allies** *npl* **the Allies** the countries that fought on the same side as the USA and Britain during World War I and II.

almanac ['ɔːlmənæk] *n* a book that is published every year and gives information about the movements of the sun, moon, tides etc as well as important dates.

almighty [ɔːl'maɪtɪ] *adj* **an almighty bang/crash** a very big or loud bang/crash (informal use) □ *We had an almighty row!*

◆ **Almighty** ◇ *adj* who has power over everything □ *Almighty God.* ◇ *n* **the Almighty** a name used to refer to God.

almond ['ɑːmənd] *n* -1. a flat oval-shaped nut that is eaten raw or used in cooking □ *roast/*

ground almonds. **-2. an almond (tree)** a tree that produces almonds.

almond paste *n* a sweet paste made from crushed almonds, sugar, and eggs that is used to cover cakes or to make candies.

almost ['ɔːlmoʊst] *adv* **almost ready** nearly ready but not completely ready □ *I've been ill, but I'm almost better now.* □ *Almost everyone agrees with me.* □ *We were late and almost missed the plane.* □ *"Have you finished?" — "Almost!"* ■ **almost nobody** very few people.

alms [ɑːmz] *npl* money, food, clothes etc that are given to poor people (old-fashioned use).

aloft [ə'lɒft] *adv* **-1.** [hold, raise] in the air and over one's head (formal use) □ *He held the child aloft.* **-2.** SAILING in the rigging of a ship.

alone [ə'loʊn] ◇ *adj* **-1. to be alone** to be without any other people present □ *He wants to be alone.* □ *I don't want to be left alone with him.* □ *They need to spend some time alone together.* **-2. to be/feel alone** to be without friends or people one knows □ *I felt I was all alone in a strange country.* **-3. you/he etc alone** only you/he etc □ *You alone know what really happened.* □ *Fear alone prevented me from speaking.* **-4.** used to say that something is only a small part of a much larger amount or number □ *Last year alone he earned $200,000.*
◇ *adv* **-1. to do sthg alone** to do sthg without the help of other people □ *She had to run the business alone and unaided.* ■ **to go it alone** to do something without the help or support of other people □ *If that's how you feel, I'll just have to go it alone.* **-2. to leave sthg alone** to stop touching sthg □ *Leave it alone!* ■ **to leave sb alone** to stop annoying sb □ *Leave me alone!*

along [ə'lɒŋ] ◇ *adv* **-1. to walk along** to walk forward, usually on a road or path, in an easy or unhurried way □ *The dog trotted along behind us.* □ *I was driving along, listening to the car radio.* ■ **the work is coming along well** the work is progressing well. **-2. he will be along soon** he will be here soon □ *There'll be another bus along shortly.* **-3. I took sb along** I took sb with me □ *Liz asked if she could bring her sister along to the concert.*
◇ *prep* **-1. she walked along the road** she walked on or beside the road in the direction that it was going. **-2. the road runs along the coast** the road goes beside the coast for its whole length □ *There were policemen placed every twenty meters along the route.* **-3. the office is along the corridor** the office is further down the corridor □ *Could you move further along the row, please?*
◆ **all along** *adv* **she was right all along** she was right all the time from the very beginning.
◆ **along with** *prep* **along with several/many others** in the same way as several/many others □ *I wrote in and complained, along with hundreds of other viewers.*

alongside [ə,lɒŋ'saɪd] ◇ *prep* **-1.** next to <sthg> □ *They moored alongside the pier.* **-2.** together with <sb/sthg> □ *He works alongside his brother.* □ *We use this alongside more*

traditional methods. ◇ *adv* [stop, park] next to somebody or something □ *The car drew up alongside.*

aloof [ə'luːf] *adj* **-1.** [person] who avoids talking to people and is unfriendly □ *He was very aloof with the staff.* **-2. to remain** OR **stay aloof** to avoid getting involved in something □ *I prefer to remain aloof from such arguments.*

aloud [ə'laʊd] *adv* [speak, read] in a voice that can be heard □ *I was just thinking aloud.*

ALP (*abbr of* **Australian Labor Party**) *n* **the ALP** the main center-left party in Australia.

alpaca [æl'pækə] *n* a type of llama found in South America that has long wool used for making clothes; the wool of this animal.

alphabet ['ælfəbet] *n* a set of letters or symbols in a fixed order that are used for writing a language.

alphabetical [,ælfə'betɪkl] *adj* [list] arranged according to the order of the alphabet □ *The files are arranged in alphabetical order.*

alphabetically [,ælfə'betɪklɪ] *adv* [classify, order] *see* **alphabetical** □ *The names are listed alphabetically.*

alphabetize, -ise ['ælfəbətaɪz] *vt* to arrange <files, data> etc in alphabetical order.

alphanumeric [,ælfənjʊ'merɪk] *adj* [data, display, keyboard] that contains both letters and numbers.

alpine ['ælpaɪn] *adj* [climate, plant, resort] that is found in the Alps or other high mountains.

Alps [ælps]: **the Alps** the biggest mountain range in Europe. It extends from the Mediterranean coast of France through northern Italy, Switzerland, and Austria to Slovenia. HIGHEST POINT: 4,807 m.

already [ɔːl'redɪ] *adv* **-1. I've already told you** I've told you before now (used to emphasize that an action is completed) □ *When we got there she'd already gone home.* **-2. we have too many guests already** we have more guests now than we want □ *You don't need the money; you're rich enough already.* **-3. they were already there** they were there and this was earlier than was expected □ *You're not leaving already, are you?*

alright [,ɔːl'raɪt] *adv* & *adj* = **all right.**

Alsatian [æl'seɪʃn] *n* a large dog with a light-brown and black coat that is often used by the police and as a guard dog.

also ['ɔːlsoʊ] *adv* **-1.** as well (used to introduce another fact about a person or thing) □ *'Also available on CD.'* **-2.** too (used to say that two people or things are similar) □ *He's a colleague, and also a good friend.* □ *Her second novel was also a success.* **-3.** moreover (used at the beginning of sentences to introduce another fact or argument) □ *I don't like her; also, I don't trust her.*

also-ran *n* a person who is unsuccessful in a competition, election etc (informal use).

altar ['ɔːltər] *n* a table where the priest or minister stands in Christian services.

alter ['ɔːltər] ◇ *vt* **-1.** [dress, jacket] to change the style, shape, size etc of <a piece of

clothing> □ *You could always alter the sleeves.* **-2.** [plan, opinion, situation] to change <sthg> slightly by changing one part of it □ *None of which alters the fact that he's a liar.* ◇ *vi* [person, weather, place] to change □ *His face had altered very little over the years.* □ *Yes, but that doesn't alter the fact that we've lost.*

alteration [ˌɔːltə'reɪʃn] *n* **-1.** [of clothes, a plan, opinion] *see* **alter** □ *The text needs some alteration before it can be published.* **-2.** a slight change □ *I've made a few alterations to today's schedule.*

altercation [ˌɔːltəʳ'keɪʃn] *n* a short noisy argument (formal use) □ *Hutchens was involved in an altercation with some reporters.*

alter ego (*pl* **alter egos**) *n* **-1.** the side of one's personality that people do not normally see. **-2.** a close friend who one trusts.

alternate [*adj* US 'ɔːltərnət, GB ɔːl'tɜːnət, *vb* 'ɔːltəʳneɪt] ◇ *adj* **-1.** following one after the other □ *He does alternate night and day shifts.* **-2.** one of every two □ *We visit her on alternate weekends.* **-3.** US = **alternative**.
◇ *vt* to make <two things, sets of people> etc follow each other in a repeated sequence □ *They try to alternate the two teams of doctors.* ■ **to alternate sthg with sthg** to make sthg follow sthg repeatedly □ *The course alternates lectures with seminars.*
◇ *vi* **to alternate with sthg** to follow sthg in a repeated sequence □ *Hard work alternated with long rest periods.* ■ **to alternate between sthg and sthg** to keep changing from sthg to sthg and back again □ *He alternates between being very rude and extremely charming.*

alternately [US 'ɔːltərnətlɪ, GB ɔːl'tɜːnətlɪ] *adv* a word used when there is a regular change from one state or action to another □ *He's alternately happy and sad.*

alternating current [ˌɔːltəʳneɪtɪŋ-] *n* an electric current that regularly changes direction as it flows.
NOTE: Compare **direct current**.

alternation [ˌɔːltəʳ'neɪʃn] *n* the regular changing from one thing or state to another, then back again □ *the alternation of day and night.*

alternative [ɔːl'tɜːʳnətɪv] ◇ *adj* **-1.** [plan, suggestion, route] that can be used instead of something else □ *We'll have to use some alternative means of transport.* **-2.** [theater, lifestyle] that is different from the traditional or established kind □ *sources of alternative energy such as wind power.* ◇ *n* something that can be done or chosen instead of something else □ *We have two alternatives, either we sell now, or we wait.* □ *They're looking for an alternative to their current computer system.* □ *If you continue to be late for work, I'll have no alternative but to ask you to leave.*

alternatively [ɔːl'tɜːʳnətɪvlɪ] *adv* as an alternative course of action □ *We could hold the meeting at ten or, alternatively, we could meet in the afternoon.*

alternative medicine *n* a way of treating illness, e.g. using homeopathy, aromatherapy, or acupuncture, that is not part of standard Western medical practices.

alternator ['ɔːltəʳneɪtəʳ] *n* a machine that produces an electric current which changes direction at regular periods.

although [ɔːl'ðoʊ] *conj* **-1.** in spite of the fact that □ *She's very knowledgeable, although she's never had any formal education.* **-2.** but □ *I don't think it will work, although it's worth a try.*

altitude ['æltɪtʲuːd] *n* the height of a place or thing, e.g. an aircraft, above sea level □ *The plane was flying at an altitude of 1500 meters.* □ *Lack of oxygen makes breathing difficult at high altitudes.*

alto ['æltoʊ] (*pl* **altos**) ◇ *n* **-1.** the highest male singing voice. **-2.** the lowest female singing voice. ◇ *comp* [saxophone, clarinet] that has the same range of notes as an alto.

altogether [ˌɔːltə'geðəʳ] *adv* **-1.** completely □ *That's a different matter altogether.* □ *It was altogether different when I worked here.* □ *The engine stopped altogether.* ■ **not altogether** used to make a negative statement less strong □ *I wasn't altogether surprised to hear he'd left.* **-2.** considering all things □ *Altogether I'd say he's not such a bad guy.* **-3.** in total □ *Altogether that makes $10.* □ *You owe me $50 altogether.*

altruism ['æltruɪzm] *n* concern for other people rather than oneself.

altruistic [ˌæltru'ɪstɪk] *adj* [action, person] *see* **altruism**.

aluminum [ə'luːmɪnəm] US, **aluminium** [ælə'mɪnjəm] GB *n* a light silver-gray metal that is easily shaped and is used e.g. for making cooking utensils, aircraft, and vehicles. SYMBOL: AL □ *aluminum cans.*

aluminum foil *n* US very thin metal in a sheet that can be used for covering food.

alumna [ə'lʌmnə] (*pl* **alumnae** [-niː]) *n* a former female student of a school, college, or university.

alumnus [ə'lʌmnəs] (*pl* **alumni** [-naɪ]) *n* a former male student of a school, college, or university.

always ['ɔːlweɪz] *adv* **-1. he always arrives late** he arrives late every time □ *You should always wear a seatbelt.* ■ **I have always liked her** I have liked her all the time I have known her □ *Have you always worn contact lenses?* **-2. I will always love you** I will never stop loving you □ *There will always be a need for trained graduates.* **-3. he's always complaining** he complains too often □ *You always think you know best!* **-4. you can always go by train** why don't you go by train (used to make suggestions) □ *We could always borrow John's car.*

Alzheimer's (disease) [US 'ɑːltshaɪməʳz-, GB 'ælts-] *n* a disease that affects a person's brain, usually in old age, and causes them to feel confused and lose their memory.

am [æm] *vb* → **be**.

a.m. (*abbr of* **ante meridiem**) between midnight and midday □ *The flight leaves at 8 a.m.*
NOTE: Compare **p.m.**

AM (*abbr of* **amplitude modulation**) *n* a system of radio broadcasting that does not always

produce a very clear sound □ *ABC National, broadcasting on 576 AM.*
NOTE: Compare **FM.**

AMA (*abbr of* **American Medical Association**) *n* **the AMA** an organization for doctors and medical researchers in the USA.

amalgam [əˈmælgəm] *n* -1. a mixture of two or more things (formal use). -2. a mixture of mercury with another metal, especially silver, often used as fillings for teeth.

amalgamate [əˈmælgəmeɪt] ◇ *vt* to join together <two or more groups, businesses> etc to form a larger one □ *Our office is to be amalgamated with the Chicago branch.* ◇ *vi* [groups, businesses] to be amalgamated.

amalgamation [ə,mælgəˈmeɪʃn] *n*: *see* **amalgamate.**

amass [əˈmæs] *vt* to collect a lot of <money, information> etc over a period of time □ *He has amassed a considerable fortune.*

amateur [US ˈæmətʃʊr, GB ˈæmətə] ◇ *n* -1. a person who does an activity for pleasure and is not paid for it □ *a keen amateur* □ *The competition is open to both amateurs and professionals.* -2. a person who is not very good at a particular activity □ *They're just a bunch of amateurs.* ◇ *adj* -1. [sport, sportsman, photographer] *He plays amateur football.* -2. [performance, attempt] = **amateurish.**

amateurish [US ,æməˈtʃʊrɪʃ, GB ˈæmətərɪʃ] *adj* [performance, attempt] not very good.

amaze [əˈmeɪz] *vt* to surprise <sb> very much □ *Jim amazed us all with his cooking.*

amazed [əˈmeɪzd] *adj* **to be amazed** to be very surprised □ *I'm amazed you never told anyone.* □ *I was amazed to discover she had been fired.*

amazement [əˈmeɪzmənt] *n* a feeling of great surprise □ *I never thought she'd agree, but to my amazement she did.* □ *He looked at me in amazement.*

amazing [əˈmeɪzɪŋ] *adj* -1. [coincidence, story] very surprising □ *It's amazing that nobody else thought of it.* -2. [dress, car, offer] very good or impressive □ *They have the most amazing house.* □ *The food was absolutely amazing.*

amazingly [əˈmeɪzɪŋlɪ] *adv* **amazingly quick/high etc** so quick/high etc that it is surprising □ *It was amazingly crowded for the time of year.* □ *Amazingly, no one was hurt.*

Amazon [US ˈæməzɑːn, GB -zən]: **the Amazon** a river in South America that starts in the Andes in Peru and flows through northern Brazil to the Atlantic. It is the second-longest river in the world □ *the Amazon basin.*

Amazonian [,æməˈzoʊnjən] *adj*: *see* **Amazon.**

ambassador [æmˈbæsədər] *n* a diplomat of the highest rank who looks after their country's interests in another country □ *the US ambassador to Britain.*

amber [ˈæmbər] ◇ *n* -1. a hard yellow resin used to make jewelry; the color of this □ *an amber brooch/necklace.* -2. GB the yellow light between the red and green lights of a traffic light □ *The lights changed from red to amber.* ◇ *adj* [eyes, light] that is the color of amber.

ambiance [US ,ɑːmbɪˈɑːns, GB ˈæmbjəns] *n* = **ambience.**

ambidextrous [,æmbɪˈdekstrəs] *adj* [person] who can use both hands with equal skill.

ambience [US ,ɑːmbɪˈɑːns, GB ˈæmbjəns] *n* the atmosphere or character of a place □ *The restaurant, I have to say, lacks ambience.*

ambiguity [,æmbɪˈgjuːətɪ] (*pl* **ambiguities**) *n* -1. the possibility of understanding a word, phrase, situation etc in more than one way □ *To avoid any ambiguity I've added some notes in the margin.* □ *There's a certain ambiguity in their relationship.* -2. a word or phrase that can be understood in more than one way □ *The text was full of ambiguities.*

ambiguous [æmˈbɪgjuəs] *adj* [reply, statement] that can be understood in more than one way and so is not clear □ *The wording of this clause is a little ambiguous.*

ambiguously [æmˈbɪgjuəslɪ] *adv*: *see* **ambiguous** □ *It was ambiguously expressed in the text.*

ambition [æmˈbɪʃn] *n* -1. the desire to be successful, e.g. by having a good job, making money, or becoming famous □ *When he was a young lawyer he was full of ambition.* -2. something that one wants to do very much □ *Her ambition is to climb Everest.*

ambitious [æmˈbɪʃəs] *adj* -1. [person] who wants very much to be successful □ *an ambitious politician/lawyer/businessman.* -2. [plan, project] that is difficult and will need great effort and skill □ *It all sounded pretty ambitious to me.*

ambivalence [æmˈbɪvələns] *n*: *see* **ambivalent.**

ambivalent [æmˈbɪvələnt] *adj* [person] who has two opposite feelings or views about somebody or something at the same time □ *He feels very ambivalent about leaving his wife.* □ *I have rather ambivalent feelings about him.*

amble [ˈæmbl] *vi* to walk in a relaxed way without hurrying □ *We ambled across the park.*

ambulance [ˈæmbjələns] *n* a vehicle with special equipment for taking sick or injured people to the hospital □ *She was taken to the hospital by ambulance.* □ *Somebody call for an ambulance!* □ *the ambulance service.*

ambush [ˈæmbʊʃ] ◇ *vt* to attack <sb> by surprise after hiding and waiting for them □ *The convoy was ambushed by rebel soldiers.* ◇ *n*: *The troops were caught in an ambush.*

ameba US, **amoeba** GB [əˈmiːbə] (US *pl* **amebas** OR **amebae** [-biː], GB *pl* **amoebas** OR **amoebae** [-biː]) *n* the smallest kind of living creature, consisting of only one cell.

ameliorate [əˈmiːljəreɪt] *vt* [working conditions] to improve <a situation> (formal use).

amen [,ɑːˈmen, ,eɪ-] *excl* the word used at the end of a Christian prayer.

amenable [əˈmiːnəbl] *adj* [person] who is willing to do what somebody else suggests. ■ **to be amenable to sthg** [to a proposal, idea] to be willing to accept sthg □ *I'm always amenable to suggestions.*

amend [əˈmend] *vt* to improve, correct, or make small changes to <a text, law, rule>

etc □ *The last paragraph should be amended to take account of recent developments.*

◆ **amends** *npl* **to make amends** to show that one is sorry for harming or offending somebody by doing something pleasant or helpful for them □ *Don was trying to make amends for having forgotten my birthday.*

amendment [ə'mendmənt] *n* -1. a correction, improvement, or small change made to a text, statement, law etc □ *A number of amendments were made to the bill before it became law.* □ *the Fifth Amendment.* -2. [to a text, law] *see* **amend** □ *The schedule needs some amendment.*

amenities [ə'mi:nətɪz] *npl* places and services, e.g. stores or transportation, that are near one's home and make life more comfortable, convenient, or pleasant □ *The apartment is close to local amenities.*

Amerasian [,æmə'reɪʒn] *n* a person who has both American and Asian ancestors.

America [ə'merɪkə] -1. = **United States.** -2. = **Americas.**

◆ **Americas**: **the Americas** North, Central, and South America.

American [ə'merɪkən] *n* & *adj*: *see* **America.**
NOTE: The term *American* usually refers to the USA rather than South America.

Americana [US ə,merɪ'kænə, GB -'kɑːnə] *n* objects, books, documents etc that are connected with American history or culture.

American Civil War *n* **the American Civil War** the war (1861 to 1865) that took place between the Northern states of the USA (the Union), and the Southern states (the Confederacy).

▼ THE AMERICAN CIVIL WAR
The American Civil War began in 1861, when eleven Southern states left the Union (the United States) to form a separate political grouping called the Confederacy, or the Confederate States of America. Fighting ended in 1865, when Robert E. Lee, the Confederate general, surrendered to Ulysses S. Grant, the leader of the Union troops. As a result of the war slavery was no longer allowed in the USA, and the states became less important than the central government.

American Dream *n* **the American Dream** the idea that everybody in the USA has the opportunity to become rich and successful.

American eagle *n* the bald eagle, especially when it is used as a symbol for the USA.

American football *n* GB a popular US sport played on a large field by two teams of eleven players who throw or carry an oval-shaped ball past each other in order to score points at the end of the field.

American Indian *n* = **Native American** (old-fashioned use).

Americanism [ə'merɪkənɪzm] *n* a word or phrase, e.g. "elevator" or "sidewalk", that is used only in American English.

Americanize, -ise [ə'merɪkənaɪz] *vt* to make <a word, place> etc American in style.

American League *n* **the American League** one of the two major US baseball leagues.

American Legion *n* **the American Legion** an association of people who have served in the US armed forces.

American Revolution, American Revolutionary War *n* **the American Revolution** OR **Revolutionary War** the war (1775 to 1783) between Great Britain and its colonies in North America. It was won by the Americans, and the USA became independent.

▼ THE AMERICAN REVOLUTION
The American Revolution began in 1775 when the thirteen British colonies in America rebelled against British rule because they no longer wanted to pay taxes without being able to participate in government. In 1776, several "Founding Fathers" sent a letter to the British king, George III, declaring that America was an independent nation. The British responded by sending an army to stop them. Although the Americans, who were led by George Washington, did not have a professional army, they finally won the war in 1781. As a result, America became recognized as the United States of America, an independent and democratic nation.

American Way *n* **the American Way** the attitude to life that is considered typical of Americans and that favors democracy, individualism, hard work etc.

America's Cup *n* **the America's Cup** an important international yacht race.

Amerindian [,æmə'rɪndjən] *n* a member of any of the peoples originally living in North, Central, or South America or the West Indies.

amethyst ['æməθɪst] *n* a purple stone used for making jewelry; the color of this stone.

Amex ['æmeks] (*abbr of* **American Stock Exchange**) *n* the second-largest stock exchange in the USA.

amiable ['eɪmjəbl] *adj* [person] who is friendly and easy to like.

amicable ['æmɪkəbl] *adj* [relationship, agreement] friendly □ *The divorce was amicable.*

amicably ['æmɪkəblɪ] *adv* [decide, settle, divorce] *see* **amicable** □ *We parted amicably enough.*

amid(st) [ə'mɪd(st)] *prep* -1. **amid(st) all the noise** with the noise going on all around □ *Share prices fell amid(st) rumors of a rise in interest rates.* -2. **amid(st) the trees** surrounded by the trees.

amino acid [ə,mi:nou-] *n* any of a group of acids that form proteins □ *essential/nonessential amino acids.*

Amish ['ɑːmɪʃ] ◇ *npl* **the Amish** a Christian group living mainly in Pennsylvania and Ohio, USA. They wear simple clothes, speak German, and live on farms. Their religion forbids them to use modern technology such as cars or electricity. ◇ *adj*: *an Amish farm/family.*

amiss [əˈmɪs] ◇ *adj* **to be amiss** to be wrong □ *Is there anything amiss?* ◇ *adv* **to take sthg amiss** to be upset or offended by sthg □ *I hope you won't take it amiss if I leave early.* ■ **it would not go** OR **come amiss** it would be very welcome □ *A little politeness would not go amiss.*

ammonia [əˈmoʊnjə] *n* a colorless liquid or gas with a very strong smell, used in making explosives, fertilizers, and domestic cleaning products. FORMULA: NH_3.

ammunition [ˌæmjəˈnɪʃn] *n* -1. bullets, bombs etc that are fired from a gun or other weapon. -2. information that can be used against somebody in an argument.

ammunition dump *n* a place where ammunition is stored.

amnesia [æmˈniːʒə] *n* MEDICINE the condition of not being able to remember anything.

amnesty [ˈæmnəstɪ] (*pl* **amnesties**) *n* -1. a pardon given by the state to prisoners, especially those in prison for political crimes □ *The government declared an amnesty for all political prisoners.* -2. a period of time during which a particular law is not applied so that people can admit their crimes or give up weapons without being arrested.

Amnesty International *n* an international organization that aims to protect human rights and particularly to help people imprisoned for their beliefs.

amniocentesis [ˌæmnɪoʊsenˈtiːsəs] *n* a test carried out on a pregnant woman in which fluid is removed from her womb and examined in order to make sure that her unborn baby is healthy.

amoeba *n* GB = ameba.

amok [əˈmʌk] *adv* **to run amok** [person, animal] to behave in a dangerous or uncontrolled way □ *The gunman ran amok, firing indiscriminately at passers-by.*

among(st) [əˈmʌŋ(st)] *prep* -1. **among(st) the crowd** in or surrounded by the crowd □ *He was hiding somewhere among(st) the trees.* □ *The letter was found among(st) her personal belongings.* -2. **it's popular among(st) teenagers** it's popular with teenagers as a group □ *They were talking among(st) themselves.* □ *There has been a lot of interest among(st) our customers.* -3. **among(st) those present** one of the people present □ *It's among(st) her most important plays.* ■ **among(st) other things** in addition to other things □ *She is, among(st) other things, an excellent cook.* -4. **to share sthg among(st) a group** to share sthg so that each person in a group gets some (usually the same amount).

amoral [ˌeɪˈmɒrəl] *adj* [person] who has no moral principles.

amorous [ˈæmərəs] *adj* [person, affair] that shows or involves love and a desire for sex.

amorphous [əˈmɔːrfəs] *adj* [mass, body] that does not have a definite shape.

amortize [US ˈæmərtaɪz, GB əˈmɔːtaɪz] *vt* [cost,

mortgage] to repay <a debt> completely by making regular payments.

amount [əˈmaʊnt] *n* -1. a word used to say how much of something there is, or how much of something one has, uses etc □ *The amount he eats is amazing.* □ *They consume an enormous amount of energy.* □ *There's a certain amount of disagreement within the party.* -2. a sum of money □ *I paid the money I owed in regular amounts over a period of a year.*

◆ **amount to** *vt fus* -1. **to amount to sthg** to come to a total of sthg □ *The bill amounts to $650 exactly.* -2. **to amount to sthg** to be the same as sthg in its effect □ *It amounts to the same thing in the end.* □ *His answer amounted to a flat refusal.* □ *What it amounts to is this: we'll have to sell everything.*

amp [æmp] *n* -1. *abbr of* **ampere**. -2. *abbr of* **amplifier** (informal use).

amperage [ˈæmpərɪdʒ] *n* the strength of an electric current measured in amps.

ampere [ˈæmpeər] *n* a unit for measuring electric current.

ampersand [ˈæmpərsænd] *n* a symbol (&) used to mean the word "and".

amphetamine [æmˈfetəmiːn] *n* a drug that stimulates the nervous system, making one more energetic and excited than normal.

amphibian [æmˈfɪbɪən] *n* an animal, e.g. a frog or toad, that can live on land and in water.

amphibious [æmˈfɪbɪəs] *adj* -1. [animal] that can live on land and in water. -2. [vehicle] that can move on land and in water.

amphitheater US, **amphitheatre** GB [ˈæmfɪθɪətər] *n* a round theater, common in ancient Rome and Greece, that has no roof and consists of a stage surrounded by rows of seats that rise one behind the other.

ample [ˈæmpl] *adj* -1. [food, time, supplies] more than enough □ *You'll have ample opportunity to explain at the interview.* -2. **it's ample room.** -2. **an ample figure/bosom** a figure/bosom that is large in an attractive way.

amplification [ˌæmpləfəˈkeɪʃn] *n*: *see* **amplify** □ *sound amplification* □ *One or two points need amplification.*

amplifier [ˈæmpləfaɪər] *n* an electronic device used to amplify sound.

amplify [ˈæmpləfaɪ] (*pt* & *pp* **amplified**) *vt* -1. to make <a sound or musical instrument> louder using electricity. -2. to explain <an idea, statement> etc better by giving more information.

◆ **amplify on** *vt fus* [idea, statement] = **amplify**.

amply [ˈæmplɪ] *adv* [rewarded, illustrated] *see* **ample** □ *an amply proportioned room.*

ampule US, **ampoule** GB [ˈæmpuːl] *n* a small container with no lid, usually made of glass, that contains medicine that is going to be used for an injection.

amputate [ˈæmpjəteɪt] ◇ *vt* to cut off all or part of <sb's arm, leg> etc in a medical operation. ◇ *vi*: *Doctors had to amputate in order to avoid further infection.*

amputation [ˌæmpjəˈteɪʃn] *n*: *see* **amputate**.

Amsterdam [,æmstər'dæm] the capital of the Netherlands. It is known for its canals. POPULATION: 702,444.

amt *abbr of* **amount**.

Amtrak™ ['æmtræk] *n* the company that runs passenger train services in the USA.

amuck [ə'mʌk] *adv* = **amok**.

amulet ['æmjʊlət] *n* a small object that somebody wears or carries in the belief that it will protect them from harm.

amuse [ə'mjuːz] *vt* -**1**. to make <sb> want to laugh or smile □ *Does the idea amuse you?* □ *Larry amused us all with his stories.* -**2**. to keep <sb> busy doing something enjoyable so that they do not feel bored □ *Can you keep the children amused while I cook lunch?* □ *He amused himself by drawing doodles.*

amused [ə'mjuːzd] *adj* -**1**. **to be amused** to find something funny □ *She was not amused at his silly jokes.* -**2**. **to keep oneself amused** to do something that stops one from feeling bored.

amusement [ə'mjuːzmənt] *n* the feeling one has when one finds somebody or something funny □ *The adults looked on in amusement.* □ *Much to everyone's amusement, he fell over.*

◆ **amusements** *npl* activities, especially at an amusement park, that are exciting and fun.

amusement arcade *n* a place where people can play games on machines by putting money into them.

amusement park *n* a large outdoor area with many stalls and special machines, e.g. rollercoasters and ferris wheels, that people can ride on.

amusing [ə'mjuːzɪŋ] *adj* [story, event, person] that one finds funny □ *I heard an amusing anecdote the other day.*

an [*stressed* æn, *unstressed* ən] *det: see* **a**.

ANA (*abbr of* **American Newspaper Association**) *n* **the ANA** a US labor union for journalists.

anabolic steroid [,ænəbɒlɪk-] *n* any of a number of drugs that make muscles and bones grow more quickly and that are sometimes used illegally by athletes to improve their performance.

anachronism [ə'nækrənɪzm] *n* -**1**. a person, thing, or attitude that seems old-fashioned to many people □ *To some people the monarchy is simply an anachronism.* -**2**. something that is placed in a period of history in which it did not exist □ *Critics spotted several anachronisms in the movie.*

anachronistic [ə,nækrə'nɪstɪk] *adj* [event, opinion] *see* **anachronism**.

anaemia *etc* GB = **anemia** *etc*.

anaesthetic *etc* GB = **anesthetic** *etc*.

anagram ['ænəgræm] *n* a word or phrase that is formed by rearranging the order of the letters in another word or phrase □ *"Ear" is an anagram of "era".*

anal ['eɪnl] *adj* [passage, sex] *see* **anus**.

analgesic [,ænəl'dʒiːzɪk] ◇ *n* a drug that makes pain less strong. ◇ *adj: an analgesic drug.*

analog ['ænəlɒg] ◇ *n* US something that is

similar to something else (formal use). ◇ *adj* [watch, clock] that has pointers moving around a dial to show the time. NOTE: Compare **digital**.

analogous [ə'næləgəs] *adj* similar □ *The organization of the school is analogous to that of an army.*

analogue ['ænəlɒg] *n* & *adj* GB = **analog**.

analogy [ə'nælədʒɪ] (*pl* **analogies**) *n* a comparison that is made between two similar things in order to explain something □ *An analogy can be drawn between the human eye and the camera.* ■ **by analogy with sthg** by making a comparison with sthg □ *He explained the workings of the memory by analogy with a computer system.*

analyse *vt* GB = **analyze**.

analysis [ə'næləsɪs] (*pl* **analyses** [-siːz]) *n* -**1**. a detailed examination of something that is made in order to explain or understand it □ *after a thorough analysis of the facts* □ *a biological analysis* □ *The sample has been sent away for analysis.* -**2**. an explanation of something that results from a detailed examination of it □ *My analysis of the situation is this...* □ *He drew up a detailed analysis of the company's accounts.* -**3**. = **psychoanalysis**. -**4**. *phrase* **in the final** OR **last analysis** a phrase used when stating what one thinks is the most basic fact about a situation □ *In the final analysis, it's his responsibility, not ours.*

analyst ['ænəlɪst] *n* -**1**. a person whose job is to analyze information □ *a political/computer/financial analyst.* -**2**. = **psychoanalyst**.

analytic(al) [,ænə'lɪtɪk(l)] *adj* [mind, approach, study] that uses logical and careful reasoning.

analyze US, **analyse** GB ['ænəlaɪz] *vt* [problem, situation, data] to examine <sthg> in detail in order to understand or explain it □ *Laboratory staff analyze the results of the tests.*

anarchic [æ'nɑːrkɪk] *adj* -**1**. [person, behavior] that does not respect authority or normal rules of behavior. -**2**. [style, scene, organization] that shows no signs of order.

anarchist ['ænərkəst] *n* a person who rejects all systems of government and authority.

anarchy ['ænərkɪ] *n* -**1**. a state of chaos and disorder □ *The country is in a state of anarchy.* -**2**. political disorder caused when there is no government.

anathema [ə'næθəmə] *n* something that one dislikes very much □ *Racism is absolute anathema to him.*

anatomical [,ænə'tɒmɪkl] *adj* [description, feature] *see* **anatomy**.

anatomy [ə'nætəmɪ] (*pl* **anatomies**) *n* -**1**. the scientific study of the structure of the human or animal body. -**2**. the structure of the human or animal body □ *the human anatomy* □ *the anatomy of the horse.* -**3**. the human body (humorous use) □ *I got hit in a tender part of my anatomy.*

ANC (*abbr of* **African National Congress**) *n* **the ANC** a South African political party that opposed apartheid and was banned from 1960 to 1990. It is now the largest party in South Africa.

ancestor ['ænsestə^r] *n* -1. a person who is related to oneself and who lived in the past. -2. a machine, vehicle etc that is a simpler and earlier version of a modern one.

ancestral home [æn,sestrl-] *n* a house, usually a very large one, where a person's ancestors lived.

ancestry ['ænsestrɪ] (*pl* **ancestries**) *n* one's ancestors or national background □ *I'm trying to trace my ancestry.*

anchor ['æŋkə^r] ◇ *n* -1. SAILING a heavy piece of metal with a hook that is attached to a boat by a chain or rope and is dropped into the water to stop the boat from moving. ■ **to drop/weigh anchor** to drop the anchor into/to pull the anchor out of the water. -2. TV a person who is in charge of a television program such as the news and who acts as a link between different parts of the program. -3. US a small, hollow, plastic object that holds a screw tightly in a hole. ◇ *vt* -1. to fix <sthg> in position to prevent it from moving □ *They anchored the garden table with a couple of heavy stones.* -2. TV to do the job of an anchor for <a television program> □ *John Thorman anchors the six o'clock news.* ◇ *vi* -1. SAILING to lower the anchor of a boat in order to stop it from moving □ *We anchored off the coast of Gibraltar.* -2. TV to work as an anchor on a television program.

anchorage ['æŋkərɪdʒ] *n* SAILING a place where boats can anchor.

anchorman ['æŋkə^rmæn] (*pl* **anchormen** [-men]) *n* TV a male anchor.

anchorwoman ['æŋkə^rwʊmən] (*pl* **anchorwomen**) *n* TV a female anchor.

anchovy [US 'æntʃoʊvɪ, GB -əvɪ] (*pl* **anchovy** OR **anchovies**) *n* a very small fish that has a strong salty taste.

ancient ['eɪnʃənt] *adj* -1. [monument, history, civilization] that belongs to the very distant past □ *ancient Greece* □ *a tradition that goes back to ancient times.* -2. [custom, tradition, belief] that has existed for a very long time. -3. [person, car, coat] that one thinks is very old (humorous use).

ancillary [æn'sɪlərɪ] *adj* **ancillary staff** people whose job is to support all the other people who work in a building or industry, e.g. by cooking or cleaning.

and [*stressed* ænd, *unstressed* ən] *conj* -1. used to join words, phrases, and clauses □ *Two and two make four.* □ *Put your shoes and socks on.* □ *I was tired and hungry.* -2. used to show that two events follow one another almost immediately □ *I got into bed and put out the light* -3. used in large numbers before the numbers "one" to "ninety-nine"; used between whole numbers and fractions □ *one hundred and eighty* □ *six and three quarters.* -4. **he cried and cried** he cried for a very long time (used for emphasis or to say that something continued for a long time) □ *He was becoming*

more and more angry. -5. **I fell downstairs and broke my leg** I fell downstairs, then I broke my leg (used to join two clauses when the second event is a result of the first). -6. **go and look for it** go in order to find it (used after verbs like "come", "go", and "try" to show intention or reason) □ *Try and be home on time.* □ *Let's wait and see.*

◆ **and all that** *adv* and things like that (informal use) □ *I'm just not ready for marriage and all that.*

◆ **and so on (and so forth)** *adv* used at the end of a list to show that other things could be added to it □ *My department deals with sales, marketing, promotion, and so on.*

Andersen ['ændə^rsən], **Hans Christian** (1805–1875) a Danish writer whose fairy tales include *The Ugly Duckling* and *The Snow Queen.*

Andes ['ændi:z]: **the Andes** a major mountain range that extends down the west side of South America. HIGHEST POINT: 6,959 m.

androgynous [æn'drɒdʒənəs] *adj* [person, appearance] that has both male and female characteristics.

android ['ændrɔɪd] *n* in science fiction stories, a robot that looks like a human being.

anecdote ['ænɪkdoʊt] *n* a short, amusing, and usually personal account of something that has happened □ *The book is full of anecdotes about his acting career.*

anemia US, **anaemia** GB [ə'ni:mjə] *n* a shortage of red blood cells that causes one to feel very tired and look pale.

anemic US, **anaemic** GB [ə'ni:mɪk] *adj* [person] who suffers from anemia; who looks very pale and weak.

anemone [ə'nemənɪ] *n* a plant with red, blue, or purple flowers on long thin stems.

anesthesia [,ænəs'θi:ʒə] US, **anaesthesia** [,ænəs-'θi:zɪə] GB *n* a state in which the whole body or part of it does not feel pain, heat, cold etc.

anesthesiologist [,ænəsθi:zɪ'ɒlədʒəst] *n* US a doctor who gives anesthetics to patients.

anesthetic US, **anaesthetic** GB [,ænəs'θetɪk] *n* a substance that stops a person from feeling pain □ *The operation was performed under anesthetic.* □ *The anesthetic soon wore off.*

anesthetist [ə'nesθətəst] US, **anaesthetist** [ə'ni:s-θətəst] GB *n* GB a doctor who gives patients anesthetics.

anesthetize [ə'nesθətaɪz] US, **anaesthetize, -ise** [ə'ni:sθətaɪz] GB *vt* to give <sb> an anesthetic.

anew [ə'nju:] *adv* again (literary use).

angel ['eɪndʒəl] *n* -1. RELIGION a messenger and servant of God, usually shown in human form with white wings. -2. a person who one thinks is very good or kind □ *Be an angel and make me a cup of coffee, will you?*

Angeleno [,ændʒə'li:noʊ] *n* a person from Los Angeles.

Angel Falls a waterfall in Venezuela, in

South America. It is the highest waterfall in the world (979 m).

angelic [æn'dʒelɪk] *adj* [person, face, smile] that seems good, pure, and beautiful.

anger ['æŋgər] ◇ *n* a strong feeling of annoyance and unhappiness with somebody that makes one want to criticize, shout at them, or hurt them in some way □ *She slammed the door in a fit of anger.* □ *Peter's family reacted with anger and disbelief at his decision.* ◇ *vt* to make <sb> angry □ *Shareholders were angered by the board's failure to act.*

angina [æn'dʒaɪnə] *n* severe pain in the chest caused when too little blood is being carried to the heart muscle.

angle ['æŋgl] ◇ *n* -1. MATH the space between two lines or surfaces at the point where they meet or cross each other, measured in degrees □ *a 60° angle* □ *The ball hit the ground at a 45° angle.* ■ **at an angle** not straight □ *The picture had been hung at an angle.* -2. a corner of a building, structure, piece of furniture, etc □ *The room has a lot of awkward angles.* -3. a point of view □ *Let's try looking at it from another angle.* □ *They have an interesting angle on the subject.* □ *The photo was taken from an unusual angle.*
◇ *vt* to present <information, a report> etc from a particular point of view □ *The program was angled to suit younger viewers.*
◇ *vi* -1. to fish with a fishing rod. -2. **to angle for sthg** [for invitation, compliment] to try to get sthg, especially in an indirect way □ *I could see she was angling for a pay raise.*

Anglepoise™ (lamp) ['æŋglpɔɪz-] *n* GB a lamp that can be adjusted to shine in any direction and that stands on a desk.

angler ['æŋglər] *n* a person who fishes with a fishing rod.

Anglican ['æŋglɪkən] ◇ *adj* [Church, bishop] that is connected with the Church of England. ◇ *n* a member of the Church of England.

Anglicism ['æŋglɪsɪzm] *n* -1. a word or phrase that is used only in British English. -2. an English word or expression that is used in a foreign language.

angling ['æŋglɪŋ] *n* the art or sport of fishing using a fishing rod.

Anglo- ['æŋgloʊ] *prefix* added to a word to mean English □ *an Anglo-French treaty.*

Anglo-American ◇ *n* an American who came from Britain, or whose family originally came from Britain. ◇ *adj* [trade, relations] that involves Britain and the USA.

Anglo-Indian *n* a person who has both British and Indian ancestors.

Anglo-Saxon ◇ *n* -1. a person whose language is English and whose culture is British or American. -2. a member of the Germanic people who settled in Britain in the 5th and 6th centuries. -3. the language spoken in Britain between the 5th and 12th centuries. ◇ *adj* [culture, attitude] that is British or American rather than European.

Angola [æŋ'goʊlə] a country in southwest Africa. SIZE: 1,246,700 sq kms. POPULATION: 9,500,000 (*Angolans*). CAPITAL: Luanda. LANGUAGE: Portuguese. CURRENCY: kwanza.

angora [æŋ'gɔːrə] *n* -1. a breed of goat, rabbit, or cat with very long soft hair. -2. wool, material, or clothing made from the hair of the angora goat or rabbit.

angrily ['æŋgrəlɪ] *adv* [stare, answer] *see* **angry** □ *The accusation was angrily disputed.*

angry ['æŋgrɪ] (*compar* **angrier**, *superl* **angriest**) *adj* [person] who is feeling anger; [look, quarrel, face] that is showing anger □ *He was very angry with me.* □ *I feel extremely angry about the whole business.* □ *There's no need to get so angry!* □ *an angry letter.*

angst [æŋst] *n* a strong feeling of anxiety, caused especially by worrying about one's general situation.

anguish ['æŋgwɪʃ] *n* very great mental pain and suffering □ *He was in terrible anguish over the loss of his son.* □ *a look of anguish.*

anguished ['æŋgwɪʃt] *adj* [cry, look, expression] that is full of anguish.

angular ['æŋgjələr] *adj* [face, jaw, body] that appears thin, with clearly visible bones.

animal ['ænɪml] ◇ *n* -1. any living creature, including human beings, that is not a plant; any mammal except human beings □ *an animal lover* □ *the animal kingdom* □ *animal fat.* -2. a rough and violent person (informal use). ◇ *adj* **an animal instinct/desire** an instinct/desire that is connected with the needs of the body, e.g. sex and food, rather than with the mind.

animate ['ænɪmət] *adj* that is living, as opposed to objects and machines, that are not.

animated ['ænɪmeɪtəd] *adj* [debate, person, face] full of life and energy □ *The discussion suddenly became very animated.*

animated cartoon *n* a cartoon film.

animation [ˌænɪ'meɪʃn] *n* -1. liveliness □ *She spoke with great animation.* -2. the photographic process by which cartoon films are made.

animosity [ˌænɪ'mɒsətɪ] (*pl* **animosities**) *n* a very strong feeling of dislike or hostility □ *There was intense animosity between them.*

aniseed ['ænɪsiːd] *n* the licorice-flavored seeds of the anise plant, used as a flavoring in cakes, drinks, and medicines.

ankle ['æŋkl] ◇ *n* the part of the body where the foot joins the leg. ◇ *comp* **ankle boots/socks** boots/socks that reach the ankle □ *an ankle-length skirt.*

annals ['ænlz] *npl* -1. a yearly record of events or activities such as the reports of the work of a society. -2. the records of the history of a country □ *the worst scandal in the annals of American political history.*

Annapolis [ə'næpəlɪs] the capital of Maryland, USA. The United States Naval Academy is based here and the name is often used to mean the academy itself. POPULATION: 33,187.

Anne, Queen (1665–1714) Queen of Great Britain and Ireland from 1702 to 1714. In her reign, England and Scotland were united. A style of furniture and architecture that was popular at the time is named after her.

annex ['æneks] ◇ *n* US a building that is joined or added to a main building such as a hospital or hotel. ◇ *vt* to take control of <a region or country>, especially by force, and add it to one's own territory.

annexation [ˌænek'seɪʃn] *n* [of a region, country] *see* **annex** □ *the annexation of Indian territory.*

annexe ['æneks] *n* & *vt* GB = **annex**.

annihilate [ə'naɪəleɪt] *vt* to destroy <a city, building, population> etc completely.

annihilation [əˌnaɪə'leɪʃn] *n: see* **annihilate** □ *The species faces annihilation.*

anniversary [ˌænɪ'vɜːʳsərɪ] (*pl* **anniversaries**) *n* a day on which one celebrates an event that happened on the same date in a previous year □ *It's my parents' 25th wedding anniversary next week.* □ *The anniversary celebrations have just begun.*

annotate ['ænəteɪt] *vt* to add notes to <a text, book> etc in order to explain it or comment on it □ *the annotated version of the text.*

announce [ə'naʊns] *vt* **-1.** to say <sthg> publicly or officially □ *The Secretary of State has announced his intention to resign.* □ *The company announced a 40 percent leap in half-year profits.* **-2.** to state <sthg> in a loud voice □ *She stood up and announced that she was going home.*

announcement [ə'naʊnsmənt] *n* **-1.** a public statement about an event that has happened or will happen □ *The announcement appeared in Friday's paper.* □ *I have an important announcement to make.* **-2.** the act of announcing something □ *after the announcement of their marriage* □ *Yesterday's announcement of the company's poor figures caused a fall in the share price.*

announcer [ə'naʊnsəʳ] *n* a person who reads the news or introduces programs on TV or radio □ *a television/radio announcer.*

annoy [ə'nɔɪ] *vt* to make <sb> feel slightly angry □ *That music is really annoying me.*

annoyance [ə'nɔɪəns] *n* a feeling of slight anger and impatience □ *a look of annoyance* □ *I found it difficult to hide my annoyance.*

annoyed [ə'nɔɪd] *adj* **to be annoyed** to be slightly angry and impatient □ *Ian felt very annoyed at the way he had been treated.* □ *I'm really annoyed with him for coming so late.*

annoying [ə'nɔɪɪŋ] *adj* [person, habit, behavior] that makes one feel annoyance.

annual ['ænjʊəl] ◇ *adj* **-1.** [event, vacation] that happens every year □ *We're holding our annual conference in Helsinki.* **-2.** [income, increase] that is calculated over a year □ *annual profits of $3 billion* □ *annual rainfall.* ◇ *n* **-1.** a plant that lives for one year. **-2.** a book or magazine that is published once a year.

annually ['ænjʊəlɪ] *adv* [meet, happen] once a year.

annual meeting US, **annual general meeting** GB *n* an annual meeting of all the important members of a company or society at

which a report of the year's business is presented.

annual report *n* the report of a company's financial position sent to all shareholders once a year.

annuity [ə'njuːɪtɪ] (*pl* **annuities**) *n* a fixed sum of money paid to somebody each year over a period of time as part of an insurance or investment policy.

annul [ə'nʌl] (*pt* & *pp* **annulled**, *cont* **annulling**) *vt* LAW to state that <a marriage, agreement, contract> etc no longer legally exists.

annulment [ə'nʌlmənt] *n: see* **annul** □ *The couple were granted an annulment by the Pope.*

annum ['ænəm] *n* **per annum** each year □ *He's paid $22,000 per annum.*

Annunciation [əˌnʌnsɪ'eɪʃn] *n* **the Annunciation** in the Christian religion, the occasion described in the Bible when an angel called Gabriel appears to tell Mary that she will give birth to Jesus Christ.

anode ['ænoʊd] *n* the positive part of an electric cell.

anoint [ə'nɔɪnt] *vt* to put oil on <a person's head> as part of a religious ceremony.

anomalous [ə'nɒmələs] *adj* [result, position] that seems different from what is usual (formal use).

anomaly [ə'nɒməlɪ] (*pl* **anomalies**) *n* something or somebody that is anomalous (formal use) □ *Several serious anomalies were found in the contract.*

anon. *abbr of* **anonymous**.

anonymity [ˌænə'nɪmətɪ] *n: see* **anonymous** □ *We try to preserve the anonymity of the winners.*

anonymous [ə'nɒnɪməs] *adj* **-1.** [person] whose name is not known □ *The author wishes to remain anonymous.* **-2.** [donation, phone call] for which the name of the person responsible is not known □ *We've received a number of anonymous letters.* **-3.** [hotel room, city] that has no special or interesting features.

anonymously [ə'nɒnɪməslɪ] *adv* [write, donate] *see* **anonymous**.

anorak ['ænəræk] *n* a short waterproof jacket, usually with a hood.

anorexia [ˌænə'reksɪə] *n* **anorexia (nervosa)** a serious illness, usually affecting young women, in which a person has an obsessive fear of becoming fat and refuses to eat.

anorexic [ˌænə'reksɪk] ◇ *adj* [person] who is suffering from anorexia nervosa. ◇ *n* a person suffering from anorexia nervosa.

another [ə'nʌðəʳ] *det* & *pron* **-1. have another drink** have one more drink of the same kind as before □ *Tina's another relative of mine.* □ *There's another train due in ten minutes.* ■ **she smoked one cigarette after another** she smoked a lot of cigarettes without stopping □ *Her three sons left home, one after another.* **-2. I'm looking for another job** I'm looking for a different or new job □ *Let's try it another way.* □ *We can do that another time.* **-3. wait another ten minutes** wait ten minutes more □ *I'll give them another half hour, then I'm going.*

Ansaphone™ [US 'ænsəfoʊn, GB 'ɑːnsə-] *n* = answering machine.

ANSI ['ænsɪ] (*abbr of* **American National Standards Institute**) *n* a US organization that sets the standards for the design and performance of technical equipment.

answer [US 'ænsr, GB 'ɑːnsə] ◇ *n* -1. the words that one says or writes, or the actions that one does as a result of somebody asking a question, sending a letter, making a request etc □ *He rang the bell but there was no answer.* □ *I've been waiting for an answer to my letter.* □ *She won't take "no" for an answer.* □ *In answer to your question, no, we do not approve of such tactics.* -2. [to a problem] a solution or way of dealing with a problem □ *The only answer is to recruit more staff.* □ *There's no easy answer to the problem.* -3. [in an exam] the words that one says or writes as a result of being asked a question in an exam or test □ *I got the wrong answer.* □ *What's the answer to number 15?*
◇ *vt* -1. to give an answer to <a question>; to write in answer to <a letter or advertisement> □ *He answered me with a smile.* □ *I answered her letter immediately.* □ *She got the job by answering an advertisement in the paper.* -2. **to answer the door** to open the door when somebody knocks or rings □ *Don't answer the door to anyone.* ▪ **to answer the phone** to pick up the phone when it rings □ *Will you answer that? I'm busy.*
◇ *vi* -1. to answer a question, letter, or advertisement □ *He asked her again, but she didn't answer.* □ *I wrote, but they never answered.* -2. to answer the door or telephone □ *I tried phoning, but nobody answered.*

◆ **answer back** ◇ *vt sep* **to answer sb back** to answer sb older or more senior in a rude way □ *Don't answer me back when I tell you to do something!* ◇ *vi:* *Don't answer back, it's rude.*

◆ **answer for** *vt fus* -1. **to answer for sb** to say that sb can be relied on to do something □ *I can answer for her ability to do the job.* -2. **to answer for sthg** to explain why sthg bad has happened and suffer for it if necessary □ *He'll have to answer for his behavior to me.* □ *Tina's got a lot to answer for.*

answerable [US 'ænsərəbl, GB 'ɑːns-] *adj* **to be answerable to sb/sthg** [to a superior, organization] to have to explain one's actions to sb/sthg □ *Their organization is answerable to the Civil Aviation Authority.* ▪ **to be answerable for sthg** [for one's actions, behavior] to be responsible for sthg □ *I am not answerable for the behavior of my employees.*

answering machine [US 'ænsərɪŋ-, GB 'ɑːns-] *n* a machine connected to one's telephone that records messages from people who telephone while one is out.

answerphone [US 'æːnsəfoʊn, GB 'ɑːnsə-] *n* GB = answering machine.

ant [ænt] *n* a small insect, often black or brown, that lives in large groups and is thought of as hard-working.

antacid [,ænt'æsəd] *n* a substance used to reduce the amount of acid in one's stomach.

antagonism [æn'tægənɪzm] *n* open and strong opposition or hostility □ *There is considerable antagonism toward the new tax/between ethnic groups.*

antagonist [æn'tægənəst] *n* a person who is against another person in a contest or fight.

antagonistic [æn,tægə'nɪstɪk] *adj* [person, behavior, speech] that shows antagonism □ *He is extremely antagonistic toward his colleagues.*

antagonize, -ise [æn'tægənaɪz] *vt* to make <sb> feel antagonism toward oneself □ *You'll only antagonize them if you keep pestering them like that.*

Antarctic [æn'tɑːʳktɪk]: **the Antarctic (Ocean)** the sea between the Antarctic Circle and Antarctica.

Antarctica [ænt'ɑːʳktɪkə] the continent around the South Pole. It is covered with ice and uninhabited except for scientific research stations.

Antarctic Circle: **the Antarctic Circle** an imaginary circle around the Antarctic region, parallel to the equator at latitude 66° 32′ S.

ante ['æntɪ] *n* **to up** OR **raise the ante** to make the amount of money involved in a bet or deal higher (informal use).

anteater ['æntiːtəʳ] *n* an animal with a long nose that eats ants.

antecedent [,æntə'siːdnt] *n* an event that happens before another event and is similar to, or related to it (formal use).

antelope ['æntəloʊp] (*pl* **antelope** OR **antelopes**) *n* a graceful animal with long legs and horns that is able to run very fast and lives in Africa or Asia.

antenatal [,æntɪ'neɪtl] *adj* [care, check-up, exercise] for women who are expecting a baby.

antenatal clinic *n* a clinic for women who are expecting a baby.

antenna [æn'tenə] (*pl sense 1* **antennae** [-niː], *pl sense 2* **antennas**) *n* -1. one of the two long thin parts attached to the head of an insect, lobster etc that are used for feeling and touching. -2. US a metal rod for receiving television or radio signals, usually attached to a building, car, or TV set.

anteroom ['æntɪruːm] *n* a small room that leads to a larger room and is often used as a waiting room.

anthem ['ænθəm] *n* -1. a song sung by a choir as part of a church service. -2. a song that praises or celebrates something □ *a national anthem.*

anthill ['ænthɪl] *n* a mound of earth in which ants live.

anthology [æn'θɒlədʒɪ] (*pl* **anthologies**) *n* a collection of poems, short stories, plays etc by different writers.

Anthony ['æntənɪ], **Susan B.** (1820–1906) a US feminist who campaigned for the right of women to have the vote and equal pay.

anthrax ['ænθræks] *n* a serious infectious disease that affects cattle and sheep and sometimes humans, causing them to have a fever and a swollen throat.

anthropologist [ˌænθrə'pɒlədʒəst] *n* an expert in anthropology.

anthropology [ˌænθrə'pɒlədʒɪ] *n* the study of human society, its origins, beliefs, and culture.

anti- ['æntɪ] *prefix* -1. added to a word to mean opposed to □ *anti-smoking*. -2. added to a word to mean preventing □ *anti-theft*.

antiaircraft [US ˌæntɪ'eərkræft, GB -'eəkrɑːft] *adj* **an antiaircraft gun/missile** a gun/missile that is designed to destroy enemy aircraft.

antiballistic missile [ˌæntɪbəlɪstɪk-] *n* a missile that is designed to destroy ballistic missiles.

antibiotic [ˌæntɪbaɪ'ɒtɪk] *n* a substance such as penicillin that is used in medicine to kill or stop the growth of bacteria □ *a course of antibiotics*.

antibody ['æntɪbɒdɪ] (*pl* **antibodies**) *n* a substance produced in the blood of a human or animal body that fights disease.

anticipate [æn'tɪsəpeɪt] *vt* -1. [event, problem] to expect and be prepared for <sthg> □ *We anticipate a fall in share prices.* □ *She hadn't anticipated having to go abroad/that she would have to go abroad.* □ *We eagerly anticipate your reply.* -2. [competitor, rival] to do something before <sb else> does it □ *They anticipated the competition by launching their product first.*

anticipation [æn,tɪsə'peɪʃn] *n* -1. a feeling of excitement about something that is going to happen soon □ *There was much anticipation surrounding the announcement.* -2. *phrases* ■ **thanking you in anticipation** a formula used at the end of a letter to thank somebody for doing something before they have done it. ■ **in anticipation of sthg** because one expects sthg to happen □ *They raised their prices in anticipation of an increase in inflation.*

anticlimax [æntɪ'klaɪmæks] *n* something that is disappointing because it comes after something more interesting or exciting; something that is not as interesting or exciting as expected □ *It was a terrible anticlimax coming home.* □ *The movie was something of an anticlimax.*

anticlockwise [ˌæntɪ'klɒkwaɪz] GB ◇ *adj* [direction, movement] that is in the opposite direction to the movement of the hands of a clock. ◇ *adv*: *Turn the wheel anticlockwise.*
NOTE: Compare **clockwise**, **counterclockwise**.

antics ['æntɪks] *npl* behavior that is considered foolish, ridiculous, or funny □ *Jerry found the clown's antics hilarious.*

anticyclone [ˌæntɪ'saɪkloʊn] *n* an area of high pressure that causes calm weather.

antidepressant [ˌæntɪdɪ'presnt] *n* a type of drug used to help people suffering from depression.

antidote ['æntɪdoʊt] *n* -1. a substance that stops or controls the effects of a poison □ *There is no known antidote to this toxin.* -2. something that helps to change or improve a difficult or unpleasant situation □ *There is no immediate antidote to stress.*

antifreeze ['æntɪfriːz] *n* a substance that is put

in a car radiator to prevent the water from freezing in winter.

antihero ['æntɪhɪəroʊ] (*pl* **antiheroes**) *n* a main character in a book, movie etc who does not behave in the way a hero is usually expected to behave.

antihistamine [ˌæntɪ'hɪstəmiːn] *n* a drug used to treat allergies, insect bites, colds etc.

antinuclear [ˌæntɪ'nʲuːkliər] *adj* **an antinuclear demonstration/policy** a demonstration/policy that is against nuclear power or weapons.

antipathy [æn'tɪpəθɪ] *n* a strong dislike □ *There is a growing sense of antipathy between them.* □ *His antipathy toward* OR *to the peace movement is well-known.*

antipersonnel [ˌæntɪpɜːˈsəˈnel] *adj* **an antipersonnel bomb/mine** a bomb/mine that is designed to injure people rather than destroy buildings or equipment.

antiperspirant [ˌæntɪ'pɜːˈspərənt] *n* a substance that is put on the skin, especially under the arms, to help stop sweating.

Antipodean [æn,tɪpə'diːən] *n* & *adj*: *see* **Antipodes**.

Antipodes [æn'tɪpədiːz]: **the Antipodes** Australia and New Zealand (formal or humorous use).

antiquarian [ˌæntɪ'kweəriən] ◇ *adj* that deals in antiques or rare books □ *an antiquarian bookshop.* ◇ *n* a person who studies, collects, or deals in antiques.

antiquated ['æntɪkweɪtəd] *adj* [machine, law, method] that seems old-fashioned and out-of-date.

antique [æn'tiːk] ◇ *adj* [furniture, object] that is very old, rare, and often valuable. ◇ *n* an antique object.

antique dealer *n* a person who buys and sells antiques.

antique shop *n* a shop that sells antiques.

antiquity [æn'tɪkwətɪ] (*pl* **antiquities**) *n* -1. the distant past, especially the time before the end of the Roman Empire □ *one of the most famous rulers of antiquity.* -2. an object, building etc that has survived from the distant past □ *a museum of antiquities.*

anti-Semitic [-sə'mɪtɪk] *adj* [person, attitude] that shows a strong and unreasonable dislike of Jewish people.

anti-Semitism [-'semətɪzm] *n* anti-Semitic beliefs or attitudes.

antiseptic [ˌæntɪ'septɪk] ◇ *n* a substance that destroys harmful bacteria and is put on cuts, wounds etc to prevent disease or infection. ◇ *adj*: *antiseptic cream/ointment.*

antisocial [ˌæntɪ'soʊʃl] *adj* -1. [habit, behavior] that annoys or upsets other people □ *It's very antisocial to smoke during a meal.* -2. [person] who does not like being with other people □ *I'm not being antisocial, but I'd rather stay at home.* -3. [job, working hours] that makes a normal social life difficult □ *Staff are paid extra for working antisocial hours.*

antistatic [ˌæntɪ'stætɪk] *adj* [device, substance,

material] that is designed to prevent static electricity from gathering on a surface.

antitank [ˌæntɪˈtæŋk] *adj* **an antitank weapon/ missile** a weapon/missile that is designed to destroy tanks.

antithesis [ænˈtɪθəsɪs] (*pl* **antitheses** [-əsiːz]) *n* the exact opposite □ *He's the complete antithesis of the average stockbroker.*

antitrust laws [ˌæntɪˈtrʌst-] *npl* in the USA, a set of laws that aim to prevent large companies from controlling all of the market for their products or services.

antlers [ˈæntlərz] *npl* the pair of horns on a male deer's head.

antonym [ˈæntənɪm] *n* a word or phrase that has the opposite meaning to another word or phrase □ *"Hard" is the antonym of "soft".* NOTE: Compare **synonym**.

anus [ˈeɪnəs] *n* the opening in the lower part of the body through which waste leaves the bowels.

anvil [ˈænvəl] *n* a solid iron block on which metal is hammered into shape.

anxiety [æŋˈzaɪətɪ] (*pl* **anxieties**) *n* -1. a feeling of concern or worry, usually caused by the fear that something bad might happen □ *It's a source of constant anxiety to him.* □ *an anxiety attack.* -2. a cause or source of anxiety □ *Her son is a great anxiety to her.* -3. an eager desire to do something □ *In her anxiety to please, she asked them to stay for dinner.*

anxious [ˈæŋkʃəs] *adj* -1. [person, look, smile] that is filled with anxiety □ *She's very anxious about losing her job.* -2. [moment, time] that causes anxiety □ *I had an anxious week waiting for the results.* -3. **to be anxious that...** to want a particular thing to happen very much □ *He was anxious that they should fully understand what was involved.* ■ **to be anxious to do sthg** to want to do sthg very much □ *She was too anxious to please.*

anxiously [ˈæŋkʃəslɪ] *adv* [look, say] with anxiety.

any [ˈenɪ] ◇ *det* -1. **I don't have any friends/ money** I have no friends/money (used in negative sentences) □ *He never does any work.* □ *I changed the battery but it didn't do any good.* -2. **do you have any witnesses/proof?** do you have some witnesses/proof? (used in questions, and clauses starting with "if" or "whether") □ *Are there any sandwiches left?* □ *She asked me whether any letters/mail had arrived.* □ *If you had any sense, you'd say no.* -3. **you can choose any number you like** it is not important which number you choose □ *If you have any other books by her, please let me know.* □ *Call me any time.* ◇ *pron* -1. **I don't have any** I have none (used in negative sentences) □ *I didn't know any of the guests/poetry.* □ *She had lots of friends/ money and I didn't have any.* -2. **do you have any?** do you have some? (used in questions, and clauses beginning with "if" or "whether") □ *Did any of them offer to help?* □ *If you find any, let me know.* ■ **if any** and perhaps none □ *Few foreign films, if any, are successful in America.* ■ **take any you like** it is not important

which you take □ *Any of our staff will be able to tell you.* ◇ *adv* -1. used for emphasis in negative sentences □ *I can't stand it any longer.* -2. used for emphasis in questions, and clauses starting with "if" or "whether" □ *Do you want any more potatoes?* □ *Tell me if this looks any better.*

anybody [ˈenɪbɒdɪ] *pron* -1. **I didn't see anybody** I saw no person (used in negative sentences) □ *There wasn't anybody else there when I arrived.* □ *Don't tell anybody.* -2. **can anybody help me?** can any person help me? (used in questions, and clauses starting with "if" or "whether") □ *Would anybody else like a drink?* □ *If anybody asks for me, tell them I'm busy.* -3. **anybody can learn French** most people can learn French.

anyhow [ˈenɪhaʊ] *adv* -1. in a careless or untidy way □ *She threw her things down just anyhow.* -2. = **anyway**.

anymore [ˌenɪˈmɔːr] *adv* US **not...anymore** no longer □ *They are not clients of ours anymore.* □ *I've lent her money in the past. Not anymore!*

anyone [ˈenɪwʌn] *pron* = **anybody**.

anyplace [ˈenɪpleɪs] *adv* US = **anywhere** (informal use).

anything [ˈenɪθɪŋ] *pron* -1. **I don't want anything** I want nothing (used in negative sentences) □ *You can't believe anything he says.* -2. **do you have anything to say?** is there something you want to say? (used in questions, and clauses starting with "if" or "whether") □ *Is there anything to eat?* □ *If anything happens, call me immediately.* -3. **take anything you want** take whatever you want □ *I'll do anything you ask.*

◆ **anything but** *adv* exactly the opposite □ *He wasn't very friendly — anything but.*

anyway [ˈenɪweɪ] *adv* -1. used when explaining why a previous statement is not important □ *I was very tired, but I went along anyway.* □ *Don't worry about losing that: it didn't work anyway.* -2. used to limit a statement to what is definitely true □ *It's all done now, well, most of it, anyway.* -3. used to show that you want to change the subject of a conversation or to return to a previous subject □ *Anyway, at least you're OK now.* □ *Anyway, there I was at the station...* -4. used to show that you want to end a conversation □ *Anyway, I have to go now.*

anywhere [ˈenɪweər] *adv* -1. **I haven't seen it anywhere** I haven't seen it in any place (used in negative sentences) □ *We haven't been anywhere exciting for years.* -2. **have you seen my keys anywhere?** have you seen my keys in any place? (used in questions, and clauses starting with "if" or "whether") □ *Did you go anywhere yesterday?* ■ **sit anywhere you like** sit in any place you like. -3. **anywhere between one and ten** OR **from one to ten** some number between one and ten.

Anzac [ˈænzæk] (*abbr of* **Australia-New Zealand Army Corps**) *n* a soldier from Australia or New Zealand during World War I.

Anzac Day *n* a public holiday in Australia and New Zealand on April 25 in memory of the Anzacs' landing in Gallipoli in 1915.

ᵇ ANZAC DAY
April 25, 1915 was the date in World War I
when the Anzacs landed at Gallipoli in Turkey. Although they failed to capture the
area for the Allies, they fought bravely, and
over 8,000 of them were killed. This was
the first international event that gave Australians a sense of national identity, and the
memory of it still makes Australians feel
proud and patriotic.

AOB, a.o.b. (*abbr of* **any other business**) *n* GB
anything that needs to be discussed at a
meeting that is not written in the list of
subjects to be discussed.

Apache [ə'pætʃɪ] *n* a member of a Native
American people who live mainly in the
southwestern USA; the language of this
people.

apart [ə'pɑːrt] *adv* **-1. to be apart** to be some
distance away from sb/sthg and separated
from them □ *The houses were only a few yards
apart (from each other).* □ *She and her husband
are now living apart.* ■ **a week apart** with a
week between □ *The weddings took place a
couple of months apart.* **-2. to come apart** to
break into several pieces □ *The clock came
apart in my hands.* □ *Our marriage is falling apart.*
■ **to take sthg apart** to undo the parts of sthg
carefully so that it is in pieces. **-3. joking
apart** if we stop joking now and consider
the matter seriously □ *Joking apart, you must
get a decent haircut.*
◆ **apart from** *prep* **-1. everyone agreed, apart
from Bob** Bob was the only person who did
not agree □ *Apart from that, everything's fine!*
-2. apart from sports, I like reading as well as
sports, I like reading □ *Quite apart from the
fact that it's expensive, it's the wrong size.*

apartheid [ə'pɑːrteɪt] *n* until 1994, the official
government policy in South Africa that kept
people of different races separate in order to
favor white people.

apartment [ə'pɑːrtmənt] *n* **-1.** a place to live
that consists of a set of rooms inside a larger building and includes a kitchen, a bathroom, and bedrooms □ *an apartment block.*
-2. a large and usually grand room inside an
important building □ *the royal apartments.*

apartment building *n* a large building that
contains a lot of apartments.

apathetic [,æpə'θetɪk] *adj* [person, attitude] that
shows little interest or enthusiasm.

apathy ['æpəθɪ] *n* lack of interest or enthusiasm □ *The election result reflected voters' apathy.* □ *It was hard to shake him out of his apathy.*

APB (*abbr of* **all points bulletin**) *n* US a police
radio message that is broadcast to all the
police in an area, and usually concerns a
wanted person.

ape [eɪp] ◇ *n* a large animal similar to a monkey, such as a gorilla or chimpanzee. ◇ *vt*
[person, behavior] to imitate <sb/sthg>, especially in an unsuccessful or ridiculous way □
Daniel is always aping his older brothers.

APEC ['eɪpek] (*abbr of* **Asia-Pacific Economic Co-**
operation) *n* an organization whose members include the countries of East and
Southeast Asia, the USA, and Canada. It
was set up to encourage economic links in
the Pacific region and aims to establish a
free-trade area by 2020.

aperitif [əperə'tiːf] *n* an alcoholic drink that is
drunk before a meal.

aperture ['æpərtʃər] *n* **-1.** a small narrow hole
or opening (formal use). **-2.** PHOTOGRAPHY the
opening in a camera or telescope through
which light passes.

apex ['eɪpeks] (*pl* **apexes** OR **apices**) *n* **-1.** MATH
the top point of a triangle, pyramid etc.
-2. the most successful part of something,
e.g. somebody's career.

APEX ['eɪpeks] (*abbr of* **advance purchase ex-**
cursion) *n* GB a reduced-price airline or rail
fare that has to be bought a certain number
of days before one travels □ *I got an APEX
(ticket) to New York for £100.*

aphid ['eɪfəd] *n* a small insect that feeds off
the juice of plants.

aphorism ['æfərɪzm] *n* a short statement that
expresses a generally accepted idea in an
amusing way.

aphrodisiac [,æfrə'dɪzɪæk] *n* a food, drug etc
that makes somebody sexually excited.

apices ['eɪpɪsiːz] *plural of* **apex**.

apiece [ə'piːs] *adv* each □ *They cost $10 apiece.*

aplomb [ə'plɒm] *n* **to do sthg with aplomb** to
do sthg well in a relaxed and confident way,
especially in difficult circumstances □ *She delivered the talk with great alomb.*

APO *n abbr of* **Army Post Office**.

apocalypse [ə'pɒkəlɪps] *n* an event of great
violence or destruction; the end of the
world.

apocalyptic [ə,pɒkə'lɪptɪk] *adj* [vision, warning]
that is concerned with future violence or destruction.

apogee ['æpədʒiː] *n* [of somebody's career, suc-
cess] the highest point (formal use).

apolitical [,eɪpə'lɪtɪkl] *adj* [person] who is not
interested in politics; [stance, attitude] that
does not favor any political party.

apologetic [ə,pɒlə'dʒetɪk] *adj* [letter, tone] that
expresses regret for something that has been
done, said etc □ *He was very apologetic about
the noise.*

apologetically [ə,pɒlə'dʒetɪklɪ] *adv* [smile, an-
swer] *see* **apologetic** □ *"I hope I'm not boring
you," he said apologetically.*

apologize, -ise [ə'pɒlədʒaɪz] *vi* to say that one
is sorry for something that has been done,
said etc □ *He never apologized for his behavior.*
□ *I must apologize to you for the other evening.*

apology [ə'pɒlədʒɪ] (*pl* **apologies**) *n* a statement that expresses regret for something
that has been done, said etc □ *Please accept
our apologies for any inconvenience caused.* □ *I
owe you an apology.* □ *a letter of apology.*

apoplectic [,æpə'plektɪk] *adj* [person] who is
very angry (informal use) □ *Matthew was apoplectic with rage when he found out.*

apoplexy ['æpəpleksɪ] *n* a stroke (old-fashioned use).

apostle [ə'pɒsl] *n* one of the 12 followers of Christ chosen to spread his message.

apostrophe [ə'pɒstrəfɪ] *n* a symbol (') used to indicate that one or more letters or numbers is missing in a word or series of numbers; this symbol when used to form the possessive in English.

appal *vt* GB = **appall**.

Appalachian [,æpə'leɪtʃɪən]: **the Appalachians, the Appalachian Mountains** a mountain range in eastern North America. HIGHEST POINT: 2,037 m.

appall US, **appal** GB [ə'pɔːl] (*pt* & *pp* **appalled**, *cont* **appalling**) *vt* to make <sb> very shocked and disgusted □ *Their lack of sensitivity appalled me.*

appalled [ə'pɔːld] *adj* [person, silence] that feels or shows shock and disgust □ *Everybody was appalled at the way things were hushed up.*

appalling [ə'pɔːlɪŋ] *adj* -1. [cruelty, conditions, waste] that one finds shocking and wrong □ *What an appalling thing to say!* -2. [movie, joke, taste] that is very bad □ *He's an appalling judge of character.*

appallingly [ə'pɔːlɪŋlɪ] *adv* -1. **appallingly slow/late etc** very slow/late etc □ *The service was appallingly slow.* -2. [behave, perform, sing] very badly.

apparatus [US ,æpə'rætəs, GB -'reɪtəs] (*pl* **apparatus** OR **apparatuses**) *n* -1. [for an activity] a set of equipment, instruments, tools etc used for a particular purpose □ *breathing apparatus* □ *a piece of apparatus.* -2. [of an organization] the complex structure of an organization □ *the apparatus of government.*

apparel [US ə'perl, GB ə'pærl] *n* clothing □ *'Ladies' apparel, 4th floor.'*

apparent [US ə'perənt, GB -'pær-] *adj* -1. **to be/become apparent** to be/become obvious □ *It soon became apparent that no further progress would be made.* ■ **for no apparent reason** for a reason that is not obvious □ *They left for no apparent reason.* -2. [interest, success, improvement] that seems to exist □ *He showed an apparent lack of concern for their feelings.*

apparently [US ə'perəntlɪ, GB -'pær-] *adv* -1. **apparently,...** a word used to introduce information that one has heard but is not certain about □ *Apparently, Sandy and Clive have split up.* □ *I couldn't go to the meeting but apparently it was quite exciting.* □ *"Has he been invited?"— "Apparently not."* -2. **apparently well/happy etc** seeming to be well/happy etc, but not necessarily so □ *Although apparently in control, she was finding the pressure hard to deal with.*

apparition [,æpə'rɪʃn] *n* a ghost (formal use).

appeal [ə'piːl] ◇ *vi* -1. **to appeal for sthg** [for help, food, understanding] to make a serious or urgent request for sthg □ *The police are appealing for witnesses.* □ *They appealed to the public for assistance.* -2. LAW to ask a court to change a decision, sentence etc □ *They're going to appeal against the verdict.* -3. [idea, suggestion, person] to be attractive or interesting □

□ *This type of humor doesn't really appeal to me.* □ *The band is hoping to appeal to a wider audience.*
◇ *vt* US LAW to ask a court to change <a decision> □ *I intend to appeal the sentence.*
◇ *n* -1. [for help, money, support] a serious or urgent request □ *She made* OR *launched an appeal on behalf of the victims.* -2. LAW a formal request to a court asking for a decision, sentence etc to be changed □ *Their appeal for a retrial was rejected.* -3. [for somebody] the characteristic of an idea, suggestion, person etc that makes them attractive or interesting □ *Traveling has lost its appeal for me.*
◆ **appeal to** *vt fus* **to appeal to sb** to use reasons or arguments that are intended to make <sb's sense of honor, common sense> etc influence their behavior or thinking □ *They appealed to his sense of decency.*

Appeal Court *n* = **Court of Appeal**.

appealing [ə'piːlɪŋ] *adj* [idea, person] attractive or interesting □ *I don't find the thought of two weeks in a tent particularly appealing.*

appear [ə'pɪəʳ] *vi* -1. [person, animal, object] to become visible; to arrive, especially suddenly and unexpectedly □ *He appeared in the doorway.* -2. [book, article] to be published; [product] to become available □ *The novel has just appeared in paperback.* □ *Their new range appeared last year.* -3. **to appear (to be) normal/finished etc** to give the impression of being normal/finished etc □ *She appeared (to be) quite happy with the results.* □ *There appears to have been a misunderstanding.* □ *These reports appear to contradict each other.* ■ **it appears (that)..., it would appear (that)...** a phrase used to introduce information that one has heard but is not certain about □ *It now appears that the operation may not be necessary after all.* □ *It would appear that our offer has been rejected.* -4. THEATER & CINEMA [actor] to perform in a play, movie etc □ *Her husband is currently appearing in a musical.* -5. **to appear before** OR **at sthg** [before a court, hearing, enquiry] to go to sthg as a witness or as somebody who is accused of doing something wrong □ *He will have to appear before a military tribunal.* □ *Weston is due to appear in court next Monday.*

appearance [ə'pɪərəns] *n* -1. [of a person, of something new] *see* **appear** □ *The appearance of our new range of products has caused a lot of excitement.* □ *Tenants were alarmed at the appearance of cracks in the outside wall.* ■ **to make an appearance** to appear in public, usually at an organized event □ *The President made a personal appearance.* ■ **to put in an appearance** to go to a party, meeting etc but only stay for a short time. -2. [of a person, thing] the way a person, place, or thing looks to other people □ *We need to improve the appearance of our upmarket range.* □ *Scott worries too much about his appearance.* □ *She certainly didn't give the appearance of being stressed.* ■ **to keep up appearances** to continue to live or behave in a way that other people expect in order to hide the fact that one's situation has become worse. -3. [of an actor] *see* **appear** □ *This was his first appearance on Australian television.*

◆ **by all appearances, to all appearances**
adv a phrase used to introduce information
that seems to be true, based on what can be
seen or on what one knows □ *By all appearances, they're pleased with the results.*

appease [ə'piːz] *vt* to make <sb> calm by giving them what they want □ *It is unlikely that
the Opposition will be appeased by what is essentially a compromise.*

appeasement [ə'piːzmənt] *n* -1. [of person] *see*
appease. -2. POLITICS the act or policy of giving one's enemies what they want in order
to avoid a dispute, war etc □ *He was convinced appeasement would never work.*

append [ə'pend] *vt* [note, signature, glossary] to
add <sthg> to the end of a piece of writing
(formal use) □ *I have appended a short bibliography to the article.*

appendage [ə'pendɪdʒ] *n* something that is
added on or joined to something more important.

appendices [ə'pendɪsiːz] *plural of* **appendix**.

appendicitis [ə,pendə'saɪtəs] *n* a medical condition in which the appendix becomes infected and usually has to be removed.

appendix [ə'pendɪks] (*pl* **appendixes** OR **appendices**) *n* -1. MEDICINE a small part of the bow-
el that has little or no use. ■ **to have one's
appendix out** OR **removed** to have one's appendix removed by an operation. -2. [of a
book] additional information shown at the
end of a book, after the main text □ *All tables
are contained in an appendix.*

appertain [,æpər'teɪn] *vi* **to appertain to sb/sthg**
to be connected with sb/sthg (formal use) □
matters appertaining to public health.

appetite ['æpətaɪt] *n* -1. [for food] a desire for
food □ *I've lost my appetite.* □ *a healthy appetite*
□ *That walk has really given me an appetite.*
-2. [for life, an activity] enthusiasm that somebody has for a particular subject, activity etc
□ *He's lost his appetite for politics.*

appetizer, -iser ['æpətaɪzər] *n* something that
one eats or drinks before the main part of a
meal.

appetizing, -ising ['æpətaɪzɪŋ] *adj* [food, smell]
that increases one's appetite □ *That fish
doesn't look very appetizing to me.*

applaud [ə'plɔːd] ◇ *vt* -1. [actor, play, speech] to
show approval of <sb/sthg> by clapping
one's hands □ *The audience warmly applauded
his performance.* -2. [decision, action] to approve of <sthg> very much □ *Their recommendations have been applauded by observers on
both sides.* ◇ *vi:* *The audience applauded enthusiastically.*

applause [ə'plɔːz] *n* -1. THEATER [for a performer,
performance] a sign of approval made by an
audience clapping their hands □ *The speaker
was greeted with enthusiastic applause.* -2. [for
an idea, action] praise given to an idea, decision, action etc □ *His suggestions received general applause from his colleagues.*

apple ['æpl] *n* -1. a hard round fruit that has
green, red, or yellow skin and a white juicy
part inside that can be eaten raw or cooked

□ *apple juice.* -2. *phrase* **to be the apple of sb's
eye** to be the person that sb loves very
much and is especially proud of.

apple pie *n* a sweet pie made with apples. ■
as American as apple pie typically American.

apple tree *n* a tree that produces apples.

appliance [ə'plaɪəns] *n* a machine or device
that is usually used in the home and is powered by gas or electricity, e.g. a washing machine.

applicable [ə'plɪkəbl] *adj* [rule, question] that is
of interest, importance etc to a particular
person, situation etc □ *'Delete where not applicable.'* □ *This rule is only applicable to members.*

applicant ['æplɪkənt] *n* a person who applies
for membership, a job, a grant etc.

application [,æplɪ'keɪʃn] *n* -1. [for membership, a
job, grant] a formal request for something,
usually in writing, that is made to an organization, institution etc □ *Her application
was turned down.* □ *We have received over 2,000
applications for the job.* -2. [of a device, machine]
a practical use □ *The machine has various applications.* -3. [of a person] hard work and concentration □ *The task requires a certain amount
of application.* -4. COMPUTING **an application
(package)** a computer program that is written to carry out a specific task, e.g. word
processing. -5. [of knowledge, skill, a lotion] *see*
apply □ *I'm not convinced this research will have
any practical application.* □ *'For external application only.'*

application form *n* a form used for making
an application for something such as a job.

applicator ['æplɪkeɪtər] *n* an object that is used
for applying lotion, paint, glue etc.

applied [ə'plaɪd] *adj* [art, linguistics, science] that
is used for a practical purpose.

appliqué [US ,æplə'keɪ, GB ə'pliːkeɪ] *n* a type of
decorative needlework that consists of
pieces of material sewn or stuck onto a larger piece □ *designer jeans with appliqués on
them.*

apply [ə'plaɪ] (*pt* & *pp* **applied**) ◇ *vt* -1.
[knowledge, skill, rule] to use <sthg> in a particular situation □ *Sadly, Tony never applied the
principle to his own life.* ■ **to apply oneself** OR
one's mind to work hard □ *Ben must learn to
apply himself in class.* -2. [lotion, paint, glue] to
spread <a substance> on the surface of
something □ *Apply the ointment to the infected
area.* -3. AUTO to operate <a brake> □ *'Apply
handbrake and leave car in gear.'* -4. [pressure,
force, heat] to use <sthg> to change something else.

◇ *vi* -1. [person] to make a formal request,
usually in writing, for membership, a job,
grant etc □ *I didn't actually apply for this post.* □
*She applied to the Julliard School for a scholar-
ship.* -2. [rule, question] to be of interest, importance etc to a particular person or situation □ *None of what I said applies to you.* □ *Do
these conditions still apply?*

appoint [ə'pɔɪnt] *vt* -1. [applicant] to choose
<sb> for a job, position etc □ *She was ap-
pointed to the post of director.* □ *He has been ap-*

pointed as head of finance. **-2. to appoint a time/place** to decide when/where something will happen (formal use) □ We met on the appointed day.

appointment [ə'pɔɪntmənt] n **-1.** [of an applicant] see **appoint** □ Crane's appointment to the post comes as a surprise to everybody. ■ **'by appointment to Her Majesty the Queen'** a phrase used on labels, packaging etc by companies who supply products to the British Royal Family. **-2.** [in a company] a job or position; a person chosen for a particular job or position □ This top-level appointment carries a competitive salary. □ the appointments page in the newspaper. **-3.** [with one's doctor, client, lawyer] an arranged meeting □ a doctor's/dentist's appointment □ Do you have an appointment? □ I'd like to make an appointment with Mr White, please. □ He sees clients by appointment only.

Appomattox [,æpə'mætəks] a town in Virginia, USA, where on April 9 1865, Robert E. Lee surrendered to Ulysses S. Grant, ending the American Civil War.

apportion [ə'pɔːʳʃn] vt [money, praise, blame] to divide <sthg> between a number of people in the way that one thinks is suitable □ The Committee will not seek to apportion blame.

apposite ['æpəzət] adj [comment, intervention] that comes at a suitable time (formal use).

appraisal [ə'preɪzl] n [of a person, situation] a statement, report, or interview in which somebody or something is appraised.

appraise [ə'preɪz] vt [person, performance, situation] to judge the quality, value, importance etc of <sb/sthg> (formal use).

appreciable [ə'priːʃəbl] adj [amount, difference, increase] large enough to be clearly noticed.

appreciably [ə'priːʃəblɪ] adv **appreciably smaller/warmer** smaller/warmer in a way that is easily noticed □ Sales have fallen appreciably.

appreciate [ə'priːʃɪeɪt] ◇ vt **-1.** [help, advice, co-operation] to be grateful for <sthg that is done or given by somebody else> □ I would appreciate a prompt reply. □ Thanks, I'd appreciate that. ■ **I'd/we'd etc appreciate it if...** a phrase used to introduce a request □ I'd appreciate it if you didn't repeat any of this. **-2.** [food, music, art] to understand and enjoy the qualities of <sthg> □ Richard appreciates good wine. **-3.** [problem, situation, difficulty] to understand the importance or nature of <sthg> □ Are you sure you appreciate the risks involved? □ I appreciate your concern, but unfortunately there's nothing we can do at this stage. ◇ vi [property, jewelry, currency] to increase in value over a period of time.

appreciation [ə,priːʃɪ'eɪʃn] n **-1.** [of somebody's help, advice, cooperation] a feeling of gratitude for something that somebody else has done or given □ Please accept this gift as a token of my appreciation. **-2.** [of food, music, art] the enjoyment of something whose qualities one understands □ They showed their appreciation by giving her a standing ovation. **-3.** [of a problem, situation, difficulty] the ability to understand the importance or nature of something □ We were impressed by his appreciation

of the key issues. **-4.** [of property, jewelry, a currency] an increase in value over a period of time □ an appreciation of 25%. **-5.** [of a novel, play] a discussion, often in writing, about the qualities of a novel, play, writer etc.

appreciative [ə'priːʃətɪv] adj [audience, remark, gesture] that shows approval or gratitude □ They are always very appreciative of his cooking.

apprehend [,æprɪ'hend] vt to arrest <a criminal or suspect> (formal use).

apprehension [,æprɪ'henʃn] n feelings of worry about a future event □ The prospect of a confrontation filled him with apprehension.

apprehensive [,æprɪ'hensɪv] adj [person, expression] that shows feelings of worry about a future event □ He was feeling rather apprehensive about the interview.

apprehensively [,æprɪ'hensɪvlɪ] adv [wait, enter, speak] see **apprehensive** □ "And what about me?" he asked apprehensively.

apprentice [ə'prentɪs] ◇ n a person who is learning a trade or craft by working with somebody who is skilled in that trade or craft □ an electrician's apprentice □ an apprentice draughtsman. ◇ vt **to be apprenticed to sb** to work as an apprentice for sb.

apprenticeship [ə'prentəsʃɪp] n the period of time spent working as an apprentice; the state of being an apprentice □ I served my apprenticeship as a carpenter.

approach [ə'prəʊtʃ] ◇ n **-1.** [to a place] a road or path that leads to a building, town etc □ All approaches to the city were flooded. **-2.** [in space] the act of moving nearer to an object or place □ Ladies and gentlemen, we are beginning our approach to Houston International Airport. **-3.** [in time] the process of becoming closer in time □ the approach of spring. **-4.** [to a problem] a way of doing something □ Let's try a different approach. **-5.** [to a person] a request, offer, or suggestion made for the first time □ He's had an approach from a rival company. ■ **to make approaches** OR **an approach** to speak to somebody in order to make a request, offer, suggestion etc for the first time □ We have made an approach to our suppliers.

◇ vt **-1.** [city, building, border] to move nearer to <a person, place, or thing> □ We'll be approaching Paris from the south. **-2.** [date, event] to move nearer in time □ He's approaching retirement. **-3.** [manager, company] to speak to <sb> about a job, deal etc for the first time □ I've been approached about a transfer. □ They approached her about giving a talk. **-4.** [problem, subject, issue] to decide to deal with <a situation> in a particular way □ That's not the way to approach it. **-5.** [level, age, maturity] to almost reach <a state or quality> □ He must be approaching 50 by now. □ The work doesn't even begin to approach our standards.

◇ vi [person, vehicle, event] to move nearer.

approachable [ə'prəʊtʃəbl] adj [person] who is easy to talk to.

approaching [ə'prəʊtʃɪŋ] adj [person, vehicle, event] that is becoming closer in distance or time □ We looked for shelter from the approaching storm. □ the sound of an approaching train.

approbation [ˌæprə'beɪʃn] *n* praise or approval (formal use).

appropriate [*adj* ə'prouprɪət, *vb* ə'prouprɪeɪt] ◇ *adj* [clothing, word, moment] that is suitable or correct for a particular occasion □ *They took the appropriate steps.* □ *the level of contribution appropriate for* OR *to each country* □ *His remarks were hardly appropriate for the occasion.* ◇ *vt* **-1.** LAW to take <money, funds> etc for one's own use, especially illegally. **-2.** BUSINESS to decide to use <money, funds> etc for a particular purpose □ *$5 billion has been appropriated for the relief work.*

appropriately [ə'prouprɪətlɪ] *adv* [dress, behave] in a suitable or correct way □ *The restaurant is appropriately named "Foodies".*

appropriation [əˌprouprɪ'eɪʃn] *n*: *see* **appropriate.**

approval [ə'pruːvl] *n* **-1.** [of a person, decision, action] a favorable opinion about somebody or something □ *a gesture of approval* □ *The Senator's approval rating has slumped.* ■ **to meet with sb's approval** to be accepted by sb as correct, good, or suitable □ *Does the report meet with your approval?* **-2.** [of a plan, proposal, agreement] official acceptance □ *We're still waiting for the chairman's approval.* ■ **to buy sthg on approval** [product, goods] to buy sthg and be able to return it without paying if it is not satisfactory.

approve [ə'pruːv] ◇ *vi* to think that a person, decision, action etc is right, good, or suitable □ *We're going ahead with the wedding even though my family doesn't approve.* □ *Her parents don't approve of her leaving college.* ◇ *vt* [plan, proposal] to officially accept <sthg> □ *We'll have to get it approved by head office.* □ *a strategy approved by the authorities.*

approved [ə'pruːvd] *adj* [method, practice] that has become accepted by many people.

approved school *n* GB = **community home.**

approving [ə'pruːvɪŋ] *adj* [look, comment, gesture] that shows support or agreement □ *Ma gave us an approving wink.*

approx. *abbr of* **approximately.**

approximate [*adj* ə'prɒksɪmət, *vb* ə'prɒksɪmeɪt] ◇ *adj* [number, time, distance] that is almost exact, but not completely □ *Could you give me an approximate idea of when you'll be arriving?* ◇ *vi* **to approximate to sthg** [to an amount, size] to be close to sthg, but not the same □ *These figures approximate to our earlier estimates.*

approximately [ə'prɒksɪmətlɪ] *adv* [calculate, draw, measure] in a way that is almost exact, but not completely □ *We're approximately halfway through the project.*

approximation [əˌprɒksɪ'meɪʃn] *n* [of a number, time, distance] an approximate calculation.

Apr. *abbr of* **April.**

APR (*abbr of* **annual percentage rate**) *n* **the APR** the interest rate payable by somebody borrowing money or buying something on credit. It includes the interest that is calculated on the original sum, and on unpaid interest, fees, and charges.

après-ski [US ˌɑːpreɪ-, GB ˌæpreɪ-] *n* the entertainment at the end of a day of skiing in a resort □ *après-ski entertainment.*

apricot ['eɪprɪkɒt] *n* **-1.** a small round fruit with soft juicy flesh and a yellow or orange furry skin □ *apricot tart.* **-2.** the color of apricots □ *white with a hint of apricot.*

April ['eɪprəl] *n* the fourth month of the year in the Western calendar; *see also* **February.**

April Fools' Day *n* April 1, when it is traditional to play tricks on people, who are then called April Fools.

▼ APRIL FOOLS' DAY
On April Fools' Day in Britain and Australia, it is traditional to play tricks on people to make them believe something that is not true, e.g. that the Prime Minister has just resigned. Even the most serious newspapers and radio and television programs give false news stories on April 1. In the USA people also play practical jokes, such as secretly attaching a sign to somebody's back that says "Kick me".

apron ['eɪprən] *n* **-1.** COOKING a piece of clothing that is tied around the waist and is worn over one's normal clothes while cooking in order to stop them from getting dirty. ■ **to be tied to sb's apron strings** to be under sb's control □ *He's still very much tied to his mother's apron strings.* **-2.** [at an airport] an area where airplanes are parked.

apropos ['æprəpou] *adj* [comment, criticism] relevant.

◆ **apropos of** *prep* a phrase used to introduce a subject that is connected with the one being discussed (formal use) □ *Apropos of what we were talking about earlier...*

apt [æpt] *adj* **-1.** [description, remark] that is suitable □ *Your comments were most apt.* **-2.** **to be apt to do sthg** to be likely to do sthg, especially because of having a particular tendency □ *He is apt to get flustered when under pressure.* **-3.** **an apt pupil/student** a pupil/student who learns quickly.

apt. *abbr of* **apartment.**

aptitude ['æptɪtjuːd] *n* a natural ability to learn something quickly □ *He has a real aptitude for languages.*

aptitude test *n* a test to measure a person's ability to do a specific task.

aptly ['æptlɪ] *adv* [describe, remark] *see* **apt** □ *As you so aptly pointed out...*

aqualung [US 'ɑːkwəlʌŋ, GB 'æk-] *n* a container of air worn by divers on their backs for breathing underwater.

aquamarine [US ˌɑːkwəmə'riːn, GB ˌæk-] *n* a greenish-blue color.

aquaplane [US 'ɑːkwəpleɪn, GB 'æk-] *vi* GB [car, truck] to slide out of control on a wet road surface.

aquarium [ə'kweərɪəm] (*pl* **aquariums** OR **aquaria** [-rɪə]) *n* **-1.** a glass tank full of water in which fish or other animals that live in water are kept. **-2.** a building, usually part of a zoo, with several aquariums.

Aquarius [əˈkweərɪəs] *n* a sign of the zodiac, often represented by a man pouring water; a person born under this sign between January 21 and February 19.

aquatic [US əˈkwɑːtɪk, GB əˈkwætɪk] *adj* **-1.** [animal, plant] that lives in water. **-2.** [sport, environment] that is connected with water.

aqueduct [ˈækwədʌkt] *n* a bridge that carries water across a valley.

Aquinas [əˈkwaɪnəs], **St. Thomas** (1225–1274) an Italian philosopher who wrote about religion and was very important in the development of Catholicism.

AR *abbr of* **Arkansas**.

ARA (*abbr of* **Associate of the Royal Academy**) *n* GB a member of the Royal Academy.

Arab [ˈærəb] ◇ *n* **-1.** a person who comes from Arabia. **-2.** a person who comes from the Middle East or North Africa. ◇ *adj*: *an Arab horse* □ *the Arab world.*

Arabia [əˈreɪbjə] a large peninsula between the Red Sea and the Persian Gulf that includes Saudi Arabia, Yemen, Oman, and the United Arab Emirates.

Arabian Peninsula [ə,reɪbjən-] = **Arabia**.

Arabian Sea *n* **the Arabian Sea** the northwestern part of the Indian Ocean, between Arabia and India.

Arabic [ˈærəbɪk] *n* a language spoken in Arabia, North Africa, and the Middle East.

Arabic numeral *n* a sign used to represent a number, e.g. 1, 2, or 3 that is different than a Roman numeral, e.g. I, II, or III.

arable [ˈærəbl] *adj* [land, area, farming] that is used for, suitable for, or connected with growing crops □ *Much of the land is given over to arable farming.*

Arab League *n* **the Arab League** an association of Arab countries established in 1945.

arbiter [ˈɑːrbɪtər] *n* a person who arbitrates in a dispute (formal use) □ *an independent arbiter.*

arbitrage [ˈɑːrbɪtrɑːʒ] *n* FINANCE the buying and selling of shares, currency etc in two different markets at almost the same time, in order to make a profit from differences in price.

arbitrary [US ˈɑːrbɪtreri, GB ˈɑːbɪtrərɪ] *adj* [attack, arrest, choice] that is made for no particular reason and is therefore often unfair □ *Many art galleries have complained that withdrawal of funding has been completely arbitrary.*

arbitrate [ˈɑːrbɪtreɪt] *vi* to act as a judge in order to settle a dispute without going to court □ *France has offered to arbitrate in the dispute.*

arbitration [,ɑːrbɪˈtreɪʃn] *n* a way of settling a dispute that uses somebody official who is not involved to judge it, and whose decision both sides have agreed they will accept. ■ **to go to arbitration** to ask somebody to settle a dispute by arbitration.

Arbor Day [ˈɑːrbər-] *n* a special day each year in the USA, New Zealand, and parts of

Canada and Australia when people plant trees.

arc [ɑːrk] *n* a curved line, e.g. part of a circle □ *Spread the seeds in a wide arc.*

ARC [ɑːrk] (*abbr of* **AIDS-related complex**) *n* a set of symptoms found in people who are HIV-positive, e.g. high temperature or weight loss.

arcade [ɑːrˈkeɪd] *n* **-1.** [with shops] a covered passage, often between two streets, with shops on either side. **-2.** ARCHITECTURE a set of arches and pillars along the side of a building.

arch [ɑːrtʃ] ◇ *n* **-1.** ARCHITECTURE a curved structure that forms an opening in a building or supports a bridge or roof. **-2.** ANATOMY the raised part of one's foot between one's toes and one's heel. ◇ *vt* [back, eyebrow] to move <a part of one's body> into a curved shape. ◇ *vi* [back, eyebrow] to form a curved shape; [rocket, missile] to move in a curved line.

arch- *prefix* added to a word to show it is the greatest and most important of its kind □ *her arch-rival* □ *an arch-criminal.*

archaeology *etc* [,ɑːrkɪˈɒlədʒɪ] = **archeology** *etc*.

archaic [ɑːrˈkeɪɪk] *adj* [language, custom, practice] that is very old-fashioned and no longer used.

archangel [ˈɑːrkeɪndʒəl] *n* an angel of the highest rank.

archbishop [,ɑːrtʃˈbɪʃəp] *n* a bishop of the highest rank. ■ **the Archbishop of Canterbury** the person who governs the Church of England. ■ **the Archbishop of Westminster** the person who governs the Roman Catholic Church in Britain.

archduchess [,ɑːrtʃˈdʌtʃəs] *n* a duchess of the highest rank.

archduke [,ɑːrtʃˈdjuːk] *n* a duke of the highest rank.

arched [ɑːrtʃt] *adj* [roof, doorway, window] that has an arch; [back] that is curved.

archenemy [,ɑːrtʃˈenəmɪ] (*pl* **archenemies**) *n* the greatest enemy of a country, hero etc.

archeological [,ɑːrkɪəˈlɒdʒɪkl] *adj* [excavation, research] *see* **archeology**.

archeologist [,ɑːrkɪˈɒlədʒəst] *n* a person who studies archeology.

archeology [,ɑːrkɪˈɒlədʒɪ] *n* the study of the remains of past societies, e.g. the buildings and the objects they made, by digging them out of the ground.

archer [ˈɑːrtʃər] *n* a person, especially a soldier, who is trained to use a bow and arrow.

archery [ˈɑːrtʃərɪ] *n* the sport, skill, or practice of shooting arrows from a bow.

archetypal [,ɑːrkɪˈtaɪpl] *adj*: *see* **archetype** □ *the archetypal nervous bridegroom.*

archetype [ˈɑːrkɪtaɪp] *n* somebody or something that is a perfect example of a particular kind of person or thing.

Archimedes [,ɑːrkɪˈmiːdiːz] (287–212 BC) a Greek mathematician and inventor. According to a popular story, he leapt out of his bath and shouted "Eureka" (I have found it) after discovering the law of physics now known as Archimedes' principle.

archipelago [ˌɑːᵏkəˈpeləgoʊ] (*pl* **archipelagoes** OR **archipelagos**) *n* a group of small islands; an area of sea where these islands are found □ *the Tuscan Archipelago.*

architect [ˈɑːᵏkətekt] *n* -1. a person whose job is to design buildings □ *a firm of architects.* -2. the person responsible for inventing a system, plan etc or planning an event □ *He was the architect of the New Deal.*

architectural [ˌɑːᵏkəˈtektʃrəl] *adj* [style, history] see **architecture** □ *an architectural firm/tour* □ *architectural studies.*

architecture [ˈɑːᵏkətektʃəʳ] *n* -1. the art of designing and constructing buildings □ *a superb piece of architecture* □ *Her son is studying architecture.* -2. [of a region, period] a particular style of building □ *Roman/Gothic/modern architecture.* -3. COMPUTING the overall design of the inside of a computer and the software that operates it.

archive file *n* the file in a computer used for storing data that is no longer being used.

archives [ˈɑːᵏkaɪvz] *npl* historical records, e.g. documents, photographs, or maps.

archivist [ˈɑːᵏkəvəst] *n* a person whose job is to collect and keep archives.

archway [ˈɑːᵏtʃweɪ] *n* a passage or entrance in the shape of an arch.

Arctic [ˈɑːᵏktɪk] ◇ **the Arctic** the region around the North Pole, including the Arctic Ocean. ◇ *adj* -1. [wildlife, plant] that is from the Arctic. -2. [weather, conditions] very cold.

Arctic Circle: **the Arctic Circle** an imaginary circle around the Arctic region, parallel to the equator, at latitude 66° 32' N.

Arctic Ocean: **the Arctic Ocean** the sea around the North Pole.

ardent [ˈɑːᵏdnt] *adj* [supporter, feminist] who is very enthusiastic.

ardor US, **ardour** GB [ˈɑːᵏdəʳ] *n* a strong feeling of love, enthusiasm etc □ *He spoke with genuine ardor about Italy.*

arduous [ˈɑːᵏdʒʊəs] *adj* [task, journey] that is very difficult and tiring and takes a long time □ *an arduous trip across the desert.*

are [*stressed* ɑːʳ, *unstressed* əʳ] *vb* → **be.**

area [ˈeərɪə] *n* -1. [of a town, country] a particular part of a place □ *in the Boston area* □ *a poor area of town* □ *The area of the crash was cordoned off.* □ *an area manager.* ■ **area of outstanding natural beauty** in Britain, any part of the countryside that is protected by law from being built on. ■ **in the area** near to a particular place □ *Come and visit when you're in the area.* -2. [of a piece of land] the amount of ground that a piece of land covers □ *The garden is 500m² in area.* -3. [in a building, room, space] a place used for a particular purpose □ *a parking/dining/smoking area.* -4. [of knowledge, interest] a particular subject or activity □ *She's an expert in the area of finance.*

area code *n* a number that must be dialed

before a telephone number if the call is being made from a different area.

arena [əˈriːnə] *n* -1. [for sports] a stadium for sports, concerts etc. -2. [of an activity] a particular area of activity, usually of conflict □ *the political/economic arena.*

aren't [ɑːnt] = **are not.**

Argentina [ˌɑːᵏdʒənˈtiːnə] a country in southern South America, between the Andes and the Atlantic Ocean. SIZE: 2,780,000 sq kms. POPULATION: 33,500,000 (*Argentines, Argentinians*). CAPITAL: Buenos Aires. LANGUAGE: Spanish. CURRENCY: peso.

Argentine [ˈɑːᵏdʒəntaɪn] ◇ **the Argentine** = **Argentina.** ◇ *n* & *adj*: see **Argentina.**

Argentinian [ˌɑːᵏdʒənˈtɪnɪən] *n* & *adj*: see **Argentina.**

arguable [ˈɑːᵏgjʊəbl] *adj* [point, idea, statement] that is not necessarily true and can be disagreed with □ *It's arguable whether the plan is actually worthwhile.*

arguably [ˈɑːᵏgjʊəblɪ] *adj* a word used to say that an opinion is probably true, although not everybody would agree with it □ *She's arguably the best manager in the company.*

argue [ˈɑːᵏgjuː] ◇ *vi* -1. [with a person] to speak angrily to somebody because one disagrees with them □ *He argued with her about his contract.* □ *They're always arguing.* □ *We usually end up arguing over who should pay.* -2. [for or against something] to give reasons for or against something □ *She argued for* OR *in favor of raising taxes.* □ *He argued against going.* ◇ *vt* **to argue (that)...** to say that something is true, and explain why it is true □ *He argued that further investment was needed.* □ *She argued her case/point convincingly.*

argument [ˈɑːᵏgjəmənt] *n* -1. [between people] a conversation in which people argue □ *Richard had an argument with his boss about overtime.* -2. [for or against something] a reason for or against doing something or allowing something to happen □ *There are good arguments against smoking/for HIV tests.* -3. [from a person] the way somebody explains why something is true □ *I didn't follow his line of argument.*

argumentative [ˌɑːᵏgjəˈmentətɪv] *adj* [person] who likes to disagree and start arguments with other people.

aria [ˈɑːrɪə] *n* a song sung by one person in an opera.

arid [ˈærɪd] *adj* -1. [land, desert] that is very dry. -2. [subject, writing] that is very boring.

Aries [ˈeəriːz] *n* a sign of the zodiac, represented by a male sheep; a person born under this sign between March 21 and April 20.

arise [əˈraɪz] (*pt* **arose**, *pp* **arisen** [əˈrɪzn]) *vi* [problem, situation] to begin to exist and be noticed □ *if the need/occasion arises.* ■ **to arise from sthg** to be created or caused by sthg □ *Several points arose from the discussion.*

aristocracy [ˌærɪˈstɒkrəsɪ] (*pl* **aristocracies**) *n* the highest social class consisting of families who are usually rich and who often have titles as part of their names.

aristocrat [US əˈrɪstəkræt, GB ˈærɪstəkræt] *n* a member of the aristocracy.

aristocratic [US ə,rɪstəˈkrætɪk, GB ,ærɪstəˈkrætɪk] *adj* [person, family] *see* **aristocracy**.

Aristotle [ˈærɪstɒtl] (384–322 BC) a Greek philosopher. His works on logic, ethics, politics, literature, and biology strongly influenced Christian and Muslim ideas.

arithmetic [əˈrɪθmətɪk] *n* the area of mathematics concerned with addition, subtraction, multiplication, and division □ *an arithmetic test/problem.*

Arizona [,ærɪˈzoʊnə] a state in the southwestern USA, with many mountainous and desert areas. ABBREVIATION: AZ. SIZE: 295,000 sq kms. POPULATION: 3,665,228 (*Arizonans*). CAPITAL: Phoenix.

ark [ɑːʳk] *n* in the Bible, the ship that Noah built to save his family and selected animals from a great flood.

Arkansas [ˈɑːʳkənsɔː] a state in the southern USA. ABBREVIATION: AR. SIZE: 138,000 sq kms. POPULATION: 2,350,725 (*Arkansans*). CAPITAL: Little Rock.

Arlington National Cemetery [,ɑːʳlɪŋtən-] a cemetery in Virginia, USA, where many US soldiers and politicians are buried.

arm [ɑːʳm] ◇ *n* **-1.** [of a person] one of the two parts of the body attached to the shoulders □ *She threw her arms around me.* ■ **to keep sb at arm's length** to avoid becoming too involved with sb. ■ **to twist sb's arm** to persuade sb to do something by insisting (informal use) □ *He refused at first, but I managed to twist his arm.* **-2.** [of a coat, sweater, shirt] the part of a piece of clothing where a person's arm goes. **-3.** [of a chair, sofa] one of the two raised parts at the side of a chair or couch where people rest their arms when sitting. **-4.** [of an organization] a section that does a particular job □ *the political arm of the IRA* □ *the Canadian arm of the electronics giant Herst.* ◇ *vt* [troops, population] to supply <sb> with weapons □ *I armed myself with a shotgun and set off.*

◆ **arms** *npl* weapons □ *an arms dealer/manufacturer* □ *arms limitation.* ■ **to be up in arms** to protest angrily □ *People are up in arms about* OR *over the new bypass.*

◆ **arm in arm** *adv* [walk, go] next to each other, with each person bending their arm around the other person's arm □ *He was walking arm in arm with her.*

armada [ɑːʳˈmɑːdə] *n* a group of ships, especially warships.

armadillo [,ɑːʳməˈdɪloʊ] (*pl* **armadillos**) *n* a small animal, found in North and South America, that has a hard shell divided into sections that allows it to roll into a ball when it is attacked.

Armageddon [,ɑːʳməˈgedn] *n* a terrible battle that, according to Christian belief, will cause the end of the world.

armaments [ˈɑːʳməmənts] *npl* a collective term for weapons and other military equipment □ *the build-up of armaments.*

arm band *n* a band of material that is worn around the top part of the arm as a symbol of something, e.g. to show respect for somebody who has died.

armchair [ˈɑːʳmtʃeəʳ] *n* a comfortable chair with arms.

armed [ɑːʳmd] *adj* **-1.** [policeman, thief, vehicle] that is carrying a weapon, especially a gun □ *He was armed with a gun/stick.* □ *The public has been warned that he is armed and dangerous.* **-2. to be armed with sthg** [with information, skills, a map] to have sthg that is useful in a particular situation □ *We arrived at the meeting armed with statistics to support our argument.*

armed forces *npl* the army, navy, and air force of a country □ *a member of the armed forces.*

armed robbery *n* a robbery in which the criminals carry guns.

Armenia [ɑːʳˈmiːnjə] a mountainous country in western Asia, in the Caucasus northeast of Turkey. SIZE: 29,800 sq kms. POPULATION: 3,600,000 (*Armenians*). CAPITAL: Yerevan. LANGUAGE: Armenian. CURRENCY: dram.

armful [ˈɑːʳmfl] *n* **an armful of sthg** the amount of sthg that can be held in one arm or both arms □ *an armful of flowers.*

armhole [ˈɑːʳmhoʊl] *n* [of a coat, shirt, sweater] one of the two holes that the arms are put through in a piece of clothing.

armistice [ˈɑːʳməstɪs] *n* an agreement between countries to stop fighting for a limited period to discuss peace.

Armistice Day *n* November 11, the anniversary of the end of World War I.

armor US, **armour** GB [ˈɑːʳməʳ] *n* **-1.** [for a soldier] protective clothes made of metal that were worn by medieval soldiers in battle □ *a suit of armor.* **-2.** [for a military vehicle] a protective metal covering for a ship, truck etc.

armored US, **armoured** GB [ˈɑːʳməʳd] *adj* [vehicle, personnel carrier] that is protected by armor.

armored car *n* a light military vehicle that is armed and armored.

armor-plated [-ˈpleɪtəd] *adj* = **armored**.

armory US, **armoury** GB [ˈɑːʳmərɪ] (*pl* US **armories**, GB **armouries**) *n* a place where weapons are stored.

armour *etc n* GB = **armor** *etc*.

armpit [ˈɑːʳmpɪt] *n* the part of one's body under one's arm where it joins the body and where hair grows.

armrest [ˈɑːʳmrest] *n* the part of a seat in a car or plane that supports one's arm and that can often be folded back to leave more space.

Armstrong [ˈɑːʳmstrɒŋ], **Louis** (1900–1971) a US jazz trumpeter and singer who had a big influence on the development of jazz.

Armstrong, Neil (1930–) a US astronaut who was the first person to land on the Moon in 1969.

army [ˈɑːʳmɪ] (*pl* **armies**) *n* **-1.** MILITARY a large organized group of soldiers trained to fight on land □ *an army officer/truck* □ *He's in the army.* **-2.** [of people] a large group of people □ *an army of tourists.*

Arnold ['ɑːʳnld], **Benedict** (1741–1801) a US soldier who betrayed his country to the British during the American Revolution.

A road *n* GB a main road between towns.

aroma [ə'rəʊmə] *n* a strong pleasant smell, especially of food or drink □ *a wonderful aroma of fresh coffee.*

aromatherapy [ə,rəʊmə'θerəpɪ] *n* a type of alternative medicine in which oils with a pleasant smell are massaged into the skin.

aromatic [,ærə'mætɪk] *adj* [substance, herb] that has a strong aroma.

arose [ə'rəʊz] *past tense of* **arise**.

around [ə'raʊnd] ◇ *adv* **-1. to walk/travel around** to walk/travel in different directions □ *I wandered around for a couple of hours, trying to decide what to do.* □ *Clothes were lying around all over the floor.* **-2. the stadium measures a mile around** the length of the outside of the stadium is a mile □ *The garden was well hidden, with a high wall all around.* **-3. the book is around somewhere** the book is somewhere near here and can be found or used □ *There was nobody around.* **-4. to be around** to exist and be noticeable □ *That song has been around for years.* **-5. phrase he's/she's been around** he/she has seen many places and things and so has knowledge and experience (informal use).
◇ *prep* **-1. to walk around a place** to walk to many different parts of a place, usually with no special purpose □ *In the evening, we strolled around the town.* **-2. they sat around the table** they sat in a circle on all sides of the table □ *The Earth moves around the Sun.* □ *He wore a scarf around his neck.* **-3. it's around the corner** it's on the other side of the corner □ *The door was somewhere around the back of the house.* **-4. it's around here** it's near here □ *Is there a bank anywhere around here?* **-5. at around 100 mph** at approximately 100 mph □ *There were around 2,000 people there.*

arousal [ə'raʊzl] *n: see* **arouse**.

arouse [ə'raʊz] *vt* **-1.** [curiosity, interest, fear] to make somebody have <a particular feeling> □ *Her sudden departure aroused their suspicions.* □ *The idea failed to arouse much interest.* **-2.** [person] to make <sb> feel sexually excited □ *sexually aroused.*

arr. *abbr of* **arrives**.

arrange [ə'reɪndʒ] ◇ *vt* **-1.** [flowers, books, furniture] to put <sthg> in a particular position to be neat, attractive etc □ *Four chairs were arranged around a table.* **-2.** [meeting, trip] to plan and organize <sthg> usually by getting somebody's agreement or permission □ *We have arranged a training course on the new software.* □ *Let's arrange a time to meet.* □ *I've arranged to meet them at the airport.* □ *She was able to arrange a loan for us.* **-3.** MUSIC to adapt <a piece of music> for different instruments or voices.
◇ *vi* to plan something together with some-

body else □ *We have arranged for the delegates to stay at the Central Hotel.* □ *I've arranged with her to meet outside the restaurant.*

arranged marriage [ə,reɪndʒd-] *n* a marriage where the partners are chosen by their parents or relatives.

arrangement [ə'reɪndʒmənt] *n* **-1.** [between people] an agreement to do something □ *I'm sure we can come to an* OR *some arrangement with the bank.* □ *He sold the stock by arrangement with the company.* **-2.** [of furniture, books] a group of things that has been arranged in a particular way □ *a flower arrangement.* **-3.** MUSIC a piece of music that has been arranged in a particular way.

◆ **arrangements** *npl* plans and preparations for doing something □ *Sophie has made all the necessary arrangements for the trip.* □ *I'll leave the arrangements to you, then.*

array [ə'reɪ] *n* **-1.** an impressive group of objects, people, or ornaments □ *There's a vast array of styles to choose from.* **-2.** COMPUTING an arrangement of data in rows and columns.

arrears [ə'rɪəʳz] *npl* money that has still not been paid and is late □ *The company collapsed, leaving arrears of $360,000.* ■ **to be in arrears** to owe arrears □ *We're six months in arrears on the loan repayments.* ■ **to be paid in arrears** to be paid for one's work after the work has been done.

arrest [ə'rest] ◇ *vt* **-1.** [criminal, suspect] to catch <sb> and not let them go free because they are suspected of committing a crime □ *They were arrested for fraud/on suspicion of fraud.* **-2. to arrest sb's attention** to attract and keep sb's attention (formal use) □ *There was something about her manner that arrested my attention.* **-3.** [development, progress] to stop <sthg> from happening or getting bigger, going further etc (formal use) □ *in an effort to arrest unemployment/inflation.* ◇ *n* the act of arresting somebody □ *The police made 50 arrests at the demonstration.* ■ **to be under arrest** to be held by the police after an arrest □ *He was put under arrest.*

arresting [ə'restɪŋ] *adj* [beauty, image] that arrests one's attention.

arrival [ə'raɪvl] *n* **-1.** [at a place] the act of arriving at a place □ *On* OR *Upon our arrival we were met by the conference organizers.* □ *We apologize for the late arrival of flight AA 251.* **-2.** [something new] the act of coming into existence or use □ *the arrival of the microchip.* **-3. a new arrival** a person who has recently moved to a new company, prison, school etc; a baby who has recently been born.

◆ **arrivals** *npl* [at an airport, station] the planes, trains etc that have just arrived after a trip □ *the arrivals board/lounge.*

arrive [ə'raɪv] *vi* **-1.** [person, train, taxi] to reach a place during a trip or at the end of a trip □ *They arrived yesterday.* □ *When you arrive at the airport...* □ *I arrived in this country in 1976.* **-2.** [letter, news] to be brought or delivered to somebody □ *The mail usually arrives at 8 o'clock.* **-3.** [product, invention] to start to exist or be used □ *The drug finally arrived on the mar-*

ket in the 1970s. -4. [baby] to be born □ *The baby arrived three weeks early.* -5. [moment, day, event] to happen □ *The time has arrived for us to take action.*

◆ **arrive at** *vt fus* **to arrive at a decision** to succeed in making à decision after a lot of thought or discussion □ *We finally arrived at the conclusion that...* □ *How did you arrive at that figure?*

arrogance [US 'erəgəns, GB 'ær-] *n: see* **arrogant** □ *That doesn't excuse his arrogance*

arrogant [US 'erəgənt, GB 'ær-] *adj* [person] who is rude and unpleasant because they think they are better, more important etc than other people □ *Her arrogant behavior made her generally unpopular.*

arrow [US 'erou, GB 'ær-] *n* -1. a thin stick with a point at one end and feathers at the other end, that is shot from a bow and used in archery or as a weapon. -2. a sign (→) that is shaped like an arrow and points to something on a page, sign, computer screen etc.

arrowroot [US 'erouruːt, GB 'ær-] *n* a natural substance, made from a West Indian plant, that is used in cooking to thicken sauces.

arsenal ['ɑːrsnəl] *n* a place for storing weapons; a large number of weapons that are stored in this place.

arsenic ['ɑːrsnɪk] *n* a very strong poison used for killing rats, insects etc. SYMBOL: As.

arson ['ɑːrsn] *n* the crime of setting fire to a building in order to cause damage □ *He was convicted of arson.*

arsonist ['ɑːrsnəst] *n* a person who commits arson.

art [ɑːrt] *n* -1. the act or process of creating paintings, sculptures, music etc □ *Shakespeare's art* □ *She is studying art.* □ *a great work of art.* -2. [in a museum] works of art, especially ones that can be seen, e.g. paintings or sculptures □ *modern/Asian/16th-century art* □ *an art collection/exhibition.* -3. something that requires skill □ *the art of survival* □ *Giving dinner parties is quite an art.*

◆ **arts** *npl* -1. EDUCATION subjects that are not scientific or technical, e.g. history, languages, or music □ *an arts degree/graduate/subject.* -2. **the arts** all the different types of art, e.g. painting, music, drama, literature, cinema etc, considered as a group.

art deco [US -deɪ'kou, GB -'dekou] *n* a style of art and design, common in the 1920s and 1930s, that is based on geometrical shapes with rounded angles □ *art deco furniture.*

artefact ['ɑːrtəfækt] *n* = **artifact**.

arterial [ɑːr'tɪərɪəl] *adj* [blood, disease, road] *see* **artery**.

arteriosclerosis [ɑːr'tɪərɪousklə'rousəs] *n* a disease that hardens the arteries and reduces the flow of blood around the body.

artery ['ɑːrtərɪ] (*pl* **arteries**) *n* -1. ANATOMY one of the tubes that carry blood from the heart around the body. -2. TRANSPORT a main road or railroad.

artful ['ɑːrtfl] *adj* [person] who is clever, usually at doing something dishonest.

art gallery *n* -1. a building where paintings and sculptures are publicly displayed. -2. a place where paintings and sculptures are sold.

arthritic [ɑːr'θrɪtɪk] *adj* [person, joint] that is affected by arthritis.

arthritis [ɑːr'θraɪtəs] *n* a disease that causes painful swelling in the joints.

Arthur ['ɑːrθər] a legendary British king who lived in Camelot and led a group of knights.

artichoke ['ɑːrtətʃouk] *n* a round green vegetable with thick pointed leaves and a soft center. When cooked, the bottom of the leaves and the center can be eaten □ *artichoke hearts.*

article ['ɑːrtɪkl] *n* -1. [of clothing, furniture] an object, especially an object of a particular type □ *articles of jewelry/of value.* -2. [in a newspaper, magazine] a piece of writing; [on television, the radio] a piece of news □ *an article on* OR *about the trade deficit.* -3. [in an agreement, contract, constitution] a section or paragraph. -4. GRAMMAR **the definite article** the word "the". ■ **the indefinite article** the words "a" and "an".

articled clerk [ˌɑːr'tɪkld-] *n* GB a person who is training to be a solicitor.

articles of association *npl* the laws that control the way in which a registered company is run; the document containing these laws.

Articles of Confederation *npl* **the Articles of Confederation** the first constitution of the USA. It was replaced by the present constitution in 1788.

articulate [*adj* ɑːr'tɪkjələt, *vb* ɑːr'tɪkjəleɪt] ◇ *adj* [person] who is good at expressing their thoughts and ideas clearly □ *a highly articulate writer/piece of writing.* ◇ *vt* [thought, idea, sound] to say or express <sthg> clearly.

articulated lorry [ɑːr'tɪkjələtəd-] *n* GB a large truck consisting of a separate part for the driver and a trailer joined by a metal bar.

artifact ['ɑːrtəfækt] *n* a tool, weapon, ornament etc that was made a long time ago and is of historical interest.

artificial [ˌɑːrtə'fɪʃl] *adj* -1. [flavoring, material] that is not made of natural materials or substances; [leg, hip, wood] that looks like or works like something real or natural □ *I don't like working in artificial light.* -2. [person] who pretends to have feelings and attitudes that are not real (disapproving use) □ *artificial behavior/tears.*

artificial insemination *n* a way of making a woman or female animal pregnant by transferring sperm with an instrument rather than through sex.

artificial intelligence *n* the part of computer science concerned with making computers do what humans can do, e.g. talk or move.

artificially [ˌɑːrtə'fɪʃlɪ] *adv* [flavor, behave, smile] *see* **artificial** □ *Prices are being kept artificially high.*

artificial respiration *n* a way of helping somebody to start breathing again when they are unconscious, usually by blowing air into their mouth.

artillery [ɑːˈtɪlərɪ] *n* big guns on wheels, used by an army □ *artillery fire.*

artisan [ˌɑːˈtəˈzæn] *n* a person whose job is to make and do things, especially traditional crafts, with their hands.

artist [ˈɑːˈtəst] *n* -1. ART a person who creates works of art, especially paintings □ *a success-ful/ commercial artist.* -2. [in an activity] a skillful and creative person in a particular field or activity □ *She's a real artist in the kitchen.*

artiste [ɑːˈtiːst] *n* a person whose job is to perform in public, e.g. a singer or dancer.

artistic [ɑːˈtɪstɪk] *adj* -1. [person] who is good at creating or appreciating art □ *James is the artistic member of the family.* -2. [freedom, style] that is connected with art or artists □ *Futur-ism was an influential artistic movement in the early part of the century.* -3. [design, work, ar-rangement] that is creative and attractive □ *Her Christmas decorations were very artistic.*

artistically [ɑːˈtɪstɪklɪ] *adv* [talented, designed] see **artistic** □ *an artistically arranged bunch of flowers.*

artistry [ˈɑːˈtɪstrɪ] *n* the creative skill of an art-ist □ *It was all done with great artistry.*

artless [ˈɑːˈtləs] *adj* [person] who is simple, honest, and does not deceive other people.

art nouveau [ˌɑːˈnuːˈvoʊ] *n* a style of art and design, common in the 1890s, that is based on flowing lines and floral shapes.

Arts Council *n* **the Arts Council** one of four organizations in the UK, supported by the British government, that gives grants to arts projects.

arugula [əˈruːgələ] *n* US a plant with small dark-green leaves that have a peppery taste and are eaten raw in salads.

ARV (*abbr of* **American Revised Version**) *n* **the ARV** an American translation of the Bible.

as [*stressed* æz, *unstressed* əz] ◇ *conj* -1. used to link two events that are happening at the same time □ *Kim called (just) as I was leaving.* □ *As he grew older, he became more bad-tempered.* -2. used to describe the way that something should happen □ *Why can't things be as they were before?* □ *Do as I say.* -3. used to introduce comparisons □ *The "h" is silent, as in "hour".* -4. used to introduce statements giving extra information □ *As you know, I lived in Africa for several years.* -5. because □ *As you weren't in, I left a message.* -6. **tired as I was...** although I was tired...
◇ *prep* -1. **he was dressed as a policeman** he was dressed so that he looked like a police-man (used to describe somebody's appear-ance). -2. **he works as a taxi driver** he has a job driving taxis (used to describe some-body's job, role, function etc) □ *my duties as a manager* □ *I lived in France as a boy.* -3. **to treat sthg as a joke** to consider sthg like a joke.
◇ *adv* used in comparisons □ *It cost twice as much as my first apartment.* □ *He's not as intelligent/handsome as his brother.*

◆ **as for** *prep* used to introduce a new topic □ *As for Arthur, he can come with me.*

◆ **as from** *prep* = **as of**.

◆ **as if** *conj* **as if I was** OR **were mad** in a way that might make people think that I am mad □ *It looks as if it's going to rain.*

◆ **as it is** *adv* already □ *You have enough work as it is, don't take on any more!*

◆ **as it were** *adv* used to show that a word is not being used precisely □ *He was, as it were, my teacher and guide.*

◆ **as of** *prep* **as of Monday** on Monday and for the time after that □ *I'll be in Madrid as of next week.*

◆ **as though** *conj* = **as if**.

◆ **as to** *prep* -1. = **as for**. -2. about □ *I am un-certain as to the best way to proceed.*

◆ **as well** *adv* also □ *Can I come as well?*

◆ **as yet** *adv* used to describe an event that has not happened but is expected soon □ *I wrote on Monday but haven't received their reply as yet.*

AS (*abbr of* **Associate in Science**) *n* a US col-lege degree.

a.s.a.p., asap *adv abbr of* **as soon as possible**.

asbestos [æsˈbestəs] *n* a gray material that does not burn. It is sometimes used in buildings, clothing etc to protect against heat and fire, but can be dangerous to peo-ple's health □ *asbestos fibers/clothing.*

asbestosis [ˌæsbeˈstoʊsəs] *n* a disease of the lungs that is caused by breathing in asbestos dust.

ascend [əˈsend] (formal use) ◇ *vt* [hill, stairs, slope] to go up <sthg>. ■ **to ascend the throne** to become king or queen. ◇ *vi* [per-son, smoke, staircase] to go upward.

ascendancy [əˈsendənsɪ] *n* a position of power over somebody.

ascendant [əˈsendənt] *n* **to be in the ascendant** to be in a powerful or dominant position.

ascending [əˈsendɪŋ] *adj* [person, smoke, stair-case] that goes up. ■ **in ascending order** ar-ranged in a list, row etc so that each one is bigger, higher, or more important than the one before it.

ascension [əˈsenʃn] *n* [to the throne] see **ascend**.

◆ **Ascension** *n* a Christian festival celebrating Christ's ascent into heaven.

ascent [əˈsent] *n* -1. [of a hill, mountain, staircase] a climb □ *the ascent of Everest* □ *Please remain seated during our ascent.* -2. a slope or path that goes upward □ *a steep ascent.* -3. [in rank, status] the process by which somebody be-comes more important, successful etc □ *He made a rapid ascent up the executive ladder.*

ascertain [ˌæsəˈteɪn] *vt* to find out <sthg>, usually by making an effort (formal use) □ *The police never managed to ascertain her true iden-tity.* □ *It is too soon to ascertain what effect this will have on the environment.*

ascetic [əˈsetɪk] ◇ *adj* [person] who lives a sim-ple life without luxuries or physical pleas-ures, usually for religious reasons (formal use) □ *an ascetic life/existence.* ◇ *n* a person who lives an ascetic life.

ASCII ['æskɪ] (*abbr of* **American Standard Code for Information Interchange**) *n* a computer code containing letters and numbers that is used for transferring information between computers □ *an ASCII file.*

ascorbic acid [ə‚skɔːˈbɪk-] *n* vitamin C (technical use). FORMULA: $C_6 H_8 O_6$.

Ascot ['æskət] *n* a race course in southern England. It is well-known for an annual race meeting called Royal Ascot, which fashionable society and the Royal Family go to.

ascribe [ə'skraɪb] *vt* **-1. to ascribe sthg to sthg** [problem, symptom, event] to think or say that sthg is responsible for sthg □ *Heart attacks are often ascribed to stress.* **-2. to ascribe sthg to sb** [quality, virtue, characteristic] to think or say that sb has sthg; [work of art, piece of music, book] to think or say that sb painted, composed, or wrote sthg □ *The statue is ascribed magical powers.* □ *The poem has been ascribed to various authors.*

ASEAN ['æsɪæn] (*abbr of* **Association of Southeast Asian Nations**) *n* an organization consisting of Malaysia, Indonesia, the Philippines, Singapore, Thailand, and Brunei that encourages economic and political cooperation between its members.

asexual [‚eɪˈsekʃʊəl] *adj* [reproduction] that takes place without sex; [animal, organism] that is neither male nor female; [person] who is not interested in sex.

ash [æʃ] *n* **-1.** [from a cigarette, fire] the soft gray powder that is left after something has been burned □ *wood/cigarette ash.* **-2.** BOTANY a tree that grows in Europe and Asia that has gray bark and seeds that are shaped like wings; the wood of this tree □ *an ash tree.*
♦ **ashes** *npl* the ash that is left after somebody has been cremated.

ASH [æʃ] (*abbr of* **Action on Smoking and Health**) *n* a British organization that tries to stop people from smoking.

ashamed [ə'ʃeɪmd] *adj* **to be ashamed** [person] to feel guilty or embarrassed because of something one has done □ *There's nothing to be ashamed of.* □ *You ought to be ashamed of yourself!* □ *I'm ashamed to say that I ate all of it.*

ash can *n* US a container for trash.

ashen-faced ['æʃnfeɪst] *adj* [person] who is very pale, usually because they have had a shock.

ashore [ə'ʃɔːr] *adv* [go, swim] to the shore from the ocean or a lake □ *We jumped out of the dinghy and waded ashore.*

ashtray ['æʃtreɪ] *n* a small dish where people put the ash from their cigarettes or cigars while smoking.

Ash Wednesday *n* the first day of Lent in the Christian calendar.

Asia [US 'eɪʒə, GB 'eɪʃə] the largest and most highly populated continent, including the eastern part of the old USSR, the Middle East, and the Far East.

Asian [US 'eɪʒn, GB 'eɪʃn] *n & adj: see* **Asia**.
NOTE: In the USA and Australia the term *Asian* usually refers to a person whose family comes from China, Japan, Vietnam, or Korea. In Britain *Asian* usually refers to a person whose family comes from India, Pakistan, or Bangladesh.

Asian American *n* an American whose family originally came from Asia.

Asia-Pacific: the Asia-Pacific (region) the countries of East Asia that border on the Pacific Ocean, e.g. Korea, Japan, and Taiwan.

aside [ə'saɪd] ◇ *adv* **-1.** [move, step, throw] to one side □ *Can you move aside, I want to get past.* ■ **to take sb aside** to take sb away from a group of people in order to talk in private. ■ **to brush** OR **sweep sthg aside** [idea, feeling, suggestion] to reject sthg that one considers unimportant □ *He simply brushed my question aside and went on talking.* **-2. work/money aside,...** a word used to show that somebody is finishing the subject of work/money and starting another subject, or that one does not want to discuss it □ *Financial concerns aside, we should start thinking about a new marketing strategy.*
◇ *n* **-1.** [in a play, movie] words spoken by a character that the other characters do not hear. **-2.** [in a conversation, discussion] a remark not directly connected with what one is talking about □ *He mentioned the bribe almost as an aside.*
♦ **aside from** *prep* apart from <sb/sthg> □ *There were no injuries, aside from a few bruises.*

ask [US æsk, GB ɑːsk] ◇ *vt* **-1.** to say <a question> to somebody; to say this question to <sb> □ *I don't know, you'll have to ask Steve about that.* □ *May I ask you something?* □ *He asked her where she was from.* □ *She asked me if I could come.* ■ **to ask sb sthg** to speak to sb to get sthg, usually information □ *I asked her the time.* ■ **if you ask me** in my opinion □ *If you ask me, they should have closed this place years ago.* **-2.** to speak to somebody to get <permission, advice, forgiveness> etc □ *He asked my opinion of the new system.* ■ **to ask sb to do sthg** to speak to sb because one wants them to do sthg □ *Please ask them to wait in the lobby.* ■ **to ask sb for sthg** to speak to sb because one wants them to give one sthg □ *I've asked the boss for a raise.* □ *She asked for more money/a glass of water.* **-3.** to invite <sb> to go somewhere with one □ *They asked her to join them.* □ *Why don't you ask him to dinner/ the party?* **-4.** to demand <a particular amount of money> for something □ *They're asking $90 per unit but I think they'll accept $85.*
◇ *vi* **-1.** to request information □ *I don't know, I didn't ask.* □ *Ask about the job.* **-2.** to speak to somebody because one wants something from them □ *I'll help you if you ask nicely.* □ *He asked if I could pass him the wine.*
♦ **ask after** *vt fus* **to ask after sb** to ask for information about sb, sb's health etc □ *There was a young man here asking after you.*
♦ **ask for** *vt fus* **to ask for sb** to ask if one can see or speak to sb □ *They asked for the manager.*
♦ **ask out** *vt sep* **to ask sb out** to invite sb to go out with one to a meal, party etc.

askance [ə'skæns] *adv* **to look askance at sb/ sthg** to look at sb/sthg with doubt or mistrust.

askew [ə'skjuː] *adj* [hat, necktie] not straight or level □ *The picture was hanging askew.*

asking price [US æskɪŋ-, GB 'ɑːskɪŋ-] *n* the amount of money that a person is hoping to get for an item that they are selling.

asleep [ə'sliːp] *adj* **to be asleep** to be sleeping. ■ **to fall asleep** to start sleeping □ *It took me a long time to fall asleep.* ■ **to be fast** OR **sound asleep** to be completely asleep □ *She was fast asleep on the sofa.*

ASLEF, Aslef ['æzlef] (*abbr of* **Associated Society of Locomotive Engineers and Firemen**) *n* a British labor union for railroad workers.

A/S Level *n* a school examination taken in a particular subject in England and Wales. An A/S level involves half the coursework of an A Level, and gives half as many points for university entrance.

asparagus [ə'spærəgəs] *n* a vegetable with long green shoots that are cooked until they are tender, and then eaten □ *asparagus soup* □ *asparagus tips.*

ASPCA (*abbr of* **American Society for the Prevention of Cruelty to Animals**) *n* **the ASPCA** a US charity that tries to prevent cruel treatment of animals.

aspect ['æspekt] *n* **-1.** [of a situation, problem] one part of something that has many parts □ *It will affect all aspects of daily life.* □ *We'll be looking at various aspects of American foreign policy.* **-2.** [of an idea, plan] a particular way of considering something □ *Meeting people is the most enjoyable aspect of my job.* □ *There's also the financial aspect to think about.* **-3.** [of a building] the direction in which a building faces □ *a house with a westerly aspect.*

aspen ['æspən] *n* a kind of poplar tree with leaves that rustle in the wind.

aspersions [ə'spɜːʳʃnz] *npl* **to cast aspersions on sb/sthg** to express doubts about or criticize sb/sthg (formal or humorous use) □ *I'm not casting aspersions on your ability to manage the situation.*

asphalt [US 'æsfɔːlt, GB -fælt] *n* a black substance used for making the surfaces of roads.

asphyxiate [əs'fɪksɪeɪt] *vt* to kill <sb> by preventing them from breathing in oxygen □ *He was asphyxiated by fumes from the fire.*

aspic ['æspɪk] *n* a clear jelly made from the juice of meat or fish and used in making cold dishes.

aspidistra [,æspə'dɪstrə] *n* a houseplant with long, hard, pointed, green leaves.

aspirate ['æspərət] *adj* [letter] pronounced by blowing out air so that the sound of the letter "h" is heard □ *an aspirate h.*

aspiration [,æspə'reɪʃn] *n* a strong desire and ambition to do or be something better □ *The international community now has to take their aspirations to independence seriously.* □ *the hopes and aspirations of the young.*

aspire [ə'spaɪəʳ] *vi* **to aspire to sthg/to do sthg**

to have a strong desire and ambition to have sthg/to do sthg better □ *young actors who aspire to wealth and fame.*

aspirin ['æsprɪn] *n* a common drug, usually in the form of a white pill, that is taken to reduce pain, fever, or inflammation □ *Do you want an* OR *some aspirin?*

aspiring [ə'spaɪərɪŋ] *adj* **an aspiring actor/ politician** an actor/politician who is trying to be successful in their profession □ *She was always getting letters from aspiring filmmakers.*

Asquith ['æskwɪθ], **H. H.** (1852–1928) British Prime Minister from 1908 to 1916. His government was responsible for the introduction of welfare benefits for old people.

ass [æs] *n* **-1.** an animal related to the horse, but smaller and with longer ears. **-2.** a foolish person (informal use) □ *You silly ass!* **-3.**▽ a person's buttocks (very informal use) □ *Move your ass!*

assail [ə'seɪl] *vt* **-1.** to attack <sb> violently (formal use). **-2.** to make <sb> very worried □ *He was assailed by doubts/fears.*

assailant [ə'seɪlənt] *n* a person who attacks somebody physically □ *He provided a detailed description of his assailant.*

assassin [ə'sæsɪn] *n* a person who assassinates somebody.

assassinate [ə'sæsɪneɪt] *vt* to murder <a political or religious leader>.

assassination [ə,sæsɪ'neɪʃn] *n: see* **assassinate** □ *an assassination attempt.*

assault [ə'sɔːlt] ◇ *n* **-1.** MILITARY [on a building, area] an attack by a large number of soldiers on a place held by enemy forces □ *an unsuccessful assault on the parliament building.* **-2.** [on a person] a physical attack on somebody □ *The number of assaults on prison officers has increased.* **-3.** LAW the crime of attacking somebody physically. ◇ *vt* **-1.** to attack <sb> physically □ *He was arrested for assaulting a police officer.* **-2.** to rape or try to rape <sb> □ *The victim had been sexually assaulted.*

assault course *n* GB an area of land on which soldiers train to get fit by climbing over walls, jumping over ditches etc.

assemble [ə'sembl] ◇ *vt* **-1.** [troops, collection, information] to gather <people or things> together □ *The company has assembled a very efficient team.* **-2.** [car, radio, shelves] to put the parts of <a piece of equipment or furniture> together □ *You have to assemble all the furniture yourself.* ◇ *vi* [people] to come together for a particular purpose □ *In the event of fire, hotel guests should assemble in the foyer.*

assembly [ə'semblɪ] (*pl* **assemblies**) *n* **-1.** EDUCATION a meeting that is held each morning at a school for all the pupils and teachers □ *The pupils go to assembly every morning.* □ *a school assembly.* **-2.** POLITICS a group of people who come together to make laws or to discuss political problems □ *the UN General Assembly.* **-3.** the act of gathering together. ■ **the right of assembly** the right to meet as a group without fear of being arrested or sent to prison. **-4.** [of shelves, a car, radio] *see* **as-**

semble □ *The kit comes with easy-to-follow assembly instructions.*

assembly language *n* COMPUTING a programing language used to code instructions for a computer.

assembly line *n* a production system where the product is assembled gradually by being passed from one worker to another, usually along a conveyor belt.

assent [əˈsent] ◇ *n* agreement to a plan, suggestion etc □ *The bill eventually obtained the assent of Parliament.* ◇ *vi* to agree to a plan, suggestion etc □ *The committee finally assented to most of their proposals.*

assert [əˈsɜːʳt] *vt* -1. **to assert (that)...** to state firmly that something is true □ *He continues to assert the truth of the claim.* □ *She asserted that she had no involvement in the affair.* -2. [right, claim] to speak or act in a way that makes other people understand that one has <sthg> □ *No longer a child, Susan had to assert her independence.* □ *You must assert your authority right from the start.* ■ **to assert oneself** to behave or speak confidently and in a way that gains people's attention and respect □ *I'm learning how to assert myself more.*

assertion [əˈsɜːʳʃn] *n*: *see* **assert** □ *I dispute their assertion that these tests are safe.*

assertive [əˈsɜːʳtɪv] *adj* [person] who states their opinions, wishes etc firmly □ *She has a confident and assertive manner.*

assess [əˈses] *vt* -1. [somebody's ability, performance] to decide the quality of <sthg> by looking at it closely □ *Staff are assessed each year on their work.* -2. [situation, development] to give one's opinion about <sthg> by thinking carefully about it □ *How would you assess the mood on the shop floor?* -3. [property, tax] to calculate the value or cost of <sthg> □ *Damages were assessed at $50,000.*

assessment [əˈsesmənt] *n*: *see* **assess** □ *student assessment* □ *What is your assessment of the current economic climate?*

assessor [əˈsesəʳ] *n* FINANCE a person whose job is to assess property, damages, or tax.

asset [ˈæset] *n* -1. a skill or quality that is valuable and useful □ *Julie's knowledge of Japanese is a real asset.* -2. a person whose skills or qualities are very useful to an organization □ *He's a great asset to the company.*
♦ **assets** *npl* BUSINESS the things of value that belong to a person or company and that can be sold to pay debts □ *The company has assets of over $3 million.*

asset-stripping [-ˌstrɪpɪŋ] *n* the practice of buying a company at a low price and then selling its assets to make a profit.

assiduous [əˈsɪdʒʊəs] *adj* [worker] who is careful and gives a lot of attention to detail.

assiduously [əˈsɪdʒʊəslɪ] *adv*: *see* **assiduous** □ *Sam has worked assiduously throughout the year.*

assign [əˈsaɪn] *vt* -1. **to assign sthg to sb/sthg** [resources, money, time] to give sthg to sb/sthg for a particular purpose □ *Most of the budget for this year has already been assigned to specific projects.* ■ **to assign sthg to sb, to assign sb sthg** [work, job] to give sb sthg to do □ *I was assigned the task of writing the report.* -2. **to assign sb to sthg** [to a job, department] to choose sb for sthg □ *Two FBI men were assigned to the case.* □ *Paul Johnson has been assigned to look into their accounts.*

assignation [ˌæsɪgˈneɪʃn] *n* a secret meeting with somebody, especially a lover (formal or humorous use).

assignment [əˈsaɪnmənt] *n* -1. a particular task given to somebody, especially as part of their work □ *My first assignment was to cover the New York Marathon.* -2. *see* **assign** □ *Her assignment to the post met with widespread approval.*

assimilate [əˈsɪməleɪt] ◇ *vt* -1. [facts, idea] to understand completely and be able to use <new information> □ *Some students find it difficult to assimilate new vocabulary.* -2. [immigrant, member, staff] to accept <sb> as part of one's group or country □ *They were gradually assimilated into the local community.* ◇ *vi* [immigrant, member, staff] *Some ethnic groups find it harder to assimilate than others.*

assimilation [əˌsɪməˈleɪʃn] *n*: *see* **assimilate**.

assist [əˈsɪst] *vt* to help <sb> to do a particular thing □ *They were sent in to assist the aid workers with the relief effort.* □ *There are a number of grants available to assist you with the initial expenses.* □ *Our staff will be happy to assist you.*

assistance [əˈsɪstəns] *n* help in doing a particular thing □ *He cannot walk without assistance.* □ *'Ring for assistance.'* □ *The industry is receiving financial assistance from the government.* ■ **to be of assistance** to help somebody □ *Can I be of any assistance?*

assistant [əˈsɪstənt] *n* -1. [in a company, organization] a person whose job is to help somebody and who works for them □ *a sales and promotions assistant* □ *an assistant producer/manager.* -2. GB [in a store] a person who works in a store, selling things to customers.

associate [*adj* & *n* əˈsəʊʃɪət, *vb* əˈsəʊʃɪeɪt] ◇ *adj* -1. **an associate member** a member who has only some of the rights and privileges held by a normal member of an organization. -2. **an associate director/partner** a director/partner who has equal or slightly lower status.
◇ *n* a person that one has contact with, especially at work □ *He's a business associate of mine.*
◇ *vt* -1. **to associate sb/sthg with sb/sthg** to connect sb/sthg with sb/sthg in one's mind □ *People associate California with sunshine and healthy living.* -2. **to be associated with sthg** to be connected with sthg □ *the problems associated with nuclear power* □ *the diseases that are associated with heavy smoking.* -3. **to be associated with sb/sthg** to be involved with sb/sthg as a partner, participant etc □ *She refused to be associated with the venture.*
◇ *vi* **to associate with sb** to spend a lot of time with sb □ *He is believed to have associated with the Mafia.*

association [əˌsəʊsɪˈeɪʃn] *n* -1. a group of people or companies with a shared interest □ *a tenants' association* □ *the American Automobile Association*. **-2.** [with a person, company] the process of being involved with somebody or something as a partner, participant etc □ *They denied any association with the terrorist group.* □ *The program was made in association with German television.* **-3.** [of an idea, place] a connection one has in one's mind with a particular memory, idea, feeling etc □ *The place has unpleasant associations for me.*

assorted [ə'sɔːrtəd] *adj* including different types of the same thing □ *cold cuts with assorted seasonings.*

assortment [ə'sɔːrtmənt] *n* a collection of similar things that have different shapes, colors, sizes etc □ *He arrived at the station with an assortment of boxes and packages.*

asst. *abbr of* **assistant**.

assuage [ə'sweɪdʒ] *vt* (formal use) **-1.** [grief, guilt] to make <a feeling> less strong □ *Laurence tried in vain to assuage the woman's fears.* **-2.** [thirst, hunger] to satisfy <a need or desire> □ *a thirst for revenge that could never be assuaged.*

assume [ə'sjuːm] *vt* **-1. to assume (that)**... to believe that something is true without having any proof □ *We can't assume (that) these figures are accurate.* □ *Let's assume interest rates will come down soon.* □ *The information is assumed to be correct.* **-2.** [post, duty] to accept or take <a position of power or responsibility> □ *He's assumed control of the firm.* □ *General Bancroft assumed command of the army.* **-3.** [tone, expression, manner] to start using <a particular way of behaving> in order to give a particular impression □ *She assumed an air of indifference.*

assumed name [ə,sjuːmd-] *n* a name used by somebody that is not their real name.

assuming [ə'sjuːmɪŋ] *conj* a word used to introduce something that one believes to be true or very likely and that is a condition for something else □ *Assuming (that) there's no delay, we should arrive at ten thirty.*

assumption [ə'sʌmpʃn] *n* **-1.** something that one believes is true without having any proof □ *Try not to make too many assumptions about what actually happened.* □ *We are working on the assumption that our bid will be successful.* **-2.** [of a post, duty] *see* **assume**.

♦ **Assumption** *n* **the Assumption** the occasion when the Virgin Mary was taken into heaven; the day when this is celebrated by Roman Catholics.

assurance [ə'ʃʊərəns] *n* **-1.** a statement in which one says that something is definitely true or promises something □ *He gave us his written assurance that it would not happen again.* □ *Despite repeated assurances, they failed to deliver the goods on time.* **-2.** calm confidence □ *She spoke with assurance.* **-3.** GB & CAN FINANCE life insurance □ *an assurance company/policy.*

assure [ə'ʃʊər] *vt* **-1. to assure sb that**... to tell sb something firmly in order to make them less worried or doubtful □ *He assured us that the building was safe.* □ *It certainly wasn't our*

mistake, I can assure you. □ *They assured us of their good intentions.* **-2. to be assured of sthg** [of success, victory] to be certain of getting sthg □ *The Danes are assured of a gold medal.*

assured [ə'ʃʊərd] *adj* [voice, manner, person] that seems calm and confident □ *a smartly-dressed and assured young man.*

AST (*abbr of* **Atlantic Standard Time**) *n* the local time used in winter in eastern Canada and parts of the West Indies.

asterisk ['æstərɪsk] *n* a symbol shaped like a star (*) that is often used to refer the reader to a note at the bottom of the page.

Asterix ['æstərɪks] a character from a French cartoon strip set in a time when France was part of the Roman Empire. Asterix and his friend Obelix fight the Romans, and often defeat them in battles.

astern [ə'stɜːrn] *adv* [stand, move] at or toward the stern.

asteroid ['æstərɔɪd] *n* a large lump of rock that moves around the Sun.

asthma [US 'æzmə, GB 'æs-] *n* a disease that causes difficulty in breathing.

asthmatic [US æz'mætɪk, GB æs-] ◇ *adj* [person, attack] *see* **asthma**. ◇ *n* a person who suffers from asthma.

astigmatism [ə'stɪɡmətɪzm] *n* imperfect vision that is caused by a problem with the lens in the eye.

astonish [ə'stɒnɪʃ] *vt* to surprise <sb> very much □ *The success of the book astonished everyone.*

astonished [ə'stɒnɪʃt] *adj* [person, look] very surprised □ *I'm astonished to hear (that) she's leaving.* □ *We were astonished at the result.*

astonishing [ə'stɒnɪʃɪŋ] *adj* [news, success, result] very surprising.

astonishment [ə'stɒnɪʃmənt] *n* a feeling of great surprise □ *To my astonishment he actually agreed.* □ *She looked at me in astonishment.*

astound [ə'staʊnd] *vt* to make <sb> feel very surprised and a little shocked □ *What really astounded me was his complete lack of interest in his patients.*

astounded [ə'staʊndəd] *adj* [person] who is very surprised at something that is hard to believe □ *I was astounded at his rudeness.*

astounding [ə'staʊndɪŋ] *adj* [behavior, result] so surprising or good that it is hard to believe □ *She's an astounding performer.*

astrakhan [,æstrə'kæn] *n* gray or black curly fur made from the wool of lambs and often used to make coats and hats.

astray [ə'streɪ] *adv* **to go astray** [letter, package] to get lost □ *My pen seems to have gone astray.* ■ **to lead sb astray** to encourage or cause sb to behave in a bad or immoral way that is not usual for them.

astride [ə'straɪd] *prep* with one leg on either side of <a horse, bicycle> etc □ *He was sitting astride a powerful-looking motorbike.*

astringent [ə'strɪndʒənt] ◇ *adj* **-1.** [lotion] that is able to tighten the skin; [drug] that is put on a wound to stop it from bleeding.

-2. [remark, criticism] severe. ◇ *n* an astringent drug or lotion.

astrologer [əˈstrɒlədʒəʳ] *n* a person who uses astrology and predicts what will happen in the future.

astrological [ˌæstrəˈlɒdʒɪkl] *adj* [sign, prediction, chart] *see* **astrology**.

astrologist [əˈstrɒlədʒəst] *n* = **astrologer**.

astrology [əˈstrɒlədʒɪ] *n* the study of the positions and movements of the Sun, Moon, stars, and planets in the belief that they influence a person's character and behavior.

astronaut [ˈæstrənɔːt] *n* a person who is trained to travel in a spacecraft.

astronomer [əˈstrɒnəməʳ] *n* a scientist who studies astronomy.

astronomical [ˌæstrəˈnɒmɪkl] *adj* -1. [instrument, research] *see* **astronomy**. -2. [amount, size, price] very large □ *She's a good lawyer, but her fees are astronomical.*

astronomy [əˈstrɒnəmɪ] *n* the scientific study of the Sun, Moon, stars, planets etc.

astrophysics [ˌæstrouˈfɪzɪks] *n* the scientific study of the physical and chemical properties of the Sun, Moon, stars, planets etc.

Astroturf ™ [ˈæstroutɜːʳf] *n* a green plastic material that looks like grass and is used as a playing surface for sports.

astute [əˈstʲuːt] *adj* [person] that shows intelligence and an ability to understand people and situations □ *an astute negotiator* □ *That was an astute move/investment.*

asunder [əˈsʌndəʳ] *adv* **to tear sthg asunder** to tear sthg apart or into pieces (literary use).

ASV (*abbr of* **American Standard Version**) *n* **the ASV** an American translation of the Bible.

asylum [əˈsaɪləm] *n* -1. protection given by a government to somebody who has left a foreign country for political reasons □ *She sought political asylum.* -2. a mental hospital.

asymmetrical [ˌeɪsɪˈmetrɪkl] *adj* that has two sides or parts which are different in size or shape.

at [*stressed* æt, *unstressed* ət] *prep* -1. used with places, especially places where an activity is taking place □ *They arrived at the airport.* □ *We met at the hotel/campsite.* □ *She studied at Harvard.* □ *I live at 23, Eton Square.* ■ **at my father's** at my father's house □ *We had dinner at Jane's last night.* -2. used to describe the exact position of something □ *The car stopped at the traffic lights.* □ *There was a door at the end of the corridor.* □ *Turn left at the post office.* -3. used with events that somebody is attending □ *I'll see you at the conference/party.* -4. **at home/ school/work** in one's home/school/work (used with places where somebody lives, studies, works etc) □ *I'm not at the office/ factory today.* □ *Their daughter is at college in the States.* -5. used to describe direction. ■ **to look at sb/sthg** to look in the direction of sb/sthg □ *The children stood gazing at the animals.* □ *She stared/shouted at him.* ■ **to shoot at sb** to shoot toward sb with the intention of hitting them □ *He threw a stone at the window.* -6. used to describe an exact time. ■ **at elev-** en o'clock/midnight when it is eleven o'clock/midnight □ *The bus arrives at 11:45 am.* □ *We set out at noon/daybreak.* □ *We arranged to meet at a later date.* ■ **at Christmas** during the period of Christmas □ *What are you doing at Easter?* -7. used to describe an exact age, speed, price etc. ■ **she retired at (the age of) 60** she retired when she was 60 years old. ■ **we sell jeans at £15 a pair** jeans cost £15 a pair to our customers. ■ **we are flying at (a height of) 30,000 feet** the plane is 30,000 feet above the ground. -8. used after certain adjectives describing feelings, abilities etc. ■ **amused at sthg** amused because of sthg □ *I was appalled/delighted at the news.* ■ **good/bad at sthg** able/not able to do sthg well □ *I'm useless at languages.* -9. **to be at work/play etc** to be working/playing etc □ *The country is at peace/war.* □ *She's out at lunch right now.* -10. *phrase* **to be at one's best** to be in one's best condition □ *I wasn't at my best on Monday night.* □ *This is French cooking at its finest.*

◆ **at all** *adv* used for emphasis in negative sentences and in questions □ *She's not at all happy about the decision.* □ *You can have anything at all.* □ *Do you know her at all?* ■ **not at all** used as a polite reply when somebody has said thank you; used as a polite way of answering a request □ *"It was kind of you to help." — "Not at all."* □ *"Do you mind if I sit here?" — "Not at all."*

◆ **at that** *adv* used to give extra information about something □ *All I got for my birthday was a bottle of wine, and a cheap one at that!*

ate [eɪt] *past tense of* **eat**.

atheism [ˈeɪθɪɪzm] *n* the belief that there is no God.

atheist [ˈeɪθɪəst] *n* a person who does not believe that God exists.

Athens [ˈæθɒnz] the capital of Greece and the largest city in both ancient and modern Greece. POPULATION: 748,110.

athlete [ˈæθliːt] *n* a person who takes part in sports that involve physical strength or speed, e.g. running or jumping.

athlete's foot *n* a disease of the foot that affects the skin between the toes and on the sole so that it becomes sore and cracked.

athletic [æθˈletɪk] *adj* -1. [person] who is physically fit and good at sports □ *a strong athletic body.* -2. [competition, excellence] that is connected with athletics.

◆ **athletics** *npl* sports that involve strength or speed, e.g. running, throwing, or jumping.

Atlanta [ætˈlæntə] the state capital of Georgia, USA. POPULATION: 394,017.

Atlantic [ətˈlæntɪk]: **the Atlantic (Ocean)** the large ocean that separates the Americas from Europe and Africa □ *the Atlantic coast/ climate/crossing.*

Atlantis [ətˈlæntɪs] an island that is supposed to have sunk into the Atlantic Ocean in ancient times.

atlas [ˈætləs] *n* a book of maps.

Atlas: the Atlas Mountains a group of mountain ranges in northwestern Africa. HIGHEST POINT: 4,165 m.

ATM (*abbr of* **automatic teller machine**) *n* a machine outside a bank that gives out cash in the form of bills to customers who key in a special code.

atmosphere ['ætməsfɪər] *n* -1. [around a planet] the gases that surround the Earth, planets, stars etc □ *the Earth's atmosphere.* -2. [in a room] the air in a particular place □ *a hot, sticky atmosphere.* -3. [of a town, house] the character or mood of a place, especially because of the people there □ *The office has a relaxed and friendly atmosphere.*

atmospheric [ˌætməs'ferɪk] *adj* -1. [pressure, pollution] that is connected with the Earth's atmosphere. -2. [movie, music, scene] that has a special mood, often a mysterious or exciting one.

ATO (*abbr of* **Australian Taxation Office**) *n* **the ATO** the Australian government department responsible for collecting taxes.

atoll ['ætɒl] *n* a circular coral reef or group of coral islands around a lagoon.

atom ['ætəm] *n* -1. PHYSICS the smallest amount of a substance that can combine and react with other substances. -2. **an atom of sthg** a very small amount of sthg □ *There's not an atom of truth in it.*

atom bomb *n* a bomb which explodes because of the energy that is released when atoms are split.

atomic [ə'tɒmɪk] *adj* -1. [power station, submarine, weapon] that uses or is produced by atomic energy □ *atomic power* □ *an atomic reactor.* -2. [structure, weight] that is connected with the atom.

atomic bomb *n* = **atom bomb**.

atomic energy *n* the energy that is released as a result of splitting or combining atoms.

Atomic Energy Authority *n* **the Atomic Energy Authority** the British government agency that controls research and development in atomic energy.

Atomic Energy Commission *n* **the Atomic Energy Commission** the US government agency that controls research and development in atomic energy.

atomic number *n* the number given to elements in the periodic table that indicates the number of protons in the nucleus of an atom.

atomizer, -iser ['ætəmaɪzər] *n* a device used to spray a liquid, e.g. a perfume or medicine, by forcing it through a small opening.

atone [ə'toʊn] *vi* **to atone for sthg** [for one's sins, crime, bad behavior] to show that one is sorry for sthg bad that one has done by doing something good □ *He was anxious to atone for his past misdeeds.*

atonement [ə'toʊnmənt] *n*: see **atone** □ *It was a gesture of atonement for wrongs committed during the war.*

A to Z *n* GB a street plan of a town, with an alphabetical list of street names.

ATP *n abbr of* **Association of Tennis Professionals**.

atrocious [ə'troʊʃəs] *adj* -1. [treatment, crime] that is very cruel and violent in a way that shocks people □ *an atrocious act of cruelty.* -2. [handwriting, conditions] that one thinks is very bad □ *The weather/His behavior was atrocious.*

atrocity [ə'trɒsətɪ] (*pl* **atrocities**) *n* a very cruel and violent act that shocks people □ *The army was accused of committing atrocities against innocent civilians.*

attach [ə'tætʃ] *vt* -1. to join or fix <sthg> to something else with a pin, clip etc □ *Please attach a recent photograph to your application.* -2. **to attach significance/importance etc to sthg** [to a fact, event, remark] to consider sthg to be significant/important etc □ *The university attaches a great deal of importance to individual tuition.*

attaché [US ˌætə'ʃeɪ, GB ə'tæʃeɪ] *n* a member of staff of an embassy who has expert knowledge of a particular subject □ *a commercial attaché.*

attaché case *n* a thin briefcase that is used for carrying documents and papers.

attached [ə'tætʃt] *adj* -1. [object] that is joined or fixed to something else □ *Please refer to the attached leaflet for further details.* □ *a baby buggy with a sunshade attached.* -2. **to be attached to sthg** [to a group, organization] to be working with sthg, usually for a short period of time □ *He was attached to the WHO for a few months.* -3. **to be attached to sb/sthg** to be fond of sb/sthg □ *I've grown very attached to this old sweater.*

attachment [ə'tætʃmənt] *n* -1. [for a device, piece of equipment] an extra part that can be attached to a machine to do a particular job □ *a food mixer with a grinder attachment.* -2. [to a person, object] a feeling of fondness for somebody or something □ *She forms attachments easily.*

attack [ə'tæk] ◇ *n* -1. [by fighting, hitting] an act of physical violence against somebody □ *The attack was racially motivated.* □ *The recent spate of attacks on tourists is causing concern.* -2. MILITARY an attempt by an army to capture or destroy a place belonging to the enemy □ *The Serbs had launched an attack on Mostar.* -3. [in words, writing] a speech, statement, or piece of writing that contains strong criticism □ *He launched a scathing attack on the press.* -4. [of an illness] a sudden and severe period of a particular kind of pain or illness □ *an attack of asthma/indigestion.* -5. **an attack of nerves/shyness etc** a sudden feeling of nervousness/shyness etc that one cannot control □ *He had a panic/an anxiety attack.*

◇ *vt* -1. [person] to use violence to hurt <sb> physically □ *He was attacked on his way home.* -2. MILITARY to try to capture or destroy <a place belonging to the enemy>. -3. [person, idea, proposal] to criticize <sb/sthg> strongly □ *She wrote an article attacking government economic policies.* -4. [body, plant, tree] to have a damaging effect on <sthg> □ *The disease at-*

tacks the immune system. **-5.** [work, question] to start to deal with <a problem or job> with energy and determination □ *Let's go and attack those dirty dishes!*
◇ *vi* **-1.** [person, animal] to try to hurt another person or animal physically. **-2.** MILITARY to start using weapons against an enemy in order to defeat them or destroy a place. **-3.** SPORT to try to score goals or points in soccer, hockey etc by moving forward against the other team.

attacker [ə'tækər] *n* **-1.** a person who physically attacks somebody □ *She described her attacker as tall, with long black hair.* **-2.** SPORT one of the players in a team whose main role is to score goals or points.

attain [ə'teɪn] *vt* [goal, success, knowledge] to get or achieve <sthg that one wants>, usually with some effort or after a period of waiting □ *She strives to attain perfection in everything she does.*

attainable [ə'teɪnəbl] *adj* [target, goal] that can be achieved □ *Set yourself attainable goals.*

attainment [ə'teɪnmənt] *n* **-1.** one's **attainments** skills that one usually acquires with some effort or over a period of time □ *literary attainments* □ *educational attainments.* **-2.** *see* **attain** □ *one of the many ways of measuring attainment in the classroom.*

attempt [ə'tempt] ◇ *n* the act of trying to do something □ *He made no attempt to help.* □ *They raised my salary in an attempt to persuade me to stay.* □ *Stephen made a faint attempt at a smile.* ■ **an attempt on sb's life** an attempt to kill sb. ◇ *vt* to try to do <sthg difficult, dangerous, or unusual> at a particular time □ *They're attempting a takeover of the MCT corporation.* □ *an attempted suicide/murder* □ *They're attempting to extradite the terrorists.*

attend [ə'tend] ◇ *vt* **-1.** [meeting, conference] to be present at <an event> □ *The service was attended by the President and his wife.* **-2.** [school, church] to go regularly to <a place where people in a particular group meet>. ◇ *vi* to be present at a meeting, conference etc □ *Unfortunately I was unable to attend.*

◆ **attend to** *vt fus* **-1.** **to attend to sthg** [to a problem, matter, one's work] to deal with sthg □ *Is there any more business to attend to?* **-2.** **to attend to sb** [to a customer, child] to take care of sb □ *Dr. Harris was attending to a patient when I arrived.*

attendance [ə'tendəns] *n* **-1.** the number of people who are present at an event or who go to a school, church etc □ *Attendance has fallen off recently.* □ *The school has a poor attendance record.* **-2.** *see* **attend** □ *We do insist on regular attendance.*

attendant [ə'tendənt] ◇ *n* a person whose job is to help the public in a particular place □ *a museum/cloakroom attendant.* ◇ *adj* [difficulties, problems] that are linked to what has just been mentioned (formal use) □ *high-speed travel and its attendant dangers.*

attention [ə'tenʃn] ◇ *n* **-1.** the state in which one is looking at and thinking about somebody or something at the same time, usually

as a sign that one is interested □ *Can I have your attention please!* □ *World attention is focused on the plight of the hostages.* □ *She likes to be the center of attention.* □ *This job requires a lot of attention to detail.* ■ **to bring sthg to sb's attention, to draw sb's attention to sthg** to make sb notice sthg such as a problem □ *She drew his attention to an error in the text.* ■ **to attract** OR **catch sb's attention** to make sb notice one □ *She tried to attract his attention by honking her horn.* ■ **to pay attention to sb/sthg** to listen to and watch sb/sthg very carefully □ *Pay no attention to him, he's in a bad mood this morning.* □ *Pay particular attention to spelling.* ■ **'for the attention of...'** a phrase used on a memo, fax, letter etc to say who it is for. **-2.** the act of taking care of or dealing with somebody or something □ *This matter requires your immediate attention.* □ *She needs medical attention.* **-3.** MILITARY **to stand to attention** to stand straight and not move.
◇ *excl* a word used to tell soldiers to stand to attention.

attentive [ə'tentɪv] *adj* **-1.** [audience, pupil] who pays attention □ *Sarah was a bright, attentive student.* **-2.** [staff] who is helpful and caring □ *We try to be attentive to the needs of our guests.* □ *a most attentive host.*

attentively [ə'tentɪvlɪ] *adv*: *see* **attentive** □ *They listened attentively to what I had to say.*

attenuate [ə'tenjʊeɪt] *vt* to reduce <the size, strength, value> etc of something (formal use).

attest [ə'test] ◇ *vt* **to attest that...** to say, show, or prove that something is true. ◇ *vi*: *His diaries attest to the fact that his family was very important to him.*

attic ['ætɪk] *n* a room or space just beneath the roof of a house, used to store things.

attire [ə'taɪər] *n* the clothes that somebody is wearing (formal use) □ *The men were in formal attire.*

attitude ['ætɪtjuːd] *n* **-1.** the way that one thinks and feels about something or somebody □ *They take a relaxed attitude to* OR *toward latecomers.* **-2.** the way that one behaves toward somebody □ *I don't like his attitude.* **-3.** a confident and slightly aggressive manner (informal use) □ *That boy has attitude!*

Attlee ['ætlɪ], **Clement** (1883–1967) British Prime Minister from 1945 to 1951. His government introduced the National Health Service, nationalized many industries, and gave independence to India and Burma.

attn *abbr of* **for the attention of.**

attorney [ə'tɜːrnɪ] *n* US a person whose job is to give people legal advice and to represent them in court.

attorney general (*pl* **attorneys general**) *n* an important government official in charge of legal affairs.

attract [ə'trækt] *vt* **-1.** [tourists, customers] to cause <sb> to come by offering something they want □ *The book fair attracts publishers from all over the world.* □ *The Chamber of Commerce is trying to attract business to the area.*

-2. **to be attracted to sb** to find sb attractive □ *I've always been attracted to older men.* -3. [criticism, interest] to be the cause of <a particular reaction from people> □ *The proposals attracted widespread support.* -4. [dust, dirt] to cause <sthg> to move near or settle □ *Magnets attract metal objects.* □ *Honey attracts wasps.*

attraction [ə'trækʃn] *n* -1. the feeling one has for somebody when one is attracted to them □ *They felt an instant attraction to each other.* -2. [of a place, idea] the quality that something has of being interesting or pleasant □ *My wife loves golf but I don't see the attraction myself.* -3. [for tourists, visitors] an event or place that attracts people to it □ *a tourist attraction.*

attractive [ə'træktɪv] *adj* -1. [person, body, face] that has a pleasant appearance, especially in a way that people find sexually interesting; [object, place] that has a pleasant appearance □ *I've always found her attractive.* □ *The house is situated in a very attractive spot.* -2. [offer, salary, investment] that makes people want it because they are likely to benefit from it □ *We offer attractive terms for borrowers.*

attractively [ə'træktɪvlɪ] *adv* -1. **attractively arranged/designed etc** arranged/designed etc in a way that is pleasant to look at □ *an attractively illustrated brochure.* -2. **attractively priced** [goods, house] not expensive.

attributable [ə'trɪbjətəbl] *adj* **to be attributable to sthg** to be likely to be caused by sthg □ *The drop in revenue is directly attributable to our declining market share.*

attribute [*vb* ə'trɪbjuːt, *n* 'ætrɪbjuːt] ◇ *vt* -1. **to attribute sthg to sthg** [success, failure, win] to believe sthg to be the result of sthg □ *The collapse of the peace talks is being attributed to extremists.* □ *What do you attribute his immense popularity to?* -2. **to attribute sthg to sb** [painting, poem, remark] to say that sthg was said, written, painted etc by sb □ *The drawing has been attributed to Mantegna.* ◇ *n* a particular qual- ity or feature of somebody or something □ *physical/mental attributes* □ *One can count honesty and fairness amongst her many attributes.*

attribution [ˌætrɪ'bjuːʃn] *n: see* **attribute**.

attrition [ə'trɪʃn] *n* -1. **a war of attrition** a fight, war, or dispute in which one side is weakened by repeated attacks. -2. US BUSINESS a reduction in the number of employees in a company because some resign, retire, or die.

attuned [ə'tʲuːnd] *adj* **to be attuned to sthg** to understand and appreciate sthg □ *I gradually became attuned to their way of thinking.*

Atty. Gen. *abbr of* **Attorney General**.

ATV (*abbr of* **all terrain vehicle**) *n* a strongly built motor vehicle with three or four wheels, for use on rough ground.

atypical [eɪ'tɪpɪkl] *adj* not typical.

aubergine ['oʊbəˈʒiːn] *n* GB a vegetable with shiny purple skin and soft white flesh.

auburn ['ɔːbəˈn] *adj* [hair] reddish-brown.

Auckland ['ɔːklənd] the largest city and main port of New Zealand, in the northern part of North Island. POPULATION: 840,000.

auction ['ɔːkʃn] ◇ *n* a sale where items are sold to the person who offers the most money □ *The house is to be sold at* OR *by auction.* ■ **to put sthg up for auction** to offer sthg for sale at an auction. ◇ *vt* [car, house, property] to sell <sthg> at an auction.

◆ **auction off** *vt sep* **to auction sthg off** to auction sthg.

auctioneer [ˌɔːkʃə'nɪəˈ] *n* a person whose job is to call out the prices that people bid at an auction and to accept the highest bid.

AUD *abbr of* **Australian dollar**.

audacious [ɔː'deɪʃəs] *adj* [person, plan, remark] that is daring and takes risks.

audacity [ɔː'dæsətɪ] *n: see* **audacious** □ *He had the audacity to say it wasn't good enough.*

Auden ['ɔːdn], **W. H.** (1907–1973) a British poet whose modern style of writing influenced many other writers in the 1930s and 1940s. He became a US citizen in 1946.

audible ['ɔːdəbl] *adj* [sound, voice] that can be heard □ *His words were barely audible.* □ *The background noise was audible on the recording.*

audience ['ɔːdjəns] *n* -1. the people listening to or watching a concert, play, TV program etc; the people who read the books of a particular author □ *She invited a member of the audience up on stage.* □ *Her novels deserve to have a wider audience.* -2. a formal meeting with an important person □ *He was granted an audience with the Pope.*

audio ['ɔːdɪoʊ] *adj* **audio equipment/tape** equipment/tape that records or reproduces sound □ *an audio recording.*

audiotypist ['ɔːdɪoʊtaɪpəst] *n* GB a person whose job is to type letters, memos etc that have been recorded on a tape recorder.

audiovisual [ˌɔːdɪoʊ'vɪʒʊəl] *adj* [equipment, material] that involves the use of pictures and recorded sounds.

audit ['ɔːdət] ◇ *n* an official examination, usually once a year, of the accounts of a company, an organization, or a person □ *a routine audit of the company's records.* ◇ *vt* -1. [company, organization, person] to carry out the audit of <sb/sthg>. -2. [class] to go to <a course> at college or university without taking exams.

audition [ɔː'dɪʃn] ◇ *n* a short performance by a performer, e.g. an actor or musician, for a possible employer. ◇ *vi* to perform in an audition □ *Laura's auditioning for a part in the new musical.*

auditor ['ɔːdɪtəˈ] *n* a person whose job is to audit accounts.

auditorium [ˌɔːdɪ'tɔːrɪəm] (*pl* **auditoriums** OR **auditoria** [-rɪə]) *n* -1. the part of a theater or concert hall where the audience sits. -2. a building for public meetings.

Audubon ['ɔːdəbɒn], **John James** (1785–1851) a US artist and naturalist, well-known for his paintings of birds.

au fait [oʊ'feɪ] *adj* **to be au fait with sthg** GB

[with a system, procedure] to know sthg □ *He didn't seem very au fait with the regulations.*

Aug. *abbr of* **August.**

augment ['ɔːg'ment] *vt* [amount, number, income] to make <sthg> bigger or larger by adding something to it (formal use) □ *a revised and augmented edition of the dictionary.*

augur ['ɔːgəʳ] *vi* **to augur well/badly** to be a sign that things will go well/badly in the future □ *These disagreements augur badly for next week's meeting.*

august [ɔː'gʌst] *adj* [gathering, person] that seems dignified and impressive (literary use).

August ['ɔːgəst] *n* the eighth month of the year in the Western calendar; *see also* **February.**

Auld Lang Syne [,ɔːldlæŋ'zaɪn] *n* a Scottish song that is sung at midnight on December 31 to celebrate the New Year.

aunt [US ænt, GB ɑːnt] *n* the sister of one's mother or father; the wife of one's uncle.

auntie, aunty [US 'ænti, GB 'ɑːnti] (*pl* **aunties**) = **aunt** (informal use).

au pair [ou'peəʳ] *n* a young woman, usually a foreigner, who lives with a family in order to learn the language, and helps with the housework or taking care of the family's children.

aura ['ɔːrə] *n* [of mystery, confidence] a particular feeling or quality that seems to surround a person or place □ *The town still has an aura of fading grandeur about it.*

aural ['ɔːrəl] *adj* [skill, ability, comprehension] that is connected with hearing.

aurally ['ɔːrəlɪ] *adv* **aurally handicapped** deaf.

auspices ['ɔːspɪsɪz] *npl* **under the auspices of sb/sthg** with the support and approval of sb/sthg.

auspicious [ɔː'spɪʃəs] *adj* [start, occasion, day] that makes one think that something will be successful in the future □ *It was hardly an auspicious beginning to the vacation.*

Aussie ['ɒzi] (informal use) ◇ *adj* Australian. ◇ *n* an Australian.

Austen ['ɒstən], **Jane** (1775–1817) a British novelist whose books, including *Emma* and *Pride and Prejudice*, describe middle-class English life.

austere [ɒ'stɪəʳ] *adj* -1. [way of life, home] that is simple and has very little comfort or pleasure; [person, manner] very serious □ *the simple and austere dress of a nun.* -2. [room, building] that is plain and has no decoration □ *The design of the house is austere and elegant, using simple geometric shapes.*

austerity [ɒ'sterətɪ] *n* -1. *see* **austere.** -2. difficult economic conditions in which the amount of money people spend, e.g. on luxuries, has to be limited □ *an austerity budget/program.*

Australasia [,ɒstrə'leɪʒə] Australia, New Zealand, Papua New Guinea, and their neighboring islands.

Australia [ɒ'streɪljə] a country that is an island lying between the Indian Ocean and

the Pacific Ocean. It consists mainly of desert, with tropical forest in the north and most major cities in the south and east. SIZE: 7,700,000 sq kms. POPULATION: 17,800,000 (*Australians*). CAPITAL: Canberra. LANGUAGE: English. CURRENCY: Australian dollar.

Australia Day *n* a public holiday in Australia, on the first Monday after January 26.

❧ AUSTRALIA DAY
Australia Day commemorates the landing of the first British convict ships in Australia in 1788. It is a relaxed, informal public holiday, when most people have a picnic or a barbecue with their family or friends. Some people hang flags outside their houses, and some cities have parades, street parties, and firework displays.

Australian [ɒ'streɪljən] *n* & *adj*: *see* **Australia.**

Australian Capital Territory a district in southeastern Australia that does not belong to any state. It contains Canberra, the capital. POPULATION: 263,085.

Australian Labor Party *n* → **ALP.**

Australian Rules football *n* an Australian game like rugby that is played on an oval pitch. Points are scored by kicking the ball between one of the two sets of posts at each end. Players are allowed to run with the ball, but they must bounce it every ten yards.

Austria ['ɒstrɪə] a mountainous country in central Europe. It used to be the center of a large empire, and is now a republic. SIZE: 84,000 sq kms. POPULATION: 7,900,000 (*Austrians*). CAPITAL: Vienna. LANGUAGE: German. CURRENCY: schilling.

Austrian ['ɒstrɪən] *n* & *adj*: *see* **Austria.**

AUT (*abbr of* **Association of University Teachers**) *n* **the AUT** a British labor union for teachers and researchers in higher education.

authentic [ɔː'θentɪk] *adj* -1. [document, painting, food] that is real rather than an imitation □ *Try Café Fidel for the authentic taste of Cuban cooking.* -2. [account, testimony] that is accurate and can be believed □ *an authentic account of life in the prison camps.*

authenticate [ɔː'θentɪkeɪt] *vt* [painting, document] to prove that <sthg> is authentic.

authenticity [,ɔːθen'tɪsətɪ] *n*: *see* **authentic** □ *Experts have confirmed the authenticity of the sculpture.*

author ['ɔːθəʳ] *n* a writer of novels, articles, poems etc; the writer of a particular novel, article, poem etc □ *the German author, Heinrich Mann* □ *The author of the book teaches at Yale.*

authoritarian [ɔː,θɒrə'teərɪən] *adj* [regime, parent, leader] who tells people what to do and does not let them make their own decisions (disapproving use).

authoritative [US ə'θɒrəteɪtɪv, GB -tətɪv] *adj* -1. [person, voice] that has authority and the power to make people obey □ *My father was a tall, authoritative figure.* -2. [study, account] that is complete and accurate and can be trusted □ *an authoritative account of events leading up to the war.*

authority [ɔː'θɒrəti] (*pl* **authorities**) *n* -1. an official group, e.g. a government department or an organization, that controls a particular activity for the public □ *the local education authority.* -2. [of a person, organization] the power or right to control and give orders to people □ *They have little respect for authority.* □ *They claim the UN has no authority to intervene.* □ *Each officer has authority over 500 men.* □ *It's for the people in authority to decide.* -3. [to do something] official permission □ *Who gave you the authority to enter the area?* -4. [on a subject] an expert □ *She's an authority on China.* -5. **to have it on good authority** to believe something because one heard it from somebody who can be trusted □ *I have it on good authority that Simpson is intending to resign.*

◆ **authorities** *npl* **the authorities** the people who are in a position of authority, e.g. the government □ *The authorities have got to do something about the state of the roads.*

authorization [ˌɔːθərai'zeiʃn] *n*: *see* **authorize** □ *These expenses need your authorization.*

authorize, -ise ['ɔːθəraiz] *vt* [payment, loan] to give official permission for <sthg>, especially by signing a document □ *She is authorized to sign checks for the company.*

Authorized Version [ˌɔːθəraizd-] *n* **the Authorized Version** the English translation of the Bible published in 1611.

authorship ['ɔːθərʃip] *n* [of a play, novel, poem] the fact of being the author of something □ *No one has yet claimed authorship of the article.*

autistic [ɔː'tistik] *adj* [person] who suffers from a form of mental illness that makes communication with other people very difficult.

auto ['ɔːtəu] (*pl* **autos**) *n* US a car □ *the auto industry* □ *an auto accident.*

autobiographical [ˌɔːtəbaiə'græfikl] *adj* [novel, account, story] that describes events that took place in the life of the author.

autobiography [ˌɔːtəbai'ɒgrəfi] (*pl* **autobiographies**) *n* the story of a person's own life that is written by that person.

autocrat ['ɔːtəkræt] *n* a person who rules a state or company with complete power without asking the opinions of other people.

autocratic [ˌɔːtə'krætik] *adj* [person, rule, attitude] *see* **autocrat** □ *As a father he was stern and autocratic.*

autocross ['ɔːtəukrɒs] *n* GB the sport of racing cars over rough grass.

Autocue™ ['ɔːtəukjuː] *n* GB a device which shows people the words they have to say on television so that they can talk while looking directly at the camera.

autofocus ['ɔːtəufəukəs] *n* a device in a camera that focuses the lens automatically.

autograph [US 'ɔːtəgræf, GB -grɑːf] ◇ *n* a famous person's signature. ◇ *vt* [photo, book] to sign <sthg> with one's autograph.

Automat™ ['ɔːtəmæt] *n* US a type of restaurant where food can be bought from vending machines.

automata [ɔː'tɒmətə] *plural of* **automaton**.

automate ['ɔːtəmeit] *vt* [process, factory] to change <sthg> so that the work is done by machines instead of people.

automatic [ˌɔːtə'mætik] ◇ *adj* -1. [machine, weapon] that can perform particular functions with little human control □ *an automatic barrier/gearbox.* -2. [gesture, response] that is done without thinking □ *My automatic reaction was to deny it.* -3. [penalty, right, increase] that always happens or follows as a result of something and cannot be avoided □ *Ticket inspectors can impose an automatic fine of £10.* □ *Customers have no automatic entitlement to a refund.*

◇ *n* -1. AUTO a car in which the gears change automatically as the speed increases and decreases □ *I learned to drive in an automatic.* -2. MILITARY a gun that keeps reloading and firing automatically when the trigger is pressed. -3. a washing machine that washes, rinses, spins etc automatically.

automatically [ˌɔːtə'mætikli] *adv* [work, smile, increase] *see* **automatic** □ *All members automatically receive free legal advice.* □ *The kettle switches off automatically.*

automatic pilot *n* -1. a device on an aircraft or ship that keeps it on course automatically. -2. **to be on automatic pilot** [person] to be doing something without thinking about it, e.g. because one is tired or has done it many times before.

automation [ˌɔːtə'meiʃn] *n* [of a process, factory] the use of machines to do jobs previously done by people □ *Automation means that far fewer miners are now needed to work underground.*

automaton [ɔː'tɒmətən] (*pl* **automatons** OR **automata**) *n* -1. a robot. -2. a person who does things without thought or emotion (disapproving use).

automobile ['ɔːtəməbiːl] *n* a car.

automotive [ˌɔːtə'məutiv] *adj* [technology, industry] that is concerned with cars.

autonomous [ɔː'tɒnəməs] *adj* [region, organization] that governs itself.

autonomy [ɔː'tɒnəmi] *n* [of a region, organization] the freedom to govern itself □ *They're fighting to regain their autonomy.*

autopilot ['ɔːtəupailət] *n* = **automatic pilot**.

autopsy ['ɔːtɒpsi] (*pl* **autopsies**) *n* a medical examination of a dead body in order to find out why the person died.

autoteller ['ɔːtəutelər] *n* US & AUS a machine outside a bank that gives out cash in the form of bills to customers who key in a special code.

autumn ['ɔːtəm] *n* the season between summer and winter when leaves change color and start to fall □ *I'm going there in the* OR *in autumn.* □ *autumn colors/leaves/weather.*

autumnal [ɔː'tʌmnəl] *adj* [colors, equinox, weather] *see* **autumn**.

auxiliary [ɔːg'ziljəri] (*pl* **auxiliaries**) ◇ *adj* -1. [staff, nurse, soldier] whose job is to provide assistance to more highly qualified people. **-2.** [equipment, generator] that is used when necessary in addition to the main equipment. ◇ *n* **-1.** a person who helps more highly qualified people, especially nurses or soldiers □ *nursing auxiliaries.* **-2.** = **auxiliary verb.**

auxiliary verb *n* a verb, e.g. *be, do,* or *have,* that is used with the main verb to show differences in tense, person, and voice.

Av. *abbr of* **avenue.**

AV ◇ *n abbr of* **Authorized Version.** ◇ *abbr of* **audiovisual.**

avail [ə'veɪl] ◇ *n* **to no avail** without success □ *We tried, but it was to little avail.* ◇ *vt* **to avail oneself of sthg** [of a facility, opportunity] to accept or use sthg □ *I availed myself of his services.*

availability [ə,veɪlə'bɪlətɪ] *n: see* **available** □ *The industry relies heavily upon the availability of raw materials.*

available [ə'veɪləbl] *adj* **-1.** [product, service] that can be used, bought, or obtained □ *We've tried all available sources.* □ *There are several options available to us.* □ *'Cars available for rent.'* **-2.** [person] who is not busy and can be met, spoken to, chosen for a job etc □ *The senator was not available for comment.* □ *I can make myself available to see him next week.*

avalanche [US 'ævəlænʃ, GB -lɑːnʃ] *n* **-1.** [of snow, rocks] a large amount of snow or rocks that falls down the side of a mountain □ *Greg was killed in an avalanche.* **-2.** [of complaints, calls] a large amount of things that arrive somewhere at the same time □ *They received an avalanche of letters after the appeal.*

avant-garde [US ,ɑːvɑːn'gɑːrd, GB ,ævɒŋ'gɑːd] *adj* [theater, artist] modern and experimental.

avarice ['ævərɪs] *n* greed, especially for money (formal use).

avaricious [,ævə'rɪʃəs] *adj* [person] who shows avarice (formal use).

avdp. (*abbr of* **avoirdupois**) a system for measuring weight that uses ounces, pounds, hundredweights etc.

Ave. *abbr of* **avenue.**

avenge [ə'vendʒ] *vt* [death, crime, wrong] to hurt or punish the person responsible for <sthg> □ *Chet swore to avenge his sister's murder.*

avenue ['ævənjuː] *n* **-1.** a wide street, often with trees or tall buildings on each side □ *Fifth Avenue.* **-2.** a possible way of achieving something □ *We need to explore every avenue that is open to us.*

average ['ævərɪdʒ] ◇ *n* **-1.** a result calculated by adding together a number of figures and dividing the total by that number □ *They produce an average of ten new models a year.* □ *The game has increased his average by 24 points.* **-2.** the normal amount or standard □ *Class sizes here are above the national average.* ■ **on average** a phrase used to describe a number that is the average of several different numbers □ *On average 100 people die every day from smoking-related diseases.*

◇ *adj* **-1.** [age, amount, salary] that represents an average □ *Average earnings are around $100 a week.* **-2.** [person, product] that is typical □ *The average American takes two weeks' vacation a year.* **-3.** [work, performance] that is neither good nor bad □ *The food was just average.* □ *This year's results were above average.*

◇ *vt* to do, make, get etc <a particular amount of sthg> on average □ *The factory averages ten machines per day.*

◆ **average out** ◇ *vt sep* to average sthg out [figures, amounts] to calculate the average of two or more numbers. ◇ *vi* to average out at sthg to represent an average of sthg when calculated over a period of time □ *The bills average out at $50 a month.*

averse [ə'vɜːrs] *adj* **not to be averse to sthg** to like sthg □ *I'm not averse to a glass of Scotch now and then.*

aversion [ə'vɜːrʃn] *n* **an aversion to sb/sthg** a strong dislike for sb/sthg □ *That cruise did nothing to cure my aversion to boats.* □ *Sport is one of my pet aversions.*

avert [ə'vɜːrt] *vt* **-1.** [danger, accident] to stop <sthg bad> from happening □ *Disaster was averted just in time.* **-2.** to turn away <one's eyes, gaze> etc in order not to see something □ *He politely averted his eyes as I opened the safe.*

aviary ['eɪvjərɪ] (*pl* **aviaries**) *n* a large cage or building where birds are kept.

aviation [,eɪvɪ'eɪʃn] *n* the science or business of designing, building, and flying aircraft.

avid ['ævɪd] *adj* **an avid reader/supporter etc** a very enthusiastic and eager reader/supporter etc □ *avid viewers of this popular TV show.*

avidly ['ævɪdlɪ] *adv* [read, listen] *see* **avid.**

avocado [,ævə'kɑːdoʊ] (*pl* **avocados** OR **avocadoes**) *n* an avocado **(pear)** a pear-shaped tropical fruit with thin, hard, dark-green skin, pale-green flesh, and a large hard seed in the middle.

avoid [ə'vɔɪd] *vt* **-1.** to prevent <a problem, accident, mistake> etc from happening □ *They are keen to avoid any kind of confrontation.* ■ **to avoid doing sthg** to deliberately not do sthg, e.g. because it may be dangerous or cause problems □ *Try to avoid giving them too much information.* **-2.** to keep away from <a person, place, or thing>; to keep the conversation away from <a subject> □ *I left early to avoid the rush hour.* □ *Stop trying to avoid the issue.*

avoidable [ə'vɔɪdəbl] *adj* [accident, result, disease] that can be avoided □ *avoidable losses.*

avoidance [ə'vɔɪdəns] *n* → **tax avoidance.**

avowed [ə'vaʊd] *adj* **-1.** **an avowed supporter/opponent etc** a person who has told everybody that they are a supporter/opponent etc of something □ *He is an avowed atheist.* **-2. an avowed belief/intention** a very strong belief/intention □ *It's my avowed belief that nuclear weapons are wrong.*

AWACS ['eɪwæks] (*abbr of* **airborne warning and control system**) *n* a US military aircraft used for watching the movements of enemy armies, planes etc.

await [ə'weɪt] *vt* **-1.** [person, event, reply] to

wait for <sb/sthg> □ *He is currently awaiting trial for drugs smuggling.* **-2.** to be going to happen to <sb> in the future □ *Who knows what discoveries await us in the next century?*

awake [ə'weɪk] (*pt* **awoke**, *pp* **awoken**) ◇ *adj* **to be awake** [person, animal] not to be sleeping □ *Hey! Are you awake?* □ *Lewis was already awake by the time I arrived.* ■ **to be wide awake** to be completely awake. ◇ *vt* **-1.** (literary use) to wake <a person or animal> up □ *I was awoken by a noise in the night.* **-2.** [curiosity, interest] to cause somebody to have <a particular feeling> □ *His suspicions were awoken by the man's strange accent.* ◇ *vi* [person, animal] to wake up.

awaken [ə'weɪkən] *vi* & *vt* = **awake**.

awakening [ə'weɪkənɪŋ] *n* the start of a particular feeling □ *the awakening of sexual desire.* ■ **to have a rude awakening** to suddenly realize something that is difficult to accept.

award [ə'wɔːrd] ◇ *n* **-1.** a prize or reward given to somebody, usually for doing something well □ *the annual movie and television awards* □ *an award ceremony.* **-2.** LAW a sum of money that a judge decides should be given to somebody □ *a compensation award.* ◇ *vt* **to award sb sthg, to award sthg to sb** to give sb sthg as an award □ *The court awarded her $1,000 in damages.* □ *The business prize was awarded to Splendid Productions.*

award wage *n* in Australia, the minimum wage that can legally be paid for a particular type of work.

aware [ə'weər] *adj* **-1. to be aware of sthg** [of a fact, situation, sb's existence] to know about sthg, especially sthg one understands □ *Are you aware of the problems/risks involved?* □ *I'm well aware that this is not the perfect solution.* **-2. to be aware of sthg/sb** to realize that sthg/sb is present because one can hear, smell, or see them □ *I gradually became aware that they couldn't understand a word of what I was saying.* **-3.** [person] who understands a lot about a particular subject because they think it is important □ *She's very politically aware.*

awareness [ə'weərnəs] *n*: *see* **aware** □ *We need to increase public awareness of the health risks.*

awash [ə'wɒʃ] *adj* **-1. to be awash** [floor] to be covered with water □ *After the floods, the whole town was awash.* **-2. to be awash with sthg** [with people, litter] to have a lot or too much of sthg □ *The room was suddenly awash with cameras and lights.*

away [ə'weɪ] ◇ *adv* **-1. to walk/move/drive away** to walk/move/drive so that one is no longer in a place □ *Go away and leave me alone!* ■ **to look** OR **turn away** to turn one's head so that one is no longer looking at something. **-2. he stood ten feet away** he stood at a distance of ten feet from me □ *I don't live far away — it's only ten minutes' walk.* □ *We live four miles away from the city center.* **-3. two days/a month away** two days/a month in the future □ *The exams are only a week away now.* **-4. to be away (from work/school)** not to be at work/school at a time when one would usually be there □ *My boss*

was away on Tuesday because he had a cold. **-5. to put sthg away** to put sthg into a safe place where it cannot be seen □ *She filed the papers away in a box on the shelf.* **-6.** used to describe something that has disappeared. ■ **the noise faded away** the noise faded so that it could no longer be heard □ *The lock on the gate had rusted away.* ■ **to give sthg away** to give sthg to somebody so that one no longer has it □ *She gave all her money away to charity.* ■ **to take sthg away** to move sthg so that it is no longer there □ *The police towed the car away.* **-7. to talk away** to keep talking □ *He was happily singing away to himself.* ◇ *adj* SPORT [team, game] at the other team's ground or stadium.

awe [ɔː] *n* a feeling of wonder and amazement mixed with fear □ *She gazed in awe at the ancient ruins above her.* □ *He was filled with awe.* ■ **to be in awe of sb** to feel great respect and admiration for sb, so that one is a little frightened of them □ *I've always been slightly in awe of Prof. Jacob.*

awesome ['ɔːsəm] *adj* [task, responsibility, power] that causes feelings of awe, especially because it is extremely difficult, large, powerful etc □ *The building was an awesome achievement and we were very proud.*

awestruck ['ɔːstrʌk] *adj* [person] who is full of awe.

awful ['ɔːfl] *adj* **-1.** [pain, weather] that one thinks is very bad □ *We had a really awful time there.* □ *You look awful!* □ *How awful for you!* **-2. an awful lot** a large amount; very much (informal use) □ *There's an awful lot of work to do.* □ *There's not an awful lot I can do about it.*

awfully ['ɔːflɪ] *adv* **awfully sorry/good/difficult etc** very sorry/good/difficult etc (informal use) □ *The weather is awfully hot.*

awhile [ə'waɪl] *adv* [stay, wait] for a short time.

awkward ['ɔːkwərd] *adj* **-1.** [person, movement] that shows no skill or grace □ *He took a few awkward steps and then fell over.* **-2.** [person, feeling] that is uncomfortable or embarrassed □ *I felt awkward about accepting his invitation.* **-3.** [person] who refuses to do what somebody wants (disapproving use) □ *He's just being awkward.* **-4.** [job, machine] that is difficult to do, use, carry etc; [shape, size, design] that makes something difficult to use, carry etc □ *It's an awkward place to find.* □ *The table was an awkward shape.* **-5.** [situation, question, silence] that is embarrassing and difficult to deal with □ *You've come at an awkward moment.* □ *I don't want to put you in an awkward position.*

awkwardly ['ɔːkwərdlɪ] *adv* [move, behave, speak] *see* **awkward** □ *She was perched awkwardly on a bar stool.*

awkwardness ['ɔːkwərdnəs] *n*: *see* **awkward** □ *I sensed a certain awkwardness in his manner.*

awl [ɔːl] *n* a pointed tool for making holes in wood or leather.

awning ['ɔːnɪŋ] *n* a piece of canvas or plastic attached to the front of a building or vehicle to provide shelter from the sun or rain.

awoke [ə'wouk] *past tense of* **awake**.

awoken [ə'woukn] *past participle of* **awake**.

AWOL ['eɪwɒl] *abbr of* **absent without leave** □ *The new recruits have gone AWOL.*

awry [ə'raɪ] *adj* **-1. to be awry** [picture, necktie] to be at an angle or twisted to one side instead of in the correct position. **-2. to go awry** [plan, test] to go wrong □ *Things started to go awry just after you left the company.*

AWU (*abbr of* **Australian Workers' Union**) *n* one of the largest labor unions in Australia.

ax US, **axe** GB [æks] ◇ *n* a tool with a sharp metal blade attached to a handle, used for chopping wood. ■ **to have an ax to grind** to have a selfish reason for being involved in a particular situation □ *I have no particular ax to grind in this matter.* ◇ *vt* to end <a project, job> etc very suddenly, especially because there is not enough money to continue it □ *Management has axed 300 jobs at the Detroit plant.*

axes ['æksiːz] *plural of* **axis**.

axiom ['æksɪəm] *n* a statement or principle that is generally accepted to be true.

axiomatic [ˌæksɪə'mætɪk] *adj* that is accepted as true by most people (formal use).

axis ['æksɪs] (*pl* **axes**) *n* **-1.** [of a planet] an imaginary straight line that passes through the center of an object such as a planet, and that the object moves around □ *The Earth rotates on its axis.* **-2.** [of a shape] a real or imaginary line that divides a regular shape into two equal parts. **-3.** [on a graph] one of the two lines along the edge of a graph, one horizontal and the other vertical. The horizontal line is usually called the X axis and the vertical line the Y axis.
◆ **Axis** *n* **the Axis (Powers)** a term used to refer to Germany, Italy, and Japan, who fought the Allies in World War II.

axle ['æksl] *n* a rod on which a wheel turns or which connects a pair of wheels in a car, truck, bus etc.

ayatollah [ˌaɪə'tɒlə] *n* a religious leader of the Iranian Shiite Muslims.

aye [aɪ] *adv* GB yes (regional use).
◆ **ayes** *npl* **the ayes** the votes in favor of something at a meeting; the people who vote this way. ■ **the ayes have it** the majority of people have said yes.

Ayers Rock ['eəʳz-] a large rock (867 m) in central Australia that is an important tourist attraction. It is a sacred place for Australian Aborigines, and their name for it is Uluru.

AYH (*abbr of* **American Youth Hostels**) *n* **the AYH** the organization that runs youth hostels in the USA.

AZ *abbr of* **Arizona**.

azalea [ə'zeɪljə] *n* a small evergreen bush with pink or purple flowers.

Azores [US 'eɪzɔːrz, GB ə'zɔːz]: **the Azores** a group of volcanic islands in the Atlantic, belonging to Portugal. SIZE: 2,247 sq kms. POPULATION: 241,794. CAPITAL: Ponta Delgada.

AZT (*abbr of* **azidothymidine**) *n* a drug that is used in the treatment of AIDS.

Aztec ['æztek] ◇ *n* a member of an Indian people who ruled central Mexico until the Spanish defeated them in 1519. ◇ *adj*: *Aztec gold.*

azure ['æʒəʳ] *adj* [sky, sea] bright blue (literary use).

B

b [biː] (*pl* **b's** OR **bs**), **B** [biː] (*pl* **B's** OR **Bs**) *n* the second letter of the English alphabet.
◆ **B** *n* **-1.** MUSIC one of the notes in Western music. **-2.** EDUCATION a grade for a piece of work that is above average but not of the highest quality.

b. *abbr of* **born**.

BA *n* **-1.** (*abbr of* **Bachelor of Arts**) a first degree from a university in an arts or social science subject; a person who has this degree □ *I have a BA in history.* □ *J. Scott BA* □ *She's a BA.* **-2.** *abbr of* **British Academy**.

babble ['bæbl] ◇ *n* the sound of several people talking at once □ *I could hear the babble of excited voices in the hall.* ◇ *vi* to talk quickly so that one's words are not clear □ *She was babbling on about some great friend of hers.*

babe [beɪb] *n* **-1.** US a word that some people use when they are speaking to somebody they are fond of □ *Hi, babe.* **-2.** a baby (literary use) □ *a babe in arms.* **-3.** an attractive young woman □ *Hollywood babes.*

baboon [bə'buːn] *n* a large monkey with a long face and long tail that is found in Africa and Asia.

baby ['beɪbɪ] (*pl* **babies**) *n* **-1.** a very young child, especially one who has not started to talk or walk; a very young animal □ *a baby boy/girl* □ *my baby brother* □ *a baby lion/chimpanzee.* **-2. baby carrots/cauliflowers etc** carrots/cauliflowers etc that are grown and picked to be eaten while they are still small. **-3.** a person who behaves in a childish way (disapproving use) □ *Don't be such a baby!* **-4.** a word used when speaking to somebody one is fond of (informal use) □ *Don't worry, baby.*

baby boomer [-buːməʳ] *n* a person born during a period when a lot of babies were born, especially just after World War II.

baby buggy *n* **-1.** US = **baby carriage**. **-2.** GB a light folding chair with small wheels and a handle that a young child can sit in to be pushed along.

baby carriage *n* US a small vehicle with four wheels and a folding cover that is pushed and in which babies are taken around.

baby food *n* food for babies, usually in the form of a thick smooth sauce, that is sold in packets or jars.

Baby-gro™ [-groʊ] *n* GB an item of clothing for babies that covers the whole body from the feet to the neck.

babyish [ˈbeɪbɪɪʃ] *adj* [person] who behaves in a childish way; [behavior, book, voice] that is not suitable for somebody who is not a baby (disapproving use) □ *Stop being so silly and babyish!* □ *These toys seem a little babyish for an 11-year-old.*

baby-sit *vi* to go to another family's home and look after the children while the parents go out □ *I used to baby-sit for my neighbor.*

baby-sitter [-sɪtəʳ] *n* a person who baby-sits.

Bach [bɑːk], **Johann Sebastian** (1685–1750) a German composer, considered one of the greatest in history. His works include the *Brandenburg Concertos*, the *St Matthew Passion*, and *The Art of Fugue*.

bachelor [ˈbætʃələʳ] *n* a man who is not married.

NOTE: Compare **spinster**.

Bachelor of Arts *n* → **BA**.

Bachelor of Science *n* → **BSc**.

bachelor's degree [ˈbætʃələʳz-] *n* a first degree from a university in any subject.

back [bæk] ◇ *adv* **-1. to move/step back** to move/step in the direction that is behind one, without turning around □ *I moved my chair back from the fire.* ■ **she looked back over her shoulder** she looked behind her over her shoulder. ■ **stand back!** stand farther away. ■ **to sit/lie back** to sit/lie in a more comfortable position, leaning backward. ■ **she tied back her hair** she tied her hair behind her head away from her face. **-2. to be/go back** to be in/go to the same place one started out from □ *Call me as soon as you get back.* □ *We'll be back home soon.* **-3. to send sthg back** to send sthg to the place or person that it has come from □ *Put the book back where you found it.* ■ **to give sthg back** to give sthg to the person who had it before □ *I want my money back!* **-4. to go back to sleep** to fall asleep again after being awake for a time □ *When will he be back at work?* □ *Things are getting back to normal after the holidays.* **-5. to write back** to write a reply to somebody □ *He's not in his office right now; I'll get him to call you back.* **-6. back in January** in January, in the past □ *Please think back and see what you can remember.* □ *Our records reach back to 1965.* **-7. to be back (in fashion)** [clothes, style] to be in fashion again □ *The miniskirt is back.*
◇ *adj* **-1. a back door/wheel etc** a door/wheel etc that is at the back, not the front, of a building or vehicle □ *She drove and he sat in the back seat.* **-2. back rent** rent that should have been paid before □ *They owe $3000 in back rent.* **-3. a back road** a road that is small and has few people and little traffic □ *We'll take one of the back roads if the traffic's bad.*
◇ *n* **-1.** the part of a person's body that goes from their neck to their bottom; the same part of an animal's body □ *She broke her back*

in an accident. ■ **to break the back of sthg** [of a task, job] to complete the most difficult part of sthg □ *I've finally managed to break the back of these accounts.* ■ **to do sthg behind sb's back** to do sthg without sb knowing about it □ *Simon has been talking about me behind my back.* ■ **to put sb's back up** to annoy sb (informal use). ■ **to stab sb in the back** to harm the position, reputation etc of sb who is a friend or colleague. ■ **to turn one's back on sb/sthg** to ignore sb/sthg that needs one's help □ *You can't just turn your back on me like this!* **-2.** [of a door, hand, envelope] the side of something that is not usually seen or used □ *I could only see the back of his head.* □ *He wrote his address on the back of the invitation.* ■ **to know a place like the back of one's hand** to know a place very well. **-3.** [of a house, car, room] the part of a building, object etc that is furthest away from its front □ *Turn to the back of the book.* □ *We sat at the back of the class.* ■ **in back of sthg** US, **at the back of sthg** GB behind sthg □ *I was in back of him in line.* ■ **the back of beyond** GB a place that is a long way from any town or city (informal use) □ *They live somewhere out in the back of beyond.* **-4.** [of a seat] the part of a chair that supports one's back when one is sitting on it □ *I hung my jacket over the back of a chair.* **-5.** SPORT [in hockey, soccer] a player whose main job is to defend their team's goal.
◇ *vt* **-1.** [car, truck] to drive <a vehicle> somewhere backward □ *She backed the car into the driveway.* **-2.** [company, proposal, politician] to support <sb/sthg> by giving one's money, approval, vote etc □ *Mr Denny is backing my proposal.* **-3.** [horse, competitor, team] to place a bet on <sb/sthg> to win a race or competition □ *I'm backing the Red Sox to win tonight.* **-4.** [curtain, cover] to put a lining on <a piece of material>.
◇ *vi* [car, truck, driver] *He backed out of/into the parking space.*

♦ **back to back** *adv* [sit, stand] with the backs facing or touching each other □ *She placed the chairs back to back.*

♦ **back to front** *adv* GB **she was wearing her sweater back to front** she was wearing her sweater with the back at the front and the front at the back.

♦ **back away** *vi* [person, animal] to move away from something while still facing it, usually because of fear.

♦ **back down** *vi* [person] to admit that one has been defeated or that one was wrong □ *The government has finally backed down and withdrawn the new tax.* □ *She had to back down on OR over the penalty clauses.*

♦ **back off** *vi* to move away from somebody while still facing them □ *Back off, Donohue! This gun's loaded and I'm ready to use it.*

♦ **back onto** *vt fus* GB **to back onto sthg** [onto a building, piece of land] to face sthg at the back □ *Our house backs onto a park.*

♦ **back out** *vi* to change one's mind about something that one had previously agreed to do □ *Unfortunately, the Argentinian firm backed out of the deal at the last minute.*

◆ **back up** ◇ *vt sep* **-1. to back sb/sthg up** [person, story, claim] to provide evidence in support of sb/sthg □ *If they don't believe you I'll back you up.* □ *She backed up the story with a lot of photographic evidence.* **-2. to back a vehicle up** to drive a vehicle backward. **-3.** COMPUTING **to back up a file** to make a copy of a file. ◇ *vi* **-1.** [vehicle, driver] *Back up some more so you're not in the way.* **-2.** COMPUTING *You should always back up before you switch off the network.*

backache ['bækeɪk] *n* pain in one's back □ *I get terrible backache.*

backbencher [ˌbæk'bentʃər] *n* a member of the British Parliament who does not hold an official post in either the Government or the Opposition.

backbenches [ˌbæk'bentʃɪz] *npl* **the backbenches** the rows of seats in the British House of Commons where backbenchers sit.

backbiting ['bækbaɪtɪŋ] *n* unkind or unpleasant things that are said about somebody who is not present □ *I hate all the backbiting that goes on at the office.*

backboard ['bækbɔːrd] *n* in basketball, the board behind the basket.

backbone ['bækboʊn] *n* **-1.** [of a person, animal] the column of small bones that is in the center of a person's or animal's back. **-2.** [of an organization] the person or thing that does most of the work in an organization □ *He's the backbone of this company.* □ *Industry has always been the backbone of our economy.* **-3.** [in a person] strength of character □ *He lacks the backbone to stand up to his boss.*

backbreaking ['bækbreɪkɪŋ] *adj* [work, job] very hard and tiring □ *Cleaning those stairs is backbreaking work.*

back burner *n* **to put sthg on the back burner** [plan, project] to stop working on sthg for a time and intend to go back to it later □ *She's put her career on the back burner while she has a family.*

backchat *n* GB = **backtalk.**

backcloth ['bækklɒθ] *n* GB THEATER = **backdrop.**

backcomb ['bækkoʊm] *vt* GB to comb <one's hair> from the ends to the roots to make it look thicker.

back copy *n* = **back number.**

back country *n* **the back country** US & AUS a country area away from any towns or cities.

backdate [ˌbæk'deɪt] *vt* [pay raise, check] to make <a payment, document, or agreement> valid from a date that is earlier than the date on which it is signed, agreed etc □ *They've backdated the increase to May.*

back door *n* a door at the back of a building. ■ **to get in through** OR **by the back door** to get a job, position etc in a secret or unfair way.

backdrop ['bækdrɒp] *n* **-1.** THEATER a painted cloth that is hung at the back of a theater stage. **-2.** the general situation that exists while a particular event is taking place □ *Negotiations took place against a backdrop of continuing violence.*

backer ['bækər] *n* a person who gives money

or support to a business, project, proposal etc □ *They had no difficulty finding financial backers for the new venture.*

backfire [ˌbæk'faɪər] *vi* **-1.** [car, truck] to make loud noises like small explosions because the engine is not working properly. **-2.** [plan, idea, joke] to have the opposite result to the one that was intended □ *The plan totally backfired on him.*

backgammon ['bækgæmən] *n* a game for two people in which they throw dice and move small disks around a board marked with long triangles.

background ['bækgraʊnd] ◇ *n* **-1.** the part of a picture or view that is behind the things that are or seem to be close to one □ *He painted her standing against a background of trees.* ■ **to be in the background** [scenery, building, figure] to be behind the main thing that one is looking at; [music, sound] to be heard at the same time as the main thing that one is listening to, but not as clearly □ *In the background was a tall building.* □ *I could hear music playing in the background.* ■ **to remain** OR **stay in the background** to try not to attract people's attention □ *He prefers to remain in the background.* **-2.** [to an event, situation] the historical, social, or political situation that explains a particular event or situation □ *the background to the war in former Yugoslavia.* **-3.** [of a person] one's family, education, or experience □ *He comes from a very poor background.* □ *She has a background in management training.*
◇ *comp* **-1. background music/noise** music/noise that is heard in the background. **-2. background reading/information etc** reading/information etc that adds to one's knowledge of the main subject.

backhand ['bækhænd] *n* [in tennis, squash] a shot made by hitting the ball with one's arm across one's body so that the back of one's hand is facing the direction of the shot □ *a backhand volley.*
NOTE: Compare **forehand.**

backhanded ['bækhændəd] *adj* **a backhanded compliment** a remark that seems to be a compliment but could also be an insult.

backing ['bækɪŋ] *n* **-1.** [for a person, project] support, usually financial or official □ *The idea has received government backing.* □ *The project has the full backing of the company chairman.* **-2.** [of an object] something that is attached to the back of an object to make it stronger or to give it a particular quality □ *The rug has a special nonslip backing.* **-3.** MUSIC the musical accompaniment to a song or singer, especially in pop music □ *backing vocals/track* □ *a backing singer/group.*

back issue *n* = **back number.**

backlash ['bæklæʃ] *n* a strong or violent reaction against an idea, belief etc, especially one that has become dominant in society □ *a feminist/conservative backlash* □ *Tax increases provoked a backlash against the government in last year's local elections.*

backless ['bækləs] *adj* [dress, top, swimsuit] that does not cover the back.

backlog ['bæklɒg] *n* [of work, papers, letters] a large amount of things that are still waiting to be dealt with □ *There's a huge backlog of correspondence to get through.*

back number *n* an old issue of a newspaper, magazine etc.

backpack ['bækpæk] *n* a bag that one carries on one's back, especially for walking, mountaineering etc.

backpacker ['bækpækəʳ] *n* a person who goes backpacking.

backpacking ['bækpækɪŋ] *n* **to go backpacking** to travel with a backpack.

back pay *n* money owed to an employee that should have been paid earlier □ *I'm owed six months' back pay.*

backpedal ['bækpedl] (US *pt* & *pp* **backpedaled**, *cont* **backpedaling**, GB *pt* & *pp* **backpedalled**, *cont* **backpedalling**) *vi* to say or do something different from what one said, promised, or did before □ *Management has been accused of backpedaling on promised pay increases.*

back seat *n* the seat in the back of a car. ■ **to take a back seat** to take a less important part than before in an activity or group □ *Your social life is just going to have to take a back seat until the exams are over.*

back-seat driver *n* a passenger in a car who gives unwanted advice to the driver on how to drive (humorous use).

backside ['bæksaɪd] *n* one's bottom (informal use) □ *He sits on his backside all day long doing nothing.*

backslapping ['bækslæpɪŋ] *n* behavior in which people praise each other too much for something successful they have done □ *There was a lot of mutual backslapping and not much serious discussion.*

backslash ['bækslæʃ] *n* the symbol (/) found on a keyboard and used to separate words, numbers, or letters.

backslide ['bækslaɪd] (*pt* & *pp* **backslid**) *vi* to start doing something bad again after having stopped doing it □ *Critics accused the government of backsliding on the issue of welfare.*

backspace ['bækspeɪs] ◇ *n* the key on the keyboard of a word processor or typewriter that moves the cursor or carriage back toward the beginning of the line. ◇ *vi* to use the backspace key.

backstage [,bæk'steɪdʒ] *adv* behind the stage in a theater, where the actors' dressing rooms are □ *We were invited backstage after the performance.*

back street *n* a small street in a town or city away from the busy areas.

back-street abortion *n* an illegal abortion, often carried out by somebody who is not properly trained to do it.

backstroke ['bækstroʊk] *n* a way of swimming in which one lies on one's back, moves one's arms backward, and kicks one's feet.

backtalk ['bæktɔːk] US, **backchat** ['bæktʃæt] GB *n* rude remarks made in reply to somebody, especially somebody in authority (informal use) □ *That's enough of your backtalk!*

backtrack ['bæktræk] *vi* = **backpedal.**

backup ['bækʌp] *n* **-1.** help or advice that is available if there is a problem □ *The company provides technical backup.* □ *a backup plan/team/supply.* **-2.** COMPUTING a copy of a file or disk, made in case the first one gets accidentally deleted or lost □ *a backup file/disk.*

back-up light *n* US a white light on the back of a vehicle that shines when the vehicle is being reversed.

backward ['bækwərd] ◇ *adj* **-1. a backward look/step etc** a look/step etc in the direction behind one □ *She threw us a bitter backward glance as she left.* **-2.** [child] slow in learning and development compared to other children of the same age; [country, society] that does not have modern industries, technology etc. ◇ *adv* US = **backwards.**

backward-looking [-lʊkɪŋ] *adj* [idea, view, action] old-fashioned (disapproving use).

backwards ['bækwərdz] *adv* **-1. to walk/step backwards** to walk/step with one's back facing in the direction that one is moving □ *He fell backwards down the stairs.* **-2. to do sthg backwards** to do sthg in the opposite way from normal, e.g. by starting at the end and going back to the beginning □ *He played the recording backwards.*

♦ **backwards and forwards** *adv* in one direction then the other, repeatedly □ *Colin paced backwards and forwards impatiently.*

backwash ['bækwɒʃ] *n* the wave of water that is created by the movement of a boat.

backwater ['bækwɔːtəʳ] *n* a place that is isolated and not affected by what is happening in the world outside (disapproving use) □ *The town is a cultural backwater.*

backwoods ['bækwʊdz] *npl* an area in the countryside that is very isolated and far from any towns or cities □ *They live out in the backwoods somewhere.*

backyard [,bæk'jɑːʳd] *n* **-1.** US an area at the back of a house, usually covered with grass. **-2.** GB an area at the back of a house, usually covered with a hard surface.

bacon ['beɪkən] *n* meat from the back or sides of a pig that is salted or smoked and often cut into thin slices □ *bacon and eggs.*

Bacon ['beɪkən], **Francis** (1909–1992) a British artist, born in Ireland, who often painted deformed human or animal shapes.

bacteria [bæk'tɪərɪə] *npl* tiny organisms that are found in animals, plants, air, soil, and water, some of which can cause disease.

bacteriology [bæk,tɪərɪ'ɒlədʒɪ] *n* the study of bacteria.

bad [bæd] (*compar* **worse**, *superl* **worst**) *adj* **-1.** [weather, smell, taste] that is unpleasant; [result, school report, grade] that is not of the right standard or quality; [decision, teacher] that is not effective □ *She's in a bad mood.* □ *I've had some bad news.* □ *He sets a very bad example to the junior staff.* □ *The job is interest-*

ing but the pay is bad. □ I blame it on bad management/government. ■ **not bad** a phrase used when the speaker is surprised that something is actually good □ "How are you feeling?" — "Not bad." □ This book is not bad at all. ■ **to go from bad to worse** [situation, health, weather] to become even worse than before □ Things went from bad to worse as the day went on. ■ **it's too bad** a phrase used to show disappointment or regret □ It's too bad (that) he couldn't come. ■ **too bad** a phrase used to show that the speaker does not think it is worth doing anything to change the situation □ "We can't go yet, Dave isn't here." — "Too bad, he'll just have to walk." **-2. to be bad at sthg** [at sports, math, languages] to be unable to do sthg well □ I'm really bad at remembering people's names. **-3.** [influence, effect, situation] that can have harmful effects □ Things are looking bad for the Republicans. □ It's been a bad day on the Stock Exchange. □ Smoking is bad for your health. **-4.** [heart, leg, circulation] that is injured or diseased or does not work properly □ She's got a bad back. **-5.** [accident, injury, cold] that is severe □ a bad case of the flu □ It's been a bad winter. **-6. to feel bad about sthg** to feel guilty about sthg □ I felt bad about letting her down. **-7.** [person, behavior] that is rude or disobedient □ You've been a very bad boy. **-8.** [egg, meat, fish] that is beginning to go rotten □ Those sausages must have been bad. □ Food goes bad very quickly in this heat.

bad blood n feelings of hate and anger between people □ There's a lot of bad blood between them.

bad check n a ·check that a bank cannot accept because the person who wrote it does not have enough money in their account.

bad debt n money that is owed but that is unlikely to be paid back.

baddy ['bædɪ] (pl **baddies**) n a character in a movie, book etc who is bad and acts against the hero (informal use).

bade [bæd, beɪd] past tense of **bid**.

bad feeling n feelings of dislike between people □ There's a lot of bad feeling between them.

badge [bædʒ] n **-1.** a small piece of metal or cloth that people wear to show their official rank or position □ a policeman's badge □ a badge of office. **-2.** GB a small piece of plastic, metal, or paper with a picture or writing on it that shows that one supports a particular cause or belongs to a particular group □ a Save the Whale badge.

badger ['bædʒəʳ] ◇ n an animal with thick gray fur and black-and-white stripes on its face that lives underground and comes out at night. ◇ vt to ask or tell <sb> repeatedly to do something □ She badgered me into going. □ The kids have been badgering me all day to take them swimming.

badlands ['bædlændz] npl areas of empty dry land, especially in the central USA and in western Canada, that have been worn into strange shapes by the weather.

bad language n swear words □ Those videos just encourage kids to use bad language.

badly ['bædlɪ] (compar **worse**, superl **worst**) adv **-1.** [play, sing, dress] in a way that is not good, pleasing, or satisfactory □ badly managed/made. ■ **to do badly** to be unsuccessful □ I did badly in the exam. □ Things are going badly at the moment. ■ **to take sthg badly** to be upset by sthg, e.g. a piece of news □ "How did she take the news?" — "Badly." ■ **to think badly of sb** to have a bad opinion of sb □ I hope you don't think badly of me for telling him. **-2.** [cut, damage, injure] seriously □ She fell badly and broke her arm. □ badly burned/wounded/affected. **-3.** [behave, treat] in a way that is not acceptable because somebody or something suffers □ Their children are so badly behaved. □ He treated all his staff very badly. **-4.** [want, need] very much □ We're badly in need of a new filing system. □ I miss you badly.

badly-off adj **-1. to be badly-off** [person, family] to be poor □ We're not so badly-off. **-2. to be badly-off for sthg** not to have enough of sthg □ I'm not too badly-off for clothes at the moment.

badminton ['bædmɪntən] n an indoor sport in which players use a racket to hit a shuttlecock over a net.

bad-mouth vt to criticize <sb> (informal use) □ Don't you go bad-mouthing me to your mother!

bad-tempered [-'tempəʳd] adj [person] angry and unfriendly □ He's always bad-tempered in the morning.

baffle ['bæfl] vt **to be baffled by sthg** to be unable to understand or explain sthg □ Their behavior completely baffles me. □ The police are baffled by the incident.

baffling ['bæflɪŋ] adj [question, problem, crime] that is hard to understand or explain □ We don't know why he disappeared — the whole thing is completely baffling.

bag [bæg] (pt & pp **bagged**, cont **bagging**) ◇ n **-1.** a container made of cloth, plastic, paper, leather etc, often with handles or straps, that is used for carrying things such as shopping or personal belongings. ■ **to be in the bag** [contract, game] to be certain of being won or successfully completed (informal use) □ Once the deal is in the bag, we're off on vacation. ■ **to pack one's bags** to leave. **-2.** [of a woman] a small bag used by women to carry small personal things and money □ Her bag was stolen. **-3.** [of potatoes, candy] the amount of something that can be held in a bag □ I ate a whole bag of cherries. □ a five-pound bag of potatoes □ Will one bag be enough between three of us?

◇ vt to put <money, food> etc into bags.

◆ **bags** npl **-1.** loose folds of skin under one's eyes, usually caused by lack of sleep □ You've got bags under your eyes. **-2. bags of sthg** [of energy, time, money] a lot of sthg (informal use) □ There's bags of space.

bagel ['beɪgl] n a hard round bread roll with a hole in the middle that is often served with a filling such as cream cheese.

baggage ['bægɪdʒ] n all the bags and cases

that one travels with □ *Do you have any baggage?*

baggage car *n* US the part of a train in which only baggage is carried.

baggage handler *n* a person whose job is to move baggage at an airport.

baggage reclaim *n* the place at an airport where passengers go to collect their baggage after a flight.

baggage room *n* US a place in a train station where baggage can be left for a period of time.

baggy ['bægɪ] (*compar* **baggier**, *superl* **baggiest**) *adj* [sweater, shirt, pants] that fits loosely on the body because it is big or too big □ *He wore an old pair of baggy corduroy pants.*

Baghdad [US 'bægdæd, GB bæg'dæd] the capital of Iraq and its largest city. POPULATION: 3,205,000.

bag lady *n* a woman who lives on the streets and carries her belongings around with her in bags (informal use).

bag lunch *n* US a lunch, especially consisting of sandwiches, that is wrapped up or put in a box to be eaten when one is away from home or outdoors.

bagpipes ['bægpaɪps] *npl* a musical instrument, traditional in Scotland, that is played by blowing into a bag and then squeezing the air out through pipes.

bagsnatcher ['bægsnætʃəʳ] *n* a person who steals somebody's bag while they are carrying it and then runs away.

baguette [bæ'get] *n* a long thin loaf of bread.

Bahamas [bə'hɑːməz]: **the Bahamas** a country consisting of a group of islands in the Caribbean. It is an important center for tourism and banking. SIZE: 13,900 sq kms. POPULATION: 300,000 (*Bahamians*). CAPITAL: Nassau. LANGUAGE: English. CURRENCY: Bahamian dollar.

Bahrain [,bɑː'reɪn] a country consisting of a group of islands in the Persian Gulf. SIZE: 660 sq kms. POPULATION: 500,000 (*Bahrainis*). CAPITAL: Manama. LANGUAGE: Arabic. CURRENCY: Bahraini dinar.

Bahraini [,bɑː'reɪnɪ] *adj* & *n*: see **Bahrain**.

Bahrein [,bɑː'reɪn] = **Bahrain**.

bail [beɪl] *n* LAW money that is paid to a court to release somebody who has been arrested as a guarantee that they will return to court for their trial. ■ **to be released on bail** to be let out of prison after bail has been paid □ *He was out on bail within a couple of days of the attack.* ■ **to grant sb bail** to allow sb to leave prison after bail is paid □ *The court refused to grant them bail.*

◆ **bail out** ◇ *vt sep* -1. LAW **to bail sb out** to pay bail for sb. -2. **to bail a person/company etc out** to help a person/company etc that is having problems, by giving them money □ *They bailed their son's business out with a large loan.* -3. **to bail water out** to remove water from a boat. ◇ *vi* [pilot] to jump out of a plane with a parachute because the plane is going to crash □ *She bailed out just in time.*

bailiff ['beɪlɪf] *n* -1. US an official in a court who looks after prisoners and keeps order. -2. GB an official employed by a court to go to the house, office etc of somebody who has not paid a debt and take their property instead of money.

Baird [beəʳd], **John Logie** (1888–1946) a British engineer who invented a system of television broadcasting.

bait [beɪt] ◇ *n* food that is used to attract animals, fish etc in order to catch them. ■ **to rise to** OR **take the bait** to react to something somebody says or does in the way they had hoped □ *I asked Jon about their date but he didn't rise to the bait.* ◇ *vt* -1. [hook, trap] to put bait on or in <sthg> to catch a fish or animal. -2. [person] to try to make <sb> angry by deliberately upsetting them □ *He's known for baiting his opponents.*

baize [beɪz] *n* thick green material that is used for covering billiard tables or card tables.

bake [beɪk] ◇ *vt* -1. [bread, cake] to cook <food> in an oven without adding fat or oil □ *Bake the mixture for 60 minutes in a warm oven.* -2. [clay, earth] to make <sthg> hard by heating it □ *The sun had baked the mud dry.* ◇ *vi* [bread, cake] *It will take two hours to bake.*

baked Alaska [,beɪkt-] *n* a dessert made from cake and ice cream covered with meringue and cooked in an oven.

baked beans *npl* a dish made from navy beans cooked in tomato sauce sometimes with bacon and molasses.

baked potato *n* a potato that has been cooked whole in the oven with its skin on.

baker ['beɪkəʳ] *n* a person who bakes bread, cakes etc to be sold in a store. ■ **a baker's (shop)** GB a store where bread, cakes etc are sold.

bakery ['beɪkərɪ] (*pl* **bakeries**) *n* a place where bread is baked and where bread, cakes etc are usually sold.

baking ['beɪkɪŋ] ◇ *adj* **to be baking** [person, place] to be very hot (informal use) □ *You must be baking in that sweater!* ◇ *adv* **baking hot** very hot (informal use) □ *It's baking hot in here.* ◇ *n* the activity of baking bread, cakes etc □ *home baking.*

baking powder *n* a powder used to make cakes rise when they are being cooked.

baking sheet *n* a tray that food is placed on for cooking in an oven.

baking soda *n* = **bicarbonate of soda**.

baking tin *n* a tin used for baking cakes, bread etc.

baking tray *n* GB = **baking sheet**.

balaclava [,bælə'klɑːvə] *n* GB a woolen hat that covers the whole head except the face.

balance ['bæləns] ◇ *n* -1. the ability to stay steady and upright and not fall over □ *a good sense of balance* □ *I tripped, but just managed to keep my balance.* □ *He lost his balance and fell off his bike.* -2. [between different elements] a situation in which all the different elements have the same importance or influence □ *We've got to get the balance right between car-*

ing for patients and cutting medical costs. **-3. the balance of evidence/opinion etc** the larger or more important part of all the evidence/opinions etc being considered □ *The balance of opinion is against her.* **-4.** [for weighing] an instrument for weighing things. **-5.** FINANCE an amount of money that remains after some has been spent □ *That leaves a balance of $30.00.* **-6.** *phrase* **to be** OR **hang in the balance** [life, fate, future] to be uncertain □ *The future of the government was hanging in the balance.*

◇ *vt* **-1.** to keep <sthg> in a steady position so that it does not fall □ *He balanced the plate on his knee.* **-2. to balance sthg against sthg** to consider the importance of sthg in relation to sthg else □ *We have to balance the need for new staff against our financial position.* **-3. to balance sthg with sthg** to give sthg the same importance as one gives sthg else □ *It's not easy trying to balance a career with the demands of a young family.* **-4. to balance the books** to make sure that the amount of money spent is the same as the amount of money received. ■ **to balance a budget** to make sure that the amount of money that one plans to spend is the same as the amount of money available.

◇ *vi* **-1.** [person, object] to keep steady □ *She balanced on one leg.* **-2.** [books, budget] to show that the amount of money spent is not more than the amount of money received □ *The figures don't balance.*

◆ **on balance** *adv* after considering all the relevant information □ *On balance, I think the first candidate was the best.*

◆ **balance out** *vt sep* **to balance sthg out** to have the same weight, value, importance etc as sthg □ *The time you save by flying balances out the extra cost.*

balanced ['bælənst] *adj* **-1.** [judgment, report, view] that considers all the aspects of something and so is fair. **-2.** [person] who is reliable and not likely to behave unreasonably.

balanced diet *n* a diet that contains the right amount and variety of food for good health.

balance of payments *n* the difference between the amount of money that a country receives and the amount it spends.

balance of power *n* a situation in which the military or political forces opposing each other have the same amount of power □ *The end of Communism upset the balance of power in Europe.*

balance of trade *n* the difference in value between the exports and imports of a country.

balance sheet *n* a statement that shows the assets, credits, and debts of a business.

balancing act ['bælənsɪŋ-] *n* an attempt to please two or more people or groups who have opposing views □ *Ivan has to perform a delicate balancing act to keep both publisher and agent happy.*

balcony ['bælkənɪ] (*pl* **balconies**) *n* **-1.** a platform attached to the outside of a building above ground level that has a wall or railings in front of it and is reached through a door from one of the rooms □ *The President*

and his wife came out onto the balcony. **-2.** a seating area, e.g. in a theater, that is raised above ground level □ *the upper/lower balcony.*

bald [bɔːld] *adj* **-1.** [person] who has little or no hair on their head □ *He's completely bald.* □ *a bald spot.* ■ **to go bald** to lose one's hair □ *He started going bald in his twenties.* **-2.** [tire] that has become very smooth and is therefore not safe to use. **-3.** [statement, account] that is very direct and has no words added to it that might soften its effect □ *He described his role in a few bald, unemotional sentences.*

bald eagle *n* a large eagle with a white head that lives in North America and is used as the symbol of the USA.

balding ['bɔːldɪŋ] *adj* [head, person] that is going bald □ *a tall man, balding.*

baldness ['bɔːldnəs] *n* [of a person] *see* **bald** □ *a cure for baldness.*

Baldwin ['bɔːldwɪn], **James** (1924–1987) a US writer who was active in the civil rights movement. His works include *Go Tell It On The Mountain* and *Another Country*.

bale [beɪl] *n* [of cloth, hay, paper] a large amount of something that is tied tightly together □ *Bales of hay stood in the middle of the field.*

◆ **bale out** GB ◇ *vt sep* **to bale water out** to remove water from a boat. ◇ *vi* to jump out of a plane with a parachute because the plane is going to crash.

Balearic Islands [,bælɪærɪk-]: **the Balearic Islands** a group of islands in the western Mediterranean that includes Majorca, Minorca, and Ibiza, and forms a province of Spain. SIZE: 5,000 sq kms. POPULATION: 739,501. CAPITAL: Palma de Mallorca.

Balearics [,bælɪ'ærɪks] = **Balearic Islands**.

baleful ['beɪlfl] *adj* **a baleful look** a look that is threatening or full of blame (literary use).

Bali ['bɑːlɪ] an island in Indonesia, east of Java. SIZE: 5,561 sq kms. POPULATION: 2,470,000 (*Balinese*). CAPITAL: Denpasar.

balk [bɔːk] *vi* to hesitate before doing something or allowing it to happen because one considers it to be wrong, unpleasant, or difficult □ *I suggested we sleep out in the open, but he balked at the idea.*

Balkans ['bɔːlkənz]: **the Balkans** the countries in southeastern Europe, between the Adriatic and the Aegean Seas, including Albania, Bosnia, Bulgaria, Croatia, Greece, Macedonia, the European part of Turkey, and the Federal Republic of Yugoslavia.

Balkan States [,bɔːlkən-] = **Balkans**.

ball [bɔːl] *n* **-1.** SPORT & GAMES a round object that can be thrown, hit, or kicked, and is used in various sports and games □ *a golf/tennis ball.* ■ **to be on the ball** to be able to react or understand quickly because one is concentrating or knows a lot about a subject □ *You really have to be on the ball if you're doing a live interview.* ■ **to play ball** to do something that somebody wants one to do □ *If you play ball with us, there may be something in it for you.* ■ **to start/keep the ball rolling** to begin/continue a discussion, meeting, project etc □

Now that we've got the ball rolling, who would like to ask Professor James a question? **-2.** [of wool, string] a mass of something that is in the shape of a ball □ *The hedgehog rolled itself up into a ball.* □ *melon balls* □ *The car was engulfed in a ball of flames.* **-3. the ball of one's foot** the rounded part underneath one's foot where it joins the big toe. **-4.** [event] a formal party at which people dance □ *a graduation ball.* **-5.** *phrase* **to have a ball** to have a wonderful time (informal use) □ *We had an absolute ball at the Levinsons' party.*

◆ **balls**▾ (vulgar use) ◇ *n* **-1.** nonsense. **-2.** courage. ◇ *npl* testicles. ◇ *excl* a word used to show that one is annoyed about something.

ballad ['bæləd] *n* **-1.** a poem or song that tells a story. **-2.** a slow romantic song.

ball-and-socket joint *n* a joint in the body that consists of a rounded bone which fits into a rounded socket.

ballast ['bæləst] *n* heavy material such as sand that is used to keep a ship stable or is carried in a hot-air balloon and thrown out to make the balloon rise.

ball bearing *n* one of a group of small metal balls that are placed between the moving parts of a machine to help them to move more easily.

ball boy *n* a boy who picks up balls that have been hit into the net or off the court during a game of tennis.

ballcock ['bɔːlkɒk] *n* a device in a water tank, e.g. in a toilet, that consists of a floating ball that is connected to a plug. When water goes out of the tank and the ball drops, the plug opens and allows more water in to refill the tank.

ballerina [,bælə'riːnə] *n* a female ballet dancer.

ballet [US bæ'leɪ, GB 'bæleɪ] *n* **-1.** a form of classical Western dance that uses movement and gestures, accompanied by music, to tell a story; a professional group of dancers who perform this type of dance □ *classical ballet* □ *the Kirov Ballet.* **-2.** a work written for ballet dancers to perform; a performance of this type of dance □ *He wrote several ballets.* □ *We're going to the ballet this evening.*

ballet dancer *n* a dancer who is professionally trained in ballet.

ball game *n* **-1.** US a baseball game □ *Are you going to the ball game?* **-2.** *phrase* **it's a whole new ball game** it's a completely different or new situation (informal use) □ *It's a whole new ball game now the company's been taken over.*

ball girl *n* a girl who picks up balls that have been hit into the net or off the court during a game of tennis.

ballistic missile [bə,lɪstɪk-] *n* a missile that is guided until it is near its target and then falls freely.

ballistics [bə'lɪstɪks] *n* the study of the movement of objects, e.g. bullets, rockets, or missiles, that are shot or thrown into the air.

balloon [bə'luːn] ◇ *n* **-1.** [for children] a small bag made of thin rubber that is filled with air and used as a children's toy or for decoration at parties □ *The room was decorated with brightly-colored balloons.* **-2.** [for flying] a large bag made of lightweight material that floats above the ground when it is filled with hot air or gas and can carry passengers in a basket attached underneath □ *a hot-air balloon.* **-3.** [in cartoons] in cartoon drawings, a circular shape containing the words that a character is saying or thinking.
◇ *vi* [costs, debts, weight] to become bigger in amount very quickly □ *His weight had ballooned to 190 pounds.*

ballooning [bə'luːnɪŋ] *n* the activity or sport of traveling in a balloon.

ballot ['bælət] ◇ *n* **-1.** a system of voting, usually secret, in which people mark a piece of paper to indicate their choice of candidate or their opinion on a particular issue □ *Members of the committee are elected by ballot.* □ *The union held a strike ballot.* □ *a secret ballot.* **-2.** = **ballot paper.** ◇ *vt* to find out the opinion or choice of <a group of people> by asking them to vote in a ballot □ *All members will be balloted on the question of funding.*

ballot box *n* **-1.** the box which ballot papers are put in during a vote □ *She put the slip of paper in the ballot box.* **-2.** the system of choosing a government by voting □ *We believe in achieving political change through the ballot box.*

ballot paper *n* the piece of paper that is marked by somebody who takes part in a ballot.

ball park *n* US a stadium where baseball is played.

ball-park figure *n* an approximate number or amount of money (informal use) □ *I don't know exactly what it would cost, but I can give you a ball-park figure.*

ballpoint ['bɔːlpɔɪnt] *n* **a ballpoint (pen)** a pen with a small ball at the tip that rolls ink onto the paper □ *Please write clearly in ballpoint.*

ballroom ['bɔːlruːm] *n* a large room, usually with bright lighting and decoration, where formal dances are held.

ballroom dancing *n* the activity of taking part in formal dances such as the tango or foxtrot.

balm [bɑːm] *n* **-1.** an oil with a strong sweet smell that comes from tropical trees and is used to reduce pain or to treat wounds. **-2.** something that makes one feel calmer and happier □ *The news was balm to his troubled mind.*

balmy ['bɑːmɪ] (*compar* **balmier**, *superl* **balmiest**) *adj* [evening, breeze] that feels warm and pleasant.

baloney [bə'ləʊnɪ] *n* **-1.** nonsense (informal use) □ *What a load of baloney!* **-2.** US a large smoked sausage.

balsa ['bɔːlsə] *n* = **balsawood.**

balsam ['bɔːlsəm] *n* an oil with a sweet smell that comes from tropical trees and is used in medicines or perfumes.

balsawood ['bɔːlsəwʊd] *n* a type of very light wood that is easy to cut and is used for making models, e.g. of airplanes.

Baltic ['bɔːltɪk]: **the Baltic (Sea)** a sea in northern Europe, between Scandinavia and the Baltic States.

Baltic States: **the Baltic States** the countries on the Baltic Sea, i.e. Estonia, Latvia, and Lithuania, that were part of the USSR until 1991.

balustrade [US 'bæləstreɪd, GB ,bæləs'treɪd] *n* a wall or railing that is fixed to the outer edge of a staircase or balcony to prevent people from falling off it.

bamboo [,bæm'buː] *n* a tall tropical plant that has thick hollow stems and shoots that can be eaten. Its stems are often used for making furniture □ *bamboo furniture/shoots.*

bamboozle [bæm'buːzl] *vt* to trick <sb> by confusing them (informal use) □ *They tried to bamboozle us into buying several more tickets.*

ban [bæn] (*pt* & *pp* **banned**, *cont* **banning**) ◇ *n* an official order saying that something is forbidden or preventing somebody from doing something □ *The government has imposed a ban on smoking in public places.* □ *He faces a lifetime ban from the sport.* ◇ *vt* [trade, drinking, smoking] to give an official order that forbids <an activity>; [person] to give an official order that prevents <sb> from doing something or going to a particular place □ *Strikes have been banned.* □ *banned goods/books* □ *He's been banned from driving for a year.*

banal [bə'nɑːl] *adj* [idea, remark, story] that one finds very ordinary and not interesting □ *The play was banal and totally lacking in originality.* □ *He made banal comments about the weather.*

banana [US bə'nænə, GB bə'nɑːnə] *n* a long, curved, tropical fruit that has yellow skin and soft, sweet, white flesh inside □ *a bunch of bananas.* ■ **to go bananas** to become very angry or excited (informal use).

banana republic *n* a small country, especially in Central or South America, that is poor and politically unstable (offensive use).

banana split *n* a banana cut in half and served as a dessert with ice cream, whipped cream, nuts etc.

band [bænd] *n* **-1.** MUSIC a group of musicians who play popular music together, or who play on brass instruments □ *The band struck up a military march.* □ *a rock band* □ *a band leader.* **-2.** [of people] a group of people who share the same aim □ *a band of thieves/rebels.* **-3.** [of cloth, steel] a long, thin, flat strip of fabric or metal that is used for fastening things together or for decorating or strengthening them □ *She'd tied a band of red ribbon in her hair.* **-4.** [of color, light] a long thin line, e.g. of color or light, that is different from the color or light around it □ *a wide band of green.* **-5. an income/age etc band** a range that people's incomes/ages etc can be divided into □ *What tax band are you in?*

◆ **band together** *vi* to join together in order to achieve a shared aim □ *Residents are banding together to form protest groups.*

bandage ['bændɪdʒ] ◇ *n* a long strip of fabric that is tied around a wound or injury in order to protect it while it heals. ◇ *vt* to wrap a bandage around <a part of one's body that has been cut or injured> □ *Let me bandage that for you.* □ *He had a bandaged knee.*

Band-Aid™ *n* a small piece of adhesive material used to protect a cut on one's body while it heals.

bandan(n)a [bæn'dænə] *n* a large brightly-colored handkerchief that is worn around the neck or head.

b and b, B and B (*abbr of* **bed and breakfast**) *n* accommodation at a house or small hotel where one can sleep and have breakfast; a place where this type of accommodation is provided □ *We stayed at a b and b.*

bandeau ['bændəʊ] (*pl* **bandeaux** ['bændəʊz]) *n* a thin band of material worn around the head by a woman to keep the hair in place.

bandit ['bændət] *n* an armed robber, especially one who attacks travelers in wild isolated places.

bandmaster [US 'bændmæstr, GB -mɑːstə] *n* the leader or conductor of a band of musicians, especially a military band or brass band.

band saw *n* an electric saw whose blade is a flexible metal band that runs over two wheels.

bandsman ['bændzmən] (*pl* **bandsmen** [-mən]) *n* a musician who plays in a brass band or military band.

bandstand ['bændstænd] *n* a raised platform with a roof, often in a park, where a brass band or military band plays.

bandwagon ['bændwægən] *n* **to jump on the bandwagon** to start doing something because it has become very popular, especially because one believes one will benefit from it □ *It's only a matter of time before other designers start jumping on the bandwagon.*

bandwidth ['bændwɪdθ] *n* COMPUTING the amount of information that can be sent through a cable, e.g. from a modem, measured in bits per second.

bandy ['bændɪ] (*compar* **bandier**, *superl* **bandiest**, *pt* & *pp* **bandied**) *adj* **bandy legs** legs that curve outward at the knees.

◆ **bandy about, bandy around** *vt sep* to **bandy sthg about** OR **around** [name, amount, word] to mention sthg frequently in a careless way, often with the intention of impressing people □ *A figure of several million was being bandied about.*

bandy-legged [-'legd] *adj* **to be bandy-legged** to have bandy legs.

bane [beɪn] *n* **the bane of sb's life** a person or thing that constantly makes sb's life difficult □ *That photocopier is the bane of my life!*

bang [bæŋ] ◇ *adv* **-1.** exactly (informal use) □ *The train was bang on time.* □ *Our predictions were bang on target.* □ *The car broke down bang in the middle of town.* **-2. bang goes** OR **go...** a phrase used when it becomes clear that a future event is not going to take place or

succeed □ *Bang goes our vacation!* □ *Bang goes my chance of making some money!*
◇ *n* **-1. to get a bang** to get hit by something □ *She got a nasty bang on the head.* **-2.** a sudden, sharp, loud noise □ *The firework went off with a loud bang.* ■ **to go with a bang** to be a success (informal use) □ *The show went (off) with a bang.*
◇ *vt* **-1.** to hit <a part of one's body> accidentally on an object □ *I banged my knee on the desk.* **-2.** to hit or move <an object> violently causing a loud noise □ *They marched by, shouting and banging drums.* □ *She banged the door shut.* □ *He banged the books down on the table.*
◇ *vi* **-1. to bang into sthg** [into a table, chair] to hit sthg accidentally □ *The room was dark, and I kept banging into things.* **-2. to bang on sthg** [on a table, door] to hit sthg, causing a loud noise □ *There was someone banging on the front door.* **-3.** to make a loud noise □ *There's someone banging around upstairs.*
◇ *excl* a word used to represent a loud noise such as a explosion or gunshot.
◆ **bangs** *npl* US a section of hair that is cut to hang over the forehead.
banger [ˈbæŋəʳ] *n* GB a type of firework that makes a loud noise.
Bangkok [ˌbæŋˈkɒk] the capital of Thailand and its largest city. POPULATION: 5,154,000.
Bangladesh [ˌbæŋɡləˈdeʃ] a country in southern Asia, near the eastern edge of India. SIZE: 143,000 sq kms. POPULATION: 116,600,000 (*Bangladeshis*). CAPITAL: Dacca. CURRENCY: taka.
Bangladeshi [ˌbæŋɡləˈdeʃɪ] *n* & *adj*: *see* **Bangladesh**.
bangle [ˈbæŋɡl] *n* a thin band of metal, plastic etc that is worn on the wrist, arm, or ankle as jewelry.
banish [ˈbænɪʃ] *vt* **-1.** [person] to order <sb> to leave a place, e.g. their country, as a punishment □ *The king banished him from the court.* □ *The children were banished upstairs.* **-2.** [thought, worries] to stop oneself from thinking about <sthg> □ *He tried to banish the memory of her face from his mind.*
banister [ˈbænɪstəʳ] *n*, **banisters** [ˈbænɪstəʳz] *npl* a rail supported by a set of posts that is fixed along the outer edge of a staircase to stop people falling.
banjo [ˈbændʒoʊ] (*pl* **banjos** OR **banjoes**) *n* a musical instrument like a small round guitar with a long neck.
bank [bæŋk] ◇ *n* **-1.** FINANCE an organization that looks after its customers' money and offers them financial services such as loans, mortgages, foreign exchange etc; a branch or office of an organization of this kind □ *I'm just going to the bank to change some money.* □ *My bank is just around the corner from here.* **-2. a blood/sperm etc bank** a place where blood/sperm etc is stored until it is needed. **-3.** [of a river] the raised ground at the edge of a river □ *A man was fishing on the river bank.* □ *on the banks of the Amazon.* **-4.** [of earth] a pile of earth, mud, snow etc that

forms a slope □ *He climbed up the grassy bank.*
-5. a bank of cloud/fog a mass of cloud/fog.
◇ *vt* FINANCE to put <money or a check> in a bank account □ *I banked your check yesterday.*
◇ *vi* **-1.** FINANCE to have a bank account □ *Where do you bank?* □ *She banks with Lloyds.*
-2. [airplane] to move so that one wing is raised higher than the other □ *The plane suddenly banked sharply.*
◆ **bank on** *vt fus* **to bank on sb/sthg** to depend on sb/sthg □ *I wouldn't bank on her coming tonight.* □ *"You will support my case, won't you?"* — *"I wouldn't bank on it."*
bank account *n* an arrangement with a bank which allows a customer to keep money in the bank and take it out when it is needed □ *I've opened a bank account.*
bank balance *n* the amount of money somebody has in their bank account □ *I'd like to buy it, but I dread to think what it would do to my bank balance.*
bankbook [ˈbæŋkbʊk] *n* a book in which one keeps a record of all the money paid into and taken out of one's bank account.
bank card *n* a card given by a bank to a customer that can be used to take money out of their account or to pay for things.
bank charges *npl* money that a customer must pay a bank for services such as loans or transfers of money.
bank draft *n* a document from one bank authorizing another bank, usually in a foreign country, to pay money to an individual or organization.
banker [ˈbæŋkəʳ] *n* a person who owns or has an important position in a bank.
banker's card *n* GB a small plastic card that a bank gives to owners of checking accounts, promising that it will pay out the money for checks up to the amount that is stated on the card.
banker's draft *n* = **bank draft**.
banker's order *n* GB an instruction from a customer to a bank to pay a particular sum to a particular person or organization at regular intervals.
bank holiday *n* GB an official public holiday, when banks and many other businesses are closed by law. Bank holidays are usually on Mondays □ *a bank holiday weekend.*
banking [ˈbæŋkɪŋ] *n* the business activities of a bank or banker □ *a career in banking* □ *banking hours.*
bank loan *n* a loan given to an individual or an organization by a bank.
bank manager *n* a person who is in charge of a branch of a bank.
bank note *n* a piece of paper issued by the national bank of a country that is worth a particular amount of money.
Bank of England *n* **the Bank of England** the central bank in Britain.
bank rate *n* the rate of interest at which a country's central bank lends money.
bankrupt [ˈbæŋkrʌpt] ◇ *adj* [person, company,

organization] who is unable to pay their debts. ■ **to go bankrupt** [person, company, organization] to be unable to pay one's debts and as a result be forced to stop doing business □ *They almost went bankrupt last year.* ◊ *n* a person who is bankrupt. ◊ *vt* to make <a person, company, or organization> go bankrupt □ *That court case nearly bankrupted us.*

bankruptcy ['bæŋkrʌptsɪ] (*pl* **bankruptcies**) *n* [of a person, company, organization] *see* **bankrupt** □ *We face bankruptcy.* □ *an increasing number of bankruptcies.*

bank statement *n* a regular statement that a bank sends to a customer about their account, and that lists all withdrawals and deposits of money over a period of time.

banner ['bænər] *n* a long strip of cloth on which a message, slogan etc is written and which is often carried by demonstrators on a march or hung across a street.

bannister ['bænəstər] *n*, **bannisters** ['bænəstərz] *npl* = **banister**.

Bannister ['bænəstər], **Sir Roger** (1929–) a British athlete who in 1954 became the first person to run a mile in less than four minutes.

banns [bænz] *npl* **to publish** OR **read the banns** to make an announcement in church that two people are going to get married.

banquet ['bæŋkwət] *n* a large formal dinner, often given for a special occasion and followed by speeches □ *a wedding banquet.*

bantam ['bæntəm] *n* a type of small chicken.

bantamweight ['bæntəmweɪt] *n* a boxer who belongs to the second-lightest of the weight categories.

banter ['bæntər] *n* friendly conversation and jokes, especially between people who are pretending to make fun of each other □ *There was a lot of good-natured banter about weddings and mother-in-laws.*

bap [bæp] *n* GB a soft white bread roll.

baptism ['bæptɪzm] *n* in the Christian religion, a ceremony in which a person has water sprinkled on their head or is covered in water as a sign of their formal acceptance into the Church. ■ **a baptism of fire** an introduction to a new activity or experience that takes place in very difficult or unpleasant conditions □ *Having to get up and speak in front of all my new colleagues was a real baptism of fire.*

Baptist ['bæptəst] *n* a member of a Christian group that believes that people should not be baptized until they are old enough to understand their religion.

baptize, -ise [US 'bæptaɪz, GB bæp'taɪz] *vt* to perform the ceremony of baptism on <sb> □ *Have you been baptized?*

bar [bɑːr] (*pt* & *pp* **barred**, *cont* **barring**) ◊ *n* -1. [of soap, chocolate, gold] a solid rectangular piece of something □ *a chocolate/candy bar* □ *a bar of soap.* -2. [of metal] a long narrow piece of metal used to strengthen or protect a window, building etc □ *an iron bar.* ■ **to be behind bars** to be in prison □ *Now that the kill-*

er *is safely behind bars...* -3. **a bar to sthg** something that makes it difficult or impossible for somebody to do sthg □ *Language is no bar to understanding.* -4. **a bar on sthg** an official order saying that sthg is forbidden □ *There's a bar on foreign imports.* -5. [for drinks] a place where alcoholic drinks are served □ *a cocktail bar.* -6. **a sandwich/snack etc bar** a small restaurant that serves sandwiches/snacks etc. -7. [in a restaurant] the counter in a bar or restaurant where drinks are served □ *You order drinks separately at the bar.* -8. MUSIC one of the units that a piece of music is divided into, containing a particular number of beats □ *There are four beats to the bar.*

◊ *vt* -1. to put an iron bar or piece of wood across <a door or window> so that people cannot get in or out □ *The door was barred.* -2. to block or obstruct <an area, path, road> etc □ *A fallen tree barred the street.* ■ **to bar sb's way** to prevent sb from going somewhere by standing in front of them □ *The way was barred by a group of demonstrators.* ■ **to bar sb from a place** to say that sb is not allowed to enter a place □ *She's been barred from the club.*

◊ *prep* except for <sthg> □ *I'd finished all my work, bar a few letters.* ■ **bar none** with no exceptions □ *He's the best boxer in the USA, bar none.*

◆ **Bar** *n* **the Bar** US the profession of a lawyer; GB the profession of a barrister. ■ **to be called to the Bar** to begin one's career as a barrister.

Barbados [US bɑːrˈbeɪdoʊs, GB -ˈbeɪdɒs] a country in the Caribbean. SIZE: 431 sq kms. POPULATION: 300,000 (*Barbadians*). CAPITAL: Bridgetown. LANGUAGE: English. CURRENCY: Barbados dollar.

barbarian [bɑːrˈbeərɪən] *n* -1. HISTORY a person belonging to a primitive tribe and considered to be rough and wild □ *barbarian hordes.* -2. a person who has very bad manners and knows nothing about art or culture (disapproving use) □ *It's no use inviting Ray, he's such a barbarian when it comes to opera.*

barbaric [bɑːrˈbærɪk] *adj* [act, behavior] very cruel □ *the barbaric treatment of prisoners of war* □ *Some of my friends think eating veal is barbaric.*

barbarous ['bɑːrbərəs] *adj* -1. [tribe, people] rough and wild. -2. [act, behavior] very cruel.

barbecue ['bɑːrbɪkjuː] ◊ *n* -1. an outdoor grill on which meat, fish etc is cooked over an open fire. -2. an outdoor party at which people eat food that has been cooked on a barbecue □ *We're invited to a barbecue.* ◊ *vt* [meat, fish] to cook <food> on a barbecue.

❧ BARBECUES

Although barbecues have become more common in the UK, they are still not as popular as in the USA and Australia, where they are an important part of social life. Barbecues can take place on any occasion, not just informal family meals, and they are a traditional way of celebrating national holidays like the Fourth of July and Australia Day. Many people have a barbecue in their backyard, and in the USA and Australia parks and campsites often have special barbecue areas. If you are invited to a barbecue, or "barbie", in Australia, you may be asked to "bring a plate" — a plateful of food — as a contribution to the meal.

barbed [bɑːʳbd] *adj* **-1.** [hook, arrow, spear] that has one or more sharp curved points. **-2.** [comment, remark] sharp and unkind □ *He kept making barbed jokes about his ex-wife.*

barbed wire *n* wire with sharp points on it that is used in a fence, on top of a wall etc to prevent people or animals from entering or leaving a place □ *a barbed-wire fence.*

barber ['bɑːʳbəʳ] *n* a man whose job is to cut men's hair. ■ **a barber's (shop)** the place where a barber works.

Barbican ['bɑːʳbɪkən]: **the Barbican (Arts Centre)** a cultural center in London that includes a concert hall, movie theater, two theaters, a library, and an art gallery.

barbie ['bɑːʳbɪ] *n* AUS & GB = **barbecue** (informal use).

barbiturate [bɑːʳbɪtʃərət] *n* a type of drug that makes people calm and helps them to sleep.

Barcelona [,bɑːʳsə'loʊnə] a city in eastern Spain, on the Mediterranean. It is the capital of Catalonia, and Spain's most important port. POPULATION: 1,643,542.

bar chart *n* GB = **bar graph**.

bar code *n* a code made up of numbers and lines that is printed on a product and gives information about its price, identity etc which can be read by a computer at a store checkout.

bare [beəʳ] ◇ *adj* **-1.** [foot, leg, arm] not covered with clothes; [tree, branch] not covered with leaves; [ground, hill] not covered with plants □ *Don't go out in your bare feet.* □ *The trees were bare and there was snow on the ground.* **-2. the bare facts** the most basic and simple facts □ *I just told him the bare facts of the situation.* **-3. the bare minimum** the smallest possible amount □ *They pay them the absolute bare minimum.* □ *I took the bare minimum of clothing/cash.* ■ **the bare necessities** OR **essentials** only the things that are completely necessary. **-4.** [room, cupboard, floorboards] not filled, covered, or decorated □ *The walls look rather bare.* ◇ *vt* **-1.** to remove clothing from <one's head, legs> etc so that one's skin can be seen □ *I wouldn't dare bare my body in public.* **-2. the dog bared its teeth** the dog showed its teeth as a sign of aggression.

bareback ['beəʳbæk] ◇ *adj* **a bareback rider** a person who rides a horse without a saddle. ■ **bareback riding** the activity of riding a horse without a saddle. ◇ *adv* **to ride bareback** to ride a horse without a saddle.

barefaced [,beəʳ'feɪst] *adj* **a barefaced lie** a lie told by somebody who does not care if other people know they are lying.

barefoot ['beəʳfʊt], **barefooted** [,beəʳ'fʊtəd]
◇ *adj* [person] who is not wearing shoes or socks. ◇ *adv*: *She walked barefoot over the pebbles.*

bareheaded [,beəʳ'hedəd] ◇ *adj* [person] who is not wearing a hat. ◇ *adv*: *Several refugees sat bareheaded in the hot sun.*

barelegged [,beəʳ'legd] ◇ *adj* [person] who is not wearing anything on their legs. ◇ *adv*: *They ran barelegged down to the stream.*

barely ['beəʳlɪ] *adv* **-1. I could barely keep awake** I kept awake, but it was very difficult □ *There's barely enough to feed four of us.* **-2. she had barely arrived** she had arrived only a very short time before □ *But we've barely met!*

bargain ['bɑːʳgən] ◇ *n* **-1.** an agreement between two people or two groups of people that each of them will do something in return for something else □ *I've kept my side of the bargain.* ■ **to make** OR **strike a bargain** to decide the terms of a bargain. **-2.** something that is on sale for a price that is cheaper than normal or than expected □ *There are some real bargains in the sale.* □ *I got a good bargain at that hardware store.* □ *What a bargain!* ◇ *vi* to discuss the terms of an agreement or sale and try to persuade the other person or people involved to accept the conditions that one wants □ *They are currently bargaining with the unions for a peaceful settlement.* □ *He's still bargaining over the price.*

◆ **into the bargain** *adv* a phrase used to emphasize an extra advantage that somebody or something provides □ *She's a great organizer and a gifted linguist into the bargain.*

◆ **bargain for, bargain on** *vt fus* **I/he/she etc hadn't bargained for sthg** I/he/she etc hadn't expected sthg □ *They hadn't bargained on so many people turning up.* □ *He got more than he bargained for when he asked Matt to stay.*

bargain basement *comp* **bargain basement prices** prices that are much lower than usual.

bargaining power ['bɑːʳgənɪŋ-] *n* the amount of power a person or group has when negotiating an agreement about prices, pay, terms etc.

barge [bɑːʳdʒ] ◇ *n* a type of long boat with a flat bottom that is used to carry heavy loads on canals or rivers. ◇ *vi* to rush in a forceful, clumsy, or rude way □ *I tried to stop him, but he barged straight past me.*

◆ **barge in** *vi* to enter in a forceful, clumsy, or rude way □ *She just barged in demanding to see the manager.* ■ **to barge in on sb/sthg** to interrupt sb/sthg rudely □ *He barged in on us/our conversation without a word of apology.*

◆ **barge into** *vt fus* **-1. to barge into sb** to bump sb heavily or clumsily. **-2. to barge into a room** to enter a room in a forceful, clumsy, or rude way.

bar graph US, **bar chart** GB *n* a graph in which rectangles of different lengths represent particular amounts.

baritone ['bærətoʊn] *n* a male singing voice that is lower than a tenor but higher than a bass □ *a rich baritone voice.*

barium meal [ˌbeərɪəm-] *n* a chemical mixture that is drunk by a patient before an X-ray in order to allow the internal organs to be seen more clearly.

bark [bɑːʳk] ◇ *n* -1. the loud harsh noise made by a dog □ *The dog gave a loud bark.* ■ **his bark is worse than his bite** he appears much more unfriendly and frightening than he really is (informal use). -2. the hard, rough, outer covering of the trunk and branches of a tree □ *a piece of tree bark.* ◇ *vt* [order, instructions, command] to shout <sthg> in a sudden unfriendly way □ *The sergeant-major was barking out orders to his men.* ◇ *vi* [dog] to make a loud harsh noise □ *The dog was barking at me.*

barking [ˈbɑːʳkɪŋ] *n* the sound of a dog that is barking □ *I'll go mad if that barking doesn't stop soon.*

barley [ˈbɑːʳlɪ] *n* a plant similar to tall grass that has long straight hairs growing from the head of each stalk; the grain of this plant grown for food and used for making beer and whiskey.

barley sugar *n* GB a type of hard candy made from boiled sugar.

barley water *n* GB a type of non-alcoholic drink made from barley that usually has a lemon or orange flavor.

barmaid [ˈbɑːʳmeɪd] *n* GB a woman who serves drinks in a bar or pub.

barman [ˈbɑːʳmən] (*pl* **barmen** [-mən]) *n* GB a man who serves drinks in a bar or pub.

bar mitzvah [ˌbɑːʳˈmɪtsvə] *n* a religious ceremony that takes place when a Jewish boy becomes 13 years old. It means he is old enough to carry out religious duties.

barn [bɑːʳn] *n* a large farm building used for storing crops or for keeping animals in.

barnacle [ˈbɑːʳnəkl] *n* a small shellfish that attaches itself to rocks, the bottom of boats etc and is very difficult to remove.

Barnardo's [bəʳˈnɑːʳdoʊz] a British charity that provides homes and schools for orphans and poor children.

barn dance *n* a party at which people do country dancing; a type of dance done at such an event.

barn owl *n* a type of owl that has brown and white feathers and a heart-shaped face.

barometer [bəˈrɒmətəʳ] *n* -1. an instrument for measuring air pressure that is used to predict changes in the weather. -2. something that gives a sign of changes or of what people think □ *These polls are always a useful barometer of public opinion.*

baron [US ˈberən, GB ˈbær-] *n* -1. a man who is a member of a low rank of the nobility and whose title can be given to his son when he dies. -2. **an oil/a press etc baron** an extremely powerful businessman who makes their money from oil/newspapers etc.

baroness [US ˈberənes, GB ˈbær-] *n* a woman who has the same rank as a baron; the wife of a baron.

baronet [US ˈberənət, GB ˈbær-] *n* a nobleman who is lower in rank than a baron, and whose title can be given to his son when he dies.

baroque [US bəˈroʊk, GB -ˈrɒk] *adj* -1. [art, architecture] typical of a detailed and dramatic style used in Europe between the sixteenth and eighteenth centuries. -2. [music] typical of a style of seventeenth and eighteenth century European composers, e.g. Bach and Vivaldi. -3. [writing, style] that contains very descriptive language and is too complicated.

barrack [US ˈberək, GB ˈbær-] ◇ *vt* GB to interrupt <a speaker> by shouting loudly. ◇ *vi* **barrack for sb/sthg** AUS [for players, a team] to shout words of encouragement to sb/sthg that one supports.

◆ **barracks** *npl* a building or group of buildings where soldiers live □ *army barracks.*

barracking [US ˈberəkɪŋ, GB ˈbær-] *n* GB the act of interrupting a speaker by shouting loudly.

barracuda [US ˌberəˈkuːdə, GB ˌbærəˈkjuːdə] *n* a large tropical fish that eats the flesh of other fish and other animals.

barrage [*senses 1 & 2* US bəˈrɑːʒ, GB ˈbærɑːʒ, *sense 3* US ˈbɑːrɪdʒ, GB ˈbærɑːʒ] *n* -1. the firing of a lot of guns, often before the start of an attack □ *a barrage of heavy artillery fire.* -2. **a barrage of complaints/criticism etc** a large number of complaints/criticisms etc that come one after the other □ *She was met with a barrage of questions.* -3. GB a structure that is built across a river to control the depth of the water, e.g. to help with irrigation or prevent flooding.

barred [bɑːʳd] *adj* **a barred window** a window that has bars across it to prevent people from getting through.

barrel [US ˈberəl, GB ˈbær-] *n* -1. a large round container that is wider in the middle than at the top or bottom, and is usually made of wood □ *a beer barrel.* -2. [of oil] a unit (159 liters) for measuring an amount of oil □ *They have a production capacity of two million barrels a day.* -3. [of a gun] the tube of a gun that the bullet travels down when it is fired.

barrel organ *n* a large musical instrument on wheels that plays a tune when the handle is turned and was often used in the past to entertain people in the street.

barren [US ˈberən, GB ˈbær-] *adj* (literary use) -1. [field, land] that cannot produce crops. -2. [discussion, time] that does not produce any useful results. -3. [woman] who is not able to have children.

barrette [bəˈret] *n* US a clip used to hold a woman's hair in place.

barricade [ˌbærəˈkeɪd] ◇ *n* a temporary barrier across a road, passage, or entrance. ◇ *vt* to block <a street, door, window> etc by building a barricade. ■ **to barricade oneself in** to put barricades across all the entrances to the building that one is in, preventing anybody else from entering.

barrier [US ˈberɪr, GB ˈbærɪə] *n* -1. something that prevents people or things from moving from one place to another, e.g. a fence or gate □ *You have to show your passport at the* barrier. -2. something that makes contact, agreement etc between people difficult or impossible □ *a language/trade barrier* □ *This change in the law removes the last barrier to a settlement.*

barrier cream *n* a cream used to protect one's skin against dirt or infection.

barrier method *n* a form of contraception that uses a physical object, e.g. a condom or diaphragm, rather than a drug.

barring ['bɑːrɪŋ] *prep* -1. except for <sb/sthg> □ *All the projects, barring one, are now complete.* -2. a word used to say that something will happen unless something else prevents it □ *Barring further complications, we start tomorrow.*

barrio [US 'bɑːrɪoʊ, GB 'bær-] *n* US a part of a US town or city where many Spanish-speaking people live.

barrister [US 'berɪstr, GB 'bærɪstə] *n* in England, Wales, and Australia, a lawyer who speaks in the higher courts of law to represent a client.

barroom ['bɑːruːm] *n* US a room or building with a bar where alcohol is served.

barrow [US 'beroʊ, GB 'bær-] *n* -1. a small cart, usually used for selling fruit and vegetables at markets. -2. = **wheelbarrow**.

bar stool *n* a high stool for people to sit on at a bar or counter.

Bart. *abbr of* **baronet**.

bartender ['bɑːrtendər] *n* US a person whose job is to serve drinks at a bar.

barter ['bɑːrtər] ◇ *vt* to exchange <goods> for other goods, without using money □ *They barter farm produce for clothes.* ◇ *vi: They come to the market to barter.* ◇ *n: a barter economy.*

base [beɪs] ◇ *n* -1. [of a tree, one's spine, a triangle] the bottom or lowest part of something □ *The bud grows at the base of the branch.* -2. [for a mixture, paint] the main part of something to which other things are added □ *The stock forms the base of your sauce.* □ *Cream is a good base color.* -3. SPORT in baseball, one of the four points on the field that players have to run around in order to score points. -4. MILITARY the place in a particular area where an army, navy etc keeps its staff and equipment and from where activities in that area are organized □ *Report back to base when you have accomplished your mission.* -5. BUSINESS the main office of a company or organization in a particular country, city etc □ *We have a base in London.* -6. [for a salesman, tourist, climber] a place where one has one's home, office etc and from which one travels to other places in the same country, region, or area □ *From her base in Hong Kong, she covers the whole of the Far East.* □ *They used our apartment as a base and took the subway into town each day.*
◇ *vt* -1. **to be based in a place** [company, employee] to have a place as a base or main location □ *Where are you based?* □ *The company's main activities are based in Paris.* -2. **to base sthg on** OR **upon sthg** to use sthg as the point from which to develop sthg □ *The plot of the novel is based on a true story.*

◇ *adj* [person, behavior] that one thinks is bad and does not deserve respect (literary use).

baseball ['beɪsbɔːl] *n* a game, played mainly in the USA, between two teams of nine players. A player from one team hits a ball with a bat and scores points by running around four points in the field, known as bases. The other team tries to prevent this by throwing the ball to a base before the batter has reached it.

baseball cap *n* a hat that fits tightly over the top of one's head and has a curved part that sticks out in front.

baseboard ['beɪsbɔːrd] *n* US the strip of wood that covers the bottom of a wall in a room or corridor.

base camp *n* the main camp used, especially by mountaineers, as a base for expeditions.

-based [beɪst] *suffix* added to a word to show where a person, organization etc has their base or to show what the most important part of something is □ *a Tokyo-based firm* □ *The mixture is water-based.*

baseless ['beɪsləs] *adj* [fears, doubts, gossip] not based on facts.

baseline ['beɪslaɪn] *n* the line that marks each end of the playing area in tennis, badminton etc.

basement ['beɪsmənt] *n* a story of a building that is below ground level.

base metal *n* a metal that is not very valuable, e.g. iron or lead (old-fashioned use).

base rate *n* the interest rate that banks use as a basis when calculating other rates.

bases ['beɪsiːz] *plural of* **basis**.

bash [bæʃ] (informal use) ◇ *n* -1. [on the head, knee] a hard blow. -2. [for a celebration] a party. ◇ *vt* [person, vehicle, head] to hit <sb/sthg> hard.

bashful ['bæʃfl] *adj* [person, smile] shy.

basic ['beɪsɪk] *adj* -1. [need, problem, aim] that is the most important part of something and that depends on or is connected with everything else □ *Her basic argument is that saving energy means saving money.* □ *These things are basic to our corporate strategy.* -2. [skill, vocabulary, food] that is simple but is necessary and can be developed or added to; [salary, model] that has nothing extra added □ *These are the basic ingredients.* -3. **to be basic** [room, accommodation] to be simple and have nothing more than is necessary □ *Their apartment is quite basic.*

◆ **basics** *npl* -1. the simplest, but often the most important parts of something □ *the basics of computing/French.* -2. the items of something, e.g. food or equipment, that are most important for a particular situation or activity □ *They learned to survive with just the basics.*

BASIC ['beɪsɪk] (*abbr of* **Beginner's All-purpose Symbolic Instruction Code**) *n* a form of language used for programing a computer.

basically ['beɪsɪklɪ] *adv* a word used when emphasizing the most important aspect of something or when giving a simple description of something complicated □ *They amount* to basically the same thing. □ He is basically a kind person. □ Basically, we're just very different.

basic rate *n* GB the standard or lowest rate of taxation or interest.

basic wage *n* a wage with no extra payments, e.g. for overtime or commission.

basil [US 'beizl, GB 'bæzl] *n* an herb with thin wide leaves that have a strong pleasant smell.

basin ['beisn] *n* -1. [in a bathroom] a small sink for washing one's hands and face in. -2. GEOGRAPHY an area where several rivers flow into a large river, a lake, or the sea □ the Amazon Basin. -3. GB [for food, liquid] a large bowl used for mixing food in; a large bowl used for washing dishes in.

basis ['beisəs] (*pl* **bases**) *n* -1. the part of a plan, idea, organization etc that everything else develops from □ the basis of his argument □ The text can be used as a basis for discussion. -2. **on the basis of sthg** a phrase used to show the reason for a particular action or decision □ We made the decision on the basis of what we had been told. □ He did it on the basis that he had nothing to lose. ■ **to do sthg on a regular/daily/weekly basis** to do sthg regularly/every day/every week.

bask [US bæsk, GB bɑːsk] *vi* -1. **to bask in the sun** to sit or lie somewhere and enjoy the heat from the sun □ The others were out basking in the sun. -2. **to bask in sthg** [in somebody's approval, praise] to enjoy sthg □ He's basking in the glory of his recent Broadway success.

basket [US 'bæskət, GB 'bɑːsk-] *n* -1. a container made of woven strips of straw, wood, plastic, wire etc and used for carrying or storing things □ a shopping basket. -2. FINANCE **a basket of currencies** the average value of several different currencies. -3. BASKETBALL a small round net that is open at the bottom and is fixed high above the ground at each end of a basketball court. Points are scored by throwing the ball through this net.

basketball [US 'bæskətbɔːl, GB 'bɑːsk-] *n* a game between two teams of five players, played on a court with a basket at each end. Points are scored by throwing a large ball through the other team's basket; the ball used in this game.

basketwork [US 'bæskətwɜːrk, GB 'bɑːskətwɜːk] *n* the craft of weaving baskets and other objects from strips of wood or cane.

basking shark [US 'bæskiŋ-, GB 'bɑːsk-] *n* a large shark that eats plankton and often swims near the surface of the sea.

Basque [bæsk] ◇ *n* a member of a people living in the Basque Country, the region between southwestern France and northeastern Spain; the language of this people. ◇ *adj*: Basque literature/traditions.

Basque Provinces: **the Basque Provinces** a self-governing region of northern Spain. SIZE: 7,250 sq kms. POPULATION: 2,099,978 (*Basques*). CAPITAL: Vitoria. MAIN CITY: Bilbao.

bass¹ [beis] ◇ *adj* [note, voice] low in sound. ◇ *n* -1. a man who sings the lowest range

of musical notes. -2. = **double bass**. -3. = **bass guitar**.

bass² [bæs] (*pl* **bass** OR **basses**) *n* a fish that lives in rivers or the sea and is eaten.

bass clef [,beis-] *n* a symbol (𝄢) at the beginning of a line of music that shows that the notes are in the lower range.

bass drum [,beis-] *n* a large drum that produces a low sound.

basset ['bæsət] *n* **a basset (hound)** a dog that has short legs, a long body, and long ears.

bass guitar [,beis-] *n* an electric guitar with four strings that is used to play bass notes.

bassoon [bə'suːn] *n* a large woodwind instrument that produces a low sound.

Bass Strait [,bæs-]: **the Bass Strait** the channel of water between Tasmania and Australia.

bastard [US 'bæstərd, GB 'bɑːstəd] *n* -1.▽ a word used to describe somebody, usually a man, in a way that seems insulting but is meant as a joke (very informal use) □ You lucky/silly/clever bastard! -2.▼ a word used to describe a man that one dislikes and finds very unpleasant (offensive use). -3. a person whose parents are not married to each other (old-fashioned use).

baste [beist] *vt* to cover <meat> with hot fat and its own juices while it is cooking to keep it moist.

bastion [US 'bæstʃən, GB 'bæstiən] *n* something that allows a principle or way of life to continue at a time when it is threatened or seems likely to disappear □ the last bastion of monetarism.

BASW (*abbr of* **British Association of Social Workers**) *n* **the BASW** a British labor union for social workers.

bat [bæt] (*pt & pp* **batted**, *cont* **batting**) ◇ *n* -1. a small flying animal that looks like a mouse with wings and hunts for its food at night. -2. SPORT a piece of wood with a particular shape and a handle at one end, that is used for hitting a ball, e.g. in baseball, cricket, or table tennis. -3. *phrases* (informal use) **right off the bat** US immediately □ Right off the bat, I knew something was wrong. ■ **to do sthg off one's own bat** GB to do sthg without being told to do it □ She did all the research off her own bat.
◇ *vt* to hit <a ball> with a bat.
◇ *vi* [baseball player, cricketer, team] to try to score runs by hitting the ball with a bat.

batch [bætʃ] *n* [of papers, products] a group of things that are similar and are produced or dealt with at the same time; [of recruits, trainees] a number of people who are dealt with by an organization as a group □ The first batch of applications/applicants was being processed by the personnel department.

batch file *n* a computer file that contains a series of commands and is used to avoid having to type in each command separately.

batch processing *n* the processing by a computer of a batch of information that has been collected together over a period of time.

bated ['beɪtəd] *adj* **with bated breath** not knowing what will happen and so very excited or nervous □ *We watched/waited with bated breath for news of the verdict.*

bath [US bæθ, GB bɑ:θ] ◇ *n* -1. a large container, usually fitted against a wall, that one sits or lies in to wash one's body □ *He forgot to clean the bath.* -2. **to have** OR **take a bath** to sit or lie in a bath that is filled with water and wash oneself □ *I had a bath when I got home.* ◇ *vt* GB [baby, old person] to wash <sb> in a bath.

◆ **baths** *npl* GB an indoor public swimming pool.

bath chair *n* a type of old-fashioned wheelchair, usually with a cover over the top.

bath cube *n* a cube of bath salts that dissolves in water.

bathe [beɪð] ◇ *vt* -1. to wash <a wound, cut> etc in water or another liquid □ *I bathed my foot in antiseptic.* -2. **to be bathed in light** to be filled or covered with light (literary use) □ *The garden was bathed in sunshine.* ◇ *vi* -1. US to have a bath. -2. GB to swim for pleasure in a lake, river etc.

bather ['beɪðəʳ] *n* GB a person who is swimming or playing in a lake, river etc.

◆ **bathers** *npl* AUS a swimsuit.

bathing ['beɪðɪŋ] *n* GB the activity of swimming for pleasure □ *'No bathing.'*

bathing cap *n* a cap that is worn to keep one's hair dry when one is swimming.

bathing suit *n* a piece of clothing made to be worn while swimming.

bathing trunks *npl* shorts worn by men when swimming (old-fashioned use).

bath mat *n* a mat placed next to a bath so that one can stand on it when drying oneself.

bath oil *n* oil that is added to bathwater to give it a pleasant smell.

bathrobe [US 'bæθroʊb, GB 'bɑ:θ-] *n* -1. a long loose piece of clothing, usually made of toweling, that is worn after having a bath or a swim. -2. US a loose piece of clothing worn over nightwear or underwear, especially after just getting out of bed.

bathroom [US 'bæθru:m, GB 'bɑ:θ-] *n* -1. a room that contains a bath or shower and usually a sink and toilet. -2. US a room in which there is a toilet.

bath salts *npl* crystals that are added to a bath to soften the water and give it a pleasant smell.

bath towel *n* a large towel.

bathtub [US 'bæθtʌb, GB 'bɑ:θ-] *n* a large container that one sits in or lies in to wash one's body.

bathwater [US 'bæθwɔ:tr, GB 'bɑ:θwɔ:tə] *n* the water that one takes a bath in □ *Add a few drops to your bathwater.*

batik [bə'ti:k] *n* a process of printing designs on cloth by putting wax on the areas that

are not to be dyed; a piece of cloth with a design printed on it in this way □ *a batik shirt/dress/scarf.*

Batman ['bætmæn] a US cartoon character who wears a black cloak and mask. He fights crime with his partner Robin.

baton [US bə'tɑ:n, GB 'bætɒn] *n* -1. MUSIC a short thin stick used by a conductor to conduct an orchestra. -2. SPORT a short stick that is passed from one runner to the next in a relay race. -3. GB [used by the police] a heavy stick used as a weapon by the police.

batsman ['bætsmən] (*pl* **batsmen** [-mən]) *n* a player in cricket who is batting, or who specializes in batting.

battalion [bə'tælɪən] *n* a large unit of soldiers made up of three or four companies.

batten ['bætn] *n* a long flat strip of wood used for strengthening things or for fixing them in place.

◆ **batten down** *vt fus* **to batten down the hatches** to prepare oneself for a difficult period in the near future.

batter ['bætəʳ] ◇ *vt* to hit <sb/sthg> hard many times with one's fists or something heavy □ *He had been battered to death.* ◇ *vi* to batter something □ *He was battering at the door.* ◇ *n* -1. SPORT in baseball, the player who hits the ball. -2. COOKING a mixture of flour, eggs, and milk, used e.g. for making pancakes or covering food before frying it □ *Dip the fish in batter.*

◆ **batter down** *vt sep* to batter sthg down [door, barrier] to batter sthg until it falls down.

battered ['bætəʳd] *adj* -1. **a battered baby/wife** a baby/wife who has been a victim of violence from somebody in their family □ *a refuge for battered wives.* -2. [car, briefcase] that looks old and in bad condition □ *Prof. Burns turned up on a battered old bicycle.*

battering ['bætərɪŋ] *n* **to take a battering** [city, building, object] to suffer damage as a result of being hit, attacked etc many times; [team, political party] to suffer a bad defeat □ *The Old Town took a real battering in the war.* □ *The Democrats took a battering in the poll.*

battering ram *n* a long heavy piece of wood used by armies in the past for breaking down doors, walls, or gates.

battery ['bætərɪ] (*pl* **batteries**) *n* -1. ELECTRICITY a device that produces electricity, e.g. for a radio or car □ *The car battery is flat again.* -2. MILITARY a group of big guns fixed in one place. -3. **a battery of tests/measures etc** a large number of tests/measures etc that come together □ *She met with a battery of insults.*

battery charger *n* a device for putting electricity into batteries.

battery hen *n* a hen that is kept with a lot of other hens in small cages to lay eggs.

battle ['bætl] ◇ *n* -1. a fight between large groups of people □ *the Battle of Waterloo/Midway* □ *a battle between police and demonstrators* □ *He was killed in battle.* -2. a situation in which somebody tries very hard to get or achieve something, especially when they are opposed by somebody or something else □ *the battle for freedom/power* □ *the battle against poverty/inflation* □ *a battle with the authorities* □ *It's a real battle to get her to do her homework.* ■ **a battle of wits** a struggle or contest between people using intelligence and not violence. ■ **to be half the battle** to be a very important step toward achieving something □ *Getting to see him is half the battle, now all you have to do is to convince him.* ■ **to be fighting a losing battle** to be trying to do something when it is obvious that one cannot succeed.

◇ *vi* to try very hard to get or achieve something, especially in difficult or unpleasant circumstances □ *She battled to save his life.* □ *He's battling against cancer/for power.*

◇ *vt* US to battle against <sb/sthg> □ *Evans had been battling the disease for 10 years.*

battledress ['bætldres] *n* GB a soldier's uniform for fighting □ *troops in battledress.*

battlefield ['bætlfiːld], **battleground** ['bætl-graund] *n* -1. a place where a battle takes place. -2. a subject that people argue about strongly □ *The health system will be the political battlefield for the next election.*

battlements ['bætlmənts] *npl* a wall around the top of a castle that has spaces through which guns or arrows can be fired.

battleship ['bætlʃɪp] *n* the largest kind of warship.

bauble ['bɔːbl] *n* a piece of cheap jewelry; a cheap ornament.

baud [bɔːd] *n* a unit for measuring the speed at which information is passed between computers.

baud rate *n* the speed at which information is passed between computers.

baulk [bɔːk] *vi* = balk.

Bavaria [bə'veəriə] a state in south Germany. SIZE: 70,550 sq kms. POPULATION: 11,220,735 (*Bavarians*). CAPITAL: Munich.

bawdy ['bɔːdi] (*compar* bawdier, *superl* bawdiest) *adj* [joke, story, song] that refers to sex in a humorous and vulgar way.

bawl [bɔːl] ◇ *vi* -1. to shout loudly and harshly □ *I could hear the two of them bawling at each other.* -2. [baby, child] to cry loudly. ◇ *vt* [command, insult] to shout <sthg> loudly and harshly □ *"Get out!" he bawled.*

bay [beɪ] ◇ *n* -1. GEOGRAPHY a part of the coast where the land curves in and surrounds the water on three sides □ *a hotel overlooking the bay.* -2. [of a building] an area in or outside a building that is marked in a particular way and used for a particular purpose □ *a parking/loading bay.* -3. [horse] a reddish-brown horse. -4. *phrase* **to keep sb/sthg at bay** to stop sb/sthg from approaching, attacking, or affecting one □ *We're desperately trying to keep our creditors at bay while we figure out our finances.* ◇ *vi* [dog, wolf] to howl.

bay leaf *n* a leaf of the bay tree, used in cooking as a flavoring.

Bay of Biscay [-'bɪskeɪ]: **the Bay of Biscay** a

large bay in the Atlantic between western France and northern Spain. The sea there is often rough.

Bay of Pigs: **the Bay of Pigs** a bay in Cuba where an invading force of Cuban exiles and US troops was defeated by Cuban troops in 1961.

bayonet ['beɪənət] *n* a knife attached to the end of a gun.

bay tree *n* a Mediterranean laurel tree that has shiny dark-green leaves.

bay window *n* a window that is rounded or has three sides and sticks out from the main wall of a building.

bazaar [bə'zɑːʳ] *n* -1. a marketplace, especially in North Africa or the Middle East. -2. a sale of goods held in order to collect money for a particular charity or organization □ *a church bazaar.*

bazooka [bə'zuːkə] *n* a long antitank gun shaped like a tube that is held on the shoulder when it is fired.

BB *n abbr of* **Boys' Brigade**.

B & B *n abbr of* **bed and breakfast**.

BBB (*abbr of* **Better Business Bureau**) *n* **the BBB** an organization that aims to defend the standards of service provided by businesses, e.g. hotels or insurance companies.

BBC (*abbr of* **British Broadcasting Corporation**) *n* **the BBC** the British state-owned radio and television company.

BBQ, bbq *abbr of* **barbecue**.

BC -1. (*abbr of* **before Christ**) before the birth of Jesus Christ, according to the modern Western calendar □ *He died in 48 BC.* -2. *abbr of* **British Columbia**.
NOTE: Compare AD.

BCG (*abbr of* **Bacillus Calmette-Guérin**) *n* a vaccine against tuberculosis.

BD (*abbr of* **Bachelor of Divinity**) *n* a degree in the study of religion; a person who has this degree.

B/D *abbr of* **bank draft**.

BDS (*abbr of* **Bachelor of Dental Science**) *n* a degree in dentistry; a person who has this degree.

be [*stressed* biː, *unstressed* bɪ] (*pt* was OR were, *pp* been) ◇ *aux vb* -1. used with the -*ing* form of the verb to make continuous tenses □ *She was cooking dinner when I arrived.* □ *They've been waiting for ages.* □ *She's starting work on Monday.* -2. used with the past participle to make passive tenses □ *The bottle had already been opened.* -3. used in various types of sentence to represent whole clauses where the main verb is "be" □ *It was fun, wasn't it?* □ *I'm sure she'll be better than he was.* □ *"Aren't you Linda's brother?" — "Yes, I am."* -4. used with "to" and the infinitive for events that will or should happen in the near future. ■ **we are to meet at 8 pm** it is planned that we will meet at 8 pm. ■ **you are not to open it** you must not open it. ■ **I was to find this out later** I found this out later (used of events that are seen as important). **-5.** used to show what might happen □ *If I were you, I'd go.*

◇ *vi* (+ *complement*) **-1.** used before adjectives, nouns, adverbs etc to describe the subject of a sentence □ *I'm Scottish/from Scotland.* □ *The children are being difficult.* □ *She's a doctor/a fine violinist.* □ *Aren't you Doreen West?* ■ **how are you?** used to say "hello" or to ask whether somebody is well □ *"Hello, how are you?" — "I'm fine thanks."* **-2.** used to show age, time, place, price etc □ *I was 16 (years old) when I left school.* □ *The concert is this evening.* □ *The café is at the end of this road, on the left.* □ *He's been at home all day.* □ *The meal was $10 a head.* □ *The shirt is pure silk.* **-3.** used with "it" to show times, dates, distances, and weather □ *It's February 7 today.* □ *It's exactly 3 o'clock.* □ *It was too hot to go out.* **-4.** used to put emphasis on the most important item □ *What I need is a drink!* □ *It was Peter who first mentioned it.* **-5.** used with "there" to show that something exists, or where it is □ *Have there been any messages for me?* □ *There's a hole in my sock.*

◆ **be that as it may** *adv* that is perhaps true, but it is not relevant and I want to change the subject □ *Be that as it may, we still have to confront the problem of corruption.*

B/E *abbr of* **bill of exchange.**

beach [biːtʃ] ◇ *n* an area of sand or pebbles at the edge of a sea or lake □ *Let's go to the beach.* □ *We spent the day at the beach.* □ *Children were playing on the beach.* □ *The area is known for its unspoilt beaches.* ◇ *vt* to force or pull <a boat> onto the beach.

beach ball *n* a large light ball for playing with at the beach.

beach buggy *n* a car with very wide wheels that is used for traveling on sandy beaches.

beachcomber ['biːtʃkoʊmə'] *n* a person who looks for valuable things left by the tide on a beach.

beachhead ['biːtʃhed] *n* a part of a beach that has been captured from the enemy, and where an army can land its soldiers and equipment □ *An advance party of marines established* OR *secured a beachhead.*

beachwear ['biːtʃweə'] *n* clothing that is designed to be worn on the beach □ *Beachwear should not be worn in the restaurant.*

beacon ['biːkən] *n* **-1.** [on land] a fire, usually on a hill or a tower, that has been lit as a signal or warning. **-2.** SHIPPING an object with a light on it, e.g. a lighthouse, that shows boats they are near land or in dangerous waters. **-3.** RADIO a transmitter that sends out radio signals so that ships and aircraft can check their position.

Beacon Hill an expensive area of Boston.

bead [biːd] *n* **-1.** a small round piece of colored glass, wood, or plastic with a hole through the middle, used in jewelry □ *a string of beads* □ *a bead necklace.* **-2.** a small drop of liquid □ *By now his forehead was covered with beads of sweat.*

beaded ['biːdəd] *adj* [dress, bag] decorated with beads.

beading ['biːdɪŋ] *n* a narrow strip of wood for decorating furniture or doors.

beady ['biːdɪ] (*compar* **beadier**, *superl* **beadiest**) *adj* **beady eyes** small, round, bright eyes that are not attractive.

beagle ['biːgl] *n* a dog with short legs and large ears, kept as a pet or for hunting.

beak [biːk] *n* the hard pointed part of a bird's mouth.

beaker ['biːkə'] *n* a large cup or glass, usually without a handle.

be-all *n* **the be-all and end-all** the main purpose or most important part of something □ *Money isn't the be-all and end-all, you know.*

beam [biːm] ◇ *n* **-1.** [of wood] a long thick piece of wood, usually used for supporting the roof of a building □ *an old house with big, thick wooden beams.* **-2.** [of light] a line of light, e.g. from a flashlight or car headlight □ *Lasers produce a very narrow beam of light.* **-3.** US AUTO **high/low beams** car lights that point straight ahead/toward the ground.

◇ *vt* to send <radio or television signals> somewhere by using electronic equipment □ *Pictures of the opening ceremony were beamed all round the world.*

◇ *vi* **-1.** [person] to smile happily □ *They were beaming with joy.* □ *She beamed at me in delight.* **-2.** [sun, light] to shine brightly □ *The spotlight was beaming down on her.*

beaming ['biːmɪŋ] *adj* [face, person] that is smiling happily □ *She turned and gave me a beaming smile.*

bean [biːn] *n* **-1.** a seed that comes from a climbing plant and that is dried and eaten as a vegetable; a long thin pod containing such seeds that is eaten fresh □ *green beans* □ *kidney beans.* **-2.** a seed that comes from a plant and is used to make certain food and drinks □ *coffee/cocoa beans.* **-3.** *phrases* **to be full of beans** [person] to be very lively (informal use) □ *You're full of beans today!* ■ **to spill the beans** to tell a secret at the wrong time or to the wrong person (informal use).

beanbag ['biːnbæg] *n* a very large and loosely filled cushion, used as a seat.

beanshoot ['biːnʃuːt], **beansprout** ['biːnspraʊt] *n* a small shoot that has grown from a mung bean, used especially in Chinese cooking.

bear [beə'] (*pt* **bore**, *pp* **borne**) ◇ *n* **-1.** a large wild animal with a big head, thick fur, and strong claws □ *a brown bear.* **-2.** FINANCE a person who sells shares in order to buy them back when the prices have fallen.

◇ *vt* **-1.** **to bear the weight of sb/sthg** to support the weight of sb/sthg □ *Metal girders bear the weight of the roof.* **-2.** [blame, responsibility, burden] to have to accept or deal with <sthg> □ *The cost of the new rail link will be borne by taxpayers.* **-3.** [mark, signs, resemblance] to have <sthg> in a way that can be seen or noticed by other people □ *He still bears the scars from his accident.* □ *The published article bears absolutely no resemblance to* *what I originally wrote*. **-4. I/he/she can't bear it** I/he/she cannot accept it because it is unpleasant □ *I can't bear that man/to see you go.* **-5.** [goods, gifts] to carry or transport <sb/sthg> somewhere (literary use) □ *A convoy of trucks bore the refugees away.* **-6. to bear fruit/flowers** [tree, plant] to produce fruit/flowers □ *The tree bears fruit in the autumn.* ■ **to bear fruit** [plan, investment] to finally be successful □ *All my efforts have finally borne fruit.* **-7.** [child] to give birth to <a baby> □ *She bore him a son.* **-8. to bear sb no ill will** OR **malice** not to feel angry with sb □ *She bears him no ill will.*

◇ *vi* **-1. to bear left/right** to turn slightly to the left/right and continue □ *Bear left at the traffic lights.* **-2. to bring pressure/influence to bear on sb** to use pressure/influence to persuade sb to do something.

◆ **bear down** *vi* **to bear down on sb/sthg** to move toward sb/sthg quickly and in a threatening way □ *Martin turned to see a huge truck bearing down on him.*

◆ **bear out** *vt sep* **to bear sthg out** [claim, story, alibi] to support the truth of sthg □ *The allegations of malpractice are borne out by the report's findings.*

◆ **bear up** *vi* to stay cheerful, despite one's difficulties □ *He's bearing up under the strain.* □ *Bear up! I'm sure things will get better soon.*

◆ **bear with** *vt fus* **bear with me** a polite phrase used when one wants somebody to be patient □ *If you'll just bear with me a moment, I'll explain the whole process.*

bearable ['beərəbl] *adj* **to be bearable** to be acceptable, even though it is unpleasant □ *This heat is just about bearable.*

beard [bɪərd] *n* hair that grows on a man's chin and cheeks □ *He decided to grow a beard.* □ *He had a long, thin beard.*

bearded ['bɪərdəd] *adj* [man, face] that has a beard.

bearer ['beərər] *n* **-1.** [of a coffin, stretcher] a person who helps to carry something □ *the official flag bearer.* **-2.** [of news, a letter] a person who brings something to somebody else □ *I hate to be the bearer of bad news.* **-3.** FINANCE a person who has a banknote or check which can be exchanged for money.

bear hug *n* **to give sb a bear hug** to put one's arms around sb very tightly, usually to show affection.

bearing ['beərɪŋ] *n* **-1. to have a bearing on sthg** to have a connection with or some effect on sthg □ *The evidence has some/no bearing on the present case.* **-2.** [of a person] the way somebody stands or moves and what that shows about their character □ *her noble/modest bearing.* **-3.** [in a machine] a part of a machine that supports the weight of a moving part. **-4.** [with a compass] the direction that one is traveling in or needs to travel in to reach somewhere, found by using a compass. ■ **to get/lose one's bearings** to know/not to know where one is □ *I lost my bearings in the maze of corridors.*

bear market *n* FINANCE a situation in which many people are selling stock market shares because they expect the prices to fall.

bearskin ['beərskɪn] *n* **-1.** the skin and fur of a bear, sometimes used as a rug. **-2.** a tall black fur hat that is worn by some British soldiers on ceremonial occasions.

beast [biːst] *n* **-1.** an animal (literary use). **-2.** a person who one thinks is cruel or unpleasant (informal use).

beastly ['biːstlɪ] (*compar* **beastlier,** *superl* **beastliest**) *adj* [person, weather, smell] that one thinks is very unpleasant (old-fashioned use).

beat [biːt] (*pt* **beat,** *pp* **beaten**) ◇ *vt* **-1.** [child, dog, metal] to hit <a person, animal, or object> hard many times □ *He beat the donkey with a stick.* **-2. to beat a drum** to hit a drum to make a sound. **-3.** [opponent, team] to defeat <sb> in a race, competition etc; [inflation, crime] to deal with <a problem> successfully over a period of time with a lot of effort □ *She beat him at poker/chess.* □ *Regular exercise can help you beat depression.* ■ **it beats me** I don't understand (informal use) □ *It beats me how she does it.* ■ **to beat sb to it** to arrive somewhere or do something before sb else does □ *I planned to get there first but she beat me to it.* **-4.** [score, record] to achieve something that is better than <sthg> □ *The sprinter beat her previous best time by a quarter of a second.* ■ **it beats walking/working etc** it is better than walking/working etc □ *You can't beat a good night out at the theater.* **-5.** COOKING to stir <eggs, cream> etc thoroughly with a fork or whisk □ *Beat the eggs into the mixture.* **-6.** [bird] to flap <its wings>. **-7. to beat time** [person] to show the speed and rhythm of a piece of music by moving one's hand or foot up and down regularly. **-8.** *phrase* **beat it!** go away! (informal use).

◇ *vi* **-1.** [rain, wind] to keep hitting the surface of something hard □ *The waves beat against the side of the boat.* **-2.** [heart, pulse] to make a regular rhythmic movement □ *Her heart had stopped beating.*

◇ *n* **-1.** [of a drum, wing] a regular blow or movement; the sound of this □ *I could hear the beat of his heart.* **-2.** MUSIC the main regular rhythm in a piece of music □ *I like dance music with a strong beat.* **-3.** [of a police officer] the area that a police officer patrols or is responsible for.

◇ *adj* **to be beat** [person] to be very tired (informal use) □ *I'm beat. Let's go to bed.*

◆ **beat down** ◇ *vi* **-1.** [sun] to shine strongly □ *The sun was beating down on my back.* **-2.** [rain] to fall heavily □ *The rain beat down on the car roof.* ◇ *vt sep* **to beat sb down** to persuade sb to accept a lower price for something □ *I beat him down to $20.*

◆ **beat off** *vt sep* **to beat sb/sthg off** to be successful in resisting sb/sthg and making them go away □ *She was somehow able to beat off her attackers.* □ *They beat off some stiff competition from their nearest rivals.*

◆ **beat up** *vt sep* **to beat sb up** to hit or kick sb until they are seriously hurt □ *My brother was badly beaten up last night.*

beaten ['biːtn] *adj* [gold, copper] that has been shaped by being hit with a hammer.

beater ['biːtə'] *n* -1. a tool or machine for beating cooking ingredients, e.g. eggs or cream. -2. a long stick with a wide flat end for beating carpets.

Beat Generation *n* the Beat Generation a group of US-writers in the 1950s who opposed the values of Western society by using drugs, practicing Buddhism and meditation, not working etc. It included writers such as Jack Kerouac.

beating ['biːtɪŋ] *n* -1. to give sb a beating to hit sb repeatedly, often as a punishment. -2. to get OR take a beating [player, team] to be easily defeated □ Detroit took a beating against Cleveland.

beat-up *adj* [car, guitar] in very bad condition (informal use).

beaut [bjuːt] (informal use) ◇ *n* a beaut a very good example of something □ Good shot! What a beaut! ◇ *adj* US & AUS very good □ That was a beaut shot!

beautician [bjuːˈtɪʃn] *n* a person whose job is to give beauty treatments for the face, nails, skin etc.

beautiful ['bjuːtəfl] *adj* -1. [woman] who is very pleasing to look at □ He has a very beautiful wife. -2. [scenery, music, dress] that one finds very pleasing to look at, listen to etc □ What a beautiful house you have! □ We had a beautiful meal. □ It's a beautiful day, isn't it? -3. [shot, pass, stroke] that one thinks is very good or skillful (informal use).

beautifully ['bjuːtəflɪ] *adv* [dress, sing, play] very well □ The house was beautifully decorated. □ You handled the situation beautifully.

beauty ['bjuːtɪ] (*pl* beauties) ◇ *n* -1. [of a person, place] the quality of being beautiful □ He had not been prepared for the sheer beauty of the scenery. -2. [person] a beautiful person, usually a woman □ She is a famous beauty. -3. the beauty of sthg the aspect of sthg that makes it so good □ The beauty of the treatment is that it has no side effects. -4. to be a beauty to be an excellent example of something (informal use) □ That boat's a real beauty! ◇ *comp* [product, treatment] that is intended to make women look more attractive.

beauty contest *n* a contest between a group of people, usually women, to judge who is the most beautiful.

beauty parlor *n* a place where beauty treatments, e.g. manicures, massage, or make-up, are carried out.

beauty queen *n* the winner of a beauty contest.

beauty salon *n* = beauty parlor.

beauty spot *n* -1. a place in the countryside that people think is very beautiful □ It's a famous beauty spot. -2. a small dark spot on a person's skin.

Beauvoir [US boʊvˈwɑːr, GB ˈboʊvwɑː], **Simone de** (1908–1986) a French existentialist writer and feminist who was closely associated with the writer Jean-Paul Sartre.

beaver ['biːvə'] *n* an animal with brown fur, large teeth, and a large, round, flat tail that builds dams on rivers to live in.

becalmed [bɪˈkɑːmd] *adj* to be becalmed [ship, boat] to be unable to move because there is no wind (literary use).

became [bɪˈkeɪm] *past tense of* become.

because [bɪˈkɒz] *conj* I came because he asked me he asked me and so I came (used to show the reason for something) □ I'm glad you're coming, because there's something I want to talk to you about.

◆ **because of** *prep* we stayed indoors because of the rain the reason why we stayed indoors was the rain.

béchamel sauce [ˌbeɪʃəmel-] *n* a thick white sauce made from milk, flour, and butter.

beck [bek] *n* to be at sb's beck and call to be ready to do whatever sb asks (disapproving use) □ If she thinks I'm going to be at her beck and call all day, she's wrong!

Beckett ['bekɪt], **Samuel** (1906–1989) an Irish writer who lived in France and wrote plays, novels, and poetry in French and English. His best-known work is Waiting for Godot.

beckon ['bekən] ◇ *vt* -1. to signal to <sb> with one's finger or hand in order to get them to come closer □ She beckoned the waiter over. -2. to attract or seem likely to involve <sb> □ A new life beckoned him. ◇ *vi* to beckon to sb to signal to sb with one's finger or hand in order to get them to come closer.

become [bɪˈkʌm] (*pt* became, *pp* become) *vi* (+ complement) he became rich he started to be rich (used before adjectives and nouns) □ The noise became louder and louder. □ Clinton became President in 1993. □ It's becoming a real problem. ■ what has become of Jim? what has happened to Jim and where is he now?

becoming [bɪˈkʌmɪŋ] *adj* [dress, color, hairstyle] that makes somebody look attractive (literary use) □ That outfit is very becoming on you.

BECTU ['bektuː] (*abbr of* Broadcasting, Entertainment, Cinematograph and Theatre Union) *n* a British labor union for film, television, and theater technicians.

bed [bed] (*pt* & *pp* bedded, *cont* bedding) *n* -1. [for a person] a piece of furniture that is used to sleep on □ I was lying in bed reading. □ He got out of bed and went to the window. □ a single/double bed. ■ to go to bed to lie down on a bed in order to sleep, usually at night □ What time do you go to bed? ■ to make the bed to arrange all the sheets, blankets etc neatly on a bed so that it is ready to sleep in □ Have you made your bed yet? ■ to go to bed with sb to have sex with sb (polite use). -2. [for plants, flowers] an area of soil where flowers, vegetables etc are planted. ■ it's not a bed of roses it is not pleasant, comfortable, or easy (informal use) □ My life isn't exactly a bed of roses, you know. -3. [of a river, the sea] the bottom of a river, sea, pond etc.

◆ **bed down** *vi* to go to bed □ She had to bed down on the couch.

BEd [biːˈed] (*abbr of* Bachelor of Education) *n* a

degree in education; a person who has this degree.

bed and breakfast *n* a type of accommodation in which a guest pays for a room for the night and breakfast the next morning; a hotel or private house that offers this type of accommodation.

🐝 BED AND BREAKFAST
Most bed and breakfasts are private houses, and they usually have a friendly atmosphere. Some provide an evening meal as well as a home-cooked breakfast. Many are in seaside resorts, but they are also found in big cities and in isolated parts of the country. In Britain and Australia they are cheaper than hotels; in the USA they tend to be more fashionable and more expensive.

---

bed bath *n* a way of washing somebody who is in bed because they are old, ill etc.

bedbug ['bedbʌg] *n* a small insect that lives in beds and feeds on human blood.

bedclothes ['bedkloʊz] *npl* = **bedding**.

bedcover ['bedkʌvəʳ] *n* = **bedspread**.

bedding ['bedɪŋ] *n* the sheets and blankets that cover a bed.

bedding plant *n* a plant that is suitable for growing in a flowerbed.

bedeck [bɪ'dek] *vt* **to be bedecked with sthg** [with flowers, flags] to be decorated with sthg (literary use).

bedevil [bɪ'devl] (US *pt* & *pp* **bedeviled**, *cont* **bedeviling**, GB *pt* & *pp* **bedevilled**, *cont* **bedevilling**) *vt* **to be bedeviled by** OR **with sthg** [with difficulties, controversy] to be continually affected by sthg unpleasant □ *The production has been bedeviled by bad luck from the start.*

bedfellow ['bedfeloʊ] *n* **strange** OR **uneasy bedfellows** two people or things that are connected in a way that is surprising or unlikely to continue because they are so different □ *The campaign groups make strange bedfellows.*

Bedfordshire ['bedfəʳdʃəʳ] a county in southern England. SIZE: 1,235 sq kms. POPULATION: 525,900. ADMINISTRATIVE CENTER: Bedford.

bedlam ['bedləm] *n* a word used to describe a noisy and uncontrolled place or situation □ *It was sheer bedlam in there.*

bed linen *n* the sheets and pillowcases that go on a bed.

Bedouin ['beduɪn] ◇ *n* a member of one of the nomadic peoples living in the deserts of Arabia, Jordan, Syria, and the Sahara. ◇ *adj*: *a Bedouin camp/costume.*

bedpan ['bedpæn] *n* a shallow bowl that can be used as a toilet by a person who cannot get out of bed.

bedraggled [bɪ'drægld] *adj* [person, hair] that looks messy after getting wet or dirty.

bedridden ['bedrɪdn] *adj* [person] who is too ill or old to get out of bed.

bedrock ['bedrɒk] *n* -1. GEOLOGY the solid rock that is underneath the loose layers of soil on the ground. -2. the principles or facts that a

belief, idea, activity etc is based on □ *This is where the bedrock of Republican support lies.*

bedroom ['bedruːm] *n* a room that one sleeps in □ *It's a three-bedroom house.*

Beds *abbr of* **Bedfordshire**.

bedside ['bedsaɪd] *n* the space by the side of a bed □ *He was at her bedside all through her illness.* □ *a bedside lamp/table.*

bedside manner *n* the way in which a doctor talks to a sick person and makes them feel less worried □ *I don't think much of his bedside manner.*

bed-sit(ter) [ˌbed'sɪt(əʳ)] *n* GB a rented room in a house that one eats and sleeps in.

bedsore ['bedsɔːʳ] *n* a sore area on somebody's skin that they get when they are unable to move from their bed for a long time.

bedspread ['bedspred] *n* a decorative cover that is placed on a bed.

bedtime ['bedtaɪm] *n* the time at which somebody normally goes to bed □ *a bedtime story* □ *It's past my bedtime.*

Beduin ['beduɪn] *n* & *adj* = **Bedouin**.

bed-wetting [-wetɪŋ] *n* the habit of urinating accidentally in bed at night.

bee [biː] *n* a flying insect with black and yellow stripes that makes honey. ■ **to have a bee in one's bonnet about sthg** to talk or think a lot about sthg because one is worried or enthusiastic about it.

beech [biːtʃ] *n* a large tree with a smooth gray trunk and dark-green leaves; the wood of this tree.

beef [biːf] *n* the meat of a cow, bull, or ox.

♦ **beef up** *vt sep* **to beef sthg up** [report, story, flavor] to improve or strengthen sthg by adding things to it (informal use).

beefburger ['biːfbɜːʳgəʳ] *n* a round flat piece of ground beef.

Beefeater ['biːfiːtəʳ] *n* one of the ceremonial guards of the Tower of London.

beefsteak ['biːfsteɪk] *n* good-quality lean beef that can be grilled or fried.

beehive ['biːhaɪv] *n* -1. a kind of box where bees are kept to make honey. -2. a woman's hairstyle, popular in the 1960s, in which the hair is piled very high on the head.

beekeeper ['biːkiːpəʳ] *n* a person who keeps bees and collects their honey.

beeline ['biːlaɪn] *n* **to make a beeline for sb/sthg** to move directly and quickly toward sb/sthg (informal use) □ *As soon as we got there, he made a beeline for the bar.*

been [biːn] *past participle of* **be**.

beep [biːp] ◇ *n* a short high-pitched noise that is made by a car horn or an electronic device such as an alarm clock. ◇ *vi* [car horn, alarm clock] to make a beep.

beeper ['biːpəʳ] *a* small, portable, electronic device that makes a noise to tell one to telephone somebody.

beer [bɪəʳ] *n* an alcoholic drink made from hops; a glass, bottle, or can of this □ *a sip/bottle of beer* □ *Would you like a beer?*

🍺 BEER

In the USA and Australia the most common type of beer is lager (a light gassy beer that is served cold), and people asking for beer will always be given lager. The type of beer that is traditionally sold in British pubs is called bitter. It is not very gassy, and has a slightly bitter taste. It is usually served in pint glasses, at room temperature. When asking for beer in Britain, you have to say if you want beer, lager, or stout (a type of very dark beer).

beer garden *n* GB an area outside a pub with seats and tables where customers can sit and drink.

beer mug *n* a large glass with a handle, usually used for drinking beer.

beeswax ['biːzwæks] *n* wax that is made by bees and is used for making furniture polish and candles.

beet [biːt] *n* -1. a root vegetable used to make sugar. -2. US a dark-red root vegetable that is cooked and often eaten cold in salads.

Beethoven [US 'beɪtoʊvn, GB 'beɪthoʊvn], **Ludwig van** (1770–1827) a German composer. Many of his greatest works, including the *Fifth Symphony*, the *Ninth Symphony*, and the *Violin Concerto*, were written after he had gone deaf.

beetle ['biːtl] *n* an insect with wings that fold under a hard shiny covering on its back.

Beeton ['biːtn], **Mrs** (1836–1865) a British writer on cookery, whose best-known book is *Household Management*.

beetroot ['biːtruːt] *n* GB [in a salad] = **beet**.

befall [bɪ'fɔːl] (*pt* **befell** [-'fel], *pp* **befallen** [-'fɔːlən]) *vt* [harm, bad luck] to happen to <sb> (literary use).

befit [bɪ'fɪt] (*pt* & *pp* **befitted**, *cont* **befitting**) *vt* to be suitable for <sb/sthg> (formal use) □ *as befits a woman of her standing.*

before [bɪ'fɔːr] ◇ *prep* -1. **they arrived before us** they arrived first and we arrived second □ *They bought lots of souvenirs before leaving the country.* □ *At 6 o'clock we have the news, but before that here is some music.* -2. **before the war** in the period leading up to the war □ *I saw him the day before yesterday.* -3. **she appeared before the judge** she appeared in the presence of the judge □ *They played before a crowd of 20,000 people.*
◇ *conj* -1. **have a drink before you go** you are going, but have a drink first □ *He took off his shoes before entering the mosque.* □ *I had to pay a fine before the police would return my car.* -2. **we had to wait an hour before the bus arrived** we had to wait an hour until the bus arrived □ *People weren't really motivated before she took over.*
◇ *adv* **I had seen the play before** I had already seen the play □ *Have we met before somewhere?* ■ **the day/week etc before** the previous day/week etc □ *We went to Broadway last night and Chinatown the night before.*

beforehand [bɪ'fɔːrhænd] *adv* **if you're coming,** let us know beforehand if you're coming, let us know before you do.

befriend [bɪ'frend] *vt* to make friends with <sb who is lonely or needs help> □ *He was befriended by a colleague in the same department.*

befuddled [bɪ'fʌdld] *adj* [person, thoughts] confused □ *He was obviously befuddled with drink when he said that.*

beg [beg] (*pt* & *pp* **begged**, *cont* **begging**) ◇ *vt* to ask for <a favor, forgiveness> etc in a very humble or anxious way □ *He begged her to let him stay.* ◇ *vi* -1. to ask for money or food from people in a public place □ *The station was full of people begging for money.* -2. to beg somebody for something or to do something □ *She begged for a second chance/to be allowed to go.*

began [bɪ'gæn] *past tense of* **begin**.

beggar ['begər] *n* a person who begs for food or money in the street.

begin [bɪ'gɪn] (*pt* **began**, *pp* **begun**, *cont* **beginning**) ◇ *vt* -1. to do the first part of <sthg> □ *Police have begun their search for the body.* □ *He began his speech with a joke.* ■ **to begin doing** OR **to do sthg** to do sthg that one was not doing before □ *He began running* OR *to run.* □ *It began to get dark.* -2. to be responsible for starting <sthg> □ *You began the argument, now it's up to you to settle it.*
◇ *vi* -1. to do or be the first part of something □ *Who's going to begin?* □ *We began by approving the minutes of the previous meeting.* ■ **to begin with** a phrase used to talk about the first stage of something or to introduce the first thing one wants to say □ *To begin with, things went well.* □ *To begin with, let me thank you all for coming here today.* -2. [event, activity] to take place from a particular time or date and continue after that □ *The talk begins at 10:00 am.* □ *Our troubles had only just begun.*

beginner [bɪ'gɪnər] *n* a person who is beginning to learn how to do something □ *I'm a real beginner at chess.* □ *They've put me in the beginners' class.* □ *That's not bad for a beginner.*

beginning [bɪ'gɪnɪŋ] *n* [of a book, movie, year] the first part of something □ *The book has a good beginning.* □ *I pay my rent at the beginning of the month.* ■ **in the beginning** a phrase used to refer to the first stage of something, especially when it changes later □ *In the beginning I was doubtful, but I eventually changed my mind.*

◆ **beginnings** *npl* the early or first part of something, which it develops from later □ *The movement has its beginnings in the 1920s.*

begonia [bɪ'goʊnjə] *n* a plant with shiny dark-green leaves and pink, red, or white flowers.

begrudge [bɪ'grʌdʒ] *vt* -1. **to begrudge sb sthg** to feel angry about sb having or doing sthg □ *I don't begrudge him his success.* -2. **to begrudge doing sthg** to do sthg unwillingly □ *I didn't begrudge giving up my time for them.*

beguile [bɪ'gaɪl] *vt* to charm <sb>, especially in order to deceive them.

beguiling [bɪ'gaɪlɪŋ] *adj* [manner, smile, person] that is charming and attractive.

begun [bɪ'gʌn] *past participle of* **begin.**

behalf [US bɪ'hæf, GB -'hɑːf] ◆ **in behalf of** US, **on behalf of** *prep* **-1.** as the representative of <sb> □ *I'm phoning on behalf of the chairman.* □ *On behalf of the whole company, I'd like to wish you good luck in the future.* **-2.** for <sb> □ *They went to a lot of trouble on my behalf.*

behave [bɪ'heɪv] ◇ *vt* **to behave oneself** to act in a way that is considered correct or acceptable □ *Behave yourselves, children!* ◇ *vi* **-1.** to act in a particular way □ *Stop behaving like a child!* **-2.** to act in a way that is considered correct or acceptable □ *Will you behave!*

behavior US, **behaviour** GB [bɪ'heɪvjəʳ] *n* the way in which somebody or something behaves □ *I thought his behavior was rather strange.* □ *animal/human behavior.* ■ **to be on one's best behavior** to behave as politely and sensibly as one can □ *Rourke was on his best behavior for the TV cameras.*

behaviorism US, **behaviourism** GB [bɪ'heɪvjərɪzm] *n* a theory that the study of a person's psychology should be based on their behavior rather than on their thoughts and emotions.

behead [bɪ'hed] *vt* to cut off the head of <sb>.

beheld [bɪ'held] *past tense & past participle of* **behold.**

behind [bɪ'haɪnd] ◇ *prep* **-1. to hide behind sthg** to hide at the back of sthg, so that one cannot be seen. ■ **to stand behind sb/sthg** to stand facing the back of sb/sthg □ *She sits behind me in class.* ■ **shut the door behind you** shut the door behind you when you go out. **-2. our problems are now behind us** our problems are now in the past and finished. **-3. the Socialists are 2% behind the Conservatives** the Socialists are 2% less successful than the Conservatives. **-4. the man behind our success** the man who caused or was responsible for our success □ *Do you know the reason behind her outburst?* **-5. we are behind our leader** we support our leader □ *Don't worry, I'm behind you all the way.*
◇ *adv* **-1. to sit/walk behind** to sit/walk facing the back of the person or thing in front of one □ *They were attacked from behind.* ■ **stay behind after the meeting** stay after all the other people in the meeting have gone □ *Hurry up, or you'll get left behind!* **-2. to leave sthg behind** to leave sthg in the place one was before □ *I left my purse behind at Kate's apartment.* **-3. to be behind with sthg** to be late with sthg □ *I'm behind with my work at the moment.* **-4. to be a point/goal etc behind** to have one point/goal etc less than one's opponent □ *New York time is five hours behind London time.*
◇ *n* the part of the body that one sits on (informal use).

behold [bɪ'hoʊld] (*pt & pp* **beheld**) *vt* to see <sb/sthg> (literary use).

beige [beɪʒ] ◇ *adj* [trousers, wall, shirt] pale brown. ◇ *n* a pale brown color.

Beijing [beɪ'dʒɪŋ] the capital of China, and its second-largest city. POPULATION: 9,830,000.

being ['biːɪŋ] *n* **-1.** something that is alive, especially a person □ *beings from another planet.* **-2. to come into being** to begin to exist □ *The new law comes into being in September.*

Beirut [beɪ'ruːt] the capital of Lebanon. It was badly damaged by wars in the 1970s and 1980s. POPULATION: 1,100,000.

Belarus [ˌbelə'ruːs] a country in eastern Europe, between Russia and Poland. SIZE: 208,000 sq kms. POPULATION: 10,200,000 (*B(y)elorussians*). CAPITAL: Minsk. LANGUAGE: Belorussian. CURRENCY: rouble.

belated [bɪ'leɪtəd] *adj* [arrival, apology] that should have happened sooner □ *I'll send her a belated birthday card.*

belch [beltʃ] ◇ *vt* to give out <smoke, fire, fumes> etc in large quantities. ◇ *vi* **-1.** [person] to make a noise by letting air from one's stomach out through one's mouth. **-2.** [smoke, fire] to come out in large quantities. ◇ *n* the act or sound of belching □ *He gave a loud belch.*

beleaguered [bɪ'liːgəʳd] *adj* **-1.** [city, army] that is surrounded and being attacked from all sides. **-2.** [person, management, government] that is continuously affected by problems, criticism, or worries.

Belfast [US 'belfæst, GB -fɑːst] the capital of Northern Ireland. It is a major port. POPULATION: 325,000.

belfry ['belfrɪ] (*pl* **belfries**) *n* the part of a church tower where the bells hang.

Belgian ['beldʒən] *n & adj*: see **Belgium.**

Belgium ['beldʒəm] a country in northwestern Europe, on the North Sea, between France, the Netherlands, and Germany. SIZE: 30,500 sq kms. POPULATION: 9,980,000 (*Belgians*). CAPITAL: Brussels. LANGUAGE: Flemish, French. CURRENCY: Belgian franc.

Belgrade [bel'greɪd] the capital of Serbia and the Federal Republic of Yugoslavia. POPULATION: 1,445,000.

Belgravia [bel'greɪvjə] a fashionable residential part of central London where there are many embassies.

belie [bɪ'laɪ] (*pt & pp* **belied**, *cont* **belying**) *vt* **-1.** [claim, statement, expectation] to show <sthg> to be wrong □ *Our own calculations belie the figures shown in the estimates.* **-2.** to hide the real nature of <sthg> □ *His polite smile belied his real intentions.*

belief [bɪ'liːf] *n* **-1.** a feeling that something definitely exists, is true, or is good □ *a belief in God/the principles of Socialism* □ *My cynicism could never shake his belief in basic human kindness.* ■ **beyond belief** so extreme, strange etc that it is difficult to believe □ *The way they behaved is simply beyond belief.* **-2.** a principle or idea that one thinks is right, good, or true □ *political beliefs* □ *She has strong religious beliefs.* □ *He holds the belief that all unemployed people are lazy.* ■ **it is my/her etc belief that...** my/her etc opinion is that... □ *It is my belief that the prisoner is guilty.* ■ **in the belief that...** thinking that... □ *They locked the door in the belief that everyone had left.*

believable [bɪ'liːvəbl] *adj* [story, account, explanation] that can be believed □ *Did you find her explanation believable?*

believe [bɪ'liːv] *vt* **-1. to believe (that)...** to think that something is true □ *I believe the entrance is at the rear.* □ *"Has the meeting started yet?" — "I believe so."* □ *We honestly believe (that) this is the best solution.* ■ **to believe sb to be sthg** to think that sb is sthg □ *She's believed to be uninjured/a millionairess/living abroad.* **-2.** [statement, story] to accept <sthg> as true □ *I don't believe a word he says.* □ *If we are to believe what the papers say, the economic recovery has already started.* ■ **believe it or not** a phrase used to introduce information that is surprising □ *Believe it or not, she actually arrived on time.* **-3.** [person] to accept what is said by <sb> as true □ *I don't believe you.* ■ **I couldn't believe my ears/eyes** I was very surprised by what I heard/saw □ *She could hardly believe her eyes when Don walked in.*

◆ **believe in** *vt fus* **-1. to believe in sthg** [in God, ghosts] to be convinced that sthg exists □ *Do you believe in reincarnation?* **-2. to believe in sthg** [in a principle, idea, approach] to be convinced of the importance and value of sthg □ *I have always believed in freedom of speech.* □ *He believes in letting people know what he thinks.* **-3. to believe in sb** [in a friend, leader] to have trust and confidence in sb □ *You've never believed in me.*

believer [bɪ'liːvəʳ] *n* **-1.** a person who believes in God. **-2.** a person who believes in the value and importance of an idea, principle etc □ *I'm a great believer in discussion as a means of resolving problems.*

Belisha beacon [bə,liːʃə-] *n* GB a round orange light on the top of a pole that marks a pedestrian crossing.

belittle [bɪ'lɪtl] *vt* [person, achievement, success] to treat <sb/sthg> as being unimportant.

Belize [bə'liːz] a country in Central America, on the Caribbean Sea. SIZE: 23,000 sq kms. POPULATION: 200,000 (*Belizeans*). CAPITAL: Belmopan. MAIN CITY: Belize City. LANGUAGE: English. CURRENCY: Belizean dollar.

bell [bel] *n* **-1.** [in a church] a round, hollow, metal object that makes a ringing sound when the rod that hangs inside hits its side □ *a church/hand bell.* **-2.** [in a house] an electric device that makes a ringing sound when a button is pressed □ *Did somebody ring the bell?* **-3.** [on a bicycle] a small metal device fitted on a bicycle that makes a ringing sound when the rider pushes a small lever. ■ **to ring a bell** to sound familiar □ *I'm not sure, but the name rings a bell.*

Bell [bel], **Alexander Graham** (1847–1922) a British inventor who moved to the USA in 1871, where he invented the telephone.

bell-bottoms *npl* pants with legs that are very wide at the bottom.

bellhop ['belhɒp] *n* US a man or boy in a hotel whose job is to carry luggage and take messages.

belligerent [bə'lɪdʒərənt] *adj* **-1.** [person, attitude, tone] that seems unfriendly and aggressive. **-2. a belligerent country** a country that is at war.

bellow ['beloʊ] ◇ *vt* [command, instruction] to shout <sthg> in a very loud deep voice. ◇ *vi* **-1.** [person] *He bellowed with pain/laughter.* **-2.** [bull] to make a deep loud sound.

bellows ['beloʊz] *npl* a device consisting of a bag with two handles that are opened and closed to blow air onto a fire to make it burn better.

bell push *n* GB a button, usually next to the front door of a building, that one presses to make the bell ring.

bell-ringer *n* a person who rings church bells.

belly ['belɪ] (*pl* **bellies**) *n* **-1.** one's stomach (informal use) □ *He crawled along on his belly.* **-2.** [of a horse, dog] the lower part of an animal's body that contains the stomach □ *the silver belly of a fish.*

bellyache ['belieɪk] (informal use) ◇ *n* stomach ache. ◇ *vi* to complain □ *He's always bellyaching about something.*

belly button *n* one's navel (informal use).

belly dancer *n* a woman who dances a Middle Eastern dance that involves movements of the stomach and hips.

belong [bɪ'lɒŋ] *vi* to be in the right place or situation □ *That file doesn't belong here.* □ *He doesn't really belong in marketing.*

◆ **belong to** *vt fus* **-1. to belong to sb** to be the property of sb □ *Does this belong to anybody?* **-2. to belong to sthg** [to a group, club, organization] to be a member of sthg □ *He belongs to a labor union.*

belongings [bɪ'lɒŋɪŋz] *npl* the things that one owns that can be carried easily □ *Make sure you take all your belongings with you when you leave the train.*

Belorussia [,beloʊ'rʌʃə] = **Belarus**.

beloved [bɪ'lʌvəd] ◇ *adj* that is loved very much □ *my beloved father.* ◇ *n* **my/your etc beloved** the person that I/you etc love very much (literary use).

below [bɪ'loʊ] ◇ *adv* **-1. the room below** the room directly underneath □ *She lives in the apartment below.* □ *The picture shows the airplane seen from below.* **-2. the items below** the items that are mentioned later in a letter, report etc □ *See below for further details.* **-3. aged five or below** aged five or less (used with numbers, amounts etc). **-4.** downstairs and inside on a ship (used by sailors) □ *He went below to his cabin.*
◇ *prep* **-1. below the horizon** lower than the horizon □ *He had a cut below his eye.* ■ **below ground** under the surface of the ground. **-2. the person below me** the person who is lower than me in rank, status, or position. **-3. below the age of 15** less than the age of 15 □ *The temperature fell to below zero.*

belt [belt] ◇ *n* **-1.** CLOTHING a long narrow piece of leather, fabric, or plastic that is worn around the waist. ■ **to be below the belt** [comment, remark] to be unfair. ■ **to have sthg under one's belt** to have already obtained sthg □ *She's got a lot of experience un-*

der her belt. ■ **to tighten one's belt** to be more careful about the amount of money one spends □ *We're going to have to tighten our belt in this department this year.* **-2.** [in a machine] a circular piece of rubber, plastic etc that is used to drive machines or to move objects along. **-3.** [of land, sea] a large area of land, air, space etc, especially one that has a particular characteristic □ *the commuter/farming belt.*
◇ *vt* to hit <sb/sthg> very hard (informal use).

◆ **belt out** *vt sep* **to belt sthg out** [song, tune] to sing or play sthg very loudly and enthusiastically (informal use).

beltway ['beltweɪ] *n* US a road that goes around a town and makes it possible for traffic to avoid the center.

bemoan [bɪ'moʊn] *vt* to complain about or show one is disappointed by <sthg> □ *Organizers bemoaned the lack of public interest in the event.*

bemused [bɪ'mjuːzd] *adj* [person, look, voice] that seems confused and slightly surprised □ *She seemed bemused when I told her.*

bench [bentʃ] *n* **-1.** [for people] a long seat for more than one person that is usually made of wood and often used outdoors □ *a park bench.* **-2.** [for working on] a long table in a laboratory or workshop that one can work on. **-3.** GB POLITICS a row of seats in the Houses of Parliament. Members of Parliament sit on different benches depending on which party they belong to and how important they are □ *the government benches.*

benchmark ['bentʃmɑːʳk] *n* something that is used as a standard for judging or measuring the quality, performance, value etc of other similar things □ *This decision will serve as a benchmark for other such cases in the future.*

bend [bend] (*pt* & *pp* **bent**) ◇ *n* a curved part of something, e.g. a road, river, or tube □ *As we came round the bend I saw the house in the distance.* ◇ *vt* **-1.** [arm, leg] to move <a part of one's body> so that it is not straight □ *Can you touch your toes without bending your knees?* **-2.** [wire, pipe, fork] to force <an object> into a curved shape □ *He took the metal bar and bent it in two.* ◇ *vi* to have or make a curved shape □ *The road bends here.* □ *The tree bent in the wind.*

◆ **bends** *npl* **the bends** muscle pains and difficulty in breathing suffered by divers when they come to the surface too quickly.

◆ **bend down** *vi* [person] to move the top of one's body nearer to the ground by bending it at the waist or knees □ *I bent down to look under the table.*

◆ **bend over** *vi* [person] to bend one's body forward at the waist. ■ **to bend over backwards to do sthg** to try everything possible to do sthg, even if this causes one difficulties □ *They'll bend over backwards to help you.*

beneath [bɪ'niːθ] ◇ *prep* **-1. the ground beneath one's feet** the ground below, and covered by, one's feet □ *The book was buried beneath a pile of papers.* □ *The ship sank beneath*

the waves. **-2. he married beneath him** he married somebody of lower rank or status. **-3. it is beneath him/her etc** he/she etc is too good or important to do it □ *He seems to think it's beneath him to make the coffee.* ◇ *adv* **the valley beneath** the valley below (formal use).

benediction [ˌbenə'dɪkʃn] *n* a prayer that gives a blessing.

benefactor ['benəfæktəʳ] *n* a person who helps somebody else or an organization, usually by giving them money.

beneficial [ˌbenə'fɪʃl] *adj* [effect, measure, treatment] that helps to improve something □ *The air is very beneficial to her health.*

beneficiary [ˌbenə'fɪʃərɪ] (*pl* **beneficiaries**) *n* **-1.** LAW a person who receives money or property from somebody in a will. **-2.** a person who is helped by something such as a change in the law □ *The main beneficiaries of the new system will be people under 25.*

benefit ['benəfɪt] ◇ *n* **-1.** something that helps somebody or brings them an advantage □ *What are the benefits of working from home?* □ *He's had the benefit of a university education.* □ *There might be some benefit in delaying the meeting.* □ *For the benefit of those who were not here yesterday, I will repeat what I said then.* □ *It can only be to your benefit to learn a new skill.* □ *This could be of great benefit to the business.* **-2.** [from the state] money that is given by the government of a country to help specific groups of people, e.g. the unemployed, sick people, or children □ *He's on unemployment benefit.* □ *You are entitled to claim a number of benefits.* **-3.** phrase **to give sb the benefit of the doubt** not to question sb's honesty in a particular situation, even if one does not completely trust or believe them.
◇ *comp* [concert, match] that is organized in order to make money for a charity.
◇ *vt* to help or give an advantage to <sb/sthg> □ *These measures could benefit small businesses.*
◇ *vi* **to benefit from sthg** to be helped or given an advantage by sthg □ *Who stands to benefit most from these changes?*

Benefits Agency *n* **the Benefits Agency** the British government agency responsible for paying unemployment and incapacity benefit, and retirement pensions.

Benelux ['benɪlʌks]: **the Benelux countries** Belgium, the Netherlands, and Luxembourg.

benevolent [bə'nevələnt] *adj* [person] who is kind and generous.

BEng [biː'en] (*abbr of* **Bachelor of Engineering**) *n* a degree in engineering; a person who has this degree.

Bengal [ben'ɡɔːl] an area covering northeastern India and Bangladesh.

Benidorm ['benɪdɔːʳm] a popular tourist resort in southeastern Spain, on the Mediterranean. POPULATION: 42,442.

benign [bə'naɪn] *adj* **-1.** [person, smile] that seems friendly and gentle. **-2.** [tumor, growth] that does not cause serious illness or death.

Ben Nevis [,ben'nevɪs] the highest mountain in Britain, in northwestern Scotland. HEIGHT: 1,343 m.

bent [bent] ◇ *past tense & past participle of* **bend**. ◇ *adj* **-1.** [wire, metal, tree] curved □ *The metal pin was bent out of shape.* **-2.** [person, part of body] not straight □ *When you do this exercise, always keep your knees slightly bent.* **-3.** GB [official, policeman] dishonest (informal use). **-4. to be bent on doing sthg** to be determined to do sthg □ *She seems to be bent on self-destruction.* ◇ *n* **to have a bent for sthg** to be naturally good at sthg □ *She has a bent for this type of work.* □ *George has a natural artistic bent.*

bequeath [bɪ'kwiːð] *vt* (formal use) **-1.** [money, property] to leave <sthg> in one's will □ *He bequeathed his fortune to his wife.* **-2.** [idea, system] to pass <sthg> on to somebody who comes after.

bequest [bɪ'kwest] *n* money, property etc that is bequeathed to somebody.

berate [bɪ'reɪt] *vt* to scold <sb> severely (formal use).

Berber ['bɜːᵣbəᵣ] ◇ *n* **-1.** a member of a Muslim people living in North Africa, mainly in Algeria and Morocco. **-2.** the language of the Berbers. ◇ *adj*: *a Berber dialect/village.*

bereaved [bɪ'riːvd] (*pl* **bereaved**) ◇ *adj* [person] whose relative or close friend has recently died □ *Our thoughts are with the bereaved family.* ◇ *npl* **the bereaved** the family and close friends of a person who has recently died.

bereavement [bɪ'riːvmənt] *n* the death of a relative or close friend.

bereft [bɪ'reft] *adj* **to be bereft of sthg** [of hope, support] to be without sthg (formal use) □ *He felt completely bereft without her.*

beret [US bə'reɪ, GB 'bereɪ] *n* a flat round cap with no peak, made of soft material.

Bering Sea [US ˌbɪrɪŋ-, GB ˌbeər-]: **the Bering Sea** the northern part of the Pacific Ocean, between Siberia and Alaska.

Bering Strait: **the Bering Strait** a strait between Siberia and Alaska that joins the Bering Sea to the Arctic Ocean.

Berks *abbr of* **Berkshire**.

Berkshire ['bɑːᵣkʃəᵣ] a county in southern England. SIZE: 1259 sq kms. POPULATION: 740,600. ADMINISTRATIVE CENTER: Reading.

Berlin [bɜːᵣ'lɪn] the capital of Germany, and its largest city. It was divided into East Berlin and West Berlin by the Berlin Wall between 1945 and 1990, when it became the capital of the reunified Germany. POPULATION: 3,409,737.

Berlin, Irving (1888–1989) a US songwriter, born in Russia, who wrote songs for many Broadway and Hollywood musicals.

Berliner [bɜːᵣ'lɪnəᵣ] *n* a person who comes from Berlin or who lives in Berlin.

berm [bɜːᵣm] *n* US a narrow path at the edge of a slope or road.

Bermuda [bəᵣ'mjuːdə] a group of islands in the western Atlantic. It is a self-governing British colony. SIZE: 53.5 sq kms. POPULATION: 70,000 (*Bermudans, Bermudians*). CAPITAL: Hamilton. LANGUAGE: English. CURRENCY: Bermuda dollar.

Bermuda shorts *npl* short trousers, usually made of thin material, that end just above the knee.

Bern [bɜːᵣn] the capital of Switzerland. POPULATION: 136,338.

berry ['berɪ] (*pl* **berries**) *n* a small, round, soft fruit that grows on some plants, bushes, and trees.

berserk [bəᵣ'zɜːᵣk] *adj* **to go berserk** to become very angry and sometimes violent (informal use) □ *The crowd went berserk when the result was announced.*

berth [bɜːᵣθ] ◇ *n* **-1.** [in a harbor] a space for a ship in a harbor. **-2.** [in a boat, train, camper] a bed in a vehicle. **-3. to give sb/sthg a wide berth** to avoid sb/sthg □ *She's in a foul mood, so we've all been giving her a wide berth.* ◇ *vt* to bring <a ship> into a berth. ◇ *vi* [ship] to come into a berth.

beseech [bɪ'siːtʃ] (*pt & pp* **besought** OR **beseeched**) *vt* to beg <sb> (literary use).

beset [bɪ'set] (*pt & pp* **beset**, *cont* **besetting**) ◇ *adj* **to be beset with** OR **by sthg** [difficulties, doubts, fears] to be continually troubled by sthg □ *The project has been beset by problems from the start.* ◇ *vt* to trouble <sb/sthg> continually □ *the crisis currently besetting the car industry.*

beside [bɪ'saɪd] *prep* **-1. I was standing beside her** I was standing next to her □ *It's on the table beside the bookcase.* **-2. to be beside oneself** to be unable to control oneself because of a strong feeling □ *He was beside himself with rage/joy.*

besides [bɪ'saɪdz] ◇ *adv* **-1.** used to give a new and more important reason or argument □ *It's too far to travel. And besides, we can't afford it.* **-2.** in addition □ *The car is economical, and a lot more besides.* ◇ *prep* **there were two other people besides myself** there were two people as well as me □ *Besides being old, he's extremely deaf.*

besiege [bɪ'siːdʒ] *vt* **-1.** [building, office] to crowd into or around <a place> □ *Fans besieged the hotel where the group was staying.* **-2.** [person, organization] to send a lot of questions, demands etc to <sb> □ *Since announcing the sale, they've been besieged with offers.* **-3.** MILITARY [castle, town] to surround <a place> in order to capture it □ *The Bosnian village was later besieged by Serb troops.*

besotted [bɪ'sɒtəd] *adj* **to be besotted** to be so fond of somebody or something that one appears foolish □ *He's completely besotted with her!*

besought [bɪ'sɔːt] *past tense & past participle of* **beseech**.

bespectacled [bɪ'spektəkld] *adj* [person] who is wearing glasses (literary use).

bespoke [bɪ'spəʊk] *adj* GB [clothes, suit] specially made to fit a particular person.

best [best] ◇ *adj* used as the superlative form

of "good" □ *They are the best team in Europe.* □ *I want the best possible education for my son.* □ *I'm only doing what is best for you.* ■ **she's my best friend** she's my closest friend.

◇ *adv* used as the superlative form of "well" □ *Which of them did you like best, Liz or her sister?* □ *The prize goes to the person who does best in the exam.* ■ **as best you can** as well as you can □ *I repaired the car as best I could.*

◇ *n* -1. **to do one's best** to make the greatest possible effort one can □ *I'll do* OR *try my best to be there on time.* -2. **the best** the person or thing of the highest quality or standard □ *Even the best of us make mistakes.* □ *Only the best will do for him.* ■ **all the best!** a phrase used when saying goodbye to somebody. ■ **it's for the best** it's the best thing to do in the circumstances. ■ **to make the best of sthg** to accept sthg cheerfully, even though it is not exactly what one wants □ *It wasn't a particularly nice hotel, but we just had to make the best of it.* -3. used in compound adjectives □ *He's the best-dressed man in the whole office.* □ *New York's best-kept secret.*

◆ **at best** *adv* if it is described in the most favorable way □ *The policy was at best a compromise.*

bestial [US 'bestʃəl, GB 'bestjəl] *adj* [cruelty, crime] very shocking and showing a lack of human feelings (literary use).

best man *n* the man who accompanies the bridegroom at a wedding.

❦ BEST MAN
In the USA, Britain, and Australia, it is traditional for a man who is getting married to choose a male friend or relative as his best man. This person looks after the wedding rings until they are exchanged during the wedding ceremony. In Britain and Australia, there is also a tradition that the best man makes a humorous speech about the bridegroom at the wedding reception. In the USA the best man is also the leader of the ushers, the men who walk in the wedding procession with the bridesmaids.

bestow [bɪ'stoʊ] *vt* **to bestow sthg on sb** to give sthg to sb (literary use) □ *She had the highest honors in the land bestowed on her.*

best-seller *n* a book that is sold in very large numbers □ *Number one on the best-seller list.*

best-selling *adj* [book] sold in very large numbers; [author] who has written one or more best-sellers.

bet [bet] (*pt* & *pp* **bet** OR **betted**, *cont* **betting**) ◇ *n* -1. an agreement made between two people to pay money to whichever one correctly predicts a future event, e.g. the result of a horse race; the money that somebody uses to make this agreement □ *I had/made a bet with Fred on which of us would get promoted first.* □ *I put a bet on Paradise Boy to win the race.* ■ **to hedge one's bets** to protect oneself from possible loss, e.g. by supporting more than one person or point of view. -2. a prediction □ *My bet is* OR *It's my bet that the*

book will be a best-seller. ■ **a good/bad bet** a person, thing, course of action etc that is likely/unlikely to be successful □ *That savings plan sounds like a good bet.* ■ **a safe** OR **sure bet** something that is almost certain to happen □ *It's a pretty safe bet he'll be elected.* ■ **one's best bet** the person, thing, course of action etc that is most likely to be successful □ *If you want financial advice, Kate's your best bet.* □ *Your best bet would be to fly via Houston.*

◇ *vt* -1. to risk <money> in a bet □ *I bet ten dollars on the last race.* □ *She bet me a week's pay that I couldn't do it.* -2. to state that <sthg> is very likely to happen or to have already happened □ *I bet you it rains tomorrow.* □ *I bet he forgot to tell her.*

◇ *vi* to risk money in a bet □ *I never bet on the favorite.* ■ **I wouldn't bet on it** I think it's unlikely. ■ **you bet!** (informal use) a phrase used to show that one agrees very strongly with what has been said; US a phrase used to say thank you □ *"Would you like to come along?" — "You bet!"*

beta-blocker ['biːtəblɒkəʳ] *n* a drug that makes the heart beat more slowly.

Bethlehem ['beθlɪhem] a town on the west bank of the Jordan River, near Jerusalem. According to the Bible, it was the birthplace of Jesus Christ.

betray [bɪ'treɪ] *vt* -1. [friend, country, voter] to harm or disappoint <sb who deserves one's loyalty>, especially by helping their enemies or opponents □ *By spying for the enemy he knew he was betraying his country.* □ *She felt betrayed by her friends.* ■ **to betray sb's trust** to disappoint or harm sb by breaking a promise or telling other people a secret. -2. [principles, ideals] to stop behaving according to <the ideas one believed in>. -3. [person, fact] to give information about <sb/sthg> to an enemy □ *She betrayed him/his secret to the police.* -4. [fear, desire] to show <an emotion> without intending to □ *She tried to sound calm, but her voice betrayed her excitement.*

betrayal [bɪ'treɪəl] *n* [of someone's trust, a secret] *see* **betray** □ *I couldn't help feeling a sense of betrayal when he left.*

betrothed [bɪ'trəʊðd] *adj* **to be betrothed to sb** to be engaged to be married to sb (old-fashioned use).

better ['betəʳ] ◇ *adj* -1. used as the comparative form of "good" □ *Your camera takes much better photos than mine.* □ *You look better without glasses.* □ *She's gotten a lot better at standing up for herself.* ■ **that's better!** used to give praise or encouragement. -2. not so ill as before □ *Are you feeling any better now?* □ *My cold is much better.* ■ **to get better** to recover □ *I hope you get better soon.*

◇ *adv* -1. used as the comparative form of "well" □ *You'll like her once you get to know her better.* -2. used in compound adjectives □ *I'm looking for a better paid job.* -3. more □ *I liked her second novel better than her first.* -4. **I'd better leave** I ought to leave, otherwise there

will be a problem □ *You'd better call your parents as soon as you get home.*
◇ *n* phrases **a change for the better** an improvement. ■ **to get the better of sb** to be too strong for sb to hide or control □ *I know I shouldn't have read it, but my curiosity got the better of me.*
◇ *vt* [offer, conditions, plan] to improve on or do better than <sthg> □ *We aim to better last year's production figures.* ■ **to better oneself** to improve one's skills, position etc.

better half *n* sb's **better half** sb's wife or husband (informal or humorous use).

better off *adj* **-1.** in a better financial position □ *We're much better off now that my wife's working.* **-2.** in a better situation than before □ *We'd be much better off without him.* □ *They'd be better off leaving the job to an expert.*

◆ **better-off** *npl* **the better-off** people who are rich compared to most people.

betting ['betɪŋ] *n* **-1.** the practice of making bets. **-2.** the odds offered on a particular race □ *The betting opened at 10-1.*

betting shop *n* GB a place where people can bet on sporting events such as horse races.

between [bɪ'twiːn] *prep* **-1. I sat between Paul and Anne** I sat with Paul on one side and Anne on the other side □ *The farm lies halfway between Charlotte and Raleigh.* □ *Leave plenty of space between each word.* **-2. the road between Palo Alto and San Francisco** the road from Palo Alto to San Francisco □ *There is a shuttle service between the airport and the city center.* **-3. we left between 6 and 7 o'clock** we left after 6 o'clock and before 7 o'clock □ *Don't eat between meals.* □ *There are three years between my sister and me.* **-4. it costs between $4 and $5** it costs more than $4 and less than $5 (used with numbers, quantities etc) □ *Temperatures today will be between 20°C and 25°C.* □ *I'd guess she's somewhere between 30 and 35 years old.* **-5.** used in phrases involving two or more people or things to show connections, relations, comparison, or choice □ *the link between smoking and lung cancer* □ *trade between Britain and the rest of Europe* □ *talks between staff and management* □ *Can you see the difference between the pictures?* □ *It's impossible to choose between them.* □ *We divided the money between the six of us.*

◆ **in between** *adv* between two people, things, times, amounts etc □ *We have appointments at two and six o'clock, but nothing in between.* □ *Read the first and last chapters, but you can leave out all the stuff in between.*

Bevan ['bevn], **Aneurin** (1897–1960) a British politician, born in Wales, who began work as a coalminer. As Minister of Health, he introduced the National Health Service in 1948.

beveled US, **bevelled** GB ['bevld] *adj* [edge, surface] that slopes rather than forming a right angle; [mirror] that has this kind of edge.

beverage ['bevərɪdʒ] *n* a drink (formal use).

Beveridge ['bevərɪdʒ], **William** (1879–1963) a British economist and social reformer. His

Beveridge Report, published in 1942, helped to create the welfare state in Britain.

Beverly Hills [‚bevə'lɪ'-] a wealthy area of Los Angeles. POPULATION: 32,367.

bevy ['bevɪ] (*pl* **bevies**) *n* **a bevy of women/admirers etc** a group of women/admirers etc (humorous use).

beware [bɪ'weər] *vi* a word used to tell somebody to be careful □ *'Beware of the dog'* □ *Tell him to beware of doing anything to annoy her.*

bewildered [bɪ'wɪldərd] *adj* [person] who is confused, e.g. because they do not understand why something is happening □ *She had a bewildered look on her face.*

bewildering [bɪ'wɪldərɪŋ] *adj* [situation, experience] confusing □ *There's a bewildering range to choose from.*

bewitched [bɪ'wɪtʃt] *adj* **to be bewitched** to be under a magic or evil spell; to be so fascinated by something that one is unable to concentrate on anything else □ *I was totally bewitched by their performance.*

bewitching [bɪ'wɪtʃɪŋ] *adj* [charm, smile] very attractive.

beyond [bɪ'jɒnd] ◇ *prep* **-1. beyond the hill** on the far side of the hill □ *We'll stop once we get beyond Paris.* **-2. beyond the age of five** later than the age of five. **-3.** phrases **it's beyond belief** it is impossible to believe □ *due to circumstances beyond our control.* ■ **it's beyond me** I cannot understand it □ *Why they ever got married in the first place is beyond me.*
◇ *adv* **-1. the hills beyond** the hills on the far side of a particular place or point. **-2. 1998 and beyond** 1998 and the period following that.

b/f [in bookkeeping] *abbr of* **brought forward**.

bhp *abbr of* **brake horsepower**.

Bhutan [buː'tɑːn] a country in the Himalayas, between China and India. SIZE: 47,000 sq kms. POPULATION: 1,400,000 (*Bhutanese*). CAPITAL: Thimbu. LANGUAGE: Tibetan, Nepali. CURRENCY: ngultrum.

bi- [baɪ] *prefix* **-1.** used to form words that involve two people or things □ *bilateral.* **-2.** used to indicate that something happens twice in every week, month etc or once in every two weeks, months etc □ *bi-weekly.*

BIA (*abbr of* **Bureau of Indian Affairs**) *n* **the BIA** a US government organization that deals with the education, health etc of Native Americans.

biannual [baɪ'ænjʊəl] *adj* [event] that happens twice a year.

bias ['baɪəs] *n* **-1.** [against a person, group] a tendency to unfairly prefer one person or group over another □ *a bias in favor of/against women.* **-2.** [toward an area, idea] a concern with one thing more than other things □ *The course has a scientific bias.*

biased ['baɪəst] *adj* **-1.** [person, decision] that unfairly prefers one person or group over another □ *The judges were heavily biased in favor of/against the local candidate.* **-2.** [system, procedure] that gives an advantage or disadvantage to a particular person or group □

The exam was biased toward people with practical skills. □Their recruitment policy is obviously biased against older applicants.

bib [bɪb] *n* a piece of cloth or plastic which is tied under a baby's chin to keep its clothes clean when it is eating.

Bible ['baɪbl] *n* **the Bible** the holy book of the Christian religion.

◆ **bible** *n* -1. a copy of the Bible. -2. any book considered to have the best information on a particular subject □ *the economists' bible.*

Bible Belt: **the Bible Belt** an area in the southeastern USA where there are many Christians who follow the teachings of the Bible very strictly.

biblical ['bɪblɪkl] *adj* [language, character, story] that is found in the Bible.

bibliography [ˌbɪblɪ'ɒɡrəfɪ] (*pl* **bibliographies**) *n* -1. [of books] a list of books or articles on a certain subject. -2. [in a book] the part of a book where all the books and articles the author consulted are listed.

bicarbonate of soda [baɪ'kɑːrbənət-] *n* a white powder used in baking to make cakes rise, or taken with water to help indigestion. FORMULA: $NaHCO_3$.

bicentennial [ˌbaɪsen'tenjəl] US, **bicentenary** [-'tiːnərɪ] GB (*pl* **bicentenaries**) *n* a 200th anniversary of an event.

biceps ['baɪseps] (*pl* **biceps**) *n* the large muscle on the front of the upper arm.

bicker ['bɪkər] *vi* to quarrel over small and unimportant things □ *They bickered constantly.*

bickering ['bɪkərɪŋ] *n*: *see* **bicker** □ *I'm tired of all this endless bickering!*

bicycle ['baɪsɪkl] ◇ *n* a two-wheeled vehicle that one rides by sitting on it and pushing two pedals round with one's feet □ *a bicycle wheel.* ◇ *vi* to ride on a bicycle.

bicycle path *n* a path for cyclists.

bicycle pump *n* a pump used to fill bicycle tires with air.

bid [bɪd] (*pt* & *pp vi all senses and vt sense 1* **bid**, *pt vt sense 2* **bid** OR **bade**, *pp vt sense 2* **bid** OR **bidden** ['bɪdn], *cont vt and vi all senses* **bidding**) ◇ *n* -1. an attempt or effort to achieve something □ *She failed in her bid to become the first woman to row across the Atlantic.* □ *Their bid for stardom began at a local radio station.* -2. [at an auction] an offer to buy something at a particular price □ *I made a bid of $500.* -3. BUSINESS an offer to do some work at a particular price □ *The firm put in a bid for the contract.*

◇ *vt* -1. to offer to pay <a particular sum of money> for something, especially at an auction □ *I ended up bidding more than I could afford.* □ *What am I bid for this handsome Ming vase?* -2. **to bid sb good morning/farewell etc** to say good morning/farewell etc to sb (formal use).

◇ *vi* -1. to offer to buy something at a particular price. -2. BUSINESS to make a formal offer to do work or provide something for a particular price □ *Several firms are currently bidding for the multi-million-dollar contract.*

bidder ['bɪdər] *n* a person who makes a bid at an auction, sale etc □ *The paintings were sold to the highest bidder.*

bidding ['bɪdɪŋ] *n* the act of making bids at an auction □ *Who'll open the bidding at $100?*

bide [baɪd] *vt* **to bide one's time** to wait patiently for the right moment to do something.

bidet [US bɪ'deɪ, GB 'biːdeɪ] *n* a low sink which one sits over to wash one's genitals and bottom.

Bielarus [bɪelə'ruːs] = **Belarus**.

biennial [baɪ'enjəl] ◇ *adj* [event] that takes place once every two years. ◇ *n* a plant that lives for two years.

bier [bɪər] *n* a movable stand on which a coffin is placed at a funeral.

bifocals [baɪ'fooklz] *npl* glasses with lenses made in two halves, the upper half for seeing things at a distance, the lower half for seeing things that are nearby.

BIFU ['bɪfuː] (*abbr of* **Banking, Insurance and Finance Union**) *n* a British labor union for people working in financial institutions, e.g. banks.

big [bɪg] (*compar* **bigger**, *superl* **biggest**) ◇ *adj* -1. [building, increase] large in size or amount □ *There'll be a big crowd at the game.* □ *The actual chip is no bigger than a postage stamp.* -2. [person] tall □ *She's big for her age.* -3. [difference, change, problem] important □ *There have been several meetings recently, but this is the really big one.* ■ **in a big way** a phrase used when somebody does something on a large scale or with a lot of enthusiasm □ *Our company is moving into Eastern Europe in a big way.* □ *She's into aerobics in a big way.* ■ **to have big ideas** to have aims or plans that are too ambitious. ■ **the/one's big day** the day on which an important event, e.g. a wedding or an exam, takes place □ *When's the big day then?* -4. **one's big brother/sister** one's older brother/sister. -5. **a big investor/spender etc** a person who invests/spends etc on a large scale □ *We can't afford to offend them, they're our biggest customer.* -6. **to be big** to be successful and popular □ *She's very big in Japan.*

◇ *adv* phrases **to make it big** to be very successful. ■ **to think big** to have ambitious ideas.

bigamist ['bɪgəmɪst] *n* a person who commits bigamy.

bigamy ['bɪgəmɪ] *n* the crime of marrying somebody when one is already married.

Big Apple: **the Big Apple** a name for New York.

Big Ben [-'ben] the bell in the clock tower of the Houses of Parliament in London; the tower itself.

Big Brother a character in the novel *Nineteen Eighty-Four*, by George Orwell. He is a dictator who is never seen but who spies on all his citizens and makes them fear him.

big business *n* -1. large companies and commercial operations, considered as a group.

-2. to be big business to be an important business activity □ *Language teaching is now big business.*

big cat *n* a member of one of the larger species in the cat family, e.g. the lion or tiger.

big deal (informal use) ◇ *n* **it's no big deal** it's not important □ *It's no big deal if they can't make it, but it would be nice to see them.* ■ **to make a big deal of sthg** to treat sthg as if it is important when it is not □ *Don't make such a big deal of it.* ◇ *excl* a phrase used to show that one is not impressed by something that has been said or done □ *What if they do sack me? Big deal!*

Big Dipper [-'dɪpəʳ] ◇ US ASTRONOMY **the Big Dipper** a group of seven bright stars in the Northern Hemisphere. ◇ *n* GB a raised railroad with steep slopes and sharp curves that people ride on for entertainment, usually at fairs.

big end *n* the part of a connecting rod in a car engine that is attached to the crankshaft.

big fish *n* an important or powerful person (informal use). ■ **to be a big fish in a small pond** to have influence and importance among a small group of people.

Bigfoot ['bɪgfʊt] *n* a mythical animal that is supposed to look like a very large hairy human and live in the mountains of northwestern North America.

big game *n* large wild animals, e.g. lions, leopards, and elephants, that are hunted for sport □ *a big-game hunter.*

bighead ['bɪghed] *n* a person who is big-headed (informal use).

bigheaded [,bɪg'hedəd] *adj* [person] who thinks they are more important or clever than they really are (informal use).

big-hearted [-'hɑːʳtəd] *adj* [person] who seems kind, generous, and friendly.

Bight [baɪt] = **Great Australian Bight.**

Big Issue: the Big Issue a weekly magazine sold in many British cities by homeless people, who can keep most of the money paid for it.

big leagues *npl* US = **major leagues.**
◆ **big-league** *adj* [banker, manager] who is at the highest level in their field of activity.

big money *n* a large amount of money (informal use).

big mouth *n* **to be** OR **have a big mouth** to reveal things that should have been kept secret (informal use) □ *Whoops! Me and my big mouth.*

big name *n* a famous or important person (informal use) □ *Several big names have been invited to the conference.* □ *some of the biggest names in advertising.*

bigot ['bɪgət] *n* a bigoted person.

bigoted ['bɪgətəd] *adj* [person] who thinks that their own opinions, especially about race, politics, or religion, are correct and that other people are always wrong.

bigotry ['bɪgətrɪ] *n* an unwillingness to accept any attitudes and opinions that are different from one's own.

big shot *n* a very powerful and important person (informal use).

Big Ten *n* **the Big Ten** a group of ten universities in the US Midwest that are considered to be the most important for college sports.

big time *n* **to hit** OR **make the big time** to become well-known and successful, especially in the entertainment industry (informal use).

big toe *n* the largest toe on one's foot.

big top *n* **-1.** a circus. **-2.** a large tent that a circus gives performances in.

big wheel *n* **-1.** a very powerful and important person (informal use). **-2.** GB a very large vertical wheel on which people ride at fairgrounds.

bigwig ['bɪgwɪg] *n* an important person (informal use).

bike [baɪk] *n* (informal use) **-1.** a bicycle. **-2.** a motorcycle.

bikeway ['baɪkweɪ] *n* US a path for cyclists.

bikini [bɪ'kiːnɪ] *n* a woman's two-piece bathing suit.

Biko ['biːkoʊ], **Steve** (1946–1977) a South African black activist and student leader who died in police custody.

bilateral [baɪ'lætrəl] *adj* [agreement, talks] involving two groups, nations etc □ *a bilateral peace treaty.*

bilberry [US 'bɪlberɪ, GB -bərɪ] (*pl* **bilberries**) *n* a small blue or blue-black berry; the bush on which these berries grow.

bile [baɪl] *n* **-1.** [in one's body] a greenish liquid that is produced by the liver and helps to digest fats in food. **-2.** [of a person] strong anger that is shown toward somebody or something (literary use).

bilingual [baɪ'lɪŋgwəl] *adj* **-1.** [person] who can speak two languages very well. **-2.** [text, dictionary] that is written in two languages.

bilious ['bɪlɪəs] *adj* **-1.** [person] who feels sick. **-2.** [color, green] that is very unpleasant to look at.

bill [bɪl] ◇ *n* **-1.** a written statement of how much somebody will have to pay for something □ *Can I have the bill, please?* □ *the electricity/gas/telephone bill* □ *She sent us a bill for the damage we caused.* **-2.** POLITICS a formal written proposal for a new law, which is presented to a legislative body such as Parliament or Congress □ *The bill became law last year.* **-3.** [of a show, concert] a list of the performers or the kinds of entertainment in a show □ *He was top of the bill at Radio City Music Hall.* **-4.** US [of money] a banknote □ *a dollar bill.* **-5.** **'post** OR **stick no bills'** a notice on a wall in a public place warning people not to put up any posters. **-6.** [of a bird] a bird's beak. **-7.** *phrase* **to be given a clean bill of health** to be told by a doctor that one's health is good.
◇ *vt* to send a bill to <a person, company> etc □ *Bill me for your travel expenses.*

billboard ['bɪlbɔːʳd] *n* a large board, often

placed near a major road, which advertisements are displayed on.

billet ['bɪlət] ◇ *n* a place, usually a private home, where soldiers stay for a short time. ◇ *vt* to provide <a soldier> with a billet.

billfold ['bɪlfould] *n* US a flat folding case, usually made of leather, that is used for keeping banknotes, credit cards etc in.

billiards ['bɪlɪəʳdz] *n* a game played on a large flat table in which two players, using long sticks, score points by knocking balls into small nets placed at certain points around the edge of the table.

billion ['bɪlɪən] *num* a thousand million □ *billions of francs* □ *a billion-dollar deal.*

billionaire [ˌbɪlɪə'neəʳ] *n* **-1.** a person who owns money or property worth at least a billion dollars, pounds, francs etc. **-2.** a very rich person.

bill of exchange (*pl* **bills of exchange**) *n* a document which tells a bank to pay a person a particular sum of money.

bill of lading [-'leɪdɪŋ] (*pl* **bills of lading**) *n* a list of goods to be sent by ship that is given by the transporter to the sender to show that the goods have been loaded.

Bill of Rights *n* **the Bill of Rights** the first ten amendments to the US Constitution, which guarantee certain rights to citizens such as the right to criticize the government, follow the religion they want, or have weapons.

bill of sale (*pl* **bills of sale**) *n* an official document which states that something has been sold by one person to another.

billow ['bɪlou] ◇ *n* a large cloud of smoke, steam etc that is moving upward. ◇ *vi* **-1.** [smoke, steam] to move in a large cloud □ *Smoke was billowing from the upstairs windows.* **-2.** [skirt, sail] to be blown into a large round shape by the wind.

billposter ['bɪlpoustəʳ] *n* a person who puts advertising notices on street walls, often illegally.

billy(can) ['bɪlɪ(kæn)] *n* GB & AUS a metal pot used by campers for boiling water.

billy goat ['bɪlɪ-] *n* a male goat.

Billy the Kid [ˌbɪlɪðə'kɪd] (1859–1881) a US outlaw, famous for the many murders and robberies he committed.

bimbo ['bɪmbou] (*pl* **bimbos** OR **bimboes**) *n* a young woman who one thinks is attractive but stupid (informal and offensive use).

bimonthly [baɪ'mʌnθlɪ] ◇ *adj* **-1.** that takes place, appears etc every two months. **-2.** that takes place, appears etc twice a month. ◇ *adv* **-1.** every two months. **-2.** twice a month.

bin [bɪn] (*pt* & *pp* **binned**, *cont* **binning**) ◇ *n* **-1.** [for grain, coal] a large container for storing grain, coal etc □ *a coal bin.* **-2.** GB [for bread] a household container, usually with a lid, for storing bread, flour etc □ *a bread bin.* **-3.** GB [for garbage] a container for putting garbage in. ◇ *vt* GB to put <sthg> into a bin □ *"What shall I do with this file now?" — "Oh, just bin it."*

binary ['baɪnərɪ] *adj* MATH & COMPUTING [system, code] that is based on the digits 0 and 1.

bind [baɪnd] (*pt* & *pp* **bound**) ◇ *vt* **-1.** [person, hands, documents] to tie rope, string etc tightly around <sb/sthg> □ *The notes were bound in bundles of fifty.* **-2.** [countries, groups] to create strong feelings of friendship, love, respect etc between <different people> □ *the cultural ties that bind Great Britain and the United States.* **-3.** [leg, head] to wrap a bandage around <a wound or part of the body>. **-4.** [copy, report] to fasten the pages of <a book> together and put on a cover □ *The book is bound in leather.* **-5.** [person] to oblige <sb> to do something □ *We are bound by contract to make four more movies for this company.* ◇ *n* **-1. to be in a bind** to be in a difficult situation. **-2.** GB an annoying and boring thing (informal use) □ *It's such a bind having to do all this paperwork.*

◆ **bind over** *vt sep* **to bind sb over** GB LAW to order sb to do something and threaten punishment if they do not obey the order □ *He was bound over to keep the peace.*

binder ['baɪndəʳ] *n* **-1.** a machine that binds books, hay etc. **-2.** a person whose job is to bind books □ *a book binder.* **-3.** a hard cover in which loose sheets of paper can be kept together.

binding ['baɪndɪŋ] ◇ *adj* [agreement, contract] that must be obeyed □ *The terms of the agreement are legally binding.* ◇ *n* **-1.** [for a book] the cover of a book. **-2.** [for cloth] a strip of material used to strengthen or decorate the edge of a piece of cloth.

binge [bɪndʒ] (informal use) ◇ *n* a period of eating a very large amount of food or drinking a very large amount of alcohol □ *She went on a binge which lasted the whole weekend.* ◇ *vi* to have a binge □ *We binged on strawberries.*

bingo ['bɪŋgou] ◇ *n* a game, played for money or prizes, in which each player has a card with numbers on it. Numbers are called out at random, and the winner is the first player who has all their numbers called and who shouts "Bingo!" or "House!" ◇ *excl* **-1.** a word called out by somebody to show that they have won a game of bingo. **-2.** a word used to show that one is pleased when something successful and unexpected happens □ *I just pressed a button and bingo, it started to print out.*

bin-liner *n* GB a plastic bag placed inside a trash can and used to collect rubbish.

binoculars [bɪ'nɒkjələʳz] *npl* an instrument that consists of two small telescopes joined together and that makes distant objects seem nearer □ *a pair of binoculars.*

biochemistry [ˌbaɪou'kemɪstrɪ] *n* the science that is connected with the study of chemical processes that take place in living things.

biodegradable [ˌbaɪoudɪ'greɪdəbl] *adj* [waste, detergent] that decays naturally and so does not cause pollution.

biodiversity [ˌbaɪoudaɪ'vɜːʳsətɪ] *n* a measure of the different types of animal and plant life that exist in a particular area.

biographer [baɪˈɒɡrəfəʳ] *n* a person who writes a biography.

biographic(al) [ˌbaɪəˈɡræfɪk(l)] *adj* [information, writing] that is connected with the story of a person's life.

biography [baɪˈɒɡrəfɪ] (*pl* **biographies**) *n* -1. an account of a person's life, written by somebody else. -2. a type of literature that is concerned with biographical writing.

biological [ˌbaɪəˈlɒdʒɪkl] *adj* -1. [process, function, system] that is connected with natural processes in living things. -2. **one's biological mother/father** one's natural mother/father. -3. [laundry detergent] that contains natural enzymes.

biological weapon *n* a weapon that uses bacteria to harm people or crops.

biologist [baɪˈɒlədʒəst] *n* a person who studies biology.

biology [baɪˈɒlədʒɪ] *n* the science that is connected with the study of living things.

biopic [ˈbaɪəʊpɪk] *n* a movie based on the story of the life of a famous person.

biopsy [ˈbaɪɒpsɪ] (*pl* **biopsies**) *n* the removal of a small quantity of cells, liquids etc from the body of a sick person to discover what illness they have.

biotechnology [ˌbaɪəʊtekˈnɒlədʒɪ] *n* the use of living organisms, e.g. bacteria and cells, to make products such as drugs or to help to recycle waste.

bipartite [baɪˈpɑːˈtaɪt] *adj* [treaty, agreement] that involves two groups, nations etc.

biplane [ˈbaɪpleɪn] *n* a plane with two sets of wings, one above the other.

birch [bɜːˈtʃ] *n* -1. a tall tree, common in northern countries, with thin branches and silver-white bark that often peels off in long strips. -2. **the birch** a stick or a bundle of twigs from the birch tree, used in the past to beat people as a punishment.

bird [bɜːˈd] *n* an animal that has feathers, wings, and two legs and can usually fly. ■ **to kill two birds with one stone** to achieve two things at the same time by doing only one thing.

birdcage [ˈbɜːˈdkeɪdʒ] *n* a cage for a bird.

birdie [ˈbɜːˈdɪ] *n* -1. a bird (used by or to children). -2. SPORT in golf, a score of one under par for a hole.

bird of paradise *n* a bird with brightly colored feathers that is found in New Guinea.

bird of prey *n* a bird that kills and eats other birds and small animals.

birdseed [ˈbɜːˈdsiːd] *n* a mixture of seeds given as food to birds.

bird's-eye view *n* a view of a place or event seen from high above.

bird-watcher [-ˌwɒtʃəʳ] *n* a person whose hobby is studying birds in their natural surroundings.

Birmingham [US ˈbɜːˈmɪŋhæm, GB -əm] -1. the largest city in Alabama, USA. POPULATION: 265,968. -2. an industrial city in the West

Midlands of England. It is the second-largest city in Britain. POPULATION: 934,900.

Biro™ [ˈbaɪrəʊ] *n* GB a ballpoint pen.

birth [bɜːˈθ] *n* -1. [of a person, baby] the process of being born; the event of somebody being born □ *It was a difficult birth.* □ *At birth he only weighed three pounds.* □ *He had been blind from birth.* ■ **to give birth** to have a baby □ *Two years later she gave birth to a son.* -2. [of a science, movement, country] the creation or beginning of something □ *the conference which gave birth to the United Nations.*

birth certificate *n* a document that officially records the details, e.g. the date and place, of a person's birth.

birth control *n* the practice of limiting and planning the number of children born, especially by using contraception.

birthday [ˈbɜːˈθdeɪ] *n* the date on which a person was born that is celebrated each year □ *My birthday is on August 16th.* □ *a birthday card/present/party.* ■ **happy birthday!** a phrase used to express one's good wishes to somebody who is celebrating their birthday.

❦ BIRTHDAYS
Birthdays are very important in many English-speaking countries, especially for children. Traditionally, the person whose birthday it is has a party where they receive birthday presents and birthday cards, and a birthday cake with a number of candles equal to their age. They have to blow out all the candles and make a wish.

birthmark [ˈbɜːˈθmɑːˈk] *n* a mark on somebody's skin, usually a red or brown patch, that they were born with.

birthplace [ˈbɜːˈθpleɪs] *n* -1. [of a person] the place where somebody, usually a famous person, was born. -2. [of a movement, idea] the place where something began or was created □ *These valleys were the birthplace of the Industrial Revolution.*

birthrate [ˈbɜːˈθreɪt] *n* the number of babies born for every thousand people in a particular area within a particular period.

birthright [ˈbɜːˈθraɪt] *n* a right that a person is considered to have from birth.

Biscay [ˈbɪskeɪ] → Bay of Biscay.

biscuit [ˈbɪskɪt] *n* -1. US a kind of bread baked in small round pieces and usually eaten with a meal □ *sausages with biscuits and gravy.* -2. GB a small, flat, crisp cake, usually sweetened and flavored □ *a chocolate/ginger biscuit* □ *a biscuit box/tin* □ *a packet of biscuits.*

bisect [baɪˈsekt] *vt* -1. MATH [line, angle] to divide <sthg> into two equal parts by drawing a line through it. -2. [town, area] to divide <a place> into two parts by going through the middle of it □ *The city is bisected by the river.*

bisexual [baɪˈsekʃʊəl] ◇ *adj* [person] who is sexually attracted to both men and women. ◇ *n* a bisexual person.

bishop [ˈbɪʃəp] *n* -1. RELIGION a senior priest

who is in charge of the churches, priests etc in a particular area □ *the Bishop of Johannesburg.* **-2.** CHESS one of the two identical pieces in chess that can only move diagonally.

bison ['baɪsn] (*pl* **bison** OR **bisons**) *n* a large wild ox with thick hair around its neck and short horns on its head. It was originally found in Europe and North America but is now less common.

bistro ['bi:strou] (*pl* **bistros**) *n* a small restaurant or bar in a French style.

bit [bɪt] *n* **-1. a bit of cake** a small piece of cake, broken, torn, or cut from the whole cake (used to make uncountable nouns countable) □ *a bit of wood/land/string* □ *There are bits of broken glass on the floor.* ■ **a bit of a book** a (small) part of a book □ *Which bits of the play/job did you like best?* **-2. a bit of equipment** a single piece, amount, or example of equipment □ *a bit of hardware/furniture/news* □ *I have a bit of shopping to do.* ■ **a bit of a problem** a problem, but not a very serious one □ *It's a bit of a mess/an improvement.* □ *The news came as a bit of a shock to us.* ■ **bits and pieces** GB small things of different sorts; (small) things that belong to somebody □ *I've put all your bits and pieces in that box.* ■ **to do one's bit** GB to do one's share of work to help one's country, an organization etc □ *I've done my bit for charity.* ■ **she's every bit as good as you** she is just as good as you in every way (used for emphasis). ■ **to fall to bits** to break into little pieces. ■ **thrilled to bits** very thrilled (informal use). **-3. a bit of food** some food, but not very much □ *We've had a bit of excitement here today.* **-4.** [for a drill] a piece of hard metal at the end of a drill, for making holes in stone, wood etc □ *a drill bit.* **-5.** [for a horse] a metal bar that goes in a horse's mouth, is fixed to the reins, and is used for guiding the horse. **-6.** COMPUTING [of information] the smallest unit of information that a computer can use or store □ *8 bits make up a byte.* □ *32-bit technology.*

◆ **a bit** *adv* **-1. for a bit** for a short time (informal use) □ *He's just gone out for a bit.* **-2.** slightly □ *"Does he help you much?"* — *"A bit, now and then."* ■ **a bit tired** rather tired □ *It's a bit difficult to explain.* ■ **not a bit** not at all. □ *"Do you mind helping?"* — *"Not a bit!"* ■ **quite a bit** quite often □ *I've seen them quite a bit recently.* ■ **it's a bit much** it is not fair or reasonable □ *I think it's a bit much being expected to work Sundays.*

◆ **bit by bit** *adv* slowly and one part at a time □ *The palace is being restored bit by bit.*

bitch [bɪtʃ] ◇ *n* **-1.** a female dog. **-2.**▽ a word used to refer to a woman who makes unpleasant and nasty remarks (very informal and disapproving use). ◇ *vi* to complain about somebody in an unfair and nasty way (informal use) □ *They're always bitching about somebody.*

bitchy ['bɪtʃɪ] (*compar* **bitchier**, *superl* **bitchiest**) *adj* [person, comment, remark] that one thinks is critical and nasty about somebody else in an unfair way (informal use).

bite [baɪt] (*pt* **bit**, *pp* **bitten**) ◇ *vt* **-1.** [person, animal] to cut or hold <sb/sthg> tightly with the teeth □ *Your dog just bit me!* □ *He bites his nails.* **-2.** [insect, snake] to make a hole in the skin of <a person or animal>, often removing blood or injecting poison □ *I've been bitten by a mosquito.*

◇ *vi* **-1.** [animal, person, insect] to bite somebody or something □ *Does your dog bite?* □ *She bit into a peach.* □ *This species does not bite.* **-2.** [tires, clutch] to grip a surface firmly. **-3.** [law, policy, sanctions] to have a noticeable effect □ *The recession is starting to bite.*

◇ *n* **-1.** the act of biting something; a piece removed from something by biting □ *She took a large bite from* OR *out of the pear.* **-2. to have a bite to eat** to have a snack or a small meal (informal use) □ *I haven't had a bite to eat all morning.* □ *Come over and have a bite to eat at our place.* **-3.** [from a person, animal, insect] a wound made by the teeth of a person or animal, or by an insect □ *a mosquito bite.* **-4.** [of food, a drink] a sharp strong flavor □ *This beer's got a real bite to it.*

◆ **bite off** *vt sep* **to bite sthg off** to remove sthg by biting. ■ **to bite off more than one can chew** to try to have or do more than is possible or reasonable.

biting ['baɪtɪŋ] *adj* **-1.** [wind, frost] very cold. **-2.** [wit, sarcasm, comment] clever, direct, and often cruel.

bit-map *vt* COMPUTING to define <the data> in a computer using a grid of bits, so that each bit has a particular function, image etc.

bit part *n* a small unimportant role for an actor or actress.

bitten ['bɪtn] *past participle of* **bite**.

bitter ['bɪtər] ◇ *adj* **-1.** [taste, flavor] that is sharp rather than sweet □ *This coffee's too bitter for my liking.* **-2.** [wind, weather] very cold □ *I had to walk home in the bitter cold.* **-3.** [disappointment, blow] that is upsetting and difficult to accept □ *I've learned from bitter experience that there's no point in arguing with him.* □ *the bitter truth.* ■ **to the bitter end** [fight, struggle] until all hope of success has gone; [stay, watch] until something is completely finished. **-4.** [argument, disagreement, opposition] that is angry and intense □ *her bitter hatred of injustice* □ *The two men are bitter enemies.* **-5.** [person] who is unable to accept or forget the suffering, injustice etc they have experienced □ *He still feels terribly bitter about being laid off/the divorce.*

◇ *n* GB a traditional dark beer that has a bitter taste and is usually drunk at room temperature □ *a pint of bitter.*

bitter lemon *n* GB a fizzy drink that contains lemon juice and is sometimes mixed with other drinks.

bitterly ['bɪtərlɪ] *adv* **-1. bitterly upset/disappointed/angry etc** very upset/disappointed/angry etc □ *It was a bitterly cold day.* □ *Turkey is bitterly opposed to lifting sanctions.* **-2.** [criticize, cry] in a way that shows one finds something upsetting and difficult to accept □ *I bitterly regret not going to college now.*

bitterness ['bɪtəʳnəs] *n*: *see* **bitter** □ *He spoke with great bitterness.*

bittersweet ['bɪtəʳswiːt] *adj* [taste, flavor] that is bitter and sweet at the same time; [memory] that is pleasant but also painful.

bitumen [US bə'tuːmən, GB 'bɪtjʊmɪn] *n* a black sticky substance used to cover roads.

bivouac ['bɪvʊæk] (*pt* & *pp* **bivouacked**, *cont* **bivouacking**) ◇ *n* a temporary shelter or camp made by mountaineers, soldiers etc. ◇ *vi* to stay in a bivouac.

biweekly [baɪ'wiːklɪ] ◇ *adj* -1. that takes place every two weeks. -2. that takes place twice a week. ◇ *adv* -1. every two weeks. -2. twice a week.

bizarre [bɪ'zɑːʳ] *adj* [behavior, remark, shape] that is strange and different from what is usual or expected □ *He suddenly made a bizarre attack on the media.* □ *She turned up wearing the most bizarre outfit.*

bk -1. *abbr of* **bank**. -2. *abbr of* **book**.

bl, B/L *abbr of* **bill of lading**.

BL *n* GB -1. (*abbr of* **Bachelor of Law(s)**) a degree in law; a person who has this degree. -2. (*abbr of* **Bachelor of Letters**) a degree in literature; a person who has this degree. -3. (*abbr of* **Bachelor of Literature**) a degree in literature; a person who has this degree.

blab [blæb] (*pt* & *pp* **blabbed**, *cont* **blabbing**) *vi* to talk about something, especially when it is a secret, in a careless way (informal use) □ *Someone must have blabbed to the police.*

black [blæk] ◇ *adj* -1. [hair, dress, sky] that is the color of coal □ *a cloud of black smoke* □ *a black limousine*. ■ **to be black and blue** to be covered in bruises □ *They beat him black and blue*. -2. [person] who belongs to a race that has dark skin, especially one of African origin; [culture, music] that is connected with black people □ *the country's first black judge* □ *a member of the black community*. -3. [tea, coffee] made without milk or cream. -4. [day, outlook] very depressing or worrying; [mood, thoughts] very depressed or worried □ *He painted a very black picture of our financial situation.* □ *The future looks black.* □ *His mind was full of black thoughts.* ■ **black humor** jokes about sad or unpleasant things. -5. **a black look** a very angry or hostile look.
◇ *n* -1. the color of coal □ *She was dressed in black.* ■ **to be in the black** [account, person, company] to be in credit and without debts. -2. a black person □ *Blacks represent 20% of the party's voters.*
◇ *vt* GB [goods, workers] to refuse to be involved with <particular people or things> in protest against something.

◆ **black out** ◇ *vt sep* -1. **to black a place out** [room, building, city] to make a place dark by covering or putting out the lights, or by cutting the electricity supply □ *Large parts of the city were blacked out by the storm.* -2. **to black sthg out** [news] to prevent information from being published or broadcast. ◇ *vi* [person] to faint for a short time □ *He blacked out after the crash, so intense was the pain.*

black and white ◇ *adj* -1. [photograph, television] that shows the colors black, white, and gray only □ *I love watching old black and white movies.* -2. [view, attitude] that treats an issue, especially a moral one, in terms of simple opposites □ *Things aren't that black and white.* ◇ *n* **to be in black and white** [agreement, contract] to be written on a piece of paper □ *I won't believe it until I've seen it in black and white.*

blackball ['blækbɔːl] *vt* to vote against allowing <sb> to become a member of a club, committee etc.

black belt *n* a black belt worn by a person who is an expert in judo or karate; a person who has the right to wear this belt.

blackberry [US 'blækberɪ, GB -bərɪ] (*pl* **blackberries**) *n* a small, soft, black fruit that grows in woods and hedges; the bush that this fruit grows on.

blackbird ['blækbɜːʳd] *n* a common American or European bird that has black feathers if it is a male.

blackboard ['blækbɔːʳd] *n* a large sheet of smooth black or dark-green material, usually found in a classroom, that a teacher writes on in chalk.

black box *n* AVIATION a device on an aircraft that records information while it is in flight and can be examined after a crash to help find the cause of the accident.

black comedy *n* comedy that uses black humor.

Black Country: the Black Country the industrial part of the West Midlands of England.

blackcurrant [US ˌblæk'kɜːrənt, GB -kʌr-] *n* a small, black, round fruit that is grown in gardens □ *blackcurrant jelly.*

black economy *n* GB the business activities in a country that take place illegally, especially to avoid paying tax.

blacken ['blækən] ◇ *vt* -1. [wall, skin] to make the surface of <sthg> black or dark □ *an old wall blackened with soot/smoke* □ *They blackened their faces.* -2. **to blacken sb's name** OR **reputation** to give people a bad opinion of sb by accusing them of criminal or immoral behavior, often falsely. -3. US COOKING to cook <meat> over a high heat so that it goes black on the outside □ *blackened chicken.* ◇ *vi* [sky] to become dark, especially before a storm.

black eye *n* a bruise that forms around somebody's eye after they have been hit there □ *He gave me a black eye.*

Blackfoot ['blækfʊt] (*pl* **Blackfeet** OR **Blackfoot**) *n* a member of a Native American people living on the northwestern plains of the USA and Canada; the language of this people.

blackhead ['blækhed] *n* a small spot on one's skin that has a black center.

black hole *n* ASTRONOMY an area in outer space where gravity is so strong that everything near it is pulled into it and not even light can escape from it.

black ice *n* GB a layer of thin ice on a road surface that is very difficult to see.

blackjack ['blækdʒæk] *n* **-1.** a card game, usually played for money, in which players try to collect cards with a total value of 21. **-2.** US a metal stick covered in leather that is used as a weapon.

blacklist ['blæklɪst] ◇ *n* a list of people, organizations, places etc that an organization or government disapproves of, does not trust, and stops using or helping. ◇ *vt* to place <a person, organization, place> etc on a blacklist □ *The company was blacklisted for using non-union workers.*

black magic *n* magic that is believed to use the power of the devil to do evil.

blackmail ['blækmeɪl] ◇ *n* **-1.** the act of getting money or favors from somebody by threatening to tell other people about something dishonest, immoral etc that they have done and want to keep secret. **-2.** the act of using a person's feelings of love, loyalty etc to make them do what one wants □ *emotional blackmail.* ◇ *vt* **-1.** to use blackmail to make <sb> give one money or favors □ *They blackmailed him into giving them the money.* **-2.** to threaten <sb> with emotional blackmail □ *If you're trying to blackmail me into staying, it won't work.*

blackmailer ['blækmeɪlə^r] *n* a person who uses blackmail to get money or favors.

black mark *n* **a black mark against sb** something that sb has done that gives people a bad opinion of them □ *If we miss this deadline, it'll be a black mark against the department.*

black market *n* a system of buying and selling goods, foreign money, or services illegally □ *These luxuries were freely available on the black market.* □ *black-market goods.*

Black Muslim *n* a member of a black Islamic movement in the USA called the Nation of Islam. It was formed in 1929, and demanded a separate state for black people.

blackout ['blækaʊt] *n* **-1.** [during a war] a period during wartime when a city, area etc is made completely dark for safety reasons. **-2.** [of electricity] a power cut □ *an electricity blackout.* **-3.** [of a person] a loss of consciousness for a short time □ *I've started getting blackouts.*

Black Panthers: the Black Panthers the members of a black political party in the USA, the Black Panther Party, founded in 1966. They wanted a separate state for black people.

Black Power *n* a political movement in the USA and Australia whose aim was to get more political and economic power for black people. It was an important part of the civil rights movement in the USA in the sixties.

black pudding *n* GB a large sausage made of pig's blood, fat, and grain.

Black Sea: the Black Sea an inland sea between southeastern Europe and Asia.

black sheep *n* **the black sheep of the family** the member of a family who is considered to be a disgrace or failure by the rest of the family.

blacksmith ['blæksmɪθ] *n* a person whose job is to make or repair things made of iron, especially horseshoes.

blackspot ['blækspɒt] *n* GB **-1.** a place where many road accidents have taken place. **-2.** a place where a particular problem is especially serious □ *an unemployment blackspot.*

black-tie *adj* [dinner, dance] where very formal dress is worn.

blacktop ['blæktɒp] *n* US a black sticky substance used to cover roads.

bladder ['blædə^r] *n* ANATOMY a bag in the body in which urine collects □ *a bladder infection.*

blade [bleɪd] *n* **-1.** [of a knife, saw] the thin part of something that cuts when it is sharp. **-2.** [of a fan, propeller, oar] the flat wide part of something that moves through the air or water. **-3. a blade of grass** a long thin piece of grass.

Blake [bleɪk], **William** (1757–1827) a British poet and artist, one of the earliest Romantics. His works include *Songs of Innocence* and *Songs of Experience.*

blame [bleɪm] ◇ *vt* **-1.** to think or say that <sb/sthg> is responsible for an accident, failure etc □ *Don't blame me if you get into trouble.* □ *Investigators blame pilot error for the crash.* ▪ **to blame sthg on sb/sthg** to put the responsibility for sthg on sb/sthg □ *They tried to blame the crash on me.* ▪ **to be to blame** to be responsible for something bad that has happened □ *I'm not to blame for the mess we're in.* **-2. I don't blame you** I think what you are doing is understandable □ *"I'm staying at home today." — "I don't blame you, you don't look very well at all!"* ◇ *n* the responsibility for something bad that has happened □ *It's not fair that you should get the blame.* □ *Don't try to put the blame on me!* ▪ **to take the blame** to be given responsibility for something bad that has happened □ *My colleagues left me to take the blame for the department's mistakes.*

blameless ['bleɪmləs] *adj* [person] who is not to blame; [life] that is entirely good and respectable.

blanch [US blæntʃ, GB blɑːntʃ] ◇ *vt* COOKING [vegetables, fruit, nuts] to put <food> into boiling water for a short time. ◇ *vi* [person] to become pale □ *He blanched when he heard the news.*

blancmange [blə'mɒndʒ] *n* a cold dessert made of sweetened and flavored milk thickened with cornstarch.

bland [blænd] *adj* **-1.** [person, style, music] that has no interesting or unusual qualities. **-2.** [food, drink] that has no strong flavor.

blank [blæŋk] ◇ *adj* **-1.** [page, screen] that has nothing written, marked, or shown on it □ *The computer screen suddenly went blank.* □ *'Leave this space blank.'* **-2.** [cassette, tape, film] that has nothing recorded on it. **-3.** [look, stare] that shows no understanding, emotion, or interest. ■ **her mind went blank** she found herself unable to think or remember. ◇ *n* -1. an empty space □ *Answer the question by filling in the blanks.* ■ **to draw a blank** to be unsuccessful in one's search for somebody or something □ *The police have drawn a blank in their search for the bombers.* -2. MILITARY a cartridge with no bullet in it.

blank check *n* -1. a signed check that does not have the amount to be paid written on it. -2. complete freedom to make the decisions one wants, especially to spend money □ *Just giving an architect a blank check is a recipe for disaster.*

blanket [US 'blæŋkət, GB -ɪt] ◇ *adj* a blanket decision/instruction etc a decision/instruction etc that includes every part of something □ *The event received blanket coverage in the media.* ◇ *n* -1. [for a bed] a warm, usually woolen, covering used on a bed. -2. **a blanket of fog/snow etc** a layer of fog/snow etc that covers an area completely.

blanket bath *n* GB a complete wash given to somebody who cannot get out of bed.

blankly ['blæŋklɪ] *adv* [look, stare] *see* **blank**.

blank verse *n* poetry that has a regular rhythm but does not rhyme.

blare [bleəʳ] *vi* [siren, radio, horn] to make a loud harsh sound □ *They drove by with their car stereo blaring.*
◆ **blare out** *vi* = **blare**.

blasé [US ˌblɑːˈzeɪ, GB ˈblɑːzeɪ] *adj* [person, attitude] that shows no interest or concern, especially about things that excite or worry other people □ *She was very blasé about it all.*

blasphemous ['blæsfəməs] *adj* [person, words] showing complete disrespect for God or religion.

blasphemy ['blæsfəmɪ] (*pl* **blasphemies**) *n* an expression or act of disrespect for God or religion.

blast [US blæst, GB blɑːst] ◇ *n* -1. an explosion, especially one caused by a bomb □ *Six people were killed in the blast.* -2. a sudden strong rush of air □ *a blast of wind.* ◇ *vt* to create <a hole, tunnel> etc using explosives □ *The bomb blasted a huge hole in the front wall of the building.* ◇ *excl* GB a word used to express anger or frustration (informal use) □ *Blast! I've left her number at home.*
◆ **(at) full blast** *adv* -1. as loudly as possible □ *He had the radio on (at) full blast.* -2. with maximum speed and energy □ *The machine was going (at) full blast.*
◆ **blast off** *vi* [spacecraft, rocket] to leave the ground.

blasted [US 'blæstəd, GB 'blɑːstəd] *adj* a word used to show one's irritation with somebody or something (informal use) □ *That blasted dog's barking again.*

blast furnace *n* a tall structure in which blasts of heated air are used to melt a substance to get metal from it.

blast-off *n* the launching of a rocket or spacecraft.

blatant ['bleɪtnt] *adj* [dishonesty, discrimination,

liar] that is obvious and shows no shame □ *a blatant disregard for human rights.*

blatantly ['bleɪtntlɪ] *adv* [lie, discriminate, cheat] *see* **blatant**. ■ **to be blatantly obvious** to be very obvious □ *It's blatantly obvious what's been going on.*

blaze [bleɪz] ◇ *n* -1. a large destructive fire □ *The blaze spread to other houses in the street.* -2. **a blaze of publicity/glory etc** an impressive display of publicity/glory etc □ *The movie was released in a blaze of publicity.* □ *The garden was a blaze of color.* ◇ *vi* -1. [fire] to burn brightly or strongly □ *The fire has been blazing for three hours.* -2. [sun, light] to be very bright □ *The garden blazed with color.* -3. [eyes] to show strong emotion, especially anger □ *Eyes blazing, he got up and stormed out of the room.* □ *She turned to face him, her eyes blazing.*

blazer ['bleɪzəʳ] *n* a jacket that is often dark blue and sometimes has a special badge on the breast pocket.

blazing ['bleɪzɪŋ] ◇ *adj* -1. **blazing sunshine/ heat etc** sunshine/heat etc that is very hot. -2. **a blazing argument/fight etc** an argument/a fight etc that is very loud and angry. ◇ *adv* **blazing hot** very hot □ *blazing hot weather.*

bleach [bliːtʃ] ◇ *n* a strong chemical which makes things white and is used for cleaning and removing germs. ◇ *vt* [clothing, hair] to cause <sthg> to become white or lighter in color by the use of chemicals or through the effects of strong sunlight □ *Their bones were bleached white in the sun.* □ *sun-bleached hair.*

bleached [bliːtʃt] *adj* [hair, cotton] lighter in color or white, because of the use of chemicals or the effects of strong sunlight.

bleachers ['bliːtʃərz] *npl* US the cheap uncovered seats at a sports stadium, especially a baseball park.

bleak [bliːk] *adj* -1. [future, prospect, outlook] that gives no cause for hope or optimism □ *These are bleak times for many shareholders.* -2. [place, landscape, building] that causes one to feel unhappy because it has no pleasant or interesting qualities □ *The city is bleak and deserted.* -3. [weather] cold, dull, and unpleasant □ *a bleak winter's day.* -4. [face, person] without any hope or enthusiasm.

bleary ['blɪərɪ] (*compar* **blearier**, *superl* **bleariest**) *adj* [eyes] that are red and not able to see well because of tiredness, crying etc.

bleary-eyed [-'aɪd] *adj* [person] who has bleary eyes.

bleat [bliːt] ◇ *n* the sound made by a sheep or goat. ◇ *vi* -1. [sheep, goat] to make a bleat. -2. [person] to complain, especially in a weak high voice.

bleed [bliːd] (*pt* & *pp* **bled** [bled]) ◇ *vi* to have blood flowing from a wound, injury etc □ *My leg is bleeding.* □ *She was bleeding from a cut on her hand.* ◇ *vt* to remove air from <a radiator>; to remove the liquid from <a brake system>.

bleeding ['bliːdɪŋ] *n* [from a cut] *see* **bleed** □ Ap-

ply pressure to the wound to stop the bleeding. □ *internal bleeding.*

bleep [bliːp] ◇ *n* a single, short, high-pitched sound made by an electronic device. ◇ *vt* to call <sb> by using a bleeper. ◇ *vi* [alarm, pager] to make a bleep.

bleeper [ˈbliːpəʳ] *n* GB an electronic device that bleeps to tell the person carrying it that they should phone someone.

blemish [ˈblemɪʃ] ◇ *n* -1. [on skin, fruit, china] a mark that spoils the appearance of something. -2. [on somebody's reputation, character] something that damages somebody's reputation. ◇ *vt* to damage <sb's reputation>.

blend [blend] ◇ *n* -1. [of coffee, whiskey] a product made by putting different types of the same thing together in a particular way □ *a blend of three different kinds of tea.* -2. [of ideas, qualities, styles] a combination, especially one that is pleasing or new □ *His speech had just the right blend of seriousness and humor.*
◇ *vt* -1. [ingredients] to mix <substances> together to produce a smooth whole □ *Blend the flour into the eggs.* -2. [coffee, tea, tobacco] to mix <different types of drink or tobacco> to produce a particular flavor □ *a blended whisky.* -3. [ideas, styles] to combine <different qualities>, especially in a pleasing or unusual way □ *The story blends fact with fiction.*
◇ *vi* [sounds, colors] to go together in a pleasing way to produce something whole □ *Their voices blended with the sound of the orchestra.*

◆ **blend in** *vi* to combine with one's surroundings so as not to be noticeable □ *The new building blends in well with the rest of the square.* □ *He tried to blend in with the crowd.*

◆ **blend into** *vt fus* to blend into sthg [into the landscape, one's surroundings] not to be very different from sthg.

blender [ˈblendəʳ] *n* an electrical appliance used to mix food or change it into liquid form.

bless [bles] (*pt* & *pp* **blessed** OR **blest**) *vt* -1. RELIGION [congregation, house] to ask God to take care of <sb/sthg>; [bread, wine, water] to make <sthg> holy in a religious ceremony. -2. **to be blessed with sthg** [with talent, good health] to be lucky enough to have sthg. -3. *phrase* **bless you!** a phrase that one says to somebody who has just sneezed.

blessed [ˈblesɪd] *adj* -1. RELIGION very holy □ *the Blessed Virgin.* -2. [relief, silence] that one feels grateful for. -3. a word used to express one's irritation with somebody or something (informal use).

blessing [ˈblesɪŋ] *n* -1. RELIGION an act of blessing somebody. ■ **a blessing in disguise** something that at first appears to be harmful or unpleasant, but is later good or helpful □ *Losing that job may prove to be a blessing in disguise.* -2. approval and support □ *The project has the blessing of the committee.*

blest [blest] *past tense & past participle of* **bless**.

blew [bluː] *past tense of* **blow**.

blight [blaɪt] ◇ *n* -1. [in plants] a disease that makes plants or crops die slowly □ *potato blight.* -2. [in buildings, towns] a state of slow decay □ *urban blight.* -3. [on somebody's hopes, chances] something that spoils something or prevents it happening or developing fully □ *Homelessness is a blight on the lives of many young people.* ◇ *vt* to spoil <sb's career, life> etc □ *The peace process has been blighted by repeated terrorist attacks.*

blind [blaɪnd] ◇ *adj* -1. [person, animal] unable to see □ *He went blind in his seventies.* -2. **to be blind** [person] not to notice or understand sthg when one should □ *People were blind to the danger of infection.* -3. **blind rage/panic etc** uncontrollable rage/panic etc. ■ **blind faith/obedience etc** faith/obedience etc that shows no doubt or uncertainty. -4. GB a word used for emphasis □ *It doesn't make a blind bit of difference to me.*
◇ *adv* **to be blind drunk** to be very drunk.
◇ *n* a covering of cloth, plastic etc that is pulled down over a window to keep light out of a room.
◇ *npl* **the blind** blind people.
◇ *vt* -1. to make <sb> unable to see □ *She was blinded by a firework.* □ *The camera flash momentarily blinded me.* -2. to stop <sb> from knowing or noticing something □ *His ambition blinded him to the needs of his family.*

blind alley *n* -1. a small street that is closed at one end. -2. something which will not in the end produce any good results.

blind corner *n* a corner at which a driver cannot see the road ahead.

blind date *n* a date with somebody one has never met before; the person one has this kind of date with.

blinders [ˈblaɪndəʳz] *npl* US two leather patches placed beside a horse's eyes so that it can only see straight ahead.

blindfold [ˈblaɪndfould] ◇ *adv* with one's eyes covered. ◇ *n* a strip of cloth used to cover somebody's eyes so that they cannot see. ◇ *vt* to stop <sb> from seeing by tying a blindfold over their eyes.

blinding [ˈblaɪndɪŋ] *adj* [light, glare, flash] so bright that one is unable to see properly because of it.

blindingly [ˈblaɪndɪŋlɪ] *adv* **blindingly obvious** very obvious.

blindly [ˈblaɪndlɪ] *adv* -1. [grope, stumble] without being able to see. -2. [guess, speculate] without the necessary knowledge or information; [follow, accept, obey] without asking questions or showing doubt.

blindness [ˈblaɪndnəs] *n* [of a person] *see* **blind** □ *her blindness to everything except her own selfish aims.*

blind spot *n* -1. AUTO an area of the road that a driver cannot easily see, especially the area that is slightly behind and to the side of the car. -2. something that somebody is always unable or unwilling to understand □ *Dealing with other people's problems has always been a blind spot for him.*

blink [blɪŋk] ◇ *vt* -1. to open and close <one's eyes> rapidly. -2. US AUTO **to blink one's**

lights to flash one's lights on and off. ◇ *vi* **-1.** [person] to open and close one's eyes quickly □ *He stood there blinking in the sunlight.* **-2.** [light] to come on and off rapidly or shine in an unsteady way □ *We could see the lighthouse blinking in the distance.* ◇ *n* **-1.** [of eyes, light] an act of blinking. **-2. to be on the blink** [machine] not to be working □ *The washing machine's on the blink again.*

blinkered ['blɪŋkəʳd] *adj* **-1.** [horse] that is wearing blinkers. **-2.** [person, attitude] who cannot understand ideas, opinions etc that are different from theirs.

blinkers ['blɪŋkəʳz] *npl* GB = **blinders**.

blip [blɪp] *n* **-1.** a short high-pitched sound made by electronic devices such as a radar or life-support system; a spot of light on a screen that flashes on and off and often makes this sound. **-2.** a temporary problem □ *The spokesperson said that the rise in interest rates was just a blip.*

bliss [blɪs] *n* very great happiness.

blissful ['blɪsfl] *adj* [day, experience] that is happy and enjoyable.

blissfully ['blɪsflɪ] *adv* **to be blissfully happy** to be extremely happy. ■ **to be blissfully unaware/ignorant** to be unaware/ignorant of something unpleasant □ *He was blissfully unaware of the dangers he faced.*

blister ['blɪstəʳ] ◇ *n* **-1.** [on one's skin] a small raised area of skin containing clear liquid that can be painful and is caused by rubbing or burning □ *My feet/hands were covered in blisters.* **-2.** [on paint, a tire] a small area like a blister caused by a small amount of air under the surface. ◇ *vi* [skin, paint] to form blisters.

blistering ['blɪstərɪŋ] ◇ *adj* **-1.** [heat, sun] very hot. **-2.** [attack, criticism] very strong and angry □ *They had a blistering row.* ◇ *adv* **blistering hot** very hot □ *a blistering hot day.*

blister pack *n* a type of packaging consisting of a piece of raised clear plastic attached to a firm piece of cardboard.

blithe [blaɪð] *adj* **-1.** [indifference, remark] that shows that one has not thought seriously or carefully about something important.

blithely ['blaɪðlɪ] *adv* [say, talk, ignore] *see* **blithe** □ *Despite their huge overdraft they went on blithely signing checks.*

BLitt [,biːˈlɪt] (*abbr of* **Bachelor of Letters**) *n* GB a degree in literature; a person who has this degree.

blitz [blɪts] *n* **-1.** MILITARY a sudden attack in which a lot of bombs are dropped from planes on a town or city. **-2.** a period when somebody tries hard to deal with a problem or job that must be finished quickly □ *an advertising blitz* □ *Let's have a blitz on the paperwork.*

blizzard ['blɪzəʳd] *n* a heavy snowstorm with strong winds.

BLM (*abbr of* **Bureau of Land Management**) *n* the US government department responsible for planning and controlling the building of roads, cities, transport systems etc.

bloated ['bloʊtəd] *adj* **-1.** [body, face] that looks very swollen. **-2.** [person] who feels uncomfortably full after eating too much.

blob [blɒb] *n* **-1.** a large drop of thick liquid □ *a blob of paint.* **-2.** a shape that is unclear or is hard to describe □ *a blob on the horizon.*

bloc [blɒk] *n* a group of people or countries that work together for political or economic reasons □ *countries of the former Communist bloc.*

block [blɒk] ◇ *n* **-1.** [in a city, town] a building or group of buildings between two streets □ *The bank is three blocks away.* □ *We walked round the block.* **-2.** [of stone, wood, ice] a large piece of something solid that usually has straight sides. **-3.** [of apartments] a large building divided into several offices, apartments etc □ *an office block* □ *a block of flats.* **-4.** [in a pipe, tube, road] something that prevents things from moving along something. **-5. a block and tackle** a system of pulleys and ropes used for lifting heavy objects.
◇ *vt* **-1.** [road, pipe] to stop things from moving along or through <sthg> □ *The highway was completely blocked by traffic.* □ *She stood in front of me, blocking the doorway.* **-2.** [light, view] to be in the way of <sthg> □ *You're blocking my view.* **-3.** [law, deal, promotion] to prevent <sthg> from happening, succeeding etc □ *The treaty was blocked by the Spanish.* □ *The courts have blocked moves to make such mergers illegal.*

◆ **block off** *vt sep* **to block sthg off** [road, pipe] to block sthg completely for a particular reason □ *The police blocked off the entrance to the street.*

◆ **block out** *vt sep* **-1. to block sthg out** [idea, memory] to prevent oneself from thinking about sthg □ *He tried to block out all thoughts of the accident.* **-2. to block out the light/sun** etc to prevent light/sunlight etc from passing through □ *Those trees block the sun out.*

◆ **block up** ◇ *vt sep* **to be blocked up** [pipe, sink] to be completely blocked by something □ *My nose is blocked up.* □ *The drains were all blocked up with dead leaves.* ◇ *vi* [pipe, sink] *The toilet keeps blocking up.*

blockade [blɒˈkeɪd] ◇ *n* an action taken to stop goods from entering or leaving a port or country, usually by surrounding it with ships □ *a blockade on arms* OR *an arms blockade.* ◇ *vt* to close <a port, country> etc with a blockade.

blockage ['blɒkɪdʒ] *n* something that prevents things from moving through a pipe, tube etc.

block booking *n* a single reservation for a large number of tickets or seats.

blockbuster ['blɒkbʌstəʳ] *n* a very successful book or movie.

block capitals *npl* capital letters □ *Please write in block capitals.*

block letters *npl* = **block capitals**.

block release *n* GB a system that allows industrial employees to study at a college for a short period □ *I'm on block release.*

block vote *n* GB a single vote made by a representative of a group such as a labor union.

Bloc Québécois [-keɪbe'kwɑː] *n* a Canadian political party that believes that Quebec should become an independent state.

bloke [bloʊk] *n* GB a man (informal use).

blond [blɒnd] *adj* [hair] light yellow; [man] who has blond hair.

blonde [blɒnd] ◇ *adj* [hair] light yellow; [woman] who has blond hair. ◇ *n* a woman who has blond hair.

blood [blʌd] *n* the red liquid that flows through one's body □ *He/His face was covered in blood.* □ *a blood disease* □ *a blood sample.* ■ **to kill sb in cold blood** to kill sb in a planned way, without emotion □ *He was shot in cold blood.* ■ **to be in sb's blood** to be an easy or natural thing for sb to do, sometimes because their family has done it before □ *Acting is in her blood.* ■ **to make sb's blood boil** to make sb very angry □ *It really makes my blood boil to hear politicians talking about morality.* ■ **to make sb's blood run cold** to make sb very frightened. ■ **new** OR **fresh blood** new members of an organization who can bring new ideas with them.

blood bank *n* a place where blood is stored until it is needed by doctors during operations.

bloodbath [US 'blʌdbæθ, *pl* -bæðz, GB -bɑːθ, *pl* -bɑːðz] *n* the violent killing of a lot of people at the same time □ *The battle turned into a bloodbath.*

blood brother *n* a man who has promised to be loyal to one or more other men, usually in a ceremony where they mix some of their blood.

blood cell *n* one of the red or white cells that are found in blood □ *a red/white blood cell.*

blood count *n* a medical test to check that somebody has the right amounts of red and white blood cells.

bloodcurdling ['blʌdkɜːˈdlɪŋ] *adj* [cry, noise, story] very frightening.

blood donor *n* a person who gives blood from their own body to be used in hospitals.

blood group *n* one of the groups into which human blood is classified.

bloodhound ['blʌdhaʊnd] *n* a large dog with a good sense of smell, used for hunting or for searching for people.

bloodless ['blʌdləs] *adj* -1. [face, cheeks] very pale. -2. [coup, victory] in which nobody is killed.

bloodletting ['blʌdletɪŋ] *n* violence and killing, usually between rival groups.

blood money *n* money that is paid to a person for murdering or helping to murder somebody.

blood orange *n* an orange with red flesh and red juice.

blood poisoning *n* a serious illness caused by an infection in one's blood.

blood pressure *n* a measure of the force with which blood moves through one's body □ *He has high/low blood pressure.*

blood relation, blood relative *n* a person who is related to somebody by birth rather than by marriage.

bloodshed ['blʌdʃed] *n* violence and killing □ *It's time to put an end to all the bloodshed.*

bloodshot ['blʌdʃɒt] *adj* [eye] that has red lines in the part that is normally white.

blood sports *npl* sports, especially hunting, in which animals are killed.

bloodstained ['blʌdsteɪnd] *adj* [clothing, floor] that is stained with blood.

bloodstream ['blʌdstriːm] *n* the blood flowing inside one's body □ *There were traces of the drug in his bloodstream.*

blood test *n* a test carried out on a sample of blood to check for diseases or the presence of drugs.

bloodthirsty ['blʌdθɜːˈstɪ] *adj* [person] who enjoys doing, watching, or reading about acts of violence; [movie, story] very violent.

blood transfusion *n* a medical operation in which a patient is given blood from another person.

blood type *n* = blood group.

blood vessel *n* any of the tubes that blood flows through in one's body.

bloody ['blʌdɪ] (*compar* **bloodier**, *superl* **bloodiest**) ◇ *adj* -1. [war, conflict] in which there is a lot of violence and killing □ *the bloody massacre of 1,200 men.* -2. [face, hand] that is covered with blood. -3.▽ GB a word used to show how strongly one feels about something (very informal use) □ *The bloody train's late again.* □ *He's got a bloody nerve.* ◇ *adv*▽ GB very (very informal use) □ *It's a bloody good film.*

bloody mary *n* a drink made from vodka and tomato juice.

bloom [bluːm] ◇ *n* a flower. ■ **to be in bloom** [flower, tree] to have flowers that are open; [place, garden] to be full of flowers. ◇ *vi* [plant, tree] to produce flowers □ *These roses will bloom twice a year.*

blooming ['bluːmɪŋ] ◇ *adj* [person] who looks attractive and healthy □ *She's positively blooming with health.*

Bloomsbury Group ['bluːmzbərɪ-] *n* **the Bloomsbury Group** a group of artists and writers with very modern ideas, including Virginia Woolf and E.M. Forster, who lived in Bloomsbury, in London, in the 1920s.

blossom ['blɒsəm] ◇ *n* the flowers of a tree that appear before the fruit □ *cherry/apple blossom.* ■ **to be in blossom** [tree] to be covered with flowers. ◇ *vi* -1. [tree] to produce blossom □ *The apple trees blossomed very late this year.* -2. [person, business, industry] to become more successful or attractive □ *She blossomed into an exceptional artist.*

blot [blɒt] (*pt* & *pp* **blotted**, *cont* **blotting**) ◇ *n* -1. [of ink, paint] a drop of liquid that somebody has spilt on something □ *an ink blot.* -2. something unpleasant that spoils a view, somebody's reputation etc □ *The tower is considered to be a blot on the landscape.* ◇ *vt* -1. to make a blot or blots on <a piece of paper>. -2. to dry <ink, writing> etc by pressing a piece of blotting paper against it.

◆ **blot out** *vt sep* **to blot sthg out** [light, idea, memories] to block sthg out □ *You just have to blot out any thought of failure.*

blotch [blɒtʃ] *n* a small mark on skin, material etc that does not have a definite shape □ *His arms were covered in red blotches.*

blotchy ['blɒtʃɪ] (*compar* **blotchier**, *superl* **blotchiest**) *adj* [complexion, skin, face] that is covered with blotches.

blotter ['blɒtər] *n* a piece of blotting paper, often with a hard backing.

blotting paper ['blɒtɪŋ-] *n* thick soft paper used for blotting ink, writing etc.

blouse [US blaʊs, GB blaʊz] *n* a type of shirt worn by women or girls.

blouson [US 'blaʊsɑːn, GB 'bluːzɒn] *n* a short jacket, usually close-fitting at the waist.

blow [bloʊ] (*pt* **blew**, *pp* **blown**) ◇ *vi* -1. [wind, draft] to make air move □ *The wind is blowing from the north.* -2. [leaves, hat] to be moved by the wind, a draft etc □ *The papers blew off the desk.* □ *Her hair was blowing in the wind.* -3. [person] to send air out of one's mouth □ *She blew on her coffee.* -4. [fuse] to stop working suddenly because too much current has passed through it. ◇ *vt* -1. [leaves, papers] to move <sthg> by a current of air, breath, or wind □ *The wind blew the door open.* □ *He blew the dust off the desk.* -2. to make <bubbles or smoke rings> by forcing one's breath through water, smoke etc. -3. [trumpet, whistle] to make a sound by blowing into <a musical instrument>. -4. **to blow one's nose** to clear one's nose by forcing air through it. -5. [wages, savings] to spend <a lot of money> irresponsibly or extravagantly (informal use) □ *She blew it all on a new car.* ◇ *n* -1. the act of hitting somebody or something with one's hand or a weapon □ *He received several blows to the head.* ■ **to come to blows** to start fighting by hitting each other □ *The two men came to blows.* ■ **to strike a blow for sthg** [for freedom, peace] to do something important in support of sthg. -2. an unpleasant and unexpected shock □ *His resignation came as a bit of a blow.* ■ **to soften the blow** to make unpleasant news easier to accept.

◆ **blow away** *vi* [leaves, hat] to be moved away by the wind, a draft etc.

◆ **blow out** ◇ *vt sep* **to blow sthg out** [candle, match] to stop sthg burning by blowing on it. ◇ *vi* -1. [candle, match] to stop burning because the wind or a draft has blown it out. -2. [tire] to burst while moving along a road.

◆ **blow over** *vi* -1. [storm] to end gradually. -2. [argument, scandal] to end gradually and be forgotten □ *It'll soon blow over.*

◆ **blow up** ◇ *vt sep* -1. **to blow sthg up** [balloon, tire] to fill sthg with air. -2. **to blow sb/sthg up** [building, vehicle, person] to destroy sb/sthg with explosives □ *The bridge was blown up during the war.* -3. **to blow sthg up** [photo, document, image] to make a bigger copy of sthg □ *This is a blown-up section of part of the map.* ◇ *vi* [building, vehicle] *The whole ship blew up.*

blow-by-blow *adj* a **blow-by-blow account/description** an account/a description that is very detailed and mentions everything in the exact order that it happened in.

blow-dry ◇ *n* a way of drying somebody's hair using a hairdryer so that it has a particular shape □ *a cut and blow-dry.* ◇ *vt* to give <sb's hair> a blow-dry.

blowfly ['bloʊflaɪ] (*pl* **blowflies**) *n* a fly that lays its eggs on meat or open wounds.

blowgun ['bloʊɡʌn] *n* US a long tube through which arrows or darts are blown that is used for hunting or as a weapon.

blowlamp ['bloʊlæmp] *n* GB = **blowtorch**.

blown [bloʊn] *past participle of* **blow**.

blowout ['bloʊaʊt] *n* -1. [of a tire] an accident in which a tire bursts □ *We had a blowout on the highway.* -2. a very big meal (informal use).

blowpipe ['bloʊpaɪp] *n* GB = **blowgun**.

blowtorch ['bloʊtɔːrtʃ] *n* a device, held in one's hand, that gives out a very hot flame and is used for removing old paint.

BLS (*abbr of* **Bureau of Labor Statistics**) *n* the US government department responsible for producing statistics on employment.

BLT *n abbr of* **bacon, lettuce, and tomato (sandwich)**.

blubber ['blʌbər] ◇ *n* the fat of particular sea animals, e.g. whales and seals. ◇ *vi* to cry noisily (disapproving use) □ *Stop blubbering!*

bludgeon ['blʌdʒən] *vt* to hit <sb> several times with a heavy object □ *He was bludgeoned to death.*

blue [bluː] ◇ *adj* -1. [eyes, clothes, sea] that is the color of the sky on a clear day □ *The walls were painted bright blue.* □ *Her hands were blue with the cold.* -2. [person] **to feel blue** to feel sad (old-fashioned use). -3. [movie, joke] that refers to sex in a way that could offend some people. ◇ *n* the color that is blue □ *She was dressed in blue.* ■ **to appear/arrive etc out of the blue** to appear/arrive etc suddenly, when one is not expecting it □ *The takeover bid came right out of the blue.*

◆ **blues** *npl* -1. MUSIC a type of music that started in the USA and is slow and sad □ *a blues guitarist.* -2. **the blues** a feeling of sadness (informal use) □ *She's got the blues again.*

🐾 BLUE

In British politics, the color blue traditionally represents the Conservative Party. At the universities of Oxford and Cambridge, a "blue" also means a special award given to a person who has played for one of the university sports teams, and who is therefore very good at sports. Oxford players traditionally wear dark blue, and Cambridge players wear light blue.

blue baby n a baby born with slightly blue skin because of a problem with its heart or lungs.

Bluebeard ['bluːbɪəʳd] a male character in European folk stories who marries and kills several women one after the other.

bluebell ['bluːbel] n a small European wild plant with blue flowers that are shaped like bells.

blueberry [US 'bluːberɪ, GB -bərɪ] (pl **blueberries**) n a small, dark-blue, North American fruit that can be cooked and eaten; the bush that this fruit grows on □ blueberry jam/pie.

bluebird ['bluːbɜːʳd] n a small, blue, North American bird.

blue-black adj very dark blue.

blue-blooded [-'blʌdəd] adj [person] who belongs to a royal or aristocratic family.

bluebottle ['bluːbɒtl] n a large fly with a dark-blue body.

blue channel n the blue channel a special way through customs at an airport or port in the EU, used by passengers who are traveling from one EU country to another.

blue cheese n a type of cheese with blue lines of mold in it.

blue chip n a share in a company that is considered to be very reliable and profitable □ a blue-chip company/investment.

blue-collar adj [worker, union, job] that is connected with people who do manual, usually industrial, work.
NOTE: Compare white-collar.

blue exit n = blue channel.

blue-eyed boy [-aɪd-] n GB a man or boy who is somebody's favorite child, student, or employee (informal use) □ Philip was always Daddy's blue-eyed boy.

bluegrass [US 'bluːgræs, GB -grɑːs] n -1. a type of bluish-green grass that grows in North America. -2. a type of country music from the southern USA that is played on stringed instruments.

blue jeans npl US = jeans.

blue law n US a law that tries to stop activities such as drinking alcohol or doing business on Sundays that some people think are immoral.

blueprint ['bluːprɪnt] n -1. CONSTRUCTION the photographic print of a plan for a building, machine etc. -2. a blueprint for sthg an explanation of how a particular plan or idea is expected to work □ a blueprint for success.

blue ribbon n US a piece of blue ribbon, given as the first prize in a competition.

bluestocking ['bluːstɒkɪŋ] n a woman who is thought to be too highly educated (old-fashioned and disapproving use).

blue tit n GB a small bird with a blue head and yellow chest.

blue whale n a bluish-gray whale that is the largest living animal.

bluff [blʌf] ◇ vi [person] to try to deceive somebody by pretending that one is going to do something, or that one is somebody

else □ He keeps threatening to resign, but I think he's bluffing. ◇ vt to bluff one's way into/out of a situation to get into/out of a situation by deceiving somebody □ He bluffed his way into the job. ◇ n -1. the act of bluffing. ■ to call sb's bluff to try to make sb do what they are threatening to do because one is sure that they are bluffing. -2. a steep bank or cliff by a river or the ocean. ◇ adj [person, manner] cheerful and direct, often in a way that some people find rude.

blunder ['blʌndəʳ] ◇ n a big mistake that shows one is careless or stupid. ◇ vi -1. to make a blunder. -2. to move clumsily and carelessly □ He blundered into the trap.

blunt [blʌnt] ◇ adj -1. [knife, pencil] that is not sharp; [object] that has rounded edges □ These scissors are too blunt. □ a blunt edge □ He had been struck by a blunt instrument. -2. [person] who says what they really think, without trying to be polite □ a blunt question/answer. ◇ vt -1. [knife, pencil, blade] to make <sthg> blunt. -2. [feeling, sense, effect] to weaken <sthg>.

bluntly ['blʌntlɪ] adv [say, reply] see **blunt** □ Put bluntly, he's saying it's a total waste of time.

blur [blɜːʳ] (pt & pp **blurred**, cont **blurring**) ◇ n something that cannot be seen or remembered clearly □ It was all a blur. ◇ vt -1. [outline, photo] to make <sthg> less clear to see. -2. [distinction, memory, vision] to make <sthg> less clear to understand or remember □ They're deliberately trying to blur the issue.

blurb [blɜːʳb] n a short description of a book that is written on its cover (informal use).

blurred [blɜːʳd] adj [photograph, distinction] that is difficult to see, understand, or remember □ She still suffers from blurred vision.

blurt [blɜːʳt] ◆ **blurt out** vt sep to blurt sthg out to say sthg secret or embarrassing suddenly, without thinking first □ I just blurted out the whole story.

blush [blʌʃ] ◇ vi to become red in the face, usually from shame or embarrassment. ◇ n -1. the red color on one's face that comes when one blushes □ His jokes caused a few blushes in the audience. -2. a wine that is a very pale pink color.

blusher ['blʌʃəʳ] n a cosmetic for coloring one's cheeks.

bluster ['blʌstəʳ] ◇ vi to speak loudly and aggressively, usually because one is angry or confused. ◇ n the things one says when one blusters.

blustery ['blʌstərɪ] adj [weather, day] windy □ blustery winds/showers.

Blvd abbr of **boulevard**.

BM n -1. (abbr of **Bachelor of Medicine**) a degree in medicine; a person who has this degree. -2. abbr of **British Museum**.

BMA (abbr of **British Medical Association**) n the BMA an organization that aims to protect the rights of British doctors.

BMus (abbr of **Bachelor of Music**) n a degree in music; a person who has this degree.

BMX (abbr of **bicycle motorcross**) n a type of

bicycle with a strong frame and small wheels that can be used on rough ground.

BO *n abbr of* body odor.

boa constrictor [ˈbouəkənstrɪktəʳ] *n* a large South American snake that kills animals or people by crushing them.

Boadicea [ˌbouədɪˈsiːə] = **Boudicca**.

boar [bɔːʳ] *n* -1. a male pig kept on a farm. -2. a wild pig that has tusks and a thick coat.

board [bɔːʳd] ◇ *n* -1. CONSTRUCTION a long flat piece of hard material, usually wood, that is used to make floors, stages etc □ *The floor was made of wooden boards.* -2. [on a wall] a flat rectangular piece of hard material used for displaying messages, announcements etc □ *a notice board.* -3. [for games] a flat piece of wood, cardboard, or plastic that has been marked specially so that a particular game can be played on it □ *a chess board.* -4. [in a school, classroom] = **blackboard.** -5. [of a company, school] a group of people who control an organization or a particular activity □ *the board of inquiry* □ *a meeting of the board* □ *The proposal was put before the board.* ■ **the board of directors** the committee of directors that controls a company. -6. [at a hotel, guesthouse] **room and board** US, **board and lodging** meals and accommodation. ■ **full/half board** accommodation and all meals/breakfast and one other meal per day. -7. *phrases* **to go by the board** [plan, arrangement] to be abandoned because it is no longer possible □ *Any hopes we had of meeting the minister just went by the board.* ■ **to sweep the board** [in an election, competition] to win everything □ *The Cubans swept the board at this week's athletics meeting.*
◇ *vt* [ship, plane, bus] to get on a <vehicle> □ *I boarded the plane at Houston.* ◇ *vi* [plane] to take passengers on board □ *Flight BA 851 to Amsterdam is now boarding at Gate 12.*
◆ **on board** ◇ *adj* on a ship, plane, train etc □ *The bus crashed with 76 passengers on board.* ◇ *adv*: *I got* OR *went on board.* ■ **to take sthg on board** GB [fact, advice] to accept sthg and take it into account □ *I don't think she's quite taken on board the fact that we're in the middle of a crisis here.*
◆ **board up** *vt sep* **to board sthg up** [window, door] to cover sthg with boards.

boarder [ˈbɔːʳdəʳ] *n* -1. [in a house] somebody who pays for meals and a room in another person's house. -2. EDUCATION a pupil who lives at school during the school terms.

board game *n* a game played on a board, e.g. chess or backgammon.

boarding card [ˈbɔːʳdɪŋ-] *n* GB = **boarding pass.**

boarding house *n* a private house that offers meals and rooms for money.

boarding pass *n* US a card that is given to passengers when they check in and that must be shown when they board their plane, ship etc.

boarding school *n* a school where pupils live during the school terms.

board meeting *n* a meeting of the members of a board, e.g. the directors of a company or the governors of a school.

boardroom [ˈbɔːʳdruːm] *n* the room where the board of directors of a company holds its meetings; the board of directors who meet in this room □ *a boardroom takeover/row* □ *boardroom talks.*

boardwalk [ˈbɔːʳdwɔːk] *n* US a footpath made of wooden boards along a beach, harbor etc.

boast [boust] ◇ *vi* to talk with too much pride about the things one has, can do etc in order to make other people admire or envy one □ *He's always boasting about some new gadget he's bought.* □ *I don't mean to boast, but it was my idea in the first place.* ◇ *vt* to have <sthg that one is proud of> □ *The town boasts an excellent conference center.* ◇ *n* something one says when boasting □ *It's our proud boast that we have never lost a client.*

boastful [ˈboustfl] *adj* [person] who often boasts; who is boasting □ *boastful words.*

boat [bout] *n* a vehicle with a sail, an engine, or oars that is used for traveling across water; a ship □ *The goods were sent by boat.* ■ **to rock the boat** to cause problems by trying to change things at a time when everything is calm and pleasant because everybody agrees on something. ■ **to be in the same boat** to be in the same unpleasant or difficult situation as somebody else □ *We're all in the same boat.*

boater [ˈboutəʳ] *n* a hard straw hat with a flat top □ *a straw boater.*

boating [ˈboutɪŋ] *n* sailing in small boats for pleasure □ *a boating trip/holiday.*

boat people *npl* refugees, especially from Vietnam, who try to escape from their country by boat.

boatswain [ˈbousn] *n* an officer on a ship whose job is to keep the ship and its equipment in good condition.

boat train *n* a train that travels to or from a ship in a port.

bob [bɒb] (*pt* & *pp* **bobbed,** *cont* **bobbing**) ◇ *n* a woman's hairstyle in which the hair is cut to the same length at the back and sides at about the same level as her chin □ *She wears her hair in a bob.* ◇ *vi* [boat, ship] to move up and down gently on the water.

bobbin [ˈbɒbɪn] *n* a small tube which thread is wound around for sewing.

bobble [ˈbɒbl] *n* a small ball of material, used as a decoration on cushions, clothes, hats etc.

bobby [ˈbɒbɪ] (*pl* **bobbies**) *n* GB a policeman (informal and old-fashioned use).

bobby pin *n* US a pin used to hold hair in position.

bobby socks, bobby sox [-sɒks] *npl* US socks that reach just above the ankle and are worn by girls.

bobsled [ˈbɒbsled], **bobsleigh** [ˈbɒbsleɪ] *n* a sled for racing downhill on ice.

Boccaccio [US bouˈkɑːtʃiou, GB bɒ-], **Giovanni** (1313–1375) an Italian writer whose major work is the *Decameron*, a collection of stories that influenced Chaucer and Shakespeare.

bode [bəʊd] *vi* **to bode well** to be a sign that something good is going to happen □ *This doesn't bode well for us.*

bodice ['bɒdɪs] *n* the part of a dress above the waist, without the sleeves.

bodily ['bɒdəlɪ] ◇ *adj* [need, harm] that is connected with one's body. ■ **bodily functions** the act of passing urine or excrement from one's body (polite use). ◇ *adv* [lift, carry, move] by taking hold of somebody's whole body □ *He was so drunk we had to carry him bodily to his room.*

body ['bɒdɪ] (*pl* **bodies**) *n* **-1.** [of a person, animal] the whole of a person or animal, including all its parts; the main or central part of a person or animal, but not the head, arms, or legs □ *I believe in taking care of my body.* □ *She's got a fantastic body!* ■ **to keep body and soul together** to earn enough money to buy the things one needs to live. **-2.** [of a man, woman] a dead person □ *the body of a young boy* □ *There were dead bodies lying in the street.* ■ **over my dead body!** an expression used to show that one very strongly opposes something that somebody has said or asked □ *"I want to marry your daughter." — "Over my dead body!"* **-3.** [of people] a group of people who work together and are usually in charge of something □ *a legislative/governing body.* **-4.** [of a car, plane, ship] the main part of a vehicle, excluding the engine, wheels, wings etc. **-5.** [of a wine] a strong rich taste. **-6. to have body** [hair] to be thick and healthy and keep its shape □ *My hair's lost all its body.* **-7.** GB = **body suit**.

body bag *n* a bag that is used for carrying a dead person away from a place.

body building *n* the activity of doing special exercises to make one's muscles bigger.

bodyguard ['bɒdɪgɑːʳd] *n* a person or group of people whose job is to protect an important person, especially in public.

body language *n* ways of sitting, standing, or moving that tell other people how one is feeling □ *I could tell from his body language that Tony was feeling defensive.*

body odor *n* the unpleasant smell of sweat that comes from a person's body.

body search *n* a search of a person's body and clothes made by police, customs, or security guards to check for hidden weapons, drugs etc.

body shop *n* **-1.** AUTO a place where the bodywork of cars is repaired.

body stocking *n* a close-fitting piece of clothing, often worn by dancers, that covers a person's whole body including their arms and legs.

body suit *n* US a close-fitting piece of clothing for women that covers the body from the shoulders to the top of the legs.

bodywork ['bɒdɪwɜːʳk] *n* the outside part of a car, bus etc without the wheels □ *The bodywork is still in very good condition.*

bog [bɒg] *n* an area of soft wet ground.

bogey ['bəʊgɪ] *n* in golf, a score for a hole of one stroke more than the standard score.

bogeyman ['bəʊgɪmæn] *n* an imaginary person often used by parents to frighten children.

bogged down [,bɒgd-] *adj* **to be/get bogged down** [person] to be/become unable to make any progress with a problem, piece of work etc; [car, vehicle] to be/become unable to move because its wheels have sunk into the ground □ *We got completely bogged down in paperwork.* □ *The trucks were bogged down in the mud.*

boggle ['bɒgl] *vi* **it boggles my mind!** US, **the mind boggles!** GB a phrase used when one finds something very strange and difficult to understand or imagine.

boggy ['bɒgɪ] (*compar* **boggier**, *superl* **boggiest**) *adj* [ground] soft and wet □ *boggy ground.*

bogus ['bəʊgəs] *adj* [identity, claim, charm] false.

bohemian [bəʊ'hiːmjən] ◇ *adj* [family, lifestyle] unconventional in a way that is associated with artists. ◇ *n* a person with a bohemian lifestyle.

boil [bɔɪl] ◇ *vi* **-1.** [liquid] to form bubbles and change into vapor by being heated. □ *The water's boiling.* **-2.** [kettle, pan] to contain liquid that is boiling □ *The kettle's boiling!* ◇ *vt* **-1.** [water, milk] to heat <a liquid> until it boils. **-2.** [pan, kettle] to heat <a container> until the contents boil. ◇ *n* **-1.** MEDICINE a painful infected swelling under one's skin. **-2.** COOKING **to bring sthg to the boil** [milk, water] to heat sthg until it boils. ■ **to come to the boil** [milk, water] to start to boil.

◆ **boil away** *vi* [liquid] to be reduced to nothing by boiling □ *The sauce had nearly boiled away.*

◆ **boil down to** *vt fus* **it boils down to this** it is really about this; it really means this □ *In the end it all boils down to money.* □ *What it boils down to is this: either he goes, or I do.*

◆ **boil over** *vi* **-1.** COOKING [soup, milk] to boil and flow over the sides of a pan, dish etc. **-2.** [situation, anger, tension] to get out of control, especially in a violent way □ *The quarrel boiled over into a full-scale brawl.*

boiled ['bɔɪld] *adj* [rice, potato, fish] that has been cooked in boiling water. ■ **a boiled egg** an egg that is cooked in its shell in boiling water until the white part is solid.

boiler ['bɔɪləʳ] *n* a container in which water is heated, e.g. to supply a central heating system.

boiler suit *n* GB a piece of clothing that consists of trousers and top in one piece and is worn over ordinary clothes to keep them clean when one is doing dirty work.

boiling ['bɔɪlɪŋ] ◇ *adj* **-1.** [water, oil] that is making bubbles because it has been heated to boiling point. **-2.** [person, weather, room] very hot □ *It's boiling in here.* **-3. to be boiling** to be very angry □ *She was boiling with rage.*

◇ *adv* **boiling hot** very hot □ *It's boiling hot to-day.*

boiling point *n* the temperature at which a liquid boils.

boisterous ['bɔɪstərəs] *adj* [child, puppy] that is noisy and full of energy, especially in an annoying way.

bold [bəʊld] *adj* **-1.** [person, plan, action] that is brave and confident □ *It was a bold move on her part.* **-2.** [line, pattern, color] that is clear and easy to see □ *a dress with a bold floral motif.* **-3. bold type** OR **print** letters that are printed in thick dark ink.

boldly ['bəʊldlɪ] *adv* **-1.** [decide, act] bravely and confidently □ *They boldly went ahead despite the danger.* **-2.** [stand out] clearly and distinctly □ *a boldly-patterned dress.*

Boleyn [bə'lɪn], **Anne** (1504–1536) Queen of England from 1533 to 1536. The second wife of Henry VIII, she was accused of adultery and executed.

Bolivia [bə'lɪvɪə] a country in western South America, that consists of the Andes in the west and the Amazon forest in the east. SIZE: 1,100,000 sq kms. POPULATION: 8,000,000 (*Bolivians*). CAPITAL: Sucre. ADMINISTRATIVE CAPITAL: La Paz. LANGUAGE: Spanish. CURRENCY: boliviano.

bollard [US 'bɒlrd, GB -aːd] *n* GB a short thick post made of concrete or metal that is used to stop vehicles entering a particular area.

bollocks▽ ['bɒləks] GB (very informal use) ◇ *npl* testicles. ◇ *excl* a word used by somebody to show they do not agree with something.

Bolshevik [US 'bəʊlʃəvɪk, GB 'bɒlʃ-] *n* **-1.** a member or supporter of the party led by Lenin which founded and ruled the USSR after the Russian Revolution of 1917 □ *the Bolshevik revolution.* **-2.** a Communist.

bolster ['bəʊlstər] ◇ *vt* = **bolster up.** ◇ *n* a long firm pillow in the shape of a tube that is usually placed underneath other pillows.

◆ **bolster up** *vt sep* **to bolster sthg up** [case, somebody's position, confidence] to support or increase sthg in order to improve it or make it stronger □ *We're recruiting some experienced people to bolster up our sales force.*

bolt [bəʊlt] ◇ *n* **-1.** [on a door, window] a metal bar or rod that slides into a socket attached to the frame in order to lock it. **-2.** a metal rod similar to a screw, but with flat ends, that is used with a nut to fasten things together.
◇ *adv* **bolt upright** completely vertical, stiff, and straight □ *She was sitting bolt upright in her chair.*
◇ *vt* **-1.** to fasten <an object> to something else with a bolt □ *The chairs were bolted to the floor.* **-2.** [door, window] to lock <sthg> with a bolt □ *All the doors were bolted.* **-3.** = **bolt down.**
◇ *vi* **-1.** [person] to run somewhere very fast, often in order to escape from somebody or something □ *He bolted along the corridor/up the stairs.* **-2.** [horse] to start moving fast suddenly, in a way that is difficult to control.

◆ **bolt down** *vt sep* **to bolt down food** to eat food very quickly □ *I bolted down my lunch.*

bomb [bɒm] ◇ *n* a container filled with explosives that is used as a weapon □ *a car bomb* □ *a bomb attack/scare.* ◇ *vt* [building, city] to attack <a place> with a bomb or bombs □ *The town had been heavily bombed.* ◇ *vi* [play, idea] to be unsuccessful.

bombard [bɒm'baːrd] *vt* **-1.** MILITARY [city, position] to attack <a place> with gunfire or bombs. **-2. to bombard sb with sthg** [with mail, criticism] to give or send a lot of sthg to sb, often in a hostile way □ *I was bombarded with questions.*

bombardment [bɒm'baːrdmənt] *n*: *see* **bombard** □ *an aerial bombardment.*

bombastic [bɒm'bæstɪk] *adj* [person, speech] that uses long complicated words in order to sound important.

Bombay [bɒm'beɪ] a port on the west coast of India. It is India's largest city. POPULATION: 12,571,720.

bomb disposal *n* GB the act of making an unexploded bomb safe □ *a bomb-disposal squad/expert.*

bomber ['bɒmər] *n* **-1.** MILITARY an aircraft that drops bombs. **-2.** a person who puts a bomb in a place in order to cause injury, damage etc.

bomber jacket *n* a short jacket, often made of leather, that fits tightly at the waist.

bombing ['bɒmɪŋ] *n* the act of attacking a place with a bomb or bombs □ *The city has been the target of a wave of bombings.* □ *a bombing raid.*

bombproof ['bɒmpruːf] *adj* [building, shelter] that is strong enough not to be destroyed by a bomb attack.

bombshell ['bɒmʃel] *n* a piece of shocking unexpected news □ *His resignation came as a complete bombshell.*

bombsite ['bɒmsaɪt] *n* an empty space in a town where the buildings have been destroyed by a bomb.

bona fide [ˌbəʊnə'faɪdɪ] *adj* [offer, contract, customer] that is genuine and can be taken seriously.

bonanza [bə'nænzə] *n* a time or situation in which very high profits are made or people suddenly become very rich □ *It's the usual pre-Chrismas bonanza for the big stores.*

bond [bɒnd] ◇ *n* **-1.** [between people] a relationship, feeling, or shared interest that brings people or groups closely together □ *the bond of friendship/trust.* **-2.** FINANCE a certificate from a government, municipality, company etc that promises to repay borrowed money at a fixed rate of interest. **-3.** AUS [for rent] an amount of money paid as a deposit, especially for rented accommodation. ◇ *vt* to join together <two things> with glue □ *The wood is bonded to the metal with a special glue.* ◇ *vi* **-1.** [materials, surfaces] to stick together very firmly □ *These two materials do not bond (together) well.* **-2.** [people] to form a close relationship □ *The child has difficulty bonding with others.*

Bond [bɒnd], **James** a character in a series of novels by Ian Fleming, later made into movies. He is a British secret agent who has many adventures in exotic places.

bondage ['bɒndɪdʒ] *n* the state of being kept as a slave (literary use) □ *The prisoners were released from bondage.*

bonded warehouse ['bɒndəd-] *n* an official storage place where goods are kept until customs duty has been paid on them.

Bondi Beach ['bɒndaɪ-] a beach in Sydney, Australia that is very popular for surfing and sunbathing.

bone [bəʊn] ◇ *n* -1. ANATOMY one of the pieces of hard white material that form the skeleton of a human or an animal □ *I broke a bone in my hand.* □ *a fish bone.* -2. [for making tools, ornaments] the substance from which the skeleton of a human or animal is made □ *a handle made out of bone* □ *a bone carving.* -3. *phrases* **a bone of contention** something that is the cause of an argument. ■ **to feel sthg in one's bones** to be sure about sthg without being able to explain or show why □ *Something's not right, I can feel it in my bones.* ■ **to make no bones about sthg** to show no hesitation or doubt when one says sthg □ *I don't approve of their policies, and I make no bones about it.* ◇ *vt* to remove the bone or bones from <fish or meat>.

bone china *n* thin china made of clay mixed with powdered bones.

bone-dry *adj* completely dry.

boneless ['bəʊnləs] *adj* [fish, chicken] that has had the bones removed.

bone marrow *n* the soft substance in the center of a bone.

bonfire ['bɒnfaɪəʳ] *n* a large fire outdoors that is built to burn trash on or as part of a celebration.

Bonfire Night *n* November 5, the anniversary of Guy Fawkes' attempt to blow up the British Parliament in 1605. In Britain, people traditionally have firework displays and bonfires with a guy on top.

🕯 BONFIRE NIGHT
November 5 is the anniversary of Guy Fawkes' failed attempt to blow up the British Parliament in 1605. It is not an official holiday in Britain, but the evening is celebrated all over the country. Large towns have public firework displays, and many people have their own bonfires and firework parties. A model of a man representing Guy Fawkes, called a "guy", is burned on bonfires. Groups of children make their own guys in early November and display them on the street, asking passers-by for "a penny for the guy."

bongo ['bɒŋgəʊ] (*pl* **bongos** OR **bongoes**) *n* a **bongo (drum)** one of two small connected drums that one hits with one's hands.

Bonn [bɒn] a city in western Germany that was the capital of West Germany from 1949 to 1990. POPULATION: 287,117.

bonnet ['bɒnət] *n* -1. CLOTHING a hat that is worn by a woman or a baby and is tied under the chin. -2. GB AUTO a metal lid at the front of a car that usually covers the engine.

Bonnie and Clyde [ˌbɒnɪənd'klaɪd] the nicknames of Bonnie Parker (1911–1934) and Clyde Barrow (1909–1934), two US criminals who committed many robberies and murders.

Bonnie Prince Charlie [ˌbɒnɪprɪns'tʃɑːˈlɪ] (1720–1788) a Scottish prince, Charles Edward Stuart, who claimed he had a right to be the British king. He led a rebellion in Scotland, but was defeated by English forces and escaped to France.

bonsai [US ˌbɒn'saɪ, GB 'bɒnsaɪ] (*pl* **bonsai**) *n* a tree or shrub that is grown in a small pot and prevented from growing to its normal size.

bonus ['bəʊnəs] (*pl* **bonuses**) *n* -1. an extra amount of money received in addition to one's normal pay □ *We got a bonus for finishing ahead of schedule.* -2. an additional pleasure or advantage □ *It was a real bonus that you were able to come with me.*

bonus issue *n* GB FINANCE a free issue of extra shares to people who already own some.

bony ['bəʊnɪ] (*compar* **bonier**, *superl* **boniest**) *adj* -1. [person, hand, face] that is so thin that the bones can be seen. -2. [fish, meat] that is full of bones.

boo [buː] (*pl* **boos**) ◇ *excl* a sudden loud sound made to surprise or frighten somebody. ◇ *n* a long shout used to express disapproval, usually of a speaker or performer □ *The announcement was greeted with boos from the audience.* ◇ *vt* [speaker, performance, decision] to express one's disapproval of <sb/sthg> by shouting the word "boo". ◇ *vi* [audience] *Whenever he came on stage, everyone booed.*

boobs [buːbz] *npl* a woman's breasts (informal use).

boob tube *n* US **the boob tube** the television (informal and humorous use).

booby prize ['buːbɪ-] *n* a prize that is given as a joke to the person who comes last in a race or competition.

booby trap *n* -1. a hidden bomb. -2. a harmless trap for somebody that is intended as a practical joke.

◆ **booby-trap** *vt* [building, car] to place a hidden bomb inside <sthg>.

book [bʊk] ◇ *n* -1. [for reading] a number of pages fastened together at one end and fixed inside a cover of stronger paper, cardboard, or plastic, to be used for writing in or reading □ *a book about* OR *on space travel* □ *a history/science/gardening book* □ *a book of essays/short stories.* ■ **to do sthg by the book** to do sthg according to the rules. ■ **to throw the book at sb** to use every possible rule, law etc in order to charge or punish sb as severely as possible. -2. [of checks, tickets, matches] a number of things fastened together at one end and fixed inside a cover.

◇ vt **-1.** [ticket, room, seat] to arrange in advance to have <sthg> available for oneself or somebody else on a particular occasion □ *I'd like to book a table for seven (people).* □ *I've booked you on an early flight.* ■ **to be fully booked** [restaurant, hotel] to have no tables, rooms etc available because they have all been reserved. **-2.** [performer, speaker] to arrange in advance for <sb> to appear on a particular occasion □ *We've booked a band for the evening.* **-3.** [driver] to take the name, address etc of <sb who has committed an offense> in order to charge them □ *I was booked for dangerous driving.* **-4.** GB SOCCER to take the name of <a player>, e.g. because of a serious foul, so that there is a record of it. ◇ vi to book a ticket, room, seat etc □ *Book early to avoid disappointment.*

◆ **books** *npl* BUSINESS the accounts or financial records of a company or organization. ■ **to do the books** to keep or check the accounts. ■ **to be in sb's good/bad books** to be liked/disliked by sb because of something one has done.

◆ **book in** GB ◇ vt sep **to book sb in** [guest] to reserve a room for sb at a hotel. ◇ vi [guest] to report one's arrival at a hotel □ *Mrs White booked in this morning.*

◆ **book up** vt sep **to be booked up** [restaurant, theater, hotel] to have no tables, seats, rooms etc available because they have all been reserved □ *We are booked up until the end of August.*

book bag *n* US = **booksack.**

bookbinding ['bʊkbaɪndɪŋ] *n* the work or art of fastening the pages of books together and putting covers on them.

bookcase ['bʊkkeɪs] *n* a piece of furniture with shelves for keeping books on.

book club *n* a club that sells books to its members at reduced prices, usually by mail order.

bookends ['bʊkendz] *npl* a pair of supports placed at either end of a row of books to hold them upright.

Booker Prize ['bʊkə-] *n* **the Booker Prize** an important British literary prize, given every year for the best novel by a writer from Britain or the British Commonwealth.

bookie ['bʊkɪ] *n* a bookmaker.

booking ['bʊkɪŋ] *n* GB **-1.** [for a seat, room] an arrangement for something to be available to use at a particular time, e.g. a hotel room or theater seat □ *I'd like to make a booking in the name of Stevens.* **-2.** SPORT in soccer, the act of taking a player's name and keeping a record of it because they have broken a rule of the game □ *One more booking and he'll be sent off.*

booking clerk *n* GB a person who works in a booking office.

booking office *n* GB an office, especially at a train or bus station or a theater, where tickets are sold and reservations can be made.

bookish ['bʊkɪʃ] *adj* [person] who likes reading and studying; whose knowledge comes from books rather than from life.

bookkeeper ['bʊkkiːpə-] *n* a person whose job is to keep a record of the money spent and received by a business.

bookkeeping ['bʊkkiːpɪŋ] *n* the work of a bookkeeper.

booklet ['bʊklət] *n* a small book, usually in a soft cover, that gives information about something.

bookmaker ['bʊkmeɪkə-] *n* a person whose job is to accept bets on a race, competition etc and to pay money to winners.

bookmark ['bʊkmɑːrk] *n* a piece of leather, card, or plastic that is put between the pages of a book so that the reader can find the page again easily.

booksack ['bʊksæk] *n* US a bag used by schoolchildren for carrying their books, pens etc.

bookseller ['bʊkselə-] *n* a person whose job is to sell books.

bookshelf ['bʊkʃelf] (*pl* **bookshelves**) *n* a shelf for keeping books on.

bookshop ['bʊkʃɒp] *n* = **bookstore.**

bookstall ['bʊkstɔːl] *n* GB a stand or kiosk that sells books, newspapers, magazines etc.

bookstore ['bʊkstɔːr] *n* US a shop that sells books.

book token *n* GB a card that contains a voucher which is bought as a present or prize and can be used to buy a book.

bookworm ['bʊkwɜːrm] *n* a person who spends a lot of time reading (humorous use).

boom [buːm] ◇ *n* **-1.** [of thunder, guns] a loud deep sound, like that of thunder, that lasts for a few seconds □ *the distant boom of artillery fire.* **-2.** [in sales, a market, the economy] a fast growth or increase in something such as the economy or population □ *There's been a boom in tourism and leisure.* □ *the boom which followed the recession* □ *an economic boom* □ *a population boom* □ *The video craze was enjoying a boom period.* **-3.** SAILING [of a boat] a long pole which the bottom of a sail is attached to. **-4.** [for a microphone, camera] a long pole which a microphone or camera is attached to. ◇ *vi* **-1. to boom (out)** [gun, thunder] to make a boom □ *The teacher's voice boomed out.* **-2. to be booming** [business, economy] to be very successful □ *Sales are booming.*

boomerang ['buːməræŋ] *n* a curved stick that was first used by Australian Aborigines for hunting and that returns to the person who throws it.

boon [buːn] *n* something that is very helpful or useful □ *My new dishwasher is a real boon.*

Boone [buːn], **Daniel** (1735–1820) a US pioneer who explored Kentucky and became a national hero.

boor [bʊər] *n* a boorish person.

boorish ['bʊərɪʃ] *adj* [person, behavior] that seems rude, unpleasant, and insensitive.

boost [buːst] ◇ *n* **-1.** [to profits, production, popularity] a sudden large increase in something □ *Productivity needs a boost if we want to achieve our target for the year.* **-2.** [to spirits, morale] an improvement in something that comes from encouragement □ *Winning the competition gave my confidence a much-needed boost.* ◇ *vt* **-1.** [profits, production, speed] to increase <sthg> by a sudden large amount or degree. **-2.** [confidence, morale, spirits] to improve <sthg> by giving encouragement.

booster ['bu:stə^r] *n* MEDICINE an extra injection of a vaccine that is given some time after the first one in order to make sure that it remains effective □ *a booster jab.*

booster seat *n* a padded support fitted onto a car seat to enable a child to travel more safely and comfortably.

boot [bu:t] ◇ *n* **-1.** CLOTHING a heavy shoe that reaches above one's ankle and is worn to protect one's feet, e.g. from bad weather or rough ground; a lighter shoe of similar shape and length that is worn as a fashion item □ *a pair of boots.* **-2.** GB SPORT a special strong shoe that is worn when playing some sports □ *football/rugby boots.* **-3.** GB AUTO [of a car] an enclosed space at the back of a car for carrying luggage. ◇ *vt* **-1.** to kick <sthg> (informal use). **-2.** COMPUTING to start <a computer>.

◆ **to boot** *adv* as well (old-fashioned or humorous use) □ *She's a first-class manager and a gifted linguist to boot.*

◆ **boot out** *vt sep* **to boot sb out** to force sb to leave a job, organization, event etc (informal use) □ *He was booted out of the club for violent behavior.*

◆ **boot up** *vi* [computer] to start working by loading the operating instructions.

boot camp *n* a training camp for people who have just joined the US armed forces.

booth [bu:ð] *n* **-1.** [at a fair] a tent or stall where items are sold or entertainment is offered. **-2.** [in a restaurant] a small enclosed or partly enclosed space that is reserved for a particular activity □ *a voting booth* □ *'Please go to the next booth.'*

Booth [bu:ð], **John Wilkes** (1839–1865) a US actor and Confederate supporter who killed President Lincoln.

bootleg ['bu:tleg] *adj* **bootleg whiskey/a bootleg recording etc** whiskey/a recording etc that is made and sold illegally.

bootlegger ['bu:tlegə^r] *n* a person who makes and sells something illegally, especially alcohol or recordings.

booty ['bu:tɪ] *n* valuable objects taken from a defeated enemy or stolen by pirates, robbers etc.

booze [bu:z] (informal use) ◇ *n* alcohol. ◇ *vi* to drink alcohol, especially a large amount.

border ['bɔ:^rdə^r] ◇ *n* **-1.** [of a country] a line separating the territory of two different countries □ *They crossed the border into India.* □ *the Swiss-Italian border* □ *the Belgian/German border* □ *a border guard/post/town* □ *a border dispute.* **-2.** [of a dress, plate] a strip, band, pat-

tern etc along or around the edge of something □ *white with a red border.* **-3.** [of a lake, field] the edge of something. **-4.** [of a garden, path] a narrow flowerbed along the edge of a garden or path. ◇ *vt* **-1.** to have the same border as <a particular country> □ *Gambia is bordered on three sides by Senegal.* **-2.** [plate, lake, garden] to form the edge of <sthg> □ *a field bordered by trees.*

◆ **Borders: the Borders** a part of southern Scotland close to the border with England, known for its attractive scenery.

◆ **border on** *vt fus* **to border on sthg** to be almost the same as sthg □ *Their support bordered on fanaticism.*

Border collie *n* a dog with a black-and-white coat that is used as a sheepdog.

borderline ['bɔ:^rdə^rlaɪn] ◇ *adj* that is close to the dividing line between two states or categories and so could be in one or the other □ *a borderline pass/failure* □ *He's very much a borderline case.* ◇ *n* **-1.** the dividing line between two different states or categories □ *It's on the borderline between good taste and bad taste.* **-2.** a border between two countries.

bore [bɔ:^r] ◇ *past tense of* **bear**. ◇ *n* **-1.** a person, task etc that one finds boring □ *Office parties can be such a bore.* **-2.** [of a hole, tube] the diameter of the inside of something, especially of the barrel of a gun □ *a twelve-bore shotgun.* ◇ *vt* **-1.** to make <sb> feel bored □ *Am I boring you?* ■ **to bore sb stiff** OR **to tears** OR **to death** to make sb feel very bored □ *They bored us all to death with their holiday photos.* **-2.** to drill <a hole> in something.

bored [bɔ:^rd] *adj* [person] who is tired, impatient, or irritable because they have lost interest or because they have nothing to do □ *I'm bored with my work/colleagues.*

boredom ['bɔ:^rdəm] *n* the state of being bored □ *He got involved in crime out of sheer boredom.*

boring ['bɔ:rɪŋ] *adj* [person, job] that is dull and uninteresting □ *It gets kind of boring when you hear the same story over and over again.*

born [bɔ:^rn] *adj* **-1. to be born** [baby] to come out of one's mother's body □ *I was born in 1965.* □ *She was born blind.* ■ **born and bred** as a result of where one was born, or the kind of family one belongs to □ *He's a Californian/a Baptist born and bred.* **-2. a born cook/leader etc** a very good cook/leader etc.

born-again *adj* **a born-again Christian** a person who has joined a Christian church which believes that everything in the Bible is completely true.

borne [bɔ:^rn] *past participle of* **bear**.

Borneo ['bɔ:^rnɪoʊ] a large island in the western Pacific, divided between Malaysia and Brunei in the north, and Indonesia in the south.

borough [US 'bɜ:roʊ, GB 'bʌrə] *n* a town or a district of a large city that has certain powers of local government.

borough council *n* the organization responsible for local government in a borough.

borrow ['bɒroʊ] *vt* to take or use <sthg that

belongs to somebody else> for a period of time with their permission □ *I had to borrow $100 from my sister to pay the bill.*

borrower ['bɒrouəʳ] *n* a person who borrows money.

borrowing ['bɒrouɪŋ] *n* the amount of money that an organization borrows □ *government borrowing from banks.*

borstal ['bɔːrstl] *n* GB a place where young offenders are sent when they are too young to go to prison (old-fashioned use).

Bosnia ['bɒznɪə] = Bosnia-Herzegovina.

Bosnia-Herzegovina [US -,hertsəgə'viːnə, GB -,hɜːts-] a country in southeastern Europe, between Croatia, Serbia, and Montenegro. After a civil war, which ended in 1995, it was divided into two parts, the Federation of Bosnia-Herzegovina and the Republika Srpska.

Bosnian ['bɒznɪən] *adj* & *n*: see **Bosnia-Herzegovina**.

bosom ['buzəm] *n* -1. [of a woman] a woman's breasts (old-fashioned use). -2. **to be in the bosom of sthg** [of a family, community, organization] to be with the other members of sthg so that one feels safe and accepted □ *She's back in the bosom of the family now.* ■ **a bosom friend** a very close friend.

Bosporus ['bɒspərəs], **Bosphorus** ['bɒsfərəs]: **the Bosporus** the channel of water between European and Asian Turkey.

boss [bɒs] ◇ *n* [of a company, department, family] the person who is in charge in a business, group of people etc □ *All right, you're the boss, we'll do it your way.* □ *media bosses.* ■ **to be one's own boss** to be self-employed; to be free to make one's own decisions, do as one likes etc. ◇ *vt* = boss about.

◆ **boss about**, **boss around** *vt sep* to boss sb about OR around to give orders to sb in a way that suggests one is in a position of authority (disapproving use) □ *Don't let the senior members boss you around.*

bossy ['bɒsɪ] (*compar* **bossier**, *superl* **bossiest**) *adj* [person] who likes taking control and giving orders (disapproving use).

Boston ['bɒstən] a city and port in the northeastern USA. POPULATION: 574,283.

Boston Tea Party *n* **the Boston Tea Party** a protest in 1773 by colonists in Boston, Massachusetts, which led to the American Revolution. The colonists threw a cargo of tea into the harbor because they felt it was unfair that they had to pay tax to the British on tea.

bosun ['bousn] *n* = boatswain.

botanic(al) [bə'tænɪk(l)] *adj* [drawing, science, book] that is connected with plants.

botanical garden *n* a garden in which plants that are rare, exotic, or interesting to scientists are grown and displayed.

botanist ['bɒtənəst] *n* a person who studies plants.

botany ['bɒtənɪ] *n* the part of biology concerned with the scientific study of plants.

botch [bɒtʃ] (informal use) *vt* to do <sthg> badly.

◆ **botch up** *vt sep* to botch sthg up to botch sthg.

Botany Bay a bay in New South Wales, Australia, where the British captain, James Cook, first landed.

both [bouθ] ◇ *det* & *predet* **both (the) houses** the two houses that are being discussed □ *Both her parents are French.* □ *Answer both (the) questions.* ◇ *pron* **I like both (of them)** I like the two people, things etc being considered □ *We both* OR *Both of us left.* □ *They were both unhappy.*

◆ **both...and...** *conj* as well as □ *Both my brother and I will be there.* □ *She is both smart and hard-working.*

bother ['bɒðəʳ] ◇ *vt* -1. to upset <sb> slightly □ *Does it bother you that I've been married before?* ■ **I/she etc can't be bothered to do it** GB I/she etc won't do it, because it would take too much time and effort □ *I wish I hadn't bothered to come.* -2. to cause <sb> to feel pain □ *My back is still bothering me.* -3. to annoy <sb> □ *It really bothers me that they haven't replied to our letters.* -4. to disturb <sb> □ *Does the noise bother you?* □ *I'm sorry to bother you, but could you help me?* □ *He keeps bothering me with technical questions.* ◇ *vi* to take time and effort to do something □ *"Shall I give you a receipt?" — "No, don't bother."* □ *He didn't bother to lock up.* □ *Don't bother asking for more money, you won't get any.* □ *He never bothers about what other people think.* ◇ *n* -1. trouble □ *It's no bother.* □ *I don't want to put you to* OR *cause you any bother.* -2. an annoying person or thing □ *I don't want to be a bother.*

bothered ['bɒðəʳd] *adj* **to be bothered** to be worried □ *I'm more bothered about how she must be feeling.*

Botswana [bɒt'swɑːnə] a country in southern Africa. SIZE: 570,000 sq kms. POPULATION: 1,300,000 (*Botswanans*). CAPITAL: Gaborone. LANGUAGE: English. CURRENCY: pula.

Botticelli [,bɒtə'tʃelɪ], **Sandro** (1444–1510) an Italian artist who was one of the earliest Renaissance painters. His works include *The Birth of Venus* and *Primavera*.

bottle ['bɒtl] ◇ *n* -1. a container for liquids, usually with a narrow part at the top and no handle, that is made of glass or plastic □ *a wine/beer bottle.* -2. [of water, wine] the amount contained in a bottle □ *We drank three bottles of wine.* -3. [for feeding babies] a small container used for feeding milk or other liquids to a baby. ◇ *vt* -1. to put drink into bottles. -2. to put <fruit> into sealed glass jars to preserve it.

◆ **bottle up** *vt sep* [anger, grief] to keep <one's feelings> inside one's mind and hidden from other people □ *His problem is that he bottles everything up.*

bottle bank *n* GB a large container for collecting glass to be recycled.

bottled ['bɒtld] *adj* **bottled water/beer etc** water/beer etc that is kept or sold in bottles.

■ **bottled gas** gas that is kept in metal containers that can be moved easily.

bottle-feed *vt* to feed <a baby> milk from a bottle rather than from its mother's breast.

bottleneck ['bɒtlnek] *n* -1. AUTO a narrow or obstructed section of a road that causes the flow of traffic to stop or become slow. -2. a part of a process, system, production line etc that is less efficient than other parts and causes delays □ *Lack of staff can create bottlenecks in processing paperwork.*

bottle-opener *n* a small tool for removing the caps from bottles.

bottle shop *n* AUS a liquor store.

bottom ['bɒtəm] ◇ *adj* -1. **the bottom floor/shelf/step etc** the lowest floor/shelf/step etc □ *The towels are in the bottom drawer.* -2. **to be bottom** [student] to get the lowest marks □ *I was always bottom in physics.*
◇ *n* -1. **the bottom** the lowest part of something □ *Could you sign it at the bottom?* □ *She was waiting at the bottom of the stairs.* -2. **the bottom** [of a garden, street, field] the part of something that is at the farthest end □ *We walked to the bottom of the road.* -3. **the bottom** [of a range, class, organization] the least successful or least important part of something □ *She started at the bottom and worked her way up.* -4. [of a person] the part of one's body on which one sits. -5. **to be at the bottom of sthg** to be the cause of sthg □ *Who's at the bottom of all this?* ■ **to get to the bottom of sthg** to discover the cause of or the truth about sthg □ *We haven't yet been able to get to the bottom of how the fire started.*

◆ **bottom out** *vi* [prices, recession] to reach the lowest point after a period of continuous decline.

bottomless ['bɒtəmləs] *adj* -1. [pit, well] that seems very deep. -2. [supply, fund] that seems to have no limit.

bottom line *n* **the bottom line** the most important factor, question, result etc □ *The bottom line is, will the product sell?*

botulism ['bɒtjʊlɪzm] *n* a serious type of food poisoning caused by eating canned or chilled food that has gone bad.

Boudicca [US buˈdɪkə, GB ˈbuːdɪkə] (died 61 AD) Queen of an ancient British people, who led a large army and defeated the Romans in several battles.

bough [baʊ] *n* a main branch of a tree.

bought [bɔːt] *past tense & past participle of* **buy**.

bouillon cube ['buːjɒn-] *n* US a small piece of dried meat and vegetable juices that is added to hot water to make a stock for cooking.

boulder ['bəʊldəʳ] *n* a big rock.

boulevard [US ˈbʊləvɑːrd, GB ˈbuːləvɑːd] *n* a wide street, often lined with trees, in a town.

bounce [baʊns] ◇ *vi* -1. [ball, object] to spring away again after hitting a surface □ *The ball bounced off a tree.* -2. [light, sound waves] to be reflected back from a surface □ *The radio sig-*nals bounce off the satellite. -3. **to bounce on sthg** [on a bed, sofa, trampoline] to jump up and down on sthg □ *The children were bouncing up and down on the bed.* -4. [person] to move energetically and in a lively happy way □ *She came bouncing into the room.* -5. [check] to be refused as payment by a bank, because there is not enough money in the account of the person who wrote it.
◇ *vt* -1. to make <a ball, stone> etc spring back off a surface □ *He bounced the ball off the wall.* ■ **to bounce ideas off sb** to tell sb one's ideas in order to get their opinion.
◇ *n* -1. [of a ball] the quality of bouncing well □ *The ball has lost its bounce.* -2. [of a person] liveliness □ *She's full of bounce.*

◆ **bounce back** *vi* to return quickly and successfully to one's former activities after an illness or setback □ *I'm amazed at the way Rose managed to bounce back after her illness.*

bouncer ['baʊnsəʳ] *n* a man employed by a nightclub, dance hall etc to prevent unwelcome people from entering.

bouncy ['baʊnsɪ] (*compar* **bouncier**, *superl* **bounciest**) *adj* -1. [person] who is lively and enthusiastic □ *She came in, all bouncy and ready to go.* -2. [ball] that bounces well □ *This ball's not very bouncy.*

bound [baʊnd] ◇ *past tense & past participle of* **bind**.
◇ *adj* -1. **to be bound to do sthg** [person, situation] to be certain to do sthg, especially because it is usual or expected □ *Interest rates are bound to go up again.* □ *Spending such long periods apart is bound to put a strain on a relationship.* □ *You're bound to feel anxious about the results.* -2. **to be bound to do sthg** [person] to have to do sthg for e.g. legal or moral reasons □ *They are bound by the treaty to take action.* □ *I feel bound to warn you of the possible pitfalls.* □ *I'm bound to say, I disagree.* -3. **to be bound for a place** [person, train, plane] to be traveling toward a place □ *on a plane bound for Tokyo.*
◇ *n* an energetic jump □ *With a single bound he was beside her.*
◇ *vt* **to be bounded by sthg** [by a river, wall] to have sthg as its boundary □ *a country bounded on two sides by the sea.*
◇ *vi* to run with energetic jumps □ *The dog bounded up to her.*

◆ **bounds** *npl* limits □ *It's not beyond/outside the bounds of possibility.* □ *We're trying to keep spending within bounds.* ■ **to be out of bounds** [area, building] to be a place that people are not allowed to enter □ *The castle gardens are out of bounds to visitors.*

◆ **bound up with** *prep* closely connected with <sb/sthg> □ *His feelings of insecurity are bound up with his fear of rejection.*

-bound *suffix* added to a word to mean traveling in a particular direction □ *northbound traffic.*

boundary ['baʊndrɪ] (*pl* **boundaries**) *n* -1. the line that divides one area of land from another □ *The river forms the boundary between the two farms.* -2. the limit of something, e.g. a science or area of knowledge □ *pushing back the boundaries of physics.*

boundless [ˈbaʊndləs] *adj* [energy, wealth] that has no limits □ *Such boundless optimism!*

bountiful [ˈbaʊntɪfl] *adj* [supply, harvest] large (literary use).

bounty [ˈbaʊntɪ] *n* generosity (literary use).

bouquet [boʊˈkeɪ] *n* -1. a bunch of flowers, specially arranged to be presented as a gift or held by a bride □ *She was presented with a bouquet of flowers.* -2. the pleasant smell of a wine or liqueur.

bouquet garni [-gɑːˈrniː] *n* a bunch of mixed herbs tied together and used in cooking.

bourbon [ˈbɜːrbən] *n* a type of American whiskey.

bourgeois [ˈbʊərˌʒwɑː] *adj* [person] who belongs to the bourgeoisie (disapproving use) □ *He's become so bourgeois since he got married.* □ *bourgeois attitudes.*

bourgeoisie [ˌbʊərˌʒwɑːˈziː] *n* **the bourgeoisie** the middle class, especially when considered to be politically conservative and too concerned with money and possessions (disapproving use).

bout [baʊt] *n* -1. [of illness] a short period of illness □ *a bout of the flu.* -2. [of activity] a short period of a particular activity □ *a bout of drinking/writing.* -3. SPORT a boxing or wrestling match.

boutique [buːˈtiːk] *n* a small store, especially one that sells fashionable clothes.

boutonniere [US ˌbuːtnˈɪr, GB bʊˌtɒnɪˈeə] *n* US a flower worn on the lapel of a jacket.

bow¹ [baʊ] ◇ *vt* to bend <one's head> forward □ *They bowed their heads in shame/prayer.* ◇ *vi* -1. to bend one's head and upper body forward, usually to show respect or gratitude □ *He bowed to her when the dance was over.* -2. **to bow to sthg** [to pressure, somebody's judgment, one's fate] to agree to accept sthg or to act according to sthg □ *I bow to your superior knowledge.* ◇ *n* -1. the act of bowing □ *The actors took several bows following the performance.* -2. the front part of a ship or boat.

◆ **bow down** *vi* to bow very low, usually as a sign of respect.

◆ **bow out** *vi* to leave a position or stop taking part in something □ *The company president is bowing out next year.*

bow² [boʊ] *n* -1. [for arrows] a weapon for shooting arrows that consists of a long, curved, flexible piece of wood with a string joining the two ends □ *a bow and arrow.* -2. MUSIC a long thin piece of wood with horsehair stretched along it, used for playing the violin, cello etc. -3. [in a ribbon] a knot with two loops, used for tying shoelaces, hair ribbons etc, and as decoration on packages □ *She tied the laces in a neat bow.*

bowels [ˈbaʊəlz] *npl* -1. the tubes below the stomach that carry waste food out of the body. -2. the deep, often mysterious, interior of e.g. a big building or machine □ *a cavern deep in the bowels of the earth.*

Bowery [ˈbaʊərɪ]: **the Bowery** an area in New York City known for its cheap hotels and bars.

bowl [boʊl] ◇ *n* -1. a deep round dish or container that curves upward at the sides and is open at the top □ *sugar/soup bowl.* -2. the amount of food or liquid contained in a bowl □ *a bowl of rice/soup.* -3. the part of a toilet or sink, or of a smoker's pipe, that is shaped like a bowl. ◇ *vt* CRICKET to throw <the ball> toward the batsman. ◇ *vi* CRICKET *He's bowling well today.*

◆ **bowls** *n* a game in which players roll big wooden balls across smooth grass toward a smaller ball. The aim is to get the large ball as close as possible to the small one □ *a game of bowls.*

◆ **bowl over** *vt sep* -1. **to bowl sb over** to knock sb down, usually by running into them. -2. **to be bowled over** to be very surprised, impressed, or pleased □ *I was completely bowled over by the news.*

bow-legged [US ˈboʊlegəd, GB ˌboʊˈlegəd] *adj* [person] who has legs that curve outwards at the knees.

bowler [ˈboʊlər] *n* -1. CRICKET a player who bowls. -2. **a bowler (hat)** a man's hat made of stiff black material with a rounded top and small brim.

bowling [ˈboʊlɪŋ] *n* an indoor game in which players roll a big heavy ball down a long strip, with the aim of knocking down as many skittles as possible at the other end.

bowling alley *n* -1. a building where the game of bowling is played. -2. the long narrow strip along which the ball is rolled in bowling.

bowling green *n* a smooth area of short grass for playing bowls.

bow tie [ˌboʊ-] *n* a tie that is tied in the shape of a bow and is worn by men, e.g. on formal occasions.

bow window [ˌboʊ-] *n* a curved window that sticks out from a straight wall.

box [bɒks] ◇ *n* -1. a container that has straight sides and often has a lid □ *a wooden/cardboard box* □ *a tool box.* -2. the amount that a box contains □ *We ate a whole box of chocolates.* -3. THEATER a small enclosed area with a few seats that is separated from the rest of the audience. -4. [on a form] a square or rectangular space on a form in which one has to write something □ *Put a cross in the appropriate box.* -5. **the box** the television (informal use) □ *What's on the box tonight?* -6. [plant] an evergreen tree with small dark leaves, often used to make hedges. ◇ *vi* to fight using one's fists, usually in a boxing match.

◆ **box in** *vt sep* -1. **to box a person/vehicle in** to surround a person/vehicle so that they cannot move any further or faster □ *The car was boxed in between two vans.* -2. **to box sthg in** [pipe, cable, machinery] to cover sthg by building a box around it.

boxed [bɒkst] *adj* that is sold in a box □ *a boxed set of Louis Armstrong records.*

boxer ['bɒksər] *n* -1. somebody who boxes as a sport or profession. -2. a large short-haired dog with a flat nose.

boxer shorts *npl* loose shorts worn as underwear by men.

boxing ['bɒksɪŋ] *n* a sport in which two men fight each other using their fists.

Boxing Day *n* December 26, a public holiday in Britain.

boxing gloves *npl* big padded gloves worn by boxers.

boxing ring *n* a square area with ropes around the sides, used for boxing matches.

box junction *n* GB an area at an intersection, marked with crossed yellow lines, that cars may not enter until their exit is clear.

box lunch *n* US a lunch that one prepares at home and takes to school, work etc in a lunchbox.

box number *n* a number used as a postal address □ *reply to Box no. 218.*

box office *n* the part of a theater or movie theater where tickets are sold.

boxroom ['bɒksruːm] *n* GB a small room in a house, usually used for storage.

boy [bɔɪ] ◇ *n* -1. a male child □ *when I was a boy.* -2. a young man □ *She met a really nice boy at the party.* -3. a son □ *We have two boys.* -4. **the boys** one's male friends (informal use) □ *He's out drinking with the boys.* ◇ *excl* **(oh) boy!** a phrase used to show excitement or admiration (informal use).

boycott ['bɔɪkɒt] ◇ *n* an act of protest in which people refuse to do something, e.g. to buy goods made by a particular manufacturer or country, or to visit a particular place □ *The boycott of South African goods ended with the election.* ◇ *vt* to refuse to do <sthg>, e.g. buy goods or go to an event, as a form of protest □ *We decided to boycott the meeting.*

boyfriend ['bɔɪfrend] *n* -1. a man or boy who is somebody's friend. -2. a man who somebody has a romantic or sexual relationship with □ *Have you met her new boyfriend?*

boyish ['bɔɪɪʃ] *adj* -1. [man] who looks or acts like a boy □ *a boyish charm.* -2. [woman] who looks like a boy □ *her boyish figure.*

Boys' Brigade *n* **the Boys' Brigade** a British Christian organization for boys that aims to encourage discipline and self-respect.

Boy Scout *n* a boy who belongs to an organization for boys between the ages of 11 and 16 that teaches them outdoor skills and how to be a good citizen.

Bp *abbr of* **bishop**.

bps (*abbr of* **bits per second**) a way of measuring the speed that information is sent using a modem.

Br RELIGION *abbr of* **brother**.

bra [brɑː] *n* a piece of underwear that women wear to support their breasts.

brace [breɪs] (*pl sense 3* **brace**) ◇ *n* -1. [for teeth] a piece of wire worn over the teeth to straighten them □ *She wears a brace.* -2. [for leg] a metal frame attached to a weak leg to give extra support. -3. [of birds] two things, especially game birds, of the same kind □ *a brace of pheasants.* ◇ *vt* -1. **to brace oneself** to steady oneself, e.g. in order to avoid falling □ *Brace yourselves, we're going to make an emergency landing.* -2. **to brace oneself** to prepare oneself for something unpleasant □ *Brace yourself for some bad news.*

◆ **braces** *npl* -1. US [for teeth] = **brace**. -2. GB two straps that are attached to the front and back of a pair of trousers and worn over the shoulders to hold the trousers up.

bracelet ['breɪslət] *n* a piece of jewelry worn around the wrist.

bracing ['breɪsɪŋ] *adj* [air, climate] that is refreshing, usually because it is cool and windy □ *a bracing sea breeze.*

bracken ['brækən] *n* a type of fern that grows on hills and in forests.

bracket ['brækət] ◇ *n* -1. an L-shaped support attached to a wall to hold up a shelf. -2. a group of people considered as a set, e.g. because they are the same age or earn the same amount of money □ *the 20–25 age bracket* □ *the high/low income bracket.* ◇ *vt* -1. to put brackets around <words, figures> etc. -2. **to bracket sb/sthg with sb/sthg** to include sb/sthg in the same group or category as sb/sthg else □ *Why bracket together two such different companies?*

◆ **brackets** *npl* a pair of symbols, usually curved, used in writing to show that the information between them is not part of the main text. In the sentence "Jim (my brother) and I", "my brother" is in brackets □ *He added a few comments in brackets.* □ *The phonetics are in square brackets.*

brackish ['brækɪʃ] *adj* [water] that is not fresh and is slightly salty.

brag [bræg] (*pt & pp* **bragged**, *cont* **bragging**) *vi* to boast □ *He's always bragging about how much he earns.*

Brahms [brɑːmz], **Johannes** (1833–1897) a German composer whose works include four symphonies and a violin concerto.

braid [breɪd] ◇ *n* -1. narrow pieces of cloth or thread used to decorate curtains or uniforms. -2. a length of hair that has been divided into three sections, twisted together, and tied at the end. ◇ *vt* to make a braid from <three sections of hair>.

braille [breɪl] *n* a system of printing that uses raised dots to represent letters so that blind people can read by touching them □ *written in braille* □ *Do you read braille?*

brain [breɪn] *n* -1. the organ in one's head that controls thought and the actions of the rest of the body □ *brain damage* □ *a brain surgeon.* -2. intelligence □ *She's got a good brain.* ■ **to have sthg on the brain** to think about sthg very often (informal use) □ *He's got sex on the brain.* -3. an intelligent person (informal use).

◆ **brains** *npl* intelligence □ *If you had any brains, you'd realize it was a waste of time.* ■ **to pick sb's brains** to ask sb for special advice or information (informal use) □ *Can I pick your brains about something?* ■ **to cudgel** US OR **rack one's**

brains to think very hard □ *I've been cudgeling my brains, but I can't think of anyone who could help you.*

brainchild ['breɪntʃaɪld] *n* somebody's invention, idea, or plan (informal use).

brain death *n* a condition in which the brain has stopped functioning while the body is kept alive by medical equipment.

brain drain *n* **the brain drain** the movement of skilled professional people to other countries where they are offered better salaries or conditions.

brainless ['breɪnləs] *adj* [person, idea, behavior] stupid.

brainstorm ['breɪnstɔːʳm] *n* US = **brainwave**.

brainstorming ['breɪnstɔːʳmɪŋ] *n* an activity in which a group of people meet to solve a problem or develop a project by thinking of new ideas and discussing them □ *a brainstorming session.*

brainteaser ['breɪntiːzəʳ] *n* a difficult mental puzzle.

brainwash ['breɪnwɒʃ] *vt* to make <sb> believe something, e.g. by using force or stopping them from thinking about anything else □ *Advertisements can brainwash people into buying virtually anything.*

brainwave ['breɪnweɪv] *n* a sudden brilliant idea.

brainy ['breɪnɪ] (*compar* **brainier**, *superl* **brainiest**) *adj* [person] who one thinks is intelligent (informal use).

braise [breɪz] *vt* [meat, vegetable] to cook <food> by frying it, then covering it and cooking it slowly in a little liquid.

brake [breɪk] ◇ *n* **-1.** a device on a vehicle or bicycle used to slow or stop it □ *Release the brake slowly.* **-2.** something that slows down or limits something □ *High interest rates acted as a brake on mortgage lending.* ◇ *vi* [driver] to use the brakes in order to slow down or stop a vehicle □ *I had to brake quickly to avoid the dog.*

brake horsepower *n* the power of an engine measured by its resistance to a brake.

brake light *n* one of the red lights at the back of a motor vehicle that indicate that the driver is braking.

brake pedal *n* the pedal in a motor vehicle that one presses to make the brakes work.

brake shoe *n* a curved metal plate that presses against the wheel of a motor vehicle when the brake is used.

brambles ['bræmblz] *npl* wild prickly bushes that produce blackberries.

bran [bræn] *n* the outer coverings of grains of wheat, oats etc that are left behind when flour is made and are often used as added fiber in breakfast cereals, bread etc.

branch [US bræntʃ, GB brɑːntʃ] ◇ *n* **-1.** [of a tree] a part of a tree that grows out from the trunk and often has leaves, flowers, or other smaller branches growing from it □ *Kit climbed up and sat on one of the branches.* **-2.** [of a river] a small part of a river or rail-

road that leads off from the main part. **-3.** [of a company] a local office of a large company or organization □ *The traveler's checks will be ready for collection at your local branch.* □ *a branch manager.* **-4.** [within an organization] a part of a government or large organization that is responsible for a particular area of work □ *the research branch of the company.* **-5.** [of a subject] a particular part of a science or an academic subject □ *a new branch of medical science.*

◇ *vi* [road, river] to divide into two parts that go in different directions □ *The road branches after about a mile.*

◆ **branch off** *vi* [person, road, path] to go in a different direction from the main road or track □ *I branched off from the main road and cut through the forest.*

◆ **branch out** *vi* to add something different to one's normal business, interests, or activities □ *The savings banks are branching out into small business loans.*

brand [brænd] ◇ *n* **-1.** BUSINESS a variety of a product that is made by a particular manufacturer □ *What brand of butter/coffee/detergent do you buy?* □ *brand image/loyalty.* **-2. a brand of humor/politics etc** a particular type or style of humor/politics etc □ *I don't like his brand of journalism.* **-3.** [on an animal] a mark made on an animal, usually by burning part of its skin, to show who the owner is. ◇ *vt* **-1.** to mark <an animal>, usually by burning part of its skin, in order to show who the owner is. **-2.** to give <sb> a bad reputation □ *He was branded a traitor/coward.* □ *They tend to brand all young people as hooligans.*

brandish ['brændɪʃ] *vt* [stick, sword] to hold or wave <sthg>, especially in a threatening way □ *He came in brandishing a gun.*

brand name *n* the name of a particular brand of product.

brand-new *adj* [car, house, coat] completely new and not used □ *Try not to spill wine on my brand-new carpet.*

brandy ['brændɪ] (*pl* **brandies**) *n* a strong alcoholic drink, usually made from wine □ *A large brandy, please.*

brash [bræʃ] *adj* [person] who is very self-confident and speaks loudly (disapproving use) □ *He still has the brash confidence of youth.*

brass [US bræs, GB brɑːs] *n* **-1.** a bright yellow metal made by mixing copper and zinc and used for making ornaments and musical instruments □ *a brass doorknob/button.* **-2.** MUSIC **the brass** a section of an orchestra consisting of all the players of instruments made of brass, e.g. the trumpets and horns.

brass band *n* MUSIC a band consisting of brass instruments.

brasserie [US bræsə'riː, GB 'bræsərɪ] *n* a café that serves snacks, light meals, and alcoholic drinks.

brassiere [US brə'zɪr, GB 'bræzɪə] *n* = **bra** (formal use).

brass knuckles *npl* US a piece of metal with

holes in it that fits over the knuckles and is used as a weapon.

brass rubbing *n* the process of making a picture by placing paper over an engraved piece of brass and rubbing the paper with a crayon so that the engraving is copied onto it; a picture that is made in this way.

brass tacks *npl* **to get down to brass tacks** to start talking about or dealing with the really important facts or business (informal use).

brat [bræt] *n* an unpleasant or badly-behaved child (informal use) □ *What a nasty little brat!*

bravado [brə'vɑːdəʊ] *n* a show of courage or confidence that is often false and designed to impress other people □ *Buying all those shares was just an act of bravado.*

brave [breɪv] ◇ *adj* [person] who is not afraid to face danger, discomfort, or difficulty □ *a brave decision.* □ *It was very brave of you to come here alone.* ◇ *n* a Native American warrior. ◇ *vt* to risk or face <sthg difficult or dangerous> □ *He braved his family's displeasure by branching out into novel-writing.*

bravely ['breɪvlɪ] *adv* [fight, continue] *see* **brave** □ *She bravely spoke out against her attackers.*

bravery ['breɪvərɪ] *n* brave actions □ *a medal/an award for bravery.*

bravo ['brɑːvəʊ] *excl* a word that people shout to show their admiration and approval of somebody's performance □ *There were cries of "bravo!" from the audience.*

brawl [brɔːl] *n* a noisy fight, often involving more than two people.

brawn [brɔːn] *n* physical strength □ *He's all brawn and no brain.*

brawny ['brɔːnɪ] (*compar* **brawnier**, *superl* **brawniest**) *adj* [person, arm] that is strong and muscular.

bray [breɪ] *vi* [donkey] to make a loud harsh cry.

brazen ['breɪzn] *adj* [person] who shows no shame and is not afraid of what other people think of them □ *a brazen lie.*

◆ **brazen out** *vt sep* **to brazen it out** to face criticism, blame etc without shame or embarrassment.

brazier [US 'breɪʒr, GB -zjə] *n* a container for burning coal or charcoal, used especially outdoors to keep people warm.

Brazil [brə'zɪl] the largest country in South America, in the east, containing most of the Amazon rainforest. SIZE: 8,512,000 sq kms. POPULATION: 153,300,000 (*Brazilians*). CAPITAL: Brasilia. MAIN CITIES: Rio de Janeiro, São Paulo. LANGUAGE: Portuguese. CURRENCY: cruzeiro.

Brazilian [brə'zɪljən] *n* & *adj*: *see* **Brazil**.

brazil nut *n* a large three-sided nut with a hard woody shell.

breach [briːtʃ] ◇ *n* -1. [of a law, agreement] the act of breaking a law, agreement, or promise □ *They sued him for breach of contract.* □ *a breach of confidence.* ■ **to be in breach of sthg** [of regulations, contract] not to be obeying or fulfilling sthg □ *You are in breach of Section 2 of the Public Order Act.* -2. [in a wall] an open-

ing in e.g. a wall or fence, usually made by attackers. ■ **to step into the breach** to do somebody's job while they are unable to do it □ *Fortunately, Merrow was there to step into the breach.* -3. [between people] a period of unfriendly relations between people, countries etc □ *The dispute over fishing rights led to a breach between the two countries.*
◇ *vt* -1. to break <a contract, agreement> etc. -2. to make a hole or gap in <a wall, fence> etc.

breach of the peace *n* LAW noisy behavior and fighting in a public place.

bread [bred] *n* a common food made from baked flour, water, and yeast □ *a loaf/slice of bread* □ *rye bread* □ *a bread roll.*

bread and butter *n* -1. a slice of bread spread with butter. -2. one's main source of income □ *Making saucepans is this company's bread and butter.*

bread bin *n* GB = **bread box**.

breadboard ['bredbɔːd] *n* a board for cutting bread on.

bread box *n* US a container for keeping bread in.

breadcrumbs ['bredkrʌmz] *npl* very small pieces of bread, used in cooking.

breaded ['bredəd] *adj* [fish, veal] that is cooked covered in breadcrumbs.

bread knife *n* a long knife with sharp points along it, used for cutting bread.

breadline ['bredlaɪn] *n* **to be on the breadline** to be very poor.

breadth [bredθ] *n* -1. [of an object] the distance from one side to the other of a solid object □ *It's seven meters in breadth.* -2. [of interest, support, vision] the quality of including many different things, ideas, or people □ *I was impressed by the breadth of his knowledge.*

breadwinner ['bredwɪnə] *n* the person who earns the money for their family to live on.

break [breɪk] (*pt* **broke**, *pp* **broken**) ◇ *n* -1. [in a conversation, one's career] a short time when activity stops before starting again □ *a coffee/lunch break* □ *a break in transmission.* ■ **to have a break from sthg** to stop doing sthg for a short time □ *Let's have a break from decorating today.* ■ **without a break** without stopping □ *We worked for four hours without a break.* -2. EDUCATION a short pause between classes at school □ *You can finish it during break.* -3. [away from home] a short vacation □ *a spring/weekend break.* -4. [in clouds, a hedge] a hole or split in something large. ■ **a break in the weather** a short period of sunshine or fine weather. -5. [in wood, china, a bone] the place where something has broken into two or more parts □ *The doctors say it's a nasty break.* -6. a chance to do something one wants to do, especially in one's career □ *a lucky break* □ *This is my big break!* -7. *phrase* **at break of day** at dawn (literary use).
◇ *vt* -1. [branch, egg, window] to cause <sthg> to separate into pieces by using force or hitting or dropping it □ *Be careful with that vase or you'll break it!* □ *He broke the cookie in half*

and gave them each a piece. **-2.** [leg, ankle, neck] to crack or split <a bone in one's body> □ *He fell and broke his arm.* **-3.** [machine, device] to cause <sthg> to stop working by damaging it □ *I lent him my camera and he broke it.* **-4.** [skin, barrier, surface] to force a way through <sthg> □ *The river has broken its banks.* ■ **to break sb's hold** to cause sb to stop holding something, using force. **-5.** [silence, train of thought] to interrupt <sthg> □ *The silence was suddenly broken by a knock at the door.* ■ **to break sb's fall** to reduce the force with which sb hits the ground after a fall □ *A pile of leaves broke her fall.* ■ **to break one's journey** to stop at a place for a short time when one is on the way to another place. **-6.** [strike, deadlock, stalemate] to cause <sthg> to end, especially sthg that has been going on for some time □ *It's not easy to break the habit of a lifetime.* **-7.** [rule, law] to fail to obey <sthg> □ *It's a movie that breaks all the conventions.* ■ **to break one's promise** OR **word** to fail to do what one has said one will definitely do. **-8. to break a record** to beat an existing record □ *He just missed breaking the world record.* **-9. to break the news** to tell somebody a piece of bad or exciting news □ *Mike offered to break the news to her.* **-10.** SPORT **to break sb's serve** to win a game in which one's opponent is serving.

◇ *vi* **-1.** [branch, egg, window] to separate into pieces as a result of being hit, dropped etc □ *Be careful with it, it might break!* □ *The vase fell and broke into pieces.* **-2.** [machinery, device] to stop working □ *The boiler has broken.* **-3.** [for a meal, rest] to stop work for a short time □ *We'll break for lunch at three.* **-4. when day** OR **dawn broke** when it began to be daylight (literary use). **-5.** [weather] to change for the worse; [storm] to begin suddenly □ *Let's hope the fine weather doesn't break before the wedding.* **-6.** [wave] to curl over and fall down □ *We watched the waves breaking against the rocks.* **-7. to break loose** OR **free** [person, animal] to get away from somebody or something by using force □ *The child struggled, trying to break free from her grasp.* **-8.** [voice] to sound unsteady because of sadness or some other strong emotion; [voice of teenage boy] to change so that it becomes permanently deeper □ *Her voice broke and tears ran down her cheeks.* □ *He gave up singing in the choir when his voice broke.* **-9.** [news, scandal] to become publicly known □ *The story broke in the national press.* **-10. to break even** [company, business] to earn just enough income to avoid making a loss □ *More jobs will be lost if the firm fails to break even this year.*

◆ **break away** *vi* [person, animal] to move away from a group, suddenly and sometimes using force □ *Her attacker broke away from the crowd and ran off down the street.*

◆ **break down** ◇ *vt sep* **-1. to break sthg down** [door, barrier] to remove sthg that is in one's way by knocking it to the ground □ *Police had to break down the door of the apartment.* **-2. to break sthg down** [figures, data, problem] to separate sthg into several parts so that it is easier to understand or do. **-3. to break sthg down** [food, fat] to change sthg into its separate parts by means of a chemical process □ *Bacteria in the soil break down the dead leaves.*

◇ *vi* **-1.** [car, machine] to stop working □ *Our bus broke down on the highway.* **-2.** [talks, relationship, resolution] to fail □ *The marriage had broken down irretrievably by then.* **-3.** [person] to start crying, especially in public, because one can no longer control one's feelings □ *In the middle of his speech he broke down (in tears).* **-4.** [substance] to separate into different parts as a result of a chemical process □ *Fat breaks down to provide the body with energy.*

◆ **break in** ◇ *vi* **-1.** [person] to enter a building illegally by force, usually to steal something □ *The thieves broke in through an open window.* **-2.** [person] to interrupt a conversation between other people □ *Sorry to break in, but you're wanted on the phone.* ◇ *vt sep* **-1. to break sb in** to get sb accustomed to a new job or situation, especially gradually □ *There's a lot to learn but we'll break you in gently!* **-2. to break sthg in** to wear sthg, e.g. new shoes, until they are comfortable.

◆ **break into** *vt fus* **-1. to break into a place** to enter a place, e.g. a building, by force, especially in order to steal □ *Someone broke into my car and stole the radio.* **-2. to break into sthg** [into song, laughter, applause] to begin doing sthg suddenly □ *He broke into a run when the bus appeared.* □ *June amazed me by breaking into fluent Spanish.* □ *The horse broke into a gallop.* **-3.** [into politics, show business, a market] to start taking part in <sthg> □ *The company is planning to break into Southeast Asia.*

◆ **break off** ◇ *vt sep* **-1. to break sthg off** [branch, fingernail] to separate a piece of sthg from the main part by breaking it □ *Break me off a bit of chocolate.* **-2. to break off sthg** [talks, relationship] to end sthg □ *They've broken off their engagement.* ◇ *vi* **-1.** [person] to stop talking suddenly □ *They broke off as I came in.* **-2.** [person] to stop an activity suddenly □ *He broke off for a moment to answer the phone.*

◆ **break out** *vi* **-1.** [fire, panic, fighting] to begin suddenly □ *Cholera has broken out in some of the refugee camps.* **-2. to break out in pimples/a rash** to become covered in spots/a rash □ *I broke out in a cold sweat.* **-3.** to escape from prison or a similar place □ *The two men broke out of Brixton jail earlier this month.*

◆ **break through** *vt fus* **to break through sthg** to force a way through sthg □ *The sun broke through the clouds.* □ *Protesters broke through the police cordon.*

◆ **break up** ◇ *vt sep* **-1. to break sthg up** to separate sthg into smaller pieces □ *Use a fork to break up the lumps.* **-2. to break sthg up** [marriage, fight, relationship] to end sthg, especially in a forceful way □ *Rosy's parents came home and broke up the party.*

◇ *vi* **-1.** to separate into smaller pieces □ *The cake broke up when I took it out of the tin.* **-2.** [marriage, relationship] to end. ■ **to break up with sb** [with one's partner, girlfriend] to end a sexual relationship with sb. **-3.** [crowd, group, demonstration] to come to an end as people begin leaving □ *The party began to break up around midnight.* **-4.** GB [school, pupil] to begin a vacation □ *When do you break up for Easter?*

◆ **break with** *vt fus* **to break with sthg** [with tradition, habit, an old friend] to end a connection with sb/sthg □ *It is time to break with the past and try a new approach.*

breakable ['breɪkəbl] *adj* [object, ornament] that breaks easily □ *Is this package breakable?*

breakage ['breɪkɪdʒ] *n* something that has been broken □ *The insurance pays for all breakages.*

breakaway ['breɪkəweɪ] *adj* **a breakaway faction** OR **group** a group that has broken away from the main group, usually through disagreement.

breakdown ['breɪkdaʊn] *n* **-1.** [of a vehicle, machine] a sudden failure to work □ *We had a breakdown on Highway 7.* **-2.** [of talks, negotiations] a failure or ending of a process □ *a breakdown in communications/in law and order.* **-3.** = **nervous breakdown.** **-4.** [of figures, data] a division of something into smaller parts so that it is easier to understand □ *Could you give me a breakdown of the costs?*

breaker ['breɪkər] *n* a big sea wave that rolls onto the beach.

breakeven [,breɪk'iːvn] *n* the point at which a business makes neither a profit nor a loss □ *We aim to reach breakeven point in two years.*

breakfast ['brekfəst] ◇ *n* the first meal of the day □ *What time is breakfast?* ◇ *vi* to eat breakfast □ *We breakfasted at the hotel.*

breakfast cereal *n* a breakfast food made from a cereal, e.g. corn or wheat, and eaten with milk.

breakfast television *n* television programs that are broadcast early in the morning.

break-in *n* the act of breaking into a building, usually in order to steal things □ *There's been a break-in at work.*

breaking ['breɪkɪŋ] *n* LAW **breaking and entering** the crime of breaking into a building.

breaking point *n* **to be at** OR **reach breaking point** to reach a point where one is no longer able to deal with a difficult and stressful situation.

breakneck ['breɪknek] *adj* **at breakneck speed** very fast □ *They drove down the street at breakneck speed.*

breakthrough ['breɪkθruː] *n* something that allows further progress to be made, e.g. a new invention, a scientific discovery, or a new idea □ *Foreign ministers have made a major breakthrough in negotiations.*

breakup ['breɪkʌp] *n* **-1.** the ending of a relationship or marriage □ *after the breakup of his marriage.* **-2.** the separation of a group, organization etc, e.g. as a result of a disagreement between the people involved □ *Internal conflict led to the breakup of the coalition.*

breakup value *n* BUSINESS the value of a company if it is split into its different parts and each part is sold separately.

breakwater ['breɪkwɔːtər] *n* a long fence or wall that is built at right angles to a beach to protect it from the waves.

bream [briːm] (*pl* **bream** OR **breams**) *n* a silver-colored freshwater fish that can be eaten.

breast [brest] *n* **-1.** [of a woman] one of the two rounded fleshy parts on the front part of a woman's body that can produce milk □ *She put the baby to her breast.* □ *breast cancer.* **-2.** [of a person] the chest (literary use) □ *He beat his breast in sorrow.* **-3.** [of a bird] the meat that comes from the front part of a bird's body □ *a chicken breast.* **-4.** *phrase* **to make a clean breast of it** to tell the whole truth about something bad that one has done.

breastbone ['brestboʊn] *n* the bone down the front of one's chest that joins the ribs together.

breast-feed ◇ *vt* to feed <a baby> by letting it suck milk directly from its mother's breast. ◇ *vi* [mother, woman] *'Not to be taken by breast-feeding mothers.'*

breast pocket *n* a pocket at the front of a shirt or jacket, at chest level.

breaststroke ['breststroʊk] *n* a way of swimming on one's stomach that involves pushing both hands forward then sweeping them down to the sides and at the same time moving the knees up to the sides and then kicking backward □ *Can you do (the) breaststroke?*

breath [breθ] *n* **-1.** the air that is taken into the lungs when one breathes □ *Take a deep breath.* ■ **to have bad breath** to have breath that smells unpleasant. ■ **to get one's breath back** to start breathing normally again after doing something tiring, e.g. running □ *Let me get my breath back first.* ■ **to hold one's breath** to hold air in one's lungs by not breathing out; to wait anxiously for news, a decision etc □ *How long can you hold your breath?* □ *He held his breath as the results were announced.* ■ **to save one's breath** not to waste time saying something to somebody because they will not listen to one's advice, argument etc □ *I'd save my breath if I were you — he's not listening.* ■ **to say sthg under one's breath** to say sthg in a very quiet voice □ *Cheryl muttered something angrily under her breath.* ■ **to take sb's breath away** [sight, news] to surprise sb very much □ *The beauty of the valley took my breath away.* ■ **to waste one's breath** to waste time saying something to somebody because they do not want to listen □ *You're wasting your breath: my mind is already made up.* ■ **to be out of breath** to have problems breathing comfortably, usually after doing something tiring □ *He ran until he was out of breath.* **-2.** **to go out for a breath of fresh air** to go outside for a short time, usually because it is hot or smoky inside.

breathalyze US, **breathalyse** GB ['breθəlaɪz] *vt* to test <sb> with a Breathalyzer (informal use).

Breathalyzer™ US, **Breathalyser**™ GB ['breθəlaɪzər] *n* a device that the police sometimes ask drivers to blow into to find out how much alcohol they have drunk.

breathe [briːð] ◇ *vi* to take air into one's lungs and then let it out □ *Breathe deeply.* ■ **to breathe more easily** to feel more relaxed after a difficult or dangerous situation □ *Investors breathed more easily after the Fed's announcement.* ◇ *vt* **-1.** to take <air, smoke> etc into one's lungs □ *It's good to breathe fresh country air.* **-2.** to say <sthg> very quietly □ *"Shh! Come in quietly," he breathed.*

◆ **breathe in** ◇ *vi* to take air into one's lungs. ◇ *vt sep* **to breathe sthg in** to take sthg into one's lungs, e.g. air or smoke.

◆ **breathe out** *vi* to let air out of one's lungs □ *Breathe in, and then breathe out.*

breather ['briːðəʳ] *n* a short rest (informal use) □ *Let's stop for a quick breather.*

breathing ['briːðɪŋ] *n* the way in which somebody breathes □ *His breathing was heavy.*

breathing space *n* a short period when one can relax between doing other things.

breathless ['breθləs] *adj* **-1.** [person] who is unable to breathe comfortably, especially after doing something tiring □ *The walk uphill left her panting and breathless.* ■ **to be breathless with sthg** [with excitement, fear] to be so strongly affected by sthg that one has difficulty in breathing. **-2.** [silence, excitement] so intense that it makes one hold one's breath □ *There was a breathless hush in the room.*

breathtaking ['breθteɪkɪŋ] *adj* [view, performance] that one admires and finds very beautiful or exciting □ *There were breathtaking views across the valley.*

breath test *n* a test carried out using a Breathalyzer.

Brecht [brekt], **Bertolt** (1898–1956) a German poet and playwright whose experimental plays were intended to make the audience think for themselves. His works include *The Threepenny Opera* and *Mother Courage.*

breed [briːd] (*pt* & *pp* **bred** [bred]) ◇ *n* **-1.** a type of animal or plant, usually developed by humans □ *a breed of cattle.* **-2.** a particular type of person or thing □ *a new breed of manager/computer/TV program.* ◇ *vt* **-1.** to keep <animals or plants> in order to produce young animals and plants or develop new types □ *She breeds labradors.* **-2.** to cause <a particular feeling> to spread among many people □ *Violence breeds violence.* ◇ *vi* [animals] to produce young animals.

breeder ['briːdəʳ] *n* a person whose job is breeding animals or plants.

breeder reactor *n* a type of nuclear reactor that produces more plutonium than it uses in its production of electricity.

breeding ['briːdɪŋ] *n* **-1.** the activity of breeding animals or plants □ *Successful breeding in captivity ensured the survival of the bird.* **-2.** good manners that somebody is taught by their family □ *a sign of good breeding.*

breeding-ground *n* **-1.** a place where a particular type of animal goes to breed □ *Oil companies have devastated the breeding-grounds*

of the gray seal. **-2.** a place or situation that encourages something, usually something bad, to develop □ *a breeding-ground for terrorists/crime.*

breeze [briːz] ◇ *n* a light wind □ *A gentle breeze was blowing.* ◇ *vi* **to breeze in/out** to go in/out quickly and in a confident way □ *He breezed in just as we were about to start.*

breezeblock ['briːzblɒk] *n* GB a large light brick made of cement and ash and used for building houses, walls etc.

breezy ['briːzɪ] (*compar* **breezier,** *superl* **breeziest**) *adj* **-1.** [weather, day] that is a little windy. **-2.** [person, personality, manner] that is cheerful, lively, and confident □ *You're very bright and breezy today.*

Breton ['bretn] ◇ *n* a person who comes from or lives in Brittany. ◇ *adj*: see **Brittany.**

brevity ['brevətɪ] *n* [of life, a visit] the short amount of time that something lasts □ *I was surprised by the brevity of his answer.*

brew [bruː] ◇ *vi* **-1.** [tea, coffee] to be in the process of being brewed □ *I'll leave the tea to brew for a few minutes.* **-2.** [trouble, storm, crisis] to be developing or likely to happen soon □ *There's trouble brewing.* ◇ *vt* **-1.** to make <beer>. **-2.** to prepare <tea, coffee> etc by mixing it with hot water.

brewer ['bruːəʳ] *n* a person whose job is making beer.

brewery ['bruːərɪ] (*pl* **breweries**) *n* **-1.** the buildings where beer is made. **-2.** a company that makes beer.

briar ['braɪəʳ] *n* a wild bush with thorns.

bribe [braɪb] ◇ *n* something, usually money, that is offered to somebody to persuade them to do something dishonest □ *Senior policemen were accused of taking bribes.* ◇ *vt* to give <sb> a bribe so that they will do something □ *We bribed the guard to let us in.*

bribery ['braɪbərɪ] *n* the act of offering somebody a bribe □ *The former prime minister was found guilty of bribery.*

bric-a-brac ['brɪkəbræk] *n* small ornaments that are usually not worth very much.

brick [brɪk] *n* a hard rectangular block of baked clay used for building houses, bridges etc □ *a brick wall/building.*

◆ **brick up** *vt sep* **to brick sthg up** [window, door] to fill in sthg with bricks □ *They bricked up the chimney.*

bricklayer ['brɪkleɪəʳ] *n* a person whose job is to build walls or buildings using bricks.

brickwork ['brɪkwɜːʳk] *n* the parts of a wall or building that are made of bricks □ *The brickwork had been cleaned.*

bridal ['braɪdl] *adj* [gown, procession] that is connected with a bride or a wedding □ *a shop that sells bridal wear.*

bride [braɪd] *n* a woman just before, during, or after her wedding.

bridegroom ['braɪdgruːm] *n* a man just before, during, or after his wedding.

bridesmaid ['braɪdzmeɪd] *n* a woman or girl who accompanies the bride to her wedding.

bridge [brɪdʒ] ◇ *n* -1. a structure built to carry a road or railroad across a valley, river, railroad track etc □ *the Golden Gate bridge* □ *a railroad bridge.* ■ **I'll cross that bridge when I come to it** I'll deal with that problem when it happens and not before. -2. [between people] a means of communication between two people or groups of people □ *a bridge between East and West.* -3. SHIPPING the raised area of a ship from which it is steered and controlled. -4. [of one's nose] the top part of one's nose, between the eyes □ *His glasses were perched on the bridge of his nose.* -5. CARDS a card game for two teams of two players similar to whist.
◇ *vt* **to bridge the gap** to reduce the differences and improve communication between people □ *We run projects which try to bridge the gap between young and old.*

bridging loan ['brɪdʒɪŋ-] *n* GB money lent by a bank for a short time, usually to help somebody buy a new house before they have sold their old house.

bridle ['braɪdl] ◇ *n* the set of straps around a horse's head that the rider uses to control the horse. ◇ *vt* to put a bridle on <a horse, pony> etc. ◇ *vi* to express one's anger by moving the head stiffly upward □ *He bridled at the accusation.*

bridle path *n* a path for horses and riders.

brief [briːf] ◇ *adj* -1. [visit, description, glance] that lasts for a short time □ *Write giving us a brief summary of your achievements to date.* - [skirt, shorts] short □ *She was wearing a very brief pair of shorts.* -3. **to be brief** to use very few words to say something □ *To be brief, there is little we can do to remedy the situation.* □ *I'll be brief, since you're in a hurry.*
◇ *n* -1. LAW a document stating all the facts of a case that is given by one lawyer to another lawyer who will argue the case in court. -2. the instructions given to somebody about what their job or duty is □ *His brief is to improve industrial relations.*
◇ *vt* to give <sb> the information, instructions etc they need to understand a situation, do a job etc □ *The US envoy has been fully briefed on the situation.*
♦ **briefs** *npl* a piece of underwear that covers the body between the waist and the tops of the legs and goes between the legs □ *a pair of briefs.*
♦ **in brief** *adv* a phrase used to indicate that one is only giving a few details about something □ *In brief, I don't think it will work.* □ *Here is the news in brief.*

briefcase ['briːfkeɪs] *n* a flat case that is usually made of leather, has one handle, and is used for carrying papers.

briefing ['briːfɪŋ] *n* a meeting where somebody is given information or instructions to prepare them for a political debate, battle, special mission etc □ *They were given a briefing before the flight.*

briefly ['briːflɪ] *adv* -1. [pause, look, wait] for a short time □ *We met briefly at the conference.*

-2. [answer, explain] using only a few words □ *Could you tell me briefly what the job entails?*

Brig. *abbr of* **brigadier.**

brigade [brɪ'geɪd] *n* -1. MILITARY one of the main groups into which an army is divided. -2. an organization that has particular duties □ *the St. John ambulance brigade.*

brigadier [ˌbrɪgə'dɪər] *n* MILITARY the officer in charge of a brigade.

bright [braɪt] ◇ *adj* -1. [light, sun] that shines strongly; [day, weather] with sunshine and few clouds; [room, office] where there is a lot of light □ *We're enjoying the bright sunshine.* □ *We had a bright morning but then it began to rain.* □ *The lamp was so bright it hurt my eyes.* -2. [color] that is strong, light, and easy to see □ *bright blue eyes.* -3. [smile, expression] that seems lively and cheerful □ *You look much brighter this morning.* -4. [person] who is intelligent and quick at learning □ *She's a bright child.* ■ **a bright idea** an idea that is original and shows intelligence □ *Does anyone have any bright ideas on how we might get around this problem?* -5. [prospects, outlook] that seems likely to bring success □ *The future's looking bright for young men like you.*
◇ *adv* **bright and early** very early in the morning.
♦ **brights** *npl* US car headlights that point straight ahead rather than toward the ground (informal use).

brighten ['braɪtn] *vi* -1. [day, weather] to become brighter □ *The weather brightened toward the end of the afternoon.* -2. [face, expression, mood] to become more cheerful □ *She brightened visibly at the news.*
♦ **brighten up** ◇ *vt sep* -1. **to brighten sthg up** [room, house, dress] to make sthg look more colorful and attractive, e.g. by painting or decorating it □ *It just needs a lick of paint to brighten it up.* -2. **to brighten sthg up** [situation, conversation] to make sthg more lively or cheerful □ *Her visit really brightened up our day.*
◇ *vi* [weather, person, face] = **brighten.**

brightly ['braɪtlɪ] *adv* [shine, smile] *see* **bright** □ *a brightly colored scarf* □ *The room was brightly lit.* □ *"Would you like some coffee?" she said brightly.*

brightness ['braɪtnəs] *n* [of a light, color] *see* **bright** □ *How do you adjust the brightness on this TV?*

brilliance ['brɪljəns] *n see* **brilliant** □ *His brilliance as a mathematician was soon apparent.*

brilliant ['brɪljənt] *adj* -1. [person, mind] that is very intelligent [idea, solution, piece of work] that shows great intelligence or skill and is very impressive □ *She's a brilliant physicist.* □ *He gave a brilliant performance as Hamlet.* -2. [color, light] that is very bright □ *We went out into the brilliant sunshine.* -3. [career, future] that is very successful □ *She has a brilliant career in politics ahead of her.* -4. GB that one thinks is very good (informal use) □ *That's brilliant news — well done!*

brilliantly ['brɪljəntlɪ] *adv* [perform, shine] *see* **brilliant** □ *brilliantly colored* □ *It was a brilliantly planned and executed maneuver.*

Brillo pad™ ['brɪloʊ-] *n* a pad, made of wire and filled with soap, that is used for cleaning pots and pans.

brim [brɪm] (*pt* & *pp* **brimmed**, *cont* **brimming**) ◇ *n* -1. the top edge of a container for liquid, e.g. a bowl or glass □ *full to the brim.* -2. the bottom part of a hat that sticks out to protect the wearer from the sun or rain. ◇ *vi* **to brim with sthg** [with emotion, enthusiasm] to be full of sthg □ *His eyes brimmed with tears.*

◆ **brim over** *vi* -1. [cup, glass] to be so full that the contents spill over the edge. -2. **to brim over with sthg** [with pride, happiness] to be full of sthg.

brine [braɪn] *n* water that contains salt and is used for preserving food.

bring [brɪŋ] (*pt* & *pp* **brought**) *vt* -1. [person, object] to take <sb/sthg> to the place one is living in, going to, talking about etc □ *Bill's bringing his boss home for dinner.* □ *Can you bring a bottle of wine (with you)?* -2. [object] to carry <sthg> to somebody □ *I've brought her some chocolates OR some chocolates for her.* □ *'Bringing you the latest in computer technology.'* -3. [happiness, sorrow, satisfaction] to cause <a particular feeling, situation, or reaction> □ *That boy brings us nothing but trouble.* □ *Tourism has brought prosperity to the region.* ■ **to bring sthg to an end/a halt** to cause sthg to end/stop □ *The chairman brought the meeting to a close.* □ *The accident brought his sporting career to an abrupt end.* ■ **to bring sthg to sb's attention** to tell sb sthg, usually in a polite way □ *The matter was brought to my attention by one of my colleagues.* -4. [person, business tourist] to cause <sb/sthg> to come to a place □ *The festival brings crowds of visitors every year.* □ *The new sales manager has brought us a lot of new customers.* -5. LAW **to bring charges against sb** to say officially that sb is believed to have broken the law. ■ **to be brought to trial** [person] to be judged in court because one is believed to have broken the law. -6. **I couldn't bring myself to do it** I was unable to do it because it was unpleasant □ *In the end I just couldn't bring myself to tell them the truth.*

◆ **bring about** *vt sep* **to bring sthg about** [change, decision, separation] to cause sthg to happen □ *All attempts to bring about a peaceful solution to the crisis have failed.*

◆ **bring along** *vt sep* **to bring sb/sthg along** [person, object] to bring sb/sthg with one when one goes to a place or event □ *Bring your wife along too.* □ *I've brought along one of our brochures.*

◆ **bring around** *vt sep* US = **bring to.**

◆ **bring back** *vt sep* -1. **to bring sthg/sb back** [object, souvenir, gift] to come back to a place with sthg; [person] to take sb back to the place where one is living, or that one is talking about □ *Look what Kate brought me back from Egypt.* □ *I'll lend you my copy if you promise to bring it back.* □ *Who brought you back here last night?* -2. **to bring back sthg** [feeling, mood, event] to make one remember sthg □ *That song always brings back my last year at college.* -3. **to bring sthg back** [fashion, custom] to

cause sthg to return after a period of time □ *Carver thinks they should bring back hanging.*

◆ **bring down** *vt sep* -1. **to bring sthg down** [bird, aircraft, tree] to cause sthg to fall to the ground □ *The storm brought down the telephone wires.* -2. **to bring down sb/sthg** [government, dictator, regime] to cause sb/sthg to lose political power □ *This scandal could bring down the ruling party.* -3. **to bring sthg down** [price, age limit, interest rates] to cause sthg to become less, especially because people want this or expect this □ *They have succeeded in bringing inflation down to 3%.*

◆ **bring forward** *vt sep* -1. **to bring sthg forward** [meeting, interview, election] to change the time or date of an event to an earlier time or date □ *The inspection was due to happen in June, but it's been brought forward two months to April.* -2. **to bring an amount forward** [in bookkeeping] to move the total amount of a list of figures to the top of a new list of figures.

◆ **bring in** *vt sep* -1. **to bring sthg in** [rule, legislation, policy] to make sthg part of the existing set of laws □ *The government is bringing in new safety regulations for buses.* -2. **to bring in money** to earn an amount of money □ *Her job can't bring in more than $15,000 a year.* -3. **to bring sb in** [person] to ask sb from outside one's work, organization etc to take part in it, especially to give help or advice □ *We've had to bring in an outside firm of consultants to solve the problem.*

◆ **bring off** *vt sep* **to bring sthg off** [plan, deal] to complete sthg difficult successfully □ *If anybody can bring it off, you can.*

◆ **bring on** *vt sep* **to bring sthg on** [crisis, fever, attack] to cause sthg to start □ *Hot weather always brings on my hay fever.* ■ **to bring sthg on oneself** to act in a way that causes sthg unpleasant to happen to one □ *There's no use complaining, you brought it on yourself.*

◆ **bring out** *vt sep* -1. **to bring sthg out** [record, book] to make sthg available for the public to buy □ *They've just brought out a new range of their successful kitchenware.* -2. **to bring out the best/worst in sb** to cause sb to behave as well/as badly as they can □ *Simon always brings out the worst in Martin — they're like two schoolboys together.*

◆ **bring round** *vt sep* GB = **bring to.**

◆ **bring to** *vt sep* **to bring sb to** to make sb conscious again, e.g. after they have fainted □ *I used smelling salts to bring her to.*

◆ **bring up** *vt sep* -1. **to bring up a child** to look after a child until it is adult and teach it particular beliefs, ways of behaving etc □ *She was left to bring up the kids on her own.* □ *He was brought up (as) a Catholic.* -2. **to bring sthg up** [subject, the past] to start to talk about sthg □ *Let's hope she doesn't bring politics up again!* -3. **to bring up food/drink** to be sick, especially soon after eating or drinking □ *I managed to eat some fruit, but brought it all up again afterwards.*

bring and buy (sale) *n* GB a charity sale where people bring things to be sold and buy things that other people have brought.

brink [brɪŋk] *n* **on the brink of sthg** [of bankruptcy, war, extinction] close to sthg dangerous; [of a discovery, breakthrough] close to sthg exciting □ *I was on the brink of telling him to get out of the house.*

Brisbane ['brɪzbən] a port in Queensland, Australia. POPULATION: 1,240,300.

brisk [brɪsk] *adj* **-1.** [walk, swim, pace] quick, lively, and energetic □ *We walked at a brisk pace towards the station.* **-2.** [business, trading] busy and successful □ *Business has been reasonably brisk recently.* **-3.** [manner, tone, person] efficient and confident □ *Her manner was brisk and businesslike.* **-4.** [wind, weather] cold and refreshing □ *There was a brisk sea breeze.*

brisket ['brɪskət] *n* the meat from the chest of a cow.

briskly ['brɪsklɪ] *adv* [walk, trade, speak] *see* **brisk**.

bristle ['brɪsl] *vi* **-1.** [an animal's hair, fur] to stand up from the body, usually because of anger or fear. **-2.** [person] to react angrily □ *She bristled at the suggestion.*

♦ **bristles** *npl* **-1.** [on a person] the short stiff hairs that grow on the skin after shaving. **-2.** [on an animal] thick stiff hair that grows on some animals. **-3.** the thick stiff hair or similar material at the end of paintbrushes, shaving brushes etc.

♦ **bristle with** *vt fus* to bristle with **people/things** to be full of people/things □ *The whole subject bristles with difficulties.* □ *The town was bristling with police.*

bristly ['brɪslɪ] (*compar* **bristlier**, *superl* **bristliest**) *adj* [chin, face] that is covered with short stiff hairs.

Brit [brɪt] (*abbr of* **Briton**) *n* a British person (informal use).

Britain ['brɪtn] **-1.** = **Great Britain. -2.** = **United Kingdom.**

Britannia [brɪ'tænjə] a figure of a female soldier, wearing a helmet and carrying a shield and trident, used as a symbol of Britain.

British ['brɪtɪʃ] ◇ *adj* [passport, subject] that belongs to Britain or the British Commonwealth. ◇ *npl* **the British** people living in Britain.

British Academy *n* **the British Academy** a British organization that funds and encourages the study of history, philosophy, and language.

British Broadcasting Corporation *n* → **BBC.**

British Columbia [-kə'lʌmbɪə] a mountainous province of western Canada on the Pacific Coast. ABBREVIATION: BC. SIZE: 950,000 sq kms. POPULATION: 3,282,061 (*British Columbians*). CAPITAL: Victoria.

British Council *n* **the British Council** an organization that promotes Britain abroad. It runs many libraries, language courses, and cultural centers in foreign countries.

British Isles: **the British Isles** Great Britain, Ireland, and the islands around their coasts.

British Museum: **the British Museum** the national museum of Britain, in London.

British Standards Institution *n* → **BSI.**

British Summer Time *n* the system of time used in Britain from March to October that is one hour ahead of the time used during the rest of the year.

Briton ['brɪtn] *n* a British person (formal use).

Brittany ['brɪtənɪ] a region of northwestern France, between the English Channel and the Bay of Biscay.

Britten ['brɪtn], **Benjamin** (1913–1976) a British composer whose works include the operas *Peter Grimes* and *Billy Budd*.

brittle ['brɪtl] *adj* [bones, twig, glass] that is hard but easy to break.

Bro RELIGION *abbr of* **brother**.

broach [broutʃ] *vt* to begin to talk about <a subject> carefully because it is difficult or unpleasant □ *I haven't broached the subject of salaries yet.*

broad [brɔːd] ◇ *adj* **-1.** [river, shoulders, grin] wide □ *a broad tree-lined avenue* □ *He gave me a broad smile.* **-2. a broad range/variety etc** a range/variety etc that includes a lot of different things or people □ *The college has a broad and wide-ranging syllabus.* □ *The program has a very broad appeal.* **-3. a broad introduction/description etc** a general introduction/description etc rather than a detailed one □ *It's art in the broadest sense of the word.* □ *I think there is broad agreement about what needs to be done.* **-4. a broad hint** a strong and clear hint □ *Bob kept dropping broad hints about birthday presents.* **-5. a broad accent** a strong accent □ *She spoke with a broad Texas accent.* **-6.** *phrase* **in broad daylight** during the daytime, when what happens can be clearly seen □ *He was shot in broad daylight.*
◇ *n* ▽ US a woman (very informal and offensive use).

B road *n* GB a road that is smaller and less important than a main road.

broad bean *n* a large, flat, green bean.

broadcast [US 'brɔːdkæst, GB -kɑːst] (*pt & pp* **broadcast**) RADIO & TV ◇ *n* something such as a speech or musical performance that is sent by radio or television □ *a live/recorded broadcast.* ◇ *vt* to send out <a TV or radio program> □ *The game will be broadcast live on Channel 5.*

broadcaster [US 'brɔːdkæstər, GB -kɑːstə] *n* a person who regularly takes part in radio or television programs.

broadcasting [US 'brɔːdkæstɪŋ, GB -kɑːst-] *n* the activity of making and sending out radio or television programs.

broaden ['brɔːdn] ◇ *vt* **-1.** to make <a road, pavement> etc wider. **-2.** to make <the scope, appeal> etc of something more general □ *She broadened the base of her writing after retirement.* ■ **to broaden one's mind** to make one more aware of other ways of life, ideas etc □ *A little more traveling could broaden your mind.* ◇ *vi* [river, road] to become wider.

♦ **broaden out** *vi* **-1.** [river, road] to become wider. **-2.** [interests, awareness] to become more general by including more people or things.

broadly ['brɔːdlɪ] *adv* -1. generally □ *I broadly agree with what Leroy has just said.* ■ **broadly speaking** generally and without going into details □ *This is, broadly speaking, what we expected.* -2. **to smile broadly** to have a wide smile on one's face.

broadly-based [-beɪst] *adj* [party, movement, course] that includes a wide range of elements, people, or points of view.

broadminded [ˌbrɔːdˈmaɪndəd] *adj* [person, attitude] that is tolerant and open to new ideas.

broadsheet ['brɔːdʃiːt] *n* a newspaper printed on large sheets of paper.
NOTE: Compare **tabloid**.

Broadway ['brɔːdweɪ] a street in New York City famous for its theaters and shows, which usually feature stars in well-known plays □ *a Broadway hit/musical.*

brocade [brouˈkeɪd] *n* a thick decorative piece of silk with a raised pattern.

broccoli ['brɒkəlɪ] *n* a vegetable with thick green stems and green or purple heads □ *Serve with broccoli and sauté potatoes.*

brochure [US broʊˈʃʊr, GB ˈbrouʃə] *n* a booklet with pictures that contains information or advertisements □ *travel/sales brochures.*

brogues [broʊgz] *npl* thick leather shoes with a pattern of small holes in the leather.

broil [brɔɪl] *vt* US [meat, chicken, fish] to cook <food> on a grill with heat directly above or below it.

broiler ['brɔɪləʳ] *n* -1. a young chicken suitable for roasting or broiling. -2. US a tray consisting of metal bars on which food is placed for broiling.

broke [broʊk] ◇ *past tense of* **break**. ◇ *adj* **to be broke** [person, company] to have no money □ *I can't go out tonight — I'm absolutely broke.* ■ **to go broke** [company] to go bankrupt. ■ **to go for broke** to risk everything in order to try and achieve a success.

broken ['broʊkən] ◇ *past participle of* **break**. ◇ *adj* -1. [window, machine, promise] that has been broken □ *The floor was covered in broken glass.* -2. **a broken marriage** a marriage that has ended in separation. ■ **a broken home** a home where the family no longer lives together because the parents have separated □ *She comes from a broken home.* -3. **to speak broken English/Chinese etc** to speak English/Chinese etc slowly and with many mistakes.

broken-down *adj* **a broken-down car/machine** a car/machine that does not work well, or that has stopped working completely □ *He drives a broken-down old Mercedes.*

broker ['broʊkəʳ] ◇ *n* a person whose job is to buy and sell things for other people □ *a commodity broker.* ◇ *vt* to arrange <a deal, agreement> etc so that all the people involved agree to the details □ *a peace accord brokered by the UN.*

brokerage ['broʊkərɪdʒ] *n* -1. the business of being a broker □ *a brokerage firm.* -2. the amount of money charged by a broker.

bronchitis [brɒŋˈkaɪtəs] *n* an illness caused by infection of the tubes that bring air to the lungs, resulting in coughing and breathing difficulties.

Bronte ['brɒntɪ], **Charlotte** (1816–1855) a British novelist whose best-known work is *Jane Eyre*. Her sisters, Anne and Emily, were also writers.

Bronte, Emily (1818–1848) a British poet and novelist whose best-known work is *Wuthering Heights*. Her sisters, Anne and Charlotte, were also writers.

Bronx [brɒŋks]: **the Bronx** a borough of New York City across the Harlem River from Manhattan. POPULATION: 1,169,000.

bronze [brɒnz] ◇ *n* -1. a yellow-brown metal made of copper and tin □ *a bronze statue.* -2. a sculpture made of bronze □ *a bronze by Donatello.* -3. = **bronze medal.** ◇ *adj* [hair, skin] that is the color of bronze.

bronzed [brɒnzd] *adj* [person, body] suntanned.

bronze medal *n* a medal made of bronze that is given to the person who comes third in a competition, especially in sports.

brooch [broʊtʃ] *n* a piece of jewelry with a pin at the back that is usually worn on a woman's jacket or blouse.

brood [bruːd] ◇ *n* -1. a family of young animals, usually birds, that were born together. -2. the children in a family (humorous use). ◇ *vi* to spend a long time thinking about something that makes one worried, upset, or angry □ *It's no use brooding over the past.*

broody ['bruːdɪ] (*compar* **broodier**, *superl* **broodiest**) *adj* -1. [person] who seems silent and sad. -2. [bird] that wants to lay or sit on eggs.

brook [brʊk] ◇ *n* a small stream. ◇ *vt* to allow or tolerate <sthg> (formal use) □ *They will brook no opposition.*

Brooklyn ['brʊklən] a borough of New York City on Long Island. It is linked to Manhattan by the Brooklyn Bridge. POPULATION: 2,231,000.

broom [bruːm] *n* -1. a brush with a long handle that is used for sweeping the floor. -2. a shrub with yellow flowers that often grows on wasteland.

broomstick ['bruːmstɪk] *n* the long handle of a broom.

Bros, bros BUSINESS *abbr of* **brothers**.

broth [brɒθ] *n* a soup that usually contains rice, vegetables, and meat or fish.

brothel ['brɒθl] *n* a house where men pay to have sex with prostitutes.

brother ['brʌðəʳ] ◇ *n* -1. [in a family] a male relative of somebody who has the same parents □ *They are brothers.* □ *Have you met my brother?* □ *This is my elder brother, Pete.* □ *She's looking after her baby brother.* -2. [at work] a word used to talk to a man who belongs to the same race, profession, labor union etc as oneself □ *Brothers, unite!* -3. RELIGION a member of a religious group, especially a Christian monk □ *Brother Peter.* ◇ *excl* US a word used to express surprise or slight annoyance (informal use) □ *Brother, was she mad!*

brotherhood ['brʌðəʳhʊd] *n* -1. the friendship and loyalty between people with the same interests or ideas. -2. an organization of men who share the same beliefs or aims, especially religious ones.

brother-in-law (*pl* **brothers-in-law**) *n* the brother of one's husband or wife; the husband of one's sister.

brotherly ['brʌðəʳlɪ] *adj* that is typical of a brother □ *brotherly advice.*

brought [brɔːt] *past tense & past participle of* **bring**.

brow [braʊ] *n* -1. the forehead. -2. an eyebrow (literary use). ■ **to knit one's brows** to frown because one is worried or thinking carefully. -3. the top part of a hill or slope.

browbeat ['braʊbiːt] (*pt* **browbeat**, *pp* **browbeaten**) *vt* to try to make <sb> do something by being aggressive toward them □ *Don't let them browbeat you into going!*

browbeaten ['braʊbiːtn] *adj* [child, employee] who seems quiet and timid because of being regularly forced to do things by somebody strict or forceful.

brown [braʊn] ◇ *adj* -1. [hair, eyes, trousers] of the color of wood or chocolate. ■ **brown bread** bread made from whole-wheat flour. -2. [skin, leg, person] tanned □ *You're looking very brown!* ◇ *n* the color of wood or chocolate □ *She never wears brown.* ◇ *vt* to cook <meat> until it becomes brown on the outside.

Brown [braʊn], **Capability** (1715–1783) a British landscape gardener who designed gardens to look natural, when the fashionable style was formal.

Brown, Charlie a US cartoon character, a boy with a large round head and very little hair. He usually feels sorry for himself and has bad luck.

Brown, John (1800–1859) a US campaigner against slavery. A song about him, *John Brown's Body*, was popular during the American Civil War.

brown-bag *vi* US to take one's lunch to school, work etc in a brown paper bag.

brownie ['braʊnɪ] *n* a flat square piece of rich chocolate cake.

◆ **Brownie** *n* a junior member of the Guides or Girl Scouts.

Brownie point *n* an amount of approval that one thinks somebody will get for doing something to help or please somebody else (informal and humorous use) □ *He's just trying to get OR score Brownie points with the boss.*

brown paper *n* strong brown paper that is normally used for wrapping packages.

brown rice *n* rice that has not had its outer covering removed.

brownstone ['braʊnstoʊn] *n* a type of house built of red-brown stone, common in New York City.

brown sugar *n* sugar that has a dark color because it has not been refined or because it has only partly been refined.

Brown v. the Board of Education of Topeka, Kansas [-tə'piːkə-] *n* a famous court case in the USA in 1954. The decision meant that black people could go to the same schools as white people.

browse [braʊz] *vi* -1. [customer] to look at the things for sale in a relaxed way without looking for anything in particular □ *"Can I help you, sir?" — "No thanks, I'm just browsing."* -2. [person] to look through a magazine, book, computer file etc quickly, reading only parts of it □ *He browsed through the newspapers.* -3. [cow, deer, goat] to eat plants, leaves etc in a slow relaxed way.

bruise [bruːz] ◇ *n* -1. [on one's face, arm] a brownish or blue mark on the skin that is the result of an injury, especially one caused by being hit by somebody or something □ *She had a dark bruise beneath her eye.* -2. [on fruit] an area on the skin of a piece of fruit that is darker and softer than the rest, e.g. because it has been dropped or squashed. ◇ *vt* -1. [knee, fruit] to make one or more bruises on <sthg>. -2. to hurt <sb's feelings, ego> etc □ *You've just bruised his ego, that's all.* ◇ *vi* [person, fruit] *Soft fruit bruises easily.*

bruised [bruːzd] *adj* -1. [face, arm, apple] that has a bruise or bruises on it. -2. [ego, feelings] hurt by a particular event or situation.

brunch [brʌntʃ] *n* a meal eaten in the late morning instead of breakfast and lunch.

Brunei ['bruːnaɪ] a country in northern Borneo. SIZE: 5,765 sq kms. POPULATION: 300,000 (*Bruneians*). CAPITAL: Bandar Seri Begawan. LANGUAGE: Malay. CURRENCY: Brunei dollar.

Brunel [bruː'nel], **Isambard Kingdom** (1806–1859) a British engineer and inventor who designed some of the world's largest bridges and ships.

brunette [bruː'net] *n* a girl or woman with brown hair.

brunt [brʌnt] *n* **to bear** OR **take the brunt of sthg** [of an attack, somebody's anger] to be affected by the worst or main part of sthg □ *The front of the building bore the full brunt of the explosion.*

brush [brʌʃ] ◇ *n* -1. an object made of hairs, fibers, or bristles attached to a handle that is used for cleaning or tidying something, or for spreading a substance, e.g. paint, on a surface □ *a dustpan and brush.* -2. **to have a brush with death/the law** to experience a situation in which one is almost killed/arrested. ◇ *vt* -1. [one's hair, an animal's coat] to tidy <sthg> with a brush; [one's teeth, shoes] to clean <sthg> with a brush. -2. **to brush sthg away/back etc** to move sthg away/back etc by touching it quickly and lightly with one's hands or fingers □ *He brushed the mosquito away.* □ *She brushed the crumbs off her sweater.* -3. [face, wall] to touch <sb/sthg>very lightly without meaning to □ *His hand brushed her cheek.*

◆ **brush aside** *vt sep* **to brush sthg aside** [complaint, accusation, worry] to treat sthg as if it is not important □ *She brushed aside doubts over her fitness with a fine win.*

◆ **brush off** *vt sep* **to brush sb off** to ignore or be rude to sb □ *I tried to speak to him, but he just brushed me off.*

◆ **brush up** *vt sep* **to brush sthg up** [one's English, math, typing] to improve one's knowledge or standard of sthg □ *You really should brush up your French before we go.*

◆ **brush up on** *vt fus* **to brush up on sthg** to brush up sthg.

brushed [brʌʃt] *adj* [nylon, cotton] that has been specially treated to make it softer.

brush-off *n* **to give sb the brush-off** to reject sb very rudely (informal use) □ *I tried to speak to James, but he just gave me the brush-off.*

brushwood ['brʌʃwʊd] *n* **-1.** small bushes and trees that grow all over an area of land. **-2.** dead branches and twigs that have broken off trees.

brushwork ['brʌʃwɜːʳk] *n* the way in which a particular artist uses a brush to paint pictures.

brusque [US brʌsk, GB brʊsk] *adj* [person] who speaks in short quick sentences and so seems impolite □ *Don't be put off by his brusque manner.*

Brussels ['brʌslz] the capital of Belgium and the headquarters of the European Commission, the European Council of Ministers, and NATO. POPULATION: 136,424.

brussels sprout *n* a green vegetable that looks like a very small cabbage and grows on the side of a tall stem.

brutal ['bruːtl] *adj* **-1.** [person, treatment] that is cruel and violent □ *the brutal murder of this young boy.* **-2.** [truth, honesty] that one cannot ignore but finds hard to accept □ *The brutal fact is, nobody will lend us any more money.*

brutality [bruːˈtælətɪ] (*pl* **brutalities**) *n* [of a person, a killing] *see* **brutal** □ *an act of brutality* □ *the brutalities he was subjected to at the hands of the enemy.*

brutalize, -ise ['bruːtəlaɪz] *vt* **-1.** to make <sb> become cruel or uncaring □ *a society brutalized by the atrocities of war.* **-2.** to treat <sb> in a brutal way.

brutally ['bruːtlɪ] *adv*: *see* **brutal** □ *He had been brutally murdered.* □ *To be brutally frank, I hated every minute of it.*

brute [bruːt] ◇ *adj* **brute strength/force** great strength/force that somebody uses without needing to use skill or thought. ◇ *n* **-1.** a large animal □ *The poor brute can hardly move.* **-2.** a man who is rough and violent □ *He looks like a real brute.*

bs *abbr of* **bill of sale.**

BS (*abbr of* **Bachelor of Science**) *n* US a science degree; a person who has this degree.

BSA (*abbr of* **Boy Scouts of America**) *n* **the BSA** the association for scouts in the USA.

BSc (*abbr of* **Bachelor of Science**) *n* a science degree; a person who has this degree.

BSE (*abbr of* **bovine spongiform encephalopathy**) *n* = **mad cow disease** (technical use).

BSI (*abbr of* **British Standards Institution**) *n* **the BSI** in Britain, the organization that sets standards for units of measurement and controls the quality of manufactured goods.

B-side *n* [of a single] the side of a record or cassette that contains a less well-known or important song.

BSkyB [ˌbiːskaɪˈbiː] (*abbr of* **British Sky Broadcasting**) a British satellite television company.

BST *abbr of* **British Summer Time.**

Bt. *abbr of* **baronet.**

btu (*abbr of* **British thermal unit**) *n* a unit (1055.06 joules) used for measuring heat.

bubble ['bʌbl] ◇ *n* a ball of air or gas inside a thin wall of liquid □ *He was blowing bubbles through his straw.* □ *soap bubbles.* ◇ *vi* **-1.** [water, soup] to produce bubbles; to make the sound of bubbles being produced in a boiling liquid □ *The percolator bubbled on the stove.* **-2.** **to bubble with sthg** [with enthusiasm, confidence, excitement] to have a lot of sthg □ *She was bubbling with excitement.*

bubble bath *n* a liquid or powder added to a bath to produce foam and a pleasant smell.

bubble gum *n* a kind of chewing gum that one can blow bubbles with.

bubblejet printer ['bʌbldʒet-] *n* a printer that sprays ink to produce letters on the paper.

bubbly ['bʌblɪ] (*compar* **bubblier**, *superl* **bubbliest**) ◇ *adj* **-1.** [water, wine] that is full of bubbles. **-2.** [person] who is lively and cheerful □ *She has a very bubbly personality.* ◇ *n* champagne (informal use).

Bucharest [ˌbjuːkəˈrest] the capital of Romania and its largest city. POPULATION: 2,064,474.

buck [bʌk] (*pl sense* 1 **buck** OR **bucks**) ◇ *n* **-1.** ZOOLOGY the male of certain animals, e.g. a rabbit, deer, or goat. **-2.** a dollar □ *It cost me fifty bucks.* ■ **to make a fast** OR **quick buck** to make money quickly and easily, especially by doing something dishonest (informal use). **-3.** *phrases* **the buck stops here** a phrase used to say that one is responsible for something and will not pass the responsibility on to somebody else. ■ **to pass the buck** to avoid taking responsibility for something by saying that somebody else is responsible for it. ◇ *vi* [horse] to jump in the air with all four feet off the ground. ◇ *vt* **-1.** [horse] to throw off <a rider> by bucking. **-2.** **to buck a trend** to do something that is different from a trend □ *True, some markets have fallen sharply, but others have bucked the trend.* ■ **to buck the system** to do something that a system tries to stop people doing.

◆ **buck up** ◇ *vt sep* (informal use) **-1.** **to buck sb up** to help sb to feel more cheerful □ *That's good news — it's really bucked me up!* **-2.** **to buck one's ideas up** to make an effort to improve one's behavior, performance etc □ *You need to buck your ideas up, young man!* ◇ *vi* (informal use) **-1.** to hurry up □ *Buck up! We're late!* **-2.** to start being more cheerful □ *Buck up! Don't look so sad!*

bucket ['bʌkət] *n* an open container with a

handle that is usually made of metal or plastic and is used for holding and carrying water, sand etc; the contents of this container □ *The bucket was full.* □ *a bucket of water.*

◆ **buckets** *npl* **buckets of sthg** a lot of sthg (informal use) □ *They've got buckets of money/time.*

Buckingham Palace ['bʌkɪŋəm-] the official home of the British royal family in central London.

Buckinghamshire ['bʌkɪŋəmʃər] a county in southern England. SIZE: 1,883 sq kms. POPULATION: 627,300. ADMINISTRATIVE CENTER: Aylesbury.

buckle ['bʌkl] ◇ *n* a metal fastener at one end of a belt or strap with a spike that fits into a hole in the other end. ◇ *vt* [belt, shoe] to fasten <sthg> with a buckle. ◇ *vi* **-1.** [wheel, metal] to make sthg bend out of shape □ *The girders buckled in the heat.* **-2.** [legs, knees] to bend because one is extremely weak or tired □ *Her legs buckled (under her) and she collapsed.*

◆ **buckle down** *vi* to start working seriously at something □ *It's about time you buckled down to those reports.*

◆ **buckle up** *vi* US to fasten one's safety belt.

Bucks *abbr of* **Buckinghamshire.**

buck's fizz *n* GB a drink made from champagne and orange juice.

buckshot ['bʌkʃɒt] *n* balls of lead that are shot from a gun, used especially for hunting animals and birds.

buckskin ['bʌkskɪn] *n* soft, strong, yellow-gray leather made from the skin of a deer □ *a pair of buckskin gloves.*

buckteeth [bʌk'tiːθ] *npl* front teeth that stick out.

buckthorn ['bʌkθɔːrn] *n* a small tree or shrub found in the Northern hemisphere that has thorns, small green flowers, and blue-black berries.

buckwheat ['bʌkwiːt] *n* cereal with a small black grain used for making flour and feeding animals.

bud [bʌd] (*pt* & *pp* **budded**, *cont* **budding**) ◇ *n* a small pointed growth on the stem of a plant that opens up to become a flower or leaf □ *a flower bud.* ■ **to nip sthg in the bud** to stop sthg at an early stage before it becomes fully developed □ *It's best to nip this sort of behavior in the bud.* ◇ *vi* [tree, plant] to grow buds.

Budapest [ˌbjuːdə'pest] the capital of Hungary and its largest city, on the Danube. POPULATION: 2,016,774.

Buddha ['budə] (563–483 BC) a name given to Gautama Siddhartha, an Indian religious teacher who founded Buddhism.

Buddhism ['budɪzm] *n* an Eastern religion based on the teachings of Buddha.

Buddhist ['budɪst] ◇ *n* a follower of Buddhism. ◇ *adj*: *a Buddhist monk/temple.*

budding ['bʌdɪŋ] *adj* **a budding poet/artist etc** a person who is trying to make a career of being a poet/an artist etc and looks as if they will become successful.

buddy ['bʌdɪ] (*pl* **buddies**) *n* a friend (informal use).

budge [bʌdʒ] ◇ *vt* to make <sb/sthg> move □ *The drawer's stuck and I can't budge it.* ◇ *vi* **-1.** to move slightly □ *The car won't budge. He hasn't budged from his chair all day.* **-2.** to change one's opinion about something □ *She refuses to budge on the issue.* □ *It's no good, his mind's made up and he won't budge.*

budgerigar ['bʌdʒərɪgɑːr] *n* a small green, yellow, or blue bird that is often kept in a cage as a pet and can copy people's voices.

budget ['bʌdʒət] ◇ *n* **-1.** a plan that shows how much money a person or organization has available and how it will be spent □ *I have drawn up a budget for the project.* **-2.** the amount of money available for a particular purpose or to a particular person or group □ *Our budget won't stretch that far.*
◇ *vt* [money, time] to plan how to spend <sthg> □ *These are our budgeted requirements for next year.*
◇ *vi* to make a plan of how one is going to spend the money that one has available □ *We'll have to budget carefully to make the money last.*
◇ *adj* [travel, vacation, price] cheap □ *budget accommodation.*

◆ **Budget** *n* POLITICS a statement made by a government that gives details about the money they will collect from taxes and how they plan to spend it.

◆ **budget for** ◇ *vt fus* **to budget for sthg** to include the cost of sthg in one's budget □ *I hadn't budgeted for two more members of staff.*

budget account *n* **-1.** an account at a department store that allows customers to make monthly payments for the things they have bought. **-2.** an account with a bank that customers can make regular payments into for household bills.

budgetary [US 'bʌdʒəterɪ, GB -ɪtrɪ] *adj* [policy, planning] that is connected with the money a person or organization has and how they spend it □ *budgetary constraints.*

budgie ['bʌdʒɪ] *n* = **budgerigar** (informal use).

Buenos Aires [ˌbweɪnəs'aɪrɪz] the capital of Argentina and its largest city. POPULATION: 2,960,976.

buff [bʌf] ◇ *adj* [envelope, file] pale brown. ◇ *n* a person who knows a lot about a particular subject and is enthusiastic about it (informal use) □ *a movie buff.*

buffalo ['bʌfələʊ] (*pl* **buffalo** OR **buffaloes** OR **buffalos**) *n* **-1.** a large animal like a cow that has curved horns and lives mainly in Africa. **-2.** an animal like a cow with a large head and a humped back that used to be common in North America.

Buffalo Bill [ˌbʌfələʊ'bɪl] (1846–1917) a US army scout who later became an entertainer, touring the USA and Europe with his *Wild West Show.* His real name was William Cody.

buffer ['bʌfər] *n* **-1.** a person or thing that protects somebody or something from harm □

The welfare state acts as a buffer against extreme poverty. **-2.** COMPUTING a part of a computer's memory where data can be stored temporarily. **-3.** GB RAIL = **bumper.**

buffer state *n* a small, usually neutral, country that is situated between two larger rival countries and reduces the chances of conflict between them.

buffet¹ [US bə'feɪ, GB 'bʊfeɪ] *n* **-1.** a meal, usually at a party or organized event, where people serve themselves prepared food from a table and often eat it standing up □ *a buffet lunch/meal.* **-2.** a place in a train or bus station where one can buy food or drink and sit down to have it □ *the station buffet.* **-3.** = **buffet car.**

buffet² ['bʌfət] *vt* to keep pushing against <sb/sthg> violently □ *We were buffeted by the wind.*

buffet car [US bə'feɪ-, GB 'bʊfeɪ-] *n* a part of a train where drinks, sandwiches etc are sold.

buffoon [bə'fuːn] *n* a person who behaves in a way one thinks is ridiculous and foolish (old-fashioned use).

bug [bʌg] (*pt* & *pp* **bugged,** *cont* **bugging**) ◇ *n* **-1.** any small insect. **-2.** MEDICINE a minor illness, e.g. a cold or a stomach infection, that is easily caught from another person □ *There's a bug going around at the moment.* □ *a stomach bug.* **-3.** TECHNOLOGY a small device that is hidden in somebody's home, telephone etc in order to listen secretly to their conversations. **-4.** COMPUTING a small fault in a computer program. **-5. the travel/gardening etc bug** a very strong and often sudden enthusiasm for travel/gardening etc (informal use) □ *He's been bitten by the music bug.* ◇ *vt* **-1.** to put a bug in <sb's room, telephone> etc. **-2.** to annoy <sb> (informal use) □ *Quit bugging me!*

bugbear ['bʌgbeəʳ] *n* something that one generally finds very annoying or worrying □ *Junk mail is a real bugbear of mine.*

bugger▽ ['bʌgəʳ] GB (very informal use) ◇ *n* **-1.** a word used to talk to or about an unpleasant person in a way that shows one is annoyed by them □ *He's a selfish bugger.* **-2.** a word used to pretend to be rude about somebody one likes as a joke □ *You silly bugger!* **-3.** a word used to describe a difficult task or job or something that causes a problem □ *Having to get up at five each morning is a real bugger.* ◇ *excl* a word used to show that one is annoyed.

♦ **bugger off**▽ *vi* **bugger off!** go away! (very informal use).

buggy ['bʌgɪ] (*pl* **buggies**) *n* **-1.** a small carriage that is pulled by one horse. **-2.** a vehicle for a baby or young child that is pushed.

bugle ['bjuːgl] *n* a small brass musical instrument, similar to a trumpet but smaller and simpler, that is used especially in the army.

build [bɪld] (*pt* & *pp* **built**) ◇ *vt* **-1.** [house, bridge, aircraft] to make <sthg> by joining separate parts together □ *They're building a new supermarket on the edge of town.* ■ **to be built of sthg** [of bricks, wood] to be built using

sthg as the main material □ *Most of these office buildings are built of reinforced concrete.* **-2.** [relationship, society] to develop or create <sthg> gradually and carefully □ *They are trying to build a better world.* **-3. to build sthg into a wall/room etc** to build sthg so that it is part of a wall/room etc and not just fixed to it □ *The lighting is built into the ceiling.* **-4. to build sthg into a system/contract etc** to make sthg part of a system/contract etc □ *A monthly allowance is built into the agreement.* ◇ *n* the shape or size of a person's body □ *a man of medium/large build.*

♦ **build on** ◇ *vt sep* **to build sthg on sthg** to use sthg as the basis of sthg else □ *This company is built on democratic principles.* ◇ *vt fus* **to build on sthg** [on success, a relationship, result] to develop sthg further □ *We must build on the progress we have made this year.*

♦ **build up** ◇ *vt sep* **-1. to build sthg up** [speed, business, reputation] to gradually increase the size or amount of sthg □ *Over the years we've built up a lot of international contacts.* **-2. to build sthg up** [trust, confidence, hatred] to develop sthg so that one feels it more strongly □ *It takes a while to build up trust between doctor and patient.* ◇ *vi* [clouds, traffic, tension] to increase or develop gradually □ *The anger was building up inside her, waiting to explode.*

♦ **build upon** *vt sep* & *vt fus* = **build on.**

builder ['bɪldəʳ] *n* a person whose job is to build or repair houses and other buildings.

building ['bɪldɪŋ] *n* **-1.** a structure, e.g. a house or factory, that has walls and a roof □ *an office building.* **-2.** the work of building houses, bridges etc □ *building materials* □ *the building industry/trade* □ *Building work began last month.*

building and loan association *n* US an organization that keeps money for people who want to save it and uses it to give loans to people who want to buy a home.

building block *n* **-1.** one of a set of wooden or plastic blocks used as a toy for a child to build things with. **-2.** one of the basic parts that go together to make something.

building contractor *n* a person whose job is to organize the building of houses, offices etc.

building site *n* a place where a building is being built.

building society *n* GB an organization that keeps money for people who want to save it and uses it to lend money to people who want to buy a home □ *a building society account.*

buildup ['bɪldʌp] *n* [of traffic, weapons, troops] a gradual increase in the number or amount of people or things at a particular time □ *There are fears of a military buildup in the region.* □ *There will be a big publicity buildup to the launch.* □ *'Prevents the buildup of limescale in kettles and irons.'*

built [bɪlt] ◇ *past tense & past participle of* **build.** ◇ *adj* **to be built for sthg/to do sthg** to be specially designed for sthg/to do sthg □ *This vehicle is not built for speed/to carry heavy loads.* □ *Our shoes are built to last.*

built-in adj [closet, clause, safety device] that has been built into something.

built-up adj a **built-up area** an area where there are a lot of buildings.

bulb [bʌlb] n -1. ELECTRICITY the rounded glass part of an electric lamp that produces light □ a 100-watt bulb □ a naked bulb. -2. [of a flower, plant] the rounded root of some plants, e.g. a daffodil, onion, or tulip, that the plant grows from □ a tulip bulb. -3. [of an object] a rounded part on an object such as a thermometer.

bulbous ['bʌlbəs] adj [nose, shape] that looks large, round, and unattractive.

Bulgaria [bʌl'geərɪə] a country in southeastern Europe, on the Black Sea, between Romania and Greece. It was a Communist state from 1947 to 1989. SIZE: 111,000 sq kms. POPULATION: 9,000,000 (Bulgarians). CAPITAL: Sofia. LANGUAGE: Bulgarian. CURRENCY: lev.

bulge [bʌldʒ] ◇ n -1. [on a surface] a rounded mass that forms on a normally flat surface □ There was a strange bulge on the wall. -2. [in the population, birthrate] a sudden, but temporary, increase. ◇ vi to stick out and form a rounded mass, especially because there is not enough space □ His stomach bulged out over his belt. ■ **to be bulging with sthg** [bag, case, folder] to be so full of sthg that it bulges □ The file was bulging with papers.

bulging ['bʌldʒɪŋ] adj [pocket, bag, file] that is so full that it bulges; [stomach, muscle] that is so large that it bulges; [eyes, veins] that seem to stick out, especially because of emotion or physical effort.

bulimia [bjʊ'lɪmɪə], **bulimia nervosa** [bjʊ,lɪm-ɪənɜː'vəʊsə] n a medical condition in which people, especially young women, eat large amounts of food, usually secretly, and then make themselves sick.

bulimic [bjʊ'lɪmɪk] ◇ adj who is suffering from bulimia. ◇ n a bulimic person.

bulk [bʌlk] ◇ n -1. [of an object] the large size of something □ The package was a problem because of its sheer bulk. -2. [of a person, animal] a body that is large and heavy □ He lowered his bulk onto the sofa. -3. **in bulk** [buy, sell] in large quantities □ We find it's cheaper to buy in bulk. -4. **the bulk of sthg** most of sthg □ The bulk of complaints came from older viewers. ◇ adj [order, sale, purchase] that involves something that is bought or sold in bulk □ We offer special bulk rates for orders of over 100 units.

bulk buying [-'baɪŋ] n the act of buying goods in bulk.

bulkhead ['bʌlkhed] n a wall inside a ship or plane that divides it into separate parts.

bulky ['bʌlkɪ] (compar **bulkier**, superl **bulkiest**) adj [package, equipment] large, heavy, and awkward to move or carry; [pullover, jacket] thick and large.

bull [bʊl] n -1. FARMING a male cow. -2. ZOOLOGY the male of some animals, e.g. an elephant or seal □ a bull elephant. -3. FINANCE a person who buys shares when they think share prices are going to rise in order to sell

them at a higher price later. -4.▽ a word used to show that one thinks something is completely untrue (very informal use) □ That's a load of bull!

bulldog ['bʊldɒg] n a small strong dog with short legs, a short neck, and a large broad head.

bulldog clip n GB a large metal clip with a spring, used for holding papers together.

bulldoze ['bʊldəʊz] vt -1. [earth, stones, trees] to move or remove <sthg> with a bulldozer in order to make a level surface □ Whole villages have been bulldozed flat. -2. [building] to destroy <sthg> with a bulldozer. -3. **to bulldoze sb into sthg** to force sb into sthg □ He was bulldozed into selling. ■ **to bulldoze one's way into/through sthg** to force one's way into/through sthg □ She bulldozed her way to the top of the business.

bulldozer ['bʊldəʊzəʳ] n a powerful vehicle with a metal blade at the front that is used to knock down buildings, move earth etc.

bullet ['bʊlɪt] n -1. [for a gun] a small metal object with a pointed end that is fired from a gun. -2. PRINTING a large dot used in texts to show the start of an important section.

bulletin ['bʊlətən] n -1. a short news report or an official public statement about a matter of public interest that is broadcast on TV or on the radio □ We will be bringing you news bulletins throughout the night. -2. a regular publication or report produced by an organization, association etc.

bulletin board n -1. a board on a wall on which notices are displayed. -2. COMPUTING a system that allows computer users to send each other messages and information.

bullet-proof adj [vest, glass, car] that is designed to stop bullets passing through.

bullfight ['bʊlfaɪt] n a traditional form of entertainment in Spain and other countries in which a man fights and usually kills a bull.

bullfighter ['bʊlfaɪtəʳ] n a man who fights bulls in bullfights.

bullfighting ['bʊlfaɪtɪŋ] n the act or sport of fighting bulls.

bullion ['bʊljən] n gold or silver in the form of bars □ gold bullion.

bullish ['bʊlɪʃ] adj FINANCE [market, trend] that shows a rise in prices; [person] who expects a rise in prices.

bull market n a situation in which people buy shares because it appears that the price of shares is going to rise.

bullock ['bʊlək] n a young bull that cannot breed.

bullring ['bʊlrɪŋ] n a round area of ground surrounded by seats where bullfights take place.

bull's-eye n the small circle at the center of a target in shooting, darts, or archery; a shot or throw with which one hits this circle.

bullshit▽ ['bʊlʃɪt] (pt & pp **bullshitted**, cont **bullshitting**) (vulgar use) ◇ n a word used to show that one thinks something is untrue or a lie. ◇ *vi* to talk nonsense.

bull terrier *n* a strong dog with short, often white, hair and a long flat nose.

bully ['bʊlɪ] (*pl* **bullies**, *pt* & *pp* **bullied**) ◇ *n* a person who acts in an aggressive and unpleasant way to somebody who is weaker, e.g. to frighten them or to make them do something □ *Don't be such a bully!* ◇ *vt* [student, staff] to behave in an aggressive and unpleasant way toward <sb who is weaker> □ *She was bullied at school.* ■ **to bully sb into doing sthg** to persuade sb to do sthg by being aggressive and forceful □ *Don't let him bully you into going.*

bullying ['bʊlɪɪŋ] *n* aggressive and unpleasant behavior toward somebody who is weaker □ *There is concern over increased bullying in schools.*

bulrush ['bʊlrʌʃ] *n* a tall plant that grows near water and has a thick stem with a soft brown part at the top.

bum [bʌm] (*pt* & *pp* **bummed**, *cont* **bumming**) (informal use) *n* **-1.** a tramp. **-2.** a person who one thinks does not do any work and is very lazy □ *You lazy bum!* **-3.** GB one's bottom.

◆ **bum around** *vi* **-1.** to spend time being lazy and doing nothing worthwhile or useful □ *He bums around at home all day watching TV.* **-2.** to travel from one place to another for pleasure, with very little money.

bum bag *n* GB a small leather or plastic bag for valuables, worn on a belt outside one's clothes.

bumblebee ['bʌmblbiː] *n* a large furry bee.

bumbling ['bʌmblɪŋ] *adj* [person] who seems clumsy, confused, and inefficient.

bumf [bʌmf] *n* GB written material containing information about an organization, service etc that is usually given out in large quantities and often considered boring (informal use).

bump [bʌmp] ◇ *n* **-1.** [on one's knee, head] a small round swelling on one's body, often caused by hitting some object; [on the ground, a slope] an uneven raised part of a flat surface □ *He's got a big bump on his head.* □ *There was a bump in the road.* **-2.** [in an accident] a knock that a vehicle gets in an accident that is not very serious □ *The car got a bump during the storm but nobody was hurt.* **-3.** the dull heavy sound of something falling onto or hitting something else □ *There was a loud bump from upstairs.*
◇ *vt* [one's head, knee, car] to hit <sthg> accidentally by knocking it against something else □ *I bumped my elbow on/against the door.*
◇ *vi* **to bump along** [car, truck] to move over an uneven surface.

◆ **bump into** *vt fus* **-1.** to bump into sb/sthg [into a table, door, child] to hit sb/sthg accidentally with a part of one's body □ *She kept bumping into things in the dark.* **-2.** to bump into sb [friend, colleague] to meet sb by chance □ *I bumped into him on my way home.*

◆ **bump off** *vt sep* **to bump sb off** to kill sb (informal use).

◆ **bump up** *vt sep* **to bump sthg up** [sales, production, price] to increase sthg (informal use).

bumper ['bʌmpər] ◇ *adj* [harvest, crop, pack] larger than usual. ◇ *n* **-1.** AUTO a bar fixed at the front and back of a car that protects it if it bumps into something. **-2.** US RAIL one of a pair of metal disks fixed to springs at both ends of a car or at the end of a railroad track to reduce the shock when cars bump against each other or when a train hits the end of the track.

bumper-to-bumper *adj* [cars, traffic] driving slowly with each vehicle very close to the next one.

bumpy ['bʌmpɪ] (*compar* **bumpier**, *superl* **bumpiest**) *adj* **-1.** [surface, road, ground] that has many bumps. **-2.** [ride, trip] that is uncomfortable because the road or surface has many bumps.

bun [bʌn] *n* **-1.** US a small round loaf of bread for one person □ *a hamburger bun.* **-2.** a small sweet roll that often contains currants or spices □ *a fruit bun.* **-3.** a hairstyle consisting of long hair gathered in a round shape at the top or back of the head □ *She wore her hair in a bun.*

bunch [bʌntʃ] ◇ *n* **-1.** [of people] a group of people who are similar in some way □ *They're a bunch of crooks.* □ *Her family are a strange bunch.* **-2. a bunch of flowers** a number of cut flowers that are tied or held together □ *a bunch of roses.* **-3. a bunch of grapes/bananas etc** a number of grapes/bananas etc that have grown together on the same stem. **-4. a bunch of keys** a number of keys that are held together with a keyring, piece of string etc. ◇ *vt* to group or gather <several things> together to form a bunch □ *We all sat bunched together in the back of the van.* ◇ *vi* [people] to form a small group with everybody very close to each other.

◆ **bunches** *npl* GB a hairstyle for women and girls consisting of long hair gathered and tied in two sections, one on either side of the head □ *She wore her hair in bunches.*

bundle ['bʌndl] ◇ *n* [of papers, clothes, wood] a number of things or pieces that are gathered, piled, or tied together □ *He carried a large bundle of papers.* ◇ *vt* to push or put <sb/sthg> somewhere quickly and without being careful □ *They were bundled into a waiting taxi.* □ *She bundled some clothes into a suitcase.* □ *We were bundled off to school in a big car.*

◆ **bundle up** *vt sep* **-1. to bundle sthg up** [papers, wood] to put sthg into bundles. **-2. to bundle sb up** to dress <sb> in warm clothes □ *She bundled the baby up in a blanket.*

bundled software ['bʌndld-] *n* the programs that are included in the price when one buys computer hardware and software together.

bung [bʌŋ] ◇ *n* a round piece of rubber, wood, plastic etc used to close the hole in a container. ◇ *vt* GB to throw or put <sthg> somewhere in a careless way (informal use).

bungalow [ˈbʌŋgəlou] *n* a house with only one story.

bunged up [bʌŋd-] *adj* **to be bunged up** [nose, drain] to be blocked (informal use).

bungee-jumping [ˈbʌndʒiːdʒʌmpɪŋ] *n* the sport of jumping from a bridge, building etc with an elastic cord attached to one's body to prevent one from hitting the ground.

bungle [ˈbʌŋgl] *vt* [job, robbery, operation] to do <sthg> badly with the result that it fails.

bunion [ˈbʌnjən] *n* a painful swelling on the first joint of one's big toe.

bunk [bʌŋk] *n* -1. [on a ship, train] a narrow bed attached to a wall. -2. = **bunk bed**. -3. a word used to describe something that one thinks is stupid and untrue (informal use) □ *What a load of bunk!*

bunk bed *n* one of two beds fixed one above the other.

bunker [ˈbʌŋkəʳ] *n* -1. MILITARY a building, often built underground, that is used to protect people from bombs and gunfire □ *a concrete bunker.* -2. [for coal] a container or place for storing coal □ *a coal bunker.* -3. GOLF a large hole on a golf course that is filled with sand □ *a sand bunker.*

Bunker Hill the place outside Boston where the first important battle of the American Revolution was fought, on June 17, 1775.

bunkhouse [ˈbʌŋkhaus, *pl* -hauzɪz] *n* a building where the workers on a ranch sleep.

bunny [ˈbʌnɪ] (*pl* **bunnies**) *n* a word used by children to refer to a rabbit.

bunny hill *n* US a ski slope for beginners.

bunny rabbit *n* = **bunny**.

Bunsen burner [ˌbʌnsn-] *n* a device used in laboratories for heating chemicals that produces a strong flame using gas.

bunting [ˈbʌntɪŋ] *n* small colored flags on a long string that are hung up in streets on special occasions □ *The streets were decorated with bunting.*

buoy [US ˈbuːɪ, GB bɔɪ] *n* a floating object that is attached to the bottom of a river or the sea by a rope or chain and marks the areas where boats can and cannot sail.

◆ **buoy up** *vt sep* **to buoy sb up** to make sb feel more cheerful or confident.

buoyancy [US ˈbuːjənsɪ, GB ˈbɔɪənsɪ] *n*: see **buoyant** □ *a feeling of buoyancy.*

buoyant [US ˈbuːjənt, GB ˈbɔɪənt] *adj* -1. [object] that can float in a liquid. -2. [person] who is optimistic and cheerful □ *He was in a buoyant mood.*

burden [ˈbɜːʳdn] ◇ *n* -1. a heavy object or load that a person or animal has to carry. -2. a person or thing that causes a lot of worry, work etc for the person who feels responsible for them □ *She has become a burden on her family.* □ *Our long-term aim is to decrease the tax burden on the public.* ◇ *vt* **to burden sb with sthg** [with a problem, a responsibility, tax] to force sb to have to deal with sthg in addi-

tion to what they already have □ *I don't want to burden you with my problems/extra work.*

bureau [ˈbjuərou] (*pl* **bureaux** OR **bureaus**) *n* -1. POLITICS in the USA, a government department. -2. BUSINESS an office or agency that collects and provides information. -3. US [for clothes] a chest of drawers. -4. GB = **writing bureau**.

bureaucracy [bjuəˈrɒkrəsɪ] (*pl* **bureaucracies**) *n* -1. a system of administration that employs a large number of officials; the officials who work in this system □ *an overworked and inefficient bureaucracy.* -2. administrative rules and procedures that are complicated and confusing □ *He hates bureaucracy.*

bureaucrat [ˈbjuərəkræt] *n* an official who works in a bureaucracy (disapproving use) □ *I'm tired of dealing with government bureaucrats.*

bureaucratic [ˌbjuərəˈkrætɪk] *adj* [system, procedure] that involves following the complicated rules of a particular organization and can be slow and frustrating □ *The whole experience was a bureaucratic nightmare.*

bureau de change [-dəʃɑːndʒ] (*pl* **bureaux de change**) *n* GB a place, e.g. a counter in a bank or travel agent's, where customers can change money into another currency.

bureaux [ˈbjuərouz] *plural of* **bureau**.

burger [ˈbɜːʳgəʳ] *n* a hamburger.

burglar [ˈbɜːʳgləʳ] *n* a person who enters buildings illegally and steals things.

burglar alarm *n* an electronic device that makes a loud ringing noise when somebody tries to enter a building secretly and illegally.

burglarize [ˈbɜːʳgləraɪz] *vt* US [house, office] to enter <a building> illegally to steal things.

burglary [ˈbɜːʳglərɪ] (*pl* **burglaries**) *n* the crime of burglarizing a building □ *We reported the burglary to the police.*

burgle [ˈbɜːʳgl] *vt* GB = **burglarize**.

burial [ˈberɪəl] *n* the act or ceremony of burying a dead person □ *Chris wasn't at the burial.*

burial ground *n* a place where people are buried □ *an ancient burial ground.*

Burke and Wills [ˌbɜːʳkəndˈwɪlz] Robert Burke (1821–1861) and William Wills (1834–1861), the first European explorers to cross Australia from the north to the south, in 1860.

Burke's Peerage [ˌbɜːʳks-] *n* a book that lists the names and titles of all the British aristocratic families.

burly [ˈbɜːʳlɪ] (*compar* **burlier**, *superl* **burliest**) *adj* [man] who is big, strong, and heavy.

Burma [ˈbɜːʳmə] = **Myanmar**.

Burmese [bɜːʳˈmiːz] (*pl* **Burmese**) *n* & *adj*: see **Myanmar**.

burn [bɜːʳn] (*pt* & *pp* **burned** OR **burnt**) ◇ *vi* -1. [paper, car, building] to produce flames and great heat and be damaged or destroyed □ *She could smell something burning upstairs.* -2. [fuel, coal] to be able to start and continue to burn □ *I can't get this wood to burn.* -3. [candle, fire] to give heat or light after being lit □ *The lamps burned brightly.* -4. [food] to be spoiled by being cooked for too long or in heat that is too great □ *The toast's burning!* **-5.** [acid, alcohol, lotion] to cause a hot painful feeling when it is drunk or put on one's skin. **-6.** [face, cheek] to feel very hot because one is ill or embarrassed. **-7.** [person, skin] to become sunburned □ *I burn easily.* **-8. to burn with sthg** [with anger, desire] to feel sthg very strongly □ *He was burning with rage.*

◇ *vt* **-1.** [object, document, building] to destroy <sthg> by fire □ *They were burning trash in the back yard.* □ *The house was burned to the ground.* **-2.** [meat, toast, cake] to spoil <food> by cooking it for too long or in heat that is too great □ *I've left the stove on and burned the vegetables!* **-3.** [coal, wood, oil] to use <sthg that burns> as a fuel □ *a wood-/coal-burning stove.* **-4.** [person, skin, hand] to damage the skin of <sb or part of sb's body> by heat, fire, or chemicals □ *I burned myself on the oven.* □ *I got badly burned in the sun.*

◇ *n* **-1.** [on a person] a wound caused by burning □ *I got a nasty burn from the iron.* □ *a burn mark.* **-2.** [on an object, fabric] a mark or hole caused by burning □ *a cigarette/acid burn.*

♦ **burn down** ◇ *vt sep* **to burn sthg down** [town, building] to destroy sthg by fire □ *Fire/An arsonist burned down the factory.* ◇ *vi* **-1.** [town, building] *His house burned down in the fire.* **-2.** [fire, candle] to burn less brightly.

♦ **burn out** ◇ *vt sep* **to burn oneself out** to make oneself ill or very tired by working or exercising too hard over a period of time (informal use). ◇ *vi* [fire] to stop burning because there is no wood, coal etc left to burn.

♦ **burn up** ◇ *vt sep* **to burn sthg up** [fuel, energy] to use a lot of <sthg> □ *Swimming is a good way of burning up excess calories.* ◇ *vi* [rocket, satellite] to be destroyed by fire, especially when re-entering the Earth's atmosphere.

burner ['bɜːrnər] *n* one of the parts of a stove that produces flames or heat.

burning ['bɜːrnɪŋ] ◇ *adj* **-1.** [desert, heat, sun] very hot □ *I could feel the burning heat of the flames.* **-2.** [face, cheek] that feels hot because one is ill or embarrassed. **-3. a burning interest/desire etc** a very strong interest/desire etc □ *It was her burning ambition to fly a plane.* ■ **a burning question** OR **issue** a subject that people are thinking about and feel strongly about at a particular time. **-4.** [car, wreckage] that is on fire □ *They pulled his body out of the burning ruins of the house.* ◇ *adv* **burning hot** very hot □ *a burning hot day.*

burnish ['bɜːrnɪʃ] *vt* [metal, surface] to polish <sthg> so that it shines.

burnout ['bɜːrnaʊt] *n* **-1.** [of a machine] a breakdown caused by overheating. **-2.** [of a person] illness or extreme tiredness that is caused by working too hard over a period of time.

Burns ['bɜːrnz], **Robert** (1759–1796) a Scottish poet who wrote many poems about love and everyday country life. He is considered the national poet of Scotland.

Burns Night *n* January 25, the anniversary of the birth of Robert Burns. Scottish people celebrate it by eating traditional Scottish food, reading Burns' poetry, and singing his songs.

burnt [bɜːrnt] *past tense & past participle of* **burn.**

burnt-out *adj* **-1.** [building, car] that has been completely destroyed by fire □ *the burnt-out shell of a house.* **-2.** [person] who is ill or very tired because they have done too much work or exercise over a period of time □ *If you're not careful, you'll be burnt-out by the time you're forty.*

burp [bɜːrp] ◇ *vi* [person] to make a noise by letting gas from the stomach out through the mouth (informal use). ◇ *vt* to make <a baby> bring up air from its stomach after eating by rubbing or gently hitting its back. ◇ *n* an act of burping (informal use) □ *He gave a loud burp.*

burrow [US 'bɜːroʊ, GB 'bʌr-] ◇ *n* a hole in the ground that an animal, e.g. a rabbit or mole, digs and uses as a place to live. ◇ *vi* **-1.** [rabbit, mole, worm] to dig a hole in the ground. **-2.** [person] to search with one's hands for something that is among other things or in a container □ *She burrowed around in her pockets for a coin.*

bursar ['bɜːrsər] *n* a person whose job is to control the money and spending of an institution □ *the school/college bursar.*

bursary ['bɜːrsərɪ] (*pl* **bursaries**) *n* GB an amount of money given to somebody by an institution or organization so that they can study.

burst [bɜːrst] (*pt & pp* **burst**) ◇ *vi* **-1.** [tire, pipe, dam] to break or split open, usually in one place, so that everything that is inside suddenly comes out □ *The balloon burst in my face.* **-2. to burst open** [door, lid] to open suddenly and violently □ *Suddenly the door burst open and Dave rushed in.* **-3. to burst into/out of a place** to enter/leave a place suddenly and noisily □ *He burst into/out of the room.* ■ **to burst in on sb** to suddenly and noisily enter a place where sb is, often interrupting something they are doing □ *Sorry to burst in on you like this.*

◇ *vt* [tire, pipe, dam] *Don't blow up the balloon too much, you'll burst it!*

◇ *n* [of gunfire, activity] a sudden period of something □ *There was a burst of applause.*

♦ **burst into** *vt fus* **-1. to burst into tears/laughter/flames** to suddenly start crying/laughing/burning. **-2. to burst into flower** OR **bloom** to produce a lot of flowers suddenly □ *Every summer the roses burst into flower.*

♦ **burst out** *vt fus* **-1. to burst out sthg** to say sthg suddenly □ *"What's going to happen to me?" she burst out.* **-2. to burst out laughing/crying** to start laughing/crying suddenly.

bursting ['bɜːrstɪŋ] *adj* **-1. to be bursting** [bag, room, town] to be so full that there is no room for anything else; [person] to feel that one has eaten so much that one cannot eat anything more □ *The room was bursting with people.* □ *I can't eat any more, I'm bursting.* **-2. to be bursting with sthg** [with excitement, pride, energy] to be very full of sthg □ *She was bursting with enthusiasm/health.* **-3. to be bursting to do sthg** to be very eager to do sthg □ *They were bursting to tell us the news.*

bury ['berɪ] (*pt & pp* **buried**) *vt* **-1.** [person] to put <sb who is dead> into a grave □ *He was buried in his home town.* **-2.** [object] to hide <sthg> by putting it in a hole in the ground and covering it with earth □ *buried treasure.* **-3. to bury one's face/head in sthg** to press one's face/head against sthg □ *She buried her face in her hands/the pillow.* **-4. to bury oneself in sthg** [in work, a book] to give all one's time or attention to sthg.

bus [bʌs] (*pl* **buses** OR **busses**, *pt & pp* **bused** OR **bussed**, *cont* **busing** OR **bussing**) ◇ *n* **-1.** a large motor vehicle that carries passengers who pay for trips along a fixed route □ *We got on/off the bus.* □ *I travel to work by bus.* □ *a bus route/service.* □ *How much is the bus fare?* **-2.** COMPUTING an electronic channel through which data is transferred between parts of a computer. ◇ *vt* **-1.** to take <students> by bus to a school in a different area. **-2. to bus tables** US to work as a busboy in a restaurant.

busboy ['bʌsbɔɪ] *n* US a young man whose job is to take away dirty dishes from tables in a restaurant.

bus conductor *n* GB a person whose job is to collect fares from passengers on a bus.

bus driver *n* a person whose job is to drive buses.

bush [bʊʃ] *n* **-1.** BOTANY a large plant with many branches that is smaller than a tree. **-2. the bush** the wild area of a hot country, e.g. in Africa or Australia, where few people live. **-3. to beat around** US OR **about** GB **the bush** to avoid saying something directly, usually because it is unpleasant or embarrassing □ *There's no need to beat around the bush, just tell me what the problem is.*

bushel ['bʊʃl] *n* a unit (US 35.24 liters, GB 36.4 liters) for measuring amounts of cereals or vegetables.

bushfire ['bʊʃfaɪər] *n* a fire that has gotten out of control in a wild area of a hot country.

bushy ['bʊʃɪ] (*compar* **bushier**, *superl* **bushiest**) *adj* [hair, beard, tail] that is very thick; [plant, tree] that has many branches and leaves growing close together.

busily ['bɪzɪlɪ] *adv: see* **busy** □ *John was busily preparing dinner when I arrived.*

business ['bɪznəs] *n* **-1.** [of a company] the activity of buying and selling goods or services to make money □ *I'm in the travel/fashion business.* □ *The firm has been in business for 25 years.* □ *She's decided to go into business on her own.* □ *He does a lot of business with German companies.* □ *How's business?* □ *We've lost business to foreign competitors.* □ *business interests/hours* □ *the business community* □ *a business trip/partner.* ■ **to be/go on business** [person] to be/go somewhere because of work and not for pleasure □ *I'm here on business.* □ *Are you traveling on business?* ■ **to go out of business** [person, company] to stop trading, usually be-

cause one is not making enough money □ *Meadgate Leisure went out of business three years ago.* **-2.** an organization that buys and sells goods or provides a service □ *He runs the family business.* □ *I'd like to set up a business of my own one day.* **-3. one's business** something that is one's responsibility, problem etc and does not concern other people □ *"Can Dan afford it?" — "That's his business."* □ *It's none of your business how I spend my time.* ■ **to have no business doing** OR **to do sthg** to have no right to do sthg □ *He had no business telling you what to do.* ■ **mind your own business!** stop taking an interest in things that do not concern you (informal use). **-4.** a word used to describe an event, activity, situation etc that one finds unusual or disapproves of □ *It's a strange/dirty business.* □ *This strike business has gone on for long enough.* **-5.** *phrase* **to mean business** to be serious about what one is doing or threatening to do (informal use) □ *When Carson says he'll take you to court, he means business.*

business address *n* the address of the company where one works.

business card *n* a card that somebody in business gives to their customers and to people they meet, and that shows their name, job, business address etc.

business class *n* the standard of service and seating on a plane that is cheaper than first class and more expensive than tourist class □ *I always fly business class.*

business hours *npl* the hours when stores and offices are open.

businesslike ['bɪznəslaɪk] *adj* [person] who is efficient and does not waste time on unnecessary things □ *in a businesslike manner.*

businessman ['bɪznəsmæn] (*pl* **businessmen** [-men]) *n* a man who is in business, especially a manager of a company.

business park *n* an area, usually outside a town, planned as a place where businesses and offices can be built.

business plan *n* a document that explains a project that a company wants to carry out, and the costs and profits involved in it.

business reply mail *n* the system in which a company pays the cost of postage for the letters it receives.

business school *n* a school or college that specializes in subjects connected with business, e.g. management and commerce.

business suit *n* US a man's suit that is worn at work rather than at a formal occasion.

businesswoman ['bɪznəswʊmən] (*pl* **businesswomen**) *n* a woman who is in business, especially a manager of a company.

busker ['bʌskər] *n* GB a person who sings or plays music in a public place such as a street or subway station in order to get money.

bus lane *n* a lane on a wide street where only buses are allowed to drive.

bus shelter *n* a structure at a bus stop that has a roof and three sides to protect people waiting there from the weather.

bus station *n* a place where buses begin and end their trips.

bus stop *n* a place, usually marked by a pole or shelter, where buses stop to let people get on or off.

bust [bʌst] (*pt & pp* **bust** OR **busted**) ◇ *n* -1. [of a woman] a woman's breasts; the measurement around a woman's body at the level of her breasts □ *Take the measurement just below the bust.* □ *What bust size are you?* -2. [by an artist] a sculpture of a person's head and shoulders □ *a marble bust.* -3. [by the police] a situation in which the police go into a place quickly and unexpectedly and arrest people there for an illegal activity (informal use) □ *a drugs bust.*
◇ *vt* (informal use) -1. [watch, machine, leg] to break <sthg> □ *She bust my calculator.* -2. [person] to arrest <sb> □ *Stein was busted by the state police for possession of heroin.* -3. [house, party] to go into <a place> quickly and unexpectedly to arrest people there for an illegal activity □ *The party was busted by the police.*
◇ *vi* [watch, machine, leg] (informal use) □ *The bag has bust.*
◇ *adj* (informal use) -1. [watch, machine] broken □ *The radio's bust.* -2. **to go bust** [person, company] to go bankrupt □ *The firm went bust.*

bustle ['bʌsl] ◇ *n* energetic and noisy activity □ *I miss the bustle of the city streets.* ◇ *vi* to move somewhere quickly in a determined and energetic way □ *She was bustling around in the kitchen.*

bustling ['bʌslɪŋ] *adj* [city, market] that is full of bustle □ *the bustling city streets.*

bust-up *n* (informal use) -1. a fight caused by an argument □ *There was a bust-up at the bar last night.* -2. [of a marriage, relationship] a quarrel that ends a relationship □ *They've had a bust-up.*

busy ['bɪzɪ] (*compar* **busier**, *superl* **busiest**) ◇ *adj* -1. [person] who has a lot to do and so is active and does not have much free time □ *She likes to keep busy.* □ *Can I call you back? I'm busy at the moment.* □ *He's busy drafting the new contracts.* -2. [week, town, office] that is full of activity □ *August is our busiest time of the year.* -3. **to be busy** [phone, line] to be already in use, so that one hears the busy signal □ *I tried to call you, but the line was busy.* ◇ *vt* **to busy oneself** to keep oneself busy □ *She busied herself looking for a new job.*

busybody ['bɪzɪbɒdɪ] (*pl* **busybodies**) *n* a person who likes to become involved in matters that concern other people and not themselves (disapproving use).

busy lizzie [-'lɪzɪ] *n* a pot plant that has pink, red, or white flowers.

busy signal *n* US the sound that one hears on the telephone when the number that one has dialed is already being used.

but [*stressed* bʌt, *unstressed* bət] ◇ *conj* -1. used before something that contrasts with what has just been said □ *Things are looking bad, but we'll pull through.* □ *I'd love to meet them, but not today.* -2. used to add something to what one has just said □ *She's like me, but taller.* □

"Have you met him?" — *"No, but I've heard a lot about him."* -3. used after "I'm sorry", "excuse me" etc □ *I'm sorry, but I still think that my idea is best.* □ *Excuse me, but I couldn't help hearing what you were saying.* -4. used to show that one is surprised, shocked, pleased, angry etc □ *"He says it's your fault."* — *"But I wasn't even there!"* -5. used when changing the subject □ *That's very interesting, but let me tell you something that'll surprise you.*
◇ *prep* **everyone but Joe** everyone except Joe □ *We've had nothing but rain and wind.* □ *You have no one to blame but yourself.* ■ **the last but one** GB the one before the last one □ *Quality control is the next item but one on the agenda.*
◇ *adv* only (old-fashioned use) □ *We can but try.*
◆ **but for** *prep* **but for her** if she had not been there □ *But for her I would have died.*
◆ **but then** *adv* used to explain why something is not surprising □ *I get on pretty well with him, but then I've known him for some time.*

butane ['bjuːteɪn] *n* a natural gas used for cooking and heating. FORMULA: C_4H_{10}.

butch [bʊtʃ] *adj* [woman] who seems more like a man than a woman (informal use).

butcher ['bʊtʃər] ◇ *n* -1. a person whose job is to sell meat. ■ **a butcher's** a store where meat is sold. -2. a person who kills somebody in a cruel and violent way. ◇ *vt* -1. to kill <an animal> for meat. -2. to kill <sb> in a cruel and violent way.

butchery ['bʊtʃərɪ] *n* the cruel and violent killing of a lot of people.

butler ['bʌtlər] *n* a man who is the head servant in a household.

butt [bʌt] ◇ *n* -1. [of a cigarette] the end of a cigarette that is left when somebody has finished smoking it □ *an ashtray full of cigarette butts.* -2. [of a gun] the end of the handle of a rifle or pistol □ *a rifle butt.* -3. **to be the butt of a joke/criticism** to be the person who other people make fun of/criticize □ *He became the butt of everybody's cruelty.* -4. US one's bottom (informal use) □ *Move your butt!* ◇ *vt* to hit <sb> with one's head.
◆ **butt in** *vi* to interrupt a conversation or join in an activity without being invited □ *Excuse me for butting in.* □ *She's always butting in on other people's conversations.*

butter ['bʌtər] ◇ *n* a yellow fat made from milk that is used in cooking or spread on bread □ *Do you want butter on your sandwich?* ■ **butter wouldn't melt in his/her mouth** a phrase used to describe somebody who behaves as if they could never possibly do anything wrong or unpleasant. ◇ *vt* [bread, toast] to spread butter on <sthg>.
◆ **butter up** *vt sep* **to butter sb up** to be very nice to sb because one wants them to do something.

butter bean *n* a large, flat, pale-yellow bean that is cooked and eaten as a vegetable.

buttercup ['bʌtərkʌp] *n* a small wild plant with bright yellow flowers, common in Europe and North America.

butter dish *n* a dish for keeping butter in.

buttered ['bʌtə'd] *adj* [toast, bread, potato] that has butter on it.

butterfingers ['bʌtə'fɪŋgə'z] (*pl* **butterfingers**) *n* a person who often drops things or is not good at catching things (informal use).

butterfly ['bʌtə'flaɪ] (*pl* **butterflies**) *n* -1. ZOOLOGY a flying insect with a thin body and large colorful wings. -2. SPORT **(the) butterfly** a way of swimming on one's front that involves bringing both arms over one's head and down into the water, while moving one's legs up and down together. -3. *phrase* **to have butterflies (in one's stomach)** to be very nervous, usually before an important event (informal use).

buttermilk ['bʌtə'mɪlk] *n* the liquid that is left after butter has been made from milk.

butterscotch ['bʌtə'skɒtʃ] *n* a type of hard candy made of butter and brown sugar □ *ice cream with butterscotch sauce.*

buttocks ['bʌtəks] *npl* the two soft rounded parts of the body between the lower part of one's back and the top of one's legs that one sits on.

button ['bʌtn] ◇ *n* -1. CLOTHING a small object, usually round and flat and made of plastic or metal, that is attached to a piece of clothing and is passed through a hole in another part in order to fasten it □ *Can you do this button up for me?* □ *a skirt with buttons up the front.* -2. [on a machine] a small round or square object that one presses to switch a machine on or off □ *Press the red button.* -3. US [on one's lapel] a small piece of metal, plastic, or cloth with a picture or writing on it. ◇ *vt* = **button up.**

◆ **button up** *vt sep* **to button sthg up** [shirt, coat] to fasten sthg by using buttons □ *He buttoned his shirt up hurriedly.*

button-down ◇ *adj* **a button-down collar** a shirt collar that has a button at each end for fastening it to the front of the shirt.

buttonhole ['bʌtnhoʊl] ◇ *n* -1. a hole that a button is passed through in order to fasten a piece of clothing. -2. GB a flower that is worn in a buttonhole on the lapel of a jacket. ◇ *vt* to stop <sb> and make them listen to one □ *She buttonholed me on my way to the coffee machine.*

button mushroom *n* a small white mushroom that can be eaten.

buttress ['bʌtrəs] ◇ *n* a stone or brick structure built against a wall or building to make it stronger. ◇ *vt* [wall, building] to support <sthg> with a buttress.

buxom ['bʌksəm] *adj* [woman, girl] who looks healthy, rounded, and attractive and has large breasts.

buy [baɪ] (*pt & pp* **bought**) ◇ *vt* -1. [food, house, car] to get <sthg> by paying money for it □ *I bought it from an antiques dealer.* ■ **to buy sb sthg, to buy sthg for sb** to pay for sthg and give it to sb, usually as a present □ *What did you buy for her for her birthday?* □ *Can I buy you a drink?* □ *I bought myself a new shirt.* -2. [judge, politician] to bribe <sb> by giving them mon-

ey □ *He can't be bought.* ◇ *n* something that one has bought or is thinking of buying □ *It's a good buy at $50.*

◆ **buy in** *vt sep* **to buy sthg in** GB [food, supply] to buy a large amount of sthg, usually to prepare for a future event or shortage.

◆ **buy into** *vt fus* **to buy into sthg** [company, industry] to buy a part of sthg, usually to get more control over it.

◆ **buy off** *vt sep* **to buy sb off** to give money to sb in order to stop them doing something that will harm one □ *They bought off the key witness.*

◆ **buy out** *vt sep* **to buy sb out** FINANCE to buy the part of a business, property etc owned by sb so that one becomes the only owner of it □ *They've offered to buy me out.*

◆ **buy up** *vt sep* **to buy sthg up** [property, goods, shares] to buy large amounts of or all of sthg □ *They have bought up all the land in the area.*

buyer ['baɪə'] *n* -1. a person who buys something □ *I think we may have found a buyer for that property.* -2. a person whose job is to buy goods or new materials for a company □ *She's a buyer for Freebodys.*

buyer's market *n* a situation in which goods are cheap because there are more goods for sale than people who want to buy them.

buyout ['baɪaʊt] *n* the act of buying enough shares to gain control of a company □ *a union/management buyout.*

buzz [bʌz] ◇ *vi* -1. [insect, machine] to make a noise like a bee flying □ *There was a fly buzzing around my head.* -2. [town, street, office] to be full of activity, excitement, or noise □ *The stock exchange was buzzing with excitement.* -3. [head, brain] to be full of ideas, thoughts etc □ *My mind was still buzzing with curiosity.* ◇ *vt* to call <sb> using a buzzer □ *Buzz me on the intercom and I'll let you in.* ◇ *n* -1. [of a bee, machine] the sound made by a bee or machine that buzzes □ *the buzz of a mosquito.* -2. [of people talking] the sound made by a lot of people talking, usually when they are excited □ *There was a sudden buzz of excitement among the crowd.* -3. **to give sb a buzz** to call sb on the telephone (informal use) □ *I'll give you a buzz tonight.*

◆ **buzz off** *vi* **buzz off!** go away! (informal use).

buzzard ['bʌzə'd] *n* -1. US a large black bird that eats animals that are already dead. -2. GB a large bird of prey belonging to the hawk family.

buzzer ['bʌzə'] *n* a device, e.g. on a clock or intercom, that makes a buzzing sound to attract somebody's attention □ *Just press the buzzer if you want to get back into the building.*

buzzing ['bʌzɪŋ] *n* [of a bee, plane, machine] the sound made by something that buzzes □ *What's that buzzing noise?*

buzzword ['bʌzwɜː'd] *n* a fashionable word or phrase (informal use).

by [baɪ] ◇ *prep* -1. **he was killed by a soldier** a soldier killed him (used in passive sentences) □ *I was shocked by his reaction.* -2. **a book by Joyce** a book written by Joyce. ■ **a speech by the President** a speech made by the Presi-

dent. **-3.** used to show the method or means □ *I paid by credit card.* □ *You turn on the machine by pressing this button.* **-4.** used to show the manner or circumstances □ *He took me by the hand.* □ *We dined by candlelight.* **-5. to travel by bus/plane** used to show the means of transportation used □ *Did you come by car?* **-6. by the window/sea** beside or near the window/sea □ *He sat by her bed.* **-7. to pass by sb/sthg** to go past sb/sthg □ *He rushed by me and shut the door.* **-8. to come in by the back door** to come in through the back door □ *We returned from France by Dover this year.* **-9. I'll be home by 8 o'clock** I'll be home at or before 8 o'clock □ *By 1918 it was all over.* □ *They should have been here by now.* **-10. by day** during the daytime □ *a postcard of Paris by night.* **-11. day by day** gradually, as each day passes (used to show the speed at which something happens) □ *The guests entered the hall one by one.* **-12.** MATH **15 divided by 3 is 5** used in calculations. ■ **the room measures 15 feet by 12** the room is 15 feet long and 12 feet wide. **-13. paid by the hour** paid at a fixed rate for each hour □ *Most fabrics are bought/sold by the meter.* **-14. prices have gone up/down by 10%** prices are 10% more/less than before. **-15. what did you understand by his comments?** what did you think his comments meant? □ *What do you mean by "funny"?* **-16. I'm a plumber by trade** my trade is being a plumber. **-17. by law** according to the law □ *You're not allowed to park here by law.* **-18.** phrases **I did it by myself** I did it without any help □ *She painted the entire house all by herself.* ■ **I'm all by myself** I'm all alone □ *What are you doing here all by yourself?*
◇ *adv* **to walk/drive etc by** to walk/drive etc past without stopping □ *He watched as the horses galloped by.*
◆ **by and large** *adv* mostly, in most cases □ *Your work is fine, by and large.* □ *By and large, business has been pretty good this year.*

bye(-bye) [US ˈbaɪ(baɪ), GB ˌbaɪ(ˈbaɪ)] *excl* = **goodbye** (informal use).

bye-election *n* = **by-election**.

byelaw [ˈbaɪlɔː] *n* = **bylaw**.

by-election *n* in Britain and Australia, a local election to choose a new Member of Parliament after the last one has retired or died. NOTE: Compare **general election**.

Byelorussia [bɪˌeloʊˈrʌʃə] = **Belarus**.

bygone [ˈbaɪɡɒn] *adj* [age, day] that existed or happened a long time ago □ *music from a bygone era.*
◆ **bygones** *npl* **to let bygones be bygones** to forget one's past quarrels with somebody.

bylaw [ˈbaɪlɔː] *n* **-1.** a local government law that only affects people in that particular area. **-2.** a rule that affects members of a particular organization.

by-line *n* a line above a newspaper or magazine article giving the writer's name.

BYO (*abbr of* **bring your own**) used to show that people can bring alcoholic drinks into a restaurant □ *a BYO restaurant.*

✌ **BYO**

In Australia most cafes and restaurants (except the most expensive ones) are BYO eating places. These places will let you drink alcohol that you have bought somewhere else, but they sometimes make a small extra charge, called corkage, for opening and serving the drink.

---

bypass [US ˈbaɪpæs, GB -pɑːs] ◇ *n* **-1.** a road that goes round the edge of a town to join the main road on the other side. **-2.** MEDICINE **a bypass (operation)** an operation in which the way that blood flows through the heart is changed so that it avoids a part that is damaged □ *a heart bypass operation.* ◇ *vt* **-1.** [town, city] to avoid <a place> by traveling round it. **-2.** [manager, procedure, law] to try to get something done more quickly by avoiding having to deal with or obey <sb/sthg> □ *I bypassed the personnel officer and went straight to the top.*

by-product *n* **-1.** INDUSTRY something that is produced as an indirect result of the manufacture of another product □ *one of the by-products of the distilling process.* **-2.** [of an event] an indirect or unexpected result of something □ *The trade deal was a useful by-product of the peace talks.*

Byron [ˈbaɪrən], **Lord** (1788–1824) a British Romantic poet, known for his wild and unconventional life, who died while fighting for Greek independence.

bystander [ˈbaɪstændər] *n* a person who is present when something, e.g. a fight or accident, takes place, but does not take part in it □ *You were just an innocent bystander.*

byte [baɪt] *n* a unit (6 or 8 bits) of computer data.

byword [ˈbaɪwɜːrd] *n* **to be a byword for sthg** to be well-known for sthg and therefore very closely connected with it in people's minds □ *That company is a byword for inefficiency.*

c[1] [siː] (*pl* **c's** OR **cs**), **C** [siː] (*pl* **C's** OR **Cs**) *n* the third letter of the English alphabet.
◆ **C** *n* **-1.** MUSIC one of the notes in Western music. **-2.** EDUCATION an average grade for a piece of work. **-3.** *abbr of* **Celsius, Centigrade**.

c[2] *abbr of* **century, cent(s), circa**.

C4 *n abbr of* **Channel 4**.

ca. *abbr of* **circa**.

c/a GB **-1.** *abbr of* **credit account**. **-2.** *abbr of* **current account**.

CA ◇ *n abbr of* **chartered accountant**. ◇ -1. *abbr of* **California**. -2. *abbr of* **Central America**.

CAA (*abbr of* **Civil Aviation Authority**) *n* the CAA the organization responsible for aircraft companies and air routes in Britain and Australia.

cab [kæb] *n* -1. a taxi □ *I took a cab to get here.* □ *They went by cab.* □ *a cab driver.* -2. [of a truck, bus, train] the part of a vehicle where the driver sits.

CAB *n abbr of* **Citizens' Advice Bureau**.

cabaret ['kæbəreɪ] *n* a type of entertainment, e.g. singing, dancing, or comedy, that is provided in a nightclub, restaurant etc □ *a cabaret artist/show.*

cabbage ['kæbɪdʒ] *n* a large round vegetable consisting of layers of dark-green, white, or purple leaves.

cabbie, cabby ['kæbɪ] (*pl* **cabbies**) *n* a taxi driver (informal use).

cabin ['kæbɪn] *n* -1. [on a ship] a room on a ship for sleeping in □ *Can you show me to my cabin?* -2. [in a plane] the area in a plane where the pilot sits; the area in a plane where the passengers sit. -3. [in a forest, on a mountain] a small house usually made of wood, with only one main room.

cabin class *n* the standard of service and accommodation on a ship that is cheaper than first class and more expensive than tourist class.

cabin crew *n* the people whose job is to look after passengers on a plane.

cabin cruiser *n* a motorboat with one or more cabins.

cabinet ['kæbɪnət] *n* a piece of furniture with shelves and doors, used for storing or displaying things □ *a display/drink cabinet.*

◆ **Cabinet** *n* the Cabinet POLITICS the most important members of a government who meet to decide policies □ *a member of the Cabinet* □ *a Cabinet minister.*

cabinetmaker ['kæbɪnətmeɪkə^r] *n* a person whose job is to make high-quality furniture.

cable ['keɪbl] ◇ *n* -1. [of metal] a strong thick rope, usually made of metal, and used to support or pull something heavy □ *a steel cable.* -2. TECHNOLOGY a telegram. -3. ELECTRICITY a wire or group of wires for carrying electricity or information □ *Pictures can now be sent via cable.* □ *a telephone/printer cable.* -4. TV = **cable television**. ◇ *vt* -1. [money, information] to send <sthg> to somebody by cable. -2. [person] to send <sb> a telegram.

cable car *n* -1. a vehicle that hangs from a moving cable and is used for taking people up mountains. -2. a car on a cable railway.

cablegram ['keɪblgræm] *n* a telegram.

cable railway *n* a railway on which the cars are pulled, usually up steep hills, by a cable under the roadway.

cable television, cable TV *n* a system of broadcasting television programs through cables □ *cable TV channels.*

caboodle [kə'buːdl] *n* the whole (kit and) caboodle everything (informal use).

cache [kæʃ] ◇ *n* -1. [of objects] a group of things that have been hidden; a place where things are hidden □ *an arms cache.* -2. COMPUTING a high-speed area of a computer's memory that stores data temporarily to make it quicker to find □ *cache memory.* ◇ *vt* COMPUTING to store <data> in a cache.

cachet [US kæ'ʃeɪ, GB 'kæʃeɪ] *n* a quality that somebody or something has that other people admire (formal use) □ *Owning a Porsche obviously has a certain cachet.*

cackle ['kækl] ◇ *n* -1. [of a hen] the noise made by a hen, usually after laying an egg. -2. [of a person] a loud harsh noise made when somebody laughs or talks □ *She let out a cackle of laughter.* ◇ *vi* -1. [hen] to make a cackle. -2. [person] to give a cackle □ *The old witch cackled with glee.*

cacophony [kə'kɒfənɪ] *n* a loud unpleasant mixture of noises.

cactus ['kæktəs] (*pl* **cactuses** OR **cacti** [-taɪ]) *n* a desert plant that is covered in spikes and has no leaves.

CAD [kæd, ˌsiːeɪ'diː] (*abbr of* **computer-aided design**) *n* the use of computers to design products, equipment, buildings etc.

caddie ['kædɪ] ◇ *n* a person whose job is to carry the clubs for somebody who is playing golf. ◇ *vi* to caddie for sb to be sb's caddie.

caddy ['kædɪ] (*pl* **caddies**) *n* a small container for tea.

cadence ['keɪdns] *n* the way a person's voice gets higher and lower as they speak.

cadet [kə'det] *n* a young person who is being trained in the police force or the armed forces □ *a police cadet.*

cadge [kædʒ] (informal use) ◇ *vt* to cadge sthg off OR from sb GB [money, cigarette, drink] to get sthg from sb for free by asking them for it □ *Can I cadge a fiver off you?* ◇ *vi*: *She's always cadging off OR from her friends.*

cadmium ['kædmɪəm] *n* a soft metal used in batteries and nuclear reactors. SYMBOL: Cd.

Caesar ['siːzə^r], **Julius** (100–44 BC) a Roman general, politician, and historian. He became a dictator, and was killed by a group of Republicans.

caesarean (section) [sɪˌzeərɪən-] *n* GB = **cesarean (section)**.

Caesar salad *n* a salad made from lettuce, eggs, and cheese with a special dressing.

CAF (*abbr of* **cost and freight**) a term in international trade that means the seller pays for the transport of goods but the buyer pays for the insurance.

cafe, café [US kæ'feɪ, GB 'kæfeɪ] *n* a place in which drinks and light meals are sold and eaten.

🐝 CAFÉ

Cafés in Britain and Australia and coffee shops in the USA are usually open all day, but closed in the evenings. They serve mainly tea, coffee, soft drinks, cakes, and snacks, and some of them also serve hot food. Cafés in the USA, and cafés in some big cities in Britain and Australia, are often more fashionable and expensive places, selling special types of tea, coffee, and cakes.

cafeteria [ˌkæfə'tɪərɪə] *n* a self-service restaurant.

caffeine [US kæ'fiːn, GB 'kæfiːn] *n* the drug in coffee, tea, and cocoa that makes people more active.

cage [keɪdʒ] *n* a structure, usually made of metal bars, in which birds or animals are kept.

caged [keɪdʒd] *adj* [bird, animal] that is kept in a cage.

cagey ['keɪdʒɪ] (*compar* **cagier**, *superl* **cagiest**) *adj* [answer, person] that seems to be trying to avoid giving away too much information (informal use) □ *He was very cagey about where they were going this weekend.*

cagoule [kə'guːl] *n* GB a thin waterproof jacket with a hood.

cahoots [kə'huːts] *n* **to be in cahoots** to be working in partnership, usually for a dishonest purpose □ *The security guard was in cahoots with the gang.*

CAI (*abbr of* **computer-aided instruction**) *n* the use of computers in education and training.

Cain [keɪn] in the Bible, the eldest son of Adam and Eve. He was jealous of his brother Abel, and killed him.

cairn [keəˈn] *n* a pile of stones used as a monument or to show a boundary or route, often on top of a mountain.

Cairns [keəˈnz] a city in Queensland, Australia, that is a popular tourist center. POPULATION: 97,640.

Cairo ['kaɪrou] the capital of Egypt and the largest city in Africa. POPULATION: 9,750,000.

cajole [kə'dʒoul] *vt* to persuade <sb> to do something by being very friendly to them, making them laugh etc □ *She cajoled them into helping her.*

Cajun ['keɪdʒən] ◇ *n* a member of a people living in Louisiana, USA. They speak a dialect of French, and are known for their lively music and spicy food. ◇ *adj*: *Cajun music/cooking.*

cake [keɪk] *n* -1. a type of sweet food made from flour, sugar, eggs, and fat, sometimes with fruit, nuts etc, that is baked in the oven and eaten cold, often as a snack or on a special occasion □ *a birthday cake/fruit cake* □ *a piece of cake.* ■ **to be a piece of cake** to be very easy (informal use). ■ **to sell like hot cakes** to sell very fast (informal use). ■ **you can't have your cake and eat it** you can't have two things when one of them means the other thing is not possible, or when it is unfair because other people do not have the choice. -2. **a fish/potato etc cake** mashed fish/potato etc that has been made into a flat round shape and then cooked. -3. **a cake of soap** a small block of soap.

caked [keɪkt] *adj* **caked with sthg** [with mud, dirt] covered with a thick hard layer of sthg.

cake pan *n* US a metal container used for baking cakes.

cake tin *n* GB -1. a metal container with a lid, used for storing cakes. -2. = **cake pan**.

cal [kæl] *n abbr of* **calorie**.

Calais ['kæleɪ] a port in northeastern France, used especially by ferries to and from Dover, England. POPULATION: 75,836.

calamine lotion [ˌkæləmaɪn-] *n* a pink lotion used for soothing irritated or burnt skin.

calamitous [kə'læmətəs] *adj* [event, result] disastrous (formal use).

calamity [kə'læmətɪ] (*pl* **calamities**) *n* a sudden terrible event that causes a lot of damage and destruction (formal use) □ *They suffered a series of calamities.*

calcium ['kælsɪəm] *n* a silver-white element that is found in bones, teeth, chalk, and limestone. SYMBOL: Ca.

calculate ['kælkjəleɪt] *vt* -1. [number, figure, result] to work out <an amount> by adding, dividing etc numbers □ *I've calculated that if our sales continue to rise, we will start making a profit in three years.* □ *He calculated the cost of employing another engineer.* -2. [effect, consequences] to find out the size, importance etc of <sthg in the future> by using information that one has □ *Have you calculated what the effect of such a plan would be?* -3. **to be calculated to do sthg** to be intended to do sthg □ *Her words were calculated to cause controversy.*

◆ **calculate on** *vt* **to calculate on sthg** to depend on sthg that one expects to happen □ *You can't calculate on them saying yes.*

calculated ['kælkjəleɪtəd] *adj* [attack, insult] that has been deliberately planned □ *It was a calculated challenge to Rosero's authority.* ■ **a calculated risk** a risk that has been carefully thought about before it is taken.

calculating ['kælkjəleɪtɪŋ] *adj* [person] who carefully plans to get what they want without caring about how much other people suffer □ *a cool, calculating murderer.*

calculation [ˌkælkjə'leɪʃn] *n* MATH the act of calculating a number or amount; a number or amount that has been calculated □ *He made a rough calculation.* □ *According to our calculations, we've only got three years left.*

calculator ['kælkjəleɪtəˈ] *n* an electronic device used for making mathematical calculations.

calculus ['kælkjələs] *n* a branch of mathematics that deals with quantities that are continually changing.

Calcutta [kæl'kʌtə] a port in eastern India, and India's largest city. POPULATION: 10,916,672.

calendar ['kæləndəˈ] *n* -1. a chart that lists all the days, weeks, and months of a particular year □ *a wall calendar.* -2. a system for dividing the year into units of months, weeks, and days □ *the Gregorian/Julian calendar.* -3. US a book with spaces for each day where one can note down the times of meetings and other events. -4. a list of events that a particular group or organization is involved in during a particular year □ *the political/arts calendar* □ *We have a number of important conferences on our calendar this year.*

calendar month *n* the period of time from a particular date in one month to the same date in the next month □ *Rent is $800 per calendar month.*

calendar year *n* a whole year, beginning on January 1 and ending on December 31.

calf [US kæf, GB kɑːf] (*pl* **calves**) *n* -1. a young cow; leather that is made from the skin of this animal □ *The book is bound in calf.* -2. the young of some animals □ *a whale/an elephant calf.* -3. ANATOMY the rounded muscular part at the back of the leg, between the knee and ankle.

calfskin [US ˈkæfskɪn, GB ˈkɑːf-] *n* leather that is made from the skin of a calf □ *calfskin leather/boots.*

caliber US, **calibre** GB [ˈkælɪbəʳ] *n* -1. [of somebody's work] the quality of something; [of a person] the ability or excellence of somebody □ *This report is of a very high caliber.* □ *We need more staff of his caliber.* -2. [of a tube, gun] the width of the inside of a tube or a gun barrel; [of a bullet] the width of a bullet.

calibrate [ˈkælɪbreɪt] *vt* -1. [instrument, scale, container] to mark <sthg> so that it can be used to measure something exactly □ *a calibrated syringe.*

calibre *n* GB = **caliber**.

calico [ˈkælɪkoʊ] ◇ *n* -1. US a light cotton fabric with a pattern. -2. GB a white cotton fabric with no pattern or design. ◇ *adj* **a calico cat** US a cat with black, brown, and white fur.

California [ˌkælɪˈfɔːrnjə] a state in the western USA. It is a major producer of fruit and wine, with important electronics and movie industries. ABBREVIATION: CA. SIZE: 411,000 sq kms. POPULATION: 29,760,021 (*Californians*). CAPITAL: Sacramento. OTHER MAJOR CITIES: Los Angeles, San Francisco.

Caligula [kəˈlɪgjʊlə] (12–41 AD) a Roman emperor who ruled from 37 to 41 AD and is known for his cruel and unjust behavior.

calipers US, **callipers** GB [ˈkælɪpəʳz] *npl* -1. an instrument for measuring the width of things that consists of two long, thin, curved pieces of metal joined at the top □ *a pair of calipers.* -2. a device consisting of metal rods and straps that supports a person's leg and helps them to walk.

call [kɔːl] ◇ *vt* -1. [person, object, animal] to give a particular name to <sb/sthg> □ *Have you decided what to call the baby?* □ *Everyone calls him Dave for short.* ■ **to be called sthg** to have sthg as one's name □ *I'm called Sara.* □ *What's her latest novel called?* -2. **to call sb/sthg sthg** [person, animal, object] to describe sb/sthg as sthg □ *$80,000? That's what I call an expensive car!* □ *Are you calling me a liar?* -3. to try and attract the attention of <a person or animal> by shouting □ *Someone called my name.* □ *She kept calling the dog but it took no notice.*

-4. [person] to telephone <sb> □ *He called me from Chicago last night.* -5. [doctor, police, plumber] to ask <a professional person> to come to the place where one is, usually by phoning them □ *Do you think we should call an ambulance?* -6. [flight, meeting, strike] to announce officially that <sthg> is going to happen □ *The President called an emergency cabinet meeting.* □ *A press conference has been called for this afternoon.*

◇ *vi* -1. [person] to shout or speak in a loud clear voice □ *He was calling for help.* -2. [animal, bird] to make its typical sound □ *I could hear a pair of owls calling to one another.* -3. [person] to telephone □ *May I ask who's calling?* □ *People have been calling for you all morning.* -4. [person] to make a visit □ *Jane said she'd call at the office on her way home.*

◇ *n* -1. [of a person] a cry or shout for attracting attention; [of an animal, bird] the typical cry or noise made by a particular bird or animal □ *the call of the owl.* -2. [by a doctor, sales representative] a short professional visit ■ **to pay a call on sb** to visit sb for a particular reason □ *The police will be paying a call on Mr Hill very shortly.* -3. **a call for sthg** a demand for sthg □ *There have been calls for her resignation.* ■ **there's not much call for it** not many people ask for it, or want to buy it □ *There isn't much call for records any more, it's all CDs.* ■ **there's no call to be rude!** it was not necessary for you to be rude. -4. **to be on call** [doctor, engineer] to be available for work whenever necessary, e.g. during the night □ *I'm on call this week.* -5. [on the phone] a telephone call □ *There's a call for you on line one.* ■ **to give sb a call** to telephone sb □ *I'll just make a quick call to my parents.* ■ **to return sb's call** to call sb back on the telephone.

◆ **call back** ◇ *vt sep* -1. **to call sb back** to make a telephone call to sb who has already phoned one □ *Tell him to call me back in an hour.* -2. **to call sb back** to ask sb to come back to the place they have just left, e.g. their home or office □ *My mother called me back as I was leaving.* □ *She was called back from abroad to deal with the crisis.* ◇ *vi* -1. [on the phone] *He said he'd call back later.* -2. [at a place] to come back to a place one has been to earlier, especially somebody's home □ *I'll call back tomorrow to see how you're feeling.*

◆ **call by** *vi* GB [person] = **call in** □ *I'll call by and pick it up on my way home tonight.*

◆ **call for** *vt fus* -1. **to call for sb/sthg** [person, package, goods] to go to a place in order to collect sb/sthg and take them somewhere else □ *I'll call for you at seven.* -2. **to call for sthg** [reform, justice, inquiry] to make a strong public demand for sthg □ *Local officials are calling for an investigation.* -3. **to call for sthg** to deserve or need sthg □ *This calls for a drink/a celebration!* □ *It was a situation that called for quick thinking.*

◆ **call in** ◇ *vt sep* -1. **to call sb in** [doctor, expert, police] to send for sb professional or official □ *The Drugs Squad has been called in.* -2. BUSINESS **to call sthg in** to make a public request for a product or goods to be returned because they have faults or are dangerous □ *The company is calling in all 1987 models.* **-3.** FINANCE **to call a loan in** to ask for a loan to be repaid. ◇ *vi* GB [person] to make a short visit, usually on the way to another place □ *Could you call in at the store and get some milk?* □ *I called in on her after work.*

◆ **call off** *vt sep* **-1. to call sthg off** [party, strike, wedding] to cancel sthg □ *The game was called off because of the rain.* **-2. to call sb/sthg off** [dog, thug] to order a person or animal to stop attacking.

◆ **call on** *vt fus* **-1. to call on sb** to pay sb a short visit □ *One of our representatives will be happy to call on you and discuss things.* **-2.** = **call upon.**

◆ **call out** *vt sep* **-1. to call sb out** [army, fire brigade, lifeboat] to order an official group to come and help one with a situation. **-2.** GB [workers, union members] to order sb to go on strike. **-3. to call sthg out** to shout sthg □ *When your name is called out, go to the desk.*

◆ **call round** *vi* GB = **call in** □ *I'll call round at Joe's on the way over.*

◆ **call up** *vt sep* **-1. to call sb up** to telephone sb □ *Why don't we call up Mario's and order a pizza?* **-2. to call sb up** GB MILITARY to order sb to join the armed forces □ *He was too old to be called up in 1939.* **-3.** COMPUTING **to call sthg up** [file, data, document] to make sthg appear on a computer screen.

◆ **call upon** *vt fus* **to call upon sb to do sthg** to publicly ask sb to do sthg □ *The women are calling upon senior churchmen and politicians to help them in their fight.*

Callas ['kæləs], **Maria** (1923–1977) a US opera singer whose parents were Greek. She is considered one of the greatest singers of her time.

call box *n* GB a telephone booth.

caller ['kɔːləʳ] *n* **-1.** a person who comes to make a short visit □ *We don't get many callers these days.* **-2.** a person who makes a telephone call □ *Several callers voiced their outrage at the views expressed on the show.* □ *Sorry, caller, that line is busy.*

call girl *n* a prostitute who makes appointments with clients by telephone.

calligraphy [kə'lɪgrəfɪ] *n* the art of handwriting; beautiful handwriting.

call-in *n* US a television or radio program in which people are invited to telephone and give their questions, opinions etc to one or more people in the studio □ *a call-in show.*

calling ['kɔːlɪŋ] *n* **-1.** a career or profession (formal use). **-2.** a strong desire to do a particular job, especially one that involves caring for other people □ *He feels a calling to the ministry.*

calling card *n* a small card with a person's name, address, and telephone number written on it that they give to people they visit.

callipers *npl* GB = **calipers.**

call letters *npl* US the letters or numbers that are used by a person who sends messages by radio to identify themselves.

callous ['kæləs] *adj* [person, remark, attitude] that shows no concern for the suffering of other people □ *The press showed a callous disregard for the family's feelings.*

callously ['kæləslɪ] *adv* [act, behave, treat] *see* **callous.**

call-out charge *n* the fee charged by somebody to travel to one's home, car etc in order to fix something.

call sign *n* GB = **call letters.**

call-up *n* GB an official order for a person to join the armed forces □ *call-up papers.*

callus ['kæləs] (*pl* **calluses**) *n* an area of hard skin that develops on one's hands, feet etc from something that has rubbed one's skin, especially as a result of hard physical work.

calm [kɑːm] ◇ *adj* **-1.** [person, voice, behavior] that is not worried, excited, or angry □ *Please keep calm.* □ *He's always calm in a crisis.* **-2.** [place, situation] peaceful □ *The streets are calm again after last night's fighting.* □ *I love this house, it's always so calm and relaxing.* **-3.** [evening, weather] not stormy or windy □ *After the morning's storm the afternoon was calm and sunny.* **-4.** [sea, lake] that has no large waves □ *the calm waters of the lake.*
◇ *n* [of a person, mind] a state in which one is not worried, excited, or angry □ *As tensions mounted, police appealed for calm.* □ *I'm trying to keep my calm.*
◇ *vt* to make <sb/sthg> calm □ *She tried to calm their fears about losing their jobs.* □ *I had a drink to calm my nerves.*

◆ **calm down** ◇ *vt sep* **to calm sb down** to make sb calm and not excited, worried, angry, or upset □ *I tried to calm her down, but she was almost hysterical.* ◇ *vi* [person, place, situation] to become calm again □ *Look, calm down and tell us what happened.* □ *When things have calmed down a little, we'll try to find another solution.*

calmly ['kɑːmlɪ] *adv* [speak, behave, act] *see* **calm** □ *People were calmly going about their normal business.*

calmness ['kɑːmnəs] *n*: *see* **calm** □ *I admire your calmness at such a difficult time.*

Calor gas™ ['kæləʳ-] *n* GB a kind of gas that is sold in metal containers and can be used when there is no main gas supply.

calorie ['kælərɪ] *n* a unit for measuring the amount of energy that a particular type of food will produce □ *Each slice contains 500 calories.*

calve [US kæv, GB kɑːv] *vi* [COW] to give birth to a calf.

calves [US kævz, GB kɑːvz] *plural of* **calf.**

Calvin ['kælvən], **John** (1509–1564) a French religious thinker who led the Protestant Reformation in France and Switzerland.

cam [kæm] *n* a projecting part on a shaft or wheel that changes circular movement into movement that goes backward and forward.

CAM (*abbr of* **computer-aided manufacturing**) *n* the use of computers to control machinery and make industrial products.

camaraderie [US ˌkɑːməˈrɑːdərɪ, GB ˌkæmə-] *n* a feeling of friendship and trust between friends or people who work together.

camber [ˈkæmbər] *n* a slight curve on a road surface that allows water to drain off it.

Cambodia [kæmˈbəʊdjə] a country in southeast Asia, between Thailand and Vietnam. SIZE: 181,000 sq kms. POPULATION: 9,000,000 (*Cambodians*). CAPITAL: Phnom Penh. LANGUAGE: Khmer. CURRENCY: riel.

Cambridge [ˈkeɪmbrɪdʒ] -1. a city near Boston, Massachusetts, USA, the site of Harvard University and MIT. POPULATION: 95,802. -2. a city in eastern England, famous for its university. POPULATION: 101,000.

Cambridgeshire [ˈkeɪmbrɪdʒʃər] a county in eastern England. SIZE: 3,409 sq kms. POPULATION: 652,740. ADMINISTRATIVE CENTER: Cambridge.

Cambs *abbr of* **Cambridgeshire**.

camcorder [ˈkæmkɔːʳdəʳ] *n* a small video camera and recorder in one unit that can be carried around.

came [keɪm] *past tense of* **come**.

camel [ˈkæml] ◇ *n* a large animal with a long neck that has one or two humps on its back and lives in deserts □ *We crossed the desert by camel.* ◇ *adj* yellow-brown in color □ *a camel coat.*

camellia [kəˈmiːlɪə] *n* a large plant with dark-green shiny leaves and large white, red, or pink flowers that look like roses.

Camelot [ˈkæmələt] -1. according to legend, the place where King Arthur had his court. Camelot was meant to be a wonderful and magical place. -2. the White House at the time J.F. Kennedy was president.

cameo [ˈkæmɪəʊ] (*pl* **cameos**) *n* -1. [for wearing] a piece of jewelry consisting of a raised design, especially a woman's face, set on a flat background of a different color □ *a cameo brooch/ring.* -2. [in a play, movie] a small part in a play or movie that is acted by a well-known actor □ *a cameo role/performance.*

camera [ˈkæmərə] *n* -1. a device used for taking photographs □ *a 35mm camera* □ *a camera lens.* -2. a device used for recording a movie or television program □ *a TV/movie camera.*

◆ **in camera** *adv* LAW [meet, discuss] privately, without members of the public or the press □ *The trial was held in camera.*

cameraman [ˈkæmrəmən] (*pl* **cameramen** [-mən]) *n* a person who operates a television or movie camera.

Cameroon [ˌkæməˈruːn] a country in West Africa on the Atlantic coast. SIZE: 475,000 sq kms. POPULATION: 12,800,000 (*Cameroonians*). CAPITAL: Yaoundé. LANGUAGE: French, English. CURRENCY: CFA franc.

camisole [ˈkæməsəʊl] *n* a woman's sleeveless top with thin straps, worn as underwear.

camomile [ˈkæməmaɪl] *n* a small plant with yellow and white flowers that are used in herbal remedies and in tea □ *camomile tea.*

camouflage [ˈkæməflɑːʒ] ◇ *n* -1. MILITARY something, e.g. leaves, paint, or clothes, that is used to disguise guns, equipment, or soldiers from the enemy □ *soldiers in camouflage* □ *a camouflage net.* -2. BIOLOGY a color or pattern on an animal that makes it look like things around it and makes it difficult to see. ◇ *vt* to make <sthg> look similar to the things around it so that it is difficult to see.

camp [kæmp] ◇ *n* -1. [for travelers] a place where people live in tents, usually for a short time, e.g. when on vacation or traveling □ *We pitched camp near the beach.* □ *They went back to camp.* -2. MILITARY a group of buildings where soldiers live or stay □ *a training/army camp.* -3. [for refugees, prisoners] a group of huts or tents, usually inside a fence, that have been put up to house a large number of people, e.g. refugees or prisoners of war □ *a refugee/labor/prison camp.* -4. POLITICS a group of people who hold a particular view or belief, especially in opposition to another group □ *He's very much part of the pro-Western camp.*

◇ *vi* to live in a tent for a short period, especially when on vacation □ *We camped in the Dordogne this summer.*

◆ **camp out** *vi* to sleep outdoors, usually in a tent.

campaign [kæmˈpeɪn] ◇ *n* -1. a series of planned actions that are intended to produce a particular result, e.g. to help sell a product or get a politician or a party elected □ *an advertising/election campaign* □ *There has been a campaign in the press against tax increases.* -2. MILITARY a series of planned actions against an enemy that are intended to achieve a particular aim □ *a bombing campaign* □ *They mounted a campaign against the German forces in Africa.* ◇ *vi* to take part in a campaign □ *They were campaigning for an end to violence.* □ *He campaigned against the use of animals in drugs tests.*

campaigner [kæmˈpeɪnəʳ] *n* a person who campaigns for or against something □ *an animal rights campaigner.*

camp bed *n* GB a folding bed, usually made of canvas with a metal frame, that can be easily carried and is used for camping.

Camp David a place in Maryland, USA, where the President goes to relax.

camper [ˈkæmpəʳ] *n* -1. a person who goes camping. -2. **a camper (van)** a van that has a living space in the back with beds, storage space, a sink etc.

campground [ˈkæmpgraʊnd] *n* US a place where people can camp and which often has toilets and showers.

camphor [ˈkæmfəʳ] *n* a white substance with a strong smell that is used in several medical and industrial products, e.g. mothballs.

camping [ˈkæmpɪŋ] *n* the activity of camping □ *a camping vacation.*

camping site, **campsite** [ˈkæmpsaɪt] *n* GB = **campground**.

camp meeting *n* an outdoor religious meeting, especially in the USA in the 19th century.

campus ['kæmpəs] (*pl* **campuses**) *n* an area where the main buildings of a university, e.g. the lecture halls, offices, and accommodation, are situated □ *Most students live on campus.* □ *a campus university.*

camshaft [US 'kæmʃæft, GB -ʃɑːft] *n* a rod that has one or more cams attached to it, especially in the engine of a motor vehicle.

can¹ [kæn] (*pt* & *pp* **canned**, *cont* **canning**) ◇ *n* -1. a sealed metal container which contains no air and keeps food or drink fresh; the contents of such a container □ *a beer can* □ *a can of lemonade/beer/tomatoes.* -2. a metal container, usually with a lid that can be removed, used for holding liquids, e.g. oil or paint; the contents of such a container □ *an oil can* □ *I used two cans of paint.* ◇ *vt* to put <food> in cans.

can² [*stressed* kæn, *unstressed* kən] (*pt* & *conditional* **could**, *negative* **cannot** OR **can't**) *modal vb* -1. **I can swim** I know how to swim □ *I didn't know you could ski.* -2. **I can come next Tuesday** I am able to come next Tuesday □ *We tried, but we couldn't lift it.* ■ **can you see anything?** do you see anything? (used with verbs like *see, hear, feel*) □ *Can you hear that noise?* -3. **you can use my car** I allow you to use my car □ *I can't talk now, I'm in a meeting.* -4. used to make offers and invitations, or polite requests for help or information □ *Can you come to lunch tomorrow?* □ *Could I see your papers, please?* -5. used to give advice, make suggestions etc □ *If we're late, we can always take a taxi.* □ *I can tell him myself, if you like.* -6. used with negatives etc to express disbelief, confusion, surprise etc □ *Surely that can't be right!* □ *He can't have left already, can he?* -7. **Scotland can be very cold in the winter** Scotland is often very cold in winter (used to make general statements) □ *The children can be a little naughty sometimes.* -8. **the plane could arrive at any time** it is possible that the plane will arrive at any time.

Canada ['kænədə] a country in North America, north of the USA. It is the second-largest country in the world, with very low temperatures in the north. SIZE: 9,975,000 sq kms. POPULATION: 28,100,000 (*Canadians*). CAPITAL: Ottawa. MAIN CITIES: Toronto, Montreal, Vancouver. LANGUAGE: English, French. CURRENCY: Canadian dollar.

Canadian [kə'neɪdjən] *n* & *adj*: see **Canada**.

Canadian French *n* the French spoken in some parts of Canada.

canal [kə'næl] *n* a man-made waterway like a straight narrow river that is used for transporting goods or for providing fields with water.

canapé ['kænəpeɪ] *n* a small cracker or piece of bread with meat, fish, cheese etc on it that is served with drinks at parties.

Canaries [kə'neərɪz] = **Canary Islands**.

canary [kə'neərɪ] (*pl* **canaries**) *n* a small yellow songbird often kept as a pet.

Canary Islands: the Canary Islands a group of

islands in the Atlantic, off the coast of Morocco, that form two provinces of Spain and contain many popular tourist resorts. SIZE: 7,300 sq kms. POPULATION: 1,601,812.

Canary Wharf an office development in London's Docklands.

Canberra [US 'kænberə, GB -bərə] the capital of Australia, in the southeast of the country. The name is often used to refer to the federal government of Australia. POPULATION: 297,300.

cancel ['kænsl] (US *pt* & *pp* **canceled**, *cont* **canceling**, GB *pt* & *pp* **cancelled**, *cont* **cancelling**) *vt* -1. [appointment, trip, performance] to decide or state that <sthg that has been planned> will not happen □ *I'll have to call my wife and cancel our dinner date.* □ *Our flight was canceled at the last minute.* -2. [reservation, order, subscription] to say that one no longer needs or wants <sthg one had asked for> □ *I canceled the rental car and took a taxi instead.* -3. [check, agreement, contract] to declare that <sthg one signed> is no longer valid □ *The agreement may be canceled by either party at any time.*

◆ **cancel out** *vt sep* to cancel sthg out to take away all the effect of sthg by having an equal but opposite effect to it □ *The extra money I earn for working at night is canceled out by the cost of having to get a taxi home.*

cancellation [,kænsə'leɪʃn] *n* -1. something, especially a ticket, that has been canceled and can be given to somebody else □ *All the tickets for tonight's play are sold out, but you can wait to see if there are any cancellations.* -2. see **cancel** □ *Cancellation of the game means thousands will be disappointed.* □ *a cancellation fee.*

cancer ['kænsər] *n* a serious disease in which the cells in a part of the body multiply abnormally to form a tumor that can cause death □ *throat/breast/lung cancer* □ *a cancer specialist/ward/patient* □ *cancer research.*

◆ **Cancer** *n* a sign of the zodiac, often shown as a crab; a person born under this sign between June 22 and July 22.

cancerous ['kænsərəs] *adj* [growth, cell] affected with cancer.

candelabra [,kændə'lɑːbrə] *n* a large decorative holder for two or more candles.

C and F = CAF.

candid ['kændəd] *adj* [person, confession, opinion] that is honest and truthful, even when the truth is unpleasant or embarrassing □ *I'll be candid with you.*

candidacy ['kændədəsɪ] *n* the fact of being a candidate for something □ *He announced his candidacy for the post.*

candidate ['kændədeɪt] *n* -1. a person who is competing with other people to get a job, political position etc □ *There are three candidates for the presidency/job.* -2. GB a person who is taking an exam □ *Candidates are required to answer three out of four questions.*

candidature ['kændədətʃər] *n* = **candidacy**.

candied ['kændɪd] *adj* [fruit, peel] that has been covered or cooked in sugar.

candle ['kændl] *n* a stick of wax with a piece

of string in the middle that gives out light when it is lit. ▪ **to burn the candle at both ends** to try to do too many things at once by staying up very late at night and getting up early in the morning.

candlelight ['kændllaɪt] *n* a light produced by a candle □ *We ate our dinner by candlelight.*

candlelit ['kændllɪt] *adj* [dinner, supper] lit by candles.

candlestick ['kændlstɪk] *n* a holder for a candle.

candor US, **candour** GB ['kændəʳ] *n* the quality of being honest and not trying to hide anything.

candy ['kændɪ] (*pl* **candies**) *n* sweet foods, e.g. chocolates, toffee, or mints, that are eaten especially by children; a piece of one of these foods □ *Mom, can I have some candy?* □ *Do you want a piece of candy?*

candy bar *n* US a bar of chocolate.

candyfloss ['kændɪflɒs] *n* GB a mass of soft, sticky, pink or white sugar threads that are eaten on a stick, often at fairs.

candy store *n* US a store where candy is sold.

cane [keɪn] ◇ *n* -1. [for furniture] strips of the stems of some plants such as reeds, used for making furniture □ *cane furniture* □ *a cane chair.* -2. [for walking] a long stick used to help somebody walk. -3. **the cane** a thin stick used by teachers, especially in the past, for hitting children as a punishment. -4. [for plants] a long thin stick used to support plants. ◇ *vt* to hit <sb> with a cane.

cane sugar *n* sugar made from sugarcane.

canine ['keɪnaɪn] ◇ *adj* that is connected with dogs. ◇ *n* **a canine (tooth)** one of four pointed teeth at the front of the mouth in humans and certain animals.

canister ['kænɪstəʳ] *n* -1. a metal container with a lid, for storing film or dry food such as tea □ *a tea/sugar/flour canister.* -2. a sealed metal container with a substance such as gas or smoke inside that breaks open when thrown or fired from a gun □ *a tear gas canister.*

cannabis ['kænəbəs] *n* a drug, illegal in some countries, that is made from the hemp plant and is usually smoked in a cigarette for pleasure and to help people relax.

canned [kænd] *adj* -1. [food, drink] that is stored in cans so that it stays fresh. -2. **canned laughter/applause** laughter/applause that has been recorded and is used in television programs to make it seem that there is a live audience (informal and disapproving use).

cannelloni [ˌkænə'ləʊnɪ] *n* a dish consisting of tubes of pasta filled with meat and served with tomato and cheese sauces.

cannery ['kænərɪ] (*pl* **canneries**) *n* a factory where food is put in cans.

cannibal ['kænəbl] *n* -1. a person who eats human flesh. -2. an animal that eats other animals of the same type.

cannibalize, -ise ['kænəbəlaɪz] *vt* to take parts from <a machine or vehicle> and use them to repair or build another machine or vehicle.

cannon ['kænən] (*pl* **cannon** OR **cannons**) *n* -1. in the past, a type of large gun, attached to two wheels, that fired a solid metal ball. -2. a gun that is fitted to an aircraft or a ship and can fire bullets continuously.

◆ **cannon into** *vt fus* GB **to cannon into sb/sthg** to accidentally hit sb/sthg, especially while running.

cannonball ['kænənbɔːl] *n* a solid metal ball fired from a cannon.

cannot ['kænɒt] *vb* a negative form of "can" □ *You cannot be serious!*

canny ['kænɪ] (*compar* **cannier**, *superl* **canniest**) *adj* [person] who is wise, careful, and not easily deceived, especially in business matters □ *a canny investment.*

canoe [kə'nuː] (*cont* **canoeing**) ◇ *n* a long, thin, light boat for one or two people that is pointed at both ends and is moved by using a paddle. ◇ *vi* to travel in a canoe.

canoeing [kə'nuːɪŋ] *n* the sport or activity of rowing a canoe □ *We went canoeing in Mexico.*

canon ['kænən] *n* -1. [of a cathedral] a Christian priest who is on the staff of a cathedral. -2. [of somebody's behavior] a basic principle or rule □ *the canons of taste and decency.* -3. **the Canon** in the Roman Catholic Church, the central prayer of the Mass.

canonize, -ise ['kænənaɪz] *vt* in the Roman Catholic Church, to declare <a dead person> to be a saint.

can opener *n* a device used for opening cans of food.

canopy ['kænəpɪ] (*pl* **canopies**) *n* -1. [on furniture] a decorative piece of material that hangs over something, especially over a bed or seat. -2. [of trees] the highest branches and leaves in a forest or jungle that form a single layer.

cant [kænt] *n* statements about morals or religion made by somebody who does not really believe what they are saying (disapproving use).

can't [US kænt, GB kɑːnt] = **cannot**.

Cantab. (*abbr of* **Cantabrigiensis**) from Cambridge University (used after university degrees).

cantaloupe ['kæntəloʊp] US, **cantaloup** ['kæntəluːp] GB *n* a large melon with orange flesh and green and yellow skin.

cantankerous [kæn'tæŋkərəs] *adj* [person] who is unfriendly and complains and quarrels a lot □ *a cantankerous old man.*

canteen [kæn'tiːn] *n* -1. a restaurant that is part of a school, workplace, military camp etc. -2. a plastic or metal container for water that is carried by people on a long walk or expedition. -3. a box containing a set of knives, forks, and spoons.

canter ['kæntəʳ] ◇ *n* a speed at which a horse moves that is faster than a trot but slower than a gallop □ *The horse broke into a canter.* ◇ *vi* [horse, rider] to move at a canter.

Canterbury [US 'kæntərberı, GB 'kæntəbərı] a city in Kent, England, that is famous for its cathedral. POPULATION: 33,000.

cantilever ['kæntəli:vəʳ] *n* a beam or girder that is fixed at one end and supports a structure, e.g. a shelf, bridge, or an arch, at the other □ *a cantilever bridge.*

Canton [kæn'tɒn] = **Guangzhou**.

Cantonese [,kæntə'ni:z] ◇ *n* the language spoken in Guangzhou. It is also the language spoken by many Chinese people living in Hong Kong, Britain, and the USA. ◇ *adj* that comes from Guangzhou □ *Cantonese food.*

Canute [kə'nʲu:t] (995–1035) King of England from 1016, Denmark from 1019, and Norway from 1028. According to a famous story he stood on a beach and ordered the waves to turn back.

canvas ['kænvəs] *n* -1. a strong heavy fabric that is used for making tents, sails, bags etc □ *a canvas rucksack.* ■ **under canvas** [sleep, live] in a tent. -2. ART a piece of canvas used for an oil painting; an oil painting.

canvass ['kænvəs] ◇ *vt* -1. POLITICS to visit <people or a place> to ask people to vote for one's party; to try to get <people's votes, support> etc in this way □ *We've canvassed the whole street/area.* □ *They're canvassing local support for the Democrats.* -2. to find out <people's opinions> by asking them questions. ◇ *vi* POLITICS *Good morning, I'm canvassing for the Green Party.*

canvasser ['kænvəsəʳ] *n* a person who canvasses votes, opinions etc.

canvassing ['kænvəsıŋ] *n* the activity of canvassing votes, opinions etc.

canyon ['kænjən] *n* a very deep narrow valley that often has a river flowing through it.

cap [kæp] (*pt* & *pp* **capped,** *cont* **capping**) ◇ *n* -1. [for one's head] a soft flat hat, usually worn by men or boys; a hat, usually flat, that sometimes has a small stiff part at the front and is worn as part of a uniform □ *a flat/cloth cap* □ *a baseball cap.* ■ **to go cap in hand to sb** to go and ask sb for something in a very humble way. -2. [for a pen, bottle, lens] an object designed to cover the end or top of a particular thing □ *a lens cap.* -3. GB **the cap** a contraceptive device used by women consisting of a small circle of rubber.

◇ *vt* -1. **to be capped with sthg** [with snow, cloud] to have its top covered with sthg □ *The mountains were capped with snow.* -2. [performance, feat] to do or say something that is better than <sthg that has been done before> □ *She capped his story with an even better one of her own.* □ *Cap that, if you can!* ■ **to cap it all** a phrase used before the last and worst thing in a list of things □ *I was lost, hungry, and to cap it all, it started to rain.*

CAP [kæp, si:eı'pi:] (*abbr of* **Common Agricultural Policy**) *n* **the CAP** the EU system for supporting farmers by keeping agricultural prices at agreed levels.

capability [,keıpə'bılətı] (*pl* **capabilities**) *n* -1. **sb's capability** OR **capabilities** the ability

that sb has to do a particular thing □ *Frankly, I think the job is beyond his capabilities.* □ *I don't doubt her capabilities.* -2. MILITARY the ability of a country to take military action of a particular kind □ *the country's nuclear capability.*

capable ['keıpəbl] *adj* -1. **to be capable of sthg** to be strong enough, fast enough, bad enough etc to do sthg □ *Is he capable of murder?* □ *The computer is capable of processing vast quantities of data.* □ *It's capable of speeds of up to 150 mph.* -2. [person] who does something well without help from other people □ *She's a very capable driver/doctor.*

capably ['keıpəblı] *adv* [perform, do, act] *see* **capable** □ *He runs the office very capably.*

capacious [kə'peıʃəs] *adj* [bag, pocket] that has a lot of space.

capacitor [kə'pæsıtəʳ] *n* a device for collecting and storing an electrical charge.

capacity [kə'pæsətı] (*pl* **capacities**) *n* -1. the maximum amount that something can contain or produce □ *The hall has a seating capacity of 700.* □ *The factory was working at full capacity.* ■ **a capacity audience/crowd** an audience/crowd that fills all the seats in a hall, theater etc □ *The band played to a capacity audience.* ■ **to be full** OR **filled to capacity** to be completely full □ *The theater was filled to capacity.* -2. an ability that somebody has to do something □ *His capacity for work is amazing.* □ *Everyone has the capacity to learn.* □ *The job is well within her capacities/capacity.* -3. a particular kind of job that somebody has □ *I can only comment in my capacity as chairman.* □ *Mr Patel works for them in an unofficial capacity.*

cape [keıp] *n* -1. GEOGRAPHY a piece of land that sticks out from the mainland into the sea. -2. a piece of clothing that is worn around the shoulders and fastened at the neck like a very short cloak.

Cape Canaveral [-kə'nævrəl] a cape in Florida, USA, that is the launching site of NASA space flights. OLD NAME: Cape Kennedy.

Cape Cod a cape in Massachusetts, USA, that is popular with tourists.

Cape Horn the cape at the southern end of South America that is well known for its bad weather and dangers to shipping.

Cape of Good Hope: the Cape of Good Hope the cape at the southern end of South Africa.

caper ['keıpəʳ] ◇ *n* -1. the flower bud of a Mediterranean plant that is pickled and used to flavor food. -2. a dangerous or dishonest activity (informal use). ◇ *vi* [child, lamb] to jump around playfully.

Cape Town the legislative capital of the Republic of South Africa, near the Cape of Good Hope. POPULATION: 1,491,000.

capillary [US 'kæpəlerı, GB kə'pılərı] (*pl* **capillaries**) *n* a thin blood vessel in the body.

capita ['kæpətə] → **per capita**.

capital ['kæpıtl] ◇ *adj* -1. [letter] written in large form, e.g. as the first letter of a sentence □ *My name was written in capital letters.* □ *capital "A".* -2. **a capital offense/crime** an offense/crime that can be punished by death.

◇ *n* -1. [of a country, state] a city that is the center of government of a country or state □ *Beijing is the capital of China.* -2. [of commerce, crime] a town or city that is the center of a particular activity □ *Paris is the capital of fashion.* □ *Germany's financial capital.* -3. = **capital letter**. -4. FINANCE money, especially money that is used to start up a business, or money that is invested in order to earn interest □ *I had to use my capital to pay it back.* □ *They've invested a lot of capital in our business.* ■ **to make capital out of sthg** to use sthg to one's own advantage □ *Much political capital was made out of the governor's mistake.*

capital allowance *n* a tax allowance given to a company for money that is spent on fixed assets.

capital assets *npl* things that a company owns, e.g. land, equipment, and buildings.

capital expenditure *n* the money that a company spends on buying or improving equipment, buildings etc.

capital gains tax *n* a tax on any profit made from the sale of an asset.

capital goods *npl* goods such as machines and raw materials that are used to help make other goods and are not sold.

capitalism ['kæpɪtəlɪzm] *n* an economic system based on private rather than state ownership of property, business, and wealth, in which companies and individuals are free to compete with each other for profit. NOTE: Compare **Communism**, **Socialism**.

capitalist ['kæpɪtəlɪst] ◇ *adj* [society, system, economy] that works according to the principles of capitalism; [person] who supports capitalism □ *the capitalist economies of the West.* ◇ *n* -1. a person who supports capitalism. -2. a person who has or controls a lot of money (disapproving use).

capitalize, **-ise** ['kæpɪtəlaɪz] *vi* **to capitalize on sthg** [on a situation, advantage] to use sthg to one's advantage □ *Our competitors have capitalized on our labor problems.*

capital letter *n* a letter written in large form, as e.g. the first letter of a sentence is written □ *My name appeared in capital letters.*

capital punishment *n* legal punishment of a crime by death.

capital stock *n* the value of all the shares that a company is allowed to issue.

capital transfer tax *n* a tax that one pays on money or property that is given to one as a gift or when somebody dies.

Capitol ['kæpɪtl]: **the Capitol** the main building where the US Congress meets, in Washington D.C.

Capitol Hill the buildings in Washington D.C. where the US Congress meets to discuss and make laws. The term is used to mean the US Congress itself □ *There will be a big debate on Capitol Hill.*

capitulate [kə'pɪtʃəleɪt] *vi* to agree to the demands of one's opponents after refusing

them for some time □ *The authorities finally capitulated in the face of growing public protest.*

capitulation [kə,pɪtʃə'leɪʃn] *n*: *see* **capitulate**.

Capone [kə'poʊn], **Al** (1899–1947) a US gangster who was very powerful in Chicago during the time of Prohibition.

cappuccino [US ,kɑːpə'tʃiːnoʊ, GB ,kæpʊ-] (*pl* **cappuccinos**) *n* a kind of coffee that is made with frothy hot milk and is sometimes served with chocolate powder on top.

capricious [kə'prɪʃəs] *adj* [person] who often changes their mind for no good reason or has sudden changes of mood or behavior.

Capricorn ['kæprɪkɔːrn] *n* a sign of the zodiac, often shown as a goat; a person born under this sign between December 23 and January 20.

caps [kæps] *npl abbr of* **capital letters**.

capsicum ['kæpsɪkəm] *n* a red, green, or yellow vegetable that is hollow and has seeds inside.

capsize [US 'kæpsaɪz, GB kæp'saɪz] ◇ *vi* [boat, ship, raft] to turn over in the water. ◇ *vt*: *The waves capsized the dinghy.*

capsule [US 'kæpsl, GB 'kæpsjuːl] *n* -1. MEDICINE a small container made of gelatin that contains medicine and is swallowed like a pill. -2. [of a spacecraft] the part of a spacecraft that the crew live and work in.

Capt. *abbr of* **captain**.

captain ['kæptən] ◇ *n* -1. MILITARY a rank in the army, navy, or US Air Force □ *Captain Jones.* -2. SHIPPING & AVIATION the officer in charge of a ship or aircraft. -3. SPORT the leader of a team □ *He's just been made captain of the football team.* ◇ *vt* -1. SHIPPING & AVIATION to be in charge of <a ship or airplane>. -2. SPORT to be the leader of <a team>.

caption ['kæpʃn] *n* the words printed below a photograph, picture, or cartoon, that describe or explain it.

captivate ['kæptəveɪt] *vt* to attract and fascinate <sb>.

captivating ['kæptəveɪtɪŋ] *adj* [smile, face, scene] that one thinks is fascinating and attractive.

captive ['kæptɪv] ◇ *adj* -1. [person, animal] that has been captured □ *He was held* OR *kept captive for three months.* -2. **a captive audience** a person or group of people that is forced to listen to somebody because they cannot leave. ◇ *n* a prisoner, especially during a war.

captivity [kæp'tɪvətɪ] *n* the state of being held in a prison, cage etc and having no freedom □ *The hostages were held in captivity for three weeks.* □ *an eagle bred in captivity.*

captor ['kæptər] *n* **sb's captor** the person who keeps sb prisoner □ *They eventually escaped their captors.*

capture ['kæptʃər] ◇ *vt* -1. [person] to catch <sb> to make them a prisoner, especially in a war □ *The two pilots are thought to have been captured.* -2. [town, castle, land] to take control of <a place> etc after defeating the people

there □ *The town was captured after a prolonged gun battle.* **-3.** [tiger, bird] to catch <an animal>, especially in order to keep it □ *a horse captured in the wild.* **-4. to capture sb's attention/imagination etc** to attract and hold sb's attention, imagination etc □ *The song captured the imagination of young people.* **-5.** [market, vote] to succeed in getting <sthg that one's competitors are also trying to get> □ *Our aim is to capture at least 15% of the soft drinks market.* □ *The socialists captured 30% of the vote.* **-6.** [scene, face, mood] to succeed in representing <sthg, especially sthg that is not easy to describe>, in words, pictures, music etc □ *The movie captures perfectly the atmosphere of the time.* **-7.** COMPUTING to enter <data> in a computer.
◇ *n* [of a person, animal, town] the act of capturing a person, animal, or place □ *a photo taken before his capture.*

car [kɑːʳ] *n* **-1.** a vehicle that is powered by an engine, usually has four wheels, and has room for a small number of passengers □ *We drove* OR *went to Boston by car.* □ *a sports/racing car* □ *a car door/engine/seat* □ *a car dealer/repairer/manufacturer* □ *the car industry.* **-2.** one of the parts of a train for passengers □ *a restaurant/sleeping/buffet car.*

carafe [kəˈræf] *n* a glass container with a wide bottom and thin neck used for serving wine or water.

caramel [ˈkærəmel] *n* **-1.** burnt sugar that is used to flavor and color food. **-2.** a chewy candy made of boiled sugar.

carat [US ˈkerət, GB ˈkær-] *n* **-1.** a unit (0.2 g) for measuring the weight of diamonds and other precious stones □ *a 44-carat diamond.* **-2.** a unit of measure for the purity of gold □ *24-carat gold.*

caravan [US ˈkerəvæn, GB ˈkær-] *n* **-1.** a long line of people, camels, wagons etc all traveling together, especially through the desert. **-2.** GB a vehicle containing beds, cooking equipment etc that can be pulled by a car and is often used by people when they are on vacation □ *a caravan holiday/park.*

caravanning [US ˈkerəvæniŋ, GB ˈkær-] *n* GB **to go caravanning** to take a vacation in a trailer.

caravan site *n* GB a place where people can park their trailers when they are on vacation.

caraway seed [US ˈkerəwei-, GB ˈkær-] *n* a seed with a strong taste, used in cooking.

carbohydrate [ˌkɑːʳbouˈhaidreit] *n* a substance that is contained in some foods, e.g. potatoes, bread, or cakes, and that gives one energy.
◆ **carbohydrates** *npl* types of food, e.g. bread and potatoes, that contain a lot of carbohydrate.

car bomb *n* a bomb that consists of explosives hidden inside a car.

carbon [ˈkɑːʳbən] *n* **-1.** a chemical element that is found in its pure form in diamonds and graphite, and is present in coal, oil, and all organic matter. SYMBOL: C. **-2.** [of a document] = **carbon copy. -3.** = **carbon paper.**

carbonated [ˈkɑːʳbəneitəd] *adj* [water, drink] that is fizzy because it contains bubbles of carbon dioxide gas.

carbon copy *n* **-1.** [of a document] a copy of a document that has been made by using carbon paper. **-2. to be a carbon copy of sb/sthg** to be exactly the same as sb/sthg else.

carbon dating *n* a method of measuring the age of very old objects by calculating the amount of radioactive carbon they contain.

carbon dioxide [-daiˈɒksaid] *n* a gas that is present in the atmosphere and is formed e.g. when animals and humans breathe out. FORMULA: CO_2.

carbon fiber *n* thin threads of carbon used for making metals, ceramics, and resins stronger.

carbon monoxide [-məˈnɒksaid] *n* a poisonous gas produced when carbon burns in very little air, e.g. in a car engine. FORMULA: CO.

carbon paper *n* a thin sheet of paper with a dark substance on one side. It is placed between two pieces of plain paper so that what is typed or written on the top piece is copied onto the bottom piece.

car-boot sale *n* GB a sale that takes place outside, e.g. in a parking lot or field, and at which people sell things from the trunk of their car.

carburetor [ˈkɑːʳbəreitr] US, **carburettor** [ˌkɑːbəˈretə] GB *n* a device that produces the mixture of air and gasoline that is burned in a car engine.

carcass [ˈkɑːʳkəs] *n* the body of a dead animal.

carcinogenic [ˌkɑːʳsɪnəˈdʒenik] *adj* [substance] that causes cancer.

card [kɑːʳd] *n* **-1.** CARDS one of a set of 52 small rectangular pieces of stiff paper with numbers or pictures on one side, used for playing games □ *a deck of cards* □ *a card game/player.* ■ **to play one's cards right** to handle a situation or behave in the right way, so that one gets something one wants □ *If you play your cards right you could end up running this place.* ■ **to put** OR **lay one's cards on the table** to tell somebody one's thoughts, plans, ideas etc, especially after one has kept these secret. **-2.** [for showing information] a small rectangular piece of stiff paper or plastic that has a name or information written on it □ *a membership/visiting/business card* □ *Do you have my card?* **-3.** [for sending a message] a piece of stiff paper, folded in half with a picture on one side, that one sends to another person on a special occasion □ *a birthday/Christmas/greeting card.* **-4.** = **postcard. -5.** GB stiff paper □ *a piece of card.*
◆ **cards** *n* any game that is played using cards □ *They were sitting playing cards.* □ *a game of cards.*
◆ **in the cards** US, **on the cards** GB *adv* likely to happen (informal use) □ *A management buyout is still in the cards.*

cardamom [ˈkɑːrdəməm] *n* the seeds of an Asian plant that are used as a spice.

cardboard [ˈkɑːrdbɔːrd] *n* thick stiff paper used for making boxes, cartons etc □ *a cardboard folder/file.*

cardboard box *n* a box that is made of cardboard.

card-carrying *adj* **a card-carrying member** an official and active member of an organization, party etc □ *For years I was a card-carrying member of the Green Party.*

card catalog *n* US a set of cards, usually in a library, that have information written on them and are arranged in alphabetical order.

cardholder [ˈkɑːrdhouldər] *n* the person who has a particular credit or debit card.

cardiac [ˈkɑːrdiæk] *adj* [disease, massage, failure] that is connected with the heart.

cardiac arrest *n* a medical condition in which one's heart stops beating.

Cardiff [ˈkɑːrdɪf] the capital of Wales and its main port. POPULATION: 272,600.

cardigan [ˈkɑːrdɪgən] *n* a knitted top like a sweater with buttons up the front.

cardinal [ˈkɑːrdənl] ◇ *adj* [principle, idea] very important and fundamental □ *a cardinal virtue/sin.* ◇ *n* a priest in the Roman Catholic Church who is next in rank to the Pope.

cardinal number, cardinal numeral *n* a number that shows quantity, e.g. 1, 2, 3, rather than order, e.g. first, second. NOTE: Compare **ordinal number**.

card index *n* GB = **card catalog**.

cardiology [ˌkɑːrdɪˈɒlədʒɪ] *n* the medical study and treatment of heart disease.

cardiovascular [ˌkɑːrdɪouˈvæskjələr] *adj* [disease, system] that is connected with the heart and the blood vessels.

cardsharp [ˈkɑːrdʃɑːrp] *n* a person who cheats at cards to make money.

card table *n* a small square table for playing cards on.

card vote *n* GB a vote by people at a labor union meeting in which each person's vote represents the votes of all the members of his or her union.

care [keər] ◇ *n* -1. the activity of providing somebody or something with what they need in order to be or stay healthy, safe, in good condition etc □ *She/This plant needs a lot of care.* □ *He has several patients in his care.* □ *care facilities.* ■ **in care** GB [child] who is being looked after by a local authority because a court has ordered this to happen □ *When she went to prison her children were taken into care.* ■ **to take care of sb** to be responsible for the comfort, safety etc of sb □ *The nurses took very good care of me.* □ *She can take care of herself.* ■ **to take care of sthg** to deal with sthg □ *That will be taken care of later.* □ *I'll take care of the bill.* ■ **take care!** a phrase used to say goodbye to somebody □ *OK, I'll see you tomorrow. Take care! Bye!* -2. attention to what one is doing so that one does not make mistakes or cause damage □ *Take more care with your writing/work.* □ *'Handle with care.'* ■ **to take care** to be careful □ *I've learned to take more care of my body.* ■ **to take care to do sthg** to make sure one does sthg □ *He always took great care to lock up the house at night.* □ *Take care not to drip water on the carpet.* -3. **a care** something that makes one worried □ *She was weighed down with cares.* □ *I walked along without a care in the world.* ◇ *vi* to be concerned about something and think it is important □ *I really do care, you know.* □ *All he cares about is his car/himself.* □ *"Do you want to go out for a drink or stay in?" — "I don't really care."* □ *Who cares?* ■ **I couldn't care less** it doesn't matter to me at all (informal use) □ *I couldn't care less what he thinks!*

♦ **care of** *prep* at the address of <sb> □ *Write to me care of my sister in Adelaide.*

♦ **care for** *vt fus* -1. **to care for sb/sthg** to like sb/sthg □ *I don't care for opera/him much.* □ *Would you care for a drink?* -2. **to care for sb** to take care of sb who is ill or too young to take care of themselves □ *He spent his life caring for the sick.*

CARE [keər] (*abbr of* **Cooperative for American Relief Everywhere**) *n* a US organization that sends packages of food, medicine, clothing, and tools to people who need help in developing countries □ *a CARE package.*

careen [kəˈriːn] *vi* = **career**.

career [kəˈrɪər] ◇ *n* -1. a job or profession that requires training and that somebody does for a long period of their life □ *a career in medicine/banking* □ *Many women are understandably worried about taking a career break.* -2. the part of one's life that one spends working □ *He has enjoyed a long career in show business/politics.* □ *Most of her career was spent abroad.* ◇ *comp* **a career diplomat/soldier etc** a diplomat/soldier etc who aims to do their job for all of their working life. ◇ *vi* to move very fast in an uncontrolled way □ *The van careered down the road.*

career counselor *n* US a person whose job is to give advice about careers, especially to students about to leave school or college.

careerist [kəˈrɪərəst] *n* a person who does their job mainly because they want to keep getting more power and success (disapproving use).

careers [kəˈrɪərz] *comp* **a careers office/service etc** an office/service etc that provides information and advice to people to help them choose a career □ *a careers advice center.*

careers adviser, careers officer *n* GB = **career counselor**.

career woman *n* a woman whose career is very important to her.

carefree [ˈkeərfriː] *adj* [person] who is cheerful and not worried because they have no problems □ *a carefree attitude/life.*

careful [ˈkeərfl] *adj* -1. [person] who is sensible and tries to avoid danger, problems, mistakes etc □ *He's a very careful driver.* □ *Be careful!* □ *He's very careful with his money.* ■ **to be careful to do sthg** to make sure that one does sthg □ *She's always careful not to offend* *people.* **-2.** [work, preparation] that is done with care so that no mistakes are made and nothing is left out □ *She's a careful and meticulous worker.* □ *I've given your proposal careful consideration.*

carefully ['keə^rflɪ] *adv* **-1.** [walk, hold, handle] in a way that avoids hurting anybody or damaging anything □ *Please drive carefully!* **-2.** [read, listen] with careful attention; [think, consider] seriously and thoroughly □ *He thought carefully before replying.* □ *a carefully thought-out plan.*

caregiver ['keə^rgɪvə^r] *n* a person who cares for a child or for somebody who is sick or disabled.

careless ['keə^rləs] *adj* **-1.** [person] who is not careful and makes mistakes, loses things etc; [work, mistake] that is done with too little thought or care □ *a careless driver* □ *That was a careless thing to do/say!* **-2.** [gesture, ease] that is relaxed and does not show any effort □ *She was dressed with careless elegance.*

carelessly ['keə^rləslɪ] *adv* [drive, speak, act] *see* **careless** □ *Books were carelessly scattered across the floor.*

carelessness ['keə^rləsnəs] *n* [of a person, somebody's work] *see* **careless** □ *Mary makes mistakes through sheer carelessness.*

carer ['keərə^r] *n* a person, especially a relative, who cares for an ill or disabled person.

caress [kə'res] ◇ *n* a gentle touch or kiss, especially as a sign of affection. ◇ *vt* to give <a person or animal> a caress.

caretaker ['keə^rteɪkə^r] *n* a person whose job is to look after a large building by keeping it clean, doing repairs etc □ *the school caretaker.*

caretaker government *n* a government that holds power for a short time after the end of one government and before the election of a new one.

car ferry *n* a ferry designed to carry cars.

cargo ['kɑːrgoʊ] (*pl* **cargoes** OR **cargos**) *n* goods that are carried by a ship, plane, truck etc □ *We have a cargo of coffee and bananas.* □ *a cargo ship/plane.*

car hire *n* GB = **car rental**.

Caribbean [US kerə'biən, GB kær-] ◇ **-1. the Caribbean (Sea)** a part of the Atlantic Ocean between North America, South America, and the West Indies. **-2. the Caribbean** the islands in the Caribbean Sea. ◇ *adj*: *Caribbean culture/cooking.*

caribou [US 'kerɪbuː, GB 'kær-] (*pl* **caribou** OR **caribous**) *n* a large deer from North America.

caricature ['kærɪkətʃʊə^r] ◇ *n* **-1.** [of a person] a picture or description of somebody that exaggerates the way they look or behave, especially in a humorous way. **-2.** [of the facts, truth] a very exaggerated account of something. ◇ *vt* to draw or describe <sb> as a caricature.

caries ['keəriːz] decay of the teeth or bones (technical use).

caring ['keərɪŋ] *adj* [person, attitude, society] that shows kindness and concern for other people □ *a caring home environment.*

caring professions *npl* **the caring professions** the professions that involve caring for people, e.g. nursing, social work, and medicine.

carnage ['kɑːrnɪdʒ] *n* the violent killing of a large number of people, especially in battle.

carnal ['kɑːrnl] *adj* [desire, pleasure] that involves sex or sexual feelings (formal and disapproving use).

carnation [kɑːr'neɪʃn] *n* a plant that has sweet-smelling pink, white, or red flowers.

Carnegie [kɑːr'neɪgɪ], **Andrew** (1835–1919) a US businessman who gave millions of dollars to education and the arts. He was responsible for building many libraries, and also Carnegie Hall in New York.

Carnegie Hall ['kɑːr'nəgɪ-] a large concert hall in New York.

carnival ['kɑːrnɪvl] *n* **-1.** a celebration that takes place in the street, usually before Easter, and often involves a large procession of people who dance to loud music in colorful costumes. **-2.** US an outdoor event with bright lights and music, where people enjoy themselves by riding on fast machines, playing games of skill or strength etc.

carnivore ['kɑːrnɪvɔː^r] *n* an animal that is carnivorous.

carnivorous [kɑːr'nɪvərəs] *adj* [animal, species] that eats the flesh of other animals.

carol [US 'kerəl, GB 'kær-] *n* a religious song that is traditionally sung at Christmas □ *a carol singer.*

carouse [kə'raʊz] *vi* to drink a lot of alcohol and have fun in a noisy way.

carousel [US ‚kerə'sel, GB ‚kær-] *n* **-1.** US [at an amusement park] a mechanical device consisting of a circular covered platform with models of animals or cars on which children can sit while the machine turns around. **-2.** [at an airport] a circular conveyor belt on which passengers' baggage is placed for collection after a flight.

carp [kɑːrp] (*pl* **carp** OR **carps**) ◇ *n* a large, edible, freshwater fish. ◇ *vi* to complain □ *He's always carping about poor service in hotels.*

car park *n* GB a place where people can leave their cars.

Carpathian Mountains = **Carpathians**.

Carpathians [kɑːr'peɪθɪənz]: **the Carpathians** a mountain range in central Europe extending from Slovakia to Romania. HIGHEST POINT: 2,655 m.

carpenter ['kɑːr'pəntə^r] *n* a person whose job is to make or repair things made of wood.

carpentry ['kɑːr'pəntrɪ] *n* the work of a carpenter.

carpet ['kɑːr'pɪt] ◇ *n* **-1.** a piece of a heavy fabric such as woven wool that is used for covering floors or stairs □ *a wall-to-wall/stair carpet.* ■ **to sweep sthg under the carpet** to keep sthg secret. **-2. a carpet of leaves/snow etc** a thick covering of leaves, snow etc on the ground. ◇ *vt* **-1.** to put a carpet on the floor of <a house, room> etc □ *I'd like to carpet the whole house in the same color.* **-2. to be car-**

peted with sthg [with snow, leaves] to be covered with a thick layer of sthg.

carpetbagger [ˈkɑːrpətbægər] *n* in US history, a Northerner who went to live in the South after the Civil War to improve their financial situation or political career (disapproving use).

carpet slipper *n* a soft shoe for wearing indoors.

carpet sweeper [-ˌswiːpər] *n* a device for sweeping the dirt from carpets.

car phone *n* a phone that is designed to be used in a car.

car pool *n* -1. US a group of people who travel to work, school etc together by sharing a car. -2. GB a group of cars owned by a company for the use of its employees.

carport [ˈkɑːrpɔːrt] *n* a shelter for a car that is attached to the side of a building and consists of a roof supported on posts.

car radio *n* a small radio fitted in a car.

car rental *n* the act or business of renting cars □ *a car rental company.*

carriage [US ˈkerɪdʒ, GB ˈkær-] *n* -1. a vehicle with four wheels that is pulled by horses. -2. [of goods] the transport of goods from one place to another; the cost of this transport. ■ **carriage paid** OR **free** GB with the cost already paid by the sender. ■ **carriage forward** GB with the cost to be paid by the receiver. -3. [on a machine] a moving part of a machine, e.g. a typewriter, that supports another part. -4. [of a person] the way that one holds one's head and body when standing, moving etc (literary use). -5. GB RAIL a vehicle forming part of a train that carries passengers □ *a railway carriage.*

carriage clock *n* a small ornamental clock with a rectangular case and a handle on top.

carriage return *n* a lever or key on a typewriter or computer for moving to the beginning of a new line.

carriageway [US ˈkerɪdʒweɪ, GB ˈkær-] *n* GB the part of a road which vehicles travel along.

carrier [US ˈkerɪər, GB ˈkærɪə] *n* -1. INDUSTRY somebody or something, e.g. an airline, that carries goods or people from one place to another. -2. MEDICINE a person, animal etc that carries a disease which they can infect others with although they do not have any symptoms of it themselves □ *carriers of the AIDS virus.* -3. MILITARY = **aircraft carrier**. -4. GB = **carrier bag**.

carrier bag *n* GB a large plastic or paper bag with handles, used for carrying shopping.

carrier pigeon *n* a pigeon that has been trained to carry messages from one place to another.

carrion [US ˈkerɪən, GB ˈkær-] *n* the rotting flesh of dead animals □ *Crows feed on carrion.*

Carroll [ˈkærəl], **Lewis** (1832–1898) a British writer and mathematician. His most famous works are the children's stories *Alice's Adventures in Wonderland* and *Through the Looking-Glass.*

carrot [US ˈkerət, GB ˈkær-] *n* -1. a long, thin,

orange-colored root vegetable that is cooked or eaten raw in salads □ *carrot cake/soup.* -2. something that is used to try to tempt somebody to do something (informal use).

carry [US ˈkerɪ, GB ˈkærɪ] (*pt* & *pp* **carried**) ◇ *vt* -1. [child, load, equipment] to take <sb/sthg> somewhere by holding them in one's hands, arms, on one's back etc so that they do not touch the ground □ *He was carrying a suitcase.* -2. [passenger, goods, information] to take <sb/sthg> from one place to another □ *My car can only carry four people.* □ *The seeds are carried for miles by the wind.* □ *The pipeline carries the oil inshore to the terminal.* -3. [gun, wallet] to have <sthg> with one all the time □ *I never carry cash when I'm abroad.* □ *The car carries a spare wheel.* -4. [person, animal, insect] to have <a disease or virus> and be likely to spread it to others □ *Mosquitoes do not carry Aids.* -5. [penalty, fine, responsibility] to have or involve <sthg> as a necessary part or result of itself; [message, warning] to contain or show <sthg> □ *All operations carry an element of risk to the patient.* □ *All our products carry a six-month guarantee.* -6. **to be carried** [motion, proposal] to be accepted after getting enough votes □ *The motion was carried by 62 votes to 30.* -7. **to be carrying a child** to be pregnant. -8. MATH to move <a number> from one column of figures to the next when doing a sum.
◇ *vi* [sound, noise, voice] to be able to be heard a long way away □ *Their laughter carried over the water.*

◆ **carry away** *vt fus* **to get carried away** to become so interested, angry, enthusiastic etc about something that one does too much □ *We went shopping and I got a little carried away!*

◆ **carry forward** *vt sep* **to carry a number forward** in bookkeeping, to move a number from the bottom of a column to the top of the next page.

◆ **carry off** *vt sep* -1. **to carry sthg off** to do <sthg difficult> successfully □ *I never thought we'd carry it off!* -2. **to carry a prize/award off** to win a prize/award □ *They carried off first prize.*

◆ **carry on** ◇ *vt fus* -1. **to carry on sthg** [conversation, tradition, relationship] to continue sthg without stopping □ *He told me to carry on taking the pills.* -2. **to carry on sthg** to start sthg again after stopping for a short time □ *I intend to carry on working after I've had the baby.* ◇ *vi* -1. to continue something □ *We carried on with our meal.* □ *We'll take a break now, then carry on after coffee.* -2. to behave in a silly, excited, or worried way (informal use).

◆ **carry out** *vt sep* **to carry sthg out** [plan, threat, instructions] to do sthg that has been ordered or planned □ *The gang carried out a series of attacks on elderly people.* □ *I'm only carrying out orders.*

◆ **carry through** *vt sep* **to carry sthg through** [plan, reform] to complete sthg successfully, even though there are problems.

carryall [US ˈkerɪɔːl, GB ˈkær-] *n* US a large soft bag that people use for carrying clothes and possessions when they travel.

carrycot [US 'kerikɒt, GB 'kær-] *n* GB a small bed with high sides and handles in which a baby can be carried.

carry-on *adj* **carry-on luggage** luggage that passengers take on to a plane with them.

carry-out *n* US & SCOT a cooked meal that one can buy at a restaurant and take away to eat.

carsick ['kɑːrsɪk] *adj* **to be carsick** to feel sick while traveling in a car.

cart [kɑːrt] ◇ *n* -1. a vehicle with two or four wheels that is used for carrying things, is pulled by a horse or by hand, and is often used on a farm. -2. US = **grocery cart.** ◇ *vt* -1. [hay, crops] to carry <sthg> to a place in a cart. -2. [person, luggage] to carry or take <sb/sthg heavy> to a place, especially with difficulty (informal use) □ *I'm not carting that suitcase around with me all day.* □ *He was carted off to the police station.*

carte blanche [ˌkɑːrt'blɑːnʃ] *n* **to give sb carte blanche** to give sb complete freedom to do what they want or think best □ *We were given carte blanche to employ whoever we wanted.*

cartel [kɑːr'tel] *n* a group of people or companies that work together as a way of limiting competition and controlling prices □ *a drugs cartel.*

carthorse ['kɑːrthɔːrs] *n* a large, very strong horse used in the past to pull carts and farm equipment.

cartilage ['kɑːrtəlɪdʒ] *n* a substance that forms most of the skeleton of young animals and humans and is found in the nose and joints of adults; a piece of this tissue □ *He fell and tore a cartilage in his knee.*

carton ['kɑːrtn] *n* -1. a strong cardboard box. -2. a cardboard or plastic container in which food or drink is sold □ *a milk/yogurt/fruit-juice carton.*

cartoon [kɑːr'tuːn] *n* -1. [in a newspaper, magazine] a humorous drawing; a series of these drawings that tell a story □ *a political cartoon.* -2. CINEMA a movie in which the characters and background are drawn by artists.

cartoonist [kɑːr'tuːnəst] *n* a person whose job is drawing cartoons.

cartridge ['kɑːrtrɪdʒ] *n* -1. [in a gun] a metal, plastic, or cardboard tube that contains a bullet and the explosive charge used to fire it. -2. [in a pen] a plastic tube that contains ink and fits inside a pen. -3. [in a camera] a container with film inside that is loaded into a camera. -4. [in a record player] the part of the arm of a record player that holds the needle. -5. [in a photocopier, printer] a small plastic device that contains ink and fits inside a printer or photocopier.

cartridge paper *n* a strong thick paper used for drawing.

cartridge pen *n* a pen that contains a small plastic tube full of ink that is replaced when empty.

cartwheel ['kɑːrtwiːl] *n* an acrobatic movement made by putting one's hands on the ground, then throwing one's legs sideways so that one lands back on one's feet.

car valeting [-vælətɪŋ] *n* GB a service offered by some garages in which a car is cleaned inside and outside.

carve [kɑːrv] ◇ *vt* -1. [sculpture, figure] to make <an object> out of wood or stone by cutting pieces off it; [wood, stone] to cut and shape <sthg> in this way □ *a carved wooden staircase* □ *He carved the wood into the form of a horse.* -2. [lamb, beef] to cut <meat> into slices. -3. [writing, pattern] to cut <a design> into wood □ *They carved their names on the tree.* ◇ *vi* to cut meat into slices.

◆ **carve out** *vt sep* **to carve sthg out** [career, niche, position] to get sthg for oneself by working hard □ *He has carved out a place for himself in politics.*

◆ **carve up** *vt sep* **to carve sthg up** [property, country] to divide sthg between a few people, especially in a greedy way □ *They carved up the profits between them.*

Carver ['kɑːrvər], **George Washington** (1864–1943) a US scientist who originally came from a slave family. He encouraged education for black people and improved farming methods in the south of the USA.

carving ['kɑːrvɪŋ] *n* -1. the art of making carved objects, sculptures, or designs. -2. an object that has been carved □ *a beautiful wood/stone carving.*

carving knife *n* a sharp knife for cutting cooked meat into slices.

car wash *n* a machine at a gas station that washes cars automatically using large brushes and hoses.

Casanova [ˌkæzə'nouvə] *n* a man who has a reputation for having a lot of lovers.

cascade [kæ'skeɪd] ◇ *n* a waterfall or series of waterfalls that flows over rocks. ◇ *vi* [water sparks] to fall downwards quickly and in large amounts □ *The water cascaded over the rocks.* □ *Her hair cascaded over her shoulders.*

case [keɪs] *n* -1. a single example or occasion of something □ *It was a case of mistaken identity.* □ *In this particular case, I felt I had no choice but to leave.* ■ **a case in point** a good example □ *This school is a case in point, with a failure rate of over 50%.* ■ **in some/most cases** on some/most occasions □ *In most cases, complaints were dealt with in less than a month.* -2. [of a doctor, lawyer] a person or problem that is being dealt with by somebody such as a doctor, lawyer, adviser, or social worker □ *Our complaints department deals with cases like these.* □ *There have been several cases of measles in the area.* -3. LAW a crime or complaint that the police are investigating; the trial in court that results from this □ *a murder/rape case* □ *Her case is due in court next week.* -4. [in an argument] the facts and arguments given in support of an opinion □ *She made a strong case for cutting taxes.* -5. [for holding something] a box or other container for holding and protecting something, especially one that can be carried □ *a violin/binocular case* □ *a case of wine/books.* -6. GB = **suitcase.** -7. *phrase* **to**

be the case to be true or correct □ *That is certainly not the case in the United States.*

◆ **in case** ◇ *conj* **take an umbrella in case it rains** take an umbrella because it might rain. ◇ *adv*: *Should I keep a spare key, just in case?*

◆ **in case of** *prep* 'in case of emergency' if there is an emergency.

◆ **in any case** *adv* used to give a new and more important reason for something □ *In any case, that's not the point.*

◆ **in that case** *adv* if what has just been said is true or correct □ *"What if it doesn't work?"* — *"In that case we'll start again."*

◆ **in which case** *conj* if this happens or is true □ *He may still come, in which case we can all leave together.*

case history *n* a record of a person's past, e.g. their medical history, that helps to explain and treat a present illness or problem that they have.

caseload ['keɪsloud] *n* the amount of work that a social worker, psychiatrist etc has to do, consisting of individual cases.

casement ['keɪsmənt] *n* **a casement (window)** a window that has hinges at one side and opens outward like a door.

case study *n* a detailed study of a person or group of people over a period of time by doctors, sociologists etc.

cash [kæʃ] ◇ *n* **-1.** money in the form of notes and coins rather than checks or credit cards □ *I've got £20 in cash.* □ *She always pays (in) cash.* □ *a cash payment.* **-2.** money (informal use) □ *I'm a little short of cash.* **-3. cash in advance** an arrangement in which goods or services are paid for before they are received. ■ **cash on delivery** → **COD**. ◇ *vt* to exchange <a check> for money.

◆ **cash in** *vi* **to cash in on sthg** to take advantage of sthg in a way that is thought by other people to be wrong or unfair (informal use) □ *Everyone is cashing in on his idea.*

cash and carry *n* a large store which sells goods in large quantities at a cheaper price.

cashbook ['kæʃbʊk] *n* a book in which a person or company keeps a record of all the money they spend and receive.

cash box *n* a metal box, usually with a lock, for keeping money in.

cash card *n* a plastic card that is used for getting money from a cash dispenser.

cash cow *n* a product or part of a business that keeps making a profit.

cash crop *n* a crop that is grown in order to be sold.

cash desk *n* GB a desk or counter in a store where goods are paid for.

cash discount *n* a discount that is offered to somebody when they pay in cash rather than by check or credit card.

cash dispenser *n* a machine, usually built into the outside wall of a bank, where one can get money by putting in a plastic card and entering a personal code number.

cashew ['kæʃuː] *n* **a cashew (nut)** a small

curved nut that grows in the tropics, often eaten roasted and salted.

cash flow *n* the movement of money into and out of a business □ *They failed to expand because of cash flow problems.*

cashier [kæ'ʃɪəʳ] *n* **-1.** a person in a store whose job is to take money as payment for goods. **-2.** a person in a bank whose job is to cash checks, take payments etc.

cash machine *n* = **cash dispenser**.

cashmere [US 'kæʒmɪr, GB 'kæʃmɪə] *n* a fine soft wool that is very expensive □ *a cashmere sweater/scarf.*

cashpoint (machine) ['kæʃpɔɪnt-] *n* GB = **cash dispenser**.

cash price *n* the price of something when it is paid for in cash rather than by check or credit card.

cash register *n* a machine in a store that is used to add up and record the prices of goods bought, with a drawer for keeping the money received.

cash sale *n* the act of selling something for cash.

casing ['keɪsɪŋ] *n* something that covers and protects something else □ *a rubber casing* □ *Remove the outer casing before use.*

casino [kə'siːnou] (*pl* **casinos**) *n* a place where people gamble by playing games, e.g. roulette or cards.

cask [US kæsk, GB kɑːsk] *n* a large wooden barrel for wine, sherry, beer etc □ *'Matured in oak casks.'*

casket [US 'kæskət, GB 'kɑːsk-] *n* **-1.** US a box in which a dead person is buried or burned. **-2.** a small box for jewels and other valuable things.

Caspian Sea [ˌkæspjən-]: **the Caspian Sea** the world's largest inland sea, between southeastern Europe and Asia.

casserole ['kæsəroul] *n* **-1. a casserole (dish)** a deep dish with a lid for cooking food in an oven. **-2.** food cooked in a casserole □ *a chicken/vegetable casserole.*

cassette [kə'set] *n* **-1.** a rectangular plastic box that holds a roll of audio or video tape and fits into a machine for playing or recording. **-2.** a container of photographic film that fits into a camera.

cassette deck *n* a machine for playing and recording audio cassettes, usually as part of a hi-fi system.

cassette player *n* a machine for playing audio cassettes.

cassette recorder *n* a machine for playing and recording audio cassettes.

cassock ['kæsək] *n* a long robe, usually black, that is worn by Christian priests in church.

cast [US kæst, GB kɑːst] (*pt* & *pp* **cast**) ◇ *vt* **-1. to cast an eye** OR **a glance over sthg** to look at sthg quickly □ *Could you cast an eye over this report?* ■ **to cast doubt on sthg** to make people doubt sthg □ *His indecision casts doubt on his ability to govern.* ■ **to cast a spell** to change somebody or something using

magic □ *The witch cast a spell on the prince.* **-2. to cast a shadow/light** to send a shadow/light somewhere □ *The flames cast a red glow around the room.* **-3.** [object] to throw <sthg> (literary use). **-4.** [person] to choose <an actor> to play a role in a play, movie etc □ *She cast him in the role of Hamlet.* **-5. to cast one's vote** to vote. **-6.** [in a mold] to make <an object> by leaving liquid metal or plastic in a mold until it hardens □ *a statue cast in bronze.*
◇ *vi* FISHING to throw a fishing line into the water.
◇ *n* **-1.** all the actors in a particular play, movie etc □ *He was in the cast of "Showboat".* □ *a member of the cast* □ *a cast of thousands.* **-2.** MEDICINE = **plaster cast**.

◆ **cast about, cast around** *vt fus* **to cast about** OR **around for sthg** to try to think of sthg to do or say □ *We're desperately casting around for ideas.*

◆ **cast aside** *vt sep* **to cast sb/sthg aside** to get rid of sb/sthg that one no longer wants □ *He later cast aside his pacifism.*

◆ **cast off** ◇ *vt sep* **to cast sthg off** [mood, burden] to get rid of sthg (formal use) □ *She cast off her old habits.* ◇ *vi* **-1.** to unfasten a boat or ship and start sailing. **-2.** to fasten the stitches tightly at the end of a piece of knitting to stop them from coming loose.

◆ **cast on** *vi* to put the first row of stitches onto a needle at the beginning of a piece of knitting.

castanets [ˌkæstəˈnets] *npl* a Spanish musical instrument that consists of two small pieces of wood that are held in the hand and knocked together.

castaway [US ˈkæstəweɪ, GB ˈkɑːst-] *n* a person who has survived a shipwreck and been carried by the sea to an empty shore or island.

caste [US kæst, GB kɑːst] *n* one of the fixed classes in some societies, especially in Hindu society □ *a caste system* □ *a low-/high-caste family.*

caster [US ˈkæstr, GB ˈkɑːstə] *n* one of the small wheels under a bed, chair, sofa etc.

caster sugar *n* GB fine white sugar used in cooking.

castigate [ˈkæstəgeɪt] *vt* to criticize <sb> severely (formal use).

casting [US ˈkæstɪŋ, GB ˈkɑːst-] *n* the process of choosing actors for a play, movie etc □ *a casting director.*

casting vote *n* the vote of the most important member of a group or committee that is used to decide an issue when there is an equal number of votes for and against it.

cast iron *n* a strong kind of iron that is made into objects by pouring it in liquid form into a mold and leaving it until it hardens.

◆ **cast-iron** *adj* **-1.** [gate, stove, railing] made of cast iron. **-2. a cast-iron will/decision** a firm and strong will/decision. **-3. a cast-iron alibi/guarantee** an alibi/a guarantee that is very certain and can be trusted.

castle [US ˈkæsl, GB ˈkɑːsl] *n* **-1.** a large and

very old building with thick walls, ditches etc to protect it against attack. **-2.** CHESS a chess piece which can move in a straight line but not diagonally.

castoff [US ˈkæstɒf, GB ˈkɑːst-] *n* a piece of clothing that is given away because it is no longer wanted or needed □ *I used to wear all my elder brother's castoffs.*

castor [US ˈkæstr, GB ˈkɑːstə] *n* = **caster**.

castor oil *n* a thick yellow oil used as a medicine.

castor sugar *n* = **caster sugar**.

castrate [US ˈkæstreɪt, GB kæˈstreɪt] *vt* to remove the testicles of <a man or animal>.

castration [kæˈstreɪʃn] *n*: *see* **castrate**.

Castro [ˈkæstroʊ], **Fidel** (1927–) the Communist revolutionary leader of Cuba, who became Prime Minister in 1959, and President in 1976.

casual [ˈkæʒʊəl] *adj* **-1.** [behavior, attitude, person] that seems not to care or be concerned □ *He tried to appear casual when talking about it.* □ *He cast a casual glance over the report.* ■ **a casual observer** a person who does not look at something in detail □ *To the casual observer this may seem like a very ordinary event.* **-2.** [relationship, affair] that is not serious and does not last for long □ *casual sex.* **-3.** [meeting] that happens without being planned. **-4.** [clothes, shoes] that are informal and comfortable □ *casual wear.* **-5.** [work, worker] that is not regular or permanent □ *a casual job/laborer.*

casually [ˈkæʒʊəlɪ] *adv* [glance, behave, dress] *see* **casual** □ *She was casually dressed.* □ *He casually mentioned he was leaving town.*

casualty [ˈkæʒʊəltɪ] (*pl* **casualties**) *n* **-1.** [in a war, accident] a person who has died or been injured in a war, accident, or disaster □ *There were heavy casualties.* **-2.** GB [in a hospital] a part of a hospital where people who have suddenly fallen ill or have been injured in accidents are taken for emergency medical treatment □ *She's in casualty.* **-3. a casualty of sthg** [of a change, policy, system] a person or thing that is lost, destroyed, or suffers as a result of sthg □ *Truth is often the first casualty in political debates.*

casualty department *n* GB [in a hospital] = **casualty**.

cat [kæt] *n* **-1.** a small furry animal with whiskers and sharp claws, often kept as a pet or to catch mice □ *a domestic cat.* ■ **to let the cat out of the bag** to tell somebody a secret, often by mistake. ■ **to be like a cat on a hot tin roof** US OR **on hot bricks** GB to be unable to stay still because one is very nervous or excited. **-2.** any animal related to the domestic cat, e.g. a lion or tiger □ *a member of the cat family.* **-3.** AUTO = **catalytic converter**.

cataclysmic [ˌkætəˈklɪzmɪk] *adj* [effect, change] that seems very big and disastrous.

catacombs [US ˈkætəkoʊmz, GB -kuːmz] *npl* a series of underground rooms and tunnels where bodies were once buried.

Catalan [ˈkætəlæn] ◇ *n* **-1.** a person who comes

from or lives in Catalonia. -2. the language of Catalonia. ◇ *adj*: see **Catalonia**.

catalog US, **catalogue** ['kætəlɒg] ◇ *n* -1. BUSINESS a book, often illustrated with photographs, listing all the items for sale in a store, at an auction, or through the mail □ *a mail-order catalog.* -2. [of a museum, gallery, library] a book listing everything in a collection □ *I bought a copy of the exhibition catalog.* -3. **a catalog of disasters/crimes etc** a series of disasters/crimes etc that happen close to each other □ *A whole catalog of errors led up to the crisis.* ◇ *vt* -1. to make a list of the <books, works of art> etc in a collection. -2. to make a list of <mistakes, crimes> etc.

Catalonia [ˌkætə'ləʊnjə] a self-governing region of northeastern Spain, with many tourist resorts and industries.

catalyst ['kætələst] *n* -1. CHEMISTRY a substance that speeds up a chemical reaction without being affected itself. -2. somebody or something that causes a social or political change □ *The shelling of unarmed civilians could act as a catalyst for UN military intervention.*

catalytic converter [ˌkætəlɪtɪkkən'vɜː'tə'] *n* a device in the exhaust of a car that reduces the amount of harmful gas produced.

catamaran [ˌkætəmə'ræn] *n* a boat or ship with two hulls joined by a single deck.

catapult ['kætəpʌlt] GB ◇ *n* -1. a weapon for shooting stones, usually used by children, which consists of a Y-shaped stick with an elastic strip fastened between the two sides. -2. a machine for launching aircraft from an aircraft carrier. ◇ *vt* -1. to fire <sthg> from a catapult. -2. to throw <sthg> very suddenly and quickly □ *The impact catapulted him through the windshield.* -3. **to be catapulted to fame/stardom etc** to suddenly become famous/a star etc because of some event □ *The show catapulted her to fame.*

cataract ['kætərækt] *n* -1. an area of the lens of the eye that has become unclear and prevents one from seeing properly □ *cataract surgery.* -2. a large waterfall (literary use).

catarrh [kə'tɑː'] *n* a condition in which a thick yellowish substance is produced in one's nose and throat, e.g. when one has a cold.

catastrophe [kə'tæstrəfɪ] *n* a terrible event that causes great suffering, destruction, or death □ *He predicted that lifting the arms embargo would lead to catastrophe.*

catastrophic [ˌkætə'strɒfɪk] *adj* [result, event, war] that causes great suffering, destruction, or death □ *Pollutants are being released unchecked with catastrophic results for the environment.*

cat burglar *n* a burglar who gets into buildings by climbing high walls and roofs.

catcall ['kætkɔːl] *n* a loud noise made by somebody in an audience to show they do not like something.

catch [kætʃ] (*pt* & *pp* **caught**) ◇ *vt* -1. [a moving object] to take hold of <an object> while it is moving through the air □ *I just managed to catch the glass before it hit the ground.*

-2. [criminal, mouse, fish] to stop and hold onto <a person or animal> that is trying to escape □ *I went fishing but didn't catch anything.* -3. [person] to surprise <sb>, especially while they are doing something wrong or illegal □ *He was caught stealing from the petty cash.* □ *Don't let me catch you telling lies again!* -4. **to catch a train/plane etc** to get onto a train/plane etc and travel somewhere □ *I caught the 7:30 train to Lille.* -5. [train, plane, program] not to be too late to get, see, or hear <sthg> □ *We just caught the last bus/the end of the movie.* ■ **to catch the post** GB to put a letter, package etc in the mailbox before it is emptied. -6. **not to catch sthg** [name, reply, word] not to hear sthg clearly □ *I didn't catch what you said.* -7. **to catch sb's attention/imagination** to make sb interested in what is happening □ *The trial has caught the public's interest/imagination.* -8. **to catch sight of sb/sthg, to catch a glimpse of sb/sthg** to see sb/sthg suddenly for a short time and not completely □ *I caught sight of him in the crowd.* -9. [cold, measles, cholera] to get <an illness or disease> □ *Put a thick sweater on or you'll catch a chill.* -10. [part of one's body, clothing] to get <sthg> trapped or stuck □ *I caught my finger in the door.* □ *She caught her sleeve on a nail.* -11. **to catch the light** to reflect the light and shine □ *Her ring sparkled as it caught the light.* -12. [person, animal, target] to hit <sb/sthg> □ *He caught me on the chin and it really hurt.*

◇ *vi* -1. [coat, sleeve, hair] to become trapped or stuck □ *My skirt caught on the barbed wire and tore.* -2. [fire, wood] to start to burn □ *The fire wouldn't catch because the wood was damp.*

◇ *n* -1. [with one's hands] the act of taking hold of an object that is moving through the air, especially a ball □ *Good catch!* -2. [of fish] an amount of fish that has been caught □ *The boat landed its catch in Dover.* -3. [on a door, window] a device used to fasten containers, windows, doors etc □ *a safety catch.* -4. [in a situation] a disadvantage or problem, especially one that has been hidden deliberately □ *The plan seems perfect, but there must be a catch in it somewhere.*

◆ **catch at** *vt fus* **to catch at sthg** [branch, rope, arm] to try to take hold of sthg □ *He caught at the railing and missed.*

◆ **catch on** *vi* -1. [fashion, craze, trend] to become popular □ *No one thought the idea would catch on.* -2. [person] to begin to understand slowly or later than everybody else (informal use) □ *Her husband eventually caught on to what was happening.*

◆ **catch out** *vt sep* **to catch sb out** GB to make sb make a mistake, especially in order to show that they are lying or doing something wrong □ *They asked a lot of questions to try and catch me out.*

◆ **catch up** ◇ *vt sep* -1. **to get caught up in sthg** [in a crime, affair, argument] to become involved in sthg, usually against one's will. -2. **to catch sb up** GB to come from behind and reach the same point as sb □ *You go on ahead, I'll catch you up in a minute.* ◇ *vi* -1. to come from behind and reach the same point as somebody □ *Our competitor is the most suc-cessful company in the market but we're catching up fast.* □ *Let's wait here for the others to catch up.* **-2. to catch up on sthg** [on work, sleep, reading] to spend time doing sthg that one has not been able to do for a while □ *We had a lot of news to catch up on.*

♦ **catch up with** *vt fus* **-1. to catch up with sb** to reach the same point or level as sb □ *We've only had two lessons so you'll soon catch up with us.* □ *I finally caught up with her at the gate.* **-2. to catch up with sb** to catch sb one has been chasing for some time □ *The police finally caught up with him in Barcelona.* □ *The taxman will catch up with you in the end!*

catch-22 [-twentɪˈtuː] *n* **a catch-22 situation** a situation that one cannot escape from be-cause one needs one thing in order to get a second thing, but cannot get the second thing unless one has the first thing.

catch-all *adj* [clause, term] that is general enough to cover all possibilities.

catcher [ˈkætʃər] *n* the baseball player behind homeplate who catches the ball when it is not hit by the batter.

catching [ˈkætʃɪŋ] *adj* **to be catching** [disease, enthusiasm] to be easily passed on to other people (informal use).

catchment area [ˈkætʃmənt-] *n* GB the area served by a school, hospital etc, which peo-ple living in the area are expected to go to.

catchphrase [ˈkætʃfreɪz] *n* a phrase that is used by somebody famous, e.g. an enter-tainer, and is associated with them.

catchword [ˈkætʃwɜːrd] *n* a well-known word or phrase that is often repeated, e.g. by a political party.

catchy [ˈkætʃɪ] *(compar* **catchier**, *superl* **catchi-est)** *adj* [tune, song] pleasant and easy to re-member.

cat door *n* US a small opening in the door of a house through which cats can enter and leave.

catechism [ˈkætəkɪzm] *n* a series of questions and answers that are used to teach Christian beliefs.

categorical [ˌkætəˈgɒrɪkl] *adj* [denial, refusal, statement] clear and firm.

categorically [ˌkætəˈgɒrɪklɪ] *adv* [deny, refuse, state] *see* **categorical** □ *She categorically denied any involvement in the affair.*

categorize, -ise [ˈkætəgəraɪz] *vt* to put <sb/sthg> into a category □ *He is categorized as a Romantic.*

category [US ˈkætəgɔːrɪ, GB -əgərɪ] *(pl* **catego-ries)** *n* a group or class of people or things with similar qualities □ *Her work doesn't fall into any neat category.*

cater [ˈkeɪtər] *vi* [person, company] to provide food and drinks.

♦ **cater for** *vt fus* **to cater for sb** GB to cater to sb.

♦ **cater to** *vt fus* **-1. to cater to sb** US to give sb what they need or want □ *The magazine caters to independent working women.* □ *We ca-ter to all levels of ability.* **-2. to cater to sthg** to

provide somebody with sthg that they want but that is thought to be bad □ *This kind of rhetoric caters to the very worst in people.*

caterer [ˈkeɪtərər] *n* a person whose job is to provide food and drink for particular occa-sions □ *a firm of caterers.*

catering [ˈkeɪtərɪŋ] *n* the service of providing food and drink for special occasions □ *A local firm did the catering.* □ *a catering college* □ *the catering industry.*

caterpillar [ˈkætəˌpɪlər] *n* a small long animal with many legs that moves slowly and de-velops into a butterfly.

caterpillar tracks *npl* a continuous band of metal plates attached to the wheels of heavy vehicles, e.g. tanks or bulldozers.

catfish [ˈkætfɪʃ] *(pl* **catfish** OR **catfishes)** *n* a fish with long thin parts around the mouth that look like whiskers.

cat flap *n* GB = **cat door**.

cat food *n* food for cats sold in cans.

catgut [ˈkætgʌt] *n* a strong cord made from the intestines of animals and used to make the strings of violins and tennis rackets.

catharsis [kəˈθɑːrsəs] *(pl* **catharses** [-siːz]) *n* the release of strong emotions in a harmless way, e.g. by talking about them or by ex-periencing them through drama or music.

cathedral [kəˈθiːdrəl] *n* the main church in an area that a bishop is in charge of □ *St Patrick's Cathedral in New York.*

Catherine the Great [ˌkæθərəndəˈgreɪt] (1729–1796) Empress of Russia from 1762 to 1796.

catheter [ˈkæθətər] *n* a thin tube that is put into an opening in the body for putting in medicine, taking out urine etc.

cathode ray tube [ˌkæθoʊd-] *n* a device used in television sets and computers that pro-duces an image by sending a beam of elec-trons onto a screen.

catholic [ˈkæθlɪk] *adj* [tastes, interests] that in-clude a wide range of things.

Catholic ◇ *n* a member of the Roman Catho-lic Church. ◇ *adj*: *a Catholic priest/school.*

Catholicism [kəˈθɒləsɪzm] *n* the Roman Catho-lic religion.

catkin [ˈkætkɪn] *n* a flower shaped like a long thin tail that hangs from some types of tree, e.g. willows or hazels.

cat litter *n* special grains that are placed in a tray in the house for cats to use as a toilet.

Catseyes™ [ˈkætsaɪz] *npl* GB small pieces of glass fixed in the middle of a road that re-flect car headlights at night and guide driv-ers.

Catskill [ˈkætskɪl]: **the Catskills, the Catskill Mountains** a mountain range in the south-east of New York State, USA. HIGHEST POINT: 1,282 m.

catsup [ˈkætsəp] *n* US a rich tomato sauce con-taining vinegar, served cold with food.

cattle [ˈkætl] *npl* cows and bulls □ *a herd of cat-tle* □ *cattle farming.*

cattle guard US, **cattle grid** GB *n* a row of metal bars over a hole in the ground that stops cows and sheep from going over it.

catty ['kætɪ] (*compar* **cattier**, *superl* **cattiest**) *adj* [person, remark] spiteful (informal use).

catwalk ['kætwɔːk] *n* **-1.** a raised path or bridge, e.g. between two parts of a large building. **-2. the catwalk** the raised path where models walk in a fashion show.

Caucasian [kɔːˈkeɪzjən] (formal use) ◇ *adj* who belongs to a white race □ *The suspect is a Caucasian male in his early twenties.* ◇ *n* a person who is Caucasian.

Caucasus ['kɔːkəsəs]: **the Caucasus** a mountainous region in southeastern Europe between the Black Sea and the Caspian Sea. HIGHEST POINT: 5,642 m.

caucus ['kɔːkəs] (*pl* **caucuses**) *n* **-1.** in some states of the USA and Australia, a large political meeting where people decide who will represent their party in an election and what their policies will be. **-2.** in Britain, a group within a political party that is strong enough to influence policy.

caught [kɔːt] *past tense & past participle of* **catch**.

cauliflower ['kɒlɪflaʊər] *n* a large vegetable consisting of a rough, round, hard, white part surrounded by green leaves.

causal ['kɔːzl] *adj* [relationship] in which one thing is caused by another □ *There is no causal link between the two events.*

cause [kɔːz] ◇ *n* **-1.** [of an event] a person, action, or event that makes something happen □ *The cause of the crash is still unknown.* □ *She died of natural causes.* □ *the law of cause and effect.* **-2. cause for sthg** a good reason for feeling or doing sthg □ *We mustn't give our clients cause for complaint.* □ *There is no cause for concern.* **-3.** something such as a charity, political movement, or principle that people fight for or support □ *Please give generously, it's for a good cause.* ◇ *vt* [delay, problem, anxiety] to be the cause of <sthg> □ *The accident was caused by faulty wiring.* □ *Who would have thought a missing fax could cause so much trouble?* □ *The traffic caused them to miss the appointment.* □ *Torrential rain caused the game to be postponed.*

causeway ['kɔːzweɪ] *n* a raised path or road, usually over water.

caustic ['kɔːstɪk] *adj* **-1.** [chemical, cleaner] that can burn or destroy materials. **-2.** [comment, wit] unkind and hurtful.

caustic soda *n* a strong chemical substance used in cleaning products.

cauterize, -ise ['kɔːtəraɪz] *vt* to close <a wound> by burning it with a hot object or caustic substance.

caution ['kɔːʃn] ◇ *n* **-1.** care that one takes to avoid danger □ *Proceed with caution.* □ *Treat everything he says with caution.* □ *'Caution: handle with care.'* □ *A word of caution, do not let the glue come into contact with your skin.* **-2.** GB LAW an official warning given by a policeman to somebody who has committed an offense, telling them not to do it again. ◇ *vt* **-1. to caution sb against doing sthg** to warn sb not to do sthg because it may be dangerous or unwise. **-2.** GB LAW to warn <sb> that they will be charged with a crime and that anything they say may be used against them at their trial □ *He was taken down to the police station and cautioned.* **-3.** GB LAW **to caution sb for sthg** to warn sb that they have done sthg wrong and should not do it again □ *She was cautioned for speeding.*

cautionary [US 'kɔːʃənerɪ, GB -ərɪ] *adj* **a cautionary tale** a story that gives a warning.

cautious ['kɔːʃəs] *adj* [person, approach, reply] that is very careful and does not take risks □ *He is cautious by nature.* □ *Here we are seeing a more cautious approach to foreign policy.*

cautiously ['kɔːʃəslɪ] *adv* [move, approach, reply] *see* **cautious** □ *I tapped the mysterious package cautiously.* □ *We are cautiously optimistic about winning the contract.*

cavalier [ˌkævəˈlɪər] *adj* [person, manner, attitude] having no respect or concern for other people's feelings.

cavalry ['kævlrɪ] *n* **-1.** soldiers who fight on horses. **-2.** the section of an army that uses armored vehicles.

cave [keɪv] *n* a large natural hole either underground with an opening to the surface or in the side of a cliff or hill.

◆ **cave in** *vi* **-1.** [roof, ceiling] to collapse. **-2.** [person] to stop opposing something, especially because one is under pressure □ *Eventually they caved in to our demands.*

caveman ['keɪvmæn] (*pl* **cavemen** [-men]) *n* a person who lived in a cave in prehistoric times.

cavern ['kævən] *n* a large cave.

cavernous ['kævənəs] *adj* [room, mouth, space] that seems very big and deep □ *The sound echoed in the cavernous depths below.*

caviar(e) ['kævɪɑːr] *n* the salted black or red eggs of the sturgeon fish that are eaten as a delicacy.

caving ['keɪvɪŋ] *n* the sport or activity of exploring caves □ *We sometimes go caving.*

cavity ['kævɪtɪ] (*pl* **cavities**) *n* **-1.** a hole or hollow space in an object or structure, or in one's body □ *the nasal cavity.* **-2.** a hole in a tooth where the tooth is decayed.

cavity wall insulation *n* GB a way of keeping out cold and noise from a room by building the walls in two separate layers and filling the space with special material.

cavort [kəˈvɔːt] *vi* to dance or behave in a noisy or sexual way.

cayenne [keɪˈen] *n* **cayenne (pepper)** a very hot red powder made from capsicum peppers and used to flavor food.

CB *n* **-1.** (*abbr of* **Citizens' Band**) = **CB radio**. **-2.** (*abbr of* **Companion of (the Order of) the Bath**) an honorary title in Britain.

CBC (*abbr of* **Canadian Broadcasting Corpora-**

tion) *n* a Canadian radio and television company that is paid for by the state.

CBD (*abbr of* **central business district**) *n* AUS the business district of a town.

CBE (*abbr of* **Companion of (the Order of) the British Empire**) *n* an award given to somebody who has achieved a lot for Britain.

CBI (*abbr of* **Confederation of British Industry**) *n* **the CBI** a federation of British companies that carries out surveys and research for its members.

CB radio *n* a set of radio frequencies used by the public to talk to one another on radios; a radio that uses these frequencies to send and receive messages.

CBS (*abbr of* **Columbia Broadcasting System**) *n* a major national TV network in the USA.

CBT (*abbr of* **computer-based training**) *n* the use of computers for training people.

cc ◇ *n abbr of* **cubic centimeter** □ *a 1300 cc engine.* ◇ [on a document] *abbr of* **carbon copy.**

CCTV *n abbr of* **closed-circuit television.**

CD ◇ *n abbr of* **compact disc** □ *a CD player.* ◇ **-1.** *abbr of* **civil defense. -2.** (*abbr of* **Corps Diplomatique**) the diplomatic corps.

CDI, CD-i (*abbr of* **compact disc interactive**) *n* a compact disc that contains test, sound, and pictures, and is used in a special machine attached to a television.

CD player *n* = **compact disc player.**

Cdr. *abbr of* **commander.**

CD-ROM [,si:di:'rɒm] (*abbr of* **compact disc read-only memory**) *n* a compact disc that contains text, sound, and pictures, and is used in a computer. The information on a CD-ROM cannot be changed □ *The dictionary is now available on CD-ROM.*

CDT (*abbr of* **Central Daylight Time**) *n* the time used in summer in the central USA and Canada.

CDV (*abbr of* **compact disc video**) *n* a compact disc that plays movies.

CDW *abbr of* **collision damage waiver.**

CE *abbr of* **Church of England.**

cease [si:s] (formal use) ◇ *vt* to stop doing <sthg> □ *The firm has ceased trading.* □ *You never cease to amaze me!* ◇ *vi* to stop happening □ *It rained without ceasing.*

cease-fire *n* an agreement by two sides in a war to stop fighting for a period of time, especially while discussions about permanent peace take place □ *The two sides agreed to a temporary cease-fire.* □ *a cease-fire resolution.*

ceaseless ['si:sləs] *adj* [rain, activity, noise] that does not stop (formal use).

cedar ['si:dər] *n* **a cedar (tree)** a tall evergreen tree with branches that spread out horizontally and leaves shaped like needles.

cede [si:d] *vt* [right, authority, land] to give <sthg> to somebody else, often unwillingly and because there is no choice □ *The territory was ceded to France in the nineteenth century.*

cedilla [sə'dɪlə] *n* an accent (¸) put under a letter, e.g. the letter "c" in French, to show that it is pronounced in a certain way.

Ceefax™ ['si:fæks] *n* the BBC teletext service.

ceilidh ['keɪlɪ] *n* an informal party in Scotland or Ireland with dancing, folk music, and singing.

ceiling ['si:lɪŋ] *n* **-1.** [of a room] the surface at the top of a room inside a building □ *From the ceiling hung a large lamp.* **-2.** [on prices] an upper limit that is put on spending, prices, wages etc by a government or official organization □ *The government has imposed a ceiling on interest rates.*

celebrate ['seləbreɪt] ◇ *vt* **-1.** [anniversary, success] to mark <an important event or date> by enjoying oneself, e.g. by having a party □ *He always celebrated his birthday with a big dinner.* □ *The company celebrated 50 years of business yesterday.* **-2.** [beauty, heroism, person] to praise <sb/sthg> (formal use). **-3.** [marriage, Mass] to perform <a religious ceremony>. ◇ *vi* to show that one is happy about an event by doing something enjoyable, e.g. having a party □ *I got the job — let's celebrate!*

celebrated ['seləbreɪtəd] *adj* [writer, actor, speech] well-known and admired.

celebration [,selə'breɪʃn] *n* **-1.** the act of celebrating something □ *There was much celebration after her promotion was announced.* **-2.** an event or occasion that celebrates something □ *The celebrations went on late into the night.*

celebrity [sə'lebrətɪ] (*pl* **celebrities**) *n* a person who is well-known, especially in the world of show business □ *TV celebrities.*

celeriac [sə'lerɪæk] *n* a kind of celery with a large round root that is eaten as a vegetable.

celery ['selərɪ] *n* a vegetable that grows in long green sticks, often eaten raw in salads □ *a stick of celery.*

celestial [US sə'lestʃəl, GB -'lestjəl] *adj* [body, sphere, being] that is connected with the sky or heaven (literary use).

celibacy ['seləbəsɪ] *n*: see **celibate** □ *a vow of celibacy.*

celibate ['seləbət] *adj* **-1.** [priest, monk] who is unmarried or does not have sex because of their religious beliefs. **-2.** [person] who is not having a sexual relationship with anybody □ *I've been celibate for three years.*

cell [sel] *n* **-1.** BIOLOGY the smallest unit of a living thing, e.g. a plant or animal, that is able to function independently □ *blood cells.* **-2.** [for prisoners] a small room in which a prisoner is kept □ *He was kept overnight in a police cell.* □ *a prison cell* □ *a cell block.* **-3.** RELIGION a small room with very simple furniture in which a monk or nun lives. **-4.** [in an organization] a small group of people who work together, often secretly, as part of a larger organization □ *a terrorist cell.*

cellar ['selər] *n* **-1.** a room underneath a house that is used for storing things □ *a coal/wine cellar.* **-2.** the stock of wine that is kept in a cellar □ *He keeps a good cellar.*

cellist ['tʃelɪst] *n* a person who plays the cello.

cello ['tʃeloʊ] (*pl* **cellos**) *n* a musical instrument

like a large violin that is held upright between the player's knees and played with a
bow □ *She plays the cello.*

Cellophane™ ['seləfeɪn] *n* a thin transparent
material that is used to wrap food and other
products.

cellphone ['selfoʊn], **cellular phone** ['seljələ^r-]
n a telephone that works without wires and
that people use while traveling around.

cellulite ['seljəlaɪt] *n* fat in the body that
makes the skin look slightly swollen and
lumpy.

Celluloid™ ['seljələɪd] *n* a type of plastic used
in the past for making film.

cellulose ['seljəloʊs] *n* the material from
which the cell walls of plants are made,
used in making paper, film, plastic etc.

Celsius ['selsɪəs] *n* a scale for measuring temperature in which water freezes at 0° and
boils at 100° □ *20 degrees Celsius.*

Celt [kelt] *n* a member of a people who lived
in the British Isles and western Europe in
ancient times.

Celtic ['keltɪk] *adj: see* **Celt** □ *Celtic art.*

cement [sə'ment] ◇ *n* -1. a gray powder made
of limestone and clay that is mixed with
sand and water and used in building. -2. a
kind of strong thick glue. ◇ *vt* -1. [floor, path]
to cover <a surface> with cement. -2. [two
objects] to glue <sthg> to something else.
-3. [relationship, tie] to make <a link or con-
nection> stronger □ *They cemented their new
friendship with a major business deal.*

cement mixer *n* a machine with a revolving
round container in which cement is mixed
with sand and water.

cemetery [US 'seməterɪ, GB -ətrɪ] (*pl* **cemeteries**)
n a place, usually not next to a church,
where dead people are buried □ *a war cemetery.*

cenotaph [US 'senətæf, GB -tɑːf] *n* a monument
built to remind people of soldiers who were
killed in a war.

censor ['sensə^r] ◇ *vt* to examine <a book,
movie, letter> etc in order to ban or remove
any parts that are considered offensive, immoral, or politically unacceptable □ *Most
newspapers printed the words in a censored
form.* ◇ *n* an official whose job is to censor
books, movies, letters etc □ *a movie censor.*

censorship ['sensə^rʃɪp] *n* the practice of cen-
soring letters, movies, books etc.

censure ['senʃə^r] ◇ *n* strong official criticism □
*The police chief's comments met with strong
censure.* ◇ *vt* to criticize <sb/sthg> officially
□ *The social services were heavily censured for
their failure to act.*

census ['sensəs] (*pl* **censuses**) *n* an official survey, made by a government, that gathers information about the number of people living
in the country, their age, occupation etc □ *A
census of the population was taken in 1991.*

cent [sent] *n* a small unit of money in many
countries, including the United States, Australia, and Canada, that is worth one hundredth of a larger unit □ *50 cents.*

centennial [sen'tenjəl] US, **centenary** [US sen-
'tenərɪ, GB -'tiːn-] GB (*pl* **centenaries**) *n* the day
or year that marks one hundred years since
an event took place □ *This year is/marks the
centennial of Van Gogh's death.* □ *centennial celebrations.*

center US, **centre** GB ['sentə^r] ◇ *n* -1. [of an
area] the point or part that is at an equal dis-
tance from all points on the edge of an area
□ *They have an office in the center of town.* □ *A
vase stood in the center of the table.* -2. a
medical/sports etc center a building where
people can have medical treatment/play
sports etc □ *a drug rehabilitation center.* -3. a
cultural/trading etc center a place that is very
important for culture/trading etc □ *New York
is one of the world's most important financial centers.* -4. **to be at the center of a row/dispute
etc** to be the most important person or
thing in a row/dispute etc □ *The government
is at the center of the dispute.* ■ **the center of
attention** somebody who everybody is interested in □ *She loves being the center of attention.* -5. **the center** POLITICS political groups
that are moderate and neither very left-wing
nor very right-wing. -6. SPORT a player who
plays mostly in the middle of the playing
field.
◇ *adj* -1. that is in the center □ *a center parting.* -2. **a center party/politician** a party/
politician that is in the middle of two more
extreme parties.
◇ *vt* [text, picture] to place <sthg> in the center of something □ *The title isn't centered.*

◆ **center around, center on** *vt fus* **to center
around** OR **on sthg** to be concentrated on or
directed at sthg □ *The controversy centered
around the workers' pay claim.* □ *Attention was
centered on the figure of the President.*

center back *n* SOCCER a player who plays in
the center of the defense positions.

center-fold *n* -1. two pages, often illustrated,
at the center of a newspaper or magazine.
-2. a picture of a naked or nearly naked
woman in the center of a magazine.

center forward *n* SPORT a player who plays in
the center of the attack positions.

center half *n* = **center back**.

center lane *n* US the middle lane of a road.

center of gravity *n* the point in an object on
which it balances.

centerpiece US, **centrepiece** GB ['sentə^rpiːs] *n*
-1. a decoration, e.g. a vase of flowers, that
is placed in the middle of a table. -2. the
most important or attractive part of something □ *The painting is the centerpiece of the
whole exhibition.*

Centers for Disease Control *npl* the **Centers
for Disease Control** a US organization, partly
funded by the government, that tries to prevent the spread of diseases and encourage
better health care for the public.

center-spread *n* the two pages, often illustrated, at the center of a magazine or newspaper.

centigrade ['sentəgreɪd] *n* a scale for measuring temperature in which water freezes at 0° and boils at 100° □ *16 degrees centigrade.*

centigram(me) ['sentəgræm] *n* one hundredth of a gram.

centiliter US, **centilitre** GB ['sentəli:tər] *n* one hundredth of a liter.

centimeter US, **centimetre** GB ['sentəmi:tər] *n* one hundredth of a meter.

centipede ['sentəpi:d] *n* a long thin crawling creature like a worm with a lot of legs.

central ['sentrəl] *adj* -1. [area, object, place] that is in the center or is the center of something or somewhere □ *They live in central Spain.* □ *The office had a large central conference room.* -2. [house, office] that is easy to reach because it is in or near the center of a town, city etc □ *My apartment is very central.* □ *The company has moved to a more central location.* -3. **a central organization/committee** an organization/a committee that is the most important and makes all the main decisions □ *The central office has refused permission.* -4. [aim, idea, person] most important □ *The minister was the central figure in the scandal.* □ *She played a central role in improving conditions for women.* □ *Education is a central issue.* ■ **to be central to sthg** [to success, a plan] to be a very important part of sthg □ *Participation is absolutely central to our new management strategy.*

Central America the strip of land connecting North and South America, consisting of Belize, Costa Rica, El Salvador, Guatemala, Honduras, Nicaragua, Panama, and parts of Mexico and Colombia.

central bank *n* a bank that is owned by a state, controls the amount of money available, and helps to decide interest rates.

Central Criminal Court → **Old Bailey.**

central government *n* the government of a whole country as opposed to local government of a region or city.

central heating *n* a system of heating buildings in which hot water, oil, or air flows through pipes into radiators □ *Does the house have central heating?*

centralization [US ˌsentrələˈzeɪʃn, GB -aɪˈzeɪʃn] *n*: *see* **centralize** □ *the process of bureaucratic centralization.*

centralize, -ise ['sentrəlaɪz] *vt* [power, government, system] to put <sthg> under central, rather than regional, control.

centralized ['sentrəlaɪzd] *adj* [power, government, system] that is controlled by one main authority rather than several regional ones.

central locking [-'lɒkɪŋ] *n* a system of locking a car in which a key turned in one lock automatically locks all the other doors too.

centrally ['sentrəlɪ] *adv* [positioned, situated] *see* **central** □ *The hotel is centrally located.*

centrally heated *adj* [office, house] that has central heating.

central nervous system *n* the part of the nervous system, consisting of the brain and spinal cord, that controls activity.

Central Park the main park in Manhattan, New York City.

central processing unit *n* the part of a computer where the main mathematical and logical operations are performed.

central reservation *n* GB a raised strip of grass or concrete that divides the two sides of a motorway.

centre *etc* GB = **center** *etc.*

centrifugal force [US senˌtrɪfjəgl-, GB sentrɪˌfjuːgl-] *n* a force that can be thought of as making objects move outward when they are traveling in a circle.

centrist ['sentrɪst] *adj* [policy, party] that is moderate rather than extreme politically.

century ['sentʃərɪ] (*pl* **centuries**) *n* -1. a period of 100 years □ *After centuries of violence, peace was finally made.* -2. a period of 100 years used in dates and calculated forwards or backwards from the year in which Jesus Christ is supposed to have been born □ *the twentieth century* □ *in the first century BC.* ■ **at the turn of the century** at the end of one century and the beginning of the next. -3. CRICKET 100 runs scored by a batsman.

CEO *n abbr of* **chief executive officer.**

ceramic [sə'ræmɪk] *adj* [pot, tile] that is made from clay that has been shaped and baked in an oven until hard.

◆ **ceramics** ◇ *npl* a collective term for ceramic objects. ◇ *n* the art or activity of making these objects.

cereal ['sɪərɪəl] *n* -1. a plant such as wheat, barley, or rice that is grown for its grains which are eaten as food □ *cereal crops.* -2. a breakfast food, e.g. cornflakes or granola, that is made from grain □ *breakfast cereal.*

cerebral ['serəbrəl] *adj* -1. [person, book, activity] that involves one's mind more than one's feelings. -2. [hemorrhage, cortex] that is connected with the brain.

cerebral palsy *n* a medical condition, caused by lack of oxygen to a baby's brain before birth, in which the muscles do not function properly and are very weak.

ceremonial [ˌserə'məʊnjəl] ◇ *adj* [uniform, function, duty] that is connected with or used in a ceremony □ *The Chancellor, in ceremonial dress, led the procession.* ◇ *n* the particular elements of a ceremony, e.g. the rules and rituals of how to behave and what to say.

ceremonious [ˌserə'məʊnjəs] *adj* [behavior, greeting] very formal and polite.

ceremony [US 'serəməʊnɪ, GB -mənɪ] (*pl* **ceremonies**) *n* -1. a special set of actions and words that are performed or spoken at an important social or religious occasion □ *The wedding ceremony was very short.* -2. the special behavior and formal words used at a ceremony □ *The president and his wife were welcomed to the palace with great ceremony.* ■ **without ceremony** in an informal and hurried way □ *She was escorted, without ceremony, towards the exit.* ■ **to stand on ceremony** to behave in a way that is too formal □ *We don't stand on ceremony in this house.*

cert. *abbr of* **certificate**.

certain ['sɜːᵗtn] *adj* **-1. to be certain** to have no doubts about something □ *I'm certain (that) things will improve.* □ *I'm not certain where we're going.* □ *You can be certain of getting good service there.* ■ **to be certain to do sthg** to be very likely to do sthg □ *He is certain to be late.* ■ **to make certain** to check something so that one does not make a mistake □ *"Did you lock the door?" — "I can't remember, I'll just go and make certain."* □ *Make certain that you take your passport with you.* ■ **to make certain of doing sthg** to take action in order to make sure that sthg happens □ *I made certain of getting a ticket by reserving in advance.* **-2.** [fact, knowledge] that is known to be true □ *It's certain now that Hitler committed suicide in his bunker.* **-3.** [result, death] that one is sure will happen □ *It's certain that she will get the job.* **-4.** a word used to refer to a particular person, thing, or amount that is known but is not named or described exactly □ *once you reach a certain level of achievement* □ *Certain people prefer this kind of arrangement.* □ *There are certain things one can't discuss openly.* **-5.** some □ *Well, that's true to a certain extent.* □ *There's a certain amount of risk involved.* **-6.** [feeling, quality] that is noticeable but is difficult to define exactly □ *She has a certain charm, don't you think?* **-7. a certain** a phrase used to refer to a person who one does not know apart from their name □ *A certain Mr Jones is asking for you.*

◆ **for certain** *adv* without doubt □ *England won't win, that's for certain.* □ *I know for certain he won't do anything about it.*

certainly ['sɜːᵗtnlɪ] *adv* **-1.** a word used to express strong agreement or approval □ *"Can I bring a friend along?" — "Certainly!"* □ *"Do you think it's true?" — "Certainly not!"* □ *"Do you agree?" — "I certainly do."* **-2.** without any doubt □ *It's certainly improved since then.*

certainty ['sɜːᵗtntɪ] (*pl* **certainties**) *n* **-1.** the state of not having any doubts about something □ *I can't say with any degree of certainty whether he'll come.* **-2.** something that is certain to happen □ *There are few certainties in life.* □ *It's an absolute certainty that she'll win.*

CertEd [sɜːᵗt'ed] (*abbr of* **Certificate in Education**) *n* a British teaching qualification.

certifiable [ˌsɜːᵗtɪˈfaɪəbl] *adj* **-1.** [person] crazy (informal use). **-2.** [person] who can be officially classed as being insane.

certificate [səᵗtɪfɪkət] *n* an official document that states that a particular event has taken place □ *a birth/death/marriage certificate* □ *a certificate of education.*

certification [ˌsɜːᵗtɪfɪˈkeɪʃn] *n* the act of certifying something; documents which certify something.

certified ['sɜːᵗtɪfaɪd] *adj* **a certified teacher/ nurse** a teacher/nurse who has successfully completed their training.

certified mail *n* US a mail service that records when and by whom a letter or package is sent.

certified public accountant *n* US a person who has qualified to work as an accountant.

certify ['sɜːᵗtɪfaɪ] (*pt & pp* **certified**) *vt* **-1.** [fact, results] to declare <sthg> to be true, especially in writing □ *This card certifies that Paul Lloyd is a member of the Civil Liberties Union.* □ *I hereby certify the information above to be correct.* **-2.** [person, goods, work] to give a certificate to <sb/sthg> that proves that they have done something or are something □ *The driver was certified dead by the doctor.* **-3.** [person] to declare <sb> officially insane.

cervical ['sɜːᵗvɪkl] *adj* **cervical cancer/screening** cancer/screening of the cervix.

cervical smear *n* a small sample of tissue taken from a woman's cervix and used as a test for cervical cancer.

cervix ['sɜːᵗvɪks] (*pl* **cervices** [səᵗvaɪsiːz]) *n* the narrow opening at the bottom of a woman's womb.

CES (*abbr of* **Commonwealth Employment Service**) *n* **the CES** the employment agency run by the Australian government.

cesarean (section) [sɪˌzeərɪən-] *n* an operation to deliver a baby through an opening cut in the mother's stomach □ *The baby was born by cesarean.*

cessation [seˈseɪʃn] *n* the end of something; a pause in something (formal use).

cesspit ['sespɪt], **cesspool** ['sespuːl] *n* **-1.** a hole or container underground into which waste, especially human waste, flows. **-2.** a place one thinks is disgusting and corrupt.

CET (*abbr of* **Central European Time**) *n* the standard time in central Europe.

cf. (*abbr of* **confer**) a word used in front of a piece of information that is to be compared with what has just been mentioned.

c/f *abbr of* **carried forward**.

C & F = **CAF**.

CFA franc (*abbr of* **Communauté financière africaine**) *n* the unit of money used in several African countries.

CFC (*abbr of* **chlorofluorocarbon**) *n* a gas used in refrigerators and aerosols that is harmful to the ozone layer □ *a CFC gas.*

cg *abbr of* **centigram(me)**.

CG *n abbr of* **coastguard**.

C & GLI *n abbr of* **City and Guilds of London Institute**.

CGT *n abbr of* **capital gains tax**.

ch. *abbr of* **chapter**.

CH (*abbr of* **Companion of Honour**) *n* an honorary title in Britain.

Chad [tʃæd] a country in central Africa. SIZE: 1,284,000 sq kms. POPULATION: 5,400,000 (*Chadians*). CAPITAL: Ndjamena. LANGUAGE: French. CURRENCY: CFA franc.

chafe [tʃeɪf] ◇ *vi* **-1.** [skin, feet] to become painful as a result of being rubbed by something. **-2. to chafe at sthg** to be impatient about sthg. ◇ *vt* [skin, feet] *The harness chafed the horse's neck.*

chaff [US tʃæf, GB tʃɑːf] *n* the outer part of wheat and other grains that is not used as food and is removed by beating.

chaffinch ['tʃæfɪntʃ] *n* a small bird found in Europe that has black and white marks on its wings and, in the male, a reddish body and gray head.

chain [tʃeɪn] ◇ *n* -1. [of metal, gold] a series of linked metal rings □ *She wore a silver chain around her neck.* □ *a bicycle chain* □ *The prisoners were kept in chains.* ■ **a chain of office** a large chain worn by an important person around their neck as a mark of their official status. -2. [of mountains, islands, people] a line of people or things that are connected □ *a mountain chain* □ *a human chain.* ■ **a chain of events** a series of events that are all connected □ *This is the chain of events that led to the historic agreement.* ■ **a chain of command** a system in an organization in which each person has more power than the person below them to give orders to everybody else. -3. [of stores, hotels] a number of stores, hotels, companies etc that are all owned by the same person or organization □ *They own a chain of clothes stores.* □ *a restaurant chain.*
◇ *vt* to keep <sb/sthg> in a particular place with a chain or chains □ *The dog was chained to the railings.*

chain letter *n* a letter, often asking for and promising money, that is sent to a number of people who are then asked to send copies of the letter to several more people.

chain reaction *n* a series of events or chemical reactions, each one of which makes the next one happen.

chain saw *n* a large saw, driven by a motor, that consists of a circular chain with sharp cutting teeth.

chain-smoke *vi* to smoke one cigarette after another without a break.

chain store *n* a large store that is one of a group of similar stores which belong to the same owner or organization.

chair [tʃeəʳ] ◇ *n* -1. [for sitting on] a piece of furniture that is designed for one person to sit on, consisting of a seat, four legs, a back, and sometimes arms □ *Is this chair free?* □ *a kitchen chair.* -2. EDUCATION the university post of a professor □ *She holds the chair in French at Yale.* -3. **the chair** [at a meeting] the position of chairperson of a meeting; a person holding this position □ *All questions must be addressed to the chair.* ■ **to take the chair** to be the chairperson at a meeting. ◇ *vt* to be the chairperson at <a meeting, discussion> etc □ *Dr. Eliot will be chairing this debate.*

chair lift *n* a machine for carrying people up mountains, ski slopes etc that consists of seats that hang from a moving cable.

chairman ['tʃeəʳmən] (*pl* **chairmen** [-mən]) *n* -1. a chairperson, usually a man, of a meeting, debate etc. -2. the person in charge of an organization or company □ *General Powell, now retired as chairman of the Joint Chiefs of Staff.*

chairmanship ['tʃeəʳmənʃɪp] *n* the position of being chairman; the period during which a person is chairman □ *She is being considered for the chairmanship.* □ *The company prospered under his chairmanship.*

chairperson ['tʃeəʳpɜːʳsn] (*pl* **chairpersons**) *n* a person who is in charge of a meeting, discussion, or debate and who decides who can speak and when.

chairwoman ['tʃeəʳwʊmən] (*pl* **chairwomen**) *n* -1. a female chairperson. -2. a woman who is in charge of a company or organization.

chaise longue [US tʃeɪs'lɑːŋ, GB ʃeɪz'lɒŋ] (*pl* **chaises longues**) *n* a piece of furniture for lying on that has a back and only one arm.

chalet [US ʃæ'leɪ, GB 'ʃæleɪ] *n* -1. a kind of house common in Switzerland that is made of wood and has window shutters and a sloping roof. -2. a small wooden house, often one of a group, built as accommodation in vacation areas.

chalice ['tʃæləs] *n* a gold or silver cup, especially one used to hold wine during the Christian service of Communion.

chalk [tʃɔːk] *n* -1. a very soft white rock □ *chalk cliffs.* -2. a piece of chalk that is used for writing or drawing on a slate or blackboard □ *written in chalk.*

◆ **chalk up** *vt sep* **to chalk up sthg** to achieve sthg successful □ *She's already chalked up three gold medals.*

chalkboard ['tʃɔːkbɔːʳd] *n* US a hard black board that is written on with chalk and is often used in teaching.

challenge ['tʃælɪndʒ] ◇ *n* -1. [in a contest] an invitation to fight or compete for something □ *Will you accept my challenge?* □ *the challenge to the leadership.* -2. [of a fact, remark] something that questions a statement, idea, or fact, or a person's right to do something □ *This is a major challenge to the new legal system.* □ *What he says is always open to challenge.* -3. [in one's work, life] a situation, job, task etc that is difficult and exciting and that will make one have to try hard to succeed □ *This new job will be a challenge for me.*
◇ *vt* -1. [person] to invite <sb> to fight or compete with one in a game, duel, competition etc □ *She challenged me to a game of chess.* ■ **to challenge sb to do sthg** to invite sb to do sthg that one thinks they cannot do or will find very difficult □ *He challenged anybody to prove he was lying.* -2. [authority, right, legality] to question <sthg> □ *They challenged the power of the court to decide such matters.*

-challenged ['tʃælɪndʒd] *suffix* added to words to say that somebody has a particular problem that they were born with □ *visually-/physically-challenged.*

challenger ['tʃælɪndʒəʳ] *n* a person who tries to win something such as a sports title from somebody who already has it □ *the Cup challengers.*

challenging ['tʃælɪndʒɪŋ] *adj* -1. [task, job] that is exciting because it is difficult □ *We offer you a challenging and rewarding career.* -2. [look, tone of voice] that challenges somebody to disagree or object to something.

chamber ['tʃeɪmbəʳ] *n* -1. a large room used for meetings of an official organization □ *the Council chamber.* -2. [in a castle, tomb] a room used for a particular purpose, especially in an old or underground building □ *a torture chamber.* -3. [in a gun] the space inside a gun where the bullet is placed. -4. [of a heart, engine] an enclosed space inside a machine or one's body □ *a combustion chamber.* -5. GOVERNMENT one of the two parts of a parliament or the US Congress □ *the Upper/Lower Chamber.*

◆ **chambers** *npl* -1. US a judge's offices. -2. GB a barrister's offices.

Chamberlain ['tʃeɪmbəʳlɪn], **Neville** (1869–1940) British Prime Minister from 1937 to 1940. He was criticized for making a deal with Hitler and Mussolini in 1938 which he said would bring "peace in our time".

chambermaid ['tʃeɪmbəʳmeɪd] *n* a woman whose job is to clean and tidy the bedrooms in a hotel or large house.

chamber music *n* classical music that is written for a small number of instruments.

chamber of commerce *n* an organization of local business people who work together to promote and protect their trade.

chamber orchestra *n* a small orchestra.

chameleon [kə'miːljən] *n* a lizard whose skin can change color to match the color of its surroundings.

chamois¹ [US ʃæm'wɑː, GB 'ʃæmwɑː] (*pl* **chamois**) *n* a small antelope with horns that lives in the mountains of Europe and South East Asia.

chamois² ['ʃæmɪ] *n* **chamois (leather)** soft leather made from the skin of chamois, goats, or sheep, often used for cleaning; a piece of this leather.

champ [tʃæmp] ◇ *n* a champion (informal use). ◇ *vi* [horse] to eat noisily.

champagne [ʃæm'peɪn] *n* an expensive, sparkling, French white wine made according to a special method and traditionally drunk to celebrate something.

champion ['tʃæmpjən] *n* -1. a person or animal that has defeated all others in a competition □ *a tennis/snooker/chess champion* □ *the world champion.* -2. a person who defends a particular cause or person □ *a champion of the underprivileged.*

championship ['tʃæmpjənʃɪp] *n* -1. a competition to find the best person in a particular sport or activity □ *The world championships were held in Helsinki.* -2. the title or status of champion □ *Do you think she'll win the championship?*

chance [US tʃæns, GB tʃɑːns] ◇ *n* -1. something that seems to happen without any cause or reason □ *It was pure chance that we got there on time.* □ *a chance encounter.* ■ **by any chance** an expression used when one is making a polite request □ *You don't by any chance have a copy of last week's report?* -2. **a chance of doing sthg** a possibility of doing sthg □ *What are our chances of winning?* □ *There was no*

chance of finding her in that crowd. ■ **to stand a chance of doing sthg** to have a possibility of doing sthg □ *Jerry Kaplan doesn't stand a chance of being promoted to manager.* ■ **the chances are...** it is likely that... □ *The chances are she's already left.* -3. **a chance to do sthg** an opportunity to do sthg □ *The meeting gave us a chance to talk to some of the competitors.* -4. **a chance that...** a risk that something might happen □ *There's just a chance that they'll pull out at the last minute.* ■ **to take a chance** to take a risk □ *I took a chance on there being a late flight home.*

◇ *vt* -1. to risk <sthg> □ *I decided to chance it.* □ *He's chancing his luck a bit, isn't he?* -2. **to chance to do sthg** to do sthg without planning it □ *If she should chance to notice, pretend you're doing something for me.*

◆ **by chance** *adv* without planning it □ *We met by chance.* □ *It was quite by chance that I happened to be there.*

chancellor [US 'tʃænslər, GB 'tʃɑːnslə] *n* -1. the head of government in some countries □ *the German chancellor.* -2. EDUCATION the head of an American university; the person who represents a British university on official occasions. -3. **the Chancellor (of the Exchequer)** GB the minister of government in charge of finance and taxes.

chancy [US 'tʃænsɪ, GB 'tʃɑːnsɪ] (*compar* **chancier**, *superl* **chanciest**) *adj* [action, matter] risky or uncertain (informal use).

chandelier [ˌʃændə'lɪəʳ] *n* a frame for holding candles or lightbulbs that hangs from the ceiling and is usually decorated with pieces of cut glass.

Chandler [US 'tʃændlr, GB 'tʃɑːndlə], **Raymond** (1888–1959) a US crime writer. His best-known character, the detective Philip Marlowe, appears in novels such as *Farewell My Lovely* and *The Long Goodbye*.

change [tʃeɪndʒ] ◇ *n* -1. [in a person, situation] the process of becoming different; the result of this process □ *They forecast a change in the weather.* □ *There has been no change in her condition.* □ *Too many changes have been introduced too quickly.* □ *ways of dealing with stressful change* □ *A few changes had been made to the wording of the document.* -2. [in one's habit, routine] a situation that is different from usual and often pleasant □ *A weekend walking in the country will be a pleasant change from my usual routine.* □ *Working from home makes a nice change.* □ *Let's go back to your place for a change.* -3. **a change of address/plan etc** a different address/plan etc that replaces the original one □ *I decided to go abroad because I wanted a change of scene.* □ *the change from public to private ownership.* ■ **a change of clothes** a clean set of clothes that one has with one for changing into later □ *I'll just need to take my toilet bag and a change of underwear with me.* -4. [after payment] the money that one gets back after paying for something with more money than it costs □ *I think you've given me too much change.* □ *Keep the change.* -5. [instead of paper money] coins not notes □ *Could you lend me some change to* *make a phone call?* **-6. change for $10/£20** coins or paper money worth $10/£20 given in exchange for a bill worth $10/£20 □ *Do you have change for a ten-dollar bill?*

◇ *vt* **-1.** [situation, plan, attitude] to make <sthg> different □ *We've changed our vacation plans; we're going to Egypt instead.* □ *The experience changed my whole outlook on life.* ■ **to change one's mind** to change one's opinion or decision about something □ *"I thought you decided to stay."* — *"I've changed my mind."* **-2.** [job, name, car] to replace <sthg> with a different one; [tire, fuse] to replace <sthg old or broken> with a new one □ *Have you changed jobs* OR *your job recently?* □ *Give me a minute to change my clothes, and I'll be with you.* □ *Change the batteries every three months.* ■ **to change direction** to start moving in a different direction □ *The wind had changed direction.* ■ **to change planes/trains etc** to get off one plane/train etc and get on another in order to continue one's trip. ■ **to change the subject** to start talking about something different □ *I tried to get her to talk about it, but she just kept changing the subject.* **-3. to change $10/$20 etc** to give somebody $10/$20 etc and get back the same value in bills or coins of a lower value □ *Can you change a $50 bill?* **-4.** [currency] to exchange <one kind of money> for another kind □ *I'd like to change my dollars into yen.* **-5. to change a bed** to take dirty sheets off a bed and put clean ones on □ *Will you help me change the sheets?* ■ **to change a baby** to take a dirty diaper off a baby and put a clean one on.

◇ *vi* **-1.** [person, situation, place] to become different □ *The color changes when the two chemicals are mixed.* □ *Bill has changed a lot since I last saw him.* □ *They say the weather's going to change.* ■ **to change into sthg** to become sthg different □ *I've watched him change from a shy teenager into a happy and well-adjusted young man.* **-2.** [person] to take off the clothes one is wearing and put on different ones □ *She went upstairs to change.* □ *I'll just change into something more casual.* **-3.** [traveler] to get off one bus, plane etc and get on another one in order to continue one's journey □ *You'll have to change at Chicago.*

◆ **change over** *vi* to stop doing or using something and start doing or using something else □ *We changed over to a computerized system last year.*

changeable ['tʃeɪndʒəbl] *adj* [mood, weather] that keeps changing very quickly □ *She's very changeable at the moment.*

changed [tʃeɪndʒd] *adj* **to be a changed man/woman** to be completely different, and usually much improved, in character or attitude as a result of something that has happened □ *He's a changed man since he got married.*

change machine *n* a machine that changes bills or high-value coins into low-value coins.

change of life *n* **the change of life** the menopause.

changeover ['tʃeɪndʒəʊvər] *n* a change to a new system or method of working □ *We are considering a changeover to computerized accounting.*

change purse *n* US a very small bag, often made of leather, used for carrying coins.

changing ['tʃeɪndʒɪŋ] *adj* [attitudes, circumstances, times] becoming different, usually over a long period of time □ *The company failed to adapt to changing market conditions.*

changing room *n* **-1.** a room at a gym, swimming pool etc, where people can change their clothes and usually take a shower. **-2.** a small room in a store where customers can try on clothes they are thinking of buying.

Chang Jiang [ˌtʃæŋˈdʒɪæŋ] = **Yangtze**.

channel ['tʃænl] (US *pt* & *pp* **channeled**, *cont* **channeling**, GB *pt* & *pp* **channelled**, *cont* **channelling**) ◇ *n* **-1.** TV & RADIO a single TV or radio station; the wavelength on which this station broadcasts its programs □ *The game is on Channel 3.* **-2.** [for water] a man-made passage that carries water and is used for drainage, irrigation etc □ *an irrigation channel.* **-3.** [in a river, sea] a long area of deep water used as a route by ships and boats □ *the Irish Channel.* **-4.** [for sending information] a system that exists for sending information, dealing with requests, questions, or complaints, or getting something done □ *Applications for export licenses must be made through the proper channels.* □ *a channel of communication/distribution.*

◇ *vt* **-1.** [water, rain] to make <a liquid> flow through man-made channels □ *The liquid plastic is channeled into molds.* **-2.** [efforts, money] to use <sthg> for one particular purpose □ *All our energies have been channeled into promoting our new range.* □ *Our aim is to channel resources to those who need them most.*

◆ **Channel** = **English Channel**.

Channel 4 *n* a commercial television channel in Britain that specializes in cultural programs.

channel-hopping *n* GB = **channel-surfing**.

Channel Islands: the Channel Islands a group of British islands in the English Channel, near the French coast, that have important banking and tourist industries. SIZE: 195 sq kms. POPULATION: 120,000.

channel-surfing *n* US the activity of changing from one TV channel to another without watching any show completely.

Channel Tunnel: the Channel Tunnel the railroad tunnel under the English Channel, between southeastern England and northeastern France.

chant [US tʃænt, GB tʃɑːnt] ◇ *n* **-1.** RELIGION a prayer or religious song that has a very simple melody with long sections sung on a single note □ *a Gregorian chant.* **-2.** a word or short sentence repeated rhythmically over and over again, usually by a crowd of people □ *A chant of "Down with apartheid" echoed around the hall.* ◇ *vt* **-1.** RELIGION [words, prayer] to sing or say <sthg> as a chant. **-2.** [insult, slogan] to say <sthg> repeatedly as a chant □

The fans were chanting slogans throughout the match. ◇ *vi* to sing or say a chant.

chaos ['keɪɒs] *n* complete confusion and lack of organization □ *The company's finances are in complete chaos.* □ *The strike will cause chaos for commuters.*

chaotic [keɪ'ɒtɪk] *adj* [system, management] that is completely confused and lacks organization □ *The room was in a chaotic state.*

chap [tʃæp] *n* GB a man (informal use).

chapat(t)i [tʃə'pɑːti] *n* a flat round piece of bread that is made without yeast and is eaten with Indian meals.

chapel ['tʃæpl] *n* -1. [in a church] a room in a church or cathedral that has its own altar and is used for private prayer, special services etc. -2. [in a prison, hospital, school] a room or small church in a larger building that is used for Christian services.

chaperon(e) ['ʃæpərəʊn] ◇ *n* an older woman who goes with a girl or unmarried woman to a party or other social event in order to protect them from sexual relationships with men. ◇ *vt* to go somewhere with <a girl or young woman> as a chaperone.

chaplain ['tʃæplɪn] *n* a Christian minister who works in a hospital, university, or other institution □ *a prison/school/army chaplain.*

Chaplin ['tʃæplɪn], **Charlie** (1889–1977) a British movie actor and director who worked mainly in the USA. Most of his movies are silent comedies in which he plays a tramp with a small mustache and a bowler hat.

chapped [tʃæpt] *adj* [skin, hands, lips] that are red, rough, cracked, and sore, usually because of cold weather or wind.

chapter ['tʃæptər] *n* -1. [of a book] a major section of a book, usually with its own number or title □ *chapter four.* -2. [of somebody's life, a history] an event or period of time seen as a part of somebody's life, a country's history etc □ *The strike is the latest chapter in this long-running dispute.*

Chapter 11 [-ɪ'levn] *n* in the USA, a law that allows a company in financial difficulty to carry on business in a reorganized form instead of closing.

char [tʃɑːr] (*pt* & *pp* **charred**, *cont* **charring**) ◇ *vt* [wood, food] to make <sthg> black by burning it.

character [US 'kerəktər, GB 'kærəktə] *n* -1. **sb's/ sthg's character** the qualities that make something or somebody special and different from other things or people □ *The whole character of our town has changed.* □ *Please tell us something about her character and attitude to work.* □ *It's a side of his character that I've never really seen.* ■ **out of/in character** not typical/ typical of the way a particular person usually behaves □ *Her reaction was really out of character.* -2. [of a place, building] interesting and unusual qualities □ *We chose this house because it had a lot of character.* -3. [of a person] good qualities such as honesty, bravery etc □ *It showed real character on his part, admitting his mistakes.* -4. [in a movie, book, play] a per-

son who appears in a story □ *The play has only three characters.* -5. [person] a person, especially a strange or unpleasant one □ *There were a couple of suspicious-looking characters outside my room.* -6. **to be a character** to have a strong, amusing, or unusual personality (informal use) □ *Have you met Wilkins? He's quite a character!* -7. [in writing] a letter, sign, or symbol used in writing □ *a 102-character keyboard* □ *Chinese characters.*

character code *n* COMPUTING a system where each character is represented by a number.

characteristic [US ˌkerəktə'rɪstɪk, GB ˌkær-] ◇ *adj* [behavior, taste, quality] that is very typical of a person, place, or thing □ *He set about the job with his characteristic energy.* □ *These mistakes are characteristic of her work.* ◇ *n* a feature or quality that makes somebody or something easy to recognize □ *She seems to have all the characteristics of a good teacher.*

characteristically [US ˌkerəktə'rɪstɪkli, GB ˌkær-] *adv* a word used to say that something is characteristic of somebody □ *Characteristically, she refused to say anything.* □ *It was a characteristically brave attempt on her part.*

characterization [US ˌkerəktəraɪ'zeɪʃn, GB ˌkær-] *n* the way in which the characters in a book, movie etc are described □ *The play is ruined by its weak characterization.*

characterize, -ise [US 'kerəktəraɪz, GB 'kær-] *vt* -1. to be the most noticeable or typical quality of <a period, place, event, or sb's work or style> □ *The building has the sense of space that characterizes all his architecture.* □ *The 19th century was characterized by a great growth in technology.* -2. to describe <sb/sthg> as having certain noticeable and typical qualities □ *The press has characterized this policy as shortsighted.*

charade [US ʃə'rɑːd, GB -'reɪd] *n* a situation or event that people pretend is normal even though they know it is false or pointless □ *Our marriage has become a charade.*

◆ **charades** *n* a game in which one person acts out a word or phrase without speaking, and others have to guess what the word or phrase is.

charcoal ['tʃɑːrkəʊl] *n* the black substance produced when wood is heated without air. It is used as fuel for barbecues and heaters, by artists for drawing, and in industrial filters □ *a charcoal drawing.*

charge [tʃɑːrdʒ] ◇ *n* -1. [for goods, services] the amount something, especially a service, costs □ *an admission charge* □ *Telephone charges are still going up.* □ *There is no charge for delivery.* ■ **to be free of charge** to cost nothing □ *We'll fix those free of charge.* -2. LAW an official statement saying that somebody is suspected of a crime □ *The charges against Benson included fraud and tax evasion.* □ *She was arrested on a charge of murder.* -3. **to take charge** to take control of or responsibility for something □ *I want you to take charge of the design department.* ■ **in charge** in control or authority □ *You'd better speak to the person in charge.* ■ **in charge of sb/sthg** [of a department, group of people] in control of or responsible for sb/ sthg □ *She was put in charge of sales and promotion.* **-4.** ELECTRICITY the amount of electricity in a substance or battery. **-5.** [by soldiers] a forceful attack made by soldiers, police, animals etc running forward at full speed □ *a police/cavalry charge.*

◇ *vt* **-1.** to ask <a customer> to pay a particular amount of money for goods, services etc; to state <a particular amount of money> as the price of goods, services etc □ *The mechanic only charged me $25 for the starter.* □ *How much do you charge?* ■ **to charge sthg to sthg** [to one's company, account] to tell a store, hotel etc to record the price of sthg so that it will be paid by sthg else at a later time □ *I charge all my expenses to the firm.* **-2.** LAW to accuse <a suspect, criminal> etc formally of a crime □ *The police intend to charge him with handling stolen goods.* **-3.** [crowd, building] to run or move quickly toward <sb/sthg>, usually in order to attack □ *The riot police charged the crowd of demonstrators.* **-4.** ELECTRICITY to put electricity into <a battery> so that it becomes stored there □ *The computer needs to be charged daily.*

◇ *vi* **-1.** [store, company] to ask for a particular amount of money in payment for goods, services etc □ *Do you charge for delivery?* **-2.** to run or move somewhere quickly □ *The children charged down the corridor.* **-3.** to run toward somebody in order to attack them □ *Suddenly the bull charged at the crowd.*

chargeable ['tʃɑːʳdʒəbl] *adj* **-1.** [costs, expenses] that can be charged to somebody or something □ *All travel expenses are chargeable to the company.* **-2.** LAW [offense, crime] that is serious enough for the police to make a criminal charge against somebody □ *They will be chargeable with contempt of court.*

charge account *n* an account at a store that allows a customer to take goods immediately and pay for them later.

charge card *n* a plastic card that a store gives to customers who have a charge account and which they show when they want to buy something and pay for it later.

charged [tʃɑːʳdʒd] *adj* [question, atmosphere] filled with emotion, tension, or excitement □ *a voice charged with emotion* □ *an emotionally charged reunion.*

chargé d'affaires [ˌʃɑːʳʒeɪdəˈfeəʳ] (*pl* **chargés d'affaires**) *n* a diplomat who does the work of an ambassador, either temporarily when the ambassador is away, or permanently in a country where there is no ambassador.

charge hand *n* GB a worker who is next in status below a foreman.

charge nurse *n* GB a nurse, especially a man, who is in charge of a hospital ward.

charger ['tʃɑːʳdʒəʳ] *n* **-1.** ELECTRICITY a device used for charging batteries. **-2.** MILITARY a large horse ridden by a soldier (literary use).

charge sheet *n* GB LAW an official form on which the police list the charges against an accused person.

chariot [US 'tʃerɪət, GB 'tʃær-] *n* a vehicle with two wheels and no seats that was pulled by horses and used in ancient times for fighting or racing.

charisma [kəˈrɪzmə] *n* the ability to attract, influence etc other people by using the strength and charm of one's own personality.

charismatic [ˌkærɪzˈmætɪk] *adj* [person] who has charisma.

charitable ['tʃærətəbl] *adj* **-1.** [person, remark, attitude] that is kind and sympathetic when judging other people □ *That's a charitable way of describing theft!* □ *That wasn't a very charitable thing to say.* **-2.** a **charitable organization/society etc** an organization/a society etc that helps poor people, sick animals etc. ■ a **charitable donation** money that is given to a charitable organization.

charity ['tʃærətɪ] (*pl* **charities**) ◇ *n* **-1.** money and donations given to help poor people, hospitals etc □ *They're organizing a concert in aid of charity.* □ *I'm not so poor that I need to accept charity.* **-2.** an organization that uses money and donations to help poor people, hospitals etc □ *The Red Cross is an international charity.* □ *a charity worker.* **-3.** kindness and sympathy when judging other people □ *Please show them a little more charity.* ◇ *comp* a **charity concert/ball etc** a concert/ball etc that is organized to raise money for charity.

charity shop *n* GB a shop where secondhand goods and clothes are sold by volunteer workers to make money for a particular charity.

charlatan ['ʃɑːlətən] *n* a person who pretends to have skills or qualifications, especially in medicine, in order to impress or cheat other people.

Charlemagne ['ʃɑːləmeɪn] (742–814) King of what is now France from 771, and Emperor of Europe from 800. He encouraged Christianity, education, and the arts.

Charles [tʃɑːlz], **Prince** (1948–) the eldest son of Queen Elizabeth II of Great Britain. His title is the Prince of Wales.

Charles I [ˌtʃɑːlzðəˈfɜːʳst] (1600–1649) King of England, Scotland, and Ireland from 1625 to 1649. His dispute with Parliament led to the English Civil War, in which he was defeated and executed.

Charles II [ˌtʃɑːlzðəˈsekənd] (1630–1685) King of England, Scotland, and Ireland. The son of Charles I, he became King after a period in exile, following the English Civil War.

charm [tʃɑːʳm] ◇ *n* **-1.** qualities which make somebody or something pleasing and attractive □ *a man of great charm* □ *The charm of her poetry lies in its simplicity.* **-2.** a word or object which people believe brings good luck □ *Many people still believe in charms and spells.* **-3.** a small ornament, usually of gold or silver, worn attached to a necklace or bracelet. ◇ *vt* to please, attract, or influence <sb> by charm □ *He charmed us with his wit and humor.*

charm bracelet *n* a bracelet that charms can be attached to and hang from.

charming ['tʃɑːʳmɪŋ] *adj* [person, smile] that one finds attractive or pleasing □ *What a charming young man!* □ *I think this little room is quite charming.* □ *"He said he wasn't going to pick you up." — "Oh, charming!"*

charmingly ['tʃɑːʳmɪŋlɪ] *adv* [smile, dress] *see* **charming** □ *a charmingly renovated cottage.*

charred [tʃɑːʳd] *adj* [paper, wood] that has been made black by heat or fire □ *She sifted through the charred remains of the letters.*

chart [tʃɑːʳt] ◇ *n* -1. a diagram or illustration which presents information, especially statistical information □ *a sales chart.* -2. a special map showing stars, oceans, weather conditions etc □ *a weather chart.* ◇ *vt* -1. [seas, weather conditions] to make a chart showing <sthg>; [position, route] to mark <sthg> on a map □ *The sales figures have been charted and analyzed in detail.* □ *The general charted the enemy's advance on the map.* -2. [events, career] to record the progress of <sthg> in writing □ *The book charts the rise of fascism in Germany.*

♦ **charts** *npl* **the charts** the weekly list that shows which pop records have sold the most copies □ *It's been in the charts for two weeks.*

charter ['tʃɑːʳtəʳ] ◇ *n* an official document issued by a government or other organization that lists the rights or functions of a group of people, institution etc, or its own aims and purposes □ *article 6 of the UN Charter.* ◇ *vt* [plane, ship] to rent <a vehicle> for a special use or service.

chartered accountant [ˌtʃɑːʳtəʳd-] *n* GB a fully qualified accountant.

charter flight *n* a flight on a charter plane that is usually cheaper than a flight on a regular service.
NOTE: Compare **scheduled flight**.

charter plane *n* a plane that is rented for special use, e.g. taking people to a resort, and is not part of a regular service.

chary ['tʃeərɪ] (*compar* **charier**, *superl* **chariest**) *adj* **to be chary of doing sthg** to be unwilling to do sthg because it seems to involve a lot of risks □ *Banks are becoming chary of lending to new businesses.*

chase [tʃeɪs] ◇ *vt* -1. to follow <a person, animal, or vehicle> quickly in order to catch them □ *The dog chased the cat down the alley.* -2. to run after <a person or animal> in order to make them go away □ *The farmer chased the children out of his field.* -3. to use a lot of time and energy trying to get <money, a job> etc □ *There are too many companies chasing too few contracts.* ◇ *n* an act of chasing somebody or something in order to catch them □ *a high-speed car chase* ■ **to give chase** to chase somebody or something in order to catch them □ *The man ran away and the policeman gave chase.*

♦ **chase after** *vt fus* **to chase after sb/sthg** to follow sb/sthg quickly in order to try to catch them □ *Chase after him and give him this message.*

♦ **chase up** *vt sep* GB -1. **to chase sb up** to re-mind sb about something that one wants from them and that they are late in supply-ing □ *Can you chase her up about the weekly figures?* -2. **to chase sthg up** to look for sthg that is wanted □ *I've chased up those reports that you needed.*

chaser ['tʃeɪsəʳ] *n* -1. a strong alcoholic drink, usually whiskey, that is drunk after beer □ *a beer with a whiskey chaser.* -2. US a drink containing little or no alcohol, e.g. beer or fruit juice, that is drunk after a strong alcoholic one, usually whiskey.

chasm ['kæzəm] *n* -1. a very deep opening in a large mass of rock or ice □ *A deep chasm opened up before them.* -2. a large difference in opinions or conditions between two groups of people □ *It will be difficult to bridge the chasm between the two sides.*

chassis ['ʃæsɪ] (*pl* **chassis** [-ɪz]) *n* the frame of a vehicle on which the body, wheels etc are fixed.

chaste [tʃeɪst] *adj* [person] who does not have sex with anybody; who only has sex with their husband or wife (literary use) □ *a chaste life/relationship.*

chasten ['tʃeɪsn] *vt* **to be chastened** to be made to realize that what one has done is wrong □ *He returned, much chastened by the experience.*

chastise [tʃæ'staɪz] *vt* to punish <sb> severely (formal use).

chastity ['tʃæstətɪ] *n: see* **chaste** (literary use) □ *a vow of chastity.*

chat [tʃæt] (*pt* & *pp* **chatted**, *cont* **chatting**) ◇ *n* a friendly conversation, especially about personal or unimportant things □ *I've just been having a chat with my brother.* ◇ *vi: She was chatting with* OR *to him about her vacation.*

♦ **chat up** *vt sep* **to chat sb up** GB to talk to sb that one is attracted to in the hope that this will lead to a romantic or sexual relationship (informal use).

chatline ['tʃætlaɪn] *n* GB a telephone service that one can call to talk to other callers.

chat show *n* GB TV & RADIO a program in which an interviewer talks in a friendly and informal way to well-known guests.

chatter ['tʃætəʳ] ◇ *vi* -1. [person] to speak rapidly and continuously about unimportant things □ *They were chattering away about some movie they'd seen.* -2. [animal, bird] to make short, quick, high-pitched sounds. -3. [teeth] to knock together rapidly as a result of cold or fear. ◇ *n* -1. [of people] informal conversation about unimportant things. -2. [of an animal, bird] the sound made by an animal or bird when it chatters.

chatterbox ['tʃætəʳbɒks] *n* a person who talks a lot about unimportant things (informal use).

chattering classes [ˌtʃætərɪŋ-] *npl* **the chattering classes** GB educated middle-class people who know a lot about topics in the news and enjoy discussing them (disapproving use).

chatty ['tʃætɪ] (*compar* **chattier**, *superl* **chattiest**) *adj* -1. [person] who likes chatting □ *The land-lord seemed very chatty.* -2. [letter] that contains a lot of personal news and is written in a friendly and informal style. □ *He writes cheerful, chatty letters.*

Chaucer ['tʃɔːsə'], **Geoffrey** (1340–1400) an English poet whose most famous work is *The Canterbury Tales.*

chauffeur [US 'ʃoufɜːr, GB 'ʃoufə] ◇ *n* a person whose job is to drive a car for somebody rich or important. ◇ *vt* to be the chauffeur for <sb>.

chauvinist ['ʃoʊvənɪst] *n* **-1.** a man who believes that men are better than women □ *a male chauvinist.* **-2.** a person who is unreasonably proud of their country and believes that it is much better than all others.

chauvinistic [ʃoʊvə'nɪstɪk] *adj* [remark, attitude] that is typical of a chauvinist.

ChE *abbr of* **chemical engineer.**

cheap [tʃiːp] ◇ *adj* **-1.** [clothing, labor] that does not cost much money □ *It was the cheapest in the shop.* □ *I bought a cheap new pen at the market.* □ *The car's economical on gas, so it's cheap to run.* **-2.** [fare, ticket] that costs less than the usual price □ *Do you have any cheap flights to the States?* □ *We should call him in the evening when it's cheaper.* **-3.** that is not expensive and is of bad quality □ *The new office furniture is cheap and ugly.* □ *cheap and nasty plastic rings.* **-4.** [joke, comment] that is unkind or unfair □ *He's only interested in scoring cheap political points.* ◇ *adv* [buy, sell] for little money □ *Work of that quality doesn't come cheap.*

cheapen ['tʃiːpən] *vt* **-1.** [goods, exports] to lower the price of <sthg> □ *The competition should cheapen the cost of travel.* **-2.** to make <sb> lose the respect other people have for them □ *Don't cheapen yourself by getting involved with this man.*

cheaply ['tʃiːplɪ] *adv* [buy, sell] for little money □ *We were able to live very cheaply in Africa.*

cheap rate *n* GB the periods, usually during the evening and at weekends, when making a phone call costs less than usual □ *a cheap-rate phone call.*

cheapskate ['tʃiːpskeɪt] *n* a person who will do anything to avoid spending money (informal and disapproving use).

cheat [tʃiːt] ◇ *vt* to get something, usually money, from <sb> by being dishonest □ *My boss cheated me out of my share of the commission.* ■ **to feel cheated** to feel that one has been treated badly because one has not got what one wanted □ *The audience felt cheated because she only sang for half an hour.* ◇ *vi* to act dishonestly or unfairly in order to get something that one wants □ *You can't trust a man who cheats at cards.* □ *She was caught cheating on* US OR *in* GB *the test.* ◇ *n* a person who cheats □ *He's a cheat and a liar.*

◆ **cheat on** *vt fus* **to cheat on sb** [on one's wife, husband, partner] to deceive sb by having a sexual relationship with another person (informal use).

cheating ['tʃiːtɪŋ] *n* the act of cheating in an exam, competition, or game □ *You can't look at my cards, it's cheating!*

check [tʃek] ◇ *n* **-1.** [for safety, accuracy] an inspection or test to make sure that something is correct, safe etc □ *The army has mounted a security check at the airport.* □ *Have you done a check on the figures?* □ *Keep a careful check on how much you spend.* **-2.** [on progress, spending, someone's ambitions] an action or circumstance that stops something from getting worse or out of control □ *The quota system should act as a check on imports.* ■ **to keep** OR **hold sthg in check** to control sthg and stop it from becoming worse or stronger □ *You must learn to keep your emotions in check.* □ *The enemy advance has been held in check.* **-3.** US FINANCE a printed form one uses to pay money to somebody from one's bank account by writing their name and the amount of money on it □ *You can pay by check, cash, or credit card.* □ *Is it OK if I write you a check?* □ *Checks should be made payable to "M. Bridges and Co."* **-4.** US [in a restaurant] a bill for food at a restaurant □ *Can I get the check, please?* **-5.** [in a pattern] a pattern made up of squares like on a chessboard □ *a check tablecloth.* **-6.** US [on a list, in a box] a written mark (✓) used to show that something has been checked and is satisfactory.

◇ *vt* **-1.** [luggage, accuracy, health] to look at or inspect <sthg> to make sure that it is correct, safe etc □ *Her secretary called to check the arrangements.* □ *I checked my watch: it was 2:00 p.m. exactly.* □ *Before you leave, check that the lights are off.* **-2.** [progress, spending, attack] to control and limit <sthg> □ *The spread of the disease has been checked.* **-3.** [person, opponent] to stop <sb> from doing or saying something □ *I had to check an impulse to slap him hard.* □ *She began to say something, but checked herself and sat in silence.* **-4.** US [box, item] to mark <sthg> with a check □ *Check this box if you are unemployed.* **-5.** [baggage] to give <one's baggage> to an official so that it can be put on a plane, train etc and sent somewhere □ *I checked my bags through to Chicago.* **-6.** US [bag, coat] to leave <one's bag, coat> etc for a short time with somebody whose job is to take care of it □ *I'll just check my coat and umbrella if we're going to eat.*

◇ *vi* to find out whether something is correct, allowed etc □ *"Can you come on Monday?" — "I'll have to check with my boss/in my calendar."* ■ **to check for sthg** [for mistakes, a disease] to try to find out whether sthg bad is present □ *Engineers were called in to check for signs of structural damage.* ■ **to check on sb/sthg** [on progress, accuracy, a patient] to look at or inspect sb/sthg to see that everything is safe, correct etc □ *I'll just go and check on the baby to see if he's asleep.*

◆ **check in** ◇ *vt sep* **to check sb/sthg in** [guest, passenger, luggage] to record the arrival of sb/sthg at a hotel, airport etc □ *The receptionist checked me/my bags in at the United counter.* □ *I checked my bags in and went for coffee.* ◇ *vi* **-1.** [guest] to register one's name, get one's key etc when one arrives at a hotel □ *She checked in the next day at the Plaza Hotel.* **-2.** [passenger] to show one's ticket and hand in one's luggage when one arrives at an airport □ *Please check in one hour before departure.*

◆ **check off** *vt sep* **to check sthg off** [name, item] to put a mark beside sthg on a list to show that it has been counted or dealt with □ *He checked their names off on the list.*

◆ **check out** ◇ *vt sep* **-1. to check sthg out** [library book] to have the removal of sthg recorded, e.g. by having it stamped. **-2. to check sthg out** [facts, story] to look for more information about sthg in order to find out whether it is true, correct, safe etc □ *Check these figures out first and then we'll decide what to do.* ■ **to check sb out** [suspect] to look for more information about sb in order to find out whether they are honest, reliable etc □ *You should have checked him out more carefully before offering him credit.* ◇ *vi* to pay one's bill at a hotel and leave □ *We checked out of our hotel at 8:00 a.m.*

◆ **check up** *vi* to check up on sb/sthg [on a person, story, the details] to find out more precise information about sb/sthg □ *I'll check up on the times of the trains.* □ *He was held in prison while the police checked up on him.*

checkbook US, **chequebook** GB ['tʃekbʊk] *n* a book of checks printed with the name of the owner and their bank.

checked [tʃekt] *adj* [trousers, tablecloth] that has a pattern of checks of two or more colors.

checkered US, **chequered** GB ['tʃekəʳd] *adj* **-1.** [trousers, tablecloth] with a pattern of checks of two or more colors. ■ **the checkered flag** a flag that has a pattern of black and white checks and that is waved to show that a racing car has won a race. **-2.** [career, history] that includes periods of success as well as failure.

checkers ['tʃekəʳz] *n* US a game played on a chessboard with 12 round white or red pieces and 12 round black pieces.

check-in *n* the place at an airport where passengers check in □ *a check-in desk.*

checking account ['tʃekɪŋ-] *n* US a bank account from which one can make payments at any time using checks or a cash card.

checklist ['tʃeklɪst] *n* a list of things to be done, people to be considered etc that can be used as a guide or reference □ *In case of breakdown, go through items 1–10 on the checklist.*

checkmate ['tʃekmeɪt] *n* the situation in a game of chess where one player is unable to move their king out of danger and has therefore lost.

checkout ['tʃekaʊt] *n* **-1.** the place in a supermarket where customers pay for goods □ *a checkout girl* □ *Pay at the checkout.* **-2.** the time before which a guest is supposed to leave a hotel room □ *Checkout time is 11 a.m.*

checkpoint ['tʃekpɔɪnt] *n* a place where travelers are stopped so that their vehicles and papers can be inspected, e.g. at the border between two countries.

checkup ['tʃekʌp] *n* an examination by a doc-

tor or dentist to check that one is healthy, e.g. after an illness □ *I've got to go for a checkup on my knee.* □ *a medical checkup.*

Cheddar ['tʃedəʳ] *n* **Cheddar (cheese)** a type of hard yellow or orange cheese.

cheek [tʃiːk] *n* **-1.** [on one's face] one of the two soft parts of one's face on either side of one's nose and mouth □ *His cheeks were red.* **-2.** [of one's bottom] a buttock (informal use). **-3.** GB [by a person] behavior that one thinks is rude or not respectful enough, especially to somebody older or more important (informal use) □ *What a cheek that man has!*

cheekbone ['tʃiːkbəʊn] *n* the bone in one's face between one's cheek and one's eye.

cheeky ['tʃiːkɪ] (*compar* **cheekier**, *superl* **cheekiest**) *adj* GB [person, answer, smile] that one thinks is rude or not respectful enough □ *He was very cheeky to me yesterday.*

cheep [tʃiːp] *vi* [young bird] to make high-pitched sounds.

cheer [tʃɪəʳ] ◇ *n* a shout of approval, support, or encouragement □ *Now please give three cheers for our new winner.* ◇ *vt* **-1.** [team, speech, leader] to shout loudly to show approval, support, or encouragement of <sb/ sthg> □ *Lake was cheered by supporters as he ran onto the field.* **-2.** [person] to make <sb> feel happier and more hopeful □ *Everyone felt cheered by the news.* ◇ *vi* to cheer a team, speech, leader etc □ *The audience clapped and cheered as the band came onto the stage.*

◆ **cheers** *excl* **-1.** a word one says to somebody else before drinking an alcoholic drink. **-2.** GB goodbye (informal use). **-3.** GB thank you (informal use).

◆ **cheer on** *vt sep* **to cheer sb on** [team, runner] to encourage sb by cheering □ *Don't worry, we'll all be there to cheer you on.*

◆ **cheer up** ◇ *vt sep* **to cheer sb up** to make sb feel less unhappy or worried □ *I've brought you some magazines to cheer you up.* ◇ *vi* to become less unhappy or worried □ *Cheer up!*

cheerful ['tʃɪəʳfl] *adj* **-1.** [person, mood, atmosphere] happy and lively □ *You're looking very cheerful.* □ *a cheerful smile.* **-2.** [music, story] that makes people feel happy and lively □ *The room was painted a cheerful red color.* **-3.** [agreement, worker] that is willing and enthusiastic □ *She shows a cheerful attitude to work.*

cheerfully ['tʃɪəʳflɪ] *adv* **-1.** [smile, sing] in a happy and lively way □ *He greeted me cheerfully on my way in.* **-2.** [admit, agree] willingly □ *She cheerfully agreed to let them bring their entire film crew into her apartment.*

cheering ['tʃɪərɪŋ] ◇ *adj* [news, story] that makes one feel happier and more hopeful □ *It was very cheering to discover that I wasn't the only one who was short of money.* ◇ *n* shouts of approval, support, or encouragement □ *Loud cheering could be heard coming from the stadium.*

cheerleader ['tʃɪəʳliːdəʳ] *n* a person, usually a girl, who wears a special uniform and leads the cheering at a sports event.

cheerless ['tʃɪəˈləs] *adj* [place, day] dull and gloomy.

cheery ['tʃɪərɪ] (*compar* **cheerier,** *superl* **cheeriest**) *adj* [person, face, hello] cheerful and friendly.

cheese [tʃiːz] *n* a type of solid food made from milk that is usually yellow or white and is often eaten with bread, crackers, or salad □ *I'd like some cheese.* □ *I like French cheeses.* □ *a cheese sandwich.*

cheeseboard ['tʃiːzbɔːˈd] *n* -1. [for cheeses] a wooden board on which cheese is cut and served. -2. [in a meal] a course consisting of different cheeses that can be ordered in a restaurant, usually at the end of a meal.

cheeseburger ['tʃiːzbɜːˈgəˈ] *n* a hamburger that has a slice of melted cheese on top of the meat.

cheesecake ['tʃiːzkeɪk] *n* a cake that consists of a thin layer of crushed cookies covered with a thick layer of sweetened cream cheese, sometimes with fruit on top □ *blackcurrant cheesecake.*

cheesy ['tʃiːzɪ] (*compar* **cheesier,** *superl* **cheesiest**) *adj* [snack, cracker] that tastes of cheese.

cheetah ['tʃiːtə] *n* a large African wild cat that is yellow with black spots, and is able to run very fast.

chef [ʃef] *n* a person whose job is to cook in a hotel or restaurant, especially the chief cook.

Che Guevara [ˌʃeɪgəˈvɑːrə] (1928–1967) an Argentinian revolutionary leader, who played an important part in the Cuban revolution. He was killed fighting with guerrillas in Bolivia.

Chekhov ['tʃekɒf], **Anton** (1860–1904) a Russian writer of plays and short stories. His works include *The Three Sisters, Uncle Vanya,* and *The Cherry Orchard.*

chemical ['kemɪkl] ◇ *adj* [reaction, composition] that is connected with chemistry. ◇ *n* a substance used in or produced by chemistry.

chemical engineering *n* the area of engineering that involves designing and operating machines used for industrial chemical processes.

chemically ['kemɪklɪ] *adv* [complex, stable] a word used when one is talking about the chemical composition of a substance.

chemical weapons *npl* poisonous gases used as weapons in war.

chemist ['kemɪst] *n* -1. a person who studies or works in chemistry. -2. GB & AUS a person who is qualified to sell drugs, medicines etc. ■ **a chemist's** a store that sells drugs, medicines, cosmetics etc.

chemistry ['kemɪstrɪ] *n* -1. [as a science] the study of substances, their composition from molecules, atoms etc, and how they react and combine with other substances □ *organic/inorganic chemistry* □ *a chemistry lesson.* -2. [of a substance] the composition of a particular substance and how it reacts with other substances □ *We are doing research into the chemistry of plant proteins.*

chemotherapy [ˌkiːmoʊˈθerəpɪ] *n* the use of chemicals to treat diseases, especially cancer.

cheque *n* GB FINANCE = **check**.

chequebook *n* GB = **checkbook**.

cheque (guarantee) card *n* GB a small plastic card that a bank gives to owners of accounts with checkbooks, promising that it will pay out the money for checks up to the amount that is stated on the card □ *'Cheques accepted only when backed by a valid cheque card.'*

chequered *adj* GB = **checkered**.

Chequers ['tʃekəˈz] the official country home of the British prime minister, in Buckinghamshire, southern England.

cherish ['tʃerɪʃ] *vt* -1. [hope, memory] to keep <sthg> in one's mind because it makes one feel happier □ *Andrew had long cherished the hope that he might one day take charge of the firm.* -2. [privilege, right, belief] to consider <sthg> to be very valuable and try to keep it □ *We cherish our democratic principles.* -3. [person, possession] to care a lot for <sb/sthg that is important to one> □ *cherishing his loved ones with fervor and loyalty.*

cherished ['tʃerɪʃt] *adj* [memory, privilege, possession] that one cherishes □ *That old car, believe it or not, is one of Colin's most cherished possessions.*

Chernobyl [tʃəˈnoʊbl] a city in central Ukraine where a nuclear reactor broke down in 1986, causing serious radioactive pollution.

Cherokee ['tʃerəkiː] *n* a member of a Native American people who used to live around the Appalachian Mountains; the language of this people.

cherry ['tʃerɪ] (*pl* **cherries**) *n* a small, round, dark-red fruit with a hard seed in the middle that grows on trees in bunches □ *cherry pie.*

cherry-picking [-pɪkɪŋ] *n* BUSINESS the act of choosing only the best of something, e.g. buying only the most profitable sectors of an industry.

cherry tomato *n* a kind of very small tomato.

cherry tree *n* the tree that cherries grow on.

cherub ['tʃerəb] *n* -1. an angel that is shown in art as a fat, naked child with wings. -2. a pretty baby or young child with a round smiling face.

chervil ['tʃɜːˈvɪl] *n* an herb with a taste like aniseed that is used in salads and soups.

Ches *abbr of* **Cheshire**.

Chesapeake Bay [ˌtʃesəpiːk-] a large bay on the east coast of the USA, between Maryland and Virginia.

Cheshire ['tʃeʃəˈ] a county in northwestern England. SIZE: 2,328 sq kms. POPULATION: 955,800. ADMINISTRATIVE CENTER: Chester.

chess [tʃes] *n* a game of skill for two players, one with 16 white pieces, the other with 16 black pieces, played on a chessboard. Each set of pieces represents a king, queen, knight etc □ *a game of chess* □ *a chess piece/set.*

chessboard ['tʃesbɔːrd] *n* a board on which chess is played with 32 white and 32 black squares.

chessman ['tʃesmæn] (*pl* **chessmen** [-men]) *n* a piece used in the game of chess, such as a king or castle.

chest [tʃest] *n* **-1.** [of a person, animal] the upper part of the front of the body, containing the lungs, heart etc □ *chest pains* □ *a chest wound* □ *chest measurement.* ■ **to get sthg off one's chest** [problem, worry] to tell somebody sthg and feel better because it is no longer secret (informal use) □ *Once I'd got it off my chest I felt so much better.* **-2.** [for clothes, tools] a large box, usually made of wood, used for storing things □ *a tool/medicine chest.*

chestnut ['tʃesnʌt] ◇ *adj* [hair, horse] dark red-brown in color. ◇ *n* a large brown nut that grows inside a spiky green covering.

chestnut tree *n* the tree that chestnuts grow on.

chest of drawers (*pl* **chests of drawers**) *n* a piece of furniture with drawers, usually used for storing clothes.

chesty ['tʃestɪ] (*compar* **chestier**, *superl* **chestiest**) *adj* **a chesty cough** a cough caused by mucus in one's lungs.

chevron ['ʃevrən] *n* **-1.** [on cloth, a road sign] a V shape or design. **-2.** [on a uniform] a V-shaped piece of material on the arm of the uniform of a soldier, a policeman etc, showing their rank.

chew [tʃuː] *vt* **-1.** [meat, candy] to crush <food> repeatedly between one's back teeth □ *He just sat there chewing gum.* **-2.** [fingernails, pencil] to tear pieces off <sthg> by biting it many times.

◆ **chew over** *vt sep* **to chew sthg over** [problem, offer] to think about sthg long and carefully □ *Give us a few days to chew it over.*

◆ **chew up** *vt sep* **to chew sthg up** [carpet, lawn, paper] to crush or twist sthg until it is completely broken up or torn □ *The photocopier has just chewed up all my documents!*

chewing gum ['tʃuːɪŋ-] *n* a sweet substance made to be chewed for a long time but not swallowed □ *a piece* OR *stick of chewing gum.*

chewy ['tʃuːɪ] (*compar* **chewier**, *superl* **chewiest**) *adj* [meat, candy] that needs to be chewed for a long time before it can be swallowed.

chic [ʃiːk] ◇ *adj* [person, clothes, restaurant] fashionable and sophisticated □ *She came in, looking extremely chic in a black Chanel suit.* ◇ *n* the quality of being chic □ *Our offices have an air of mid-fifties chic.*

Chicago [ʃə'kɑːgoʊ] the third-largest city in the USA, on Lake Michigan in Illinois. POPULATION: 2,783,726.

Chicago Board of Trade *n* **the Chicago Board of Trade** an important financial market in Chicago where futures and other commodities are traded.

Chicana [tʃɪ'kɑːnə] *n* in the USA, a girl or woman whose family came from Mexico.

chicane [ʃɪ'keɪn] *n* a series of sharp bends in a motor-racing track.

chicanery [ʃɪ'keɪnərɪ] *n* tricks and dishonesty, especially in politics, business etc.

Chicano [tʃɪ'kɑːnoʊ] *n* in the USA, a boy or man whose family came from Mexico.

chick [tʃɪk] *n* **-1.** a young bird, especially a young chicken. **-2.** a young woman (informal and offensive use).

chicken ['tʃɪkən] *n* **-1.** a common farm bird kept for its meat and the eggs it produces; the meat of this bird eaten as food □ *I ordered roast chicken.* □ *a chicken sandwich/salad.* ■ **a chicken and egg situation** a situation where it is impossible to tell which of two things came first and caused the other. **-2.** a person one thinks is a coward (informal use).

◆ **chicken out** *vi* to decide not to do something because one is afraid (informal use) □ *I chickened out of meeting them face to face.*

chickenfeed ['tʃɪkənfiːd] *n* a very small amount of money (informal and disapproving use) □ *You earned $20,000? That's chickenfeed!*

chickenpox ['tʃɪkənpɒks] *n* an infectious disease, usually caught by children, that causes a high temperature and red, itchy spots which can leave scars.

chicken wire *n* wire netting with holes which have six sides □ *a chicken wire fence.*

chickpea ['tʃɪkpiː] *n* a hard pale-yellow seed shaped like a pea that is soaked in water, cooked, and eaten.

chicory ['tʃɪkərɪ] *n* **-1.** US a plant whose curly green leaves are eaten raw in salads. **-2.** GB a plant whose long, crisp, pale-green leaves are eaten raw in salads or stewed; a powder made from the dried roasted roots of this plant and used to add a bitter flavor to coffee.

chide [tʃaɪd] *vt* to speak angrily to <sb> about something they have done wrong (literary use).

chief [tʃiːf] ◇ *adj* **-1.** [aim, concern, problem] that is the most important □ *Foreign imports are the chief cause of falling sales figures.* **-2.** [officer, clerk, engineer] who is the highest in rank □ *the chief rabbi/librarian.* ◇ *n* **-1.** a person with the highest authority or rank in an organization □ *the Chief of Police* □ *union chiefs.* **-2.** the leader of a tribe or clan.

chief constable *n* the head of the police force in a British county or region.

Chief Executive *n* US **the Chief Executive** the president of the United States.

chief executive officer *n* the most important person in charge of running a company.

chief justice *n* **-1.** US the chief judge of the Supreme Court. **-2.** GB & AUS the title given to a senior judge in a high court.

chiefly ['tʃiːflɪ] *adv* mainly □ *My work is chiefly administrative.* □ *They invested chiefly in gold.*

chief of staff *n* **-1.** the senior officer of a commander's advisory staff. **-2.** the senior officer of one of the branches of the armed forces of a particular country.

chieftain ['tʃiːftən] *n* the leader of a tribe or clan.

chiffon ['ʃɪfɒn] *n* a very thin, almost transparent fabric made of silk or nylon and used to make blouses, dresses etc □ *a chiffon scarf.*

chihuahua [tʃɪ'wɑːwə] *n* a very small dog with smooth hair and large eyes.

chilblain ['tʃɪlbleɪn] *n* a painful itchy swelling, usually on one's fingers or toes, caused by cold weather.

child [tʃaɪld] (*pl* **children**) *n* **-1.** a boy or girl before they start to develop into adults □ *children's books/toys/clothes* □ *Stop treating me like a child.* □ *child labor.* **-2.** a person's son or daughter at any age □ *My children are all grown-up now.*

child abuse *n* cruel treatment of a child, usually by somebody in the same family, that involves being violent to them, or having a sexual relationship with them.

childbearing ['tʃaɪldbeərɪŋ] *n* the process of giving birth to a child □ *a woman of child-bearing age.*

child benefit *n* GB money paid regularly by the state to parents who have a child or children under a certain age.

childbirth ['tʃaɪldbɜːrθ] *n* the act of giving birth to a child □ *She died in childbirth.*

childcare ['tʃaɪldkeəʳ] *n* GB the work involved in taking care of young children while their parents are at work □ *The company has excellent childcare facilities.*

childhood ['tʃaɪldhʊd] *n* the period of somebody's life during which they are a child □ *I spent most of my childhood in Switzerland.* □ *childhood experiences/memories.*

childish ['tʃaɪldɪʃ] *adj* [behavior, fantasy] that is silly because it makes an adult seem like a child (disapproving use) □ *I think you're being very childish.*

childishly ['tʃaɪldɪʃlɪ] *adv* [behave, react] *see* **childish.**

childless ['tʃaɪldləs] *adj* [couple, person] that has no children.

childlike ['tʃaɪldlaɪk] *adj* [trust, faith, face] that is typical of a child.

childminder ['tʃaɪldmaɪndəʳ] *n* GB a person whose job is to take care of children while their parents are at work.

child prodigy *n* a child who has an extraordinary talent or skill.

childproof ['tʃaɪldpruːf] *adj* [lock, container] that is designed so that it cannot be opened by children.

children ['tʃɪldrən] *plural of* **child.**

children's home *n* a place where children are sent to live, e.g. when their parents are dead or cannot look after them very well.

child support *n* US money that a person has to pay to their former wife or husband in order to support their children.

Child Support Agency *n* the **Child Support Agency** the British government department responsible for finding absent parents and making them pay for the maintenance of their children.

Chile ['tʃɪlɪ] a country in western South America, between the Andes and the Pacific Ocean. SIZE: 757,000 sq kms. POPULATION: 13,400,000 (*Chileans*). CAPITAL: Santiago. LANGUAGE: Spanish. CURRENCY: peso.

Chilean ['tʃɪlɪən] *n* & *adj*: *see* **Chile.**

chili ['tʃɪlɪ] (*pl* **chilies**) *n* a small red or green vegetable that has a hot spicy taste and is used to flavor food □ *chili sauce.*

chili con carne [-kɒn'kɑːrnɪ] *n* a dish made from beans, ground beef, and chili powder.

chili powder *n* ground dried chilies used as a spice in cooking.

chill [tʃɪl] ◇ *vt* **-1.** to make <food or drink> colder without freezing it □ *The wine should be chilled before serving.* **-2. to chill sb to the bone** OR **to the marrow** [cold weather] to make sb feel very cold; [story, noise] to frighten sb. ◇ *vi* [food, drink] to become colder without freezing □ *Leave the wine to chill.* ◇ *n* **-1.** an illness that causes one to shiver □ *I think I've caught a chill.* **-2. there's a chill in the air** the weather is cold. **-3.** a feeling of coldness, usually caused by fear or shock □ *A sudden chill ran down my spine.* ◇ *adj* [wind, air] cold.

✦ **chill out** *vi* **chill out!** relax and calm down (informal use).

chilli ['tʃɪlɪ] *n* GB = **chili.**

chilling ['tʃɪlɪŋ] *adj* **-1.** [wind] very cold. **-2.** [story, experience] that makes one feel frightened □ *I found his calm quite chilling.*

chilly ['tʃɪlɪ] (*compar* **chillier**, *superl* **chilliest**) *adj* **-1.** [weather, water, day] cold □ *It's rather chilly out on deck.* **-2.** [stare, atmosphere] unfriendly □ *He got a chilly reception.*

Chiltern Hundreds [ˌtʃɪltəʳn'hʌndrədz] an administrative district in England that does not legally exist. According to tradition, British MPs apply for the Chiltern Hundreds when they want to resign.

chime [tʃaɪm] ◇ *vi* [bell, clock] to make a pleasant ringing sound. ◇ *vt* to show <the time> by chiming □ *The clock chimed five.* ◇ *n* the sound made by a bell or clock when it chimes.

✦ **chime in** *vi* to join in a conversation by saying or asking something suddenly.

chimney ['tʃɪmnɪ] (*pl* **chimneys**) *n* a narrow vertical passage that takes the smoke from a fire out of the roof of a building.

chimneypot ['tʃɪmnɪpɒt] *n* a short pipe fitted on a roof to the top of a chimney.

chimneysweep ['tʃɪmnɪswiːp] *n* a person whose job is to clean chimneys, usually with a long brush.

chimp [tʃɪmp] *n* = **chimpanzee** (informal use).

chimpanzee [ˌtʃɪmpæn'ziː] *n* a small brown African ape whose appearance and behavior are sometimes similar to those of humans.

chin [tʃɪn] *n* the lowest part of one's face below one's mouth.

china ['tʃaɪnə] *n* **-1.** a type of clay used to make high-quality pottery; the pottery made from this clay □ *a china cup/plate.* **-2.** a collective term for cups, plates etc made of china □ *They brought out the family china.* □ *a piece of china.*

China ['tʃaɪnə] a large country in eastern Asia, with the highest population and one of the oldest civilizations in the world. It has had a Communist government since 1949. SIZE: 9,600,000 sq kms. POPULATION: 1,178,500,000 (*Chinese*). CAPITAL: Beijing. LANGUAGE: Mandarin (Chinese). CURRENCY: yuan.

china clay *n* the fine white clay that china is made from.

China Sea: the China Sea part of the Pacific Ocean off the coast of China. It is divided into the East China Sea and the South China Sea.

Chinatown ['tʃaɪnətaʊn] *n* a district of a Western city where many people of Chinese origin live and work.

chinchilla [tʃɪn'tʃɪlə] *n* a small South American animal that is similar to a squirrel, with soft silver-gray fur; the fur of this animal, used to make clothes.

Chinese [,tʃaɪ'niːz] ◇ *n* any of the languages spoken in China, e.g. Mandarin or Cantonese, that are all written the same way but spoken differently. ◇ *npl* & *adj: see* **China**.

Chinese cabbage *n* GB a type of cabbage whose leaves are used in salads and in Chinese cooking.

Chinese lantern *n* a folding lantern made of thin colored paper.

Chinese leaves *npl* GB the edible leaves of a Chinese cabbage.

chink [tʃɪŋk] ◇ *n* **-1.** [in a wall] a long narrow opening □ *He peeped through a chink in the wall.* ■ **a chink of light** a narrow beam of light shining through an opening in something. **-2.** [of coins, glasses] a light ringing sound made by objects hitting one another. ◇ *vi* [coins, money, glasses] to make a light ringing sound when knocked together.

chinos ['tʃiːnoʊz] *npl* trousers made of strong cotton fabric □ *a pair of chinos.*

chintz [tʃɪnts] *n* a shiny, patterned, cotton fabric used for covering furniture or making curtains □ *chintz curtains.*

chip [tʃɪp] (*pt* & *pp* **chipped**, *cont* **chipping**) ◇ *n* **-1.** COOKING US a thin slice of potato that is fried until crisp, usually sold in packages and eaten cold as a snack; GB a long thin piece of potato that is deep-fried and eaten hot □ *fish and chips.* **-2.** [of stone, wood] a small piece of wood, stone, pottery etc that has broken off a larger object; the mark left on this object □ *a wood chip* □ *There's a chip in this cup.* ■ **to have a chip on one's shoulder** to always be angry and aggressive because one feels inferior or unfairly treated □ *Larry's got a real chip on his shoulder about being small.* **-3.** ELECTRONICS a thin piece of silicon with electric circuits on it, used as part of a computer. **-4.** GAMES a plastic object used to represent money in gambling. ■ **when the chips are down** in a serious or difficult situation

(informal use) □ *But, when the chips are down, will she still support you?*
◇ *vt* [cup, plate, glass] to damage <sthg> by breaking a small piece off it □ *I fell and chipped my tooth.*

◆ **chip in** (informal use) ◇ *vi* **-1.** to say something in the middle of a conversation between other people □ *David suddenly chipped in with the suggestion that we should all go out.* **-2.** to give a sum of money toward something that a group of people are buying together □ *We're all going to chip in and buy her something nice.* ◇ *vt fus* **to chip in sthg** to pay sthg toward something that a group of people are buying together □ *We all chipped in $50 toward Miriam's present.*

◆ **chip off** *vt sep* **to chip sthg off** [piece, bit, flake] to break sthg small off an object made of wood, stone, pottery etc □ *I chipped off a bit of paint from the wall.*

chip-based [-beɪst] *adj* [technology, system] that uses microchips.

chipboard ['tʃɪpbɔːʳd] *n* a building material made from wood chips and glue that are pressed together and shaped into boards □ *shelves made of chipboard.*

chipmunk ['tʃɪpmʌŋk] *n* a small North American animal like a squirrel that has light and dark stripes down its back and lives in holes underground.

chipolata [,tʃɪpə'lɑːtə] *n* a small sausage.

chipped [tʃɪpt] *adj* [mug, cup, plate] that has a small piece broken out of it.

Chippendale ['tʃɪpəndeɪl] *n* a style of furniture made in England in the 18th century by Thomas Chippendale □ *a Chippendale chair.*

chippings ['tʃɪpɪŋz] *npl* very small pieces of wood, stone etc. ■ **'Loose chippings'** GB a sign that warns drivers that a road has been recently resurfaced with stone chippings.

chip shop *n* GB a shop that sells hot fish and chips, chicken, sausages etc to take out.

chiropodist [kə'rɒpədɪst] *n* a person whose job is to care for people's feet.

chiropody [kə'rɒpədɪ] *n* the profession of a chiropodist.

chiropractor ['kaɪroʊpræktəʳ] *n* a person whose job is to treat medical conditions by working on people's backs and joints with their hands.

chirp [tʃɜːʳp] *vi* [bird, grasshopper] to make a short high-pitched sound.

chirpy ['tʃɜːʳpɪ] (*compar* **chirpier**, *superl* **chirpiest**) *adj* [person, attitude] cheerful and lively (informal use) □ *You're very chirpy this morning!*

chisel ['tʃɪzl] (US *pt* & *pp* **chiseled**, *cont* **chiseling**, GB *pt* & *pp* **chiselled**, *cont* **chiselling**) ◇ *n* a tool that has a flat blade with a squared sharp end that is used for cutting and shaping wood or stone. ◇ *vt* [groove, slot, wood] to cut or shape <sthg> using a chisel.

Chisholm ['tʃɪzm], **Shirley** (1924–) a US politician who was the first black woman to be elected to Congress.

chit [tʃɪt] *n* a short written note that shows how much money one owes or has paid.

chitchat ['tʃɪttʃæt] *n* informal talk about unimportant things (informal use) □ *I wasn't really in the mood for Sara's chitchat.*

chivalrous ['ʃɪvlrəs] *adj* [man, attitude, behavior] polite, helpful, and unselfish, especially when dealing with women □ *It was very chivalrous of you to offer to help.*

chivalry ['ʃɪvlrɪ] *n* -1. the combination of good qualities expected of medieval knights, such as honor, loyalty, courage etc. -2. chivalrous behavior, especially toward women □ *And who says the age of chivalry is dead?*

chives [tʃaɪvz] *npl* the long, thin, hollow leaves of a particular plant that taste like onions and are used as an herb.

chivy, chivvy ['tʃɪvɪ] (*pt & pp* **chivied** OR **chivvied**) *vt* **to chivy sb along** to encourage sb to do something faster by telling them several times to hurry up (informal use).

chloride ['klɔːraɪd] *n* a chemical compound of chlorine and another substance.

chlorinated ['klɔːrɪneɪtəd] *adj* [water] that has chlorine added to it.

chlorine ['klɔːriːn] *n* a chemical element that is a strong-smelling, greenish-yellow gas, used mainly for purifying water. SYMBOL: Cl.

chlorofluorocarbon [ˌklɔːroʊfluərouˈkɑːrbən] *n* → CFC.

chloroform ['klɔrəfɔːrm] *n* a colorless chemical liquid used as an anesthetic. FORMULA: $CHCl_3$.

chlorophyll ['klɒrəfɪl] *n* the green substance in plants that uses energy from sunlight to help them grow.

choc-ice ['tʃɒkaɪs] *n* GB a small block of ice cream covered in a thin layer of chocolate.

chock [tʃɒk] *n* a wedge-shaped block that is placed under a wheel, barrel etc to stop it from moving.

chock-a-block, chock-full *adj* **to be chock-a-block** OR **chock-full** to be completely full (informal use) □ *The corridor was chock-a-block with packing cases.*

chocolate ['tʃɒklət] *n* -1. a solid brown food made from cocoa beans that is usually sweetened and eaten as a candy or used as a flavoring □ *a bar/piece of chocolate* □ *a chocolate bar/cake.* -2. a small candy that is covered with chocolate □ *a box of chocolates.*

Choctaw ['tʃɒktɔː] (*pl* **Choctaw** OR **Choctaws**) *n* a member of a Native American people who used to live in the southeastern USA; the language of this people.

choice [tʃɔɪs] ◇ *n* -1. **to make** OR **take one's choice** to choose one of several things available □ *You must make* OR *take your choice, you can't have both.* ■ **to do sthg by** OR **from choice** to do sthg because one wants to □ *I didn't come here by choice.* -2. **one's choice** the thing or person that one chooses □ *She'd be my choice as the new manager/for the position.* □ *This model was my first/second choice.* -3. **to have a choice** to be able to choose □ *If I had the choice, I'd go by car.* □ *It was a choice between going to university and finding a job.* □ *"Why did you join?" — "I didn't really have a*

choice." ■ **to have no choice but to do sthg** to be forced to do sthg □ *Unfortunately I have no choice but to report you to the principal.* -4. **a choice of things** a range or variety of things to choose from □ *There's a choice of several different styles.* □ *We offer a wide choice of leisure activities.*
◇ *adj* [wine, meat, fruit] that is of high quality.

◆ **of one's choice** *adv* that one chooses □ *You will be flown there by an airline of your choice.*

choir ['kwaɪər] *n* an organized group of singers, especially one that sings in a church.

choirboy ['kwaɪərbɔɪ] *n* a boy singer in a church choir.

choke [tʃoʊk] ◇ *n* a valve which makes it easier to start a vehicle's engine by reducing the amount of air going into the carburetor. ◇ *vi* to be unable to breathe because one's windpipe is blocked □ *She choked on a fishbone.* ◇ *vt* -1. [person] to cause <sb> to choke □ *The fumes choked me.* -2. [road, pipe, gutter] to cause <sthg> to be blocked □ *Our cities are choked with traffic.*

◆ **choke back** *vt fus* **to choke back sthg** [one's tears, sobs, anger] to prevent sthg one is feeling from being seen or heard.

choker ['tʃoʊkər] *n* a necklace or a band of decorative material that is worn by women and that fits around their throat.

cholera ['kɒlərə] *n* a highly infectious and serious disease of the intestines that is caught from contaminated water or food and is common in hot countries.

cholesterol [US kəˈlestəroʊl, GB -rɒl] *n* a fatty substance found in body tissues and fluids, which can cause heart disease if there is too much of it □ *a high/low cholesterol level.*

chomp [tʃɒmp] *vi* to chew food noisily □ *He was chomping away on a hamburger.*

choose [tʃuːz] (*pt* **chose**, *pp* **chosen**) ◇ *vt* -1. to decide to have or take <sthg/sb> from the number of things or people that are available □ *Will you help me choose a suitable present for the boss?* □ *You were chosen for your communications skills.* □ *Who would you choose as* OR *to be our representative?* ■ **there's little** OR **not much to choose between them** it is difficult to choose one of them because they are almost the same. -2. **to choose to do sthg** to do sthg because one wants to □ *I didn't choose to come on this trip.* ◇ *vi* to make a decision from a number of possibilities □ *We had to choose from ten possible titles.*

choos(e)y ['tʃuːzɪ] (*compar* **choosier**, *superl* **choosiest**) *adj* **to be choos(e)y** to be difficult to please when making a choice □ *You can't afford to be too choosey about the hotels in this town.*

chop [tʃɒp] (*pt & pp* **chopped**, *cont* **chopping**) ◇ *n* -1. COOKING a piece of meat, usually pork or lamb, attached to a rib □ *Cut the fat off the lamb chops.* -2. [with the hand] a single blow with a knife, ax etc, or with the hand. ◇ *vt* -1. [meat, wood] to cut up <sthg> into pieces using a knife, ax etc □ *Steve was outside chopping wood.* -2. [budget, funding] to reduce <sthg> by a very large amount (informal use).

chopper

◇ *vi* **to chop and change** GB to change one's plans, opinion, attitude etc continually.

◆ **chops** *npl* one's mouth and cheeks (informal use).

◆ **chop down** *vt sep* **to chop a tree down** to cut down a tree with an ax.

◆ **chop up** *vt sep* **to chop sthg up** [meat, vegetables, wood] to cut sthg into small pieces using a knife, ax etc.

chopper ['tʃɒpər] *n* -1. a knife with a blade like an ax, used for cutting wood or meat. -2. AVIATION a helicopter (informal use).

chopping block, chopping board ['tʃɒpɪŋ-] *n* a board which is used to chop food on in the kitchen.

choppy ['tʃɒpɪ] (*compar* **choppier**, *superl* **choppiest**) *adj* [sea, water] that is rough and covered in small waves.

chopsticks ['tʃɒpstɪks] *npl* two thin sticks that are held in one hand and used for eating Chinese, Japanese etc food.

choral ['kɔːrəl] *adj* [music, work] that is performed by a choir □ *a choral symphony*.

chord [kɔːrd] *n* a number of musical notes that are played or sung together at the same time. ■ **to strike a chord** to be something that one is familiar with and can sympathize with □ *What she said about parents' responsibilities struck a chord with me.*

chore [tʃɔːr] *n* an unpleasant boring task, especially one that has to be done regularly □ *It's a real chore having to go to this meeting.* □ *domestic chores.*

choreographer [ˌkɒrɪ'ɒɡrəfər] *n* a person whose job is to create and teach the movements to be performed by dancers.

choreography [ˌkɒrɪ'ɒɡrəfɪ] *n* the profession of a choreographer.

chortle ['tʃɔːrtl] *vi* to laugh loudly with pleasure.

chorus ['kɔːrəs] *n* -1. [in a song] a part of a song which is repeated after each verse and is usually sung by all the singers □ *...then we'll all join in with the chorus.* -2. a choir. -3. [of singers, dancers] a group of singers or dancers who take part in the action of an opera or musical. -4. **a chorus of sthg** [of disapproval, complaints] sthg expressed by many people at the same time □ *The joke was met with a chorus of laughter.*

chose [tʃouz] *past tense of* **choose**.

chosen ['tʃouzn] *past participle of* **choose**.

choux pastry ['ʃuː-] *n* very light pastry made with eggs that is used to make éclairs, profiteroles etc.

chow [tʃau] *n* -1. a breed of dog, originally from China, that has a thick coat and a blue-black tongue. -2. US food (informal use).

chowder ['tʃaudər] *n* thick soup made with seafood or fish and vegetables.

Christ [kraɪst] ◇ = **Jesus Christ**. ◇ *excl* ▽ a word used to express annoyance or frustration (very informal use) □ *For Christ's sake, calm down!*

christen ['krɪsn] *vt* -1. RELIGION [baby, child] to

give a Christian name to <sb> at a christening □ *She was christened Naomi.* -2. [person, place, car] to give a name to <sb/sthg> (informal use) □ *We christened it 'the treehouse'.*

christening ['krɪsnɪŋ] *n* the religious ceremony at which a person is given a Christian name and made a member of a Christian church □ *a christening cake/gown/present.*

Christian ['krɪstʃən] ◇ *adj* -1. RELIGION [person] who believes that Jesus Christ is the Son of God and follows his teachings; [doctrine, church] that is based on the teachings of Jesus Christ □ *a Christian family* □ *the Christian religion.* -2. [act, thought] kind (informal use). ◇ *n* RELIGION a Christian person.

Christian Aid *n* a British aid organization, supported by many Christian churches, that supports development projects in poor countries.

Christian Democrat *n* a member or supporter of a moderate conservative party that exists in several European countries.

Christianity [ˌkrɪstɪ'ænətɪ] *n* a religion based on the teachings of Jesus Christ.

Christian name *n* a person's first name, given to them when they are born or when they are christened.

Christian Science *n* a Christian group founded in the USA in 1883. Members believe that illness is cured by religion, not by medicine or doctors.

Christie ['krɪstɪ], **Agatha** (1891–1976) a British writer of detective novels who created the characters Hercule Poirot and Miss Marple. Her works include *Murder on the Orient Express* and *Death on the Nile*.

Christmas ['krɪsməs] *n* -1. December 25, a public holiday in Christian countries, when the anniversary of the birth of Jesus Christ is celebrated □ *I last saw them at Christmas.* □ *a Christmas present/party.* ■ **Happy** OR **Merry Christmas** a phrase used to express one's good wishes when one meets somebody at Christmas or when one sends somebody a Christmas card. -2. = **Christmastime**.

Christmas cake *n* GB a cake containing dried fruit and covered with icing that is eaten at Christmas.

Christmas card *n* a greeting card sent at Christmas.

Christmas cracker *n* GB a tube made of colored paper that makes a loud noise when pulled apart by two people and usually contains a small toy and a paper hat.

Christmas Day *n* December 25, the anniversary of the birth of Jesus Christ.

Christmas Eve *n* December 24.

Christmas pudding *n* GB a heavy, sweet, boiled pudding, full of dried fruit, that is eaten as a dessert at dinner on Christmas Day.

Christmas stocking *n* a large sock that children hang up empty on Christmas Eve and find full of presents on Christmas morning.

Christmastime ['krɪsməstaɪm] *n* the days before and after December 25, when people celebrate Christmas.

Christmas tree *n* a real or artificial fir tree that is decorated with lights, ornaments, tinsel etc in people's homes at Christmas.

chrome [krəʊm] *n* = **chromium** (non-technical use) □ *chrome taps.*

chromium ['krəʊmjəm] *n* a shiny silver-colored metal that is used especially for covering other metals. SYMBOL: Cr.

chromosome ['krəʊməsəʊm] *n* the part of a living cell that contains its genes.

chronic ['krɒnɪk] *adj* -1. [illness, unemployment] that lasts for a long time and does not improve □ *There's a chronic shortage of teachers.* -2. [alcoholic, invalid] who has an illness, problem, or habit that has lasted for a long time.

chronically ['krɒnɪklɪ] *adv* **to be chronically sick/ ill etc** to have been sick/ill etc for a long time □ *a chronically depressed person.*

chronic fatigue syndrome *n* an illness causing tiredness and aching muscles that sometimes lasts for years.

chronicle ['krɒnɪkl] ◇ *n* a record of events in the order in which they happened. ◇ *vt* [life, history] to record <a series of events> in the order in which they happened □ *The book chronicles their adventures across India in the 1920s.*

chronological [,krɒnə'lɒdʒɪkl] *adj* **in chronological order** in the order in which something happened □ *The events are listed in chronological order.*

chronologically [,krɒnə'lɒdʒɪklɪ] *adv* [list, order] see **chronological** □ *The list of his writings is laid out chronologically.*

chronology [krə'nɒlədʒɪ] *n* a list of events in the order in which they happened.

chrysalis ['krɪsəlɪs] *n* a stage in the development of a butterfly or moth when it is inside a hard protective case and is changing from a caterpillar into an adult.

chrysanthemum [krɪ'sænθəməm] (*pl* **chrysanthemums**) *n* a flower with a large, round, brightly colored head made up of many thin petals.

chub [tʃʌb] (*pl* **chub** OR **chubs**) *n* a freshwater fish with a dark-green body, found in Europe.

chubby ['tʃʌbɪ] (*compar* **chubbier**, *superl* **chubbiest**) *adj* [face, cheeks, person] fat and rounded in an attractive way.

chuck [tʃʌk] (informal use) *vt* -1. [ball, book] to throw <sthg> in a careless way □ *Could you chuck me the lighter?* -2. **to chuck a job** to resign from a job. -3. [boyfriend, girlfriend] to end a relationship with <sb> because one does not want it to continue.

♦ **chuck away, chuck out** *vt sep* **to chuck sthg away** OR **out** to throw sthg away.

chuckle ['tʃʌkl] ◇ *n* a quiet laugh □ *He gave a little chuckle of delight.* ◇ *vi* to laugh quietly □ *He sat in a corner, chuckling away to himself.*

chuck wagon *n* US a wagon where food was stored and prepared, used by cowboys in the Western USA.

chug [tʃʌg] (*pt* & *pp* **chugged**, *cont* **chugging**) *vi* [train, car] to move slowly and steadily, making low throbbing sounds; [engine, motor] to make low throbbing sounds □ *The little boat was chugging slowly toward the shore.*

chum [tʃʌm] *n* a friend (informal use).

chummy ['tʃʌmɪ] (*compar* **chummier**, *superl* **chummiest**) *adj* [person] friendly (informal use).

chump [tʃʌmp] *n* a person who one thinks is silly (informal use).

chunk [tʃʌŋk] *n* -1. [of bread, cheese, meat] a large thick piece of food. -2. **a chunk of sthg** a large amount of sthg (informal use) □ *Rehearsals are taking up a huge chunk of my time.*

chunky ['tʃʌŋkɪ] (*compar* **chunkier**, *superl* **chunkiest**) *adj* -1. [person] short and rather fat. -2. [sweater, jewelry] large and heavy.

Chunnel ['tʃʌnl] = **Channel Tunnel**.

church [tʃɜːrtʃ] *n* -1. a building where Christian services are held and where Christians can go to pray □ *There's a small village church nearby.* ▪ **to go to church** to attend services regularly at a church. -2. an organized group of Christians, e.g. the Roman Catholic Church □ *the conflict between Church and State.*

churchgoer ['tʃɜːrtʃgəʊər] *n* a person who regularly goes to church to attend religious services.

Churchill ['tʃɜːrtʃɪl], **Sir Winston** (1874–1965) British Prime Minister from 1940 to 1945, and from 1951 to 1955. He is famous for his strong leadership during World War II, and for his speeches and writing.

churchman ['tʃɜːrtʃmən] (*pl* **churchmen** [-mən]) *n* a clergyman (formal use).

Church of England *n* **the Church of England** the official branch of the Christian religion in England.

❦ THE CHURCH OF ENGLAND
The Church of England is one of two official state churches in the UK. It is a branch of the Christian religion that separated from the Roman Catholic Church in the 16th century. The head of the Church is the King or Queen, and its religious head is the Archbishop of Canterbury. Priests of the Church are allowed to marry, and since 1994, women have been accepted as priests.

Church of Scotland *n* **the Church of Scotland** the official church in Scotland.

❦ THE CHURCH OF SCOTLAND
The Church of Scotland is one of the two official state churches in the UK. It is a Presbyterian church that was established as a branch of the Christian religion in Scotland in the 16th century. Both men and women may be ministers. It has a strong missionary tradition and supports many Protestant Churches in developing countries.

churchyard ['tʃɜːᵊtʃjɑːᵊd] *n* an area close to a church where dead people can be buried.

churlish ['tʃɜːᵊlɪʃ] *adj* [person, manner, behavior] that seems rude and unfriendly □ *It would seem churlish to refuse.*

churn [tʃɜːᵊn] ◇ *n* **-1.** [for butter] a container that is used for making butter from milk. **-2.** [for milk] a metal container that is used for transporting or storing milk. ◇ *vt* = **churn up.** ◇ *vi* [stomach, water, mud] to move about violently □ *The smell was enough to make my stomach churn.*

◆ **churn out** *vt sep* **to churn sthg out** [goods, programs] to produce a lot of sthg quickly and without much care.

◆ **churn up** *vt sep* **to churn sthg up** [water, mud] to make sthg move around violently.

chute [ʃuːt] *n* a long sloping tube or passage along which water, rubbish, coal etc can be passed from one place high up to another lower down.

chutney ['tʃʌtnɪ] *n* a mixture of fruit, spices, and sugar that is eaten with meat, cheese etc □ *lime/mango chutney.*

CI *abbr of* **Channel Islands.**

CIA (*abbr of* **Central Intelligence Agency**) *n* **the CIA** the US government department that is responsible for finding out information about people or countries that might harm the interests of the USA.

cicada [US sɪ'keɪdə, GB -'kɑːdə] *n* a large winged insect that lives in warm countries and makes a loud high-pitched noise.

CID (*abbr of* **Criminal Investigation Department**) *n* **the CID** the detective branch of the British police force.

cider ['saɪdəᵊ] *n* **-1.** US a nonalcoholic drink made with apples. **-2.** GB an alcoholic drink made with apples.

CIF (*abbr of* **cost, insurance, and freight**) a condition of international trade, where the seller pays the cost of insurance and transport.

cigar [sɪ'ɡɑːᵊ] *n* a thick roll of uncut dried tobacco leaves that is smoked for pleasure.

cigarette [,sɪɡə'ret] *n* a thin roll of finely-cut, dried, rolled tobacco covered in paper that is smoked for pleasure.

cigarette butt *n* the part of a cigarette that is left after it has been smoked.

cigarette end *n* GB = **cigarette butt.**

cigarette holder *n* a thin tube that one puts on the end of a cigarette and sucks in order to smoke it.

cigarette lighter *n* a small device that produces a flame for lighting a cigarette, pipe, or cigar.

cigarette paper *n* a very thin piece of paper that can be rolled around cut tobacco to make a cigarette.

C-in-C *n abbr of* **commander in chief.**

cinch [sɪntʃ] *n* **it's a cinch** it's easy to do (informal use).

cinderblock ['sɪndəᵊblɒk] *n* US a large gray brick with a lot of small air spaces.

Cinderella [,sɪndə'relə] a character in a fairy tale. She is treated badly by her stepmother and two ugly sisters, but with the help of her fairy godmother, she goes to a ball, where a prince falls in love with her.

cinders ['sɪndəᵊz] *npl* small pieces of burnt wood, coal etc that remain after a fire has gone out.

cinecamera ['sɪnɪkæmərə] *n* GB a camera that is used for making movies.

cine-film *n* GB film that is used in a cinecamera.

cinema ['sɪnəmə] *n* **-1.** the art or business of making movies □ *This is Italian cinema at its best.* □ *a cinema director.* **-2.** GB a place where people go to watch movies □ *What's on at the cinema tonight?*

cinematic [,sɪnə'mætɪk] *adj* [effect, quality, art] that is connected with or is typical of the art of cinema.

cinnamon ['sɪnəmən] *n* a brown spice that is used as a powder or in small sticks to give flavor to cooked apples, cakes, curries etc.

cipher ['saɪfəᵊ] *n* a secret code.

circa ['sɜːᵊkə] *prep* a word used to indicate that the date which follows is not exact □ *The company was founded circa 1800.*

circle ['sɜːᵊkl] ◇ *n* **-1.** a two-dimensional shape consisting of a curved line on which any point is the same distance from the center; anything that has this shape □ *He drew a circle on the paper.* □ *They stood in a circle.* ■ **to come full circle** to reach the point at which something first began after a long series of changes or events □ *So, after 200 years, events came full circle.* □ *I felt as if my life had come full circle.* ■ **to go around in circles** to keep coming back to the same point where one was before without making any progress. **-2.** [of people] a group of people who have similar tastes, interests, or backgrounds □ *He moves in very chic circles these days.* □ *I have a very small circle of good friends.* **-3.** [in a theater] the seats in a theater or cinema that are arranged in a curve above ground level.
◇ *vt* **-1.** [word, mistake] to draw a circle around <sthg> □ *He circled the passage in red.* **-2.** [place, object] to move in a circle in the sky around <sthg> □ *The plane circled the airport.*
◇ *vi* [plane, bird] to fly in a circle in the sky □ *The vultures circled overhead.*

circuit ['sɜːᵊkɪt] *n* **-1.** ELECTRICITY a continuous path which an electric current can flow around □ *an electrical circuit.* **-2.** SPORT a trip around a particular route □ *She completed the circuit in four minutes.* **-3.** RACING a circular route that cars, runners etc race around □ *a racing circuit.* **-4.** EDUCATION, SPORT, & THEATER a series of events where a group of people meet regularly for professional or social reasons □ *the fringe theater/tennis/lecture circuit* □ *He's very well known on the cabaret circuit.*

circuit board *n* a board made of insulating material that holds an electronic circuit.

circuit breaker *n* a device that can stop people from getting an electric shock by stopping the electricity if there is a fault.

circuitous [səˈrkjuːətəs] *adj* **a circuitous route** a long and indirect way of going to a place.

circular [ˈsɜːrkjələr] ◇ *adj* -1. [table, pond] that is shaped like a circle. -2. [route, journey] that involves going to a place and coming back by a different route. -3. [argument, discussion] that keeps coming back to the same point and makes no progress. ◇ *n* a letter, notice, or advertisement that is sent to a large number of people.

circulate [ˈsɜːrkjəleɪt] ◇ *vi* -1. [blood, virus, drug] to move around the body; [air, smell] to move around a room. -2. [money, document, goods] to be passed around among a group of people □ *Illegal copies of the software have been circulating in Asia.* -3. [rumor, story] to spread among a large number of people □ *There's a rumor circulating that she's leaving.* -4. [guest, host] to talk to a lot of different people at a party □ *I'd better go and circulate.* ◇ *vt* -1. [money, document] *Please circulate this memo.* -2. [rumor, story] *Find out who's been circulating these rumors.*

circulation [ˌsɜːrkjəˈleɪʃn] *n* -1. MEDICINE & BIOLOGY the movement of blood in the body □ *I've got very poor circulation.* -2. **to be in circulation** [money] to be in public use □ *They've taken the old $5 note out of circulation.* -3. JOURNALISM the number of copies of a newspaper or magazine that are sold each time it is published □ *The paper has a circulation of 60,000.* -4. [of heat, air] the movement of heat, air etc within a place. -5. [of information] the movement of documents, information etc within a group of people □ *the free circulation of ideas.*

circumcise [ˈsɜːrkəmsaɪz] *vt* -1. [boy, man] to remove the foreskin from the penis of <a male>. -2. [girl, woman] to cut away the clitoris of <a female>.

circumcision [ˌsɜːrkəmˈsɪʒn] *n* the act or ceremony of circumcising somebody or of being circumcised.

circumference [səˈrkʌmfərəns] *n* the outside edge of a circle, lake, garden etc; the distance around this □ *How do you calculate the circumference of the Earth?*

circumflex [ˈsɜːrkəmfleks] *n* **a circumflex (accent)** an accent (ˆ) that is placed over certain vowels in some languages, e.g. French □ *"Rôle" is sometimes spelled with an "o" circumflex.*

circumnavigate [ˌsɜːrkəmˈnævɪgeɪt] *vt* to sail or fly completely around <the world>.

circumscribe [ˈsɜːrkəmskraɪb] *vt* [freedom, movement, activity] to limit or restrict <sthg>.

circumspect [ˈsɜːrkəmspekt] *adj* [behavior, manner, person] cautious □ *We must be extremely circumspect about who we tell.*

circumstances [ˈsɜːrkəmstænsɪz] *npl* the conditions in which an event takes place or in which something exists □ *They were investigating the circumstances of her disappearance.* □ *These are exceptional circumstances.* ■ **under** OR

in no circumstances an expression used to emphasize that something must not happen □ *Don't, under any circumstances, open the door.* □ *Under no circumstances may deposits be returned.* ■ **under** OR **in the circumstances** considering the situation □ *Under the circumstances, I think it would be better if you left.*

circumstantial [ˌsɜːrkəmˈstænʃl] *adj* **circumstantial evidence** facts that make it seem likely that something happened but do not prove that it did happen (formal use).

circumvent [ˌsɜːrkəmˈvent] *vt* to avoid following <a law or rule> in a clever way (formal use).

circus [ˈsɜːrkəs] *n* -1. a group of acrobats, clowns, and sometimes animals, who travel around and give performances in a large tent; a performance given by this group □ *a traveling circus* □ *Can we go to the circus?* □ *a circus clown/act.* -2. GB an open area where several streets meet □ *Piccadilly Circus.*

cirrhosis [səˈrousɪs] *n* **cirrhosis (of the liver)** a serious disease of the liver, often caused by drinking too much alcohol.

CIS (*abbr of* **Commonwealth of Independent States**): **the CIS** a union of 11 of the countries that used to be republics of the USSR, formed in 1991. It includes Armenia, Azerbaijan, Belarus, Kazakhstan, Kyrgyzistan, Moldavia, Russia, Tadjikistan, Turkmenistan, Ukraine, and Uzbekistan.

cissy [ˈsɪsɪ] (*pl* **cissies**) *n* a boy who one thinks is weak or cowardly (informal use).

cistern [ˈsɪstərn] *n* -1. [in a roof] a tank in the roof of a house in which water is stored. -2. [of a toilet] a tank attached to a toilet in which water for flushing the toilet is stored.

citation [saɪˈteɪʃn] *n* -1. [for a person] an official statement that praises somebody for something brave or good that they have done □ *He received a citation for his services to the nation.* -2. [from a book] a quotation. -3. US LAW a summons to appear in court.

cite [saɪt] *vt* -1. [passage, words] to quote <sthg>; [factor, problem] to mention <sthg> as the reason for something □ *His employers cited his frequent absences as the reason for firing him.* -2. LAW to mention <sb/sthg> as part of a case in court □ *His lover was cited in the divorce proceedings.*

citizen [ˈsɪtɪzən] *n* -1. [of a country] a person who belongs to a particular country □ *a US/British citizen.* -2. [of a city] a person who is a permanent resident of a particular town or city □ *citizens of Toronto.*

Citizens' Advice Bureau *n* **the Citizens' Advice Bureau** an organization with offices in many British and Australian towns that gives free advice to people about problems such as divorce, housing, money etc.

Citizens' Band *n* → **CB.**

Citizen's Charter *n* **the Citizen's Charter** a set of proposals made by the British government in 1991 that stated the standards of service that government departments should provide and the compensation that people can claim for poor service.

citizenship ['sɪtɪzənʃɪp] *n* the state of being a citizen of a particular country □ *He was given French citizenship after 5 years.*

citric acid [,sɪtrɪk-] *n* a weak acid that comes from citrus fruits.

citrus fruit ['sɪtrəs-] *n* a fruit, e.g. an orange or grapefruit, that has a sharp acidic taste.

city ['sɪtɪ] (*pl* **cities**) *n* -1. a large town where a lot of people live and where a lot of business and social activity takes place □ *Mexico City is one of the biggest cities in the world.* □ *City life is so stressful these days.* -2. US the local government of a city.
◆ **City** *n* GB **the City** a small area in the center of London where all the major banks, including the Bank of England, and the stock exchange are situated □ *She works in the City.* □ *a City stockbroker.*

❦ THE CITY
The City, London's financial district, is like a small independent city with its own administration and police force. People often talk about "the City" when they mean the world of finance in Britain generally.

City and Guilds *n* -1. **the City and Guilds (of London Institute)** a British organization that gives qualifications in technical subjects. -2. a qualification given by the City and Guilds.

city center *n* the center of a city, where all the main stores, businesses etc are.

city government *n* US the work involved in running the affairs of a city; the officials who do this work.

city hall *n* US a building used by a city's administration; the administration itself.

city planner *n* US a person who is responsible for city planning.

city planning *n* US the work of planning, designing, and developing the buildings, roads, parks etc in a town or city.

city technology college *n* a type of secondary school in Britain that specializes in technological subjects, is based in inner-city areas, and is funded by industry.

civic ['sɪvɪk] *adj* [leader, duty, pride] that is connected with a city or its citizens.

civic center *n* the buildings in a town that belong to the local government, e.g. the offices or sports facilities.

civil ['sɪvl] *adj* -1. [disorder, strife] that involves the different groups of people who live in a country; [aviation] that is not military but is for the ordinary citizens of a country; [ceremony] that is not religious. -2. [person] who is polite in a formal way □ *He could at least have been more civil.*

civil defense *n* the organization and training of ordinary citizens to deal with enemy attack.

civil disobedience *n* the refusal of people to obey a particular law, pay a tax etc as a pro-

test against something the government has done or wants to do.

civil engineer *n* an engineer who is qualified to plan, build, and repair public buildings, roads, bridges etc.

civil engineering *n* the work or profession of a civil engineer □ *She's studying civil engineering.*

civilian [sə'vɪlɪən] *n* a person who does not belong to the armed forces □ *civilian clothes/life* □ *a civilian organization.*

civility [sə'vɪlətɪ] *n* the quality of being polite in a formal way.
◆ **civilities** *npl* polite remarks.

civilization [US ,sɪvlə'zeɪʃn, GB -aɪ'zeɪʃn] *n* -1. the state of having a very developed society and economy □ *Mesopotamia is believed to be the birthplace of civilization.* □ *This could be the end of civilization as we know it.* -2. a society which is culturally, socially, and economically advanced □ *an ancient civilization.*

civilize, -ise ['sɪvəlaɪz] *vt* to change <a person, society> etc from being badly educated, organized etc to a more advanced state □ *His wife has a civilizing influence on him.*

civilized ['sɪvəlaɪzd] *adj* -1. [society, people, tribe] that has a high level of civilization □ *This shouldn't happen in a civilized country.* -2. [person] polite and cultured; [discussion] polite rather than angry or violent □ *It was a pleasantly civilized dinner.* □ *Let's talk about this in a civilized manner.*

civil law *n* a collective term for the laws connected with personal matters, e.g. divorce, property, and business, rather than criminal behavior.

civil liberties *npl* the rights of individual people to do what they like so long as this does not affect other people's rights.

civil list *n* **the civil list** GB the money that is given by Parliament to the Royal Family every year.

civil rights *npl* the rights of individual people to be treated equally, regardless of their race, sex, or religion □ *a civil rights campaigner.*

Civil Rights Movement *n* **the Civil Rights Movement** a movement that began in the USA in the 1950s in order to fight for equal rights for minorities, especially blacks.

❦ CIVIL RIGHTS MOVEMENT
The Civil Rights Movement in the USA began in 1954, when the Supreme Court passed a law that said that black people could go to the same schools as white people. Later, in the 1960s, many peaceful protests were organized by leaders like Martin Luther King to try to win better treatment for black people. The Civil Rights Act (1964) and the Voting Rights Act (1965) made it illegal to treat minorities such as black people differently from white people, either at work or in public places.

---

civil servant *n* a person who works in the civil service □ *a high-grade civil servant.*

civil service *n* the non-political organization that is responsible for the administrative work of a government, but not including the military or judicial departments.

civil war *n* a war that is fought between citizens of the same country.

cl *n abbr of* **centiliter.**

clad [klæd] *adj* **to be clad in white/silk etc** to be dressed in white/silk etc (literary use).

claim [kleɪm] ◇ *n* -1. **a claim to sthg** [to somebody's land, money] the right to have or own something □ *He has a rightful claim to the inheritance.* ■ **to lay claim to sthg** to state that one has a right to sthg. -2. **a claim on sb** the right one feels one has to ask sb for something, especially their time or attention □ *He acts as if he has some kind of claim on you.* -3. [for money] a request for money that one believes one has a right to □ *a pay/insurance claim* □ *Don't forget to put in a claim for expenses.* □ *The owner has made a claim for the damage to his property.* -4. [by somebody] a statement made by somebody before other people know if it is true □ *His claim of unfair dismissal was rejected by the court.*

◇ *vt* -1. [money, property, right] to ask for <sthg that one believes one has a right to> □ *He claimed the money back on expenses.* □ *She claimed the umbrella from lost and found.* □ *You should be able to claim it on your insurance.* -2. **to claim responsibility/credit for sthg** to state that the responsibility/credit for sthg belongs to oneself □ *You can't claim all the credit for the idea.* -3. **to claim (that)...** to declare that something is true before other people know if it is true □ *She claimed (that) the company had made an illegal deal.* ■ **to claim to do sthg** to claim that one does sthg. □ *The cult claims to have a membership of 500,000.* -4. **the accident claimed 50 lives** 50 people died in the accident.

◇ *vi* **to claim for sthg** [for postage, damage] to officially ask for the money to pay for sthg □ *Remember to claim for expenses.* ■ **to claim on one's insurance** to ask an insurance company to pay for the loss or damage of something.

claimant ['kleɪmənt] *n* a person who is claiming something □ *one of the claimants to the title* □ *All claimants should wait at the counter.*

claim form *n* a form that one has to fill in in order to claim something such as an insurance payment.

clairvoyant [kleə'vɔɪənt] ◇ *adj* [person] who is thought to be able to see the future. ◇ *n* a person who is clairvoyant.

clam [klæm] (*pt & pp* **clammed**, *cont* **clamming**) *n* an animal that lives on the bottom of the sea and has a soft edible body protected by a hard shell that can open and close.

◆ **clam up** *vi* to stop talking because one is afraid or does not want to talk (informal use).

clamber ['klæmbər] *vi* to climb with difficulty, using one's hands and feet □ *We clambered up the tree/down the slope.*

clammy ['klæmɪ] (*compar* **clammier**, *superl* **clammiest**) *adj* [hand, forehead] cold and wet; [weather] humid and unpleasant.

clamor US, **clamour** GB ['klæmər] ◇ *n* -1. a loud and continuous noise of many voices talking or shouting together □ *I could hardly hear what he was saying above the clamor.* -2. a very strong expression of a demand, complaint, or anger made by a large number of people □ *the growing clamor for a change to the tax system.* ◇ *vi* **to clamor for sthg** to demand sthg very strongly and insistently □ *The public is clamoring for change.*

clamorous ['klæmərəs] *adj* [applause, voices, demands] very loud.

clamour *n & vi* GB = **clamor.**

clamp [klæmp] ◇ *n* -1. [for carpentry, surgery] a tool that has two metal parts joined by a screw, spring etc that closes two things together or forces two things apart. -2. a wheelclamp. ◇ *vt* -1. to put a clamp on <sthg> □ *My car's been clamped!* -2. to hold <sthg> in position firmly using a clamp.

◆ **clamp down** *vi* to begin to take strong measures to control or prevent something □ *The police are clamping down on drunk driving.*

clampdown ['klæmpdaʊn] *n* the act of clamping down on something □ *a clampdown on crime.*

clan [klæn] *n* a group of families, especially in Scotland, that have the same name and are originally descended from the same family □ *the clan tartan* □ *a clan gathering.*

clandestine [klæn'destən] *adj* [movement, meeting, organization] that is secret, often because it is not legal □ *Nobody knows how many clandestine immigrants there are in the city.*

clang [klæŋ] ◇ *n* a loud ringing noise that is made when something that is made of metal hits something else □ *The gates made a loud clang.* □ *the clang of the bell.* ◇ *vi* [bell, gate, gong] to make a clang □ *The iron doors clanged shut behind her.*

clank [klæŋk] ◇ *n* a sharp, loud, metallic noise like that of a chain being moved □ *the clank of chains.* ◇ *vi* [chain, machinery] to make a sharp, loud, metallic noise □ *machines clanking all around.*

clap [klæp] (*pt & pp* **clapped**, *cont* **clapping**) ◇ *n* -1. the sound made by a person hitting the flat part of their hands together, often to show approval; the act of hitting one's hands together in this way. -2. **a clap of thunder** a sudden loud noise made by thunder.

◇ *vt* -1. to hit <one's hands> together once or repeatedly, often to show approval □ *"Let's begin!" she said, clapping her hands.* -2. to put <sb/sthg> somewhere firmly □ *She clapped her hand to her mouth.* ◇ *vi* [audience, crowd] to clap one's hands □ *Everybody clapped wildly when she finished singing.*

clapboard [US 'klæbrd, GB 'klæpbɔːd] *n* US wooden boards fixed in rows to the outside of a building to protect it from the weather □ *a clapboard house.*

clapperboard ['klæpərbɔːd] *n* a small black board, made of two pieces of wood that make a loud noise at the beginning of each scene when a movie is being made, so that the picture can be matched with the sound.

clapping ['klæpɪŋ] *n* the act or sound of hitting the flat part of one's hands together, often to show approval.

claptrap ['klæptræp] *n* nonsense (informal use).

claret [US 'klerət, GB 'klær-] *n* **-1.** a type of red wine that comes from the Bordeaux region in France. **-2.** a deep red color.

clarification [US ,klerɪfɪ'keɪʃn, GB ,klær-] *n*: see **clarify** □ Your statement requires some clarification.

clarify [US 'klerɪfaɪ, GB 'klær-] (*pt* & *pp* **clarified**) *vt* [matter, point, statement] to make <sthg> clear □ Could you clarify an earlier point for me...

clarinet [US ,klerə'net, GB ,klær-] *n* a long thin musical instrument that is played by blowing into a mouthpiece with a reed in it.

clarity [US 'klerətɪ, GB 'klærətɪ] *n* **-1.** [of an explanation, text] the quality of being clear and easy to understand □ I find this report somewhat lacking in clarity. **-2.** [of one's mind] the ability to understand something clearly □ I could now see things with greater clarity.

clash [klæʃ] ◇ *n* **-1.** [of personalities] a strong contrast □ There is a personality clash between us. **-2.** [between people] a fight □ There were renewed clashes with the police. **-3.** [between forces] a disagreement □ a clash of interests. **-4.** [of metal] a loud noise like metal hitting metal □ the clash of cymbals.
◇ *vi* **-1.** [opinions, beliefs, policies] to be in conflict with each other □ This statement clashes with what was previously said. **-2.** [colors, styles] to look unpleasant together □ That sofa clashes with the carpet. **-3.** [protesters, rival groups] to fight □ Demonstrators clashed with police. **-4.** [colleagues, politicians] to argue with each other □ We clashed on a number of points. □ I've clashed with him about policy before. **-5.** [appointments, events] to happen at the same time, so that it is not possible to go to both □ The conference clashes with our meeting. **-6.** [cymbals] to make a loud metallic noise.

clasp [US klæsp, GB klɑːsp] ◇ *n* a metal fastener that holds the two ends or sides of a belt, necklace, bracelet etc together. ◇ *vt* to hold <sb/sthg> tightly □ She clasped the table as if she was going to fall.

class [US klæs, GB klɑːs] ◇ *n* **-1.** [in a school, college] a group of students who are learning together □ They're a good class. □ In my class there were only 10 students. **-2.** [in a subject] a lesson or series of lessons □ a French/evening class. **-3.** [in society] a group in society whose members have similar status □ He comes from the lower/upper class. □ a member of the middle classes □ the class system □ class conflict. **-4.** [of animals, plants, objects] a group of things that share the same set of characteristics □ A lion is an animal of the class "Mammalia". **-5.** a particular level of quality □ business class passengers □ second-class accommodations ■ **to be in a class of one's own** to be much better at something than other

people □ As far as translations go, she's in a class of her own. **-6. to have class** to have style and elegance (informal use) □ He's got a lot of class.
◇ *vt* **to class sb as sthg** to consider sb to be sthg □ Even though he's been playing for two years, he's still classed as a beginner.

classic ['klæsɪk] ◇ *adj* **-1.** [example, mistake, case] very typical □ What you are seeing here are the classic symptoms of schizophrenia. **-2.** [book, work of art, movie] that is of very high quality and is used as a standard in judging other works of a similar kind □ Charles Dickens' classic story of nineteenth-century England. ◇ *n* a classic book, movie, play etc □ a classic in French cinema.

◆ **classics** *npl* Latin and Greek language, literature, and culture as a subject of study.

classical ['klæsɪkl] *adj* **-1.** [literature, ballet, architecture] that is based on traditional methods or principles. **-2.** [poetry, civilization, sculpture] that is connected with the civilizations of Ancient Greece and Rome.

classical music *n* a serious traditional kind of music played only on instruments invented a long time ago.

classification [,klæsɪfɪ'keɪʃn] *n* **-1.** the act or system of putting information, things, facts etc into groups so that they can be found easily or understood better □ What is now needed is classification of the relevant documents. **-2.** a group into which information, things, facts etc are put □ They've added a new classification.

classified ['klæsɪfaɪd] *adj* [information, document, material] that has been declared secret by a government.

classified ad *n* a small advertisement in a newspaper, usually placed by an individual or small business, that offers goods for sale, employment, services etc, or which asks for employment, goods etc.

classify ['klæsɪfaɪ] (*pt* & *pp* **classified**) *vt* [plant, animal, book] to put <sthg> in a particular group of things of a similar type so that it can be found easily or understood better □ Cars are classified according to engine capacity and value. □ Such people are usually classified as villains.

classless [US 'klæsləs, GB 'klɑːs-] *adj* [society] in which divisions between social classes are not important.

classmate [US 'klæsmeɪt, GB 'klɑːs-] *n* a person who one studies with in the same class.

classroom [US 'klæsruːm, GB 'klɑːs-] *n* a room in a school where teaching takes place.

classy [US 'klæsɪ, GB 'klɑːsɪ] (*compar* **classier**, *superl* **classiest**) *adj* [car, person] that one thinks is stylish and attractive (informal use).

clatter ['klætər] ◇ *n* the unpleasant noise made by several hard objects knocking against each other or against something else □ the clatter of pots and pans. ◇ *vi* to make a clatter □ The carriage clattered over the cobblestones.

clause [klɔːz] *n* **-1.** LAW a section in a legal

document □ *They've added a clause to protect maternity rights.* **-2.** GRAMMAR a part of a sentence that contains at least a verb and a subject □ *a subordinate/main clause.*

claustrophobia [ˌklɔːstrəˈfoʊbjə] *n* a strong feeling of anxiety one has when one is in a small enclosed space or among a crowd of people.

claustrophobic [ˌklɔːstrəˈfoʊbɪk] *adj* **-1.** [room, atmosphere] that gives one a feeling of claustrophobia □ *It's getting rather claustrophobic in here.* **-2. to be claustrophobic** to suffer from claustrophobia □ *I began to feel extremely claustrophobic.*

claw [klɔː] ◇ *n* **-1.** [of an animal, bird] one of the sharp curved nails at the end of an animal's paw or a bird's foot. **-2.** [of an insect] a curved part at the end of the legs of some insects and sea animals, e.g. a crab or scorpion, that opens and closes and is used mainly for catching food. ◇ *vt* to tear <sb/sthg> using claws □ *The cat was clawing the sofa.* ◇ *vi* **to claw at sthg** to pull or tear sthg using claws.

◆ **claw back** *vt sep* **to claw money back** GB to get money back, especially through taxation.

clay [kleɪ] *n* a substance, found in soil, that is soft and sticky when wet and hard when dry and is used to make pots, bricks etc.

clay pigeon shooting *n* the sport of shooting at small clay disks that are fired into the air by a machine.

clean [kliːn] ◇ *adj* **-1.** [shirt, room, floor] that has no marks or dirt; that has been washed or cleaned; [person] who keeps themselves and the place where they live free from dirt □ *Are your hands clean?* □ *There are clean glasses on the shelf.* □ *He's very clean and neat.* **-2.** [page, piece of paper] that has not been written on. □ *Have you a clean sheet of paper?* **-3.** LAW [record, driver's license] that does not have any legal offences recorded on it. ■ **to come clean about sthg** to admit sthg (informal use). **-4.** [joke, humor] that does not involve sex or anything considered immoral □ *Look, it was just some good clean fun, nothing more.* **-5.** [outline, design] simple in design □ *The apartment is full of clean lines and white surfaces.* **-6.** [cut, break] neat and regular. □ *It's a clean fracture, so it will mend easily.* **-7. to be clean** [person] to have stopped taking illegal drugs (informal use). ◇ *adv* completely (informal use) □ *The bullet went clean through his chest.* □ *I clean forgot we were going out tonight.* ◇ *vt* [house, window, clothes] to make <sthg> clean by washing, sweeping, scrubbing etc □ *Don't forget to clean the car.* ◇ *vi* **-1.** to make something clean □ *I've been cleaning all day.* **-2.** to work as a cleaner □ *She cleans for the Joneses.* ◇ *n* the act of cleaning □ *This room needs a good clean.*

◆ **clean out** *vt sep* **-1. to clean sthg out** [room, cupboard, drawer] to make sthg clean and tidy, especially by throwing out all the things that one no longer needs. **-2. to clean**

sb/sthg out [person, house] to take or steal everything, e.g. money or possessions, from sb/sthg (informal use).

◆ **clean up** *vt sep* **to clean sthg up** [room, house] to make sthg clean and neat □ *I tried to clean everything up before they came home.* □ *You really should clean yourself up.* ■ **to clean sthg up** [mess, debris] to get rid of sthg by washing, wiping etc.

clean-cut *adj* [boy, man] who looks neat and tidy in a way that makes one think they are honest.

cleaner [ˈkliːnəʳ] *n* **-1.** [in a house, office] a person whose job is to clean people's houses, offices etc □ *an office cleaner.* **-2.** [for a kitchen, bathroom] a substance that is used for cleaning □ *a floor cleaner* □ *oven cleaner.* **-3.** a machine that is used for cleaning something □ *a carpet cleaner.* **-4. the cleaner's** the dry cleaner's □ *My coat is at the cleaner's.*

cleaning [ˈkliːnɪŋ] *n* the activity of making a house, office etc clean □ *I have to do the cleaning before I leave.*

cleaning lady *n* a woman whose job is to clean people's houses, offices etc.

cleanliness [ˈklenlɪnəs] *n* the habit of keeping things or oneself clean □ *Cleanliness is something I'm particularly fussy about.*

clean-living *adj* [person] who leads a healthy life and does not smoke, drink, take drugs etc.

cleanly [ˈkliːnlɪ] *adv* [cut, break] *see* **clean** □ *The plate broke cleanly down the middle.*

cleanse [klenz] *vt* **-1.** [wound, skin] to make <sthg> completely clean □ *He cleansed the cut with disinfectant.* **-2.** to make <sb/sthg> free of something unpleasant or impure □ *He felt the need to cleanse himself of the memory of this terrible weekend.*

cleanser [ˈklenzəʳ] *n* a lotion or liquid that is used for cleaning something, especially one's face □ *a skin cleanser.*

clean-shaven [-ˈʃeɪvn] *adj* [man] who has no beard or moustache.

cleanup [ˈkliːnʌp] *n* the process of cleaning up □ *a cleanup campaign/operation.*

clear [klɪəʳ] ◇ *adj* **-1.** [light] that is strong and pure, and makes it easy to see; [sky, day] that is light and has no clouds; [color] light and bright; [eyes] that are not red, and look honest and calm; [water, air] that looks clean and fresh □ *Everything looked different in the clear light of day.* □ *On a clear day you can see right across to the bay.* □ *His eyes were a beautiful clear blue.* □ *She had attractive eyes, clear and expressive.* □ *clear mountain streams.* **-2.** [signal, explanation, argument] that is easy to understand □ *The report's recommendations were brief and clear.* □ *I want you to leave, is that clear?* ■ **to make sthg clear to sb** [feelings, opinion] to make sb understand sthg by using words, or in other ways □ *I'd like to make clear my thoughts on the subject.* ■ **to make it clear that...** to explain in a way that is easy to understand that... □ *I made it clear that if her work didn't improve, she would have to go.* ■

to make oneself clear to explain what one is trying to say, especially when this is unpleasant, in a way that is easy to understand □ *Do I make myself clear?* □ *You've made yourself abundantly clear.* **-3.** [difference, answer, improvement] that is easy to see, notice, or recognize □ *It's clear to me that you haven't understood.* □ *We need to win by a clear majority.* □ *It's a clear case of racial prejudice.* **-4.** [sound, voice, speaker] that is easy to hear □ *The telephone line to Australia was amazingly clear.* **-5.** [glass, plastic, liquid] that one can see through completely □ *a clear gel.* **-6.** [skin, complexion] that is healthy and has no spots. **-7.** [mind, thinking, idea] that is not confused □ *I need a clear head to deal with statistics.* □ *I'm not quite clear on your reasons for leaving.* **-8.** [road, desk, space] that is free of blockages or things that take up space; [week, hour] when one does not have work to do □ *My garden is now clear of weeds.* □ *The highway is now clear after the accident.* □ *There's a clear view of the Alps.* □ *Please keep Fridays clear.* **-9. my/his conscience is clear, I have/he has a clear conscience** I have/he has not done anything to feel guilty about. **-10.** a word used to say that a particular sum of money is what is left after expenses, taxes etc have been taken off □ *We made a clear profit of $6000.*

◇ *adv* **to jump/stand clear** to jump to/stand in another place so that one is not in the way □ *Stand clear of the doors!* ▪ **to steer clear of sb/sthg** not to go near sb/sthg □ *Steer clear of him — he's a bad influence.*

◇ *n* **to be in the clear** not to be in danger □ *The doctors told her she was now in the clear.* ▪ **to put sb in the clear** to show that sb cannot be guilty □ *New evidence puts him in the clear.*

◇ *vt* **-1.** [road, desk, space] to remove the blockages or things that take up space in or on <sthg> □ *We cleared the table and sat down with a glass of whiskey.* ▪ **to clear one's throat** to cough to prepare oneself to speak, or to tell people that one is going to speak. **-2.** [fallen tree, ruins, mess] to remove <sthg that is in the way> □ *The snow has now been cleared from main roads.* **-3.** [fence, hurdle] to jump over <sthg> without touching it □ *The pole-vaulter cleared three meters.* **-4. to clear a debt** to pay money that one owes so that one does not have a debt any more. **-5.** [plan, proposal] to give permission for <sthg> □ *The Governor has cleared the new airport.* □ *The plane was cleared for take off.* **-6. to be cleared of sthg** [of a crime] to be not guilty of sthg □ *Simpson was finally cleared of murder.* □ *She was cleared of all charges.* ▪ **to clear one's name** to prove that one has not committed a crime. **-7. to be cleared** [check] to be accepted by a bank after it has made sure that one has enough money in one's account.

◇ *vi* **-1.** [fog, mist, smoke] to gradually disappear □ *When the mist cleared, the rocks were plainly visible.* **-2.** [weather, sky] = **clear up.**

◆ **clear away** *vt sep* **to clear sthg away** [plates, books, mess] to remove sthg that is in the

way □ *If I clear away these magazines you can sit here.*

◆ **clear out** ◇ *vt sep* **to clear sthg out** [room, drawer] to remove objects that are not useful any more from sthg; [belongings, clothes] to throw away sthg in this way □ *I'm clearing out all my old books.* □ *I cleared out my office before I went on vacation.* ◇ *vi* to leave a place (informal use) □ *They cleared out without paying their bills.*

◆ **clear up** ◇ *vt sep* **-1. to clear sthg up** [room, house] to make sthg tidy and clean; [mess, dishes] to remove sthg to make a place tidy and clean □ *You'd better clear up your bedroom before your mother sees it.* □ *It'll take ages to clear up this mess.* **-2. to clear sthg up** [dispute, misunderstanding] to end sthg by making or helping people to agree or understand each other; [mystery, problem] to find the answer to sthg that is difficult to understand or solve □ *Let's clear up this matter once and for all.* □ *There's just one point I'd like you to clear up.*

◇ *vi* **-1.** [weather, sky] to become sunny after a period of bad weather □ *The rain cleared up and the sun came out.* **-2.** [illness, infection] to be cured □ *The rash will clear up in a few days.* **-3.** [person] to make a place tidy and clean □ *Don't forget to clear up after you've finished!*

clearance ['klɪərəns] *n* **-1.** [of garbage, furniture] the removal of things that are not wanted or needed □ *a company that organizes house clearances.* **-2.** [to do something] permission □ *The airplane was waiting for clearance to land.* **-3.** [for a vehicle] the amount of space around a vehicle that allows it to move without hitting an object, building, or another vehicle.

clearance sale *n* a sale in which goods are sold at a reduced price, e.g. because a store is closing or because the owner wants to sell the stock quickly.

clear-cut *adj* [issue, division, advantage] that is simple and clear □ *The choice is clear-cut: do we accept or not?*

clear-headed [-'hedəd] *adj* [person] who is able to think clearly, especially in a difficult situation □ *You need to stay clear-headed when you're under pressure.*

clearing ['klɪərɪŋ] *n* an open space in the middle of a forest or wood.

clearing bank *n* GB a bank that serves ordinary customers, e.g. by transferring checks and money.

clearing house *n* **-1.** an organization that collects and distributes information □ *a university clearing house.* **-2.** FINANCE an institution where banks exchange checks, settle accounts etc.

clearing-up *n* the tidying and cleaning that is done after a meal, party etc.

clearly ['klɪərlɪ] *adv* **-1.** [speak, think, explain] see **clear.** **-2.** a word used when one expects people to agree with what one is saying, or when something is easy to understand or see □ *Frances Chadwick is clearly the best candidate for the job.* □ *The man was clearly nervous.* □ *Clearly there has been a mistake.*

clearout ['klɪəraʊt] *n* the act of throwing away a lot of unwanted things from one's house, office, room etc.

clear-sighted [-'saɪtəd] *adj* [person] who can understand things clearly and make sensible decisions.

clearway ['klɪəˈweɪ] *n* GB a road on which cars are not allowed to stop unless they have problems.

cleavage ['kliːvɪdʒ] *n* the space between a woman's breasts, especially when shown by a low-cut top or dress □ *a dress that shows some cleavage.*

cleaver ['kliːvəˈ] *n* a wide metal blade with a handle that is used especially for chopping meat □ *a meat cleaver.*

clef [klef] *n* a symbol (𝄞) or (𝄢) that is written at the beginning of a piece of music to indicate the pitch of the music.

cleft [kleft] *n* a crack or narrow opening in the ground or in a rock.

cleft palate *n* a medical condition in which somebody has a split along the roof of their mouth that makes it difficult to talk.

clematis ['klemətəs] *n* a plant with brightly-colored flowers that grows on walls or on other plants.

clemency ['klemənsɪ] *n* **to show clemency** to treat a criminal in a way that is not severe (formal use).

clementine ['kleməntaɪn] *n* GB a fruit similar to a small orange.

clench [klentʃ] *vt* to hold or squeeze <sthg> tightly ■ **to clench one's fist** to close one's fist tightly. ■ **to clench one's teeth** to close one's teeth together tightly.

Cleopatra [ˌkliːəˈpætrə] (69–30 BC) Queen of Egypt from 51 to 48 BC and 47 to 30 BC, and the lover of Julius Caesar and Mark Antony. She committed suicide.

clergy ['klɜːˈdʒɪ] *npl* **the clergy** all the people who are specially trained to serve in the Christian Church, e.g. priests and bishops.

clergyman ['klɜːˈdʒɪmən] (*pl* **clergymen** [-mən]) *n* a man who is a member of the clergy.

cleric ['klerɪk] *n* a member of the clergy.

clerical ['klerɪkl] *adj* **-1.** [work, staff, job] that is connected with the routine administration of an office. **-2.** RELIGION [duty, matter] *see* **clergy.**

clerk [US klɜːrk, GB klɑːk] *n* **-1.** [in an office] a person whose job is to do the routine administrative tasks in an office, e.g. filing and keeping records □ *an office/a filing clerk.* **-2.** [in a court] a person who is in charge of keeping records in a court. **-3.** US [in a store] a sales assistant.

Cleveland ['kliːvlənd] **-1.** an industrial city in Ohio, USA, on Lake Erie. POPULATION: 505,616. **-2.** a county in northeastern England until 1996. SIZE: 583 sq kms. POPULATION: 554,500. ADMINISTRATIVE CENTER: Middlesbrough.

clever ['klevəˈ] *adj* **-1.** [idea, invention] that works well and shows the skill and intelli-gence of the person who thought of it □ *a really clever little device.* **-2.** [person] who is physically skillful □ *I'm not very clever with my hands.* **-3.** [politician, lawyer] who is good at using their intelligence to get what they want, sometimes in an unfair way □ *It was a clever move, marrying the boss's daughter!* **-4.** GB [person] who is quick to understand and learn things; [action, behavior] that shows intelligence □ *She was always clever at school.* □ *That wasn't a very clever thing to do!*

cleverly ['klevəˈlɪ] *adv* [arrange, manage] in a way that shows skill and intelligence □ *a very cleverly worded statement.*

cliché [US kliːˈʃeɪ, GB 'kliːʃeɪ] *n* something that has been done, said, or thought so often before that it is not considered interesting or useful □ *I was tired of hearing the same old cli-chés about equality and democracy.*

click [klɪk] ◇ *n* a short quiet sound like a camera taking a picture □ *I heard the click of the door behind me.* ◇ *vt* to move or hit <one's fingers, heels> etc against each other to make a click □ *"Waiter!" he said, clicking his fingers.* ■ **to click one's tongue** to make a noise like a click with one's tongue against the top of one's mouth. ◇ *vi* **-1.** [camera, heels, telephone] to make a click □ *The gate clicked shut behind him.* **-2.** **it suddenly** OR **all clicked** it suddenly became clear (informal use) □ *It suddenly clicked what was going on.*

◆ **click on** *vt fus* COMPUTING **to click on sthg** [icon, word] to press the button on a mouse in order to select sthg on a screen □ *Click on "maximize".*

client [ˌklaɪənt] *n* a person or organization that buys services or goods from a business or individual □ *Manfred & Co are one of our best clients.*

clientele [US 'klaɪən'tel, GB ˌkliːɒn-] *n* the customers or clients of a business or individual □ *They have a very select clientele.*

client-server *comp* [technology, database] that uses a central computer to provide services for other computers on the same network.

cliff [klɪf] *n* a wall or very steep slope made of rock, especially on a coast.

cliffhanger ['klɪfhæŋəˈ] *n* a part of a book, movie etc in which it seems that something very dramatic is going to happen, but that makes one wait to see what happens.

climactic [klaɪˈmæktɪk] *adj* [moment, point] that is especially exciting or important, usually because it is near or at the end of something.

climate ['klaɪmət] *n* **-1.** WEATHER the kind of weather conditions that an area, country etc normally has □ *a cold/warm/tropical climate.* **-2.** [in society] the kind of situation created by the way a group of people feel about a particular subject at a particular time □ *I don't think that would be wise, given the current political climate.*

climatic [klaɪˈmætɪk] *adj* [conditions, change] that is connected with the climate of a place □ *climatic changes owing to the greenhouse effect.*

climax ['klaɪmæks] *n* **-1.** [of an event] the most exciting or important point in an experience, event, or series of events, which usually comes at or near the end □ *The climax of his career came when he won the Nobel Prize.* **-2.** [during sex] the point at which a person reaches the highest level of physical pleasure during sex.

climb [klaɪm] ◇ *n* **-1.** [by a person] the act of climbing □ *The climb took three hours.* **-2.** a hill, slope etc that one climbs □ *a steep climb.* ◇ *vt* [tree, ladder, mountain] to go up <sthg> toward the top □ *the first woman to climb K2.* ◇ *vi* **-1.** [person] **to climb up/over/into etc sthg** to move carefully up/over/into etc sthg, often with difficulty □ *She climbed out of bed.* **-2.** [plant] to grow in an upward direction □ *The ivy had started to climb up the walls.* **-3.** [road, plane] to go upward □ *The path began to climb steeply.* **-4.** [price, cost] to increase □ *Our profits have been steadily climbing all year.*

◆ **climb down** *vi* GB [person] to change one's plans or admit that one was wrong, especially to avoid a serious conflict □ *The newspaper finally climbed down over the allegations.*

climb-down *n* GB an act of climbing down □ *The company's change of policy should not be seen as a climb-down.*

climber ['klaɪmə^r] *n* a person who climbs mountains, hills, rocks etc □ *an experienced climber.*

climbing ['klaɪmɪŋ] *n* the activity or sport of going up mountains, hills, rocks etc □ *I took up climbing ten years ago.*

climbing frame *n* GB a metal, plastic, or wooden structure of bars on which children can play and climb.

climbing plant *n* a plant that grows upward on walls or other plants.

climes [klaɪmz] *npl* **sunnier/warmer etc climes** a sunnier/warmer etc part of the world (literary use).

clinch [klɪntʃ] *vt* [argument, deal, victory] to finally succeed in winning <sthg> □ *We're about to clinch a deal with a Polish company to supply the parts.* □ *The team clinched the title with a last-minute goal.*

cling [klɪŋ] (*pt* & *pp* **clung**) *vi* **-1.** [person] to hold on very tightly to somebody or something □ *We clung on, hoping to be rescued.* **-2.** [clothes, smell] to stick or stay close to somebody □ *His wet shirt was clinging to his chest.* **-3. to cling to sb** to be very dependent on sb emotionally and spend a lot of time with them so that they have little freedom □ *She's five, but she still clings to her mother.* ■ **to cling to sthg** [to a principle, hope, idea] to continue to believe in sthg even if it is no longer appropriate □ *He had clung for so long to a belief in the value of honesty and hard work.*

clingfilm ['klɪŋfɪlm] *n* GB very thin transparent plastic that is put over food to keep it fresh.

clinging ['klɪŋɪŋ] *adj* **-1.** [child, wife] who clings to somebody. **-2.** [clothing] that fits or sticks closely to the body □ *a clinging dress.*

clinic ['klɪnɪk] *n* a place, often part of a hospital, where people go to be treated and to receive advice for particular medical problems □ *a baby/a chest/an eye clinic.*

clinical ['klɪnɪkl] *adj* **-1.** MEDICINE [training, examination, test] that is connected with real patients rather than theory □ *She works as a clinical psychologist.* **-2.** [person, approach] that shows no emotion □ *The program dealt with the issue in a fairly clinical way.* **-3.** [room, furniture] that is simple, practical, and has no character or warmth □ *Her plain white walls simply looked clinical.*

clinically ['klɪnɪklɪ] *adv* [examine, test, approach] *see* **clinical** □ *He was clinically depressed at the time.*

clink [klɪŋk] ◇ *n* a short quiet sound like that of two bottles hitting each other lightly □ *the clink of glasses.* ◇ *vi* [cups, glasses, bottles] to make a clink.

clip [klɪp] (*pt* & *pp* **clipped**, *cont* **clipping**) ◇ *n* **-1.** a small device for holding things such as pieces of paper together, or for keeping something such as one's hair in place. □ *She fastened the papers together with a clip.* **-2.** a short part of a movie or TV program that is shown separately, e.g. for publicity. □ *They showed a clip of "Star Wars".* ◇ *vt* **-1.** [paper, badge] to fasten <sthg> to something else with a clip □ *He clipped the papers together.* **-2.** [hedge, hair] to cut <sthg> so that it is short and tidy □ *The blackberry bushes need clipping.* ■ **to clip an article** to cut an article out of a newspaper, magazine etc. **-3.** [person, animal] to hit <sb/sthg> lightly (informal use) □ *The ball just clipped the edge of the post.*

◆ **clip on** *vi* [tie, microphone, earring] to be designed so that it can be fixed to something else with a clip.

clipboard ['klɪpbɔː^rd] *n* a small board with a clip at the top that holds pieces of paper in place so that one can write on them while standing.

clip-on *adj* [earring, bow-tie, badge] that clips on to something.

clipped [klɪpt] *adj* **-1.** [voice, speech, accent] that makes words sound very short. **-2.** [hair, moustache] that is cut to a short tidy length.

clippers ['klɪpə^rz] *npl* a tool or machine for clipping hair, nails, or grass □ *a pair of nail clippers.*

clipping ['klɪpɪŋ] *n* an article or section that has been cut from a newspaper or magazine □ *a pile of newspaper clippings.*

clique [kliːk] *n* a group of people who behave as if they are special and do not accept other people as part of their group.

clitoris ['klɪtərəs] *n* a part of the woman's sexual organs that is found just above the vagina and that causes pleasurable feelings and orgasm during sex.

cloak [kləʊk] ◇ *n* **-1.** a piece of clothing like a coat without sleeves that is worn around the shoulders and fastened at the neck. **-2.** something that is used to keep an activity, intention etc secret □ *The business is a* *cloak for drug-dealing.* ◇ *vt* **to be cloaked in sthg** [in mist, mystery] to be covered by sthg in a way that hides it.

cloak-and-dagger *adj* [behavior, story] that involves mystery and secrecy in a way that is often unnecessary.

cloakroom ['kloʊkruːm] *n* -1. a place in a restaurant, museum, theater etc where one can leave one's coat, hat, or bags □ *a cloakroom attendant.* -2. GB a toilet in a public building (polite use).

clobber ['klɒbər] *vt* (informal use) -1. [with one's fists, a stick] to hit <sb> hard. -2. SPORT & GAMES to beat <sb> easily in a race, competition etc.

clock [klɒk] *n* -1. [for telling the time] an instrument that is usually kept in one place to show the time, especially one that has the numbers 1 to 12 arranged in a circle with two separate pieces that point to the numbers □ *the church clock* □ *The clock said five to four.* □ *That clock is fast/slow.* □ *a digital clock.* ■ **around** OR **round the clock** [work] all day and all night □ *Our lines are kept open around the clock.* ■ **to do sthg against the clock** to do sthg as quickly as possible, because one is running out of time □ *It was a race against the clock.* ■ **to put the clock forward/back** to change the time on a clock to be later/earlier than it was. ■ **to turn** OR **put back the clock** to return to a situation that existed in the past □ *Things are different now. You can't turn back the clock.* -2. AUTO **the clock** the device in a car that shows how far the car has traveled or the speed the car is traveling at □ *The car has 60,000 miles on the clock.* □ *We were doing 180 mph by the clock.*

◆ **clock in** *vi* [worker] to record the time at which one arrives at work, usually by putting a card into a device that marks the time on it.

◆ **clock off** *vi* GB = **clock out.**

◆ **clock on** *vi* = **clock in.**

◆ **clock out** *vi* US [worker] to record the time at which one leaves work, usually by putting a card into a device that marks the time on it.

◆ **clock up** *vt fus* **to clock up a number/amount** to achieve or reach a total number/amount □ *We clocked up 800 miles in just one day.* □ *They've clocked up a whole series of victories.*

clock radio *n* a type of alarm clock with a radio that can be set to switch itself on at a particular time.

clockwise ['klɒkwaɪz] ◇ *adj* [direction, movement] that is in the same direction as the movement of the hands of a clock □ *Traffic circulates in a clockwise direction.* ◇ *adv* [move, turn, walk] *Turn the switch clockwise.*

NOTE: Compare **anticlockwise, counterclockwise.**

clockwork ['klɒkwɜːrk] ◇ *n* **to go like clockwork** [operation, event] to happen as planned and without problems. ◇ *comp* [toy, model] that has a mechanism which is operated by turning a key to make it move.

clod [klɒd] *n* a lump of earth □ *a clod of earth.*

clog [klɒg] (*pt* & *pp* **clogged**, *cont* **clogging**) *vt* [road, pipe, mechanism] to block or fill <sthg> so that it does not work properly and movement is very difficult □ *The gears on my bike are completely clogged with oil.*

◆ **clogs** *npl* shoes that have a wooden bottom and leather upper part or are made only of wood □ *a pair of clogs.*

◆ **clog up** ◇ *vt sep* = **clog** □ *The amount of mail has clogged up our delivery system.* ◇ *vi* [road, pipe, mechanism] *Every winter the drains clog up with leaves.*

clogged [klɒgd] *adj* [road, pipe, mechanism] that does not work properly because it is blocked.

cloister ['klɔɪstər] *n* a covered passage that goes around a square garden or courtyard in a church, monastery etc.

cloistered ['klɔɪstərd] *adj* **to lead a cloistered life** OR **existence** to live without seeing or having the problems or fun of ordinary life (literary use).

clone [kloʊn] ◇ *n* -1. SCIENCE an animal or plant that has been artificially produced from the cells of another animal or plant and is exactly the same as the original one. -2. [of a person] a person who looks or acts exactly like somebody else and so is not taken seriously. -3. COMPUTING a copy of a computer or circuit that operates in the same way as the original one. ◇ *vt* TECHNOLOGY to produce <an animal or plant> artificially as a clone of another animal or plant.

close¹ [kloʊs] ◇ *adj* -1. **to be close** [person, event, place] to be only a short distance away in time or space □ *I was so close I could have touched him.* □ *Christmas is getting closer.* □ *Stay close to me.* ■ **to be close to tears** to be almost crying. ■ **that was a close shave** OR **thing** OR **call** something unpleasant or dangerous almost happened □ *I had a close shave with a bus on the way here.* ■ **close up, close to** [be, come, stand] very near, so that one can see or hear properly □ *The shoes looked really cheap when I saw them close up.* ■ **to be close by, close at hand** [person, place, thing] to be very near □ *Luckily, help was close at hand.* □ *Two women were sunbathing close by.* -2. **to be close** [friends, family] to like each other, spend a lot of time together, and know each other well □ *My sister and I are very close.* □ *He grew closer to his father during his last days.* -3. [relative] who is one of the main members of one's family, e.g. a parent, brother, or sister. □ *I'm a close relative of Miles Barraclough.* -4. [involvement, cooperation] that involves people talking to each other regularly and often; [connection, resemblance] very strong □ *The text was drawn up on close consultation with Mr Marsh himself.* □ *The organization has close links with the Church.* □ *She bears a very close resemblance to her father.* -5. [observation, questioning, study] that is detailed and careful □ *Let's take a closer look.* □ *The police are keeping a close watch on him.* □ *Closer examination revealed traces of blood on the clothing.* -6. [weather, atmosphere, room] that is too warm and lacks fresh air □ *It's very close in here; do* *you mind if I open a window?* **-7.** [fight, race, vote] in which both sides have almost the same number of points □ *It's going to be a close contest.*

◇ *adv* [stay, come, live] near □ *We all stood close together.* □ *Hold me close.* □ *They live quite close to London.*

◇ *n* GB a quiet road with houses, closed at one end.

◆ **close on, close to** *prep* slightly less than <a particular amount or number> □ *Close on 4,000 people turned up.*

close² [kləʊz] ◇ *vt* **-1.** [door, lid, book] to shut <sthg> so there is no longer a gap, passage etc □ *They've closed the road through the mountains.* □ *Close your eyes and go to sleep.* **-2.** [factory, mine, store] = **close down** □ *There are plans to close five more hospitals.* ■ **to close an account** to remove all the money from an account and stop using it. **-3.** [speech, meeting, case] to make <sthg> finish □ *Let's close the subject, shall we?*

◇ *vi* **-1.** [door, lid, eyes] to move so that there is no longer a gap, passage etc □ *I heard the door close behind me.* **-2.** [store, library, museum] to stop being open to the public, usually for a short time □ *What time does the bank close?* **-3.** [factory, mine, store] = **close down** □ *The shipyard closed last year with the loss of 500 jobs.* **-4.** [discussion, performance, offer] to come to an end □ *We close with a piece of music by Bach.* □ *'Sale closes March 31.'* **-5.** FINANCE [shares, currency] to be worth a particular price at the end of a day's trading □ *The dollar closed at 0.5c down on the Mark.*

◇ *n* **the close of business/play** the end of business/play on a particular occasion □ *The pound stood at $1.53 at close of business yesterday.* □ *The meeting was drawing to a close.* □ *The chairman brought the debate to a close.*

◆ **close down** ◇ *vt sep* **to close sthg down** [factory, company, mine] to cause sthg to stop operating permanently □ *They had to close down the family business.* ◇ *vi* [factory, company, mine] *When did the steelworks close down?*

◆ **close in** *vi* **to close in on sb/sthg** to surround sb/sthg gradually from all sides in a threatening way □ *Government forces are closing in on the rebels.* □ *The darkness closed in around them.*

◆ **close off** *vt sep* **to close sthg off** [room, road, area] to stop people from using or going into sthg □ *Security men closed off the surrounding streets.*

close-cropped [ˌkləʊsˈkrɒpt] *adj* [hair] that has been cut very short.

closed [kləʊzd] *adj* **-1.** [door, window, eyes] not open □ *Keep the window closed — it's cold otherwise.* **-2.** [store, bank, library] not open to the public □ *I'm sorry, we're closed for lunch.* □ *This road is closed to traffic.* **-3.** [society, world] that is not open to outside influences or to other people □ *They have a fairly closed circle of friends.*

closed-circuit television *n* a television system that is used to observe people, usually

for security purposes, inside a store, parking lot etc.

closedown [ˈkləʊzdaʊn] *n* **-1.** the act of stopping all work, e.g. in a factory. **-2.** GB the time when a TV or radio station stops broadcasting for the night.

closed shop *n* a workplace, e.g. a factory or company, where workers must belong to a particular labor union.

close-fitting [ˌkləʊs-] *adj* [dress, top] that is tight and shows the shape of one's body □ *She was wearing a pair of close-fitting pants.*

close-knit [ˌkləʊs-] *adj* [family, village, community] closely united by social, political, or religious connections.

closely [ˈkləʊslɪ] *adv* [follow, watch, listen] *see* **close** □ *He's closely related to the Kennedy family.* □ *She's very closely involved with our work.*

closeout [ˈkləʊzaʊt] *n* US a sale of all the goods of a business that is closing down, usually at reduced prices.

close quarters [ˌkləʊs-] *npl* **at close quarters** from a position that is very near □ *The building looks very different at close quarters.*

close season [ˈkləʊs-] *n* GB a period during each year when particular animals, birds, or fish are not allowed to be killed for sport.

closet [ˈklɒzət] ◇ *n* a cabinet or small room that is used for hanging and storing clothes, tools etc □ *Hang it up in the closet.* ◇ *vt* **to be closeted with sb** to be in a room with sb and have a private conversation with them. ◇ *comp* [belief, feeling] that one hides from other people as a secret. ■ **a closet homosexual/fascist etc** a person who is a homosexual/fascist etc but who does not want to admit it □ *He's suspected of being a closet socialist.*

close-up [ˈkləʊs-] *n* a photo or way of filming that shows somebody or something from a short distance away so that one can see a lot of detail □ *Here we see a photo of the wing in close-up.* □ *a close-up shot.*

closing [ˈkləʊzɪŋ] *adj* [remark, speech, stage] that comes near the end of something □ *We are now in the closing stages of the competition.*

closing date *n* the last date on which people can ask for something □ *The closing date for applications is May 6.*

closing price *n* the final price of shares at the end of the day on a stock exchange.

closing time *n* the time at which a store, bar etc closes in the evening.

closure [ˈkləʊʒəʳ] *n* **-1.** [of a business] the act of closing a business, company etc permanently □ *factory closures* □ *After the closure of the Detroit plant...* **-2.** [of a road] the act of blocking a road, railroad track etc in order to stop people from using it □ *lane closures on the highway.*

clot [klɒt] (*pt* & *pp* **clotted,** *cont* **clotting**) ◇ *n* a lump that forms in a liquid such as blood or milk □ *a blood clot.* ◇ *vi* [blood, milk] to form clots.

cloth [klɒθ] *n* **-1.** a fabric that is made by weaving or knitting materials such as cotton, wool, or nylon □ *a piece of cloth.* **-2.** a piece of cloth used for a particular purpose, e.g. cleaning, drying, or covering something □ *Wipe it up with a cloth.* □ *a floor cloth.*

cloth cap *n* a soft flat cap, worn by men and usually made of wool. It is often used as a symbol of the British working class.

clothe [kloʊð] *vt* (formal use) **-1.** to provide clothes for <sb>. **-2.** to dress <sb> in clothes.

clothes [kloʊz] *npl* the things that a person wears to cover parts of their body, e.g. trousers, shirt, or socks □ *Andrea took off all her clothes and jumped in.* □ *He had no clothes on.*

clothes basket *n* a basket in which one puts clothes that need to be washed.

clothes brush *n* a brush that is used to remove dust, mud, hairs etc from clothes.

clotheshorse ['kloʊzhɔːʳs] *n* a frame on which one hangs wet clothes inside a house until they are dry.

clothesline ['kloʊzlaɪn] *n* a piece of rope or cable on which one hangs wet clothes outside until they are dry.

clothespin ['kloʊzpɪn] US, **clothes peg** GB *n* a small device made of wood or plastic that is used for holding clothes on a clothesline.

clothing ['kloʊðɪŋ] *n* the things that a person wears to cover parts of their body □ *You'll need warm clothing.* □ *a piece of clothing* □ *items* OR *articles of clothing* □ *the clothing industry.*

clotted cream [ˌklɒtəd-] *n* thick cream that is made by heating milk slowly and taking the cream from the top.

cloud [klaʊd] ◇ *n* **-1.** [in the sky] a white or gray mass of water vapor that floats in the sky □ *The sun disappeared behind a cloud.* □ *There was not a cloud in the sky.* □ *a thunder cloud.* ■ **to be under a cloud** to be disliked and not trusted because of something one has done □ *I'm afraid he left under a cloud.* **-2.** [of smoke, dust] a mass of smoke, dust, gas etc that floats in the air. ◇ *vt* **-1.** [window, glass] to cover <sthg> with mist so that one can no longer see through it □ *The steam clouded the mirror.* **-2.** [memory, happiness, day] to spoil <sthg> by making it sad □ *My happiness was clouded only by the thought that Lewis could not be with us.* **-3. to cloud the issue** to make something more complicated and difficult to understand or deal with.

◆ **cloud over** *vi* **-1.** [sky] to become covered with clouds. **-2.** [face] to become sad or worried.

cloudburst ['klaʊdbɜːʳst] *n* a sudden heavy fall of rain.

cloudless ['klaʊdləs] *adj* [sky] that has no clouds in it □ *a sunny cloudless day.*

cloudy ['klaʊdɪ] (*compar* **cloudier**, *superl* **cloudiest**) *adj* **-1.** [day, sky] that has a lot of clouds □ *It looks pretty cloudy today.* **-2.** [beer, water] not clear.

clout [klaʊt] (informal use) ◇ *n* **-1.** [with one's hand] a blow with one's hand or with an object in one's hand. **-2.** [of a person] the ability to get things done using one's influence □

Irving has a lot of clout with the local authorities. ◇ *vt* to hit <sb> with one's hand or with an object in one's hand.

clove [kloʊv] *n* **-1.** a kind of spice that is brown and hard, looks like a tiny twig, and is a dried flower bud. **-2. a clove of garlic** one of the small parts of a bulb of garlic.

clover ['kloʊvəʳ] *n* a small wild plant with three or sometimes four leaves on each stem and pink or white flowers.

clown [klaʊn] ◇ *n* **-1.** [in a circus] a performer, usually in a circus, who wears loose brightly-colored clothes, has a painted face, and does silly things to make people laugh □ *a circus clown.* **-2.** a person who one thinks behaves in a silly way. ◇ *vi* to behave in a silly way □ *Will you stop clowning around!*

cloying ['klɔɪɪŋ] *adj* [smell, sentiment] that is intended to be pleasant but is too sweet or sentimental.

club [klʌb] (*pt* & *pp* **clubbed**, *cont* **clubbing**) ◇ *n* **-1.** [for people] an organization that people belong to because they have the same interest or do the same activity; a place where the members of this organization meet □ *a sports/bridge/theater club* □ *a club member.* **-2.** [for dancing] = **nightclub**. **-3.** [for hitting a person] a kind of thick stick made of wood, metal etc with a rounded end that is used as a weapon □ *a wooden club.* **-4.** [for golf] a long thin stick with a rounded head made of metal or wood that is used for hitting golf balls. ◇ *vt* to hit <a person or animal> with a club □ *The seals are clubbed to death with sticks.*

◆ **clubs** *npl* one of the four suits in a set of playing cards whose symbol (♣) is black and looks like three round leaves on a stem.

◆ **club together** *vi* GB [group of people] to join together to pay for something together □ *We're clubbing together to buy him a present.*

club car *n* US a section of a train where food and drink are sold.

clubhouse ['klʌbhaʊs, *pl* -haʊzɪz] *n* a building where members of a sports club meet.

club sandwich *n* a sandwich made of three slices of bread with food in between.

club soda *n* = **soda water**.

cluck [klʌk] *vi* **-1.** [hen] to make a short quiet noise. **-2.** [person] to make a short quiet noise with one's tongue to express an emotion, e.g. sympathy or disapproval.

clue [kluː] *n* something, e.g. an object or a piece of information, that helps one to solve a problem, crime, or mystery □ *No clues were found on the body.* □ *Could you just give me a clue?* □ *The clue to understanding her is her family.* □ *a crossword clue.* ■ **not have a clue** an expression used to emphasize the fact that one does not know something □ *I don't have a clue where she went.* ■ **he doesn't have a clue** he is very bad at doing something □ *You don't have a clue how to treat people!*

clueless ['kluːləs] *adj* [person] who does not know anything about a particular subject or is unable to do something practical (informal use).

clump [klʌmp] ◇ *n* -1. [of plants] a small group of trees, bushes, flowers etc that grow together. -2. [of feet] a heavy dull noise □ *the clump of boots.* ◇ *vi* to walk very heavily and slowly.

clumsily ['klʌmzɪlɪ] *adv* [move, apologize] *see* **clumsy** □ *a clumsily worded statement.*

clumsy ['klʌmzɪ] (*compar* **clumsier**, *superl* **clumsiest**) *adj* -1. [person, movement, gesture] that is awkward, careless, and may cause an accident □ *How clumsy of me! I'm so sorry.* -2. [machine, tool] that has a shape which makes it difficult to use □ *a clumsy-looking device.* -3. [remark, apology] that is careless and likely to offend or annoy somebody □ *He made a clumsy attempt to apologize.*

clung [klʌŋ] *past tense & past participle of* **cling**.

clunk [klʌŋk] *n* a deep low sound made when two heavy objects hit against each other.

cluster ['klʌstər] ◇ *n* [of people, objects] a small group of people, houses, trees etc that stand close together; [of fruit] a number of grapes, flowers etc that grow together. ◇ *vi* [people] to gather close together in groups; [houses, trees] to stand close together in groups □ *They clustered around the table, waiting for food.*

clutch [klʌtʃ] ◇ *n* the pedal in a car that one presses before changing gear; the mechanism operated by this pedal. ◇ *vt* to hold <sthg> tightly, often because one is anxious or afraid □ *Tom clutched his mother's hand in the crowd.* □ *She was clutching her bag nervously.* ◇ *vi* **to clutch at sb/sthg** to try to catch hold of sb/sthg.

◆ **clutches** *npl* **in the clutches of sb** under the control of sb □ *I managed to escape from the clutches of my relatives.*

clutch bag *n* a handbag with no handle that is usually carried under one's arm or in one's hand.

clutter ['klʌtər] ◇ *n* a lot of untidily arranged and often useless things in a room, drawer etc □ *The room was filled with clutter.* ◇ *vt* **to be cluttered** [room, space, mind] to be filled with useless things in a disordered way.

Clyde¹ [klaɪd]: **the Clyde** a river in Scotland that flows through Glasgow.

Clyde² [klaɪd] → **Bonnie and Clyde**.

cm *n abbr of* **centimeter**.

CND (*abbr of* **Campaign for Nuclear Disarmament**) *n* a British organization that is against the use of nuclear weapons.

CNN (*abbr of* **Cable News Network**) *n* an American cable television station that only broadcasts news.

co- [kəʊ] *prefix* added to words to show that something is shared or done with another person □ *a co-worker.*

c/o *abbr of* **care of**.

Co. [kəʊ] -1. *abbr of* **company**. -2. *abbr of* **county**.

CO ◇ *n* -1. *abbr of* **commanding officer**. -2. (*abbr of* **Commonwealth Office**) the British government department responsible for Commonwealth affairs. -3. *abbr of* **conscientious objector**. ◇ *abbr of* **Colorado**.

coach [kəʊtʃ] ◇ *n* -1. a large closed vehicle pulled by horses. -2. RAIL a vehicle for carrying passengers that forms part of a train. -3. SPORT a person who is in charge of training and who improves the skills of a player or team □ *a football/tennis coach.* -4. EDUCATION a teacher who gives somebody lessons in a particular skill or prepares them for an examination □ *a voice/drama coach.* -5. US AVIATION = **coach class**. -6. GB a bus used on long-distance routes and for touring, trips etc □ *a coach driver/trip/station.* ◇ *vt* -1. SPORT [player, team] to act as a coach to <sb>. -2. EDUCATION [student] to give <sb> special help in preparing for an examination.

coach class *n* US a standard of service that provides the cheapest seats on a plane.

coaching ['kəʊtʃɪŋ] *n* SPORT & EDUCATION the activity or profession of being a coach.

coagulate [kəʊ'ægjəleɪt] *vi* [milk, blood] to thicken and form solid lumps.

coal [kəʊl] *n* -1. a hard black substance, dug from the ground, that is burned to provide heat and power □ *a piece of coal* □ *coal dust* □ *a coal fire* □ *the nation's coal reserves.* -2. a piece of coal □ *A red-hot coal fell out of the fire.*

coalesce [ˌkəʊə'les] *vi* [ideas, systems, parties] to mix and form a single thing.

coalface ['kəʊlfeɪs] *n* the rock surface from which coal is cut in a mine.

coalfield ['kəʊlfiːld] *n* an area of a country that has a lot of coal underground.

coal gas *n* gas that comes from coal and is used for heating and lighting.

coalition [ˌkəʊə'lɪʃn] *n* two or more nations, political parties, groups etc that are working together for a common aim □ *a coalition of environmentalist groups* □ *a coalition government.*

coalman ['kəʊlmæn] (*pl* **coalmen** [-men]) *n* GB a person whose job is to deliver coal to people's houses.

coal merchant *n* a company that sells coal to people and delivers it to their houses.

coalmine ['kəʊlmaɪn] *n* a mine that coal is dug from.

coalminer ['kəʊlmaɪnər] *n* a person whose job is to dig for coal in a mine.

coalmining ['kəʊlmaɪnɪŋ] *n* the work or business of getting coal from a mine □ *an important coalmining area.*

coarse [kɔːrs] *adj* -1. [hair, sandpaper, fabric] that is rough and not fine, smooth, or delicate □ *If the edges are too coarse, smooth them down first.* -2. [remark, laugh, joke] that is vulgar and likely to be offensive; [person, behavior] that shows a lack of manners and politeness □ *There's no need to use coarse language.* □ *Don't be so coarse.*

coarse fishing *n* GB the activity of fishing for any freshwater fish apart from salmon or trout.

coarsen ['kɔːrsn] ◇ *vt* [person, skin, texture] to make <sb/sthg> coarse. ◇ *vi* [person, texture] to become coarse.

coast [kəʊst] ◇ *n* the area of land in a country

that is beside the sea □ *the East/West Coast of the USA* □ *an island off the coast of British Columbia* □ *a network covering the country from coast to coast.* ◇ *vi* [vehicle] to move by going downhill without using the engine; [person] to continue one's work, life etc without effort and in a relaxed happy way □ *We coasted down the hill.* □ *He was just coasting along, enjoying life.*

coastal ['koʊstl] *adj* [town, district, area] that is on or near the coast.

coaster ['koʊstəʳ] *n* a small mat that is placed under a glass or bottle to protect the surface of a table.

coastguard ['koʊstɡɑːʳd] *n* -1. **the coastguard** an organization whose job is to watch the coast and the sea close to the shore of a particular country. -2. GB a member of the coastguard.

coastline ['koʊstlaɪn] *n* the edge or shape of a coast.

coat [koʊt] ◇ *n* -1. [for a person] a piece of clothing that is usually quite long and warm, has sleeves, and is worn over other clothing □ *a winter/summer coat* □ *I left my keys in my coat pocket.* -2. [of an animal] the fur or hair that covers an animal □ *The dog had a glossy, healthy coat.* -3. [of paint] a thin layer of paint, wax, varnish etc used to cover and protect a surface □ *The wall will need two coats of paint.* ◇ *vt* [surface, top] to cover <sthg> with a layer of paint, wax, varnish etc □ *a chocolate-coated wafer* □ *Coat each surface thoroughly with glue.*

coat check *n* US a place in a museum, theater etc where one can leave one's coat.

coat hanger *n* an object, usually in the shape of a triangle with a hook on top, that is used for hanging clothes on rails.

coating ['koʊtɪŋ] *n* a layer of something that is spread evenly over a surface □ *There was a thick coating of soot in the chimney* □ *a crisp sugar coating.*

coat of arms (*pl* **coats of arms**) *n* a design, usually on a shield, that represents a family, organization, town etc.

coat stand *n* a tall pole with small hooks at the top to hang coats on.

coauthor [ˌkoʊˈɔːθəʳ] *n* one of two or more people who write a book together.

coax [koʊks] *vt* [child, horse] to persuade <a person or animal> to do something by speaking to them pleasantly and gently; [information, smile] to get <sthg> from somebody in this way □ *He tried to coax them to sign* OR *into signing the document.* □ *I managed to coax the cat down from the tree.* □ *Eventually I coaxed the full story out of her.*

coaxial cable [koʊˌæksjəl-] *n* an electrical cable that is used to carry high frequency signals for televisions or computers.

cob [kɒb] *n* → **corn on the cob**.

cobalt ['koʊbɔːlt] *n* -1. a green-blue color. -2. CHEMISTRY a hard silver-white metal used to make things blue or used with other metals to make alloys. SYMBOL: Co.

cobble ['kɒbl] ◆ **cobbles** *npl* = **cobblestones**.

◆ **cobble together** *vt sep* GB **to cobble sthg together** [agreement, draft, report] to make or prepare sthg when one does not have much time, many materials etc.

cobbled ['kɒbld] *adj* [road, street] that has a surface made of cobblestones.

cobbler ['kɒbləʳ] *n* a person whose job is to mend shoes.

cobblestones ['kɒblstoʊnz] *npl* rounded stones that are laid down as a surface for streets, courtyards etc.

Cobol ['koʊbɒl] (*abbr of* **Common Business Oriented Language**) *n* a computer programing language used mainly in business software.

cobra ['koʊbrə] *n* a poisonous snake found in Africa and Asia that can spread the skin of its neck into a kind of hood.

cobweb ['kɒbweb] *n* a net of threads made by a spider in order to catch insects □ *The cellar was full of cobwebs.*

Coca-Cola™ [ˌkoʊkəˈkoʊlə] *n* a sweet, brown, fizzy, non-alcoholic drink from the USA.

cocaine [koʊˈkeɪn] *n* an addictive drug that is usually illegal and is taken through the nose in the form of a white powder.

cock [kɒk] ◇ *n* -1. a male chicken. -2. the male of a species of bird □ *a cock pheasant.* ◇ *vt* -1. **to cock a gun** to pull back the hammer of a gun to make it ready to shoot. -2. **to cock one's head/hat etc** to place one's head/hat etc at an angle.

◆ **cock up**▽ *vt sep* GB **to cock sthg up** to do sthg very badly (very informal use).

cock-a-hoop *adj* GB **to be cock-a-hoop** [person] to be extremely pleased and excited, usually because one has won or achieved something (informal use).

cockatoo [ˌkɒkəˈtuː] (*pl* **cockatoos**) *n* an Australian parrot with a crest of feathers on its head.

cockerel ['kɒkrəl] *n* a young male chicken.

cocker spaniel [ˌkɒkəʳ-] *n* a small dog with a round head, long ears, and a silky coat.

cockeyed ['kɒkaɪd] *adj* (informal use) -1. [picture, hat] not straight. -2. [idea, plan] foolish and unlikely to work.

cockfight ['kɒkfaɪt] *n* a fight, usually illegal, between two cocks with sharp metal spurs attached to their feet.

cockle ['kɒkl] *n* a small edible shellfish in a rounded shell.

Cockney ['kɒknɪ] (*pl* **Cockneys**) *n* -1. a working-class person born in London, especially in the East End of London. -2. the dialect or accent spoken by Cockneys □ *a Cockney accent.*

cockpit ['kɒkpɪt] *n* the compartment in a plane where the controls are situated.

cockroach ['kɒkroʊtʃ] *n* a large insect with a flat body that eats decaying food and is regarded as a pest in houses.

cocksure [US ˌkɒkˈʃʊər, GB -ˈʃɔː] *adj* [person] who is confident or certain in an arrogant way □ *I dislike his cocksure attitude.*

cocktail ['kɒkteɪl] *n* a drink that is a mixture of various drinks shaken together in a container □ *a cocktail bar/lounge.*

cocktail dress *n* a woman's dress, usually short and elegant, that is worn at formal parties.

cocktail party *n* a party in the early evening, often quite formal and short, where cocktails and snacks are served.

cocktail shaker *n* a metal container in which a mixture of drinks is shaken together to make a cocktail.

cocktail stick *n* a small, thin, sharp stick of wood or plastic used for putting cherries, olives etc into cocktails or for serving small pieces of food at parties.

cock-up▽ *n* GB something that has been done badly (very informal use).

cocky ['kɒkɪ] (*compar* **cockier**, *superl* **cockiest**) *adj* [person] who is very confident and too proud of themselves (informal and disapproving use).

cocoa ['koʊkoʊ] *n* -1. a brown powder made from a plant and used to make chocolate □ *cocoa powder.* -2. a hot drink made by mixing cocoa with milk or water.

coconut ['koʊkənʌt] *n* the large, egg-shaped, hairy nut of a kind of palm tree; the white part inside this nut that can be eaten □ *coconut oil/milk.*

cocoon [kə'kuːn] ◇ *n* -1. [around an insect] the protective covering of silk threads formed around the larva of an insect or the eggs of spiders. -2. [around a person] something that forms a protective environment for a person □ *The family house was a cocoon which he found it hard to leave.* ◇ *vt* to make <sb> feel safe and protected □ *In his little room, he felt cocooned from the outside world.*

Cocos Islands ['koʊkəs-]: **the Cocos Islands** a group of 27 coral islands in the Indian Ocean that belongs to Australia. POPULATION: 550.

cod [kɒd] (*pl* **cod** OR **cods**) *n* a large fish with white flesh that is mainly found in the North Atlantic and is eaten as food.

COD -1. (*abbr of* **cash on delivery**) a term that describes an arrangement in which goods are paid for when they are delivered. -2. *abbr of* **collect on delivery**.

code [koʊd] ◇ *n* -1. [for communicating] a set of letters or symbols used in place of the ordinary alphabet to communicate information in a way that cannot be understood by other people □ *a secret code.* □ *The message was sent in code.* -2. [of rules] a set of rules that tell people the correct or sensible way to act in particular situations □ *a code of behavior/conduct.* -3. [in addresses, phone numbers] a set of letters, numbers, or symbols that identifies an address, phone number, credit card etc □ *The code for that project is LE0916* □ *a code number.*
◇ *vt* -1. [message, signal] to translate <sthg> into a code. -2. [product, file] to identify or classify <sthg> using a code □ *All documents are coded for ease of location.*

coded ['koʊdəd] *adj* [message, signal] that is written or sent in a code so that other people cannot understand it.

codeine ['koʊdiːn] *n* a drug made from morphine that is used to relieve pain.

code name *n* a name used to keep the identity or nature of somebody or something a secret from other people.

code of practice *n* a set of rules that states how people in a particular profession or organization are supposed to conduct their business.

cod-liver oil *n* a type of oil, made from the liver of the cod, that contains a large amount of vitamins.

coed ['koʊed] ◇ *adj abbr of* **coeducational** (informal use). ◇ *n* -1. US (*abbr of* **coeducational student**) a female student at a mixed college. -2. GB *abbr of* **coeducational school**.

coeducational [ˌkoʊedʒə'keɪʃnəl] *adj* [school] that has members of both sexes as students.

coefficient [ˌkoʊɪ'fɪʃnt] *n* -1. MATH a number or factor by which a variable is multiplied in an equation. -2. PHYSICS a number that represents a particular quality of a substance under particular conditions □ *the coefficient of expansion/viscosity.*

coerce [koʊ'ɜːrs] *vt* to force <sb> to do something by using threats □ *I was coerced into agreeing to the takeover.*

coercion [koʊ'ɜːrʃn] *n see* **coerce** □ *You will never achieve your aims by coercion.*

coexist [ˌkoʊɪg'zɪst] *vi* [conditions, factors] to exist together at the same time or in the same place □ *Cooperation can never coexist with suspicion.*

coexistence [ˌkoʊɪg'zɪstəns] *n*: *see* **coexist** □ *a peaceful coexistence between North and South.*

C of C *n abbr of* **chamber of commerce**.

C of E *n abbr of* **Church of England**.

coffee ['kɒfɪ] *n* -1. a drink made by adding boiling water to roasted and ground coffee beans; a cup of this drink □ *a cup of instant/filter coffee.* □ *Will you come for (a) coffee?* -2. = **coffee beans**. -3. the brown granules or powder made from coffee beans and used to make coffee to drink □ *a jar/can of coffee.*

coffee bar *n* GB a café that serves coffee, other non-alcoholic drinks, and snacks.

coffee bean *n* the seed of a tropical plant that is collected, dried, and roasted in order to be used for making coffee.

coffee break *n* a rest period during work when people drink coffee.

coffee cup *n* a small cup for drinking coffee.

coffee grinder *n* = **coffee mill**.

coffee-maker *n* a small machine used for making coffee from ground coffee beans.

coffee mill *n* a machine for grinding coffee beans.

coffee morning *n* GB a social event in the morning at which coffee is served and which is often used as a way of raising money for a church or charity.

coffeepot ['kɒfɪpɒt] *n* a tall pot with a lid, used for serving coffee.

coffee shop *n* -**1.** a small restaurant on its own or inside a department store, hotel etc that serves drinks and light snacks. -**2.** a store that sells ground coffee, beans etc and sometimes serves drinks and snacks at tables.

coffee table *n* a low table usually placed in front of a sofa or chairs in a sitting room.

coffee-table book *n* a large attractive book, usually containing many pictures, that is meant to be looked at, not read.

coffer ['kɒfəʳ] *n* a large strong box for keeping money in. ▪ **the coffers are full/empty** there is a lot of money/no money to spend.

coffin ['kɒfn] *n* a long wooden box used for burying or cremating a dead person in.

cog [kɒg] *n* a wheel that has teeth around its edge that connect with similar teeth on another wheel to make a machine work. ▪ **a cog in the machine** a person who plays an unimportant part in, and feels exploited by, a large organization.

cogent ['koʊdʒənt] *adj* [argument, reason] that is very persuasive and convincing.

cogitate ['kɒdʒəteɪt] *vi* to think very carefully about something (formal use).

cognac [US 'koʊnjæk, GB 'kɒn-] *n* a type of French brandy; a glass of this drink.

cognitive ['kɒgnətɪv] *adj* [process, faculty] that is connected with the mind and its ability to learn □ *cognitive psychology.*

cogwheel ['kɒgwiːl] *n* = **cog**.

cohabit [koʊ'hæbət] *vi* [two people] to live together like a married couple (formal use) □ *He was, at the time, cohabiting with his girlfriend.*

coherent [koʊ'hɪərənt] *adj* [argument, answer, speech] that is organized in a clear and logical way; [person] who is able to talk clearly and can be easily understood □ *The article is organized in a perfectly coherent fashion.* □ *The more he drank, the less coherent he became.*

coherently [koʊ'hɪərəntlɪ] *adv* [argue, answer, speak] *see* **coherent** □ *The first candidate expressed herself clearly and coherently.*

cohesion [koʊ'hiːʒn] *n*: *see* **cohesive** □ *We need greater cohesion among our local branches.*

cohesive [koʊ'hiːsɪv] *adj* [structure, group] that fits together well □ *The new students now form a very cohesive group within the college.*

cohort ['koʊhɔːrt] *n* a group of people who follow or support somebody (disapproving use).

COI (*abbr of* **Central Office of Information**) *n* **the COI** the British government department responsible for producing information about Britain for the public.

coil [kɔɪl] ◇ *n* -**1. a coil of wire/rope/hair** one of a series of circular sections into which a length of wire/rope/hair is wound □ *Her hair fell in black coils.* -**2.** ELECTRICITY a coil of wire carrying an electric current that is used in electric motors. -**3.** GB a contraceptive device that is fitted inside a woman's womb. ◇ *vt* [wire, rope, hair] to wind <sthg> into a coil □

He coiled the rope around his arm. ◇ *vi* [snake, rope, smoke] to form itself into a coil.

◆ **coil up** *vt sep* **to coil sthg up** [hose, wire, rope] to wind all of sthg into a coil.

coiled [kɔɪld] *adj* [rope, spring] that is wound into a coil.

coin [kɔɪn] ◇ *n* a piece of money in the form of a small, round, flat piece of metal □ *a dollar coin.* ◇ *vt* to invent <a word, expression> etc. ▪ **to coin a phrase** a phrase used humorously when one says something that is not original and has been said many times before □ *There was a free and frank exchange of views, to coin a phrase.*

coinage ['kɔɪnɪdʒ] *n* -**1.** [of a country] the metal money used in a particular country. -**2.** [in speech, writing] a word or phrase that has been recently invented.

coin-box *n* GB a public telephone that is operated by coins but not by a card.

coincide [ˌkoʊɪn'saɪd] *vi* -**1.** [events, meetings] to happen at the same time, usually by chance □ *His arrival coincided with my visit.* -**2.** [ideas, opinions] to be the same □ *Her views coincided with mine.*

coincidence [koʊ'ɪnsɪdəns] *n* a situation where something happens by chance at the same time as something else □ *By a strange coincidence, I found I was staying in the same hotel.* □ *It is no coincidence that they both turned up at the same time.* □ *What a coincidence!*

coincidental [koʊˌɪnsə'dentl] *adj* that happens, exists etc by chance at the same time as something else □ *Any similarity between the two designs is purely coincidental.*

coincidentally [koʊˌɪnsə'dentlɪ] *adv* a word used to say that something is coincidental □ *Coincidentally, I was thinking exactly the same thing.*

coin-operated [-ɒpəreɪtəd] *adj* [machine, phone] that works when one puts a coin into it.

coitus ['kɔɪtəs] *n* sexual intercourse (formal use).

coke [koʊk] *n* -**1.** [for burning] a solid fuel used in fires that is made by removing gas from coal. -**2.**▽ = **cocaine** (drugs slang).

Coke™ [koʊk] *n* Coca-Cola; a glass, can, or bottle of this.

Col. *abbr of* **colonel**.

cola ['koʊlə] *n* a sweet, brown, non-alcoholic drink with bubbles.

COLA ['koʊlə] (*abbr of* **cost-of-living adjustment**) *n* US an amount of money added to salaries or social security payments to cover increases in the cost of living.

colander ['kʌləndəʳ] *n* a bowl with holes in the bottom and sides that is used for washing food or separating it from liquid.

cold [koʊld] ◇ *adj* -**1.** [drink, weather, room] that has a low temperature □ *Turn the heat up, it's cold in here.* ▪ **to be** OR **feel cold** [person] to feel uncomfortable because the temperature is low. ▪ **to get cold** [person] to begin to feel cold; [food, room, air] to lose heat. -**2.** [eyes, voice, stare] unfriendly and without emotion

□ *He was given a cold reception by his colleagues.* -3. [person] who does not seem to care about other people.

◇ *n* -1. MEDICINE a common illness whose symptoms are a sore throat, sneezing, coughing, and a headache □ *I've got a cold.* ■ **to catch (a) cold** to become ill with a cold □ *Put your coat on or you'll catch a cold.* -2. **the cold** cold air or weather □ *Come in out of the cold.*

cold-blooded [-ˈblʌdɪd] *adj* -1. [animal] whose body temperature goes up or down depending on the temperature of its surroundings. -2. [murder, crime] that is done in an intentional and cruel way. -3. [person] who does not seem to care if other people suffer or are upset.

cold call *n* BUSINESS a visit or phone call made by a salesperson to somebody who is not expecting it.

cold cream *n* a cosmetic cream used to clean and soften the skin, especially on the face.

cold cuts *npl* US slices of cooked meat, such as ham or salami, served cold.

cold feet *npl* **to have/get cold feet** to feel/start feeling that one does not want to do something one has planned, usually because one is afraid of failing (informal use) □ *There are signs that the Australians are getting cold feet and may pull out of the deal.*

cold front *n* the front of a mass of cold air that is moving into a mass of warmer air. NOTE: Compare **warm front.**

cold-hearted [-ˈhɑːrtəd] *adj* [person, refusal] that does not show any concern for people's feelings and so seems unkind.

coldly [ˈkoʊldlɪ] *adv* [look, speak, behave] *see* **cold** □ *"It's not my fault," she said coldly.*

coldness [ˈkoʊldnəs] *n*: *see* **cold** □ *Kate was puzzled by his coldness toward her.*

cold shoulder *n* **to give sb the cold shoulder** to ignore sb and be unfriendly to them (informal use).

cold sore *n* a blister on the edge of one's lips that sometimes appears when one has a cold.

cold storage *n* storage, especially of food, at a low temperature in a refrigerator or freezer □ *Food lasts longer if kept in cold storage.*

cold sweat *n* sweat that is a result or sign of nervousness or fear □ *I woke up in a cold sweat.*

Cold War *n* **the Cold War** the political struggle between the USA and the USSR that started after World War II, and ended in 1990. Although both countries regarded each other as enemies, there was no actual fighting.

Coleridge [ˈkoʊlərɪdʒ], **Samuel Taylor** (1772–1834) a British poet and critic. He was a friend of Wordsworth, and one of the Romantics.

coleslaw [ˈkoʊlslɔː] *n* a salad made of chopped raw cabbage, carrots, onions, and mayonnaise.

colic [ˈkɒlɪk] *n* a medical condition that causes

sharp pains in the stomach and abdomen, and is usually suffered by young babies.

collaborate [kəˈlæbəreɪt] *vi* -1. [partners, colleagues] to work together on a particular project □ *I'm collaborating with John* OR *John and I are collaborating on the basic design.* -2. [person] to help or cooperate with an enemy who is occupying one's country □ *He was accused of collaborating with the Nazis.*

collaboration [kə,læbəˈreɪʃn] *n*. *see* **collaborate** □ *The timetable was worked out in close collaboration with our partners.* □ *He was accused of collaboration with the occupying forces.*

collaborative [kəˈlæbərətɪv] *adj* [effort, project] that involves people or groups working together □ *It's a collaborative venture between the USA and Mexico.*

collaborator [kəˈlæbəreɪtər] *n* -1. [with other people] a person who collaborates with another person or other people on a project □ *Sarah was my main collaborator on the encyclopedia.* -2. [with the enemy] a person who collaborates with the enemy □ *He was accused of being a collaborator.*

collage [US kəˈlɑːʒ, GB ˈkɒlɑːʒ] *n* a method of making pictures by sticking photographs, pieces of paper, fabric etc onto a background; a picture made by this method.

collagen [ˈkɒlədʒən] *n* a type of protein that is used in women's face creams and can be injected into their lips to make them bigger.

collapse [kəˈlæps] ◇ *vi* -1. [building, structure, roof] to fall down suddenly □ *The roof collapsed under the weight of the snow.* -2. [company, government, marriage] to become unable to continue □ *The bank collapsed last May with millions owed in bad debts.* -3. MEDICINE [person] to fall down because one is tired or suddenly ill □ *He collapsed in the street and was rushed to the hospital.* -4. [table, chair, bed] to have the ability to fold so that it can be stored more easily □ *The tripod collapses for easy storage.*

◇ *n* -1. [of a building, structure] the act of collapsing □ *What caused the bridge's collapse?* -2. [of a company, government, marriage] a failure □ *The system is on the verge of collapse.* □ *the changes that followed the collapse of the Soviet Union.* -3. MEDICINE an inability to continue living normally because of mental or physical exhaustion; the act of falling over because one suddenly becomes ill.

collapsible [kəˈlæpsəbl] *adj* [table, chair, bed] that can collapse.

collar [ˈkɒlər] ◇ *n* -1. [of a shirt] the part of a shirt, jacket, coat etc that fits around the neck and that is usually folded □ *My collar's too tight.* □ *What is your collar size?* -2. [of a dog, cat] a band, usually made of leather, that is fitted around the neck of an animal. -3. [in a machine] an object shaped like a ring and used in a machine around a pipe, tube etc to hold something in place. ◇ *vt* to catch or capture <sb>, especially because they have done something wrong (informal use).

collarbone [ˈkɒlərboʊn] *n* the long bone that

connects one's shoulder to the bottom of one's neck.

collate [kə'leɪt] *vt* -1. [information, evidence] to bring <facts> together and compare them. -2. [pages, photocopies] to put <pieces of paper> in the correct order.

collateral [kə'lætərəl] *n* something such as property, money, or goods that are used as security for a loan □ *This stock was used as collateral for the loan.*

colleague ['kɒliːg] *n* a person one works with □ *May I introduce my colleague, Bruce Roberts?*

collect [kə'lekt] ◇ *vt* -1. [wood, files, information] to bring or gather <sthg> together from different places □ *The teacher collected the exam papers.* ■ **to collect one's thoughts, to collect oneself** to become calm and get one's thoughts into order. -2. [stamps, coins, butterflies] to get and keep <several things of the same type>, usually as a hobby □ *My father collects antiques.* -3. [washing, photographs, car] to go to a place in order to take <sb/sthg> from there to another place □ *Can you collect me from the station?* -4. [taxes, contributions, donations] to ask for and get <money> from people. ■ **collect on delivery** US a term that describes an arrangement in which goods are paid for when they are delivered. ◇ *vi* -1. [crowd, people] to gather together and form a group □ *Several fans had collected outside the hotel.* -2. [dust, leaves, dirt] to form a pile, layer etc over a period of time □ *Rainwater had collected in the bottom of the trough.* -3. [person] to ask people for money, usually for charity or to buy a gift for somebody □ *I'm collecting on behalf of sick children.* ◇ *adv* **to call (sb) collect** US to call somebody on the telephone so that the person who receives the call pays for it.

◆ **collect up** *vt sep* **to collect things up** to bring things together in one place □ *Can you help me collect up the empty bottles?*

collectable [kə'lektəbl] ◇ *adj* [antique, book] that is worth keeping or buying because it is valuable or interesting □ *Early examples of her work are proving to be highly collectable.* ◇ *n* a collectable object.

collected [kə'lektəd] *adj* -1. **to be collected** [person] to be calm and self-controlled □ *He always stays cool, calm, and collected.* -2. [works, poems] that are published together in one book □ *"The Collected Writings of Joseph Roth."*

collecting [kə'lektɪŋ] *n* the hobby of getting and keeping many examples of the same object □ *coin collecting.*

collecting tin *n* GB a box, usually with a slot in the top, into which people are asked to put donations for a charity.

collection [kə'lekʃn] *n* -1. [of stamps, coins, antiques] a group of objects of the same type that somebody has collected □ *a stamp/record collection.* -2. [of stories, poems] a group of short stories, poems etc, published in one book, by the same writer or on the same subject. -3. [of wood, files, information] the act of coming and taking something away □ *Your photos will be ready for collection on Mon-*

day. □ *The next (mail) collection is at noon.* -4. [of money] money that is collected from many people for a charity, to buy somebody a present, or during a church service □ *We're having a collection for her leaving present.* -5. [of people] a group of people who have gathered together; [of objects] a group of things that have been gathered together □ *a collection of strange-looking characters* □ *I've got to go through the collection of papers on my desk.*

collective [kə'lektɪv] ◇ *adj* [decision, responsibility] that belongs to all the members of a group □ *the industrial nations' collective share of fossil fuel emissions.* ◇ *n* a business or farm that is owned by all the people who work there.

collective bargaining *n* discussions between labor unions and employers about the pay and working conditions of employees.

collectively [kə'lektɪvlɪ] *adv* -1. [decide, own] *see* **collective** □ *They are all collectively responsible.* □ *The three states collectively spend $20 million on law enforcement.* -2. **to be collectively known as sthg** to be called sthg when they are in a group □ *A group of fish is collectively known as a "school".*

collective ownership *n* the ownership of a business by the people who work in it.

collector [kə'lektər] *n* -1. [of stamps, coins, antiques] a person who collects things as a hobby □ *a stamp/record collector.* -2. [of taxes, garbage] a person whose job is to collect money, garbage etc □ *a rent/debt collector.*

collector's item *n* a thing that collectors would want because it is rare or valuable.

college ['kɒlɪdʒ] *n* -1. a place where one can go after leaving school in order to study for further qualifications and that often specializes in one particular subject; the people who work and study there □ *When does John start college?* □ *I go to art/nursing/agricultural college* □ *college life* □ *a college professor/scarf.* -2. [of a university] one of the parts that some universities are divided into, where students live and study; the people who work and study there □ *King's College, Cambridge* □ *an all-female college.* -3. a group of people who have the same professional, educational, or religious duties □ *the Royal College of Nursing* □ *an electoral college.*

college of education *n* a college where people train to become teachers.

collide [kə'laɪd] *vi* [people, vehicles, planets] to crash □ *They collided in the corridor.* □ *The bus collided with a car.*

collie ['kɒlɪ] *n* a type of dog that has black and white hair and is often used to control sheep.

colliery ['kɒljərɪ] (*pl* **collieries**) *n* a coalmine.

Collins ['kɒlɪnz], **Michael** (1890–1922) an Irish revolutionary, and MP. He was a leader of Sinn Féin, and founder of the IRA.

collision [kə'lɪʒn] *n* -1. [between vehicles] a crash between two vehicles traveling fast □ *Their car was in a head-on collision with a truck* □ *a collision between two trains.* -2. [between peo-*

ple] a serious disagreement between two or more people or things □ *a collision of interests.* ■ **to be on a collision course** to be very likely to disagree strongly with somebody about something □ *Their stance has put them on a collision course with the anti-abortion lobby.*

collision damage waiver *n* a section that is added to an insurance contract when one rents a car, stating that damage caused to the car will be paid for by the insurer.

colloquial [kə'loʊkwɪəl] *adj* [word, expression, English] that is used only in informal conversation.

collude [kə'luːd] *vi* [people] to work together in secret to do something dishonest □ *They were accused of colluding with the enemy.*

collusion [kə'luːʒn] *n* **to be in collusion with sb** to be colluding with sb.

cologne [kə'loʊn] *n* a mild perfume.

Colombia [kə'lʌmbɪə] a country in northwestern South America, with Pacific and Caribbean coasts. SIZE: 1,140,000 sq kms. POPULATION: 33,600,000 (*Colombians*). CAPITAL: Bogotá. LANGUAGE: Spanish. CURRENCY: peso.

colon ['koʊlən] *n* -1. ANATOMY the part of the large intestine that leads to the anus. -2. GRAMMAR a symbol (:) used before a list, explanation, or quotation.

colonel ['kɜːrnl] *n* an officer of high rank in the army.

colonial [kə'loʊnjəl] *adj* [rule, power] that is connected with countries that are colonies; [style, period, building] that is connected with a country when it was a colony.

colonialism [kə'loʊnjəlɪzm] *n* the practice of colonizing other countries.

colonist ['kɒlənɪst] *n* a person who starts a colony.

colonize, -ise ['kɒlənaɪz] *vt* [country, region] to make <an area of land> a colony.

colonnade [,kɒlə'neɪd] *n* a row of columns.

colony ['kɒlənɪ] (*pl* **colonies**) *n* -1. [of another country] a country or area that is controlled by a more powerful country that is usually far away; the people who live there □ *They spent the day visiting the former Portuguese colony.* -2. [of people] a group of people who live together because they have the same interest, problem etc □ *a nudist/leper colony.* -3. [of ants, birds] a group of the same kind of animal or insect that lives together □ *an ant colony.*

color US, **colour** GB ['kʌlər] ◇ *n* -1. the appearance that the reflection of light gives to an object, e.g. red, blue, or green □ *It looks like a different color in this light.* ■ **to be in color** [movie, magazine, photograph] to be made showing different colors, not just black and white □ *The brochure is printed in full color.* -2. a particular color □ *Red is my favorite color.* □ *What color is it?* □ *This model comes in a wide range of colors.* -3. the color of one's skin when this shows one's race or state of health □ *Her skin was a lovely color after her holiday in Spain.* □ *He has faced much discrimination on account of his color* □ *people of color.*

◇ *vt* -1. [picture, drawing] = **color in** □ *I colored it blue.* -2. [hair, food] to change the color of <sthg> using dyes or chemicals. -3. [opinion, judgment] to influence <sthg> □ *His narrow-minded comments colored my attitude toward him from then on.*

◇ *vi* [person, cheeks] to blush.

◆ **colors** *npl* -1. [of a team, school] a piece of clothing, e.g. a tie or a badge, that shows which team, club, school etc one belongs to. -2. [of a country, regiment] the flag of a country, ship, or regiment.

◆ **color in** *vt sep* **to color sthg in** [picture, drawing] to fill in the outline of sthg with color.

Colorado [US ,kɒlə'rædoʊ, GB -'rɑːd-] a mountainous state in the western USA. ABBREVIATION: CO. SIZE: 270,000 sq kms. POPULATION: 3,294,394 (*Coloradans, Coloradoans*). CAPITAL: Denver.

colorado beetle *n* a black and yellow insect that eats potato plants.

color bar *n* the rule or custom in some places that does not allow people of different colors to mix.

color-blind *adj* [person] who cannot see the difference between particular colors, especially red and green.

color-coded *adj* [system, wiring] that has different colors to identify different parts.

colored US, **coloured** GB ['kʌlərd] *adj* -1. [pen, sheet] that has one or more colors, not just black or white. -2. [jacket, hair, bird] that has a particular color □ *straw-colored hair* □ *a brightly-colored shirt.* -3.▼ [person] who belongs to a race whose skin is not white (old-fashioned and offensive use).

colorfast ['kʌlrfæst] US, **colourfast** ['kʌləfɑːst] GB *adj* [garment, fabric] that does not lose its color when washed.

colorful US, **colourful** GB ['kʌlərfl] *adj* -1. [dress, picture, procession] that has one or more bright colors □ *The parade made a colorful sight.* -2. [story, career, life] that is full of interesting or exciting details □ *a person with a colorful past.* -3. [person] who is interesting, unusual, and amusing □ *I met lots of colorful characters along the way.*

coloring US, **colouring** GB ['kʌlərɪŋ] *n* -1. [food, drink] a substance or chemical used to color food or drink □ *This orange juice contains no artificial coloring.* -2. [of a person] the color of a person's hair, eyes, and skin □ *With your coloring you only need a low-factor suncream.* -3. [of an animal] the color of an animal's skin or fur □ *The male's bright coloring is designed to attract the hen.*

colorless US, **colourless** GB ['kʌlərləs] *adj* -1. [ink, complexion, liquid] that has no color. -2. [person, voice, place] that is not interesting and has no strong qualities.

color scheme *n* the combination of colors used in the decoration of a room, house etc.

color television, color TV *n* a television that can show pictures in color.

colossal [kə'lɒsl] *adj* [statue, amount, building]

very large □ *Most of their colossal profits are reinvested.*

colostomy [kə'lɒstəmɪ] (*pl* **colostomies**) *n* a medical operation that passes the colon through a hole made in the abdomen, so that feces can be collected in a bag □ *a colostomy bag.*

colour *etc* GB = **color** *etc.*

colour supplement *n* GB a free color magazine that comes with a newspaper, especially at weekends.

colt [koʊlt] *n* a young male horse.

Columbus [kə'lʌmbəs], **Christopher** (1451–1506) an Italian-born explorer who, supported by the Spanish royal family, was the first European to discover the West Indies and the South American mainland.

Columbus Day *n* a US public holiday on the second Monday in October, in memory of Christopher Columbus.

column ['kɒləm] *n* -1. ARCHITECTURE a very tall rounded structure, usually made of stone, that is used to support a roof. -2. **a column of smoke** a long straight line of smoke that goes upwards. -3. [of people, vehicles, animals] a long straight line that is moving forwards □ *a column of tanks* OR *tank column.* -4. [of text, numbers] a vertical block on a page □ *Add up each column of figures.* -5. [in a newspaper, magazine] a section that is always written by the same person or is always about the same subject □ *the sports column.*

columnist [US 'kɒləmnəst, GB 'kɒləməst] *n* a person who writes a regular column in a newspaper or magazine □ *a gossip columnist.*

coma ['koʊmə] *n* **to be in a coma** to be unconscious for a long time, especially after an accident □ *She's gone into a deep coma.*

Comanche [kə'mæntʃɪ] *n* a member of a Native American people who used to live in the southwestern USA; the language of this people.

comatose ['koʊmətoʊs] *adj* **to be comatose** to be in a coma.

comb [koʊm] ◇ *n* a thin flat object made of plastic or metal with a row of sharp points along one side that are moved through one's hair to make it look neater. ◇ *vt* -1. **to comb one's hair** to arrange one's hair more neatly using a comb. -2. [field, city, country] to search <a large area> very carefully for somebody or something □ *The police combed the countryside for clues/the missing man.*

combat ['kɒmbæt] ◇ *n* -1. fighting between two or more people or armies □ *The young soldier was killed in combat* □ *combat aircraft/troops.* -2. a struggle between two systems, ideas etc □ *the combat between good and evil.* ◇ *vt* [crime, disease, inflation] to struggle to stop <sthg>.

combative [US kəm'bætɪv, GB 'kɒmbətɪv] *adj* [person] who is always ready to fight or argue.

combination [ˌkɒmbɪ'neɪʃn] *n* -1. the act of combining two or more things □ *The alloy can be produced by combination with copper.* ■

in combination together □ *Running, cycling, and swimming in combination provide a comprehensive training program.* -2. [of colors, people, ideas] something that is made by combining two or more things, especially something that works well □ *a winning combination* □ *A combination of printing techniques was used to produce the book.* □ *His success is due to a combination of business flair and an understanding of the consumer.* -3. [for a lock, safe] the numbers or letters in a particular order that are needed to open something.

combination lock *n* a lock that can only be opened using a particular combination of numbers.

combination skin *n* skin on one's face that is partly dry and partly oily.

combine [*vb* kəm'baɪn, *n* 'kɒmbaɪn] ◇ *vt* [groups, classes, efforts] to join together <two or more things>; [activities] to do <two or more things> at the same time; [two qualities or features] to have <two or more different qualities or features> □ *Let's combine forces.* □ *How do you combine having a career with looking after four children?* □ *I try to combine business with pleasure whenever possible.* □ *Our new model combines speed and reliability.*

◇ *vi* [groups, activities, qualities] *The two parties combined to form the Alliance Party.* □ *Events combined to leave her penniless.*

◇ *n* -1. a group of organizations that have joined together □ *an industrial combine.* -2. = **combine harvester.**

combined [kəm'baɪnd] *adj* [effort, operation] that is made by two or more groups of people.

combine harvester [ˌkɒmbaɪn'hɑːrvɪstəʳ] *n* a large vehicle used on a farm that cuts, sorts, and cleans grain as it is driven across a field.

combustible [kəm'bʌstəbl] *adj* [substance, material] that can start to burn easily.

combustion [kəm'bʌstʃən] *n* the act of starting to burn.

come [kʌm] (*pt* **came**, *pp* **come**) *vi* -1. [person, car, train] to move toward the place where one is sitting, standing etc □ *The bus came round the corner.* □ *She came running down the stairs to meet me.* ■ **coming!** I shall be there soon (used as a reply when somebody is called to dinner, the telephone etc). -2. [guest, visitor] to go to one's home for a visit, usually for a short time □ *Some friends are coming to dinner.* -3. [person] to go somewhere with one □ *Come with me, I've got something to show you.* -4. [person, bus, news] to arrive at the place where one is □ *She came home late.* □ *The train came into the station.* □ *You'll feel better when summer comes.* □ *Letters of complaint came flooding in.* ■ **the time has come to leave** it is now the right time to leave. -5. [level, flood, person] to reach a particular point or place □ *The water came up over his boots.* □ *Keep going until you come to some traffic lights.* -6. [announcement, change] to happen or be done at a particular time □ *The strike comes at a bad time for the company.* ■ **the news came as a shock** somebody had a shock when the news came □ *It comes as no* surprise to me to hear that he's been fired. -7. **to come first/second etc in a competition** to be first/second etc compared to all the other people in a competition. ■ **P comes before Q** P is before Q in order. -8.▽ [person] to have an orgasm during sex (very informal use). -9. **to come to do sthg** to start to do sthg gradually and over a period of time □ *Over the years I came to enjoy living in New York.* ■ **how did you come to lose it?** explain to me how you lost it. ■ **come to think of it** a phrase used when one suddenly remembers or realizes something □ *Come to think of it, he did sound strange on the phone.* -10. **her dream came true** what she had dreamed about happened. ■ **to come loose/undone** to become loose/unfastened slowly or gradually. ■ **come again?** a phrase used to ask somebody to repeat something because one did not hear it or is surprised by it (informal use).

◆ **to come** *adv* **in (the) days/years to come** in the days/years that follow □ *We do not expect any improvement for some time to come.*

◆ **come about** *vi* [discovery, crisis, situation] to happen, usually by chance □ *We still don't know how the problem came about.*

◆ **come across** ◇ *vt fus* **to come across sb/sthg** to find or meet sb/sthg by chance □ *Years later, I came across him in Beirut.* ◇ *vi* **to come across well** to make a good impression on people □ *She came across as being more nervous than she really was.* ■ **the main point comes across clearly** people can clearly understand the main point.

◆ **come along** *vi* **-1.** [bus, opportunity, job] to arrive, often unexpectedly and by chance □ *We're waiting for the right candidate to come along.* □ *Everything was going fine till you came along!* **-2. the project is coming along well** the project is going or progressing well □ *How's your new secretary coming along?* **-3.** *phrase* **come along!** a phrase used to encourage somebody to hurry up or to do something that they do not want to do □ *Come along or you'll be late for school.*

◆ **come apart** *vi* [shoes, package, machine] to become broken or fall to pieces □ *The toy just came apart in my hands.*

◆ **come around** *vi* **-1.** [guest, visitor] to visit one in one's home, usually for a short time □ *Do come around for a game of bridge.* **-2.** [Christmas, birthday, summer] to happen (used of regular events) □ *The local elections are coming around in May.* **-3.** [patient] to become conscious again after being unconscious. **-4. to come around to sthg** to change one's opinion and start agreeing with sthg □ *He's very stubborn, but he'll come around to our way of thinking in the end.*

◆ **come at** *vt fus* **to come at sb** to move toward sb in order to attack them □ *He came at me with a knife.*

◆ **come back** *vi* **-1.** [person] to return to the place where one is or lives □ *She came back from work early.* □ *Call me if the pain comes back.* **-2. it all came back (to me)** I remembered it all suddenly □ *I can't remember her name but I'm sure it will come back (to me).*

-3. to come back into fashion to become fashionable again.

◆ **come back to** *vt fus* **to come back to sthg** [question, topic, idea] to consider or discuss sthg again □ *That's an interesting point and I'll come back to it later.*

◆ **come by** *vt fus* **-1. to come by sthg** [money, name, idea] to get or find sthg, usually by chance □ *How did you come by that nasty cut?* □ *Jobs aren't easy to come by.* **-2. they came by the house** US they came to visit, unexpectedly and for a short time.

◆ **come down** *vi* **-1.** [fog, barrier, building] to fall, drop, or be taken down; [plane, parachute] to land, usually not in the place intended □ *That tree is dangerous, it's got to come down.* □ *Barriers to free trade are coming down all over the world.* □ *The helicopter came down in a field.* **-2.** [unemployment, prices, spending] to become lower or less. **-3.** [person] to visit somebody, usually when this involves going southwards or into the countryside □ *The Tylers are coming down next weekend.*

◆ **come down to** *vt fus* **it comes down to cost in the end** cost is the most important thing that matters in the end □ *It came down to a choice between the Fiat and the Renault.*

◆ **come down with** *vt fus* **to come down with an illness** to catch an illness □ *She's come down with a cold.*

◆ **come for** *vt fus* **to come for sb/sthg** to come to collect sb/sthg and take them away.

◆ **come forward** *vi* [volunteer, expert] to offer help or information, especially because somebody has asked for it publicly □ *The police have asked for witnesses to come forward.*

◆ **come from** *vt fus* **-1. to come from a place** to be born or live in a place □ *I come from Chicago.* □ *Where do you come from?* **-2. to come from sthg** to have sthg as its source □ *Milk comes from cows.* □ *The picture comes from one of her movies.* □ *I don't know where the money is going to come from.*

◆ **come in** *vi* **-1.** [person] to enter a house or room where one is □ *I was in the kitchen when John came in.* ■ **come in!** a phrase used to ask somebody to come into one's office, room etc. □ *Come in out of the cold and get warm.* **-2.** [news, information, message] to be received by people who are waiting for it □ *Reports are coming in of riots in Tokyo.* **-3. to have money coming in** to earn money regularly. **-4. where do I come in?** how am I involved? □ *The plan is fine, but I don't see where I come into it.* **-5.** [clothes, custom] to become fashionable or popular □ *These shoes first came in in the fifties.*

◆ **come in for** *vt fus* **to come in for criticism/praise** to get a lot of criticism/praise from people.

◆ **come into** *vt fus* **-1. to come into sthg** [into money, an inheritance] to inherit sthg when somebody dies □ *She came into a fortune when her father died.* **-2. to come into sight** OR **view** to appear a long way away. ■ **to come into being** OR **existence** to start to exist.

◆ **come of** *vt fus* **nothing came of it** it did not happen □ *We did have plans to work abroad, but* *nothing came of it.* ■ **that's what comes of smoking** that is the result of smoking □ *''I feel sick.'' — ''That's what comes of eating too much!''*

◆ **come off** ◇ *vi* -1. [button, label, lid] to become separated or broken off from the main part of something □ *The chain has come off my bike, can you fix it back on?* -2. [stain, dirt] to be possible to remove □ *Will the paint come off?* -3. [wedding, attempt, trip] to take place as planned □ *Let's hope the deal comes off.* -4. **to come off well/badly** to be in a good/bad situation as a result of something □ *They came off badly from the deal and lost a lot of money.*
◇ *vt* -1. **to come off sthg** [horse, bike, roof] to fall off sthg. -2. **to come off sthg** [medicine, drug] to stop taking sthg □ *I've had to come off the Pill.* -3. *phrase* **come off it!** a phrase used when one does not believe what somebody is saying □ *Oh, come off it, you must have known what was going on!*

◆ **come on** *vi* -1. **to be coming on** [cold, headache] to be starting □ *I can feel a cold coming on.* -2. [light, heating] to start working, usually automatically □ *I set the radio to come on at 8 am.* -3. [project, person] to be making good progress □ *Her Russian has come on well this term.* -4. *phrase* **come on!** a phrase used to encourage somebody or to tell them to hurry up □ *Come on, don't give up, you can do it! Come on or we'll miss the bus.*

◆ **come out** *vi* -1. [person] to leave a room or building and move toward where one is □ *Can Sam come out to play?* □ *He came out of prison after two years.* -2. [Sun, Moon, stars] to appear in the sky □ *The clouds parted and the Sun came out.* -3. [stain, dirt] to be removed by washing □ *The mark will come out if you soak it.* -4. [photograph, recording] to be produced successfully and clearly □ *Only a few of our wedding pictures came out.* -5. [information, fact] to become known after being secret or hidden □ *The truth eventually came out.* -6. [newspaper, book] to be published; [movie, product] to become available to the public □ *The magazine comes out on Tuesdays.* □ *The video is coming out next month.* -7. **to come out for/against sthg** to state publicly that one is in favor of/against sthg. -8. to publicly admit that one is homosexual. -9. GB [workers, union] to go on strike.

◆ **come out in** *vt fus* **to come out in pimples** to become covered in pimples □ *I come out in a rash if I eat strawberries.*

◆ **come over** ◇ *vt fus* **a change came over her** a change made her behave in an unusual way □ *I'm sorry about that, I don't know what came over me.* ◇ *vi* -1. [person] to arrive at the place where one is, usually by crossing a bridge, the sea etc □ *They came over from France on the night ferry.* -2. **she comes over well** people get a good impression of her □ *He came over as being very efficient in the interview.* -3. GB [guest, visitor] to visit one at home, usually for a short time □ *You must come over for tea some time.*

◆ **come round** *vi* = **come around**.

◆ **come through** ◇ *vt fus* **to come through sthg** [crisis, recession, war] to reach the end of sthg difficult without being hurt, harmed, or killed □ *He came through the divorce fairly well.* ◇ *vi* [news, document] to arrive after going through the necessary procedures or stages □ *My passport hasn't come through yet.*

◆ **come to** ◇ *vt fus* -1. **to come to a place** to arrive at a place one has not been to before □ *We carried on walking until we came to a crossroads.* □ *They came to England in 1962.* -2. **to come to an end** to end, usually after some time □ *The war finally came to an end in 1919.* □ *We have not yet come to a decision/ conclusion.* ■ **to come to a halt** OR **stop** to stop moving □ *The ball came to rest at the bottom of the stairs.* ■ **to come to power** to start to rule or govern a country. -3. **the bill came to $15** the bill was $15 in all. ◇ *vi* [person] to become conscious again after being unconscious □ *When he came to there was a nurse standing over him.*

◆ **come under** *vt fus* -1. **to come under sthg** to be controlled or managed by sthg □ *The state police comes under the authority of the Governor.* -2. **to come under a category** to belong in a particular category □ *This book comes under the heading of fiction.* -3. **to come under attack/criticism** to be attacked/criticized □ *The Fed is coming under pressure from the banks to raise interest rates.*

◆ **come up** *vi* -1. [person, train] to go to or arrive at the place where one is □ *My mother came up yesterday by train.* □ *He came up to me and asked for a cigarette.* -2. **to be coming up** [Christmas, birthday] to be happening soon □ *It's coming up to Easter/six o'clock.* -3. [subject, person] to be mentioned or discussed □ *Your name came up in the conversation.* -4. [Sun, Moon] to appear in the sky from below the horizon. -5. [situation, problem] to happen unexpectedly □ *Sorry I'm late, but something came up at work.*

◆ **come up against** *vt fus* **to come up against sthg** [opposition, prejudices] to meet sthg that causes problems □ *We've come up against a few snags.*

◆ **come upon** *vt fus* **to come upon sb/sthg** to find or meet sb/sthg by chance □ *I came upon some errors in your report.*

◆ **come up to** *vt fus* **to come up to a standard** to reach or equal a standard.

◆ **come up with** *vt fus* **to come up with sthg** [plan, idea, solution] to think up, invent, or suggest sthg □ *What excuse did he come up with?*

comeback ['kʌmbæk] *n* a return to being as popular, fashionable, or successful as before □ *She made her comeback in the stage version of ''Sunset Boulevard''.* □ *a comeback record.*

comedian [kə'miːdjən] *n* a person whose job is to tell jokes and make people laugh.

comedienne [kə,miːdɪ'en] *n* a female comedian.

comedown ['kʌmdaʊn] *n* something that is less exciting or important than something one has had or felt before (informal use) □

This place is a real comedown after my usual room at the Ambassador!

comedy ['kɒmədɪ] (*pl* **comedies**) *n* **-1.** THEATER & CINEMA a play or movie that is meant to be funny □ *a comedy actor.* **-2.** [of a situation] the quality in a situation, play etc that makes it funny □ *She's an actress with a gift for comedy.*

comely ['kʌmlɪ] *adj* [woman] attractive (literary use).

come-on *n* **to give sb the come-on** to show sb in a very obvious way that one would like to have sex with them (informal use).

comet ['kɒmət] *n* an object that looks like a star with a long bright tail and that travels around the Sun.

come-uppance [ˌkʌm'ʌpəns] *n* **to get one's come-uppance** to get the punishment one deserves (informal use).

comfort ['kʌmfət] ◇ *n* **-1.** the feeling of being comfortable; the state of having everything that one needs to live □ *clothes designed for comfort and style* □ *They live in comfort.* □ *This service is provided for your comfort and convenience.* ■ **to be too close for comfort** to be so close that one feels frightened □ *That truck came a little too close for comfort.* **-2.** [in the home] something used in the home that makes one's life easier and more pleasant □ *I like my comforts.* □ *a home with every modern comfort.* **-3.** **to be a comfort** to make one feel less worried or unhappy □ *It's a great comfort to know you're around.* □ *That's not much comfort to me now, is it!*
◇ *vt* to make <sb> feel less worried or unhappy □ *She comforted me when I was really down.* □ *It comforted him to know she was safe.*

comfortable ['kʌmftəbl] *adj* **-1.** **to be comfortable** to be in a position or place in which one is relaxed because it is pleasant □ *Sit down and make yourself comfortable.* □ *I had just got comfortable when the phone rang.* **-2.** [chair, room, trip] that makes one feel comfortable □ *Those shoes look comfortable.* **-3.** MEDICINE [patient] who is not in too much pain or danger after an accident or operation □ *Both mother and baby were said to be comfortable.* **-4.** [lead, win] that is large enough for one to be sure about winning □ *He won by a comfortable margin.* **-5.** [family] that has enough money to pay for things easily □ *He comes from a comfortable, middle-class background.* **-6.** **to be comfortable about** OR **with sthg** not to be worried about sthg □ *I don't really feel comfortable with the idea, frankly.*

comfortably ['kʌmftəblɪ] *adv* **-1.** **to be comfortably off** [person] to be quite rich. **-2.** [sleep, win] *see* **comfortable** □ *Are you sitting comfortably?* □ *I can live comfortably on $100 a week.* □ *By half-time, Brazil was comfortably in the lead.*

comforter ['kʌmfətər] *n* **-1.** a person who comforts somebody. **-2.** US a thick warm bedcover that is filled with feathers or another soft material.

comforting ['kʌmfətɪŋ] *adj* [thought, news,

voice] that comforts one □ *It's comforting to know help is never far away.*

comfort station *n* a public restroom (polite use).

comfy ['kʌmfɪ] (*compar* **comfier**, *superl* **comfiest**) *adj* [shoes, chair, room] comfortable (informal use).

comic ['kɒmɪk] ◇ *adj* [event, performance, actor] that is intended to make people laugh. ◇ *n* **-1.** THEATER & TV a person whose job is to tell jokes and make people laugh. **-2.** [for children] a magazine, usually for children, containing stories in the form of cartoons.

♦ **comics** *npl* US the part of a newspaper that contains stories in the form of cartoons.

comical ['kɒmɪkl] *adj* [appearance, person, event] that is funny but was not intended to be.

comic strip *n* a series of cartoons that tell a story.

coming ['kʌmɪŋ] ◇ *adj* **the coming storm/election etc** the storm/election etc that will happen soon □ *We're hoping to negotiate a deal in the coming days/weeks.* ◇ *n* **comings and goings** the movement of people arriving and leaving somewhere.

comma ['kɒmə] *n* a symbol (,) used between the items in a list or to divide up a sentence.

command [US kə'mænd, GB -'mɑːnd] ◇ *n* **-1.** [to a person] an order that is given by somebody in a position of authority □ *His commands were always carried out promptly.* □ *At her command* OR *When she gave the command everybody stood up.* **-2.** [of an army, country, situation] control over particular people, events etc □ *The troops were under his command.* □ *He has command of 30,000 men.* □ *We are looking to take command of the market.* ■ **to be in command** to have command over somebody or something □ *Who's in command here?* □ *She is in total command of the situation.* □ *I'm only second in command.* **-3.** [of a language, subject] knowledge of something and the ability to use it □ *His command of detail is outstanding.* □ *She has a poor/an excellent command of French.* ■ **to have sthg at one's command** [language, resource] to have sthg that one can use □ *With Japanese and Korean at her command, she's perfect for the job.* **-4.** COMPUTING an instruction to a computer.
◇ *vt* **-1.** **to command sb to do sthg** to order sb to do sthg when one has the authority to do this □ *He commanded us to wait.* **-2.** [regiment, troops] to be in a position of control over <people>. **-3.** [respect, attention] to get <sthg that one deserves> from other people □ *He no longer commands the respect of his staff.* ■ **to command a high fee/salary** to get a high fee/salary □ *Consultants now command a five-figure salary.*

commandant ['kɒməndænt] *n* an officer who is in charge of a particular place or group of soldiers.

commandeer [ˌkɒmən'dɪər] *vt* [vehicle, building, property] to take <sthg> without paying for it for the use of the army.

commander [US kə'mændr, GB kə'mɑːndə] *n*

-1. an officer in charge of a military campaign or group. -2. GB an officer in the Royal Navy.

commander in chief (*pl* **commanders in chief**) *n* the officer in charge of all the military groups in a particular area.

commanding [US kə'mændɪŋ, GB -'mɑːnd-] *adj* -1. **to be in a commanding position** to be in a position that allows one to have a lot of control over other people and events. ■ **to have a commanding lead** to be far ahead of other people in a race or competition. -2. [voice, manner, look] that commands respect and obedience □ *He was a commanding presence in his uniform.* -3. **a commanding view/ height** a view/height that allows one to see for a great distance all around.

commanding officer *n* the officer who is in charge of a group of soldiers.

commandment [US kə'mændmənt, GB -'mɑːnd-] *n* one of the ten rules in the Bible that Jews and Christians believe God told people to obey □ *the Ten Commandments.*

command module *n* the part of a spacecraft where the controls are situated.

commando [US kə'mændou, GB -'mɑːnd-] (*pl* **commandos** OR **commandoes**) *n* a group of soldiers who have been specially trained to carry out surprise attacks on enemy territory; a member of this group □ *a commando of marines* □ *a commando unit.*

command performance *n* a performance at a theater that has been requested by a king or queen and is attended by a member of their family.

commemorate [kə'meməreɪt] *vt* -1. to do something that shows one remembers and respects <a person or event> □ *Hundreds turned up at the ceremony to commemorate the end of the war.* □ *a series of programs commemorating the 100th anniversary of the author's death.* -2. to remind people officially of <a person or event> □ *The statue was erected to commemorate those who died in the war.*

commemoration [kə,memə'reɪʃn] *n: see* **commemorate** □ *a statue in commemoration of the dead soldiers.*

commemorative [kə'memərətɪv] *adj* [stamp, service, plaque] that commemorates a person or event.

commence [kə'mens] (formal use) ◇ *vt* [trip, speech, work] to begin <sthg> □ *They commenced construction of the bridge in 1992.* ◇ *vi* [meeting, work] *'Sale commences January 3rd.'*

commencement [kə'mensmənt] *n* -1. the start of something (formal use). -2. **a commencement (ceremony)** US EDUCATION a graduation ceremony.

commend [kə'mend] *vt* -1. to praise <sb> officially, especially for something brave they have done □ *He was highly commended on* OR *for his actions.* -2. [restaurant, person, place] to praise <sthg/sb> to somebody because they may want to use it, employ them etc (formal use) □ *I can certainly commend her to you.* □ *The policy has little to commend it.*

commendable [kə'mendəbl] *adj* [action, achievement, effort] that deserves praise.

commendation [,kɒmən'deɪʃn] *n* a special award given to somebody because of something they have done that deserves praise □ *a commendation for bravery.*

commensurate [kə'mensərət] *adj* **commensurate with sthg** at a level that is appropriate to sthg (formal use) □ *Salary is commensurate with experience.*

comment ['kɒment] ◇ *n* a statement that gives one's opinion about something, sometimes in public □ *Does anyone have any comments?* □ *She made a few useful comments on how we had handled the incident.* □ *His wife was unavailable for comment.* ■ **no comment** a phrase used when one does not want to give an opinion or talk about something, especially to the press. ◇ *vt* **to comment that...** to say that something is true in one's opinion □ *Officials commented that the proposed pay increases were unrealistic.* ◇ *vi* to make a comment about something □ *I'm afraid I cannot comment on this matter.*

commentary [US 'kɒməntərɪ, GB -əntərɪ] (*pl* **commentaries**) *n* -1. RADIO & TV a spoken description of a game, ceremony etc that is given while it is happening □ *a news/sports commentary.* -2. [on a book, situation] a written discussion or explanation of something.

commentate ['kɒmənteɪt] *vi* RADIO & TV to give a spoken commentary on something □ *She commentates on tennis matches.*

commentator ['kɒmənteɪtəʳ] *n* -1. RADIO & TV a person whose job is to commentate on a sports game, ceremony etc □ *a sports commentator.* -2. JOURNALISM an expert who writes or talks about a particular subject □ *a political commentator.*

commerce ['kɒmɜːʳs] *n* the activity of buying and selling goods, especially between different countries or companies □ *the enormous benefits of commerce between our two countries* □ *My father went into commerce.*

commercial [kə'mɜːʳʃl] ◇ *adj* -1. [venture, movie, television] that is intended to make money □ *The song has a very commercial sound.* □ *The idea is just not commercial.* □ *a commercial success.* -2. [law, district, correspondence] *see* **commerce.** ◇ *n* an advertisement on the television or radio □ *I made a cup of coffee during the commercials.*

commercial bank *n* a bank that lends money to businesses for a short period of time, using money from savings accounts.

commercial break *n* the time during a television or radio program, or between programs, when advertisements are shown.

commercial college *n* GB a college where skills needed for business are taught, e.g. accounting.

commercialism [kə'mɜːʳʃəlɪzm] *n* the attitude that is based on the belief that making a profit is the most important thing (disapproving use).

commercialized [kə'mɜːʳʃəlaɪzd] *adj* [place, record] that is too concerned with making a profit (disapproving use) □ *Christmas has become very commercialized.*

commercially [kə'mɜːrʃəlɪ] *adv* [sell, print, produce] see **commercial** □ *They are commercially very successful.* □ *a commercially viable business* □ *Commercially, it was a disaster.*

commercial television, commercial TV *n* GB television that gets money from the advertisements it shows and not from the government.

commercial vehicle *n* a vehicle used to carry goods along roads.

commie ['kɒmɪ] *n* & *adj* = **Communist** (informal and disapproving use).

commiserate [kə'mɪzəreɪt] *vi* to show sympathy to somebody about something bad that has happened to them □ *I commiserated with them over their defeat.*

commiseration [kə,mɪzə'reɪʃn] *n* the sympathy one shows when one commiserates with somebody □ *a look of commiseration* □ *Our commiserations go to the losers.*

commission [kə'mɪʃn] ◇ *n* **-1.** BUSINESS an amount of money that one earns for selling something □ *She gets a 5% commission on each item she sells.* □ *The bank charges 10% commission.* □ *I work on a commission basis.* □ *a commission fee.* **-2.** ART & MUSIC a piece of work that an artist, architect, musician etc is officially chosen to make. **-3.** POLITICS a special group of people chosen to carry out a particular duty or examine a particular subject □ *the Equal Opportunities Commission.*
◇ *vt* [painting, building, book] to officially choose somebody to make <sthg>; [artist, architect] to officially choose <sb> to make something □ *City Hall has commissioned a suite of new offices from him.* □ *We commissioned her to create the costumes for the play.*

commissionaire [kə,mɪʃə'neər] *n* GB a person whose job is to help customers and open the doors of a theater, hotel etc.

commissioned officer [kə,mɪʃnd-] *n* an officer in the army or navy of middle or high rank.

commissioner [kə'mɪʃnər] *n* **-1.** [of the church, police, a government department] a person in charge of an organization □ *a police commissioner.* **-2.** POLITICS a member of a commission.

Commission for Racial Equality *n* the **Commission for Racial Equality** the British government organization responsible for making sure that people of all races are treated equally by the law.

commit [kə'mɪt] (*pt* & *pp* **committed**, *cont* **committing**) *vt* **-1.** [crime, sin, offense] to do <sthg bad or illegal> □ *He was sent to prison for a murder he never committed.* **-2.** [money, resources, staff] to promise to provide or use <sb/sthg> for a particular purpose □ *The US has committed several thousand troops to the peace-keeping process.* ■ **to commit oneself to sthg** to promise to do sthg □ *The Government has committed itself to market reforms.* **-3.** LAW to order <sb> to be put in prison or a men-

tal hospital. **-4. to commit sthg to memory** [information, poem] to learn sthg so that one remembers it exactly (formal use).

commitment [kə'mɪtmənt] *n* **-1.** [to a person, charity, one's job] the hard work, activity, or involvement in something that comes from a real interest or belief in it □ *Her enthusiasm and commitment to the project were crucial to its success.* □ *They would like to see a greater commitment to AIDS research.* **-2.** [of a person] something that one must do or agrees to do and that takes some of one's time, money etc □ *a financial commitment* □ *I have too many commitments at the moment.*

committed [kə'mɪtəd] *adj* [supporter, socialist] who shows a strong belief in something and who works hard to help it succeed □ *committed to innovation and change.*

committee [kə'mɪtɪ] *n* a group of specially chosen people who discuss, make decisions, or give advice about a particular subject □ *A committee was formed to deal with the problem.* □ *Who is on the committee?* □ *a committee meeting/member.*

commode [kə'məʊd] *n* a piece of furniture like a chair or stool with a pot inside that is used as a toilet by sick people.

commodity [kə'mɒdətɪ] (*pl* **commodities**) *n* a product, such as oil or sugar, that can be bought or sold for profit, usually in large quantities.

commodity exchange *n* the central market where commodities are bought and sold.

common ['kɒmən] ◇ *adj* **-1.** [occurrence, experience, problem] that happens often, in large numbers, or in many different places □ *Foxes are quite a common sight in some cities.* □ *It's very common to see people using cellular phones nowadays.* ■ **common practice** a way of doing things that is usual and accepted □ *Polygamy used to be common practice among Mormons.* **-2.** [aim, feature, language] that is shared by two or more people or things □ *We share a common belief that education ought to be free for everyone.* □ *This type of experience is common to many.* **-3.** [cold, man] ordinary and with no special characteristics □ *the common toad.* **-4.** [person] a word used to describe a person who one thinks has bad manners and bad taste (disapproving use) □ *She thought her son-in-law was common.*
◇ *n* an area of grassy land in a town or village that all the local people can use.
♦ **in common** *adv* **to have sthg in common** to have the same characteristics or interests □ *I no longer have much in common with my brother.* □ *We have such a lot in common.*

Common Agricultural Policy *n* → CAP.

commoner ['kɒmənər] *n* a person who is not a member of the nobility □ *It is no longer unusual for royalty to marry commoners.*

common good *n* **for the common good** in order to benefit people in general.

common ground *n* something that the different people involved in an argument or dispute already agree about □ *Let's try to find some common ground.*

common knowledge *n* something that is known by most people □ *It is common knowledge that Stephen only got the job because of family connections.*

common land *n* a piece of land in a particular area that all the local people can use.

common law *n* the system of law that is based on the past decisions of a court rather than on written laws.

◆ **common-law** *adj* **a common-law husband/wife** a husband/wife who is living with somebody as their husband/wife but is not legally married to them □ *a common-law husband/wife/marriage.*

commonly ['kɒmənlɪ] *adv* a word used to say what many people do, think, say etc □ *Oysters are commonly thought to be an aphrodisiac.*

Common Market *n* **the Common Market** the name used to refer to the European Union in its original form as an economic community.

commonplace ['kɒmənpleɪs] *adj* [object, event, activity] that is not unusual or special in any way □ *Satellite dishes are now becoming commonplace.*

common room *n* a room in a school or college where students can meet and relax during breaks and free time.

Commons ['kɒmənz] *npl* = **House of Commons** □ *a Commons debate.*

common sense *n* **-1.** the ability to think sensibly or logically about a problem or situation and make practical decisions □ *Use your common sense!* **-2. it's common sense** it's something that seems obvious to most people for logical reasons □ *It's just a matter of common sense.*

Commonwealth ['kɒmənwelθ] *n* **the Commonwealth** the association of countries that used to be part of the British Empire and still have special relations with Britain and each other.

👋 THE COMMONWEALTH
In Britain, the term "the Commonwealth" refers to the group of 50 independent countries, founded in 1931, that used to be British colonies. The official name for this is the Commonwealth of Nations, but it is often called the British Commonwealth.
In Australia, people use the term "the Commonwealth" when they are referring to the federal government, or when they want to distinguish the federal government from the governments of each state. The term comes from the official name for Australia, which is the Commonwealth of Australia.

Commonwealth Employment Service *n* → **CES**.

Commonwealth of Independent States *n* → **CIS**.

commotion [kə'məʊʃn] *n* the sudden noise and movement of people who are excited,

confused, or angry □ *Suddenly we heard a tremendous commotion outside.*

communal [kə'mju:nl, 'kɒmjʊnl] *adj* [garden, kitchen, land] that is shared by a group of people who live in the same house, area etc □ *Communal baths are popular in Japan.*

commune [*n* 'kɒmju:n, *vb* kə'mju:n] ◇ *n* a group of people living together who share everything equally, including food and money □ *He was brought up in a hippy commune.* ◇ *vi* **to commune with nature/God** to become spiritually close to nature/God (literary use).

communicate [kə'mju:nɪkeɪt] ◇ *vt* [information, opinion, feeling] to make <sthg> known to somebody using words, images etc □ *I find it hard to communicate what I really feel in a foreign language.* ◇ *vi* *It's important to communicate with your staff.*

communicating [kə'mju:nɪkeɪtɪŋ] *adj* [rooms] that are connected by a door; [door] that connects two rooms.

communication [kə,mju:nɪ'keɪʃn] *n* **-1.** □ *There has been a breakdown in communication.* □ *good communication skills.* **-2.** [from a person] a message, letter, or telephone call (formal use).

◆ **communications** *npl* the various systems and methods of communication between people and places, such as the telephone, mail, and computers □ *the communications industry.*

communications satellite *n* a satellite in space that uses radio signals to make it possible to communicate over long distances by television, telephone, and computer.

communicative [kə'mju:nəkeɪtɪv] *adj* [person] who likes to talk to people and can communicate well □ *You're not being very communicative.*

communicator [kə'mju:nɪkeɪtər] *n* **a good/bad communicator** a person who communicates well/badly with other people.

communion [kə'mju:njən] *n* a feeling of being spiritually close to somebody or something, especially when emotions, ideas etc are exchanged □ *a feeling of communion with Nature.*

◆ **Communion** *n* a Christian service in which people eat bread and drink wine as a symbol of Christ's death and resurrection.

communiqué [kə'mju:nɪkeɪ] *n* an official statement made by a government, organization etc to the media.

Communism ['kɒmjənɪzm] *n* a political system in which the state has complete control of the sources of wealth, e.g. land and factories, and in which there is no private property and no difference in social classes. NOTE: Compare **Capitalism, Socialism**.

Communist ['kɒmjənɪst] ◇ *n* a person who believes in Communism. ◇ *adj*: *a member of the Communist Party* □ *a Communist state.*

community [kə'mju:nətɪ] (*pl* **communities**) *n* [of people] a group of people who are connected to each other because they live in the same area or have a particular religion, nationality, interests etc □ *The business community has welcomed the move.* □ *the English-speaking com-*

munity in Rome □ an organization to help prisoners released into the community □ the international community.

community association *n* one of many local voluntary groups in Britain that works to help the local neighborhood.

community care *n* the British government program of taking people out of institutions, e.g. mental hospitals, and sending them home, to be cared for by their families or local welfare organizations.

community center *n* a building used by the people of an area for meetings and entertainment or sports.

community college *n* in the USA and Australia, an undergraduate college where students, who generally live at home, receive a technical qualification after two years of study.

community home *n* in Britain, a special school for children who have broken the law.

community service *n* -1. [by volunteers] voluntary work done to benefit the local community as part of an organized program. -2. LAW unpaid work for the local community that a criminal is ordered to do, instead of going to prison.

community spirit *n* the feeling of friendliness and helpfulness that exists between people who live in the same area.

commutable [kə'mjuːtəbl] *adj* LAW [sentence] that can be made less severe.

commutation ticket [,kɒmjʊ'teɪʃn-] *n* US a ticket for a fixed number of trips on a train along a route during a limited period.

commute [kə'mjuːt] ◇ *vt* to make <a criminal sentence> less severe □ The sentence was later commuted to life imprisonment. ◇ *vi* to travel to and from work every day □ He commutes to work by train.

commuter [kə'mjuːtər] *n* a person who commutes to work □ a commuter train/town.

commy ['kɒmɪ] (*pl* **commies**) *adj* & *n* = **commie**.

compact [*adj* & *vb* kəm'pækt, *n* 'kɒmpækt] ◇ *adj* [bag, apartment, car] that is not large and is smaller than other ones of the same kind. ◇ *n* -1. a small flat case that contains face powder and a mirror. -2. US **a compact (car)** a small car. ◇ *vt* [earth, sand, mixture] to force <sthg> into a smaller space by pressing it together (formal use).

compact disc [,kɒmpækt-] *n* a small plastic disk that stores recorded music in the form of numbers that are changed back to music by a special machine □ The album is now available on compact disc.

compact disc player *n* a machine used for playing compact discs.

companion [kəm'pænjən] *n* a person who one spends a lot of time with as a friend or to avoid feeling bored, lonely etc □ I offered to go with her as a traveling companion.

companionable [kəm'pænjənəbl] *adj* [person, occasion] that seems pleasant and friendly.

companionship [kəm'pænjənʃɪp] *n* the friendly relationship that exists between people who know each other well □ Pets provide much-needed companionship for elderly people.

company ['kʌmpənɪ] (*pl* **companies**) *n* -1. BUSINESS a group of people who work together in business under one name □ They decided to set up a company together. □ company profits. -2. [of performers] a group of actors or dancers who work together on a production, sometimes traveling around a country □ a touring company. -3. [for a person] the presence of somebody who helps to pass the time □ I'd be glad of your company. □ Cats make good company. ■ **to have/expect company** to have/expect guests □ We have company this weekend so we can't come to dinner. ■ **to keep sb company** to spend time with sb so that they are not lonely □ Stay here and keep me company. ■ **to part company** to go in separate directions after meeting, traveling together etc; to come to the end of a personal or business relationship, especially because of a disagreement □ He parted company with the firm last year.

company car *n* a car that a company provides for an employee, especially one who travels a lot in their job.

company director *n* one of the group of people who control a company at the highest level.

company secretary *n* GB an important member of a company who is responsible for the accounts and the legal side of the company's business.

comparable ['kɒmpərəbl] *adj* that is similar enough in size, quality etc to be able to be compared with something else □ The car's fuel consumption is comparable to OR with that of a much smaller car. □ This is the only comparable case that I can think of.

comparative [kəm'pærətɪv] *adj* -1. [wealth, luxury, safety] that has the particular quality mentioned when it is compared to something similar □ After Moscow I enjoyed the comparative warmth of Prague. -2. **a comparative study** a study that shows the differences and similarities between two or more related things □ They carried out a comparative study between males and females. -3. GRAMMAR a word used to refer to the form of an adjective or adverb that shows a difference in size, quality etc between two related things or people □ "Older" is the comparative form of "old".

comparatively [kəm'pærətɪvlɪ] *adv* **comparatively poor/wealthy etc** poor/wealthy etc when compared with other things or people of a similar kind □ The weather has been comparatively mild for the time of year.

compare [kəm'peər] ◇ *vt* to find the similarities or differences between <two or more people or things> □ If we compare the increase with OR to last year's, we can see a big difference. ■ **compared with** OR **to** a phrase used to introduce the difference(s) between two or more people or things □ Compared to most laptops, it has a large keyboard. ◇ *vi* to be of a similar standard □ *The two just don't compare.* □ *Nothing can compare with the awesome splendor of the Grand Canyon.* ■ **to compare favorably/unfavorably with sb/sthg** to seem good/bad when compared with sb/sthg else.

comparison [US kəm'perɪsən, GB -'pær-] *n* [of people, things] *see* **compare** □ *He made* OR *drew an interesting comparison between US and Japanese marketing strategies.* □ *Domestic sales are low by* OR *in comparison.*
◆ **in comparison with** *prep* a phrase used to introduce the differences between two or more people or things □ *My problems seem small in comparison with yours.*

compartment [kəm'pɑːrtmənt] *n* **-1.** a separate space in a car, refrigerator, bag etc where things are kept □ *Salad should be kept in a separate compartment.* **-2.** RAIL a divided section of a train carriage □ *We found an empty compartment.* □ *a smoking compartment.*

compartmentalize, -ise [ˌkɒmpɑːrt'mentəlaɪz] *vt* to divide <sthg> into separate sections.

compass ['kʌmpəs] *n* **-1.** a device for showing directions that consists of a magnetized needle that always points to the north. **-2.** a device used with a pencil for drawing circles and measuring distances that has two bars attached at one end that can be moved apart to form a "V" shape. **-3. the compass of sthg** the limited area of activity, ability, knowledge, importance etc of sthg (formal use) □ *This issue does not lie within the compass of the committee.*

compassion [kəm'pæʃn] *n* a strong feeling of sympathy and pity that one has for somebody who is suffering □ *He felt no compassion for his victims.*

compassionate [kəm'pæʃənət] *adj* [person] who shows compassion.

compatibility [kəmˌpætə'bɪlətɪ] *n* the quality of being suited to each other; the ability to work well together.

compatible [kəm'pætəbl] *adj* **-1.** [people] who are able to have a good relationship because they have the same interests or personalities □ *We were never compatible.* **-2.** [methods, ideas] that can work well together □ *Is this compatible with official guidelines?* **-3.** COMPUTING [hardware, software] that can be used with particular machines or programs without causing problems □ *IBM-compatible* □ *The printer is not compatible with my computer.*

compatriot [US kəm'peɪtrɪət, GB -'pætr-] *n* a person of the same nationality as oneself.

compel [kəm'pel] (*pt* & *pp* **compelled**, *cont* **compelling**) *vt* **-1.** to make <sb> do something, especially by threatening them □ *I feel compelled to justify myself.* **-2.** [admiration, attention] to cause <sthg, especially a feeling>, in a way that is difficult to resist or prevent (formal use).

compelling [kəm'pelɪŋ] *adj* **-1.** [argument, reason] that is so strong and powerful it is difficult to disagree with □ *The writer builds up his case with compelling logic.* **-2.** [story, movie,

book] that is extremely interesting or exciting □ *Her biography makes compelling reading.*

compendium [kəm'pendjəm] (*pl* **compendiums** OR **compendia** [-'pendjə]) *n* a short but detailed book on a subject (formal use).

compensate ['kɒmpənseɪt] ◇ *vt* LAW to pay <sb> money because of something bad that has happened to them, e.g. an accident or unfair dismissal from a job □ *He was compensated for loss of earnings.* ◇ *vi* to cancel the effect of something bad □ *The good food compensated for the lousy weather.*

compensation [ˌkɒmpən'seɪʃn] *n* **-1.** LAW money that is paid to compensate somebody □ *The victims' families are demanding compensation for the suffering caused.* **-2. it has its compensations** there are good points that make it less unpleasant □ *Working on short-term contracts has its compensations.*

compere ['kɒmpeər] GB ◇ *n* a person whose job is to introduce the performers in a show and entertain the audience between the different sections of the show. ◇ *vt* to be the compere of <a show> □ *Tonight's show was compered by Frank Greenhouse.*

compete [kəm'piːt] *vi* **-1.** [athlete, team, contestant] to try to obtain something for oneself and to prevent other people from having it □ *Eight teams will be competing for the title.* □ *Christie will be competing with* OR *against Lewis in the final.* **-2.** BUSINESS to try to be more successful than one's rivals □ *We're competing with some of the top brand names.* □ *With everyone competing for a share in the market, it's going to be tough.* **-3.** [in a competition] to take part in a competition or race □ *She competed in the last Olympics.*

competence ['kɒmpətəns] *n* the ability to do something correctly and to a satisfactory standard □ *I don't doubt your competence, I'm simply questioning your attitude.*

competent ['kɒmpətənt] *adj* [person] who is able to do something correctly and to a satisfactory standard □ *She's a competent enough worker.* □ *I'm competent in three languages.*

competently ['kɒmpətəntlɪ] *adv*: *see* **competent** □ *He plays the piano competently.*

competing [kəm'piːtɪŋ] *adj* [views, ideas] that are different and opposed to each other.

competition [ˌkɒmpə'tɪʃn] *n* **-1.** [between people] a situation in which two or more people try to be better or more successful than each other, usually to obtain something; the person or people one is competing against in this situation □ *There's stiff competition for the contract.* □ *I'm finding it hard to keep up with the competition.* **-2.** BUSINESS the process of trying to be more successful than one's rivals □ *Once again, the two firms are in competition with each other.* **-3.** [between teams, players] an event that people try to win by being better than everybody else in some way □ *a skating competition.*

competitive [kəm'petətɪv] *adj* **-1.** [person] who likes to try to win or be better than everybody else □ *Our students are encouraged to be competitive.* **-2.** [match, sport, exam] that involves competition; [atmosphere, spirit] that involves the desire to win □ *She's involved in competitive swimming.* □ *It's very competitive at work.* **-3.** [price, goods] that is not expensive compared to rival products or services and so is likely to attract customers □ *I think you'll find our prices very competitive.* □ *Reducing overheads is one way of remaining competitive in today's market.*

competitively [kəm'petətɪvlɪ] *adv* **-1.** [play] *see* **competitive.** **-2. competitively priced** that is not too expensive compared to rival products.

competitor [kəm'petətər] *n* **-1.** BUSINESS a person or company that is competing with another □ *We're looking for anything that will give us an edge over our competitors.* **-2.** [in a competition] a person who takes part in a competition or race.

compilation [ˌkɒmpɪ'leɪʃn] *n* **-1.** a book, record, TV program, or report that contains a collection of work from different sources. **-2.** *see* **compile.**

compile [kəm'paɪl] *vt* [book, record, report] to make <sthg> from information, work etc that has been collected together □ *The program was compiled from archive film.*

complacency [kəm'pleɪsnsɪ] *n* the state of being complacent about something □ *There's no room for complacency here.*

complacent [kəm'pleɪsnt] *adj* [person] who is not worried about something or does not make an effort when they should □ *Despite good progress we can't afford to be complacent.*

complain [kəm'pleɪn] *vi* **-1.** [customer, passenger, worker] to say that one is unhappy or not satisfied with a situation, product, or service □ *Despite the constant pain, he never complained.* □ *Oh, stop complaining!* □ *She complained about the smell.* □ *As usual, he's complaining about his job.* **-2.** MEDICINE **to complain of sthg** [of a pain, illness] to say that one is suffering from sthg □ *He's been complaining of chest pains for some time.*

complaint [kəm'pleɪnt] *n* **-1.** [about a problem] a statement in which somebody complains about somebody or something; the reason for making this statement □ *Following the program, they received several complaints about bad language.* □ *If you like, you can make an official complaint.* □ *I have no cause for complaint.* **-2.** MEDICINE an illness or pain that is usually not very serious □ *a chest complaint.*

complement ['kɒmpləmənt] ◇ *vt* to improve <sb/sthg> by adding something that has different qualities □ *They complement each other perfectly.* ◇ *n* **-1.** something that helps one to appreciate the qualities of the thing it is combined with □ *Red wine is the ideal complement to this type of dish.* **-2. a full complement** the number or amount needed to make something complete □ *We now have our full complement of staff.* **-3.** GRAMMAR a word or phrase that comes after a verb and describes the subject of the verb, e.g. "late" in the sentence, "He is late."

complementary [ˌkɒmplə'mentərɪ] *adj* that makes something complete or more effective □ *Their skills, though different, are complementary.*

complementary medicine *n* a way of treating illness, e.g. homeopathy or acupuncture, that is not part of standard Western medical practices.

complete [kəm'pliːt] ◇ *adj* **-1.** [story, collection, version] that has every part of something with nothing missing □ *No visit to Athens would be complete without a tour of the Acropolis.* □ *"The Complete Works of Oscar Wilde."* **-2. to be complete** [work, report, plan] to be finished and ready □ *At last everything is complete.* **-3.** a word used for emphasis □ *It was a complete disaster!*

◇ *vt* **-1.** [collection, set] to add to and make <sthg> whole or finished □ *A diamond necklace completed the outfit.* □ *His failure to notice the flowers completed her misery.* **-2.** [report, painting, job] to finish <a piece of work> □ *I plan to travel as soon as I complete my studies.* **-3.** [questionnaire, application] to write the necessary information in the spaces provided on <a form> □ *Complete the coupon below and send it to the following address ...*

◆ **complete with** *prep* including or with the addition of <sthg> □ *The TV comes complete with remote control.*

completely [kəm'pliːtlɪ] *adv* **completely finished/wrong etc** finished/wrong etc in every way □ *I completely forgot about it.* □ *My attitude toward him has changed completely.*

completion [kəm'pliːʃn] *n* [of work, a collection, a test] *see* **complete** □ *Work is nearing completion.*

complex ['kɒmpleks] ◇ *adj* [problem, system, character] that is not simple and has many different connected parts; [language, calculation] difficult to understand □ *The plot of the movie is highly complex.* □ *It's too complex for me.* ◇ *n* **-1.** ARCHITECTURE a very large building with different parts, or a number of connected buildings, used for a particular purpose □ *a shopping complex.* **-2.** PSYCHOLOGY a set of feelings, beliefs, or worries that develops unconsciously from experiences or childhood memories, and that affects one's behavior □ *an inferiority complex* □ *After failing three times, I'm starting to get a complex.*

complexion [kəm'plekʃn] *n* **-1.** [of a person] the nature and appearance of the skin on one's face □ *an oily complexion.* **-2.** [of a problem, situation] the nature or character of a problem, matter, or situation □ *This of course puts an entirely different complexion on the issue.*

complexity [kəm'pleksətɪ] (*pl* **complexities**) *n* **-1.** [of a problem, system, character] the state of being complex. **-2. the complexities of sthg** the many different connected parts of sthg that make it difficult to understand.

compliance [kəm'plaɪəns] *n*: *see* **comply** □ *We acted in compliance with your wishes.*

complicate ['kɒmpləkeɪt] *vt* [matter, situation, life] to make <sthg> more difficult to understand or deal with □ *Don't change the schedule now, it will only complicate things.*

complicated ['kɒmpləkeɪtəd] *adj* [situation, process, problem] that consists of so many different parts that it is difficult to understand or deal with □ *The case is so complicated I don't know where to start.*

complication [ˌkɒmplə'keɪʃn] *n* -1. an extra fact or detail that makes a situation or problem more difficult to understand or deal with □ *The car broke down on the way, which was an added complication.* -2. MEDICINE a condition that develops as a result of another illness or treatment, and makes it more difficult for the patient to get better □ *She died of complications following a minor infection.*

complicity [kəm'plɪsətɪ] *n* involvement in something bad or illegal (formal use) □ *His complicity in the scandal was never proved.*

compliment [*n* 'kɒmpləmənt, *vb* 'kɒmpləment] ◇ *n* a pleasing statement praising one's appearance, work etc □ *He's always paying me compliments.* ■ **to take sthg as a compliment** to decide that sthg somebody says or does shows that they like or respect one. ◇ *vt* to tell <sb> that one likes or admires their work, appearance etc □ *She complimented him on his good taste.*

◆ **compliments** *npl* a word used to express respect or good wishes (formal use) □ *The liqueurs came with the compliments of the house.* □ *My compliments to the chef!*

complimentary [ˌkɒmplə'mentərɪ] *adj* -1. [remark, look] that shows admiration or liking for something □ *She was most complimentary about my work.* -2. [drink, copy] that is given free to somebody □ *I have two complimentary tickets for tonight's show.*

compliments slip ['kɒmpləmənts-] *n* GB a small piece of paper with a company's name on it that is put in an envelope with letters, documents etc sent from that company.

comply [kəm'plaɪ] (*pt* & *pp* **complied**) *vi* **to comply with sthg** [with the law, rules] to do something that is ordered or requested by sthg □ *The new model complies with all safety regulations.*

component [kəm'pəʊnənt] *n* one of the parts in a machine or system □ *The car is assembled in Europe from Japanese components.*

compose [kəm'pəʊz] *vt* -1. **to be composed of sthg** to have sthg as its parts or members □ *The chamber is composed of 650 members.* -2. [music, letter] to write <sthg>, thinking very carefully about what to include and how to arrange it. -3. **to compose oneself** to make oneself calm after being upset.

composed [kəm'pəʊzd] *adj* [person] who is calm, especially in a difficult situation □ *I felt calm and composed before the interview.*

composer [kəm'pəʊzər] *n* a person who writes music □ *a composer of musicals.*

composite [US kəm'pɑːzət, GB 'kɒmpəzɪt] ◇ *adj* [picture, account] that is made up of several different parts □ *We used various sources to produce a composite program.* ◇ *n* something that is made up of different parts □ *The article is a composite of three people's statements.*

composition [ˌkɒmpə'zɪʃn] *n* -1. a piece of music or poetry; the act of composing this □ *one of Mahler's later compositions.* -2. [of a chemical, committee] the way that different parts are combined to make a whole thing. -3. EDUCATION a piece of writing on a particular subject, done as an exercise, especially at school.

compost [US 'kɒmpəʊst, GB -pɒst] *n* a mixture of decayed material, e.g. cut grass or dead leaves, that is used to improve the quality of soil □ *a compost heap.*

composure [kəm'pəʊʒər] *n* the ability to stay calm, especially in a difficult situation □ *She was clearly embarrassed, but quickly regained her composure.*

compound [*adj* & *n* 'kɒmpaʊnd, *vb* kəm'paʊnd] ◇ *adj* -1. [eye, problem] that has two or more parts. -2. GRAMMAR [noun, adjective] that is formed by two or more words.
◇ *n* -1. CHEMISTRY a substance that is made by mixing two or more simple chemical elements together □ *a chemical compound.* -2. [of factors, conditions, ingredients] a mixture of two or more things. -3. [in a prison, military camp] an enclosed area with a wall or fence around it that is used for a particular purpose □ *a military compound.* -4. GRAMMAR a noun or adjective that is formed by joining two or more words together □ *"Coffee table" is a compound.*
◇ *vt* -1. **to be compounded of sthg** to be a mixture of sthg (formal use). -2. [problem, mistake, difficulty] to make <sthg bad> worse □ *My apologies only compounded her irritation.*

compound fracture ['kɒmpaʊnd-] *n* MEDICINE a type of bone fracture in which the bone goes through the flesh, causing a wound on the surface of the body.

compound interest ['kɒmpaʊnd-] *n* the interest that is paid on the total of the original amount of money and the interest it has already made.

comprehend [ˌkɒmprɪ'hend] *vt* [action, idea, significance] to understand <sthg> completely □ *I fail to comprehend what good that will do.*

comprehension [ˌkɒmprɪ'henʃn] *n* -1. [of an action, idea] the ability to understand a situation, problem, or process □ *Why they do it is beyond my comprehension.* -2. EDUCATION a reading or listening exercise to check a student's ability to understand something □ *reading/listening comprehension.*

comprehensive [ˌkɒmprɪ'hensɪv] ◇ *adj* -1. [report, list] that includes everything that is necessary or important. □ *We offer a comprehensive range of services.* -2. **comprehensive insurance** insurance that pays for all types of damage that is caused by oneself or somebody else. -3. GB [teacher, system] that is connected with comprehensive schools. ◇ *n* GB = **comprehensive school.**

comprehensively [ˌkɒmprɪ'hensɪvlɪ] *adv* [cover, study, treat] paying attention to the details, so that everything necessary or important is included.

comprehensive school *n* a school in Britain

that provides free education to children of all abilities between the ages of 11 and 18.

compress [*n* 'kɒmpres, *vb* kəm'pres] ◇ *vt* **-1.** [air, gas, metal] to squeeze or press <sthg> together so that it takes up a smaller space □ *compressed air.* **-2.** [text, information, file] to make <sthg> shorter so that it takes up less space or time □ *A three-hour debate was compressed into two minutes of television.* ◇ *n* a hot or cold pad of material placed on a part of the body to reduce pain, fever etc.

compression [kəm'preʃn] *n*: see **compress**.

comprise [kəm'praɪz] *vt* **-1.** to be <a particular amount of something> □ *Women comprise 60% of the workforce.* **-2. to be comprised of sthg** to have sthg as its parts or members □ *The USA is comprised of 50 states.*

compromise ['kɒmprəmaɪz] ◇ *n* an agreement or situation in which somebody accepts less than they really want □ *The two parties reached a compromise late last night.* ◇ *vt* [person, position, party] to make <sb/sthg> appear insincere, dishonest, or immoral □ *I didn't want to compromise my principles by taking part.* ◇ *vi* to reach a compromise with somebody in order to end a disagreement □ *We compromised on the deadline.*

compromising ['kɒmprəmaɪzɪŋ] *adj* [position, circumstances, letter] that can make one seem insincere, dishonest, or immoral □ *I don't think Howard realized what a compromising situation he was putting himself in.*

compulsion [kəm'pʌlʃn] *n* **-1.** a strong desire or need to do something that is often impossible to control □ *I felt a sudden compulsion to hit him.* **-2. to be under no compulsion to do sthg** to have no obligation to do a particular thing □ *He is under no compulsion to sell.*

compulsive [kəm'pʌlsɪv] *adj* **-1.** [gambling, smoking, behavior] that somebody does often and finds difficult to stop or control. ■ **a compulsive liar/gambler etc** a person who lies/gambles etc very often because they cannot stop doing it. **-2.** [book, program] that is so interesting one does not want to stop reading, watching, listening etc □ *This study makes compulsive reading.*

compulsory [kəm'pʌlsəri] *adj* [education, military service] that one must do because of a law, regulation, or rule □ *It's compulsory to wear a seat belt.*

compulsory purchase *n* GB the buying of land or property by a local council or the government for public use, whether the owner wishes to sell it or not.

compunction [kəm'pʌŋkʃn] *n* **to have** OR **feel no compunction** to not feel guilty at all about doing something (formal use) □ *I felt absolutely no compunction in asking him for money.*

compute [kəm'pjuːt] *vt* [number, quantity, total] to calculate <sthg>, especially with a computer □ *After the results have been computed we will make the necessary changes.*

computer [kəm'pjuːtə'] *n* an electronic machine that is used e.g. for calculations and for storing and providing information, and

that is operated by a programmed set of instructions □ *The information is kept on computer.* □ *a computer program* □ *computer graphics.*

computer dating [-deɪtɪŋ] *n* a service provided by an agency that uses personal information about somebody, e.g. their interests or appearance, to help them find a partner for a personal relationship.

computer game *n* a game that is played using a computer.

computerization [US kəm,pjuːtərə'zeɪʃn, GB -əraɪ'zeɪʃn] *n*: see **computerize**.

computerize, -ise [kəm'pjuːtəraɪz] *vt* [system, firm, information] to change <sthg> so that computers control all the information that is dealt with.

computerized [kəm'pjuːtəraɪzd] *adj* [system, process] that is controlled by a computer; [information, database] that is stored on a computer □ *The accounts department is fully computerized.* □ *computerized files/invoices.*

computer language *n* the language used in the writing of a computer program.

computer-literate *adj* [person] who understands and knows how to use computers.

computer science *n* the study of computers and their uses.

computing [kəm'pjuːtɪŋ] *n* the activity of using a computer; the study of computers and their uses □ *a course in computing* □ *a computing manual.*

comrade [US 'kɒmræd, GB -reɪd] *n* **-1.** POLITICS a word used by a Communist or Socialist to address somebody who belongs to the same organization, especially in speeches. **-2.** a person who is close to another person, especially because they are together in the same situation, e.g. a war (old-fashioned use).

comradeship [US 'kɒmrædʃɪp, GB -reɪd-] *n* the friendship that exists between people who are together in a particular situation, e.g. a war or expedition.

comsat ['kɒmsæt] *n* abbr of **communications satellite**.

con [kɒn] (*pt* & *pp* **conned**, *cont* **conning**) (informal use) ◇ *n* a situation or deal in which somebody is deceived and often loses money. ◇ *vt* to deceive <sb> in order to achieve or obtain something, especially money □ *He conned her out of $200,000.*

Conan Doyle [,kəʊnən'dɔɪl], **Sir Arthur** (1859–1930) a British writer well known for his stories about the detective Sherlock Holmes.

concave [kɒn'keɪv] *adj* [lens, mirror] that curves inward in the middle.

NOTE: Compare **convex**.

conceal [kən'siːl] *vt* **-1.** [building, smell, weapon] to cover or hide <sthg> □ *The house was partly concealed from the road by trees.* □ *The drugs were concealed in a consignment of paper goods.* **-2.** [feeling, information] to stop somebody from knowing <sthg>, especially by lying □ *She even concealed the truth from her husband.*

concede [kən'siːd] *vt* **-1. to concede (that)...** to admit that something is true even though one does not want to □ *He eventually conced-*

concession

ed that a mistake had been made. **-2. to concede defeat** to admit that one has lost a game, an argument etc □ *They were finally forced to concede defeat.*

conceit [kən'siːt] *n* a conceited attitude (disapproving use) □ *He was puffed up with conceit.*

conceited [kən'siːtəd] *adj* [person] who feels too proud of their abilities, talents etc (disapproving use) □ *Don't tell him you like it, he's conceited enough already.*

conceivable [kən'siːvəbl] *adj* [reason, means] that one thinks is possible but not very likely □ *It's just conceivable that she may be right.*

conceivably [kən'siːvəblɪ] *adv* a word used to show that one thinks something is possible but not very likely □ *We could conceivably win.*

conceive [kən'siːv] ◇ *vt* **-1.** [plan, idea] to form and develop <sthg> in one's mind. **-2. to conceive a child** to become pregnant. ◇ *vi* **-1.** [woman] to become pregnant. **-2. to conceive of sthg** to imagine sthg □ *It's hard to conceive of anything more stupid.*

concentrate ['kɒnsntreɪt] ◇ *vt* **-1.** [attention, effort, mind] to use all of <sthg that one has> in order to do or achieve something □ *We're concentrating all our energy on developing existing markets.* **-2. to be concentrated in a place** [power, industry] to be situated in one place, especially in large amounts □ *Most of the population is concentrated in the north.* ◇ *vi* to use all one's attention, effort etc to do or achieve something □ *I can't concentrate with all this noise.* □ *The government should concentrate on improving the economy.*

concentrated ['kɒnsntreɪtəd] *adj* **-1.** [fruit juice, detergent] that is very strong, e.g. because it contains very little water, so that only a little needs to be used. **-2.** [effort, work] that is done with a lot of determination □ *a period of concentrated activity.*

concentration [,kɒnsn'treɪʃn] *n* **-1.** [of one's attention] the act or state of fixing one's thoughts and attention on something so that one deals with it properly □ *Don't disturb my concentration.* **-2.** [of power, industry] *see* **concentrate** □ *the concentration of political power in the hands of a few individuals.*

concentration camp *n* a prison camp for large numbers of people who are usually placed there because of their race or political beliefs.

concentric [kən'sentrɪk] *adj* **concentric circles** circles that have the same center but are of different sizes.

concept ['kɒnsept] *n* a basic idea or principle that is connected with a particular thing □ *He has redefined the concept of socialism.* □ *an interesting concept.*

conception [kən'sepʃn] *n* **-1.** an understanding of something □ *He has no conception of the problems involved.* □ *a book that alters our conception of man's recent past.* **-2.** [of a plan, idea, child] *see* **conceive** □ *all the joys of motherhood, from conception to early infancy.*

conceptualize, -ise [kən'septʃuəlaɪz] *vt* [idea,

theory] to put <sthg> into the form of a concept that can be understood.

concern [kən'sɜːᵊn] ◇ *n* **-1.** a feeling of worry about a particular thing □ *There is no cause for concern.* □ *She showed little concern for their welfare.* **-2. to be sb's concern** to be something that interests, involves, or is important to sb □ *It's of no concern to me* OR *It's not my concern.* □ *This is a matter of great concern to everybody.* **-3.** BUSINESS a company or business □ *It's a profitable concern.*
◇ *vt* **-1. to be concerned** to be worried about somebody or something □ *They're very concerned about her health.* □ *We're concerned to make sure there is no misunderstanding.* □ *I'm only concerned for your health.* **-2.** to involve <sb/sthg> □ *This doesn't concern you.* □ *Where human rights are concerned, we cannot sit back and do nothing.* □ *It was a difficult time for everybody concerned.* ■ **to be concerned with sthg** to be interested and involved in sthg □ *Our main job is concerned with identifying future markets.* ■ **to concern oneself with sthg** to get involved with sthg because one thinks it is important □ *I don't concern myself too much with details.* ■ **as far as sb/sthg is concerned** a phrase used to introduce somebody's opinion; a phrase used to introduce the subject being talked about □ *As far as I'm concerned, he's just an idiot.* □ *Their record is good as far as safety is concerned.* **-3.** [subject, topic] to be about <sb/sthg> □ *The first paragraph concerns the budget for next year.*

concerning [kən'sɜːᵊnɪŋ] *prep* on the subject of <sthg> □ *I wrote to her concerning the lease.*

concert ['kɒnsəᵊt] *n* a live performance of music for an audience □ *We went to a rock concert last night.*
◆ **in concert** *adv* **-1.** [sing, play] at a concert □ *Have you ever seen them in concert?* **-2. to act in concert** to do something in close cooperation with other people (formal use).

concerted [kən'sɜːᵊtəd] *adj* **-1.** [attempt, effort] that shows a lot of determination □ *We've made a concerted effort to improve on last year's figures.* **-2.** [attack, campaign] that happens in close cooperation with other people □ *They launched a concerted attack on the enemy.*

concertgoer ['kɒnsəᵊtgəʊəᵊ] *n* a person who often goes to concerts.

concert hall *n* a building where concerts are held.

concertina [,kɒnsəᵊ'tiːnə] (*pt* & *pp* **concertinaed**, *cont* **concertinaing**) ◇ *n* a musical instrument that consists of a bag of air that folds and unfolds as its ends are pushed together or pulled apart, and notes are played by pressing small buttons. ◇ *vi* GB AUTO to be pressed into a smaller shape during an accident □ *The front of the car concertinaed.*

concerto [kən'tʃɜːᵊtoʊ] (*pl* **concertos**) *n* a piece of music written for a solo instrument and orchestra □ *a piano concerto.*

concession [kən'seʃn] *n* **-1.** [to an opponent] something that one lets one's opponents have, usually in order to end a disagreement □ *Neither side seems willing to make conces-*

sions on any of these points. -2. BUSINESS the right to carry out a particular business or activity on somebody's property; the stand or area where this business is carried out. -3. GB [for unemployed or retired people] a reduced price for some events and services, e.g. for unemployed or retired people □ *Is there a concession for students?*

concessionaire [kən,seʃə'neəʳ] *n* BUSINESS a person who has been given a concession.

concessionary [US kən'seʃənerɪ, GB -'seʃnərɪ] *adj* [ticket, fare, rate] that is cheaper because it is reduced in price, e.g. for unemployed or retired people □ *'Concessionary rates for students.'*

conciliation [kən,sɪlɪ'eɪʃn] *n* the act or process of ending a dispute □ *There is no hope of conciliation between the two sides.*

conciliatory [US kən'sɪlɪətɔːrɪ, GB -ətrɪ] *adj* [phrase, tone, approach] that is intended to help end a disagreement.

concise [kən'saɪs] *adj* [book, speech, report] that is short and only uses the words that are necessary □ *Please be as concise as possible.*

concisely [kən'saɪslɪ] *adv* [explain, write, speak] *see* **concise** □ *Please state concisely your reasons for applying for this post.*

conclave ['kɒnkleɪv] *n* a secret and private meeting.

conclude [kən'kluːd] ◇ *vt* -1. [meeting, speech, article] to end or represent the end of <sthg> □ *He concluded the report with a list of next year's targets.* □ *That concludes tonight's programs.* -2. **to conclude that...** to decide or suppose that something is true because of what one has seen, heard, or discovered □ *They concluded that military intervention was a grave mistake.* □ *I conclude from your statements that you're not in favor.* -3. [settlement, deal, sale] to arrange and agree the final terms of <sthg> □ *The treaty was concluded in the early hours of last night.* ◇ *vi* [meeting, speaker, book] to end □ *The report concludes with a message of hope for the future.*

conclusion [kən'kluːʒn] *n* -1. a decision or theory based on what one has seen, heard, or discovered □ *People are free to draw their own conclusions from today's news.* □ *I've come to the conclusion that I'll never learn to drive.* ■ **to jump to conclusions** to suppose or decide something too soon, without having all the necessary information □ *Don't go jumping to the wrong conclusions.* -2. [of a meeting, speech, book] the last part of something □ *In conclusion, I'd like to thank everybody for taking the time to come here today.* -3. [of a settlement, deal, sale] *see* **conclude** □ *Martin saw the deal was brought to a successful conclusion.*

conclusive [kən'kluːsɪv] *adj* [evidence, proof] that proves something so that there is no doubt.

concoct [kən'kɒkt] *vt* -1. [story, excuse] to invent <sthg that is not true> □ *He concocted some story about an accident on his way home.* -2. [meal, dish, drink] to prepare <sthg> by mixing several ingredients, especially in an

unusual way □ *What will he have concocted for us this evening, I wonder?*

concoction [kən'kɒkʃn] *n* a mixture of food, drink, or medicine that is unusual or unpleasant.

concord ['kɒnkɔːrd] *n* a state of peaceful agreement, usually between two countries.

Concord a village in Massachusetts, USA, where the first fighting of the American Revolution took place in 1775.

concourse ['kɒnkɔːrs] *n* a large hall, e.g. in an airport or station.

concrete ['kɒnkriːt] ◇ *adj* -1. [fact, evidence] that is definite and based on reality rather than imagined or vague. -2. [object] that is real rather than in the mind, and can be touched, seen etc. ◇ *n* a building material made of a mixture of sand, cement, small stones, and water □ *a concrete slab/wall.* ◇ *vt* [path, garden] to cover <sthg> with concrete.

concrete mixer *n* = cement mixer.

concur [kən'kɜːʳ] (*pt* & *pp* **concurred**, *cont* **concurring**) *vi* to say that one agrees □ *Everyone concurred with the views expressed.*

concurrently [US kən'kɜːrəntlɪ, GB -'kʌr-] *adv* [happen, develop] at the same time □ *I'm working on two projects concurrently.*

concussed [kən'kʌst] *adj* **to be concussed** to have a concussion.

concussion [kən'kʌʃn] *n* damage to the brain, usually temporary, that results from a blow to the head and can make one faint or feel dizzy □ *The doctors said she was suffering from concussion.*

condemn [kən'dem] *vt* -1. [opponent, policy, decision] to express very strong disapproval of <sb/sthg> □ *She was widely condemned for her comments.* □ *The decision was condemned as unfair and harsh.* -2. **to condemn sb to sthg/to do sthg** to force sb into sthg/to do sthg unpleasant or undesirable □ *people condemned to live in poverty.* -3. LAW **to condemn sb to sthg** [to imprisonment, death] to sentence sb to sthg as punishment. -4. [house, block] to state officially that <a building> is unsafe.

condemnation [,kɒndem'neɪʃn] *n* the act of expressing strong disapproval □ *There was widespread condemnation of the killings.*

condemned [kən'demd] *adj* -1. [building] that has been officially declared unsafe. -2. [criminal, prisoner] who is in prison waiting to be killed as an official punishment.

condensation [,kɒnden'seɪʃn] *n* small drops of water that form when steam condenses on a cold surface such as a window.

condense [kən'dens] ◇ *vt* -1. [steam, alcohol, vapor] to cause <a gas> to become a liquid, usually by cooling it. -2. [report, ideas, message] to put <sthg> into a shorter or smaller form so that only the important points are included □ *These points need to be condensed into one paragraph.* ◇ *vi* [gas, steam] to become a liquid □ *On cold days water vapor condenses on the windows.*

condensed milk [kən,denst-] *n* milk that has

been thickened and sweetened and is sold in cans.

condescend [ˌkɒndɪ'send] *vi* **-1. to condescend to sb** to treat sb in a way that suggests one thinks they are inferior. **-2. to condescend to do sthg** to agree to do sthg in a way that suggests one considers it unimportant or not worth one's attention □ *He finally condescended to write a reply.*

condescending [ˌkɒndɪ'sendɪŋ] *adj* [person, attitude, tone] that shows a belief that other people are inferior □ *She's very condescending toward her employees in the factory.*

condiment ['kɒndɪmənt] *n* a substance, e.g. salt or mustard, that is used to add flavor to food (formal use).

condition [kən'dɪʃn] ◇ *n* **-1.** [of a person, building, car] the state that somebody or something is in at a particular time □ *The house is in very good/bad condition.* □ *The patient is in a critical condition.* ■ **to be out of condition** [person, animal] to be unfit. **-2.** MEDICINE an illness or disorder □ *He has a heart condition.* □ *a serious medical condition.* **-3.** [for improvement, talks, growth] something that must be done or must exist in order for something else to happen □ *She agreed to go on one condition, that she could take a friend with her.* □ *He'll do it on condition that he's paid well.*
◇ *vt* **-1.** to influence <sb> over a period of time to think or behave in a particular way □ *Society conditions us to believe/into believing that money is the key to happiness.* **-2. to be conditioned by sthg** to be directly influenced by sthg □ *The market is conditioned by changes in interest rates.* **-3. to condition one's hair** to put conditioner on one's hair.

◆ **conditions** *npl* **-1.** the physical surroundings or circumstances in which people live or work □ *The working/living conditions are appalling.* **-2.** the circumstances under which something happens □ *The conditions are right for economic growth.* □ *The team struggled against appalling weather conditions.*

conditional [kən'dɪʃnəl] *adj* [offer, acceptance, agreement] that depends on something else happening □ *The ceasefire is conditional on OR upon the withdrawal of troops.*

conditionally [kən'dɪʃnəlɪ] *adv*: *see* **conditional** □ *I've agreed conditionally to the offer.*

conditioner [kən'dɪʃnər] *n* a liquid used for softening hair after washing it with shampoo □ *hair conditioner.*

conditioning [kən'dɪʃnɪŋ] *n* the influences or training somebody has had that make them think or behave in a particular way.

condo ['kɒndoʊ] *n* US *abbr of* **condominium** (informal use).

condolences [kən'doʊlənsɪz] *npl* sympathy that is expressed to somebody who has experienced something sad, especially the death of a close friend or relative □ *I would like to offer you my condolences on the death of your husband.*

condom [US 'kʌndəm, GB 'kɒnd-] *n* a thin rubber cover that a man wears on his penis

during sex as a contraceptive and as protection against disease.

condominium [ˌkɒndə'mɪnjəm] *n* US an apartment block in which each apartment is owned by the people living in it; an apartment in such a block.

condone [kən'doʊn] *vt* [practice, drugs, war] to accept or allow <sthg bad or wrong> □ *We cannot condone such immoral behavior.*

condor ['kɒndɔːr] *n* a type of large American vulture.

conducive [kən'djuːsɪv] *adj* **to be conducive to sthg** to make sthg easier or more likely to happen □ *It's hardly conducive to a relaxing weekend, is it?*

conduct [*n* 'kɒndʌkt, *vb* kən'dʌkt] ◇ *n* **-1.** [of a person] the way somebody behaves □ *He was dismissed for conduct unbecoming to an officer.* **-2.** [of business, talks] the way something is organized and done. ◇ *vt* **-1.** [investigation, survey] to carry out <sthg> □ *The inquiry was conducted in a fair and open manner.* **-2. to conduct oneself well/badly** to behave well/badly. **-3.** [orchestra, choir] to direct <a group of singers or musicians> in a performance. **-4.** PHYSICS [metal] to allow <heat or electricity> to move through it. ◇ *vi* [conductor] to direct an orchestra or choir in a performance.

conducted tour [kən,dʌktəd-] *n* a tour of a place in which a guide explains the points of interest to a group of people.

conductor [kən'dʌktər] *n* **-1.** MUSIC a person whose job is to conduct an orchestra or choir. **-2.** [on a bus] a person whose job is to check and sell tickets on a bus, streetcar etc □ *a bus conductor.* **-3.** US [on a train] a railroad official in charge of a train.

conduit ['kɒndjuɪt] *n* a pipe or channel that something such as water can pass through.

cone [koʊn] *n* **-1.** a three-dimensional shape with a circular base and rounded sides that narrow to a point at the other end. **-2.** [for ice cream] a wafer in the shape of a cone that is used for holding ice cream. **-3.** [of a tree] the fruit of a coniferous tree that is made up of a lot of small wooden pieces □ *pine cones.*

Coney Island ['koʊnɪ-] a popular resort for tourists on the Atlantic Ocean at Brooklyn, New York.

confectioner [kən'fekʃnər] *n* a person whose job is to make or sell candy, cakes etc.

confectioner's sugar *n* US a type of very fine sugar used to make icing.

confectionery [US kən'fekʃənerɪ, GB -ərɪ] *n* a collective term for sweet food that can be bought in a store, e.g. candy, cakes, or ice cream.

Confederacy [kən'fedərəsɪ] *n* **the Confederacy** the eleven Southern US states that left the Union in 1861 to form an independent country, officially called the Confederate States of America. They were defeated in the American Civil War.

Confederate [kən'fedərət] *adj* that belongs to the Confederacy □ *the Confederate States.*

confederation [kən,fedə'reɪʃn] *n* an organization that consists of smaller groups, usually for business or political purposes.

Confederation of British Industry *n* → CBI.

confer [kən'fɜːʳ] (*pt* & *pp* **conferred**, *cont* **conferring**) ◇ *vt* [honor, title, award] to give <sthg> to somebody (formal use). ◇ *vi* to talk with somebody else in order to exchange ideas or opinions □ *I need to confer with my management team on* OR *about this matter.*

conference ['kɒnfrəns] *n* an organized event at which a large group of people meets to discuss a particular subject, usually for a number of days □ *the annual sales conference.* ■ **to be in conference** GB to be in a meeting □ *She can't come to the phone now, she's in conference.*

conference call *n* a telephone call that allows three or more people to talk to each other at the same time.

conference center *n* a building where conferences are held.

conference hall *n* a large room where conferences are held.

conferencing ['kɒnfrənsɪŋ] *n* the facility on a telephone that allows conference calls to be made.

confess [kən'fes] ◇ *vt* -1. RELIGION to tell a priest about <a sin one has committed>. -2. [crime, truth, mistake] to admit <sthg> to somebody □ *I must confess (that) I've never been there.* ◇ *vi* to confess a crime, sin etc □ *She confessed to the murders.* □ *I confess to not really having understood what he said.*

confession [kən'feʃn] *n* -1. [of a crime, mistake, the truth] a statement that somebody makes when they confess something □ *I have a confession to make. I forgot to reserve the seats.* □ *Fielding made a full confession to all three murders.* -2. RELIGION a religious act where one confesses one's sins to a priest □ *I haven't been to confession recently.*

confessional [kən'feʃnl] *n* a small enclosed place in a church in which a person can confess to a priest in private.

confetti [kən'fetɪ] *n* small pieces of colored paper that are thrown in the air at a celebration, especially over the bride and groom at a wedding □ *They were showered in confetti.*

confidant [US ,kɒnfɪ'dɑːnt, GB -'dænt] *n* a man one trusts enough to discuss secret or personal matters with □ *Alan was my friend and confidant for many years.*

confidante [US ,kɒnfɪ'dɑːnt, GB -'dænt] *n* a woman who acts as a confidant.

confide [kən'faɪd] ◇ *vt* [thought, fear] to tell <sthg secret or personal> to somebody because one trusts them. ◇ *vi* **to confide in sb** to tell sb about something secret or personal because one trusts them.

confidence ['kɒnfɪdəns] *n* -1. [in oneself] the belief that one has in one's ability to do something well □ *He spoke with confidence.* -2. [in a person, plan, machine] the belief one has that a person or thing will do what one expects of them □ *We have every confidence (that) you'll*

succeed. □ *I have great confidence in her abilities.* □ *Consumer confidence is building slowly.* -3. **to tell sthg to sb in confidence** to tell sthg to sb as a secret because one trusts them not to tell anybody else □ *I'm telling you this in the strictest confidence, you understand.* -4. something that is told in confidence □ *She'd never betray a confidence.*

confidence trick *n* a trick in which somebody deceives somebody else in order to get money or property from them.

confident ['kɒnfɪdənt] *adj* [person] who has confidence in their own ability to do something; who has confidence in somebody or something □ *You should be more confident.* □ *I feel confident (that) we will succeed.* □ *We are confident of success.*

confidential [,kɒnfɪ'denʃl] *adj* -1. [document, information, arrangement] that is secret and should not be told to anybody else □ *I have no need to add that this matter is strictly confidential.* -2. [tone, voice, look] showing that what is being said is supposed to be secret □ *"This is just between you and me," she said with a confidential wink.*

confidentiality [,kɒnfɪdenʃɪ'æləti] *n* [of information, a document] *see* **confidential**.

confidentially [,kɒnfɪ'denʃəlɪ] *adv* [tell, whisper] *see* **confidential** □ *All enquiries are treated confidentially.*

confidently ['kɒnfɪdəntlɪ] *adv* [speak, smile, predict] in a way that shows one is confident □ *I think I can confidently say we've never had such a response before.*

configuration [kən,fɪgjə'reɪʃn] *n* -1. a shape formed by arranging things, or parts of something, in a particular way. -2. COMPUTING a particular arrangement of the different parts and programs of a computer and their connections.

confine [kən'faɪn] *vt* -1. **to confine sthg to sthg** [comments, criticism] to limit sthg so that it only mentions or concerns sthg □ *The allegations are not confined to bribery alone.* ■ **to confine oneself to sthg** to limit one's thoughts or actions to sthg □ *I suggest we confine ourselves to discussing the most urgent issues.* -2. to keep <sb> in a place that they cannot leave □ *He's confined to his room/a wheelchair.*

♦ **confines** *npl* **within the confines of sthg** [of a system, place, building] inside the limits and boundaries of sthg; [of space, time, system] inside the limits and restrictions that are fixed by sthg □ *Inmates must not leave the confines of the hospital.* □ *We have to work within the confines of what the local planning laws allow.*

confined [kən'faɪnd] *adj* -1. [space, area] that seems small and enclosed. -2. **to be confined to sb** [problem, attitude] to only affect or involve sb □ *This behavior is confined to a small minority of fans.* -3. **to be confined to a place** [animal, plant, event] to only exist or happen in a particular place □ *This species is now confined to a few remote areas.*

confinement [kən'faɪnmənt] *n* -1. [of a prisoner] the period when somebody is in prison or in a place that they are not free to leave. -2. [of a pregnant woman] the period between the beginning of labor and the birth of a child (old-fashioned use).

confirm [kən'fɜːᵊm] *vt* **-1.** [reservation, appointment, decision] to make <an arrangement> definite □ *Please confirm your flight two days prior to departure.* **-2.** [report, suspicion, news] to state or prove the truth of <sthg> □ *I can confirm (that) I will be retiring next year.* **-3.** RELIGION to accept <sb> officially as a member of a Christian church.

confirmation [ˌkɒnfəᵊ'meɪʃn] *n* **-1.** [of a reservation, appointment] *see* **confirm.** □ *We have not yet received confirmation of this report.* **-2.** RELIGION a church ceremony at which people are confirmed.

confirmed [kən'fɜːᵊmd] *adj* **a confirmed bachelor/teetotaler etc** a person who has been a bachelor/teetotaler etc for a long time and is unlikely to change.

confiscate ['kɒnfɪskeɪt] *vt* to take <sthg that is not allowed> away from somebody, when one has the necessary authority □ *Police confiscated a number of weapons before the game.*

confiscation [ˌkɒnfɪ'skeɪʃn] *n*: *see* **confiscate** □ *powers of confiscation.*

conflagration [ˌkɒnfləˈɡreɪʃn] *n* a large fire that causes a lot of damage (formal use).

conflict [*n* 'kɒnflɪkt, *vb* US 'kɒnflɪkt, GB kən'flɪkt] ◇ *n* **-1.** [between countries, people] a period of fighting between countries or groups of people □ *an armed conflict.* **-2.** [between ideas, beliefs] a serious difference between ideas, beliefs etc, that makes it difficult for them to exist or be used together; a serious argument or disagreement between people □ *a conflict between her private and her public life* □ *Their policies are in conflict with their manifesto.* □ *I often came into conflict with my boss.* ■ **a conflict of interest** a situation in which a person is working for two competing clients, organizations etc, or has goals that are different and opposed. ◇ *vi* [ideas, interests] to be different or opposed in a way that makes it difficult to be used or to exist together □ *This appears to conflict with their earlier statement.*

conflicting [US 'kɒnflɪktɪŋ, GB kənˈflɪktɪŋ] *adj* [account, advice, evidence] that conflicts with something else of the same kind □ *There were conflicting reports in the press.*

conform [kənˈfɔːᵊm] *vi* **-1.** [person] to behave the way one is expected to or the way most other people in the same group behave □ *School puts a lot of pressure on kids to conform.* **-2.** [object, action] to be done in a way that obeys particular rules or standards □ *All new windows must conform to* OR *with current building regulations.*

conformist [kənˈfɔːᵊmɪst] ◇ *adj* [person, behavior, attitude] that is not original and follows what is expected, or what is already established (disapproving use) □ *He reacted against the conformist views of his parents.* ◇ *n* a person whose behavior or attitude is conformist (disapproving use).

conformity [kənˈfɔːᵊmətɪ] *n* [of a person, action, behavior] *see* **conform.**

confound [kənˈfaʊnd] *vt* to confuse and surprise <sb> □ *Your expectations are likely to be confounded.*

confounded [kənˈfaʊndəd] *adj* a word used to show that one is annoyed about something (old-fashioned and informal use) □ *It's a confounded nuisance!*

confront [kənˈfrʌnt] *vt* **-1.** [problem, truth] to consider <sthg unpleasant> and start to deal with it. **-2.** [person] to present <sb> with a difficulty that they have to deal with □ *This year, many more problems/obstacles are confronting the company.* **-3. to confront sb with sthg** [with evidence, the truth, an allegation] to accuse or criticize sb by showing or talking to them about sthg.

confrontation [ˌkɒnfrʌnˈteɪʃn] *n* a situation in which there is strong disagreement or violence between two people or groups □ *We don't want to risk confrontation with the bosses.*

Confucius [kənˈfjuːʃəs] (551–479 BC) a Chinese philosopher whose ideas on the importance of order and duty influenced Chinese society.

confuse [kənˈfjuːz] *vt* **-1.** [person] to cause <sb> to be uncertain about something or unable to think clearly □ *The instructions in the manual just confused me even more.* **-2.** [people, objects, places] to make a mistake about <two or more people or things> because one cannot tell the difference between them □ *You seem to be confusing me with someone else.* □ *This new software should not be confused with earlier versions.* **-3.** [situation, problem] to make <sthg> more complicated or unclear than it was before □ *To confuse the issue further, there are several different departments involved.*

confused [kənˈfjuːzd] *adj* [person] who is unable to understand something or think clearly; [idea, thought, situation] that is unclear and difficult to understand □ *I'm confused about which one to choose.* □ *His argument was confused and poorly structured.*

confusing [kənˈfjuːzɪŋ] *adj* [instruction, story, description] that is not clear or simple enough to understand □ *I found the plot very confusing.*

confusion [kənˈfjuːʒn] *n* **-1.** [of a person] the state of being confused □ *There is a lot of confusion about* OR *over who exactly is eligible under the new law.* **-2.** [of people, objects, places] *see* **confuse** □ *To avoid confusion, please state your full name.* **-3.** [in a place] a state of disorder, usually with a lot of noise and a lot of things happening at the same time □ *The house was in total confusion.*

conga ['kɒŋɡə] *n* **the conga** a Latin American dance performed by people in a line, one behind the other.

congeal [kənˈdʒiːl] *vi* [milk, fat, sauce] to become thick and sticky □ *congealed blood.*

congenial [kənˈdʒiːnjəl] *adj* [atmosphere, work] that is pleasant and makes one feel relaxed □ *an evening spent in congenial company.*

congenital [kənˈdʒenətl] *adj* [disease, defect, deafness] that has affected somebody since birth, but was not inherited □ *He has a congenital heart condition.*

conger eel [ˌkɒŋgəʳ-] *n* a large eel that lives in seawater.

congested [kənˈdʒestəd] *adj* -1. [road, area] that is very crowded or blocked with traffic or people. -2. MEDICINE [lung, nose] that is blocked because it is full of liquid.

congestion [kənˈdʒestʃən] *n* [of a road, somebody's nose] the state of being congested □ *the problems of traffic congestion.*

conglomerate [kənˈglɒmərət] *n* BUSINESS a large company made up of several smaller companies.

conglomeration [kənˌglɒməˈreɪʃn] *n* an unusual mixture of many different things (formal use).

Congo [ˈkɒŋgoʊ] -1. **the Congo (Republic)** a country in the western part of central Africa. SIZE: 342,000 sq kms. POPULATION: 2,400,000 (*Congolese*). CAPITAL: Brazzaville. LANGUAGE: French. CURRENCY: CFA franc. -2. **the Congo (River)** = Zaïre River.

Congolese [ˌkɒŋgəˈliːz] *adj* & *n*: see **Congo**.

congratulate [kənˈgrætʃəleɪt] *vt* to express one's pleasure or praise to <sb> when they have done something well or when something pleasant has happened to them □ *They congratulated her on her promotion/being promoted.* ■ **to congratulate oneself** to be proud of a quality one has or of one's actions □ *You can congratulate yourself on a job well done.*

congratulations [kənˌgrætʃəˈleɪʃənz] ◇ *npl* a message given to congratulate somebody on something □ *Give him my congratulations.* □ *a letter of congratulations.* ◇ *excl* a word used to congratulate somebody □ *"We won the contract!" — "Congratulations!"* □ *Congratulations on your new baby!*

congratulatory [US kənˈgrætʃələtɔːri, GB -ˌgrætʃ-əˈleɪtəri] *adj* [message, smile] that congratulates somebody.

congregate [ˈkɒŋgrɪgeɪt] *vi* to gather together and form a large group □ *A large crowd had congregated around the scene of the accident.*

congregation [ˌkɒŋgrɪˈgeɪʃn] *n* the people at a church service; the people who regularly go to a particular church □ *the congregation of St Mark's.*

congress [ˈkɒŋgres] *n* a meeting of representatives of large organizations or countries, usually held to discuss ideas and policies □ *the party's annual congress.*
◆ **Congress** *n* US the elected group of politicians that makes laws in the USA □ *The Democrats had a majority in Congress.*

☙ CONGRESS
The US Congress, which meets in the Capitol building in Washington, D.C., consists of the Senate and the House of Representatives. A proposed new law must be approved by both houses separately, and then by the President. If the President refuses the proposal, it can still be made law if two-thirds of the members of Congress agree.

---

congressional [kənˈgreʃnəl] *adj* [hearing, election, committee] that is connected with the US Congress.

Congressional Record *n* **the Congressional Record** the official written record of everything that takes place in the US Congress, including speeches and the results of votes.

congressman [ˈkɒŋgresmən] (*pl* **congressmen** [-mən]) *n* a man who is a member of the US House of Representatives.

congresswoman [ˈkɒŋgreswʊmən] (*pl* **congresswomen**) *n* a woman who is a member of the US House of Representatives.

conical [ˈkɒnɪkl] *adj* [shape, hat] that is shaped like a cone.

conifer [ˈkɒnəfəʳ] *n* an evergreen tree that produces cones, e.g. pine, fir, or sequoia.

coniferous [US koʊˈnɪfərəs, GB kə-] *adj* [tree, forest] see **conifer**.

conjecture [kənˈdʒektʃəʳ] ◇ *n* an idea or opinion that is based on incomplete or uncertain information □ *At this stage, it's a matter of pure conjecture.* ◇ *vt* **to conjecture (that)...** to suggest that something is true without having all the necessary information □ *Police conjectured that a terrorist organization was responsible.* ◇ *vi: We can only conjecture where/how the money was spent.*

conjugal [ˈkɒndʒəgl] *adj* [happiness, right] that is connected with a marriage, especially the sexual relationship between a husband and wife (formal use).

conjugate [ˈkɒndʒəgeɪt] *vt* to list the different grammatical forms of <a verb>.

conjugation [ˌkɒndʒəˈgeɪʃn] *n* -1. a class of verbs that are conjugated in the same way. -2. a way of conjugating a particular verb.

conjunction [kənˈdʒʌŋkʃn] *n* GRAMMAR a word that connects other words or phrases, e.g. "and", "but", or "while".
◆ **in conjunction with** *prep* together with <sb/sthg> □ *They work in conjunction with the U.N.*

conjunctivitis [kənˌdʒʌŋktɪˈvaɪtəs] *n* an infection of one's eye that causes the thin skin covering one's eyeball and the inside of one's eyelid to become red and swollen.

conjure [ˈkʌndʒəʳ] ◇ *vt* to make <sthg> appear in a way that seems like magic □ *He conjured a rabbit out of a hat.* ◇ *vi* to perform conjuring tricks.
◆ **conjure up** *vt sep* **to conjure sthg up** [memory, picture] to make sthg appear in somebody's imagination □ *The thought of India still conjures up for many images of its colonial past.*

conjurer [ˈkʌndʒərəʳ] *n* a person who performs conjuring tricks.

conjuring trick [ˈkʌndʒərɪŋ-] *n* a trick in which somebody makes something appear or disappear, especially by using their hands cleverly in a way that looks like magic.

conjuror [ˈkʌndʒərəʳ] *n* = **conjurer**.

conk [kɒŋk] ◆ **conk out** *vi* (informal use) **-1.** [person] to collapse from exhaustion. **-2.** [vehicle, machine] to break down.

conker ['kɒŋkə'] *n* GB a horse chestnut.

conman ['kɒnmæn] (*pl* **conmen** [-men]) *n* a person who gets money from people by deceiving them □ *a professional conman.*

connect [kə'nekt] ◇ *vt* **-1.** to join or attach <two things> to each other □ *The island is connected to the mainland by a bridge.* □ *The rooms were connected by a hidden door.* **-2.** [by telephone] to allow <sb> to speak to another person by joining two lines, e.g. on a switchboard □ *I'm trying to connect you now, sir.* **-3. to connect sb/sthg with sb/sthg** to realize that there is a link between sb/sthg and sb/sthg else; to succeed in finding a link between sb/sthg and sb/sthg else □ *Many people would never connect libraries with fun.* □ *The police were unable to connect him with the previous attacks.* **-4.** [machine, appliance, wire] to join <sthg> to the main supply of electricity, gas, or water □ *Have you had your phone connected yet?*
◇ *vi* [train, plane, bus] to arrive in time for passengers to transfer to another train, plane etc in order to continue their journey □ *This flight connects with AA112 to Amsterdam.*

connected [kə'nektəd] *adj* [event, idea, person] that is linked to somebody or something □ *Is he connected with the robbery/place/project?* □ *The two religions are closely connected.*

Connecticut [kə'netɪkət] a state in the northeastern USA. ABBREVIATION: CT. SIZE: 13,000 sq kms. POPULATION: 3,287,116. CAPITAL: Hartford.

connecting [kə'nektɪŋ] *adj* **a connecting flight/train etc** a flight/train etc that takes passengers from one part of their trip to another.

connecting rod *n* a rod in the engine of a car, truck etc that connects the piston to the crankshaft.

connection [kə'nekʃn] *n* **-1.** [between two facts, events] a link or relationship between two things □ *Does this have any connection with what happened yesterday?* □ *the connection between interest rates and unemployment.* **-2.** [between two wires] something that joins two wires in an electrical circuit □ *a loose connection.* **-3.** [on a telephone] the link between people when they are talking to each other by telephone □ *It's a bad connection.* **-4.** TRANSPORT a train, plane, or bus that leaves after passengers have transferred to it from another one in order to continue their trip □ *I missed my connection.*
◆ **connections** *npl* people who one knows and who may be useful to one, e.g. because they are in important positions □ *He has connections in the government.*
◆ **in connection with** *prep* about <sthg> □ *Two men have been arrested in connection with the murder.* □ *I am writing in connection with your comments yesterday.*

connective tissue [kə,nektɪv-] *n* animal tissue that supports organs and connects limbs.

connive [kə'naɪv] *vi* to plan secretly with oth-er people to do something dishonest in order to get something for oneself □ *She connived with his enemies to have him discredited.*
◆ **connive at** *vt fus* **to connive at sthg** to allow sthg bad to happen even though one knows that one ought to prevent it □ *teachers who had connived at students' absence from school.*

conniving [kə'naɪvɪŋ] *adj* [person] who is cunning and dishonest.

connoisseur [,kɒnə'sɜː'] *n* a person who enjoys and knows a lot about art, music, wine etc, and can tell when it is of good quality □ *He's a connoisseur of antique porcelain.* □ *a wine connoisseur.*

connotation [,kɒnə'teɪʃn] *n* an idea or quality that is suggested by a word □ *The word clearly has political connotations.*

conquer ['kɒŋkə'] *vt* **-1.** [country, town, people] to take <a place> by fighting and beating the people there □ *The invaders conquered most of modern Mexico.* **-2.** [fear, shyness, inflation] to bring <a problem> under control □ *It took me six months to conquer my addiction to smoking.*

conqueror ['kɒŋkərə'] *n* a person who has conquered a place or group of people.

conquest ['kɒŋkwest] *n* **-1.** [of a country, town] success in conquering something □ *the conquest of North Africa.* **-2.** something that has been conquered, usually land □ *They added France to their list of conquests.*

Conrad ['kɒnræd], **Joseph** (1857–1924) a British novelist, born in Poland. His stories of adventures at sea include *Lord Jim* and *Heart of Darkness.*

cons [kɒnz] *npl* **-1.** → mod cons. **-2.** → pro.

Cons. *abbr of* **Conservative.**

conscience ['kɒnʃns] *n* a sense of right and wrong; a sense of having done something wrong that makes one feel guilty □ *She has no conscience about letting people down.* □ *It's something that has been weighing on my conscience for a long time.* □ *What you decide to do in the end is a matter of conscience.* ■ **to have a guilty conscience** to feel guilty about something. ■ **I cannot, in all conscience** I cannot, because I think it is wrong □ *In all conscience, I couldn't have said yes.*

conscientious [,kɒnʃɪ'enʃəs] *adj* [student, worker] who is thorough, careful, and serious in the way they do things □ *It can't have been Jenny, she's usually so conscientious.*

conscientiously [,kɒnʃɪ'enʃəslɪ] *adv* [study, work] *see* **conscientious.**

conscientious objector *n* a person who refuses to join the armed forces for moral or religious reasons.

conscious ['kɒnʃəs] *adj* **-1. to be conscious** [person] to be alive and aware of things around one rather than asleep or unconscious □ *He's fully conscious now.* **-2. to be conscious of sthg** to be aware of sthg □ *She was very conscious of him watching her.* **-3. a conscious decision/effort** a decision/an effort that has been thought about and is deliberate □ *I've never*

made a conscious attempt to win people's respect.
-4. [mind, memory] that one is aware of.

-conscious *suffix* **class-/health- etc conscious**
aware of or concerned about class/health etc
□ *Al's pretty safety-conscious these days.*

consciously [ˈkɒnʃəslɪ] *adv* [decide, try] *see* **con-scious** □ *I wasn't consciously aware I was taking
a risk.* □ *I didn't consciously avoid the subject.*

consciousness [ˈkɒnʃəsnəs] *n* **-1.** the state of
being awake and aware of things around
one □ *She lost/regained consciousness.* **-2.**
everything that somebody thinks and be-lieves, especially about a particular subject □
They are trying to raise levels of political con-sciousness.

conscript [*vb* kənˈskrɪpt, *n* ˈkɒnskrɪpt] ◇ *vt* to
make <sb> join one of the armed forces □
He was conscripted into the navy. ◇ *n* a person
who has been conscripted.

conscription [kənˈskrɪpʃn] *n* the official system
that makes people join the armed forces,
e.g. because a war is being fought.

consecrated [ˈkɒnsɪkreɪtəd] *adj* RELIGION [church,
bread] that has been officially declared to be
holy in a religious ceremony □ *His body was
buried in consecrated ground.*

consecration [ˌkɒnsɪˈkreɪʃn] *n* **-1.** [of a church,
bread] *see* **consecrated.** **-2.** a religious ceremo-ny in which somebody is made a priest or
bishop.

consecutive [kənˈsekjətɪv] *adj* [days, occasions]
that happen one after the other without any
breaks □ *America won the championship for the
fourth consecutive year.*

consecutively [kənˈsekjətɪvlɪ] *adv*: *see* **consecu-tive** □ *The tickets are numbered consecutively.*

consensus [kənˈsensəs] *n* general agreement
among a group of people □ *Delegates failed to
reach (a) consensus on arms limitation.*

consent [kənˈsent] ◇ *n* **-1.** official permission
for something □ *Because of her age she need-ed her parents to give their consent to the mar-riage.* □ *They used my name without my consent.*
-2. by common OR **general consent** a phrase
used to say what most people think is true
□ *He is, by general consent, the best worker on
the team.* ◇ *vi* to agree to do something or to
allow something to happen □ *They consented
to the plan/marriage/interview.* □ *After much delib-eration, she consented to take part.*

consenting [kənˈsentɪŋ] *adj* **consenting adults**
adults who are old enough to decide they
will have sex together.

consequence [ˈkɒnsɪkwəns] *n* **-1.** a result or ef-fect of something □ *The policy had terrible con-sequences for the poor.* ■ **in consequence** as a
result □ *The work is undervalued and, in conse-quence, underpaid.* **-2. of little/no etc conse-quence** of little/no etc importance (formal
use) □ *a person of consequence* □ *It's of little
consequence.*

consequent [ˈkɒnsɪkwənt] *adj* [difficulty, event]
that happens as a result of something □ *the
political disagreements and consequent splits
within the party.*

consequently [ˈkɒnsɪkwəntlɪ] *adv* as a result of

something that has just been mentioned □
We took on extra work, and consequently, an ad-ditional member of staff had to be hired.

conservation [ˌkɒnsəˈveɪʃn] *n* **-1.** [of nature, a
painting, building] the preservation and protec-tion of something □ *a conservation project.*
-2. [of energy, water] the careful use of some-thing to stop it being wasted or lost □ *energy
conservation.*

conservation area *n* in Britain, an area that
is officially protected because of its natural
beauty, or its historical or architectural im-portance.

conservationist [ˌkɒnsəˈveɪʃnəst] *n* a person
who works or campaigns to protect the en-vironment.

conservatism [kənˈsɜːrvətɪzm] *n* [of attitudes,
ideas, methods] the state of being conserva-tive.

◆ **Conservatism** *n* the policies and ideas of a
Conservative Party.

conservative [kənˈsɜːrvətɪv] ◇ *adj* **-1.** [person]
who likes established and traditional things
and dislikes change □ *conservative ideas/
attitudes.* **-2. a conservative estimate/guess etc**
an estimate/a guess etc that one deliberately
makes lower than one thinks the real
amount is to avoid exaggerating □ *At a con-servative estimate, we should make $3 million in
the next year.* ◇ *n* a conservative person.

◆ **Conservative** ◇ *n* a member or supporter
of a Conservative Party. ◇ *adj*: *a Conservative
MP/policy.*

Conservative Party *n* **the Conservative Party**
in Britain, Australia, and Canada, a center-right political party that is in favor of free
enterprise and against Socialism.

conservatory [US kənˈsɜːrvətɔːrɪ, GB -ˈsɜːvətrɪ]
(*pl* **conservatories**) *n* a room, usually at-tached to a house, with glass walls and a
roof that is used for sitting in or growing
plants in.

conserve [*vb* kənˈsɜːrv, *n* ˈkɒnsɜːrv] ◇ *vt* [energy,
water, electricity] to prevent <sthg> from be-ing wasted or lost by using it carefully □
More can be done to conserve the Earth's re-sources. ◇ *n* jam that contains whole fruit or
large pieces of fruit □ *raspberry conserve.*

consider [kənˈsɪdər] *vt* **-1.** [proposal, possibility]
to think carefully about <sthg>, especially
before making a decision about it □ *She's be-ing considered for the post of manager.* □ *I need
time to consider my future.* **-2.** [budget, conse-quences, somebody's feelings] to remember
<sb/sthg> and think about how they will be
affected before making a decision □ *You
have your family to consider above all.* ■ **all
things considered** when everything has been
thought about carefully □ *We haven't done too
badly, all things considered.* **-3. to consider
(that)...** to believe that something is the case
□ *He considered (that) the use of firearms in this
case was justified.* □ *I have always considered her
to be a friend.* □ *This sort of behavior would be
considered unacceptable by most people.*

considerable [kənˈsɪdrəbl] *adj* [damage, number,

expense] that is large in amount or size □ *He lost a considerable sum of money.*

considerably [kən'sɪdrəblɪ] *adv* **considerably greater/less etc** much greater/less etc □ *We were considerably better-off before the move.* □ *Relations between locals and the police have improved considerably.*

considerate [kən'sɪdərət] *adj* [person] who is kind and thoughtful to other people.

consideration [kən,sɪdə'reɪʃn] *n* **-1.** careful thought about something □ *After due consideration the proposal was rejected.* ■ **to take sthg into consideration** [fact, factor] to think about sthg before one makes a decision □ *It was a good performance, taking into consideration the problems he faced.* **-2.** [for other people] kind attention and care shown to other people □ *He showed no consideration for their feelings.* **-3. a financial/political etc consideration** a financial/political etc aspect of something that should be thought about, especially when making a decision □ *Money is an important consideration.* **-4. to be under consideration** [question, matter] to be in the process of being considered □ *Your application for a loan is presently under consideration.*

considered [kən'sɪdəd] *adj* **a considered opinion/response etc** an opinion/a response etc that is the result of careful thought □ *It's my considered opinion that military action at this time would serve no useful purpose.*

considering [kən'sɪdərɪŋ] ◇ *prep* & *conj* a word used to show that one is taking a particular fact into account □ *Considering all the problems we had, it's amazing that we finished on time.* □ *Considering (that) they'd never met before, they got along very well.* ◇ *adv* a word used at the end of a sentence to show that one did not expect things to turn out as well as they have □ *The results are pretty good, considering.*

consign [kən'saɪn] *vt* **-1. to consign sthg to sb** [goods, supplies] to send sthg to sb. **-2. to consign sthg to a place** to get rid of sthg by putting it in a place □ *It's time that old coat was consigned to the trash can!* **-3. to consign sb to sb** to put sb into sb's care or control.

consignee [,kɒnsaɪ'niː] *n* the person that something is being sent to.

consignment [,kən'saɪnmənt] *n* a quantity of goods that is being sent to somebody □ *a large consignment of medical supplies.*

consignment note *n* the documents that accompany a consignment of goods.

consignor [kən'saɪnəʳ] *n* a person who consigns goods.

consist [kən'sɪst] ◆ **consist in** *vt fus* **to consist in sthg** to have sthg as a base or main element (formal use) □ *The plan's success consists largely in its simplicity.*

◆ **consist of** *vt fus* **to consist of sb/sthg** to be made up of sb/sthg □ *The panel consists of five executive managers.*

consistency [kən'sɪstənsɪ] (*pl* **consistencies**) *n* **-1.** [of a person, argument] *see* **consistent** □ *Consistency is vital when disciplining young children.* **-2.** [of a substance] the degree of thickness,

smoothness, or firmness of something, e.g. food or a liquid □ *Add the liquid until the mixture has the consistency of thin cream.*

consistent [kən'sɪstənt] *adj* **-1.** [person, behavior, quality] that does not vary □ *His performance has been consistent all year.* □ *a consistent approach to punishment.* **-2.** [growth, improvement] that develops in a regular way □ *This year has seen a consistent increase in sales.* **-3.** [idea, argument] whose different parts agree with each other □ *The new measure is entirely consistent with the government's tough approach to crime.*

consistently [kən'sɪstəntlɪ] *adv* [behave, improve, argue] in a way that does not vary □ *They have consistently denied the accusation.* □ *We produce work to a consistently high standard.*

consolation [,kɒnsə'leɪʃn] *n* a person or thing that consoles somebody □ *If it's any consolation, you're not the only one who got cheated.* □ *Her work with charities was a great consolation to her after her husband died.*

consolation prize *n* a small prize given to somebody who has failed to win a competition.

console [*n* 'kɒnsoʊl, *vb* kən'soʊl] ◇ *n* a panel where the controls for a piece of equipment are situated. ◇ *vt* to comfort <sb> when they are sad or disappointed □ *He consoled himself with the thought that he had learned a lot from the experience.*

consolidate [kən'sɒlɪdeɪt] ◇ *vt* **-1.** [position, power, knowledge] to strengthen one's control over <sthg that one has won or gained> □ *Rebel forces have consolidated their earlier gains.* **-2.** BUSINESS to join <two or more companies> together □ *consolidated accounts.* ◇ *vi* BUSINESS *The two companies have recently consolidated.*

consolidation [kən,sɒlɪ'deɪʃn] *n*: *see* **consolidate** □ *ACL is concentrating on the consolidation of its existing position in the market.*

consols ['kɒnsɒlz] *npl* FINANCE bonds issued by the British government.

consommé [US ,kɒnsə'meɪ, GB kɒn'sɒmeɪ] *n* a clear soup made of meat stock.

consonant ['kɒnsənənt] *n* a sound made when one is talking that is not a vowel and is made by stopping the air in the mouth; a letter that represents such a sound, e.g. "r", "p", or "t".

consort [*vb* kən'sɔːt, *n* 'kɒnsɔːt] ◇ *vi* **to consort with sb** to spend a lot of time with sb (disapproving use). ◇ *n* the husband or wife of a king or queen.

consortium [kən'sɔːtjəm] (*pl* **consortiums** OR **consortia** [-tjə]) *n* a group of people or businesses working together on a project □ *an American consortium* OR *a consortium of American companies.*

conspicuous [kən'spɪkjʊəs] *adj* [color, building, failure] that is easy to see and attracts attention □ *Such conspicuous wealth attracts envy, of course.* □ *Simon was conspicuous by his absence at the meeting.*

conspicuously [kən'spɪkjʊəslɪ] *adv* [dress, fail]

see **conspicuous** □ *Any mention of an apology was conspicuously absent.* □ *Officials have conspicuously avoided any mention of compensation.*

conspiracy [kən'spɪrəsɪ] (*pl* **conspiracies**) *n* a secret plan by a group of people to do something harmful or dishonest together □ *He became convinced there was a conspiracy against him.*

conspirator [kən'spɪrətəʳ] *n* a person who takes part in a conspiracy.

conspiratorial [kən,spɪrə'tɔːrɪəl] *adj* [look, smile, whisper] that shows one shares a secret with somebody.

conspire [kən'spaɪəʳ] *vi* -1. [people] to take part in a conspiracy □ *They conspired to kill him.* □ *They have been accused of conspiring with/against the unions.* -2. [events, circumstances] to combine to cause a particular result □ *Various factors have conspired to bring about the latest crisis.*

constable ['kʌnstəbl] *n* GB the lowest rank of police officer.

Constable ['kʌnstəbl], **John** (1776–1837) a British artist, well known for his paintings of English landscapes. His most famous picture is *The Haywain.*

constabulary [kən'stæbjələrɪ] (*pl* **constabularies**) *n* GB the police force of a particular area □ *the Sussex constabulary.*

constancy ['kɒnstənsɪ] *n*: *see* **constant.**

constant ['kɒnstənt] *adj* -1. [temperature, speed, support] that stays at the same level □ *Demand for our services has remained fairly constant.* -2. [attacks, arguments] that happen very often or that never stop □ *I've had to put up with constant criticism.* □ *He's in constant pain.* -3. [friend, husband, wife] who is always faithful (literary use).

Constantine (the Great) [,kɒnstəntaɪn(ðə'greɪt)] (280?–337) a Roman emperor who established the city of Constantinople and the Byzantine Empire, and made Christianity the official religion.

constantly ['kɒnstəntlɪ] *adv* in a way that stays at the same level or happens often □ *The world is constantly changing.* □ *My job keeps me constantly busy.*

constellation [,kɒnstə'leɪʃn] *n* ASTRONOMY a group of stars that has been given a name.

consternation [,kɒnstəʳ'neɪʃn] *n* a feeling of worry or fear □ *The statement caused consternation among community leaders.*

constipated ['kɒnstɪpeɪtəd] *adj* [person] who has difficulty emptying their bowels.

constipation [,kɒnstɪ'peɪʃn] *n* the condition of being constipated □ *Eat a high-fiber diet to avoid constipation.*

constituency [kən'stɪtʃʊənsɪ] (*pl* **constituencies**) *n* the area of a country, region etc that elects somebody to represent it in parliament; the people who vote in this area.

constituency party *n* GB a regional section of a political party.

constituent [kən'stɪtʃʊənt] ◇ *adj* **the constituent parts/members etc of sthg** the parts/

members etc that combine to form sthg □ *All of the alliance's constituent countries are taking part.* ◇ *n* -1. POLITICS a voter in a constituency. -2. one of the parts that something is made from □ *The constituents of water are hydrogen and oxygen.*

constitute ['kɒnstɪtʲuːt] *vt* -1. to form or make up <sthg> □ *This is a challenge for all the countries that constitute the European Union.* □ *Women constitute less than 10% of applicants.* -2. [threat, victory] to mean the same as <sthg> □ *This constitutes a breach of privacy.* -3. [committee, panel] to create <sthg> □ *A working party was constituted to investigate the problem.*

constitution [,kɒnstə'tʲuːʃn] *n* -1. [of a country] the set of laws that describe the way a country is governed and the rights of its citizens. -2. [of a person] one's general health □ *He has a strong constitution.* -3. [of a committee, working party] the way in which different elements combine to form something.

ℰ CONSTITUTION
In the USA and Australia, the system of government is described in a written constitution. The US Constitution was written in 1787, and the Australian one in 1901. Changes to the US Constitution have to be approved by the Supreme Court. In Australia, people vote to approve any proposed change, which must have the support of the majority of voters in at least four states.
The British Constitution has no written form. It has developed through history, as laws have been made and changed.

constitutional [,kɒnstə'tʲuːʃnəl] *adj* -1. [change, crisis, right] that is connected with the constitution of a country or organization □ *It's all part of the constitutional process.* -2. [government, right] that is allowed by the constitution of a country □ *The king can only be deposed by constitutional means.*

constitutional monarch *n* a king or queen who is the head of a constitutional monarchy.

constitutional monarchy *n* a system of government with a king or queen whose power is limited by a constitution and in which most important decisions are made by elected politicians; a country that has this system.

constrain [kən'streɪn] *vt* -1. **to be constrained to do sthg** to be or feel forced to do something one does not want to do □ *He felt constrained to agree to the decision.* -2. [feeling, freedom, development] to limit the size, expression, or growth of <sthg> □ *They were constrained from expressing their true opinions by an outdated law.*

constrained [kən'streɪnd] *adj* [manner, smile] that is awkward and seems forced.

constraint [kən'streɪnt] *n* -1. something that limits or controls what somebody does □ *They are subject to the constraints of time and money.* □ *There are certain constraints on their activities.* -2. self-control □ *He showed remark-*

able constraint. **-3. to do sthg under constraint** to do sthg because one has been forced to do it □ *I'll do it, but under constraint.*

constrict [kən'strɪkt] *vt* **-1.** [neck, wrist, blood vessel] to make <sthg> narrower or tighter □ *The bandage can be tightened to constrict the flow of blood.* **-2.** [person] to limit the actions of <sb> □ *I felt very constricted in my role as Chairman.*

constriction [kən'strɪkʃn] *n*: *see* **constrict** □ *Remove any tight articles of clothing that may cause constriction.*

constricting [kən'strɪktɪŋ] *adj* **-1.** [clothes, shoes] that are too tight and limit the way one moves □ *This jacket is very constricting.* **-2.** [circumstances, system, situation] that constricts somebody □ *Army life is very constricting.*

construct [*vb* kən'strʌkt, *n* 'kɒnstrʌkt] ◇ *vt* **-1.** [building, boat, bridge] to build <sthg> □ *The floor was constructed out of blocks of wood.* **-2.** [sentence, argument, theory] to form <sthg> by putting parts together □ *The new evidence demolishes their carefully constructed case.* ◇ *n* a complex idea that is formed in one's mind (formal use) □ *Some philosophers believe that religion is just a mental construct.*

construction [kən'strʌkʃn] *n* **-1.** [of a building, bridge] the act of building something □ *The tunnel's construction will be financed privately.* □ *Construction work begins next month.* ■ **to be under construction** to be in the process of being built □ *Several major new buildings are under construction.* **-2.** the area of work and business connected with the construction of buildings, bridges etc □ *the construction industry* □ *a construction worker/site/company.* **-3.** something, e.g. a building or bridge, that has been built; the way that this has been built □ *a massive brick construction* □ *a model ship of elaborate construction.*

constructive [kən'strʌktɪv] *adj* [criticism, attitude, person] that is useful and helpful rather than damaging or negative □ *Both sides described the talks as "constructive."*

construe [kən'struː] *vt* [word, behavior] to understand <sthg> in a particular way (formal use) □ *In fact, their words could be construed as a challenge to the West.*

consul ['kɒnsl] *n* an official who is appointed by the government of a country to help and protect its citizens and its business interests in a foreign city □ *the US consul in Athens.*

consular [US 'kɒnslər, GB 'kɒnsjʊlə] *adj* [office, section, duties] *see* **consul**.

consulate [US 'kɒnslət, GB 'kɒnsjʊlət] *n* the building where a consul lives or works.

consult [kən'sʌlt] ◇ *vt* **-1.** [friend, doctor, lawyer] to ask <sb, especially an expert>, for advice on something serious □ *I consult her about everything.* **-2.** [dictionary, map] to read <sthg> for information □ *After consulting our records, it appears you still have not paid the amount due.* ◇ *vi* **to consult with sb** to talk to and exchange ideas with sb, especially sb who knows a lot about a particular subject.

consultancy [kən'sʌltənsɪ] (*pl* **consultancies**) *n* BUSINESS a company whose business is to give advice on a particular subject □ *a design/management consultancy.*

consultancy fee *n* a fee paid to a person or company for professional advice.

consultant [kən'sʌltənt] *n* **-1.** BUSINESS a person whose job is to give expert professional advice □ *a management/design consultant.* **-2.** GB MEDICINE a senior hospital doctor who specializes in a particular field of medicine □ *a consultant pediatrician.*

consultation [,kɒnsəl'teɪʃn] *n* **-1.** [before a decision] a discussion, usually held in order to make a decision about something □ *Parents can now make better choices for their children in consultation with schools.* **-2.** [for advice] a discussion in which somebody is consulted for advice. **-3.** [of a dictionary, map] *see* **consult**.

consulting room [kən'sʌltɪŋ-] *n* GB a room where a doctor sees patients.

consumables [kən'suːməblz] *npl* goods that people need to buy, often because they have to be replaced after being used.

consume [kən'sjuːm] *vt* **-1.** [food, drink] to eat or drink <sthg> (formal use) □ *The device shows how much alcohol you have consumed.* □ *As a nation, we consume far too much fat.* **-2.** [fuel, time, resource] to use <sthg> □ *We are consuming the world's supply of solid fuels at an alarming rate.* □ *These heaters consume far less energy than the old ones.* **-3.** [person] to fill the thoughts or feelings of <sb> (literary use) □ *He was consumed by jealousy.*

consumer [kən'sjuːmər] *n* a person who buys and uses goods and services □ *consumer advice/protection/rights.*

consumer credit *n* personal credit that allows somebody to buy goods.

consumer durables *npl* goods, e.g. cars or televisions, that people do not buy often because they are expected to last a long time.

consumer goods *npl* goods that people buy and use in everyday life.

consumerism [kən'sjuːmərɪzm] *n* **-1.** the idea that buying and selling a lot of consumer goods is desirable for a strong economy. **-2.** the protection of the rights and interests of consumers.

consumer price index *n* US a system of figures that shows how the prices of a list of goods have increased over a period of time, used to show changes in the cost of living.

consumer society *n* a society in which the production and buying of consumer goods is very important.

consumer spending *n* money spent on consumer goods.

consuming [kən'sjuːmɪŋ] *adj* **a consuming interest/passion etc** an interest/a passion etc that one gives all of one's energy and enthusiasm to □ *Dance was her consuming passion.*

consummate [*adj* 'kɒnsəmət, *vb* 'kɒnsəmeɪt] ◇ *adj* (formal use) **-1.** [skill, happiness] that is very great □ *The champion won with consummate ease.* **-2.** [liar, politician, actor] who is very

skillful □ *She's a consummate actress.* ◇ *vt* **-1. to consummate a marriage** to make a marriage complete by having sexual intercourse. **-2.** [deal, achievement] to complete <sthg>.

consummation [ˌkɒnsə'meɪʃn] *n* [of a marriage] see **consummate**.

consumption [kən'sʌmpʃn] *n* [of food, fuel] *see* **consume** □ *We must reduce our consumption of imported timber.* □ *fuel consumption charges.*

cont. **-1.** *abbr of* **continued. -2.** GRAMMAR *abbr of* **continuous.**

contact ['kɒntækt] ◇ *n* **-1.** the act or state of touching somebody or something □ *physical contact* □ *Keep one foot in contact with the ground.* **-2.** [by telephone, letter] the act of communicating with somebody, especially by telephoning or writing to them □ *Have you been in contact with them?* □ *We are no longer in contact.* ■ **to lose contact with sb** to no longer see sb or hear from them. ■ **to make contact with sb** to begin to communicate with sb. **-3. to come into contact with sb/sthg** to know or be affected by sb/sthg as a result of one's experiences □ *It's not known when she came into contact with the disease.* **-4.** [in a country, organization] a person who one knows and who may be useful □ *a business contact* □ *He's got lots of contacts in the movie business.*
◇ *vt* to communicate with <sb> by phone, fax etc, especially in order to give or ask for information □ *We'll contact you when we have the results.* □ *You can contact me at this number.*

contact lens *n* a small lens that fits directly onto one's eye and is worn instead of glasses as a way of improving one's eyesight.

contact number *n* a telephone number where somebody can be contacted.

contact sport *n* a sport such as football in which players are allowed to touch each other during games, and which can be rough.

contagious [kən'teɪdʒəs] *adj* **-1.** [disease] that is spread by physical contact. **-2.** [laughter, enthusiasm] that spreads quickly to other people.

contain [kən'teɪn] *vt* **-1.** to hold or to have <sthg> inside □ *Each pack contains twenty cigarettes.* **-2.** [message, sugar, fat] to have <sthg> as a part □ *The food contains additives and preservatives.* □ *This movie contains scenes of a sexually explicit nature.* □ *Her story does contain some truth.* **-3.** [one's anger, excitement] to keep <a feeling> hidden and under control □ *He could hardly contain his enthusiasm.* ■ **to contain oneself** to control a particular strong feeling, so that other people do not notice it. **-4.** [epidemic, fire, revolt] to limit <sthg> so that it does not spread □ *Firemen fought to contain the blaze.*

container [kən'teɪnəʳ] *n* **-1.** something that is designed to contain things, e.g. a box or bottle □ *a plastic/glass container.* **-2.** TRANSPORT a large rectangular box, usually made of metal, used for transporting goods on trucks

and ships; the amount of something contained in this box.

containerize, -ise [kən'teɪnəraɪz] *vt* **-1.** to transport <goods, cargo> etc in containers. **-2.** to make changes to <a port> so that containers can be used there.

container ship *n* a ship that is designed to transport goods in containers.

containment [kən'teɪnmənt] *n* **-1.** [of one's excitement, an epidemic, enemy] *see* **contain. -2.** POLITICS the process or policy of limiting the power of another country □ *a policy of containment.*

contaminate [kən'tæmɪneɪt] *vt* [water, blood, food] to make <sthg> dangerous or harmful by adding something dirty or poisonous to it, often by accident □ *rivers contaminated with* OR *by sewage.*

contaminated [kən'tæmɪneɪtəd] *adj* [water, blood, food] that has been made dangerous or harmful by the addition of something dirty or poisonous □ *The buildings had been erected on contaminated land.*

contamination [kənˌtæmɪ'neɪʃn] *n: see* **contaminate** □ *the contamination of rivers by agricultural runoff.*

cont'd *abbr of* **continued.**

contemplate ['kɒntəmpleɪt] ◇ *vt* **-1.** [idea, thought] to think deeply and seriously about <sthg>, especially when it is connected with what one might do in the future □ *They are contemplating selling the company.* **-2.** [sunset, flower] to look at <sthg> thoughtfully (literary use).

contemplation [ˌkɒntəm'pleɪʃn] *n* the act of thinking deeply about something □ *She was lost in contemplation.*

contemplative [kən'templətɪv] *adj* [person, life] that is thoughtful and quiet.

contemporary [US kən'tempərerɪ, GB -rərɪ] (*pl* **contemporaries**) ◇ *adj* **-1.** [art, design] that is modern and belongs to the present time □ *He also writes a lot of contemporary music.* **-2.** [account, report, event] that belongs to the same period □ *He was contemporary with Lincoln.* ◇ *n* a person living at the same time as another person; a person who is the same age as another person □ *She was a contemporary of Frank Pugh.* □ *He's a contemporary of yours, I believe.*

contempt [kən'tempt] *n* **-1.** dislike for something or somebody that one thinks is unpleasant, unimportant, and worthless □ *I feel nothing but contempt for him/his policies.* ■ **to hold sb in contempt** to feel contempt for sb. **-2.** LAW **contempt (of court)** the crime of disobeying the rules of a court, e.g. by being rude to a judge or by failing to appear in court when requested.

contemptible [kən'temptəbl] *adj* [person, manner, behavior] that one feels deserves contempt □ *I think it's contemptible the way he's behaved toward her.*

contemptuous [kən'temptʃuəs] *adj* [person, look, remark] that shows contempt □ *He's contemptuous of anyone else's work.*

contend [kən'tend] ◇ *vi* **-1. to have to contend with sb/sthg, to have sb/sthg to contend with** to have to deal with sb/sthg that may cause one difficulty or problems □ *Don't do it again, or you'll have me to contend with.* **-2. to contend for sthg** [for power, a trophy] to compete for sthg. ■ **to contend with sb** to compete with sb for something. ◇ *vt* **to contend (that)...** to claim that something is true □ *He contended (that) his client could not have known the firm was exporting military equipment.*

contender [kən'tendəʳ] *n* a person who is competing with other people for something, e.g. a job or sports title □ *He was a leading contender for the post.*

content [*adj* & *vb* kən'tent, *n* 'kɒntent] ◇ *adj* [person] who is happy and satisfied with what they have □ *He seems quite content with his new life.* ■ **to be content to do sthg** to be happy to do sthg and not wish to do more. ◇ *n* **-1.** the amount of a particular substance contained in something □ *food with a high fiber content.* **-2.** the things that are written or spoken about in a book, program, speech etc □ *His movies are all style and no content.* ◇ *vt* **to content oneself with sthg** to be satisfied with sthg □ *We've never contented ourselves with coming second.*

◆ **contents** *npl* **-1.** [in a bottle, bag] everything that is contained inside something □ *He emptied the contents of the bin on the floor.* **-2.** [of a letter, document] everything that is said in a piece of writing □ *I haven't yet seen the contents of the report.* **-3.** [in a book, magazine] a list at the beginning of a book or magazine which gives the title of each chapter or article and its page number □ *the contents page.*

contented [kən'tentəd] *adj* [person] who is satisfied, happy, and does not want things to be changed □ *She gave a contented smile.*

contentedly [kən'tentədlɪ] *adv* [smile, sit] *see* **contented** □ *Gary hummed contentedly as we drove along.*

contention [kən'tenʃn] *n* (formal use) **-1.** [by a person] an opinion or idea that is expressed, e.g. during an argument or discussion □ *It is my contention that the other proposal offers better opportunities.* **-2.** [among people] angry disagreement or argument □ *Privatization is an issue of contention within the government.* **-3. to be in contention for sthg** to be in a competition and have a chance of winning sthg.

contentious [kən'tenʃəs] *adj* [issue, subject, decision] that is likely to cause a lot of disagreement and argument.

contentment [kən'tentmənt] *n* a feeling of quiet happiness and satisfaction with one's situation □ *a feeling of peace and contentment.*

contest [*n* 'kɒntest, *vb* kən'test] ◇ *n* **-1.** a competition, usually decided by specially chosen judges, in which two or more people try to win something □ *a fishing contest.* **-2.** a struggle between different people who want to win power □ *She has little chance in the contest for the leadership of the party.* ◇ *vt* **-1.** [leadership, election, competition] to try to win <sthg> □ *a hotly contested tennis tournament.*

-2. [decision, statement, claim] to argue against <sthg> because one believes it is wrong or unreasonable (formal use).

contestant [kən'testənt] *n* a person who takes part in a competition, game, quiz etc in order to try to win □ *Our third contestant is Mr Knight from Stockton.*

context ['kɒntekst] *n* **-1.** the words and sentences that come before and after a word, sentence etc and affect or help to explain its meaning □ *Try to work out the meaning from the context.* ■ **to use/quote etc sthg out of context** to use/quote etc sthg without its context, with the result that it is likely to be misunderstood □ *These comments should not be taken out of context.* **-2.** the circumstances in which something happens and which one needs to know about to understand it completely □ *Seen in a world context, these shortages have little importance.*

continent ['kɒntɪnənt] *n* one of the earth's large areas of land, e.g. Europe, Asia, or Africa □ *the continent of Africa* OR *the African continent.*

◆ **Continent** *n* **the Continent** GB a phrase used by people in Britain to talk about the rest of western Europe □ *a holiday on the Continent.*

continental [,kɒntɪ'nentl] *adj* **-1.** [waters, crust] *see* **continent. -2.** GB [food, city] that belongs to or is part of the Continent □ *a continental holiday.*

continental breakfast *n* a light breakfast consisting of bread, rolls or buns, and coffee or tea, but no hot cooked dish.

NOTE: Compare **English breakfast**.

continental climate *n* GB a climate that is very hot in summer, very cold in winter, and usually quite dry.

Continental Congress *n* **the Continental Congress** the law-making body of the thirteen North American colonies before and during the American Revolution.

continental quilt *n* GB a large bag filled with feathers or synthetic fiber that is used instead of blankets on a bed.

contingency [kən'tɪndʒənsɪ] (*pl* **contingencies**) *n* an event that might happen in the future and might cause problems if it does □ *You must be prepared for all contingencies.*

contingency plan *n* a plan that is ready to be used if something goes wrong.

contingent [kən'tɪndʒənt] ◇ *adj* **to be contingent on** OR **upon sthg** to depend on sthg that may or may not happen (formal use). ◇ *n* **-1.** MILITARY a group of soldiers, police, vehicles etc that is part of a larger group. **-2.** [at a conference, meeting] a group of people representing a country, organization etc □ *There was a large Australian contingent at our sales promotion.*

continual [kən'tɪnjʊəl] *adj* **-1.** [noise, growth, fear] that continues without stopping, often for a long time □ *We lived under the continual threat of starvation.* **-2.** [demands, interruptions, warnings] that happen many times, often over a long period of time □ *There have been continual calls for his release.*

continually [kən'tɪnjuəlɪ] *adv* [grow, change, demand] *see* **continual** □ *He was continually complaining about the food.*

continuation [kən,tɪnju'eɪʃn] *n* **-1.** [of talks, work, a game] *see* **continue** □ *We are unable to offer you a continuation of your contract.* **-2.** [of a road, book, voyage] something which is added to something else and makes it longer □ *My lecture today is a continuation of last week's.*

continue [kən'tɪnjuː] ◇ *vt* **-1.** [studies, talks, supper] to keep doing <sthg> without stopping □ *I intend to continue my career in France.* □ *The band continued to play* OR *playing late into the night.* **-2.** [concert, game, work] to start doing <sthg> again after a break or interruption □ *'To be continued'* □ *"And so we move on to our next topic," he continued.*

◇ *vi* **-1.** [noise, fighting, rain] to go on happening or existing for some time without stopping □ *If interest rates continue to rise, we'll be bankrupt before long.* □ *She will continue to be the director until we find a replacement.* □ *I no longer wish to continue as an employee of the company.* □ *The doctor told me to continue with the treatment.* **-2.** [concert, game, speaker] to start again after a break or interruption □ *The article continues on page 15.* □ *The chairman made a few comments and then asked me to continue.* **-3.** [person, vehicle, road] to keep moving, traveling, or going somewhere □ *We continued along the path.*

continuity [,kɒntə'nʲuːətɪ] *n* **-1.** the quality of something that develops and continues in a smooth way without any sudden unwanted changes □ *The party has to ensure continuity in its political programs.* **-2.** CINEMA & TV the correct arrangement of scenes in a movie or television program so that one follows another logically and without sudden breaks.

continuous [kən'tɪnjuəs] *adj* **-1.** [rain, supply, line] that continues all the time without stops or breaks □ *There has been a continuous stream of telephone calls to protest.* **-2.** GRAMMAR a word used to refer to the form of a verb that describes an action while it is still happening. This form is made using the verb "to be", as in the phrases "she is thinking" and "I was working".

continuous assessment *n* EDUCATION the system of judging students' progress regularly throughout a course rather than by an examination at the end of it.

continuously [kən'tɪnjuəslɪ] *adv* [rain, complain, increase] *see* **continuous** □ *Their TV is on continuously from morning till night.*

contorted [kən'tɔːrtəd] *adj* [body, image] that is twisted or bent so that it becomes an unnatural and unattractive shape □ *His face was contorted with anger.*

contortion [kən'tɔːrʃn] *n* a position or shape produced when something becomes contorted.

contour ['kɒntuər] *n* **-1.** [of a face, coastline] the shape of the outside edge of something, especially something that has a lot of curves □

Her dress showed off the contours of her body. **-2.** [on a map] a line on a map showing how high places are above sea level □ *a contour map/line.*

contraband ['kɒntrəbænd] ◇ *adj* [cigarettes, goods] that are brought into a country illegally, usually to avoid paying tax. ◇ *n* contraband goods □ *Customs officials seized $3 million worth of contraband.*

contraception [,kɒntrə'sepʃn] *n* methods used to prevent a woman from becoming pregnant □ *What form of contraception do you use?*

contraceptive [,kɒntrə'septɪv] ◇ *adj* [method, device] that is intended to prevent a woman from becoming pregnant. ◇ *n* a contraceptive device, pill etc □ *an oral contraceptive.*

contraceptive pill *n* a small pill containing hormones that a woman takes regularly to prevent her from becoming pregnant.

contract [*n* 'kɒntrækt, *vb* kən'trækt] ◇ *n* a formal agreement, usually in writing, that often concerns money in return for work, services etc □ *a contract of employment* □ *The two parties then signed the contract.* □ *We won the contract for the new bridge.* ■ **to put work out to contract** to employ a firm or person to do some work instead of doing it oneself.

◇ *vt* **-1.** BUSINESS [company, builder] to get <sb> to do some work according to conditions written down in a contract □ *We contracted Vincents to do the cleaning.* **-2.** MEDICINE [malaria, measles] to get <a disease> (formal use) □ *She contracted hepatitis in the tropics.* **-3.** [name, word] to make <sthg> shorter by removing some letters. **-4.** ANATOMY to make <a muscle in one's body> tighter and shorter.

◇ *vi* [metal, muscle, sales] to become smaller □ *Our business is contracting as demand falls.*

◆ **contract in** *vi* GB to agree formally, and usually in writing, to join or take part in something □ *You have the opportunity to contract in to the company pension plan.*

◆ **contract out** ◇ *vt sep* **to contract sthg out** [services, work] to have sthg done by somebody from outside one's organization, according to conditions written down in a contract □ *The university has contracted out security to a private company.* ◇ *vi* GB to agree formally, and usually in writing, not to join or take part in something □ *We are contracting out of the company pension plan.*

contraction [kən'trækʃn] *n* **-1.** [of a metal, muscle, sales] *see* **contract** □ *a muscular contraction.* **-2.** [of a name, word] a shortened form of a word or words.

contractor [kən'træktər] *n* a person or company that does a particular job for another company, especially building or public works □ *a cleaning contractor.*

contractual [kən'træktʃuəl] *adj* [obligations, agreement] that is described or listed in a contract □ *The company was accused of failing to fulfil its contractual obligations to employees.*

contradict [,kɒntrə'dɪkt] *vt* **-1.** [person, statement, opinion] to show that one thinks <sb/sthg> is wrong, by saying something very different or disagreeing □ *Why do you contradict everything I say?* **-2.** [statement, claim, idea] to be different from <sthg> and make it seem wrong □ *Their statements contradict each other.*

contradiction [ˌkɒntrəˈdɪkʃn] *n* **-1.** a difference between two statements, facts etc that shows that they cannot both be true □ *There seems to be a contradiction between our records and your invoice.* ■ **a contradiction in terms** a phrase or sentence that is meaningless because it contains two different ideas that cannot both be true. **-2.** a difference between parts of somebody's character, behavior etc that is difficult to understand or accept □ *She's full of contradictions.*

contradictory [ˌkɒntrəˈdɪktəri] *adj* [statements, reports] that are so different that they cannot both be true.

contraflow [ˈkɒntrəfloʊ] *n* **a contraflow (system)** GB AUTO a temporary system on a road where traffic going in both directions uses one side of the road only, usually because the other side is being repaired.

contralto [US kənˈtræltoʊ, GB -ˈtrɑːltoʊ] (*pl* **contraltos**) *n* a woman's singing voice that is quite low; a woman who has this kind of voice.

contraption [kənˈtræpʃn] *n* a strange or complicated machine or piece of equipment.

contrary [ˈkɒntrəri, *adj sense 2* kənˈtreəri] ◇ *adj* **-1.** [ideas, attitudes, directions] that are completely different from each other □ *His opinions are contrary to mine and we'll never agree.* **-2.** [person] who likes disagreeing with other people and behaving unreasonably □ *My boss can be so contrary at times.*
◇ *n* **the contrary** the opposite □ *He always says the contrary to what I say.* □ *"Were you upset?" — "Quite the contrary, I was delighted."* ■ **on the contrary** a phrase used to introduce a statement or opinion that corrects what has just been said or suggested by somebody else □ *She's not fat; on the contrary, she's rather thin.* ■ **to the contrary** a phrase used to say that the opposite of what has been arranged, said etc is true □ *Despite evidence to the contrary, many people still believe the drug is effective.* □ *If you don't hear anything to the contrary, aim to arrive at about 7pm.*

◆ **contrary to** *prep* a phrase used to emphasize that something is true even if something else makes it seem unlikely or wrong □ *Contrary to all advice, she married him.* □ *Contrary to what people say, she's not that bad to work for.*

contrast [*n* US ˈkɒntræst, GB -ˈtrɑːst, *vb* US kənˈtræst, GB -trɑːst] ◇ *n* **-1.** a difference that can be seen when two things are compared with each other □ *the contrast between summer and winter* □ *This year's performance makes a striking contrast with* OR *to last year's.* ■ **by** OR **in contrast** a phrase used to emphasize the differences between two things □ *Last year we did badly, but this year, by contrast, we have made a profit.* ■ **in contrast with** OR **to sb/sthg** in a way that is very different than sb/sthg

□ *In contrast to his sister, he works very hard.* □ *In marked contrast to earlier statements, the General adopted a conciliatory tone.* **-2.** something or somebody that is very different to something or somebody else □ *Their new house is a complete contrast to their old one.*
◇ *vt* to compare <two things> in order to show how different they are □ *It's interesting to contrast the styles of the two players.* □ *If we contrast this year's figures with last year's, we can see an improvement.*
◇ *vi* [actions, statements] to be very different from each other when compared □ *Blue contrasts well with yellow.* □ *The two reports contrast sharply.*

contrasting [US kənˈtræstɪŋ, GB -ˈtrɑːstɪŋ] *adj* [colors, personalities, views] that are very different when compared with each other □ *The room was painted in contrasting shades of red and blue.*

contravene [ˌkɒntrəˈviːn] *vt* [law, treaty] to be against the rules or terms of <sthg> (formal use).

contravention [ˌkɒntrəˈvenʃn] *n: see* **contravene** □ *They attacked the town, in direct contravention of the ceasefire agreement.*

contribute [US kənˈtrɪbjət, GB -juːt] ◇ *vt* **-1.** [to a fund, cause] to give <money> to help pay for something □ *We contributed $150 toward the cost of the trip.* **-2.** [to a discussion, debate] to make <comments, suggestions> etc as part of a discussion or debate □ *I have nothing more to contribute to this conversation.* **-3.** [to a magazine, book] to write <sthg> for a magazine, book etc □ *Dr Williams has contributed several articles to the journal.*
◇ *vi* **-1.** [to a collection, charity, conversation] to contribute something that makes something increase, develop, or get better □ *Everyone contributed in their own individual way.* □ *Your work has contributed greatly to our increase in profits.* **-2. to contribute to sthg** [to an event, change, problem] to be one of the causes of sthg □ *Unemployment is contributing to the increase in crime.* **-3. to contribute to sthg** [to a magazine, book] to write articles for sthg.

contributing [US kənˈtrɪbjətɪŋ, GB -jutɪŋ] *adj* [factor, cause] that is part of the reason why something happens □ *Poverty is one of the contributing factors in the rise of urban crime.*

contribution [ˌkɒntrɪˈbjuːʃn] *n* **-1.** [to a fund, cause] money given to help pay for or support something □ *They agreed to make a contribution to charity.* □ *a contribution of $3,000.* **-2.** [to science, safety, peace] something, e.g. help, work, or a service, that somebody or something gives to help something to succeed □ *She has made a valuable contribution to medical science.* **-3.** [to a debate, discussion] something, e.g. an idea or comment, that one contributes to a discussion or debate □ *Thank you for that most interesting contribution to the discussion.* **-4.** [to a magazine, book] an article, essay, poem etc written for a magazine or book □ *We have received contributions from journalists all over the world.* **-5.** GB FINANCE money that the government takes from people's wages to pay for public health and pensions □ *National Insurance contributions.*

contributor [kən'trɪbjətəʳ] *n* -1. [to funds, a cause] a person who gives money to help pay for something □ *Britain is a major contributor to EU funds.* -2. [to a magazine, book] a person who writes for a magazine, book etc □ *Christine Lowe is a regular contributor to the magazine.*

contributory [US kən'trɪbjətɔːrɪ, GB -trɪbjətərɪ] *adj* [factor, cause] = **contributing.**

contributory pension scheme *n* GB a pension scheme for employees in which pensions are paid for partly by themselves and partly by their employers.

contrite [US kən'traɪt, GB 'kɒntraɪt] *adj* [person] who is sorry and apologetic for something they have done (formal use).

contrition [kən'trɪʃn] *n* the feeling one has when one is contrite.

contrivance [kən'traɪvns] *n* -1. a machine or piece of equipment, especially an unusual one made for a particular purpose. -2. a clever plan or trick that is usually dishonest or unfair (disapproving use).

contrive [kən'traɪv] *vt* (formal use) -1. [meeting, scheme] to arrange <sthg> in a clever way, often secretly and by using tricks or dishonesty □ *The scandal has been deliberately contrived by the media.* -2. **to contrive to do sthg** to succeed in doing sthg difficult □ *Despite the rain, the Finnish team contrived to produce its best performance all season.*

contrived [kən'traɪvd] *adj* [plot, ending] that does not seem natural or believable.

control [kən'trəʊl] (*pt* & *pp* **controlled,** *cont* **controlling**) ◇ *n* -1. [of a country, organization, machine] the power or ability to make something work or happen the way one wants it to □ *The director has control of OR over the budget.* □ *a control switch* □ *She lost control of the steering wheel.* □ *They have made a bid to gain control of the business.* ■ **to take control** [of a situation, game] to start to have control of something □ *You must learn to take control of your own life.* ■ **beyond** OR **outside one's control** that one has no power over and is unable to change □ *Payments will be delayed due to circumstances beyond our control.* ■ **to be in control** to have control □ *Who's in control here?* □ *They are fully in control of the situation.* ■ **to be out of control** [car, crowd, disease] to be impossible to deal with and likely to cause harm □ *His drinking is getting out of control.* ■ **to be under control** [horse, crowd, fire] to have been dealt with and made less dangerous □ *The government claims to have brought inflation under control.* □ *Don't worry, everything's under control.* ■ **to be under the control of sb** [town, area] to be ruled or directed by sb □ *The south of the country is under enemy control.* -2. [of one's emotions] the ability to stop oneself from becoming too excited, angry, or emotional □ *They just lost control and started shooting.* -3. [of immigration, spending] a system or method used to limit or prevent something that is harmful or unwanted □ *pest/*

traffic control □ *The administration has imposed controls on* OR *over defense spending.* -4. [in an experiment] something used in an experiment as a standard against which the results of the experiment are compared. -5. COMPUTING = **control key.**

◇ *vt* -1. [country, company, budget] to have the power to direct, manage, rule, or make decisions about <sthg> □ *He controls his business interests from his home in Switzerland.* □ *a US-controlled company.* -2. [crowd, traffic, emotion] to prevent <sb/sthg> from becoming too violent or harmful □ *He found it hard to control his anger.* ■ **to control oneself** to stop oneself becoming too excited or emotional. -3. [machine, car, heating] to make <a device> work in the way intended □ *This lever controls the supply of fuel.* □ *They were living in an artificially controlled environment.* -4. [inflation, costs, spending] to keep <sthg> at a particular level; [disease, epidemic, pollution] to prevent <sthg> from spreading or getting worse □ *The tax is intended to control the rise in imports.* □ *measures designed to control the spread of AIDS.*

◆ **controls** *npl* **the controls** the switches, buttons etc used to make a machine work □ *She suddenly found herself sitting at the controls of a 120-seater jet.*

control code *n* an instruction given to a computer using the control key and at least one other key.

control group *n* a group of people used in an experiment to provide a standard against which the results of the experiment are compared.

control key *n* a key on a computer keyboard used with other keys to enter commands and perform different operations.

controlled [kən'trəʊld] *adj* -1. [person] who is able to stop themselves from getting too excited or emotional □ *He spoke in a calm, controlled voice.* -2. **a controlled economy** an economy that is directed and limited by the government.

controller [kən'trəʊləʳ] *n* the head or most important manager of a large organization or department □ *The Controller of the national network stood by the decision to broadcast the show.*

controlling [kən'trəʊlɪŋ] *adj* [factor, influence] that is very important in deciding the way in which something happens.

controlling interest *n* FINANCE ownership of enough shares in a company to be able to direct its policies.

control panel *n* a board or surface containing the switches and buttons used to operate a machine, car, plane etc.

control room *n* the part of a factory, power station etc where the central controls for equipment are kept, and where operations can be observed and checked, often on TV screens.

control tower *n* a building at an airport from which pilots are given instructions about taking off and landing via radio.

controversial [ˌkɒntrə'vɜːʳʃl] adj [movie, person, decision] that causes controversy □ The allegations are made in his controversial new book.

controversy ['kɒntrəvɜːʳsɪ] (pl **controversies**) n a lot of argument and discussion caused by something that makes people feel very strongly □ The mayor's speech was the subject of much controversy. □ the controversy over the sale of arms to Iran.

conundrum [kə'nʌndrəm] (pl **conundrums**) n a confusing problem that is hard to solve.

conurbation [ˌkɒnɜːʳ'beɪʃn] n a large urban area that has been formed by individual towns growing until they join together.

convalesce [ˌkɒnvə'les] vi to rest for a period of time in order to get completely better after a serious illness or operation.

convalescence [ˌkɒnvə'lesns] n the period of time in which somebody convalesces.

convalescent [ˌkɒnvə'lesnt] n a person who is convalescing.

convalescent home n a place where people who are convalescing stay.

convection [kən'vekʃn] n the movement of heat through air, water etc, that happens as a result of warm parts rising and colder parts sinking □ convection currents.

convector (heater) [kən'vektəʳ-] n a heater that heats air that then moves around a room by convection.

convene [kən'viːn] ◇ vt [meeting, conference] to ask people to come to <sthg> □ The meeting was convened last week. ◇ vi [court, parliament] to come together for a formal meeting □ Members of the Board convened last May.

convener [kən'viːnəʳ] n a person who organizes a meeting and asks people to come to it.

convenience [kən'viːnjəns] n -1. the quality of being suitable or useful for somebody by saving them time and trouble □ I keep my datebook in my car for convenience. -2. sb's convenience sb's personal comfort or advantage □ A telephone is provided for your convenience. ■ **at your convenience** when it is easiest for you (formal use). ■ **at your earliest convenience** as soon as you can (formal use) □ Please reply at your earliest convenience. -3. a machine or piece of equipment that is useful and makes life easier □ The house has every modern convenience.

convenience food n food, especially canned or frozen food, that is easy to store and quick to prepare.

convenience store n a small local store that is open late and sells food, drink, and other basic items.

convenient [kən'viːnjənt] adj [time, date, place] that is suitable for one's needs or plans and helps one to avoid wasting time or effort □ Will Tuesday be convenient for you? □ I find a bicycle a convenient way to get around town. ■ **to be convenient for sthg** [for stores, facilities] to be close to sthg □ I chose this area because it's convenient for work.

conveniently [kən'viːnjəntlɪ] adv: see **convenient** □ The hotel is conveniently situated downtown.

convent ['kɒnvənt] n a building where a group of nuns live.

convention [kən'venʃn] n -1. the way of behaving or doing something that is accepted by most people □ He defied convention by wearing jeans. □ a social convention. -2. POLITICS an international agreement about how countries should behave □ international conventions on human rights. -3. [of teachers, doctors] a large meeting of an organization or political party that is usually held once a year □ the Democratic convention.

❦ CONVENTION
The most important political conventions in the USA are the national party conventions, which take place every four years to choose the candidates for president. Party members come from all over the country to represent their state and nominate, or choose, the candidates for president and vice-president; they also help to decide party policies. Conventions usually take place in large halls filled with red, white, and blue signs and balloons. Important party members make speeches during the days before the voting, and there are informal parties in the evenings.

conventional [kən'venʃnəl] adj -1. [person, style, taste] that is normal and traditional, in a way that some people may think is boring □ She wears very conventional clothes. -2. [education, medicine, method] that has been used for a long time and is accepted by most people. -3. MILITARY [weapon, warfare] that does not involve nuclear weapons.

conventional oven n an ordinary oven rather than a microwave oven.

conventionally [kən'venʃnəlɪ] adv [dress, behave] see **conventional** □ She was conventionally educated at public school.

convent school n a school for girls run by nuns.

converge [kən'vɜːʳdʒ] vi -1. [rivers, paths, roads] to come together and meet □ The paths converge at the top of the hill. ■ **to converge on a place** [people, traffic] to come to a place in large numbers from many different directions □ Rock fans from all over Europe are converging on London for the event. -2. [interests, societies, views] to become more similar □ The Mexican economy is beginning to converge with those of its neighbors.

conversant [kən'vɜːʳsnt] adj **to be conversant with sthg** [with a method, idea] to know and be familiar with sthg (formal use) □ I'm fully conversant with the latest network systems.

conversation [ˌkɒnvəʳ'seɪʃn] n an informal talk between two or more people □ I had a long conversation with him over the phone. □ They were deep in conversation. ■ **to make conversation** to make an effort to talk to somebody, usually in order to be polite.

conversational [ˌkɒnvəˈseɪʃnəl] *adj* [style, tone] that is used in friendly conversation.

conversationalist [ˌkɒnvəˈseɪʃnəlɪst] *n* a person who is interesting and entertaining when they have conversations.

converse [*adj* US kənˈvɜːrs, GB ˈkɒnvɜːs, *n* ˈkɒnvɜːrs, *vb* kənˈvɜːrs] (formal use) ◇ *adj* [opinion, view] that is opposite to something. ◇ *n* **the converse** the opposite of something else, especially something that has just been said. ◇ *vi* to have a conversation with somebody □ *I find it very difficult to converse with her.*

conversely [kənˈvɜːrslɪ] *adv* a word used to introduce a situation or statement that is the opposite of the one just mentioned (formal use) □ *The demand for new housing in the area has fallen over recent years. Conversely, the interest in older properties has shown a marked increase.*

conversion [kənˈvɜːrʃn] *n* -1. [to a new system, method] the process of changing from one system, method, or form to another □ *Conversion from electric to gas heating could be expensive.* -2. CONSTRUCTION a room, house etc that has been changed or rebuilt for a new use □ *a loft conversion.* -3. [to a new belief, religion] a major change in somebody's religious or political beliefs □ *His conversion to Catholicism came late in his life.* -4. SPORT the act of kicking a rugby ball over the bar between the goalposts after scoring a try to score more points.

conversion table *n* a list that shows values in one system converted to values in another, e.g. dollars to pounds.

convert [*n* ˈkɒnvɜːrt, *vb* kənˈvɜːrt] ◇ *vt* -1. **to convert sthg to** OR **into sthg** [currency, machine] to change sthg completely so that it becomes sthg else and can be used in a different way □ *The process converts crude oil into petroleum.* -2. [person] to persuade <sb> to change their religious or political beliefs or opinions □ *At college she was converted to Marxism.* -3. [room, house] to change or rebuild <a building or part of a building> for a new use □ *We converted our basement into another bedroom.* -4. SPORT **to convert a try** to score points with a successful conversion. ◇ *vi* -1. [person] to change one's opinion, religious beliefs, way of doing things etc to something very different □ *We're converting from gas to electricity.* □ *She converted to Islam.* -2. [equipment, material] to be able to be changed and used in a different way □ *The sofa converts into a bed.* ◇ *n* a person who has been converted to a new opinion, or to a new religious or political belief □ *a recent convert to Christianity/the benefits of exercise.*

converted [kənˈvɜːrtəd] *adj* [room, building] that has been changed or rebuilt for a new use.

convertible [kənˈvɜːrtəbl] ◇ *adj* -1. [bed] that becomes a sofa when it is folded; [sofa] that becomes a bed when it is opened out. -2. [currency] that can easily be exchanged for a different currency. -3. [car] that has a roof that can be folded down or removed. ◇ *n* a car that is convertible.

convex [kɒnˈveks] *adj* [lens, mirror, surface] that curves outward in the middle. NOTE: Compare **concave**.

convey [kənˈveɪ] *vt* -1. [people, cargo, luggage] to take <sb/sthg> from one place to another (formal use) □ *The goods will be conveyed by boat.* -2. [idea, opinion, thought] to communicate <sthg> to somebody, often indirectly □ *I was unable to convey to them what I thought.* □ *His manner conveyed a slight nervousness.*

conveyancing [kənˈveɪənsɪŋ] *n* LAW the process by which the ownership of a house, property etc is legally transferred from one person to another.

conveyer belt, conveyor belt [kənˈveɪəʳ-] *n* a long strip of plastic, rubber etc that moves continuously and is used for moving objects from place to place, especially in factories.

convict [*vb* kənˈvɪkt, *n* ˈkɒnvɪkt] ◇ *vt* to find <sb> guilty of a crime in a court of law □ *She was convicted of fraud and tax evasion.* ◇ *n* a person who has been convicted of a crime and sent to prison □ *an escaped convict.*

convicted [kənˈvɪktəd] *adj* **a convicted killer/rapist etc** a person who has been found guilty of killing/raping etc somebody.

conviction [kənˈvɪkʃn] *n* -1. a strong belief □ *It is my conviction that there is no such thing as a limited war.* -2. the quality that somebody shows when they believe something strongly, and that helps them to persuade other people □ *His words lacked conviction.* -3. LAW a decision made by a court of law that somebody is guilty of a crime □ *She has several previous convictions for shoplifting.*

convince [kənˈvɪns] *vt* to make <sb> believe or realize something is true, especially when they doubted it before □ *She convinced me (that) she was telling the truth.* □ *I was unable to convince them of the importance of these findings.* ■ **to convince sb to do sthg** to persuade sb to do sthg □ *I tried to convince him not to leave.*

convinced [kənˈvɪnst] *adj* [person] who believes something totally □ *I'm not convinced of the need to buy a new one.* □ *Lorna was convinced (that) she'd seen the man someplace before.*

convincing [kənˈvɪnsɪŋ] *adj* -1. [person, argument, evidence] that convinces people that something is true □ *He didn't sound very convincing to me.* -2. [win, victory] that is big enough to show that somebody deserved it □ *China won the event by a convincing margin.*

convincingly [kənˈvɪnsɪŋlɪ] *adv* [argue, win] *see* **convincing** □ *He spoke convincingly in favor of lifting the ban.*

convivial [kənˈvɪvɪəl] *adj* [group, atmosphere, welcome] that seems cheerful and friendly (formal use).

convoluted [ˈkɒnvəluːtəd] *adj* [sentence, plot, reasoning] that is complicated and difficult to understand (formal use).

convoy [ˈkɒnvɔɪ] *n* a group of ships or vehicles traveling together, often for protection □ *a naval convoy* □ *a convoy of trucks.* ■ **in convoy** [drive, travel] together, one behind the other.

convulse [kən'vʌls] *vt* **to be convulsed with sthg** [with pain, laughter] to shake suddenly and uncontrollably because of sthg.

convulsion [kən'vʌlʃn] *n* a sudden and uncontrollable movement of the muscles □ *After taking the drug, she went into convulsions.*

convulsive [kən'vʌlsɪv] *adj* [movement, laughter, shiver] that is sudden, violent, and cannot be controlled.

coo [ku:] *vi* **-1.** [dove, pigeon] to make a soft sound. **-2.** [person] to speak in a very soft voice, usually lovingly.

cook [kʊk] ◇ *vt* **-1.** [meat, vegetables, meal] to prepare <food> to eat by heating it □ *Let me cook you dinner* OR *cook dinner for you.* **-2. to cook the books** to change the figures in a company's accounts in order to deceive people (informal use). ◇ *vi* [person] to cook food; [food] to become cooked □ *I don't mind cooking tonight.* □ *Put the pie in a preheated oven and leave it to cook for 20 minutes.* ◇ *n* a person who cooks food, often as a job □ *Her husband is an excellent cook.*

◆ **cook up** *vt sep* **to cook sthg up** [plan, excuse] to spend time inventing sthg (informal use) □ *What are they cooking up now?*

Cook [kʊk], **Captain James** (1728–1779) a British explorer who was the first European to discover Australia, New Zealand, and many Pacific islands.

cookbook ['kʊkbʊk] *n* a book that shows one how to cook particular dishes.

cooked [kʊkt] *adj* [food, meal] that has been prepared for eating by heating □ *The chicken's only half-cooked.*

cooked breakfast *n* GB a meal of bacon, sausages, fried eggs, tomatoes etc eaten for breakfast.

cooker ['kʊkər] *n* GB a piece of equipment used in a kitchen for cooking food that consists of a grill, an oven, and some rings, and that uses gas or electricity.

cookery ['kʊkərɪ] *n* GB the activity and skills of cooking food □ *She teaches cookery.*

cookery book *n* GB = cookbook.

cookie ['kʊkɪ] *n* US a small flat cake, usually sweetened and flavored and baked until crisp □ *a chocolate cookie.*

cooking ['kʊkɪŋ] *n* **-1.** the activity of cooking food □ *cooking utensils.* **-2.** a style of cooking food □ *French/vegetarian cooking* □ *Don't you like my cooking?*

cooking apple *n* a large sour apple used for cooking.

cooking oil *n* oil taken from a plant or animal that is used for cooking food.

cookout ['kʊkaʊt] *n* US an event where people cook and eat outdoors.

cool [ku:l] ◇ *adj* **-1.** [room, drink, weather] pleasantly cold □ *Store in a cool place.* **-2.** [clothing] made of material that is suitable for wearing in hot weather □ *I should change into something cooler.* **-3.** [person] who is calm and does not show their emotions, especially when other people do □ *Throughout the crisis she re-*

mained cool and in control. ■ **to keep a cool head** to stay calm in a difficult situation □ *You'll need to keep a cool head during the negotiations.* **-4.** [person, welcome, relationship] that is less friendly and enthusiastic than one expects □ *The proposals have met with a cool response from the public.* **-5.** [idea, suggestion] that one approves of and thinks is good (informal use) □ *"Why don't we head out of town for a while?" — "Hey, that'd be cool!"* **-6.** [person, clothes, car] that seems attractive and fashionable (informal use) □ *Evan looked so cool in his tuxedo!*

◇ *vt* to make <sthg> less hot □ *The engine is cooled by air.*

◇ *vi* **-1.** to become less hot □ *Leave the pot to cool.* **-2.** [friendship, anger, love] to become less powerful and intense □ *My feelings toward him have cooled since then.*

◇ *n* (informal use) **to keep one's cool** to remain calm in a difficult situation. ■ **to lose one's cool** to become excited or angry.

◆ **cool down** ◇ *vt sep* **-1. to cool sb/sthg down** to make sb/sthg less hot. **-2. to cool sb down** to make sb less angry or excited.

◇ *vi* **-1.** [food, engine, person] to become less hot □ *I drank some water to cool down after the game.* **-2.** [person] to become less angry or excited □ *Let him go and cool down first and then we can talk about it.*

◆ **cool off** *vi* = cool down.

coolant ['ku:lənt] *n* a liquid used to keep a machine from becoming too hot.

cool bag *n* GB a bag made of plastic and used for keeping food cool on a picnic, trip etc.

cooler ['ku:lər] US, **cool box** GB *n* a box for keeping food cool on a picnic, trip etc.

cool-headed [-'hedɪd] *adj* [person, decision] calm and unexcited in a difficult situation.

cooling-off period [,ku:lɪŋ-] *n* a period of time in which two sides in a dispute can think more calmly about the situation before deciding how to act.

cooling tower *n* a large round tower at a power station or factory in which water is cooled as part of an industrial process.

coolly ['ku:lɪ] *adv* **-1.** [behave, react] in a calm way and without becoming excited. **-2.** [welcome, say] in a way that is less friendly and enthusiastic than one expects.

coolness ['ku:lnəs] *n* [of the weather, a person, welcome] *see* cool □ *The Chief was praised for his coolness under pressure.* □ *He felt hurt by her coolness toward him.*

coop [ku:p] *n* a cage for small animals or birds □ *a chicken coop.*

◆ **coop up** *vt sep* **to be cooped up** to be kept in a small space so that one feels uncomfortable and wants to get out.

co-op ['kəʊɒp] *n* = cooperative (informal use).

Cooper ['ku:pər], **James Fenimore** (1789–1851) a US writer who described life in the Wild West. He wrote the novel *The Last of the Mohicans.*

cooperate, co-operate [kəʊ'ɒpəreɪt] *vi* **-1.** [people, companies, countries] to work together for a purpose that will be good for everybody in-volved □ *The two firms are cooperating on a joint venture to build tramways.* □ *The USA is cooperating with Canada to find the criminals.* **-2.** [public, wit-ness] to do what somebody else wants in order to help them achieve something □ *He refused to cooperate with the police investigation.*

cooperation [kou,ɒpə'reɪʃn] *n* **-1.** [between peo-ple, companies, countries] *see* **cooperate** □ *We need more cooperation among staff members.* □ *Our new pump was designed in cooperation with a company in Mexico.* **-2.** the act of willingly doing what one is asked in order to help somebody achieve something □ *I would like more cooperation from some employees.*

cooperative, co-operative [kou'ɒpərətɪv] ◇ *adj* **-1.** [child, witness] who is helpful and willing to do what they are asked □ *The staff there are helpful and cooperative.* **-2.** [work, activity] that is carried out by several people working together □ *The project was a cooperative effort.* **-3. a cooperative factory/farm etc** a factory/farm etc that is owned and run by the peo-ple who work there. ◇ *n* a cooperative fac-tory, farm, store etc □ *an agricultural coopera-tive.*

co-opt [kou'ɒpt] *vt* **to be co-opted onto a com-mittee** to be made a member of a committee as the result of being asked by the other members rather than by being elected □ *She was co-opted onto the planning committee.*

coordinate, co-ordinate [*n* kou'ɔːᵈdnət, *vt* kou-'ɔːᵈdəneɪt] ◇ *n* one of two numbers or letters that give the precise position of a point on a map or graph. ◇ *vt* **-1.** [project, mission, cam-paign] to organize <sthg> so that all its dif-ferent parts work well together □ *She's re-sponsible for coordinating policy initiatives across the various divisions.* **-2.** to control <move-ments, muscles> etc so that they work smoothly together □ *I found it hard to coordi-nate both hands when I started playing the piano.*

◆ **coordinates** *npl* two or more articles of women's clothing that are designed to be worn together.

coordination [kou,ɔːᵈdən'eɪʃn] *n* **-1.** [of a proj-ect, mission] *see* **coordinate** □ *Mr Evans will be responsible for the coordination of the campaign.* **-2.** [in a person] the ability to move different parts of one's body together in a controlled way.

coot [kuːt] *n* a water bird with black feathers.

co-ownership *n* ownership of something by two or more people or groups of people.

cop [kɒp] (*pt* & *pp* **copped**, *cont* **copping**) (infor-mal use) *n* a policeman or policewoman □ *Who called the cops?*

◆ **cop out** *vi* to avoid doing something that one ought to do □ *You can't just cop out at the last minute.*

cope [koup] *vi* to deal successfully with a diffi-cult situation □ *I can't cope any more.* □ *The system can't cope with so much traffic.*

Copenhagen [US 'koupənheɪɡən, GB ,koupən-'heɪɡən] the capital of Denmark and its larg-est city. POPULATION: 482,000.

Copernicus [kou'pɜːᵈnɪkəs], **Nicolas** (1473–1543) a Polish astronomer who was the first person to suggest that the sun was at the center of the solar system.

copier ['kɒpɪəᵣ] *n* = **photocopier**.

copilot ['koupaɪlət] *n* the assistant pilot of an aircraft.

copious ['koupjəs] *adj* [notes, tears, supply] that exists or is produced in large amounts □ *We drank copious amounts of coffee.*

Copland ['kouplənd], **Aaron** (1900–1990) a US classical composer who used traditional folk music and jazz in his work.

cop-out *n* something that somebody does to avoid doing something that they ought to do (informal use) □ *Instead of camping they stayed in a hotel; what a cop-out!*

copper ['kɒpəᵣ] *n* **-1.** a soft reddish-brown metal that is a good conductor of heat and electricity. SYMBOL: Cu □ *a copper mine/coin* □ *copper piping/wire.* **-2.** GB a coin that is worth 1p or 2p.

copperhead ['kɒpəᵣhed] *n* a poisonous snake found in the eastern USA.

coppice ['kɒpəs], **copse** [kɒps] *n* a small group of trees and bushes.

copulate ['kɒpjəleɪt] *vi* [people, animals] to have sex (formal use).

copulation [,kɒpjə'leɪʃn] *n* the act of copulat-ing (formal use).

copy ['kɒpɪ] (*pt* & *pp* **copied**) ◇ *n* **-1.** [of a work of art, product] something that has been made to look similar to, or exactly like, something that somebody else has already made or de-signed □ *It's a copy of the original drawing.* □ *Lo-cal workshops make cheap copies of expensive watches imported from the West.* **-2.** [of a letter, document, print] something that looks exactly the same as something else because it has been printed or photocopied from it □ *Can you give me a copy of the report?* **-3.** [of a book, newspaper, record] a single example of some-thing of which many have been printed or made □ *There's a copy in the library.*

◇ *vt* **-1.** [person] to try to be like <sb>, e.g. by dressing or behaving like them; [action, behavior] to do <sthg that somebody else has done> in order to be like them □ *There is a danger of children copying the violence they see on TV.* **-2.** [idea, piece of work, signature] to make or produce something that is the same as <sthg else>, sometimes in order to cheat □ *I copied it from the original.* **-3.** [letter, docu-ment, report] to photocopy <sthg>.

◇ *vi* to cheat during a test, examination etc by copying what somebody else has written.

◆ **copy down** *vt sep* [notes, information] to make a written copy of sthg that is said or written □ *He spoke so fast that we didn't have time to copy down what he said.*

◆ **copy out** *vt sep* GB = **copy over**.

◆ **copy over** *vt sep* **to copy sthg over** [notes, re-port] to write sthg again completely, using the same words □ *I copied over the relevant in-formation.*

copycat ['kɒpɪkæt] *n* a person who copies other people's behavior, ideas, dress etc (informal and disapproving use) □ *a copycat killer/murder.*

copy-protect *vt* COMPUTING to format <a program> so that it cannot be copied.

copyright ['kɒpɪraɪt] *n* the right to publish, sell, perform etc an original piece of work for a period of time □ *They own the copyright on the software.* □ *The work/invention is protected by copyright.* □ *'Copyright reserved'* □ *copyright laws.* ■ **to be in/out of copyright** to be protected/not protected by copyright.

copy typist *n* GB a typist who copies written material by typing it.

copywriter ['kɒpɪraɪtəʳ] *n* a person whose job is to write the words of advertisements.

coral ['kɒrəl] *n* a kind of rock found on the seabed that is formed by the skeletons of small sea creatures and is used to make jewelry □ *a coral island/necklace.*

coral reef *n* a reef formed from coral, found in the tropics.

cord [kɔːʳd] *n* **-1.** [for tying things] thick strong string □ *She tied the package up with cord.* **-2.** ELECTRICITY a cable that contains two or three insulated wires for carrying electricity to electrical appliances □ *an electric cord.* **-3.** = **corduroy** □ *a cord jacket.*
◆ **cords** *npl* corduroy trousers (informal use) □ *a pair of cords.*

cordial [US 'kɔːrdʒəl, GB 'kɔːdjəl] ◇ *adj* [reception, welcome, smile] that is warm and friendly. ◇ *n* a drink made from fruit juice and sugar to which water is added before drinking □ *a lime cordial.*

cordially [US 'kɔːrdʒəlɪ, GB 'kɔːdjəlɪ] *adv* [greet, welcome] *see* **cordial** □ *You are cordially invited to the wedding of...*

cordless ['kɔːʳdləs] *adj* [shaver, drill, phone] that works without an electric cord.

cordon ['kɔːʳdn] *n* a barrier formed by police officers, soldiers, vehicles etc to prevent people entering and leaving an area □ *a police cordon.*
◆ **cordon off** *vt sep* **to cordon sthg off** [area, street] to put a cordon around sthg.

cordon bleu [US kɔːr,dɒn'blu, GB ,kɔːdɒn'blɜː] *adj* [cook, cooking, recipe] of the highest standard.

corduroy ['kɔːʳdərɔɪ] *n* a thick cotton cloth with parallel raised lines on it, used for making clothes □ *a corduroy jacket.*

core [kɔːʳ] ◇ *n* **-1.** [of an apple, pear] the hard part in the middle of some fruits that contains the seeds □ *an apple core.* **-2.** [of a cable, planet, nuclear reactor] the central part of something □ *the temperature at the Earth's core.* ■ **to the core** completely □ *The system is rotten to the core.* **-3.** [of a problem, argument, business] the most important part of something □ *These proposals form the core of the campaign.* ◇ *comp* **-1. a core business/industry** the most important business/industry etc. **-2. core subjects/a core curriculum** EDUCATION subjects/a curriculum that everybody must

study, including e.g. math and English. ◇ *vt* to cut out the core of <an apple>.

CORE [kɔːʳ] (*abbr of* **Congress on Racial Equality**) *n* a US organization against racism.

corer ['kɔːrəʳ] *n* a device for coring apples.

corespondent [,kɔʊrɪ'spɒndənt] *n* a person accused of committing adultery with the partner of a person who wants a divorce.

core time *n* GB the central period of the day in a flextime system when everybody must be at work.

Corfu [kɔː'fuː] a Greek island, off the northwestern coast of the mainland, that is popular with tourists.

corgi ['kɔːʳgɪ] (*pl* **corgis**) *n* a breed of small dog with short legs and a long body.

coriander [,kɒrɪ'ændəʳ] a plant whose leaves and seeds are used as a flavoring, especially in Asian food.

cork [kɔːʳk] *n* **-1.** the light springy bark of a kind of oak tree, used to make tiles, mats etc □ *a cork mat/tile.* **-2.** a round piece of cork or plastic that is used to block the open end of bottles □ *a champagne cork.*

Cork [kɔːʳk] **-1.** a county in the south of the Republic of Ireland. SIZE: 7,459 sq kms. POPULATION: 279,427. ADMINISTRATIVE CENTER: Cork. **-2.** a port on the south coast of Ireland. POPULATION: 127,024.

corkage ['kɔːʳkɪdʒ] *n* GB a charge made by a restaurant for allowing people to drink wine they have brought with them.

corked [kɔːʳkt] *adj* [wine] that tastes and smells bad because the cork has mold in it.

corkscrew ['kɔːʳkskruː] *n* a device for pulling corks out of bottles.

cormorant ['kɔːʳmərənt] *n* a large black seabird with a long neck and hooked beak.

corn [kɔːʳn] *n* **-1.** US & AUS a tall plant with large yellow seeds that is grown for food. **-2.** [on one's foot] an area of hard skin formed on the foot that can be painful. **-3.** GB any plant such as barley, oats, or wheat that is grown as a crop for its seeds; the seeds of such a plant □ *vast fields of corn* □ *a grain of corn.*

Corn *abbr of* **Cornwall**.

Corn Belt: **the Corn Belt** an agricultural area of the American Midwest, including Iowa and Illinois, that produces large quantities of corn.

corn bread *n* a kind of bread made from corn.

cornea ['kɔːʳnɪə] (*pl* **corneas**) *n* the transparent outer covering of the eye.

corned beef [,kɔːʳnd-] *n* beef that has been cut into little pieces, cooked, pressed, and preserved in salt and usually canned.

corner ['kɔːʳnəʳ] ◇ *n* **-1.** [of a table, page, painting] the angle formed where two lines, edges, or surfaces meet □ *She stood in the corner of the room.* ■ **to cut corners** to do something carelessly or ignore rules in order to save time or money □ *We'll have to cut a few corners to meet the deadline.* **-2.** [of a street] the place where two streets or roads meet □ *I'll meet you on* OR *at the corner of 76th and Lincoln.* □ *kids hanging around on street corners.* **-3.** [in a road, path] a sharp bend □ *A car appeared around the corner.* **-4.** [of the earth, a country] a remote or distant place □ *Politicians from all (four) corners of the earth met in Rio.* **-5.** SPORT in soccer and field hockey, a shot taken from one of the corners of the field □ *The referee awarded a corner.*

◇ *vt* **-1.** to put <a person or animal> in a position from which it is difficult to escape; to stop <sb> so that they have to talk to one □ *He lashed out like a cornered animal.* □ *I managed to corner him as he was leaving the office.* **-2. to corner the market** to gain complete control of a particular market by being the only, or the main, supplier □ *They've cornered the market in rubber goods.*

corner flag *n* a flag that marks the corner of a playing field in soccer, rugby etc.

corner kick *n* SPORT [in soccer] = **corner**.

corner shop *n* GB = **corner store**.

cornerstone ['kɔːʳnəʳstoʊn] *n* **the cornerstone of sthg** [of one's success, a policy, argument] the most basic or essential part of sthg that makes it possible, successful, or true □ *One of the cornerstones of our education policy is parental choice.*

corner store *n* US a small store, often on a street corner, that sells food and household goods and is used especially by the people who live nearby.

cornet [US kɔːrˈnet, GB 'kɔːnɪt] *n* **-1.** MUSIC a brass musical instrument similar to a trumpet but smaller. **-2.** GB a thin crisp wafer shaped like a cone in which ice cream is served.

cornfield ['kɔːʳnfiːld] *n* a field in which corn is growing.

cornflakes ['kɔːʳnfleɪks] *npl* a breakfast cereal of flakes made from corn and eaten with milk and sometimes sugar □ *a box of cornflakes.*

cornflour *n* GB = **cornstarch**.

cornice ['kɔːʳnɪs] *n* a decorative border on the top edge of the wall of a building or room.

Cornish ['kɔːʳnɪʃ] ◇ *npl* **the Cornish** people from Cornwall. ◇ *adj: see* **Cornwall.** ◇ *n* the ancient language of Cornwall.

Cornishman ['kɔːʳnɪʃmən] (*pl* **Cornishmen** [-mən]) *n* a man from Cornwall.

Cornish pasty *n* GB a small semicircular pie containing meat and vegetables.

Cornishwoman ['kɔːʳnɪʃwʊmən] (*pl* **Cornishwomen**) *n* a woman from Cornwall.

corn oil *n* oil made from corn and used in cooking, especially to fry food.

corn on the cob *n* the long, round, sweet-tasting part of the corn plant, cooked and eaten as a vegetable.

cornstarch ['kɔːʳnstɑːʳtʃ] US, **cornflour** ['kɔːʳnflaʊəʳ] GB *n* flour made from corn, often used in cooking to thicken sauces.

cornucopia [ˌkɔːʳnʲəˈkoʊpjə] *n* a large number or amount of good things (literary use).

Cornwall ['kɔːʳnwɔːl] a county in the far southwest of England. It is a popular tourist area. SIZE: 3,564 sq kms. POPULATION: 453,100. ADMINISTRATIVE CENTER: Truro.

corny ['kɔːʳnɪ] (*compar* **cornier**, *superl* **corniest**) *adj* [joke, movie] that one thinks is bad because it is not original (informal use) □ *That sounds so corny!*

corollary [US 'kɔːrəlerɪ, GB kəˈrɒlərɪ] (*pl* **corollaries**) *n* something that follows logically from something else □ *The obvious corollary to increased costs is lower profits.*

coronary [US 'kɔːrənerɪ, GB 'kɒrənrɪ] (*pl* **coronaries**), **coronary thrombosis** [-θrɒmˈboʊsəs] (*pl* **coronary thromboses** [-iːz]) *n* a heart attack caused when the flow of blood to the heart is blocked.

coronation [ˌkɒrəˈneɪʃn] *n* the ceremony at which a king or queen is crowned □ *a coronation ceremony.*

coroner ['kɒrənəʳ] *n* an official who investigates the cause of violent or suspicious deaths □ *a coroner's inquest/report.*

Corp *abbr of* **corporation**.

corpora ['kɔːʳpərə] *plural of* **corpus**.

corporal ['kɔːʳprəl] *n* an officer in the army or air force who is higher in position than a private but lower than a sergeant.

corporal punishment *n* a form of punishment in which somebody is hit with a stick or a whip.

corporate ['kɔːʳpərət] *adj* **-1.** [boss, affairs, strategy] that is connected with a large business □ *a corporate borrower.* **-2.** [existence, responsibility, effort] that is made or created by all the members of a group.

corporate hospitality *n* things that a large company provides free for the entertainment of its clients, e.g. theater tickets or meals.

corporate identity, corporate image *n* the image a large business tries to give to the public; the image that the public has of a large business.

corporation [ˌkɔːʳpəˈreɪʃn] *n* **-1.** BUSINESS a large company □ *the British Broadcasting Corporation.* **-2.** POLITICS a group of people elected to run a city or town □ *the Corporation of the City of Boston.*

corporation tax *n* GB a tax on profits that is paid by large businesses.

corps [kɔːʳ] (*pl* **corps**) *n* **-1.** MILITARY a part of the army which has special duties □ *the medical/intelligence corps.* **-2.** a group of people involved in a particular activity together □ *the press/diplomatic corps.*

corpse [kɔːʳps] *n* a dead body.

corpulent ['kɔːʳpjələnt] *adj* [person, body] fat (formal use).

corpus ['kɔːʳpəs] (*pl* **corpora** OR **corpuses**) *n* a collection of texts.

corpuscle ['kɔːʳpʌsl] *n* ANATOMY a red or white blood cell □ *red blood corpuscles.*

corral [US kə'ræl, GB -'rɑːl] *n* an enclosed area for horses, cattle etc on a ranch or farm.

correct [kə'rekt] ◇ *adj* **-1.** [answer, forecast, time] that is right and accurate □ *Yes, that's correct, the answer is ten.* **-2.** [temperature, amount] that is required or is the most suitable □ *Rearrange the letters in the correct order.* **-3.** [behavior, dress, views] respectable or socially acceptable □ *It was all very correct and proper.* ◇ *vt* **-1.** [mistake, eyesight, behavior] to make correct <sthg that is not correct> □ *Correct me if I'm wrong, but don't I know you?* □ *We have to correct people's impression that we're a failure.* **-2.** [work, spelling] to write corrections on <sthg> □ *Teachers have to correct homework in their own time.*

correcting [kə'rektɪŋ] *n* US the activity of checking and correcting a piece of homework or an exam and giving it a grade to show how good or bad it is.

correction [kə'rekʃn] *n* **-1.** [of a mistake, one's eyesight, work] the act of correcting somebody or something □ *There are a few passages that are in need of correction.* **-2.** a mark written on a piece of writing that corrects a mistake □ *My teacher has made several corrections on my paper.*

correctly [kə'rektlɪ] *adv* [answer, behave] *see* **correct** □ *They didn't even spell my name correctly.*

correlate ['kɒrəleɪt] ◇ *vt* to find a connection between <two things> □ *Research has clearly correlated smoking and lung cancer.* ◇ *vi:* *These figures do not correlate with our findings.*

correlation [ˌkɒrə'leɪʃn] *n* a connection between two things □ *There's a close/strong correlation between smoking and lung cancer.*

correspond [ˌkɒrə'spɒnd] *vi* **-1.** [names, numbers, handwriting] to be the same or closely connected □ *Their versions do not correspond.* □ *The minutes must correspond with* OR *to what was actually said.* **-2.** [words, ideas, jobs] to have the same effect, position, importance etc □ *What does that word correspond to in English?* □ *The reality didn't correspond with the description in the brochure.* **-3.** [person] to write letters to somebody who writes back □ *We've been corresponding for years.*

correspondence [ˌkɒrə'spɒndəns] *n* **-1.** [between people] letters that have been sent to somebody; the act of writing letters to somebody □ *I have a lot of correspondence to answer.* □ *There has been no correspondence between us.* □ *the poet's correspondence with his mistress.* **-2.** [between names, numbers, handwriting] an agreement or similarity between two facts, situations etc □ *It bears no correspondence to what was actually said.*

correspondence course *n* a course in which a student studies at home, receiving work from a teacher and mailing it back.

correspondent [ˌkɒrə'spɒndənt] *n* a journalist who reports from a particular place, usually abroad, or on a particular subject □ *a foreign correspondent* □ *a report from our Moscow correspondent, James White.*

corresponding [ˌkɒrə'spɒndɪŋ] *adj* that is the same, but in a different situation, position etc or at a different time □ *In the corresponding month last year, inflation stood at 7%.*

corridor [US 'kɔːrədr, GB 'kɒrɪdɔː] *n* a long narrow passage in a building or train, often with doors on either side □ *She followed him along* OR *down the corridor.*

corroborate [kə'rɒbəreɪt] *vt* [statement, theory, view] to support or confirm <sthg> □ *Their story is corroborated by the evidence.*

corrode [kə'roʊd] ◇ *vt* [pipe, metal] to damage or destroy <sthg> gradually by chemical action. ◇ *vi* [pipe, metal] *The batteries had corroded completely.*

corrosion [kə'roʊʒn] *n* the damage caused when something corrodes.

corrosive [kə'roʊsɪv] *adj* [substance, chemical] that can corrode something.

corrugated ['kɒrəgeɪtəd] *adj* [cardboard, roof, paper] that has rows of curved ridges and grooves to make it stronger □ *a sheet of corrugated iron.*

corrupt [kə'rʌpt] ◇ *adj* **-1.** [government, politician, official] who uses their power, job etc to do illegal or dishonest things, especially by helping people who give them money or presents □ *We intend to stamp out these corrupt practices.* **-2.** [person, society] that is sexually immoral. **-3.** COMPUTING [disk, data] that contains errors. ◇ *vt* **-1.** [politician, official, morals] to make <sb/sthg> corrupt □ *They were corrupted by wealth/power.* **-2.** [society, young person] to cause or encourage <sb> to become involved in immoral sexual activities □ *He was accused of corrupting a minor.* **-3.** COMPUTING [disk, file, data] to cause <sthg> to contain errors □ *The virus had corrupted the entire database.*

corruption [kə'rʌpʃn] *n* corrupt activities or behavior □ *official/police corruption.*

corsage [kɔːr'sɑːʒ] *n* a small bunch of flowers worn on the front of a woman's dress.

corset ['kɔːrsət] *n* **-1.** a tight piece of clothing worn in the past, especially by women, around the waist to look slimmer. **-2.** a tight piece of clothing that is used to support one's back after an injury.

Corsica ['kɔːrsɪkə] a large mountainous island in the Mediterranean, north of Sardinia, belonging to France. SIZE: 8,680 sq kms. POPULATION: 250,371 (*Corsicans*). CAPITAL: Ajaccio.

cortege [US kɔːr'teʒ, GB kɔː'teɪʒ] *n* a procession of people or cars accompanying a body at a funeral □ *a funeral cortege.*

cortisone ['kɔːrtəzoʊn] *n* a hormone used as a drug in the treatment of arthritis, allergies, skin diseases etc □ *a cortisone injection.*

cos [kɒs] *n* GB = **cos lettuce**.

cosh [kɒʃ] GB ◇ *n* a long piece of thick rubber or metal used as a weapon. ◇ *vt* to hit <sb>, usually on the head, with a cosh.

cosignatory [US ˌkoʊ'sɪgnətɔːrɪ, GB -trɪ] (*pl* **cosignatories**) *n* one of two or more people, countries etc who have signed a document.

cosine ['koʊsaɪn] *n* the ratio of the length of the side of a right-angled triangle that is next to an acute angle to the length of the hypotenuse.

cos lettuce *n* GB a type of lettuce with long crisp leaves.

cosmetic [kɒz'metɪk] ◇ *n* a substance, e.g. lipstick or powder, used on the face or body, especially by women, to make them more attractive □ *a cosmetic cream.* ◇ *adj* [measure, change, reform] that only makes something look better without really changing what it is or what happens.

cosmetic surgery *n* surgery that improves somebody's physical appearance.

cosmic ['kɒzmɪk] *adj* -1. [ray, dust, force] that is connected with the cosmos □ *those who believe in cosmic order.* -2. [scale, importance] that is extremely big and affects a large number of people □ *a scandal/disaster of cosmic proportions.*

cosmonaut ['kɒzmənɔːt] *n* an astronaut from the former Soviet Union.

cosmopolitan [,kɒzmə'pɒlɪtn] *adj* -1. [city, gathering] where there are a lot of people from all over the world □ *I love New York because it's so cosmopolitan.* -2. [person] who has been to many different countries and respects people's different ways of life □ *She has a very cosmopolitan outlook.*

cosmos [US 'kɒzməs, GB -mɒs] *n* **the cosmos** the universe considered as a system □ *the mysteries of the cosmos.*

Cossack ['kɒsæk] *n* a member of a people living mainly in southern Russia and the Ukraine. In the past they were well-known for their military and horse-riding skills.

cosset ['kɒsət] *vt* to protect <sb> too much □ *She was cosseted as a child.*

cost [kɒst] (*pt* & *pp* senses *1* & *3* cost, sense *2* costed) ◇ *n* -1. [of damage, replacement, transport] the amount of money needed or paid to buy, do, or make something □ *The total cost will be about $50,000.* □ *The cost of repairs can be high.* □ *The stadium was built at a cost of $1 million.* □ *The cost to the taxpayer is put at billions.* □ *A replacement will be provided at no extra cost.* ■ **at cost** at cost price. -2. [of one's health, marriage] the loss, damage, sacrifice etc of something that is caused by doing something □ *He continued to work, but at great cost to his health.* □ *The cost in terms of human lives was terrible.* □ *She is determined to succeed whatever the cost.* ■ **at all costs** a phrase used to say that everything possible must be done in order to avoid or achieve something □ *We must avoid conflict at all costs.*
◇ *vt* -1. to have <a particular price> □ *It cost me $300/a lot of money.* □ *How much does it cost?* □ *It won't cost much to run.* □ *It costs £55.* -2. BUSINESS [job, service, project] to estimate the price of <sthg> in advance □ *The work was costed at $650.* ■ **to cost a product** to calculate how much a product will cost to make, so that its price can be decided. -3. [job, health, marriage] to cause somebody to lose <sthg> □ *His political views cost him his life.* □ *It wouldn't cost him much to be polite.* □ *We must succeed whatever it costs.*

◆ **costs** *npl* LAW -1. the expenses involved in a court case. -2. **sb's costs** BUSINESS the money sb has to spend on running their business or a particular part of their business □ *Our costs are still far too high.* □ *production/fuel costs.*

Costa Brava [,kɒstə'brɑːvə]: **the Costa Brava** part of the Mediterranean coast of northeastern Spain. It includes many popular tourist resorts.

cost accountant *n* a person who keeps a record of a business's expenses.

Costa del Sol [US ,kɒstədel'soul, GB -'sɒl]: **the Costa del Sol** part of the Mediterranean coast of southern Spain. It includes many popular tourist resorts.

co-star ◇ *n* a famous actor or actress who appears in a movie with another famous actor or actress. ◇ *vt* to have <a particular actor or actress> as a co-star □ *The movie co-stars Anthony Hopkins and Debra Winger.* ◇ *vi* [actor, actress] *She co-starred with Bogart in "Casablanca".*

Costa Rica [US ,kɒstə'riːkə, GB ,kɒstə'riːkə] a country in Central America. SIZE: 51,000 sq kms. POPULATION: 3,300,000 (*Costa Ricans*). CAPITAL: San José. LANGUAGE: Spanish. CURRENCY: colón.

cost-benefit analysis *n* a study of the relationship between the cost of something and the benefits it offers.

cost-effective *adj* [business, plan, project] that gives enough profit in comparison with the money spent □ *The business is not being run in a cost-effective way.*

costing ['kɒstɪŋ] *n* an official estimate of costs or prices □ *We need a detailed costing for the proposed extension.*

costly ['kɒstlɪ] (*compar* costlier, *superl* costliest) *adj* -1. [operation, business] that is expensive and wastes money □ *The car is very costly to run.* -2. [mistake, war] that causes great loss or damage □ *It proved to be a costly error.*

cost of living *n* the money needed to pay for the things people need to live, including their food, home, heating, travel etc □ *The cost of living has gone up dramatically.*

cost-of-living index *n* **the cost-of-living index** an index that shows relative changes in the cost of living at different times.

cost price *n* the price of an article when it is bought by a retailer from the maker □ *I had to sell it at cost price.*

costume ['kɒstjuːm] *n* -1. [for an actor] the clothes, often typical of a particular period, worn by an actor in a movie, play etc □ *The costumes were the best thing about the movie.* -2. [of a period, country] the clothes that are typical of a particular period, group etc □ *medieval/traditional/national costume* □ *They were dressed in costume.* -3. [for a party] a set of clothes that make one look like somebody or something famous, funny etc □ *He appeared in a gorilla costume.* -4. GB [for swimming] an item of clothing worn for swimming, especially by women □ *a one-piece swimming costume.*

costume jewelry *n* cheap jewelry that looks valuable or is large and decorative.

costume party *n* US a party where everybody wears clothes that make them look like somebody or something famous, funny etc.

cosy *adj* & *n* GB = **cozy**.

cot [kɒt] *n* -1. US a folding bed, usually made of canvas with a metal frame, that can be easily carried and is used for camping. -2. GB a bed for a baby or small child, usually with bars or sides to stop the child from falling out.

cot death *n* GB the sudden death of a baby while it is asleep and not suffering from any illness.

Cotswolds ['kɒtswouldz]: **the Cotswolds** a hilly area in southwestern England, famous for its attractive scenery and villages.

cottage ['kɒtɪdʒ] *n* a small house, especially in the countryside.

cottage cheese *n* a kind of soft, white, lumpy cheese.

cottage hospital *n* GB a small hospital in the countryside.

cottage industry *n* a small business based in somebody's home.

cottage pie *n* GB a hot dish consisting of ground beef covered with mashed potato.

cotton ['kɒtn] ◇ *n* -1. FARMING a plant grown as a crop whose seeds are surrounded by soft white fibers used for making thread, cloth etc; the fibers that come from this plant □ *a field of cotton* □ *cotton fibers.* -2. [for clothes] cloth made from cotton □ *a cotton dress/shirt/sheet.* -3. [for sewing] thread made from cotton □ *a needle and cotton.* -4. US [for cleaning part of one's body] a mass of soft cotton used for cleaning wounds, removing make-up etc □ *a piece of cotton* □ *a cotton pad.* ◇ *comp* [mill, industry] that produces cotton.

◆ **cotton on** *vi* GB to understand or realize something, especially without being told (informal use) □ *It took me ages to cotton on to the fact he was lying.*

Cotton Belt: **the Cotton Belt** an area of the southeastern USA where cotton is grown.

cotton bud *n* GB = **cotton swab**.

cotton candy *n* US a mass of soft, sticky, pink or white sugar threads that are eaten on a stick, often at fairs.

cotton swab *n* US a short, thin, plastic or wooden stick with a small piece of cotton on each end, used for cleaning ears, noses etc.

cottonwood ['kɒtnwʊd] *n* a tree with seeds like balls of white cotton that grows in North America.

cotton wool *n* GB a mass of soft cotton used for cleaning wounds, removing make-up etc □ *a piece of cotton wool.*

couch [kaʊtʃ] ◇ *n* a long piece of furniture which more than one person can sit on, and which usually has a back and sides for leaning on. ◇ *vt* [reply, idea, thought] to express

<sthg> in a particular way (formal use) □ *The statement was couched in very polite terms.*

couchette [kuːˈʃet] *n* a bed on a train that folds against the wall of the compartment when it is not being used.

couch potato *n* a person who spends a lot of time watching television because they are lazy (informal and humorous use).

cougar ['kuːgəʳ] (*pl* **cougar** OR **cougars**) *n* a large wild cat with brown fur that lives in the mountain regions of North and South America.

cough [kɒf] ◇ *vi* to force air out of one's throat with a rough sound, often to clear one's lungs or throat □ *I could hear him coughing in the next room.* □ *She coughed quietly.* ◇ *vt* [blood, phlegm, food] = **cough up.** ◇ *n* -1. an act of coughing; the sound of coughing □ *She gave a discreet cough.* -2. an illness that makes one cough a lot □ *He has a bad/chesty cough.*

◆ **cough up** ◇ *vt sep* **to cough sthg up** [blood, phlegm, food] to clear sthg from one's lungs or throat by coughing □ *He told the doctor he'd been coughing up thick green phlegm.* ◇ *vt fus* **to cough up an amount of money** to pay an amount of money for something, usually unwillingly (informal use) □ *I won the bet, so Philip had to cough up.*

cough drop *n* a candy containing ingredients to make a cough feel better.

coughing ['kɒfɪŋ] *n* the act or sound of coughing.

cough mixture *n* GB = **cough syrup**.

cough sweet *n* GB = **cough drop**.

cough syrup *n* a type of liquid medicine that one swallows to make a cough feel better.

could [kʊd] *past tense of* **can**.

couldn't ['kʊdnt] = **could not**.

could've ['kʊdəv] = **could have**.

council ['kaʊnsl] ◇ *n* -1. [of a city] a group of people elected to run the affairs of a city, county, large organization etc □ *She works for the council.* □ *the city/student council* □ *a council meeting/leader.* -2. [of representatives, members] a group or organization elected or appointed to give advice, make rules, manage affairs etc □ *The UN Security Council is meeting tomorrow.* ◇ *comp* GB [housing, flat] that has been built by the local council for people who pay rent to the council □ *a council tenant.*

council estate *n* GB an estate consisting of council houses or apartments.

councilor US, **councillor** GB ['kaʊnsləʳ] *n* a member of a council □ *Councilor Williams* □ *a local councilor.*

Council of Europe *n* **the Council of Europe** an organization established in 1949 to promote European cooperation and defend human rights. It includes 39 European states and is based in Strasbourg.

council of war *n* a meeting held to decide how to deal with a particular problem, threat, emergency etc.

council tax *n* GB a local tax in Great Britain based on the value of a building.

counsel ['kaʊnsl] (US *pt* & *pp* **counseled**, *cont* **counseling**, GB *pt* & *pp* **counselled**, *cont* **counselling**) ◇ *n* -1. advice that is given after thinking carefully (formal use). -2. LAW a lawyer or group of lawyers who represent somebody in a court of law □ *counsel for the defense/prosecution.* ◇ *vt* **to counsel sb to do sthg** to advise sb to do sthg (formal use) □ *My attorney counseled me not to say anything.*

counseling US, **counselling** GB ['kaʊnslɪŋ] *n* professional help and advice, especially for emotional or personal problems □ *Counseling will be available for the families of the crash victims.* □ *debt counseling.*

counselor US, **counsellor** GB ['kaʊnslər] *n* -1. US a lawyer. -2. a person trained to give counseling □ *a marriage guidance counselor.*

count [kaʊnt] ◇ *vt* -1. [money, children] to add up the total number of <things or people> □ *I counted 60 people in the line.* -2. **to count sb as sthg** to consider sb as part of sthg □ *I don't count him as one of the family.* -3. to include <sb/sthg> when one is counting things □ *There are six, not counting the broken ones.*
◇ *vi* -1. [person] to say all the numbers in order up to a particular number □ *I'll count (up) to a hundred.* -2. [age, sex, intelligence] to be important or valuable □ *Enthusiasm is what really counts.* □ *I'd like to feel my work counted for something.* □ *That doesn't count, you cheated!* -3. [test, mark, expenses] to be considered in a particular way □ *After 6 o'clock all work counts as overtime.* □ *All coursework counts toward your final grade.*
◇ *n* -1. the total number reached by counting □ *The count has risen to over a million.* □ *At the last count he'd moved nine times.* ■ **to keep/lose count** to remember/forget how many there are, especially when the number keeps changing □ *There are so many it's impossible to keep count of them.* □ *I've lost count of the number of times he's been late.* -2. **on this/that count** a phrase used to refer to a particular point in a discussion □ *I disagree with him on both counts.* -3. LAW a charge which a person is accused of □ *She was convicted on three counts of theft and shoplifting.* -4. [as a title] a European nobleman □ *Count Lowenstahe.*

◆ **count against** *vt fus* **to count against sb/sthg** to cause people to have a less favorable opinion of sb/sthg □ *Do you think my lack of experience will count against me?*

◆ **count in** *vt sep* **count me in!** I want to be involved too (informal use).

◆ **count on** *vt fus* -1. **to count on sb/sthg** [on a friend, relative] to rely on sb/sthg □ *You can count on me for help if you need it.* □ *I was counting on you to back me up.* -2. **to count on sthg** [on somebody's help, support] to expect sthg □ *I didn't count on so many guests coming.*

◆ **count out** *vt sep* -1. **to count money out** [coins, change] to count money so that it comes to a particular amount □ *The cashier counted out $16 in change.* -2. **count me out!** I don't want to be involved (informal use).

◆ **count up** *vt fus* **to count things/people up** to count all the things/people up in order to find out how many there are □ *I've counted up the number of days that are left.*

◆ **count upon** *vt fus* = **count on**.

countdown ['kaʊntdaʊn] *n* -1. [to lift-off] the act of counting backward in seconds to zero before a spacecraft, missile etc is launched □ *They had to stop the countdown.* -2. [to an event] the period of time just before an important event, when people think or talk about it a lot □ *The countdown to the presidential race has begun.*

countenance ['kaʊntənəns] ◇ *n* a person's face, especially when it shows a particular feeling or character (literary use). ◇ *vt* [idea, use] to allow <sthg> to happen (formal use).

counter ['kaʊntər] ◇ *n* -1. [in a store, bank] a long flat surface that salesclerks, office clerks etc stand at to serve customers □ *Please pay at the counter.* -2. US [in a kitchen] a flat surface on top of a piece of kitchen furniture, used e.g. for preparing food. -3. [in a game] a small disk used by each player in some board games. ◇ *vt* [criticism, argument, trend] to do something that reduces the effect of <sthg bad> □ *They countered the threat with an even stronger display of their own power.* ◇ *vi: He countered with more scandalous accusations of his own.*

◆ **counter to** *prep* **to run counter to sthg** to be the complete opposite of sthg □ *What he did ran counter to everything he had been taught.*

counteract [,kaʊntər'ækt] *vt* [effect, influence, trend] to reduce the effect of <sthg bad> by doing something that has the opposite effect □ *Our new face cream helps counteract the effects of aging.*

counterattack [,kaʊntərə'tæk] ◇ *n* an attack made to defend oneself against somebody who has just attacked one. ◇ *vt* to make a counterattack against <sb/sthg>. ◇ *vi* [army, soldiers] *The opposition counterattacked in the media.*

counterbalance [,kaʊntər'bæləns] *vt* [effect, influence, amount] to correct or balance <sthg> with something else that has an opposite effect.

counterclaim ['kaʊntərkleɪm] *n* a legal claim made against somebody who has brought a claim against one.

counterclockwise [,kaʊntər'klɒkwaɪz] US ◇ *adj* [movement, direction] that is in the opposite direction to the movement of the hands of a clock. ◇ *adv: Turn the lid counterclockwise.*
NOTE: Compare **anticlockwise, clockwise**.

counterespionage [,kaʊntər'espɪənɑːʒ] *n* action taken by a government to limit or prevent espionage.

counterfeit ['kaʊntərfɪt] ◇ *vt* [money, signature] to make an illegal copy of <sthg> so that people will think it is real □ *These coins have been counterfeited by an expert.* ◇ *adj* [money, coin] that has been counterfeited □ *There are counterfeit banknotes in circulation.*

counterfoil ['kaʊntəʳfɔɪl] *n* the part of a check or receipt that the payer keeps as a record of how the money was spent.

counterintelligence [ˌkaʊntərɪn'telɪdʒəns] *n* = **counterespionage.**

counter lunch *n* US & AUS a small meal bought at a bar, e.g. in a hotel.

countermand [US 'kaʊntərmænd, GB ˌkaʊntə'mɑːnd] *vt* to give an order to cancel <an earlier order, instruction> etc.

countermeasure ['kaʊntəʳmeʒəʳ] *n* something that is done in order to prevent a situation from becoming worse or more dangerous.

counteroffensive [ˌkaʊntərə'fensɪv] *n* a large counterattack.

counterpane ['kaʊntəʳpeɪn] *n* a decorative cover placed on top of the sheets, blankets etc of a bed (old-fashioned use).

counterpart ['kaʊntəʳpɑːʳt] *n* a person or thing that has the same function as another person or thing but in a different organization, country etc □ *The Secretary of State is having discussions with his French counterpart.*

counterpoint ['kaʊntəʳpɔɪnt] *n* the use of two different melodies in one piece of music at the same time.

counterproductive [ˌkaʊntəʳprə'dʌktɪv] *adj* [action, decision] that has the opposite result from what was intended □ *I think it would be counterproductive to confront him with it now.*

counter-revolution *n* a political or military action that is intended to defeat a government that came to power as a result of a previous revolution.

countersank ['kaʊntəʳsæŋk] *past tense of* **countersink.**

countersign ['kaʊntəʳsaɪn] *vt* [document, check] to sign <sthg that somebody else has already signed>, usually to show that their signature is correct or legal □ *The invoice must be countersigned by an authorized signatory.*

countersink ['kaʊntəʳsɪŋk] (*pt* **countersank,** *pp* **countersunk** [-sʌŋk]) *vt* to give a slope to the head of <a screw> so that it fits a hole exactly; to give a slope to the shape of <a hole> so that a screw fits exactly.

countess ['kaʊntəs] *n* a woman of high status with the same rank as a count or earl, either by birth or marriage.

countless ['kaʊntləs] *adj* **countless people/opportunities** very many people/opportunities □ *He told me so on countless occasions.*

countrified ['kʌntrɪfaɪd] *adj* [area, person] that is typical of the countryside or has been made to seem typical of the countryside.

country ['kʌntrɪ] (*pl* **countries**) *n* **-1.** [of the world] a part of the world with its own government, language, culture etc □ *What country are you from?* □ *all the countries of* OR *in the world* □ *She's out of/in the country on a state visit.* **-2. the country** the people who live in a country □ *The country will not accept this new tax.* **-3. the country** land that is away from towns or cities and is often used for farming □ *They live in the country.* □ *a country boy/town* □ *country life.* **-4.** [for walking, farming] land of a particular type, usually outside towns □ *mountainous/farming country.*

country and western *n* a style of popular music developed from the folk music of white people in the south of the USA □ *country and western music* □ *a country and western song/singer.*

country club *n* an expensive club outside a city or in suburban areas where people can play golf and outdoor sports and take part in social activities.

country code *n* TELECOMMUNICATIONS a number that one dials before the main part of a telephone number if one is calling from outside a particular country.

country dancing *n* in Britain, a traditional style of dancing by several pairs of dancers arranged in rows or circles.

country house *n* a large old house in the country with land around it, usually owned by a rich or aristocratic person.

countryman ['kʌntrɪmən] (*pl* **countrymen** [-mən]) *n* **-1.** a person from the same country as oneself □ *my fellow countrymen.* **-2.** a man who has lived in the countryside for a long time.

country music *n* country and western music □ *a country music singer.*

country park *n* in Britain, a park in the country, often around a large private house, where people can walk, have picnics etc.

countryside ['kʌntrɪsaɪd] *n* land away from towns and cities, including fields, woods etc □ *We enjoy taking walks in the countryside.*

Countryside Commission *n* **the Countryside Commission** a British government agency responsible for protecting the countryside, and for making it accessible to the public.

countrywoman ['kʌntrɪwʊmən] (*pl* **countrywomen**) *n* a woman who has lived in the countryside for a long time.

county ['kaʊntɪ] (*pl* **counties**) *n* **-1.** in the USA, one of several areas of a state that has its own local government □ *The county boundaries have been changed again.* **-2.** in Britain and Ireland, one of several areas of a country that has its own local government.

county council *n* in Britain, a group of people elected to govern a county.

county court *n* a local court of law that deals with less important crimes, e.g. when somebody fails to pay a debt or fine.

county seat US, **county town** GB *n* the main town of a county, where the local government has its offices.

coup [kuː] *n* **-1. a coup (d'état)** an attempt by a small group of people who have not been elected, often army officers, to get rid of their government and take power for themselves □ *He came to power in the coup of 1976.* □ *There are fears of a military coup.* **-2.** [for a person, business] something that is very successful and surprises people because it was very intelligent or difficult □ *Winning the contract would be a real coup for us.*

coupé [US kuːˈpeɪ, GB ˈkuːpeɪ] *n* a car with two doors and a sloping back.

couple [ˈkʌpl] ◇ *n* **-1.** two people who have a romantic or sexual relationship; a husband and wife □ *a married couple.* **-2. a couple of people/things** two people/things; a small number of people/things □ *I was stopped by a couple of policemen.* □ *I'll see you in a couple of minutes.* ◇ *vt* **-1.** RAIL [wagons, cars] to join <two parts of a train> together □ *They coupled the car to the engine.* **-2. to couple sb/sthg with sthg** to think of sb/sthg as being closely connected with sthg □ *People tend to couple young people with crime.*

◆ **coupled with** *prep* together with <sthg> □ *Unemployment, coupled with high interest rates, is at the root of the problem.*

couplet [ˈkʌplət] *n* two lines of poetry that are next to each other, are of the same length, and contain a rhyme at the end.

coupon [ˈkuːpɒn] *n* **-1.** a piece of paper that gives somebody the right to buy something, to buy something more cheaply, or to get it free □ *book/butter coupons* □ *a coupon for 10 cents off your next hamburger.* **-2.** a small form in a newspaper, catalog etc that people can send away to order goods, ask for information, or enter a competition.

courage [US ˈkɜːrɪdʒ, GB ˈkʌr-] *n* the ability to control one's fear when doing something difficult or dangerous □ *I wish I had the courage to tell him what I think of him.* ■ **to take courage** to feel more hopeful or confident because of something □ *You should take courage from the fact that many people share your views.* ■ **to have the courage of one's convictions** to say or do what one thinks is right, even though it is difficult or dangerous.

courageous [kəˈreɪdʒəs] *adj* [person, action, fight] that shows courage □ *It was a courageous decision.*

courageously [kəˈreɪdʒəslɪ] *adv* [act, fight] *see* **courageous** □ *She battled courageously against cancer.*

courgette [US kʊrˈʒet, GB kɔː-] *n* GB a long, thin, green vegetable that is fairly small, has white flesh, and is soft and watery when cooked.

courier [ˈkʊrɪər] *n* **-1.** [for letters, packages] a person or company that delivers letters, goods, packages etc □ *We will send the papers by motorcycle courier.* **-2.** GB [for a travel company] a person whose job is to work for a travel company looking after groups of tourists □ *a travel courier.*

course [kɔːrs] ◇ *n* **-1.** [of study, lectures] a series of lessons on a particular subject □ *I'm doing* OR *taking a course in computing.* □ *a science/language course.* **-2.** [of treatment, injections, drugs] a series of things that are planned as a treatment over a period of time □ *My doctor put me on a course of antibiotics.* **-3.** [of a ship, plane] the direction in which something is moving; [of negotiations, one's life, a country's history] the way in which something happens □ *The ship changed course to avoid the rocks.* □ *In the normal course of events, I would* have finished by now. ■ **to run** OR **take its course** [disease, war] to develop naturally and come to a natural end □ *You must allow events to take their natural course.* ■ **to be on course** [ship, plane] to be moving in the right direction; [person, plan] to be going or developing the right way to achieve something □ *We're on course for Jamaica.* □ *The company is on course to win the contract.* ■ **to be off course** [ship, plane] to be moving away from the right direction □ *The boat was blown off course by the storm.* **-4. a course (of action)** something one can do in a particular situation □ *Your only course now is to resign.* □ *We took the only course of action open to us.* **-5. in due course** at some time in the future □ *Everything will become clear in due course.* ■ **in** OR **during the course of sthg** at some time during sthg □ *I'll see you in the course of the next few days.* □ *Kay Barnes has achieved much during the course of her long and fruitful career.* **-6.** [of a meal] a part of a meal served separately from the other parts □ *The main course was lamb.* □ *the first/second/dessert course* □ *a three-course meal.* **-7.** SPORT a piece of open land or water where a particular sport or game is played □ *a golf course.*
◇ *vi* [tears, blood, water] to flow quickly (literary use).

◆ **of course** *adv* **-1.** a phrase used to show that one expects people to know about or agree with what one is saying □ *Of course, that's not her real name.* □ *That's my advice, but it's up to you, of course.* **-2.** a phrase used to introduce information that is the obvious result of another action or event □ *If it rains the trip will, of course, have to be canceled.* **-3.** a phrase used as an emphatic way to say yes □ *"Can I come?" — "Of course you can."* □ *"Do you love me?" — "Of course (I do)."* **-4. of course not** a phrase used as an emphatic way of saying no □ *"Do you want me to tell her?" — "Of course not."*

coursebook [ˈkɔːrsbʊk] *n* GB a book written for students studying a particular course.

coursework [ˈkɔːrswɜːrk] *n* work done as part of a course of study.

court [kɔːrt] ◇ *n* **-1.** LAW a place where crimes and other legal cases are judged □ *I'll see you in court!* ■ **to appear in court** [defendant, lawyer, witness] to take part in a trial in a court □ *Mrs Edwards will appear in court charged with manslaughter.* ■ **to go to court** to have a legal case heard and decided by a court □ *I am prepared to go to court over this matter.* ■ **to take sb to court** to ask a court to decide a legal case or complaint against sb □ *They've threatened to take us to court if we don't pay.* **-2.** LAW **the court** the people in a court, especially the judge and jury □ *This is a matter for the courts to decide.* **-3.** SPORT an area where tennis and similar games are played □ *a tennis/badminton/squash court* □ *The players come out onto the court.* ■ **to be on court** [player] to be playing on a court. **-4.** [of a building] a courtyard. **-5.** [of a king, queen] the official home of a king or queen; the officials and advisers who work there □ *a court painter/jester.*

◇ *vt* [danger, disaster] to behave in a way that makes <sthg bad> likely to happen; [favor, popularity] to try to win <sthg good> from somebody (formal use).

◇ *vi* [man and woman] to spend a lot of time together with the intention of getting married (old-fashioned use) □ *a courting couple.*

court circular *n* GB a column in a newspaper that says what the Royal Family will be doing on a particular day.

courteous ['kɔːˡtjəs] *adj* [person, reply, letter] that shows courtesy toward somebody.

courtesan [US 'kɔːrtəzn, GB ˌkɔːtɪˈzæn] *n* a prostitute for wealthy men or men of high status (old-fashioned use).

courtesy ['kɜːˡtəsɪ] ◇ *n* good manners and polite respectful behavior; something polite that somebody says or does □ *He didn't even have the courtesy to say "please".* □ *You should ask their permission first, as a matter of courtesy.*
◇ *adj* **a courtesy bus/car etc** a bus/car etc provided free by a company or hotel for the use of its customers, guests etc.

◆ **courtesy of** *prep* **-1.** with the permission of <sb> who has provided a favor, usually without cost □ *'This painting is displayed courtesy of the National Gallery.'* **-2.** because of <sthg> that has made something possible □ *The Dutch won courtesy of a last-minute goal.*

◆ **by courtesy of** *prep* GB = **courtesy of.**

courthouse ['kɔːˡthaʊs, *pl* -haʊzɪz] *n* a building containing a court of law.

courtier ['kɔːˡtjəˡ] *n* a noble advisor or assistant at the court of a king or queen.

court-martial (*pl* **court-martials** OR **courts-martial,** US *pt* & *pp* **court-martialed,** *cont* **court-martialing,** GB *pt* & *pp* **court-martialled,** *cont* **court-martialling**) ◇ *n* a court in which officers judge a member of the armed forces who is accused of breaking military law; a trial at this court □ *Corporal Havering was tried by court-martial.* ◇ *vt* to try <a soldier> by court-martial □ *He was court-martialed for insubordination.*

Court of Appeal *n* **the Court of Appeal** the highest court of law in England and Wales, apart from the House of Lords, where appeals against decisions made in other courts are considered.

court of appeals *n* in the USA, a court of law that reconsiders a decision made in another court if somebody makes an appeal.

court of inquiry *n* an official investigation into a serious accident, riot etc; a group of people officially appointed to carry out this investigation.

court of law *n* a place where crimes and other law cases are judged.

courtroom ['kɔːˡtruːm] *n* a room where trials are held □ *The case will be held in courtroom number 12.*

courtship ['kɔːˡtʃɪp] *n* **-1.** [of people] the time during which a man and woman are courting □ *We had a long courtship.* **-2.** [of animals] the things that a male animal does to attract a female before they mate □ *an elaborate courtship ritual.*

court shoe *n* GB a woman's shoe of a simple design with a low heel and no fastening.

courtyard ['kɔːˡtjɑːˡd] *n* a flat area of ground without a roof that is surrounded by walls or buildings, and is part of a large house, castle etc.

cousin ['kʌzn] *n* a son or daughter of one's uncle or aunt.

couture [kʊˈtjʊəˡ] *n* **(haute) couture** the business of designing, making, and selling expensive and fashionable women's clothes.

cove [kəʊv] *n* a small bay on a coast □ *We had a picnic in a quiet cove.*

coven ['kʌvn] *n* a group of witches; a meeting of this group.

covenant ['kʌvənənt] *n* **-1.** LAW a formal written promise to pay a certain amount of money every year, especially to a charity □ *If you pay by covenant, more money actually reaches the charity.* **-2.** [between people, countries] a formal agreement between two or more people, groups, countries etc □ *They made a solemn covenant never to mention it again.*

Covent Garden [US ˌkʌvnt-, GB ˌkɒv-] *n* **-1.** a square in central London that used to be a fruit and vegetable market. **-2.** another name for the Royal Opera House in London.

🌑 COVENT GARDEN

Covent Garden, once the fruit, flower, and vegetable market for central London, is now an enormous covered shopping area with many restaurants and small stores. It attracts performers who entertain the crowds with street theater, mime, and magic shows. The Royal Opera House, next to the old market, is also known as "Covent Garden".

Coventry [US 'kʌvntrɪ, GB 'kɒv-] **-1.** an industrial city in the Midlands, central England. POPULATION: 292,600. **-2.** *phrase* **to send sb to Coventry** GB to refuse to talk to sb as a punishment or sign of disapproval.

cover ['kʌvəˡ] ◇ *n* **-1.** [of a machine, piece of furniture] something made of material that is put on top of or around something else, usually to protect it or keep it clean □ *a seat cover.* **-2.** [of a pan] a lid that fits a pan. **-3.** [of a book, magazine] the outside page that is usually thicker than the pages inside □ *the front/back cover.* **-4.** [for a bed] a sheet or blanket that keeps a person warm in bed □ *the bed covers.* **-5.** [from attacks, the weather] something that provides shelter or protection from attacks, the weather etc □ *Fighter planes provided air cover.* □ *We looked for cover from the storm.* ■ **to break cover** to come out of a place where one has been hiding. ■ **to take cover** [from the rain, weather] to go somewhere where one will be sheltered; [from gunfire, a bomb] to go somewhere where one will be safe □ *Take cover!* ■ **under cover** under a roof as a protection from bad weather. ■ **to do sthg under cover of darkness** OR **night to**

do sthg at night so that one will not be noticed. **-6.** [for an illegal activity] a way of hiding an illegal activity □ *The freight business is a cover for drug smuggling.* **-7.** [against a risk] insurance that will provide repayment if there is a fire, accident etc □ *insurance/accident cover* □ *I took out cover against theft of my belongings.* **-8.** [of a song] = **cover version**.
◇ *vt* **-1.** [table, book, one's face] to put or spread something over or around <sthg> to protect or hide it □ *We've had the sofa covered.* □ *The prisoner arrived covered in* OR *with a blanket.* **-2.** [ground, mountain, floor] to lie over the surface of <sthg> □ *Snow covered the fields.* □ *Her hands were covered with* OR *in paint.* **-3.** [county, country] to spread over <a particular area> □ *The forest covers 20 square kilometers.* □ *His interests cover a wide field.* **-4.** [case, situation] to apply to <sb/sthg> □ *All workplaces are covered under the act.* **-5. to cover a particular distance** to travel a particular distance □ *We had covered most of the distance by lunchtime.* **-6.** [insured person] to provide <sb> with insurance cover against something □ *Does this policy cover me against breakages?* **-7.** [subject, details] to discuss or deal with <sthg> □ *That particular point is covered in paragraph three.* □ *Well, I think that covers everything. Any questions?* **-8.** JOURNALISM to report <a news story> for radio, TV, a newspaper etc. **-9.** [cost, price] to be enough to pay for <sthg> □ *$5 won't even cover the taxi fare.*

◆ **cover up** *vt sep* **-1. to cover sthg up** [machine, face] to cover sthg so that it cannot be seen or damaged □ *Cover yourself up with this blanket.* **-2. to cover sthg up** [fact, scandal] to hide sthg so that people will not know about it □ *The company tried desperately to cover up news of the disaster.*

coverage ['kʌvərɪdʒ] *n* the amount of time or space given to a news story by radio, TV, a newspaper etc □ *The President's tour has been given saturation coverage on TV.*

coveralls ['kʌvərɔːlz] *npl* US outer clothing worn by people in factories, on building sites etc for protection and to keep their other clothes clean.

cover charge *n* **-1.** US a fee paid to get into some bars, concerts, or discos. **-2.** GB a charge made by a restaurant that is added to the cost of food, drinks, and service.

covered wagon *n* a wagon with a canvas roof that was pulled by horses or oxen. It was used especially by families traveling to the west of the USA in the 19th century.

cover girl *n* an attractive woman whose photograph appears on the front of a magazine.

covering ['kʌvərɪŋ] *n* something that covers or hides something □ *a thin covering of snow/dust* □ *a type of floor covering.*

cover letter US, **covering letter** GB *n* a note or letter sent with a package, goods, documents etc, giving information or explanations.

cover note *n* GB a short printed statement from an insurance company stating that insurance has been paid for and giving protection until the full contract or policy is ready.

cover price *n* the price of a book, magazine, or newspaper that is printed on its cover.

covert ['koʊvɜːrt] *adj* [operation, look] that is secret or not intended to be noticed by other people □ *a covert military operation.*

cover-up *n* an attempt or plan to prevent the public from finding out about something criminal, dishonest, or embarrassing □ *a police cover-up.*

cover version *n* a performance or recording of a song that has been made famous by another performer or group.

covet ['kʌvət] *vt* to want <sthg> very much, especially when it belongs to somebody else (formal use).

cow [kaʊ] ◇ *n* **-1.** FARMING a large female animal kept on farms for its milk □ *a herd of cows* □ *cow's milk.* **-2.** [of an elephant, whale] the female of some types of large mammals. ◇ *vt* to make <sb> do what one wants by frightening or threatening them □ *The workers were cowed into accepting the terms by threats of dismissal.*

coward ['kaʊərd] *n* a cowardly person □ *She accused him of being a coward.*

cowardice ['kaʊərdɪs] *n* lack of courage □ *an act of cowardice.*

cowardly ['kaʊərdlɪ] *adj* [person, decision, behavior] that shows fear and a lack of courage in a dishonorable way □ *That was a cowardly thing to do.*

cowboy ['kaʊbɔɪ] *n* **-1.** a man who looks after cattle, especially one who rides horses in North America □ *a cowboy movie.* **-2.** GB a man who gives customers bad service because he is careless, dishonest, or does not have enough experience (informal use) □ *cowboy builders/taxi drivers.*

cower ['kaʊər] *vi* to bend down or move back because one is afraid □ *The child, terrified, sat cowering in a corner of the room.*

Cowes Week ['kaʊz-] *n* a series of yacht races that takes place once a year off the port of Cowes, Isle of Wight, in England. It is an important social event.

cowhand ['kaʊhænd] *n* a person whose job is to look after cattle.

cowhide ['kaʊhaɪd] *n* strong leather from the skin of a cow.

cowl neck ['kaʊl-] *n* a neckline of a woman's sweater or dress that forms loose folds at the front.

cowshed ['kaʊʃed] *n* a building in which cows are kept or milked.

cox [kɒks], **coxswain** ['kɒksn] *n* a person who steers a rowboat, especially one with four or eight rowers.

coy [kɔɪ] *adj* [person] who pretends to be shy or modest, especially in order to attract more interest or avoid saying something □ *a coy smile.*

coyly ['kɔɪlɪ] *adv* [smile, answer, behave] *see* **coy**.

coyote [kaɪˈoʊtɪ] *n* a small wolf from the plains of North America.

cozy US, **cosy** GB [ˈkoʊzɪ] (US *compar* **cozier**, *superl* **coziest**, GB *compar* **cosier**, *superl* **cosiest**) ◇ *adj* -1. [room, apartment, sweater] warm and comfortable □ *It was so cozy indoors, I didn't want to go out.* -2. [atmosphere, chat, gathering] that is friendly because people feel close to each other □ *It's a pity to interrupt our cozy get-together.* ◇ *n* = **tea cozy.**

cp. (*abbr of* **compare**) a word used in front of a piece of information that is to be compared with what has just been mentioned.

c/p GB *abbr of* **carriage paid.**

CPA *n abbr of* **certified public accountant.**

CPI (*abbr of* **Consumer Price Index**) *n* a scale that shows how much the prices of consumer goods have risen over a fixed period.

Cpl *abbr of* **corporal.**

cps (*abbr of* **characters per second**) *n* COMPUTING the number of characters of text, information etc that can be printed or processed in a second.

CPS *n abbr of* **Crown Prosecution Service.**

CPSA (*abbr of* **Civil and Public Services Association**) *n* a British labor union for public employees.

CPU *n abbr of* **central processing unit.**

cr -1. *abbr of* **credit.** -2. *abbr of* **creditor.**

crab [kræb] *n* a sea creature with a flat shell and five pairs of legs, with strong claws on the front pair; the meat of this animal eaten as food □ *crab meat/paté.*

crab apple *n* a small sour apple; the tree that this apple grows on.

crabby [ˈkræbɪ] (*compar* **crabbier**, *superl* **crabbiest**) *adj* [person] who gets cross easily and is unpleasant to people.

crack [kræk] ◇ *n* -1. [in a glass, cup, the ground] a long thin line where something has broken, but not into separate pieces □ *There's a crack in this window/the paint.* -2. [in the curtains, a door] a long narrow gap between two objects □ *We watched through a crack in the fence.* ■ **at the crack of dawn** very early in the morning. -3. [of twigs, a whip] a loud sharp sound. -4. [about a person] a clever joke or funny comment, usually critical of or rude about somebody. -5. **to have a crack at sthg** to do or take part in sthg that one tries to win or do well at (informal use) □ *I'd like a crack at the World Championship.* -6.▽ **crack (cocaine)** concentrated and very addictive cocaine in hard lumps (drugs slang). ◇ *vt* -1. [glass, paint, cup] to damage <sthg> so that it has a crack or cracks □ *The frost had cracked the pipe.* -2. [nut, safe] to open <sthg> using force, sometimes by breaking it □ *Crack the eggs on the side of the cup.* ■ **to crack open a bottle** to open a bottle of wine, champagne etc to celebrate something. -3. [whip, one's fingers] to make a sharp sound with <sthg>. -4. [head, knee] to hit <part of one's body> sharply and painfully against something hard □ *He fell over and cracked his head on the chair.* -5. [problem, code]

to solve or find the answer to <sthg> after much time and effort □ *We've cracked it!* -6. **to crack a joke** to make a joke (informal use). ◇ *vi* -1. [glass, paint, cup] *The ice cracked under my feet.* □ *My lips are cracking in the cold.* -2. [whip] *The dry twigs cracked beneath our feet.* -3. [person] to lose one's self-control as a result of great difficulty, stress, or pressure □ *His voice cracked with emotion.* -4. [marriage, system] to stop working properly as a result of difficulties that have existed for a long time. -5. **to get cracking** to start doing something immediately; to speed up when doing something (informal use) □ *Come on, let's get cracking!* ◇ *adj* [troops, regiment, team] that is highly trained and very skillful □ *He's a crack shot with a rifle.*

◆ **crack down** *vi* [police, government] to take strong action to try to stop something that is wrong □ *The administration intends to crack down on crime.*

◆ **crack up** *vi* to go crazy as a result of stress or pressure (informal use).

crackdown [ˈkrækdaʊn] *n* [on crime, drugs] strong official action to try to stop illegal activities □ *The government is planning a crackdown on tax-evaders.*

cracked [krækt] *adj* -1. [glass, paint, skin] that is damaged with a crack or cracks. -2. **to be cracked** to be crazy (informal use).

cracker [ˈkrækər] *n* -1. a thin hard biscuit that is not sweet and is usually eaten with cheese. -2. GB = **Christmas cracker.**

crackle [ˈkrækl] ◇ *n* a series of loud very short sounds made by a fire, or by a telephone or radio that does not work correctly □ *There's a lot of crackle on the line.* ◇ *vi* [fire, radio, loudspeaker] to make a crackle.

crackling [ˈkræklɪŋ] *n* -1. [on a telephone, radio] crackles □ *We could hear the crackling of the fire.* -2. COOKING the crispy skin on roasted pork.

crackpot [ˈkrækpɒt] ◇ *adj* [idea, scheme, letter] that is crazy in an impractical way (informal use). ◇ *n* a person with crackpot ideas (informal use).

cradle [ˈkreɪdl] ◇ *n* -1. [for a baby] a small bed, usually shaped like a box with a curved base so that it can be rocked from side to side. -2. **the cradle of sthg** [of civilization, a movement] the place where something began. -3. [on a building, ship] an open box that can be moved on ropes up and down the outside of tall buildings and ships so that people can paint, do repairs, clean windows etc. ◇ *vt* [baby, bottle, glass] to hold <sb/sthg> gently and carefully in one's arms, especially rocking them from side to side □ *She cradled the child in her arms.*

craft [US kræft, GB krɑːft] (*pl sense 2* **craft**) *n* -1. a job or activity that involves making things with one's hands, especially a traditional skill such as making pottery or furniture; the work produced by such a skill □ *a* *craft fair/exhibition.* -2. a boat, ship, hovercraft, or other vehicle used on or under water.

craftsman [US 'kræftsmən, GB 'krɑːfts-] (*pl* **craftsmen** [-mən]) *n* a person who knows a craft and does skilled work with their hands; a person who uses great skill, thought, and care in any activity, e.g. music or sports □ *Skilled craftsmen who can do this kind of work are fast disappearing.* □ *He's a real craftsman.*

craftsmanship [US 'kræftsmənʃɪp, GB 'krɑːfts-] *n* the skill or ability of a craftsman; the skilled work that a craftsman produces.

crafty [US 'kræftɪ, GB 'krɑːftɪ] (*compar* **craftier**, *superl* **craftiest**) *adj* [person] who is good at deceiving other people in order to get what they want □ *That was a crafty move!*

crag [kræg] *n* a high steep rock or cliff.

craggy ['krægɪ] (*compar* **craggier**, *superl* **craggiest**) *adj* -1. [mountain, slope] that is steep and rocky. -2. [face, features] that looks attractive in a rough way, with large bones and deep lines.

cram [kræm] (*pt* & *pp* **crammed**, *cont* **cramming**) ◇ *vt* to push or force <clothes, food, people> etc into a small space with the result that it is full □ *He crammed the cake into his mouth.* □ *We were all crammed into one small car.* □ *His head is crammed with useless facts.* □ *I crammed in as much as I could during the trip.* ◇ *vi* [for an examination, test] to learn a lot of facts as quickly as possible □ *She was up all night cramming for her final exam.*

cramp [kræmp] ◇ *n* pain and an inability to move that is caused by a muscle suddenly becoming very stiff □ *stomach cramps* □ *I've got a cramp* US OR *cramp* GB *in my leg.* ◇ *vt* [somebody's progress, movement, prospects] to stop <sthg> from developing or working as well as it could.

cramped [kræmpt] *adj* [room, office] that is too small. ■ **to be cramped (for space)** [person] not to have enough space □ *We're beginning to feel cramped in our present house.*

crampon ['kræmpɒn] *n* a piece of metal with sharp spikes that is fixed under shoes to make climbing or walking on ice easier.

cranberry [US 'krænberɪ, GB -bərɪ] (*pl* **cranberries**) *n* a small red berry with a sour taste that grows on a low bush and is used in sauces for turkey and duck □ *cranberry sauce.*

crane [kreɪn] ◇ *n* -1. a large machine for lifting heavy objects that has a cable fixed to a long movable arm. -2. a tall bird with long legs and a long neck that lives near water. ◇ *vt* to stretch <one's neck or head> forward, usually in order to see something. ◇ *vi*: *I craned forward to get a better view.*

crane fly *n* an insect with wings and very long legs that can fly.

cranium ['kreɪnɪəm] (*pl* **craniums** OR **crania** [-nɪə]) *n* the curved part of the skull that covers the brain.

crank [kræŋk] ◇ *n* -1. TECHNOLOGY a handle which, when it is turned, causes something to move. -2. a person who behaves in a strange way and often has unusual ideas (informal use) □ *Some crank rang up claiming he was a terrorist.* ◇ *vt* -1. to cause <sthg> to move by turning a handle □ *She cranked the shutters down.* -2. AUTO [engine, car] to try to start <sthg> by turning a crank.

crankshaft [US 'kræŋkʃæft, GB -ʃɑːft] *n* a metal rod in the engine of a vehicle that is turned by the pistons and so makes the wheels in the gearbox turn.

cranky ['kræŋkɪ] (*compar* **crankier**, *superl* **crankiest**) *adj* -1. US [person] bad-tempered □ *There's no need to get cranky with me.* -2. [person, ideas, habits] strange and unusual (informal use) □ *a cranky old man.*

cranny ['krænɪ] (*pl* **crannies**) *n* → **nook**.

crap [kræp] *n* -1.▼ excrement (vulgar use). -2.▽ something worthless, untrue, or unimportant (very informal use) □ *What a load of crap!*

crappy▽ ['kræpɪ] (*compar* **crappier**, *superl* **crappiest**) *adj* [movie, party, idea] that one thinks is very bad (very informal use).

crash [kræʃ] ◇ *n* -1. [in a vehicle] an accident in which a moving vehicle hits something, e.g. another vehicle, and is badly damaged □ *He was killed in a car/plane crash.* □ *They had a crash on the way to work.* -2. [of something breaking] a sudden loud noise, usually caused by something hitting something or by something breaking □ *From the kitchen came a sudden crash.* -3. FINANCE the sudden and serious failure of a company or business institution □ *the Wall Street Crash.* ◇ *vt* [car, airplane] to have a crash in <a vehicle> □ *She crashed her car into a tree.* ◇ *vi* -1. [car, airplane, person] to have a crash □ *She crashed into the car in front.* -2. [object] to hit or fall onto something, making a sudden loud noise □ *The bottle crashed to the floor.* -3. FINANCE [company, stock market] to fail suddenly and seriously; [currency] to fall suddenly in value by a large amount □ *The firm crashed with debts of $7 million.* □ *The Spanish peseta crashed on the currency markets yesterday.* -4. COMPUTING [computer, system] to stop working suddenly.

crash barrier *n* a strong low fence that is designed to hold back crowds, stop cars leaving a road etc.

crash course *n* a course of lessons intended to teach the most important aspects of a subject as quickly as possible □ *a crash course in computing.*

crash diet *n* a diet intended to make somebody lose a lot of weight as quickly as possible.

crash-dive *vi* [submarine, plane] to move suddenly downward, usually to avoid an attack.

crash helmet *n* a strong hat worn by motorcyclists, racing drivers etc to protect their heads.

crash-land ◇ *vt* to land <an airplane> in an emergency, trying to cause as little damage as possible. ◇ *vi* [airplane, pilot] *They were forced to crash-land in a field.*

crash landing *n*: *see* **crash-land** □ *We were forced to make a crash landing in the ocean.*

crass [kræs] *adj* [person, remark, behavior] that is stupid and shows a lack of sympathy or respect for other people.

crate [kreɪt] *n* a large box, usually made of wood or plastic, that is used for transporting and storing things; the contents of a crate □ *a milk crate* □ *a crate of milk.*

crater ['kreɪtəʳ] *n* -1. a round hole in the ground, especially one made by an explosion; a similar hole on the surface of the Moon □ *The meteorite left a 200m-wide crater.* □ *a bomb crater.* -2. a deep round hole in the top of a volcano.

cravat [krə'væt] *n* a piece of clothing worn by men around their neck and folded inside the top of a shirt.

crave [kreɪv] ◇ *vt* [affection, wealth, cigarette] to want <sthg> very much, especially in a way that is difficult to control □ *He never gave her the love she craved.* ◇ *vi* **to be craving for sthg** to want sthg very much.

craving ['kreɪvɪŋ] *n* a strong desire for something that is difficult to control □ *I had a sudden craving for chocolate.* □ *a constant craving for attention.*

crawl [krɔːl] ◇ *vi* -1. [person] to move slowly on one's hands and knees or with one's body on the ground □ *He crawled along the window ledge.* -2. [insect, worm] to move slowly along a surface. -3. [car, traffic, crowd] to move somewhere very slowly □ *We crawled along at 15 miles an hour.* -4. **to be crawling with tourists/maggots etc** to be covered with or full of tourists/maggots etc (informal use) □ *When we got there, the place was crawling with police/reporters.* -5. **to crawl to sb** to try to become liked by sb more important by praising them, agreeing with them etc all the time (informal and disapproving use) □ *Stop crawling!*
◇ *n* -1. **a crawl** a very slow speed □ *We drove at a crawl.* □ *Traffic had slowed to a crawl.* -2. **the crawl** a way of swimming on one's stomach by moving one's arms over one's head, one after the other, and kicking one's legs.

crawler lane ['krɔːləʳ-] *n* GB a lane on a road that is for vehicles which are moving slowly, especially on a hill.

crayfish ['kreɪfɪʃ] (*pl* **crayfish** OR **crayfishes**) *n* a small shellfish, similar to a lobster, that lives in rivers and lakes; the meat of this shellfish eaten as food.

crayon ['kreɪɒn] *n* a colored pencil or stick of colored wax or chalk that is used for drawing □ *a box of crayons.*

craze [kreɪz] *n* something such as an activity or a way of dressing that is very popular for a short time, especially among young people □ *the latest dance craze.*

crazed [kreɪzd] *adj* [mob, gunman, behavior] who is wild and excited in a way that is frightening □ *They were half crazed with fear.*

crazy ['kreɪzɪ] (*compar* **crazier**, *superl* **craziest**) *adj* (informal use) -1. [person, idea, behavior]
that is very foolish □ *It would be crazy to give up now.* ■ **to drive sb crazy** to annoy sb very much □ *That noise is driving me crazy.* ■ **to go crazy** to become very angry □ *When I told him he went crazy and started shouting.* -2. **to be crazy about sthg** to be very interested in and enthusiastic about sthg □ *I'm not crazy about the idea.* ■ **to be crazy about sb** to be in love with sb in a way that one cannot control.

Crazy Horse (1849–1877) a leader of the Sioux people, who defeated the US army at the battle of the Little Bighorn.

crazy paving *n* GB pieces of flat stone that have irregular shapes and are fitted together to make a path or garden terrace.

CRE *n abbr of* **Commission for Racial Equality**.

creak [kriːk] ◇ *n* a sound like the one that is made by a loose floorboard when somebody steps on it. ◇ *vi* [door, bed] to make creaks □ *The floorboards creak when you walk on them.*

creaky ['kriːkɪ] (*compar* **creakier**, *superl* **creakiest**) *adj* [door, bed, floorboard] that creaks.

cream [kriːm] ◇ *n* -1. [in milk] the thick yellow-white liquid that rises to the top of milk; an artificial mixture with a similar taste and appearance that is used in making food □ *a fresh cream cake* □ *strawberries and cream* □ *cream of chicken soup.* -2. [for one's skin] a thick liquid or smooth paste that one rubs into one's skin as a cosmetic or medicine □ *a tube of suntan cream.* -3. a food, candy, or cookie containing cream or a similar smooth mixture □ *chocolate creams.* -4. [color] a white color with a little yellow in it □ *Do you have the same dress in cream?* -5. **the cream** the best people or things in a group □ *We recruit from the cream of British graduates.*
◇ *vt* [potatoes, ingredients] to mix <food> so that it becomes smooth and soft, often by adding milk, cream, or butter □ *creamed potatoes* □ *Cream the butter and sugar in a bowl.*
◇ *adj* [wall, shirt] that is the color of white with a little yellow in it.

◆ **cream off** *vt sep* **to cream off the profits/the best students etc** to separate the profits/the best students etc from the rest for one's own benefit.

cream cake *n* a cake or roll containing cream.

cream cheese *n* a soft white cheese with a rich flavor.

cream cracker *n* GB a dry unsweetened cracker that is often eaten with cheese.

cream of tartar *n* a white powder that is mixed with baking soda to make baking powder.

cream tea *n* GB an afternoon meal that consists of tea with scones, jam, and whipped cream.

creamy ['kriːmɪ] (*compar* **creamier**, *superl* **creamiest**) *adj* -1. [coffee, pudding] that tastes of or contains cream. -2. [liquid, soup, paint] that is thick and smooth □ *This cheese has a deliciously creamy texture.* -3. [silk, flower] that is yellow-white in color.

crease [kriːs] ◇ *n* -1. a straight line on a piece of clothing that is made by folding and pressing it □ *I can never get the creases right when I iron my pants.* -2. an irregular line where cloth, paper etc has been folded or crushed in a way that is not intentional □ *I'll just iron these jeans quickly to get rid of the creases.* ◇ *vt* [skirt, paper] to make a crease or creases in <sthg>. ◇ *vi* [skirt, paper] to become creased □ *The beauty of this shirt is that it doesn't crease.* -2. [face, forehead] to get lines on it because one is frowning, smiling etc.

creased [kriːst] *adj* [skirt, paper] that has irregular lines in it as a result of being crushed □ *My jacket got creased on the plane.*

crease-resistant *adj* [fabric, shirt] that does not crease easily.

create [kriːˈeɪt] *vt* -1. [poem, painting, style] to produce <sthg new>, especially using one's imagination □ *In the 1960s, he created a look that was to last a generation.* -2. [employment, risk, problem] to cause <sthg> to exist or develop □ *A number of new jobs have been created.* □ *It's important to create a good impression.*

creation [kriːˈeɪʃn] *n* -1. *see* **create** □ *the creation of a new training program.* -2. the whole universe and everything in it (literary use). -3. something created with imagination or skill, e.g. a work of art, a hairstyle, or a meal □ *The Paris fashion designers are showing their latest creations.*

creative [kriːˈeɪtɪv] *adj* [person, design, writing] that uses new, original, and imaginative ideas, especially in an artistic way □ *a designer with creative flair.*

creativity [ˌkriːeɪˈtɪvəti] *n* [of a person, idea] the quality of being creative □ *We're looking for somebody with flair and creativity.*

creator [kriːˈeɪtər] *n* [of a story, idea] a person who makes, produces, or invents something □ *a new film from the creators of "Delicatessen".*

creature [ˈkriːtʃər] *n* -1. a living animal, bird, fish, insect etc □ *sea creatures.* -2. a word used to describe a person who has a particular quality □ *What an extraordinary creature your mother is!* □ *Most of us are creatures of habit.*

crèche [kreʃ] *n* GB a place, especially one provided at a place of work, where babies and small children are looked after while their parents work □ *With our crèche facilities, you can shop with peace of mind.*

credence [ˈkriːdns] *n* **to give** OR **lend credence to sthg** [to a story, claim, promise] to make sthg seem more likely to be true □ *This evidence lends further credence to his case.*

credentials [krəˈdenʃlz] *npl* -1. sb's credentials ability, knowledge, experience etc that show that somebody is suitable for a job or position or has reached a high standard □ *No one doubts her credentials as an artist.* -2. a letter or other document that proves that somebody is who or what they say they are □ *The receptionist asked him for his credentials.*

credibility [ˌkredəˈbɪləti] *n*: *see* **credible** □ *She's lost all political credibility.*

credible [ˈkredəbl] *adj* [excuse, person, policy] that can be believed, trusted, or taken seri-

ously □ *The company has no credible strategy for market development.*

credit [ˈkredət] ◇ *n* -1. [with a store, bank] a system of paying for goods or services some time after they have been received; an arrangement for somebody to pay in this way □ *'We regret that we are unable to give credit.'* ■ **to be in credit** [bank account, customer] to have money available for use and not be overdrawn. ■ **to buy sthg on credit** to take sthg and use it immediately without having to pay for it until later. -2. [for an achievement] praise or approval given to somebody for something they have done □ *She took* OR *got all the credit for the invention.* ■ **to sb's credit** a phrase used to draw attention to something good that somebody has done, especially when they are also being criticized for something else □ *To his credit, he was quick to rectify the mistake.* ■ **to do sb credit** [action, attitude] to make sb deserve praise or approval □ *Your honesty does you credit.* ■ **to give sb credit for sthg** to say or admit that sb has done sthg good □ *She works much harder than people give her credit for.* ■ **to have sthg to one's credit** to have already achieved or completed sthg successfully □ *With three hit musicals to his credit, he is now going into movies.* -3. EDUCATION a pass in one part of a course at a college or university. -4. FINANCE a sum of money that is added to somebody's account □ *The statement shows a credit of $90.* □ *a credit transfer.*

◇ *vt* -1. FINANCE to add <a sum of money> to an account □ *We have credited the dividend to your account.* □ *Your account has been credited with $100.* -2. [statement, story] to believe <sthg unlikely or unexpected> □ *Can you credit it? The package still hasn't arrived!* -3. **to credit sb with sthg** [with common sense, tact] to believe or say that sb has sthg □ *Credit me with at least some intelligence!* ■ **to be credited with sthg** to be generally believed to be responsible for sthg □ *He's credited with having invented television.*

◆ **credits** *npl* the list of people who helped to make a movie or TV program that appears at the beginning or end of it.

creditable [ˈkredətəbl] *adj* [effort, attempt, performance] that is good enough to deserve praise or approval □ *She gave a creditable performance in the preliminary rounds.*

credit account *n* GB an account at a store that allows a customer to take goods away and pay for them later.

credit broker *n* a person or company whose job is to find the best place for people to borrow money.

credit card *n* a small plastic card that is given to a customer by a bank, finance company, or store and is used to buy goods on credit □ *Can I pay by credit card?* □ *a credit-card purchase/customer.*

credit control *n* -1. a company's system of control for checking that customers do not spend more than their credit limit. -2. limits on the amount of money a bank can lend that are decided by the government.

credit facilities *npl* an arrangement with a bank, supplier etc that allows a customer to buy things on credit.

credit line US, **credit limit** GB *n* the largest amount of money that a customer of a bank, store, company etc can have on credit, especially when using a credit card or credit account.

credit note *n* -1. a piece of paper that a store gives instead of money to a customer who returns goods, and that allows the customer to buy other goods of the same value. -2. a letter sent by a supplier to a customer to tell them the supplier owes them money.

creditor ['krɛdətə^r] *n* a person or company that somebody owes money to.

credit rating *n* an estimate of how likely a person is to pay back money that they borrow, used to calculate their credit line.

credit squeeze *n* a period when the government makes it difficult to borrow money, usually to reduce spending or inflation.

credit transfer *n* a payment of money directly from one bank account to another, rather than by cash, check etc.

credit union *n* US & AUS a kind of savings bank that gives better terms to particular kinds of people, e.g. students or members of a labor union.

creditworthy ['krɛdətwɜː^rði] *adj* [person, company, project] that it is safe to lend money or give credit to.

credulity [krə'dju:lətɪ] *n: see* **credulous** (formal use).

credulous ['krɛdʒələs] *adj* [person] who is too willing to believe what other people say without real proof □ *He somehow duped dozens of credulous investors.*

Cree [kri:] *n* a member of a Native American people living mainly in Canada and Montana; the language of this people.

creed [kri:d] *n* -1. a set of beliefs and principles that are usually shared by many people □ *They embraced the creed of socialism.* -2. a religion □ *people of every color and creed.* -3. **the Creed** a short statement of Christian beliefs that is spoken as part of some church services.

creek [kri:k] *n* -1. US a small narrow river or stream. -2. GB a long narrow area of water that reaches inland from the sea.

Creek *n* a member of a Native American people who used to live in Georgia and Alabama; the language of this people.

creep [kri:p] (*pt* & *pp* **crept**) ◇ *vi* -1. [person, animal] to move somewhere quietly and carefully to avoid being noticed □ *The burglar crept through the house.* □ *The cat crept toward the mouse.* -2. [cloud, traffic, time] to move in a particular direction very slowly □ *The cars crept along at a walking pace.* □ *Our debts have crept up to over $1 million.* -3. **to creep (up) to sb** to try to become liked by sb important by praising them, agreeing with them etc all

the time (informal and disapproving use) □ *I see you've been creeping (up) to the boss again.* ◇ *n* a person who one dislikes (informal use) □ *He's a real creep!*

◆ **creeps** *npl* **to give sb the creeps** to make sb feel fear, disgust, or strong dislike (informal use) □ *There's something about that guy that gives me the creeps.*

◆ **creep in** *vi* [mistakes, idea, fear] to begin to appear □ *A hint of doubt crept into his voice.*

◆ **creep up on** *vt fus* -1. **to creep up on a person/an animal** to creep toward another person/animal, usually from behind. -2. **to creep up on sb** [feeling, time] to get slowly closer to sb in a way that is not always noticeable □ *Old age is creeping up on me.* □ *The deadline is creeping up on us.*

creeper ['kri:pə^r] *n* a long plant that grows along the ground, up walls etc.

creeping ['kri:pɪŋ] *adj* [inflation, paralysis] that increases or spreads slowly and causes damage.

creepy ['kri:pɪ] (*compar* **creepier**, *superl* **creepiest**) *adj* [story, person, place] that makes one feel fear, disgust, or strong dislike (informal use) □ *Their house is dark and creepy.*

creepy-crawly [-'krɔ:lɪ] (*pl* **creepy-crawlies**) *n* an insect that one finds unpleasant or that makes one nervous or afraid (informal use).

cremate [US 'kri:meɪt, GB krə'meɪt] *vt* to burn <the body of a dead person>.

cremation [krə'meɪʃn] *n: see* **cremate** □ *After the cremation, we all went back to my uncle's house.*

crematorium [US ˌkri:mə'tɔ:rɪəm, GB ˌkrem-] (*pl* **crematoriums** OR **crematoria** [-rɪə]) *n* a building where the bodies of dead people are cremated.

crematory [US 'kri:mətɔ:rɪ, GB 'kremətrɪ] (*pl* **crematories**) *n* US = **crematorium**.

creosote ['krɪəsoʊt] ◇ *n* a brown liquid with a strong smell that is used to preserve wood. ◇ *vt* [fence, shed] to paint <sthg made of wood> with creosote.

crepe [kreɪp] *n* -1. CLOTHING a light thin fabric such as cotton or wool that has an uneven surface □ *a crepe blouse/dress.* -2. [for shoes] a kind of strong rubber with an uneven surface that is used for making the soles of shoes. -3. COOKING a thin pancake.

crepe bandage *n* GB a long piece of white flexible fabric with an uneven surface that is used for covering and protecting cuts and injuries.

crepe paper *n* thin brightly-colored paper with an uneven surface that is used for making decorations and wrapping gifts.

crepe-soled shoes [-soʊld-] *npl* shoes with thick soles made of crepe rubber.

crept [krept] *past tense & past participle of* **creep**.

Cres *abbr of* **crescent**.

crescendo [krɪ'ʃendoʊ] (*pl* **crescendos**) *n* -1. [of noise, applause] a sudden increase in the loudness of something □ *There was a crescendo of clapping and cheering from the audience.* -2. **to rise to** OR **reach a crescendo** [noise, protest] to increase gradually and reach a climax □ *The music reached a crescendo, then suddenly stopped.*

crescent [US 'kresnt, GB 'krez-] ◇ *n* -1. a curved shape like that of the Moon when it is less than half full. -2. a street or line of houses that forms a curve. ◇ *adj* [shape, Moon] that has the shape of a crescent.

cress [kres] *n* a very small plant with small leaves that have a strong taste and are eaten raw in salads and sandwiches.

crest [krest] *n* -1. [of a bird] a group of feathers growing upward on a bird's head. -2. [of a hill, wave] the top or highest part of a hill or wave. -3. [of a family, institution] a small design used on furniture, writing paper etc as the symbol of a family, town, or organization □ *the family crest.*

crestfallen ['krestfɔːlən] *adj* [person] who is disappointed and sad □ *She looked crestfallen when I told her the news.*

Crete [kriːt] a Greek island in the eastern Mediterranean. SIZE: 8,336 sq kms. POPULATION: 536,980 (*Cretans*).

cretin [US 'kriːtn, GB 'kretɪn] *n* a person who one thinks is very stupid (informal use).

crevasse [krə'væs] *n* a long deep hole in thick ice.

crevice ['krevəs] *n* a long narrow space or hole in a rock, wall etc.

crew [kruː] *n* -1. the people who work on a ship, plane, ambulance or other vehicle □ *an ambulance crew* □ *a crew member.* -2. a group of people, usually with special skills, who work together on a task or project □ *a movie/camera crew.*

crew cut *n* a hairstyle in which the hair is cut very short all over one's head.

crewman ['kruːmən] (*pl* **crewmen** [-mən]) *n* a member of a crew.

crew-neck(ed) [-nek(t)] *adj* [sweater, pullover] that has a round collar and is close-fitting at the neck.

crib [krɪb] (*pt* & *pp* **cribbed**, *cont* **cribbing**) ◇ *n* a bed with high sides for a baby. ◇ *vt* to copy <sthg written> from somebody else and pretend it is one's own idea, work etc (informal use) □ *He cribbed the answer off OR from the girl next to him.*

cribbage ['krɪbɪdʒ] *n* a card game in which the players keep their scores by putting small sticks into holes on a wooden board.

crib death *n* US the sudden death of a baby while it is asleep and is not suffering from any illness.

crick [krɪk] ◇ *n* a pain in one's neck or back caused by the muscles suddenly becoming stiff. ◇ *vt* to get a crick in <one's neck or back>.

cricket ['krɪkət] *n* -1. an outdoor sport that is played by two teams of eleven players who dress in white and score points by hitting a small hard ball with a wooden bat and running between two sets of small posts □ *a cricket ball/match/pitch.* -2. a small brown insect that jumps in the air and makes short loud sounds by rubbing its wings together.

cricketer ['krɪkətəʳ] *n* a person who plays cricket.

cried [kraɪd] *past tense & past participle of* **cry**.

crime [kraɪm] *n* -1. acts and behavior which are against the law □ *The government is worried about the increase in violent crime.* □ *crime prevention* □ *a crime novel.* -2. an act which is against the law □ *a minor* OR *petty crime.* -3. something that one thinks it is wrong to do or let happen □ *It would be a crime to tear down that old church.*

Crimea [kraɪ'mɪə]: **the Crimea** an area of land in the Ukraine on the Black Sea.

crime wave *n* a sudden increase in crime that lasts for a particular period of time.

criminal ['krɪmɪnl] ◇ *adj* -1. [offense, behavior, lawyer] that is connected with acts which are against the law □ *Shoplifting is a criminal offense.* -2. [waste, neglect] that one thinks is wrong to do or let happen □ *It's a criminal waste of taxpayers' money.* ◇ *n* a person who has committed a crime.

criminalize, -ise ['krɪmɪnəlaɪz] *vt* to make <an activity> a criminal offense.

criminal law *n* the laws of a country that deal with crimes that are punished, rather than with people's rights, disagreements etc.

criminology [,krɪmɪ'nɒlədʒɪ] *n* the study of the causes and prevention of crime.

crimped [krɪmpt] *adj* [hair] that has been made to look wavy.

crimson ['krɪmzn] ◇ *adj* -1. [dress, flower] that is dark purple-red in color. -2. **to be/turn crimson** [face] to be/become very red because one is embarrassed or angry. ◇ *n* a dark purple-red color.

cringe [krɪndʒ] *vi* -1. to have a very unpleasant feeling of shame or embarrassment that is clear from the expression on one's face (informal use) □ *It makes me cringe (with embarrassment) when I think about it.* -2. to move backward because of fear.

crinkle ['krɪŋkl] ◇ *n* a small line, wave, or fold in the surface of paper, cloth, skin etc. ◇ *vi* [clothes, leaf, face] to become covered with crinkles.

crinkly ['krɪŋklɪ] *adj* [surface, face] that is covered with crinkles.

cripple ['krɪpl] ◇ *n*▼ a person who is permanently unable to walk or move properly as a result of an injury or disease in their back or legs (old-fashioned and offensive use). ◇ *vt* -1. [person] to cause <sb> to become a cripple □ *He was crippled in a riding accident.* -2. [country, economy, ship] to prevent <sthg> from continuing to work properly □ *The company was crippled by debts.*

crippling ['krɪplɪŋ] *adj* -1. [disease, pain] that prevents somebody from walking or moving properly. -2. [debt, price, tax] very large and difficult to deal with.

crisis ['kraɪsəs] (*pl* **crises** [-iːz]) *n* -1. a point in a situation when it has become very difficult, dangerous, and uncertain □ *The govern-*

ment is in crisis. □ We need international measures to combat the energy crisis. □ Relations between the two countries have reached crisis point. **-2.** a time in a person's life when they are unable to deal with their problems □ He'll start drinking again at the first sign of crisis.

crisp [krɪsp] adj **-1.** [toast, bacon, leaves] hard, dry, and easily broken; [apple, lettuce] firm and fresh □ He handed over a wad of crisp dollar bills. **-2.** [weather, wind] pleasantly fresh, cold, and dry □ It was a fine, crisp morning. **-3.** [tone, manner] quick, confident, and often unfriendly □ "Good morning," said a clear crisp voice over the telephone.

◆ **crisps** npl GB thin slices of potato that are fried until they are hard and break easily, and that are eaten cold.

crispbread ['krɪspbred] n a plain, dry, unsweetened cracker that is eaten in place of bread, e.g. by people on diets.

crispy ['krɪspɪ] (compar **crispier**, superl **crispiest**) adj [bacon, toast] that has been fried, grilled etc until it is hard and breaks easily; [apple, lettuce] firm and fresh.

crisscross ['krɪskrɒs] ◇ adj [pattern, design] that has many straight lines that cross each other. ◇ vt to cross <a landscape, map> etc in many different directions □ The region is crisscrossed by a network of canals. ◇ vi [lines, roads] to form a crisscross pattern.

criterion [kraɪ'tɪərɪən] (pl **criteria** [-rɪə]) n a measure or standard that people use to make decisions or to judge somebody or something □ Wealth is not the only criterion of success. □ All new products will have to meet the criteria laid down by the authorities.

critic ['krɪtɪk] n **-1.** a person whose job is to give their opinion of movies, books, music etc □ The critics loved the new show. □ an art/a film critic. **-2.** a person who criticizes somebody or something publicly □ He is an outspoken critic of the regime.

critical ['krɪtɪkl] adj **-1.** [stage, moment] that is very important in deciding what will happen □ The discussions had reached a critical point. □ The next few weeks will be critical for the company's future. **-2.** [illness, situation, condition] that is very serious and may suddenly get worse or lead to somebody's death □ The patient is still critical. **-3.** [person, article, attitude] that expresses or shows disapproval □ The chairman was highly critical of our department's performance. □ The play met with critical acclaim. **-4.** [study, analysis] that examines and judges carefully somebody or something's good and bad qualities □ The report provides a critical assessment of potential markets. **-5.** [success, acclaim] that is connected with what critics have said.

critically ['krɪtɪklɪ] adv **-1.** critically important/ill etc very important/seriously ill etc □ She was critically injured in the explosion. **-2.** [look, judge] in a way that shows disapproval □ She often speaks critically about her husband.

criticism ['krɪtəsɪzm] n **-1.** [of a book, play] serious discussion of something, especially what its

good and bad points are □ literary criticism. **-2.** [of a person, decision] disapproval that is expressed about somebody or something; a comment that expresses this □ They've had a lot of criticism lately. □ These tactics are open to criticism. □ I have a few small criticisms to make.

criticize, -ise ['krɪtəsaɪz] ◇ vt [person, policy] to express disapproval of <sb/sthg> □ She always criticizes the way I drive. ◇ vi: All he ever does is criticize.

critique [krɪ'tiːk] n an article, book, speech etc that carefully examines and judges something □ She's writing a critique of Borges' work.

croak [krəʊk] ◇ n **-1.** [of a frog, bird] a deep harsh sound. **-2.** [of a person] a low, harsh, rough voice that is caused by a sore throat, tiredness, thirst, fear etc. ◇ vi **-1.** [frog, bird] to make a croak. **-2.** [person] to speak with a croak.

Croat ['krəʊæt] n & adj: see **Croatia**.

Croatia [krəʊ'eɪʃə] a country in southeastern Europe, on the Adriatic Sea, that was part of Yugoslavia until 1991. SIZE: 56,500 sq kms. POPULATION: 4,400,000 (Croats, Croatians). CAPITAL: Zagreb. LANGUAGE: Croatian. CURRENCY: Croatian dinar.

Croatian [krəʊ'eɪʃn] adj & n: see **Croatia**.

crochet [US krəʊ'ʃeɪ, GB 'krəʊʃeɪ] ◇ vt [sweater, tablecloth] to make <sthg> from wool or thread using a short needle with a hook on the end □ I'm going to crochet a nice scarf for you. ◇ n the art of crocheting things.

crockery ['krɒkərɪ] n a collective term for plates, cups, saucers etc.

Crockett ['krɒkət], **Davy** (1786–1836) a US hero from the Wild West who later became a politician. He died at the battle of the Alamo.

crocodile ['krɒkədaɪl] (pl **crocodile** OR **crocodiles**) n a large reptile with a long mouth and many sharp teeth that lives in rivers and lakes in Africa, Australia, and Asia. It eats meat and can attack people.

crocus ['krəʊkəs] (pl **crocuses**) n a small garden plant that produces white, yellow, or purple flowers early in the spring.

Croesus ['kriːsəs] a king who ruled in the 6th century BC in what is now Turkey. He is famous for being very rich.

croft [krɒft] n GB a small farm, especially in Scotland.

croissant [US kwɑː'sɑːnt, GB 'kwæsɒŋ] n a crescent-shaped piece of light flaky pastry that is sometimes eaten for breakfast.

Cromwell ['krɒmwəl], **Oliver** (1599–1658) a British soldier and politician who led the Parliamentary army against the Royalists in the English Civil War. He established a republic, which he governed until his death.

crony ['krəʊnɪ] (pl **cronies**) n sb's crony sb's close friend or companion (informal and disapproving use) □ We think it was John and some of his cronies that did it.

crook [krʊk] ◇ n **-1.** a dishonest person (informal use). **-2.** [of one's arm, leg] the soft part where somebody's elbow or knee bends.

-3. [of a shepherd] a long stick with a curved end that is used by shepherds for catching sheep. ◇ *vt* to bend <one's finger or arm>. ◇ *adj* AUS ill (informal use).

crooked ['krʊkəd] *adj* -1. [path, branch, tie] that is not straight □ *I've always had crooked teeth.* -2. [person, deal] dishonest (informal use).

croon [kruːn] ◇ *vt* [song, tune, words] to sing or say <sthg> softly and gently. ◇ *vi: She was crooning over the baby.*

crop [krɒp] (*pt* & *pp* **cropped**, *cont* **cropping**) ◇ *n* -1. FARMING a plant grown in large amounts on farms, e.g. grain, vegetables, or fruit; the amount of a crop that is grown and collected in a year or season in one particular place □ *This land is no good for growing crops.* □ *We expect a good crop of apples this year.* □ *The wheat crop was damaged by the storm.* -2. [of people, results, problems] a group of similar people or things that all appear at the same time (informal use) □ *I don't think much of this year's crop of students/recruits.* □ *the latest crop of official figures.* -3. [for horse riding] a short whip used by horse riders.
◇ *vt* -1. [hairdresser] to cut <sb's hair> very short. -2. [animal] to bite the tops off <plants, grass> etc and eat them.
◆ **crop up** *vi* [problem, subject] to happen or appear unexpectedly (informal use) □ *I'm afraid something's cropped up at the office so I'll have to meet you later.* □ *Your name cropped up during the conversation.*

crop spraying [-spreɪɪŋ] *n* the treatment of crops with chemicals that kill insects, usually using low-flying airplanes.

croquet [US kroʊ'keɪ, GB 'kroʊkeɪ] *n* a game in which players use long sticks with heavy heads to hit wooden balls through metal arches fixed into a grass lawn.

croquette [kroʊ'ket] *n* a ball of crushed potato, fish etc that is covered in breadcrumbs and fried or baked □ *a potato croquette.*

cross [krɒs] ◇ *adj* [person, look, reply] angry □ *I'm sorry I was so cross with you.* □ *He got cross with me when I told him so.*
◇ *n* -1. [on a map] a symbol (×) used e.g. on a map to indicate where something is or on a piece of work to indicate that an answer is wrong □ *Please put a cross in the relevant boxes.* -2. [in Christianity] a symbol (+) that is often used to represent the Christian religion □ *She wore a little silver cross on a chain around her neck.* -3. [of animals, plants] a mixture of two different things, especially two types of animal or plant □ *A mule is a cross between a horse and a donkey.*
◇ *vt* -1. [street, room, river] to go from one side of <sthg> to the other □ *We crossed the border into Spain.* ■ **to cross sb's face** [look, expression] to appear for a short time on sb's face □ *A look of anxiety crossed his face.* -2. **to cross one's arms/legs** to place one arm/leg over the other □ *I sat on the floor with my legs crossed.* -3. RELIGION **to cross oneself** to make the sign of a Christian cross by touching one's head, chest, and shoulders with one's hand. -4. **to cross a cheque** GB to draw two

lines across a check so that it must be deposited into a bank account and cannot be exchanged for cash □ *a crossed cheque.* -5. [person] to annoy <sb> by opposing them or preventing them from getting what they want □ *You'd better be careful with the manager; he doesn't like being crossed.*
◇ *vi* -1. [lines, streets] to come together and go across each other □ *The roads cross just south of Detroit.* -2. [pedestrian, vehicle] to cross a street, room, the sea etc □ *It's best to cross at the traffic lights.*
◆ **cross off** *vt sep* **to cross sthg off** to delete sthg from a list □ *You may as well cross Jenny's name off; she won't even be here.*
◆ **cross out** *vt sep* **to cross sthg out** [word, sentence] to draw a line through sthg to show that it is incorrect or unnecessary □ *Please cross out the words that do not apply.*

crossbar ['krɒsbɑːr] *n* -1. SPORT the horizontal bar between the two upright posts of a goal. -2. the horizontal bar on a man's bicycle that is between the saddle and the handlebars.

crossbencher ['krɒsbentʃər] *n* a member of the British parliament who sits on the crossbenches.

crossbenches ['krɒsbentʃɪz] *npl* **the crossbenches** the seats in the House of Lords and the House of Commons for members who do not belong to the Government or to the Opposition.

crossbow ['krɒsboʊ] *n* a weapon that consists of a small horizontal bow whose string is pulled back along a central shaft and released by a trigger.

crossbreed ['krɒsbriːd] *n* a type of animal or plant that is produced by mixing two different types.

cross-Channel *adj* **a cross-Channel ferry/route etc** a ferry/route etc that crosses the English Channel between England and mainland Europe.

cross-check *n* a check of something that is carried out to make sure that no mistakes have been made and that uses a different method from the one originally used □ *Can you please run a cross-check on these figures?*
◆ **crosscheck** *vt* [data, calculation, statement] to carry out a cross-check on <sthg>.

cross-country ◇ *adj* [running, skiing] that involves crossing fields, open country etc; [route, service] that uses less important roads, railroad lines etc rather than main routes. ◇ *adv* [walk, travel] by crossing fields, open country etc or using cross-country routes. ◇ *n* the sport of running races across fields and open country; one of these races.

cross-cultural *adj* [study, music, conflict] that involves two or more different cultures.

cross-dressing *n* the practice of wearing clothes that are usually worn by the opposite sex.

crossed line [,krɒst-] *n* a fault on a telephone line in which one can hear somebody else's conversation on another line.

cross-examination *n*: see **cross-examine** □ *The second witness was called for cross-examination.*

cross-examine *vt* **-1.** LAW to ask <a witness> a lot of detailed questions in a court of law to check that they give the same answers as the previous time they were questioned □ *You can expect to be cross-examined at length about this.* **-2.** to ask <sb> a lot of detailed questions, often because one does not believe them □ *I hate being cross-examined.*

cross-eyed [-aɪd] *adj* [person] who has eyes that seem to look toward their nose.

cross-fertilize *vt* to fertilize <a female plant> using the male pollen of a different type of plant.

crossfire ['krɒsfaɪəʳ] *n* gunfire that comes from two or more places. ■ **to be/get caught in the crossfire** to be/become unwillingly involved in an argument between two other people.

crosshead ['krɒshed] *adj* GB **a crosshead screwdriver** a screwdriver that has a pointed end in the shape of a cross. ■ **a crosshead screw** a screw that has a slot in the shape of a cross at one end.

crossing ['krɒsɪŋ] *n* **-1.** [for pedestrians, cars] a safe place to cross a road, railroad etc. **-2.** [between countries] an official place to cross from one country to another □ *a border crossing.* **-3.** [across water] a trip by boat or ship across a sea, lake etc □ *We had a rough/pleasant crossing.*

cross-legged [-legd] *adv* to **sit cross-legged** to sit with one leg placed on top of the other so that one's knees point to each side; with one leg placed on top of the other.

crossly ['krɒslɪ] *adv* [say, reply, frown] in an angry way □ *"No it isn't!" she said crossly.*

crossply ['krɒsplaɪ] (*pl* **crossplies**) ◇ *adj* a **crossply tire** a tire that is made stronger by having wires or cords arranged crosswise inside the rubber. ◇ *n* a crossply tire.

cross-purposes *npl* to **be at cross-purposes** [two people] to be talking about different things without realizing it so that there is confusion and misunderstanding □ *We seem to be talking at cross-purposes.*

cross-question *vt* = **cross-examine**.

cross-refer ◇ *vt* to send <a reader> to another part of a book or document using a cross-reference. ◇ *vi*: *An arrow is used to cross-refer to related topics.*

cross-reference *n* a note in a book or document that tells readers that there is more information on a subject in another part of the book or document.

crossroads ['krɒsrəʊdz] (*pl* **crossroads**) *n* a place where two roads meet and cross each other □ *When you come to the crossroads, turn left.* ■ **to be at a crossroads** to be at an important point in one's life or career where one has to make a decision that will affect one's future.

cross-section *n* **-1.** [of a plant, brain, pipe] the inside surface that can be seen when something is cut in half; a picture of this □ *The drawing shows a cross-section of the building.* □ *The beam is shown in cross-section.* **-2.** [of students, the community, population] a group chosen as being typical of a larger group □ *Our market researchers have tested the product on a cross-section of consumers.*

crosswalk ['krɒswɔ:k] *n* US a specially marked part of a road where vehicles have to stop to allow pedestrians to cross.

crossways ['krɒsweɪz] *adv* = **crosswise**.

crosswind ['krɒswɪnd] *n* a wind blowing across the direction in which an airplane, ship, car etc is traveling.

crosswise ['krɒswaɪz] *adv* [lie, lay, arrange] across each other; from corner to corner across something.

crossword (puzzle) ['krɒswɜ:ʳd-] *n* a word game found in newspapers, magazines etc in which one has to find words from information that is given and write the answers in squares on a special pattern.

crotch [krɒtʃ] *n* the place where one's legs meet at the front of one's body; the part of a pair of trousers, pantyhose etc that cover this place.

crotchet ['krɒtʃət] *n* GB MUSIC a note (♩) that is a quarter as long as a whole note.

crotchety ['krɒtʃətɪ] *adj* [person] who is bad-tempered (informal use).

crouch [kraʊtʃ] *vi* [person, animal] to lower the body close to the ground by bending the legs, especially in order to hide □ *I crouched down in the bushes, hoping no one had seen me.*

◆ **crouch over** *vt fus* to **crouch over sthg** to lean forward so that one's body is very close to sthg.

croup [kru:p] *n* **-1.** MEDICINE a children's disease which causes coughing and breathing problems. **-2.** [of a horse] the fleshy part above the back legs of a horse.

croupier ['kru:pɪəʳ] *n* a person whose job is to spin the roulette wheel, deal the cards, take in and pay out money etc in a casino.

crouton ['kru:tɒn] *n* a small square of fried bread that is eaten in soups or salads.

crow [krəʊ] ◇ *n* a large black bird with a loud harsh cry. ■ **as the crow flies** a phrase used to give the distance between two places if one travels in a straight line □ *It's two miles, as the crow flies.* ◇ *vi* **-1.** [cock] to make a loud high call, especially at dawn. **-2.** [person] to talk proudly about something, especially to somebody who has not been as successful (disapproving use) □ *He's been crowing about* OR *over his promotion all week.*

Crow *n* a member of a Native American people living in Montana; the language of this people.

crowbar ['krəʊbɑ:ʳ] *n* a long, heavy, iron bar with a bent end that is used for lifting heavy objects and breaking open boxes.

crowd [kraʊd] ◇ *n* **-1.** a large group of people who have gathered together, usually outdoors □ *There was a crowd of people waiting to get in.* □ *a football crowd.* **-2.** a particular group of people, e.g. friends or people who work together (informal use) □ *"Who was at the party?" — "The usual crowd."*

◇ *vi* [people] to come together somewhere in large numbers □ *Everyone crowded around as the salesman demonstrated the machine.* □ *The fans crowded into the stadium.*

◇ *vt* -1. to fill <a place> □ *Tourists crowded the streets.* -2. to force <people> into a small space □ *We were just able to crowd everybody in.* □ *The delegates were crowded into a tiny room.*

crowded ['kraʊdəd] *adj* -1. [train, room] that is filled with a lot of people so that it is often difficult to move, find a seat etc □ *The beach was very crowded.* □ *The hall was crowded with photographers.* -2. [timetable, schedule] that is full of events □ *The agenda is starting to look very crowded.*

crown [kraʊn] ◇ *n* -1. [of a king, queen] a decorative hat, often of silver or gold, worn as a symbol of royal power. -2. [of a hill, hat, somebody's head] the top or highest part of something. -3. [of a tooth] a cover of gold or porcelain fixed over the top of a broken tooth. ◇ *vt* -1. to make <sb> a king or queen by placing a crown on their head □ *Charles V was crowned king of Spain in 1516.* -2. [dentist] to put a crown on <a tooth>. -3. **to be crowned with sthg** to be covered with sthg at the top □ *His head was crowned with soft white hair.*

◆ **Crown** *n* **the Crown** the monarchy in a particular country □ *a Crown estate/property.*

crown court *n* GB a local court in England or Wales where serious criminal cases are judged.

crowning ['kraʊnɪŋ] *adj* **sb's crowning achievement** sb's best or most important achievement.

crown jewels *npl* the crowns and other jewels and valuable objects that are worn or carried by a king or queen at official ceremonies.

crown prince *n* the prince who will become king when the present king or queen dies.

Crown Prosecution Service *n* **the Crown Prosecution Service** the government department responsible for bringing legal charges for serious crimes in England and Wales.

crow's feet *npl* lines or folds in the skin at the outside corners of the eyes that one usually gets as one becomes older.

crow's nest *n* a small box high up on the mast of a ship from which one can look for land, danger etc.

crucial ['kruːʃl] *adj* [decision, factor, moment] that is extremely important, because the success of something depends on it □ *This deal is crucial to* OR *for the future of the company.* □ *It is absolutely crucial that no one else hears about this.*

crucially ['kruːʃlɪ] *adv* **to be crucially important** to be very important.

crucible ['kruːsəbl] *n* a container used to heat metals to very high temperatures.

crucifix ['kruːsəfɪks] *n* a cross with a figure of Christ on it.

Crucifixion [,kruːsə'fɪkʃn] *n* **the Crucifixion** the death of Christ by being crucified.

crucify ['kruːsɪfaɪ] (*pt* & *pp* **crucified**) *vt* -1. to kill <sb> by tying or nailing them to a cross. -2. to treat, defeat, or criticize <sb> very severely (informal use) □ *He'll be crucified in the press for this.*

crude [kruːd] ◇ *adj* -1. [sugar, rubber] that is in its natural state and is not yet treated and cannot be used □ *The crude oil is piped ashore to a refinery.* -2. [person, joke, remark] rude and vulgar □ *There's no need to be so crude, Roger.* -3. [sketch, guess] that is not completely accurate because it has been made quickly, is not finished, or is not skilled □ *Making a crude guess, I'd say there were over 50 people there.* ◇ *n* crude oil.

crudely ['kruːdlɪ] *adv* [behave, express, sketch] see **crude** □ *a crudely carved sculpture* □ *Put crudely, they want more money.*

crude oil *n* oil that is in the natural state in which it comes from the ground.

cruel [kruːəl] (*compar* **crueller**, *superl* **cruellest**) *adj* -1. [person, treatment, remark] that deliberately causes pain or suffering □ *Don't be cruel to animals.* -2. [disappointment, winter, wind] that causes pain or suffering □ *Losing the contract was a cruel blow for the company.*

cruelly ['kruːəlɪ] *adv* [treat, speak] see **cruel** □ *They were cruelly tortured.* □ *His hopes were cruelly shattered.*

cruelty ['kruːəltɪ] *n* cruel behavior or actions □ *They argue that such practices expose the animals to unnecessary cruelty.*

cruet ['kruːət] *n* a stand containing pots or bottles of salt, pepper, oil, vinegar etc that is put on a table at mealtimes.

Cruft's [krʌfts] *n* an annual competition for dogs in Britain, where prizes are given for the best dog in each breed.

cruise [kruːz] ◇ *n* a vacation spent traveling on a large ship □ *We're going on a cruise.* ◇ *vi* -1. [ship, passenger] to sail from one place to another on a cruise □ *I like the idea of cruising around the Caribbean for a few weeks.* -2. [car, plane] to move at a speed that is quite fast but that can be continued over a long distance □ *We will be cruising at an altitude of 30,000 feet.*

cruise missile *n* a missile which carries a nuclear bomb, flies quite low, and is guided by its own computer.

cruiser ['kruːzər] *n* -1. MILITARY a large fast warship. -2. SAILING a motorboat that has a room where people can sleep and eat and is used for pleasure trips.

crumb [krʌm] *n* -1. [of bread, cake, a cookie] a very small piece of dry food □ *You left crumbs all over the table.* -2. **a crumb of knowledge/information etc** a very small amount of knowledge/information etc, especially when it is not enough to be useful □ *He hung on, waiting for whatever crumbs of information the hospital might be able to give.*

crumble ['krʌmbl] ◇ *n* a dessert of cooked fruit covered with a loose mixture of butter, flour, and sugar □ *apple/rhubarb crumble.* ◇ *vt* [bread, cheese] to break <sthg> into very small pieces. ◇ *vi* **-1.** [building, plaster, cliff] to break slowly into pieces because it is weak or old □ *We came across the crumbling ruins of a church.* **-2.** [relationship, hope, opposition] to become slowly weaker and start to fail or disappear □ *Support for the party is crumbling.*

crumbly ['krʌmblɪ] (*compar* **crumblier**, *superl* **crumbliest**) *adj* [bread, cake] that one thinks is easily broken into little pieces.

crummy ['krʌmɪ] (*compar* **crummier**, *superl* **crummiest**) *adj* [place, book, idea] that is of poor quality (informal use).

crumpet ['krʌmpət] *n* GB a flat and round kind of bread with holes in one side that is eaten hot with butter.

crumple ['krʌmpl] ◇ *vt* [clothes, paper] to crush or squash <sthg> so that it has a lot of lines or folds □ *He was wearing a crumpled shirt.* ◇ *vi* **-1.** [clothes, car] *This skirt crumples easily.* **-2.** [person] to suddenly fall or lie down because one is weak, helpless, or has had a shock; [team, regime] to suddenly become weak and so be easily defeated □ *She crumpled on the sofa in exhaustion.* □ *The army crumpled under the attack.*

◆ **crumple up** *vt sep* **to crumple sthg up** [clothes, paper] to crumple sthg □ *She crumpled up the letter and threw it on the fire.*

crunch [krʌntʃ] ◇ *vt* **-1.** [cracker, bone] to crush <food> noisily with one's teeth □ *He sat crunching a cookie.* **-2.** [gravel, snow] to cause <sthg hard or rough> to make a noise by stepping on it, driving over it, crushing it etc. ◇ *n* the sound of something being crunched □ *There was a crunch of gears and the car raced away.* ■ **if/when it comes to the crunch...** if/when the important time comes when one has to decide or take action... □ *I can't find work, but if it came to the crunch I could always go back to teaching.*

crunchy ['krʌntʃɪ] (*compar* **crunchier**, *superl* **crunchiest**) *adj* **-1.** [apple, cracker] that makes a noise when it is eaten because it is hard. **-2.** [gravel, snow] that crunches when somebody steps or drives on it.

crusade [kruː'seɪd] ◇ *n* **-1.** HISTORY one of the wars fought by Christians to win Jerusalem and Palestine from the Muslims between about 1100 and 1300 AD. **-2.** a campaign to improve the way people live or behave □ *The government has launched a crusade against crime.* □ *They're on a moral/political crusade.* ◇ *vi* **to crusade for/against sthg** to lead or take part in a crusade for/against sthg.

crusader [kruː'seɪdər] *n* **-1.** HISTORY a Christian soldier who went on a crusade. **-2.** [for change, against war] a person who takes part in a campaign to improve the way people live or behave □ *a human rights crusader.*

crush [krʌʃ] ◇ *n* **-1.** a crowd of people packed tightly together in a way that makes it difficult to move □ *I forced my way through the* crush. **-2. to have a crush on sb** to have an uncontrolled feeling of love for sb, especially an older person, that does not last (informal use). **-3. orange/lemon crush** GB a drink made from orange/lemon juice, sugar, and water.

◇ *vt* **-1.** [car, hat] to push or press <sthg> so that it becomes flat, broken, or damaged □ *The box got crushed in the mail.* □ *He was crushed to death by falling rocks.* **-2.** [seeds, garlic] to make <sthg> into a powder or paste by squashing it. **-3.** [army, opposition, hopes] to defeat or destroy <sthg> completely □ *The army was sent to crush the rebels.*

crush barrier *n* GB a strong fence used in a stadium, street etc to stop people from becoming crushed in a crowd.

crushing ['krʌʃɪŋ] *adj* **-1.** [defeat, blow] that destroys somebody's hopes completely. **-2.** [remark, indifference] that makes one feel very hurt, upset, or embarrassed.

crust [krʌst] *n* **-1.** [on bread] the hard outer covering of a loaf of bread □ *a piece of crust.* **-2.** [on a pie] a layer of pastry on a pie, tart etc □ *the pie crust.* **-3.** [on a surface] a hard covering that has formed on top of something or on the outside of it □ *There was a crust of ice on the window.* □ *the Earth's crust.*

crustacean [krʌ'steɪʃn] *n* an animal such as a crab, shrimp, or lobster that has a hard outer shell and usually lives in water.

crusty ['krʌstɪ] (*compar* **crustier**, *superl* **crustiest**) *adj* **-1.** [food] that has a hard crust. **-2.** [person] who is bad-tempered.

crutch [krʌtʃ] *n* **-1.** [for walking] a stick with a piece at the top that fits under the arm and is used by injured people as a support when walking □ *He was walking on* OR *with crutches.* **-2.** [for help] a person or thing that provides help or support (disapproving use) □ *She uses her mother as an emotional crutch.* **-3.** [of one's body, a pair of pants] = **crotch.**

crux [krʌks] *n* **the crux of the issue/problem etc** the most important or difficult part of the issue/problem etc □ *Now we come to the crux of the matter: how much will it cost?*

cry [kraɪ] (*pl* **cries**, *pt* & *pp* **cried**) ◇ *vi* **-1.** [person] to produce tears because one is sad, in pain, scared, laughing etc □ *The baby was crying for its mother.* □ *I cried with pain.* **-2.** [person] to shout □ *He cried for help.*

◇ *n* **-1. to have a cry** to cry because one is sad, in pain, or scared □ *You'll feel better if you have a good cry.* **-2.** [of a person] a shout or loud call □ *a cry of pain* □ *a cry for help.* ■ **to be a far cry from sthg** to be very different from sthg □ *The hotel was a far cry from what the brochure had promised.* **-3.** [of a bird, animal] the sound made by some birds and animals, especially if it is loud and high-pitched.

◇ *vt* **-1. to cry tears of joy/relief** to cry because one is happy/relieved. ■ **to cry oneself to sleep** to cry until one falls asleep. **-2.** to shout <sthg> □ *"Help!" he cried.*

◆ **cry off** *vi* GB to say that one will not do something that one has promised or agreed to do □ *I arranged an interview with her but she cried off at the last moment.*

◆ **cry out** ◇ *vt sep* **to cry sthg out** to shout or call sthg suddenly and loudly □ *"Be careful!" he cried out.* ◇ *vi* to shout, call, or make a sound suddenly and loudly because of fear, excitement, or surprise □ *She cried out in pain when I tried to lift her.*

◆ **cry out for** *vt fus* **to be crying out for sthg** to need sthg very much and very soon □ *The system is crying out for change.*

crybaby ['kraɪbeɪbɪ] (*pl* **crybabies**) *n* a person, especially a child, who cries too much and without a good reason (informal and disapproving use).

crying ['kraɪɪŋ] ◇ *adj* **-1. it's a crying shame** a phrase used to show that one thinks something is wrong or unfair (informal use) □ *It's a crying shame, the way she treats her husband.* **-2. a crying need for sthg** a very great and urgent need for sthg □ *There is a crying need for reforms.* ◇ *n* the act of crying or the sound of somebody crying □ *I could hear crying coming from the next room.*

crypt [krɪpt] *n* a room under a church.

cryptic ['krɪptɪk] *adj* [message, comment, smile] that is mysterious because its meaning is hidden or difficult to understand.

crypto- ['krɪptəʊ] *prefix* added to words to mean secret □ *a crypto-communist/crypto-fascist.*

crystal ['krɪstl] *n* **-1.** a hard object with many flat sides that forms naturally when substances such as minerals or sugar become solid □ *a rock/quartz crystal* □ *ice/sugar crystals.* **-2.** high-quality colorless glass that is used to make bowls, wine glasses etc and whose surface is often cut so that it shines in the light □ *lead crystal* □ *a crystal chandelier/bowl.*

crystal ball *n* a clear glass ball in which fortune-tellers try to see future events.

crystal clear *adj* **-1.** [water, air, glass] that is completely clear and bright, and that one can see through. **-2.** [meaning, statement] that is completely clear, so that there is no doubt or misunderstanding □ *I have made my reasons crystal clear.* **-3.** [voice, sound] that is heard very clearly.

crystallize, -ise ['krɪstəlaɪz] ◇ *vi* **-1.** [liquid, substance] to form crystals. **-2.** [idea, plan] to become clear, fixed, and definite in somebody's mind. ◇ *vt* [idea, plan] to cause <sthg> to crystallize.

crystallized ['krɪstəlaɪzd] *adj* **crystallized fruit** fruit that has been preserved by covering it with sugar □ *crystallized orange/ginger.*

CSC (*abbr of* **Civil Service Commission**) *n* **the CSC** the British government department responsible for recruiting civil servants.

CS gas *n* a type of tear gas that is used by the police to stop riots and makes one's eyes water and makes breathing difficult.

CST (*abbr of* **Central Standard Time**) *n* the local winter time in the central USA and Canada; the local time in central Australia.

ct *abbr of* **carat**.

CT *abbr of* **Connecticut**.

CTC *n abbr of* **city technology college**.

CTP (*abbr of* **compulsory third party**) *n* car insurance that all drivers in Australia must have.

cu. *abbr of* **cubic**.

cub [kʌb] *n* **-1.** a young fox, bear, lion etc □ *a tiger cub.* **-2.** = **Cub Scout**.

Cuba ['kjuːbə] a country in the Caribbean, south of Florida. The largest island in the West Indies, it has been a Communist country since 1959. SIZE: 111,000 sq kms. POPULATION: 10,700,000 (*Cubans*). CAPITAL: Havana. LANGUAGE: Spanish. CURRENCY: Cuban peso.

Cuban ['kjuːbən] *n* & *adj*: *see* **Cuba**.

Cuban missile crisis *n* **the Cuban missile crisis** a period of tension between the USA and the USSR in 1962, when the USSR started to build military bases for nuclear missiles in Cuba. As a result of threats by the USA, the USSR removed the bases.

cubbyhole ['kʌbɪhəʊl] *n* a very small room or space for storing things in (informal use).

cube [kjuːb] ◇ *n* **-1.** a shape or object that has six square sides all of the same size □ *a sugar cube.* **-2.** MATH the number made by multiplying a number by itself twice □ *The cube of 3 is 27.* ◇ *vt* MATH to calculate the cube of <a number> □ *3 cubed is 27.*

cube root *n* the number that makes a particular number when it is cubed □ *3 is the cube root of 27.*

cubic ['kjuːbɪk] *adj* **a cubic centimeter/foot etc** a unit used for measuring the space inside something, equal in size to a cube whose sides are all a centimeter/foot etc long.

cubicle ['kjuːbɪkl] *n* a very small room shaped like a box and separated from the rest of a larger room, e.g. for dressing and undressing at a swimming pool.

Cubism ['kjuːbɪzm] *n* an early 20th-century style of painting developed by Picasso and Braque that presents objects as simple geometrical shapes.

Cubist ['kjuːbəst] *n* an artist who uses Cubism.

cub reporter *n* a young journalist who is still learning their job.

Cub Scout *n* a member of the Cub Scouts, an organization for boys aged 8–11 that teaches boys practical skills and organizes outdoor activities.

cuckoo ['kʊkuː] *n* a gray European bird that has a call that sounds like "cuckoo" and lays its eggs in other birds' nests.

cuckoo clock *n* a type of clock that has a wooden cuckoo that comes out and says "cuckoo" every hour.

cucumber ['kjuːkʌmbər] *n* a long thin vegetable that is dark green on the outside, light green inside, and is eaten raw in salads.

cud [kʌd] *n* **to chew the cud** [cow] to chew food slowly in the mouth again after already having swallowed it once.

cuddle ['kʌdl] ◇ *vt* to put one's arm around <sb/sthg> and hold them close to show love, sympathy etc. ◊ *vi: They sat cuddling on the sofa.* ◊ *n* an act of cuddling somebody or something □ *She gave him a cuddle.*

◆ **cuddle up** *vi* [people] to sit or lie close together, holding each other □ *Jonathon cuddled up to me and fell asleep.*

cuddly ['kʌdlɪ] (*compar* **cuddlier,** *superl* **cuddliest**) *adj* [person, animal] that is small, soft, and harmless and looks pleasant to cuddle □ *He's so cute and cuddly!*

cuddly toy *n* a soft furry children's toy such as a teddy bear.

cudgel ['kʌdʒəl] (US *pt* & *pp* **cudgeled,** *cont* **cudgeling,** GB *pt* & *pp* **cudgelled,** *cont* **cudgelling**) ◊ *n* a short, thick, heavy stick used as a weapon. ■ **to take up the cudgels for sb/sthg** to support or defend sb/sthg strongly. ◊ *vt* to hit <sb> with a cudgel.

cue [kjuː] *n* **-1.** THEATER a word or action from one actor that is a signal for another actor to speak or do something □ *That's the cue for Simon to come on.* ■ **on cue** exactly at the expected or most appropriate moment □ *We were talking about John when, right on cue, he came in through the door.* ■ **to take one's cue from sb** to follow the way sb behaves or reacts by behaving or reacting in the same way □ *The audience took its cue from the chairman and started to applaud.* **-2.** [for a new event, situation] an event or situation that acts as a signal for something else □ *I took it as my cue to leave.* □ *The fall in spending could be a cue for inflation to ease.* **-3.** SPORT a long wooden stick used for hitting the ball in snooker, pool etc.

cuff [kʌf] ◊ *n* **-1.** [of a shirt] the end of a sleeve, especially a shirt sleeve, where it goes around the wrist □ *a shirt cuff.* **-2.** US [on trousers] the bottom of a trouser leg where the material is turned upwards □ *a trouser cuff.* **-3.** [with one's hand] the act of hitting somebody lightly. ◊ *vt* to hit <sb> lightly with one's hand, especially on the head.

cuff link *n* one of a pair of small decorative objects that can be attached to shirt cuffs to fasten them □ *a pair of gold cuff links.*

cu. in. *abbr of* **cubic inch(es).**

cuisine [kwɪˈziːn] *n* the style of cooking of a particular country, region, restaurant etc □ *I love Italian cuisine.*

cul-de-sac ['kʌldəsæk] *n* a street that is only open to traffic at one end.

culinary [US 'kʌlənerɪ, GB -ɪnərɪ] *adj* [skills, expertise] that is connected with cooking □ *We had a chance to sample the local culinary delights.*

cull [kʌl] ◊ *vt* **-1.** [seals, deer] to reduce the numbers of <a group of animals> by killing some of them. **-2.** [facts, details] to collect <information> from different sources and choose the useful parts □ *The data is culled from a number of official reports.* ◊ *n* an operation to cull seals, deer etc □ *a seal cull.*

culminate ['kʌlmɪneɪt] ◆ **culminate in** *vt fus* **to culminate in sthg** [in disaster, triumph] to result in sthg important after a period of gradual development □ *The series of one-day stoppages culminated in an all-out strike.*

culmination [ˌkʌlmɪˈneɪʃn] *n* **the culmination of sthg** [of a period, process] something important that happens at the end of a long period of activity □ *The award was the culmination of his life's work.*

culottes [US 'kuːlɒts, GB kjuːˈlɒts] *npl* wide knee-length or short trousers that look like a skirt and are worn by women □ *a pair of culottes.*

culpable ['kʌlpəbl] *adj* **-1.** [person, negligence] that deserves blame (formal use). **-2. culpable homicide** LAW manslaughter.

culprit ['kʌlprɪt] *n* a person who has committed a particular crime or done something wrong □ *The money is missing but we know who the culprit is.*

cult [kʌlt] *n* **-1.** RELIGION a religious group that is often small and secretive and has its own rituals and beliefs, especially when these are considered strange or dangerous by most of society. **-2.** a person, movie, activity etc that is very popular or fashionable among a particular group in society, especially among young people □ *a cult figure/movie* □ *The band has a cult following among the young.*

cultivate ['kʌltɪveɪt] *vt* **-1.** FARMING to prepare and use <land> for growing crops; to grow <a crop>. **-2.** [friendship, skill] to try hard to improve or develop <sthg> □ *My job is to cultivate links with potential overseas partners.* □ *a carefully cultivated image.* **-3.** [person] to try to win the friendship or support of <sb>, usually in order to gain some advantage.

cultivated ['kʌltɪveɪtəd] *adj* **-1.** [land, plant] that is developed or grown by a farmer □ *a patch of cultivated land.* **-2.** [person, accent] that shows good manners, taste, and education.

cultivation [ˌkʌltɪˈveɪʃn] *n* [of land, crops, a skill] *see* **cultivate** □ *Hundreds of acres have been brought under cultivation.*

cultural ['kʌltʃrəl] *adj* [difference, event, activity] that is connected with the culture of a particular group of people □ *India has a great cultural diversity/heritage.* □ *My cultural background is mixed.*

culture ['kʌltʃəʳ] *n* **-1.** [of a group of people] the way of life, ideas, traditions, arts etc produced and shared by a particular group of people □ *We are all products of our culture.* □ *Their songs have become part of popular culture.* □ *Japanese culture is very different in this respect.* **-2.** [in a part of the world] a society that shares a particular culture □ *all cultures of the world practice some form of religion* □ *a primitive culture.* **-3.** ARTS art, music, literature, and all other aspects of society that require education and thought □ *There isn't much culture in the town where I live.* □ *a center of culture.* **-4.** BIOLOGY a group of bacteria, cells etc grown in a laboratory, e.g. to see whether a disease is present.

cultured ['kʌltʃəʳd] *adj* [person] who is well-educated and knows a lot about literature, art etc □ *She comes from a very cultured background.*

cultured pearl *n* a pearl produced artificially by putting a piece of sand into an oyster.

culture shock *n* the confusion, loneliness etc felt by somebody who has moved from one country to live in another one that has a different culture.

culture vulture *n* a person who is always eager to attend concerts, visit exhibitions, read books etc (informal and disapproving use).

culvert ['kʌlvəʳt] *n* a pipe that carries water under a road, railroad etc.

cumbersome ['kʌmbəʳsəm] *adj* -1. [package, machine] big, heavy, and difficult to carry or handle □ *These suitcases are too cumbersome for traveling around with.* -2. [system, process] slow, complicated, and inefficient □ *I find their accounting methods outdated and cumbersome.*

Cumbria ['kʌmbrɪə] a county in northwestern England. SIZE: 6,810 sq kms. POPULATION: 486,900. ADMINISTRATIVE CENTER: Carlisle.

cumin ['kʌmɪn] *n* a dark-yellow spice that has a sweet smell and is used especially in Indian cooking.

cummings ['kʌmɪŋz], **e. e.** (1894–1962) a US poet known for his experimental style.

cumulative ['kjuːmjələtɪv] *adj* [interest, effect] that increases gradually over a period of time □ *The changes are cumulative, and are far-reaching when taken together.*

cunning ['kʌnɪŋ] ◇ *adj* [person] who is clever and is able to deceive people in order to get things □ *It was a cunning trick/plan.* ◇ *n* the ability of somebody to be cunning □ *a man of great cunning.*

cup [kʌp] (*pt* & *pp* **cupped**, *cont* **cupping**) ◇ *n* -1. [for a drink] a small round container that is made of pottery, usually has a small handle, and is used for drinking hot drinks; a small round container made of paper or plastic that has no handle, is used for any drink, and is thrown away after it has been used □ *a paper/plastic cup.* -2. [of coffee, tea] a drink contained in a cup □ *Would you like a cup of coffee/tea?* ■ **it's not my cup of tea** a phrase used to say that something is not the kind of thing that one likes. -3. [for measuring] the amount that a cup holds □ *Mix one cup of sugar and two cups of flour.* -4. SPORT a decorative metal bowl or cup given as a prize to the winner of a competition; a competition to win this □ *Hungary reached the fifth round of the World Cup.* -5. [of a bra] one of the two parts of a bra that covers a woman's breasts □ *What is your cup size, ma'am?* □ *a bra cup.* ◇ *vt* **to cup one's hands** to put one's hands together in the shape of a cup or bowl.

cupboard ['kʌbəʳd] *n* -1. a piece of furniture fixed to a wall that has one or two doors, often with shelves inside, and is used for storing clothes, food, tools etc □ *a kitchen cupboard* □ *a wall cupboard.* -2. GB a small part of a room that has one or two doors and is used for storing things □ *a broom cupboard* □ *There's a cupboard under the stairs.*

cupcake ['kʌpkeɪk] *n* a small sweet cake baked in a paper container shaped like a cup and covered with frosting □ *a cupcake tin.*

Cup Final *n* **the Cup Final** the final game to decide the winners of an annual soccer competition.

cup holder *n* SPORT a team that is the champion of a sport at a particular time and has been given a trophy as a prize.

Cupid ['kjuːpɪd] the Roman god of romantic love, usually shown as a boy with wings and a bow and arrow. When the arrow hits somebody's heart, they fall in love.

cupola ['kjuːpələ] (*pl* **cupolas**) *n* a small dome on the top of a roof or larger dome.

cup tie *n* GB a game, especially in soccer, between two teams that are competing in a competition for which the prize is a trophy.

curable ['kjʊərəbl] *adj* [illness, disease] that can be cured.

curate ['kjʊərət] *n* a priest who helps the main priest of a church in a particular area.

curator [kjʊ'reɪtəʳ] *n* the person who is in charge of the objects in a museum, art gallery etc.

curb [kɜːʳb] ◇ *n* -1. US the raised edge of a sidewalk where it meets the road. -2. a way of limiting or controlling something in order to prevent it from increasing or continuing □ *They ought to put a curb on cheap imported goods.* ◇ *vt* [spending, powers] to control or limit <sthg> in order to reduce it □ *He did his best to curb his son's extravagances.*

curd cheese [ˌkɜːʳd-] *n* GB a soft, white, mild cheese made from sour milk.

curdle ['kɜːʳdl] *vi* [milk, cream] to become thicker and form lumps, e.g. as a result of being left to go sour.

cure [kjʊəʳ] ◇ *n* -1. MEDICINE a medicine or treatment that cures an illness □ *As yet, there is no cure for Alzheimer's disease.* -2. a solution to a problem, difficulty etc □ *There is no easy cure for the country's economic ills.* ◇ *vt* -1. MEDICINE to make <a sick person> better by medical or other treatment; to cause a person to no longer have <an illness> □ *He was cured of cancer.* □ *It was the antibiotics that cured me.* □ *a disease that cannot be cured.* -2. [problem, difficulty] to cause <sthg bad> to stop □ *At least it's cured his habit of smoking at mealtimes.* -3. **to cure sb of sthg** to cause sb to no longer be influenced by sthg □ *It cured me of any ideas I had about being a teacher.* -4. [meat, fish] to preserve <food> by hanging it to dry, smoking it, or salting it □ *a piece of cured pork.*

cure-all *n* something that people think can cure any illness, problem etc □ *They look upon low inflation as a kind of general cure-all.*

curfew ['kɜːʳfjuː] *n* a rule or law that forbids people to be outside their houses after a certain time of day, usually from when it is dark until the next morning □ *The military government imposed a curfew.*

Curie ['kjʊərɪ], **Marie** (1867–1934) a French scientist, born in Poland. With her husband, Pierre, she studied radioactivity, and discovered the elements radium and polonium.

curio ['kjʊərɪoʊ] (*pl* **curios**) *n* a small object

such as an ornament that is valued because it is unusual, rare, or beautiful.

curiosity [ˌkjʊərɪ'ɒsətɪ] *n* -1. the desire to know about somebody or something □ *I'd like to see the house, just out of curiosity.* -2. a rare and unusual object □ *The shop was full of curiosities.*

curious ['kjʊərɪəs] *adj* -1. [person] who wants to know about somebody or something because they are interested □ *I'm curious to know why he was late.* □ *I'm curious about his past life.* -2. [noise, coincidence, object] that seems strange and unusual □ *I saw a very curious sight as I crossed the bridge.*

curiously ['kjʊərɪəslɪ] *adv* -1. [look, watch, ask] with a desire to know more about something □ *She stared curiously at the child.* -2. **curiously (enough),...** a phrase used to introduce a fact that one finds strange or unusual □ *Curiously enough, they had already met.*

curl [kɜːrl] ◇ *n* -1. a piece of hair that is not straight but forms a curved or circular shape □ *Her hair fell in dark curls over her shoulders.* -2. a shape similar to that of a curl of hair □ *A curl of smoke rose above the house.*
◇ *vt* -1. to make curls in <sb's hair> □ *I went to the hairdresser's and had my hair curled.* -2. to move <sthg> so that it makes a curved shape □ *The cat curled its tail around its body.*
◇ *vi* -1. [hair] to form curls. -2. [leaf, paper] to change shape so that the edges move toward the center in a curl. ■ **to curl into a ball** [person, animal] to lie with the body rolled up, forming a rounded shape. -3. [snake, tail] to move in a way that forms curved shapes □ *Smoke curled from the chimney.*
◆ **curl up** *vi* [person, animal] to lie in a way that forms a curved shape with the legs pulled closely to the rest of the body □ *I like nothing better than to curl up with a good book.*

curler ['kɜːrlər] *n* a small hollow cylinder made of metal or plastic that one rolls wet hair around so that it dries in the shape of a curl.

curling ['kɜːrlɪŋ] *n* a winter sport played in countries such as Scotland and Canada that consists of sliding heavy stones across ice toward a target.

curling irons US, **curling tongs** GB *npl* a heated metal rod with a flat movable part on the side that is used to hold wet hair in place and make it curly as it dries.

curly ['kɜːrlɪ] (*compar* **curlier**, *superl* **curliest**) *adj* [hair] that is not straight but forms curved or circular shapes.

currant [US 'kɜːrənt, GB 'kʌr-] *n* -1. a small dried grape that is often used in making cakes, cookies etc □ *a currant bun.* -2. the small round fruit of one of a number of bushes.

currency [US 'kɜːrənsɪ, GB 'kʌr-] (*pl* **currencies**) *n* -1. the type of money that is used in a particular country □ *The yen was up two points against a wide range of currencies.* □ *the currency markets* □ *foreign/local currency.* -2. **to gain currency** to become accepted and popular with

an increasing number of people □ *His ideas have gained currency over the years.*

current [US 'kɜːrənt, GB 'kʌr-] ◇ *adj* [year, price, crisis] that is happening, exists etc now but is certain or likely to change in the future □ *We are confident of surviving the current recession.* □ *The practice is no longer current over here.*
◇ *n* -1. [of water, air] the continuous movement of water, air, or gas in a particular direction □ *Be careful, there's a strong current.* -2. [of opinion, thought] the pattern of the way a situation, set of opinions etc is changing □ *The policy goes against the current of public opinion.* -3. ELECTRICITY the flow of electricity through a conductor such as a wire □ *The electric current was getting weaker.*

current account *n* GB a type of bank account that earns little or no interest and from which one can take money at any time using a check or card.

current affairs *npl* events, especially in politics, that are considered important and receive attention in newspapers, on TV etc.

current assets *npl* financial assets that can be changed into cash within a year.

current liabilities *npl* the debts of a company that must be paid within a year.

currently [US 'kɜːrəntlɪ, GB 'kʌr-] *adv* at this particular time □ *He's currently chairman of the board.* □ *Talks are currently in progress.*

curriculum [kə'rɪkjələm] (*pl* **curriculums** OR **curricula** [-lə]) *n* the different courses that can be studied at a school, university etc; one of these courses □ *Italian isn't on the school curriculum.*

curriculum vitae [US -'vaɪtɪ, GB -'viːtaɪ] (*pl* **curricula vitae**) *n* → **CV**.

curried [US 'kɜːrɪd, GB 'kʌr-] *adj* **curried chicken/beans etc** chicken/beans etc flavored with curry powder.

curry [US 'kɜːrɪ, GB 'kʌrɪ] (*pl* **curries**) *n* an Indian dish that is made of meat, vegetables etc flavored with spices, and tastes hot.

curry powder *n* a mixture of hot spices made into a powder, used especially in Indian cooking.

curse [kɜːrs] ◇ *n* -1. **to put a curse on sb** to ask God or some magical force to make something unpleasant happen to sb □ *The wicked witch put a curse on the whole land.* -2. a vulgar or offensive word that somebody uses when they are angry □ *He uttered a curse under his breath.* -3. **to be a curse** to be a cause of problems □ *Those rabbits are a real curse, they've eaten all the lettuce.* ◇ *vt* -1. to put a curse on <sb>. -2. to say vulgar or offensive things to <sb> because one is angry with them □ *I cursed the train for being late.*
◇ *vi* to use vulgar or offensive language because one is angry □ *She cursed loudly as she bumped her head on the shelf.*

cursor ['kɜːrsər] *n* COMPUTING a point of light or symbol that can be moved around a screen and is used to indicate where one is working.

cursory ['kɜːʳsrɪ] *adj* [look, glance] that is quick and does not give much attention to detail.

curt [kɜːʳt] *adj* [person, reply, manner] that uses few words and so seems quite rude.

curtail [kɜːʳ'teɪl] *vt* -1. [visit, vacation] to make <sthg> shorter than was planned □ *His career was curtailed by injury.* -2. [spending, service, powers] to reduce or limit <sthg> □ *We need to curtail expenditure.* □ *The new measures are designed to curtail crime severely.*

curtailment [kɜːʳ'teɪlmənt] *n*: see **curtail** □ *The Governor announced the curtailment of privileges long enjoyed by inmates at the prison.*

curtain ['kɜːʳtn] *n* -1. [for a window] a piece of material that hangs in front of a window inside a house, apartment etc to prevent people seeing in or to keep the light out □ *She drew the curtains.* -2. [in a theater] a large piece of material that hangs down from above the stage at a theater and is raised when the play begins □ *As the curtain fell, there was a loud burst of applause.* -3. **a curtain of smoke/dust etc** a layer of smoke/dust etc that one cannot see through □ *We hit a thick curtain of fog as we approached the Bay area.*

◆ **curtain off** *vt sep* **to curtain sthg off** to separate sthg from the rest of a room by using a curtain □ *The bed had been curtained off.*

curtain call *n* the moment at the end of a theater performance when the actors come to the front of the stage to receive the audience's applause.

curtain raiser [-reɪzəʳ] *n* an event that comes before another event that is more important, especially one that is organized.

curts(e)y ['kɜːʳtsɪ] (*pt & pp* **curtsied**) ◇ *n* a sign of respect given by a woman in which she bends her knees, keeping one foot behind the other. ◇ *vi* to make a curtsy.

curvaceous [kɜːʳ'veɪʃəs] *adj* [woman] whose body has curves that make it attractive.

curvature ['kɜːʳvətʃəʳ] *n* [of the Earth, Moon] the curved shape of something. ■ **curvature of the spine** MEDICINE a condition in which the spine is curved in the wrong place.

curve [kɜːʳv] ◇ *n* -1. a line that is not straight at any point and bends smoothly □ *The graph showed a steady upward curve.* □ *The car drove fast, following the curve of the road.* -2. US SPORT a throw in baseball in which the ball curves unexpectedly as it moves through the air. ◇ *vi* [road, river, surface] to form a curve □ *The path curved slightly to the left.*

curved [kɜːʳvd] *adj* [shape, surface, line] that is in the form of a curve.

curvy ['kɜːʳvɪ] (*compar* **curvier**, *superl* **curviest**) *adj* [line, shape] curved; [woman] whose body has curves that make it attractive.

cushion [kʊʃn] ◇ *n* -1. a round or square piece of fabric filled with soft material on which one can sit, rest one's head etc. -2. a layer of something that protects an object or person from the impact of being hit in some way □ *a cushion of air.* ◇ *vt* [impact, shock] to make <sthg violent or unpleasant> feel softer or less severe □ *The snow cushioned his fall.* □ *The reduction in income tax cushioned the blow of an increase in sales tax.* ■ **to cushion sb against sthg** [against change, reality] to protect sb against sthg □ *We've been cushioned against the full effects of the recession.*

cushy ['kʊʃɪ] (*compar* **cushier**, *superl* **cushiest**) *adj* [job, life] that is very easy and involves little effort (informal use) □ *Sean's having a cushy time living with his parents.*

custard ['kʌstəʳd] *n* -1. US a sweet food that consists of a mixture of milk, sugar, and eggs baked until it is solid. -2. GB a sweet yellow sauce made from milk, sugar, eggs, and flour that is put on puddings and fruit.

custard pie *n* an open pie made with custard that is used by clowns, comedians etc to throw at each other on stage.

custard powder *n* a powder that is mixed with milk and sugar to make custard.

Custer ['kʌstəʳ], **General George Armstrong** (1839–1876) a US soldier who was successful in the American Civil War. He was killed by a force of Native Americans at the battle of the Little Bighorn, also known as Custer's Last Stand.

custodian [kʌ'stoʊdjən] *n* a person who is in charge of a building, museum etc.

custody ['kʌstədɪ] *n* -1. the legal right to be responsible for bringing up a child, given to a father or mother in a divorce case □ *She was given custody of the children.* -2. **to be in custody** to be held by the police □ *The suspect is now in police custody.*

custom ['kʌstəm] *n* -1. [of a society] a tradition or usual practice of a particular society or community □ *It's a local/an ancient custom.* □ *It's the custom to write a note of thanks to the hostess.* -2. [of a person] the habit of a particular person (literary use) □ *It's his custom to invite people for a drink before dismissing them.* -3. BUSINESS the act of regularly buying goods or services from a particular store or business □ *Thank you for your custom.*

◆ **customs** *n* the place at the border of a country or at an airport or port where people arriving from a foreign country must declare certain goods that they have brought with them, e.g. alcohol or tobacco, and where officials search baggage to look for these goods □ *We went through customs without any problems.* □ *customs officials.*

customary [US 'kʌstəmerɪ, GB -əmərɪ] *adj* [behavior, way, time] usual and expected □ *You'll need to go through the customary procedures.*

custom-built *adj* [car, machine] that has been built to suit a particular person's needs.

customer ['kʌstəməʳ] *n* -1. a person who buys goods or services from a store or business □ *She's a valued customer.* -2. **an awkward/a strange etc customer** a person who one thinks is awkward/strange etc (informal use).

customer services *npl* a department in a company, store etc that deals with requests, inquiries, and complaints from customers.

customize, -ise ['kʌstəmaɪz] *vt* to make or change <a car, machine> etc to suit a particular person's needs.

custom-made *adj* [shoes, suit, car] made to suit a particular person's needs.

Customs and Excise *n* a British government department that collects duty on imported goods and collects taxes on certain goods made in Britain.

customs duty *n* an amount of money that has to be paid for bringing certain goods from one country into another.

customs officer *n* an official who works at customs.

cut [kʌt] (*pt* & *pp* **cut**, *cont* **cutting**) ◇ *vt* -1. [bread, meat] to separate <sthg> into pieces using a knife or other sharp instrument; [slice, piece] to separate <one piece of sthg> from the rest, using a knife or other sharp instrument □ *Cut the cake in half/in three pieces.* □ *She cut her articles from the paper.* -2. [finger, leg, wrists] to wound <a part of one's body> by making an opening in the skin □ *He fell and cut his knee.* □ *I cut myself with the can opener.* -3. [prices, workforce] to reduce <sthg> □ *We cut our costs by half.* □ *They will cut taxes in the run-up to the election.* -4. [grass, hair] to make <sthg> shorter by removing part of it using a sharp tool □ *He was cutting his toenails.* □ *You've had your hair cut.* -5. [article, film] to remove part of <sthg> before it is published or broadcast; [line, scene] to remove <sthg> so that it is not published or broadcast □ *The censors cut all scenes of violence.* -6. **to cut a tooth** [child] to grow a tooth □ *The baby is cutting his first tooth.* -7. **to cut the cards** to divide a pack of cards into two sections before starting to play. -8. [meeting, class] to be deliberately absent from <sthg>.
◇ *vi* -1. [knife, blade] to make an opening in something, or to remove a piece of something when pressed into it; [bread, cake] to be able to be cut □ *These scissors don't cut very well.* □ *The rope cut into my wrists.* □ *This meat cuts easily.* -2. CINEMA to stop filming a scene □ *"Cut!" cried the director.*
◇ *n* -1. [in wood, cloth] a narrow opening made by cutting; [in skin, a finger] a narrow wound □ *She had a nasty cut on her leg.* -2. [of beef, lamb] a piece of meat that has been cut in a particular way, usually before cooking. -3. [in salary, personnel] a reduction; [in an article, a film] a part of something that is removed before it is published or broadcast □ *He is calling for cuts in government spending/tax cuts.* -4. [of the deal, the spoils] a share (informal use) □ *What's his cut (of the profits)?* -5. [of hair, clothes] the shape or style of something. -6. *phrase* **a cut above the rest** better than the other things or people □ *Nine Elms is full of good restaurants but this one is a cut above the rest.*

◆ **cut across** *vt fus* -1. **to cut across sthg** [across a field, forest] to go across sthg instead of around it, in order to save time □ *We got there early by cutting across the square.* -2. [across party lines, social divisions] to affect people on both sides of <sthg> □ *The issue cuts across party lines.*

◆ **cut back** *vt sep* -1. **to cut sthg back** [tree, bush] to remove some of the branches of sthg. -2. **to cut sthg back** [expenditure, budget] to reduce sthg □ *The factory is cutting back production.* ◇ *vi* [on education, advertising] to spend less money on sthg; [on spending, staff] to reduce sthg □ *They had to cut back on business travel.* □ *We are cutting back at the moment.*

◆ **cut down** ◇ *vt sep* -1. **to cut a tree down** to cut through the trunk of a tree until it falls to the ground. -2. **to cut sthg down** [expenses, intake] to reduce sthg □ *He cut his smoking down to ten a day.* ◇ *vi* **to cut down on sthg** [on smoking, drinking, spending] to do less of sthg □ *They have cut down on eating out in restaurants.*

◆ **cut in** *vi* -1. [in a conversation] to interrupt □ *She cut in on their discussion.* -2. [in a car] to move into a different lane in front of a moving vehicle □ *The taxi cut in on them.* -3. SPORT to move in front of another player or players moving in the same direction.

◆ **cut off** *vt sep* -1. **to cut sthg off** [finger, branch, piece of meat] to remove sthg by cutting □ *They cut the king's head off.* □ *She cut off a big lump of cheese.* -2. **to cut sthg off** [gas, electricity] to stop the supply of sthg □ *They've had their water cut off.* □ *They have cut off all military aid to the region.* ■ **to be cut off** [on the telephone] to lose one's connection □ *"What happened?" — "I don't know, we just got cut off."* -3. **to be cut off** [place] to have no contact with other places, because they are far away or difficult to reach; [person] to have no contact with other people □ *The house was cut off by snow drifts.* □ *He felt cut off from his family.*

◆ **cut out** ◇ *vt sep* -1. **to cut sthg out** [photograph, tumor] to remove sthg by cutting □ *advertisements cut out of magazines.* -2. SEWING **to cut sthg out** [pattern, dress] to make sthg into a particular shape by cutting. -3. **to be cut out for sthg** to have the necessary qualities or abilities for sthg □ *He's not cut out to be a politician.* -4. **to cut sthg out** [smoking, drinking] to stop doing sthg; [meat, chocolate] to stop eating sthg. ■ **cut it out!** stop it! (informal use). -5. **to cut sthg out** [light, sound] to prevent sthg from reaching somewhere □ *The blinds cut out the sunlight.* -6. **to cut sb out of one's will** to remove sb's name from one's will. ◇ *vi* [engine] to stop working.

◆ **cut up** *vt sep* **to cut sthg up** [meat, vegetables] to cut sthg into small pieces.

cut-and-dried *adj* [argument, result] clear and definite □ *There is no cut-and-dried solution to this issue.*

cut and paste COMPUTING ◇ *vi* to take pieces of text from one part of a document and put them in another part. ◇ *vt* to cut and paste in order to move <text>.

cutback ['kʌtbæk] *n* a reduction in the amount of money that is spent on something □ *cutbacks in defense/health/education.*

cute [kju:t] *adj* [child, dress, animal] that one thinks is pretty and has an innocent or simple quality □ *What a cute little girl!*

cut glass *n* glass that is decorated with patterns that have been cut into it □ *a cut-glass bowl.*

cuticle ['kju:tɪkl] *n* an area of dead skin at the lower part of a fingernail or toenail.

cutlery ['kʌtlərɪ] *n* GB a collective term for knives, forks, spoons etc that are used for eating.

cutlet ['kʌtlət] *n* -1. a small piece of meat, e.g. lamb or pork, joined to a bone. -2. **a nut/vegetable cutlet** a flat mass of chopped nuts/vegetables that is grilled or fried.

cut lunch *n* AUS a light lunch, usually of sandwiches (informal use).

cutoff (point) ['kʌtɒf-] *n* a point or level that one fixes and decides not to go beyond □ *Our cutoff is $45,000 — we can't afford any more.*

cutout ['kʌtaʊt] *n* -1. a device in a machine that automatically stops the machine functioning when there is a fault or if there is too much electric current passing through it □ *a cutout switch/mechanism.* -2. a shape that has been cut from paper, card etc □ *a cardboard cutout.*

cut-rate US, **cut-price** *adj* [offer, goods, gasoline] sold at a reduced price □ *a store offering cut-rate cigarettes.*

cutter ['kʌtər] *n* a tool that is used for cutting things such as wire or glass.

cutthroat ['kʌtθrəʊt] *adj* [competition, campaign] that is aggressive and shows a great determination to succeed □ *The price war is becoming increasingly cutthroat.*

cutting ['kʌtɪŋ] ◇ *adj* [comment, remark] that is unkind and is intended to hurt somebody □ *Nathan can be very cutting at times, but don't let it get to you.* ◇ *n* -1. [of a plant] a part of a plant, e.g. a leaf or part of a stem, that is put in soil or water to grow into a new plant. -2. [from a newspaper, magazine] an article, piece of news, photograph etc that has been cut out of a newspaper or magazine. -3. GB [in a hill] an area of land cut from a hill to allow a road or railroad to pass through □ *a railway cutting.*

cuttlefish ['kʌtlfɪʃ] (*pl* **cuttlefish**) *n* a sea creature with a broad soft body, tentacles, and a flat bony part inside.

CV (*abbr of* **curriculum vitae**) *n* a summary of one's education, background, achievements, and employment history that one sends to a company, institution etc when one is trying to get a job.

C & W *n abbr of* **country and western (music)**.

cwo (*abbr of* **cash with order**) a term that indicates that something has to be paid for in cash when the order is placed.

cwt. *abbr of* **hundredweight**.

cyanide ['saɪənaɪd] *n* a strong poisonous substance.

cybernetics [ˌsaɪbərˈnetɪks] *n* a science that is concerned with studying how electronic and mechanical devices are controlled and comparing them to the way humans do the same tasks.

cyberspace ['saɪbərspeɪs] *n* a word used to describe the space in which electronic messages travel or exist when computer users send or receive them, e.g. via the Internet.

cyclamen ['sɪkləmən] (*pl* **cyclamen**) *n* a plant that has red, pink, or white flowers with petals that curl backward.

cycle ['saɪkl] ◇ *n* -1. [of events, processes] a series of events, actions, or processes that happen repeatedly, always in the same order □ *people trapped in a cycle of poverty and violence* □ *This machine completes three cycles per hour.* □ *the growth cycle of a plant.* -2. = **bicycle** □ *a cycle path/shop/race.* -3. [of poems, songs] a series of poems, songs etc that form one continuous story about a particular person or event □ *Schubert's song cycles.* ◇ *vi* to ride a bicycle □ *I usually cycle to work.*

cyclic(al) ['sɪklɪk(l)] *adj* [change, process] that happens in cycles □ *the cyclic(al) pattern of boom and bust.*

cycling ['saɪklɪŋ] *n* the activity of riding a bicycle □ *We went cycling through Belgium.* □ *a cycling vacation.*

cycling helmet *n* a hard hat worn by cyclists as a protection for the head.

cyclist ['saɪkləst] *n* a person who rides a bicycle.

cyclone ['saɪkləʊn] *n* a violent tropical storm that moves air very fast in a circle.

cygnet ['sɪgnət] *n* a young swan.

cylinder ['sɪlɪndər] *n* -1. [shape] a shape that has long straight sides and flat circular ends. -2. [container] a cylinder-shaped container, usually made of metal, that is used especially for keeping gas in. -3. [in a machine] the tube through which a piston moves in an engine or a piece of machinery.

cylinder block *n* the metal casing that holds the cylinders in the engine of a motor vehicle.

cylinder head *n* a piece of metal that fits onto the top of a cylinder block in a motor vehicle.

cylinder-head gasket *n* a piece of material that joins the cylinder block and the cylinder head in a motor vehicle.

cylindrical [səˈlɪndrɪkl] *adj* [object] that is shaped like a cylinder.

cymbals ['sɪmblz] *npl* a musical instrument consisting of two metal disks that are hit together or hit with a stick or metal brush.

Cymru ['kʌmrɪ] the Welsh name for Wales.

cynic ['sɪnɪk] *n* a person who believes that people only care about themselves and so does not expect good things to happen □ *Don't be such a cynic — I'm sure it's true!*

cynical ['sɪnɪkl] *adj* [remark, person, attitude] that shows cynicism □ *People get to a certain age and they become cynical.*

cynically ['sɪnɪklɪ] *adv* [say, talk] *see* **cynical**.

cynicism ['sɪnɪsɪzm] *n* the attitude of a cynic □ *I find his cynicism rather depressing.*

CYO (*abbr of* **Catholic Youth Organization**) *n* **the CYO** an organization for young Catholics in the USA.

cypher ['saɪfər] *n* = **cipher**.

cypress ['saɪprəs] *n* an evergreen tree with dark-green leaves.

Cypriot ['sɪprɪət] *n* & *adj*: *see* **Cyprus**.

Cyprus ['saɪprəs] an island in the eastern Mediterranean that is divided into the Republic of Cyprus in the south, controlled by Greek Cypriots, and the Turkish Republic of Northern Cyprus. SIZE: 9,251 sq kms. POPULATION: 700,000 (*Cypriots*). CAPITAL: Nicosia. LANGUAGE: Greek, Turkish. CURRENCY: Cypriot pound.

cyst [sɪst] *n* a bubble of liquid that can form in or on various parts of the body.

cystic fibrosis [ˌsɪstɪkfaɪˈbrousəs] *n* an inherited disease that causes lung infections, difficulties in absorbing food, and restricted growth in children.

cystitis [sɪˈstaɪtəs] *n* an infection of the bladder that is especially common in women and makes urination frequent and painful.

cytology [saɪˈtɒlədʒɪ] *n* the study of plant and animal cells.

CZ (*abbr of* **canal zone**) the Panama Canal and the land on each side of it. It was controlled by the USA until 1979, when Panama took it over.

czar [zɑːr] *n* a hereditary male ruler of Russia before the revolution of 1917.

Czech [tʃek] *n* & *adj*: *see* **Czech Republic**.

Czechoslovakia [US ˌtʃekəslouˈvɑːkɪə, GB -ˈvæk-] a country in central Europe until 1993, when it was divided into two independent states, the Czech Republic and Slovakia.

Czech Republic: **the Czech Republic** a country in central Europe that was part of Czechoslovakia until it became an independent republic in 1993. SIZE: 79,000 sq kms. POPULATION: 10,350,000 (*Czechs*). CAPITAL: Prague. LANGUAGE: Czech. CURRENCY: koruna.

D

d¹ [diː] (*pl* **d's** OR **ds**), **D** [diː] (*pl* **D's** OR **Ds**) *n* the fourth letter of the English alphabet.

◆ **D** ◇ *n* -1. EDUCATION a low grade for a piece of work. -2. MUSIC one of the notes in Western music. ◇ US *abbr of* **Democrat(ic)**.

d.² *abbr of* **died**.

DA *n abbr of* **district attorney** □ *the DA's office.*

dab [dæb] (*pt* & *pp* **dabbed**, *cont* **dabbing**) ◇ *n* a small amount of cream, paint, powder etc that is put on a surface with a quick gentle stroke. ◇ *vt* [wound, skin] to put cream, an ointment etc on <sthg> with quick gentle strokes □ *She dabbed his knee with antiseptic.* ■ **to dab sthg on(to) sthg** [cream, ointment] to put sthg on sthg with quick gentle strokes □ *He dabbed some paint on(to) the canvas.* ◇ *vi* **to dab at sthg** to touch sthg with quick gentle strokes □ *He dabbed at the cut with antiseptic.*

dabble ['dæbl] ◇ *vt* to put <one's toes or fingers> in a liquid and move them about gently. ◇ *vi* to be interested or involved in something without being very serious about it □ *He dabbles in astrology.*

dachshund [US 'dɑːkshʊnd, GB 'dæksnd] *n* a small dog with a long body and short legs.

dad [dæd], **daddy** ['dædɪ] (*pl* **daddies**) *n* a father (informal use).

daddy longlegs [-ˈlɒŋlegz] (*pl* **daddy longlegs**) *n* GB an insect that has very long legs and can fly.

daffodil ['dæfədɪl] *n* a bright yellow flower that is shaped like a trumpet and blooms in the spring.

daft [US dæft, GB dɑːft] *adj* GB [person, behavior, idea] that seems silly (informal use).

dagger ['dægər] *n* a small, sharp, pointed knife that is used as a weapon.

dahlia [US 'dælɪə, GB 'deɪl-] *n* a brightly colored flower with a lot of pointed petals.

Dáil [dɔɪl] *n* **the Dáil (Eireann)** in the Republic of Ireland, the lower chamber of parliament.

daily ['deɪlɪ] (*pl* **dailies**) ◇ *adj* -1. **a daily occurrence/routine etc** an occurrence/a routine etc that happens every day □ *They kept us up to date with daily reports on his progress.* -2. **a daily newspaper** a newspaper that is published every day except Sunday. -3. **a daily rate/wage etc** a rate/wage etc that is based on a single day □ *They paid us on a daily basis.* ◇ *adv* every day □ *The mail is distributed twice daily.* ◇ *n* a daily newspaper.

daintily ['deɪntɪlɪ] *adv* [eat, walk, move] in a delicate way.

dainty ['deɪntɪ] (*compar* **daintier**, *superl* **daintiest**) *adj* [person, dress, ornament] delicate or pretty.

dairy ['deərɪ] (*pl* **dairies**) *n* -1. the part of a farm where milk is kept or is made into butter or cheese. -2. a store where butter, cheese, milk, cream etc are sold.

dairy cattle *npl* cows that are kept on a farm to produce milk.

dairy farm *n* a farm that specializes in producing milk, butter, cheese etc.

dairy products *npl* products made from milk, e.g. cheese, butter, and yogurt.

dais ['deɪəs] *n* a raised platform in a hall that speakers stand on to address people.

daisy ['deɪzɪ] (*pl* **daisies**) *n* a small flower with white petals and a yellow center that often grows in grass.

daisy wheel *n* in some typewriters and printers, a disk for printing characters that is made up of a lot of thin rods with different letters of the alphabet on them.

daisy-wheel printer *n* a printer that uses a daisy wheel.
NOTE: Compare **dot-matrix printer**.

Dakota [də'kəʊtə] → **North Dakota, South Dakota**.

Dalai Lama [US ˌdɑːlaɪ'lɑːmə, GB 'dæl-] *n* the **Dalai Lama** the title of the religious and political leader of Tibet. The present Dalai Lama (1935–) has lived in exile since the Chinese invasion of Tibet in 1959.

dale [deɪl] *n* a valley.

Dali ['dɑːlɪ], **Salvador** (1904–1989) a Spanish Surrealist painter, famous for his eccentric behavior and thin mustache.

Dallas ['dæləs] a city in Texas, USA, that is an important center of the oil industry. POPULATION: 1,006,877.

dalmatian [dæl'meɪʃn] *n* a large dog with short white hair and black or brown spots.

dam [dæm] (*pt* & *pp* **dammed**, *cont* **damming**) ◇ *n* a barrier that is built across a river to control the flow of water. ◇ *vt* to build a dam across <a river>.
◆ **dam up** *vt sep* **-1. to dam a river up** to block a river by building a dam across it. **-2. to dam one's feelings up** to control one's feelings.

damage ['dæmɪdʒ] ◇ *n* **-1.** physical harm that spoils the condition of something or stops it from working properly □ *The fire caused a lot of damage.* □ *You'll have to pay for the damage to the kitchen.* □ *He suffered damage to his ligaments.* **-2.** a harmful effect □ *This scandal has done a lot of damage to his career.* ◇ *vt* **-1.** [building, structure] to destroy part of <sthg> □ *The house was badly damaged by the explosion.* **-2.** [reputation, career] to have a harmful effect on <sthg> □ *This has severely damaged her chances of becoming mayor.*
◆ **damages** *npl* LAW an amount of money that a person is ordered by a court to pay to somebody after being found guilty of damaging their property or reputation or injuring them □ *She was awarded $15,000 in damages.*

damaging ['dæmɪdʒɪŋ] *adj* [scandal, affair] that has harmful effects □ *This could be very damaging to your reputation/chances.*

Dame [deɪm] *n* a title given by the British monarch to a woman as a reward for important work or services □ *Dame Margot Fonteyn.*

damn [dæm] (informal use) ◇ *adj* a word used to emphasize how annoyed one is about something □ *What a damn nuisance!* ◇ *adv* very □ *You know damn well I'm right!* ◇ *n* **I don't give** OR **care a damn** I don't care at all. ◇ *vt* **-1.** RELIGION to send <sb> to hell. **-2.** a word used to show that one is annoyed about somebody or something □ *Damn it!* ◇ *excl* a word used to show that one is annoyed.

damnation [dæm'neɪʃn] *n* RELIGION the state of being damned.

damned [dæmd] (informal use) ◇ *adj* a word used to show how strongly one feels about something □ *It's a damned shame.* ■ **I'm damned if...** a phrase used to show that one does not intend to do something □ *I'm damned if I'm going to give up my Saturdays for him!* ■ **well I'll be** OR **I'm damned!** a phrase used to express surprise □ *Well I'll be damned, look who's here!* ◇ *adv:* *This kitchen needs a damned good clean.*

damning ['dæmɪŋ] *adj* **a damning statement/report etc** a statement/report etc that shows that somebody has done something very bad or wrong □ *The number of homeless people is a damning indictment of our society.*

damp [dæmp] ◇ *adj* [clothes, building, weather] that feels slightly wet □ *a damp cold room.* ◇ *n* slight wetness that affects areas of walls, ceilings etc □ *There's a patch of damp above the window.* ◇ *vt* to make <sthg> damp □ *She damped the cloth and wiped the table.*
◆ **damp down** *vt sep* **to damp sthg down** [unrest, panic, enthusiasm] to make sthg less intense.

damp course *n* GB a layer of special material that is placed near the bottom of a wall to prevent damp rising through its bricks.

dampen ['dæmpən] *vt* **-1.** [cloth, surface] to make <sthg> damp. **-2.** [excitement, enthusiasm, hope] to make <sthg> less strong □ *Nothing could dampen her high spirits.*

damper ['dæmpər] *n* a metal plate in front of a fire or furnace that can be moved to control the flow of air, making the fire burn more or less brightly. ■ **to put a damper on sthg** [on a party, somebody's enthusiasm] to make sthg less lively or enjoyable □ *The news put a damper on things, didn't it?*

damp-proof course *n* = **damp course**.

damson ['dæmzn] *n* a small purple plum.

dance [US dæns, GB dɑːns] ◇ *n* **-1.** a rhythmical way of moving one's body and feet, usually in time to music □ *Dance is a good form of exercise.* **-2.** a particular set of movements performed in time to music, e.g. the tango or the waltz □ *Would you like a dance?* □ *a fast dance.* **-3.** a social occasion where there is music and dancing □ *Are you coming to the dance?* **-4.** an art form in which performers move in time to music, e.g. ballet □ *classes in contemporary dance and ballet.* ◇ *vi* **-1.** [person] to perform a dance □ *Can you dance?* **-2.** [shadows, flowers, flames] to move quickly, as if dancing □ *The daffodils danced in the wind.*

dance floor *n* an area of a club, restaurant etc where there are no chairs, tables etc and people can dance □ *There were only two people on the dance floor.*

dance hall *n* a public hall that can be rented for parties and where people dance.

dancer [US 'dænsr, GB 'dɑːnsə] *n* a person who dances □ *You're a good dancer.* □ *She used to be a professional dancer.*

dancing [US 'dænsɪŋ, GB 'dɑːns-] *n* the activity of dancing □ *dancing lessons.*

D and C (*abbr of* **dilatation and curettage**) *n*

MEDICINE an operation in which the inside of the womb is scraped to remove a growth or tissue for a sample, or to carry out an abortion.

dandelion ['dændəlaɪən] *n* a common wild plant that has yellow flowers that become soft balls of white seeds.

dandruff ['dændrʌf] *n* small white pieces of dead skin that come from people's heads and can be seen in their hair or on their clothing.

dandy ['dændɪ] (*pl* **dandies**) *n* a man who pays a lot of attention to his clothing and appearance.

Dane [deɪn] *n* a person who comes from or lives in Denmark.

danger ['deɪndʒər] *n* -1. the possibility of being hurt or killed □ *He sensed danger.* □ *'Danger, keep out.'* ■ **to be in danger** to be in a situation where one may be killed or hurt □ *They/Their lives are in great danger.* ■ **to be out of danger** to be safe, after having been in danger or seriously ill. -2. something that may cause harm □ *the dangers of smoking/of making hasty judgments* □ *The power station is a danger to public safety.* -3. **to be in danger of doing sthg** to be in a situation in which one might do sthg bad □ *We're in danger of exceeding the budget.* -4. **there's no danger of that** a phrase used to say that something bad will not happen □ *There's no danger of that happening.*

danger list *n* **to be on the danger list** to be so ill that one may die □ *She's off the danger list now.*

danger money *n* GB = **danger pay**.

dangerous ['deɪndʒərəs] *adj* [animal, person, situation] that may cause harm or a problem □ *It would be dangerous to invest everything in one type of stock.*

dangerous driving *n* the act of driving a motor vehicle in a way that is likely to cause injury or damage.

dangerously ['deɪndʒərəslɪ] *adv* -1. [live, drive] see **dangerous** □ *This building is dangerously close to collapse.* -2. **dangerously ill** very ill and close to death.

danger pay *n* US extra money that is paid to somebody for doing a dangerous job.

danger zone *n* a dangerous area.

dangle ['dæŋgl] ◇ *vt* -1. to let <sthg> hang loosely so that it can move □ *She dangled her legs over the arm of the sofa.* -2. **to dangle sthg in front of sb** to offer sthg as an attractive possibility to sb in order to encourage them to do something. ◇ *vi* [legs, chain] to hang loosely in a way that allows movement □ *Let your arms dangle by your side.*

Daniel ['dænjəl] in the Bible, a Jew who was captured and put into a lions' den to be killed. He survived because God protected him.

Danish ['deɪnɪʃ] ◇ *adj: see* **Denmark**. ◇ *n* a roll made of sweet pastry and filled with apple or almond paste □ *an apple Danish.* ◇ *npl* **the Danish** the people of Denmark.

Danish blue *n* a strong white cheese with lines of blue mold in it.

Danish pastry *n* = **Danish**.

dank [dæŋk] *adj* [room, cellar, atmosphere] that is unpleasantly damp and cold □ *The basement was dank and cold.*

Danube ['dænjuːb]: **the Danube** a river in central Europe that starts in southern Germany and flows into the Black Sea.

dapper ['dæpər] *adj* [man] who is small and neat in appearance.

dappled ['dæpld] *adj* -1. [light, shade] that consists of small patches of shadow and light. -2. **a dappled horse** a horse that is marked with spots of a different color from the rest of its coat.

Dardanelles [,dɑːrdə'nelz]: **the Dardanelles** a narrow channel between European and Asian Turkey, connecting the Mediterranean and the Sea of Marmara.

dare [deər] ◇ *vt* -1. **to dare (to) do sthg** to be brave enough to do sthg (used as a modal verb) □ *I didn't dare argue.* □ *He lay hidden, hardly daring to breathe.* ■ **I dare say you are right** you are probably right □ *I dare say you're hungry after your journey.* ■ **don't you dare!** if you do that I shall be very angry and upset □ *Don't you dare tell him what I said!* ■ **how dare you!** what you have done makes me feel very angry because it is unfair □ *How dare he speak to me like that!* -2. **to dare sb to do sthg** to persuade sb to do sthg dangerous in order to show how brave they are □ *Go on, I dare you to ask him!* ◇ *n* a challenge made to somebody to do something dangerous in order to show how brave they are □ *He stole the radio on a dare.*

daredevil ['deərdevl] *n* a person who enjoys doing dangerous activities or sports.

daren't ['deərnt] GB = **dare not**.

daring ['deərɪŋ] ◇ *adj* -1. [person] who is not afraid to take risks or do something dangerous; [action, feat, attempt] that is brave and involves risk □ *a daring bid to get into the record books.* -2. [comment, movie, dress] that is unusual or unexpected and likely to shock people □ *It was very daring of you to suggest a complete rethink.* ◇ *n* the courage to take risks □ *a man of great daring.*

dark [dɑːrk] ◇ *adj* -1. [room, street, night] with little or no light □ *It gets dark at 3:00 p.m. in wintertime.* -2. [color, material] that is nearer to black than to white □ *a dark-blue suit.* -3. [person] who has dark skin and dark brown or black hair □ *Is she dark or fair?* -4. [story, thought] sad and depressing □ *during the dark days of the Depression.* -5. [look, comment] that is unpleasant and threatening □ *There's a dark side to him.*

◇ *n* -1. **the dark** a situation where there is no light □ *He's afraid of the dark.* ■ **to be in the dark about sthg** to know nothing about sthg □ *I'm afraid we're as much in the dark about Joel's intentions as you are.* □ *Even her aides were kept in the dark about the deal until the last* minute. -2. **before/after dark** before/after sunset □ *Make sure you're back before dark.*

Dark Ages *npl* **the Dark Ages** the period of European history from about 500 AD to 1000 AD.

darken ['dɑːˤkən] ◇ *vt* [color, room] to make <sthg> darker □ *A large thunder-cloud darkened the sky.* ◇ *vi* -1. [sky, room] to become darker. -2. [face] to start looking angry.

dark glasses *npl* glasses that have dark lenses to keep one's eyes protected or hidden.

dark horse *n* a person who keeps their thoughts, intentions, or talents secret □ *You're a dark horse, I didn't know you could speak Italian.*

darkness ['dɑːˤknəs] *n* [of a room, street, night] the state of being dark □ *Thousands of homes were plunged into darkness.* □ *Darkness fell.*

darkroom ['dɑːˤkruːm] *n* a room that does not let any light in and is used for developing photographs.

darling ['dɑːˤlɪŋ] ◇ *adj* -1. [person] a word used to somebody who one loves very much □ *To my darling husband on his birthday.* -2. [child, cottage] that one thinks is attractive or likes very much □ *What a darling little puppy!* ◇ *n* -1. a term of affection for somebody one loves □ *I'm home, darling!* -2. a word used to address somebody, usually of the opposite sex, in a friendly way (informal use) □ *Hello, darling.* -3. **to be the darling of...** to be popular among a particular group of people at a particular time □ *the darling of the media/party conference.*

darn [dɑːˤn] ◇ *adj* a word used to show that one is annoyed about something (informal use) □ *That darn dog!* ◇ *adv* very (informal use) □ *I came darn close to having an accident.* ◇ *vt* to mend a hole in <a piece of clothing> by sewing long stitches across it; to mend <a hole> in a piece of clothing in this way. ◇ *excl* a word used by somebody to show that they are annoyed (informal use) □ *Darn it!*

darning needle *n* a long needle used for darning.

dart [dɑːˤt] ◇ *n* -1. a small arrow that is thrown at a board in games, or fired from a gun or blowpipe as a weapon. -2. SEWING a fold that is made in a piece of clothing to make it fit more closely. ◇ *vt* **to dart a look** OR **glance at sb** to look very quickly at sb. ◇ *vi* to move somewhere suddenly and quickly □ *She darted behind a tree.*

◆ **darts** *n* a game in which darts are thrown at a dartboard.

dartboard ['dɑːˤtbɔːˤd] *n* a round board divided into numbered sections that is used as a target in the game of darts.

Dartmoor ['dɑːˤtmʊəˤ] -1. a large area of high land in southwestern England that is a national park. -2. a famous prison on Dartmoor.

Darwin[1] ['dɑːˤwən] the capital of the Northern Territory of Australia. POPULATION: 78,139.

Darwin[2] ['dɑːˤwən], **Charles** (1809–1882) a British scientist whose book, *The Origin of Species*, stated that people are descended from animals. His theory of evolution caused controversy because it disagreed with Christian ideas.

dash [dæʃ] ◇ *n* -1. **a dash of sthg** a small amount of sthg that is mixed with or added to some other substance □ *Add a dash of tabasco sauce.* -2. GRAMMAR a punctuation mark (–) that is usually used to separate a phrase from the rest of a sentence. -3. AUTO = **dashboard.** -4. **to make a dash for sthg** [for a train, building] to run suddenly and quickly toward sthg □ *We made a dash for the nearest doorway to try and shelter from the rain.*
◇ *vt* -1. to break <sthg> by throwing it against a hard surface (literary use) □ *The waves dashed the boat against the rocks.* -2. to destroy <sb's hopes> □ *His letter dashed any hopes I had of a reconciliation.*
◇ *vi* to go somewhere quickly □ *I've got to dash back to the office.* ■ **I must dash** I am in a hurry and have to leave now.

◆ **dash off** *vt sep* **to dash sthg off** [letter, memo] to write sthg quickly because one is in a hurry to finish it.

dashboard ['dæʃbɔːˤd] *n* AUTO the panel in a motor vehicle in front of the driver that contains instruments and switches.

dashing ['dæʃɪŋ] *adj* [person] who is lively, stylish, and attractive.

DAT [dæt, ˌdiːeɪˈtiː] (*abbr of* **digital audio tape**) *n* a high-quality cassette tape that records sounds in digital form.

data ['deɪtə] *n* -1. information, usually in the form of facts and figures, that helps people to understand something quickly □ *I haven't had time to process all the data yet.* -2. COMPUTING information that is stored in a computer □ *data entry/input/protection.*

databank ['deɪtəbæŋk] *n* = **database.**

database ['deɪtəbeɪs] *n* a collection of data that is stored in a computer in such a way that related types of data can be identified.

data capture *n* the act of entering data into a computer system, usually using a keyboard, diskette, or scanner.

Datapost™ ['deɪtəpoust] *n* a British mail service for sending letters, packages etc more quickly than the usual mail.

data processing *n* the act of selecting or organizing data in a computer in order to produce or analyze information.

data protection *n* the protection of people's privacy by legally controlling the use of data about them that is stored on computers.

data transmission *n* the process of sending computer data from one place to another, e.g. by using a modem.

date [deɪt] ◇ *n* -1. a particular point in time, usually shown by the number of the day, the name of the month, and the number of the year □ *"What's today's date?"* OR *"What date is it today?" — "It's June ninth."* □ *We can look at the figures again at a later date.* -2. [with a friend] an arrangement to meet somebody at a particular time □ *Shall we make a date for lunch?* **-3.** [with a boyfriend, girlfriend] an arrangement to go out with a boyfriend or girlfriend, or with somebody that one hopes to have a romantic relationship with □ *My daughter's going out on her first date tonight.* **-4.** [boyfriend, girlfriend] the person one goes out with as a boyfriend or girlfriend on a date □ *Can I bring a date to the party?* **-5.** [fruit] a small, sweet, dark-brown fruit that grows on palm trees.

◇ *vt* **-1.** to estimate the age of <sthg> □ *The church can be dated from the stonework.* **-2.** [letter, check] to write the present date on <sthg> □ *The invoice was dated August 24th.* **-3.** [person] to go out regularly with <sb that one is having a romantic relationship with> □ *Is Jim still dating Anne?*

◇ *vi* to go out of fashion □ *It's the sort of style that never dates.*

◆ **to date** *adv* up to the present time □ *Enclosed is a list of all our transactions to date.* □ *To date, I've only met him once.*

◆ **date back to, date from** *vt fus* **to date back to the 14th/15th etc century** to have been in existence since the 14th/15th etc century □ *The church dates from Norman times.*

datebook ['deɪtbʊk] *n* US **-1.** a newspaper editor's record of events that have to be reported in the future. **-2.** a small book with spaces marked for each day or week of the year where one can write down appointments etc.

dated ['deɪtəd] *adj* that is no longer fashionable □ *That look seems rather dated these days.*

dateline ['deɪtlaɪn] *n* = **international date line.**

date of birth *n* the date on which somebody was born □ *Give your name, age, and date of birth.*

date rape *n* a situation in which a man rapes a woman who he knows socially and who he has usually just spent the evening with.

date stamp *n* **-1.** a rubber stamp used for marking the date on documents. **-2.** a date marked by a date stamp.

daub [dɔːb] *vt* [surface, wall, face] to spread a substance on <sthg> unevenly and carelessly □ *The door was daubed with paint.* ■ **to daub sthg on sthg** [paint, mud] to spread sthg unevenly and carelessly on sthg □ *He daubed paint on the wall.*

daughter ['dɔːtəʳ] *n* somebody's female child □ *Our youngest daughter is still at school.*

daughter-in-law (*pl* **daughters-in-law**) *n* the wife of one's son.

daunt [dɔːnt] *vt* to make <sb> worried and uncertain about whether they can succeed in what they are trying to do □ *I felt daunted by the prospect.*

daunting ['dɔːntɪŋ] *adj* [task, prospect] that daunts somebody □ *Meeting Charles' huge family was very daunting.*

David ['deɪvəd] (10th century BC) King of Israel. In the Bible, he killed the giant Goliath with a stone. The names David and Goliath

are often used to describe battles between weak and strong people.

Davis ['deɪvəs], **Jefferson** (1808–1889) President of the Confederacy from 1861 to 1864.

dawdle ['dɔːdl] *vi* to waste time by doing something or going somewhere very slowly □ *She dawdled over her breakfast.* □ *Hurry up and stop dawdling!*

dawn [dɔːn] ◇ *n* **-1.** the time at the beginning of a day when the first light appears in the sky □ *He woke up at dawn.* □ *They work from dawn to dusk.* **-2. the dawn of an age/era etc** the beginning of an age/era etc □ *the dawn of civilization.* ◇ *vi* **-1.** [day] to begin □ *The day dawned bright and sunny.* **-2.** [period, hope] to begin to develop □ *A new era of peace dawned.*

◆ **dawn (up)on** *vt fus* **to dawn (up)on sb** to become slowly clear to sb □ *It finally dawned on me that they were taking advantage of me.*

dawn chorus *n* GB **the dawn chorus** the sound of birds singing at dawn.

day [deɪ] *n* **-1.** one of the seven periods that a week is divided into □ *the day before/after the conference* □ *What day is it today?* ■ **the day before yesterday** two days ago. **-2.** a period of 24 hours □ *It will take three days for the check to clear your account.* ■ **any day now** at any time soon in the next few days □ *We're expecting to hear something any day now.* ■ **to call it a day** to stop doing something, usually working □ *I suggest we call it a day now and finish up tomorrow.* ■ **to make sb's day** to make sb very happy (informal use) □ *Getting the chance to meet up with you really made my day.* ■ **to save sthg for a rainy day** to keep sthg, especially money, so that one can use it later when it is more needed. ■ **it's early days yet** GB it's too soon to be certain □ *The new product seems to be selling well, but it's early days yet.* ■ **his days are numbered** he has not got much time left to live or keep his job, power etc. ■ **in this day and age** in the present time □ *In this day and age you can hardly expect your wife to do all the cooking and cleaning for you.* ■ **one day, some day, one of these days** at some time in the future □ *One of these days I'm going to tell him what I think of him.* **-3.** a period in the past □ *In those days there were no cars.* ■ **in sb's day** during the time when sb was alive, active, or famous □ *In my day, children were expected to be polite to their elders.* □ *He was well known in his day.* **-4.** the time when it is light and when people are usually active □ *He sleeps by day and works at night.* □ *I've had a miserable day at the office.* □ *Lovely day, isn't it!* □ *I was trying to phone you all day!* ■ **day and night** [work] all or almost all the time, without stopping □ *We've been working day and night trying to get this finished in time.*

◆ **days** *adv* [work] during the day.

dayboy ['deɪbɔɪ] *n* GB a male pupil who goes to a boarding school but lives at home.

daybreak ['deɪbreɪk] *n* the time at the beginning of the day when the first light appears in the sky □ *I left the house at daybreak.*

daycare center ['deɪkeə^r-] *n* a nursery where young children can be taken care of while their parents are at work.

daycenter ['deɪsentə^r] *n* GB a place where children or elderly or disabled people can be taken care of during the day.

daydream ['deɪdriːm] ◇ *n* a pleasant thought or fantasy somebody has when they are awake. ◇ *vi* to have daydreams □ *What are you daydreaming about?*

daygirl ['deɪgɜː^rl] *n* GB a female pupil at a boarding school who lives at home.

Day-Glo™ [-gloʊ] *adj* a Day-Glo color a color, e.g. pink, orange, or green, that is very bright when light shines on it.

daylight ['deɪlaɪt] *n* -1. natural light during the day □ *It looks different in daylight.* -2. [in the morning] the time at the beginning of a day when the first light appears in the sky □ *We set off before daylight.* -3. **to scare the (living) daylights out of sb** to scare sb very much.

daylight robbery *n* an expression used to show that one thinks something is much more expensive than it should be (informal use) □ *$50 for a notebook? That's daylight robbery!*

daylight saving (time) [-'seɪvɪŋ-] *n* the practice of setting all the clocks in a country or region one hour later than the local standard time in the summer in order to have more daylight hours.

day nursery *n* GB = daycare center.

Day of Atonement *n* = Yom Kippur.

day off (*pl* **days off**) *n* a working day when one does not go to work □ *She took a day off to go to the dentist.* □ *I could meet you on Monday — it's my day off.*

day pupil *n* GB a pupil who goes to a boarding school but lives at home.

day release *n* GB a system that allows employees to take time off work, e.g. one day a week, to study at college.

day return *n* GB a travel ticket to go somewhere and come back the same day that costs less than the standard round trip fare.

dayroom ['deɪruːm] *n* a room in an institution, e.g. a hospital, where people can read, write, relax etc.

day school *n* a school where the students return home at the end of each day rather than stay to sleep there.

day shift *n* a shift in which one works during the day.

day student *n* US a student who goes home in the evening rather than living at the school or college where they are studying.

daytime ['deɪtaɪm] *n* the time during the day when it is light □ *a daytime job* □ *daytime TV.*

day-to-day *adj* -1. **day-to-day activities/duties etc** activities/duties etc that are a regular part of one's life and are not special in any way □ *She is in charge of the day-to-day running of the organization.* -2. **to live a day-to-day ex-**

istence to live each day as it happens without planning ahead.

day trip *n* a sightseeing excursion in which one goes to a place and comes back the same day.

day tripper *n* a person on a day trip.

daze [deɪz] ◇ *n* **to be in a daze** to be unable to think clearly, e.g. after a shock or a blow to the head □ *I went around in a daze for weeks after she left.* ◇ *vt* to put <sb> in a daze.

dazed [deɪzd] *adj* [person] who is in a daze □ *He seemed dazed and confused.*

dazzle ['dæzl] *vt* -1. [light, sun] to make <sb> unable to see for a short time because of being so bright □ *I was dazzled by the car's headlights.* -2. [beauty, skill, wit] to impress <sb> very much □ *She dazzled everyone with her wit and humor.*

dazzling ['dæzlɪŋ] *adj* [light, beauty, skill] that dazzles somebody □ *She gave a dazzling performance.*

DBE (*abbr of* **Dame Commander of the Order of the British Empire**) *n* a British honorary title for women.

DBS (*abbr of* **direct broadcasting by satellite**) *n* a system of broadcasting television programs via a satellite into homes equipped with special satellite dishes.

DC ◇ *n abbr of* **direct current.** ◇ -1. *abbr of* **District of Columbia.** -2. = **Washington D.C.** NOTE: Compare **AC.**

DD (*abbr of* **Doctor of Divinity**) *n* a postgraduate degree in religious studies; a person who has this degree.

D/D *abbr of* **direct debit.**

D-day *n* -1. the day (June 6, 1944) when the Allied forces invaded German-occupied Europe by landing on the beaches of northern France. -2. a day when a particular important event is planned to happen.

DDS (*abbr of* **Doctor of Dental Science**) *n* a postgraduate degree in dentistry; a person who has this degree.

DDT (*abbr of* **dichlorodiphenyltrichloroethane**) *n* a chemical used for killing insects that is also harmful to people and animals. It is now banned in many countries.

DE *abbr of* **Delaware.**

DEA (*abbr of* **Drug Enforcement Administration**) *n* **the DEA** the US government department responsible for controlling the use and sale of dangerous drugs.

deacon ['diːkən] *n* -1. in some Christian churches, a person who is below a priest in rank. -2. in some Protestant churches, a person who helps the minister.

deaconess [,diːkə'nes] *n* in some Christian churches, a woman who performs some of the duties of a priest.

deactivate [diː'æktɪveɪt] *vt* to make <a bomb> safe.

dead [ded] ◇ *adj* -1. [person, animal, plant] that is no longer alive □ *The family refuse to accept that she might be dead.* ■ **to shoot sb dead** to kill sb by shooting them. ■ **he wouldn't be seen dead in that restaurant/wearing those**

clothes **etc** he would never go to that restaurant/wear those clothes etc (informal use). **-2. to go dead** [leg, arm, finger] to lose all feeling □ *My hand's gone dead.* **-3.** [telephone, battery, radio] that does not work because there is no electrical power in it □ *I tried to phone but the line was dead.* **-4. dead silence/ calm etc** complete silence/calm etc □ *The train came to a dead stop.* **-5.** [town, party] that is boring because there is nothing exciting happening □ *This place is completely dead at night.* **-6.** [voice, eyes] showing no excitement or emotion.
◇ *adv* **-1.** completely; very (informal use) □ *I'm dead against it.* □ *I'm dead tired.* ■ **to be dead set on/against sthg** to be determined to do or have sthg/prevent sthg from happening. **-2. to stop dead** to stop suddenly. **-3.** GB exactly □ *They arrived dead on time/on six o'clock.* □ *dead in the middle.*
◇ *n* **in the dead of night/winter** in the middle of the night/winter.
◇ *npl* **the dead** people who have died □ *a memorial service for the war dead.*

deadbeat ['dedbiːt] *n* US a person who does not want to live and work in the way that most people in society do and so is considered to be lazy (informal use).

dead center *n* **the dead center** the exact center of something.

dead duck *n* a person, plan, or idea that is thought to have no chance of success or survival (informal use) □ *His plan to run for the presidency is now a dead duck.*

deaden ['dedn] *vt* [pain, hunger, noise] to make <sthg> less extreme so that one notices it less.

dead end *n* **-1.** a street that does not lead to other streets because one end of it is permanently closed. **-2.** an activity or situation that does not lead to any further development □ *The talks have reached a dead end.*

dead-end job *n* a job with no possibilities of future progress or promotion.

dead heat *n* a situation in which two or more competitors finish as equal winners.

dead letter *n* **-1.** a letter that has not been delivered. **-2.** a rule or law that still exists, but is no longer enforced or obeyed.

deadline ['dedlaɪn] *n* the time after which it is too late for something to be done □ *The deadline for applications is August 26th.* □ *We'll have to work overtime to meet the deadline.*

deadlock ['dedlɒk] *n* a situation in a dispute in which no agreement can be reached between the two sides □ *The talks between the two parties have reached a deadlock.* ■ **to break the deadlock** to end the deadlock □ *Last-minute negotiations failed to break the deadlock.*

deadlocked ['dedlɒkt] *adj* **to be deadlocked** [talks, negotiations] to have reached a deadlock.

deadly ['dedlɪ] (*compar* **deadlier**, *superl* **deadliest**) ◇ *adj* **-1.** [poison, weapon] that can kill people. **-2. deadly enemies** people who hate each other and want to harm each other □ *They became deadly enemies.* **-3.** [accuracy, force] that is complete and capable of causing a lot of damage □ *His aim is deadly.* ◇ *adv* **deadly boring/serious etc** very boring/serious etc □ *His speech was deadly dull.*

deadly nightshade [-'naɪtʃeɪd] *n* a plant with purple bell-shaped flowers and very poisonous black berries.

deadpan ['dedpæn] ◇ *adj* [expression, manner, humor] that deliberately seems serious while intending to be funny. ◇ *adv* [look, act] in a deadpan way.

Dead Sea: **the Dead Sea** a large lake between Israel and Jordan. The water in it is so salty that people can float in it easily.

deadwood ['dedwʊd] US, **dead wood** GB *n* people or things in an organization that are no longer considered useful or profitable □ *The new management plans to get rid of any deadwood.*

deaf [def] ◇ *adj* **-1.** [person] who is unable to hear □ *She was born deaf in one ear.* **-2. to be deaf to sthg** [to somebody's demands, criticism] to refuse to take notice of sthg □ *The government was deaf to our requests for aid.* ◇ *npl* **the deaf** deaf people □ *a school for the deaf.*

deaf-aid *n* GB = hearing aid.

deaf-and-dumb *adj* [person] who cannot hear or speak.

deafen ['defn] *vt* to make <sb> unable to hear □ *We were deafened by the noise from outside.*

deafening ['defnɪŋ] *adj* [noise, crash] very loud □ *the deafening roar of planes overhead.*

deaf-mute ◇ *adj* [person] who is unable to hear or speak. ◇ *n* a deaf-mute person.

deafness ['defnəs] *n* [of a person] *see* **deaf** □ *She overcame her deafness, eventually becoming a successful percussionist.*

deal [diːl] (*pt* & *pp* **dealt**) ◇ *n* **-1. a good** OR **great deal** a lot □ *I miss her a great deal.* □ *There's a great deal of work to be done.* **-2.** [between people, organizations, countries] an agreement, usually in business □ *I assume the deal is going ahead.* ■ **to do** OR **strike a deal with sb** to make an agreement with sb □ *We struck a good deal with the distribution company.* □ *The government does not do deals with terrorists.* **-3. a good/bad etc deal** (informal use) good/bad etc treatment □ *The legislature promised to give small businesses a better deal.* □ *At least we can say we got a fair deal.*
◇ *vt* **-1. to deal sb/sthg a blow, to deal a blow to sb/sthg** to hit sb/sthg □ *They dealt him several blows to the head.* □ *The closure of the plant dealt a terrible blow to the community.* **-2.** to give <cards> to the players in a card game.
◇ *vi* **-1.** to give cards to the players in a card game. **-2.** to buy and sell drugs, weapons etc.

◆ **deal in** *vt fus* **to deal in sthg** [in drugs, furniture, commodities] to buy and sell sthg to make money □ *They deal in second-hand books.*

◆ **deal out** *vt sep* **-1. to deal cards out** to give cards to the players in a card game. **-2. to deal sthg out** [food, money] to share sthg out among several people. ■ **to deal punishment out** to punish somebody.

◆ **deal with** *vt fus* **-1. to deal with sthg** [with a problem, situation] to take action in order to bring sthg to an acceptable or desirable conclusion □ *We are dealing with your complaint.* **-2. to deal with sb** [with a customer, patient] to take action to meet the needs of sb □ *The job involves dealing with the public.* **-3. to deal with sthg** to be about sthg □ *The book/movie deals with corruption in high places.* **-4. to deal with sthg** [with a problem, emergency] to be faced with sthg □ *We are dealing with what is potentially a major disaster.*

dealer ['diːlər] *n* **-1.** a person who buys and sells particular goods to make money □ *a drugs/an arms/an antiques dealer.* **-2.** a person who deals the cards in a card game.

dealership ['diːlərʃɪp] *n* a place where particular types of goods are bought and sold □ *a car dealership.*

dealing ['diːlɪŋ] *n* BUSINESS the activity of buying and selling of goods, shares etc □ *Dealing in futures was down yesterday.*

◆ **dealings** *npl* personal involvement or a business relationship that one has with somebody □ *I don't know, I've never had any dealings with him.*

dealt [delt] *past tense & past participle of* **deal**.

dean [diːn] *n* **-1.** [at a university, college] a teacher who is in charge of a faculty or college, or who looks after the welfare of students. **-2.** [in the Church of England] a priest who is in charge of other priests and of running a cathedral.

Dean [diːn], **James** (1931–1955) a US movie actor who was killed in a car crash. He appeared in *East of Eden* and *Rebel without a Cause*, and became a symbol of angry youth.

Dean's List *n* **the Dean's List** at some US universities, a list of the top students.

dear [dɪər] ◇ *adj* **-1. a dear friend/sister etc** a friend/sister etc who one loves very much □ *She's a very dear friend.* □ *I've always been fond of dear old Shirley.* ■ **to be dear to sb** to be very important to sb □ *You are very dear to me.* **-2.** GB **to be dear** to cost a lot of money □ *Property is dear in this area.* **-3. Dear Sir/ Madam/John etc** a phrase used at the beginning of a letter to show who one is writing to.

◇ *n* **-1.** a word used when speaking to somebody one likes or loves, especially one's husband or wife □ *Hello, dear, I'm home!* □ *I do understand, my dear.* **-2.** a kind and helpful person □ *John is such a dear.*

◇ *excl* **oh dear!** a phrase used to show disappointment or sympathy □ *Oh dear! I seem to have broken it.*

Dear Abby™ [-'æbɪ] *n* the name of a personal advice column in many US newspapers.

dearly ['dɪərlɪ] *adv* **to love sb dearly** to love sb very much □ *I've always loved you very dearly, Sam.* ■ **I would dearly love** OR **like to know** I would very much like to know.

dearth [dɜːʳθ] *n* **a dearth of sthg** a shortage of sthg that is needed □ *There is a dearth of good restaurants in this area.*

death [deθ] *n* **-1.** [of a person, animal] the end of a person's or animal's life □ *What was the cause of death?* ■ **to be crushed/beaten etc to death** to be crushed/beaten etc so much that one dies. ■ **to fall/jump etc to one's death** to die by falling/jumping etc. **-2. an agonizing/a horrible etc death** an agonizing/horrible etc way to die □ *It was a cruel death!* **-3.** a person who has died or been killed □ *The number of road deaths has increased rapidly.* **-4.** [of a tradition, idea] the end of something □ *Videos will be the death of cinema.* **-5.** *phrases* **to frighten/ worry sb to death** to frighten/worry sb a lot □ *Where have you been? I was worried to death.* ■ **to be bored to death with sb/sthg** to be very bored by sb/sthg (informal use). ■ **to be sick to death of sthg** to be very annoyed or bored by sthg (informal use) □ *I'm sick to death of listening to Tony complaining the whole time!* ■ **to put sb to death** to kill sb, usually after an official order □ *He was put to death for his religious views.* ■ **to be at death's door** to be very ill and close to death.

deathbed ['deθbed] *n* **to be on one's deathbed** to be about to die □ *a deathbed confession.*

death certificate *n* an official document written by a doctor that states where and when a person died and what caused their death.

death duty *n* GB = **death tax.**

death knell *n* **to sound the death knell for sthg** to cause sthg to end soon □ *Another scandal could sound the death knell for the party.*

deathly ['deθlɪ] ◇ *adj* **a deathly silence** OR **hush** a total silence. ◇ *adv* **deathly pale/cold etc** very pale/cold etc □ *It was deathly quiet.*

death penalty *n* **the death penalty** the punishment of a serious crime by death.

death rate *n* the number of deaths within a particular area or group of people in proportion to the population of that area or group.

death row [-'rou] *n* **to be on death row** [prisoner, inmate] to have been sentenced to death □ *Collins has been on death row for 10 years.*

death sentence *n* a punishment of death given by a court □ *In some countries, drug trafficking carries the death sentence.*

death squad *n* a group of people employed by a political party or military force to kill people who oppose them.

death tax *n* US a tax that has to be paid on money and property left by a person who has died.

death toll *n* the number of people who have died in a war, massacre, earthquake etc.

death trap *n* something, e.g. a vehicle or building, that is so unsafe that anybody who goes in it could be killed.

Death Valley an area of desert between California and Nevada. It is the lowest, hottest, and driest part of the USA.

deathwatch beetle [ˌdeθwɒtʃ-] *n* a kind of beetle that eats holes in wood and makes a tapping or clicking noise.

death wish *n* to have a death wish to take such big risks that one seems not to care if one dies.

deb [deb] *n* = debutante (informal use).

débâcle [deɪ'bɑːkl] *n* an event that ends in total failure.

debar [diː'bɑːʳ] (*pt* & *pp* **debarred**, *cont* **debarring**) *vt* to prevent <sb> from doing something or going somewhere □ *Foreigners are debarred from applying for these posts.*

debase [dɪ'beɪs] *vt* to lower the value or quality of <sb/sthg>. ■ **to debase oneself** to act in a way that makes people lose respect for one.

debatable [dɪ'beɪtəbl] *adj* [question, point, issue] that one does not know the answer to because people have different views about it □ *It's debatable whether the Germans are even interested joining.*

debate [dɪ'beɪt] ◇ *n* -1. a discussion about something by two or more people who hold different views □ *a heated debate* □ *There has been a lot of debate about* OR *over the issue of embryo research.* ■ **to be open to debate** [question, matter] to be debatable □ *Whether that would have achieved anything is open to debate.* -2. a formal meeting at which people have a debate about something □ *There will be a live debate on television.*
◇ *vt* -1. [issue, question, subject] to have a debate about <sthg> □ *The origins of the virus are much debated.* -2. [course of action] to discuss and think about <sthg> before making a decision □ *We're just debating whether to go ahead with the deal or not.*
◇ *vi*: *I debated with my boss about the merits of the idea.* □ *I debated a little about which color was best.*

debating society [dɪ'beɪtɪŋ-] *n* a society that organizes formal debates.

debauched [dɪ'bɔːtʃt] *adj* [person] who treats themselves and other people badly, e.g. by getting drunk or using people for sex (formal use).

debauchery [dɪ'bɔːtʃərɪ] *n* debauched behavior (formal use).

debenture [dɪ'bentʃəʳ] *n* a loan to a company or government agency that is made for a fixed period and has a fixed rate of interest.

debenture stock *n* GB money lent to a company in the form of debentures.

debilitate [dɪ'bɪlɪteɪt] *vt* to make <sb> weaker □ *a country debilitated by war.*

debilitating [dɪ'bɪlɪteɪtɪŋ] *adj* [disease, heat] that is unpleasant and makes one weaker.

debility [dɪ'bɪlətɪ] *n* weakness, usually as the result of illness.

debit ['debɪt] ◇ *n* a sum of money that somebody takes out of their account; a record of this money □ *a debit of $548* □ *Several debits appeared on last month's statement.* ◇ *vt* to take money out of <an account>; to withdraw <a sum of money> from an account □ *We have debited your account with $100.* □ *$50 will be debited from your account.*

debit card *n* a plastic card that one can use

to pay for goods and that takes money directly out of one's bank account.

debit note *n* a note that shows that a customer owes money.

debonair [ˌdebə'neəʳ] *adj* [man] well-dressed, confident, and charming.

Debrett's Peerage [də'brets-] *n* a book that lists the names and titles of all the British aristocratic families.

debrief [ˌdiː'briːf] *vt* [soldier, hostage] to get information from <sb> after a mission, task etc that they have carried out or after an experience they have had □ *The released hostages are being debriefed first.*

debriefing [ˌdiː'briːfɪŋ] *n* a meeting or series of meetings in which somebody is debriefed □ *a debriefing session/meeting.*

debris [US də'briː, GB 'debriː] *n* pieces of material, e.g. bricks, broken glass, that remain after something has been destroyed □ *Various personal belongings were found in the debris.*

debt [det] *n* -1. money that is owed by a person or organization to somebody else □ *The company has debts of over $100,000.* -2. the state of owing money to somebody □ *the worry of debt and possible bankruptcy.* ■ **to be in debt** to owe money to somebody □ *The company is $3 million in debt.* □ *He's in debt to the bank.* □ *She went deeper and deeper into debt.* -3. [of gratitude] a feeling one has that one owes something to somebody for something they have done □ *I wish we could repay our debt of gratitude to you.* ■ **to be in sb's debt** to feel grateful to sb for something they have done □ *I am very much in your debt for your help and advice.*

debt collector *n* a person whose job is to collect debts for a creditor.

debtor ['detəʳ] *n* a person or business that owes money to somebody.

debug [ˌdiː'bʌg] (*pt* & *pp* **debugged**, *cont* **debugging**) *vt* -1. TECHNOLOGY to remove hidden microphones from <a room, building> etc. -2. COMPUTING to remove faults from <a program>.

debunk [ˌdiː'bʌŋk] *vt* [idea, theory] to show that <sthg that a lot of people believe> is not true.

debut [US deɪ'bjuː, GB 'deɪbjuː] *n* the first time that somebody performs publicly as a singer, actor, athlete etc □ *She made her debut at the Met.* □ *a debut appearance/speech.*

debutante ['debjʊtɑːnt] *n* a young upper-class woman who makes her first formal appearance in high society by attending a series of balls, parties etc.

Dec *abbr of* **December**.

decade ['dekeɪd] *n* a period of ten years.

decadence ['dekədəns] *n*: *see* **decadent** □ *It was an age of decadence.*

decadent ['dekədənt] *adj* [person, society] that only cares about pleasure and does not take life seriously □ *It feels very decadent having breakfast in bed on a weekday!*

decaff ['diːkæf] *n* decaffeinated coffee (informal use).

decaffeinated [dɪ'kæfɪneɪtəd] *adj* [coffee, drink] that has had the caffeine removed from it.

decal ['diːkæl] *n* US a small sticker used as an advertisement.

decamp [dɪ'kæmp] *vi* to leave somewhere in a hurry, often secretly (informal use).

decant [dɪ'kænt] *vt* [wine, whiskey] to pour <an alcoholic drink> from a bottle into a jug, decanter etc before serving it.

decanter [dɪ'kæntəʳ] *n* a glass bottle or jug used to serve wine, whiskey etc.

decapitate [dɪ'kæpɪteɪt] *vt* to cut off the head of <sb>.

decathlete [dɪ'kæθliːt] *n* an athlete who competes in the decathlon.

decathlon [dɪ'kæθlɒn] *n* a competition in which athletes compete in ten different events.

decay [dɪ'keɪ] ◇ *n* -1. the natural chemical process that slowly destroys something, e.g. a tooth, plant, or dead body □ *tooth decay.* -2. the process of getting into a worse condition □ *The house has fallen into decay.* ◇ *vi* -1. [tooth, plant, dead body] to become rotten. -2. [building] to get into a worse condition.

deceased [dɪ'siːst] (*pl* **deceased**) (formal use) ◇ *adj* [person] who has died recently □ *his deceased wife.* ◇ *n* **the deceased** a phrase used to refer to somebody who has recently died □ *The family of the deceased has been informed.*

deceit [dɪ'siːt] *n* something dishonest that somebody says or does that is intended to make somebody else believe something that is not true.

deceitful [dɪ'siːtfl] *adj* [person] who tries to deceive people.

deceive [dɪ'siːv] *vt* to deliberately make <sb> believe something that is not true □ *She's been deceiving him all these years.* □ *Unless my eyes deceive me, that's him over there.* ■ **to deceive oneself** to choose to believe something although one knows it is not true.

decelerate [ˌdiː'seləreɪt] *vi* [car, machine] to slow down.

December [dɪ'sembəʳ] *n* the twelfth month of the year in the Western calendar; *see also* **February**.

decency ['diːsnsɪ] *n* -1. **to have the decency to do sthg** to have enough good manners to do sthg □ *He didn't even have the decency to apologize.* -2. acceptable moral behavior □ *standards of public decency in broadcasting.*

decent ['diːsnt] *adj* -1. [person] who shows respect for accepted standards of behavior and morality □ *decent, law-abiding folk* □ *After her husband died she left a decent interval before remarrying.* ■ **are you decent?** are you dressed? (humorous use). -2. **a decent wage/home etc** a wage/home etc that is acceptable □ *Why don't you get yourself a decent winter coat?* -3. [movie, restaurant] that is of good quality □ *Can you recommend a decent hotel?* -4. [person] who one likes because they are kind □ *She's a decent kid.* □ *It was decent of her to offer.*

decentralization [US ˌdiːsentrələ'zeɪʃn, GB -aɪ-'zeɪʃn] *n*: *see* **decentralize.**

decentralize, -ise [diː'sentrəlaɪz] *vt* [government, company] to remove some part of <a large organization> from one central place to several smaller places so that decisions are made locally □ *Asian governments are pushing ahead toward decentralized economic structures.*

deception [dɪ'sepʃn] *n* -1. something that deceives somebody □ *It was a cruel deception.* -2. the act of deceiving somebody, especially by telling lies □ *He was charged with obtaining money by deception.*

deceptive [dɪ'septɪv] *adj* [behavior, appearance] that deceives one □ *First impressions can be deceptive.* □ *The building's quite deceptive: it looks much bigger than it actually is.*

deceptively [dɪ'septɪvlɪ] *adv* **to look deceptively simple/easy** to look simpler/easier than it actually is.

decibel ['desɪbel] *n* a measurement of the loudness of a sound.

decide [dɪ'saɪd] ◇ *vt* -1. to make a choice about <sthg> after thinking about it □ *They've decided (that) the offices should be closed.* □ *I couldn't decide whether to go or not.* □ *You need to decide if it's big enough.* □ *They've decided to accept the offer.* □ *What have you decided?* -2. [question, case] to make a judgment about <sthg> so that people cannot disagree about it any more □ *The court decided the issue.* -3. [result, future] to influence <sthg> and cause a particular result to happen □ *Talks with union leaders will decide the outcome of the dispute.* □ *The battle was decided by superior fire power.* -4. [person] to cause <sb> to make a particular choice □ *So what finally decided you?* ◇ *vi* to make a choice about something after thinking about it □ *I can't decide between them.* □ *You'll have to decide for yourself.* □ *We have decided against economic sanctions.*

◆ **decide (up)on** *vt fus* **to decide (up)on sthg** [plan, choice] to choose sthg after thinking about it □ *They've decided on the new location for the offices.*

decided [dɪ'saɪdəd] *adj* **a decided change/advantage etc** a clear and definite change/advantage etc.

decidedly [dɪ'saɪdədlɪ] *adv* **decidedly unhappy/uncomfortable etc** very unhappy/uncomfortable etc □ *The future looks decidedly bleak.*

deciding [dɪ'saɪdɪŋ] *adj* **to have the deciding vote** to have the last vote, so that one decides what the result of an election, ballot, debate etc will be.

deciduous [dɪ'sɪdʒʊəs] *adj* [tree, shrub] that loses its leaves in the autumn.
NOTE: Compare **evergreen.**

deciliter US, **decilitre** GB ['desɪliːtəʳ] *n* one tenth of a liter.

decimal ['desəml] ◇ *adj* **a decimal system** a system of counting based on the number ten. ◇ *n* a fraction in which tenths, hundredths, and thousandths are shown as figures after a decimal point, e.g. 0.03 or 0.12.

decimal currency *n* a currency in which each

coin or note is either a tenth of or ten times the value of another coin or note.

decimalize, -ise ['desəməlaɪz] *vt* [currency, number] to change <sthg> to a decimal system.

decimal place *n* one of the positions after a decimal point □ *Calculate the answer to within three decimal places.*

decimal point *n* a symbol (.) in a decimal used to separate whole numbers from fractions.

decimate ['desəmeɪt] *vt* to reduce the number of <animals, people, plants> etc by destroying many of them.

decipher [dɪ'saɪfəʳ] *vt* [code, piece of writing] to work out the meaning of <sthg that is difficult to understand or read>.

decision [dɪ'sɪʒn] *n* **-1.** a choice that one makes about something after thinking about it □ *Have they reached a decision yet?* □ *His decision to leave took us all by surprise.* □ *You've made* OR *taken the right decision.* **-2.** the ability to make choices or judgments quickly and with determination □ *a man of decision.*

decision-maker *n* a person whose job is to make important decisions.

decision-making *n* the activity of making decisions □ *I was not involved in the decision-making process.*

decisive [dɪ'saɪsɪv] *adj* **-1.** [person] who is good at making decisions quickly □ *Be decisive for once.* **-2.** [factor, moment, defeat] that makes the result of something certain □ *It was a decisive victory for the Allies.*

decisively [dɪ'saɪsɪvlɪ] *adv* [act, speak, beat] *see* **decisive** □ *He was decisively beaten.*

deck [dek] ◇ *n* **-1.** [of a ship] one of the floors or levels of a large ship; the flat open areas on each of these floors or levels □ *We were sitting on deck.* □ *the car deck of a ferry.* **-2.** [of a bus] one of the two floors of a bus □ *the top/lower deck.* **-3.** [for playing records] a piece of equipment designed to play records □ *a record deck.* **-4.** [of cards] a complete set of playing cards. **-5.** [of a house] a wooden entrance at the front or back of a house that is raised above the ground and has no roof. ◇ *vt* **to be decked with sthg** [with flags, jewelry] to be decorated with sthg in a colorful and attractive way.

◆ **deck out** *vt sep* **-1. to be decked out with** OR **in sthg** [with flags, ribbons] to be decorated with sthg colorful and attractive. **-2. to be decked out in sthg** [in clothes, jewelry] to be wearing sthg colorful and attractive □ *She was decked out in an ermine coat and pearls.*

deckchair ['dektʃeəʳ] *n* a folding chair that consists of a wooden frame covered with canvas and that is used outdoors, e.g. on a beach or in a park.

deckhand ['dekhænd] *n* a person who works on the deck of a ship doing various jobs.

declaration [,deklə'reɪʃn] *n* **-1.** a statement that makes one's thoughts, feelings, intentions etc very clear to other people □ *He made a declaration of love.* **-2.** an official an-

nouncement □ *a declaration of war/independence.*

Declaration of Independence *n* **the Declaration of Independence** a document written in 1776 by Thomas Jefferson. It stated that the American colonies were no longer ruled by Britain.

declare [dɪ'kleəʳ] *vt* **-1. to declare (that)...** to say very clearly that something is true, especially because one believes it or feels it strongly □ *He declared (that) he would find a way to solve the problem.* □ *He declared his love to her.* **-2.** [news, war, state of emergency] to announce <sthg> officially □ *They declared war on Britain.* **-3.** [goods, money] to tell a government official, e.g. at a border, at customs, or on a form, about <sthg that one has> so that the correct tax can be paid □ *Go through the green channel if you have nothing to declare.*

declared [dɪ'kleəʳd] *adj* **one's declared intention/belief etc** an intention/belief etc that one makes known officially to other people □ *It's their declared aim to double production in 10 years.*

declassify [diː'klæsɪfaɪ] (*pt* & *pp* **declassified**) *vt* to officially change the status of <information, a document> etc so that it is no longer secret.

decline [dɪ'klaɪn] ◇ *n* a gradual change from a good, healthy etc position to a worse or lower one □ *Increased competition hastened the company's decline.* □ *a decline in numbers/the population* □ *There has been a sharp decline in the quality of journalism.* ■ **to be in decline** [number, quality, health] to be gradually becoming smaller or worse. ■ **to be on the** OR **in decline** to be gradually changing from a good, healthy etc position to a worse or lower one □ *The coal industry is in decline.*

◇ *vt* [offer, request, invitation] to refuse <sthg> □ *She declined to say what their plans were.*

◇ *vi* **-1.** [number, quality, health] to gradually change from a good, healthy etc position to a worse or lower one □ *The amount of business we do overseas has declined rapidly.* **-2.** [person] to refuse an invitation, offer, or request □ *We asked him to speak at the conference, but he declined.*

declutch [diː'klʌtʃ] *vi* to disconnect the clutch of a vehicle before changing gear.

decode [diː'kəʊd] *vt* [message, text] to find out the meaning of <sthg that is written in code> by changing it to normal language.

decoder [diː'kəʊdəʳ] *n* a device for decoding messages, texts etc.

decommission [,diːkə'mɪʃn] *vt* [nuclear reactor, warship, weapon] to stop using <a piece of equipment>.

decompose [,diːkəm'pəʊz] *vi* [body, food] to rot by a process of chemical change.

decomposition [,diːkɒmpə'zɪʃn] *n*: *see* **decompose** □ *the process of decomposition* □ *The body was in an advanced stage of decomposition.*

decompression chamber [,diːkəm'preʃn-] *n* a special room in which divers can be brought slowly and safely back to normal air pressure.

decompression sickness *n* a sickness that affects divers if they return to normal air pressure too quickly.

decongestant [ˌdiːkənˈdʒestənt] *n* a medicine used for treating colds, flu etc that helps to clear the nose and chest.

decontaminate [ˌdiːkənˈtæmɪneɪt] *vt* to make <a building, area, or object> safe by removing harmful substances, e.g. germs, poison, or radioactivity.

decor [US deɪˈkɔːr, GB ˈdeɪkɔː] *n* the way in which a room or house is decorated, including the design, colors, furniture etc □ *I liked the simple decor.*

decorate [ˈdekəreɪt] *vt* -1. [room, wall, card] to make <sthg> look more attractive by adding things, e.g. ornaments, balloons, flags etc □ *She decorated his birthday cake with candles.* -2. [bedroom, hall] US to make <the inside of a room or building> more attractive by putting furniture, curtains etc in it; GB to make <the inside of a room or building> more attractive by painting the walls, ceiling, or woodwork, putting up wallpaper etc □ *I spent the day decorating the living-room.* -3. [soldier] to give <sb> a medal for something they have done □ *He was twice decorated for bravery.*

decoration [ˌdekəˈreɪʃn] *n* -1. [for a cake, street] something that is added to something else to make it look more attractive □ *cake/Christmas decorations.* -2. the way in which a room, house, building etc is decorated □ *I like the decoration.* -3. MILITARY a medal □ *a military decoration.* -4. [of a room, building] the process of painting, papering etc a room or building □ *Work has begun on the decoration of the upstairs rooms.*

decorative [ˈdekərətɪv] *adj* [ornament, effect] that makes something more attractive □ *The drape is purely decorative.*

decorator [ˈdekəreɪtər] *n* a person whose job is to decorate houses or buildings □ *a firm of painters and decorators.*

decorous [ˈdekərəs] *adj* [behavior, manner, appearance] that shows decorum (formal use).

decorum [dɪˈkɔːrəm] *n* proper and correct behavior that respects society's customs.

decoy [ˈdiːkɔɪ] *n* -1. something or somebody that is used to distract another person's attention or lead them into danger □ *The attack was a decoy for the main assault further north.* -2. a model of an animal, especially a duck, that is used by hunters to attract animals of the same kind in order to shoot or catch them □ *a decoy duck.*

decrease [*n* ˈdiːkriːs, *vb* diːˈkriːs] ◇ *n* -1. a reduction in the size, number, or strength of something □ *There has been a sharp decrease in foreign trade.* -2. the amount by which something decreases □ *a 10% decrease in profits.* ◇ *vt* to reduce the size, number, or strength of <sthg> □ *They've decreased the budget for*

next year. ◇ *vi:* *The population has steadily decreased.*

decreasing [diːˈkriːsɪŋ] *adj* **a decreasing number/amount etc** a number/amount etc that is becoming less □ *We now have decreasing unemployment for the first time in five years.*

decree [dɪˈkriː] ◇ *n* -1. a command or decision that is made by a state, ruler etc. -2. US a judgment made in a court of law. ◇ *vt* **to decree that...** to officially decide that something must happen □ *The judge decreed that he should be sentenced to death.*

decree absolute (*pl* **decrees absolute**) *n* GB a court order stating that a marriage is finally and legally ended.
NOTE: Compare **decree nisi**.

decree nisi [-ˈnaɪsaɪ] (*pl* **decrees nisi**) *n* GB a court order that states that a marriage will be ended at a future date with a decree absolute unless some reason is given why this may not take place.
NOTE: Compare **decree absolute**.

decrepit [dɪˈkrepɪt] *adj* [person, building] that is very old and in poor condition.

decry [dɪˈkraɪ] (*pt* & *pp* **decried**) *vt* [situation, decline] to criticize and show disapproval of <sthg bad> (formal use).

dedicate [ˈdedɪkeɪt] *vt* -1. **to dedicate sthg to sb** [book, song, poem] to say that sthg was written, composed etc especially for sb □ *I'd like to dedicate the next song to the late, great Bill Morris.* -2. to give <all one's time, energy> etc to a particular purpose □ *He dedicated his life to trying to find a cure for cancer.* ■ **to dedicate oneself to sthg** to give all one's time and energy to sthg □ *She dedicated herself to looking after him/to the revolutionary cause.*

dedicated [ˈdedɪkeɪtəd] *adj* -1. [person] who gives a lot of time and energy to something and believes it is important, useful etc □ *She's very dedicated to her work.* □ *He's a dedicated musician.* -2. **to be dedicated to sb/sthg** to be officially declared or designed to honor or deal with sb/sthg □ *The church is dedicated to St. Francis.* □ *It's the only museum in the country dedicated to the history of the theater.* ■ **a dedicated computer/phone line etc** a computer/phone line etc that has only one particular use □ *a dedicated lounge and check-in area.*

dedication [ˌdedɪˈkeɪʃn] *n* -1. the state of being dedicated □ *He shows great dedication to his work.* -2. the words at the beginning of a book, poem, song etc that state who it is written or composed for.

deduce [dɪˈdjuːs] *vt* **to deduce (that)...** to decide that something is true because of something one knows, finds out, notices etc □ *He deduced that she had already left.* ■ **to deduce sthg from sthg** to deduce sthg by using sthg else as evidence □ *I deduce from your expression that the meeting did not go well.*

deduct [dɪˈdʌkt] *vt* to take <a number, a sum of money> etc from a total □ *The money will be deducted from your wages.*

deductible [dɪˈdʌktəbl] ◇ *adj* [sum of money]

that can be deducted. ◇ *n* US an amount of money that one does not pay tax on.

deduction [dɪˈdʌkʃn] *n* -1. the process of deducing something □ *By a process of deduction I was able to work out the exact location.* -2. the act of deducting something; an amount that has been deducted □ *after the deduction of tax* □ *My income is $58,000 after all deductions.* □ *a tax deduction.*

deed [diːd] *n* -1. something that somebody does, especially something very good or very bad □ *dark deeds.* -2. LAW an official document that contains the details of an agreement, especially a contract involving property □ *a deed of covenant.*

deed poll (*pl* **deed polls** OR **deeds poll**) *n* GB **to change one's name by deed poll** to change one's name legally.

deem [diːm] *vt* **to deem sb/sthg to be sthg** to consider sb/sthg to be sthg (formal use) □ *He deemed it wise/best to keep quiet.* □ *The building was deemed to be unsafe.* □ *They deem that the time is not yet ripe.*

deep [diːp] ◇ *adj* -1. [water, sea, hole] that goes a long way down from the surface □ *That's a very deep cut, you may need stitches.* ■ **to be thrown in at the deep end** to start a new job by having to do something very difficult. -2. [shelf, drawer] that goes a long way in from the outer edge □ *They live deep in the mountains.* -3. [used in measurements] a word used to say how far it is from the top of something to the bottom or from the outer edge of something to the inner edge □ *The water/cupboard is two feet deep.* -4. [sorrow, disappointment, resentment] that is strongly felt □ *It is with deep regret that I tender my resignation.* □ *Please accept my deepest sympathy.* -5. **to be in a deep sleep** to be completely asleep and difficult to wake. -6. [blue, green, red] dark and strong □ *a deep blue sea* □ *a deep shade of pink.* -7. [sound, voice] low □ *a rich, deep voice.* -8. [conversation, movie] that explores things that are difficult to understand □ *They were having a deep theological discussion.* -9. **to take a deep breath** to breathe in a lot of air and then breathe it out again □ *She gave a deep sigh.*

◇ *adv* [dig, advance, move] a long way from the top of something toward the bottom, or from the outer edge of something toward the inner edge □ *They went deep into the jungle.* ■ **to be deep in thought** to be completely absorbed in thinking about something. ■ **deep down** OR **inside** a phrase used to describe somebody's true character or feelings that are not obvious from the way they look or behave □ *Deep down, he doesn't really want the job.* □ *He's a nice guy, deep down.*

deepen [ˈdiːpən] ◇ *vt* [hole, channel] to make <sthg> deeper. ◇ *vi* -1. [river, sea, channel] to become deeper □ *The lake deepens considerably in the middle.* -2. [crisis, recession] to become worse; [love, hatred] to be felt more strongly □ *Their love deepened over the years.* -3. [darkness, color] to become darker.

deepening [ˈdiːpənɪŋ] *adj* **a deepening crisis/recession** a crisis/recession that is becoming worse.

deep-fat fryer [-ˈfraɪəʳ] *n* a deep cooking pan that holds enough oil to cover food and fry it completely.

deep freeze *n* a refrigerator that freezes food.
♦ **deep-freeze** *vt* to freeze or keep <food> in a deep freeze.

deep-fry *vt* to fry <food> in fat or oil so that it is completely covered.

deeply [ˈdiːplɪ] *adv* -1. **to be deeply involved/offended etc** to be very involved/offended etc □ *I'm deeply indebted to you.* □ *He'll be deeply missed when he's gone.* -2. **to dig deeply** to dig a long way down into something. -3. **to breathe deeply** to breathe in a lot of air and then breathe it out again.

deep-rooted *adj* [prejudice, hatred, affection] that has been felt by a person, society etc for a long time and is unlikely to stop.

deep-sea *adj* **deep-sea diving/fishing** diving/fishing that takes place a long way out at sea.

deep-seated *adj* **a deep-seated belief/fear etc** a belief/fear etc that is very strong and difficult to change.

deep-set *adj* **deep-set eyes** eyes that have deep sockets.

Deep South: the Deep South the southeastern states of the USA, including Louisiana, Mississippi, and Alabama.

deer [dɪəʳ] (*pl* **deer**) *n* a large animal that eats grass, often lives in forests, and can run fast. The male has two long horns with several points on them.

deerstalker [ˈdɪəˌstɔːkəʳ] *n* a kind of hat made of thick cloth with flaps that cover the ears or can be tied together on top.

de-escalate [diːˈeskəleɪt] ◇ *vt* [crisis, violence] to make <a situation> less dangerous and less harmful. ◇ *vi: The arms race shows no signs of de-escalating.*

deface [dɪˈfeɪs] *vt* [picture, wall, notice] to spoil <sthg> by marking it in some way, e.g. by writing or drawing on it.

defamation [ˌdefəˈmeɪʃn] *n* the act of publicly saying or writing something about a person that could damage their reputation (formal use).

defamatory [US dɪˈfæmətɔːrɪ, GB -ətərɪ] *adj* [remark, statement] that is damaging to a person's reputation (formal use).

default [dɪˈfɔːlt] ◇ *n* -1. a failure to do something, e.g. to pay a debt or to appear in court □ *Default on loan repayments would lead to the banks laying down even stricter conditions in the future.* ■ **to happen by default** to happen because somebody failed to do something that would have prevented it □ *Our opponents didn't turn up, so we won by default.* -2. COMPUTING a system for performing operations when no specific instructions have been given. ◇ *adj* COMPUTING [position, setting] that is automatically used by a computer if the user has not given different instructions.

◇ *vi* to fail to do something, especially to pay a debt □ *He defaulted on his mortgage.*

defaulter [dɪˈfɔːltəʳ] *n* a person who fails to do something, especially to pay a debt.

default value *n* COMPUTING a value that is automatically used by a computer if the user has not chosen another value.

defeat [dɪˈfiːt] ◇ *vt* -1. [opponent, rival] to beat <sb> in a contest, sport, argument etc □ *The Russian army was defeated at the Battle of Austerlitz.* -2. [motion, proposal] to win enough votes to stop <sthg that one is opposed to> from being accepted □ *The motion was defeated by a majority of 132 votes.* -3. [plan, project] to cause <sthg> to fail □ *Rescue attempts have so far been defeated by the weather.* ◇ *n* a failure to win or achieve something □ *The prime minister refused to admit defeat.* □ *The Battle of Waterloo was Napoleon's final defeat.*

defeatism [dɪˈfiːtɪzm] *n* the attitude of a person who expects to fail or be defeated.

defeatist [dɪˈfiːtəst] ◇ *n* a person who expects to fail or be defeated. ◇ *adj: That's a very defeatist attitude.*

defecate [ˈdefəkeɪt] *vi* to get rid of feces from one's body (formal use).

defect [*n* ˈdiːfekt, *vi* dɪˈfekt] ◇ *n* a fault that makes something or somebody not perfect □ *There's a slight defect in this appliance/your argument.* ◇ *vi* to leave one's country or political party and move to an opposing one □ *He's defected to the other side.*

defection [dɪˈfekʃn] *n*: see **defect** □ *after his defection to the West* □ *There has been a rise in the number of defections.*

defective [dɪˈfektɪv] *adj* [appliance, product] that has a defect and so does not work properly.

defector [dɪˈfektəʳ] *n* a person who defects to another country or party.

defence *etc* GB = **defense** *etc.*

defend [dɪˈfend] ◇ *vt* -1. [person, city, country] to take action to protect <a person or place> against physical attack □ *Troops were sent in to defend the capital.* □ *He used his cane to defend himself against his attackers.* -2. [action, opinion, decision] to argue in support of <sthg> that is accused of being wrong □ *I'm not trying to defend what she did.* □ *In a letter to the press, she vigorously defended herself against the accusations of corruption.* -3. LAW to represent <sb> in court to argue against an accusation that has been made against them. -4. SPORT to take action to prevent somebody from attacking <one's goal, position> etc. -5. **to defend one's title** to play against somebody and try to prevent them from taking a title that one holds □ *They will be defending their title in the World Championships next week.* ◇ *vi* SPORT to take action against an opponent who is attacking.

defendant [dɪˈfendənt] *n* the person in a trial who is accused of a crime. NOTE: Compare **plaintiff**.

defender [dɪˈfendəʳ] *n* -1. [of a country, city] a person who defends a place against attack.

-2. SPORT a player who tries to prevent the other side from scoring points. -3. **a defender of sthg** [of a cause, policy] a person who defends sthg.

defense US, **defence** GB [dɪˈfens] *n* -1. [of oneself, a country] the act of defending oneself or one's country against attack □ *She carries a weapon for defense against attackers/mugging.* -2. MILITARY the armed forces of a country and their equipment □ *How much do we spend on defense?* -3. [against an illness, attack] a device or system that protects a person, animal, or thing □ *the body's natural defenses against infection* □ *Attack is often the best defense.* -4. LAW an argument or arguments used to deny a charge in court □ *Lawyers are preparing her defense.* ■ **the defense** the lawyers who are defending somebody in court; the case presented by these lawyers □ *He was cross-examined by the defense.* □ *a witness for the defense* □ *a defense witness.* ■ **in sb's defense** as a way of defending sb against criticism or an accusation □ *It must be said in her defense that she's always been kind to us.* -5. SPORT the players who defend against the opposing team □ *He managed to break through the Irish defense.*

◆ **defenses** US, **defences** GB *npl* the armed forces and equipment available to defend a country, town, or building □ *They broke through the city's defenses.*

defenseless US, **defenceless** GB [dɪˈfensləs] *adj* [person] who is unable to defend themselves, e.g. because they are weak or have no weapon □ *They even attacked defenseless women and children.*

defensive [dɪˈfensɪv] ◇ *adj* -1. [weapon, tactic] that is intended to be used in defense □ *Parts of the defensive walls remain.* -2. [person] who is ready to defend themselves against criticism □ *Why are you getting all defensive?* ◇ *n* **to be/go on the defensive** to be/make oneself ready to defend oneself against criticism or attack.

defer [dɪˈfɜːʳ] (*pt* & *pp* **deferred**, *cont* **deferring**) ◇ *vt* [decision, action, payment] to delay <sthg> until later □ *I've decided to defer my entry to university and spend a year doing voluntary work.* ◇ *vi* **to defer to sb** to accept sb's decision, even if one does not agree with it, because one respects them or because they are in a position of authority.

deference [ˈdefrəns] *n* polite and respectful behavior, usually toward somebody older or in authority □ *I wore a tie in* OR *out of deference to tradition.*

deferential [ˌdefəˈrenʃl] *adj* [behavior, treatment, person] that shows great respect for a person, their wishes etc.

defiance [dɪˈfaɪəns] *n* behavior that shows that one refuses to obey a law, a rule, or somebody's wishes □ *She tore up the letter in a gesture of defiance.* ■ **to do sthg in defiance of sb/sthg** to do sthg even though one has been told not to do it □ *They are continuing to test chemical weapons in defiance of the ban.*

defiant [dɪˈfaɪənt] *adj* [person, action, behavior]

that shows defiance of somebody or something □ *She gave him a defiant look.*

defiantly [dɪ'faɪəntlɪ] *adv* [say, refuse] *see* **defiant** □ *He laughed defiantly.*

deficiency [dɪ'fɪʃnsɪ] (*pl* **deficiencies**) *n* [in vitamins, person, system] *see* **deficient** □ *a Vitamin A deficiency.*

deficient [dɪ'fɪʃnt] *adj* -1. **to be deficient in sthg** to have too little of sthg that is necessary for health, growth etc □ *a diet deficient in vitamins.* -2. [person, system, process] that is not good enough for a particular activity or purpose □ *They must be mentally deficient to think that.*

deficit ['defəsɪt] *n* the amount by which something, usually a sum of money, is less than what is necessary, correct, or expected □ *The government faces a trade deficit of $20 billion.*

defile [dɪ'faɪl] *vt* to spoil <sthg> by treating it with disrespect or by making it less pure or good □ *She felt his memory had been defiled.*

define [dɪ'faɪn] *vt* -1. [word, phrase, concept] to explain or show the meaning of <sthg> □ *It's a difficult word to define.* □ *How would you define happiness?* -2. [problem, feeling, function] to explain the nature of <sthg> in a precise way □ *It's hard to define how I feel right now.* □ *Their role is clearly defined in their contract.*

definite ['defənət] *adj* -1. [plan, date] firm and clear □ *We're supposed to be meeting next week but it's not definite.* □ *When can you give me a definite answer?* -2. [improvement, advantage] very noticeable □ *There has been a definite change in his behavior.* -3. **to be definite** to be firm and confident about one's wishes, opinion etc □ *Briggs was very definite about the need for punctuality.*

definitely ['defənətlɪ] *adv* a word used to show that one is certain about something □ *He's definitely the man I saw.* □ *He has definitely decided to resign.* □ *"Are you going to the show?" — "Definitely!"*

definition [,defə'nɪʃn] *n* -1. an explanation of the meaning of a word or phrase, especially in a dictionary □ *It's not a very clear definition.* ■ **by definition** a phrase used to say that a word has a particular quality because that quality is part of the meaning of the word □ *Jealousy is by definition a destructive feeling.* -2. the quality of being clear □ *the improved definition of computer screens.*

definitive [dɪ'fɪnətɪv] *adj* -1. **a definitive answer/decision etc** an answer/decision etc that is final and cannot be questioned or changed. -2. **a definitive book/study etc** a book/study etc that is considered to be the best of its kind □ *the definitive work on the history of the American Civil War.*

deflate [diː'fleɪt] ◇ *vt* -1. to let the air out of <a balloon, tire> etc. -2. to make <sb> less proud or self-confident □ *He came back from the meeting looking a little deflated.* -3. to cause deflation in <an economy>. ◇ *vi* [balloon, tire] to lose air and become flat.

deflation [diː'fleɪʃn] *n* ECONOMY a reduction in the supply of money, leading to less eco-

nomic activity, lower prices, and lower levels of investment and employment.
NOTE: Compare **inflation**.

deflationary [diː'fleɪʃnərɪ] *adj* [policy, measure] that is intended to cause deflation.
NOTE: Compare **inflationary**.

deflect [dɪ'flekt] *vt* -1. [ball, stream, bullet] to make <sthg> change direction, e.g. by blocking its path □ *The ball was deflected off another player's legs.* -2. [criticism, anger] to avoid <sthg> by directing it toward somebody or something else □ *The war was partly an attempt to deflect attention away from domestic problems.*

deflection [dɪ'flekʃn] *n*: *see* **deflect** □ *The deflection sent the ball just wide of the goal.*

defog [,diː'fɒg] *vt* US to remove mist from <a car window>.

defogger [,diː'fɒgər] *n* US a device that blows air onto the front window of a car so that one can see clearly through it; a set of wires that heat the back window of a car so that one can see clearly through it.

deforest [,diː'fɒrɪst] *vt* to cut down all the trees in <an area>.

deforestation [diː,fɒrɪ'steɪʃn] *n*: *see* **deforest** □ *Since the 1970s the rainforests have suffered massive deforestation.*

deform [dɪ'fɔːm] *vt* to change the shape or appearance of <a person, animal, or thing> so that it is no longer normal, especially because of a disease or injury □ *His face was hideously deformed in the attack.*

deformed [dɪ'fɔːmd] *adj* [person, animal, limb] that does not have a normal shape or appearance, especially because of a disease or injury.

deformity [dɪ'fɔːmətɪ] (*pl* **deformities**) *n* the state of being deformed; a part of the body that is deformed.

defraud [dɪ'frɔːd] *vt* to get money or goods illegally by deceiving <a person, company> etc.

defray [dɪ'freɪ] *vt* to provide money to pay for <costs, expenses> etc □ *The company is hoping that these measures will defray future pension costs.*

defrost [,diː'frɒst] ◇ *vt* -1. [fridge, icebox] to turn off or adjust <a refrigerator or freezer> so that the ice melts. -2. [meat, vegetables] to allow <frozen food> to become warmer gradually before eating or cooking it □ *I defrosted the fish overnight.* -3. US [window, windshield] to remove ice or mist from <a car window>. ◇ *vi* -1. [fridge, freezer] to be turned off so that the ice can melt □ *The fridge is defrosting.* -2. [food] to pass from a frozen state to its usual state □ *Allow the meat 4 hrs to defrost.*

deft [deft] *adj* -1. [movement, maneuver, shot] that looks quick and skillful □ *his deft handling of the ball.* -2. [handling, leadership] that is skillful and shows an ability to think quickly □ *deft use of the media.*

deftly ['deftlɪ] *adv* [move, manage, handle] *see* **deft** □ *Mr Robinson deftly avoided the question.*

defunct [dɪ'fʌŋkt] *adj* [project, organization, company] that no longer exists or has importance □ *the now defunct Greater London Council.*

defuse [ˌdiː'fjuːz] *vt* -1. to remove the fuse from <a bomb> to prevent it from exploding □ *The device was defused by bomb disposal experts.* -2. [tension, argument] to make <a dangerous or tense situation> calmer □ *Diplomats are hurriedly trying to defuse the row.*

defy [dɪ'faɪ] (*pt* & *pp* **defied**) *vt* -1. [person, order, law] to refuse openly to respect or obey <sb/sthg> □ *The union defied the court order.* -2. **to defy sb to do sthg** to say that one thinks sb is unable to do sthg in order to make them try to do it □ *I defy you to prove otherwise.* -3. [description, attempts] to make <sthg> very difficult or impossible □ *Some of the things they did defy belief.*

de Gaulle [də'gəʊl], **Charles** (1890–1970) a French general and politician who was president from 1959 to 1969. During World War II he led French opposition to the Nazis while he was based in England. As president he was responsible for the independence of the French colonies in Africa.

degenerate [*adj* & *n* dɪ'dʒenərət, *vb* dɪ'dʒenəreɪt] ◇ *adj* [person] who has low standards of behavior and morals. ◇ *n* a degenerate person. ◇ *vi* [discussion, situation] to go from one state to a worse one □ *The meeting degenerated into a brawl.*

degradation [ˌdegrə'deɪʃn] *n* a state of extreme poverty or shame □ *a life of misery and degradation.*

degrade [dɪ'greɪd] *vt* -1. to make <sb> feel worthless and not respected by other people □ *She felt degraded by their treatment of her.* -2. to cause damage to <sthg> □ *chemicals that degrade the environment.*

degrading [dɪ'greɪdɪŋ] *adj* [comment, experience] that degrades somebody □ *the degrading treatment of prisoners.*

degree [dɪ'griː] *n* -1. [for measuring temperature] a unit of measurement for temperature □ *30 degrees Centigrade.* -2. [for measuring angles] a unit of measurement for angles □ *a 90-degree angle.* -3. [for measuring positions] a unit of measurement for positions on a map □ *a latitude of 52 degrees north.* -4. EDUCATION a qualification, usually from a university □ *She has a degree in economics.* -5. [of truth, risk, luck] an amount or level of something □ *There is a degree of risk in this venture.* ■ **to a certain degree** partly □ *To a certain degree he's right.* ■ **by degrees** gradually □ *The economy is improving by degrees.*

dehumanize, **-ise** [diː'hjuːmənaɪz] *vt* to treat <sb> in a way that causes them to lose their dignity or individuality.

dehydrated [ˌdiːhaɪ'dreɪtəd] *adj* -1. [food] that has been preserved by drying. -2. [person] whose body is suffering from a lack of water.

dehydration [ˌdiːhaɪ'dreɪʃn] *n* a medical condition in which one feels weak or ill because one's body does not contain enough water.

de-ice [ˌdiː'aɪs] *vt* to remove ice from <a windshield>.

de-icer [ˌdiː'aɪsər] *n* a chemical used for removing ice from a windshield.

deign [deɪn] *vi* **to deign to do sthg** to do sthg one considers to be below one's status or abilities □ *So you've deigned to join us.*

deity ['deɪtɪ] (*pl* **deities**) *n* a god or goddess.

déjà vu [ˌdeɪʒɑː'vuː] *n* the feeling that one is experiencing something that one has already experienced before at some time in the past.

dejected [dɪ'dʒektəd] *adj* [look, face, person] unhappy and disappointed □ *He looked sad and dejected.*

dejection [dɪ'dʒekʃn] *n* a feeling of unhappiness caused by something very disappointing.

del *abbr of* **delete**.

Delaware ['deləweər] a state in the eastern USA, on the Atlantic coast. ABBREVIATION: DE. SIZE: 5,004 sq kms. POPULATION: 666,168 (*Delawareans*). CAPITAL: Dover.

delay [dɪ'leɪ] ◇ *vt* -1. [passenger, traffic, trip] to cause <sb/sthg> to be late □ *The flight was delayed for three hours.* -2. [meeting, payment, decision] to make <sthg> happen at a later time □ *She delayed telling him the truth until it was too late.* ◇ *vi* to be slow or late in doing something □ *Don't delay in giving him your answer.* ◇ *n* -1. an act of delaying □ *Delays may occur as a result of the fog.* □ *We should buy now, without delay.* -2. the length of time that something is delayed □ *There is a three-hour delay on all flights.*

delayed [dɪ'leɪd] *adj* happening at a later time than usual or expected □ *a delayed start* □ *He had a delayed reaction to the news.*

delayed-action *adj* [response, fuse] that happens or works after a delay. ■ **a delayed-action shutter** PHOTOGRAPHY a camera shutter that works a short time after it is operated.

delectable [dɪ'lektəbl] *adj* -1. [food, meal] that tastes very good. -2. [person, dress] that one thinks is very attractive (informal use).

delegate [*n* 'delɪgət, *vb* 'delɪgeɪt] ◇ *n* a person chosen to represent a country, organization etc at a conference or meeting. ◇ *vt* -1. to give <sb> the authority or responsibility to do something as one's representative □ *Sarah was delegated to represent us at the meeting.* -2. to give somebody <a job, task> etc to do as one's representative; to give somebody <authority or responsibility> so they can act as one's representative □ *I've delegated most of my secretarial work to Chuck.* ◇ *vi* to delegate responsibility, a task etc □ *We would be more efficient if we delegated more often.*

delegation [ˌdelɪ'geɪʃn] *n* -1. a group of delegates □ *the Korean/trade delegation.* -2. [of power, responsibility] the act of delegating something.

delete [dɪ'liːt] ◇ *vt* to remove <a word, line, phrase> etc from a text by crossing it out, erasing it, or removing it from a computer screen. ◇ *vi*: *'Delete where not applicable.'*

deletion [dɪ'liːʃn] *n*: see **delete** □ We'll need to make a few deletions.

Delhi ['delɪ] a city in central northern India consisting of Old Delhi, an ancient walled city, and New Delhi, the capital of India. POPULATION: 8,375,188.

deli ['delɪ] *n* = **delicatessen** (informal use).

deliberate [*adj* dɪ'lɪbərət, *vb* dɪ'lɪbəreɪt] ◇ *adj* -1. [act, rudeness, insult] that happens because somebody intends it to happen, and not by accident or chance □ It was a deliberate attempt to embarrass the guests. -2. [movement, speech] slow and careful. ◇ *vi* [jury, committee] to think about something very seriously before making a decision □ She deliberated for several minutes before answering.

deliberately [dɪ'lɪbərətlɪ] *adv* [act, insult, move] see **deliberate** □ He deliberately kept us waiting, I'm sure! □ Police said the fire had been started deliberately.

deliberation [dɪ,lɪbə'reɪʃn] *n* -1. careful consideration □ After much deliberation, it was decided that he should be allowed to join. -2. **with deliberation** [act, speak] slowly and carefully.

◆ **deliberations** *npl* serious discussion by a group of people about something (formal use).

delicacy ['delɪkəsɪ] (*pl* **delicacies**) *n* -1. [of a hand, situation] see **delicate** □ a matter of the utmost delicacy. -2. [of a person] a way of acting or speaking to somebody that avoids offending them. -3. COOKING something that is very pleasant to eat but is rare or expensive □ Snails are a delicacy here.

delicate ['delɪkət] *adj* -1. [hand, work, movement] small, attractive, and graceful □ a small delicate woman. -2. [flavor, color] that is pleasant and not strong □ a delicate hint of saffron. -3. [glass, china] that is fragile and breaks easily □ Don't drop it, it's very delicate. -4. [person] who becomes ill easily □ He was a delicate child. □ Her health is becoming increasingly delicate. -5. [situation, subject, issue] that needs to be treated in a careful and sensitive way, e.g. because it is uncertain or likely to cause problems □ Talks have reached a very delicate stage. -6. [instrument, equipment] that is very sensitive and shows small changes.

delicately ['delɪkətlɪ] *adv* -1. **delicately drawn/ carved etc** drawn/carved etc in a delicate way □ a piece of delicately made china. -2. **delicately colored/flavored etc** pleasantly and not strongly colored/flavored etc □ delicately spiced with cinnamon. -3. [hint, suggest] in a careful and sensitive way □ He put it very delicately, but it was quite clear that he wanted us to leave.

delicatessen [,delɪkə'tesn] *n* a store that sells cold fresh food of good quality that is often imported, e.g. cheese and cooked meat.

delicious [dɪ'lɪʃəs] *adj* -1. [food, drink, flavor] that tastes very good □ This pasta is absolutely delicious! □ What a delicious smell! -2. [feeling] that one finds very enjoyable or satisfying.

delight [dɪ'laɪt] ◇ *n* -1. a feeling of great pleasure □ He discovered to his delight that his shares had doubled in value. ■ **to take delight in doing sthg** to enjoy doing sthg very much □ Simon takes a great delight in teasing his younger sister. -2. a thing or person that gives great pleasure □ the delights of country life. ◇ *vt* to please <sb> very much □ The news should delight enthusiasts everywhere. ◇ *vi* **to delight in sthg** to enjoy sthg very much □ He delights in annoying me.

delighted [dɪ'laɪtəd] *adj* **to be delighted** to be very happy about something □ We were delighted with the news. □ She was delighted to see him. □ "Can you come?" — "I'd be delighted." □ We were delighted (that) you could come.

delightful [dɪ'laɪtfl] *adj* [person, place, evening] very pleasant or enjoyable □ We had a delightful time while we were there.

delightfully [dɪ'laɪtflɪ] *adv*: see **delightful** □ a delightfully amusing book.

Delilah [dɪ'laɪlə] → **Samson**.

delimit [diː'lɪmət] *vt* [powers, scope] to fix the limits of <sthg> □ The role of the commission is delimited by law.

delineate [dɪ'lɪnɪeɪt] *vt* [plan, policy, problem] to describe <sthg>.

delinquency [dɪ'lɪŋkwənsɪ] *n* delinquent behavior.

delinquent [dɪ'lɪŋkwənt] ◇ *adj* [child] who breaks the law, usually by committing minor crimes against society. ◇ *n* a delinquent child.

delirious [dɪ'lɪrɪəs] *adj* -1. who is suffering from delirium □ He was delirious with fever. -2. who is very excited and happy □ She was delirious with joy. □ He'll be delirious at the news.

delirium [dɪ'lɪrɪəm] *n* an inability to think or speak in a clear sensible way, usually caused by fever □ suffering from delirium.

deliver [dɪ'lɪvəʳ] ◇ *vt* -1. [goods, mail, newspapers] to take <sthg> to somebody's home or office, usually because one is paid to do this □ Can you deliver these photos to the press office by 11 am? -2. [speech, lecture, warning] to say <sthg> in public □ The jury delivered a verdict of guilty. -3. to help a woman while she gives birth to <a baby> □ Her husband helped to deliver the baby. -4. **to deliver sb from sthg** [from captivity, danger] to help sb escape from sthg unpleasant (literary use). -5. US POLITICS to succeed in getting <the votes of a group of people> □ Can he deliver the Black vote? -6. **to deliver a blow** to hit somebody □ He delivered a heavy blow to the back of her head. ◇ *vi* -1. to take things to somebody's home, office etc, usually in return for payment □ We deliver 24 hours a day. -2. to do what one has promised or been asked to do □ The Administration has failed to deliver on tax reform/its promises.

delivery [dɪ'lɪvərɪ] (*pl* **deliveries**) *n* -1. [of letters, goods] the act of delivering something □ Mail deliveries are fairly irregular. □ 'Allow two weeks for delivery.' □ 'Payment on delivery' □ 'Free delivery.' ■ **to take delivery of sthg** to accept sthg that has been delivered, usually by signing for it. -2. [of stationery, stock] something that is delivered □ *Another delivery of spare parts has just arrived.* **-3.** [of a speech] somebody's way of speaking, especially when making a speech or acting □ *He needs to work on his delivery.* **-4.** [of a baby] the act of giving birth to a baby □ *the delivery room.*

delivery note *n* a document signed by somebody who receives a package, goods etc to prove that they have been delivered.

delivery truck US, **delivery van** *n* a small van used for delivering goods.

delphinium [del'fɪnɪəm] (*pl* **delphiniums**) *n* a tall garden plant with blue flowers growing along its stem.

delta ['deltə] (*pl* **deltas**) *n* a triangular area where a river divides into many parts before reaching the sea □ *the Pearl River delta.*

delude [dɪ'luːd] *vt* to persuade <sb> to believe something that is not true □ *If he thinks they can survive the recession he's deluding himself.*

deluge ['deljuːdʒ] ◇ *n* **-1.** a flood; a large amount of heavy rain. **-2.** [of questions, letters] a very large amount of things that arrive at the same time. □ *We've received a deluge of complaints.* ◇ *vt* **to be deluged with sthg** [with letters, questions] to receive a large amount of sthg □ *The band has been deluged with fan mail.*

delusion [dɪ'luːʒn] *n* something that somebody believes, but that is not true □ *She is under the delusion that her illness isn't serious.* ■ **to have delusions of grandeur** to believe that one is more important than one really is.

de luxe [də'lʌks] *adj* [hotel, car] that is of high quality and expensive.

delve [delv] *vi* **-1. to delve into sthg** [into a mystery, the past] to investigate sthg in detail in order to get information □ *I don't want to delve too deeply into his reasons for not going.* **-2.** to search in a place, especially in something that is deep or filled with things □ *She had to delve inside her bag to find it.*

Dem *abbr of* **Democrat(ic).**

demagogue ['deməgɒg] *n* a political leader who tries to win support by appealing to people's emotions and prejudices.

demand [US dɪ'mænd, GB -'mɑːnd] ◇ *n* **-1.** a firm request for something, usually for something that another person does not want to give □ *There have been demands for the president's resignation.* ■ **a wage demand** a request for an increase in wages. ■ **on demand** whenever anybody asks for it □ *Abortion is now available on demand.* **-2. demands on sb** the things that use up sb's time and energy □ *His family makes huge demands on his time.* ■ **a demand for sthg** a need or desire for sthg □ *There's not much demand for luxury goods in this area.* ■ **to be in demand** to be very popular and wanted by many people □ *American jeans are in great demand.*

◇ *vt* **-1.** [apology, explanation, wage increase] to ask firmly and forcefully for <sthg> □ *He demanded to see the report.* **-2.** to ask <sthg> firmly □ *"What's wrong with that?" she demanded.* **-3.** [attention, dedication, time] to need

<sthg> □ *He has the courage that the job demands.*

demanding [US dɪ'mændɪŋ, GB -'mɑːnd-] *adj* **-1.** [job, task, situation] that is difficult and needs a lot of effort, concentration, time etc □ *It's extremely demanding being on duty 14 hours a day.* **-2.** [person] who needs a lot of attention and is not easily satisfied □ *She's a very demanding child.*

demarcation [ˌdiːmɑːˈkeɪʃn] *n* a boundary or line of separation, e.g. between two pieces of land or between different types of work □ *a demarcation line.*

demarcation dispute *n* a dispute between labor unions about which jobs should be done by their members.

demean [dɪ'miːn] *vt* to cause <sb/sthg> to lose the respect of other people □ *Pornography demeans women.*

demeaning [dɪ'miːnɪŋ] *adj* [work, experience] that demeans somebody □ *a demeaning, sexist remark.*

demeanor US, **demeanour** GB [dɪ'miːnəʳ] *n* the way that somebody behaves (formal use) □ *I didn't like his haughty demeanor.*

demented [dɪ'mentəd] *adj* [person] crazy.

dementia [dɪ'menʃə] *n* serious mental illness that is caused by a disease or injury of the brain □ *people suffering from dementia.*

demerara sugar [ˌdeməreərə-] *n* GB a type of brown sugar.

demigod ['demɪgɒd] *n* a mythological being who is half-human and half-god.

demijohn ['demɪdʒɒn] *n* a large bottle with a narrow neck that is used for making wine.

demilitarized zone [diː'mɪlɪtəraɪzd-] *n* an area from which military forces have been removed.

demise [dɪ'maɪz] *n* **-1.** [of a company, empire] the end of something that was successful or important □ *the demise of the Welfare State.* **-2.** the death of somebody (formal use) □ *after the tragic demise of his wife.*

demist [ˌdiː'mɪst] *vt* GB to remove mist from <a car window>.

demister [ˌdiː'mɪstəʳ] *n* GB a device that blows air onto the front window of a car so that one can see clearly through it; a set of wires that heat the back window of a car so that one can see clearly through it.

demo ['deməʊ] (*pl* **demos**) *n* = **demonstration** (informal use).

demobilize, -ise [ˌdiː'məʊbəlaɪz] *vt* to release <troops, soldiers> etc from the armed forces, usually after a war.

democracy [dɪ'mɒkrəsɪ] (*pl* **democracies**) *n* **-1.** a system of government in which people choose leaders to govern them by voting in elections □ *We are working to bring back democracy.* **-2.** a country whose government is elected by the people □ *a fragile democracy.*

democrat ['deməkræt] *n* a person who believes in democracy.

◆ **Democrat** *n* a person who supports or is a

member of the Democratic Party in the USA.

democratic [ˌdeməˈkrætɪk] *adj* [country] that has a government elected by the people; [government, system, election] that is found in this kind of country □ *Western liberal democratic values.*

◆ **Democratic** *adj* that is connected with the Democratic Party in the USA □ *the Democratic election campaign.*

democratically [ˌdeməˈkrætɪklɪ] *adv* [decide, discuss] by asking everybody for their opinion □ *a democratically elected leader.*

Democratic Party *n* the Democratic Party one of the two main political parties in the USA. It is considered to be more left-wing than the Republican Party.

demographic [ˌdeməˈgræfɪk] *adj* [change, trend] that is connected with the population of a particular country and where people live.

demolish [dɪˈmɒlɪʃ] *vt* **-1.** [house, block] to pull down <a building>, usually to provide space for something new □ *The old cinema was demolished and a new one built in its place.* **-2.** [theory, case] to prove that <an idea or argument> is wrong □ *By the end of the trial the prosecution had completely demolished Mrs Baxtor's defense.* **-3.** [meal, course] to eat <food> very quickly so that there is no more left (informal use) □ *Frank demolished the contents of his plate in five minutes flat.*

demolition [ˌdeməˈlɪʃn] *n* [of a house, block] *see* **demolish** □ *Demolition work is already underway on the site.*

demon [ˈdiːmən] ◇ *n* an evil spirit or devil. ◇ *comp* **a demon player/cyclist etc** an extremely skilled player/cyclist etc.

demonstrable [dɪˈmɒnstrəbl] *adj* [fact, change, improvement] that can be shown to be true or exist □ *a demonstrable link between smoking and lung cancer.*

demonstrably [dɪˈmɒnstrəblɪ] *adv* [true, better] *see* **demonstrable** □ *Their claims are demonstrably wrong.*

demonstrate [ˈdemənstreɪt] ◇ *vt* **-1.** [theory, principle] to prove that <sthg> is true or exists □ *The findings clearly demonstrate a link between poverty and crime.* □ *You must demonstrate that you are able to do the work.* **-2.** [machine, technique] to show how <sthg> works by operating it and giving an explanation at the same time □ *Can you demonstrate how it works?* **-3.** [ability, skill, quality] to show that one has <sthg> □ *This clearly demonstrates her organizational skills.* ◇ *vi* **to demonstrate for/against sthg** to take part in a demonstration for/against sthg.

demonstration [ˌdemənˈstreɪʃn] *n* **-1. to give a demonstration** to show how something works or is done □ *She gave us a demonstration of how it operated.* **-2.** [for something, against something] a public meeting or march held by people who feel strongly about a particular subject and want their opinions to be known □ *They held/staged a massive demonstration against the new highway.* **-3. a demon-**

stration of affection/support etc an act of showing affection/support etc.

demonstrative [dɪˈmɒnstrətɪv] *adj* [person] who shows their feelings openly, especially by hugging and kissing people.

demonstrator [ˈdemənstreɪtər] *n* **-1.** a person who shows and explains how a machine, appliance etc works. **-2.** a person who takes part in a demonstration for or against something □ *Over a thousand demonstrators gathered to protest the measures.*

demoralize, -ise [dɪˈmɒrəlaɪz] *vt* to make <sb> lose confidence in what they are doing □ *It demoralized many teachers to see cuts being made in key areas.*

demoralized [dɪˈmɒrəlaɪzd] *adj* [person, workforce, army] who has lost confidence in what they are doing □ *They returned from the meeting tired and demoralized.*

demote [diːˈməʊt] *vt* to put <sb> into a lower rank or position, often as a punishment □ *He was demoted to the rank of sergeant.*

demotion [diːˈməʊʃn] *n*: *see* **demote** □ *Miss Taft's behavior improved after her demotion.*

demotivate [ˌdiːˈməʊtəveɪt] *vt* to make <workers, students> etc lose their enthusiasm for what they are doing.

demure [dɪˈmjʊər] *adj* [woman, child] who seems shy and careful to behave correctly □ *She looked very demure in her long white dress.*

demystify [ˌdiːˈmɪstəfaɪ] (*pt* & *pp* **demystified**) *vt* to make <sthg> less mysterious and easier for ordinary people to understand.

den [den] *n* a home made by wild animals such as foxes.

denationalize, -ise [ˌdiːˈnæʃnəlaɪz] *vt* to sell <an industry> to private owners so that it no longer belongs to the state.

denial [dɪˈnaɪəl] *n* **-1.** [of an accusation, allegation, rumor] a statement that says something is not true □ *The Prime Minister issued a firm denial today.* **-2.** [of a right, privilege] a refusal to allow somebody to have something they want.

denier [ˈdenjər] *n* GB a measurement of how fine the thread is in pantyhose or stockings □ *15-denier tights.*

denigrate [ˈdenɪgreɪt] *vt* [person, achievement, character] to speak or write very unfavorably about <sb/sthg> especially when they deserve to be praised (formal use).

denim [ˈdenɪm] *n* a strong cloth made of cotton that is usually blue and is used to make clothes □ *denim jeans.*

◆ **denims** *npl* jeans made of denim □ *a pair of denims.*

denim jacket *n* a short casual jacket made of denim.

denizen [ˈdenɪzən] *n* an inhabitant of a particular place (literary use).

Denmark [ˈdenmɑːrk] a country in northern Europe, between the Baltic and the North Sea. SIZE: 43,000 sq kms. POPULATION: 5,100,000 (*Danes, Danish*). CAPITAL: Copenhagen. LANGUAGE: Danish. CURRENCY: Danish krone.

denomination [dɪ,nɒmə'neɪʃn] *n* **-1.** RELIGION one of the main groups of believers in a particular religion. **-2.** FINANCE the value of a coin or bill □ *We cannot change denominations smaller than 2000 lire.*

denominator [dɪ'nɒməneɪtər] *n* the part of a fraction that is below the line and that the top number is divided by.

denote [dɪ'nout] *vt* (formal use) to mean <sthg>; to be a sign or symbol for <sthg>.

denouement [US ,deɪnuː'mɑːŋ, GB deɪ'nuːmɒŋ] *n* the end of a book, movie, or play, when everything is explained □ *I found the denouement of the plot rather unsatisfactory.*

denounce [dɪ'naʊns] *vt* [person, idea, policy] to criticize <sb/sthg> severely in public □ *He was denounced as a traitor to his country.*

dense [dens] *adj* **-1.** [crowd, traffic, forest] where there are many people or things with very little space between them; [fog, mist, smoke] that is difficult to see through. **-2.** [person] who one thinks is stupid and slow in understanding (informal use).

densely ['densli] *adv* **densely populated** that has a lot of people living in a small area.

density ['densəti] (*pl* **densities**) *n* **-1.** [of traffic, a crowd, forest] the degree to which people or things are very close together; [of fog, mist, smoke] the fact of being difficult to see through □ *a map showing population density.* **-2.** PHYSICS the relationship between an object's mass and its volume □ *Water has a higher density than oil.*

dent [dent] ◇ *n* a hollow area on a surface where it has been hit by something and damaged □ *I noticed a small dent in my car.* ◇ *vt* [surface, metal, car] to make a dent in <sthg>.

dental ['dentl] *adj* [hygiene, decay] that is connected with one's teeth □ *a dental appointment.*

dental floss *n* thread covered in wax that is used to clean the spaces between one's teeth.

dental plate *n* the part of a set of dentures that fits against the top of the mouth.

dental surgeon *n* = **dentist**.

dental surgery *n* GB the place where a dentist works and gives treatment to patients.

dental treatment *n* something done by a dentist to one's teeth to keep them healthy or attractive.

dented ['dentəd] *adj* [car, surface] that has a dent in it.

dentist ['dentəst] *n* a person whose job is to treat people's teeth. ■ **a dentist's** the place where a dentist works □ *I've got to go to the dentist's.*

dentistry ['dentəstri] *n* the work done by a dentist.

dentures ['dentʃərz] *npl* artificial teeth that are used to replace teeth that have fallen out or been removed □ *a set of dentures.*

denude [dɪ'njuːd] *vt* **to be denuded of sthg** [of leaves, flowers] to have all of sthg removed so that it is completely bare (formal use).

denunciation [dɪ,nʌnsɪ'eɪʃn] *n* [of a person, organization, decision] a statement that denounces somebody or something □ *Brandon's denunciation of the behavior of the press.*

deny [dɪ'naɪ] (*pt* & *pp* **denied**) *vt* **-1.** [accusation, allegation, rumor] to say that <sthg> is not true □ *He denied all knowledge of the takeover bid.* □ *She denied driving while under the influence of alcohol.* □ *A spokesman denied (that) the company had knowingly damaged the environment.* **-2.** **to deny sb sthg** [right, access, chance] to refuse to allow sb to have sthg that they want □ *You cannot deny me the right to speak to my own wife!*

deodorant [dɪ'oʊdərənt] *n* a substance, usually a liquid or a spray, that is used to reduce body smells, especially under one's arms □ *a spray/roll-on deodorant* □ *He doesn't use deodorant.*

depart [dɪ'pɑːrt] *vi* (formal use) **-1.** [train, plane, person] to leave □ *The train for Pisa will depart from platform 16.* **-2.** **to depart from sthg** [from normal procedure, a custom, script] not to follow sthg □ *Departing from tradition, the Queen traveled on a scheduled flight.*

department [dɪ'pɑːrtmənt] *n* **-1.** [of a company] a section of a company or organization that has a particular function □ *the company's personnel/sales department.* **-2.** [of a store] a section of a large store that sells a particular kind of goods □ *the menswear/china department.* **-3.** EDUCATION a group of teachers in a school, college, or university who teach a particular subject □ *the psychology department.* **-4.** [of a government] a section of a government that has responsibility for a particular activity, service etc □ *the Department of Health/Industry/Transport.*

departmental [,diːpɑːrt'mentl] *adj* [meeting, staff, manager] that is connected with a particular department of a company, government etc.

department store *n* a large store made up of different sections selling many kinds of goods.

departure [dɪ'pɑːrtʃər] *n* **-1.** [from a place] the act of leaving a place; a plane, train, ferry etc that leaves a particular place at a particular time □ *Passengers are advised to confirm their return flight 24 hours before departure.* □ *There are three departures a day for Dublin.* □ *the departure gate/time.* **-2.** **a departure from sthg** [from normal procedure, a custom] a change from the usual way of doing sthg □ *In a departure from his normal practice, the commissioner gave a press conference immediately.* **-3.** **a new departure** a change in the kind of things one does □ *This is a new departure for me in my career.*

departure lounge *n* the room at an airport where passengers wait until they can get on their plane.

depend [dɪ'pend] *vi* **it depends** a phrase used to say that one is not certain about something because other factors must be taken into consideration.

◆ **depending on** *prep* a phrase used to introduce information that will affect a future decision, course of action etc □ *Depending on when I finish work, I'll either call for you at the hotel or meet you at the theater.*

◆ **depend on** *vt fus* **-1. to depend on sb/sthg** [on a parent, salary] to need sb/sthg because one cannot survive, cope, succeed etc without them □ *I depend on public transportation to get to work.* ■ **you can depend on him/her** you can trust him/her to do what he/she says □ *You can always depend on me.* **-2. to depend on sb/sthg** to be affected, controlled, or decided by sb/sthg □ *Whether you succeed in business depends on your attitude.* □ *"Do you think you'll ever get married?" — "It depends (on) whether I meet the right person."*

dependable [dɪ'pendəbl] *adj* [person, income, car] that one can trust □ *John's a solid, dependable kind of guy.*

dependance [dɪ'pendəns] *n* US = **dependence**.

dependant [dɪ'pendənt] *n* a person who depends on another person or organization for money □ *Does the applicant have any dependants under the age of 18?*

dependence [dɪ'pendəns] *n* [on charity, alcohol, a person] the state of needing somebody or something and not being able to survive, succeed etc without them □ *alcohol dependence.*

dependent [dɪ'pendənt] *adj* **-1.** [person, organization, country] that needs somebody or something else in order to continue or survive □ *We are entirely dependent on the government for getting us contracts.* **-2. to be dependent on sthg** [on drugs, alcohol, cigarettes] to be addicted to sthg □ *the problem of young people dependent on hard drugs.* **-3. to be dependent on sb/sthg** [on a result, the time] to be affected, controlled, or decided by sb/sthg □ *Pay is dependent on age and experience.*

depict [dɪ'pɪkt] *vt* **-1.** [person, scene] to show <sb/sthg> in a picture □ *The painting depicts a battle scene.* **-2.** [person, place, way of life] to describe <sb/sthg>, usually by writing about them, in a way that creates a clear and detailed impression of them □ *The biography depicts him as a cold and ruthless traitor.*

depilatory [US dɪ'pɪlətɔːrɪ, GB -ətərɪ] *adj* [cream, wax] that is used to remove unwanted hair from one's body.

deplete [dɪ'pliːt] *vt* to reduce <supplies, resources> etc to a level that is very low and sometimes dangerous □ *His energy levels have been seriously depleted.*

depletion [dɪ'pliːʃn] *n: see* **deplete** □ *As we near the depletion of our coal stocks...*

deplorable [dɪ'plɔːrəbl] *adj* [state, condition, treatment] that one finds bad or wrong, and unacceptable □ *It is deplorable that people should have to wait so long to see a doctor.* □ *The service at the restaurant was simply deplorable.*

deplore [dɪ'plɔːʳ] *vt* to disapprove of <sthg>

very strongly □ *This company deplores the use of animals to test cosmetics.*

deploy [dɪ'plɔɪ] *vt* to organize <troops, weapons, resources> in a way that makes them ready to be used when necessary.

deployment [dɪ'plɔɪmənt] *n: see* **deploy** □ *the deployment of nuclear missiles.*

depopulated [diː'pɒpjəleɪtəd] *adj* [country, area] where there are far fewer people living than there were before.

depopulation [diːˌpɒpjə'leɪʃn] *n: see* **depopulated** □ *the rural crisis triggered by depopulation.*

deport [dɪ'pɔːt] *vt* to make <sb> leave a country where they are not a citizen because they have done something illegal or are not wanted by the government □ *Illegal immigrants risk being deported.*

deportation [ˌdiːpɔːˈteɪʃn] *n: see* **deport**.

deportation order *n* an official order that tells somebody that they must leave a country.

depose [dɪ'pəʊz] *vt* to remove <a monarch, ruler> etc from power □ *The King was deposed by the military in 1967.*

deposit [dɪ'pɒzət] ◇ *n* **-1.** FINANCE [at a bank] an amount of money placed in a bank account □ *I'd like to make a deposit of $5,000.* **-2.** [on a house, car] a sum of money that one gives as a first part of a payment when buying a house, car etc to make sure that nobody else can buy it □ *We put down a deposit on a new television.* **-3.** [on equipment, an apartment] a sum of money that one gives when one rents something and that is returned if the thing one rented is used without being damaged □ *The deposit on the apartment is equivalent to one month's rent.* **-4.** GEOLOGY a layer of a substance formed underground by natural processes □ *oil deposits.* **-5.** [in a liquid] a solid substance left behind at the bottom of a container of liquid, or by a river, flood etc. ◇ *vt* **-1.** [liquid, river] to leave behind <sand, dust, mud> etc on a surface. **-2.** FINANCE [customer] to put <money or valuables> in a bank □ *I'd like to deposit $150 in my savings account.* **-3.** [person] to put <sthg> down somewhere □ *She deposited her luggage at my feet.*

deposit account *n* GB a bank account that pays interest on the money saved in it.

depositor [dɪ'pɒzətəʳ] *n* a person who saves money in a deposit account.

depot [*sense 1* 'depəʊ, *sense 2* US 'diːpəʊ, GB 'dep-] *n* **-1.** [for goods] a place where equipment or goods are stored □ *an ammunition depot.* **-2.** [for buses, trains] a bus or train station at the end of a route or line.

depraved [dɪ'preɪvd] *adj* [person, habit, behavior] that is very evil or corrupt.

depravity [dɪ'prævətɪ] *n* behavior that is depraved.

deprecate ['deprəkeɪt] *vt* to express disapproval of <sthg> (formal use).

deprecating ['deprəkeɪtɪŋ] *adj* [remark, gesture] that expresses disapproval.

depreciate [dɪ'priːʃieɪt] *vi* [currency, investment, property] to go down in value.

depreciation [dɪˌpriːʃi'eɪʃn] *n*: *see* **depreciate** □ *the depreciation of shares.*

depress [dɪ'pres] *vt* -1. [news, event, situation] to make <sb> feel very sad and hopeless □ *Hearing him talk about the war just depressed me.* -2. ECONOMICS to make <a market or the economy> less active; to make <prices, values, sales> etc go down.

depressant [dɪ'presnt] *n* a substance that reduces the activity of the brain or body □ *Alcohol acts as a depressant.*

depressed [dɪ'prest] *adj* -1. [person] who is very sad and has lost hope □ *I felt so depressed I couldn't get out of bed.* -2. **a depressed market** a market in which there is not much demand for the goods and services offered for sale. -3. **a depressed area** an area that suffers from a lack of economic activity and jobs.

depressing [dɪ'presɪŋ] *adj* [person, news, story] that makes one depressed □ *It's depressing to think that you may never work again.*

depression [dɪ'preʃn] *n* -1. MEDICINE a feeling of extreme unhappiness that causes one to believe that there is no hope for one in the future and that prevents one from living an active life □ *He's having treatment for depression.* -2. ECONOMICS a period when economic activity is low and unemployment is high □ *The country is in the grip of a severe depression.* -3. [in a surface] a hole or hollow in a surface caused by something pressing down on it.

◆ **Depression** *n* = **Great Depression.**

depressive [dɪ'presɪv] *adj* [person] who sometimes suffers from depression; [effect] that causes depression.

deprivation [ˌdeprə'veɪʃn] *n* the state of not being able to have something one needs to live properly □ *sleep deprivation.*

deprive [dɪ'praɪv] *vt* **to deprive sb/sthg of sthg** to prevent sb/sthg from having sthg □ *If people are deprived of sleep, they become irritable.* □ *His captors deprived him of all contact with the outside world.*

deprived [dɪ'praɪvd] *adj* [background, area] where the people are poor and living conditions are bad □ *He had a deprived childhood.*

dept. *abbr of* **department.**

depth [depθ] *n* -1. the distance between the top and the bottom of a lake, mine, hole etc; the distance between the front and back of a solid object or a space □ *The submarine can dive to a depth of 500m.* □ *Make sure you measure the depth of the refrigerator before you buy it.* ■ **to be out of one's depth** [in the ocean, a swimming pool] to be in water where one's feet do not touch the bottom; [in a situation, discussion] not to know enough to be able to deal with or understand what is being done or said □ *I felt a bit out of my depth among all those specialists.* -2. [of one's feelings, knowledge] the strength or intensity of one's feelings, knowledge etc □ *We were impressed by the depth of his understanding.* □ *We have studied the matter in (great) depth.*

◆ **depths** *npl* **the depths** the deepest parts of something, or the parts that are most difficult to get to; the worst part of something □ *the depths of the ocean/forest* □ *in the depths of winter/despair.*

depth charge *n* an underwater bomb used to destroy submarines.

deputation [ˌdepjə'teɪʃn] *n* a group of people who are chosen to be representatives of a larger group, and to speak or complain to somebody in authority on their behalf.

deputize, -ise ['depjətaɪz] *vi* to do somebody else's job or replace them at a meeting when they are unable to be there □ *I had to deputize for my boss while she was away.*

deputy ['depjətɪ] (*pl* **deputies**) ◇ *n* -1. BUSINESS a person who is next below a chairman, manager etc in rank, and who often has to represent them when they are not there. -2. US LAW a person who is second-in-command to a sheriff. ◇ *adj* [leader, head, chairman] who acts as deputy □ *Mrs Cowling, the Deputy Chairman of the Committee.*

derail [diː'reɪl] *vt* to make <a train> go off the tracks.

derailment [diː'reɪlmənt] *n*: *see* **derail** □ *Trains are running late following an earlier derailment.*

deranged [dɪ'reɪndʒd] *adj* [person] who acts in a crazy and sometimes dangerous way.

derby [US 'dɜːrbɪ, GB 'dɑːbɪ] (*pl* **derbies**) *n* -1. US a round stiff hat, usually black and worn by men. -2. SPORT a sports event between two teams from the same area or city.

Derby *n* **the Derby** an important horserace held every year at Epsom, southern England.

Derbyshire [US 'dɜːrbɪʃr, GB 'dɑːbɪʃə] a county in northern central England. SIZE: 2,631 sq kms. POPULATION: 918,700. ADMINISTRATIVE CENTER: Matlock.

deregulate [ˌdiː'regjəleɪt] *vt* to remove government controls from <a company, industry, or market>.

deregulation [ˌdiːregjə'leɪʃn] *n*: *see* **deregulate** □ *plans for deregulation of the country's broadcasting services.*

derelict ['derəlɪkt] *adj* [building, site, area] that is in very bad condition because it is no longer used.

deride [dɪ'raɪd] *vt* [person, suggestion, idea] to speak about <sb/sthg> in a way that makes them seem ridiculous or worthless □ *She has been much derided for her outdated views.*

derision [dɪ'rɪʒn] *n* things that are said about somebody or something and that make them seem ridiculous or worthless □ *His ideas were greeted with derision.*

derisive [dɪ'raɪsɪv] *adj* [laughter, smile, comment] that shows that one thinks somebody or something is ridiculous or worthless.

derisory [dɪ'raɪsərɪ] *adj* -1. [amount, increase] that is so small or unimportant that it cannot be taken seriously (disapproving use) □ *I* was paid the derisory sum of $20. **-2.** [laughter, smile, comment] derisive.

derivation [ˌderə'veɪʃn] *n* the source or origin of a word.

derivative [də'rɪvətɪv] ◇ *adj* [idea, work, style] that is not new or original, and is based on another person's ideas (disapproving use) □ *I quite like his paintings, but they're very derivative.* ◇ *n* something which is developed from something else □ *Many cosmetics are petroleum derivatives.*

derive [dɪ'raɪv] ◇ *vt* **-1.** **to derive sthg from sthg** [pleasure, satisfaction, amusement] to get sthg from sthg □ *She derived great pleasure from telling him that the work would have to be done again.* **-2.** **to be derived from sthg** to have developed from sthg □ *The word is derived from the Latin term.* ◇ *vi* **to derive from sthg** to be the result of sthg □ *His confidence in speaking in public derives from considerable experience.* □ *The word "table" in English derives from the French word.*

dermatitis [ˌdɜːmə'taɪtəs] *n* a medical condition in which the skin becomes sore and irritated.

dermatologist [ˌdɜːmə'tɒlədʒəst] *n* a doctor who specializes in dermatology.

dermatology [ˌdɜːmə'tɒlədʒɪ] *n* the branch of medicine that deals with diseases of the skin.

derogatory [US dɪ'rɒgətɔːrɪ, GB -ətərɪ] *adj* [remark, comment] that criticizes somebody or something in a harsh and unfriendly way □ *He was sitting there in front of me, making derogatory remarks about my furniture!*

derrick ['derɪk] *n* **-1.** a kind of crane that lifts cargo onto a ship. **-2.** a structure built over an oil well that moves the drill up and down.

Derry ['derɪ] = **Londonderry**.

derv [dɜːv] *n* GB the fuel used in diesel vehicles.

desalination [diːˌsælə'neɪʃn] *n* the process of removing salt from sea water to make it suitable for drinking □ *a desalination plant.*

Descartes [US deɪ'kɑːrt, GB 'deɪkɑːt], **René** (1596 – 1650) a French philosopher and mathematician who developed a complete system of philosophy based on scientific reasoning. He is famous for the phrase "I think therefore I am."

descend [dɪ'send] ◇ *vi* **-1.** [sun, vehicle, person] to move in a downward direction (formal use). **-2.** [silence, sadness, darkness] to become noticeable among a group of people or over an area □ *A strange hush descended on the guests.* **-3.** **to descend on a place** [crowd, tourists] to arrive in a place suddenly and in large numbers □ *Thousands of visitors descend on the town each summer.* □ *My relations are going to descend on us this weekend.* **-4.** **to descend to sthg** to do sthg that is below one's usual moral standards □ *How could you descend to lying to me like that?* ◇ *vt* [stairs, hill, ladder] to go down <sthg> (formal use).

descendant [dɪ'sendənt] *n* a person who is the child, grandchild, great-grandchild etc of another person □ *a descendant of George Washington.*

descended [dɪ'sendəd] *adj* **to be descended from sb** to be directly related to sb who lived in the past □ *Man is descended from the apes.*

descending [dɪ'sendɪŋ] *adj* **in descending order** going from a high number or value to a lower one.

descent [dɪ'sent] *n* **-1.** [from a high place] a movement downward □ *We will shortly be commencing our descent to La Guardia.* **-2.** [of a person] the origins of one's family □ *She is of mixed French and Cherokee descent.*

describe [dɪ'skraɪb] *vt* to give an account of the appearance, quality etc of <sb/sthg> □ *Would you be able to describe him to the police?* □ *It's difficult to describe what it was like because it all happened so quickly.*

description [dɪ'skrɪpʃn] *n* **-1.** [of a person, thing, place, event] *see* **describe** □ *There was a description of the man in this morning's paper.* □ *The beauty of Alaska defies description.* **-2.** **of every/any/some description** of every/any/some etc type □ *Are you carrying an aerosol or anything of that description?*

descriptive [dɪ'skrɪptɪv] *adj* [passage, language] that gives a detailed description of somebody or something, especially one that is expressed in a pleasing way □ *One of our assignments was to do a descriptive piece of writing.*

Desdemona [ˌdezdə'məʊnə] the heroine of Shakespeare's play *Othello.* She is killed by her jealous husband, Othello.

desecrate ['desɪkreɪt] *vt* [church, grave] to damage <sthg> deliberately as an insult to something that is holy and sacred.

desecration [ˌdesɪ'kreɪʃn] *n*: *see* **desecrate** □ *The attack was condemned as the desecration of a holy place.*

desegregate [diː'segrɪgeɪt] *vt* to make sure that people of different races, sexes, or religions are no longer kept apart in <a place, institution> etc □ *desegregated schools.*

deselect [ˌdiːsə'lekt] *vt* GB [constituency] to decide not to choose and support <an MP> as a candidate at the next election.

desert [*n* 'dezəʳt, *vb* & *npl* dɪ'zɜːʳt] ◇ *n* **-1.** GEOGRAPHY an area of land with very little water, or plant or animal life □ *the Sahara Desert.* **-2.** a place with few facilities for people □ *a cultural desert.* ◇ *vt* **-1.** [town, building] to abandon <a place> and leave it empty. **-2.** [wife, friend] to leave <a person or group of people> and stop supporting them □ *He deserted his wife and children.* □ *People are deserting the party in droves.* ◇ *vi* [soldier] to leave one's job in the armed forces without permission □ *He deserted from the army.*

♦ **deserts** *npl* **to get one's just deserts** to receive the punishment one deserves.

deserted [dɪ'zɜːʳtəd] *adj* [town, street, beach] that has very few or no people □ *When we arrived, the place was deserted.*

deserter [dɪˈzɜːʳtəʳ] *n* a soldier who has deserted.

desertion [dɪˈzɜːʳʃn] *n* [by a soldier, husband] *see* **desert** □ *a man wanted for desertion.*

desert island [ˌdezəʳt-] *n* a small, uninhabited, tropical island that has no contact with the outside world □ *He was shipwrecked on a desert island.*

deserve [dɪˈzɜːʳv] *vt* [reward, prize, punishment] to have done something for which one should get <sthg> in return or as a result □ *You've been working very hard and deserve a rest.* □ *She deserves to lose her job for speaking to you like that.* □ *I know he can be difficult, but he doesn't deserve to be treated like that.*

deserved [dɪˈzɜːʳvd] *adj* [reward, punishment] that somebody deserves □ *The performers received a well-deserved round of applause.*

deservedly [dɪˈzɜːʳvədlɪ] *adv*: *see* **deserved** □ *She was deservedly beaten in the final.* □ *He has been described as a genius, and deservedly so.*

deserving [dɪˈzɜːʳvɪŋ] *adj* [cause, charity] that deserves to be helped, rewarded, or praised. ■ **to be deserving of sthg** to deserve sthg (formal use).

desiccated [ˈdesɪkeɪtəd] *adj* **desiccated coconut** coconut that has been grated and dried.

design [dɪˈzaɪn] ◇ *n* -1. [for a building, product] a plan for a new building, construction, or manufactured object that has been drawn to show what it will look like □ *The architect showed us her designs.* -2. ART the work or art of planning and drawing the form of things that are going to be made □ *industrial design.* -3. [on wallpaper, fabric] a decorative pattern on a surface □ *an intricate floral design.* -4. [of an object] the form or shape that is given to a manufactured object □ *The chair has a simple but practical design.* -5. [of a person] an intention. ■ **by design** intentionally □ *Was it left here by accident or by design?* ■ **to have designs on sthg** to plan to get and use sthg that belongs to somebody else, often in a dishonest way □ *He's got designs on that plot of land behind the house.* ■ **to have designs on sb** to be intending to seduce sb. ◇ *vt* -1. [building, dress, car] to draw plans for <sthg> so that it can be made or built □ *The chair was designed by Le Corbusier.* -2. **to be designed for sthg** [product, system, layout] to be planned or made in a particular way so that it can be used for sthg □ *The apartments are specially designed for old people.* □ *The car is designed to perform well in the most difficult conditions.*

designate [*adj* ˈdezɪgnət, *vb* ˈdezɪgneɪt] ◇ *adj* **the President/director etc designate** the person who has been appointed to be President/ director etc but who has not yet started doing the job. ◇ *vt* to officially choose <a person or place> for a particular purpose □ *The earthquake zone has been officially designated a disaster area.* □ *I have been designated to chair the committee.* □ *Mr Townsend has been designated as the next chairman.*

designation [ˌdezɪgˈneɪʃn] *n*: *see* **designate** □ *the designation of safe havens by the UN.*

designer [dɪˈzaɪnəʳ] ◇ *n* a person whose job is to design clothes, manufactured goods, buildings etc □ *a dress/interior designer.* ◇ *adj* **designer jeans/jewelry etc** jeans/jewelry etc that have been designed or produced by a famous designer or company □ *Everything she wears has to be a designer label.*

desirable [dɪˈzaɪərəbl] *adj* -1. [result, approach] that is what one wants □ *It would not be desirable to comment further at this stage.* -2. [house, place, object] that is attractive and that people want □ *This has become a highly desirable area to live in.* -3. [person] who is sexually attractive □ *She looked extremely desirable in that evening dress.*

desire [dɪˈzaɪəʳ] ◇ *n* -1. a strong wish □ *I have no desire to see him again.* □ *There is a genuine desire for an improvement in relations.* -2. a strong feeling of wanting to have sex with somebody □ *He was filled with desire for her.* ◇ *vt* -1. to want <sthg> □ *You can have anything you desire.* ■ **to leave a lot to be desired** [person, service, quality] to be of a low standard □ *The food was good, but the service left a lot to be desired.* -2. to want to have sex with <sb>.

desirous [dɪˈzaɪərəs] *adj* **to be desirous of sthg** to want sthg (formal use).

desist [dɪˈzɪst] *vi* **to desist from doing sthg** to stop doing sthg (formal use).

desk [desk] *n* -1. [for writing] a kind of table that one sits at to write or work □ *Steve's not at his desk right now.* -2. [for information] a place in a public building where one can obtain a particular service □ *the information desk* □ *the Air France desk at the airport.*

desk clerk *n* US a hotel receptionist.

desk diary *n* GB a large book used in an office for writing business appointments in.

desk lamp *n* a lamp for use on a desk.

desktop [ˈdesktɒp] *adj* **a desktop computer** a computer designed to fit on top of a desk.

desktop publishing *n* a system of producing documents, books etc that uses a desktop computer.

desolate [ˈdesələt] *adj* -1. [place, scene] that is empty and makes one feel sad □ *I never expected to meet anyone in this desolate spot.* -2. [person] who is lonely and feels sad.

desolation [ˌdesəˈleɪʃn] *n*: *see* **desolate** □ *a scene of utter desolation.*

despair [dɪˈspeəʳ] ◇ *n* a feeling of not having any hope □ *She looked at me in despair.* ◇ *vi* to lose hope □ *Don't despair!* □ *He began to despair of ever finding a job.*

despairing [dɪˈspeərɪŋ] *adj* [look, gesture] that expresses despair.

despairingly [dɪˈspeərɪŋlɪ] *adv* [look, appeal] *see* **despairing** □ *"We'll never get there on time," she said despairingly.*

despatch [dɪˈspætʃ] *n* & *vt* = **dispatch**.

desperate [ˈdesprət] *adj* -1. [person] who needs or wants something very much and is ready to try anything to get it; [attempt, measure] that is tried because one is in this state □ *He asked James for money? He must be desperate!*

□ This calls for desperate measures. □ a desperate gang of criminals. **-2.** [situation, lack, need] that is very serious and needs to be dealt with very soon □ There is a desperate shortage of teachers in science subjects. **-3.** [person] who feels completely helpless □ She felt desperate and alone. **-4. to be desperate for sthg** [for money, a drink, rest] to need sthg very badly □ They're desperate for staff down at Palmer's. □ I'm desperate to go to the toilet.

desperately ['desprətlɪ] adv **-1.** [want, need] so much that one will try anything □ They desperately want to have children. **-2.** [fight, struggle] very fiercely because one is in a dangerous or unpleasant situation. **-3. desperately ill/ unhappy etc** very ill/unhappy etc.

desperation [ˌdespə'reɪʃn] n the state of being desperate □ In desperation, I turned to Franklin for help.

despicable [dɪ'spɪkəbl] adj [person, behavior, act] that deserves to be despised □ I thought his behavior was absolutely despicable.

despise [dɪ'spaɪz] vt [person, idea, activity] to dislike <sb/sthg> and consider them to be of little importance or worth □ Sometimes I feel that she despises me for the kind of job I do.

despite [dɪ'spaɪt] prep **we had a good time despite the rain** the fact that it was raining did not stop us from having a good time □ She remains cheerful despite all her problems.

♦ **despite the fact that** conj although □ Despite the fact that I was very tired, I offered to drive us home.

despondent [dɪ'spɒndənt] adj [person] who feels sad and without hope □ Sam came back from the interview looking tired and despondent.

despot ['despɒt] n a person, especially the ruler of a country, who uses their control over people in a cruel and unfair way.

despotic [dɪ'spɒtɪk] adj [person] who uses their control over other people in a cruel and unfair way □ despotic behavior.

dessert [dɪ'zɜːt] n sweet food that is eaten as the last part of a meal □ Would you like to see the dessert menu?

dessertspoon [dɪ'zɜːˈtspuːn] n a large spoon used to eat dessert; the amount of food or liquid that can be contained in this.

dessert wine n a type of sweet wine that is drunk with a dessert.

destabilize, -ise [ˌdiː'steɪbəlaɪz] vt [government, country, economy] to make <sthg> less secure □ rumors of a plot to destabilize the regime.

destination [ˌdestɪ'neɪʃn] n the place where a person, package, aircraft etc is supposed to arrive at the end of a journey □ After three days of traveling we finally reached our destination. □ Feingold's eventual destination was not known.

destined ['destɪnd] adj **-1. to be destined for sthg** [for fame, success] to be certain to have or achieve sthg in the future □ She is destined for a successful career in advertising. ■ **to be destined to do sthg** to be certain to do sthg in the future □ We were destined never to meet again. **-2. to be destined for a place** [person, air-

craft, package] to be traveling to a particular place □ a plane destined for Bangkok.

destiny ['destənɪ] (pl **destinies**) n **-1.** one's future, especially when this is considered to be controlled by events and circumstances rather than by oneself □ I just hate feeling that our destiny is in their hands. **-2.** the force that some people believe controls their lives □ Destiny brought us together.

destitute ['destɪtjuːt] adj [person] who has no money or possessions, and often no home □ It left him destitute and with no one to turn to.

destroy [dɪ'strɔɪ] vt **-1.** [evidence, building, friendship] to damage <sthg> so severely that it no longer exists in its original form □ The station was completely destroyed by the bombing. **-2.** [person] to affect <sb> badly so that they cannot continue the kind of life they were living before □ He was financially/emotionally destroyed. **-3.** [dog, horse] to kill <an animal> because it is suffering too much from an illness or injury, or because it is dangerous.

destroyer [dɪ'strɔɪəʳ] n MILITARY a small fast warship.

destruction [dɪ'strʌkʃn] n [of evidence, a building, friendship] the act of destroying something □ scenes of death and destruction.

destructive [dɪ'strʌktɪv] adj [person, behavior, feeling] that causes serious damage to somebody or something □ The scandal had a destructive effect on the election campaign.

desultory [US 'desltɔːrɪ, GB -ərɪ] adj [attempt, conversation] that has no plan or purpose and shows little enthusiasm (formal use) □ They made a few desultory comments, then lapsed into awkward silence.

Det. abbr of **detective**.

detach [dɪ'tætʃ] vt **-1.** [handle, collar, label] to remove <sthg that is fixed to something else> □ You can detach the hood from the rest of the jacket. **-2. to detach oneself from sthg** [from reality, a discussion] to try to avoid being involved in or affected by sthg □ It's impossible to detach myself from what's happening at home.

detachable [dɪ'tætʃəbl] adj [handle, collar, hood] that can be removed.

detached [dɪ'tætʃt] adj [view, attitude, person] that is not affected by personal feelings about something □ As a doctor, one has to at least try to remain detached.

detached house n a house that stands alone and is not attached to any other houses.

detachment [dɪ'tætʃmənt] n **-1.** [of a person] the state of being detached □ As an outsider, she was able to look at the situation with a certain degree of detachment. **-2.** MILITARY a group of soldiers who are sent on a mission separately from the rest of a larger group.

detail [US dɪ'teɪl, GB 'diːteɪl] ◇ n **-1.** a small point that is part of a story, discussion, plan, design etc; many of these points when they are part of something more complete □ No further details on the decision are available yet. □ My assistant will take care of the details for you. □ She's got a good eye for detail. □ I looked more closely to admire the detail. ■ **to go into detail**

to include a lot of points or facts about something □ *The report goes into great detail on where the money would come from.* ■ **in detail** [examine, study, speak] in a careful and thorough way □ *I would welcome the opportunity to look into these proposals in detail.* **-2.** MILITARY a small group of soldiers chosen for a particular mission.

◇ *vt* [costs, plan] to give all the details of <sthg> □ *Expenses should be detailed on the yellow form attached.* □ *Mr Bryant's relationship with Miss Walker has been detailed in the press.*

◆ **details** *npl* GB personal information about somebody, e.g. their name, address, and occupation □ *Can I take down your details, sir?*

detailed [US dɪ'teɪld, GB 'diːteɪld] *adj* [map, report, plan] that is carefully prepared and contains a lot of details □ *He gave us very detailed instructions about how to get there.*

detain [dɪ'teɪn] *vt* **-1.** [suspect] to keep <sb> in a police station for questioning. **-2.** to delay <sb>, especially by talking to them or keeping them working (formal use).

detainee [ˌdiːteɪ'niː] *n* a person who is held by the authorities of a country because they are suspected of doing something illegal.

detect [dɪ'tekt] *vt* **-1.** to notice <sthg that is not obvious> □ *Do I detect a note of irony in your voice?* **-2.** [smoke, aircraft, submarine] to find and show the presence of <sthg> □ *The aircraft was detected by radar.*

detection [dɪ'tekʃn] *n* **-1.** [of an aircraft, submarine] *see* **detect.** **-2.** the act of finding out who committed a crime □ *The criminals have so far managed to escape detection.* □ *The detection rate for burglary went up last year.*

detective [dɪ'tektɪv] *n* a person whose job is to find out who committed a crime.

detective novel *n* a book that tells the story of a detective who tries to solve a crime.

detector [dɪ'tektər] *n* a piece of equipment that shows the presence of something □ *a smoke/metal detector.*

détente [deɪ'tɒnt] *n* a period of more friendly relations between two countries that have had bad relations for a long time.

detention [dɪ'tenʃn] *n* **-1.** [of a suspect, criminal] the act of detaining somebody. ■ **to be in detention** to be held by the authorities of a country because one is suspected of a crime, especially when the crime is a political one. **-2.** [of a student] a form of punishment in which a student has to stay at school after normal classes and do extra work □ *He was given detention for misbehaving in class.*

detention centre *n* GB a place where young criminals are kept for a period of time as a punishment.

deter [dɪ'tɜːr] (*pt & pp* **deterred,** *cont* **deterring**) *vt* to stop <sb> from doing something by showing the bad things that will happen if they do it □ *Her parents' warnings did not deter her from going out every night.*

detergent [dɪ'tɜːrdʒənt] *n* a chemical product in the form of a liquid or powder that is used for cleaning things such as clothes.

deteriorate [dɪ'tɪərɪəreɪt] *vi* [health, situation, weather] to become worse, usually over a period of time □ *Relations between the two countries have deteriorated in recent months.*

deterioration [dɪˌtɪərɪə'reɪʃn] *n*: *see* **deteriorate** □ *There has been a marked deterioration in* OR *of living standards.*

determination [dɪˌtɜːrmɪ'neɪʃn] *n* **-1.** the quality of being prepared to try hard to do something that one has decided to do □ *I was impressed by his determination to succeed.* **-2.** [of a cause, boundary] *see* **determine.**

determine [dɪ'tɜːrmɪn] *vt* **-1.** [location, cause] to find out <sthg> for certain □ *We need to determine whether it is worth continuing in this way.* **-2.** [result, outcome, success] to control or decide <sthg> □ *These elections could determine the future of the President's domestic policy for the next two years.* **-3. to determine to do sthg** to decide to do sthg (formal use). **-4.** [price, wage, boundary] to officially decide what <sthg> will be.

determined [dɪ'tɜːrmɪnd] *adj* **-1.** [person] who has decided to do something and is prepared to try very hard to do it □ *a very determined young man* □ *You two are determined to ruin the day, aren't you?* **-2. determined efforts/ resistance etc** efforts/resistance etc showing a desire to succeed □ *a determined fight for survival.*

deterrent [US dɪ'tɜːrənt, GB -'ter-] ◇ *adj* **a deterrent effect/action** an effect/action that deters somebody from doing something. ◇ *n* something, e.g. a punishment or weapon, that stops people from doing something by making them afraid of what will happen to them if they do it □ *They believe capital punishment acts as a deterrent to crime.* □ *the nuclear deterrent.*

detest [dɪ'test] *vt* to dislike <sb/sthg> very much □ *I detest lies and hypocrisy.*

detestable [dɪ'testəbl] *adj* [person, behavior, attitude] that one detests or finds very unpleasant.

dethrone [dɪ'θroʊn] *vt* to remove <a king or queen> from their position of power.

detonate ['detəneɪt] ◇ *vt* [bomb, explosive device] to make <sthg> explode. ◇ *vi*: *The package detonated in his face.*

detonator ['detəneɪtər] *n* a device that is used to make a bomb explode.

detour ['diːtʊər] *n* an indirect route between two places that is chosen for a particular purpose, e.g. to avoid traffic □ *We made a detour so we could stop off at the gas station.*

detox [ˌdiː'tɒks] *n* = **detoxification** (informal use).

detoxification [ˌdiːtɒksɪfɪ'keɪʃn] *n* treatment for addiction to alcohol or drugs.

detract [dɪ'trækt] *vi* **to detract from sthg** [from a quality, achievement] to make the good aspects of sthg less noticeable or enjoyable □ *I'm not going to let that detract from my enjoyment of the evening.*

detractor [dɪ'træktər] *n* **one's detractors** people who criticize one's achievements.

detrain [ˌdiː'treɪn] *vi* [passenger] to get off a train.

detriment ['detrɪmənt] *n* **to do sthg to the detriment of sb/sthg** to do sthg that affects sb/sthg badly without intending to □ *We have concentrated on exports to the detriment of our domestic market.*

detrimental [ˌdetrɪ'mentl] *adj* [policy, effect] that causes damage or harm □ *This type of image could be detrimental to our sales in certain countries.*

detritus [dɪ'traɪtəs] *n* **-1.** pieces of waste that are left after something has been used or after something has happened (formal use). **-2.** GEOLOGY loose material left behind when rocks have eroded.

Detroit [dɪ'trɔɪt] a city in Michigan, USA that is famous for its car industry and popular music. POPULATION: 1,027,974.

deuce [djuːs] *n* the score of 40 points each in a game of tennis.

Deutschmark ['dɔɪtʃmɑːʳk], **Deutsche Mark** ['dɔɪtʃəmɑːʳk] *n* the unit of currency used in Germany.

devaluation [ˌdiːvæljʊ'eɪʃn] *n* the reduction of the value of something, especially a national currency □ *the devaluation of the pound.*

devalue [ˌdiː'væljuː] *vt* **-1.** FINANCE to reduce the value of <a currency>. **-2.** [person, achievement] not to treat <sb/sthg> with the respect they deserve.

devastate ['devəsteɪt] *vt* **-1.** [area, city] to damage <a place> very badly so that most of the things there are destroyed □ *The country has been devastated by floods.* **-2.** to upset and shock <sb> very badly □ *He was devastated by the news.*

devastated ['devəsteɪtəd] *adj* **-1.** [area, city] that has been very badly damaged. **-2. to be devastated** [person] to be very upset and shocked □ *I felt completely devastated when I heard what had happened.*

devastating ['devəsteɪtɪŋ] *adj* **-1.** [hurricane, earthquake, disaster] that causes a lot of destruction □ *the devastating effects of the drought.* **-2.** [remark, argument, shot] that is very effective and difficult for an opponent to deal with □ *The Swede responded with a devastating volley.* **-3.** [news, experience] very upsetting and shocking □ *It was a devastating blow to the family.* **-4.** [looks, charm] very attractive.

devastation [ˌdevə'steɪʃn] *n* [of an area, city] *see* **devastate** □ *scenes of devastation.*

develop [dɪ'veləp] ◇ *vt* **-1.** [business, country, system] to make <sthg> better, more successful, complete etc □ *We need to develop our overseas market.* □ *There are plans to develop tourism in this area.* □ *We are developing new approaches to the care of the elderly.* **-2.** CONSTRUCTION to build new buildings in <a place> so that it becomes more useful and valuable □ *They're developing the old docks as a new residential area.* **-3.** [fault, habit, illness] to gradually get <sthg> □ *You've developed a nasty cough.* □ *The engine developed a problem.*

-4. [idea, point] to think, speak, or write about <sthg> so that it becomes clearer and more complete □ *a well-developed argument.* **-5.** PHOTOGRAPHY to use a chemical process to make a photograph appear from <film>; to make <a photograph> by developing a film □ *When I've had the photos developed, I'll bring them over for you.*
◇ *vi* **-1.** [business, country, story] to become bigger, more advanced, complex etc □ *Our friendship developed from that chance meeting/developed into love.* **-2.** [person] to grow physically or become more mature. **-3.** [problem, trouble] to appear and increase gradually □ *Tensions soon developed between the two countries.* **-4.** PHOTOGRAPHY to be developed □ *It'll take a few minutes for the film to develop.*

developer [dɪ'veləpəʳ] *n* **-1.** CONSTRUCTION a person or company that uses land for building on or does work to improve existing buildings in order to make a profit. **-2. an early/a late developer** a person, especially a child, who develops more quickly/slowly than other people of the same age. **-3.** PHOTOGRAPHY a chemical used to make photographs from film.

developing country [dɪˌveləpɪŋ-] *n* a poor country that is trying to improve its industry and agriculture in order to become stronger economically.

development [dɪ'veləpmənt] *n* **-1.** [of a product, idea, industry] the process of making something better, more successful, complete etc □ *Investment is needed to finance the development of tourism in the region.* **-2.** CONSTRUCTION a project in which land is developed in a particular way; an area of land that is developed by this project □ *plans for development of the old docks* □ *a new property development.* **-3.** [in a situation] a new event or element in a situation, problem etc □ *We will be keeping you informed of the latest developments in the hostage crisis.* □ *a worrying development.* **-4.** [of an illness, habit, fault] the process of getting something gradually.

development area *n* GB an area with a high level of unemployment that the government tries to encourage companies to invest in.

deviant ['diːvɪənt] ◇ *adj* [behavior, tendency] that is different from what is accepted or usual in society □ *sexually deviant.* ◇ *n* a person who is deviant in their behavior, especially a criminal or sexual way.

deviate ['diːvɪeɪt] *vi* to move away from what is usual, decided, agreed etc □ *This deviates from the original agreement.*

deviation [ˌdiːvɪ'eɪʃn] *n* **-1.** [in a person] behavior or ideas that are different from what is usual or accepted in society □ *sexual deviation.* **-2.** [from a plan] a change from something that is usual, agreed etc □ *There must be no deviation from the party line.*

device [dɪ'vaɪs] *n* **-1.** a small piece of equipment that has a particular purpose □ *a safety/listening device.* **-2.** a plan that is designed for a particular purpose, especially a dishonest one □ *It was just a device to get my* attention. ■ **to leave sb to their own devices** to allow sb to think about or do something alone and without interference □ *Left to my own devices, I think I'd have done the same.*

devil ['devl] *n* **-1.** RELIGION an evil spirit □ *devil-worship.* **-2.** a word that is used to address or refer to somebody, especially when commenting on something that has happened to them or that they have done (informal use) □ *You silly/lucky/poor devil!* **-3. who/where/why the devil...** a phrase used to give emphasis to a question (informal use) □ *What the devil are you doing here?*

◆ **Devil** *n* **the Devil** in Christianity, the most powerful evil spirit, which is believed to be directly opposed to God.

devilish ['devlɪʃ] *adj* [scheme, plan] that aims to do something bad in a clever way.

devil-may-care *adj* [approach, attitude] that seems relaxed and careless.

devil's advocate *n* a person who presents the opposing point of view in an argument without necessarily supporting it themselves.

devious ['diːvɪəs] *adj* **-1.** [person] who tries to get what they want dishonestly, usually by using a secret and complicated plan □ *a devious plan/method.* **-2.** [route] that is not direct and so is longer than necessary.

devise [dɪ'vaɪz] *vt* [plan, system, method] to create <sthg> by thinking carefully about it □ *We've devised a way of keeping costs down.*

devoid [dɪ'vɔɪd] *adj* **to be devoid of sthg** [of humor, sense, meaning] to be completely without sthg (formal use) □ *The conference wasn't entirely devoid of interest.*

devolution [US ˌdevə'luːʃn, GB ˌdiːvə-] *n* the transfer of power from a central organization, especially from a government, to an organization at a lower level.

devolve [dɪ'vɒlv] *vi* **to devolve (up)on sb** [responsibility, duty, work] to be sb's responsibility (formal use) □ *It devolves on you to make good use of the available funds.*

Devon ['devn] a county in southwestern England. SIZE: 6,712 sq kms. POPULATION: 1,021,100. ADMINISTRATIVE CENTER: Exeter.

devote [dɪ'vəʊt] *vt* **to devote time/energy etc to sthg** to give a lot of time/energy etc to sthg □ *They've devoted a lot of money to advertising the new product.* ■ **to devote oneself to sthg** to give all of one's time, energy etc to sthg □ *She devoted herself to her work/studies.*

devoted [dɪ'vəʊtəd] *adj* [person] who cares a lot about somebody or something and so gives them a lot of time, energy etc □ *a devoted mother/friend/follower* □ *He's devoted to his work/children.*

devotee [ˌdevə'tiː] *n* a person who likes somebody or something a lot □ *Devotees of Miles Davis will recognize this next track.*

devotion [dɪ'vəʊʃn] *n* **-1.** [to an ideal, person] a feeling of love and loyalty toward somebody or something □ *His devotion to the cause cannot be questioned.* **-2.** [to God, a religion] strong religious belief.

devour [dɪ'vaʊər] *vt* **-1.** [person, animal] to eat <food> quickly and greedily □ *He devoured one plateful, and then asked for more.* **-2.** [reader] to read <a book, letter, magazine> etc quickly and with great interest. **-3.** [fire] to destroy <a place, building> etc quickly.

devout [dɪ'vaʊt] *adj* [person] who believes strongly in a particular religion □ *a devout Catholic/Muslim.*

dew [djuː] *n* the drops of water that form on outdoor surfaces during the night.

dexterity [dek'sterətɪ] *n* skill, especially in using one's hands □ *a test of manual dexterity.*

dexterous ['dekstərəs] *adj* [person] who shows skill with their hands.

dextrose ['dekstrəʊz] *n* a form of sugar that is found in fruit and honey.

dextrous ['dekstrəs] *adj* = **dexterous**.

DFEE (*abbr of* **Department for Education and Employment**) *n* **the DFEE** the British government department responsible for education, employment policy, and unemployment benefits.

DI (*abbr of* **donor insemination**) *n* the process of artificial insemination using semen from a donor.

diabetes [US ˌdaɪə'biːtəs, GB -iːz] *n* a medical condition in which one has too much sugar in one's blood.

diabetic [ˌdaɪə'betɪk] ◇ *adj* **-1.** [person] who suffers from diabetes. **-2.** [jam, chocolate] that is suitable for a diabetic. ◇ *n* a person who suffers from diabetes.

diabolic(al) [ˌdaɪə'bɒlɪk(l)] *adj* **-1.** [plan, treatment, nature] evil and cruel. **-2.** [traffic, service] very bad (informal use) □ *The food was absolutely diabolical!*

diaeresis *n* GB = **dieresis**.

diagnose [US 'daɪəgnoʊs, GB -noʊz] *vt* **-1.** MEDICINE to decide that a patient has <a particular illness>, especially after examining the symptoms □ *Her illness was diagnosed as tonsillitis.* **-2.** [problem, fault] to find or decide the nature of <sthg>.

diagnosis [ˌdaɪəg'noʊsɪs] (*pl* **diagnoses** [-iːz]) *n*: *see* **diagnose** □ *The doctor gave a diagnosis of pneumonia.*

diagnostic [ˌdaɪəg'nɒstɪk] *adj* MEDICINE [test, investigation, equipment] that is used to find out what illness somebody has.

diagonal [daɪ'ægnəl] ◇ *adj* [line, path] that is straight and goes between two points that are in opposite corners of a shape, area etc. ◇ *n* a diagonal line.

diagonally [daɪ'ægnəlɪ] *adv* [move, go] *see* **diagonal** □ *The houses are diagonally opposite each other.*

diagram ['daɪəgræm] *n* a drawing that shows how something works or that represents scientific, technical etc information.

diagrammatic [ˌdaɪəgrə'mætɪk] *adj* [form, representation] that is in the form of a diagram.

dial ['daɪəl] (US *pt* & *pp* **dialed**, *cont* **dialing**, GB *pt* & *pp* **dialled**, *cont* **dialling**) ◇ *n* **-1.** [on a clock] the front part of a watch, clock, meter

etc that has a pointer and numbers on it and is used for showing measurements of time, speed etc □ *I couldn't see the dial clearly in the dark.* -**2.** [on a radio] the round control on a device such as a radio that is turned by hand in order to change the station □ *She fiddled with the dial.* -**3.** [on a telephone] the circular part on the front of some telephones that has holes for one's fingers.
◇ *vt* to choose <a number or code> on a telephone by pressing buttons or turning the dial □ *Dial 911 for the emergency services.* □ *I'm sorry, I must have dialed the wrong number.*

dialect ['daɪəlekt] *n* the form of a language that is spoken in a particular region.

dialling code ['daɪəlɪŋ-] *n* GB the first part of a telephone number, representing a town or area □ *The dialling code for central London is 0171.*

dialling tone *n* GB = dial tone.

dialog US, **dialogue** ['daɪəlɒg] *n* -**1.** [between people] discussions between people or groups of people who have different opinions, e.g. labor unions and management □ *We need dialog in order to find a lasting settlement.* -**2.** [in a play, book] a written conversation, e.g. in a play, book, or movie □ *There's a lot of dialog and not much action.*

dial tone US, **dialling tone** GB *n* the sound that tells a telephone user that it is possible to make a call.

dialysis [daɪ'æləsəs] *n* the process used for removing waste and fluid from the body of a person suffering from kidney problems.

diamanté [US ˌdiːəmɑːn'teɪ, GB ˌdaɪə'mɒnteɪ] *adj* [jewelry] that is covered with small sparkling decorations that look like diamonds.

diameter [daɪ'æmətər] *n* the length of a straight line that passes from one side of a circle to the other and through its center.

diametrically [ˌdaɪə'metrɪklɪ] *adv* **diametrically opposed** [ideas, points of view] that are exactly the opposite of each other.

diamond ['daɪmənd] *n* -**1.** a hard precious stone that is transparent and without color, and is used to make expensive jewelry □ *a diamond ring/necklace.* ■ **a diamond in the rough** US a person who has good qualities, but whose appearance or behavior makes them seem aggressive, rude etc. -**2.** the shape (◇) that is similar to a square but that rests on one of its corners. -**3.** SPORT the field that a baseball game is played on; the area of the field between the four bases.
♦ **diamonds** *npl* one of the four suits in a pack of playing cards, with red diamond shapes printed on each card of the suit □ *the queen of diamonds.*

diamond anniversary *n* US a married couple's sixtieth wedding anniversary.

diamondback ['daɪməndbæk] *n* **a diamondback (rattlesnake)** a large poisonous snake that lives in the southern USA.

diamond wedding *n* GB = diamond anniversary.

diaper ['daɪpər] *n* US a piece of material, e.g.

cloth or paper, that is wrapped around the waist and between the legs of a baby to collect urine and feces □ *Do you know how to change a diaper?*

diaphanous [daɪ'æfənəs] *adj* [cloth, dress] that looks very thin and almost transparent.

diaphragm ['daɪəfræm] *n* -**1.** ANATOMY the muscle that is between the chest and the stomach and is used when breathing deeply. -**2.** MEDICINE a contraceptive used by women that is made of rubber and shaped like a dome, and that fits inside the vagina to prevent sperm from getting into the womb.

diarrhea US, **diarrhoea** GB [ˌdaɪə'rɪə] *n* an illness that makes one's feces very liquid and makes it necessary to go to the toilet very often.

diary ['daɪərɪ] (*pl* **diaries**) *n* -**1.** a written personal record of events, feelings etc that happen to one in one's day-to-day life □ *He kept a diary all his life.* -**2.** GB a book in which space is provided for each day of the year so that appointments and other things to remember can be written in it.

diatribe ['daɪətraɪb] *n* a long attack on somebody or something that is written or spoken and expressed in strong terms (formal use) □ *He launched into a diatribe against the EU.*

dice [daɪs] (*pl* **dice**) ◇ *n* a small wooden or plastic cube with between one and six dots on each of its sides, used in games □ *Throw the dice to see who starts.* ■ **no dice** US (informal use) a phrase used to say "no" when refusing a request; a phrase used to say that an attempt was unsuccessful □ *"What did he say?" — "No dice. He's not going to give us the money."* ◇ *vt* [vegetable, meat, cheese] to cut <sthg> into small cubes.

dicey ['daɪsɪ] (*compar* **dicier**, *superl* **diciest**) *adj* [situation, plan, activity] that could be dangerous or unsuccessful (informal use) □ *I wouldn't trying skiing down there, it looks dicey to me.*

dichotomy [daɪ'kɒtəmɪ] (*pl* **dichotomies**) *n* a large difference between two things, e.g. ideas or groups of people (formal use).

Dickens ['dɪkənz], **Charles** (1812–1870) a British novelist whose writing drew attention to the conditions of the poor in Victorian Britain. His works include *Oliver Twist* and *David Copperfield*.

Dickinson ['dɪkənsən] , **Emily** (1830–1886) a US poet, who wrote in an experimental style. She is sometimes called "The Belle of Amherst".

Dictaphone™ ['dɪktəfoʊn] *n* a piece of equipment used for recording what somebody wants to say, e.g. in a letter or report, so that it can be written down or typed later.

dictate [*vb* dɪk'teɪt, *n* 'dɪkteɪt] ◇ *vt* -**1.** [letter, passage] to read or say <sthg> aloud so that somebody else can hear it and copy it into written or typed form □ *She dictated a letter to her secretary.* -**2.** [terms, conditions] to decide and state <what one wants> in a way that does not allow any opposition □ *He dictated when/where the meetings would take place.*

-3. [result, outcome, events] to affect or control <sthg> □ *Circumstances will dictate whether we get a second chance.*

◇ *vi* **-1.** to dictate a letter, passage etc □ *He was in the middle of dictating to his secretary.* **-2.** to tell somebody what to do in a way that makes it seem that they have to obey □ *Stop trying to dictate to me.*

◇ *n* an order or idea that one feels one has to follow, especially one that is based on a particular ideology □ *the dictates of modern society/Marxism.*

dictation [dɪk'teɪʃn] *n* **-1.** [of a letter, passage] see **dictate** □ *Can you take* OR *do dictation?* **-2.** [to students] an exercise used in teaching in which students must write down as accurately as possible a text that is read aloud to them □ *a French dictation.*

dictator [dɪk'teɪtər] *n* a leader of a country who has complete power and allows no opposition.

dictatorship [US 'dɪkteɪtərʃɪp, GB dɪk'teɪtəʃɪp] *n* a form of government in which a dictator has power; a country that is ruled by this form of government □ *The country has been living under a dictatorship for 50 years.* □ *It's not the first time they've done business with a dictatorship.*

diction ['dɪkʃn] *n* the quality of somebody's way of speaking □ *She's got very good diction.*

dictionary [US 'dɪkʃənerɪ, GB -ʃənrɪ] (*pl* **dictionaries**) *n* a reference book that contains translations, definitions, or explanations of words in a particular language or specialized subject, in alphabetical order □ *an English-Spanish dictionary* □ *Look it up in the dictionary.*

did [dɪd] *past tense of* **do**.

didactic [daɪ'dæktɪk] *adj* [play, story] that is designed to educate people, especially on a moral subject.

diddle ['dɪdl] *vt* to take or keep money from <sb> unfairly (informal use) □ *I've been diddled!*

didn't ['dɪdnt] = **did not**.

die [daɪ] (*pt* & *pp* **died** [daɪd], *cont* **dying**, *pl* sense 2 only **dice**) ◇ *vi* **-1.** [person, animal, plant] to stop living □ *He died of cancer.* ■ **to be dying** to be coming closer to death □ *She continued to work as normal while her father lay dying in the hospital.* ■ **to be dying for sthg/to do sthg** to want sthg/to do sthg very much (informal use) □ *I'm dying for a drink/cigarette.* □ *They're all dying to meet you.* **-2.** [love, hope, memory] to stop existing □ *All hope finally died when I saw her with another man.*

◇ *n* **-1.** a block of hard metal with a special shape or design on it that is used to make a design on another softer metal. **-2.** a dice (old-fashioned use).

◆ **die away** *vi* [sound, wind] to disappear gradually □ *The sound of the police sirens gradually died away.*

◆ **die down** *vi* [wind, fire, trouble] to become less intense □ *When all the fuss has died down, people will forget all about it.*

◆ **die out** *vi* [language, tradition, species] to stop existing gradually □ *The local dialect is in danger of dying out in some areas.*

diehard ['daɪhɑːrd] *n* a person who continues to support or believe in something because of loyalty or unwillingness to accept change □ *Republican diehards* □ *a diehard supporter.*

dieresis US, **diaeresis** GB [daɪ'erəsəs] (*pl* US **diereses**, GB **diaereses** [-əsiːz]) *n* the mark (¨) that is placed above a vowel to show that it is pronounced separately from a vowel immediately before it, as in "naive".

diesel ['diːzl] *n* **-1.** [fuel, oil] a type of fuel that is used especially in trains and trucks and sometimes in cars. **-2.** [vehicle] a vehicle that uses this fuel.

diesel engine *n* a car or rail engine that uses diesel as fuel.

diesel fuel, diesel oil *n* = **diesel**.

diet ['daɪət] ◇ *n* **-1.** the type and quantity of the food and drink that a person usually eats and drinks □ *He eats* OR *has a fairly balanced diet.* **-2.** a plan that states what somebody should eat and drink during a period of time, e.g. in order to help them to lose weight or for medical reasons □ *a fruit/seven-day diet.* ■ **to be/go on a diet** to eat and drink/start eating and drinking in a controlled way in order to lose weight □ *I'll have to go on a diet before my vacation.*

◇ *comp* [food, drink] that contains few calories and is produced for people who are trying to lose weight □ *diet cola.*

◇ *vi* to follow a diet □ *Susan is always dieting.*

dietary [US 'daɪəterɪ, GB -ətərɪ] *adj* [requirements, intake] that is connected with what somebody eats and drinks □ *Do any of your guests have special dietary needs?*

dietary fiber *n* fiber in fruit and vegetables that passes through the body without being digested. It can help one's digestion and prevent certain diseases.

dieter ['daɪətər] *n* a person who is on a diet.

dietician [ˌdaɪə'tɪʃn] *n* a person whose job is to advise people on what to eat and drink in order to be healthy.

differ ['dɪfər] *vi* **-1.** [people, ideas, approaches] to be different □ *They differ in appearance, but not in character.* □ *In what way does this text differ from the first?* **-2.** [person] to disagree □ *I must differ with you about* OR *on that point.* ■ **to agree to differ** to accept that there is disagreement on a subject and to stop arguing □ *Well, we'll just have to agree to differ on that point.*

difference ['dɪfrəns] *n* **-1.** [between people, things] a way in which one person or thing is not the same as another □ *The big difference is that I know what I'm doing.* **-2.** [in a person, thing] a way in which a person or thing is not the same as they were at another time □ *I've noticed a difference in your writing.* **-3.** [amount] the amount or degree to which people, things, or numbers are not the same □ *There's not much difference between the two parties.* ■ **to make a difference** to affect or change a situation in some way □ *The extra hour made quite a difference.* □ *It makes no dif-*

ference to me what time you come. ■ **to make all the difference** to have an effect that changes something completely in a good way □ *Having a new car makes all the difference.* **-4.** [in ideas] a cause of disagreement between people □ *We have our differences.* □ *a difference of opinion.*

different ['dɪfrənt] *adj* **-1.** [person, thing] that is not the same as something or somebody else □ *You look different with that haircut.* □ *It's very different than US OR from any other city I've visited.* **-2. different kinds/times etc** more than one separate kind/time etc □ *We wrote to him on five different occasions.* □ *There are a variety of different ways you can cook pork.*

differential [,dɪfə'renʃl] ◇ *adj* [rate, charge] that is different for different people, things etc, depending on factors such as age, experience etc. ◇ *n* **-1.** a difference in the amount of something, especially in the rate of pay for different workers or for different types of work □ *the price differential* □ *pay differentials.* **-2.** MATH the difference between two values on a scale.

differentiate [,dɪfə'renʃɪeɪt] ◇ *vt* to make <two things> different from each other □ *What differentiates this car from its competitors?* ◇ *vi* to find the difference between two things □ *I'm unable to differentiate between the two.*

differently ['dɪfrəntlɪ] *adv* [feel, think, act] *see* **different** □ *I look at it differently from you.*

difficult ['dɪfɪklt] *adj* **-1.** [task, question, language] that is not easy and requires effort or skill □ *We find ourselves in a difficult situation.* **-2.** [marriage, period] that is affected by problems and so causes unhappiness or stress □ *He's had a difficult life.* **-3.** [person] who is unfriendly or unhelpful, and so is not easy to deal with □ *My father can be very difficult.*

difficulty ['dɪfɪkltɪ] (*pl* **difficulties**) *n* **-1.** a problem that affects a process or situation □ *We are experiencing financial difficulties at the moment.* □ *We got him upstairs but not without some difficulty.* **-2. to have difficulty (in) doing sthg** to find it difficult to do sthg □ *You should have no difficulty finding the place.*

diffidence ['dɪfɪdəns] *n*: *see* **diffident**.

diffident ['dɪfɪdənt] *adj* [person, manner, voice] that shows a lack of confidence, especially in relation to personal opinions, abilities, and achievements □ *He was a quiet, diffident man.*

diffuse [*adj* dɪ'fju:s, *vb* dɪ'fju:z] ◇ *adj* **-1.** [light, population] that is spread out over a large space and is not concentrated in one small area. **-2.** [thought, speech] vague and unclear. ◇ *vt* [light, information] to spread <sthg> out in different directions. ◇ *vi*: *These ideas gradually diffused to other parts of Europe.*

diffusion [dɪ'fju:ʒn] *n*: *see* **diffuse**.

dig [dɪg] (*pt* & *pp* **dug**, *cont* **digging**) ◇ *vt* **-1.** [grave, well, tunnel] to make <a hole> by removing the earth □ *They dug a trench.* **-2.** [garden, flowerbed] to break up earth in <a place> in order to remove weeds, plant seeds etc. **-3. to dig sthg into sb/sthg** to press sthg against or into sb/sthg □ *She dug*

her nails into his hand. □ *He dug me in the ribs with his elbow.*
◇ *vi* **-1.** to break up or remove earth, rock, sand etc □ *They used to dig for gold in those hills.* □ *Archeologists are digging near the castle.* **-2. to dig into sthg** to press into sthg □ *These shoes are digging into my heels.*
◇ *n* **-1.** [at a person] an unkind remark. **-2.** ARCHEOLOGY a place where archeologists are digging.

◆ **dig out** *vt sep* **-1. to dig sb/sthg out** [victim, car] to rescue sb/sthg that is covered with earth, snow etc □ *It took rescuers three hours to dig the family out from under the rubble.* **-2. to dig sthg out** [letter, photograph, file] to find sthg that has been left somewhere for a long time (informal use).

◆ **dig up** *vt sep* **-1. to dig sthg up** [tree, potato, bone] to remove sthg from the earth. **-2. to dig sthg up** [fact, information] to discover sthg that has been hidden or forgotten for a long time (informal use) □ *They've dug up all kinds of old stories about her when she was young.*

digest [*n* 'daɪdʒest, *vb* daɪ'dʒest] ◇ *vt* **-1.** [meal, fat, starch] to break down <food> inside the body so that it can be used by the body □ *I don't digest onions very well.* **-2.** [news, information] to think about and understand <sthg> □ *It took me a few minutes to digest what he said.*
◇ *n* a magazine or book that contains pieces of writing that have been made shorter so they are easier to read.

digestible [daɪ'dʒestəbl] *adj* [food] that can be easily digested.

digestion [daɪ'dʒestʃn] *n* **-1.** [of food] the process of digesting food □ *A liqueur can aid digestion.* **-2.** [in the body] the digestive system.

digestive [daɪ'dʒestɪv] *adj* [disorder, juice] *see* **digestion**.

digestive biscuit *n* GB a round wholemeal cookie.

digestive system *n* the part of the body that digests food, including the stomach and intestine in humans.

digger ['dɪgər] *n* a machine that is used for digging □ *a mechanical digger.*

digit ['dɪdʒɪt] *n* **-1.** MATH a number between 0 and 9, written as a figure. **-2.** ANATOMY a finger or toe (formal use).

digital ['dɪdʒətl] *adj* **-1.** that is in the form of numbers. **-2.** [clock, device, screen] that shows information by displaying numbers on a screen □ *a digital display.* **-3. digital radio/TV** a method of transmitting radio/TV programs that provides a high quality reception and makes it possible to have a large number of stations, and to receive special services.
NOTE: Compare **analog**.

digital recording *n* a high-quality recording made by changing sounds into thousands of tiny signals.

digital watch *n* a watch that has a digital screen.

digitize, -ise ['dɪdʒətaɪz] *vt* to convert <information> into numbers so that it can be processed by a computer.

dignified ['dɪgnəfaɪd] *adj* [person, response, behavior] that shows dignity □ *It wasn't exactly dignified running after him like that.*

dignitary [US 'dɪgnəterɪ, GB -ərɪ] (*pl* **dignitaries**) *n* a person who has an important position in a government or Church □ *a visiting/foreign dignitary.*

dignity ['dɪgnətɪ] *n* -1. [of a person] a calm and serious appearance or manner that makes people have respect for one □ *He should be allowed to die with dignity.* -2. **one's dignity** the sense one has of being important □ *She felt that typing letters was beneath her dignity.*

digress [daɪ'gres] *vi* [writer, lecturer, passage] to talk or write about something that is not relevant to one's main subject □ *Try not to digress from the main point.*

digression [daɪ'greʃn] *n* a part of a conversation, report etc that digresses □ *After numerous digressions, she finally got around to telling us what had actually happened.*

dike [daɪk] *n* -1. a thick wall or bank, especially one built to control flooding. -2.▼ a lesbian (informal and offensive use).

diktat [US 'dɪktɑːt, GB -tæt] *n* a harsh order given by a government or ruler.

dilapidated [dɪ'læpədeɪtəd] *adj* [house, furniture, car] that is old and in bad condition.

dilate [daɪ'leɪt] ◇ *vt* [pupils, blood vessel, cervix] to make <a part of the body> bigger or more open, usually for a short time. ◇ *vi*: *These eye drops will make your pupils dilate.*

dilated [daɪ'leɪtəd] *adj* [blood vessel, cervix] that has become bigger and wider.

dilemma [dɪ'lemə] *n* a situation in which one cannot decide whether to do one thing or another thing □ *It's put me in a terrible dilemma; I now can't decide whether to go or not.* □ *a moral dilemma.*

dilettante [US ˌdɪlə'tɑːnt, GB -'tæntɪ] (*pl* **dilettantes** [US -'tɑːnts, GB -'tæntɪz] OR **dilettanti** [US -'tɑːntɪ, GB -'tæntɪ]) *n* a person who one thinks is not very interested in an activity or not very good at it (disapproving use).

diligent ['dɪlɪdʒənt] *adj* [student, official] who is careful and works hard □ *I appreciate your diligent efforts on my behalf.*

dill [dɪl] *n* a herb with green leaves, used to add flavor to food such as soup or pickle.

dillydally ['dɪlɪdælɪ] (*pt* & *pp* **dillydallied**) *vi* to waste time (informal use).

dilute [daɪ'luːt] ◇ *vt* [acid, drink] to make <a liquid> less strong by adding another liquid to it, usually water □ *wine diluted with water* □ *'Dilute to taste.'* ◇ *adj* [acid, drink] that has been diluted.

dilution [daɪ'luːʃn] *n*: *see* **dilute.**

dim [dɪm] (*compar* **dimmer**, *superl* **dimmest**, *pt* & *pp* **dimmed**, *cont* **dimming**) ◇ *adj* -1. [light, room] that is not very bright □ *The room was lit by one dim light bulb.* -2. [shape, outline] that cannot be seen clearly; [feeling, memory] that is not clear in one's mind □ *a dim figure on the horizon* □ *I had only a dim recollection of having been there before.* -3. [eyes] that do not see clearly because one is old or is crying □

His sight is growing dim. -4. **to take a dim view of sthg** to disapprove of sthg □ *Your boss would take a dim view of you being late if he knew.* -5. [person, idea] that is not intelligent (informal use).
◇ *vt* -1. [light, room] to make <sthg> less bright. -2. **to dim one's headlights** OR **lights** US to switch one's car headlights so that they point downward and not in the eyes of other drivers.
◇ *vi* -1. [light, room] *The lights dimmed all around the hall.* -2. [hope, memory] to become weaker.

DiMaggio [də'mædʒɪoʊ], **Joe** (1914–) a US baseball player who was married to Marilyn Monroe.

dime [daɪm] *n* US -1. a small coin worth 10 cents. -2. **they're a dime a dozen** they're not valuable or special, because there are a lot of them.

dimension [daɪ'menʃn] *n* -1. [of an object, room] a measurement of the height, length, width, or depth of something □ *He wrote down the dimensions of the bookcase.* -2. [of a problem, subject] a particular aspect of something that can be thought about □ *The book opens up a whole new dimension of thought.*

diminish [dɪ'mɪnɪʃ] ◇ *vt* [importance, popularity, feeling] to make <sthg> smaller or weaker □ *Nothing can never diminish the horror of what those people suffered.* ◇ *vi* [importance, popularity, feeling] *Their share of the market has diminished.*

diminished [dɪ'mɪnɪʃt] *adj* [profit, role] that has become smaller.

diminished responsibility *n* LAW the fact that a person was mentally ill when they committed a crime, so that they deserve a less severe punishment □ *He was found not guilty on the grounds of diminished responsibility.*

diminishing returns [dɪˌmɪnɪʃɪŋ-] *npl* the idea that it is not worth continuing something because a lot of work is always needed to do it, and the results will keep getting smaller.

diminutive [dɪ'mɪnjətɪv] ◇ *adj* [person, animal, object] very small (literary use). ◇ *n* a word formed by adding an ending to a word to show that it is small, e.g. piglet, duckling.

dimly ['dɪmlɪ] *adv* [see, remember] *see* **dim** □ *I dimly remembered her mentioning something when we were at the party.* ■ **dimly-lit** [room, bar] that has little light.

dimmer ['dɪmər] *n* -1. a device that makes it possible to change the brightness of an electric light. -2. a switch that makes the headlights on a car point downward.

dimmer switch *n* = **dimmer.**

dimple ['dɪmpl] *n* a small hollow in one's cheek or chin that is usually considered attractive.

dimwit ['dɪmwɪt] *n* a person who is not very intelligent (informal use).

dim-witted [-'wɪtəd] *adj* [person] who is not very intelligent (informal use).

din [dɪn] *n* a loud unpleasant noise that lasts a long time (informal use) □ *What a din!*

dine [daɪn] *vi* to eat dinner (formal use).

◆ **dine out** *vi* to eat dinner in a restaurant or at somebody else's house □ *Do you want to eat in or dine out tonight?*

diner ['daɪnər] *n* -1. a person who is eating a meal, especially in a restaurant. -2. US a small restaurant where meals are cooked and served quickly.

ể DINER
Diners are found mainly on highways in the USA, but most towns also have a diner. They are open for breakfast, lunch, and dinner, and specialize in cheap hot food such as hamburgers and ham and eggs. The first diners were converted railroad cars, and many modern diners are still designed in the same way.

dingdong ['dɪŋdɒŋ] *n* a word used to represent the noise made by a bell ringing.

dinghy ['dɪŋgɪ] (*pl* **dinghies**) *n* a small boat for rowing or sailing or a motorboat.

dingo ['dɪŋgoʊ] (*pl* **dingoes**) *n* an Australian wild dog.

dingy ['dɪndʒɪ] (*compar* **dingier**, *superl* **dingiest**) *adj* [room, area] that looks dirty and dark □ *They live in a dark and dingy little apartment.*

dining car ['daɪnɪŋ-] *n* a car on a train where meals are served.

dining room *n* a room in a house or hotel where meals are eaten.

dining table *n* a large table on which meals are eaten.

dinkum ['dɪŋkəm] *adj* AUS genuine or honest (informal use).

dinner ['dɪnər] *n* -1. [at home] the main meal of the day, eaten in the evening or the middle of the day; [in a restaurant, hotel] the meal served in the evening □ *Come on, I'll take you out for dinner!* □ *What's for dinner?* -2. [at a club, organization] a formal evening meal □ *Are you going to the annual dinner?*

dinner dance *n* a formal evening meal for a large number of people, usually at a restaurant or hotel, followed by dancing.

dinner jacket *n* a man's black jacket worn for formal evening occasions.

dinner lady *n* GB a woman whose job is to prepare and serve meals in a school.

dinner party *n* an evening party at somebody's house for a small number of guests at which dinner is served □ *I'm having a dinner party next week.*

dinner service *n* a set of matching plates, bowls, cups etc.

dinner table *n* **at the dinner table** while dinner is being eaten □ *You shouldn't read at the dinner table.*

dinnertime ['dɪnərtaɪm] *n* the time at which dinner is eaten □ *Come on, Joe, it's dinnertime!*

dinosaur ['daɪnəsɔːr] *n* any of several types of often very large reptiles that lived on the Earth millions of years ago and no longer exist □ *dinosaur bones.*

dint [dɪnt] *n* **by dint of sthg** by means of sthg (formal use) □ *She succeeded by dint of sheer courage and determination.*

diocese ['daɪəsəs] *n* the area under the control of a bishop.

diode ['daɪoʊd] *n* a device used in electrical circuits to change alternating current to direct current.

Dionysus [ˌdaɪə'naɪsəs] the Greek god of wine and fertility.

dip [dɪp] (*pt* & *pp* **dipped**, *cont* **dipping**) ◇ *vt* -1. **to dip sthg in(to) sthg** [in water, a drink] to put sthg into sthg for a short time □ *Dip the strawberries in melted chocolate.* -2. **to dip one's headlights** OR **lights** GB to switch one's car headlights so that they shine downward and not in the eyes of other drivers.
◇ *vi* -1. [plane, bird] to move downward suddenly. -2. [road, ground, sales] to drop in level suddenly.
◇ *n* -1. [in the ground] a slight drop in the level of the ground □ *There's a dip in the road just ahead.* -2. [for food] a thick sauce eaten with small pieces of food that are dipped into it □ *a cheese/avocado dip.* -3. **to go for a dip** to go for a short swim.

Dip GB *abbr of* **diploma.**

diphtheria [dɪf'θɪərɪə] *n* a serious disease that makes the throat swell and makes breathing difficult.

diphthong ['dɪfθɒŋ] *n* a sound in speech made by pronouncing two vowels one after the other as if they were one vowel, e.g. "ou" in "shout".

diploma [dɪ'ploʊmə] (*pl* **diplomas**) *n* -1. a document showing that a student has completed their studies at high school or college. -2. GB a document given to somebody who has successfully completed a course of study or passed an exam.

diplomacy [dɪ'ploʊməsɪ] *n* -1. [between countries] the process of keeping peaceful relations between countries. -2. [with people] the ability to deal skillfully and politely with people in difficult situations □ *He acted with great tact and diplomacy.*

diplomat ['dɪpləmæt] *n* -1. [of a country] an official representative of a government in a foreign country □ *a career diplomat.* -2. a tactful person □ *You're such a diplomat.*

diplomatic [ˌdɪplə'mætɪk] *adj* [service, behavior, person] *see* **diplomacy** □ *Diplomatic efforts are being stepped up on their behalf.* □ *You could have been more diplomatic about telling her she was wrong.*

diplomatic bag *n* a bag, used to send documents to and from an embassy or consulate, that customs officials are not allowed to open.

diplomatic corps *n* all the diplomats living and working in a country.

diplomatic immunity *n* the right of diplomats not to pay taxes or be charged with a criminal offense in the country where they are working.

diplomatic relations *npl* the relationship between two governments that exists when they have diplomats in each other's country □ *They have established/broken off diplomatic relations with Iraq.*

dipsomaniac [ˌdɪpsə'meɪnɪæk] *n* a person who cannot control their desire for alcohol.

dipstick ['dɪpstɪk] *n* AUTO a stick with a scale marked on it to show how much liquid is in a container, especially how much oil is in a car engine.

dipswitch ['dɪpswɪtʃ] *n* GB the device used to make car headlights shine downward.

dire ['daɪəʳ] *adj* [need, consequences, warning] very serious □ *a dire shortage of medical supplies* □ *These socks are in dire need of mending.*

direct [də'rekt] ◇ *adj* **-1.** [route, line] that goes straight to a particular place without stopping or changing direction □ *a direct flight to Cairo.* **-2.** [access, contact, control] that does not involve anybody or anything else in between □ *As manager, she has direct control over finances and forward planning.* □ *I've had direct experience of such problems myself.* □ *Public opinion has a direct influence over policy.* **-3.** [result, response] that follows immediately and only from a particular thing □ *The product was withdrawn as a direct consequence of the protests.* **-4.** [answer, manner, person] that is clear and easy to understand, but can offend people by not being polite enough □ *She asked some very direct questions.* **-5.** [attack, challenge, threat] that goes straight to the person or place it is aimed at □ *The move is seen as a direct attack on the premier's leadership.* **-6. direct sunlight/heat** strong sunlight/ heat that can damage people or things □ *'Do not store in direct sunlight.'* **-7. the direct opposite** something that is completely the opposite of something else □ *That's the direct opposite of the truth!* **-8. a direct descendant of sb** a person who is descended from sb through their parents, grandparents etc □ *Hulse is a direct descendant of the 16th-century Admiral Hulse.*

◇ *vt* **-1.** [question, message, attention] to aim <sthg> at a particular person, thing, or place □ *The campaign is directed at teenagers.* □ *Our efforts should be directed toward helping these people more.* **-2.** [tourist, foreigner] to tell <sb> how to get to a particular place □ *Can you direct me to the station, please?* **-3.** [project, company, campaign] to be in charge of <sthg> □ *Mr Bonnell, 38, is directing research on behalf of L.R.C.* **-4.** CINEMA, TV & THEATER to be the director of <a play, movie, or TV program> □ *He's directing "Aida" at the Sydney Opera House.* **-5. to direct sb to do sthg** to tell sb to do sthg, especially officially.

◇ *adv* [come, go] without stopping or going anywhere else on the way □ *We flew direct to Houston.* □ *I came direct from the hospital.* **-2.** BUSINESS [buy, sell] without involving another company, so that there are fewer costs □ *We buy all our equipment direct from the*

factory. **-3.** [call, dial] without having to go through a switchboard or operator first □ *You can ring me direct on extension 0448.*

direct action *n* action, e.g. strikes, organized by unions or groups of workers in order to get what they want from their employers or the government.

direct current *n* an electric current that is continuous and flows from a battery in one direction only.

direct debit *n* GB an arrangement that somebody can have with their bank to pay money from their account to an organization or person at regular times □ *I pay all my bills by direct debit.*

direct dialing [-'daɪəlɪŋ] *n* the system that allows one to make long-distance telephone calls without the help of the operator.

direct hit *n* the act of hitting all of something with a bomb or other missile.

direction [də'rekʃn] *n* **-1.** the way that somebody or something goes when they move toward a particular place or state □ *She went in the direction of the river.* □ *European military policy is taking a new direction.* □ *His life lacks direction.* **-2. under the direction of sb/sthg** under the control of sb/sthg □ *The project was completed under the direction of the company head, Malcolm McManus.* **-3.** [of a play, movie, TV program] *see* **direct.**

◆ **directions** *npl* **-1.** [to a place] instructions telling somebody how to get to a place □ *Can you give me directions from here to Fifth Avenue?* **-2.** [for a product] instructions on the box, jar etc of a product that tell one how to use it □ *Read the directions before use.*

directive [də'rektɪv] *n* an official order □ *an EU directive.*

directly [də'rektlɪ] *adv* **-1.** [look, travel, go] in a straight line, and without stopping or changing direction □ *She looked directly at me.* □ *He's directly descended from Leo Tolstoy.* **-2.** [answer, say] in a way that is easy to understand and does not hide anything □ *I can't answer that question directly.* **-3. directly behind/above etc** exactly behind/above etc □ *My apartment is directly underneath hers.* □ *The bank is directly opposite the mosque.* **-4. directly before/after** immediately before/after □ *He left directly before you arrived.* **-5.** [arrive, start] very soon □ *I'll be with you directly.*

direct mail *n* a way of selling products or services by sending letters that contain advertisements to people.

director [də'rektəʳ] *n* **-1.** [of a company, project] a person chosen by the people who own a company, whose job is to help run it □ *the board of directors.* **-2.** CINEMA, TV & THEATER the person who tells the actors, cameramen etc what to do when rehearsing a play or making a movie.

directorate [də'rektərət] *n* a group of directors who control a company or organization.

director-general (*pl* **directors-general** OR **director-generals**) *n* the head of a large organization □ *the Director-General of the BBC.*

Director of Public Prosecutions *n* GB **the Director of Public Prosecutions** the government official who prosecutes in all cases brought by the police and advises government departments whether prosecutions should be started.

directorship [də'rektəʳʃɪp] *n* the position of director of a company; the period of time spent by somebody in this position.

directory [də'rektərɪ] (*pl* **directories**) *n* **-1.** a book containing a list of the names, addresses, and telephone numbers of people, companies, organizations etc □ *a telephone directory* □ *a business directory.* **-2.** COMPUTING a list of files that have been put in the same area of a disk to make them easier to find.

directory assistance US, **directory enquiries** GB *n* the service one calls to find out somebody's telephone number.

direct rule *n* a system in which a government in one place rules an area somewhere else that used to rule itself.

direct selling *n* a way of selling in which manufacturers sell products to customers without selling them to stores first.

direct speech *n* the way of telling people what somebody else has said or written by writing their exact words.

direct taxation *n* the system by which taxes are paid by people, companies etc and not on goods and services that are sold.

dire straits *npl* **to be in dire straits** to be in a difficult or dangerous situation □ *Peel's has been in dire financial straits for some time now.*

dirge [dɜːʳdʒ] *n* a slow sad song, usually sung when somebody has died.

dirt [dɜːʳt] *n* **-1.** [on clothes, a person] any substance such as mud, dust, or soil that one removes from a surface, fabric, or part of the body in order to keep it clean □ *She came in covered in dirt.* **-2.** [on the ground] loose earth, e.g. in a garden or field.

dirt cheap (informal use) ◇ *adj* very cheap. ◇ *adv*: *I bought it dirt cheap.*

dirt track *n* a track used for some types of motorcycle race.

dirty ['dɜːʳtɪ] (*compar* **dirtier**, *superl* **dirtiest**, *pt* & *pp* **dirtied**) ◇ *adj* **-1.** [hands, floor] not clean □ *Try not to get your clothes dirty.* **-2.** [business, deal] dishonest; [trick] cruel. **-3.** [book, language] that is connected with sex in an offensive way □ *He told a dirty joke.* ◇ *vt* [floor, hands] to make <sthg> dirty.

disability [,dɪsə'bɪlətɪ] (*pl* **disabilities**) *n* the state of being unable to use one's body completely or move around normally; a physical illness or condition that causes this, e.g. deafness □ *a disability allowance.*

disable [dɪs'eɪbl] *vt* [illness, accident] to cause <sb> to have a physical disability □ *Kevin was left disabled after a motorcycle accident.*

disabled [dɪs'eɪbld] ◇ *adj* [person] who has a disability □ *She's severely disabled.* ◇ *npl* **the disabled** people who are disabled □ *parking/ access for the disabled.*

disablement [dɪs'eɪblmənt] *n*: *see* **disable**.

disabuse [,dɪsə'bjuːz] *vt* **to disabuse sb of sthg** [of an idea, belief] to tell sb that sthg that they believe is wrong (formal use) □ *I soon disabused him of THAT idea!*

disadvantage [US ,dɪsəd'væntɪdʒ, GB -'vɑːnt-] *n* something that causes somebody or something to have a problem that other people or things do not have □ *The major disadvantage of this model is its size.* ■ **to be at a disadvantage** to have a particular disadvantage □ *Women are at a disadvantage when it comes to lifting heavy weights.* ■ **to be to one's disadvantage** to cause one to be at a disadvantage □ *His lack of experience was to his disadvantage.*

disadvantaged [US ,dɪsəd'væntɪdʒd, GB -'vɑːnt-] *adj* [person] who lives in bad conditions because they are poor.

disaffected [,dɪsə'fektəd] *adj* [member, soldier] who no longer supports an organization, a political party etc.

disaffection [,dɪsə'fekʃn] *n* [of a member, soldier] the state of being disaffected.

disagree [,dɪsə'griː] *vi* **-1.** [person] to have different opinions or argue about something □ *We disagree on most issues.* □ *My parents and I disagree about* OR *over politics.* □ *I disagree with him/the proposals.* **-2.** [statements, accounts, results] to be different from each other □ *Our totals disagree.* **-3. to disagree with sb** [food, drink] to make sb feel ill □ *Something I ate disagreed with me.*

disagreeable [,dɪsə'griːəbl] *adj* [smell, job, person] unpleasant.

disagreement [,dɪsə'griːmənt] *n* an argument or situation in which people disagree about something □ *We're in disagreement over the new sales policy.* □ *They had a disagreement over money.*

disallow [,dɪsə'laʊ] *vt* **-1.** [appeal, claim] to refuse to allow <sthg> (formal use). **-2.** SPORT to refuse to allow <a goal>.

disappear [,dɪsə'pɪəʳ] *vi* **-1.** [person, object, car] to no longer be able to be seen or found □ *The plane gradually disappeared from sight.* □ *The sun disappeared behind a cloud.* □ *Mrs Schneider disappeared while on vacation.* □ *My pencil keeps disappearing from my desk.* □ *Where did you disappear to?* **-2.** [custom, threat, species] to stop existing □ *Dinosaurs disappeared from the Earth millions of years ago.*

disappearance [,dɪsə'pɪərəns] *n*: *see* **disappear** □ *Officials are investigating the disappearance of large sums of money from the account.*

disappoint [,dɪsə'pɔɪnt] *vt* to make <sb> disappointed □ *I didn't want to disappoint them by not going to the party.* □ *I was disappointed by the result.*

disappointed [,dɪsə'pɔɪntəd] *adj* [person] who is unhappy because somebody has not done what they want or something has not happened the way they want □ *She was disappointed in* OR *with her exam results.* □ *We were disappointed at* OR *about the news.*

disappointing [,dɪsə'pɔɪntɪŋ] *adj* [result, performance, behavior] that makes one disappointed □ *The response has been disappointing.*

disappointment [ˌdɪsəˈpɔɪntmənt] *n* -1. the feeling that one has when one is disappointed □ *I tried to hide my disappointment.* -2. **to be a disappointment** to be disappointing □ *The vacation was a real disappointment.* □ *I hope I wasn't a disappointment to you.*

disapproval [ˌdɪsəˈpruːvl] *n* the feeling one has when one disapproves of somebody or something □ *He frowned in disapproval.*

disapprove [ˌdɪsəˈpruːv] *vi* **to disapprove of sb/ sthg** to dislike sb/sthg because one thinks they are not acceptable or suitable □ *My mother's always disapproved of the way I dress.*

disapproving [ˌdɪsəˈpruːvɪŋ] *adj* [look, person] that shows disapproval.

disarm [dɪsˈɑːrm] ◇ *vt* -1. [criminal, attacker] to take a weapon from <sb>. -2. [critic, audience] to stop <sb> from being angry with one or not liking one, usually by being pleasant. ◇ *vi* [country] to reduce the size and power of its armed forces.

disarmament [dɪsˈɑːrməmənt] *n* [of a country] see **disarm** □ *nuclear disarmament.*

disarming [dɪsˈɑːrmɪŋ] *adj* [smile, person, honesty] that makes somebody like or trust one immediately.

disarray [ˌdɪsəˈreɪ] *n* **to be in disarray** [clothes, hair] to be untidy; [organization, government] to be in a state of confusion and not know what to do (formal use) □ *When I returned, the room was in complete disarray.* □ *The election has left the Republicans in disarray.*

disassociate [ˌdɪsəˈsoʊʃieɪt] *vt* **to disassociate oneself from sb/sthg** [from an organization, policy] to show that one is not connected with sb/sthg □ *Campbell had moved to disassociate himself from the more extreme wing of his party.*

disaster [US dɪˈzæstr, GB -ˈzɑːstə] *n* -1. a harmful or destructive event □ *an air disaster* □ *The area is prone to natural disasters.* -2. something which has very serious consequences for somebody □ *The recession meant financial disaster for a number of small enterprises.* -3. a failure (informal use) □ *You're/It's a complete disaster!*

disaster area *n* an area where a disaster such as an earthquake has just occurred.

disastrous [US dɪˈzæstrəs, GB -ˈzɑːst-] *adj* [event, results, effect] extremely bad □ *The fax was never sent, with disastrous consequences.*

disastrously [US dɪˈzæstrəsli, GB -ˈzɑːst-] *adv* [fail, perform] see **disastrous** □ *It happened at a disastrously bad time.* □ *Everything went disastrously wrong.*

disband [dɪsˈbænd] ◇ *vt* [group, army] to stop <an organization> from existing. ◇ *vi:* *The group disbanded.*

disbelief [ˌdɪsbɪˈliːf] *n* **in** OR **with disbelief** in a way that shows that one does not believe something is true □ *Monica looked at him in sheer disbelief.*

disbelieve [ˌdɪsbɪˈliːv] *vt* [person, story] to refuse to believe <sb/sthg>.

disc *n* GB -1. = **disk.** -2. MUSIC a record for playing on a record player.

discard [dɪsˈkɑːrd] *vt* [object, clothes] to get rid of <sthg that is useless>.

discarded [dɪsˈkɑːrdəd] *adj* [object, piece of clothing] that has been left somewhere by somebody who has discarded it.

disc brake *n* a type of brake that works by two disks pressing against each other in the center of a car wheel.

discern [dɪˈsɜːrn] *vt* -1. [figure, shape] to see <sthg> by looking carefully □ *I could just discern a vague shape in the darkness.* -2. [difference, improvement, reason] to notice or understand <sthg> □ *I had discerned a small change in his attitude during recent weeks.*

discernible [dɪˈsɜːrnəbl] *adj* [shape, improvement, difference] that can be discerned □ *The scar was barely discernible under his hair.*

discerning [dɪˈsɜːrnɪŋ] *adj* [person] who has good taste or judgment.

discharge [*n* ˈdɪstʃɑːrdʒ, *vt* dɪsˈtʃɑːrdʒ] ◇ *n* -1. [from an organization] the release of somebody from an institution or organization, e.g. a hospital, prison, or the armed services. -2. [of one's duty] the act of doing one's duty, responsibility etc completely and properly (formal use). -3. [of sewage] the release into the surrounding area of sewage, pollution, chemicals etc. -4. MEDICINE any liquid that is released from a wound or an opening in one's body when one has an infection □ *a nasal/vaginal discharge.* -5. [of a debt] payment (formal use).
◇ *vt* -1. [patient, prisoner] to allow <sb> to leave a hospital, prison etc; [soldier, sailor] to allow <sb> to leave the army, navy etc □ *He was discharged from hospital yesterday.* -2. [duty, responsibility] to do <sthg that one has to do> completely and properly (formal use). -3. [smoke, sewage, pollution] to release <sthg> into the air or the surrounding area □ *These chemicals are discharged directly into the atmosphere.* -4. **to discharge a debt** to pay a debt (formal use).

discharged bankrupt [dɪsˌtʃɑːrdʒd-] *n* a person who was bankrupt and can legally do business again.

disciple [dɪˈsaɪpl] *n* -1. [in Christianity] one of the 12 early followers of Jesus Christ. -2. a follower of a great teacher of religion, political thought etc □ *a disciple of Karl Marx.*

disciplinarian [ˌdɪsəplɪˈneərɪən] *n* a person who makes people behave in a disciplined way □ *My father was a strict disciplinarian.*

disciplinary [US ˈdɪsəpləneri, GB -plɪnəri] *adj* [measure, procedure] that is designed to punish people for not obeying rules, or to force them to obey rules. ■ **to take disciplinary action against sb** to punish sb formally for having done something wrong, especially at work □ *Disciplinary action will be taken.*

discipline [ˈdɪsəplɪn] ◇ *n* -1. good behavior which comes from obeying rules □ *Teachers must maintain discipline in the classroom.* □ *good discipline.* -2. [in an activity] the use of rules that make people behave correctly and do what one thinks is right □ *Discipline is essential to the smooth running of the company.* □ *He im-*

poses strict discipline on team members. **-3.** [at school] a subject that people study □ *a scientific discipline.* ◇ *vt* **-1.** [children, staff, regiment] to impose a system of rules for behavior on <sb>. **-2.** [employee, child, pupil] to punish <sb> in order to maintain control.

disciplined ['dɪsəplɪnd] *adj* [person, routine] that follows a fixed system of rules □ *Our soldiers are highly disciplined.* □ *a strict, disciplined diet.*

disc jockey *n* a person whose job is to introduce and play records on the radio or at a disco.

disclaim [dɪs'kleɪm] *vt* [knowledge, responsibility] to refuse to accept that one has <sthg> (formal use) □ *The company disclaims all responsibility for customers' private property.*

disclaimer [dɪs'kleɪmər] *n* a statement that disclaims knowledge, responsibility etc □ *The newspaper issued a disclaimer.*

disclose [dɪs'kloʊz] *vt* [evidence, detail, information] to tell somebody about <sthg that is secret> □ *I am not at liberty to disclose the source of my information.*

disclosure [dɪs'kloʊʒər] *n* **-1. to make a disclosure** to disclose a fact to a newspaper, interviewer etc. **-2.** [of evidence, information] *see* **disclose.**

disco ['dɪskoʊ] (*pl* **discos**) *n* **-1.** a party where people dance to records □ *We're having a disco on Saturday night.* **-2.** MUSIC a type of dance music that became popular in the 1970s. **-3.** a place where people dance to recorded music (old-fashioned use).

discolor US, **discolour** GB [dɪs'kʌlər] ◇ *vt* [teeth, fabric, surface] to make <sthg> lose its original color, especially so that it looks unpleasant □ *The poster was faded and discolored by the sun.* ◇ *vi* [teeth, fabric, paint] *This material may discolor if exposed to direct sunlight.*

discoloration [dɪs,kʌlə'reɪʃn] *n*: *see* **discolor** □ *Bleach may cause slight discoloration.*

discolored US, **discoloured** GB [dɪs'kʌlərd] *adj* [teeth, fabric, surface] that has changed color because something has discolored it.

discomfort [dɪs'kʌmfərt] *n* **-1.** [in one's back, feet] slight pain □ *New shoes often cause a little discomfort at first.* □ *You will feel some discomfort after the operation.* **-2.** [of a person] a feeling of embarrassment or anxiety □ *Their kindness only added to my discomfort.*

disconcert [,dɪskən'sɜːrt] *vt* to make <sb> feel uncomfortable or worried □ *Her silence disconcerted me considerably.*

disconcerting [,dɪskən'sɜːrtɪŋ] *adj* [silence, stare] that disconcerts one □ *He had a disconcerting habit of laughing after everything he said.*

disconnect [,dɪskə'nekt] *vt* **-1.** [hosepipe, wire] to undo <sthg> □ *Disconnect the nozzle from the end of the pipe.* **-2.** [washing machine, heater] to remove the plug of <an appliance or device> from a socket so that no electricity or gas reaches it □ *'Disconnect plug before removing cover.'* **-3.** [gas, electricity, telephone] to stop <sthg> from working in a building because the people there have not paid their bills or are leaving □ *Our phone's been discon-*

nected. **-4.** [caller] to end a conversation on the telephone of <sb> by interrupting the line □ *We were suddenly disconnected.*

disconnected [,dɪskə'nektəd] *adj* **-1.** [thoughts, remarks] that are not connected in a logical way □ *The poem is a series of seemingly disconnected images.* **-2.** [telephone, wire] that has been disconnected □ *One of the wires had become disconnected.*

disconsolate [dɪs'kɒnsələt] *adj* [person] who is very unhappy or disappointed □ *Don't look so disconsolate!*

discontent [,dɪskən'tent] *n* a feeling one has when one is not satisfied □ *There is growing discontent among senior staff.*

discontented [,dɪskən'tentəd] *adj* [staff, youth] who is not satisfied with something □ *I became increasingly discontented with married life.*

discontinue [,dɪskən'tɪnjuː] *vt* [service, supply] to stop <sthg> after it has happened regularly or existed for a period of time □ *This product has been discontinued.*

discontinued line [dɪskən,tɪnjuːd-] *n* a product that is no longer being sold or made.

discord ['dɪskɔːrd] *n* **-1.** a lack of agreement between people that causes problems. **-2.** MUSIC the strange or unpleasant sound made when notes that do not go well together are played at the same time.

discordant [dɪs'kɔːrdnt] *adj* [opinions, points of view, music] *see* **discord.**

discotheque ['dɪskətek] *n* a place where people dance to recorded pop music (old-fashioned use).

discount [*n* 'dɪskaʊnt, *vb* US 'dɪskaʊnt, GB dɪs'kaʊnt] ◇ *n* a reduction in the price of something □ *a 10% discount* □ *We offer a discount on all goods over $50.* □ *a staff discount.* ◇ *vt* **-1.** [report, claim, story] to say or decide that <sthg> is unimportant or untrue and no longer consider it. **-2.** BUSINESS to lower the price of <a product>.

discount house *n* **-1.** = **discount store. -2.** a financial organization that specializes in discounting bills of exchange.

discount store *n* a store that sells goods at a low price.

discourage [US dɪs'kɜːrɪdʒ, GB -'kʌr-] *vt* **-1.** [person] to make <sb> lose their enthusiasm and willingness to do something □ *I felt discouraged by their lack of interest.* **-2.** [action, behavior] to try to stop <sthg> by making it difficult or by showing one's disapproval □ *We are trying to discourage smoking.* □ *They've installed closed-circuit television to discourage shoplifters.* □ *This type of diet should be discouraged.* □ *They discouraged him from seeing her.*

discouraging [US dɪs'kɜːrɪdʒɪŋ, GB -'kʌr-] *adj* [result, remark, sign] that discourages one □ *The response so far has been discouraging.*

discourse ['dɪskɔːrs] *n* **-1.** [about something] a serious speech or piece of writing about a particular subject (formal use) □ *a lengthy discourse on the subject of Eastern philosophy.* **-2.** [between people] spoken or written discussion between people (formal use). **-3.**

LINGUISTICS written or spoken units of language of more than one sentence.

discourteous [dɪs'kɜːˈtjəs] *adj* [person, behavior] that is not polite (formal use).

discourtesy [dɪs'kɜːˈtəsɪ] *n*: *see* **discourteous**.

discover [dɪ'skʌvəˈ] *vt* -1. [continent, process, product] to be the first person to find <sthg that is important and that already existed> □ *When was the planet Pluto discovered?* -2. [object, person] to find <sb/sthg>, especially when one is not looking for them; [fact] to learn or realize <sthg> □ *The money was discovered in a disused warehouse.* □ *Have you discovered the cause of the problem?* □ *When did you discover that the keys were missing?* -3. [country, activity] to visit, learn etc <sthg> oneself for the first time □ *'Discover the Greek Islands.'* □ *I discovered the joys of painting.* -4. [artist, athlete] to recognize the ability or talent of <sb> and help them to become successful □ *He's still waiting to be discovered.*

discoverer [dɪ'skʌvərəˈ] *n* the first person to discover a continent, process etc.

discovery [dɪ'skʌvərɪ] (*pl* **discoveries**) *n* -1. something that has been discovered □ *Scientists have made an important scientific discovery.* -2. *see* **discover** □ *The discovery of the murder weapon gave the police a vital clue.*

discredit [dɪs'kredət] ◇ *vt* -1. [politician, company] to make <sb> lose the respect and trust of other people □ *The government has been discredited by the recent spate of scandals.* -2. [idea, theory] to make people lose their trust or belief in <sthg> □ *Their findings have been largely discredited by more recent research.* ◇ *n* a loss of respect or the trust of other people □ *He brought discredit on the company.* □ *Much to his discredit, he lied about the money.*

discreet [dɪ'skriːt] *adj* [person] who is careful about what they say or do in order to avoid attracting too much attention, upsetting other people etc □ *I made a few discreet enquiries about her background.*

discreetly [dɪ'skriːtlɪ] *adv* [enquire, enter, leave] *see* **discreet** □ *I coughed discreetly.*

discrepancy [dɪs'krepənsɪ] (*pl* **discrepancies**) *n* a difference between two things that one expects to be the same □ *a discrepancy in the figures* □ *There were a number of discrepancies between the two versions.*

discrete [dɪ'skriːt] *adj* [objects, units, ideas] that are separate and independent (formal use).

discretion [dɪ'skreʃn] *n* -1. [of a person] good judgment or tact □ *a man of discretion.* -2. **one's discretion** the ability to decide what it is best to do in a particular situation □ *I'll leave the timing of the announcement to your discretion.* □ *Use your discretion in borderline cases.* ■ **at the discretion of sb** depending on the decision of sb □ *Visitors are admitted at the discretion of the management.*

discretionary [US dɪ'skreʃənerɪ, GB -ənrɪ] *adj* [award, payment] that is given when it is considered to be appropriate rather than according to any particular rules.

discriminate [dɪ'skrɪmɪneɪt] *vi* -1. **to discriminate between people/things** to see or make a difference between people/things □ *He seems unable to discriminate between right and wrong.* -2. **to discriminate against sb** to treat sb differently from other people in a way that is unfair □ *Many people are still being racially/sexually discriminated against.*

discriminating [dɪ'skrɪmɪneɪtɪŋ] *adj* [person, taste, audience] that shows an ability to judge the difference between good and bad quality □ *I would hardly call his taste in women discriminating.*

discrimination [dɪˌskrɪmɪ'neɪʃn] *n* -1. [against a person] different treatment of a person or group that is unfair □ *She was a victim of racial/sexual discrimination.* -2. [in choosing something] the ability to judge the quality of something accurately □ *He shows no discrimination in the company he keeps.*

discus ['dɪskəs] (*pl* **discuses**) *n* a disk thrown by athletes in a competition.

discuss [dɪ'skʌs] *vt* [subject, plan] to exchange opinions and ideas about <sthg> in speech or writing, usually in order to make a decision □ *The issue was never properly discussed.* □ *I'll have to discuss that with my partners first.*

discussion [dɪ'skʌʃn] *n* -1. the act of exchanging opinions on a subject, plan etc, usually in order to make a decision □ *There was much discussion about which route would be the best.* ■ **to be under discussion** to be being discussed □ *The plans are under discussion.* -2. an exchange of opinions on a subject, plan etc, usually in order to make a decision □ *Many discussions on this matter have been held.* □ *The report contained a discussion of the recent findings.*

disdain [dɪs'deɪn] (formal use) ◇ *n* a feeling of dislike or disapproval for somebody or something that one thinks is not worth considering. ◇ *vt* -1. [invitation, offer, attempt] to show disdain for <sthg>. -2. **to disdain to do sthg** to refuse to do sthg because one thinks that it is not worth considering.

disdainful [dɪs'deɪnfl] *adj* [person, look, manner] that shows disdain for somebody or something.

disease [dɪ'ziːz] *n* -1. [of a person, animal] an illness in a human, animal, or plant that is usually caused by an infection rather than an accident □ *Cholera is a common tropical disease.* □ *It is hoped that the vaccination program will help halt the spread of the disease.* -2. [of society] a condition, situation etc that is considered to be harmful □ *Violent crime is largely a disease of the inner city.*

diseased [dɪ'ziːzd] *adj* -1. [body, organ, plant] that is suffering from a disease. -2. [mind] that is not normal or healthy.

disembark [ˌdɪsɪm'bɑːˈk] *vi* to leave a plane or ship.

disembarkation [ˌdɪsembɑːˈ'keɪʃn] *n* the act of leaving a plane or ship.

disembodied [ˌdɪsɪm'bɒdɪd] *adj* [voice, spirit,

head] that exists or seems to exist separately from a real person or body.

disembowel [ˌdɪsɪmˈbaʊəl] (US *pt* & *pp* **disemboweled**, *cont* **disemboweling**, GB *pt* & *pp* **disembowelled**, *cont* **disembowelling**) *vt* to remove the bowels of <a person> in a violent act.

disenchanted [US ˌdɪsɪnˈtʃæntəd, GB -ˈtʃɑːnt-] *adj* [person] who is disappointed with something that they used to admire or consider worthwhile □ He's become utterly disenchanted with city life.

disenfranchise [dɪsɪnˈfræntʃaɪz] *vt* = **disfranchise**.

disengage [ˌdɪsɪnˈgeɪdʒ] *vt* -1. to free or release <sthg> from something □ She politely disengaged herself from her companion and walked over to me. -2. AUTO to press <the clutch> down, usually before changing gear, in order to stop the power from the engine going to the wheels.

disengagement [ˌdɪsɪnˈgeɪdʒmənt] *n* the process of becoming less involved with an activity or organization.

disentangle [ˌdɪsɪnˈtæŋgl] *vt* [hair, string] to remove the tangles from <sthg>. ■ **to disentangle sb/sthg from sthg** to free sb/sthg from sthg so that they are no longer trapped, tangled etc □ They had to disentangle the rope from the propellor. □ She disentangled herself from his arms.

disfavor US, **disfavour** GB [dɪsˈfeɪvəʳ] *n* -1. **to look on sthg with disfavor** to disapprove of sthg. -2. **to fall into disfavor with sb** to become disliked or disapproved of by sb.

disfigure [dɪsˈfɪgəʳ] *vt* [person, face, view] to spoil the appearance of <sb/sthg> by causing permanent damage □ He was horribly disfigured in an accident.

disfranchise [dɪsˈfræntʃaɪz] *vt* to remove the right to vote from <sb>.

disgorge [dɪsˈgɔːʳdʒ] *vt* -1. to bring up <food> from one's stomach (formal use). -2. [smoke, chemicals] to pour <sthg> out in large quantities □ The wreck is disgorging oil into the sea at an alarming rate.

disgrace [dɪsˈgreɪs] ◇ *n* -1. a loss of the respect of other people □ She brought disgrace on her family. ■ **to be in disgrace** to be regarded with strong disapproval because one has done something wrong □ He resigned in disgrace. -2. [to one's family, profession] a person or thing that causes one to feel embarrassed or ashamed □ This new building's a disgrace. □ She's a disgrace to the university. ◇ *vt* [family, employer] to cause <sb> to lose the respect of other people □ He disgraced himself in front of everyone.

disgraceful [dɪsˈgreɪsfl] *adj* [behavior, condition] that is very bad and causes one to feel shock or disapproval □ It's a disgraceful waste of public money.

disgruntled [dɪsˈgrʌntld] *adj* [person] who is unhappy and annoyed about something □ Disgruntled readers wrote in to complain about the new style layout of the paper.

disguise [dɪsˈgaɪz] ◇ *n* something that one wears to make one's appearance different from usual, usually in order to deceive people □ He attended in disguise to hide his identity from the press. ◇ *vt* -1. **to be disguised** to be dressed in a disguise □ He was disguised as a policeman. ■ **to disguise oneself** to put on a disguise □ They disguised themselves as journalists to gain entry. -2. [appearance, smell] to prevent <sthg> from being recognized by changing it □ She put on a funny accent to disguise her voice. -3. [fact, feeling] to prevent <sthg> from being noticed by hiding it or making it seem different □ He didn't even try to disguise his disappointment. □ You can't disguise the fact that he's just not up to the job.

disgust [dɪsˈgʌst] ◇ *n* the feeling one has when one finds something shocking and unacceptable or disgusting □ I was filled with disgust at the sight. □ She resigned/left in disgust. ◇ *vt* to cause <sb> to feel disgust □ I am disgusted by their attitude.

disgusting [dɪsˈgʌstɪŋ] *adj* [person, behavior, food] that one thinks is extremely unpleasant □ It was a disgusting sight. □ It's disgusting the way they've been treated.

dish [dɪʃ] *n* -1. a container for serving food in that is not as deep as a bowl and often has a lid □ Put the beans in that dish. -2. food prepared in a particular way for a meal □ He loves Mediterranean dishes.

◆ **dishes** *npl* a collective term for the plates, cups, bowls etc that have been used for a meal and need to be washed □ Can you take the dishes into the kitchen? ■ **to do** OR **wash the dishes** to clean the plates, cups, bowls etc after a meal.

◆ **dish out** *vt sep* **to dish sthg out** [money, advice] to give a lot of sthg to different people (informal use).

◆ **dish up** *vt sep* **to dish sthg up** [food] to serve sthg at the beginning of a meal.

dish antenna US, **dish aerial** *n* a device shaped like a dish that is used for receiving signals that are sent by satellite.

disharmony [ˌdɪsˈhɑːʳmənɪ] *n* an unpleasant atmosphere that is caused by disagreement between people.

dishcloth [ˈdɪʃklɒθ] *n* a cloth used for washing dishes.

disheartened [dɪsˈhɑːʳtnd] *adj* **to be disheartened** to no longer have confidence or hope □ Don't be disheartened — I'm sure you'll pass next time.

disheartening [dɪsˈhɑːʳtnɪŋ] *adj* [experience, result, remark] that makes one lose confidence or hope.

disheveled US, **dishevelled** GB [dɪˈʃevld] *adj* [clothes, hair] untidy □ Ian arrived late, looking very disheveled.

dishonest [dɪsˈɒnəst] *adj* [person, behavior] that is not honest □ It would be dishonest of me to say I was satisfied. □ It never occurred to him he was doing anything dishonest.

dishonesty [dɪsˈɒnəstɪ] *n* behavior or an action that shows a lack of honesty.

dishonor US, **dishonour** GB [dɪs'ɒnəʳ] ◇ *n* a loss of the honor or respect of other people □ *He brought dishonor on his country.* ◇ *vt* [family, country, institution] to make <sb/sthg> lose the honor and respect of other people.

dishonorable US, **dishonourable** GB [dɪs'ɒnərəbl] *adj* [person, behavior] that is not honorable.

dishonour *etc* GB = **dishonor** *etc.*

dish rack *n* a frame on which plates, cups etc are placed to dry after being washed.

dish soap *n* US a soapy liquid added to hot water for cleaning dirty dishes.

dish towel *n* a cloth for drying dishes after they have been washed.

dishwasher ['dɪʃwɒʃəʳ] *n* a machine for washing dishes.

disillusioned [,dɪsɪ'luːʒnd] *adj* [person] who is disappointed with somebody or something that they used to admire or respect □ *The members have grown* OR *become disillusioned with the leadership.*

disillusionment [,dɪsɪ'luːʒnmənt] *n* the state of being disillusioned with somebody or something.

disincentive [,dɪsɪn'sentɪv] *n* something that makes somebody less willing or likely to do something.

disinclined [,dɪsɪn'klaɪnd] *adj* **to be disinclined to do sthg** to be unwilling to do sthg □ *I felt disinclined to cooperate.*

disinfect [,dɪsɪn'fekt] *vt* [cut, toilet, instrument] to clean <sthg> with a disinfectant.

disinfectant [,dɪsɪn'fektənt] *n* a substance used to kill germs in order to prevent disease or infection □ *It contains a powerful disinfectant.* □ *disinfectant soap/fluid.*

disinformation [,dɪsɪnfəʳ'meɪʃn] *n* untrue information that is given especially by a government, in order to confuse an enemy or to deceive people.

disingenuous [,dɪsɪn'dʒenjʊəs] *adj* [person] who is insincere because they know something they are not admitting.

disinherit [,dɪsɪn'herət] *vt* to stop <sb> from inheriting something by changing one's will □ *He was disinherited by his family.*

disintegrate [dɪs'ɪntəgreɪt] *vi* **-1.** [object] to break into many small pieces □ *The plane disintegrated on impact.* **-2.** [project, marriage] to gradually fail □ *Their marriage gradually disintegrated.*

disintegration [dɪs,ɪntə'greɪʃn] *n*: *see* **disintegrate** □ *We are witnessing the disintegration of the country.*

disinterested [,dɪs'ɪntrəstəd] *adj* **-1.** [observer, party] who is not influenced by the possibility of getting something for themselves from a situation □ *It's difficult to remain completely disinterested.* □ *Let me give you some disinterested advice.* **-2.** **to be disinterested** to have or show no interest in something (informal use) □ *I'm completely disinterested in football.*

disinvestment [,dɪsɪn'vestmənt] *n* a reduction

or removal of the money that has been invested in something.

disjointed [dɪs'dʒɔɪntəd] *adj* [speech, style] that does not follow a clear logical order □ *Her speech was confused and disjointed.*

disk US, **disc** GB [dɪsk] *n* **-1.** an object that is flat and round. **-2.** MEDICINE a round flat piece of cartilage between the bones of the spine. **-3.** COMPUTING a square, flat, plastic object on which information is recorded for use by a computer □ *How much free disk space is there left?*

diskette [dɪ'sket] *n* COMPUTING = **floppy disk**.

diskette drive *n* US a device that transfers information between a computer's memory and the disk.

disk operating system *n* COMPUTING → **DOS**.

dislike [dɪs'laɪk] ◇ *n* **-1.** a feeling of not liking somebody or something □ *a look of dislike* □ *his dislike of travel/computers.* ■ **to take a dislike to sb** to begin to dislike sb, usually after knowing them for only a short time □ *I took an instant dislike to him.* **-2.** **sb's dislikes** the things that sb dislikes □ *It was hard to remember all his likes and dislikes.* ◇ *vt* to have a feeling of dislike for <sb/sthg>.

dislocate ['dɪsləkeɪt] *vt* **-1.** MEDICINE [shoulder, hip] to move <a bone> out of its correct position in a joint □ *I think I've dislocated my finger.* **-2.** [business, service] to prevent <sthg> from operating properly.

dislodge [dɪs'lɒdʒ] *vt* to succeed in removing <sb/sthg> from their position □ *They dislodged their rivals from the top of the division.*

disloyal [,dɪs'lɔɪəl] *adj* [friend, colleague] who is not loyal □ *forces disloyal to the regime.*

dismal ['dɪzməl] *adj* **-1.** [weather, future, place] that is depressing □ *February is always a dismal time of year.* **-2.** [attempt, failure] very bad □ *The whole party was a dismal failure.*

dismantle [dɪs'mæntl] *vt* [machine, building, system] to separate the parts of <sthg> so that it is no longer whole □ *I dismantled the radio, but I can't put it back together again.*

dismay [dɪs'meɪ] ◇ *n* a feeling of shock and loss of confidence that is caused by a disappointment □ *To our dismay, the decision was no.* □ *She looked at him in dismay.* ◇ *vt* to fill <sb> with dismay □ *We were dismayed at the cost of the repairs.*

dismember [dɪs'membəʳ] *vt* to remove the limbs of <a person or animal>.

dismiss [dɪs'mɪs] *vt* **-1.** [worker, employee] to make <sb> leave their job □ *He was dismissed for incompetence.* **-2.** [idea, plan, person] to refuse to think about <sb/sthg> because it is not serious □ *He was dismissed as a crank.* **-3.** [class, troops] to allow <sb> to leave □ *Class was dismissed early because of the weather.* **-4.** LAW [case, appeal, charges] to refuse to consider <sthg> in a court of law □ *Case dismissed.*

dismissal [dɪs'mɪsl] *n*: *see* **dismiss**.

dismissive [dɪs'mɪsɪv] *adj* [letter, attitude, tone] that refuses to take somebody or something seriously and is slightly rude □ *He was very dismissive of the whole idea.*

dismount [ˌdɪs'maʊnt] *vi* [rider, jockey] to get off a horse, bicycle etc.

Disney ['dɪznɪ], **Walt** (1901–1966) a US movie maker who specialized in animated cartoons. His work, popular with children, includes *Bambi, Fantasia,* and *Mary Poppins.*

disobedience [ˌdɪsə'biːdjəns] *n* behavior that involves refusing to do what one is told or ordered to do □ *I will not tolerate disobedience from my children.*

disobedient [ˌdɪsə'biːdjənt] *adj* [child, dog] that is not obedient.

disobey [ˌdɪsə'beɪ] ◇ *vt* [officer, rule, order] to refuse to obey <sb/sthg> □ *She decided to disobey the command.* ◇ *vi:* *He did not dare to disobey.*

disorder [dɪs'ɔːrdər] *n* **-1. in disorder** in a state of confusion and disorganization □ *After a noisy quarrel, the meeting broke up in disorder.* □ *Everything was scattered over the floor in disorder.* **-2.** [in the streets] riots or fighting in the streets □ *outbreaks of public disorder.* **-3.** MEDICINE a failure of part of the mind or body to work properly □ *a heart/psychiatric/mental disorder.*

disordered [dɪs'ɔːrdərd] *adj* [room] in a state of confusion and disorganization.

disorderly [dɪs'ɔːrdərlɪ] *adj* **-1.** [room, appearance] that is untidy. **-2.** [behavior, person] that is uncontrolled and aggressive.

disorderly conduct [-'kɒndʌkt] *n* the crime of behaving in an uncontrolled and aggressive way.

disorganized, -ised [dɪs'ɔːrgənaɪzd] *adj* **-1.** [person] who is bad at organizing and planning things. **-2.** [system, company, event] that is badly organized □ *The whole department is extremely disorganized.*

disoriented [dɪs'ɔːrɪəntəd] US, **disorientated** [dɪs'ɔːrɪənteɪtəd] GB *adj* **-1.** [person] who is unsure of where they are □ *The hostages stepped out of the plane, looking tired and disoriented.* **-2.** [person] who is confused and does not know what to think □ *Old people can easily become disoriented.*

disown [dɪs'oʊn] *vt* [relative, friend, work] to show that one does not want to be connected with or considered responsible for <sb/sthg> □ *I could never tell my parents — they'd disown me!*

disparaging [US dɪ'sperɪdʒɪŋ, GB -'spær-] *adj* [comment, remark] that shows one disapproves of somebody or something or does not value them □ *He's very disparaging about his brother.*

disparate ['dɪspərət] *adj* [groups, reasons] that are very different from each other (formal use) □ *It's difficult to unite such disparate elements within one party.*

disparity [dɪ'spærɪtɪ] (*pl* **disparities**) *n* a large difference between two or more things □ *the disparity between town and country* □ *disparities in pay and conditions.*

dispassionate [dɪ'spæʃnət] *adj* [judge, observer] who is able to judge somebody or something fairly because they are not influenced by emotion □ *a dispassionate account of events leading up to the crime.*

dispatch [dɪ'spætʃ] ◇ *n* an official or military message. ◇ *vt* [person, letter, goods] to send <sb/sthg> somewhere □ *Your order was dispatched yesterday, Mr Nolan.*

dispatch box *n* **the dispatch box** POLITICS the place where ministers stand in the British parliament to speak.

dispatch rider *n* **-1.** a soldier who acts as a messenger and travels by motorcycle. **-2.** a person whose job is to deliver documents, packages etc by motorcycle.

dispel [dɪ'spel] (*pt* & *pp* **dispelled,** *cont* **dispelling**) *vt* [doubt, fear, illusion] to remove <an idea> from somebody's mind □ *The announcement did little to dispel fears of a takeover.*

dispensable [dɪ'spensəbl] *adj* [staff, luxury] that one can get rid of because it is not important □ *Don't buy anything that's dispensable.*

dispensary [dɪ'spensərɪ] (*pl* **dispensaries**) *n* a place in a hospital, school etc where medicines are prepared and given to people.

dispensation [ˌdɪspen'seɪʃn] *n* special permission to do something that is against the normal rules □ *He received a special dispensation from the Pope to get married in St Peter's.*

dispense [dɪ'spens] *vt* **-1.** [justice, advice] to make sure that people receive <sthg>. **-2.** [drug, medicine] to prepare and give <sthg> to people.

◆ **dispense with** *vt fus* **-1. to dispense with sb/sthg** to continue without sb/sthg because they are not necessary □ *We can dispense with the formalities.* **-2. to dispense with the need for sthg** to make sthg unnecessary □ *Decent public transport would dispense with the need for a car.*

dispenser [dɪ'spensər] *n* a machine in a public place that one can get soap, drinks, cash etc from □ *a drink dispenser* □ *a cash dispenser.*

dispensing chemist [dɪ'spensɪŋ-] *n* GB a pharmacist who prepares and gives people medicines, drugs etc that have been prescribed by a doctor.

dispersal [dɪ'spɜːrsl] *n:* *see* **disperse** □ *The grain is collected here for dispersal to each village.*

disperse [dɪ'spɜːrs] ◇ *vt* **-1.** [crowd, seeds] to make <a group of people or things> separate and go in different directions. **-2.** [gas, chemical] to make <sthg> spread out over a wide area. ◇ *vi* **-1.** [crowd, seeds] *The police told the demonstrators to disperse.* **-2.** [gas, chemical] *The smoke quickly dispersed.*

dispirited [dɪ'spɪrətəd] *adj* **to be dispirited** to have lost one's enthusiasm, usually because of something bad that has happened.

dispiriting [dɪ'spɪrətɪŋ] *adj* [result, performance, experience] that makes one dispirited □ *Last year's results were most dispiriting.*

displace [dɪs'pleɪs] *vt* **-1.** [leader, champion] to remove <sb> from a position □ *She has been displaced as financial director.* **-2.** PHYSICS to cause <a liquid> to move by putting a solid object in it.

displaced person [,dɪspleɪst-] *n* a person who has been forced to leave their home, area, or country because of war, a natural disaster etc.

displacement [dɪs'pleɪsmənt] *n* **-1.** the removal of people from their home, area, or country by war, natural disasters etc. **-2.** PHYSICS [of liquid] *see* **displace.**

display [dɪ'spleɪ] ◇ *n* **-1.** [of goods, works of art] an arrangement of objects for the public to see □ *a display of weapons from the Bronze Age* □ *a window display* □ *It's on display in the window.* □ *a display cabinet/unit.* **-2.** [of courage, intelligence] the act of showing an emotion, skill etc to other people □ *a display of affection* □ *a public display of support.* **-3.** [of acrobatics, dancing] a public demonstration or exhibition □ *an aerobatics display.* **-4.** COMPUTING a screen on which information or images can be seen.
◇ *vt* **-1.** [painting, object] to put <sthg> in a particular place so that it can be seen □ *All goods displayed in the window are in the sale.* **-2.** [emotion, skill, attitude] to show <sthg> clearly by what one says or does □ *He displayed a remarkable understanding of the subject.*

display advertising *n* printed or written advertisements that are designed to attract people's attention, e.g. by having a border or a special typeface.

displease [dɪs'pliːz] *vt* to make <sb> angry or upset □ *He was far from displeased by what he heard.*

displeasure [dɪs'pleʒəʳ] *n* a feeling of annoyance or anger □ *I was careful not to arouse his displeasure!*

disposable [dɪ'spəʊzəbl] *adj* [razor, lighter, diaper] that is intended to be thrown away after it has been used once or a few times □ *You can now buy disposable contact lenses.*

disposable income *n* the money from one's salary or earnings that one has for spending after one has paid tax, housing bills etc.

disposal [dɪ'spəʊzl] *n* **-1.** [of garbage, waste] the removal of something that is not wanted or necessary □ *a waste disposal unit.* **-2. to be at sb's disposal** [person] to be available for sb to help them; [house, vehicle] to be available for sb so that they can use it □ *I'm entirely at your disposal.* □ *The car was left at their disposal for the weekend.*

dispose [dɪ'spəʊz] ◆ **dispose of** *vt fus* **-1. to dispose of sthg** [garbage, waste] to get rid of sthg. **-2. to dispose of sthg** [problem, question] to deal with and find an answer to sthg.

disposed [dɪ'spəʊzd] *adj* **-1. to be disposed to do sthg** to be willing to do sthg □ *He was not disposed to help/linger/comment.* **-2. to be well disposed to** OR **toward sb** to have a friendly attitude toward sb.

disposition [,dɪspə'zɪʃn] *n* **-1.** a particular way that somebody usually behaves because of their character □ *She has a very sweet disposi-*tion. **-2. a disposition to do sthg** a willingness or tendency to do sthg.

dispossess [,dɪspə'zes] *vt* **to dispossess sb of sthg** to take away from sb sthg that they own, especially land or property (formal use) □ *dispossessed families.*

disproportion [,dɪsprə'pɔːʳʃn] *n* lack of proportion.

disproportionate [,dɪsprə'pɔːʳʃnət] *adj* [level, amount] that is bigger than it should be □ *a disproportionate amount of time.*

disprove [,dɪs'pruːv] *vt* [theory, idea, belief] to show <sthg> to be false □ *The statistics disprove your argument.*

dispute [dɪ'spjuːt] ◇ *n* **-1.** [between people, countries] an argument, usually about who owns something or who has the right or responsibility to do something □ *a border dispute* □ *a dispute over ethnic rights.* **-2.** INDUSTRY a disagreement between workers and employers, usually about pay, working conditions etc □ *a pay dispute* OR *dispute over pay.* **-3. to be open to dispute** to be likely to be disagreed with □ *A lot of what he said is open to dispute.* ■ **to be in dispute** [person] to be involved in an argument, usually about money, ownership, rights etc; [case, fact, opinion] to be the subject of an argument or disagreement □ *We're in dispute with the supplier over a consignment of faulty goods.* □ *It is not your figures that are in dispute.*
◇ *vt* **-1.** [opinion, fact, figure] to say that one thinks <sthg> is not true or correct □ *I don't dispute (that) she may be right.* **-2.** [right, method, ownership] to argue about <sthg>, usually over a long period □ *It's a hotly-disputed issue.* **-3.** [territory, championship] to fight against somebody for the right to have <sthg> □ *the disputed border area.*

disqualification [dɪs,kwɒlɪfɪ'keɪʃn] *n*: *see* **disqualify** □ *Foul play will result in disqualification from the competition.*

disqualify [,dɪs'kwɒlɪfaɪ] (*pt* & *pp* **disqualified**) *vt* **-1.** [court, judge] to take away from <sb> the right to do something, usually because that person has done something dishonest or illegal □ *The judge disqualified her from driving for a year.* **-2.** [one's age, sex, criminal record] to make it impossible for <sb> to do or obtain something □ *His poor eyesight disqualified him from going into the army.* **-3.** SPORT [referee] to take away from <an athlete, team> etc the right to take part in a sport or sports event, usually because they have done something that breaks the rules □ *Two swimmers were disqualified for taking drugs.*

disquiet [dɪs'kwaɪət] *n* fear that people feel when they do not know what is going to happen □ *a vague feeling of disquiet.*

Disraeli [dɪz'reɪlɪ], **Benjamin** (1804–1881) a British politician and writer. He was prime minister in 1868, and from 1874 to 1880.

disregard [,dɪsrɪ'gɑːʳd] ◇ *n* the act of not paying enough care and attention to something □ *He shows a complete disregard for the feelings of his staff.* ◇ *vt* [law, advice, warning] to ignore

<sthg> □ *He has completely disregarded the feelings of those around him.*

disrepair [ˌdɪsrɪ'peəʳ] *n* **to fall into disrepair** [building] to become gradually more broken or ruined as a result of not being repaired.

disreputable [dɪs'repjətəbl] *adj* [person, company] that has a bad reputation and is thought to be dishonest □ *He's a thoroughly disreputable character.*

disrepute [ˌdɪsrɪ'pjuːt] *n* **to bring sthg into disrepute** [profession, sport] to damage the reputation of sthg by acting dishonestly. ■ **to fall into disrepute** [work, theory, institution] to become less admired or accepted than before.

disrespectful [ˌdɪsrɪ'spektfl] *adj* [person, attitude] that does not show enough respect.

disrupt [dɪs'rʌpt] *vt* [meeting, procedure, traffic] to stop <sthg> from continuing as normal □ *The celebrations were disrupted by political protests.*

disruption [dɪs'rʌpʃn] *n: see* **disrupt** □ *The accident caused severe disruption to rush-hour traffic.*

disruptive [dɪs'rʌptɪv] *adj* [effect, child, behavior] *see* **disrupt** □ *A disruptive child can upset a whole class of pupils.*

dissatisfaction [ˌdɪssætəs'fækʃn] *n* a feeling of unhappiness that one gets when something is not as good as it should be □ *There is widespread dissatisfaction at OR with the efficiency of the service.*

dissatisfied [ˌdɪs'sætəsfaɪd] *adj* [customer, worker] who feels dissatisfaction; [comment, look] that shows dissatisfaction □ *The guest claimed that he was dissatisfied with his room/at his treatment.*

dissect [dɪ'sekt] *vt* **-1.** [body, corpse, rat] to cut up <a dead person, animal> etc in order to examine what is inside for scientific or medical purposes. **-2.** [book, movie, proposal] to study <a work of art, idea> etc very carefully in order to understand its meaning.

disseminate [dɪ'semɪneɪt] *vt* [news, information] to spread <sthg> so that as many people as possible know about it □ *New ideas were disseminated by word of mouth.*

dissemination [dɪˌsemə'neɪʃn] *n* [of news, information] *see* **disseminate.**

dissension [dɪ'senʃn] *n* disagreement and arguments □ *The program is likely to cause a great deal of dissension among ethnic communities.*

dissent [dɪ'sent] (formal use) ◇ *n* strong disagreement with an official policy or with an opinion that a lot of people have. ◇ *vi* to show one's dissent.

dissenter [dɪ'sentəʳ] *n* a person who dissents.

dissenting [dɪ'sentɪŋ] *adj* **a dissenting voice** a person who disagrees strongly with an opinion that a lot of other people have.

dissertation [ˌdɪsəʳ'teɪʃn] *n* a long essay on a particular subject, especially one written as part of a university degree □ *a dissertation on Brecht.*

disservice [ˌdɪs'sɜːʳvɪs] *n* **to do sb a disservice** to do something that harms sb □ *You could*

do yourself a great disservice by antagonizing people like that.

dissident ['dɪsədənt] *n* a person who openly protests against a government, especially when this is not allowed □ *Dissidents were thrown into jail.*

dissimilar [dɪ'sɪmɪləʳ] *adj* [person, opinion, experience] that is very different from somebody or something else □ *They come from completely dissimilar backgrounds.* □ *Her views are not dissimilar to mine.*

dissipate ['dɪsəpeɪt] (formal use) ◇ *vt* **-1.** [heat, fog] to make <sthg> spread so much that it disappears. **-2.** [one's money, time, energy] to gradually waste <sthg> in a silly way. ◇ *vi* [crowd, heat, fog] *The mist finally dissipated.*

dissipated ['dɪsəpeɪtəd] *adj* [person] who has spent a lot of time doing things for pleasure that are harmful, e.g. drinking □ *a dissipated youth.*

dissociate [dɪ'səʊʃɪeɪt] *vt* to consider or make <sthg> separate from something else □ *I try to dissociate my working life from my family life.* □ *I cannot dissociate the two ideas in my mind.* ■ **to dissociate oneself from sb/sthg** to end one's involvement with sb/sthg, usually in order to avoid trouble.

dissolute ['dɪsəluːt] *adj* [person, way of life] that is considered to be immoral.

dissolution [ˌdɪsə'luːʃn] *n* [of an organization, relationship] the official ending of something by breaking it up or sending its members away □ *the dissolution of Parliament.*

dissolve [dɪ'zɒlv] ◇ *vt* **-1.** [sugar, aspirin, chlorine] to mix <a solid or gas> so completely with a liquid that it becomes part of it □ *Dissolve the tablets in water.* **-2.** [partnership, link, parliament] to end <an organization, campaign> etc officially by making its members separate (formal use) □ *Their marriage was finally dissolved.* ◇ *vi* **-1.** [sugar, aspirin, chlorine] *Hydrogen does not dissolve in water.* **-2.** [resistance, opposition, courage] to become weaker and finally disappear.

◆ **dissolve in(to)** *vt fus* **to dissolve in(to) laughter/tears** to start laughing/crying in a way that one cannot control.

dissuade [dɪ'sweɪd] *vt* to persuade <sb> not to do something □ *We were dissuaded from leaving until the next day.*

distance ['dɪstəns] ◇ *n* **-1.** [between places] the amount of space between one place and another □ *It is quite a distance from here to the bus station.* □ *We walked for a distance of five miles.* □ *The school is within easy walking distance.* □ *Distances in Europe are measured in kilometers.* **-2. the distance** a point that is far away from one □ *She stared into the distance.* ■ **at a distance** quite far away □ *We remained at a safe distance from the protest march.* □ *The radio should be placed at a distance of at least four meters from the screen.* ■ **from a distance** from quite far away □ *Peter watched from a distance.* □ *The building looks even more impressive from a distance.* □ *It can still be seen from a distance of five miles.* ■ **in the distance** far away, but able to be seen or heard □ *I could* hear thunder in the distance. □ There, in the distance, stood our home.

◇ **vt** **to distance oneself** to deliberately become less involved with or less sympathetic to people, actions, beliefs etc □ He later distanced himself from his more radical comments/colleagues.

distance learning *n* a method of studying, often for a degree, in which one studies at home and sends work to a teacher.

distant ['dɪstənt] *adj* **-1.** [place, country] that is far away □ We could hear the sound of distant guns. **-2. in the distant past/future** a long time ago/in the future □ I hope to see them again in the not-too-distant future. **-3.** [relative, cousin] who is not closely related to one □ I have some distant relations in Canada. **-4.** [person, manner] that is not very friendly □ She seemed cold and distant, unlike her usual self.

distaste [dɪs'teɪst] *n* a feeling of dislike, especially of something that is considered vulgar, unpleasant, or immoral □ The scandal left me with a deep distaste for the world of politics.

distasteful [dɪs'teɪstfl] *adj* [experience, action, scene] that makes one feel distaste □ I consider it distasteful to discuss people's private affairs.

Dist Atty *abbr of* **district attorney**.

distemper [dɪ'stempər] *n* [in animals] a serious infectious disease of dogs and some other animals.

distended [dɪ'stendəd] *adj* MEDICINE [stomach, vein] that is larger and rounder than usual, often because there is too much air inside.

distill US, **distil** GB [dɪ'stɪl] (*pt* & *pp* **distilled**, *cont* **distilling**) *vt* **-1.** [water] to purify <a liquid> by heating it until it evaporates, and then cooling it until it becomes liquid again; [whiskey, brandy, vodka] to make <a strong alcoholic drink> from a liquid in this way. **-2.** to produce <information, an idea> by choosing the most useful parts from several places or from one much longer source.

distiller [dɪ'stɪlər] *n* a person or company that produces whiskey, brandy etc.

distillery [dɪ'stɪlərɪ] (*pl* **distilleries**) *n* a factory that produces whiskey, brandy etc.

distinct [dɪ'stɪŋkt] *adj* **-1.** that is different enough to be considered a separate thing or type □ The legal system in Scotland is distinct from that in England. □ Try to keep these two facts distinct in your mind. **-2.** [improvement, possibility, impression] that is definite and clearly noticeable □ A distinct smell of burning came from the kitchen. □ There are distinct advantages to buying now.

◆ **as distinct from** *prep* a phrase used to help explain what something is by saying what it is not □ Sales of footwear, as distinct from clothing, have actually increased.

distinction [dɪ'stɪŋkʃn] *n* **-1.** [between things] a small difference between things that are similar □ The main distinction between sales tax and other taxes is in its method of collection. ■ **to draw** OR **make a distinction between two things** to say that two similar things are different or show how they are different □ We

need to draw a clear distinction between financial and personal motives in this case. **-2. of distinction** of high quality □ wines of distinction. **-3.** EDUCATION the highest possible grade in some types of examination, degree etc □ He passed with a distinction in math.

distinctive [dɪ'stɪŋktɪv] *adj* [flavor, sound, voice] that has its own individual, special, and recognizable character □ This pattern is quite distinctive of Irish glassware. □ I heard the distinctive sound of Jan's voice in the corridor.

distinctly [dɪ'stɪŋktlɪ] *adv* **-1.** [see, remember, speak] clearly □ I distinctly recall the day I started school. **-2. distinctly rude/colder etc** rude/colder etc in a way that is noticeable □ It's grown distinctly warmer in the last two days.

distinguish [dɪ'stɪŋgwɪʃ] ◇ *vt* **-1.** [tastes, smells, colors] to recognize <people or things> as being different from each other □ He was unable to distinguish certain colors. □ Can you honestly distinguish her from her twin sister? **-2.** [shape, plane, word] to be able to see <a distant, small, or unclear object> □ If you look closely you can just distinguish the line of the scar. **-3.** [person, one's work] to show <sb/sthg> to be different or separate from other people or things □ What distinguishes her from the other staff is her willingness to learn. ■ **to distinguish oneself** to work, perform etc so well that other people notice and praise one □ She distinguished herself in the field of international law.

◇ *vi* **to distinguish between two things** to be able to see or to explain the difference between two things □ These children are unable to distinguish between right and wrong.

distinguished [dɪ'stɪŋgwɪʃt] *adj* [visitor, politician, career] that is highly respected and successful □ Please welcome our distinguished guest, Professor Bryant.

distinguishing [dɪ'stɪŋgwɪʃɪŋ] *adj* [feature, mark, characteristic] that allows something or somebody to be recognized as different from other things or people □ the town's only distinguishing feature being a large town hall.

distort [dɪ'stɔːrt] *vt* **-1.** [shape, sound] to change <sthg> so that it becomes unclear, strange, or ugly □ Turning up the volume tends to distort the sound still further. **-2.** [meaning, account, truth] to change <sthg> so that it is different from what was true or what was meant □ The press tend to distort the real nature of the problem.

distorted [dɪ'stɔːrtəd] *adj* [shape, sound, view] that has been distorted □ He has somehow acquired a distorted impression of the facts.

distortion [dɪ'stɔːrʃn] *n*: *see* **distort** □ The article is a complete distortion of the truth.

distract [dɪ'strækt] *vt* to prevent <sb> from concentrating on what they are doing □ I was distracted by a dog barking. □ Try to distract his attention while I finish what I'm doing.

distracted [dɪ'stræktəd] *adj* [person] who is unable to concentrate properly because they are scared, worried etc.

distraction [dɪ'strækʃn] *n* **-1.** something that prevents one from concentrating on what one is doing; something that helps one to stop thinking or worrying too much so that one can relax □ *There are fewer distractions working at home.* □ *The party provided a welcome distraction from pressures at work.* **-2. to drive sb to distraction** [noise] to make <sb> very annoyed.

distraught [dɪ'strɔːt] *adj* [person] who is very upset or anxious and cannot think clearly or act sensibly □ *The child's parents were distraught with worry.*

distress [dɪ'stres] ◇ *n* **-1.** [of a person, animal] great mental or physical suffering □ *The child was clearly in distress.* **-2. to be in distress** [ship, plane] to be in a state of great danger or difficulty □ *The ship was in distress and drifting with the tide.* ◇ *vt* to make <sb> feel very unhappy and worried □ *It distresses me to see you like this.*

distressed [dɪ'strest] *adj* [person, animal] that feels distress.

distressing [dɪ'stresɪŋ] *adj* [news, thought, sight] that causes distress □ *Some people may find these images distressing.*

distress signal *n* a message or signal sent from a ship or plane, usually by radio, to say that it is in serious danger.

distribute [US dɪ'strɪbjət, GB -juːt] *vt* **-1.** [leaflets, prizes, tests] to give or send <sthg> to several people □ *The memo should be distributed to* OR *among all members of the staff.* **-2.** [money, food, blankets] to give <things> to people who need them □ *Aid is distributed by several relief agencies working in the region.* **-3.** BUSINESS to send out <goods> to stores, customers, retailers etc.

distribution [ˌdɪstrɪ'bjuːʃn] *n: see* **distribute** □ *The supplies are stored in the capital for distribution later.*

distributor [dɪ'strɪbjətəʳ] *n* **-1.** BUSINESS a person or company that sends out goods to stores, customers, retailers etc □ *Our main distributor in this area is in Jersey City.* **-2.** AUTO a device in a car, motorbike etc that sends electric current to the spark plugs.

district ['dɪstrɪkt] *n* **-1.** an area of a city that has a particular character □ *They have offices in the business district of Milan.* **-2.** an area into which a country or city is divided for a particular purpose □ *the city's historical district* □ *a postal district.*

district attorney *n* in the USA, the lawyer who represents the local or state government and brings legal charges against criminals.

district council *n* in the UK, a group of people elected to govern a district.

district court *n* a court in the USA that deals with cases involving national laws.

district nurse *n* in the UK, a nurse who visits people in their homes to give them treatment.

District of Columbia: the District of Columbia a special district in the eastern USA that is not part of any of the states. It includes the US capital, Washington, and covers the same area as it. ABBREVIATION: D.C. SIZE: 175 sq kms. POPULATION: 606,900. CAPITAL: Washington.

distrust [dɪs'trʌst] ◇ *n* the feeling that one cannot trust somebody or something □ *They have a deep distrust of the police.* ◇ *vt* [person, motive, method] to feel distrust of <sb/sthg> □ *It's not that I distrust his motives, but...*

distrustful [dɪs'trʌstfl] *adj* **to be distrustful of sb/sthg** to distrust sb/sthg □ *I'm still distrustful of his motives.*

disturb [dɪ'stɜːʳb] *vt* **-1.** [person, concentration] to interrupt <sb/sthg> by making a noise or causing problems; [person, baby] to wake <sb> up when they need to sleep □ *I'm sorry to disturb you, but could I have a word?* □ *'Do not disturb.'* **-2.** [person] to upset and worry <sb> a lot □ *It disturbs me greatly to know that he was lying.* **-3.** [branches, sand, papers] to cause <sthg> to change its position □ *There was no wind to disturb the trace of his footsteps in the sand.* **-4.** [peace and quiet, calm] to spoil <the silence> □ *Not a whisper disturbed the silence in the great round reading room.*

disturbance [dɪ'stɜːʳbəns] *n* **-1.** [in public] a fight or noisy argument in public, usually involving several people □ *Local residents reported a disturbance in the park.* **-2. disturbance of the peace** the crime of being violent in public (legal use). **-3.** [in a person] mental upset leading to behavior that is not normal □ *severe emotional disturbance in childhood.*

disturbed [dɪ'stɜːʳbd] *adj* **-1.** [child] who suffers from a mental illness, especially one caused by something unpleasant that has happened to them; [childhood, behavior] that is typical of a person in this state □ *She became emotionally disturbed.* **-2.** [person] who feels worried and upset □ *I was disturbed to hear he had not been attending school.*

disturbing [dɪ'stɜːʳbɪŋ] *adj* [news, thought, photograph] that is worrying and upsetting □ *It's disturbing to see the number of young women who smoke.*

disunity [ˌdɪs'juːnətɪ] *n* lack of agreement and cooperation among people.

disuse [dɪs'juːs] *n* **to fall into disuse** [building, regulation, custom] to stop being used, usually over a long period, because it is no longer needed □ *The factory had gradually fallen into disuse.*

disused [ˌdɪs'juːzd] *adj* [factory, railroad, mine] that is no longer used □ *The performance was staged in a disused warehouse.*

ditch [dɪtʃ] ◇ *n* a long channel dug into the ground beside a road or field, usually to allow water to flow away. ◇ *vt* (informal use) **-1.** [boyfriend, girlfriend, wife] to end one's relationship with <a partner> □ *He just ditched his girlfriend because he was going away.* **-2.** [plan, proposal] to stop considering <sthg> □ *The council have finally ditched their plans to build a golf course there.* **-3.** [car, garbage] to get rid of <sthg that one no longer wants> by leaving it somewhere.

dither ['dɪðəʳ] *vi* to hesitate and waste time because one is confused or unable to decide what to do □ *Stop dithering and make up your mind!*

ditto ['dɪtoʊ] *adv* -1. a word used to refer to a thing that has just been mentioned, to avoid repeating it. It can be represented in writing by the symbol (″) written under the word that is being repeated □ *Red wine: 2 bottles; white wine: ditto.* -2. a word used to express agreement (informal use) □ *"I'm in favor of leaving." — "Ditto."*

diuretic [US ,daɪjə'retɪk, GB -jʊ-] *n* a substance or drug that makes people urinate more.

diva ['diːvə] (*pl* **divas**) *n* a female opera star.

divan [dɪ'væn] *n* a long, low, soft seat with no back or arms.

divan bed *n* a bed that has a thick base under the mattress and no frame or springs.

dive [daɪv] (US *pt* **dived** OR **dove**, *pp* **dived**, GB *pt* & *pp* **dived**) ◇ *vi* -1. [into water] to jump headfirst into water with one's arms stretched out; [bird, airplane, fish] to go down headfirst; [submarine] to leave the surface and go underwater □ *Sally dived from the bank into the canal.* -2. [underwater] to swim underwater using special breathing apparatus to go diving. -3. [into a place] to jump or move quickly, usually in order to catch or avoid something □ *She dived after the child as it ran into the road.* □ *We dived into a doorway to get out of the rain.* -4. [into a bag] to put one's hands quickly into a bag, cupboard etc in order to find something □ *Simon dived into the cupboard and brought out a large can of beans.* ◇ *n* -1. [of a person, submarine, bird] the act of diving □ *She made a sudden dive for the door.* -2. a bar or club that has a bad reputation (informal and disapproving use).

dive-bomb *vt* [plane] to move downward suddenly and drop bombs on <people, a city> etc.

diver ['daɪvəʳ] *n* a person who works or explores underwater using special equipment for breathing.

diverge [daɪ'vɜːʳdʒ] *vi* -1. [opinions, interests, statements] to be or become different □ *His account of the accident diverges from mine in significant details.* □ *At this point our interests diverge.* -2. [roads, paths] to separate into two and go in different directions.

divergence [daɪ'vɜːʳdʒəns] *n* [of opinions, interests] *see* **diverge** □ *There is no divergence between his views and mine.*

divergent [daɪ'vɜːʳdʒənt] *adj* [opinions, attitudes] that diverge from each other.

diverse [daɪ'vɜːʳs] *adj* [opinions, topics, nationalities] that are very different from one another □ *The guests included people as diverse as politicians and hairdressers.* □ *people from diverse backgrounds.*

diversification [daɪ,vɜːʳsəfə'keɪʃn] *n*: *see* **diversify**.

diversify [daɪ'vɜːʳsəfaɪ] (*pt* & *pp* **diversified**) ◇ *vt* [company, manager] to introduce <new products, services> etc in order to increase business. ◇ *vi*: *Many farmers are now diversifying into new areas such as tourism.*

diversion [daɪ'vɜːʳʃn] *n* -1. [from an activity] an action or event that turns people's attention away from what they should be doing or noticing □ *The incident provided an amusing diversion from the day's business.* -2. GB [of traffic] a special route that is made for traffic because the usual route is closed. -3. [of funds, resources, a river] *see* **divert**.

diversionary [US daɪ'vɜːʳʒəneɪ, GB -'vɜːʳʃnəri] *adj* [tactic, bid] that is intended to turn people's attention away from something more important □ *This is just a diversionary tactic on the part of the government.*

diversity [daɪ'vɜːʳsətɪ] *n* a range of many different people or things □ *The area boasts a huge diversity of plant life.*

divert [daɪ'vɜːʳt] *vt* -1. [traffic, river] to change the usual direction of <sthg> □ *All flights are being diverted to Hartford.* -2. [funds, resources] to use <money> for a purpose different from the one originally intended □ *Funds will be diverted away from schools to the universities.* -3. **to divert sb** OR **sb's attention** to deliberately turn sb's attention away from what they should be doing or noticing □ *The festival was intended to divert people's attention from the damage caused by the fire.* -4. **to divert sb** to amuse sb by giving them entertainment of some kind.

divest [daɪ'vest] *vt*: **to divest sb/sthg of sthg** [of their role, importance] to take sthg away from sb/sthg (formal use). ■ **to divest oneself of sthg** [of a feeling, idea, responsibility] to get rid of sthg.

divide [də'vaɪd] ◇ *vt* -1. [one's money, work, time] to break <sthg> up into parts and give some to one person or activity and some to another □ *He divided his property between* OR *among his three children.* □ *She divides her time between New York and Barcelona.* □ *Divide the money with your brother.* -2. [area, house, book] to split <sthg> up into smaller parts □ *Let's divide the class into two groups.* -3. GEOGRAPHY to form a boundary between <two places> □ *The Pyrenees divide France from Spain.* -4. MATH to calculate how many times bigger one number is than another □ *15 divided by 3 equals 5.* -5. [question, controversy, law] to make <people> disagree □ *The party is divided on this issue.* ◇ *vi* -1. [road, river, branch] to separate into two or more parts □ *The river divides in two around an island.* -2. [group, class] to form smaller groups, which sometimes disagree with each other □ *The nation divides into two camps on the issue of capital punishment.* ◇ *n* a difference or disagreement that breaks up a large group of people into smaller groups □ *the North-South divide between rich and poor countries.*

◆ **divide up** *vt sep* [one's money, work, time] = **divide**.

divided [də'vaɪdəd] *adj* [people, nation, meeting] that has separated into groups that disagree with each other. ■ **to have divided loyalties** to be unsure who one should be loyal to □ *My loyalties were divided between my company* and my sense of justice. ■ **opinions are divided over sthg** people have different opinions about sthg.

dividend ['dıvıdend] *n* -1. an unexpected benefit □ *Politicians speak of a peace dividend now that we do not need to spend so much on defense.* ■ **to pay dividends** to produce benefits at a later time □ *The long nights of studying paid dividends when it came to the exams.* -2. FINANCE a payment from company profits to each of the company's shareholders.

dividers [də'vaıdəʳz] *npl* a tool used by draftsmen for measuring lines, angles etc, consisting of two metal pieces with points at one end and joined at the other □ *a pair of dividers.*

dividing line [də'vaıdıŋ-] *n* something that marks the boundary between two different ideas or principles, e.g. between right and wrong or reality and fiction □ *There's a fine dividing line between being patriotic and being downright bigoted.*

divine [də'vaın] ◇ *adj* -1. [being, inspiration, worship] that is connected with or has the qualities of a god □ *divine retribution.* -2. [meal, weather] that one thinks is very good (old-fashioned and informal use) □ *Her blueberry pie is absolutely divine!* ◇ *vt* -1. [fact, meaning, the future] to guess <sthg> (literary use) □ *I divine from your comments that you don't agree.* -2. [underground water, mineral] to look for or find <sthg> using a stick of wood in the shape of a "Y".

diving ['daıvıŋ] *n* -1. the sport or activity of jumping headfirst into water with one's arms stretched out. -2. the sport or activity of swimming underwater using special equipment for breathing.

diving board *n* a raised platform from which people can dive into a swimming pool.

diving suit *n* a piece of clothing made of rubber or plastic, worn by divers to keep warm or for protection.

divinity [də'vınətı] (*pl* **divinities**) *n* -1. [of a god] the state of being a god □ *belief in Christ's divinity.* -2. EDUCATION the study of religion, especially Christianity. -3. [of a tribe, people, religion] a god or goddess □ *one of several Hindu divinities.*

divisible [də'vızəbl] *adj* MATH **to be divisible by a number** to be able to be divided by another number into smaller whole numbers that are all the same □ *35 is divisible by 7.*

division [də'vıʒn] *n* -1. [of a country, object] the act of separating or breaking something up into smaller parts; [between places, objects] something that separates one thing from another □ *The division of Europe into countries is the result of its complicated history.* □ *This wall marks the division between our land and theirs.* -2. [of work, money] the way in which something, e.g. work, responsibilities, or money, is divided up and shared out □ *They argued over the division of the spoils.* -3. MATH the act of dividing numbers; the method used to divide numbers. -4. [between people] a strong disagreement between two or more groups

of people □ *The country has a history of strife and division among its ethnic groups.* -5. [of a company] an important department, smaller company etc that operates on its own as part of a large company or organization □ *the company's engineering division.* -6. SPORT a group of teams that forms part of a larger league, especially in soccer. -7. MILITARY one of the sections that an army is divided into. -8. POLITICS a vote for or against something in the British parliament. Those who are voting in favor of a proposed law go to one division lobby, and those voting against it go to another.

division bell *n* **the division bell** POLITICS the bell that is rung to warn MPs in the British parliament that there is going to be a division.

division lobby *n* POLITICS one of the two places where MPs in the British parliament go in order to vote in a division.

division sign *n* MATH a symbol ($\div$) used between two numbers to indicate that the first number is to be divided by the second number.

divisive [də'vaısıv] *adj* [policy, issue, influence] that produces disagreement among a group of people □ *Holding down public-sector pay while the private sector enjoys a healthy increase is bound to be divisive.*

divorce [də'vɔːʳs] ◇ *n* the official and legal ending of a marriage □ *The marriage ended in divorce.* □ *a divorce settlement.* ◇ *vt* -1. [husband, wife] to legally end one's marriage to <sb> □ *He divorced her on the grounds of adultery.* -2. [idea, activity] to consider <sthg> to be completely separate from something else □ *It's difficult to divorce one's personal feelings from this case.*

divorced [də'vɔːʳst] *adj* -1. [man, woman] who is no longer married □ *He's been divorced since 1992.* -2. **to be divorced from sthg** [from a subject, the truth] to be different and completely separate from sthg □ *Her ideas are utterly divorced from reality.*

divorcee [US də,vɔːr'seı, GB dı,vɔː'siː] *n* a person who is divorced.

divot ['dıvət] *n* a piece of grass and earth that is dug out of the ground when a player hits the ball in golf.

divulge [daı'vʌldʒ] *vt* [secret, information, plan] to let other people know <sthg that has been secret> □ *I can now divulge (that) they were married last week.*

Dixie ['dıksı] a name used to refer to the Southern states of the USA.

Dixieland ['dıksılænd] ◇ *n* a type of jazz music that originally came from New Orleans. ◇ *adj*: *a Dixieland rhythm.*

DIY (*abbr of* **do-it-yourself**) *n* GB the activity of improving the appearance of one's home and repairing things in it oneself, without skilled help □ *a DIY store.*

dizziness ['dızınəs] *n* the feeling one has when one is dizzy □ *I have been suffering from headaches and dizziness lately.*

dizzy ['dɪzɪ] (*compar* **dizzier**, *superl* **dizziest**) *adj* -1. [person] who feels unsteady or confused, e.g. because they are looking down from a great height or have been turning around quickly □ *The blow made me feel dizzy.* □ *a dizzy spell.* -2. [height, speed] that makes one feel dizzy.

DJ *n* -1. *abbr of* **disc jockey**. -2. GB *abbr of* **dinner jacket**.

DJIA *n abbr of* **Dow Jones Industrial Average**.

dl *abbr of* **deciliter**.

DLit(t) [di:'lɪt] (*abbr of* **Doctor of Letters**) *n* GB a postgraduate degree in literature; a person who has this degree.

DM *abbr of* **Deutschmark**.

DMA (*abbr of* **direct memory access**) *n* a direct link between a piece of computer equipment, e.g. a printer, and a computer's main memory.

DMus [di:'mʌz] (*abbr of* **Doctor of Music**) *n* a postgraduate degree in music; a person who has this degree.

DMV *n abbr of* **Department of Motor Vehicles**.

DMZ *n abbr of* **demilitarized zone**.

DNA (*abbr of* **deoxyribonucleic acid**) *n* the chemical in the cells of living things that carries genetic information.

do¹ *abbr of* **ditto**.

do² [du:] (*pt* **did**, *pp* **done**, *pl* **dos** OR **do's** [du:z]) ◇ *aux vb* -1. used in negative sentences □ *Don't leave it there.* □ *I didn't want to see him.* -2. used in questions □ *Does she know you're here?* □ *What did he want?* □ *When do you think she'll come?* -3. used in question tags □ *You speak Italian, don't you?* □ *I surprised you, didn't I?* -4. used to refer back to a previous verb □ *She reads more than I do.* □ *"I don't smoke."* — *"Neither do I."* -5. used for emphasis □ *You're wrong, I DO know him.* □ *Do sit down.* □ *Oh do shut up!* □ *If you do decide to come, let me know.* ◇ *vt* -1. to perform <an activity or task> □ *It took her minutes to do the crossword.* □ *Yesterday I did something that I'd never done before.* ■ **do as you're told!** do what you have been told to do! -2. to perform <some regular activity> □ *It's your turn to do the cooking/cleaning.* -3. **what do you do?** what is your job? □ *What does Jill want to do when she leaves college?* -4. **I must do something** I must try to help or to solve this problem □ *We're going to have to do something about our overdraft.* □ *Is there anything I can do to help?* -5. to make <sthg> happen □ *What does this switch do?* □ *I didn't mean to do any damage.* ■ **to do sb good** to help sb or make them feel better □ *I think a long vacation would do you good.* ■ **it didn't do any good** it did not help the situation at all. -6. [physics, art, Spanish] to study <sthg> □ *She did an MBA at Harvard.* □ *He's doing a management training course.* -7. to travel or perform at <a particular speed> □ *This car can do 200 kph.* □ *The printer does 50 sheets a minute.* -8. *phrase* **that will do me** that is (good) enough for me □ *"I can only let you have $10 at the moment. Will that do you?"*

◇ *vi* -1. **to do well/badly** to act or perform well/badly in an exam, test etc □ *He did really badly in the interview.* □ *"How did you do in the exam?"* — *"OK, but I could have done better."* ■ **you would do well to do sthg** I advise you to do sthg □ *You'd do well to forget the whole affair.* -2. **that will do** that is (good) enough □ *"Will $6 do?"* — *"Yes, that will do nicely."*

◇ *n* a large party, dinner, or other formal social event (informal use) □ *They're having a big do for their 25th wedding anniversary.*

◆ **dos** *npl* **dos and don'ts** things that somebody must and must not do in a particular situation.

◆ **do away with** *vt fus* **to do away with sthg** [system, method] to put an end to sthg or remove it □ *It's time to do away with such old-fashioned practices.*

◆ **do down** *vt sep* GB **to do sb down** to criticize sb (informal use) □ *He's always doing me down.*

◆ **do for** *vt fus* **to be done for** to be in a hopeless situation (informal use) □ *If the boss finds out, we're done for.*

◆ **do in** *vt sep* **to do sb in** to kill sb deliberately (informal use).

◆ **do out of** *vt sep* **to do sb out of sthg** to cheat sb so that they lose sthg that they expected to have (informal use) □ *He did me out of $500.*

◆ **do up** *vt sep* -1. **to do sthg up** [shoelaces, buttons, coat] to fasten sthg □ *Your shirt's not done up.* -2. **to do sthg up** [house, room, car] to repair or improve the appearance of sthg □ *We've done up the spare bedroom.* -3. **to do sthg up** [package, gift] to wrap or tie up sthg in paper, string etc □ *The box was all done up with pink ribbon.*

◆ **do with** *vt fus* -1. **I could do with a drink** I need or want a drink □ *We could have done with some help.* -2. **I had nothing to do with it** I was not in any way connected with it. ■ **it's nothing to do with you** it does not concern you. ■ **he is** OR **has something to do with banking** his job is connected with banking.

◆ **do without** ◇ *vt fus* **to do without sthg** [help, car, dishwasher] to succeed in doing something or living even though one does not have sthg □ *I couldn't do without a washing machine.* ◇ *vi*: *If there's no cream for the strawberries, we'll just have to do without.*

DOA (*abbr of* **dead on arrival**) *adj* an official term used to describe somebody who has died while being taken to hospital.

doable ['du:əbl] *adj* [job, plan] that can be done (informal use) □ *Well, it's just about doable in the time we have available.*

dob, DOB *abbr of* **date of birth**.

Doberman ['doʊbərmən] (*pl* **Dobermans**) *n* a **Doberman (pinscher)** a large type of dog with a square face and pointed ears, often used as a guard dog.

docile [US 'dɒsl, GB 'doʊsaɪl] *adj* [person, animal] that is not aggressive and is easy to control.

dock [dɒk] ◇ *n* -1. [in a harbor] a part of a harbor where ships are loaded, unloaded, and repaired □ *The ship is in dock.* -2. **the dock** the place in a court of law where the accused person sits or stands □ *The prisoner stood nervously in the dock.* ◇ *vt* **to dock sb's wages** to reduce the amount of money sb is paid, usually because they have done something wrong. ◇ *vi* [ship, passenger] to arrive at a port by sea □ *The ship docked in New York.*

docker ['dɒkər] *n* a person who works at a harbor loading and unloading ships.

docket ['dɒkət] *n* GB a label or ticket sent with a package or cargo listing its contents, use, owner etc.

docklands ['dɒkləndz] *npl* GB the area around the harbor of a town or city.

◆ **Docklands** a new housing and office development in an area of east London that used to be docks.

dockworker ['dɒkwɜːrkər] *n* = **docker**.

dockyard ['dɒkjɑːrd] *n* a place where ships are built or repaired.

doctor ['dɒktər] ◇ *n* **-1.** MEDICINE a person who is qualified to treat sick or injured people □ *I went to see my doctor yesterday about my leg.* □ *I think we'd better call a doctor.* ■ **to go to the doctor's** to go to the place where a doctor works to get medical advice or treatment. **-2.** EDUCATION [of philosophy, divinity, music] a person who has the highest university degree in a particular subject. ◇ *vt* [results, text, photograph] to change <sthg> secretly and dishonestly so that it will seem more favorable.

doctorate ['dɒktərət], **doctor's degree** *n* the highest university degree, usually given for research done over at least three years □ *a doctorate in political science.*

doctrinaire [,dɒktrə'neər] *adj* [person] who has views that they refuse to change in any way despite all arguments and practical difficulties (disapproving use).

doctrine ['dɒktrɪn] *n* a belief or set of beliefs that is accepted as true by a religion, political party etc □ *Christian/Marxist doctrine.*

docudrama [US 'dɒkjədræmə, GB -jʊdrɑːmə] (*pl* **docudramas**) *n* a television play that tells a true story.

document ['dɒkjəmənt] ◇ *n* a paper, set of papers, book etc that contains official evidence or information □ *travel documents, including passport and visa.* ◇ *vt* [event, situation, life] to record all the facts about <sthg important> in writing, pictures, film etc □ *There are only three documented cases of the disease.*

documentary [,dɒkjə'mentəri] (*pl* **documentaries**) ◇ *adj* [evidence, proof] that depends on or consists of recorded factual information rather than opinion, guessing etc □ *We will need some documentary evidence if the case is to stand up in court.* ◇ *n* a TV program, radio program, or movie that gives factual information.

documentation [,dɒkjəmen'teɪʃn] *n* documents that give evidence or proof of something □ *He was unable to provide any documentation to support his claim.*

DOD (*abbr of* **Department of Defense**) *n* the US

government department responsible for the armed forces.

doddering ['dɒdərɪŋ], **doddery** ['dɒdəri] *adj* [old person] who is weak and unsteady on their feet (informal and disapproving use).

dodge [dɒdʒ] ◇ *n* a clever trick to avoid having to do something (informal use) □ *a tax dodge.* ◇ *vt* **-1.** [car, stone, person] to move suddenly to one side or downward to avoid being hit or caught by <sb/sthg> □ *I've had enough of dodging bullets in various guerrilla wars.* **-2.** [taxes, responsibility, question] to avoid <sthg> in a dishonest or dishonorable way □ *Mr Rossi accused Senator Moore of dodging the issue.* ◇ *vi* to move suddenly to one side or downward to avoid being hit, caught, or seen □ *Barry had to dodge to avoid the car.*

Dodgem™ ['dɒdʒəm] *n* **the Dodgems** GB a fairground ride consisting of small electric cars that can bump into each other without causing damage.

doe [dəʊ] *n* **-1.** a female deer. **-2.** a female rabbit.

DOE *n* **-1.** (*abbr of* **Department of Energy**) **the DOE** the US government department responsible for energy. **-2.** (*abbr of* **Department of the Environment**) **the DOE** the British government department responsible for local government, housing, city planning, protection of the countryside, and anti-pollution laws.

doer ['duːər] *n* a person who gets things done quickly without wasting time (informal use) □ *I want a doer, not a complainer!*

does [*stressed* dʌz, *unstressed* dəz] *vb* → **do**.

doesn't ['dʌznt] = **does not**.

dog [dɒg] (*pt* & *pp* **dogged** [dɒgd], *cont* **dogging**) ◇ *n* **-1.** a very common animal that is kept as a pet or used to guard places, keep sheep together, or for hunting □ *my pet dog.* ■ **it's a dog's life** a phrase used to say that life is very difficult or unpleasant (informal use). ■ **to go to the dogs** to develop into something bad or worse (informal use) □ *The company is going to the dogs.* **-2.** US a hot dog. ◇ *vt* **-1.** [person] to follow <sb> closely and without giving up □ *He dogged Mary's footsteps all the way to the entrance of her apartment.* **-2.** [problems, misfortune] to affect <a person, career, event> etc in a continuous way □ *The whole enterprise was dogged by bad luck from the start.*

dog biscuit *n* a biscuit for dogs.

dog collar *n* **-1.** [on a dog] a collar placed around the neck of a dog which a leash can be attached to. **-2.** [on a priest] a white collar worn by Christian priests (informal use).

dog-eared [-ɪərd] *adj* [book, page] that is in bad condition because the corners have been bent over a lot.

dog-end *n* GB the part of a cigarette that is left after it has been smoked (informal use).

dogfight ['dɒgfaɪt] *n* **-1.** [between planes] a fight between fighter planes in the sky. **-2.** [between dogs] a fight between two dogs, especially an illegal fight organized as a sport on which bets are placed.

dogfish ['dɒgfɪʃ] (*pl* **dogfish**) *n* a small European shark with spots on its skin.

dog food *n* food for dogs, especially meat sold in cans.

dogged ['dɒgɪd] *adj* [resistance, refusal] that shows determination to continue although the situation is very difficult □ *He shared a dogged determination to win.*

doggone ['dɒgɒn], **doggoned** ['dɒgɒnd] *adj* US a word used to show that one is annoyed or surprised (informal use) □ *a doggone waste of time.*

doggy ['dɒgɪ] (*pl* **doggies**) *n* a dog (used by children).

doggy bag *n* a bag, box etc that one is given in a restaurant for food that one has not finished, so that one can eat it later at home.

dogma ['dɒgmə] *n* a belief or rule that people are not allowed to question □ *religious dogma.*

dogmatic [dɒg'mætɪk] *adj* [person] who is convinced they are right and does not listen to other ideas □ *She believed in her policies, to the point of being dogmatic.* □ *a dogmatic belief/idea.*

do-gooder [-'gʊdər] *n* a person who tries to help people with problems but who one thinks is interfering or naive.

dog paddle, **doggy paddle** *n* a way of swimming, often used by people learning to swim, in which the whole head stays above the water and the arms and legs move quickly up and down close to the body.

dogsbody ['dɒgzbɒdɪ] (*pl* **dogsbodies**) *n* GB a person who does unskilled and boring jobs for somebody (informal use).

dog tag *n* a small disk worn by a soldier so that people will know who he is if he is killed or injured.

DOH (*abbr of* **Department of Health**) *n* **the DOH** the British government department responsible for health care for the public and the National Health Service.

doing ['duːɪŋ] *n* **is this your doing?** did you do this?

◆ **doings** *npl* activities that one does at a particular time □ *She was constantly telling us stories of Mary's marvelous doings.*

do-it-yourself *n* → DIY.

doldrums ['dɒldrəmz] *npl* **to be in the doldrums** [person] to feel depressed and without energy; [business, economy, market] to be unsuccessful because there is little activity.

dole [dəʊl] (informal use) *n* in Britain and Australia, the money paid to unemployed people by the state. ■ **to be on the dole** to get dole money in regular payments □ *Thousands more will be forced to join the dole queue.*

◆ **dole out** *vt sep* **to dole sthg out** [food, money] to give sthg in fixed amounts to all the people in a group.

doleful ['dəʊlfl] *adj* [look, voice] unhappy.

doll [dɒl] *n* a small model of a person, especially of a female, used as a toy by children.

dollar ['dɒlər] *n* **-1.** the standard unit of money

in the USA, Australia, and some other countries □ *It cost fifty dollars.* □ *How many dollars to the pound?* **-2.** a bill or coin with the value of one dollar □ *He handed me two dollars.* □ *a dollar bill.*

dolled up [,dɒld-] *adj* **to be dolled up** [woman] to be wearing make-up and attractive clothes, usually for a special occasion (informal use) □ *Where are you going all dolled up like that?*

dollhouse ['dɒlhaʊs] US, **doll's house** GB *n* a toy house that contains small dolls and toy furniture.

dollop ['dɒləp] *n* a large spoonful of soft food, e.g. ice cream or mashed potato.

doll's house *n* GB = **dollhouse**.

dolly ['dɒlɪ] (*pl* **dollies**) *n* **-1.** a doll (used by children). **-2.** CINEMA & TV a small platform with wheels that is used to move a TV or movie camera.

dolphin ['dɒlfɪn] *n* a sea mammal with a long nose and mouth that swims in groups and often seems friendly to people.

domain [dəʊ'meɪn] *n* **-1.** [of study] the area of interest or responsibility of somebody or something □ *This problem lies outside the domain of ordinary science.* **-2.** [of a ruler] the land ruled or controlled by a person or government.

dome [dəʊm] *n* the rounded roof of a building or room.

Domesday Book ['duːmzdeɪ-] *n* **the Domesday Book** a survey of all the land in England, giving details of ownership, size, value etc. It was carried out in 1086.

domestic [də'mestɪk] ◇ *adj* **-1.** [policy, flight, production] that is connected with a particular country and does not involve other countries; that is not international □ *There is good news on the domestic front.* □ *domestic sales.* **-2.** [chore, water supply, violence] that is connected with a family and their home □ *'For domestic use only.'* **-3.** [person] who enjoys home life □ *He's very domestic — he does all the cooking and cleaning.* **-4.** [animal] that is tame and is kept as a pet in a home or on a farm □ *the domestic cat.* ◇ *n* a servant in a house.

domestic appliance *n* an electrical device designed to be used in a house, e.g. a vacuum cleaner or refrigerator.

domesticated [də'mestəkeɪtəd] *adj* **-1.** [animal] that is no longer wild and is kept as a pet or on a farm. **-2.** [person] who is used to home life (humorous use).

domesticity [,dəʊme'stɪsətɪ] *n* the state of living at home with one's family; a love of this kind of life.

domestic science *n* the school subject that deals with the work that needs to be done in a house, e.g. cooking and sewing.

domicile ['dɒməsaɪl] *n* the place where a person lives (formal use).

dominance ['dɒmənəns] *n* **-1.** [of a person, country] power and influence that a person, nation etc has over another □ *Russia's domi-*

nance in Eastern Europe. **-2.** [of a system, idea] influence that a system, idea etc has over all others in a particular field.

dominant ['dɒmənənt] *adj* **-1.** [idea, group] that is the most important or powerful □ *The dominant literary influence at that time was Jean-Paul Sartre.* **-2.** [color, feature] that is the most noticeable □ *The dominant mood is one of gloom.* **-3.** [personality, person] that tries to control or influence other people □ *a very dominant woman.*

dominate ['dɒməneɪt] *vt* **-1.** [event, situation] to have the most important place or role in <sth> □ *The news is dominated this week by events in the Far East.* **-2.** [country] to have control over <a person or place> □ *For years they were dominated by their more powerful neighbors.* **-3.** [building] to be taller than <sth>; [town, area] to be the tallest thing in <a place> □ *The square is dominated by the enormous Renaissance palace in its center.*

dominating ['dɒməneɪtɪŋ] *adj* [person, personality] that tries to control or influence other people.

domination [ˌdɒmɪ'neɪʃn] *n*: see **dominate** □ *Japan's domination of OR over world markets.*

domineering [ˌdɒmə'nɪərɪŋ] *adj* [person] who tries to control other people by telling them what to think, do etc □ *He has a very domineering personality.*

Dominica [dɒ'mɪnɪkə] a country in the eastern Caribbean. SIZE: 751 sq kms. POPULATION: 100,000 (*Dominicans*). CAPITAL: Roseau. LANGUAGE: English. CURRENCY: East Caribbean dollar.

Dominican Republic [dəˌmɪnɪkən-]: **the Dominican Republic** a country in the Caribbean, situated in the eastern part of the island of Hispaniola. SIZE: 48,400 sq kms. POPULATION: 7,300,000 (*Dominicans*). CAPITAL: Santo Domingo. LANGUAGE: Spanish. CURRENCY: Dominican peso.

dominion [də'mɪnjən] *n* **-1.** the authority and power of a ruler or government □ *Your government has no dominion over the islands.* **-2.** the land under the control of a ruler or government □ *one of the Empire's many dominions.*

domino ['dɒmɪnoʊ] (*pl* **dominoes**) *n* a small rectangular block of wood or plastic divided into two halves, each marked with a number of spots. ◆ **dominoes** *npl* a game in which players try to place their dominoes next to other dominoes that have the same number of spots.

domino effect *n* a situation in which one bad thing that happens makes several other things happen one after the other.

don [dɒn] (*pt & pp* **donned**, *cont* **donning**) ◇ *n* GB a teacher at a university, especially at Oxford or Cambridge. ◇ *vt* [hat, coat] to put on <a piece of clothing>.

Donald Duck [ˌdɒnld'dʌk] a cartoon character representing a duck that appears in many movies by Walt Disney.

donate [doʊ'neɪt] *vt* [money, clothes, blood] to give <sth> to a charity or other organization to help other people □ *He donates a tenth of his income to charity.*

donation [doʊ'neɪʃn] *n* something, e.g. money or food, that is donated □ *Would you like to make a donation?*

done [dʌn] ◇ *past participle of* **do.** ◇ *adj* **-1. to be done** [work, job] to be finished; [person] to have finished something; [food, meat] to be cooked and ready to eat □ *"Have you finished?" — "No, but I'm almost done." □ Aren't those potatoes done yet?* **-2. it's not the done thing** it's not socially acceptable. ◇ *excl* a word used to show that one agrees on a price, deal etc with somebody else □ *"I'll give you half now and the rest later." — "OK, done!"*

Donegal [ˌdɒnɪ'gɔːl] a county in the northwest of the Irish Republic, on the Atlantic. SIZE: 4,830 sq kms. POPULATION: 129,428. ADMINISTRATIVE CENTER: Lifford.

Don Juan [ˌdɒn'wɑːn] a character who seduces many women and who appears in several poems, plays, and operas.

donkey ['dɒŋkɪ] (*pl* **donkeys**) *n* an animal with long ears that looks like a small horse.

donkey jacket *n* GB a short thick coat, worn especially by workmen.

donkeywork ['dɒŋkɪwɜːʳk] *n* GB work that one finds hard and uninteresting (informal use) □ *I have to do all the donkeywork around here.*

donor ['doʊnəʳ] *n* **-1.** [of blood] a person who gives blood or a body organ for the medical treatment of another person □ *a kidney/blood donor.* **-2.** [of money] a person who gives money, clothes etc to help other people □ *an anonymous donor.*

donor card *n* a card carried by a person that says they want their organs to be used in transplants after their death.

Don Quixote [ˌdɒn'kwɪksət] a character in the novel *Don Quixote de la Mancha* (1605) by Cervantes. He thinks he is a romantic hero and does many foolish things, such as attacking windmills because he thinks they are monsters.

don't [doʊnt] = **do not.**

doodle ['duːdl] ◇ *n* a picture or pattern one draws because one is bored or is thinking about something else. ◇ *vi* to draw doodles.

doom [duːm] *n* something very bad that happens to somebody and that they cannot avoid, especially death □ *an overriding sense of doom* □ *The news was all doom and gloom.*

doomed [duːmd] *adj* [plan, mission, person] that is certain to end in failure, death, or disaster □ *The scheme was doomed to failure/doomed to fail right from the start.*

doona ['duːnə] *n* US & AUS [on a bed] = **comforter.**

door [dɔːʳ] *n* **-1.** a flat piece of wood, metal, glass etc that is attached to an opening in a building, room, car, piece of furniture etc, that can be opened or closed so that people can get in or out, or get something in or out □ *The door was open/closed.* □ *Don't forget to lock the door behind you!* □ *Suddenly there was a* knock on the door. □ *There must be somebody at the door.* ■ **to open the door to sthg** [to success, prosperity] to make sthg possible □ *I'll show* OR *see you to the door.* -2. = **doorway** □ *I came in through the door.*

doorbell ['dɔːrbel] *n* a bell at the entrance to a building that visitors ring to tell the people inside that they are there □ *There was a ring at the doorbell.*

doorhandle ['dɔːrhændl] *n* a handle on a door that is turned to open and close the door.

doorknob ['dɔːrnɒb] *n* a round handle on a door that is pushed or pulled to open and close the door.

doorknocker ['dɔːrnɒkər] *n* a metal object that is attached to a door by a hinge and is used by visitors to knock at the door.

doorman ['dɔːrmən] (*pl* **doormen** [-mən]) *n* a man whose job is to help visitors when they arrive at hotels, office buildings, theaters etc.

doormat ['dɔːrmæt] *n* -1. a mat placed near a door for people to wipe their shoes on when they enter. -2. a person who one thinks is weak because they allow themselves to be treated badly by other people.

doorstep ['dɔːrstep] *n* a step outside a front door or a back door.

doorstop ['dɔːrstɒp] *n* a device or object used to stop a door from closing.

door-to-door *adj* [selling, survey] that involves going to every house in an area and speaking to the people there □ *a door-to-door salesman.*

doorway ['dɔːrweɪ] *n* an entrance to a room or building that can be closed by a door □ *Don't stand in the doorway, come in!*

dope [doʊp] ◇ *n* -1. cannabis (drugs slang). -2. a person who one thinks is stupid (informal use). ◇ *vt* to give a drug to <a person or animal> in order to affect their performance or behavior (informal use).

dope test *n* a test carried out on the urine or blood of a person or animal in a sporting competition to make sure they have not taken or been given illegal drugs.

dopey ['doʊpɪ] (*compar* **dopier**, *superl* **dopiest**) *adj* (informal use) -1. **to feel dopey** to feel not completely awake. -2. [person] who is stupid.

dormant ['dɔːrmənt] *adj* -1. [volcano] that is not active, but may become active in the future. -2. [idea, plan, law] that still exists but is not used or applied □ *The idea had lain dormant for many years.*

dormer (window) ['dɔːrmər-] *n* a vertical window in a sloping roof.

dormice ['dɔːrmaɪs] *plural of* **dormouse**.

dormitory [US 'dɔːrmətɔːrɪ, GB 'dɔːmətrɪ] (*pl* **dormitories**) *n* -1. [at a school] a large room, especially in a boarding school, containing several beds for sleeping. -2. US [at a college, camp] a building at a college or camp where people live and sleep.

dormitory town *n* GB a town outside a larger town or city from which large numbers of people travel to work every day.

Dormobile™ ['dɔːrməbiːl] *n* GB a kind of van that people can live and sleep in while they travel.

dormouse ['dɔːrmaʊs] (*pl* **dormice**) *n* a small field mouse with a furry tail that hibernates in winter.

Dors *abbr of* **Dorset**.

Dorset ['dɔːrsət] *n* a county in southwestern England, on the English Channel. SIZE: 2,654 sq kms. POPULATION: 655,700. ADMINISTRATIVE CENTER: Dorchester.

DOS [dɒs] (*abbr of* **disk operating system**) *n* a program that loads itself automatically when a computer is switched on. It lets the user operate the computer, and use other software □ *It runs on DOS.*

dosage ['doʊsɪdʒ] *n* the right amount of a drug or medicine that one must take at particular times.

dose [doʊs] ◇ *n* -1. [of medicine, a drug] a measured amount of something taken at one time □ *What's the correct dose for adults?* -2. [of flu] an amount or period of something, especially something unpleasant □ *I caught a dose of food poisoning.* ◇ *vt* to give medicine to <sb> □ *He dosed himself with medicine and went to bed.*

Dos Passos [US doʊs'pæsoʊs, GB dɒs'pæsɒs], **John** (1896–1970) a US writer whose best-known work is a collection of three novels called *U.S.A.*

doss [dɒs] ◆ **doss down** *vi* GB to sleep in a place that is uncomfortable and is not one's usual bed (informal use).

dossier ['dɒsɪeɪ] *n* a file containing papers or documents about a particular person or subject.

Dostoyevsky [US ˌdɒstə'jefskɪ, GB -ɔɪ'ef-], **Fyodor** (1821–1881) a Russian novelist whose books show a great understanding of human behavior and had a strong influence on 20th-century literature. His major works are *Crime and Punishment* and *The Brothers Karamazov.*

dot [dɒt] (*pt & pp* **dotted**, *cont* **dotting**) ◇ *n* -1. [on material] a small round mark □ *a blue fabric with white dots.* -2. [on a page] a symbol (·) used in punctuation, mathematics, and music. ◇ *vt* -1. **to be dotted over an area** to be scattered over a wide area □ *We have branches dotted all over the country.* -2. **to be dotted with sthg** [with trees, houses] to have a lot of sthg in different places all over it □ *The hills were dotted with trees.*

◆ **on the dot** *adv* [arrive, leave] exactly on time or at the time stated (informal use) □ *We left at three o'clock on the dot.*

DOT (*abbr of* **Department of Transportation**) *n* **the DOT** the US government department responsible for transportation.

dotage ['doʊtɪdʒ] *n* **to be in one's dotage** to be old, so that one is weak and one's mind is slow.

dote [doʊt] ◆ **dote on** *vt fus* **to dote on sb** to love sb very much, often so much that one is thought to be stupid or weak □ *He absolutely dotes on his granddaughter.*

doting ['dəʊtɪŋ] *adj* [mother, husband] who dotes on somebody.

dot-matrix printer *n* a printer used with a computer in which the shape of each character is formed by a series of dots. NOTE: Compare **daisywheel printer**.

dotted line ['dɒtəd-] *n* a line made up of a series of dots □ *Cut along dotted line.* ■ **to sign on the dotted line** to sign a contract or official document to show that one agrees to it.

dotty ['dɒtɪ] (*compar* **dottier**, *superl* **dottiest**) *adj* [person] who one thinks is slightly crazy in an amusing way (informal use) □ *a wonderfully dotty idea.*

double ['dʌbl] ◇ *adj* **-1.** [episode, murder] that includes or is made up of two similar things □ *Go through the double doors.* **-2. to have a double meaning** to have a meaning that can be understood in two different ways; [purpose, danger, advantage] that has two parts □ *Sending him abroad could serve a double purpose.* **-3.** [portion, whiskey] that is twice the normal amount or size □ *A double gin, please.* **-4.** [letter, number] a word used to show that a letter or number is repeated, e.g. when spelling a word or telling somebody a phone number □ *Apple is spelled with a double "p".* ◇ *adv* & *predet* **-1.** twice as much □ *He asked for double the amount.* **-2. to be seeing double** to see two of the same thing when there is only one thing there. **-3.** in two equal parts □ *He folded the sheet double.* ■ **to be bent double** to bend one's body bent forward and down □ *He was bent double with pain.* ◇ *n* **-1.** [an amount] something that is twice the amount, size etc of something else □ *I earn double what I used to.* **-2. a double** an alcoholic drink that is twice the normal size □ *Make it a double.* **-3. sb's double** a person who looks exactly like sb □ *You're the double of your mother.* **-4.** CINEMA a person whose job is to take the place of a movie actor in dangerous scenes. ◇ *vt* [price, number, figure] to make <sthg> twice as large in amount, size etc □ *They doubled their offer.* ◇ *vi* **-1.** [price, number, figure] *Profits have doubled over the last five years.* **-2. to double as sthg** to have sthg as a second job, function, or use □ *The manager doubles as our PR man.* □ *The dining room doubles as a study.*

◆ **doubles** *n* a game of tennis, badminton etc in which two people play together against two other people □ *a doubles match.*

◆ **double up** *vt sep* **to be doubled up in** OR **with sthg** [in pain, with laughter] to bend one's body because one is in pain or because one is laughing.

double act *n* a pair of performers, especially comedians, who work together.

double agent *n* a spy who pretends to work for one country, while in fact working for that country's enemy.

double-barreled US, **double-barrelled** GB [US -'berəld, GB -'bær-] *adj* **-1.** [shotgun, rifle] that

has two barrels. **-2.** GB [name, surname] that has two surnames joined by a hyphen.

double bass [-beɪs] *n* the largest and the lowest in pitch of the instruments in the violin family.

double bed *n* a large bed for two people. NOTE: Compare **single bed**.

double-breasted [-'brestəd] *adj* [jacket, coat] that has two flaps at the front and is closed by crossing one side over the other side. NOTE: Compare **single-breasted**.

double-check ◇ *vt* [detail, fact, arrangement] to check <sthg> again in order to make sure that it is correct or safe □ *Don't forget to double-check the reservation.* ◇ *vi: I'd better double-check.*

double chin *n* a fold of loose skin under the chin that fat people sometimes have.

double cream *n* GB thick cream. NOTE: Compare **single cream**.

double-cross *vt* to betray <sb> by helping their enemies or breaking an agreement.

double-dealer *n* a person who betrays or tricks somebody.

double-decker [-'dekər] *n* a bus with two floors.

double-density *adj* [disk] that can store twice the amount of information that a normal disk stores.

double-dutch *n* words that one does not understand (humorous use) □ *It's all double-dutch to me.*

double-edged [-'edʒd] *adj* **-1.** [sword, blade] that has two sharp cutting edges. **-2.** [remark, success] that can be either good or bad.

double entendre [ˌduːblɒn'tɒndrə] *n* a word or phrase that can be understood in two ways, one of which is usually sexual.

double fault *n* in tennis, two mistakes made one after the other when serving the ball that result in the loss of a point.

double figures *npl* **to be in double figures** to be any number higher than nine and lower than a hundred □ *Inflation will soon reach double figures.*

double-glazing [-'ɡleɪzɪŋ] *n* a system used in windows and doors in which there are two panes of glass to keep a room warmer and quieter.

double-jointed [-'dʒɔɪntəd] *adj* [person] whose joints can bend backward and forward further than those of most other people.

double-park *vi* to park a car next to another parked car that is between one's own car and the curb.

double-quick GB (informal use) ◇ *adj* extremely fast; as fast as possible. ◇ *adv: Let's get out of here double-quick!*

double room *n* a large bedroom for two people in a hotel. NOTE: Compare **single room**, **twin room**.

double-sided [-'saɪdəd] *adj* [disk] that can store information on both sides; [tape] that is sticky on both sides.

double standard *n* an idea about what is

right and wrong that is applied to some people but not to others, and so is unfair.

double take *n* **to do a double take** to suddenly show surprise, shock etc after hearing or seeing something.

double-talk *n* something that somebody says that has two meanings so that it is confusing or deceiving.

double time *n* **to be on double time** to earn twice the usual wages for working on weekends, public holidays etc.

double vision *n* a medical condition caused by a head injury or by drinking too much alcohol, in which a person sees two images of every object.

double whammy [-'wæmɪ] *n* two bad things that happen to somebody one after the other (informal use).

doubly ['dʌblɪ] *adv* **-1. doubly sure/difficult etc** more sure/difficult etc than usual or than expected. **-2. doubly complicated/important etc** complicated/important etc for two reasons.

doubt [daʊt] ◇ *n* a feeling that something is perhaps not true □ *They think they've found the ideal location, but I have my doubts.* □ *There's some doubt about the final result.* ■ **there is no doubt (that)...** it is absolutely certain that... □ *There's no doubt in my mind that he stole the money.* ■ **to cast doubt on sthg** to act or speak in a way that makes other people uncertain about sthg □ *This new evidence casts doubt on the verdict.* ■ **no doubt** a phrase used when one suspects that something is true □ *No doubt you're tired after your journey.* ■ **without (a) doubt** certainly. ■ **beyond (all) doubt** definitely □ *It has been proved beyond all doubt.* ■ **to be in doubt** [person] to feel unsure about something; [result, future] to be uncertain □ *I am in no doubt that this would have saved his life.* □ *I don't think your job is in doubt.*

◇ *vt* **-1.** [person, somebody's motives, word] to have little confidence in <sb/sthg> □ *I don't doubt his sincerity at all.* **-2. I doubt it** I think that it is unlikely □ *"Do you think they'll agree?" — "I doubt it."* ■ **to doubt whether** OR **if...** to consider it unlikely that... □ *I doubt if they'll come now.*

doubtful ['daʊtfl] *adj* **-1.** [result, possibility] unlikely □ *"Will he come?" — "It seems doubtful."* **-2.** [person, truth, origin] uncertain □ *I'm rather doubtful about* OR *of their chances of success.* **-3. of doubtful value** that is probably worthless. ■ **of doubtful character** that is probably dishonest □ *an account of doubtful authenticity.*

doubtless ['daʊtləs] *adv* almost certainly □ *Doubtless it will rain tomorrow.*

dough [doʊ] *n* **-1.** a mixture of flour and water used to make bread, pastry etc □ *Give the dough time to rise.* **-2.** money (informal use).

doughnut ['doʊnʌt] *n* a small round cake of dough cooked in fat and covered in sugar.

Douglass ['dʌgləs], **Frederick** (1817–1895) a former slave who fought against slavery in the American Civil War. He later became a politician.

dour [dʊəʳ] *adj* [person] who shows little humor and seems unfriendly □ *a dour expression.*

douse [daʊs] *vt* **-1.** [flames, blaze] to put <a fire> out with water. **-2.** [cloth, one's body] to pour liquid over <sthg> □ *They doused the floor with gasoline and then set fire to it.*

dove[1] [dʌv] *n* a white bird like a pigeon, often used as a symbol of peace.

dove[2] [doʊv] US *past tense of* **dive**.

dovecot(e) ['dʌvkoʊt] *n* a small structure, usually made of wood, for doves and pigeons to live in.

Dover ['doʊvəʳ] *n* a port in Kent, England, used especially by ferries going to and from France. POPULATION: 34,000.

dovetail ['dʌvteɪl] ◇ *vt* to join <two pieces of wood> together using a dovetail joint. ◇ *vi* [arrangements, plans] to fit together neatly □ *That dovetails nicely with my other duties that day.*

dovetail joint *n* a wedge-shaped joint used in carpentry to make two pieces of wood fit together.

dowager ['daʊədʒəʳ] *n* a widow who got a title or property from her husband when he died.

dowdy ['daʊdɪ] (*compar* **dowdier**, *superl* **dowdiest**) *adj* [piece of clothing] that is not colorful, is old-fashioned, and is not attractive; [woman] who wears dowdy clothes and is not interesting.

Dow Jones [,daʊ'dʒoʊnz] *n* **the Dow Jones (Industrial Average)** a daily list showing the average of the price of the shares of thirty companies sold on the New York Stock Exchange. It is used as a guide to how the stock market is performing.

down [daʊn] ◇ *adv* **-1. to look down** to look from a higher position toward a lower one, or toward the ground □ *He bent down and whispered in my ear.* □ *Come down off that ladder!* □ *He was knocked down by a car.* ■ **down in the valley** in the valley below □ *They live two floors down from us.* **-2. 21 down** the word in a crossword written from top to bottom and with the number 21. **-3. I'm going down to the mall** I'm going from here to the mall. **-4. to travel down to the coast** to travel south from one's home or another place to the coast □ *We traveled down to London together.* **-5. prices have gone down** prices have become lower □ *I have gotten my weight down to under 120 pounds.* □ *That radio's too loud, turn it down!* **-6. to write sthg down** to write sthg on paper □ *Don't worry, it's down in my calendar.*

◇ *prep* **-1. to run down the hill** to run from the top to the bottom of the hill □ *She came down the stairs to meet me.* □ *Tears ran down his face.* ■ **to fall down a hole** to fall into a hole. **-2. to walk down the street** to walk along the street □ *Guess who I saw coming down the path!* ■ **to go down the river** to go along the river in the direction of the sea.

◇ *adj* **-1. prices are down** prices are lower. **-2. two points down** losing by two points □

Faldo is four strokes down on the leaders. **-3. to feel down** to feel a little depressed or unhappy (informal use) □ *Don't let them get you down!* **-4. to be down** [computer system, telephones] to be not working because of a temporary fault □ *I'm sorry, all our phones are down at the moment.*

◇ *n* **-1.** [on a bird] small soft feathers used to fill bed covers, pillows etc; [on a person] small soft hairs on the face, arms etc. **-2.** SPORT **first down** the first part of a game in football.

◇ *vt* **-1.** [opponent] to knock or hit <sb> to the ground. **-2.** [beer, dinner] to eat or drink <sthg> quickly □ *He downed his drink quickly and left.*

◆ **downs** *npl* a region of low, gentle, grassy hills.

◆ **down to** *prep* **-1. to be down to sb/sthg** to be the responsibility of sb/sthg □ *It's all down to you now.* **-2. correct down to the last detail** correct including every detail. **-3. I am down to my last dollar** I have only one dollar left.

◆ **down with** *excl* a phrase used to show one is against somebody or something □ *Down with the Government!*

down-and-out ◇ *adj* [person] who is poor and has no home. ◇ *n* a down-and-out person.

down-at-heel *adj* [person] who is badly dressed and in poor condition because they have little money.

downbeat ['daʊnbiːt] *adj* **-1.** [person, message, ending] that feels there is little hope for the future. **-2.** [person] who shows little emotion and does not try to attract attention.

downcast [US 'daʊnkæst, GB -kɑːst] *adj* **-1. to be downcast** [person] to be sad and disappointed □ *Don't be too downcast about it.* **-2.** [eyes] looking toward the ground, because one is sad, embarrassed, confused etc (formal use).

downer ['daʊnər] *n* **-1.**▽ a drug or substance that makes one feel calm and sleepy, such as a tranquilizer (drugs slang). **-2.** a depressing event or person (informal use).

downfall ['daʊnfɔːl] *n* **sb's downfall** the reason why sb loses power, money, success etc □ *Gambling was his downfall.*

downgrade ['daʊngreɪd] *vt* [job, status, role] to make <sthg> less important; [employee] to give <sb> a less important job.

downhearted [,daʊn'hɑːˤtəd] *adj* [person] who feels sad and discouraged.

downhill [,daʊn'hɪl] ◇ *adj* **-1.** [slope, stretch, path] that goes downward □ *It's mostly downhill from here to town.* **-2. downhill skiing** the sport of skiing down slopes. ■ **downhill skier** a skier who skies down slopes. **-3.** *phrase* **it's downhill all the way** the most difficult part of the job, project etc has been completed and things will now become easier. ◇ *adv* **-1.** [run, race, walk] down a slope □ *We cycled downhill then walked uphill.* **-2. to go downhill** [person, career, marriage] to become weaker or less successful; [quality, area, hotel] to get worse □ *His health went downhill rapidly after that.* □ *The place had gone downhill since the*

time I lived there. ◇ *n* the sport of skiing down slopes.

Downing Street ['daʊnɪŋ-] *n* the street in London where the British Prime Minister lives.

❧ DOWNING STREET
Number 10 Downing Street is the official home of the British Prime Minister, while the Chancellor of the Exchequer lives at number 11. The term "Downing Street" is often used to mean the Prime Minister and his officials.

download ['daʊnloʊd] *vt* to copy or send <data, a file, a program> etc from one computer to another □ *I'll just download this file onto the hard disk.*

down-market ◇ *adj* [product, restaurant] that is cheap and of poor quality. ◇ *adv*: *The area has really gone down-market.*

down payment *n* the first payment, made at the time of buying, for something that one will pay for over a period of time.

downplay [,daʊn'pleɪ] *vt* [event, situation] to make <sthg> seem less important than it really is.

downpour ['daʊnpɔːˤ] *n* a heavy fall of rain.

downright ['daʊnraɪt] ◇ *adj* **-1. a downright lie/insult etc** a very clear and upsetting lie/insult etc □ *He's a downright cheat!* **-2.** [person] who is honest and says immediately what they think. ◇ *adv* **downright rude/unfriendly** very rude/unfriendly □ *That's downright insulting!*

downside ['daʊnsaɪd] *n* the aspect of something that is bad or less useful □ *The downside of the new offices is that we'll be paying more rent.*

downsize [,daʊn'saɪz] *vt* [company, business, industry] to make <a business> smaller in size, e.g. by firing employees or by selling part of it.

Down's syndrome *n* a condition that causes people to be born with a flat forehead and sloping eyes, and to be less intelligent and physically developed than normal.

downstairs [,daʊn'steəˤz] ◇ *adj* [apartment, room] that is on a lower floor or on the ground floor. ◇ *adv* [come, go, live] to or on a lower floor □ *"Does Tom live here?" — "No, try downstairs."*

downstream [,daʊn'striːm] *adv* [drift, sail, swim] in the direction of the current and toward the mouth of the river □ *The boat floated gently downstream.*

downtime ['daʊntaɪm] *n* the time during which a machine or computer is not working or being used.

down-to-earth *adj* [person, approach, manner] practical and realistic □ *You'll like her — she's very sensible and down-to-earth.*

downtown [,daʊn'taʊn] ◇ *adj* [shop, office] that is in the center of a town or city □ *downtown Moscow.* ◇ *adv* [go, live] to or in the center of a town or city □ *It's downtown, by the bridge.*

downtrodden ['daʊntrɒdn] *adj* [people, workers]

who are treated badly by people in positions of power.

downturn ['daʊntɜːʳn] *n* a decrease in success or in the production of something □ *a downturn in the economy/productivity.*

down under *adv* [live, go] in or to Australia or New Zealand.

downward ['daʊnwəʳd] ◇ *adj* **-1.** [movement, glance] in the direction of the ground. **-2.** [trend, spiral] that is becoming lower or less □ *the continuing downward spiral in employment figures.* ◇ *adv* [move, look] into a lower position or toward the ground □ *The cave extends downward to a depth of 1,000 meters.*

downwards ['daʊnwəʳdz] *adv* **-1.** = **downward. -2. everyone from the President downwards** the President and everyone of lower rank, position, or status.

downwind [,daʊn'wɪnd] *adv* [drift, blow] in the same direction that the wind is blowing.

dowry ['daʊrɪ] (*pl* **dowries**) *n* in some societies, the money or property that a husband receives from his wife's family when he gets married.

doz. *abbr of* **dozen.**

doze [doʊz] ◇ *n* a short light sleep □ *I was just having a little doze.* ◇ *vi* to have a doze □ *Grandma sat dozing in her chair.*

◆ **doze off** *vi* to fall asleep without intending to □ *I must have dozed off.*

dozen ['dʌzn] (*pl* **dozen**) *num* **a dozen** twelve □ *a dozen eggs* □ *They cost $4.25 a dozen.*

◆ **dozens** *pron* used to refer to very many people or things (informal use) □ *I've met him dozens of times.* □ *"How many do you need?" — "Dozens."*

DP *n abbr of* **data processing.**

DPh, DPhil [,diː'fɪl] *n* = **PhD.**

DPP *n abbr of* **Director of Public Prosecutions.**

Dr. -1. [in a street name] *abbr of* **drive. -2.** [in a person's title] *abbr of* **doctor.**

drab [dræb] (*compar* **drabber**, *superl* **drabbest**) *adj* [color, room, life] that seems dull and uninteresting.

draconian [drə'koʊnjən] *adj* [measure, punishment, law] very severe.

Dracula ['drækjələ] a character in a novel (published in 1897) by Bram Stoker. He is a count who wears a black cape and drinks human blood.

draft [dræft] US, **draught** [drɑːft] GB ◇ *n* **-1.** [of a speech, contract, letter] a first version of a text that may be changed or corrected □ *This is just the first draft.* □ *a draft speech/contract/ letter.* **-2.** FINANCE a money order □ *a banker's draft.* **-3. the draft** US MILITARY the system of making men of a particular age serve in the army, navy etc, especially during a war. **-4.** [in a room] a current of air, usually in a room □ *Can you close the window? There's a terrible draft.* **-5.** [of water, beer] a large amount of liquid that is swallowed by somebody; [of air] a large amount of air that is breathed in by somebody □ *He took a deep draft of his beer.* **-6. on draft** [beer] that is

served by pumping it from a barrel through a special tap.

◇ *vt* **-1.** [speech, contract, letter] to write a draft of <a text> □ *I've drafted a letter of acceptance — see what you think.* **-2.** MILITARY to order <sb> to join the army, navy etc. **-3.** [employee, manager] to transfer <sb> to another job, department, or country □ *I've been drafted to help out in the accounting department.*

draft beer *n* beer that is pumped from a barrel.

draft dodger [-dɒdʒəʳ] *n* US a person who avoids doing their military service.

draftee [US ,dræf'tiː, GB ,drɑː'f-] *n* US a person who joins the armed forces by being drafted, rather than by volunteering.

draftsman ['dræftsmən] US, **draughtsman** ['drɑːftsmən] GB (*pl* US **draftsmen** [-mən], GB **draughtsmen** [-mən]) *n* a person whose job is to make technical drawings, e.g. plans of machines or buildings.

draftsmanship ['dræftsmənʃɪp] US, **draughtsmanship** ['drɑːftsmənʃɪp] GB *n* the work or skill of a draftsman.

drafty ['dræftɪ] US, **draughty** ['drɑːftɪ] GB (US *compar* **draftier**, *superl* **draftiest**, GB *compar* **draughtier**, *superl* **draughtiest**) *adj* [room, house] that has drafts blowing through it.

drag [dræg] (*pt* & *pp* **dragged**, *cont* **dragging**) ◇ *vt* **-1.** [chair, feet, suitcase] to pull <sthg heavy> along the ground; [prisoner, hostage] to pull <a person or animal> roughly □ *She dragged the trunk up the stairs.* □ *They had to practically drag him onto the plane.* **-2.** [person] to force or persuade <sb> to go somewhere they do not want to go □ *I'm sorry to drag you out on such a cold night.* **-3.** [river, lake] to search <an area of water> for something by pulling nets or hooks along the bottom □ *The police dragged the canal for the body.*

◇ *vi* **-1.** [dress, coat] to touch the ground and be pulled along. **-2.** [time, meeting] to seem to happen more slowly than usual because one is bored □ *After the first week the vacation started to drag.*

◇ *n* **-1.** a boring or annoying job, activity etc (informal use) □ *What a drag!* **-2. to take a drag** to breathe in smoke from a cigarette, pipe etc that one is smoking (informal use). **-3.** [of the wind] the resistance caused by the wind. **-4. to be in drag** to be wearing the clothes of the opposite sex, usually as entertainment □ *a drag artist/queen.*

◆ **drag down** *vt sep* **to drag sb down** to bring sb down to a lower position in society or standard of behavior □ *Marrying that man has really dragged her down.*

◆ **drag in** *vt sep* **to drag sb/sthg in** [name, issue, question] to involve sb/sthg in something they have no connection with; to involve sb in something they do not want to be involved in □ *There's no need to drag my mother into it.* □ *Don't drag me into your argument!*

◆ **drag on** *vi* [meeting, time, day] to seem to go very slowly □ *The meeting/Their speeches just dragged on and on all afternoon.*

◆ **drag out** *vt sep* **-1. to drag sthg out** [talks, negotiations, meeting] to make sthg last longer than necessary. **-2. to drag sthg out of sb** [fact, truth, information] to force sb to tell one sthg that they do not want to tell □ *I finally dragged it out of her.*

dragnet ['drægnet] *n* **-1.** [for objects] a net that is dragged along the bottom of a river or lake in order to try to find something. **-2.** [for criminals] a system or plan for catching criminals.

dragon ['drægən] *n* **-1.** in children's stories, an animal that has wings and skin like a snake's and can breathe fire. **-2.** a woman who one thinks is fierce and unpleasant (informal use).

dragonfly ['drægənflaɪ] (*pl* **dragonflies**) *n* a large brightly-colored insect with a long thin body and two pairs of wings. It lives near rivers and lakes.

dragoon [drə'guːn] ◇ *n* in the past, a soldier who fought on a horse. ◇ *vt* **to dragoon sb into doing sthg** to force sb to do sthg that they do not want to do.

drag racing *n* a type of racing in which special cars are timed over a fixed distance.

dragster ['drægstər] *n* a car that has been built or adapted for drag racing, usually with a large engine and back wheels, and small front wheels.

drain [dreɪn] ◇ *n* **-1.** [for water] a pipe for carrying away water or sewage. ■ **to go down the drain** [money, work] to be wasted □ *Well, that's $500 down the drain!* **-2. to be a drain on sthg** [on resources, funds, time] to use up sthg that is needed for other people or things □ *The creative department is an unnecessary drain on our resources.*
◇ *vt* **-1.** [carrots, tank, marsh] to remove the liquid from <food, a container, place> etc □ *Drain the vegetables and serve with rice.* **-2.** [energy, funds, resources] to use <sthg> up □ *This last project drained almost all of our funds.* **-3. to be drained** to be very tired and have no energy □ *I feel drained.* **-4.** [glass, bottle] to drink all the liquid in <a container> □ *He drained his glass in one gulp.*
◇ *vi* **-1.** [dishes, vegetables] to become dry because one lets the water or liquid drip off. **-2.** [blood, water] to flow away □ *The color drained from her face.*

drainage ['dreɪnɪdʒ] *n* **-1.** a system for draining something □ *a drainage ditch.* **-2.** the process of draining something.

drainboard ['dreɪnbɔːrd] US, **draining board** ['dreɪnɪŋ-] GB *n* a sloping surface, usually next to a sink, where dishes can drain.

drainpipe ['dreɪnpaɪp] *n* a pipe that carries away water or sewage, usually fixed to the side of a building.
◆ **drainpipes** *npl* = drainpipe trousers.

drainpipe trousers *npl* GB trousers with narrow straight legs.

drake [dreɪk] *n* a male duck.

Drake [dreɪk], **Sir Francis** (1540–1596) the

first British sea captain to sail around the world.

dram [dræm] *n* a small glass of an alcoholic drink, usually Scotch whisky □ *a dram of whisky.*

drama ['drɑːmə] *n* **-1.** TV & RADIO a serious play □ *a TV/radio drama.* **-2.** THEATER the art of writing or performing plays □ *Greek/modern drama* □ *a drama school/student/critic.* **-3.** a serious and exciting situation □ *a real-life courtroom drama.*

dramatic [drə'mætɪk] *adj* **-1.** [work, production] connected with the theater □ *the dramatic arts.* **-2.** [event, gesture, escape] that is exciting and makes people notice □ *one of the most dramatic discoveries since DNA.* **-3.** [change, recovery, improvement] that is sudden and noticeable □ *Don't worry, nothing dramatic has happened — just a few changes, that's all.*

dramatically [drə'mætɪklɪ] *adv* **-1.** [change, recover, improve] *see* **dramatic.** **-2.** [say, announce, enter] in a way that is intended to be exciting or to make people notice.

dramatist ['dræmətɪst] *n* a person who writes plays.

dramatization [,dræmətaɪ'zeɪʃn] *n* [of a book, story] *see* **dramatize.**

dramatize, -ise ['dræmətaɪz] *vt* **-1.** THEATER [book, story] to adapt <a piece of writing> so that it can be performed as a play or movie. **-2.** [situation, event] to make <sthg that has happened> seem more exciting than it really is (disapproving use) □ *There's no need to dramatize the situation.*

drank [dræŋk] *past tense of* **drink.**

drape [dreɪp] *vt* to hang <cloth, material> etc in folds, so that it covers something in an attractive way. ■ **to be draped with** OR **in sthg** [with silk, in a cloak] to be covered with sthg.
◆ **drapes** *npl* US pieces of material that can be pulled in front of a window to keep out light or stop people from seeing in □ *Open/Close the drapes, will you?*

draper ['dreɪpər] *n* GB a person who sells cloth.

drastic ['dræstɪk] *adj* **-1.** [measure, cut] that is extreme and needed urgently because the situation is serious □ *Drastic steps must be taken.* □ *She's threatening to do something drastic.* **-2.** [change, improvement] that seems very big and noticeable □ *I didn't notice any drastic differences.*

drastically ['dræstɪklɪ] *adv* [change, improve] *see* **drastic** □ *Our funding has been cut drastically.*

draught *etc* GB = **draft** *etc.*

draughtboard [US 'dræftbɔːrd, GB 'drɑːftbɔːrd] *n* GB = **checkerboard.**

draught excluder [-eksklu:dər] *n* GB a strip of foam or other material fixed to the edge of a door or window to stop drafts in a house.

draughts [US dræfts, GB drɑːfts] *n* GB a game for two people, played on a board with 64 black and white squares, in which each player has twelve round pieces that move diagonally.

draw [drɔː] (*pt* **drew**, *pp* **drawn**) ◇ *vt* **-1.** [object,

shape, scene] to represent <sthg> by making marks on a surface, especially with a pencil on a piece of paper; [portrait, sketch] to make <a picture>, usually with a pencil or pen □ *He drew a tree/map on the back of the envelope.* **-2.** [cart, person, object] to pull <sb/sthg> in a particular direction □ *He drew her gently toward him.* ■ **to draw the curtains** to open or close the curtains by pulling them. **-3. to draw breath** to breathe in. **-4. to draw a gun/knife** to pull a gun/knife out of its holder and be ready to use it □ *He drew a gun from his pocket.* **-5. to draw a conclusion** to reach a conclusion about something □ *You must draw your own conclusions.* **-6. to draw a distinction/comparison etc** to make a distinction/comparison etc □ *I don't want to draw any comparisons between Mary and her sister.* **-7.** [criticism, praise] to attract <sb/sthg> □ *The event drew crowds of people.* ■ **to be drawn to sb/sthg** to feel attracted to sb/sthg. ■ **to draw sb's attention to sthg** to make sb notice sthg □ *May I draw your attention to page six of the contract?*
◇ *vi* **-1.** [person] to make a picture, usually with a pencil or pen □ *I can't draw very well.* **-2. to draw away/near etc** [person, animal] to move away/near etc gradually or slowly □ *He drew away from/nearer to the fire.* □ *The date for the contest drew closer.* ■ **to draw to an end** OR **a close** to finish gradually □ *The game was drawing to its conclusion.* **-3.** GB SPORT to end a game or sporting event with the same number of points as one's opponent □ *Italy and Nigeria drew.* □ *Italy drew with Nigeria.*
◇ *n* **-1.** SPORT the result of a game or sporting event in which two teams or opponents draw □ *The match ended in a draw.* **-2.** GAMBLING a lottery; the act of choosing the winner of a lottery □ *a prize draw* □ *That's the luck of the draw.* **-3. to be a (big) draw** to be something which attracts a lot of people □ *The show proved to be a big draw.*

◆ **draw in** *vi* [nights] to become dark earlier as winter approaches □ *It's October and the nights are already drawing in.*

◆ **draw into** *vt sep* **to draw sb into sthg** [into a dispute, discussion] to involve sb in sthg □ *I refused to be drawn into the argument.*

◆ **draw on** *vt fus* **-1.** = **draw upon.** **-2. to draw on sthg** [on a cigarette, pipe] to breathe in smoke from sthg.

◆ **draw out** *vt sep* **-1. to draw sb out** [newcomer, shy person] to make sb feel less nervous or shy □ *Go and talk to her and try to draw her out a little.* **-2. to draw sthg out** [meeting, speech] to make sthg last longer than necessary □ *Professor Newman drew his speech out endlessly.* **-3. to draw money out** FINANCE to take money out of a bank account □ *I drew out $100 only last week.*

◆ **draw up** ◇ *vt sep* **to draw sthg up** [plan, list, contract] to prepare and write sthg □ *Draw up a list of the people you want to contact, then I'll type it out for you.* ◇ *vi* [vehicle] to stop □ *A large Mercedes drew up outside.*

◆ **draw upon** *vt fus* **to draw upon sthg** [information, reserves, knowledge] to use sthg in

order to do something better □ *I was able to draw upon my previous experience.*

drawback ['drɔːbæk] *n* a disadvantage, especially one of several □ *The main drawback to the plan is its cost.*

drawbridge ['drɔːbrɪdʒ] *n* a bridge that can be pulled up to stop people from crossing it, or to allow ships to pass beneath it.

drawer [drɔːʳ] *n* a part of a desk or chest that slides out so that clothes, papers etc can be put in or taken out.

drawing ['drɔːɪŋ] *n* **-1.** [of a person, object] a picture that has been drawn □ *I did a quick drawing of the house.* **-2.** the art or skill of making pictures with a pen or pencil □ *I'm terrible at drawing.* □ *drawing materials.*

drawing board *n* a large board, usually fixed on a frame, where architects or draftsmen put their paper when drawing or designing something. ■ **back to the drawing board!** a phrase used when an idea or project has failed and one has to start again (informal use).

drawing pin *n* GB a short pin with a round flat head, used for attaching papers to bulletin boards or walls.

drawing room *n* a living room (old-fashioned use).

drawl [drɔːl] ◇ *vi* to speak slowly using long vowel sounds. ◇ *vt:* "Hi there," she drawled. ◇ *n* the way somebody speaks when they drawl □ "I sure do," he said in a Southern drawl.

drawn [drɔːn] ◇ *past participle of* **draw.** ◇ *adj* **-1. to be drawn** [curtain, blind] to be closed □ *The curtains were drawn.* **-2. to look drawn** [person] to look thin because one is tired, ill, or worried □ *Shona returned, looking tired and drawn.*

drawn-out *adj* [meeting, speech] that lasts longer than necessary □ *The party was a long-drawn-out affair.*

drawstring ['drɔːstrɪŋ] *n* a string that goes around the opening of something such as a bag, and closes it when pulled.

dread [dred] ◇ *n* a feeling of fear and deep worry about something bad that might happen □ *He lived in dread of the Mafia/losing his business.* ◇ *vt* [meeting, exam] to feel afraid and worried about <sthg> because it is likely to be unpleasant □ *She's dreading the trip/going into the hospital.* ■ **I dread to think** a phrase used to show that one is worried about something, or imagines that something will be unpleasant □ *I dread to think what our losses will be.* □ *"I wonder what Nick will be wearing." — "I dread to think!"*

dreaded ['dredəd] *adj* [disease, person] that causes a feeling of dread □ *You didn't have to talk to the dreaded Mike Pearsons, did you!*

dreadful ['dredfl] *adj* **-1.** [accident, pain, illness] that is very serious □ *The passengers on board suffered dreadful injuries.* ■ **to feel dreadful** [person] to feel ill □ *This headache is making me feel dreadful.* **-2. to feel dreadful about sthg** to feel embarrassed and guilty about sthg □ *I feel dreadful about it now!* **-3.** [waste, behavior, noise] that one thinks is very bad □ *Do you have to keep making that dreadful noise!*

dreadfully ['dredflɪ] *adv* **-1.** [hurt, behave, perform] very badly. **-2. dreadfully sorry/boring etc** very sorry/boring etc (informal use) □ *Tessa will be dreadfully upset when she hears you can't make it.*

dreadlocks ['dredlɒks] *npl* long hair that is twisted into small braids, often worn by Rastafarians.

dream [dri:m] (*pt* & *pp* **dreamed** OR **dreamt**) ◇ *n* **-1.** a series of images that one experiences during sleep □ *I had a bad dream last night.* **-2.** something that one wants very much □ *His dream is to become the next CEO.* □ *the woman/job of his dreams.* ■ **to be beyond one's wildest dreams** to be better than one ever imagined □ *wealth beyond one's wildest dreams!* ◇ *adj* **a dream trip/job etc** a trip/job etc that one thinks would be very enjoyable and that one wants very much. ◇ *vt* to experience <imaginary events> during sleep □ *I dreamt (that) I was in a strange house.* ■ **I never dreamed this would happen** I did not think that this would happen. ◇ *vi* **-1.** to have a dream □ *I dreamed of* OR *about my grandparents.* ■ **I wouldn't dream of it!** I wouldn't do it because I think it would be wrong or inappropriate □ *"Don't tell anybody." — "I wouldn't dream of it."* □ *She wouldn't dream of complaining.* **-2. to dream of sthg** to wish very much for sthg □ *He'd always dreamed of having his own business.*

♦ **dream up** *vt sep* **to dream sthg up** [excuse, story, idea] to invent sthg, especially sthg that other people do not take seriously □ *What excuse has he dreamed up this time?*

dreamer ['dri:məʳ] *n* a person whose ideas are not realistic or practical □ *James? He's always been a dreamer, hasn't he.*

dreamily ['dri:mɪlɪ] *adv* [look, walk] slowly and without concentrating □ *Michela stared dreamily out at the falling snow.*

dreamt [dremt] *past tense & past participle of* **dream**.

Dreamtime ['dri:mtaɪm] *n* in Australian Aboriginal mythology, the period when the world was formed.

🏵 DREAMTIME

All the ancient stories of the Australian Aborigines are about Dreamtime, the time when the Earth, and living things, were formed. Each people has its own story that describes how the particular landscape around them was created, and each generation is taught how to "read" the story in the features of the landscape, such as trees, animals, and rocks. Most traditional Aboriginal art is based on stories about Dreamtime.

dream world *n* an imaginary world □ *He must be living in a dream world.*

dreamy ['dri:mɪ] (*compar* **dreamier**, *superl* **dreamiest**) *adj* **-1.** [smile, expression] that shows one is thinking about something pleasant, and not concentrating □ *He had that dreamy look that he always has when he's in love.* **-2.** [music, feeling] peaceful and like a dream □ *The movie had an odd, dreamy kind of atmosphere.*

dreary ['drɪərɪ] (*compar* **drearier**, *superl* **dreariest**) *adj* **-1.** [weather, day] that is dark and makes one feel sad □ *Another dreary Sunday afternoon.* **-2.** [person, life, work] that one thinks is boring □ *the same old dreary routine.*

dredge [dredʒ] *vt* to remove the mud from the bottom of <a river, harbor> etc to make it deeper or to look for something.

♦ **dredge up** *vt sep* **-1. to dredge sthg up** [mud, body, treasure] to bring sthg up from the bottom of a river or harbor. **-2. to dredge sthg up** [memory, crime, relationship] to remember or remind somebody of sthg from the past □ *They've been dredging up all kinds of odd facts about Pablo's past.*

dredger ['dredʒəʳ] *n* a ship or machine for dredging rivers or harbors.

dregs [dregz] *npl* **-1.** [of tea, coffee, wine] the solid particles and the last few drops of liquid at the bottom of a glass or cup □ *"Is there any coffee left?" — "Just the dregs."* **-2. the dregs of society** the people in a society who are considered to be the most unpleasant and useless.

drench [drentʃ] *vt* to make <sb/sthg> completely wet □ *He was drenched in* OR *with sweat.*

dress [dres] ◇ *n* **-1.** [for a woman] a woman's piece of clothing that consists of a skirt and top in one piece □ *a wedding/summer dress.* **-2.** [for an occasion, of a people] a particular type of clothing □ *They were wearing evening/national/traditional dress.* ◇ *vt* **-1.** [child, invalid] to put clothes on <sb>. ■ **to be dressed** to have clothes on; to be wearing the clothes that one intends to wear for the day □ *Aren't you dressed yet?* ■ **to be dressed in black/blue etc** to be wearing black/blue etc clothes. ■ **to get dressed** to put all one's clothes on. **-2.** MEDICINE to clean <a wound> and cover it with a bandage. **-3.** COOKING to cover <a salad> with dressing. ◇ *vi* **-1.** to put all one's clothes on □ *I quickly washed, dressed, and cleaned my teeth.* **-2.** to wear a particular style of clothes □ *She always dresses very fashionably.*

♦ **dress up** ◇ *vt sep* **to dress sthg up** [facts, statements] to make sthg seem more interesting or attractive than it really is □ *They accused the management of dressing up old ideas in a new format.* ◇ *vi* **-1.** [as somebody] to put on different or unusual clothes in order to disguise oneself or for amusement □ *She dressed up as a clown.* □ *He dressed up in his father's old clothes.* **-2.** [for an occasion] to put on elegant or formal clothes for a special occasion □ *There's no need to dress up — it should be fairly informal.*

dressage [US drə'sɑ:ʒ, GB 'dresɑ:ʒ] *n* a competition in which a rider has to make a horse perform particular movements.

dress circle *n* the first balcony upstairs in a theater.

dress code *n* a set of rules or instructions

that say what one should wear in a particular situation, e.g. at work or at a social event.

dresser ['dresər] *n* **-1.** US [for clothes] a piece of furniture with a mirror on top that has drawers for storing clothes. **-2. a smart/casual etc dresser** a person who dresses in a smart/casual etc way □ *He's a flashy/sloppy dresser.* **-3.** GB [for dishes] a piece of furniture that has open shelves in the top part and cupboards in the bottom for storing dishes.

dressing ['dresɪŋ] *n* **-1.** MEDICINE something that covers a wound, e.g. a bandage or antiseptic cream □ *This will need a clean dressing.* **-2.** [for salad] a kind of sauce, e.g. of oil and vinegar, that one puts on a salad □ *Do you want some dressing on your salad?* **-3.** US [for turkey] a mixture of small pieces of food that is put inside a turkey before cooking.

dressing gown *n* a loose piece of clothing like a coat, usually worn immediately after getting out of bed.

dressing room *n* **-1.** SPORT a room in a sports stadium where athletes or players can change clothes. **-2.** THEATER a room in a theater, film studio etc where actors or performers can change their clothes.

dressing table *n* a piece of furniture that has a drawer, a flat top, and small mirror, and is usually used in a bedroom.

dressmaker ['dresmeɪkər] *n* a person whose job is to make women's or children's clothes.

dressmaking ['dresmeɪkɪŋ] *n* the skill or activity of making women's or children's clothes.

dress rehearsal *n* the last rehearsal of a play, opera etc in which the performers wear their costumes, and the stage is lit and decorated as if for a public performance.

dress shirt *n* a shirt, usually white with a decorated front, worn by men on formal occasions.

dressy ['dresɪ] (*compar* **dressier**, *superl* **dressiest**) *adj* [piece of clothing, person, occasion] that looks elegant and fashionable.

drew [druː] *past tense of* **draw**.

dribble ['drɪbl] ◇ *n* **-1.** [of saliva] saliva that is coming from somebody's mouth. **-2.** a small amount of liquid that is moving, e.g. blood or water. ◇ *vt* **-1.** to spill small amounts of <liquid> □ *Careful, you're dribbling soup all down your front.* **-2.** SPORT in soccer, basketball etc, to move <the ball> as one moves forward, by giving it frequent short kicks or bounces. ◇ *vi* [baby] to let small amounts of saliva come out of one's mouth.

dribs [drɪbz] *npl* **in dribs and drabs** in small irregular amounts, rather than all together □ *People kept arriving in dribs and drabs.*

dried [draɪd] ◇ *past tense & past participle of* **dry.** ◇ *adj* [food, flower] that has been preserved by drying □ *dried apricots/pears.*

dried fruit *n* fruit, especially grapes, figs, dates etc, that has been preserved by drying.

dried-up *adj* [well, river] that has no water.

drier ['draɪər] *n* = **dryer.**

drift [drɪft] ◇ *n* **-1.** [of people, animals, a current] a general movement in a particular direction □ *a drift back to home ownership* □ *a population drift.* **-2.** [of snow, sand, leaves] a large mass of something that has been formed into a pile by the wind □ *The snow lay in drifts.* **-3.** [of a conversation, remark] the general meaning of something □ *I don't think I catch your drift.* ◇ *vi* **-1.** [boat] to be carried along by the current or the wind □ *We drifted downstream/toward the shore.* **-2.** [snow] to be blown into piles by the wind. **-3.** [person] to gradually go somewhere, do something, or get into a situation, often without planning or intending to □ *He drifted from one job to another.* □ *He drifted into a life of crime.*

◆ **drift apart** *vi* [couple, friends] to gradually see each other less often and become less close □ *We just drifted apart over the years.*

◆ **drift off** *vi* [person] to fall asleep gradually □ *I must have drifted off.*

drifter ['drɪftər] *n* a person who drifts between places, jobs etc (disapproving use).

driftwood ['drɪftwʊd] *n* wood that drifts in a river or the ocean, or that has drifted to the shore □ *a piece of driftwood.*

drill [drɪl] ◇ *n* **-1.** [for making holes] a tool or machine with a sharp end that spins around and is used for making holes, e.g. in a wall, in the road, or in an oilfield □ *a dentist's/an electric drill.* **-2.** [for soldiers, students] a training exercise □ *a fire/battle drill.*

◇ *vt* **-1.** [tooth, rock] to make a hole in <sthg> using a drill. **-2.** [oil well, tunnel] to make <a hole> using a drill. **-3.** [students, soldiers] to teach <sb> by making them repeat the same exercise many times. ■ **to drill sthg into sb** to make sb learn sthg by repeating it to them many times □ *We had it drilled into us that we shouldn't talk at the table.*

◇ *vi* **-1.** to make a hole in something using a drill. ■ **to drill into sthg** [into wood, a tooth, the ground] to drill a hole in sthg. **-2.** to make a deep hole in the ground or in the ocean bed using a drill. ■ **to drill for sthg** [for oil, water] to drill a deep hole in the hope of finding sthg.

drilling platform ['drɪlɪŋ-] *n* a structure built above the surface of the ocean to house the people and support the equipment needed to drill below the ocean bed.

drily ['draɪlɪ] *adv* = **dryly.**

drink [drɪŋk] (*pt* **drank**, *pp* **drunk**) ◇ *vt* [water, coffee, wine] to fill one's mouth with <liquid> and swallow it □ *What would you like to drink?* □ *Would you like something to drink?* ◇ *vi* **-1.** to drink a liquid □ *I prefer to drink from the bottle.* **-2.** to drink alcoholic drinks □ *She doesn't drink.* ◇ *n* **-1.** [of water, lemonade] an amount of a liquid that is drunk □ *I had a drink of water/milk.* **-2.** [of alcohol] an alcoholic drink, e.g. beer, wine, or whiskey □ *Let's go for/have a drink after work.* **-3.** alcoholic drinks □ *I'm off drink for the time being.*

◆ **drink to** *vt fus* **to drink to sb/sthg** [to a person, plan, idea] to hold up one's glass before drinking and express one's good wishes to or approval of <sb/sthg> □ *We drank to their success.* □ *I'll drink to that!*

drinkable ['drɪŋkəbl] *adj* **-1.** [water] that is safe to drink □ *Is the water here drinkable?* **-2.** [wine] that is good enough to drink □ *"What's the wine like?" — "Well, it's just about drinkable."*

drink-driving *n* GB = **drunk-driving**.

drinker ['drɪŋkəʳ] *n* **-1.** a person who drinks alcohol, especially a lot of alcohol □ *a heavy drinker.* **-2. a tea/coffee etc drinker** a person who drinks tea/coffee etc □ *I'm not a big coffee drinker.*

drinking ['drɪŋkɪŋ] *n* the act or habit of drinking alcohol □ *His drinking is becoming a problem.* □ *a drinking companion/session.*

drinking fountain *n* a device that provides drinking water, usually in public places.

drinking-up time *n* GB the time that customers in pubs are given to finish their drinks after the landlord has stopped serving.

drinking water *n* water that is safe to drink.

drink machine US, **drinks machine** GB *n* a machine that automatically produces drinks such as coffee, lemonade etc.

drip [drɪp] (*pt* & *pp* **dripped**, *cont* **dripping**) ◇ *n* **-1.** [of water, a faucet] the flow of drops of liquid falling one after the other □ *the steady drip of water on the roof.* **-2.** MEDICINE a piece of medical equipment that gradually lets small amounts of liquid into a patient's bloodstream through a tube. **-3.** [person] somebody who one thinks is weak and dull (informal use) □ *He's such a drip, that boy.* ◇ *vt* to drop small amounts of <water, blood, paint> etc. ◇ *vi* **-1.** [water, rain, blood] to fall in small drops, one after the other □ *Don't let the paint drip on the carpet.* **-2.** [faucet] to let water drip. **-3.** [nose] to let mucus drip. **-4. to be dripping with sthg** [with sweat, blood] to have a lot of sthg liquid on one's clothes or body.

drip-dry *adj* [clothing] that dries without creases if it is hung up wet after being washed, and does not need to be ironed.

dripping ['drɪpɪŋ] ◇ *adj* [faucet] that loses water in drips. ◇ *adv* **dripping wet** very wet. ◇ *n* the fat that comes from meat when it is cooked.

drive [draɪv] (*pt* **drove**, *pp* **driven**) ◇ *n* **-1.** [in a car, bus] a trip in a vehicle, sometimes only for pleasure; the distance traveled during this trip □ *We went for a drive in the country.* □ *How was the drive?* □ *The house is a 100-mile drive from here.* **-2.** [of a person] a particular strong desire or need that all people have □ *sex drive.* **-3.** [of a company] a determined effort to do something, usually by a group of people □ *a drive to clean up the neighborhood.* **-4. to have drive** to have the energy and determination to do things □ *She's got real drive.* **-5.** = **driveway**. **-6.** SPORT the act of hitting a ball, e.g. in golf, so that it travels fast or a long distance. **-7.** US [in an automatic car] the position of the controls in an automatic car that allows it to move forward.

◇ *vt* **-1.** [car, bus, truck] to make <a vehicle> move by sitting inside it and controlling the engine, steering wheel etc □ *I drove the car over to Matt's and left it there.* **-2.** [passenger] to take <sb> somewhere in a vehicle, especially a car □ *She drove me to the airport.* □ *He always drives the children to school.* **-3.** [generator, engine] to provide power for <a machine> □ *It's driven by solar power.* **-4.** [army, cattle] to force <a person or animal> to move in a particular direction □ *The attackers were driven back.* □ *The farmer drove his sheep back to their pen.* **-5.** [ambitious person, politician, scientist] to give <sb> a great desire to do something □ *What is it that drives her?* □ *He was driven by greed and ambition.* **-6. to drive sb to sthg** [to murder, drink] to force sb to do sthg after a long time; [to despair, desperation] to force sb to feel sthg after a long time □ *Those kids are driving me to distraction.* ■ **to drive sb crazy** OR **mad** to make sb insane; to irritate sb very much □ *His wife's jealousy drove him crazy.* □ *That noise is driving me crazy.* **-7.** [nail, stake] to push or hit <sthg> in a particular direction using a lot of strength □ *He drove the pole into the ground.* **-8.** SPORT to hit <a ball> very hard so that it travels very fast in a particular direction.

◇ *vi* **-1.** to drive a vehicle □ *He drove off in his car.* **-2.** to travel somewhere in a vehicle □ *We're driving down to Miami.*

◆ **drive at** *vt fus* **what are you driving at?** what are you trying to say? □ *What I'm driving at is that all these incidents must somehow be related.*

◆ **drive out** *vt sep* **to drive sb/sthg out** [person, thought, evil spirit] to force sb/sthg to go away □ *You've got to drive these thoughts right out of your mind.*

drive-in ◇ *adj* **a drive-in restaurant/movie theater etc** a restaurant/movie theater etc that provides a service for people while they stay in their cars. ◇ *n* **-1.** [for food] a restaurant that serves food to customers while they stay in their cars. **-2.** [for movies] an outdoor movie theater where people watch the movie from their cars.

drivel ['drɪvl] *n* words that make no sense; a very bad piece of writing (informal use) □ *Don't talk such drivel!*

driven ['drɪvn] *past participle of* **drive**.

driver ['draɪvəʳ] *n* **-1.** [of a car, bus] a person who drives a car, bus etc; a person whose job is to drive a bus, car etc □ *The driver was not hurt in the accident.* **-2.** COMPUTING a computer program used to control a connected device.

driver's license US, **driving licence** GB *n* an official document that shows that one is legally allowed to drive.

drive shaft *n* the shaft that carries power from the gearbox to the wheels of a vehicle.

driveway ['draɪvweɪ] *n* a private road that goes from a public road to a house or garage.

driving ['draɪvɪŋ] ◇ *adj* **driving wind/ambition** very strong wind/ambition □ *The climbers* *struggled against the driving wind and rain.* ◇ *n* the activity of driving a vehicle.

driving force *n* the most important person or thing that influences something □ *She was the driving force behind the movement.*

driving instructor *n* a person whose job is to teach other people how to drive.

driving lesson *n* a lesson in which somebody is taught how to drive.

driving licence *n* GB = **driver's license**.

driving school *n* a company that teaches people how to drive.

driving test *n* a test that a person must pass before they are legally allowed to drive alone.

drizzle ['drɪzl] ◇ *n* very fine rain. ◇ *v impers* to rain very gently □ *It's been drizzling all day.*

droll [drəʊl] *adj* [humor, remark] that is funny in an unusual way.

dromedary [US 'drɒmədəri, GB -ədəri] (*pl* **dromedaries**) *n* a camel with one hump.

drone [drəʊn] ◇ *n* -1. [of an insect, airplane, voice] a low humming sound that stays the same □ *The drone of the engine made her sleepy.* -2. ZOOLOGY a male honeybee. ◇ *vi* [insect, engine, airplane] to make a sound like a drone.

◆ **drone on** *vi* to speak for a long time in a boring way □ *She droned on for an hour about insurance claims.*

drool [druːl] *vi* -1. [person] to let saliva fall from the mouth. -2. **to drool over sb/sthg** to admire sb/sthg in a way that makes one look ridiculous □ *Everyone was drooling over the new baby.*

droop [druːp] *vi* -1. [head, eyelids, flower] to hang downward, especially because of tiredness, weakness etc □ *His eyelids began to droop.* -2. [spirits, person] to become less lively □ *She began to droop noticeably toward the end of the evening.*

drop [drɒp] (*pt & pp* **dropped**, *cont* **dropping**) ◇ *n* -1. [of liquid] a very small amount of a liquid that has formed a round shape and falls somewhere □ *a drop of blood.* -2. [of whiskey, milk] a small amount of a drink □ *Would you like a drop of wine?* -3. [for sucking] a small round candy that is made to be sucked □ *a cough/fruit drop.* -4. [in value, level] a decrease in the value or amount of something □ *There's been a sharp drop in temperature today.* □ *a price drop.* -5. [from a high place] the distance from the top to the bottom of something that a person or object can fall □ *It was a sheer drop to the bottom.* □ *a 20-foot drop.*

◇ *vt* -1. [glass, plate, wallet] to let <sb/sthg that one is holding or carrying> fall, especially accidentally □ *Be careful not to drop it!* □ *They dropped two bombs over the harbor.* -2. [level, price, amount] to make the amount or value of <sthg> lower □ *He dropped his speed.* □ *You're going to have to drop your prices.* -3. **to drop one's voice** to talk more quietly □ *She dropped her voice to a confidential whisper.* -4. [idea, plan] to stop considering or talking about <sthg>; [math, history] to stop studying <sthg>; [friend] to stop being friendly to

<sb>; [player] to leave <sb> out of a team □ *Look, let's just drop the subject, okay?* □ *If I were you, I'd drop the whole idea.* □ *When he heard the news, he dropped everything and rushed home.* □ *I dropped French and studied German instead.* -5. [passenger] to leave <sb> at a place after driving them there □ *She dropped me at the airport.* -6. [remark, hint] to mention <sthg> without saying it directly or making it seem important □ *He kept dropping hints about Christmas and gifts and things.* -7. SPORT to lose <a set, game> etc. -8. **to drop sb a note** OR **line** to send sb a short letter □ *Drop me a line when you know more about it.*

◇ *vi* -1. [cup, stone] to fall straight down to the ground; [person] to fall down or feel as if one is going to fall down because one is tired or ill; [ground] to go down to a lower level □ *Her keys dropped out of her bag.* □ *We walked until we dropped.* □ *The cliffs drop down to the ocean.* -2. [temperature, price, wind] to become less big, high, strong etc □ *Attendance has been dropping all season.* -3. [voice] to become quieter □ *Her voice dropped to a whisper.*

◆ **drops** *npl* liquid medicine that is taken or used in small amounts with a dropper □ *eye/ear drops.*

◆ **drop by** *vi* to make an informal visit, usually without arranging it first □ *Why don't you drop by if you're in town again next Wednesday?*

◆ **drop in** *vi* = **drop by** □ *He dropped in on me quite unexpectedly.*

◆ **drop off** ◇ *vt sep* **to drop sb off** to leave sb at a place after driving them there □ *Can you drop me off at the corner, please?* ◇ *vi* -1. [person] to fall asleep, sometimes without intending to □ *The baby gradually dropped off to sleep.* -2. [number, level] to become less high; [interest, support] to become less strong □ *Sales are/Business is beginning to drop off.*

◆ **drop out** *vi* to stop going to something or taking part in it, with no plans to go back □ *He dropped out of school at 16.*

dropcloth ['drɒpklɒθ] *n* US a large cloth used to cover furniture to protect it from dust.

drop-in centre *n* GB a place run by the social services or a charity where people can go for company, advice etc.

droplet ['drɒplət] *n* a very small drop.

dropout ['drɒpaʊt] *n* -1. [from college] a person who has dropped out of school or college before finishing their studies. -2. [from society] a person who has chosen to live and behave in a way that is different from the way most people live and behave, e.g. by refusing to do a full-time job.

dropper ['drɒpər] *n* a short glass tube with a rubber cap at one end, used for measuring out small amounts of liquid.

droppings ['drɒpɪŋz] *npl* the excrement of birds and animals.

drop shot *n* a shot in tennis, badminton etc in which the ball is hit gently so that it falls to the ground just after it crosses the net.

dross [drɒs] *n* -1. something that has been

very badly made, written etc (disapproving use) □ *Most of the book is complete dross.* **-2.** INDUSTRY the waste material that appears on the surface of a metal when it melts.

drought [draʊt] *n* a long period of time in which little or no rain falls and there is not enough water □ *The effects of the drought are starting to be felt.*

drove [droʊv] ◇ *past tense of* **drive.** ◇ *n* **in droves** in large numbers □ *The crowds were arriving in droves.*

drown [draʊn] ◇ *vt* **-1.** to kill <a person or animal> by keeping them underwater so that they cannot breathe □ *They drowned the kittens when they were born.* **-2.** [speech, sound] to prevent <sb/sthg> from being heard □ *His voice was drowned out by cries of protest.* ◇ *vi* [person, animal] to die because one is underwater and unable to breathe □ *Two men are missing, believed drowned.*

drowsy ['draʊzɪ] *(compar* **drowsier,** *superl* **drowsiest)** *adj* [person, animal] that is sleepy and unable to think clearly □ *The pills make you feel drowsy, so don't drive when you take them.*

drudge [drʌdʒ] *n* a person who does a lot of hard boring work.

drudgery ['drʌdʒərɪ] *n* work that is hard and boring but that must be done.

drug [drʌg] *(pt & pp* **drugged,** *cont* **drugging)** ◇ *n* **-1.** MEDICINE a substance used to treat a person who is ill. **-2.** a substance, usually illegal, that people smoke, sniff, swallow, or inject for pleasure or excitement or because they are addicted to it □ *It was clear that he was on drugs.* □ *She started taking drugs at fifteen.* □ *a drug problem.* ◇ *vt* **-1.** [prisoner, patient] to make <a person or animal> sleepy or unconscious by giving them a drug. **-2.** [meal, coffee] to add a drug to <food or drink> to make somebody unconscious or sleepy.

drug abuse *n* the use of drugs, especially illegal drugs, for pleasure or excitement.

drug addict *n* a person who cannot stop taking drugs.

drug addiction *n* the state of being addicted to a particular drug.

druggist ['drʌgɪst] *n* US a person who prepares and sells medicines.

drug pusher *n* a person who sells illegal drugs.

drugstore ['drʌgstɔːr] *n* US a shop that sells medicines and drugs, and items such as beauty products, office supplies, and snacks.

druid ['druːɪd] *n* a priest of a religion that existed in Britain, Ireland, and France before Christianity; a modern follower of this religion.

drum [drʌm] *(pt & pp* **drummed,** *cont* **drumming)** ◇ *n* **-1.** MUSIC a musical instrument consisting of a skin stretched over a hollow round frame that is played by hitting the skin with a stick or with one's hand. **-2.** [for a liquid] a large cylindrical container made of metal or plastic, used for storing liquids □ *an*

oil drum. ◇ *vt* **to drum one's fingers** to hit a surface with one's fingers one after another, usually as a sign that one is impatient. ◇ *vi* **-1.** [person] to play a drum. **-2.** [rain, fingers, hoofs] to make a continuous sound like a drum □ *the sound of the rain drumming on the roof.*

◆ **drums** *npl* **the drums** a set of drums played by one person in popular music.

◆ **drum into** *vt sep* **to drum sthg into sb** to make sb remember sthg by saying it to them many times □ *These principles were drummed into us in early childhood.*

◆ **drum up** *vt sep* **to drum sthg up** [support, trade] to get sthg by attracting a lot of people □ *We really need to drum up some more business.*

drumbeat ['drʌmbiːt] *n* the sound made by hitting a drum.

drum brake *n* a type of brake attached to the wheels of a vehicle that works by pressing against the wheel when it is used.

drummer ['drʌmər] *n* a person who plays a drum or the drums.

drum roll *n* a series of drumbeats that follow each other very quickly and sound like one long sound.

drumstick ['drʌmstɪk] *n* **-1.** [for a drum] a stick used for playing a drum or the drums. **-2.** [of a chicken] the bottom part of the leg of a bird, especially a chicken, that is cooked and eaten.

drunk [drʌŋk] ◇ *past participle of* **drink.** ◇ *adj* **-1.** [person] who has drunk too much alcohol and can no longer speak or think clearly □ *We got drunk on home-made wine.* ■ **drunk and disorderly** LAW drunk and acting in a noisy or violent way. **-2. to be drunk with sthg** [with success, power] to feel very excited because of sthg one has. ◇ *n* a person who is drunk or who often gets drunk □ *A drunk stopped me in the street and asked me for money.*

drunkard ['drʌŋkərd] *n* a person who often gets drunk.

drunk-driving *n* the offense of driving a car, truck etc while one is drunk □ *He was caught for drunk-driving and lost his license.*

drunken ['drʌŋkən] *adj* [person] who is drunk and behaves in a way that shows it; [party, laughter] that is caused by or that involves somebody who has drunk a lot of alcohol □ *I could hear a lot of loud drunken laughter from the room below.* □ *He fell into a drunken stupor.*

drunken driving *n* = **drunk-driving.**

dry [draɪ] *(compar* **drier,** *superl* **driest,** *pt & pp* **dried)** ◇ *adj* **-1.** [wood, paint, towel] that contains no water or liquid; [hands, glass, plate] not wet □ *The clothes should be dry now.* □ *The ink isn't dry yet.* **-2.** [weather, day, area] that is without rain □ *It's the longest dry spell since records began.* **-3.** [river, well, soil] that has no water. **-4.** [person] who feels thirsty; [mouth, throat] that needs water □ *My mouth felt parched and dry.* **-5.** [humor, comment] that is amusing in a way that is not too obvious □ *his dry sense of humor.* **-6.** [book, subject] that

one finds boring □ *dry medical textbooks.*
-7. [sherry, wine] that does not taste sweet □
a dry white wine.
◇ *vt* [face, hair, dishes] to make <sthg> dry □
He dried his hands on the towel.
◇ *vi* [clothes, hair] *The ink hasn't dried yet.* □
quick-drying paint.

◆ **dry out** ◇ *vt sep* **to dry sthg out** [clothes,
wood] to make sthg completely dry. ◇ *vi*
[clothes, wood, person] to become completely
dry □ *The paint takes days to dry out.*

◆ **dry up** ◇ *vt sep* **to dry sthg up** [cup, dish] to
dry sthg by wiping it with a cloth. ◇ *vi*
-1. [lake, river, well] to become dry. **-2.** [supply]
to finish or stop □ *The money dried up pretty
quickly after Sandra left.* **-3.** [speaker] to stop
speaking because one cannot think what to
say □ *In the middle of his speech, Grant just
dried up.* **-4.** [person] to dry the dishes.

dry-clean *vt* to clean <a piece of clothing>
with chemicals instead of water.

dry cleaner *n* **a dry cleaner's** a store where
clothes are dry-cleaned.

dry-cleaning *n* the process or work of dry-
cleaning clothes; clothes that have been
cleaned in this way.

dry dock *n* a dock where the water can be
removed so that ships can be repaired or
kept safe.

dryer ['draɪə'] *n* a machine that dries clothes.

dry ginger *n* a fizzy drink that tastes of ginger, often served with whiskey.

dry goods *npl* **-1.** US goods such as cloth,
clothes, and household goods. **-2.** GB goods
such as tea, coffee, and flour.

dry ice *n* solid carbon dioxide, used on stage,
in a movie etc to look like mist.

dry land *n* land, when it is contrasted with
the sea □ *It was good to be back on dry land.*

dryly ['draɪlɪ] *adv* [comment, remark] *see* **dry.**

dry rot *n* a disease caused by fungus that
turns wood into powder.

dry run *n* a complete rehearsal or practice of
something that is done without an audience.

dry ski slope *n* a slope with an artificial surface instead of snow, where people can
practice skiing.

dry-stone wall *n* a wall made of stones fitted
together without mortar.

DSc (*abbr of* **Doctor of Science**) *n* a postgraduate science degree; a person who has this
degree.

DSS (*abbr of* **Department of Social Security**) *n*
the DSS the British government department
responsible for the running of social security
agencies.

DST (*abbr of* **daylight saving time**) *n* the system of time used in the USA in the summer,
which is usually one hour ahead of the local
standard time.

DT *abbr of* **data transmission.**

DTI (*abbr of* **Department of Trade and Industry**)
n **the DTI** the British government department
responsible for trade and industry.

DTP *n abbr of* **desktop publishing.**

DT's [,diː'tiːz] (*abbr of* **delirium tremens**) *npl* **the
DT's** a medical condition, caused by alcohol-
ism, in which somebody shakes all over and
sees things that are not there.

dual ['djuːəl] *adj* **a dual function/purpose etc** a
function/purpose etc that has two aspects or
parts □ *dual citizenship.*

dual carriageway *n* GB a road on which vehicles
traveling in opposite directions are separated
by a barrier or a narrow strip of grass.

dual control *n* [of a machine, organization] the
state of being under the control of two people or groups of people at the same time.

dual nationality *n* the state of being a citizen
of two countries and having the right to live
in both.

dub [dʌb] *vt* **-1.** CINEMA [movie, soundtrack] to replace <the original voices in a movie> by
the voices of other actors speaking a different language. **-2.** [person, place] to give <sb>
a particular nickname □ *It is dubbed "the Venice of the North".*

Dubai [,duː'baɪ] a state in southeastern Arabia,
on the Persian Gulf, consisting mainly of the
port of Dubai. It is one of the United Arab
Emirates. POPULATION: 300,000. CAPITAL: Dubai.

dubious ['djuːbjəs] *adj* **-1.** [character, activity,
deal] that does not seem completely honest;
[distinction, honor] that has no value □ *I have
had the dubious distinction of working for them!*
-2. to be dubious about sthg to be uncertain
about sthg because it is perhaps not a good
idea □ *I'm a little dubious about going there, myself.*

Dublin ['dʌblɪn] the capital of the Irish Republic and its largest city, on the Irish Sea. POPU-
LATION: 477,675.

Dublin Bay prawn *n* a large prawn, usually
eaten fried as scampi.

Dubliner ['dʌblɪnə'] *n* a person who comes
from Dublin, or who lives in Dublin.

duchess ['dʌtʃəs] *n* the title of a woman who
is equal in rank to a duke; a woman who is
married to a duke.

duchy ['dʌtʃɪ] (*pl* **duchies**) *n* the land ruled by
a duke.

duck [dʌk] ◇ *n* a common water bird with
short legs and a flat beak that is sometimes
kept for its eggs, meat, or feathers; the meat
of this bird, eaten as food □ *duck à l'orange.* ■
to take to sthg like a duck to water to adapt
to or learn sthg easily and naturally. ◇ *vt*
-1. to lower <one's head> quickly, usually
to hide or to avoid being hit. **-2.** [duty, responsibility, question] to avoid <sthg>.
-3. [person] to push <sb> underwater. ◇ *vi*
-1. to lower one's head quickly, usually to
hide or to avoid being hit □ *Quick! Duck!*
-2. to move somewhere quickly, usually to
avoid danger □ *They ducked behind the rocks.*

◆ **duck out** *vi* **to duck out of sthg** to avoid doing sthg □ *Don't try to duck out of it.*

duckling ['dʌklɪŋ] *n* a young duck; the meat of
this duck, eaten as food.

duct [dʌkt] *n* **-1.** CONSTRUCTION a pipe or tube

dump

for liquids, gases etc to pass through □ *a heating/water duct.* **-2.** ANATOMY a tube in the body that air or a liquid passes through □ *a tear duct.*

dud [dʌd] ◇ *adj* **-1. a dud coin/check etc** a coin/check etc that is false and has no value □ *They gave me a dud dollar bill.* **-2. a dud machine/bullet etc** a machine/bullet etc that does not work □ *That's a dud engine.* ◇ *n* **-1.** a person who is not good at doing something. **-2.** a dud coin, bill etc; a dud shell, bullet etc □ *Fortunately, the bomb was a dud.*

dude [dʲuːd] *n* US a man (informal use).

dude ranch *n* US a ranch where tourists can stay, ride horses etc.

due [dʲuː] ◇ *adj* **-1. to be due** [event, plane, person] to be expected to take place, appear, or arrive at a particular time; [baby] to be expected to be born □ *I'm due at a meeting in ten minutes.* □ *She's due back at four o'clock.* □ *The book is due out in May.* □ *I'm due to give a talk there tonight.* □ *When is the baby due?* **-2. due care/consideration etc** the amount of care/consideration etc that is suitable or necessary □ *He was charged with driving without due care and attention.* ■ **in due course** after the proper amount of time □ *Your new card will be sent to you in due course.* **-3. to be due** [payment, sum] to have to be paid □ *This bill is due for payment now.* ■ **to be due to sb** [money, respect] to be owed to sb. ■ **to be due sthg** to be owed sthg □ *We're due a pay increase.* **-4. to be due to sthg** to be caused by sthg □ *The delay was due to mechanical problems.* ◇ *n* **to give him his due** a phrase used to mention a good point about somebody who one generally disapproves of □ *I don't like her, but to give her her due, she's very generous.* ◇ *adv* **due north/south etc** exactly north/south etc.

◆ **dues** *npl* money or fees that one pays to belong to a club, organization etc □ *I've paid my dues to the union.*

◆ **due to** *prep* because of <sthg> □ *'Canceled due to illness.'*

due date *n* the latest date that something can be paid, delivered etc.

duel [dʲuːəl] *n* a fight between two people with swords or guns, often to decide a quarrel.

duet [dʲuːˈet] *n* a piece of music that is written for two players or singers.

duffel bag [ˈdʌfl-] *n* a canvas bag, worn over one's shoulder, that is round at the bottom and closed at the top with string.

duffel coat *n* a heavy coat that has long wooden buttons and usually a hood.

duffle bag [ˈdʌfl-] *n* = **duffel bag.**

duffle coat *n* = **duffel coat.**

dug [dʌg] *past tense & past participle of* **dig.**

dugout [ˈdʌgaʊt] *n* **-1. a dugout (canoe)** a boat made from a log that has been hollowed out. **-2.** SPORT a covered section of seating beside a playing field where managers, trainers etc sit during a game.

DUI (*abbr of* **driving under the influence**) *n* US the crime of driving after drinking too much alcohol □ *It's his second DUI.*

duke [dʲuːk] *n* the title of a nobleman of the highest rank □ *the Duke of York.*

dull [dʌl] ◇ *adj* **-1.** [person, conversation, evening] that is not interesting or exciting □ *We're so busy there's never a dull moment.* **-2.** [gray, light, glow] that is not bright □ *A dull, blue light shone through the curtains.* **-3.** [weather, day] that is cloudy □ *It was a dull, cloudy day.* **-4.** [sound, thud, boom] that is not loud or clear □ *There was a dull explosion somewhere far away.* **-5.** [ache, pain] that is felt all the time but never becomes suddenly painful □ *All I could feel was a constant dull pain in my jaw.* ◇ *vt* **-1.** [pain, feeling] to make <sthg> weaker □ *I took some aspirin to dull the pain.* **-2.** [color, metal] to make <sthg> less bright □ *a dull grayish color.*

duly [ˈdʲuːlɪ] *adv* **-1.** in the proper or correct way □ *Your proposal has been duly noted.* **-2.** as expected □ *We duly received her letter of acknowledgment.*

dumb [dʌm] *adj* **-1.** [person] who cannot speak □ *She was born deaf and dumb.* **-2.** [person] who one thinks is stupid (informal use) □ *Don't be so dumb, of course he's coming!*

dumbbell [ˈdʌmbel] *n* a metal bar with weights at both ends that is lifted in one hand to exercise one's muscles.

dumbfound [dʌmˈfaʊnd] *vt* **to be dumbfounded** to be so surprised that one does not know what to say □ *He just stared at me, utterly dumbfounded.*

dumbstruck [ˈdʌmstrʌk] *adj* **to be dumbstruck** to be so surprised and shocked that one cannot speak.

dumb waiter *n* an elevator for carrying food, plates, garbage etc between the floors of a building.

dumdum (bullet) [ˈdʌmdʌm-] *n* a bullet that expands when it hits a person's body.

dummy [ˈdʌmɪ] (*pl* **dummies**) ◇ *adj* **a dummy gun/drawer etc** a gun / drawer etc that looks real but cannot be used. ◇ *n* **-1.** [in a store window] a model of a person, usually used for displaying clothes □ *a tailor's dummy* □ *a ventriloquist's dummy.* **-2.** [of a gun, door] something that looks real but is in fact a toy or model. **-3.** GB [for babies] a specially shaped piece of rubber that is given to a baby to suck. **-4.** SPORT a trick in which a player pretends to move or pass the ball in order to make an opponent move in the wrong direction. ◇ *vt* SPORT to make <sb> move in the wrong direction by using a dummy.

dummy run *n* a rehearsal or trial of something new to find out if it works.

dump [dʌmp] ◇ *n* **-1.** [for garbage] a place, usually an area of open ground, where garbage and waste materials can be left □ *a garbage dump.* **-2.** [for weapons] a place where weapons, military supplies etc are stored □ *an ammunition dump.* **-3.** a place that one thinks is dirty and unpleasant (informal use) □ *This hotel's a real dump.*

◇ *vt* **-1.** [bag, laundry, suitcase] to put <sthg> down in a careless and untidy way; [load, sand] to unload <sthg> □ *She dumped her* books on my desk. □ *The truck dumped its load of coal.* -2. [garbage, car] to throw <sthg> away, especially in a careless or dangerous way □ *Radioactive waste is being dumped off our shores.* -3. BUSINESS [meat, butter, cars] to sell <goods> abroad in large quantities and at low prices. -4. COMPUTING to transfer <data> from the memory of a computer to a disk or printer. -5. [girlfriend, boyfriend] to finish a relationship with <sb> (informal use).

♦ **dumps** *npl* **to be (down) in the dumps** to feel sad and depressed.

dumper (truck) *n* GB = dump truck.

dumping ['dʌmpɪŋ] *n* the act of throwing away something that is no longer wanted or useful □ *nuclear dumping.* ■ **'No dumping'** a phrase used on signs to show that dumping of waste materials is not allowed there.

dumping ground *n* a place where garbage or unwanted objects are left.

dumpling ['dʌmplɪŋ] *n* a ball of dough cooked and served with meat or soup or as a dessert.

Dumpster™ ['dʌmpstə'] *n* US a large container that is used for putting garbage in, e.g. during building work.

dump truck US, **dumper (truck)** ['dʌmpə'-] GB *n* a truck with a container for carrying its load that can be tilted so that the load slides out.

dumpy ['dʌmpɪ] (*compar* **dumpier**, *superl* **dumpiest**) *adj* [person] who looks short and fat (informal use).

dunce [dʌns] *n* a person who one thinks is slightly stupid and unable to learn things very quickly.

dune [dʲuːn] *n* a hill of sand in the desert or near the ocean, made by the wind.

dung [dʌŋ] *n* excrement from animals such as cows and horses.

dungarees [,dʌŋɡə'riːz] *npl* -1. US heavy jeans. -2. GB trousers made of strong material that have a piece of material covering the chest and are held up by shoulder straps.

dungeon ['dʌndʒən] *n* an underground prison, often in a castle.

dunk [dʌŋk] *vt* [cookie, cake] to dip <sthg> into a cup of tea, coffee etc before eating it.

Dunkirk [dʌn'kɜː'k] a port in northern France, on the English Channel. Many Allied soldiers were rescued from Dunkirk in a military operation in World War II. POPULATION: 71,071.

duo ['dʲuːoʊ] *n* -1. [of performers] two actors, singers, musicians etc who perform together. -2. [of people] two people, when they are talked about together.

duodenal ulcer [,dʲuːoʊdiːnl-] *n* an ulcer in the part of the small intestine that is just below the stomach.

dupe [dʲuːp] ◇ *vt* to trick <sb> into doing something □ *He duped me into believing him.* ◇ *n* a person who is duped.

duplex ['dʲuːpleks] *n* US -1. an apartment that has rooms on two floors. -2. a house that shares a wall with a neighboring house.

duplicate [*adj* & *n* 'dʲuːplɪkət, *vb* 'dʲuːplɪkeɪt]

◇ *adj* **a duplicate copy/key etc** a copy/key etc that is an exact copy of something and looks just like it. ◇ *n* a duplicate copy of something. ■ **in duplicate** with a duplicate copy □ *Applications should be submitted in duplicate.* ◇ *vt* -1. [key, document] to make an exact copy of <sthg>. -2. [work] to do <sthg that has already been done>, so that it is done twice.

duplication [,dʲuːplɪ'keɪʃn] *n* [of work, a key, document] *see* **duplicate** □ *an unnecessary duplication of effort.*

duplicity [dʲuː'plɪsətɪ] *n* deceitful behavior (formal use).

Dur *abbr of* **Durham.**

durability [,dʲʊərə'bɪlətɪ] *n* [of a car, material, relationship] the ability of something to last for a long time.

durable ['dʲʊərəbl] *adj* [product, material] that is strong and can last for a long time.

duration [dʲʊ'reɪʃn] *n* [of a war, the winter, an illness] the period of time that something lasts □ *He kept silent for the duration of the meeting.*

duress [dʲʊ'res] *n* **to do sthg under duress** to do sthg because one has been forced to do it.

Durex™ ['dʲʊəreks] *n* -1. GB a condom. -2. AUS clear sticky tape used for sticking paper onto something.

Durham [US 'dɜːrəm, GB 'dʌrəm] -1. a county in northeastern England. SIZE: 2,436 sq kms. POPULATION: 598,700. ADMINISTRATIVE CENTER: Durham. -2. a city in the county of Durham, England, famous for its cathedral and university. POPULATION: 26,000.

during ['dʲʊərɪŋ] *prep* -1. **I worked there during the summer** I worked there all through the summer. -2. **she died during the night** she died at some point in the night.

dusk [dʌsk] *n* the last period of daylight, just before it becomes completely dark.

dusky ['dʌskɪ] (*compar* **duskier**, *superl* **duskiest**) *adj* [skin, complexion] that is dark rather than light or bright (literary use).

dust [dʌst] ◇ *n* -1. [in the road] very small pieces of earth or sand □ *The cars disappeared in a cloud of dust.* -2. [on furniture] fine powder made up of particles of dirt □ *There was dust everywhere.* ■ **to gather dust** [ornaments, books] to become dusty; [idea, plan] to remain unused for a long period. -3. [from a substance] fine powder made up of tiny pieces of substances such as gold, coal etc □ *chalk/coal/gold dust.* ◇ *vt* -1. [furniture, ornament] to clean <sthg> by wiping it with a cloth or brush to remove the dust. -2. **to dust sthg with sthg** [with powder, sugar] to cover sthg with a thin layer of sthg.

♦ **dust off** *vt sep* -1. **to dust sb/sthg off** to clean the dust or dirt from sb/sthg □ *I got up off the floor and dusted myself off.* -2. **to dust sthg off** [suit, speech, plan] to try to make sthg appear new by cleaning it or by making a few changes.

dustbin ['dʌstbɪn] *n* GB a large container that is kept outside a house and is used for putting household garbage into.

Dust Bowl: the Dust Bowl the states in the central USA, including Oklahoma and Kansas, that suffered from dust storms and drought in the 1930s.

🎯 THE DUST BOWL
The Dust Bowl was an ecological disaster that affected the US states of Oklahoma, Kansas, Nebraska, and North and South Dakota. It was caused mainly by poor farming methods: farmers had removed millions of acres of grass to plant wheat, which does not hold the soil together well. When a drought came in the 1930s, the winds picked up the loose soil, causing dust storms that forced 60% of the population to leave the region. Most of these people, called "Okies," went to the West Coast of America to settle.

dustcart ['dʌstkɑːᵗt] *n* GB a truck that is used to collect the garbage from people's garbage cans.

dust cover *n* = dust jacket.

duster ['dʌstəʳ] *n* -1. [for dusting] a cloth for dusting. -2. US [for keeping clean] an item of clothing that is worn over ordinary clothes to keep them clean while one is working.

dust jacket *n* a paper cover that is wrapped around the hard covers of a book and often gives information about the book and its author.

dustman ['dʌstmən] (*pl* **dustmen** [-mən]) *n* GB a person whose job is to empty garbage from people's garbage cans.

dust mite *n* a very small insect that lives in carpets, beds etc and can cause attacks of asthma or allergies.

dustpan ['dʌstpæn] *n* a small flat container with a handle that is used with a small brush to sweep up dirt and garbage □ a dustpan and brush.

dustsheet ['dʌstʃiːt] *n* GB a large cloth used to cover furniture to protect it from dust.

dust storm *n* a violent weather condition where strong winds blow clouds of dust around.

dusty ['dʌstɪ] (*compar* **dustier**, *superl* **dustiest**) *adj* [room, furniture, surface] that is covered with dust because it has not been used or cleaned for a long time □ It's probably dusty, so be careful with your coat!

Dutch [dʌtʃ] ◇ *npl* **the Dutch** people who come from the Netherlands. ◇ *n* the language of the Dutch. ◇ *adj*: Dutch bulbs/cheese. ◇ *adv* **to go Dutch** to share the cost of tickets, a meal etc when one goes out with somebody.

Dutch barn *n* GB a structure consisting of a metal frame with no walls and a curved roof that is used for storing crops on a farm.

Dutch courage *n* false courage that one gets by drinking alcohol (informal use).

Dutch elm disease *n* a disease that kills elms.

Dutchman ['dʌtʃmən] (*pl* **Dutchmen** [-mən]) *n* a man who comes from the Netherlands.

Dutchwoman ['dʌtʃwʊmən] (*pl* **Dutchwomen**) *n* a woman who comes from the Netherlands.

dutiful ['djuːtɪfl] *adj* [son, daughter] who is obedient and respectful, especially toward their family □ She gave a dutiful smile.

duty ['djuːtɪ] (*pl* **duties**) *n* -1. [of a person] a moral or legal responsibility □ As a citizen it's your duty to report the crime. □ Have you no sense of duty to your parents? ■ **to do one's duty** to do what one feels it is one's responsibility to do □ I was only doing my duty, please don't take it personally. -2. [of a job] the work that somebody has to do as part of their job □ The policeman/soldier/nurse reported for duty. ■ **to be on/off duty** [policeman, nurse] to be working/not working □ She goes off duty at 11 o'clock. -3. [on goods] a tax paid on goods or services □ customs/stamp/death duty.
◆ **duties** *npl* the particular tasks or responsibilities that are part of somebody's job □ Your duties will include dealing with customers.

duty bound *adj* **to be duty bound to do sthg** to have to do sthg because one feels it is one's responsibility □ Susan felt duty bound to tell me exactly what happened.

duty-free *adj* [alcohol, tobacco, perfume] that is sold without tax, usually in airports or on ships.

duty officer *n* GB [in the police, army] the officer on duty or in charge.

duvet [US duˈveɪ, GB ˈduːveɪ] *n* GB a large bed cover that is filled with feathers or man-made fiber □ a duvet cover.

DVLA (*abbr of* **Driver and Vehicle Licensing Agency**) *n* **the DVLA** the British government department responsible for collecting road tax and keeping records of drivers' licenses and vehicles.

DVM (*abbr of* **Doctor of Veterinary Medicine**) *n* a postgraduate degree in veterinary medicine; a person who has this degree.

dwarf [dwɔːᵗf] (*pl* **dwarfs** OR **dwarves** [dwɔːᵗvz]) ◇ *adj* **a dwarf plant/animal** a plant/animal that never grows to be as large as other members of the same species. ◇ *n* -1. ▼ a person who does not grow to normal height (offensive use). -2. in folk legends, a small man with a beard and a pointed hat who often have magical powers. ◇ *vt* to be much bigger in size than <sthg>, and so make it look very small □ The house is dwarfed by the new office buildings.

dwell [dwel] (*pt* & *pp* **dwelt** OR **dwelled**) *vi* to live in a particular place (literary use).
◆ **dwell on** *vt fus* **to dwell on sthg** [on the past, a problem] to think or talk for too long about sthg □ Try not to dwell on it.

-dweller [-ˈdweləʳ] *suffix* **a city/cave-dweller** a person who lives in a city/cave.

dwelling ['dwelɪŋ] *n* a place where somebody lives (literary use).

dwelt [dwelt] *past tense & past participle of* **dwell**.

DWI *n* US *abbr of* **driving while intoxicated**.

dwindle ['dwɪndl] *vi* [supply, money, number of people] to gradually become smaller in amount or number □ *Movie audiences started to dwindle with the introduction of video.*

dwindling ['dwɪndlɪŋ] *adj* [supply, money, number] that is gradually becoming smaller in amount or number □ *our ever-dwindling group of unmarried friends.*

dye [daɪ] ◇ *n* a substance for changing the color of hair, clothes etc. ◇ *vt* to change the color of <clothes, hair> etc using dye □ *She dyed her hair red.*

dyed [daɪd] *adj* [cloth, wool, hair] that has been dyed □ *Her hair was obviously dyed.*

dying ['daɪɪŋ] ◇ *cont* → **die**. ◇ *adj* -1. [person, animal, plant] that is going to die soon □ *He visited his dying father in the hospital.* -2. [language, tradition, industry] that is becoming less important and does not seem likely to continue in the future. ◇ *npl* **the dying** people who are dying.

dyke [daɪk] *n* = **dike**.

dynamic [daɪ'næmɪk] *adj* [person] who has a lot of energy and ideas.

◆ **dynamics** *npl* the study of movement, forces, and energy.

dynamism ['daɪnəmɪzm] *n*: see **dynamic**.

dynamite ['daɪnəmaɪt] ◇ *n* -1. an explosive, often in the form of a stick, that is used e.g. in mining □ *a stick of dynamite.* -2. **to be dynamite** [person, story, piece of news] to be very exciting or impressive □ *You were dynamite!* ◇ *vt* [building, bridge, mountain] to make <sthg> explode using dynamite.

dynamo ['daɪnəmoʊ] (*pl* **dynamos**) *n* a device that converts the movement of a machine or vehicle into electricity.

dynasty [US 'daɪnəstɪ, GB 'dɪn-] (*pl* **dynasties**) *n* a series of rulers of a country who are all from the same family.

dysentery [US 'dɪsnterɪ, GB -ntrɪ] *n* a disease of the intestines that causes severe diarrhea.

dyslexia [dɪs'leksɪə] *n* a disorder that makes it hard for people to see the difference between letters, and so makes reading difficult.

dyslexic [dɪs'leksɪk] *adj* [person] who suffers from dyslexia.

dyspepsia [dɪs'pepsɪə] *n* indigestion (formal or technical use).

E

e [iː] (*pl* **e's** OR **es**), **E** [iː] (*pl* **E's** OR **Es**) *n* the fifth letter of the English alphabet.

◆ **E** ◇ *n* MUSIC one of the notes in Western music. ◇ *abbr of* **east**.

E111 [ˌiːwʌnɪ'levn] *n* a form that an EU citizen fills out to get the right to health care while they are visiting other EU countries.

ea. *abbr of* **each**.

each [iːtʃ] ◇ *det* **each child** all the children in a group considered separately (used of a group of two or more people or things) □ *Each contestant has to answer three questions.* □ *Each time I see that movie I cry.* ◇ *pron: Each of them has his/her/their own ideas.* ◇ *adv: We were each given a present.* □ *We can't share it; we need one each.* □ *The books cost £10 each.*

◆ **each other** *pron* **Tom and Carol love each other** Tom loves Carol and Carol loves Tom (used of two or more people in a group) □ *Mike and I have known each other for years.* □ *We were getting on each other's nerves.*

eager ['iːgər] *adj* [person, expression, behavior] that shows enthusiasm about something □ *He is eager for success/eager to meet you.*

eagerly ['iːgəlɪ] *adv* [talk, plan] see **eager** □ *We waited eagerly for the results.*

eagle ['iːgl] *n* a large bird of prey with broad wings and a hooked beak.

eagle-eyed [-'aɪd] *adj* [person] who has very good eyesight or is good at noticing small details.

Eagle Scout *n* in the USA, the highest rank for a boy scout.

eaglet ['iːglət] *n* a young eagle.

Ealing comedy ['iːlɪŋ-] *n* one of several movies made at Ealing Studios, London, in the 1940s and 1950s, that are known for their gentle humor.

E and OE (*abbr of* **errors and omissions excepted**) a phrase written on an invoice to show that the company is not responsible for any mistakes in it.

ear [ɪər] *n* -1. [of a person, animal] one of the two parts of the body on each side of the head that are used for hearing. ■ **to play by ear** MUSIC to play a piece of music on an instrument without any written music. ■ **to play it by ear** to go into a situation without a fixed plan and to decide what to do according to what happens □ *Let's play it by ear and see what happens when we get there.* ■ **to go in one ear and out the other** [advice, information] to be forgotten immediately (informal use) □ *You can talk to him all you like, but it just goes in one ear and out the other.* ■ **to have** OR **keep one's ear to the ground** to pay attention in order to find out information about something □ *I don't know of anything right now, but I'll keep my ear to the ground for you.* ■ **to have sb's ear** to be able to influence sb important. ■ **to have an ear for sthg** [for music, languages] to be good at appreciating, learning, or reproducing sthg that is connected with sound □ *Jenny has a very good ear for music.* -2. [of wheat] the top part of a stem of wheat or corn that contains the grains used for food.

earache ['ɪəreɪk] *n* a pain inside the ear.

eardrum ['ɪədrʌm] *n* a piece of tightly-stretched skin inside the ear that helps one to hear sounds.

Earhart ['eəhɑːrt], **Amelia** (1898–1937) a US

pilot who was the first woman to fly across the Atlantic Ocean alone.

earl [ɜːʳl] *n* a British nobleman who ranks below a marquess and above a viscount.

earlier [ˈɜːʳlɪəʳ] ◇ *adj* -1. a word used to refer to a period or point in time before the present one, or before one in the past □ *as I said on an earlier occasion.* -2. [version, model, interview] that existed, happened etc before something similar that has already been mentioned □ *according to earlier reports.* ◇ *adv* at a point in time before the present one, or before one in the past □ *as I mentioned earlier* □ *earlier that day.* ■ **earlier on** at an earlier time □ *He was here earlier on.*

earliest [ˈɜːʳlɪəst] ◇ *adj* -1. first □ *I'll speak to her at the earliest opportunity.* ■ **at your earliest convenience** as soon as you can. -2. that happens, exists etc before everybody or everything else of the same type □ *The earliest train doesn't leave until 8 a.m.* ◇ *adv* **at the earliest** not before the time stated □ *I won't be there until Monday at the earliest.*

earlobe [ˈɪəʳloʊb] *n* the soft rounded piece of flesh at the bottom of the ear.

early [ˈɜːʳlɪ] (*compar* **earlier**, *superl* **earliest**) ◇ *adj* -1. **to be early** to arrive before the expected or usual time □ *John was early for his appointment.* □ *She was ten minutes early.* -2. [hour, breakfast, train] that exists, happens etc at the beginning of the day □ *I've got an early start tomorrow.* -3. [memory, invention, movie] that is from the beginning of a particular period of time, e.g. somebody's life or career □ *I prefer her early poems.* □ *the early morning mist* □ *The vase is early Victorian.* ◇ *adv* -1. [leave, arrive] before the time that is expected or usual □ *Mail early for Christmas.* □ *The meeting ended early.* -2. [set off, rise] at the beginning of the morning □ *I got up early.* -3. at or near the beginning of a period □ *She's flying over in early November.* □ *She's arriving early this evening.* □ *We should hear early next week.* ■ **as early as** at a time that is sooner than is usual or expected □ *The job could be finished as early as Friday.* ■ **early on** at or near the beginning □ *It was something she wrote early on in her career.*

early closing day *n* in Britain, the one day each week on which most of the shops in a town close earlier than normal.

early retirement *n* **to take early retirement** to retire before the official retirement age.

early warning system *n* a military radar system that is designed to notice signs of an enemy attack as soon as possible.

earmark [ˈɪəʳmɑːʳk] *vt* **to be earmarked for sthg** [money, land] to be reserved for a particular purpose in the future.

earn [ɜːʳn] *vt* -1. [wage, salary] to receive <a sum of money> as a payment for working □ *She earns £30,000 a year.* -2. BUSINESS to produce <interest, a profit, or a sum of money> for a person, company etc □ *His investments earned him a lot of money.* -3. [respect, praise, reputation] to get <sthg that one deserves> as

a result of one's actions □ *She earned her place in the people's affections.*

earned income [ˌɜːʳnd-] *n* money that one receives for work one does.

earner [ˈɜːʳnəʳ] *n* -1. a person who earns money by working. -2. GB **a nice little earner** something that produces profits easily, e.g. a business (informal use).

earnest [ˈɜːʳnəst] *adj* [person, expression, attempt] that is serious and sincere □ *It is my earnest wish to make up for the damage I have done.*
◆ **in earnest** ◇ *adj* **to be in earnest** to be serious and not intended as a joke or to deceive somebody □ *Do you think he is in earnest?* ◇ *adv* [speak, begin] seriously; [rain, snow] heavily.

earnings [ˈɜːʳnɪŋz] *npl* the money that a person, company, or country earns □ *Do you have earnings from any other sources?*

earnings-related *adj* [payment, benefit] that is calculated in relation to one's earnings while one is in work.

Earp [ɜːʳp], **Wyatt** (1849–1929) a US lawman from the Wild West. He won a famous gun battle at the O.K. Corral in Tombstone, Arizona.

earphones [ˈɪəʳfoʊnz] *npl* a piece of equipment that fits directly over one's ears and is used for listening to recorded music or speech in private.

earplugs [ˈɪəʳplʌgz] *npl* small pieces of wax or foam that fit inside one's ears to protect them from loud noise or water □ *I wear earplugs in bed.* □ *a pair of earplugs.*

earring [ˈɪərɪŋ] *n* a piece of jewelry that people wear attached to their earlobe.

earshot [ˈɪəʳʃɒt] *n* **within/out of earshot** close enough/too far away to hear something that is being said □ *They moved out of earshot of the others.*

earsplitting [ˈɪəʳsplɪtɪŋ] *adj* [scream, noise] that is very loud and unpleasant to hear.

earth [ɜːʳθ] ◇ *n* -1. ASTRONOMY the planet that we live on □ *The Earth revolves around the Sun.* □ *the planet earth.* ■ **who/what/where etc on earth** a phrase used when asking a question to emphasize that one does not know or understand something, or that one is annoyed or surprised □ *Where on earth did I put those keys?* □ *What on earth is he talking about?* □ *How on earth did you do that?* ■ **to cost/charge the earth** GB to cost/charge a very large amount of money. -2. [in an area] the surface of an area of land □ *The explosion made the earth shake.* -3. [on the ground] the substance that covers the surface of land in which plants grow □ *The carrots still had earth on them.* -4. ELECTRICITY the wire that connects an electrical appliance or plug to the ground. ◇ *vt* GB to connect <an appliance, plug> etc to the ground with an electrical wire □ *All appliances must be earthed.*

earthenware [ˈɜːʳθnweəʳ] ◇ *adj* [vase, casserole,

plate] made of baked clay. ◇ *n* objects made of baked clay, e.g. vases or plates.

earthling ['ɜːθlɪŋ] *n* in science fiction, a human being who lives on the Earth.

earthly ['ɜːθlɪ] *adj* -1. [life, power] that is connected with material things rather than with the spirit □ *leaving behind all her earthly possessions.* -2. **no earthly reason/purpose etc** no possible or real reason/purpose etc □ *There is no earthly reason why I shouldn't go.* □ *He doesn't have an earthly chance.*

earthquake ['ɜːθkweɪk] *n* a movement below the surface of the earth that causes the ground to shake.

earthshattering ['ɜːθʃætərɪŋ] *adj* [news, event] that seems very important and surprising or shocking (informal use) □ *It's hardly earthshattering news.*

earth tremor *n* a small earthquake.

earthward(s) ['ɜːθwəd(z)] *adv* [fly, fall] down toward the earth.

earthworks ['ɜːθwɜːks] *npl* in the past, masses of earth that were built for defense.

earthworm ['ɜːθwɜːm] *n* a common type of worm that lives in soil.

earthy ['ɜːθɪ] (*compar* **earthier**, *superl* **earthiest**) *adj* -1. [person, humor] that is open about subjects that embarrass some people □ *She has a really earthy sense of humor.* -2. [taste, smell] that is like earth.

earwax ['ɪəwæks] *n* the natural wax in people's ears.

earwig ['ɪəwɪg] *n* a small thin insect with two sharp points at the end of its tail.

ease [iːz] ◇ *n* -1. a lack of difficulty in doing something □ *The new entrance is designed for ease of access.* ■ **to do sthg with ease** to do sthg easily □ *Her horse jumped the fence with ease.* -2. **a life of ease** a life of comfort and relaxation. ■ **to be** OR **feel at ease** to feel confident and relaxed □ *Try to make the candidates feel at ease during the interview.* ■ **to be** OR **to feel ill at ease** to feel nervous and uncomfortable □ *Simon felt very ill at ease surrounded by all those strange people.* ◇ *vt* -1. [pain, tension] to make <sthg> less severe □ *The codeine should help to ease the pain.* -2. [patient, piano, sculpture] to move <sb/sthg> carefully and slowly into a particular position □ *She eased the window open.* □ *She eased herself into the armchair.* ◇ *vi* [problem, pain, rain] to become less severe □ *The rain showed no sign of easing.*

◆ **ease off** *vi* [problem, pain, rain] = **ease** □ *The rain started to ease off slightly.*

◆ **ease up** *vi* -1. [pressure, work, traffic] to become less intense □ *Things at work should ease up in a day or two.* -2. [person] to become less active; to relax □ *You should really ease up or you'll give yourself an ulcer.* ■ **to ease up on sb** to treat sb less severely (informal use) □ *Try to ease up on David a little — he's only a boy.*

easel ['iːzl] *n* a piece of equipment that is used to support a picture while it is being painted.

easily ['iːzəlɪ] *adv* -1. [cope, succeed, win] with-out difficulty □ *That problem is easily solved.* -2. **easily the best** the best without doubt □ *She's easily the most suitable of the three candidates.* -3. [speak, behave] in a confident way without showing tension or worry.

east [iːst] ◇ *n* -1. the direction the sun rises in □ *He looked toward the east.* -2. **the east** the part of a country or region that is nearest to the direction the sun rises in □ *The weather is worse in the east.* ◇ *adj* [side, coast] that is in or faces the east. ■ **an east wind** a wind that comes from the east. ◇ *adv* [face, travel] toward the east. ■ **east of sthg** situated to the east of sthg □ *We live 180 km east of the capital.*

◆ **East** *n* **the East** the eastern part of a country or region; the continent of Asia, especially when it is contrasted with Europe and the West; the countries of Eastern Europe and the area that used to be the USSR □ *East-West relations.*

East Anglia [-'æŋglɪə] a region of eastern England consisting of the counties of Norfolk and Suffolk, and parts of Essex and Cambridgeshire.

East Asia = Far East.

eastbound ['iːstbaʊnd] *adj* [road, direction] that leads toward the east; [train, traffic] that travels toward the east.

East Coast the eastern coast of the USA.

NOTE: When Americans refer to *the East Coast*, they usually mean the northeastern cities of Boston, New York, Philadelphia, and Washington D.C.

East End: the East End the eastern part of London, which was traditionally a working-class area.

Easter ['iːstər] *n* a Christian religious festival that is held to celebrate the resurrection of Christ after his death.

♥ EASTER

Easter is one of the most important religious festivals in the USA, Britain, and Australia, and Good Friday and Easter Monday are public holidays. Both the USA and Australia have the tradition of the Easter Bunny, who comes during the night and leaves Easter baskets or chocolate Easter eggs for children to find on Easter Sunday. Parents also hide colored hard-boiled eggs or chocolate Easter eggs in the house and backyard for children to "hunt." In the USA big parades are also held in cities like New York.

Easter basket *n* US a basket filled with candy that is left for children on Easter morning.

Easter bunny *n* US & AUS an imaginary rabbit that children believe brings Easter eggs.

Easter egg *n* a decorated egg, usually made of chocolate, that is given as a present at Easter.

Easter Island an island in the South Pacific Ocean, belonging to Chile. It is famous for the ancient stone statues found there. SIZE: 162.5 sq kms. POPULATION: 2,770.

easterly ['iːstəlɪ] *adj* -1. [place] that is in the

east; [direction] that is toward the east. **-2.** [wind] that comes from the east.

eastern ['iːstə^rn] *adj* that is in or from the east of a country or region.

◆ **Eastern** *adj* **-1.** [religion, philosophy, culture] that is found in or comes from Asia. **-2.** that relates to the countries in the east of Europe □ *Eastern European languages.*

Eastern bloc: the Eastern bloc the USSR and the countries of Eastern Europe that used to have close political and economic links with each other □ *Eastern bloc countries.*

Eastern Europe the eastern part of Europe, consisting of countries that used to have Communist governments, e.g. Poland, the Czech Republic, Slovakia, Hungary, Romania, and the Balkan states.

Eastern Seaboard *n* **the Eastern Seaboard** the regions along the east coast of the USA or Australia.

Easter Sunday *n* the day every year when Christians celebrate the resurrection of Christ.

East Germany the eastern part of Germany that was a Communist republic from 1949 until the reunification of Germany in 1990.

East River: the East River the river between Manhattan and Long Island, USA.

East Timor [-'tiːmɔː^r] the eastern part of the island of Timor, in southeast Asia, that was annexed by Indonesia in 1975.

eastward ['iːstwə^rd] ◇ *adj* [side, slope] that faces the east; [direction, journey] that goes toward the east. ◇ *adv* toward the east.

eastwards ['iːstwə^rdz] *adv* toward the east □ *You can travel eastwards for days and see no one.*

easy ['iːzɪ] (*compar* **easier**, *superl* **easiest**) ◇ *adj* **-1.** [task, question, victory] that is not difficult or complicated and causes no problems □ *The new material is very easy to clean/use.* □ *She's nice, and extremely easy to get on with.* **-2. an easy time/life** a time/life that is pleasant and relaxing, and involves no problems or effort □ *I'll do anything for an easy life.* **-3.** [person, manner, conversation] that is relaxed and shows no tension or worry.
◇ *adv* (informal use) **to go easy on sb** to treat sb less severely than usual, especially because they are having problems □ *Go easy on Anthony, he's not been too well recently.* ■ **to go easy on sthg** not to use too much of sthg □ *Go easy on the chili sauce, won't you?* ■ **to take it** OR **things easy** to relax □ *Why don't you take it easy for a while and I'll make dinner.*

easy chair *n* a large comfortable armchair.

easygoing [ˌiːzɪ'gəʊɪŋ] *adj* [person, attitude] that is tolerant and relaxed.

eat [iːt] (*pt* **ate**, *pp* **eaten**) ◇ *vt* to take in <food> through one's mouth □ *He was eating a sandwich.* ◇ *vi* to eat food; to have a meal □ *She was too sick to eat.* □ *Where should we eat tonight?*

◆ **eat away** *vt sep* **-1. to eat sthg away** [metal, paint, plastic] to remove the surface of sthg

slowly. **-2. to eat sthg away** [savings, capital] to use all of sthg slowly.

◆ **eat into** *vt fus* **to eat into sthg** to eat sthg away.

◆ **eat out** *vi* to eat a meal, especially an evening meal, at a restaurant □ *Let's eat out this evening.*

◆ **eat up** *vt sep* **-1. to eat sthg up** [meal, vegetables] to eat all of sthg. **-2. to eat sthg up** [money, time, energy] to use a lot of sthg very quickly.

eaten ['iːtn] *past participle of* **eat.**

eater ['iːtə^r] *n* a person who eats something or who eats in a particular way □ *He's a slow/messy/meat eater.*

eatery ['iːtrɪ] (*pl* **eateries**) *n* a place where people pay to have a meal, e.g. a restaurant or café.

eating apple ['iːtɪŋ-] *n* an apple that is sweet enough to be eaten without being cooked.

eau de cologne [ˌəʊdəkə'ləʊn] *n* a type of light perfume that makes one feel fresh.

eaves [iːvz] *npl* the bottom edges of a roof.

eavesdrop ['iːvzdrɒp] (*pt* & *pp* **eavesdropped**, *cont* **eavesdropping**) *vi* to listen secretly to what is being said □ *I caught him eavesdropping on us/our conversation.*

ebb [eb] ◇ *n* [of the sea] the movement of water away from the shore when the tide is going out. ■ **the ebb and flow of sthg** the good and bad periods of sthg that follow each other. ■ **to be at a low ebb** [person] to be unhappy; [business, relationship] to be less successful than before or than usual. ◇ *vi* **-1.** [sea, tide] to flow away from the shore. **-2.** [strength, feeling] to become weaker and disappear gradually (literary use) □ *The pain ebbed away.*

ebb tide *n* a tide that is going out.

ebony ['ebənɪ] ◇ *adj* [hair, skin] black (literary use). ◇ *n* a very hard dark wood.

ebullient [ɪ'bʊlɪənt] *adj* [person, wit, manner] that is lively, cheerful, and enthusiastic.

EC *n abbr of* **European Community.**

eccentric [ɪk'sentrɪk] ◇ *adj* [person, behavior, appearance] that people think is strange, especially in an amusing way. ◇ *n* an eccentric person □ *He's a harmless eccentric.*

eccentricity [ˌeksen'trɪsətɪ] (*pl* **eccentricities**) *n* **-1.** *see* **eccentric. -2.** an eccentric habit, action, or way of thinking □ *It's just one of his little eccentricities.*

ecclesiastic(al) [ɪˌkliːzɪ'æstɪk(l)] *adj* [music, architecture] that is connected with the Christian church.

ECG *n abbr of* **electrocardiograph.**

ECGD (*abbr of* **Export Credits Guarantee Department**) *n* the British government department that protects British exporters against nonpayment by their clients.

echelon ['eʃəlɒn] *n* a level in an organization or a society where people have a particular amount of power or responsibility □ *a member of the upper echelons of society.*

echo ['ekəʊ] (*pl* **echoes**, *pt* & *pp* **echoed**, *cont* echoing) ◇ *n* -1. [of a sound] a sound that is a repetition of another sound reflected off a surface in a large area such as a cave □ *Shout something to see if there's an echo.* -2. [of a past event] something that reminds people of somebody or something in the past □ *The situation had unfortunate echoes of my previous marriage.* ◇ *vt* [comment, phrase] to repeat <sb's words or opinion>, usually to show agreement □ *I'd like to echo what's just been said.* ◇ *vi* -1. [sound] to be repeated as an echo, often a number of times □ *His voice echoed around the building.* -2. [place] to be filled with echoes □ *The corridor echoed with footsteps.*

éclair [eɪ'kleəʳ] *n* a long thin cake made of light pastry, filled with cream, and often with chocolate on the top □ *a chocolate éclair.*

eclectic [ɪ'klektɪk] *adj* [style, method, taste] that includes what seems best from many different systems or traditions □ *He has very eclectic tastes in music.*

eclipse [ɪ'klɪps] ◇ *n* -1. ASTRONOMY [of the Sun] a natural event in which the light of the Sun is blocked when the Moon passes between the Sun and the Earth □ *a solar eclipse.* -2. [of the Moon] a natural event in which the light of the Moon is blocked by the Earth moving between the Sun and Moon □ *a lunar eclipse.* ■ **a total/partial eclipse** an eclipse in which the Sun or Moon is completely/partially blocked from view. -3. [of a person, organization] a loss of importance or status. ◇ *vt* [person, organization, success] to become more important or influential than <sb/sthg> □ *The announcement was completely eclipsed by the news from the war zone.*

ecological [,iːkə'lɒdʒɪkl] *adj* -1. [balance, damage, study] that is connected with ecology. -2. [group, movement] that aims to preserve the environment.

ecologically [,iːkə'lɒdʒɪklɪ] *adv* **ecologically friendly** [product] that does not damage the environment.

ecologist [ɪ'kɒlədʒɪst] *n* -1. SCIENCE a person who studies ecology. -2. a person who believes that the environment should be preserved.

ecology [ɪ'kɒlədʒɪ] *n* -1. [of an area] the balance of relationships between plants, animals, people, and their environment □ *the ecology of the region.* -2. SCIENCE the scientific study of the balance of the environment.

economic [,iːkə'nɒmɪk] *adj* -1. [policy, forecast, crisis] that is connected with the financial state of a country or region □ *The government is leading us into economic ruin.* -2. [service, rate] that makes enough money to be worthwhile □ *It isn't economic to sell at that price.*

economical [,iːkə'nɒmɪkl] *adj* -1. [car, method, product] that saves money because it is cheap to use □ *an economical use of resources* □ *It is more economical to buy in bulk.* -2. [person] who is careful not to waste money □ *I try to be as economical as possible with my grant.*

economics [,iːkə'nɒmɪks] ◇ *n* the study of

how wealth is created and used in a society. ◇ *npl* [of a plan, business] the economic facts that need to be considered □ *You have to get the economics right.*

economist [ɪ'kɒnəmɪst] *n* a person who studies or writes about economics.

economize, -ise [ɪ'kɒnəmaɪz] *vi* to save money or resources by only buying or using things that are necessary. ■ **to economize on sthg** to use less of sthg than before; to spend less money on sthg than before □ *We're going to have to economize on fuel.*

economy [ɪ'kɒnəmɪ] (*pl* **economies**) *n* -1. the financial state or system of a country or region □ *the Far Eastern economies.* -2. a careful use of money, time, or effort in order to avoid waste □ *We'll have to introduce some economy measures to stay within the budget.* □ *Buying small packages is a false economy.* □ *We need to make some economies.* ■ **economies of scale** savings that are made by producing something in large quantities.

economy class *n* the cheapest class of travel by plane.

economy drive *n* an effort, especially by a company, to save money □ *We're on an economy drive at the moment.*

economy-size(d) *adj* [pack, jar] that is bigger than the usual size and contains goods that cost less than they do in a smaller container.

ecosystem ['iːkəʊsɪstəm] *n* all the people, animals, and plants in an area, and their relationships with each other and with their environment.

ecstasy ['ekstəsɪ] (*pl* **ecstasies**) *n* -1. a feeling of very great happiness and enjoyment. ■ **to go into ecstasies about sthg** to be full of enthusiasm and praise for sthg □ *Laura was in ecstasies over the new furniture.* -2. DRUGS an illegal stimulant drug in the form of pills, taken especially by young people who are dancing to loud rhythmic music.

ecstatic [ek'stætɪk] *adj* [person, feeling, shout] that shows great happiness and excitement about something □ *The crowd was ecstatic when the band came back onstage for an encore.*

ecstatically [ek'stætɪklɪ] *adv* [shout, dance] *see* **ecstatic.**

ECT (*abbr of* **electroconvulsive therapy**) *n* a method of treating mental illness by passing an electric current through the brain.

ectopic pregnancy [ek'tɒpɪk-] *n* a pregnancy in which the fetus grows outside the womb.

ECU, ecu [US eɪ'kuː, GB 'ekjuː] (*abbr of* **European Currency Unit**) *n* a unit of money based on the value of several currencies in the European Union. It was replaced in 1995 by the Euro.

Ecuador ['ekwədɔːʳ] a country in northwestern South America, on the Pacific Ocean. SIZE: 270,670 sq kms. POPULATION: 10,800,000 (*Ecuadoreans*). CAPITAL: Quito. MAIN CITY: Guayaquil. LANGUAGE: Spanish. CURRENCY: sucre.

ecumenical [,ekjə'menɪkl] *adj* [service, movement] that aims to unite different Christian churches □ *ecumenical dialog between churches.*

eczema [US ɪg'ziːmə, GB 'eksɪmə] *n* a skin disease that produces rough, red, itchy patches.

ed. -1. *abbr of* **edited. -2.** *abbr of* **edition. -3.** *abbr of* **editor.**

eddy ['edɪ] (*pl* **eddies**, *pt* & *pp* **eddied**) ◇ *n* a circular movement in water or in the air. ◇ *vi* [water, wind] to move in eddies.

Eddy ['edɪ], **Mary Baker** (1821–1910) a US religious leader who started the Christian Science Church.

Eden ['iːdn]: **(the Garden of) Eden** in the Bible, the garden where Adam and Eve lived happily until God told them to leave because they had disobeyed him.

edge [edʒ] ◇ *n* **-1.** [of a place, surface] the place where something, e.g. a cliff, table, or garden, stops or finishes □ *They built the factory at the edge of the town/at the water's edge.* ▪ **to be on the edge of sthg** [of war, disaster] to be at a point where sthg bad is likely to happen unless somebody does something to stop it □ *The country is on the edge of financial ruin.* **-2.** [of a blade] the sharp side of a blade that is used for cutting □ *This knife has a very sharp edge.* **-3. to have an edge over sb/sthg, to have the edge on sb/sthg** to have an advantage over sb/sthg; to be slightly better than sb/sthg □ *His experience abroad gives him an edge over the other applicants.* **-4.** [in somebody's voice] a tone of voice that shows impatience or anger □ *There was an unfamiliar edge to her voice.*
◇ *vi* to move very slowly and carefully in a particular direction □ *She edged along the crowded platform.*
◇ *vt* **to edge one's way = to edge.**
♦ **on edge** *adj* **to be on edge** to be tense and nervous and likely to become angry or upset □ *I was feeling slightly on edge.*

edged [edʒd] *adj* **to be edged with sthg** [with lace, blue] to have edges consisting of sthg □ *The lake was edged with reeds.*

edgeways ['edʒweɪz], **edgewise** ['edʒwaɪz] *adv* sideways □ *Try getting it through the door edgewise.*

edging ['edʒɪŋ] *n* [of paper, a blouse, tablecloth] something decorative that is along the edges of something else.

edgy ['edʒɪ] (*compar* **edgier**, *superl* **edgiest**) *adj* [person, manner, voice] that is nervous and anxious □ *I could see Paul was becoming a little edgy.*

edible ['edəbl] *adj* [food, plant] that is safe to eat □ *"Are these mushrooms edible?" — "I think so."*

edict ['iːdɪkt] *n* an order or instruction that is given by somebody in authority (formal use).

edifice ['edəfəs] *n* a large and impressive building (formal use).

edifying ['edəfaɪɪŋ] *adj* [talk, experience, book] that one learns from and finds helpful.

Edinburgh [US 'edɪnbɜːrə, GB -bərə] the capital of Scotland, in the southeast of the country. It is a financial center, and is famous for its annual arts festival. POPULATION: 420,000.

Edinburgh, Duke of the title given to Prince Philip, husband of Queen Elizabeth II.

Edinburgh Festival *n* **the Edinburgh Festival** an important arts festival that takes place every year in Edinburgh. It includes concerts, operas, plays, and alternative exhibitions and performances in informal venues.

Edison ['edɪsən], **Thomas Alva** (1847–1931) a US scientist and inventor whose most important inventions are the light bulb and the gramophone.

edit ['edɪt] *vt* **-1.** [book, article, text] to make corrections and improvements to <a piece of writing>. **-2.** [collection, anthology, series] to select material for <a book>. **-3.** TV, RADIO, & CINEMA to make <a movie, TV or radio program> etc by choosing pieces of recorded material and putting them together in a particular order. **-4.** JOURNALISM to be in charge of <a newspaper, magazine> etc.
♦ **edit out** *vt sep* **to edit sthg out** [word, section] to remove sthg from a film, recording, or piece of writing.

edition [ɪ'dɪʃn] *n* **-1.** [of a book, newspaper] a version of a book or newspaper that is printed at a particular time or place □ *Monday's edition of the "Herald Tribune"* □ *I've got the first edition in hardback.* **-2.** TV & RADIO one of a series of TV or radio shows that is broadcast at a particular time □ *tonight's edition of "Front Page".*

editor ['edɪtər] *n* **-1.** [of a newspaper] the person in charge of a newspaper or magazine. **-2.** [of a newspaper section] the journalist who is responsible for a particular section of a newspaper or magazine □ *the business/travel editor.* **-3.** [of a book] a person whose job is to edit text, e.g. books or articles. **-4.** [of an anthology] a person whose job is to select material for a book or series of books. **-5.** TV, RADIO, & CINEMA a person whose job is to edit movies, or TV or radio programs.

editorial [,edɪ'tɔːrɪəl] ◇ *adj* **-1.** [department, staff, budget] that is concerned with the production of written material, e.g. for a newspaper or series of books. **-2.** [outlook, change, policy] that concerns the content of a publication or broadcast. ◇ *n* a newspaper article that gives the opinion of the editor or owner on one of the stories in the newspaper.

EDP *n abbr of* **electronic data processing.**

EDT (*abbr of* **Eastern Daylight Time**) *n* the local daylight saving time in the eastern USA, Quebec, and Ontario.

educate ['edʒəkeɪt] *vt* **-1.** [pupil, student] to teach <sb> several subjects over a long period, usually at a school or college □ *He was educated privately.* **-2.** [people, the public] to tell <sb> about something, so that they will change the way they think or behave □ *a campaign to educate people about AIDS.*

educated ['edʒəkeɪtɪd] *adj* [person] who has had a good education, is intelligent, and knows a lot □ *a highly educated young woman.*

education [,edʒə'keɪʃn] *n* the process or result of being educated; the activity or profession of educating people □ *She had a good/an ex-*

pensive education. □ primary/secondary/higher education □ health education □ education cuts.

educational [ˌedʒə'keɪʃənl] adj -1. [toy, talk, experience] that teaches somebody something, especially because it is meant to do this. -2. [establishment, policy] see **education** □ I first came here on an educational visit.

educationalist [ˌedʒə'keɪʃnəlɪst] n a person who studies and writes about theories and methods of education.

educator ['edʒəkeɪtəʳ] n a teacher (formal use).

edutainment [ˌedʒə'teɪnmənt] n television programs, computer games etc that are designed to educate people in an entertaining way.

Edward VIII [ˌedwəʳdəɪ'eɪtθ] (1894–1972) King of Great Britain and Northern Ireland from January to December 1936, when he abdicated in order to marry a US divorcée, Mrs Wallis Simpson.

Edwardian [ed'wɔːʳdɪən] ◇ adj [building, style] that existed or was fashionable in Britain in the reign of Edward VII (1901–1910). ◇ n a person who lived in the Edwardian period.

EEC (abbr of **European Economic Community**) n **the EEC** the term that was used to refer to the EC when it consisted of six countries.

EEG n abbr of **electroencephalograph**.

eel [iːl] n a long thin fish that looks like a snake and lives in both fresh and salt water.

EENT (abbr of **eye, ear, nose, and throat**) n a department in a hospital that deals with diseases of the eyes, ears, nose, and throat □ an EENT specialist.

EEOC (abbr of **Equal Employment Opportunity Commission**) n **the EEOC** a US government body responsible for making sure that people of different sexes, races, colors etc are treated equally and fairly by employers.

eerie ['ɪərɪ] adj [place, music, atmosphere] that seems strange and slightly frightening □ The resemblance was eerie.

EET (abbr of **Eastern European Time**) n the standard local time in Eastern Europe.

efface [ɪ'feɪs] vt -1. [graffiti, footprint, word] to remove or cover up <a mark> so that it can no longer be seen. -2. [memory, thought] to get rid of <sthg> completely so that one no longer thinks about it.

effect [ɪ'fekt] ◇ n -1. [on a person, place] a result of an action, attitude, policy etc that changes somebody or something □ The effects on the local population were disastrous. □ This could have the effect of improving performance. ■ **to have an effect on sb/sthg** to influence or produce some change in sb/sthg □ His words had no effect on them at all. □ The campaign had an immediate effect on sales. ■ **to take effect** [law, rule] to become officially valid □ The new regulations take effect as of next April. ■ **to put sthg into effect** [policy, law, rule] to make sthg start working □ The embargo was put into effect with limited success. -2. [of lighting, a gesture, color] an impression that is given by the way somebody or something looks, sounds etc □ The lights created an eerie

effect. ■ **for effect** in order to create a particular impression or atmosphere, or get somebody's attention □ She just did it for effect. -3. **to the effect that...** with the meaning that... □ a statement to the effect that no action would be taken. ■ **to that effect** with that general meaning □ She called me an incompetent old fool, or words to that effect. ◇ vt [change, improvement] to succeed in making <sthg> happen (formal use).

effective [ɪ'fektɪv] adj -1. [method, system, policy] that works well and has the result that was wanted □ There's supposed to be a ban on the drugs, but it's not very effective. -2. [head, command, control] that exists or has a particular job, although this is not official □ He has effective control over the entire ship. -3. **to be effective** [law, ceasefire, policy] to be officially valid □ The changes become effective January 1.

effectively [ɪ'fektɪvlɪ] adv -1. [manage, work] well. -2. a word used to explain what the effect of something is □ Management refused to negotiate, effectively prolonging the strike. □ John is now effectively head of our department.

effectiveness [ɪ'fektɪvnəs] n [of a method, system, policy] see **effective** □ This demonstrates the effectiveness of our methods.

effeminate [ɪ'femɪnət] adj [man, boy] who behaves or sounds like a woman or girl (disapproving use).

effervesce [ˌefəʳ'ves] vi [drink, liquid] to produce bubbles.

effervescent [ˌefəʳ'vesnt] adj [drink, liquid] that has bubbles in it.

effete [ɪ'fiːt] adj [person] weak and powerless (disapproving use).

efficacious [efɪ'keɪʃəs] adj [medicine, method, solution] that achieves the result that is wanted (formal use).

efficacy ['efɪkəsɪ] n: see **efficacious**.

efficiency [ɪ'fɪʃnsɪ] n: see **efficient** □ Calls for greater efficiency are likely to be ignored.

efficient [ɪ'fɪʃnt] adj [person, machine, method] that works well and does not make mistakes or waste time, money etc □ Their organization is highly efficient. □ an efficient use of time/resources.

efficiently [ɪ'fɪʃntlɪ] adv [work, function] see **efficient** □ Tuning the engine makes it run more efficiently.

effigy ['efɪdʒɪ] (pl **effigies**) n -1. a figure or model made to look like a person one hates. -2. a statue or carving of somebody.

effluent ['efluənt] n liquid waste from a factory, sewage plant etc.

effort ['efəʳt] n -1. energy or time spent by somebody in trying to do something □ We put a lot of effort into making the conference a success. ■ **to be worth the effort** to be worth doing □ We could write to complain, but it isn't worth the effort. ■ **to make the effort to do sthg** to try more than usual to do sthg □ I decided to make the effort and go there myself. ■ **with effort** with difficulty □ He won their backing without too much effort. -2. an attempt to do something □ Despite all their efforts, they *lost the contract.* □ *Your essay was a pretty good/poor effort.* ■ **to make an/no effort to do sthg** to try/not try to do sthg □ *We're making a big effort to improve our performance.* □ *Some/No effort was made to improve output.*

effortless ['efə'tləs] *adj* [win, movement, success] that is done easily and without much effort, especially because one has a lot of skill □ *She danced with effortless grace.*

effortlessly ['efə'tləslı] *adv* [win, move, succeed] *see* **effortless** □ *He ran effortlessly past the winning post.*

effrontery [ı'frʌntərı] *n* behavior that one finds rude or disrespectful (formal use).

effusive [ı'fjuːsıv] *adj* [person, welcome, praise] that shows enthusiasm □ *We were given a most effusive welcome.*

EFL (*abbr of* **English as a foreign language**) *n* English taught to people who do not speak it as their first language □ *an EFL teacher.*

EFTA ['eftə] (*abbr of* **European Free Trade Association**) *n* an association of European countries that includes Austria, Finland, Iceland, Norway, Sweden, and Switzerland, and that has no restrictions on imports among members.

EFTPOS ['eftpɒs] (*abbr of* **electronic funds transfer at point of sale**) *n* a system that moves money from somebody's bank account by computer when they pay for goods using a credit card or debit card.

e.g. (*abbr of* **exempli gratia**) *adv* for example.

EGA (*abbr of* **enhanced graphics adapter**) *n* a system for displaying color graphics that is used in many personal computers.

egalitarian [ı,gælı'teərıən] *adj* [system, society] in which everybody has equal rights and opportunities; [person] who believes in equal rights and opportunities for everybody.

egg [eg] *n* -1. [of a bird, insect] a smooth rounded object produced by female birds, reptiles, fish, and insects, with an outer shell to protect the young creature that grows inside. -2. COOKING an egg, usually from a hen, when it is used as food □ *boiled/fried/poached eggs* □ *Beat the eggs and sugar together.* -3. BIOLOGY the reproductive cell in female mammals □ *an egg cell.*

◆ **egg on** *vt sep* **to egg sb on** to encourage sb to do something stupid or dangerous □ *He climbed onto the track, egged on by the others.*

eggcup ['egkʌp] *n* a small cup with no handle that is used for holding a boiled egg.

eggplant [US 'egplænt, GB -plɑːnt] *n* US a vegetable with shiny purple skin and soft white flesh.

eggshell ['egʃel] *n* the hard outer layer of an egg.

egg timer *n* a device for measuring the amount of time it should take for an egg to boil, often in the form of a glass cylinder that is half-filled with sand and has a narrow middle section.

egg whisk *n* a kitchen utensil that is used for beating eggs, cream etc.

egg white *n* the part of an egg that is clear and becomes white when cooked.

egg yolk *n* the yellow part of an egg.

EGM (*abbr of* **extraordinary general meeting**) *n* a meeting of a company's shareholders that is specially called to discuss an urgent matter such as a takeover bid.

ego ['iːgoʊ] (*pl* **egos**) *n* one's opinion of oneself □ *He has a big ego.*

egocentric [,iːgoʊ'sentrık] *adj* [person, behavior] selfish.

egoism ['iːgoʊızm] *n* = **egotism**.

egoist ['iːgoʊıst] *n* = **egotist**.

egoistic [,iːgoʊ'ıstık] *adj* [person, attitude, behavior] = **egotistic(al)**.

egotism ['iːgətızm] *n* the belief that one is better, more important, or more interesting than other people; behavior that shows this (disapproving use).

egotist ['iːgətıst] *n* a person who shows egotism □ *Tim? He's a terrible egotist, but he's OK.*

egotistic(al) [,iːgə'tıstık(l)] *adj* [person, attitude, behavior] *see* **egotist**.

ego trip *n* something one does only to make other people admire one more (informal and disapproving use) □ *The whole thing was just a big ego trip for her.*

Egypt ['iːdʒıpt] a country in North Africa, on the Mediterranean and the Red Sea, consisting mainly of desert. SIZE: 1,000,000 sq kms. POPULATION: 58,300,000 (*Egyptians*). CAPITAL: Cairo. LANGUAGE: Arabic. CURRENCY: Egyptian pound.

Egyptian [ı'dʒıpʃn] *n & adj*: *see* **Egypt**.

eh [eı] *excl* GB (informal use) -1. a word used to ask somebody to reply to or agree with what one has just said □ *Pretty impressive, eh?* -2. a word used to ask somebody to repeat something □ *"Your tea's ready, Grandad!"* — *"Eh?"*

eiderdown ['aıdə'daʊn] *n* a quilted bedcover, usually filled with feathers and placed on top of blankets and sheets.

eight [eıt] *num* the number 8; *see also* **five**.

eighteen [,eı'tiːn] *num* the number 18; *see also* **fifteen**.

eighteenth [,eı'tiːnθ] *num* 18th, number 18 in a series; *see also* **fifteenth**.

eighth [eıtθ] *num* 8th, number 8 in a series; *see also* **fifth**.

eighth note *n* US a musical note that lasts for an eighth of the time of a whole note.

eightieth ['eıtıəθ] *num* 80th, number 80 in a series; *see also* **fiftieth**.

eighty ['eıtı] (*pl* **eighties**) *num* the number 80; *see also* **fifty**.

Einstein ['aınstaın], **Albert** (1879–1955) a German physicist who became a Swiss citizen in 1901, and a US citizen in 1940. He is famous for his theories of relativity, and is considered one of the greatest scientists of the 20th century.

Eire ['eərə] the Irish Gaelic name for Ireland. It is often used to mean the Irish Republic.

Eisenhower ['aɪzənhaʊəʳ], **Dwight D.** (1890–1969) US President from 1953 to 1961, and an important general in World War II.

either [US 'iːðr, GB 'aɪðə] ◇ *det* -1. **take either book** take one of the two books, it does not matter which one □ *Either solution is perfectly feasible.* ■ **either way** whichever of two possible things happens □ *We can go out or stay in, I don't mind either way.* -2. **on either side** on both of the two sides □ *There was a door at either end of the corridor.* □ *I don't support either team.*
◇ *pron*: *"Which would you like?" — "Either will do."* □ *I've met both her sisters and I don't like either of them.* □ *Do/Does either of you want to come?*
◇ *adv* a word used at the end of negative statements that add information to other negative statements □ *Kim doesn't smoke and I don't either.*

◆ **either...or...** *conj* a phrase used to say what the only two possibilities are □ *Either we go today or we don't go at all.* □ *He's arriving either tomorrow or Monday.* ■ **I don't like either him or his wife** I don't like him and I also don't like his wife □ *I don't want either Chris or Mike to find out.*

ejaculate [ɪ'dʒækjəleɪt] ◇ *vt* to say or shout <sthg> suddenly (literary use). ◇ *vi* [man] to release semen through the penis during orgasm.

eject [ɪ'dʒekt] *vt* -1. [cassette, video, pilot] to send or push <sb/sthg> out from somewhere. -2. [intruder, troublemaker] to force <sb> to leave a building, club, or position of authority.

ejection seat [ɪ'dʒekʃn-] US, **ejector seat** [ɪ'dʒektəʳ-] GB *n* a special seat in some aircraft that can eject the pilot in an emergency.

eke [iːk] ◆ **eke out** ◇ *vt sep* to **eke sthg out** [food, money, fuel] to make one's supply of sthg last longer by using it carefully. ◇ *vt fus* to **eke out a living** OR **an existence** to live with very little money or supplies.

EKG *n* US = **ECG**.

el [el] (*abbr of* **elevated railroad**) *n* US **the el** a railway in Chicago, USA, that is built on supports above the streets (informal use).

elaborate [*adj* ɪ'læbərət, *vb* ɪ'læbəreɪt] ◇ *adj* [carving, ceremony, plan] that seems very complicated and detailed □ *Her designs were too elaborate.* ◇ *vi* to give more details about something to explain it more clearly □ *Would you care to you elaborate on that statement?*

elapse [ɪ'læps] *vi* [time, minute, day] to pass □ *How much time elapses between the dropping of the bomb and the explosion?*

elastic [ɪ'læstɪk] ◇ *adj* -1. [material] that stretches easily and then returns to its previous shape and size □ *the elastic properties of skin.* -2. [idea, plan, timetable] that can change easily so that there are no problems if something else changes □ *My views on the whole issue are fairly elastic.* ◇ *n* an elastic material, usually made partly of rubber, used in particular parts of clothes, e.g. around the waist or wrist □ *a piece of elastic.*

elasticated [ɪ'læstɪkeɪtəd] *adj* [sock, waistband] that has elastic in it so that it can stretch.

elastic band *n* GB a small thin band of rubber used to hold things together tightly.

elasticity [ˌiːlæ'stɪsətɪ] *n* [of a material] *see* **elastic** □ *The skin begins to lose its elasticity.*

elated [ɪ'leɪtəd] *adj* who is very happy and excited □ *I felt elated on hearing the news.*

elation [ɪ'leɪʃn] *n* a feeling of great happiness and excitement □ *a sense of elation.*

elbow ['elbəʊ] ◇ *n* -1. [of one's arm] the part where a joint lets one's arm bend. ■ **to rub elbows with sb** US to meet sb, especially a famous person, and socialize with them as an equal. -2. [of one's sleeve] the part of a sleeve that covers one's elbow. ◇ *vt* **to elbow sb aside** to push sb out of the way with one's elbow.

elbow grease *n* the effort needed to do hard physical work, especially when it involves rubbing (informal use).

elbowroom ['elbəʊruːm] *n* the space needed to move or work in easily, without being uncomfortable (informal use) □ *Everyone sat very close together, with very little elbowroom.*

elder ['eldəʳ] ◇ *adj* **sb's elder brother/sister** sb's brother/sister who is older than them □ *I have an elder sister.* ◇ *n* -1. an older person □ *You should show more respect for your elders.* -2. [in a tribe] an older person in a tribe who has a position of influence or authority □ *a tribal/village elder.* -3. RELIGION an official in some Protestant Churches □ *a Church elder.* -4. [tree] a small tree with white flowers and black berries.

elderberry ['eldəʳberɪ] (*pl* **elderberries**) *n* the black berry of the elder tree, often used to make wine.

elderly ['eldəʳlɪ] ◇ *adj* [person] old (polite use). ◇ *npl* **the elderly** old people □ *accommodation for the elderly.*

elder statesman *n* an old, respected, and influential person who is a member or was once a member of a government or organization.

eldest ['eldəst] *adj* [brother, sister] oldest.

El Dorado, Eldorado [ˌeldə'rɑːdəʊ] a place that is thought to offer great wealth and opportunities.

elect [ɪ'lekt] ◇ *vt* -1. [president, leader, candidate] to choose <sb> by voting □ *She was elected (as) chairperson.* □ *Mr Pyke was elected to the board/Senate two years before.* -2. **to elect to do sthg** to choose to do sthg (formal use). ◇ *adj* **the president/governor etc elect** the person who has been elected president/governor etc but has not yet officially taken up the position.

elected [ɪ'lektəd] *adj* **an elected body/representative etc** a body/representative etc that has been elected.

election [ɪ'lekʃn] *n* -1. the process of electing a president, leader etc □ *We will have* OR *hold an election next month.* □ *the European/local elections.* -2. [of a president, leader] *see* **elect** □ *a week after his election as President.*

❦ ELECTIONS
US presidental elections take place every four years, and there is a law which states that a president cannot be in power for more than two four-year periods. British general elections take place every five years, but the prime minister can call an election at any time within this period. Australian general elections are held every three years, but an early election can be called, as in Britain. Australians must vote by law in general and local elections, but US and British citizens do not have to vote if they do not want to.

election campaign *n* a campaign organized by a political party or candidate before an election to tell people their views and persuade people to vote for them.

electioneering [ɪ,lekʃəˈnɪərɪŋ] *n* activities intended to persuade people to vote for a particular party in an election.

elective [ɪˈlektɪv] *n* a course at a school or college that students can choose to take.

elector [ɪˈlektərʳ] *n* a person who has the right to vote in an election.

electoral [ɪˈlektərəl] *adj* **an electoral campaign/system etc** a campaign/system etc that is connected with an election.

electoral college *n* a group of electors, especially in the USA, chosen by the voters to elect the president.

electoral register, electoral roll *n* **the electoral register** the official list of voters in a particular area.

electorate [ɪˈlektərət] *n* **the electorate** all the people in a country who have the right to vote in elections.

electric [ɪˈlektrɪk] *adj* **-1.** [appliance] that works by using electricity □ *an electric heater/fan.* **-2.** [cable, wire] that is designed to carry electricity; [current, charge] that is produced by electricity □ *an electric plug/socket* □ *an electric power line.* **-3.** [situation, atmosphere] exciting.

◆ **electrics** *npl* **the electrics** GB the electric wiring and equipment in a car or machine (informal use).

electrical [ɪˈlektrɪkl] *adj* [equipment, appliance, device] that uses electricity; [fault, energy] that is connected with electricity □ *the electrical goods department of a store.*

electrical engineer *n* a person whose job is to make or look after electrical equipment, wiring etc.

electrical engineering *n* the profession of an electrical engineer.

electrically [ɪˈlektrɪklɪ] *adv* **electrically heated/powered etc** heated/powered etc using electricity.

electrical shock US, **electric shock** GB *n* a painful feeling caused when one touches a source of electricity.

electric blanket *n* a blanket heated by electric wires inside it.

electric chair *n* **the electric chair** a special chair that is used in some US states for executing people, using a strong electric current.

electric current *n* GB the flow of electricity through a wire or circuit.

electric fire *n* GB a device that heats a room by using electricity.

electric guitar *n* a guitar that can only be heard when it is connected to an amplifier.

electrician [ɪ,lekˈtrɪʃn] *n* a person whose job is to install or repair electrical wiring, appliances etc.

electricity [ɪ,lekˈtrɪsətɪ] *n* **-1.** a form of energy that can be produced by a battery or generator and is used for heating, lighting, and for making machines work □ *the electricity supply.* **-2.** an exciting atmosphere □ *There was real electricity between them when they met.*

electric light *n* a light that works by using electricity.

electric shock *n* GB = **electrical shock**.

electric shock therapy *n* a method of treating mental illness by giving electric shocks to the brain.

electric storm *n* a storm with thunder and lightning, sometimes without rain, that is caused by static electricity in the air.

electrify [ɪˈlektrɪfaɪ] (*pt & pp* **electrified**) *vt* **-1.** [railroad line, fence] to adapt <sthg> so that it can use electric power. **-2.** [person, audience] to make <sb> very excited.

electrifying [ɪˈlektrɪfaɪɪŋ] *adj* [atmosphere, speech, performance] very exciting.

electro- [ɪˈlektrəʊ] *prefix* added to words to show that something uses or involves electricity.

electrocardiograph [US ɪ,lektrəʊˈkɑːʳdɪəgræf, GB -grɑːf] *n* an instrument that records the electrical activity of the heart.

electrocute [ɪˈlektrəkjuːt] *vt* **to electrocute oneself, to be electrocuted** to be injured or killed by touching a source of electricity.

electrode [ɪˈlektrəʊd] *n* a point through which electric current leaves or enters a source of power, piece of equipment etc.

electroencephalograph [US ɪ,lektrəʊɪnˈsefələgræf, GB -grɑːf] *n* an instrument that records the electrical activity of the brain.

electrolysis [ɪ,lekˈtrɒləsɪs] *n* **-1.** PHYSICS the process of passing an electric current through a substance to make chemical changes in it. **-2.** a method of removing hair by destroying the roots with electric current.

electromagnet [ɪ,lektrəʊˈmægnət] *n* a magnet that is made more powerful by having an electric current passed through a coil of wire around it.

electromagnetic [ɪ,lektrəʊmægˈnetɪk] *adj* [force, field] *see* **electromagnet**.

electron [ɪˈlektrɒn] *n* a very small piece of matter that is one of the parts of an atom and has a negative charge.

electronic [ɪ,lekˈtrɒnɪk] *adj* **-1.** [device, equipment, system] that uses transistors, chips, or valves to control an electric current. **-2.**

[surveillance, music] that uses electronic devices.

◆ **electronics** ◇ *n* the science concerned with electronic devices and systems. ◇ *npl* electronic equipment.

electronic data processing *n* data processing carried out by electronic equipment such as computers.

electronic mail *n* → **email**.

electron microscope *n* a microscope that uses a beam of electrons to magnify very small things.

electroplated [ɪ'lektroʊpleɪtəd] *adj* [knife, spoon] that has been covered with a layer of metal by electrolysis.

elegance ['elɪgəns] *n*: *see* **elegant** □ *an age in which elegance and manners were all-important.*

elegant ['elɪgənt] *adj* -1. [person, dress] that is attractive and has a lot of style □ *You're looking very elegant tonight.* -2. [theory, plan] that works or is clear, even though it is simple.

elegantly ['elɪgəntlɪ] *adv* **elegantly dressed/planned etc** dressed/planned etc in an elegant way.

elegy ['elədʒɪ] (*pl* **elegies**) *n* a sad poem or song, usually for somebody who has died.

element ['elɪmənt] *n* -1. [of a whole] a part of something □ *One of the key elements in their success was their willingness to invest in new technology.* -2. [in society] a small group of people in a society or organization who are disapproved of by other members □ *antisocial elements in society* □ *They're a disruptive element.* -3. **an element of luck/danger etc** a small amount of luck/danger etc □ *There is an element of truth/jealousy in what he says.* -4. CHEMISTRY one of 105 substances that cannot be reduced to simpler substances because they contain only one type of atom, e.g. hydrogen, oxygen, or gold. -5. [in a heater] the piece of metal that heats up in an electric heater or kettle. -6. **to be in one's element** to be in a situation that one enjoys; to be doing something that one does well □ *Oh, Rod will be in his element, surrounded by adoring fans!*

◆ **elements** *npl* -1. the most basic or important aspects of something □ *the elements of computing.* -2. **the elements** the weather, especially wind, rain etc □ *battling against the elements.*

elementary [,elɪ'mentərɪ] *adj* -1. [precautions, answer, question] simple □ *"What do I do?" — "It's elementary, you just say you don't want to carry on."* -2. **elementary math/education etc** basic math/education etc.

elementary school *n* in the USA, a school where children go for the first six or seven years of their education.

elephant ['elɪfənt] (*pl* **elephant** OR **elephants**) *n* a very large African or Indian animal with wide flat ears, two tusks, and a long nose.

elevate ['elɪveɪt] *vt* -1. **to elevate sb/sthg to sthg** to raise the status of sb/sthg to sthg that is higher and more important □ *He was elevated to the rank of Colonel.* -2. [road, garden,

structure] to raise <sthg> up so that it is higher than the things around it □ *The street level was elevated to prevent flooding.*

elevated ['elɪveɪtəd] *adj* -1. [job, role] that is important and has a high status (formal use). -2. [sentiment, language, idea] that belongs to a level that is morally or intellectually higher than the level used in ordinary life (formal use). -3. [platform, section, land] that is higher than the things around it □ *an accident on the elevated section of the motorway.*

elevated railroad *n* a railroad that is built above street level in a town or city.

elevation [,elə'veɪʃn] *n* -1. the act of raising somebody or something to a higher level (formal use) □ *her elevation to the peerage.* -2. the height of land, a hill etc above sea level □ *Elevation is shown in meters.*

elevator ['elɪveɪtər] *n* a device like a large box that carries people or goods from one floor to another in a building □ *Shall we take the elevator, or walk up?*

eleven [ɪ'levn] *num* the number 11; *see also* **five**.

elevenses [ɪ'levnzɪz] *n* GB a cup of coffee or tea and something to eat that people sometimes have between breakfast and lunch, at around 11 o'clock (informal use).

eleventh [ɪ'levnθ] *num* 11th, number 11 in a series; *see also* **fifth**.

eleventh hour *n* **at the eleventh hour** at the last possible moment □ *An eleventh hour compromise has been reached.*

elf [elf] (*pl* **elves**) *n* an imaginary creature in folk tales that looks like a small human with pointed ears and plays tricks on people.

Elgin Marbles [,elgɪn-] *npl* **the Elgin Marbles** a collection of ancient Greek marble sculptures that were brought to Britain in 1803.

El Greco [el'grekoʊ] (1541–1614) a Spanish artist, born in Crete, famous for his portraits and religious paintings.

elicit [ɪ'lɪsət] *vt* [response, comment, fact] to get <a reaction or information> from somebody because of something one says or does (formal use).

eligibility [,elɪdʒə'bɪlətɪ] *n* [of an applicant, candidate] *see* **eligible** □ *We must check the eligibility of all candidates.*

eligible ['elɪdʒəbl] *adj* -1. [applicant, candidate] who is suitable and qualified for something. ■ **to be eligible for sthg/to do sthg** to have the right qualifications or be the right age for sthg/to do sthg □ *You're not eligible to vote yet.* -2. [bachelor, man, woman] who is suitable as a marriage partner, especially because they are very rich or attractive □ *Paul was considered the most eligible young man in town.*

eliminate [ɪ'lɪməneɪt] *vt* -1. [mistake, need] to remove <sthg that is not wanted or needed> □ *We have eliminated all other possibilities.* □ *The program will eliminate spelling errors from the text.* -2. SPORT **to be eliminated from sthg** [from a competition, election] to be defeated in sthg so that one can no longer take part in it.

Eliot ['elɪət], **George** (1819–1880) a British

novelist, well known for her realistic novels of provincial English life, including *The Mill on the Floss* and *Middlemarch*.

Eliot, T. S. (1888–1965) a US poet and playwright, who became a British citizen in 1927. His best-known works include *The Waste Land* and *Murder in the Cathedral*.

elite [ɪˈliːt] ◇ *adj* [school, group, army] that is the best of its kind with higher standards than other people or things □ *He attended an elite business school in the USA.* ◇ *n* a small group of people who are more talented, rich, or powerful than the rest of their community □ *the country's business elite.*

elitism [ɪˈliːtɪzm] *n* an attitude or way of behaving that is elitist (disapproving use) □ *This whole thing smacks of elitism.*

elitist [ɪˈliːtəst] (disapproving use) ◇ *adj* [society, policy] that favors an elite and does not give the same advantages or attention to those who do not belong to it □ *The college is accused of having an elitist admissions policy.* ◇ *n* a person who is elitist.

elixir [ɪˈlɪksər] *n* a drink that is thought to have magical powers, e.g. keeping people young forever or curing all illnesses.

Elizabeth I [ɪˌlɪzəbəθðəˈfɜːrst] (1533–1603) Queen of England from 1558 to 1603. She was called "The Virgin Queen."

Elizabeth II [ɪˌlɪzəbəθðəˈsekənd] (1926–) Queen of Great Britain and Northern Ireland from 1952.

Elizabethan [ɪˌlɪzəˈbiːθn] ◇ *adj* [drama, architecture] that existed or was fashionable in Britain in the reign of Elizabeth I (1558–1603). ◇ *n* a person who lived during the Elizabethan period.

elk [elk] (*pl* **elk** OR **elks**) *n* a type of large deer that has very big flat antlers and is found in Northern Europe, North America, and Asia.

ellipse [ɪˈlɪps] *n* a shape that is like a circle that has been flattened into an oval.

elliptical [ɪˈlɪptɪkl] *adj* -1. [path, object] that is like an ellipse. -2. [phrase, remark] that is difficult to understand because it does not include all the words that make it complete.

Ellis Island [ˌelɪs-] an island near New York City where, from the 1890s, foreign immigrants had to go to find out if they would be allowed to live in the USA.

elm [elm] *n* a tall tree found north of the equator that has broad leaves and seeds that spin as they fall to the ground; the hard heavy wood of this tree □ *an elm tree.*

elocution [ˌeləˈkjuːʃn] *n* the art of speaking in public with a clear voice and correct pronunciation □ *She took elocution lessons before becoming a newsreader.*

elongated [US ɪˈlɒŋɡeɪtəd, GB ˈiːlɒŋ-] *adj* [face, shape, finger] that is thin and long in a way that looks as if it has been stretched □ *a fruit shaped like an elongated melon.*

elope [ɪˈloʊp] *vi* [couple] to leave a place secretly to get married, especially when other

people do not approve of the marriage □ *She eloped with the gardener.*

eloquence [ˈeləkwəns] *n*: see **eloquent** □ *She was taken in by his charm and eloquence.*

eloquent [ˈeləkwənt] *adj* -1. [speech, gesture, style] that expresses something fluently and well, especially in a way that persuades people of something □ *We were impressed by his eloquent defense of their position.* -2. [person] who can speak or write in an eloquent way □ *It's a pleasure to hear such an eloquent speaker.*

eloquently [ˈeləkwəntlɪ] *adv* [speak, write, describe] see **eloquent** □ *The report eloquently reminds us of the need for tolerance.*

El Salvador [ˌelˈsælvədɔːr] a country in Central America, on the Pacific Ocean. SIZE: 21,000 sq kms. POPULATION: 5,400,000 (*Salvadoreans*). CAPITAL: San Salvador. LANGUAGE: Spanish. CURRENCY: colón.

else [els] *adv* **somewhere/something else** somewhere/something different from the place/thing that has just been mentioned □ *Let's go somewhere else.* □ *Do you need anything else?* □ *I've just thought of someone else we forgot to invite.* ■ **who else knows?** who knows in addition to the people just mentioned? (used after question words) □ *What else did he say?* ■ **everyone/everything else** all the other people/things apart from the one that has just been mentioned □ *I didn't enjoy myself, but everyone else seemed to have a good time.* □ *We had to stay in a motel, because everywhere else was full.*

◆ **or else** *conj* -1. **hurry up or else we'll be late** if you do not hurry up we'll be late (used to show what might go wrong if something is not done) □ *You'd better stop now or else you'll be too tired.* -2. a phrase used to threaten somebody □ *Get out of this house, or else I'll call the police!* □ *You'd better pay up, or else!* □ *"Shut up!" — "Or else what?"* -3. a phrase used to show the second of two things that might happen or be true □ *We could go there by train, or else fly.*

elsewhere [US ˈelswer, GB ˌelsˈweə] *adv* [look, go, buy] in or to a different place □ *The snow is just as heavy elsewhere in the country.*

ELT (*abbr of* **English language teaching**) *n* the teaching of English to people who do not speak it as their mother tongue.

elucidate [ɪˈluːsɪdeɪt] (formal use) ◇ *vt* to make <a point, comment> etc clearer by giving more information □ *Could you elucidate one or two things?* ◇ *vi*: *Allow me to elucidate.*

elude [ɪˈluːd] *vt* -1. [police, authorities] to avoid being caught or found by <sb>, especially over a long period of time □ *How has he managed to elude capture for so long?* -2. **the answer eludes me** I cannot remember the answer; I cannot think of the answer □ *The name eludes me for the moment.*

elusive [ɪˈluːsɪv] *adj* -1. [person, animal] that is difficult to find □ *I finally found my elusive colleague.* -2. [quality] that is difficult to define or describe; [solution] that is difficult to work out □ *the elusive smile of the Mona Lisa* □ *The answer remained elusive.*

elves [elvz] *plural of* **elf**.

'em [əm] = **them** (informal use).

emaciated [ɪ'meɪʃɪeɪtəd] *adj* [person, arm, leg] that is very thin, especially because of illness or hunger □ *The dog looked emaciated.*

email, e-mail ['i:meɪl] (*abbr of* **electronic mail**) ◇ *n* a system that links computers together so that users can send messages to each other's computers; information that is sent in this way □ *an email message* □ *Can I contact you by email?* ◇ *vt* to send <sb> a message by email.

emanate ['eməneɪt] ◇ *vt* to have a large amount of <a feeling, quality> etc in such a way that other people are aware of it □ *She/ The building emanates power.* ◇ *vi* **to emanate from sb/sthg** [smell, idea, noise] to come from sb/sthg □ *There was a pleasant smell of garlic emanating from the kitchen.*

emancipate [ɪ'mænsɪpeɪt] *vt* to give <sb> more political rights and freedom.

emancipated [ɪ'mænsɪpeɪtɪd] *adj* [woman] who does not follow traditional ideas about how women should behave.

emancipation [ɪ,mænsɪ'peɪʃn] *n*: *see* **emancipate** □ *She campaigned for the emancipation of women.*

Emancipation Proclamation *n* **the Emancipation Proclamation** a speech made by President Abraham Lincoln on January 1, 1863 in which he said that all slaves in the United States were to be free.

ｅ EMANCIPATION PROCLAMATION
In a speech on January 1, 1863, in the middle of the American Civil War, President Abraham Lincoln stated that all slaves in the Confederation (i.e. the Southern states that were rebelling against the government) would now be free. The proclamation did not become law until the war ended in 1865, when it became the Thirteenth Amendment to the US Constitution.

---

emasculate [ɪ'mæskjəleɪt] *vt* [bill, organization] to remove the power of <sb/sthg> so that it is no longer effective (formal use).

embalm [ɪm'bɑːm] *vt* to treat <a dead body> with oils or chemicals to prevent it from decaying.

embankment [ɪm'bæŋkmənt] *n* **-1.** [for a road, railroad] a long section of raised earth or stone that is built to carry a road or railroad over low ground. **-2.** [along a river, sea, lake] a long section of raised earth or stone that is built to stop water from spreading over the land beside it.

embargo [ɪm'bɑːrgoʊ] (*pl* **embargoes**, *pt & pp* **embargoed**, *cont* **embargoing**) ◇ *n* **-1.** BUSINESS & POLITICS an order made by a government or group of governments that forbids trade with another country, often used as a way of punishing that country □ *The UN has placed/imposed an embargo on oil shipments.* □ *an arms/oil embargo.* **-2.** an order made by one person to another person that tells them not

to do something □ *a news embargo.* ◇ *vt* BUSINESS & POLITICS to place an embargo on <a product or activity>.

embark [ɪm'bɑːrk] *vi* **-1.** to get on a ship □ *A signal told us it was time to embark.* **-2. to embark on** OR **upon sthg** [on a trip, project, explanation] to begin sthg that is important or likely to take a long time □ *Think carefully before you embark on such an ambitious plan.*

embarkation [,embɑːr'keɪʃn] *n* the act of getting onto a ship □ *Passports must be shown before embarkation.*

embarkation card *n* GB a ticket given to a passenger when they get on a ship.

embarrass [US ɪm'berəs, GB -'bær-] *vt* to make <sb> feel ashamed, or nervous and uncomfortable □ *I don't want to embarrass her.*

embarrassed [US ɪm'berəst, GB -'bær-] *adj* [person, silence, smile] that shows embarrassment □ *She was too embarrassed to speak.*

embarrassing [US ɪm'berəsɪŋ, GB -'bær-] *adj* [moment, remark] that causes embarrassment □ *It was so embarrassing having to leave like that!* □ *There was an embarrassing silence.*

embarrassment [US ɪm'berəsmənt, GB -'bær-] *n* **-1.** a feeling of being nervous and uncomfortable because of something that has been said or done □ *It has been a great source of embarrassment for us.* **-2.** a person or thing that causes embarrassment □ *Honestly, you're such an embarrassment!*

embassy ['embəsɪ] (*pl* **embassies**) *n* a group of government officials who work in a foreign country as representatives of their country, with an ambassador as their head; the building where this group is based □ *the American Embassy in Paris* □ *embassy staff.*

embattled [ɪm'bætld] *adj* [government, economy, regime] that has many opponents or enemies and continually has problems □ *New scandals have hit the embattled party.*

embedded [ɪm'bedəd] *adj* **-1. to be embedded in sthg** [in rock, wood, mud] to be firmly fixed in sthg □ *The car's wheels were embedded in the mud.* **-2.** [feeling, guilt] that is deeply and strongly fixed in a person, culture, society etc □ *a deeply-embedded prejudice.*

embellish [ɪm'belɪʃ] *vt* **-1. to embellish sthg with sthg** to make sthg more attractive by adding sthg decorative □ *a facade embellished with statues.* **-2.** [story, the truth] to make <sthg> more interesting by adding details to it that are often false □ *He always tends to embellish what really happened.*

embers ['embəz] *npl* the small pieces of very hot coal or wood that remain after a fire has almost stopped burning.

embezzle [ɪm'bezl] *vt* [funds, profits] to take <money> and use it illegally for one's own profit by using one's position in a company or organization.

embezzlement [ɪm'bezlmənt] *n* the crime of embezzling money □ *They were arrested for embezzlement.*

embittered [ɪm'bɪtəd] *adj* [person] who has become bitter because of bad experiences that they have had □ *She had become embittered by failure.*

emblazoned [ɪm'bleɪznd] *adj* **to be emblazoned on sthg** [symbol, design, emblem] to be drawn, painted, or fixed on sthg so that it is very noticeable □ *The jacket had the emblem of the school emblazoned on the pocket.* ■ **to be emblazoned with sthg** [tie, jacket, flag] to be decorated with sthg, especially in a way that is very clear or noticeable □ *His necktie was emblazoned with the club crest.*

emblem ['embləm] *n* an object or design that is used as a symbol to represent a particular country or organization □ *The bald eagle is the national emblem of the United States.*

embodiment [ɪm'bɒdɪmənt] *n* a person or thing that represents a particular quality or idea in a very strong or typical way □ *He was the embodiment of evil.*

embody [ɪm'bɒdɪ] (*pt* & *pp* **embodied**) *vt* **-1.** to express or represent <a quality, ideal, or principle> in a physical or noticeable way □ *To us, he embodied all the ideals to which we aspired.* **-2. to be embodied in sthg** to be included as a basic and necessary part of sthg □ *The right to vote is embodied in our Constitution.*

embolism ['embəlɪzm] *n* something, e.g. a clot of blood or a bubble of air, that blocks a vein or artery.

embossed [ɪm'bɒst] *adj* **-1.** [paper, leather] that has a raised pattern on its surface that one can feel with one's fingers. **-2. to be embossed on sthg** [title, design, symbol] to be printed so that it forms a raised pattern on sthg □ *She had her initials embossed on her suitcase.*

embrace [ɪm'breɪs] ◇ *vt* **-1.** [child, friend] to put one's arms around <sb> as a sign of love or affection, especially when meeting or saying goodbye □ *Kathy embraced her daughter warmly.* **-2.** [religion, belief, idea] to start believing in <sthg> in a way that shows one accepts it completely (formal use). **-3.** [features, types] to include <sthg> (formal use) □ *The conference will embrace all aspects of biotechnology.* ◇ *vi* [two people] *The lovers embraced, then parted.* ◇ *n* the act of embracing somebody or something □ *He held her in a lingering embrace.*

embrocation [,embrə'keɪʃn] *n* a cream that is rubbed into the skin to reduce muscle pain (formal use).

embroider [ɪm'brɔɪdər] ◇ *vt* **-1.** SEWING [tablecloth, blouse] to decorate <sthg> by sewing a design, picture etc onto it; [design, picture] to sew <sthg> onto a piece of material. **-2.** [story, account] to make <sthg> more interesting by adding some details that are not completely true (disapproving use) □ *Alex always tends to embroider his stories a little.* ◇ *vi* SEWING *I'm learning to embroider.*

embroidered [ɪm'brɔɪdəʳd] *adj* [tablecloth, design, blouse] that has been decorated with embroidery □ *a handkerchief with an embroidered edge.*

embroidery [ɪm'brɔɪdərɪ] *n* **-1.** the skill or activity of embroidering □ *I've taken up embroidery.* **-2.** designs or pictures that have been

embroidered onto something □ *She does beautiful embroidery.*

embroil [ɪm'brɔɪl] *vt* **to get/be embroiled in sthg** [in an argument, scandal] to get/be involved in sthg that is difficult to stop being involved in □ *You don't want to get embroiled in their marital problems.*

embryo ['embrɪoʊ] (*pl* **embryos**) *n* BIOLOGY an unborn human being or animal in the very earliest stages of development inside the mother's body.

embryonic [,embrɪ'ɒnɪk] *adj* [movement, idea] that is at an early stage in its development □ *Then, television was still in its embryonic form.*

emcee [,em'siː] *n abbr of* **master of ceremonies**.

emend [ɪ'mend] *vt* [text, translation] to remove the mistakes from <sthg written> □ *an emended version of the speech.*

emerald ['emərəld] ◇ *adj* bright green □ *an emerald green hat.* ◇ *n* a precious stone that is a bright green color.

emerge [ɪ'mɜːʳdʒ] *vi* **-1.** [person, animal, vehicle] to come out from a hidden place, or from inside a room, house, car etc □ *She finally emerged from the meeting at 2pm.* **-2.** [from an experience, situation] to come out of an experience, situation etc in a particular way □ *Buendia emerged as the most important new opposition figure after the death of Munada.* □ *She emerged from the scandal with her reputation intact.* **-3.** [truth, fact, information] to become known, usually gradually □ *A picture of the killer is emerging from eye-witness accounts.* **-4.** [writer, movement, organization] to become increasingly important or well-known □ *New talent is constantly emerging.* **-5. it emerges that...** it is now known or clear that... □ *It soon emerged that the President had given the order himself.*

emergence [ɪ'mɜːʳdʒəns] *n*: *see* **emerge** □ *the emergence of China as a world industrial power.*

emergency [ɪ'mɜːʳdʒənsɪ] (*pl* **emergencies**) ◇ *n* a difficult or dangerous situation, e.g. an accident, that happens suddenly and unexpectedly and that needs to be dealt with very quickly □ *'In case of emergency, pull handle.'* ◇ *adj* [meeting, action, equipment] that is intended or needed to deal with an emergency □ *We must take emergency steps to deal with the crisis.*

emergency brake *n* US a device in a vehicle that stops it from moving and is used when the main brake does not work or when the vehicle is parked.

emergency exit *n* an exit in a building, store etc that is used only when there is an emergency, such as a fire.

emergency landing *n* a landing that an aircraft has to make when something has gone wrong □ *The pilot had to make an emergency landing a mile short of the airport.*

emergency number *n* a telephone number that people ring to call one of the emergency services.

emergency room *n* US the part of a hospital

where people are treated if they have an accident or suddenly become ill.

emergency services *npl* the public services, e.g. the fire brigade or ambulance service, that deal with emergencies.

emergency stop *n* a sudden stop that one makes in a car, usually to avoid having an accident.

emergent [ɪ'mɜːrdʒənt] *adj* [nation, power, political group] that is only just beginning to have power or to be noticed.

Emerson ['eməʳsən], **Ralph Waldo** (1803–1882) a US poet whose writing had a strong influence on the philosophy and religion of his time.

emery board ['eməri-] *n* a flat stick of wood or cardboard with a rough surface like sandpaper on it, used for filing one's nails.

emetic [ɪ'metɪk] *n* something that one drinks or eats in order to make oneself vomit, especially as a medicine.

emigrant ['emɪgrənt] *n* a person who has emigrated or is emigrating.

emigrate ['emɪgreɪt] *vi* [person] to leave one's own country to live permanently in another □ They emigrated from America after the war.

emigration [,emɪ'greɪʃn] *n*: see **emigrate** □ He received help with his emigration papers.

émigré ['emɪgreɪ] *n* a person who has left their country for political reasons.

eminence ['emɪnəns] *n*: see **eminent** □ a professor of such eminence.

eminent ['emɪnənt] *adj* [scientist, doctor] who is important, respected, and well-known □ She holds an eminent position in the organization.

eminently ['emɪnəntlɪ] *adv* **eminently sensible/fair/practical** very sensible/fair/practical (formal use).

emir [e'mɪəʳ] *n* a Muslim leader, especially in parts of Africa and Southwest Asia.

emissary [US 'eməserɪ, GB -ɪsərɪ] (*pl* **emissaries**) *n* a person who has been sent to a foreign country on a specific mission, usually as the representative of a government or country.

emission [ɪ'mɪʃn] *n* **-1.** [of heat, sound, smoke] see **emit**. **-2.** a substance that is emitted □ toxic emissions.

emit [ɪ'mɪt] (*pt* & *pp* **emitted**, *cont* **emitting**) *vt* [heat, sound, smoke] to produce <sthg> and send it out into the surrounding area (formal use) □ The radar emits a signal.

Emmy ['emɪ] *n* an award given to outstanding television actors and programs in the USA.

emollient [ɪ'mɒlɪənt] *n* a liquid that one puts on one's skin to soften it (formal use).

emolument [ɪ'mɒljəmənt] *n* money or some other payment that a person receives for work they have done (formal use).

emotion [ɪ'məʊʃn] *n* **-1.** strong feelings that are often difficult to control □ She showed no emotion when she heard the news. **-2. one's emotions** strong feelings that one has, e.g. love, fear, or anger □ He was unable to contain his emotions.

emotional [ɪ'məʊʃnəl] *adj* **-1.** [person] who has strong feelings that are shown often or easily □ He got very emotional and started to cry. **-2.** [scene, reunion, farewell] that is filled with emotion □ It was an emotional moment for us. **-3.** [speech, music, plea] that appeals to one's emotions □ The princess made an emotional plea on behalf of the orphans. **-4.** [need, problem] that concerns the emotions □ The job will make emotional demands on you.

emotionally [ɪ'məʊʃnəlɪ] *adv* [react, answer] see **emotional** □ The child is emotionally disturbed. □ Avoid becoming too involved emotionally.

emotive [ɪ'məʊtɪv] *adj* [remark, issue, language] that makes people feel strongly about something □ These are extremely emotive terms that you are using.

empathy ['empəθɪ] *n* the ability to understand and share other people's feelings □ I felt enormous empathy with their situation.

emperor ['empərəʳ] *n* a man who rules an empire □ a Roman emperor.

emphasis ['emfəsɪs] (*pl* **emphases** [-siːz]) *n* a particular force or importance that is given to something that one says or does □ The emphasis is on training in a practical context. ■ **to lay** OR **place emphasis on sthg** to give special importance to sthg □ Here at Langhill we put special emphasis on acquiring management skills.

emphasize, -ise ['emfəsaɪz] *vt* [point, feature, word] to give emphasis to <sthg> □ I want to emphasize that we do not allow smoking here.

emphatic [ɪm'fætɪk] *adj* [statement, tone, refusal] that is clear and forceful □ She was emphatic that they should not leave.

emphatically [ɪm'fætɪklɪ] *adv* **-1.** [say, declare, state] see **emphatic** □ I emphatically deny the allegations against me. **-2.** definitely □ This is emphatically not the right thing to do.

emphysema [,emfə'siːmə] *n* a medical condition in which the lungs become filled with too much air, causing difficulty in breathing.

empire ['empaɪəʳ] *n* **-1.** POLITICS & HISTORY a group of separate countries that are all ruled by one person or country □ the Roman Empire. **-2.** BUSINESS a powerful group of companies that are all controlled by one person □ He controls a huge publishing empire.

empire-building *n* the attempt to increase one's power by adding more and more companies, staff etc to one's business or department.

empirical [ɪm'pɪrɪkl] *adj* [proof, knowledge] that is based on real facts or practical experience rather than on theory □ the empirical study of language.

empiricism [ɪm'pɪrɪsɪzm] *n* the belief that knowledge should be based on practical experience rather than on theory.

employ [ɪm'plɔɪ] *vt* **-1.** [worker, staff] to give paid work to <sb> regularly □ The company employs 500 people at its plant. □ The company employs me to handle sales. ■ **to be employed as sthg** to have a job as sthg □ He had been employed as an accountant. **-2.** [machine, device, tool] to use <sthg> (formal use).

employable [ɪm'plɔɪəbl] *adj* [person] who is

suitable to be employed □ *Mark? I would have thought he was eminently employable.*

employee [ɪm'plɔɪiː] *n* a person who is employed by a particular person, company etc □ *a government/company employee* □ *I'm an employee of Globax Inc.*

employer [ɪm'plɔɪəʳ] *n* a person or company that employs other people □ *The dispute between employers and the workforce continues.*

employment [ɪm'plɔɪmənt] *n* **-1.** the state of being employed □ *His future employment is threatened.* **-2.** paid work that somebody does □ *I'm looking for employment.*

employment agency *n* an agency that finds jobs for people and finds employees to fill vacancies for companies, businesses etc.

employment office *n* GB a government office that provides information about jobs that are available and helps people to find work.

emporium [em'pɔːrɪəm] *n* a large store that sells a lot of different things (old-fashioned and formal use).

empower [ɪm'paʊəʳ] *vt* **to be empowered** to be given the legal authority to do something □ *The police have been empowered to arrest suspects on sight.*

empress ['emprəs] *n* **-1.** the wife of an emperor. **-2.** a woman who rules an empire.

emptiness ['emptɪnəs] *n* **-1.** [of a desert, ocean] the state of being empty □ *the awful emptiness of space.* **-2.** [of a person] a feeling of having nothing interesting or valuable in one's life.

empty ['emptɪ] (*compar* **emptier**, *superl* **emptiest**, *pt* & *pp* **emptied**, *pl* **empties**) ◇ *adj* **-1.** [bottle, glass, pocket] that has nothing inside it; [room, street] where there are no people □ *My stomach's completely empty.* □ *It was a holiday and the city was empty.* **-2.** [threat, speech, promise] that seems to have meaning but does not □ *These are just empty words.* **-3.** [existence, life] that seems to have no meaning or importance □ *Things seemed somehow empty now Jamie had gone.* **-4.** [person] who feels very tired and has little energy, especially after a strong emotional experience □ *Sarah sat back in her chair, tired and empty after a demanding day.*
◇ *vt* **-1.** [bag, pocket, can] to remove the contents of <sthg> □ *He emptied the bottle in one gulp.* **-2.** [trash, water, food] to remove <the contents> from a container □ *He emptied the trash into/out of the can.*
◇ *vi* [room, theater, street] to become empty □ *The auditorium gradually emptied.*
◇ *n* an empty bottle (informal use) □ *Did you take the empties back?*

empty-handed [-'hændəd] *adv* [return, arrive, come] with nothing □ *They were sent away empty-handed.*

empty-headed [-'hedəd] *adj* [person] who seems silly and does not think about things seriously.

EMS *n abbr of* **European Monetary System**.

EMT (*abbr of* **emergency medical technician**) *n* a person whose job is to give medical help

to people at the scene of an accident or in an ambulance.

emu ['iːmjuː] (*pl* **emu** OR **emus**) *n* a large Australian bird with long legs that cannot fly.

EMU ['iːmjuː, ˌiːem'juː] *n abbr of* **Economic and Monetary Union**.

emulate ['emjəleɪt] *vt* to try to copy <sb> because one admires them and wants to be like them (formal use).

emulsion [ɪ'mʌlʃn] ◇ *n* **-1.** PHOTOGRAPHY the substance on the surface of photographic film that makes the film sensitive to light. **-2. emulsion (paint)** GB a water-based paint that is not shiny and is used for painting walls, ceilings etc inside a building. ◇ *vt* GB to paint <a room, wall> etc with emulsion.

enable [ɪ'neɪbl] *vt* **to enable sb to do sthg** to give sb the ability or opportunity to do sthg □ *The pass will enable you to enter without paying.*

enabling [ɪ'neɪblɪŋ] *adj* **enabling legislation** a law that makes it possible for something to happen.

enact [ɪ'nækt] *vt* **-1.** LAW to pass <a law, bill> etc so that it becomes legal □ *The bill will be enacted before the end of this session.* **-2.** [role, scene, situation] to perform <sthg> by acting.

enactment [ɪ'næktmənt] *n*: *see* **enact**.

enamel [ɪ'næml] *n* **-1.** a substance similar to glass that is used in decorating pots, glass etc, or to protect the surface of saucepans. **-2.** [on teeth] the hard white outer covering of one's teeth. **-3.** = **enamel paint**.

enameled US, **enamelled** GB [ɪ'næmld] *adj* [pot, handle, box] that is covered or decorated with enamel.

enamel paint *n* a kind of shiny paint used especially on wood surfaces.

enamored US, **enamoured** GB [ɪ'næməʳd] *adj* **to be enamored of sb/sthg** to like sb/sthg very much (literary use).

en bloc [ɒn'blɒk] *adv* GB [resign, leave, arrive] as a group □ *The delegates walked out en bloc.*

enc BUSINESS **-1.** *abbr of* **enclosure**. **-2.** *abbr of* **enclosed**.

encamp [ɪn'kæmp] *vi* [army, soldiers] to set up a camp.

encampment [ɪn'kæmpmənt] *n* a place where there is a camp, especially a military camp.

encapsulate [ɪn'kæpsjəleɪt] *vt* [idea, theory] to express <sthg> in a short clear form □ *I think this article pretty well encapsulates what I want to say.*

encase [ɪn'keɪs] *vt* **to be encased in sthg** [in armor, plaster] to be completely covered by sthg hard.

encash [ɪn'kæʃ] *vt* GB to cash <a check> (formal use).

enchanted [US ɪn'tʃæntəd, GB -'tʃɑːnt-] *adj* **-1. to be enchanted by sb/sthg** [person] to be delighted and fascinated by sb/sthg □ *He sat listening, enchanted by her voice.* **-2.** [forest, princess, apple] that is under the influence of a magic spell.

enchanting [US ɪn'tʃæntɪŋ, GB -'tʃɑːnt-] *adj* [person, child] that one thinks is charming and delightful □ *He had the most enchanting smile.*

encircle [ɪn'sɜːʳkl] *vt* [city, camp, area] to surround <a person, place, or thing> completely □ *The building was encircled by troops/trees.*

enclave ['enkleɪv] *n* a part of a country or area where people belong to a nationality, race, culture etc that is different from that of the people around it □ *a small Serb enclave.*

enclose [ɪn'kləʊz] *vt* -1. [garden, city, space] to surround <sthg> with a wall, fence, or other solid object so that it is separate from everything else □ *The field was enclosed by* OR *with hedges.* □ *enclosed spaces.* -2. [check, document] to put <sthg> in an envelope with something else □ *Please find enclosed a copy of the report.*

enclosure [ɪn'kləʊʒəʳ] *n* -1. FARMING an area that has been enclosed □ *The cattle were kept in an enclosure.* -2. BUSINESS something that has been enclosed with a letter.

encompass [ɪn'kʌmpəs] *vt* to include <a range of things, activities, interests> etc □ *The course encompasses all aspects of computer programming.*

encore ['ɒŋkɔːʳ] ◇ *n* a short extra performance that is given by a musician, singer etc at the end of a performance after the audience has applauded a lot □ *The pianist gave two encores.* ◇ *excl* the word that is used to call for more music, singing etc by the same performers at the end of a musical performance □ *"Encore!" they shouted.*

encounter [ɪn'kaʊntəʳ] ◇ *n* -1. [with a person] a meeting that is unexpected □ *a chance encounter with an old friend.* -2. [with an idea, group] an experience of a particular thing □ *It was her first encounter with danger.* ◇ *vt* -1. to meet <sb> when one is not expecting to □ *She encountered Paul, quite by chance, in the street.* -2. [resistance, hostility] to experience <a difficulty> when trying to do something □ *She encountered a lot of opposition.*

encourage [US ɪn'kɜːrɪdʒ, GB -'kʌr-] *vt* -1. [child, student, sportsperson] to give <sb> one's support, especially in something they are trying to do □ *My mother always encouraged me in what I did.* ■ **to encourage sb to do sthg** to try to make sb do sthg by giving them support or by being very positive about it □ *I always tried to encourage my children to study hard.* □ *She encouraged me to apply for the job.* □ *Success encouraged us to expand.* -2. [good relations, independence] to give positive support to <an activity or idea> □ *The company does not encourage political activities among its employees.*

encouragement [US ɪn'kɜːrɪdʒmənt, GB -'kʌr-] *n* the act of encouraging somebody □ *You'll get no encouragement from me.*

encouraging [US ɪn'kɜːrɪdʒɪŋ, GB -'kʌr-] *adj* [news, progress, sign] that gives one a feeling of encouragement □ *She was very encouraging about my work.* □ *Well, I think that's a very encouraging sign if he liked your script.*

encroach [ɪn'krəʊtʃ] *vi* **to encroach on** OR **upon sthg** [on somebody's property, land] to gradually take possession of sthg that belongs to somebody else; [on somebody's time, privacy] to take up more of sthg than is acceptable □ *Forest clearances have gradually encroached on the birds' habitat.* □ *My work is beginning to encroach on the time I spend with my family.*

encrusted [ɪn'krʌstəd] *adj* **to be encrusted with sthg** [with jewels, mud, dirt] to be covered with a hard layer of sthg.

encumber [ɪn'kʌmbəʳ] *vt* **to be encumbered with sthg** [with luggage] to be carrying sthg heavy so that it is difficult to move □ *He was encumbered with large bags and boxes.*

encyclop(a)edia [ɪn,saɪklə'piːdjə] *n* a book or set of books giving information in alphabetical order on all aspects of knowledge or on all aspects of a particular subject □ *an art encyclop(a)edia* □ *Look it up in the encyclop(a)edia.*

encyclop(a)edic [ɪn,saɪklə'piːdɪk] *adj* [knowledge, memory] that contains very full and complete information on a subject or subjects.

end [end] ◇ *n* -1. [of a story, period, relationship] the last part of a story, event, period of time etc □ *I have until the end of July/the year to find a new job.* □ *We watched the video right through to the end.* ■ **to be at an end** [period of time, event, situation] to be finished (formal use) □ *His days as a carefree student were now at an end.* ■ **to come to an end** [period of time, event, situation] to stop □ *I didn't want the evening to come to an end.* □ *Funding for the project will come to an end in July.* ■ **to put an end to sthg** [to a situation, activity] to make sthg stop, especially sthg that should not be happening □ *It is time to put an end to the violence.* ■ **at the end of the day** a phrase used to sum up what is important after all the facts have been considered □ *At the end of the day, only you can decide if you want the job.* -2. [of a stick, table, road] the part or point of something that is furthest away from one, or from the center □ *We were sitting at opposite ends of the room.* □ *Stand the box on its end.* ■ **the other end** the place a person is telephoning or traveling to □ *Will someone be there to meet you at the other end?* ■ **end to end** [lay, place, arrange] with the points or narrowest edges touching □ *The path was marked out with bricks laid end to end.* ■ **to make ends meet** to have just enough money for food, clothes, somewhere to live etc □ *I have scarcely enough money to make ends meet at the moment, let alone lend you any.* -3. [of a cigarette, loaf, lipstick] a small piece that has been left after something has been used. -4. **to** OR **for an end** for a particular reason (formal use) □ *We are all working to that end.* ■ **to be an end in itself** to be a good enough reason for doing something even though nothing useful may be achieved as a result. -5. *phrase* **to meet one's end** to die (literary use).
◇ *vt* to cause <an event, situation, or state> to finish □ *Both sides are eager to end the dispute.* □ *They ended the meeting early.* □ *We ended the meal with coffee and liqueurs.*
◇ *vi* [event, story, situation] *The novel ends hap-*

pily. □ *I remember the day the war ended.* □ *The party didn't end until 4 a.m.* ■ **to end with sthg** to finish with sthg □ *The concert ended with the national anthem.* ■ **to end in failure/disaster/tears** to have failure/disaster/tears as a result □ *I warn you, it'll end in tears!*

◆ **in the end** *adv* after a long series of events □ *Everything turned out all right in the end.* □ *In the end we decided to fly.*

◆ **no end** *adv* [amuse, please] very much (informal use) □ *Oh yes, it amused my children no end.*

◆ **no end of** *prep* [bother, worry, trouble] a lot of <sthg> (informal use) □ *Your visitor seems to be causing you no end of complications.*

◆ **on end** *adv* -1. to stand on end [hair] to stick up vertically □ *It's the kind of story that makes your hair stand on end.* -2. **for hours/days on end** continuously for hours/days without stopping □ *He works for days on end without a break.*

◆ **end up** *vi* to be in a particular situation or state, especially one which has not been planned, after many things have happened □ *I knew they'd end up getting married.* □ *If you don't drive more carefully, you'll end up in the hospital!*

endanger [ɪn'deɪndʒəʳ] *vt* to act in a way that causes danger to <sb's life, health> etc □ *This could endanger our position as a company.*

endangered species [ɪn,deɪndʒəʳd-] *n* a type of animal or plant that is in danger of being destroyed completely □ *The panda is an endangered species.*

endear [ɪn'dɪəʳ] *vt* **to endear sb/oneself to sb** to cause sb/oneself to be liked by sb □ *You're hardly going to endear yourself to him by criticizing his work, are you?*

endearing [ɪn'dɪərɪŋ] *adj* [smile, habit] that causes somebody to be liked by another person □ *I think his efforts to please you are rather endearing, don't you?*

endearment [ɪn'dɪəʳmənt] *n* a word or phrase that shows affection for somebody (formal use) □ *a term of endearment.*

endeavor US, **endeavour** GB [ɪn'devəʳ] (formal use) ◇ *n* an attempt to do something, especially something new or difficult □ *Despite all my endeavors, my proposals were rejected.* ◇ *vt* **to endeavor to do sthg** to try to do sthg □ *We endeavor to provide a consistently high standard of service.*

endemic [en'demɪk] *adj* -1. MEDICINE [disease] that is very common in a particular area or country and spreads quickly and easily. -2. [problem] that is very common in a particular area or country □ *Poverty is endemic in the Indian subcontinent.*

ending ['endɪŋ] *n* the way that a story, movie, play etc finishes □ *a happy ending.*

endive ['endaɪv] *n* -1. a plant with crisp, curly, green leaves that is often eaten raw in salads. -2. US a plant with long, crisp, pale green leaves that is often eaten raw in salads and has a slightly bitter taste.

endless ['endləs] *adj* -1. [journey, complaining, patience] that continues for a long time and

never seems likely to end □ *The possibilities are endless.* -2. [desert, supplies] very large in size or amount □ *We do not have endless supplies of alcohol, you know.*

endlessly ['endləslɪ] *adv* continuously for a long time and in a way that seems likely never to end □ *The rain fell endlessly.* □ *She's been endlessly patient.*

endorse [ɪn'dɔːʳs] *vt* -1. [plan, proposal, candidacy] to give official or public support to <sb/sthg>, especially by voting in favor of them □ *My ideas were endorsed by the boss.* -2. FINANCE **to endorse a check** to put one's signature on the back of a check. -3. **to endorse sb's licence** GB to record a conviction for a driving offense on sb's driver's license.

endorsement [ɪn'dɔːʳsmənt] *n* GB *see* **endorse** □ *He got an endorsement for speeding.*

endow [ɪn'daʊ] *vt* -1. **to be endowed with sthg** [with beauty, talent, intelligence] to have sthg that is considered to give one an advantage □ *Nature had endowed her with brains as well as beauty.* -2. [school, charity, hospital] to give a large amount of money to <an institution or organization>.

endowment [ɪn'daʊmənt] *n* -1. [of a person] a natural ability or quality that somebody has □ *one of his many endowments.* -2. [for a school, hospital] a gift of money made to an institution or organization □ *He made an endowment to his old college.*

endowment insurance *n* a type of insurance policy that guarantees the payment of a certain sum of money to the insured person on a fixed date.

endowment mortgage *n* a mortgage in which the borrower pays interest on the loan, and also makes payments into a life insurance policy designed to provide enough money at the end of the mortgage to repay the sum borrowed.

end product *n* the result or final product of a process or activity □ *Yes, but it's the end product that's important, not the process.*

end result *n* the final result produced by a process or activity □ *The end result was a dispute that lasted several months.*

endurance [ɪn'djʊərəns] *n* the ability to tolerate pain, suffering, difficulty etc for a long time □ *Their suffering was beyond endurance.*

endurance test *n* a test to find out how strong and resistant a machine or person is.

endure [ɪn'djʊəʳ] ◇ *vt* [pain, hardship] to suffer <sthg> with patience, especially for a long time □ *I cannot imagine the suffering those people have had to endure.* ◇ *vi* [fame, memory] to last for a long time (formal use).

enduring [ɪn'djʊərɪŋ] *adj* [peace, fame, love] that lasts for a long time (formal use).

end user *n* the person, organization etc that will eventually use a product.

endwise ['endwaɪz] US, **endways** ['endweɪz] GB *adv* -1. with the end upward or forward □ *She placed the carton endwise on the table.* -2. with the end of one thing touching the

end of another □ *They were stacked endwise on the floor.*

end zone *n* US in football, the area at the end of the field where players take the ball to score points.

enema ['enəmə] *n* a liquid that is put into somebody's rectum in order to make them empty their bowels.

enemy ['enəmi] (*pl* **enemies**) *n* -1. a person who strongly dislikes another person and speaks or acts against them □ *They are bitter enemies.* -2. MILITARY **the enemy** the army or country that one is fighting against in a war □ *enemy troops/forces/aircraft.*

energetic [,enə'dʒetik] *adj* -1. [person] who is full of energy and very active □ *Since she was feeling energetic, she started immediately.* -2. [sport, game] that involves a lot of physical activity □ *You should take up an energetic activity such as swimming.* -3. [campaigner, supporter] who is enthusiastic and works hard for a particular purpose □ *an energetic campaigner for human rights.*

energy ['enədʒi] (*pl* **energies**) *n* -1. the physical and mental strength to be active, to work hard, to play a sport etc without getting tired very quickly □ *He's got lots of energy.* □ *I haven't got the energy to go out tonight.* -2. the power produced by electricity, coal etc that makes machines work and provides heat □ *nuclear/solar energy* □ *Save energy by turning off the lights.* ■ **the Department of Energy** → DOE.
◆ **energies** *npl* the effort and will of a person or group to do something □ *I've been putting all my energies into doing up the house.*

energy-saving *adj* [device, policy] that is designed to save energy □ *energy-saving devices, such as time-controlled light switches.*

enervating ['enəveitiŋ] *adj* [atmosphere, weather] that causes one to feel weak and lose one's enthusiasm (formal use).

enfold [in'fould] *vt* to surround <sb/sthg> with something (literary use) □ *She enfolded him in her arms.*

enforce [in'fɔːʳs] *vt* [law, discipline] to make <sthg> be obeyed, often by using the threat of punishment □ *The referee has to enforce the rules.*

enforceable [in'fɔːʳsəbl] *adj* [law, rule] that can be enforced □ *This law is only enforceable if the person is over 18.*

enforced [in'fɔːʳst] *adj* [inactivity, discipline, solitude] that is forced to happen, exist etc by somebody or something else □ *After a period of enforced rest, Kate was eager to play again.*

enforcement [in'fɔːʳsmənt] *n*: *see* **enforce** □ *law enforcement officers.*

enfranchise [in'fræntʃaiz] *vt* -1. [citizen] to give <sb> the right to vote in elections □ *the newly enfranchised electorate of the East.* -2. [slave] to free <sb> from slavery.

engage [in'geidʒ] ◇ *vt* -1. **to engage sb's interest/attention** to attract and keep the interest/attention of sb □ *My attempts to engage the attention of my young audience were*

fruitless. ■ **to engage sb in conversation** to start and continue a conversation with sb □ *He engaged Paul in conversation about gardening for over an hour.* -2. TECHNOLOGY [wheel, gear, clutch] to cause <a mechanism> to operate. -3. [staff] to employ <sb> (formal use) □ *If the economy picks up, we'll engage more workers.*
◇ *vi* **to engage in sthg** to take part in sthg □ *He was suspected of engaging in criminal activity.*

engaged [in'geidʒd] *adj* -1. [fiancé] who has formally agreed to marry somebody □ *She's engaged to Henry.* □ *They're engaged.* □ *They got engaged over the summer.* -2. **to be engaged** to be involved in a particular activity □ *The unions and management are still engaged in lengthy negotiations.* -3. GB [telephone, number, toilet] that is already being used □ *I tried calling, but it was engaged.*

engaged tone *n* GB the sound that one hears on a telephone when the number one has dialed is busy.

engagement [in'geidʒmənt] *n* -1. [to one's fiancé] a formal agreement between two people to get married; the period of time during which a couple are engaged □ *They announced their engagement at Christmas.* -2. [with a person] an arrangement to do something or to see somebody at a particular time □ *a business/social engagement.*

engagement ring *n* a ring given by a man to a woman to show that they are engaged.

engaging [in'geidʒiŋ] *adj* [smile, manner, personality] that seems attractive and interesting □ *The poems were simple and engaging.*

engender [in'dʒendəʳ] *vt* [hope, conflict] to make <sthg> happen or exist (formal use).

engine ['endʒin] *n* -1. [of a car, truck, bus] the part of a vehicle that produces power from gasoline, electricity etc to make it move □ *a car engine.* -2. RAIL the vehicle that pulls a train. -3. COMPUTING in a piece of software, the part of a program that operates a set of instructions.

engine driver *n* GB a person who drives a train.

engineer [,endʒi'niəʳ] ◇ *n* -1. a person who is trained to design, build, and repair roads, electrical equipment, machines etc □ *a road engineer.* -2. [on a ship] a person who is trained to make sure the engines on a ship continue working properly. -3. US RAIL a person who drives a train. ◇ *vt* -1. [bridge, building] to design and build <sthg>. -2. [event, meeting] to make <sthg> happen by planning it secretly or in a clever way.

engineering [,endʒi'niəriŋ] *n* the work or science of designing and building roads, buildings, machines etc; a product that is the result of this □ *He works in engineering.* □ *an engineering degree* □ *a fine piece of engineering.*

England ['iŋglənd] a country in the United Kingdom, consisting of the southern part of Great Britain. SIZE: 130,400 sq kms. POPULATION: 46,170,300 (*English*). CAPITAL: London. LANGUAGE: English. CURRENCY: pound sterling.

English ['iŋgliʃ] ◇ *npl* **the English** the people who live in England. ◇ *n* a language spoken in Britain, the USA, Canada, Australia, New Zealand, and many other countries. ◇ *adj*: see **England**.

English breakfast *n* a breakfast which includes hot food, especially bacon, sausage, eggs, and toast, with tea or coffee □ *a full English breakfast.*

🍴 ENGLISH BREAKFAST
The traditional English breakfast, consisting of cereal or porridge, a hot dish such as bacon and eggs, and toast and marmalade, is served in most hotels, bed and breakfasts, and cafés in the UK. At home, most people eat a much lighter breakfast, typically cereal or muesli and toast, although many have a full English breakfast on weekends.

English Channel: **the English Channel** the sea between England and France, connecting the North Sea and the Atlantic Ocean.

English Civil War *n* **the English Civil War** a war (1642–1651) between the supporters of the English parliament, led by Oliver Cromwell, and the army of King Charles I, who refused Parliament's demands for reform. Cromwell's army won the war, and the King was executed.

English Heritage *n* a British organization that looks after important historical buildings.

Englishman ['ɪŋglɪʃmən] (*pl* **Englishmen** [-mən]) *n* a man who comes from or lives in England.

English muffin *n* US a type of round bread roll that is sliced in half and toasted before eating, and served with butter, jam etc.

Englishwoman ['ɪŋglɪʃwʊmən] (*pl* **Englishwomen**) *n* a woman who comes from or lives in England.

engrave [ɪn'greɪv] *vt* **-1.** [metal, glass, cup] to cut writing, a design etc into the surface of <sthg>; [design, inscription] to cut <sthg> into the surface of glass, metal etc □ *an engraved bracelet* □ *His name was engraved on the cup.* **-2. to be engraved on sb's mind/heart etc** [day, event] to have a quality that affects one's mind/heart etc for a long time □ *The incident was engraved on her memory.*

engraver [ɪn'greɪvə^r] *n* a person whose job is to engrave designs on objects made of glass, metal etc.

engraving [ɪn'greɪvɪŋ] *n* **-1.** a design engraved on an object or surface; a picture that has been printed from an engraved surface. **-2.** the skill or activity of an engraver.

engrossed [ɪn'grəʊst] *adj* **to be engrossed in sthg** [person] to be paying so much attention to sthg that one does not notice anything else □ *She was engrossed in a book.*

engulf [ɪn'gʌlf] *vt* [fire, sea, waves] to completely surround and cover <a person or building>, often very suddenly or quickly □ *The building was engulfed in flames.*

enhance [US ɪn'hæns, GB -'hɑːns] *vt* [reputation, beauty, chances] to improve <sthg> by add-ing something or developing it in some way □ *A little wine will enhance the flavor of the fish.*

enigma [ɪ'nɪgmə] *n* a person or thing whose characteristics, qualities etc make them unusual and difficult to understand, often in a way that makes them interesting □ *After 15 years, her disappearance is still an enigma.*

enigmatic [,enɪg'mætɪk] *adj* [person, smile, silence] mysterious and difficult to understand □ *His only answer was an enigmatic smile.*

enjoy [ɪn'dʒɔɪ] ◇ *vt* **-1.** [trip, life, meal] to get pleasure from <sthg> □ *He enjoyed watching TV.* □ *I don't really enjoy energetic sports.* ■ **to enjoy oneself** to get pleasure and feel happy when one is doing something □ *I'm enjoying myself here in Florida.* □ *You should get out and enjoy yourself more.* **-2.** [privileges, good health, respect] to be lucky enough to have or receive <sthg> (formal use) □ *Members can enjoy the many advantages of the club.* ◇ *vi* **enjoy!** US a word used to say that one hopes that somebody will enjoy something such as a meal, vacation, or gift (informal use).

enjoyable [ɪn'dʒɔɪəbl] *adj* [day, trip, work] that gives one pleasure □ *I had a very enjoyable time there.*

enjoyment [ɪn'dʒɔɪmənt] *n* **-1.** [from an activity] a feeling of pleasure that one gets from a particular activity, event etc □ *I get a lot of enjoyment from my radio.* **-2.** [an enjoyable activity] something that gives somebody pleasure or satisfaction □ *His greatest enjoyment is golf.* **-3.** [of privileges, advantages] the use or possession of something that is good.

enlarge [ɪn'lɑːrdʒ] *vt* [business, building, photograph] to make <sthg> larger □ *The supermarket has a new enlarged parking lot.*

◆ **enlarge (up)on** *vt fus* to enlarge (up)on sthg [on a comment, story] to speak or write about sthg in greater detail □ *Could you enlarge on your previous statement?*

enlargement [ɪn'lɑːrdʒmənt] *n* **-1.** [of a building, photograph] *see* **enlarge**. **-2.** PHOTOGRAPHY a photograph that has been made larger.

enlighten [ɪn'laɪtn] *vt* [reader, audience] to give <sb> more knowledge and a greater understanding of something (formal use) □ *Would you care to enlighten us as to your intentions?*

enlightened [ɪn'laɪtnd] *adj* [person, approach, policy] that is very practical and shows a good understanding of people's needs and problems □ *Their approach to motherhood is hardly what I'd call enlightened.*

enlightening [ɪn'laɪtnɪŋ] *adj* [person, book] that gives one more knowledge and a greater understanding of something □ *"I found his speech most enlightening," said the professor.*

enlightenment [ɪn'laɪtnmənt] *n*: *see* **enlighten**.

◆ **Enlightenment** *n* **the Enlightenment** in 18th-century Europe, a philosophical movement which emphasized the importance of reason and put the role of Christianity into doubt.

enlist [ɪn'lɪst] ◇ *vt* **to enlist sb's help/support** to get sb's help/support □ *Can I enlist your help for tomorrow's visit?* ◇ *vi* MILITARY to join one of the armed forces □ *He enlisted in the army/ navy/air force.*

enlisted man [ɪnˌlɪstəd-] *n* US a man in the army or navy who is not an officer.

enliven [ɪnˈlaɪvn] *vt* [meeting, event] to make <sthg> more interesting and lively □ *The lecture was enlivened by some controversial remarks.*

en masse [ɒnˈmæs] *adv* all together or in a group □ *The workers left en masse.*

enmeshed [ɪnˈmeʃt] *adj* **to be enmeshed in sthg** [in a dispute, difficult situation] to be involved in sthg and unable to escape.

enmity [ˈenmətɪ] (*pl* **enmities**) *n* a strong feeling of dislike that somebody has for another person □ *I feel no enmity toward him.*

ennoble [ɪˈnoʊbl] *vt* **-1.** to make <sb> a member of the nobility. **-2.** to make <sb/sthg> seem more honorable and dignified.

enormity [ɪˈnɔːˈmətɪ] *n* the great size or seriousness of a problem, crime, danger etc □ *She did not seem to understand the enormity of what she had done.*

enormous [ɪˈnɔːˈməs] *adj* **-1.** [object, building, animal] extremely large in size, number, or amount □ *an enormous cat/crowd/investment program.* **-2.** [luck, patience, number] a word used to indicate the large degree of something □ *The launch was an enormous success.*

enormously [ɪˈnɔːˈməslɪ] *adv* **-1. enormously successful/rich/popular** very successful/rich/popular □ *She's enormously pleased with the results.* **-2.** [improve, change, admire] a lot □ *Prices have risen enormously.*

enough [ɪˈnʌf] ◇ *det* **-1. to have/be enough money** to have/be as much money as is wanted or needed □ *There isn't enough time for us to finish the job.* **-2. I have enough problems** I have a lot of problems and do not want any more □ *I have enough difficulty understanding what he says without you trying to interrupt all the time!* □ *There are enough bad drivers on the roads as it is.*

◇ *pron* **-1. to have enough** to have as much or as many as one wants or needs □ *That's enough for me, thanks.* □ *Have you all had enough to eat?* **-2. five children is (quite) enough** five children is a lot and I do not want any more. ■ **more than enough** too much □ *I have more than enough to worry about already.* ■ **to have had enough of sthg** to be angry, annoyed, or bored because sthg has continued too long □ *I've had (about) enough of listening to your complaints.* ■ **that's enough (of that)!** stop behaving in this stupid, rude, or unpleasant way!

◇ *adv* **-1. to be warm/big/fast enough** to be as warm/big/fast as is needed for a particular purpose □ *You're not old enough to vote.* **-2. I've suffered enough already** I have suffered too much already and do not want to suffer any more □ *I think I've already done quite enough to help them.* **-3. strangely/interestingly etc enough** used to show that the speaker finds something strange/interesting etc □ *Funnily enough, all my family are left-handed.*

enquire [ɪnˈkwaɪəʳ] *vt* & *vi* = **inquire.**

enquiry [ɪnˈkwaɪərɪ] (*pl* **enquiries**) *n* **-1.** the act of asking a question in order to get some information □ *I'll make some enquiries about the available options.* ■ **'Enquiries'** GB a desk or department where one can go for information □ *I'll put you through to Customer Enquiries.* **-2.** an official investigation to find out why an event, accident etc happened □ *An enquiry has been set up into the bank's foreign dealings.*

enraged [ɪnˈreɪdʒd] *adj* [person, animal] very angry □ *Enraged animal rights activists protested outside the company's offices.*

enrich [ɪnˈrɪtʃ] *vt* **-1.** [person, nation] to make <sb/sthg> rich. **-2.** [life, mind, soil] to improve the quality of <sthg> by adding something to it □ *vitamin-enriched cereals* □ *baby food enriched with calcium.*

enroll US, **enrol** GB [ɪnˈroʊl] (*pt* & *pp* **enrolled,** *cont* **enrolling**) ◇ *vt* to accept <a student> on a course or at a university, college etc by adding their name to an official list. ◇ *vi* [student] to join a course, university, college etc by adding one's name to an official list □ *I've enrolled on a publishing course.*

enrollment US, **enrolment** GB [ɪnˈroʊlmənt] *n* **-1.** [of a student] *see* **enroll. -2.** [at a college] the total number of people enrolled at a university, college etc or on a course □ *Enrollment is up this year.*

en route [ɒnˈruːt] *adv* on the way to or from a place □ *They stopped en route for something to eat.* □ *We were en route to/from the airport.*

ensconced [ɪnˈskɒnst] *adj* **to be ensconced** to be settled comfortably somewhere (humorous use) □ *There I was, safely ensconced in my corner, when Ralph came up and disturbed me.*

enshrine [ɪnˈʃraɪn] *vt* **to be enshrined** [privilege, idea] to be permanent and unchangeable in law □ *The right to bear arms is enshrined in the Constitution.*

ensign [ˈensaɪn] *n* **-1.** a flag that is flown on a ship to show its nationality. **-2.** US a junior officer in the US navy.

enslave [ɪnˈsleɪv] *vt* **-1.** to make <sb> a slave. **-2.** [society, consumers, workers] to put <sb> into a situation they do not like but cannot escape from □ *enslaved by social pressures.*

ensue [ɪnˈsjuː] *vi* [peace, legal battle] to happen or start existing after something, especially as a result of it (formal use) □ *The problems which then ensued have still not been resolved.*

ensuing [ɪnˈsjuːɪŋ] *adj* [conflict, controversy] that ensues (formal use) □ *The ensuing clashes were violent and bloody.*

en suite [ɒnˈswiːt] *adj* **an en suite bathroom** GB a bathroom that is joined onto a bedroom.

ensure [ɪnˈʃʊəʳ] *vt* [safety, success] to make <sthg> certain □ *Get there early to ensure (that) you get a good seat.*

ENT (*abbr of* **ear, nose, & throat**) *n* a hospital department that deals with diseases of the ears, nose, and throat □ *an ENT specialist.*

entail [ɪnˈteɪl] *vt* [risk, expense, difficulty] to involve <sthg> as a necessary part □ *Merging* the two departments would entail a lot of job losses. □ What exactly does the work entail?

entangled [ɪn'tæŋgld] adj -1. **to be entangled in sthg** [in bushes, a net] to be caught or twisted in sthg so that it is difficult to move or escape; [in a conflict, dispute, difficulty] to be involved in sthg that is difficult to escape from □ He got entangled in the ropes. □ We don't want to become entangled in a legal battle. -2. **to be entangled with sb** to be involved in a relationship with sb that is difficult or bad □ How did you get entangled with those criminals?

entanglement [ɪn'tæŋglmənt] n a relationship with somebody, usually sexual, that is harmful or complicated □ romantic entanglements.

enter ['entər] ◇ vt -1. [room, house, country] to come or go into <a place, building> etc □ On entering the boardroom I felt strangely confident. □ Harry entered the room with a smile on his face. -2. [university, Congress, army] to become a member of <a profession or institution> □ She entered politics soon after she got out of college. -3. [competition] to say officially that one will take part in <a race or competition> □ She's entered the student fiction competition. -4. **to enter sb/sthg for sthg** to say officially that sb/sthg will take part in sthg □ He entered his horse in the race. □ She entered her poem in the competition. -5. [figure, name] to type or write <sthg> on a form, list, register etc □ Please enter your name in block capitals. -6. [situation, mind] to appear suddenly in <sthg> □ A note of panic entered her voice. -7. [era, stage, talks] to begin <a period or process> □ The war entered a deadly new phase. -8. COMPUTING to type <data> into a computer.
◇ vi -1. to come or go into a room or place □ 'Please knock and enter.' -2. to say officially that one will take part in a race, competition etc □ I don't think I'll enter for it this year.

◆ **enter into** vt fus -1. **to enter into sthg** [negotiations, a debate] to become involved in sthg, especially in a serious or official way □ The government has refused to enter into discussions with the terrorists. -2. **to enter into sthg** to influence or be an important part of sthg □ Money doesn't enter into it.

enteritis [,entə'raɪtəs] n a medical condition in which one's intestine becomes inflamed.

enter key n the button on a computer keyboard that is pressed in order to confirm an instruction or to start a new line.

enterprise ['entərpraɪz] n -1. a company or firm □ a small-scale enterprise. -2. [of a company, partnership] a project or plan that is original, bold, and often difficult □ Have you heard about their latest enterprise? -3. [of a person] a willingness and determination to do original and bold things □ He's full of enterprise. -4. business activity □ capitalist enterprise.

enterprise culture n a type of society that encourages and values business and enterprise, especially when it involves private companies.

enterprise zone n in Britain, a special region that the government tries to attract new business to by giving firms financial rewards and privileges if they go there.

enterprising ['entərpraɪzɪŋ] adj [person, plan, company] that shows a willingness to try new ideas and methods □ We are looking for an enterprising young college graduate.

entertain [,entər'teɪn] ◇ vt -1. [audience, reader] to interest and amuse <sb> □ The audience was thoroughly entertained. -2. [guests, clients] to provide food and drink for <sb> □ I'm entertaining my boss at home tonight. -3. [idea, proposal] to be willing to consider <sthg> (formal use) □ I would never even entertain the possibility of something like that happening. -4. [hope, ambition, suspicion] to have <sthg> in one's mind, usually over a long period (formal use). ◇ vi to invite people to one's home for a meal □ We like entertaining.

entertainer [,entər'teɪnər] n a person whose job is to entertain audiences by singing, dancing, telling jokes etc □ a TV entertainer.

entertaining [,entər'teɪnɪŋ] ◇ adj [person, story, movie] that one finds interesting and amusing □ His account of the wedding was highly entertaining. ◇ n the activity of entertaining guests □ She does a lot of entertaining.

entertainment [,entər'teɪnmənt] n -1. the act of giving or getting amusement or pleasure □ the entertainment world/business. -2. THEATER, CINEMA, & TV a show, movie etc that people watch for pleasure □ an entertainments guide.

entertainment allowance n the money that a company allows employees to spend to entertain clients.

enthrall US, **enthral** GB [ɪn'θrɔːl] (pt & pp en-thralled, cont enthralling) vt to completely hold the attention of <sb> by being interesting or exciting □ We listened enthralled as she recounted stories from her childhood.

enthralling [ɪn'θrɔːlɪŋ] adj [story, movie] that enthralls somebody □ She gave an enthralling performance.

enthrone [ɪn'θroʊn] vt to mark the beginning of the authority or rule of <a king, queen, or bishop> with a ceremony in which they are placed on a throne (formal use).

enthuse [ɪn'θjuːz] vi to express great excitement and satisfaction about something □ He was enthusing about his new car.

enthusiasm [ɪn'θjuːzɪæzm] n -1. a strong feeling of excitement and eagerness about something □ His enthusiasm for athletics was infectious. -2. an activity or subject that one is very interested in (formal use).

enthusiast [ɪn'θjuːzɪæst] n a person who very much enjoys a particular subject or hobby □ an opera enthusiast.

enthusiastic [ɪn,θjuːzɪ'æstɪk] adj [crowd, supporter, response] that shows great enthusiasm for something □ You don't sound very enthusiastic about my news.

enthusiastically [ɪn,θjuːzɪ'æstɪklɪ] adv [talk, applaud] see **enthusiastic** □ Everybody clapped enthusiastically.

entice [ɪn'taɪs] vt to persuade <sb> to leave one person, company etc and go to another by offering them something better □ They tried to entice him away from his company.

enticing [ɪn'taɪsɪŋ] *adj* [offer, invitation, smile] very attractive or tempting □ *The thought of a vacation was very enticing.*

entire [ɪn'taɪəʳ] *adj* [country, area, career] whole; [support, agreement] complete □ *We've reduced the prices of our entire range.* □ *We're in entire agreement.*

entirely [ɪn'taɪəʳlɪ] *adv* completely □ *That's entirely different.* □ *I agree entirely.*

entirety [ɪn'taɪrətɪ] *n* **in its entirety** with nothing missing or left out (formal use) □ *They bought the hotel chain in its entirety.*

entitle [ɪn'taɪtl] *vt* **to entitle sb to sthg** to give sb the right to have or do sthg □ *This ticket entitles you to free admission.*

entitled [ɪn'taɪtld] *adj* **-1. to be entitled to sthg/to do sthg** to have the right to sthg/to do sthg □ *I think I'm entitled to an explanation.* **-2. to be entitled sthg** [book, report] to have sthg as a title □ *a new musical entitled "Miracle".*

entitlement [ɪn'taɪtlmənt] *n* the right of a person to have or do something □ *You have no entitlement to maternity benefit.*

entity ['entətɪ] (*pl* **entities**) *n* something that exists on its own and is separate from other things □ *The publishing side of the business is a completely separate entity.*

entomology [,entə'mɒlədʒɪ] *n* the scientific study of insects.

entourage [,ɒntʊ'rɑːʒ] *n* the group of people who work for and travel with a politician, performer etc □ *The Princess arrived, surrounded by her usual entourage.*

entrails ['entreɪlz] *npl* the intestines of a person or animal.

entrance [*n* 'entrəns, *vt* US ɪn'træns, GB -'trɑːns] ◇ *n* **-1.** [to a building] the opening or way that one goes through to get into a place, e.g. a door or gate □ *The entrance is over there, on the right.* □ *the entrance to the White House.* **-2.** [of a person] the arrival of a person in a room or building, especially when it makes other people notice them; the appearance of an actor on stage during a play □ *Her entrance caused a sensation.* **-3. to gain entrance to sthg** [to a building] to be allowed to enter sthg (formal use); [to a society, university] to be accepted as a member of sthg. ◇ *vt* **to be entranced by sb/sthg** [by somebody's beauty, a performer, performance] to feel delight and wonder because of sb/sthg □ *We sat silently, entranced by the music.*

entrance examination *n* an examination that a person takes to become a member of a profession, school etc.

entrance fee *n* a sum of money that one pays to be allowed to enter a museum, zoo etc.

entrance ramp *n* US a road for joining a highway.

entrancing [US ɪn'trænsɪŋ, GB -'trɑːns-] *adj* [music, singer, performance] that causes feelings of delight and wonder.

entrant ['entrənt] *n* **-1.** [to a competition] a person who officially enters a competition, ex-

amination etc □ *All entrants will be required to present a portfolio of their recent work.* **-2.** [to a university] a person who is joining or has recently joined a university, profession etc.

entreat [ɪn'triːt] *vt* to ask <sb> seriously and sincerely to do something □ *He entreated me to help him.*

entreaty [ɪn'triːtɪ] (*pl* **entreaties**) *n* an urgent request (formal use).

entrenched [ɪn'trentʃt] *adj* [idea, attitude, custom] that is firmly established and hard to change □ *He has become more and more entrenched in his views.*

entrepreneur [,ɒntrəprə'nɜːʳ] *n* a person who runs their own business and is prepared to try new ideas and take risks in order to make a profit.

entrepreneurial [,ɒntrəprə'nɜːrɪəl] *adj* [skills, spirit] *see* **entrepreneur.**

entrust [ɪn'trʌst] *vt* **to entrust sthg to sb, to entrust sb with sthg** to give sb the responsibility for sthg □ *I was entrusted with the job of taking care of her plants while she was away.* □ *He entrusted the file to one of his assistants.*

entry ['entrɪ] (*pl* **entries**) *n* **-1.** the act of entering a building, room etc □ *Entry to the office is by the back door.* ■ **to gain entry** to succeed in entering a building or part of a building, usually by using force □ *The police/intruders gained entry through a door at the back of the house.* **-2.** [of a person] the arrival of a person in a room, building etc □ *Nobody noticed his entry into the building.* □ *I'll make my entry unannounced.* **-3.** the right to enter a building, country etc □ *Entry to the reception is by invitation only.* □ *He was refused entry into the country.* □ *'No entry.'* **-4.** the act of joining a group, organization, event etc □ *At 24, he made his entry into politics.* □ *Spain's entry into the EU.* **-5.** [for a competition] a person or thing that is entered for a competition □ *There were hundreds of entries for this month's competition.* **-6.** [in a diary, dictionary] a piece of information that appears in a list, e.g. in a set of accounts, a diary, or a dictionary □ *See the entry under "foot".* **-7.** COMPUTING the process of putting information into a computer. **-8.** US a door, gate, passage etc that one goes through to enter a room, building etc.

entry fee *n* = **entrance fee.**

entry form *n* a form that one writes information on to enter a competition.

entry phone *n* a doorbell connected to a kind of telephone that allows the people inside a building to talk to visitors before letting them come in.

entryway ['entrɪweɪ] *n* US a passage that one goes through to enter a place.

entwine [ɪn'twaɪn] *vt* **to be entwined** [arms, stems] to be twisted around each other tightly.

E number *n* a number with the prefix "E" that is used as a symbol for a particular food additive.

enumerate [ɪ'njuːməreɪt] *vt* to list <a number of things> one after the other.

enunciate [ɪ'nʌnsɪeɪt] ◇ vt -1. [word, consonant] to say <sthg> clearly so that each sound can be heard. -2. [opinion, idea] to explain <sthg> clearly and logically (formal use). ◇ vi [person] to say words, consonants etc clearly.

envelop [ɪn'veləp] vt **to envelop sb/sthg in sthg** to completely cover or surround sb/sthg in sthg □ The top of the hill was enveloped in mist. □ He enveloped her in his arms.

envelope ['envələup] n a paper cover in which letters are mailed.

enviable ['envɪəbl] adj [success, skill, reputation] that other people would like to have for themselves □ She's in the enviable position of having two job offers to choose from.

envious ['envɪəs] adj [person, look] full of envy □ She became envious of her sister's good looks.

enviously ['envɪəslɪ] adv [look, speak] see **envious** □ Karl watched enviously as I climbed onto the gleaming bike.

environment [ɪn'vaɪrənmənt] n -1. [of a person] a particular situation that somebody spends a lot of time in and which affects their behavior, attitude, development etc □ I grew up in a happy home environment. □ Rose is used to working in an electronic environment. -2. **the environment** the natural world around us, including the air, seas, forests etc □ The protection of the environment must be a priority. ■ **the Department of the Environment** → DOE. -3. COMPUTING a system, program, or group of programs that provides everything that is necessary for a particular task □ a word processing environment.

environmental [ɪn,vaɪrən'mentl] adj [pollution, awareness] connected with the natural world □ the growing number of environmental hazards.

environmentalist [ɪn,vaɪrən'mentləst] n a person whose job is to help protect the environment.

environmentally [ɪn,vaɪrən'mentlɪ] adv **to be environmentally aware** to be concerned about the environment. ■ **environmentally friendly** [policy, product] that does not have a harmful effect on the environment □ All our detergents are environmentally friendly.

Environmental Protection Agency n → EPA.

environs [ɪn'vaɪrənz] npl the area that is near to and around a particular place □ the city and its environs.

envisage [ɪn'vɪzɪdʒ] vt to imagine that <sthg> is likely to happen in the future □ Do you envisage any problems? □ I don't envisage (that) there will be any difficulty.

envision [ɪn'vɪʒn] vt US = envisage.

envoy ['envɔɪ] n a messenger who is sent overseas, especially by a government, to discuss something with a foreign government.

envy ['envɪ] (pt & pp envied) ◇ n the feeling one has toward somebody else when they have something that one would like to have very much □ He was motivated by envy of OR toward his more successful colleagues. ■ **to be the envy of sb** to be envied by sb □ She was the envy of all her friends. ■ **to be green with envy** to be full of envy. ◇ vt to feel envy toward <sb> □ I can't say I envy him. □ I envied her for her patience. ■ **to envy sb sthg** to feel envy toward sb because of sthg they have □ I don't envy you that job!

enzyme ['enzaɪm] n a liquid produced in living things that is active in certain chemical processes, e.g. in digesting food in human beings; a chemical substance in some detergents that helps to remove stains.

EOC (abbr of **Equal Opportunities Commission**) n **the EOC** a British government body responsible for making sure that people of a different sex, race, color etc are treated equally and fairly by employers.

eon ['iːən] n a very long period of time.

EPA (abbr of **Environmental Protection Agency**) n **the EPA** a US government department responsible for protecting the environment from pollution.

epaulet(te) [,epə'let] n a decoration on the part of a uniform that covers the shoulder.

ephemeral [ɪ'femrəl] adj [success, fashion, happiness] that lasts only for a very short time.

epic ['epɪk] ◇ adj [journey, story, contest] that is long and impressive, and often involves courage or adventure. ◇ n a long book, movie, poem etc that is impressive, and often contains scenes of courage or adventure.

epicenter US, **epicentre** GB ['epɪsentər] n the point where an earthquake starts.

epidemic [,epɪ'demɪk] n a situation in which a very large number of people are affected by an infectious disease that is spreading in a particular area □ a flu epidemic.

epidural [,epɪ'djʊərəl] n an injection that is given in the spine to reduce pain in the lower part of the body, especially during childbirth.

epigram ['epɪgræm] n a saying or poem that is short, amusing, and clever.

epilepsy ['epɪlepsɪ] n a disease of the central nervous system that causes sudden violent and uncontrolled movements of the body and loss of consciousness.

epileptic [,epɪ'leptɪk] ◇ adj [fit, attack, person] see **epilepsy**. ◇ n a person who suffers from epilepsy.

epilogue ['epɪlɒg] n a short section at the end of a book, play, movie etc that is used as a conclusion.
NOTE: Compare **prologue**.

Epiphany [ɪ'pɪfənɪ] n **(the) Epiphany** a Christian festival held on January 6th that commemorates, in the Western Church, the visit of the Magi to Christ and, in the Eastern Church, the baptism of Christ.

episcopal [ɪ'pɪskəpl] adj [palace, authority, duties] connected with a bishop.

episode ['epɪsəʊd] n -1. an event or period of time that forms part of a longer story or series of events □ I'd rather forget the whole episode. □ an unfortunate episode. -2. a part of a longer story that appears at regular intervals on the radio or TV, or in a magazine □ I missed last week's episode.

episodic [ˌepɪ'sɒdɪk] *adj* [story, book, movie] that is presented in the form of a number of episodes.

epistle [ɪ'pɪsl] *n* a letter (literary use).

epitaph [US 'epɪtæf, GB -tɑːf] *n* the words written about somebody who is dead, usually on their tombstone.

epithet ['epɪθet] *n* a word or short phrase that describes a person and is used as part of or instead of their name.

epitome [ɪ'pɪtəmɪ] *n* **to be the epitome of sthg** to be a perfect example of sthg □ *His approach/He is the epitome of laziness.*

epitomize, -ise [ɪ'pɪtəmaɪz] *vt* to be the most typical example of <a quality, attitude, type of person> etc □ *She epitomizes all the good qualities of this company.*

epoch [US 'epək, GB 'iːpɒk] *n* a period in history that is remembered for its important changes.

epoch-making *adj* [event, discovery, invention] that is important and influences a particular period of history.

eponymous [ɪ'pɒnɪməs] *adj* **the eponymous hero** the hero in a book, play etc whose name appears in the title.

EPOS ['iːpɒs] (*abbr of* **electronic point of sale**) *n* a system that uses a computer terminal to record each sale that is made, so that stock can be controlled and money can be transferred electronically.

equable ['ekwəbl] *adj* [person] who is not easily annoyed or upset □ *Tom's a very equable sort of guy.*

equal ['iːkwəl] (US *pt* & *pp* **equaled**, *cont* **equaling**, GB *pt* & *pp* **equalled**, *cont* **equalling**) ◇ *adj* **-1.** [amount, share] that is the same size, value etc as something else □ *Mix equal parts of cement and sand.* □ *The two men are equal in ability.* □ *One inch is equal to 2.54 cm.* **-2.** [right, access, pay] that is the same for everybody □ *Both teams have an equal chance of winning.* ■ **on equal terms, on an equal basis** [talk, compete] without one side being in a stronger position than the other □ *When we next meet, it must be on equal terms.* **-3. to be equal to sthg** to be able to deal successfully with sthg □ *He was more than equal to the task.*
◇ *n* a person who has the same abilities, rights, or opportunities as another □ *He's hardly my intellectual equal!*
◇ *vt* **-1.** MATH to be the same as <an amount or number> □ *2 times 4 equals 8.* **-2.** [person, record, score] to reach the same level or standard as <sb/sthg> □ *His bad manners are only equaled by his ignorance.* □ *Her generosity equals her father's.*

equality [ɪ'kwɒlətɪ] *n* the same rights or status as other people □ *racial equality.*

equalize, -ise ['iːkwəlaɪz] ◇ *vt* [rights, pay] to make <sthg> more equal and fair for everybody. ◇ *vi* GB SPORT to reach the same score as one's opponent by scoring a goal or point.

equalizer ['iːkwəlaɪzəʳ] *n* GB SPORT a goal, shot etc which makes the score equal.

equally ['iːkwəlɪ] *adv* **-1. equally acceptable/ difficult** acceptable/difficult to the same degree □ *Equally important is the new emphasis on safety features.* □ *Both were held equally responsible.* **-2.** [divide, share, distribute] in equal parts □ *Blame was allocated equally between the police and security staff.* **-3. equally,...** a word used to introduce a piece of information, an argument etc that is opposed to what has just been mentioned but is of the same importance □ *The area is economically deprived, but equally there is hope for improvement.*

equal opportunities *npl* a policy that guarantees equal rights to higher education, employment etc to people of all ethnic origins, both genders etc □ *an equal opportunities employer.*

Equal Opportunities Commission *n* → EOC.

Equal Rights Amendment *n* → ERA.

equal(s) sign *n* a symbol (=) used to show that two figures are equal.

equanimity [ˌekwə'nɪmətɪ] *n* a calm attitude □ *He viewed the decision with his usual equanimity.*

equate [ɪ'kweɪt] *vt* **to equate sb/sthg with sb/ sthg** to connect sb/sthg with sb/sthg in one's mind, because one thinks they are similar □ *You don't normally equate politicians with humility.*

equation [ɪ'kweɪʒn] *n* MATH a statement in which two amounts are given as being the same.

equator [ɪ'kweɪtəʳ] *n* **the equator** an imaginary line around the world, halfway between the North and South Poles.

equatorial [US ˌiːkwə'tɔːrɪəl, GB ˌekwə-] *adj* [region, climate] near or at the equator.

equestrian [ɪ'kwestrɪən] *adj* [sport, event, statue] that is connected with horses or horseriding.

equidistant [ˌiːkwɪ'dɪstənt] *adj* **to be equidistant** [points, places] to be the same distance from a particular place □ *The capital is equidistant from the east and west coasts.*

equilateral triangle [ˌiːkwɪlætrəl-] *n* a triangle whose sides are all the same length.

equilibrium [ˌiːkwɪ'lɪbrɪəm] *n* a situation in which there is a balance between different influences, forces, or emotions with the result that there are no sudden and unexpected changes □ *These spending cuts will help keep the economy in equilibrium.*

equine [US 'iːkwaɪn, GB 'ek-] *adj* [disease, family] that is connected with horses; [features, face] similar to that of a horse.

equinox ['iːkwɪnɒks] *n* one of the two times of year when day and night are the same length in every part of the world.

equip [ɪ'kwɪp] (*pt* & *pp* **equipped**, *cont* **equipping**) *vt* **-1.** to provide <sb/sthg> with what is useful or necessary for a particular situation or purpose □ *The hospital is not equipped to deal with emergency cases.* □ *This car comes equipped with its own hi-fi system.* □ *a fully-equipped kitchen.* **-2.** to give <sb> experience, knowledge etc that helps to prepare them for something □ *In what way do you feel your previous experience equips you for this post?*

equipment [ɪˈkwɪpmənt] *n* the objects that one must use to do a particular job, hobby etc □ *office/kitchen equipment* □ *a piece of equipment.*

equitable [ˈekwɪtəbl] *adj* [system, arrangement, share] that is fair to everybody.

equity [ˈekwəti] *n* FINANCE the market value of a property after the debts of its owner have been subtracted from it. ■ **negative equity** a situation in which the value of a property has fallen so that it is worth less than the amount of money that was borrowed to buy it.

◆ **equities** *npl* shares whose rate of interest is not fixed.

Equity *n* in Britain, the labor union for actors and actresses.

equivalent [ɪˈkwɪvələnt] ◇ *adj* that has the same size, value, or function as something else □ *Their wage was equivalent to $2 per day in today's money.* □ *There's no equivalent organization in the UK.* ◇ *n* a person or thing that is equivalent to somebody or something else □ *The Queen is Britain's nearest equivalent of* OR *to a president.*

equivocal [ɪˈkwɪvəkl] *adj* [statement, reply, person] that is deliberately vague in order to avoid stating the truth □ *He was very equivocal about his travel arrangements.*

equivocate [ɪˈkwɪvəkeɪt] *vi* [person] to speak in a vague way in order to avoid stating the truth (formal use).

er [ɜːʳ] *excl* -1. a word used to express hesitation before one speaks or continues speaking □ *Er, let's see.* -2. a word used to attract somebody's attention □ *Er, excuse me.*

ER (*abbr of* **Elizabeth Regina**) Queen Elizabeth.

era [ˈɪərə] (*pl* **eras**) *n* a period in history that is remembered for a particular fashion, event, invention, ruler etc □ *His death marked the end of an era.* □ *This is the era of the computer.*

ERA *n* -1. (*abbr of* **Equal Rights Amendment**) **the ERA** a proposed change to US law that was intended to give equal rights to men and women. It was rejected in 1982. -2. (*abbr of* **earned run average**) in baseball, the average number of times a pitcher has allowed batters to hit the ball and make a run.

eradicate [ɪˈrædɪkeɪt] *vt* [crime, disease] to completely remove <sthg harmful or unpleasant> from a place so that it no longer exists □ *This party is committed to eradicating poverty.*

eradication [ɪˌrædɪˈkeɪʃn] *n*: *see* **eradicate** □ *The eradication of this practice is long overdue.*

erase [ɪˈreɪz] *vt* -1. [writing, drawing, graffiti] to remove <sthg> from paper, a surface etc, especially using an eraser. -2. to remove <a recording> from a tape; to remove <a file> from a computer memory. -3. [feeling, thought, problem] to remove <sthg> so that it no longer affects somebody or something □ *He tried hard to erase the whole incident from his mind/memory.*

eraser [ɪˈreɪzəʳ] *n* a piece of rubber for removing pencil marks.

erect [ɪˈrekt] ◇ *adj* -1. [person] who sits or stands in a straight upright position. -2. [penis, nipple] that is stiff and stands up or out, rather than in its normal position. ◇ *vt* -1. [building, statue, barrier] to build or make <sthg> □ *A monument is to be erected in his memory.* -2. [tent, chair] to put the different parts of <sthg> together so that it is upright and can be used.

erection [ɪˈrekʃn] *n* -1. [of a building, statue, barrier] *see* **erect**. -2. **to have an erection** to have an erect penis.

ergonomics [ˌɜːgəˈnɒmɪks] *n* the study of how machines, equipment, working areas etc can be improved so that people can work with them more efficiently.

Erie [ˈɪərɪ]: **Lake Erie** one of the Great Lakes between Canada and the USA.

ERM (*abbr of* **Exchange Rate Mechanism**) *n* **the ERM** an agreement between EU countries to keep their exchange rates within certain limits.

ermine [ˈɜːʳmɪn] *n* the white fur of the stoat in winter, which has black spots and is used to decorate royal robes and crowns.

erode [ɪˈrəʊd] ◇ *vt* -1. **to be eroded** [rock, soil, coastline] to be removed gradually by the action of wind, water, rain etc. -2. [confidence, rights, support] to reduce or destroy <sthg> gradually □ *Voters' trust has been eroded by a series of political scandals.* ◇ *vi* [rock, soil, confidence] to be eroded □ *Much of the cliff had eroded away.* □ *His power base among local blacks had eroded over the years.*

erogenous zone [ɪˈrɒdʒənəs-] *n* an area of the body that can cause one to feel sexual excitement when it is touched.

erosion [ɪˈrəʊʒn] *n*: *see* **erode** □ *the effects of erosion on the coastline* □ *We are witnessing the erosion of people's right to privacy.*

erotic [ɪˈrɒtɪk] *adj* [art, movie, dream] that presents or involves sexual desire.

eroticism [ɪˈrɒtɪsɪzm] *n* the erotic quality of a work of art, movie, scene etc.

err [ɜːʳ] *vi* to make a mistake (formal use). ■ **to err on the side of caution** to be more cautious than is necessary in order to avoid making a mistake.

errand [ˈerənd] *n* a short trip to do a small job such as buying something from a store or delivering a message, often for somebody else □ *I have a few errands to do before lunch.* ■ **to go on** OR **run an errand** to do an errand □ *Do you mind running an errand for me?*

errand boy *n* a boy whose job is to run errands.

erratic [ɪˈrætɪk] *adj* [behavior, service, performance] that often changes in an irregular and unpredictable way and does not stay the way that one would prefer □ *He's a very erratic player.*

erroneous [ɪˈrəʊnjəs] *adj* [belief, statement, conclusion] that is not correct, because of a lack of understanding or knowledge (formal use).

error [ˈerəʳ] *n* -1. a mistake that is made during a process or activity □ *a typing error.* ■ **an error of judgment** a decision in which one makes a mistake because of the way one considers a situation □ *I admit I made an error of judgment.* **-2.** the act of making mistakes □ *There's no room for error when you're driving that fast.* ■ **in error** by mistake □ *The letter was delivered to me in error.*

error message *n* a message on a computer screen that shows there has been an error during an operation.

erstwhile ['ɜːˈstwaɪl] *adj* **sb's erstwhile colleague/opponent etc** a person who used to be sb's colleague/opponent etc (literary or humorous use).

erudite [US 'erjədaɪt, GB 'eru-] *adj* [person, book] that has or shows knowledge that comes from studying and reading a lot □ *She gave a very erudite speech on the origins of language.*

erupt [ɪˈrʌpt] *vi* **-1.** [violence, war, fighting] to start suddenly in an uncontrolled way □ *Violence has erupted in parts of the city.* **-2.** [volcano] to explode and start sending ash, lava etc out into the air.

eruption [ɪˈrʌpʃn] *n: see* **erupt** □ *The eruption of violence onto the streets has alarmed community leaders.*

ESA (*abbr of* **European Space Agency**) *n* **the ESA** the organization responsible for Europe's space program.

escalate ['eskəleɪt] *vi* [conflict, violence, cost] to increase quickly and in a way that is serious and worrying □ *Prices have escalated to unprecedented levels.*

escalation [ˌeskəˈleɪʃn] *n: see* **escalate** □ *We want to avoid an escalation of hostilities.*

escalator ['eskəleɪtəʳ] *n* a moving staircase in a large building, public area etc.

escalator clause *n* a clause in a contract that allows for price increases if costs increase.

escapade ['eskəpeɪd] *n* an act that involves bravery, excitement, or breaking rules.

escape [ɪˈskeɪp] ◇ *vt* **-1.** [death, injury, punishment] to avoid <sthg unpleasant> □ *She narrowly escaped injury/being killed.* **-2.** [details, facts] to be difficult for <sb> to remember □ *His name escapes me for the moment.* ■ **to escape sb's notice** [mistake, error] not to be noticed by sb □ *It hasn't escaped my notice that a number of employees have been arriving late.* ◇ *vi* **-1.** [person] to succeed in getting away from a person, place, or situation that one thinks is unpleasant or dangerous □ *He escaped from prison/his captors.* □ *We escaped to Italy.* **-2.** [person] to live through a dangerous experience without being killed or hurt □ *Luckily, we escaped unharmed.* □ *The pilot escaped with minor injuries.* **-3.** [gas, water] to pass from a closed space into the area around or near it. ◇ *n* **-1.** [from prison, boredom] the act of escaping from a person, place, or situation □ *The men made their escape in a red van.* □ *For many, these books are a means of escape from their boring routine.* **-2.** [from injury, death] the act of living through an experience without being killed or badly hurt □ *We had a lucky escape.* **-3.** [of gas, water] an amount of gas,

water etc that escapes from somewhere. **-4.** = **escape key**.

escape clause *n* a clause in a contract that allows one of the people or groups involved to stop following the terms of the contract under certain conditions.

escape key *n* a key on a computer keyboard that is used to cancel the previous command.

escape route *n* **-1.** [in a building] the safest and quickest way for people to leave a building if there is a fire. **-2.** [of a prisoner, robber] the direction that a prisoner, robber etc takes after escaping from prison or committing a crime.

escapism [ɪˈskeɪpɪzm] *n* an activity, way of thinking etc that helps one forget the boring or unpleasant things in one's real life □ *This movie is pure escapism.*

escapist [ɪˈskeɪpɪst] *adj* [story, movie, fantasy] that involves or encourages escapism □ *romantic escapist fiction.*

escapologist [ˌeskəˈpɒlədʒəst] *n* a performer who entertains people by escaping from chains and locked containers.

escarpment [ɪˈskɑːʳpmənt] *n* a wide steep slope on the side of a hill or mountain.

eschew [ɪsˈtʃuː] *vt* [idea, policy, violence] to avoid or reject <sthg> because one disagrees with it strongly (formal use).

escort [*n* 'eskɔːʳt, *vb* ɪˈskɔːʳt] ◇ *n* **-1.** one or more people or vehicles that travel with somebody or something to guard them □ *Mr Cooke arrived under police escort.* **-2.** a person who accompanies somebody of the opposite sex at a social occasion. ◇ *vt* to accompany <sb> to a place to be sure that they leave or that they arrive safely □ *Make sure he escorts you home.*

escort agency ['eskɔːʳt-] *n* an agency that provides escorts for social occasions.

Eskimo ['eskɪmoʊ] (*pl* **Eskimos**) *n & adj* = **Inuit**.

Esky™ ['eskɪ] *n* AUS a plastic box designed to keep food and drink cool.

ESL (*abbr of* **English as a Second Language**) *n* = **ESOL**.

ESOL ['iːsɒl] (*abbr of* **English for Speakers of Other Languages**) *n* the subject of English taught to people who live in an English-speaking country and who do not speak English as their mother tongue.

esophagus US, **oesophagus** GB [ɪˈsɒfəgəs] *n* the tube that carries food from the mouth to the stomach.

esoteric [ˌesəˈterɪk] *adj* [fact, knowledge] that is known or understood by very few people, especially because information about it is hard to find □ *an interest in esoteric religions.*

esp. *abbr of* **especially**.

ESP *n* **-1.** *abbr of* **extrasensory perception**. **-2.** (*abbr of* **English for special purposes**) English that is taught to people who need it for a particular purpose, e.g. business, finance, or information technology.

espadrille ['espədrɪl] *n* a cotton or canvas shoe with a sole made of rope.

especial [ɪ'speʃl] *adj* **especial care/interest etc** more care/interest etc than normal or usual (formal use) □ *Please take especial notice of this announcement.*

especially [ɪ'speʃlɪ] *adv* **-1.** a word used to emphasize that something which has already been mentioned is most true in the case of a particular person or thing □ *The town attracts many tourists, especially in summer.* □ *This was especially true of the others.* **-2. especially cold/difficult etc** colder/more difficult etc than is usual □ *It has been an especially satisfying year.* □ *She was especially nice to me.* **-3.** [choose, buy] for a particular person or thing □ *I got it especially for you.*

espionage ['espɪənɑːʒ] *n* the activities of a spy □ *industrial espionage.*

esplanade [US 'esplənɑːd, GB esplə'neɪd] *n* a straight wide path or road, usually on a seafront, that people walk along for pleasure.

espouse [ɪ'spaʊz] *vt* [cause, principle] to openly discuss and support <sthg> (formal use).

espresso [e'spresoʊ] (*pl* **espressos**) *n* a strong coffee made with steam on a special machine and served without milk in a small cup; a cup of this coffee □ *an espresso machine* □ *Could I have an espresso please?*

Esq. *n abbr of* **Esquire**.

Esquire [ɪ'skwaɪəʳ] *n* GB a formal title used after the name of a man if he has no other title, and instead of "Mr", especially above the address on an envelope; US this title used after the name of a man or woman who is a lawyer.

essay ['eseɪ] *n* **-1.** EDUCATION a short piece of writing on a particular subject by a student. **-2.** [for a publication] a short piece of writing that somebody does on a particular subject and which is published.

essayist ['eseɪəst] *n* a person who writes essays which are published.

essence ['esns] *n* **-1. the essence of sthg** [of an argument, problem] the main idea in sthg that is important in relation to the rest of it □ *That was the essence of her speech.* **-2.** a concentrated liquid used to flavor food □ *vanilla essence.*
◆ **in essence** *adv* a phrase used to emphasize the most important and basic aspect of something □ *The agreement was, in essence, a compromise.*

essential [ɪ'senʃl] *adj* **-1.** [item, reading, requirement] that is absolutely necessary □ *It's essential that it gets there on time.* □ *The project's success is essential to OR for our reputation.* **-2.** [difference, feature] that is most important and basic □ *I jotted down the essential points of her argument.*
◆ **essentials** *npl* **-1.** [for life, survival] the most basic items needed for a particular situation □ *We can only afford to buy the essentials.* **-2.** [of a language, subject] the basic elements of something □ *It wouldn't take you long to learn the essentials of the system.*

essentially [ɪ'senʃlɪ] *adv* a word used to show that one is making a basic general statement about something □ *Essentially, I agree with you.*

Essex ['esɪks] a county in southeastern England. SIZE: 3,672 sq kms. POPULATION: 1,521,800. ADMINISTRATIVE CENTER: Chelmsford.

est. -1. *abbr of* **established**. **-2.** *abbr of* **estimated**.

EST (*abbr of* **Eastern Standard Time**) *n* the local time in the eastern parts of the USA, Canada, and Australia.

establish [ɪ'stæblɪʃ] *vt* **-1.** [organization, business, procedure] to create <sthg that one expects to exist or continue for a long time> □ *'Established in 1847.'* **-2. to establish contact with sb** to make contact with sb □ *They managed to establish radio contact with the ship.* **-3.** [facts, cause, truth] to find out <sthg> for certain by asking questions, doing research etc □ *Police are trying to establish when/why the accident happened.* **-4.** [person, reputation, authority] to cause <sb/sthg> to be accepted or respected by other people □ *She soon established herself as an expert in the field.*

established [ɪ'stæblɪʃt] *adj* **-1.** [custom, practice, system] that has become accepted and fixed over a period of time □ *Female circumcision is still an established practice in some societies.* **-2.** [person, firm, reputation] that is well-known and respected □ *Once you're established, the work will come pouring in.*

establishment [ɪ'stæblɪʃmənt] *n* **-1.** a shop, business, institution etc that is based in a particular building □ *a research establishment.* **-2.** [of an organization, business, procedure] *see* **establish**.
◆ **Establishment** *n* **the Establishment** a term used to describe the various people in powerful jobs who control a particular country or profession □ *the medical Establishment* □ *He's a well-known Establishment figure.*

estate [ɪ'steɪt] *n* **-1.** [in the countryside] a large area of land in the countryside that is owned by one person. **-2.** GB an area of land with buildings of one kind only, especially for housing or industry. **-3.** LAW the money and property left by a dead person.

estate agency *n* GB a company that sells or rents houses and apartments for the owners.

estate agent *n* GB a person who works in an estate agency. ■ **an estate agent's** an estate agency.

estate car *n* GB a car that has a long body, a door at the back end, and a large space behind the back seats instead of a separate trunk.

estd., est'd. *abbr of* **established**.

esteem [ɪ'stiːm] (formal use) ◇ *n* a good opinion of somebody that is based on respect □ *She rapidly won the esteem of her fellow workers in the field.* ■ **to hold sb/sthg in high esteem** to have a good opinion of sb/sthg that one respects. ◇ *vt* [person, work, talents] to respect

<sb/sthg> very much □ *She's highly esteemed by her colleagues.*

esthetic [US es'θetɪk, GB iːs-] *etc* US = **aesthetic** *etc.*

estimate [*n* 'estɪmət, *vb* 'estɪmeɪt] ◇ *n* -1. [of an amount, the time] an approximate idea, calculation, or judgment of something □ *Do you think you could give me a rough estimate?* -2. BUSINESS a statement given by somebody for the charge they are likely to make for doing a particular job □ *We got three separate companies to do an estimate for repairs.*

◇ *vt* [cost, time, damage] to calculate <sthg> approximately □ *She estimated that it would take her three more days.* □ *The damage was estimated at OR to be around £3 million.* □ *It's hard to estimate how long a full recovery could take.*

◇ *vi* BUSINESS **to estimate for sthg** to provide somebody with an estimate for sthg □ *I'll get them to estimate for the repairs before we decide anything.*

estimated ['estɪmeɪtəd] *adj* [cost, value, number] that is approximate and thought to be likely □ *Our estimated time of arrival is 14:00 hours.*

estimation [,estɪ'meɪʃn] *n* -1. **in my/his/her etc estimation** in my/his/her etc opinion □ *In my estimation, more could have been done.* ■ **to go up/down in sb's estimation** to become more/less respected by sb □ *When I heard what he had done, he went up/down in my estimation.* -2. [of cost, time, damage] *see* **estimate**.

Estonia [e'stəʊnjə] a country in northeastern Europe, on the Baltic Sea. SIZE: 45,000 sq kms. POPULATION: 1,600,000 (*Estonians*). CAPITAL: Tallinn. LANGUAGE: Estonian. CURRENCY: kroon.

estranged [ɪ'streɪndʒd] *adj* [person] who is no longer in contact with somebody because of a disagreement □ *He became increasingly estranged from his family/friends.* ■ **sb's estranged husband/wife** a husband/wife who is no longer living with sb.

estrogen ['estrədʒən] US, **oestrogen** ['iːstrədʒən] GB *n* a hormone in females which causes changes in the sexual and reproductive parts of the body.

estuary [US 'estʃʊərɪ, GB -tʃʊrɪ] (*pl* **estuaries**) *n* the very wide part of a river where it meets a sea or ocean.

ETA *n abbr of* **estimated time of arrival**.

et al. ['etæl] (*abbr of* **et alii**) a phrase used after a name, or list of names, to show that other people are included but not mentioned.

etc. (*abbr of* **et cetera**) a word used after a list to show that other similar things or people are included but not mentioned.

et cetera [ɪt'setərə] → **etc.**

etch [etʃ] *vt* -1. [scene, picture] to draw <sthg> by cutting lines into the surface of a piece of metal, glass, or stone. -2. **to be etched on sb's memory** [experience, event] to be impossible for sb to forget because it is important to them or because of the effect it has had on them.

etching ['etʃɪŋ] *n* a picture printed from an image etched on a metal plate.

ETD *n abbr of* **estimated time of departure**.

eternal [ɪ'tɜːrnl] *adj* -1. [life, youth] that lasts forever □ *Some believe that the human spirit is eternal.* -2. [complaints, discussion] that seems never to stop, in a way that one finds annoying □ *I'm fed up with these eternal arguments about what we're going to do next.* -3. [truth, value] that never changes and is appropriate in all situations □ *These are eternal principles which every man can live by.*

eternally [ɪ'tɜːrnlɪ] *adv* [live, complain] *see* **eternal**. ■ **to be eternally grateful** to be very grateful for a long time □ *I am eternally grateful to you.*

eternity [ɪ'tɜːrnətɪ] *n* -1. a period of time that never ends. -2. [after death] the never-ending state that some people believe one exists in after death □ *Their love would last, they said, for eternity.* □ *damned to hell for eternity.* -3. **an eternity** a period of time that seems very long, especially because one is bored or worried □ *We waited for what seemed OR felt like an eternity.*

eternity ring *n* GB a ring given by somebody to their husband or wife when they have been married a long time as a symbol of their love.

ether ['iːθər] *n* a colorless liquid that was used in hospitals in the past as an anesthetic.

ethereal [iː'θɪərɪəl] *adj* [beauty, music] that is so delicate that it does not seem to belong to this world.

ethic ['eθɪk] *n* a moral principle that affects the way people think and act □ *the work/Christian ethic.*

◆ **ethics** ◇ *n* the study of the moral principles and rules that affect people's behavior. ◇ *npl* a set of moral principles and rules that a person or group believes in □ *medical ethics.*

ethical ['eθɪkl] *adj* -1. [problem, dilemma] that is connected with the question of what is morally right or wrong □ *She refused to give the information on ethical grounds.* -2. [approach, practice] that is morally right or good □ *To invest in this way is simply not ethical.*

Ethiopia [,iːθɪ'əʊpɪə] a mountainous country in northeastern Africa, between Sudan, Kenya, and Somalia. SIZE: 1,100,000 sq kms. POPULATION: 53,700,000 (*Ethiopians*). CAPITAL: Addis Ababa. LANGUAGE: Amharic. CURRENCY: birr.

ethnic ['eθnɪk] *adj* -1. [unrest, violence] that exists or happens between people of different races or cultures who live in the same place □ *ethnic tension in our cities.* -2. [group, origin] that is connected with a particular racial and cultural tradition □ *Please indicate the ethnic group to which you belong.* -3. [clothing, food] that is typical of a traditional culture and that people think is exotic because it is so different to their own culture □ *I like these ethnic earrings.*

ethnic cleansing [-'klenzɪŋ] *n* the act of forcing people of a different race, religion etc to leave an area of land, often using violence, in order to have complete control over it.

ethnic minority *n* a group of people whose race, religion, or culture is different from the race, religion, or culture of the majority of people in a community or country.

ethnology [eθ'nɒlədʒɪ] *n* the study and comparison of different racial and cultural groups.

ethos ['iːθɒs] *n* the particular beliefs, attitudes, and values of a certain group of people.

etiquette ['etɪkət] *n* the rules of proper and acceptable behavior in society or in a particular profession □ *professional/courtroom etiquette.*

etymology [,etɪ'mɒlədʒɪ] (*pl* **etymologies**) *n* -1. the study of the origins and development of words. -2. the origins and history of a particular word or phrase.

EU *n abbr of* **European Union** □ *Austrians have today given the EU a vote of confidence.*

eucalyptus [,juːkə'lɪptəs] (*pl* **eucalyptuses**) *n* a tall evergreen tree with round, gray-green leaves that produces an oil with a strong smell that is often used in cough medicines □ *eucalyptus oil.*

Euclid ['juːklɪd] (3rd century BC) a Greek mathematician who invented a system of geometry known as Euclidean geometry.

eulogize, -ise ['juːlədʒaɪz] *vt* to praise <sb/sthg> very much.

eulogy ['juːlədʒɪ] (*pl* **eulogies**) *n* a speech or piece of writing that eulogizes somebody or something.

eunuch ['juːnək] *n* a man whose testicles have been removed.

euphemism ['juːfəmɪzm] *n* a polite word or expression used to describe something that some people might find offensive or embarrassing □ *"Advanced in years" is just a euphemism for "old".*

euphemistic [,juːfə'mɪstɪk] *adj* [language, word] *see* **euphemism.**

euphoria [juː'fɔːrɪə] *n* a feeling of great excitement and happiness.

euphoric [juː'fɒrɪk] *adj* [person, feeling, occasion] *see* **euphoria.**

Eurasia [juə'reɪʒə] Europe and Asia considered together.

Eurasian [juə'reɪʒən] *n* a person who has both European and Asian ancestors.

eureka [juː'riːkə] *excl* a word that somebody says when they suddenly discover something or find the answer to a difficult problem.

Euro ['juərou] *n* the unit of currency for countries in the European Union.

Euro- *prefix* added to words to show that they relate to Europe or the European Union.

Eurocheque™ ['juəroutʃek] *n* a check that can be used in most European countries.

Eurocrat ['juərəkræt] *n* an important official in the European Union (disapproving use).

Eurocurrency ['juəroukʌrənsɪ] (*pl* **Eurocurrencies**) *n* a currency that is held in banks in Western Europe outside its country of origin

and is used especially to finance international trade.

Eurodollar ['juəroudɒlər] *n* a US dollar held in European banks.

Euro-elections *npl* the elections to membership of the European Parliament.

Euro MP *n* a member of the European Parliament in Strasbourg.

Europe ['juərəp] -1. the continent between the Atlantic, the Mediterranean, and the Ural Mountains, including the British Isles and Iceland. -2. GB the mainland of Europe, excluding the British Isles. -3. GB POLITICS the European Union.

European [,juərə'piːən] ◇ *n* a person who comes from or lives in Europe. ◇ *adj*: *see* **Europe** □ *European ministers meet today to discuss fishing quotas.*

European Commission *n* **the European Commission** the administrative body of the EU. It is responsible for proposing new policies and making sure that existing policies are carried out.

European Community *n* **the European Community** an organization of European states designed to encourage closer links between its members.

European Court of Human Rights *n* **the European Court of Human Rights** the court of the Council of Europe.

European Court of Justice *n* **the European Court of Justice** the court of the European Union.

European Currency Unit *n* → ECU.

European Monetary System *n* **the European Monetary System** a system set up by the European Union to control the exchange rates among the currencies of the member countries.

European Parliament *n* **the European Parliament** the parliament of the European Union, based in Strasbourg.

European Union *n* **the European Union** the union of European countries that was formed in 1993 when the member states of the European Community signed the Maastricht Treaty and agreed to closer political and economic cooperation.

Eurydice [juː'rɪdɪsɪ] → **Orpheus.**

euthanasia [,juːθə'neɪʒə] *n* the practice of killing very ill or old people without causing them pain so that they do not continue to suffer.

evacuate [ɪ'vækjueɪt] *vt* to get <people> to leave a place because it is dangerous; to empty <a place> in this way □ *Staff and customers were evacuated from the store shortly before the explosion.* □ *Police were called in to evacuate the area.*

evacuation [ɪ,vækjʊ'eɪʃn] *n*: *see* **evacuate** □ *McArthur ordered the evacuation of the city.*

evacuee [ɪ,vækjʊ'iː] *n* a person who has been evacuated from a dangerous place, especially during a war.

evade [ɪ'veɪd] *vt* -1. [issue, question] to avoid

dealing with <sthg>, especially because one is trying to hide something; [responsibility, problem] to avoid dealing with <sthg> because it is difficult or unpleasant □ *I think you're evading the issue here.* □ *You cannot continue to evade your responsibilities in this way.* **-2.** [tax, punishment, capture] to avoid <sthg that is required by law> □ *He managed to evade capture for several days.* **-3.** [pursuer] to avoid being caught by <sb>.

evaluate [ɪ'væljʊeɪt] *vt* [success, difficulty, evidence] to judge the value of <sthg> by considering it carefully □ *It would be wrong to evaluate his contribution in purely financial terms.*

evaluation [ɪ,væljʊ'eɪʃn] *n*: see **evaluate** □ *I would appreciate your evaluation of the situation.* □ *Each student gets an evaluation of his or her coursework.*

evangelical [,iːvæn'dʒelɪkl] *adj* [church, sermon] that is connected with a kind of Christian belief that emphasizes the importance of studying the Gospels and accepting Christ as one's personal savior □ *an evangelical preacher.*

evangelism [ɪ'vændʒəlɪzm] *n* the practice of teaching Christianity, especially to people who are not Christians.

evangelist [ɪ'vændʒələst] *n* a person who tries to persuade people to become Christians, especially at large public meetings.

evangelize, -ise [ɪ'vændʒəlaɪz] *vt* to try to persuade <sb> to become a Christian.

evaporate [ɪ'væpəreɪt] *vi* **-1.** [water, solution] to change into gas or steam. **-2.** [hopes, confidence, fears] to gradually become less strong and then disappear.

evaporated milk [ɪ,væpəreɪtəd-] *n* unsweetened milk that has been made thicker by removing water from it and which is sold in cans.

evaporation [ɪ,væpə'reɪʃn] *n*: see **evaporate** □ *water loss due to evaporation.*

evasion [ɪ'veɪʒn] *n* **-1.** the act of avoiding doing something that one is supposed to do, especially by using deception □ *This is an evasion of your responsibilities as a citizen.* **-2.** a way of using words so that one does not really give an answer to the question asked □ *Lies and evasion are his speciality.*

evasive [ɪ'veɪsɪv] *adj* **-1.** [person, answer] that avoids dealing with a question directly and honestly □ *She was being deliberately evasive.* **-2. to take evasive action** MILITARY to move away in order to avoid being attacked, injured etc □ *Our pilots were forced to take evasive action.*

eve [iːv] *n* **the eve of sthg** the day before sthg important happens □ *on the eve of the election.*

Eve [iːv] → **Adam.**

even¹ ['iːvn] *adj* **-1.** [speed, rate, temperature] that remains the same □ *The spacing between the letters has to be even.* **-2.** [ground, surface, road] smooth, flat, and level □ *You need to make the floor even before laying tiles or carpet.* **-3.** [temper, tone] that does not show great

changes in feelings and emotions □ *He spoke in a slow even tone.* **-4.** [contest, scores] equal □ *After their win on Saturday, Dallas is now even with the leaders.* ■ **to be even** [teams, players] to have an equal amount of skill or ability. **-5.** [division, share] shared out equally or fairly □ *The party is committed to a more even distribution of wealth.* ■ **to have an even chance of doing sthg** to be as likely to do sthg as not to do it □ *We've got an even chance of winning.* **-6.** *phrase* **to get even with sb** to do as much harm to sb as they have done to one □ *He vowed he'd get even with them one day.* **-7. an even number** a number that divides by two, e.g. 2, 4, or 6.
NOTE: The opposite of an *even number* is an *odd number.*

even² *adv* **-1.** a word used to show that a fact is surprising or unexpected □ *Even I could do better than that!* □ *Nobody knows, not even my mother.* **-2.** a word used for extra emphasis in comparisons □ *£5 is fine, but £10 would be even better.* □ *You're even more stupid than I first thought.*

◆ **even if** *conj* **we'll go for a walk, even if it's raining** it might rain, but if this happens it will make no difference and we will still go for a walk □ *I'm glad I bought the car, even if I can't really afford it.*

◆ **even out** ◇ *vt sep* [surface, water supply, prices] to make the differences between <two or more amounts, levels> etc smaller or less noticeable □ *Go over the ground with a roller after digging to even out any bumps.* □ *A final coat of paint should even out any light or dark patches.* ◇ *vi* [differences, rates] *The costs will even out if we pay a regular monthly amount.*

◆ **even so** *adv* **he was ill, but even so he came** in spite of the fact that he was ill, he came □ *I know he's busy at the moment. Even so, he could have offered to help.*

◆ **even though** *conj* **we enjoyed the game, even though we didn't win** it is surprising that we enjoyed the game, because we didn't win □ *I get nervous going there, even though I've been there before.*

even-handed [-'hændəd] *adj* [person, approach] that treats everybody fairly □ *I have tried to be reasonably even-handed in my treatment of the candidates.*

evening ['iːvnɪŋ] *n* **-1.** the part of the day between the end of the afternoon and the beginning of the night □ *an evening show* □ *I could meet you this/tomorrow evening.* □ *We could go out in the evening.* □ *I spent all evening at home.* **-2.** a social event or entertainment that takes place in the evening □ *a musical evening* □ *Thanks for a wonderful evening!*

◆ **evenings** *adv* US in the evening □ *I tend to be fairly busy evenings.*

evening class *n* an educational class for adults that takes place in the evening.

evening dress *n* **-1.** special clothes worn for formal events in the evening □ *Mark was wearing evening dress.* **-2.** a dress, usually long, that is worn by a woman for a formal event in the evening □ *She was wearing a beautiful black evening dress.*

Evening Star *n*: **the Evening Star** a bright planet, usually Venus, seen in the western sky just after the sun goes down.

evenly ['iːvnlɪ] *adv* -1. **to breathe evenly** to breathe in a way that is regular and stays at the same level. ■ **to be evenly spaced** [objects, letters] to have the same amount of space between each other. -2. [divide, distribute] in a way that gives an equal amount to every part of something □ *Apply the paint evenly.* ■ **to be evenly matched** [teams, players] to be even. -3. [talk, speak] in a way that does not show one's emotions.

evensong ['iːvnsɒŋ] *n* a service held in the evening in Anglican churches.

event [ɪ'vent] *n* -1. something that happens and is usually interesting or important □ *historical events* □ *The party was quite an event!* -2. SPORT a race or activity that is part of an organized competition □ *track and field events.* -3. **in that event** if that happens □ *In that event, I should withdraw my application.*
◆ **in any event** *adv* a phrase used to emphasize that something will happen even if something else makes it seem uncertain or unlikely □ *I'll try to phone tomorrow, but in any event I'll write next week.*
◆ **in the event** *adv* GB when something actually happened or took place □ *We thought there would be problems, but in the event everything went smoothly.*
◆ **in the event of** *prep* if <sthg> happens □ *'In the event of fire, break glass.'*
◆ **in the event that** *conj* if a particular thing happens □ *In the event that the show is canceled, a refund will be issued.*

even-tempered *adj* [person] who is calm and does not get angry easily □ *He's a fairly even-tempered boy.*

eventful [ɪ'ventfl] *adj* [life, day] in which a lot of interesting or exciting things happen □ *It wasn't exactly an eventful trip.*

eventing [ɪ'ventɪŋ] *n* GB SPORT a horse riding competition that lasts three days and involves cross-country riding and show jumping.

eventual [ɪ'ventʃʊəl] *adj* [outcome, improvement, choice] that is the final result of a process □ *The eventual winner was Deborah Fields from Toronto.*

eventuality [ɪ,ventʃʊ'ælətɪ] (*pl* **eventualities**) *n* a possible event or result in the future □ *We must be prepared for such an eventuality/all eventualities.*

eventually [ɪ'ventʃʊəlɪ] *adv* -1. after a long time, especially after a lot of difficulties or delays □ *Eventually, somebody came to answer the door.* □ *I eventually realized what a waste of time it was.* -2. at some point in the future when a particular process or situation comes to an end □ *Interest rates should come down eventually.*

ever ['evər] *adv* -1. **have you ever been to France?** have you been to France at any time? (used in commands, questions, negative sentences, and clauses beginning with "if") □ *No one ever calls these days.* □ *Don't ever speak to me like that!* □ *He denied ever having been there.* □ *If you ever need any help, ask me.* -2. a word used in comparisons and after superlatives □ *Business is better than ever.* □ *It's the worst play I've ever seen.* -3. a word used in questions to emphasize one's surprise □ *What ever makes you think that?*
◆ **as ever** *adv* in the usual way □ *As ever, he was charming and witty.*
◆ **ever since** ◇ *adv* a phrase used to show that a situation has existed since a particular event, and that it still exists □ *I decided not to take the job and have regretted it ever since.* ◇ *prep* **ever since the 1920s** all the time from the 1920s until now. ◇ *conj*: *She's been getting headaches ever since she had the accident.*
◆ **ever so** *adv* very (informal use) □ *Thank you ever so much.*
◆ **ever such** *det* **ever such nice people** very nice people (informal use).
◆ **for ever** *adv* for all time in the future □ *I'm not going away for ever, just for a year.*

Everest ['evərəst]: **(Mount) Everest** a mountain in the Himalayas, the highest in the world. HEIGHT: 8,846 m.

Everglades ['evəgleɪdz]: **the Everglades** a large area of marshland in Florida, USA. It includes a national park that is famous for its alligators.

evergreen ['evəgriːn] ◇ *adj* [tree, shrub] that never loses its leaves. ◇ *n* an evergreen tree, shrub etc.
NOTE: Compare **deciduous**.

everlasting [US ,evər'læstɪŋ, GB ,evə'lɑːstɪŋ] *adj* [life, peace] that never ends □ *The promise of everlasting happiness.*

every ['evrɪ] *det* -1. **every child** all the children in the group □ *Every room in the hotel has a TV.* □ *They argue every time they meet.* □ *Every word of it is true.* -2. **every three months** regularly, once in every period of three months □ *I think of him every hour/day of my life.* □ *They stopped and rested every five miles.* -3. **every tenth girl** one girl out of ten □ *The Olympics are held every fourth year.* -4. a word used for emphasis □ *Every attempt was made to save them.* □ *There's every chance she'll make a full recovery.*
◆ **every now and then, every so often** *adv* sometimes but not often □ *I like to go out dancing every so often.*
◆ **every which way** *adv* US in all directions (informal use) □ *People were running about every which way.*

everybody ['evrɪbɒdɪ] *pron* -1. all the people in a particular group □ *I get on well with everybody at work.* □ *Has everybody had enough to eat?* -2. all the people who are important or relevant □ *She's the kind of person who gets on well with everybody.* □ *It's the movie that everybody is talking about at the moment.*

everyday ['evrɪdeɪ] *adj* [routine, occurrence, use] that happens regularly as a part of ordinary life and is not unusual or interesting □ *This kind of thing is hardly an everyday occurrence.* □ *It doesn't happen often in everyday life.*

everyone ['evrɪwʌn] *pron* = **everybody**.

everyplace ['evrɪpleɪs] *adv* US = **everywhere** (informal use).

everything ['evrɪθɪŋ] *pron* -1. all the objects, facts, actions etc in a particular place or situation □ *Don't believe everything you read in the newspapers!* □ *Everything in the house is for sale.* -2. the whole situation □ *Don't worry, everything's under control.* -3. all the possible things that might happen or be needed □ *I can't do everything at once!*

everywhere ['evrɪweəʳ] *adv* -1. all the places somebody goes to □ *Her dog follows her around everywhere.* -2. in every part of the world □ *And here is a song for Elvis fans everywhere.* -3. in every part of a particular building, area, or country □ *There were flames in the kitchen and smoke everywhere.* □ *We've been everywhere in London.* -4. in all possible places □ *Oh here you are, I've been looking everywhere for you!*

evict [ɪ'vɪkt] *vt* [tenant, resident] to make <sb> leave the house, apartment etc where they are living, because they no longer have the legal right to be there □ *We want to evict them from our land.*

eviction [ɪ'vɪkʃn] *n: see* **evict** □ *The number of evictions has grown in the past year.*

eviction notice *n* a formal warning to somebody that they are going to be evicted.

evidence ['evɪdəns] *n* -1. objects, words, or events which make somebody believe a statement or theory □ *This latest move is evidence of a change in government thinking.* -2. LAW objects or words used to prove that something is true □ *There's no evidence to prove that he was there that night.* ■ **to give evidence** GB to say what one knows about a particular person or event during a trial in a court of law.
◆ **in evidence** *adj* to be in evidence to be present and noticeable in a particular place or situation □ *The police were much in evidence at the demonstration.*

evident ['evɪdənt] *adj* [enjoyment, uneasiness] that can be clearly seen, noticed etc □ *It soon became evident that he was a sick man.*

evidently ['evɪdəntlɪ] *adv* -1. **evidently,...** a word used to show that one thinks something is probably true because of what one already knows □ *She's evidently forgotten to fax us.* -2. a word used to show that one thinks something is certainly true because of what one can see □ *He was evidently in great pain.*

evil ['iːvl] ◇ *adj* [person, torture, practice] very bad, harmful, or unpleasant. ◇ *n* -1. the quality of being very bad and harmful □ *Evil is all around us.* -2. something that is considered to be unpleasant or harmful □ *the evils of drink* □ *These parking regulations are a necessary evil.*

evil-minded [-'maɪndəd] *adj* [person] who

wants unpleasant or harmful things to happen to other people.

evince [ɪ'vɪns] *vt* [interest, desire] to show <a feeling, attitude> etc clearly (formal use).

evocation [,iːvou'keɪʃn] *n* something which causes somebody to have a memory or picture of something in their mind.

evocative [ɪ'vɒkətɪv] *adj* [smell, poem] that makes somebody think of something else, usually from the past □ *The photographs were very evocative of my early childhood.*

evoke [ɪ'vouk] *vt* -1. to bring into one's mind <a memory, feeling> etc □ *The movie evoked memories of summer vacations long ago.* -2. to cause <a response, reaction> etc □ *The appeal evoked little response from the audience.*

evolution [,iːvə'luːʃn] *n* -1. BIOLOGY the gradual process of development by which plants and animals change their forms over millions of years. -2. [of society, a system] a gradual development of something.

evolve [ɪ'vɒlv] ◇ *vt* [system, style] to develop <sthg> gradually □ *We've evolved our own method of filing.* ◇ *vi* -1. [model, style] to gradually develop and become more advanced or complex □ *Technology is continually evolving.* -2. BIOLOGY to change gradually from one form into another □ *Birds evolved from reptiles.*

ewe [juː] *n* a female sheep.

ex- [eks] *prefix* added to words to show that a person or thing no longer has the status they used to have □ *his ex-wife* □ *an ex-serviceman/president.*

exacerbate [ɪg'zæsəʳbeɪt] *vt* [difficulty, pain] to make <sthg> worse (formal use) □ *Maxwell's anxious presence only exacerbated the situation.*

exact [ɪg'zækt] ◇ *adj* [amount, copy, time] that is correct and includes every necessary detail □ *What is your exact location?* ■ **to be exact** a phrase used when one is giving more detailed or accurate information about a subject □ *He comes from the North, Boston, to be exact.* ◇ *vt* [promise, payment] to demand and get <sthg> from somebody, usually because one is stronger or more powerful than them (formal use) □ *The gang exacts money from local storekeepers under the threat of violence.*

exacting [ɪg'zæktɪŋ] *adj* [job, person] that demands hard work and effort □ *Her team had to live up to her own exacting standards.*

exactitude [ɪg'zæktɪtｊuːd] *n* the quality of being exact (formal use).

exactly [ɪg'zæktlɪ] ◇ *adv* -1. a word used to refer to an amount, location etc in a way that is correct and includes every necessary detail □ *Where exactly do you live?* □ *That's exactly $10, please.* □ *What exactly happened?* ■ **at nine/ten etc o'clock exactly** neither earlier nor later than nine/ten etc o'clock. ■ **not exactly** a phrase used to show that something is not completely true or correct □ *It's not exactly a disaster but it's not a success either.* □ "*So you were ill yesterday?*" — "*Not exactly, but I felt pretty low.*" -2. [copy, calculate] *see* **exact**.
◇ *excl* a word used to show that a person is

in complete agreement with what has just been said □ *Exactly! That's just what I was thinking.*

exaggerate [ɪɡ'zædʒəreɪt] ◇ *vt* [truth, problem, effect] to make <sthg> seem bigger, better, more important etc than it really is □ *The scale of the problem has been grossly exaggerated.* ◇ *vi: Don't exaggerate! It's not that bad!*

exaggerated [ɪɡ'zædʒəreɪtəd] *adj* **-1.** [claim, report] that is made to seem bigger, better, more important etc than it really is □ *Her claims to be the new Jane Fonda are somewhat exaggerated.* **-2.** [sigh, gesture] that is done in a way that is more obvious than it needs to be in order to create a particular effect □ *"Be quiet," she said in an exaggerated whisper.*

exaggeration [ɪɡ,zædʒə'reɪʃn] *n: see* **exaggerate** □ *He's prone to exaggeration.* □ *It would be no exaggeration to say that we all felt betrayed.*

exalted [ɪɡ'zɔːltəd] *adj* [person, position] that seems very important.

exam [ɪɡ'zæm] (*abbr of* **examination**) *n* a formal test of somebody's knowledge or ability in a particular subject, usually given at the end of a course of study □ *an oral/English exam.* ■ **to take** OR GB **sit an exam** to do a test in order to get an official qualification.

examination [ɪɡ,zæmɪ'neɪʃn] *n* **-1.** = **exam.** **-2.** a careful and detailed check of something such as a document or vehicle to make sure that everything is the way it is supposed to be □ *On closer examination, it turned out to be a fake.* **-3.** MEDICINE the process of looking at a person's body to find out how healthy they are □ *The doctor sent the patient to her local hospital for an examination.* **-4.** [of a plan, proposal, idea] a detailed consideration of something □ *The offer is still under examination.*

examination board *n* an organization responsible for preparing and grading exams for students.

examination paper *n* GB a set of printed questions used as an examination; the set of pages on which answers to these questions are written.

examine [ɪɡ'zæmɪn] *vt* **-1.** [document, painting] to look at <sthg> carefully □ *Professor Martin examined the manuscript closely.* **-2.** MEDICINE to look at <sb> to find out whether they are healthy or not. **-3.** [idea, proposal, evidence] to consider <sthg> carefully, especially in order to make a decision about it □ *We cannot come to a conclusion until all the evidence has been examined.* **-4.** [pupil, student] to give <sb> a test □ *Students will be examined on a number of subjects.* **-5.** LAW to ask <sb> questions during a trial in a court of law □ *It was the prosecution's turn to examine the witness.*

examiner [ɪɡ'zæmɪnər] *n* **-1.** a person who writes questions for an exam. **-2.** a person who grades the answers to an exam. ■ **an internal/external examiner** GB an examiner from the institution where the exam is taken/from a separate institution.

example [US ɪɡ'zæmpl, GB -'zɑːmpl] *n* **-1.** a thing which is mentioned when one is trying to show the typical qualities of a larger group of things □ *This is a perfect example of the kind of attitude I'm talking about.* **-2.** a person or a type of behavior that other people are encouraged to copy □ *Her courage is an example to us all.* ■ **to follow sb's example** to copy what sb else has done in one's own behavior □ *I followed your example and complained about the service.* ■ **to make an example of sb** to punish sb severely to stop other people from copying their behavior.

◆ **for example** *adv* a phrase used to introduce an example of what is being shown or discussed □ *Cycling, for example, is an excellent way of building up stamina.*

exasperate [ɪɡ'zæspəreɪt] *vt* to make <sb> very frustrated and annoyed □ *He was exasperated by his daughter's lack of enthusiasm.*

exasperating [ɪɡ'zæspəreɪtɪŋ] *adj* [person, day] that makes one feel frustrated and annoyed □ *I find him really exasperating.*

exasperation [ɪɡ,zæspə'reɪʃn] *n: see* **exasperate** □ *She looked at him in exasperation.*

excavate ['ekskəveɪt] *vt* **-1.** [building site, area] to remove earth from <a piece of land> by digging; to make <a hole> by doing this. **-2.** [object, pottery, bone] to find <sthg> by digging a hole in the ground; [settlement, site, hill] to show <sthg> as it was in the past by removing earth from it.

excavation [,ekskə'veɪʃn] *n* **-1.** [of site, hole] *see* **excavate.** **-2.** a site or area of land that is being excavated.

excavator [,ekskə'veɪtər] *n* GB a large machine for digging and moving earth, e.g. on a construction site.

exceed [ɪk'siːd] *vt* **-1.** [amount, number] to be greater than <sthg> in quantity □ *The number of applicants far exceeds the number of places available.* **-2.** [speed limit, expectations] to go beyond <sthg> □ *The trip certainly exceeded all my expectations.*

exceedingly [ɪk'siːdɪŋlɪ] *adv* **exceedingly complicated/good etc** very complicated/good etc.

excel [ɪk'sel] (*pt* & *pp* **excelled,** *cont* **excelling**) ◇ *vi* to be very good at something □ *She excels in OR at music.* ◇ *vt* **to excel oneself** to do better than usual □ *You've excelled yourself tonight, Mark.*

excellence ['eksələns] *n* the quality of being extremely good □ *As a company we pride ourselves on setting standards of excellence.* □ *the excellence of the food.*

Excellency ['eksələnsɪ] (*pl* **Excellencies**) *n* a title used for officials of very high rank such as ambassadors □ *Your/His/Her Excellency.*

excellent ['eksələnt] ◇ *adj* [meal, idea, athlete] extremely good □ *What an excellent program!* ◇ *excl* a word used to show one's approval of something □ *Excellent! That's a great plan!*

except [ɪk'sept] ◇ *prep* a word used to introduce the only thing or person not included in the previous statement □ *I can make any day except Monday.* □ *We know nothing except what you've already told us.* ◇ *conj* **except (that)...** a word used to introduce one slight difference between two things or people □ *The twins look the same, except (that) Jane has green eyes.*

◆ **except for** *prep* = **except** □ *We told everyone, except for Ian.*

excepted [ɪk'septəd] *prep* with the exception of <sb/sthg> □ *Dan excepted, everyone agreed.*

excepting [ɪk'septɪŋ] *prep* & *conj* a word used to indicate the only thing that stops one's general statement from being completely true □ *Everyone agreed, excepting Ron.*

exception [ɪk'sepʃn] *n* **-1.** a person, thing, or situation that is not included in a general statement, rule, or pattern □ *an exception to the rule* □ *I'll make an exception in your case.* ■ **with the exception of sb/sthg** a phrase used to introduce a person, thing, or situation not included in a general statement □ *Everybody was there, with the notable exception of Tom.* ■ **without exception** a phrase used to show that something is true for every one of the people or things mentioned □ *I want everyone, without exception, in the office at eight-thirty tomorrow.* **-2. to take exception to sthg** [to a remark, attitude] to show that one does not accept sthg because one finds it annoying or offensive □ *He took exception to being called "Sonny".*

exceptional [ɪk'sepʃənl] *adj* **-1.** [musician, work] very good □ *The food was good, but I wouldn't say it was exceptional.* **-2.** [case, circumstances] very unusual and unlikely to happen or exist often □ *Only under exceptional circumstances will employees be allowed to leave before 5:00pm.*

exceptionally [ɪk'sepʃnəlɪ] *adv* **exceptionally kind/cold etc** very kind/cold etc.

excerpt ['eksɜːʳpt] *n* a small part of a book, movie, piece of music etc □ *This is an excerpt from Copland's "Appalachian Spring."*

excess [ɪk'ses, *before nouns* 'ekses] ◇ *adj* [weight, fat] more than is allowed, necessary, or usual □ *Drain off any excess water.* ◇ *n* an amount that is greater than what is necessary, usual, or allowed □ *She was driving with an excess of alcohol in her blood.*

◆ **in excess of** *prep* more than <sthg> □ *He spent in excess of $2,000.*

◆ **to excess** *adv* too much □ *He drinks to excess.*

excess baggage *n* baggage that weighs more than the limit that a passenger is allowed to take onto a plane; the money paid by a passenger in order to be allowed to take this baggage onto a plane.

excess fare *n* GB extra money that one has to pay if one's train ticket does not cover the fare for the entire trip.

excessive [ɪk'sesɪv] *adj* [interest, demand, price] that is much greater in amount or degree than is necessary or desirable □ *$50 for lunch seems a little excessive.*

excess luggage *n* = **excess baggage**.

exchange [ɪks'tʃeɪndʒ] ◇ *vt* **-1.** [addresses, gifts] to give <things of the same kind> to each other at the same time □ *We exchanged letters for years.* □ *I exchanged jobs with a German*

colleague for a few months. **-2.** [currency, goods] to replace <sthg> with something else of the same value □ *Merchandise can only be exchanged with a receipt.* □ *I'd like to exchange this shirt for one in a smaller size.*

◇ *n* **-1.** [of two things] the act of exchanging something for something else □ *the free exchange of information* □ *an exchange of goods/views.* **-2.** [for telephones] a building or part of an office, where connections are made between telephone lines. **-3.** [between two families, students] an arranged visit in which two people go to each other's home town □ *I went to Moscow on a cultural exchange.* □ *an exchange visit.* **-4.** [during a meeting, discussion] a short argument, especially in a public meeting or a political debate (formal use) □ *There was a heated exchange.*

◆ **in exchange** *adv* a phrase used when giving something to somebody in return for something else that is similar or of the same value □ *I'll give you my bike in exchange for your skis.*

exchange rate *n* the official rate at which money in one currency is exchanged for money in another currency.

excise ['eksaɪz] ◇ *n* **excise (tax)** a tax that a government puts on goods such as alcohol that are produced and sold within its country. ◇ *vt* [passage of text, tumor] to cut out and remove <sthg> (formal use).

excise duty *n* = **excise tax**.

excitable [ɪk'saɪtəbl] *adj* [person, animal] that gets excited or nervous easily.

excite [ɪk'saɪt] *vt* **-1.** to make <sb> excited □ *Try not to excite yourself too much.* **-2.** to cause <interest, suspicion, admiration> etc □ *The movie failed to excite my imagination.*

excited [ɪk'saɪtəd] *adj* [person] who is full of strong feelings of enthusiasm and interest and unable to relax, usually because of something good that they think is going to happen □ *We were very excited about OR at the news.* □ *What are you getting so excited about?*

excitement [ɪk'saɪtmənt] *n* **-1.** the feeling of being excited □ *I've had enough excitement for one day, thanks!* □ *In my excitement, I forgot to thank him.* **-2.** something that causes one to feel excited □ *the excitements of a trip to Paris.*

exciting [ɪk'saɪtɪŋ] *adj* [movie, idea, race] that makes one feel excited □ *I think it's very exciting to be going away to India.* □ *an exciting new discovery.*

excl *abbr of* **excluding.**

exclaim [ɪk'skleɪm] ◇ *vt* to say <sthg> suddenly and in a loud voice when one is surprised, shocked, disappointed etc □ *"That's ridiculous!" he exclaimed.* ◇ *vi*: *She exclaimed at how much work there was to be done.*

exclamation point US, **exclamation mark** GB *n* a symbol (!) at the end of a sentence, phrase, or word that shows that it is an exclamation.

exclude [ɪk'skluːd] *vt* **-1.** to deliberately prevent <sb/sthg> from being part of something □ *Try to exclude all dairy products from* your diet. ▫ People under 16 are excluded from taking part. **-2.** [reason, option] not to consider <sthg> when one is trying to find a solution, answer etc ▫ We cannot exclude the possibility that they might change their minds.

excluding [ɪk'skluːdɪŋ] prep not including <sb/sthg> ▫ There were ten of us in the bus, excluding the driver.

exclusion [ɪk'skluːʒn] n [from a place, group] see **exclude** ▫ Complaints were received about the exclusion of stockholders from the meeting. ■ **to the exclusion of all else** a phrase used when somebody is involved in a particular activity to such an extent that there is no time for anything else ▫ He is obsessed with work to the exclusion of everything else.

exclusion clause n a clause in a contract that states what is not covered by the terms of the contract.

exclusive [ɪk'skluːsɪv] ◇ adj **-1.** [club, hotel, district] that is only for people who are considered socially acceptable or who have enough money ▫ They are staying in a rather exclusive hotel on the left bank. **-2.** [use, ownership, property] that is limited to one person or group of people and is not shared with anybody else ▫ Our company has exclusive rights on this publication. ▫ an offer exclusive to our readers. **-3.** [interview, news story] only covered by one TV company, radio station, or newspaper ▫ Tonight we have exclusive coverage of the game between Sweden and Italy. ◇ n an exclusive news story ▫ The paper ran an exclusive on the latest talks.

◆ **exclusive of** prep not including <sthg> ▫ The total comes to $515, exclusive of sales tax.

exclusively [ɪk'skluːsɪvlɪ] adv only ▫ We deal exclusively with foreign clients. ▫ He works exclusively for our company.

excommunicate [ˌekskə'mjuːnəkeɪt] vt to say publicly that <sb> is no longer a member of the Roman Catholic Church.

excommunication [ˌekskəmjuːnə'keɪʃn] n: see **excommunicate**.

excrement ['ekskrəmənt] n human or animal waste passed from the bowels (formal use).

excrete [ɪk'skriːt] vt [feces, urine, sweat] to pass <waste matter> from the body, especially through the anus.

excruciating [ɪk'skruːʃɪeɪtɪŋ] adj **-1.** [pain, ache] that is very intense and hurts a lot ▫ Sam was in excruciating pain. **-2.** [performance, experience] that is extremely bad, distressing, or embarrassing ▫ "How was the concert?" — "Excruciating!"

excursion [ɪk'skɜːʃn] n a short trip, especially one that is made for pleasure or relaxation, or as part of a vacation ▫ There are daily excursions to nearby places of interest.

excusable [ɪk'skjuːzəbl] adj [behavior, mistake, oversight] that can be forgiven ▫ It's perfectly excusable for him to be late this one time.

excuse [n ɪk'skjuːs, vb ɪk'skjuːz] ◇ n a reason one gives for doing something wrong, especially when asking to be forgiven ▫ I made an excuse and left early. ▫ Her excuse was (that)

she'd been delayed in traffic. ▫ The only excuse I could think of was that I had been ill. ▫ I'm trying to think of an excuse not to go to the meeting. ■ **that's/there's no excuse for sthg** a phrase used to show that one disapproves of sthg ▫ That's no excuse for rudeness.

◇ vt **-1.** [somebody's behavior] to make <sthg> seem less bad ▫ That does not excuse his absence/the fact that he was late! **-2.** [person] to forgive <sb> for something bad they have done ▫ Please excuse me for not coming to the party. ▫ I can't excuse what you've done. **-3. to excuse sb from sthg** to give sb permission not to do sthg ▫ I was excused from attending the meeting. **-4. would you excuse me?** a phrase used to say politely that one is about to leave ▫ If you would excuse me for a moment, I'll go and see to dinner. ■ **to excuse oneself** to say politely that one is about to leave ▫ She excused herself and went to talk to the other guests. **-5. excuse me** an expression used to attract somebody's attention or to apologize for something one has done that might seem rude; US an expression used to show that one has not heard what somebody has said ▫ Excuse me! I think you've forgotten something. ▫ Excuse me, could I squeeze past you? ▫ Oh, excuse me, I didn't see you. ▫ Excuse me? Did you say you were Canadian?

ex-directory adj GB [phone number, person] that is not listed in the public telephone directory ▫ My number's ex-directory.

exec [ɪg'zek] n abbr of **executive**.

execrable ['eksɪkrəbl] adj [performance, taste, cooking] that one thinks is very bad (formal use) ▫ The whole joke was in execrable taste.

execute ['eksəkjuːt] vt **-1.** [prisoner, criminal] to kill <sb>, especially as a punishment for a crime ▫ The group has threatened to execute one of the hostages each day. **-2.** [plan, order, movement] to carry out <sthg> (formal use) ▫ That was a beautifully executed maneuver.

execution [ˌeksə'kjuːʃn] n: see **execute** ▫ His execution is due to take place tomorrow morning. ▫ She was meticulous in her execution of her brief.

executioner [ˌeksə'kjuːʃnər] n a person whose job is to kill somebody as a punishment for a crime.

executive [ɪg'zekjətɪv] ◇ n **-1.** BUSINESS a person who holds a senior position in a business and is responsible for making decisions, running a department etc ▫ company/advertising executives. **-2.** [of an organization] the committee of an organization that has the power to make decisions and carry them out ▫ the Labour Party executive. **-3. the executive** POLITICS the part of the government of a country that is responsible for carrying out laws or decrees ▫ The three branches of government in the USA are the legislative, the executive, and the judiciary.

◇ adj **-1.** [power, board, section] that is connected with making decisions and running an organization, especially a business ▫ involved in an executive capacity. **-2.** [chair, washroom, desk] that is expensive or luxurious and is intended for executives or people of a similar social position □ *an executive car.*

executive director *n* a director who works in the running of a business or organization.

executive toy *n* a small toy that is designed for executives and is supposed to help relieve stress.

executor [ɪgˈzekjətəʳ] *n* a person who one names to carry out the instructions in one's will after one's death.

exemplary [ɪgˈzemplərɪ] *adj* [behavior, employee] that is extremely good and an example to other people □ *Jonathan's conduct throughout the trial was exemplary.*

exemplify [ɪgˈzemplɪfaɪ] (*pt* & *pp* **exemplified**) *vt* -1. [skill, belief, situation] to be a typical example of <sthg> □ *I think this book exemplifies the kind of publication we can expect from a small firm.* -2. [point, usage] to give an example of <sthg>.

exempt [ɪgˈzempt] ◇ *adj* **to be exempt** to be freed from or not affected by a payment, rule etc □ *Students are exempt from taxes/ military service.* ◇ *vt* to make <sb> exempt from something □ *He was exempted from military service on health grounds.*

exemption [ɪgˈzemptʃn] *n: see* **exempt** □ *tax exemptions for married couples.*

exercise [ˈeksəʳsaɪz] ◇ *n* -1. [for part of the body] a set of movements that one does in order to keep a particular part of the body fit, or before playing a sport □ *You need to do stomach/chest exercises.* -2. [for general health] physical activities, e.g. walking or swimming, that one does to keep one's body in good condition □ *You must take more exercise.* □ *Twenty minutes' exercise a day is enough to keep most people in shape.* -3. MILITARY a military operation that is part of training for war □ *They're on exercises in Dartmouth at the moment.* -4. EDUCATION an activity that a student does, usually a piece of writing, in order to develop a skill, e.g. spelling, math, or a foreign language □ *a book of grammar exercises.* -5. **the exercise of power/authority etc** the act of using power/authority etc.
◇ *vt* -1. [dog, horse] to make <an animal> take exercise □ *Dogs need to be exercised regularly.* -2. [shoulder, leg] to move <a part of the body> regularly and in a special way to make it stronger and fitter □ *Try jogging to exercise your leg muscles.* -3. [power, authority] to use <sthg> (formal use) □ *Police officers were asked by community leaders to exercise restraint.* ◇ *vi* to get exercise □ *Try to exercise regularly.*

exercise bike *n* a bicycle that is fixed on a base and used indoors, e.g. in a gym or in one's home, for getting exercise.

exercise book *n* -1. a notebook used by schoolchildren for doing their schoolwork in. -2. a book of exercises that are done as part of a written course.

exert [ɪgˈzɜːʳt] *vt* to use <influence, pressure> etc to achieve a particular purpose □ *He exerted all his charm in persuading her to agree to his plan.* ■ **to exert oneself** to make a great effort physically or mentally.

exertion [ɪgˈzɜːʳʃn] *n* physical effort □ *There's a lot of physical exertion involved in this job.* □ *After the morning's exertions I was exhausted.*

ex gratia [eksˈɡreɪʃə] *adj* **an ex gratia payment** a payment that is made as a favor.

exhale [eksˈheɪl] ◇ *vt* [person] to breathe out <smoke, air> etc □ *He exhaled a cloud of cigarette smoke.* ◇ *vi* [person] to breathe out □ *Take a deep breath in, then exhale slowly.*

exhaust [ɪgˈzɔːst] ◇ *n* -1. the gases that are produced by an engine while it is being used □ *exhaust fumes.* -2. = **exhaust pipe.** ◇ *vt* -1. [person] to make <sb> very tired □ *That walk completely exhausted me!* -2. [fuel, funds, patience] to use all of <sthg> so that there is none left □ *We seem to have exhausted all possibilities.*

exhausted [ɪgˈzɔːstəd] *adj* [person] who is very tired □ *You look exhausted! What have you been doing?*

exhausting [ɪgˈzɔːstɪŋ] *adj* [day, job, trip] that is very tiring □ *He's quite an exhausting person to talk to.*

exhaustion [ɪgˈzɔːstʃn] *n* extreme tiredness □ *Two of the runners were taken to the hospital suffering from exhaustion.*

exhaustive [ɪgˈzɔːstɪv] *adj* [search, study] that covers all aspects of something □ *This list is by no means exhaustive, but it should give you a general idea.*

exhaust pipe *n* a pipe attached to the bottom of a car, truck etc that carries gases away from the engine into the air.

exhibit [ɪgˈzɪbət] ◇ *n* -1. ART something that is put in an exhibition, museum, or art gallery for people to look at. -2. LAW something that is shown in court as a piece of evidence in a case. ◇ *vt* -1. [emotion, tendency] to show <sthg> (formal use) □ *Investors have so far not exhibited any signs of panic following the board's announcement.* -2. ART [painting, statue, collection] to show <sthg> to the public, especially in an art gallery or museum. ◇ *vi* [artist] to show one's work in public.

exhibition [ˌeksɪˈbɪʃn] *n* -1. ART an organized event where paintings, sculptures, prints etc are put in a public place, e.g. in a museum or art gallery, so that people can look at them □ *I went to see a very interesting exhibition on* OR *of women's photography.* □ *an art/a sculpture exhibition.* -2. [of emotion, behavior] *see* **exhibit.** ■ **to make an exhibition of oneself** GB to act in a foolish and ridiculous way that other people notice □ *Did you have to make an exhibition of yourself in front of my friends?*

exhibitionist [ˌeksɪˈbɪʃnəst] *n* a person who likes attracting people's attention in public, especially by wearing strange clothes or talking loudly.

exhibitor [ɪgˈzɪbətəʳ] *n* a person whose work is being shown at an exhibition.

exhilarating [ɪgˈzɪləreɪtɪŋ] *adj* [experience, walk, sight] that makes one feel very happy and full of energy □ *There's something quite exhilarating about traveling at that speed.*

exhort [ɪgˈzɔːʳt] *vt* **to exhort sb to do sthg** to

try hard to persuade sb to do sthg (formal use) □ *General McVane exhorted the troops to fight on.*

exhume [eks'hju:m] *vt* **to exhume sb's body** to take sb's dead body out of a grave.

exile ['eksaɪl] ◇ *n* **-1.** a person who is forced, often for political reasons, to live in a country that is not their own and is unable to return home □ *Harrison now lives in the Cayman Islands as a tax exile.* **-2.** the state of living as an exile □ *He lived for many years in exile.* □ *The disgraced leader was sent into exile.* ◇ *vt* to send <sb> away from a country as an exile □ *He was exiled from/to France.*

exiled ['eksaɪld] *adj* [monarch, writer, leader] who is forced, often for political reasons, to live in a country that is not their own □ *The exiled guerrilla leader arrived in Washington today.*

exist [ɪg'zɪst] *vi* to live or be present in the world as something real, rather than as something imaginary □ *I'm sure he doesn't even know I exist.* □ *The law has existed for centuries.*

existence [ɪg'zɪstəns] *n* **-1.** the state of existing □ *They have been trying to prove the existence of a black hole.* □ *This kind of technology has been in existence for years.* □ *The law came into existence in 1964.* **-2.** a particular type of life □ *They led a miserable existence.*

existentialism [ˌegzɪ'stenʃəlɪzm] *n* the belief that because there seems to be no meaning in the universe, people are free to act as they like and are therefore responsible for their own actions.

existentialist [ˌegzɪ'stenʃələst] ◇ *n* a person who believes in existentialism. ◇ *adj*: *existentialist philosophy/writing.*

existing [ɪg'zɪstɪŋ] *adj* [system, structure, government] that exists now □ *The existing guidelines are simply inadequate.*

exit ['eksət] ◇ *n* **-1.** a way out of a movie theater, store, subway etc □ *Please leave the building by the nearest available exit.* **-2.** the act of leaving a place □ *I made a quick exit.* ◇ *vi* to go out of a place □ *Exit, stage right.* ◇ *vt*: *'Exit the station to your right for the piazza.'*

exit poll *n* a process of asking people how they have voted in an election in order to be able to estimate what the result of the election will be.

exit ramp *n* US a road for leaving a highway.

exit visa *n* a visa that allows somebody to leave a country.

exodus ['eksədəs] *n* the departure of a large number of people from a region, country etc at the same time, e.g. for economic or political reasons □ *the exodus of young people from rural areas* □ *a mass exodus.*

ex officio [eksə'fɪʃɪoʊ] ◇ *adj* a phrase used to show that somebody has a particular right because of their position □ *an ex officio member/chairman.* ◇ *adv*: *She acted ex officio.*

exonerate [ɪg'zɒnəreɪt] *vt* to show or state officially that <sb> is not to blame for something □ *She was exonerated from all blame.*

exorbitant [ɪg'zɔːrbətənt] *adj* [cost, price] much higher than is reasonable □ *They were asking for an exorbitant sum of money.*

exorcism ['eksɔːrsɪzm] *n* [of a ghost, spirit] see **exorcize.**

exorcist ['eksɔːrsəst] *n* a person who exorcizes ghosts, spirits etc.

exorcize, -ise ['eksɔːrsaɪz] *vt* to force <a ghost or spirit> out of somewhere or somebody by using special prayers and ceremonies □ *By going back, he hoped to exorcize the memory of that terrible time.*

exotic [ɪg'zɒtɪk] *adj* [fruit, smell, setting] that one finds unusual and exciting because it comes from or makes one think of a distant place.

expand [ɪk'spænd] ◇ *vt* to make <sthg> larger in size, number, or amount □ *They've expanded their business to include two new offices.* ◇ *vi* [business, population, market] □ *Our department has expanded enormously in the last three years.* □ *Metal expands as you heat it.*

◆ **expand (up)on** *vt fus* **to expand (up)on sthg** [on a subject, argument] to say more about sthg □ *Would you care to expand on that?*

expanse [ɪk'spæns] *n* a wide stretch of sky, sea, desert etc □ *a vast expanse of sand.*

expansion [ɪk'spænʃn] *n*: see **expand** □ *We hope to press ahead with the expansion of our marketing operation.*

expansion card *n* a printed circuit board that is added to a computer to make it perform extra operations or make it more powerful.

expansionism [ɪk'spænʃənɪzm] *n* the policy or practice of expanding the economy, influence, or land of a country (disapproving use).

expansionist [ɪk'spænʃənəst] *adj* [policy, tendency] see **expansionism.**

expansion slot *n* a slot in a computer into which an expansion card is fitted.

expansive [ɪk'spænsɪv] *adj* [person] who is relaxed and willing to talk a lot □ *I found him, for once, in an expansive mood.*

expatriate [eks'pætrɪət] ◇ *n* a person who lives or works in a foreign country □ *British expatriates in the area are being flown home.* ◇ *adj*: *the expatriate community.*

expect [ɪk'spekt] ◇ *vt* **-1.** to think that <sthg> is going to happen □ *When do you expect it to be ready?* □ *That's just the kind of thing I'd expect him to do.* □ *Of course I'm angry, what do you expect?* □ *We expect to be there by 4 o'clock.* **-2. to be expecting sb/sthg** [letter, phone call] to be ready for sb/sthg because one thinks or knows that they are going to come □ *Go straight through, Mr Jay is expecting you.* □ *We are expecting a delivery from India.* **-3.** [loyalty, good manners] to consider it right or necessary to have <sthg> □ *She expects a great deal of all her employees.* ■ **to expect sb to do sthg** to feel that it is reasonable or necessary for sb to do sthg □ *I expect you to be punctual at all times.* **-4. I expect** a phrase used to introduce information that one thinks is probably true □ *"Is Steve coming?"* — *"I expect so."* □ *I expect (that) she's got stuck* *in traffic.* **-5. to be expecting a baby** to be pregnant □ *My sister's expecting her first child.* ◇ *vi* **to be expecting** to be pregnant (informal use).

expectancy [ɪk'spektənsɪ] *n* → **life expectancy.**

expectant [ɪk'spektənt] *adj* [person, crowd] that is waiting eagerly for something to happen □ *An expectant hush fell over the auditorium.*

expectantly [ɪk'spektəntlɪ] *adv* [smile, listen] *see* **expectant** □ *The audience waited expectantly for the concert to begin.*

expectant mother *n* a woman who is expecting a baby.

expectation [ˌekspek'teɪʃn] *n* **-1.** a hope that something will happen □ *He has every expectation of getting the job.* **-2.** a belief that something will happen □ *It is my expectation that the election will be in June.*

◆ **expectations** *npl* the belief that something good is going to happen □ *He has very high expectations of his son.* ■ **to live up to sb's expectations** to be as good or successful as sb has expected □ *The play didn't really live up to our expectations.* ■ **against** OR **contrary to all expectations** in a way that is different to everything that was expected □ *Contrary to all expectations, the UK team has won a place in the finals.*

expectorant [ɪk'spektərənt] *n* a cough medicine that helps to remove phlegm from one's lungs.

expedient [ɪk'spiːdjənt] ◇ *adj* [plan, measure] that is convenient or appropriate in a particular situation, even if it is morally wrong. ◇ *n* an expedient idea, plan, measure etc.

expedite ['ekspədaɪt] *vt* to make <sthg> happen more quickly (formal use).

expedition [ˌekspə'dɪʃn] *n* **-1.** a long trip that is organized for a specific purpose, e.g. to climb a mountain or explore a region □ *They're going on a climbing expedition in the Himalayas.* **-2.** the people who take part in an expedition.

expeditionary force [ˌekspə'dɪʃenərɪ-, GB -nərɪ] *n* an army or part of an army that is sent to fight abroad.

expel [ɪk'spel] (*pt* & *pp* **expelled,** *cont* **expelling**) *vt* **-1.** [student, member] to make <sb> leave a school, organization etc because they have behaved badly □ *She was expelled from school for smoking.* **-2.** [diplomat, journalist] to force <a foreigner> to leave a country □ *He was eventually expelled from the capital.* **-3.** [substance] to force <a gas or liquid> from a container, one's body etc □ *Wind is expelled through the mouth or anus.*

expend [ɪk'spend] *vt* [time, money, energy] to use up or spend <sthg> □ *The army was reluctant to expend any more of its limited resources on defending the border posts.*

expendable [ɪk'spendəbl] *adj* [person, resource, item] that is not thought to be essential and can be got rid of, fired etc □ *Sophisticated computer systems have made pilots expendable, in theory at least.*

expenditure [ɪk'spendɪtʃəʳ] *n* **-1.** the amount of money that is spent on services, food, wages etc □ *government/public expenditure.* **-2.** [of time, money, energy] *see* **expend.**

expense [ɪk'spens] *n* the amount of money that is spent on something □ *Our day-to-day expenses are not high.* □ *The new bridge was built at great public expense* OR *at great expense to the public.* ■ **to go to great expense, to spare no expense** to spend a lot of money in order to do something. ■ **at the expense of sb/sthg** in a way that causes sb/sthg to be affected badly □ *He finished the book on time, but at the expense of his social life.* □ *She only succeeded at the expense of other people.* ■ **at sb's expense** [travel, entertain] using sb else's money to pay; [make a joke, have fun] in a way that makes sb look foolish □ *I arranged for you to be flown here at great personal expense.* □ *Sandy felt that everyone was having a laugh at her expense.*

◆ **expenses** *npl* BUSINESS the money that one spends on restaurants, taxis etc as part of one's work, that is later paid back by the company, employer etc □ *There's a special form for claiming back expenses.* □ *a trip to Paris with all expenses paid.* ■ **on expenses** [travel, entertain] using the money of one's company or employer to pay □ *We can put this lunch on my expenses.*

expense account *n* an arrangement between an employer and employee in which any money spent by the employee for work purposes, e.g. for travel or entertaining clients, is paid back by the employer □ *I'll put it on my expense account.* □ *an expense-account lunch.*

expensive [ɪk'spensɪv] *adj* [meal, car, coat] that costs a lot of money □ *She has very expensive tastes.*

experience [ɪk'spɪərɪəns] ◇ *n* **-1.** knowledge or skill that one has gained in life or in one's job over a period of time □ *It was difficult to find a job since I had no work experience.* □ *Do you have any experience of working in an office?* □ *Experience tells me that he'll be late.* □ *I know from my own experience how difficult it can be.* □ *It'll become easier with experience.* □ *'No previous experience necessary.'* **-2.** an event that happens to somebody and usually affects them in a particular way □ *She told us about her wartime experiences in Italy.* □ *That must have been a memorable experience!* ◇ *vt* **-1.** [event, change, difficulty] to live through or be affected by <sthg> directly □ *I've never experienced anything like this before.* **-2.** [sadness, pain] to feel <sthg> □ *You may experience slight dizziness.*

experienced [ɪk'spɪərɪənst] *adj* [doctor, driver, worker] who has a lot of experience □ *She's very experienced at* OR *in teaching young children.*

experiment [ɪk'sperɪmənt] ◇ *n* **-1.** SCIENCE a test that is done in order to see what happens to somebody or something in particular conditions □ *The students carry out* OR *do experiments on dead mice.* **-2.** an act of putting a new idea or theory into practice to see how it works in the real world □ *It was a*

disastrous experiment in social engineering. ◇ vi
-1. SCIENCE to carry out an experiment □
They've been experimenting with weightlessness.
□ *He's experimenting on the human brain.* **-2.** to
try something new to see what result it will
produce or if it will work □ *He started experimenting with drugs when he was 17.*

experimental [ɪk,sperɪ'mentl] *adj* **-1.** [method,
test] that is connected with or used in an experiment □ *He's an experimental psychologist.*
-2. [person, technique, music] that uses new
methods, principles etc, especially when
these are not yet completely accepted □ *her
acclaimed and highly experimental production of
"La Bohème."*

expert ['ekspɜːt] ◇ *n* a person who has a very
high level of skill or knowledge in a particular activity or field □ *a computer/gardening expert* □ *an expert in* OR *on computer-aided design.*
◇ *adj* [cook, technician, performer] who is an
expert; [advice, knowledge] of an expert □ *He's
become very expert at spotting fakes.*

expertise [,ekspɜː'tiːz] *n* skill or knowledge in
a particular activity or field □ *managerial expertise.*

expert system *n* COMPUTING a computer that
gives advice and information and makes decisions in a way that is similar to that of the
human mind.

expiate ['ekspɪeɪt] *vt* [crime, sin] to show that
one is sorry for <sthg> by doing something
good (formal use).

expiration [ekspə'reɪʃn] *n* US *see* **expire**.

expiration date *n* US the date after which a
credit card, passport etc cannot be used, or
food should not be eaten.

expire [ɪk'spaɪəʳ] *vi* [credit card, contract, membership] to become invalid at the end of a
particular period of time □ *My car insurance
expires in March.*

expiry [ɪk'spaɪərɪ] *n* GB *see* **expire** □ *These conditions cease to apply on expiry of the lease.*

expiry date *n* GB the date on which a membership, credit card, license etc expires.

explain [ɪk'spleɪn] ◇ *vt* **-1.** [meaning, situation,
story] to make <sthg> clear by giving information about it □ *Could you explain to me how
the device works?* □ *They explained what to do.* □
*The rules ought to be explained to people more
clearly.* **-2.** [one's behavior, absence, decision] to
give a reason for <sthg> □ *Could you explain
why you were so late?* ■ **to explain oneself** to
give a reason for something one has done,
especially something other people think is
wrong □ *He tried to explain himself but was
shouted down.* □ *Come on then, explain yourself!*
◇ *vi* **-1.** to explain a meaning, situation etc □
She explained to me that the company had expanded too fast. **-2.** to explain one's behavior,
decision etc □ *You've got some explaining to do.*

◆ **explain away** *vt sep* **to explain sthg away** [a
mistake, one's behavior] to give a reason for
sthg in order to make it seem less important, or to stop somebody from thinking
one has done something wrong □ *He tried to
explain away the stains on the carpet.*

explanation [,eksplə'neɪʃn] *n* **-1.** [for one's behavior] something that explains an action,
meaning, decision etc □ *He gave no explanation as to why he was late.* □ *I'm sure there's a
perfectly simple explanation for all this.* □ *Duncan
pointed to the figures on the chart by way of explanation.* **-2.** [of a process, machine] a description that explains how something works or
how to do something □ *He gave a long and
complicated explanation of the machine's functions.*

explanatory [US ɪk'splænətɔːrɪ, GB -ətərɪ] *adj*
[note, leaflet] that is intended to help one
understand something □ *There's a brief explanatory passage at the beginning.*

expletive [ɪk'spliːtɪv] *n* a swearword (formal
use).

explicit [ɪk'splɪsət] *adj* **-1.** [permission, reason, order] that is completely clear and does not allow any doubt □ *I left explicit instructions not
to tell them.* □ *Could you be more explicit about
the purpose of the visit?* **-2.** [scene, passage, description] that gives all the details, especially
about sex □ *sexually explicit material.*

explode [ɪk'spləʊd] ◇ *vi* **-1.** [bomb, building] to
break up into tiny pieces with great force
and a loud noise □ *The airplane exploded on
impact.* **-2.** [person] to express feelings suddenly and strongly □ *He exploded with anger/
laughter.* ◇ *vt* **-1.** [bomb, mine] to make <sthg>
explode. **-2.** [theory, idea] to prove <sthg> to
be false □ *The book explodes many myths about
the Aztecs.*

exploit [*n* 'eksplɔɪt, *vb* ɪk'splɔɪt] ◇ *n* something
that somebody has done that is brave, interesting, or amusing □ *Uncle Jack was only too
willing to recount tales of his exploits as a young
man.* ◇ *vt* **-1.** [person] to use and benefit from
<sb> while giving them very little in return
(disapproving use) □ *I feel exploited.* **-2.** [resources, area, idea] to use or develop <sthg>
in order to make money □ *Our competitors
will, of course, try to exploit the situation.*

exploitation [,eksplɔɪ'teɪʃn] *n*: *see* **exploit** □ *The
company has been criticized for its exploitation of
local workers.* □ *The exploitation of mineral deposits is sure to boost the economy.*

exploration [,eksplə'reɪʃn] *n*: *see* **explore** □ *the
researchers' explorations into the possibility of
isolating the gene* □ *space exploration.*

exploratory [US ɪk'splɒrətɔːrɪ, GB -ətərɪ] *adj* [examination, discussion, operation] that is carried
out in order to find out more about something before further action is taken □ *Exploratory talks are likely to continue for some time.*

explore [ɪk'splɔːʳ] ◇ *vt* **-1.** [country, area, city] to
travel around <a place> that one does not
know in order to find out about it □ *We
went exploring in the caves.* **-2.** [possibility, theory] to examine <an idea> in order to find out
more about it □ *We need to explore the
matter/question further.* ◇ *vi*: *Let's go exploring.*

explorer [ɪk'splɔːrəʳ] *n* a person who travels to
places about which little is known in order
to explore them.

explosion [ɪk'spləʊʒn] *n* **-1.** [of a bomb, building]
see **explode** □ *There were several explosions in*

the Kensington area. **-2.** [of interest, crime] a sudden and large increase in the amount or degree of something □ There's been a huge explosion in the demand for video games. **-3.** [of anger, violence] a sudden and powerful expression of anger, violence, protest etc □ There was an explosion of incredulous laughter at his words.

explosive [ɪk'splousɪv] ◇ adj **-1.** [material, substance] that can cause an explosion □ Be careful, this stuff can be highly explosive. **-2.** [temper, personality] that can easily show strong anger □ Juan has a very explosive temper, so watch out. **-3.** [issue, situation] that is likely to have serious or dangerous effects □ The situation is highly explosive and could erupt into violence at any time. ◇ n a substance or device that causes something to explode □ The bomb contains several tons of high explosive. □ Explosives experts were called to the scene.

explosive device n a device that is designed to explode, e.g. a bomb or mine (formal use).

exponent [ɪk'spounənt] n **-1. an exponent of sthg** [of a theory, method] a person who supports, practices, and praises sthg □ She's a great exponent of socialism. **-2.** [of a skill, activity] a person who is good at sthg □ a superb exponent of Chopin/the sonnet. **-2.** MATH a number written small and placed next to and above another to show how many times the other number must be multiplied by itself.

exponential [ˌekspə'nenʃl] adj [increase, growth] that happens very rapidly (formal use) □ The growth in sales has been exponential.

export [vb ɪk'spɔːrt, n 'ekspɔːrt] ◇ vt **-1.** BUSINESS to send <goods> to another country to be sold □ They export a lot of wine to Britain. **-2.** [idea, system] to take <sthg> to another country and try to encourage people to use it □ Cricket could never be successfully exported to the rest of Europe. **-3.** COMPUTING to change <data, a file> etc so that one can use it with different software. ◇ n a product or service that is sold by one country to another country □ a ban on exports to/from the country.
NOTE: Compare **import**.

exportation [ˌekspɔːr'teɪʃn] n [of goods, a system] see **export**.

exporter [ek'spɔːrtər] n a person or company that exports goods.

export licence n in Britain, a license that somebody must get before they can sell certain goods abroad.

expose [ɪk'spouz] vt **-1.** to uncover <sthg that is usually not visible> □ The paint had peeled off, exposing the plaster underneath. ■ **to be exposed to sthg** [to heat, the wind, sun] to be uncovered and not protected against sthg; [to danger, disease] to experience sthg unpleasant □ She had been exposed to scenes of terrible poverty. ■ **to expose oneself** to show one's sexual parts in a public place □ He was arrested for exposing himself at a public swimming pool. **-2.** [person, scandal] to make known the truth about <sb/sthg immoral> □ He was finally exposed as a leading drug trafficker.

-3. PHOTOGRAPHY to allow light onto <film> when taking a photograph.

exposé [eks'pouzeɪ] n a report, e.g. in a newspaper, that makes the truth about somebody or something known, especially if it is shocking and has been kept secret.

exposed [ɪk'spouzd] adj [place, house] that has no protection from the weather; [position, defenses] without protection from danger, an attack etc □ We left ourselves exposed each time we moved forward against the other team.

exposition [ˌekspə'zɪʃn] n **-1.** [of a subject, theory] a detailed explanation or description of something (formal use) □ a brief exposition of the theory of quantum mechanics. **-2.** [of goods, art] a large public exhibition.

exposure [ɪk'spouʒər] n **-1. exposure to sthg** the state of being exposed to sthg, e.g. light, radiation, or danger □ Avoid exposure to sunlight. **-2.** MEDICINE the harmful effects on the body of being exposed to the cold for a long time □ He died of exposure. **-3.** [of a secret] the act of showing the truth about a dishonest person, a crime, scandal etc □ He disappeared after the public exposure of his part in the crime. **-4.** PHOTOGRAPHY the length of time that film is exposed to light; a length of film on which one photograph can be taken □ Set the exposure to 1/90 of a second. □ I've got six exposures left. □ the exposure time. **-5.** [in the media] publicity that is given in the media to somebody or something □ The book was given a lot of exposure in the media.

exposure meter n an instrument on a camera that measures how strong the light is so that the correct setting can be chosen.

expound [ɪk'spaund] (formal use) ◇ vt to explain <one's theories, views> etc in detail □ Professor Medina expounded his thoughts on the benefits of genetic engineering. ◇ vi **to expound on sthg** to speak in detail about sthg □ She expounded at some length on her plans to change and improve the system.

express [ɪk'spres] ◇ adj **-1.** [letter, parcel] that is sent by a fast delivery service. **-2.** [service, bus] that is fast and does not have many stops. **-3.** [request, purpose] that is clearly and deliberately stated (formal use) □ It was her express wish that the money should go to charity. ◇ adv [send, deliver] using a fast service □ I'll mail it to you express first thing in the morning. ◇ n **an express (train)** a train that travels very fast and does not stop very often. ◇ vt **-1.** to make known <a thought, idea, opinion> etc by putting it into words □ I'd like to express my gratitude to you. □ These concepts are difficult to express in another language. □ Words cannot express how I feel. ■ **to express oneself** to put one's thoughts, feelings, ideas etc into words □ Because of her poor German, she found it hard to express herself clearly. **-2.** MATH to show <a quantity, result> etc by using a symbol or formula □ In the diagram, figures are expressed as percentages.

expression [ɪk'spreʃn] n **-1.** a word or phrase, especially one that is unusual or that is used more when speaking than when writing □

What's the expression? "Better late than never"? **-2.** [of pain, surprise] the look on somebody's face that shows a particular feeling □ She had a slightly bemused expression on her face. **-3.** [in a dancer, musician] the ability to express feelings through art □ She plays the piano with a lot of expression. **-4.** [of an idea, opinion] see **express** □ There's little freedom of expression in the press there. □ The meeting ended with expressions of hope and goodwill on all sides.

Expressionism [ɪk'spreʃənɪzm] n an artistic and literary movement that is based on the belief that expressing emotions is more important than describing the outside world in a realistic way.

Expressionist [ɪk'spreʃənɪst] ◇ n an artist who practices Expressionism. ◇ adj: an Expressionist painting/film.

expressionless [ɪk'spreʃənləs] adj [voice, face] that does not show somebody's feelings.

expressive [ɪk'spresɪv] adj [face, poem, quality] that expresses feelings, meanings etc clearly and well.

expressly [ɪk'spresli] adv [tell, order] clearly and deliberately □ I expressly asked for a room overlooking the lake.

expressway [ɪk'spresweɪ] n US a very wide major road designed for long-distance travel at high speeds.

expropriate [eks'prouprɪeɪt] vt to take away <sb's property> for public use (formal use).

expropriation [eks,prouprɪ'eɪʃn] n: see **expropriate** (formal use).

expulsion [ɪk'spʌlʃn] n: see **expel** □ There have been three expulsions for bad behavior already this semester.

exquisite [ɪk'skwɪzɪt] adj **-1.** [painting, face, jewelry] that is very beautiful, especially because it is so delicate, refined, or colorful □ the most exquisite Chinese porcelain. **-2.** [taste, behavior] that is extremely sensitive and cannot be faulted □ He has exquisite taste in clothes. **-3.** [pleasure, pain] very great.

exquisitely [ɪk'skwɪzɪtlɪ] adv **exquisitely beautiful/dressed etc** beautiful/dressed etc in a very delicate refined way.

ex-serviceman n GB a man who previously belonged to the armed forces.

ex-servicewoman n GB a woman who previously belonged to the armed forces.

ext [telephone] abbr of **extension**.

extant [ek'stænt] adj [building, document, evidence] that still exists (formal use).

extemporize, -ise [ɪk'stempəraɪz] vi to give a speech, performance etc without doing any preparation for it in advance (formal use).

extend [ɪk'stend] ◇ vt **-1.** [building, area] to make <sthg> larger by adding something to it □ The Blooms have extended their garden terrace. **-2.** [road, route] to make <sthg> longer in distance □ The freeway is to be extended as far as Baltimore. **-3.** [visit, visa] to make <sthg> last longer □ They extended the deadline to fit my schedule. **-4.** [control, rule, law] to make <sthg> include more than it did before so that it is more powerful □ They've extended

the powers of the police. **-5.** [arm, leg] to stretch out <a part of one's body> (formal use) □ He extended an arm to help her up. **-6.** [friendship, help, welcome] to offer <sthg> to somebody □ I would like to extend my thanks to all those involved.

◇ vi **-1.** [road, railroad, runway] to reach a particular point □ The expressway now extends to the northern suburbs. **-2.** [event, period, stay] to last until a particular time □ Meetings often extend into the evening. **-3. to extend to sb/sthg** to include sb/sthg □ This restriction does not extend to club members. □ The regulations now extend to people living abroad. **-4.** to stick out from a surface or object □ The counter extends two feet from the wall.

extendable [ɪk'stendəbl] adj **-1.** [contract, visa, permit] that can be made to last longer □ They've given me a six-month extendable visa. **-2.** [ladder, antenna] that can be made longer.

extension [ɪk'stenʃn] n **-1.** [of a building] an extra part that has been added on to a building □ They've built an extension onto the back of their house. **-2.** [of a visa, law] see **extend** □ He's asked for an extension on his permit/the deadline. □ the extension of government powers to include military affairs. **-3.** [at home] an additional telephone that has the same number as one's main telephone; [at work] a telephone that is connected to the switchboard of a company, institution etc and that has its own number □ Can you put me through to extension 3295? □ "What's your extension?" — "It's 297." **-4.** = **extension cord. -5.** COMPUTING a short code, usually three letters, used after a computer filename to describe the format or purpose of the file.

extension cord US, **extension lead** GB n a long electric cable that is connected to the cable of an electrical appliance so that it can be used further away from the socket.

extensive [ɪk'stensɪv] adj **-1.** [property, land] that covers a large area □ They own extensive areas of land near the state border. **-2.** [damage, effect] that affects many people or things □ They've made extensive changes to the program. **-3.** [coverage, knowledge, list] that is detailed and includes many different things □ We had extensive talks on possible ways of developing the idea.

extensively [ɪk'stensɪvlɪ] adv [cover, discuss, travel] see **extensive** □ I've borrowed extensively from her notes.

extent [ɪk'stent] n **-1.** the area that something covers □ From the air you can see the full extent of the flood damage. □ Open the table out to its full extent. **-2. the extent of sthg** [of harm, difficulty, knowledge] how great sthg is □ It's hard to know the true extent of the problem. **-3. to what extent...** a phrase used when asking how far something is true □ To what extent is there a link between smoking and cancer? □ It is not yet clear to what extent they were involved in the scandal. ■ **to the extent that...** a phrase that introduces a statement that shows how true, good, bad etc something is □ The dis-

agreement has gotten worse, to the extent that they're no longer speaking to each other.

♦ **to a certain extent, to some extent** *adv* in some ways but not completely □ *I agree with you to a certain extent.* □ *To some extent, what he says is true.* □ *I think the problem was to some extent their own fault.*

♦ **to a large extent, to a great extent** *adv* almost completely □ *The work that's been done is to a large extent due to her.*

extenuating circumstances [ɪk'stenjʊeɪtɪŋ-] *npl* circumstances that make a crime, somebody's bad behavior etc likely to be judged less severely □ *There are extenuating circumstances that could operate in your favor.*

exterior [ɪk'stɪərɪəʳ] ◇ *adj* [wall, light, paintwork] that is on the outside of something. ◇ *n* -1. the outside surface of a car, building etc □ *The exterior of the house had been painted pink.* -2. **sb's confident/cold etc exterior** sb's confident/cold etc way of behaving, which usually hides their true feelings or character □ *Beneath her smiling exterior she was tough, even ruthless.*

exterminate [ɪk'stɜːʳmɪneɪt] *vt* to kill all the members of <a group of people, animals, or insects> □ *The entire species will be exterminated unless the destruction of the rainforests is halted.*

extermination [ɪkˌstɜːʳmɪ'neɪʃn] *n: see* **exterminate** □ *extermination camps.*

external [ɪk'stɜːʳnl] *adj* -1. [appearance] that shows the outside of something or somebody; [wound, bleeding, wall] that is on the outside of something □ *The external part of the wall did not appear to have been damaged by the blast.* -2. [pressure, influence, examiner] that comes from outside an object, group, organization etc □ *'This medicine is for external use only.'* □ *External events had long ceased to influence them.* -3. [affairs, politics, relations] connected with foreign countries □ *the minister in charge of external trade.*

♦ **externals** *npl* the appearance of a situation when it is seen from the outside.

externally [ɪk'stɜːʳnəlɪ] *adv* [operate, exist, function] on the outside of or separately from something □ *Externally, it's in very good condition.* □ *Your exam papers will be marked externally.*

extinct [ɪk'stɪŋkt] *adj* -1. [animal, species] that no longer exists □ *The dodo became extinct in the 17th century.* -2. [volcano] that is no longer likely to erupt.

extinction [ɪk'stɪŋkʃn] *n* [of a species, animal] the state of being extinct □ *The tiger is now threatened with extinction.*

extinguish [ɪk'stɪŋɡwɪʃ] *vt* (formal use) -1. [fire, cigarette, flame] to put out <sthg burning> □ *Please extinguish all cigarettes before takeoff.* -2. [memory, feeling] to destroy <sthg> □ *When we saw his face, we knew all hope had finally be extinguished.*

extinguisher [ɪk'stɪŋɡwɪʃəʳ] *n* = **fire extinguisher.**

extn [telephone] *abbr of* **extension.**

extol [ɪk'stoul] (*pt* & *pp* **extolled,** *cont* **extolling**) *vt* [person, excellence, benefits] to praise <sb/sthg> greatly (formal use) □ *Michael was busy extolling the virtues of private education.*

extort [ɪk'stɔːʳt] *vt* **to extort sthg from sb** [money, information] to get sthg from sb by using force, threats etc.

extortion [ɪk'stɔːʳʃn] *n* the crime of extorting something from somebody □ *He was charged with extortion.*

extortionate [ɪk'stɔːʳʃnət] *adj* [price, rent, bill] that one thinks is too high □ *The taxi ride cost an extortionate amount of money.*

extra ['ekstrə] ◇ *adj* [charge, cost] more than is usual or essential □ *You'll need some extra cash/an extra suitcase.* □ *Take extra care when you cross.* ◇ *n* -1. something that is added to something else and is not a usual or essential part of it □ *The cocktail cabinet is an optional extra.* □ *an all-in package tour with no hidden extras.* -2. a person who has a very small part as an actor in a movie or TV program and does not usually have to speak. ◇ *adv* -1. [pay, charge] in addition to the normal amount □ *They made us pay extra because we were late.* -2. **extra long/special etc** longer/more special etc than usual □ *I've been working extra hard.*

extra- *prefix* -1. added to words to emphasize a particular quality □ *extra-big* □ *extra-long* □ *extra-special.* -2. added to words to show that something happens outside something else □ *extra-territorial* □ *extra-judicial.*

extract [*n* 'ekstrækt, *vb* ɪk'strækt] ◇ *n* -1. a short piece that is taken from a book, poem, piece of music etc □ *Here is an extract from the speech.* -2. CHEMISTRY a concentrated form of a substance that has been removed from another substance using a special process □ *malt extract.* ◇ *vt* -1. to take <sthg> out of something else with difficulty □ *He had his wisdom teeth extracted.* □ *They tried to extract the spoon from behind the fridge.* -2. [confession, information] to get <sthg> from somebody with difficulty □ *I found it very difficult to extract any information at all from her.* -3. [coal, oil, juice] to remove <sthg> from plants, the ground etc using an industrial process □ *Salt used to be extracted from these mines.*

extraction [ɪk'strækʃn] *n* -1. the place where one's family originally comes from □ *a Pole of Rumanian extraction.* -2. [of coal, a confession, tooth] *see* **extract.**

extractor (fan) [ɪk'stræktəʳ-] *n* GB a device that removes air which is hot or unpleasant from a room or building.

extracurricular [ˌekstrəkə'rɪkjələʳ] *adj* EDUCATION [activity] that does not form part of the school or college schedule.

extradite ['ekstrədaɪt] *vt* to send <sb> from a foreign country to their home country to be tried for a crime □ *The government has asked for the terrorists to be extradited to Europe.*

extradition [ˌekstrə'dɪʃn] *n: see* **extradite** □ *an extradition treaty/order.*

extramarital [ˌekstrə'mærətl] *adj* [affair, sex]

that a married person has with somebody who is not their husband or wife.

extramural [ˌekstrə'mjʊərəl] *adj* [course, studies] organized by a university or college either for people who are not full-time students or as an addition to students' main studies.

extraneous [ɪk'streɪnjəs] *adj* [detail, matter, issue] that is not directly connected with what is being discussed, considered etc.

extraordinary [US ɪk'strɔːrdnerɪ, GB ɪk'strɔːdnrɪ] *adj* -1. [person, beauty, success] that is very special or unusual □ *He had an extraordinary gift for music.* -2. [behavior, remark, event] that one finds very strange or surprising □ *What an extraordinary coincidence!* -3. [meeting, session] that is not part of the regular schedule and is organized for a special purpose □ *There will be an extraordinary meeting of shareholders tomorrow at 9:00am.*

extraordinary general meeting *n* a special meeting of shareholders in a particular company to discuss an urgent and important matter.

extrapolate [ɪk'stræpəleɪt] ◇ *vt* **to extrapolate sthg from sthg** [figure, fact] to calculate or guess sthg from sthg that one knows already (formal use). ◇ *vi: These figures are arrived at by extrapolating from last year's sales.* □ *You cannot simply extrapolate from what you know of much smaller businesses.*

extrasensory perception [ˌekstrəsensərɪ-] *n* an ability that some people are believed to have that allows them to know things without using their sense of sight, touch etc.

extraterrestrial [ˌekstrətə'restrɪəl] *adj* [being, life] that comes from somewhere outside the Earth.

extra time *n* GB SPORTS a period of thirty minutes that is added onto a soccer game at the end if the teams' scores are equal and it is necessary for one team to win.

extravagance [ɪk'strævəgəns] *n* -1. the act of spending too much money, especially on things that one cannot really afford and does not need □ *One could certainly never accuse him of extravagance.* -2. something that one does not really need, but that one enjoys spending money on □ *Expensive perfume is my one extravagance.*

extravagant [ɪk'strævəgənt] *adj* -1. [person] who spends too much money, especially on things that they cannot afford □ *She's surprisingly extravagant with her money.* -2. [entertainment, present, dinner] that involves spending a lot of money in a way that seems unnecessary □ *He lives a life of extravagant luxury.* □ *The couple next door have very extravagant tastes.* -3. [behavior, claim, expectation] that is extreme and seems unreasonable □ *an extravagant display of affection.*

extravaganza [ɪkˌstrævə'gænzə] *n* an expensive and impressive public entertainment, e.g. a large fireworks display.

extreme [ɪk'striːm] ◇ *adj* -1. [danger, caution, cold] that is very great □ *There is extreme concern about the outcome of the talks.* -2. [idea,

policy, reaction] that goes beyond what is reasonable □ *He has very extreme views on women priests.* □ *We don't want to do anything extreme.* -3. [point, edge, south] that is the furthest out or away from something □ *in the extreme north of the country.*

◇ *n* the most exaggerated or unreasonable in a range of opinions, actions, behavior etc □ *He goes from one extreme to the other.* □ *Well, you could go to the other extreme and say they should all be banned.* ■ **to extremes** to an extreme point □ *Yes, but do you have to take everything to such extremes?*

◆ **in the extreme** *adv* very □ *That was tactless in the extreme.*

extremely [ɪk'striːmlɪ] *adv* **extremely happy/ difficult etc** very happy/difficult etc □ *It was extremely kind of you to invite me here.*

extremism [ɪk'striːmɪzm] *n* extreme behavior, ideas, or opinions, especially in politics □ *Some party members may be guilty of political extremism.*

extremist [ɪk'striːməst] ◇ *n* a person who has very extreme opinions □ *Extremists protested outside as the funeral took place.* ◇ *adj*: *extremist left-wing groups.*

extremity [ɪk'stremətɪ] (*pl* **extremities**) (formal use) *n* -1. a situation of extreme difficulty or suffering □ *You can always, in extremity, call the police.* -2. [of a country, region] the point of a place that is furthest from the center □ *the northern extremity of the Carpathians.*

◆ **extremities** *npl* the parts of one's body that are at the ends, especially one's fingers and toes.

extricate ['ekstrɪkeɪt] *vt* to free <sb/sthg> from a place or situation □ *Firemen extricated him from the wreckage.* □ *I managed to extricate myself from what was a very embarrassing situation.*

extrovert ['ekstrəvɜː't] *n* a person who enjoys being with other people and who is very active and lively □ *She's a real extrovert.* ◇ *adj* [person] who is an extrovert; [behavior] that is typical of an extrovert □ *an extrovert child.*

extruded [ɪk'struːdəd] *adj* [metal, plastic] that is produced in a particular shape by being forced through a small hole in a block of metal.

exuberance [ɪg'zjuːbərəns] *n* exuberant behavior □ *He could scarcely contain his exuberance.*

exuberant [ɪg'zjuːbərənt] *adj* [person, mood, behavior] very cheerful, lively, and excited □ *She was in an exuberant mood.*

exude [ɪg'zjuːd] ◇ *vt* -1. [substance, animal, plant] to produce <a smell or liquid> □ *The stem exuded a strange gray liquid.* -2. [person] to have a lot of <a quality> in a very noticeable way □ *Melanie exudes confidence/charm.* ◇ *vi* [liquid, smell] *An unpleasant odor exudes from its body.*

exult [ɪg'zʌlt] *vi* to show great happiness, especially because of somebody else's defeat or failure □ *She exulted in her victory.* □ *Rival fans exulted at the team's defeat.*

exultant [ɪg'zʌltənt] *adj* [smile, person, tone] that shows great happiness, especially because of somebody else's defeat or failure □ *She was exultant in her victory.*

eye [aɪ] *(cont* **eyeing** OR **eying)** ◇ *n* -1. one of the two parts of the body that people and animals use for seeing □ *She has green/blue/brown eyes.* □ *He opened his eyes wide in surprise.* ■ **before one's (very) eyes** right in front of one □ *It all happened right before my eyes!* ■ **in his/her etc eyes** as far as he/she etc is concerned □ *In his eyes, she can do no wrong.* ■ **to cast** OR **run one's eye over sthg** to have a quick look at sthg □ *Could you cast an eye over this letter and tell me if it's OK?* ■ **to catch one's eye** to attract one's attention □ *A red dress in the window caught my eye.* ■ **to catch sb's eye** to do something in order to attract sb's attention □ *I tried unsuccessfully to catch the waiter's eye.* ■ **to lay** OR **set** OR **clap eyes on sb** to see sb (informal use) □ *It was the first time I'd ever set eyes on him.* ■ **to cry one's eyes out** to cry a lot because one is extremely upset (informal use). ■ **to feast one's eyes on sthg** to enjoy looking at sthg pleasant or attractive. ■ **to have an eye for sthg** [for quality, detail, a bargain] to have the ability to find or notice sthg □ *She has an eye for a bargain, I'll say that!* ■ **to have one's eye on sb** to watch sb carefully whenever possible because one is suspicious of or interested in them □ *I've got my eye on you!* ■ **to have one's eye on sthg** to be very interested in buying sthg □ *We've got our eye on a place down near the harbor.* ■ **to keep one's eyes open, to keep an eye out** to watch carefully □ *Remember to keep your eyes open for a large blue van.* ■ **to keep an eye on sb/sthg** to watch sb/sthg to make sure that they are safe or not causing any problems □ *Can you keep an eye on my suitcase for a minute?* ■ **there is more to this than meets the eye** this is more complicated, difficult etc than it seems. ■ **to open sb's eyes** to make sb realize something □ *It opened his eyes to the difficulties of raising a family alone.* ■ **not to see eye to eye** [two people] to disagree with each other □ *I never saw eye to eye with Ray.* ■ **to close** OR **shut one's eyes to sthg** [to a danger, problem, the truth] to ignore sthg and pretend that it does not exist □ *You can't just close your eyes to what's happening!* ■ **to turn a blind eye** to pretend that one has not noticed something that would normally need punishment or some kind of action □ *I can't just turn a blind eye to what they're doing.* ■ **to be up to one's eyes in sthg** to be very busy with sthg (informal use) □ *I'm up to my eyes in work at the moment.* -2. [of a needle] the small hole at the top of a needle where the thread goes. -3. [on a potato] a black spot on a potato. -4. **the eye of a hurricane/storm etc** the center of a hurricane/storm etc, where everything is calm.
◇ *vt* to look at <sb/sthg> in a particular way □ *The dog eyed the bone hungrily.* □ *She eyed him suspiciously.*

♦ **eye up** *vt sep* **to eye sb up** to look at sb in a way that shows one finds them attractive (informal use).

eyeball ['aɪbɔːl] ◇ *n* the whole eye, both in-side and outside the head. ◇ *vt* to look at <sb> directly (informal use).

eyebrow ['aɪbraʊ] *n* the line of hair that one has over each eye. ■ **to raise one's eyebrows** to be surprised or shocked □ *He didn't even raise an eyebrow when I told him.*

eyebrow pencil *n* a pencil that is used for making one's eyebrows darker.

eye-catching *adj* [car, dress, building] that attracts one's attention, especially by being very impressive, beautiful etc □ *He was wearing a very eye-catching outfit.*

eye contact *n* **to make/avoid eye contact** to look/avoid looking directly at somebody □ *Try to maintain eye contact with each other at all times.*

eyedrops ['aɪdrɒps] *npl* medicine for treating eye infections that is put into the eye in the form of drops.

eyeglasses [US 'aɪglæsɪz, GB -glɑːs-] *npl* US = **glasses**.

eyelash ['aɪlæʃ] *n* one of the fine hairs that grow on one's eyelids.

eyelet ['aɪlət] *n* a small hole with a metal ring around it that is made in a piece of material so that a shoelace, piece of string, rope etc can be passed through it.

eye-level *adj* [grill, picture, mirror] that is at the same height as one's eyes □ *The painting was hung just above eye-level.*

eyelid ['aɪlɪd] *n* the skin that covers one's eye when it is closed. ■ **not to bat an eyelid** to show no signs of surprise (informal use) □ *He didn't even bat an eyelid when I told him about the robbery.*

eyeliner ['aɪlaɪnəʳ] *n* a dark substance, often in the form of a pencil, that women put at the edge of their eyelids to make their eyes look larger and more attractive.

eye-opener *n* an experience that teaches one something surprising or interesting (informal use) □ *Working in a hospital proved to be a real eye-opener for me.*

eyepatch ['aɪpætʃ] *n* a small piece of material that one wears over an eye that has been damaged, or is healing after an operation, injury etc.

eye shadow *n* a powder or cream that one puts on one's eyelids to make them a particular color.

eyesight ['aɪsaɪt] *n* the ability to see □ *I have very bad/good eyesight.*

eyesore ['aɪsɔːʳ] *n* something, especially a building, that one thinks is very ugly and spoils the appearance of the things around it □ *That new shopping mall is a real eyesore.*

eyestrain ['aɪstreɪn] *n* pain or tiredness of one's eyes that is caused by too much work or reading.

eyeteeth ['aɪtiːθ] *npl* **I'd give my eyeteeth for sthg/to do sthg** I want very much to have sthg/to do sthg (informal use) □ *I'd give my eyeteeth for a job like that.*

eyewitness [ˌaɪ'wɪtnəs] *n* a person who sees an accident or crime happen and is able to give a description of it afterward □ *an eye-witness account/report.*

eyrie ['ɪərɪ] *n* the nest of a bird of prey such as an eagle that is built in a very high place and is difficult to reach.

f [ef] (*pl* **f's** OR **fs**), **F** [ef] (*pl* **F's** OR **Fs**) *n* the sixth letter in the English alphabet.
◆ **F** ◇ *n* MUSIC one of the notes in Western music. ◇ *abbr of* **Fahrenheit**.

FA (*abbr of* **Football Association**) *n* **the FA** the organization in charge of professional and amateur soccer in England and Wales.

FAA (*abbr of* **Federal Aviation Administration**) *n* **the FAA** the US government department responsible for aircraft and airport safety.

fable ['feɪbl] *n* a traditional story that teaches a moral lesson, especially one that has animals as its characters.

fabled ['feɪbld] *adj* [hero, character, victory] that is spoken about by many people or is in an old story and so has been well-known for a long time □ *the fabled city of Atlantis.*

fabric ['fæbrɪk] *n* **-1.** cloth that is produced by weaving threads of cotton, wool etc together □ *a luxurious silk fabric* □ *a piece of fabric.* **-2. the fabric of a building** the structure of a building including its walls, roof etc. **-3. the fabric of society** the basic structure of society, including its laws and institutions □ *This new phenomenon threatens the very fabric of our society.*

fabricate ['fæbrɪkeɪt] *vt* **-1.** [evidence, story] to invent <sthg> in order to deceive people □ *There have been claims that the police fabricated the whole thing.* **-2.** [object, structure] to make or construct <sthg>.

fabrication [,fæbrɪ'keɪʃn] *n* [of evidence, a story, object] *see* **fabricate** □ *The story is (a) complete fabrication.*

fabric softener US, **fabric conditioner** GB *n* a special liquid that is added to the water that clothes are washed in to make them soft.

fabulous ['fæbjələs] *adj* **-1.** [day, party, news] that one thinks is very good or enjoyable (informal use) □ *That's a really fabulous dress.* **-2.** [wealth, beauty] a word used to emphasize how great something is. **-3.** [beast, hero] that only exists in fables (literary use).

fabulously ['fæbjələslɪ] *adv* **fabulously rich/ successful etc** very rich/successful etc.

facade [fə'sɑːd] *n* **-1.** ARCHITECTURE the front of a building □ *a fine Renaissance facade.* **-2.** [of a person, organization] an outward appearance

that is false □ *a facade of generosity* □ *Her confidence is all a facade.*

face [feɪs] ◇ *n* **-1.** [of a person, animal] the front part of somebody's head, where the eyes, nose, and mouth are □ *She has a nice/friendly face.* □ *His face went bright red.* □ *I recognize his face.* ■ **face to face with sb** facing sb □ *There I was, face to face with him at last.* ■ **face to face with sthg** [with a situation, problem] in a position where one cannot avoid dealing with sthg □ *We came face to face with the same frustrating lack of organization.* ■ **to fall flat on one's face** to fall down and onto one's front. ■ **to look sb in the face** to look at sb directly without feeling uncomfortable or embarrassed □ *How can I ever look him in the face again?* ■ **to say sthg to sb's face** to say sthg directly to sb, rather than to somebody else □ *If you've got something on your mind, why can't you just say it to my face?* ■ **to show one's face** to appear in public or in a particular place so that people can see one □ *Don't show your face around here again!* ■ **it was staring me in the face** the answer, reason etc was so obvious that at first I didn't realize it □ *All that time the answer had been staring me in the face.* **-2. sb's face** the expression that somebody has on their face □ *You should have seen his face!* ■ **to make** OR **pull a face** to make an expression with one's face to show that one is angry or in order to be funny □ *When I told Chris, he just pulled a face and walked off.* ■ **her/his face fell** she/he looked suddenly disappointed □ *Her face fell when I told her the trip had been canceled.* **-3.** [of a cliff, mountain, building] the front surface of something vertical □ *They climbed up via the north face of the mountain.* **-4.** [of a clock, watch] the front part of a clock or watch that shows the numbers □ *a clock face.* **-5. the face of sthg** [of society, technology, a town] the appearance or character of sthg □ *ambitious plans that will change the face of politics/the capital forever.* **-6.** phrases **to disappear** OR **vanish off the face of the earth** [species, animal, person] to disappear completely □ *He seems to have disappeared off the face of the earth.* ■ **to lose face** to lose people's respect □ *I was afraid of losing face with my colleagues.* ■ **to save face** to avoid losing people's respect or one's good reputation □ *In order to save face, both sides claimed to have made substantial gains in the treaty.* ■ **to fly in the face of sthg** to seem to say that sthg is not correct or true □ *His beliefs fly in the face of traditional theories.*
◇ *vt* **-1.** to be turned or pointing in the direction of <sthg> □ *She turned and faced them.* □ *Stand and face the wall.* □ *The house faces the river.* **-2. to face** OR **be faced with sthg** [with a problem, dilemma] to have to deal with sthg difficult; to be about to experience sthg unpleasant □ *You are now facing a very tough choice.* □ *Sanderson now faces two years in jail.* ■ **to face facts/the truth** not to try to ignore or avoid the facts/the truth □ *You've got to face facts: you didn't get the job, so you're stuck here for now.* □ *Let's face it, we've no hope of winning.* **-3. I can't face it** I feel unable to do

it □ *I can't face another omelet!* □ *He simply couldn't face going in to work that day.*

◇ *vi* **to face north/south etc** to point toward the direction of north/south etc.

◆ **in the face of** *prep* [difficulty, opposition] despite <sthg> □ *They remained optimistic in the face of defeat.*

◆ **on the face of it** *adv* judging by appearances □ *On the face of it, it looks like a good idea.*

◆ **face down/up** *adv* [lie, float] with the front part of one's body facing downward/upward; [put, lay] with the front part of an object turned toward/away from the surface of the floor, a table etc □ *The body was lying face down in the water.* □ *She put the watch face down on the table.*

◆ **face up to** *vt fus* **to face up to sthg** [a problem, the truth] to have the courage to accept and deal with sthg □ *It's time to face up to the fact that you're not getting any younger.*

facecloth ['feɪsklɒθ] *n* GB a small piece of cloth that one uses to wash one's face, hands etc.

face cream *n* a cream that one uses to make the skin on one's face softer, or to protect it against the cold, wind etc.

faceless ['feɪsləs] *adj* [person] who has no character or personal identity □ *soulless dance music played by faceless DJ's.*

face-lift *n* -1. a surgical operation to make the face look younger. -2. **to give sthg a face-lift** [place, building] to make sthg look more attractive, e.g. by cleaning or renovating it □ *They've given City Hall a face-lift.*

face pack *n* a cream for improving the skin that one leaves on one's face for several minutes and then removes.

face powder *n* a powder that one puts on one's face to make the skin look smooth.

face-saving [-seɪvɪŋ] *adj* [agreement, intervention, action] that allows one to keep one's reputation and other people's respect □ *a face-saving compromise.*

facet ['fæsɪt] *n* -1. [of a problem, issue, somebody's character] a particular aspect or part of something □ *This anger is just one of the many facets of her complex personality.* -2. [of a jewel, gem] one of the flat surfaces on something such as a diamond.

facetious [fə'siːʃəs] *adj* [person] that tries to be funny at the wrong time or in the wrong situation □ *This is no time for facetious remarks!*

face-to-face *adj* [meeting, discussion, talks] in which people meet and talk to each other directly.

◆ **face to face** *adv*: *She came face to face with her attacker.*

face value *n* the value of a coin, bill, or stamp as shown on the front of it. ■ **to take sthg at face value** to accept that sthg is true without questioning it □ *I wouldn't take what he says at face value; he's probably bluffing.*

facial ['feɪʃl] ◇ *adj* [expression, muscle, hair] that is part of the face or is found on the face. ◇ *n* a beauty treatment in which the face is massaged and treated with special creams.

facile [US 'fæsl, GB 'fæsaɪl] *adj* [remark, argument] that one thinks is too simple and has not been thought about deeply or carefully enough (disapproving use) □ *The whole discussion seemed to me to be rather facile.*

facilitate [fə'sɪləteɪt] *vt* to make <sthg> easier (formal use) □ *This will facilitate communication between departments.*

facility [fə'sɪlətɪ] (*pl* **facilities**) *n* -1. **to have a facility for sthg** to be able to do sthg well and easily □ *She's always had a facility for languages.* -2. [on a machine] something useful that is added to a piece of equipment or a service □ *The phone has a call-indication facility.* -3. = **facilities** □ *a nuclear facility.*

◆ **facilities** *npl* buildings or equipment used for a particular activity □ *washing/sports facilities.*

facing ['feɪsɪŋ] *adj* [page, side] opposite.

facsimile (machine) [fæk'sɪmɪlɪ-] *n* = **fax** (formal use).

fact [fækt] *n* -1. [about a subject] a true piece of information about somebody or something □ *Several interesting facts have come to light.* □ *It's a fact that he earns more than me.* □ *I don't want to hear your opinions, just stick to the facts.* □ *The fact that you speak fluent Spanish should give you an advantage over the other candidates.* -2. what is true or real □ *How much of the story is based on fact, and how much is invented?* -3. *phrases* **the fact (of the matter) is,...** a phrase used to emphasize the main point about a situation, especially when this is the opposite of what has been said or believed before □ *The fact is, nobody cares what I do as long as I don't cause trouble.* ■ **the fact remains that...** a phrase used to introduce something true but unpleasant that has to be accepted □ *Even if the operation is successful, the fact remains that he may never walk again.* ■ **to know sthg for a fact** to be absolutely sure about sthg □ *I know for a fact that you were there.*

◆ **in fact** *adv* a phrase used to introduce a piece of information that is different, surprising, or more precise □ *She doesn't enjoy teaching much, in fact, she hates it.*

fact-finding [-faɪndɪŋ] *adj* **a fact-finding tour/trip** a tour/trip that one does in order to find out information about something □ *They've been sent on a fact-finding mission to Kenya.*

faction ['fækʃn] *n* a group of people who are part of a larger group but who disagree with some of their ideas □ *There were competing factions struggling for power in the university.*

factional ['fækʃnəl] *adj* [dispute, fighting] that takes place between factions of the same group.

fact of life *n* a situation that cannot be changed, even though one might not like it □ *It's an unpleasant fact of life, but everyone has to work for a living.*

◆ **facts of life** *npl* **the facts of life** the subject of sex and how babies are born (polite use).

factor ['fæktər] *n* -1. one of the things that affect an event, decision, or situation □ *High growth rates could be a major factor in the outcome of the election.* -2. MATH a whole number that can be multiplied by another whole number to give a particular number □ *2 and 3 are factors of 6.*

factory ['fæktrɪ] (*pl* **factories**) *n* a building where goods are made in large quantities using machines □ *a shoe factory* □ *Our factory's closing down.*

factory farming *n* a method of farming in which large numbers of animals are kept in small cages and given special food and drugs to make them grow faster or produce more eggs or milk.

factory ship *n* a large ship where fish can be cleaned and frozen or canned immediately after they are caught.

factotum [fæk'toutəm] (*pl* **factotums**) *n* a servant whose job is to do many different kinds of work (formal use) □ *I was employed as housekeeper, nanny, and general factotum.*

fact sheet *n* GB a short document that lists the most important details of a subject.

factual ['fæktʃʊəl] *adj* [account, report] that is based on facts and not on somebody's opinions, ideas etc □ *My diary is not just a factual record of what happens every day.*

faculty ['fækltɪ] (*pl* **faculties**) *n* -1. [of a person] the ability to carry out a normal human function, e.g. to speak, hear, or walk □ *the faculty of speech/sight.* -2. [of a school, college] a group of related departments; the teachers who work there □ *the Faculty of Arts/Science* □ *There is a meeting of the faculty today.*

FA Cup *n* **the FA Cup** in Britain, an important soccer competition, involving English and Welsh teams from different leagues.

fad [fæd] *n* something which is very fashionable for a short time □ *I'm hoping this dieting of Susan's is just a fad.*

faddy ['fædɪ] (*compar* **faddier**, *superl* **faddiest**) *adj* [person] who is too fussy, especially about food (informal and disapproving use).

fade [feɪd] ◇ *vi* -1. [color, material, piece of clothing] to become paler □ *The drapes faded the first time I washed them.* -2. [light, daylight] to become gradually less bright □ *I quietly sipped my drink as the last light faded.* -3. [sound, noise] to become gradually quieter □ *The music faded into the distance.* -4. [memory, feeling, interest] to become less strong □ *Hopes are fading for the remaining victims.* -5. [smile, expression] to disappear slowly □ *The smile slowly faded from his face.* ◇ *vt* [jeans, drapes, paint] to make <sthg> paler.

◆ **fade away, fade out** *vi* [sound, image, anger] to fade and then disappear.

faded ['feɪdəd] *adj* [color, material, piece of clothing] that has faded, usually because it has been in sunlight or has been washed □ *a pair of faded jeans.*

faeces *npl* GB = **feces**.

fag [fæg] *n* -1.▼ US a male homosexual (informal and offensive use). -2. GB a cigarette (informal use).

fagot▼ ['fægət] *n* US a male homosexual (offensive use).

Fahrenheit ['færənhaɪt] *n* a scale for measuring temperature on which water freezes at 32 degrees and boils at 212 degrees.

fail [feɪl] ◇ *vt* -1. **to fail to do sthg** not to do sthg, especially when one is expected to do it or is trying to do it □ *I fail to see what this has to do with me.* □ *I failed to convince her that she was wrong.* □ *The missing child failed to arrive home last night.* -2. [test, exam] to be unsuccessful in <sthg> by not scoring enough points; [candidate] to give <sb> fewer points than they need to pass an exam or test □ *Robbie failed the exam by eight points.* □ *The professor failed me again.* -3. **her courage/memory failed her** her courage/memory was not there when she needed it. □ *Halfway up the mountain his strength failed him.*

◇ *vi* -1. [person] to be unsuccessful when trying to do something □ *I tried to fix the TV but failed.* -2. [student, candidate] to be unsuccessful in a test or exam by not scoring enough points □ *"How did you do in history?" — "I failed."* -3. [lights, engine] to stop working □ *The brakes suddenly failed.* -4. [health, daylight, memory] to become weaker □ *His eyesight is failing.*

◆ **without fail** *adv* -1. a phrase used to say that something must happen □ *I want it finished by this evening without fail.* -2. a phrase used to say that something is always the case □ *She rings every day without fail.*

failed [feɪld] *adj* **a failed singer/writer etc** a person who has not been a successful singer/writer etc.

failing ['feɪlɪŋ] ◇ *n* a fault or weakness that somebody or something has □ *She has few failings, but one of them is a tendency to be late.* ◇ *prep* **failing that,...** a phrase used to suggest something else, in case something just mentioned is impossible □ *The information can be found in our files or, failing that, in the main library.*

fail-safe *adj* -1. **a fail-safe device/mechanism etc** a device/mechanism etc that prevents anything dangerous from happening if a machine or system stops working or goes wrong. -2. **a fail-safe plan** a plan that is certain to succeed.

failure ['feɪljər] *n* -1. [in doing something] a lack of success □ *The attempt at resolving the conflict ended in failure.* -2. **to be a failure** to be unsuccessful □ *I'm a hopeless failure.* □ *The conference was a complete failure.* -3. **failure to do sthg** the act of not doing sthg □ *I was surprised by her failure to attend the meeting.* -4. [of lights, an engine] an occasion when something stops working □ *She died of liver/kidney failure.*

faint [feɪnt] ◇ *vi* to lose consciousness, usually because of shock, pain, heat, or hunger □ *Several soldiers fainted while on parade.* ◇ *adj* -1. [sound, smell, shape] that is not clear or definite and is difficult to see, hear, smell etc □ *The ink had faded, and the writing was very faint.* -2. [smile, chance, hope] that is not strong at all □ *Hopes of finding the missing boy grew fainter as the day progressed.* □ *I don't have the faintest idea what you're talking about!* -3. **to**

feel faint to feel as if one is going to faint □ *I suddenly felt faint, and had to sit down.*

faint-hearted [-'hɑːᵣtəd] *adj* [person] who does not have enough courage or confidence.

faintly ['feɪntlɪ] *adv* -1. **faintly absurd/ridiculous** slightly absurd/ridiculous □ *Looking back the whole thing seems faintly ridiculous.* -2. [hear, recall, smile] *see* **faint** □ *The clothes smelled faintly of lavender.*

fair [feəᵣ] ◇ *adj* -1. [treatment, description, person] that treats somebody correctly because everybody else is treated in the same way; [comment, criticism] that is reasonable for one to make □ *It's not fair, he's got more than me!* □ *That's a fair point.* □ *The rules are not fair on* OR *to people on lower incomes.* ■ **to be fair,...** a phrase used to show that one is taking another person's point of view into account □ *To be fair, he was under a lot of stress.* -2. **a fair amount/distance etc** a fairly large amount/distance etc □ *We had a fair number of applicants.* □ *The house is a fair size.* -3. [standard, guess] that is quite good □ *They have a fair chance of winning.* □ *I have a fair idea of what they've been up to.* -4. [hair, skin] light in color □ *She has a very fair complexion.* -5. [weather, sky] clear, dry, and pleasant □ *As long as the weather's fair tomorrow, we can go.*
◇ *adv* **to play fair** to act fairly.
◇ *n* -1. a market where goods are bought and sold. -2. an exhibition where e.g. farm animals and hand-made goods are judged □ *a state fair.* -3. = **funfair.** -4. = **trade fair.**

◆ **fair enough** *adv* a phrase used to show that one understands somebody's opinion, decision, or wish, though perhaps one does not agree with it □ *Well, fair enough, he did ask you beforehand.*

fair copy *n* a corrected copy of a piece of writing.

fair game *n* a person or thing that it is acceptable to criticize □ *After such behavior he was fair game for the press.*

fairground ['feəᵣgraʊnd] *n* a place where a fair is being held.

fair-haired [-'heəᵣd] *adj* [person] who has light-colored hair.

fair-haired boy *n* US a man or boy who is liked better than anybody else by somebody in authority (informal and disapproving use).

fairly ['feəᵣlɪ] *adv* -1. **fairly difficult/large/sure** rather difficult/large/sure □ *It was a fairly important meeting, but I didn't mind being interrupted.* -2. [treat, describe, distribute] *see* **fair** □ *We try to ensure that all clients are fairly treated.*

fair-minded [-'maɪndəd] *adj* [person] who makes fair decisions □ *You have to admit, as a judge she's very fair-minded.*

fairness ['feəᵣnəs] *n* [of a person, comment] *see* **fair.** ■ **in (all) fairness to sb** a phrase used to introduce a statement that defends somebody from a criticism that they do not deserve □ *In all fairness to him, he did try to apologize.*

fair play *n* behavior that is fair □ *That's just not fair play — they didn't give us any warning.*

fairway ['feəᵣweɪ] *n* an area of short grass on a golf course between a tee and a green.

fairy ['feərɪ] (*pl* **fairies**) *n* in children's stories, a small person with wings who has magical powers.

fairy lights *npl* GB small, colored, electric lights, usually used for decorating a Christmas tree.

fairy tale *n* a story, usually for children, about fairies or other imaginary magical creatures.

fait accompli [US ˌfeɪtəkɒm'pliː, GB ˌfeɪtə-'kɒmpliː] (*pl* **faits accomplis**) *n* something that somebody has already done and that cannot be changed □ *Why not present them with a fait accompli rather than asking their permission?*

faith [feɪθ] *n* -1. a belief that somebody or something can be trusted □ *I have faith in her/her ability/human nature.* □ *They're beginning to lose faith in the unions.* ■ **to do sthg in good faith** to do sthg honestly and without trying to deceive somebody □ *I sold this to you in good faith.* -2. a particular religion; one's belief in this □ *the Christian faith* □ *He has a strong faith.*

faithful ['feɪθfl] ◇ *adj* -1. [friend, support, promise] loyal □ *The party remained faithful to its principles.* -2. [copy, account, translation] accurate □ *The movie adaptation is faithful to the book.* -3. [husband, wife, partner] who does not have sex with anybody else □ *Yes, he's always been faithful to me.* ◇ *npl* **the faithful** the people who believe in a particular religion.

faithfully ['feɪθflɪ] *adv* [support, promise] *see* **faithful** □ *She promised me faithfully that she'd come.* ■ **Yours faithfully** GB a phrase used at the end of a formal letter that begins with the phrase "Dear Sir" or "Dear Madam."

faith healer [-hiːləᵣ] *n* a person who claims to be able to cure illness by prayer and religious faith.

faithless ['feɪθləs] *adj* [person] who is not loyal or honest (formal use).

fake [feɪk] ◇ *adj* [copy, gun, jewelry] that is not genuine and is intended to deceive □ *He is traveling on a fake passport.* ◇ *n* -1. a fake copy of something □ *This painting is a fake.* -2. a person who pretends to be something that they are not (disapproving use) □ *He's just a fake.* ◇ *vt* -1. to produce a fake copy of <a picture, document, signature> etc □ *She faked his signature on the note.* -2. to pretend to have <an illness, feeling> etc in order to deceive somebody □ *He faked ignorance of the affair.* ◇ *vi* to pretend in order to deceive somebody □ *Ignore him, he's just faking.*

falcon [US 'fælkən, GB 'fɔːlk-] *n* a bird of prey that can be trained to hunt.

Falkland Islands ['fɔːklənd]: **the Falkland Islands** a group of British islands in the South Atlantic Ocean, off the coast of Argentina. Argentina invaded them in 1982, but they were recaptured by British forces. SIZE: 12,173 sq kms. POPULATION: 2,000 (*Falkland Islanders*). CAPITAL: Stanley.

Falklands ['fɔːkləndz] = **Falkland Islands.**

fall [fɔːl] (*pt* **fell**, *pp* **fallen**) ◇ *vi* **-1.** [person, object] to drop to the ground □ *She fell off the stool/out of the window.* □ *The plate fell to the ground with a smash.* ■ **to fall flat** [joke] to fail to make people laugh with the result that the person telling the joke is embarrassed. **-2.** [snow, leaves] to drop from the sky □ *The first drops of rain began to fall.* **-3.** [demand, temperature] to decrease in amount or value □ *Unemployment has fallen for the third month in a row.* □ *The pound has fallen against the dollar.* **-4. to fall ill/silent/pregnant** to become ill/silent/pregnant. ■ **to fall asleep** to begin sleeping □ *I fell asleep on the sofa.* ■ **to fall in love** to begin to love somebody □ *They fell in love on vacation.* ■ **to fall open** [book] to open □ *The book fell open at the very page I was looking for.* **-5. to fall into a particular group/category** to belong to a particular group/category □ *Our customers fall into two groups.* ■ **to fall under a particular heading** to belong under a particular heading □ *The matter does not fall under our jurisdiction.* **-6. to fall to bits** OR **pieces** [car, book, chair] to gradually get broken so that pieces fall off it □ *The old shed is falling to pieces.* **-7.** [government, leader] to lose power □ *The ruling party has fallen after 20 years in power.* **-8.** [town, region] to be taken over by enemy forces □ *Constantinople fell to the Turks.* **-9.** GB [political constituency] to pass into the control of a different political party □ *Hillhead has fallen to Labour.* **-10.** [night, darkness, silence] to begin to be present □ *A hush fell over the audience.* **-11.** [light, shadow] to reach a particular place or object □ *A shadow fell across the bay.* **-12.** [soldier, fighter] to die in battle (literary use).
◇ *n* **-1.** [of a person, object] the act of falling to the ground □ *She slipped and had a nasty fall.* **-2.** [of snow, rocks] the act of falling from somewhere higher up □ *There's been a big rock fall.* **-3.** [of a government, leader] the act of losing power □ *A defeat on this issue could result in the fall of the Government.* **-4.** [of a city, region] the act of being taken over by the enemy □ *the fall of Paris to the Allies.* **-5.** [in unemployment, demand, temperature] a decrease □ *the fall in the value of the pound.* **-6.** US [the season between summer and winter] □ *New England is beautiful in the fall.*

◆ **falls** *npl* a waterfall.

◆ **fall apart** *vi* **-1.** [car, book, chair] to break into smaller pieces, especially because it is old □ *My copy of "Tom Sawyer" is so old it's starting to fall apart.* **-2.** [country, organization, marriage] to become disorganized or stop working properly; [person] to become emotionally disturbed □ *The social fabric of our country is gradually falling apart.* □ *He just fell apart when his wife left him.*

◆ **fall away** *vi* **-1.** [paint, plaster] to break off from the surface it was attached to. **-2.** [land, slope] to slope downward □ *At this point the path falls away sharply down to the sea.*

◆ **fall back** *vi* **-1.** [person, crowd] to move backward away from somebody or something □ *The police fell back as the demonstrators advanced.* **-2.** [person] to move more slowly than the other people in a group so that one walks behind them □ *Danny fell back so that he could walk with Ruth.*

◆ **fall back on** *vt fus* **to fall back on sb/sthg** [a plan, resources, friends] to use sb/sthg because somebody or something else has not been good enough □ *If John loses his job, he has nothing to fall back on.*

◆ **fall behind** *vi* **-1.** [in a race] to go more slowly than the other people so that one is left behind □ *Can't you walk any faster? We don't want to fall behind.* **-2.** [with the rent, one's work] to owe something to somebody because one has not given it to them at the agreed times □ *He fell behind with the payments.*

◆ **fall down** *vi* **-1.** [person, building] to collapse; [picture, shelf] to drop to the ground □ *He fell down and hurt himself.* □ *The sign's fallen down again.* **-2.** [idea, plan, argument] to no longer work or be convincing because of a particular weakness in it □ *That's where your theory falls down.*

◆ **fall for** *vt fus* **-1. to fall for sb/sthg** [for a person, place, house] to fall in love with sb/sthg □ *I fell for that dress as soon as I saw it.* **-2. to fall for sthg** [for a trick, lie, story] to be deceived by sthg □ *You didn't fall for that old excuse, did you?*

◆ **fall in** *vi* **-1.** [roof, ceiling] to collapse. **-2.** [soldiers] to line up in a military formation for inspection.

◆ **fall in with** *vt fus* **to fall in with an idea/a suggestion etc** to accept and act in agreement with an idea/a suggestion etc □ *I'm happy to fall in with whatever you plan to do.*

◆ **fall off** *vi* **-1.** [branch, tile] to become separated from the thing it was attached to □ *Pieces of the plaster kept falling off.* **-2.** [demand, numbers] to decrease □ *Interest in the bond market has fallen off recently.*

◆ **fall on** *vt fus* **-1. to fall on sthg** [eyes] to notice sthg □ *By chance, her gaze fell on the letter.* **-2. to fall on sb/sthg** [attackers, robbers] to attack sb/sthg □ *The gang fell on him as he left the bar.*

◆ **fall out** *vi* **-1.** [hair, tooth] to become separated from one's body □ *an old woman whose teeth had fallen out.* **-2.** [friends] to quarrel □ *She's fallen out with her boyfriend.* **-3.** [soldiers] to leave their positions in a formation.

◆ **fall over** ◇ *vt fus* **to fall over sthg** [over a step, object] to fall down after hitting sthg with one's feet when walking □ *I fell over his bag and twisted my ankle.* ■ **to be falling over oneself to do sthg** to be very enthusiastic about doing sthg (informal use) □ *All the men were falling over themselves to carry her baggage.* ◇ *vi* [person, chair] to fall from an upright position to the ground □ *I fell over and hurt my knee.*

◆ **fall through** *vi* [plan, deal] not to happen or be carried out as expected □ *My trip to the Bahamas fell through.*

◆ **fall to** *vt fus* **to fall to sb** to be the responsibility of sb □ *It fell to me to tell her the news.*

fallacious [fəˈleɪʃəs] *adj* [idea, theory, argument] that is based on a fallacy (formal use).

fallacy ['fæləsɪ] (*pl* **fallacies**) *n* something a lot of people think is true, but which is not □ *It's a fallacy that children learn languages more quickly than adults.*

fallen ['fɔːlən] *past participle of* **fall**.

fall guy *n* a person who is blamed for something bad that has happened, even though it is not their fault (informal use) □ *I'm just being used as the fall guy in this.*

fallible ['fæləbl] *adj* [person, method, plan] that is not perfect and can be wrong or make mistakes □ *This just proves that everybody is fallible.*

falling ['fɔːlɪŋ] *adj* **falling demand/unemployment etc** decreasing demand/unemployment etc □ *Falling prices have led to an increase in consumer spending.*

fallopian tube [fə,loupɪən-] *n* one of two tubes in a woman's body through which eggs pass from the ovaries to the uterus.

fallout ['fɔːlaʊt] *n* radioactive dust that is the result of a nuclear explosion.

fallout shelter *n* a shelter designed to protect people from fallout.

fallow ['fæloʊ] *adj* [land, field] that has been dug or plowed but left with nothing planted in it, in order to improve the soil quality □ *The land lay fallow for a year.*

false [fɔːls] *adj* **-1.** [statement] that is not true; [impression, idea, assumption] that is based on a belief or on information that is wrong □ *Wearing a helmet can give you a false sense of security.* **-2.** [eyelash, beard, nail] that is not real but is worn to look like something real. ■ **a false ceiling** a ceiling that has been built below the actual ceiling □ *The suitcase had a false bottom.* **-3.** [passport, name] that is not genuine and is intended to deceive somebody □ *They were traveling under a false name.* **-4.** [smile, modesty] that is not sincere and is intended to deceive somebody □ *There was a false note in his voice.* **-5.** [person] who pretends to care but does not really care □ *I find her really false, actually.*

false alarm *n* a situation in which somebody believes there is an emergency when there is not □ *It's OK, it was only a false alarm.*

falsehood ['fɔːlshʊd] *n* **-1.** a lie (formal use). **-2.** the fact of being a lie or not being true.

falsely ['fɔːlslɪ] *adv* **-1.** [state, imprison] incorrectly or for reasons that are not just and right □ *He was falsely accused of the murder.* **-2.** [smile, laugh] in a way that is not sincere.

false start *n* **-1.** SPORT a situation where one contestant, horse etc starts a race before the signal is given. **-2.** a failed attempt to start something □ *After a few false starts the project finally got under way.*

false teeth *npl* artificial teeth worn by people who have lost all their own teeth.

falsetto [fɔːl'setoʊ] (*pl* **falsettos**) ◇ *adv* [sing, speak] with a very high-pitched voice, higher than one's normal voice. ◇ *n* a man who sings falsetto.

falsify ['fɔːlsɪfaɪ] (*pt* & *pp* **falsified**) *vt* [document, accounts, evidence] to change <sthg> with the intention of deceiving somebody □ *The entries in the diary had been falsified.*

Falstaff [US 'fɔːlstæf, GB -stɑːf] a character in Shakespeare's plays *Henry IV* and *The Merry Wives of Windsor*. He is fat, greedy, dishonest, and drinks too much, but is also funny and lovable.

falter ['fɔːltər] *vi* **-1.** [person, animal] to move unsteadily and seem about to fall □ *The wounded deer faltered, staggered, and finally fell.* **-2.** [voice] to become weak and hesitant □ *His voice faltered and he fell silent for a moment.* **-3.** [interest, demand] to lose strength, energy etc and seem about to stop or decrease; [person] to become unsure what to do □ *Throughout those years, her courage never faltered.* □ *He did what he thought was right without faltering.*

faltering ['fɔːltərɪŋ] *adj* **a faltering step/attempt etc** an unsure and hesitant step/attempt etc □ *Malcolm read from the letter in a low, faltering voice.*

fame [feɪm] *n* the state of being famous □ *He left for Hollywood in search of fame and fortune.*

familiar [fə'mɪljər] *adj* **-1.** [face, surroundings, sight] that one knows well or recognizes □ *Our brand names are familiar to millions of consumers.* **-2. to be familiar with sthg** [with a book, the law] to know or understand sthg well □ *She's familiar with the situation/type of work.* ■ **to be on familiar terms with sb** to know sb well enough to behave informally with them □ *I'm hardly on familiar terms with them — why don't YOU ask?* **-3.** [tone, manner, person] that one thinks is too friendly (disapproving use).

familiarity [fə,mɪlɪ'ærətɪ] *n: see* **familiar** □ *I found his sudden familiarity alarming.* ■ **familiarity breeds contempt** a phrase used to say that people often lose respect for people, places, or things that they know very well.

familiarize, -ise [fə'mɪljəraɪz] *vt* **to familiarize oneself with sthg** to learn or find out about sthg. ■ **to familiarize sb with sthg** to tell sb about sthg so that they know more about it □ *You'd probably like to familiarize yourself with the layout of the building first.*

family ['fæmlɪ] (*pl* **families**) ◇ *n* **-1.** [of people] a group of people who are related by birth or marriage □ *a family of four* □ *How is your family?* □ *Have you got any family?* □ *She is bringing up a family on her own.* □ *Heart disease runs in the family.* **-2.** BIOLOGY a group of animals or plants that are classified together because they have similar characteristics □ *the cat family.* ◇ *comp* **family entertainment/viewing etc** entertainment/viewing etc that is designed or suitable for both parents and children □ *His latest movie makes good family viewing.* □ *a family house/car* □ *a family-size packet of cornflakes.*

family business *n* a business owned and run by members of the same family.

family credit *n* in Britain, an allowance paid by the state to families who do not have enough money to live on.

family doctor *n* a doctor who treats all common illnesses and deals with people who live in a particular area.

family life *n* life at home with one's family □ *She doesn't get much time for family life.*

family planning *n* the use of contraception to control the number of children born in a family □ *a family planning clinic.*

family practitioner *n* US a doctor who provides general medical care and does not specialize in one area of medicine.

family tree *n* a diagram showing several generations of a family and the way its members are related.

famine ['fæmɪn] *n* a serious shortage of food in a large area, usually resulting in many deaths □ *There is widespread famine in the country areas.*

famished ['fæmɪʃt] *adj* **to be famished** to be very hungry (informal use).

famous ['feɪməs] *adj* [person, place, painting] that is very well known □ *The region is famous for its wine.*

famously ['feɪməslɪ] *adv* **to get along** OR **on famously** to get on very well (informal use).

fan [fæn] (*pt* & *pp* **fanned**, *cont* **fanning**) ◇ *n* -1. a flat piece of paper, cloth etc that one holds in one's hand and waves near one's face in order to cool oneself. -2. an electrical device with blades that spin around to blow air in a particular direction □ *an electric/a ceiling fan.* -3. [of a sport, team] a very enthusiastic follower or supporter of a sport, type of music, particular performer, program etc □ *a football/rock fan.*
◇ *vt* -1. to cool <sb> with a fan, or something like a fan □ *She fanned herself with a newspaper.* -2. [blaze, flames] to wave something like a fan at <a fire> to make it burn more strongly □ *He fanned the fire to stop it from going out.* -3. [somebody's love, desire] to make <a feeling> stronger □ *The fact that she avoided him simply fanned his passion for her.*

✦ **fan out** *vi* [people, searchers] to spread out while moving forward, usually when looking for something □ *I suggest we fan out and search the woods.*

fanatic [fə'nætɪk] *n* -1. a person who has extreme religious or political views (disapproving use). -2. a person who is very enthusiastic about a particular activity or subject □ *a football/health fanatic.*

fanatical [fə'nætɪkl] *adj* -1. [supporter, belief, devotion] very loyal and enthusiastic □ *She's a fanatical believer in the power of crystals.* -2. [regime, leader, sect] that has extreme ideas or beliefs (disapproving use) □ *a fanatical group of right-wing extremists.*

fanaticism [fə'nætɪsɪzm] *n* fanatical ideas or beliefs.

fan belt *n* a continuous belt that turns a fan to cool the engine of a car, truck etc.

fanciful ['fænsɪfl] *adj* -1. [idea, explanation] that does not seem true, real, or possible □ *Don't you think this all sounds a little fanciful?* -2. [design, name] that is unusual and attracts

attention □ *a fanciful design on the side of his car.*

fan club *n* a club formed by or for the fans of a particular celebrity, sports team etc.

fancy ['fænsɪ] (*compar* **fancier**, *superl* **fanciest**, *pl* **fancies**, *pt* & *pp* **fancied**) ◇ *vt* (informal use) -1. GB [something to eat, drink] to want <sthg> □ *Do you fancy a piece of cake?* □ *I fancy going out tonight.* -2. GB [man, woman] to be sexually attracted to <sb> □ *She told her schoolfriends she didn't fancy him.* ■ **to fancy oneself** to have a high opinion of oneself (disapproving use) □ *That guy over there really fancies himself.* ■ **to fancy oneself as sthg** to think that one is sthg or could be sthg that one is not □ *She fancies herself as an artist.* -3. a word used to show that one is surprised by something □ *Fancy meeting you here!* □ *"And I never saw him." — "Fancy that!"*
◇ *n* -1. **to take a fancy to sb/sthg** to begin to desire sb/sthg (informal use) □ *Robert's taken a fancy to your younger sister.* ■ **to take** OR **catch sb's fancy** to attract sb (informal use) □ *The dress took her fancy so she went in and bought it.* ■ **a passing fancy** a liking or desire for somebody or something that lasts for a short time. -2. a fantasy □ *a childish fancy.*
◇ *adj* (informal use) -1. [food, clothes, price] more expensive, colorful, or elaborate than usual □ *I've just prepared a few things for dinner — you know, nothing fancy.* -2. [restaurant, hotel] expensive and luxurious □ *his taste for fancy cars.*

fancy dress *n* GB a special costume, usually worn at a party, that makes somebody look like a person, animal etc that is well-known, amusing, unusual etc, e.g. a pirate or a gorilla □ *You have to come in fancy dress.* □ *a fancy-dress party.*

fancy goods *npl* GB small items in a shop that are used as gifts or kept as ornaments.

fanfare ['fænfeər] *n* a short loud piece of music, usually played on trumpets at the beginning of an important event or when an important person arrives.

fang [fæŋ] *n* one of the long sharp teeth of a wolf, snake, vampire etc.

fan heater *n* an electrical device that uses a fan to blow hot air into a room.

fanlight ['fænlaɪt] *n* a small window in the shape of a half circle above a door or larger window.

fan mail *n* letters sent to a famous person by their fans.

fanny ['fænɪ] *n* US one's bottom (informal use).

fanny pack *n* US a small bag that is attached to the waist by a belt and used to carry personal belongings, especially money.

fantasize, -ise ['fæntəsaɪz] *vi* to think or talk about something very pleasant that is unlikely to happen □ *He fantasized about going to live in the country.*

fantastic [fæn'tæstɪk] *adj* -1. [person, movie, idea] very good □ *We had a fantastic time in Europe this summer.* -2. [number, amount, profit] that seems very large □ *They're paying him a* fantastic salary. -3. [story, plan] unbelievable □ fantastic tales of aliens and spaceships.

fantastically [fæn'tæstıklı] adv -1. **fantastically expensive/high etc** very expensive/high etc. -2. [colored, designed, decorated] in a very strange and unusual way.

fantasy ['fæntəsı] (pl **fantasies**) n -1. an event, activity, or situation which one thinks about, especially because one wants it to happen, but which will never happen □ a childhood/sexual fantasy □ My fantasy is to captain a football team. -2. something that does not exist and is only part of somebody's imagination □ It is difficult to separate fact from fantasy in this report. □ He lives in a fantasy world.

fanzine ['fænziːn] n a magazine for fans of a particular type of music, sport etc.

fao abbr of **for the attention of.**

FAO (abbr of **Food and Agriculture Organization**) n **the FAO** the UN department responsible for improving food production and combating hunger, especially in developing countries.

far [fɑːr] (compar **farther** OR **further**, superl **farthest** OR **furthest**) ◇ adv -1. **to go/travel far** to go/travel a long way (used mainly in questions and negative sentences). ■ **it's not far** it's not a long distance from here □ It's too far to walk. □ The house is down a sidestreet, not far from the main road. □ How much further is it? □ How far away do you live? ■ **I would go so far as to say I enjoyed it** this will sound surprising, but I enjoyed it □ I wouldn't go so far as to say I actually like him... ■ **to go too far** to behave in a way that is not reasonable and that upsets or annoys other people □ Now you've gone too far this time! -2. [in the past, future] a long time in the past or future □ We worked far into the night. □ This story takes us far back in time. -3. **far better** very much better (used with comparatives) □ The room looks far brighter now. □ I enjoyed it far more than I thought I would. □ It's far too late to go out. -4. used to show extent or degree □ I wouldn't trust him very far. □ How far have you gotten with your work? ■ **it's not far wrong** OR **off** OR **out** it's very nearly correct □ "26?" — "You're not far off, he's 29." ◇ adj -1. **the far side of the road** the side of the road that is the greater distance away from where one is □ It's the door on the far left, at the end of the corridor. -2. **the far right/left** the most right-wing/left-wing supporters of a political party. -3. [country, mountains] distant (literary use).

◆ **as far as** ◇ prep **we walked as far as the river** we walked to the river (but not farther). ◇ conj -1. **as far as I can remember** this is what I remember (but I am not totally certain) □ As far as I can recall, he had brown hair and blue eyes. -2. **as far as possible** as much as possible □ We'll try to help you as far as we can. -3. **as far as it goes** only to a limited extent □ This kind of thing is alright as far as it goes, but it soon gets pretty boring.

◆ **as far back as** ◇ prep **this was known as far back as 1880** this has been known since

1880, which is a long time ago. ◇ conj for as long in the past as □ There's been a shop here as far back as I can remember.

◆ **by far**, **far and away** adv **it is by far the biggest** it is the biggest by a great amount (used with comparatives and superlatives) □ She's far and away the best player in the team.

◆ **far and wide**, **far and near** adv **people came from far and wide** people came from many places, some of them a long way away □ They searched far and wide for a similar lamp, but could never find one.

◆ **far away**, **far off** adv a long way away in place or time □ Summer isn't far off now.

◆ **far from** prep **I am far from certain** I am not at all certain □ "Was she angry?" — "Far from it, she thought it was a good idea."

◆ **so far** adv -1. [walk, go] only a little distance; [believe, agree] only to a limited extent □ We'll go so far and then turn back. □ You can only trust him so far. ■ **so far so good** things have been going well up to now, but this may not continue □ "How are things going?" — "So far so good, but you never know, do you?" -2. until now □ So far we've had twenty applications for the job.

◆ **so far as** conj = **as far as.**

faraway [,fɑːrə'weı] adj -1. **a faraway country/land etc** a country/land etc that is a long distance away □ They heard the faraway sound of gunfire. -2. **a faraway look** a look on one's face that shows one is thinking about something that is not connected to where one is or what is happening □ She had that faraway look in her eyes that tells you you're wasting your time.

farce [fɑːrs] n -1. THEATER a comic play in which the characters get into ridiculous situations; this style of drama. -2. an event that should be serious or useful but that becomes ridiculous or useless, e.g. because it is not organized or carried out properly □ The whole thing was a complete farce.

farcical ['fɑːsıkl] adj [episode, situation] that is ridiculous □ It's farcical the way his ex-wife carries on.

fare [feər] ◇ n -1. the money one pays to travel by bus, taxi, airplane, boat, train etc for one trip □ How much is the air fare? □ They charge very high fares. □ Bus/train fares are due to go up. -2. food (formal use) □ farm fare. ◇ vi **to fare well/badly** to be successful/unsuccessful; to be treated well/badly □ Our business has fared well despite the recession.

Far East: **the Far East** the countries of eastern Asia, including China and Japan.

farewell [,feər'wel] ◇ n the act or process of saying goodbye to somebody □ He said his farewells and left. □ a farewell party/speech/dinner. ◇ excl a word that is used to say goodbye (literary use).

farfetched [,fɑːr'fetʃt] adj [idea, suggestion, story] that is difficult to believe because it seems very unlikely or unrealistic □ I found the ending very farfetched.

far-flung adj -1. [outpost, country] that is a long distance away from the center of an empire, organization etc □ *He's always flying off to far-flung places.* **-2.** [empire, network] that includes a lot of different places that are far-flung.

farm [fɑːʳm] ◇ *n* an area of land and buildings where animals are kept to be sold as food or crops are grown □ *They live on a farm.* □ *fresh farm produce* □ *farm animals.* ◇ *vt* to use <an area of land> for keeping animals to be sold as food or for growing crops □ *He farms 1,000 acres in Alberta.* ◇ *vi*: *His family has been farming for generations.*

◆ **farm out** *vt sep* **to farm work out** to send work to different people to do.

farmer [ˈfɑːʳməʳ] *n* a person who owns a farm or who organizes the work done on the farm.

Farmer [ˈfɑːʳməʳ], **Fannie** (1857–1915) a US cookery expert and writer whose cookbooks were the first to use exact measurements in recipes.

farmhand [ˈfɑːʳmhænd] *n* a person who is employed to do general work on a farm.

farmhouse [ˈfɑːʳmhaʊs, *pl* -haʊzɪz] *n* the house on a farm where the farmer lives.

farming [ˈfɑːʳmɪŋ] *n* the activity of keeping animals to be sold as food or growing crops □ *sheep/pig/cattle farming.*

farmland [ˈfɑːʳmlænd] *n* land that is used for farming □ *It's a waste of good farmland.*

farmstead [ˈfɑːʳmsted] *n* US a farm.

farmyard [ˈfɑːʳmjɑːʳd] *n* the area near farm buildings or a farmhouse.

far-off *adj* **-1.** [event, time] that happened long ago or will happen a long time in the future □ *It's still only a far-off possibility.* **-2.** [country, town] that is a long distance away □ *I'd love to travel to far-off places.*

far-reaching [-ˈriːtʃɪŋ] *adj* [change, effect, implication] that affects many people or things, usually in an important way □ *The closure of the coal mine has had far-reaching consequences for the local community.*

farsighted [ˌfɑːʳˈsaɪtəd] *adj* **-1.** [person, plan, decision] that gives proper consideration to future events or problems □ *The government has shown itself to be anything but farsighted in its policy-making.* **-2.** US [person] whose eyes can see things that are further away more clearly than things that are near □ *I've become increasingly farsighted as I've gotten older.*

fart▽ [fɑːʳt] (very informal use) ◇ *vi* to release air from the anus in a way which often makes a noise and smells unpleasant. ◇ *n* **-1.** an act of farting. **-2.** a word used to describe a silly or boring person.

farther [ˈfɑːʳðəʳ] *comparative of* **far.**

farthest [ˈfɑːʳðəst] *superlative of* **far.**

FAS (*abbr of* **free alongside ship**) at a price that includes all costs of transportation and insurance of goods until they reach the ship and are ready for loading.

fascia [ˈfeɪʃə] *n* **-1.** [of a store] the board above the front of a store that has the store's name on it. **-2.** GB [in a car, boat, aircraft] the

board in front of the driver or pilot that has the instruments on it.

fascinate [ˈfæsəneɪt] *vt* [idea, story] to interest <sb> so much that they keep looking at it, thinking about it etc □ *The children are fascinated by the tropical fish.*

fascinating [ˈfæsəneɪtɪŋ] *adj* [person, country, idea] that one thinks is extremely interesting □ *He has led a fascinating life.* □ *Did you really? How fascinating!*

fascination [ˌfæsəˈneɪʃn] *n* a feeling of being fascinated □ *Chemistry holds a great fascination for me.* □ *He watched in fascination.*

fascism [ˈfæʃɪzm] *n* a political philosophy or system of government that supports total government control, an active role for the army, and aggressive opposition to other nationalities or political ideas, especially Communism.

fascist [ˈfæʃəst] ◇ *adj* [ideology, policy, tactics] that is based on fascism; [dictator, regime] that believes in fascism. ◇ *n* a person who supports fascism.

fashion [ˈfæʃn] ◇ *n* **-1.** [in clothes] the business or activity that is connected with different styles of clothing and appearance; a style of clothing, appearance etc that is popular at a particular time □ *the fashion industry* □ *a fashion model* □ *Short hair is the fashion.* ■ **to be in/out of fashion** [style, music, word] to be fashionable/no longer fashionable □ *The mini-skirt is back in fashion.* □ *The group went out of fashion in the early 90s.* **-2.** [behavior] the way in which somebody does something □ *He drove in his usual fashion: very badly!* ■ **after a fashion** in a way that is not satisfactory or correct □ *He can speak German after a fashion.* ◇ *vt* to make <sthg>, usually with one's hands (formal use) □ *She fashioned a pot out of clay.*

fashionable [ˈfæʃnəbl] *adj* [style, place, clothes, activity] that is popular at a particular time, but not usually for very long; [person] who wears fashionable clothes □ *Aerobics was very fashionable in the 1980s.* □ *a fashionable area of Sydney* □ *It was fashionable to believe that at the time.*

fashion-conscious *adj* [person] who tries to dress in a way that follows the most recent fashions.

fashion designer *n* a person whose job is to design fashionable clothes.

fashion show *n* an event at which a new collection of clothes is shown to the public.

fast [US fæst, GB fɑːst] ◇ *adj* **-1.** [person, vehicle] that runs, moves, works etc at high speed □ *This is the fastest car I've ever driven.* □ *a fast worker.* ■ **to pull a fast one** to trick somebody in a clever way, especially by taking money from them (informal use). **-2. to be fast** [clock, watch] to show a time that is later than the real time □ *My watch is ten minutes fast.* **-3.** [dye, color] that stays in a material, especially clothing, when it is wet.
◇ *adv* **-1.** [move, talk, change] at high speed □ *How fast can this car go?* □ *I need help fast.* □

Telecommunications is one of the world's fastest-growing industries. **-2.** [make, tie, stick] **firmly** □ *I can't dislodge it, it's stuck fast.* ■ **to hold fast to sthg** [to a rope, handle] to grip sthg firmly; [to an idea, ambition] to keep sthg firmly in one's mind, even in difficult times □ *Hold on fast and I'll see if I can get help.* □ *She held on fast to the belief that one day he'd return.* ■ **to be fast asleep** to be completely asleep □ *I fell fast asleep on the couch.*
◇ *n* a period of time during which one eats no food, usually for religious or health reasons □ *She stuck firmly to her three-day fast.*
◇ *vi* to spend a long time without eating, usually for religious or health reasons □ *They were fasting for Ramadan.*

fast breeder reactor *n* a nuclear reactor that produces more plutonium than it uses.

fasten [US 'fæsn, GB 'fɑːsn] ◇ *vt* **-1.** [seatbelt, jacket, bag] to close <sthg> using a zipper, button, clasp etc □ *She fastened her coat right up to the neck.* **-2. to fasten sthg to sthg** to attach sthg to sthg □ *She fastened her photo to the application.* **-3. to fasten one's hands/teeth etc around sthg** to close one's hands/teeth etc around sthg in order to hold it □ *He fastened his hands around the pulley and jumped.*
◇ *vi* **to fasten onto sb/sthg** to give all one's attention and concentration to sb/sthg □ *He fastened on to me at the reception and after that I couldn't get rid of him.*

fastener [US 'fæsnr, GB 'fɑːsnə] *n* a part of something, especially of clothing, that is used to close it, e.g. a zipper or button.

fastening [US 'fæsnɪŋ, GB 'fɑːs-] *n* [of clothing, a door, window] something that is used to keep something else closed.

fast food *n* food that is prepared quickly and served and paid for when it is ordered □ *a fast food take-out.*

fast-forward ◇ *n* the button on a video or cassette player that makes it possible to make the tape in a cassette move forward more quickly than usual □ *the fast-forward button.* ◇ *vt* to make <a tape or cassette> go faster in order to reach a particular point on it. ◇ *vi*: *I fast-forwarded to the end of the movie.* NOTE: Compare **rewind.**

fastidious [fə'stɪdɪəs] *adj* [person] who is difficult to please, especially in relation to tidiness, food etc □ *She's always been a fastidious eater.*

fast lane *n* **-1.** [on a freeway] the lane on a freeway in which drivers can go fastest. **-2. to live in the fast lane** to have a life in which one has many exciting experiences and takes risks □ *She lives life in the fast lane.*

fast track *n* a system that allows some people in an organization to be promoted to important positions more quickly than usual.

fat [fæt] (*compar* **fatter**, *superl* **fattest**) ◇ *n* **-1.** [on people, animals] the layer of flesh under the skin that keeps the body warm □ *body fat.* **-2.** [on meat] the layer of soft white or yellowish substance that surrounds a piece of meat □ *bacon fat.* **-3.** COOKING a solid or liquid substance that is taken from animals or plants and used in cooking □ *pork/beef fat.* **-4.** [in food] a substance contained in many foods which the body uses to produce energy □ *full fat milk* □ *Animal fats should be eaten in moderation.*
◇ *adj* **-1.** [person, animal, face] that has a lot of extra flesh and is overweight □ *This is the fattest I've ever been.* □ *a fat stomach* □ *I don't want to eat too much, or I'll get fat.* **-2.** [book, wallet, report] that is thick because it is full of something □ *He pulled out a fat wad of $10 bills.* **-3. a fat profit/fee etc** a large profit/fee etc □ *I got a nice fat check for my contribution to the book.* **-4. to be a fat lot of good** OR **use** not to be useful in any way (informal use) □ *Well, a fat lot of good you are!* ■ **fat chance!** a phrase used to say that something is impossible or unlikely (informal use).

fatal ['feɪtl] *adj* **-1.** [mistake, decision, attraction] that has a bad or very serious result □ *Canceling this deal could be fatal to our business future.* **-2.** [accident, illness, wound] that causes death □ *Cancer can be fatal to certain sufferers.* □ *The blow proved fatal.*

fatalism ['feɪtəlɪzm] *n* the belief that everything is decided by fate and that nobody can influence or change what happens to them □ *Jo's fatalism always struck me as being somewhat out of character.*

fatalistic [ˌfeɪtə'lɪstɪk] *adj* [person] who believes that everything is decided by fate and that nobody can influence or change what happens to them □ *He's always had a very fatalistic outlook on life.*

fatality [fə'tæləti] (*pl* **fatalities**) *n* the death of a person that is the result of an accident or act of violence □ *The attack resulted in one fatality and several serious injuries.*

fatally ['feɪtli] *adv* **-1. fatally flawed** flawed in a way that will cause harm or danger and cannot be avoided □ *Her argument is fatally flawed.* **-2. fatally ill/wounded** ill/wounded in a way that causes death.

fate [feɪt] *n* **-1.** the power that is believed to decide one's future and which cannot be controlled □ *I believe in fate.* ■ **to tempt fate** to do or say something that is likely to have bad consequences □ *"Well, at least we didn't break down." — "Don't tempt fate, we haven't arrived yet!"* □ *Don't you think going there would be rather tempting fate?* **-2. sb's fate** the things that are going to happen to sb which they cannot control and which are usually unpleasant □ *My fate is in their hands.*

fated ['feɪtəd] *adj* **to be fated to happen** [meeting, disaster, death] to be certain to happen because of fate □ *They seemed fated to keep missing each other.*

fateful ['feɪtfl] *adj* [day, decision, announcement] that is very important and often has a bad result in the future □ *The fateful moment had finally arrived.*

fathead ['fæthed] *n* a person who one thinks is foolish (informal use).

father ['fɑːðər] ◇ *n* **-1.** [of a child] a male parent □ *My father lives in Canada.* **-2.** [of a discovery, invention] the person who invents something or who starts something, usually when this is good or respected □ *Freud is the father of modern psychoanalysis.* ◇ *vt* to make a woman pregnant and become the father of her <child> □ *King Henry VIII fathered three children by different wives.*

◆ **Father** *n* -1. a word used to address or refer to a Catholic priest □ *Father Wilson.* -2. **Our Father** a phrase used to address or refer to God.

Father Christmas *n* GB an old man that children believe is dressed in red, has a long white beard, and comes down the chimney to leave presents for them the night before Christmas Day.

fatherhood ['fɑːðəʰhʊd] *n* the state of being a father □ *Many teenagers are simply not ready for fatherhood.*

father-in-law (*pl* **father-in-laws** OR **fathers-in-law**) *n* the father of one's husband or wife.

fatherly ['fɑːðəʰlɪ] *adj* [attitude, advice] that is typical of a kind father □ *He was always ready to give fatherly love and affection.*

Father's Day *n* the day in the year on which people have celebrations, give cards etc in order to show appreciation of their fathers □ *Happy Father's Day!*

fathom ['fæðəm] ◇ *n* a unit (1.8 m) used for measuring the depth of water □ *The wreck was ten fathoms down.* ◇ *vt* to understand the character or nature of <sb/sthg> □ *I can't fathom her at all.*

fatigue [fə'tiːg] ◇ *n* -1. [of a person] extreme tiredness □ *muscle fatigue* □ *Symptoms often include constant fatigue.* -2. [in a metal] a weakness in a material which may cause it to break □ *metal fatigue.* ◇ *vt* to make <sb> very tired (formal use).

◆ **fatigues** *npl* the clothes worn by soldiers when they are working or fighting.

fatten ['fætn] *vt* [pig, sheep, cow] to give <an animal> a lot of food to make it fat □ *The farmer was fattening his turkeys for Christmas.*

◆ **fatten up** *vt sep* to fatten a person/an animal up to give a person/an animal a lot of food to make them fatter □ *His wife tried to fatten him up a bit after they got married.*

fattening ['fætnɪŋ] *adj* [food] that makes one fat □ *Chocolate can be very fattening.*

fatty ['fætɪ] (*compar* **fattier**, *superl* **fattiest**, *pl* **fatties**) ◇ *adj* -1. [meat, food] that contains a lot of fat □ *Try to avoid fatty foods.* -2. [acid, tissue, deposit] that contains or consists of fat (technical use). ◇ *n* a word used to address or refer to somebody who is fat (informal and offensive use) □ *Move over, fatty!*

fatuous [US 'fætʃʊəs, GB 'fætjʊ-] *adj* [remark, manner, comment] that one thinks is stupid and unnecessary □ *If I have to sit there listening to any more of his fatuous remarks I'll scream!*

fatwa, fatwah ['fætwɑː] *n* a religious order given by a Muslim leader, especially for somebody to be killed.

faucet ['fɔːsɪt] *n* US a device that controls the flow of a gas or liquid from a container or pipe.

Faulkner ['fɔːknəʰ], **William** (1897–1962) a US novelist who described life in the South. His work includes *The Sound and the Fury* and *As I Lay Dying.*

fault [fɔːlt] ◇ *n* -1. **it's my/your etc fault** the responsibility for something bad that has happened is mine/yours etc □ *It's all my fault (that) she left home.* □ *It's your own silly/stupid fault, I did warn you.* ■ **to be at fault** [company, person] to be responsible for something bad that has happened □ *It's the owner that's at fault, not you.* ■ **through no fault of one's own** not because of something one has done □ *Through no fault of my own I missed the train.* -2. [in a person] a weakness or negative quality in somebody's character □ *I love him despite his faults.* □ *She has many faults, as we all do, but she's a good manager.* -3. [in a machine, system, calculation] a problem or mistake □ *There must be a fault on the line; I can't get any reply.* □ *a manufacturing fault.* ■ **to find fault with sb/sthg** to criticize sb/sthg, especially when there is no reason □ *Perhaps instead of sitting there finding fault you could help us for once!* -4. GEOLOGY a crack in the Earth's surface □ *the San Andreas Fault.* -5. TENNIS the act of serving the ball wrongly □ *a double fault.*
◇ *vt* [person, performance, technique] to criticize <sb/sthg> because there is something not perfect □ *I can't fault him on his work.*

faultless ['fɔːltləs] *adj* [performance, technique] that cannot be criticized because it is perfect □ *His manners are faultless.* □ *She addressed the conference in faultless French.*

faulty ['fɔːltɪ] (*compar* **faultier**, *superl* **faultiest**) *adj* -1. [machine, system] that is not working properly; [workmanship, job] that has not been done properly □ *Faulty wiring can cause house fires.* -2. [reasoning, logic] not correct □ *Your argument is basically faulty.*

fauna ['fɔːnə] *n* a collective term for the animal life of a particular area □ *The island supports a rich fauna.*

Faust [faʊst] a legendary character who appears in many different plays, novels, and operas, who sells his soul to the devil in exchange for knowledge and power.

faux pas [,fəʊ'pɑː] (*pl* **faux pas** [-'pɑːz]) *n* a mistake that involves doing or saying something that is socially unacceptable □ *They committed/made a terrible faux pas by forgetting to thank the hostess.*

favor US, **favour** GB ['feɪvəʰ] ◇ *n* -1. **to win sb's favor** to get the liking and approval of sb □ *Don't try too hard to win her favor, just be yourself.* ■ **to be in sb's favor** to give support or an advantage to sb □ *The odds are in her favor.* □ *The decision went in her favor.* □ *"What's your opinion of the company?" — "Well, there's a lot to be said in their favor."* ■ **to be in/out of favor** [person, idea, attitude] to be popular/unpopular for a period of time □ *I don't know what she said to Robert, but she's certainly out of favor with him.* ■ **to curry favor with sb** to try to please sb by doing things for them or being very pleasant, in order to get something from them in return. -2. [for a person] an act of helping somebody □ *Do you mind if I ask you a favor?* □ *Can I borrow your car? You owe me a favor or two anyway.* ■ **to do sb a favor** to help sb when they ask one to do something for them □ *Can you do me a favor and mail this letter?* -3. **to show sb favor** to show a preference for sb by giving an unfair advantage to them □ *The teacher didn't show her own students any favor.* -4. **to rule in sb's favor** to officially decide that sb is right □ *The court ruled in favor of the father.*

◇ *vt* -1. [option, choice, possibility] to like <sthg> more than the other things of a similar type that are available □ *We favor the more traditional method of teaching.* -2. [child, person, team] to prefer <sb> and treat them better than other people □ *A referee should not favor one team more than the other.* -3. [enemy, candidate, event] to help by giving <sb/sthg> an advantage □ *The extremely hot weather favored the African athletes.*

♦ **in favor** *adv* in agreement □ *All those in favor please raise their hands.*

♦ **in favor of** *prep* -1. a phrase used to show that one person or thing is chosen or preferred in the place of another □ *She was rejected in favor of a more experienced candidate.* -2. in support of <sthg> □ *They voted in favor of the strike.*

favorable US, **favourable** GB ['feɪvərəbl] *adj* -1. [weather, position, moment] that is suitable because it makes something easier □ *If wind conditions are favorable, we'll sail tomorrow.* -2. [review, comparison, impression] that shows or encourages approval of somebody or something □ *She spoke of you in very favorable terms.* □ *His account of events showed himself in a favorable light, of course.*

favorably US, **favourably** GB ['feɪvərəblɪ] *adv* [review, compare, speak] *see* **favorable** □ *I was favorably impressed.*

favored US, **favoured** GB ['feɪvəˈd] *adj* that has special advantages □ *the favored few.*

favorite US, **favourite** GB ['feɪvərət] ◇ *adj* [food, person, music] that one likes more than any other of the same type □ *What's your favorite color?* ◇ *n* -1. somebody's favorite person or thing □ *Of all her grandchildren, James was her favorite.* □ *These candies are my favorite.* -2. the person or animal that is expected to win a race, competition etc □ *the hot favorite* □ *He's the favorite to win.*

favoritism US, **favouritism** GB ['feɪvərətɪzm] *n* special treatment that somebody gives to another person and that shows an unfair preference □ *Teachers must avoid showing favoritism at all costs.*

favour *etc* GB = **favor** *etc.*

Fawkes [fɔːks], **Guy** (1570–1606) a British Catholic who was hanged for his involvement in the secret plan to blow up the Houses of Parliament and the King; *see box at* **Bonfire Night**.

fawn [fɔːn] ◇ *adj* [coat, trousers] pale yellow-brown in color. ◇ *n* a young deer. ◇ *vi* **to**

fawn on sb to try to please sb by doing whatever they want and by giving them a lot of attention, usually because one hopes to get something from them.

fax [fæks] ◇ *n* -1. the method of sending a message using a fax machine □ *Most of my work is done by fax.* □ *a fax link.* -2. a copy of a message or drawing that is sent using a fax machine □ *Can you send the fax again?* ◇ *vt* [person] to send <sb> a letter, document etc using a fax machine; [letter, document] to send <sthg> using a fax machine □ *I'll fax you tomorrow.* ■ **to fax sb sthg, to fax sthg to sb** [letter, document] to send sthg to sb by fax □ *Would you fax the details to her immediately?*

fax machine *n* a machine that sends a copy of a written message or drawing to another machine using a telephone line.

fax number *n* the series of numbers that is pressed on a fax machine in order to send a fax to a particular place.

faze [feɪz] *vt* to confuse or upset <sb> (informal use).

FBH *abbr of* **Federation of Bosnia-Herzegovina**.

FBI (*abbr of* **Federal Bureau of Investigation**) *n* **the FBI** in the USA, a police organization that deals mainly with crimes against the government, such as fraud and spying. It is part of the Department of Justice.

FC *n abbr of* **Football Club**.

FCC (*abbr of* **Federal Communications Commission**) *n* **the FCC** the US government department responsible for radio and television broadcasting laws and standards.

FCO (*abbr of* **Foreign and Commonwealth Office**) *n* **the FCO** in Britain, the official name of the Foreign Office.

FD *n abbr of* **Fire Department**.

FDA *n* -1. (*abbr of* **Food and Drug Administration**) **the FDA** the US government department responsible for deciding which foods and drugs can legally be sold in the USA, and what information has to be supplied with them. -2. (*abbr of* **Association of First Division Civil Servants**) a British labor union for senior civil servants.

FE *n abbr of* **Further Education**.

fear [fɪəˈ] ◇ *n* -1. [of danger, water, the dark] the nervous feeling one has when one thinks that something very unpleasant or dangerous is going to happen □ *She felt no fear as she opened the door.* □ *He was full of fear.* □ *a fear of heights/spiders.* -2. [that something will happen] the thought in one's mind that something frightening or bad might happen; something that causes one to have one of these thoughts □ *He told me of his worst fears.* □ *My fear is that it may be too late.* -3. **there's no fear of...** there is no possibility of something bad happening □ *There's no fear of it happening again.* ■ **for fear of sthg** because of the possibility that sthg bad might happen □ *We couldn't watch TV for fear of waking the children.* □ *She wouldn't come with us for fear of being late.*

◇ *vt* -1. [death, one's opponent] to feel nervous

and worried about <sb/sthg> □ *He fears nothing.* □ *I've always feared living alone.* **-2. to fear (that)...** to think that something bad has happened or will happen □ *Many fear (that) an uprising is likely.* □ *He feared the worst.*

◇ *vi* **to fear for sb/sthg** to be afraid that sb/sthg is in danger □ *She feared for her life.* □ *He feared for the passengers' safety.*

fearful ['fɪəˈfl] *adj* **-1. to be fearful** to be afraid or worried (formal use). **-2.** [consequence, storm, risk] very bad □ *There was a fearful bang, then a lot of smoke.*

fearless ['fɪəˈləs] *adj* [person, courage, attack] that shows no fear □ *He was fearless in his defense of his beliefs.*

fearlessly ['fɪəˈləslɪ] *adv* [act, attack] *see* **fearless** □ *She'd always campaigned fearlessly against nuclear weapons.*

fearsome ['fɪəˈsəm] *adj* [temper, sight] that is very frightening □ *She's a fearsome opponent.*

feasibility [ˌfiːzəˈbɪlətɪ] *n*: *see* **feasible** □ *I'm not sure about the feasibility of publishing the book.*

feasibility study *n* a report that is done to decide whether it is feasible to do a particular thing.

feasible ['fiːzəbl] *adj* [idea, plan] that one believes it is realistically possible to do □ *The project sounds feasible enough to me.*

feast [fiːst] ◇ *n* a large meal that consists of many special and different foods, usually organized to celebrate an important occasion □ *Our hosts had prepared a huge feast for us.* ◇ *vi* **to feast on** OR **off sthg** to eat a lot of sthg □ *Their guests feasted on roast duck.*

feat [fiːt] *n* an action or achievement that is very impressive because of the skill, courage etc involved □ *Trapeze artists perform great feats of daring.* □ *a feat of strength.*

feather ['feðə] *n* one of the many parts that form the covering of a bird and that is like a set of light thin hairs on either side of a long stem □ *The bird's feathers were covered with oil.* □ *a pillow stuffed with duck feathers* □ *a feather mattress.* ■ **a feather in one's cap** something one does that people see as a sign of one's abilities and that deserves respect □ *Well, a nomination for the prize is certainly a feather in your cap.*

feather bed *n* a mattress filled with small soft feathers.

featherbrained ['feðəˈbreɪnd] *adj* [person, idea, scheme] silly and not practical.

featherweight ['feðəˈweɪt] *n* a boxer who belongs to one of the lightest weight categories.

feature ['fiːtʃə] ◇ *n* **-1.** [of a device, style, landscape] an interesting or important part or quality that something has □ *a safety/natural feature* □ *We would like to point out the special features of this model.* **-2.** [of one's face] a part of one's face, e.g. one's eyes, nose, or mouth □ *Her eyes are her best feature.* □ *delicate features.* **-3.** JOURNALISM a piece of writing in a newspaper or magazine that is not about a news story □ *a feature writer* □ *I enjoyed the feature on women in today's society.*

-4. RADIO & TV a special report, interview etc that is part of a program and looks at a particular subject. **-5.** CINEMA = **feature film**.

◇ *vt* [person, actor, work] to give <sb/sthg> an important part in a movie, exhibition etc □ *a series of movies featuring James Dean.*

◇ *vi* to be present in a particular place or situation □ *The president featured prominently in the evening news coverage.* □ *His work is currently featuring at the Mall Gallery.*

feature film *n* a full-length movie that is usually shown as the main movie at a movie theater.

featureless ['fiːtʃələs] *adj* [landscape, land, plain] that has no interesting features.

Feb. *abbr of* **February**.

February ['februərɪ] ◇ *n* the second month of the year in the Western calendar □ *I was born on February ninth* US OR *on the ninth of February* GB. □ *It snowed at the beginning/end of February.* □ *He goes skiing every February.* □ *She joined the firm last February.* □ *I'm leaving next February.* ■ **in February** during the month of February □ *We'll be moving into the new office in February.* □ *They met in February.* ◇ *adj*: *I don't like the cold February nights/weather.*

feces US, **faeces** GB ['fiːsiːz] *npl* solid waste material produced from the anus (formal use).

feckless ['fekləs] *adj* [person] who does not take responsibility seriously and is disorganized □ *feckless behavior.*

fed [fed] *past tense & past participle of* **feed**.

Fed [fed] ◇ *n* (informal use) **-1. the Fed** the Federal Reserve Board. **-2. the Fed** the Federal Reserve System. **-3.** a person who works for the FBI or the IRS. ◇ **-1.** *abbr of* **federal**. **-2.** *abbr of* **federation**.

federal ['fedərəl] *adj* **-1.** [republic, state, system] that is controlled by a central government but consists of smaller states which are independent in many ways. **-2.** [law, funding, tax] that is connected with the central government of a country and not with the governments of the individual states.

Federal Bureau of Investigation *n* → **FBI**.

federal court *n* in the USA, a court that deals with federal law rather than state law.

federalism ['fedərəlɪzm] *n* the belief in a federal system of government.

Federal Parliament *n* **the Federal Parliament** the Australian national parliament. It consists of a lower house, known as the House of Representatives, and an upper house, known as the Senate.

Federal Reserve Bank *n* **the Federal Reserve Bank** one of the 12 banks that are part of the Federal Reserve System.

Federal Reserve Board *n* **the Federal Reserve Board** the organization, consisting of seven governors, that is in charge of the Federal Reserve System.

Federal Reserve System *n* **the Federal Reserve System** the central bank of the USA. It divides the country into 12 areas, each with its own Federal Reserve Bank.

Federal Trade Commission *n* → FTC.

federation [ˌfedəˈreɪʃn] *n* -1. POLITICS a group of states that is controlled by a central government but where each state has its own government to decide many of its own affairs. -2. [of groups, organizations] a collection of groups or organizations that have joined together to form one large organization.

fed up *adj* **to be fed up** to be bored or irritated □ *She's fed up with him.* □ *I'm so fed up with sitting here all day doing nothing.* □ *I'm fed up of having to do the accounts.*

fee [fiː] *n* the amount of money that is paid to a person, organization etc in order to receive a service or be allowed to .do something □ *doctor's/school fees* □ *He receives over $1,000 per week in fees.* □ *the annual membership fee.*

feeble [ˈfiːbl] *adj* -1. [person, voice] that is very weak □ *Surely you're not too feeble to lift a couple of books?* -2. [excuse, attempt] that is not effective, usually because of a lack of effort □ *Stop being so feeble!* □ *What a feeble joke!*

feebly [ˈfiːblɪ] *adv* [smile, shine, try] *see* **feeble** □ *"I feel dreadful," he said feebly.*

feed [fiːd] (*pt* & *pp* **fed**) ◇ *vt* -1. [child, dog] to give food to <a person or animal>; [prisoner, delegate] to provide food for <a person or group of people> □ *Our son can feed himself now.* □ *We have three hungry mouths to feed.* □ *The aid workers fed the refugees with all surplus stocks available.* -2. [fire, machine] to regularly supply <sthg> with something that it needs in order to continue working or existing □ *Don't forget to feed the parking meter.* -3. [fear, rumor, river] to make <sthg> become stronger, larger etc by adding something to it □ *The newspapers only fed the nation's paranoia.* -4. **to feed sthg into sthg** [data, information, paper] to put sthg into sthg regularly or continuously □ *The results have to be fed into the computer.* ◇ *vi* -1. [person, baby, animal] to take in food or drink through the mouth □ *Lions feed on* OR *off raw meat.* -2. **to feed on** OR **off sthg** [off one's emotion, anger, prejudice] to become stronger because of sthg □ *These are the kind of social conditions that racism feeds on.* ◇ *n* -1. a meal that is taken by a baby or animal □ *He's ready for his two o'clock feed.* -2. food for animals □ *cattle feed.*

feedback [ˈfiːdbæk] *n* -1. [on one's work, performance, a product] useful advice and criticism given to somebody about something they have done □ *positive/negative feedback* □ *Any feedback on my work would be very welcome.* -2. ELECTRICITY loud high-pitched noises from an amplifier.

feedbag [ˈfiːdbæg] *n* US a bag that contains a horse's food and is hung around the horse's head and mouth so that it can eat.

feeder [ˈfiːdər] ◇ *n* a baby or animal that eats food in a particular way □ *a noisy/messy/slow feeder.* ◇ *comp* [road, route, flight] that leads to something of the same type that is larger.

feeding bottle [ˈfiːdɪŋ-] *n* GB a special bottle used for giving milk to a baby.

feel [fiːl] (*pt* & *pp* **felt**) ◇ *vt* -1. [surface, face, material] to touch <sthg> with one's fingers in order to find out something about it □ *The doctor felt her pulse.* -2. [tension, presence] to be aware of <sthg> without seeing or hearing it □ *You could feel the hostility between them.* -3. **to feel that...** to believe that something is true, right etc □ *She felt that she was a failure.* □ *I feel (that) I should warn you about the dangers.* □ *How do you feel about it?* -4. [anger, fear, pity] to experience <an emotion>; [wind, cold, heat] to experience <a sensation> □ *He felt the touch of her hand on his arm.* □ *She could feel her heart beating.* □ *She felt a sense of loss.* □ *I felt a sudden desire to scream.* -5. [effect, consequence, difference] to notice or be affected by <sthg> □ *The damage caused by closing the factory will still be felt years from now.* ■ **to feel oneself doing sthg** to feel or realize that one is doing sthg □ *She felt herself shaking/falling/blushing.* -6. **I'm not feeling myself today** I feel slightly ill today. ◇ *vi* -1. to experience a particular physical feeling □ *I feel hungry.* □ *I'm not feeling very well.* ■ **to feel like sthg** to want to have or do sthg □ *Do you feel like a drink?* □ *She said she felt like eating out.* □ *I feel like a change.* -2. to experience a particular emotion or state of mind □ *I felt angry/curious.* ■ **it feels odd/good** etc the situation makes me feel odd/good etc □ *It feels strange to be back.* □ *What does it feel like to win?* -3. to have a particular quality when one touches it □ *The cover feels like leather.* -4. to look for something by using one's hands or fingers □ *I felt under the sofa for my keys.* ◇ *n* -1. [of a fabric, surface] the quality of the surface of something that one notices when one touches it □ *the luxurious feel of silk* □ *The paper has a smooth feel.* -2. [of a room, house, movie] the atmosphere of something □ *The town had the feel of an 18th-century fishing village.* -3. **to have a feel for sthg** to have a good ability in or understanding of sthg □ *I'm finally getting a feel for the work now.*

feeler [ˈfiːlər] *n* [of an insect, snail] a long thin part on the head of an animal that is used to touch and sense objects.

feeling [ˈfiːlɪŋ] *n* -1. [of happiness, sadness, anger] an emotion □ *I know the feeling.* □ *a feeling of anger/urgency/loss* □ *His voice was full of feeling.* ■ **bad** OR **ill feeling** anger or resentment □ *There's been a lot of bad feeling over the pay cuts.* -2. [of sickness, dizziness] a physical sensation, e.g. of pain or pleasure □ *a feeling of nausea/exhaustion* □ *He lost all feeling in his legs after the accident.* -3. **to have a feeling** to have an impression or belief □ *I have a feeling this isn't going to work.* □ *I had a nasty feeling that he was lying.* -4. **with feeling** in an emotional way □ *She spoke with great feeling.* -5. **to have a feeling for sthg** [for poetry, music] to enjoy and understand sthg well □ *The writer has a wonderful feeling for the rhythms of American speech.*

◆ **feelings** *npl* **one's feelings** the emotions one feels □ *She always hides her feelings.* ■ **to hurt sb's feelings** to say or do something that upsets and offends sb □ *I didn't mean to hurt* *your feelings.* ■ **no hard feelings!** a phrase used to try to stop somebody from feeling angry because of something one has done or said or to show that one does not feel this way toward them.

fee-paying [-'peɪɪŋ] *adj* GB [school] that charges fees; [student, parent] who pays fees.

feet [fiːt] *plural of* **foot.**

feign [feɪn] *vt* [anger, surprise, illness] to pretend to be affected by <an emotion or physical feeling> (formal use).

feint [feɪnt] ◇ *n* [in a fight, sport] the act of pretending to move in a particular direction or way in order to trick or confuse one's opponent. ◇ *vi* [in fight, sport] to use a feint against one's opponent.

feisty ['faɪstɪ] (*compar* **feistier,** *superl* **feistiest**) *adj* [person] who is forceful and able to defend themselves in an argument (informal use) □ *My mother was then a feisty sixty-year-old.*

felicitous [fə'lɪsɪtəs] *adj* [choice, combination] that is well-chosen or produces the perfect result (formal use).

feline ['fiːlaɪn] ◇ *adj* [appearance, movement, grace] that is like that of a cat. ◇ *n* a member of the cat family (formal use).

Felix the Cat [,fiːlɪksðə'kæt] a cartoon cat in children's movies and books.

fell [fel] ◇ *past tense of* **fall.** ◇ *vt* **-1.** to cut down <a tree>. **-2.** to make <sb> fall down, e.g. by pushing or hitting them □ *Bob felled the other man with a single blow.*

◆ **fells** *npl* an area of hills or low mountains.

fellow ['feləʊ] ◇ *adj* one's **fellow students/ passengers etc** the people who study/travel etc with one □ *What do your fellow workers think?* ■ one's **fellow man** other people in general □ *Man should help his fellow man.* ◇ *n* **-1.** a word used to address or refer to a man (old-fashioned use) □ *How are you, my old fellow?* □ *He's a funny fellow.* **-2.** [of a college, society] a very important member of an institution such as a college or university □ *a Fellow of the Royal Society* □ *a research fellow.*

fellowship ['feləʊʃɪp] *n* **-1.** a feeling of friendship between people who are doing something together and giving each other support □ *a symbol of their fellowship.* **-2.** a group of people who come together for a particular reason or purpose □ *a Christian fellowship.* **-3.** [of a society, college] the position held by a fellow; an award made to a postgraduate student, usually to enable them to do research □ *a Royal Society/research fellowship.*

felony ['felənɪ] (*pl* **felonies**) *n* a very serious crime.

felt [felt] ◇ *past tense & past participle of* **feel.** ◇ *n* a soft thick fabric that is often used to make men's hats.

felt-tip *n* a **felt-tip (pen)** a pen with a point made of felt which is full of ink of a particular color.

female ['fiːmeɪl] ◇ *n* **-1.** a person or animal that produces either babies or eggs □ *the female of the species.* **-2.** a woman. ◇ *adj* [employee, student, animal] that is a female; [population, influence, voice] that is connected with females □ *This measure won't be popular among female students.* ■ **the female sex** women in general.

feminine ['femənɪn] ◇ *adj* **-1.** [appearance, woman, charm] that is typical of a woman, especially in an attractive way □ *a feminine touch* □ *She's very feminine.* **-2.** GRAMMAR [noun, pronoun, form] that belongs to or is connected with a particular class of words □ *The feminine plural ending is "-es."* ◇ *n* GRAMMAR the form that relates to a feminine subject □ *in the feminine* □ *The feminine of "lion" is "lioness."*

femininity [femə'nɪnətɪ] *n* the quality of being feminine □ *He felt she was lacking in femininity.*

feminism ['femənɪzm] *n* the belief that men and women should have equal opportunities and rights □ *the changes in feminism since the 1960s.*

feminist ['femənəst] *n* a person who supports feminism □ *the feminist movement* □ *He considers himself a feminist.*

fence [fens] ◇ *n* an object made of wood or wire that separates one piece of land from another □ *a garden fence.* ■ **to sit on the fence** to avoid supporting one particular side in an argument, dispute etc □ *You can't just sit on the fence, you have to decide.* ◇ *vt* [garden, field] to put a fence around <an area of land>.

◆ **fence in** *vt sep* **-1.** **to fence sthg in** [garden, field] to put a fence around sthg. **-2.** **to fence sb in** to be so close to sb that they cannot move or leave.

◆ **fence off** *vt sep* **to fence sthg off** [garden, field] to put a fence around sthg so that it is separated from something else □ *They've fenced off the entire area.*

fencing ['fensɪŋ] *n* **-1.** SPORT a sport in which two people fight using long thin swords. **-2.** the pieces of wood, metal etc used for making fences □ *wooden fencing.*

fend [fend] *vi* **to fend for oneself** to take care of oneself without help from other people, especially by finding food to eat □ *We were left to fend for ourselves.*

◆ **fend off** *vt sep* **-1.** **to fend sb/sthg off** [attacker, blow] to protect oneself against sb/sthg by using one's arms or an object □ *I fended the dog off with a stick.* **-2.** **to fend sb/sthg off** [reporter, question] to avoid answering sb/sthg directly □ *Politicians are very good at fending off awkward questions.*

fender ['fendər] *n* **-1.** US AUTO the part of a car or bicycle that is above the wheels; the bar at the front and back of a car that is designed to protect its body. **-2.** [around a fire] a metal barrier around the bottom of a fireplace that is used to stop wood or coal from falling out onto the floor. **-3.** SAILING an object such as a car tire that is hung over the side of a boat to act as a cushion if it hits other boats.

fennel ['fenl] *n* a vegetable similar to celery that is round at the bottom. Its seeds are used as an herb.

fens [fenz] *npl* an area of low wet land.

feral ['ferəl] *adj* [animal] that has become wild after living among people and then escaping □ *a feral cat.*

ferment [*n* 'fɜːrment, *vb* fər'ment] ◇ *n* political or social unrest caused by change. ∎ **to be in ferment** to be in a state of unrest. ◇ *vi* [wine, beer] to change chemically because yeast or bacteria change the sugar in it to alcohol.

fermentation [,fɜːrmen'teɪʃn] *n*: see **ferment** □ *The yeast allows fermentation to take place.* □ *the fermentation process.*

fern [fɜːrn] *n* a green plant that has leaves that look like feathers but no flowers.

ferocious [fə'rouʃəs] *adj* [animal, attack, criticism] violent and uncontrolled □ *They had a ferocious row.* □ *He launched a ferocious attack on the government.* □ *scenes of ferocious violence.*

ferocity [fə'rɒsətɪ] *n*: see **ferocious** □ *Witnesses were shocked by the ferocity of the attack.*

ferret ['ferət] *n* a small fierce animal with a long thin body that hunts rats and rabbits in their holes.

◆ **ferret around, ferret about** *vi* to look around a place without permission in order to find out information (informal use) □ *I came in to find Raoul ferreting around in my desk.*

◆ **ferret out** *vt sep* **to ferret sthg out** [information, truth] to discover sthg by looking for it carefully for a long time (informal use) □ *We've managed to ferret out some rather interesting information about the president.*

ferris wheel ['ferəs-] *n* a large revolving wheel at a fairground that has seats attached to it and that people ride on for entertainment.

ferry ['ferɪ] (*pl* **ferries**, *pt* & *pp* **ferried**) ◇ *n* a boat for carrying people and vehicles over water between two or more places, usually along the same regular route □ *We went by ferry.* ◇ *vt* to carry <sb/sthg> from one place to another □ *Buses ferried in troops from surrounding areas.*

ferryboat ['ferɪbout] *n* = **ferry.**

ferryman ['ferɪmən] (*pl* **ferrymen** [-mən]) *n* a man who drives a ferry.

fertile [US 'fɜːrtl, GB 'fɜːtaɪl] *adj* **-1.** [soil, land, valley] that is able to grow plants easily □ *the fertile valleys of the South.* **-2.** [imagination, brain] that is able to produce a lot of original thoughts, ideas etc □ *You must have a very fertile imagination to have thought up something like that.* **-3.** [person] who is able to produce babies □ *Women are at their most fertile at around 18.*

fertility [fɜːr'tɪlətɪ] *n*: see **fertile** □ *Manure is used to improve the soil's fertility.*

fertility drug *n* a drug for infertile women to help them to have babies.

fertilization [US ,fɜːrtələ'zeɪʃn, GB ,fɜːtɪlaɪ'zeɪʃn] *n*: see **fertilize.**

fertilize, -ise ['fɜːrtəlaɪz] *vt* **-1.** to make <soil, an area of land> etc produce crops more successfully by adding manure or chemicals to it □ *He still fertilizes his fields with manure.* **-2.** to provide <an egg> with sperm to start reproduction; to provide <a plant, flower> etc with pollen to start reproduction.

fertilizer ['fɜːrtəlaɪzər] *n* a substance that is put on soil to make crops and plants grow more successfully.

fervent ['fɜːrvənt] *adj* [belief, wish] that is strong and intense; [believer, supporter] who has very strong and intense feelings, beliefs etc □ *It is my fervent hope that when my son grows up he will study at Harvard.*

fervor US, **fervour** GB ['fɜːrvər] *n* strong and intense feeling or belief □ *revolutionary/religious fervor.*

fester ['festər] *vi* **-1.** [wound, sore] to become infected □ *a festering wound.* **-2.** [feeling, quarrel] to become worse or more bitter, usually because it is not dealt with or discussed over a long period of time □ *We don't want to allow the situation to fester.*

festival ['festɪvl] *n* **-1.** a series of artistic shows or events organized in a particular place over a particular period of time □ *a music/dance festival.* **-2.** a day or series of days when people are on vacation, usually because of a religious event □ *a religious festival.*

festive ['festɪv] *adj* [atmosphere, occasion] where people are very happy, usually because of a holiday or celebration.

festive season *n* **the festive season** the period of the year when people celebrate Christmas.

festivities [fe'stɪvətɪz] *npl* the events or activities that are organized to celebrate a special event □ *the wedding festivities.*

festoon [fe'stuːn] *vt* **to be festooned with sthg** [with flags, balloons, garlands] to be decorated with sthg that is hanging □ *The hall was festooned with brightly colored flags.*

fetal US, **foetal** GB ['fiːtl] *adj* [death, heartbeat] that is connected with the fetus □ *fetal distress* □ *curled up in the fetal position.*

fetch [fetʃ] *vt* **-1.** to go somewhere in order to take <sb/sthg> from there back to the place one started out from □ *Fetch me a glass of water!* □ *Could you fetch down that book for me?* □ *Shall I go and fetch the doctor?* **-2.** to be sold for <a particular amount of money> □ *The painting fetched $1,000 at auction.*

fetching ['fetʃɪŋ] *adj* [dress, person] attractive □ *You're looking very fetching tonight.*

fete, fête [feɪt] ◇ *n* GB an outdoor event where there are competitions and homemade food and goods for sale, and that is usually organized to make money for a special purpose □ *the church/village fete.* ◇ *vt* **to be feted** [visitor, writer, artist] to get a lot of praise or friendly attention from the public.

fetid ['fetəd] *adj* [water, air] that has a strong unpleasant smell □ *The air smelled fetid and stale.*

fetish ['fetɪʃ] *n* **-1.** a liking for a particular thing or activity that provides sexual excitement □ *a leather fetish.* **-2.** something that is not important but that somebody spends a lot of time doing or thinking about □ *She's got a fetish about keeping things clean.*

fetlock ['fetlɒk] *n* the part of a horse's leg just above the back part of its hoof.

fetter ['fetər] *vt* to stop <sb> from acting or moving freely □ *The court order fettered his movements.*

◆ **fetters** *npl* chains that are placed around a person's feet to prevent them from moving; things that prevent a person from acting or moving freely.

fettle ['fetl] *n* **to be in fine fettle** to be healthy or in good condition (old-fashioned use).

fettucine [fetʊ'tʃiːnɪ] *n* long, flat, narrow strips of pasta.

fetus US, **foetus** GB ['fiːtəs] *n* an unborn human or animal.

feud [fjuːd] ◇ *n* a long angry quarrel or dispute between two people, families etc □ *There's a bitter feud within the board over plans for a merger.* ◇ *vi* to have a feud with somebody □ *They've been feuding with their neighbors for years.*

feudal ['fjuːdl] *adj* [system, society, lord] that is connected with the political system in medieval Europe in which people were given land and protection by a person of higher rank if they worked and fought for them.

fever ['fiːvər] *n* -**1.** MEDICINE a condition in which one has a very high temperature □ *Symptoms include fever and vomiting.* □ *He has a fever.* -**2.** a state of great excitement or nervous activity □ *a fever of anticipation.* □ *The country is gripped by election fever.*

fevered ['fiːvərd] *adj* -**1. a fevered brow** a forehead that is hot because of a fever, hard physical work etc. -**2. to have a fevered imagination** to imagine strange things that are not true or do not exist.

feverish ['fiːvərɪʃ] *adj* -**1.** MEDICINE [person] who has a fever □ *I felt feverish all day.* -**2.** [excitement, activity] that shows that people are very excited and nervous □ *in a state of feverish excitement.*

fever pitch *n* a state of extreme and intense excitement □ *Tension was at fever pitch.*

few [fjuː] ◇ *det* -**1. few cars** only a small number of cars; not as many cars as expected (used with plural nouns) □ *Few people know this.* □ *We get very few visitors in winter.* □ *They are one of the few really good groups around.* -**2. a few days** some days, but not many (used with plural nouns) □ *The train will be here in a few minutes.* □ *I only know a few people there but Dave knows lots.* ■ **quite a few, a good few** many □ *I found quite a few mistakes in his work.* -**3. the first few days** the first days (some but not many) □ *We meet every few weeks.* □ *Then I read the last few pages of the report.* ◇ *pron* -**1.** only a small number of people or things; not as many people or things as expected □ *There used to be a lot of coal mines in the area, but few (of them) remain.* □ *Few could have predicted what would happen.* -**2. a few** some people or things, but not many □ *A few (of us) were still working.* ■ **quite a few, a good few** rather a lot □ *Of the books on the list, she's already read quite a few.*

◆ **few and far between** *adj* not often seen or happening □ *Restaurants in Dufftown are few*

and far between, I'm afraid. □ *Such moments of glory are few and far between now.*

fewer ['fjuːər] *(compar of few)* ◇ *det* not as many people or things; less in number (used with plural nouns) □ *The party received fewer votes in 1992 than in 1987.* ◇ *pron:* *Few people know about it, and even fewer care.*

◆ **no fewer than** *det* **no fewer than five** five, which is a surprisingly big number □ *We received no fewer than 50 complaints about the program.*

fewest ['fjuːəst] *(superl of few)* ◇ *det* least in number □ *This plan seems to have the fewest problems.* ◇ *pron:* *Some departments have lots of computers; ours has (the) fewest.*

FH GB *abbr of* **fire hydrant.**

fiancé [US ˌfiːɒn'seɪ, GB fɪ'ɒnseɪ] *n* the man who a woman is engaged to.

fiancée [US ˌfiːɒn'seɪ, GB fɪ'ɒnseɪ] *n* the woman who a man is engaged to.

fiasco [fɪ'æskoʊ] *(US pl* **fiascos** OR **fiascoes,** GB *pl* **fiascos)** *n* an event or situation that is a complete failure and causes embarrassment □ *The event turned into a fiasco.* □ *the Landsdowne fiasco.*

fib [fɪb] *(pt & pp* **fibbed,** *cont* **fibbing)** *(informal use)* ◇ *n* a lie that is not serious because it is about something unimportant □ *Have you been telling me fibs again?* ◇ *vi* to tell fibs.

fibber ['fɪbər] *n* a person who tells fibs.

fiber US, **fibre** GB ['faɪbər] *n* -**1.** [of cotton, wool] a narrow thread of a natural or artificial substance, such as cotton, wool etc; cloth or other material made from such threads □ *plant fibers* □ *a cotton fiber* OR *a fiber of cotton* □ *glass fibers* □ *man-made fibers.* -**2.** [in food] parts of plants that move quickly through the body when they are eaten and are good for people's health □ *Cereals contain a lot of fiber.* -**3.** ANATOMY tiny thin pieces of flesh that make up muscles and connect nerves in the body □ *nerve and muscle fiber.* -**4.** [of a person] the strength of one's character □ *moral fiber.*

fiberboard US, **fibreboard** GB ['faɪbərbɔːrd] *n* a material used in building that is made from very small pieces of wood stuck together.

fiberglass ['faɪbrglæs] US, **fibreglass** ['faɪbəglɑːs] GB *n* a material made from plastic and glass fibers □ *a fiberglass boat/deck.*

fiber optics *n* the technology of carrying information in the form of light along long fibers of glass.

fibre *etc* GB = **fiber** *etc.*

fibrositis [ˌfaɪbrə'saɪtəs] *n* MEDICINE a condition in which the tissue in somebody's muscles is inflamed.

FICA ['faɪkə] *(abbr of* **Federal Insurance Contributions Act)** *n* in the USA, money that is taken from people's salaries to be used for welfare.

fickle ['fɪkl] *adj* [voter, lover] who changes their mind often about what they like □ *The British public can be very fickle.*

fiction ['fɪkʃn] *n* -**1.** LITERATURE the type of

writing that uses characters and stories that are not real □ *Do you like reading fiction?* **-2.** something that a person claims to be true when they know that it is false □ *What he told you was a complete fiction.*

fictional ['fɪkʃnəl] *adj* [character, event, account] that is not real or true but is found in a story □ *a fictional account of events that occurred during the Spanish Civil War.*

fictionalize, -ise ['fɪkʃnəlaɪz] *vt* [autobiography, true story] to change <sthg>, e.g. by adding imaginary events or characters, so that it is more like a work of fiction.

fictitious [fɪk'tɪʃəs] *adj* [address, account] that is not true or does not exist □ *His version of events was entirely fictitious.*

fiddle ['fɪdl] ◇ *n* a violin, especially one that is played for folk music or dancing. ■ **to be (as) fit as a fiddle** to be in excellent health. ■ **to play second fiddle to sb** to have a less important role in something than sb. ◇ *vt* GB to deliberately give wrong information about <one's accounts, expenses> etc in order to get money for oneself (informal use). ◇ *vi* **-1.** to move one's hands in a way that shows one is bored, worried etc □ *Stop fiddling (around) with your pen.* **-2. to fiddle with sthg** to move or adjust sthg with one's hands □ *Try fiddling with the antenna and you might get a better picture.*

fiddler ['fɪdlə^r] *n* a person who plays the violin, especially for folk music or dancing.

fiddly ['fɪdlɪ] (*compar* **fiddlier**, *superl* **fiddliest**) *adj* GB [job] that is difficult to do, because it requires delicate and precise movements of one's hands (informal use).

fidelity [fɪ'delətɪ] *n* **-1.** the quality of being loyal to a friend; the state of being faithful to a lover, husband, or wife in a sexual relationship □ *I would never doubt her fidelity.* **-2.** [of information, a report, account] the degree of accuracy of something that has been copied, translated, or written down.

fidget ['fɪdʒət] *vi* to make small movements with one's hands or other parts of one's body because one is bored or nervous □ *He sat fidgeting with his pen.* □ *Stop fidgeting!*

fidgety ['fɪdʒətɪ] *adj* [person] who fidgets.

fiduciary [fə'dju:ʃɪərɪ] (*pl* **fiduciaries**) ◇ *adj* [duty, capacity] that is connected with the legal responsibility of controlling property for another person. ◇ *n* a person who legally controls property for another person.

field [fi:ld] ◇ *n* **-1.** FARMING an area of land on a farm, usually surrounded by a fence or hedge, that is used for growing crops or keeping animals on □ *a field of cabbages* □ *open fields.* **-2.** SPORT an area of grassy land used for playing sport □ *a hockey/soccer field.* **-3.** [of knowledge] an area of knowledge or activity □ *an expert in the field of social history* □ *Politics isn't really my field.* **-4. in the field** in the sort of place or situation where real events occur, rather than in theory or in a laboratory. **-5.** PHYSICS the area in which a particular force is felt □ *a magnetic/gravitational field.* **-6. one's field of vision** the area one can

see without moving one's head □ *The building was outside my immediate field of vision.* **-7.** COMPUTING a section of a database that contains a particular type of information □ *The employee record has fields for "age", "name", "address" etc.*

◇ *vt* to deal with <a question or comment>, especially in a skillful way □ *Senator Hart fielded questions from the press.*

◇ *vi* [in cricket, baseball] to stand on the field and try to stop or catch the ball when players from the opposing team hit it.

field day *n* **-1.** a day when all the children in a school take part in sports competitions, usually watched by their parents. **-2.** *phrase* **to have a field day** to enjoy oneself very much, because one gets the opportunity to do something one cannot usually do □ *The newspapers will have a field day when they learn about this.*

fielder ['fi:ldə^r] *n* [in cricket, baseball] a player who is fielding.

field event *n* an event in athletics, e.g. the javelin or long jump, that does not take place on a track.

field glasses *npl* binoculars □ *a pair of field glasses.*

field hockey *n* US hockey that is played on grass, not ice.

field marshal *n* an officer who has the most senior rank in the British army.

field mouse *n* a mouse with a long tail that lives in woods and fields.

field trip *n* a trip to a particular place to study something that is found there □ *Dr Brown made the discovery while on a field trip to Borneo.* □ *a geography field trip.*

fieldwork ['fi:ldwɜ:^rk] *n* research into a subject that is done by going out of the classroom, laboratory etc and collecting information about it directly.

fiend [fi:nd] *n* **-1.** an evil and cruel person (literary use) □ *an evil fiend.* **-2.** a person who is very interested in or fond of a particular activity, food, drink etc (informal use) □ *a jogging/health fiend.*

fiendish ['fi:ndɪʃ] *adj* **-1.** [criminal, murder, plan] evil and cruel. **-2.** [problem, puzzle] that one finds very difficult (informal use).

fierce [fɪə^rs] *adj* **-1.** [dog, person] that has an aggressive and violent nature □ *The guards looked fierce and menacing.* **-2.** [storm, temper, blaze] that is violent and stronger than usual □ *fierce winds from the north.* **-3.** [fighting, battle] that involves a lot of violent activity; [loyalty, criticism, heat] that is very strong □ *He is a fierce critic of the scheme.* □ *There is always fierce competition for places.*

fiercely ['fɪə^rslɪ] *adv* **-1. fiercely loyal/independent** very loyal/independent □ *It's a fiercely competitive business.* **-2.** [argue, criticize, fight] see **fierce** □ *The dog barked fiercely.* □ *The fire was burning fiercely.*

fiery ['faɪərɪ] (*compar* **fierier**, *superl* **fieriest**) *adj* **-1.** [explosion, heat] that is very hot or burning □ *a fiery ball of flame.* **-2.** [food] that has a very hot flavor. **-3.** [temper, speech, person] that shows strong emotion □ *The fiery Spaniard fought back to win by three shots.* **-4. fiery (red)** [hair, sunset] bright red.

FIFA ['fiːfə] (*abbr of* **Fédération Internationale de Football Association**) *n* the organization in charge of international soccer. It also organizes the World Cup.

fifteen [ˌfɪf'tiːn] ◇ *n* **-1.** the number 15 □ *Three fives are fifteen.* **-2.** the age of 15 years □ *He left school at (the age of) fifteen.* **-3.** a person or object represented by the number 15 □ *Their number fifteen is playing well.* □ *If I were you, I'd take the number fifteen (bus).* ◇ *adj*: *a fifteen-hour flight.* □ *I knew her when she was fifteen (years old).* □ *I take a size fifteen collar.* ◇ *pron*: *"How many people have you got coming?" — "Fifteen."*

fifteenth [ˌfɪf'tiːnθ] ◇ *n* **-1.** one of fifteen equal parts of something □ *A fifteenth of the population lives in the capital.* **-2.** day fifteen of a particular month □ *She was born on May fifteenth* US OR *on the fifteenth of May* GB. □ *I'll see you on the fifteenth.* ◇ *adj* [week, floor] 15th, number fifteen in a series □ *That's the fifteenth takeover bid this year to be referred to the Monopolies and Mergers Commission.* □ *on his fifteenth birthday* □ *It was written in the fifteenth century.* ■ **Louis the Fifteenth** the fifteenth king of a particular country to be called Louis. ◇ *adv*: *They were placed fifteenth in the top 100 companies.*

fifth [fɪfθ] *n* **-1.** one of five equal parts of something □ *a fifth of a mile* □ *A fifth of our production goes for export.* **-2.** day five of a particular month □ *I was born on July fifth* US OR *on the fifth of July* GB. □ *The meeting is on the fifth.* **-3. the Fifth = the Fifth Amendment** □ *He took the Fifth.*
◇ *adj* [week, floor] 5th, number five in a series □ *It's the fifth door on the right.* □ *It's the fifth time this year that interest rates have gone up.* ■ **to feel like a fifth wheel** US to feel that one is not wanted or needed in a particular situation (informal use). ■ **Henry the Fifth** the fifth king of a particular country to be called Henry.
◇ *adv*: *He came fifth in the 100 meters.*

Fifth Amendment *n* **the Fifth Amendment** an article of the US Bill of Rights that says that a person does not have to give evidence at their own trial.

Fifth Avenue a street in New York known for its expensive stores and restaurants.

fifth column *n* a group of people within a country who secretly support and work for its enemies.

fiftieth ['fɪftɪəθ] ◇ *n* one of fifty equal parts of something □ *A fiftieth of a gram can be written 0.02g.* ◇ *adj* [week, floor] 50th, number fifty in a series □ *It's his fiftieth birthday.* ◇ *adv*: *They were placed fiftieth in the top 100 companies.*

fifty ['fɪftɪ] (*pl* **fifties**) ◇ *n* **-1.** the number 50 □ *Five tens are fifty.* □ *Turn to page fifty.* ■ **the fifties** the years between 1950 and 1960 □ *It was made in the early/late fifties.* ■ **to be in one's fifties** to be between 50 and 60 years

old. ■ **to be in the fifties** [temperature] to measure between 50° and 60° Fahrenheit or Celsius. ■ **to do fifty** to drive a motor vehicle at 50 miles per hour □ *He was doing fifty when he was stopped by the police.* **-2.** the age of 50 years □ *He will be fifty next year.* **-3.** a person or object represented by the number 50 □ *Caller number fifty will win a weekend in Hawaii.* ◇ *adj*: *There were about fifty people there.* ◇ *pron*: *There were about fifty (of them).*

fifty-fifty ◇ *adj* **a fifty-fifty chance** an equal possibility that something will or will not happen □ *Doctors gave him a fifty-fifty chance of survival.* ◇ *adv* into two equal parts □ *Let's split the bill fifty-fifty.*

fig [fɪg] *n* a soft, sweet, green or purple fruit full of seeds that is often sold dried □ *a dried fig.*

fight [faɪt] (*pt* & *pp* **fought**) ◇ *n* **-1.** [to hurt somebody physically] a situation or event in which two or more people try to hurt each other by punching, kicking, using weapons etc □ *Fights broke out between rival fans.* □ *Do you want a fight about it?* □ *a street fight.* ■ **to have a fight** to take part in a fight with somebody □ *He had a fight with another boy in his class.* ■ **to put up a fight** to try hard to resist somebody who is much stronger or much more powerful □ *He didn't even put up a fight.* **-2.** [to achieve something] a serious attempt to stop something or to achieve something □ *the fight against crime/for liberty.* **-3.** [using words] a quarrel or argument □ *There were a number of fights over money.* □ *He's just had a fight with his wife.*
◇ *vt* **-1.** [army, country] to take part in a war with <an enemy> □ *The two countries fought each other for control of the islands.* **-2.** [person] to punch and kick <sb> in order to hurt them. **-3.** [battle, war] to take part in <sthg> in order to defeat an enemy □ *The battle was fought and lost in France.* **-4.** [election, campaign] to take part in <sthg> in order to defeat an opponent □ *Two candidates will go forward to fight the next round.* **-5.** [racism, drugs, fire] to try to stop <sthg> from developing or taking control □ *The police should spend more of their time fighting crime.*
◇ *vi* **-1.** to take part in a fight or war □ *My brother and I used to fight constantly as children.* □ *He fought against Germany in World War II.* **-2. to fight for/against sthg** to try hard to get/prevent sthg □ *I had to fight for the right to work normal office hours.* **-3.** to argue □ *They were always fighting about/over money.*

◆ **fight back** ◇ *vt fus* **to fight back sthg** [tears, laughter, anger] to try hard not to show sthg that one feels □ *She was fighting back the tears as they said goodbye.* ◇ *vi* to resist somebody who is attacking one or trying to beat one in a competition □ *Norman fought back courageously in the next election.*

◆ **fight off** *vt sep* **-1. to fight sb off** [thief, mugger] to make sb go away by fighting back □ *Somehow, he found the strength to fight off his attacker.* **-2. to fight sthg off** [illness, desire, sadness] to succeed in resisting sthg □ *Their bodies are no longer able to fight off infection.*

fighter

◆ **fight out** *vt sep* **to fight it out** to end a conflict, argument etc by fighting or arguing □ *You'll have to fight it out among yourselves.*

fighter ['faɪtəʳ] *n* -1. **a fighter (plane)** a military aircraft used for attacking other aircraft □ *a fighter pilot.* -2. [in a war] a person who takes part in a fight or war □ *a guerrilla fighter.* -3. a person who continues to try to do something despite great difficulties, opposition etc □ *He's a born fighter.*

fighting ['faɪtɪŋ] *n* the activity of taking part in a fight or war □ *There was too much fighting in the movie.*

fighting chance *n* **to have a fighting chance** to have a chance of doing or achieving something if one tries very hard □ *We still have a fighting chance of winning this contract.*

figment ['fɪgmənt] *n* **a figment of sb's imagination** something that has been imagined by sb and is not real or true.

figurative ['fɪgjərətɪv] *adj* -1. [sense, expression] that uses a word or words in a way that is different from their literal or most obvious meaning, often in an imaginative way □ *I'm using the word in its figurative sense, of course.* -2. ART [painting, sculpture, artist] that copies the real shapes or appearance of things □ *I tend to prefer figurative painting to abstract art.*

figuratively ['fɪgjərətɪvlɪ] *adv* [express, paint] *see* **figurative** □ *Figuratively speaking, he's a giant among men.*

figure ['fɪgjəʳ] ◇ *n* -1. [a number] an amount of something expressed as a number □ *unemployment figures.* ■ **to put a figure on sthg** to say the precise amount or cost of sthg □ *It's hard to put a figure on it.* -2. [a symbol] any of the symbols from 0 to 9 used to represent a number □ *She drew a figure seven.* □ *He was paid a six-figure sum.* ■ **in double figures** between 10 and 99 □ *Inflation will soon be in double figures.* ■ **in single figures** between 0 and 9. -3. [of a person] the shape of a person that one sees from a distance or in the dark □ *a shadowy figure.* -4. [an important person] a person who is important because of what they do or the qualities they have □ *He's a senior figure in the party.* □ *a media figure* □ *sports figures of the fifties* □ *a father figure.* -5. [a person's body] the shape of a person's body □ *Dieting won't necessarily improve your figure.* □ *She has a fantastic figure!* -6. [in a book, article] a picture or diagram used to show or explain something □ *See figure 2.*
◇ *vt* **to figure (that)...** to suppose or believe that something is true □ *I figure he had his reasons.* □ *I figured that she'd call if she wanted to.*
◇ *vi* -1. to appear or be included in something □ *They figure in the financial news again.* -2. **that figures** that is logical or not surprising □ *I suppose it figures that they'd call the police.*

◆ **figure out** *vt sep* **to figure sthg out** [puzzle, problem] to find the answer to sthg; [answer, reason] to work sthg out □ *I couldn't figure out what went wrong.*

figure eight US, **figure of eight** GB *n* something that has the shape of the number 8, e.g. a knot □ *We drove around in a figure eight.*

figurehead ['fɪgjəhed] *n* -1. [on a ship] an ornament, usually in the shape of a person, on the front of a sailing ship. -2. [of a country, organization] a leader of a group of people who has no real power □ *The Queen is more of a figurehead than anything else.*

figure of eight *n* GB = **figure eight**.

figure of speech *n* a word or phrase that has a figurative meaning □ *It's just a figure of speech.*

figure skating *n* ice-skating in which a person makes attractive patterns by turning, jumping etc.

figurine [,fɪgjə'riːn] *n* a small model in the shape of a person, used as an ornament.

Fiji ['fiːdʒiː] a country in the South Pacific, east of Australia, consisting of many islands. SIZE: 18,300 sq kms. POPULATION: 727,000 (*Fijians*). CAPITAL: Suva. LANGUAGE: English. CURRENCY: Fijian dollar.

filament ['fɪləmənt] *n* the thin piece of wire that produces light in an electric light bulb.

filch [fɪltʃ] *vt* to steal <sthg> (informal use).

file [faɪl] ◇ *n* -1. [of papers] a box or folded piece of cardboard used for keeping documents and papers in □ *a file copy.* -2. [on a subject] a collection of documents or information about a particular person, group, or subject □ *a file on economic growth* □ *They can't find my file.* □ *a police file.* ■ **to be on file** OR **on the files** to be recorded in writing in a collection of documents about somebody or something □ *I've kept your letter on file.* -3. COMPUTING pieces of information that are related and stored together under one name on a computer □ *a computer data file* □ *How do you open/close the file?* -4. [for rubbing things] a tool that one rubs against hard or rough surfaces to make them smooth □ *a nail file* □ *a metal file.* -5. **in single file** [wait, stand] one behind the other in a line □ *They entered the room in single file.*
◇ *vt* -1. [document, paper, account] to put <sthg> in a file □ *The letter was filed away for future reference.* -2. LAW [accusation, complaint, lawsuit] to present <sthg> officially □ *I'm going to file a suit for libel.* -3. [fingernail, wood, metal] to make <sthg> smooth or give it a particular shape using a file □ *The rivets are then filed down until they are smooth.*
◇ *vi* -1. [people] to walk somewhere one behind the other □ *The mourners filed into the church.* -2. LAW **to file for divorce** to ask for a divorce officially.

file clerk US, **filing clerk** GB *n* a person whose job is to file documents and papers in an office.

filename ['faɪlneɪm] *n* a code used to identify a computer file.

filet [fɪ'leɪ] *n* US = **fillet**.

filibuster ['fɪlɪbʌstəʳ] *vi* POLITICS to deliberately speak for a very long time so that a law cannot be passed because there is no time for a vote □ *The senator denied filibustering.*

filigree ['fɪlɪgriː] ◇ *n* an ornament in gold or silver wire □ *a piece of gold filigree.* ◇ *adj* [earrings, jewelry] made with filigree.

filing cabinet ['faɪlɪŋ-] *n* a set of metal drawers for keeping files in, usually in an office.

filing clerk *n* GB = **file clerk**.

Filipino [ˌfɪləˈpiːnəʊ] (*pl* **Filipinos**) *n* & *adj*: see **Philippines**.

fill [fɪl] ◇ *vt* **-1.** [glass, tank, bag] to make <a container> full □ *He filled the basin with water.* **-2.** [building, area] to be in <a place> in large numbers or amounts so that there is little space left □ *People filled the streets.* **-3.** [crack, gap] to repair <a hole> by putting a substance in it □ *You'll need to have this tooth filled.* **-4.** [post, position, role] to take <a job> □ *The vacancy has now been filled.* **-5.** [requirement, demand] to satisfy <a need> □ *Television fills a gap in many people's lives.* ◇ *vi* to become full of something □ *His eyes filled with tears.*
◇ *n* **to have had one's fill of sthg** to be unwilling to do or experience sthg any more □ *I've had my fill of political in-fighting.* ■ **to eat one's fill** to eat as much food as one wants □ *They sat down and ate their fill of roast meat and vegetables.*
◆ **fill in** ◇ *vt sep* **-1. to fill sthg in** [form, coupon, questionnaire] to complete the spaces on it □ *Fill in the form with your name and address.* **-2. to fill sb in** to give sb more information about something □ *I filled him in on the situation.* □ *I'll fill you in later about what happens at the meeting.* ◇ *vt fus* **to be filling in time** GB to be doing something unimportant while one is waiting for something more important. ◇ *vi* to do somebody else's job for a limited period of time □ *She filled in for me when I was off sick.*
◆ **fill out** ◇ *vt sep* [form, coupon, questionnaire] = **fill in.** ◇ *vi* [person] to get fatter or more physically developed □ *Sandy's certainly filled out since she was a teenager.*
◆ **fill up** ◇ *vt sep* **to fill sthg up** [container, place] to make sthg completely full □ *I filled the car up with gasoline.* ◇ *vi* [room, town] to become full □ *The theater soon filled up with people.*

filled [fɪld] *adj* **-1. to be filled with sthg** [with a feeling, emotion] to be full of sthg □ *He's still filled with resentment because of the divorce.* **-2.** [roll, pastry] that has a different kind of food in the middle □ *a doughnut filled with jam.*

filler ['fɪlər] *n* a substance for filling holes or cracks in walls, car bodies etc □ *wood filler.*

fillet [US frˈleɪ, GB ˈfɪlət] *n* **-1.** a piece of meat or fish to be eaten that contains no bones □ *a fillet of pork/cod.* **-2.** meat cut from near the ribs of a cow or the buttocks of other animals and used in cooking □ *fillet of beef.*

fillet steak *n* fillet of beef; a slice of this for grilling, frying etc.

filling ['fɪlɪŋ] ◇ *adj* [meal, food] that makes a person feel full or satisfied when it is eaten □ *I don't find salad very filling.* ◇ *n* **-1.** [for a tooth] a small amount of a substance used to fill a hole in a tooth to stop it from decaying

□ *a gold filling.* **-2.** [in a pie, cake, sandwich] any food put inside another kind of food □ *a sponge with a chocolate filling.*

filling station *n* a place that sells gasoline and oil for vehicles.

fillip ['fɪlɪp] *n* a sudden or unexpected improvement □ *The move gave a much-needed fillip to the retail sector.*

filly ['fɪlɪ] (*pl* **fillies**) *n* a young female horse.

film [fɪlm] ◇ *n* **-1.** CINEMA & TV a story, report etc in the form of moving pictures and usually with sound that is shown on a television or cinema screen □ *a horror film* □ *They made a film about his life.* □ *a film critic.* **-2.** PHOTOGRAPHY a strip of plastic placed in a camera for taking photographs on; a roll of this □ *color film* □ *a roll of film.* **-3.** CINEMA & TV a series of moving pictures that record an event, battle etc which can be shown on a television or cinema screen □ *old film footage* □ *a film sequence.* **-4.** [of powder, grease] a very thin layer of something that covers the surface of something else □ *a film of dust/oil.*
◇ *vt* [scene, riot, discussion] to use a camera to take moving pictures of <sb/sthg> so that they can be shown on a television or cinema screen □ *He was filmed leaving his house at 2 a.m.*
◇ *vi* to make a movie □ *I don't think you'll be allowed to film on Brooklyn Bridge.*

filming ['fɪlmɪŋ] *n* the activity of making a movie.

film-maker *n* a person whose job is to make movies for television or the cinema.

film star *n* an actor or actress who is famous for their appearances in movies.

filmstrip ['fɪlmstrɪp] *n* a piece of film with a series of pictures on it that are shown one after another as stills on a screen.

Filofax™ ['faɪləfæks] *n* a small book for writing personal information such as appointments and addresses in.

filter ['fɪltər] ◇ *n* **-1.** [for coffee, air] a device for cleaning or removing unwanted particles from a liquid or gas that is passed through it □ *a coffee/oil/air filter.* **-2.** [on a camera, telescope] a piece of glass, used on a camera, telescope etc, that changes the quality or quantity of light that passes through it □ *an orange filter* □ *a filter on a camera/lamp.* ◇ *vt* [coffee, water, air] to clean or remove unwanted particles from <a liquid or gas> by passing it through a filter. ◇ *vi* [people] to move somewhere gradually and in small numbers □ *Delegates filtered into the conference room from 9 o'clock onward.*
◆ **filter out** *vt sep* **to filter sthg out** [substance, gas, light] to remove sthg from a different substance, gas, or kind of light because one does not want it □ *This device filters out the harmful ultraviolet rays.*
◆ **filter through** *vi* [news, information] to become known gradually or slowly □ *News of the earthquake gradually filtered through to the world's media.*

filter coffee *n* a hot drink made by passing

boiling water through coffee beans that have been ground and placed in a filter.

filter lane *n* GB a special lane for vehicles turning left or right.

filter paper *n* paper used to filter liquids.

filter-tipped [-'tɪpt] *adj* **a filter-tipped cigarette** a cigarette that has a small device attached to the end that reduces the amount of nicotine and tar breathed in by the person who smokes it.

filth [fɪlθ] *n* **-1.** dirt that one finds very unpleasant to look at, smell etc □ *He was covered in filth.* **-2.** something such as words or pictures that people find offensive, particularly because it is connected with sex □ *I'm not letting my children watch that filth!*

filthy ['fɪlθɪ] (*compar* **filthier**, *superl* **filthiest**) *adj* **-1.** [shoes, clothes, room] very dirty □ *His hands were absolutely filthy!* **-2.** [joke, movie, magazine] that one thinks is offensive, especially because of the way it shows or describes sex □ *You've got a filthy mind!*

filtration plant [fɪl'treɪʃn-] *n* a place where water is cleaned before people use it.

fin [fɪn] *n* **-1.** [on a fish, whale] any of the parts attached to the surface of a fish's body that it uses for swimming □ *a dorsal fin.* **-2.** US [for one's feet] a rubber shoe shaped like a fish's fin that is sometimes worn by swimmers, especially underwater □ *a pair of fins.*

final ['faɪnl] ◇ *adj* **-1.** [day, page, word] that comes at the end of a series of things □ *She's in her final year at college.* **-2.** [score, result] that happens or exists at the end of something □ *during the final stages of the war.* **-3.** [decision, offer] that cannot be changed □ *I'm leaving and that's final!* ◇ *n* the last part of a competition that decides who wins □ *Holland is through to the final.*

◆ **finals** *npl* EDUCATION **-1.** US the exams taken at the end of a semester. **-2.** GB the exams taken at the end of a university degree course □ *When do you take* OR *sit your finals?*

final demand *n* the last letter that a company sends to a customer to demand payment of a bill or invoice before legal action is taken.

finale [US fɪ'nælɪ, GB -'nɑːlɪ] *n* the last part of a piece of music, that is often impressive or exciting □ *The concert ended in a grand finale.*

finalist ['faɪnləst] *n* a person who takes part in the final of a competition.

finalize, -ise ['faɪnəlaɪz] *vt* [date, deal] to finish discussing or planning <sthg> by agreeing about it or by making it definite □ *We need to finalize the arrangements for next month's conference.*

finally ['faɪnəlɪ] *adv* **-1.** after a long time, especially after some difficulty or delay □ *The delivery finally came at three in the afternoon.* **-2.** a word used to introduce the last point in a list of ideas, information etc □ *Finally, I would like to speak about our plans for the future.*

finance [*n* US fə'næns, GB 'faɪnæns, *vb* US fə'næns, GB faɪ'næns] ◇ *n* **-1.** the money that makes a project, development, or deal possible □ *The city government had to raise extra finance.* **-2.** the management of money in a company, organization, or government □ *the finance department* □ *the Finance Minister.* ◇ *vt* [project, development, deal] to provide money for <sthg> □ *Construction of the dam was financed by an IMF loan.*

◆ **finances** *npl* the amount of money that a person, company etc has; the way this money is organized □ *I need to check my finances first.* □ *I leave the finances to Sara.*

financial [fə'nænʃl] *adj* [security, difficulties, success] that involves or is connected with money □ *Frankfurt is a major financial center.* □ *I'm having financial problems.*

financial adviser *n* a person or company that gives advice to clients on how to manage or invest their money.

financially [fə'nænʃlɪ] *adv* [stable, secure] *see* **financial** □ *Financially, they're not doing very well.* □ *The project simply isn't financially viable.*

financial services *npl* a selection of services provided by banks, insurance companies, etc to help people or companies with financial matters such as pensions and insurance.

financial year *n* GB = **fiscal year.**

financier [US ˌfɪnən'sɪr, GB faɪ'nænsɪə] *n* a person who provides large sums of money for projects, new businesses etc.

finch [fɪntʃ] *n* a small songbird with a short wide beak.

find [faɪnd] (*pt* & *pp* **found**) ◇ *vt* **-1.** [missing person, object] to discover by chance or by searching <sb/sthg that was lost, missing, or not known> □ *The police eventually found the man they were looking for.* □ *I found a note pinned on the door.* ■ **to find one's way** to go somewhere, especially without directions from somebody else □ *I found my way to the hotel.* **-2.** [time, money, job] to get or discover <sb/sthg that one needs> □ *Have you found anywhere to live yet?* □ *When are you going to find a wife?* **-3. to find (that)...** to discover or realize that something is true or has happened □ *When did you find (that) your purse was missing?* □ *It pays to be honest with people, I always find.* **-4. to find sb/sthg attractive/useful etc** to think that sb/sthg is attractive/useful etc □ *How do you find Tokyo?* □ *I found her very interesting to talk to.* □ *I find it impossible to be angry with him.* **-5. to be found somewhere** to exist somewhere □ *The plant is found throughout the southern hemisphere.* **-6.** LAW **to be found guilty/not guilty of sthg** to be judged guilty/not guilty of sthg in a court of law.

◇ *n* something or somebody that is found, especially by chance, and that is interesting, useful, or valuable □ *That restaurant was a real find!*

◆ **find out** ◇ *vt fus* **-1. to find out sthg** [fact, information] to discover sthg, especially by asking people about it □ *Did you manage to find out their address?* □ *Find out who did it!* **-2. to find out sthg** [truth, reason] to learn or get to know sthg □ *I wonder if we'll ever find out what really happened to them.* ◇ *vi*: *I'll try and find* *out.* ◇ *vt sep* **to find sb out** to discover that <sb> is dishonest □ *One day he'll be found out.*

findings ['faɪndɪŋz] *npl* the important information collected by a report, study, or investigation, or the conclusions drawn from this □ *The Commission will publish its findings in the autumn.*

fine [faɪn] ◇ *adj* **-1.** [person, work, example] that one admires □ *It's a fine building.* □ *The house is a fine example of late 18th-century architecture.* **-2.** [arrangement, agreement] that one thinks is completely satisfactory □ *That's fine by me.* □ *I'm sure it'll be fine if you're a little late.* **-3. to be fine** [person] to feel well or happy □ *"How are you?" — "Fine, thanks."* □ *"Are you feeling better?" — "Yes, I'm fine now, thank you."* **-4.** [weather, day] sunny and dry □ *It's turned out fine again.* **-5.** [hair, point, tip] that is very thin and delicate □ *The surface is coated with a fine layer of silver.* **-6.** [powder, sand, rain] that is light and made up of very small parts □ *The water comes out in a fine spray.* **-7.** [adjustment, distinction, detail] that is small, exact, and not obvious □ *I'll need to explain some of the finer points to you.* ◇ *adv* very well □ *Everything went fine.* ◇ *n* a sum of money that somebody must pay as a punishment, usually because they have broken the law □ *He got a parking fine.* ◇ *vt* to make <sb> pay a fine □ *They were fined $2,000 for criminal damage.*

fine arts *npl* forms of art such as painting and sculpture in which objects are produced not for any practical function but simply to be appreciated for their beauty.

finely ['faɪnlɪ] *adv* **-1.** [slice, cut] into small pieces; [grind] into powder form □ *finely chopped onions.* **-2.** [judge, time] delicately and accurately □ *a delicate, finely formed face* □ *a finely tuned engine.* ■ **finely balanced** evenly balanced □ *a finely balanced competition.*

finery ['faɪnərɪ] *n* clothing or jewelry that is impressive and usually only worn on special occasions.

finesse [fɪ'nes] *n* skill and elegance.

fine-tooth comb *n* **to go over sthg with a fine-tooth comb** to examine sthg very carefully.

fine-tune *vt* [engine, system, method] to make very small changes to <sthg> so that it works as well as possible.

finger ['fɪŋgə^r] ◇ *n* one of the five movable parts at the end of one's hand □ *He pointed at me with his finger.* □ *I've cut my finger.* ■ **to keep one's fingers crossed** to hope that one will be lucky and that something will happen in the way one wants □ *I should be alright, fingers crossed!* ■ **she didn't lay a finger on him** she didn't touch or hurt him in any way (informal use). ■ **he didn't lift a finger to help** he made no effort to help at all (informal use). ■ **to point a OR the finger at sb** to accuse sb of something □ *Don't point the finger at me!* ■ **to put one's finger on sthg** [on a problem, feeling, the reason] to recognize and point out sthg □ *Yes, exactly, you've put your finger on it.* □ *I can't quite put my finger on it.* ■

to twist sb around one's little finger to be able to get sb to do exactly what one wants, especially because they like one a lot. ◇ *vt* to touch <sthg> using one's fingers □ *She fingered the soft fabric enviously.*

fingermark ['fɪŋgə^rmɑː^rk] *n* a mark caused by a finger touching the surface of something.

fingernail ['fɪŋgə^rneɪl] *n* the hard part at the end of a finger that can grow long if it is not cut.

fingerprint ['fɪŋgə^rprɪnt] *n* the mark made by the lines on the skin at the end of a finger. It can be used by the police to identify people □ *The police took his fingerprints.*

fingertip ['fɪŋgə^rtɪp] *n* the end of a finger. ■ **to have sthg at one's fingertips** [information, knowledge] to know sthg very well and be able to answer questions about it quickly.

finicky ['fɪnɪkɪ] *adj* [person] who is very fussy about unimportant details (disapproving use) □ *Jake is very finicky about his food.*

finish ['fɪnɪʃ] ◇ *vt* **-1.** [book, work] to reach the end of <sthg> □ *They finished filming last week.* □ *When do you finish college?* **-2.** [food, drink, cigarette] to use up the last part of <sthg> □ *We finished the rest of the ice-cream.* ◇ *vi* **-1.** [work, movie, party] to come to an end □ *My contract finishes early next year.* **-2.** [person] to reach the end of something □ *I can't believe you still haven't finished.* **-3.** [horse, runner] to be in a particular position at the end of a race or competition □ *"Where did you finish?" — "Fifth."* ◇ *n* **-1.** [of a race] the end or last part of something □ *It was a harrowing experience from start to finish.* **-2.** the quality of a surface that has been painted, polished, glazed etc □ *We used a gloss finish on the woodwork.*

◆ **finish off** *vt sep* **-1. to finish sthg off** [task, report, letter] to complete the last part of sthg □ *Can you finish that off now, please?* **-2. to finish sthg off** [food, drink, cigarette] to finish sthg □ *I'm afraid I finished off the last of the chocolate mousse.*

◆ **finish up** *vi* to be in a particular state, situation, or place at the end of something □ *If you're not careful, you'll finish up in hospital!*

◆ **finish with** *vt fus* **to finish with sb** [one's boyfriend, girlfriend] to end a relationship with sb.

finished ['fɪnɪʃt] *adj* **-1.** [job, task] completely done; [activity, situation] ended □ *I'm glad that's finished.* **-2. to be finished** [person] to have stopped doing a particular task or activity □ *When do you think you'll be finished?* **-3. to be finished with sthg** to be no longer using sthg or interested in sthg □ *Have you finished with the screwdriver?* □ *I'm finished with college.* **-4. to be finished** [person] to be no longer important, successful, useful etc (informal use) □ *Dubinsky is finished as a politician.*

finishing school ['fɪnɪʃɪŋ-] *n* a private school where girls from wealthy families are sent to complete their education and learn the skills needed for socializing and entertaining.

finish line US, **finishing line** GB *n* the part of a racecourse or track that the competitors try to be the first to cross at the end of a race in order to win □ *Sanchez was the first to cross the finish line.*

finite ['faɪnaɪt] *adj* -1. [number, possibilities] limited (formal use) □ *Unfortunately, we only have a finite amount of resources.* -2. GRAMMAR [verb] in a form that shows a particular tense or subject, rather than being an infinitive or participle.

Finland ['fɪnlənd] a country in northern Europe, on the Baltic Sea, between Sweden and Russia. SIZE: 338,000 sq kms. POPULATION: 5,100,000 (*Finns*). CAPITAL: Helsinki. LANGUAGE: Finnish, Swedish. CURRENCY: markka.

Finn [fɪn] *n* a person who lives in or comes from Finland.

Finn [fɪn], **Huckleberry** a character in Mark Twain's novels *The Adventures of Huckleberry Finn* and *Tom Sawyer*. He has many adventures on the Mississippi River with his friend Jim, a runaway slave.

Finnish ['fɪnɪʃ] ◇ *adj: see* **Finland**. ◇ *npl* the **Finnish** the people of Finland. ◇ *n* the language spoken in Finland.

fiord [fɪ'ɔːrd] *n* = fjord.

fir [fɜːr] *n* an evergreen tree that grows especially in cold countries and has thin sharp leaves and brown cones.

fire ['faɪər] ◇ *n* -1. hot, bright, yellow or orange flames that are produced by something that is burning; these flames when they are out of control and causing damage □ *The building was destroyed by fire.* □ *There were fires throughout the city.* □ *a forest fire.* ■ **to be on fire** to be burning with flames □ *By now, all his clothes were on fire.* ■ **to catch fire** to start to burn with flames, especially by accident □ *The whole building caught fire.* ■ **to set fire to sthg** to make sthg start burning □ *I set fire to the bedding by accident.* -2. [in a fireplace, at a camp] a pile of coal, wood etc that is being burnt to keep a room warm or to cook food □ *They sat by the fire to keep warm.* □ *a wood/log/coal fire.* -3. GB a device that uses electricity or gas to keep a place warm □ *I'll put the fire on.* -4. [from a gun] shots from a gun □ *Our troops came under fire.* ■ **to open fire** to start shooting at somebody □ *The police suddenly opened fire on the demonstrators.*

◇ *vt* -1. [person] to use <a weapon> and make it shoot bullets, ammunition etc; [weapon] to shoot <bullets, missiles> etc □ *A number of shots were fired.* -2. to direct <questions, accusations> etc at somebody very quickly, especially in order to confuse them or make them admit to something □ *Two officers kept firing questions at the prisoner.* -3. [employee, staff] to tell <sb> to leave their job, especially because they have done something wrong (informal use) □ *Scott was fired from ADN Inc. in 1978.* □ *You're fired!*

◇ *vi* to fire a gun at somebody □ *He gave the order to fire on OR at the protesters.*

fire alarm *n* a device that makes a loud noise, e.g. by ringing a bell, to warn people when there is a fire.

firearm ['faɪərɑːrm] *n* a small gun such as a pistol or revolver □ *the illegal possession of firearms* □ *He was charged with several firearms offenses.*

fireball ['faɪərbɔːl] *n* a round mass of fire, especially one at the center of a very big explosion.

firebomb ['faɪərbɒm] ◇ *n* a bomb that burns after exploding. ◇ *vt* to attack <a building> using a firebomb.

firebreak ['faɪərbreɪk] *n* a ditch or an area of land that has been cleared of trees and that stops fires spreading in a forest or wood.

fire brigade *n* GB = fire department.

fire chief US, **fire master** GB *n* the most important officer of a fire department.

firecracker ['faɪərkrækər] *n* a firework that makes several loud exploding noises.

fire-damaged ['dæmɪdʒd] *adj* [product, stock] that has been damaged by a fire and is therefore sold at a reduced price.

fire department US, **fire brigade** GB *n* the emergency service that people call when there is a fire or somebody is trapped somewhere.

fire door *n* a strong door in a building that is kept closed to stop a fire from spreading quickly through the building.

fire drill *n* an exercise in a school or workplace to practice what to do if there is a fire.

fire-eater *n* an entertainer who does dangerous tricks with fire, such as putting burning torches in their mouth.

fire engine *n* a special large vehicle that is used to carry firemen and their equipment for putting out fires.

fire escape *n* a metal staircase on the outside of a building that people can use to escape down if there is a fire inside.

fire extinguisher *n* a metal cylinder containing a special powder or liquid that is sprayed onto a fire to put it out.

fire fighter *n* a person who is involved in controlling or putting out fires, especially as part of their job.

fireguard ['faɪərgɑːrd] *n* a wire screen that is placed in front of a fireplace when the fire is burning, to prevent accidents.

fire hazard *n* something that could cause a fire or be dangerous if there is a fire.

fire hydrant *n* a pipe next to a street that provides water that the fire department can use to put out a fire.

firelight ['faɪərlaɪt] *n* **the firelight** the light that comes from a burning fire □ *I could see his face in the firelight.*

firelighter ['faɪərlaɪtər] *n* a piece of a substance that burns easily and is used to help to light a fire.

fireman ['faɪərmən] (*pl* **firemen** [-mən]) *n* a person whose job is to put out fires.

fire master *n* GB = fire chief.

fireplace ['faɪərpleɪs] *n* the space in the wall of a room that leads to the chimney and where a wood or coal fire can be lit.

fireplug *n* US = **fire hydrant**.

firepower ['faɪəˌpaʊər] *n* the amount of weapons such as guns and missiles that a person, army, or country is able to use against other people □ *NATO now has enough firepower in the region to back up its threats.*

fireproof ['faɪəˌpruːf] *adj* [clothing, door] that cannot be easily damaged by fire.

fire regulations *npl* official rules that are used to try and prevent fires, especially in public places.

fire service *n* GB = **fire department**.

fireside ['faɪəˌsaɪd] *n* **by the fireside** near the fire in a room.

fire station *n* a building where fire fighters and their vehicles are based.

firewood ['faɪəˌwʊd] *n* wood that is used for burning on a fire.

firework ['faɪəˌwɜːrk] *n* an object that contains an explosive and other chemicals and is used to entertain people. When it is lit it explodes or spins around, making colorful sparks and loud bangs □ *a firework display* □ *Kids were letting off fireworks in the street.*

♦ **fireworks** *npl* an angry reaction to something (informal use).

firing ['faɪərɪŋ] *n* MILITARY the shooting of guns □ *We could hear firing outside.*

firing squad *n* a group of soldiers ordered to shoot and kill somebody, usually as punishment for a crime.

firm [fɜːrm] ◊ *adj* **-1.** [fruit, soil, body] that is not very soft but is not completely hard either □ *a firm mattress.* **-2.** [foundation, foothold] that is secure and does not move easily □ *Make sure the ladder is firm.* **-3.** [handshake, pressure] that is strong and forceful; [discipline, rule] that is strict □ *His grip was firm.* □ *I've always been very firm with my kids.* ■ **to stand firm** to refuse to change one's mind about something despite pressure □ *She intends to stand firm on this issue.* **-4.** [answer, denial, agreement] definite; [belief, decision] that will not change □ *There is no firm evidence to back up the charge.* □ *They remain firm friends.* **-5.** FINANCE [investment, trade] that does not lose its value □ *The franc stayed firm against the dollar.* □ *Prices remained firm.*

◊ *n* BUSINESS a company, especially a small one □ *a firm of accountants* □ *an advertising firm.*

♦ **firm up** ◊ *vt sep* **-1. to firm sthg up** [body, muscle] to make sthg firm through exercise □ *Running is a good way to firm up your leg muscles.* **-2. to firm sthg up** [agreement, deal] to make sthg definite □ *These are just rough plans and need to be firmed up.* ◊ *vi* [trade, investment] to become firm □ *Prices are firming up.*

firmly ['fɜːrmlɪ] *adv* [hold, press, believe] *see* **firm** □ *He firmly denies any involvement.* □ *She has very firmly held beliefs.*

firmness ['fɜːrmnəs] *n*: *see* **firm** □ *I was surprised by the firmness of her handshake.*

first [fɜːrst] ◊ *adj* 1st, number 1 in a series □ *Take the first turning on the left.* □ *the first time we met.* ■ **first thing** at the beginning of a particular period of time □ *It will be delivered*

first thing tomorrow morning. ■ **first things first** a phrase used to introduce the most important things that have to be dealt with before anything else □ *First things first: let's talk about salary.* ■ **I don't know the first thing about it** I don't know anything about it □ *I don't know the first thing about cooking.* ■ **Henry the First** the first king of a particular country to be called Henry.

◊ *adv* **-1.** before anybody or anything else □ *I saw it first!* □ *He came first in the boat race/French exam.* □ *She always puts her family/career first.* **-2. first (of all)** a phrase used to introduce the first point in a speech or argument □ *First of all I'd like to say thank you to everyone.*

◊ *n* **-1.** [person] the person or group of people before all others □ *They were the first to realize the full potential of the discovery.* **-2.** day one of a particular month □ *I was born on May first* US OR *on the first of May* GB. □ *The meeting is on the first.* **-3.** [event] something that has never happened before □ *That's a notable first for Australia.* **-4.** AUTO the gear that one puts a vehicle in to start it moving □ *I drove off in first.* **-5.** GB & AUS EDUCATION a first-class degree □ *She has a first in engineering from Durham University.*

♦ **at first** *adv* a phrase used to describe the way that something is at the beginning of a particular time, situation, or event, before it changes □ *It will be cloudy at first, with sunny spells later on.* □ *At first I thought he was her boss.* □ *He was a little nervous at first.*

♦ **(at) first hand** *adv* a phrase used to describe a way of learning about something by seeing or experiencing it directly, rather than by hearing or reading other people's reports □ *It's important to see these things (at) first hand.*

first aid *n* the treatment that is given to somebody immediately after an accident or sudden attack of illness, and that can often help to save that person's life □ *He was given first aid by the roadside.* □ *first-aid treatment.*

first-aid kit *n* a box containing bandages, band aids, antiseptic cream etc for treating minor injuries.

First Amendment *n* **the First Amendment** an article of the US Bill of Rights that gives Americans freedom of speech and the right to have public meetings and to choose their own religion.

❧ FIRST AMENDMENT

The First Amendment is considered very important by US citizens, who see it as a guarantee of their personal freedoms: freedom of speech, freedom of religion, freedom of the press, and freedom to hold public meetings. Added to the US Constitution in 1791 as part of the Bill of Rights, it is often reexamined in US courts. For example, when journalists or political activists are accused of breaking the law, the courts must decide what free speech is, and when it is being abused.

first-class ◇ adj -1. [meal, performance] of the highest quality □ The service here is always first-class. -2. [ticket, compartment] that is the most expensive and provides most comfort □ First-class passengers are offered a free glass of champagne. ■ a first-class stamp a stamp that is more expensive and guarantees a quicker service □ Send it by first-class mail. -3. GB & AUS EDUCATION a first-class degree a university degree of the highest standard that can be achieved. ◇ adv: If you send it first-class, it should get there tomorrow. □ We traveled first-class.

first course n a small portion of food that is eaten at the start of a meal.

first cousin n the son or daughter of one's uncle and aunt.

first-day cover n a card or envelope with a set of special stamps on it that is stamped by the post office with the date of issue of the stamps.

first-degree adj -1. MEDICINE a first-degree burn the least serious type of burn. -2. US LAW first-degree murder murder that is committed deliberately.

First Family n the First Family the family of the president of a country, especially the USA.

first floor n -1. US the part of a building that is at ground level □ She lives on the first floor. □ a first-floor apartment. -2. GB the first level of a building that is above ground level □ I live on the first floor. □ a first-floor flat.

first gear n AUTO = first.

firsthand [ˌfɜːˈrstˈhænd] ◇ adj [information, knowledge] that somebody gets directly, rather than from reports by other people □ Having lived in China, Clayton has firsthand experience of life there. ◇ adv [learn, hear, see] I like to find out things for myself firsthand.

First Lady n the First Lady the wife of the president of a country, especially the USA.

first language n the language that one learned as a child before any other language and that one speaks most easily □ My first language is Dutch.

first lieutenant n an officer below the rank of captain in the US army, air force, or marine corps.

firstly [ˈfɜːrstlɪ] adv a word used to introduce the first point in a list of subjects, reasons, pieces of information etc □ Firstly, let me welcome you all here. □ Firstly I don't have the money, and secondly I'm too tired.

first mate n SAILING a member of a ship's crew, next in rank below the captain.

first name n the name that is not one's family name, but the one used by friends, family, and other people one knows fairly well □ Surname: Rossi; first name: Paola.

◆ **first-name** adj to be on a first-name basis US OR on first-name terms with sb to know sb well enough to call them by their first name □ Well, I'm hardly on a first-name basis with her, am I?

first night n the first public performance of a play, show, musical etc □ Did you go to the first night of La Traviata?

first offender n LAW a person found guilty of a crime for the first time.

first officer n = first mate.

first-past-the-post system n GB a system that gives a political party representation in parliament for each local election it wins, rather than in proportion to the percentage of votes it receives in the country as a whole.

first-rate adj [performance, player] that one thinks is extremely good □ The doctors did a first-rate job on my knee.

first refusal n to give sb first refusal GB to let sb decide whether they want to buy something before one sells it to somebody else □ They said they'd give us first refusal on the house.

first-time buyer n a person who is buying a house or apartment for the first time.

First World War n the First World War the war that took place mainly in Europe and the Middle East between 1914 and 1918.

fir tree n = fir.

fiscal [ˈfɪskl] adj [control, policy, measure] that is connected with the public money controlled by a government, especially money from taxes.

fiscal year n US the period of twelve months over which a company, government etc plans its calculations of profits, taxes, and budgets.

✷ FISCAL YEAR
The fiscal year in the USA is from April 16 to April 15. In Britain it is from April 6 to April 5, and in Australia it is from July 1 to June 30.

fish [fɪʃ] (pl fish) ◇ n an animal that lives in water only and uses its tail and fins to swim; this animal eaten as food □ I caught two fish. □ He didn't catch much fish. □ Do you eat fish? □ a fish bone. ◇ vi -1. to try to catch fish in a sea, river, lake etc □ He is fishing for trout. -2. to fish for sthg [for compliments, information] to try to get sthg without asking for it directly □ Stop fishing for compliments! ◇ vt [river, lake] to fish in <an area of water>.

◆ **fish out** vt sep to fish sthg out to find and take sthg from a place (informal use) □ She fished her keys out of her bag.

fish and chips n a popular traditional British meal of fried fish and potatoes, often bought at a fast-food restaurant and wrapped in paper.

fish and chip shop n GB a takeout restaurant that sells fish and chips.

fishbowl [ˈfɪʃbəʊl] n a glass bowl in which fish are kept as pets.

fishcake [ˈfɪʃkeɪk] n a small, round, flat cake made of fish and mashed potatoes covered in breadcrumbs, which is fried or grilled.

fisherman [ˈfɪʃərmən] (pl fishermen [-mən]) n a person who catches fish as a job or sport.

fishery ['fɪʃərɪ] (*pl* **fisheries**) *n* an area of the sea used by the fishermen of a particular region or country to catch fish for selling.

fish-eye lens *n* a camera lens that makes it possible to photograph a wide space and that makes everything in the photograph look curved.

fish farm *n* an enclosed area of water for breeding fish that are sold as food.

fish fingers *npl* GB = **fish sticks**.

fishhook ['fɪʃhʊk] *n* the hook at the end of a fishing line, used for catching fish.

fishing ['fɪʃɪŋ] *n* the activity of trying to catch fish as a job, sport, or pastime □ *Why don't we go fishing?* □ *a fishing fleet* □ *the fishing industry.*

fishing boat *n* a boat used for catching fish in, especially in order to sell them.

fishing line *n* a long piece of cord attached to a rod, with a hook at the end that is used for catching fish.

fishing rod *n* a long thin pole with a fishing line attached to it, used for catching fish.

fishmonger ['fɪʃmʌŋgəʳ] *n* a person who works in a store that sells fresh fish. ■ **a fishmonger's (shop)** GB a store that sells fresh fish.

fishnet ['fɪʃnet] *n* -1. a net used for catching fish. -2. **fishnet stockings** stockings made of threads that cross over each other to form holes.

fish pond *n* a pond in a garden that has fish in it.

fish slice *n* GB a kitchen tool with a long handle attached to a flat wide section with holes in it.

fish sticks US, **fish fingers** GB *npl* short, narrow, flat pieces of fish in breadcrumbs or batter that are fried or grilled.

fish tank *n* a tank in which fish are kept, e.g. as pets.

fishwife ['fɪʃwaɪf] (*pl* **fishwives** [-waɪvz]) *n* a word used to refer to a woman who is loud, uses vulgar language, and is often bad-tempered (disapproving use).

fishy ['fɪʃɪ] (*compar* **fishier**, *superl* **fishiest**) *adj* -1. [smell, taste] that is like fish □ *It had a funny fishy smell.* -2. [story, excuse] that seems dishonest or untrue and makes one suspicious (informal use) □ *There's something very fishy about all this.*

fission ['fɪʃn] *n* PHYSICS the scientific process of splitting an atom in order to produce nuclear energy □ *atomic/nuclear fission.*

fissure ['fɪʃəʳ] *n* a deep crack in a rock or the earth's surface.

fist [fɪst] *n* one's hand when it is tightly closed □ *a clenched fist.*

fit [fɪt] (US *pt* & *pp* **fitted** OR **fit**, *cont* **fitting**, GB *pt* & *pp* **fitted**, *cont* **fitting**) ◇ *adj* -1. [person, building, equipment] good enough or suitable for a particular use or purpose □ *This place isn't fit for human habitation.* □ *He's not fit to marry my daughter.* □ *Is he fit to rule?* ■ **to see** OR **think fit** to think that something is right or necessary □ *She apparently didn't see fit to inform us.* □ *You must do as you think fit.* -2. [person] who is in good physical condition, usually because they have regular exercise □ *I keep fit by cycling to work.*

◇ *n* -1. [of clothes, shoes] the way that something looks or feels because of its size in relation to somebody or something □ *The dress is not a very good fit.* □ *These shoes are a tight fit.* -2. **to have a fit** MEDICINE to suffer an attack of epilepsy; to become very angry (informal use) □ *He'll have an absolute fit when he finds out.* -3. [of rage, laughter, panic] a short intense period of activity or feeling that is difficult to control □ *She broke the vase in a fit of temper.* □ *a coughing fit.* ■ **in fits and starts** with short irregular periods of activity □ *I worked on the book in fits and starts while the kids were little.* □ *The rain came in fits and starts throughout the day.*

◇ *vt* -1. to be the right size and shape for <sb> □ *It doesn't fit me any more.* -2. **to fit sthg into sthg** to place sthg in sthg else so that it is in the correct position □ *You fit the shelf bracket into this slot here.* -3. [device, equipment] to put <sthg> in a particular place or position, so that it can work; to provide <sthg> with a piece of equipment or an extra part □ *Fitting locks on all the windows would help.* □ *It comes fitted with speakers.* -4. [occasion] to be suitable for <sthg>; [description, requirement] to match <sthg> □ *The punishment should fit the crime.* □ *He fits the description of the man the police want to interview.* -5. **to be fitted for an item of clothing** to try on an item of clothing to see if any changes need to be made □ *I'm being fitted for a new suit.*

◇ *vi* -1. [shoe, dress] to be the right size and shape for somebody or something □ *It fits perfectly.* □ *This shirt/lid doesn't fit properly.* -2. to be designed and shaped to be put in a particular place □ *The steamer fits over the pan like this.* -3. to be the right size or shape to go in a particular place □ *The books won't all fit into one box.*

◆ **fit in** ◇ *vt sep* **to fit sthg/sb in** to find time to do sthg/see sb even though one has a lot of other things to do □ *I just don't know how she fits it all in.* □ *I can fit you in on Tuesday.* ◇ *vi* -1. [person] to be accepted by a group of people because one has the same behavior, appearance, or attitudes □ *At college he never seemed to fit in with the other students.* -2. **to fit in with sthg** to happen at the same time as sthg else without causing problems □ *That doesn't really fit in with my plans.*

◆ **fit out** *vt sep* **to fit sb/sthg out** [ship, person] to provide sb/sthg with all the equipment or things that they need □ *They were fitted out with new clothes.*

◆ **fit together** ◇ *vt sep* **to fit sthg together** to join various pieces together to make sthg □ *How do you fit this bed together?* ◇ *vi* **it all fits together** everything is clear and makes sense.

fitful ['fɪtfl] *adj* **fitful sleep** sleep that is interrupted and not continuous □ *Finally, Karen fell into a fitful sleep.*

fitment ['fɪtmənt] *n* GB a piece of furniture, especially a cabinet, that is designed to fit in a particular place.

fitness ['fɪtnəs] *n* [of an athlete, candidate, phrase] *see* **fit** □ *a health and fitness club.*

fitted ['fɪtəd] *adj* **-1. to be fitted for sthg** [for a job, environment] to be suited to sthg. **-2.** [skirt, suit, jacket] that is cut in order to fit somebody exactly. **-3.** GB [cupboard, wardrobe] that is designed for a particular space and fixed in place □ *fitted shelves.*

fitted carpet *n* GB a carpet that is cut to cover the floor of a room exactly and is fixed in place.

fitted kitchen *n* GB a kitchen in which the cupboards are fixed in place and match each other.

fitted sheet *n* a sheet that is made with elasticated corners to fit a mattress tightly.

fitter ['fɪtər] *n* GB a person whose job is to install or put particular machinery or equipment together for use □ *a shop-/carpet-fitter.*

fitting ['fɪtɪŋ] ◇ *adj* [end, tribute] right and suitable (formal use) □ *It is fitting that such a great musician should be remembered in this way.* ◇ *n* **-1.** [on a machine] a small part attached to a piece of equipment or furniture □ *a light fitting.* **-2.** [with a tailor] an appointment that somebody arranges with a tailor so that they can be measured for new clothes □ *She's gone for a fitting for her wedding dress.*

◆ **fittings** *npl* GB the parts in a building that are fixed in place but that can be removed when people move out of it, e.g. radiators or shelves.

fitting room *n* a small room in a store where one can try on clothes before deciding whether to buy them.

Fitzgerald [fɪts'dʒerəld], **F. Scott** (1896–1940) a US novelist who described fashionable life in the 1920s. His best-known work is *The Great Gatsby.*

five [faɪv] ◇ *n* **-1.** the number 5 □ *Two and three are five.* ■ **Meet me at five** meet me at five o'clock. **-2.** the age of 5 years □ *Most children start school at (the age of) five.* **-3.** a person or object represented by the number 5 □ *A great goal by City's number five...* □ *I'm waiting for a number five (bus).* ◇ *adj*: *I'll be back in five minutes.* □ *It weighs five kilos.* □ *a five-door car.* ◇ *pron*: *There are five (of them).*

five-and-ten *n* a **five-and-ten (cent store)** a store that sells a large selection of inexpensive goods.

five-day week *n* a week in which one works five days, usually Monday through Friday □ *We work a five-day week.*

Five Nations *n* **the Five Nations** a political union of five Iroquois peoples.

fiver ['faɪvər] *n* (informal use) **-1.** US five dollars; a five-dollar bill. **-2.** GB five pounds; a five-pound bill.

five-star *adj* a **five-star hotel/restaurant etc** a hotel/restuarant etc of the highest quality.

fix [fɪks] ◇ *vt* **-1. to fix sthg to sthg** [sign, mirror] to attach sthg to sthg else so that it does not move □ *The picture had been fixed to the wall with screws.* **-2. to fix sthg on sb/sthg** [one's mind, attention, eyes] to concentrate sthg on sb/sthg □ *Try to fix your attention on the job in hand.* **-3.** [price, quota] to agree or decide <sthg>; [date, time] to arrange <sthg> for a future event □ *We need to fix a pass mark for the test.* □ *Could you fix it for me to fly direct?* **-4.** [car, photocopier] to repair <sthg>; [problem] to solve <sthg> □ *Hasn't the computer been fixed yet?* □ *They sent somebody to fix the phone.* □ *I had a problem with my car, but it's been fixed.* **-5.** [vote, trial, race] to arrange the result of <sthg>, often illegally, so that one gets the result one wants (informal use) □ *Claims that the electoral results were fixed have been denied.* **-6.** US [breakfast, dinner, cocktail] to prepare <a meal or drink> □ *Can I fix you a drink?*

◇ *n* **-1. to be in a fix** to be in a difficult situation, especially one that is hard to get out of (informal use) □ *How did you get yourself into such a fix?* **-2.** [of a drug] an amount of an illegal drug that is taken (drugs slang).

◆ **fix up** *vt sep* **-1. to fix sb up** to arrange for sb to have something □ *He kindly fixed me up with a bed for the night.* **-2. to fix sthg up** [vacation, visit, meeting] to make all the arrangements for sthg to happen □ *The conference organizer fixed up a tour of the city.*

fixation [fɪk'seɪʃn] *n* an unhealthy or unreasonable interest in somebody or something □ *He's got a real fixation about her.*

fixed [fɪkst] *adj* **-1.** [sign, mirror] that stays permanently in one position and cannot be moved □ *There was a bulletin board fixed above the desk.* **-2.** [charge, price] that is always the same; [idea, belief] that never changes, even if it is wrong or unreasonable □ *a fixed-price meal* □ *a fixed-rate mortgage* □ *Lawyers tend to have fixed ideas about what their clients want.* **-3.** [smile] that lasts longer than normal and seems insincere; [stare, glare] that lasts a long time □ *He had a fixed expression on his face.*

fixed assets *npl* property that is owned and used by a company but cannot be sold, e.g. buildings and machinery.

fixed costs *npl* costs involved in running a business that do not change.

fixture ['fɪkstʃər] *n* **-1.** [in a building] an object in a building, e.g. a light switch or sink, that is not removed when people move out. **-2.** [in a place] a person or thing that is always in a particular place □ *Bob's photography equipment has become a permanent fixture in the bathroom.* **-3.** SPORT a regular event that is arranged for a particular date.

fizz [fɪz] ◇ *vi* **-1.** [lemonade, champagne] to produce a lot of small bubbles. **-2.** [firework] to give off a lot of small sparks. ◇ *n* the bubbles in a drink that make a sound.

fizzle ['fɪzl] ◆ **fizzle out** *vi* [fire, firework] to stop burning gradually so that no more noise is made; [interest, enthusiasm, fun] to become less strong or intense; [party] to become less lively □ *Interest in the case slowly fizzled out over the following weeks.*

fizzy ['fɪzɪ] (*compar* **fizzier**, *superl* **fizziest**) *adj* [drink] that has a lot of small bubbles in it □ *fizzy mineral water.*

fjord [fɪ'ɔːʳd] *n* a part of a coast, especially in Norway, where there is a steep cliff on both sides of a narrow area of sea.

FL *abbr of* **Florida.**

flab [flæb] *n* unwanted fat on a person's body □ *I'm desperate to get rid of some of this flab.*

flabbergasted [US 'flæbrgæstəd, GB 'flæbəgɑːstəd] *adj* **to be flabbergasted** to be very surprised and not know what to say or do (informal use) □ *I was flabbergasted when I heard they were getting married.*

flabby ['flæbɪ] (*compar* **flabbier**, *superl* **flabbiest**) *adj* [person, stomach] that has flab □ *It's easy to get flabby if you don't take regular exercise.*

flaccid ['flæsɪd] *adj* [part of the body] that is soft when it should be hard and firm □ *flaccid muscles.*

flag [flæg] (*pt* & *pp* **flagged**, *cont* **flagging**) ◇ *n* a piece of cloth attached to a pole that usually has a printed design or symbol to indicate a particular country, organization etc □ *the Japanese flag.* ◇ *vi* [person] to start to become tired, usually after a long time; [interest, enthusiasm, conversation] to become less lively □ *After the tour of the city, everybody was starting to flag.* □ *Games are useful if the party starts to flag.*

◆ **flag down** *vt sep* **to flag sb/sthg down** [driver, car, taxi] to ask sb/sthg to stop by waving one's arm at them □ *Try flagging down a passing motorist.*

◆ **flag up** *vt sep* **to flag sthg up** [problem, difficulty] to draw attention to sthg.

Flag Day *n* in the USA, the day (June 14) when people display the US flag.

flag of convenience *n* the flag of a country used by a foreign ship that has registered there to avoid the regulations of its own country.

flagon ['flægən] *n* **-1.** [for wine, cider] a large bottle in which a drink is sold □ *a flagon of cider.* **-2.** [for beer, wine] a kind of jug in which a drink is served.

flagpole ['flægpoʊl] *n* a pole that a flag is attached to, and that allows the flag to be raised and lowered.

flagrant ['fleɪgrənt] *adj* [violation, lie, injustice] that is very shocking because it is done in an open and obvious way and shows no shame □ *The country shows a flagrant disregard of human rights.*

flagship ['flægʃɪp] *n* **-1.** [of a company] the most important product, branch etc of a company, that is intended to present a good image □ *a flagship hotel.* **-2.** [of a fleet] the most important ship in a fleet.

flagstone ['flægstoʊn] *n* a large flat stone used for paving.

flail [fleɪl] ◇ *vt* [arms, legs] to swing <sthg> wildly in the air □ *He flailed his arms around like a windmill.* ◇ *vi* [arms, legs] *The animal was caught, its legs flailing wildly.*

flair [fleəʳ] *n* **-1.** a natural ability to do something well or in an interesting or imaginative way □ *Ann has a great flair for languages.* **-2.** a sense of style □ *His dinner parties always have such flair.*

flak [flæk] *n* **-1.** strong criticism, especially from a lot of people □ *Yes, but if something goes wrong, I'll be the one to take the flak.* **-2.** MILITARY gunfire aimed at aircraft.

flake [fleɪk] ◇ *n* [of snow, paint, skin] a small flat piece of something □ *The cake was covered with flakes of chocolate.* ◇ *vi* [skin, paint, plaster] to come off in flakes.

◆ **flake out** *vi* [person] to fall asleep or collapse because one is very tired (informal use) □ *When I got home afterward I just flaked out.*

flaky ['fleɪkɪ] (*compar* **flakier**, *superl* **flakiest**) *adj* **-1.** [skin, paint, plaster] that comes off in flakes. **-2.** US [person] who behaves in a way that one thinks is strange but amusing (informal use).

flaky pastry *n* a type of pastry that has several thin layers.

flambé [US flɒm'beɪ, GB 'flɒmbeɪ] (*pt* & *pp* **flambéed**, *cont* **flambéing**) ◇ *vt* [steak, crepe] to cook or serve <sthg> in burning brandy, rum etc. ◇ *adj* [steak, crepe] that has been flambéed.

flamboyant [flæm'bɔɪənt] *adj* **-1.** [person, behavior] that appears confident, interesting, and unusual and attracts the attention of other people □ *Humphrey is a flamboyant presence in the gray world of banking.* □ *She tends to dress in a rather flamboyant way.* **-2.** [clothes, design, building] that has unusual exaggerated features that attract attention □ *the flamboyant designs of Philippe Stark.*

flame [fleɪm] ◇ *n* the bright, orange-yellow, moving mass of burning gas produced by a fire □ *Flames were coming from the second floor.* ▪ **to burst into flames** to start burning suddenly and very strongly □ *The car went over the edge and burst into flames.* ▪ **to go up in flames** [building] to be destroyed by fire □ *The whole building just went up in flames.* ▪ **to be in flames** [building] to be on fire □ *After the bombing, half the city was in flames.* ◇ *vi* **-1.** [gas, fire] to suddenly start burning brightly. **-2.** [cheeks, face] to be red or suddenly turn red.

flameproof ['fleɪmpruːf] *adj* [dish, material] that is not easily damaged by flames.

flame-retardant [-rɪtɑːʳdnt] *adj* [foam, material] that has been treated with a special chemical so that it does not burn easily or quickly.

flame-thrower [-θroʊəʳ] *n* a kind of gun that shoots out streams of burning liquid.

flaming ['fleɪmɪŋ] *adj* **-1.** **flaming red** a very bright red □ *She has flaming red hair.* **-2.** **a flaming argument/temper** a very angry argument/very bad temper □ *I walked in when they were in the middle of a flaming row.*

flamingo [flə'mɪŋgoʊ] (*pl* **flamingos** OR **flamingoes**) *n* a large bird that lives near water and has pink feathers, long very thin legs, and a curved beak.

flammable ['flæməbl] *adj* [liquid, material, gas] that starts to burn easily.

flan [flæn] *n* -1. US a baked dessert made of milk, eggs, and sugar. -2. GB an open tart that is made from pastry or cake □ *a strawberry flan.*

Flanders [US 'flændrz, GB 'flɑːndəz] a region of mainly flat land that covers parts of southwestern Netherlands, Belgium, and northeastern France.

flange [flændʒ] *n* the raised edge of an object, e.g. a train wheel, that holds it firmly onto something else, e.g. a track.

flank [flæŋk] ◇ *n* -1. [of a person, animal] the side of a person or animal between the hip and the ribs □ *Laura patted her pony on his flanks.* -2. MILITARY the side of an army in battle □ *The army's left flank was exposed.* ◇ *vt* **to be flanked by sb/sthg** to have sb/sthg on both sides □ *We found ourselves flanked by hundreds of tourists.*

flannel ['flænl] *n* -1. [for a suit] a kind of soft woolen material □ *a gray flannel suit.* -2. GB [for one's face] a cloth used for washing one's body and face with.

♦ **flannels** *npl* flannel trousers worn by men □ *a pair of flannels.*

flannelette [flænl'et] *n* a kind of soft cotton cloth □ *flannelette sheets.*

flap [flæp] (*pt* & *pp* **flapped**, *cont* **flapping**) ◇ *n* -1. [of skin, cloth, paper] a loose piece of something thin that is attached along one edge and hangs down or sticks out □ *The wing flaps are raised to slow down the aircraft.* -2. **to be in a flap** to be in a state of confusion and panic (informal use) □ *It's not worth getting in a flap about.* ◇ *vt* [wing, arm] to move <sthg> up and down or from side to side, usually making a noise □ *"Like this," he said, flapping his arms like a bird.* ◇ *vi* -1. [wing, flag, curtain] *The sails flapped in the breeze.* -2. [person] to panic (informal use).

flapjack ['flæpdʒæk] *n* -1. US a pancake. -2. GB a cookie made with oats.

flare [fleəʳ] ◇ *vi* -1. **to flare (up)** [violence, anger, temper] to suddenly start or become more intense □ *Fighting has flared up in the capital again.* -2. **to flare (up)** [fire, flames] to suddenly start burning more strongly □ *The fire flared up in the breeze.* -3. [trousers, skirt] to become wider at the bottom. -4. [nostrils] to become wider. ◇ *n* a device that produces a bright flame and is used as a signal, especially when somebody is in danger.

♦ **flares** *npl* trousers that are flared at the bottom □ *He was wearing flares.*

flared [fleəʳd] *adj* [trousers, skirt] that is designed so that it is wider at the bottom than higher up.

flash [flæʃ] ◇ *n* -1. [of light, lightning] a sudden bright light that lasts only for a short time; [of color] a small area of color that is very noticeable □ *There was a flash and then everything went dark.* □ *All we saw of the rabbit was a*

flash of its white tail. -2. PHOTOGRAPHY a device that produces a flash of light and is used when a place is too dark to take a photograph in □ *'Flashes are forbidden.'* □ *flash photography.* -3. [of inspiration, anger] a sudden and unexpected thought or feeling □ *Colin suddenly had a flash of genius.* ■ **in a flash** very suddenly and quickly □ *It was all over in a flash.* ■ **quick as a flash** immediately □ *The answer came back quick as a flash.*

◇ *vt* -1. [light, flashlight] to make flashes with <sthg> □ *The other car flashed its lights at me.* -2. [smile, look, glance] to send <sthg> quickly and for a short time in a particular direction □ *She flashed a smile at the waiting journalists.* -3. [information, picture] to show <sthg> on a screen for a short time □ *The results were flashed up on the monitor.* -4. [passport, ticket, identity card] to show <sthg> quickly to somebody □ *He flashed his pass at the driver.*

◇ *vi* -1. [light, lightning, camera] to produce flashes of light □ *When the green light flashes it means the machine is ready.* -2. [eyes] to suddenly show a strong emotion, usually anger □ *"Get out!" he said, his eyes flashing angrily.* -3. **to flash by/past etc** [train, car] to move by/past etc almost too quickly to be seen □ *The President's car flashed by and was gone.* -4. **to flash into** OR **through one's mind** [idea, thought, image] to suddenly come into one's mind for a short time. -5. [picture, image, face] to appear somewhere for a short time □ *The results flashed up on the screen.*

flashback ['flæʃbæk] *n* a scene in a movie, book etc that shows or describes an earlier event □ *There are frequent flashbacks to the hero's childhood* □ *Most of the story was shown in flashback.*

flashbulb ['flæʃbʌlb] *n* a light attached to a camera that flashes to give extra light for taking photographs.

flashcube ['flæʃkjuːb] *n* four flashbulbs in a small cube used to take four photographs.

flasher ['flæʃəʳ] *n* a man who deliberately shows his penis to strangers in public (informal use).

flash flood *n* a sudden and often very large flood.

Flash Gordon [ˌflæʃ'gɔːʳdn] a science fiction cartoon character in the 1930s. He fights many battles in space to save the world from evil characters.

flashgun ['flæʃgʌn] *n* a device attached to a camera that automatically switches on a flashbulb when a photograph is taken.

flashlight ['flæʃlaɪt] *n* a small electric light that one can carry in one's hand and works with a battery.

flash point *n* -1. [in a city] a place where violence is likely to start and from where it can spread. -2. [during a disturbance] the moment when people become violent, especially after a time of tension or disagreement.

flashy ['flæʃɪ] (*compar* **flashier**, *superl* **flashiest**) *adj* [car, clothes, person] that looks expensive and fashionable, especially in an obvious or exaggerated way (informal use) □ *He's a very flashy dresser!*

flask [US flæsk, GB flɑːsk] *n* **-1.** CHEMISTRY a glass bottle with a narrow neck that is used in a laboratory. **-2.** [for whiskey, rum] a flat metal bottle that is used for keeping alcohol in and is designed to be carried in a pocket. **-3.** GB [for tea, coffee] a container with a double wall that keeps drinks either hot or cold.

flat [flæt] (*compar* **flatter,** *superl* **flattest**) ◇ *adj* **-1.** [surface, ground, stomach] that is smooth and level rather than curved, rounded, bumpy, or sloping □ *Until then, people thought the earth was flat.* □ *a calm, flat sea.* ■ **to have flat feet** to have feet that rest flat on the ground because the arches are too low. **-2.** **a flat fare/rate etc** a fare/rate etc that is the same for everybody □ *Banks charge a flat fee of 2% on all transactions.* **-3.** [voice, performance, style] that is not exciting or interesting □ *He read the poem in a dull, flat voice.* **-4.** [rejection, denial] that is definite and unlikely to be changed □ *Their requests were met with a flat refusal.* **-5.** BUSINESS [sales, business, trade] that shows little activity □ *Despite generally flat passenger revenue, business is good.* **-6.** [battery] that has lost its power □ *The battery keeps going flat.* **-7.** [tire] that does not have enough air in it, e.g. because of a puncture □ *I got a flat tire on the way home.* **-8.** [music, note] that is slightly lower than the correct note; [singer, instrument] that produces flat notes by mistake; that is a half step lower than the stated note □ *a waltz in E flat.* **-9.** [beer, cola] that is no longer fizzy □ *The beer had gone flat overnight.* **-10.** [shoe] that has a low heel or no heel; [heel] that is low.
◇ *adv* **-1.** [press, roll, iron] so as to be level or smooth; [lie, place] so as to be in a horizontal position □ *The can was squashed flat by the traffic.* □ *He fell flat on his back.* **-2.** a word used to emphasize how fast something happens or is done □ *They did it in five minutes flat.* **-3.** a word used to emphasize that a refusal, rejection, denial etc is definite and unlikely to be changed □ *They turned me down flat.* **-4.** **to be flat broke** to have no money at all (informal use). **-5.** MUSIC [sing, play, sound] slightly lower than is correct.
◇ *n* **-1.** MUSIC a symbol (♭) used to show a note should be sung or played a half-step lower; a note of this type. **-2.** GB a home that consists of several rooms that are part of a larger building □ *a two-bedroomed flat.*

◆ **flat out** *adv* [work, drive, run] as fast as possible (informal use) □ *We'll have to go flat out to make that deadline.*

flat cap *n* GB a cloth cap with a stiff part at the front that is usually worn by men.

flat-chested [-'tʃestəd] *adj* [woman] who has small breasts.

flatfish ['flætfɪʃ] (*pl* **flatfish**) *n* a fish with a flat body, e.g. a sole or flounder.

flat-footed [-'fʊtəd] *adj* [person] who has flat feet.

flatlet ['flætlət] *n* GB a small apartment.

flatly ['flætlɪ] *adv* **-1.** [refuse, deny, reject] definitely and in a way that suggests one will not change one's mind □ *He flatly refused to talk to me.* **-2.** [speak, write, perform] in a way that shows little emotion.

flatmate ['flætmeɪt] *n* GB a person one shares an apartment with.

flat racing *n* a type of horseracing in which the horses do not jump over fences.

flatten ['flætn] *vt* **-1.** [paper, crease, bump] to make <sthg> flat or flatter, especially by pressing it □ *John flattened himself against the wall.* **-2.** [building, city, tree] to destroy <sthg> □ *Many houses have been completely flattened by the earthquake.* **-3.** [opponent, attacker] to beat <sb> in a fight (informal use) □ *Miami flattened Detroit in the play-off last night.*

◆ **flatten out** ◇ *vt sep* **to flatten sthg out** [paper, crease, bump] to make sthg flatter. ◇ *vi* [land, countryside, graph] to become flat or flatter □ *The road flattened out a little and the cyclists started to relax.*

flatter ['flætər] *vt* **-1.** [person] to praise <sb> in order to please them, usually because one wants something from them in return □ *Stop trying to flatter me!* ■ **to flatter oneself** to take pride in something one has done, sometimes mistakenly □ *We flatter ourselves (that) we provide the best service available.* □ *Don't flatter yourself, I wasn't talking about you.* **-2.** [clothes, color] to make <sb> appear more attractive □ *That dress really flatters you.*

flatterer ['flætərər] *n* a person who flatters somebody □ *Oh, you're such a flatterer!*

flattering ['flætərɪŋ] *adj* **-1.** [interest, concern, comment] that makes somebody feel happier and more confident about themselves □ *I found the attention of a younger man very flattering.* **-2.** [dress, color, picture] that makes somebody appear more attractive □ *Harsh studio lights are never very flattering.*

flattery ['flætərɪ] *n* flattering remarks or behavior □ *Flattery will get you nowhere!*

flatulence ['flætʃələns] *n* too much gas in one's body that comes out of one's mouth or anus, sometimes in a noisy way.

flatware ['flætweər] *n* US a collective term for knives, forks, and spoons.

flaunt [flɔːnt] *vt* [money, success] to show <sthg that one has> openly to other people in order to impress them (disapproving use) □ *I could never flaunt my body like that in public.*

flautist ['flɔːtəst] *n* GB = **flutist.**

flavor US, **flavour** GB ['fleɪvər] ◇ *n* **-1.** [of food, drink] the taste that a drink or kind of food has □ *If you cook vegetables too much they lose their flavor.* **-2.** [of a place] the particular atmosphere of music, an area, festival etc □ *We had a walk around to get the flavor of the old town.* ◇ *vt* [food, wine, sweets] to give <sthg> a particular taste by adding something to it □ *The wine was flavored with cinnamon.* □ *fruit-flavored yoghurt.*

flavoring US, **flavouring** GB ['fleɪvərɪŋ] *n* something added to food to improve the flavor □ *'No artificial flavorings.'*

flaw [flɔː] *n* **-1.** [in a plan, argument, design] a

mistake or weakness that prevents something from working properly □ *There is just one flaw in his theory.* **-2.** [in glass, material, a diamond] a mark or fault that spoils the appearance or quality of something; [in somebody's character, personality] an unpleasant or undesirable quality that a person with many good qualities has □ *The jacket was reduced in price because there was a flaw in the sleeve.* □ *David has many flaws, but dishonesty is not one of them.*

flawed ['flɔːd] *adj* [argument, glass, character] that has a flaw □ *Richardson's analysis is fundamentally flawed.*

flawless ['flɔːləs] *adj* [performance, skin] that is perfect and has no flaws □ *Her technique was flawless.*

flax [flæks] *n* a plant with a thick stem, oily seeds, and blue flowers; thread made from this plant that is used to make linen.

flay [fleɪ] *vt* to remove the skin from <a dead animal>.

flea [fliː] *n* a small insect that lives on animals and people, eats their blood, and can jump very high □ *Our dog has fleas again.* ■ **to send sb away with a flea in their ear** to scold sb angrily and send them away (informal use).

flea market *n* a sale of old and used goods, especially ones that people like to collect.

fleck [flek] ◇ *n* [of color, paint] a tiny mark or spot; [of dandruff, powder] a tiny piece; [of rain] a tiny drop □ *Sandra brushed some flecks of face powder from her lapel.* ◇ *vt* **to be flecked with sthg** to be covered with very small or thin amounts of sthg □ *His hair was flecked with gray.*

fled [fled] *past tense & past participle of* **flee**.

fledg(e)ling ['fledʒlɪŋ] ◇ *adj* [industry, democracy, movement] that has not existed for long and has not developed very much yet □ *Paula remembered the days when she had been a fledgling reporter.* ◇ *n* a young bird that is learning to fly.

flee [fliː] (*pt* & *pp* **fled**) ◇ *vt* to escape from <a danger, person, or place> very quickly because one feels afraid or threatened □ *He was arrested just as he was about to flee the country.* ◇ *vi*: *The inhabitants had fled from the advancing troops.*

fleece [fliːs] ◇ *n* the wool that covers a sheep; a material made from this, especially when it is used to line coats and jackets □ *a fleece-lined jacket.* ◇ *vt* to take a lot of money from <sb> by deceiving them or charging them too much (informal use).

fleet [fliːt] *n* **-1.** [of ships] a group of ships that is put together and organized for a particular purpose, e.g. for war or business □ *A fleet is heading for the Gulf even as we speak.* **-2.** [of cars, buses] a group of motor vehicles that belongs to a single company □ *We've added three new trucks to our fleet.* □ *a car fleet.*

fleet admiral *n* the officer of the highest rank in the US navy.

fleeting ['fliːtɪŋ] *adj* [glimpse, visit, moment] that

lasts for a very short time □ *I caught only a fleeting glimpse of them as they passed by.*

Fleet Street a street in central London where many newspapers used to be published.

❦ FLEET STREET
The area around Fleet Street, in the City of London, used to be where most national British newspapers had their offices. Today, most of these newspapers have moved to new locations, particularly in Docklands. However, the term "Fleet Street" is still used to mean the newspaper industry and the world of journalism.

Fleming ['flemɪŋ] *n* a person from Flanders, especially a Flemish-speaking Belgian.

Fleming ['flemɪŋ], **Sir Alexander** (1881–1955) a British scientist whose most famous discovery was the medical use of penicillin.

Flemish ['flemɪʃ] ◇ *adj* that belongs to or comes from Flanders. ◇ *n* a language closely related to Dutch, spoken in parts of Belgium and northeastern France.

flesh [fleʃ] *n* **-1.** [of an animal, person] the soft part of the body that covers the bones and is under the skin □ *human flesh.* ■ **one's (own) flesh and blood** somebody who is part of one's own family □ *How can you do that to your own flesh and blood!* ■ **in the flesh** in person □ *That was the first time I'd seen him in the flesh.* **-2.** [of a fruit, vegetable] the soft part of a vegetable or piece of fruit that can be eaten □ *Her teeth sank into the peach's soft ripe flesh.*
♦ **flesh out** *vt sep* **to flesh sthg out** [facts, argument, report] to add extra details and information to sthg □ *Try fleshing your essay out with a few quotations.*

flesh wound *n* a wound that does not damage the bones or the main organs of one's body.

fleshy ['fleʃɪ] (*compar* **fleshier**, *superl* **fleshiest**) *adj* [arm, cheek, fruit] that has a lot of soft flesh □ *He was a big man, who looked fleshy and unfit.*

flew [fluː] *past tense of* **fly**.

flex [fleks] ◇ *n* GB a cord consisting of electrical wires in a tube of plastic that carry electricity to an appliance □ *Be careful you don't trip over the flex.* ◇ *vt* [muscle, arm, leg] to stretch <a part of the body> by bending it, especially as a form of exercise □ *He flexed his muscles before picking up the weight.*

flexibility [ˌfleksə'bɪlətɪ] *n*: *see* **flexible** □ *The new contracts offer us greater flexibility in planning.*

flexible ['fleksəbl] *adj* **-1.** [plan, hours, person] that can change easily to suit particular needs or circumstances □ *We need to be flexible in our approach.* **-2.** [wire, tree, body] that bends easily without breaking □ *The light is on a flexible arm that is fully adjustable.*

flextime ['flekstaɪm] US, **flexitime** ['fleksitaɪm] GB *n* a system that lets people start or finish work at different times, as long as they work the necessary number of hours □ *Some of our employees work flextime.*

flick [flɪk] ◇ n -1. [of a whip] a single sudden movement made with a whip, towel etc □ He gave a sharp flick of the whip to the horse's rump. -2. [of one's fingers] a single sudden movement made with one's finger and thumb □ One flick and the paper pellet landed on the teacher's desk. ◇ vt -1. to hit <sthg> with a flick, usually to remove it □ She flicked the ash off her cigarette. □ The children were flicking pieces of paper at each other. -2. [tail, whip, towel] to move <sthg> with a flick □ She flicked the cloth quickly over the floor. -3. [switch] to turn <sthg> on or off □ Just flick the switch and the ice cream is ready in ten minutes.

◆ **flick through** vt fus **to flick through sthg** [through a book, magazine] to turn the pages of sthg quickly, without reading it thoroughly or looking at it closely □ I've only had time to flick through it quickly.

flicker ['flɪkə r] ◇ vi -1. [candle, flame, light] to burn or shine in a weak irregular way □ The candle flickered in the wind. -2. [shadow, eyelids] to make small irregular movements in different directions □ The image flickered on the screen. ◇ n -1. [of hope, interest] a short and not very strong sign of something □ Bill didn't show the slightest flicker of recognition when we met again. -2. [of a candle, flame, light] the act of flickering □ There was a brief flicker, and then the fire went out.

flick knife n GB a kind of knife that has a blade, kept inside the handle, that opens out when a button is pressed.

flier ['flaɪə r] n an advertising leaflet that is given to people in the street.

flight [flaɪt] n -1. [in a plane] a trip by plane □ I made several flights to Johannesburg last year. -2. a regular service that takes people to a particular place by plane □ Air America flight 109 to Boston. ■ **a flight of fancy** OR **of the imagination** an imaginative idea, suggestion etc that is not very practical or realistic □ Not another of her flights of fancy! -3. **a flight of steps/stairs** a row of steps/stairs that joins two different levels. -4. [of a bird] the act of flying □ a bird in flight. -5. [from danger] the act of running away from danger, a threat etc □ criminals in flight from the law. ■ **to take flight** to run away or escape from something □ The birds took flight as soon as they saw me.

flight attendant n a person whose job is to take care of passengers during a flight.

flight crew n the people who work on an aircraft during a flight.

flight deck n -1. SHIPPING the part of a ship that is used by aircraft for landing and taking off. -2. AVIATION the part of a large aircraft where the pilot sits and operates the controls.

flight path n the route taken by an aircraft.

flight recorder n a device on an aircraft that records information about each flight.

flighty ['flaɪtɪ] (compar **flightier**, superl **flightiest**) adj [person] who often changes their mind, partner, behavior etc and so is not reliable.

flimsy ['flɪmzɪ] (compar **flimsier**, superl **flimsiest**) adj -1. [excuse, evidence, argument] that is not convincing □ The defense only has a flimsy case. -2. [structure] that is weak or badly made □ The chalet looked too flimsy to resist the mountain storms. -3. [dress, material] that is thin, light, and gives little protection □ She wore a flimsy summer dress.

flinch [flɪntʃ] vi to move back suddenly as a result of pain, shock, or embarrassment □ Bill listened to the insults without flinching. ■ **to flinch from sthg** to try to avoid sthg unpleasant □ He didn't flinch from calling the police.

fling [flɪŋ] (pt & pp **flung**) ◇ n a sexual relationship that is not serious and lasts a short time □ She had a fling with Marcus last year. ◇ vt [garbage, money, stone] to throw <sb/sthg> somewhere in a careless or violent way □ He flung himself into an armchair. □ She flung her arms around his neck.

flint [flɪnt] n -1. a hard gray stone that has very sharp edges when it breaks and makes sparks when it is hit with something □ a piece of flint. -2. the part of a cigarette lighter that produces sparks □ All it needs is a new flint.

flip [flɪp] (pt & pp **flipped**, cont **flipping**) ◇ vt -1. [page, pancake, mattress] to turn <sthg/sb> over quickly □ She flipped open the book. ■ **to flip through sthg** to read sthg very quickly and not in detail □ Mr Holland flipped through the report quickly before the meeting. -2. [switch, headlights] to turn <sthg> on or off □ He flipped on/off the radio. -3. **to flip a coin** to send a coin into the air with one's fingers so that it spins, usually to see which side faces up when it lands in order to decide something. ◇ vi to become very angry or excited suddenly (informal use) □ When Colin heard about it, he just flipped. ◇ n -1. **the flip of a coin** the act of flipping a coin to decide something □ Are you saying that this whole decision was based on the flip of a coin? -2. GYMNASTICS the act of spinning one's body in the air. -3. **at the flip of a switch** by turning a switch on □ I can control the whole thing at the flip of a switch.

flipchart ['flɪptʃɑː rt] n large sheets of paper held together on a stand, used for writing on during presentations, meetings etc.

flip-flop n a light shoe made of soft rubber that is held in place by a strap between one's toes.

flippant ['flɪpənt] adj [remark, reply, person] that is not serious and shows no concern about a serious matter, usually deliberately □ This is no time for being flippant.

flippantly ['flɪpəntlɪ] adv [remark, reply] see **flippant**.

flipper ['flɪpə r] n -1. [of a seal, dolphin] one of the flat limbs of an animal that help it swim underwater. -2. [for swimming] a long flat rubber shoe that makes it easier to swim and dive underwater □ a pair of flippers.

flip side n the side of a record that does not have the main song on it.

flirt [flɜː rt] ◇ vi -1. to behave toward or speak to somebody in a way that suggests one is sexually attracted to them, often not in a very serious way □ *She flirts with every man she meets!* **-2. to flirt with sthg** [with an idea, possibility] to think about sthg as a possibility rather than as a serious plan □ *I'm flirting with the idea of a career change.* ◇ *n* a person who flirts with other people □ *He's such a flirt!*

flirtation [flɜːˈteɪʃn] *n* **-1. a flirtation with sthg** an interest or involvement in sthg that lasts for a short time □ *After a brief flirtation with politics, he went into business.* **-2.** [with a man, woman] a short romantic or sexual relationship □ *They had a brief flirtation, nothing serious.*

flirtatious [flɜːˈteɪʃəs] *adj* [person] who likes to flirt with people □ *After several glasses of champagne, Eve was in a flirtatious mood.*

flit [flɪt] (*pt* & *pp* **flitted**, *cont* **flitting**) *vi* [bat, bird] to fly with short sudden movements □ *A butterfly flitted past.*

float [fləʊt] ◇ *vi* **-1.** [boat, cork, swimmer] to stay on or near the surface of a liquid □ *The pond was full of leaves floating on the surface.* **-2.** [sound, smell, balloon] to be carried through the air □ *Her perfume floated across the room to me.*
◇ *vt* **-1.** [boat, timber] *They floated the logs downstream.* **-2.** FINANCE to offer <shares in a company> for sale on the stock exchange for the first time. **-3.** [idea, project] to suggest <sthg> in order to find out what other people think of it □ *Plenty of names have been floated for the new job.*
◇ *n* **-1.** [for fishing] a piece of cork or light material used to hold up a fishing hook or fishing net; [for swimming] a piece of light material used to help people float in water. **-2.** [in a parade] a large vehicle specially decorated for a street parade or procession. **-3.** GB money given to somebody to use for expenses, or as change to give to customers.

floating [ˈfləʊtɪŋ] *adj* **-1.** [population] that is not permanently settled in a particular place. **-2.** [restaurant, hotel] that is built on a boat.

floating voter *n* GB a person who has not yet decided who to vote for in an election.

flock [flɒk] ◇ *n* **-1.** [of sheep, birds] a group of birds or sheep □ *The shepherd rounded up his flock.* **-2.** [of people] a large crowd of people.
◇ *vi* **to flock to a place** [people] to go to a place in large numbers over a period of time, usually because of something exciting or interesting □ *Everybody is flocking to the new Thai restaurant.*

flog [flɒg] (*pt* & *pp* **flogged**, *cont* **flogging**) *vt* **-1.** to beat <a person or animal> with a whip or stick □ *He was flogged to death.* **-2.** GB to sell <sthg> quickly (informal use).

flood [flʌd] ◇ *n* **-1.** a large amount of water that suddenly spreads over the ground or in a building □ *Floods in the north are making roads impassable.* **-2.** [of people, letters] a large number of people, letters etc that all arrive at a particular place at the same time □ *They've received floods of complaints.* ■ **to be in floods of tears** to be crying a lot □ *When she heard the news, Denise broke down in floods of tears.*
◇ *vt* **-1.** [street, valley, bathroom] to fill or cov-

er <sthg> with a large amount of water □ *The rains flooded the whole area.* **-2.** [country, city, streets] to arrive in <a place> in large numbers at the same time □ *Eastern Germany has been flooded with cheap consumer goods.* ■ **to be flooded with letters/complaints** [person, office] to receive very many letters/complaints □ *Viewers flooded the channel with complaints after the show.* ■ **to flood the market** [goods, products] to fill the whole market for a particular product □ *The market is flooded with cheap imports.* **-3. to be flooded in light** [room, valley] to be filled with light □ *The stage was flooded in bright green light.* **-4.** AUTO **to flood the engine** to cause too much gasoline to enter an engine, usually when one is trying to start a vehicle.
◇ *vi* **-1.** [river, bath, drain] to become filled with so much water that some of it escapes over a wide area □ *Her eyes flooded with tears.* **-2.** [street, valley, bathroom] *The house flooded during the storm.* **-3.** [people, letters, complaints] to arrive in large numbers □ *Applications flooded in after our advert.* **-4. to come flooding back** [memories, emotions] to return suddenly and be experienced intensely □ *The horror of it all came flooding back.*

floodgates [ˈflʌdgeɪts] *npl* **to open the floodgates** to make it possible for something to happen for the first time in a way that is difficult to control □ *The new bill could open the floodgates to thousands of requests for compensation.*

flooding [ˈflʌdɪŋ] *n* a situation where a street, field etc becomes covered in water from a river or heavy rain □ *Flooding has caused serious damage to crops.*

floodlight [ˈflʌdlaɪt] *n* a very bright light used outside at night to light up e.g. public buildings or sports events.

floodlit [ˈflʌdlɪt] *adj* [sports ground, match, building] that is lit by floodlights □ *a floodlit baseball game.*

flood tide *n* a rising tide.

floor [flɔːr] ◇ *n* **-1.** [in a room] the horizontal surface that people walk on in a room □ *Don't leave your clothes lying on the floor.* □ *a floor tile.* **-2.** [of a valley, the sea] the bottom part of a place like a valley, forest, or sea □ *animals that live on the forest floor.* **-3.** [of a building] one of the levels on which the rooms of a building are arranged □ *My office is on the seventh floor.* **-4.** [at a conference] the place where people stand when they make a speech at a debate or meeting □ *Mrs Darcy stood up to take the floor.* **-5.** [for dancing] the area of a club, restaurant etc where people can dance □ *By 12 o'clock there were still only a few people on the floor.* **-6.** FINANCE the place at a stock exchange where stocks and shares are bought and sold □ *The fall of the dollar created panic on the floor.*
◇ *vt* (informal use) **-1.** [opponent, attacker] to make <sb> fall down by hitting them hard □ *He floored him with a punch to his jaw.* **-2.** [interviewee, speaker, expert] to cause <sb> to be so confused, surprised etc that they

are unable to say anything □ *His question completely floored me.*

floorboard ['flɔːrbɔːrd] *n* a long flat piece of wood that forms part of the floor in a room □ *We had to take up the floorboards to put in central heating.*

floor cloth *n* GB a piece of material used for cleaning floors.

flooring ['flɔːrɪŋ] *n* material used for making floors □ *vinyl flooring.*

floor lamp *n* US a kind of tall lamp that stands on the floor of a room.

floor show *n* a performance or series of performances given by singers, dancers etc at a nightclub.

floorwalker ['flɔːrˌwɔːkər] *n* a supervisor in a department store.

flop [flɒp] (*pt* & *pp* **flopped**, *cont* **flopping**) ◇ *n* a failure (informal use) □ *The new Hardenberger movie was a complete flop in the States.* ◇ *vi* **-1.** [movie, play, plan] to be unsuccessful □ *If the show doesn't flop in the first week, we'll be OK.* **-2.** [person, hair] to fall down as if one has no support □ *She flopped down exhausted on the sofa.*

floppy ['flɒpɪ] (*compar* **floppier**, *superl* **floppiest**) *adj* [hair, hat] that is soft and hangs loosely □ *a dog with long floppy ears.*

floppy (disk) *n* a thin, flat, square object that holds information for use on a computer, and that is inserted into the computer when it is being used. NOTE: Compare **hard disk.**

flora ['flɔːrə] *n* a collective term for all the plants found in a particular place □ *flora and fauna* □ *the flora of the Greek islands.*

floral ['flɔːrəl] *adj* **-1.** [arrangement, decoration] that consists of flowers □ *a floral bouquet.* **-2.** [pattern, dress] that has a design of flowers □ *It was printed with a floral design.*

Florence ['flɒrəns] a city in central Italy, famous for its paintings, churches, and palaces. POPULATION: 402,316.

Florentine [US 'flɒrəntiːn, GB -taɪn] ◇ *n* a person who comes from or lives in Florence. ◇ *adj*: *Florentine architecture.*

floret ['flɒrət] *n* a small piece of a vegetable such as a cauliflower.

florid ['flɒrɪd] *adj* **-1.** [style, language] complicated and elaborate □ *His speech was somewhat florid.* **-2.** [complexion, face] red □ *a little old man with florid cheeks.*

Florida ['flɒrɪdə] a state in the southeastern USA, between the Atlantic Ocean and the Gulf of Mexico. ABBREVIATION: FL. SIZE: 151,670 sq kms. POPULATION: 12,937,926 (*Floridans, Floridians*). CAPITAL: Tallahassee. MAJOR CITIES: Miami, Orlando.

florist ['flɒrəst] *n* a person who sells flowers in a store. ■ **a florist's** the store where a florist works □ *I'll order a bouquet from the florist's.*

floss [flɒs] ◇ *vt* to clean <one's teeth> with dental floss. ◇ *vi*: *Remember to floss after meals.*

flotation [floʊ'teɪʃn] *n* FINANCE the sale of shares in a company to the public for the first time.

flotilla [floʊ'tɪlə] *n* a group of small ships, often warships.

flotsam ['flɒtsəm] *n* **flotsam and jetsam** [on a beach] broken pieces of wood, plastic etc from the ocean that are left on the seashore; [in society] people who do not have homes or jobs and have lost control of their lives.

flounce [flaʊns] ◇ *n* SEWING a piece of material sewn onto something such as a dress for decoration. ◇ *vi* to move in an exaggerated way that shows anger □ *She flounced angrily out of the room.*

flounder ['flaʊndər] (*pl* **flounder** OR **flounders**) ◇ *n* a kind of flat fish. ◇ *vi* **-1.** [person] to make large uncontrolled movements to try to avoid sinking in water, mud etc □ *I could see a small figure floundering in the snow.* **-2.** [person] to lose control and feel less confident □ *As the questions got more difficult, he began to flounder.*

flour ['flaʊər] *n* a white or brown powder made from wheat that is used to make bread, cakes etc □ *You'll need to add some flour to the mixture.*

flourish [US 'flɜːrɪʃ, GB 'flʌr-] ◇ *vi* **-1.** [plant, garden, child] to grow in a healthy pleasing way □ *My tomatoes are flourishing since I moved them.* **-2.** [company, market, activity] to be successful or strong □ *areas where violent crime flourishes.* ◇ *vt* [letter, document] to wave <sthg> so that people notice it □ *Diane flourished her first check proudly under his nose.* ◇ *n* an exaggerated confident movement □ *He signed the contract with a flourish.*

flourishing [US 'flɜːrɪʃɪŋ, GB 'flʌr-] *adj* [company, market, activity] successful □ *We also own a flourishing textile business in the south.*

flout [flaʊt] *vt* [law, rule, order] to do something that breaks <sthg> deliberately and openly.

flow [floʊ] ◇ *n* **-1.** [of water, air, a river] the continuous movement of a liquid or gas □ *The condition affects the flow of blood around the body.* **-2.** [of traffic, people] a steady movement forward; [of information, work, funds] a regular supply; [of words, ideas] a steady production □ *Measures have been introduced to ensure the flow of information between the two institutes.* ◇ *vi* **-1.** [liquid, electric current, air] to move in a continuous stream □ *The river flows through the center of the city.* **-2.** [traffic, people] to move steadily without any obstructions; [words, ideas] to occur one after the other in a steady stream □ *Traffic is flowing freely in both directions.* □ *One day flowed into another.* **-3.** [hair, clothes] to hang loosely in an attractive way □ *The dress flows beautifully around your ankles.* **-4. to flow from sthg** to be the result of sthg □ *A better understanding of the problem should flow from this experience.*

flowchart ['floʊtʃɑːrt], **flow diagram** *n* a diagram that shows how the individual steps in a process work together.

flower ['flaʊər] ◇ *n* **-1.** [of a plant] the part of a plant that produces seeds or fruit, only lives for a short time, and often has a bright color or colors and a pleasant smell □ *the flowers of the tomato plant* □ *We picked flowers in the garden.* ■ **to be in flower** [tree, plant] to have flowers on it. **-2.** [in a pot] a plant that is grown for its flowers; [in a vase] a stem of such a plant that has been cut and has one or more flowers on it □ *a bunch of flowers* □ *a flower arrangement.* ◇ *vi* **-1.** [plant] to produce flowers □ *a late-flowering variety.* **-2.** [person, art, genius] to reach a mature stage of development □ *This style of painting flowered in the 15th century.*

flowerbed ['flaʊəˌbed] *n* an area of soil in a garden or park where flowers are planted and grown.

flowered ['flaʊəd] *adj* [material, wallpaper] that has a pattern of flowers.

flowering ['flaʊərɪŋ] ◇ *adj* [plant, tree] that produces flowers. ◇ *n* [of talent, an artistic movement] the period in which something starts to develop and grow in a pleasing and impressive way.

flowerpot ['flaʊəˌpɒt] *n* a container in which plants are grown.

flowery ['flaʊərɪ] (*compar* **flowerier**, *superl* **floweriest**) *adj* **-1.** [dress, material, wallpaper] that has a pattern of flowers □ *I think a flowery pattern would be nice for the drapes.* **-2.** [language, style] that uses long descriptive words (disapproving use) □ *Does it have to be so flowery?* **-3.** [perfume, scent] that smells like flowers.

flowing ['fləʊɪŋ] *adj* [movement, gesture] loose and free; [hair, clothes] that is loose, elegant, and able to move freely; [writing, style] that flows in a pleasant way □ *She wore a long, flowing, silk dress* □ *beautiful, flowing prose.*

flown [fləʊn] *past participle of* **fly**.

fl oz *abbr of* **fluid ounce**.

flu [fluː] *n* **to have flu** GB OR **the flu** to have a common infectious illness like a cold but more serious, in which one feels very weak □ *I think I must have the flu.* □ *a flu epidemic.*

fluctuate ['flʌktʃʊeɪt] *vi* [price, number, value] to go up and down in an unpredictable way □ *The temperature doesn't fluctuate much in winter.*

fluctuation [ˌflʌktʃʊ'eɪʃn] *n see* **fluctuate** □ *There has been a lot of fluctuation in the exchange rate.*

flue [fluː] *n* a chimney of a factory, boiler etc □ *a chimney flue.*

fluency ['fluːənsɪ] *n: see* **fluent** □ *Fluency in two foreign languages is required.* □ *Reading fluency is a priority at this school.*

fluent ['fluːənt] *adj* **-1.** [person] who is able to speak a language without hesitating too much or making too many mistakes □ *He's a fluent Japanese speaker.* □ *She's fluent in French and English.* □ *He speaks fluent Spanish.* **-2.** [style, writing] that flows in a pleasant way □ *clear, fluent written style.*

fluently ['fluːəntlɪ] *adv* [speak, write] *see* **fluent** □ *My little boy can read French fluently.*

fluff [flʌf] ◇ *n* **-1.** the soft warm material that covers the bodies of young birds and animals □ *baby chicks covered with fluff.* **-2.** the light and soft material made up of very small threads that collects in corners of a room, on people's clothes etc □ *There's a piece of fluff on your jacket.* ◇ *vt* **-1.** [cushion, hair] to shake or move <sthg soft> to get some air into it and make it appear larger □ *The swan fluffed up its feathers.* **-2.** [catch, opportunity] to do <sthg> badly (informal use) □ *I really fluffed the interview.*

fluffy ['flʌfɪ] (*compar* **fluffier**, *superl* **fluffiest**) *adj* [animal, fur, sweater] that is soft and is or seems to be covered with fluff □ *a few fluffy white clouds.*

fluid ['fluːɪd] ◇ *n* a liquid □ *brake/cleaning fluid* □ *body fluids.* ◇ *adj* **-1.** [style, movement, technique] that can flow easily from one part to another □ *With one fluid movement she circled and skated back.* **-2.** [situation] that tends to change easily or unexpectedly □ *Things are still pretty fluid right now.*

fluid ounce *n* a unit (28.4 ml) for measuring liquids.

fluke [fluːk] *n* something surprising or unlikely that happens by chance (informal use) □ *It was a complete fluke that I found this place.*

flummox ['flʌməks] *vt* to confuse <sb> so that they do not know what to say or think (informal use) □ *I was completely flummoxed.*

flung [flʌŋ] *past tense & past participle of* **fling**.

flunk [flʌŋk] (informal use) ◇ *vt* **-1.** [exam, course, interview] to fail <sthg> □ *She flunked math.* **-2.** [student, candidate] to give <sb> a bad grade for an exam so that they fail □ *They flunked Donald at the exam.* ◇ *vi* [student] to fail in an exam or course □ *I flunked again!*

◆ **flunk out** *vi* to be ordered to leave a college because one's work is not good enough □ *Miriam flunked out of Michigan State in her second year.*

fluorescent [flɔː'resnt] *adj* [color, clothing] that is very bright, reflects light, and can be seen very easily, even when there is little light.

fluorescent light *n* an electric light, usually in the form of a long tube, that gives a bright harsh light.

fluoride ['flʊəraɪd] *n* a chemical compound that is thought to strengthen the teeth and is sometimes added to toothpaste and water supplies.

fluorine ['flʊəriːn] *n* a poisonous yellow gas. SYMBOL: F.

flurry [US 'flɜːrɪ, GB 'flʌrɪ] (*pl* **flurries**) *n* **-1.** [of snow] a short heavy period of snow or rain. **-2.** [of activity] a sudden intense period of activity □ *There was a flurry of excitement as the star's car pulled up.*

flush [flʌʃ] ◇ *n* **-1.** [of a toilet] the mechanism in a toilet that sends water into the bowl and carries away waste material. **-2.** [of a person] a hot feeling accompanied by redness in one's face, often experienced when one is embarrassed □ *a flush of embarrassment.* **-3.** [of anger, excitement] a sudden strong feeling. ■ **to be in the first flush of sthg** to be in the first stage of sthg that is more intense than later stages (literary use) □ *in the first flush of youth.*

◇ *vt* **to flush the toilet** to make a toilet flush by using the flush mechanism. ■ **to flush sthg down the toilet** to get rid of sthg by putting it in the toilet and flushing it.

◇ *vi* **-1.** [toilet] to send a strong stream of water to carry away waste □ *The toilet won't flush.* **-2.** [person] to become red in the face with embarrassment □ *He flushed at the mention of her name.*

◇ *adj* **-1. to be flush with sthg** [with a surface] to be at the same level as sthg □ *The washing machine fits flush with the sink unit.* **-2. to be flush** [person] to have a lot of money or more money than usual (informal use) □ *I'm feeling flush tonight!*

◆ **flush out** *vt sep* to flush a person/an animal out to force a person/an animal to leave the place where they are hiding □ *The hijackers were flushed out with tear gas.*

flushed [flʌʃt] *adj* **-1.** [person, face] that is red because of embarrassment, physical activity etc □ *You look a little flushed.* **-2. to be flushed with sthg** to be excited or happy because of sthg □ *They returned home, flushed with success.*

fluster ['flʌstər] ◇ *n* a feeling of confusion and embarrassment caused by something outside one's control □ *Try not to get into a fluster.* ◇ *vt* to make <sb> feel confused and embarrassed □ *They tried to fluster me by not giving me time to answer.*

flustered ['flʌstərd] *adj* [person] who is confused and embarrassed and unable to concentrate □ *He looked pretty flustered when I asked him to explain.*

flute [fluːt] *n* MUSIC a musical instrument consisting of a metal or wooden tube with holes in it that is played by holding it so that it points to the side and blowing across a hole at one end □ *She plays the flute.*

fluted ['fluːtəd] *adj* [column, glass] that has a pattern of vertical grooves cut into it.

flutist ['fluːtəst] *n* US a person who plays the flute.

flutter ['flʌtər] ◇ *n* **-1.** [of wings] a small fast movement up and down □ *I could hear the flutter of its wings.* **-2.** [of one's heart, pulse] a quick irregular beat □ *His heart gave a flutter when she walked in the room.* **-3.** [of excitement] a sudden nervous and excited feeling (informal use) □ *There was a brief flutter of excitement as the president took his seat.*

◇ *vt* [wings, eyelashes] to move two parts of <sthg> rapidly up and down □ *She fluttered her eyelashes coquettishly.*

◇ *vi* **-1.** [bird, insect, wings] to move through the air with small quick movements □ *A robin fluttered down to the grass.* **-2.** [flag, clothes] to move gently in the wind □ *The washing was fluttering in the wind.* **-3.** [heart, pulse] to beat quickly and irregularly □ *The sight of her made my heart flutter.*

flux [flʌks] *n* **to be in a state of flux** [situation, market, prices] to be changing constantly □ *Things at work are still in a state of flux.*

fly [flaɪ] (*pl* **flies,** *pt* **flew,** *pp* **flown**) ◇ *n* **-1.** any small insect with two wings □ *The kitchen was full of flies.* ■ **a fly in the ointment** a person or thing that spoils a situation, occasion etc □ *So, is he the only fly in the ointment?* **-2.** [on one's trousers] the opening at the front of a pair of trousers where there is a zipper or set of buttons □ *Hey, your fly's open.*

◇ *vi* **-1.** [bird, insect, bat] to move through the air by moving its wings; [plane, helicopter] to travel through the air □ *The geese are flying south for the winter.* □ *Holiday Air flies to Spain three times a week.* **-2.** [pilot] to steer and control an aircraft in the air □ *I learned to fly during the war.* **-3.** [passenger] to travel by aircraft □ *I prefer flying to traveling by train.* **-4.** [person, vehicle, ball] to move somewhere very quickly □ *She flew across the room* □ *The door flew open.* ■ **I must fly** I must leave immediately. **-5.** [time, event] to pass quickly □ *My vacation just flew past.* □ *Doesn't time fly!* **-6. to fly at sb** to attack sb physically or with words □ *Is there any reason why she flew at you like that?* **-7.** [flag] to be displayed □ *If the flag is flying, it means the Queen's there.*

◇ *vt* **-1.** [plane, helicopter, balloon] to make <sthg> move through the air □ *I learnt how to fly a glider.* **-2.** [passengers, goods] to carry <sb/sthg> somewhere in an aircraft □ *Supplies were flown into the famine area.* **-3. to fly a flag** to display a flag at the top of a pole.

◆ **fly away** *vi* [bird, insect] to leave a place by flying □ *I tried to get closer but they flew away.*

◆ **fly in** ◇ *vt sep* to fly sb/sthg in [supplies, troops] to bring sb/sthg to a place by aircraft □ *Reinforcements were flown in from the mainland.* ◇ *vi* [person] to arrive somewhere by aircraft □ *She's flying in next week to visit us.*

◆ **fly into** *vt fus* **to fly into a rage** OR **temper** to become angry very suddenly □ *He suddenly flew into a rage and started shouting.*

◆ **fly out** ◇ *vt sep* **to fly sb/sthg out** to take <sb/sthg> somewhere by aircraft. ◇ *vi* [person] to leave somewhere by aircraft □ *They're flying out of La Guardia this morning.* □ *I'll fly out to join you next Monday.*

flyby ['flaɪbaɪ] *n* a display performed by aircraft flying together, often in somebody's honor.

fly-fishing *n* the activity of fishing using an artificial fly as bait.

fly half *n* a position in rugby; a person who plays in this position.

flying ['flaɪɪŋ] ◇ *adj* [animal, insect] that can fly □ *The air was thick with flying ants.* ■ **to take a flying leap** OR **jump** to make a jump after running a short distance so that one passes further through the air □ *He took a flying jump and landed in the water.* ◇ *n* **-1.** the activity of traveling by aircraft □ *I hate flying.* **-2.** the activity or sport of flying an airplane □ *Nick goes flying every weekend.*

flying colors *npl* **to pass with flying colors** to do very well in an exam or test.

flying doctor *n* a doctor, especially in Australia, who has to visit patients by plane because they are spread over such a large area.

flying officer *n* a commissioned officer in the British Royal Air Force.

flying picket *n* a group of people belonging to a labor union who travel to a different place to persuade the workers there to go on strike.

flying saucer *n* a disk-shaped object thought to be a spaceship from another planet.

flying squad *n* GB a group of policemen who can get to the scene of a crime quickly.

flying start *n* **to get off to a flying start** to start something very well and successfully □ *Well, we didn't exactly get off to a flying start, did we?*

flying visit *n* a very short visit, especially one that somebody makes when they are traveling to another place □ *I'm afraid this will have to be a flying visit.*

flyleaf ['flaɪliːf] (*pl* **flyleaves** [-liːvz]) *n* a blank page at the beginning or end of a book □ *The author's notes are on the flyleaf.*

flyover ['flaɪəʊvəʳ] *n* GB a road built high above other roads that allows traffic to avoid busy areas.

flypast [US 'flaɪpæst, GB -pɑːst] *n* GB = **flyby**.

flysheet ['flaɪʃiːt] *n* the outer layer of a tent that stops rain from getting inside.

fly spray *n* a spray used to kill insects.

flyweight ['flaɪweɪt] *n* a boxer in the lightest official weight category.

flywheel ['flaɪwiːl] *n* a heavy wheel that keeps the speed of a machine constant.

FM *n* -1. (*abbr of* **frequency modulation**) a system of radio broadcasting that produces a very clear sound. -2. *abbr of* **field marshal**. NOTE: Compare **AM**.

FO *n abbr of* **Foreign Office**.

foal [fəʊl] *n* a young horse.

foam [fəʊm] ◇ *n* -1. a mass of small bubbles □ *bath foam.* -2. **foam (rubber)** a soft material filled with small air bubbles that is used in making mattresses, cushions etc □ *a foam cushion.* ◇ *vi* [water, champagne, beer] to produce foam □ *The dog was foaming at the mouth.*

foamy ['fəʊmɪ] (*compar* **foamier**, *superl* **foamiest**) *adj* [sea, bathwater, drink] full of small bubbles □ *I lay reading in a hot foamy bath.*

fob [fɒb] (*pt* & *pp* **fobbed**, *cont* **fobbing**) ♦ **fob off** *vt sep* **to fob sb off** to tell sb something that is not true or useful in order to stop them complaining, asking questions etc □ *When I went to complain, the manager just tried to fob me off. □ She tried to fob me off with some excuse.* ■ **to fob sthg off on sb** to give or sell sb sthg that one no longer wants and that one knows is not useful to them □ *I managed to fob that old sofa off on them.*

FOB, fob (*abbr of* **free on board**) *adv* at a price that includes all the seller's costs up to the delivery of goods to a particular place □ *The books are being shipped fob Chicago.*

fob watch *n* a watch attached to a chain and kept in a pocket.

foc *adv abbr of* **free of charge**.

focal point *n* -1. [of a view, room] the part of something that attracts most attention □ *The fireplace is the focal point of the room.* -2. [of a report, study, somebody's life] the part of something that is most important □ *What this essay really lacks is a focal point.*

focus ['fəʊkəs] (*pl* **focuses** OR **foci** [-saɪ], *pt* & *pp* **focused** OR **focussed**) ◇ *n* -1. [of a camera, telescope] the mechanism in a camera, telescope etc that makes the image clear and sharp. ■ **to be out of/in focus** [photograph] to be blurred/clear; [camera] to give a blurred/clear image □ *The people in the foreground were out of focus.* -2. PHYSICS the point where lines, rays of light, sound waves etc come together. -3. [of an argument] the most important part of an argument, discussion, campaign etc that attracts people's attention and interest □ *They are trying to shift the focus of the debate. □ The focus is on quality rather than quantity.* ■ **the focus of attention** the person or thing that everybody is watching, interested in, or concentrating on □ *However, the main focus of attention was the new Fiat range. □ She loves to be the focus of attention.* ◇ *vt* -1. [camera, telescope] to adjust <sthg> to produce a clear sharp image. ■ **to focus sthg on sb/sthg** [camera, eyes] to direct sthg toward sb/sthg □ *All eyes were focused on the defendant as she took the witness stand.* -2. **to focus one's attention on sb/sthg** to give all of one's attention to sb/sthg □ *Try to focus your attention on what we're discussing.* ◇ *vi* -1. [eyes, camera] *I have difficulty focussing on things that are far away.* -2. [attention] *It's impossible to focus on two problems at the same time.*

focus(s)ed ['fəʊkʌst] *adj* [person] who does something in a very careful way that shows they are determined to succeed □ *Adam is very focused on his work.*

fodder ['fɒdəʳ] *n* food for farm animals □ *cattle fodder.*

foe [fəʊ] *n* an enemy (literary use).

FOE *n* -1. *abbr of* **Friends of the Earth**. -2. (*abbr of* **Fraternal Order of Eagles**) **the FOE** a US charitable organization.

foetus *etc* GB = **fetus** *etc.*

fog [fɒg] *n* a mass of cloud near the ground that makes it difficult to see things that are not very near □ *There will be fog tonight. □ fog patches.*

fogbound ['fɒgbaʊnd] *adj* [airport, aircraft, passenger] that cannot work or travel as usual because of fog.

fogey ['fəʊgɪ] *n* = **fogy**.

foggiest ['fɒgɪəst] *n* **I haven't the foggiest** a phrase used to emphasize that one does not know the answer to a question (informal use) □ *I haven't the foggiest idea where he could be.*

foggy ['fɒgɪ] (*compar* **foggier**, *superl* **foggiest**) *adj* [weather, day, area] *see* **fog** □ *Foggy conditions are making driving difficult.*

Foggy Bottom *n* the US Department of State (informal use).

foghorn ['fɒghɔːʳn] *n* a piece of equipment that makes a very loud noise to warn ships of danger caused by fog.

fog lamp, fog light *n* one of the powerful lights on the front of a vehicle that can be used when one is driving in fog.

fogy ['fougɪ] (*pl* **fogies**) *n* **an old fogy** a person whose ideas are considered to be old-fashioned.

foible ['fɔɪbl] *n* a weakness or failing in a person's character that is not very serious □ *one of his many little foibles.*

foil [fɔɪl] ◇ *n* -1. [of metal] a very thin sheet of metal □ *silver/kitchen foil.* -2. a person or thing that acts as a contrast to emphasize the characteristics of some other person or thing □ *The white walls are a foil for the brightly-colored pictures.* ◇ *vt* [plan, attempt, criminal] to prevent <sthg/sb bad> from succeeding □ *The raid was foiled by a security guard.*

foist [fɔɪst] *vt* **to foist sthg on sb** to give or sell sb sthg they do not really want □ *Don't try to foist your political views on me.*

fold [fould] ◇ *vt* -1. [piece of paper, cloth, sheet] to bend a part of <sthg> so that it covers another part □ *He folded the letter in half.* ■ **to fold one's arms** to hold one's arms so that they are crossed over each other against one's chest □ *She leaned back, arms folded, and said nothing.* -2. [table, chair, umbrella] to bend or close parts of <sthg> so that it takes up less space □ *The bench can be folded when not in use.* -3. **to fold sb in one's arms** to put one's arms around sb.
◇ *vi* -1. [table, chair, bed] to be able to be bent or closed, so that it takes up less space. -2. [company, show] to fail and close (informal use) □ *The show folded after only a week.*
◇ *n* -1. [in paper] the line or edge that is made in a piece of material, paper etc when it is folded □ *Cut along the fold.* -2. [for animals] an enclosed part of a field where animals spend the night. -3. **the fold** the place or institution where someone belongs or feels at home □ *It's good to welcome Professor Barclay back to the fold.*

◆ **fold up** ◇ *vt sep* -1. **to fold sthg up** [cloth, sheet] to fold sthg several times in order to make it smaller □ *Fold up your clothes and put them away.* -2. **to fold sthg up** [table, chair, umbrella] to bend or close parts of sthg so that it takes up less space □ *I've got one of those beds that you can fold up.* ◇ *vi* -1. [table, chair, umbrella] to be able to be bent or closed, so taking up less space □ *The umbrella folds up to fit in your purse.* -2. [company, business] to fail and close (informal use) □ *The company folded up after only a year in business.*

foldaway ['fouldəweɪ] *adj* [bed, table] that can be folded for storage.

folder ['fouldər] *n* -1. [for documents] a folded piece of cardboard or plastic that is designed to hold documents, papers etc. -2. COMPUTING an area of a disk that contains a particular type of information.

folding ['fouldɪŋ] *adj* [table, chair, bicycle] that can be folded in order to use less space □ *A folding bed is perfect for a studio apartment.*

foliage ['fouliɪdʒ] *n* the leaves of a tree or bush □ *the dense foliage of the laurel tree.*

folk [fouk] ◇ *adj* [art, dancing, medicine] that is traditional and popular among the people of a particular country, region etc □ *a traditional folk remedy for headaches.* ◇ *n* = **folk music**. ◇ *npl* people □ *city/country folk.*

◆ **folks** *npl* (informal use) -1. **one's folks** one's parents or relatives □ *I rarely go back to see my folks.* -2. a word used to address a group of people one knows well □ *See you, folks!*

folklore ['fouklɔːr] *n* the traditional customs, music, stories etc of the people of a particular country or region □ *His adventures have become a part of local folklore.*

folk music *n* -1. a traditional kind of music that has been passed down from generation to generation and has no known composer. -2. a kind of music that uses traditional instruments, especially acoustic guitars, and sounds like folk music.

folk singer *n* a person who sings folk songs.

folk song *n* a song that has been passed down from generation to generation and has no known composer.

folksy ['fouksɪ] (*compar* **folksier**, *superl* **folksiest**) *adj* US that seems simple and informal in manner or appearance (informal use).

follicle ['fɒlɪkl] *n* a very small hole in the skin that a hair grows out of □ *a hair follicle.*

follow ['fɒlou] ◇ *vt* -1. [guide, person in front] to go after <sb> □ *A dog followed me all the way home.* -2. [event] to happen after <sthg> □ *The lecture will be followed by a question and answer session.* -3. [river, path, trend] to go the same way as <sthg> □ *The road follows the coast for 20 miles, then veers inland.* -4. [suspect, criminal] to go after <sb> in order to catch them □ *I had the feeling I was being followed.* -5. [movement, development] to watch <sthg> □ *I've followed his progress with great interest.* -6. [argument, logic] to understand the connections between the parts of <sthg> □ *I'm sorry, I don't follow you.* -7. [instructions, advice] to act according to <sthg> □ *Just follow my example.*
◇ *vi* -1. [person, package, letter] to come after □ *We have dispatched your order, and an invoice will follow.* □ *We heard nothing in the weeks that followed.* ■ **as follows** a phrase used to introduce a list of people or things or a description of the way in which something should be done □ *The report's recommendations are as follows...* □ *Please complete the form as follows...* -2. [success, victory] to be a logical result of something □ *His death follows a long illness.* -3. [conclusion, argument] to be logical □ *Just because this one is useless, it doesn't necessarily follow that they all are.* -4. [person] to understand □ *I'm sorry, I don't quite follow.*

◆ **follow up** *vt sep* -1. **to follow sthg up** [idea, suggestion, hunch] to explore or develop sthg further □ *I want you to follow this complaint up with the people concerned.* □ *The company is following up last year's success with three new products.* -2. **to follow sthg up** [meal, study, job] to finish sthg in a way which makes it complete □ *He followed up a perfect performance with a brilliant encore.*

follower ['fɒloʊə'] *n* a person who supports the ideas of a particular person □ *He's a faithful follower of the latest economic guru.*

following ['fɒloʊɪŋ] ◇ *adj* -1. [time, flight, day] that comes next in a sequence □ *I went back the following week.* -2. a word used to refer to something that is about to be mentioned □ *The following candidates have been successful: Mark Chadwick, Jane Moore.* ◇ *n* a group of supporters □ *He has built up a devoted following.* ◇ *prep* after and as a result of <sthg> □ *Following heavy rain, the game has been canceled.*

follow-up ◇ *adj* [visit, treatment, study] that deals with something started earlier □ *We had a follow-up meeting to monitor the progress that had been made.* ◇ *n* a meeting, visit, lesson etc that deals with something started earlier □ *I missed the follow-up to last week's lecture.*

folly ['fɒlɪ] *n* foolishness □ *It would be sheer folly to give up now.*

foment [foʊ'ment] *vt* **to foment trouble/rebellion etc** to encourage people to make trouble/to rebel etc (formal use).

fond [fɒnd] *adj* -1. [smile, embrace, farewell] that expresses affection □ *One last fond kiss, and then they parted.* -2. **to be fond of sb** to like sb very much, especially when one has known them for a long time □ *I'm very fond of you, but I can't marry you.* ■ **to be fond of sthg** to like sthg very much □ *I'm very fond of chocolate liqueurs.* □ *I've grown very fond of my old car.* -3. **a fond hope/wish** a hope/wish that is not likely to happen, and so seems foolish (literary use) □ *It was his fond ambition that I become a surgeon.*

fondle ['fɒndl] *vt* to touch or stroke <a person, animal, or thing> several times in a gentle way that shows affection □ *He tried to fondle her in the back of the car.*

fondly ['fɒndlɪ] *adv* -1. [smile, remember] with affection □ *I often think fondly of those days.* -2. [believe, hope] *see* **fond** □ *Her parents fondly imagined that she would get married.*

fondness ['fɒndnəs] *n* a liking □ *He has a fondness for rich food.*

fondue [US fɒn'duː, GB 'fɒnduː] *n* a dish consisting of hot oil or a hot cheese sauce into which pieces of bread, meat, or vegetables are dipped and eaten.

font [fɒnt] *n* -1. [in a church] the stone structure in a church that consists of a container at the top that holds water for baptizing people. -2. [of characters] a set of letters of a particular size and style used in printing, word processing etc.

food [fuːd] *n* something that people or animals eat □ *How much do you spend on food?* □ *I love Italian food!* ■ **food for thought** something that makes one think seriously about something □ *Well, that's certainly given us food for thought.*

food chain *n* the relationship that exists between living things that eat each other □ *Plankton play a vital role in the food chain.*

food mixer *n* an electrical appliance used in the kitchen to mix ingredients together, or chop or grind them.

food poisoning *n* an illness in which harmful organisms in food cause stomach pains, vomiting, and diarrhea □ *an outbreak of food poisoning.*

food processor *n* an appliance used in the kitchen to mix food or cut it into smaller pieces.

food stamps *npl* in the USA, coupons given by the government to poor people that they can use to buy food.

foodstuffs ['fuːdstʌfs] *npl* particular kinds of food that people eat □ *All foodstuffs must be stored in accordance with the instructions.*

fool [fuːl] ◇ *n* -1. a person who one thinks is stupid □ *I felt like such a fool.* ■ **to make a fool (out) of sb** to make sb appear ridiculous □ *Are you trying to make a fool of me?* ■ **to make a fool of oneself** to act in a way that makes one appear ridiculous □ *I think I made rather a fool of myself last night.* ■ **to act** OR **play the fool** to behave in a silly way to make people laugh □ *Oh John, stop acting the fool.* -2. GB a kind of dessert made from fruit puree and cream □ *a fruit fool.* ◇ *vt* to trick <sb> □ *You can't fool me so easily!* □ *He was fooled into thinking the intruders were repairmen.* ◇ *vi* to do or say something as a joke □ *I was only fooling!* □ *Quit fooling!*

◆ **fool around** *vi* -1. [child, student] to behave in a foolish way. -2. [husband, wife] to have sex with somebody who is not one's usual partner □ *I had no idea she was fooling around with another man.* -3. **to fool around with sthg** [with a radio, computer] to use or make changes to sthg, especially without permission □ *If I catch you fooling around with my computer again I'll stop your pocket money!*

foolhardy ['fuːlhɑːʳdɪ] *adj* [person] who takes foolish and unnecessary risks □ *It was foolhardy to drive in such conditions.*

foolish ['fuːlɪʃ] *adj* -1. [person] who is not sensible and does not consider the results of their actions □ *That was a foolish thing to do.* -2. **to look/feel foolish** to look/feel stupid, especially in a way that is likely to make people laugh at one □ *We've all been made to look foolish in front of the shareholders.*

foolishly ['fuːlɪʃlɪ] *adv* -1. a word used to show that one thinks something was foolish □ *Foolishly, I believed him.* -2. [behave, act] *see* **foolish** □ *She grinned foolishly.*

foolproof ['fuːlpruːf] *adj* [system, machine, plan] that is simple to use or understand and cannot go wrong □ *This new system is supposed to be foolproof.*

foolscap ['fuːlskæp] *n* a size of paper (340×430mm) □ *a piece of foolscap.*

foot [fʊt] (*pl* **feet**) ◇ *n* -1. [of a person, animal, bird] the part of the body at the end of the leg that is used for standing on, walking etc □ *I've got a blister on my right foot.* □ *a foot massage.* ■ **to be on one's feet** to be standing. □ *I've been on my feet all day.* ■ **to get to one's feet** to stand up □ *Frederick got slowly to his*

feet. ■ **on** OR **by foot** by walking □ *They come to work on foot.* ■ **to be back on one's feet** [person] to be well again after an illness or operation; [company, economy] to be successful again after a period of difficulty □ *We'll have you back on your feet in no time.* □ *The business will take years to get back on its feet again.* ■ **to have cold feet** to be scared of doing something frightening, dangerous etc after having agreed to do it (informal use) □ *You're not getting cold feet about this, are you?* ■ **to have itchy feet** to feel like moving from one home or job to another one (informal use). ■ **to put one's foot down** to demand that something must stop and not happen □ *I had to put my foot down and demand better service.* ■ **to put one's foot in it** to cause a difficult or embarrassing situation by saying something that upsets somebody or that is a secret □ *Oh dear, have I put my foot in it again?* ■ **to put one's feet up** to relax by sitting or lying down and supporting one's legs on something □ *When I get home all I want is to sit down and put my feet up.* ■ **to be rushed off one's feet** to have a lot of work to do very quickly. ■ **to set foot in a place** to enter a place □ *Never set foot in my house again!* ■ **to stand on one's own two feet** to survive without help from anybody else □ *It's time you learned to stand on your own two feet.* -2. **the foot of sthg** [of a page, hill, stairs] the bottom of sthg □ *The village is at the foot of the hill.* -3. [in measurements] a unit (0.3048m) used for measuring length □ *I'm five foot five (inches).* □ *That wall is two foot* OR *feet high.*
◇ *vt* **to foot the bill** to pay for something (informal use).

footage ['fʊtɪdʒ] *n* a part of a film that shows a particular event □ *They showed some footage of the first televised Olympic Games.*

foot-and-mouth disease *n* a very serious disease that affects the mouth and hooves of cattle, pigs, sheep etc.

football ['fʊtbɔːl] *n* -1. US a game played on a large field by two teams of 11 players who throw or carry an oval-shaped ball past each other in order to score points at the end of the field □ *Do you play football?* -2. GB a game, also called soccer, played by two teams of 11 players who kick a ball around a large field with a goal at each end. The aim is to kick the ball into the opponents' goal □ *Let's have a game of football.* -3. a ball used for playing any kind of football.

footballer ['fʊtbɔːləʳ] *n* GB a person who plays soccer, usually as a job.

football field *n* US an area of ground, 300 feet long, used for playing football.

football game *n* US a game of football.

football ground *n* GB the field and buildings used by people playing or watching soccer.

football match *n* GB a game of soccer.

football player *n* = footballer.

football pools *npl* GB a game in which money is bet on the results of soccer matches that have not yet been played.

🏆 FOOTBALL POOLS
In Britain, "doing the pools" means trying to guess which soccer matches will end in a draw, and betting a small amount of money on them. It is also possible to gamble on which teams will win home or away games. People who do the pools regularly listen eagerly to the results of soccer matches on the radio or television on Saturday evenings. Large cash prizes are won every week by people who guess the results correctly.

footbrake ['fʊtbreɪk] *n* a brake in a car, truck etc that is operated by one's foot.

footbridge ['fʊtbrɪdʒ] *n* a bridge that is designed for people to walk across.

footer ['fʊtəʳ] *n* COMPUTING information such as a page number that is programmed to appear at the bottom of each page.

foot fault *n* a fault in tennis where a player steps over the back line of the court while serving.

foothills ['fʊthɪlz] *npl* low hills at the bottom of a mountain or range of mountains.

foothold ['fʊthəʊld] *n* a place to put one's foot when climbing up or down a mountain □ *You should be able to find a foothold further up.* ■ **to get a foothold in sthg** [in a company, market] to get a job or position from which one can make good progress □ *The company is trying to get a foothold in southeast Asia.*

footing ['fʊtɪŋ] *n* -1. **to lose one's footing/balance** to slip, with the result that one falls or nearly falls □ *She lost her footing on the steps.* -2. **to be on a business/an official etc footing** to have a business/official etc relationship with somebody. ■ **to be on an equal footing** to be treated or considered in the same way as somebody else □ *Western companies will soon be able to compete on an equal footing with their Asian rivals.*

footlights ['fʊtlaɪts] *npl* the row of lights along the front of a stage in a theater.

footman ['fʊtmən] (*pl* **footmen** [-mən]) *n* a male servant who opens doors, serves food etc.

footmark ['fʊtmɑːʳk] *n* a mark made by a foot or shoe on a surface.

footnote ['fʊtnəʊt] *n* information at the bottom of a page that says more about a particular point, shown by a number or letter in the text.

footpath [US 'fʊtpæθ, *pl* -pæðz, GB -pɑːθ, *pl* -pɑːðz] *n* a narrow path for people to walk along □ *'Keep to the footpath.'*

footprint ['fʊtprɪnt] *n* the mark made by a shoe or by a person's or animal's foot on a soft or wet surface □ *There were fresh footprints in the snow.*

Footsie ['fʊtsɪ] *n* = FT-SE 100 (informal use).

footsore ['fʊtsɔːʳ] *adj* [person] who has tired and painful feet because they have been walking a lot.

footstep ['fʊtstep] *n* -1. the sound made by a foot on the ground when somebody is walking □ *She heard footsteps behind her.* -2. a mark made by a foot or shoe on a surface □ *footsteps in the sand.* ■ **to follow in sb's footsteps** to do the same job or activity that sb else has done in the past, especially an older relative □ *She hopes to follow in her father's footsteps.*

footwear ['fʊtweəʳ] *n* a collective term for shoes, boots, sandals etc □ *Bring sensible footwear with you.*

footwork ['fʊtwɜːʳk] *n* movements or steps made by the feet, especially when playing sports or dancing.

for [*stressed* fɔːʳ, *unstressed* fəʳ] ◇ *prep* -1. **a present for my sister** a present to be given to or used by my sister (used to show who something is meant for) □ *Are there any messages for me?* -2. **to do sthg for sb** to do sthg to be useful, helpful, or pleasant to sb (used for the indirect objects of some verbs) □ *Let me carry that bag for you.* □ *He bought a book for his brother.* □ *I cooked lunch for twelve people.* -3. **to work for sb** to be employed by sb □ *She writes for a newspaper.* ■ **to act for sb** to act on behalf of sb; to represent sb □ *She played tennis for England.* -4. **a knife for cutting paper** a knife designed, used, or intended to cut paper □ *a gadget for opening cans* □ *We need a new carpet for the living room.* ■ **what's it for?** what is its use?; what does it do? □ *Do you have anything for a sore throat?* -5. **in prison for burglary** in prison because of burglary (used to show why something has happened or is true) □ *I apologized for my rudeness.* □ *The zoo closed for lack of funds.* □ *Burgundy is famous for its wines.* ■ **the reason for my question** the reason why I asked. ■ **what...for?** why? □ *What did you do that for?* -6. **I'm going out for a walk** I'm going out in order to have a walk □ *We had to run for the bus.* □ *I came here for a rest.* -7. **we talked for two hours** used to show how long something goes on □ *She'll be away for a month.* □ *They've lived here for years.* -8. **I'll be back for lunch** I shall be back in time to have lunch. -9. **the meeting planned for the 30th** the meeting planned to take place on the 30th. ■ **I got a watch for Christmas/my birthday** I got a watch at Christmas/on my birthday (used for special occasions). -10. **the plane for Phoenix** the plane that goes to Phoenix □ *She left for Paris yesterday.* -11. used to show distances □ *We drove for miles.* -12. **I bought/sold it for $10** the price was $10 when I bought/sold it □ *You can eat there for under $30.* -13. used to show who is affected or concerned by something □ *The work should be easy for someone like you.* □ *I have enormous respect for her.* -14. **she's tall for her age** she is surprisingly tall when you consider her age. -15. **the old name for London** the old name that means or describes London □ *What's the Greek for "mother"?* -16. **to vote for sb/sthg** to vote in favor of or in support of sb/sthg. ◇ *conj* because (literary use).

◆ **for all** ◇ *prep* -1. in spite of <sthg> □ *He's a very unhappy man for all his money.* -2. when you consider how little... □ *For all the good it's done me, I might as well have stayed at* home. □ *He can go to hell, for all I care.* ◇ *conj* **for all I know, she's already left** she has perhaps already left.

FOR (*abbr of* **free on rail**) *adv* at a price that includes all the seller's costs up to the delivery of goods to the railroad for shipment.

forage ['fɒrɪdʒ] *vi* [person, animal] to search for food □ *They foraged for roots and berries to stay alive.*

foray ['fɒreɪ] *n* -1. [into enemy area] a sudden short attack on enemy land by soldiers. -2. [into politics, publishing, television] an attempt to enter a new field of work or activity □ *After a brief foray into journalism she went into business.*

forbad, forbade [fəʳ'bæd] *past tense of* **forbid**.

forbearing [fɔːʳ'beərɪŋ] *adj* [person] who is patient and forgives people □ *a forbearing nature/attitude.*

forbid [fəʳ'bɪd] (*pt* **forbade** OR **forbad**, *pp* **forbid** OR **forbidden**, *cont* **forbidding**) *vt* [action, activity] to tell somebody firmly or officially not to do <sthg> □ *I forbid it.* □ *The government continues to forbid the use of these drugs.* □ *I am forbidden to disclose that information.* □ *I forbid you to leave the house.* ■ **God** OR **Heaven forbid!** a phrase used to show one hopes very much that something will not happen.

forbidden [fəʳ'bɪdn] ◇ *past participle of* **forbid**. ◇ *adj* -1. [place] that one is not allowed to visit □ *Certain areas were forbidden to foreigners.* -2. [subject] that one is not allowed to talk or write about □ *For this writer there is no such thing as a forbidden topic.* -3. [activity] that one is not allowed to do □ *Smoking is strictly forbidden.*

forbidding [fəʳ'bɪdɪŋ] *adj* [person, place] that looks unfriendly or frightening □ *The house looked dark and forbidding.* □ *a forbidding task.*

force [fɔːʳs] ◇ *n* -1. [of an explosion, earthquake] strength and power □ *We felt the force of the blast from five miles away.* □ *Her singing voice has lost some of its legendary force.* -2. [of a person] physical strength or violence □ *The police used force to enter the building.* ■ **by force** using physical strength or violence □ *We had to open the door by force.* -3. [of gravity, magnetism] the pushing or pulling effect of one thing on another □ *the force of gravity* □ *the magnetic force.* -4. somebody or something that has a strong influence or powerful effect over people or things □ *the forces of evil.* ■ **to do sthg from force of habit** to do sthg without thinking because one has done it many times before □ *I still refer to the store by its old name from force of habit.* -5. **to be in/come into force** [law, regulation, agreement] to be used/start being used □ *The ban will come into force as of tomorrow.*

◇ *vt* -1. [person] to make <sb> do something they do not want to do □ *They forced him to resign.* □ *I was forced to admit I was wrong.* □ *I had to force myself to get out of bed this morning.* □ *The company was forced into bankruptcy.* -2. [door, lock, case] to use physical strength to open <sthg> □ *The burglars had forced an entry through the bathroom window.* □ *They had* to *force open the window lock.* **-3. to force one's way through/into sthg** to use physical strength to get through/into sthg □ *A few demonstrators managed to force their way through the police cordon.* □ *He forced his way into the building.* **-4.** [decision, issue] to cause <sthg> to be dealt with more quickly. **-5. to force a smile/laugh** to smile/laugh unwillingly or with difficulty.

◆ **forces** *npl* **-1. the forces** a collective term for the army, navy, and airforce. **-2. to join forces** to work together in order to achieve something □ *We are joining forces with the government to promote AIDS awareness.*

◆ **in force** *adv* in large numbers □ *The fans turned out in force.*

◆ **by force of** *prep* as a result of doing or using <sthg> □ *She won the argument by sheer force of reason.*

◆ **force back** *vt sep* **-1. to force a group of people back** to use force to move a group of people backward □ *The police forced the demonstrators back.* **-2. to force an emotion back** to control an emotion so that other people do not notice it □ *She forced back the tears.*

◆ **force down** *vt sep* **-1. to force sthg down** to eat or drink sthg that one does not really want. **-2. to force an aircraft down** to make an aircraft land before it arrives at the place where it was going.

forced [fɔːrst] *adj* **-1. forced labor** work done by prisoners in very bad conditions. **-2.** [humor, conversation] that is not enjoyable because it takes a lot of effort; [smile, laugh] that does not show real pleasure because it is not sincere.

forced landing *n* the sudden landing of an aircraft that has developed problem.

force-feed *vt* to make <a person or animal> eat when they do not want to.

forceful [ˈfɔːrsfl] *adj* **-1.** [person] who expresses opinions strongly and gets other people to agree with them □ *She has a strong and forceful personality.* **-2.** [argument] that is very convincing; [impression] that has a strong effect on somebody □ *The whole scene made a very forceful impression on me.*

forcefully [ˈfɔːrsflɪ] *adv* [express, argue, speak] *see* **forceful** □ *He spoke out forcefully against the country's human rights abuses.*

forceps [ˈfɔːrseps] *npl* a medical instrument like a pair of scissors with curved ends, used for holding things firmly □ *a pair of forceps.*

forcible [ˈfɔːrsəbl] *adj* **-1.** [removal, detention] that is done using physical force □ *the forcible repatriation of illegal immigrants.* **-2. to be a forcible reminder of sthg** to remind people of sthg in a strong and clear way □ *The iron gates stood as a forcible reminder of what the camp had once been.*

forcibly [ˈfɔːrsəblɪ] *adv* [enter, impose, remind] *see* **forcible.**

ford [fɔːrd] ◇ *n* a place in a river or stream where the water is not very deep and where one can cross by foot or in a car. ◇ *vt* to cross <a river or stream> at a ford.

Ford [fɔːrd], **Henry** (1863–1947) a US businessman and car manufacturer. He was the first person to use a production line to make cars in large numbers.

fore [fɔːr] ◇ *adj* [wing, deck] that is at the front of an animal, ship, or aircraft. ◇ *n* **to come to the fore** to become popular or important □ *This technology came to the fore during the 1980s.*

forearm [ˈfɔːrɑːrm] *n* the part of the arm between the hand and the elbow.

forebears [ˈfɔːrbeərz] *npl* one's ancestors (formal use).

foreboding [fɔːrˈboudɪŋ] *n* [of evil, disaster, danger] a feeling that something bad will happen □ *She had a foreboding that things would go seriously wrong.*

forecast [US ˈfɔːrkæst, GB ˈfɔːkɑːst] (*pt* & *pp* **forecast** OR **forecasted**) ◇ *n* a statement, usually official, about a particular subject that says what one thinks will happen in the future □ *a sales/economic forecast.* ◇ *vt* [weather, result, level] to make a forecast about <sthg> □ *Economists have forecasted 3% growth next year.*

forecaster [US ˈfɔːrkæstr, GB ˈfɔːkɑːstə] *n* a person whose job is to forecast profits, economic growth etc □ *an economic forecaster.*

foreclose [fɔːrˈklouz] ◇ *vt* **to foreclose a mortgage** to stop a mortgage and take possession of the property it was used to buy, because the money has not been repaid as agreed. ◇ *vi*: *The bank has threatened to foreclose on him/his mortgage.*

foreclosure [fɔːrˈklouʒər] *n: see* **foreclose** □ *The bank has threatened me with foreclosure.*

forecourt [ˈfɔːrkɔːrt] *n* GB the open area in front of a large building, especially a garage or station.

forefathers [ˈfɔːrfɑːðərz] *npl* one's ancestors.

forefinger [ˈfɔːrfɪŋɡər] *n* the finger next to one's thumb.

forefront [ˈfɔːrfrʌnt] *n* **to be in** OR **at the forefront of sthg** [of research, a struggle, campaign] to be among the people leading sthg □ *She's at the forefront of the pro-choice campaign.* □ *Pro-Impex, a company at the forefront of communications technology.*

forego [fɔːrˈgou] *vt* = **forgo.**

foregoing [fɔːrˈgouɪŋ] (formal use) ◇ *adj* [information, analysis] that has just been mentioned □ *The foregoing statement was issued by the department's spokesperson.* ◇ *n* **the foregoing** a phrase used to refer to something that has just been mentioned.

foregone conclusion [ˌfɔːrgɒn-] *n* **a foregone conclusion** something that has not yet happened but that one believes must happen and cannot be avoided □ *The outcome of the election was a foregone conclusion.*

foreground [ˈfɔːrɡraund] *n* the part of a picture, view, photograph etc that is or seems nearest to one □ *A tree stood in the foreground.*

forehand [ˈfɔːrhænd] *n* [in tennis, squash, badminton] a shot in which the palm of the hand

faces the ball as it is hit □ *a forehand smash.*
NOTE: Compare **backhand**.

forehead ['fɒrəd] *n* the part of the face above the eyebrows and below the top of the head.

foreign ['fɒrən] *adj* -1. [country] that is not one's own; [person, language, import] that is from a foreign country □ *He sounded foreign to me.* □ *She had a foreign accent.* -2. [policy, news, vacation] that deals with or involves foreign countries □ *our foreign news desk.* -3. **a foreign object/substance** an object/a substance that has entered something by accident and can cause harm. -4. **to be foreign to sb** not to be typical of sb's character, behavior etc □ *Such thinking is entirely foreign to them.*

foreign affairs *npl* issues that concern one's own country's relations with other countries.

foreign aid *n* help, e.g. money, food, or goods, that is given to poorer foreign countries □ *foreign aid workers/shipments/supplies.*

foreign body *n* a small object or insect that has entered somewhere, e.g. part of the body, by accident □ *Irritation in the eye may be caused by a foreign body.*

foreign competition *n* BUSINESS competition in a particular business or industry from other countries.

foreign correspondent *n* a journalist who reports news from a foreign country.

foreign currency *n* money that is used in another country.

foreigner ['fɒrənər] *n* a person who comes from a foreign country □ *Foreigners are not allowed into the country without a visa.*

foreign exchange *n* the system of buying and selling money from different countries □ *The dollar has fallen sharply against the yen on foreign exchange markets.* □ *Foreign exchange rates are fluctuating wildly.*

foreign investment *n* money invested in foreign countries; the act of investing in foreign countries.

foreign minister *n* a minister who is responsible for their country's relations with other countries.

Foreign Office *n* **the Foreign Office** the British government department that deals with relations with other countries.

Foreign Secretary *n* the British government minister who is head of the Foreign Office.

foreign service *n* US the people who are employed by their government to work in embassies abroad.

foreleg ['fɔːleg] *n* one of the front legs of an animal.

foreman ['fɔːmən] (*pl* **foremen** [-mən]) *n* -1. an experienced worker who is in charge of other workers in a factory, on a building site etc, and reports to a manager. -2. a member of a jury who tells the court their verdict at the end of a trial.

foremost ['fɔːmoust] ◇ *adj* **the foremost writer/expert etc** the best or most important writer/expert etc □ *It is one of the country's foremost research centers.* ◇ *adv* **first and foremost** most importantly □ *Although a successful writer, she is, first and foremost, a teacher.*

forename ['fɔːneɪm] *n* one's first name, chosen by one's parents (formal use).

forensic [fə'rensɪk] *adj* [department, evidence, scientist] that is concerned with the use of forensic science.

forensic medicine *n* the use of medical knowledge to help solve crimes.

forensic science *n* the use of scientific techniques to help solve crimes.

forerunner ['fɔːrʌnər] *n* a person, thing, or idea that started something that later developed into something bigger or better □ *one of the forerunners of modern psychology.*

foresee [fɔː'siː] (*pt* **foresaw** [-'sɔː], *pp* **foreseen**) *vt* [change, problem, event] to know <that something will or will probably happen> before it does happen □ *I can't foresee any reasons why they would refuse this contract.* □ *Nobody could have foreseen that the bridge would collapse.*

foreseeable [fɔː'siːəbl] *adj* [accident, problem] that can be expected to happen and is therefore not surprising. ■ **for the foreseeable future** as far ahead in the future as one can see or plan □ *He will be staying with the company for the foreseeable future.* ■ **in the foreseeable future** quite soon □ *I don't think any changes will be made in the foreseeable future.*

foreseen [fɔː'siːn] *past participle of* **foresee**.

foreshadow [fɔː'ʃædoʊ] *vt* [event, development] to be a sign of <sthg that is going to happen> □ *The company's sell-off was foreshadowed by the recent decline in profits.*

foreshortened [fɔː'ʃɔːtnd] *adj* that has been drawn, painted etc as it looks in real life, so that part of it looks smaller or shorter because it is further away or is at an angle.

foresight ['fɔːsaɪt] *n* the ability to see what is likely to happen in a particular situation and to do something about it □ *Fortunately, they had the foresight to take out full insurance.*

foreskin ['fɔːskɪn] *n* a piece of skin that covers the end of the penis.

forest ['fɒrəst] *n* a large area of trees that grow close together □ *a pine forest.*

forestall [fɔː'stɔːl] *vt* [person, attempt, criticism] to prevent <sb> from doing something, or prevent <sthg> from happening, by doing something else first □ *There were large numbers of policemen there to forestall any trouble.*

forestation [ˌfɒrə'steɪʃn] *n* the practice of planting trees over a wide area.

forestry ['fɒrəstrɪ] *n* the profession of growing and looking after forests.

Forestry Commission *n* **the Forestry Commission** in Britain, the organization in charge of the management of forests.

foretaste ['fɔːteɪst] *n* **to be a foretaste of sthg** to be a small example of sthg that will happen later □ *As a foretaste of your trip, let me show you a few photographs of the area.*

foretell [fɔː'tel] (*pt & pp* **foretold**) *vt* to say

<that something will happen in the future>, before it actually does happen □ *Who could have foretold that prices would fall so sharply?*

forethought ['fɔːrθɔːt] *n* careful thought that is given to something before it happens in order to make it more successful or avoid problems □ *A little forethought can save a lot of time and trouble.*

foretold [fɔːrˈtould] *past tense & past participle of* **foretell**.

forever [fərˈevər] *adv* **-1.** from now until the end of time □ *I'll love you forever.* □ *The days of the great Hollywood legends are gone forever.* **-2. to be forever doing sthg** to do sthg too often in a way that annoys people (informal use) □ *He's forever telling me how broke he is!*

forewarn [fɔːrˈwɔːrn] *vt* to warn <sb> about something bad that is going to happen so that they can be prepared □ *The gang appears to have been forewarned of the raid.*

foreword ['fɔːrwɜːrd] *n* a text at the beginning of a book that tells people about the author and the book.

forfeit ['fɔːrfət] ◇ *n* something one loses or has to do as a punishment □ *If you lose, you have to pay a forfeit.* ◇ *vt* [property, deposit, right] to lose <sthg>, especially because one has broken an agreement or done something wrong □ *You understand that in signing this contract, you forfeit your right to the estate?*

forgave [fərˈgeɪv] *past tense of* **forgive**.

forge [fɔːrdʒ] ◇ *n* a place where metal is heated and made into objects, such as horseshoes and gates. ◇ *vt* **-1.** [metal, iron] to heat and shape <sthg> by hammering it. **-2.** [friendship, alliance] to create <sthg> with a lot of effort and determination □ *We have forged strong links with churches in Johannesburg.* **-3.** [money, passport, signature] to make an illegal copy of <sthg> in order to deceive people; [painting, work of art] to make <sthg> that copies the style of a famous artist so that people pay a lot of money for it.

◆ **forge ahead** *vi* to make progress quickly, especially more quickly than other people □ *They are forging ahead with plans to open up ten new stores.*

forger ['fɔːrdʒər] *n* a person who forges money, passports etc.

forgery ['fɔːrdʒərɪ] (*pl* **forgeries**) *n* **-1.** something that has been forged, e.g. a signature, passport, or painting □ *The painting was discovered to be a forgery.* **-2.** [of money, passport] *see* **forge** □ *He was accused of forgery.*

forget [fərˈget] (*pt* **forgot**, *pp* **forgotten**, *cont* **forgetting**) ◇ *vt* **-1.** [person, name, fact] not to remember <sb/sthg> □ *I'll never forget you, Jack.* □ *I always forget to turn the alarm on.* □ *He completely forgot (that) we were coming.* □ *I never forget a face.* □ *I forget which company he works for.* □ *I'll never forget buying my first car.* ■ **to forget oneself** to behave in an unusual or uncontrolled way, as a result of a strong emotion □ *Professor Marget forgot himself to the extent of hitting the student over the head with a book.* **-2.** [scarf, book] to leave <sthg> behind in a place when one goes away, without intending to leave it □ *Don't forget your umbrella.* **-3.** [idea, event] to deliberately stop thinking about or doing <sthg> □ *We might as well forget the whole thing!* □ *Let's forget our differences.* □ *Oh, forget it!*

◇ *vi* **-1.** not to remember something □ *Sorry, I had completely forgotten about it.* □ *And try not to forget in future!* **-2.** to deliberately stop thinking about something □ *I can forgive but I can't forget.* □ *How could I ever forget!* □ *We agreed to forget about the outburst.*

forgetful [fərˈgetfl] *adj* [person] who forgets things easily, especially things that have to be done □ *She became forgetful in her old age.*

forget-me-not *n* a plant with tiny blue flowers.

forgive [fərˈgɪv] (*pt* **forgave**, *pp* **forgiven** [-ˈgɪvn]) *vt* **-1.** to say or feel that one is no longer angry with <sb>; to say or feel that one is no longer angry with somebody about <sthg> □ *Can you ever forgive me?* □ *I can never forgive him for what he did.* □ *Please forgive his behavior.* **-2. one could be forgiven for thinking…** a phrase used to say that it is very easy to understand why somebody might think a particular thing □ *If you didn't know him very well you could be forgiven for thinking that making money was his only interest in life.*

forgiveness [fərˈgɪvnəs] *n* the act of forgiving somebody □ *They asked his forgiveness.*

forgiving [fərˈgɪvɪŋ] *adj* [person] who forgives people easily.

forgo [fɔːrˈgou] (*pt* **forwent**, *pp* **forgone** [-ˈgɒn]) *vt* [opportunity, vacation] to decide not to have <sthg> □ *I had to forgo my trip to India because of work pressures.*

forgot [fərˈgɒt] *past tense of* **forget**.

forgotten [fərˈgɒtn] *past participle of* **forget**.

fork [fɔːrk] ◇ *n* **-1.** [for eating] a small tool used for eating with that has three or four points at one end and is often used with a knife held in the other hand □ *a knife and fork.* **-2.** [for digging] a tool with a handle at one end and three or four large metal points at the other, used for digging □ *a garden fork.* **-3.** [in a road] a place where a road, river etc separates into two parts; one of these parts □ *We came to a fork in the road.* □ *Take the right fork for Craster.* ◇ *vi* [road, path, river] to separate into two parts.

◆ **fork out** (informal use) ◇ *vt fus* **to fork out money** to pay money for something, especially a lot of money or too much money □ *Some parents fork out $10,000 a year for private school fees.* ◇ *vi*: *We've just had to fork out for a new computer.*

forklift ['fɔːrklɪft] *n* **a forklift (truck)** a vehicle with two metal arms at the front that are placed under heavy goods and used to lift and move them.

forlorn [fərˈlɔːrn] *adj* **-1.** [person, face, expression] that looks lonely and sad □ *He stood there looking lost and forlorn.* **-2.** [place, landscape, building] that is empty and looks depressing □ *a forlorn-looking house on the edge of the lake.* **-3. a forlorn hope/attempt** a hope/attempt

form 412

that has very little chance of success □ *Jack made a forlorn attempt at a smile.*

form [fɔːʳm] ◇ *n* **-1.** [of a mountain, building, object] the shape of something □ *The cake was in the form of a heart.* □ *The drug is also available in tablet form.* **-2.** [of government, travel, exercise] a type of something □ *It's a rare form of cancer.* ■ **in the form of sthg** a phrase used to give more precise information about something that one has just mentioned □ *Help soon appeared in the form of Mr Gray.* □ *His major sugar intake is in the form of chocolate.* ■ **to take the form of sthg** a phrase used to give details about the way in which something is presented or takes place □ *The interview took the form of an informal chat.* **-3.** [of a person] a person's physical condition; a person's level of performance □ *Given their current form, they're unlikely to win.* ■ **to be on form** GB to be performing well; to be feeling well. **-4.** [for writing on] an official document that one writes one's details on for a particular purpose □ *a booking form* □ *Please fill in* OR *out the enclosed form.* **-5.** [of a man, woman, child] a person's figure □ *her slender/tiny form.* **-6.** GB EDUCATION a class in a school □ *She's in the first form.* **-7.** *phrase* **true to form** a phrase used to say that something that somebody did is typical of them □ *Clark, true to form, arrived half an hour late.*

◇ *vt* **-1.** [organization, friendship, alliance] to create <sthg> □ *The company was formed in 1987.* □ *Valleys are most commonly formed by the action of rivers.* **-2.** [circle, line] to make <a shape> by moving into particular positions □ *The applicants formed a line.* **-3.** to be a particular part of something □ *These ads will form the basis of our campaign.* □ *Exports form 60% of our sales.*

◇ *vi* **-1.** [cloud, line, crowd] to begin to exist and grow □ *Doubts began to form in my mind.* **-2. to form into a circle/line etc** to come together and make a circle/line etc □ *We formed into groups.*

formal [ˈfɔːʳml] *adj* **-1.** [language, speech, behavior] that is correct, serious, and suitable for official situations □ *I wrote them a formal letter of complaint.* □ *She was very formal, addressing us by our surnames only.* **-2. a formal occasion/dinner etc** an occasion/a dinner etc that follows socially correct rules and requires special clothes to be worn □ *They are having a formal wedding.* **-3. formal clothes** special clothes worn on official occasions □ *Guests are required to wear formal dress.* **-4. a formal decision/offer** an official decision/offer □ *A formal announcement will be made this afternoon.* □ *Formal talks are being held in Washington.* **-5. formal education/training etc** education/training etc that is given in a school or college □ *He has no formal qualifications.*

formality [fɔːʳˈmælətɪ] (*pl* **formalities**) *n* **-1.** correct formal behavior and attention to accepted rules □ *She treated him with cold formality.* **-2.** something that must be done because it is a rule, although it will not affect a particular person, decision, or result □ *There are just a few formalities I have to observe, sir.* □ *The*

interview was just a formality. □ *customs formalities.*

formalize, -ise [ˈfɔːʳməlaɪz] *vt* [plan, agreement, arrangement] to make <sthg> official □ *The deal has yet to be formalized.*

formally [ˈfɔːʳməlɪ] *adv* [behave, dress, decide] see **formal** □ *The proposal has now been formally accepted.* □ *He greeted us very formally.*

format [ˈfɔːʳmæt] (*pt* & *pp* **formatted**, *cont* **formatting**) ◇ *n* **-1.** [of a book] the size, shape, number of pages etc of a book or magazine □ *A4 format.* **-2.** [of a meeting] the way in which a meeting, television program etc is organized and presented. □ *The show is back in a new format.* **-3.** COMPUTING the way in which data is arranged on a disk. ◇ *vt* to prepare <a computer disk or diskette> so that it can have data entered onto it in a particular way.

formation [fɔːʳˈmeɪʃn] *n* **-1. in formation** arranged in a particular order or pattern □ *The planes flew past in formation.* **-2.** [of plans, rocks, an idea] the gradual creation and development of something □ *unusual rock formations.* **-3.** [of an alliance, government, company] the process of forming something □ *the formation of self-help groups.*

formative [ˈfɔːʳmətɪv] *adj* **a formative influence/experience etc** an influence/experience etc that greatly affects one's character or the way one thinks. ■ **formative years** the years during which a person's character is formed □ *They say that one to three are a child's most formative years.*

former [ˈfɔːʳməʳ] ◇ *adj* **-1. a former president/teacher etc** a person who used to be a president/teacher etc, but is not any more □ *the former prime minister of Australia, Bob Hawke* □ *There are still strong links with the former colony.* ■ **one's former boss/job etc** a boss/job etc that one used to have □ *I met a former student of mine yesterday.* **-2. in former times** OR **days** in the past. **-3.** that relates to the first of two people or things that have just been mentioned □ *I prefer the former idea to the latter.* ◇ *n* **the former** the first of the two people or things that have just been mentioned □ *Of the two options, I prefer the former.*

formerly [ˈfɔːʳməʳlɪ] *adv* in the past, but not now □ *The house was formerly owned by a priest.*

form feed *n* COMPUTING a command to a printer to move to the next sheet of paper.

Formica™ [fɔːʳˈmaɪkə] *n* a hard plastic that is used to cover tables and kitchen surfaces.

formidable [ˈfɔːʳmɪdəbl] *adj* **-1.** [person, voice, opponent] that is very impressive and causes a feeling of fear and respect □ *She's a formidable woman.* □ *a formidable intellect.* **-2.** [task, challenge] that is difficult to deal with and makes one worried □ *We face formidable obstacles.* □ *They succeeded against formidable odds.*

formless [ˈfɔːʳmləs] *adj* [clothes, structure] without a clear and definite shape.

Fortune 500

formula ['fɔːʳmjələ] (*pl* **formulas** OR **formulae** [-liː]) *n* -**1.** MATH & SCIENCE a sequence of letters, figures, and signs that represents a particular rule or fact □ *a mathematical formula* □ *What's the formula for calculating the area of a triangle?* -**2.** CHEMISTRY a sequence of letters, figures, and signs that represent what a substance is made up of □ *The formula for sulfuric acid is* H_2SO_4. □ *The fuel is made to a secret formula.* -**3.** [for success] a way of doing or saying something that will make something difficult work successfully □ *a formula for success* □ *We must find a formula that is acceptable to both sides.* -**4.** RACING a word used before a number to refer to a particular type of racing car or car race □ *Formula One.*

formulate ['fɔːʳmjəleɪt] *vt* -**1.** [question, answer, idea] to choose particular words to express <sthg> □ *It took Gerard some time to formulate a reply.* -**2.** [policy, strategy, plan] to decide the details of <sthg> □ *The party had only recently formulated its financial strategy.*

formulation [ˌfɔːʳmjəˈleɪʃn] *n*: *see* **formulate** □ *the formulation of new policies.*

fornicate ['fɔːʳnɪkeɪt] *vi* to have sex with a person one is not married to (literary use).

forsake [fəʳˈseɪk] (*pt* **forsook**, *pp* **forsaken**) *vt* [person, habit, place] to abandon <sb/sthg> completely (literary use).

forsaken [fəʳˈseɪkən] *past participle of* **forsake**.

forsook [fəʳˈsʊk] *past tense of* **forsake**.

Forster ['fɔːʳstəʳ], **E.M.** (1879–1970) a British novelist whose works include *A Passage to India* and *A Room with a View.*

forsythia [US fəʳˈsɪθɪə, GB fɔːʳˈsaɪθɪə] *n* a kind of bush with yellow flowers that bloom in early spring.

fort [fɔːʳt] *n* a strong building or group of buildings designed to provide defense against a military attack. ▪ **to hold the fort** to look after something or somebody temporarily □ *I'm holding the fort for my parents while they're away.*

forte [US fɔːʳt, GB 'fɔːteɪ] *n* something that one is especially good at □ *Music was never my forte.*

forth [fɔːʳθ] *adv* -**1.** [go, bring, send] out from a place (literary use) □ *We set forth on our adventure.* -**2. from that day forth** from that day onward □ *And from that day forth, they never spoke again.*

forthcoming [fɔːʳθˈkʌmɪŋ] *adj* -**1. a forthcoming meeting/election etc** a meeting/an election etc that has been planned to happen soon □ *A cabaret and a Christmas party are among the forthcoming attractions.* -**2. to be forthcoming** [help, answer, information] to be made available or be given to somebody □ *The necessary resources are rarely forthcoming.* -**3.** [person] who is willing to give somebody information □ *I found him very open and forthcoming.* □ *I tried to ask her about it, but she wasn't very forthcoming.*

forthright ['fɔːʳθraɪt] *adj* [person] who says what they think honestly.

forthwith [ˌfɔːʳθˈwɪθ] *adv* immediately (formal use).

fortieth ['fɔːʳtɪəθ] *num* 40th; number 40 in a series; *see also* **fiftieth**.

fortification [ˌfɔːʳtɪfɪˈkeɪʃn] *n* [of a town, building] *see* **fortify**.
◆ **fortifications** *npl* walls, ditches etc that are built around a town or building in order to protect or defend it □ *Some of the city's old fortifications still remain.*

fortified wine [ˌfɔːʳtəfaɪd-] *n* a drink such as port or sherry made from wine to which extra alcohol has been added.

fortify ['fɔːʳtəfaɪ] (*pt* & *pp* **fortified**) *vt* -**1.** [city, coast, town] to make <a place> strong, e.g. by building a wall around it to defend it against attack. -**2.** [resolve, determination, person] to make <sb/sthg> stronger □ *I took a large gulp of wine to fortify myself before going in.*

fortitude ['fɔːʳtətjuːd] *n* the mental strength and courage one needs when one has to deal with a difficult or painful situation □ *She bore her misfortune with great fortitude.*

Fort Knox [-ˈnɒks] a fort in Kentucky where the US gold supply is kept. It is used as a symbol for a place that cannot be broken into easily.

fortnight ['fɔːʳtnaɪt] *n* GB a period of two weeks □ *I'll see you again in a fortnight.*

fortnightly ['fɔːʳtnaɪtlɪ] GB ◇ *adj* **a fortnightly newspaper/edition etc** a newspaper/an edition etc that appears every two weeks. ▪ **a fortnightly visit/meeting etc** a visit/meeting etc that happens every two weeks □ *Meetings take place at fortnightly intervals.* ◇ *adv* [appear, visit, meet] *She sends in a report fortnightly on a Monday.*

fortress ['fɔːʳtrəs] *n* a large fort or fortified town.

fortuitous [fɔːʳˈtjuːətəs] *adj* [meeting, decision] that happens by chance and has a good result (formal use) □ *It was quite fortuitous the way we met.*

fortunate ['fɔːʳtʃənət] *adj* [person, event, choice] lucky □ *You're very fortunate to have such wonderful children.*

fortunately ['fɔːʳtʃənətlɪ] *adv* a word used to show that one believes that something is fortunate □ *Nobody was injured, fortunately.* □ *Fortunately for him, the store was still open.*

fortune ['fɔːʳtʃən] *n* -**1.** a large amount of money □ *He earns a fortune.* □ *That car must have cost a fortune.* -**2.** luck □ *good/bad fortune* □ *Fortune smiled on us.* -**3. to tell sb's fortune** to say what sb's future life will be like by looking at the palm of their hand, a crystal ball, a deck of cards etc.
◆ **fortunes** *npl* **sb's fortunes** the good or bad events that happen to sb in their life □ *The book traces the changing fortunes of its hero, Charlie Snow, and his family.*

Fortune 500 [-faɪvˈhʌndrəd] *n* a list made each year of the 500 largest and most successful companies in the USA.

fortune-teller *n* a person who tells people's fortunes, usually for money.

forty ['fɔːtɪ] *num* the number 40; *see also* **fifty.**

forum ['fɔːrəm] (*pl* **forums**) *n* -1. HISTORY the open space where public business was carried out in ancient Rome. -2. [for a debate] a place, TV program, magazine etc where subjects of interest can be discussed □ *The conference provides a useful forum for debate.*

forward ['fɔːrwərd] ◇ *adv* -1. **to move/step forward** to move/step in the direction that one is already facing □ *She leaned forward and whispered something in his ear.* -2. **to bring sthg forward** to change the date of sthg to an earlier time □ *We'll have to bring July's meeting forward to next week.* -3. **to look forward** to look toward the future or a later time. ■ **to put the clock forward** to change the clock so that it shows a later time.
◇ *adj* -1. [movement, seat on train] toward the front □ *I asked for a forward cabin.* -2. toward the future □ *The project is no farther forward now than it was last year.* ■ **forward planning** planning for the future, especially in business. -3. [person] who is too confident and does not show enough respect □ *I hope you don't think I'm being forward.*
◇ *n* SPORT [in soccer, rugby, hockey] a player who plays closer to the other team's goal than the other players in their team.
◇ *vt* [goods, information] to send <sthg> to the person who has asked for it; [letters, mail] to send <sthg> on to somebody's new address when they have moved □ *Please forward all correspondence to our new address.*

forwarding address ['fɔːrwərdɪŋ-] *n* the new address a person leaves with the people at their old address so that their mail can be sent to them after they have moved □ *They went without leaving a forwarding address.*

forward-looking [-'lʊkɪŋ] *adj* [person] who has modern ideas and thinks that it is important to plan for the future □ *a forward-looking attitude/policy.*

forwards ['fɔːrwərdz] *adv* GB = **forward.**

forwent [fɔː'went] *past tense of* **forgo.**

fossick ['fɒsək] *vi* AUS to search somewhere for something by moving things around roughly.

fossil ['fɒsl] *n* the print or part of a plant or animal that died long ago and has been preserved in rock, ice etc.

fossil fuel *n* a fuel, e.g. coal, petroleum, or natural gas, that is found in the earth and is made of the remains of plants and animals that died long ago.

fossilized, -ised ['fɒsəlaɪzd] *adj* [animal, plant, bone] that has become a fossil.

foster ['fɒstər] ◇ *adj* a **foster mother/father** a woman/man who looks after somebody else's child as a member of their own family for a period of time □ *He was taken into a foster family.* ◇ *vt* -1. to look after <somebody else's child> as a foster parent. -2. to help <an idea, illusion, hope> etc to grow or develop □ *policies aimed at fostering economic growth/the arts/friendly relations.*

foster child *n* a child who is fostered.

foster parent *n* a person who fosters somebody else's child.

fought [fɔːt] *past tense & past participle of* **fight.**

foul [faʊl] ◇ *adj* -1. [water, air] dirty □ *The air in this city is really foul.* -2. [weather, smell, person] very unpleasant □ *She's in a foul mood today.* □ *Mark was quite foul to me earlier.* □ *What a foul smell!* -3. **foul language** language that is rude and is full of swear words. -4. **to fall foul of sb** to do something that makes sb angry with one. ■ **to fall foul of sthg** [of the law, police] to do something that makes trouble for one from sthg □ *Individuals who fail to obtain a license could fall foul of the new regulations.*
◇ *n* SPORT an action that is against the rules.
◇ *vt* -1. [sea, beach] to make <a place> dirty □ *'Please do not allow dogs to foul the footpath.'* -2. SPORT [opponent] to do something to <another player> that is against the rules. -3. [propeller, anchor] to stop <a device> from working by getting twisted around it.
◆ **foul up** *vt sep* **to foul sthg up** [plan, life, project] to spoil sthg (informal use).

foul-mouthed [-'maʊðd] *adj* [person] who swears a lot and uses rude words.

foul play *n* -1. SPORT actions that are against the rules. -2. criminal activity that results in something serious, especially in somebody's death □ *The police suspect foul play.*

found [faʊnd] ◇ *past tense & past participle of* **find.** ◇ *vt* -1. [hospital, school, organization] to cause <sthg> to exist by paying for it □ *The company was founded in 1846.* -2. [town, building, castle] to start building <sthg>. -3. **to be founded on sthg** [on fact, a belief] to be based on sthg □ *The article is founded entirely on rumor.*

foundation [faʊn'deɪʃn] *n* -1. [of a friendship, education, belief] the important fact or idea on which something is based □ *Our marriage is built on solid foundations.* -2. [for charity, research] an organization that provides money for charity, research etc □ *a science foundation.* -3. [for one's face] a cream that is rubbed into the face as a base for make-up □ *foundation cream.* -4. [of a hospital, company, school] *see* **found** □ *since the bank's foundation in 1896.*
◆ **foundations** *npl* the solid layer of concrete, stones etc that a building stands on □ *They're laying the foundations of the new library.*

foundation stone *n* a block of stone that is part of the wall of a public building, has words on it, and is often uncovered at a special ceremony when the building is completed.

founder ['faʊndər] ◇ *n* a person who founds a company, school, organization etc. ◇ *vi* -1. [ship, boat] to fill with water and sink. -2. [plan, hope, project] to fail □ *The plan foundered in its early stages.*

founder member *n* = **founding member.**

founding father [,faʊndɪŋ-] *n* a person who establishes an important company, organization, idea etc (formal use).

◆**Founding Father** *n* the Founding Fathers the group of men who wrote the US Constitution in 1787. They include George Washington and Thomas Jefferson.

founding member *n* one of the first members of a society, club, company, movement etc.

foundry ['faʊndrɪ] (*pl* **foundries**) *n* a place where metal or glass is melted and made into particular shapes.

fount [faʊnt] *n* **a fount of knowledge/information etc** a person who is the source of knowledge/information etc (literary use).

fountain ['faʊntən] *n* -1. a structure that sends jets of water into the air and is often used to decorate public places or gardens. -2. a jet of water, oil etc that rises into the air.

fountain pen *n* a pen with a container inside that one fills with ink.

four [fɔːr] *num* the number 4; *see also* **five.** ■ **on all fours** on one's hands and knees.

four-leaf clover, **four-leaved clover** [-liːvd-] *n* a clover plant with four leaves instead of three that is believed to bring luck to the person who finds it.

four-letter word *n* any short word that people find offensive, usually because it relates to sex or one's body in an unpleasant way.

four-poster (bed) *n* a large bed with a post at each corner supporting a frame that curtains hang down from.

foursome ['fɔːrsəm] *n* a group of four people who do something together, especially for fun.

four-star *adj* **a four-star hotel/restaurant** a hotel/restaurant that is of a high standard.

fourteen [ˌfɔːrˈtiːn] *num* the number 14; *see also* **fifteen.**

fourteenth [ˌfɔːrˈtiːnθ] *num* 14th; number 14 in a series; *see also* **fifteenth.**

fourth [fɔːrθ] *num* 4th; number 4 in a series; *see also* **fifth.**

Fourth of July *n* the Fourth of July a US national holiday that marks the anniversary of the Declaration of Independence.

🐝 THE FOURTH OF JULY
The Fourth of July, also known as Independence Day, is one of the most important public holidays in the USA. Many cities organize street parades and displays of red, white, and blue fireworks at night. Buildings are covered with red, white, and blue decorations, or with US flags. Most people spend the day with their families having picnics, which traditionally include hot dogs and watermelon.

four-way stop *n* US a place where four roads meet. All vehicles must stop here and priority is given to the first vehicle that arrived.

four-wheel drive *n* a system in a vehicle in which all four wheels are connected directly to the engine; a vehicle that uses this system □ *a four-wheel drive car.*

fowl [faʊl] (*pl* **fowl** OR **fowls**) *n* a bird that is eaten for food, e.g. a chicken or pheasant; the meat of this bird eaten as food.

fox [fɒks] ◇ *n* a wild animal like a dog, with a pointed nose and ears, reddish fur, and a thick tail. ◇ *vt* [person] to trick <sb> by being more clever than them □ *That'll fox them!*

foxcub ['fɒkskʌb] *n* a young fox.

foxglove ['fɒksglʌv] *n* a tall plant with purple, pink, or white bell-shaped flowers growing on either side of a straight stem.

foxhole ['fɒkshoʊl] *n* a hole in the ground in which soldiers hide to shoot at the enemy.

foxhound ['fɒkshaʊnd] *n* a dog used to find and kill foxes.

foxhunt ['fɒkshʌnt] *n* an occasion when a fox is hunted by people on horses with dogs for sport.

foxhunting ['fɒkshʌntɪŋ] *n* the practice of hunting foxes with dogs.

fox terrier *n* a small dog with a white coat and dark markings.

foxy ['fɒksɪ] (*compar* **foxier**, *superl* **foxiest**) *adj* [woman] sexy (informal use).

foyer [US 'fɔɪr, GB 'fɔɪeɪ] *n* -1. [of a theater, hotel] the entrance hall of a public building. -2. [of a house] the entrance hall of a house.

FP *n* -1. *abbr of* **former pupil.** -2. *abbr of* **fireplug.**

FPA (*abbr of* **Family Planning Association**) *n* the FPA a British organization that gives free advice on family planning.

fr *abbr of* **franc.**

Fr RELIGION *abbr of* **father.**

fracas [US 'freɪkəs, GB 'frækɑː] (US *pl* **fracases** ['freɪkəsɪz], GB *pl* **fracas** ['frækɑːz]) *n* a noisy argument, often ending in a fight (formal use).

fraction ['frækʃn] *n* -1. MATH a part of a whole number, e.g. a half or a quarter. -2. a very small part or amount □ *a fraction of a second* □ *Lift it up a fraction higher.*

fractionally ['frækʃnəlɪ] *adv* **fractionally better/lower etc** very slightly better/lower etc.

fractious ['frækʃəs] *adj* [child, baby] who gets annoyed easily, usually because they are tired.

fracture ['fræktʃər] MEDICINE ◇ *n* a slight break or crack in a bone in one's body □ *a hip/skull fracture.* ◇ *vt* [arm, leg] to slightly break or crack <a bone in one's body> □ *She fractured her leg in the fall.* □ *He suffered a fractured skull.*

fragile [US 'frædʒl, GB -aɪl] *adj* -1. [cup, plate, structure] that is not strong and is easily broken □ *Careful, those ornaments are fragile.* -2. [health, relationship, peace] that is weak and is easily damaged or hurt □ *a fragile alliance.*

fragility [frəˈdʒɪlətɪ] *n*: *see* **fragile.**

fragment [*n* 'frægmənt, *vb* fræg'ment] ◇ *n* -1. [of glass, paper, rock] a small piece of something that has broken off a larger object □ *She gathered up the fragments and tried to piece them together.* -2. [of a conversation, piece of writing] a small part of something □ *Only fragments of her writing remain.* ◇ *vi* [paper, glass, rock] to break into small pieces.

fragmentary [US 'frægmənterı, GB -ərı] *adj* [information, knowledge, memory] that is not complete and consists of pieces or parts that are not connected with each other □ *Our understanding of their civilization is still fragmentary.*

fragmented [fræg'mentəd] *adj* [account, structure, society] that is made up of different parts that are not connected.

fragrance ['freigrəns] *n* -1. a pleasant smell □ *the fragrance of lavender.* -2. a perfume □ *a new fragrance for men.*

fragrant ['freigrənt] *adj* [flower, air, room] that has a pleasant smell that is not very strong.

frail [freil] *adj* -1. [person] who is weak and delicate, especially because of old age □ *a frail old woman.* -2. [structure, boat, shelter] that is easily broken.

frailty ['freiltı] (*pl* **frailties**) *n* a fault or weakness in somebody's character □ *ordinary human frailties.*

frame [freim] ◇ *n* -1. [of a picture, mirror] a solid structure, usually rectangular and made of wood, metal, or plastic, that surrounds a picture or a mirror □ *I think it would look better in a black frame.* □ *a picture frame.* -2. [of a door, window] the outer case which something fits inside; [of a bed, bicycle, boat] the main structure of an object to which other parts are added □ *a door/window frame* □ *The frame is made of aluminum.* -3. [of a person] the shape or size of somebody's body (literary use) □ *his large frame.*
◇ *vt* -1. [picture, photograph] to put <sthg> in a frame □ *I'd like to get this picture framed.* -2. [window, face] to surround <sthg> like a frame □ *Her face was framed with tight curls.* -3. [reply, question, apology] to put <sthg> into words (formal use) □ *Her reply was framed in the dull, official language of the courts.* -4. [person] to make <sb who is innocent> appear to be guilty of a crime by providing false evidence (informal use) □ *I was framed by the police!*

♦ **frames** *npl* the metal or plastic part of a pair of glasses that holds the lenses in place □ *I prefer round frames.*

frame of mind *n* the way a person is feeling and thinking at a particular time □ *I have to be in the right frame of mind for writing letters.*

framework ['freimwɜːrk] *n* -1. [of a ship, building] the main structure that supports something. -2. [of society, democracy] a set of ideas, beliefs, rules etc that allows people to deal with a particular question or matter □ *The document will provide a framework for negotiations.*

France [US fræns, GB frɑːns] a country in western Europe, with coastlines on the English Channel, the Atlantic Ocean, and the Mediterranean. SIZE: 549,000 sq kms. POPULATION: 57,500,000 (*French*). CAPITAL: Paris. LANGUAGE: French. CURRENCY: French franc.

franchise ['fræntʃaiz] *n* -1. POLITICS the right of a person to vote in public elections. -2. BUSINESS the right to sell a particular company's goods or services in a particular

place in their name; a store that has bought this right □ *a franchise-holder* □ *The firm is signing up around three franchises a month.*

franchisee [,fræntʃai'ziː] *n* the person or company that buys a franchise.

franchisor [,fræntʃai'zɔːr] *n* the company that sells a franchise.

Franco ['fræŋkoʊ], **General Francisco** (1892–1975) a Spanish soldier who led the right-wing Nationalist Party to victory in the Spanish Civil War in 1939. He ruled Spain as a dictator from then until his death.

frank [fræŋk] ◇ *adj* [person, discussion] honest and direct □ *To be perfectly frank, I never liked him anyway.* ◇ *vt* to put a special mark on <a letter> instead of a stamp, to show that the cost of mailing it has been paid.

Frankenstein ['fræŋkənstain] the title of a novel whose main character, Dr Frankenstein, creates a living man, or monster, that tries to destroy him. The name is often used to describe the monster.

Frankfurt ['fræŋkfɜːrt]: **Frankfurt (am Main)** an industrial city and important banking center in western Germany. POPULATION: 635,151.

frankfurter ['fræŋkfɜːrtər] *n* a smoked sausage, often served in a bread roll as a hot dog.

frankincense ['fræŋkinsens] *n* a substance that is burned, especially during religious ceremonies, to make a sweet smell.

franking machine ['fræŋkiŋ-] *n* a machine used in offices to frank letters.

Franklin ['fræŋklin], **Benjamin** (1706–1790) a US scientist, businessman, writer, and politician. He discovered that lightning was electricity, and helped to write the Declaration of Independence.

frankly ['fræŋkli] *adv* -1. (**quite) frankly,...** a word used to show that one is saying what one really believes □ *Frankly, I don't care what you think.* -2. [speak, tell] *see* **frank** □ *He talks openly and frankly about his sexuality.*

frankness ['fræŋknəs] *n*: *see* **frank** □ *I admire your frankness.*

frantic ['fræntik] *adj* -1. [person] who is very worried and frightened about something; [cry, voice] that sounds frightened, excited, or desperate □ *Where were you?* □ *We were frantic with worry.* □ *I could hear the frantic barking of their dog.* -2. [day, rush, pace] hurried and disorganized (informal use) □ *There was a lot of frantic activity.*

frantically ['fræntikli] *adv* [scream, rush] *see* **frantic** □ *She searched frantically in her bag.*

frappé [US fræ'pei, GB 'fræpei] *n* -1. US a thick milkshake. -2. a strong alcoholic drink served with ice.

fraternal [frə'tɜːrnl] *adj* -1. [relationship] like that that exists between brothers. -2. [greeting, feeling] friendly.

fraternity [frə'tɜːrnəti] (*pl* **fraternities**) *n* -1. at US universities, a club for male students. -2. a group of people with the same profession or interests □ *the legal fraternity.* -3. the state of being brothers; the state of showing support and friendship for other people.

❦ FRATERNITIES
Fraternities (for men) and sororities (for women) play an important part in the social life of many US universities. Many students join these social clubs in their first year, and continue as members even after they have finished their studies. Each club has a name made up of Greek letters, and is based in one building, where most of the members live. The clubs do work for charity and are well known for their drinking parties and their secret ceremonies. Some universities have banned these clubs because their ceremonies for new students are considered cruel or dangerous.

fraternize, -ise ['frætəˈnaɪz] *vi* **to fraternize with sb** [with a colleague, the enemy] to meet and talk to sb in a friendly way, as an equal.

fraud [frɔːd] *n* -1. the crime of getting money or goods by deceiving somebody; deceitful behavior □ *Credit card fraud is on the increase.* □ *She obtained nearly $4,000 by fraud.* -2. a person who is not who they say they are (disapproving use) □ *He turned out to be a fraud.*

fraudulent ['frɔːdʒələnt] *adj* [means, behavior, promise] that is dishonest and usually done to get money illegally □ *fraudulent use of stolen credit cards.*

fraught [frɔːt] *adj* -1. **fraught with sthg** [with problems, difficulty] full of sthg □ *The expedition was fraught with danger.* -2. [time, situation, person] that seems tense and anxious □ *Christmas with the in-laws was always fraught.*

fray [freɪ] ◇ *vi* -1. [material, cuff, hem] to become damaged because some threads are loose, especially at the edges □ *The scarf was fraying at the edges.* -2. **tempers began to fray** people began to get angry. ◇ *n* **to enter** OR **join the fray** to join the fight (literary use).

frayed [freɪd] *adj* -1. [material, cuff] that has frayed. -2. **frayed nerves** a feeling of nervousness that is caused by a difficult or stressful situation □ *The noise was beginning to play on his already frayed nerves.*

frazzled ['fræzld] *adj* [person] who is mentally and physically tired as a result of hard work or problems (informal use).

FRB *n abbr of* **Federal Reserve Board.**

FRCP (*abbr of* **Fellow of the Royal College of Physicians**) a title given to members of a professional body for British doctors.

FRCS (*abbr of* **Fellow of the Royal College of Surgeons**) a title given to members of a professional body for British surgeons.

freak [friːk] ◇ *adj* **a freak storm/accident etc** a very unusual and unexpected storm/accident etc □ *The islands are experiencing freak weather conditions.* ◇ *n* -1. a person, animal, or plant that has an unusual appearance or behaves in an unnatural way □ *a freak of nature.* -2. an unexpected and unusual event □ *It was a complete freak that we met like that.* -3. a person who is extremely interested in a particular thing and does it as often as possible (informal use) □ *a fitness freak.*

freak out (informal use) ◇ *vi* -1. to become very angry □ *She freaked out when she heard the news.* -2. to panic. ◇ *vt sep* **to freak sb out** to make sb very upset or frightened.

freakish ['friːkɪʃ] *adj* [person, appearance] that is a freak or looks like a freak.

freckle ['frekl] *n* a small brown spot on a person's skin, especially on the face.

free [friː] (*compar* **freer**, *superl* **freest**, *pt* & *pp* **freed**) ◇ *adj* -1. [person] who can do as they like □ *I'm young, free, and single.* ■ **free movement/access/choice etc** movement/access/choice etc that is not limited in any way. ■ **a free country** a country where people are allowed to express any opinion. ■ **a free press/society** a press/society that is not controlled by the government. ■ **to be free to do sthg** to have the right to do sthg □ *You're free to go now.* ■ **feel free** a phrase used to give somebody permission to do something in an informal way □ *"Do you mind if I take this chair?" — "Feel free!"* □ *Please feel free to ask questions.* -2. [person, animal] that is not held captive □ *The hostages are free at last.* ■ **to set a person/an animal free** to release a person/an animal □ *The animals were set free in the wild.* ■ **to cut sb free** to release sb by cutting the rope, metal etc that is preventing them from moving □ *Firemen cut her free from the wreckage.* -3. [drink, ticket] that does not cost any money □ *'Buy one, get one free.'* ■ **free of charge** without payment □ *All repairs will be carried out free of charge.* -4. [person] not busy □ *Are you free for dinner on Thursday?* ■ **a free moment/afternoon etc** a moment/an afternoon etc when one is not working and can do what one likes -5. **to be free** [seat, place, parking space] to be empty and not being used by somebody □ *Is this seat free?* -6. **to be** OR **hang free** [rope, chain, string] not to be fixed to anything □ *The rope was hanging free.* -7. **free from** OR **of sthg** [from care, worry, dirt] without sthg □ *This product is guaranteed free from additives.* -8. **to be free with sthg** [with money, affection] to be generous with sthg □ *He's very free with his advice.*
◇ *adv* -1. [travel, get in, ride] without paying. ■ **for free** without paying □ *We got it for free.* □ *He's going to paint the kitchen for free.* -2. [run, roam] without being limited in any way □ *The animals are allowed to roam free.*
◇ *vt* -1. to release <a prisoner, slave, animal> etc; to remove an unwanted ruler, army etc from <a city, country> etc □ *He was freed after being detained for questioning.* □ *The rebels were driven out and the city was freed.* ■ **to free sb of sthg** [of disease, hunger, a problem] to remove sthg unpleasant from sb □ *At last he was freed of the responsibilities of being a parent.* -2. [person, time, money] to make time, money, staff etc available for somebody □ *Could you free some of your men for tomorrow?* -3. [arm, rope] to move <sthg> from the place where it is stuck or fixed □ *Olaf carefully freed his coat from the doorhandle.* ■ **to free sb from sthg** to move sb from sthg which is trapping them □ *Survivors were freed from the wreckage.* □ *freed from an unhappy marriage.*

-free *suffix* added to words to show that something does not contain any of a particular substance or thing □ *sugar-free chewing gum* □ *a trouble-free vacation.*

freebie ['fri:bɪ] *n* something that is given to somebody, e.g. by a company, as a free gift (informal use).

Freecall ['fri:kɔːl] *n* AUS a system by which a company or organization pays the cost of telephone calls made to it.

freedom ['fri:dəm] *n* -1. [of action, thought, choice] the state of being able to do what one likes without being limited in any way □ *The hostages have finally gained their freedom.* □ *restrictions on freedom of movement and association.* ■ **freedom of speech** the right to express one's beliefs and opinions. -2. **freedom from sthg** [from pain, hunger, care] the state of being free from sthg unpleasant.

freedom fighter *n* a person who uses violence to try and overthrow the government of their country.

Freedom of Information Act *n* **the Freedom of Information Act** a US law that gives the public access to government information.

free enterprise *n* an economic system in which business and trade are carried out without much government control.

free-fall *n* the action of falling through the air or space without being attached to anything or held back in any way.

Freefone™ ['fri:foʊn] *n* GB a system in which a company or organization pays the cost of telephone calls made to it.

free-for-all *n* a noisy situation, argument, or fight in which a lot of people take part.

free gift *n* a product given free of charge when another product is bought.

freehand ['fri:hænd] ◇ *adj* [drawing, map] that is drawn by hand without compasses, a ruler etc. ◇ *adv* [draw] *I sketched it freehand.*

freehold ['fri:hoʊld] ◇ *n* the status of being the only owner of a building or piece of land for an unlimited time □ *a freehold property.* ◇ *adv* [buy, sell] with a freehold. NOTE: Compare **leasehold**.

❦ FREEHOLD

In Britain, the freehold of a property, e.g. a house, office, or store, is the right to own it for an unlimited amount of time. Most apartments in large buildings are leasehold, which means you buy the lease (the right to live in that apartment for a fixed period, usually 99 years) and become the leaseholder. The freeholder, who owns the whole building, has the right to collect money from the leaseholders to pay for cleaning, repairs to the building, insurance etc. When a lease ends, the leaseholder has to leave the building, or take out a new lease. The laws affecting freehold have changed recently, making it easier for leaseholders to renew their lease, or to buy the freehold of the property they live in.

freeholder ['fri:hoʊldəʳ] *n* a person who owns the freehold of a building or piece of land. NOTE: Compare **leaseholder**.

free house *n* GB a pub that can sell as many types of beer as it likes and not just the beer produced by a particular company.

free kick *n* in soccer, a kick given to one team that the other team is not allowed to try and prevent, as a punishment for a foul □ *They were awarded a free kick in the closing minutes of the first half.*

freelance [US 'fri:læns, GB -lɑːns] ◇ *adj* [worker] who works for more than one company, but is not a full-time employee of any company; [writing, photography] that is done by a freelance worker □ *a freelance journalist/translator* □ *I'm looking for freelance work.* ◇ *n* a person who does freelance work. ◇ *adv* [work] as a freelance □ *I write freelance for several publications.* ◇ *vi* to work as a freelance □ *She freelances for various companies.*

freelancer [US 'fri:lænsr, GB -lɑːnsə] *n* a person who does freelance work.

freeloader ['fri:loʊdəʳ] *n* a person who accepts money and goods from other people without offering anything in return (informal and disapproving use).

freely ['fri:lɪ] *adv* -1. [admit, confess] willingly and without being asked □ *He freely acknowledges his part in the affair.* -2. [talk, mix, travel] without being limited in any way □ *Traffic is moving freely again.* □ *Alcohol is freely available in this country.* -3. [spend, give] generously □ *She gave freely of her time.*

freeman ['fri:mən] (*pl* **freemen** [-mən]) *n* a person who has been granted special rights in a city.

free-market economy *n* an economic system in which prices and wages are controlled by the needs of the economy, not by the government.

Freemason ['fri:meɪsn] *n* a member of a secret society of men who try to help one another and use secret signs and words to recognize each other.

Freemasonry ['fri:meɪsnrɪ] *n* the organization, beliefs, or activities of the Freemasons.

Freephone ['fri:foʊn] *n* = **Freefone**.

Freepost ['fri:poʊst] *n* GB the system in which a company pays the cost of postage for the letters it receives.

free-range *adj* GB [hen] that is kept outdoors so that it can move around freely; [egg] that is produced by a free-range hen.

free sample *n* a small amount of a new product that is given to people free of charge to encourage them to buy it in the future.

freesia ['fri:ʒə] *n* a plant with yellow, purple, pink, red, or white flowers that smell sweet.

free speech *n* the right to express one's beliefs and opinions freely about subjects such as politics and religion.

freestanding [ˌfri:'stændɪŋ] *adj* [statue, stove] that stands on its own and is not supported by or attached to anything.

freestyle ['fri:staɪl] *n* a race in which the swimmers may swim in any style.

freethinker [ˌfri:'θɪŋkə^r] *n* a person who has developed their own views, particularly about religion.

free time *n* the time during which one does not have to work but when one can do what one wants □ *I don't really have much free time.* □ *What do you do in your free time?*

free trade *n* a system in which the amount of foreign goods entering a country is not limited and high charges do not have to be paid.

freeway ['fri:weɪ] *n* US a road with several lanes, used by vehicles traveling long distances.

freewheel [ˌfri:'wi:l] *vi* [cyclist] to ride a bicycle downhill without using the pedals; [driver] to drive a car downhill without using the engine.

freewheeling [ˌfri:'wi:lɪŋ] *adj* [person] who is relaxed and does not behave or do things in the same way as everybody else (informal use).

free will *n* the ability to choose freely what one does. ■ **to do sthg of one's own free will** to do sthg that one has chosen freely to do □ *He went there of his own free will.*

free world *n* **the free world** a term used to refer to the non-Communist countries of the world during the Cold War.

freeze [fri:z] (*pt* froze, *pp* frozen) ◇ *vt* **-1.** [water, pond] to make <a liquid> so cold that it becomes hard or solid. **-2.** [engine, lock] to make <sthg> so cold that it cannot move or work properly. **-3.** [meat, fish, vegetables] to preserve <food> by keeping it at a temperature below freezing point □ *'Suitable for freezing.'* **-4.** [assets, shares, bank account] to legally prevent <sthg> from being used, spent, sold etc □ *The bank froze all the company's assets until the debts were paid.* **-5.** [wages, prices] to keep <sthg> at a particular level for a fixed period of time □ *The government is threatening to freeze wages at last year's level.*
◇ *vi* **-1.** [water, river, ground] to become hard or solid because ice has formed in it or on it □ *The pipes froze overnight.* **-2.** WEATHER to become so cold that the temperature drops to freezing point or below □ *The forecast says it will freeze tomorrow.* **-3.** [person] to stop moving and stay very still, e.g. because one is frightened □ *"OK, everybody freeze!"* **-4.** [person] to feel very cold (informal use) □ *You'll freeze in that thin dress!*
◇ *n* **-1.** a period of very cold weather. **-2.** the act of freezing wages or prices; a period in which this happens □ *a wage/price freeze.*

◆ **freeze over** *vi* [pond, river, lake] to become completely covered in ice because the weather is so cold □ *Next morning, all the puddles had frozen over.*

◆ **freeze up** *vi* [pond, river] to become completely covered in ice; [lock, engine] to become completely blocked with ice.

freeze-dried *adj* [vegetables, coffee] that has been preserved by being frozen then quickly dried.

freeze frame *n* a device for stopping a video tape or film at a particular picture □ *the freeze-frame button.*

freezer ['fri:zə^r] *n* an electrical appliance for storing food at a temperature below freezing point.

freezing ['fri:zɪŋ] ◇ *adj* [weather, person, place] very cold (informal use) □ *It's freezing in here!* ◇ *adv* (informal use): *It's freezing cold outside.* ◇ *n* = **freezing point** □ *The temperature is down to freezing.*

freezing point *n* the temperature (0° Celsius, 32° Fahrenheit) that water freezes at; the temperature that a particular liquid freezes at □ *Temperatures tonight will drop to below freezing point.*

freight [freɪt] *n* the transportation of goods over a long distance by ship, train, plane etc; goods transported in this way □ *air/rail/freight* □ *freight charges* □ *a freight plane/train.*

freighter ['freɪtə^r] *n* a ship or aircraft designed to carry goods.

French [frentʃ] ◇ *npl* **the French** people who come from France. ◇ *adj*: *French customs/currency.* ◇ *n* a language spoken in France, parts of Belgium, Canada, Switzerland, and many African countries.

French bean *n* a thin green bean that is cooked and eaten as a vegetable; the plant that these beans grow on.

French bread *n* white bread in the form of long, thin, crusty loaves.

French Canadian ◇ *n* a Canadian whose first language is French. ◇ *adj*: *a French Canadian accent.*

French doors *npl* = **French windows.**

French dressing *n* US a salad dressing made from mayonnaise and ketchup; GB a salad dressing made from oil, vinegar, and seasonings.

French fries *npl* long thin pieces of potato that have been deep-fried in oil.

French horn *n* a brass musical instrument shaped like a coil.

Frenchman ['frentʃmən] (*pl* **Frenchmen** [-mən]) *n* a man who comes from France.

French polish *n* a type of varnish that gives wood a very shiny surface.

French Polynesia five groups of French islands in the southern Pacific, including Tahiti, Moorea, the Marquesas, and the Austral Islands. SIZE: 4,000 sq kms. POPULATION: 188,814 (*French Polynesians*). CAPITAL: Papeete. LANGUAGE: French, Tahitian. CURRENCY: Pacific franc.

French Revolution *n* **the French Revolution** the revolution in France (1789 to 1799) during which the king, Louis XVI, was killed and a republic was declared.

French Riviera: the French Riviera the Mediterranean coast of southeastern France.

French stick *n* GB a loaf of French bread.

French toast *n* pieces of bread that are dipped in an egg mixture and then fried.

French windows *npl* a pair of doors that look like windows, usually leading from a house to its yard.

Frenchwoman ['frentʃwʊmən] (*pl* **Frenchwomen**) *n* a woman who comes from France.

frenetic [frə'netɪk] *adj* [pace, speed, activity] that is very fast and busy, and seems uncontrolled □ *Life can be too frenetic at times.*

frenzied ['frenzɪd] *adj* [activity, crowd] very excited and uncontrolled; [attack] wild and uncontrolled □ *a period of frenzied activity.*

frenzy ['frenzɪ] (*pl* **frenzies**) *n* a frenzied state; frenzied behavior □ *The crowd was in a frenzy of excitement.*

frequency ['friːkwənsɪ] (*pl* **frequencies**) *n* **-1.** [of an event, occurrence, action] the state of happening often; the number of times that something happens □ *This sort of attack is happening with such frequency that people are no longer shocked by it.* □ *The frequency of the phone calls increased.* **-2.** RADIO a particular rate of radio waves per second at which a radio station broadcasts its programs □ *Which frequency is WKLP on?*

frequent [*adj* 'friːkwənt, *vb* frɪ'kwent] ◇ *adj* [visits, storms, mistakes] that happen often □ *He was a frequent visitor to the apartment.* ◇ *vt* [bar, restaurant] to go to <a place> often, usually to relax or enjoy onself □ *a club frequented by local teenagers.*

frequent flyer *comp* a **frequent flyer program** a system of benefits that an airline provides for customers who travel with them regularly.

frequently ['friːkwəntlɪ] *adv* often □ *Daniel is frequently mistaken for his brother.*

fresco ['freskoʊ] (*pl* **frescoes** OR **frescos**) *n* a picture painted on plaster on a wall when the plaster is still wet.

fresh [freʃ] ◇ *adj* **-1.** [fruit, vegetable, meat] that has been picked or cut recently and has not been frozen, canned, or dried; [bread, coffee] that has been made recently; [flowers] that have been picked recently and are still in good condition □ *You should eat plenty of fresh fruit.* □ *There's some fresh coffee on the stove if you want.* **-2. fresh air** clean air from outside a room or building □ *I'm just going out for a breath of fresh air.* **-3. fresh water** water that is found in streams, lakes etc and is not salty. **-4.** [news, outbreak] that has happened recently □ *Write it down while it's still fresh in your mind.* **-5.** [paint, snow] that has been added recently to an existing layer □ *a fresh covering of snow.* **-6.** [drink, evidence, information] that is new and replaces or is added to something □ *Here, use a fresh towel.* □ *Fresh talks have started between the two sides in the dispute.* ■ **to make a fresh start** to start to do something again or to live in a different way. **-7.** [person, horse] not tired □ *What's the secret in looking so fresh after a hard day's work?* **-8.** [complexion, face] that looks clear, clean, and healthy □ *Her skin looked fresh and clean.* □ *a fresh-faced young boy.* **-9.** [taste, smell] that is pleasant because it is clean and natural □ *There was a lovely, fresh, lemony smell.* **-10.** [approach, style] new and interesting □ *The author takes a fresh look at family relationships.* **-11.** [weather, wind, day] pleasantly cold □ *a fresh sea breeze.* **-12. to be/get fresh** to be/start being too friendly to somebody and not polite enough, sometimes to show them that one finds them sexually attractive (informal and disapproving use) □ *Don't get fresh with me.* **-13.** [color, room] that seems bright and pleasant. **-14.** *phrases* **to be fresh from a place** to have recently been in a place □ *young graduates fresh from college.* ■ **to be fresh out of sthg** to have no more of sthg left (informal use) □ *I'm sorry, we're fresh out of napkins!*

fresh- *prefix* **fresh-made/baked** that has been made/baked recently.

freshen ['freʃn] ◇ *vt* [air, room] to make <sthg> more clean and pleasant. ◇ *vi* [wind, breeze] to become stronger.

◆ **freshen up** ◇ *vi* to wash and make oneself more pleasant to look at □ *Just give me a few minutes to freshen up and I'll be ready to go.* ◇ *vt sep* **-1. to freshen oneself up** to freshen up. **-2. to freshen sthg up** [room, clothes] to make sthg cleaner and more pleasant.

freshly ['freʃlɪ] *adv* **freshly made/baked etc** that has been made/baked etc recently □ *freshly picked tomatoes.*

freshman ['freʃmən] (*pl* **freshmen** [-mən]) *n* US a first-year student at college or in high school.

freshwater ['freʃwɔːtər] *adj* [pool, lake] that consists of water that is not salty; [fish] that lives in rivers, lakes etc and not in the sea.

fret [fret] (*pt* & *pp* **fretted**, *cont* **fretting**) *vi* worry □ *It's not worth fretting about* OR *over.* □ *Don't fret, I'm sure they'll be back soon.*

fretful ['fretfl] *adj* [baby, child, sleep] that is not comfortable or relaxed.

fretsaw ['fretsɔː] *n* a saw with a thin blade and small teeth, used for cutting patterns in thin sheets of wood.

Freud [frɔɪd], **Sigmund** (1856–1939) an Austrian doctor who developed the science of psychoanalysis. His studies of the unconscious mind had a strong influence on 20th-century thought.

Freudian slip [ˌfrɔɪdɪən-] *n* a word or phrase that one says accidentally, but that often shows what one is really thinking.

FRG (*abbr of* **Federal Republic of Germany**) the official name of Germany.

Fri. *abbr of* **Friday**.

friar ['fraɪər] *n* a member of a Catholic religious order who used to travel around begging for food and teaching people about Christianity.

Friar Tuck one of Robin Hood's outlaws in English folk stories. He is a fat monk who enjoys eating and drinking.

friction ['frɪkʃn] *n* **-1.** PHYSICS the force that prevents one surface from sliding smoothly over another. **-2.** [between two objects, surfaces] the act of one thing rubbing against another. **-3.** [between people] conflict between two people or groups of people □ *It's likely to cause friction between them.*

Friday ['fraɪdeɪ] ◇ *n* the day between Thursday and Saturday □ *It's Friday today.* □ *I was born on a Friday.* □ *There's a sale every Friday.* □ *I'd like to reserve a room for Friday May 6.* □ *I have an appointment next Friday/the Friday after next.* □ *I saw her last Friday/the Friday before last.* □ *I'm leaving Friday* US OR *on Friday* GB. ▪ **Fridays** US, **on Fridays** each Friday □ *The cleaning woman comes (on) Fridays.* ▪ **a week from** US OR **on** GB **Friday, Friday week** GB the Friday after next Friday □ *We'll meet again a week from Friday.* ▪ **on the Friday** the Friday of a particular week □ *We arrived on the Friday and left on the Sunday.* ◇ *adj*: *Friday morning/afternoon/night.*

fridge [frɪdʒ] *n* an electrical appliance for storing food and drinks at low temperatures.

fridge-freezer *n* GB a large kitchen appliance consisting of a refrigerator and a freezer in two separate sections.

fried [fraɪd] ◇ *past tense & past participle of* **fry**. ◇ *adj* [onion, egg, fish] that has been cooked in hot oil, butter etc.

friend [frend] *n* **-1.** a person one knows well, likes, and trusts and who is not a member of one's family □ *She is my best friend.* □ *You've always been a good friend to me.* □ *I'd like you to meet a friend of mine.* ▪ **to be friends with sb** to have a friendship with sb □ *They're very close friends.* ▪ **to make friends** to begin a friendship □ *She made friends with him during a trip to Israel.* □ *You need to go out, meet people, make some new friends!* **-2.** [of a charity, cause, country] a person, country etc that helps somebody or something by supporting them □ *The troubled president will be looking to friends abroad for financial aid.*

friendless ['frendləs] *adj* [person] who has no friends.

friendly ['frendlɪ] (*compar* **friendlier,** *superl* **friendliest,** *pl* **friendlies**) ◇ *adj* **-1.** [person, attitude, animal] that is kind and pleasant □ *The neighbors were always very friendly toward me.* □ *a relaxed, friendly bunch of people.* ▪ **to be friendly with sb** to know sb as a friend □ *While we were there, we got quite friendly with a few of the locals.* **-2.** [nation, government] that is not an enemy. **-3.** [game, argument] that is not serious and involves no aggression or unpleasant feelings. ◇ *n* GB SPORT a game between two teams in which the result is not important because it is not part of a competition.

-friendly *suffix* added to words to mean not damaging or harmful to a particular thing, or suitable for a particular person □ *ozone-friendly products* □ *learner-friendly books.*

friendship ['frendʃɪp] *n* **-1.** the feeling that exists between friends □ *He values her friendship.* □ *The aim is to promote friendship between nations.* **-2.** a particular relationship that exists between friends □ *That incident marked the end of their friendship.*

Friends of the Earth *n* an international organization that tries to make governments and the public more aware of harm being done to the environment.

fries [fraɪz] *npl* = **French fries.**

Friesian (cow) ['friːʒn-] *n* a type of a black and white cow that gives a lot of milk.

frieze [friːz] *n* a long, narrow, decorative border along the top of the walls of a room.

frigate ['frɪgət] *n* a small, fast, military ship, used for protecting other ships.

fright [fraɪt] *n* **-1.** a feeling of fear □ *His face was pale with fright.* ▪ **to take fright** to suddenly feel afraid □ *They took fright and ran off.* **-2.** a shock □ *She got a terrible fright when she heard noises downstairs.*

frighten ['fraɪtn] *vt* to make <a person or animal> afraid □ *The explosion frightened the life out of me.* ▪ **to frighten sb into sthg** to make sb do sthg by frightening them □ *They frightened local residents into paying up.*

◆ **frighten away** *vt sep* **to frighten sb away** to make sb go away by frightening them □ *Don't do that! You'll frighten the birds away.*

◆ **frighten off** *vt sep* **to frighten sb off** to make sb stop doing sthg by frightening them □ *Don't allow yourself to be frightened off by all this talk of failure.*

frightened ['fraɪtnd] *adj* [person, animal] that feels worried and afraid because they think something bad is going to happen □ *Don't be frightened of the dog, it won't bite you.* □ *I'm frightened (that) I might make a mistake.* □ *People were too frightened to protest.*

frightening ['fraɪtnɪŋ] *adj* [experience, movie] that makes one feel afraid □ *It was really frightening the way he just stared at us.*

frightful ['fraɪtfl] *adj* [weather, noise, mess] that one thinks is very bad or unpleasant (old-fashioned use).

frigid ['frɪdʒɪd] *adj* [person] who does not easily become sexually excited.

frill [frɪl] *n* **-1.** a piece of cloth with many folds in it that is attached to the edges of clothes, cushions etc as decoration. **-2.** an extra thing that is not essential (informal use) □ *a cheap basic washing machine with no frills.*

frilly ['frɪlɪ] (*compar* **frillier,** *superl* **frilliest**) *adj* [dress, skirt, blouse] that is decorated with many frills.

fringe [frɪndʒ] ◇ *n* **-1.** [on a lampshade, dress, curtain] a decorative edge made of threads that hang down. **-2.** [of a crowd, town, forest] one of the parts of something that is furthest from the middle □ *a quiet suburb on the fringes of Geneva.* **-3.** [of society, a political party] a small group of people whose ideas or behavior make them different from everybody else in the group, especially because they are more extreme □ *Such people live on the fringes of society.* **-4.** GB [of hair] hair that is cut in a way that makes it hang down over one's forehead. ◇ *vt* [beach, town] to surround the edge of <a place>.

fringe benefit *n* something that is offered by

an employer in addition to a salary to attract people to a job, e.g. a car or pension.

fringed [frɪndʒd] *adj* **to be fringed with sthg** to have sthg all around the edge □ *a beach fringed with palm trees.*

fringe group *n* a small group of people in a larger organization, e.g. a political party, who have different or more extreme ideas.

fringe theatre *n* GB a kind of drama that uses new techniques and ideas and is not as popular as traditional drama.

Frisbee™ ['frɪzbɪ] *n* a plastic disk that people throw to each other as a game.

frisk [frɪsk] ◇ *vt* to search <sb> by quickly moving one's hands over every part of their body to see if they are hiding something under their clothes, especially a weapon □ *Fans are frisked by security staff as they enter the stadium.* ◇ *vi* [lamb, puppy, child] to run or jump around in a happy playful way.

frisky ['frɪskɪ] (*compar* **friskier**, *superl* **friskiest**) *adj* [animal, person] that is lively and playful (informal use) □ *Our dog gets quite frisky at times.*

fritter ['frɪtər] *n* a slice of fruit, vegetable, or meat that has been covered in batter and then fried □ *pineapple fritters.*

◆ **fritter away** *vt sep* **to fritter sthg away** [money, time] to waste sthg by using small amounts of it on unnecessary things □ *He frittered his savings away on cars.*

frivolity [frɪ'vɒlətɪ] (*pl* **frivolities**) *n* **-1.** a frivolous thing or activity □ *Don't waste your money on such frivolities.* **-2.** [of a person] *see* **frivolous.**

frivolous ['frɪvələs] *adj* [person] who is not sensible or serious enough; [hobby, pastime] that is done for fun and not for serious reasons □ *I found his attitude rather frivolous.* □ *He had no time for frivolous pursuits such as dancing.*

frizzy ['frɪzɪ] (*compar* **frizzier**, *superl* **frizziest**) *adj* [hair] that has a lot of tight curls □ *My hair always goes frizzy after I wash it.*

fro [frou] *adv* → **to.**

frock [frɒk] *n* a dress (old-fashioned use).

frog [frɒg] *n* a small animal that lives on land and in water and has smooth greenish skin and long back legs for swimming and jumping. ■ **to have a frog in one's throat** to have difficulty speaking because of phlegm in one's throat.

frogman ['frɒgmən] (*pl* **frogmen**) *n* a person who swims underwater using breathing equipment and a rubber suit and flippers.

frogmarch ['frɒgmɑːrtʃ] *vt* GB to take <sb> somewhere by force, holding their arms to their sides or behind their back □ *Jackson was frogmarched out of the hall.*

frogmen ['frɒgmən] *plural of* **frogman.**

frogspawn ['frɒgspɔːn] *n* a mass of frog's eggs in a soft jelly.

frolic ['frɒlɪk] (*pt* & *pp* **frolicked**, *cont* **frolicking**) ◇ *vi* [lamb, puppy, person] to move around or play in a lively and happy way. ◇ *n* a silly

enjoyable activity or game □ *We had fun and frolics on the beach.*

from [*stressed* frɒm, *unstressed* frəm] *prep* **-1. the flight from Miami** the flight that started in Miami (used to show the point where something begins) □ *the road from here to Paris* □ *the latest news from America* □ *A light bulb hung from the ceiling.* □ *It's a quotation from Shakespeare.* **-2. she's from Spain** she was born or grew up in Spain □ *He comes from Houston originally.* ■ **where are you from?** what is your nationality? **-3. a letter from his wife** a letter sent by his wife (used to show who gave, sent, or provided something) □ *I heard the story from George.* □ *I got this jacket from Webbers on Main Street.* **-4. wine is made from grapes** wine is made using grapes (used to show the material used to make something) □ *It's made from a mixture of copper and brass.* **-5. the man from the tax office** the man who works for the tax office □ *The people from the gas company were here yesterday.* **-6.** used to indicate a change from one state or condition to another □ *The industry has switched from coal to nuclear fuel.* □ *She translates from Spanish to English.* **-7.** used when saying how far away something is □ *We're still a long way from home.* **-8.** used to show the time when something begins □ *I lived there from 1989 to 1993.* □ *I liked her from the moment I met her.* **-9.** used to show something is being removed from a place □ *He snatched the purse from my hand.* □ *Tax will be deducted from your salary.* □ *If you take 5 from 9 you get 4.* ■ **to escape from prison** to escape so that one is no longer in prison □ *I'll be away from home for a few days.* **-10.** used to indicate the position from which one views something □ *You look thinner from this angle.* **-11. from what you say** according to or judging by what you say □ *From her accent, I'd guess she was French.* ■ **from my point of view** as it affects me □ *Obviously from my point of view any delay would be disastrous.* **-12. to suffer from cold/hunger** to suffer because of or as a result of cold/hunger □ *These problems result from your failure to listen correctly to what is said.*

frond [frɒnd] *n* [of seaweed, a fern, a palm tree] a long leaf.

front [frʌnt] ◇ *n* **-1.** [of a house, car, person] the part of something that is furthest forward □ *We had seats at the front.* □ *Can I sit in the front?* **-2.** MILITARY a line that can be drawn on a map where two opposing armies face each other □ *Troops are massing on the eastern front.* ■ **on the domestic/employment etc front** as far as the situation at home/work etc is concerned □ *The news is no better on the political front.* □ *We haven't made much progress on that front, I'm afraid.* **-3. the (sea) front** a road beside the sea, usually in a town □ *We went for a walk on the sea front.* **-4.** [for hiding something] behavior that is intended to deceive people; a business that is used to hide an illegal activity □ *He put on a bold* OR *brave front.* □ *The business is just a front for a drugs ring.* **-5.** WEATHER a line where a mass of cold air meets a mass of warm air □ *a cold/warm front.*

◇ *adj* [tooth, garden, page] that is at the front of or in front of something ▫ *the front wheels of the car.*

◇ *vt* -1. [house, hotel] to be outside and in front of <sthg> ▫ *The building is fronted by extensive gardens.* -2. to be the leader of <an organization> ▫ *He fronts the country's leading consumer group.* -3. to be the presenter of <a radio or TV program>.

◇ *vi* **to front onto sthg** [onto a garden, road] to have sthg outside and in front of it ▫ *The hotel fronts onto the beach.*

◆ **in front** *adj* & *adv* -1. [walk, sit] further forward ▫ *The people in front got served first.* ▫ *You go in front; we'll be right behind.* -2. **to be in front** to be winning ▫ *Schumacher is still in front with a two-second lead.*

◆ **in front of** *prep* -1. close to the front part of <a person, object, or place> ▫ *She was sitting in front of me/the TV.* -2. when <sb> is present ▫ *Don't tell me off in front of the staff.*

frontage ['frʌntɪdʒ] *n* the part of a building or piece of land that faces a street or river ▫ *prime commercial frontage.*

frontal ['frʌntl] *adj* -1. [attack, assault, collision] that happens directly and from the front of something. -2. [lobe, view] that is of or at the front of something.

front bench *n* **the front benches** in the British and Australian parliaments, the two front rows of seats on each side of the upper and lower house. The prime minister and members of the government sit in one row, and the leaders of the Opposition sit in the opposite row ▫ *a front-bench spokesman.*

front desk *n* a reception desk in a hotel or office building.

front door *n* the main entrance to a house, usually at the front.

frontier [US frʌn'tɪər, GB 'frʌntɪə] *n* -1. new land that is wild and unexplored and is next to areas where people already live; land like this in the western USA, especially in the 19th century ▫ *a frontier post.* -2. [of a country] a border where one country meets another country ▫ *the French-German frontier.*

◆ **frontiers** *npl* the limit of knowledge in a particular field of study ▫ *the frontiers of science.*

frontispiece ['frʌntɪspiːs] *n* a picture at the beginning of a book, usually facing the title page.

front line *n* **the front line** MILITARY the area where fighting is taking place ▫ *a front-line reporter.*

front man *n* -1. [for an organization] a person who represents a group of people when dealing with other people or organizations (disapproving use) ▫ *He's a front man for the Mafia.* -2. TV & RADIO the presenter of a program. -3. MUSIC the member of a group of musicians, usually the singer, who gets most attention from an audience.

front-page *adj* [news, headline, article] that is important enough to be printed on the front page of a newspaper.

front room *n* a room, usually at the front of a house, used as the living room.

front-runner *n* the person or organization that seems most likely to win a contest, contract etc.

front-wheel drive *n* a system in a vehicle in which only the front two wheels are connected directly to the engine; a vehicle that uses this system ▫ *a front-wheel drive car.*

frost [frɒst] *n* -1. a thin white layer of ice that forms on the ground and other surfaces when the temperature is below freezing point ▫ *There was frost on the window pane.* -2. weather conditions when the temperature is below freezing point and frost forms ▫ *There is a heavy frost forecast for tonight.*

Frost [frɒst], **Robert** (1874–1963) a US poet whose works include the poem *Stopping by Woods on a Snowy Evening.*

frostbite ['frɒstbaɪt] *n* a condition in which one's fingers, toes, ears, nose etc are damaged by extreme cold.

frostbitten ['frɒstbɪtn] *adj* [toe, finger] that is affected by frostbite.

frosted ['frɒstəd] *adj* -1. [glass, window] that has a raised pattern on its surface so that people cannot see through it clearly. -2. [cake] that is covered with frosting.

frosting ['frɒstɪŋ] *n* a covering for cakes, made from powdered sugar and liquid ▫ *chocolate fudge frosting.*

frosty ['frɒstɪ] (*compar* **frostier**, *superl* **frostiest**) *adj* -1. [morning, weather] that is very cold ▫ *It was a cold, frosty morning.* -2. [field, window] that is covered with frost. -3. [person] who is unfriendly, especially because they do not like or approve of one ▫ *She gave me a very frosty welcome.*

froth [frɒθ] ◇ *n* a layer of small bubbles on the surface of something, e.g. on the sea or a glass of beer. ◇ *vi* [beer, sea] to form froth ▫ *The dog was frothing at the mouth.*

frothy ['frɒθɪ] (*compar* **frothier**, *superl* **frothiest**) *adj* [beer, sea] that has a lot of froth.

frown [fraʊn] ◇ *vi* to bring one's eyebrows closer together so that there are lines on one's forehead, usually when one is annoyed, worried, or confused ▫ *She frowned as I told her of my plans.* ◇ *n* the expression on somebody's face when they frown ▫ *a worried frown.*

◆ **frown (up)on** *vt fus* **to frown (up)on sthg** to disapprove of sthg ▫ *This kind of behavior is frowned upon at the Academy.*

froze [frəʊz] *past tense of* **freeze.**

frozen ['frəʊzn] ◇ *past participle of* **freeze.** ◇ *adj* -1. [ground, field] that is hard, because the temperature is below freezing point ▫ *The ground was frozen hard.* -2. [lake, river, pond] that is covered with ice. -3. [food] that has been preserved by freezing ▫ *frozen fish/vegetables.* -4. [person, fingers] very cold ▫ *I'm absolutely frozen!* -5. [prices, salaries] that cannot be increased for a period of time; [assets] that a person, company etc is not allowed to use for a period of time ▫ *with prices fro-*

zen at 1990 levels. **-6. to be frozen with sthg**
[with fear, terror] to be unable to move because of sthg □ *Mandy stood rooted to the spot,*
frozen with terror.

FRS *n* **-1.** (*abbr of* **Federal Reserve System**) the
system of central banks in the USA.
-2. (*abbr of* **Fellow of the Royal Society**) a title
given to members of a professional body for
British scientists.

frugal ['fruːgl] *adj* **-1.** [meal] that is small and
simple □ *Dinner at Aunt Olive's was always a*
frugal affair. **-2.** [person] who avoids spending
a lot of money, usually because they are not
rich □ *They have a fairly frugal lifestyle.*

fruit [fruːt] (*pl* **fruit** OR **fruits**) ◇ *n* **-1.** something
that grows on a tree or bush, that contains
seeds, and can usually be eaten, e.g. apples,
oranges, and bananas □ *Would you like some*
fruit? □ *a fruit bowl/cocktail/tree.* **-2. the fruit(s)**
of sthg [of somebody's experience, hard work]
the successful result of sthg □ *The book is the*
fruit of years of research. ■ **to bear fruit** [work,
idea] to be successful and produce results
that are useful □ *Their efforts have never really*
borne fruit. ◇ *vi* [tree, plant] to produce fruit.

fruitcake ['fruːtkeɪk] *n* a cake that contains
small pieces of dried fruit.

fruiterer ['fruːtərəʳ] *n* GB a person who has a
store that sells fruit.

fruitful ['fruːtfl] *adj* [meeting, collaboration, peri-
od] that is useful and produces good results
□ *Our partnership with the German company*
GMB has proved extremely fruitful.

fruition [fruːˈɪʃn] *n* **to come to fruition** [plan,
idea] to be successful and produce the result
that one wanted □ *One day, when this project*
finally comes to fruition, you'll understand what I
mean.

fruit juice *n* a drink made from the juice of
one or more types of fruit.

fruitless ['fruːtləs] *adj* [discussion, search] that
does not produce the results that one want-
ed □ *There have been a number of fruitless at-*
tempts to restart the talks.

fruit machine *n* GB a machine for gambling
that pays out money when a particular combination of symbols, usually fruit, appears
on its screen.

fruit salad *n* a dessert that consists of pieces
of different types of fruit in juice.

frumpy ['frʌmpɪ] (*compar* **frumpier**, *superl*
frumpiest) *adj* [person, clothes] that one finds
boring, unattractive, and old-fashioned (informal use).

frustrate [US 'frʌstreɪt, GB frʌ'streɪt] *vt* **-1.**
[person] to annoy or disappoint <sb> by
stopping them from doing what they want
to do □ *Stephen's attitude really frustrates me*
sometimes! **-2.** [plan, attempt] to prevent <sb/
sthg> from succeeding □ *The President has*
been frustrated in his efforts to push the bill
through Congress.

frustrated [US 'frʌstreɪtəd, GB frʌ'streɪt-] *adj*
-1. a frustrated poet/artist etc a person who
would like to be a successful poet/artist etc
but has not been able to achieve this.

-2. [person] who is annoyed or disappointed
because they cannot do what they what □
It's easy to get frustrated and give up.

frustrating [US 'frʌstreɪtɪŋ, GB frʌ'streɪt-] *adj*
[person, situation, time] that makes one feel
frustrated □ *It's so frustrating not being able to*
help.

frustration [frʌˈstreɪʃn] *n* a feeling of being
frustrated; something that frustrates somebody □ *I snapped at him out of sheer frustration.*
□ *It's one of the many frustrations of working at*
home.

fry [fraɪ] (*pt* & *pp* **fried**) ◇ *vt* [egg, steak, pota-
toes] to cook <food> in hot fat, oil etc. ◇ *vi*
[egg, steak, fish] to be fried □ *While the onions*
are frying, prepare the steak.

FRY *n abbr of* **Federal Republic of Yugoslavia**.

frying pan ['fraɪɪŋ-] *n* a shallow pan with a
long handle, used for frying food. ■ **to jump**
out of the frying pan into the fire to go from a
bad situation to one that is even worse.

ft [in measurements] *abbr of* **foot**.

FT (*abbr of* **Financial Times**) *n* a British business and financial newspaper, printed on
pink paper in London and Frankfurt.

FTC (*abbr of* **Federal Trade Commission**) *n* **the**
FTC the US government department responsible for making sure that competition between businesses is fair.

FT index (*abbr of* **Financial Times-Ordinary**
Share Index) *n* **the FT index** a figure based on
the daily average prices of the shares of 30
companies on the London Stock Exchange.

FTP (*abbr of* **file transfer protocol**) *n* a way of
moving files from one site to another.

FT-SE 100 (*abbr of* **Financial Times - Stock Ex-**
change 100 Share Index) *n* **the FT-SE 100 (In-**
dex) a figure based on the average prices
every hour of 100 important companies on
the London Stock Exchange. It is the most
important London Stock Exchange index.

fuchsia ['fjuːʃə] *n* a plant with red, purple, or
white flowers that hang downward.

fuck▼ [fʌk] (vulgar use) ◇ *vt* to have sex with
<sb>. ◇ *vi* to have sex. ◇ *excl* a word used
to show that one is annoyed.

◆ **fuck off** ◇ *vi* to go away. ◇ *excl* a phrase
used to tell somebody to go away.

fucking▼ ['fʌkɪŋ] *adj* a word used to show
how strongly one feels about something
(vulgar use).

fuddy-duddy ['fʌdɪdʌdɪ] (*pl* **fuddy-duddies**) *n* a
boring and old-fashioned person who does
not like new ideas (informal use).

fudge [fʌdʒ] ◇ *n* a soft brown candy made of
sugar, butter, and milk □ *a piece of fudge.*
◇ *vt* [issue, figures] to deliberately avoid
making a clear decision or statement about
<sthg> (informal use) □ *Stop trying to fudge the*
issue!

fuel ['fjuːəl] (US *pt* & *pp* **fueled**, *cont* **fueling**, GB
pt & *pp* **fuelled**, *cont* **fuelling**) ◇ *n* something
that can be used to make heat or energy,
e.g. coal, petrol, or plutonium □ *fuel*
consumption/costs. ■ **to add fuel to the flames**

to make an unpleasant or difficult situation worse. ◇ vt -1. [boiler, engine] to supply <sthg> with fuel. -2. [argument, inflation, violence] to cause <sthg> to continue and become worse □ *Mayor Tomlin's words merely served to fuel tensions in the district.*

fuel pump n a mechanical pump that sends fuel to the carburetor of an engine.

fuel tank n a container for storing fuel in a motor vehicle.

fugitive ['fjuːdʒətɪv] n a person who is running away or hiding from an enemy, the police etc.

fugue [fjuːg] n a piece of music in which one or two tunes are repeated, with variations, by different voices or instrumental parts.

fulcrum ['fʊlkrəm] (pl **fulcrums** OR **fulcra** [-krə]) n the central point that something turns on or is balanced on.

fulfill US, **fulfil** GB [fʊlˈfɪl] (pt & pp **fulfilled**, cont **fulfilling**) vt -1. [promise, ambition, duty] to carry out <sthg> □ *It was not the first time he had failed to fulfill his promise to us.* -2. [need, requirement, condition] to satisfy <sthg> □ *I'm afraid most of these candidates fail to fulfill the basic entrance requirements of the school.* □ *I don't really think she feels she has fulfilled herself in her job.*

fulfilling [fʊlˈfɪlɪŋ] adj [job, life] that makes one feel satisfied and happy because one is making good use of one's abilities □ *We can promise you a fulfilling career with plenty of opportunity for promotion.*

fulfillment US, **fulfilment** GB [fʊlˈfɪlmənt] n -1. a feeling of satisfaction or happiness that comes from making good use of one's abilities or from personal development □ *a deep sense of fulfillment.* -2. [of an ambition, promise, requirement] see **fulfill** □ *Seeing the new design in operation was the fulfillment of a dream.*

full [fʊl] ◇ adj -1. [glass, parking lot, hotel] that cannot contain any more □ *I'm sorry, but the hotel is full all weekend.* ■ **to be full of sthg** [of things, people] to contain a large amount or number of sthg; [of enthusiasm, imagination] to have a lot of sthg □ *Rome was full of tourists.* □ *She was full of questions.* -2. **to be full** [person] to feel full of food and not want to eat any more □ *I'm so full I couldn't eat another thing!* -3. [employment, details, name] complete □ *You don't have to pay the full amount.* □ *I want a full and frank assessment of the situation.* -4. [price, control, volume] maximum □ *We must make the fullest possible use of the facilities.* -5. [schedule, day] in which one is very busy and has little spare time □ *I have a very full week ahead of me.* ■ **to have a full life** to have a busy and satisfying life □ *Marsha leads a very full life for a woman of her age.* -6. [flavor, sound] strong and rich in quality □ *a full-flavored Brazilian coffee.* -7. [lips, figure] that looks attractively round and fat □ *She had full, rounded hips.* -8. [skirt, sleeves] that is made with a lot of material □ *She wore a long, full skirt.*
◇ adv -1. directly and with force □ *She took the impact full in the face.* -2. **to know full well**

that... to know very well that... □ *You know full well that I'm unable to help you right now.* -3. **full on** GB at maximum power, speed, volume etc □ *The heating was full on.*
◆ **in full** adv completely □ *Please write your name out in full.* □ *The money has been repaid in full.*
◆ **to the full** adv as much as is possible □ *She lived life to the full.*

fullback ['fʊlbæk] n a soccer, rugby, or hockey player who plays at the back of the defense.

full-blooded [-ˈblʌdɪd] adj [support, attack, defense] that is strong and committed □ *He wrote a full-blooded attack on the monarchy.*

full-blown adj [war, argument] that has all the elements that make it complete and is therefore serious □ *The drug can slow down the development of full-blown AIDS.*

full board n an arrangement at a hotel or guesthouse in which guests pay to have all their meals there.

full-bodied [-ˈbɒdɪd] adj [wine] that has a strong pleasant taste.

full dress n formal clothes worn for a special occasion, e.g. by soldiers on parade.

full-face adj [portrait, photo] that shows somebody's face from the front rather than from the side.

full-fledged US, **fully-fledged** GB [-ˈfledʒd] adj [doctor, member, movement] that has all the qualifications or characteristics necessary to be taken seriously □ *Miss Johnson is well on her way to becoming a full-fledged Hollywood star.*

full-frontal adj [photo, nudity] that shows all of the front part of a naked person's body.

full-grown adj [man, woman, animal] that is fully developed and will not grow any bigger.

full house n a situation in a theater, cinema etc when every seat is taken □ *We have a full house tonight.*

full-length ◇ adj -1. [mirror, portrait] that is big enough to show the whole of a person's body. -2. [dress, skirt, coat] that reaches down to the feet; [curtain] that reaches down to the floor. -3. [movie, novel] that is of the usual or standard length. ◇ adv [lie] with one's body stretched out to its greatest length.

full moon n the moon when it appears completely round.

fullness ['fʊlnəs] n -1. [of details, somebody's lips, clothing] see **full**. -2. phrase **in the fullness of time** at the right moment in the future □ *"When can we see it?" — "All in the fullness of time."*

full-page adj [advertisement, photo] that covers a whole page of a magazine or newspaper.

full-scale adj -1. [model, drawing, copy] that is the same size as the original object. -2. [war, investigation, attack] that uses all possible means □ *We want at all costs to avoid this conflict developing into a full-scale war.*

full-size(d) [-ˈsaɪz(d)] adj -1. [model] full-scale. -2. [animal, plant] full-grown. -3. US AUTO **a full-size car** a large sedan.

full stop GB ◇ *n* the punctuation mark (.) that comes after the last word of a sentence to show that the sentence is finished. ◇ *adv* a phrase used at the end of a statement to show that one refuses to discuss a subject further □ *I'm not going, full stop.*

full time *n* GB the moment when a sports game, especially a game of soccer, comes to an end.

◆ **full-time** ◇ *adj* [job, employment, course] that takes up all of the usual working hours of the week □ *Is your course full- or part-time?* □ *The number of people in permanent, full-time jobs is decreasing rapidly.* □ *full-time staff.* ◇ *adv* *She's going back to working full-time next month.*

full up *adj* **to be full up** [person] to feel full of food and not want to eat any more; [bus, train, hotel] not to have space to hold any more people □ *I'm full up after that meal.* □ *All the hotels were full up.*

fully ['fʊlɪ] *adv* **-1.** [understand, agree, satisfy] completely □ *We haven't fully decided our plans yet.* □ *He's not fully qualified yet.* **-2.** [describe, answer] in a way that includes everything that is necessary □ *We made every attempt to comply fully with their demands.*

fully-fledged *adj* GB = **full-fledged**.

fulsome ['fʊlsəm] *adj* [apology, praise] that seems exaggerated and not sincere (formal use).

fumble ['fʌmbl] ◇ *vt* **-1.** [catch, pass, ball] to handle <sthg> in an awkward and uncertain way. ◇ *vi* to use one's hands in an awkward and uncertain way. ■ **to fumble for sthg** to search for sthg with one's hands in an awkward and uncertain way □ *I held the flashlight while Steve fumbled for the switch.* **-2.** SPORT to drop <a ball> after catching it.

fume [fjuːm] *vi* to show or feel anger very strongly □ *When we eventually got there, Gina was fuming.*

◆ **fumes** *npl* strong-smelling gases or smoke □ *Mr Hobart, 58, was overcome by the fumes.* □ *gasoline fumes.*

fumigate ['fjuːmɪgeɪt] *vt* [room, building] to remove germs, disease, or insects from <a place>, using chemicals.

fun [fʌn] ◇ *n* **-1.** pleasure and enjoyment; something that provides this □ *We had a lot of fun.* □ *It's no fun working with her!* □ *Come on, join in the fun!* ■ **for fun, for the fun of it** for pleasure or enjoyment, rather than for any serious reason □ *We just went for the fun of it.* **-2. to be fun** [person] to have the ability to enjoy oneself and amuse others □ *I like Paul, he's great fun.* □ *She's really fun to be with.* **-3.** *phrase* **to make fun of sb, to poke fun at sb** to make sb look foolish by making jokes or unkind comments about them □ *Are you making fun of me?* ◇ *adj* [person, activity] that provides pleasure or enjoyment (informal use) □ *He's a real fun person.* □ *a fun thing to do.*

function ['fʌŋkʃn] ◇ *n* **-1.** [of a person, thing] the special purpose of somebody or something □ *It is the function of a lawyer to provide sound legal advice.* **-2.** [of the heart, brain] the way that something works □ *This may eventu-*

ally impair the function of the liver. **-3.** [at a place] a formal or official dinner or party □ *The President will attend a number of official functions during his visit.* **-4.** MATH a value that varies according to the changes of other values that affect it. **-5.** COMPUTING a series of instructions that tell a computer to perform a particular task. **-6.** COMPUTING a special feature available on a computer.

◇ *vi* **-1.** [machine, system] to work properly □ *After the operation, your knee should soon be functioning normally again.* **-2. to function as sthg** to perform the role of sthg □ *This room also functions as a workshop.*

functional ['fʌŋkʃnəl] *adj* **-1.** [furniture, design] that is made to be used for a practical purpose only and is simple and without decoration □ *The furniture in his room is all plain and functional.* **-2.** [machine, system] that is working properly □ *The network is no longer functional.*

functionary ['fʌŋkʃnərɪ] (*pl* **functionaries**) *n* a person whose job involves official duties.

function key *n* a key on a computer keyboard that is pressed to perform a particular operation.

fund [fʌnd] ◇ *n* **-1.** a large amount of money that is collected for a particular purpose, especially to help people □ *The money collected will go to the Lifeboat Fund.* □ *My parents set up a trust fund for me when I was still in school.* **-2. a fund of experience/knowledge etc** a large amount of experience/knowledge etc □ *You will have access to staff with a fund of expertise in the fields of economics and finance.* ◇ *vt* [project, research] to provide money for <sthg> □ *The center is funded by a local charity.*

◆ **funds** *npl* money that is available to an organization, a government etc, and can be spent in particular ways □ *Funds are low, so don't expect too much!*

fundamental [ˌfʌndə'mentl] *adj* **-1.** [belief, change, mistake] that is basic and important □ *There's a fundamental difference between the two approaches.* **-2. to be fundamental to sthg** to be essential for making sthg possible or complete □ *This research is fundamental to our understanding of the human brain.*

◆ **fundamentals** *npl* things which are basic and important □ *the fundamentals of chemistry.*

fundamentalism [ˌfʌndə'mentlɪzm] *n* belief in a very strict basic form of a particular religion.

fundamentalist [ˌfʌndə'mentlɪst] *n*: *see* **fundamentalism** □ *Christian/Islamic fundamentalists.*

fundamentally [ˌfʌndə'mentlɪ] *adv* **-1.** [right, flawed, incompatible] **fundamentally,...** a word used to show that one is talking about the basic nature of something □ *Fundamentally, it's the same system we had before.* □ *Professor Weiss's argument is, however, fundamentally flawed.* □ *The message is fundamentally one of hope.* **-2.** [change, alter, disagree] in an important way that cannot be ignored.

funding ['fʌndɪŋ] *n* money that a government, organization etc provides for something □

I'm trying to get funding for a further degree. □ *Where will the funding come from?*

fund manager *n* a person whose job is to invest money on behalf of clients.

fund-raising [-reɪzɪŋ] *n* the activity or job of collecting money for a purpose, especially to help people □ *a fund-raising campaign/event.*

funeral ['fjuːnrəl] *n* a ceremony at which a dead person is buried or burned □ *Only close relatives attended the funeral.* □ *a funeral procession.*

funeral director *n* a person whose job is to organize funerals.

funeral parlor *n* the place where a funeral director receives clients and prepares the body of a dead person before a funeral.

funeral service *n* a religious service that is held before a dead person is buried or burned.

funereal [fjuːˈnɪərɪəl] *adj* [music, atmosphere] that is sad and reminds one of funerals or death □ *a funereal silence.*

funfair ['fʌnfeəʳ] *n* GB an outdoor event with bright lights and music, where people enjoy themselves by riding on fast machines and playing games of skill or strength.

fungus ['fʌŋɡəs] (*pl* **fungi** [-ɡaɪ] OR **funguses**) *n* a type of plant, e.g. a mushroom, that does not have any flowers, leaves, or green coloring □ *There was fungus growing all over the wall.*

funk [fʌŋk] *n* MUSIC a type of modern dance music with a strong beat and guitar rhythms.

funky ['fʌŋkɪ] (*compar* **funkier**, *superl* **funkiest**) *adj* [music, rhythm, beat] *see* **funk**.

funnel ['fʌnl] (US *pt* & *pp* **funneled**, *cont* **funneling**, GB *pt* & *pp* **funnelled**, *cont* **funnelling**) ◇ *n* -1. a tube that is wide at the top and narrow at the bottom and is used for pouring liquids or powders into a container with a narrow neck. -2. a metal chimney on a ship. ◇ *vt* -1. [water, oil] to make <a liquid> go through a narrow space. -2. [crowd, money] to make <sthg> go somewhere in a controlled way. ◇ *vi* [people] to move somewhere through a narrow space □ *The crowd funneled out of the gates.*

funnily ['fʌnɪlɪ] *adv* [smile, act] in a strange way □ *I thought Steve was behaving funnily when I last saw him.* ■ **funnily enough,...** a phrase used to introduce a piece of information that one thinks is strange or surprising □ *Funnily enough, I ran into her just yesterday.*

funny ['fʌnɪ] (*compar* **funnier**, *superl* **funniest**) *adj* -1. [joke, story, person] that is amusing and makes people laugh □ *I don't see what's so funny about it!* □ *He's the funniest man I've ever heard!* -2. [situation, person] that one finds interesting, surprising, or worrying □ *It's a funny world.* □ *The funny thing is, I'd never even met him before.* -3. **to feel funny** to feel slightly ill or slightly worried (informal use).

◆ **funnies** *npl* **the funnies** US the comic strips in a newspaper.

funny bone *n* the sensitive part of the elbow that hurts very much if it is hit.

funny farm *n* a mental hospital (informal and humorous use).

fun run *n* an event in which people run a certain distance in order to collect money for a particular purpose, especially for charity.

fur [fɜːʳ] *n* -1. [of a cat, fox, rabbit] the soft thick hair that covers the body of some animals □ *a piece of rabbit fur.* -2. [for clothes] the skin of an animal that is covered with fur; an item of clothing, especially a coat, that is made from this or from an artificial material that looks like it □ *a fur collar* □ *a fur-lined hat* □ *She was wrapped in expensive fur.* -3. [on one's tongue] a white coating on one's tongue.

fur coat *n* a coat made from the fur of an animal.

Furies ['fjʊərɪz]: **the Furies** in Roman and Greek mythology, three goddesses who punished people who had done something wrong.

furious ['fjʊərɪəs] *adj* -1. [person] who is very angry □ *Mary will be furious with us if we're late.* -2. [effort, activity, discussion] that is very energetic and uncontrolled □ *The runners set off at a furious pace.*

furiously ['fjʊərɪəslɪ] *adv* -1. [shout, deny, react] very angrily □ *an accusation which she furiously denied.* -2. [run, try, fight] in a wild or uncontrolled way □ *The cat was scrabbling furiously at the door.*

furled [fɜːʳld] *adj* [flag, umbrella, sail] that is rolled or folded up because it is not being used.

furlong ['fɜːʳlɒŋ] *n* a unit (201 meters) used mainly in horse racing for measuring distance.

furnace ['fɜːʳnɪs] *n* a very large oven used for industrial purposes, e.g. in iron and steel production.

furnish ['fɜːʳnɪʃ] *vt* -1. [room, house, office] to provide <a place> with furniture □ *They had furnished the apartment with beautiful antiques.* -2. [goods, proof] to provide <sthg that somebody wants> □ *They furnished us with all the information we needed.*

furnished ['fɜːʳnɪʃt] *adj* [apartment, room] that contains furniture □ *We're looking for somewhere that's fully furnished.*

furnishings ['fɜːʳnɪʃɪŋz] *npl* a collective term for the furniture and fittings in a room or house □ *soft furnishings.*

furniture ['fɜːʳnɪtʃəʳ] *n* a collective term for the movable objects, e.g. tables and chairs, that are found in a room and have particular uses □ *a piece of furniture* □ *We had hardly any furniture when we moved in.*

furniture polish *n* a polish that is used for cleaning the surface of wooden furniture so that it shines.

furor ['fjʊərɔːʳ] US, **furore** [fjʊəˈrɔːrɪ] GB *n* a situation in which a lot of anger or excitement is expressed by people who are reacting to something □ *His comments caused a furor in the national press.*

furphy ['fɜːʳfɪ] (*pl* **furphies**) *n* AUS a rumor or untrue story (informal use).

furrier ['fʌriər] *n* a person who makes or sells clothes made from fur.

furrow ['fʌrou] *n* -1. a long deep line in a field, caused by the soil being turned over by a plow. -2. a deep line in the skin of somebody's face, especially on the forehead.

furrowed ['fʌroud] *adj* -1. [field, land] that has furrows. -2. [brow] that is covered with wrinkles because one is frowning.

furry ['fɜːrɪ] (*compar* **furrier**, *superl* **furriest**) *adj* -1. [animal, coat] that is covered with fur □ *I felt something furry rub against my leg.* -2. [material, toy] that is made from something that is similar to fur.

further ['fɜːrðər] (*compar of* **far**) ◇ *adv* -1. [walk, travel, jump] a greater distance □ *How much further is it?* □ *My next trip took me even further from home.* -2. [complicate, develop] to a greater extent □ *We need to cut costs still further.* ■ **to go further with sthg, to take sthg further** to continue with sthg □ *I'm not sure that I want to take this case any further.* ■ **this must not go any further** you must not tell this to anybody else.
◇ *adj* [information, assistance, developments] more, extra □ *Any further questions?* ■ **until further notice** until you receive different instructions □ *The service has been suspended until further notice.*
◇ *vt* [career, cause] to help <sthg> to develop and become more successful □ *We hope to further our aims by writing to all the papers.*
♦ **further to** *prep* BUSINESS **further to your letter of the 6th** on the subject of your letter of the 6th (formal use).

further education *n* GB education received after leaving school, but not at university.

furthermore [,fɜːrðər'mɔːr] *adv* a word used to introduce another important point in an argument or explanation □ *Furthermore, Jonson had no authority to give these instructions.*

furthermost ['fɜːrðərmoust] *adj* that is furthest away (formal use).

furthest ['fɜːrðɪst] (*superl of* **far**) ◇ *adv* -1. [walk, travel, jump] the greatest distance □ *It's the furthest I've ever been from home.* -2. [develop, advance] in the greatest detail or to the greatest extent □ *Who got the furthest with solving the problem?* ◇ *adj* [house, outpost] that is the greatest distance away □ *It's the large white one, the furthest on your left.*

furtive ['fɜːrtɪv] *adj* [person] who acts as if they are keeping something secret, especially something they should not be doing □ *He gave her a furtive glance.*

furtively ['fɜːrtɪvlɪ] *adv* [look, behave] *see* **furtive** □ *I furtively removed the empty wine bottle from the table.*

fury ['fjʊərɪ] *n* extreme anger □ *She was white with fury.* ■ **in a fury** very angry □ *He left in a fury, slamming the door behind him.*

fuse [fjuːz] ◇ *n* -1. ELECTRICITY a device in a plug or electric system containing a short thin piece of wire that melts and breaks the circuit if too much electricity passes through it. -2. [of a firework, bomb] a piece of wire,

rope, paper etc that carries fire to a firework or bomb and causes it to explode after a certain period of time.
◇ *vt* -1. to join <pieces of metal> together using heat. -2. to combine <ideas, systems, styles> etc to create something new.
◇ *vi* -1. GB ELECTRICITY [plug, light] to stop working because a fuse has melted. -2. [pieces of metal] *The girders had fused into a single mass.* -3. [ideas, systems, styles] *The three religions fused into a single creed.*

fusebox ['fjuːzbɒks] *n* a box that is usually found on an inside wall of a building and that contains the fuses for the electric circuits in the building.

fused [fjuːzd] *adj* GB [appliance, plug] that has a fuse □ *Is this plug fused?*

fuselage ['fjuːzəlɑːʒ] *n* the main part of an airplane, but not the wings, tail, or nose.

fuse wire *n* the wire that is used in fuses.

fusillade [US 'fjuːsəleɪd, GB ,fjuːzə'leɪd] *n* a large number of shots fired from several guns in a short period of time.

fusion ['fjuːʒn] *n* -1. [of ideas, systems, styles] *see* **fuse** □ *a fusion of jazz and hard rock.* -2. PHYSICS a reaction in which two nuclei combine and release energy □ *atomic fusion.*

fuss [fʌs] ◇ *n* unnecessary excitement, anxiety, or anger □ *What's all the fuss about now?* ■ **to kick up** OR **make a fuss** to show that one is excited, anxious, or annoyed, often about something that is not very important, by talking loudly or shouting to attract people's attention □ *They made a big fuss about the size of the bill.* ■ **to make a fuss of sb** to show sb a lot of attention, hospitality, or affection □ *Grandma loves to make a fuss of the children when they come to see her.* ◇ *vi* to behave in an excited or anxious way, especially when it is unnecessary □ *You're always fussing about something, try to relax!*
♦ **fuss over** *vt fus* **to fuss over sb** to show sb too much attention in an excited or anxious way □ *Quit fussing over the poor boy and give him a chance to get his coat off.*

fussy ['fʌsɪ] (*compar* **fussier**, *superl* **fussiest**) *adj* -1. [person, eater, customer] who is very particular about details and is difficult to please □ *He's very fussy about who he lends his CDs to.* -2. [dress, furniture] that is decorated with too much detail □ *a white blouse with lots of fussy little bows and ribbons on it.*

fusty ['fʌstɪ] (*compar* **fustier**, *superl* **fustiest**) *adj* -1. [room, clothing] that smells old and unpleasant because it has been kept away from fresh air for a long time. -2. [person, idea, attitude] old-fashioned.

futile [US 'fjuːtl, GB -aɪl] *adj* [attempt, action, question] that does not achieve any useful results □ *It's futile trying to reason with him.*

futility [fjʊ'tɪlətɪ] *n*: *see* **futile** □ *The movie depicts the futility of war.*

futon ['fuːtɒn] *n* a thin cotton mattress for sleeping on that can be folded when it is not being used.

future ['fjuːtʃər] ◇ *n* -1. [in time] the time that

comes after the present □ *We must look to the future, not to the past.* ■ **in the future** at a time after now □ *Sometime in the future, I would like to be my own boss.* □ *I hope to hear from you in the near future.* **-2.** [of a person] the things that will happen to somebody or something in the future □ *You have to think of your future.* □ *You have a great future ahead of you.* ■ **to have a future** to be likely to be successful □ *This kind of hardware has no future.* **-3.** GRAMMAR **the future (tense)** the tense of the verb that is used to refer to future actions and states.
◇ *adj* **-1.** [date, generation] that will exist in the future; [event, occasion] that will happen in the future □ *It may not help us, but it's something that future generations will benefit from.* □ *I kept the document for future reference.* **-2.** [president, wife] who is soon to have a particular job or role □ *Meet your future boss.*
◆ **in (the) future** *adv* on the next similar occasion and on all other similar occasions after that □ *In the future, I will personally be checking the accounts.* □ *Try to be more careful in future.*
◆ **futures** *npl* FINANCE contracts to buy commodities, currencies etc at prices fixed in the present, with payment and delivery made at a time in the future.

futuristic [ˌfjuːtʃəˈrɪstɪk] *adj* [architecture, design, world] that appears very modern, as if it belonged to the future.

fuzz [fʌz] *n* **-1.** short, soft, light hairs on somebody's skin. **-2. the fuzz** the police (informal and old-fashioned use).

fuzzy [ˈfʌzɪ] (*compar* **fuzzier**, *superl* **fuzziest**) *adj* **-1.** [hair] that forms a soft curly mass. **-2.** [image, sound] not clear. **-3.** [idea, mind] confused □ *My head feels fuzzy after last night.*

fwd. *abbr of* **forward.**

fwy *abbr of* **freeway.**

FY *n abbr of* **fiscal year.**

FYI *abbr of* **for your information.**

G

g¹ [dʒiː] (*pl* **g's** OR **gs**), **G** [dʒiː] (*pl* **G's** OR **Gs**) *n* the seventh letter of the English alphabet.
◆ **G** ◇ *n* MUSIC one of the notes in Western music. ◇ **-1.** *abbr of* **good.** **-2.** (*abbr of* **general audience** OR **exhibition**) a symbol used in the USA and Australia to show that a movie or videotape is suitable for everybody to watch.

g² **-1.** *abbr of* **gram.** **-2.** *abbr of* **gravity.**

G7 [ˌdʒiːˈsevn] *adj* (*abbr of* **Group of Seven**) a group of seven major industrial nations: the USA, Japan, Canada, France, Germany, Italy, and Britain.

GA *abbr of* **Georgia.**

gab [gæb] *n* → **gift.**

gabardine [ˈgæbərdiːn] *n* **-1.** a thick, soft, waterproof material that is used for making clothes □ *a gabardine suit/coat.* **-2.** a coat made from gabardine.

gabble [ˈgæbl] ◇ *vi* to speak quickly and in an unclear way □ *He was gabbling on about nothing as usual.* ◇ *vt*: *She gabbled (out) her story.* ◇ *n* the sound of a person or people gabbling.

gable [ˈgeɪbl] *n* the top part of a wall of a house that forms a triangle under the roof.

Gabriel [ˈgeɪbrɪəl] in the Bible, the angel sent by God to tell Mary that she would be the mother of Jesus.

gad [gæd] (*pt* & *pp* **gadded**, *cont* **gadding**)
◆ **gad about** *vi* to move or travel around enjoying oneself, rather than doing something useful (informal and old-fashioned use).

gadget [ˈgædʒɪt] *n* any small device, especially one that is used in people's homes, e.g. a can opener □ *a kitchen gadget.*

gadgetry [ˈgædʒɪtrɪ] *n* gadgets.

Gaelic [ˈgeɪlɪk] ◇ *n* a language spoken in Ireland and parts of Scotland. ◇ *adj*: *Gaelic poetry/speakers.*

gaffe [gæf] *n* an embarrassing mistake made in a social situation □ *I made a terrible gaffe at Sarah's wedding.*

gag [gæg] (*pt* & *pp* **gagged**, *cont* **gagging**) ◇ *n* **-1.** a piece of material used to cover or block somebody's mouth so that they cannot speak or shout. **-2.** a joke, especially one told by a professional comedian (informal use). ◇ *vt* **-1.** [person] to put a gag on or in the mouth of <sb> □ *He was found in the cellar, tied up and gagged.* **-2.** [journalist, newspaper] to stop <sb/sthg> from telling people something that is an official secret. ◇ *vi* to choke as if one is going to vomit □ *The smell made him gag.*

Gagarin [gəˈgɑːrɪn], **Yuri** (1934–1968) a Russian cosmonaut who became the first person to go into space in 1961.

gage [geɪdʒ] *n* & *vt* US = **gauge.**

gaiety [ˈgeɪətɪ] *n* an atmosphere or feeling of fun and happiness.

gaily [ˈgeɪlɪ] *adv* **-1.** [talk, laugh, walk] in a cheerful way. **-2. gaily colored/dressed etc** brightly colored/dressed etc.

gain [geɪn] ◇ *n* **-1.** BUSINESS a financial profit □ *We made a net gain of $300,000.* **-2.** [for oneself] the improvement of one's own situation □ *Financial gain was her sole motive.* **-3.** [in output, weight, popularity] an increase or improvement in quality or quantity □ *There has been a considerable gain in productivity.*
◇ *vt* **-1.** [support, advantage, reputation] to get <sthg useful>, especially over a period of time □ *He has gained the respect of his colleagues.* □ *There's nothing to be gained by staying.* **-2.** [confidence, speed, weight] to get more

of <sthg> □ *I'm gaining strength every day.*
-3. [watch, clock] to go ahead of time by <seconds, minutes, or hours> □ *For some reason, my watch gains a few minutes a day.*
◇ *vi* **-1. to gain in sthg** [in strength, experience] to gradually get or develop more of sthg □ *Every day the party is gaining in popularity.* **-2.** [from a deal, change] to get something useful from an event or situation □ *We hope to gain from* OR *by the removal of tariffs.* **-3.** [watch, clock] to go too fast □ *My watch keeps gaining!*
◆ **gain on** *vt fus* **to gain on sb** [on a rival, opponent, competitor] to reduce the space between oneself and sb who is ahead □ *Can't you go any faster? They're gaining on us!*

gainful ['geɪnfl] *adj* **to be in gainful employment** to be doing a job for which one is paid (formal use).

gainfully ['geɪnflɪ] *adv* **to be gainfully employed** to be doing a job for which one is paid (formal use).

gainsay [ˌgeɪn'seɪ] (*pt* & *pp* **gainsaid** [ˌgeɪn'sed]) *vt* [statement, fact] to deny or contradict <sthg> (formal use).

Gainsborough [US 'geɪnzbɜːrou, GB -brə], **Thomas** (1727–1788) a British artist, well known for his landscapes and portraits of people in fashionable society.

gait [geɪt] *n* the particular way in which somebody walks (formal use) □ *I immediately recognized Luther's slow, rambling gait.*

gaiters ['geɪtərz] *npl* cloth or leather coverings for the lower front part of one's legs, usually worn by skiers, climbers, or walkers to keep water or snow out.

gal. *abbr of* **gallon.**

gala [US 'geɪlə, GB 'gɑːlə] *n* **-1.** a special event organized to entertain people □ *a gala performance/occasion.* **-2.** GB SPORT a sports meeting □ *a swimming gala.*

galah [gə'lɑː] *n* a pink and gray cockatoo that is found in most parts of Australia and is popular as a cage bird.

Galahad ['gæləhæd], **Sir** in English legends, one of King Arthur's knights, known for being kind and honorable.

Galapagos Islands [US gə'lɑːpəgous-, GB -'læpəgəs-]: **the Galapagos Islands** a group of islands in the Pacific Ocean that form a province of Ecuador. They are famous for their giant tortoises. SIZE: 7,800 sq kms. POPULATION: 6,000.

galaxy ['gæləksɪ] (*pl* **galaxies**) *n* a large group of planets and stars.

gale [geɪl] *n* **-1.** a very strong wind □ *gale-force winds.* **-2. gales of laughter** a lot of loud laughter.

Galileo [ˌgælɪ'leɪou] (1564–1642) an Italian scientist, mathematician, and astronomer who built the first modern telescope and made many important discoveries.

gall [gɔːl] ◇ *n* **to have the gall to do sthg** to do sthg that seems rude or unfair □ *He had the gall to say I'd done nothing to help.* ◇ *vt* to make <sb> angry or annoyed because they

feel unfairly treated □ *What really galls me is watching him take the credit for all my hard work!*

gall. *abbr of* **gallon.**

gallant [*sense 1* 'gælənt, *sense 2* gə'lænt, 'gælənt] *adj* (old-fashioned use) **-1.** [fight, soldier] that is brave and honorable. **-2.** [man, gesture, behavior] that is very polite and helpful to other people, especially women □ *It was very gallant of you to give up your seat!*

gallantry ['gæləntrɪ] *n* gallant behavior (old-fashioned or formal use).

gall bladder *n* a part of one's body like a small bag that holds liquid produced by the liver.

galleon ['gælɪən] *n* a large sailing ship used in the past.

gallery ['gælərɪ] (*pl* **galleries**) *n* **-1.** [for exhibitions] a place where people go to see exhibitions of works of art □ *an art gallery.* **-2.** [for buying] a place where works of art are sold □ *a commercial gallery.* **-3.** [in a court] an area of seats or standing space above a room or hall, e.g. in a court or parliament, where people can watch and listen to what is happening □ *a public gallery* □ *the visitors' gallery.* **-4.** [in a theater] the highest section of seats facing the stage in a theater.

galley ['gælɪ] (*pl* **galleys**) *n* **-1.** a long low ship, often rowed by slaves, that was used in the past for trading or as a warship. **-2.** [on a ship] the kitchen in a ship or aircraft. **-3. a galley (proof)** PRINTING a copy of the pages of a book, printed on a continuous sheet, on which corrections can be made before printing the final pages.

Gallic ['gælɪk] *adj* [charm, style, humor] that is typically French.

galling ['gɔːlɪŋ] *adj* that one finds very annoying because it seems unfair □ *It's so galling knowing that all this trouble could have been avoided.*

Gallipoli [gə'lɪpəlɪ] a peninsula in Turkey where Allied troops tried unsuccessfully to land in World War I.

gallivant ['gælɪvænt] *vi* to go from one place to another enjoying oneself, rather than doing something useful (informal and old-fashioned use).

gallon ['gælən] *n* a unit (US 3.79 liters, GB 4.55 liters) used for measuring liquids, e.g. gasoline or water.

gallop ['gæləp] ◇ *n* **-1.** the fastest pace of a horse □ *The horse broke into a gallop.* **-2.** a ride on a horse that is running at its fastest pace □ *We went for a gallop.* ◇ *vi* **-1.** [horse] to run very fast, lifting all four legs off the ground once in every stride. **-2.** [person] to run fast □ *She came galloping down the stairs with excitement.*

galloping ['gæləpɪŋ] *adj* that is increasing very quickly □ *galloping inflation.*

gallows ['gælouz] (*pl* **gallows**) *n* a wooden structure on which criminals are killed by hanging.

gallstone ['gɔːlstoun] *n* a small hard lump that can form in the gall bladder and cause pain.

Gallup poll™ ['gæləp-] *n* a survey of a typical selection of the people in a country in which they are asked for their opinions on something or how they will vote in the next election.

galore [gə'lɔːʳ] *adv* **opportunities/money etc galore** a large number or amount of opportunities/money etc □ *Help yourself, there's food galore.*

galoshes [gə'lɒʃɪz] *npl* special rubber shoes that are used to cover normal shoes and protect them from rain or snow.

galvanize, -ise ['gælvənaɪz] *vt* **-1.** TECHNOLOGY to give <iron> a covering of zinc as a protection against rust. **-2. to galvanize sb into action** to make sb start doing something suddenly by making them feel shocked, angry, frightened etc □ *It took an election defeat to finally galvanize the party into action.*

Galway ['gɔːlweɪ] **-1.** a county in the west of the Republic of Ireland. SIZE: 5,939 sq kms. POPULATION: 178,180. ADMINISTRATIVE CENTER: Galway. **-2.** a port on the west coast of Ireland. POPULATION: 47,008.

Gama ['gɑːmə], **Vasco da** (1469–1525) a Portuguese explorer who discovered the sea route to India, around the Cape of Good Hope.

Gambia ['gæmbɪə]: **(the) Gambia** a country in West Africa, surrounded by Senegal. SIZE: 11,300 sq kms. POPULATION: 900,000 (*Gambians*). CAPITAL: Banjul. LANGUAGE: English. CURRENCY: dalasi.

gambit ['gæmbɪt] *n* **-1.** something that somebody does at the beginning of a game or situation in order to gain an advantage. **-2.** a phrase, statement, question etc used to start a conversation, argument etc □ *His favorite opening gambits usually involve saying something to shock people.*

gamble ['gæmbl] ◇ *n* an action or decision that involves a risk, but could produce a good result □ *Sometimes you've just got to take a gamble.* ◇ *vi* to risk money on something, e.g. the result of a horse race or game of cards □ *She's been known to gamble on the stock exchange.*

◆ **gamble on** *vt fus* **to gamble on sthg** to take a risk on sthg □ *She might come, but I wouldn't gamble on it.*

gambler ['gæmbləʳ] *n* a person who gambles regularly.

gambling ['gæmblɪŋ] *n* the activity of trying to make money by risking it on a horse race, game of cards etc □ *gambling debts.*

gambol ['gæmbl] (US *pt* & *pp* **gamboled**, *cont* **gamboling**, GB *pt* & *pp* **gambolled**, *cont* **gambolling**) *vi* [child, dog] to jump or run around in an excited playful way (literary use).

game [geɪm] ◇ *n* **-1.** a sport or test of skill, knowledge, chance etc that one takes part in to win against an opponent or to gain personal satisfaction □ *What's your favorite game?* **-2.** [for children] an activity, done especially by children, that involves pretending, following rules, using special toys etc; the equipment used for this □ *Let's play a game.* □ *Did you get any new games for Christmas?* **-3.** [of football, cards, chess] an event in which players or teams play against each other in order to win □ *How about a game of tennis?* **-4.** TENNIS one of the short sections that make a set in a tennis match □ *Game, set, and match to Navratilova.* **-5.** HUNTING wild animals or birds that are hunted and killed, especially for sport □ *game pie.* **-6.** *phrases* **to beat sb at their own game** to use the same tricks as sb in order to be in a better position than them □ *You'll just have to beat Owen at his own game, that's all.* ■ **what's your/his etc game?** a phrase used to ask why somebody is behaving in a particular way, usually because it appears to be dishonest. ■ **the game's up** a phrase used to tell somebody that their plan or activity is no longer a secret and that they cannot continue in the same way. ■ **to give the game away** to reveal a secret plan or activity.

◇ *adj* **to be game** [person] to be willing to do something unusual, difficult, or dangerous □ *He's always game for a laugh.*

◆ **games** ◇ *npl* an organized event in which competitions in a number of different sports take place □ *the Olympic Games.* ◇ *n* GB sports that are played at a school as part of the regular timetable.

gamekeeper ['geɪmkiːpəʳ] *n* a person whose job is to look after the animals and birds on a private area of land before they are hunted for sport.

gamely ['geɪmlɪ] *adv* [fight, continue] bravely □ *He very gamely attempted to finish the race, despite his injury.*

game reserve *n* an area of land on which wild animals and birds are kept and hunted for sport.

game show *n* a TV program where people play games or answer questions to try and win prizes.

gamesmanship ['geɪmzmənʃɪp] *n* the practice of distracting one's opponent or destroying their confidence to win a game.

gamma rays ['gæmə-] *npl* rays of very short wavelength from a radioactive source.

gammon ['gæmən] *n* meat from the cured back leg of a pig □ *a gammon steak.*

gamut ['gæmət] *n* **the gamut of sthg** the complete range of sthg □ *the whole gamut of emotions.* ■ **to run the gamut of sthg** [of emotion] to experience every possible kind of sthg.

gander ['gændəʳ] *n* a male goose.

Gandhi ['gændɪ], **Mahatma** (1869–1948) an Indian lawyer and religious leader who led the movement to make his country independent from Britain. He is famous for his policy of avoiding violence.

gang [gæŋ] *n* **-1.** [of criminals, workmen] an organized group of people, especially men, who work together □ *a criminal gang.* **-2.** [of friends, young people] a group of young people who often do things or go out together. **-3.** a group of young people who go around together and often cause trouble □ *a street gang.*

◆ **gang up** *vi* to act together as a group, e.g. to attack or frighten somebody □ *He complained that his workmates had been ganging up on him.*

Ganges ['gændʒiːz]: **the Ganges** a river in Asia that begins in the Himalayas and flows into the Bay of Bengal. It is a sacred river to Hindus.

gangland ['gæŋlænd] *adj* that is connected with criminal gangs □ *a gangland murder/racket.*

gangling ['gæŋglɪŋ], **gangly** ['gæŋglɪ] (*compar* **ganglier**, *superl* **gangliest**) *adj* [person, animal] that is tall and thin, has long legs, and moves awkwardly.

gangplank ['gæŋplæŋk] *n* a plank used by people for walking on or off a boat.

gangrene ['gæŋɡriːn] *n* the decay of a part of the body that is caused when disease, injury etc stops blood getting to it □ *Gangrene had set in in his foot.*

gangrenous ['gæŋɡrɪnəs] *adj* [wound, limb] that is affected by gangrene.

gangster ['gæŋstər] *n* a person who belongs to an organized gang of violent criminals.

gangway ['gæŋweɪ] *n* **-1.** = **gangplank**. **-2.** GB a passage between rows of seats, e.g. on a bus or in a theater.

gannet ['gænət] (*pl* **gannet** OR **gannets**) *n* a large white seabird that dives to catch fish.

gantry ['gæntrɪ] (*pl* **gantries**) *n* a high metal structure, built like a frame, that supports e.g. railroad signals, a crane, or a space rocket.

GAO *n abbr of* **General Accounting Office**.

gaol [dʒeɪl] *n* & *vt* GB = **jail**.

gap [gæp] *n* **-1.** [between two objects] an empty space between two things or in the middle of something □ *The dog disappeared through a gap in the hedge.* □ *There's a gap between the two seats.* **-2.** [in time] a short period of time when nothing is being done □ *I've got a gap in my schedule tomorrow afternoon.* **-3.** [in knowledge, report] something that is missing and makes something incomplete □ *There are large gaps in my knowledge of current affairs.* □ *Her death left a terrible gap in our lives.* **-4.** [between two ideas, people] a great difference between two things, people, or groups of people □ *There's a huge gap between one's dreams and reality.*

gape [geɪp] *vi* [person] to stare at somebody or something with one's mouth open in a way that shows one is stupid or surprised □ *He gaped at me in amazement.* □ *He just stood there gaping.*

gaping ['geɪpɪŋ] *adj* **a gaping hole/wound** a very wide hole/wound.

garage [US ɡə'rɑːʒ, GB 'gærɑːʒ] *n* **-1.** a building, often attached to a house, where a car is kept □ *a garage door.* **-2.** a place where cars are serviced, repaired, and sold, and where gasoline is sometimes sold □ *My car's at the garage.* □ *a garage mechanic.*

garage sale *n* a sale of unwanted clothes, books, records etc, usually held in somebody's garage.

❤ GARAGE SALE
Garage sales are very popular in the USA and Australia. When people want to get rid of things in their home that they no longer want, for example because they are moving, they hold a garage sale, which can include furniture, clothes, books, and tools. The sale may take place in their garage, inside their house, in their yard, or even on the street outside the house. Garage sales are advertised in local newspapers or on signs around the neighborhood.

garb [ɡɑːrb] *n* clothing (formal use).

garbage ['gɑːrbɪdʒ] *n* **-1.** US things that people no longer want and throw away, e.g. waste food, used paper, and empty cans. **-2.** nonsense (informal use).

garbage bag *n* US a plastic bag placed inside a trash can and used to collect trash.

garbage can *n* US a container with a lid, usually kept in the kitchen or outside the house, in which people put their garbage.

garbage collector *n* US a person whose job is to collect people's garbage and take it away.

garbage disposal *n* US a device fitted to the drain of a kitchen sink that breaks up waste food so that it can go down the drain with water.

garbage truck *n* US a truck that is used for collecting garbage from people's houses.

garbled ['gɑːrbld] *adj* [message, explanation] that is confused and difficult to understand □ *He left a garbled message on my answering machine.*

Garda ['gɑːrdə] *n* **the Garda (Síochána)** the police force of the Irish Republic.

garden ['gɑːrdn] ◇ *n* **-1.** an area of private ground in front of or behind a house that usually has a lawn and flowerbeds, bushes, trees etc and is used for relaxation and to look at □ *a front/back garden* □ *a garden plant* □ *garden furniture/tools.* **-2.** = **vegetable garden**. ◇ *vi* to take care of a garden by keeping it tidy, weeding, planting flowers etc.

◆ **gardens** *npl* a public area containing lawns, trees, flowerbeds etc.

garden center *n* a store that sells gardening equipment, seeds, plants etc.

garden city *n* GB a town that has been specially designed to have a lot of open green spaces and trees.

gardener ['gɑːrdnər] *n* a person whose job is to look after gardens; a person who enjoys gardening as a hobby or pastime.

gardenia [gɑːr'diːnjə] *n* a plant with dark-green leaves and white or yellow flowers that smell very sweet.

gardening ['gɑːrdnɪŋ] *n* the activity of taking care of a garden □ *gardening gloves/equipment.*

garden party *n* a formal party held outdoors on a lawn or in a garden.

gargantuan [gɑːˈgæntʃʊən] *adj* enormous (literary use).

gargle [ˈgɑːgl] *vi* to wash one's throat by holding liquid in it and breathing out so that one blows bubbles through the liquid □ *Try gargling with an antiseptic solution.*

gargoyle [ˈgɑːgɔɪl] *n* a decoration in the form of an ugly person's or animal's head, that is part of a roof gutter on old buildings and which the rainwater flows out of.

Garibaldi [ˌgærɪˈbɔːldɪ], **Giuseppe** (1807–1882) an Italian soldier and nationalist leader.

garish [ˈgeərɪʃ] *adj* [piece of clothing, furniture] that is too brightly colored and is unpleasant to look at.

garland [ˈgɑːlənd] *n* a ring of flowers, leaves etc that is worn around one's head or neck or used as a decoration.

garlic [ˈgɑːlɪk] *n* a vegetable that looks like a small onion divided into segments, has a strong taste and smell, and is often used in cooking □ *a clove of garlic* □ *crushed garlic.*

garlic bread *n* pieces of cooked bread spread with garlic and butter.

garlicky [ˈgɑːlɪkɪ] *adj* [food, breath] that tastes or smells of garlic (informal use).

garment [ˈgɑːmənt] *n* a piece of clothing.

garner [ˈgɑːnər] *vt* [truth, news, support] to get <sthg>, often from several different places (formal use).

garnet [ˈgɑːnət] *n* a deep-red semi-precious stone.

garnish [ˈgɑːnɪʃ] ◇ *n* a vegetable, fruit, herb etc used to decorate food or to improve its taste □ *a salad garnish.* ◇ *vt* to decorate <food> with vegetables, fruit, herbs etc □ *Garnish the fish with lemon and parsley.*

garret [US ˈgerət, GB ˈgær-] *n* a small room below the roof of a house.

garrison [US ˈgerɪsən, GB ˈgær-] ◇ *n* troops who live in a town, base, fort etc to protect it. ◇ *vt* to protect <a place> as a garrison.

garrulous [US ˈgerələs, GB ˈgær-] *adj* [person] who talks too much □ *Pete tended to become garrulous when he was nervous.*

garter [ˈgɑːtər] *n* -1. a band worn around one's leg to keep socks or stockings in place. -2. US one of the four straps that are attached at one end to a woman's underwear and at the other end to her stockings to keep them up □ *a garter belt.*

gas [gæs] (*pl* **gases** OR **gasses**, *pt* & *pp* **gassed**, *cont* **gassing**) ◇ *n* -1. CHEMISTRY a kind of substance that is neither solid nor liquid and usually cannot be seen □ *the emission of poisonous gases into the atmosphere.* -2. [for heating, lighting, cooking] gas used as a fuel □ *There is no gas supply in the village.* -3. US = **gasoline**. ■ **to step on the gas** to make a vehicle go faster; to hurry up (informal use). -4. US excess gas produced in the stomach. ◇ *vt* to poison or kill <a person or animal> by making them breathe in poisonous gas.

gas can *n* US a plastic or metal container with

a handle and a long spout for keeping gasoline in, e.g. in one's car.

gas cap *n* US the cap or lid that covers the hole used for putting gasoline into a vehicle.

gas chamber *n* a room in which people or animals are killed using poisonous gas.

gas cooker *n* GB = **gas stove**.

gas cylinder *n* a cylindrical metal container for gas.

gaseous [US ˈgæsəs, GB ˈgæsɪ-] *adj* [substance] that is in the form of a gas.

gas fire *n* GB a heater in a room that uses gas for fuel.

gas fitter *n* GB a person whose job is to fit and repair gas appliances and pipes.

gas gage *n* US a gage that shows how much gas is left in a tank.

gash [gæʃ] ◇ *n* a large deep cut or wound □ *She has a nasty gash in her knee.* ◇ *vt* [arm, leg] to make a gash in <a part of one's body>.

gasket [ˈgæskət] *n* a seal used in a joint between metal surfaces to stop gas, oil, water etc from escaping.

gasman [ˈgæsmæn] (*pl* **gasmen**) *n* a person who checks gas meters.

gas mask *n* a mask worn as protection against poisonous gas.

gasmen [ˈgæsmen] *plural of* **gasman**.

gas meter *n* a meter in a building that measures how much gas has been used.

gasoline [ˈgæsəliːn] *n* US a liquid made from natural oil that is used as a fuel in motor cars and other engines.

gasometer [gæˈsɒmətər] *n* a very large, round, tall tank in a city in which gas for use as fuel is stored.

gas oven *n* -1. a kitchen oven that uses gas for fuel. -2. = **gas chamber**.

gasp [US gæsp, GB gɑːsp] ◇ *n* the act or sound of suddenly breathing in, that one makes when one feels pain, a shock, surprise etc □ *She gave a gasp of surprise.* ◇ *vi* -1. to breathe quickly and deeply through the mouth because one isn't able to get enough air into one's lungs □ *She emerged from under the water gasping for air.* -2. to give a gasp □ *The audience gasped at his audacity.* □ *We gasped in* OR *with amazement.*

gas pedal *n* US the pedal in a motor vehicle that one presses with one's foot in order to go faster.

gas station *n* US a place that sells gasoline for vehicles.

gas station attendant *n* US a person whose job is to fill cars with gas at a gas station.

gas stove *n* a kitchen stove that uses gas for fuel.

gassy [ˈgæsɪ] (*compar* **gassier**, *superl* **gassiest**) *adj* [water, beer] that contains too much gas in the form of carbon dioxide bubbles.

gas tank *n* US a container that supplies gasoline to the engine of a vehicle.

gas tap *n* a tap on a gas pipe that is used to turn a supply of gas on or off.

gastric ['gæstrɪk] *adj* **a gastric complaint** an illness of the stomach. ▪ **gastric juices** the acids in one's stomach that help to digest food.

gastric ulcer *n* an ulcer in the stomach.

gastritis [gæ'straɪtəs] *n* inflammation of the lining of the stomach.

gastroenteritis [,gæstrɒuentə'raɪtəs] *n* inflammation of the stomach and intestine.

gastronomic [,gæstrə'nɒmɪk] *adj*: see **gastronomy** □ *gastronomic delights.*

gastronomy [gæ'strɒnəmɪ] *n* the art and practice of cooking and enjoying very good-quality food.

gasworks ['gæswɜːʳks] (*pl* **gasworks**) *n* a place where gas for use as fuel is produced.

gate [geɪt] *n* **-1.** a barrier in a wall, fence, hedge etc that opens and closes on hinges □ *We climbed over the gate into the next field.* **-2.** an entrance in an airport which passengers go through to their airplane □ *Flight AI101 is now boarding at Gate 19.*

gâteau [US gæ'tou, GB 'gætou] (*pl* **gâteaux** [US gæ'touz, GB 'gætouz]) *n* GB a type of cake with cream in the middle and on top.

gatecrash ['geɪtkræʃ] ◇ *vt* to attend <a party, meeting> etc without an invitation. ◇ *vi*: *We tried to gatecrash but they wouldn't let us in.*

gatecrasher ['geɪtkræʃəʳ] *n* a person who has gatecrashed or tried to gatecrash a party, meeting etc.

gatehouse ['geɪthaus, *pl* -hauzɪz] *n* a house built next to a gate that is the entrance to a park, castle, estate etc.

gatekeeper ['geɪtkiːpəʳ] *n* a person whose job is to let people in and out of a gate next to a gatehouse.

gatepost ['geɪtpoust] *n* one of the two posts which a gate is attached or tied to.

gateway ['geɪtweɪ] *n* **-1.** [of a building] an entrance or exit which has a gate. **-2.** [to success] a means of getting something □ *An MBA is seen as a gateway to a career in management consultancy.* **-3.** [to a country] a route to a place □ *Singapore, gateway to the East.*

gather ['gæðəʳ] ◇ *vt* **-1.** [people, firewood, information] to bring <several people or things> together in one place from several different places □ *We gathered together all our belongings and piled them into the truck.* □ *He gathered the whole family together before making his announcement.* **-2. to gather speed** OR **momentum** to get faster □ *The reform process has been steadily gathering momentum.* ▪ **to gather force** OR **strength** [movement, party, campaign] to get stronger. **-3. to gather (that)...** to know that something is true because one has read it or heard it from somebody else □ *I gather (that) he won't be coming after all.* □ *I gather you told Emily I was sick.* **-4.** [cloth, garment] to pull <a piece of material> together to form folds or pleats □ *The skirt is gathered at the waist.*
◇ *vi* [people, animals, clouds] to come together in one place □ *A large crowd had gathered in the square to watch the fireworks.*

◆ **gather up** *vt sep* **to gather things up** to collect several things and put them all together.

gathering ['gæðərɪŋ] *n* a meeting of people; the people at this meeting □ *a social gathering.*

GATT [gæt] (*abbr of* **General Agreement on Tariffs and Trade**) *n* an international organization that was established in 1947 to encourage trade between its members. It was replaced in 1995 by the WTO.

Gatwick ['gætwɪk] a major international airport in England, south of London.

gauche [gouʃ] *adj* [person] who behaves in a clumsy way toward other people because they are not confident in social situations.

gaudy ['gɔːdɪ] (*compar* **gaudier**, *superl* **gaudiest**) *adj* [piece of clothing, color, jewelry] that is too bright and colorful and looks ugly and cheap.

gauge [geɪdʒ] ◇ *n* **-1.** [for measuring things] an instrument for measuring the amount or level of pressure, fuel, rain etc □ *a fuel gauge.* **-2.** [of a cable, wire] a standard measure of thickness. **-3.** RAIL the distance between the rails of a railroad. ◇ *vt* **-1.** [temperature, distance] to measure <sthg> by using an instrument. **-2.** to try to guess or judge sthg in advance □ *I'll try to gauge how much it'll cost.* □ *It's difficult to gauge how she'll respond.*

gaunt [gɔːnt] *adj* **-1.** [person, face, figure] that looks very thin, pale, and unhealthy □ *She looked pale and gaunt.* **-2.** [landscape, outline, building] that looks bare and depressing.

gauntlet ['gɔːntlət] *n* a strong protective glove that covers one's wrist. ▪ **to run the gauntlet of sthg** [of danger, criticism] to face sthg. ▪ **to throw down the gauntlet** to invite somebody to argue or compete with one.

gauze [gɔːz] *n* a very thin light cloth that is used especially to dress wounds.

gave [geɪv] *past tense of* **give**.

gawky ['gɔːkɪ] (*compar* **gawkier**, *superl* **gawkiest**) *adj* [person] who moves in a nervous awkward way □ *a gawky teenager.*

gawp [gɔːp] *vi* to stare in a stupid or rude way without any expression on one's face □ *They just stood there gawping.*

gay [geɪ] ◇ *adj* **-1.** [person] homosexual □ *Is he gay?* □ *gay men and women* □ *a gay bar.* ▪ **gay rights** the rights of gay people. **-2.** [person, place, music] cheerful and lively. **-3.** [color, piece of clothing] bright. ◇ *n* a homosexual person, especially a homosexual man □ *lesbians and gays.*

Gaza Strip [US ,gæzə-, GB ,gɑːzə-]: **the Gaza Strip** a strip of land on the Mediterranean between Egypt and Israel. It was occupied by Israel in 1967 and in 1993 plans were begun for limited Palestinian self-rule of the region.

gaze [geɪz] ◇ *n* a long fixed look □ *He returned her gaze.* ◇ *vi* to look steadily at somebody or something for a long time □ *They gazed at him/his work in admiration.*

gazebo [US gə'zeɪbou, GB -'ziːb-] (*pl* **gazebos**) *n* a decorative wooden structure like a hut, usually used in a garden for sitting and relaxing in.

gazelle [gə'zel] (*pl* gazelle OR gazelles) *n* a small type of antelope.

gazette [gə'zet] *n* an official news publication □ *The Evening Gazette.*

gazetteer [,gæzə'tɪəʳ] *n* an alphabetical list of places and their location.

gazump [gə'zʌmp] *vt* GB to refuse to sell one's house to <sb> after one has accepted their offer, because somebody else has offered more money.

GB *abbr of* **Great Britain**.

GBH *n* GB *abbr of* **grievous bodily harm**.

GC *n abbr of* **George Cross**.

GCH GB *abbr of* **gas central heating**.

GCHQ (*abbr of* **Government Communications Headquarters**) *n* the British government department that gathers information about other countries by listening to their radio broadcasts.

GCSE (*abbr of* **General Certificate of Secondary Education**) *n* in England and Wales, a school examination taken at the age of 16 in one of many subjects.

Gdns GB *abbr of* **Gardens**.

GDP *n abbr of* **gross domestic product**.

GDR (*abbr of* **German Democratic Republic**) = **East Germany**.

gear [gɪəʳ] ◇ *n* **-1.** TECHNOLOGY a system of wheels that sends power from an engine to the vehicle or machine it drives and allows changes in speed □ *a gear system/mechanism.* **-2.** [of a car, bicycle] a particular position of the gear system of a car or bicycle □ *I was driving along in fourth gear.* □ *You have to keep changing gear.* ■ **in/out of gear** with the gear system engaged/in neutral. **-3.** [for activity, sport] the equipment, clothes etc required for a particular activity or occasion □ *camping/fishing/football gear.* ◇ *vt* **to gear sthg to sb/sthg** to change sthg to suit sb/sthg □ *The course is geared to the needs of non-native speakers.*

◆ **gear up** *vt sep* **to gear sb/sthg up** to prepare sb/sthg □ *We're gearing ourselves up to meet the rise in demand.*

gearbox ['gɪəʳbɒks] *n* the part of a motor vehicle that contains the gear mechanism.

gearing ['gɪərɪŋ] *n* the way in which the speed ratios in a gear mechanism are set.

gear lever, **gear shift** US, **gear stick** GB *n* a lever used to change gear in a vehicle.

gear wheel *n* a cog wheel in a gear mechanism.

gee [dʒiː] *excl* **-1.** gee (whizz)! US a phrase used to show that one is surprised, impressed etc (informal use) □ *Gee! That sure looks great, Mrs Maine!* **-2.** gee up! GB a phrase used to tell a horse to start or go faster.

geek [giːk] *n* (informal use) **-1.** a boring unfashionable person. **-2.** a person who is very interested in computers.

geese [giːs] *plural of* **goose**.

Geiger counter ['gaɪgəʳ-] *n* a device for measuring levels of radioactivity.

geisha (girl) ['geɪʃə-] *n* a Japanese woman whose job is to entertain men.

gel [dʒel] (*pt* & *pp* gelled, *cont* gelling) ◇ *n* any substance like jelly, especially one used to wash hair or treat one's hair or body □ *shower gel.* ◇ *vi* **-1.** [idea, thought, plan] to become more clearly formed in one's mind. **-2.** [liquid] to become thicker like a jelly.

gelatin ['dʒelətɪn], **gelatine** ['dʒelətiːn] *n* a clear tasteless substance like jelly that is used in making jelly, soups etc.

gelding ['geldɪŋ] *n* a horse that has been castrated.

gelignite ['dʒelɪgnaɪt] *n* a powerful explosive □ *a stick of gelignite.*

gem [dʒem] *n* **-1.** a precious stone. **-2.** a person or thing that is highly valued.

Gemini ['dʒemɪnaɪ] *n* a sign of the zodiac, usually represented by a pair of twins; a person born under this sign between May 23 and June 21.

gemstone ['dʒemstoʊn] *n* a precious stone.

gen [dʒen] (*pt* & *pp* genned, *cont* genning) GB *n* information (informal use).

◆ **gen up** *vi* to find out as much as possible about something (informal use).

gen. *abbr of* **general, generally**.

Gen. MILITARY *abbr of* **General**.

gender ['dʒendəʳ] *n* **-1.** [of a person] one of the sexes, male or female, that a person or animal belongs to □ *gender issues.* **-2.** GRAMMAR one of the groups, masculine, feminine, or neuter, which nouns and pronouns in some languages belong to □ *What gender is the word "chaise"?*

gene [dʒiːn] *n* the part of a cell that contains the information that is passed from a parent to its children and that is responsible for a particular physical or mental feature □ *Scientists are trying to isolate the gene responsible for the disease.*

genealogist [US ,dʒiːnɪ'ɑːlədʒəst, GB -'æl-] *n* a person who studies or is an expert in genealogy.

genealogy [US ,dʒiːnɪ'ɑːlədʒɪ, GB -'æl-] (*pl* genealogies) *n* the study of the history of a family and the members of the family that lived a long time ago; the history of the family of a particular person.

genera ['dʒenərə] *plural of* **genus**.

general ['dʒenrəl] ◇ *adj* **-1.** [improvement, description, impression] a word used to summarize a situation, feeling, idea etc when one is not concerned with details or exceptions □ *The general effect is quite pleasing.* □ *I think I've got the general idea.* ■ **as a general rule** a phrase used to say what happens most of the time. **-2.** [interest, use, concern] a word used to refer to something that affects or concerns most people □ *We do not admit latecomers as a general rule.* □ *I think most people would agree that these measures are for the general good.* **-3.** [question, education] that is not

connected with one particular subject only □ *I have a few general inquiries to make.* □ *a book of interest to the general reader.* **-4.** [costs] a word used to refer to a number of things when there are too many to list separately □ *Stationery can be put under general expenses.*
◇ *n* MILITARY an army officer of high rank.

◆ **in general** *adv* **-1.** a phrase used to summarize a situation □ *In general, I think that's true.* **-2.** a phrase used to refer to most of the people or things in a group □ *society/the population/mankind in general.* **-3.** a phrase used to say that something happens or is true in most cases □ *In general, books are more expensive in Europe than in the States.*

General Accounting Office *n* the General Accounting Office the US government department that supervises the financial affairs of public organizations and local government.

general anesthetic *n* an anesthetic designed to make a patient unconscious.
NOTE: Compare **local anesthetic.**

general delivery *n* in the USA, a service that allows people to receive their mail at the post office.

general election *n* a national election for a new government.
NOTE: Compare **by-election.**

general hospital *n* a large hospital designed to treat all kinds of ill people.

generality [ˌdʒenəˈrælətɪ] (*pl* **generalities**) *n* a statement that does not contain any details.

generalization [US ˌdʒenrələˈzeɪʃn, GB -aɪˈzeɪʃn] *n* a vague general statement □ *The report is full of sweeping generalizations.*

generalize, -ise [ˈdʒenrəlaɪz] *vi* to make a generalization □ *You can't generalize about such a complex issue.*

general knowledge *n* knowledge of a wide variety of subjects □ *We had to answer questions on general knowledge, sport, and history.*

generally [ˈdʒenrəlɪ] *adv* **-1.** usually □ *Generally, we go shopping once a week.* □ *I don't generally like to discuss my ideas until they're more developed.* **-2. generally accepted/believed etc** accepted/believed etc by most people □ *I think it is generally agreed now that change is inevitable.* **-3.** [talk, discuss] without speaking about the details of a situation □ *Mrs Blackwell spoke generally about the problems facing the industry.*

general manager *n* a person in charge of a company, store etc who takes care of the everyday running of the business.

general practice *n* the work done by a GP.

general practitioner *n* → **GP** (formal use).

general public *n* the general public ordinary people in general.

general-purpose *adj* **general-purpose tools/clothes etc** tools/clothes etc suitable for several different uses etc.

general store *n* a store that sells several different kinds of goods.

general strike *n* a strike affecting all or most of a country's industries and services.

General Synod *n* the General Synod (of the Church of England) the group of church members who meet regularly and make decisions concerning the Church of England.

generate [ˈdʒenəreɪt] *vt* **-1.** [energy, electricity, heat] to produce <sth> □ *wind-generated power.* **-2.** [interest, excitement, business] to create <sth> □ *The project will generate hundreds of jobs in the area.*

generation [ˌdʒenəˈreɪʃn] *n* **-1.** [in a family, society] the people in a family or country who are about the same age □ *the younger generation.* ■ **first/second generation** [Italian, black] who is an immigrant/whose parents were immigrants □ *second-generation Irish immigrants.* **-2.** the period of time, usually considered to be about 25 to 30 years, that it takes for a person to grow up and have their own family □ *For generations the city was in decline.* **-3.** TECHNOLOGY a stage in the development of a product □ *the new generation of computers* □ *fourth-generation word processors.* **-4.** [of business, interest, energy] *see* **generate.**

generation gap *n* the difference in attitudes, customs, taste etc between younger and older generations of people.

generator [ˈdʒenəreɪtər] *n* a machine that produces electricity.

generic [dʒəˈnerɪk] *adj* [term, name] that applies to a whole group of similar things.

generosity [ˌdʒenəˈrɒsətɪ] *n* [of a person] the quality of being generous □ *We appreciate your generosity.*

generous [ˈdʒenrəs] *adj* **-1.** [person, nature] willing to give money, help etc freely □ *He's a very generous person.* **-2.** [gift, meal, portion] larger than is usual or expected □ *generous helpings of food.*

generously [ˈdʒenrəslɪ] *adv* **-1.** [agree, offer] willingly and kindly □ *Marc very generously offered to help.* **-2.** [pay, contribute] more than is usual or expected □ *Please give generously.*

genesis [ˈdʒenəsɪs] (*pl* **geneses** [-siːz]) *n* the genesis of sthg [of an idea, the world] the origin of sthg (formal use).

genetic [dʒəˈnetɪk] *adj* [characteristic, code, map] that is connected with genes or genetics.

◆ **genetics** *n* the scientific study of the way the characteristics of living things are passed from one generation to the next through the genes.

genetic engineering *n* the science of changing the characteristics of a living thing by altering its genes.

genetic fingerprinting [-ˈfɪŋɡərprɪntɪŋ] *n* a method of identifying an individual by studying the unique genetic structure of a sample of their blood, hair, saliva etc.

Geneva [dʒəˈniːvə] **-1.** a city in Switzerland, on Lake Geneva. It is an important banking center and many international organizations have their headquarters there. POPULATION: 171, 042. **-2. Lake Geneva** a lake in southern Europe, between France and Switzerland.

Geneva Convention *n* the Geneva Convention an international agreement on the treatment of wounded soldiers and prisoners during periods of war, signed in Geneva, Switzerland in 1864.

Genghis Khan [ˌdʒeŋgɪsˈkɑːn] (1162–1227) a Mongol emperor and soldier, known for his cruelty.

genial [ˈdʒiːnjəl] *adj* [person, remark, smile] that seems cheerful and friendly.

genie [ˈdʒiːnɪ] (*pl* **genies** OR **genii** [-ɪaɪ]) *n* a magical spirit in Arabian stories.

genitals [ˈdʒenɪtlz] *npl* the sex organs that are outside the body.

genius [ˈdʒiːnɪəs] (*pl* **geniuses**) *n* -1. a person who has a rare and great natural intelligence, ability, or talent □ *He's a mathematical genius.* -2. a rare and great natural ability or talent □ *That idea was a stroke of genius.* □ *She has a real genius for organization.*

genocide [ˈdʒenəsaɪd] *n* the planned or organized killing of a whole community, race etc.

genre [ˈʒɒnrə] *n* a particular type of literature, music, or other work of art □ *a master of the genre of crime writing.*

gent [dʒent] *n* GB = **gentleman** (informal use).
◆ **gents** *n* GB a men's public toilet (informal use) □ *Can you tell me where the gents is?*

genteel [dʒenˈtiːl] *adj* -1. [person] who seems respectable and refined. -2. [manner, voice] that is polite in an unnatural exaggerated way.

gentile [ˈdʒentaɪl] ◇ *adj* [person] who is not Jewish. ◇ *n* a person who is not Jewish.

gentle [ˈdʒentl] *adj* -1. [person, smile, manner] that is calm and kind □ *He was a kind, gentle man.* -2. [movement, touch] that is pleasant and light, and is not rough or violent □ *There was a gentle breeze blowing.* -3. [slope, curve] that is gradual, not steep or sharp □ *a gentle incline.* -4. [hint, reminder] that is mild and subtle □ *She dropped a few gentle hints.*

gentleman [ˈdʒentlmən] (*pl* **gentlemen**) *n* -1. a man who treats other people with politeness and consideration □ *He behaved like a real gentleman.* ■ **a gentleman's agreement** an agreement that is not written down and is made between people who trust each other. -2. a word used as a polite way of talking about a man □ *There's a gentleman to see you, Mrs Smith.*

gentlemanly [ˈdʒentlmənlɪ] *adj* [behavior, manners] polite and considerate.

gentlemen [ˈdʒentlmən] *plural of* **gentleman**.

gently [ˈdʒentlɪ] *adv* -1. [smile, touch, slope] *see* **gentle** □ *She gently reminded him it was time to leave.* -2. [move, heat] slowly and without sudden movements □ *a gently flowing river.*

gentry [ˈdʒentrɪ] *n* a collective term for people of a high social class.

genuflect [ˈdʒenjəflekt] *vi* to bend down with one knee on the ground as a sign of respect (formal use).

genuine [ˈdʒenjuɪn] *adj* -1. [antique, work of art] that is really what it seems to be and is not a copy □ *a genuine Ming vase.* -2. [person, feel-

ing, effort] that is sincere and not a pretense □ *Their intentions seem genuine enough.*

genuinely [ˈdʒenjuɪnlɪ] *adv* [feel, believe] *see* **genuine** □ *I was genuinely surprised/shocked/disappointed.* □ *a genuinely honest man.*

genus [ˈdʒiːnəs] (*pl* **genera**) *n* BIOLOGY a class of animals or plants within a family.

geographer [dʒɪˈɒgrəfəʳ] *n* an expert in geography.

geographical [dʒɪəˈgræfɪkl] *adj* [feature, survey, area] *see* **geography** □ *the town's geographical location.*

geography [dʒɪˈɒgrəfɪ] *n* -1. the study of the earth's surface, physical features, political boundaries, climate, populations, resources etc. -2. the way in which the parts of a place are arranged □ *I haven't quite worked out the geography of the area yet.*

geological [ˌdʒiːəˈlɒdʒɪkl] *adj* [feature, fault] *see* **geology** □ *a geological survey of the area.*

geologist [dʒɪˈɒlədʒəst] *n* an expert in geology.

geology [dʒɪˈɒlədʒɪ] *n* -1. the study of the rocks, soil etc that form the earth's crust and of the way in which they change and develop over long periods of time. -2. the characteristics of the rocks, soil etc in a particular area.

geometric(al) [ˌdʒiːəˈmetrɪk(l)] *adj* [shape, design, pattern] that consists of basic shapes such as triangles, circles, and squares.

geometry [dʒɪˈɒmətrɪ] *n* a mathematical science that deals with the measurement of lines, angles, curves, and shapes.

geophysics [ˌdʒiːoʊˈfɪzɪks] *n* the study of the physical qualities of the earth and the physical processes that happen in, on, and above it.

geopolitical [ˌdʒiːoʊpəˈlɪtɪkl] *adj: see* **geopolitics.**

geopolitics [ˌdʒiːoʊˈpɒlɪtɪks] *n* the study of the way in which a country's location, population etc affects its influence and power in the world.

Geordie [ˈdʒɔːʳdɪ] (informal use) ◇ *n* -1. a person from Tyneside, England. -2. a dialect of English spoken in Tyneside. ◇ *adj: a Geordie accent.*

George III [ˌdʒɔːʳdʒəˈθɜːʳd] (1738–1820) King of Great Britain and Ireland from 1760 to 1820. He suffered from insanity, especially toward the end of his reign.

George VI [ˌdʒɔːʳdʒəˈsɪksθ] (1895–1952) King of Great Britain and Northern Ireland from 1936 to 1952.

George Cross [ˌdʒɔːʳdʒ-] *n* **the George Cross** in Britain, a medal given to somebody who has done something very brave.

georgette [dʒɔːʳˈdʒet] *n* a thin strong material used for making clothes.

Georgia [ˈdʒɔːʳdʒə] -1. a country in western Asia, on the Black Sea, between Russia and Turkey. SIZE: 70,000 sq kms. POPULATION: 5,400,000 (*Georgians*). CAPITAL: Tblisi. LANGUAGE: Georgian. CURRENCY: rouble. -2. a state in the southeastern USA, north of Florida. ABBREVIATION: GA. SIZE: 152,488 sq kms. POPULATION: 6,478,216 (*Georgians*). CAPITAL: Atlanta.

Georgian ['dʒɔːˈdʒən] ◊ *adj* -1. [architecture, furniture] that is in the style of the period of the British kings George I to George IV (1714 to 1830). -2. *see* **Georgia**. ◊ *n*: *see* **Georgia**.

geranium [dʒəˈreɪnjəm] (*pl* **geraniums**) *n* a pot plant or garden plant with small red, pink, or white flowers and round leaves.

gerbil ['dʒɜːˈbl] *n* a small furry animal with long hind legs that is often kept as a pet.

geriatric [ˌdʒerɪˈætrɪk] *adj* -1. **a geriatric ward/ hospital etc** a ward/hospital etc for old people □ *My sister is a geriatric nurse.* -2. [infrastructure, system] that is very old and inefficient.

germ [dʒɜːˈm] *n* -1. a bacterium or virus that causes disease □ *a disinfectant guaranteed to kill all known germs.* -2. **the germ of an idea/a plan** the beginning of an idea/a plan that may develop.

German ['dʒɜːˈmən] ◊ *n* -1. a person who comes from or lives in Germany. -2. a language spoken in Germany, Austria, and Switzerland. ◊ *adj*: *the German economy.*

Germanic [dʒɜːˈrˈmænɪk] *adj* [style, feature, language] that is typical of Germany or the German people.

German measles *n* an infectious disease in which red spots appear on the body, and which is harmful to the unborn children of pregnant women.

German shepherd (dog) *n* a large dog that looks like a wolf and is often used by the police to help them catch criminals.

Germany ['dʒɜːˈmənɪ] a country in central Europe. It was divided into East and West Germany from 1945 to 1990. SIZE: 357,000 sq kms. POPULATION: 81,000,000 (*Germans*). CAPITAL: Berlin. LANGUAGE: German. CURRENCY: Deutschmark.

germicide ['dʒɜːˈmɪsaɪd] *n* a substance that kills germs.

germinate ['dʒɜːˈmɪneɪt] ◊ *vt* to make <a seed> start growing. ◊ *vi* -1. [seed] *The seeds need the right conditions to germinate.* -2. [idea, feeling] to start to develop □ *New concepts are germinating all the time.*

germination [ˌdʒɜːˈmɪˈneɪʃn] *n*: *see* **germinate** □ *Moisture is vital for germination.*

germ warfare *n* a method of fighting that involves using germs to spread disease among enemy troops.

Geronimo [dʒəˈrɒnəmoʊ] (1829–1909) a Native American chief of the Apache people who fought against Americans who came to settle on his land.

gerrymandering ['dʒerɪmændərɪŋ] *n* the changing of electoral boundaries to give one party an unfair advantage.

Gershwin ['gɜːˈʃwɪn], **George** (1898–1937) a US composer who used jazz, blues, and pop in his music. He wrote *Porgy and Bess* and *Rhapsody in Blue*.

gerund ['dʒerənd] *n* a noun formed from a verb that, in English, ends in *-ing*.

gestation [dʒeˈsteɪʃn] *n* the development of a baby or young animal in its mother's body before birth.

gestation period *n* -1. the period of time during which a baby or young animal develops in its mother's body. -2. the period of time during which an idea or plan is developed.

gesticulate [dʒesˈtɪkjəleɪt] *vi* [person] to move one's hands and arms in an angry or excited way to emphasize what one is saying or instead of using words □ *He gesticulated angrily.*

gesture ['dʒestʃər] ◊ *n* -1. a movement of a part of the body to express a particular emotion or idea □ *a hand gesture* □ *He made a large sweeping gesture with his hand.* □ *an insulting gesture.* -2. something that one says or does to show a particular feeling to somebody □ *a kind gesture* □ *a gesture of friendship/ defiance.* ◊ *vi* to make a gesture □ *He gestured to me to step forward.*

get [get] (US *pt* **got**, *pp* **gotten**, *cont* **getting**, GB *pt* & *pp* **got**, *cont* **getting**) ◊ *aux vb* **he got killed** he was killed (used with the past participle to form the passive) □ *Be careful, somebody could get hurt!* □ *Where did they get married?*

◊ *vt* -1. **he got a present from his wife** his wife gave, sent etc him a present □ *I got a letter/phone call from my sister.* □ *When did you get the news?* -2. **she got a surprise/shock** she had a surprise/shock, she was surprised/ shocked □ *I get the feeling that he doesn't like us.* □ *I get a real thrill out of driving fast.* -3. **I got a cold/the flu** I caught a cold/the flu □ *You can't get AIDS from kissing.* -4. **I must get a car** I must buy, find, win etc a car □ *He can't get a job anywhere.* □ *They got me a book for my birthday.* □ *She got a good grade.* -5. **I'll get my coat** I'll go to the place where my coat is and bring it back here □ *I'll just get you a drink from the bar.* □ *Could you go and get your sister, she's upstairs.* -6. **to get a person/an animal** to capture or kill a person/an animal □ *Did the police get him yet?* -7. **to get a rest** to have a rest, especially when this is needed □ *I need to get more exercise.* ■ **to get a look at sthg** to be able or allowed to look at sthg □ *I got a quick glimpse of his face.* ■ **to get the time/ opportunity to do sthg** to have or find the time/opportunity to do sthg □ *I don't often get the time to go to the theater.* □ *Visit the Louvre if you get the chance.* -8. **to get a bus/train** to find a bus/train in order to travel on it □ *Where do you get the bus?* □ *We got a flight to Athens.* -9. **to get dinner/lunch** to make or prepare dinner/lunch □ *Darren was in the kitchen getting (the) breakfast.* □ *We'll find a café and get some lunch there.* -10. **to get money/a salary** to be paid or earn money/a salary □ *He gets about $12,000 a year.* □ *We only got $5 for the picture.* -11. **to get a joke/an idea** to understand a joke/an idea □ *I don't get it — I thought she was your friend.* □ *They seemed to get the point I was trying to make.* -12. **what gets me...** what annoys me (informal use) □

What really gets me is that he never listens!
-13. to get sb/sthg to a place to move or
bring sb/sthg to a place □ *It's time to get the
children to bed.* □ *Get that report to me by 2
o'clock!* **-14. to get sb ready/worried etc** to
make sb ready/worried etc □ *The news got
me really worried.* □ *He got her pregnant.* □ *I
can't get this piece to fit.* **-15. to get sthg done**
to do what has to be done to make sthg
happen □ *We'll have to get the TV repaired.*
-16. to get sb to do sthg to employ or persuade sb to do sthg □ *I'll get my secretary to
make an appointment.* **-17. you get a lot of rain
here** there is a lot of rain here.
◇ *vi* **-1.** (*+ complement*) to become □ *I got really enthusiastic about it.* □ *My cold's getting better.* □ *It's time we got dressed.* **-2. we got home**
we came or arrived home □ *How do you get
to the station?* □ *The party was over by the time I
got there.* **-3. I got (up) to page 10** I reached
or made progress as far as page 10 □ *Life becomes easier when you get to my age.* □ *We got
as far as buying the paint.* ■ **to be getting somewhere** to be having some success □ *The work
started slowly, but now we're really getting somewhere.* **-4. to get to do sthg** to do sthg,
usually after having to wait, get permission,
or make an effort □ *Did you get to speak to
her?* □ *In the end we got to be very close friends.*
-5. to get going OR **moving** to start moving,
working, or being active □ *We'd better get going if we're going to finish the work today; see
also* **got.**
◆ **get about** *vi* = **get around.**
◆ **get across** *vt sep* **to get sthg across** [idea,
message] to succeed in making people understand sthg □ *We've failed to get our policies
across to the public.*
◆ **get ahead** *vi* [person] to be successful in
one's work or career □ *She really wants to get
ahead in life.*
◆ **get along** *vi* **-1.** [person] to make good progress □ *How are you getting along with the
work?* **-2.** [two people] to have a friendly relationship □ *My boss and I get along really well.* □
*I've just never gotten along with him, for some
reason.*
◆ **get around** ◇ *vt fus* **-1. to get around sthg**
[problem, obstacle, law] to find a way of dealing with or avoiding the problems caused by
sthg □ *It's a tricky situation, but we'll get around
it somehow.* **-2. to get around sb** to persuade
sb to do what one wants by being pleasant
to them □ *She really knows how to get around
her parents.* ◇ *vi* **-1.** [person] to go to different
places and see people □ *I don't get around
much any more.* □ *Having a car makes it easier to
get around.* **-2.** [news, information] to become
known by a large number of people □ *The
story soon got around that he'd been fired.*
◆ **get around to** *vt fus* **to get around to sthg**
to find time to do sthg that one should have
done before □ *I finally got around to fixing the
radiator.*
◆ **get at** *vt fus* **-1. to get at sthg** [book, branch]
to succeed in reaching sthg that is difficult
to reach; [information] to succeed in finding
out sthg that is hidden or not generally

known □ *Put the cake somewhere where the
children can't get at it.* □ *He was determined to
get at the truth.* **-2. what are you getting at?**
used to ask somebody to say clearly what
they mean, often when one thinks they
have said something unpleasant or unfair.
-3. to get at sb to keep criticizing sb in an
annoying way (informal use) □ *Stop getting at
me!*
◆ **get away** *vi* **-1.** [person] to succeed in leaving a place □ *I won't get away from the meeting
before six.* **-2.** [person] to go away on a vacation □ *I need to get away for a few days.* ■ **to
get away from it all** to have a complete
change from one's usual surroundings and
activities □ *It was great to get away from it all
for a few days.* **-3.** [robber, prisoner, animal] to
succeed in escaping □ *Thieves got away with
thousands of dollars in used bills.*
◆ **get away with** *vt fus* **to get away with sthg**
to do sthg bad and not to be punished for it
□ *He's so pushy, I don't know how he gets away
with it!*
◆ **get back** ◇ *vt sep* **-1. to get sb/sthg back**
[money, book, husband] to have sb/sthg that
one has lost or given to someone □ *She got
her old job back.* **-2. to get sb back** to do
something unpleasant to sb because of
something unpleasant that they have done
to oneself □ *I'll get you back for what you said!*
◇ *vi* **-1.** to move away □ *The police were telling everyone to get back.* **-2.** to arrive back at
the place one has left, especially one's home
□ *When did you get back from your vacation?*
◆ **get back to** *vt fus* **-1. to get back to sthg** to
start doing sthg again □ *Now, to get back to
what I was saying...* ■ **to get back to sleep** to
fall asleep again after waking up. ■ **to get
back to normal** to become normal again. ■ **to
get back to work** to start working again after
a rest, illness etc. **-2. to get back to sb** to
phone or write to sb at a later time, usually
because one cannot answer their question
straight away □ *Can I get back to you on that,
I'll need to think about it.*
◆ **get behind** *vi* to fail to do something by
the time that it should be done □ *You've gotten behind with your work/payments.*
◆ **get by** *vi* to have just enough money for
the things one needs to live normally □
*"How do you survive on $80 a week?" — "Oh,
we get by."*
◆ **get down** ◇ *vt sep* **-1. to get sb down** to
make sb unhappy or depressed □ *Don't let it
get you down.* **-2. to get sthg down** to take
sthg from a higher place □ *She got the book
down from the shelf.* ◇ *vi* **-1.** to bend or lower
oneself toward the ground □ *I got down on
my knees to pray.* **-2.** to climb down from
something □ *She got down from OR off the ladder.*
◆ **get down to** *vt fus* **to get down to sthg** to
start to do sthg important that one has been
unable to do earlier □ *Right, let's get down to
work/business.*
◆ **get in** ◇ *vi* **-1.** [person] to get inside a vehicle or a building □ *She opened the car door,
got in, and drove away.* □ *The burglar got in*

through an open window. **-2.** [train, plane] to arrive at its destination; [person] to arrive home □ *What time does your flight get in?* □ *He was out drinking and didn't get in until 3 o'clock.* **-3.** [politician, party] to win an election □ *It doesn't look as if the Republicans will get in this time.* ◇ *vt sep* **-1. to get sthg in** [washing, harvest, shopping] to go out and find, buy, or collect sthg and then bring it home □ *We'd better get in some food for the weekend.* **-2. to get sb in** [electrician, plumber] to get sb to come and do a job □ *We'll have to get someone in to fix the heater.*

◆ **get in on** *vt fus* **to get in on sthg** to become involved in sthg that other people have started to do □ *He's trying to get in on the deal.*

◆ **get into** *vt fus* **-1. to get into a vehicle/building** to get inside a vehicle/building □ *I had to borrow a key to get into the apartment.* **-2. to get into a piece of clothing** to be the right size for a piece of clothing □ *I've put on so much weight I can't get into this dress any more.* **-3. to get into sthg** [into a conversation, fight, profession] to become involved in an activity □ *He got into an argument with his boss.* □ *How do you get into advertising?* **-4. to get into a temper/mess** to start to be in a temper/mess □ *He got into trouble with the police.* **-5. to get into a school/college** to be accepted as a student at a school/college, usually by passing an exam □ *She got into Yale.* **-6. what's got into you?** why are you behaving so badly or strangely? □ *I don't know what's gotten into her lately.*

◆ **get off** ◇ *vt sep* **-1. to get a piece of clothing off** to remove a piece of clothing, often with difficulty □ *Get those wet shoes off.* **-2. to get sthg off** [letter, package] to put sthg in the mail, usually by a particular time □ *I'll get the tickets off to you today.* ◇ *vt fus* **-1. to get off sthg** [chair, horse, bicycle] to move or climb down from sthg □ *He told the children to get off the roof.* **-2. to get off sthg** [train, bus, plane] to leave sthg □ *She got off the streetcar at the next stop.* ◇ *vi* **-1.** [passenger] to leave a train, bus, plane etc □ *You need to get off at the next stop.* **-2.** [person, train] to leave a place because one has to go somewhere else □ *Did the kids get off to school OK this morning?* **-3.** [person] to be given a punishment that is not as severe as it could be □ *She got off with a fine.* ■ **he got off lightly** his punishment was not severe.

◆ **get on** ◇ *vt sep* **to get a piece of clothing on** to put a piece of clothing on □ *Get your coats on, boys, we're going.* ◇ *vt fus* **-1. to get on sthg** [train, bus, plane] to go inside sthg in order to travel on it □ *I told him to get on the next flight to New York.* **-2. to get on sthg** [horse, bicycle, roof] to go or climb up onto sthg □ *He got on his motorcycle and rode away.* ◇ *vi* **-1.** [passenger] to get on a train, bus, plane etc □ *I got on at Springfield.* **-2.** [person] to have a friendly relationship □ *I get on really well with his family.* **-3.** [person] = **get ahead.** **-4.** [job, person] to make progress □ *How are you getting on with your new computer?* **-5. to get on with sthg** to continue to do sthg seri-

ously, especially after a break or interruption □ *I'll call you back later, I must get on with this report.* **-6. to be getting on** [person] to be rather old □ *He's getting on now.*

◆ **get on for** *vt fus* **to be getting on for a particular amount/time/age** to be nearly or approximately a particular amount/time/age (informal use) □ *There were getting on for 2,000 people at the concert.* □ *She's getting on for retirement age.*

◆ **get on to, get onto** *vt fus* **-1. to get on to** OR **onto sthg** [a train, plane, horse] = **get on** □ *How did you get onto the roof?* **-2. to get on to** OR **onto sthg** [subject, topic] to start talking about sthg, usually by chance □ *How did we get onto the subject of marriage?* **-3. to get on to** OR **onto sb** to speak or write to sb in order to ask for or give information, or to complain □ *I'll get on to the manager right away.*

◆ **get out** ◇ *vt sep* **-1. to get sthg out** [gun, notebook] to take sthg out of a pocket, drawer etc □ *I opened my bag and got a pen out.* **-2. to get sthg out** [mark, dirt] to remove sthg by cleaning □ *How do you get wine stains out?* ◇ *vi* **-1.** [news, truth] to become known publicly after being kept secret □ *Word got out that he was leaving the company.* **-2.** [passenger, driver] to leave or come out of a car, bus, plane etc □ *We get out at the next stop.*

◆ **get out of** ◇ *vt fus* **-1. to get out of sthg** [car, boat, train] to leave or come out of sthg □ *I had to get out of the car and walk to the nearest gas station.* **-2. to get out of sthg** [jail, cage] to escape or be released from sthg □ *He gets out of prison next week.* **-3. to get out of sthg** [work, commitment, agreement] to avoid doing sthg one has promised to do □ *You're not getting out of doing the housework!* □ *"It's Jane's party tonight." — "Can't you get out of it?"* ◇ *vt sep* **to get sthg out of sb** to make sb tell or say sthg □ *I couldn't get a word out of her.*

◆ **get over** ◇ *vt sep* **to get sthg over** [message, idea, point] = **get across.** ◇ *vt fus* **-1. to get over sthg** [an illness, shock, disappointment] to recover from sthg that was a bad experience □ *It's taken me ages to get over that cold.* □ *He never got over the death of his son.* **-2. to get over a problem** to find a way of dealing with a problem □ *We got over the difficulty by renting a second car.*

◆ **get over with** *vt sep* **to get sthg over with** [operation, meeting, examination] to do and finish sthg which is unpleasant but must be done □ *I'll be glad to get the interview over with.*

◆ **get round** *vt fus* & *vi* = **get around.**

◆ **get round to** *vt fus* = **get around to.**

◆ **get through** ◇ *vt fus* **-1. to get through sthg** [job, task, book] to manage to finish sthg, usually sthg that takes a lot of effort □ *I don't know how we're going to get through all this work by tomorrow.* **-2. to get through sthg** [exam, test] to pass sthg □ *I got through my driving test on the second attempt.* **-3. to get through sthg** [food, money, supplies] to use up a lot of sthg □ *We'll never get through all this wine!* **-4. to get through a difficult period or situation** to come to the end of a difficult period or situation without being harmed □

Somehow he got through the funeral without breaking down.

◇ *vi* **-1. to get through to sb** to succeed in making sb understand what one wants to tell them □ *I just can't seem to get through to him.* **-2. to get through to sb** to succeed in contacting sb by telephone □ *It took me ages to get through to the operator.*

◆ **get to** *vt fus* **to get to sb** to make sb feel depressed or irritated (informal use) □ *I know he's rude, but don't let it get to you.*

◆ **get together** ◇ *vt sep* **to get sthg together** [team, project] to organize sthg by collecting all the parts needed to make it □ *She's getting a panel of advisors together.* □ *Get your things together and be ready to leave at 6 o'clock.* ◇ *vi* to meet somebody for pleasure or to discuss something □ *Let's get together for lunch one day.* □ *Can you get together with Dave to arrange the transport?*

◆ **get up** *vi* **-1.** [person] to stand up from a sitting or lying position □ *She got up from her desk.* **-2.** [person] to leave one's bed, usually after sleeping □ *What time do you get up in the morning?* □ *I got up and took a shower.*

◆ **get up to** *vt fus* **to get up to sthg** to do sthg that people disapprove of (informal use) □ *We got up to all sorts of things when I was at college.*

getaway ['getəweɪ] *n* an escape that somebody makes, especially after committing a crime □ *They made their getaway in a stolen car.*

getaway car *n* a car used by criminals to make a getaway after a crime.

get-together *n* a friendly social meeting or party □ *We're having a small get-together tonight, if you'd like to come.*

Gettysburg Address [ˌgetɪzbɜːˈr-g-] *n* **the Gettysburg Address** a famous speech made by Abraham Lincoln in 1863, at the opening of a cemetery for victims of the American Civil War.

⛉ THE GETTYSBURG ADDRESS

The Gettysburg Address is one of the most famous speeches in American history. It was made by President Abraham Lincoln on November 19, 1863, at Gettysburg, Pennsylvania, at a cemetery for soldiers who had died in a recent battle in the Civil War. In the speech Lincoln talked about democracy, freedom, and equality. Many Americans know parts of it by heart, especially the ending where he said that "government of the people, by the people, and for the people shall not perish from the earth".

---

getup ['getʌp] *n* a strange or unusual set of clothes that somebody is wearing (informal use).

get-up-and-go *n* energy and initiative (informal use).

get-well card *n* a card sent to wish somebody a quick recovery when they are ill.

geyser [US 'gaɪzr, GB 'giːzə] *n* **-1.** a natural hot spring that from time to time throws up hot water and steam into the air. **-2.** GB a gas

heater used in kitchens and bathrooms for heating water.

Ghana ['gɑːnə] a country in West Africa, on the Atlanic coast. SIZE: 240,000 sq kms. POPULATION: 16,400,000 (*Ghan(a)ians*). CAPITAL: Accra. LANGUAGE: English. CURRENCY: cedi.

Ghan(a)ian [US 'gɑːnɪən, GB gɑːˈneɪən] *n & adj*: see **Ghana**.

ghastly [US 'gæstlɪ, GB 'gɑːst-] (*compar* **ghastlier**, *superl* **ghastliest**) *adj* **-1.** [weather, man, experience] that one thinks is very unpleasant (informal use) □ *I've made a ghastly mistake!* **-2.** [crime, murder, sight] that one finds very frightening. **-3. to look/feel ghastly** to look/feel very ill.

gherkin ['gɜːˈkɪn] *n* a small pickled cucumber.

ghetto ['getoʊ] (*pl* **ghettos** OR **ghettoes**) *n* a poor part of a city where a group of people of the same race, religion etc lives □ *a black ghetto.*

ghetto blaster [US -blæstr, GB -blɑːstə] *n* a large portable radio cassette player (informal and humorous use).

ghost [goʊst] *n* the spirit of a dead person that is supposed to haunt living people □ *Do you believe in ghosts?* ■ **he doesn't have a ghost of a chance** he has no chance at all.

ghostly ['goʊstlɪ] (*compar* **ghostlier**, *superl* **ghostliest**) *adj* [figure, sight, sound] that is, looks, or sounds like something connected with ghosts.

ghost town *n* a town that has been abandoned by everybody who used to live there □ *The resort is like a ghost town in winter.*

ghostwriter ['goʊstraɪtər] *n* a person who writes something for somebody else who then publishes it under their own name.

ghoul [guːl] *n* a person who gets pleasure from death, suffering, and other unpleasant things (disapproving use).

ghoulish ['guːlɪʃ] *adj* **a ghoulish interest/ pleasure** an interest/pleasure that somebody takes in death, suffering, and other unpleasant things (disapproving use).

GHQ (*abbr of* **general headquarters**) *n* the main base of a large military operation.

GI (*abbr of* **government issue**) *n* a US soldier, especially in World War II.

giant ['dʒaɪənt] ◇ *adj* [size, organization, plant] unusually large □ *We saw the movie on a giant screen.* ◇ *n* **-1.** a person of great size and strength, in myths and children's stories. **-2.** an unusually tall person. **-3.** a person of great ability and importance □ *a literary giant.* **-4.** a very large business or organization □ *an advertising giant.*

giant-size(d) [-saɪz(d)] *adj* larger than usual □ *a giant-size(d) package of detergent.*

gibber ['dʒɪbər] *vi* to talk very quickly without making sense □ *a gibbering idiot.*

gibberish ['dʒɪbərɪʃ] *n* words that do not make sense □ *This is complete gibberish.*

gibbon ['gɪbən] *n* an ape with long arms and no tail that is found in southeast Asia.

gibe [dʒaɪb] ◇ *n* a remark intended to make

somebody or something look foolish □ *He made one or two unpleasant gibes at my expense.* ◇ *vi* **to gibe at sb/sthg** to say unpleasant things about sb/sthg in order to make them look foolish.

giblets ['dʒɪbləts] *npl* the internal organs of a chicken or turkey that are removed before cooking and sometimes cooked separately.

Gibraltar [dʒɪ'brɔːltəʳ] a British territory on the south coast of Spain consisting of a large rock that is used mainly as a military base. Spain also claims it owns Gibraltar. SIZE: 5.9 sq kms. POPULATION: 29,000 (*Gibraltarians*). LANGUAGE: English, Spanish. CURRENCY: pound sterling.

giddy ['gɪdɪ] (*compar* **giddier**, *superl* **giddiest**) *adj* **to feel giddy** to have the unpleasant feeling that things are moving around one and that one is going to fall or be sick □ *I had a giddy feeling.*

gift [gɪft] *n* **-1.** something that is given freely and willingly, usually without anything expected in return □ *The vase was a gift from my grandmother.* **-2.** a natural ability or talent □ *He has a gift for music/for making people relax.* ■ **the gift of the gab** the ability to speak easily and convincingly.

GIFT [gɪft] (*abbr of* **gamete in fallopian transfer**) *n* a type of artificial insemination in which egg cells are removed from a woman's ovary, mixed with sperm, and placed in one of her fallopian tubes.

gift certificate *n* US a token or voucher that is given as a present and can be taken to a particular store and exchanged for goods.

gifted ['gɪftəd] *adj* **-1.** [actor, writer, politician] who has great natural ability in a particular area or field □ *one of the country's most gifted politicians.* **-2. a gifted child** a child who is unusually intelligent.

gift token, gift voucher *n* GB = **gift certificate.**

gift wrap *n* patterned paper used for wrapping up presents.

gift-wrapped [-ræpt] *adj* [present, book] that has been specially wrapped in a decorative way □ *Would you like it gift-wrapped?*

gig [gɪg] *n* a performance by a pop or jazz musician or group (informal use).

gigabyte ['gɪgəbaɪt] *n* one thousand million bytes.

gigantic [dʒaɪ'gæntɪk] *adj* that seems extremely big □ *The ship was hit by a gigantic waves.*

giggle ['gɪgl] ◇ *n* a quiet laugh that is nervous, childish, or silly □ *He gave a nervous giggle.* ◇ *vi* to laugh quietly in a nervous, childish, or silly way □ *She couldn't stop giggling.*

giggly ['gɪglɪ] (*compar* **gigglier**, *superl* **giggliest**) *adj* [person, schoolchild] who giggles a lot.

GIGO ['gaɪgoʊ] (*abbr of* **garbage in, garbage out**) *n* a term meaning that the information produced by a computer system is only as good as the information put into it.

gigolo ['dʒɪgəloʊ] (*pl* **gigolos**) *n* a man who is paid to be the lover or companion of a usually rich older woman (disapproving use).

GI Joe [-'dʒoʊ] a name for a US soldier (informal use).

Gilbert ['gɪlbɜːʳt], **Sir W. S.** (1836–1911) a British writer who worked with the composer Sir Arthur Sullivan on many famous operettas, including *The Pirates of Penzance* and *The Mikado.*

gilded ['gɪldəd] *adj* = **gilt.**

gill [dʒɪl] *n* a unit (0.142 liters) used for measuring liquids.

gills [gɪlz] *npl* the organs through which a fish breathes.

gilt [gɪlt] ◇ *adj*: **a gilt frame/clock/statue etc** a frame/clock/statue etc that is covered in a thin layer of gold or gold paint. ◇ *n* a thin layer of gold or gold paint.
♦ **gilts** *npl* gilt-edged stocks, shares, and securities.

gilt-edged [-edʒd] *adj* **gilt-edged stocks/shares/securities** stocks/shares/securities that are sold by a government and give a low rate of interest but are considered to be a safe investment.

gimme ['gɪmɪ] = **give me** (informal use).

gimmick ['gɪmɪk] *n* something that is used to attract attention or publicity, especially in order to sell something (disapproving use) □ *It's just a sales gimmick.*

gin [dʒɪn] *n* a colorless alcoholic drink made from grain and flavored with juniper berries □ *I'll have a gin and tonic, please.*

ginger ['dʒɪndʒəʳ] ◇ *n* **-1.** a plant root used as a hot spicy flavoring in foods. **-2.** powdered ginger. ◇ *adj* GB [hair, cat] that is close to orange in color.

ginger ale *n* a non-alcoholic soft drink flavored with ginger and often mixed with spirits.

ginger beer *n* a slightly alcoholic soft drink flavored with ginger.

gingerbread ['dʒɪndʒəʳbred] *n* a cake flavored with ginger.

ginger group *n* GB a group of people inside a political party, labor union etc, who urge a more active or radical policy.

ginger-haired [-'heəʳd] *adj* [person] who has ginger hair.

gingerly ['dʒɪndʒəʳlɪ] *adv* [walk, touch, hold] very cautiously, especially because one is afraid of hurting oneself or damaging something.

gingham ['gɪŋəm] *n* cotton cloth with a check pattern on it, used for tablecloths, dresses, curtains etc □ *a gingham dress/tablecloth.*

gingivitis [,dʒɪndʒɪ'vaɪtəs] *n* inflammation of the gums.

ginseng ['dʒɪnseŋ] *n* the root of a Chinese plant, used as medicine in some parts of the world.

Giotto ['dʒɒtoʊ] (1267–1337) an Italian artist and architect who painted many religious frescoes. He introduced a more realistic style of painting.

gipsy ['dʒɪpsɪ] (*pl* **gipsies**) *n* & *adj* GB = **gypsy.**

giraffe [US dʒɪ'ræf, GB -'rɑːf] (*pl* **giraffe** OR **giraffes**) *n* an African animal with a very long neck and dark patches on yellow or orange skin.

gird [gɜːʳd] (*pt* & *pp* **girded** OR **girt**) *vt* → **loin**.

girder [ˈgɜːʳdəʳ] *n* a long metal bar used in buildings, bridges etc to give them extra strength □ *a metal/iron girder.*

girdle [ˈgɜːʳdl] *n* a piece of women's underwear that makes the stomach and hips look slimmer.

girl [gɜːʳl] *n* -1. a female child □ *I can remember when I was a little girl.* □ *a twelve-year-old/baby girl.* -2. a young woman, usually who is not married or who does a particular job □ *a teenage girl* □ *the checkout girl* □ *Look where you're going, girl!* □ *He's going out with a French girl.* -3. a daughter □ *I've got a little girl called Sarah.* -4. **the girls** the women that a person works with or sees often (informal use) □ *I'm having an evening out with the girls.*

girl Friday *n* a young woman who does general office work.

girlfriend [ˈgɜːʳlfrend] *n* -1. a girl or woman that a person is having a romantic or sexual relationship with □ *Have you met his new girlfriend?* -2. a female friend, usually of a woman.

girl guide *n* in Britain, a member of an organization, the Girl Guide Association, that teaches young girls useful skills and to be good citizens.

girlie magazine [ˈgɜːʳlɪ-] *n* a magazine for men that has erotic pictures of naked or partly naked women (informal use).

girlish [ˈgɜːʳlɪʃ] *adj* [laughter, dress] that is typical of a young girl.

girl scout *n* in the USA, a member of an organization, the Girl Scouts, that teaches young girls useful skills and to be good citizens.

giro [ˈdʒaɪroʊ] (*pl* **giros**) *n* GB -1. a banking system that transfers money between accounts without the need for a check □ *I'll pay by bank giro.* □ *a giro account/check.* -2. = **girocheque.**

girocheque [ˈdʒaɪroʊtʃek] *n* GB a check that is given to people who get money from the state, e.g. to the unemployed or disabled.

girt [gɜːʳt] *past tense & past participle of* **gird**.

girth [gɜːʳθ] *n* -1. the size of somebody's stomach, when this is large □ *his ample girth.* -2. the strap attached to a saddle that goes around a horse's stomach.

gist [dʒɪst] *n* **the gist of sthg** [of a conversation, speech, article] the main points or basic idea of sthg that does not include the details □ *I was just able to get* OR *catch the gist of what he was saying.*

give [gɪv] (*pt* **gave**, *pp* **given**) ◇ *vt* -1. **to give sb sthg, to give sthg to sb** to hand or send sthg to sb as a present □ *He gave me a watch for my birthday.* □ *"Did you buy that skirt?" — "No, it was given to me."* -2. **to give sb sthg, to give sthg to sb** to hand or pass sthg to sb for them to look at or use □ *Give me that book.* □ *She gave her ticket to the inspector.* -3. **to give a sum of money for sthg** to pay a sum of money for sthg □ *I'll give you $50 for it.* -4. **to give sb sthg** [treat, pay increase, support] to let sb have sthg that they want or need □ *Can you give me the name of your dentist?* □ *We were given a room on the third floor.* -5. **to give sb sthg, to give sthg to sb** [message, information, greetings] to tell sb sthg; to let sb know or hear sthg □ *You didn't give him your telephone number, did you?* □ *Let me give you some advice.* -6. **to give sb time/power etc** to cause sb to have time/power etc □ *She was given half an hour to collect her things and leave the building.* □ *What gives you the right to talk to me like that?* □ *She'd love to do it, given the opportunity/chance.* -7. **to give sb a feeling/problem etc** to cause sb to have a feeling/problem etc □ *I hope the children don't give you any trouble.* □ *The walk has given me an appetite.* □ *The news gave me a shock.* □ *Donald gives the impression of not caring.* -8. **to give a smile/wave etc** to smile/wave etc once (used to show that somebody performs an action) □ *She gave a shrug.* ■ **to give sb/sthg sthg** to do sthg to sb/sthg □ *He gave me a grin.* □ *I gave the car a good clean.* -9. **to give a speech/lecture etc** to speak/lecture etc in public □ *Mr Kowalski gave a press conference after the meeting.* □ *The band will be giving a couple of concerts in London.* -10. **I was/we were given to believe that...** I/we thought that something was true because somebody said so (formal use).

◇ *vi* [branch, rope, bridge] to bend, stretch, or break because of pressure or strain □ *The platform finally gave under their weight.*

◇ *n* the ability of something to bend or stretch under pressure □ *These shoes don't seem to have much give.*

◆ **give or take** *prep* **it's 60 miles, give or take a mile** it is 60 miles, or perhaps a mile more or less.

◆ **give away** *vt sep* -1. **to give sthg away** [books, old clothes] to give sthg to somebody as a present because one does not want or need it any more □ *She gave away all her furniture when she went abroad.* -2. **to give sthg away** [information, secret, truth] to let people know sthg that should be kept secret, usually by mistake □ *It was your accent that gave you away.*

◆ **give back** *vt sep* **to give sthg back** [present, book, pen] to return sthg to its owner or to the person who had it before □ *I gave him back the $20 that he had lent me.*

◆ **give in** ◇ *vi* -1. [person] to admit that one has been beaten □ *We will continue to fight and never give in.* -2. **to give in to sthg** to agree to do sthg unwillingly □ *I was determined not to give in to their demands.* ◇ *vt sep* **to give sthg in** [report, paper] to hand sthg to the proper person or place □ *All room keys must be given in to the receptionist on departure.*

◆ **give off** *vt fus* **to give off sthg** [heat, fumes, smell] to produce sthg and send it into the air, often because of a chemical reaction □ *When foam rubber catches fire, it gives off toxic fumes.*

◆ **give out** ◇ *vt sep* **to give sthg out** [presents, leaflets] to hand sthg to everyone in a group

□ *Someone was giving out free samples of make-up to shoppers in the store.* ◇ *vi* [strength, car] to stop working, usually due to tiredness or a mechanical fault □ *My legs gave out after ten miles.*

♦ **give over** *vt sep* to be given over to sthg to be used only for sthg □ *The building is given over to sports on Monday nights.*

♦ **give up** ◇ *vt sep* **-1. to give sthg up** [alcohol, chocolate] to stop doing, using, eating etc sthg □ *My doctor has told me to give up smoking.* □ *I gave up my seat to an old lady.* ■ **to give up hope** to stop hoping. ■ **to give up one's job** to leave one's job. **-2. to give oneself up** to go to the police and allow them to arrest one □ *The terrorists gave themselves up to the police.* ◇ *vi* to admit that one cannot do something and stop doing it □ *She was forced to give up after twelve miles because of blisters.*

♦ **give up on** *vt fus* **to give up on sb/sthg** to stop believing that one can understand sb/sthg □ *Don't give up on me now!* ■ **to give up on sthg** to stop believing that one can do sthg.

give-and-take *n* a willingness by two people or groups of people to let each other decide what to do □ *There has to be a certain amount of give-and-take in any relationship/negotiation.*

giveaway ['gɪvəweɪ] ◇ *n* something that somebody does, without intending to, that makes one realize the truth □ *That blush was a real giveaway.* ◇ *adj* **giveaway prices** very cheap prices.

given ['gɪvn] ◇ *past participle of* **give.** ◇ *adj* **-1. a given date/moment etc** a date/moment etc that is fixed and decided in advance □ *At a given signal everyone will stop what they are doing.* **-2. at any given time** at any time one chooses □ *We should be able to know where they are at any given time.* **-3. to be given to sthg** [to exaggerating, lying] to do sthg often, especially sthg bad □ *I'm not given to telling lies.* ◇ *prep* taking <sthg> into account □ *Given his background, it's no surprise.* □ *I was lucky to get a prize, given the number of people who entered.*

given name *n* a person's first name, chosen by their parents when they are born.

glacé cherry [US glæ'seɪ-, GB 'glæseɪ-] *n* a cherry that has been kept in sugar and is used in cakes and cocktails.

glacial ['gleɪsjəl] *adj* **-1. a glacial look/stare etc** a look/stare etc that is cold and unfriendly. **-2.** [landscape, deposit, period] that is connected to or made by glaciers.

glacier [US 'gleɪʃr, GB 'glæsjə] *n* a large mass of ice that moves slowly over land.

glad [glæd] (*compar* **gladder**, *superl* **gladdest**) *adj* **-1. to be glad** to be happy and pleased □ *I'm glad to hear he's better.* □ *I'm glad (that) you phoned.* □ *I'm glad about your new job!* **-2. to be glad to do sthg** to be very willing to do sthg for somebody □ *Nonsense, I was glad to be of help.* □ *"Could you give me a hand?"* — *"I'll be glad to."* **-3. to be glad of sthg** to be grateful for sthg □ *To be honest, I was glad of the*

company/chance/help. □ *I'd be very glad if you would let me know.*

gladden ['glædn] *vt* **to gladden sb's heart** to make sb very happy (literary use).

glade [gleɪd] *n* a small area in a forest that has grass and no trees (literary use).

gladiator ['glædɪeɪtə'] *n* in ancient Rome, a man, often a slave, trained to entertain a crowd by fighting other men or animals.

gladioli [,glædɪ'oʊlaɪ] *npl* a garden plant that has a long thick stem with bright flowers on each side.

gladly ['glædlɪ] *adv* [help, listen, kill] willingly, and even at some cost to oneself □ *They'd gladly die rather than suffer the humiliation.* □ *I'd gladly help, but I'm going out that night.*

Gladstone [US 'glædstoʊn, GB -stən], **W. E.** (1809–1898) British Prime Minister from 1864 to 1874, 1880 to 1885, in 1886, and from 1892 to 1894.

glamor US, **glamour** GB ['glæmə'] *n* [of a person, place, job] the quality of being more attractive, exciting, or interesting than somebody or something ordinary □ *the glamor of the fashion world.*

glamorize, -ise ['glæməraɪz] *vt* [truth, job, place] to make <sthg> appear glamorous when it is not □ *I think you're glamorizing what I do — most of the time the work's really boring.*

glamorous ['glæmərəs] *adj* [person, place, job] that has glamor □ *Traveling around the world on business is not as glamorous as it sounds.*

glamour *n* GB = **glamor.**

glance [US glæns, GB glɑːns] ◇ *n* a quick look □ *He had* OR *took a glance at his watch.* □ *She cast* OR *threw a glance in my direction.* ■ **at a glance** without having to look or think carefully □ *You can tell at a glance it's a fake.* ■ **at first glance** before one looks or thinks more carefully about it □ *At first glance I thought it was a dog.* ◇ *vi* to look quickly □ *He glanced over his shoulder/around the room/in the mirror.* □ *He glanced at her/his watch.* □ *I haven't read it, I've only glanced at* OR *through it.*

♦ **glance off** *vt fus* **to glance off sb/sthg** [head, shoulder, wall] to hit sb/sthg at an angle and bounce off again □ *The stone glanced off the window.*

glancing [US 'glænsɪŋ, GB 'glɑːns-] *adj* **a glancing blow** a blow that hits somebody or something at an angle.

gland [glænd] *n* an organ in humans, animals, and plants that produces and releases chemical substances that are needed, or that have to be got rid of □ *the thyroid gland* □ *sweat glands.*

glandular fever [,glændʒələ'-] *n* GB an infectious disease that gives people fever, a sore throat, and swollen glands and makes them feel weak.

glare [gleə'] ◇ *n* **-1.** [of a person] an angry look □ *a fierce/an angry glare.* **-2.** [of the sun, a light, headlight] a very bright light that is difficult to look at □ *She shaded her eyes from the glare.* **-3. in the glare of sthg** [of publicity, the media] in public so that the media show everybody what is happening □ *The trial will be held in the full glare of television cameras.* ◇ *vi* -1. [person] to look in an angry way at somebody or something □ *He glared at me.* -2. [sun, light, headlight] to shine very brightly so that it is difficult to look at □ *The sun glared down from a cloudless sky.*

glaring ['gleərɪŋ] *adj* -1. [mistake, injustice, abuse] that is obvious and very bad □ *His speech contained a number of glaring errors.* -2. [sun, light, headlight] that glares.

Glasgow [US 'glæsgoʊ, GB 'glɑːz-] the largest city in Scotland, in the southwest of the country. POPULATION: 684,000.

glasnost [US 'glɑːsnoʊst, GB 'glæznɒst] *n* a policy that began in the former USSR of making government less secret and giving the people more power over it.

glass [US glæs, GB glɑːs] *n* -1. a hard transparent substance that is used to make windows, bottles etc and that breaks easily □ *a piece of broken glass* □ *a glass bottle/door/bowl.* -2. a small glass container, usually without a handle, used for drinks; the amount of drink that is contained in this □ *a beer glass* □ *I had* OR *drank a few glasses last night.* □ *Can I have a glass of water, please?* -3. objects made of glass □ *All the glass and china is kept in the kitchen.*

◆ **glasses** *npl* a device consisting of two glass lenses in a frame that is worn in front of one's eyes to help one see better □ *a pair of glasses* □ *reading glasses.*

glassblowing [US 'glæsbloʊɪŋ, GB 'glɑːs-] *n* the art of blowing air through a tube into liquid glass to make vases and other shapes.

glass fibre *n* GB a material made from tiny glass threads, used to make plastic stronger or to keep heat in.

glasshouse [US 'glæshaʊs, GB 'glɑːs-, *pl* -haʊzɪz] *n* GB a building with glass walls used for growing plants in.

glassware [US 'glæsweər, GB 'glɑːsweə] *n* objects made of glass, especially drinking glasses and things used in a house.

glassy [US 'glæsɪ, GB 'glɑːsɪ] (*compar* **glassier**, *superl* **glassiest**) *adj* -1. **glassy eyes, a glassy stare** eyes that show no emotion or understanding □ *a glassy-eyed stare.* -2. [sea, surface] that looks smooth, shiny, and hard, like glass.

Glastonbury [US 'glæstənberɪ, GB -bərɪ] a town in southwestern England where, according to legend, King Arthur was buried.

Glaswegian [US glæs'wiːdʒən, GB glɑːz-] ◇ *n* -1. a person who comes from or lives in Glasgow. -2. a dialect of English spoken in Glasgow. ◇ *adj*: *see* **Glasgow**.

glaucoma [glɔː'koʊmə] *n* an eye disease that causes gradual blindness.

glaze [gleɪz] ◇ *n* -1. a smooth shiny layer on the surface of a piece of pottery. -2. COOKING a thin layer of beaten egg, milk etc, that is brushed onto food, e.g. bread, pastry, and meat, before it is cooked to make it look shiny and attractive. ◇ *vt* -1. [vase, tile, pot-

tery] to cover <a piece of pottery> with a smooth shiny layer. -2. COOKING [pie, pastry] to cover <food> with a layer of beaten egg, milk etc, especially before baking it.

◆ **glaze over** *vi* [eyes, expression] to start showing signs of boredom.

glazed [gleɪzd] *adj* -1. **a glazed look** OR **expression** a look that shows no signs of feeling or understanding, because one is bored, drunk, ill etc. -2. [pottery, pastry] that has a glaze on it. -3. [window, door, picture] that has been fitted with glass.

glazier ['gleɪzjər] *n* a person whose job is to cut and fit glass for windows, doors etc.

gleam [gliːm] ◇ *n* -1. [of metal, the sun, a candle] a soft light, sometimes reflected off something else □ *a gleam of light.* -2. [of triumph, pride, anger] a particular feeling that can be seen in somebody's eyes or face and that comes and goes very quickly □ *The mention of money brought a gleam to his eye.* ◇ *vi* -1. [metal, glass] to reflect light because it is shiny and clean □ *He polished the windows until they gleamed.* -2. [sun, star, candle] to shine faintly. -3. [eyes] to shine and show a particular feeling □ *Her eyes gleamed with malice.*

gleaming ['gliːmɪŋ] ◇ *adj* [light, metal, face] that gleams □ *rows of gleaming copper pans.* ◇ *adv*: *a gleaming new car* □ *a gleaming white bathroom.*

glean [gliːn] *vt* [fact, information] to find out <sthg> gradually or indirectly □ *Did you manage to glean anything from their conversation?*

glee [gliː] *n* a feeling of great happiness and excitement, often at somebody else's bad luck or at one's own good luck □ *He rubbed his hands with glee at the thought.*

gleeful ['gliːfl] *adj* [expression, person, smile] that shows glee.

glen [glen] *n* a deep narrow valley in Scotland.

Glenn [glen], **John** (1921–) a US astronaut who was the first American to go around the Earth in a spaceship.

glib [glɪb] (*compar* **glibber**, *superl* **glibbest**) *adj* [remark, answer] that is difficult to believe because it is said quickly and easily, without much thought; [person] who speaks in a glib way.

glide [glaɪd] *vi* -1. [dancer, person, boat] to move smoothly, easily, and quietly over a surface □ *The skater glided across* OR *over the ice.* -2. [bird] to fly without flapping its wings; [plane] to fly without power from an engine □ *The eagle glided across the sky/through the air.*

glider ['glaɪdər] *n* a very light aircraft with no engine that uses air currents to fly.

gliding ['glaɪdɪŋ] *n* the sport of flying gliders.

glimmer ['glɪmər] ◇ *n* -1. [of light, dawn] a faint light that is often unsteady □ *The first glimmers of light were beginning to appear on the horizon.* -2. **a glimmer of hope/interest/emotion** etc a faint sign of hope/interest/emotion etc. ◇ *vi* [light] to shine faintly and often unsteadily □ *A light glimmered in the distance.*

glimpse [glɪmps] ◇ *n* -1. a quick look at somebody or something that is not long enough for one to see or remember all the details □ *I only caught a glimpse of the driver.* **-2.** [of the truth, future, somebody's character] a brief experience of something that helps one to understand it better □ *glimpses of what life was like in the 1940s.* ◇ *vt* **-1.** [person, object, building] to see <sb/sthg> for only a moment so that one cannot remember all the details □ *I glimpsed a figure in the doorway.* **-2.** [truth, character, future] to experience <sthg> for a short time and begin to understand it □ *I really only glimpsed the truth behind all of this.*

glint [glɪnt] ◇ *n* **-1.** [of light, metal] a brief flash, usually from a shiny surface □ *the cold glint of steel.* **-2.** [of humor, mischief] a sign in somebody's eyes that shows a particular feeling, especially an unpleasant one □ *There was an evil glint in his eyes.* ◇ *vi* **-1.** [water, metal] to reflect or produce brief flashes of light □ *The knife glinted in the sun.* **-2.** [eyes] to show a particular, usually unpleasant, feeling □ *Her eyes glinted with spite.*

glisten [ˈglɪsn] *vi* [body, gold, sweat] to shine all over because it is wet, oily, or polished and reflects light, especially in an attractive way □ *The wet grass glistened in the sunlight.* □ *His eyes glistened with tears.*

glitch [glɪtʃ] *n* a small problem that stops something from working (informal use).

glitter [ˈglɪtər] ◇ *n* **-1.** [of stars, jewelry] light that glitters □ *the bright glitter of diamonds.* **-2.** [for decoration] very small squares of shiny paper, used as cheap decoration □ *She had stuck glitter on the card in the shape of a Christmas tree.* ◇ *vi* **-1.** [star, jewelery, lights] to shine attractively with many small bright points of reflected light □ *The sky glittered with stars.* □ *The sunlight glittered on the surface of the lake.* **-2.** [eyes] to shine with a particular feeling □ *Her eyes glittered with greed.*

glittering [ˈglɪtərɪŋ] *adj* **-1.** [stars, jewels, eyes] that glitter. **-2.** [occasion, cast] that is impressive and exciting because many famous and beautiful people are there □ *The festival hosts a glittering line-up of stars.* **-3.** [career, success] that is very successful and impressive.

glitzy [ˈglɪtsɪ] (*compar* **glitzier**, *superl* **glitziest**) *adj* [occasion, dress, woman] that looks attractive and fashionable in a showy and obvious way.

gloat [gloʊt] *vi* to show somebody that one is pleased that one has been more lucky or successful than them, in order to make them feel worse □ *I didn't come here to gloat over your bad luck.*

global [ˈgloʊbl] *adj* **-1.** [market, importance, warfare] that reaches or involves people and places all over the world □ *global security and the new world order.* **-2.** [view, picture] that includes all aspects of a situation □ *We've tried to take a global view of the situation.*

globally [ˈgloʊbəlɪ] *adv*: see **global** □ *Sales have exceeded three million globally.* □ *Think globally, act locally.*

global warming [-ˈwɔːrmɪŋ] *n* the general increase in the world's temperature, thought

to be caused by damage to the Earth's atmosphere.

globe [gloʊb] *n* **-1. the globe** the world □ *people all over the globe.* **-2.** a small model of the world, usually on a stand, used as a map. **-3.** an object that is round like a ball.

globetrotter [ˈgloʊbtrɒtər] *n* a person who travels a lot to different countries.

globule [ˈglɒbjuːl] *n* [of oil, wax] a tiny drop of thick liquid.

gloom [gluːm] *n* **-1.** [of a house, forest, room] darkness □ *I could hardly see anything in the gloom.* **-2.** [of a person, atmosphere] a feeling of unhappiness and hopelessness □ *There's a feeling of gloom in the stock market tonight.*

gloomy [ˈgluːmɪ] (*compar* **gloomier**, *superl* **gloomiest**) *adj* **-1.** [house, forest, room] that does not have or get much light and makes people feel sad □ *She lives in a gloomy little apartment.* **-2.** [weather, sky, day] that is very cloudy and dull □ *a gloomy winter's day.* **-3.** [person, atmosphere] that is unhappy and shows no signs of hope □ *The movie paints a very gloomy picture of life in downtown LA.* □ *I think he's feeling gloomy about his chances of success.* **-4.** [outlook, forecast, future] that offers little hope for the future □ *She faced the gloomy prospect of losing her home.*

glorified [ˈglɔːrəfaɪd] *adj* that is no more exciting than something else, although it is described as something different and better □ *The "plush hotel" was just a glorified motel.*

glorify [ˈglɔːrəfaɪ] (*pt & pp* **glorified**) *vt* **-1.** [war, virtue] to praise <sthg> and make it seem more important than it really is □ *Violence should not be glorified, but deplored.* **-2. to glorify God** to praise God greatly.

glorious [ˈglɔːrɪəs] *adj* **-1.** [sight, countryside] beautiful, especially to look at □ *We saw some glorious sunsets.* **-2.** [feeling, vacation, moment] very enjoyable and wonderful □ *We had a glorious time.* **-3. glorious weather/sunshine** weather/sunshine that is hot and sunny □ *It was a glorious summer's day.* **-4.** [victory, death, king] that has, brings, or deserves great glory □ *He died a glorious death in battle.*

glory [ˈglɔːrɪ] (*pl* **glories**) *n* **-1.** fame and honor that one earns by doing something impressive □ *Those brave men died for the greater glory of France.* □ *She believes in working as a team, not for personal glory.* **-2.** the natural beauty of somebody or something □ *Come back in summer and see the garden in all its glory.* **-3. the glory of sb/sthg** the most beautiful or impressive feature of sb/sthg □ *The glory of the idea lies in its very simplicity.* □ *The real glory of the collection is the piece by Rodin.* □ *the glories of Renaissance art.*

◆ **glory in** *vt fus* **to glory in sthg** [success, freedom, violence] to enjoy sthg very much, especially a new feeling or situation, or an activity that harms other people □ *They seem to glory in their reputation for crass commercialism.*

Glos *abbr of* **Gloucestershire**.

gloss [glɒs] *n* **-1.** the shiny appearance of something smooth and flat, new, or in good condition that can show things as reflections □ *The woodwork had an attractive gloss finish.* **-2.** = **gloss paint**.

◆ **gloss over** *vt fus* **to gloss over sthg** [fact, problem] to talk about sthg unpleasant quickly and not in detail □ *He glossed over the possible closure of the school.*

glossary ['glɒsərɪ] (*pl* **glossaries**) *n* an alphabetical list of words used in a particular field of knowledge, together with an explanation of their meanings.

gloss paint *n* paint that produces a very smooth and shiny surface.

glossy ['glɒsɪ] (*compar* **glossier**, *superl* **glossiest**) ◇ *adj* **-1.** [surface] that looks smooth and shiny; [hair] that is shiny because it is in good condition □ *a healthy cat with a nice glossy coat.* **-2.** [photo, cover, page] that is printed on shiny paper. **-3.** [display, packaging] that is attractive but often has no real use □ *It's all very glossy, but what would you use it for?* ◇ *n* = **glossy magazine**.

glossy magazine *n* a magazine full of glossy pages and color photos of fashion, famous people, expensive homes etc.

Gloucestershire ['glɒstəʳʃəʳ] a county in southwestern England. SIZE: 2,643 sq kms. POPULATION: 522,200. ADMINISTRATIVE CENTER: Gloucester.

glove [glʌv] *n* a piece of clothing that fits one's hand and is worn for warmth or protection □ *a pair of gloves.*

glove compartment *n* a small compartment in a car underneath the windshield, used to keep small articles in.

glove puppet *n* GB a puppet that fits on the hand and is moved by it.

glow [gləʊ] ◇ *n* **-1.** [of the sun, a fire] a soft light □ *a soft/gentle glow.* **-2.** [of somebody's face] a pink color on a person's face that shows they are healthy or have just finished exercising □ *a healthy glow.* **-3.** [of pride, satisfaction] the feeling one has when one is pleased about something □ *Inside, Sue felt a warm glow of satisfaction.* ◇ *vi* **-1.** [light, star, sun] to shine with a soft steady light; [fire, cigarette] to shine with light but without flames □ *a plastic toy that glows in the dark* □ *His eyes glowed with pleasure/anger.* **-2.** [walls, place] to shine in light that comes from somewhere else □ *The whole valley glowed in the sunset.* **-3.** [leaves, color] to be very bright, especially with red and orange colors □ *Her paintings glow with color.* □ *The forest glowed red and gold.* **-4.** [face, cheeks, person] to have a healthy glow, usually because of excitement or pride □ *He was positively glowing with health!*

glower ['glaʊəʳ] *vi* to look at somebody or something in an angry way.

glowing ['gləʊɪŋ] *adj* **a glowing report/tribute etc** a report/tribute etc that praises somebody or something very much □ *He's always spoken of you in glowing terms.*

glow-worm *n* GB a flying insect that can be seen in the dark because it produces a small amount of light.

glucose ['glu:kəʊs] *n* a form of sugar found in fruit and used by the body for energy. FORMULA: $C_6H_{12}O_6$.

glue [glu:] (*cont* **glueing** OR **gluing**) ◇ *n* any thick liquid that is used to stick thing together □ *The whole thing was stuck together with glue.* ◇ *vt* to attach <sthg> to something else using glue □ *Glue the broken pieces together.* □ *The photo was glued to the page.* ■ **to be glued to sthg** [to the TV, radio] to be so interested in sthg that one never stops listening to or watching it □ *He just sits there all day glued to his computer screen.* ■ **to be glued to the spot** to be unable to move because of a strong emotion □ *He stood glued to the spot, not daring to move.*

glue-sniffing [-snɪfɪŋ] *n* the use of glue and similar substances as drugs, by breathing in their fumes.

glum [glʌm] (*compar* **glummer**, *superl* **glummest**) *adj* [expression, face] that shows that one is unhappy and not hopeful □ *Why are you looking so glum?*

glut [glʌt] *n* [of produce, oil, houses] a situation in which there is too much of something available, so it becomes difficult to sell □ *There's a glut in the property market.*

gluten ['glu:tn] *n* a protein found in wheat flour.

glutinous ['glu:tnəs] *adj* [rice, stew, mud] that is thick, sticky, and can become solid.

glutton ['glʌtn] *n* a person who eats more than they need. ■ **to be a glutton for punishment** to choose to keep suffering although one could avoid it (humorous use).

gluttony ['glʌtnɪ] *n* the habit of eating more than one needs.

glycerin ['glɪsərɪn], **glycerine** ['glɪsəri:n] *n* a thick colorless or yellow liquid that tastes sweet and is used to make medicine, antifreeze, and explosives.

Glyndebourne ['glaɪndbɔːʳn] *n* an opera house in the country in southeastern England, where a famous opera festival takes place every year; the festival itself.

gm *abbr of* **gram**.

GMAT (*abbr of* **Graduate Management Admissions Test**) *n* in the USA, a test taken by students who have finished their degree and want to study business at graduate school.

GMB (*abbr of* **General, Municipal, and Boilermakers**) *n* a large British labor union for administrative, clerical, and industrial workers.

GMT (*abbr of* **Greenwich Mean Time**) *n* the time in Greenwich, London. Local times around the world are described by comparing them with GMT.

gnarled [nɑːʳld] *adj* [tree, hand, face] that has hard lumps or is twisted out of shape because it is old.

gnash [næʃ] *vt* **to gnash one's teeth** to close and move one's teeth together noisily; to be very angry or frustrated about something.

gnat [næt] *n* a very small fly that bites people and animals.

gnaw [nɔ:] ◇ *vt* -1. [bone, fingernail] to bite <sthg> continuously □ *Mice have gnawed through the electric cables.* -2. **to gnaw a hole in sthg** to make a hole in sthg by gnawing it. ◇ *vi* **to gnaw (away) at sb** [fear, doubt, problem] to make sb feel worried all the time □ *I could feel a vague anxiety gnawing away at the back of my mind.*

gnome [noʊm] *n* in stories for children, a very small old man with white hair, a white beard, and a pointed hat; a small brightly painted statue of this type of man that is used as a decoration in gardens □ *a garden gnome.*

GNP *n abbr of* **gross national product**.

gnu [nu:] (*pl* **gnu** OR **gnus**) *n* an antelope with curved horns and a beard that comes from South Africa.

go [goʊ] (*pt* **went**, *pp* **gone**, *pl* **goes**) ◇ *vi* -1. [person, bus] to move or travel toward a particular place, usually away from the speaker □ *Let's go home, it's late.* □ *Where are you going?* □ *We went on foot/by bus.* -2. [person] to move from one place to another in order to do some activity □ *I'm going for a walk.* □ *Are you going to the party on Saturday?* ■ **to go (and) do sthg** to go somewhere in order to do sthg □ *Go and see if she's ready.* ■ **to go swimming/dancing** to go somewhere in order to swim/dance for pleasure or to relax □ *Last summer we went walking in the Pyrenees.* -3. [person, bus] to leave a place □ *I must be going.* □ *What time does the bus go?* ■ **he's gone** he has left and is no longer here. ■ **let's go!** let's start now! -4. [path, line] to lead toward a particular place or follow a particular direction □ *Where does this road go?* □ *The tunnel goes under the river.* -5. **to go to school/college/church** to attend school/college/church regularly □ *What time do you go to work?* -6. [period of time] to pass □ *Time goes slowly in prison.* □ *The years went very fast.* -7. **to go well/badly** [event] to be successful/unsuccessful □ *How did the interview go today?* □ *Things are going much better now.* -8. [car, clock, watch] to work as it is supposed to; [washing machine, tape recorder] to be switched on and operating □ *The car won't go.* -9. [bell, siren] to sound suddenly and loudly □ *At that point, the alarm went.* -10. **to go on** OR **into sthg** [money, time] to be spent on or used for sthg □ *Most of our income goes on rent.* -11. **to go to sb** [prize, job] to be won by or given to sb □ *The contract went to another agency.* □ *All profits will go to charity.* -12. [employee] to be made to leave a job □ *He'll have to go!* ■ **'everything must go'** everything must be sold (used in a store where there is a sale). -13. [light bulb, fuse] to stop working because it has become weak or worn-out □ *The battery's going in my camera.* □ *My voice has gone.* ■ **his sight/hearing is going** he is becoming blind/deaf. -14. **to go (together)** to be suitable to be put, used etc together □ *Wine and chocolate don't really go (together).* □ *This blouse goes well with that skirt.* -15. [box,

clothes] to be small enough to fit in a particular place □ *The turkey's too big to go in the freezer.* -16. [book, piece of machinery] to have somewhere as its proper or usual place □ *The plates go in this cupboard.* □ *Where does this piece go?* -17. used when repeating a song, poem etc □ *How does that tune go?* □ *His version of what happened goes like this.* -18. MATH **10 goes into 50 five times** 50 can be divided by 10 five times. -19. (+ *complement*) **to go naked/hungry** to be or remain naked/hungry □ *Our cries for help went unnoticed.* ■ **to go mad/blind** to become mad/blind □ *He went pale with fear.* □ *The company went bankrupt.* -20. **don't go doing sthg** don't do sthg (informal use) □ *Don't go blaming yourself/catching cold!*

◇ *vt* **ducks go "quack"** ducks make the sound "quack".

◇ *modal vb* **I'm going to leave** I intend to leave □ *We're going to eat out this evening.* □ *We're going to go to the States in June.* ■ **it's going to rain** it will rain soon □ *She's going to have a baby.* □ *You're going to regret this!*

◇ *n* -1. **it's my/your go** [in a game] it's my/your turn or time to do something, e.g. play a card □ *Whose go is it?* -2. **to have a go** to make an attempt (informal use) □ *I decided I'd have a go at sailing.* □ *At least have a go!* -3. *phrases* **to make a go of sthg** to do what is needed to make sthg successful (informal use) □ *They're trying to make a go of their business/marriage.* ■ **to be on the go** to be busy (informal use) □ *I've been on the go all day.*

◆ **to go** *adv* -1. **there are five miles to go** there are five miles left or remaining □ *There are only three days to go* OR *before the deadline.* -2. **a pizza to go** a pizza to be taken out rather than eaten at the restaurant.

◆ **go about** ◇ *vt fus* -1. **to go about sthg** [job, problem] to start to deal with sthg □ *How do you intend going about it?* □ *I think they went about it in completely the wrong way.* -2. **to go about one's business** to do what one normally does □ *I want to be left alone to go about my business.* ◇ *vi* [person, story] = **go around**.

◆ **go after** *vt fus* **to go after sthg** to try to get sthg □ *We both went after the same job/prize.*

◆ **go against** *vt fus* -1. **to go against one's principles/wishes** to be opposed to or in conflict with what one believes/wants □ *You know what will happen if you go against your father's wishes.* -2. **to go against sb's advice** to do something different from what sb has advised □ *She went against our advice and reported it to the police.* -3. **to go against sb** [decision, judgment, verdict] to be unfavorable to sb □ *We were worried that the result of the ballot might go against us.*

◆ **go ahead** *vi* -1. **to go ahead with sthg** to do or carry out <sthg that has already been planned> □ *It looks as if they're going ahead with the project.* ■ **go ahead!** do it! □ *Go ahead and sue me: I don't care.* -2. [event, game] to take place as planned □ *The concert will go ahead without her.*

◆ **go along** *vi* [meeting, talk] to attend <an event> □ *Are you going along to the party?*

◆ **go along with** *vt fus* **to go along with sb/ sthg** [person, suggestion, decision] to accept that sb/sthg is right and do what they want □ *I'm happy to go along with everyone else.* □ *He agreed to go along with our ideas.*

◆ **go around** *vi* **-1. to go around doing sthg** [person] to do sthg often or as a habit □ *There's no need to go around telling everyone!* **-2.** [wheels, record, dancer] to move in a circular direction. **-3.** [story, joke] to be told by many different people □ *There's a rumor going around that the business is up for sale.* **-4. to be enough to go around** [money, food] to be enough for everybody present □ *Do we have enough chairs to go around?*

◆ **go around with** *vt fus* **to go around with sb** to spend a lot of time going to places with sb □ *She's been going around with Joel.*

◆ **go away** *vi* **-1.** [person] to leave a place or person □ *Go away! I'm reading.* **-2.** [person] to spend a period of time away from home, usually for relaxation □ *Why don't we go away for a few days?* **-3.** [feeling, smell] to disappear □ *I can't get this stain to go away.*

◆ **go back** *vi* [person] to return to the place one has left, especially one's own home □ *I've left him and I'm never going back!*

◆ **go back on** *vt fus* **to go back on sthg** [promise, agreement] to fail to do sthg that one has said that one will do □ *She never goes back on her word.*

◆ **go back to** *vt fus* **-1. to go back to sthg** [job, reading] to start doing sthg again after doing something different for a time □ *He went back to scribbling in his notebook.* □ *He went back to work.* ■ **to go back to sleep** to fall asleep again after waking up. **-2. to go back to sthg** [topic, subject, point] to start talking about sthg again after talking about something different for a time □ *Going back* OR *To go back to what you were saying earlier...* **-3. to go back to a particular time in the past** [building, plan] to have existed since a particular time in the past □ *The firm goes back to 1952.*

◆ **go before** *vi* to exist or happen before □ *We wanted to forget what had gone before.*

◆ **go by** ◇ *vt fus* **to go by sb/sthg** to be guided by sb/sthg when deciding what to do or believe □ *Don't go by what he says: he's lying.* □ *Going by her accent, I'd say she was Hungarian.* ◇ *vi* **-1.** [car, people] to move past □ *She stared at the crowds going by outside.* **-2.** [period of time] to pass □ *Whole days went by without any news.*

◆ **go down** *vi* **-1.** [level, liquid] to become lower □ *We must wait until the floodwaters go down.* **-2.** [sun] to sink below the horizon and disappear □ *We stood on the beach and watched the sun go down.* **-3.** [tire, balloon] to lose air and become less swollen and firm □ *My tire's gone down again.* **-4.** [rate, output] to become less □ *Prices/Interest rates are going down.* □ *The average age of participants is going down.* **-5. it went down well/badly** people liked it/did not like it □ *His comment about overtime went down badly with the staff.*

◆ **go down with** *vt fus* **to go down with an illness** to catch an illness, usually one that is

not very serious (informal use) □ *She's gone down with chickenpox.*

◆ **go for** *vt fus* **-1. to go for a walk/ride** to go out to walk/ride for pleasure □ *She goes for a run every morning.* **-2. to go for sthg/sb** [type of product, method, person] to choose sthg/sb, especially because one likes them □ *In the end we decided to go for a second-hand car.* □ *I don't really go for tall women.* **-3. to go for sthg** [job, championship] to try to get sthg □ *She's going for the world record.* **-4. to go for sb/sthg** [person, part of the body] to suddenly attack sb/sthg □ *He went for me with a knife.* **-5. that goes for you/it as well** that is true about you/it as well as other people or things □ *You're a fool, and the same goes for your sister.*

◆ **go in** *vi* **-1.** [person] to enter a building, especially one's own home □ *She opened the door and went in.* **-2.** [sun] to disappear behind a cloud.

◆ **go in for** *vt fus* **-1. to go in for sthg** [competition, exam] to arrange to take part in sthg □ *Are you going in for the New York Marathon?* **-2. to go in for sthg** [sport, music, dancing] to enjoy sthg and do it often □ *I don't really go in for jazz.*

◆ **go into** *vt fus* **-1. to go into sthg** [subject, problem] to describe or discuss sthg in a detailed way □ *The report goes into her family background.* □ *I'd rather not go into that now.* **-2. to go into sthg** [crime, question] to examine sthg in order to decide what to do about it □ *We intend to go into the matter of the missing money very thoroughly.* **-3. to go into a career/an occupation** [teaching, journalism] to start a particular career/occupation □ *Have you ever thought of going into advertising?* **-4. a lot of time/money went into that** a lot of time/money was used to make or do that □ *Most of our resources went into promoting the book.* **-5. to go into a dive/spin** [car, plane] to start to dive/spin.

◆ **go off** *vi* **-1.** [person] to leave a place in order to do something □ *"Where's Ann?" — "She went off to look for a gas station."* **-2.** [bomb, hand grenade] to explode; [gun] to fire □ *A bomb was planted in the car but failed to go off.* **-3.** [alarm, siren] to sound suddenly and loudly □ *Suddenly, the car alarm went off.* **-4.** [device, lamp] to switch off, usually automatically □ *The central heating goes off at night.* **-5. to go off well/badly** [concert, meeting] to be successful/unsuccessful □ *"How was the speech?" — "Oh, it didn't go off too badly."* **-6.** GB [milk, meat, fish] to start to become bad or rotten.

◆ **go off with** *vt fus* **to go off with sb/sthg** to take sb/sthg that belongs to somebody else and take them away □ *Who's gone off with my map?* □ *He went off with his best friend's wife.*

◆ **go on** ◇ *vi* **-1. to be going on** to be happening □ *There's a fight going on outside.* □ *I began to suspect that something was going on.* **-2.** [device, lamp] to start to operate, usually automatically □ *A light went on upstairs.* **-3.** [battle, argument] to continue to happen □ *The air raids went on through the night.* **-4. to go on** doing sthg, **to go on with sthg** to continue doing sthg, especially after one has been interrupted □ *I ignored them and went on (with my) reading.* **-5.** [person] to continue talking □ *"Shall I tell you about it?" — "Go on."* **-6.** [person] to talk about something too long or too much □ *Don't keep going on about it!* **-7.** [time] to pass □ *As time went on, I came to like him better.* **-8.** [traveler, walker] to continue traveling while others stay behind □ *You go on ahead, I'll wait here.* **-9. to go on to a place** to go to a place after doing something else □ *We went on to a nightclub afterward.* **-10. to go on to do sthg** to do sthg next or later □ *She went on to win the gold medal.*

◇ *vt fus* **to go on sthg** [evidence, information] to use sthg as a basis for judgments or opinions □ *The police only have a few clues to go on.*

◇ *excl* used to encourage somebody to do something □ *Go on, have another drink!*

◆ **go on at** *vt fus* **to go on at sb** to keep telling sb to do something in an annoying way □ *I wish you'd stop going on at me about my hair!*

◆ **go out** *vi* **-1.** [person] to leave a building, often one's own home □ *I went out at seven o'clock.* **-2.** [person] to go to places away from one's home for pleasure or entertainment □ *We don't go out much since the baby was born.* **-3.** [two people] to have a romantic or sexual relationship but not live together □ *She's not going out with anyone at present.* **-4.** [candle, cigarette] to stop burning □ *You let the fire go out.* **-5.** [light] to be switched off □ *Suddenly, all the lights went out.* **-6.** [TV program, radio program] to be broadcast □ *The interview went out live.* **-7.** [clothes, style] to stop being fashionable □ *Flares went out (of fashion) years ago.*

◆ **go over** *vt fus* **-1. to go over sthg** [document, event, figures] to look at and think about sthg carefully □ *She went over my work with me afterward.* **-2. to go over sthg** [explanation, theory] to repeat sthg so that it is easier to understand □ *The police asked me to go over my statement again.*

◆ **go over to** *vt fus* **-1. to go over to sthg** [system, method] to change to sthg that is new or different □ *The USA still hasn't gone over to the metric system.* **-2.** POLITICS **to go over to a group** to leave one organization and join a group that has very different beliefs and principles □ *He's gone over to the enemy.* **-3. to go over to a place** TV & RADIO to change the place that a broadcast is coming from □ *We're going over to the scene of the accident.* □ *And now let's go over to our Omaha studio.*

◆ **go round** *vi* = **go around.**

◆ **go through** ◇ *vt fus* **-1. to go through sthg** [problem, bad time, war] to experience or live through sthg unpleasant □ *I couldn't bear to go through all that again.* **-2. to go through sthg** [money, supplies] to spend or use sthg until it is finished □ *I've gone through all my savings already.* **-3. to go through sthg** [archives, drawer, desk] to search through sthg carefully, often in order to find something □ *She found the letter as she was going through his pockets.* **-4. to go through sthg** [document, report] to read sthg from beginning to end, often to

check it is correct □ *She went through the list, checking off each item.*

◇ *vi* [law, motion, proposal] to be agreed or accepted officially □ *The divorce went through without any problems.*

◆ **go through with** *vt fus* **to go through with sthg** [plan, action, threat] to do sthg that one has planned or promised to do even though one has doubts about it □ *She decided that she couldn't go through with the marriage.*

◆ **go toward** *vt fus* **to go toward sthg** to help to pay for sthg □ *Most of the money will go toward rebuilding the school.*

◆ **go under** *vi* **-1.** [ship, swimmer] to sink below the water. **-2.** [business, company] to go bankrupt □ *A lot of businesses went under in the recession.*

◆ **go up** ◇ *vi* **-1.** [person, aircraft] to move or rise to a higher position □ *We went up onto the roof.* □ *The escalator goes up to the fifth floor.* **-2.** [inflation, value, output] to become more or greater □ *House prices are going up.* □ *Standards have gone up since then.* **-3.** [house, office block] to be built; [advertisement, poster] to be put up in public places □ *Notices began to go up all around town.* **-4.** [building, ship] to explode and be destroyed, usually by fire □ *The whole factory went up.* **-5. a cheer went up** many people cheered at the same time. ◇ *vt fus* **to go up sthg** [mountain, stairs, building] to climb to the top of sthg □ *We went up the Eiffel Tower.*

◆ **go with** *vt fus* **to go with sthg** to be included as a natural part or result of sthg □ *The uniform goes with the job.*

◆ **go without** ◇ *vt fus* **to go without sthg** [sleep, food] not to have sthg that one usually has □ *For the last week they had to go without an evening meal.* ◇ *vi:* *They don't serve wine here, so you'll just have to go without.*

goad [goud] *vt* to cause <sb> to do something they are unwilling to do by continually annoying them, criticizing them etc □ *Their constant teasing finally goaded him into action/fighting back.*

go-ahead ◇ *adj* [company, organization, person] that uses new methods, ideas etc in order to be successful □ *Their go-ahead attitude will take them far in today's competitive market.* ◇ *n* **to get/be given the go-ahead** to get/be given official permission to start something □ *We hope to get the go-ahead soon.* □ *The project finally got the go-ahead in June.*

goal [goul] *n* **-1.** SPORT in games such as soccer and hockey, the space within the playing area, usually marked by posts, where the ball must go in order to score a point; the point scored when the ball enters this space □ *They scored four goals in the second half.* ■ **to score a goal** to win a point by making the ball enter the goal. **-2.** something that one wants to achieve □ *I've set myself two goals for next year: to lose weight and pass my driving test.* □ *Our goal is world peace.* □ *What is your goal in life?*

goalie ['gouli] *n* = **goalkeeper** (informal use).

goalkeeper ['goulki:pər] *n* in soccer and hockey, the player in a team who stays near the goal in order to stop the ball from entering.

goalless ['gɔʊlləs] *adj* **a goalless draw** [in soccer, hockey] the result of a game in which neither team scores a goal.

goalmouth ['gɔʊlmaʊθ, *pl* -maʊðz] *n* [in soccer] the area in front of the goal.

goalpost ['gɔʊlpɔʊst] *n* [in soccer, football, hockey] one of the two upright posts that form part of a goal.

goat [gɔʊt] *n* an animal with short horns and a rough hairy coat that lives wild on mountains and hills or is kept on farms for its milk and wool.

goatee [gɔʊ'tiː] *n* **a goatee (beard)** a small pointed beard that covers the chin only.

goat's cheese *n* cheese that is made from goat's milk.

gobble ['gɒbl] *vt* to eat <food> very quickly and often noisily.

◆ **gobble down, gobble up** *vt sep* **to gobble food down** OR **up** to eat food very quickly and often noisily until there is no more left.

gobbledygook ['gɒbldɪguːk] *n* formal and official language that is very difficult or impossible to understand.

go-between *n* a person who takes messages from one person to another when these people cannot meet or do not want to meet □ *Stein acted as a go-between in the dispute.*

Gobi ['gɔʊbɪ]: **the Gobi Desert** a large desert in central Asia, covering parts of Mongolia and China.

goblet ['gɒblət] *n* a cup without a handle, usually made of metal or glass, that has a stem and is used for drinking wine.

goblin ['gɒblɪn] *n* a small ugly fairy in children's stories who is usually bad and unkind.

go-cart [-kɑːʳt] *n* a small low car with very little covering for the engine or driver that is used for racing.

god [gɒd] *n* a male being that is or was believed to have power over a particular part of nature or over human life □ *the god of love/war/the Sun* □ *Apollo was a Greek god.*

◆ **God** ◇ *n* the being worshiped in the Christian, Muslim, and Jewish religions for creating and ruling the world □ *Do you believe in God?* ■ **God knows** a phrase used to emphasize that one does not know something □ *"What's she doing?" — "God only knows."* □ *God knows the money I've spent on those kids.* ◇ *excl* **God!** a word used to express surprise, excitement, or fear □ *Oh/My/Good God, what happened?*

godchild ['gɒdtʃaɪld] (*pl* **godchildren**) *n* a child that somebody agrees to be the godparent of.

goddam(n) ['gɒdæm] (informal use) ◇ *adj* a word used to express annoyance, anger, or excitement □ *The goddam(n) car won't start!* ◇ *excl* a word used to express annoyance or surprise □ *Goddam(n) it!*

goddaughter ['gɒddɔːtəʳ] *n* a female godchild.

goddess ['gɒdəs] *n* a female god □ *Artemis, the Greek goddess of the Moon.*

godfather ['gɒdfɑːðəʳ] *n* a male godparent.

godforsaken ['gɒdfəʳseɪkn] *adj* **a godforsaken place/town etc** a place/town etc that is depressing and has no interesting or attractive qualities.

Godiva [gə'daɪvə], **Lady** (1040–1080) an English noblewoman who, according to legend, rode naked on her horse through Coventry to protest against the taxes her husband was making people pay.

godmother ['gɒdmʌðəʳ] *n* a female godparent.

godparent ['gɒdpeərənt] *n* in the Christian religion, a person who promises to be responsible for the religious or moral education of somebody's child at that child's baptism.

godsend ['gɒdsend] *n* somebody or something that arrives, happens etc unexpectedly and that one finds very useful at a particular time □ *That check was a real godsend.*

godson ['gɒdsʌn] *n* a male godchild.

goes [gɔʊz] *vb* → **go**.

Goethe ['gɜːtə], **Johann Wolfgang von** (1749–1832) a German poet, dramatist, and scientist who is considered the greatest German writer. His best-known work is *Faust.*

gofer ['gɔʊfəʳ] *n* a person whose job is to do small tasks for other people, such as taking messages and fetching or carrying things (informal use).

go-getter [-getəʳ] *n* a person who is very ambitious and determined, works hard, and tries to use every opportunity to succeed, especially in their job.

goggle ['gɒgl] *vi* **to goggle at sb/sthg** to stare at sb/sthg with one's eyes open wide in surprise, admiration etc.

goggles ['gɒglz] *npl* a pair of glass or plastic lenses attached to an elastic strap, worn around the head to protect the eyes from water, wind, dirt etc □ *driving/protective/swimming/skiing goggles* □ *a pair of goggles.*

go-go dancer *n* a person at a nightclub, bar etc whose job is to dance to fast music in a sexy way while wearing few clothes.

going ['gɔʊɪŋ] ◇ *adj* **-1. the going rate** the salary or wage that is being paid for a particular job or in a particular area □ *What's the going rate for this kind of work?* **-2. the biggest/best etc thing going** the biggest/best etc example of a particular thing □ *He's the biggest idiot going.* **-3. to be going** GB [food, wine] to be available □ *Are there any jobs going?*

◇ *n* **-1.** the speed at which somebody or something moves or progresses □ *The going is pretty slow on the expressway due to a pileup at the Maple Street exit.* ■ **good going** a phrase used to show that one is impressed at something's speed or progress □ *Have you finished already? That's pretty good going.* **-2.** GB **to be hard** OR **heavy going** to be difficult to do or deal with □ *It was hard going on the way up the mountain.* □ *This novel is heavy going.*

going concern *n* a business that is making money □ *The firm was sold as a going concern.*

goings-on *npl* events in a particular place or involving particular people over a period of time that one finds interesting, amusing etc or disapproves of (informal use).

go-kart [-kɑːʳt] *n* GB = **go-cart**.

Golan Heights [US ˌɡoʊluːn-, GB ˌɡoʊlæn-]: **the Golan Heights** a range of hills in the Middle East, on the eastern bank of the Jordan. They were occupied by Israel in 1967 and are likely to be returned to Syria

gold [ɡoʊld] ◇ *n* -1. a valuable soft metal that is yellow in color and is used for making coins, jewelry etc. SYMBOL: Au □ *The price of gold is dropping.* □ *a gold ring/coin/watch.* ■ **to be as good as gold** [child] to be very well-behaved. -2. = **gold medal.** ◇ *adj* [paint, star, car] that is gold in color.

Gold Coast: **the Gold Coast** an area off the coast of southern Queensland, Australia, famous for its beaches and tourist resorts.

golden [ˈɡoʊldən] *adj* -1. [ring, crown] that is made of gold. -2. [hair, shine, pastry] that has the color of gold.

golden age *n* a period of great success, achievements etc in a particular field of activity that people remember for a long time □ *the golden age of science-fiction/the cinema.*

golden eagle *n* a large golden-brown eagle that lives in mountains in northern parts of the world.

golden handshake *n* a large amount of money given to reward or thank somebody for their services when they leave a job after many years, usually to retire.

golden opportunity *n* a perfect chance to do something, especially one that probably will not happen again □ *Don't turn down his invitation, it's a golden opportunity to meet the company bosses.*

golden retriever *n* a type of medium-sized dog with a soft, wavy, yellow coat.

golden rule *n* the most important thing to remember to do if one wants to be successful in a particular situation.

golden wedding *n* the fiftieth anniversary of somebody's wedding.

goldfish [ˈɡoʊldfɪʃ] (*pl* **goldfish**) *n* a bright orange fish that is often kept as a pet.

goldfish bowl *n* a round glass bowl used for keeping goldfish in.

gold leaf *n* gold in very thin sheets that is used for covering things or to decorate pictures, writing etc.

gold medal *n* a medal that is gold in color and that is given to the winner of a competition, especially in sport.

goldmine [ˈɡoʊldmaɪn] *n* -1. a place where gold is mined. -2. a business, invention, plan etc that makes or is likely to make a big profit □ *The woman who invented the system is sitting on a goldmine.*

gold-plated [-ˈpleɪtəd] *adj* [frame, clock, jewelry] that is covered in a very thin layer of gold.

gold rush *n* the sudden arrival of large numbers of people who have come to look for gold in an area where gold has just been found. ■ **the Gold Rush** the first and most famous gold rush, in California, in 1849.

☙ THE GOLD RUSHES
There have been three major gold rushes in North American history, when large numbers of people moved to an area hoping to find gold there. The first one was in California in 1849, the second one in Colorado in 1858, and the third one in the Klondike region of Canada in 1897. The arrival of hundreds of thousands of people, and the wealth of those who found gold, were responsible for the rapid development of many western US cities and states in the 19th century.

goldsmith [ˈɡoʊldsmɪθ] *n* a person whose job is to make things out of gold.

gold standard *n* **the gold standard** the system in which the value of gold is used as a fixed basis for deciding the value of a currency.

golf [ɡɒlf] *n* a game in which each player tries to send a small white ball into a series of holes by hitting it through the air or along the ground as few times as possible using special sticks □ *a round of golf.*

golf ball *n* -1. a small, hard, white ball used for playing golf. -2. **a golf ball (typewriter)** an electric typewriter with the letters and symbols arranged on a small metal ball.

golf club *n* -1. a club for golf players that usually has its own golf course and buildings; the buildings and land used by this club. -2. a long wooden or metal stick with a heavy curved bottom that is used to hit the ball in golf □ *a set of golf clubs.*

golf course *n* an area of grassy land used to play a game of golf.

golfer [ˈɡɒlfəʳ] *n* a person who plays golf.

Goliath [ɡəˈlaɪəθ] → David.

golly [ˈɡɒlɪ] *excl* a word used to express surprise (informal and old-fashioned use).

gondola [ˈɡɒndələ] *n* a long narrow boat with high curved ends that is used in Venice, Italy, and is moved through water by a person standing at one end using a long pole.

gondolier [ˌɡɒndəˈlɪəʳ] *n* a person whose job is to give tourists tours in a gondola.

gone [ɡɒn] ◇ *past participle of* go. ◇ *adj* **to be gone** [person] to be no longer present in a particular place; [money, time] to have been completely used or finished □ *"Is there any cake left?" — "No, it's all gone."* □ *The days when I used to go out every night are long gone.* ◇ *prep* GB later than <a particular time>; older than <a particular age> □ *It's gone lunchtime.* □ *It's just gone 12 o'clock.* □ *He's gone fifty, you know.*

gong [ɡɒŋ] *n* a round flat piece of metal that is hung in a frame and is hit with a stick to make a long, loud, and deep ringing noise, e.g. to attract people's attention.

gonna ['gɒnə] = **going to** (informal use).

gonorrhea US, **gonorrhoea** GB [gɒnə'riːə] *n* a disease of the sex organs that is passed from one person to another during sexual intercourse.

goo [guː] *n* any substance that is thick and sticky (informal use).

good [gʊd] (*compar* **better**, *superl* **best**) ◇ *adj* **-1.** [event, experience, period of time] that is pleasant or enjoyable □ *Did you have a good time in Spain?* □ *It's good to see you.* □ *She's not in a very good mood today.* □ *It feels good to be out in the fresh air.* **-2.** [education, manners, result] that is of a high quality or standard □ *The firm doesn't have a very good reputation.* □ *The steak's very good here.* **-3.** [idea, suggestion, plan] that is desirable or suitable □ *It's good that she finally got promoted.* □ *It's a really good house for children.* **-4.** [writer, actor, translation] that is skillful □ *He isn't a very good swimmer.* ■ **to be good at sthg** [at French, cooking, sport] to be able to do sthg well □ *She's always been good at organizing.* ■ **to be good with sthg/sb** [with animals, engines, children] to be skillful at doing things with sthg/sb □ *I'm not much good with computers.* **-5.** [person] who is kind and considerate □ *It was very good of you to come.* □ *They were very good to me when I was sick.* ■ **to be good enough to do sthg** a polite phrase used to ask somebody to do something or to say that they have done something helpful □ *Would you be good enough to open the door for me?* □ *This gentleman was good enough to find us a taxi.* **-6.** [person, life, act] that is honest, moral, and concerned with the health and happiness of other people □ *She devoted herself to good works.* **-7.** [child, dog] that is well-behaved □ *His prison sentence was reduced on the grounds of good behavior.* ■ **be good!** behave well! **-8. it's good for you** [milk, fresh air, exercise] it makes one more healthy or prevents one from becoming ill □ *Fried food isn't good for you.* **-9.** [looks, legs, figure] that is physically attractive □ *She came back from vacation looking really good.* **-10.** [opportunity, sign, news] that is favorable □ *There's never been a better time to invest.* □ *a job with good prospects.* **-11.** [chance, way, distance] used to show that the speaker thinks an amount is large □ *It took us a good hour to get there.* ■ **a good many people** a lot of people □ *A good many people would agree with him.* **-12.** [cry, look, clean] that is thorough □ *I gave him a good talking-to.* **-13.** phrases **it's a good thing** OR **job (that)...** GB it's lucky (that)... □ *It's a good thing no one saw us.* ■ **good for you!** a phrase used to show approval and pleasure at something another person has done □ *"I won first prize!"* — *"Good for you!"* ■ **to make sthg good** to repair or replace sthg lost or damaged. ◇ *n* **-1.** something that benefits or improves somebody □ *In the end, you might do more harm than good by telling him.* ■ **for the good of sb/sthg** [one's health, the nation] for the benefit or improvement of sb/sthg □ *She spent her life working for the good of other people.* □ *I'm telling you this for your own good.* ■ **it will**

do you/him etc good it will have a positive effect on your/his etc mind or body □ *It will do you good to have a rest.* **-2. will this be any good?** will this be useful? □ *"We need something to stand on."* — *"Will this be any good?"* ■ **to be no good** to be of poor quality or unsatisfactory □ *This corkscrew is no good.* ■ **to be no good at sthg** not to be able to do sthg □ *He's no good at dancing.* ■ **it's no good** it will not make any difference □ *It's no good crying, that won't help us.* □ *I'd come along if I thought it would do any good.* **-3.** behavior and actions that are moral, help other people, and are usually based on religious teachings □ *He could always see the good in people.* □ *the choice between good and evil.* ■ **to be up to no good** to be doing or planning to do something wrong □ *I knew they were up to no good when I saw them hanging around the car.*

◇ *excl* a word used to express pleasure, satisfaction, or approval □ *Oh good, you're here.*

◆ **goods** *npl* objects which are made to be bought and sold □ *consumer/leather/duty-free goods.* ■ **to come up with** OR **deliver the goods** to do successfully what one has agreed or been asked to do (informal use) □ *They may be well-known, but are they going to deliver the goods?*

◆ **as good as** *adv* almost □ *He as good as promised to come.*

◆ **for good** *adv* forever □ *I left home for good when I was 18.*

good afternoon *excl* a phrase used to greet somebody in the afternoon □ *Good afternoon, Sally. Is the boss free?*

good behavior *n* LAW good and lawful behavior by a prisoner that can result in a shortening of their sentence □ *He was released early for good behavior.*

goodbye [ˌgʊd'baɪ] ◇ *excl* a word used by people when they are leaving each other or finishing a telephone conversation □ *Please come again, goodbye.* □ *Goodbye, Mom. See you soon.* ◇ *n* the things one says or one's actions when leaving or being left by somebody □ *We quickly said our goodbyes and I ran to catch the train.* □ *She waved/hugged me goodbye.* □ *a goodbye kiss.*

good day *excl* a phrase used to say hello or goodbye (old-fashioned use).

good deed *n* something one does to help another person that proves one is a helpful member of society □ *I've done my good deed for the day!*

good evening *excl* a phrase used to greet somebody in the evening □ *Good evening. May I speak to Mr Jones, please?*

good-for-nothing ◇ *n* a person, usually a man, who is lazy and not good at anything □ *He's just a lazy good-for-nothing.* ◇ *adj*: *that good-for-nothing brother of yours.*

good fortune *n* luck that brings something pleasant, useful etc □ *a piece of good fortune* □ *By good fortune we managed to catch the train after all.*

Good Friday *n* the Friday before Easter Sunday, on which Christians remember the death of Jesus Christ.

good-humored [-'hju:mərd] *adj* [person] who does not get angry easily and is always friendly and pleasant even in difficult situations □ *He was very good-humored about the damage.*

good-looking [-'lʊkɪŋ] *adj* [person] who has an attractive face □ *He's a good-looking guy.*

good manners *npl* polite behavior that follows the accepted rules of how one should act toward other people.

good morning *excl* a phrase used to greet somebody in the morning □ *Good morning, everyone!*

good-natured [-'neɪtʃərd] *adj* [person, animal] that does not get angry easily, and is always friendly, calm, and pleasant; [rivalry, argument] that is friendly and does not involve anger.

goodness ['gʊdnəs] ◇ *n* -1. the quality of being kind and thoughtful □ *I shall never forget their goodness to me.* -2. the quality in fruit, vegetables etc that makes them good for one's health □ *Milk is full of goodness.* □ *Vegetables lose their goodness if you overcook them.* ◇ *excl* **(my) goodness!** a word or phrase used to express surprise □ *My goodness me! What have you been doing? You're filthy!* □ *Goodness gracious!* ■ **for goodness' sake!** a phrase used to express annoyance □ *For goodness' sake hurry up, or we'll be late!* ■ **thank goodness** a phrase used to express relief □ *Thank goodness he's safe.*

good night *excl* a phrase used by people to say goodbye at the end of an evening or before they go to bed at night □ *Good night, and see you tomorrow!* □ *She wished us good night and went upstairs.*

goods train *n* GB a train that transports goods rather than passengers.

good-tempered [-'tempərd] *adj* [person, meeting] that is calm and friendly.

good turn *n* **to do sb a good turn** to do something to help sb.

goodwill [,gʊd'wɪl] *n* -1. kind feelings or a friendly helpful attitude toward a person, organization etc □ *The treaty they proposed showed their goodwill to the Canadians.* □ *feelings of goodwill* □ *a goodwill gesture/message.* -2. BUSINESS an asset earned by a company or business through its reputation, customer relations etc that helps decide its value.

goody ['gʊdɪ] (*pl* **goodies**) ◇ *n* the hero or any other character in a story who supports what is morally right and who the audience or reader wants to succeed (informal use). ◇ *excl* a word used especially by children to express their pleasure at something.
♦ **goodies** *npl* (informal use) -1. delicious food or candies. -2. desirable objects.

gooey ['gu:ɪ] (*compar* **gooier**, *superl* **gooiest**) *adj* [cake, dessert, chewing gum] that is soft and sticky (informal use).

goof [gu:f] US (informal use) ◇ *n* a stupid mistake. ◇ *vi* to make a goof.

♦ **goof off** *vi* to be lazy and waste time, especially when one is supposed to be working.
♦ **goof up** *vi* to goof.

goofy ['gu:fɪ] (*compar* **goofier**, *superl* **goofiest**) *adj* [idea, behavior, person] that one finds silly or awkward and unusual (informal use) □ *a goofy smile.*

goose [gu:s] (*pl* **geese**) *n* a large bird with webbed feet and a long neck that lives on farms or near ponds and is kept for its eggs, meat, and feathers.

gooseberry [US 'gu:sberɪ, GB 'gʊzbərɪ] (*pl* **gooseberries**) *n* -1. a small, rounded, pale-green fruit with small hairs on its skin that grows on bushes, has a sour taste, and is used to make desserts □ *a gooseberry bush/pie.* -2. **to play gooseberry** GB to be the third person with a couple who are in love and who want to be alone together.

goose bumps *npl* US the tiny lumps that appear when the hairs on one's skin stand up straight as a result of cold, fear etc.

gooseflesh ['gu:sfleʃ] *n* GB = **goosebumps**.

goose pimples *npl* GB = **goose bumps**.

goosestep ['gu:sstep] (*pt* & *pp* **goosestepped**, *cont* **goosestepping**) ◇ *n* **the goosestep** a way of marching used by soldiers in some armies, in which each step is made by lifting the leg up high and straight. ◇ *vi* to do the goosestep □ *The soldiers goosestepped across the square.*

GOP (*abbr of* **Grand Old Party**) *n* **the GOP** a nickname for the Republican Party in the USA.

gopher ['goʊfər] *n* a small animal that looks like a rat with large cheeks and lives underground in northern and central America.

gore [gɔ:r] ◇ *n* blood from a serious wound □ *a movie full of blood and gore.* ◇ *vt* to seriously wound <a person or animal> using horns or tusks □ *He was gored to death by a bull.*

gorge [gɔ:rdʒ] ◇ *n* a deep narrow valley that often has a river running along the bottom. ◇ *vt* **to gorge oneself on** OR **with sthg** to eat sthg greedily and in such quantity that one cannot eat anything else □ *We gorged ourselves on chocolate mousse.*

gorgeous ['gɔ:rdʒəs] *adj* -1. [food, beach, weather] very beautiful □ *What a gorgeous view of the countryside!* □ *She always wears absolutely gorgeous clothes.* -2. [man, woman] who is very sexually attractive (informal use) □ *She has a gorgeous figure.*

gorilla [gə'rɪlə] *n* an African animal that is the largest of the apes.

gorse [gɔ:rs] *n* a wild European bush that has prickles and yellow flowers.

gory ['gɔ:rɪ] (*compar* **gorier**, *superl* **goriest**) *adj* -1. [movie, scene, death] that involves a lot of blood and violence □ *There was an extremely gory battle scene.* -2. **the gory details** too many details □ *Spare me the gory details!*

gosh [gɒʃ] *excl* a word used to express surprise or admiration (old-fashioned and informal use) □ *Gosh! Did you really?*

go-slow *n* GB an official protest by workers in which they work as slowly as possible.

gospel ['gɒspl] ◇ *n* -1. a set of ideas that somebody believes in very strongly and tries to make other people believe in □ *She's off preaching her Socialist/feminist gospel.* -2. **gospel (truth)** something that is completely true □ *You mustn't take it as gospel.* ◇ *comp* **gospel music** a style of religious music that is powerful and rhythmic and is sung especially by black American Christians.

◆ **Gospel** *n* any one of the four books in the Bible that describe the life and works of Jesus Christ □ *St Mark's Gospel* □ *the Gospel according to St Luke.*

gossamer ['gɒsəmər] *n* the long fine threads produced by a spider to make its web.

gossip [US 'gɒsəp, GB -ɪp] ◇ *n* -1. the things people say or write to each other about the behavior and private lives of other people, whether it is true or not □ *Have you heard any good gossip lately?* □ *It's just idle gossip, don't take any notice.* □ *We only had time for a quick gossip and then I had to go.* -2. a person who likes to talk gossip (disapproving use) □ *He's a terrible gossip.* ◇ *vi* to talk about the behavior and private lives of other people □ *She's always gossiping about the neighbors.*

gossip column *n* a section in a newspaper or magazine in which the behavior and private lives of famous people are written about.

got [gɒt] *past tense & past participle of* **get.** ■ **I have got sthg** GB I have sthg □ *He's got blue eyes/flu/a nice house.* ■ **I have got to do sthg** I must do sthg □ *I've got to finish this today.*

Gotham ['gɒθm] US an informal name for New York City.

Gothic ['gɒθɪk] *adj* -1. [architecture, church, window] that is in a style of architecture that was popular between the 12th and 16th centuries in Western Europe. Gothic buildings have high ceilings, pointed arches and windows, and tall columns. -2. **a Gothic novel/story etc** a novel/story etc that is set in a ruin or castle and contains mystery, horror, or supernatural elements. Gothic novels were popular in Britain in the 18th and 19th centuries. -3. [lettering, script, writing] that is printed or written in a style in which the letters are thick, pointed, and angular.

gotta ['gɒtə] = **got to** (informal use).

gotten ['gɒtn] US *past participle of* **get.**

gouge [gaʊdʒ] *vt* -1. **to gouge a hole (out)** to make a hole in something hard using a sharp object, especially using a lot of effort □ *Someone had gouged a hole in the desk.* -2. **to gouge sb's eyes out** to force sb's eyes out using a sharp object.

goulash [US 'guːlɑːʃ, GB -æʃ] *n* a type of meat stew, traditionally from Hungary, that contains paprika.

gourd [gɔːrd] *n* a type of round fruit which cannot be eaten and has a hard outer covering; a container made from this fruit.

gourmet ['gʊərmeɪ] ◇ *n* a person who knows a lot about food and wine, and enjoys food and wine of a high quality. ◇ *adj* **gourmet food/meal** food/a meal of very high quality.

gout [gaʊt] *n* a disease that causes the toes, knees, and fingers to swell and become painful.

govern ['gʌvərn] ◇ *vt* -1. POLITICS to legally control <a country, state, people> etc and have the power to make decisions about laws, taxes, the economy etc □ *This party is not fit to govern the country.* -2. to influence or control <a price, one's behavior, destiny> etc □ *There are strict rules governing the sale of alcohol and tobacco.* ◇ *vi* POLITICS [party, politician] *We need a leader who can govern efficiently.*

governess ['gʌvərnəs] *n* a woman who, especially in the past, lived with a family in order to teach the children.

governing ['gʌvərnɪŋ] *adj* **the governing party** the political party that is in power at a particular time.

governing body *n* the group of people who are in charge of making decisions and taking actions concerning a public organization □ *the governing body of the University/hospital.*

government ['gʌvərnmənt] *n* -1. the group of people who govern a country or state □ *the Australian government* OR *government of Australia* □ *The government has signed the treaty.* □ *On the Prime Minister's resignation, his successor had to form a new government very quickly.* □ *a government official/department* □ *government spending/funding/policy.* -2. the act of governing a country or state □ *The Social Democrats are in government/out of government.* □ *We want democratic government.*

governmental [ˌgʌvərn'mentl] *adj* [decision, measure] that is taken by the government.

government stock *n* certificates issued by the government when it borrows money from members of the public.

governor ['gʌvərnər] *n* -1. POLITICS a person who governs a particular colony, country etc; in the USA, a person who governs a particular state □ *He's running for governor at the next elections.* -2. [of a school, bank, hospital] a member of the group that is in charge of making decisions and taking actions concerning a particular organization □ *the Board of Governors.*

governor-general (*pl* **governor-generals** OR **governors-general**) *n* the person who represents the British king or queen in a country that is in the Commonwealth and is not a republic □ *the Canadian Governor-General.*

govt *abbr of* **government.**

gown [gaʊn] *n* -1. a long dress worn on special or formal occasions □ *an evening/bridal gown.* -2. an item of clothing like a cloak, worn by academics and lawyers. -3. a loose tunic worn by patients or surgeons in a hospital □ *a hospital gown.*

Goya ['gɔɪə], **Francisco de** (1746–1828) a Spanish artist who is famous for his portraits, especially of Spanish royalty.

GP (*abbr of* **general practitioner**) *n* a doctor

who treats all kinds of illness and does not specialize in any particular type.

GPA (*abbr of* **Grade Point Average**) *n* the score given to US high school and college students that is the average grade for all their courses.

GPMU (*abbr of* **Graphical, Paper and Media Union**) *n* a British labor union for people working in printing and publishing.

GPO *n* (*abbr of* **Government Printing Office**) **the GPO** the US government department responsible for publishing government documents.

gr. *abbr of* **gross**.

grab [græb] (*pt* & *pp* **grabbed**, *cont* **grabbing**) ◇ *vt* **-1.** [person, money, arm] to take hold of <sb/sthg> with a sudden and sometimes violent movement; [opportunity, chance] to eagerly take <sthg> because there will probably not be another one □ *Sally grabbed the knife from the baby just in time.* □ *The thief grabbed the bag and ran off.* **-2.** [sandwich, meal] to get <sthg to eat or drink> quickly because one is very busy or in a hurry (informal use) □ *We can grab a bite to eat on the way to the station.* **-3. to grab a few hours'** OR **some sleep** to stop and sleep for a short period of time when one is very busy or has very little time (informal use). **-4. how does that grab you?** a phrase used when asking if somebody would like to do something (informal use) □ *How does a weekend in Paris grab you?*
◇ *vi* **to grab at sthg** to make a sudden movement with one's hand to try to take hold of or pick up sthg □ *He grabbed at my sleeve.*
◇ *n* **to make a grab at** OR **for sthg** to grab at sthg □ *I made a grab for the control lever.*

grab bag *n* US a container filled with small prizes that children put their hand into and pick a prize out of without looking.

grace [greɪs] ◇ *n* **-1.** [of a dancer, animal, movement] smooth, elegant, and controlled movement that is pleasing to watch and appears to be without effort □ *She dances with style and grace.* **-2. to have the grace to do sthg** to be fair and considerate enough to do sthg □ *At least she had the grace to apologize.* ■ **to do sthg with good grace** to do sthg without complaining and without showing that one would prefer not to do it □ *She accepted the decision with good grace.* **-3. a day's/week's grace** an extra day/week to do or finish something that one is given as a favor □ *We've been given a week's grace.* **-4.** RELIGION a prayer thanking God for the meal one is about to eat □ *Father always said grace in the evenings.*
◇ *vt* **-1.** to be present at <a meeting or event>, usually with the result that people there feel honored or grateful (formal or ironic use) □ *So you've decided to grace us with your presence!* **-2.** [room, shelf, table] to act as an attractive decoration in or on <sthg> □ *His paintings now grace the walls of the town hall.*
◆ **Grace** *n* **His/Her/Your Grace** a title used when talking to a duke, duchess, or archbishop.

Grace [greɪs], **W. G.** (1848–1915) a British

cricketer, considered to be the greatest of his time.

graceful ['greɪsfl] *adj* **-1.** [dancer, movement, step] that moves in a smooth, elegant, and attractive way and apparently without effort; [line, curve] that is smooth, controlled, and attractive to look at □ *She made a graceful exit.* □ *the graceful curve of her neck.* **-2.** [refusal, apology] that is polite, pleasant, and dignified □ *He gave a very graceful apology for his mistake.*

graceless ['greɪsləs] *adj* **-1.** [city, place] that is ugly and without elegance or charm. **-2.** [person] who is impolite and does not have dignity or good manners.

gracious ['greɪʃəs] ◇ *adj* **-1.** [person] who is polite and kind, especially to somebody who has less money or a lower social position □ *a gracious refusal.* **-2.** [house, residence] that has the elegance and comfort that a lot of money can provide □ *gracious living.* ◇ *excl* **(good) gracious!** a word or phrase used to express surprise □ *Good gracious! What on earth is that?*

graciously ['greɪʃəslɪ] *adv* [accept, invite, thank] *see* **gracious**.

gradation [grə'deɪʃn] *n* [of color, light, a feeling] a slight difference in size, intensity etc in a series or scale.

grade [greɪd] ◇ *n* **-1.** [of wool, gasoline, paper] the level or quality of a person or product □ *a high-/low-grade employee* □ *grade A eggs.* ■ **to make the grade** [person] to achieve the necessary standard, especially in one's job. **-2.** US a group of classes at school for students who are of a particular age or level □ *I'm in sixth grade.* **-3.** [for homework, exam] the mark, usually a letter or number, that represents the quality of a student's work □ *What grade did you get for math?* ◇ *vt* **-1.** to separate <potatoes, eggs, fruit> etc into different groups of similar size, quality etc □ *We grade our beer according to strength.* **-2.** to give <homework, an exam paper> etc a grade.

grade crossing *n* US a place where a road crosses a railroad, that usually has gates and warning signals to stop traffic when a train is approaching.

grade point average *n* → **GPA**.

grade school *n* US a school for children aged between 5 and 11 □ *a grade school teacher.*

gradient ['greɪdjənt] *n* a slope; the angle of a slope □ *a hill with a steep gradient.*

gradual ['grædʒʊəl] *adj* [change, increase, improvement] that happens slowly and in small stages □ *His recovery was gradual.*

gradually ['grædʒʊəlɪ] *adv*: *see* **gradual** □ *The economy gradually began to improve.*

graduate [*n* 'grædʒʊət, *vb* 'grædʒʊeɪt] ◇ *n* **-1.** [of a college] a person who has a first degree from a university or college □ *an English/a chemistry graduate.* **-2.** US [of a high school] a person who has successfully completed high school.
◇ *comp* **a graduate course** a course of further studies after a first degree. ■ **a graduate stu-**

dent a student who is doing further studies after a first degree.

◇ *vi* **-1.** [from college] to receive a certificate for successfully completing a degree at a university or college □ *He graduated from Oxford, you know.* **-2.** US [from high school] to receive a certificate for successfully completing high school □ *I graduated from high school last year.* **-3. to graduate from sthg to sthg** to move from sthg less important or difficult to sthg more important or difficult □ *He's graduated from a moped to a motorcycle.*

graduated ['grædʒʊeɪtəd] *adj* **-1.** [pension, tax] in which the amount that people pay depends on the amount that they earn. **-2.** [ruler, container] that is marked with lines to show measurements. **-3.** [exercises] that are arranged in order from the easiest to the most difficult. **-4.** [colors] that blend gradually into each other.

graduate school *n* US the part of a university where students who already have a first degree are taught.

graduation [,grædʒʊ'eɪʃn] *n* **-1.** the ceremony at which students receive their certificates for completing a university degree; US the ceremony at which students receive their certificates for completing high school □ *a graduation ceremony/photograph.* **-2.** [from university, college, high school] *see* **graduate** □ *After graduation I got a job with a bank.*

♻ GRADUATION
When students at a university or college or a US high school complete their course of studies, they are given their degree or diploma at a public ceremony called graduation. Their family and friends usually come to the graduation ceremony, at which students wear a cap (a round hat, usually with a flat board on top) and a gown (a long loose garment like a cloak). In the USA, the student with the best grades, called the valedictorian, makes a speech, and at the end of the ceremony everyone throws their cap up in the air.

---

graffiti [grə'fiːtɪ] *n* words or pictures that are written or drawn on walls, posters etc in public places □ *The side of the subway train was covered in graffiti.*

graft [US græft, GB grɑːft] ◇ *n* **-1.** GARDENING a part cut from one plant and joined onto another plant so that it can continue growing on the new plant. **-2.** MEDICINE a piece of healthy skin or bone taken from a person's body and used to replace skin or bone that has been damaged □ *a skin graft.* **-3.** POLITICS the act of getting money dishonestly by using one's power or authority (informal use).
◇ *vt* **-1.** GARDENING [branch, twig] to join <part of a plant> to another plant as a graft □ *It's the result of grafting a cutting onto a hardier variety.* **-2.** MEDICINE [skin, bone, organ] to attach <a graft> to a damaged part of the body in an operation □ *He had to have some skin grafted to* OR *onto his leg.* **-3.** [idea, system] to add <sthg> to something else when the two

things are very different □ *They're trying to graft Socialist ideals onto a market economy.*

Graham ['greɪəm], **Martha** (1894–1991) a US dancer and choreographer who had a great influence on modern dance.

grain [greɪn] *n* **-1.** [of wheat, rice] a seed of wheat, rice, or a similar plant □ *a grain of corn/rice.* **-2.** a collective term for wheat, corn, or any similar crop from a cereal plant □ *stocks of grain.* **-3.** [of salt, sand] a single very small piece of a hard substance □ *a grain of salt/sand/gold.* **-4.** [of truth, humor] a very small amount □ *There's not a grain of truth in what he says.* **-5.** [in wood] the natural pattern of lines or fibers in a piece of wood, rock etc □ *This wood has a beautiful grain.* ■ **to go against the grain** to be difficult to accept or do, because it feels unusual and is not what one usually does □ *I'll do it for you, but it goes against the grain.*

gram [græm] *n* a unit (0.001 kilogram) for measuring weight □ *250 grams of butter.*

grammar ['græmər] *n* **-1.** [of a language] the rules of a language that describe how words are put together in sentences □ *English/French grammar* □ *His grammar is terrible.* **-2.** a book that describes the rules of a language □ *a French grammar.*

grammar school *n* **-1.** in the USA, a school where children go for the first six to eight years of their education. **-2.** in Britain, a school that teaches some children aged between 11 and 18 who have been chosen because they are good at academic subjects.

grammatical [grə'mætɪkl] *adj* **-1.** [rule, structure] *see* **grammar. -2.** [English, French] that is correct according to the rules of grammar.

gramme [græm] *n* GB = **gram.**

Grammy ['græmɪ] *n* in the USA, an award given to outstanding members of the music industry.

gramophone ['græməfoʊn] *n* a record player (old-fashioned use).

gran [græn] *n* GB a word used to talk to or about one's grandmother (informal use).

granary ['grænərɪ] (*pl* **granaries**) *n* a building in which grain is stored.

granary bread *n* GB a type of brown bread that contains whole grains of wheat.

grand [grænd] (*pl* **grand**) ◇ *adj* **-1.** [style, house, sight] that is impressive in size or appearance □ *This place is much too grand for me.* **-2.** [plan, design, scale] that is ambitious and intended to achieve impressive results □ *My partner has some very grand ideas for expanding the company.* **-3.** [person, title, job] that is socially or professionally important □ *She sounds very grand, but she's really quite friendly.* **-4.** [time, party, day] very enjoyable (informal and old-fashioned use). ◇ *n* a thousand dollars or pounds (informal use) □ *"How much will it cost?" — "Two grand, minimum."*

grandad ['grændæd] *n* a word used to talk to or about one's grandfather (informal use).

Grand Canyon: the Grand Canyon a very long and deep valley that has been made in the rock of northwest Arizona by the Colorado River. It is a popular tourist attraction.

grandchild ['grænt∫aɪld] (*pl* **grandchildren**) *n* the child of somebody's son or daughter □ *her two grandchildren.*

granddad ['grændæd] *n* = **grandad**.

granddaughter ['grændɔːtəʳ] *n* the daughter of somebody's son or daughter.

grand duchess *n* the wife of a grand duke; a noblewoman who has the same rank as a grand duke.

grand duke *n* a nobleman who rules a state or large area of land.

grandeur ['grændʒəʳ] *n* **-1.** [of an occasion, ceremony] a quality that something has that makes it impressive and beautiful □ *the severe grandeur of the Rockies.* **-2.** [of a person] great importance.

grandfather ['grændfɑːðəʳ] *n* the father of somebody's father or mother.

grandfather clock *n* a piece of furniture consisting of a clock in a tall wooden case.

grandiose ['grændɪəʊs] *adj* [building, plan] that is bigger or designed to be more impressive than is necessary or useful (disapproving use) □ *He had some rather grandiose ideas about changing it into an opera house.*

grand jury *n* in the USA, a jury of 12 to 24 people who decide whether there is enough evidence to charge somebody with a crime and hold a trial.

grandma ['grænmɑː] *n* a word used to talk to or about one's grandmother (informal use).

grand master *n* a player of the very highest level in chess.

grandmother ['grænmʌðəʳ] *n* the mother of somebody's mother or father.

Grand National *n* **the Grand National** an important horse race that takes place each year at Aintree race course, near Liverpool, northwestern England.

Grand Ole Opry [-ʊʊl'ɒprɪ] *n* a country music show that takes place near Nashville, Tennessee.

grandpa ['grænpɑː] *n* a word used to talk to or about one's grandfather (informal use).

grandparents ['grænpeərənts] *npl* the parents of somebody's mother or father.

grand piano *n* a large piano in which the frame and strings are horizontal.

grand prix [,grɒn'priː] (*pl* **grands prix** [,grɒn-'priː]) *n* one of a series of races in an international competition for very powerful racing cars.

grand slam *n* the act of winning all the important matches or tournaments in a particular season, especially in tennis, golf, or rugby.

grandson ['grænsʌn] *n* the son of somebody's son or daughter.

grandstand ['grændstænd] *n* a large structure consisting of rows of seats and a roof, where people sit to watch sports matches and races □ *We had grandstand seats.*

grand total *n* the final amount of something when everything has been added together □ *That makes a grand total of $78.*

granite ['grænɪt] *n* a very hard rock, usually gray in color, that is used for buildings.

granny ['grænɪ] (*pl* **grannies**) *n* a word used to talk to or about one's grandmother (informal use).

granny flat *n* GB part of a house where somebody, especially an old relative of the family, can live separately from the other people in the house.

granola [grə'nəʊlə] *n* US a mixture of oats, chopped nuts, and fruits that is usually served with milk and eaten as a cereal for breakfast □ *a granola bar.*

grant [US grænt, GB grɑːnt] ◇ *n* an amount of money given by the state or local government to a person or organization for a special purpose □ *a grant toward relocation* □ *a student grant.*

◇ *vt* **-1.** [request, wish, permission] to agree officially that somebody can have or do <sthg that they have asked for> □ *She was granted an audience with the Pope.* □ *The prisoner's request to see his wife was granted.* □ *a movie star who rarely grants interviews.* **-2.** [logic, truth] to admit <sthg> to be true or correct (formal use). ■ **I grant (that)...** I admit (that)... (formal use) □ *I grant you it's a risk, but it's worth it.* **-3.** *phrases* **to take sb for granted** to expect that sb will always be there to help, even though one never thanks them □ *Once they start taking you for granted, it's time to leave.* ■ **to take sthg for granted** to expect that sthg will always be there and rely on it □ *I had somehow always taken mother's interest in my life for granted.* ■ **to take it for granted that...** to accept without questioning or thinking about it that... □ *Don't take it for granted that I'll be there to help you.*

Grant [US grænt, GB grɑːnt], **Ulysses S.** (1822–1885) US President from 1869 to 1877. He was the general in command of the Union army during the American Civil War.

granulated sugar [,grænjəleɪtəd-] *n* sugar in the form of tiny grains.

granule ['grænjuːl] *n* a very small piece of something hard, especially of a food that dissolves □ *a granule of sugar/coffee/salt.*

grape [greɪp] *n* a small green or purple fruit that grows in bunches and is eaten raw or used for making wine □ *a bunch of grapes* □ *the grape harvest.*

grapefruit ['greɪpfruːt] (*pl* **grapefruit** OR **grapefruits**) *n* a large, round, yellow fruit that is like an orange but bigger and has a sourer taste.

grape picking [-pɪkɪŋ] *n* the activity of picking grapes when they are ripe.

grapevine ['greɪpvaɪn] *n* **-1.** a plant that produces grapes. **-2. to hear sthg through** OR **on the grapevine** to get to know sthg because people have told each other about it in conversation □ *I heard through the grapevine that you were thinking of leaving us.*

graph [US græf, GB grɑːf] *n* a diagram that gives information about numbers, measurements etc in the form of lines or blocks □ *The results are then plotted on a graph.*

graphic ['græfɪk] *adj* **-1.** [description, account] that is detailed and clear □ *The movie contains graphic scenes of violence.* **-2.** [art, work] that is concerned with drawing and printing.

◆ **graphics** *npl* drawings and diagrams that give information □ *computer graphics* □ *graphics options.*

graphic design *n* the profession of designing books, magazines etc so that they are attractive to look at.

graphic designer *n* a person who uses graphic design in their job.

graphic equalizer *n* a device for increasing and decreasing particular frequencies, e.g. on a stereo system.

graphics card *n* a piece of equipment in a computer that allows graphics to be used.

graphite ['græfaɪt] *n* a hard black substance that is a type of carbon and is used to make tennis rackets, fishing rods, and the part of a pencil that makes a mark.

graphology [græ'fɒlədʒɪ] *n* the study of people's handwriting to find out their personality.

graph paper *n* paper with small squares printed on it, used for drawing graphs on.

grapple ['græpl] ◆ **grapple with** *vt fus* **-1. to grapple with sb** [with an attacker, thief] to take hold of sb and fight them, usually without letting go □ *The old lady grappled unsuccessfully with her assailant.* **-2. to grapple with sthg** [with a problem, difficulty] to try hard to find the answer to sthg □ *I found Alan grappling with a particularly complicated algebra problem.*

grappling iron ['græplɪŋ-] *n* a metal bar with several hooks at one end that is attached to a rope and sometimes used to tie a ship to something else.

grasp [US græsp, GB grɑːsp] ◆ *n* **-1.** [on an object] a firm hold □ *Stephen's arm began to tire and gradually, slowly, he loosened his grasp.* **-2. to be in** OR **within one's grasp** to be easily possible for one to have or do □ *Success was finally within our grasp.* **-3.** [of a subject] an understanding and knowledge of a situation, language, subject etc □ *I have a reasonable grasp of what the job involves.* ◆ *vt* **-1.** [rope, hand] to take a firm hold of <sthg>. **-2.** [point, significance] to be able to understand <sthg> □ *I don't quite grasp your reasons for doing this.* **-3.** [chance, opportunity] to use <sthg> □ *You should grasp the opportunity to visit Japan while you can.*

grasping [US 'græspɪŋ, GB 'grɑːsp-] *adj* [person] who always tries to get as much money as possible (disapproving use).

grass [US græs, GB grɑːs] ◆ *n* **-1.** a common green plant that covers areas of ground, e.g. gardens and parks □ *fields of lush grass.* **-2.**▽ marijuana (very informal use). ◆ *vi*▽ **to grass on sb** GB to tell the police about a crime that sb has planned or committed (very informal use).

grasshopper [US 'græshɒpr, GB 'grɑːshɒpə] *n* an insect that can jump high into the air and that makes a loud noise by rubbing its long legs against its wings.

grassland [US 'græslænd, GB 'grɑːs-] *n* an area of land covered with grass, especially when it is used to feed cattle on.

grass roots *npl* all the ordinary people who belong to a political party or organization but are not the leaders □ *grass-roots opinion/support.*

grass snake *n* a harmless European snake with a green-brown body.

grassy [US 'græsɪ, GB 'grɑːsɪ] (*compar* **grassier**, *superl* **grassiest**) *adj* [bank, field] that is covered with grass.

grate [greɪt] ◆ *n* a frame of metal bars for holding the coal or wood in a fireplace. ◆ *vt* [cheese, carrots, nutmeg] to rub <sthg> against a rough and sharp surface to cut it into small pieces □ *250g of grated cheese.* ◆ *vi* [noise, laugh] to make a sharp unpleasant sound; [manner] to be annoying or irritating □ *The lecturer's voice soon began to grate.* □ *It really grates on me the way she's always smiling and smirking.* ■ **to grate on sb's nerves** to irritate sb very much □ *After a while the children's constant noise began to grate on my nerves.*

grateful ['greɪtfl] *adj* [person] who feels they want to thank somebody for something that person has done for them □ *I'm very grateful to you for all your help.* □ *We've received hundreds of letters from grateful listeners.*

gratefully ['greɪtflɪ] *adv*: *see* **grateful** □ *He accepted the loan gratefully.*

grater ['greɪtər] *n* a metal instrument with a rough sharp surface with holes for grating food □ *a cheese grater.*

gratification [grætɪfɪ'keɪʃn] *n* [of one's desire, appetite, curiosity] *see* **gratify.**

gratify ['grætɪfaɪ] (*pt & pp* **gratified**) *vt* **-1. to be gratified** to be pleased and satisfied □ *I was very gratified to see so many people here.* **-2.** [desire, appetite, curiosity] to satisfy <sthg> □ *I'm not going to gratify your curiosity by telling you what he said.*

gratifying ['grætɪfaɪɪŋ] *adj* [response, change] that makes one feel pleased and satisfied □ *It was so gratifying when he actually came and apologized.*

grating ['greɪtɪŋ] ◆ *adj* [noise, voice] that sounds sharp and unpleasant. ◆ *n* a frame of metal bars, used to cover a hole or window.

gratitude ['grætɪtjuːd] *n* the feeling of being grateful □ *I'd like to express my gratitude to my colleagues for all their help.*

gratuitous [grə'tjuːɪtəs] *adj* [insult, violence] that is done for no reason and harms or offends people □ *movies full of gratuitous sex and violence.*

gratuity [grə'tjuːɪtɪ] (*pl* **gratuities**) *n* an amount of money given to somebody for a service (formal use). □ *'Total does not include gratuity.'*

grave¹ [greɪv] ◇ *adj* -1. [face, expression] serious and solemn □ *Tom looked suddenly grave.* -2. [danger, news] that is very serious and causes worry □ *The driver of the vehicle is said to be in a very grave condition in the hospital.* ◇ *n* a hole in the ground where a dead person is buried □ *The victim was buried in a shallow grave.*
■ **he would turn in his grave** he would be very upset or would disapprove if he were alive now □ *Shakespeare would turn in his grave if he saw what they'd done to "Hamlet"!*

grave² [grɑːv] *adj* **e grave** a letter e with a grave accent.

grave accent [ˌgrɑːv-] *n* a symbol (ˋ) that is put above a letter in some languages to show that it is pronounced in a certain way.

gravedigger [ˈgreɪvdɪgəʳ] *n* a person whose job is to dig graves.

gravel [ˈgrævl] *n* very small stones used as a surface for paths and roads □ *a gravel path.*

graveled US, **gravelled** GB [ˈgrævld] *adj* [path] that is covered with gravel.

gravestone [ˈgreɪvstəʊn] *n* a large stone that has the name of a dead person written on it, and is placed on their grave.

graveyard [ˈgreɪvjɑːʳd] *n* an area of ground where people are buried.

gravitate [ˈgrævɪteɪt] *vi* **to gravitate toward sb/sthg** to be attracted by sb/sthg and gradually move toward them/it □ *Everybody inevitably gravitated toward the kitchen.*

gravity [ˈgrævətɪ] *n* -1. PHYSICS the force that makes things fall toward the ground when they are dropped □ *the law of gravity.* -2. [of a situation, illness, remark] *see* **grave** □ *Given the gravity of the situation, I think the police should be informed.*

gravy [ˈgreɪvɪ] *n* -1. COOKING a sauce served with meat that is made using the juices from the meat. -2. US money or profit that somebody gets without effort.

gravy boat *n* a small long dish used for serving gravy.

gravy train *n* **the gravy train** something, e.g. a job or position, that allows somebody to get a lot of money for very little work (disapproving use).

gray US, **grey** GB [greɪ] ◇ *adj* -1. [clouds, sky, beard] that has a color that is like black and white mixed together □ *a small man with light-gray hair.* -2. **to go gray** [hair] to become gray, usually because one is old; [person] to have hair that is going gray □ *He* OR *His hair is starting to go gray at the sides.* -3. [face, skin] that looks pale and unhealthy because of fear, illness etc □ *Her face looked gray with tiredness.* -4. [sky, light, day] that is not bright because there is no sun; [image, lifestyle, town] that is not interesting or exciting □ *It was gray and wet all day.* □ *a dull, gray little man with little to say for himself.*
◇ *n* the color that is like black and white mixed together □ *schoolboys all dressed in gray.*
◇ *vi* [hair, person] to go gray.

gray area *n* an aspect of a subject, law, activity etc that is not clearly defined or understood and that people have difficulty dealing with □ *The issue of compensation is something of a gray area.*

gray-haired [-ˈheəʳd] *adj* [person] who has gray hair □ *a little gray-haired old lady.*

graying US, **greying** GB [ˈgreɪɪŋ] *adj* [hair] that is becoming gray □ *a tall man with thin, graying hair.*

gray matter *n* -1. MEDICINE the material that the brain is made of. -2. intelligence (informal use) □ *I don't think Bob's got too much in the way of gray matter upstairs.*

grayscale US, **greyscale** GB [ˈgreɪskeɪl] *n* the shades of gray that represent colored information when it is shown on a black and white screen.

gray squirrel *n* a type of squirrel with gray fur.

graze [greɪz] ◇ *vt* -1. [knee, elbow] to break the surface of the skin of <a part of the body> by accidentally rubbing it against something rough or hard □ *She fell and grazed her knee.* -2. [surface, treetops, roof] to touch <sthg> lightly when passing it □ *The plane just grazed the treetops as it began to land.* -3. [cattle, sheep] to keep <animals> in a particular area so that they can eat grass; [field, meadow] to feed on the grass in <an area of land> □ *Cows grazed the nearby field.* ◇ *vi* [cattle, sheep] to eat grass in a field, meadow etc □ *sheep grazing in the field.* ◇ *n* a slight wound or injury on somebody's skin □ *It's nothing, just a graze, that's all.*

GRE (*abbr of* **Graduate Record Examination**) *n* in the USA, an exam taken by graduates who want to go to graduate school.

grease [griːs] ◇ *n* -1. [from an animal] the soft fat of an animal when it is cooked. -2. [for machines] a thick oily substance that is put on the moving parts of engines and machines to make them work more smoothly □ *Hal wiped the grease from his hands before picking up the phone.* -3. [on one's skin] an oily substance, especially that produced by somebody's skin. ◇ *vt* [engine, machine, baking tray] to put grease on <sthg> □ *Grease the dish before adding the cake mixture.*

grease gun *n* a device for putting grease in special holes in machines to make them work more smoothly.

greasepaint [ˈgriːspeɪnt] *n* an oily substance used as make-up by actors.

greaseproof paper [ˌgriːspruːf-] *n* GB paper that does not let grease pass through it, used in cooking.

greasy [ˈgriːsɪ] (*compar* **greasier**, *superl* **greasiest**) *adj* [tools, fingers, clothes] that is covered in grease; [food] that contains a lot of grease because it has been cooked in oil, fat etc; [skin, hair] that produces a lot of grease □ *Don't touch that with your greasy hands!* □ *The rolls were nice, if a little greasy.* □ *an adolescent with bad skin and greasy hair.*

greasy spoon *n* a cheap restaurant where fried food is served (informal use).

great [greɪt] ◇ *adj* **-1.** [care, pleasure, friend] large in degree; [age, number, majority] large in amount; [object, animal] large in size □ *The exhibition was a great success.* □ *It would give me great pleasure if you would join us for dinner.* □ *A great crowd of people had gathered outside the theater.* □ *A great number of the people who were here already knew the result.* □ *a great big bear.* **-2.** [leader, city, achievement] very impressive or important □ *This is a great day for our country.* **-3.** [idea, party, vacation] very good (informal use) □ *I had a great time on vacation in Florida.* □ *"We could go to the movies."* — *"What a great idea!"* □ *Are you coming too? That's great!*
◇ *npl* **the greats** people, e.g. movie stars or writers, who everybody agrees are the best in their field □ *one of the all-time greats of basketball.*
◇ *excl* a word used to show one approves of something that has just been said or done □ *"We've won!"* — *"Great!"*

Great Barrier Reef: **the Great Barrier Reef** the largest coral reef in the world, 30 to 90 miles off the northeastern coast of Australia. It is a popular tourist attraction.

Great Britain a term used to refer to England, Scotland, and Wales, considered as a political unit.
NOTE: Compare **United Kingdom**.

greatcoat ['greɪtkoʊt] *n* a thick overcoat, worn especially by soldiers.

Great Dane *n* a type of very large dog with a smooth coat.

Great Depression *n* **the Great Depression** a serious economic crisis that began in the USA in 1929 and lasted until the 1940s.

❧ THE GREAT DEPRESSION
During the Great Depression of the 1930s, millions of people throughout the world lost their jobs when businesses failed and there was little demand for goods. One of the causes of these bad business conditions was the Wall Street Crash in 1929, when a huge number of stocks on the New York Stock Exchange lost their value. The period that followed was especially difficult in the USA, where about 17 million people were unemployed and had no government money to help them.

Greater ['greɪtər] *adj* that includes the areas surrounding the center of a particular city □ *Greater Atlanta/London.*

great-grandchild *n* the child of somebody's grandson or granddaughter.

great-grandfather *n* the grandfather of somebody's mother or father.

great-grandmother *n* the grandmother of somebody's mother or father.

Great Lakes: **the Great Lakes** a group of five lakes in North America, between Canada and the USA: Lake Superior, Lake Huron, Lake Erie, Lake Ontario, and Lake Michigan.

greatly ['greɪtlɪ] *adv* very much □ *I greatly ad-* mire your work. □ *Her singing has improved greatly.*

greatness ['greɪtnəs] *n* [of a leader, city, achievement] see **great**.

Great Plains: **the Great Plains** an area of high plains in North America, east of the Rocky Mountains.

Great Salt Lake: **the Great Salt Lake** a large shallow lake in Utah, USA, that contains very salty water.

Great Wall of China: **the Great Wall of China** a very long wall built across northern China in ancient times as a defense against invaders.

Great War *n* = World War I.

Grecian ['griːʃn] *adj* [vase, temple, style] that was made in ancient Greece or in the style of ancient Greece.

Greece [griːs] a country in southeastern Europe that includes many Mediterranean islands as well as the most southeasterly part of the Greek mainland. SIZE: 132,000 sq kms. POPULATION: 10,500,000 (*Greeks*). CAPITAL: Athens. LANGUAGE: Greek. CURRENCY: drachma. OFFICIAL NAME: Hellenic Republic.

greed [griːd] *n* the desire for more of something than one needs □ *He was motivated purely by greed.*

greedily ['griːdɪlɪ] *adv* [eat, drink] see **greedy** □ *Mo was looking greedily at the cake.*

greedy ['griːdɪ] (*compar* **greedier**, *superl* **greediest**) *adj* **-1.** [person, animal] that wants more food than they need or should have □ *Don't be so greedy!* **-2.** [person] who wants more of something than they need or should have □ *He was greedy for power.*

Greek [griːk] ◇ *n* **-1.** a person who lives in or comes from Greece. **-2.** the language spoken in Greece in ancient or modern times. ◇ *adj*: *a Greek temple/meal.*

green [griːn] ◇ *adj* **-1.** [paint, eyes, fields] that has the same color as grass or leaves □ *green and white stripes* □ *a pale-green dress.* **-2.** [tomato, banana] that is not ripe; [wood] that is not ready to be used □ *The wood won't burn if it's green.* **-3.** [activist, politics, issues] that is concerned with the protection of the environment □ *They belong to a green organization.* □ *a green detergent.* **-4.** [person, face] that looks pale or unhealthy, especially because of fear or illness (informal use) □ *You're looking a little green this morning! Do you have a hangover?* **-5.** [worker, youngster, recruit] who does not have much experience (informal use). **-6. to be green (with envy)** to be very envious □ *Teresa will be green with envy when she sees my new dress.*
◇ *n* **-1.** the color of grass or leaves. ■ **in green** in green paint, materials, clothes etc □ *She was dressed in green.* **-2.** [in a village] an area of grass in a village or town, usually in the center □ *cricket on the village green.* **-3.** SPORT on a golf course, the area of smooth grass around each hole.
◆ **Green** *n* a member of a political movement concerned with the protection of the environment. ■ **the Greens** the political move-

ment concerned with the protection of the environment.

◆ **greens** *npl* the leaves of green vegetables such as cabbage that are cooked and eaten □ *Eat up your greens — they're good for you.*

greenback ['gri:nbæk] *n* US a dollar bill (informal use).

green bean *n* a plant that has thin green pods that are eaten as a vegetable.

green belt *n* GB an area of land around a town or city where no factories or houses are allowed to be built.

Green Beret *n* **the Green Berets** the members of the American or British army that are specially trained as commandos (informal use).

green card *n* -1. an official document that allows a foreigner to work in the USA. It is usually temporary. -2. in Britain, a document used by motorists when they go abroad that shows they have insurance for their car.

Green Cross Code *n* GB a set of rules to help children to cross the road safely.

Greene [gri:n], **Graham** (1904–1991) a British writer who became a Catholic. Many of his novels, such as *Brighton Rock* and *The Power and the Glory*, have religious themes.

greenery ['gri:nəri] *n* green plants that make a room or area look attractive □ *All we could see was a huge expanse of greenery.*

green fingers *npl* GB **to have green fingers** to be good at growing plants and flowers.

greenfly ['gri:nflaɪ] (*pl* **greenfly** OR **greenflies**) *n* a tiny green insect with wings that harms plants.

greengage ['gri:ngeɪdʒ] *n* a juicy light-green fruit like a plum.

greengrocer ['gri:ngrəʊsəʳ] *n* a person who has a store that sells fruit and vegetables. ■ **a greengrocer's** a store that sells fruit and vegetables □ *Can you get me some lettuce at the greengrocer's?*

greenhouse ['gri:nhaʊs, *pl* -haʊzɪz] *n* a building with glass walls and a glass roof, used for growing plants that need heat, light, and protection from bad weather.

greenhouse effect *n* **the greenhouse effect** the gradual increase in the temperature of the air around the Earth, caused by gases such as carbon dioxide.

greenish ['gri:nɪʃ] *adj* [color, eyes] slightly green.

Greenland ['gri:nlənd] a large, self-governing Danish island in the Arctic Ocean, northeast of Canada.

green light *n* **to give sb the green light** to give sb permission to do something □ *We've gotten the green light to go ahead with the project.*

green onion *n* US a small onion with a long green stem, usually eaten raw.

green paper *n* a document, published by the British government, that contains ideas about a particular subject that it wants people, including Parliament, to study and discuss. NOTE: Compare **white paper**.

Green Party *n* **the Green Party** a political party that is concerned with the protection of the environment.

Greenpeace ['gri:npi:s] *n* an international organization that takes action to stop people who are harming the environment, e.g. people who are killing whales or dumping poisonous waste.

green salad *n* a salad consisting mostly of green vegetables such as lettuce, often served with another dish.

green thumb *n* US **to have a green thumb** to be good at growing plants and flowers.

Greenwich Village [,grenɪtʃ-] an area in New York City, USA, famous for its artists and writers.

greet [gri:t] *vt* -1. [friend, colleague, family member] to say something to <sb>, or do something, to show that one is happy to meet or see them □ *When I arrived at the train station there was nobody there to greet me.* -2. [speech, announcement, remark] to react to <sthg> in a particular way □ *The banks greeted the news with enthusiasm.* -3. [person] to be immediately noticeable to <sb> when they arrive somewhere □ *The sound of heavy gunfire greeted us on our arrival.*

greeting ['gri:tɪŋ] *n* something that one says, such as "Good morning", or does when meeting somebody □ *He smiled in friendly greeting.*

◆ **greetings** *npl* a word written on something, e.g. a greeting card, to express one's good wishes to somebody □ *'Birthday greetings.'*

greeting card US, **greetings card** GB *n* a card with a picture on the front and a friendly message inside, sent to somebody on a special occasion such as their birthday.

✵ GREETING CARDS
In large towns in the USA, Britain, and Australia, there are stores that sell nothing but greeting cards. People send these cards to their friends or family on special occasions such as Christmas or Easter, or on Mother's Day or Father's Day. They can also be sent to someone on their birthday, or when they have got married or had a baby. In the USA, there are also cards for occasions such as Grandparents' Day and Secretaries' Day.

gregarious [grɪ'geərɪəs] *adj* [person] who likes being with other people.

gremlin ['gremlɪn] *n* a small imaginary being that is said to cause problems in machines (informal use).

Grenada [grə'neɪdə] a country in the Caribbean consisting of the island of Grenada and several neighboring islands. SIZE: 344 sq kms. POPULATION: 100,000 (*Grenadians*). CAPITAL: St. George's. LANGUAGE: English. CURRENCY: East Caribbean dollar.

grenade [grə'neɪd] *n* a small bomb designed to be thrown by hand.

grenadier [,grenə'dɪəʳ] *n* a soldier who is a

member of a special regiment in the British army.

grew [gru:] *past tense of* **grow**.

grey *adj* & *n* GB = **gray**.

greyhound ['greɪhaʊnd] *n* a dog with a thin body and long legs that can run very fast.

Greyhound™ *n* a bus belonging to a large bus company in the USA that travels long distances □ *I'll take a Greyhound to San Francisco.*

greying *n* GB = **graying**.

greyscale ['greɪskeɪl] *n* GB = **grayscale**.

grid [grɪd] *n* **-1.** [of bars] a framework of metal bars, used to cover a hole or window. **-2.** [of lines] a system of straight lines that cross each other to form little squares.

griddle ['grɪdl] *n* a flat, heavy, metal plate on which food can be cooked directly □ *griddle cakes.*

gridiron ['grɪdaɪəʳn] *n* **-1.** COOKING a framework of metal bars, used for cooking meat or fish over a fire. **-2.** US SPORT an area of ground with white markings on it, where football is played.

gridlock ['grɪdlɒk] *n* a traffic jam in which cars cannot move in any direction.

grid reference *n* the letters and numbers that help one to find a place on a map by following the lines printed on it and seeing where they meet.

grief [gri:f] *n* **-1.** [of a person] extreme sadness, caused especially by somebody's death □ *You will have to learn to come to terms with your grief.* **-2. to give** OR **cause sb grief** to make trouble for sb (informal use) □ *That guy's caused us a lot of grief over this Pepsi deal.* **-3. to come to grief** GB [person] to get hurt; [plan, deal, company] to fail □ *The whole project came to grief when they were refused a bank loan.* ■ **good grief!** an exclamation used to show one is surprised or shocked.

grief-stricken *adj* [person] who feels grief because something bad has happened recently.

grievance ['gri:vns] *n* something that causes somebody to complain, especially because they feel they have been badly treated at work □ *The workers would welcome a chance to air their grievances.*

grieve [gri:v] ◇ *vt* **it grieves me to...** it makes me sad to... (informal use) □ *It grieves me to hear you talk in this way.* ◇ *vi* to feel extremely sad, especially because somebody has died □ *She was grieving for her dead child.*

grieving ['gri:vɪŋ] *n*: *see* **grieve** □ *a group of grieving relatives.*

grievous bodily harm [,gri:vəs-] *n* GB LAW serious physical harm or injury done by one person to another.

Griffith ['grɪfɪθ], **D. W.** (1875–1948) a US movie maker, who experimented with new techniques. His work includes *The Birth of a Nation.*

grill [grɪl] ◇ *n* **-1.** GB [in an oven] a metal shelf where food can be cooked quickly under direct heat from above □ *Give the fish five minutes under the grill.* **-2.** [over a fire] a frame of metal bars, used for cooking food over a fire. **-3.** food that has been grilled, especially bacon, chops, sausages etc □ *a mixed grill.* ◇ *vt* **-1.** [meat, fish, vegetables] to cook <food> using strong direct heat from above or below □ *grilled peppers.* **-2.** [prisoner, suspect, interviewee] to ask <sb> a lot of questions in an aggressive way □ *The interview panel grilled candidates on their career goals.*

grille [grɪl] *n* a frame of metal bars or wires over a window or door or in front of a piece of machinery.

grim [grɪm] (*compar* **grimmer**, *superl* **grimmest**) *adj* **-1.** [face, expression] that looks serious and worried □ *Sam came out of the meeting looking grim.* **-2.** [place, day] that is unpleasant and depressing; [situation, news] that is serious and not likely to get better □ *The weather was cold and grim.* □ *Things are looking grim.*

grimace [grɪ'məs] ◇ *n* a look on a person's face that shows they are angry, annoyed, in pain etc □ *"How disgusting!" she said with a grimace.* ◇ *vi* to make a grimace □ *He grimaced with pain.*

grime [graɪm] *n* dirt that covers a surface in a dark layer □ *The miners' faces were covered in grime.*

grimly ['grɪmlɪ] *adv* **-1.** [think, smile, watch] in a way that shows no pleasure at all □ *"Yes," he said, nodding grimly.* **-2.** [struggle, defend] with a strong desire to succeed □ *She struggled grimly to keep a hold on the rope.*

Grim Reaper *n* **the Grim Reaper** a symbol of death, usually shown as a skeleton wearing a hood and carrying a scythe.

grimy ['graɪmɪ] (*compar* **grimier**, *superl* **grimiest**) *adj* [surface, city, hand] that is covered with a layer of dirt □ *All we could see was one grimy factory after another.*

grin [grɪn] (*pt* & *pp* **grinned**, *cont* **grinning**) ◇ *n* a very wide smile □ *"Hello there!" he said with a grin.* ◇ *vi* to give a very wide smile □ *What are you grinning at?* □ *Ma was grinning from ear to ear.* ■ **to grin and bear it** to experience difficulties or an unpleasant situation without complaining.

grind [graɪnd] (*pt* & *pp* **ground**) ◇ *vt* **-1.** [wheat, coffee, pepper] to crush <sthg> into small pieces or a fine powder □ *Our coffee is ground by hand.* **-2.** [dirt, ash, cigarette] to press <sthg> with great force against the surface of something else □ *He ground the cigarette into the carpet.* ■ **to grind one's teeth** to move one's upper and lower teeth against each other with one's mouth closed. ◇ *vi* [car gears, engine] to make a sharp scraping sound. ◇ *n* **-1.** hard boring work that one hates doing □ *the daily grind.* **-2.** US a person who studies hard for exams (informal use).

◆ **grind down** *vt sep* **to grind sb down** [enemy, worker] to make sb weak and obedient by treating them badly.

◆ **grind up** *vt sep* **to grind sthg up** [glass, powder] to crush sthg into small pieces or a fine powder.

grinder ['graɪndəʳ] *n* a device or machine for

crushing substances into small pieces □ *a coffee/pepper grinder.*

grinding ['graɪndɪŋ] *adj* **grinding poverty/misery** very great poverty/misery.

grinning ['grɪnɪŋ] *adj* [person, face] that has a grin.

grip [grɪp] (*pt* & *pp* **gripped**, *cont* **gripping**) ◇ *n* -1. [on an object] the act of holding something firmly; [on a situation, of the facts] the act of controlling something well □ *He has a strong grip.* □ *He's got a good grip on the situation.* ■ **to be in the grip of sthg** [of winter, recession] to be influenced or controlled by sthg □ *The country was in the grip of a deep recession.* ■ **to come** OR **get to grips with sthg** [with a job, situation] to begin to understand and deal with sthg new or difficult □ *She can't seem to get to grips with the fact that Mike has left for good.* ■ **to get a grip on oneself** to control oneself and stop being very excited, angry, or upset □ *Look, get a grip on yourself, you're acting like a hysterical child!* ■ **to lose one's grip** to lose one's ability to deal with difficult situations or with life in general □ *I'm sorry to say it, but Matt is really losing his grip.* -2. [of tires, shoes] the ability to grip the surface of something such as the road, and not to slip □ *These boots are losing their grip.* -3. [of handlebars, a camera] the handle or the part of something by which it is held. -4. [for holding things] a bag in which somebody keeps their belongings when they are traveling. ◇ *vt* -1. [hand, steering wheel, arm] to take <sthg> and hold it firmly □ *He gripped me by the arm.* -2. [road] to hold the surface of <sthg> firmly and not slip □ *These tires grip the road well.* -3. [imagination, attention, country] to affect <sthg> powerfully □ *The whole class was gripped by Mr Saunders' story.*

gripe [graɪp] (informal use) ◇ *n* a complaint □ *Students always have some gripes about their classes.* ◇ *vi* to complain all the time □ *Stop griping and get on with it!*

gripping ['grɪpɪŋ] *adj* [story, movie, play] that holds all of one's attention □ *I found it really gripping, right up until the end.*

grisly ['grɪzlɪ] (*compar* **grislier**, *superl* **grisliest**) *adj* [scene, sight, story] that is very unpleasant because it involves death, corpses, etc □ *There was a grisly bit when he gets his eyes poked out.*

grist [grɪst] *n* **to be (all) grist to one's** OR **the mill** to be useful for a particular purpose that one has □ *Oh, any information's welcome — it's all grist to the mill.*

gristle ['grɪsl] *n* the tough part of meat that cannot be eaten.

gristly ['grɪslɪ] (*compar* **gristlier**, *superl* **gristliest**) *adj* [meat, pork] that contains a lot of gristle.

grit [grɪt] (*pt* & *pp* **gritted**, *cont* **gritting**) ◇ *n* -1. [on a road] very small pieces of stone. -2. [of a person] courage and a strong desire to do something (informal use) □ *You have to have a lot of grit to survive here.* ◇ *vt* [road, surface, path] to put grit on <sthg> to make it less slippery in icy weather.

◆ **grits** *npl* US finely ground corn served as a cereal or with other food.

gritty ['grɪtɪ] (*compar* **grittier**, *superl* **grittiest**) *adj* -1. [surface, road, floor] that is covered with grit □ *sitting on the sand eating gritty cheese sandwiches.* -2. [person, determination, performance] that shows a lot of courage (informal use).

grizzled ['grɪzld] *adj* [hair, beard] that is gray or partly gray; [person] who has gray hair.

grizzly ['grɪzlɪ] (*pl* **grizzlies**) *n* **grizzly (bear)** a large bear with gray and brown fur that lives in North America.

groan [grəʊn] ◇ *n* a long low shout or cry of pain, disappointment, or sadness □ *We heard a groan coming from the other room.* ◇ *vi* -1. [person] to make a groan □ *He groaned loudly in his sleep.* -2. [table, door] to make a loud, harsh, creaking sound □ *The table was literally groaning with food.*

grocer ['grəʊsər] *n* a person who sells groceries in a store. ■ **a grocer's** a store that sells groceries □ *I need to get some sugar from the grocer's.*

groceries ['grəʊsərɪz] *npl* food that is bought from a store fresh, or in cans, packets etc □ *We get all our groceries from the supermarket.*

grocery cart ['grəʊsərɪ-] *n* US a metal basket on wheels used to collect groceries in a supermarket.

grocery store *n* US a large store that sells food and household goods where customers serve themselves and pay at the exit.

grog [grɒg] *n* AUS alcoholic drink (informal use).

groggy ['grɒgɪ] (*compar* **groggier**, *superl* **groggiest**) *adj* [person] who feels weak, tired, and confused □ *He was still groggy after the anesthetic.*

groin [grɔɪn] *n* the area of the body where the legs join the body at the front □ *She kneed him in the groin.*

groom [gruːm] ◇ *n* -1. a person whose job is to look after horses. -2. = **bridegroom**. ◇ *vt* -1. [horse, dog] to look after <an animal> by cleaning and brushing it. -2. to prepare <sb> for a particular role or position □ *I've groomed him for the top job.*

groomed [gruːmd] *adj* **well/badly groomed** [person] who is well/badly dressed and looks neat/messy.

groove [gruːv] *n* a narrow line cut into the surface of something such as a record or a piece of wood □ *The water runs along a narrow groove in the stone.*

grope [grəʊp] ◇ *vt* -1. **to grope one's way** to try to get somewhere by feeling with one's hands because one cannot see □ *Suzi groped her way carefully along the corridor.* -2. to touch the body of <sb> for sexual pleasure, usually against their will (informal and disapproving use) □ *My boss tried to grope me.* ◇ *vi* **to grope (about) for sthg** [for a flashlight, switch] to search for sthg that one cannot see by using one's hands; [for an answer, word] to try but fail to find sthg that one wants to say □

I groped around in the dark for a candle. □ *It was obvious she was just groping for an excuse.*

gross [grous] (*pl* **gross**) ◇ *adj* -**1. gross weight** total weight, including the box, container etc. ■ **one's gross salary/earnings etc** one's total salary/earnings etc, before money has been taken off it, e.g. for tax □ *$10,000? Do you mean net or gross?* -**2. gross misconduct/ negligence** very serious and unacceptable misconduct/negligence (formal use) □ *He was accused of gross professional misconduct.* -**3.** [person, behavior, idea] disgusting (informal use) □ *How gross!* -**4.** very fat (informal use) □ *Fat? He was gross!* ◇ *n* a group or set of 144 things □ *five gross.* ◇ *vt* to earn <a sum of money> as a total amount that is gross □ *They were grossing $3,000,000 a year.*

gross domestic product *n* the total value of all goods and services produced by a country in a year, not including goods and services it produces abroad.

grossly ['grousli] *adv* **grossly unfair/overweight etc** extremely unfair/overweight etc □ *I think these city bankers are grossly overpaid.*

gross national product *n* the total value of all goods and services produced by a country in a year.

gross profit *n* the total amount of profit made by a company before taxes and other deductions.

grotesque [grou'tesk] *adj* [figure, appearance] very ugly and unpleasant in a way that is frightening or funny □ *It was grotesque the way she tried to make herself look younger.*

grotto ['grɒtou] (*pl* **grottoes** OR **grottos**) *n* a cave, usually man-made, that is small and attractive.

grotty ['grɒti] (*compar* **grottier**, *superl* **grottiest**) *adj* GB [apartment, room, town] that looks dirty and in bad condition (informal use) □ *a grotty bedsit.*

grouchy ['grautʃi] (*compar* **grouchier**, *superl* **grouchiest**) *adj* [person] who is bad-tempered, complains a lot, and is rude (informal use) □ *Ignore Alan, he's always grouchy in the mornings.*

ground [graund] ◇ *past tense & past participle of* **grind**.
◇ *n* -**1.** the surface of the earth. ■ **above ground** on or above the surface of the earth. ■ **below ground** below the surface of the earth □ *He lay there on the ground, very still.* □ *I could see tiny figures standing waving on the ground below us.* ■ **to be thin on the ground** to be rare □ *Good decorators are thin on the ground.* ■ **to get sthg off the ground** to start sthg □ *We've been trying for a long time to get this project off the ground.* -**2.** an area of empty land □ *This is holy ground.* □ *waste ground.* -**3.** an area of land used for a particular purpose □ *a football/sports ground* □ *a parade ground.* -**4. to be on dangerous/safe ground** to feel unsure/sure about what one is dealing with or talking about □ *I knew I was on dangerous/safe ground.* ■ **to break fresh** OR **new ground** to make a new discovery or to start something that has not been done before □ *Well, you're scarcely breaking new ground, are*

you? -**5. to gain ground** to make progress or to gain an advantage □ *The jeeps were rapidly gaining ground on us.* ■ **to lose ground** to lose an advantage or not make enough progress □ *Smith's are losing ground to their competitors.* -**6.** US ELECTRICITY a wire that connects an electrical appliance with the ground. -**7.** *phrases* **to cut the ground from under sb's feet** to make a situation difficult for sb by preventing them from saying or doing what they intended to. ■ **to go to ground** GB to hide for a period of time. ■ **to run sb/sthg to ground** GB to find sb/sthg after a long and careful search. ■ **to stand one's ground** not to let oneself be forced to do what one does not want to do.
◇ *vt* -**1. to be grounded on** OR **in sthg** [on fact, certainty, knowledge] to be based on sthg □ *Our success is grounded on years of experience.* -**2.** AVIATION to stop <a pilot, aircraft> etc from flying □ *He's been grounded.* -**3.** [son, daughter] to stop <a young person> from going out for a period of time as a punishment □ *My best friend has been grounded for a week.* -**4.** US ELECTRICITY **to be grounded** to be connected to the ground with a wire.

◆ **grounds** *npl* -**1.** [for doing something] a good reason for doing or thinking something □ *Such behavior constitutes grounds for divorce.* □ *You have no grounds for complaint/complaining.* ■ **on the grounds of** because of □ *The case was dismissed on the grounds of insufficient evidence.* ■ **on the grounds that** because □ *She asked him to leave on the grounds that he was encouraging disruption in the class.* -**2.** [of a building] the land that surrounds and belongs to a building □ *the school/hospital grounds.* -**3.** [for an activity] an area of land where a particular activity, e.g. hunting or fishing, takes place □ *fishing/hunting grounds.* -**4.** [of coffee] the small pieces of coffee beans that are left at the bottom of a pot, cup etc when the coffee has been drunk □ *coffee grounds.*

ground beef *n* finely chopped beef.

groundcloth ['graundklɒθ] *n* US = **groundsheet**.

ground control *n* the people and equipment that guide the flights of aircraft and spacecraft.

ground cover *n* the layer of thick low plants that cover the surface of the ground.

ground crew *n* the people whose job is to take care of and repair aircraft and spacecraft when they are on the ground and to monitor their flights.

ground floor *n* the part of a building that is level with the ground outside □ *a ground-floor office.*

groundhog ['graundhɒg] *n* a small furry animal in North America that lives in holes in the ground.

Groundhog Day *n* in the USA, a holiday celebrated on February 2.

ground-in *adj* [dirt, grease] that has been rubbed deeply into the surface of something.

grounding ['graundɪŋ] *n* a knowledge of the basic principles or skills of a particular subject □ *I acquired a good grounding in chemistry.*

groundless ['graʊndləs] *adj* [fear, suspicion] that is not necessary because there is no reason for it □ *The doctor told her that her worries were groundless.*

ground level *n* **at ground level** on the floor of a building that is level with the ground; at the level of the ground.

groundnut ['graʊndnʌt] *n* GB a peanut.

ground plan *n* a plan of the street level of a building.

ground rent *n* rent paid by the owner of a building to the owner of the land which it is built on.

ground rules *npl* the basic rules or principles that control the way a particular thing must be done.

groundsheet ['graʊndʃiːt] *n* a piece of waterproof material placed on the ground, especially in a tent.

groundskeeper ['graʊndskiːpər] *n* US a person whose job is to look after a park or sports field.

groundsman ['graʊndzmən] (*pl* **groundsmen** [-mən]) *n* GB = **groundskeeper**.

ground staff *n* -1. the people whose job is to take care of a sports ground. -2. GB the people whose job is to take care of and repair aircraft and monitor their flights.

groundswell ['graʊndswel] *n* **a groundswell of feeling/opinion** a rapid growth in the number of people who have the same feeling or opinion.

groundwork ['graʊndwɜːrk] *n* the important work that is done before a plan, study, activity etc can be successfully completed □ *Our marketing department is laying the groundwork for the company's expansion.*

group [gruːp] ◇ *n* -1. [of people, things] a number of people or things that are together at a particular moment □ *A small group of people stood waiting outside.* □ *The teacher told the students to form a group.* -2. [of protesters, activists, feminists] an organization of people who share an interest or aim □ *an action group* □ *a drama group.* -3. BUSINESS a number of companies joined together in the same organization □ *a newspaper group.* -4. [in society] a number of people or things that are similar because they share a quality, skill etc □ *an age/income group.* -5. MUSIC a small number of people who play music together □ *a member of a rock group.*
◇ *vt* to put <one or more people or things> into a group or groups somewhere □ *The students are grouped according to ability.*
◇ *vi* **to group (together)** to come to a particular place at the same time, or form an organization for a particular purpose □ *They were all grouped together under the heading "Lilies".*

group captain *n* in the UK, a senior officer in the air force, above a wing commander but below an air commodore in rank.

groupie ['gruːpɪ] *n* a person who is a fan of somebody famous, especially a girl who follows a pop star on tour to have sex with him (informal use).

group practice *n* a group of doctors who work together as a business in the same building.

group therapy *n* a form of treatment for a group of people who come together to discuss a problem they all have.

grouse [graʊs] (*pl sense 1* **grouse** OR **grouses**, *pl sense 2* **grouses**) ◇ *n* -1. a bird that is shot for sport, especially on the Scottish moors; the meat of this bird eaten as food. -2. [about a problem] a complaint (informal use) □ *I have just one small grouse to make.* ◇ *vi* to complain (informal use) □ *There's no use grousing about it.*

grove [grəʊv] *n* an area planted with trees □ *an orange/a lemon grove* □ *a grove of trees.*

grovel [US 'grʌvl, GB 'grɒvl] (US *pt* & *pp* **groveled**, *cont* **groveling**, GB *pt* & *pp* **grovelled**, *cont* **grovelling**) *vi* to show too much eagerness to please somebody, especially because they are powerful or important (disapproving use) □ *He was groveling to his boss as usual.* □ *Do you expect me to grovel?*

grow [grəʊ] (*pt* **grew**, *pp* **grown**) ◇ *vi* -1. [person, animal, company] to become bigger □ *The children have grown so much, I hardly recognize them!* □ *The town has grown a lot in the last few years.* -2. [hair, beard] to become longer. -3. [traffic, feeling, investment] to increase □ *Our friendship grew over the years.* □ *Sales are growing at a rate of 3% per annum.* -4. [plant, flower, mold] to be alive in a particular place □ *There were poppies growing in the fields.* -5. to become □ *It grew dark.* □ *He grew tired/faint/angry.* □ *I've grown used to the noise now.* -6. **to grow to like/hate etc sthg** to begin to like/hate etc sthg after a long period of time □ *I've grown to respect him.*
◇ *vt* -1. [fruit, vegetable, crop] to put <a plant> in the ground and help it to grow □ *They grow potatoes around these parts.* -2. **to grow one's hair** to allow one's hair to grow long. ■ **to grow a beard/mustache** to allow a beard/mustache to grow on one's face.

◆ **grow apart** *vi* [people, family, friends] to begin to be less close and to have different ideas and interests □ *Gradually, she began to grow apart from Jake.*

◆ **grow into** *vt fus* -1. **to grow into sthg** [into one's shoes, shirt] to become big enough to be able to wear sthg □ *I know it's a little big, honey, but you'll soon grow into it.* -2. **to grow into sthg** [into a man, woman, adult] to become sthg over a long period of time □ *She's grown into a good-looking girl!*

◆ **grow on** *vt fus* **to grow on sb** [idea, name] to become gradually more liked by sb (informal use) □ *It sounded stupid to begin with, but gradually the idea began to grow on me.*

◆ **grow out** *vi* [hairstyle, dye] to disappear gradually from one's hair as it grows □ *How long will it take my perm to grow out completely?*

◆ **grow out of** *vt fus* -1. **to grow out of sthg** [out of one's trousers, shirt, shoes] to become too big for sthg □ *Jamie grows out of all his* clothes so quickly these days! **-2. to grow out of sthg** [out of a hobby, interest, habit] to become too old to be interested in sthg □ Don't worry, he'll soon grow out of it.

◆ **grow up** vi **-1.** [person] to become an adult □ What do you want to do when you grow up? □ Why don't you just grow up and stop being so stupid! **-2.** [custom, feeling] to develop gradually; [town, city] to gradually get larger □ The tea ceremony was something that had grown up over the centuries.

grower ['grouəʳ] n a person who grows plants, vegetables etc in order to sell them.

growl [graul] ◇ n **-1.** [of an animal] a deep unfriendly sound made by an animal, e.g. a dog or lion □ The dog gave a low growl. **-2.** [of a machine] a low noise made by an engine or piece of machinery that sounds like the growl of an animal. **-3.** [of a person] a harsh angry sound made by a person □ "Take your hands off!" he said with a growl. ◇ vi **-1.** [dog] to make a growl. **-2.** [engine] to make a sound like the growl of an animal. **-3.** [person] to speak in a low angry voice □ "Hurry up!" he growled.

grown [groun] ◇ past participle of **grow**. ◇ adj [man, woman] adult □ To think that a grown man could behave like that!

grown-up ◇ adj **-1.** [son, daughter] adult □ We have two grown-up children. **-2.** [girl, boy] who behaves in a mature way □ She seemed very grown-up for her age. ◇ n an adult □ Tonight you can eat with the grown-ups, Billy.

growth [grouθ] n **-1.** [of the economy, population, a person] an increase or development in size, value, importance, or ability □ After a short period of rapid growth, the economy went into recession again. **-2.** MEDICINE a lump that is not normal, e.g. a tumor that grows in or on a person's body.

growth rate n the rate or speed at which something is increasing or developing in size or value.

GRSM (abbr of **Graduate of the Royal Schools of Music**) n a title given to music graduates in Britain.

grub [grʌb] n **-1.** an insect at the stage when it still looks like a small white worm. **-2.** food (informal use) □ Does anyone want some grub?

grubby ['grʌbɪ] (compar **grubbier**, superl **grubbiest**) adj [hand, piece of clothing, child] that has become dirty over a period of time, and needs washing □ Don't put your grubby hands on my nice clean tablecloth.

grudge [grʌdʒ] ◇ n a feeling of dislike and anger one has toward somebody because of something they have done to one. ■ **to bear sb a grudge, to bear a grudge against sb** to continue to dislike sb and be angry with them because of something they have done in the past □ You've borne a grudge against me ever since. ◇ vt **to grudge sb sthg** [success, popularity] to be unhappy that sb has got sthg □ I don't grudge you your happiness. ■ **to grudge doing sthg** to be unwilling to do sthg

□ I don't grudge cleaning up, but it would be nice to get some thanks.

grudging ['grʌdʒɪŋ] adj [praise, admiration, respect] that is given or felt unwillingly □ She had won the grudging respect of her department.

grudgingly ['grʌdʒɪŋlɪ] adv [accept, admit, thank] see **grudging** □ "Well, it's not bad," she said grudgingly.

grueling US, **gruelling** GB ['gruːəlɪŋ] adj [trip, job, race] that is very tiring and takes a lot of effort □ We got home after a grueling drive.

gruesome ['gruːsəm] adj [scene, sight, tale] that is unpleasant to look at or hear about, often because death or injury is involved □ There was a gruesome bit about dead bodies, but apart from that it was fine.

gruff [grʌf] adj **-1.** [voice] that has a deep rough quality. **-2.** [manner, reply] that seems rough and unfriendly □ Don't be put off by his gruff exterior.

grumble ['grʌmbl] ◇ n **-1.** [about a problem] a small complaint □ I have a few grumbles regarding what was said. **-2.** [of stomach] a low rumbling sound in one's stomach that is heard when one is hungry. ◇ vi **-1.** to complain in a bad-tempered way □ He was grumbling about the trains again. □ Oh, stop grumbling, for goodness' sake! **-2.** [stomach] to make a low rumbling sound because one is hungry.

grumpy ['grʌmpɪ] (compar **grumpier**, superl **grumpiest**) adj [person] who is bad-tempered and rude to people who talk to them (informal use) □ You're in a grumpy mood today!

grunt [grʌnt] ◇ n **-1.** [of a pig] the low sound made by a pig. **-2.** [of a person] a short sound made by a person, often with their mouth closed, to show they disapprove of something or are not interested in something □ He gave a short grunt, which I took to mean yes. ◇ vi [pig, person] to make a grunt.

G-string n a narrow strip of material worn over one's genitals and held in place by a piece of string attached around the waist.

Guadeloupe [ˌgwɑːdəˈluːp] a group of islands in the Caribbean belonging to France, including Basse-Terre and Grande-Terre.

Guangzhou [ˌgwɑːŋˈdʒou] a major port and industrial center in southeastern China. POPULATION: 4,000,000. OLD NAME: Canton.

guarantee [US ˌgerənˈtiː, GB ˌgær-] ◇ n **-1.** BUSINESS [of a radio, TV, watch] a written promise by a company that it will repair or replace goods made by it if they break or stop working within a certain period of time □ The radio comes with a six-month guarantee. ■ **to be under guarantee** [goods, product] to be protected by a guarantee □ If it's still under guarantee you can send it back. **-2.** [of a job, good behavior] a promise or official statement that something will definitely happen; [of quality, success] something that makes it certain that something else is true or will happen □ There's no guarantee (that) it's going to be sunny. □ A good education used to be a guarantee of success. □ What guarantees can you give me?

◇ *vt* -1. BUSINESS [TV, watch] to give a formal promise that one will replace or repair <a product> if it stops working within a certain period of time □ *They guarantee all their products for three years.* -2. [delivery, success] to promise or make sure that <sthg> will happen; [satisfaction, happiness] to promise or make sure that somebody will feel <sthg> □ *I can't guarantee I'll be there on time, but I'll try.* □ *We guarantee (that) you'll be completely satisfied.*

guarantor [US ,gerən'tɔːr, GB ,gærən'tɔː] *n* a person who gives a guarantee or who agrees to be responsible for something such as the payment of a debt □ *She asked Henry if he would act as her guarantor.*

guard [gɑːd] ◇ *vt* -1. [house, president] to protect <a person, object, or place> by staying near and watching them □ *The premises are guarded by a private security firm.* -2. [prisoner, criminal] to stay near and watch <sb> to prevent them from escaping □ *The prisoner was guarded by three police officers.* -3. [information, knowledge] to keep <sthg> secret by not telling anybody about it □ *a closely guarded secret.*

◇ *n* -1. [of a person, place] a person, e.g. a policeman or soldier, who guards a person or place; a group of people who guard a person or place □ *a prison guard* □ *an armed guard.* -2. [in a place] a planned operation to guard a person or place □ *a 24-hour guard.* ■ **to be on guard** to be guarding a person or place □ *There were three soldiers on guard outside.* ■ **to stand guard** to guard a person or place. ■ **to be on (one's) guard** to be careful to prevent something from happening, or to avoid it □ *I would advise you to be on your guard against any unexpected visitors.* ■ **to catch sb off guard** to surprise sb by doing or saying something they do not expect □ *Her questions caught me off guard.* -3. GB RAIL the person whose job is to help passengers and check their tickets on a train. -4. [for one's mouth, head, knee] a protective pad used in sport; [on a machine] a protective part on a machine.

◆ **Guards** *npl* **the Guards** a group of regiments in the British army. They are considered to be among the best soldiers in the armed forces.

◆ **guard against** *vt fus* **to guard against sthg** [against a danger, threat, infection] to be very careful to try to prevent sthg bad from happening □ *New checks are being introduced to guard against smuggling.*

guard dog *n* a fierce dog that has been trained to protect places.

guarded ['gɑːdəd] *adj* [person, reply, statement] that is careful not to give much information □ *She gave me a guarded smile.*

guardian ['gɑːdjən] *n* -1. [of a child] a person who is legally responsible for taking care of a child, especially after their parents have died □ *The child's legal guardian will have to be asked first.* -2. [of democracy, virtue, morality] a person or organization that protects or de-

fends something □ *I would hardly consider Jasper a guardian of morality!*

guardian angel *n* a good spirit believed to protect somebody.

guardianship ['gɑːdjənʃip] *n* the position of being the guardian of somebody.

guardrail ['gɑːdreɪl] *n* a railing along a path, passageway etc that stops people from going where there is danger.

guardsman ['gɑːdzmən] (*pl* **guardsmen** [-mən]) *n* -1. a member of the National Guard. -2. a member of the Guards.

guard's van *n* GB RAIL the car of a train that the guard travels in.

Guatemala [,gwɑːtə'mɑːlə] a country in Central America, between Mexico, El Salvador, and Honduras. SIZE: 109,000 sq kms. POPULATION: 10,000,000 (*Guatemalans*). CAPITAL: Guatemala City. LANGUAGE: Spanish. CURRENCY: quetzal.

guava ['gwɑːvə] *n* a round, yellow, tropical fruit with pink or white flesh and hard seeds.

gubernatorial [,guːbərnə'tɔːriəl] *adj* US POLITICS [campaign, elections] that is connected with the governor of a state.

guerilla [gə'rilə] *n* = guerrilla.

Guernsey[1] ['gɜːnzɪ] one of the Channel Islands. Some British people keep their money in banks there because the taxes are lower than in mainland Britain. SIZE: 63 sq kms. POPULATION: 53,000. CAPITAL: St. Peter Port. LANGUAGE: English, French. CURRENCY: pound sterling.

Guernsey[2] *n* -1. a heavy, knitted, woolen sweater. -2. a type of cow that produces very rich and creamy milk.

guerrilla [gə'rilə] *n* a member of an unofficial military group that is fighting against the official government of their country for political reasons.

guerrilla warfare *n* the activity of fighting against an official army or the state by making small attacks or planting bombs.

guess [ges] ◇ *n* an attempt to give the right answer to something without being sure what the answer is □ *I don't know, I'll have to make* OR *take a guess.* □ *Well, at a guess, I'd say there were about a hundred people there.* ■ **it's anybody's guess** nobody knows what is true or what will happen □ *It's anybody's guess how many will come to the party.*

◇ *vt* [answer, number, identity] to say what <sthg> is without being certain that one is right □ *Try and guess the meaning of the word.* □ *Guess who I saw yesterday!* ■ **guess what!** a phrase used to draw attention to something exciting or surprising that one is about to say □ *Guess what! I got a new job!*

◇ *vi* -1. *We can only guess at what happened.* ■ **to keep sb guessing** to refuse to tell sb what is going to happen or what they want to know. -2. **I guess...** I suppose... □ *"I think we should inform them." — "I guess so."* □ *I guess they decided not to come after all.*

guesstimate ['gestəmət] *n* a calculation of the

value, size, or amount of something when one is not really sure (informal use).

guesswork ['geswɜːrk] *n* the process or result of trying to work something out by guessing □ *It's guesswork, but I think he'll accept.*

guest [gest] *n* -1. [in one's home] a person who has been invited to stay or eat in one's home □ *We have guests for dinner tonight.* -2. [at a restaurant] a person one invites to the theater, restaurant etc and whom one pays for □ *No, you're my guest tonight. Let me pay.* -3. [at a hotel] a person who is staying in a hotel or guesthouse □ *a paying guest.* -4. [on a show] an actor or performer who has been invited to take part in a show as a special visitor □ *a guest artist/speaker.* -5. phrase **be my guest!** a phrase used to tell somebody that they may do what they have asked one's permission to do □ *"Do you mind if I sit here?" — "Be my guest!"*

guesthouse ['gesthaʊs, *pl* -haʊzɪz] *n* a private house where people pay to sleep and eat.

guest of honor *n* the most important guest at a dinner or social occasion.

guestroom ['gestruːm] *n* a bedroom in a house where visitors can sleep.

guest star *n* a famous actor, performer etc who appears in a movie, TV program etc, but who is not one of the main members of the cast □ *With special guest star, Mandy Philips.*

guffaw [gʌ'fɔː] ◇ *n* a loud laugh □ *He gave a loud guffaw.* ◇ *vi* to laugh loudly because something seems ridiculous.

Guggenheim ['gʊɡənhaɪm]: **the Guggenheim (Museum)** a museum of modern art in New York City. It is famous for its spiral shape.

guidance ['gaɪdns] *n* -1. [of a teacher, friend, parent] help and advice on how to run one's private or working life □ *Can you give some guidance on how to invest my money?* □ *spiritual guidance.* -2. [of a leader, director] leadership. ■ **under the guidance of sb** led or directed by sb □ *Students write their thesis under the guidance of a tutor.*

guide [gaɪd] ◇ *n* -1. a person who takes tourists around museums and other places of interest and tells them about them; a person who leads other people through an area or country □ *a tour/tourist guide* □ *a mountain guide* -2. = **guide book.** -3. [to a subject] a book that describes how to do something or gives information about a particular subject □ *a user's guide* □ *a guide to gardening.* -4. something that provides a model for people to base opinions or actions on □ *These figures are no more than a rough guide.* -5. = **girl guide.**

◇ *vt* -1. [tourist, stranger, newcomer] to show <sb> how to get somewhere □ *The waiter guided us to our table.* -2. [learner, student, beginner] to show <sb> how to do something correctly □ *The booklet guides you through the complexities of buying your own home.* -3. [plane] to control the movements or actions of <sthg>; [country] to give political leadership to <sthg> □ *We need a leader who can guide our country through this difficult time.*

-4. **to be guided by sb/sthg** to be influenced in one's actions or opinions by sb/sthg □ *I shall be guided by my conscience.*

guide book *n* a book that gives tourists information about a place.

guided missile [,gaɪdəd-] *n* a missile whose course can be changed while it is in the air.

guide dog *n* a dog that has been trained to help a blind person walk around safely.

guidelines ['gaɪdlaɪnz] *npl* advice or rules about how to do something □ *The Department of Health has issued new guidelines on health care for the elderly.*

guiding ['gaɪdɪŋ] *adj* **a guiding principle/light** a principle/light that provides somebody with guidance about how they should act/where to go.

guild [gɪld] *n* -1. in the past, an organization of people who produced the same kinds of goods, that helped its members, and kept standards high. -2. an organization of people who have the same profession or who share an interest □ *the local women's guild.*

guildhall ['gɪldhɔːl] *n* a building near the center of a town where members of a guild used to meet, now often used for official meetings and public events.

guile [gaɪl] *n* skill at deceiving people (literary use).

guileless ['gaɪlləs] *adj* [person] who is honest and never tries to deceive people (literary use).

guillotine ['gɪlətiːn] ◇ *n* -1. [for executing people] an apparatus for chopping off people's heads, consisting of a heavy blade that is dropped down between two posts. It was first used in France during the French Revolution. -2. GB [for cutting paper] a device consisting of a long blade attached to a lever, used for cutting paper. -3. GB & AUS POLITICS a system that limits the time MPs spend discussing a bill in parliament. ◇ *vt* to execute <sb> using a guillotine.

guilt [gɪlt] *n* -1. an unhappy feeling that one has because one has done something bad or shameful □ *I don't feel any guilt about what I did.* □ *a sense of guilt.* -2. LAW the fact of having done something illegal □ *This new evidence establishes her guilt beyond all doubt.*

guiltily ['gɪltɪlɪ] *adv* [behave, blush] see **guilty.**

guilty ['gɪltɪ] (*compar* **guiltier**, *superl* **guiltiest**) *adj* -1. [person] who feels guilt □ *I feel guilty about not going to their party.* ■ **to have a guilty conscience** to feel guilty about something that one has done. ■ **a guilty secret** a secret that one feels guilty about. ■ **a guilty look/smile etc** a look/smile etc that shows that somebody feels guilty. -2. LAW [person] who has been judged to have committed a particular crime □ *He was found guilty/not guilty of rape.* □ *The defendant is innocent until proved guilty.* -3. **to be guilty of sthg** to have done sthg that is wrong □ *The hospital is guilty of gross negligence.*

guinea ['gɪnɪ] *n* a British coin that is no longer used, worth £1.05.

guinea fowl *n* a large, gray, African bird with white spots and a bald head and neck.

guinea pig *n* -1. a small furry animal with short ears and no tail, often kept as a pet or used in laboratory experiments. -2. a person who is used in an experiment to test something new.

Guinevere ['gwɪnəvɪəʳ] (6th century) a legendary British queen, the wife of King Arthur and lover of Sir Lancelot.

guise [gaɪz] *n* the way somebody or something looks that hides what they really are and is intended to deceive people (formal use) □ *Their philosophy is simply fascism in a new guise.*

guitar [gɪ'tɑːʳ] *n* a musical instrument made of wood that usually has six strings stretched over a long, flat, narrow section, and is played by moving one's fingers over the strings □ *a guitar string.*

guitarist [gɪ'tɑːrəst] *n* a person who plays the guitar.

Gujarati, Gujerati [,gudʒə'rɑːtɪ] *n* a member of a people living in western India; the language of this people. There are now many Gujaratis living in Britain.

gulch [gʌltʃ] *n* US a narrow valley with steep sides.

gulf [gʌlf] *n* -1. GEOGRAPHY a large area of deep sea that goes a long way into the land and is almost enclosed □ *the Gulf of Aden.* -2. a big difference or separation between two people, groups, or points of view □ *the widening gulf between the rich and the poor.* -3. a deep hole or crack in the Earth's surface.

◆ **Gulf** = Persian Gulf.

Gulf of Mexico: the Gulf of Mexico part of the Atlantic Ocean between Mexico, the USA, and Cuba.

Gulf States: the Gulf States the countries around the Persian Gulf, including Iran, Iraq, Kuwait, Saudi Arabia, Bahrain, Qatar, the UAE, and Oman; the states on the Gulf of Mexico: Alabama, Florida, Louisiana, Mississippi, and Texas.

Gulf Stream: the Gulf Stream a current of warm water flowing northeastward across the Atlantic, from the Gulf of Mexico to Europe.

Gulf War *n* the Gulf War a conflict between the UN and Iraq in 1991 which started when Iraq invaded Kuwait. Most of the UN forces were American.

gull [gʌl] *n* one of several types of common gray or black-and-white sea birds.

gullet ['gʌlət] *n* the tube leading from the mouth to the stomach.

gullible ['gʌləbl] *adj* [person] who is easy to trick because they believe what people tell them.

gully ['gʌlɪ] (*pl* **gullies**) *n* -1. a narrow valley, especially one made in the side of a hill by rainwater. -2. a deep ditch.

gulp [gʌlp] ◇ *vt* [food, liquid, air] to swallow a large amount of <sthg> quickly. ◇ *vi* to swallow suddenly when one is surprised or nervous □ *I gulped nervously.* ◇ *n* an act of gulping □ *Simon took a large gulp of water.*

◆ **gulp down** *vt sep* to gulp sthg down [food, drink] to eat or drink sthg quickly and in large amounts □ *He was gulping down his food as if he had a train to catch.*

gum [gʌm] (*pt* & *pp* **gummed**, *cont* **gumming**) ◇ *n* -1. = chewing gum. -2. a sticky substance used for gluing things together such as pieces of paper. -3. ANATOMY the area of firm pink flesh that surrounds one's teeth. -4. = gum tree. ◇ *vt* -1. to put gum on <sthg> □ *gummed envelopes.* -2. [paper, label] to stick <sthg> to something else using gum.

gumbo ['gʌmbou] *n* a spicy stew made with okra.

gumboil ['gʌmbɔɪl] *n* a painful swelling on one's gum, usually caused by tooth decay.

gumboots ['gʌmbuːts] *npl* GB long rubber boots that are worn to keep one's feet dry.

gumption ['gʌmpʃn] *n* the ability to decide what the best thing to do in a particular situation is, and to do it (informal use).

gumshoe ['gʌmʃuː] *n* a detective (informal use).

gum tree *n* = eucalyptus.

gun [gʌn] (*pt* & *pp* **gunned**, *cont* **gunning**) -1. a weapon that fires bullets at high speed from a metal tube □ *The men were carrying guns.* □ *He pointed a gun at her head.* □ *gun control laws.* ■ **to stick to one's guns** not to change one's original aim, decision, opinion etc, despite what other people do or say □ *She's sticking to her guns on this one.* -2. SPORT a device that makes a loud noise and is used to signal the start of a race. ■ **to jump the gun** to do something before the proper time, with the result that one may make a mistake □ *Don't you think you're jumping the gun a little?* -3. a tool that forces a particular substance or object out under pressure □ *a spray/grease/staple gun.*

◆ **gun down** *vt sep* to gun sb down to injure sb badly or kill them by shooting them with a gun.

gunboat ['gʌnbout] *n* a small ship that has large guns on board.

gundog ['gʌndɒg] *n* a dog trained to find and bring back birds that have been shot by hunters.

gunfight ['gʌnfaɪt] *n* a fight between two or more people who are using guns, especially one taking place in the Wild West.

gunfire ['gʌnfaɪəʳ] *n* the sound of guns being fired □ *the distant sound of gunfire.*

gunge [gʌndʒ] *n* GB any messy, sticky, unpleasant substance (informal use).

gung-ho [,gʌŋ'hou] *adj* [attitude, policy] that shows too much eagerness to do something, especially to go to war (informal use).

gunk [gʌŋk] *n* any slimy, oily, or unpleasant substance (informal use) □ *The car was covered in some kind of revolting gunk.*

gunman ['gʌnmən] (*pl* **gunmen** [-mən]) *n* a criminal who is armed with a gun □ *He was kidnapped by masked gunmen.*

gunner ['gʌnəʳ] *n* a member of the armed forces who is trained to use guns.

gunpoint ['gʌnpɔɪnt] *n* **at gunpoint** under the threat of being shot □ *The hostages were held at gunpoint.*

gunpowder ['gʌnpaʊdəʳ] *n* an explosive powder, used especially in fireworks.

gunrunning ['gʌnrʌnɪŋ] *n* the activity of bringing guns or other weapons into a country secretly and illegally.

gunshot ['gʌnʃɒt] *n* the firing of a gun □ *the sound of gunshots* □ *a gunshot wound.*

gunsmith ['gʌnsmɪθ] *n* a person whose job is to make or repair guns.

gurgle ['gɜːʳgl] ◇ *vi* **-1.** [water] to make a low uneven sound, especially when flowing through a narrow space or over rocks □ *Somewhere nearby a stream gurgled peacefully.* **-2.** [baby] to make a happy sound in the back of the throat like gurgling water □ *The baby lay gurgling quietly.* ◇ *n* [of water, baby] the sound made when water or a baby gurgles □ *The water disappeared down the plughole with a loud gurgle.*

guru ['guːruː] *n* **-1.** RELIGION a Hindu or Sikh religious leader or teacher. **-2.** a person whose ideas are followed by many people □ *a fashion guru.*

gush [gʌʃ] ◇ *n* a sudden flow of a large amount of liquid □ *It all came out in a big gush.* ◇ *vt* [blood, oil, water] to send <a liquid> out in gushes □ *The pipe was gushing oil.* ◇ *vi* **-1.** [blood, oil] *The water gushed out of the pipe.* **-2.** [person] to praise somebody or something in a very enthusiastic way that seems insincere to other people (disapproving use) □ *"Darling, you were wonderful!" she gushed.*

gushing ['gʌʃɪŋ] *adj see* **gush** (disapproving use) □ *I find her rather gushing, I'm afraid.*

gusset ['gʌsət] *n* a piece of cloth, shaped like a triangle, that is sewn into a garment to make it stronger, larger, or more comfortable, e.g. between the legs.

gust [gʌst] ◇ *n* a sudden strong movement of wind □ *a gust of wind.* ◇ *vi* [wind, snow] to blow in gusts.

gusto ['gʌstoʊ] *n* **with gusto** with energy and enthusiasm □ *He sat down and began to eat with great gusto.*

gusty ['gʌstɪ] (*compar* **gustier**, *superl* **gustiest**) *adj* [day, weather] in which there are many strong gusts of wind □ *It was a cold, gusty autumn day.*

gut [gʌt] (*pt* & *pp* **gutted**, *cont* **gutting**) ◇ *n* the tube inside the body that food passes through when it is being digested. ◇ *vt* **-1.** to remove the internal organs from <an animal or fish>, usually to prepare it for cooking. **-2.** to destroy everything inside <a building>, leaving only the outer walls □ *The house was completely gutted by the fire.*

◆ **guts** *npl* **-1.** one's bowels or intestines (informal use) □ *My guts are aching!* ■ **to hate sb's guts** to hate sb very much (informal use). **-2.** **to have guts** to be brave and determined

□ *It takes a lot of guts to ignore that kind of threat.*

gut feeling *n* a strong feeling about somebody or something that cannot be explained in a logical way □ *My gut feeling is that business will improve next year.*

gut reaction *n* a natural or instinctive reaction that cannot be explained in a logical way □ *No, it's just a gut reaction — there's something about her I don't like.*

gutter ['gʌtəʳ] *n* **-1.** [along a road] a channel at the side of a road that allows water to drain away. **-2.** [along a roof] a curved plastic or metal channel along the edge of a roof that collects rainwater and sends it through pipes down to the ground.

guttering ['gʌtərɪŋ] *n* all the gutters and drainpipes of a building.

gutter press *n* **the gutter press** newspapers that contain a lot of stories about people's personal lives (disapproving use).

guttural ['gʌtərəl] *adj* [speech, sound, accent] that sounds harsh because it is produced at the back of somebody's throat.

guy [gaɪ] *n* **-1.** a man or boy (informal use) □ *He's a great guy!* □ *I heard it from some guy on the radio.* **-2.** in the UK, the model of a man that is burned on a bonfire on Guy Fawkes Night.

◆ **guys** *npl* a word used to talk to or about a group of men or women □ *Hey, you guys!*

Guyana [gaɪˈænə] a country in northern South America, between Venezuela and Surinam, on the Atlantic Ocean. SIZE: 215,000 sq kms. POPULATION: 800,000 (*Guyanans, Guyanese*). CAPITAL: Georgetown. LANGUAGE: English. CURRENCY: Guyanese dollar.

Guy Fawkes Night [ˌgaɪˈfɔːks-] *n* = **Bonfire Night**.

guy rope *n* a rope that is stretched from part of a tent to the ground, to keep the tent in position.

guzzle ['gʌzl] ◇ *vt* [food, beer] to eat or drink a large amount of <sthg> quickly and greedily. ◇ *vi*: *You'll feel sick if you guzzle like that.*

Gwyn [gwɪn], **Nell** (1650–1687) an English actress and the mistress of King Charles II. She is supposed to have sold oranges on the streets of London.

gym [dʒɪm] *n* **-1.** a building or large room for physical exercise, usually containing special equipment, e.g. weights, mats, and bars. □ *I work out at my local gym.* **-2.** physical exercises done inside a building □ *gym shorts/lessons.*

gymkhana [dʒɪmˈkɑːnə] *n* GB an event with horse riding displays and competitions.

gymnasium [dʒɪmˈneɪzjəm] (*pl* **gymnasiums** OR **gymnasia** [-jə]) *n* a gym (formal use).

gymnast ['dʒɪmnæst] *n* a person who is skilled or trained in gymnastics.

gymnastics [dʒɪmˈnæstɪks] *n* exercises, often using mats, ropes, or bars, that develop or display physical strength and agility.

gym shoes *npl* light shoes, usually with canvas tops and flat rubber soles.

gymslip ['dʒɪmslɪp] *n* GB a sleeveless dress that used to be worn by schoolgirls as part of their uniform.

gynaecology *etc* [ˌgaɪnə'kɒlədʒɪ] GB = **gynecology** *etc*.

gynecological [ˌgaɪnəkə'lɒdʒɪkl] *adj*: see **gynecology**.

gynecologist [ˌgaɪnə'kɒlədʒəst] *n* a doctor who specializes in gynecology.

gynecology [ˌgaɪnə'kɒlədʒɪ] *n* the branch of medicine concerned with diseases that affect women's reproductive organs.

gypsy ['dʒɪpsɪ] (*pl* **gypsies**) *n* a member of a race of people that travels from place to place, mainly in Europe, and lives in caravans. ◇ *adj*: *a gypsy caravan/dance/camp*.

gyrate [dʒaɪ'reɪt] *vi* -1. [object] to keep turning around. -2. [dancer, body] to dance in a sexually exciting way.

gyration [dʒaɪ'reɪʃn] *n* a spinning movement.

gyroscope ['dʒaɪrəskoʊp] *n* a device containing a disk that spins freely inside a fixed frame, used for keeping ships and aircraft steady, and as a children's toy.

h [eɪtʃ] (*pl* **h's** OR **hs**), **H** [eɪtʃ] (*pl* **H's** OR **Hs**) *n* the eighth letter of the English alphabet.

ha [hɑː] *excl* a word used to express triumph, surprise, or amusement □ *Ha! I knew it!*

habeas corpus [ˌheɪbjəs'kɔːʳpəs] *n* a law that states that a person being kept in prison must appear in court so that a judge can decide if the imprisonment is lawful or not □ *the law of habeas corpus.*

haberdashery ['hæbəʳdæʃərɪ] (*pl* **haberdasheries**) *n* -1. US men's clothing. -2. GB small articles used in sewing, e.g. pins, thread, and buttons. -3. a store or a part of a store that sells haberdashery □ *the haberdashery department.*

habit ['hæbɪt] *n* -1. something that somebody does often as a normal or usual action; something that somebody does often and is unable to stop doing □ *She has a habit of sticking out her tongue when she is concentrating.* □ *a nasty/bad habit* □ *I do it out of habit.* □ *She finally beat her drug habit.* ■ **to be in the habit of doing sthg** to do sthg regularly or often □ *I'm not in the habit of eating late in the evening.* □ *I got into/out of the habit of checking my finances.* ■ **to make a habit of doing sthg** to do sthg regularly or often □ *I try to make a habit of calling her once a week.* □ *"I'm sorry I'm late." — "Yes, well, try not to make a habit of it."* -2. RELIGION a loose piece of clothing reaching the ground, worn by a monk or nun.

habitable ['hæbɪtəbl] *adj* [house, room, region] that is good enough or suitable for people to live in □ *That apartment is barely habitable.*

habitat ['hæbɪtæt] *n* the natural environment that an animal or plant normally lives in □ *the destruction of the eagle's natural habitat.*

habitation [ˌhæbɪ'teɪʃn] *n* -1. the act of living in a place □ *The building is unfit for human habitation.* -2. a place where somebody lives (formal use).

habit-forming [-fɔːʳmɪŋ] *adj* [activity, drug] that is easy to become addicted to.

habitual [hə'bɪtʃʊəl] *adj* [lateness, rudeness] that is a usual state or part of somebody's regular behavior □ *I couldn't live with his habitual swearing.* ■ **a habitual criminal/smoker/drinker** *etc* a person who often commits crimes/smokes/drinks etc and seems not to be able to stop.

habitually [hə'bɪtʃʊəlɪ] *adv* [late, rude] see **habitual** □ *They habitually argue.* □ *He is habitually drunk.*

hack [hæk] ◇ *n* -1. a writer or journalist whose writing is dull or of average quality. -2. US a taxi (informal use). ◇ *vt* to cut <sb/sthg> roughly, using short violent movements □ *He was hacked to death with a sword.* ■ **to hack one's way through sthg** to cut a rough path for oneself through sthg. ◇ *vi*: *He hacked at a branch with an ax.*

◆ **hack into** *vt fus* **to hack into a system** COMPUTING to enter the computer system of a large organization illegally from another computer.

◆ **hack off** *vt sep* **to hack sthg off** to cut sthg off using heavy uneven blows.

hacker ['hækəʳ] *n* a person who hacks into somebody else's computer system in order to use or change the information stored there.

hackie ['hækɪ] *n* US the driver of a taxi (informal use).

hacking ['hækɪŋ] *n* COMPUTING the activity of hacking into an organization's computer system.

hacking cough *n* a painful cough with a rough unpleasant sound.

hackles ['hæklz] *npl* the hairs on the back of the neck of some animals that rise when the animal is angry. ■ **to make sb's hackles rise** to make sb angry.

hackney cab, **hackney carriage** ['hæknɪ-] *n* a taxi (formal use).

hackneyed ['hæknɪd] *adj* [phrase, word, remark] that is boring or meaningless because it has been used too often (disapproving use).

hacksaw ['hæksɔː] *n* a saw with a narrow blade fixed in a frame, used for cutting metal.

had [*stressed* hæd, *unstressed* həd] *past tense & past participle of* **have**.

haddock ['hædək] (*pl* **haddock**) *n* an edible white fish, like cod but smaller, that lives in the North Atlantic.

hadn't ['hædnt] = **had not**.

haematology *n* GB = **hematology**.

haemoglobin *n* GB = **hemoglobin**.

haemophilia *n* GB = **hemophilia**.

haemophiliac *n* GB = **hemophiliac**.

haemorrhage *n* & *vi* GB = **hemorrhage**.

haemorrhoids *npl* GB = **hemorrhoids**.

hag [hæg] *n* a woman who one thinks is ugly or unpleasant.

haggard ['hægəʳd] *adj* [face, person] that has lines and hollows around the eyes, caused by tiredness, anxiety, or starvation □ *Liam came to the door looking pale and haggard.*

haggis ['hægɪs] *n* a Scottish dish made of the internal organs of a sheep mixed with oatmeal and spices and then boiled in a bag made from the animal's stomach.

haggle ['hægl] *vi* to argue, usually about the cost of something □ *The street traders expect you to haggle over the price of their goods.*

Hague [heɪg]: **The Hague** the administrative capital of the Netherlands and the place where the International Court of Justice meets.

hail [heɪl] ◇ *n* -1. WEATHER small round pieces of ice that fall like rain □ *Apparently there's going to be hail today.* -2. **a hail of bullets/ arrows etc** a lot of bullets/arrows etc that are fired at somebody or something at the same time □ *He died in a hail of bullets.* -3. **a hail of abuse/criticism etc** a lot of abuse/ criticism etc that somebody receives at a particular time ◇ *vt* -1. [taxi, waiter] to call or attract the attention of <sb/sthg> □ *See if you can hail a cab for us.* -2. **to hail sb/sthg as sthg** to describe sb/sthg as sthg good □ *He's been hailed as the greatest athlete this century.* ◇ *v impers* WEATHER **it's hailing** hail is falling.

Haile Selassie [ˌhaɪlɪsəˈlæsɪ] (1891–1975) Emperor of Ethiopia from 1930 to 1936 and 1941 to 1974. He lived in exile in England from 1936 to 1941, when his country was occupied by Italy. He is worshipped as a god by Rastafarians. He is also called Ras Tafari Makonnen.

hailstone ['heɪlstoʊn] *n* a piece of hail.

hailstorm ['heɪlstɔːʳm] *n* a storm during which a lot of hail falls.

hair [heəʳ] *n* -1. one of the long fine strands that grow from the skin of people and some animals □ *The dog has left hairs all over the rug.* -2. a mass of hairs, especially on a person's head □ *She has beautiful long hair.* □ *Mike has gone to get his hair cut.* □ *body/underarm/facial hair* □ *a dog with smooth hair* □ *hair oil/ conditioner.* ■ **to do one's hair** to arrange one's hair in a particular style □ *She gets her hair done once a week at the hairdresser's.* ■ **to let one's hair down** to relax and enjoy oneself, especially after a period of restrained behavior □ *Come on, let your hair down for once.* ■ **to make sb's hair stand on end** to make sb very afraid □ *It quite makes my hair stand on end just thinking about that race.* ■ **to split hairs** to point out unnecessary or unimportant differences or details (disapproving use) □ *Now you're just splitting hairs.*

hairbrush ['heəʳbrʌʃ] *n* a brush used for brushing one's hair.

haircut ['heəʳkʌt] *n* -1. the act of cutting somebody's hair □ *I need a haircut.* -2. the style that somebody's hair is cut in □ *I like your new haircut.*

hairdo ['heəʳduː] (*pl* **hairdos**) *n* = **hairstyle** (informal use).

hairdresser ['heəʳdresəʳ] *n* a person whose job is to cut and style people's hair. ■ **a hairdresser's (salon)** a place where hairdressers work □ *She goes to the hairdresser's once every month.*

hairdressing ['heəʳdresɪŋ] *n* the activity, job, or study of cutting and styling people's hair □ *a hairdressing shop/salon/course.*

hairdryer ['heəʳdraɪəʳ] *n* a machine that blows out warm air and is used for drying or styling people's hair.

hair gel *n* gel that is used for fixing hair in a particular style.

hairgrip ['heəʳgrɪp] *n* GB a hairpin with sides that are pressed closely together.

hairline ['heəʳlaɪn] *n* the line at the top of the forehead where the hair starts to grow □ *a receding hairline.*

hairline fracture *n* a very thin fracture, especially of a bone.

hairnet ['heəʳnet] *n* a net that some women wear over their hair to keep it in place.

hairpiece ['heəʳpiːs] *n* a section of false hair that some people wear on their head to cover a bald patch, make their hair seem longer etc.

hairpin ['heəʳpɪn] *n* a thin metal pin, bent into a narrow U-shape, used especially by women to keep their hair in position.

hairpin turn US, **hairpin bend** GB *n* a very sharp bend on a road.

hair-raising [-reɪzɪŋ] *adj* [movie, experience, trip] very frightening □ *Getting through customs was pretty hair-raising!*

hair remover *n* a substance for removing the hair from a part of one's body.

hair restorer *n* a substance that is supposed to make hair grow again on bald people's heads.

hair's breadth *n* **by a hair's breadth** by a very small distance, degree, or amount □ *He won by a hair's breadth.*

hair slide *n* GB a decorative clip, used for keeping hair in position.

hair-splitting *n* the act of pointing out unnecessary or unimportant differences or details (disapproving use) □ *This endless hair-splitting will get us nowhere.*

hairspray ['heəʳspreɪ] *n* a spray that is used for keeping hair in a particular style.

hairstyle ['heəʳstaɪl] *n* the style that a person's hair is cut or arranged in □ *I like your new hairstyle.*

hairstylist ['heəʳstaɪləst] *n* = **hairdresser**.

hairy ['heərɪ] (*compar* **hairier**, *superl* **hairiest**) *adj* -1. [animal, person] that has a lot of hair □ *I don't like men with hairy chests.* -2. [ride, moment, situation] dangerous and frightening (informal use) □ *Things were looking a little bit hairy.*

Haiti ['heɪtɪ] a country in the Caribbean, in the western part of the island of Hispaniola. It was invaded by US troops in 1994 after the government was overthrown in a coup d'état. SIZE: 27,750 sq kms. POPULATION: 6,500,000 (*Haitians*). CAPITAL: Port-au-Prince. LANGUAGE: French, Creole. CURRENCY: gourde.

Haitian ['heɪʃn] *n* & *adj*: *see* **Haiti**.

hake [heɪk] (*pl* **hake** OR **hakes**) *n* one of several types of edible white fish, living mainly in northern seas.

halal [hə'lɑːl] ◇ *n* meat from an animal that has been killed in accordance with Muslim law. ◇ *adj*: *halal meat/butchers*.

halcyon ['hælsɪən] *adj* **halcyon days** a happy and peaceful time, especially when remembered at a later, less happy time (literary use).

hale [heɪl] *adj* **hale and hearty** [old person] healthy and active (old-fashioned use) □ *Henry's still hale and hearty and going strong*.

Hale [heɪl], **Nathan** (1755–1776) a US revolutionary. He was killed by the British for being a spy during the American Revolutionary War.

half [US hæf, GB hɑːf] (*pl* **halves**) ◇ *predet* that is one of the two equal parts that an amount, object, distance etc can be divided into □ *Just give me half a glass of wine.* □ *I'll be there in half an hour.* □ *She spends half the week in the city.* ■ **half a dozen** six □ *She bought half a dozen of them.*
◇ *adj* *I got it for half price.* □ *There are buses every half hour.* □ *a half chicken* □ *They serve half portions here if you ask them.*
◇ *adv* **-1.** [closed, open, asleep] partly □ *The bottle was half full/empty.* □ *I half expected her to say no.* □ *This meat's only half cooked!* ■ **to be half English, half French** to have one English parent and one French parent. ■ **half and half** made with equal amounts of two things □ *"How do you like your orange and soda?" — "Half and half, please."* **-2.** [used in telling the time] **it's half after ten** US, **it's half past ten** GB it's 10:30.
◇ *n* **-1.** one of the two equal parts that an amount, object, distance etc can be divided into □ *Profits were down in the first half of the year.* ■ **by half** by half the full amount □ *We had to reduce/increase the price by half.* ■ **in half** into two equal parts □ *Cut it in half and give a piece to your sister.* ■ **she doesn't do things by halves** she always does things very thoroughly, and sometimes too thoroughly □ *There's no point doing things by halves.* ■ **to go halves** to each pay for half the cost of something □ *You buy it, and I'll go halves with you* □ *Let's go halves on this.* **-2.** SPORT [of a match] one of the two equal periods of time a sports match is divided into □ *The score was even at the end of the first/second half.* **-3.** GB TRANSPORT a ticket, usually for a child, that costs half the price of the normal fare □ *One and two halves to Kew, please.* **-4.** GB [of beer] a half pint of draught beer or lager.
◇ *pron*: *I've eaten half of it.* □ *Half of us were late for the meeting.*

half-and-half *n* US a mixture of cream and milk used in coffee.

halfback [US 'hæfbæk, GB 'hɑːf-] *n* a midfield player in some sports, e.g. in football and rugby.

half-baked [-'beɪkt] *adj* [idea, project, opinion] that is silly because it has not been thought about carefully enough (informal use) □ *Not another of his half-baked schemes.*

half board *n* a type of accommodation at a hotel in which guests are given breakfast and an evening meal.
NOTE: Compare **full board**.

half-brother *n* a man or boy who shares only one of the same parents as another person.

half-caste▼ [US -kæst, GB -kɑːst] (offensive use) ◇ *n* a person whose parents are of different races. ◇ *adj* [person] whose parents are of different races.

half cock *n* **to go off half-cocked** OR **at half cock** to happen without being fully planned or thought about carefully.

half-day *n* a day when a school, store, office etc is closed, either in the morning or in the afternoon □ *We have half-days on Wednesdays.*

half-fare *n* a reduced fare for a child traveling on a bus, train etc.

half-hearted [-'hɑːrtəd] *adj* [support, attempt, smile] that shows very little interest or effort □ *Somebody had made a rather half-hearted attempt at cleaning up.*

half-heartedly [-'hɑːrtədlɪ] *adv* [support, attempt, smile] *see* **half-hearted** □ *The audience clapped rather half-heartedly.*

half hour *n* a period of thirty minutes □ *You must take one pill every half hour.*

◆ **half-hour** *adj* a **half-hour trip/appointment** etc a trip/an appointment etc that lasts half an hour □ *It's a half-hour walk, no more.*

half-hourly *adj* [visits, broadcasts] that happen every half hour □ *We give him half-hourly feeds.*

half-leaded petrol *n* AUS a type of gasoline that contains a reduced amount of lead and can be used by cars that cannot use unleaded gasoline.

half-length *adj* [portrait] that shows only the upper half of somebody; [coat, jacket] that covers only the upper half of somebody.

half-light *n* **the half-light** the dull light of early morning or evening, or of a room that is badly lit □ *I could barely make him out in the half-light.*

half-mast *n* **to be (flying) at half-mast** [flag] to be flying near the middle of the pole, as a sign of respect for a person who has died.

half measures *npl* actions that are not strong or complete enough to deal with a problem, difficult situation etc □ *It's no use doing things by half measures.*

half moon *n* **-1.** the part of the Moon that is seen from the Earth as the shape of half a circle. **-2.** the shape of half a circle.

half note *n* US MUSIC a note (♩) that lasts for half as long as a whole note.

halfpenny ['heɪpnɪ] (*pl* **halfpennies** OR **halfpence** ['heɪpəns]) *n* in Britain, a small bronze coin used in the past that was worth one half of a penny.

half-price *adj* a half-price meal/ticket etc a meal/ticket etc that can be bought for half of the usual price □ *This card entitles you to half-price train travel.*

◆ **half price** *adv* [sell, buy, pay] *We got it half price.*

half-sister *n* a woman or girl who shares only one of the same parents as another person.

half step *n* US MUSIC the difference in pitch between any two notes that are next to each other on a piano.

half term *n* GB a short period in the middle of a school term when the school is closed □ *a half-term holiday.*

half time *n* in soccer, rugby etc, a short break for a rest between the two halves of a game or match □ *The score was 2 - 1 at half time.* □ *the half-time score.*

half tone *n* US = **half step**.

half-truth *n* a statement that contains some truth but is intended to deceive somebody by not including important details.

halfway [US ˌhæf'weɪ, GB ˌhɑːf-] ◇ *adj* the halfway stage OR mark OR point the middle point of a distance or period of time. □ *We're now at the halfway mark in the competition.* ◇ *adv* **-1.** at the middle point of a distance or period of time □ *New Haven is halfway between Boston and New York.* □ *I was halfway there/home before I realized.* □ *The movie was halfway through before he turned up.* **-2.** *phrase* to meet sb halfway to agree to do part of what sb wants in order to reach an agreement, solve a problem etc □ *Look, I'm prepared to meet you halfway on this.*

half-wit *n* a person who one thinks is stupid □ *What a complete half-wit!*

half-yearly *adj* [profits, accounts, results] that are calculated six months after the beginning of a calendar year, tax year etc □ *a half-yearly forecast.*

◆ **half yearly** *adv* [calculate, assess] every six months □ *our profits are calculated half yearly.*

halibut ['hælɪbət] (*pl* **halibut** OR **halibuts**) *n* a large flat fish that lives in the sea and is eaten as food.

halitosis [ˌhælɪ'təʊsəs] *n* the condition of having breath that smells unpleasant.

hall [hɔːl] *n* **-1.** [in a house] the area or corridor that leads from the front door of a house to other rooms □ *an entrance hall.* **-2.** [for meetings, concerts, dances] a large room or building where many people can meet together for particular events □ *a dining hall* □ *the church/school hall* □ *We've hired a hall for the party.* □ *Carnegie Hall.* **-3.** GB EDUCATION = **hall of residence**. ■ to live in hall to live in a hall of residence. **-4.** GB a very large country house with a lot of land (used in names) □ *Bizley Hall is open to the public.*

halleluja(h) [ˌhælɪ'luːjə] *excl* a word used, es-pecially in songs, to express praise and thanks to God.

hallmark ['hɔːlmɑːᵏk] *n* **-1.** a very typical feature of somebody's work or way of behaving □ *This bears all the hallmarks of a terrorist attack.* **-2.** an official mark that is stamped on objects made of platinum, silver, or gold to show their origin, the quality of the metal etc □ *a silver hallmark.*

hallo [hə'ləʊ] *excl* = **hello**.

Hall of Fame *n* US a building that contains information about the most famous people connected with a sport or activity.

hall of residence (*pl* **halls of residence**) *n* a building or buildings owned by a college or university, where students live.

hallowed ['hæləʊd] *adj* [building, memory] that is highly respected □ *as we stepped into the hallowed halls of Trinity College.*

Halloween, Hallowe'en [ˌhæləʊ'iːn] *n* the night of October 31, which was believed in the past to be the time when ghosts and witches could be seen, and when children of today wear disguises and play tricks on people.

☝ HALLOWEEN
On October 31 in the USA, Britain, and Australia, children celebrate Halloween by dressing up as witches or ghosts and going from door to door asking "Trick or treat?" People have to give the children "treats", such as candy, otherwise the children play a "trick" on them, for example covering their windows with soap. Halloween is most popular in the USA, where many adults also dress up as witches, and some even go to work in their disguise.

hallucinate [hə'luːsɪneɪt] *vi* to believe that one is seeing strange and frightening things that do not really exist, as a result of illness, taking drugs etc.

hallucination [hə,luːsɪ'neɪʃn] *n* the experience of hallucinating; something that one sees when one hallucinates □ *You can't convince me that this was a hallucination.*

hallucinogenic [hə,luːsɪnə'dʒenɪk] *adj* [drug, substance] that causes hallucinations.

hallway ['hɔːlweɪ] *n* the area just inside the main entrance to a house or building □ *Don't stand in the hallway, come in!*

halo ['heɪləʊ] (*pl* **haloes** OR **halos**) *n* **-1.** a ring of light that is shown above or around the heads of saints, angels etc in paintings. **-2.** a bright circle of light above or around something □ *a halo of light.*

halogen ['hælədʒen] *n* any one of the elements astatine, bromine, chlorine, fluorine, or iodine □ *a halogen lamp.*

halt [hɔːlt] ◇ *n* to come to a halt [car, train, person] to slow down and stop; [work, progress, meeting] to stop before being completed because of a problem □ *All traffic in the city came to a complete halt.* □ *All building work came to a halt during the vacation.* ■ to call a halt to sthg [to a dispute, negotiation, practice] to order sthg to stop □ *Protests have forced the government to call a halt to further tests.* ■ **to grind to a halt** [car, train, truck] to gradually and noisily slow down and stop; [economy, project, country] to gradually stop making progress because of great difficulty □ *There was a loud bang and the engine slowly ground to a halt.* □ *Everything just seemed to grind to a halt because Pia wasn't there.*

◇ *vt* [growth, activity, process] to stop <sthg> from continuing □ *A solution must be found to halt the widespread smuggling of heroin into the country.*

◇ *vi* [person, train, soldier] to stop moving or walking □ *The car halted at the traffic lights.*

halter ['hɔːltər] *n* a length of rope or band of leather that is put round a horse's head so that it can be led somewhere.

haltertop US, **halterneck** GB ['hɔːltərnek] *n* a piece of clothing that is worn by a woman and is tied behind the neck with a narrow band of cloth, so that the shoulders, arms, and back are not covered □ *a haltertop dress.*

halting ['hɔːltɪŋ] *adj* [voice, progress, explanation] that keeps stopping and starting, often because of uncertainty or lack of confidence □ *He spoke in halting English.*

halve [US hæv, GB hɑːv] *vt* -1. [budget, time, price] to reduce <sthg> by half □ *The new road will halve the time it takes to complete the journey.* -2. [apple, cake, money] to divide <sthg> into two equal parts □ *The two men agreed to halve the profits.*

halves [US hævz, GB hɑːvz] *plural of* **half.**

ham [hæm] (*pt* & *pp* **hammed,** *cont* **hamming**) ◇ *n* -1. COOKING meat from the upper part of a pig's leg that has been salted, smoked, or boiled □ *a slice of ham* □ *roast ham* □ *a ham sandwich.* -2. THEATER an actor or actress whose acting is exaggerated, with the result that it seems unnatural. -3. TECHNOLOGY a person who sends and receives radio messages using their own equipment. ◇ *vt* **to ham it up** [actor, actress] to perform with too much expression and movement □ *I think they were hamming it up on purpose.*

Hamburg ['hæmbɜːrg] an industrial city in northern Germany. It is Germany's main port, and an important commercial and cultural center. POPULATION: 1,626,220.

hamburger ['hæmbɜːrgər] *n* -1. a flat circle of ground beef that is cooked and served in a round bread roll, often with sauces and salad. -2. US ground or chopped meat.

ham-fisted [-'fɪstəd] *adj* GB [person] who one thinks is clumsy at doing things with their hands; who one thinks is not skillful at dealing with people □ *He made a rather ham-fisted attempt at apologizing.*

Hamilton ['hæmltən], **Alexander** (1757–1804) a US politician. He helped to write the US Constitution.

hamlet ['hæmlət] *n* a small village.

Hamlet ['hæmlət] the hero of Shakespeare's play *Hamlet.* He kills his uncle, who had killed his father, the King of Denmark, and married his mother.

hammer ['hæmər] ◇ *n* a tool with a long wooden handle and a heavy metal head, used especially for hitting nails into wood.

◇ *vt* -1. [nail, plank] to hit <sthg> with a hammer □ *Make sure you hammer all the nails in straight.* -2. [door, wall, table] to hit <sthg> loudly and with force several times, usually with one's hand and because one is angry or impatient □ *He hammered the desk with his fist.* -3. [opponent, team] to beat <sb/sthg> extremely easily (informal use) □ *Did we lose? We were absolutely hammered!*

◇ *vi* -1. [at a nail, plank] *He was hammering (away) at that shelf.* -2. [at a door, on a wall] *He was hammering at the door, demanding to be let in.* -3. **to hammer away at sthg** [at a problem, contract, agreement] to keep working hard at sthg □ *Keep hammering away and you'll eventually get a job.*

◆ **hammer into** *vt sep* **to hammer sthg into sb** [message, fact, importance] to repeat sthg several times to sb so that they will remember or learn it □ *You have to keep hammering the message into these kids — drugs are dangerous.*

◆ **hammer out** ◇ *vt fus* **to hammer out sthg** [agreement, policy, solution] to spend a long time discussing sthg and reach a final agreement □ *We finally managed to hammer out an agreement.* ◇ *vt sep* **to hammer a dent/bump out** to remove a dent/bump by hitting it with a hammer.

Hammerstein ['hæmərstaɪn], **Oscar** (1895–1960) a US songwriter. He worked with Richard Rodgers on musicals such as *South Pacific, Oklahoma,* and *The Sound of Music.*

Hammett ['hæmɪt], **Dashiell** (1894–1961) a US crime writer, the first to have a private detective as a hero. His work includes *The Maltese Falcon.*

hammock ['hæmək] *n* a large piece of cloth that is hung between two poles or trees and is used for lying in.

hamper ['hæmpər] ◇ *n* -1. [for food] a large basket with a lid and a handle that is used for carrying food, e.g. for a picnic □ *a picnic hamper.* -2. US [for clothes, washing] a large basket in which dirty clothes, towels, sheets etc are put before being washed. ◇ *vt* [progress, movement] to make <sthg> difficult □ *The rescue attempt was hampered by wind and rain.*

Hampshire ['hæmpʃər] a county in southern England, on the English Channel. SIZE: 3,777 sq kms. POPULATION: 1,542,900. ADMINISTRATIVE CENTER: Winchester.

hamster ['hæmstər] *n* a small animal that looks like a mouse but has a short tail and stores food in its cheeks. Hamsters are often kept as pets.

hamstring ['hæmstrɪŋ] ◇ *n* a tendon at the back of one's knee that joins the muscles at the back of one's thigh to the bones below it □ *He's suffering from a pulled hamstring.* □ *a hamstring injury.* ◇ *vt* [person] to make it very difficult for <sb> to do something; [project, process] to stop <work> from making progress ☐ *The company is hamstrung by staff short-ages.*

Hancock ['hænkɒk], **John** (1737–1793) a US revolutionary. He was the first person to sign the Declaration of Independence.

hand [hænd] ◇ *n* **-1.** the part of one's body that is at the end of one's arm, has four fingers and a thumb, and is used for holding things, picking them up, touching etc ☐ *She held the pen/ring/letter in her hand.* ☐ *He led her forward by the hand.* ☐ *my left/right hand.* ■ **to hold hands with sb** to hold sb's hand with one's own hand ☐ *They sat holding hands in the back row.* ■ **by hand** [sew, knit, make] using one's hands rather than a machine; [write] in handwriting and without using a typewriter or printer; [deliver, give] to somebody directly without using the postal system ☐ *All our garments are finished by hand.* ☐ *Applications must be written by hand.* ☐ *This letter was delivered by hand yesterday.* ■ **hand in hand** [walk, sit] holding hands, especially to show affection for each other ☐ *They walked hand in hand down the street.* ■ **with one's bare hands** without using a weapon or tool ☐ *I'll kill him with my bare hands!* **-2.** a **hand** help given to somebody to do a particular thing ☐ *Do you need a hand?* ■ **to give** OR **lend sb a hand** to help sb to do a particular thing ☐ *I gave him a hand with his homework.* ☐ *Can I give you/lend a hand with those bags?* **-3. to have a problem on one's hands** to have to deal with a problem ☐ *Saira's got quite a lot on her hands right now.* ■ **in the hands of sb** under the responsibility of sb ☐ *It's all in Jenny's hands now.* ■ **to take sb in hand** to take responsibility for controlling sb who has not been behaving correctly ☐ *Somebody's got to take that child in hand before he gets into trouble.* **-4. the hand of sb** the influence or participation of sb in an event or situation ☐ *She could detect the hand of the Personnel Manager behind the suggestion.* ■ **to have a hand in sthg** to be partly responsible for sthg ☐ *I had no hand in arranging the meeting.* **-5.** [on a farm, ship] a person whose job is to do general physical work ☐ *a stable/factory hand.* **-6.** [of a clock, watch] one of the long thin pieces of metal or plastic that move to indicate the hour, minutes, or seconds ☐ *a clock hand* ☐ *the minute/hour hand.* **-7. in sb's hand** in sb's handwriting ☐ *She has an elegant hand.* **-8.** CARDS the group of cards that one receives at the beginning of a game of cards ☐ *a strong/weak hand.* **-9.** phrases ■ **at the hands of sb** while under the control of sb ☐ *They received terrible treatment at the hands of the enemy.* ■ **hands up!** a phrase used by a person holding a gun to order somebody to raise their arms above their heads. ■ **to change hands** [car, company, house] to become the property of somebody else ☐ *This car has already changed hands several times.* ■ **to force sb's hand** to make sb do something they do not want to or are not yet ready to do ☐ *I would recommend that you wait a bit longer; don't try to force his hand.* ■ **to get** OR **lay one's hands on sb** to catch sb and deal with them ☐ *Wait till I get my hands on that little idiot!* ■ **to**

get OR **lay one's hands on sthg** to finally find or get sthg ☐ *Where can I get my hands on a cheap used car?* ■ **to give sb a free hand** to let sb do a particular thing in exactly the way they want ☐ *They've given me a completely free hand to organize things the way I want.* ■ **to give sb a big hand** [speaker, performer] to welcome or show one's approval of sb by clapping (informal use) ☐ *Give a big hand for our special guest.* ■ **to go hand in hand with sthg** to exist or happen together with sthg else, because of a very close connection with it ☐ *Crime often goes hand in hand with poverty.* ■ **to have one's hands full** to be very busy ☐ *He has his hands full with the children and finishing his work in time.* ■ **to try one's hand at sthg** to try sthg for the first time, especially when a particular skill is involved ☐ *I've always wanted to try my hand at hang gliding.* ■ **to wait on sb hand and foot** to serve sb everything they need and do everything for them (disapproving use). ■ **to wash one's hands of sb/sthg** to refuse to be responsible for or be connected with sb/sthg any longer ☐ *I wash my hands of the whole lot of you!*

◇ *vt* **to hand sthg to sb, to hand sb sthg** to give sthg to sb with one's hand ☐ *He handed her the letter.*

◆ **(close) at hand** *adv* very close ☐ *Help/The wedding/The phone was close at hand.*

◆ **in hand** *adv* **-1. to have sthg in hand** GB [time, money] to still have an amount of sthg available to be used ☐ *There's no rush, we have two days in hand.* **-2. to have sthg in hand** [problem, situation] to have sthg under control ☐ *Matters are now well in hand.*

◆ **on hand** *adv* near enough or ready to help or be used if necessary ☐ *The police were on hand in case of trouble.*

◆ **on the other hand** *conj* a phrase used to introduce a contrasting aspect of a subject ☐ *This deal will increase revenue. On the other hand it will certainly mean losing valued clients.*

◆ **out of hand** ◇ *adj* to get out of hand [situation, person] to become difficult to control ☐ *The rioting soon got out of hand.* ☐ *They've let their kids get completely out of hand.* ◇ *adv* [reject, dismiss] completely and immediately ☐ *The appeal was rejected out of hand.*

◆ **to hand** *adv* GB near and ready for use ☐ *Do you have a phone directory to hand?*

◆ **hand down** *vt sep* **to hand sthg down** [heirloom, knowledge, clothing] to give sthg to somebody who is younger or leave it to them after one has died ☐ *The brooch had been handed down from generation to generation.*

◆ **hand in** *vt sep* **-1. to hand sthg in** [wallet, book] to give or return sthg to somebody in authority so that it is safe ☐ *Please hand in your key at reception before leaving the hotel.* **-2. to hand sthg in** [essay, application] to give sthg to somebody in authority who will read it and make a decision about it ☐ *I told him I was ready to hand in my resignation.*

◆ **hand on** *vt sep* **to hand sthg on** [piece of clothing, memo, knowledge] to give sthg to somebody else because one has finished with it, no longer needs it etc □ *It's time for me to hand on my job to someone new.*

◆ **hand out** *vt sep* **-1. to hand sthg out** [money, food, papers] to give sthg to each member of a group of people □ *People were handing out leaflets to passers-by.* **-2. to hand sthg out** [advice, punishment] to give sthg to somebody, especially when one does this often □ *Inspectors can now hand out fines to passengers traveling without a ticket.*

◆ **hand over** ◇ *vt sep* **-1. to hand sb/sthg over** [prisoner, money, gun] to give sb/sthg to somebody else because one has been asked or forced to do so □ *Hand over that book, it's mine!* **-2. to hand sthg over** [job, matter] to officially give sthg to somebody else to have or deal with □ *He's now ready to hand over power to an interim government.* **-3. to hand sb over** to let sb that one is speaking to speak to somebody else by handing them the receiver □ *I'll hand you over to Sue.* ◇ *vi* to give somebody else a job, responsibility etc that one has had □ *We're handing over to the new directors next week.*

handbag ['hændbæg] *n* a small bag in which a woman carries things that she needs during the day, e.g. money, make-up, or keys □ *a leather handbag.*

handball ['hændbɔːl] *n* a game played by two teams of seven players with a goal at each end of the court. The ball has to be thrown or bounced but players cannot make more than three steps while they have the ball.

handbill ['hændbɪl] *n* a small printed advertisement that is given to people by hand.

handbook ['hændbʊk] *n* a short book that gives useful information and instructions about a particular subject or product.

handbrake ['hændbreɪk] *n* a brake in a car, truck etc which is worked with the hand.

handclap ['hændklæp] *n* **a slow handclap** GB slow clapping by an audience to show that it is waiting for something or not satisfied with something.

handcrafted [US 'hændkræftəd, GB -krɑːftəd] *adj* [sweater, pottery, toy] that is designed and made by hand rather than by a machine.

handcuff ['hændkʌf] *vt* [criminal, suspect] to put handcuffs on <sb>.

handcuffs ['hændkʌfs] *npl* two metal rings, joined by a chain, that are used by the police to hold a prisoner's wrists.

Handel ['hændl], **George** (1685–1759) a German composer who lived mainly in London. His works include the *Water Music* and the *Messiah.*

handful ['hændfl] *n* **-1.** [of sand, hair, rice] a quantity that can easily be held in one's hand □ *He picked up a handful of stones.* **-2.** [of people, places] a very small number □ *Only a handful of companies have shown an interest in our product.* **-3. to be a handful** [child, dog] to be lively and difficult to control (informal use) □ *He's a real handful now that he's learnt to walk.*

hand grenade *n* a small bomb designed to be thrown by hand.

handgun ['hændgʌn] *n* a small gun that can be fired using only one hand.

hand-held *adj* [tool, device] that one holds when using it □ *a hand-held camera.*

handicap ['hændɪkæp] (*pt* & *pp* **handicapped**, *cont* **handicapping**) ◇ *n* **-1.** damage to the mind or body that prevents a person from living a normal life □ *a physical/mental handicap* □ *Sue, now eight, was born with a severe handicap.* **-2.** a disadvantage that makes something more difficult □ *His greatest handicap is his lack of confidence.* □ *Her car was stolen, which has been a handicap to her business.* **-3.** SPORT [in a race] a disadvantage that is given to the stronger competitor or team to make the competition more equal; [in golf] the number of extra strokes one takes to complete one's home golf course, compared to the number of strokes that is needed by a good player □ *The horse was running with a slight weight handicap.* □ *I'm trying to improve my handicap.*

◇ *vt* [progress, work] to make <sthg> more difficult to do or achieve; [person] to prevent <sb> from doing or achieving something easily □ *Attempts at negotiating have been handicapped by continuing disturbances.* □ *Poor management has severely handicapped our company's progress.*

handicapped ['hændɪkæpt] ◇ *adj* [person] who has a mental or physical handicap □ *She is physically/mentally handicapped.* ◇ *npl* **the handicapped** people who have a physical or mental handicap.

handicraft [US 'hændɪkræft, GB -krɑːft] *n* any skilled activity, e.g. sewing or pottery, in which one uses one's hands to make something.

◆ **handicrafts** *npl* things that have been made by somebody using their hands in a skilled way.

handiwork ['hændɪwɜːrk] *n* **my/your etc handiwork** something that I/you etc have done or made □ *He stepped back from the canvas to admire his handiwork.* □ *The explosion looks like the handiwork of militant extremists.*

handkerchief ['hæŋkərtʃɪf] (*pl* **handkerchiefs** OR **handkerchieves** [-tʃiːvz]) *n* a square of thin cloth or soft paper, used for blowing one's nose, drying one's eyes etc.

handle ['hændl] ◇ *n* a part of an object that is used to hold, carry, or open it □ *a door/knife/cup handle* □ *She grabbed the suitcase by the handle.* ■ **to fly off the handle** to suddenly become angry about something □ *Sometimes she'll just fly off the handle for no reason.*

◇ *vt* **-1.** to hold, feel, or touch <sthg> with one's hands □ *Please do not handle the fruit.* □ *'Handle with care.'* **-2.** [car, horse] to be able to control <a vehicle or animal> well; [gun, language] to know how to use <a piece of equipment or information> □ *He looks as if he could handle himself in a fight.* □ *Have you ever handled this kind of machinery before?* **-3.** [complaint, order] to be responsible for dealing with <sthg>, especially on a regular basis □ *Who handles the company's publicity?* □

He's been accused of handling stolen goods. **-4.** [person, situation, crisis] to deal with <sb/sthg> successfully so that a problem is avoided or solved □ *You handled that very well.* ◇ *vi* **to handle well/badly** [car, boat] to be easy/difficult to control.

handlebars ['hændlɑːʳz] *npl* the part of a bicycle or motorbike that one holds in each hand to steer it.

handler ['hændləʳ] *n* [of dog] a person whose job is to control an animal □ *a dog handler.*

handling charges ['hændlɪŋ-] *npl* money charged by a bank for providing some services or by companies for packaging or transporting goods.

hand lotion *n* a lotion used on hands to keep them soft.

hand luggage *n* the small items of luggage that one is allowed to keep with one on a plane, coach etc.

handmade [ˌhænd'meɪd] *adj* [clothes, furniture, ornament] made by hand, without using a machine □ *a box of handmade chocolates.*

hand-me-down *n* an item of clothing that has belonged to somebody and that they give to somebody else, especially a younger relative (informal use).

handout ['hændaʊt] *n* **-1.** a small amount of money, food, or clothing given free to poor people □ *a free handout* □ *He lives on government handouts.* **-2.** a piece of paper with a list of the points or facts that are dealt with in a class, meeting etc, given to each person taking part □ *Did you get one of these handouts?*

handover ['hændəʊvəʳ] *n* [of power, responsibility] the act of transferring somebody or something from one person or organization to another □ *The handover went very smoothly.*

handpick [ˌhænd'pɪk] *vt* [team, staff] to chose <sb> very carefully as the best for a particular purpose □ *He was handpicked for the mission.*

handrail ['hændreɪl] *n* a long piece of metal or wood for people to hold on to, usually where there are several steps.

handset ['hændset] *n* the part of a telephone that one holds to speak into and to listen to □ *'Replace the handset after use.'*

handshake ['hændʃeɪk] *n* the act of shaking somebody's right hand with one's own right hand to say hello or goodbye, or to confirm a deal □ *He has a firm/limp handshake.*

hands-off *adj* **a hands-off approach/policy etc** an approach/a policy etc that involves letting other people deal with situations or problems without interference □ *a hands-off management style.*

handsome ['hænsəm] *adj* **-1.** [man] who has a very attractive and masculine face. **-2.** [woman] who has an attractive face because it looks strong and healthy. **-3.** [reward, tip] that is large or generous □ *a handsome profit.*

handsomely ['hænsəmlɪ] *adv* [reward, pay] *see* **handsome** □ *Those who work hard will be handsomely rewarded.*

hands-on *adj* **hands-on training/a hands-on approach etc** training/an approach etc that involves practical use of equipment or methods □ *She has a hands-on management style.* □ *We offer trainees plenty of hands-on experience with all the latest equipment.*

handstand ['hændstænd] *n* a gymnastic exercise in which one holds one's body and legs straight up in the air and touches the floor only with one's hands.

hand-to-mouth *adj* **to live a hand-to-mouth existence** to have just enough money and food to live. ◆ **hand to mouth** *adv*: *They live very much hand to mouth.*

hand towel *n* a towel for drying one's hands after washing them.

handwriting ['hændraɪtɪŋ] *n* the particular way somebody writes □ *I don't recognize this handwriting.*

handwritten ['hændrɪtn] *adj* [letter, invitation, apology] that has been written by hand and not using a typewriter or printer.

handy ['hændɪ] (*compar* **handier**, *superl* **handiest**) *adj* (informal use) **-1.** [size, book, gadget] that is useful and convenient □ *The microwave is so handy for preparing food quickly.* ■ **to come in handy** [money, advice, tool] to be useful, especially at a particular time □ *a few extra clothes might come in handy for the trip.* **-2.** [person] who can do practical tasks well □ *She's very handy with a needle/pair of shears.* **-3.** [place, transport, person] very near and convenient to reach □ *The office is handy for local stores.* □ *Bus services are very handy where we live.* ■ **to keep sthg handy** to keep sthg in a place that is near and easy to reach.

handyman ['hændɪmæn] (*pl* **handymen** [-men]) *n* a person who is good at repairing things and doing other practical jobs around the house.

hang [hæŋ] (*pt* & *pp sense 1* **hung**, *sense 2* **hanged** OR **hung**) ◇ *vt* **-1.** [curtain, picture, towel] to put the top part of <sthg> on or against something that supports its weight and lets the bottom part move freely above the ground □ *Where should I hang my coat?* □ *He hung his wet socks in front of the fire.* □ *Together they hung decorations on the tree.* □ *Try hanging it from the ceiling.* **-2.** [criminal, prisoner] to kill <sb> by putting a rope around their neck and letting them fall, usually as a legal punishment for a serious crime □ *the last woman to be hanged in Britain.*

◇ *vi* **-1.** [curtain, picture, towel] *A portrait of her father hung over the fireplace.* □ *A bare light bulb hung from the ceiling.* **-2.** [criminal, prisoner] *All four men have been sentenced to hang.*

◇ *n* **to get the hang of sthg** [of a system, machine, activity] to begin to understand how to do sthg (informal use) □ *I'm just about beginning to get the hang of it.*

◆ **hang about, hang around** *vi* to stay in one place without doing anything, especially because one is waiting for someone or something □ *After a while we got tired of hang-*

ing around and went home. □ *There were a few bored teenagers hanging around outside the café.*

◆ **hang on** ◇ *vt fus* **to hang on sb/sthg** to depend on sb/sthg □ *The success of the peace initiative hangs on the willingness of both sides to cooperate.* □ *There's a lot hanging on the result.* ◇ *vi* **-1.** to keep on holding something tightly in case one loses it or to keep one's balance □ *He hung on tightly as the winch pulled him up toward the helicopter.* **-2.** to wait for a short time (informal use) □ *Hang on, I'll be with you in a minute.*

◆ **hang onto** *vt fus* **-1.** to hold sthg with one's hands and not let go [rope, ledge, branch] □ *Here, hang onto my arm.* □ *Hang onto your handbags, there are pickpockets around.* **-2. to hang onto sthg** [onto power, money, belief] to try to keep sthg, especially because somebody is trying to take it away from one □ *He was trying desperately to hang onto his job.*

◆ **hang out** ◇ *vt sep* **to hang out the washing** to hang clean wet washing on a clothesline to dry. ◇ *vi* to spend time relaxing in a particular place (informal use) □ *We just hung out at Mike's all day.*

◆ **hang round** *vi* = **hang about**.

◆ **hang together** *vi* [parts of an explanation, argument, story] to be connected in a logical and convincing way □ *Somehow her explanation of what happened just doesn't hang together.*

◆ **hang up** ◇ *vt sep* **to hang sthg up** [coat, decorations] to hang sthg, especially from a hook or nail □ *Hang up your clothes, don't leave them lying around on the floor!* ◇ *vi* to end a telephone call by replacing the receiver □ *He hung up as soon as he heard my voice.*

◆ **hang up on** *vt fus* **to hang up on sb** to hang up when sb is talking, usually because one is angry □ *Don't ever hang up on me again!*

hangar ['hæŋə^r] *n* a large building where aircraft are kept or repaired □ *an aircraft hangar.*

hangdog ['hæŋdɒg] *adj* [expression, look] that makes somebody seem miserable or ashamed.

hanger ['hæŋə^r] *n* a shaped piece of metal, wood, or plastic used for hanging clothes on.

hanger-on (*pl* **hangers-on**) *n* a person who spends time with a richer or more important person or group, trying to be friendly in order to get things from them for free.

hang glider *n* a piece of equipment for gliding through the air that does not have an engine and consists of a large frame covered in cloth with a harness underneath for the pilot.

hang gliding *n* the sport of flying a hang glider.

hanging ['hæŋɪŋ] *n* **-1.** the form of punishment in which a criminal is killed by being hanged; a death caused by this punishment □ *A minority of people are in favor of hanging.* □ *A crowd gathered to watch the hanging.* **-2.** a piece of cloth such as a curtain that is hung on a wall or at a window as a decoration □ *a wall hanging.*

hangman ['hæŋmən] (*pl* **hangmen** [-mən]) *n* a man whose job is to hang criminals.

hangover ['hæŋoʊvə^r] *n* **-1.** [after drinking] a bad headache and feeling of sickness that somebody has the day after drinking too much alcohol □ *I woke up with an awful hangover.* **-2.** [from the past] something that remains or results from a practice, event, or situation in the past □ *a hangover from the past.*

Hang Seng [,hæŋ'seŋ] *n* **the Hang Seng (Index)** the average of the current price of shares on the Hong Kong Stock Exchange.

hang-up *n* something, e.g. an activity or a personal physical feature, that makes one worry too much (informal use) □ *She's got a hang-up about her looks/going to the dentist.*

hank [hæŋk] *n* a long piece of wool, string, or rope that has been loosely wound into several loops.

hanker ['hæŋkə^r] ◆ **hanker after, hanker for** *vt fus* **to hanker after** OR **for sthg** to continuously think about having sthg that one wants or misses □ *Those days are gone and there's no point hankering after them.*

hankering ['hæŋkərɪŋ] *n* **to have a hankering after** OR **for sthg** [for foreign travel, new clothes, success] to have a constant wish for sthg, especially when one cannot have it.

hankie, hanky ['hæŋkɪ] (*pl* **hankies**) *n* = **handkerchief** (informal use).

hanky-panky [-'pæŋkɪ] *n* behavior involving or suggesting sexual activity between two people (informal and humorous use).

Hanoi [hæ'nɔɪ] the capital city of Vietnam. POPULATION: 3,100,000.

Hansard ['hænsɑː^rd] *n* the official written report of what is said and decided by the British parliament.

Hants *abbr of* **Hampshire**.

haphazard [,hæp'hæzə^rd] *adj* [arrangement, distribution, guess] not exact or planned □ *He has a very haphazard way of doing things.*

haphazardly [,hæp'hæzə^rdlɪ] *adv* [arrange, distribute, guess] *see* **haphazard** □ *Clothes were scattered haphazardly all over the floor.*

hapless ['hæpləs] *adj* [person] unfortunate (literary use) □ *The snake crushes its hapless victim to death.*

happen ['hæpən] *vi* **-1.** [accident, change, mistake] to take place □ *What happened next?* □ *Make sure it doesn't happen again.* ■ **to happen to sb/sthg** to take place and have an effect on sb/sthg □ *I'm afraid something awful has happened to him.* □ *What's happened to your hand?* **-2. to happen to do sthg** to do sthg by chance □ *She happened to meet him in the bar.* □ *Do you happen to know the way to the post office?* ■ **as it happens** a phrase used to show that what is being said is rather surprising □ *We've met before, as it happens.* □ *As it happened, we were on the same flight to Milan.*

happening ['hæpənɪŋ] *n* an event.

happily ['hæpəlɪ] *adv* **-1.** [laugh, talk, play] in a happy way □ *They are happily married.* □ *We were happily driving along when suddenly the engine started smoking.* **-2. happily,...** fortunately

□ *Happily, no one was hurt.* **-3.** [help, come, stay] willingly □ *I'd happily go with you, but I'm busy that night.*

happiness ['hæpɪnəs] *n* the state of being satisfied or pleased □ *a feeling of happiness* □ *I wish you health and happiness.*

happy ['hæpɪ] (*compar* **happier,** *superl* **happiest**) *adj* **-1.** [person] who feels or shows satisfaction or pleasure; [smile, face] that shows satisfaction or pleasure □ *She looked so happy when I told her.* **-2.** [day, story] that makes somebody feel satisfied or pleased □ *a movie with a happy ending* □ *They had a very happy marriage.* ■ **Happy Christmas/New Year/Birthday** the words used to express the wish that somebody has a pleasant Christmas/New Year/birthday. **-3.** [customer, staff] who is satisfied with the way things are □ *Nick is happy at school/in his job.* □ *She's not very happy about the new arrangement* ■ **to be happy with** OR **about sthg** [with a decision, situation, result] to be satisfied with sthg □ *Are you happy with your new secretary?* **-4.** [chance, coincidence, choice] fortunate (formal use). **-5. to be happy to do sthg** to be willing to do sthg □ *I'd be happy to help.*

happy event *n* the birth of a child (informal and humorous use) □ *And when can we expect this happy event?*

happy-go-lucky *adj* [person] who is cheerful and not affected by worries about the future □ *He's just an easy-going, happy-go-lucky kind of guy.*

happy hour *n* a time, usually early in the evening, when a bar sells alcoholic drinks at reduced prices (informal use).

happy medium *n* **to find** OR **strike a happy medium** to do something in a way that is not too extreme, or that provides a balance between two different things □ *We're trying to strike a happy medium between saving money and compromising on quality.*

harangue [hə'ræŋ] ◇ *n* a long and often angry speech that somebody gives on a subject they feel strongly about, especially when they want to make people agree with them or do something they want. ◇ *vt* [troops, staff] to give a harangue to <sb>.

harass [US hə'ræs, GB 'hærəs] *vt* to trouble <sb> by repeatedly asking questions, causing problems, or making comments about sex □ *Mrs Ewart complained she was sexually harassed by her boss.*

harassed [US 'herəst, GB 'hær-] *adj* [person] who has a lot of problems and looks worried and unhappy □ *a harassed expression/reply.*

harassment [US 'herəsmənt, GB 'hær-] *n*: see **harass** □ *police/racial/sexual harassment.*

harbinger ['haːrbɪndʒər] *n* [of war, doom, a crisis] a warning or sign that something, often something unpleasant or important, is going to happen soon (literary use).

harbor US, **harbour** GB ['haːrbər] ◇ *n* an area of water on the coast, sheltered from the sea, where boats can be loaded and unloaded. ◇ *vt* **-1.** [doubt, misgiving, ambition] to have <sthg> in one's mind for a long time, espe-

cially without showing it □ *She's harbored a grudge against me since we were at school.* **-2.** [refugee, criminal] to keep <sb> secretly in one's house, especially if they are hiding from the police.

harbor master *n* the official in charge of a harbor.

hard [haːrd] ◇ *adj* **-1.** [bed, ground, surface] that is not soft and does not change its shape when something presses on or against it; [food] that is difficult to chew or bite because it is not soft enough □ *marine animals with hard shells* □ *hard candy* □ *The bread had gone hard.* **-2.** [exam, question] difficult □ *It's hard to believe.* □ *You're a hard man to please.* □ *He learned about life the hard way.* **-3.** [work, job, day] that requires effort and is tiring □ *She's intelligent and also a very hard worker.* □ *I had a very hard day at the office.* **-4.** [push, kick] that has a lot of force □ *She gave him a hard slap in the face.* **-5.** [person, comment] that shows no kindness □ *There was a hard edge to her voice.* ■ **to be hard on sb/sthg** to treat sb/sthg in a severe way □ *Don't be too hard on her, she's very young.* □ *All this walking is very hard on the feet.* **-6.** [life, time] unpleasant and difficult □ *These are hard times for the aircraft industry.* **-7.** [winter, frost] very cold and severe □ *It was a hard winter, and many of the animals died.* **-8.** [water] that contains a lot of lime and so leaves a white substance inside water pipes and kettles, and stops soap from making a lot of bubbles. **-9.** [news, fact, evidence] that is true and can be shown to be true □ *We need some hard evidence to support our claim.* **-10.** GB POLITICS **the hard left/right** the extremists in the Labour/Conservative party □ *He is facing opposition from politicians on the hard right of the party.* ◇ *adv* **-1.** [try, work] with a lot of effort □ *He ran as hard as he could.* □ *He thought hard before answering.* □ *She looked at him long and hard.* **-2.** [push, kick] with a lot of force □ *He was hit hard in the stomach.* **-3.** [rain, snow] heavily □ *Outside, it was raining hard.* **-4.** [bake, set] until it is hard □ *The glue had set hard.* **-5.** *phrases* **to be hard pushed** OR **pressed to do sthg** to be unlikely to do sthg, because of difficulty or a lack of time □ *We'll be hard pressed to finish the job by Friday.* ■ **to feel hard done by** to feel as though one has been treated unfairly □ *He always feels hard done by.*

hard-and-fast *adj* **a hard-and-fast rule** a fixed rule.

hardback ['haːrdbæk] ◇ *adj* [book, edition, copy] that has a strong hard cover. ◇ *n* a hardback book □ *Is it available in hardback?*
NOTE: Compare **paperback.**

hard-bitten *adj* [businessman, journalist] who is not kind because they have had a hard career and are determined to succeed.

hardboard ['haːrdbɔːrd] *n* a kind of board that bends slightly, made of very small pieces of wood pressed into thin sheets □ *a piece of hardboard.*

hard-boiled *adj* **-1.** [egg] that has been boiled until the yolk is hard. **-2.** [person] who does not show their feelings, especially because they have had a hard life.

hard cash *n* money in the form of bills and coins.

hard cider *n* US apple juice that has been fermented to become alcoholic.

hard copy *n* information that is printed from a computer onto paper instead of being kept on a disk.

hard-core *adj* [pornography] that shows or describes sexual acts in a detailed and unpleasant way; [magazine, video] that contains this kind of pornography.

◆ **hard core** *n* the members of a political party or a group who are the most active or who do not want anything to change □ *We have a hard core of about 200 members.*

hard court *n* a tennis court made of clay or concrete rather than grass.

hard currency *n* a kind of money that is likely to keep its value and can be exchanged between countries.

hard disk *n* the device inside a computer, that is used to store large amounts of information □ *I saved it on the hard disk.* □ *How much hard disk space does your computer have?* NOTE: Compare **floppy (disk)**.

hard drugs *npl* drugs, e.g. heroin or cocaine, that are thought to be dangerous and addictive. NOTE: Compare **soft drugs**.

harden ['hɑːrdn] ◇ *vt* -**1.** [concrete, glue] to make <sthg> become hard □ *The heat hardens the clay.* -**2.** [person] to make <sb> hard □ *His years in the army had hardened him.* -**3.** [attitude, opinion, view] to make <sthg> stronger □ *The public's attitude has been hardened by repeated cases of corruption.* ◇ *vi* -**1.** [concrete, glue] to become hard □ *The earth had dried and hardened in the sun.* -**2.** [person] to become hard □ *Her heart gradually hardened against him.* -**3.** [attitude, opinion, view] to grow stronger □ *Opposition to federalism has hardened in recent months.*

hardened ['hɑːrdnd] *adj* [person] who has experienced something for so long that it no longer has an effect on them □ *a hardened criminal* □ *She became hardened to their taunts.*

hardening ['hɑːrdnɪŋ] *n*: *see* **harden** □ *The statement reflects the hardening of US opinion on the issue.*

hard hat *n* a strong hard hat which workmen and horse riders wear to protect their heads.

hardheaded [,hɑːrd'hedəd] *adj* [person] who is practical and determined and does not allow their emotions to affect their actions □ *a hardheaded approach/decision.*

hard-hearted [-'hɑːrtəd] *adj* [person] who is not kind or sympathetic to other people and does not care about their feelings □ *How can you be so hard-hearted?*

hard-hitting [-'hɪtɪŋ] *adj* [report, account] that contains strong opinions and makes people think carefully about something □ *a hard-hitting documentary about government corruption.*

Harding ['hɑːrdɪŋ], **Warren G.** (1865–1923) US President from 1921 to 1923.

hard labor *n* a form of punishment which makes criminals do hard work, e.g. digging or building, while they are in prison □ *He was sentenced to three years' hard labor.*

hard line *n* **to take a hard line on sthg** to have a fixed opinion and way of dealing with sthg □ *He takes a hard line on under-age drinking.*

◆ **hard-line** *adj* [Communist, separatist] who has fixed and often extreme views on a subject, and is unlikely to change them □ *The USA is taking a hard-line stance on immigration.*

hard-liner *n* a person who has fixed and often extreme views, usually about politics.

hardly ['hɑːrdlɪ] *adv* -**1.** almost not □ *I hardly care what happens now.* □ *You can hardly expect him to come now, can you?* ■ **hardly ever/anything** almost never/nothing □ *I hardly ever go to the movies.* □ *I've hardly eaten a thing all day.* -**2.** a word used to show that one thing happens very soon after another, often in an unexpected way □ *We'd hardly left the theater when it started to snow.*

hardness ['hɑːrdnəs] *n* [of water, a bed, person] *see* **hard.**

hard-nosed [-'nouzd] *adj* [businessman, approach] that is practical, determined, and not kind to other people.

hard sell *n* **to give sb the hard sell** to try to make sb buy something by putting a lot of pressure on them.

hardship ['hɑːrdʃɪp] *n* a difficult or unpleasant situation that is often caused by a lack of money □ *The family suffered financial hardship.*

hard shoulder *n* the area at the edge of a highway where drivers can stop in an emergency □ *'Please use hard shoulder.'*

hard up *adj* (informal use) **to be hard up** to have very little money. ■ **to be hard up for sthg** to be in need of sthg □ *We're always hard up for volunteers.*

hardware ['hɑːrdweər] *n* -**1.** a collective term for tools or equipment, e.g. saucepans, hammers, or nails, sold for use in the home and garden. -**2.** COMPUTING the machinery that is part of a computer, rather than the programs the computer can operate. NOTE: Compare **software.**

hardware store *n* US a store where hardware for the home is sold.

hardwearing [,hɑːrd'weərɪŋ] *adj* GB [shoes, clothes] that can last a long time, even if they are used often □ *a hardwearing carpet.*

hardwood ['hɑːrdwʊd] *n* hard, strong, heavy wood, e.g. teak or mahogany, that is used to make good-quality furniture that will last a long time □ *a hardwood table.*

hardworking [,hɑːrd'wɜːrkɪŋ] *adj* [pupil, employee] who works hard □ *Laura is a diligent and hardworking student.*

hardy ['hɑːrdɪ] (*compar* **hardier**, *superl* **hardiest**) *adj* -**1.** [person, animal] that is strong and healthy, even under difficult conditions, e.g. lack of food, sleep, or warmth □ *Even the har-*

diest of climbers would have found this difficult. **-2.** [plant] that can live outside during the winter □ *a hardy annual.*

hare [heəʳ] ◇ *n* an animal like a large rabbit that has long ears and powerful back legs and can run very fast. ◇ *vi* GB **to hare off** to move away very quickly.

harebell ['heəʳbel] *n* a plant with thin stems and blue flowers that are shaped like bells.

harebrained ['heəʳbreɪnd] *adj* [person, scheme, idea] silly and impractical □ *They've got some harebrained scheme about going off to Morocco for the weekend.*

harelip [ˌheəʳ'lɪp] *n* a break in the top lip, which some babies are born with, and which can usually be repaired by an operation.

harem [US 'hærəm, GB hɑːˈriːm] *n* the part of a Muslim house where the women live and which only certain men are allowed to enter; the women who live in this place.

haricot (bean) [US 'herɪkoʊ-, GB 'hærɪ-] *n* a small white bean, usually sold in a dried form, that can be cooked and eaten.

hark [hɑːʳk] *vi* **to hark back to sthg** [to one's schooldays, youth] to talk or think about sthg which happened in the past; [to an era, style] to be similar to sthg from the past □ *I was harking back to my time in the army.* □ *The movie harks back to the days of the great Hollywood musicals.*

Harlem ['hɑːʳləm] an area of northeastern Manhattan, New York City, with a large Black and Hispanic community.

harlequin ['hɑːʳləkwɪn] *n* in the past, a humorous character in plays who usually wore clothes with a diamond pattern in many colors and a black mask.

Harley Street ['hɑːʳlɪ-] a street in central London where there are many expensive private doctors and medical clinics □ *a Harley Street doctor/clinic.*

harm [hɑːʳm] ◇ *n* [to a person, animal] physical or psychological damage; [to a plant, sb's reputation, clothes] damage. ■ **to do harm to sb/ sthg, to do sb/sthg harm** to affect sb/sthg badly □ *It could do you more harm than good.* □ *No harm done.* ■ **to mean no harm** to have no intention of hurting somebody or damaging something because of what one does □ *Ignore his teasing, he means no harm by it.* ■ **there's no harm in it** it will not hurt anybody or cause any damage □ *There's no harm in having a look.* □ *Where's the harm in that?* ■ **to be out of harm's way** [person, animal, object] to be safe □ *I've put the glass stuff out of harm's way for the party.* ■ **to come to no harm** to suffer no injury during an event or experience □ *Do what I say and you won't come to any harm.* ◇ *vt* [person, animal] to hurt <sb/sthg> physically or psychologically; [reputation, clothes] to damage <sthg> □ *I would never want to harm you/our relationship.* □ *It remains to be seen whether their comments will harm the peace process.*

harmful ['hɑːʳmfl] *adj* [substance, drug, effect] that can cause physical or psychological

harm □ *Drinking and smoking during pregnancy are harmful to your baby.*

harmless ['hɑːʳmləs] *adj* [animal, person, substance] that does not cause harm □ *It was just harmless fun.*

harmlessly ['hɑːʳmləslɪ] *adv* [fall, explode] without causing harm □ *The bomb exploded harmlessly in the ocean.*

harmonic [hɑːˈʳmɒnɪk] *adj* [quality, effect] that is caused by two or more notes being played or sung together to make a pleasant sound.

harmonica [hɑːˈʳmɒnɪkə] *n* a small musical instrument that is moved from side to side across one's lips and blown or sucked to make a sound.

harmonious [hɑːˈʳmoʊnjəs] *adj* **-1.** [relationship, meeting] peaceful and pleasant □ *policies for a more caring harmonious society.* **-2.** MUSIC [notes, sounds] that sound pleasant when heard together □ *a very harmonious tune.* **-3.** [effect, building, layout] that is made up of parts that fit together well to make something that looks good or works □ *The design of the house is a harmonious blend of old and new.*

harmonium [hɑːˈʳmoʊnjəm] (*pl* **harmoniums**) *n* a musical instrument that has keys and pedals like a piano and is worked by air that is pumped through it.

harmonize, -ise ['hɑːʳmənaɪz] ◇ *vt* [policies, styles, approaches] to join <two or more things> so that they go well together □ *Inflation rates must be harmonized before economic integration can occur.* ◇ *vi* **-1.** [sounds, colors, methods] to go well together. ■ **to harmonize with sthg** to go well with sthg □ *The new gallery was designed to harmonize with the surrounding buildings.* **-2.** MUSIC to sing in harmony with a piece of music.

harmony ['hɑːʳmənɪ] (*pl* **harmonies**) *n* **-1.** [between people, animals, organizations] a state of peaceful agreement □ *racial harmony* □ *The two peoples had lived together in harmony for generations.* ■ **to be in harmony with sthg** to have the same qualities or ideas as sthg □ *Her novels were not in harmony with the attitudes of her time.* **-2.** MUSIC notes sung or played together to make a pleasant sound □ *two voices singing in harmony.* **-3.** [of proportions, colors, a building] the pleasant effect produced by two or more things, or the parts of something, which go together well to make a single thing □ *a certain lack of harmony in the design of the building.*

harness ['hɑːʳnəs] ◇ *n* **-1.** [for a horse] the pieces of leather and metal put on a horse in order to control it or fasten it to a vehicle. **-2.** [for a person, child] the set of bands used to attach somebody to a seat, parachute etc □ *a safety harness* □ *a children's harness.* ◇ *vt* **-1.** to attach a harness or vehicle to <a horse>. **-2.** [energy, power, skills] to make good practical use of <sthg> □ *Man is now able to harness the power of the sun and the winds.*

harp [hɑːʳp] *n* a large musical instrument with strings which run from the top to the bottom of a frame and which are plucked to make a sound.

◆ **harp on** *vi* **to harp on about sthg** to talk about sthg very often, in an annoying way □ *For goodness sake, stop harping on about it!*

harpist ['hɑːrpəst] *n* a person who plays the harp.

harpoon [hɑːrˈpuːn] ◇ *n* a large spear attached to a rope, used to kill large creatures that live in the sea. ◇ *vt* [whale, shark] to fire or push a harpoon into <an animal>.

harpsichord ['hɑːrpsɪkɔːrd] *n* a musical instrument that was an early form of the piano and that was popular in the 17th and 18th centuries.

harrowing [US 'heroʊɪŋ, GB 'hær-] *adj* [experience, report, story] that is very unpleasant and upsetting because somebody involved suffers □ *We had a pretty harrowing trip here.*

harry [US 'heri, GB 'hærɪ] (*pt* & *pp* **harried**) *vt* **-1.** [person] to put pressure on <sb> so that they become annoyed or anxious □ *The landlord was harrying them for the rent.* **-2.** MILITARY [enemy, troops] to keep attacking <a group of soldiers> □ *Fighter planes continually harried supply lines.*

harsh [hɑːrʃ] *adj* **-1.** [life, existence, reality] severe and unpleasant; [punishment, criticism, person, measures] unfairly severe □ *I think you're being too harsh on him.* **-2.** [weather, conditions] that is unpleasant and difficult to deal with □ *Very few animals can survive in this harsh climate.* **-3.** [cry, breathing, voice] that is unpleasant to hear because it is loud, forced, or rough □ *an ugly harsh laugh.* **-4.** [color, contrast, light] that is very strong and unpleasant to the eyes □ *The harsh sunlight made her blink.* **-5.** [terrain] extreme and difficult to travel across or live in. **-6.** [taste, flavor, smell] strong and unpleasant □ *It tasted bitter and harsh.*

harshly ['hɑːrʃlɪ] *adv* [punish, cry, shine] *see* **harsh** □ *We mustn't judge her too harshly.*

harshness ['hɑːrʃnəs] *n*: *see* **harsh** □ *Her voice had lost something of its harshness.* □ *the harshness of an Arctic winter.*

harvest ['hɑːrvɪst] ◇ *n* **-1.** the act of picking crops at the end of a growing season □ *at harvest time.* **-2.** the crops that have been picked at the end of a particular growing season □ *a good/bad harvest.* ◇ *vt* [corn, wheat, grapes] to pick <all of a crop> and put it somewhere safe □ *The fruit is harvested in late summer.*

harvest festival *n* a Christian celebration that takes place in churches and some schools to thank God for the harvest.

has [*stressed* hæz, *unstressed* həz] *vb* → **have**.

has-been *n* a person or thing that is no longer as popular or successful as they were in the past (informal and disapproving use) □ *Face it, Gloria, you're a has-been!*

hash [hæʃ] *n* **-1.** COOKING small pieces of cooked meat served in a sauce □ *beef hash.* **-2.** **to make a hash of sthg** to do sthg badly and unsuccessfully (informal use) □ *I'm sorry, I*

seem to have made a real hash of things. **-3.** hashish (informal use).

hash browns *npl* potatoes cut into small pieces, shaped into round pieces, and fried in oil until they are brown.

hashish ['hæʃiːʃ] *n* a drug, made from the leaves of the cannabis plant, which is smoked and is illegal in many countries.

hasn't ['hæznt] = **has not**.

hassle ['hæsl] (informal use) ◇ *n* something that is annoying or difficult and causes a lot of extra work □ *They gave us a lot of hassle at customs.* ◇ *vt* to annoy <sb>, especially by trying to make them do something □ *She's always hassling me to stop smoking.*

haste [heɪst] *n* **-1.** rush. ■ **to do sthg in haste** to do sthg quickly, often with bad results □ *In his haste to leave, he dropped the precious envelope on the ground.* **-2.** speed. ■ **to make haste** to hurry (old-fashioned use).

hasten ['heɪsn] (formal use) ◇ *vt* [end, downfall, development] to make <sthg> happen more quickly □ *Her drinking served merely to hasten her death.* ◇ *vi* to hurry □ *They hastened to close the windows.* □ *It wasn't me, I hasten to add.*

hastily ['heɪstəlɪ] *adv* **-1.** [discuss, decide] too quickly, so that something may go wrong later □ *The bridge was rather hastily built.* **-2.** [eat, dress, wash] quickly □ *"At least, so I've heard," he added hastily.*

hasty ['heɪstɪ] (*compar* **hastier**, *superl* **hastiest**) *adj* **-1.** [decision, judgment] that is made too quickly and often has bad results; [person] who does something too quickly, without considering something carefully □ *We mustn't be too hasty.* **-2.** [meal, letter] that is eaten, written etc quickly because there is not much time □ *Hasty preparations were being made for the visit.*

hat [hæt] *n* an item of clothing that is worn on one's head and often has a section around the bottom that sticks outward. ■ **keep it under your hat** keep it a secret (informal use). ■ **to be talking through one's hat** to be talking nonsense (informal use). ■ **to be old hat** to be so well-known that it has become boring and old-fashioned (informal use) □ *Violence on TV? Oh, come on now, that's old hat!*

hatbox ['hætbɒks] *n* a round box for carrying and storing a hat.

hatch [hætʃ] ◇ *vt* **-1.** [bird] to sit on <an egg> until it breaks open and a baby bird comes out □ *The mother sits on the eggs to hatch her chicks.* **-2.** FARMING to make <a baby bird> come out of its shell at the right time □ *The eggs are hatched in an incubator.* **-3.** [person] to make <a plan, plot> etc in secret □ *They're hatching some kind of plot, I can tell.* ◇ *vi* [chick, animal, insect] to come out of an egg; [egg] to be broken open when a baby bird, animal, or insect is born. ◇ *n* an opening in a wall, usually between the kitchen and the dining room, through which food and dishes are passed □ *a serving hatch.*

hatchback ['hætʃbæk] *n* a car with an extra door at the back which opens upwards.

hatchet ['hætʃət] *n* a small ax with a short handle, used for chopping wood. ■ **to bury the hatchet** to become friendly again after a quarrel, especially one a long time ago □ *What do you say we bury the hatchet and be friends again?*

hatchet job *n* **to do a hatchet job on sb/sthg** to say or write very cruel things about sb/sthg (informal use).

hatchway ['hætʃweɪ] *n* an opening in a wall, floor, or ceiling, especially on a ship, through which people and things can pass.

hate [heɪt] ◇ *n* a feeling of very strong dislike □ *You could hear the hate in his voice.* ◇ *vt* **-1.** [person, violence, rudeness] to dislike <sb/sthg> very much □ *I hate you!* □ *He's the country's most hated man.* **-2.** [food, activity, situation] to find <sthg> unpleasant and undesirable □ *I hate going to the dentist's.* □ *I hate to tell you, but you forgot to save that file.* □ *She hates it when her parents argue.*

hateful ['heɪtfl] *adj* [person, job, remark] very unpleasant □ *That was a hateful thing to say.*

hate mail *n* unkind letters sent to somebody by a person who dislikes them □ *We've been receiving hate mail again.*

hatred ['heɪtrəd] *n* a feeling of very strong dislike □ *He had an intense hatred of the police.* □ *a feeling of hatred.*

hat trick *n* SPORT [in soccer, hockey] three goals scored by one person in one game.

haughty ['hɔːtɪ] (*compar* **haughtier**, *superl* **haughtiest**) *adj* [person] who shows a feeling of superiority and a low opinion of other people □ *a haughty tone of voice.*

haul [hɔːl] ◇ *n* **-1.** an amount of stolen goods □ *The gang got away with a huge haul of stolen jewels.* **-2. a long haul** a long difficult trip or process □ *It was a long haul up to the summit.* □ *the long haul towards democracy.* ◇ *vt* **-1.** [rope, bag, log] to move <sthg> with a lot of effort in a particular direction by pulling it, lifting it etc □ *She hauled the suitcase into the car.* □ *Ben hauled himself to his feet.* **-2.** [goods] to transport <sthg> by truck over a long distance.

haulage ['hɔːlɪdʒ] *n* the business, activity, or cost of transporting goods by road □ *haulage costs.*

haulage contractor *n* a person or company that transports goods by road.

hauler ['hɔːlr] US, **haulier** ['hɔːlɪəʳ] GB *n* **-1.** a business that transports goods by truck; a person who runs this kind of business □ *a firm of road haulers.* **-2.** a driver who transports goods by truck.

haunch [hɔːntʃ] *n* the hip, buttock, and top part of the leg on one side of a person's or animal's body.

haunt [hɔːnt] ◇ *n* a place that somebody visits often □ *The club was one of his favorite haunts.* ◇ *vt* **-1.** [ghost] to visit <a person or place> in the form of a ghost □ *He claimed that his father had come back to haunt him.* **-2.** [memory, fear] to return often to the thoughts of <sb> □ *He is haunted by the past.*

haunted ['hɔːntəd] *adj* **-1.** [house, castle] where a ghost or ghosts can be seen or heard □ *They say this house is haunted.* **-2.** [look, expression] worried □ *Brian developed a kind of permanently haunted look.*

haunting ['hɔːntɪŋ] *adj* [tune, image, memory] that is so beautiful or sad that one remembers it for a long time □ *the haunting melody of the solo violin.*

Havana [hə'vænə] the capital of Cuba and its largest city. POPULATION: 1,925,000.

have [hæv] (*pt & pp* **had**) ◇ *aux vb* **-1.** used to form the past tenses of verbs □ *I have been ill.* □ *We had gone to bed early that evening.* □ *They will have forgotten all about it by next week.* □ *If I'd known, I wouldn't have said anything.* **-2.** used in question tags □ *She hasn't left yet, has she?* □ *"You've told him, haven't you?" — "Yes, I have."*

◇ *vt* **-1.** used to describe things or qualities that are owned by somebody, or are part of their appearance, way of life etc □ *They have a lot of friends/money.* □ *He had dark hair and brown eyes.* □ *We don't have a car/dishwasher.* **-2. to have a swim/shower/nap** to swim/shower/nap (used to describe actions) □ *Let's not have an argument about it.* □ *Why don't we have a party?* ■ **to have a sandwich/beer** to eat a sandwich/drink a beer (used instead of more specific verbs) □ *Let's have something to eat!* **-3. to have cancer/the flu** to be ill with cancer/the flu □ *I have a terrible headache.* **-4. to have a baby** to give birth to a baby. ■ **to be having a baby** to be pregnant. **-5.** to be sent or told <sthg> □ *Have you had any news yet?* □ *I had a phone call from John.* **-6. to have sthg done** to employ somebody to do sthg for one □ *I'm having the outside of the house painted.* □ *I have my hair cut once a month.* **-7. I had my car stolen** my car was stolen (used to describe something unpleasant that happens to one). **-8. to have sthg to do** to have sthg that must be done or that one is responsible for □ *We have a deadline to meet.* □ *She had a large family to feed.* □ *I'll come with you. I don't have anything to do today.* **-9. it has to do with money** it involves money □ *All this has nothing to do with you.* **-10.** *phrases* **you've been had!** you have been cheated or tricked. ■ **it's had it** [car, machine, dress] it is too old or worn-out to be usable □ *These shoes have really had it.* ■ **I won't have it!** I won't allow it □ *I won't have you going out dressed like that!* ■ **to have it in for sb** to dislike sb and try to find ways to treat them badly □ *He really has it in for you!*

◇ *modal vb* **to have to do sthg** to be forced to do sthg because of reasons one cannot control □ *Did you have to wait long?* □ *I might have to leave work early today.* ■ **he doesn't have to come** it is not necessary for him to come □ *I told him I'd have to think about it.*

◆ **haves** *npl* **the haves and the have-nots** the rich and the poor people in society.

◆ **have on** *vt sep* **-1. to have sthg on** [dress, shoes] to be wearing sthg □ *Don't come in, I have nothing on!* □ *She had on a pair of gold ear-*

rings. -2. **to have a lot on/nothing on** to be busy/not busy □ *I don't have much on this weekend, so why not come around for a meal?* -3. **you're having me on!** you're teasing me! (informal use).

◆ **have out** *vt sep* -1. **to have one's tonsils/ appendix out** to have one's tonsils/appendix taken out of one's body by a doctor because they are making one ill □ *Have you had your wisdom teeth out?* -2. **to have it out with sb** to have a frank and thorough discussion with sb in order to end a disagreement or misunderstanding that has existed □ *I'm determined to have it out with him once and for all.*

haven ['heɪvn] *n* a peaceful and safe place □ *The refugees were just looking for some kind of haven over the border.*

haven't ['hævnt] = **have not.**

haversack ['hævərsæk] *n* GB a canvas bag, usually carried over one shoulder by a hiker, soldier etc.

havoc ['hævək] *n* disorder, confusion, and damage □ *There was havoc as everybody stampeded for the doors.* □ *scenes of sheer havoc.* ■ **to play havoc with sthg** to cause a lot of problems and confusion for sthg □ *The weather is playing havoc with flight departures again.*

Hawaii [hə'waɪiː] a state of the USA consisting of a group of islands in the central Pacific Ocean. ABBREVIATION: HI. SIZE: 16,600 sq kms. POPULATION: 1,108,229 (*Hawaiians*). CAPITAL: Honolulu.

Hawaiian [hə'waɪən] *n* & *adj:* see **Hawaii**.

hawk [hɔːk] ◇ *n* -1. one of several types of large birds of prey with very good eyesight. ■ **to watch sb like a hawk** to watch sb very carefully □ *You have to watch those kids like a hawk!* -2. POLITICS a person who supports the use of force when dealing with other countries, especially in order to settle disputes □ *the hawks in the Pentagon.* ◇ *vt* to try to sell <sthg> by offering it to different people, e.g. in the street or by visiting their homes.

hawker ['hɔːkər] *n* a person who stands in the street or goes from house to house hawking goods.

Hawksmoor ['hɔːksmʊər], **Nicholas** (1661–1736) a British architect who designed many churches in London.

hawthorn ['hɔːθɔːrn] *n* a small tree with red or white flowers, thorns, and red berries.

Hawthorne ['hɔːθɔːrn], **Nathaniel** (1804–1864) a US writer of novels and short stories. His work includes *The Scarlet Letter* and *The House of the Seven Gables.*

hay [heɪ] *n* grass that has been cut and dried to be used for feeding animals □ *a bale of hay.* ■ **to make hay while the sun shines** to enjoy or take advantage of a situation as much as possible before it ends.

hay fever *n* a medical condition caused by an allergy to pollen that causes irritation to the eyes, nose, and throat, and makes people sneeze a lot.

haymaking ['heɪmeɪkɪŋ] *n* the process of cut-

ting and drying grass to make hay □ *the hay-making season.*

haystack ['heɪstæk] *n* a large pile of cut hay.

haywire ['heɪwaɪər] *adj* **to go haywire** [plan, machine, system] to become disordered, confused, or out of control □ *Suddenly the dials went haywire.*

hazard ['hæzərd] ◇ *n* something that could be dangerous to somebody or something □ *The wreck is* OR *poses a hazard to other ships.* □ *a health hazard.* ◇ *vt* -1. to put <sb's life, health, reputation> etc in a situation that might be dangerous or harmful. -2. **to hazard a guess** to make a guess □ *If I were to hazard a guess, I'd say there were 60 of them.*

hazardous ['hæzərdəs] *adj* [venture, waste] dangerous.

hazard (warning) lights *npl* the indicators on a motor vehicle when they are all operated at the same time to warn other road users of a problem such as a breakdown.

haze [heɪz] *n* -1. air that is difficult to see through because of the effects of heat, smoke, or mist □ *a heat haze.* -2. **to be in a haze** [person, mind] to be confused because one's thoughts are not clear.

hazel ['heɪzl] ◇ *adj* [eyes] green brown in color. ◇ *n* a small tree that produces hazelnuts.

hazelnut ['heɪzlnʌt] *n* a small round nut that can be eaten.

hazy ['heɪzɪ] (*compar* **hazier**, *superl* **haziest**) *adj* -1. [sky, weather, view] that is caused by haze □ *The light's very hazy today.* -2. [understanding, memory, facts] that is not very clear and not completely correct □ *I'm a bit hazy about the details, though.*

H-bomb *n abbr of* **hydrogen bomb.**

h & c *abbr of* **hot and cold (water).**

he [hiː] ◇ *pron* -1. (used as the subject of a verb) the man, boy, or male animal that has just been mentioned, seen etc □ *"I'm looking for Kevin." — "He's over there, talking to Jane."* -2. used in statements where no specific person has been identified □ *A parent can only do what he thinks is right.* ◇ *n* a male animal or baby □ *Is it a he or a she?*

he- *prefix* added to words to refer to the male of a particular type of animal □ *a he-goat.*

HE -1. *abbr of* **high explosive.** -2. *abbr of* **His (or Her) Excellency.**

head [hed] ◇ *n* -1. [of a person, animal] the top part of the body that includes the eyes, ears, nose, mouth, brain etc □ *She turned/nodded her head.* □ *I bumped my head on the door.* ■ OR **per head** for each person □ *Tickets cost $50 a head.* ■ **to say sthg off the top of one's head** to say sthg without thinking about it first and without being sure it is correct □ *Just off the top of my head, I'd say we'd need around $10,000.* ■ **to bite** OR **snap sb's head off** to speak very angrily to sb, especially when they do not expect it or when there is no strong reason for it (informal use) □ *There's no need to bite my head off, I was only asking.* ■ **to laugh/sing/shout one's head off** to laugh/sing/ shout in a very noisy and energetic way (informal use). ■ **to be banging one's head against a brick wall** to keep trying to do something but without success, because it is impossible (informal use) □ *I feel as if I'm just banging my head against a brick wall.* ■ **I couldn't make head or tail of it** I couldn't understand it at all. ■ **on your (own) head be it** you will have to take all the responsibility for it □ *You can go, but on your own head be it.* -2. a person's mind or their ability to use their brain for a particular kind of work □ *Don't put silly ideas into his head.* □ *I can't get that tune out of my head.* □ *She has a good head for figures/business.* □ *Use your head.* ■ **to have a head for heights** to be able to stay up in a high place or position without feeling dizzy, falling etc. ■ **to be out of one's head** US, **to be off one's head** GB to be crazy or foolish (informal use) □ *You must be out of your head to want to go there now!* ■ **we put our heads together** we exchanged opinions and information, and thought of a plan □ *Why don't we put our heads together and come up with a plan?* ■ **to go to one's head** [alcohol] to make one feel drunk; [success, praise] to make one feel too proud of oneself □ *I think all this media attention has gone to his head.* ■ **to keep one's head** to stay calm and able to think clearly, especially in a dangerous situation □ *We need somebody who is able to keep their head in a stressful situation.* ■ **to lose one's head** to panic or stop thinking clearly □ *He just lost his head and started screaming.* ■ **to be soft in the head** to be stupid or crazy (informal use) □ *Have you gone soft in the head or something?* -3. [of a nail, page, bed] the top part of something □ *My name appeared at the head of their list.* □ *the head of a hammer* □ *a screw head.* -4. [of a flower, cabbage] the top part where the petals or leaves grow □ *a flower head.* -5. [of a company, department, family] the person who is in charge of an organized group of people □ *Fifteen heads of government attended the meeting.* -6. ELECTRONICS a device in a tape recorder, video recorder, computer etc, that records signals on tape or disk, or plays them back □ *tape heads.* -7. GB EDUCATION = **head teacher.** -8. *phrase* **to come to a head** [problem, dispute, issue] to come to a point when something urgent has to be done □ *Matters came to a head last June.*

◇ *vt* **-1.** [procession, convoy] to be at the front of <sthg> □ *Members of the family headed the march.* **-2.** [delegation, company, organization] to be officially in charge of <sthg> □ *the UN troops, headed by General Janvier.* **-3.** [list, group] to be the first in <sthg> □ *In the 1970s, Lawson headed the FBI's "most wanted" list.* **-4.** SPORT [in soccer] to hit <a ball> with one's head.

◇ *vi* to move in a particular direction □ *We gave up and headed home.* □ *The ship was heading due north* □ *Where are you headed? Maybe I can give you a ride.*

◆ **heads** *npl* the side of a coin that has an image of a head on it. ■ **heads or tails?** a phrase used by people when tossing a coin to decide something. The aim is to guess which side of the coin will face upward when it lands.

◆ **head for** *vt fus* **-1. to head for a place** to go towards a place □ *I'm heading for Toronto.* **-2. to be heading for sthg** [for trouble, victory] to behave or happen in a way that makes sthg very likely □ *I'm heading for financial ruin at this rate.*

◆ **head off** ◇ *vt sep* **-1. to head off sb/sthg** [person, vehicle] to make sb/sthg change direction by moving toward or in front of it □ *The police headed him off on Galena Road.* **-2.** to do something to stop <a disaster, rebellion> etc from happening. ◇ *vi* [person] to leave a place □ *The car headed off east.*

headache ['hedeɪk] *n* **-1.** a pain in the head □ *I have a headache.* **-2.** an annoying problem (informal use) □ *Publication of the details would present a big headache for the party in power.*

headband ['hedbænd] *n* a strip of fabric that one wears across one's forehead to keep one's hair or sweat out of one's eyes.

headboard ['hedbɔːʳd] *n* an upright board at the top end of a bed.

head boy *n* GB EDUCATION a boy pupil chosen to lead the prefects and represent the school at public events.

head cold *n* a cold that causes headaches and a blocked or runny nose.

head count *n* the act or process of counting how many people are present in a particular place □ *I did a quick head count when everybody was back on the bus.*

headdress ['heddres] *n* a piece of clothing that is worn on the head as a decoration, especially at important ceremonies.

header ['hedəʳ] *n* **-1.** SPORT [in soccer] the act of heading a ball. **-2.** COMPUTING information at the beginning of a list of data that is connected with the rest of the data.

headfirst [hed'fɜːʳst] *adv* [fall, dive] with the rest of the body following the head □ *He crashed and plunged headfirst into the ditch.*

headgear ['hedgɪəʳ] *n* a collective term for things that are worn on one's head, e.g. hats, caps, or scarves □ *Protective headgear should be worn by all cyclists.*

head girl *n* GB EDUCATION a girl pupil chosen to lead the prefects and represent the school at public events.

headhunt ['hedhʌnt] *vt* to try to persuade <sb> to leave their job and take another one, usually by offering more money or status.

headhunter ['hedhʌntəʳ] *n* a person whose job is to headhunt people for particular jobs.

heading ['hedɪŋ] *n* the title given at the top of a piece of writing, e.g. of a report, chapter, or paragraph □ *The information appeared under the heading "miscellaneous".*

headlamp ['hedlæmp] *n* GB = **headlight.**

headland ['hedlənd] *n* a narrow piece of land that sticks out into the sea.

headlight ['hedlaɪt] *n* a powerful light at the

front of a car, truck, motorcycle etc □ *'Dip your headlights.'*

headline ['hedlaɪn] *n* -1. [in a newspaper] the title of a newspaper article printed in large letters above it □ *I only saw the headline.* -2. TV & RADIO the most important details of one of the main news stories, often read at the beginning of a news program □ *Here are today's headlines.* □ *the news headlines.* -3. *phrase* **to hit the headlines** [person, scandal] to be the subject of one of the main news stories □ *Unemployment has hit the headlines again.*

headlong ['hedlɒŋ] ◇ *adv* -1. [run, rush] very quickly and out of control □ *The truck hurtled headlong down the road.* -2. **to rush headlong into sthg** to become involved in sthg quickly and without thinking about what one is doing □ *I don't want to rush headlong into marriage.* -3. [fall, dive] headfirst □ *He was thrown headlong into a bush.* ◇ *adj* [rush, dash] that one does without thinking about what one is doing □ *The crowd made a headlong dash for the exit.*

headmaster [US ˌhed'mæstr, GB -'mɑːstə] *n* the male teacher who runs a school.

headmistress [ˌhed'mɪstrəs] *n* the female teacher who runs a school.

head office *n* GB the main office of a business or organization where important decisions are made; the people who work in this office.

head of state (*pl* **heads of state**) *n* a person who is the official leader of a country □ *The President met with Commonwealth heads of state.*

head-on ◇ *adj* -1. [collision, crash] in which the front parts of two vehicles hit each other □ *The car was involved in a head-on collision with a truck.* -2. [confrontation, disagreement] that is direct and in which people are not willing to compromise □ *The stage is set for a head-on clash between the President and Congress.* ◇ *adv* [meet, collide] *The car drove head-on into a lamp-post.* □ *Management confronted the union head-on.*

headphones ['hedfoʊnz] *npl* small loudspeakers that fit over the ears, are usually held in place by a band across the head, and are used for listening to recorded sounds in private, e.g. from a personal stereo □ *a pair of headphones* □ *She was wearing headphones.*

headquarters [ˌhed'kwɔːrtərz] *npl* [of a company, army, the police] the main office, building etc where the leaders of an organization work and important decisions are made □ *Their headquarters are in Bonn.* □ *the UN headquarters.*

headrest ['hedrest] *n* the soft part at the top of a seat, usually in a car, that can be used for resting the back of one's head on.

headroom ['hedruːm] *n* -1. [below a bridge, barrier] the amount of space between the top of a vehicle and something it needs to pass under □ *'Max Headroom: 8 ft.'* -2. [in a car] the amount of space above somebody's head □ *There's not much headroom in here.*

headscarf ['hedskɑːrf] (*pl* **headscarves** [-skɑːrvz]

OR **headscarfs**) *n* a scarf worn on the head, usually by women.

headset ['hedset] *n* a pair of headphones, especially one that has a microphone attached.

headship ['hedʃɪp] *n* GB the position held by the head of an organization, especially the head teacher of a school.

headstand ['hedstænd] *n* the act of balancing on one's head and hands, with one's feet in the air.

head start *n* an important advantage that somebody has in a situation such as a race, competition etc □ *Being bilingual gives her a head start on* OR *over the other applicants.*

headstone ['hedstoʊn] *n* the stone at the end of a grave that has the dead person's name on it.

headstrong ['hedstrɒŋ] *adj* [person] who is determined and unwilling to listen to other people's advice □ *Sarah can be extremely headstrong at times.*

head teacher *n* GB the teacher who runs a school.

head waiter *n* the waiter who is in charge of the other waiters in a restaurant.

headway ['hedweɪ] *n* **to make headway** [project, person] to make progress, often after there have been a lot of problems □ *Talks are finally beginning to make headway.*

headwind ['hedwɪnd] *n* a wind that is blowing in the opposite direction to the one somebody is moving in.

headword ['hedwɜːrd] *n* in a dictionary, a word or short group of words that is followed by a definition or a translation, and sometimes by an example, to show its meaning.

heady ['hedɪ] (*compar* **headier**, *superl* **headiest**) *adj* -1. [time, atmosphere, experience] that makes one feel very excited and hopeful □ *After the heady days of last August, the government now has to produce results.* -2. [perfume, drink] that is very strong and makes one feel drunk or dizzy □ *a heady wine.*

heal [hiːl] ◇ *vt* -1. [person, wound] to make <sb/sthg> healthy again □ *This man claims to be able to heal the sick.* -2. [damage, discord] to repair <sthg> □ *Is Jospin the man to heal the Party's divisions?* ◇ *vi* [wound, broken bone] *The emotional scars will take even longer to heal.*

♦ **heal up** *vi* [wound, injury] = **heal**.

healing ['hiːlɪŋ] ◇ *adj* [power, treatment] that can heal a person or wound □ *The herb has many healing properties.* ◇ *n* [of a person, wound] *see* **heal** □ *The healing process will take time.*

health [helθ] *n* -1. [of a person] the condition of a person's body □ *Smoking is bad for your health.* □ *The prisoners are all in good/poor health.* ■ **the Department of Health and Human Services** the US government department responsible for the welfare system. ■ **the Department of Health** the British government department responsible for the National Health Service. ■ **to drink to sb's health** to raise one's glass, say that one hopes sb continues to have good health, and then drink.

-2. [of an economy, organization, industry] the state of being successful and working well □ *measures to improve the health of the economy.*

health care *n* the system of hospitals, doctors, pharmacies etc that exist in a particular place □ *healthcare workers* □ *healthcare plan* □ *France has excellent health care.*

health center *n* a place where a group of doctors provide medical treatment and advice for the people of a particular area.

health club *n* a private club where people go to exercise.

health-conscious *adj* [person] who tries to have good health by exercising, eating healthy food, not smoking etc.

health farm *n* a place where people pay to stay and are encouraged to become more healthy, especially by dieting and exercising.

health food *n* food that is thought to be good for one's health, e.g. because it has more fiber or fewer artificial additives than most normal food.

health food store *n* a store that sells health food.

health hazard *n* something such as pollution that might harm people's health.

health insurance *n* a form of insurance that is used to pay for medical treatment.

health service *n* the combined social services in a country that are concerned with people's health.

health visitor *n* GB a nurse whose job is to visit people at home, e.g. people with babies, or people who are handicapped or elderly, to give help and advice on matters concerning their health.

healthy ['helθɪ] (*compar* **healthier,** *superl* **healthiest**) *adj* **-1.** [person, animal, plant] that is in good health □ *She was looking tanned and healthy.* **-2.** [appetite, skin, color] that shows that somebody is in good health. **-3.** [climate, food, lifestyle] that is good for one's health □ *a healthy diet* □ *healthy red cheeks* □ *It's not healthy to eat too much fat.* **-4.** [economy, organization, industry] that is successful and works well □ *Our business is healthy again.* **-5.** [profit, amount, increase] that is large and pleasing □ *He made a healthy profit on the deal.* **-6.** [attitude, respect, skepticism] that is natural and sensible □ *I've always had a healthy mistrust of political extremists like him.*

heap [hiːp] ◇ *n* an untidy pile □ *a heap of rubble/clothes* □ *His books lay in a heap on the floor.* □ *a compost heap.* ■ **to fall down** OR **collapse in a heap** [person] to fall down with a lot of force and not move □ *Simon came in and just collapsed in a heap on the floor.* ◇ *vt* **-1.** [rubbish, coal] to make a heap of <sthg> □ *He heaped food on* OR *onto his plate.* **-2.** **to heap praise/scorn etc on sb** to praise/scorn etc sb a lot.

◆ **heaps** *npl* **heaps of sthg** [of money, time] a large amount of sthg (informal use) □ *He has heaps of experience.*

hear [hɪəʳ] (*pt* & *pp* **heard** [hɜːʳd]) ◇ *vt* **-1.** [voice, person, sound] to become aware of, recognize, or understand <sb/sthg> through one's ears □ *Can you hear me?* □ *I heard that song again.* **-2.** [news, result, rumor] to find <sthg> out by being told by somebody else or from the radio or television □ *I heard (that) he made $12 million on the deal.* **-3.** LAW [case, evidence] to listen to <sthg> in order to make an official decision □ *The court will now hear the case for the prosecution.*

◇ *vi* **-1.** to become aware of, recognize, or understand sounds through one's ears □ *I couldn't hear very well.* **-2.** **to hear about sthg** to find out about sthg, especially because people are talking about it; to get news about sthg □ *Did you hear about the takeover bid?* □ *Have you heard about your interview yet?* ■ **to hear from sb** to be contacted by sb, e.g. by letter or telephone □ *Have you heard from Simon recently?* **-3.** *phrases* **to have heard of sb/sth** to know about the existence or reputation of sb/sthg □ *I've never heard of him/them/it.* ■ **I won't hear of it** I won't allow it □ *I offered to pay, but she wouldn't hear of it.*

◆ **hear out** *vt sep* **to hear sb out** to listen to sb without interrupting until they have finished speaking, especially even when one disagrees with them or does not believe them □ *Look, just hear me out first and then make up your mind.*

hearing ['hɪərɪŋ] *n* **-1.** the sense that makes it possible for people and animals to hear □ *I think there's something wrong with my hearing.* ■ **in** OR **within sb's hearing** close enough to sb for them to be able to hear what is being said □ *She'd never dare say that in my hearing.* ■ **to be hard of hearing** to be permanently unable to hear properly. **-2.** an official inquiry or trial □ *The hearing is on the 12th.* ■ **to get a fair hearing** to be allowed to say what one thinks or explain one's actions.

hearing aid *n* a device fitted in or around somebody's ear to help them hear □ *He wears a hearing aid.*

hearsay ['hɪəʳseɪ] *n* something that somebody is told, but which they cannot prove to be true □ *That's just hearsay.*

hearse [hɜːʳs] *n* a special car that carries the coffin at a funeral.

Hearst [hɜːʳst], **William Randolph** (1863–1951) a US newspaper owner. His newspapers were sometimes criticized for being too sensationalist.

heart [hɑːʳt] *n* **-1.** ANATOMY the organ in one's chest that pumps blood around one's body □ *Her heart was beating fast.* □ *He suffers from a heart complaint.* **-2.** the part of a person where their deepest feelings and emotions are supposed to be. ■ **to have a heart of gold** to be a very kind person. ■ **his/her heart isn't in it** he/she is not enthusiastic about it □ *I did my best, but my heart wasn't in it.* ■ **it's a subject close to my heart** it's something I am very interested in or concerned about. ■ **to say sthg from the heart** OR **from the bottom of one's heart** to say sthg that one really means and feels strongly □ *I thank you from the bottom of my heart.* ■ **in one's heart of hearts** in one's most secret private thoughts □ *Deep down, in his heart of hearts, he knew she was right.* ■ **to do sthg to one's heart's content** to do sthg as much as one wants □ *Look, once I've gone you can sing away to your heart's content.* ■ **my heart leapt/sank** I became suddenly very happy or excited/sad or disappointed. □ *Her heart leapt when she saw the envelope lying on the floor.* ■ **to break sb's heart** to make sb very sad □ *It broke his heart to sell the car.* ■ **to set one's heart on sthg** to want sthg very much and to be determined to have or do it □ *What a shame, I'd really set my heart on going.* ■ **to take sthg to heart** [comment, insult, criticism] to be upset by sthg because one takes it too seriously □ *Don't take what John says too much to heart.* -3. courage and determination □ *I didn't have the heart to tell her the bad news.* ■ **to lose heart** to become discouraged □ *After all the effort I'd made, I was really beginning to lose heart.* -4. [of a city, issue, problem] the central or most important part □ *Now we're getting to the heart of the matter.* □ *Yeltsin's former power base in the heart of the Urals.* -5. a shape (♥) used for representing love □ *He had drawn a heart on the front of the card.* -6. [of a lettuce, cabbage] the leaves at the center of some vegetables □ *artichoke hearts.*

◆ **hearts** *npl* one of the four suits in a deck of cards, marked by a heart shape □ *the nine of hearts.*

◆ **at heart** *adv* a phrase used to show that one is talking about the way a person really is, even if they seem different □ *I voted Democrat, although I'm a Republican at heart.*

◆ **by heart** *adv* **to learn/know sthg by heart** to learn/know sthg so well that one can remember how to say it exactly □ *I learned the words by heart.*

heartache ['hɑːˤteɪk] *n* a feeling of great sadness.

heart attack *n* a serious medical problem in which the heart stops working or does not work very well, often resulting in death.

heartbeat ['hɑːˤtbiːt] *n* the sound or action of the heart as it pumps blood around the body; the sound or action of one of the heart's movements □ *He had a regular heartbeat.*

heartbreaking ['hɑːˤtbreɪkɪŋ] *adj* [story, news] that makes one feel very sad or disappointed □ *It's absolutely heartbreaking to see those young kids out on the streets like that.*

heartbroken ['hɑːˤtbrəʊkən] *adj* [person] who is very sad or disappointed □ *Jenny was heartbroken when he left.*

heartburn ['hɑːˤtbɜːˤn] *n* a burning pain in one's chest that is caused by indigestion □ *Do you suffer from heartburn?*

heart disease *n* an illness that stops the heart working properly.

heartening ['hɑːˤtnɪŋ] *adj* [news, change, decision] that is encouraging and makes one feel happier or more hopeful □ *It was very heartening to hear that they liked our work.*

heart failure *n* a serious medical condition in which the heart stops working properly, e.g.

when it does not pump enough blood around the body □ *He died of heart failure.*

heartfelt ['hɑːˤtfelt] *adj* [plea, apology, thanks] sincere and showing strong feelings □ *Please send her my heartfelt condolences.*

hearth [hɑːˤθ] *n* -1. the floor of a fireplace. -2. the place that is somebody's home and where their family life is.

heartland ['hɑːˤtlænd] *n* the area of a country or continent that is the most important for a particular group of people, organization, or activity □ *Germany's industrial heartland* □ *The region is one of America's Republican heartlands.*

heartless ['hɑːˤtləs] *adj* [person, refusal, decision] that is unkind and shows no concern or sympathy for people □ *How can you be so heartless?*

heartrending ['hɑːˤtrendɪŋ] *adj* [cry, plea] that makes one feel great sadness or pity.

heart-searching *n* the process of thinking carefully about one's feelings about something □ *After a lot of heart-searching, I decided to leave.*

heartthrob ['hɑːˤtθrɒb] *n* an attractive man (humorous use) □ *He's her latest heartthrob.*

heart-to-heart ◇ *adj* **a heart-to-heart talk/chat** a talk/chat in which two people speak openly and sincerely to each other about their feelings □ *I had a heart-to-heart conversation with him.* ◇ *n* a heart-to-heart conversation.

heartwarming ['hɑːˤtwɔːˤmɪŋ] *adj* [story, response, news] that makes one feel happy because it shows that people can be kind □ *It was very heartwarming to see how many people had offered to help.*

hearty ['hɑːˤtɪ] (*compar* **heartier**, *superl* **heartiest**) *adj* -1. [person, welcome, laughter] cheerful, enthusiastic, and energetic □ *He gave a hearty laugh.* -2. [meal, appetite] large □ *He ate a hearty breakfast.* -3. **a hearty dislike/distrust etc** a strong dislike/distrust etc □ *I've always had a hearty contempt for self-appointed "experts".*

heat [hiːt] ◇ *n* -1. the quality of being hot □ *You shouldn't expose the equipment to excessive heat and cold.* □ *The radiator gives out a lot of heat.* -2. a particular temperature □ *Cook at a high/low heat.* □ *blood/body heat.* -3. a source of heat □ *Don't leave diskettes near heat.* -4. WEATHER hot weather □ *in the heat of the day/desert.* -5. strong emotional pressure or excitement □ *He couldn't stand the heat of being in charge.* □ *He called me a liar in the heat of the argument/moment.* -6. SPORT a part of a competition whose winners qualify to take part in the next stage □ *Schmidt won her heat to go through to the next round.* -7. **to be in heat** US OR **on heat** GB [female animal] to be sexually excited and ready to mate.

◇ *vt* [water, food, house] to make <sthg> warm or hot □ *The building is heated by gas.*

◆ **heat up** ◇ *vt sep* **to heat sthg up** [meal, food, water] to make sthg hot □ *I'll just heat up some soup for us.* ◇ *vi* [air, water] The soup will only take a minute to heat up.

heated ['hiːtəd] *adj* -1. [room, swimming pool]

that has been made warm by heating. -2. [person, argument, discussion] that shows strong feelings, usually of anger □ *The conversation became more and more heated.*

heater [ˈhiːtəʳ] *n* an appliance for heating a room, car, the water in a tank etc □ *a gas/ electric/kerosene heater* □ *a wall heater.*

heath [hiːθ] *n* an open area of land that is covered with grass or heather, has very few trees, and is not used for farming □ *We went for a walk on the heath.*

heathen [ˈhiːðn] (old-fashioned and disapproving use) ◇ *n* a person who does not belong to one's own religion. ◇ *adj*: *a heathen country/ custom.*

heather [ˈheðəʳ] *n* an evergreen plant with small purple, pink, or white flowers that grows wild on hills.

Heathrow [ˌhiːθˈrou] a major international airport, west of London, England.

heating [ˈhiːtɪŋ] *n* the system and equipment used to heat a building □ *Can you turn the heating down, please?* □ *a heating system/ engineer* □ *heating bills.*

heat rash *n* a red rash on the skin that itches and is caused by too much heat □ *Saunas always give me a heat rash.*

heat-resistant *adj* [plate, china] that is not easily damaged by heat.

heat-seeking [-siːkɪŋ] *adj* **a heat-seeking missile/rocket** a missile/rocket that has a device that guides it toward something hot, especially an aircraft.

heatstroke [ˈhiːtstrouk] *n* a medical condition with symptoms of fever and weakness, caused by too much heat □ *Ten people were taken to the hospital suffering from heatstroke.*

heat wave *n* a period of weather that is a lot hotter than usual.

heave [hiːv] ◇ *vt* -1. to lift, pull, push, or -throw <sth heavy> in a particular direction using a lot of effort □ *He heaved himself to his feet.* -2. **to heave a sigh** to sigh very deeply □ *We all heaved a sigh of relief.* ◇ *vi* -1. [person] to lift, pull, or push something using a lot of effort □ *He heaved on the rope with all his strength.* -2. [boat, waves] to move up and down with long regular movements. -3. [person] to want to vomit □ *My stomach heaved at the sight.* ◇ *n* **to give sth a heave** to lift, pull, or push sth heavy.

heaven [ˈhevn] *n* -1. the place where God or gods are believed to live, and where good people are believed to go after they die □ *all the saints in heaven.* ■ **heaven (alone) knows** a phrase used to show that one does not know something or that one is surprised or confused by something □ *She bought books, magazines, and heaven knows what else.* -2. a state of happiness; something that makes one very happy □ *I was in absolute heaven.* □ *That music's just heaven.*

◆ **heavens** *npl* **the heavens** the sky (literary use). ◇ *excl* **(good) heavens!** a phrase used to show that one is surprised or impressed □ *Good heavens! Did she really?*

heavenly [ˈhevnlɪ] *adj* -1. [view, eyes, setting] very beautiful (informal use) □ *The weather was heavenly!* -2. [body, configuration, voyage] that is in the sky or in space (literary use).

heavily [ˈhevəlɪ] *adv* -1. [rain, smoke, drink] a lot □ *They are heavily in debt.* □ *a heavily populated area* □ *We are heavily dependent on foreign trade.* -2. **heavily built** [person] who has a big and solid build. -3. [breathe, sigh] noisily □ *He was breathing heavily as he climbed up the stairs.* -4. [fall, sit down] *see* **heavy.** -5. [sleep] deeply □ *She slept heavily for several hours.*

heaviness [ˈhevɪnəs] *n* [of rain, breathing, a blow] *see* **heavy.**

heavy [ˈhevɪ] (*compar* **heavier,** *superl* **heaviest**) *adj* -1. [weight, bag, piece of equipment] that weighs a lot □ *It's too heavy for me to lift/carry.* -2. [rain, fighting, traffic] that there is a lot of □ *Heavy rains are forecast for tomorrow.* ■ **to be heavy on sth** [on fuel, salt] to use a lot or too much of sth (informal use) □ *The meal was fine, but a little heavy on the pepper.* ■ **a heavy smoker/drinker** a person who smokes a lot/ drinks a lot of alcohol. ■ **a heavy sleeper** a person who sleeps deeply. -3. [person] who weighs a lot. ■ **how heavy are you?** how much do you weigh? ■ **heavy build** a big and solid build. -4. **to be heavy with sth** [with fruit, blossom] to be full of or have a lot of sth (literary use). -5. [liquid, mixture, layer] thick □ *a heavy coat of paint.* -6. [food] that is difficult to digest and makes one's stomach feel full □ *I like German food, but I find it a bit heavy.* -7. [step, movement, fall] that uses a lot of force and is awkward. □ *I could hear his heavy steps coming up the stairs.* -8. [irony, humor, style] that is too obvious to work properly □ *There were some pretty heavy jokes about their wedding night.* ■ **heavy breathing** breathing that is deep and loud, especially by somebody on the telephone who is making an obscene call. -9. [schedule, week] busy □ *I've got a pretty heavy month ahead of me at work.* -10. [work, job] that is physically demanding and tiring □ *I have a very heavy workload.* -11. [air, weather] still, hot, and damp; [sky] that looks like it will rain □ *dark heavy rainclouds.* -12. **with a heavy heart** with great sadness □ *It was with a heavy heart that Angela stepped into Mr Mason's office.* -13. [responsibility] serious □ *I don't want to impose too heavy a burden upon you.*

heavy-duty *adj* [machine, tool, clothing] that is made to be stronger than normal so that it can be used a lot and treated roughly without getting damaged.

heavy goods vehicle *n* GB a large vehicle, e.g. a truck, that is allowed to carry heavy loads.

heavy-handed [-ˈhændəd] *adj* [person, treatment, policy] that is forceful and shows little consideration of how people are affected □ *You have to admit they were rather heavy-handed in the way they dealt with the protests.*

heavy industry *n* industry that processes raw materials, e.g. coal or steel, or produces large goods such as ships or cars.

heavy metal *n* a type of rock music that is played loudly on electric guitars and drums.

heavyweight ['hevɪweɪt] ◇ *adj* SPORT [boxer, champion, fight] in the heaviest official weight category. ◇ *n* -1. SPORT a heavyweight boxer or wrestler. -2. a person who is serious, important, and has a lot of influence in their field □ *a literary/political heavyweight.*

Hebrew ['hiːbruː] *n* the language of the Jews in ancient times; a modern version of this, used as the official language of Israel.

Hebrides ['hebrədiːz]: **the Hebrides** a group of British islands in the Atlantic Ocean off the west coast of Scotland.

heck [hek] *excl* (informal use) -1. **what/where/why the heck...?** a phrase used to show irritation or surprise in questions □ *Who the heck is he?* □ *Where the heck did that come from?* -2. **a** OR **one heck of a...** a phrase used to show how strongly one feels something □ *a heck of a nice guy/lot of people.*

heckle ['hekl] ◇ *vt* [speaker, comedian, singer] to deliberately interrupt <sb> by making unfriendly comments. ◇ *vi: Some of the audience started heckling.*

heckler ['heklər] *n* a person who heckles.

hectare ['hekteər] *n* a unit (10,000 m²) used for measuring an area of land.

hectic ['hektɪk] *adj* [meeting, day] very busy and full of hurried activity □ *Hectic preparations were underway.* □ *Things are pretty hectic at the moment.*

hector ['hektər] ◇ *vt* to try to persuade <sb> to do something by talking aggressively to them. ◇ *vi: Try talking to him gently instead of hectoring.*

he'd [hiːd] = **he had, he would.**

hedge [hedʒ] ◇ *n* a row of bushes along the edge of a road or field. ◇ *vi* to avoid answering a question directly; to avoid committing oneself to doing something.

hedgehog ['hedʒhɒg] *n* a small brown animal that has a lot of sharp spikes on its back.

hedgerow ['hedʒrəʊ] *n* a row of bushes, trees, and plants growing along a country road, or between two fields.

hedonism ['hiːdnɪzm] *n* the belief that pleasure is the most important thing in life; the practice of living purely for pleasure.

hedonist ['hiːdnəst] *n* a person who practices or believes in hedonism.

heed [hiːd] ◇ *n* -1. **to pay heed to sb/sthg** [to advice, an instruction, warning] to pay careful attention to sb/sthg and change what one does because of what one is told □ *My daughter pays no heed to what I say.* -2. **to take heed of sthg** [of advice, criticism, a warning] to think carefully about sthg that somebody has said □ *You'd be wise to take heed of what I say.* ◇ *vt* to pay heed to <sb/sthg> (formal use).

heedless ['hiːdləs] *adj* **to be heedless of sthg** [of advice, a warning, danger] not to pay any attention to sthg □ *Heedless of the risks to her health, she refused to stop smoking.*

heel [hiːl] *n* -1. [of one's foot] the back part of the foot below the ankle □ *I've got a blister on my heel.* ■ **to dig one's heels in** to firmly refuse to do what somebody wants. ■ **to follow hard on the heels of sb/sthg** [of a criminal, car] to follow very closely behind sb/sthg; [of an event, performer, speaker] to happen or appear very soon after sb/sthg □ *The police were following hard on Grayson's heels.* □ *Their second child followed hard on the heels of the first.* ■ **to take to one's heels** to run away quickly, especially in order to escape □ *The burglar took to his heels and fled.* ■ **to turn on one's heel** to turn around suddenly and walk away, especially because one is angry. -2. [of a shoe] the raised part at the back of the sole of a shoe.

hefty ['heftɪ] (*compar* **heftier**, *superl* **heftiest**) *adj* -1. [person] who is big, looks strong, and is often slightly fat; [blow, punch, knock] that is very hard □ *The star was protected by two hefty bodyguards.* □ *She gave the door a hefty push.* -2. [salary, price, fee] that is very large, often unfairly □ *The telephone company are proposing some pretty hefty increases.*

heifer ['hefər] *n* a young female cow.

height [haɪt] *n* -1. [of a person, building] the distance from head to foot of a person, or from the top to the bottom of an object □ *What is your height?* OR *What height are you?* □ *The statue is about five meters in height.* -2. [of a policeman, basketball player, skyscraper] the fact of being tall □ *His height gives him an advantage.* -3. [of an aircraft, cloud, window] the distance of something above the ground □ *We will be flying at a height of 20,000 feet.* □ *at chest/shoulder/head height.* ■ **to gain height** [aircraft] to gradually move up to a higher distance above the ground. ■ **to lose height** [aircraft] to gradually move down to a lower distance above the ground. -4. [of summer, the tourist season, somebody's fame] the point or period of time when something is most intense, successful, or powerful; [of ignorance, stupidity] the highest degree or a shocking example of something □ *when the storm/conflict was at its height* □ *They are now at the very height of their success.* □ *I consider it the height of bad manners.*

◆ **heights** *npl* -1. [of passion, inspiration, absurdity] the highest possible level of something □ *A perfectionist, she reached great heights in her art.* -2. GEOGRAPHY an area of high ground. -3. high places □ *I'm scared of heights.*

heighten ['haɪtn] ◇ *vt* [mood, fear, awareness] to make <sthg> increase so that it is felt more strongly □ *The recent attacks heighten the need for caution.* ◇ *vi: Tension heightened after the bomb attack.*

heinous ['heɪnəs] *adj* [crime, criminal] that one thinks is very bad (formal use).

heir [eər] *n* -1. [to a position, property, fortune] a person who inherits or will inherit something when somebody dies □ *the heir to the throne.* -2. [of a thinker, movement] a person who continues the ideas or works of another person or thing.

heir apparent (*pl* **heirs apparent**) *n* an heir

whose claim to inherit something, especially the throne of a country, cannot be stopped by the birth of any other heir.

heiress ['eərəs] *n* a female heir, especially one who inherits a large fortune.

heirloom ['eəᴿluːm] *n* an object that has belonged to a family for many generations, especially a valuable one □ *This necklace is a family heirloom.*

heist [haɪst] *n* a robbery, usually of a lot of money or very valuable objects (informal use) □ *an art/a jewel heist.*

held [held] *past tense & past participle of* **hold**.

Helen of Troy [ˌhelənəv'trɔɪ] a very beautiful woman in Greek mythology. The Trojan War was fought because of her.

helices ['helɪsiːz] *plural of* **helix**.

helicopter ['helɪkɒptəᴿ] *n* an aircraft that is lifted and driven by propeller blades which spin around above it □ *a helicopter pilot/flight* □ *The President arrived by helicopter.*

heliport ['helɪpɔːʳt] *n* an airport used by helicopters.

helium ['hiːlɪəm] *n* a very light gas which has no color or smell and is used inside balloons. SYMBOL: He.

helix ['hiːlɪks] (*pl* **helixes** OR **helices**) *n* a spiral.

hell [hel] ◇ *n* -1. RELIGION a place of punishment and torture, to which the souls of bad people are believed to be sent after death. -2. **to be hell** [place, experience] to be very unpleasant or cause a lot of suffering □ *It was sheer hell out there.* -3. (informal use) [used for emphasis] **what/where/why etc the hell...?** a phrase used to show irritation or surprise in questions □ *Who the hell does he think he is?* ■ **a** OR **one hell of a sthg** a phrase used to emphasize something □ *It cost a hell of a lot of money.* ■ **like hell** [hurt, sting] very badly; [run, work] very hard. ■ **like hell you will!** a phrase used to show that one disagrees strongly with somebody. ■ **to get the hell out of a place** to leave a place □ *Let's get the hell out of here!* -4. *phrases* **to hell with sb/sthg** a phrase used to show that one does not care about sb/sthg any more, especially because one is angry (informal use) □ *To hell with Jonathan and his stupid plans!* ■ **all hell broke loose** there was suddenly a lot of violence and confused movement; people suddenly became very angry about a particular issue or event (informal use) □ *All hell will break loose when she finds out!* ■ **to do sthg for the hell of it** to do sthg only for fun, excitement, or to cause trouble (informal use) □ *The gang destroyed the children's playground just for the hell of it.* ■ **to give sb hell** [person] to talk angrily to sb because of something they have done; [back, blister] to cause sb a lot of pain (informal use) □ *The boss will give you hell when she finds out.* □ *My tooth is giving me hell.* ■ **go to hell!**▽ a rude phrase used to tell somebody to go away (very informal use). ■ **to play hell with sthg** [with a schedule, budget] to stop sthg from working properly or happening as it should; [with one's back, rheumatism] to make

sthg painful or more painful than it was (informal use).
◇ *excl* a word used to show how annoyed, frustrated, surprised etc one is (informal use) □ *Oh hell, I've missed the bus!*

he'll [hiːl] = **he will**.

hell-bent *adj* **to be hell-bent on sthg** to be totally determined to do sthg.

hellish ['helɪʃ] *adj* [noise, mess, weather] very bad and unpleasant (informal use) □ *I felt hellish the next morning.*

hello [hə'loʊ] *excl* -1. a greeting used when one meets, sees, or is introduced to somebody; a word used when answering the telephone to begin a conversation □ *Hello, Polly, how are you?* □ *Hello, Claire speaking.* -2. a word used to attract somebody's attention □ *Hello, is there anyone at home?*

helm [helm] *n* -1. SAILING the wheel or bar used to steer a boat or ship. -2. **to be at the helm** to be in control.

helmet ['helmət] *n* a hard hat that one wears on one's head for protection □ *a policeman's/fireman's helmet.*

helmsman ['helmzmən] (*pl* **helmsmen** [-mən]) *n* the person who is steering a boat or ship.

help [help] ◇ *vt* -1. to do something with or for <sb> so that a particular job becomes easier □ *Could you help me (to) lift this crate, please?* □ *I offered to help Mary with the dishes.* ■ **can I help you?** a phrase used by people working in stores, theaters, banks etc to ask customers or vistors if they need to be served. -2. **to help sb (to) do sthg** to make it easier for sb to do sthg □ *These pills will help you sleep.* □ *Further training will help you get a better job.* -3. **to help (to) do sthg** to be useful in doing sthg or making it more likely to happen □ *I offered to help clean up.* -4. **I can't help it** I can't stop a particular thing from happening □ *I tried not to cry, but I couldn't help it.* □ *You can't help the way you feel about him.* ■ **I can't help doing sthg** I cannot stop myself from doing sthg □ *I can't help feeling sad about what happened.* □ *I couldn't help overhearing what you said.* -5. **to help oneself** [to food] to serve oneself; [to objects, property] to take what one wants, with or without permission □ *He helped himself to some more dessert.* □ *"Could I have some envelopes, please?" — "Help yourself."*
◇ *vi* -1. [person] to do something with or for somebody to make a job easier □ *I'm very willing to help with the clearing up after the party.* □ *If everyone helped, we'd get the job done much quicker.* -2. [money, advice, treatment] to make a particular problem, job etc easier to deal with □ *That book you lent me helped a lot.* □ *Making a lot of fuss won't help.* □ *It helps to talk about your problems.*
◇ *n* -1. [with a job] something one does or uses to make a particular job easier □ *He gave me a lot of help with my financial problems.* □ *We need your help if we're going to finish on time.* □ *With the help of a mechanic/the handbook, I soon managed to restart the engine.* ■ **to be of help** to help □ *Perhaps I can be of some*

help to you. **-2.** [in an emergency] somebody or something that can save somebody in danger □ *Jane stayed with the injured man while I ran to get help.* □ *Help will arrive soon.* **-3. to be a help** to be a useful or helpful person or thing □ *My daughter's been such a help to me while I've been ill.* □ *It's a great help having a word processor to write my report with.*
◇ *excl* a word that people shout when they are in danger or urgently need help □ *Help! I can't get out!*

◆ **help out** ◇ *vt sep* **to help sb out** to give a particular kind of help to sb at a time when they need it □ *I can help you out with a loan, if you like.* ◇ *vi: My children help out when the restaurant is very busy.*

helper ['helpər] *n* **-1.** a person who helps somebody to do something, especially because they want to □ *I'd like to say thank you to all the helpers who made this event possible.* **-2.** US a person who is paid to do the housework in somebody's house.

helpful ['helpfl] *adj* **-1.** [person, organization] that helps people □ *The firm was very helpful to my mother after my father died.* **-2.** [advice, information, suggestion] that is useful because it helps one to do something □ *This month's issue has some helpful tips on dieting.*

helping ['helpɪŋ] *n* [of food] an amount of food that is given to one person at a meal □ *Can I have an extra helping of meat/potatoes?*

helping hand *n* **to give sb a helping hand** to give sb some help □ *She gave me a helping hand at a time when I really needed it.*

helpless ['helpləs] *adj* **-1.** [old person, patient, child] who does not have the strength, ability, knowledge etc to do things for themselves or protect themselves; [look, gesture] that shows that one can do nothing about what is happening □ *I felt so helpless.* **-2.** [laughter, giggle] uncontrollable □ *They collapsed in helpless laughter.*

helplessly ['helpləslɪ] *adv*: *see* **helpless** □ *I could only look on helplessly as the boat was swept out to sea.*

helpline ['helplaɪn] *n* a special telephone number belonging to an organization that people can call to get help with particular problems □ *They've set up a special helpline for relatives of the victims.*

Helsinki [hel'sɪŋkɪ] the capital of Finland and its main port and largest city. POPULATION: 484,000.

helter-skelter [ˌheltər'skeltər] ◇ *n* GB a tower at a fairground in the shape of a spiral that people slide down for fun. ◇ *adv* [run, gather] in a hurried and disorganized way.

hem [hem] (*pt* & *pp* **hemmed**, *cont* **hemming**) ◇ *n* an edge which has been turned over and sewn down, especially the bottom edge of a skirt or dress. ◇ *vt* [bottom, border] to turn <an edge> over and sew it down; [skirt, dress] to put a hem on <a piece of clothing>.

◆ **hem in** *vt sep* **-1. to hem sb/sthg in** [suspect, animal] to surround sb/sthg and stop them moving freely. **-2. to hem sb in** to limit sb in

what they can do □ *We feel completely hemmed in by rules and regulations.*

he-man *n* a very strong man who has big muscles (informal and humorous use).

hematology [ˌhiːmə'tɒlədʒɪ] *n* the study of diseases of the blood.

Hemingway ['hemɪŋweɪ], **Ernest** (1899–1961) a US writer who is well known for his clear concise style. His work includes *A Farewell to Arms* and *For Whom the Bell Tolls.*

hemisphere ['hemɪsfɪər] *n* one half of a sphere, especially one half of the earth □ *the Northern/Southern/Eastern/Western hemisphere.*

hemline ['hemlaɪn] *n* the bottom edge of a skirt or dress □ *Hemlines are higher this season.*

hemoglobin [ˌhiːmə'gloubɪn] *n* a red substance in the blood that carries oxygen to the tissues.

hemophilia [ˌhiːmə'fɪlɪə] *n* a disease, passed from parents to their sons, that prevents the blood from clotting normally.

hemophiliac [ˌhiːmə'fɪlɪæk] *n* a person who suffers from hemophilia.

hemorrhage ['hemərɪdʒ] ◇ *n* a sudden heavy flow of blood from a burst blood vessel. ◇ *vi* [person] to bleed heavily; [blood, liquid] to pour out; [money, assets] to be lost or used very quickly.

hemorrhoids ['hemərɔɪdz] *npl* a condition in which the veins near the anus are swollen and painful and sometimes bleed.

hemp [hemp] *n* an Asian plant which can be used to make some narcotic drugs; the fiber of this plant used in making ropes and canvas.

hen [hen] *n* **-1.** a female chicken. **-2.** the female of any species of bird □ *a hen blackbird/sparrow.*

hence [hens] *adv* (formal use) **-1.** for this reason □ *They have made their business more efficient and hence more successful.* **-2.** from now □ *Ten years hence, the situation will be totally different.*

henceforth [ˌhens'fɔːrθ] *adv* from now on (formal use).

henchman ['hentʃmən] (*pl* **henchmen** [-mən]) *n* a person who is paid by a powerful criminal to help them in their illegal activities (disapproving use).

henna ['henə] ◇ *n* a reddish-brown dye used especially for coloring one's hair; the plant from which this dye is obtained. ◇ *vt* to color <one's hair> using henna.

hen party *n* GB a party for women only, often held before a woman gets married.

henpecked ['henpekt] *adj* [husband, man] who is completely controlled by his wife or girlfriend, so that he does whatever she says (humorous and disapproving use).

Henry V [ˌhenrɪðə'fɪfθ] (1387–1422) King of England from 1413 to 1422. He defeated the French at the Battle of Agincourt, conquered Normandy, and was recognized as the heir to the French throne.

Henry VIII [ˌhenrɪðɪ'eɪtθ] (1491–1547) King of

England from 1509 to 1547. He broke away from the Roman Catholic Church, and founded the Church of England in order to divorce his first wife, Catherine of Aragon. He is well known for having six wives.

Henry ['henrɪ], **Patrick** (1736–1799) a US revolutionary. He made speeches against British rule before the American Revolution.

hepatitis [,hepə'taɪtəs] *n* a serious disease causing inflammation of the liver.

her [hɜːʳ] ◇ *pron* -**1.** (used as the object of a verb and after prepositions) the woman, girl, or female animal that has just been mentioned, seen etc □ *"Do you know June?"* — *"Yes, I met her at your party."* □ *That's for her to decide.* □ *I sent her a letter.* -**2.** used to refer to a car or ship that has just been mentioned □ *Fill her up!* ◇ *det* -**1.** used to show that something belongs to or is connected with the woman, female animal, car, or ship that has just been mentioned, seen etc □ *What's her name?* □ *I know her brother.* □ *The ship sank with all her crew on board.* -**2.** used in titles to refer to a woman □ *Her Majesty Queen Elizabeth.*

herald ['herəld] ◇ *vt* (literary or formal use) -**1.** [birth, dawn, arrival] to show or indicate that <sthg> is going to happen soon □ *The invention of the telephone heralded a new age in communications.* -**2.** to publicly declare <sb/sthg> to be good, important etc □ *This little-known actress is already being heralded as the star of the future.* ◇ *n* in the past, an official announcer or messenger.

heraldry ['herəldrɪ] *n* the study of the symbols used in coats of arms, and of the histories of noble families.

herb [US ɜːrb, GB hɜːb] *n* a plant used as a flavoring in cooking or as a medicine □ *I grow my own herbs.* □ *an herb garden.*

herbaceous [hɜːʳ'beɪʃəs] *adj* -**1.** [plant] that has fleshy rather than woody leaves and stems. -**2. a herbaceous border** part of a garden that mainly contains plants which flower every year.

herbal [US 'ɜːrbl, GB 'hɜːbl] *adj* [medicine, remedy, tobacco] that is made from herbs □ *an herbal preparation that is an effective painkiller.*

herbalist [US 'ɜːrbələst, GB 'hɜːb-] *n* a person who sells or uses herbs, especially as medicines.

herbicide ['hɜːʳbəsaɪd] *n* a chemical that is used to kill plants, especially weeds.

herbivore ['hɜːʳbəvɔːʳ] *n* an animal that eats only plants.

herb tea *n* a drink made by soaking herbs in hot water.

Hercules ['hɜːʳkjəliːz] in Greek mythology, a very strong man. He had to perform twelve very difficult tasks, known as the Twelve Labors of Hercules.

herd [hɜːʳd] ◇ *n* -**1.** [of cattle, goats, elephants] a large group of animals that move and feed together □ *a herd of antelope.* -**2.** [of people] a large group that moves in the same direction at the same time or has the same opin-

ions □ *the herd instinct.* ◇ *vt* -**1.** [cattle, sheep] to drive <animals> along in a herd. -**2.** [prisoners, tourists] to make <people> move all together in a tight group as if they were animals □ *The refugees were herded into open trucks and driven off.*

herdsman ['hɜːʳdzmən] (*pl* **herdsmen** [-mən]) *n* a person who owns or looks after a herd of cattle.

here [hɪəʳ] *adv* -**1.** in or to the place where one is □ *Come here and I'll show you something.* -**2.** in or near the place one is pointing to □ *"Where are my keys?"* — *"They're here, by the sink."* -**3.** in or to the place where one lives, works etc □ *What time did they get here?* □ *There are lots of parks around here.* -**4.** used when one is handing something to somebody □ *Here, take my coat for me, will you?* -**5.** used to draw attention to what one is saying □ *Here is the news from Bob Dunckley.* -**6.** *phrases* **here it is/they are!** I've found it/them. ■ **here and there** in a few different places □ *There are still a few problems here and there.* ■ **here's to...** a phrase used when one is having a drink to wish somebody good luck □ *Here's to your new job!*

hereabouts [,hɪərə'baʊts], **hereabout** [,hɪərə'baʊt] *adv* US near where one is □ *It must be somewhere hereabouts.*

hereafter [US ,hɪər'æftr, GB ,hɪər'ɑːftə] ◇ *adv* from this point on (used in legal documents) □ *Emily Swift, hereafter referred to as "the deceased".* ◇ *n* **the hereafter** a life after death □ *a belief in the hereafter.*

hereby [,hɪəʳ'baɪ] *adv* used in formal written or spoken statements to make them more official and to show that they are true from that point on □ *I hereby declare you husband and wife.*

hereditary [US hɪ'redətɪ, GB -ətrɪ] *adj* -**1.** [disease, condition] that can be given to a child before it is born by one parent or both parents □ *Color-blindness is hereditary.* -**2.** [title, right, peerage] that is inherited by the legal heir when the holder dies □ *The leadership of the tribe is hereditary.*

heredity [hə'redətɪ] *n* the process by which certain characteristics, diseases, instincts etc are given to children before they are born by their parents.

Hereford and Worcester [,herɪfəʳdən'wʊstəʳ] a county in western central England. SIZE: 3,926 sq kms. POPULATION: 671,000. ADMINISTRATIVE CENTER: Worcester.

herein [,hɪəʳ'ɪn] *adv* in this particular piece of writing (formal use) □ *this document and all the information contained herein.*

heresy ['herəsɪ] (*pl* **heresies**) *n* -**1.** RELIGION a belief or set of beliefs that disagrees in an important way with the beliefs of a particular religion; the sin of holding such beliefs □ *He was accused of heresy.* -**2.** a belief or set of beliefs that is very different from what most people accept as true □ *It's heresy to suggest there might be another way of doing things.*

heretic ['herətɪk] *n* -**1.** RELIGION a person who believes in or spreads a heresy. -**2.** any person who has unusual views which people disapprove of □ *Those who do not accept the party leader's opinions are considered heretics.*

herewith [ˌhɪərˈwɪð] *adv* used in formal business letters to say that a particular document or piece of information is enclosed □ *I attach herewith a copy of the contract.*

heritage [ˈherɪtɪdʒ] *n* [of a family, nation] all the things that have been passed down from one generation to the next, especially things that are thought to be important or valuable, e.g. art, literature, and traditions □ *These ancient buildings are part of Mexico's cultural/national heritage.*

heritage centre *n* GB a museum or exhibition for visitors at a site that is historically interesting.

hermaphrodite [hɜːˈmæfrədaɪt] ◇ *adj* [animal, person] that has the sexual characteristics of both male and female. ◇ *n*: *Worms are hermaphrodites.*

hermetic [hɜːˈmetɪk] *adj* a hermetic seal a seal that does not let air in or out.

hermetically [hɜːˈmetɪklɪ] *adv* hermetically sealed [container, jar, bottle] that is closed in such a way that no air can get in or out.

hermit [ˈhɜːmət] *n* a person who lives alone, usually in a remote place, to avoid seeing or meeting other people.

hernia [ˈhɜːnjə] *n* a medical condition in which part of an organ, especially an intestine, sticks out through the part of the body that contains it.

hero [ˈhɪərəʊ] (*pl* **heroes**) *n* -1. [of a story, book, movie] the main character, especially the main male character, whom the reader or audience usually admires or sympathizes with □ *The hero eventually marries the boss's daughter.* -2. [in a battle, crisis, emergency] a person who shows great courage and determination and does something that people admire a lot, e.g. saving or helping other people □ *What a hero!* -3. [to an admirer, young person] a person one particularly admires and would like to copy, especially because they are very good at something □ *He's my hero.*

Herod [ˈherəd] in the Bible, the king who ordered all the young boys of Bethlehem to be killed, because he wanted to kill Jesus.

heroic [həˈrəʊɪk] *adj* -1. [person, act, rescue] that is admired for being very courageous □ *Their heroic stand against injustice will always be remembered.* -2. [effort, attempt] that involves a lot of determination and commitment □ *They made a heroic attempt to save the ship.*

♦ **heroics** *npl* action that is intended to be brave, but that is not sensible and can make things worse (disapproving use) □ *Look, this is no time for heroics.*

heroin [ˈherəʊɪn] *n* a narcotic drug made from morphine that people can become addicted to easily □ *a heroin addict.*

heroine [ˈherəʊɪn] *n* -1. [of a story, book, movie] the main female character whom the reader or audience usually admires or sympathizes with □ *The writer's heroines tend to be strong women in control of their lives.* -2. [in a battle, crisis, emergency] a woman or girl who shows great courage and determination and does something that people admire a lot, e.g. saving or helping other people □ *one of the heroines of the 20th century.*

heroism [ˈherəʊɪzm] *n* great courage □ *an act of heroism.*

heron [ˈherən] (*pl* **heron** OR **herons**) *n* a bird with long thin legs, a long neck, and a large bill, that lives near water.

hero worship *n* a strong feeling of admiration that somebody has for somebody else whom they want to be like.

herpes [ˈhɜːpiːz] *n* a disease, caused by a virus, that has several forms and causes painful blisters on one's skin.

herring [ˈherɪŋ] (*pl* **herring** OR **herrings**) *n* a silver-colored seafish that swims in large groups; the flesh of this fish eaten as food.

herringbone [ˈherɪŋbəʊn] *n* a pattern in the form of parallel rows of Vs, usually in alternating colors □ *a herringbone pattern/jacket.*

hers [hɜːz] *pron* used to show that something belongs to or is connected with the woman, girl, or female animal that has just been mentioned, seen etc □ *She borrowed my pen because hers doesn't work.* □ *He's been a friend of hers for years.*

herself [hɜːˈself] *pron* -1. used as the object of a verb to refer to the same person as the subject "she"; used after a preposition □ *She sat down and made herself comfortable.* □ *She was annoyed with herself for being late.* -2. used to emphasize "she", or the name of a girl or woman that is the object of a verb □ *I didn't speak to Ruth herself, just her secretary.* □ *Her husband is vegetarian, but she herself eats meat.* -3. she did it herself she did it without any help from anyone else □ *She made her wedding dress herself.* ■ by herself alone □ *She was sitting by herself on the beach.*

Hertfordshire [ˈhɑːtfədʃər] a county in southeastern England, north of London. SIZE: 1,634 sq kms. POPULATION: 986,800. ADMINISTRATIVE CENTER: Hertford.

Herts *abbr of* **Hertfordshire**.

he's [hiːz] = he is, he has.

hesitant [ˈhezətənt] *adj* [person] who pauses slightly before doing or saying something, usually because they are unsure or worried about it; [speech] that is slow and has pauses in it, showing that one is nervous or unsure; [smile, applause, guess] that shows that one is nervous or unsure about something □ *Don't be hesitant, everybody is with you.* □ *Her words were slow and hesitant.* □ *She gave him a hesitant tap on the shoulder.* ■ to be hesitant about doing sthg to be unwilling to do sthg, especially because one is worried or unsure about it □ *I'd be extremely hesitant about committing myself so early on.*

hesitate [ˈhezəteɪt] *vi* [person] to pause, usually because one is unsure whether to do something or not □ *She hesitated for a moment be-*

fore signing the contract. ■ **to hesitate to do sthg** not to do sthg immediately because one does not want to do it □ *I hesitate to disturb him on a Sunday.* ■ **don't hesitate to...** a phrase used to show that one willingly gives somebody permission to do something □ *Don't hesitate to contact me if you need more information.*

hesitation [ˌhezəˈteɪʃn] *n* **-1.** a pause before somebody does something, often because they are uncertain □ *After a slight/a moment's hesitation he began.* **-2.** the act of pausing or delaying, usually because one is unsure, or does not want to do something □ *Hesitation can lead to mistakes.* ■ **without hesitation** immediately and willingly □ *I would recommend her without hesitation.* ■ **to have no hesitation in doing sthg** to do sthg immediately and willingly □ *She had no hesitation in volunteering for the task.*

hessian [US ˈheʃn, GB ˈhesɪən] *n* GB a type of strong coarse cloth, often used to make sacks □ *a hessian rug.*

heterogeneous [ˌhetərouˈdʒiːnɪəs] *adj* [mixture, collection, group] that has many different kinds of things or people in it (formal use). NOTE: Compare **homogeneous**.

heterosexual [ˌhetərouˈsekʃʊəl] ◇ *adj* [person] who is sexually attracted to the opposite sex; [relationship, behavior] that involves sexual attraction between the two sexes. ◇ *n* a heterosexual person.

het up [ˌhet-] *adj* **to be het up about sthg** to be angry, upset, or worried about sthg (informal use) □ *There's no need to get so het up about it.*

hew [hjuː] (*pt* **hewed**, *pp* **hewed** OR **hewn** [hjuːn]) *vt* [wood, stone] to cut <sthg> with an ax, large knife etc, especially in a rough way □ *a roughly-hewn statue.*

hex [heks] *n* a curse that makes things go wrong (humorous use).

hexagon [US ˈheksəɡɑːn, GB -əɡən] *n* an object or shape that has six straight sides.

hexagonal [hekˈsæɡənl] *adj* [shape, building] that has six straight sides.

hey [heɪ] *excl* **-1.** a word used to attract somebody's attention, especially by shouting □ *Hey you, come here!* **-2.** a word used to show surprise, worry, interest, or admiration □ *Hey, what's going on here?*

heyday [ˈheɪdeɪ] *n* **the heyday of sb/sthg** the time when sb/sthg is most successful, powerful, or popular □ *In its heyday, the movement had thousands of supporters.*

hey presto *excl* GB = **presto.**

HF (*abbr of* **high frequency**) a radio frequency between 3 and 30 MHz.

HGV GB *abbr of* **heavy goods vehicle** □ *an HGV licence.*

hi [haɪ] *excl* a word used when one meets, sees, or is introduced to somebody; a word used to begin a conversation with somebody one knows (informal use) □ *Hi, how are you?*

HI *abbr of* **Hawaii.**

hiatus [haɪˈeɪtəs] (*pl* **hiatuses**) *n* (formal use) [in a conversation, discussion, in negotiations] a time when nothing happens and nobody says or does anything; [in a text] a gap where something is missing □ *There was a hiatus between the departure of the old principal and the arrival of the new one.*

Hiawatha [ˌhaɪəˈwɒθə] (16th century) the Native American chief who was responsible for organizing the alliance of Native American peoples called the Five Nations.

hibernate [ˈhaɪbərneɪt] *vi* [animal] to spend the winter months asleep or in a state like sleep □ *Bears hibernate in winter.*

hibernation [ˌhaɪbərˈneɪʃn] *n: see* **hibernate** □ *My tortoise is still in hibernation.*

hiccough, hiccup [ˈhɪkʌp] (*pt & pp* **hiccupped**, *cont* **hiccupping**) ◇ *n* **-1.** a sudden sound in the throat and movement in the chest that one cannot control, often caused by eating or drinking too quickly □ *She gave a loud hiccough.* ■ **to have (the) hiccoughs** to keep giving hiccoughs. **-2.** [in a process, operation] a slight mistake or problem, especially when it causes a short delay but is not very serious □ *There's been a slight hiccough in the arrangements.* ◇ *vi* [person] to give a hiccough.

hick [hɪk] *n* a person from a country area who doesn't know much about city life (informal and disapproving use).

Hickok [ˈhɪkɒk], **Wild Bill** (1837–1876) a US lawman and hero from the Wild West.

hid [hɪd] *past tense of* **hide.**

hidden [ˈhɪdn] ◇ *past participle of* **hide.** ◇ *adj* [meaning, cost, disadvantage] that is not immediately obvious or has been deliberately concealed □ *The move to New York could bring some hidden benefits.*

hidden agenda *n* a secret plan that is not mentioned because it would be criticized □ *The President failed to reassure Congress that there was no hidden agenda behind the reforms.*

hide [haɪd] (*pt* **hid**, *pp* **hidden**) ◇ *vt* [object, money, person] to put <sb/sthg> in a place where they cannot be seen or found; [emotion, fact, truth] to keep <sthg> secret; [scar, mark] to cover <sthg> with something □ *She hid the letter behind a cushion/in a book.* □ *They tried to hide their true financial situation from the auditors.* □ *He couldn't hide his delight/disappointment at the news.* □ *The hotel was hidden away up a quiet side street.* □ *She hid her face in her hands.*
◇ *vi* [person] to put oneself in a place where one cannot be seen or found very easily □ *I saw her coming and hid in a doorway.* □ *You can't hide from the law for ever.*
◇ *n* **-1.** [of an animal] a skin that can be used to make leather □ *buffalo/elephant hide.* **-2.** [in a game park, bird sanctuary] a small shelter which people can watch animals or birds from without being seen by them.

hide-and-seek *n* a children's game in which one person hides and the other people have to look for them.

hideaway [ˈhaɪdəweɪ] *n* a place where people go to be away from other people.

hidebound ['haɪdbaʊnd] *adj* [person, institution] that has very old-fashioned ideas and ways of doing things and does not want to change them.

hideous ['hɪdɪəs] *adj* -1. [monster, face] very ugly and frightening; [crime, wound] that is shocking □ *He had a hideous scar.* -2. [clothes, color, noise] very unpleasant; [mistake] very serious and upsetting □ *What a hideous tie!* □ *What a hideous thing to happen!*

hideout ['haɪdaʊt] *n* a place where somebody goes to hide from somebody else, especially from the police or from somebody who wants to harm them.

hiding ['haɪdɪŋ] *n* -1. **to be in hiding** to be in a place where one hopes one cannot be found □ *She went into hiding as soon as the story appeared in the press.* -2. **to get a (good) hiding** [person] to be beaten hard, especially as a punishment; [team, competitor] to be defeated completely (informal use). ■ **to give sb a (good) hiding** to beat sb hard (informal use) □ *If you don't shut up, I'll give you a (good) hiding.*

hiding place *n* a place where one can hide somebody or something, or hide oneself.

hierarchical [,haɪ'rɑːˈkɪkl] *adj* [system, society] in which there are strict levels or ranks and in which the higher levels or ranks have power over the lower ones.

hierarchy ['haɪrɑːˈkɪ] (*pl* **hierarchies**) *n* -1. [in an organization, company] a system that is organized in a hierarchical way. -2. the people who have power in a particular organization □ *the party/company hierarchy.*

hieroglyphics [,haɪrə'glɪfɪks] *npl* symbols and pictures that are used as words in ancient systems of writing such as Egyptian.

hi-fi ['haɪfaɪ] *n* -1. sound reproduction of very high quality. -2. a piece of equipment that plays records, tapes etc so that they sound almost like the original performance □ *a hi-fi system.*

higgledy-piggledy [,hɪgldɪ'pɪgldɪ] (informal use) ◇ *adj* [houses, papers, books] that are not neat or in order. ◇ *adv*: *The clothes were scattered higgledy-piggledy all over the floor.*

high [haɪ] ◇ *adj* -1. [wall, mountain] that rises a long way above the ground or its base □ *The yard was surrounded by a high fence.* -2. a word used to say what the height of something is □ *The statue is three feet high.* □ *How high is it?* -3. [shelf, window, position] that is placed or is moving a long way above the ground □ *The cupboard is too high for me to reach.* -4. [degree, amount, figure] greater than average or usual □ *They charge very high prices.* □ *a time of high unemployment* □ *The risks are high, but so are the potential rewards.* □ *I suffer from high blood pressure.* ■ **to be high in sthg** [in fiber, protein] to contain a lot of sthg. -5. [position, office, rank] that has a lot of power and influence □ *I have friends in high places.* -6. [standard, quality] very good. ■ **to have a high opinion of sb/sthg** to respect and admire sb/sthg very much, especially because they are very good at something □ *You seem to have a very high opinion of yourself!* -7. [ideals, sentiments] that

people agree with because they think they are right and good □ *I've always admired her high principles.* -8. [note, voice] that is near the top note that a voice or instrument can produce □ *She can reach a high C.* -9. **to be high** to be very happy, excited, and full of energy because one has taken drugs □ *He was high on LSD.* -10. **to be high** US to be drunk (informal use).
◇ *adv* -1. [climb, lift, fly] in or toward a high position □ *She threw the ball high above her head.* □ *They live high up on a hill.* -2. [aim, rise] in or toward an important level □ *He's risen high in his profession.*
◇ *n* the highest point, level, or number □ *Temperatures have fallen from a high of 24 degrees to around 17 degrees.* ■ **to reach a new high** to reach a higher point on a scale than has ever been reached before □ *Sales last year reached a new high.*

highball ['haɪbɔːl] *n* a drink containing an alcoholic drink, ice, water, soda etc in a tall glass.

highbrow ['haɪbraʊ] *adj* [book, play, music] that is enjoyable and interesting only for intelligent and educated people and is often hard to understand.

high chair *n* a chair with long legs and a tray attached that small children use when eating so that they are on the same level as adults.

High Church *adj* belonging to the part of the Church of England that is most like the Roman Catholic Church, and that considers ceremony and tradition to be important.

high-class *adj* [hotel, restaurant] that is of very good quality; [performance, job] excellent.

high command *n* the commander-in-chief and most senior officers in an army.

high commission *n* an embassy belonging to one Commonwealth country and situated in another.

high commissioner *n* an ambassador who is in charge of a high commission.

High Court *n* **the High Court** GB the highest court for civil cases □ *a High Court judge.*

high-density *adj* COMPUTING [diskette, storage] that can store a very large amount of information.

higher ['haɪəˈ] *adj* EDUCATION [degree, mathematics] of an advanced level.

◆ **Higher** *n* a school examination taken in a particular subject at the end of secondary education in Scotland.

higher education *n* education and training at universities and colleges.

high explosive *n* a powerful explosive.

high-fidelity *adj* [equipment, speaker] that plays music which sounds almost like the original performance.

high finance *n* the process of lending, borrowing, and investing large sums of money.

high-flier *n* a person who has the necessary ability and ambition to be very successful in their career □ *We're looking for a high-flier with plenty of ambition and drive.*

high-flying *adj* [academic, manager, executive] who is a high-flier.

high-handed [-'hændəd] *adj* [person] that uses power without considering other people and their opinions □ *Any complaints tend to be dealt with in a very high-handed way.*

high-heeled [-hi:ld] *adj* [shoe, boot] that has a high heel □ *She looked funny in her mother's high-heeled shoes.*

high horse *n* **to get on one's high horse** to become angry about something because one thinks that one's opinion is more useful or important than other people's (informal use) □ *There's no need to get on your high horse!*

high jump *n* a sporting event in which one jumps over a bar without using a pole □ *Ferguson came first in the high jump.*

Highlander ['haɪləndə'] *n* a person from the Highlands of Scotland.

Highland Games [ˌhaɪlənd-] *npl* **the Highland Games** one of several festivals that take place every year in towns in Scotland and where there are competitions in Scottish sports, music, and dancing.

Highlands ['haɪləndz]: **the Highlands** the mountainous part of northwestern Scotland.

high-level *adj* [talks, negotiations] between important officials; [diplomat, official, delegation] important □ *The US President has decided to resume high-level talks.*

high life *n* **the high life** the life of rich and famous people, full of fun and expensive activities.

highlight ['haɪlaɪt] ◇ *vt* **-1.** [aspect, problem, danger] to make <sthg> more obvious to people by explaining it in detail or by giving a lot of attention to it □ *I want to highlight the importance of this point.* □ *The tragedy highlights the need for greater safety measures.* **-2.** [word, sentence] to make <a piece of text> more noticeable on a page, screen etc by marking it in a particular way □ *The main points were highlighted in red.* ◇ *n* the most interesting, exciting, or amusing part of an event or occasion □ *His speech was the highlight of the conference.* □ *You can see the highlights of the game on TV tonight.*

◆ **highlights** *npl* parts of a person's hair that have been made lighter in color than the rest of their hair using a chemical process □ *I've had highlights put in my hair.*

highlighter ['haɪlaɪtə'] *n* **a highlighter (pen)** a pen with a thick tip that is used to mark parts of a text in a bright color in order to make them more noticeable.

highly ['haɪlɪ] *adv* **-1. highly unlikely/enjoyable/successful etc** very unlikely/enjoyable/successful etc □ *a highly profitable venture.* **-2. highly paid/placed** paid/placed at a level that is near the top of a scale □ *a highly placed official.* **-3.** [speak, rate] in a way that shows a very good opinion of somebody or something □ *This hotel was highly recommended by a colleague of mine.* □ *You know she thinks highly of you.*

highly-strung *adj* GB = **high-strung.**

high mass *n* a mass in the Catholic religion in which the ceremonies are very formal and there are parts sung by the priest.

high-minded [-'maɪndəd] *adj* [person] who has moral principles that are considered to be too high □ *I've had enough of her high-minded moralizing.*

Highness ['haɪnəs] *n* a word used to address or refer to a member of a royal family □ *His/Her/Your Royal Highness.*

high-octane *adj* [fuel, gasoline] that is of high quality.

high-pitched *adj* [sound, scream, voice] that is nearer than usual to the highest sound that can be heard □ *He called his dog with a high-pitched whistle.*

high point *n* [of an occasion, vacation, movie] the most enjoyable, exciting, or important part of something □ *For me the high point of the evening was when Lucy persuaded Matthew to dance.* □ *The award marked a high point in her career.*

high-powered [-'paʊə'd] *adj* **-1.** [car, telescope, rifle] very powerful □ *The bacteria can only be seen with a high-powered microscope.* **-2.** [businessman, businesswoman] very busy, successful, and ambitious; [job, course] that makes it necessary for one to have these qualities □ *Tom wants to give the impression he's a high-powered executive.* □ *Barbara's got a high-powered job in sales.*

high-pressure *adj* **-1.** [job, position, work] that puts workers under pressure □ *As a trader, I'm used to working in a high-pressure environment.* **-2.** [selling, technique] that is very forceful and is intended to persuade somebody to buy something. **-3.** [cylinder, canister] that contains gas under pressure.

high priest *n* the most important priest in a religious organization.

high-ranking *adj* [official, officer] who has a high position, especially in a public organization.

high-resolution *adj* [screen, graphics] able to show detailed images □ *a high-resolution monitor.*

high-rise *adj* [building, apartments] that is very tall and consists of many floors □ *the structural problems in many high-rise blocks.*

high-risk *adj* **-1.** [investment, business, strategy] that deliberately takes risks to get high rewards □ *The bank refused my high-risk business plan.* **-2.** [group, category, occupation] in which people are at risk from something □ *Skiing is a high-risk sport.*

high school *n* **-1.** in the USA, a school for students between 13 or 14 and 18 □ *a high-school diploma.* **-2.** in Britain, a school for students between 11 and 18.

high seas *npl* **the high seas** the parts of the oceans that do not belong to one particular country.

high season *n* the time of year when hotels, resorts etc, where people go on vacation, are most busy and prices are highest. NOTE: Compare **low season.**

high-speed *adj* **-1.** [train, link] that moves or happens very quickly □ *a high-speed car chase.* **-2.** PHOTOGRAPHY [film, exposure] that only needs a short exposure time.

high-spirited *adj* [person] who shows a love of fun and excitement.

high spot *n* the most enjoyable, exciting, or important part of an event or occasion.

high street *n* GB the main shopping street in a town □ *high-street sales/prices/shops.*

high-strung *adj* US [person] who is nervous and likely to become angry or upset easily □ *I've never met anybody so high-strung.*

hightail ['haɪteɪl] *vt* **to hightail it** to go somewhere in a great hurry (informal use) □ *Let's hightail it out of here!*

high tea *n* GB a meal that usually consists of tea and cooked food and is eaten in the early part of the evening instead of dinner.

high-tech [-'tek] ◇ *n* **-1.** a style of decorating a room or building that is based on the appearance of modern industrial equipment. **-2.** the use of advanced science, especially in electronics and computers. ◇ *adj* **-1.** [furniture, style] □ *Their new place is really high-tech.* **-2.** [industry, methods] □ *We are desperately trying to become more high-tech.*

high-tension *adj* [cable, pylon] that carries a powerful electrical current.

high tide *n* the time of day when the sea level reaches its highest point on the coast □ *We had to wait for high tide before the ship could leave.*

NOTE: Compare **low tide.**

high treason *n* the crime of being disloyal to one's country by helping its enemies.

high water *n* the time when a river or sea is at its highest level.

highway ['haɪweɪ] *n* **-1.** US a main road that joins towns and cities. **-2.** GB a road or street (formal use) □ *This is a public highway.*

Highway Code *n* **the Highway Code** the rules for drivers, cyclists etc in Britain.

Highway Patrol *n* **the Highway Patrol** a US police organization that controls traffic on the highways.

high wire *n* a form of entertainment in which somebody walks along a tightrope high in the air.

hijack ['haɪdʒæk] ◇ *vt* [plane, bus] to take control of <a vehicle> illegally and by force, usually to get money or to make a government do what one wants. ◇ *n* [of a plane, bus] the act of hijacking something □ *The hijack began at 7pm.*

hijacker ['haɪdʒækər] *n* a person who hijacks a plane, bus etc.

hike [haɪk] ◇ *n* **-1.** a long walk in the countryside for pleasure □ *I enjoy going on hikes.* **-2.** FINANCE a sudden large rise in a tax or a price □ *a tax hike.* ◇ *vi* to go for a hike □ *We hiked across the countryside.*

hiker ['haɪkər] *n* a person who hikes □ *The place attracts a lot of hikers in summer.*

hiking ['haɪkɪŋ] *n* the activity of going on hikes □ *We went hiking in the hills.*

hilarious [hɪ'leəriəs] *adj* [joke, person] that is very funny and makes one laugh a lot □ *It was absolutely hilarious when he fell off his chair.*

hilarity [hɪ'lærəti] *n* great amusement and loud laughter (formal use) □ *The idea caused great hilarity among the assembled crowd.*

hill [hɪl] *n* **-1.** a sloping area of land that is higher than the land around it and is smaller than a mountain □ *I live on the other side of the hill.* □ *We went walking in the hills.* **-2.** a part of a road that slopes up or down □ *Go up the hill and turn left at the top.*

hillbilly ['hɪlbɪlɪ] (*pl* **hillbillies**) *n* a person from one of the remote mountainous parts of North America, often considered to be unintelligent (offensive use).

hillock ['hɪlək] *n* a small hill □ *The tower was on a grassy hillock.*

hillside ['hɪlsaɪd] *n* the side of a hill □ *a hillside village.*

hill start *n* the act of starting a car, bus etc when it is facing upward on a slope.

hilltop ['hɪltɒp] ◇ *n* the top of a hill. ◇ *adj* [village, view, church] that is on a hilltop □ *the small hilltop towns of Tuscany.*

hilly ['hɪlɪ] (*compar* **hillier,** *superl* **hilliest**) *adj* [country, region] that is full of hills □ *The countryside becomes very hilly further north.*

hilt [hɪlt] *n* the handle of a sword, dagger etc □ *a sword with a jeweled hilt.* ■ **to back/defend etc sb to the hilt** to support/defend etc sb as much as one can □ *My colleagues have promised to back me to the hilt over this issue.* ■ **to be mortgaged to the hilt** to have a very big mortgage.

him [hɪm] *pron* the man, boy, or male animal that has just been mentioned, seen etc (used as the object of a verb and after prepositions) □ *"Do you know Dave?" — "Yes, I met him at your party."* □ *They sent him a letter.* □ *I'm very grateful to him.*

Himalayas [,hɪmə'leɪəz]: **the Himalayas** a mountain range in southern Asia, covering most of Nepal, Bhutan, southern Tibet, and northern India. It includes Mount Everest. HIGHEST POINT: 8,846 m.

himself [hɪm'self] *pron* **-1.** used as the object of a verb to refer to the same person as the subject "he" used after a preposition □ *He hates himself for what he did.* □ *Joe looked at himself in the mirror.* **-2.** used to emphasize "he", or the name of a man or boy that is the object of a verb □ *I asked to speak to the manager himself.* **-3. he did it himself** he did it without any help from anyone else □ *He built this house himself.* ■ **by himself** alone □ *He was sitting by himself on a park bench.*

hind [haɪnd] (*pl* **hind** OR **hinds**) ◇ *adj* [leg, feet] at the back part of an animal's body. ◇ *n* a female deer, especially a red deer.

hinder ['hɪndər] *vt* [progress, attempt] to make it difficult or impossible for <sthg> to develop or happen by causing problems □ *Bad weather hindered them from delivering supplies.*

Hindi ['hɪndɪ] *n* a language spoken in northern central India □ *Hindi speakers.*

hindmost ['haɪndməʊst] *adj* that is nearest to the back end of something (old-fashioned use).

hindquarters ['haɪndkwɔːˈtəʳz] *npl* the back part and back legs of an animal.

hindrance ['hɪndrəns] *n* [to progress, an attempt] a person or thing that hinders somebody or something □ *Actually, he was more of a hindrance than a help.*

hindsight ['haɪndsaɪt] *n* **with** OR **in hindsight** looking back at the past and knowing now what one did not know then □ *Now, with the benefit of hindsight, I can see I made the wrong decision.*

Hindu ['hɪnduː] (*pl* **Hindus**) ◇ *adj* [god, temple, faith] that is connected with Hinduism. ◇ *n* a person who believes in Hinduism.

Hinduism ['hɪnduːɪzm] *n* one of the main religions in India that has several gods and promises life after death.

hinge [hɪndʒ] (*cont* **hingeing**) *n* a device, usually made of two flat metal parts held together by a pin, that allows a door, lid etc to swing open and shut.

◆ **hinge (up)on** *vt fus* **to hinge (up)on sthg** [upon an outcome, somebody's support] to depend on sthg completely □ *Success hinges on whether we can get the funds.*

hint [hɪnt] ◇ *n* **-1.** [to a person] a statement that gives a suggestion or clue about something but does not say anything clear about it □ *The speech contained a few hints as to the proposed policy changes.* □ *There was no hint that one day he would achieve greatness.* ■ **to drop a hint** to deliberately give a hint to somebody □ *I was desperately trying to drop him a hint to leave.* ■ **to take a hint** to understand a hint and do what is suggested □ *OK, I can take a hint!* **-2.** [about a subject] a helpful piece of advice about a particular subject or activity □ *The book is packed with hints on houseplants.* **-3.** [of color, summer, victory] a small sign of something □ *As he spoke, there was a hint of sadness in his voice.*
◇ *vi* to give a clue or suggestion to somebody about something □ *The statement hints at some kind of compromise.*
◇ *vt*: *The President hinted that interest rates may rise soon.*

hinterland ['hɪntəʳlænd] *n* **the hinterland** the land further back from a coast, river, or port; the poorer areas away from large towns and cities.

hip [hɪp] ◇ *n* the part at either side of the human body above the legs and below the waist □ *Stand with your hands on your hips.* ◇ *adj* [music, clothes] fashionable (informal use).

hip bath *n* a small bath that one can sit in but not lie down in.

hipbone ['hɪpbəʊn] *n* the main bone in the hip.

hip flask *n* a small metal container for strong alcoholic drinks that one carries in one's pocket or joined to one's belt.

hip-hop *n* a kind of black American dance music that is more spoken than sung, has more beat than tune, and uses and repeats parts of other songs.

hippie ['hɪpɪ] *n* = **hippy**.

hippo ['hɪpəʊ] (*pl* **hippos**) *n* = **hippopotamus** (informal use).

Hippocrates [hɪ'pɒkrətiːz] (460–377 BC) a Greek doctor who was the first person to develop a scientific approach to medicine.

hippopotamus [ˌhɪpə'pɒtəməs] (*pl* **hippopotamuses** or **hippopotami** [-maɪ]) *n* a large African river animal with a large head, wide mouth, short legs, and hard gray skin.

hippy ['hɪpɪ] (*pl* **hippies**) *n* a person who does not accept the traditional values of society, has long hair, and dresses in loose brightly-colored clothes. Hippies are especially associated with the late 1960s.

hire ['haɪəʳ] ◇ *n* GB [of equipment, a car, hall] the use of something for a period of time in return for money □ *'Bicycles for hire'* □ *It's not mine, it's only on hire.* ◇ *vt* **-1.** [plumber, assassin, performer] to pay <sb> to do a particular job; [staff, agent] to employ <sb> □ *We hired a painter to do the bedrooms.* □ *You're hired!* **-2.** GB [car, equipment, hall] to pay to use <sthg> for a short time □ *Let's hire bikes.*

◆ **hire out** *vt sep* **to hire sthg out** [car, equipment, hall] to offer sthg to people by allowing them to hire it □ *Freelancers work by hiring out their services to others.*

hire car *n* GB a car that is rented.

hired help ['haɪəʳd-] *n* temporary staff employed to do a particular job, e.g. on a farm or in a house; a temporary worker.

hire purchase *n* GB a method of buying something by paying for it gradually, so that one is able to use the product before one has paid for it completely □ *We bought the car/video on hire purchase.*

Hirohito [ˌhɪrəʊ'hiːtəʊ] (1901–1989) Emperor of Japan from 1926 to 1989.

Hiroshima [US ˌhɪrəʊ'ʃiːmə, GB hɪ'rɒʃɪmə] a city in southwest Japan where the first atomic bomb was dropped in 1945.

his [hɪz] ◇ *det* **-1.** used to show that something belongs to or is connected with the man, boy, or male animal that has just been mentioned, seen etc □ *He put on his coat and went out.* □ *Joe was eating his lunch when I arrived.* **-2.** used in statements where no specific person has been identified □ *Everyone coming to the conference must make his own travel arrangements.* **-3.** used in titles to refer to a man □ *His Excellency will see you now.*
◇ *pron* used to show that something belongs to or is connected with the man, boy, or male animal that has just been mentioned, seen etc □ *A friend of his told him about it.* □ *I ate all my lunch, but he hardly touched his.*

Hispanic [hɪ'spænɪk] ◇ *n* a person in the USA whose family originally came from Latin America. ◇ *adj*: *a Hispanic dish/district.*

Hispaniola [ˌhɪspæn'jəʊlə] an island in the Caribbean, southeast of Cuba. It is divided into Haiti and the Dominican Republic. SIZE: 76,150 sq kms. OLD NAME: Santo Domingo.

hiss [hɪs] ◇ *vi* -1. [machine, snake, fire] to make a sound like a long "s" □ *The hot pan hissed under the cold water.* -2. [person] to speak in a strong whisper, often to show anger or disapproval □ *The crowd booed and hissed at the police.* ◇ *vt* [performance, speaker] to show that one dislikes or disapproves of <sb/sthg> by hissing. ◇ *n* the sound of somebody or something hissing □ *There was a hiss of escaping steam.*

histogram ['hɪstəgræm] *n* a chart in which figures are represented by vertical rectangular boxes of different lengths.

historian [hɪ'stɔːrɪən] *n* a person who studies and writes about history □ *a medieval historian.*

historic [hɪ'stɒrɪk] *adj* [event, occasion, decision] important in history □ *This is a historic day for our country.*

historical [hɪ'stɒrɪkl] *adj* -1. [event, fact, figure] that is part of the past □ *The book is faithful to historical reality.* -2. [novel, setting] that shows people and things of the past □ *a historical drama for TV.*

history ['hɪstrɪ] (*pl* **histories**) *n* -1. [of a country] the past events in the life of people, a country, or activity, especially the most important events, considered all together in the order they happened □ *Three men who changed the course of human history.* □ *Throughout history man has fought wars.* ■ **to go down in history** to be remembered by people much later on for doing something important □ *Yeltsin will go down in history for standing up to the coup leaders.* ■ **to make history** to be remembered by people much later on for doing something for the first time □ *The athlete made history by breaking three records in the same day.* -2. EDUCATION the subject that involves the study of history □ *a degree in ancient/modern history.* -3. [of art, science] a written description of the development of something in particular □ *I'm reading a history of Hollywood/space travel.* -4. [of a patient, criminal] information that has been recorded about somebody or something and is used to have a clearer idea of them □ *a crook with a history of petty crime.* □ *He has a history of heart trouble.*

histrionics [ˌhɪstrɪ'ɒnɪks] *npl* very emotional behavior that is usually not sincere □ *There were the usual histrionics when the time came for us to leave.*

hit [hɪt] (*pt* & *pp* **hit**, *cont* **hitting**) ◇ *vt* -1. [person, ball, nail] to bring one's hand or an object held in the hand into violent contact with <sb/sthg> □ *She hit me with her bag.* □ *Don't hit your brother!* □ *He hit the ball right over the fence.* -2. [person, tree, target] to come into violent contact with <sb/sthg> □ *The car hit the wall at 50 mph.* □ *He was hit by a bullet.* □ *He hit his head on the window.* -3. [target, note, level] to reach <sb/sthg> □ *The storm hit the city at 3 am.* □ *The news soon hit TV screens all*

over the world. □ *Sales have hit an all-time low.* ■ **to hit the headlines** [person, story] to suddenly receive a lot of attention in newspapers. -4. [person, area, company] to affect <sb/sthg> badly □ *Immediate aid was promised for regions worst hit by the famine.* -5. *phrase* **to hit it off** [two people] to form a friendly relationship soon after meeting □ *He immediately hit it off with my dad.* □ *I had a feeling you two would hit it off.*
◇ *n* -1. [against a wall, car, door] the act of hitting a person, ball etc □ *Give the ball a good hard hit.* -2. [of a target] the act of successfully hitting a target □ *I scored a direct hit with my second shot.* -3. [with the public] a record, movie, play etc that is very popular □ *a hit record.*

◆ **hit back** *vi* to reply to criticism from somebody by criticizing them □ *She angrily hit back at those who had criticized her.*

◆ **hit on** *vt fus* -1. = **hit upon.** -2. **to hit on sb** US to speak to sb with the intention of attracting them and possibly having sex (informal use).

◆ **hit out** *vi* **to hit out at sb/sthg** to physically attack sb/sthg; to criticize sb/sthg strongly in speech or writing □ *The old lady bravely hit out at her attackers.* □ *The coach hit out at suggestions he should retire.*

◆ **hit upon** *vt fus* **to hit upon sthg** [answer, idea, plan] to think of sthg, especially the solution to a problem, after thinking about it for a long time.

hit-and-miss *adj* = **hit-or-miss.**

hit-and-run *adj* [accident] that involves a driver who drives away immediately after an accident; [driver] who causes an accident but drives away immediately afterwards □ *Their daughter was killed in a hit-and-run accident.*

hitch [hɪtʃ] ◇ *n* [in proceedings, plans] a small problem that causes a short delay □ *a technical hitch* □ *There's one small hitch: who's going to pay?* ◇ *vt* -1. **to hitch a ride** OR **lift** to get a free ride somewhere in somebody's car, truck etc, by sticking out one's thumb at the roadside □ *Can I hitch a ride to the nearest gas station?* -2. [horses, rope] to fasten <sthg> on to something else in a particular way □ *Walter hitched the pony to the cart.* ◇ *vi* to travel somewhere by hitching a ride (informal use) □ *We hitched all the way to Sacramento.*

◆ **hitch up** *vt sep* **to hitch sthg up** [skirt, trousers] to pull the top part of sthg up to a higher level □ *She hitched up her skirt and waded into the river.*

Hitchcock ['hɪtʃkɒk], **Sir Alfred** (1899–1980) a British movie director who created movies full of suspense such as *Psycho* and *The Birds.*

hitchhike ['hɪtʃhaɪk] *vi* to travel by hitching rides □ *They plan to hitchhike across the country.*

hitchhiker ['hɪtʃhaɪkər] *n* a person who travels by hitching rides □ *I never give rides to hitchhikers.*

hi-tech [ˌhaɪ'tek] *adj* = **high-tech.**

hither ['hɪðər] *adv* to this place (literary use). ■

hither and thither in all directions at once □ *Everybody was running hither and thither.*

hitherto [ˌhɪðəˈtuː] *adv* up until then; up until now (formal use) □ *Hitherto, it has not been possible to envision a peace settlement.*

Hitler [ˈhɪtləʳ], **Adolf** (1889–1945) the leader of the German Nazi Party, and head of state from 1933 to 1945. His invasions of neighboring countries led to World War II.

hit list *n* a list of people who have to be killed, places that have to be damaged etc by a terrorist organization □ *The minister's name was discovered on the terrorists' hit list.*

hit man *n* a person who is paid to kill somebody.

hit-or-miss *adj* that may or may not be successful □ *It all sounds a little hit-or-miss to me.*

hit parade *n* the list of pop records that have sold the most copies each week or month (old-fashioned use).

HIV (*abbr of* **human immunodeficiency virus**) *n* the virus that causes AIDS □ *an HIV test.* ■ **to be HIV-positive** to have HIV.

hive [haɪv] *n* a container for bees to live in. ■ **a hive of activity** a place where a lot of people are busy working.

◆ **hive off** *vt sep* **to hive sthg off** [business, assets] to sell sthg that is part of a larger group.

HK *abbr of* **Hong Kong**.

hl (*abbr of* **hectoliter**) *n* a unit (*100 liters*) for measuring liquids.

HM *abbr of* **Her (or His) Majesty**.

HMG (*abbr of* **Her (or His) Majesty's Government**) an expression used on official documents to refer to the British government.

HMI (*abbr of* **Her (or His) Majesty's Inspector**) *n* a British government official whose job is to check that schools are being run properly.

HMO (*abbr of* **health maintenance organization**) *n* one of many organizations in the USA that own one or more hospitals and offer health insurance. People can pay regular amounts in order to get treatment in them when they are sick.

HMS (*abbr of* **Her (or His) Majesty's Ship**) used in the title of a ship in the British navy □ *HMS Ark Royal.*

HMSO (*abbr of* **Her (or His) Majesty's Stationery Office**) *n* the British government department responsible for publishing government documents.

HNC (*abbr of* **Higher National Certificate**) *n* a British technical qualification.

HND (*abbr of* **Higher National Diploma**) *n* a British technical qualification that is the equivalent of an ordinary degree.

hoard [hɔːʳd] ◇ *vt* [food, money, paper] to save <sthg> and keep it for later, either in secret or in larger amounts than is necessary □ *People started hoarding sugar in case there was a shortage.* ◇ *n* [of coins, arms, food] a collection of things that have been hoarded secretly □ *Workmen came across a hoard of jewelry that had been buried there long ago.*

hoarding [ˈhɔːʳdɪŋ] *n* GB a large board next to a road that is used for large advertisements.

hoarfrost [ˈhɔːʳfrɒst] *n* white frost that forms during the night.

hoarse [hɔːʳs] *adj* [voice, cry] that sounds rough and is not strong, especially because one has been shouting or singing too much □ *The boys were hoarse from cheering.*

hoax [həʊks] *n* an attempt by somebody to make people believe something that is not true, especially by saying that something dangerous is going to happen □ *a hoax call.*

hoaxer [ˈhəʊksəʳ] *n* a person who makes a hoax.

hob [hɒb] *n* GB the horizontal surface on top of a stove where things are put to cook □ *an electric hob.*

Hobart [ˈhəʊbɑːʳt] a seaport and the capital of Tasmania, Australia. It was founded as a penal colony in 1804. POPULATION: 179,900.

hobble [ˈhɒbl] *vi* to walk with difficulty because one has a sore foot or leg □ *Randy hobbled toward me on crutches.*

hobby [ˈhɒbɪ] (*pl* **hobbies**) *n* something one does in one's free time for pleasure and relaxation □ *What are your hobbies?* □ *My hobby is gardening.*

hobbyhorse [ˈhɒbɪhɔːʳs] *n* **-1.** [of a person] a subject one likes to talk about whenever possible □ *He's off on his hobbyhorse again.* **-2.** [for children] a toy that consists of a model of a horse's head at the top of a stick.

hobnob [ˈhɒbnɒb] (*pt & pp* **hobnobbed**, *cont* **hobnobbing**) *vi* **to hobnob with sb** to spend time with sb socially, especially if they are in a higher social position □ *There was Pete, hobnobbing with all the important guests.*

hobo [ˈhəʊbəʊ] (*pl* **hoboes** OR **hobos**) *n* US a man without a home or family who travels around and sleeps in different places.

Ho Chi Minh City [ˌhəʊtʃiːmɪnˈsɪtɪ] a seaport in southern Vietnam. POPULATION: 3,500,000. OLD NAME: Saigon.

hock [hɒk] *n* a dry white wine from Germany □ *a bottle/glass of hock.*

hockey [ˈhɒkɪ] *n* **-1.** US a game played on ice between two teams of players who try to score points by using a long curved stick to hit a small rubber disk into each other's goal □ *a game of hockey.* **-2.** GB = **field hockey**.

hockey stick *n* a curved stick used to hit the puck or ball in hockey.

hocus-pocus [ˌhəʊkəsˈpəʊkəs] *n* confusing or meaningless words or actions intended to hide the truth from people.

hod [hɒd] *n* a small open box on a pole that is used for carrying bricks.

hodgepodge [ˈhɒdʒpɒdʒ] US, **hotchpotch** [ˈhɒtʃpɒtʃ] GB *n* a mixture of different things, not arranged in any order (informal use).

hoe [həʊ] ◇ *n* a gardening tool with a long pole and small blade that is used to break up lumps of earth and to remove small plants. ◇ *vt* to work <land> with a hoe.

hog [hɒg] (*pt & pp* **hogged**, *cont* **hogging**) ◇ *n*

-1. a pig, especially a male one that is kept for its meat. -2. **to go the whole hog** to do something as completely as possible, often by spending a lot of money (informal use) □ *We might as well go the whole hog and order champagne.* ◇ *vt* [road, food, attention] to take or keep <sthg> so that other people cannot have or use it (informal use) □ *Stop trying to hog the wine.*

Hogarth [ˈhoʊgɑːrθ], **William** (1697–1764) a British artist who made a famous set of engravings called *The Rake's Progress* that show human vice and weakness.

Hogmanay [ˈhɒgməneɪ] *n* the name for New Year's Eve in Scotland.

hoi-polloi [ˌhɔɪpəˈlɔɪ] *npl* **the hoi-polloi** the ordinary common people, rather than the wealthy people of society (disapproving and humorous use).

hoist [hɔɪst] ◇ *vt* -1. [sack, child, furniture] to lift <sb/sthg> up using one's hands, by pulling ropes, or with a machine □ *They had to hoist the piano in through the window.* -2. [flag, sail] to pull <sthg> up along a pole using ropes. ◇ *n* a piece of equipment for lifting heavy objects.

Hokkaido [US hoʊˈkaɪdoʊ, GB hɒ-] the second largest island of Japan, in the north. SIZE: 78,500 sq kms. POPULATION: 5,643,647. MAIN CITY: Sapporo.

hokum [ˈhoʊkəm] *n* US nonsense (informal use).

hold [hoʊld] (*pt* & *pp* **held**) ◇ *vt* -1. [cup, book, gun] to have <sthg> in one's hand or hands □ *He was holding a bunch of flowers.* □ *Could you hold my bag for a second?* -2. [baby, kitten, bundle] to have <sb/sthg> in one's arms; [person] to put one's arms around <sb> and bring them close to one's body, especially to comfort them or show affection □ *a woman holding a child* □ *He held her tightly in his arms until she stopped crying.* -3. to keep <sthg> in a particular place or position □ *Hold the lid down.* □ *Lee held the plank in place while I hammered in the nail.* □ *She held her head high.* -4. [prisoner, hostage] to keep <sb> in a place against their wishes, especially for a short time □ *He is being held by police for questioning.* ■ **to hold sb prisoner/hostage** to keep sb in a place as a prisoner/hostage □ *The gunmen are said to be holding five people hostage.* -5. to be able to contain <a particular amount or number of sthg> □ *The main hall holds 300 people.* □ *Each bottle holds about six glasses.* -6. [power, land, money] to possess <sthg>; [license, permit, certificate] to have an <official document> □ *He holds a position of great responsibility.* □ *Those holding shares/an interest in the company may vote.* -7. [meeting, debate, talks] to cause <sthg> to take place □ *Excuse me, we're trying to hold a private conversation.* □ *Protesters held a demonstration outside the embassy.* -8. **please hold the line** a phrase used in business or official telephone calls to ask the caller to wait. -9. **to hold sb's attention/interest** to keep sb's attention/interest □ *his desperate attempts to hold the attention of a group of five-year-olds.* -10. MILITARY [area, town]

to control <a place> □ *southern villages being held by the security forces* -11. [documents, files] to contain <sthg> □ *This handy rack will hold all your CDs.* -12. **what does the future hold?** what lies ahead in the future? -13. **to hold an opinion/a belief** to have a particular opinion/belief □ *She holds strong views on the subject.* ■ **to hold (that)...** to consider that something is true □ *The Constitution holds that all citizens are born equal.* ■ **to hold sb responsible for sthg** to blame sb for sthg bad because one feels they should have prevented it □ *I'll hold you personally responsible if anything goes wrong.* ■ **to hold sthg dear** to be fond of sthg (formal use). -14. *phrases* **hold it!**, **hold everything!** a phrase used to tell somebody to stop what they are doing □ *Hold everything! Here comes Sacha now.* ■ **to hold one's own** to do as well as other people who one is competing with □ *He seems to be holding his own at his new school.*

◇ *vi* -1. [luck, weather, objection] to remain as it is, without changing □ *The offer still holds.* □ *We can go tomorrow, if the weather holds.* -2. **to hold still** OR **steady** to keep still □ *Hold still while I fasten your coat!* -3. [on the telephone] to wait □ *The line's busy, will you hold?*

◇ *n* -1. [of a person] the way in which somebody holds something □ *He kept a tight hold on her arm.* ■ **to get hold of sthg** to get sthg that is difficult to find □ *Everyone's dying to get hold of her autobiography.* ■ **to get hold of sb** to manage to find sb or talk to them on the phone □ *I'm trying to get hold of the sales manager.* □ *Where can we get hold of you over the weekend?* ■ **to keep hold of sthg** to continue holding sthg in one's hand □ *Keep hold of my hand.* ■ **to take** OR **lay hold of sthg** to put one's hands around sthg and hold it □ *Here, take hold of this rope.* -2. [in a ship, aircraft] the place in a ship or aircraft where goods are stored. -3. **to have a hold on** OR **over sb** to be able to control sb because one knows something bad about them or is in a powerful position □ *That man seems to have some sort of hold on her!* -4. *phrase* **to take hold** [fire, blaze] to start burning strongly.

◆ **hold against** *vt sep* **to hold sthg against sb** to continue to feel angry towards sb because of sthg bad they did in the past □ *I didn't give her the job and she's held it against me ever since.* □ *Go if you like, I won't hold it against you.*

◆ **hold back** ◇ *vi* [person] not to do something because one is not sure what the result will be □ *He held back from telling me what he really thought.* ◇ *vt sep* -1. **to hold sthg back** [rage, laughter] to try not to show sthg □ *She struggled to hold back the tears.* -2. **to hold sthg back** [news, information, fact] to keep sthg secret □ *You're holding something back from me!* -3. **to hold sb back** [crowd] to prevent sb from moving forward; [employee, pupil] to prevent sb from doing what they want to do □ *Police tried to hold back the demonstrators.* □ *Don't let me hold you back from working.*

◆ **hold down** *vt sep* -1. **to hold down a job** to stay employed in a job □ *He's never managed* to hold down a job for more than six months. **-2. to hold sthg down** [prices, rates] to prevent sthg from rising □ *Tight monetary policies have held inflation down to 2%.*

◆ **hold off** ◇ *vt sep* **to hold sb off** [attacker, army] to stop sb from getting too close to one □ *I can't hold off the reporters any longer.* ◇ *vi* **the rain held off** it looked as if it would rain but it didn't.

◆ **hold on** *vi* to wait for a short time □ *We'll have to hold on until Tuesday for the results.* □ *Hold on a moment and I'll go and get him for you.*

◆ **hold onto** *vt fus* **-1. to hold onto sthg** [onto a rope, bannister, the reins] to hold sthg firmly with one's hand or hands □ *Hold onto the rail or you'll fall!* **-2. to hold onto sthg** [onto power, a belief, one's job] to keep sthg and not lose it or throw it away □ *You should have held onto those old records, they'd be worth a fortune now.*

◆ **hold out** ◇ *vt sep* **to hold sthg out** [hand, arm, object] to move sthg away from one's body, usually when offering it to another person □ *She came up to us, holding out two glasses of wine.* ◇ *vi* **-1.** [food, water, supply] to last □ *We'll stay as long as the money holds out.* **-2.** [rebel, striker, union] to fight for as long as possible against a stronger enemy or an undesirable change □ *The garrison held out for another month before surrendering.*

◆ **hold out for** *vt fus* **to hold out for sthg** not to accept something one has been offered and wait for sthg better □ *Nurses have turned down the 3% offer and are holding out for 4.5%.*

◆ **hold up** *vt sep* **-1. to hold sthg up** [hand, object] to raise sthg in the air so that it can be seen □ *She held up the photograph to the light.* **-2. to hold sthg up** [production, traffic, person] to delay sb/sthg □ *Sorry I'm late, I got held up at the office.* **-3. to hold a bank/store/train etc up** to threaten people in a bank/store/train etc with a weapon and then steal money from them □ *He was held up at gunpoint by masked raiders.*

◆ **hold with** *vt fus* **to hold with sthg** to approve of sthg □ *I don't hold with that kind of behavior!*

holdall ['hoʊldɔːl] *n* a large bag with handles in which people carry their clothes and other personal things when traveling.

holder ['hoʊldər] *n* **-1.** something that is designed to hold a particular object □ *a cigarette holder* □ *a CD holder.* **-2.** a person who owns or has a particular thing □ *'Ticket holders only.'*

holding ['hoʊldɪŋ] ◇ *n* **-1.** FINANCE an investment or share in a company □ *We have a 30% holding in the company.* **-2.** FARMING a piece of land that is farmed by the person who owns or rents it. ◇ *adj* **a holding operation** OR **action** something that one does to try to stop a situation from getting worse □ *The best we can do is a holding operation.*

holding company *n* a company that has most of the shares in another company.

holdup ['hoʊldʌp] *n* **-1.** a robbery where people are threatened with a gun □ *This is a*

holdup! **-2.** a delay □ *I'm sorry about the holdup in sending you the information.*

hole [hoʊl] *n* **-1.** a hollow or empty space in something solid □ *You've got a hole in your sleeve.* □ *The workmen dug a deep hole in the ground.* ■ **to pick holes in sthg** [in a theory, argument] to find faults in sthg □ *He's always picking holes in my ideas.* **-2.** SPORT in golf, one of the small round holes that the ball is hit into. ■ **a hole in one** a successful attempt to hit the ball into one of the holes with only one stroke. **-3.** a place one thinks is unattractive or boring (informal use) □ *This town's a real hole!* **-4.** a situation that is difficult to get out of (informal use).

◆ **hole up** *vi* to hide in a particular place to avoid trouble (informal use) □ *Do you mind if I hole up with you for a while?*

holiday ['hɒlədeɪ] *n* **-1.** GB a time when one can rest and enjoy oneself away from home; a time when one does not have to go to work or school □ *We're spending our holidays in Spain this year.* □ *I have two weeks' holiday coming up.* □ *a walking/cycling holiday* □ *I'm on holiday!* ■ **to go on holiday** to go to a place away from home for one's holiday □ *The neighbors have gone on holiday.* **-2.** a day when everyone who does not do essential work has a rest □ *Monday is a public holiday.*

holiday camp *n* GB a place that provides accommodation and entertainment, where people can go to spend their vacation □ *They stayed at a holiday camp in Wales.*

holiday loading *n* in Australia, an extra payment given to most employees when they take their main vacations.

holidaymaker ['hɒlədeɪmeɪkər] *n* GB a person who is on vacation □ *The plane was full of holidaymakers.*

holiday pay *n* GB pay that one receives from one's employer when one is on vacation □ *There is no mention of holiday pay in my contract.*

holiday resort *n* GB a place where people go on vacation □ *What was a sleepy coastal village has become a fashionable holiday resort.*

holiday season *n* GB the period of the year, usually in the summer, when most people go on vacation.

holiness ['hoʊlɪnəs] *n: see* **holy** □ *the holiness of God.*

◆ **Holiness** *n* **His/Your Holiness** the words used when talking about/to the Pope and some other religious leaders.

holistic [hoʊ'lɪstɪk] *adj* [solution, approach] that is based on the idea that a person or thing should be considered as a whole and not just as a collection of different parts. ■ **holistic medicine** a way of treating people by looking at not only their illness but also their social background, mental state etc.

Holland ['hɒlənd] = **Netherlands**.

hollandaise sauce [ˌhɒləndeɪz-] *n* a rich sauce made with eggs and butter.

holler ['hɒlər] (informal use) ◇ *vi* to shout loudly □ *He just stood there, hollering at me.* ◇ *vt:* "Watch out!" he hollered.

hollow ['hɒloʊ] ◇ *adj* -1. [tree, bracelet, statue] that has an empty space inside □ *There was a hollow space behind the wall.* □ *All that remained of the house was a hollow shell.* -2. [cheeks, eyes] that have sunk inward. -3. [sound, noise] that echoes □ *The door closed with a hollow thud.* -4. [promise, threat, victory] that has no real value or meaning □ *With so much lost already, any victory is likely to prove hollow.* ■ **a hollow laugh** a laugh that shows that one does not really find something funny.
◇ *n* -1. an empty space in something such as a tree □ *He had great hollows in his cheeks.* -2. a part of something, especially the ground, that is lower than the surrounding area □ *The cottage was in a hollow in the woods.*

◆ **hollow out** *vt sep* **to hollow sthg out** [tree trunk, log] to remove the inside part of sthg; [shape, canoe] to make sthg by removing the inside part of something else.

holly ['hɒlɪ] *n* an evergreen bush with dark green prickly leaves and red berries.

hollyhock ['hɒlɪhɒk] *n* a tall garden plant with a thick hairy stem and large white, red, yellow, or purple flowers.

Hollywood ['hɒlɪwʊd] -1. an area of Los Angeles, California. It is the center of the US movie industry. -2. the movie industry in the USA □ *a Hollywood movie star* □ *Hollywood studios.*

Holmes [hoʊmz], **Sherlock** the hero of the detective stories by Sir Arthur Conan Doyle. He smokes a pipe, plays the violin, and is very good at solving mysteries.

holocaust ['hɒləkɔːst] *n* great destruction and the killing of many people □ *a nuclear holocaust.*

◆ **Holocaust** *n* **the Holocaust** the organized killing of many Jews in Europe by Nazi Germany □ *She lost her entire family in the Holocaust.*

hologram [US 'hoʊləgræm, GB 'hɒl-] *n* a three-dimensional picture made with lasers.

Holst [hoʊlst], **Gustav** (1874–1934) a British composer, whose major orchestral work is *The Planets.*

holster ['hoʊlstəʳ] *n* a holder for a gun, attached to a belt.

holy ['hoʊlɪ] (*compar* **holier**, *superl* **holiest**) *adj* -1. [book, image, place] that is connected with God and is therefore considered to be special □ *Jerusalem is the holy city of three religions.* -2. [person] who leads a good and religious life □ *He always led a pure and holy life.*

Holy Communion *n* a Christian service in which bread and wine are shared to represent Christ's last meal with his 12 disciples.

Holy Family *n* **the Holy Family** Jesus, Mary, and Joseph.

Holy Ghost *n* **the Holy Ghost** in the Christian religion, the presence of God, often pictured as a white dove.

Holy Grail [-'greɪl] *n* **the Holy Grail** the cup that Christ is said to have drunk from at the Last Supper and that many legendary characters have searched for.

Holy Land: **the Holy Land** a term for a region of the Middle East, between the Jordan River and the Mediterranean, where most of the Bible stories took place.

holy orders *npl* **to take holy orders** to become a priest.

Holy Spirit *n* = **Holy Ghost**.

homage ['hɒmɪdʒ] *n* something that one says or does that shows great respect for a person in authority or whom one admires (formal use) □ *The movie is intended as a homage to Chandler.* ■ **to pay homage to sb/sthg** to show great respect to sb/sthg □ *Mr Nikolov paid homage to the bravery of ordinary Russians.*

home [hoʊm] ◇ *n* -1. the building or place where one lives □ *the family home* □ *London's my home now.* □ *They made their home in Milan for a while.* □ *The marshes are home to thousands of wading birds.* ■ **a home away from home** US, **a home from home** GB a place that is as comfortable, well-equipped, pleasant etc as one's own home □ *Our place on Long Island has always been a home away from home for the kids.* -2. [of a movement, style] the place where somebody or something comes from □ *New Orleans is the home of jazz.* -3. [family] a person's house and family □ *a broken/happy home* □ *She came from a normal middle-class home.* ■ **to leave home** to stop living with one's family, especially because one is old enough to live alone □ *She left home at 16 to work in a factory.* -4. [for children, old people] a place where a particular group of people or animals that cannot look after themselves are cared for □ *a children's/dogs' home* □ *She wants to put her mother in an old people's home.*
◇ *adj* -1. **home life** one's life with one's family ■ **home furnishings** furnishings designed for the home ■ **home cooking** cooking that is done at home □ *a few home comforts.* -2. **home news/affairs** news/affairs connected with one's own country, not foreign countries □ *our home affairs correspondent* □ *We are having to cater for an expanding home market.* -3. SPORT **a home game** a game that is played at a team's own field □ *another home win for Juventus.*
◇ *adv* -1. [go, walk, hurry] to or at one's house □ *He took her home to meet his parents.* □ *She should be home shortly.* -2. [return, fly] to one's own country from abroad □ *Illegal immigrants were being sent home.* -3. **to bring sthg home to sb** to make sb understand how important sthg is □ *Recent price increases have brought home to the public the risks of inflation.* ■ **to drive** OR **hammer sthg home** to make sthg clearly understood in a forceful way □ *Her speech really hammered home the message.*

◆ **at home** *adv* -1. [be, stay, work] in one's house □ *I've left my briefcase at home.* -2. **to feel at home** to feel relaxed and comfortable □ *I never feel very at home in their apartment.* ■ **to be** OR **feel at home with sthg** to be familiar with sthg so that one uses or does it with confidence □ *I feel quite at home with a left-hand drive car.* ■ **to make oneself at home** to behave in a relaxed manner as if one was in one's own house □ *Make yourselves at home* *while I put the coffee on.* **-3.** in one's own country □ *The stores don't shut in the middle of the day at home.* **-4.** SPORT **to play at home** [team, player] to play at the ground where one is based.

◆ **home in on** *vt fus* **to home in on sthg** [fact, problem, mistake] to give all one's attention to sthg small; [target, prey] to find sthg or be aimed at it and attack it □ *I'd like to home in on something you just said.* □ *The missiles are homing in on their target.*

home address *n* the address of the house or apartment where one lives □ *Please send the check to my home address.*

home banking *n* a system of banking where all business is done by home computer or telephone, so that one does not need to go to the bank.

home base *n* the fourth and last base on a baseball field, that is also the homeplate.

home brew *n* beer that one makes oneself at home.

homecoming ['houmkʌmɪŋ] *n* **-1.** somebody's return to a place they have not seen for a long time □ *It was an emotional homecoming for me.* **-2.** EDUCATION an annual celebration at a college or university in the USA for people who used to be students there.

home computer *n* a small computer for personal use at home.

home cooking *n* food that one prepares and cooks oneself at home.

Home Counties: **the Home Counties** the counties in southeastern England around London.

home economics *n* a subject at school that deals with cooking, sewing, and how to run a home.

home fries *npl* US boiled potatoes that have been sliced and fried.

home ground *n* **-1. to be on home ground** to be in a place that one knows very well □ *When the train crossed the border, I felt like I was on home ground.* **-2. to be on home ground** to be dealing with a subject that one knows very well □ *If you've studied computing before, you'll be on home ground here.* **-3.** SPORT the stadium, field etc that belongs to a particular team and which is their local base □ *The team will be playing on (its) home ground.*

homegrown [,houm'groun] *adj* [fruit, vegetable] that one has grown in one's own garden; that has been grown in one's country □ *These tomatoes are homegrown.*

home help *n* GB a person employed by the social services to go to the homes of sick or old people and help them with cleaning and cooking.

home improvements *npl* work that one does to one's home to make it more comfortable or attractive.

homeland ['houmlænd] *n* **-1.** the country where one was born. **-2.** one of the areas that were set aside for the Black population under the apartheid system in South Africa.

homeless ['houmləs] ◇ *adj* [person, family] that has nowhere to live □ *Thousands of people were made homeless by the storms.* ◇ *npl* **the homeless** people, especially in a city, who have nowhere to live □ *New York's homeless.*

homelessness ['houmləsnəs] *n*: see **homeless** □ *the growing problem of homelessness.*

home loan *n* a loan that one gets in order to buy a house.

homely ['houmlɪ] *adj* **-1.** US [person, face] unattractive □ *She's a rather homely girl.* **-2.** GB [place, food, atmosphere] simple but comfortable □ *The house looked small and homely.*

homemade [,houm'meɪd] *adj* [jam, bread, wine] that has been made by somebody in their own home, not bought in a store □ *homemade marmalade.*

home movie *n* a movie that one makes of a family occasion, vacation etc and that is intended to be shown at home, not in a movie theater.

Home Office *n* **the Home Office** the British government department that deals with law and order, immigration, and broadcasting.

homeopath ['houmɪəpæθ] *n* a person qualified to practice homeopathy.

homeopathic [,houmɪə'pæθɪk] *adj* [remedy, treatment, medicine] see **homeopathy**.

homeopathy [,houmɪ'ɒpəθɪ] *n* a kind of alternative medicine that treats illness with very small amounts of natural substances.

homeowner ['houmounəʳ] *n* a person who owns their house or apartment.

homeplate ['houmpleɪt] *n* in baseball, the place where the umpire, the catcher, and the batter stand.

Homer ['houməʳ] (8th century BC) a Greek poet, whose long poems the *Iliad* and the *Odyssey* are very important in the history of Western literature.

Homer, Winslow (1836–1910) a US painter who is well known for his paintings of the sea.

home rule *n* government of an area or country by its own citizens.

home run *n* a long hit in baseball that allows the player to score a run.

Home Secretary *n* **the Home Secretary** the British government minister in charge of the Home Office.

home shopping *n* a way of buying things by ordering them by telephone or computer after seeing them on a special TV channel or computer link.

homesick ['houmsɪk] *adj* [person] who is unhappy because they are away from home □ *Don't you ever get homesick?*

homesickness ['houmsɪknəs] *n* [of person] see **homesick** □ *I used to suffer from terrible homesickness when I was working overseas.*

homespun ['houmspʌn] *adj* [philosophy, idea] simple and ordinary □ *Dave's homespun theories about how to run the country really annoy me.*

homestay ['houmsteɪ] *n* AUS **homestay (accom-**

modation) bed and breakfast accommodation in a private home.

homestead ['hoʊmsted] *n* US a farmhouse and the land around it.

Homestead Act *n* the Homestead Act a law passed in 1862 that aimed to encourage agricultural development in the west of the USA by giving land to settlers to farm.

home straight *n* GB = home stretch.

home stretch *n* US the home stretch [of a race] the final part of a race; [of a job, trip] the last stage of something.

hometown [ˌhoʊm'taʊn] *n* the town where one was born or grew up.

home truth *n* an unpleasant fact about somebody that somebody else tells them □ *It's about time he was told a few home truths.*

homeward ['hoʊmwərd] ◇ *adj* [trip] in the direction of home. ◇ *adv* = homewards.

homewards ['hoʊmwərdz] *adv* [go, travel] in the direction of home □ *I headed homewards.*

homework ['hoʊmwɜːrk] *n* -1. EDUCATION the work that teachers give their students to do at home □ *I do my homework regularly.* -2. **to do one's homework** to find out information about something so that one is prepared for something one does later.

homey ['hoʊmɪ] (*compar* homier, *superl* homiest) *adj* US [restaurant, atmosphere] that is relaxed and comfortable.

homicidal [ˌhɒmɪ'saɪdl] *adj* [person] who is likely to murder somebody □ *a homicidal maniac.*

homicide ['hɒmɪsaɪd] *n* the crime of murder (formal use).

homily ['hɒməlɪ] (*pl* homilies) *n* a long boring talk in which somebody usually criticizes another person and tells them how to behave □ *She gave me the usual homily about respecting one's elders.*

homing ['hoʊmɪŋ] *adj* -1. the homing instinct the ability that a bird or animal has to remember its way back home after traveling long distances. -2. a homing device a device in a weapon that guides it to its target.

homing pigeon *n* a pigeon that can find its way back home after flying long distances.

homoeopath *etc* ['hoʊmɪəpæθ] = homeopath *etc*.

homogeneous [ˌhoʊmə'dʒiːnɪəs] *adj* [group, class, community] that is made up of people or things of the same kind □ *The region is culturally homogeneous.*
NOTE: Compare **heterogeneous**.

homogenize, -ise [hə'mɒdʒənaɪz] *vt* to mix <milk> so that the cream is evenly spread.

homosexual [ˌhoʊmə'sekʃʊəl] ◇ *n* a person who is sexually attracted to people of the same sex as themselves. ◇ *adj*: *a homosexual man/woman/relationship.*

homosexuality [ˌhoʊməsekʃʊ'ælətɪ] *n*: *see* homosexual.

homy ['hoʊmɪ] *adj* US = homey.

Hon. -1. *abbr of* **Honourable**. -2. *abbr of* **Honorary**.

Honduras [hɒn'djʊərəs] a country in Central America, between Guatemala and Nicaragua. SIZE: 112,000 sq kms. POPULATION: 5,600,000 (*Hondurans*). CAPITAL: Tegucigalpa. LANGUAGE: Spanish. CURRENCY: lempira.

hone [hoʊn] *vt* -1. [knife, blade] to sharpen <sthg> □ *a honed sword.* -2. [one's skill, intellect] to develop and improve <sthg> over a long period of time □ *Rees honed his journalistic skills writing for a local paper.*

honest ['ɒnəst] ◇ *adj* -1. [person] who does not break the law and can be trusted □ *an honest law-abiding citizen.* -2. [person, answer, opinion] frank and truthful □ *Let's be honest with each other, we've both behaved badly.* ■ **to be honest,...** a phrase used to show that one is giving a frank opinion □ *To be honest, I don't care.* -3. [means, living] that does not involve breaking the law □ *The honest thing to do would be to hand the wallet in to the police.* ◇ *adv* a word used to emphasize that one is not lying (informal use) □ *I didn't do it, honest!*

honestly ['ɒnəstlɪ] ◇ *adv* -1. [live, act] truthfully or according to the law □ *I'll try to answer the questions honestly.* -2. a word used to emphasize that one is not lying □ *I did try, honestly!* ◇ *excl* a word used to express impatience or annoyance □ *Honestly, this is so unfair!*

honesty ['ɒnəstɪ] *n* [of a person, answer, opinion] *see* honest □ *Honesty is the best policy.*

honey ['hʌnɪ] *n* -1. a sweet sticky substance made by bees, often eaten on bread and used in cooking □ *I take honey in my tea rather than sugar.* -2. US a word used to talk to a person one is fond of (informal use) □ *Honey, I'm home!*

honeybee ['hʌnɪbiː] *n* a kind of bee which makes honey.

honeycomb ['hʌnɪkoʊm] *n* -1. a wax structure made by bees in which they store honey. -2. a pattern like a honeycomb.

honeymoon ['hʌnɪmuːn] ◇ *n* -1. the vacation which a couple take immediately after getting married □ *We went there on our honeymoon.* -2. the short period of time at the beginning of a new administration, business deal etc when everybody involved is happy and enthusiastic □ *The new President is enjoying a honeymoon period with the electorate.* ◇ *vi* [couple] to go on honeymoon □ *They're honeymooning in Paris.*

honeysuckle ['hʌnɪsʌkl] *n* a climbing plant with pale-yellow flowers that smell sweet.

Hong Kong [ˌhɒŋ'kɒŋ] a British colony in southeastern China, consisting of a group of islands and part of the mainland. A major banking, commercial, and industrial center, it will be given back to China in 1997. SIZE: 1,034 sq kms. POPULATION: 5,800,000. CAPITAL: Victoria. LANGUAGE: English, Cantonese. CURRENCY: Hong Kong dollar.

honk [hɒŋk] ◇ *n* -1. [of a car] the loud noise made by a car horn. -2. [of a goose] the loud noise made by a goose. ◇ *vt* [driver, car] to sound <a horn>. ◇ *vi* -1. [driver, car] *The bus honked at me to move.* -2. [goose] *The geese honked at the passing boats.*

honky▼ ['hɒŋkɪ] (*pl* **honkies**) *n* US a white person (offensive use).

Honolulu [ˌhɒnə'luːluː] the capital of Hawaii. It is a major port and tourist center. POPULATION: 365,272.

honor US, **honour** GB ['ɒnər] ◇ *n* -1. great respect and admiration that people have for somebody; morally correct behavior □ *He did it for the honor of the family.* □ *a man of honor.* -2. **to be an honor to sthg** [to one's school, family] to bring respect to sthg □ *She's an honor to her country.* -3. a pleasure □ *It would be an honor.* ◇ *vt* -1. [contract, agreement] to keep to the terms of <a promise> □ *Both sides agreed to honor the ceasefire.* -2. **to be honored** to be proud and pleased (formal use) □ *I'm honored to meet you.*

◆ **Honor** *n* **His/Her/Your Honor** the words used when talking about/to a judge.

◆ **honors** *npl* -1. marks of respect □ *The soldier was buried with full military honors.* -2. EDUCATION a level of a degree which is higher than the basic level □ *She passed her degree with honors.* -3. **to do the honors** to act as a host to one's guests by e.g. serving them food or drink; to introduce people to each other □ *I'll do the honors, shall I?*

◆ **in honor of** *prep* as a mark of respect for <sb/sthg> □ *A holiday was declared in honor of the President's visit.*

honorable US, **honourable** GB ['ɒnərəbl] *adj* [action, decision, conduct] that is worthy of respect; [person] who behaves in a morally correct way □ *He made an honorable withdrawal from the contest.*

◆ **Honourable** *adj* **the Honourable** a title used when talking to or about a Member of the British House of Commons □ *the Honourable member for Cambridge.*

honorably US, **honourably** GB ['ɒnərəblɪ] *adv* [act, behave, treat] *see* **honorable** □ *If we lose, we must lose honorably.*

honorary [US 'ɒnərerɪ, GB 'ɒnrərɪ] *adj* -1. [membership, title] that is given as a mark of respect □ *He was awarded an honorary degree by Oxford University.* -2. [position, treasurer] that is not paid □ *I'm acting as honorary secretary.*

honor bound *adj* **to be honor bound to do sthg** to feel that it is right to do sthg even though it may not be in one's interest □ *I felt honor bound to tell the truth.*

honor roll *n* US a list of people at a school, college, or some other institution who have performed well.

honors degree *n* a degree which is higher than the basic level.

honour *etc* GB = **honor** *etc*.

honours list *n* in Britain, a list of people who are to be given titles by the Queen as a sign of respect for the things they have done.

Hons. GB *abbr of* **honours degree**.

Hon. Sec. *abbr of* **honorary secretary**.

Honshu ['hɒnʃuː] the largest island of Japan, containing most of its main cities. SIZE: 230,000 sq kms. POPULATION: 99,254,194.

hooch [huːtʃ] *n* a strong alcoholic drink that is brewed illegally (informal use).

hood [hʊd] *n* -1. CLOTHING the part of a coat or jacket that can be put up to cover one's head □ *Put your hood up, it's raining.* -2. a part of a car, baby carriage etc that covers it and that can be put up and down □ *We drove along with the hood down.* -3. US AUTO the metal panel that covers the engine in a car □ *I'll take a quick look under the hood.*

hooded ['hʊdəd] *adj* -1. [gunman, robber] who has a hood or hat pulled over their face to avoid being recognized. -2. **hooded eyes** eyes that look partly closed because they have large eyelids.

hoodlum ['huːdləm] *n* a violent person who belongs to a gang or criminal organization.

hoodwink ['hʊdwɪŋk] *vt* to trick <sb> by behaving in a clever way □ *The old lady was hoodwinked into handing over her life savings.*

hooey ['huːɪ] *n* US nonsense (informal use).

hoof [huːf] (*pl* **hoofs** OR **hooves**) *n* the hard part of the feet of some animals, e.g. cows and horses □ *a horse's hoof.*

hook [hʊk] ◇ *n* -1. [for hanging things] a curved piece of metal, plastic etc for hanging things on □ *I hung up my jacket on a hook.* □ *a clothes/picture hook.* -2. [for catching fish] a bent piece of metal that is attached to a line and used for catching fish. -3. CLOTHING a metal fastener on a dress, skirt etc. ■ **a hook and eye** a type of fastener for clothes that consists of a metal hook held in place by a metal loop. ◇ *vt* -1. to attach <sthg> to something else with a hook □ *You can hook the exercise machine to a door handle.* -2. to catch <a fish> with a hook □ *We've hooked several trout today.* -3. to put <an arm, leg> etc around something □ *He hooked his arm around my neck.*

◆ **off the hook** *adv* -1. **to take/leave the phone** OR **receiver off the hook** to take/leave the receiver off the phone so that it cannot ring □ *Either the line's busy or the phone's off the hook.* -2. **to get off the hook** to avoid being punished □ *His lawyer succeeded in getting him off the hook.*

◆ **hook up** *vt sep* **to hook sb/sthg up** [person, computer, telephone] to connect sb/sthg to a larger system □ *We're hooked up to our head office by satellite.*

Hook [hʊk], **Captain** a character in *Peter Pan* by J.M. Barrie. He is an evil pirate, who has a hook instead of one of his hands.

hooked [hʊkt] *adj* -1. [nose, claw] that is shaped like a hook. -2. **to be hooked on sthg** to be addicted to sthg (informal use) □ *Kids today are hooked on TV.*

hooker ['hʊkər] *n* a prostitute (informal use).

hook(e)y ['hʊkɪ] *n* US **to play hook(e)y** to stay away from school without permission (informal use) □ *We were caught playing hookey.*

hooligan ['huːlɪgən] *n* a noisy violent young person who causes trouble in public □ *a gang of hooligans* □ *the hooligan element in society.*

hooliganism ['huːlɪgənɪzm] *n* the violent behavior of hooligans □ *an attempt to stamp out hooliganism in our streets.*

hoop [hu:p] *n* -1. a large circle of metal, wood, plastic etc □ *a metal hoop.* -2. GAMES a children's toy in the shape of a hoop.

hoop-la ['hu:plɑ:] *n* GB a game where people try to throw small hoops over objects to win them.

hooray [hʊ'reɪ] *excl* a word used to show that one is happy and excited □ *Hooray! I've won!*

Hoosier ['hu:ʒəʳ] *n* a person who comes from Indiana (informal use).

hoot [hu:t] ◇ *n* -1. [of an owl] the sound made by an owl. -2. [of a horn, car, truck] the loud noise made by the horn of a car or truck. -3. a loud high-pitched laugh □ *She gave a loud hoot of laughter.* -4. **to be a hoot** to be very enjoyable and funny (informal use) □ *What a hoot!* ◇ *vi* -1. [owl] to make a hoot. -2. [horn] to make a hoot; [driver] to sound a horn □ *Why is he hooting at me?* -3. to laugh with a loud high-pitched voice (informal use) □ *He hooted with laughter.* ◇ *vt* **to hoot one's horn** to sound the horn of one's car □ *Everyone started hooting their horns at each other.*

hooter ['hu:təʳ] *n* GB the horn of a car □ *'Press here to sound the hooter.'* □ *a car hooter.*

Hoover™ ['hu:vəʳ] *n* GB a vacuum cleaner.

◆ **hoover** GB ◇ *vt* [floor, room, carpet] to clean <sthg> with a vacuum cleaner. ◇ *vi*: *The maid dusts, hoovers, irons, and cooks for us.*

Hoover ['hu:vəʳ], **Herbert** (1874–1964) US President from 1929 to 1933.

Hoover, J. Edgar (1895–1972) a US lawyer who was director of the FBI from 1924 to 1972.

hooves [hu:vz] *plural of* **hoof**.

hop [hɒp] (*pt & pp* **hopped**, *cont* **hopping**) ◇ *n* -1. [of a person] a jump on one leg □ *He took a couple of hops, then asked for his crutches.* -2. [of a frog, rabbit, bird] a jump on two legs. -3. a short trip □ *From London to Paris is now just a short hop across the Channel.* ◇ *vi* -1. [person] to jump on one leg □ *He was hopping from foot to foot to keep warm.* -2. [frog, rabbit, bird] to jump on two legs □ *A robin hopped onto the lawn.* -3. to go to a place nearby quickly and for a short time □ *I'm just hopping over to the post office to buy a stamp.* ◇ *vt* (informal use) -1. US to ride on <a bus, train> etc. -2. *phrase* **hop it!** go away!

◆ **hops** *npl* the dried flowers of a plant that are used to flavor beer.

hope [həʊp] ◇ *vi* to want something that is outside one's control to happen or to be true □ *We're hoping for a baby girl.* □ *I'm hoping for a pay raise next year.* ■ **I hope so/not** a phrase used when one wants/does not want something that another person has said to happen or to be true □ *"Is James coming?" — "I hope so."* □ *"You didn't forget your wallet, did you?" — "I hope not."* ■ **to hope for the best** to want something to happen even though one is not very confident that it will □ *All we can do is hope for the best.*

◇ *vt*: *I hope (that) you've enjoyed your visit.* □ *I hope to finish the job by tomorrow.*

◇ *n* -1. a desire for something that is beyond one's control to be true or to happen □ *My hope is that one day we'll find the answer.* □ *our hopes and dreams for the future.* ■ **I don't hold out much hope** I don't have many reasons to be hopeful. -2. a chance that makes something possible; belief in this chance □ *They've no hope of winning now.* □ *Never lose hope.* □ *Hopes are fading for those still trapped underground.* ■ **in the hope** because one hopes for a particular thing □ *I went in the hope of meeting new friends* OR *in the hope that I'd meet new friends.* ■ **to pin one's hopes on sb/sthg** to make sb/sthg one's main hope. □ *Try not to pin all your hopes on this one project.* ■ **to raise sb's hopes** to make sb have more hope that something will happen □ *I said nothing because I didn't want to raise his hopes.* -3. a person or thing that can help somebody in a difficult situation □ *You're my last hope.* □ *Stein is America's best hope in the men's 100 m.*

hope chest *n* US things that are useful in a house that a woman collects before she gets married.

hopeful ['həʊpfl] ◇ *adj* -1. [person] who feels confident that something they want to happen will happen □ *Both sides in the dispute are hopeful that a settlement can be reached.* □ *We are hopeful of having our offer accepted.* -2. [sign, future, news] that makes one feel that what one wants to happen will happen □ *Things don't look too hopeful right now.* ◇ *n* a person who wishes to be chosen for a particular job, especially an acting role □ *Dozens of young hopefuls lined up for the auditions.*

hopefully ['həʊpflɪ] *adv* -1. **hopefully,...** a word used to show that one hopes something is true or will happen □ *Hopefully I'll have been paid by next week.* -2. [smile, look] *see* **hopeful** □ *He looked up hopefully as Mr Lee walked in.*

hopeless ['həʊpləs] *adj* -1. [person] who has lost all hope □ *I felt completely hopeless and alone.* -2. [situation, case, life] that has no chance of succeeding or improving □ *Thousands of viewers were moved by the hopeless plight of these starving children.* -3. [person] who is not good at something (informal use) □ *I've always been hopeless at math.*

hopelessly ['həʊpləslɪ] *adv* -1. [weep, speak] without hope □ *"It's over!" she said hopelessly.* -2. **hopelessly bad/lost etc** very bad/lost etc □ *We're hopelessly in debt.*

Hopi ['həʊpi:] *n* a Native American people living in Arizona; the language of this people.

hopper ['hɒpəʳ] *n* a large container, shaped like a funnel, for cereals, coal etc.

Hopper, Edward (1882–1967) a US painter. He is known for his realistic pictures of city life.

hopping ['hɒpɪŋ] *adv* **to be hopping mad** to be very angry (informal use).

hopscotch ['hɒpskɒtʃ] *n* a children's game played by jumping on squares marked on the ground.

horde [hɔːʳd] *n* a large group of people (disapproving use) □ *Hordes of tourists invade the beaches in summer.*

horizon [hə'raɪzn] *n* the line far away between the highest part of the sea or land and the sky □ *The sun rose above the horizon.* ■ **to be on the horizon** [ship, figure] to be visible on the horizon; [prospect, opportunity] to be going to happen quite soon □ *A cloud appeared on the horizon.* □ *The rumor is that a promotion may be on the horizon.*

◆ **horizons** *npl* the limits of one's ambitions or experience □ *Foreign travel always broadens one's horizons.*

horizontal [ˌhɒrɪ'zɒntl] ◇ *adj* [line, position] that is flat and parallel to the ground □ *The body lay horizontal on the floor.* ◇ *n* **the horizontal** a horizontal line or position □ *Raise your arm to the horizontal.*

hormone ['hɔːʳmoʊn] *n* a chemical produced by a gland in the body that causes specific changes in the body □ *He was injected with a hormone to promote growth.*

hormone replacement therapy *n* a medical treatment given to some women when their periods stop in middle age. It replaces the hormones no longer produced by the body and reduces the unpleasant effects some women experience when their periods stop.

horn [hɔːʳn] *n* -1. [of a cow, sheep, bull] a long hard growth on either side of an animal's head that is usually curved and pointed at the end; the hard material that this is made of □ *The male has horns on its head.* □ *a horn spoon/handle.* -2. MUSIC any instrument made of metal or horn that is blown to make a sound □ *the horn section.* -3. [of a car, ship] a device on a vehicle that makes a loud noise as a warning or signal □ *a car horn* □ *He sounded the horn.*

hornet ['hɔːʳnət] *n* a large wasp that stings.

Horn of Africa: **the Horn of Africa** a region of east Africa that includes Somalia, Djibouti, Eritrea, and part of Ethiopia.

horn-rimmed ['-rɪmd] *adj* **horn-rimmed spectacles** OR **glasses** glasses that have frames made of horn or plastic that is colored to look like horn.

horny ['hɔːʳnɪ] (*compar* **hornier**, *superl* **horniest**) *adj* -1. [substance] that is hard and made of horn or of a material like horn □ *a horny claw/fingernail.* -2. [hand, skin] that is hard and rough. -3. ▽ [person] who feels sexually excited (very informal use).

horoscope ['hɒrəskoʊp] *n* information about a person's character and future life, based on the position of the planets when they were born or at any particular time □ *Do you want me to read your horoscope?*

horrendous [hɒ'rendəs] *adj* -1. [murder, violence, scene] frightening and very unpleasant □ *It was a horrendous experience.* -2. [weather, mess, waste] that is very bad especially because there is so much of it (informal use) □ *a horrendous traffic jam* □ *There's a horrendous amount of work to do.*

horrible ['hɒrəbl] *adj* -1. [accident, murder] un-

pleasant and shocking. -2. [person, place, experience] very unpleasant □ *You horrible little boy!* □ *I've had a horrible day today.* □ *horrible weather.*

horribly ['hɒrəblɪ] *adv* -1. **to be horribly killed/ tortured etc** to be killed/tortured etc in an unpleasant and shocking way. -2. **horribly late/expensive etc** very late/expensive etc (informal use) □ *It all went horribly wrong!*

horrid ['hɒrɪd] *adj* [person, place, idea] very unpleasant □ *She's being horrid to me.*

horrific [hɒ'rɪfɪk] *adj* [scene, murder, violence] very shocking and unpleasant □ *He had horrific injuries to his legs.*

horrify ['hɒrɪfaɪ] (*pt* & *pp* **horrified**) *vt* to shock <sb> very much □ *The news horrified the whole nation.*

horrifying ['hɒrɪfaɪɪŋ] *adj* [violence, picture, idea] shocking and unpleasant □ *It was a horrifying thought.*

horror ['hɒrəʳ] *n* -1. a strong feeling of shock and fear □ *The thought filled me with horror.* □ *a feeling of horror.* ■ **to my/his etc horror** a phrase used to show that an event, piece of information etc is shocking and unpleasant for somebody □ *To her horror, a brick came crashing through the window.* -2. **to have a horror of sthg** to have a strong dislike for sthg □ *She has a horror of spiders.* -3. a frightening experience □ *the horrors of war.*

horror movie *n* a frightening movie, usually one that deals with supernatural things, e.g. ghosts or vampires.

horror-struck *adj* **to be horror-struck** to be very shocked.

hors d'oeuvre [ˌɔːʳ'dɜːʳv] (*pl* **hors d'oeuvres**) *n* -1. US a small amount of cold food, e.g. pieces of meat or cheese, served with drinks before a meal. -2. GB a small amount of food eaten at the beginning of a meal.

horse [hɔːʳs] *n* a large four-legged animal with hooves that people ride or use to pull things.

horseback ['hɔːʳsbæk] ◇ *adj* **a horseback rider** a rider on a horse. ■ **horseback riding** the activity of riding a horse as a sport or pastime. ◇ *n* **to be on horseback** [person] to be on a horse □ *He rode there on horseback.*

horsebox ['hɔːʳsbɒks] *n* GB = **horse trailer**.

horse chestnut *n* -1. **a horse chestnut (tree)** a large tree with big leaves made up of several parts and white or pink flowers. -2. the shiny brown nut produced by a horse chestnut tree.

horse-drawn *adj* **a horse-drawn carriage/cart** a carriage/cart that is pulled by one or more horses.

horsefly ['hɔːʳsflaɪ] (*pl* **horseflies**) *n* a large fly that bites people, horses, and cattle.

horsehair ['hɔːʳsheəʳ] *n* hair from the tail or mane of a horse that in the past was used in the soft parts of furniture or to make cloth □ *a horsehair sofa/blanket.*

horseman ['hɔːʳsmən] (*pl* **horsemen** [-mən]) *n* a man who rides a horse □ *He's a fine horseman.* □ *a group of horsemen.*

horseplay ['hɔːˈspleɪ] *n* rough noisy behavior by young people who are enjoying themselves.

horsepower ['hɔːˈspauəʳ] *n* a unit (745.7 watts) used for measuring the power of an engine □ *a 300-horsepower engine.*

horse racing *n* the sport of racing horses, in which the owner of the horse that wins usually receives a large sum of money.

horseradish ['hɔːˈsrædɪʃ] *n* a plant with a white root which has a strong flavor and is used to make a sauce usually eaten with meat □ *horseradish sauce.*

horse riding *n* the activity of riding horses as a sport or pastime □ *We sometimes go horse riding at weekends.*

horseshoe ['hɔːˈsʃuː] *n* **-1.** a piece of metal shaped like the letter "U" that is attached to each of a horse's four feet to protect them against hard surfaces. **-2.** a shape like a horseshoe; a piece of card or plastic in this shape that is given to people as a symbol of good luck □ *a lucky horseshoe.*

horse show *n* a sports competition in which riders on horseback take part in one or more different events indoors or outdoors.

horse-trading *n* the process of trying to reach an agreement (disapproving use).

horse trailer *n* US a large container on wheels that is pulled by a vehicle and is used for transporting horses in.

horse trials *npl* a sports competition held outdoors in which riders on horseback all take part in the same three events.

horsewhip ['hɔːˈswɪp] (*pt* & *pp* **horsewhipped**, *cont* **horsewhipping**) *vt* to hit <sb> with a whip used for controlling horses.

horsewoman ['hɔːˈswumən] (*pl* **horsewomen**) *n* **she's a good horsewoman** she's good at riding horses.

horticultural [,hɔːˈtɪˈkʌltʃrəl] *adj* [society, skill, expert] that is connected with horticulture.

horticulture ['hɔːˈtɪkʌltʃəʳ] *n* the practice of growing flowers, fruit, and vegetables in gardens.

hose [houz] ◇ *n* a long, flexible, plastic pipe that is attached to a faucet at one end and used to spread water onto gardens, cars, fires etc □ *a garden hose* □ *a fireman's hose.* ◇ *npl* US a piece of clothing worn by women, usually made of very fine nylon material, that covers the legs from the waist to the toes and fits close to the skin □ *a pair of hose.* ◇ *vt* [garden, lawn] to water <sthg> using a hose.

◆ **hose down** *vt sep* **to hose sthg down** [car, path] to clean sthg using a hose □ *Dad was outside, hosing down the car.*

hosepipe ['houzpaɪp] *n* GB = **hose**.

hosiery [US 'houʒərɪ, GB 'houzɪərɪ] *n* a collective term used in stores for socks, stockings, and tights.

hospice ['hɒspəs] *n* a place that is like a hospital where people who cannot be cured of serious diseases can be looked after until they die □ *hospice care.*

hospitable [hɒˈspɪtəbl] *adj* [person, place] that makes one feel welcome.

hospital ['hɒspɪtl] *n* a place where people who are sick or injured go to be treated □ *My grandmother is in the hospital* US OR *in hospital* GB. □ *He was taken to the hospital* US OR *to hospital* GB *last night.*

hospitality [,hɒspɪˈtælətɪ] *n* behavior that makes guests feel welcome □ *Thank you so much for your hospitality.*

hospitality suite *n* one or more rooms at a special event where alcoholic drinks are served free of charge.

hospitalize, -ise ['hɒspɪtlaɪz] *vt* **to be hospitalized** to be taken to the hospital for treatment □ *Did you know he was hospitalized for three weeks afterwards?*

host [houst] ◇ *n* **-1.** a person who invites guests □ *He's a wonderful host.* **-2.** a place or organization that provides equipment and buildings for a special event □ *Barcelona was the host of the 1992 Olympics.* ■ **the host country** the country that organizes and provides the location for a particular international event. **-3.** RADIO & TV a person who introduces a radio or TV program and talks to the people taking part □ *a talk show host.* **-4.** COMPUTING any computer that contains information that other computers can access on the Internet. **-5. a host of sthg** [of people, places, questions] a large number of sthg (literary use) □ *Tonight's show brings you a host of stars.*

◇ *vt* **-1.** RADIO & TV [show, quiz] to introduce <a program> and talk to the people taking part in it □ *She's now hosting her own show.* **-2.** [conference, games] to be the place where <an event> is held and provide the facilities for it □ *Birmingham is hosting this year's trade fair.*

◆ **Host** *n* **the Host** RELIGION the bread given to people during Communion in a Christian church service.

hostage ['hɒstɪdʒ] *n* somebody who is the prisoner of a person or organization and who may be hurt or killed if that person or organization does not get what they want □ *The gunman has taken a woman hostage.* □ *He was held hostage for over three years.*

hostel ['hɒstl] *n* **-1.** a building, managed by an organization, where certain types of people, such as students or nurses, can live cheaply for a short time □ *a student hostel.* **-2.** a place where young people who are traveling can spend the night.

hostess ['houstəs] *n* **-1.** a woman who invites guests. **-2.** US a woman who takes people to their tables in restaurants.

hostile [US 'hɒstl, GB 'hɒstaɪl] *adj* **-1.** [person, attitude, atmosphere] aggressive and unfriendly □ *Mr Bayer got a very hostile reception at the meeting.* ■ **to be hostile to sb/sthg** to show dislike or disapproval of sb/sthg □ *Most people are hostile to the idea of higher taxes.* **-2.** [weather, climate] that is difficult to live or work in □ *hostile conditions.* **-3.** MILITARY [army, territory] that belongs to the enemy □ *a hostile plane*.

hostility [hɒ'stɪlətɪ] *n* a feeling of dislike or disapproval that is shown in the form of aggressive or unfriendly behavior □ *You could sense his hostility to the proposals.*

◆ **hostilities** *npl* MILITARY fighting between two countries or groups of people □ *a fresh outbreak of hostilities.*

hot [hɒt] (*compar* **hotter**, *superl* **hottest**) *adj* **-1.** [water, oven, room] that has a high temperature; [day, weather, summer] that has a lot of sun and high temperatures □ *I'm too hot in this sweater.* □ *It's getting hot in here.* **-2.** [food, meal, soup] that has been heated □ *The bread was still hot from the oven.* **-3.** [dish, curry] that has a strong spicy taste which burns one's mouth □ *hot chili pepper.* **-4. to be hot on** OR **at sthg** to know a lot about sthg (informal use) □ *Sue's pretty hot on computers.* **-5.** [news, scandal, gossip] new and exciting, so that people want to know about it (informal use) □ *Do you have any hot gossip?* **-6. to have a hot temper** to become angry easily

hot-air balloon *n* a very large balloon filled with hot air that sometimes has a container underneath to carry people.

hotbed ['hɒtbed] *n* **to be a hotbed of sthg** [of crime, violence, vice] to be a place where there is a lot of sthg unpleasant.

hotchpotch *n* GB = **hodgepodge**.

hot-cross bun *n* a small, round, sweet bread roll, usually eaten at Easter, that contains dried fruit and has a mark in the shape of a cross on the top.

hot dog *n* a long bread roll with a sausage in it.

hotel [hoʊ'tel] *n* **-1.** a large building where people pay money to eat and sleep when they are away from home □ *We stayed in a five-star hotel.* □ *a hotel room* □ *the hotel staff/industry.* **-2.** AUS a building where people go to buy and drink alcohol.

hotelier [US ˌoʊtl'jeɪ, GB hoʊ'telɪə] *n* a person who owns or runs a hotel.

hot flash US, **hot flush** GB *n* a sudden feeling of hotness in the skin, often experienced by middle-aged women around the time when their periods stop.

hotfoot ['hɒtfʊt] *adv* [go, run, arrive] as quickly as possible (informal use) □ *I ran hotfoot to the nearest phone.*

hotheaded [ˌhɒt'hedəd] *adj* [person] who does things too quickly, without first considering the consequences □ *a hotheaded young boy.*

hothouse ['hɒthaʊs, *pl* -haʊzɪz] *n* a building with a glass roof and walls where the air is kept at a high temperature so that special plants can grow in it □ *a hothouse plant.*

hot line *n* **-1.** POLITICS a direct telephone line between the heads of government of two countries that is used in emergencies. **-2.** a special telephone number that people can call for information or help on a particular subject, problem etc at any time □ *an information hot line* □ *an AIDS hot line.*

hotly ['hɒtlɪ] *adv* **-1.** [debate, deny] in an angry and determined way □ *It was a hotly-contested point.* □ *The accusation was hotly denied by Clancy.* **-2. hotly pursued by sb** chased by sb close behind □ *They drove off, hotly pursued by five patrol cars.*

hotplate ['hɒtpleɪt] *n* **-1.** a small device used for cooking food on that has only one or two burners. **-2.** GB a round, flat, metal surface on top of an electric stove on which food can be cooked in a pan.

hotpot ['hɒtpɒt] *n* GB a dish that consists of pieces of meat or vegetables in a sauce that are covered with thin pieces of potato and cooked slowly in a pot □ *Lancashire hotpot.*

hot potato *n* a difficult problem that nobody wants to deal with (informal use) □ *a political hot potato.*

hot rod *n* AUTO a car that has an engine which has been changed to make it much more powerful and that is used in races.

hot seat *n* **to be in the hot seat** to be in a position of responsibility that involves dealing with difficult problems, questions etc (informal use).

hot spot *n* (informal use) **-1.** an exciting place such as a nightclub □ *She knows all the hot spots in Paris.* **-2.** an area where political problems are likely to develop □ *the hot spots of Eastern Europe.*

hot-tempered *adj* [person] who gets angry easily □ *his hot-tempered Italian cousin.*

hot water *n* **to be in/get into hot water** to be in/get into trouble (informal use) □ *Graham's got himself into hot water again!*

hot-water bottle *n* a rubber container that is filled with hot water and used to warm a bed or a part of one's body.

hot-wire *vt* to start <a car> by making two electrical wires touch each other in the device that starts the engine (informal use).

hound [haʊnd] ◇ *n* a kind of dog used for hunting or racing. ◇ *vt* **-1.** to deliberately annoy or worry <sb> by constantly following them, criticizing them, or asking questions that they do not want to answer □ *The Royal Family are constantly hounded by the press.* **-2. to hound sb out of a place/job** to force sb to leave a place/job □ *They were hounded out of the neighborhood.* □ *I will not be hounded out of office.*

houndstooth check ['haʊndztuːθ-] *n* a pattern of jagged checks, especially on cloth.

hour ['aʊər] *n* **-1.** a period of time that lasts for sixty minutes □ *Stockholm's only an hour away by plane.* □ *It took us two hours to get here.* □ *I work a 40-hour week.* ■ **half an hour** thirty minutes □ *We'll be there in about half an hour.* ■ **at 70 miles per** OR **an hour** at a speed which makes it possible to travel seventy miles in one hour □ *He drove at 120 km an hour.* **-2.** a particular time of day or night □ *What are you doing here at this hour?* □ *She woke us up at some unearthly hour of the morning.* ■ **on the hour** at exactly two o'clock/three o'clock etc □ *The bus leaves every hour, on the hour.* ■ **in**

the wee OR **small hours** in the early hours of the morning, between midnight and dawn □ *We didn't get back till the small hours of the morning.* **-3.** a period of time for doing a particular thing □ *a lunch hour.* **-4. sb's hour of glory/need** a time when sb is very successful/needs help badly (literary use) □ *Where were you in my hour of need?*

◆ **hours** *npl* **-1.** the period of time when a particular activity happens □ *We can't sell alcohol after hours.* □ *during visiting hours* □ *He works long hours.* **-2. to keep late hours** to go to bed late regularly. ■ **to keep regular/irregular hours** to go to bed at the same/a different time each night.

hourly ['aʊə^{r}lɪ] ◇ *adj* **-1.** [inspection, service] that happens every hour □ *an hourly news broadcast* □ *at hourly intervals.* **-2.** [earnings, wages] that somebody earns for every hour they work □ *an hourly pay of $20.* ◇ *adv* **-1.** [check, inspect, report] every hour □ *The President gets updated hourly.* **-2. to pay sb hourly** to pay sb for every hour they work □ *I get paid hourly.* **-3.** [change, remember] all the time □ *The situation is changing hourly.*

house [*n* & *adj* haʊs, *pl* 'haʊzɪz, *vb* haʊz] ◇ *n* **-1.** a building in which people live □ *a red-brick/stone house.* ■ **to put** OR **set one's house in order** to solve one's problems and make one's affairs more organized □ *But first, Greece must set its own economic house in order.* **-2.** the people who live in a house □ *The whole house was asleep.* **-3.** a royal or noble family □ *the House of Windsor.* **-4.** BUSINESS a company involved in a particular business □ *a publishing/fashion house.* ■ **to be on the house** [drinks, food] to be given free to a customer by a hotel or bar □ *Drinks are on the house!* **-5.** POLITICS a group of people who make the laws in a country □ *She now sits in the upper house.* **-6.** GB the people at a debate □ *This house believes in democracy.* **-7.** [in a cinema, theater] the audience at a particular performance □ *The show's been playing to packed houses.* □ *We've been playing to a full house every night.* ■ **to bring the house down** [play, joke] to make people laugh and clap their hands a lot (informal use). **-8.** EDUCATION one of the groups that a school is divided into and that competes with the other groups, especially in sports. **-9.** = **house music.**

◇ *vt* [person, family] to give <sb> a place to live; [offices, library] to contain <sthg> □ *The refugees are being housed in special camps.* □ *This building will house the new art collection.*

◇ *adj* **-1.** [magazine, style] that belongs to a particular company. **-2. the house wine** the cheapest red or white wine sold in a restaurant □ *A bottle of house white, please.*

house arrest *n* **to be under house arrest** to be made to stay at home as a form of punishment, rather than being held in prison.

houseboat ['haʊsboʊt] *n* a boat which stays in one place and is used as a house.

housebound ['haʊsbaʊnd] *adj* **to be housebound** to be unable to leave one's house because one is too ill or old.

housebreaking ['haʊsbreɪkɪŋ] *n* the crime of going into somebody else's house to steal things.

housebroken ['haʊsbroʊkən] *adj* US **to be housebroken** [dog, cat] to have been trained only to empty its bowels or bladder outdoors or in a special tray.

housecoat ['haʊskoʊt] *n* a long loose item of clothing like a dressing-gown that is worn by women when they are at home.

household ['haʊshoʊld] ◇ *n* the people who live together in a house □ *You'll wake the whole household!* ◇ *adj* **-1. a household chore/product etc** a chore/product etc that is connected with looking after a house. **-2. a household name/word** a name/word that is very well known □ *The group became a household name in the 80s.*

householder ['haʊshoʊldə^r] *n* GB the person who owns or lives in a house.

househunting ['haʊshʌntɪŋ] *n* the process of looking for a house to buy or rent □ *We've been househunting all week.*

house husband *n* a married man who stays at home during the day, doing the cleaning, cooking etc, and taking care of his children.

housekeeper ['haʊskiːpə^r] *n* a person whose job is to take care of a house by doing the cleaning, cooking etc for the person or people that live there.

housekeeping ['haʊskiːpɪŋ] *n* **-1.** the job or activity of taking care of a house by doing the cleaning, cooking etc □ *My husband does all the housekeeping.* **-2. housekeeping (money)** the money for buying food and things needed to clean and manage a house.

houseman ['haʊsmən] (*pl* **housemen** [-mən]) *n* GB MEDICINE a man or woman who has recently become a doctor and is working and often living in a hospital to get experience.

house martin *n* a small black and white bird with a forked tail that makes its nest on part of a building.

house music *n* a kind of dance music with a regular beat, sounds made by electronic machines, and words which are often spoken rather than sung.

House of Commons *n* **the House of Commons** in Britain and Canada, the second and more powerful part of the parliament, made up of members chosen by the people of the country.

❦ HOUSE OF COMMONS

The House of Commons in London is made up of 650 Members of Parliament (MPs), who are elected for a five-year term. The government consists of MPs belonging to the party that won a majority of seats at the last election. The Speaker, who controls debates, sits at one end of the debating chamber. Members of the government sit along the side to the right of the Speaker; the Opposition sit along the side to the left.

House of Lords *n* **the House of Lords** the part

of the British Parliament that is made up of members of noble families or people with titles of honor.

✸ HOUSE OF LORDS
The House of Lords in London has over one thousand members, none of whom are elected. Most of them are people who inherited their noble titles, and the rest are life peers, who have a special title for life only, or bishops of the Church of England. The House of Lords is less powerful than the House of Commons, but it has the power to change some bills that have been passed in the House of Commons. It is also the highest court of appeal in the UK (apart from Scotland, which has its own legal system).

House of Representatives *n* **the House of Representatives** in the USA and Australia, the lower, more powerful one of the two houses that make the country's laws.

✸ HOUSE OF REPRESENTATIVES
In the USA there are 435 members of the House of Representatives, called Representatives or Congressmen (and Congresswomen). They are elected for two years by the people of each US state. The number of members per state is based on the size of the state's population. In Australia there are 148 members, called Members of Parliament (MPs), each representing a local area. They are elected for three years by the people of that area.

houseplant [US 'haʊsplænt, GB -plɑ:nt] *n* a plant that can be grown in a container indoors.

house-proud *adj* GB [person] who likes their house to be very clean and tidy.

Houses of Parliament *npl* **the Houses of Parliament** the British House of Commons and the House of Lords considered together; the building in which these are located.

house-to-house *adj* **a house-to-house search** a search that involves visiting every house in an area one after the other □ *Police are making house-to-house inquiries in the area.*

house-train *vt* to teach <a pet cat, dog> etc to go outside or use a special tray to empty its bowels or bladder □ *Is your dog house-trained?*

housewarming (party) ['haʊswɔːˈmɪŋ-] *n* a party given by people who have recently moved to a new house □ *Rachel's having a housewarming tonight.*

housewife ['haʊswaɪf] (*pl* **housewives**) *n* a married woman who stays at home during the day, doing the cleaning, cooking etc, and taking care of her children □ *I'm a full-time housewife and mother.*

housework ['haʊswɜːˈk] *n* the task or activity of cleaning a house □ *They never seem to do any housework.*

housing ['haʊzɪŋ] *n* -1. places for people to live in □ *a housing policy/shortage.* -2. a part that contains or covers part of a machine.

housing association *n* GB an organization that builds or improves houses and rents them at fair prices or helps people to buy them.

housing benefit *n* GB the money a person can get from the government to help them pay for a place to live in.

housing development *n* a large number of houses or apartments planned and built close together at the same time.

housing estate *n* GB = **housing development**.

housing project US *n* an area of housing, often with its own stores and playgrounds, that is owned by the government and rented to families with low incomes.

Houston ['hjuːstən] a city in Texas, USA. It is a major port and a center for the oil industry, and the headquarters of NASA. POPULATION: 1,630,553.

HOV (*abbr of* **high occupancy vehicle**) *n* **an HOV lane** a lane on a highway that is reserved for cars that are carrying more than one person in them.

hovel [US 'hʌvl, GB 'hɒvl] *n* a place for living in that is small, dirty, or in bad condition.

hover [US 'hʌvər, GB 'hɒvə] *vi* -1. [bird, helicopter] to stay in one place in the air □ *seagulls hovering over the fishing boats.* -2. [person, animal] to stay near somebody or something in an uncertain or annoying way □ *Nervous security guards were hovering in the background.* -3. [person, country, organization] to be in a particular state or situation that is uncertain □ *They're hovering on the brink of disaster.*

hovercraft [US 'hʌvərkræft, GB 'hɒvəkrɑːft] (*pl* **hovercraft** OR **hovercrafts**) *n* a large vehicle that moves across land or water on a layer of air and carries people and cars.

hoverport [US 'hʌvərpɔːrt, GB 'hɒvəpɔːt] *n* a port for hovercraft.

how [haʊ] *adv* -1. used in questions that ask for information about the way something is done or the way it happens □ *How is he going to get here?* □ *"How did you manage to do it?" — "Jean helped me."* -2. used in questions that ask about the state of somebody's health, job etc at that moment □ *How's work/the new house?* □ *"How are you?" — "Not too bad, thanks."* -3. **how tall/old/heavy is it?** what is its height/age/weight? (used with adjectives and adverbs to ask about amounts) □ *How often do you see him?* □ *How long did you have to wait?* -4. used in exclamations to show how strongly one feels something to be true □ *How I hate ironing!* □ *How pretty you look!* ■ **how can** OR **could...?** used when one is surprised or finds something difficult to believe □ *How could you forget my birthday?*
◆ **how about** *adv* **how about a drink?** shall we have a drink? (used to make suggestions) □ *How about going away for the weekend?*
◆ **how many** *det* **how many people/times...?** what number of people/times...? (used with

plural nouns) □ *How many people were at the party?* □ *How many times have you been there?*

◆ **how much** ◇ *pron* **how much does it cost/weigh?** what is the amount that it costs/weighs? ◇ *det* used with singular nouns □ *How much bread do we have left?* ◇ *conj* used to describe the way in which something happens or is done □ *She's learning how to read.* □ *I need more information on how it works.*

howdy ['haʊdɪ] *excl* US hello (informal use).

however [haʊ'evər] *adv* -1. the previous statement is not totally true, because... □ *1995 has been a difficult one for the company. Profits, however, are up compared to 1994.* -2. **however good/bad the weather** it does not matter how good/bad the weather is, it will make no difference (used with adjectives and adverbs) □ *We'll never manage it, however hard we try.* □ *All contributions, however small, will be welcome.* -3. used in questions to show surprise □ *However did you find out I was here?*

howl [haʊl] ◇ *n* [of pain, anger, grief] a long loud cry that expresses a strong feeling □ *howls of laughter.* ◇ *vi* -1. [dog, wolf, jackal] to make a long loud cry. -2. [person] to make a long loud sound to show one is in pain, angry, or very unhappy □ *Stop howling and tell me what's wrong.* ■ **to howl with laughter** to laugh in a loud uncontrolled way. -3. [wind] to blow strongly with a long loud noise.

howler ['haʊlər] *n* a silly mistake, especially in what somebody says or writes (informal use) □ *This is fine apart from a couple of howlers.*

howling ['haʊlɪŋ] *adj* **a howling success** a very great success (informal use).

hp *n abbr of* **horsepower**.

HP *n* GB *abbr of* **hire purchase** □ *They bought their car on HP.*

HQ *n abbr of* **headquarters**.

hr *abbr of* **hour**.

HRH *abbr of* **Her (His) Royal Highness**.

hrs *abbr of* **hours**.

HRT *n abbr of* **hormone replacement therapy**.

HS US *abbr of* **high school**.

HSE (*abbr of* **Heath and Safety Executive**) *n* **the HSE** in Britain, a government organization that controls health and safety at work.

HST (*abbr of* **Hawaiian Standard Time**) *n* the local standard time in Hawaii.

ht *abbr of* **height**.

HT *abbr of* **high-tension**.

HTML (*abbr of* **HyperText Markup Language**) *n* COMPUTING the computing code used to write documents for the World Wide Web.

hub [hʌb] *n* -1. [of a wheel] the central part of a wheel □ *a wheel hub.* -2. [of a network, country] the part of a place, organization that is most important or has most activity □ *the hub of the empire/community* □ *Kingstown is the commercial/social hub of the island.*

hub airport *n* a major airport that has many planes passing through it.

hubbub ['hʌbʌb] *n* a loud noise made by a lot of people talking at the same time.

hubcap ['hʌbkæp] *n* a round metal plate that covers the hub of a car wheel.

HUD [hʌd] (*abbr of* **Department of Housing and Urban Development**) *n* the US government department responsible for housing and city planning.

huddle ['hʌdl] ◇ *vi* -1. [person] to lie, sit etc somewhere with one's arms and legs close to one's chest, especially when one is cold or frightened □ *She huddled under the blanket.* -2. [people] to move or stay close to each other □ *We huddled together for warmth.* □ *They huddled around the fire.* ◇ *n* a group of houses, trees, people etc that are all close together □ *Everyone was standing in a huddle in the corner.*

Hudson Bay [,hʌdsn-] a large bay in northeastern Canada, on the Atlantic Ocean.

Hudson River: the Hudson River a river in New York State, USA, that flows into the Atlantic Ocean at New York City.

hue [hjuː] *n* a shade of a color (literary or technical use) □ *green of a brilliant hue.*

huff [hʌf] ◇ *n* **to be in a huff** to be in a bad temper (informal use) □ *He went off in a huff.* ◇ *vi* **to huff and puff** to show that one is annoyed about something □ *After much huffing and puffing, he finally agreed.*

huffy ['hʌfɪ] (*compar* **huffier**, *superl* **huffiest**) *adj* (informal use) -1. in a bad temper □ *What's put you in such a huffy mood?* -2. easily offended □ *She tends to be rather huffy.*

hug [hʌg] (*pt* & *pp* **hugged**, *cont* **hugging**) ◇ *n* the act of putting one's arms tightly around someone as a sign of affection □ *He gave me a big hug.* ◇ *vt* -1. [mother, boyfriend, friend] to give <sb> a hug □ *They hugged and kissed each other.* -2. [bag, cushion] to hold close to one's chest with one's arms □ *I hugged the package to myself all the way home.* -3. [coast, ground] to stay close to <sthg> while moving □ *Try not to hug the curb so tightly.*

huge [hjuːdʒ] *adj* -1. [house, appetite, success] that is very large in size □ *They live in one of those huge apartment blocks downtown.* -2. [subject, problem, task] that is very large in extent □ *It's a huge responsibility to take on.* -3. [profit, amount] that is very large in volume □ *huge numbers of refugees.*

Hughes [hjuːz], **Howard** (1905–1976) a US businessman and movie producer. He lived completely away from society during the last years of his life.

Hughes, Langston (1902–1967) a black US poet and writer. His best-known work is *The Panther and the Lash.*

Hugo ['hjuːgoʊ], **Victor** (1802–1885) a French writer, and the leader of the Romantic movement in France. His work includes *Les Misérables* and *The Hunchback of Notre Dame.*

huh [hʌ] *excl* -1. a word used to change a statement into a question □ *You must be tired, huh?* -2. a word that expresses surprise or confusion □ *"I'm getting married." — "Huh?"* -3. a word used to show disapproval □ *"She calls herself a feminist." — "Huh!"* -4. a word used to ask somebody to repeat something (informal use) □ *"I'm going out." — "Huh?"*

hulk [hʌlk] *n* **-1.** SHIPPING an old ship that is at sea but is no longer used □ *a rotting hulk.* **-2.** a large awkward person.

hulking ['hʌlkɪŋ] *adj* large, heavy, and awkward □ *He's a hulking brute of a man.*

hull [hʌl] *n* SAILING the main part of a ship.

hullabaloo [,hʌləbə'luː] *n* a loud noise made by people who are shouting or protesting (informal use) □ *What's all the hullabaloo about?*

hullo [hə'loʊ] *excl* = **hello.**

hum [hʌm] (*pt* & *pp* **hummed,** *cont* **humming**) ◇ *vi* **-1.** [bee, machine, engine] to make a low continuous noise □ *I could hear the bees humming.* **-2.** [person] to sing with one's mouth closed □ *Kevin was quietly humming to himself.* **-3.** [office, party, room] to be busy □ *The kitchen was humming with activity.* **-4. to hum and haw** to hesitate in an annoying way □ *He hummed and hawed for about half an hour before deciding.* ◇ *vt* to sing <a tune> with one's mouth closed □ *She was humming an Irish ballad.* ◇ *n* [of a bee, conversation, engine] a low continuous noise □ *the distant hum of traffic.*

human ['hjuːmən] ◇ *adj* **-1.** [voice, life, expression] that is connected with human beings □ *That place isn't fit for human habitation.* **-2.** [weakness, failing] that shows characteristics which are typical of ordinary people □ *He's only human.* ◇ *n* **a human (being)** a man, woman, or child, rather than an animal □ *What differentiates human beings from animals?*

humane [hjuː'meɪn] *adj* [treatment] that is kind and not cruel □ *killed by humane methods.*

humanely [hjuː'meɪnlɪ] *adv* [treat, kill] *see* **humane.**

human error *n* a mistake or mistakes caused by a person or people, not by a machine □ *They put the accident down to human error.*

humanist ['hjuːmənəst] *n* a person who believes in a system based on the needs of people rather than on religious ideas.

humanitarian [hjuː,mænɪ'teərɪən] ◇ *adj* [approach, policy, organization] that aims to improve the lives of other people rather than make a profit □ *The UN mission is to deliver humanitarian aid to refugees.* ◇ *n* a person who works to improve the lives of other people.

humanity [hjuː'mænətɪ] *n* **-1.** kind and sympathetic behavior □ *Can't you show a little humanity for once?* **-2.** a collective term for human beings □ *crimes against humanity.*

◆ **humanities** *npl* **the humanities** subjects of study that are concerned with literature, history etc rather than science.

humanly ['hjuːmənlɪ] *adv* **it's not humanly possible** it's not something that a human being can do □ *We've done everything humanly possible to find her.*

human nature *n* the way humans usually think and behave □ *It's human nature to be lazy.*

human race *n* **the human race** the species that people belong to.

human resources *n* the department in a company that deals with its employees □ *Mrs Olrod is in charge of human resources.*

human rights *npl* the basic things in life that a person should be able to expect from the state or society □ *Violations of human rights have been reported.* □ *human-rights abuses* □ *a human-rights activist.*

human shield *n* people, often of the same nationality as the enemy in a war, who are forced to stay in a place where they would be hurt or killed if the place were attacked.

humble ['hʌmbl] ◇ *adj* **-1.** [position, job, origins] low in status □ *He rose from a humble background to become the nation's President.* **-2.** [person] who has a modest opinion of themselves; [opinion, apology, request] that shows that one feels humble □ *In my humble opinion the chairman should resign.* ◇ *vt* to make <sb> feel unimportant or worthless. ■ **to humble oneself** to behave in a way which shows that one accepts that another person is superior (formal use).

humbly ['hʌmblɪ] *adv* **-1.** [speak, beg, apologize] *see* **humble** □ *"Sorry," she said humbly.* **-2.** [live, dine] without spending much money.

humbug ['hʌmbʌg] *n* **-1.** nonsense (old-fashioned use). **-2.** GB a hard boiled candy.

humdrum ['hʌmdrʌm] *adj* [life, existence, job] that is ordinary, changes very little, and is not interesting or exciting.

Hume [hjuːm], **David** (1711–1776) a British philosopher and historian.

humid ['hjuːməd] *adj* [climate, weather, air] that is warm and wet, often in an unpleasant way □ *It's very humid today.*

humidity [hjuː'mɪdətɪ] *n* the amount of water in the air □ *Humidity will be high tomorrow.*

humiliate [hjuː'mɪlɪeɪt] *vt* to publicly say or do something to make <sb> feel that they are worthless and no longer respected □ *They tried to humiliate me in front of all those people.*

humiliating [hjuː'mɪlɪeɪtɪŋ] *adj* [experience, defeat] that is embarrassing and makes one feel worthless and no longer respected □ *It was humiliating to be told off like that.*

humiliation [hjuː,mɪlɪ'eɪʃn] *n* the feeling of embarrassment and upset that one feels when one is humiliated; a humiliating experience □ *The team suffered humiliation at the hands of their opponents.* □ *It was one humiliation after another.*

humility [hjuː'mɪlətɪ] *n* [of a person] *see* **humble.**

hummingbird ['hʌmɪŋbɜːrd] *n* a small tropical bird with a long pointed beak that makes a low continuous noise by beating its wings very fast.

hummus ['homəs] *n* a food that is made from crushed chick peas, olive oil, and garlic and is spread on bread.

humor US, **humour** GB ['hjuːmər] ◇ *n* **-1. (a sense of) humor** the ability to find things amusing □ *She has a great sense of humor.* **-2.** [of a situation, comment] the quality of being funny □ *He didn't really appreciate the humor of the situation.* ◇ *vt* to keep <sb> happy by appearing to agree with what they say or want, even if it is wrong or silly □ *Just hu-mor me this once.*

humorist ['hju:mərəst] *n* a person who writes stories, cartoons etc that make people laugh.

humorous ['hju:mərəs] *adj* [person, comment, play] that makes one laugh □ *The book takes a humorous look at the American way of life.*

humour *n* & *vt* GB = humor.

hump [hʌmp] ◇ *n* -1. [of earth, sand] a small, round, raised area of ground that is higher than the surrounding area □ *There's a slight hump in the road.* -2. [on somebody's back] a lump on the back of a person, or of some animals, e.g. a camel. ◇ *vt* GB [boxes, luggage] to carry or move <sthg heavy> in a particular direction (informal use) □ *I hate having to hump my bags from one place to another.*

humpbacked bridge [ˌhʌmpbækt-] *n* GB a kind of small bridge which is much higher in the middle than at the ends.

Humpty Dumpty [ˌhʌmptɪ'dʌmptɪ] a character in a nursery rhyme, shaped like an egg, who falls off a wall and cannot be mended.

humus ['hju:məs] *n* the top layer of soil that consists of rotting leaves, plants etc.

hunch [hʌntʃ] ◇ *n* an idea that one believes is correct because of a feeling one has and not because of something one knows (informal use) □ *I've got a hunch (that) it will work.* ◇ *vt* to move <one's shoulders or back> into a round shape □ *Don't hunch your shoulders like that.* ◇ *vi*: *It's bad to hunch when you read.*

hunchback ['hʌntʃbæk] *n* a person whose back has a hump between the shoulders.

hunched [hʌntʃt] *adj* [person] who has moved their back into a rounded position □ *She sat hunched over a book.*

hundred ['hʌndrəd] *num* the number 100 □ *There were at least a hundred people at the meeting.* □ *Water boils at one hundred degrees centigrade.* □ *several hundred people.*

◆ **hundreds** *pron* used to refer to very many people or things □ *There were hundreds of people waiting for her to arrive.* □ *Letters were arriving in the hundreds.*

hundredth ['hʌndrədθ] *num* 100th, number 100 in a series.

hundredweight ['hʌndrədweɪt] *n* a unit (US 100 pounds, GB 112 pounds) for measuring weight.

Hundred Years' War *n* the Hundred Years' War a series of wars (1337–1453) between England and France.

hung [hʌŋ] ◇ *past tense & past participle of* hang. ◇ *adj* [parliament, jury] that has no absolute majority.

Hungarian [hʌŋ'geərɪən] *n* & *adj*: *see* Hungary.

Hungary ['hʌŋgərɪ] a country in central Europe, between Austria and Romania. It was a Communist state from 1949 to 1990. SIZE: 93,000 sq kms. POPULATION: 10,300,000 (*Hungarians*). CAPITAL: Budapest. LANGUAGE: Hungarian. CURRENCY: forint.

hunger ['hʌŋgəʳ] *n* -1. [for food] the feeling that one has when one needs to eat □ *a feeling of hunger.* -2. a lack of food that causes illness or death □ *Thousands of refugees are dying of hunger.* -3. [for success, revenge] a strong desire for something (literary use).

◆ **hunger after**, **hunger for** *vt fus* to hunger after OR for sthg [after success, revenge] to have a strong desire for sthg (literary use).

hunger strike *n* a form of protest in which somebody refuses to eat for a long time □ *Several men have gone on hunger strike over conditions in the prison.*

hung over *adj* to be hung over to have a headache, feel sick etc as a result of drinking too much alcohol the night before (informal use) □ *I felt very hung over this morning.*

hungry ['hʌŋgrɪ] (*compar* hungrier, *superl* hungriest) *adj* -1. [person, animal] that feels a need to eat □ *I always feel hungry by 11 o'clock.* □ *I'm not very hungry at the moment.* ■ **to go hungry** to continue to be hungry because one has not eaten any food. -2. **to be hungry for sthg** [for success, revenge] to have a strong desire for sthg (literary use).

hung up *adj* to be hung up to have a fixed idea about something that one cannot change and that stops one from behaving normally (informal use) □ *She's always been hung up about the way she looks.*

hunk [hʌŋk] *n* -1. [of bread, cheese] a large piece of a particular food □ *a hunk of meat.* -2. a muscular and good-looking man (informal use) □ *What a hunk!*

hunky-dory [ˌhʌŋkɪ'dɔːrɪ] *adj* to be hunky-dory to be satisfactory and without problems (informal use) □ *Everything's just hunky-dory.*

hunt [hʌnt] ◇ *vt* -1. [lion, whale] to chase and kill <an animal> for food or sport □ *Tigers are being hunted to extinction.* -2. [killer, murderer] to try to find and capture <a criminal> □ *The gang is being hunted by the FBI.* ◇ *vi* -1. [animal, hunter] to hunt animals □ *They're out hunting for rabbits.* □ *The owl hunts mainly at night.* -2. [person] to search carefully in order to find something □ *I've been hunting high and low for my pen.* ◇ *n* -1. [for animals] an act of hunting animals □ *a fox hunt.* -2. [for a person, object, place] a search for something or somebody □ *Police have begun the hunt for the murderer.*

◆ **hunt down** *vt sep* to hunt sb/sthg down to find sb/sthg after looking very carefully □ *I finally hunted him down in the bar.*

hunter ['hʌntəʳ] *n* -1. a person who chases and kills animals for food or sport □ *a lion-hunter.* -2. a person who spends time trying to find a particular thing □ *an autograph hunter* □ *a bargain hunter.*

hunting ['hʌntɪŋ] *n* -1. the activity of chasing and killing animals for food or sport □ *He goes hunting every weekend.* □ *a hunting knife.* -2. the activity of spending time trying to find something □ *bargain-hunting.* -3. GB = foxhunting.

huntsman ['hʌntsmən] (*pl* huntsmen [-mən]) *n* a hunter.

hurdle ['hɜːʳdl] ◇ *n* -1. SPORT a type of fence

for jumping over in a race. -2. something that makes things difficult for somebody □ *If we can get over this hurdle, the rest is easy.* ◇ *vt* [fence, gate] to jump over <sthg>.

◆ **hurdles** *npl* a type of race in which runners or horses jump over a series of hurdles that are placed on the track □ *the 400 m hurdles.*

hurl [hɜːˈl] *vt* -1. [book, brick, stick] to throw <sthg> violently in a particular direction □ *She hurled the book at me in a rage.* -2. **to hurl sthg at sb** [abuse, threats] to shout sthg at sb □ *The protesters hurled insults at the police.*

Huron [ˈhʊərən]: **Lake Huron** one of the Great Lakes between Canada and the USA.

hurrah [hʊˈrɑː] *excl* = **hurray** (old-fashioned use).

hurray [hʊˈreɪ] *excl* a word used to show pleasure or approval □ *"Hurray!" she exclaimed, "We've won!"*

hurricane [US ˈhɜːrəkeɪn, GB ˈhʌrɪkən] *n* a storm with a very strong wind that can cause a lot of damage □ *a hurricane wind.*

hurried [US ˈhɜːrɪd, GB hʌr-] *adj* [departure, decision, attempt] that is done quickly and without much care □ *After a rather hurried meal we rushed home.*

hurriedly [US ˈhɜːrɪdlɪ, GB hʌr-] *adv* [say, leave, eat] *see* **hurried** □ *"It's not that I don't like her," she added hurriedly.*

hurry [US ˈhɜːrɪ, GB ˈhʌrɪ] (*pt* & *pp* **hurried**) ◇ *vi* to move quickly or do something quickly □ *If you hurry you'll catch the bus.* □ *Everyone hurried to help.* □ *Hurry! Sale on while stocks last!*
◇ *vt* [person] to make <sb> move or act quickly; [process, decision] to make <sthg> happen quickly □ *I'm sorry to hurry you, but it's getting late.* □ *She was hurried into making the decision.* □ *They hurried him into a waiting car.*
◇ *n* pressure to do something quickly □ *There's no hurry to get the work finished.* ■ **to be in a hurry** to have to do something or go somewhere quickly □ *I'm in a real hurry.* ■ **to do sthg in a hurry** to do sthg quickly and perhaps carelessly □ *They left in a hurry.* □ *You could tell it had been written/built in a hurry.* ■ **to be in no hurry to do sthg** to be unwilling to do sthg □ *My tenants are in no hurry to move out.*

◆ **hurry off** *vi* to leave quickly □ *They hurried off down the hill.*

◆ **hurry up** ◇ *vi* to do something or move more quickly than before □ *Tell him to hurry up.* □ *Hurry up! We're late!* ◇ *vt sep* **to hurry sb up** to make sb hurry up □ *I'm always having to hurry the children up in the mornings.*

hurt [hɜːt] (*pt* & *pp* **hurt**) ◇ *vt* -1. [person, arm, leg] to cause physical pain or damage to <sb/sthg> □ *Did you hurt yourself badly?* -2. **to be** OR **get hurt** to be injured in an accident □ *Ten people were hurt in the crash.* □ *Someone's going to get hurt if you're not careful.* -3. [person] to make <sb> suffer emotionally □ *Of course it hurts me to admit the truth.* ■ **to hurt sb's feelings** to say or do something that hurts sb emotionally □ *I don't want to hurt anybody's feelings.* -4. **it won't/wouldn't hurt to...** a phrase used to suggest that somebody does something that they have not done before

or do not usually do □ *It wouldn't hurt you to get up early for once.* □ *It won't just to talk to her, will it?*
◇ *vi* -1. [leg, arm, foot] to be painful; [shoes, punch] to make somebody suffer physical pain □ *My shoulder is hurting a lot.* □ *Ouch! That hurts!* □ *It hurts to move my arm/when I move my arm.* -2. [insult, love] to make somebody suffer emotionally □ *Divorce always hurts.* □ *It really hurts to be called a liar.* -3. to cause problems for somebody □ *It wouldn't hurt to have one more drink.*
◇ *adj* -1. **to be hurt** [person, arm, leg] to be injured □ *He's seriously hurt.* -2. **to be hurt** [person] to be suffering emotional pain □ *I felt very hurt when she refused to speak to me.* □ *There was a hurt expression on his face.*
◇ *n* emotional pain □ *The hurt will last a long time.*

hurtful [ˈhɜːtfl] *adj* [remark, action] that can cause emotional pain □ *That was a very hurtful thing to say.*

hurtle [ˈhɜːtl] *vi* [stone, car, person] to be thrown or to fall at great speed in a particular direction □ *Their sled overturned and they came hurtling down the hill.*

husband [ˈhʌzbənd] *n* the man that a woman is married to □ *Have you met my husband?*

husbandry [ˈhʌzbəndrɪ] *n* farming (formal use).

hush [hʌʃ] ◇ *n* quietness □ *A hush fell on the room.* ◇ *excl* a word used to tell somebody to be quiet □ *Hush! The baby's sleeping!*

◆ **hush up** *vt sep* -1. **to hush sthg up** [affair, news, rumor] to keep sthg secret so that the public does not know about it □ *News of the disaster was quickly hushed up by the government.* -2. **to hush sb up** to stop sb talking loudly □ *Will somebody hush that guy up before I hit him?*

hushed [hʌʃt] *adj* [person, crowd] that is not talking or making a noise; [voice, conversation] that is very quiet.

hush money *n* money paid to somebody in return for not revealing facts that one does not want other people to know (informal use).

husk [hʌsk] *n* the dry outside part of a seed or grain.

husky [ˈhʌskɪ] (*compar* **huskier**, *superl* **huskiest**, *pl* **huskies**) ◇ *adj* [voice] that sounds quiet and rough in an attractive way □ *a deep husky voice.* ◇ *n* a breed of dog found in the Arctic and used to pull sleds.

hustings [ˈhʌstɪŋz] *npl* GB the activity of trying to influence people's opinions before an election.

hustle [ˈhʌsl] ◇ *vt* -1. to force <sb> to move quickly in a particular direction □ *The police hustled the man into a doorway.* -2. US **to hustle sb into doing sthg** to persuade sb to do sthg they do not really want to do. ◇ *n* **hustle and bustle** a lot of busy movement and activity involving people and traffic □ *the hustle and bustle of modern life.*

hut [hʌt] *n* a simple house or shelter made of wood, mud etc □ *a mud hut* □ *a mountain hut.*

hutch [hʌtʃ] *n* a wooden cage in which pet rabbits are kept □ *a rabbit hutch.*

hyacinth ['haɪəsɪnθ] *n* a plant that grows from a bulb and has small white, blue, or pink flowers that grow in a cone shape and have a pleasant smell.

hybrid ['haɪbrəd] ◇ *adj* -1. [plant, animal] that is a hybrid □ *a hybrid rose.* -2. [system, form] that is mixed. ◇ *n* -1. a plant or animal that is the result of breeding between different species or breeds □ *A mule is a hybrid of a donkey and a horse.* -2. a mixture □ *Her new novel is a hybrid of detective story and romance.*

hydrangea [haɪ'dreɪndʒə] *n* a garden bush that has large bunches of white, pink, or blue flowers with round flat petals.

hydrant ['haɪdrənt] *n* = **fire hydrant.**

hydraulic [haɪ'drɔːlɪk] *adj* [pump, brake] that works by the pressure of a liquid in a pipe.
♦ **hydraulics** *n* the science that studies how liquids flow.

hydrocarbon [,haɪdrə'kɑːrbən] *n* an organic compound of hydrogen and carbon.

hydrochloric acid [,haɪdrəklɔːrɪk-] *n* an acid that contains hydrogen chloride. FORMULA: HCl.

hydroelectric [,haɪdrouɪ'lektrɪk] *adj* [dam, power station] that uses hydroelectricity □ *hydroelectric power.*

hydroelectricity [,haɪdrouɪlek'trɪsəti] *n* electricity produced by the pressure of falling water.

hydrofoil ['haɪdrəfɔɪl] *n* a kind of boat that can go very fast by raising itself above the water.

hydrogen ['haɪdrədʒən] *n* a colorless gas that burns very easily and is the lightest element. SYMBOL: H.

hydrogen bomb *n* a type of bomb that produces an explosion caused by nuclear fusion.

hydrophobia [,haɪdrə'foubjə] *n* = **rabies** (technical use).

hydroplane ['haɪdrəpleɪn] ◇ *n* -1. a fast motorboat with a flat bottom. -2. a type of hydrofoil. ◇ *vi* US [car, truck] to slide out of control on a wet road surface.

hyena [haɪ'iːnə] *n* an African animal like a dog that makes a noise that sounds like a laugh.

hygiene ['haɪdʒiːn] *n* the practice of keeping oneself and one's surroundings clean to prevent disease □ *Doctors stress the importance of personal hygiene.*

hygienic [US ,haɪdʒɪ'enɪk, GB haɪ'dʒiːnɪk] *adj* [container, practice] that keeps things clean and stops the spread of disease □ *The sauce comes in a hygienic wipe-clean bottle.* □ *Conditions there are far from hygienic.*

hygienist [haɪ'dʒiːnəst] *n* a person whose job is to clean people's teeth □ *a dental hygienist.*

hymn [hɪm] *n* a song sung to praise god in Christianity and other religions.

hymn book *n* a book containing hymns for use in a Christian church.

hype [haɪp] ◇ *n* publicity that exaggerates the benefits or qualities of a product, movie, book etc □ *Don't believe all the hype.* ◇ *vt* [product, movie, book] to try to make people buy <sthg> using hype □ *the much-hyped Bond movie.*

hyped up [,haɪpd-] *adj* [person] who is in a state of extreme excitement, often in preparation for something (informal use) □ *I'm all hyped up at the moment.*

hyper ['haɪpər] *adj* **to be hyper** to be too active or too excited (informal use) □ *She gets pretty hyper when she's nervous.*

hyperactive [,haɪpər'æktɪv] *adj* [person] who is often too excited and keeps moving about more than is normal □ *a hyperactive child.*

hyperbole [haɪ'pɜːrbəli] *n* a way of speaking or writing that is exaggerated in order to have a particular effect.

hyperinflation [,haɪpərɪn'fleɪʃn] *n* ECONOMICS extremely high inflation.

hypermarket ['haɪpərmɑːrkət] *n* GB a very large supermarket.

hypersensitive [,haɪpər'sensətɪv] *adj* -1. [person] who is too sensitive to criticism □ *She's hypersensitive to criticism.* -2. MEDICINE [tooth, person] that is more sensitive to temperature, drugs etc than is normal.

hypertension [,haɪpər'tenʃn] *n* very high blood pressure.

hypertext ['haɪpərtekst] *n* a system of linking information in a computer document by showing some words in a special form. When one selects these words, one is sent to another document where there is more information about the word □ *Some words are written in hypertext.* □ *a hypertext document.*

hyperventilate [,haɪpər'ventɪleɪt] *vi* to breathe too often or too deeply, so that one gets a headache and feels dizzy.

hyphen ['haɪfn] *n* a punctuation mark (-) like a short line that is used to join two or more words together or to separate parts of a word split between two lines of text □ *His surname is Mars-Jones, spelt with a hyphen.*

hyphenate ['haɪfəneɪt] *vt* to use a hyphen to join two parts of <a word> □ *The word "high-level" is usually hyphenated.*

hypnosis [hɪp'nousəs] *n* a state of relaxation in which a person seems to be sleeping but can hear what is being said, answer questions etc □ *He remembered his childhood under hypnosis.*

hypnotic [hɪp'nɒtɪk] *adj* [trance, effect, stare] *see* **hypnosis.**

hypnotism ['hɪpnətɪzm] *n* the technique of using hypnosis to influence a person's behavior □ *She tried hypnotism to stop smoking.*

hypnotist ['hɪpnətəst] *n* a person who can use hypnotism.

hypnotize, -ise ['hɪpnətaɪz] *vt* to put <sb> under the effects of hypnosis.

hypoallergenic [,haɪpouælər'dʒenɪk] *adj* [make-up, earring] that is designed to reduce the risk of an allergic reaction.

hypochondriac [,haɪpə'kɒndriæk] *n* a person who worries too much about their health, and often thinks they are ill when they are not.

hypocrisy [hɪˈpɒkrəsɪ] *n* something somebody says or does that is different to what they really believe (disapproving use) □ *The report criticized the hypocrisy and double standards prevalent in the council.*

hypocrite [ˈhɪpəkrɪt] *n* a person who does or feels the opposite of what they say (disapproving use) □ *Don't be such a hypocrite!*

hypocritical [ˌhɪpəˈkrɪtɪkl] *adj* [person, attitude, words] *see* **hypocrite** □ *It would be hypocritical of me to criticize others for bad timekeeping when I'm so often late myself.*

hypodermic [ˌhaɪpəˈdɜːmɪk] *n* **-1. a hypodermic (needle)** a hollow needle. **-2. a hypodermic (syringe)** a plastic tube with a hollow needle, used for injecting drugs or taking blood.

hypothermia [ˌhaɪpoʊˈθɜːmɪə] *n* a medical condition in which the body's temperature falls dangerously low □ *Old people are at risk from hypothermia in this severe weather.*

hypothesis [haɪˈpɒθəsəs] (*pl* **hypotheses** [-θəsiːz]) *n* an idea, based on a few facts, that attempts to explain something but cannot yet be shown to be true □ *I'd like to put forward a new hypothesis.* □ *It's pure hypothesis.* □ *a working hypothesis.*

hypothesize, -ise [haɪˈpɒθəsaɪz] ◇ *vt* [cause, reason] to suggest a possible explanation for <sthg> □ *We can only hypothesize the cause of the crash.* ◇ *vi* to make a hypothesis about something □ *We can only hypothesize about what might have happened.*

hypothetical [ˌhaɪpəˈθetɪkl] *adj* [question, situation] that is talked about as a possibility □ *And what will you do once you find this hypothetical job?*

hysterectomy [ˌhɪstəˈrektəmɪ] (*pl* **hysterectomies**) *n* a medical operation in which a woman's womb is removed.

hysteria [hɪˈstɪərɪə] *n* **-1.** a strong uncontrolled feeling of panic, anger etc that affects a large group of people □ *In the newsroom there was an atmosphere of excitement bordering on hysteria.* **-2.** MEDICINE a condition in which a person becomes very emotional, behaves strangely, and has symptoms of illnesses that have no obvious cause.

hysterical [hɪˈsterɪkl] *adj* **-1.** [person] who is shouting or crying in an uncontrolled way because they feel panic, anger etc □ *People were getting hysterical with fear.* □ *hysterical laughing/shouting.* **-2.** [comedian, story] very funny (informal use) □ *The sketch was hysterical!*

hysterically [hɪˈsterɪklɪ] *adv* **-1.** [laugh, scream] *see* **hysterical. -2. hysterically funny** very funny (informal use).

hysterics [hɪˈsterɪks] *npl* (informal use) **-1. to be in hysterics** to laugh in an uncontrolled way □ *He had me in hysterics.* **-2. to have hysterics** GB to become very angry or worried □ *My mother will have hysterics when she finds out.*

Hz (*abbr of* **hertz**) a unit used for measuring the frequency of sound waves that is equal to one cycle per second.

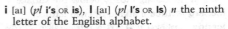

i [aɪ] (*pl* **i's** OR **is**), **I** [aɪ] (*pl* **I's** OR **Is**) *n* the ninth letter of the English alphabet.

I¹ *abbr of* **Island, Isle.**

I² [aɪ] *pron* the person who is speaking or writing (used as the subject of a verb) □ *I'm leaving.* □ *Ann and I were at college together.* □ *It is I who should apologize* (formal use).

IA *abbr of* **Iowa.**

IAEA (*abbr of* **International Atomic Energy Agency**) *n* **the IAEA** an international organization that controls how much atomic energy is used and produced.

Iberian [aɪˈbɪərɪən] *n* & *adj*: *see* **Iberian Peninsula.**

Iberian Peninsula: the Iberian Peninsula Spain and Portugal considered together.

ibid (*abbr of* **ibidem**) a word written after something to show it is in the same book, article, chapter etc that has already been mentioned.

Ibiza [ɪˈbiːθə] one of the Balearic Islands, southwest of Majorca. It is a popular tourist area. SIZE: 541 sq kms. POPULATION: 57,000. MAIN CITY: Ibiza.

IBRD (*abbr of* **International Bank for Reconstruction and Development**) *n* = **World Bank.**

i/c *abbr of* **in charge.**

ICA (*abbr of* **Institute of Contemporary Art**) *n* **the ICA** a center for modern art in London that presents exhibitions of visual art and performances of film, theater, music, and dance.

Icarus [ˈɪkərəs] in Greek mythology, a man who tried to fly using wings made of wax and feathers. When he flew too near the sun, the wax melted and he fell and died.

ICBM *n abbr of* **intercontinental ballistic missile.**

ICC *n* **-1.** *abbr of* **International Chamber of Commerce. -2.** (*abbr of* **Interstate Commerce Commission**) **the ICC** in the USA, the government department that looks after business among all the states.

ice [aɪs] ◇ *n* **-1.** [on a window, pond, road] water which is frozen solid □ *The water in the bucket had turned to ice.* □ *We had to scrape the ice off the windshield before leaving.* ■ **to break the ice** to do or say something to help people who do not know each other to relax with each other, e.g. at the beginning of a party or meeting □ *Party games can help to break the ice.* ■ **to put sthg on ice** [plan, project] to decide to wait for a period of time before using or continuing with sthg □ *We've put the Deema project on ice for the time being.*

-2. ice in the form of cubes for putting in drinks □ *Would you like ice in your juice?* **-3.** GB an ice cream. ◇ *vt* [cake, cookie] to cover <sthg> with icing.

◆ **ice over, ice up** *vi* [road, window, pond] to become covered with ice □ *The car windows had iced over.*

ice age *n* one of the periods in history when the polar ice caps covered a much larger area than they do now.

iceberg ['aɪsbɜːʳg] *n* a large mass of ice floating in the ocean, mostly below the surface.

iceberg lettuce *n* a kind of crisp lettuce.

icebox ['aɪsbɒks] *n* **-1.** US a refrigerator. **-2.** GB the part of a refrigerator that is used for keeping ice and frozen food in.

icebreaker ['aɪsbreɪkəʳ] *n* a ship that can cut through ice.

ice bucket *n* a plastic container from which ice is served for drinks; a metal container in which one puts ice and water to keep wine cold during a meal.

ice cap *n* the areas around the North and South Poles that are always covered with ice.

ice-cold *adj* [drink, hands, wind] very cold □ *a glass of ice-cold milk.*

ice cream *n* a soft frozen dessert made from milk or cream that is flavored with fruit, vanilla, chocolate etc □ *two scoops of ice cream.* □ *a strawberry ice cream.*

ice cream bar *n* US ice cream on a stick that is covered in chocolate.

ice cream truck US, **ice cream van** GB *n* a truck that drives around residential areas, parks etc selling ice cream. It usually plays a loud tune so that people know it is coming.

ice cube *n* a small piece of ice in the shape of a cube for putting in drinks.

iced [aɪst] *adj* **-1.** [drink, tea] that has been made cold with ice □ *an iced coffee.* **-2.** [cake, cookie] that is covered with icing.

ice floe *n* a sheet of ice floating in the ocean.

ice hockey *n* a kind of hockey played on ice with a rubber disk instead of a ball.

Iceland ['aɪslənd] a country in the north Atlantic Ocean, just below the Arctic Circle, with many volcanoes and hot springs. SIZE: 103,000 sq kms. POPULATION: 260,000 (*Icelanders*). CAPITAL: Reykjavik. LANGUAGE: Icelandic. CURRENCY: Icelandic krona.

Icelander ['aɪsləndəʳ] *n* a person who comes from or lives in Iceland.

Icelandic [aɪs'lændɪk] ◇ *adj: see* **Iceland**. ◇ *n* the language spoken in Iceland.

ice lolly *n* GB a type of candy made of water that is flavored with fruit and frozen onto a stick.

ice pick *n* a tool with a sharp point for making holes in ice in order to travel over it.

ice rink *n* a building or area where a surface of ice is provided for people to skate on.

ice skate *n* a special boot that has a blade at-

tached to the bottom for skating on ice □ *a pair of ice skates.*

◆ **ice-skate** *vi* to move across ice wearing ice skates.

ice-skater *n* a person who skates on ice as a sport or hobby.

ice-skating *n* the sport or hobby of skating on ice.

icicle ['aɪsɪkl] *n* a stick of ice formed when water runs off the edge of something and freezes.

icily ['aɪsɪlɪ] *adv* [say, greet, stare] in a very unfriendly way.

icing ['aɪsɪŋ] *n* a mixture of sugar and water, used to cover and decorate cakes, that becomes hard when it is dry □ *a cake with chocolate icing.* ■ **the icing on the cake** something that makes a good situation even better (informal use) □ *A celebrity to present the award really would be the icing on the cake!*

icing sugar *n* GB a type of very fine sugar used to make icing.

ICJ (*abbr of* **International Court of Justice**) *n* **the ICJ** a court in the Hague, Netherlands, that makes judgments on matters brought to it by members of the UN.

icon ['aɪkɒn] *n* **-1.** RELIGION a religious picture, especially in the Orthodox Church □ *a religious icon.* **-2.** COMPUTING a symbol like a small picture that represents a function on a computer screen □ *Double click on the icon to activate the program.*

iconoclast [aɪ'kɒnəklæst] *n* a person who strongly criticizes or rejects accepted traditions or beliefs.

ICR (*abbr of* **Institute for Cancer Research**) *n* **the ICR** in Britain, an important center for cancer research, education, and treatment.

ICU *n abbr of* **intensive care unit**.

icy ['aɪsɪ] (*compar* **icier**, *superl* **iciest**) *adj* **-1.** [wind, weather, cold] very cold □ *It's icy out there today.* **-2.** [road, sidewalk] covered with ice □ *Look out for icy patches on the roads.* **-3.** [look, stare] very unfriendly □ *They received an icy reception.*

id [ɪd] *n* the part of one's unconscious mind that is related to one's primitive instincts such as hunger and emotions.

I'd [aɪd] = **I would, I had.**

ID ◇ *n abbr of* **identification** □ *We can't cash the check if you haven't got any ID.* ◇ *abbr of* **Idaho**.

Idaho ['aɪdəhoʊ] a state in the northwestern USA, consisting mainly of the Rocky Mountains. ABBREVIATION: ID. SIZE: 216,412 sq kms. POPULATION: 1,006,749 (*Idahoans*). CAPITAL: Boise.

ID card *n* a card with one's name, photograph etc that proves who one is.

IDD (*abbr of* **international direct dialing**) *n* a system that allows people to make international telephone calls without going through an operator.

idea [aɪ'dɪə] *n* **-1.** [of how to do something] a plan or suggestion that comes into one's mind suddenly □ *I've just had an idea to im-*

prove our services. □ That's a good idea. **-2.** [in somebody's mind] a picture or representation of something in one's mind □ My ideas on the subject are still rather vague. □ He introduced the idea that the world was round. □ The idea of a month in the sun appeals to most people. ■ **to get the idea** to understand something; to get a particular feeling □ Don't worry, you'll soon get the idea of how it works. □ I'm beginning to get the idea (that) no-one likes me. ■ **to have an idea of sthg** to have an understanding of sthg □ Do you have any idea of the trouble you've caused? ■ **to have no idea** not to know something at all □ Sorry, I've no idea where he is. **-3.** a thought that is based on a feeling and not on fact □ It's just an idea, but it might work. □ I have an idea that she'll agree to it. **-4.** [about something] a belief or opinion □ He has his own ideas on OR about how to run a business. □ People have conflicting ideas about how the money should be spent. **-5.** [to do something] an intention or purpose □ My original idea was to use recycled paper. □ The idea is to finish the game with the highest possible score. **-6. an idea of sthg** [of the cost, number, time] an estimate of sthg □ Can you give me a rough idea of the price?

ideal [aɪ'dɪəl] ◇ adj [person, weather, place] that one finds perfect for one's needs □ My ideal partner would be tall, dark, and handsome. □ Those curtains would be ideal for my bedroom. □ In an ideal world, such measures would not be necessary. ◇ n **-1.** a belief, principle, way of behaving etc that one believes is right and tries to follow □ She has very high ideals. **-2.** a person or thing that one finds perfect for one's needs □ My present house is far from the ideal.

idealism [aɪ'dɪəlɪzm] n a belief in ideals □ the idealism of youth.

idealist [aɪ'dɪələst] n a person whose behavior and thoughts are based on ideals □ She likes to think of herself as something of an idealist.

idealize, -ise [aɪ'dɪəlaɪz] vt to think of <sb/ sthg> as being perfect, especially when this is not true or realistic □ Her memories of being a student are somewhat idealized.

ideally [aɪ'dɪəlɪ] adv **-1. ideally situated/suited etc** situated/suited etc in a way that cannot be improved □ The hotel is ideally located for sight-seeing. **-2. ideally,...** a word used to show that one would like something but knows or thinks it is not possible □ Ideally, I'd like to take four weeks off work.

identical [aɪ'dentɪkl] adj [color, feature, voice] that is exactly the same □ Their hats were identical. □ The new model is identical to the old one in most respects.

identical twins npl twins who come from the same fertilized egg and who look exactly the same.

identifiable [aɪ'dentəfaɪəbl] adj [person, object, characteristic] that can be recognized □ The bag is easily identifiable.

identification [aɪˌdentəfɪ'keɪʃn] n **-1.** see **identify** □ There will need to be a formal identification of the body. □ These kids' identification with their

rock star role models is almost total. **-2.** documents that prove who one is □ Can I see your identification, sir?

identify [aɪ'dentəfaɪ] (pt & pp **identified**) ◇ vt **-1.** to recognize <sb/sthg> and say who or what they are □ I was able to identify my coat from the pile that lay on the floor. **-2.** to prove the identity of <sb/sthg> □ The car's license plate identifies it as a local one. **-3. to identify sb/sthg with sthg** to associate sb/sthg with sthg □ Most people identify Italy with fine art and great food. ◇ vi **to identify with sb/sthg** to feel that one understands sb/sthg because one has the same feelings, is in the same situation etc □ We are supposed to identify with the main character in the story.

Identikit picture™ [aɪ'dentɪkɪt-] n a picture of a person's face that police make using separate sections for the eyes, mouth, nose etc after being given a description of the person by a witness.

identity [aɪ'dentətɪ] (pl **identities**) n **-1.** the state of being a particular person or thing □ The police have no clues to the attacker's identity. □ The former spy assumed a new identity. **-2.** one's sense of being a particular person □ He found a sense of identity when he became a father. □ an identity crisis.

identity card n a card with one's name, photograph etc that proves who one is.

identity parade n GB a row of people put together by police that includes a person suspected of a crime and that a witness looks at in order to see if they can recognize the suspect.

ideological [ˌaɪdɪə'lɒdʒɪkl] adj [dispute, approach, issue] see **ideology** □ We must approach the issue in a pragmatic rather than an ideological way.

ideology [ˌaɪdɪ'ɒlədʒɪ] (pl **ideologies**) n a set of ideas that are held by a particular political, religious, or social group □ It's all part of Christian/socialist ideology. □ I don't agree with the ideology of capitalism.

idiom ['ɪdɪəm] n **-1.** a group of words with a meaning that is different from the meaning of the words when they are separate □ a book of English idioms. **-2.** a form of expression that is used by a particular group of people or in a particular kind of activity (formal use) □ the idiom of dance/paint.

idiomatic [ˌɪdɪə'mætɪk] adj [expression, language] that contains words which mean something different when they are used together, and so can be difficult to translate □ I had a few problems with the idiomatic parts.

idiosyncrasy [ˌɪdɪə'sɪŋkrəsɪ] (pl **idiosyncrasies**) n an unusual habit or way of behaving that somebody has and that can be difficult for other people to understand or accept □ You must forgive my little idiosyncrasies.

idiot ['ɪdɪət] n a person who one thinks is foolish (disapproving use) □ You idiot! □ I'm not an idiot, you know!

idiotic [ˌɪdɪ'ɒtɪk] adj [idea, question, behavior] that one thinks is foolish (disapproving use) □ What an idiotic comment!

idle ['aɪdl] ◇ *adj* -1. [person] who is lazy and avoids doing work that needs to be done □ *They're an idle bunch of scroungers!* -2. **to be** OR **stand** OR **lie idle** [factory, machine, equipment] not to be used because there is no work; [worker] not to be doing anything because there is no work □ *The plant has lain idle for months.* □ *The men have been kept idle, waiting for the equipment to arrive.* -3. **an idle threat/boast** a threat/boast that is not serious □ *Is this another one of his idle threats?* -4. [glance, curiosity] that has no particular purpose □ *It was just an idle remark.* -5. [gossip, rumor] that is not based on facts and so has no use or value □ *That's just idle speculation.*
◇ *vi* [engine] to turn slowly and quietly □ *He left the engine idling while he ran into the store.*

◆ **idle away** *vt sep* **to idle the time away** to spend one's time without doing anything useful □ *He idles away the hours doodling.*

idler ['aɪdlə'] *n* a person who does nothing, or does something in a slow lazy way.

idly ['aɪdlɪ] *adv* -1. [sit, stand] in a lazy way and without doing anything useful □ *I'm not prepared to stand idly by and not help.* -2. [ask, wonder, look] without any particular purpose □ *I was idly glancing through the papers.*

idol ['aɪdl] *n* -1. a person, usually famous, who is greatly admired by people, e.g. for their achievements, personality, or appearance □ *a teenage idol.* -2. RELIGION an image or statue of a being that is worshipped as a god.

idolize, -ise ['aɪdəlaɪz] *vt* -1. [star, leader, father] to admire or love <sb> very much □ *She's idolized by fans all over the world.* -2. [god] to worship <sb/sthg> as part of a religion.

idyl(l) [US 'aɪdl, GB 'ɪdl] *n* an idyllic place, time, or situation □ *a rural idyll.*

idyllic [US aɪ'dɪlɪk, GB ɪ'dɪlɪk] *adj* [place, time, life] that seems perfect and makes one feel very happy, especially because it is peaceful □ *The hotel is set in idyllic surroundings.* □ *a scene of idyllic calm.*

i.e. (*abbr of* **id est**) namely (used in front of information that explains something more clearly) □ *all members, i.e. those who have paid the subscription.*

if [ɪf] ◇ *conj* -1. **if she calls, let me know** she might call, and when she does, let me know □ *If we started work today we could be finished by the weekend.* ■ **if I were you** a phrase used to give advice □ *If I were you I'd tell her.* -2. **if we had left earlier we would have gotten there on time** we did not leave earlier, and so we did not get there on time. ■ **if it hadn't been so expensive I'd have bought it** it was expensive, and so I did not buy it. -3. used to introduce reported questions □ *She asked me if I knew him.* □ *Do you know if she's left yet?* -4. although □ *The meal was good, if expensive.* -5. used to introduce a polite suggestion or request □ *I'd be very grateful if you would let me know.* □ *If you could just wait here for a few moments.*
◇ *npl* **ifs, ands, or buts** US, **ifs and buts** GB reasons for not doing something □ *I don't want any ifs, ands, or buts, just do it!*

◆ **if anything** *adv* used to introduce a statement that is the opposite of something that has just been mentioned □ *He doesn't look any slimmer. If anything, he's put on weight.*

◆ **if ever** *conj* used to emphasize how appropriate a description is □ *There's a hopeless case if ever I saw one!* □ *If ever I saw a man driven by ambition, it's him.*

◆ **if not** *conj* used to suggest that something might be more or less than is stated □ *I'll have it ready by Friday, if not sooner.* □ *It should arrive tomorrow. If not, give me a call.*

◆ **if only** ◇ *conj* -1. used to give a reason for doing something □ *We'll have to talk to him, if only to hear his side of things.* -2. used to say what one would like to happen, especially when one knows it is very unlikely to happen □ *If only he wouldn't drink so much!* ◇ *excl*: a phrase used to say that one would like something to happen *"Are you going abroad this summer?" — "If only!"*

iffy ['ɪfɪ] (*compar* **iffier**, *superl* **iffiest**) *adj* [person, plan, situation] that is uncertain (informal use) □ *The whole idea sounds iffy to me.*

igloo ['ɪgluː] (*pl* **igloos**) *n* a small round house made from blocks of hard snow and used by Inuits.

ignite [ɪg'naɪt] ◇ *vt* [fuel, gas] to cause <sthg> to start burning □ *He lit a match and ignited the fire.* ◇ *vi* [fuel, gas] *The crash caused the gas inside to ignite.*

ignition [ɪg'nɪʃn] *n* **the ignition** AUTO the electrical device in a car, truck etc that ignites the fuel and starts the engine □ *I must have left the key in the ignition!*

ignition key *n* a key that is used to turn the ignition of a car in order to start the engine.

ignoble [ɪg'nəʊbl] *adj* [person, action, thought] that is morally wrong and dishonorable (formal use).

ignominious [ˌɪgnə'mɪnɪəs] *adj* [defeat, behavior] that causes shame or embarrassment, especially because it happens in public (formal use) □ *democracy's most ignominious day.*

ignominy ['ɪgnəmɪnɪ] *n* a state or feeling of shame or embarrassment, especially because of something that has happened in public (formal use) □ *I couldn't bear the ignominy of it.*

ignoramus [ˌɪgnə'reɪməs] (*pl* **ignoramuses**) *n* a person who one thinks is very stupid (disapproving use) □ *I felt such an ignoramus!*

ignorance ['ɪgnərəns] *n* [of a fact, the law] a lack of knowledge or awareness of something, especially of something that one should know about □ *He showed his complete ignorance of local customs.* ■ **ignorance is bliss** a phrase used to say that it is better not to know something unpleasant in a particular situation.

ignorant ['ɪgnərənt] *adj* -1. [person] who knows little or nothing about something, especially something that they should know about □ *I'm pretty ignorant about politics.* -2. **to be ignorant of sthg** [of a fact, event] not to know about sthg □ *I was completely ignorant of its existence until now.* -3. [person, behavior] that shows a lack of politeness □ *You ignorant oaf!*

ignore [ɪgˈnɔːʳ] *vt* [advice, fact, person] to be aware of, but not pay attention to, <sb/sthg> □ *He pretended not to see me, but I knew he was ignoring me.* □ *We cannot continue to ignore the accusations that have been made against him.*

iguana [ɪˈgwɑːnə] (*pl* **iguana** OR **iguanas**) *n* a large gray-green lizard found in Latin America.

ikon [ˈaɪkɒn] *n* = **icon**.

IL *abbr of* **Illinois**.

ileum [ˈɪlɪəm] (*pl* **ilea**) *n* the lower part of one's small intestine.

ilk [ɪlk] *n* **of that ilk** of the kind that has been mentioned □ *bank robbers, burglars, and people of that ilk.*

ill [ɪl] ◇ *adj* **-1. to be ill** [person, animal] to be in bad health □ *I've been feeling ill for a few days now.* ■ **to fall** OR **be taken ill** to become ill □ *He fell ill and was taken to the hospital.* **-2.** [effects, luck] bad. ◇ *adv* **-1.** badly □ *We were ill-prepared for such news.* ■ **to speak/think ill of sb** to say/think something unpleasant about sb □ *We mustn't speak ill of the dead.* **-2. I/you etc can ill afford...** I/you etc cannot very easily afford... □ *We can ill afford such luxuries.*
◆ **ills** *npl* [of a society, system] problems (formal use) □ *social ills such as unemployment.*

ill. *abbr of* **illustration**.

I'll [aɪl] = **I will, I shall**.

ill-advised [-ədˈvaɪzd] *adj* [remark, action] that is foolish and likely to have bad results or cause problems □ *You would be ill-advised to invest all your money in one venture.*

ill at ease *adj* **to be ill at ease** not to be comfortable or relaxed, especially in a social situation □ *He felt rather ill at ease in his new surroundings.*

ill-bred *adj* [person] who shows a lack of politeness □ *What an ill-bred young man!*

ill-considered *adj* [remark, action, decision] that has not been thought about very carefully and is not very sensible □ *He made a rather ill-considered move into the timber trade.*

ill-disposed *adj* [person] who does not have a good opinion of a particular person or group of people and so is not willing to support or help them □ *They are not ill-disposed toward young people, they're just old-fashioned.*

illegal [ɪˈliːgl] ◇ *adj* [drug, parking] that is not allowed by the law of a country □ *It's illegal to carry an offensive weapon.* □ *the illegal possession of drugs.* ■ **an illegal immigrant** OR **alien** a person who has come from abroad to live in a particular country without official permission ◇ *n* an illegal immigrant.

illegally [ɪˈliːgəlɪ] *adv*: *see* **illegal** □ *He entered the country illegally.* □ *Your car is illegally parked.*

illegible [ɪˈledʒəbl] *adj* [handwriting, text, letter] that is unclear and so is impossible to read □ *This is totally illegible!*

illegitimate [ˌɪləˈdʒɪtəmət] *adj* **-1.** [son, daughter] whose parents are not married to each other □ *The composer had three illegitimate children.* **-2.** [activity, aim] that is not allowed or accepted because of rules, customs etc □ *The elections were declared illegitimate by the UN.*

ill-equipped [-ɪˈkwɪpt] *adj* **to be ill-equipped** [person, institution, organization] to be unable to do something because of not having the necessary qualities, equipment, skills etc □ *He felt ill-equipped to deal with the pressures of the job.*

ill-fated *adj* [mission, trip, attempt] that ended badly or in failure □ *their ill-fated climb to the summit.*

ill feeling *n* feelings of anger or dislike between two or more people, e.g. as the result of a disagreement □ *I don't want there to be any ill feeling between us.*

ill-founded [-ˈfaʊndəd] *adj* [fear, confidence, rumor] that is not based on facts or the real situation □ *The rumors proved to be ill-founded.*

ill-gotten gains *npl* something somebody has got from doing something immoral or illegal (formal use).

ill health *n* bad health or illness that continues over a long period of time □ *She suffered from ill health for many years.*

illicit [ɪˈlɪsət] *adj* [activity, affair, drug] that is illegal or disapproved of in a particular society and is usually secret □ *He was involved in an illicit arms deal/trade.*

illicitly [ɪˈlɪsətlɪ] *adv* [deal, sell] *see* **illicit**.

ill-informed *adj* [person, opinion, argument] that shows very little knowledge about a particular subject □ *People over here are very ill-informed about what's going on.*

Illinois [ˌɪləˈnɔɪ] a state in the Midwest of the USA, consisting mainly of agricultural prairies. ABBREVIATION: IL. SIZE: 146,075 sq kms. POPULATION: 11,430,602 (*Illinoisans*). CAPITAL: Springfield. MAIN CITY: Chicago.

illiteracy [ɪˈlɪtərəsɪ] *n* the inability of a large group of people to read or write □ *Since the beginning of the civil war, illiteracy has increased dramatically.* □ *child/adult illiteracy.*

illiterate [ɪˈlɪtərət] ◇ *adj* [person] who cannot read or write; who knows little about a particular subject □ *an illiterate peasant* □ *technologically illiterate.* ◇ *n* an illiterate person.

ill-mannered *adj* [person] who is not polite.

illness [ˈɪlnəs] *n* **-1.** [of person, animal] a period or state of being ill □ *The show has been canceled due to illness.* □ *His illness has been widely reported in the press.* **-2.** a disease of the body or mind □ *mental illness* □ *She's suffering from an incurable illness.*

illogical [ɪˈlɒdʒɪkl] *adj* [statement, idea, behavior] that has no sensible reason or explanation □ *It all seems most illogical to me.*

ill-suited *adj* **to be ill-suited** [couple] not to be right for each other, e.g. because of different interests or beliefs □ *They're most ill-suited.*

ill-tempered *adj* [person] who becomes angry easily and often □ *an ill-tempered old man.*

ill-timed *adj* [comment, action, event] that happens at the wrong time and could offend people or have bad results □ *Their decision to publish the memoirs was somewhat ill-timed.*

ill-treat *vt* [child, worker, horse] to treat <a person or animal> badly or cruelly □ *She complained of having been ill-treated by other staff.*

ill-treatment *n*: *see* **ill-treat**.

illuminate [ɪˈluːmɪneɪt] *vt* **-1**. [street, building, scene] to provide light to make <sthg> easier to see □ *The room was illuminated solely by candlelight.* **-2**. [subject, concept, problem] to help somebody to understand <sthg> more clearly by explaining or giving examples □ *This story helps to illuminate why the mission failed.*

illuminated [ɪˈluːmɪneɪtəd] *adj* **-1**. [sign, notice, building] that can be seen clearly because electric lights shine on it or in it. **-2**. ART [book, manuscript] that is decorated in bright colors, including gold or silver.

illuminating [ɪˈluːmɪneɪtɪŋ] *adj* [book, talk, experience] that helps somebody to understand something much more clearly.

illumination [ɪˌluːmɪˈneɪʃn] *n* [of a street, building, scene] *see* **illuminate**.

◆ **illuminations** *npl* in Britain, colored lights that are used to decorate part of a town or city, especially during a holiday period or on a special occasion.

illusion [ɪˈluːʒn] *n* **-1**. [about something] a false idea that seems real. ■ **to have no illusions about sb/sthg** to see sb/sthg in a realistic way, without any false ideas or expectations □ *I have no illusions about myself as an artist.* ■ **to be under the illusion that...** to wrongly believe that... □ *He was under the illusion that the service was offered free.* **-2**. [of space, depth] something that seems different from the way it really is □ *The mirror perspective gives an illusion of depth.* **-3**. [for entertaining people] a magic trick in which somebody uses a special technique or skill to make other people think they see something impossible or surprising.

illusionist [ɪˈluːʒənəst] *n* a person who performs illusions as entertainment (formal use).

illusory [ɪˈluːsərɪ] *adj* [hope, belief, victory] that one realizes after a period of time is false or impossible (formal use).

illustrate [ˈɪləstreɪt] *vt* **-1**. **to be illustrated** [book, text] to contain pictures, diagrams etc □ *The book is heavily illustrated with photos and drawings.* □ *an illustrated guide to Rome.* **-2**. [point, fact, quality] to be proof or a good example of <sthg> □ *The results clearly illustrate the need for improvement.* □ *Allow me to illustrate what I mean.*

illustration [ˌɪləˈstreɪʃn] *n* **-1**. [in a book, text, magazine] a picture, diagram etc in a book or next to a piece of writing □ *a color/black and white illustration.* **-2**. [of a point, fact, quality] an example used to help explain something □ *That's an illustration of his generosity.*

illustrator [ˈɪləstreɪtər] *n* a person whose job is to draw pictures for books, greeting cards etc □ *an illustrator of children's books.*

illustrious [ɪˈlʌstrɪəs] *adj* [career, name, achievement] that is known and admired by many people (formal use).

ill will *n* anger or dislike that one feels toward somebody, e.g. because of a disagreement □ *I don't bear him any ill will.*

ill wind *n* **it's an ill wind (that blows nobody any good)** a phrase used to say that a situation or event that seems bad may in fact bring some good luck.

ILO (*abbr of* **International Labor Organization**) *n* **the ILO** a branch of the UN concerned with pay, employment, and working conditions.

I'm [aɪm] = **I am**.

image [ˈɪmɪdʒ] *n* **-1**. [in one's mind] a picture or idea that one has in one's mind about how somebody or something looks or what they are like □ *What's your image of the typical English person?* □ *Most people's image of modeling is of glamor and excitement.* **-2**. [in a mirror, through a lens] the scene that one can see in a mirror or through the lens of a camera □ *Make sure the image is focused properly.* **-3**. [on a screen, in a picture] a picture or scene that appears on a TV, movie theater, or computer screen or in a painting, photograph etc □ *shocking images of violence.* **-4**. [of a star, party, company] the way that the public sees a person, organization etc, especially because of appearance, behavior, or advertising □ *She's got a good/bad public image.* □ *The Governor is trying to create a new, caring image with the public.* □ *an image consultant.* **-5**. [in a poem, song] a written description of something physical that is used to represent an idea or feeling □ *The image of the snake signifies danger.* **-6**. **to be the image of sb** to look exactly like sb □ *You're the exact image of your father!*

imagery [ˈɪmɪdʒərɪ] *n* **-1**. language in writing, especially poetry, that describes something physical in order to represent an idea or feeling □ *the use of religious imagery.* **-2**. the use of pictures or scenes in a movie, painting etc to represent particular ideas or feelings □ *I don't understand the imagery.*

imaginable [ɪˈmædʒɪnəbl] *adj* that one can imagine or think of □ *She's done everything imaginable, from mountain climbing to deep-sea diving.*

imaginary [US ɪˈmædʒəneri, GB -ɪnrɪ] *adj* [character, weapon, world] that exists in somebody's mind, but is not real □ *The equator is an imaginary line going around the middle of the Earth.*

imagination [ɪˌmædʒɪˈneɪʃn] *n* **-1**. the ability to imagine things, especially when they are new or unusual □ *Use your imagination!* □ *Her writing shows great imagination.* **-2**. the part of the mind that imagines things □ *I think your imagination is running away with you!* **-3**. something, e.g. an idea, that comes from somebody's imagination and is not really true □ *The whole affair is pure imagination.*

imaginative [ɪˈmædʒənətɪv] *adj* **-1**. [writer, artist] who uses their imagination □ *She's a very imaginative student.* **-2**. [writing, design, idea] that shows imagination □ *We need a more imagina-*

tive approach to creating jobs. □ a highly imaginative work of art.

imagine [ɪˈmædʒɪn] vt -1. [scene, event, situation] to form an idea or picture of <sthg> in one's mind, especially without knowing or experiencing it □ I can't imagine (myself) getting the job. □ I can imagine what she said. ■ **imagine (that)!** a phrase used to react to surprising or unusual news □ Twins! Just imagine! -2. to experience <sthg> in a way that seems real, but only exists in one's mind □ Don't be silly, you're just imagining things! -3. **to imagine (that)...** to think that something is probably true □ I imagine (that) you're tired after your trip.

imaginings [ɪˈmædʒɪnɪŋz] npl things that are not real and only exist in the mind (literary use).

imbalance [ˌɪmˈbæləns] n a state in which two closely connected things are not equal, with the result that there can be problems □ a hormone imbalance.

imbecile [US ˈɪmbəsl, GB -siːl] n a person who one thinks is stupid (disapproving use).

imbue [ɪmˈbjuː] vt **to imbue sb with sthg** [with a quality, feeling] to influence sb so that sthg becomes part of their character or behavior □ Our students are imbued with a sense of respect.

IMF n abbr of **International Monetary Fund**.

imitate [ˈɪmɪteɪt] vt -1. [person] to copy the behavior, voice etc of <sb> in order to annoy them or entertain other people □ He's always imitating his sister. -2. [person, organization, method] to copy <sb/sthg> in one's way of doing things, usually in order to achieve something similar □ Very few companies have been able to imitate their success.

imitation [ˌɪmɪˈteɪʃn] ◇ n -1. [of a person] an act of imitating somebody in order to annoy them or entertain other people □ She does a great imitation of the boss. -2. [of a piece of jewelry, machinery, clothing] a copy of something that is usually cheaper but not as good as the original item □ He only sells cheap imitations. -3. [of a person, method] see **imitate** □ Children learn to speak by imitation. ◇ adj [leather, jewelry] that is a copy of something more well-known or expensive.

imitator [ˈɪmɪteɪtər] n a person who copies somebody else in their way of doing things or in the way they look.

immaculate [ɪˈmækjələt] adj -1. [appearance, person, room] that is very clean and tidy □ an immaculate suit □ Mary looked immaculate that night. -2. [behavior, technique, timing] that is of a very high standard and cannot be criticized in any way □ It was an immaculate performance.

immaculately [ɪˈmækjələtlɪ] adv **immaculately dressed/presented** very well dressed/presented □ The house was immaculately clean.

immaterial [ˌɪmɪˈtɪərɪəl] adj [event, detail, information] that is not important in relation to a particular question □ Whether or not he was actually there at the time is immaterial.

immature [ˌɪmɪˈtjʊər] adj -1. [person, behavior,

response] that is not as sensible as one expects of an adult or of somebody of a particular age □ Don't be so immature! -2. [plant, animal, person] that is not yet fully developed □ an emotionally immature young man.

immaturity [ˌɪmɪˈtjʊərətɪ] n: see **immature**.

immeasurable [ɪˈmeʒərəbl] adj [damage, difference, wealth] that is too large to be measured □ His importance to the company is immeasurable.

immediacy [ɪˈmiːdjəsɪ] n the quality in a picture or piece of writing that makes one feel very involved in what is shown or described.

immediate [ɪˈmiːdjət] adj -1. [action, response, attention] that comes very soon after a particular event, situation etc has been noticed; [need, problem] that must receive attention very soon □ There were immediate shouts of protest. □ The money should be enough for our immediate needs. -2. [future, aim] that is nearest in time; [area, neighborhood] that is nearest in distance □ Our immediate goal is simply to survive. □ Residents in the immediate vicinity of the blast were evacuated. -3. **one's immediate family** one's closest family, including parents, brothers, and sisters □ Members of the victim's immediate family were informed.

immediately [ɪˈmiːdjətlɪ] ◇ adv -1. [act, stop, agree] without any delay □ It wasn't immediately clear what had happened. -2. [affect, concern] without any other person, consideration etc coming before □ Priority is given to patients more immediately at risk. -3. [following, above, behind] with little space in between □ I followed immediately behind the others. □ Someone had written a note in pencil immediately below. ◇ conj GB as soon as □ Immediately I mentioned it she started shouting.

immemorial [ˌɪməˈmɔːrɪəl] adj **from** OR **since time immemorial** for longer than anybody can remember □ That building's been there since time immemorial.

immense [ɪˈmens] adj [improvement, importance, satisfaction] that is great in quantity, size, or degree □ The dam is an immense structure. □ I've immense respect for all he's achieved.

immensely [ɪˈmenslɪ] adv **immensely enjoyable/popular/difficult etc** very enjoyable/popular/difficult etc □ He's immensely wealthy. □ an immensely successful artist □ I enjoyed my stay immensely.

immensity [ɪˈmensətɪ] n [of a building, task, the universe] the great size of something; [of an achievement] the great importance or seriousness of something □ I couldn't quite take in the immensity of what had happened.

immerse [ɪˈmɜːrs] vt -1. to put <sthg> in a liquid, especially water, so that it is completely covered □ For best results, ensure that the garment is completely immersed in the dye. -2. **to immerse oneself in sthg** [in one's work, reading] to give all one's attention to sthg □ She's immersing herself in her work to forget about him.

immersion heater [ɪˈmɜːrʒn-] n GB an electric heater that is used to provide hot water for use in the home.

immigrant ['ımıgrənt] *n* a person who comes from abroad to live permanently in a country, especially in order to have a better life □ *a Turkish immigrant* OR *an immigrant from Turkey* □ *the immigrant population.*

immigration [,ımı'greıʃn] *n* -1. the process of coming into a country in order to live there permanently □ *There's a lot of immigration into Europe/from the Third World.* □ *immigration restrictions/laws.* -2. **immigration (control)** the part of an airport, port etc where people's passports, visas etc are checked before they can enter a country □ *All passengers must go through immigration.*

Immigration and Naturalization Service [US -nætʃrələ'zeıʃn-, GB -aı'zeıʃn-] *n* the US government agency that deals with foreigners' requests to live and work in the USA.

imminence ['ımınəns] *n* the closeness of an event in the future, especially one that is important or unpleasant.

imminent ['ımınənt] *adj* [arrival, danger, disaster] that is very near in the future □ *With elections now imminent, speculation is running high.*

immobile [US ı'moʊbl, GB -'moʊbaıl] *adj* [person, body, animal] that is not moving or is not able to move □ *He stood/sat immobile before me.* □ *The line of traffic was immobile.*

immobilization [US ı,moʊbələ'zeıʃn, GB -aı'zeıʃn] *n: see* **immobilize.**

immobilize, -ise [ı'moʊbəlaız] *vt* [attacker, machine] to stop <sb/sthg> from moving; [system, process] to stop <sthg> from working properly □ *Security guards immobilized the man.* □ *The alarm automatically immobilizes the car.*

immodest [ı'mɒdəst] *adj* -1. [person] who emphasizes their own achievements, skills, qualities etc in a way that seems unnecessary. -2. [dress, behavior] that shocks people for moral reasons.

immoral [ı'mɒrəl] *adj* [behavior, action, idea] that is morally wrong or unacceptable; [book, movie] that shocks many people because of its sexual content □ *It's immoral to make people pay so much tax.*

immorality [,ımə'rælətı] *n: see* **immoral.**

immortal [ı'mɔːrtl] ◇ *adj* -1. [being, god] that will never die □ *the immortal universe.* -2. [play, phrase, line] that is very famous and is remembered for a long time □ *In the immortal words of Shakespeare,...* ◇ *n* -1. a being, especially a god, that never dies. -2. a person, e.g. a movie or sports star, who will be remembered for a long time because of their achievements, abilities, qualities etc □ *Ali is one of the immortals in boxing history.*

immortality [,ımɔːr'tælətı] *n* -1. life that will never end □ *He believes in the immortality of the human spirit.* -2. [of a movie star, sports personality] fame that will last for a long time □ *Monroe achieved immortality.*

immortalize, -ise [ı'mɔːrtlaız] *vt* [person, event] to do something that means that people will remember or know about <sb/sthg> for a long time □ *The duchess was immortalized in a famous painting by Van Dyck.*

immovable [ı'muːvəbl] *adj* -1. [object, table, statue] that is firmly fixed and cannot be moved. -2. [person, opinion] that cannot be changed by persuasion □ *He was immovable on the subject.*

immune [ı'mjuːn] *adj* -1. MEDICINE [person, animal] that cannot be affected by a particular illness because of the body's natural resistance or because of substances injected into the body □ *If you've had the illness already, you should be immune to it.* -2. **to be immune to** sthg [to criticism, flattery, a danger] not to be affected by sthg □ *I'm not immune to persuasion.* □ *They were immune to our cries for help.*

immune system *n* the system inside one's body that helps fight infections and prevent illness.

immunity [ı'mjuːnətı] *n: see* **immune** □ *There is no such thing as immunity to the common cold.*

immunization [US ,ımjənə'zeıʃn, GB -jʊnaı'zeıʃn] *n: see* **immunize** □ *The vaccine gives five years' immunization to* OR *against infection.*

immunize, -ise [US 'ımjənaız, GB -jʊnaız] *vt* to give <a person or animal> protection from a disease by injecting a substance into the body □ *You should be immunized against typhoid before you go.*

immunodeficiency [US ,ımjənoʊdı'fıʃnsı, GB -jʊnoʊdı'fıʃnsı] *n* the inability of somebody's immune system to work properly.

immunology [US ,ımjə'nɒlədʒı, GB -jʊ'nɒlədʒı] *n* the area of science that is connected with the body's immunity to disease.

immutable [ı'mjuːtəbl] *adj* [law, decision, attitude] that cannot be changed (formal use) □ *an immutable fact of life.*

imp [ımp] *n* -1. a small creature, especially in children's stories, that uses its special powers to cause trouble. -2. a naughty child.

impact [*n* 'ımpækt, *vb* ım'pækt] ◇ *n* -1. the force of something hitting another thing □ *The impact of the crash caused considerable damage.* ■ **on impact** at the moment of impact □ *The shell exploded on impact.* -2. the important effect that an event, change, person, piece of information etc has □ *The movie made a huge impact on audiences all over the world.* ◇ *vt* -1. to press <sthg> firmly into something else. -2. to affect <sthg>.

impair [ım'peər] *vt* [hearing, efficiency, flavor] to affect <sthg> badly so that it is not as good as before □ *We allow nothing to impair the quality of our products.*

impaired [ım'peərd] *adj* [vision, hearing] that has been damaged □ *She suffers from impaired eyesight.*

-impaired *suffix* added to words to show that somebody has a disability □ *visually-impaired.* ■ **mobility-impaired** physically disabled.

impale [ım'peıl] *vt* to cause <sb/sthg> to be pierced by a sharp pointed object □ *There was an empty can impaled on the fence outside the house.*

impart [ım'pɑːrt] *vt* (formal use) -1. [information, knowledge] to give <sthg> to somebody, especially by telling them. -2. [feeling, quality, flavor] to pass <sthg> on to somebody or something □ *The cardamom imparts a certain exotic flavor to the dish.*

impartial [ɪmˈpɑːrʃl] *adj* [observer, news report, judge] that does not favor one side more than the other in a situation and so is fair □ *A good critic should remain impartial.*

impartiality [ɪmˌpɑːrʃiˈælətɪ] *n*: *see* **impartial** □ *Can you guarantee the impartiality of the jury in this case?*

impassable [US ɪmˈpæsəbl, GB -ˈpɑːs-] *adj* [road, bridge] that no person or vehicle can travel on or across □ *The snow rendered the bridge impassable.*

impasse [US ˈɪmpæs, GB æmˈpɑːs] *n* a point in a situation or process that cannot be passed because of a problem or disagreement □ *The talks have reached an impasse.*

impassioned [ɪmˈpæʃnd] *adj* [plea, debate, speech] that is full of strong feelings □ *The politician made an impassioned plea on behalf of the victims.*

impassive [ɪmˈpæsɪv] *adj* [face, expression, person] that does not show any emotion.

impatience [ɪmˈpeɪʃns] *n*: *see* **impatient** □ *There is growing impatience with the government's failure to act.*

impatient [ɪmˈpeɪʃnt] *adj* **-1.** [person, crowd, customer] that cannot wait without becoming annoyed □ *The audience was starting to become impatient.* **-2.** [person] who wants to have or do something very much □ *She's impatient to finish.* □ *They were impatient for success/news.* **-3.** [person] who becomes annoyed easily □ *Don't be so impatient.* □ *I get very impatient with people who don't think before they talk.*

impatiently [ɪmˈpeɪʃntlɪ] *adv* [wait, react] *see* **impatient** □ *"Well?" she said impatiently.*

impeach [ɪmˈpiːtʃ] *vt* [official, politician, president] to accuse <sb> of committing a serious crime in connection with their job while they were in an important public position.

impeccable [ɪmˈpekəbl] *adj* [behavior, appearance, performance] that cannot be criticized in any way because of being perfect □ *He has impeccable manners.*

impeccably [ɪmˈpekəblɪ] *adv* [dress, behave] *see* **impeccable** □ *an impeccably dressed young man.*

impecunious [ˌɪmpəˈkjuːnjəs] *adj* [person] who has very little money (formal use).

impede [ɪmˈpiːd] *vt* [person, progress, investigation] to make it difficult for <sb/sthg> to go ahead as planned or desired □ *The salvage operation was impeded by the weather.*

impediment [ɪmˈpedɪmənt] *n* **-1.** a situation, fact etc that makes it difficult for somebody to do something or for something to happen (formal use) □ *There is no legal impediment to their marriage.* **-2.** a physical problem that makes walking or talking difficult □ *a speech impediment.*

impel [ɪmˈpel] (*pt* & *pp* **impelled**, *cont* **impelling**) *vt* to make <sb> feel that they must do something □ *I felt impelled to call and ask them what had gone wrong.*

impending [ɪmˈpendɪŋ] *adj* [disaster, danger, trial] that is going to happen soon □ *Mike had a sense of impending doom.*

impenetrable [ɪmˈpenɪtrəbl] *adj* **-1.** [barrier, darkness, forest] that is difficult or impossible to move through or see through; [mystery] that is impossible to solve □ *To the north lay impenetrable jungle.* **-2.** [writing, theory, law] that is very difficult or impossible to understand □ *The way the book's written makes it pretty impenetrable stuff.*

imperative [ɪmˈperətɪv] ◇ *adj* urgent □ *It's imperative that we take action now to prevent disaster.* ◇ *n* **-1.** something that must be done quickly and urgently □ *Immediate action is now an absolute imperative.* **-2.** GRAMMAR the verb form that is used to give an order or instruction, e.g. "come in!" or "stop!" □ *The verb is in the imperative.*

imperceptible [ˌɪmpərˈseptəbl] *adj* [change, movement] that is so small or slight that it is not noticed or felt □ *an almost imperceptible flinch.*

imperfect [ɪmˈpɜːrfɪkt] ◇ *adj* [work, copy, knowledge] that is not perfect □ *All imperfect goods have been reduced by 50%.* ◇ *n* **the imperfect (tense)** the verb form that is used to refer to a continuous action in the past, e.g. in the sentence "It was raining."

imperfection [ˌɪmpərˈfekʃn] *n* **-1.** [on skin, a piece of china] a small mark or damaged part of something. **-2.** [in a person, system] a fault in somebody or something that stops them from being perfect □ *You'll have to learn to live with his imperfections.*

imperial [ɪmˈpɪərɪəl] *adj* **-1.** [guard, palace, past] that is connected with an emperor or an empire □ *imperial China.* **-2.** [gallon, pint] that is connected with the British system of measurements for weight, size, and quantity □ *an imperial measure* □ *the imperial system of weights and measures.*

❦ IMPERIAL

The imperial system of weight and measurement, based on the pound, gallon, and yard, is used in the USA in all contexts apart from scientific ones. Americans use pounds to talk about their weight, and distances are calculated in miles.

In Britain, the imperial system has officially been replaced by the metric system, based on the kilogram, liter, and meter. However, older people still use imperial terms and describe their weight in stones and pounds, and distances are still shown in miles and kilometers on maps.

The US and British imperial systems have different quantities for ounces, pints, and gallons (the British measures are about 20% larger).

---

imperialism [ɪmˈpɪərɪəlɪzm] *n* the system by which one country controls other, usually weaker countries for its own purposes □ *cultural imperialism.*

imperialist [ɪmˈpɪərɪələst] ◇ *adj* [regime, ruler,

idea] *see* **imperialism**. ◇ *n* a person who believes in or is responsible for imperialism.

imperil [ɪm'perəl] (US *pt* & *pp* **imperiled**, *cont* **imperiling**, GB *pt* & *pp* **imperilled**, *cont* **imperilling**) *vt* [life, project] to put <sb/sthg> in danger (formal use).

imperious [ɪm'pɪərɪəs] *adj* [manner, voice, person] that demands attention or obedience.

impersonal [ɪm'pɜːrsnəl] *adj* -1. [person, manner, letter] that does not show any emotions or personal feelings □ *The letter should be as impersonal as possible.* -2. [place, atmosphere] where people feel they are not treated as individuals □ *It was a large impersonal building.* -3. GRAMMAR **an impersonal verb** a verb that is only used after "there" or "it" and that has no subject, as in "It is snowing." ■ **an impersonal pronoun** a pronoun that does not refer to a person or object, e.g. "it" in the sentence "It is going to rain."

impersonate [ɪm'pɜːrsəneɪt] *vt* -1. to copy the behavior and appearance of <sb> in order to amuse people □ *Janet started her stage career impersonating well-known public figures.* -2. to pretend to be <sb> in order to deceive people □ *Stevens was arrested for impersonating a police officer.*

impersonation [ɪm,pɜːrsə'neɪʃn] *n*: *see* **impersonate** □ *You should see her impersonation of Madonna!* ■ **to do impersonations** to impersonate famous people in order to amuse people.

impersonator [ɪm'pɜːrsəneɪtər] *n* a person who impersonates famous people to amuse an audience.

impertinence [ɪm'pɜːrtnəns] *n* behavior that one thinks is rude and disrespectful □ *I've never come across such impertinence before!*

impertinent [ɪm'pɜːrtnənt] *adj* [person, remark, behavior] that one thinks is rude and disrespectful □ *Don't be impertinent!*

imperturbable [,ɪmpər'tɜːrbəbl] *adj* [person] who is calm and is not easily upset by problems □ *He gave his usual imperturbable smile.*

impervious [ɪm'pɜːrvjəs] *adj* **to be impervious to sthg** [to criticism, new ideas] not to be influenced or changed by sthg □ *I'm not impervious to flattery, you know.*

impetuous [ɪm'petʃʊəs] *adj* [person] who acts too quickly and without thinking about the possible consequences □ *I admit I was rather impetuous as a young man.*

impetus ['ɪmpətəs] *n* -1. an influence that encourages something to develop more quickly □ *A fresh injection of cash will give us the impetus we need.* □ *With all the media coverage it's getting, the movement is gaining impetus.* -2. PHYSICS the force with which an object moves.

impinge [ɪm'pɪndʒ] *vi* **to impinge on sthg** to have an effect on sthg, usually limiting it in some way □ *The new laws will in no way impinge on people's freedom of speech.*

impish ['ɪmpɪʃ] *adj* [person, behavior, grin] that makes one think of a naughty playful child.

implacable [ɪm'plækəbl] *adj* [opponent, hatred] that cannot be changed or made less extreme.

implant [*n* US 'ɪmplænt, GB -'plɑːnt, *vb* US ɪm'plænt, GB -'plɑːnt] ◇ *n* something, such as tissue, that is placed in somebody's body in a medical operation □ *a breast implant* □ *hair implants.* ◇ *vt* -1. **to implant sthg in** OR **into sb** [idea, feeling, attitude] to fix sthg very firmly in sb □ *These prejudices were implanted in people's minds by years of propaganda.* -2. [tissue, electrode] to put <sthg> in somebody's body in a medical operation.

implausible [ɪm'plɔːzəbl] *adj* [story, theory] that is difficult to believe because it is very unusual or seems unlikely to be true □ *It seems highly implausible that no one saw her leave.*

implement [*n* 'ɪmpləmənt, *vb* 'ɪmpləment] ◇ *n* a small piece of equipment □ *farm implements.* ◇ *vt* [suggestion, policy, law] to put <sthg> into practice □ *This is our last chance before the new law is implemented.*

implementation [,ɪmpləmən'teɪʃn] *n* [of a suggestion, policy, law] *see* **implement**.

implicate ['ɪmplɪkeɪt] *vt* [person] to show that <sb> is involved in something, especially in a crime □ *The new evidence implicates you in the fraud.*

implication [,ɪmplɪ'keɪʃn] *n* -1. [of a person] *see* **implicate** □ *The senator's implication in the affair is likely to cause problems.* -2. a possible consequence of an action or decision □ *It took him a moment to realize the full implications of what he had said.* ■ **by implication** by indirect suggestion.

implicit [ɪm'plɪsət] *adj* -1. [meaning, acknowledgment, criticism] that is suggested or understood but not stated directly □ *Implicit in his statement was a condemnation of the director's conduct.* -2. [faith, belief, trust] that is complete and not doubted □ *The governor had the implicit confidence of his staff.*

implicitly [ɪm'plɪsətlɪ] *adv* [criticize, believe] *see* **implicit** □ *I trusted Anne implicitly.*

implied [ɪm'plaɪd] *adj* [criticism, rejection] that is suggested but not expressed directly □ *There was an implied threat in what she had said.*

implode [ɪm'pləʊd] *vi* to collapse or burst inward.

implore [ɪm'plɔːr] *vt* to beg <sb> to do something or to change their mind about something □ *Don't do it, I implore you!*

imply [ɪm'plaɪ] (*pt* & *pp* **implied**) *vt* -1. **to imply that...** to suggest that something is true without stating it directly □ *Are you implying that I've made a mistake?* -2. [responsibility, need] to make it seem that <sthg> is a likely or necessary result □ *What does this imply for future relations between the two countries?*

impolite [,ɪmpə'laɪt] *adj* [person, behavior, remark] that one finds rude □ *It would be impolite to refuse.*

imponderable [ɪm'pɒndərəbl] *adj* [question, law, force] whose importance is difficult to guess or measure.

◆ **imponderables** *npl* things that are imponderable □ *There are too many imponderables.*

import [n 'impɔːʳt, vt ɪm'pɔːʳt] ◇ n -1. BUSINESS a product or service brought into a country from another country □ *Imports are down on last year.* -2. **the import of sthg** [of a speech, document] the meaning that is contained in sthg (formal use). -3. **of great/little etc import** very/not very etc important (formal use). ◇ vt -1. [goods, produce] to bring <sthg> into a country from another country □ *These cars are imported from Europe.* -2. [ideas, values, word] to bring <sthg> into a system or society from outside. -3. COMPUTING [file, document] to transfer <data> from one type of software into a type that one can use.

importance [ɪm'pɔːʳtns] n the value or significance of something □ *Don't worry, it's of no great importance.* □ *It's a matter of some importance.*

important [ɪm'pɔːʳtnt] adj -1. [meeting, work, day] that is special or necessary and likely to have serious effects, e.g. on one's life □ *What's important is that you keep a detailed record of events.* □ *It's important for you all to know this.* □ *She said it was important to get plenty of rest.* □ *This contract is very important to me.* -2. [person, country, organization] that has a lot of power or influence □ *He's not as important as he'd like to think he is.* □ *She's something important in retail management.*

importantly [ɪm'pɔːʳtntlɪ] adv **more importantly** a phrase used to introduce and emphasize the second part of an argument or explanation □ *The children are healthy now but, more importantly, they're happy.*

importation [ˌɪmpɔːʳ'teɪʃn] n a product, service etc that is imported; the act of importing something □ *restrictions on the importation of manufactured goods.*

imported [ɪm'pɔːʳtəd] adj [produce, fashion] that has been brought into a country from another country; [ideas, values, word] that has been brought into a system or society from outside □ *Imported goods are heavily taxed.*

importer [ɪm'pɔːʳtəʳ] n a person, company, or country that buys goods or services from another country to use or sell them in their own country □ *a coffee/wine importer.*

import licence n in Britain, a license that somebody must get before they can bring certain goods into the country to sell them.

impose [ɪm'pəʊz] ◇ vt [discipline, beliefs, limit] to force somebody or something to accept <sthg> □ *They've imposed further tax increases on the electorate.* □ *I won't allow you to impose your ideas on my child.* ◇ vi to cause inconvenience to somebody □ *I wouldn't want to impose on you.* □ *I hope I'm not imposing in any way.*

imposing [ɪm'pəʊzɪŋ] adj [person, building] that is impressive in appearance, and is usually taller or larger than normal □ *The general was an imposing figure.*

imposition [ˌɪmpə'zɪʃn] n -1. [of beliefs, a limit] see **impose.** -2. [on a person] something that is expected of somebody but may not be convenient for them □ *I know it's a bit of an impo-*sition, but could you watch the kids for ten minutes?

impossibility [ɪmˌpɒsə'bɪlətɪ] (pl **impossibilities**) n: see **impossible** □ *It's an absolute impossibility.*

impossible [ɪm'pɒsəbl] ◇ adj -1. [task, dream] that one feels cannot be achieved □ *It's an impossible goal.* -2. [situation, person] that is very difficult to deal with □ *He's quite impossible!* -3. [event, story] that one thinks is unlikely or unbelievable □ *But that's impossible!* ◇ n **to do the impossible** to succeed in doing something that is very difficult.

imposter US, **impostor** [ɪm'pɒstəʳ] n a person who claims to be somebody else in order to get something they want □ *This woman is an imposter!*

impotence ['ɪmpətəns] n -1. the inability of a man to have sex because he cannot get an erection □ *Depression can be a cause of impotence.* -2. a lack of power and influence over people or events □ *a feeling of impotence in the face of overwhelming bureaucracy.*

impotent ['ɪmpətənt] adj -1. [man] who is unable to have sex because he cannot get an erection. -2. [person, government] that has no power to influence people or events □ *I felt utterly impotent to help.*

impound [ɪm'paʊnd] vt [goods, car] to legally take <sthg> away from somebody and keep it until they are allowed to collect it.

impoverished [ɪm'pɒvərɪʃt] adj -1. [country, people] that has been made very poor □ *his impoverished relations.* -2. [imagination, language] that has become worse in quality □ *the impoverished state of modern literature.*

impracticable [ɪm'præktɪkəbl] adj [idea, plan] that is impossible to do □ *It's completely impracticable.*

impractical [ɪm'præktɪkl] adj [idea, suggestion, plan] that is not sensible or easy to carry out; [person] who is not good at dealing sensibly with ordinary practical problems or tasks □ *John's highly intelligent but totally impractical.*

imprecise [ˌɪmprɪ'saɪs] adj [term, idea] that is not clear or exact □ *The details of the contract are still very imprecise.*

impregnable [ɪm'pregnəbl] adj [fortress, defenses] that is very strong and impossible to attack successfully.

impregnate [ɪm'pregneɪt] vt -1. to make a substance spread through <sthg> □ *A small pad impregnated with chloroform was used as an anesthetic.* -2. to make <a woman or female animal> pregnant (technical use).

impresario [ˌɪmprɪ'sɑːrɪəʊ] (pl **impresarios**) n a person who organizes theatrical or musical performances.

impress [ɪm'pres] ◇ vt -1. to cause <sb> to admire and respect one's abilities, achievements, appearance etc □ *I was really impressed by her application.* -2. **to impress sthg on sb** to make sb understand the importance of sthg □ *I tried to impress on her the need for absolute discretion.* ◇ vi to impress somebody with one's abilities, achievements etc □ *I often sing that song at parties — it never fails to impress.*

impression [ɪmˈpreʃn] *n* -1. [on a person] the effect that a person, an event etc has on somebody □ *Try to create a good impression.* ■ **to make an impression** to have a strong, usually positive, effect on somebody □ *It made quite an impression on me, I must say.* -2. [of a person, situation] what one thinks about somebody or something □ *I don't want you to get the wrong impression.* □ *I have the distinct impression she's annoyed.* ■ **to be under the impression (that)...** to believe, especially wrongly, (that)... □ *I was under the impression (that) you weren't coming.* -3. [of somebody's appearance, behavior] an imitation of a famous person's appearance and way of speaking and behaving that is intended to amuse and entertain people □ *He does a very good impression of James Cagney.* -4. [on a surface] a mark left by the pressure of something on the surface of a stamp, book etc □ *the impressions of his boots in the sand.*

impressionable [ɪmˈpreʃnəbl] *adj* [person] who is easily influenced □ *He's at that impressionable age.*

Impressionism [ɪmˈpreʃnɪzəm] *n* a style of painting, developed in France between 1870 and 1900, that is concerned with showing the effects of light on a subject rather than with giving clear and precise detail.

impressionist [ɪmˈpreʃnəst] *n* a person who imitates the appearance, speech, and behavior of well-known people to entertain other people.
◆ **Impressionist** ◇ *adj* [painting, art, painter] that uses the style of Impressionism. ◇ *n* a person who painted according to the ideas of Impressionism in the late 19th century.

impressive [ɪmˈpresɪv] *adj* [performer, achievement, building] that impresses one because it is very well done, very large, important etc □ *Her list of contacts was pretty impressive.*

imprint [*n* ˈɪmprɪnt, *vt* ɪmˈprɪnt] *n* -1. a mark left on something by an object pressing down on it □ *the imprint of a tire in the mud.* -2. a name used by a publishing company, printed at the front of a book □ *published by Larousse under the Chambers imprint.*

imprinted [ɪmˈprɪntəd] *adj* **to be imprinted on one's mind** OR **memory** to have made a strong impression on one and be difficult to forget □ *That day will be forever imprinted on my mind.*

imprison [ɪmˈprɪzn] *vt* to put <sb> in prison □ *They've been imprisoned here for 20 years.*

imprisonment [ɪmˈprɪznmənt] *n* a period of time spent in prison □ *Both men were sentenced to ten years' imprisonment.*

improbable [ɪmˈprɒbəbl] *adj* -1. [story, excuse, ending] that is unlikely to be true or to happen □ *It seems highly improbable that he could have done it on his own.* -2. [outfit, hat, machine] that looks strange or ridiculous.

impromptu [ɪmˈprɒmptˈjuː] *adj* [party, meeting, speech] that happens without being planned in advance.

improper [ɪmˈprɒpəʳ] *adj* -1. [conduct, dealings] illegal or dishonest □ *They were accused of making improper use of state funds.* -2. [sugges-tion, behavior] that seems rude and shocking in a particular situation □ *That was rather improper of you, asking a question like that.*

impropriety [ˌɪmprəˈpraɪətɪ] *n* illegal or socially unacceptable behavior.

improve [ɪmˈpruːv] ◇ *vi* -1. [weather, one's chances, one's health] to become better □ *The standard of students has improved greatly over the past year.* -2. **to improve oneself** to increase one's knowledge or qualifications by studying. ◇ *vt* [conditions, one's performance, one's chances] to make <sthg> better □ *How can I improve my Spanish?*
◆ **improve on, improve upon** *vt fus* **to improve on** OR **upon sthg** to produce something better or of higher value than sthg that already exists □ *How can we improve on last year's results?* □ *DRI improved on the offer made by its rival.*

improved [ɪmˈpruːvd] *adj* [product, conditions, relations] better than before □ *the new, improved public transportation system.*

improvement [ɪmˈpruːvmənt] *n* -1. the act of improving something, or the state of being improved □ *There's been no improvement in the weather so far.* □ *It's a vast improvement on last year's pay deal.* -2. a change made to a building, room etc in order to make it more attractive or comfortable □ *home improvements.*

improvisation [US imˌprɒvəˈzeɪʃn, GB ˌɪmprəvaɪˈzeɪʃn] *n*: see **improvise** □ *He played an improvisation on "Yesterday."*

improvise [ˈɪmprəvaɪz] ◇ *vt* [shelter, meal] to make <sthg> using whatever is available, because one does not have the proper materials or equipment □ *We had to improvise a sofa out of an old bed and some cushions.* ◇ *vi* [musician, actor] to produce words or music that has not been written down before or prepared beforehand □ *The cast was encouraged to improvise rather than use a script.*

imprudent [ɪmˈpruːdnt] *adj* [behavior, person, remark] that one thinks is not sensible □ *It would be imprudent to talk of future plans.*

impudence [ˈɪmpjədəns] *n*: see **impudent** □ *And he had the impudence to complain!*

impudent [ˈɪmpjədənt] *adj* [person, remark] that one thinks is rude and disrespectful □ *You impudent little brat!*

impugn [ɪmˈpjuːn] *vt* [honesty, claim] to criticize <sthg> by suggesting that it is false or dishonest (formal use).

impulse [ˈɪmpʌls] *n* -1. [in a person] a sudden strong desire to do something. ■ **to do sthg on impulse** to do sthg because of a sudden strong desire and without planning it □ *I bought it on impulse.* -2. [in a nerve, wire] an electrical signal that is sent through a nerve or wire, or through the air □ *These impulses are then sent to the brain.*

impulse buying [-baɪɪŋ] *n* the act of buying goods on impulse.

impulsive [ɪmˈpʌlsɪv] *adj* [person] who does things suddenly without thinking about the consequences.

impunity [ɪmˈpjuːnətɪ] *n* **with impunity** without

being punished □ *The main offenders go about their business with relative impunity.*

impure [ɪm'pjʊəʳ] *adj* **-1.** [substance] that is not pure, because it is mixed with another substance □ *This is an example of the chemical in its impure state.* **-2.** [thought, act, person] that is connected with sex and considered immoral.

impurity [ɪm'pjʊərətɪ] (*pl* **impurities**) *n* a substance that is present in another substance and that makes it less strong, valuable etc □ *This process should remove all impurities.*

IMRO ['ɪmrəʊ] (*abbr of* **Investment Management Regulatory Organization**) *n* a British organization that controls the activities of merchant banks and the managers of pension funds.

in [ɪn] ◇ *prep* **-1. it's in a box/bag/drawer** it is enclosed by a box/bag/drawer, so that it cannot be seen from the outside □ *What have you got in your mouth?* □ *I found it in the pocket of my raincoat.* **-2.** used to indicate the place where something or somebody is or where something happens □ *He's in the bedroom/garden.* □ *They met in Paris/the States.* □ *Our head office is in Tokyo.* **-3. to be in a suit/dress** to be wearing a suit/dress □ *She was still in her nightclothes.* □ *She was dressed in white.* **-4. to be in a book/movie** to appear in a book/movie □ *I read it in today's paper.* □ *His name is mentioned in Chapter 2.* ■ **to be in a race/play** to take part in a race/play □ *I'm running in the New York Marathon.* **-5. to arrive in the morning/the afternoon/January** to arrive at some point during the morning/the afternoon/January □ *We're getting married in June.* □ *In 1921 she moved to Canada.* □ *Start feeding plants in late spring.* **-6. to meet in two hours/three weeks** to meet after a period of two hours/three weeks is ended □ *Hurry up, the park closes in ten minutes.* □ *I'll call you back in twenty minutes.* **-7. to do sthg in an hour/six months** to take an hour/six months to do sthg □ *He learned to type in two weeks.* □ *I'll be ready in five minutes.* **-8. we haven't seen each other in years/months** several years/months have passed since the last time we met □ *I haven't been out at all in the last week.* **-9. to go out in the rain/snow** to go out while it is raining/snowing □ *Don't stay out too long in the sun.* ■ **to be in danger/difficulty** to be in a dangerous/difficult situation □ *He's in trouble with the police.* □ *She died in poverty.* □ *The castle was in ruins.* **-10. to speak in a loud/soft voice** to speak loudly/softly. ■ **to talk in English/French** to use English/French to talk. ■ **to write in pencil/ink** to use a pencil/ink to write with. **-11. in my excitement/anger** because I was excited/angry □ *She stared at me in amazement.* **-12. to be in business/politics** to have business/politics as one's work or career □ *My son's in computers.* □ *I started out in publishing.* ■ **advances in science/medicine** scientific/medical advances. **-13. to be in love/pain** to be feeling love/pain □ *I could see she was in some distress.* **-14. to be in one's twenties** [person] to be between 20 and 29 years old □ *The temperature was up in the forties.* □ *She retired in her late fifties.* **-15. to be in a line/row/circle** to be arranged as a line/row/circle. **-16. to buy sthg in large/small quantities** to buy large/small quantities of sthg. ■ **people came in large numbers/in their thousands** large numbers/thousands of people came □ *Fans were arriving in droves.* **-17. to be three yards in length/width** to be three yards long/wide. **-18. one in ten people** one person out of every group of ten. ■ **a tax of 15 cents in the dollar** a tax that takes 15 cents from every dollar that is earned. **-19.** used after superlatives □ *She's the tallest girl in her class.* □ *It's the longest river in the world.*

◇ *adv* **-1. to put sthg in** to put sthg inside a container □ *He opened the oven door and put the pie in.* **-2. to look/go in** to look/go into a room, building, or car □ *It started raining and we all went in.* ■ **come in!** used to give somebody permission to come into one's office, bedroom etc. **-3. to stay/be in** [person] to stay/be at home or the place where one works □ *She's not in right now.* □ *You're never in when I call.* **-4. to be in** [train, boat, plane] to have arrived □ *Is the ferry in yet?* **-5. the tide is coming in** the sea is coming toward the shore and covering it. **-6.** *phrases* **to be in for sthg** to be about to experience sthg, usually something bad □ *He's in for a shock!* □ *We're in for some nasty weather.* ■ **to be in on sthg** to know about sthg secret and be included in it □ *Who else is in on this?*

◇ *adj* **to be in** to be fashionable □ *Short skirts are in again.*

◆ **ins** *npl* **the ins and outs of sthg** all the facts and details about sthg □ *I'm interested in the deal, but I'd like to know more about the ins and outs of it.*

◆ **in all** *adv* in total □ *In all I'd say there must have been fifty people there.*

◆ **in that** *conj* used to explain the previous statement □ *It might be difficult in that we're away all that week.*

in. *abbr of* **inch**.

IN *abbr of* **Indiana**.

inability [ˌɪnə'bɪlətɪ] *n* the state of not being able to do something □ *He was surprised at his friend's inability to deal with the situation.*

inaccessible [ˌɪnək'sesəbl] *adj* **-1.** [village, house, area] that is impossible to reach □ *The cove is inaccessible by road.* **-2.** [movie, book, music] that is very difficult for most people to enjoy or understand □ *This kind of humor is inaccessible to people from other cultures.*

inaccuracy [ɪn'ækjərəsɪ] (*pl* **inaccuracies**) *n* **-1.** [of a statement, report, figure] *see* **inaccurate** □ *They apologized for the inaccuracy of their article.* **-2.** a mistake or something that is not entirely correct □ *There were several inaccuracies in the text.*

inaccurate [ɪn'ækjərət] *adj* [statement, report, figure] that is not completely correct □ *These statistics are wildly inaccurate.*

inaction [ɪn'ækʃn] *n* the failure of somebody to do something to deal with a situation □ *political inaction.*

inactive [ɪn'æktɪv] *adj* [person, animal] that does

very little or nothing □ *The movement remained inactive for several years.*

inactivity [ˌɪnæk'tɪvətɪ] *n* [of a person, animal] a lack of movement or action □ *after months of inactivity.*

inadequacy [ɪn'ædɪkwəsɪ] (*pl* **inadequacies**) *n*: see **inadequate** □ *the inadequacy of funding* □ *feelings of inadequacy.*

inadequate [ɪn'ædɪkwət] *adj* **-1.** [supplies, funding] not enough in amount for a particular purpose; [equipment, excuse] not good enough for a particular purpose □ *The sum of money offered is inadequate for our needs.* □ *There's inadequate cover for troops to attack on the ground.* □ *Their response to the problem was inadequate.* **-2. to feel inadequate** [person] to feel unable to deal with particular situations or circumstances, especially because one thinks that one does not have certain skills, qualities etc □ *He felt inadequate to deal with such a serious case.*

inadmissible [ˌɪnəd'mɪsəbl] *adj* **inadmissible evidence** evidence that cannot be used in a court of law.

inadvertently [ˌɪnəd'vɜː'tntlɪ] *adv* in a way that is not intentional □ *Cooper inadvertently gave away his whereabouts to the police.*

inadvisable [ˌɪnəd'vaɪzəbl] *adj* **to be inadvisable** not to be a sensible thing to do because of possible risks □ *It would be inadvisable to set off in this weather.*

inalienable [ɪn'eɪlɪənəbl] *adj* **an inalienable right** a right that cannot be taken away (formal use).

inane [ɪ'neɪn] *adj* [remark, act] that one thinks is silly and without purpose or meaning □ *His inane comments drove me crazy!*

inanely [ɪ'neɪnlɪ] *adv* [grin, smile] see **inane** □ *He grinned inanely at her.*

inanimate [ɪn'ænɪmət] *adj* [object] not living.

inanity [ɪ'nænətɪ] *n*: see **inane** □ *The inanity of their humor started to get on my nerves.*

inapplicable [ɪn'æplɪkəbl] *adj* [rule, question] that is not relevant to a particular subject or situation □ *The rule is inapplicable in this case.*

inappropriate [ˌɪnə'prəʊprɪət] *adj* [choice, time, remark] not suitable for a particular purpose or occasion □ *It would be inappropriate to comment further on the situation.* □ *Sarah's behavior and appearance were totally inappropriate to what was basically a very formal event.* □ *The timing of the decision could not have been more inappropriate for us.*

inarticulate [ˌɪnɑː'tɪkjələt] *adj* **-1.** [person] who is not able to express ideas or feelings well in speech because they cannot think of the best or proper words to use. **-2.** [speech, sound] that is not well or clearly expressed.

inasmuch [ˌɪnəz'mʌtʃ] ◆ **inasmuch as** *conj* a phrase used to introduce something that explains what has just been said or that limits it in some way (formal use) □ *We're satisfied with the decision inasmuch as it brings with it a degree of protection for our families.*

inattention [ˌɪnə'tenʃn] *n* a lack of attention or care □ *His writing shows inattention to detail.*

inattentive [ˌɪnə'tentɪv] *adj* [person] who does not pay attention when they are supposed to □ *Your son has been tired and inattentive in class.*

inaudible [ɪn'ɔːdəbl] *adj* [sound, voice, person] that is not loud enough to be heard □ *She spoke in a whisper that was almost inaudible.*

inaugural [ɪ'nɔːgjərəl] *adj* [meeting, edition, speech] that marks the beginning of something new □ *The President's inaugural address was watched on TV by an audience of millions.*

inaugurate [ɪ'nɔːgjəreɪt] *vt* **-1.** [leader, president] to give <sb> an important position at an official ceremony □ *The President will be inaugurated at a ceremony in the Winter Palace tomorrow.* **-2.** [building, event] to open <sthg> with an official ceremony □ *The Queen inaugurated the new museum.*

inauguration [ɪˌnɔːgjə'reɪʃn] *n*: see **inaugurate** □ *the inauguration ceremony.*

inauspicious [ˌɪnɔː'spɪʃəs] *adj* [event, beginning, day] that seems unlucky and makes one think that something will be unsuccessful.

in-between *adj* [size, stage] that comes between two other things □ *Jamie's at that in-between age.*

inboard ['ɪnbɔː'd] *adj* **an inboard motor** a motor that is inside the main part of a boat instead of outside it.

inborn [ˌɪn'bɔː'n] *adj* [ability, mistrust] that a person has as part of their nature from birth or from an early age □ *an inborn sense of social justice.*

inbound ['ɪnbaʊnd] *adj* US [flight, passenger] that is coming toward a place □ *All inbound flights to JFK have been canceled.*

inbred [ˌɪn'bred] *adj* **-1.** [mistrust, liking, charm] that is part of a person's nature from an early age □ *an inbred dislike of authority.* **-2.** [animal, plant] that is produced by inbreeding.

inbreeding ['ɪnbriːdɪŋ] *n* the breeding of people, animals, or plants that are closely related □ *Various mental defects can result from inbreeding.*

inbuilt [ˌɪn'bɪlt] *adj* **-1.** [device, mechanism] that is included as part of something when it is produced □ *It's got an inbuilt alarm.* **-2.** [quality, defect] that is a basic part of something or somebody □ *an inbuilt defense mechanism.*

inc. *abbr of* **inclusive.**

Inc. *abbr of* **incorporated.**

incalculable [ɪn'kælkjələbl] *adj* [damage, effect] that cannot be measured, usually because it is too great.

incandescent [ˌɪnkən'desnt] *adj* [metal] that gives out a bright light when it is heated.

incantation [ˌɪnkæn'teɪʃn] *n* words that are spoken or sung as a magic spell.

incapable [ɪn'keɪpəbl] *adj* **-1. to be incapable of sthg** to be unable to do sthg because one does not have the necessary ability or qualities □ *He's incapable of deciding for himself.* **-2.** [person] who is too weak or stupid to do something.

incapacitate [ˌɪnkə'pæsəteɪt] *vt* to weaken or injure <sb> so that they are unable to do something □ *He was totally incapacitated by the accident.*

incapacitated [ˌɪnkəˈpæsəteɪtəd] *adj* **to be incapacitated** [person] to be unable to function as normal, e.g. because of illness or injury □ *I'm afraid Mr Jay is temporarily incapacitated.*

incapacity [ˌɪnkəˈpæsətɪ] *n* a lack of ability or power to do something □ *his incapacity for leadership.*

incapacity benefit *n* in Britain, money paid by the government to people who are too ill to work and who do not receive sick pay from an employer.

incarcerate [ɪnˈkɑːʳsəreɪt] *vt* to put <sb> in prison (formal use).

incarceration [ɪnˌkɑːʳsəˈreɪʃn] *n: see* **incarcerate** (formal use) □ *a period of incarceration.*

incarnation [ˌɪnkɑːʳˈneɪʃn] *n* **-1. the incarnation of sthg** [of beauty, evil] a person or thing that represents sthg to an extreme degree. **-2.** [of a person] one of several lives or existences that the same person has according to certain religions □ *in a previous incarnation.*

incendiary device [US ɪnˈsendɪərɪ-, GB -ɪərɪ-] *n* a bomb that is designed to start a fire.

incense [*n* ˈɪnsens, *vt* ɪnˈsens] ◇ *n* a substance that is burned to give off a sweet smell, especially during a religious ceremony. ◇ *vt* to make <sb> very angry □ *Commuters were incensed by the latest price increase.*

incentive [ɪnˈsentɪv] *n* a benefit or advantage that is offered to somebody to encourage them to do something □ *Potential buyers are being offered tax incentives.* □ *He has no incentive to work harder.*

inception [ɪnˈsepʃn] *n* the beginning of an organization, activity etc (formal use) □ *Since its inception, the paper has expanded and is now sold in a number of cities.*

incessant [ɪnˈsesnt] *adj* [noise, activity] that never stops □ *His incessant moaning started to annoy me.*

incessantly [ɪnˈsesntlɪ] *adv* [talk, complain, smoke] *see* **incessant** □ *They argue incessantly.*

incest [ˈɪnsest] *n* sex between two people in the same family who are too closely related to get married, e.g. between a brother and sister □ *He had committed incest with his daughter.*

incestuous [ɪnˈsestjʊəs] *adj* **-1.** [relationship, act] that involves incest □ *an incestuous affair.* **-2.** [group, relationship] that is not good because the people involved are too close to one another □ *It all seems rather incestuous to me.*

inch [ɪntʃ] ◇ *n* a unit (2.54 cm) for measuring length □ *It's about six inches wide.* ◇ *vi* to move somewhere very slowly and carefully, usually because one has very little space or because one does not want to be noticed □ *I inched toward the edge of the cliff.*

incidence [ˈɪnsədəns] *n* [of crime, a problem, illness] the frequency with which something bad happens □ *There is a higher incidence of burglary/leukemia in the area than at any time in the last ten years.*

incident [ˈɪnsədənt] *n* **-1.** something that happens which is unusual or unpleasant □ *Let's forget the whole incident.* □ *The meeting went off without incident.* **-2.** POLITICS a minor event that could lead to a more serious dispute between two countries □ *a frontier/diplomatic incident.*

incidental [ˌɪnsɪˈdentl] *adj* that exists or takes place in connection with something else which is much more important □ *The meeting is incidental to the main talks, which start tomorrow.*

incidentally [ˌɪnsɪˈdentlɪ] *adv* a word used to add new information or to introduce a new subject of conversation □ *Incidentally, did you finish that report?*

incidental music *n* the music played in the background in a movie, play etc.

incinerate [ɪnˈsɪnəreɪt] *vt* to destroy <sthg> by burning it.

incinerator [ɪnˈsɪnəreɪtəʳ] *n* a device for burning rubbish in.

incipient [ɪnˈsɪpɪənt] *adj* [revolt, decline] that is starting to happen or exist (formal use).

incision [ɪnˈsɪʒn] *n* a cut made in something, e.g. by a surgeon during an operation.

incisive [ɪnˈsaɪsɪv] *adj* [person, comment, mind] that is clear and deals directly with the most important part of a subject □ *Their criticisms were incisive and intelligent.*

incisor [ɪnˈsaɪzəʳ] *n* any of the teeth at the front of the mouth used for biting into food.

incite [ɪnˈsaɪt] *vt* [violence, riot] to cause or encourage <sthg> to take place. ■ **to incite sb to sthg/to do sthg** to encourage sb to do sthg wrong or bad by making them angry or excited □ *They were accused of inciting racial hatred.* □ *The killings incited people to take up arms and revolt.*

incitement [ɪnˈsaɪtmənt] *n* the act of encouraging a particular action or feeling, especially actions or feelings that are wrong or bad □ *His words were seen as an incitement to violence/murder.*

incl. *abbr of* **including.**

inclement [ɪnˈklemənt] *adj* [weather, conditions] stormy or cold (formal use).

inclination [ˌɪnklɪˈneɪʃn] *n* **-1.** a desire to do something □ *I have no inclination to go whatsoever.* □ *I came more by chance than by inclination.* **-2.** a tendency that somebody has to do something, especially because they have a particular kind of character □ *He has an inclination to be lazy.*

incline [*n* ˈɪnklaɪn, *vb* ɪnˈklaɪn] ◇ *n* a slope □ *a sharp incline.* ◇ *vt* to bend <one's head> forward.

inclined [ɪnˈklaɪnd] *adj* **-1. artistically/politically etc inclined** [person] who has an interest or ability in art/politics etc □ *I'm not really that way inclined.* **-2. to be inclined to do sthg** to be likely to do sthg, usually because of one's personality □ *He's inclined to worry.* **-3. I'm inclined to agree/disagree etc** my natural reaction is to agree/disagree etc, though I do not feel it very strongly (formal use) □ *I'd be inclined to resign, if I were in your position.*

include [ɪnˈkluːd] *vt* -1. to contain <sb/sthg> as one of its parts □ *The price includes sales tax.* -2. to make <sb/sthg> part of a larger group or set of things or people □ *Don't forget to include the check.* □ *They never include me in their discussions.*

included [ɪnˈkluːdəd] *adj* a word used to show that somebody or something is part of something else being talked about □ *'Batteries not included'* □ *Everybody went, myself included.*

including [ɪnˈkluːdɪŋ] *prep* a word used to show that somebody or something is part of, or an example of, something that is being talked about □ *There are eight members, including the President of the USA and the British Prime Minister.*

inclusion [ɪnˈkluːʒn] *n* the act of making somebody or something part of a larger group □ *Franklin's inclusion in the team comes as a surprise.*

inclusive [ɪnˈkluːsɪv] *adj* [price, list] that includes all the items mentioned □ *I'll be away from the 3rd to the 9th inclusive.* □ *$147 inclusive of postage and handling.*

incognito [ˌɪnkɒgˈniːtoʊ] *adv* [travel, remain] with one's identity hidden or one's appearance disguised so that one is not recognized or known by other people □ *Richardson is believed to have turned up at the lunch incognito.*

incoherent [ˌɪnkoʊˈhɪərənt] *adj* -1. [person] who expresses ideas in a way that is difficult to understand, especially because they are ill, drunk, or very angry □ *She was so angry she was practically incoherent.* -2. [story, argument] that has parts that do not go together in a logical way □ *It was an incoherent speech with no clear message.*

income [ˈɪŋkʌm] *n* the money that a person or country earns or receives because of work, business etc □ *They have a joint income of $60,000 a year.* □ *The number of families on a low income has risen again.*

incomes policy *n* GB an economic policy that aims to control inflation by limiting increases in the amount of money that people earn.

income support *n* GB an amount of money paid by the state to people with no income or a very low income who cannot claim other benefits such as unemployment benefit.

income tax *n* the tax that a person pays to the state and that is a percentage of the amount of money they earn.

incoming [ˈɪnkʌmɪŋ] *adj* -1. [mail, report, phone call] that a person, company etc receives □ *Please hold all incoming calls.* -2. [plane, flight] that is coming toward a place □ *All incoming flights are subject to delay.* -3. [government, official] that has just been elected or given a particular job □ *the incoming President.* -4. [tide, wave] that is coming toward the shore □ *They were cut off by the incoming tide.*

incommunicado [ˌɪnkəmjuːnɪˈkɑːdoʊ] *adv* **to be kept incommunicado** [person] to be kept in a place or state in which one is not allowed to communicate with other people □ *Sara's been incommunicado for a while.*

incomparable [ɪnˈkɒmpərəbl] *adj* [skill, beauty, stupidity] so great that nothing can be compared with it.

incompatible [ˌɪnkəmˈpætəbl] *adj* -1. [people] who are not suited, because they are too different from each other □ *They divorced because they were basically incompatible.* -2. [demands, roles] that are not able to be successfully combined □ *Such a position is incompatible with her responsibilities as a political representative.* -3. [computers, systems] that are not designed to be linked or used together.

incompetence [ɪnˈkɒmpətəns] *n*: see **incompetent** □ *He left the company amid accusations of incompetence and mismanagement.*

incompetent [ɪnˈkɒmpətənt] *adj* [doctor, driver] who is not able to do their job properly □ *As a manager he's totally incompetent.*

incomplete [ˌɪnkəmˈpliːt] *adj* [set, story, list] not complete □ *It's incomplete without the final volume.*

incomprehensible [ɪnˌkɒmprɪˈhensəbl] *adj* [action, behavior, speech] that is impossible to understand □ *I found the whole play completely incomprehensible.*

inconceivable [ˌɪnkənˈsiːvəbl] *adj* that is impossible to believe or imagine □ *To give up now would be inconceivable.* □ *It is inconceivable that someone can have entered the palace and left without being seen.*

inconclusive [ˌɪnkənˈkluːsɪv] *adj* [meeting, evidence, outcome] that does not lead to a definite decision or result □ *The findings of the report have proved inconclusive.*

incongruous [ɪnˈkɒŋgruəs] *adj* [person, clothing, act] that seems strange and out of place in a particular situation, often in an amusing way □ *The painting looked slightly incongruous in its new setting.*

inconsequential [ɪnˌkɒnsɪˈkwenʃl] *adj* [event, person] that is not important.

inconsiderable [ˌɪnkənˈsɪdərəbl] *adj* **not inconsiderable** fairly large □ *a not inconsiderable amount of money.*

inconsiderate [ˌɪnkənˈsɪdərət] *adj* [person, attitude] that does not show consideration for people's feelings, needs etc □ *It was so inconsiderate of you to just leave us there!*

inconsistency [ˌɪnkənˈsɪstənsɪ] (*pl* **inconsistencies**) *n* -1. [of a person, performance, account] see **inconsistent** □ *The coach blames his team's inconsistency on injury problems.* -2. something that says the opposite of something else so that they cannot both be right or true □ *His story was full of inconsistencies.*

inconsistent [ˌɪnkənˈsɪstənt] *adj* -1. [person] who behaves in a particular situation sometimes in one way and sometimes in a very different way. -2. [performance, effort, work] that changes in quality, being sometimes good and sometimes bad. -3. [translation, account] that contains parts that do not agree with one another □ *These statements are inconsistent.* □ *The Secretary's decision is inconsistent with his earlier statements.*

inconsolable [ˌɪnkən'soʊləbl] *adj* [person] who is too sad to be comforted □ *The victim's wife was inconsolable after hearing the verdict.*

inconspicuous [ˌɪnkən'spɪkjuəs] *adj* [person, clothes] not easily noticed □ *I tried to make my entrance as inconspicuous as possible.*

incontinence [ɪn'kɒntənəns] *n* the inability of somebody to control their bowels or bladder □ *incontinence pads.*

incontinent [ɪn'kɒntənənt] *adj* [person] who is unable to control their bowels or bladder.

incontrovertible [ˌɪnkɒntrə'vɜːˈtəbl] *adj* [evidence, fact] that is true and cannot be shown to be false.

inconvenience [ˌɪnkən'viːnjəns] ◇ *n* difficulty caused by something that interferes with one's plans or activities □ *We would like to apologize for any inconvenience caused by this delay.* □ *I don't want to put you to any inconvenience.* ◇ *vt* to cause inconvenience to <sb> □ *We hope the noise from the building work will not inconvenience you too much.*

inconvenient [ˌɪnkən'viːnjənt] *adj* [time, date, arrangement] that causes difficulty because it does not suit one's plans □ *I can change the date if Friday is inconvenient for you.* □ *Have I called at an inconvenient time?*

incorporate [ɪn'kɔːˈpəreɪt] *vt* -1. **to incorporate sthg in** OR **into sthg** to make sthg part of sthg larger □ *We'd already incorporated that suggestion into our plans.* -2. to include or contain <sthg> as one of its parts □ *The new designs incorporate daycare facilities.*

incorporated [ɪn'kɔːˈpəreɪtəd] *adj* BUSINESS a word used to show that a company has been legally formed into a corporation □ *an incoporated company.*

incorporation [ɪnˌkɔːˈpə'reɪʃn] *n* -1. [of a suggestion, of facilities] *see* **incorporate**. -2. BUSINESS [of a company] the act of making a company part of a larger group.

incorrect [ˌɪnkə'rekt] *adj* [assumption, total] that can be shown to be wrong □ *The information I gave you was incorrect.*

incorrigible [ɪn'kɒrɪdʒəbl] *adj* [person] who is bad in some way and will never change, but whom one finds slightly amusing at the same time □ *He's an incorrigible liar!*

incorruptible [ˌɪnkə'rʌptəbl] *adj* [official, politician] who is too honest to be persuaded or bribed to do something they should not do.

increase [*n* 'ɪŋkriːs, *vb* ɪŋ'kriːs] ◇ *n* a rise in the degree, amount, or number of something □ *a huge increase in overseas trade* □ *an increase of 15%* □ *a tax increase.* ■ **to be on the increase** to be becoming more frequent or common □ *Crime is on the increase again.* ◇ *vt* [price, output, speed] to make <sthg> greater in amount; [anxiety, efforts] to make <sthg> more intense □ *The reports only increased speculation in the press about the divorce.* ◇ *vi* [price, unemployment] to become greater in

amount; [anxiety, pain] to become more intense; [tendency, problem] to become more common □ *Inflation has increased at an alarming rate in recent years.*

increased [ɪŋ'kriːst] *adj* [efficiency, speculation, demand] that is larger in amount or size than before □ *increased trade and foreign aid.*

increasing [ɪŋ'kriːsɪŋ] *adj* [unemployment, crime rate] that is becoming greater in amount; [anxiety, concern] that is becoming more intense; [tendency, use] that is becoming more common □ *an increasing tendency among young people not to vote.*

increasingly [ɪŋ'kriːsɪŋlɪ] *adv* more and more □ *It's getting increasingly difficult to find good staff.* □ *Increasingly, companies are issuing short-term contracts.*

incredible [ɪn'kredəbl] *adj* -1. [car, victory] that one thinks is very good or impressive (informal use) □ *They live in the most incredible house.* -2. [amount of money] that is very large (informal use) □ *They spent incredible sums of money doing up the house.* -3. [story, achievement, coincidence] that one finds difficult to believe □ *That's incredible!*

incredulous [ɪn'kredʒələs] *adj* [person] who cannot believe something because they think it is so surprising or unlikely □ *Everyone was incredulous at the news of her resignation.*

increment ['ɪŋkrəmənt] *n* an increase in one's salary that happens regularly, e.g. once a year □ *a yearly increment of 3%.*

incriminate [ɪn'krɪmɪneɪt] *vt* to make <sb> appear responsible for a crime □ *You're going to end up incriminating yourself even further.*

incriminating [ɪn'krɪmɪneɪtɪŋ] *adj* [evidence, testimony] that makes somebody appear responsible for a crime □ *The DNA tests are highly incriminating.*

incubate ['ɪŋkjəbeɪt] ◇ *vt* to keep <an egg> warm until the young bird inside it is ready to come out. ◇ *vi* -1. [egg] to stay warm until the young bird inside it is ready to come out. -2. MEDICINE [infection, virus] to be present in somebody's body before developing into a disease □ *Cold germs take several days to incubate.*

incubation [ˌɪŋkjə'beɪʃn] *n* [of an egg, infection] *see* **incubate** □ *the incubation period for cholera.*

incubator ['ɪŋkjəbeɪtəˈ] *n* a piece of equipment in a hospital in which small and weak babies are kept until they become stronger.

inculcate [ɪn'kʌlkeɪt] *vt* to fix <sthg> in somebody's mind by saying it very often (formal use) □ *The school aims to inculcate moral values in its pupils* OR *to inculcate its pupils with moral values.*

incumbent [ɪn'kʌmbənt] (formal use) ◇ *adj* -1. **to be incumbent on** OR **upon sb to do sthg** to be sb's duty or responsibility to do sthg □ *It is incumbent on senior politicians to set an example for the rest of the party.* -2. **the incumbent president/mayor etc** the current president/ mayor etc. ◇ *n* a person who has a particular job, especially an official one □ *the present incumbent, Revd. Hodgson.*

incur [ɪnˈkɜːr] (*pt* & *pp* **incurred**, *cont* **incurring**) *vt* [loss, expenses] to experience <sthg unpleasant> as a result of one's actions □ *The company had incurred serious losses on the stock market.* ■ **to incur sb's wrath** to make sb very angry □ *The rider has incurred the wrath of the racing establishment.*

incurable [ɪnˈkjʊərəbl] *adj* **-1.** [disease, illness] that is impossible to cure □ *She's suffering from an incurable form of the disease.* **-2. an incurable optimist/romantic** a person who is very optimistic/romantic and will never change in this way.

incursion [ɪnˈkɜːrʒn] *n* an unexpected entrance by somebody or something into a place where they do not usually belong □ *There have been a number of incursions into enemy territory.*

indebted [ɪnˈdetəd] *adj* **to be indebted to sb** to be very grateful to sb for their help □ *I'm greatly* OR *deeply indebted to you for everything you've done.*

indecency [ɪnˈdiːsnsɪ] *n* [of a joke, suggestion, somebody's behavior] *see* **indecent**.

indecent [ɪnˈdiːsnt] *adj* **-1.** [joke, suggestion, behavior] that is offensive, usually in a sexual way □ *an indecent proposal.* **-2.** [speed, amount] that is not suitable or acceptable in a particular situation □ *He remarried with indecent haste.*

indecent assault *n* a criminal sexual attack that takes place without the victim's consent but is less serious than a rape.

indecent exposure *n* the crime of deliberately showing one's sexual parts in a public place.

indecipherable [ˌɪndɪˈsaɪfərəbl] *adj* **-1.** [signature, message, handwriting] that is impossible to read. **-2.** [look, reason] that one cannot understand.

indecision [ˌɪndɪˈsɪʒn] *n* the state of being unable to decide what to do □ *I was racked with indecision.*

indecisive [ˌɪndɪˈsaɪsɪv] *adj* **-1.** [person] who finds it difficult to make decisions □ *She's very indecisive.* **-2.** [conclusion, victory] that does not give a clear and definite result □ *The election result proved indecisive.*

indeed [ɪnˈdiːd] *adv* **-1.** a word used to confirm or agree with something that has just been said in an emphatic way □ *"Are you coming tonight?" — "Indeed I am!"* **-2.** a word used to make an additional point that emphasizes what one has just said □ *I think, indeed I know, that this is the case.* □ *You couldn't have predicted this, indeed I don't think anybody could.* **-3.** a word used to give extra force to the word "very" □ *It was very cold indeed.* **-4.** a word used to show surprise, disbelief, or annoyance □ *"He thinks he's going to get your job." — "Does he indeed!"* □ *"I've decided to leave banking and go to India." — "Indeed?"*

indefatigable [ˌɪndɪˈfætɪgəbl] *adj* [worker, campaigner] who never seems to get tired □ *She was indefatigable in her attempts to rally support.*

indefensible [ˌɪndɪˈfensəbl] *adj* [behavior, posi-

tion] that is impossible to defend or justify, because it is morally wrong □ *Your conduct in this matter has been thoroughly indefensible.*

indefinable [ˌɪndɪˈfaɪnəbl] *adj* [feeling, quality] that cannot easily be described or explained in words □ *an indefinable sense of loss.*

indefinite [ɪnˈdefənət] *adj* **-1.** [period, time, number] that has no fixed limit. **-2.** [answer, opinion] that is not clear.

indefinitely [ɪnˈdefənətlɪ] *adv* [wait, continue] for a period of time which has no fixed limit □ *The meeting has been postponed indefinitely.*

indelible [ɪnˈdeləbl] *adj* **-1.** [mark, stain] that cannot be removed. **-2.** [ink, pen] that leaves a mark that cannot be removed. **-3.** [memory, influence] that cannot be forgotten.

indelicate [ɪnˈdelɪkət] *adj* [behavior, action, remark] that is slightly rude or offensive □ *It was rather indelicate of him to raise the subject of money over dinner.*

indemnify [ɪnˈdemnəfaɪ] (*pt* & *pp* **indemnified**) *vt* **-1.** to insure <sb> □ *We are indemnified for* OR *against fire and theft.* **-2. to indemnify sb for sthg** to pay sb compensation for sthg.

indemnity [ɪnˈdemnətɪ] *n* **-1.** insurance or protection against loss or damage, usually in the form of a financial payment □ *It provides indemnity against loss of employment.* **-2.** an amount of money paid to somebody as compensation for money and goods that have been lost or damaged □ *an indemnity of $60,000.*

indent [ɪnˈdent] *vt* [text, paragraph] to start <a line of writing> further in from the margin than the other lines.

indentation [ˌɪndenˈteɪʃn] *n* **-1.** a space left between the margin and the beginning of a line of writing. **-2.** a small dent in something.

indenture [ɪnˈdentʃər] *n* a contract, especially in the past, between an apprentice and their employer.

independence [ˌɪndɪˈpendəns] *n*: *see* **independent** □ *Zimbabwe gained independence in 1980.* □ *Old people value their independence.*

Independence Day *n* = **Fourth of July.**

independent [ˌɪndɪˈpendənt] *adj* **-1.** [country, organization] not controlled or ruled by another country, organization etc □ *The company became independent of its corporate owners in 1991.* **-2.** [person] who does not rely on other people for help or advice □ *Children are quite independent by the age of 15.* □ *She's now financially independent.* □ *It's about time I was more independent of my parents.* **-3.** [study, inquiry] that is not connected with or influenced by people who are directly involved in a situation or matter and so is expected to be fair □ *An independent inquiry investigated the affair.*

independently [ˌɪndɪˈpendəntlɪ] *adv* [decide, arrange, organize] without the help or influence of other people or things □ *The choice was made independently of what happened at the meeting.* □ *Students must make their travel arrangements independently.*

independent school *n* GB a school that receives no money from the government and is not controlled by it.

in-depth *adj* [analysis, study, report] that contains a lot of detail and examines something closely □ *We'll be bringing you in-depth coverage of the US Masters tournament.*

indescribable [ˌɪndɪˈskraɪbəbl] *adj* [sadness, joy, poverty] too extreme to be described in words □ *The sense of relief among these people is indescribable.*

indestructible [ˌɪndɪˈstrʌktəbl] *adj* [toy, furniture] that cannot be destroyed.

indeterminate [ˌɪndɪˈtɜːrmɪnət] *adj* [number, amount, period] not clear or fixed □ *The killer was given an indeterminate sentence.*

index [ˈɪndeks] (*pl senses 1 and 2* **indexes**, *pl sense 3* **indexes** OR **indices**) ◇ *n* **-1.** [in a book] an alphabetical list at the back of a book that gives the page numbers to help one find names and subjects mentioned in it □ *Look it up in the index.* **-2.** [in a library] an alphabetical list of writers, book titles etc, written on index cards or stored on a computer, that shows where they can be found □ *a card index.* **-3.** ECONOMICS a table of figures that allows the changes in cost or value of something to be compared □ *the Hang Seng Index.* ◇ *vt* to provide an index for <a book>; to put <information> in an index.

index card *n* a card on which information about somebody or something is written so that it can be kept and used for reference.

index finger *n* the finger that is next to one's thumb.

index-linked [-ˈlɪŋkt] *adj* GB [salary, interest rate, pension] that is linked to the cost of living so that it increases automatically as everything gets more expensive.

India [ˈɪndjə] a large densely-populated country in southern Asia, divided into 25 states and 7 territories, each with their own laws and languages. SIZE: 3,268,000 sq kms. POPULATION: 897,400,000 (*Indians*). CAPITAL: New Delhi. LANGUAGE: Hindi. CURRENCY: rupee.

India ink US, **Indian ink** GB *n* a black ink often used for drawing.

Indian [ˈɪndjən] ◇ *n* **-1.** a person who comes from or lives in India. **-2.** = **Native American.** ◇ *adj see* **India** □ *an Indian restaurant* □ *the Indian subcontinent.*

Indiana [ˌɪndɪˈænə] a state in the Midwest of the USA, consisting mainly of farmland. ABBREVIATION: IN. SIZE: 94,000 sq kms. POPULATION: 5,544,159 (*Indianians*). CAPITAL: Indianapolis.

Indianapolis 500 [ˌɪndɪəˌnæpələsfaɪvˈhʌndrəd] *n* **the Indianapolis 500** a car race that covers a distance of 500 miles and takes place once a year in Indianapolis, Indiana, USA.

Indian ink *n* GB = **India ink.**

Indian Ocean: the Indian Ocean the ocean between Africa, India, Australia, and Antarctica.

Indian summer *n* a period of warm weather in the autumn that is not usual.

Indian Wars *npl* **the Indian Wars** wars that took place in the USA in the 17th, 18th, and 19th centuries between Native Americans and Europeans who went to live in North America.

india rubber *n* rubber used for making toys, balls, and erasers.

indicate [ˈɪndɪkeɪt] ◇ *vt* **-1.** to point to <sb/sthg> □ *He indicated where he wanted me to sign.* **-2.** [change, link] to show that <a fact or situation> exists, is true, or is likely □ *The figures indicate that 1998 will be a crucial year.* **-3.** [one's preference, desire] to make <one's intention or wish> clear □ *Indicate your choice of color by circling the appropriate letter.* ◇ *vi* GB [driver] to show which way one is going to turn in a vehicle, by using lights or hand signals □ *He indicated right but turned left.*

indication [ˌɪndɪˈkeɪʃn] *n* a statement, action, or sign that suggests that something is the case or may be the case □ *He gave me no indication of what he intended to do.* □ *There are indications that the economy will pick up.* □ *There is every indication that the Director will resign.*

indicative [ɪnˈdɪkətɪv] ◇ *adj* **to be indicative of sthg** to show or suggest sthg □ *These figures may be indicative of a turnaround in the economy.* ◇ *n* the verb form used for making statements or describing events □ *Put the verb in the indicative.*

indicator [ˈɪndɪkeɪtəʳ] *n* **-1.** a fact, situation, figure etc that indicates something □ *economic/performance indicators.* **-2.** GB one of the lights used to show which way a vehicle is going to turn.

indices [ˈɪndɪsiːz] *plural of* **index.**

indict [ɪnˈdaɪt] *vt* to charge <sb> officially with a crime □ *A mother of two has been indicted on a murder charge.*

indictable [ɪnˈdaɪtəbl] *adj* [offense] for which one can be indicted.

indictment [ɪnˈdaɪtmənt] *n* **-1.** LAW a formal accusation made against somebody. **-2. to act as** OR **be an indictment of sthg** to be a clear sign of how bad sthg is □ *The state of the housing market is a clear indictment of government policy.*

indie [ˈɪndɪ] *adj* [band, label, music] that is independent and not connected with the large established record companies (informal use).

indifference [ɪnˈdɪfrəns] *n* a lack of interest in somebody or something □ *Calls for action in the community met with general indifference.* □ *the growing indifference to the political process.*

indifferent [ɪnˈdɪfrənt] *adj* **-1.** [person, manner] that shows no interest in somebody or something □ *Ben was totally indifferent to her needs.* **-2.** [quality, player] not very good □ *The place was nice but the food was indifferent.*

indigenous [ɪnˈdɪdʒənəs] *adj* [population, plant, animal] that was found originally in a particular place □ *Rabbits are not indigenous to Australia.*

indigestible [ˌɪndɪˈdʒestəbl] *adj* **-1.** [food] very difficult to digest. **-2.** [book, report] that is very difficult to understand.

indigestion [ˌɪndɪˈdʒestʃən] *n* discomfort or

pain that one feels when one's stomach cannot easily digest the food that one has eaten □ *I have indigestion from eating those oysters.*

indignant [ɪn'dɪgnənt] *adj* [person, expression, face] that shows shock and anger at something which seems wrong or unfair □ *She was most indignant at the treatment she had received.*

indignantly [ɪn'dɪgnəntlɪ] *adv* [say, reply] *see* **indignant** □ *"How dare you!" she said indignantly.*

indignation [,ɪndɪg'neɪʃn] *n* feelings of shock and anger that somebody has about something which they think is wrong or unfair □ *There was widespread indignation at the singer's remarks.*

indignity [ɪn'dɪgnətɪ] *(pl* **indignities)** *n* an event that causes somebody to lose their self-respect and feel ashamed □ *They had to suffer the indignity of a visit from the bailiffs.*

indigo ['ɪndɪgoʊ] ◇ *adj* that is dark blue-purple in color. ◇ *n* the color that is between blue and violet in the spectrum.

indirect [,ɪndə'rekt] *adj* -**1.** [route, flight] that does not go straight from one place or point to another □ *We took what seemed a very indirect route to get here.* -**2.** [compliment, answer] that is not openly stated. -**3. an indirect result/effect etc** a result/an effect etc that is connected with something else but not in a direct way.

indirect costs *npl* BUSINESS costs such as rent and heating that are not directly connected with making a product.

indirectly [,ɪndə'rektlɪ] *adv* [cause, affect] *see* **indirect** □ *He was only indirectly responsible.* □ *I heard about it indirectly.*

indirect speech *n* the grammatical construction used to report what is said or written by somebody without repeating their exact words, e.g. by using verbs such as "say", "tell", or "ask" and changing verb tenses and pronouns. In indirect speech, the statement "I am tired" is reported as "She told me (that) she was tired."

indirect taxation *n* the system of taxing people indirectly, e.g. by adding tax to the price of goods so that it is paid by the customer rather than the producer.

indiscreet [,ɪndɪ'skriːt] *adj* [person] who says or does something openly that they should keep secret □ *It was very indiscreet of you to mention our plans.*

indiscretion [,ɪndɪ'skreʃn] *n* -**1.** [of a person] *see* **indiscreet** □ *His indiscretion cost him his job.* -**2.** something slightly shocking or embarrassing that somebody has done □ *She admitted to one or two youthful indiscretions.*

indiscriminate [,ɪndɪ'skrɪmɪnət] *adj* [killing, attack, condemnation] that affects everybody or everything and shows no thought or planning (disapproving use) □ *indiscriminate remarks.*

indiscriminately [,ɪndɪ'skrɪmɪnətlɪ] *adv* [kill, shoot, fire] *see* **indiscriminate.**

indispensable [,ɪndɪ'spensəbl] *adj* [person, tool, guide] that is absolutely necessary for a par-

ticular situation or purpose □ *Nobody's indispensable, you know.*

indisposed [,ɪndɪ'spoʊzd] *adj* **to be indisposed** to be unwell and so unable to do something one had planned (formal use).

indisputable [,ɪndɪ'spjuːtəbl] *adj* [fact, proof] that is true and cannot be shown to be wrong or false □ *That she knew where the gun was is indisputable.*

indistinct [,ɪndɪ'stɪŋkt] *adj* [picture, memory] that is difficult to see because it is unclear.

indistinguishable [,ɪndɪ'stɪŋgwɪʃəbl] *adj* -**1.** [people, things] that look so much like each other that one cannot see any difference between them □ *The two versions are practically indistinguishable.* □ *His handwriting is indistinguishable from his brother's.* -**2.** [figure] that cannot be seen clearly.

individual [,ɪndɪ'vɪdʒʊəl] ◇ *adj* -**1.** [person, part, case] that is considered separately and singly, rather than as part of a group or whole □ *We treat each complaint on an individual basis.* □ *Is this an individual or a group application?* -**2.** [attention, tuition] that is given to or suitable for one person, rather than a group □ *The cheese is sold whole, or in individual portions.* □ *an individual fruit pie.* -**3.** [approach, clothing, style] that is unusual and different from anyone else's □ *He has got a very individual look.* ◇ *n* a single separate person □ *the right of each individual to vote.*

individualist [,ɪndɪ'vɪdʒʊələst] *n* a person who thinks and does things independently and in their own way.

individualistic [,ɪndɪvɪdʒʊə'lɪstɪk] *adj* [person] *see* **individualist.**

individuality [,ɪndɪvɪdʒʊ'ælətɪ] *n* the quality in somebody or something that makes them different from others □ *the sense of one's own individuality.*

individually [,ɪndɪ'vɪdʒʊəlɪ] *adv* separately □ *The gifts were all individually wrapped.* □ *She spoke to everybody individually.*

indivisible [,ɪndɪ'vɪzəbl] *adj* [number, unit] that is impossible to divide into separate parts.

indoctrinate [ɪn'dɒktrɪneɪt] *vt* to teach <sb> to accept an idea or belief so that they do not question it (disapproving use) □ *We don't want our children being indoctrinated with religious propaganda.*

indoctrination [ɪn,dɒktrɪ'neɪʃn] *n*: *see* **indoctrinate** □ *The book's all about the indoctrination of the young by the media.*

indolent ['ɪndələnt] *adj* [person] who is lazy □ *He's an indolent, good-for-nothing waste of time.*

indomitable [ɪn'dɒmətəbl] *adj* [will, person] that is very strong and cannot be destroyed or defeated □ *his indomitable spirit.*

Indonesia [,ɪndə'niːʒə] a country in Southeast Asia, consisting of over 3,000 islands that lie between the Indian Ocean and the Pacific Ocean. It includes Sumatra, Java, Sulawesi, and parts of Borneo and New Guinea. SIZE: 1,900,000 sq kms. POPULATION: 187,600,000 *(Indonesians).* CAPITAL: Jakarta. LANGUAGE: Indonesian. CURRENCY: rupiah.

Indonesian [ˌɪndəˈniːʒn] *n* & *adj*: see **Indonesia**.

indoor [ˈɪndɔːʳ] *adj* [swimming pool, tennis court] that is located inside a building; [tennis, soccer, cycling] that takes place inside a building; [shoes, clothing] that are intended to be used inside, rather than outside.

indoors [ˌɪnˈdɔːʳz] *adv* inside a building, rather than in the open air □ *Let's go indoors.* □ *I don't like being indoors all day.*

indubitably [ɪnˈdjuːbətəblɪ] *adv* without any doubt (formal use) □ *This is indubitably the best book on the subject.*

induce [ɪnˈdjuːs] *vt* -1. **to induce sb to do sthg** to cause sb to decide to do sthg □ *Nothing would induce me to live abroad!* -2. MEDICINE [labor, birth] to start <sthg> by medical means. -3. [sleep, anger] to cause somebody to experience <sthg> □ *The illness was induced by a long period of stress and lack of sleep.*

inducement [ɪnˈdjuːsmənt] *n* something, e.g. a financial payment, that is intended to persuade or encourage somebody to do something □ *With the right inducements, he may agree to come and work for us* □ *They offered us financial inducements for our story.*

induction [ɪnˈdʌkʃn] *n* -1. [of an official] the process or ceremony during which somebody starts a new job in an official post □ *the induction of the new mayor.* -2. MEDICINE [of labor, a birth] see **induce**. -3. [of an employee] the process of introducing somebody to a new job or activity □ *Allow at least two days for induction.* -4. ELECTRICITY the production of electricity or magnetism in one object or circuit by another without physical contact.

induction course *n* a course that introduces people to a new job, activity etc and gives them essential information about it □ *She's on an induction course.*

indulge [ɪnˈdʌldʒ] ◇ *vt* -1. [whim, passion] to allow oneself to have or do <sthg that one enjoys> □ *Our vacation in the countryside allowed Bobby to indulge his interest in wildlife.* -2. [child, person] to allow <sb> to have or do what they want □ *He indulges them in whatever they want.* ■ **to indulge oneself** to allow oneself to enjoy something that one particularly likes □ *Indulge yourself for once!* ◇ *vi* **to indulge in sthg** [in good food, wine] to allow oneself to enjoy sthg that one particularly likes □ *"Have a chocolate?" — "I suppose I might indulge, just this once!"*

indulgence [ɪnˈdʌldʒəns] *n* -1. see **indulgent** □ *Theo was treated with far more indulgence than he deserved.* -2. something enjoyable that one allows oneself to have or do □ *My only indulgence is expensive shoes.*

indulgent [ɪnˈdʌldʒənt] *adj* [parent, friend] who is not strict enough with somebody, especially a child □ *an indulgent smile.*

industrial [ɪnˈdʌstrɪəl] *adj* -1. [development, architecture, process] that is connected with industry □ *industrial pollution* □ *an industrial disease.* -2. [city, country, area] where industry is important and highly developed □ *The region is very industrial.*

industrial action *n* action, especially a strike, that workers use to try to force their employers to agree to what they want □ *Firefighters in the capital have decided to take industrial action.*

industrial estate *n* GB = **industrial park**.

industrial injury *n* an injury received by somebody while they are doing their job.

industrialist [ɪnˈdʌstrɪələst] *n* a person who owns or controls an important industrial company.

industrialization [US ɪnˌdʌstrɪələˈzeɪʃn, GB -aɪˈzeɪʃn] *n*: see **industrialize**.

industrialized, -ised [ɪnˈdʌstrɪəlaɪzd] *adj* [country, area] that has a lot of highly developed industries □ *a highly industrialized region.*

industrial park US, **industrial estate** GB *n* a special area, often outside a town, for small businesses, offices, and light industry.

industrial relations *npl* relations between employers and employees in a business or organization.

Industrial Revolution *n* **the Industrial Revolution** the period in the 18th and 19th centuries when a lot of machines were invented and factories were built in Britain.

industrial tribunal *n* a court of law that deals with cases involving disputes between employers and particular employees □ *She took the firm to an industrial tribunal and sued for wrongful dismissal.*

industrious [ɪnˈdʌstrɪəs] *adj* [person] who works hard □ *a diligent industrious student.*

industry [ˈɪndəstrɪ] (*pl* **industries**) *n* -1. the activity of producing large quantities of goods in factories; the people involved in this □ *More and more graduates are working in industry.* □ *Industry has backed the government's new initiative.* -2. an area of industry involved in one activity, or in making one particular product □ *the aircraft/oil/tourist industry.* -3. **hard work** (formal use) □ *Your industry will be richly rewarded.*

inebriated [ɪˈniːbrɪeɪtəd] *adj* [person] who is drunk (formal use).

inedible [ɪnˈedəbl] *adj* -1. [food, meal] that is so badly cooked, or of such poor quality, that one cannot eat it □ *The beef was inedible.* -2. [plant, mushroom] that is not safe for one to eat, e.g. because it is poisonous.

ineffective [ˌɪnɪˈfektɪv] *adj* [treatment, policy] that does not produce the desired effect or result □ *These measures have proved ineffective in combating the problem.*

ineffectual [ˌɪnɪˈfektʃʊəl] *adj* [person, attempt, plan] that does not have the necessary qualities to get something done □ *They just stood around looking ineffectual.*

inefficiency [ˌɪnɪˈfɪʃnsɪ] *n*: see **inefficient** □ *It's the height of inefficiency.*

inefficient [ˌɪnɪˈfɪʃnt] *adj* -1. [process, machine] that does not work as well as possible, often wasting time or resources □ *The industry has largely discarded its inefficient and outdated working methods.* -2. [person] who is bad at organizing things and getting things done □ *He's hopelessly inefficient!*

inelegant [ɪnˈelɪgənt] *adj* [posture, person] that lacks style and grace.

ineligible [ɪnˈelɪdʒəbl] *adj* **to be ineligible** [person] not to be allowed to have or take part in something □ *He was ineligible for the competition because he was too old.*

inept [ɪˈnept] *adj* -1. [person] who lacks the skill or ability to do something properly □ *She showed herself to be socially/physically inept.* -2. [comment, remark] that is unsuitable in a particular situation □ *He was severely criticized for his inept handling of the crisis.*

ineptitude [ɪˈneptɪtjuːd] *n*: *see* **inept** □ *I was amazed at their complete ineptitude in dealing with such a trivial matter.*

inequality [ˌɪnɪˈkwɒlətɪ] (*pl* **inequalities**) *n* an unfair difference in the way particular groups of people are treated in society □ *social/racial inequality* □ *We have to try and iron out these inequalities.*

inequitable [ɪnˈekwətəbl] *adj* [system, distribution] that is not equally fair to everybody (formal use).

inert [ɪˈnɜːt] *adj* -1. [person] who is lying or sitting very still. -2. CHEMISTRY [gas, substance] that does not react with other substances.

inertia [ɪˈnɜːrʃə] *n* -1. [in a person, system, institution] the state of not doing anything or not making any changes □ *I'd hate to stay in the same job out of sheer inertia.* -2. [of an object, body] the tendency of something to stay still or to keep moving unless something else affects it.

inertia-reel seat belt *n* a car seat belt that stops a person moving forward if they move suddenly.

inescapable [ˌɪnɪˈskeɪpəbl] *adj* [fact, truth, feeling] that exists or is true and cannot be ignored □ *The inescapable conclusion is that Johnson is lying.*

inessential [ˌɪnɪˈsenʃl] *adj* [item, details] that is not needed □ *You should throw away anything that is inessential.*

inestimable [ɪnˈestɪməbl] *adj* [value, worth] that is too great to be put into figures or words (formal use) □ *The benefit to us is inestimable.*

inevitable [ɪnˈevətəbl] ◇ *adj* [result, conclusion] that cannot be avoided or prevented; that is so common or obvious that one expects it □ *It was inevitable that someone was going to get hurt.* □ *I was asked the inevitable question about my long-term career plans.* ◇ *n* **the inevitable** something that is inevitable □ *We have to learn to accept the inevitable.*

inevitably [ɪnˈevətəblɪ] *adv* a word used to show that one believes something cannot be stopped from happening □ *Inevitably, some jobs will be lost.*

inexact [ˌɪnɪgˈzækt] *adj* [science, measurement] that is not exact or precise □ *Some of the figures turned out to be inexact.*

inexcusable [ˌɪnɪkˈskjuːzəbl] *adj* [behavior] that cannot be excused because there is no good

reason for it to happen □ *Turning up late for such an important meeting is inexcusable.*

inexhaustible [ˌɪnɪgˈzɔːstəbl] *adj* [supply, patience, energy] that is so great that it cannot be used up completely □ *She seems to have an inexhaustible source of energy.*

inexorable [ɪnˈeksərəbl] *adj* [rise, progress, pressure] that continues and cannot be stopped, even though people sometimes do not want it to continue (formal use) □ *the inexorable march of time.*

inexorably [ɪnˈeksərəblɪ] *adv* [rise, progress, approach] *see* **inexorable** (formal use).

inexpensive [ˌɪnɪkˈspensɪv] *adj* [item, meal] that does not cost very much but is good and is worth the price □ *a good inexpensive restaurant.*

inexperience [ˌɪnɪkˈspɪərɪəns] *n* [of a young person, employee, climber] the state of not having much or any experience □ *I put his mistakes down to inexperience.*

inexperienced [ˌɪnɪkˈspɪərɪənst] *adj* [driver, climber] who has little or no experience of a particular job or activity, or of life in general □ *He was young and inexperienced in these matters.*

inexpert [ɪnˈekspɜːrt] *adj* [attempt, person, technique] that shows very little skill.

inexplicable [ˌɪnɪkˈsplɪkəbl] *adj* [behavior, decision, incident] that cannot be understood and explained □ *For some inexplicable reason, they've dropped the charges.*

inextricably [ˌɪnɪkˈstrɪkəblɪ] *adv* **inextricably linked/joined etc** linked/joined etc in a way that makes it impossible to separate the different parts □ *His life and work are inextricably bound up with each other.*

infallible [ɪnˈfæləbl] *adj* -1. [person, instinct] that is never wrong □ *No one is infallible.* -2. [method, cure] that always works □ *No security system is infallible.*

infamous [ˈɪnfəməs] *adj* [act, person, occasion] that is well-known for being bad, especially for being immoral or evil □ *one of America's most infamous criminals.*

infamy [ˈɪnfəmɪ] *n* -1. the state of being well-known for something bad or evil. -2. something that is bad or evil.

infancy [ˈɪnfənsɪ] *n* the first few years of a child's life □ *illnesses common during infancy.* ■ **to be in its infancy** to be in its very early stages □ *The science/project/club is still in its infancy.*

infant [ˈɪnfənt] *n* a child in its first few years of life □ *an infant child.*

infantile [US ˈɪnfəntl, GB -taɪl] *adj* -1. [behavior, humor, person] that is more typical of a child than of an adult (disapproving use) □ *He kept making silly infantile remarks.* -2. **an infantile disease** a disease that very young children suffer from.

infant mortality *n* the death rate among very young children and babies □ *Infant mortality here is high.*

infantry [ˈɪnfəntrɪ] *n* the soldiers of an army who fight on foot or in small vehicles □ *a* *soldier in the infantry* □ *an infantry soldier/regiment.*

infantryman ['ɪnfəntrɪmən] (*pl* **infantrymen** [-mən]) *n* a soldier in the infantry.

infant school *n* GB a school for children aged between five and seven.

infatuated [ɪn'fætʃʊeɪtəd] *adj* **to be infatuated** to be very attracted to somebody in a way that is not sensible because one does not know enough about them □ *He became infatuated with her.*

infatuation [ɪnˌfætʃʊ'eɪʃn] *n* the feeling one has, or the period of time, when one is infatuated with somebody □ *It was just a teenage infatuation.*

infect [ɪn'fekt] *vt* **-1.** [person, wound, food] to cause <sb/sthg> to have an illness, virus etc, especially a serious one □ *A carrier can infect other people without actually getting the disease himself.* **-2.** to make <sb/sthg> feel the same way about something as oneself □ *His enthusiasm infected the rest of the staff.*

infected [ɪn'fektəd] *adj* [person, wound, food] that has an illness, virus etc □ *The foot had become infected with gangrene.*

infection [ɪn'fekʃn] *n* **-1.** a disease caused by a germ, virus etc that has entered one's body □ *a chest infection.* **-2.** [of food, water, a wound] *see* **infect** □ *Strict hygiene can reduce the risk of infection.*

infectious [ɪn'fekʃəs] *adj* **-1.** [disease, illness] that spreads easily from one person or animal to another □ *Is it infectious?* **-2.** [laugh, humor] that affects other people, especially because it is attractive or enjoyable.

infer [ɪn'fɜːr] (*pt* & *pp* **inferred**, *cont* **inferring**) *vt* **-1. to infer that...** to think or decide that something is true because of something else one knows already □ *What are we to infer from such behavior?* □ *From what he said I inferred that he wasn't married any more.* **-2.** = **imply** (informal use) □ *What are you inferring?*

inference ['ɪnfrəns] *n* a conclusion based on what one already knows and what seems likely □ *What inferences can be drawn from this?* ■ **by inference** judging from everything that is known □ *If Williams is guilty then so, by inference, are his associates.*

inferior [ɪn'fɪərɪər] ◇ *adj* **-1.** [quality, goods, performance] that is not as good as other things of the same kind □ *I'm not prepared to pay for inferior service!* **-2.** [person, position, rank] that is less important or has less power than somebody or something else □ *His background made him feel inferior to everybody else.* □ *socially inferior.* ◇ *n* a person who is inferior to somebody else.

inferiority [ɪnˌfɪərɪ'ɒrətɪ] *n* [of goods, a person, quality] *see* **inferior** □ *feelings of inferiority.*

inferiority complex *n* a feeling one has all the time that one is less attractive, talented, important etc than everybody else □ *He's got an inferiority complex about not having been to college.*

inferno [ɪn'fɜːrnou] (*pl* **infernos**) *n* a very large and dangerous fire.

infertile [US ɪn'fɜːrtl, GB -'fɜːtaɪl] *adj* **-1.** [person, animal] that cannot have babies. **-2.** [soil, land] that is of poor quality and is not able to produce good crops.

infertility [ˌɪnfər'tɪlətɪ] *n* [of a woman, animal, soil] *see* **infertile** □ *She has just started receiving infertility treatment.*

infestation [ˌɪnfe'steɪʃn] *n: see* **infested** □ *an infestation of rats.*

infested [ɪn'festəd] *adj* **to be infested with sthg** [house, place, river] to be full of a large number or amount of sthg dangerous or unpleasant □ *shark-infested waters* □ *The kitchen is infested with cockroaches.*

infidelity [ˌɪnfɪ'delətɪ] *n* the act of being unfaithful to one's wife, husband, or usual partner by having sex with somebody else □ *He accused her of infidelity.*

infighting ['ɪnfaɪtɪŋ] *n* quarrels and competition that take place between members of the same organization □ *political infighting.*

infiltrate [US ɪn'fɪltreɪt, GB 'ɪnfɪltreɪt] ◇ *vt* [government, territory] to secretly enter <a place or organization> as an enemy in order to find out more about it or to damage it □ *police attempts to infiltrate the rebel organization.* ◇ *vi*: *They infiltrated into enemy territory.*

infinite ['ɪnfɪnət] *adj* **-1.** [patience, wisdom] very great □ *He took infinite care not to disturb them.* **-2.** [space, number, variety] that has or seems to have no end or limit □ *There's an infinite number of possible combinations.*

infinitely ['ɪnfɪnətlɪ] *adv* **infinitely better/preferable etc** very much better/more preferable etc □ *You would be infinitely more comfortable at home.*

infinitesimal [ˌɪnfɪnɪ'tesɪml] *adj* [amount, difference, chance] that is extremely small and very difficult to see or notice □ *The risk of catching the disease is infinitesimal.*

infinitive [ɪn'fɪnətɪv] *n* the basic form of a verb that can be used with "to" in English, as for example "have" in "I want to have" and "you may have".

infinity [ɪn'fɪnətɪ] *n* **-1.** a point that is an infinite distance away so that it can never be reached □ *The rows of houses seemed to go on and on into infinity.* **-2.** MATH an infinite number that can never be expressed in figures.

infirm [ɪn'fɜːrm] ◇ *adj* [person] who is weak or not very well, especially because they are old. ◇ *npl* **the infirm** people who are infirm.

infirmary [ɪn'fɜːrmərɪ] (*pl* **infirmaries**) *n* **-1.** a hospital, especially when it is part of a larger building □ *a prison infirmary.* **-2.** a room in a building where people who are unwell are taken care of □ *a school infirmary.*

infirmity [ɪn'fɜːrmətɪ] (*pl* **infirmities**) *n* a weakness or illness that a person has, usually for a long time; the state of being weak and ill.

inflamed [ɪn'fleɪmd] *adj* [eye, wound] that is red, painful, and usually hot and swollen because of an injury or infection □ *The cut had become inflamed.*

inflammable [ɪn'flæməbl] *adj* [material, chemical,

gas] that is dangerous because it catches fire very easily □ *'Highly inflammable.'*

inflammation [ˌɪnfləˈmeɪʃn] *n* a painful swelling and redness on a part of the body, caused by disease, injury etc □ *an inflammation of the ear.*

inflammatory [US ɪnˈflæmətɔːrɪ, GB -ətərɪ] *adj* [remark, speech] that is likely to make people very angry or violent □ *inflammatory criticisms.*

inflatable [ɪnˈfleɪtəbl] *adj* [life jacket, raft, toy] that needs to be filled with air before it can be used □ *an inflatable dinghy.*

inflate [ɪnˈfleɪt] *vt* **-1.** [balloon, raft, life jacket] to fill <sthg> with air and make it bigger, often so that it can float. **-2.** ECONOMICS to increase <a price, salary> etc, usually by making it too high; to make <the economy> more active by increasing the money supply.

inflated [ɪnˈfleɪtəd] *adj* **-1.** [tire, life jacket, balloon] that is full of air □ *The raft was only partially inflated.* **-2.** [price, salary] that is higher than is necessary or fair □ *executives on grossly inflated salaries.* **-3. to have an inflated opinion of oneself** to think one is more important than one really is □ *He's got an inflated view of his own importance.*

inflation [ɪnˈfleɪʃn] *n* ECONOMICS a general increase in the prices of things that leads to a fall in the value of money; the rate at which this happens, measured as a percentage □ *a period of low inflation* □ *Inflation is running at 4%.* NOTE: Compare **deflation**.

inflationary [US ɪnˈfleɪʃənerɪ, GB -nərɪ] *adj* [policy, effect] that tends to increase inflation.

inflationary spiral *n* a situation in which inflation causes wages to go up so that the inflation gets even worse.

inflation-proof *adj* [pension, mortgage] that changes to take inflation into account so that one does not lose any money.

inflection [ɪnˈflekʃn] *n* GRAMMAR a change in the form of a word to show a difference in grammatical use, e.g. a change to make a noun plural.

inflexible [ɪnˈfleksəbl] *adj* **-1.** [material] that is stiff and cannot be bent or turned. **-2.** [person] who does not want to change their ideas or the way they do things, even though it would be better □ *His attitude is very inflexible.* **-3.** [rule, hours, system] that cannot be changed, even in new situations when a change would be better □ *inflexible working hours.*

inflict [ɪnˈflɪkt] *vt* **to inflict sthg on sb** [pain, responsibility, problem] to force sb to accept sthg unpleasant □ *The harsh economic measures have inflicted great hardship on the people.*

in-flight *adj* [entertainment, meal, magazine] that is provided for passengers during a plane trip □ *Our in-flight movie will follow shortly.*

inflow [ˈɪnfləʊ] *n* [of information, goods, immigrants] a constant movement of things or people arriving in a place.

influence [ˈɪnfluəns] ◇ *n* **-1.** [of a person, drug] the power to affect the way somebody else behaves, thinks etc □ *She seems to have no influence on OR over her own children.* □ *Her father used his influence to help get her the job.* □ *He was found guilty of driving while under the influence of alcohol/drugs.* **-2.** [on somebody's health, painting, writing] an effect that something has on a person or thing that usually lasts a long time □ *We can see the influence of Cubism in the artist's early work.* □ *As chairman he had a great influence on OR over policy-making.* **-3. to be a good/bad influence** to have a good/bad effect on the way somebody or something develops or behaves □ *I think David is a bad influence on you!*

◇ *vt* [result, person, work] to have an effect on <sb/sthg> that usually lasts a long time □ *He's easily influenced.*

influential [ˌɪnfluˈenʃl] *adj* [person, work, idea] that has an important influence on somebody or something □ *She's an influential woman/writer/film maker.*

influenza [ˌɪnfluˈenzə] *n* = **flu** (formal or technical use).

influx [ˈɪnflʌks] *n* [of tourists, immigrants, foreign goods] the arrival of a large number of people or things in a place at the same time □ *a large influx of refugees.*

info [ˈɪnfəʊ] *n* = **information** (informal use).

inform [ɪnˈfɔːm] *vt* to tell <sb> officially or formally about something □ *If you see anything suspicious, inform a member of staff immediately.* □ *We regret to inform you that your application has not been successful.* □ *Why wasn't I informed of OR about this decision earlier?*

◆ **inform on** *vt fus* **to inform on sb** to tell a person in authority, often secretly, that sb has done something illegal or wrong.

informal [ɪnˈfɔːml] *adj* **-1.** [atmosphere, occasion] that is relaxed, friendly, and not official □ *The ministers met for informal talks on the conflict.* **-2.** [clothing, language] that is suitable when one is with family and friends but not on more formal occasions □ *informal dress.*

informally [ɪnˈfɔːmlɪ] *adv* [dress, meet, discuss] see **informal**.

informant [ɪnˈfɔːmənt] *n* **-1.** a person who gives information about a criminal, especially to the police □ *a police informant.* **-2.** a person who gives information about something to somebody else, especially to somebody who is doing research.

information [ˌɪnfəˈmeɪʃn] *n* **-1.** useful facts about somebody or something □ *tourist/flight information* □ *Do you have any information on OR about loans, please?* □ *an interesting piece of information* □ *For further information, please contact your nearest branch.* **-2. 'information'** a word used on a sign at a desk, office etc to show that one can get useful details about a particular service, e.g. about transport or hotels □ *'Ask at information.'* ■ **for your information** so that you may know all the facts you need to know □ *I enclose a leaflet for your information.* □ *For your information I haven't had a single beer since Friday!* **-3.** US the service one calls to find out somebody's telephone number □ *Information didn't have the number.*

information desk *n* a counter in a hotel, airport etc that gives information to people, especially tourists or visitors.

information office *n* an office that gives information to people, especially tourists or visitors.

information retrieval *n* the process of storing and finding data in a computer.

information superhighway [-suːpəˈhaɪweɪ] *n* **the information superhighway** a collective term for all the forms of information that are available on an on-line computer system.

information technology *n* the study or activity of storing, showing, and controlling information by using electronic devices, especially computers.

informative [ɪnˈfɔːrmətɪv] *adj* [person, book, account] that gives a lot of useful information □ *Your letters are always so informative.*

informed [ɪnˈfɔːrmd] *adj* **-1.** [person, opinion, source] that shows knowledge about particular events; that shows knowledge about what is happening in the world □ *He's very informed on the subject of foreign policy.* **-2. an informed decision/choice etc** a decision/ choice etc that is based on knowledge that one has □ *I don't know, but I can make an informed guess.*

informer [ɪnˈfɔːrmər] *n* a person who gives information about criminals to the police.

infotainment [ˌɪnfoʊˈteɪnmənt] *n* TV programs that are designed to inform people about serious subjects or current affairs in an entertaining way.

infrared [ˌɪnfrəˈred] *adj* [light] that gives out heat but cannot be seen; [photograph, lamp] that uses infrared light.

infrastructure [ˈɪnfrəstrʌktʃər] *n* all the different systems and equipment, e.g. roads, telephone lines, or buildings, that people in a country, organization etc need in order to work properly.

infrequent [ɪnˈfriːkwənt] *adj* [visitor] who does not come often; [service, contact] that does not happen often □ *on one of our infrequent visits to Paris* □ *Trains to the village are very infrequent.*

infringe [ɪnˈfrɪndʒ] *(cont* **infringeing)** ◇ *vt* **-1.** [law, agreement, copyright] to break <sthg> by doing something that is not allowed □ *Don't print too much or you risk infringing copyright regulations.* **-2.** [right, liberty] to act in a way that ignores or restricts <sthg> □ *This new law infringes citizens' rights to free speech.* ◇ *vi:* *The new measures infringe on people's right to demonstrate.*

infringement [ɪnˈfrɪndʒmənt] *n* [of a law, copyright, right] *see* **infringe** □ *peace treaty infringements.*

infuriate [ɪnˈfjʊərieɪt] *vt* to make <sb> extremely angry □ *Ken always manages to infuriate me.*

infuriating [ɪnˈfjʊərieɪtɪŋ] *adj* [person, habit, behavior] that makes one very angry and an-

noyed □ *He has an infuriating habit of arguing just for the sake of it.*

infuse [ɪnˈfjuːz] ◇ *vt* **to infuse sb with sthg** [with desire, life, energy] to fill sb with sthg. ◇ *vi* [tea leaves] to soak in hot water and give it flavor □ *Leave the tea to infuse for four minutes.*

infusion [ɪnˈfjuːʒn] *n* **-1.** [of ideas, quality, money] the addition of something that helps a person or thing to develop □ *The project needs an infusion of funds.* **-2.** a liquid made by soaking herbs in hot water, used as a drink or medicine □ *a herbal infusion.*

ingenious [ɪnˈdʒiːnjəs] *adj* [device, solution] that is very clever, useful, and imaginative □ *This ingenious little gadget can help you save on your electricity costs.*

ingenuity [ˌɪndʒəˈnjuːətɪ] *n* the ability to think of new ideas or ways of doing things □ *I admired her ingenuity.*

ingenuous [ɪnˈdʒenjʊəs] *adj* [person] who is honest, believes what people say, and cannot deceive other people (formal use).

ingest [ɪnˈdʒest] *vt* [food, poison, pills] to put <sthg> in one's mouth and swallow it so that it enters one's stomach (formal use).

ingot [ˈɪŋɡət] *n* a bar of metal that has a particular size, shape, and weight □ *gold ingots.*

ingrained [ɪnˈɡreɪnd] *adj* **-1.** [habit, belief] that is very fixed in somebody's nature and difficult to change □ *It's a notion that is deeply ingrained in society.* **-2.** [dirt, stain] that goes deeply into the surface of something and is difficult to remove □ *This detergent removes ingrained dirt.*

ingratiate [ɪnˈɡreɪʃieɪt] *vt* **to ingratiate oneself with sb** to try to get sb to like one, often because one wants something from them.

ingratiating [ɪnˈɡreɪʃieɪtɪŋ] *adj* [smile, person, manner] that deliberately tries to please others in the hope of getting something in return □ *an ingratiating tone of voice.*

ingratitude [ɪnˈɡrætəˈtjuːd] *n* lack of gratitude or thanks that somebody shows or feels □ *He was stung by their ingratitude.*

ingredient [ɪnˈɡriːdjənt] *n* **-1.** COOKING one of the types of food used to make a particular meal or dish □ *You should be able to find most of the ingredients in a good supermarket.* **-2.** [of a success, process, situation] one of the things that helps something to happen or to work □ *Their relationship had all the ingredients of a successful business partnership.*

ingrowing [ˈɪnɡroʊɪŋ] GB, **ingrown** [ɪnˈɡroʊn] *adj* **an ingrown toenail** a toenail that grows into the toe and is painful.

inhabit [ɪnˈhæbət] *vt* [town, house, region] to live in <a place>, especially for a long time or for all of one's life □ *The forest is inhabited by various forms of wildlife.*

inhabitant [ɪnˈhæbətənt] *n* [of a city, country, region] a person or animal that lives in a particular place □ *The island has only a few hundred inhabitants.*

inhalation [ˌɪnhəˈleɪʃn] *n*: *see* **inhale.**

inhale [ɪnˈheɪl] ◇ *vt* [smoke, fumes] to breathe in <sthg> □ *'Warning: Deliberately inhaling con-*

tents can be fatal.' ◇ *vi* to breathe in □ *Inhale deeply, then exhale slowly.*

inhaler [ɪn'heɪlə^r] *n* a small device used by people with asthma, hay fever etc that sprays a dose of medicine into their mouth.

inherent [ɪn'hɪərənt] *adj* [danger, problem, feature] that is a natural part of somebody or something, is always there, and cannot be avoided □ *A degree of error is inherent in the system.*

inherently [ɪn'hɪərəntlɪ] *adv*: *see* **inherent** □ *The system is inherently inefficient.*

inherit [ɪn'herət] ◇ *vt* **-1.** [problem, tradition, attitude] to have <sthg> because there were other people who made it, used it, or had it before one □ *the trade deficit inherited from the previous decade.* **-2.** [money, house, title] to get <sthg> from a person who has died □ *She didn't inherit a thing from them.* **-3.** [disease, characteristic, good looks] to be born with <sthg> because one's parents or ancestors had it □ *I'm afraid he didn't inherit his father's business sense.* ◇ *vi*: *If there's no will, then the closest relative automatically inherits.*

inheritance [ɪn'herətəns] *n* the property or money that somebody gets from a person who has died, e.g. a friend or relative □ *inheritance tax* □ *He will come into his inheritance at the age of 18.*

inheritor [ɪn'herətə^r] *n* [of property, a tradition] a person who inherits something.

inhibit [ɪn'hɪbət] *vt* [progress, breathing] to make <sthg> happen slowly or stop happening □ *Too much alcohol may inhibit the growth of the fetus.* ■ **to inhibit sb from doing sthg** to prevent sb from doing sthg, even though sometimes they want to do it □ *Feelings of shame often inhibit rape victims from reporting their attackers.*

inhibited [ɪn'hɪbətəd] *adj* **to be** OR **feel inhibited** to be unable to show one's real feelings or do what one likes because one is always worried about what other people will think □ *I felt inhibited in his presence.* □ *There's no need to be inhibited about sex!*

inhibition [ˌɪnhɪ'bɪʃn] *n* a feeling or state in which it is very difficult to show one's real feelings and behave naturally □ *He talked freely and without inhibition.* □ *After a few drinks, people began to lose their inhibitions.*

inhospitable [ˌɪnhɒ'spɪtəbl] *adj* **-1.** [person] who does not welcome visitors in a polite or friendly way. **-2.** [climate, place] that is unpleasant and difficult to stay or live in, especially because there is no shelter □ *the inhospitable desert.*

in-house ◇ *adj* [member of staff] who works inside a company's office or building; [report, magazine] that is produced by a company for its staff □ *She's an in-house translator.* □ *in-house training.* ◇ *adv* [work, produce] inside a company's own office, building etc and not in another place or company □ *Most of the work is done in-house.*

inhuman [ɪn'hjuːmən] *adj* **-1.** [person, behavior] that is very cruel and shows no pity and no

feelings for other people □ *You can't ask them to work in these conditions — it's inhuman!* **-2.** [machine, sound] that is strange and frightening because it is very different from the way people look, sound etc.

inhumane [ˌɪnhjuː'meɪn] *adj* [treatment, law, person] that does not show any concern for the suffering of other people or of animals □ *The prisoners are kept in inhumane conditions.*

inimitable [ɪ'nɪmətəbl] *adj* [person, way, quality] that cannot be copied by anybody else with the same effect □ *I'm sure you'll make your views known in your usual inimitable fashion.*

iniquitous [ɪ'nɪkwətəs] *adj* [policy, system, behavior] very unfair and wrong (formal use).

iniquity [ɪ'nɪkwətɪ] (*pl* **iniquities**) *n* the quality of being unfair and wrong (formal use).

initial [ɪ'nɪʃl] (US *pt* & *pp* **initialed**, *cont* **initialing**, GB *pt* & *pp* **initialled**, *cont* **initialling**) ◇ *adj* **-1.** [reaction, stage, shyness] that happens at the beginning of a process or event, before something that happens later □ *We hope to recoup the initial investment within three years.* **-2. an initial letter** the letter at the beginning of a word □ *An acronym is formed from the initial letters of a term.* ◇ *vt* [document, agreement, change] to sign one's initials on <sthg> □ *If you could just initial this for me.* ◇ *n* the first letter of one's first name or names □ *The name's Mason, initial J.*

◆ **initials** *npl* the initial letters of one's names, or of one's first name or names □ *Kennedy was often known just by his initials: JFK.* □ *My name is Patel, initials, LM.*

initialize, -ise [ɪ'nɪʃəlaɪz] *vt* COMPUTING to make <a diskette> ready for use in a computer by running it through a special program; to make <a printer> ready for use by defining all its various settings.

initially [ɪ'nɪʃəlɪ] *adv* at the beginning □ *Initially, I really liked the idea.*

initiate [*vb* ɪ'nɪʃieɪt, *n* ɪ'nɪʃiət] ◇ *vt* **-1.** [talks, scheme, improvements] to start <sthg>; to cause <sthg> to start □ *We have initiated an exchange program with Russian scientists.* **-2. to initiate sb into sthg** [into a skill, knowledge] to teach sb about sthg that they did not know about before □ *I was initiated into the mysteries of cyberspace.* **-3.** [into a group, club] to allow somebody to join something, usually by holding a special ceremony. ◇ *n* a person who is in the process of being initiated, or who has recently been initiated, into a skill, secret, or group.

initiation [ɪ,nɪʃɪ'eɪʃn] *n* **-1.** [of talks, a program] *see* **initiate** □ *the initiation of peace talks.* **-2.** [into knowledge, a skill, a group] *see* **initiate** □ *his initiation into the world of crime* □ *an initiation ceremony.*

initiative [ɪ'nɪʃətɪv] *n* **-1.** a new plan or action that deals with something, especially a problem □ *a government/peace initiative.* ■ **to take the initiative** to take action or do something useful, important etc before anybody else. **-2. to have the initiative** to have the advantage □ *They lost the initiative to foreign competition.* **-3.** the ability to make decisions and take action without being told what to do □ *She has a lot of initiative.* □ *He acted on his own initiative.* □ *You'll have to use your initiative.*

inject [ɪn'dʒekt] *vt* **-1.** MEDICINE **to inject sb with sthg** [with a drug, substance] to put sthg into sb's bloodstream using a syringe. **-2. to inject sthg into sthg** to give sthg that is missing or needed to sthg else □ *They've injected billions of dollars into the economy.* □ *I tried to inject some humor into the situation.*

injection [ɪn'dʒekʃn] *n* **-1.** MEDICINE the act of injecting somebody with a medicine □ *I was given injections against hepatitis and typhoid.* **-2.** the act of providing more money for a country, project etc □ *The company needs large injections of money to stay afloat.*

injudicious [ˌɪndʒʊ'dɪʃəs] *adj* [remark, plan, behavior] that shows bad judgment (formal use).

injunction [ɪn'dʒʌŋkʃn] *n* LAW an official order made by a court □ *a court injunction.*

injure ['ɪndʒər] *vt* **-1.** to cause physical damage to <a person, animal, or part of the body> □ *He injured himself/his back while climbing.* □ *A number of people were seriously injured in the explosion.* **-2. to injure sb's pride/feelings** to upset sb by being unkind or unfair to them.

injured ['ɪndʒərd] ◇ *adj* [person, knee, pride] that is hurt or damaged □ *Which leg is injured?* ◇ *npl* **the injured** the people who have been injured, e.g. in an explosion or car crash □ *The injured were airlifted to the nearest hospital.*

injurious [ɪn'dʒʊərɪəs] *adj* [result, effect, strike] harmful (formal use).

injury ['ɪndʒərɪ] (*pl* **injuries**) *n* physical damage done to a person or animal □ *He received severe injuries to the head.* □ *an insurance policy against injury at work.* ■ **to do oneself an injury** to hurt oneself, e.g. while lifting something heavy □ *You'll do yourself an injury carrying that thing on your own!*

injury time *n* extra playing time at the end of a soccer game that makes up for time lost when injured players were being treated.

injustice [ɪn'dʒʌstɪs] *n* an unfair act or situation □ *to campaign against injustice* □ *the injustices of the old apartheid regime.* ■ **to do sb an injustice** to judge sb harshly or unfairly □ *It would be doing him an injustice to say that he was indifferent to their suffering.*

ink [ɪŋk] *n* a colored liquid used for writing and printing □ *an ink drawing* □ *an ink stain.*

◆ **ink in** *vt sep* **to ink sthg in** [writing, drawing] to make sthg drawn in pencil more complete or permanent by drawing over it in ink.

ink-jet printer *n* a computer printer that shoots small amounts of ink onto paper to form letters.

inkling ['ɪŋklɪŋ] *n* **to have an inkling** to have a slight knowledge about something that is happening or going to happen □ *She had no inkling that he was going to leave.*

inkpad ['ɪŋkpæd] *n* a piece of absorbent material filled with ink, used for putting ink onto a stamp, e.g. for stamping the date on a document.

inkwell ['ɪŋkwel] *n* a container for ink, used on a desk when writing.

inlaid [ˌɪn'leɪd] *adj* **-1.** [gold, silver] that has been set in holes in the surface of something to make a flat decorated surface. **-2.** [box, table] that is decorated with inlaid gold, silver, wood etc □ *The cabinet was inlaid with mother-of-pearl.*

inland [*adj* 'ɪnlənd, *adv* ɪn'lænd] ◇ *adj* [town, waterway] that is inside a country or continent, rather than on the coast. ◇ *adv* [go, head] away from the coast and toward the middle of a country or continent.

Inland Revenue *n* **the Inland Revenue** the British government department responsible for collecting taxes.

in-laws *npl* the family of one's husband or wife (informal use) □ *We're spending Christmas with the in-laws.*

inlet ['ɪnlet] *n* **-1.** [of a lake, sea] a narrow strip of water cutting into a coast, or between two islands. **-2.** an opening in a piece of machinery for letting in air, fuel, or water.

inmate ['ɪnmeɪt] *n* a person who is being kept in a prison or mental hospital □ *Several inmates have escaped.*

inmost ['ɪnmoʊst] *adj* **one's inmost feelings/secrets etc** one's most private feelings/secrets etc (literary use).

inn [ɪn] *n* a small old hotel that serves food and drink and is usually found in a village or in the countryside.

innards ['ɪnərdz] *npl* **-1.** [of a person, animal] the organs inside the body. **-2.** [of a machine] the internal parts.

innate [ˌɪ'neɪt] *adj* **an innate talent/ability etc** a talent/an ability etc that somebody is born with and so does not need to learn.

inner ['ɪnər] *adj* **-1. an inner room/layer etc** a room/layer etc that is inside something else □ *the inner ear.* **-2. inner calm** OR **peace** peace that one feels deep inside oneself. **-3. inner thoughts/feelings etc** thoughts/feelings etc that are secret, private, or not expressed.

inner city *n* **the inner city** the areas close to the center of a big city where many people live and where there are often social or economic problems □ *an inner city area/problem/school.*

innermost ['ɪnərmoʊst] *adj* = **inmost**.

inner tube *n* a tube that fits inside a tire and can be filled with air.

inning ['ɪnɪŋ] (*pl* **innings**) *n* the period of time when a team is batting in baseball or softball.

◆ **innings** *n* the period of time when a team is batting in cricket.

innocence ['ɪnəsəns] *n* **-1.** LAW the state of not being guilty of a crime □ *She has always maintained her innocence.* **-2.** the quality of having little experience of life, especially of its unpleasant aspects □ *the loss of innocence.*

innocent ['ɪnəsənt] ◇ *adj* **-1.** LAW [person] who is not guilty of a crime □ *He was innocent of the crime.* **-2.** [person, child] who has little experience of life, especially of its unpleasant aspects □ *I was very innocent in those days.* **-3.** [remark, question, fun] that is not intended to cause any harm □ *It was just a little innocent fun.* ◇ *n* a person who has little experience of life □ *My, what an innocent you are!*

innocuous [ɪ'nɒkjʊəs] *adj* [remark, substance] that is not harmful or offensive.

innovation [,ɪnə'veɪʃn] *n* **-1.** a new idea, method, or device □ *one of Lou Selsdon's many innovations in the engineering world.* **-2.** the introduction of new ideas, methods, or devices □ *They have a reputation for innovation.*

innovative ['ɪnəveɪtɪv] *adj* **-1.** [plan, design, technique] that is new and original □ *an innovative way of raising money.* **-2.** [person, company] that introduces or encourages innovations □ *We need strong innovative designers on our staff.*

innovator ['ɪnəveɪtər] *n* an innovative person.

Inns of Court *npl* **the Inns of Court** in London, the four societies for lawyers that have the right to make somebody a barrister; the buildings occupied by these societies.

innuendo [,ɪnju'endoʊ] (*pl* **innuendoes** OR **innuendos**) *n* a remark that suggests something, usually unpleasant or sexual, without stating it directly; the act of making such remarks □ *sexual innuendoes* □ *an article full of speculation and innuendo.*

innumerable [ɪ'nʲuːmərəbl] *adj* [problems, visitors, phone calls] too many to be counted □ *We suffered innumerable setbacks but eventually finished on time.*

inoculate [ɪ'nɒkjəleɪt] *vt* **to inoculate sb with sthg** [with a virus, vaccine] to inject sb with sthg to protect them against a disease. ■ **to inoculate sb against sthg** [against cholera, measles] to protect sb from sthg by giving them a weak form of it in an injection.

inoculation [ɪ,nɒkjə'leɪʃn] *n* **-1.** an injection that inoculates somebody. **-2.** the practice of inoculating people against disease.

inoffensive [,ɪnə'fensɪv] *adj* [person, manner, remark] that does not offend or hurt people □ *The joke was pretty inoffensive.*

inoperable [ɪn'ɒpərəbl] *adj* [tumor, cancer] that cannot be cured or removed in a surgical operation.

inoperative [ɪn'ɒpərətɪv] *adj* **-1.** [law, rule, tax] that does not work or cannot be put into practice. **-2.** [machine] that is not working.

inopportune [US ɪn,ɒpr'tuːn, GB ɪn'ɒpətjuːn] *adj* [moment, remark, visit] that is not convenient or suitable (formal use).

inordinate [ɪ'nɔːrdnət] *adj* [pride, pleasure] that is greater than is reasonable □ *an inordinate amount of money.*

inordinately [ɪ'nɔːrdnətlɪ] *adv*: *see* **inordinate** □ *He's never been inordinately ambitious.*

inorganic [,ɪnɔːr'gænɪk] *adj* [substance, matter, fertilizer] that is not made of organic material such as plants.

in-patient *n* a person staying in a hospital for treatment.

input ['ɪnpʊt] (*pt* & *pp* **input** OR **inputted**, *cont*

inputting) ◇ *n* **-1.** [of money, effort, resources] something that is added or given by somebody to something, e.g. a machine, project, or discussion, to help it to work better □ *I'd like to have some input at the planning stage.* **-2.** [of data] information that is put into a computer. **-3.** ELECTRICITY current that supplies a component or circuit. ◇ *vt* to put <data> into a computer, usually by typing it on a keyboard.

input/output *n* the data that passes into or out of a computer.

inquest ['ɪŋkwest] *n* an official inquiry to find out about the cause of somebody's death, especially when it is sudden or violent □ *An inquest is being held into her death.*

inquire [ɪn'kwaɪər] ◇ *vi* to ask for information □ *He telephoned to inquire about the latest prices.* ◇ *vt*: *She inquired when/whether/how they had arrived.*

♦ **inquire after** *vt fus* **to inquire after sb** to ask for news about sb.

♦ **inquire into** *vt fus* **to inquire into sthg** [crime, problem] to try to find out information about sthg by asking questions □ *Officials are inquiring into the causes of the disaster.*

inquiring [ɪn'kwaɪərɪŋ] *adj* **-1. an inquiring mind** a mind that is eager to learn about things. **-2. an inquiring look/tone etc** a look/tone etc that shows that one wants to know something.

inquiry [US 'ɪŋkwərɪ, GB ɪn'kwaɪrɪ] (*pl* **inquiries**) *n* **-1.** a question that one asks in order to get some information □ *I'd like to make an inquiry.* **-2.** an official investigation, e.g. into the causes of an accident □ *The relatives are calling for an official inquiry.*

inquisition [,ɪŋkwɪ'zɪʃn] *n* an attempt to find out information in which it seems that the people being questioned are being treated harshly.

♦ **Inquisition** *n* **the Inquisition** an organization created by the Roman Catholic Church (1232–1820) to find and punish people whose beliefs were not approved of by the Church.

inquisitive [ɪn'kwɪzətɪv] *adj* [person] who wants to find things out, especially about other people, and so asks a lot of questions □ *She was an inquisitive little girl.*

inroads ['ɪnroʊdz] *npl* **to make inroads into sthg** [into leisure hours, time] to begin to use up or take away large amounts of sthg □ *We are now making inroads into foreign markets.*

insane [ɪn'seɪn] ◇ *adj* **-1.** MEDICINE [person] who is severely mentally ill. **-2.** [jealousy, behavior] that one thinks is very foolish or stupid □ *I think it's an insane idea.* ◇ *npl* **the insane** MEDICINE people who are insane.

insanitary [US ɪn'sænəterɪ, GB -tərɪ] *adj* [housing, conditions] that is dirty and dangerous to people's health.

insanity [ɪn'sænətɪ] *n*: *see* **insane** □ *He was acquitted on the grounds of insanity.* □ *It's sheer insanity to lend them all that money!*

insatiable [ɪn'seɪʃəbl] *adj* [appetite, curiosity, person] that cannot be satisfied □ *Jan's insatiable appetite for gossip.*

inscribe [ɪnˈskraɪb] *vt* **-1.** [plaque, headstone] to cut a word, message etc into the surface of <sthg> □ *He inscribed her name on the ring.* □ *The cigar case was inscribed with his name.* **-2.** [name, message] to write <sthg> at the front of a book.

inscription [ɪnˈskrɪpʃn] *n* [on a headstone, ring, in a book] something, e.g. a message or name, that has been inscribed □ *Would you like an inscription?*

inscrutable [ɪnˈskruːtəbl] *adj* [person] whose face shows no emotion, so that it is impossible or difficult to know what they are thinking □ *his inscrutable manner/expression.*

insect [ˈɪnsekt] *n* a very small creature with six legs, e.g. a fly, beetle, or ant.

insect bite *n* a bite from an insect; a mark or wound caused by such a bite.

insecticide [ɪnˈsektɪsaɪd] *n* a chemical substance used for killing insects.

insect repellent *n* a chemical substance used to keep insects away.

insecure [ˌɪnsɪˈkjʊəʳ] *adj* **-1.** [person] who is not confident about their ability to deal with a particular situation or about the opinion other people have of them □ *a shy and insecure child* □ *I felt very insecure after two months without a job.* **-2.** [wall, structure] that is likely to collapse. **-3.** [investment, job] that is likely to be lost □ *The financial future of the company looks rather insecure.*

insecurity [ˌɪnsɪˈkjʊərətɪ] *n* [of a person, job, situation] *see* **insecure** □ *His feelings of insecurity go back to his childhood fears of rejection.*

insensitive [ɪnˈsensətɪv] *adj* **-1.** [person, remark, behavior] that does not consider other people's feelings and so is likely to upset them □ *Mark can be a little insensitive at times.* **-2. to be insensitive to sthg** [to somebody's feelings] to pay no attention to sthg; to not respond to sthg □ *She accused me of being insensitive to her needs/problems.*

insensitivity [ɪnˌsensəˈtɪvətɪ] *n*: *see* **insensitive**.

inseparable [ɪnˈsepərəbl] *adj* **-1.** [ideas, parts] that are very closely connected or impossible to separate □ *The two issues are inseparable.* □ *The future of the party is inseparable from the issue of proportional representation.* **-2.** [friends, couple] who are very close and spend a lot of time together □ *Sam and Kate are inseparable.*

insert [*vb* ɪnˈsɜːʳt, *n* ˈɪnsɜːʳt] ◇ *vt* **-1.** [key, finger, coin] to put <sthg> inside something else through a narrow space □ *Insert your card in* OR *into the machine.* **-2.** [note, comment, paragraph] to add <sthg> to a piece of writing □ *She inserted a few extra points in* OR *into her speech.* ◇ *n* something, e.g. an advertisement, on a loose piece of paper that is put between the pages of a book or magazine.

insertion [ɪnˈsɜːʳʃn] *n* **-1.** [of a coin, paragraph] *see* **insert**. **-2.** something that is inserted, e.g. an advertisement or announcement in a newspaper □ *a last-minute insertion.*

in-service training *n* training that is given to people to improve their skills in the job they are doing.

inset [ˈɪnset] *n* a small map or diagram that is printed inside a larger one.

inshore [*adj* ˈɪnʃɔːʳ, *adv* ɪnˈʃɔːʳ] ◇ *adj* **inshore waters/fishing etc** waters/fishing etc near the shore. ◇ *adv* [sail, swim, row] toward the shore.

inside [ɪnˈsaɪd] ◇ *adv* **-1. to be/look inside** to be/look in the part of an object or container that is enclosed or hidden □ *The jacket had a label inside.* **-2. to go/step inside** to go/step into a room or building from somewhere outside □ *Come inside and get warm!*
◇ *adj* **-1.** [pocket] that cannot be seen from the outside. **-2.** [toilet] that is in a house rather than outside it.
◇ *n* **-1. the inside** [of a house, room] the part that is enclosed by sides, walls etc; [of a piece of clothing] the part that cannot be seen from the outside □ *The door was locked from the inside.* □ *The inside of the cave was damp and dark.* **-2. the inside** AUTO the side of a car that is furthest from the middle of the road □ *A truck overtook him on the inside.*
◇ *prep* **-1. inside the box/envelope** in the box/envelope and completely hidden or enclosed by it (used of containers) □ *There was a letter inside the birthday card.* □ *I left it inside my jacket pocket.* ■ **inside the room/building/ town** in the room/building/town (used when one is coming to or viewing a place from the outside) □ *It was raining, so we went inside the house.* □ *He was parachuted inside enemy territory.* **-2. inside the organization** among the people working in the organization □ *Despite the company's successful results, morale inside Acme is low.* **-3. inside an hour/three weeks** before an hour is over/three weeks are over □ *We should be with you inside a couple of hours.*
◆ **insides** *npl* **one's insides** the organs in one's body, especially one's stomach or intestines (informal use) □ *Instant coffee can do terrible things to your insides.*
◆ **inside of** *prep* = **inside**.
◆ **inside out** *adv* **to be inside out** [clothes] to have the part that is usually on the inside facing outside □ *Your sweater's on inside out!* ■ **to know sthg inside out** to have a thorough knowledge of sthg □ *She knows her job inside out.*

inside information *n* information about something, e.g. a project or organization, that only somebody who is part of it has □ *Police believe the criminals must have had inside information.*

inside job *n* a crime committed against a group or organization by somebody who is connected with it □ *It looks like an inside job.*

inside lane *n* **-1.** the lane on a large road that is nearest to the side of the road □ *We were driving in the inside lane.* **-2.** the part of a racing track that is nearest to the center.

insider [ˌɪnˈsaɪdəʳ] *n* a person who belongs to a particular organization or who is involved in a particular project and knows more about it than most people.

insider dealing, insider trading *n* the illegal practice of buying and selling shares in a company when one has inside information about the company's plans □ *accusations of insider dealing.*

inside story *n* a version of events told by somebody who knows what really happened □ *I'd like to hear the inside story.*

insidious [ın'sıdıəs] *adj* [change, trend, process] that develops so gradually that people do not notice, and later causes undesirable results □ *the insidious nature of the disease.*

insight ['ınsaıt] *n* -1. the ability to understand the nature of something clearly, especially something complicated or difficult □ *The book shows remarkable insight into the problem.* -2. a sudden understanding □ *I was able to gain an insight into her real character.*

insignia [ın'sıgnıə] (*pl* **insignia**) *n* a badge or sign that shows that a person or vehicle belongs to a particular organization, especially one that is military.

insignificance [,ınsıg'nıfıkəns] *n: see* **insignificant.**

insignificant [,ınsıg'nıfıkənt] *adj* [person, fact, amount] that is not very noticeable or has very little importance □ *My own troubles seem insignificant when I think about what some people are going through.*

insincere [,ınsın'sıəʳ] *adj* [person, smile, remark] that seems to be friendly, kind etc but is not □ *Her apology sounded insincere.*

insincerity [,ınsın'serətı] *n: see* **insincere.**

insinuate [ın'sınjueıt] *vt* **to insinuate (that)** ... to indirectly suggest that something unpleasant is true (disapproving use) □ *Are you insinuating that it's my fault?* □ *What are you trying to insinuate?*

insinuation [ın,sınju'eıʃn] *n* a spoken or written statement, comment etc that insinuates something; the use of such statements, comments etc to insinuate something (disapproving use) □ *I've had enough of your insinuations.* □ *a campaign of lies and insinuation.*

insipid [ın'sıpəd] *adj* -1. [person, color, music] dull and boring (disapproving use) □ *insipid conversation.* -2. [food, drink] that does not have a strong enough taste.

insist [ın'sıst] ◇ *vt* -1. **to insist (that)**... to state firmly that something is true, especially when other people disagree with one □ *She insisted that he had been with her all evening.* -2. **to insist (that)**... to state firmly that one wants somebody to do something or wants something to happen □ *I insist (that) you go to see a doctor.* ◇ *vi* to state firmly that one wants somebody to do something or wants something to happen □ *Oh, very well, if you insist!* ■ **to insist on sthg** to demand sthg □ *I insist on the best from my employees.* □ *She insisted on coming.*

insistence [ın'sıstəns] *n* the act of insisting on something □ *I came at his insistence.* □ *their insistence on absolute secrecy.*

insistent [ın'sıstənt] *adj* -1. **to be insistent** to keep stating very firmly that somebody should do something □ *I tried to get out of going, but they were most insistent.* □ *David was insistent that we all wear fancy dress.* -2. [noise] that constantly or continually demands one's attention □ *I could no longer ignore his insistent banging at the door.*

in situ [US ın'saıtuː, GB -'sıtjuː] *adv* [repair, inspect] in the place where a particular thing is, without moving it (formal use).

insofar [,ınsou'fɑːʳ] ◆ **insofar as** *conj* to the extent that □ *The accident was not serious insofar as nobody was killed.*

insole ['ınsoul] *n* a piece of flat material shaped like the sole of a foot that is fitted inside a shoe to make it more comfortable.

insolence ['ınsələns] *n: see* **insolent.**

insolent ['ınsələnt] *adj* [child, remark, tone] that is rude and does not show the proper respect for somebody in authority.

insoluble [ın'sɒljəbl] *adj* -1. [problem, crime] that cannot be solved □ *It's a difficult situation but not an insoluble one.* -2. [substance] that cannot be dissolved.

insolvable [ın'sɒlvəbl] *adj* US [problem, crime] = **insoluble.**

insolvency [ın'sɒlvənsı] *n: see* **insolvent.**

insolvent [ın'sɒlvənt] *adj* [person, bank, company] that does not have enough money to pay their debts □ *The company was declared insolvent.*

insomnia [ın'sɒmnıə] *n* inability to sleep □ *Do you suffer from insomnia?*

insomniac [ın'sɒmnıæk] *n* a person who suffers from insomnia.

insomuch [,ınsə'mʌtʃ] ◆ **insomuch as** *conj* = **inasmuch as.**

inspect [ın'spekt] *vt* -1. to examine <sthg> in detail to find out what it is like or to check that it is the way one wants it to be □ *I went up on the roof to inspect the damage.* -2. to visit <a place, organization> etc officially to check that no rules are being broken or that it is of a certain standard □ *The kitchens are regularly inspected.*

inspection [ın'spekʃn] *n* -1. an official visit made to a place, organization etc in order to check that no rules are being broken or that it is of a certain standard □ *An inspection will be carried out at 9 am.* □ *The school is due for an inspection.* -2. a detailed examination of something □ *On closer inspection, the fuel pump was found to be leaking.*

inspector [ın'spektəʳ] *n* -1. a person whose job is to inspect things, e.g. schools, factories, or people's tickets on buses □ *a health and safety inspector* □ *a school inspector.* -2. a police officer of middle rank.

inspector of taxes *n* GB a government official whose job is to calculate how much tax people should pay.

inspiration [,ınspə'reıʃn] *n* -1. the enthusiastic feeling that makes one want to do something, especially something creative; something or somebody that gives one this feeling □ *She gets her inspiration from desert land-scapes.* □ *The riots were the inspiration for the novel.* **-2.** a sudden good idea that one has □ *I had an inspiration!*

inspire [ɪn'spaɪəʳ] *vt* **-1.** to give <sb> the enthusiasm or idea that causes them to do something □ *She was inspired by her experiences to become a doctor.* **-2. to inspire sb with sthg, to inspire sthg in sb** [passion, enthusiasm] to fill sb with sthg □ *Their past record doesn't exactly inspire confidence.*

inspired [ɪn'spaɪəʳd] *adj* [artist, performance] that is very good and impressive □ *a superb and truly inspired piece of writing* □ *It was an inspired guess.*

inspiring [ɪn'spaɪərɪŋ] *adj* [music, book, example] that makes one feel interested and enthusiastic □ *I'm afraid the conference wasn't very inspiring.*

instability [ˌɪnstə'bɪlətɪ] *n* lack of stability.

install [ɪn'stɔːl] *vt* **-1.** [computer, heating, telephone line] to put <sthg> in a place and connect it so that it is ready to be used □ *We're having central heating installed.* **-2.** to give <sb> a new position or job officially □ *Once you're installed in your new job, we'll come and visit.* **-3.** to put <sb> in a place so that they are comfortable and can stay there for a long time □ *She installed herself in front of the fire.* □ *My family is now installed in Hong Kong.*

installation [ˌɪnstə'leɪʃn] *n* **-1.** [for a particular activity] a base or site containing equipment and personnel for a particular purpose □ *a military/gas/nuclear installation.* **-2.** [of software, heating] *see* **install**.

installment US, **instalment** GB [ɪn'stɔːlmənt] *n* **-1.** FINANCE one of a series of regular payments that are made over an agreed period of time until the cost of something is covered completely □ *He paid for the car in monthly installments.* **-2.** [of a story, TV program, radio program] an episode □ *Tune in on Monday for the next exciting installment.*

installment plan *n* US a system of buying something by paying for it gradually □ *Do you offer installment plans?*

instance ['ɪnstəns] *n* an example of a particular situation □ *Instances of violent crime are rare in this area.* ■ **in the first instance** as the first of a series of actions (formal use).

◆ **for instance** *adv* a phrase used to introduce an example of what one has just mentioned □ *You could always take up a sport — golf, for instance.*

instant ['ɪnstənt] ◇ *adj* **-1.** [success, dislike] immediate □ *You can't expect instant results.* **-2. instant coffee/soup etc** coffee/soup etc that is in the form of a powder and can be prepared very quickly and easily, usually by adding boiling water. ◇ *n* a moment □ *I'll be with you in an instant.* ■ **the instant** as soon as □ *Call me the instant (that) you arrive.* ■ **at that** OR **the same instant** at exactly the same time □ *At that instant the lights went out.* ■ **this instant** at once □ *Do it this instant!*

instantaneous [ˌɪnstən'teɪnjəs] *adj* [death, reac-

tion] that happens at once □ *There was instantaneous applause.*

instantly ['ɪnstəntlɪ] *adv* immediately after something else, and often as a result of it □ *He was killed instantly when his car hit a tree.*

instant replay *n* US a slow replay of part of a sports event on television.

instead [ɪn'sted] *adv* as an alternative □ *The trains were on strike so I drove instead.*

◆ **instead of** *prep* in the place of <sthg>; as an alternative to <sthg> □ *I had an apple instead of lunch.* □ *You can have cheese instead of dessert if you prefer.*

instep ['ɪnstep] *n* the middle part of the top of one's foot, between the toes and the ankle.

instigate ['ɪnstɪgeɪt] *vt* [discussion, meeting, investigation] to make <sthg> begin to happen □ *Who instigated the argument?*

instigation [ˌɪnstɪ'geɪʃn] *n* **at sb's instigation** because sb has suggested or demanded that it happen □ *A public inquiry was held at the instigation of the Attorney General.*

instigator ['ɪnstɪgeɪtəʳ] *n* the person who instigates something.

instill US, **instil** GB [ɪn'stɪl] (*pt* & *pp* **instilled**, *cont* **instilling**) *vt* **to instill sthg in** OR **into sb** [loyalty, sense of duty, fear] to cause sb to have an idea or feeling by teaching it to them or treating them in a particular way over a period of time □ *She had instilled a strong sense of justice in her family.*

instinct ['ɪnstɪŋkt] *n* **-1.** a natural tendency to react in a particular way in particular situations without thinking about it □ *The fox finds its prey by instinct.* □ *the maternal/survival/killer instinct.* **-2.** one's natural reaction to a particular situation □ *My first instinct was to tell him the truth.*

instinctive [ɪn'stɪŋktɪv] *adj* [distrust, reaction, dislike] that is caused by instinct □ *I took an instinctive dislike to him.*

instinctively [ɪn'stɪŋktɪvlɪ] *adv* [know, react, dislike] *see* **instinctive** □ *I felt instinctively that something was wrong.*

institute ['ɪnstɪtjuːt] ◇ *n* an organization formed to do a particular type of work, especially for the purpose of education or research; the building used by such an organization □ *the Massachusetts Institute of Technology.* ◇ *vt* to start <a system, rule, legal process> etc □ *The government has instituted a series of reforms.*

institution [ˌɪnstɪ'tjuːʃn] *n* **-1.** a very old custom or tradition that is accepted by most people □ *the institution of marriage.* **-2.** a large and important organization that has existed for a long time, e.g. a university or bank □ *educational/financial institutions.* **-3.** a place where people, such as old or mentally ill people, are kept and taken care of □ *They've put her in an institution.*

institutional [ˌɪnstɪ'tjuːʃnəl] *adj* [reform, care, food] that is connected with an institution.

institutionalized, -ised [ˌɪnstɪ'tjuːʃnəlaɪzd] *adj* **-1.** [person] who has become too dependent on the care of an institution, e.g. a mental hospital □ *Such patients run the risk of becoming institutionalized.* **-2.** [custom, tradition] that has become an accepted part of life in a particular society or organization □ *institutionalized sexism/racism.*

instruct [ɪn'strʌkt] *vt* **-1. to instruct sb to do sthg** to tell sb to do sthg officially □ *We've been instructed to let no one into the building.* **-2. to instruct sb in sthg** to teach sb sthg □ *She instructs people in the art of flower arranging.*

instruction [ɪn'strʌkʃn] *n* **-1.** an order □ *She gave instructions for the papers to be destroyed.* **-2.** teaching □ *'Driver under instruction.'*

◆ **instructions** *npl* a list of details of how to do or use something □ *Read the instructions on the back of the packet.*

instruction manual *n* a book giving details of how something works and how to use it.

instructive [ɪn'strʌktɪv] *adj* [experience, book, talk] that gives one useful information □ *The whole experience was highly instructive.*

instructor [ɪn'strʌktər] *n* **-1.** a teacher of an activity □ *a ski/driving instructor.* **-2.** US EDUCATION a teacher at a college.

instrument ['ɪnstrəmənt] *n* **-1.** a tool or device that is often made up of a number of small delicate parts and used for purposes where accuracy is important, e.g. in medicine or science □ *A thermometer is an instrument for measuring temperature.* **-2.** = **musical instrument.** **-3.** [person, thing] something or somebody that is used to achieve a particular aim (literary use).

instrumental [ˌɪnstrə'mentl] ◇ *adj* **-1. to be instrumental in doing sthg** to have an important and helpful role in making sthg happen □ *She/Her work was instrumental in reforming the profession.* **-2.** [music] that is written for or played on instruments rather than intended to be sung. ◇ *n* MUSIC a piece of instrumental music.

instrumentalist [ˌɪnstrə'mentəlɪst] *n* MUSIC a person who plays a musical instrument.

instrument panel *n* the panel in a car, aircraft, or motor boat containing the speedometer and other dials and switches.

insubordinate [ˌɪnsə'bɔːrdnət] *adj* [person, behavior] that is rude and disobedient, usually to somebody of higher rank (formal use).

insubordination [ˌɪnsəbɔːrdə'neɪʃn] *n* behavior that is insubordinate (formal use).

insubstantial [ˌɪnsəb'stænʃl] *adj* **-1.** [structure, frame] that is not very big, strong, or solid. **-2.** [meal, book] that is not very satisfying □ *a good, if rather insubstantial, first novel.*

insufferable [ɪn'sʌfərəbl] *adj* [person, rudeness, arrogance] that one finds annoying and cannot tolerate □ *He's an insufferable bore!*

insufficient [ˌɪnsə'fɪʃnt] *adj* [evidence, research, interest] that is not enough □ *The course had to be canceled due to insufficient numbers.*

insular ['ɪnsjələr] *adj* [person] who is not interested in finding out about other places or other ways of life different from their own (disapproving use) □ *an insular outlook.*

insulate ['ɪnsjəleɪt] *vt* **-1.** [loft, tank, wall] to pre-vent heat, sound etc from passing through <sthg> by covering it with a special material. **-2.** [person] to keep <sb> away from situations, experiences, or knowledge that might frighten or upset them □ *As a child, I was insulated against/from the harsh realities of life.* **-3.** [cable, wire, tool] to cover <sthg> with material that does not conduct electricity, in order to make it safe to use.

insulating tape ['ɪnsjəleɪtɪŋ-] *n* plastic tape that is wrapped around electrical wiring to insulate it and make it safe to use.

insulation [ˌɪnsjə'leɪʃn] *n* any thick soft material such as foam that is put on the inside of a wall, roof, or door to stop heat or noise from escaping from a room or building.

insulin ['ɪnsjəlɪn] *n* a substance produced in the body that helps to turn sugar into energy, and sometimes needs to be injected if a person is diabetic.

insult [*vt* ɪn'sʌlt, *n* 'ɪnsʌlt] ◇ *vt* to say or do something that offends <sb> personally □ *I've never been so insulted in all my life!* ◇ *n* something that somebody says or does that offends somebody personally □ *The suggestion is an insult to our good name.* □ *The latest pay offer was described as "an insult".* ■ **to add insult to injury** a phrase used to refer to something that makes an upsetting or annoying situation even worse □ *He just walked out of the restaurant, and to add insult to injury, I had to pay the bill!*

insulting [ɪn'sʌltɪŋ] *adj* [gesture, remark] that insults somebody □ *I consider this advert insulting to women.*

insuperable [ɪn'suːprəbl] *adj* [obstacle, problem] that cannot be overcome (formal use).

insurance [ɪn'ʃʊərəns] *n* **-1.** FINANCE an arrangement in which a person makes fixed payments to a company which agrees to pay the costs which that person might have in the future because of an illness, accident, fire, theft etc □ *We've taken out insurance against fire* OR *fire insurance.* □ *an insurance plan/company.* **-2.** an action or plan that is supposed to prevent something unwanted from happening □ *The deposit is an insurance against tenants leaving without paying.*

insurance adjuster *n* US a person whose job is to calculate how much insurance should be paid for a particular claim.

insurance broker *n* a person who works as an agent for an insurance company and sells the services of the company to new clients.

insurance policy *n* a document that states the terms of an agreement between an insurance company and a client.

insurance premium *n* an amount of money paid regularly by a client to an insurance company.

insure [ɪn'ʃʊər] ◇ *vt* **-1.** FINANCE [car, house, life] to provide insurance for <sb/sthg> □ *I hope you've insured your equipment against theft.* □ *The painting has been insured for $20 million.* **-2.** US [safety, success, outcome] to make <sthg> certain □ *We try to insure that all our* *passengers have a safe and comfortable trip.* ◇ *vi* **to insure against sthg** to do what is possible in order to prevent sthg from happening.

insured [ɪn'ʃʊərd] ◇ *adj* **-1.** FINANCE [person, car, house] that is protected by insurance ◻ *Are you insured against* OR *for theft?* **-2.** US [safety, success] that is certain. ◇ *n* **the insured** FINANCE the person or people insured by an insurance company.

insurer [ɪn'ʃʊərər] *n* a company that provides insurance.

insurgent [ɪn'sɜːrdʒənt] *n* a person who fights against the government of their country.

insurmountable [ˌɪnsər'maʊntəbl] *adj* [obstacle, problem, difficulty] that cannot be overcome ◻ *None of these problems is insurmountable.*

insurrection [ˌɪnsə'rekʃn] *n* an attempt by a group of people in a country to remove the government from power by using violence ◻ *an armed insurrection.*

intact [ɪn'tækt] *adj* **to be intact** [collection, reputation] that is not damaged or broken in any way despite bad conditions or rough treatment ◻ *Few houses were left intact by the bombing.*

intake ['ɪnteɪk] *n* **-1.** [of food, drink] the amount of food or drink that a person takes into their body during a certain period of time ◻ *You should cut down on your alcohol intake.* **-2.** [of students, recruits] the number of people who join an institution or organization at a particular period of time ◻ *We have had to reduce this year's intake of students.* **-3.** [for water, fuel] a space where air, water, or fuel passes into a tube, pipe, or container ◻ *The fuel intake is blocked.*

intangible [ɪn'tændʒəbl] *adj* [quality, feeling, idea] that one knows exists but is unable to identify exactly or explain ◻ *Love is something intangible.*

integral ['ɪntɪgrəl] *adj* [part, feature] that is an essential part of something larger ◻ *Developing new strategies is integral to my role as marketing director.* ◻ *a house with integral garage.*

integrate ['ɪntəgreɪt] ◇ *vi* [person] to enter a society or group of people and become part of it, often by adapting to their way of life, habits, customs etc ◻ *They have not yet fully integrated into the community.* ◻ *She's had problems integrating with other pupils.*
◇ *vt* **-1. to be integrated into sthg** [into a society, country, school] to mix with and join a group of people who are different ◻ *It is difficult for these children to integrate into normal family life.* **-2.** [school, university] to allow all races or groups to use <an institution> ◻ *They tried to integrate all inner-city schools.* **-3.** [system, process, activity] to make <sthg> part of something else ◻ *It's important to integrate some fun with* OR *into the class work.* ◻ *We've decided to integrate the packing and dispatch departments.*

integrated ['ɪntəgreɪtəd] *adj* [school, society] that has a mixture of people from different social or racial groups.

integrated circuit *n* a very small electronic

circuit contained on a single piece of semiconductor material, usually silicon.

integration [ˌɪntə'greɪʃn] *n: see* **integrate** ◻ *They voted in favor of closer European integration.*

integrity [ɪn'tegrətɪ] *n* **-1.** [of a person] the quality of being honest and having moral principles ◻ *a woman of great integrity* ◻ *I have no doubts about his integrity.* **-2.** [of a nation, society] the state of being whole and united (formal use) ◻ *The treaty reaffirms the integrity of our borders.*

intellect ['ɪntəlekt] *n* **-1.** the ability to think and reason ◻ *The children are taught to use their intellect.* **-2.** high intelligence ◻ *It's easy to understand for a man of your intellect.* **-3.** a very intelligent person ◻ *one of France's greatest intellects.*

intellectual [ˌɪntə'lektʃuəl] ◇ *adj* **-1.** [topic, discussion] that requires the use of the mind, usually in a complex way ◻ *intellectual stimulation.* **-2.** [person] who is well educated and often uses their ability to think and reason in complex ways, especially in work or study ◻ *She has an intellectual approach to theater.* ◇ *n* an intellectual person ◻ *He's a real intellectual.*

intellectualize, -ise [ˌɪntə'lektʃuəlaɪz] *vt* [subject, problem] to think about <sthg> in a rational way and without considering emotions ◻ *She has a tendency to intellectualize everything.*

intelligence [ɪn'telɪdʒəns] *n* **-1.** [of a person] the ability to think clearly, solve problems, and understand things ◻ *He hasn't much intelligence.* **-2.** [of a country, army] a government department in charge of spying on enemy countries or organizations; the information gathered by such a department ◻ *He worked for military intelligence.* ◻ *an intelligence-gathering organization/operation* ◻ *the intelligence services.*

intelligence quotient *n* → IQ.

intelligence test *n* a test designed to find out the level of somebody's intelligence.

intelligent [ɪn'telɪdʒənt] *adj* **-1.** [person, animal] that has a high level of intelligence; [question, answer, idea] that shows a high level of intelligence ◻ *She's a highly intelligent child.* ◻ *That wasn't very intelligent of him, was it!* **-2.** COMPUTING [device, terminal] that can run a program by using simple reasoning to make decisions.

intelligentsia [ɪn,telɪ'dʒentsɪə] *n* **the intelligentsia** the well-educated people of a country or society, such as writers and scientists.

intelligible [ɪn'telɪdʒəbl] *adj* [writing, speech, report] that can be understood ◻ *The phone line was so bad his voice was barely intelligible.*

intemperate [ɪn'tempərət] *adj* **-1.** [person] who drinks too much alcohol (formal use). **-2.** [behavior, haste] that is too extreme and not controlled (formal use) ◻ *I must apologize for my intemperate language.* **-3.** [climate] that has extreme temperatures.

intend [ɪn'tend] *vt* **-1.** to have <sthg> in one's mind as a plan ◻ *We intend to increase our sales.* ◻ *I intend telling her what I really think.* ◻ *His statement was intended to mislead people.*

-2. to have a particular purpose in mind for <sthg> □ *This book is intended for the children's market.* □ *It was intended as a joke.*

intended [ɪnˈtendəd] *adj* [result] planned; [meaning] that is meant □ *Sorry, no pun intended.*

intense [ɪnˈtens] *adj* **-1.** [competition, concentration, activity] that involves a lot of effort □ *The battle for first place is becoming increasingly intense.* **-2.** [color, light] that is very bright or deep □ *an intense shade of blue.* **-3.** [heat, pain, emotion] that is very strong □ *He felt intense hatred toward her.* **-4.** [person] who has strong feelings or opinions and expresses them in a serious way □ *a very intense young man* □ *an intense look/stare.*

intensely [ɪnˈtenslɪ] *adv* **-1. intensely painful/boring etc** very painful/boring etc □ *She was intensely suspicious of everyone.* **-2.** [feel, dislike] deeply □ *He was concentrating intensely.*

intensify [ɪnˈtensəfaɪ] (*pt* & *pp* **intensified**) ◇ *vt* [efforts, activities, attacks] to increase <sthg>; [impression, feeling] to make <sthg> stronger □ *Military commanders agreed to intensify the bombing campaign.* ◇ *vi*: *Fighting has intensified in the last few days.* □ *As we traveled further north, the cold intensified.*

intensity [ɪnˈtensətɪ] *n*: *see* **intense** □ *He was surprised by the intensity of the public's interest.*

intensive [ɪnˈtensɪv] *adj* [training, course] that involves a lot of work, activity etc in a short time □ *a period of intensive study.*

-intensive *suffix* added to words to show that a large amount of a particular thing is involved □ *labor-intensive* □ *capital-intensive.*

intensive care *n* a form of hospital treatment for people who are seriously ill, involving many nurses, special equipment, and constant supervision □ *He's still in intensive care* □ *The intensive care unit.*

intent [ɪnˈtent] ◇ *adj* **-1.** [face, look] that is full of concentration. **-2. to be intent on** OR **upon doing sthg** to be very determined to do sthg □ *He's intent on* OR *upon spoiling the evening.* ◇ *n* an intention □ *That was not my intent.*

♦ to all intents and purposes *adv* in nearly every way □ *The campaign is, to all intents and purposes, over.*

intention [ɪnˈtenʃn] *n* a desire and plan to do something □ *I have no intention of resigning.* □ *They bought it with the intention of selling it later on for a profit.* □ *It was always my intention to replace it.* □ *I'm sorry if I sounded critical, that was not my intention.*

intentional [ɪnˈtenʃnəl] *adj* [insult, similarity] that is planned and deliberate □ *The omission of your name was not intentional.*

intentionally [ɪnˈtenʃnəlɪ] *adv* [insult, omit] *see* **intentional** □ *I didn't kick him intentionally.* □ *She was intentionally rude to me.*

intently [ɪnˈtentlɪ] *adv* [watch, study, listen] with a lot of concentration and interest □ *He was staring at me intently.*

inter [ɪnˈtɜːr] (*pt* & *pp* **interred**, *cont* **interring**) *vt* to bury <sb> (formal use).

interact [ˌɪntərˈækt] *vi* **-1.** [people] to talk with each other and do things together □ *She*

interacts very well with other children of her age. **-2.** [forces, ideas] to have an influence on each other.

interaction [ˌɪntərˈækʃn] *n* [of people, forces, ideas] *see* **interact** □ *social interaction.*

interactive [ˌɪntərˈæktɪv] *adj* [program, software, video] that makes it possible for a computer and its user to exchange information □ *an interactive CD-ROM/encyclopedia.*

intercede [ˌɪntərˈsiːd] *vi* to speak to somebody in order to represent or defend somebody else (formal use) □ *Mr Goldberg is set to intercede on behalf of the US hostages.*

intercept [ˌɪntərˈsept] *vt* [thief, message, missile] to find and stop <sb/sthg that is going from one place to another> □ *The drugs were intercepted at the border.*

interchange [*n* ˈɪntərˌtʃeɪndʒ, *vb* ˌɪntərˈtʃeɪndʒ] ◇ *n* **-1.** [of ideas, staff, information] an exchange. **-2.** TRANSPORT a group of small roads that connect two or more larger roads □ *Get off at the next interchange, and take the State Route 62.* ◇ *vt* to cause <people or things> to change places with each other □ *The suit has a skirt and trousers, which means you can interchange the two.*

interchangeable [ˌɪntərˈtʃeɪndʒəbl] *adj* [parts, people, terms] that can be interchanged with each other without making any difference □ *"Nobody" is interchangeable with "no one".* □ *This food processor has several interchangeable graters.*

intercity [ˌɪntərˈsɪtɪ] ◇ *adj* [train, bus] that provides fast direct transport from one city to another without stopping at many stations. ◇ *n* an intercity train or bus.

intercom [ˈɪntərkɒm] *n* a machine that people speak into, in order to communicate with people in a different part of a building □ *The message came through* OR *over the intercom.* □ *an intercom system.*

interconnect [ˌɪntərkəˈnekt] *vi* [systems, buildings] to be connected with each other.

interconnecting [ˌɪntərkəˈnektɪŋ] *adj* [rooms, wires] that are joined to each other.

intercontinental [ˌɪntərkɒntəˈnentl] *adj* [trade] that takes place between two or more continents; [flight] from one continent to another □ *the intercontinental movement of goods* □ *an intercontinental trip.*

intercontinental ballistic missile *n* a missile that can be fired a long distance from one part of the world to another.

intercourse [ˈɪntərkɔːrs] *n* = **sexual intercourse.**

interdenominational [ˌɪntərdɪnɒməˈneɪʃnəl] *adj* RELIGION [service, conference] that involves different religious groups.

interdepartmental [ˌɪntərdiːpɑːrtˈmentl] *adj* [report, meeting, conflict] between departments of a company, institution, or organization.

interdependent [ˌɪntərdɪˈpendənt] *adj* [departments, systems, countries] that are closely connected and dependent on each other □ *Man and nature are interdependent.*

interdict [ˈɪntərdɪkt] *n* **-1.** LAW an order that forbids something. **-2.** RELIGION in the Roman

Catholic Church, a punishment that forbids a person or group of people from taking part in important ceremonies, e.g. baptism.

interest ['ɪntrəst] ⋄ *n* -1. [in somebody or something] the desire to know about or be involved with something or somebody □ *He's lost interest in his work.* □ *The show was canceled through lack of interest.* -2. [outside of work] a thing that one gives time and attention to because it is enjoyable □ *My main interests are squash, golf, and motor racing.* -3. **to be of interest** to have a quality that makes one want to give one's time and attention □ *There's nothing of interest in the report.* □ *Politics holds no interest for me.* -4. **to be in sb's interest(s)** to give a possible advantage to sb □ *It's in your interest to apply.* ■ **in the interests of sthg** in order to help sthg; in order to achieve sthg □ *The government censored the book in the interests of national security.* □ *In the interests of hygiene, please wash your hands.* -5. FINANCE the money that somebody pays as a charge for borrowing money; the money that somebody earns when they invest money in something □ *I paid back the money with interest.* □ *Interest on the loan is charged at 12%.* □ *I'm paying 10% interest.* □ *Why don't you transfer your savings to a high-interest account?* -6. BUSINESS a financial share in a company or business activity □ *I have a 40% interest in the company.* □ *a financial interest.*
⋄ *vt* -1. to make <sb> feel interested □ *Football just doesn't interest me.* -2. **to interest sb in sthg** to persuade sb to do or buy sthg □ *Can I interest you in a drink/in coming out to lunch?*

interested ['ɪntrəstəd] *adj* -1. [person] who wants to know about or be involved with somebody or something □ *Would you be interested in this job/in meeting him?* □ *Sorry, I'm not interested.* -2. **an interested party/group** a person/group that is affected by something □ *Developers will be contacting all interested parties to discuss their plans.*

interest-free *adj* [loan, credit] that is given without any interest being charged □ *We offer six months' interest-free credit on any purchase over $500.*

interesting ['ɪntrəstɪŋ] *adj* [person, idea, question] that attracts and holds one's attention □ *That sounds interesting; let's try it!* □ *I'm reading a very interesting book.* □ *It's interesting that you should mention her name.* □ *That's interesting, that's not what she told me!*

interest rate *n* the percentage that is used by a bank to calculate the interest charged on a loan □ *Interest rates have gone up again.*

interface [*n* 'ɪntərfeɪs, *vb* ˌɪntər'feɪs] ⋄ *n* -1. COMPUTING a device or system that enables two parts of a computer to communicate with each other and transfer information. -2. the point at which two separate things or groups of people meet and become connected in some way □ *the management-employee interface.* ⋄ *vt* COMPUTING to connect together <two or more devices, programs> etc that have different characteristics.

interfere [ˌɪntər'fɪər] *vi* -1. to become involved in and try to affect a situation that concerns other people and not oneself □ *I never interfere in their quarrels.* -2. to affect the progress of something in a bad way □ *It's interfering with her work.*

interference [ˌɪntər'fɪərəns] *n* -1. [in a situation, quarrel] *see* **interfere** □ *She won't tolerate interference in* OR *with her private life.* -2. TECHNOLOGY a buzzing or crackling sound on a radio caused by crossed radio signals □ *I can't hear it properly, there's a lot of interference.*

interfering [ˌɪntər'fɪərɪŋ] *adj* [person] who interferes in other people's affairs (disapproving use) □ *She's just an interfering old busybody.*

intergalactic [ˌɪntərgə'læktɪk] *adj* [space, mission] that travels between galaxies.

interim ['ɪntərɪm] *adj* **an interim government/report** a government/report that is not permanent but deals with a situation until something final or complete is ready.
◆ **in the interim** *adv* in the time between two events □ *In the interim, I have plenty to do.*

interior [ɪn'tɪərɪər] ⋄ *adj* -1. [wall, lining, space] that is on the inside of a building or vehicle □ *interior furnishings.* -2. POLITICS [minister, ministry] that relates to a country's own affairs and not to those of other countries. ■ **the (United States) Department of the Interior** the US government department responsible for the management of public land and natural resources, especially national parks. ⋄ *n* -1. [of a building, vehicle] the inside part of something □ *The car has a very comfortable interior.* -2. **the interior** the part of a country that is not near the ocean.

interior decorator *n* a person whose job is to paint and decorate houses, rooms etc.

interior designer *n* a person whose job is to decide the way that a house, room etc is decorated and furnished.

interject [ˌɪntər'dʒekt] (formal use) ⋄ *vt* to say <sthg> in the middle of what somebody else is saying. ⋄ *vi*: *I couldn't say a single sentence without somebody interjecting.*

interjection [ˌɪntər'dʒekʃn] *n* -1. a sudden remark that interrupts somebody else who is speaking □ *There were constant interjections from the audience.* -2. GRAMMAR a word or phrase that is used to express a strong feeling, e.g. "ouch!"

interlock [ˌɪntər'lɒk] ⋄ *vt* [wheels, gears, chairs] to join <things> together into a fixed position □ *She sat with her chin on her hands, and her fingers interlocked.* ⋄ *vi* [wheels, gears, chairs] *The different parts interlock with each other.* □ *a series of interlocking cogwheels.*

interloper ['ɪntərloʊpər] *n* a person who tries to become involved with other people's affairs or enters a place when they have no right to (formal use).

interlude ['ɪntərluːd] *n* -1. a short break in an activity or situation, when something different happens □ *At this point in the meeting there was a brief interlude while Frank went to make coffee.* -2. CINEMA & THEATER a break between two parts of a movie, play, or performance

□ *There will be a short interlude before Act 2.* **-3.** MUSIC a short piece of music between two parts of another performance □ *a musical interlude.*

intermarry [ˌɪntəˈmærɪ] (*pt* & *pp* **intermarried**) *vi* **-1.** [people] to marry people from their own family, tribe, race etc. **-2.** [tribes, races] to become connected by marriage.

intermediary [ˌɪntəˈmiːdjərɪ] (*pl* **intermediaries**) *n* a person who helps to solve a dispute by talking to the people involved □ *a government intermediary.*

intermediate [ˌɪntəˈmiːdjət] *adj* **-1. an intermediate stage** a stage that is between two other stages. **-2. an intermediate level** EDUCATION a level in between beginners' and advanced level □ *a class for intermediate students.*

interminable [ɪnˈtɜːrmɪnəbl] *adj* [trip, speech] that seems very long and boring □ *We had to sit listening to Dad's interminable war stories.*

intermingle [ˌɪntəˈmɪŋgl] *vi* [people] to mix with each other □ *The settlers rarely intermingled with members of the local population.*

intermission [ˌɪntəˈmɪʃn] *n* a short break between two parts of a movie, play etc.

intermittent [ˌɪntəˈmɪtənt] *adj* [noise, rain, pain] that is not constant, but stops and starts □ *The weather will be cloudy with intermittent showers.*

intern [*vb* ɪnˈtɜːrn, *n* ˈɪntɜːrn] ◇ *vt* [terrorist, criminal] to limit the freedom of <sb>, e.g. by putting them in prison, especially for political reasons □ *The men were interned in a prison camp.* ◇ *n* US a person who is going through the final stages of training as a doctor or teacher.

internal [ɪnˈtɜːrnl] *adj* **-1.** [injury, bleeding] that happens inside a person's body □ *internal organs.* **-2.** [wall, door] that exists inside a building. **-3.** [affairs, politics, flight] that is connected with or takes place in a particular country and does not involve other countries □ *The rebellion is described as a purely internal problem.* **-4.** [memo, inquiry, dispute] that exists or happens within an organization □ *The company is carrying out an internal investigation into the incident.*

internal-combustion engine *n* an engine that produces power by burning a mixture of fuel and air.

internally [ɪnˈtɜːrnəlɪ] *adv* [bleed, circulate] *see* **internal** □ *The job was advertised internally.*

Internal Revenue Service *n* → IRS.

international [ˌɪntəˈnæʃnəl] ◇ *adj* [agreement, community, law] that happens in or involves several countries in different parts of the world □ *He became an international star.* ◇ *n* SPORT a sports match, e.g. a soccer or rugby match, between the teams of two countries; a player who represents their country in such a match.

International Chamber of Commerce *n* **the International Chamber of Commerce** an international organization that aims to promote and protect its members' business interests.

international date line *n* **the international**

date line the imaginary line that runs from the North Pole to the South Pole, the date of countries to the west of it being one day ahead of countries to the east.

internationally [ˌɪntəˈnæʃnəlɪ] *adv* **internationally recognized/famous** recognized/famous in many different countries of the world □ *Internationally, the situation is improving.*

International Monetary Fund *n* **the International Monetary Fund** a UN organization whose role is to help world trade and countries that have financial problems.

international relations *npl* the way that different countries deal with each other.

internecine [US ˌɪntrˈniːsn, GB ˌɪntəˈniːsaɪn] *adj* [struggle, fighting] that happens within the same country or community □ *internecine warfare.*

internee [ˌɪntɜːrˈniː] *n* a prisoner, especially a political prisoner.

Internet [ˈɪntənet] *n* **the Internet** an international computer network, consisting of smaller linked networks, on which business, academic, and private users can have access to information and communicate with each other.

internist [ˈɪntənəst] *n* US a doctor who knows about general medical problems but does not perform operations.

internment [ɪnˈtɜːrnmənt] *n* [of a terrorist, criminal] *see* **intern** □ *an internment camp.*

interpersonal [ˌɪntəˈpɜːrsnəl] *adj* [skills, relationships] that involve communication with other people □ *Managers need to develop good interpersonal skills.*

interplay [ˈɪntəpleɪ] *n* the way that people or things react and affect each other □ *the interplay between social and political factors.*

Interpol [US ˈɪntrpoʊl, GB ˈɪntəpɒl] *n* an international organization for cooperation between the police forces of different countries.

interpolate [ɪnˈtɜːrpəleɪt] *vt* (formal use) **-1.** to add <a word or words> to a conversation or text. **-2.** to interrupt somebody by saying <sthg>.

interpose [ˌɪntəˈpoʊz] *vt* (formal use) **-1.** [comment, question] to add <sthg> to a conversation. **-2.** [comment, question] to interrupt somebody by adding <sthg>.

interpret [ɪnˈtɜːrprət] ◇ *vt* **-1.** [remark, result, behavior] to understand <sthg> in a particular way □ *How would you interpret that?* □ *Their statement is being interpreted as a willingness to cooperate.* **-2.** [speech, dialogue] to put <sthg spoken in one language> into a different language □ *Would you interpret that last section for me?* **-3.** [piece of music, role] to perform <sthg> in a way that shows one's ideas about it (formal use). ◇ *vi* to put something spoken in one language into a different language □ *Luckily my colleague was able to interpret for me.*

interpretation [ɪnˌtɜːrprəˈteɪʃn] *n* **-1.** a meaning chosen from several possible meanings □ *Well, John, what's your interpretation of these* events? **-2.** [of a role, piece of music] the way something is performed.

interpreter [ɪn'tɜːˡprətəʳ] *n* a person whose job is to put what is said, e.g. during meetings or conferences, from one language into another.

interpreting [ɪn'tɜːˡprətɪŋ] *n* the job of an interpreter □ *simultaneous interpreting.*

interracial [ˌɪntəˡreɪʃl] *adj* [tension, conflict, harmony] that exists or happens between people of different races.

interrelate [ˌɪntəˡrɪ'leɪt] *vt* **to be interrelated** [factors, questions] to be connected with each other □ *The problems of crime and poverty are interrelated.*

interrogate [ɪn'terəgeɪt] *vt* **-1.** [suspect, prisoner] to question <sb> about a crime, sometimes in a threatening or aggressive way □ *The men were interrogated by the police for several hours.* **-2.** COMPUTING to get information from <a computer>.

interrogation [ɪnˌterə'geɪʃn] *n* [of a suspect, prisoner] *see* **interrogate** □ *She was taken away for interrogation.* □ *The confession was extracted under interrogation.*

interrogation mark *n* a question mark (formal use).

interrogative [ˌɪntə'rɒgətɪv] ◇ *adj* [pronoun, form] that is used to form a question. ◇ *n* **-1. the interrogative** the form of a verb or grammatical construction that is used to make a question. **-2.** a word, e.g. "why" or "where", that is used to form a question.

interrogator [ɪn'terəgeɪtəʳ] *n* a person who questions a suspect, prisoner etc during an interrogation.

interrupt [ˌɪntə'rʌpt] ◇ *vt* **-1.** [speaker] to do or say something that causes <sb> to stop speaking □ *I was interrupted at several points during my speech.* □ *I'm sorry to interrupt your conversation.* **-2.** [work, activity, process] to do something that causes <sthg> to stop for a period of time; [person] to do or say something that causes <sb> to stop working □ *We interrupt this program to bring you a newsflash.* □ *Don't let me interrupt you!* ◇ *vi:* *I've told you before not to interrupt.*

interrupter [ˌIntə'rʌptəʳ] *n* ELECTRICITY a device that opens and closes an electric circuit.

interruption [ˌɪntə'rʌpʃn] *n* **-1.** something that somebody says or does that causes an activity or process to stop for a period of time □ *The rehearsal took longer than usual as there were several interruptions.* **-2.** [of work, an activity, process] *see* **interrupt** □ *We were able to work without interruption.*

intersect [ˌɪntəˡsekt] ◇ *vi* [lines, streets] to cross each other. ◇ *vt* [line, street] to cut across <sthg> at a particular point □ *This is the point where the two roads intersect.*

intersection [ˌɪntəˡsekʃn] *n* the point at which two lines, roads etc meet and cross each other □ *We stopped at a busy intersection.*

intersperse [ˌɪntəˡspɜːʳs] *vt* **to be interspersed with sthg** to contain sthg at various points □ *Her speech was interspersed with witty remarks.*

interstate (highway) [ˌɪntəʳsteɪt-] *n* in the USA, a major highway going from one state to another □ *You can get there on the interstate (highway).* □ *Interstate 75.*

interval ['ɪntəvl] *n* **-1.** [between two events] a period of time between two events or situations □ *There was an interval of three months between the attacks.* ■ **at intervals** on repeated occasions with periods of time in between □ *There are buses to town at regular intervals.* ■ **at monthly/yearly intervals** once a month/year □ *The patient's temperature is taken at 30-minute intervals.* **-2.** GB [in a play, concert] a short break between two parts of a performance. **-3.** MUSIC the difference between two notes that do not have the same pitch.

intervene [ˌɪntəˡviːn] *vi* **-1.** [police, government] to become involved in an argument or fight to try and help end it □ *The UN is reluctant to intervene in the dispute.* **-2.** [war, strike] to occur just when something else is supposed to happen, and as a result stop it from happening □ *However, an unexpected event was to intervene and upset all his carefully laid plans.* **-3.** [hours, days, months] to pass □ *Several hours intervened between Lou's arrival and that of Mabel.* **-4.** [person] to interrupt somebody in order to say something □ *Could I intervene a moment just to say a few words about the arrangements for lunch?*

intervening [ˌɪntəˡviːnɪŋ] *adj* **in the intervening days/months etc** in the days/months etc that come between two events or points in time □ *Little had changed in the intervening period.*

intervention [ˌɪntəˡvenʃn] *n* [by the police, a government] *see* **intervene** □ *Governments in the region are calling for UN intervention.* □ *military intervention.*

interventionist [ˌɪntəˡvenʃnəst] POLITICS ◇ *adj* [policy, stance] that favors the involvement of a government, especially in the affairs of another country. ◇ *n* a person or state that is interventionist.

interview ['ɪntəvjuː] ◇ *n* **-1.** a formal meeting in which an employer asks somebody questions to discover how suitable they are for a job □ *a job interview* □ *How did the interview go?* □ *an interview room.* **-2.** MEDIA a conversation in which a journalist or TV presenter asks somebody well-known or interesting about themselves or about an event, situation etc □ *The reporter managed to get an interview with the released hostages.* □ *She hasn't given an interview for years.* ◇ *vt* [candidate, politician, star] to ask <sb> questions in an interview □ *He was interviewed by police for over an hour.*

interviewee [ˌɪntəvjuː'iː] *n* a person who is interviewed by an employer, journalist etc.

interviewer ['ɪntəvjuːəʳ] *n* the employer, journalist etc who asks questions in an interview.

interweave [ˌɪntəˡwiːv] (*pt* **interwove** [-'wəʊv], *pp* **interwoven** [-'wəʊvn]) *vt* [threads, lives] to join <two or more things> together so that they are closely connected □ *The branches were interwoven with each other.* □ *From that point on, their lives became closely interwoven.*

intestate [ɪn'testeɪt] *adj* **to die intestate** to die without making a will.

intestine [ɪn'testɪn] *n* an organ in one's body that consists of a long tube divided into a large and a small section and that carries food and water out of the body.

◆ **intestines** *npl* = **intestine** □ *an infection of the intestines.*

intimacy ['ɪntəməsɪ] (*pl* **Intimacies**) *n* [of a relationship, dinner] *see* **intimate** □ *Much has been said of the intimacy between them.*

◆ **intimacies** *npl* personal thoughts that are usually only exchanged between people who have a very close relationship.

intimate [*adj* & *n* 'ɪntəmət, *vb* 'ɪntəmeɪt] ◇ *adj* **-1.** [friend, relationship] very close □ *We're on intimate terms.* **-2.** [bar, dining room] that is small and has an atmosphere that allows people to speak to each other privately □ *an intimate little restaurant.* **-3.** [dinner, evening] that involves or suggests a romantic closeness between two people □ *an intimate tête à tête.* **-4. to be intimate with sb** to have sex with sb (formal use). **-5. intimate details/thoughts etc** very personal details/thoughts etc. **-6. an intimate knowledge/understanding** a detailed and correct knowledge/understanding □ *You must have an intimate awareness of the needs of small, rural communities.* **-7. an intimate link** OR **connection** a close link OR connection.

◇ *n* a person who is a close friend of somebody (formal use).

◇ *vt* **to intimate (that)...** to suggest that something is true or exists by saying something indirectly (formal use) □ *She intimated that she would support our campaign.*

intimately ['ɪntəmətlɪ] *adv* [know, talk] *see* **intimate** □ *I'm not intimately acquainted with him/the details.*

intimation [,ɪntə'meɪʃn] *n* [of a feeling, event] an indirect sign of something (formal use) □ *There was no intimation of the coming storm/war.*

intimidate [ɪn'tɪmədeɪt] *vt* to frighten <sb>, especially by behaving aggressively □ *Don't be intimidated into doing what they're asking.*

intimidation [ɪn,tɪmə'deɪʃn] *n* the act of frightening somebody, often in order to make them do something □ *I refuse to give in to intimidation.*

into [*stressed* 'ɪntuː, *unstressed* 'ɪntə, *before vowel* 'ɪntʊ] *prep* **-1. to go/step into a place** to go/step inside a place from the outside □ *She got into the car.* ■ **to put sthg into sthg** to put sthg inside sthg □ *Pour the mixture into a baking dish.* **-2. to bump into sb/sthg** to hit sb/sthg accidentally with one's body □ *He walked straight into a lamppost.* **-3. to change** OR **develop into sthg** to become sthg different □ *The novel was translated into Spanish.* □ *I tore the letter into tiny pieces.* **-4. to get** OR **change into a piece of clothing** to put on a piece of clothing □ *I got home from work and changed into my jeans.* **-5. an inquiry/investigation into sthg** an inquiry/investigation that is about sthg □ *We need more research into the causes of family breakdown.* **-6.** MATH **4 into 8** 8 divided by 4 □ *2 into 6 goes 3 times.* **-7. to get into trouble/difficulties** to begin experiencing trouble/difficulties □ *You've got yourself into a real mess.* **-8.** used to show that a particular period of time has passed □ *I was a week into my training program before I met my new boss.* **-9.** *phrase* **to be into sthg** to be interested in sthg and enjoy it (informal use) □ *He's really into jazz/tennis.*

intolerable [ɪn'tɒlərəbl] *adj* [situation, cruelty, injustice] that is so bad that one cannot accept it □ *This is intolerable!*

intolerance [ɪn'tɒlərəns] *n* the attitude of somebody who does not accept or respect other people's behavior or beliefs.

intolerant [ɪn'tɒlərənt] *adj* [person, attitude] that shows intolerance □ *He's terribly intolerant of women drivers.*

intonation [,ɪntə'neɪʃn] *n* the way a person's voice gets higher and lower, e.g. when they are asking a question or expressing anger or excitement.

intone [ɪn'təʊn] *vt* to say <sthg> without making one's voice higher or lower (literary use).

intoxicated [ɪn'tɒksɪkeɪtəd] *adj* **-1.** [person] who is drunk (formal use). **-2. to be intoxicated by** OR **with sthg** [by success, fame] to feel so happy or excited about sthg that one does not behave in a sensible way □ *He became intoxicated by the idea of power.*

intoxicating [ɪn'tɒksɪkeɪtɪŋ] *adj* **-1. intoxicating drink** drinks that can cause somebody to be drunk □ *'Licensed for the sale of intoxicating liquor.'* **-2.** [atmosphere, beauty, perfume] that makes one feel very happy or excited.

intoxication [ɪn,tɒksɪ'keɪʃn] *n* (formal use) **-1.** the state of being drunk. **-2.** a strong feeling of happiness, excitement etc □ *a feeling of intoxication.*

intractable [ɪn'træktəbl] *adj* (formal use) **-1.** [person] who has a strong will and is difficult to control □ *I tried to be persuasive, but he was intractable.* **-2.** [problem] that seems impossible to solve.

intramural [,ɪntrə'mjʊərəl] *adj* [course, studies] that involves different departments or areas of study within the same university, college etc.

intransigent [ɪn'trænsɪdʒənt] *adj* [person] who is not willing to change their attitude or behavior (formal use).

intransitive [ɪn'trænsətɪv] *adj* [verb] that has a subject but no direct object □ *The verb "open" is intransitive in "the door opened" and transitive in "I opened the door".*

intrauterine device [,ɪntrəjuːtəraɪn-] *n* a small plastic or metal device that is placed inside a woman's uterus to stop her from becoming pregnant.

intravenous [,ɪntrə'viːnəs] *adj* **an intravenous injection/drip** an injection/a drip that goes into a person's vein.

in-tray *n* an open plastic or metal container on somebody's desk that holds all the letters and papers that they must deal with □ *The letter was sitting in my in-tray.*

intrepid [ɪn'trepɪd] *adj* [traveler, explorer] who is not afraid in dangerous situations (literary use).

intricacy ['ɪntrɪkəsɪ] (*pl* **intricacies**) *n* [of a pattern, plan] *see* **intricate**.

◆ **intricacies** *npl* [of a situation, system, subject] the small details that make something complicated □ *He is acquainted with all the intricacies of the case.*

intricate ['ɪntrɪkət] *adj* [pattern, plan, mechanism] that is complicated and made up of many small parts □ *The workings are very intricate.* □ *The report discusses, in intricate detail, the causes of the crisis.*

intrigue [*n* 'ɪntriːg, *vb* ɪn'triːg] ◇ *n* -1. the act of making a secret plan, usually to gain power □ *political intrigue.* -2. a secret plan made by two or more people. ◇ *vt* **to be intrigued by sthg** to be very interested in sthg and want to know more about it □ *I was intrigued to hear you're emigrating.* ◇ *vi* **to intrigue against sb** to make a secret plan to do sb harm.

intriguing [ɪn'triːgɪn] *adj* [person, idea, story] that is very interesting because it is unusual and one knows little about it or does not understand it □ *an intriguing tale of love and revenge.*

intrinsic [ɪn'trɪnsɪk] *adj* [merit, value, goodness] that is part of the nature of somebody or something □ *The vase has little intrinsic value.*

intro ['ɪntrou] (*pl* **intros**) *n* = **introduction** (informal use).

introduce [,ɪntrə'djuːs] *vt* -1. [guest, friend, husband] to make <sb> known to another person or people for the first time, usually by saying their name □ *Have you all been introduced?* □ *Let me introduce myself.* □ *Can I introduce you to my wife?* □ *I'd like to introduce you to a colleague of mine.* -2. [speaker, performer, contestant] to tell the audience the name of and a few details about <sb>, just before they take part in an event □ *I'd like to introduce my next guest tonight.* -3. to bring an animal or plant to a place so that it becomes part of the environment □ *This species was introduced into Britain by the Romans.* -4. [law, method, change] to make <sthg> so that it becomes part of a system □ *They're planning to introduce an airport tax.* □ *Modern business practices are gradually being introduced into the country.* -5. **to introduce sb to sthg** [to a subject, idea] to cause sb to experience sthg for the first time □ *In Japan I was introduced to the delights of sushi.* □ *This introduced a period of conflict that lasted several years.* -6. RADIO & TV [show, movie] to talk to the audience at the beginning of and during a program to tell them what it is about □ *The "Tonight" show is introduced by Ron Miller.*

introduction [,ɪntrə'dʌkʃn] *n* -1. **an introduction to sthg** [to music, food, art] a first experience of sthg □ *That job was my first introduction to banking.* -2. [to a book, lecture] the words at the beginning of something that say what it is about. -3. [to a subject] a book that gives the basic facts about a subject □ *"An Introduc-*

tion to Physics." -4. [to a person, of a law, method] the act of introducing somebody or something □ *He was hoping for an introduction to the ambassador.* □ *Our guest tonight needs no introduction.* □ *Several jobs will be lost after the introduction of new technology.*

introductory [,ɪntrə'dʌktərɪ] *adj* [course, remark, chapter] that is intended to introduce people to something □ *an introductory offer.*

introspective [,ɪntrə'spektɪv] *adj* [person] who tends to spend a lot of time thinking about their own feelings and ideas.

introvert ['ɪntrəvɜːʳt] *n* an introverted person.

introverted [,ɪntrə'vɜːʳtəd] *adj* [person] who thinks a lot about themselves and finds it hard to talk to other people □ *She had always been the more introverted of the two sisters.*

intrude [ɪn'truːd] *vi* -1. [person] to disturb somebody by entering a place or situation where one is not wanted or should not be □ *I hope I'm not intruding.* □ *He complained that the press was intruding into his family life.* -2. [noise, smell, feeling] to have an unwelcome effect on something □ *A voice intruded on my thoughts.* □ *Work was beginning to intrude on his private life.*

intruder [ɪn'truːdəʳ] *n* a person who enters a place illegally, usually in order to steal things.

intrusion [ɪn'truːʒn] *n*: *see* **intrude** □ *I resent these intrusions on our privacy.*

intrusive [ɪn'truːsɪv] *adj* [person, noise] that intrudes □ *intrusive methods of journalism.*

intuition [,ɪntjuː'ɪʃn] *n* the ability to know or feel that something is true even though it cannot be explained or proved; a sudden feeling that something is true that is caused by this ability □ *female intuition* □ *I had a sudden intuition that something was wrong.*

intuitive [ɪn'tjuːɪtɪv] *adj* [feeling, understanding] that shows intuition; [artist, writer, tennis player] who is able to use their intuition well □ *She's a very intuitive player.*

Inuit ['ɪnʊɪt] ◇ *n* a member of a Native American people living in northern Canada, Alaska, and Greenland; the language of this people. ◇ *adj*: *an Inuit custom.*

inundate ['ɪnʌndeɪt] *vt* -1. [village, plain] to flood <an area of land> (formal use). -2. **to be inundated with sthg** [with messages, offers, requests] to receive a lot of sthg in a short time, with the result that it is difficult to deal with □ *Our office has been inundated with calls/mail.*

inured [ɪ'njʊəʳd] *adj* **to be inured to sthg** [to violence, pain] to be used to sthg unpleasant □ *As a doctor you get inured to the sight of blood.*

invade [ɪn'veɪd] *vt* -1. MILITARY [army, troops] to enter <an area> using military force with the intention of taking control of it □ *France was invaded by Germany.* -2. [tourists, insects, fans] to enter <a place> in great numbers and fill it □ *Each year thousands of visitors invade our shores.* -3. **to invade sb's privacy/peace** to arrive suddenly and stop sb from having any privacy/peace.

invader [ɪn'veɪdər] *n* a country, army, or person that invades a place □ *Viking invaders.*

invading [ɪn'veɪdɪŋ] *adj* MILITARY [troops, tanks] that are invading a country or city □ *an invading army.*

invalid [*adj* ɪn'væləd, *n* & *vb* 'ɪnvəlɪd] ◇ *adj* -1. [election, ticket, document] that cannot be used because it is not legal or correct □ *Their marriage was pronounced invalid.* -2. [result, theory, argument] that is not correct because it is based on a mistake □ *The results were declared invalid and recounted.* ◇ *n* a person who is permanently ill or disabled □ *He has an invalid mother.*

♦ **invalid out** *vt sep* **to be invalided out of the army/navy/air force** GB to be allowed to leave the army/navy/air force because of illness or injury.

invalidate [ɪn'vælədeɪt] *vt* -1. [result, theory, claim] to show that <sthg> is not true or correct □ *The theory has been invalidated by more recent research.* -2. [election, marriage] to stop <sthg> from being legal or correct □ *Illegible applications will be automatically invalidated.*

invaluable [ɪn'væljuəbl] *adj* [experience, information, help] very useful □ *She has been invaluable to the company for many years.*

invariable [ɪn'veərɪəbl] *adj* [quantity, number, routine] that never changes.

invariably [ɪn'veərɪəblɪ] *adv* a word used to say that something always happens □ *Invariably, he was right/late.*

invasion [ɪn'veɪʒn] *n*: see **invade** □ *the annual tourist invasion* □ *The attention of the press constitutes an invasion of my privacy.*

invective [ɪn'vektɪv] *n* rude and insulting words used to attack somebody □ *a stream of invective* □ *racist invective.*

inveigle [ɪn'veɪgl] *vt* **to inveigle sb into doing sthg** to persuade sb to do sthg in a clever or subtle way (formal use).

invent [ɪn'vent] *vt* -1. [machine, method, word] to think of and create <sthg new> □ *The first radar device was invented in Britain.* -2. [excuse, reason, story] to think of and tell somebody <sthg that is not true> □ *The figures were invented to disguise huge losses on the open market.*

invention [ɪn'venʃn] *n* -1. something that has been invented □ *He was unable to sell his invention.* -2. [of a machine, method, word] see **invent** □ *the invention of the steam engine.* -3. the ability to invent things □ *It tested her powers of invention to the limit.* -4. an excuse, reason etc that is not true □ *His story turned out to be a complete invention.*

inventive [ɪn'ventɪv] *adj* [person] who is good at finding new and better ways of doing something □ *a highly inventive solution* □ *He's an extremely inventive musician.*

inventor [ɪn'ventər] *n* a person who invents things.

inventory [US 'ɪnvəntɔːrɪ, GB -trɪ] (*pl* **inventories**) *n* -1. a detailed list of the goods, equipment etc that can be found in a particular place. -2. US BUSINESS the total amount of goods available for sale by a business.

inventory control *n* a system of checking the amount of goods, equipment etc held by an organization.

inverse [ɪn'vɜːrs] ◇ *adj* **to increase in inverse proportion** OR **relation to sthg** to increase by the same amount as sthg decreases □ *There is an inverse relationship between the amount of money people spend and the amount they save.* ◇ *n* **the inverse** the opposite of something (formal use) □ *In fact, the inverse is true.*

invert [ɪn'vɜːrt] *vt* [cup, chair] to turn <sthg> upside down or back to front (formal use) □ *an inverted triangle* □ *The order of the words needs to be inverted.*

invertebrate [ɪn'vɜːrtɪbrət] *n* one of a group of animals, including insects and worms, that have no backbone.

inverted commas [ɪn,vɜːrtəd-] *npl* GB the marks (' ' or " ") used in writing to show where the exact words that somebody said or wrote begin and end.

inverted snob [ɪn,vɜːrtəd-] *n* GB a person who says that they admire lower-class things or people and dislike upper-class things or people.

invest [ɪn'vest] ◇ *vt* -1. FINANCE [savings, capital] to put <money> into a bank account, business, stocks etc in order to make a profit □ *He invested $5,000 in a property company.* -2. to use <a lot of time or energy> in order to achieve something □ *He invested all his hopes in this project.* -3. **to invest sb with sthg** [with an authority, power] to give sb sthg formally. ◇ *vi* -1. to invest money in something □ *Hansen has invested heavily in government bonds.* -2. **to invest in sthg** to buy sthg useful that will last a long time □ *You'd better invest in a new watch.*

investigate [ɪn'vestɪgeɪt] ◇ *vt* [suspect, situation, crime] to try to find out information about <sb/sthg> □ *Police are investigating the causes of the accident.* ◇ *vi* [police, doctor, expert] *Investigating magistrates now wish to interview the company's finance director.*

investigation [ɪn,vestɪ'geɪʃn] *n* -1. **an investigation into sthg** [into allegations, activities, a crime] an official examination of sthg □ *a police investigation.* -2. the process of trying to find out information □ *Some of his activities require further investigation.*

investigative [US ɪn'vestəgeɪtɪv, GB -ɪgətɪv] *adj* **an investigative journalist/reporter** a journalist/reporter who tries to discover the truth about important issues □ *investigative journalism.*

investigator [ɪn'vestɪgeɪtər] *n* a person whose job is to find out information about something, e.g. a crime or accident □ *an insurance investigator.*

investiture [ɪn'vestətʃər] *n* [of a mayor, archbishop] an official ceremony in which somebody is given an important job or position.

investment [ɪn'vestmənt] *n* -1. [of savings, capital] see **invest** □ *The railroad network desperately* needs investment. -2. an amount of money invested in something □ The company offers you a good return on your investment. -3. FINANCE the stocks, shares etc in which money is invested □ The company has investments all over the world. -4. [for the future] something bought in order to make a profit □ When house prices went up, this cottage turned out to be a good investment. -5. [of time, energy] the amount of time, energy etc spent on something □ a huge personal investment.

investment analyst n a person who says how much money investments are likely to be worth by looking carefully at the activities of different companies.

investment bank n US a bank that organizes the sale of shares in new companies.

investment trust n a limited company that buys and sells shares in other companies in order to make a profit for the people investing in it.

investor [ɪn'vestər] n a person who invests money □ The government is trying to lure foreign investors into the region. □ a small investor.

inveterate [ɪn'vetərət] adj -1. an inveterate dislike/hatred etc dislike/hatred etc that is unlikely to change □ an inveterate dislike of parties. -2. an inveterate liar/gambler etc a person who is unlikely to stop lying/gambling etc.

invidious [ɪn'vɪdɪəs] adj [task, duty, position] that is unpleasant for one to have or do because it is likely to make other people jealous or angry.

invigilate [ɪn'vɪdʒəleɪt] ◇ vt GB to observe <an exam> to stop people from cheating. ◇ vi: Mr Harris will be invigilating.

invigilator [ɪn'vɪdʒəleɪtər] n GB a person who invigilates.

invigorating [ɪn'vɪgəreɪtɪŋ] adj [air, walk, swim] that makes one feel fresh and full of energy □ an invigorating shower.

invincible [ɪn'vɪnsəbl] adj [army, champion, record] that cannot be beaten □ No one is invincible.

inviolate [ɪn'vaɪələt] adj [reputation, happiness] that cannot be threatened or harmed in any way (literary use).

invisible [ɪn'vɪzəbl] adj that cannot be seen □ It was so small as to be almost invisible.

invisible assets npl things of value that belong to a company but are not physical objects, e.g. the right to make and sell a certain product.

invisible earnings npl foreign money earned by a country from investments or services but not from selling goods.

invisible ink n a liquid used for writing that cannot be seen until it is heated, treated with a chemical, or looked at under a special light.

invitation [ˌɪnvɪ'teɪʃn] n -1. [to a dinner, party, wedding] a spoken or written offer to somebody to go to a place for a particular purpose or activity □ I refused his invitation. □ 'By invitation only' □ a wedding invitation □ I received an invitation to the ball. -2. an invitation to sthg

a situation, action etc that encourages somebody to do sthg □ Prison conditions are an (open) invitation to violence.

invite [ɪn'vaɪt] vt -1. [person] to ask <sb> to come, especially to a social event □ There's a party tonight and you're all invited! □ He invited us in for coffee/out for dinner/over for drinks. □ We've been invited to their wedding. -2. **to invite sb to do sthg** to ask sb politely to do sthg □ You are invited to attend an interview. □ I will invite the audience to ask questions at the end of the lecture. -3. [comments, suggestions, questions] to ask people to give or make <sthg> □ Offers/Donations are invited. -4. [trouble, gossip, criticism] to make <sthg> likely to happen □ Her technique invites comparison with the late Maria Callas.

inviting [ɪn'vaɪtɪŋ] adj [offer, food, smell] attractive □ He held out the inviting prospect of a two-week Caribbean cruise.

in vitro fertilization [ɪn'viːtroʊ-] n the process of making a human egg develop outside the body using special equipment.

invoice ['ɪnvɔɪs] ◇ n a piece of paper showing goods or services that have been provided and the amount of money that has to be paid for them □ Have we received their invoice yet? ◇ vt to give or send an invoice to <a customer or client>; to write an invoice for <goods or a service> □ We invoiced you for the goods on June 8. □ Has that last consignment been invoiced?

invoke [ɪn'voʊk] vt -1. [law, act, right] to use <sthg> as a reason for doing something (formal use). -2. [grief, enthusiasm] to cause somebody to have <a particular feeling> □ The case has invoked a great deal of public sympathy.

involuntary [US ɪn'vɒləntəri, GB -əri] adj [movement, shudder, gasp] that one makes without a conscious effort.

involve [ɪn'vɒlv] vt -1. [work, study, traveling] to have <sthg> as a necessary part □ The job involves overseas travel/visiting clients. -2. to affect <sb/sthg> directly □ We looked at several cases involving young children. -3. **to involve sb in sthg** [in a plan, argument, problem] to arrange for sb to take part in sthg □ I'd like to involve you more in dealing with clients.

involved [ɪn'vɒlvd] adj -1. **to be involved in sthg** [in politics, research] to take part in sthg □ He was involved in secret talks with opposition leaders. ■ **to be involved in a fight/an accident etc** to be in a fight/an accident etc □ He was involved in a financial scandal. -2. [explanation, story] that is complicated □ The story is very long and involved. -3. **to be involved with sb** to have a close relationship with sb, especially a sexual one □ I don't want to get emotionally involved. -4. **to be involved** to be a necessary part of a process, job etc □ The amount of work involved is enormous.

involvement [ɪn'vɒlvmənt] n -1. [in politics, a fight, scandal] see **involved** □ Morris denied any involvement in the affair. -2. a desire or willingness to give a lot of enthusiasm and effort to something □ Thanks to your involvement we finished the project on time.

invulnerable [ɪn'vʌlnərəbl] *adj* to be invulnerable [machine, weapon, person] to be impossible to harm □ *He felt invulnerable.*

inward ['ɪnwəʳd] ◇ *adj* -1. [thoughts, feelings] that one feels but does not show to other people □ *He had an inward sense of failure.* -2. [flow, movement] toward the inside of a room, building etc. ◇ *adv* to turn/open inward to turn/open toward the inside of a room, building etc □ *The door opens inward.*

inward investment *n* money that is invested in a town, country, company etc by investors from outside.

inwardly ['ɪnwəʳdlɪ] *adv* a word used to say that one feels something without showing it to other people □ *Inwardly, she was angry/pleased.*

inwards ['ɪnwəʳdz] *adv* = inward.

I/O *abbr of* input/output.

IOC (*abbr of* International Olympic Committee) *n* the IOC the international body responsible for organizing the Olympic Games.

iodine [US 'aɪədaɪn, GB -diːn] *n* a chemical used in medicine to kill germs □ *Paint the wound with iodine.*

ion ['aɪən] *n* PHYSICS an atom that is electrically charged.

iota [aɪ'outə] *n* a very small amount of something □ *There's not one iota of truth in the story.*

IOU (*abbr of* I owe you) *n* a document that a person has signed and that states that they owe a particular person a particular amount of money □ *an IOU for $100.*

IOW *abbr of* Isle of Wight.

Iowa ['aɪəwə] a state in the Midwest of the USA, consisting mainly of farmland. ABBREVIATION: IA. SIZE: 146,000 sq kms. POPULATION: 2,776,755 (*Iowans*). CAPITAL: Des Moines.

IPA (*abbr of* International Phonetic Alphabet) *n* the IPA a system of symbols that represent the sounds people make when they say words.

IQ (*abbr of* intelligence quotient) *n* a measure of somebody's intelligence, calculated using a special test □ *She has a high IQ/an IQ of 110.*

IRA *n* -1. (*abbr of* Irish Republican Army) the IRA an illegal organization whose aim is to make Northern Ireland and the Republic of Ireland into one country. -2. (*abbr of* individual retirement account) a personal pension plan for people who live in the USA.

Iran [ɪ'rɑːn] a country in southwestern Asia, between the Caspian Sea and the Persian Gulf. In the 1970s it became an Islamic fundamentalist state. SIZE: 1,650,000 sq kms. POPULATION: 62,800,000 (*Iranians*). CAPITAL: Tehran. LANGUAGE: Farsi. CURRENCY: rial. OLD NAME: Persia.

Iran-Contra Affair *n* the Iran-Contra Affair a political scandal that happened during the presidency of Ronald Reagan. The President was accused of selling arms to Iran to have US hostages released, and giving the money to right-wing groups in Nicaragua.

Irangate [ɪ'rɑːngeɪt] *n* = Iran-Contra Affair.

Iranian [ɪ'reɪnjən] *n* & *adj*: *see* Iran.

Iraq [ɪ'rɑːk] a country in southwestern Asia, between Arabia and Iran. In 1990 it invaded Kuwait, which led to the Gulf War. SIZE: 434,000 sq kms. POPULATION: 17,100,000 (*Iraqis*). CAPITAL: Baghdad. LANGUAGE: Arabic. CURRENCY: Iraqi dinar.

Iraqi [ɪ'rɑːkɪ] *n* & *adj*: *see* Iraq.

irascible [ɪ'ræsəbl] *adj* [person] who gets angry easily (formal use).

irate [aɪ'reɪt] *adj* [person, letter] very angry □ *He got very irate about it.* □ *an irate phone call.*

Ireland ['aɪəʳlənd] -1. GEOGRAPHY an island in northwestern Europe in the Atlantic Ocean, west of Great Britain, consisting of the Irish Republic and Northern Ireland. -2. POLITICS = Irish Republic.

iridescent [,ɪrɪ'desnt] *adj* [color, feather, fish] that shows different bright colors when light shines on it (literary use).

iris ['aɪrɪs] (*pl* irises) *n* -1. a tall purple or yellow flower with long pointed leaves that often grows near water. -2. ANATOMY the colored part of one's eye.

Irish ['aɪrɪʃ] ◇ *npl* the Irish the people of Ireland. ◇ *n* the Gaelic language spoken in Ireland. ◇ *adj*: *see* Ireland □ *an Irish accent.*

Irish coffee *n* coffee with cream and whiskey added.

Irishman ['aɪrɪʃmən] (*pl* Irishmen [-mən]) *n* a man who comes from or lives in Ireland.

Irish Republic: the Irish Republic a country covering all the island of Ireland except the northeastern part. SIZE: 70,000 sq kms. POPULATION: 3,500,000 (*Irish*). CAPITAL: Dublin. LANGUAGE: English, Irish.

Irish Sea: the Irish Sea the part of the Atlantic Ocean between Great Britain and Ireland.

Irish setter *n* a dog that has a slim body and a coat of long, smooth, red-brown hair.

Irish stew *n* a dish that consists of meat cooked with potatoes, onions, and carrots.

Irish wolfhound [-'wʊlfhaʊnd] *n* a large dog that has a slim body, small ears, and a thick gray coat.

Irishwoman ['aɪrɪʃwʊmən] (*pl* Irishwomen) *n* a woman who comes from or lives in Ireland.

irk [ɜːʳk] *vt* to annoy <sb>.

irksome ['ɜːksəm] *adj* [task, duty, responsibility] annoying.

IRN (*abbr of* Independent Radio News) *n* a company that produces news programs for commercial radio stations in Britain.

IRO (*abbr of* International Refugee Organization) *n* the IRO a US organization that gives help to refugees.

iron ['aɪəʳn] ◇ *n* -1. a very hard metal used to make steel. SYMBOL: Fe □ *vast iron ore deposits.* -2. [for clothes] an electrical appliance with a flat base, a point at one end, and a handle on top, that is moved over clothes to make them smooth before they are worn □ *an electric/a steam iron.* -3. SPORT a special stick with a piece of shaped iron on the end, used for hitting a ball in golf □ *an 8 iron.*

◇ *adj* -1. [bridge, bar, railing] made of iron □ *a pair of huge iron gates.* -2. [will, discipline] very strong □ *I was very impressed by her iron self-discipline.* ■ **an Iron Man/Woman contest** in the USA and Australia, a sporting event that takes place at a beach, including swimming, surfing, and running contests.

◇ *vt* [shirt, sheet, trousers] to make <a piece of clothing or material> smooth by moving an iron across it □ *My shirt needs ironing.*

◆ **iron out** *vt sep* to iron problems/differences out to solve problems/differences, especially when these are small □ *They'll give me the contract once we've ironed out the details.*

Iron Age *n* **the Iron Age** the time, about 3,000 years ago, when people began to use iron to make tools and weapons □ *an Iron Age site/arrowhead.*

Iron Curtain *n* **the Iron Curtain** a phrase used to refer to the border between the Communist countries of Eastern Europe and the rest of Europe during the Cold War.

ironic(al) [aɪˈrɒnɪk(l)] *adj* -1. [remark, smile, laugh] that shows that one means the opposite of what one has said □ *an ironic tone of voice.* -2. [situation, outcome, result] that is the opposite of what one would expect, especially in a strange or amusing way □ *How ironic that it should finish like this!*

ironically [aɪˈrɒnɪklɪ] *adv* -1. a word used to show that something is not what one would expect, especially in a strange or amusing way □ *Ironically enough, his wife was having an affair at the same time as he was.* -2. [remark, smile, laugh] *see* **ironic.**

ironing [ˈaɪərnɪŋ] *n* -1. the activity of making clothes, sheets etc smooth by moving an iron over them □ *Let him do the ironing for once!* -2. the clothes, sheets etc that need to be ironed or that have just been ironed.

ironing board *n* narrow table with a soft cover and folding legs on which one irons clothes.

Iron Lady: the Iron Lady a nickname for Margaret Thatcher.

iron lung *n* a large metal device used in the past by doctors to help paralyzed patients breathe.

ironmonger [ˈaɪərnmʌŋgəʳ] *n* GB a person who sells metal tools, locks etc. ■ **an ironmonger's** the store where an ironmonger works.

ironworks [ˈaɪərnwɜːʳks] (*pl* **ironworks**) *n* a factory in which iron is prepared and shaped.

irony [ˈaɪrənɪ] (*pl* **ironies**) *n* -1. the use of words to express the opposite of what they usually mean in order to be humorous or show annoyance □ *There was irony in her voice.* -2. an element of a situation, story etc that is the opposite of what one would expect, especially in a strange or amusing way □ *The irony is that it might be true.*

Iroquois [ˈɪrəkwɔɪ] *n* a member of a Native American people who now live in Quebec and New York State; the language of this people.

irradiate [ɪˈreɪdɪeɪt] *vt* -1. MEDICINE [tumor] to treat <sthg> with radiation. -2. [fruit, vegetables] to treat <food> with radiation to make it last longer by killing bacteria.

irrational [ɪˈræʃnəl] *adj* [person, behavior, decision] that shows no logic and seems strange or unreasonable □ *an irrational fear.*

irreconcilable [ˌɪrekənˈsaɪləbl] *adj* [views, opinions] that cannot be made to agree □ *The differences between the two sides now seemed irreconcilable.*

irredeemable [ˌɪrɪˈdiːməbl] *adj* [loss, disaster, failure] that cannot be changed or made less extreme (formal use).

irrefutable [ˌɪrɪˈfjuːtəbl] *adj* [evidence, argument, proof] that cannot be shown to be false (formal use).

irregular [ɪˈregjələʳ] *adj* -1. [shape, surface, features] that is not smooth, even, or regular in pattern □ *an irregular-shaped room.* -2. [work, income] that is not continuous and secure; [intervals, hours] that are not always the same □ *They pay me more because I have to work irregular hours.* -3. [procedure, behavior] that does not obey the usual rules (formal use) □ *I don't think I should allow this, it is highly irregular.* -4. GRAMMAR [verb, noun] that does not follow the normal pattern.

irregularity [ɪˌregjəˈlærətɪ] (*pl* **irregularities**) *n* -1. [in accounts, papers] something that does not obey the usual rules and so is not acceptable □ *The company was cleared of financial irregularities.* -2. [of a shape, work, hours] *see* **irregular.**

irregularly [ɪˈregjələʳlɪ] *adv* [work, eat, breathe] at irregular intervals □ *I get paid irregularly.* □ *an irregularly shaped room.*

irrelevance [ɪˈreləvəns], **irrelevancy** [ɪˈreləvənsɪ] (*pl* **irrelevancies**) *n* -1. *see* **irrelevant.** -2. something irrelevant □ *Don't waste your time on irrelevancies.*

irrelevant [ɪˈreləvənt] *adj* [information, comment] that is not connected with the subject being discussed and so is not useful □ *What he says is irrelevant; it's what he does that matters.*

irreligious [ˌɪrɪˈlɪdʒəs] *adj* [person, attitude] that does not accept or have respect for religious beliefs.

irremediable [ˌɪrɪˈmiːdjəbl] *adj* [damage, situation] that cannot be put right (formal use).

irreparable [ɪˈrepərəbl] *adj* [damage, harm] that cannot be put right.

irreplaceable [ˌɪrɪˈpleɪsəbl] *adj* [jewelry, vase] that is so special that it cannot be replaced; [person] who is so well loved or good at their job that nobody else can replace them.

irrepressible [ˌɪrɪˈpresəbl] *adj* [person] who is always cheerful and lively □ *His enthusiasm is irrepressible.*

irreproachable [ˌɪrɪˈprəʊtʃəbl] *adj* [character, conduct] that cannot be criticized because it is so good.

irresistible [ˌɪrɪˈzɪstəbl] *adj* -1. [person, charm] very attractive. -2. [desire, pressure] that is extremely strong or too strong to fight against □ *Ralph felt an irresistible urge to start* giggling. □ *There is now irresistible public demand for reform.*

irresolute [ɪˈrezəluːt] *adj* [person] who finds it hard to make decisions or take action (formal use).

irrespective [ˌɪrɪˈspektɪv] ◆ **irrespective of** *prep* [age, creed, sex] without <sthg> being taken into account □ *We believe that everyone, irrespective of their financial status, has the right to a decent education.*

irresponsible [ˌɪrɪˈspɒnsəbl] *adj* [person, behavior] that shows a lack of concern for other people and might put them in danger □ *It's irresponsible to let young kids go out alone at night.*

irretrievable [ˌɪrɪˈtriːvəbl] *adj* -1. [loss, harm, situation] that is so bad that it cannot be put right. -2. [data, object] that has been lost and so cannot be used again.

irreverent [ɪˈrevrənt] *adj* [person, comment, humor] that shows little or no respect for important people or things □ *an irreverent sense of humor.*

irreversible [ˌɪrɪˈvɜːrsəbl] *adj* [judgment, decision] that cannot be changed; [change, damage] that cannot be removed and so has a permanent effect □ *The operation is irreversible.*

irrevocable [ɪˈrevəkəbl] *adj* [decision, commitment] that cannot be changed □ *They have taken the first irrevocable step toward peace/war.*

irrigate [ˈɪrɪgeɪt] *vt* [field] to supply <an area of land> with water from specially made ditches so that crops can be grown; [wheat, bushes] to supply water for <crops> in this way.

irrigation [ˌɪrɪˈgeɪʃn] *n* the act of irrigating land or crops; a system that does this □ *an irrigation canal/system.*

irritable [ˈɪrɪtəbl] *adj* [person] who is easily annoyed; [voice, reply] that shows irritation □ *He's been very irritable lately.*

irritant [ˈɪrɪtənt] *n* -1. something that causes irritation □ *The continuous noise of traffic is an added irritant.* -2. a substance that irritates the skin, eyes etc.

irritate [ˈɪrɪteɪt] *vt* -1. [person] to make <sb> annoyed, especially over a long period of time □ *What irritates me most is the way she seems to look down on me.* -2. [skin, eye, bowel] to make <part of one's body> painful □ *The smoke irritated her throat.*

irritated [ˈɪrɪteɪtəd] *adj* -1. [person] annoyed □ *I get very irritated with people who talk while I'm speaking.* -2. [skin, eye] painful and red.

irritating [ˈɪrɪteɪtɪŋ] *adj* -1. [person, habit, noise] that irritates other people □ *It's irritating when people don't put things back where they belong.* -2. [substance, material] that makes one's skin, eyes etc painful and red.

irritation [ˌɪrɪˈteɪʃn] *n* -1. a feeling of annoyance and impatience; something that causes this feeling □ *I found to my irritation that there was none left.* □ *Hudson is likely to prove an irritation to the URP at the next election.* -2. pain and redness of one's skin, eyes etc.

IRS (*abbr of* **Internal Revenue Service**) *n* the IRS the US government department responsible for collecting taxes.

Irving [ˈɜːrvɪŋ], **Washington** (1783–1859) a US writer who is famous for his short stories. They include *Rip Van Winkle* and *The Legend of Sleepy Hollow.*

is [ɪz] *vb* → **be**.

Isaiah [US aɪˈzeɪə, GB -ˈzaɪə] in the Bible, one of the leading Hebrew prophets.

ISBN (*abbr of* **International Standard Book Number**) *n* an identification number that is printed on all published books. Each book has its own number.

ISDN (*abbr of* **integrated services digital network**) *n* a digital communications network that allows data to be sent from one computer to another by video or voice.

Islam [ˈɪzlɑːm] *n* the religion of the Muslims that is based on the teachings of Muhammad, and has the Koran as its holy book.

Islamic [ɪzˈlæmɪk] *adj* [fundamentalist, country, law] that follows Islam.

island [ˈaɪlənd] *n* -1. GEOGRAPHY a piece of land that is completely surrounded by water □ *the island of Corfu* □ *a tropical island.* -2. TRANSPORT = **traffic island**.

islander [ˈaɪləndər] *n* a person who lives on an island.

isle [aɪl] *n* -1. a word used to refer to an island as part of its name □ *the Western Isles.* -2. an island (literary use).

Isle of Man: **the Isle of Man** a British island in the Irish Sea that has its own government and laws. Some British people keep their money there because the taxes are lower than on the mainland of Britain. SIZE: 570 sq kms. POPULATION: 64,000 (*Manx*). CAPITAL: Douglas. LANGUAGE: English, Manx. CURRENCY: pound sterling.

Isle of Wight [-ˈwaɪt]: **the Isle of Wight** an English county consisting of an island in the English Channel.

isn't [ˈɪznt] = **is not**.

isobar [ˈaɪsəbɑːr] *n* a line on a map that joins two areas with the same air pressure.

isolate [ˈaɪsəleɪt] *vt* -1. [person] to keep <sb> apart from other people □ *His lack of English isolated him from the rest of the group.* -2. MEDICINE [patient, dog] to keep <a sick person or animal> apart from others so that they do not pass on a disease. -3. CHEMISTRY [bacteria, gene] to find and separate <sthg> from something else in order to use or examine it.

isolated [ˈaɪsəleɪtəd] *adj* -1. [area, cottage, village] that is a long way from other places □ *Deep snow has made it impossible to reach isolated farmhouses.* -2. [person] who is lonely and has no contact with other people □ *She felt very isolated and alone.* -3. [example, incident, case] that happens only once and is not typical □ *a few isolated protests/showers.*

isolation [ˌaɪsəˈleɪʃn] *n*: see **isolate** □ *I experienced an overwhelming feeling of isolation.* □ *40 days of isolation.* ■ **in isolation** [live, work] separately from other people; [happen, exist] separately from other things □ *The patients were kept in isolation while tests were carried out.* □ *The problem should not be considered in isolation.*

isolationism [ˌaɪsə'leɪʃənɪzm] *n* a political policy in which a country does not take part in the affairs of other countries.

isosceles triangle [aɪ'sɒsəliːz-] *n* a triangle that has two sides of the same length.

isotope ['aɪsətoʊp] *n* any of at least two atoms that are of the same chemical type but have a different number of neutrons.

Israel [US 'ɪzrɪəl, GB 'ɪzreɪl] a country in the Middle East, on the Mediterranean Sea between Syria, Egypt, Jordan, and Lebanon, that was set up as a Jewish state in 1948. Tension with Palestinian groups and neighboring Arab countries has led to several wars in the region. SIZE: 21,000 sq kms. POPULATION: 5,100,000 (*Israelis*). CAPITAL: Jerusalem. LANGUAGE: Hebrew, Arabic. CURRENCY: shekel.

Israeli [ɪz'reɪlɪ] *n* & *adj*: see **Israel**.

issue ['ɪʃuː] ◇ *n* -1. an important subject that often causes disagreement □ *These are important political/social issues.* □ *A key issue in the debate will be the government's record on healthcare.* ■ **at issue** [point, question] that is being discussed because it is important □ *What's at issue is the whole future of the Middle East.* ■ **to make an issue of sthg** to treat sthg as important so that other people pay a lot of attention to it. -2. MEDIA a particular edition of a magazine, newspaper etc that is printed regularly □ *'Free with this week's issue.'* -3. [of money, shares] a number of new banknotes, stamps, shares etc that are supplied or sold at the same time □ *a new share issue.*
◇ *vt* -1. [statement, warning, order] to make <sthg> known officially □ *The police have issued a description of the attacker.* -2. [stamp, banknote, shares] to make <sthg> available, e.g. to the public. -3. [passport, document, uniform] to provide <sthg> officially □ *The Norwegians won't issue her a new visa.* □ *We will be issuing a number to each candidate.*
◇ *vi* **to issue from a place** [voice, sound, smoke] to come out of a place (formal use).

Istanbul [ˌɪstæn'bʊl] a city in northwestern Turkey, on the Bosporus. It is Turkey's largest city and its main port. POPULATION: 6,620,241. OLD NAME: Constantinople.

ISTC (*abbr of* **Iron and Steel Trades Confederation**) *n* **the ISTC** a British labor union for metalworkers.

isthmus ['ɪsməs] *n* a narrow piece of land with water on each side that joins two much larger pieces of land.

it [ɪt] *pron* -1. the thing that has just been mentioned, seen etc; the baby or animal that has just been mentioned, seen etc (used as the subject or object of a verb, or after prepositions) □ *"Did you enjoy your meal?"* — *"It was OK."* □ *The house is small, but it's comfortable.* □ *Is it a boy or a girl?* □ *Take a casserole dish and arrange the vegetables in it.* -2. used to show how one feels about a situation or

fact □ *Cheer up, it's not that bad!* □ *It's a waste of time arguing with him.* -3. used to refer to the time, date, or weather □ *It's still raining.* □ *It's half past five.* □ *"What's the date today?"* — *"It's Friday, June 12."* -4. used to emphasize part of a sentence □ *It's Philip I'm really worried about, not her.* -5. used to identify who is present, or talking on the telephone □ *Hello, it's me, Mary!* □ *Who is it on the phone?* ■ **what is it?** what is the problem?

IT *n abbr of* **information technology**.

Italian [ɪ'tæljən] *n* & *adj*: see **Italy**.

italic [ɪ'tælɪk] *adj* [lettering, script] that slopes to the right, and is usually used to make a particular word or phrase stand out in a printed text.
◆ **italics** *npl* italic letters □ *This example is in italics.*

Italy ['ɪtəlɪ] a country in southern Europe, consisting of a long peninsula in the Mediterranean Sea and the islands of Sicily and Sardinia. SIZE: 301,000 sq kms. POPULATION: 57,700,000 (*Italians*). CAPITAL: Rome. LANGUAGE: Italian. CURRENCY: lira.

ITC (*abbr of* **Independent Television Commission**) *n* **the ITC** the organization that gives broadcasting licences to British commercial television companies.

itch [ɪtʃ] ◇ *n* a feeling of slight discomfort or irritation on the skin that makes one want to scratch it □ *I've got an itch on my leg.* ◇ *vi* -1. [arm, rash] to cause an itch; [person] to feel an itch □ *My legs are itching.* □ *I'm itching all over.* -2. **to be itching to do sthg** to be impatient to do sthg □ *Go on, I know you're itching to tell me.*

itchy ['ɪtʃɪ] (*compar* **itchier**, *superl* **itchiest**) *adj* that causes one to itch □ *This sweater is itchy.*

it'd ['ɪtəd] = **it would**, **it had**.

item ['aɪtəm] *n* -1. one of the things on a list or in a group of things □ *The first item on today's agenda is the advertising budget.* □ *an item of clothing.* -2. an article in a newspaper or magazine □ *There's an item about it in the local paper.*

itemize, -ise ['aɪtəmaɪz] *vt* [goods, contents] to make a list of <things>.

itemized bill ['aɪtəmaɪzd-] *n* a bill that lists all the items that make up the total, rather than just showing the total.

itinerant [ɪ'tɪnərənt] *adj* **an itinerant worker/ preacher etc** a worker/preacher etc who travels around and works for short periods in different places.

itinerary [US aɪ'tɪnəreri, GB -rəri] (*pl* **itineraries**) *n* a plan of a journey with a list of the places that will be visited □ *A full itinerary will be sent to you nearer the date of departure.*

it'll [ɪtl] = **it will**.

ITN (*abbr of* **Independent Television News**) *n* a company that produces news programs for ITV.

its [ɪts] *det* -1. that belongs to or is connected with the thing or place that has just been mentioned, seen etc □ *The house and all its contents were sold.* □ *The committee will prod-*

uce its report next month. **-2.** that belongs to or is connected with a child or animal that has just been mentioned, seen etc □ *The baby had dropped its toy.*

it's [ɪts] = **it is, it has.**

itself [ɪt'self] *pron* **-1.** used as the object of a verb to refer to the same animal or thing as the subject of the verb; used after a preposition □ *The committee has given itself two months to prepare its final recommendations.* □ *The oven switches off by itself.* **-2.** used to emphasize "it", or the name of an animal or thing that is the subject or object of a verb □ *The surrounding countryside is pretty, and the town itself has many interesting old buildings.* ■ **in itself** if one thinks about the particular situation only □ *The island has very little night life, though this in itself is not a disadvantage.*

ITV (*abbr of* **Independent Television**) *n* a system of regional commercial television companies forming one national broadcasting channel in Britain.

IUD *n abbr of* **intrauterine device.**

IV *adj abbr of* **intravenous.**

I've [aɪv] = **I have.**

IVF *n abbr of* **in vitro fertilization.**

ivory ['aɪvərɪ] ◇ *n* the hard white substance that elephants' tusks are made of □ *an ivory carving/ring.* ◇ *adj* of the color of ivory.

ivory tower *n* **to live in an ivory tower** to refuse to face the problems and unpleasant aspects of everyday life.

ivy ['aɪvɪ] *n* an evergreen plant with dark-green shiny leaves that grows up walls and trees.

Ivy League *n* **the Ivy League** a group of eight important US universities. They are located in the northeast and are very highly respected □ *an Ivy League college/education.*

❦ IVY LEAGUE
The term Ivy League is used in the USA to refer to Dartmouth College and the universities of Brown, Columbia, Cornell, Harvard, Pennsylvania, Princeton, and Yale. They are among the oldest universities in the USA (the name refers to the ivy growing on the walls of the old buildings). An Ivy League diploma is a recognized sign of success.

J

j [dʒeɪ] (*pl* **j's** OR **js**), **J** [dʒeɪ] (*pl* **J's** OR **Js**) *n* the tenth letter of the English alphabet.

J/A *abbr of* **joint account.**

jab [dʒæb] (*pt & pp* **jabbed,** *cont* **jabbing**) ◇ *n*

-1. a sudden forceful push □ *He gave her a jab in the ribs.* **-2.** GB an injection (informal use). ◇ *vt* **to jab sthg into sb/sthg** [finger, knife] to push sthg into sb/sthg with a short, quick, forceful movement □ *The nurse jabbed the needle into my arm.* ■ **to jab one's finger at sb** to make short, quick, forceful movements with one's finger in the direction of sb. ◇ *vi* **to jab at sb/sthg** to hit sb/sthg with short, quick, forceful blows □ *"That's where we are,"* she said, jabbing at the map with her pencil.*

jabber ['dʒæbəʳ] ◇ *vt* [apology, excuse] to say <sthg> quickly and unclearly, usually because one is excited. ◇ *vi*: *He was jabbering away in some foreign language.*

jack [dʒæk] *n* **-1.** a mechanical or hydraulic device for raising a heavy object such as a car off the ground. **-2.** a playing card with a picture of a young man on it that is below the queen in value and above the ten □ *the jack of hearts.* **-3.** ELECTRICITY an electric plug with a single pin.

◆ **jack up** *vt sep* **-1. to jack a car up** to raise a car off the ground with a jack. **-2. to jack a price up** to raise a price a lot □ *They jack up their prices in the tourist season.*

jackal ['dʒækl] *n* a wild animal related to the dog that lives in Africa and Asia and often feeds on dead animals.

jackaroo [,dʒækə'ruː] *n* AUS a young male worker on a cattle or sheep farm who is training to be a farm manager.

❦ JACKAROO
Most Australian sheep and cattle farms, or "stations", are very large, with many thousands of animals spread over thousands of square kilometers of land. Traditionally, jackaroos (and jillaroos, their female equivalent) used to spend many months of each year traveling around a station on horseback, gathering the animals on a station together. Now they do most of this work by helicopter and motorcycle.

jackdaw ['dʒækdɔː] *n* a large black and gray bird of the crow family that is believed to like stealing bright objects.

jacket ['dʒækət] *n* **-1.** CLOTHING a short coat □ *a denim/leather jacket.* **-2.** [of a book] the paper cover of a book □ *There's a picture of JFK on the jacket.* **-3.** US [of a record] the envelope in which a record is kept.

jacket potato *n* GB a potato baked in its skin.

Jack Frost [,dʒæk-] an imaginary person, used as a symbol for frost or winter.

jackhammer ['dʒækhæməʳ] *n* US a type of drill that is worked by compressed air and is used to break up hard materials such as road surfaces.

jack-in-the-box *n* a children's toy that consists of a box with a doll inside that jumps out when the lid is opened.

jack knife *n* a knife with a blade that can be folded away into the handle.

◆ **jack-knife** *vi* [semitrailer] to go out of control

and stop with the trailer at a sharp angle to the cab.

jack-of-all-trades (*pl* **jacks-of-all-trades**) *n* a person who can do many different types of work.

jack plug *n* GB ELECTRICITY = **jack**.

jackpot ['dʒækpɒt] *n* the biggest prize in a game, competition, or lottery.

Jack Russell (terrier) [-rʌsl-] *n* a small dog with short legs and a white coat with dark or pale markings.

Jackson ['dʒæksən], **Andrew** (1767–1845) a US soldier, who was President from 1829 to 1837. He is famous for defending New Orleans from the British in 1815.

Jackson, Stonewall (1824–1863) a Confederate general in the American Civil War.

Jack the Ripper a murderer who killed several prostitutes in the East End of London in the 19th century.

Jacob ['dʒeɪkəb] in the Bible, one of the grandchildren of Abraham. His twelve sons started the twelve tribes of Israel, the ancestors of the Jewish people.

Jacobean [,dʒækə'bɪən] *adj* that is connected with the period when James I was king of England (1603–1625).

Jacobite ['dʒækəbaɪt] *n* a supporter of James II of England after power was taken from him in 1688.

Jacuzzi™ [dʒə'kuːzɪ] *n* a bath or pool that has jets under the water that keep the water moving.

jade [dʒeɪd] ◇ *n* -1. a semiprecious stone, usually green, used for making jewelry and ornaments □ *a jade ring*. -2. the green color of jade. ◇ *adj* of the color of jade.

jaded ['dʒeɪdəd] *adj* [person] who is tired and unenthusiastic about something, especially because they have experienced it many times □ *He used to enjoy presenting the program, but he seems so jaded nowadays.*

jagged ['dʒægəd] *adj* [edge, outline, surface] that is rough and uneven with sharp points □ *We climbed over the jagged rocks.*

jaguar [US 'dʒægwɑːr, GB -juə] *n* a large wild cat with spotted fur, similar to the leopard, that lives in Central and South America.

jail [dʒeɪl] ◇ *n* a prison □ *He was sent to jail.* □ *He spent 15 years in jail.* ◇ *vt* to put <sb> in jail □ *He was jailed for 15 years/for murder.*

jailbird ['dʒeɪlbɜːrd] *n* a person who is in prison, or who has been in prison (informal use).

jailbreak ['dʒeɪlbreɪk] *n* an escape from prison.

jailer ['dʒeɪlər] *n* a prison officer.

jam [dʒæm] (*pt* & *pp* **jammed**, *cont* **jamming**) ◇ *n* -1. a sweet food made of fruit boiled with sugar, usually kept in jars and spread on bread □ *strawberry jam* □ *a jam sandwich.* -2. a long line of vehicles on a road that cannot move forward, or which is moving very slowly □ *We were stuck in a jam for over an hour.* -3. **to get into a jam** to get into a difficult situation (informal use) □ *Sue's got herself into another jam at work.*

◇ *vt* -1. **to jam sthg on** OR **onto sthg** to push sthg quickly and roughly on sthg so that it stays in place □ *He jammed the lid on firmly.* -2. [piece of machinery, door, window] to cause <sthg> to stay fixed in one position □ *Jam the window open.* □ *I jammed the brakes on.* -3. **to be jammed** [place] to be very full of people or things □ *The streets were jammed with traffic/shoppers.* -4. **to jam a switchboard** to stop a switchboard from working properly because there are too many telephone calls to it at one time □ *The switchboards were jammed after the program.* -5. RADIO to prevent <a radio signal, broadcast> etc from being heard properly by broadcasting noise on the same wavelength □ *The authorities have been jamming all our broadcasts.*

◇ *vi* [machine, door] to get stuck □ *The lever has jammed.*

Jamaica [dʒə'meɪkə] a country in the Caribbean, south of Cuba. SIZE: 11,425 sq kms. POPULATION: 2,500,000 (*Jamaicans*). CAPITAL: Kingston. LANGUAGE: English. CURRENCY: Jamaican dollar.

Jamaican [dʒə'meɪkən] *n* & *adj*: see **Jamaica**.

jamb [dʒæm] *n* the side part of a door frame or window frame.

jamboree [,dʒæmbə'riː] *n* a large party or celebration.

James I [,dʒeɪmzðə'fɜːrst] (1566–1625) King of England from 1603 to 1625, and King James VI of Scotland from 1567 to 1625.

James II [,dʒeɪmzðə'seknd] (1633–1701) King of England and Ireland from 1685 to 1688, and King of Scotland, as James VII. He became a Catholic, and had to give up his right to be king and live in exile.

James [dʒeɪmz], **Henry** (1843–1916) a US novelist who lived in England from 1869. He is well-known for his elegant style. His work includes *The Portrait of a Lady* and *The Ambassadors*.

James, Jesse (1847–1882) a US criminal who robbed banks and trains and had his own gang.

jam-packed *adj* **to be jam-packed** [street, room, suitcase] to be very full (informal use).

jam session *n* an informal performance of jazz or rock music that has not been planned.

Jan. *abbr of* **January**.

Jane Doe [,dʒeɪn'dəu] a term used in US law for a woman whose name is not known, or which cannot be made public for legal reasons.

jangle ['dʒæŋgl] ◇ *n* a ringing, unpleasant, metallic sound, e.g. of keys or pans being knocked together. ◇ *vt* [keys, pans, bells] to cause <sthg> to make a jangling sound. ◇ *vi* [keys, pans, bells] *I knew there was money in the bag because it jangled when I shook it.*

janitor ['dʒænɪtər] *n* US & SCOT a person whose job is to take care of a building, e.g. an office or school.

January ['dʒænjuerɪ] *n* the first month of the

year in the Western calendar; *see also* **Febru-ary**.

Japan [dʒə'pæn] a country in eastern Asia, consisting of four main islands (Hokkaido, Kyushu, Honshu, and Shikoku) and many smaller islands. SIZE: 373,000 sq kms. POPULA-TION: 124,800,000 (*Japanese*). CAPITAL: Tokyo. LANGUAGE: Japanese. CURRENCY: yen.

Japanese [,dʒæpə'ni:z] (*pl* **Japanese**) ◊ *npl* **the Japanese** people who come from Japan. ◊ *n* the language spoken in Japan. ◊ *adj*: see **Japan** □ *the Japanese economy*.

jar [dʒɑːr] (*pt & pp* **jarred**, *cont* **jarring**) ◊ *n* a glass container, usually with a lid that can be sealed, for keeping preserved food in, e.g. jam or honey □ *a jam jar*. ◊ *vt* to shake <sb/sthg> sharply □ *I jarred my back when I jumped off the wall*. ◊ *vi* **-1.** [noise, voice, accent] to be annoying or irritating □ *His laugh began to jar on her*. **-2.** [colors, opinions] to clash.

jargon ['dʒɑːrgən] *n* words and expressions that are used by particular groups of people, e.g. doctors and lawyers, and that are difficult for other people to understand □ *computer/legal jargon*.

jarring ['dʒɑːrɪŋ] *adj* [noise, sight, colors] that is unpleasant and irritating.

Jarrow March [,dʒærou-] *n* **the Jarrow March** a demonstration in 1936, when many unemployed workers walked from Jarrow, in northeastern England, to London to protest about unemployment in their area.

jasmine ['dʒæzmən] *n* a climbing plant with small yellow or white flowers that have a sweet smell.

jaundice ['dʒɔːndəs] *n* an illness that makes the skin and the whites of the eyes turn yellow.

jaundiced ['dʒɔːndəst] *adj* [view, opinion] pessimistic and cynical □ *Oscar's been in the business so long he's got a jaundiced view of it*.

jaunt [dʒɔːnt] *n* a trip that is taken for pleasure.

jaunty ['dʒɔːntɪ] (*compar* **jauntier**, *superl* **jauntiest**) *adj* [clothing, gesture] that shows that one is feeling cheerful and confident □ *She wore her hat at a jaunty angle*.

Java ['dʒɑːvə] an island that forms part of Indonesia. SIZE: 130,000 sq kms. POPULATION: 108,000,000.

javelin ['dʒævlən] *n* a light spear that is thrown in sports events.

jaw [dʒɔː] ◊ *n* one of the two bones in the head that the teeth are attached to □ *the lower jaw*. ◊ *vi* to talk, usually for a long time and about unimportant things (informal use).

jawbone ['dʒɔːboun] *n* the bone in the lower jaw.

jay [dʒeɪ] *n* a noisy and colorful bird belonging to the crow family.

Jaycee [,dʒeɪ'si:] *n* in the USA, a member of the junior chamber of commerce, an organization that holds social activities.

jaywalk ['dʒeɪwɔːk] *vi* to cross the road in a careless way and ignore pedestrian crossings.

jaywalker ['dʒeɪwɔːkər] *n* a person who jaywalks.

jazz [dʒæz] *n* **-1.** a type of music, originally black American music, that is usually played on trumpets, saxophones, a piano, and drums, has a strong beat, and allows the musicians to improvise □ *a famous jazz musician*. **-2.** *phrase* **and all that jazz** and all that kind of thing (informal use) □ *honor, duty to one's country and all that jazz*.

◆ **jazz up** *vt sep* **to jazz sthg up** [room, building, appearance] to make sthg more interesting, bright, or exciting (informal use) □ *You could jazz it up with some posters on the wall*.

jazz band *n* a group of jazz musicians who play together.

jazzy ['dʒæzɪ] (*compar* **jazzier**, *superl* **jazziest**) *adj* **-1.** [colors, clothes] bright and striking. **-2.** [music, tune] that is in the style of jazz.

JCR (*abbr of* **junior common room**) *n* a common room for students in some British universities.

JCS *n abbr of* **Joint Chiefs of Staff**.

JD *n abbr of* **Justice Department**.

jealous ['dʒeləs] *adj* **-1.** [person] who feels anger and dislike toward a person because that person has something that they would like □ *He is jealous of her/of her success*. □ *You're just jealous!* **-2.** [husband, wife] who feels angry and unhappy because they are afraid that somebody they love may love somebody else more than them □ *a jealous lover* □ *He gets jealous easily*. **-3.** **to be jealous of sthg** to be protective of sthg that one has and wants to keep □ *He is very jealous of his reputation*.

jealously ['dʒeləslɪ] *adv* [look, watch] see **jealous** □ *The recipe is a jealously guarded secret*.

jealousy ['dʒeləsɪ] *n* a jealous feeling □ *Jealousy is a more destructive feeling than envy*.

jeans [dʒi:nz] *npl* casual trousers made of strong, usually blue, cloth □ *a pair of jeans*.

Jedda ['dʒedə] a city in Saudi Arabia and its main port, on the Red Sea. POPULATION: 1,500,000.

Jeep™ [dʒi:p] *n* a small open car with four-wheel drive, originally used by the American army.

jeer [dʒɪər] ◊ *vt* [performer, speaker] to show one's disapproval of <sb> by shouting insults or making rude noises. ◊ *vi* [audience, spectators] *The crowd jeered at him*.

◆ **jeers** *npl* insults shouted or noises made by people to show their disapproval of somebody □ *There were loud jeers from the fans as Lukas was sent off*.

jeering ['dʒɪərɪŋ] ◊ *n* jeers. ◊ *adj*: *jeering crowds*.

Jeeves [dʒi:vz] in the comic novels of P. G. Wodehouse, a servant who is more intelligent than his master, Bertie Wooster.

Jefferson ['dʒefərsən], **Thomas** (1743–1826) US President from 1801 to 1809. He wrote most of the Declaration of Independence and made the Louisiana Purchase.

Jehovah [dʒɪ'houvə] a name for God in the Old Testament.

Jehovah's Witness *n* a member of a religious organization that believes that everything in the Bible is true and that the world is going to end soon.

Jekyll ['dʒekl], **Dr** a character in R. L. Stevenson's story *The Strange Case of Dr. Jekyll and Mr. Hyde*, who turns into the evil Mr. Hyde when he experiments with drugs.

jell ['dʒel] *vi* **-1.** [ideas, plans] to become clearer and more definite. **-2.** [liquid] to become thick or solid.

Jello™ ['dʒelou] *n* US a dessert made from gelatine and fruit juice that wobbles when it is shaken.

jelly ['dʒelɪ] (*pl* **jellies**) *n* **-1.** GB = **Jello**. **-2.** a type of thick jam that does not contain any pieces of fruit □ *blackberry jelly*.

jelly bean *n* a small soft candy made in the shape of a bean.

jellyfish ['dʒelɪfɪʃ] (*pl* **jellyfish** OR **jellyfishes**) *n* a sea animal with a clear soft body and long tentacles that hang in the water below it and often sting.

jelly roll *n* US a thin sponge cake that has been spread with jam and rolled up.

jemmy GB *n* = **jimmy**.

jeopardize, -ise ['dʒepərdaɪz] *vt* [future, career, relationship] to put <sthg> in danger of being damaged, harmed, or lost □ *This latest setback could jeopardize their chances of winning the championship*.

jeopardy ['dʒepərdɪ] *n* **to be in jeopardy** [person, plan, future] to be in danger of being damaged, harmed, or lost □ *This recent spate of attacks puts the whole peace process in jeopardy*.

jerk [dʒɜːˈrk] ◇ *n* **-1.** a short sudden movement □ *The train stopped with a jerk.* □ *She gave the handle a jerk.* **-2.** [person] a stupid person (informal use) □ *What a jerk!* ◇ *vt* to pull <sthg> suddenly and forcefully for a short distance □ *The door was jerked open.* ◇ *vi* [train, person] to move suddenly and quickly □ *The truck jerked to a halt.* □ *Her hand jerked up instinctively.*

jerkily ['dʒɜːˈrkɪlɪ] *adv* [move, drive] *see* **jerky**.

jerkin ['dʒɜːˈrkɪn] *n* a short sleeveless jacket.

jerky ['dʒɜːˈrkɪ] (*compar* **jerkier**, *superl* **jerkiest**) *adj* [movement] that is not smooth because it is caused or interrupted by jerks □ *Your driving is pretty jerky, but you'll be OK with practice*.

jerry-built ['dʒerɪ-] *adj* [house, apartment] that has been built quickly and cheaply, without paying attention to safety or quality.

jerry can *n* a container with flat sides for keeping gasoline in, often kept in vehicles.

jersey ['dʒɜːˈrzɪ] (*pl* **jerseys**) *n* **-1.** a piece of clothing with sleeves, usually made of knitted wool and worn over a shirt. **-2.** a fine slightly stretchy cloth, usually used for making women's dresses.

Jersey ['dʒɜːˈrzɪ] **-1.** the largest of the Channel Islands, famous for its dairy produce. Some

British people keep their money there because the taxes are lower than on the British mainland. SIZE: 116 sq kms. POPULATION: 77,000. CAPITAL: St Helier. **-2.** US = **New Jersey** (informal use).

Jerusalem [dʒə'ruːsələm] the largest city in Israel, and a very important place in the history of the Christian, Jewish, and Muslim religions. It was declared the capital of Israel in 1980. POPULATION: 398,200.

Jerusalem artichoke *n* the root of a sunflower plant that has an irregular lumpy shape and is eaten as a vegetable.

jest [dʒest] *n* **to say sthg in jest** to say sthg as a joke.

jester ['dʒestəˈr] *n* a person who, in former times, was often employed by a king or queen to amuse them by telling jokes, performing tricks etc.

Jesuit ['dʒezʲuət] ◇ *n* a member of the Society of Jesus, a male religious order in the Catholic church which is very loyal to the Pope and does a lot of missionary work. ◇ *adj*: *a Jesuit priest/school*.

Jesus (Christ) ['dʒiːzəs-] a Hebrew preacher who founded the Christian religion. His life is described in the New Testament.

jet [dʒet] (*pt* & *pp* **jetted**, *cont* **jetting**) ◇ *n* **-1.** AVIATION a plane that has jet engines □ *She arrived here by jet.* □ *a private/passenger jet.* **-2.** [of water, steam] a thin stream of a liquid or gas that comes from a small hole with great force □ *A jet of ink is sprayed onto the paper.* **-3.** [for water, steam] a small hole in a piece of equipment that a jet of water, steam etc comes out of □ *a gas jet.* ◇ *vi* AVIATION to travel by jet □ *She's jetting off to New York again.*

jet-black *adj* [hair] very dark black.

jet engine *n* a powerful engine, usually used for modern aircraft, that forces out a stream of hot air and gases behind it.

jet foil *n* a boat that is built on structures like two legs and that rises out of the water when it is traveling fast.

jet lag *n* a feeling of tiredness and confusion that one experiences after flying long distances across several time zones.

jet plane *n* AVIATION = **jet**.

jet-propelled [-prə'peld] *adj* [rocket, plane] powered by jet engines.

Jetsam ['dʒetsəm] *n* → **flotsam**.

jet set *n* **the jet set** rich and fashionable people who travel a lot and have a luxurious lifestyle.

jettison ['dʒetɪsən] *vt* **-1.** [plan, idea, chance] to give <sthg> up. **-2.** [cargo, goods] to throw <sthg> away from a moving vehicle.

jetty ['dʒetɪ] (*pl* **jetties**) *n* a wall or pier built out into the water in a harbor, for loading and unloading ships.

Jew [dʒuː] *n* a person whose religion is Judaism.

jewel ['dʒuːəl] *n* a precious stone, e.g. a diamond or emerald □ *a jewel box/chest*.

jeweler US, **jeweller** GB ['dʒuːələʳ] *n* a person whose job is to make, repair, or sell jewelry.

jewelry US, **jewellery** GB ['dʒuːəlrɪ] *n* decorative objects that are attached to the body, hair, or clothes, e.g. rings or necklaces □ *She wore very little jewelry.*

Jewish ['dʒuːɪʃ] *adj*: see **Jew** □ *He/His wife is Jewish.*

Jezebel ['dʒezəbel] *n* a woman who seduces men (disapproving or humorous use).

JFK -1. *abbr of* **John Fitzgerald Kennedy.** -2. (*abbr of* **John Fitzgerald Kennedy International Airport**) the main international airport for New York City.

jib [dʒɪb] (*pt* & *pp* **jibbed**, *cont* **jibbing**) ◇ *n* -1. the horizontal arm of a crane. -2. a sail shaped like a triangle that is set in front of the mast on a yacht. ◇ *vi* **to jib at sthg** to be reluctant to do or accept sthg.

jibe [dʒaɪb] *n* an insulting remark.

Jiddah ['dʒɪdə] = **Jedda.**

jiffy ['dʒɪfɪ] *n* **in a jiffy** quickly and very soon (informal use) □ *I'll be back in a jiffy.*

Jiffy bag™ *n* GB a padded envelope for sending delicate objects in the mail.

jig [dʒɪg] (*pt* & *pp* **jigged**, *cont* **jigging**) ◇ *n* a lively folk dance. ◇ *vi* -1. to dance a jig. -2. to move up and down with quick, uneven movements.

jiggle ['dʒɪgl] *vt* [key, handle] to move <sthg> from side to side with quick, short movements □ *He jiggled the key in the lock.*

jigsaw (puzzle) ['dʒɪgsɔː-] *n* a game that consists of a picture on cardboard or wood that has been cut up into small irregular pieces that one must put back together.

jihad [US dʒɪ'hɑːd, GB -'hæd] *n* a holy war fought by Muslims to defend Islam.

jillaroo [ˌdʒɪlə'ruː] *n* a young female worker on a cattle or sheep farm who is training to be a farm manager; *see box at* **jackaroo.**

jilt [dʒɪlt] *vt* [boyfriend, girlfriend, lover] to suddenly end one's relationship with <sb>.

Jim Crow Laws [ˌdʒɪm'krou-] *npl* racist laws that existed in the south of the USA from the end of the American Civil War until the 1950s. These laws kept black people from going into the same places as white people.

jimmy ['dʒɪmɪ] US, **jemmy** ['dʒemɪ] GB (US *pl* **jimmies**, GB *pl* **jemmies**) *n* a short metal bar that is curved at one end and is used, especially by criminals, to force doors or windows open.

jingle ['dʒɪŋgl] ◇ *n* -1. a light metallic sound, like that of small bells ringing. -2. a short simple piece of music used in radio and TV advertisements. ◇ *vi* [keys, coins] *I could hear the keys jingling in his pocket.*

jingoism ['dʒɪŋgouɪzm] *n* an unreasonable belief that one's country is superior to others, often expressed in an eagerness for war with other countries.

jinx [dʒɪŋks] *n* a force that is believed to bring bad luck □ *So many things have gone wrong with this car — I'm sure there's a jinx on it.*

jinxed [dʒɪŋkst] *adj* **to be jinxed** [house, car, family] to suffer from or bring bad luck.

jitters ['dʒɪtəʳz] *npl* **to have/get the jitters** to be/become very nervous (informal use) □ *Exams give me the jitters.*

jittery ['dʒɪtərɪ] *adj* [person] who seems nervous and worried □ *The Stock Market is jittery again today following the news on interest rates.*

jive [dʒaɪv] ◇ *n* -1. a fast lively dance, performed to swing or rock and roll music, that was popular in the 1940s and 1950s. -2. US words that are meant to deceive somebody (informal use) □ *jive talk* ◇ *vi* to dance the jive.

Joan of Arc [ˌdʒoʊnəv'ɑːʳk] (1412–1431) a young French woman who dressed as a soldier and led an army against the English. Later, she was captured and burnt as a witch by the English. She was made a saint in 1920.

job [dʒɒb] *n* -1. the regular work that somebody does to earn money, especially when they are employed by somebody □ *He's looking for a new job.* □ *Hundreds of jobs have been lost.* □ *He had a job interview on Tuesday.* -2. a particular task or piece of work □ *Come on, we've got a job to do.* □ *We need to concentrate on the job at hand.* ■ **to do a good job** to do a job well. ■ **to make a good/bad job of sthg** to do sthg well/badly □ *You made a good job of fixing the car.* -3. **to have a job doing sthg** to have difficulty doing sthg □ *We had a job getting the piano upstairs.* -4. **sb's job** sb's duty, function, or responsibility □ *It's not my job to answer questions.* -5. **to have a nose job** to have an operation to improve the shape of one's nose (informal use).

Job [dʒoʊb] in the Bible, a very patient man who suffered many terrible things.

jobbing ['dʒɒbɪŋ] *adj* GB **a jobbing gardener/ tailor etc** a gardener/tailor etc who does not work full-time for anybody, but does jobs as required.

Jobcentre ['dʒɒbsentəʳ] *n* in Britain, one of many government offices, set up by the government in towns and cities, where people can look for jobs or ask for advice on finding jobs.

job creation *n* the act by a government of providing new jobs for unemployed people □ *a job creation program.*

job description *n* a document that lists the duties and responsibilities of a particular job.

jobless ['dʒɒbləs] ◇ *adj* [person] who has no job. ◇ *npl* **the jobless** people without jobs.

job lot *n* a number of cheap things that are sold together as one item, e.g. at an auction □ *I bought them as a job lot at the sale.*

job satisfaction *n* the pleasure that somebody feels as a result of doing their job.

job security *n* the feeling that one will not lose one's job.

jobsharing ['dʒɒbʃeərɪŋ] *n* an arrangement in which a job is shared by more than one person, each working part-time.

Joburg, Jo'burg ['dʒoubɜːʳg] = **Johannesburg** (informal use).

jockey ['dʒɒkɪ] (*pl* **jockeys**) ◇ *n* a person who rides horses in horse races. ◇ *vi* **to jockey for position** to try to gain an advantage over one's competitors.

jockstrap ['dʒɒkstræp] *n* a tight-fitting piece of underwear worn by male athletes to support their genitals.

jocular ['dʒɒkjələʳ] *adj* [person] cheerful and amusing; [reply, remark] that is intended to be amusing □ *a jocular manner.*

jodhpurs ['dʒɒdpəʳz] *npl* trousers, designed for riding on horses, that are loose above the knee and tight below the knee.

Joe Bloggs [,dʒouʹblɒgz] GB = **Joe Blow.**

Joe Blow [,dʒouʹblou] US a typical or average man (informal use).

Joe Public [,dʒouʹpʌblɪk], **Joe Soap** [,dʒou-ʹsoup] GB = **Joe Blow.**

jog [dʒɒg] (*pt* & *pp* **jogged**, *cont* **jogging**) ◇ *n* a slow steady run, done as a form of exercise □ *They go for a jog every evening.* ◇ *vt* to push <sthg>, especially with one's arm, so that it moves slightly □ *Watch you don't jog my elbow, I've got a glass in my hand.* ■ **to jog sb's memory** to help sb to remember something □ *Perhaps this photo will help to jog your memory.* ◇ *vi* to run slowly and steadily, usually as a form of exercise □ *He jogged down the road.*

jogger ['dʒɒgəʳ] *n* a person who jogs for exercise.

jogging ['dʒɒgɪŋ] *n* the sport practiced by joggers □ *I go jogging every morning.*

joggle ['dʒɒgl] *vt* to shake <sb/sthg> gently, usually up and down.

Johannesburg [dʒəʹhænəsbɜːʳg] the largest city in South Africa, in the northeast of the country. POPULATION: 1,566,000.

john [dʒɒn] *n* US a toilet (informal use).

John [dʒɒn] (1167–1216) King of England from 1199 to 1216. He was an unpopular king, and in 1215 he was forced to sign the Magna Carta, the basis of the English constitution.

John Barleycorn [-ʹbɑːʳlɪkɔːʳn] an imaginary person, used as a symbol for alcoholic drink.

John Birch Society [-ʹbɜːʳtʃ-] *n* an extreme right-wing group in the USA that is strongly anti Communist. It was particularly influential in the 1950s and 1960s.

John Bull an imaginary person, used as a symbol for England or the typical Englishman. He is pictured as a fat man wearing a Union Jack flag.

John Doe [-ʹdou] a term used in US law for a man whose name is not known, or which cannot be made public for legal reasons.

John Hancock [-ʹhænkɒk] *n* US a person's signature (informal use).

John O'Groats [-əʹgrouts] a village in Scotland that is considered the most northerly place on the British mainland.
NOTE: Compare **Land's End.**

John Q Public US = **Joe Blow.**

Johnson ['dʒɒnsn], **Amy** (1903–1941) a British pilot who broke records when she flew alone from England to Australia, and from England to South Africa.

Johnson, Samuel (1709–1784) a British writer and critic, also known as Dr Johnson. He is best-known for his *Dictionary of the English Language.*

John the Baptist = **Saint John the Baptist.**

join [dʒɔɪn] ◇ *vt* **-1.** [two objects] to connect or attach <two or more pieces, edges> etc together □ *You have to join (together) the two wires.* **-2.** [person] to get together with <sb> □ *Will you join me for* OR *in a drink?* □ *I'll join you later.* **-3.** [club] to become a member of <a group, club, political party> etc □ *I joined Amnesty International last year.* **-4.** [activity] to take part in <an activity> that other people are doing □ *Come and join the dancing!* **-5. to join a line** to stand at the end of a line of people who are waiting for something □ *I joined the line at the post office.*
◇ *vi* **-1.** [rivers, edges, pieces] to meet or come together □ *The roads join right here.* **-2.** [person] to become a member of a group, club etc □ *You can join at a reduced rate if you're a student.*
◇ *n* the line where two things are joined together □ *She has repaired the vase so well that I can't see the join.*

◆ **join in** ◇ *vt fus* **to join in sthg** [work, activity, fun] to take part in sthg that other people are already doing □ *She never joins in the conversation.* ◇ *vi:* **Ann started singing and the others joined in.**

◆ **join up** *vi* [person] to join one of the armed forces.

joiner ['dʒɔɪnəʳ] *n* a person whose job is to make wooden doors, door frames, window frames etc.

joinery ['dʒɔɪnərɪ] *n* the work of a joiner.

joint [dʒɔɪnt] ◇ *adj* **a joint decision/effort etc** a decision/effort etc that involves two or more people or groups together □ *a joint operation involving the army and the police* ■ **a joint owner/manager etc** a person who owns/manages etc something with one or more other people.
◇ *n* **-1.** ANATOMY a part of the body where two bones meet, e.g. at the elbow □ *I have pains in my joints.* □ *the elbow joint.* **-2.** [between two objects] the place where two things, such as two pipes or pieces of wood, are connected together □ *The pipes have started to leak at the joint.* **-3.** GB COOKING a large piece of meat for roasting □ *a joint of lamb/pork.* **-4.** a place such as a bar or nightclub that is usually not very pleasant, e.g. because it is dirty or dangerous (informal use) □ *Let's get out of this joint.* **-5.**▽ [for smoking] a cigarette that contains cannabis (drugs slang).

joint account *n* a bank account shared by two or more people.

Joint Chiefs of Staff *npl* **the Joint Chiefs of Staff** in the USA, the leaders of the Army, Navy, and Air Force.

jointed ['dʒɔɪntəd] *adj* [doll, puppet] that has joints that can be moved.

jointly ['dʒɔɪntlɪ] *adv* [own, act] together □ *We're jointly responsible for its success.*

joint ownership *n* [of business, property] the state of being owned by two or more people, groups etc.

joint resolution *n* a law or decision that is agreed by both houses of the US Congress.

joint-stock company *n* a company jointly owned by all the people who have bought shares in it.

joint venture *n* a business venture that involves two or more companies together.

joist [dʒɔɪst] *n* a long piece of wood, metal, or concrete used to support the floor or roof of a building.

jojoba [hou'houbə] *n* a small tree or bush that grows in North America and produces an oil used in cosmetics □ *jojoba oil/shampoo.*

joke [dʒouk] ◇ *n* -1. something said or done to make people laugh, e.g. a funny story or trick □ *Let me tell you a joke.* ■ **to go beyond a joke** to become serious and worrying □ *The situation has gone beyond a joke now.* ■ **to play a joke on sb** to trick or deceive sb to amuse people. ■ **it's no joke** a phrase used to refer to a job or situation that is very difficult or unpleasant □ *It's no joke bringing up three kids as a single parent.* -2. **to be a joke** [person, idea] to be too foolish or ridiculous to be taken seriously □ *He was a complete joke as chairman.* ◇ *vi* to tell funny stories; to speak about something in a way that is not serious □ *I'm only joking!* □ *You shouldn't joke about that sort of thing.* □ *He likes to joke with us.*

joker ['dʒoukər] *n* -1. a person who likes to joke about things. -2. an extra playing card that does not belong to any of the four suits.

jollity ['dʒɒlətɪ] *n* laughter and fun.

jolly ['dʒɒlɪ] (*compar* **jollier**, *superl* **jolliest**) ◇ *adj* [person, laugh, time] that seems happy and lively. ◇ *adv* GB a word used to emphasize something, especially to show approval (informal use) □ *Jolly good!* □ *It's jolly difficult to get hold of her.*

jolt [dʒoult] ◇ *n* -1. a sudden violent movement □ *The bus stopped with a jolt.* -2. an unpleasant surprise □ *The collapse of the bank gave financial institutions a sharp jolt.* ◇ *vt* -1. to cause <sb/sthg> to move suddenly and violently □ *The bus braked suddenly and jolted us forward.* -2. to shock or surprise <sb> □ *The news jolted him into action.* ◇ *vi* [cart, car, bike] to shake violently □ *We jolted along the dirt track.*

Jonah ['dʒounə] in the Bible, a man who was swallowed by a whale, and survived.

Jones [dʒounz], **Inigo** (1573–1652) a British architect who designed many great houses and gardens in London.

Joneses ['dʒounzəz] *npl* **to keep up with the Joneses** to make sure that one does not appear to have less money, success etc than one's neighbors by buying expensive things.

Jonson ['dʒɒnsən], **Ben** (1572–1637) a British playwright, whose satirical comedies include *Volpone* and *The Alchemist.*

Jordan ['dʒɔːrdn] -1. a country in the Middle East, between Israel and Saudi Arabia. SIZE: 92,000 sq kms. POPULATION: 3,800,000 (*Jordanians*). CAPITAL: Amman. LANGUAGE: Arabic. CURRENCY: Jordanian dinar. -2. **the Jordan (River)** a river in the Middle East, flowing through Israel and Jordan to the Dead Sea.

Jordanian [dʒɔːrˈdeɪnjən] *n* & *adj*: see **Jordan**.

Joseph ['dʒouzəf] in the Bible, the husband of Mary, the mother of Jesus.

joss stick ['dʒɒs-] *n* a thin stick covered with incense that produces smoke and an attractive smell when it is lit.

jostle ['dʒɒsl] ◇ *vt* to push or knock against <sb>, especially in a crowd □ *People jostled and pushed each other in order to try and get a better view.* ◇ *vi*: *The photographers were jostling for a better view.*

jot [dʒɒt] (*pt* & *pp* **jotted**, *cont* **jotting**) *n* [of truth, sympathy] a very small amount of something □ *There's not a jot of truth in what he says!*

◆ **jot down** *vt sep* **to jot sthg down** [answer, names, notes] to write sthg down in a quick informal way □ *Could you just jot your address down for me?*

jotter ['dʒɒtər] *n* GB a pad of paper or a notebook for jotting things down in.

jottings ['dʒɒtɪŋz] *npl* short notes that have been written about something, usually quickly.

joule [dʒuːl] *n* PHYSICS a unit of energy or work.

journal ['dʒɜːrnl] *n* -1. a serious magazine that deals with a particular subject or profession □ *a medical/scientific journal.* -2. an account that one writes of one's daily activities □ *I often keep a journal when on vacation.*

journalese [,dʒɜːrnəˈliːz] *n* a style of writing only found in newspapers (disapproving use).

journalism ['dʒɜːrnəlɪzm] *n* the profession of reporting or writing for newspapers, magazines, television, or radio □ *a career in journalism.*

journalist ['dʒɜːrnəlɪst] *n* a person whose profession is journalism □ *She's a great journalist.*

journey ['dʒɜːrnɪ] (*pl* **journeys**) *n* GB the process of traveling from one place to another □ *a train journey* □ *Have a nice/safe journey!* □ *I went on a journey from Paris to Istanbul.* □ *It's only a short journey from here.*

joust [dʒaust] ◇ *n* in the Middle Ages, a fight on horseback using lances. ◇ *vi* to fight a joust.

Jove [dʒouv] another name for Jupiter. ■ **by Jove!** an expression used by somebody to show that they are surprised or impressed (old-fashioned use).

jovial ['dʒouvjəl] *adj* [person, smile] cheerful.

jowls [dʒaulz] *npl* [of a person, dog] the lower parts of the sides of the face, especially the loose skin covering the jaw.

joy [dʒɔɪ] *n* -1. a feeling of great happiness □ *To my great joy, he said "yes."* -2. a person or thing that gives somebody happiness or pleasure □ *His performance was a joy to watch.*

Joyce [dʒɔɪs], **James** (1882–1941) an Irish writer whose experimental style had a great influence on 20th-century literature. His work includes *Ulysses* and *Finnegans Wake.*

joyful ['dʒɔɪfl] *adj* [person, scene, shout] very happy □ *It was a joyful occasion.*

joyfully ['dʒɔɪflɪ] *adv* [welcome, shout] *see* **joyful**.

joyous ['dʒɔɪəs] *adj* [song, occasion] very happy (literary use).

joypad ['dʒɔɪpæd] *n* a control device with buttons and levers that is used for playing computer games.

joyride ['dʒɔɪraɪd] ◇ *n* the act of driving dangerously fast in a car that one has just stolen for fun and excitement □ *The boys, 16 and 17, had gone for a joyride.* ◇ *vi* **to go joyriding** to go for a joyride.

joyrider ['dʒɔɪraɪdər] *n* a person who joyrides.

joystick ['dʒɔɪstɪk] *n* -1. AVIATION a lever used to control the movement of a plane. -2. COMPUTING a device with a lever that can be moved in different directions to control a computer or video game.

JP *n abbr of* **Justice of the Peace.**

JP
In Britain, Justices of the Peace, or JPs, are magistrates who are not professional lawyers or judges. They work part-time and are not paid for their work. They are usually respected local people, such as doctors or teachers, who are chosen by the Lord Chancellor. Usually three JPs hear a case at the same time in a magistrates' court.

Jr. *abbr of* **junior.**

jubilant ['dʒuːbɪlənt] *adj* [person] who is very happy and excited, usually because they have had good news or success □ *a jubilant shout/cheer.*

jubilation [,dʒuːbɪ'leɪʃn] *n* a feeling of happiness and excitement, usually caused by good news or success.

jubilee ['dʒuːbɪliː] *n* a celebration to mark the anniversary of an important event or occasion, especially a 25th or 50th anniversary □ *a silver/golden jubilee.*

Judaism ['dʒuːdeɪɪzm] *n* the religion of the Jews, who believe in the god of the Old Testament of the Bible.

Judas (Iscariot) [,dʒuːdəs (ɪ'skærɪət)] in the Bible, the man who betrayed Jesus. He was paid 30 pieces of silver for helping to arrange his arrest.

judder ['dʒʌdər] *vi* GB [vehicle, machine] to keep shaking violently □ *The truck juddered to a halt.*

judge [dʒʌdʒ] ◇ *n* -1. LAW a person whose job is to decide how to use the law in a court to show whether a person accused of a crime is guilty, and who decides what punishment to give them if they are found guilty □ *a High Court judge* □ *Judge Watkins.* -2. a person responsible for deciding who has won a competition or contest □ *The judges took a long time to choose the winner.*
◇ *vt* -1. LAW to make a decision about <a case> in a court of law □ *The case will be judged in a civil court.* -2. [contest, competition] to decide the result of <sthg> □ *The competition will be judged by a distinguished panel of experts.* -3. [person, situation] to form and give an opinion about <sb/sthg> based on the evidence that one has □ *You can't judge people by their appearances.* □ *They judged that he had failed in his duty.* □ *The house was judged to be unsafe.* -4. [age, distance] to guess <sthg> □ *It's difficult to judge how long it would take.*
◇ *vi* -1. to form and give an opinion about something □ *It's not for me to judge.* ■ **to judge from** OR **by sthg, judging from** OR **by sthg** [by behavior, evidence] a phrase used to introduce one's opinion based on something in particular □ *Judging by their attitude, it seems they think very little of our plan.* -2. to guess something □ *"How far is it?" — "It's hard to judge."*

judgment, judgement ['dʒʌdʒmənt] *n* -1. LAW an official decision made by a judge or court of law. -2. [opinion] an opinion given after considering all available information □ *It was a harsh judgment to make in the circumstances.* □ *In my judgment, he was wrong.* ■ **to pass judgment** to give one's opinion of somebody or criticize them □ *The voters will pass judgment on the government tonight.* ■ **to reserve judgment** to refuse to give an opinion about somebody or something until one knows more about them □ *I'll reserve judgment until I've seen all the entrants.* -3. [ability] the ability to make sensible and fair decisions □ *I really trust her judgment.* ■ **against my better judgment** a phrase used to show that one does something although one thinks that it would probably be more sensible or reasonable not to do it □ *I agreed to let them go, against my better judgment.*

judgmental, judgemental [dʒʌdʒ'mentl] *adj* [person, attitude] that one thinks is too critical of other people □ *Don't be so judgmental!*

judicial [dʒuː'dɪʃl] *adj* [decision, ruling, system] that is connected with a court of law.

judiciary [US dʒuː'dɪʃɪeri, GB -'dɪʃəri] *n* **the judiciary** the group of people in a country consisting of all the judges in all the courts, whose job is to deal with legal matters.

judicious [dʒuː'dɪʃəs] *adj* [choice, move, use] that is wise and shows good judgment.

judo ['dʒuːdou] *n* a Japanese form of wrestling in which two people try to throw each other to the ground.

jug [dʒʌg] *n* -1. US a container with a narrow neck, a handle, and a cap or stopper. -2. GB a container with a handle and a spout, used for holding and pouring liquids. -3. the amount of liquid that is held in a jug □ *a milk jug* □ *a jug of milk/water.*

juggernaut ['dʒʌgərnɔːt] *n* GB a very large truck for carrying heavy loads over long distances.

juggle ['dʒʌgl] ◇ *vt* -1. to keep <two or more

objects> in the air at the same time by catching each one as it falls and throwing it up again immediately □ *Pop was juggling oranges to amuse the children.* -2. to rearrange <numbers, ideas, or figures> carefully so that they appear in the form that one wants □ *We had to juggle the figures to make the books balance.* ◇ *vi: The clown juggled while riding a horse.* □ *I've had to juggle with the figures.*

juggler ['dʒʌglə^r] *n* a person who entertains people by juggling.

jugular (vein) ['dʒʌgjələr-] *n* a large vein in one's neck that carries blood back from the head to the heart.

juice [dʒuːs] *n* -1. the liquid part of a fruit or vegetable, often used to make drinks □ *carrot/orange juice.* -2. the liquid produced by a piece of meat when it is being cooked.

◆ **juices** *npl* the liquid in a person's stomach that helps them to digest food □ *gastric juices.*

juicy ['dʒuːsɪ] (*compar* **juicier**, *superl* **juiciest**) *adj* -1. [fruit, orange] that has a lot of juice in it. -2. [story, piece of news] that is interesting, often because it is slightly shocking or rude (informal use) □ *juicy gossip.*

jujitsu [dʒuː'dʒɪtsuː] *n* a sport and a way of fighting that started in Japan and in which one tries to hold, throw, and hit one's opponent.

jukebox ['dʒuːkbɒks] *n* a machine found in places such as bars that plays the record or CD that one selects after one has put money into it.

Jul. *abbr of* **July.**

Juliet [US 'dʒuːljət, GB -ɪət] → **Romeo.**

July [dʒuː'laɪ] *n* the seventh month of the year in the Western calendar; *see also* **February.**

jumble ['dʒʌmbl] ◇ *n* [of objects, sounds, colors] a lot of things that are mixed together in a careless or disorganized way □ *Her clothes lay in a jumble on the floor.* ◇ *vt* = **jumble up.**

◆ **jumble up** *vt sep* to jumble things up to mix things up so that they are not in any order □ *I always get their names jumbled up!*

jumble sale *n* a sale of second-hand things to raise money for a special purpose such as a charity.

jumbo ['dʒʌmbou] *adj* a jumbo meal/sausage etc a meal/sausage etc that is bigger than normal.

jumbo jet *n* a very large plane for carrying passengers.

jump [dʒʌmp] ◇ *vi* -1. [person, animal] to move up into the air so that one's feet leave the ground, usually by bending one's legs and pushing against the ground with one's feet □ *He jumped across the river.* □ *She jumped over the wall.* □ *He jumped down the stairs.* -2. [person, body] to make a sudden movement because one is surprised or frightened □ *You made me jump! I didn't hear you come in.* -3. [price, population, level] to increase by a large amount in a short period of time □ *Profits have jumped by 20% since May.*

◇ *vt* -1. [fence, stream] to cross <sthg> by

jumping over it □ *Do you think you can jump that ditch?* -2. [person] to attack <sb> suddenly (informal use) □ *Two guys jumped me in the subway.* -3. **to jump a train/bus** US to travel on a train/bus illegally, without paying.

◇ *n* -1. an act of jumping □ *a parachute jump.* -2. SPORT an object such as a fence that a horse must jump over as part of a course. -3. [in price, profits] a large increase in amount in a very short period of time □ *There was a sudden jump in property prices.* -4. *phrase* **to keep one jump ahead of sb** [of one's rival, competitor] to be prepared for what sb will do next and so have an advantage over them □ *Remember: always try to keep one jump ahead of your competitors.*

◆ **jump at** *vt fus* to jump at a chance OR opportunity to accept a chance OR opportunity immediately.

jumped-up ['dʒʌmpt-] *adj* GB [civil servant, clerk] who thinks that they are more important than they really are (informal and disapproving use).

jumper ['dʒʌmpə^r] *n* -1. US a dress without sleeves that is worn over a sweater or blouse. -2. GB a piece of knitted clothing covering the upper part of one's body and one's arms.

jumper cables *npl* US two thick wires with heavy clips at both ends, used to start a vehicle that has a dead battery by connecting it to the battery of another vehicle.

jump jet *n* a plane that takes off and lands by going straight up and down in the air.

jump leads *npl* GB = **jumper cables.**

jump rope *n* US a long rope with handles, used e.g. by children to jump over as a game.

jump-start *vt* to start <the engine of a car whose battery does not have enough power> by connecting it to the battery of another car.

jumpsuit ['dʒʌmpsuːt] *n* a single piece of clothing that consists of trousers and a top.

jumpy ['dʒʌmpɪ] (*compar* **jumpier**, *superl* **jumpiest**) *adj* who feels nervous and worried.

Jun. *abbr of* **June.**

junction ['dʒʌŋkʃn] *n* the place where two or more roads, tracks etc join or cross □ *a busy road junction.*

junction box *n* a box in which wires can be safely connected because it has a wire connected to the ground.

juncture ['dʒʌŋktʃər] *n* at this juncture at this particular time (formal use).

June [dʒuːn] *n* the sixth month of the year in the Western calendar; *see also* **February.**

Jung [jʊŋ], **Carl Gustav** (1875–1961) a Swiss psychiatrist who worked with Freud before developing his own theories of the subconscious.

jungle ['dʒʌŋgl] *n* -1. a forest in a very hot country, in which a lot of tall trees grow very close together □ *the Amazon jungle.* -2. [of laws, politics] a complicated or uncontrolled mass of things □ *a jungle of rules and regulations.*

jungle gym *n* US a frame made up of bars that children can climb and play on.

junior ['dʒuːnjə^r] ◇ *adj* -1. a word used after the name of a man who has the same name as his father as a way of avoiding confusion □ *John Grant Junior.* -2. **a junior executive/officer etc** an employee who holds a low or less important position in an organization or profession □ *a junior partner in the firm.* ◇ *n* -1. a person who holds a low rank or position □ *an office junior.* -2. a person who is younger than somebody else □ *He is five years her junior.* -3. EDUCATION in the USA, a student who is in their third year of high school or college.

junior college *n* in the USA, a place for higher education where students receive a technical degree after studying for two years.

junior doctor *n* GB a doctor who has recently qualified and who is getting experience in a hospital.

junior high school *n* in the USA, a school for children aged between 11 and 15.

junior minister *n* in Britain, a member of the government with a low rank.

junior school *n* in Britain, a school for children aged between 7 and 11.

juniper ['dʒuːnɪpə^r] *n* a small evergreen bush with purple berries that are used in cooking and in making gin.

junk [dʒʌŋk] ◇ *n* things that are old and that nobody wants any more (informal use). ◇ *vt* [car, computer] to throw <sthg> away because it is old and is not wanted □ *I had to junk my bed in the end.*

junket ['dʒʌŋkət] *n* a trip made by an official and paid for with public money (informal and disapproving use) □ *Politicians are always off on a junket.*

junk food *n* food that contains a lot of chemicals, sugar, fat etc and is not good for one's health but is quick to prepare (disapproving use).

junkie ['dʒʌŋkɪ] *n* a person who is addicted to drugs, especially heroin (informal use).

junk mail *n* letters, brochures etc that advertise goods and services and are sent to people without them asking for it (disapproving use).

junk shop *n* a shop that sells second-hand things at very cheap prices.

Juno ['dʒuːnəʊ] the Roman goddess of women and marriage.

Junr *abbr of* **junior.**

junta [US 'hʊntə, GB 'dʒʌntə] *n* a military government that has come to power in a country not as a result of being elected but by force.

Jupiter ['dʒuːpɪtə^r] -1. the ruler of the Roman gods, who could throw thunderbolts. -2. the planet in the solar system that is the largest and the fifth-furthest from the Sun.

jurisdiction [,dʒʊərɪs'dɪkʃn] *n* the right of an official, organization, or court of law to make legal judgments about something □ *That area is not under my jurisdiction.* □ *This territory comes within the jurisdiction of Canada.*

jurisprudence [,dʒʊərɪs'pruːdəns] *n* the study or science of law.

juror ['dʒʊərə^r] *n* a member of a jury.

jury ['dʒʊərɪ] (*pl* **juries**) *n* -1. LAW a group of usually twelve people who hear all the evidence in a case and decide whether the accused person is innocent or guilty. -2. [in a contest] a group of people who decide the winners in a competition.

jury box *n* the place in a court where the jury sits.

jury duty US, **jury service** GB *n* **to be on** OR **do jury duty** to spend a period of time as a member of a jury.

just [dʒʌst] ◇ *adv* -1. **he just left** he left a very short time ago □ *I've just seen her in the corridor.* □ *It had just stopped raining when we set out.* -2. **I'm just getting dressed** I am getting dressed now and will very soon be finished □ *Ann was just leaving when we got there.* ■ **I'm just about to go out** I am going to go out very soon. -3. only □ *"What do you want to eat?" — "Just a sandwich."* □ *These are just a few examples of the problems we've been having.* ■ **just a minute** OR **second** OR **moment!** a phrase used to tell somebody to wait for a short time □ *I'll be with you in just a minute.* -4. **I just got there on time** I got there on time, but I very nearly did not □ *He only just missed his train.* □ *We have just enough time for one more question.* -5. **I might just manage to get there** there is a chance that I will get there, but it is a very small chance □ *It's just possible that John will know.* -6. used for emphasis □ *I just know I'm right.* □ *The food here is just wonderful.* □ *Just do what you're told!* -7. **that's just right** that's exactly right □ *I'll plant a rose bush just here.* □ *You're just the person I need to talk to.* □ *That's just what I wanted.* -8. used with "can" and "could" to make polite requests □ *Could you just move over, please?* ◇ *adj* [person, decision, punishment] fair and reasonable.

◆ **just about** *adv* very nearly □ *I'm just about finished.* □ *We'll just about get there on time if we leave by noon.*

◆ **just as** *adv* -1. at the moment when □ *They arrived just as I was leaving.* -2. used in comparisons □ *She speaks French just as well as you do.*

◆ **just now** *adv* -1. a short time ago □ *I was talking to her just now.* -2. at this exact moment □ *I'm sorry, but I can't speak to you just now.*

◆ **just the same** *adv* in spite of that □ *She probably can't come, but I'll invite her just the same.*

◆ **just then** *adv* at that exact time □ *I didn't want to tell her just then.*

justice ['dʒʌstəs] *n* -1. fair treatment of other people □ *We demand justice for these prisoners.* -2. [system] the system in a country by which laws are made and crimes are punished □ *the courts of justice*. **-3.** [of a cause, claim] the quality of being reasonable and fair. **-4.** US [person] a judge □ *a Supreme Court justice*. **-5.** GB [title] the title of a judge in a High Court □ *Mr Justice Thomas*. **-6. the Justice Department, the Department of Justice** the US government department that gives legal advice to the President. Its chief officer is called the Attorney General. **-7.** *phrases* **to do justice to sthg** to deal with sthg properly and fully □ *The movie doesn't really do justice to the book*. ■ **to do justice to sb** [photograph, description] to make sb look or seem as good or attractive as they really are □ *The photo doesn't really do you justice*. ■ **to do oneself justice** to perform well in an exam, competition etc in a way that shows how good one is □ *She didn't really do herself justice in the exam*.

Justice of the Peace (*pl* **Justices of the Peace**) *n* a person who judges cases in the lower courts of law and, in the USA, can marry people.

justifiable ['dʒʌstɪfaɪəbl] *adj* [pride, anger, action] that is reasonable because there is a good cause for it □ *His reaction was perfectly justifiable in the circumstances*.

justifiable homicide *n* a lawful act of killing, e.g. in self-defense.

justifiably ['dʒʌstɪfaɪəblɪ] *adv*: *see* **justifiable** □ *You can be justifiably proud of your achievements*.

justification [,dʒʌstɪfɪ'keɪʃn] *n* a good reason or explanation for doing something □ *There was no justification for the level of violence used*.

justify ['dʒʌstɪfaɪ] (*pt* & *pp* **justified**) *vt* **-1.** [decision, behavior, action] to give a good reason or explanation for <sthg> □ *How can you justify spending so much money?* □ *He made no attempt to justify his violent behavior*. **-2.** COMPUTING & PRINTING [document, column, file] to arrange the words of <a piece of text> so that the left and right edges are straight □ *Justify left/right*.

justly ['dʒʌstlɪ] *adv* **-1.** [act, behave] in a fair and reasonable way □ *They have not been treated justly*. **-2.** a word used to say that something is fair and right □ *a justly deserved reputation for excellence*.

jut [dʒʌt] (*pt* & *pp* **jutted**, *cont* **jutting**) *vi* **to jut (out)** [balcony, cliff] to stick out □ *A rocky peninsula juts out into the sea*.

jute [dʒuːt] *n* the fiber of a particular plant, used in making rope, sacks, rough cloth etc.

juvenile ['dʒuːvənaɪl] ◇ *adj* **-1.** LAW [crime, delinquency] that relates to a young person not old enough to be treated like an adult □ *juvenile offenders*. **-2.** [behavior, sense of humor] that seems childish or silly (disapproving use) □ *How juvenile!* ◇ *n* LAW a young person not old enough to be treated like an adult.

juvenile court *n* a court which deals with crimes committed by juveniles.

juvenile delinquent *n* a young person who has committed a minor crime.

juxtapose [,dʒʌkstə'pəʊz] *vt* [objects, ideas, features] to put <two things> next to each other, often to show more clearly how different they are □ *Look at the way the artist juxtaposes these two images*.

juxtaposition [,dʒʌkstəpə'zɪʃn] *n*: *see* **juxtapose** □ *The juxtaposition of dark and light colors produces a very striking effect*.

k [keɪ] (*pl* **k's** OR **ks**), **K** [keɪ] (*pl* **K's** OR **Ks**) *n* the eleventh letter of the English alphabet.
◆ **K -1.** *abbr of* **kilobyte**. **-2.** *abbr of* **thousand**.

Kafka ['kæfkə], **Franz** (1883–1924) a Czech writer well known for his novels, such as *The Trial* and *The Castle*, about people faced with large impersonal organizations.

kaftan ['kæftæn] *n* a long loose piece of clothing with wide sleeves, worn by men in Arab countries and by women in America and Europe.

Kakadu [,kækə'duː] a national park in Northern Territory, Australia, that was opened in 1979 and is a big tourist attraction.

kale [keɪl] *n* a type of dark green cabbage with curly leaves.

kaleidoscope [kə'laɪdəskəʊp] *n* **-1.** a toy that consists of a tube held in the hand, through which one can see a changing pattern of colors when a disc at one end of it is turned. **-2.** a pattern of colors or images or a mixture of things that changes all the time □ *a kaleidoscope of cultures*.

Kampuchea [,kæmpuː'tʃɪə] = **Cambodia**.

kangaroo [,kæŋgə'ruː] *n* a large Australian animal with powerful back legs for jumping and a long thick tail, the female of which carries its young in a pocket on its stomach.

Kansas ['kænzəs] a state in the central USA consisting mainly of farmland. ABBREVIATION: KS. SIZE: 213,063 sq kms. POPULATION: 2,477,574 (*Kansans*). CAPITAL: Topeka.

Kant [US kɑːnt, GB kænt], **Immanuel** (1724–1804) a German philosopher who believed that human knowledge and morals should be governed by reason.

kaolin ['keɪəlɪn] *n* a fine white clay used for making cups, dishes etc and in medicine.

kaput [kə'pʊt] *adj* **to be kaput** [car, TV, washing machine] to be broken (informal use) □ *"Is the TV not working?" — "No, it's kaput."*

karaoke [,kærɪ'əʊkɪ] *n* a form of entertainment that started in Japan in which people sing pop songs, e.g. in a bar, using a recorded version of the music without the voices □ *a karaoke night/machine*.

karat [US 'kerət, GB 'kær-] *n* US = **carat**.

karate [kə'rɑːtɪ] *n* a sport and a way of fighting that started in Japan in which people use their hands, arms, legs, and feet.

Kashmir [kæʃ'mɪəʳ] a mountainous region of northern India and Pakistan.

Katar = **Qatar**.

kayak ['kaɪæk] *n* a type of canoe used by Inuits or in sport.

KB *n abbr of* **kilobyte(s)**.

KC (*abbr of* **King's Counsel**) *n* a title given to some British barristers when a king is ruling.

kcal (*abbr of* **kilocalorie**) a unit (4.18 kilojoules) for measuring the amount of energy in food.

Keats [kiːts], **John** (1795–1821) a British Romantic poet whose works include *To a Nightingale* and *To Autumn*.

kebab [US kɪ'bɑːb, GB -'bæb] *n* a dish consisting of small pieces of meat and vegetables put on a stick and grilled.

kedgeree ['kedʒəriː] *n* GB a dish consisting of rice, boiled eggs, and fish.

keel [kiːl] *n* -1. a long piece of wood or metal along the bottom of a ship onto which the rest of the structure is fitted. -2. *phrase* **to be on an even keel** to be steady and stable □ *Our finances are now on an even keel.*

◆ **keel over** *vi* [ship, person] to fall onto one side □ *He staggered in, then keeled over and fell straight to sleep.*

keen [kiːn] *adj* -1. **to be keen on sthg** to enjoy doing sthg and do it often □ *She's very keen on squash/skating.* □ *He's a keen gardener/tennis player.* -2. **to be keen on sb** GB to like sb and be attracted to them. -3. **to be keen to do** OR **on doing sthg** to want to do sthg very much □ *She seemed very keen to help.* □ *They aren't so keen on going out tonight.* □ *You don't seem very keen.* -4. [interest, desire] strong □ *She took a keen interest in the affair.* □ *There is keen competition for places on the course.* -5. [eye, sense of smell] good □ *He has a keen sense of hearing.* -6. **to have a keen mind** to be quick to understand things.

keenly ['kiːnlɪ] *adv* -1. **keenly contested/debated etc** contested/debated etc with great energy and determination □ *a keenly fought contest.* -2. **to be keenly aware/interested** to be very aware/interested □ *I was keenly aware of the dangers.* -3. [watch, listen] very carefully and with great concentration.

keep [kiːp] (*pt & pp* **kept**) ◇ *vt* -1. to continue to have <sthg> and not give it back, lose it etc □ *Here's $10 — keep the change.* □ *You can keep the book if you like.* □ *Luckily I managed to keep my job.* -2. **to keep sthg in a place** to store sthg in a place so that it can be found and used later □ *Where do you keep the teabags?* □ *Keep your passport in a safe place.* -3. **to keep sb/sthg in a place or state** to make sb/sthg stay in a particular place or state □ *I kept my hands in my pockets.* □ *They kept us waiting all afternoon.* □ *Regular spraying will keep the plants free from disease.* **-4.**

to keep forgetting/apologizing etc to forget/apologize many times □ *The photocopier keeps breaking down.* □ *I keep telling myself things will be OK.* **-5. to keep walking/talking etc** to continue to walk/talk etc without stopping □ *Keep stirring the mixture until all the lumps have gone.* **-6. to keep sb/sthg from doing sthg** to stop sb/sthg from doing sthg □ *Put the butter in the refrigerator to keep it from melting.* □ *Remember to shut the gate to keep the dog from getting out.* □ *I hope I'm not keeping you from your work.* **-7. to keep sb** to delay sb and cause them to be late □ *I'll only keep you a minute.* **-8. to keep sthg from sb** not to tell sb sthg □ *His family tried to keep the news from him.* **-9.** [sheep, hens, dog] to own and look after <farm animals or pets>. **-10.** [family, mistress] to look after <sb> by providing them with food, clothes, money etc □ *He barely earns enough to keep himself.* **-11. to keep a promise/an appointment** to carry out a promise/an appointment as agreed or planned □ *Don't make promises you can't keep.* **-12. to keep a record/diary etc** to make a record/diary etc by writing down information in a regular or organized way □ *I kept a note of how much we spent.* **-13. to keep a secret** not to tell other people a secret □ *Can you keep a secret?*

◇ *vi* -1. (+ *complement*) **to keep quiet** to continue to be quiet □ *She does aerobics to keep in shape.* □ *I like to keep in touch with my family.* **-2. keep straight ahead** continue to go straight ahead □ *Keep left until you get to the traffic lights.* □ *Pedestrians should keep on the sidewalk.* **-3.** [food] to stay fresh and not go bad □ *Fish only keeps for a couple of days in this hot weather.*

◇ *n* **to earn/pay for one's keep** to earn/pay for the cost of one's food, rent etc.

◆ **for keeps** *adv* permanently (informal use) □ *I'm coming back home for keeps.*

◆ **keep at** *vt fus* **to keep at it** to continue to work hard, even though it is difficult or tiring □ *If you want to pass these exams, you'll have to keep at it.*

◆ **keep back** *vt sep* **to keep a sum of money back** to keep a sum of money oneself, so that one does not give all of a large amount to somebody □ *They kept back 10% of my wages.* ■ **to keep something back** not to tell somebody everything □ *I could tell they were keeping something back from me.*

◆ **keep down** *vt sep* **to keep sthg down** [numbers, prices, costs] to stop sthg from increasing □ *This year we've managed to keep down travel costs.*

◆ **keep off** ◇ *vt sep* **to keep sb/sthg off** [sun, attacker, blow] to prevent sb/sthg from touching or harming something else □ *an umbrella to keep the rain off.* ◇ *vt fus* **to keep off sthg** [flowerbed, road] not to touch or walk on sthg. ■ **'keep off the grass'** do not walk on the grass.

◆ **keep on** *vt fus* -1. **to keep on doing sthg** to experience sthg repeatedly □ *I keep on getting headaches.* -2. **to keep on doing sthg** to continue to do sthg without stopping □ *We kept on working till late into the night.*

◆ **to keep on about** *vt fus* **to keep on about sthg** to talk about sthg repeatedly in an irritating way □ *Don't keep on at me about buying you a new bike!*

◆ **keep out** ◇ *vt sep* **to keep sb/sthg out** [burglar, goal] to stop sb/sthg from getting into a place □ *a fence to keep out sheep.* ◇ *vi* **'keep out'** you may not enter this place.

◆ **keep to** ◇ *vt fus* **to keep to sthg** [plan, rule, budget] to follow or obey sthg when performing a duty or doing a job □ *It is essential that we keep strictly to the deadline.* ◇ *vt sep* **-1. to keep sthg to a particular limit** not to allow sthg to rise above a particular limit □ *We must keep costs to a minimum.* **-2. to keep sthg to oneself** not to tell anybody about sthg □ *I kept these doubts to myself.* **-3.** *phrase* **they keep themselves to themselves** they spend a lot of time on their own and do not mix much with other people.

◆ **keep up** ◇ *vt sep* **to keep sthg up** [output, speed] to make sthg continue at a good or high level □ *Keep up the good work!* □ *I found it hard to keep up my enthusiasm/spirits.* ■ **keep it up!** a phrase used to encourage somebody to continue working or trying.
◇ *vi* **-1.** to move, work, produce, increase etc as fast as somebody or something □ *You're walking too fast — I can't keep up with you.* □ *Supply has failed to keep up with demand.* **-2. to keep up with sthg** [with fashion, the news] to take an interest in the latest developments affecting sthg □ *I try to keep up with current affairs.* **-3. to keep up with sb** to stay in contact with sb, e.g. by writing or phoning regularly □ *I've kept up with all my old school friends.*

keeper ['kiːpə'] *n* **-1.** a person who takes care of animals in a zoo □ *a zoo/an elephant keeper.* **-2.** a person who takes care of objects in a museum.

keep-fit *n* GB physical exercise to keep the body in good condition □ *keep-fit classes/exercises.*

keeping ['kiːpɪŋ] *n* **-1. to be in sb's keeping** [document, property] to be kept by sb so that it is safe □ *Can we leave the car in your keeping until we get back?* **-2. to be in/out of keeping with sthg** [rule, decision] to be based/not based on the same principles as sthg; [clothes, style] to be suitable/unsuitable for sthg □ *His speech was entirely in keeping with government policy.* □ *In keeping with tradition, the winners will be announced in reverse order.* □ *The columns at the front seemed out of keeping with the style of the rest of the house.*

keepsake ['kiːpseɪk] *n* a small present given to somebody so that they will remember the person who gave it □ *My mother gave me this locket as a keepsake.*

keg [keg] *n* a small barrel, especially for keeping beer in.

Kelly ['kelɪ], **Ned** (1854–1880) an Australian outlaw who committed many robberies and murders. He was eventually caught and hanged.

kelp [kelp] *n* a type of large brown seaweed.

ken [ken] *n* **beyond one's ken** beyond one's knowledge or understanding (old-fashioned use).

Kennedy ['kenədɪ], **Jackie** (1929–1994) the wife of John F. Kennedy.

Kennedy, John F. (1917–1963) US President from 1961 to 1963. He was shot and killed by Lee Harvey Oswald, though there are still many theories about his death.

Kennedy, Robert (1925–1968) a US politician who was the brother of John F. Kennedy. He was shot and killed while he was trying to become president.

Kennedy Center: the Kennedy Center a large concert hall in Washington, D.C.

kennel ['kenl] *n* **-1.** a small hut for a dog to sleep in. **-2.** = **kennels**.

◆ **kennels** *npl* a place where dogs are left when their owners go on vacation; a place where dogs are bred.

Kent [kent] a county in southeastern England, on the English Channel. SIZE: 3,731 sq kms. POPULATION: 1,520,400. ADMINISTRATIVE CENTER: Maidstone.

Kent State Incident *n* **the Kent State Incident** an incident at Kent State University, USA, in 1970. The National Guard shot at students who were protesting about the Vietnam War and killed four of them.

Kentucky [ken'tʌkɪ] a state in the southern central USA, famous for its bluegrass. ABBREVIATION: KY. SIZE: 104,623 sq kms. POPULATION: 3,685,296 (*Kentuckians*). CAPITAL: Frankfort.

Kentucky Derby *n* **the Kentucky Derby** an important horse race that happens every year in Louisville, Kentucky.

Kenya ['kenjə] a country in East Africa, on the Indian Ocean between Somalia and Tanzania. SIZE: 583,000 sq kms. POPULATION: 27,700,000 (*Kenyans*). CAPITAL: Nairobi. LANGUAGE: English, Swahili. CURRENCY: Kenyan shilling.

Kepler ['keplə'], **Johannes** (1571–1630) a German astronomer. His three laws describing how the planets move around the Sun were important for the development of modern astronomy.

kept [kept] *past tense & past participle of* **keep**.

kerb [kɜːᵇ] *n* GB a line of concrete or stones that marks the edge of a sidewalk.

kerb crawler [-krɔːlə'] *n* GB a person who drives slowly along a road looking for a prostitute to have sex with.

kernel ['kɜːᵣnl] *n* the part of a nut that is inside the shell.

kerosene ['kerəsiːn] *n* a liquid made from petroleum or coal and used as fuel in heaters, lamps, and jet engines.

Kerouac ['keruæk], **Jack** (1922–1969) a US writer who was one of the Beat Generation. His best-known novel is *On the Road*.

kestrel ['kestrəl] *n* a type of small falcon that feeds on small animals.

ketch [ketʃ] *n* a sailing ship with two masts.

ketchup ['ketʃəp] *n* a rich tomato sauce containing vinegar that is served cold with food □ *Would you like some tomato ketchup?*

kettle ['ketl] *n* a container with a lid, handle, and spout that is used for boiling water □ *I'll just put the kettle on and make some coffee.*

kettledrum ['ketldrʌm] *n* a large drum with a round bottom that is played in orchestras.

Kew Gardens [,kjuː-] a large botanical garden in southwest London, England. It is famous for its collection of plants from all over the world.

key [kiː] (*pl* **keys**) ◇ *n* -1. [for a door, engine] a specially shaped piece of metal that is used to open and close a lock in a door, drawer etc or to stop and start an engine □ *I've lost my keys.* -2. [on a computer, typewriter] any of the buttons that one presses to operate a computer, typewriter etc □ *Which key do I press?* -3. [for a map] a list of symbols and abbreviations used in a map or diagram together with explanations of their meanings □ *There should be a key at the front of the book.* -4. **the key to sthg** the way of understanding or achieving sthg □ *What's the key to success for a budding writer, then?* □ *Patience is the key.* -5. [on a piano, clarinet] one of the parts on a musical instrument that are pressed to produce particular notes. -6. MUSIC a series of notes based on a particular note □ *This song is in the key of F.*
◇ *adj* **a key industry/player** a very important industry/player.
◆ **key in** *vt sep* **to key sthg in** [data, information] to type sthg into a computer □ *First, key in the filename.*

keyboard ['kiːbɔːʳd] ◇ *n* -1. [on a typewriter, computer] the set of keys on a typewriter, computer etc that are pressed to operate it. -2. [on a piano] the set of black and white keys on a piano or organ that are pressed to play it. ◇ *vt* to type <text or data> into a computer using a keyboard.

keyboarder ['kiːbɔːʳdəʳ] *n* a person whose job is to key information into a computer.

keyed up [,kiːd-] *adj* **to be keyed up** [person] to be nervous or excited □ *I was all keyed up before the game.*

keyhole ['kiːhəʊl] *n* a hole in a lock for putting a key in.

keyhole surgery *n* surgery that is carried out through a small hole made in a person's body.

Keynes [keɪnz], **John Maynard** (1883–1946) a British economist. His idea that governments should spend more to keep people employed has had a strong influence on 20th-century economics.

keynote ['kiːnəʊt] *n* the most important or central part of something □ *a keynote speech.*

keypad ['kiːpæd] *n* a small keyboard that can be held in the hand and used for operating a calculator, television etc.

key ring *n* a ring that keys can be attached to so that they are kept together.

keystone ['kiːstəʊn] *n* -1. ARCHITECTURE the central stone at the top of an arch which keeps all the other stones in place. -2. [of a policy, ideology] the central idea in a theory, philosophy etc on which the rest is based.

keystroke ['kiːstrəʊk] *n* COMPUTING the action of pressing a key down once on a keyboard.

Key West an island off the coast of Florida, USA. It is an important tourist center. POPULATION: 24,000.

kg *abbr of* **kilogram(me)**.

KGB *n* **the KGB** the government department that was responsible for state security, espionage, and intelligence in the former USSR.

khaki [US 'kækɪ, GB 'kɑːkɪ] ◇ *adj* [shorts, dress, uniform] yellow-brown in color. ◇ *n* -1. a yellow-brown color. -2. a tough cloth that is khaki in color and is used especially for making military uniforms.

Khomeini [kʊʊ'meɪnɪ], **Ayatollah** (1900–1989) an Iranian religious and political leader. Under him Iran became a fundamentalist Islamic republic.

Khyber Pass [,kaɪbəʳ-]: **the Khyber Pass** a mountain pass between Pakistan and Afghanistan that used to be the main route by land from Europe to India.

kibbutz [kɪ'bʊts] (*pl* **kibbutzim** [,kɪbʊt'siːm] OR **kibbutzes**) *n* a farm or other place of work in Israel where the workers live together and share all duties and profits.

kick [kɪk] ◇ *vt* -1. [person, ball, door] to hit <sb/sthg> hard with one's foot □ *I saw him kick that dog!* ■ **to kick oneself** to be very annoyed with oneself for missing an opportunity or for doing something badly □ *I could have kicked myself when I found out.* □ *You'll kick yourself when you hear the answer.* -2. **to kick the habit** to stop doing something that one has been doing for a long time, especially smoking or drinking (informal use) □ *I've been trying to kick the habit for years.*
◇ *vi* to move one's legs forcefully, e.g. when swimming □ *Don't try and kick too hard.*
◇ *n* -1. the act of kicking something □ *He gave the door a kick.* -2. **to do sthg for kicks** to do sthg because it is exciting and enjoyable (informal use) □ *When asked why they committed the crime, the boys answered that it was just for kicks.* ■ **to get a kick from sthg** to get pleasure and excitement from sthg (informal use) □ *He seems to get a kick out of insulting other people.* -3. **to have a kick** to have a strong flavor, especially because of alcohol (informal use) □ *This vodka's got a real kick!*
◆ **kick about, kick around** *vi* to lie unused or forgotten somewhere (informal use) □ *If you're interested, I think I've got some old chairs kicking around in the cellar.*
◆ **kick in** *vi* [drug, device] to begin to have an effect or operate □ *If the electricity supply fails, a backup generator kicks in.*
◆ **kick off** *vi* -1. SPORT [players, teams] to start a game of soccer □ *The game kicks off at 3 o'clock.* -2. **to kick off with sthg** [with a discussion, explanation] to start an event, e.g. a

meeting, with sthg (informal use) □ *We kicked off with a brief outline of our plans.*

◆ **kick out** *vt sep* **to kick sb out** to force sb to leave a place or job (informal use) □ *She was kicked out of school for bullying.*

◆ **kick up** *vt fus* **to kick up a fuss** to get upset or complain loudly about something □ *Tina will kick up a fuss when she hears about this.*

kickoff ['kɪkɒf] *n* the start of a game of soccer □ *'Kickoff at 7pm.'*

kick-start *vt* -1. to start <a motorcycle> by kicking a pedal downwards. -2. to take forceful action in order to help <a process, situation> etc get started or develop quickly □ *measures to kick-start the economy.*

kid [kɪd] (*pt* & *pp* **kidded**, *cont* **kidding**) ◇ *n* -1. a child (informal use) □ *They've got four kids.* -2. a young goat; leather produced from the skin of a young goat.
◇ *comp* **one's kid brother/sister** one's younger brother/sister (informal use).
◇ *vt* (informal use) -1. to say something untrue to <sb> as a joke □ *Don't worry, I'm only kidding you!* -2. **to kid oneself** to allow oneself to believe something that is not true □ *Don't kid yourself, he'll never agree to it!*
◇ *vi* (informal use) **to be kidding** to be joking □ *I'm not kidding, he must have weighed 350 pounds.* □ *I was only kidding!* ■ **no kidding!** a phrase used to show one's surprise about something that has been said □ *"I won it in a raffle." — "No kidding!"*

kiddie, kiddy ['kɪdɪ] (*pl* **kiddies**) *n* a very young child (informal use).

kid gloves *npl* **to treat** OR **handle sb with kid gloves** to treat sb very carefully or gently because one does not want to upset them.

kidnap ['kɪdnæp] (US *pt* & *pp* **kidnaped**, *cont* **kidnaping**, GB *pt* & *pp* **kidnapped**, *cont* **kidnapping**) *vt* to take <sb> away from a place by force, keep them as a prisoner, and demand that somebody gives money or does something before they are released □ *The three men were kidnaped by separatists last year.*

kidnaper US, **kidnapper** GB ['kɪdnæpə'] *n* a person who has kidnaped somebody □ *The kidnapers have asked for a ransom of $2 million.*

kidnaping US, **kidnapping** GB ['kɪdnæpɪŋ] *n* the crime of kidnaping somebody □ *The kidnaping took place last Wednesday.*

kidney ['kɪdnɪ] (*pl* **kidneys**) *n* -1. ANATOMY one of the two organs in the body that remove waste from the bloodstream and produce urine. -2. COOKING an animal's kidney eaten as food.

kidney bean *n* a dark-red bean that is shaped like a small kidney and can be eaten.

kidney machine *n* a machine that does the job of the kidneys for people whose own kidneys no longer work or have been removed.

Kilimanjaro [ˌkɪlɪmən'dʒɑːrəʊ]: **(Mount) Kilimanjaro** a mountain in Tanzania which is the highest in Africa. HEIGHT: 5,895 m.

kill [kɪl] ◇ *vt* -1. to cause <a person, animal, or plant> to die □ *He tried to kill himself by tak-* ing sleeping pills. □ *The plane crashed into a mountain, killing 200 passengers.* -2. **it's killing me** it's causing me great pain (informal use) □ *These shoes/My feet are killing me!* -3. [hope, chances] to bring <sthg> to an end in a way that is very disappointing □ *That remark really killed the conversation.* -4. **to kill time** to pass the time by doing something unimportant, usually while waiting for something to happen □ *I went for a walk to kill time.*
◇ *vi* to cause death □ *'Smoking kills.'*
◇ *n* -1. **the kill** the act of killing an animal or bird after hunting it □ *The dogs moved in for the kill.* -2. a bird or animal that has been hunted and killed.

◆ **kill off** *vt sep* **to kill sthg off** [species, plants, business] to destroy most of or all of sthg □ *High prices could kill off the tourist trade.* □ *The character of Harvey has been killed off by the scriptwriters of the series.*

killer ['kɪlə'] *n* -1. a person or animal that kills □ *The killer is believed to be a woman.* -2. something, such as a disease, that causes death □ *a killer virus.*

killer whale *n* a whale with teeth whose body is white underneath and dark on top and that feeds on fish, squid etc.

killing ['kɪlɪŋ] ◇ *adj* [pain, work] that is very tiring (informal use). ◇ *n* -1. the act of causing somebody's death deliberately, usually with violence □ *There has been a spate of revenge killings.* □ *With this agreement, the killing may at last come to an end.* -2. **to make a killing** to make a lot of money very easily (informal use) □ *You'll make a killing on this deal, I promise.*

killjoy ['kɪldʒɔɪ] *n* a person who wants to stop other people from enjoying themselves.

kiln [kɪln] *n* an oven for baking bricks or pots.

kilo ['kiːləʊ] (*pl* **kilos**) *n abbr of* **kilogram** □ *I've lost six kilos in three weeks.*

kilobyte ['kɪləbaɪt] *n* a unit of 1,024 bytes of computer information.

kilogram(me) ['kɪləgræm] *n* a unit (1,000 grams) for measuring weight.

kilohertz ['kɪləhɜː'ts] (*pl* **kilohertz**) *n* a unit (1,000 hertz) for measuring radio waves.

kilojoule ['kɪlədʒuːl] *n* a unit (1,000 joules) for measuring energy or work.

kilometer [kɪ'lɒmɪtr] US, **kilometre** ['kɪləmiːtə] GB *n* a unit (1,000 meters) for measuring distance □ *I ran in a ten-kilometer road race.*

kilowatt ['kɪləwɒt] *n* a unit (1,000 watts) for measuring electrical power.

Kilroy ['kɪlrɔɪ] a name used for an unknown person, mentioned in graffiti in the phrase "Kilroy was here".

kilt [kɪlt] *n* a knee-length pleated skirt, usually made from tartan and sometimes worn by Scottish men as part of their national costume.

kimono [kɪ'məʊnəʊ] (*pl* **kimonos**) *n* a Japanese piece of clothing shaped like a loose coat and with wide sleeves.

kin [kɪn] *n* → **kith, next of kin**.

kind [kaɪnd] ◇ *adj* [person, gesture] that is

friendly and helpful toward other people and shows concern for them □ *It's a kind thought.* □ *It's so kind of you to help.* □ *He was so kind to me when I was ill.* ■ **would you be so kind as to...** a phrase used to ask somebody very politely to do something □ *Would you be so kind as to tell me how to get to the bank?*

◇ *n* [of person, object, animal] a group whose members have particular characteristics that make them different from others; a person, animal, or thing that belongs to such a group □ *What kind of dog is that?* □ *Their objections were of a different kind.* □ *This is definitely my kind of place!* ■ **a kind of...** a phrase used when one cannot describe something precisely but wants to give somebody an approximate idea of what is is like □ *They used a kind of enormous fishing net.* ■ **kind of** a phrase used to show that one is not completely sure about something or that something is only partly true (informal use) □ *"Do you miss him?" — "Kind of."* □ *It was kind of interesting.* ■ **of a kind** a phrase used to show that something is of a poor quality or is not the way one wants it to be □ *It's an agreement of a kind.* ■ **to be two of a kind** to be of the same sort □ *They're two of a kind.* ■ **to pay sb in kind** to pay sb by giving them something they need rather than money □ *Don't worry about cash, you can pay me in kind.*

kindergarten ['kɪndəˈgɑːˈtn] *n* a school for very young children who are usually between four and six years of age.

kind-hearted [-ˈhɑːˈtəd] *adj* [person] who is helpful and sympathetic.

kindle ['kɪndl] *vt* **-1.** to cause <a fire> to start burning by lighting wood or paper □ *We crouched over the fire, kindling the flames.* **-2.** to cause somebody to begin to have an idea or feeling □ *This trip kindled in him a desire to visit his birthplace.*

kindling ['kɪndlɪŋ] *n* dry wood, leaves etc used to start a fire.

kindly ['kaɪndlɪ] (*compar* **kindlier**, *superl* **kindliest**) ◇ *adj* [person] who is friendly and caring □ *a kindly old man.* ◇ *adv* **-1.** [speak, smile, treat] in a friendly caring way. ■ **to look kindly on sb/sthg** to approve of sb/sthg □ *The courts don't look kindly on this type of offense.* ■ **not to take kindly to sthg** to dislike sthg. □ *George didn't take kindly to my criticisms of his work.* **-2.** a word used as part of a request, especially to show that one is annoyed □ *Would you kindly give me my book back now?*

kindness ['kaɪndnəs] *n* **-1.** [of a person, gesture] see **kind** □ *I didn't expect such kindness.* **-2.** a helpful and kind act □ *You have done me a great kindness.*

kindred ['kɪndrəd] *adj* [ideas, subjects] similar to each other. ■ **a kindred spirit** a person who shares the same ideas, desires etc as somebody else □ *They're kindred spirits.*

kinetic [kɪˈnetɪk] *adj* [energy, art] that is connected with movement.

kinfolk(s) ['kɪnfoʊk(s)] US *npl* the members of one's family.

king [kɪŋ] *n* **-1.** [of a country] a man who is a

member of a royal family and who is the official ruler of a country without being elected □ *King Henry the Eighth.* □ *the King of Spain/ Belgium.* **-2.** [in a particular activity] a person, company, product etc that people think is the most important one in a particular field □ *the fast-food king.* **-3.** CHESS the most important piece in a game of chess. **-4.** [in cards] any of the four playing cards with a picture of a king on it □ *the king of spades.*

King [kɪŋ], **Martin Luther** (1929–1968) a US black civil rights leader. He encouraged people to demonstrate against racism without using violence. He was shot and killed.

kingdom ['kɪŋdəm] *n* **-1.** a country whose ruler or official head of state is a king or queen □ *News of her death soon spread throughout the kingdom.* **-2.** one of the three categories into which all natural objects can be divided □ *the animal/plant/mineral kingdom.*

kingfisher ['kɪŋfɪʃəˈ] *n* a small bird with greenish-blue feathers that feeds on fish in rivers and lakes.

King Kong [-ˈkɒŋ] a giant gorilla in the film *King Kong*, made in 1933. It escapes into New York and climbs the Empire State Building.

King Lear [-ˈlɪəˈ] the hero of Shakespeare's play *King Lear*. He makes the mistake of giving his kingdom to two of his daughters who do not love him, and rejecting the one who loves him.

kingpin ['kɪŋpɪn] *n* **-1.** [in an engine] a pin that is part of the structure in a vehicle and that connects the steering column with the wheels. **-2.** the most important person in an organization, group of people etc.

king prawn *n* GB a large prawn.

king-size(d) *adj* [bed, cigarette] that is much larger than is usual.

kink [kɪŋk] *n* a twist in something, e.g. in a rope or in somebody's hair, that is usually straight.

kinky ['kɪŋkɪ] (*compar* **kinkier**, *superl* **kinkiest**) *adj* [idea, behavior] that is strange and unusual and usually involves sex (informal use).

Kinsey ['kɪnzɪ], **A. C.** (1894–1956) a US scientist who studied human sexual behavior.

kinsfolk ['kɪnzfoʊk] *npl* = **kinfolk(s)**.

kinship ['kɪnʃɪp] *n* **-1.** the relationship that exists between members of a family. **-2.** a feeling of closeness with another person or group □ *I felt a strong kinship with her.*

kiosk ['kiːɒsk] *n* **-1.** a small hut on the street from which newspapers, candy etc are sold. **-2.** GB a telephone booth.

Kipling ['kɪplɪŋ], **Rudyard** (1865–1936) a British writer whose many stories and poems are set in colonial India. His best-known work is the *Jungle Book*.

kipper ['kɪpəˈ] *n* a herring that has been salted and smoked.

Kirk [kɜːˈk] *n* **the Kirk** SCOT an informal name for the Church of Scotland.

kirsch [kɪəʳʃ] *n* an alcoholic drink made from cherries.

kiss [kɪs] ◇ *vt* [person, hand, lips] to touch <sb/sthg> with one's lips as a greeting or a way of showing affection □ *She kissed me on the cheek before leaving.* ■ **to kiss sb goodbye** to say goodbye to sb by kissing them. ◇ *vi* [two people] to kiss each other as a sign of affection or love, or when greeting each other □ *They kissed passionately.* ◇ *n* the act of kissing somebody □ *He gave her a farewell kiss.*

kissagram ['kɪsəgræm] *n* a person, usually in costume, who is paid to visit somebody on a special occasion such as their birthday and kiss them.

kiss curl *n* GB a curl of a person's hair pressed flat against their cheek or forehead.

kiss of death *n* **the kiss of death** something that causes the complete failure or end of something □ *His resignation will be the kiss of death.*

kiss of life *n* **to give sb the kiss of life** to try to save somebody's life by breathing into their mouth to make them start breathing again, e.g. after a serious accident.

kit [kɪt] (*pt* & *pp* **kitted**, *cont* **kitting**) *n* -1. [of tools, equipment] a group of tools or pieces of equipment kept together and used for the same purpose or activity. -2. [for soldiers, a sport] the clothes and equipment used by soldiers, sailors etc and by people who play sport □ *a soccer kit.* -3. [for making something] a set of parts that have to be put together to make something □ *a model boat kit.*

◆ **kit out** *vt sep* GB **to kit sb/sthg out** to provide sb/sthg with everything they need, especially clothes and equipment (informal use).

kit bag *n* GB a long narrow bag used by sailors and soldiers for keeping their clothes and equipment in.

kitchen ['kɪtʃən] *n* a room used for preparing and cooking food.

Kitchener ['kɪtʃənəʳ], **Lord** (1850–1916) a British soldier and politician. His face appeared on a famous poster encouraging people to join the armed forces in World War I.

kitchenette [,kɪtʃə'net] *n* a small kitchen or a part of a room used as a kitchen.

kitchen garden *n* a garden used for growing fruit and vegetables in.

kitchen roll *n* GB thick paper that is wrapped around a cardboard tube and used in the kitchen, e.g. for wiping surfaces.

kitchen sink *n* a sink in a kitchen.

kitchen unit *n* a piece of kitchen furniture, e.g. a cupboard, that is installed together with other pieces of the same type.

kitchenware ['kɪtʃənweəʳ] *n* a collective term for items of kitchen equipment such as pans, bowls, and spoons.

kite [kaɪt] *n* -1. a toy consisting of a light wooden or metal frame covered in paper, plastic, or cloth, that is held by a long string while it flies in the sky with the help of wind □ *The weather is perfect for flying kites.* -2. a large bird with a long tail that feeds on small animals.

Kite mark *n* GB an official mark that is put on goods that are of a high enough quality to be approved by the British Standards Institution.

kith [kɪθ] *n* **one's kith and kin** one's friends and relatives.

kitsch [kɪtʃ] *n* decorative objects or works of art that are tasteless and not taken seriously.

kitten ['kɪtn] *n* a young cat.

kitty ['kɪtɪ] (*pl* **kitties**) *n* -1. an amount of money given by several people to pay for something they do or use together □ *It makes more sense to organize a kitty for food.* -2. an amount of money provided by the players in a game of cards and taken by the winner. -3. a cat (informal use).

kiwi ['kiːwiː] *n* -1. a bird with a long beak and no wings or tail that cannot fly and is found only in New Zealand. -2. a person from New Zealand (informal use).

kiwi fruit *n* a small oval-shaped fruit with rough brown skin and soft green flesh.

KKK *n abbr of* Ku Klux Klan.

KL *abbr of* Kuala Lumpur.

klaxon ['klæksən] *n* a loud horn used, especially in the past, by motor vehicles.

Kleenex™ ['kliːneks] *n* a soft paper tissue.

kleptomaniac [,kleptə'meɪnɪæk] *n* a person who has a mental illness that makes them unable to stop stealing things.

Klondike ['klɒndaɪk]: **the Klondike** a river and region in the Yukon, Canada. It is famous for the gold rush that happened there in the 1890s.

km *abbr of* kilometer.

km/h (*abbr of* kilometers per hour) a way of measuring the speed of a vehicle.

knack [næk] *n* a special skill or ability that is needed to do something difficult □ *There's a knack to opening this door.* □ *It's easy, once you get the knack (of it).*

knackered ['nækəʳd] *adj* GB (informal use) -1. **to be knackered** [person] to be very tired. -2. [car, stereo, TV] that is broken or old and in bad condition.

knapsack ['næpsæk] *n* a leather or canvas bag that is worn on the back and used, especially by hikers, to carry food and belongings.

knave [neɪv] *n* GB a playing card with a picture of a young man on it that is below the queen in value and above the ten.

knead [niːd] *vt* [dough, clay] to press <sthg> repeatedly with one's hands in order to make it smooth and flexible.

knee [niː] *n* the joint in the middle of the leg where it bends □ *I hurt my knee.* ■ **to be on one's knees** to be kneeling; to be very tired physically (informal use) □ *By the end of the day, I was on my knees.* ■ **to bring sb to their knees** [country, government, army] to cause the defeat of sb by making them too weak to continue fighting, doing a particular job etc

□ *The administration was brought to its knees by a series of damaging scandals.*

kneecap ['niːkæp] *n* the bone in the front part of one's knee.

knee-deep *adj* **-1.** [snow, water] that reaches as high as one's knees □ *The mud was knee-deep in some places.* **-2. to be knee-deep in sthg** [in water, mud] to be standing in sthg that reaches as high as one's knees □ *Richard waded knee-deep into the river.*

knee-high *adj* [undergrowth, grass] that is high enough to reach one's knees.

knee-jerk *adj* [reaction, opinion] that results from habit rather than careful thought □ *a knee-jerk feminist.*

kneel [niːl] (*pt* & *pp* **knelt** OR **kneeled**) *vi* to lower one's body by bending one's legs until one or both of one's knees is resting on the ground; to stay in this position for a period of time □ *She was kneeling in prayer.*

◆ **kneel down** *vi* to lower one's body so that one is kneeling □ *He knelt down to tie his shoelace.*

knee-length *adj* [skirt, boots] long enough to reach the knees.

knell [nel] *n* the sound of a bell rung to mark a death or funeral.

knelt [nelt] *past tense & past participle of* **kneel**.

knew [n^{j}uː] *past tense of* **know**.

knickers ['nɪkə^{r}z] *npl* **-1.** GB a piece of underwear worn by women and girls that covers the area of the body between the waist and the top of the legs and passes between the legs □ *a pair of knickers.* **-2.** US loose short trousers that reach down to the knees, worn especially in the past by women.

knick-knack ['nɪknæk] *n* a small decorative object for the house.

knife [naɪf] (*pl* **knives**) ◇ *n* an object consisting of a sharp metal blade fixed to a handle and used for cutting or as a weapon □ *a fish knife.* ◇ *vt* to injure <sb> deliberately with a knife □ *He was knifed in the stomach.*

knifing ['naɪfɪŋ] *n* an incident in which somebody is attacked and injured with a knife (informal use).

knight [naɪt] ◇ *n* **-1.** HISTORY in medieval times, a nobleman who fought for his lord on horseback, usually in armor. **-2.** [as a title] a man who has been given a knighthood by his king or queen. A knight is entitled to use the word "Sir" in front of his name □ *He was made a knight for his services to British theater.* **-3.** CHESS a chess piece shaped like the head of a horse. ◇ *vt* to give <sb> a knighthood.

knighthood ['naɪthʊd] *n* the title or rank of a knight given to a man by his king or queen as a mark of honor □ *He has since been stripped of his knighthood for spying.*

Knightsbridge ['naɪtsbrɪdʒ] a fashionable area of central London that is well known for its expensive shops.

knit [nɪt] (*pt* & *pp* **knit** OR **knitted**, *cont* **knitting**) ◇ *adj* **closely** OR **tightly knit** [group, community] whose members know each other very well and often act together or help each other □ *the close-knit communities of the islands.* ◇ *vt* [sweater, scarf, hat] to make <an item of clothing> using yarn and a knitting machine or needles □ *Mom's knitting me a cardigan.* ◇ *vi* **-1.** [person] *She sits knitting in front of the television.* **-2.** [broken bones] to join or grow together.

knitted ['nɪtəd] *adj* [sweater, scarf, hat] that has been made by knitting □ *a knitted sweater.*

knitting ['nɪtɪŋ] *n* **-1.** the activity of knitting something □ *I hate knitting.* **-2.** something that is being knitted □ *She put her knitting down on the table for a moment.*

knitting machine *n* a machine used for knitting clothes.

knitting needle *n* a thin plastic or metal stick used for knitting.

knitting pattern *n* a set of instructions that tell one how to knit a particular piece of clothing.

knitwear ['nɪtweə^r] *n* a collective term for clothing that has been knitted □ *He's designed a new range of ladies' knitwear.*

knives [naɪvz] *plural of* **knife**.

knob [nɒb] *n* **-1.** [on a door, drawer] a round handle on a door or drawer □ *The knob came off in his hand.* **-2.** [on a stick, post] a round lump used as decoration at the end of a stick or post □ *a bedstead with brass knobs on.* **-3.** [on a radio] a round button on a piece of electrical equipment such as a radio, used for switching it on and off, changing the volume etc □ *Turn the knob on the left in a clockwise direction.*

knobby ['nɒbɪ] US (*compar* **knobbier**, *superl* **knobbiest**), **knobbly** ['nɒblɪ] GB (*compar* **knobblier**, *superl* **knobbliest**) *adj* [surface] that has hard lumps on it □ *knobby knees.*

knock [nɒk] ◇ *vt* **-1.** [table, elbow, fender] to hit <sthg> with a sharp movement, often by accident □ *I knocked my leg against the chair.* **-2.** [ball, peg] to hit <sthg> hard deliberately so that it moves in a particular direction □ *She was knocking a nail into the wall.* ■ **to knock a hole into a wall** to make a hole in a wall by hitting it very hard. **-3.** [person, performance] to criticize <sb/sthg>, especially in a way that seems harsh or unfair (informal use) □ *Don't knock it!*

◇ *vi* **-1. to knock at** OR **on sthg** [on a door, window] to hit sthg, usually with one's hand, in order to attract attention □ *Somobody was knocking at the door.* **-2.** [engine, pipes] to make a harsh noise that shows something is wrong.

◇ *n* **-1.** the act of knocking something; the sound made by knocking on something □ *They heard a knock at the door.* **-2.** a piece of bad luck (informal use) □ *She's taken a few hard knocks recently.*

◆ **knock about, knock around** (informal use) ◇ *vt sep* **to knock sb about** OR **around** to hit sb hard several times □ *She's been knocked around by her husband a lot.* ◇ *vi* **-1.** to travel around in a relaxed way and experience different places and situations □ *They've been* *knocking around Europe over the summer.* **-2. to knock around with sb** to spend time with sb, usually as a friend □ *How long have you been knocking around with them?*

◆ **knock back** *vt sep* (informal use) **-1. to knock sthg back** to drink sthg very quickly □ *"Let's go," she said, knocking back her drink.* **-2. to knock sb back a sum of money** to cost sb a particular sum of money □ *The new tires knocked me back $100.*

◆ **knock down** *vt sep* **-1. to knock sb down** GB [pedestrian] to hit sb while one is driving with the result that they are hurt or killed □ *He was knocked down by a car.* **-2. to knock sthg down** [building] to destroy and remove sthg; [product] to make the price of sthg lower □ *They've knocked down the old church.* □ *Prices have been knocked down by 20%.*

◆ **knock off** ◇ *vt sep* **to knock an amount of money off a price** to lower a price by an amount of money □ *I'll knock $6 off the price.* ◇ *vi* [worker, staff] to stop working (informal use) □ *The day shift knocks off at 6 pm.*

◆ **knock out** *vt sep* **-1. to knock sb out** [person] to hit sb else so hard that they become unconscious; [drug] to make sb unconscious. **-2. to knock sb out** [player, team] to defeat sb in a competition so that they cannot compete in the later rounds □ *Simpson was knocked out in the quarter-final.*

◆ **knock over** *vt sep* **-1. to knock sthg over** [glass, bottle] to hit sthg so that it falls over □ *I nearly knocked over their expensive vase.* **-2. to knock sb over** [pedestrian] to hit sb while one is driving □ *Their son was knocked over by a car.*

◆ **knock up** *vi* SPORT [players] to practice together before beginning a tennis match.

knocker ['nɒkəʳ] *n* a piece of metal on a door that one strikes against the door to make a loud noise to show that one wants the door to be opened.

knocking ['nɒkɪŋ] *n* the sound made by somebody knocking on a door, window etc □ *I can't hear with all that knocking going on.*

knock-kneed [-'niːd] *adj* [person, animal] that has knees that turn inwards so that they appear to touch each other.

knock-on effect *n* GB **to have a knock-on effect** to start a series of events in which each one is caused by the one directly before it □ *The Bank's decision will have a knock-on effect on interest rates.*

knockout ['nɒkaʊt] *n* **-1.** SPORT the act of hitting one's opponent in a boxing match so hard that they become unconscious. **-2.** a person who one thinks is extremely impressive or attractive (informal use) □ *He/She was an absolute knockout!*

knockout competition *n* GB a competition in which only the players or teams that win each game are allowed to play in the next stage.

knock-up *n* GB the period before a tennis match in which the players practice by hitting the ball to one another.

knot [nɒt] (*pt & pp* **knotted,** *cont* **knotting**) ◇ *n* **-1.** [of a rope, shoelace] a way of fastening or tying two ends of rope, string etc together by winding them tightly around each other □ *The knot in my shoelace came undone.* ■ **to tie/untie a knot** to make/remove a knot. **-2.** [of people] a group of people standing together □ *People stood around in small knots, observing the discussion that was going on.* **-3.** [in wood] a hard spot in a piece of wood where a branch used to grow. **-4.** SHIPPING a unit (1.85km per hour) used for measuring the speed of ships □ *We got up to 15 knots once we reached open sea.* ◇ *vt* [string, rope] to make a knot in <sthg>.

knotted ['nɒtəd] *adj* [handkerchief, scarf, rope] that has a knot in it.

knotty ['nɒtɪ] (*compar* **knottier,** *superl* **knottiest**) *adj* [issue, question] that is difficult to solve.

know [nəʊ] (*pt* **knew,** *pp* **known**) ◇ *vt* **-1.** to be familiar with <a person, place, or thing> because one has met or seen them before □ *I know New York very well.* □ *She'd known Alfred for six months.* ■ **to get to know sb/sthg** to learn about sb/sthg □ *How did you get to know each other?* □ *I got to know their names very quickly.* **-2.** [name, reason, answer] to have <sthg> in one's mind and be sure that it is correct or true □ *It's important to know your rights as a tenant.* □ *Do you know what time the play starts?* □ *He knew (that) he had seen her before; but where?* **-3.** [subject, technique] to understand and have knowledge of <sthg> through personal experience or through studying it □ *"Do you know German?" she asked.* □ *He knows an enormous amount about the army.* □ *Of course I know how to change a fuse!* ■ **to know sthg backwards** to know or understand sthg extremely well □ *I know my job backwards.* **-4.** to recognize sb □ *I knew her the moment I saw her.* **-5. to know sthg from sthg** to be able to tell the difference between sthg and sthg else □ *They're old enough to know right from wrong.* **-6. to be known as...** to be called a particular name □ *Stalingrad, now known as Volgograd.*

◇ *vi* **-1.** to know a fact or piece of information □ *"Luis is coming over next week." — "Yes, I know. He called me yesterday to tell me."* ■ **to know of sb/sthg** to have heard about sb/sthg □ *I've never met him, but I know of him.* ■ **to know about sthg** to be aware of sthg; to have learned about sthg and understand it □ *Do you know about the new guidelines?* **-2.** *phrases* **you know** a phrase used in conversation to emphasize something, or when one is trying to make something clearer □ *You know, she's still young, it's not her fault.* □ *We were in the restaurant, you know, the one by the town hall.* ■ **there is no knowing...** it is impossible to know... □ *There's no knowing when this killer will strike next!* ■ **to know better** to be sensible or old enough not to behave foolishly □ *You should know better at your age!*

◇ *n* **to be in the know** to have more information about something than most other people □ *You seem to be in the know, maybe you can tell me what's going on?*

know-all *n* GB = **know-it-all.**

know-how *n* the skill and ability to do something, particularly in a scientific or industrial field □ *It is not just terrorist groups that have the know-how to make these bombs.*

knowing ['nəʊɪŋ] *adj* [look, smile] that suggests that one knows about something even though one has not spoken of it openly □ *She gave him a knowing wink.*

knowingly ['nəʊɪŋlɪ] *adv* **-1.** [smile, say] *see* **knowing. -2.** [hurt, betray] intentionally □ *I would never knowingly cause my husband pain.*

know-it-all *n* a person who thinks they know more than other people (disapproving use) □ *You're such a know-it-all!*

knowledge ['nɒlɪdʒ] *n* **-1.** information and understanding about something □ *She has a great thirst for knowledge.* ■ **it's common knowledge that...** everybody knows that... □ *It's common knowledge that they're leaving.* **-2.** the state of knowing about something □ *He did it without my knowledge.* ■ **not to my knowledge** a phrase used when one thinks that what someone is saying is not true □ *"Did the accused threaten Mr Lee?" — "Not to my knowledge, no."* ■ **to the best of my knowledge** a phrase used when one believes that what one is saying is true but that one's information may not be accurate or complete □ *To the best of my knowledge, he left two weeks ago.*

knowledgeable ['nɒlɪdʒəbl] *adj* [person] who knows a lot about a particular subject or about many things □ *Laura's very knowledgeable about local landmarks.*

known [nəʊn] ◇ *past participle of* **know.** ◇ *adj* **a known criminal/expert etc** a criminal/an expert etc that people know about □ *There is, as yet, no known cure for the disease.*

Knox [nɒks], **John** (1513–1572) a Scottish religious reformer who established the Presbyterian Church of Scotland.

knuckle ['nʌkl] *n* ANATOMY one of the joints where one's fingers bend or where they join one's hand.

◆ **knuckle down** *vi* to begin to do something seriously □ *It's time to knuckle down to work.* □ *You should knuckle down to finding a job.*

◆ **knuckle under** *vi* to accept that one has to do what somebody or something demands □ *You have no choice but to knuckle under and get on with it.*

knuckle-duster *n* a piece of metal worn over the knuckles and used for hitting people with.

KO *n abbr of* **knockout.**

koala (bear) [kəʊ'ɑːlə-] *n* an Australian animal like a small bear that can climb trees and that feeds on eucalyptus leaves.

kohl [kəʊl] *n* a substance used to make the edges of one's eyelids darker.

kook [kuːk] *n* US a kooky person (informal use).

kooky ['kuːkɪ] (*compar* **kookier,** *superl* **kookiest**) *adj* US [person, idea] that one thinks is slightly strange and unusual (informal use).

Koran [kɒ'rɑːn] *n* **the Koran** the holy book on which the Islamic religion is based.

Korea [kə'rɪə] a peninsula in northeastern Asia, between China and Japan. Since 1948 it has been divided into North Korea and South Korea.

Korean [kə'rɪən] *n* & *adj*: *see* **North Korea, South Korea.**

Korean War *n* **the Korean War** a war (1950–1953) between South Korea and Communist North Korea which neither side won. North Korea was helped by the Chinese and South Korea by the USA and other UN forces.

Kosciusko [,kɒsɪ'ʌskəʊ]: **(Mount) Kosciusko** a mountain in the Australian Alps, New South Wales, which is the highest in Australia. HEIGHT: 2,228m.

kosher ['kəʊʃəʳ] *adj* **-1.** [food, meat] that is prepared in a way that is acceptable to Jewish religious laws about food. **-2.** [person, deal] that one thinks is honest and acceptable (informal use) □ *Do we know for sure that these guys are kosher?*

kowtow [,kaʊ'taʊ] *vi* **to kowtow to sb** to show too much respect for sb □ *It's no good kowtowing to these people.*

Kremlin ['kremlɪn] ◇ **the Kremlin** the castle and palace in the center of Moscow where the government of the former Soviet Union used to be based. ◇ *n* **the Kremlin** a term used to refer to the government of the Soviet Union.

Kriss Kringle [,krɪs'krɪŋgl] US = **Santa Claus.**

KS *abbr of* **Kansas.**

KT *abbr of* **Knight.**

Kuala Lumpur [,kwɑːlə'lʊmpʊəʳ] the capital of Malaysia. POPULATION: 1,103,000.

Kublai Khan [,kuːblə'kɑːn] (1216–1294) Mongol Emperor of China from 1279 to 1294. The grandson of Genghis Khan, he ruled over a very large empire.

kudos [US 'kuːdoʊz, GB 'kjuːdɒs] *n* praise or respect that somebody gains by doing something □ *I did it for the kudos, not the money.*

Ku Klux Klan [,kuːklʌks'klæn] *n* **the Ku Klux Klan** a secret right-wing group of white Protestant people in the USA who believe that people of other races or religions should not have the same political rights as them. At meetings they wear special long white robes and pointed hoods over their heads.

kumquat ['kʌmkwɒt] *n* a fruit like a very small orange.

kung fu [,kʌŋ'fuː] *n* a style of fighting from China in which opponents hit each other using their hands and feet.

Kurd [kɜːʳd] *n* a member of a people living mainly in Kurdistan.

Kurdish ['kɜːʳdɪʃ] ◇ *n* the language of the Kurds. ◇ *adj*: *see* **Kurd** □ *a Kurdish village/song.*

Kurdistan [US 'kɜːrdəstæn, GB ,kɜːdɪ'stɑːn] a mountainous region of western Asia, mainly in eastern Turkey, northern Iraq, and western Iran.

Kuwait [kʊ'weɪt] a country on the Persian Gulf, between Iraq and Saudi Arabia. It is a major producer of oil. In 1990 it was invaded by Iraq, which led to the Gulf War. SIZE: 17,800 sq kms. POPULATION: 1,400,000 (*Kuwaitis*). CAPITAL: Kuwait City. LANGUAGE: Arabic. CURRENCY: Kuwaiti dinar.

Kuwaiti [kʊ'weɪtɪ] *n* & *adj*: see **Kuwait**.

kW, kw *abbr of* **kilowatt**.

kWh (*abbr of* **kilowatt hour**) the amount of energy produced by one kilowatt in one hour, used as a unit for measuring the consumption of electricity.

KY *abbr of* **Kentucky**.

l¹ [el] (*pl* **l's** OR **ls**), **L** [el] (*pl* **L's** OR **Ls**) *n* the twelfth letter of the English alphabet.
◆ **L -1.** *abbr of* **lake. -2.** *abbr of* **large. -3.** *abbr of* **left. -4.** *abbr of* **learner driver.**

l² *abbr of* **liter.**

la [lɑː] *n* the sixth note in the scale of Western music.

LA ◇ *n abbr of* **Los Angeles.** ◇ *abbr of* **Louisiana.**

lab [læb] *n* = **laboratory** (informal use) □ *a lab coat/technician.*

label ['leɪbl] (US *pt* & *pp* **labeled**, *cont* **labeling**, GB *pt* & *pp* **labelled**, *cont* **labelling**) ◇ *n* **-1.** [on luggage, clothes, a bottle] a small piece of paper, cloth etc, that is attached to something in order to identify it or give information about it □ *a washing label* □ *an address label.* **-2.** MUSIC the name that a record company is known by □ *My sister's band has been approached by a number of record labels.* □ *a single released on an independent label.*
◇ *vt* **-1.** [luggage, sample, clothing] to attach a label to <sthg> □ *The jelly can then be bottled and labeled.* **-2.** [person, writer, decision] to describe <sb/sthg> in a particular way, often unfairly □ *Ever since, people have labeled him (as) a failure.*

labor US, **labour** GB ['leɪbəʳ] ◇ *n* **-1.** [by a person] work, especially when it involves physical effort □ *The job involves a lot of manual labor.* □ *The team is exhausted after its labors.* □ *The repair bill was $200 for parts and labor.* **-2.** [in an industry] workers, especially people who do physical work, when they are considered as a group or a resource □ *There is a shortage of skilled labor.* □ *unskilled labor.* **-3.** MEDICINE the last stage of pregnancy, when the baby is pushed out of the womb □ *She was in labor for ten hours.* □ *She went into labor at 3 o'clock.*
◇ *vt* **to labor the point** to keep talking about or explaining something after one has already said enough for it to be clearly under-

stood □ *There's no need to keep laboring the point!*
◇ *vi* **-1.** [workman, peasant] to work hard, especially when doing a physical task □ *Teams of workers labored to get the bridge finished in time.* **-2. to labor over sthg** [over a job, decision, letter] to spend a lot more time and effort than normal doing sthg □ *The committee is still laboring over the report.* **-3. to labor under a delusion** OR **misapprehension** to continue to believe something that is wrong or false.

Labor *n* **the Department of Labor** the US government department responsible for working conditions and labor relations.

laboratory [US 'læbrətɔːrɪ, GB lə'bɒrətrɪ] (*pl* **laboratories**) *n* a room or building that contains special equipment for scientific experiments and research □ *laboratory equipment/tests.*

labor camp *n* a prison camp where prisoners have to do hard physical work.

labor costs *npl* the money needed to pay workers, especially to produce a particular product or carry out a particular service.

Labor Day *n* in the USA and Canada, a public holiday that is celebrated on the first Monday of September.

labored US, **laboured** GB ['leɪbəʳd] *adj* [joke, writing, style] that is not natural and shows signs of too much effort; [breathing, movement] that is slow and made difficult by physical problems □ *His breathing was slow and labored.*

laborer US, **labourer** GB ['leɪbərəʳ] *n* a person who does unskilled work involving physical effort outdoors, e.g. on a building site or a farm.

labor force *n* all the people in a particular country who are in employment or available for employment; all the employees in a particular company.

labor-intensive *adj* [industry, process] that needs a lot of workers.

laborious [lə'bɔːrɪəs] *adj* [task, process] that takes a lot of effort.

labor market *n* the supply of people available for work in a country.

labor of love *n* a job one does for pleasure without getting money or a reward.

labor pains *npl* the pain felt by a pregnant woman just before giving birth.

Labor Party *n* = **ALP.**

labor relations *npl* the relationship between workers and employers.

laborsaving US, **laboursaving** GB ['leɪbəʳseɪvɪŋ] *adj* **a laborsaving device** a device that makes a job, especially a physical job, much easier to do.

labor union *n* US an organization that represents the interests of workers who all do a similar type of job.

labour *etc n* GB = **labor** *etc.*

Labour GB POLITICS ◇ *adj* [MP, member, voter] who belongs to or supports the Labour Party; [policy, motion] that is suggested and supported by the Labour Party. ◊ *n* GB = **Labour Party** □ *Labour is* OR *are fighting back.*

Labour Party *n* **the Labour Party** one of the two main British political parties. It used to be a Socialist party, closely linked with the labor unions, and is now a center-left party.

Labrador¹ [ˈlæbrədɔːʳ] *n* a large dog with a smooth coat of black or yellow hair.

Labrador² the eastern part of the large Canadian peninsula that lies between Hudson Bay and the Atlantic. It belongs to the province of Newfoundland.

laburnum [ləˈbɜːʳnəm] *n* a small tree that has poisonous yellow flowers that hang on long stems.

labyrinth [ˈlæbərɪnθ] *n* a complicated network of roads, passages, tunnels etc in which it is easy to get lost □ *The museum is a labyrinth of underground passages and rooms.*

lace [leɪs] ◊ *n* -1. a delicate cloth made from fine thread that is woven into patterns with many small holes □ *trimmed with lace* □ *a lace tablecloth.* -2. a piece of string used to tie up a shoe or boot □ *Your laces are undone.* ◊ *vt* -1. [shoe, boot] = **lace up.** -2. **to lace food or drink with sthg** [with alcohol] to add a small amount of sthg to food or drink □ *He laced my orange juice with gin.*

♦ **lace up** *vt sep* **to lace sthg up** [shoe, boot] to fasten <sthg> by tying the laces together.

lacemaking [ˈleɪsmeɪkɪŋ] *n* the art of making lace.

laceration [ˌlæsəˈreɪʃn] *n* a rough and uneven cut on somebody's skin.

lace-up ◊ *adj* [shoe, boot, corset] that is fastened with laces □ *a pair of lace-up shoes.* ◊ *n* GB a lace-up shoe or boot.

lack [læk] ◊ *n* **(a) lack of sthg** [of time, money, understanding] a situation in which there is none or not enough of sthg that is needed □ *The project was stopped for* OR *through lack of funds.* □ *There was no lack of effort on my part.* ◊ *vt* [time, confidence, experience] not to have enough of <sthg>; not to have <sthg> at all □ *We lack the necessary equipment.* □ *I lack variety in my job* OR *My job lacks variety.*

lackadaisical [ˌlækəˈdeɪzɪkl] *adj* [person, approach, attitude] that shows little interest, enthusiasm, or energy (disapproving use).

lackey [ˈlækɪ] (*pl* **lackeys**) *n* a person who follows the orders of somebody else without thinking (disapproving use) □ *Don't think you can treat me like one of your lackeys.*

lacking [ˈlækɪŋ] *adj* **to be lacking** to be too small in number or amount, or not available or present at all □ *Good jobs have been sadly lacking recently.* ■ **to be lacking in sthg** not to have enough of sthg that is needed or desirable □ *The food was lacking in flavor.* □ *She's not lacking in confidence.*

lackluster US, **lacklustre** GB [ˈlæklʌstəʳ] *adj* [speech, event] that is not lively or exciting □ *a lackluster performance by the Chicago Bulls.*

laconic [ləˈkɒnɪk] *adj* [person, reply, style] that uses few words □ *This response was typical of the writer's laconic wit.*

lacquer [ˈlækəʳ] ◊ *n* -1. a substance that is painted onto objects made of wood or metal in order to give them a hard shiny surface. -2. a sticky substance that is sprayed onto hair in order to keep it in place. ◊ *vt* [wood, metal, hair] to put lacquer on <sthg>.

lacrosse [ləˈkrɒs] *n* an outdoor sport played with a small hard ball that is thrown and caught using a stick with a net at the end.

lactic acid [ˈlæktɪk-] *n* an acid that forms in sour milk.

lacy [ˈleɪsɪ] (*compar* **lacier**, *superl* **laciest**) *adj* [shirt, curtain, underwear] that has lace on it or has a pattern like lace.

lad [læd] *n* -1. a boy or young man (informal use). -2. GB a boy or man who takes care of horses in a stable.

ladder [ˈlædəʳ] ◊ *n* -1. a piece of equipment made of wood, metal, or rope that people climb up and down and that has horizontal steps for the feet between two vertical pieces. -2. GB a tear in a pair of stockings or pantyhose. ◊ *vt* GB to make a ladder in <pantyhose or stockings>. ◊ *vi* GB [pantyhose, stockings] to develop a ladder □ *These tights ladder easily.*

laden [ˈleɪdn] *adj* [person, truck, ship] that is carrying a large amount of something □ *She came in laden with shopping.* □ *The vessel weighs sixty tons when fully laden.*

ladies [ˈleɪdɪz] ◊ *plural of* **lady.** ◊ *n* GB = **ladies' room.**

ladies' room *n* US a public toilet for women □ *Could you tell me where the ladies' room is, please?*

lading [ˈleɪdɪŋ] *n* → **bill of lading.**

ladle [ˈleɪdl] ◊ *n* a large deep spoon with a long handle, used especially for serving soup. ◊ *vt* to pour <sthg> into a bowl, dish etc using a ladle □ *The cook was ladling steaming mounds of rice onto plates.*

lady [ˈleɪdɪ] (*pl* **ladies**) *n* -1. a word used instead of "woman" to show politeness and respect □ *She's a very dynamic lady.* □ *Ask the lady if she'd like to sit down.* □ *Ladies and gentlemen, can I have your attention.* □ *Fourth floor, ladies' underwear.* □ *a lady doctor.* -2. an upper-class woman. -3. a woman who is ladylike □ *Ann's a real lady.* -4. US a word sometimes used to address a woman that one does not know (informal use) □ *Hey, lady!*

♦ **Lady** *n* -1. a title given to a woman who belongs to the aristocracy or whose husband has a knighthood or a peerage □ *Lady Elizabeth Bowes-Lyon.* -2. RELIGION **Our Lady** a title of the Virgin Mary, mother of Christ.

ladybug [ˈleɪdɪbʌg] US, **ladybird** [ˈleɪdɪbɜːʳd] GB *n* a small round insect that is red with black spots on its back and can fly.

lady-in-waiting (*pl* **ladies-in-waiting**) *n* a woman who accompanies and assists a queen or princess.

lady-killer *n* a man who is attractive to many women but upsets them by ending relationships with them after a short time (informal use).

ladylike ['leɪdɪlaɪk] *adj* [behavior, woman, girl] that shows qualities such as politeness and elegance that some people expect from women and girls.

Lady of the Lake: the Lady of the Lake in English legends, a goddess whose hand came out of a lake to catch the sword thrown by King Arthur before he died.

Ladyship ['leɪdɪʃɪp] *n* her/your Ladyship a title used when talking about or to a Lady.

lag [læg] (*pt* & *pp* lagged, *cont* lagging) ◇ *vi* [person, country, economy] to move or develop more slowly than the others in a group □ *He soon got tired and started to lag behind.* □ *We now lag far behind the rest of the world in new technology.* ◇ *vt* [pipe, tank, roof] to cover <sthg> with a material that keeps heat in. ◇ *n* a period of time between two events that is often the result of a delay □ *a time lag.*

lager ['lɑːgəʳ] *n* a beer that is light in color and has bubbles.

lager lout *n* GB a young man who disturbs other people by being noisy or violent, usually because of drinking alcohol (informal use).

lagging ['lægɪŋ] *n* material used to lag a pipe, tank etc to keep the heat in.

lagoon [lə'guːn] *n* a lake of sea water that is separated from the sea by sand banks or rocks.

laid [leɪd] *past tense* & *past participle of* lay.

laid-back *adj* [person, attitude, approach] that seems calm, relaxed, and not easily affected by problems or by the behavior of other people □ *He sounded very laid-back about the prospect of losing his job!*

lain [leɪn] *past participle of* lie.

lair [leəʳ] *n* a hole or covered place where a wild animal lives.

laissez-faire [ˌleɪseɪ'feəʳ] ◇ *adj* [approach, policy, attitude] that believes it is wrong to interfere in the activities of individual companies or people. ◇ *n* a laissez-faire policy.

laity ['leɪətɪ] *n* the laity all the members of a religious group who are not members of the clergy.

lake [leɪk] *n* a large area of water in the middle of land □ *the Great Lakes.*

Lake District: the Lake District a region of lakes and mountains in northwestern England, famous for its attractive scenery and for the Romantic poets who lived there.

lakeside ['leɪksaɪd] *adj* [resort, complex] that is by the side of a lake.

lama ['lɑːmə] (*pl* lamas) *n* a Buddhist priest or monk.

lamb [læm] *n* a young sheep; the flesh of this animal eaten as food □ *roast lamb* □ *a lamb kebab.*

lambast [læm'bæst], **lambaste** [læm'beɪst] *vt* [person, book] to criticize <sb/sthg> strongly.

lamb chop *n* a small piece of meat on a bone, cut from a lamb.

lambing ['læmɪŋ] *n* the time of year when sheep give birth to lambs.

Lamb of God = Jesus.

lambskin ['læmskɪn] *n* a kind of leather, often with wool on one side, that is made from the skins of lambs □ *a lambskin coat.*

lambswool ['læmzwʊl] *n* a soft wool that comes from lambs and is used for making knitted clothes □ *a lambswool sweater/scarf.*

lame [leɪm] *adj* -1. [person, horse] that cannot walk properly because at least one leg or foot is damaged □ *He went lame in both legs.* -2. [excuse, argument] that shows a lack of thought or effort and is not good enough to be taken seriously □ *He came up with a pretty lame excuse about the traffic.*

lamé [US lɑː'meɪ, GB 'lɑːmeɪ] *n* a material containing gold or silver threads □ *a gold lamé dress.*

lamebrain ['leɪmbreɪn] *n* US a person who one thinks is stupid (informal use).

lame duck *n* -1. a person or business that continually needs help and never seems likely to succeed. -2. US POLITICS an official who has not been re-elected and is about to be replaced.

lamely ['leɪmlɪ] *adv* [say, argue] *see* lame □ *"Well, I did my best," he said lamely.*

lament [lə'ment] ◇ *n* something that somebody says, writes, or sings to show sadness, regret, or disappointment about something □ *The poem is a lament for the loss of so many young lives.* ◇ *vt* [death, decline, change] to express sadness, regret, or disappointment about <sthg> □ *This is not the first book to lament the decline of educational standards.*

lamentable ['læməntəbl, lə'mentəbl] *adj* [situation, mistake, performance] that one finds very bad and unsatisfactory □ *It is surely a lamentable state of affairs when a nurse has to go elsewhere to find a job.*

laminated ['læmɪneɪtəd] *adj* [wood, glass, steel] that is made of several thin sheets stuck together.

lamp [læmp] *n* a device that produces light using electricity, oil, or gas □ *a bedside lamp* □ *a desk/table/an oil/a gas lamp.*

lamplight ['læmplaɪt] *n* the light from a lamp □ *I got a glimpse of her face in the lamplight.*

lampoon [læm'puːn] ◇ *vt* to criticize <sb/sthg> in public by making them seem funny instead of serious □ *articles lampooning the official's behavior.* ◇ *n* a piece of writing, a cartoon etc that lampoons somebody or something.

lamppost ['læmppəʊst] *n* a tall metal or concrete pole with a light at the top that stands next to a road.

lampshade ['læmpʃeɪd] *n* a decorative cover of material, paper, glass etc around a light bulb.

LAN [læn] *n abbr of* local area network.

Lancashire ['læŋkəʃəʳ] a county in northwestern England, situated on the Irish Sea. SIZE: 3,063 sq kms. POPULATION: 1,381,300. ADMINISTRATIVE CENTER: Preston.

lance [US læns, GB lɑːns] ◇ *vt* **to lance a boil** to cut a hole in a boil to let the fluid out. ◇ *n* a long spear used in the past as a weapon by soldiers on horses.

lance corporal *n* in the British Army or US Marines, an officer of the lowest rank.

Lancelot [US ˈlænsəlɔːt, GB ˈlɑːnsəlɒt], **Sir** in English legends, the bravest of King Arthur's knights. He was also the lover of Arthur's queen, Guinevere.

lancet [US ˈlænsət, GB ˈlɑːn-] *n* a sharp knife with two edges that is used by surgeons.

Lancs *abbr of* **Lancashire**.

land [lænd] ◇ *n* **-1.** [not sea] the part of the surface of the Earth that is not sea □ *They traveled by land.* □ *It's good to be back on dry land!* □ *After three weeks at sea, they sighted land.* **-2.** [for crops, houses] ground used for building or farming □ *good grazing land.* **-3.** [as property] ground that belongs to somebody or can be bought and sold □ *They bought thirty acres of land.* □ *land prices.* **-4.** a country (literary use) □ *America, the Land of the Free.*
◇ *vt* **-1.** [helicopter, glider] to bring <an aircraft> back onto the ground at the end of a flight □ *Dan had to land the plane himself.* **-2.** [passengers, cargo] to unload <goods or people> somewhere at the end of a trip by sea or air □ *They landed the cargo in San Francisco.* **-3.** [contract, prize, job] to win <sthg> after trying for some time and against a lot of competition (informal use) □ *INC have landed the Phillips contract.* □ *Mary's landed herself a fantastic job in California.* **-4.** [fish] to catch <a fish> and bring it out of the water. **-5.** **to land sb in sthg** [in trouble, debt, jail] to cause sb to find themselves in a difficult situation (informal use) □ *You'll land yourself in prison.* □ *You've really landed me in it this time!* ■ **to land sb with sthg** [with a job, responsibility] to give sb sthg that is not wanted (informal use) □ *I was landed with the job of watching my sister's kids.*
◇ *vi* **-1.** [plane, person] to arrive on land after a trip by air □ *I'll be landing at JFK at 10 a.m.* □ *The plane will be landing shortly.* **-2.** [bomb, ball, person] to fall onto something after moving through the air □ *A raindrop landed on my head.* □ *She slipped and landed on the floor/on her back/in the water.* **-3.** [ship, person] to arrive on land after traveling by sea □ *We landed in Calais.*

◆ **land up** *vi* to reach a particular place or state without intending to after a long trip or series of events □ *Our luggage landed up in Cairo.* □ *If you're not careful, you'll land up in serious trouble.*

landed gentry [ˈlændəd-] *npl* **the landed gentry** upper-class people who own land, especially people whose families have owned land for a very long time.

landing [ˈlændɪŋ] *n* **-1.** [in a building] the area at the top of a flight of stairs that leads to different rooms □ *We always leave the landing light on.* **-2.** [of a plane] the act of landing □ *a smooth landing.* **-3.** [for boats] = **landing stage**.

landing card *n* an official document that peo-

ple of particular nationalities on a ship or plane have to fill out in order to be able to enter another country.

landing craft *n* a boat that can open at one end and is used to bring troops and military equipment on shore.

landing gear *n* the wheels and other equipment on the lower part of a plane that support it when it is on the ground, landing, or taking off.

landing stage *n* a wooden platform over water where boats stop to let passengers and goods go onto land.

landing strip *n* a long area of land that is used by planes for taking off from and landing on.

landlady [ˈlændleɪdɪ] (*pl* **landladies**) *n* **-1.** [of a house, apartment, building] a woman who owns a building and allows somebody to live or work there in return for payment. **-2.** [of a hotel, pub] a woman who runs a small hotel or pub.
NOTE: Compare **landlord, tenant**.

landlocked [ˈlændlɒkt] *adj* [country] that is surrounded on all sides by land and has no coastline.

landlord [ˈlændlɔːrd] *n* **-1.** [of a house, apartment, building] a man who owns a building and allows somebody to live or work there in return for payment. **-2.** [of a hotel, pub] a man who runs a small hotel or pub.
NOTE: Compare **landlady, tenant**.

landmark [ˈlændmɑːrk] *n* **-1.** [in a city, area] something that is noticeable as part of the landscape and is therefore used when giving directions or checking one's position □ *the Statue of Liberty, one of New York's great landmarks.* **-2.** [in history, sb's life] a very important event or idea in the history of somebody or something, especially one that marks a change □ *a landmark court case.*

land mass *n* a large area of land, e.g. a continent.

landmine [ˈlændmaɪn] *n* a bomb hidden in or under the ground that explodes when somebody walks or drives over it.

landowner [ˈlændoʊnər] *n* a person who owns land, especially a large amount.

land rights *npl* the right to own an area of land.

🐾 LAND RIGHTS
In Australia, discussions of land rights, or the ownership of land, often refer to the important High Court decision made in 1992, when Torres Straits Islander Ernie Mabo made a land rights claim on behalf of his tribe. The judges decided that Aboriginal people were still the owners of land that had later been taken over by European settlers. This has allowed Aboriginal peoples throughout Australia to claim areas of land taken by European settlers and governments during the past 200 years.

Land Rover™ [-roʊvər] *n* a large powerful car

designed for traveling over very rough, steep, or wet ground.

landscape ['lændskeɪp] ◇ *n* the view across an area of land that includes hills, rivers, buildings etc; a painting of such an area □ *Stephen stared out across the dull, flat landscape.* ◇ *vt* to design <a garden or park> to make it look attractive and interesting, e.g. by adding different levels or planting bushes □ *a beautifully landscaped park.*

landscape gardener *n* a person whose job is to landscape gardens, parks etc.

Land's End a place on the coast of Cornwall, southwest England, that people think is the most southerly place on the British coast. NOTE: Compare **John O'Groats**.

landslide ['lændslaɪd] *n* -1. the sudden movement of a lot of earth, rocks etc down the side of a hill or mountain □ *The road was blocked by a landslide.* -2. POLITICS an easy win in an election by a large number of votes □ *He won a landslide victory.*

landslip ['lændslɪp] *n* a small landslide.

lane [leɪn] *n* -1. a narrow road in the country; part of the name of a street □ *a country lane* □ *I live in Cooper Lane.* -2. TRANSPORT [of a road] one of the parts of a road that cars drive along, that is marked by lines painted on the road □ *the passing/fast lane.* ■ **'get/keep in lane'** GB a highway sign that tells drivers to move into the correct lane/stay in the lane they are in. -3. SPORT [of a pool, track] one of the parts of a swimming pool or a race track marked by ropes or white lines for each competitor in a race □ *He's running in lane three.* -4. SHIPPING & AVIATION a route across the sea or in the air that ships or planes regularly follow.

language ['læŋgwɪdʒ] *n* -1. a particular system of spoken or written communication that is used e.g. by all the people in a particular country □ *He speaks several languages, including French.* □ *animal language* □ *the language barrier.* -2. the human system of communicating through words □ *language acquisition* □ *a natural flair for language.* -3. [of a novel, article, person] a particular way of speaking or talking, using particular kinds of words □ *legal/business language.*

language laboratory *n* a room that contains tape recorders and headphones and is used by students learning and practicing a foreign language.

languid ['læŋgwəd] *adj* [person, gesture] that is slow and shows no sign of effort or interest.

languish ['læŋgwɪʃ] *vi* -1. to suffer for a long period of time in a particular place or situation □ *She languished in prison/in obscurity for many years.* -2. [plant, person] to become weak.

languorous ['læŋgərəs] *adj* [feeling, afternoon, person] that is pleasantly relaxed.

lank [læŋk] *adj* [hair] that is flat, hangs down straight, and looks unattractive.

lanky ['læŋkɪ] (*compar* **lankier**, *superl* **lankiest**) *adj* [person] who is very tall and thin with long legs.

lanolin(e) ['lænəlɪn] *n* an oily substance from sheep's wool that is used to make skin creams, cosmetics etc.

lantern ['læntərn] *n* a light that consists of a candle, flame, or bulb in a metal and glass container that is hung outside a house or carried on a pole.

Laos [US 'lɑːoʊs, GB laʊs] a country in Southeast Asia, between Thailand and Vietnam. SIZE: 236,800 sq kms. POPULATION: 4,600,000 (*Laotians*). CAPITAL: Vientiane. LANGUAGE: Laotian. CURRENCY: kip.

Laotian [US leɪˈoʊʃn, GB ˈlaʊʃn] *n* & *adj*: see **Laos**.

lap [læp] (*pt* & *pp* **lapped**, *cont* **lapping**) ◇ *n* -1. [of a person] the flat area made by the upper part of one's thighs when one is sitting down □ *She sat on her mother's lap.* -2. SPORT the distance of one complete journey around a race track □ *They were on the final lap when Schulz crashed.* ◇ *vt* -1. [milk, water] to drink <sthg> by using quick movements of the tongue □ *The cat lapped the milk with its tongue.* -2. SPORT to pass <another competitor> so that one has completed one lap more than them. ◇ *vi* [water, waves] to move gently all the time against a boat, over land etc, making soft sounds □ *The sea lapped against the shore.*

◆ **lap up** *vt sep* -1. **to lap sthg up** [milk, water] to lap sthg. -2. **to lap sthg up** [attention, praise, story] to eagerly accept sthg, even if it is not true or sincere □ *They lapped up everything she told them.*

laparoscopy [ˌlæpəˈrɒskəpɪ] (*pl* **laparoscopies**) *n* an examination of the inside of one's body using a special tube with a light attached to it so that a doctor can see through it.

lapdog ['læpdɒg] *n* any small dog that is kept as a pet in order to look decorative.

lapel [ləˈpel] *n* the part of a coat or jacket that folds from the collar onto the front of it □ *He grabbed Joe suddenly by the lapels.*

Lapland ['læplænd] a region of northern Europe, consisting of parts of Norway, Sweden, Finland, and Russia, north of the Arctic Circle.

Laplander ['læplændər] *n* a person who comes from or lives in Lapland.

Lapp [læp] *n* -1. = **Laplander**. -2. the language spoken by the people of Lapland.

lapse [læps] ◇ *n* -1. **a lapse of sthg** a short period of time during which one forgets sthg or stops concentrating on sthg □ *a lapse of memory/concentration.* -2. [in behavior] a small example of incorrect behavior, especially from a person who usually behaves properly □ *I hope that you will forgive this little lapse on my colleague's part.* -3. **a lapse of time** a period of time between two events □ *after a lapse of six months.*

◇ *vi* -1. [agreement, law, membership] to become no longer valid □ *Your subscription lapsed two weeks ago.* -2. [standards, quality] to be allowed to become worse; [tradition] to happen much less than before □ *The usually excellent standards in this restaurant have lapsed considerably over the past few years.* **-3. to lapse into sthg** [into silence, a coma] to gradually pass into sthg, especially into a less active state; [into bad habits] to start to do sthg, often sthg less good or desirable □ *He would sometimes lapse into dialect.* □ *It's so easy to lapse back into old habits.*

lapsed [læpst] *adj* **a lapsed Catholic/Jew** a Catholic/Jew who no longer follows or practices their religion.

laptop (computer) ['læptɒp-] *n* a computer that is small enough to be carried and used on one's lap.

larceny ['lɑːʳsənɪ] *n* LAW the crime of stealing.

larch [lɑːʳtʃ] *n* a tall tree with needles instead of leaves, and pink or red cones that become brown as they get older.

lard [lɑːʳd] *n* soft white fat from pigs that is used in cooking.

larder ['lɑːʳdəʳ] *n* a closet or small room where food is stored on shelves.

large [lɑːʳdʒ] *adj* [house, person, area] that is great in size compared to other things of the same type; [number, family] that is great in amount or quantity □ *We live in a large town.* □ *Benefits are usually much better in a large company.*

◆ **at large** ◇ *adj* **to be at large** [criminal, animal] to still be free, with the result that people do not feel safe. ◇ *adv* **as a whole** □ *The world/country at large has a lower infant mortality rate than 50 years ago.*

◆ **by and large** *adv* a phrase used to show that a statement is not completely true but mostly true □ *By and large, I think you'll find most people are happy with the changes.*

largely ['lɑːʳdʒlɪ] *adv* mostly □ *This is largely true in outlying areas.* □ *She left the company, largely because she didn't agree with their new sales policy.*

large-scale *adj* **-1.** [investment, operation, damage] that involves a large area or a large number of people or things □ *a large-scale rescue mission* □ *large-scale shipments of emergency supplies.* **-2.** [map, diagram] that shows a small area in great detail □ *a large-scale map of Bavaria.*

largess, largesse [lɑːʳˈdʒes] *n* generosity to people poorer than oneself.

lark [lɑːʳk] *n* **-1.** a small brown bird that is found in country areas and sings pleasantly. **-2.** something that is done because it is amusing and enjoyable (informal use) □ *It was a real lark!* ■ **on a lark** US, **for a lark** GB as a joke. □ *On a lark, he pretended he was her chauffeur.*

◆ **lark about** *vi* to do silly things to amuse oneself.

larva ['lɑːʳvə] (*pl* **larvae** [-viː]) *n* the young form of an insect, that often looks like a soft thick worm, before it changes its shape completely to become an adult.

laryngitis [ˌlærɪnˈdʒaɪtəs] *n* a painful swelling

and infection of the larynx that makes it difficult to speak.

larynx ['lærɪŋks] (*pl* **larynxes**) *n* the hollow part of one's throat in which the sounds of one's voice are produced.

lasagna, lasagne [US ləˈzɑːnjə, GB -ˈzænjə] *n* an Italian dish made with large flat layers of pasta covered with meat sauce and white sauce.

lascivious [ləˈsɪvɪəs] *adj* [look, person] that shows strong or uncontrolled sexual desire (disapproving use).

laser ['leɪzəʳ] *n* a machine that produces a very powerful narrow beam of light that is used to cut through hard materials, and in medical operations; the narrow beam of light produced by this machine □ *laser surgery.*

laser beam *n* the powerful narrow beam of light that is produced by a laser.

Laser Disc™ *n* a small flat disc that is used for showing television pictures of a higher quality than on videotape.

laser printer *n* a computer printer that uses laser beams to produce high-quality words or pictures.

laser show *n* a form of entertainment that uses colored laser beams.

lash [læʃ] ◇ *n* **-1.** [of one's eye] = **eyelash. -2.** [from a whip] a blow from a whip, especially as a form of punishment. **-3.** [of a whip] the long, thin, leather part of a whip that is attached to the handle. ◇ *vt* **-1.** to beat <a person or animal> with a whip. **-2.** to tie <sthg> firmly into a particular position □ *They had to lash the crates to the truck to prevent them from falling off.* ◇ *vi* **to lash against sthg** [wind, rain] to beat violently against sthg □ *Waves lashed against the shore.*

◆ **lash out** *vi* **-1.** [at a person] to suddenly and violently swing one's arm, leg, or a weapon at somebody in order to hurt them □ *She lashed out at him with her fists.* **-2.** [against a person, idea] to speak very angrily about somebody or something, especially publicly □ *He lashed out at OR against the government in an interview on the news.*

lashings ['læʃɪŋz] *npl* **lashings of sthg** [of food, drink] a large quantity of sthg (informal use).

lasso [US 'læsoʊ, GB læ'suː] (*pl* **lassos**, *pt & pp* **lassoed**, *cont* **lassoing**) ◇ *n* a long rope that is tied at one end to make a circle and is thrown around the necks of horses or cattle to catch them. ◇ *vt* to catch <cattle or horses> using a lasso.

last [US læst, GB lɑːst] ◇ *det* **-1. last week/Tuesday/March** the week/Tuesday/March before this present one (used with dates and periods of time) □ *This year's results show a considerable improvement over last year's.* □ *We've been in Maine for the last four years.* **-2. his last girlfriend/car/job** the girlfriend/car/job he had before this one □ *The last time I saw him was over a week ago.* □ *Their policies haven't changed since the last election.* **-3. the last bus/page/chance** the bus/page/chance that comes after all the others, and after which there are no more □ *It was the last novel he wrote before he died.* □ *It's the last turn on the left.* ■ **last thing at night** just before bedtime.

◇ *adv* **-1. to arrive/finish last** to arrive/finish after everyone else □ *Put on your lipstick last, after all your other makeup.* **-2. I last saw her ten years ago** I have not seen her since that time ten years ago □ *The suspect was last seen driving a blue van.*

◇ *pron & n* **-1. he was the last to arrive** he arrived after everyone else. ■ **to leave sthg till last** to do sthg after one has finished everything else □ *I'm always the last to find out these things!* □ *I left the dirty pans till last.* **-2. the week/Tuesday before last** the week/Tuesday before the one that has just ended. ■ **the last but one** the one before the last one in a series. ■ **that was the last I saw of him** I have not seen him since that particular time.

◇ *vi* **-1.** [event] to happen over a particular period of time □ *The performance lasts for three hours.* □ *The meeting won't last long.* **-2.** [luck, feeling] to continue □ *They're happy now, but it won't last.* **-3.** [flowers, clothes] to stay in a good condition □ *My new shoes won't last five minutes in that rain!* **-4.** [money, food] to be enough for somebody to use during a particular period of time □ *The roast should last for two days.*

◇ *vt* [money, food] *I have enough cash to last me until the weekend.*

◆ **at (long) last** *adv* after one has been waiting for a long time □ *Free at last!* □ *At long last she has found a job she enjoys.*

last-ditch *adj* **a last-ditch attempt/effort** an attempt/effort that is the last of several attempts/efforts before one gives up □ *The Republican Party are making a last-ditch campaign to win over the electorate.*

lasting [US 'læstɪŋ, GB 'lɑːst-] *adj* [feeling, effect] that lasts for a very long time or for ever □ *This injection will cut down the pain, but it is not a lasting cure* □ *a lasting peace.*

lastly [US 'læstlɪ, GB 'lɑːst-] *adv* **-1. lastly,...** a word used to introduce the end of a speech or a piece of writing □ *Lastly, I would like to thank everyone who has come along to support us today.* **-2.** a word used to introduce the last comment, fact, question etc that one wants to make □ *In the third place it is an unrealistic aim, and lastly it is too costly.*

last-minute *adj* [decision, cancellation, goal] that happens just before it is too late □ *I had to run around town doing last-minute shopping before Christmas.*

last name *n* = **surname**.

last post *n* GB **-1.** the final daily collection of mail from a mailbox or post office □ *What time's (the) last post on a Saturday?* **-2. the last post** MILITARY a tune played on a bugle at funerals or to call soldiers back to camp.

last rites *npl* **the last rites** a religious ceremony performed by a priest for a Catholic who is about to die.

last straw *n* **the last straw** the last in a series of problems, unfortunate events etc that

finally makes a situation unacceptable □ *When he started shouting, that really was the last straw.*

Last Supper *n* **the Last Supper** in the Bible, the last meal that Jesus Christ shared with all his disciples before his death.

last word *n* **to have the last word** to make the final comment in an argument □ *You know he always likes to have the last word.*

Las Vegas [US lɑːs'veɪɡəs, GB ˌlæs-] a city in Nevada, USA, famous for its casinos. POPULATION: 258,295.

latch [lætʃ] *n* a piece of metal attached to a door, gate, or window that fits into a piece of metal in the frame so that it is kept closed □ *a door latch.* ■ **to be on the latch** [door, window] to be closed but not locked, so that one can open it with the handle.

◆ **latch onto** *vt fus* **to latch onto sb** to meet sb and stay with them, especially when they do not want one to do this. ■ **to latch onto sthg** [idea, phrase] to become very interested in sthg □ *The public have been slow to latch onto the slogan.*

latchkey ['lætʃkiː] (*pl* **latchkeys**) *n* a key used for opening the outside or main doors of a house or apartment.

late [leɪt] ◇ *adj* **-1.** [person, bus, flight] that does not arrive at the necessary or fixed time □ *My car broke down, so I was very late for the meeting.* □ *Please don't be late!* □ *We apologize to customers for the late arrival of this train.* **-2.** [evening, December] that is near the end of a particular period of time □ *The late afternoon sun shone warmly across the garden.* □ *We should leave — it's getting late.* □ *a late night* □ *She's in her late twenties.* **-3.** [supper, application] that happens later than is normal or expected □ *We had a late breakfast.* **-4. the late king** the king who has died □ *The late Mrs Nuffield left $3 million.* □ *her late husband* □ *My late wife loved this park.* **-5. the late leader/director** the leader/director before this present one.

◇ *adv* [arrive, wake up, work] *The train pulled in 20 minutes late.* □ *Don't go to bed too late.* □ *We dine late on a Friday night.* □ *It was late in the day/in August before they contacted me.*

◆ **of late** *adv* recently □ *I've been feeling much better of late.*

latecomer ['leɪtkʌməʳ] *n* a person who arrives somewhere later than other people or after the arranged time.

lately ['leɪtlɪ] *adv* recently □ *She's been calling me a lot just lately.*

late-night *adj* [movie, show] that is broadcast late at night; [visitor] who arrives late at night; [pharmacist] that is open until late at night. ■ **late-night opening** GB an evening when a shop, library etc is open later than usual □ *'Late-night opening till 8pm.'*

latent ['leɪtənt] *adj* [threat, anger, meaning] that exists but is hidden and not yet noticeable □ *latent aggression.*

later ['leɪtəʳ] ◇ *adj* [date, edition, flight] that happens/exists etc at a time further in the future; that happens/exists etc at the end part of a period of time □ *I'll have to catch a later plane.* □ *In later life she went back to learning the piano.* ◇ *adv* **later (on)** at a later time □ *They met up again later on at the theater.* □ *I'll read it later, just leave it on my desk.*

lateral ['lætərəl] *adj* [growth, root] that is joined to the side of something.

lateral thinking *n* solving problems by using one's imagination to think of answers that are not obvious or expected □ *a brilliant piece of lateral thinking.*

latest ['leɪtəst] ◇ *adj* [news, fashion, book] the most recent □ *Have you seen his latest movie?* ◇ *n* **at the latest** no later than a particular time □ *She told me to be there by 6 pm at the latest.*

latex ['leɪteks] *n* a substance that comes from a type of tree and is used to make rubber, glue etc □ *latex gloves.*

lath [US læθ, GB lɑːθ] *n* a long thin piece of wood that is used as a support for plaster on walls or tiles on roofs.

lathe [leɪð] *n* a machine that turns wood or metal around as it is held against a sharp object in order to shape it.

lather [US 'læðr, GB 'lɑːðə] ◇ *n* a light mass of bubbles formed by rubbing soap, shampoo, or detergent against something in water □ *His face/hair was covered in lather.* ◇ *vt* [hair, body] to cover <sthg> with a lather. ◇ *vi* [soap, shampoo] to produce a lather.

Latin ['lætn] ◇ *adj* -1. [temperament, character] that is connected with any of the nations that speak French, Spanish, Italian, or Portuguese. -2. [studies, scholar, language] that is connected with the language spoken by the ancient Romans. ◇ *n* the language spoken by the ancient Romans.

Latin America Central and South America considered together.

Latin American *n* & *adj*: see **Latin America**.

Latino [læ'tiːnou] (*pl* **Latinos**) *n* a person living in the USA whose family came from Latin America.

latitude ['lætɪtjuːd] *n* -1. GEOGRAPHY a position on the Earth, or on a map, measured in degrees north or south of the Equator □ *The island lies at a latitude of ten degrees north.* □ *Few animals live in these latitudes.* -2. freedom to do as one chooses (formal use) □ *Students are allowed a certain degree of latitude in their subject choices.*
NOTE: Compare **longitude**.

latrine [lə'triːn] *n* a toilet in a place where soldiers live.

latter ['lætər] ◇ *adj* -1. **the latter period** the period nearer the end of a particular period of time □ *in the latter years of the war.* -2. **the latter part** the part that happens in the second part of a period of time; the part that was the second one to be mentioned □ *the latter half of the year* □ *I preferred the latter part of the movie.* ◇ *n* **the latter** the second of the two people or things that have been mentioned

□ *If I had to choose between a small house or a large apartment, I'd choose the latter.*

latter-day *adj* a word used to describe a person or place that exists now and is like a particular person or place that existed in the past □ *He stood there feeding the birds like a latter-day St. Francis.*

Latter-day Saint *n* = **Mormon** (formal use).

latterly ['lætəlɪ] *adv* recently (formal use) □ *Latterly, things had not been going so well.*

lattice ['lætəs] *n* a flat structure that consists of long thin pieces of wood or metal that cross over each other diagonally to create spaces in the shape of diamonds.

lattice window *n* a window with flat pieces of glass in the shape of diamonds that are held together by long thin pieces of metal.

Latvia ['lætvɪə] a country in northeastern Europe, on the Baltic Sea. SIZE: 64,000 sq kms. POPULATION: 2,700,000 (*Latvians, Letts*). CAPITAL: Riga. LANGUAGE: Latvian, Russian. CURRENCY: lat.

laudable ['lɔːdəbl] *adj* [behavior, intention] that deserves to be praised □ *I think it's very laudable of him to do it for free.*

laugh [US læf, GB lɑːf] ◇ *vi* to make a sound with one's voice that shows that one finds something funny, and to smile at the same time □ *He laughed loudly.* □ *You never laugh at my jokes.* □ *We laughed about it afterward.* ◇ *n* -1. an act or sound of laughing □ *He gave a long laugh.* □ *She has a loud laugh.* ■ **to have the last laugh** to finally be successful or be proved right after other people have criticized or laughed at one earlier. -2. something that is fun, or that is done because it is amusing (informal use) □ *I had a great laugh last night.* □ *It was a really good laugh.* ■ **to do sthg for laughs** OR **a laugh** to do sthg because it is amusing and enjoyable.

◆ **laugh at** *vt fus* **to laugh at sb/sthg** [person, behavior, suggestion] to treat sb/sthg as foolish.

◆ **laugh off** *vt sep* **to laugh sthg off** [insult, suggestion] to try and make sthg seem less important than it is by joking about it □ *The man was unbelievably rude, but Simon just laughed it off.*

laughable [US 'læfəbl, GB 'lɑːf-] *adj* [attempt, situation] that cannot be taken seriously (disapproving use) □ *It's laughable to think he can do the job as well as Ian.*

laughing gas [US 'læfɪŋ-, GB 'lɑːf-] *n* a gas that can make people laugh if it is breathed in, and that is used to anesthetize patients.

laughingstock [US 'læfɪŋstɒk, GB 'lɑːf-] *n* **to become a laughingstock** to start to seem ridiculous and stop being treated seriously □ *The country has become the laughingstock of the Western world.*

laughter [US 'læftr, GB 'lɑːftə] *n* the sound of a person or people laughing □ *She roared with laughter at his joke.* □ *I could hear the sound of laughter.*

launch [lɔːntʃ] ◇ *n* -1. [of a boat, ship] the act of putting a new ship into water for the first

time and making it sail. **-2.** [of a rocket, missile, satellite] the act of sending a device into the air or into space □ *a rocket launch.* **-3.** [of an attack, campaign] the start of something □ *When's the company's official launch date?* **-4.** BUSINESS [of a newspaper, car, book] the act of putting a new product onto the market □ *We've been invited to the press launch of her autobiography.* **-5.** a large motorboat for carrying passengers for short distances, especially on rivers and lakes or in harbors.
◇ *vt* **-1.** [boat, ship, submarine] to put <sthg> into water for the first time and make it sail. **-2.** [rocket, missile, satellite] to send <sthg> into the air or into space. **-3.** [attack, campaign, inquiry] to start <sthg> □ *An appeal was launched to raise funds.* **-4.** BUSINESS [newspaper, car, book] to put <a new product> onto the market □ *The marketing department needs to know when to launch the book.*
◆ **launch into** *vt fus* **to launch into sthg** [attack, task, story] to start sthg suddenly with enthusiasm and energy □ *She launched into a lecture on the importance of manners.*

launching ['lɔːntʃɪŋ] *n* the act of launching something.

launch(ing) pad ['lɔːntʃ(ɪŋ)-] *n* a platform from which a rocket, missile, satellite etc is launched.

launder ['lɔːndər] *vt* **-1.** to wash and iron <clothing, linen> etc □ *freshly laundered towels.* **-2.** to move <money> into a bank or legal business in order to hide the fact that it was made illegally □ *a money-laundering operation.*

Laundromat™ ['lɔːndrəmæt] US, **Launderette**™ [ˌlɔːndəˈret] GB *n* a type of shop where there are machines that people put coins in to wash and dry their laundry.

laundry ['lɔːndri] (*pl* **laundries**) *n* **-1.** clothes, sheets etc that are ready to be washed or have just been washed □ *a pile of fresh laundry.* **-2.** BUSINESS a business that launders clothes, sheets etc for its customers. **-3.** = **laundry room.**

laundry basket *n* a container where dirty laundry is kept until washed.

laundry detergent *n* US a chemical substance in the form of a powder or liquid that is used for washing clothes.

laundry room *n* a room in a house where clothes, sheets etc are washed.

laureate ['lɔːriət] *n* = **poet laureate.**

laurel ['lɒrəl] *n* a small evergreen tree with shiny leaves □ *a laurel leaf.*
◆ **laurels** *npl* **to rest on one's laurels** to feel satisfied with one's achievements and therefore make no more effort to succeed.

Lautro ['lautrou] (*abbr of* **Life Assurance and Unit Trust Regulatory Organization**) *n* a British organization that was set up to control the activities of life assurance companies and unit trusts. In 1994 it merged with Fimbra to become the Personal Investment Authority.

lava ['lɑːvə] *n* rock in a very hot liquid state that comes out of the top of a volcano and becomes hard as it cools □ *molten/volcanic lava.*

lavatory [US 'lævətɔːrɪ, GB -ətrɪ] (*pl* **lavatories**) *n* **-1.** a toilet. **-2.** a room or small building that contains a lavatory □ *a public lavatory.*

lavatory paper *n* GB = **toilet paper.**

lavender ['lævəndər] ◇ *adj* [ribbon, dress] that is pale purple in color. ◇ *n* **-1.** a plant that has pale purple flowers that smell very pleasant □ *a bunch of lavender* □ *lavender water/oil/soap.* **-2.** pale purple.

lavish ['lævɪʃ] ◇ *adj* **-1.** [gift, hospitality, person] that is very generous □ *She's always very lavish with her money/time.* **-2.** [party, decoration, suite] that shows a lot of wealth or too much wealth □ *He used to entertain people on a lavish scale.* ◇ *vt* **to lavish sthg on sb** [attention, affection, money] to give sthg to sb very generously or in large amounts □ *She lavished gifts on her nieces and nephews.*

lavishly ['lævɪʃlɪ] *adv* [entertain, pay, decorate] *see* **lavish.**

law [lɔː] *n* **-1.** a system of rules that has been decided by a government, that tells people what they can or must do and what they cannot or must not do, and that states how crimes will be punished; a part of this system that deals with a particular subject □ *It looks like the bill will become law next year.* □ *All aliens must register with the police by law.* □ *contract/civil/business/divorce law* □ *a law-making body* □ *There are strict laws on party financing.* ■ **to break the law** to do something that is illegal □ *Owners who fail to register their dogs are breaking the law.* ■ **to be against the law** to be illegal □ *It's against the law to smoke cannabis.* ■ **law and order** a situation in which the law is respected and obeyed □ *Law and order must be maintained/restored.* **-2.** a rule in a system of laws that deals with a particular kind of activity □ *immigration laws* □ *Is there a law against smoking in restaurants?* **-3. (the) law** the profession that is connected with the legal system and how it works □ *a law firm.* **-4.** EDUCATION the subject of the legal system and how it works that is studied □ *I did a degree in law.* □ *a law degree/student.* **-5.** [of nature] a natural or scientific process that always has the same result in particular conditions □ *a scientific law* □ *the law of gravity.* **-6. the law** the police (informal use). **-7.** *phrases* **to lay down the law** to give orders and insist that particular things are done in the way one wants. ■ **the law of the jungle** the principle that only the strongest survive or achieve anything in life and so one should only consider one's own interests.

law-abiding *adj* [citizen] who obeys the law □ *decent, law-abiding members of the public.*

law-breaker *n* a person who has broken the law.

law court *n* a place where a person who has been accused of a crime has their case judged by a jury or a judge.

law-enforcement *adj* **a law-enforcement agency/officer etc** an agency/a person etc responsible for making sure that the law is obeyed.

lawful ['lɔːfl] *adj* [marriage, method] that is legal (formal use).

lawfully ['lɔːflɪ] *adv* **to be lawfully married/killed** to be legally married/killed (formal use) □ *Police officers were found to have acted lawfully in obtaining the evidence.*

lawless ['lɔːləs] *adj* -1. [act, activity] that is illegal and violent □ *lawless behavior* □ *a lawless terrorist.* -2. [society, town] where laws have little influence or control and there is a lot of crime.

Law Lords *npl* **the Law Lords** in Britain, members of the House of Lords who are lawyers and who form the highest court of appeal.

lawmaker ['lɔːmeɪkəʳ] *n* a person who makes laws.

lawn [lɔːn] *n* an area of grass that is kept very short in a yard, garden, or park.

lawnmower ['lɔːnmoʊəʳ] *n* a machine that is pushed or driven across a lawn to cut it.

lawn party *n* US a party that happens outside on a lawn, especially in somebody's yard.

lawn tennis *n* tennis, especially when it is played on grass (technical use).

Lawrence ['lɔːrəns], **D. H.** (1885–1930) a British writer. His works include *Sons and Lovers* and *Lady Chatterley's Lover* which was banned until 1960 because of its descriptions of sex.

Lawrence, T. E. (1888–1935) a British soldier and writer, known as Lawrence of Arabia. He fought with the Arabs against Turkey in World War I. His best-known work, *The Seven Pillars of Wisdom*, is an account of his experiences in the desert.

law school *n* a part of a university where law is taught.

Lawson ['lɔːsn], **Henry** (1867–1922) an Australian poet and short-story writer. His best-known work, *When the Billy Boils*, describes life in the outback.

lawsuit ['lɔːsuːt] *n* a case in a court of law about a problem between two individual parties, not between the police and a criminal □ *She brought a lawsuit against her former employer.*

lawyer ['lɔːjəʳ] *n* a person who has studied law and who gives people legal advice or represents them in court.

lax [læks] *adj* [discipline, security] that is not as good and as strict as is required or expected □ *People here are very lax about safety.*

laxative ['læksətɪv] *n* a medicine, food, or drink that helps to stop constipation.

laxity ['læksətɪ], **laxness** ['læksnəs] *n*: see **lax**.

lay [leɪ] (*pt* & *pp* **laid**) ◇ *vt* -1. to place <sb/sthg> in a particular position so that it is flat □ *He laid a hand on the girl's forehead.* □ *She laid her dress over the bed.* -2. [trap, mine] to get <a device> ready and put it in a place where it can do damage. ■ **to lay plans** to prepare plans. ■ **to lay the table** to arrange the silverware, plates, cloth etc on the table in prepa-

ration for a meal. -3. [bricks, cable, carpet] to place <sthg> in its correct position and fix it there □ *Fifty kilometers of pipeline have been laid so far.* -4. to produce <an egg> and leave it in a place to hatch. -5. **to lay the blame on sb** to blame sb □ *You can't lay all the blame for the mistake on the secretary.* ■ **to lay the emphasis on sthg** to emphasize sthg.

◇ *adj* -1. RELIGION **a lay preacher** a preacher who does not have an official position within their religion □ *a lay member of the Church.* -2. [person] who is not trained in a particular subject □ *My job is to make medical articles accessible to a lay audience.*

◆ **lay aside** *vt sep* -1. **to lay sthg aside** [food, money] to save sthg so that one can use it later □ *One fifth of the budget is laid aside for grants.* -2. **to lay sthg aside** [book, knitting] to put down sthg that one is working on. -3. **to lay sthg aside** [one's fears, doubts, beliefs] to stop feeling or believing in sthg in order to make it easier to do something □ *We've learnt to lay aside our differences in the interest of peace.*

◆ **lay before** *vt sep* **to lay sthg before sb** [idea, situation, case] to present sthg to sb so they can approve or give advice on it □ *She laid her proposal before the client.*

◆ **lay down** *vt sep* -1. **to lay sthg down** [rules, terms, guidelines] to state sthg firmly or officially □ *As laid down in the contract, the buyer keeps exclusive rights.* -2. **to lay sthg down** [weapon, tool] to put down sthg, usually because one has finished using it □ *Mr Boaz laid down his knife and fork.*

◆ **lay into** *vt fus* **to lay into sb** (informal use) to start hitting sb violently; to start criticizing sb, usually by shouting.

◆ **lay off** ◇ *vt sep* **to lay sb off** [worker, employee] to take sb's job away because one can no longer pay them □ *We've had to lay off a third of our staff/workforce.* ◇ *vt fus* (informal use) -1. **to lay off sb** to stop treating sb in an unkind or aggressive way □ *Lay off him, he's done nothing wrong.* -2. **to lay off doing sthg** to stop doing sthg annoying or unpleasant □ *Lay off kicking that chair!* -3. **to lay off sthg** [alcohol, cigarettes] to stop taking, using, or doing sthg that harms one's health □ *You should lay off smoking for a while.*

◆ **lay on** *vt sep* **to lay sthg on** [transport, food] to provide sthg for a lot of people □ *The drinks were laid on free by the sponsors.*

◆ **lay out** *vt sep* -1. **to lay sthg out** [clothes, ingredients, tools] to arrange sthg in an organized way on a flat surface □ *Mary laid the dress out carefully on the bed.* -2. **to lay sthg out** [garden, town, office] to design sthg in a particular way □ *The house was laid out according to the owner's specifications.*

◆ **lay over** *vi* US to stop somewhere for a short period of time during a trip, usually one by plane.

layaway ['leɪəweɪ] *n* US **to put sthg on layaway** to pay for sthg in installments and collect it from the store only when one has paid for it in full.

lay-by (*pl* **lay-bys**) *n* -1. GB a space next to a

main road where people can park for a short time. -2. AUS = **layaway**.

layer ['leɪəʳ] *n* -1. [of cheese, mud, clothing] a piece of amount of something that covers a surface or is between two other things □ *Several thin layers of clothing keep you much warmer than one thick sweater.* □ *She spread a layer of cream on the cake.* -2. [of meaning, bureaucracy] one of many levels in a statement, organization etc that are all different in meaning or purpose.

layette [leɪ'et] *n* a complete set of things, e.g. clothes, that are needed for a new-born baby.

layman ['leɪmən] (*pl* **laymen** [-mən]) *n* -1. a person who is not trained in a particular subject □ *the layman's guide to psychology.* -2. RELIGION a person who does not have an official position within their religion.

layoff ['leɪɒf] *n* the act of laying off a worker □ *The takeover will mean layoffs for the company.*

layout ['leɪaʊt] *n* [of a building, garden, page] the way in which something is designed and arranged □ *I can recall the exact layout of the house.*

layover ['leɪəʊvəʳ] *n* US a short stop during a trip.

Lazarus ['læzərəs] in the Bible, a man who died and was brought back to life by Jesus Christ.

laze [leɪz] *vi* to spend time doing nothing and relaxing □ *She's been lazing around all day.*

lazily ['leɪzɪlɪ] *adv* [sit, yawn, glance] slowly and without effort □ *They strolled lazily around the park in the hot sun.*

laziness ['leɪzɪnəs] *n*: *see* **lazy**.

lazy ['leɪzɪ] (*compar* **lazier**, *superl* **laziest**) *adj* -1. [person] who dislikes work or physical activity and avoids it (disapproving use). -2. [day, afternoon] that is spent relaxing and doing very little □ *We had a wonderfully lazy time at home.*

lazybones ['leɪzɪbəʊnz] (*pl* **lazybones**) *n* a lazy person (informal use) □ *Come on, lazybones!*

lb *abbr of* **pound** (used with weights).

LB *abbr of* **Labrador**.

L/C *abbr of* **letter of credit**.

LCD (*abbr of* **liquid crystal display**) *n* [for a digital watch, radio alarm, calculator] numbers, letters etc on a small screen that become visible when an electric current passes through a special liquid.

Ld *abbr of* **Lord**.

L-driver *n abbr of* **learner driver**.

LDS *n* -1. (*abbr of* **Licentiate in Dental Surgery**) a qualification in dentistry, lower than a BDS. -2. *abbr of* **Latter-day Saint**.

LEA (*abbr of* **local education authority**) *n* the organization responsible for education in a particular region of Britain.

lead¹ [liːd] (*pt* & *pp* **led**) ◇ *n* -1. **the lead** [in a race, match, election] the position that is ahead of everybody else □ *Coming into the final lap, Brown moved into the lead.* ■ **to be in** OR **have the lead** to be in the position that is

ahead of everybody else □ *The latest opinion poll results show the Democrats to be in the lead by a narrow margin.* -2. [over one's rivals, opponents] the amount of time, distance, or points by which one person is ahead of the next □ *The Spanish cyclist has a lead of thirty meters/seconds.* □ *The Wellcome Trust has a good lead over its rivals in the search for a cure for the disease.* -3. [example] a good example that can help to guide other people's actions □ *It's up to city hall to give a lead on housing policy.* ■ **to take the lead** to do something first, often setting a good example for other people □ *He took the lead in asking questions.* □ *It's up to us to take the lead in providing child-care facilities for working parents.* -4. **the lead** [in a play, movie] the most important role □ *They gave the lead to a French actor.* -5. [in a case, investigation] information that may be useful in solving a crime or making a discovery □ *Police sources announced that several leads were being followed up.* -6. GB [for a dog] a leash for a dog □ *a dog lead* □ *'Please keep your dog on a lead.'* -7. ELECTRICITY a wire that supplies electricity to a piece of equipment.

◇ *adj* [singer, actor, news story] that is the most important □ *The lead story in the Times tells of the proposed IRA ceasefire.*

◇ *vt* -1. [procession, group, crowd] to be at the front of <sthg> □ *The youngest members led the parade.* -2. [person, animal] to take or guide <sb> to a place, especially by walking in front □ *Sean led me by the hand.* □ *I led the dog by its collar.* -3. [team, investigation] to organize or be in charge of <sthg> □ *How will he successfully lead such a split party?* ■ **to lead the way** to lead people in the direction they should go; to be more advanced or more successful than other people □ *You lead the way and I'll follow you.* □ *They seem to be leading the way toward a more united Europe.* □ *The Japanese are still leading the way in technology.* -4. **to lead a busy/happy life** to have a busy/happy life □ *He led a life of debauchery.* -5. **to lead sb to do sthg** to cause sb to do sthg □ *It was his efficiency that led her to promote him.* □ *She led me to believe she was married.*

◇ *vi* -1. [path, stairs, pipe] to take one to a particular place □ *This road leads through the quiet part of town.* □ *That door leads to the kitchen.* □ *This scene will lead nicely into Act Two.* -2. [team, party, candidate] to be in the lead □ *He is leading by 240 votes to 189 at this halfway stage.*

◆ **lead off** ◇ *vt fus* **to lead off a room** to be joined to a room by a door □ *The bathroom leads off the bedroom.* ◇ *vi* -1. [road, corridor] to go away from a place □ *The path leads off from the main road.* -2. [in a discussion, meeting] to start.

◆ **lead to** *vt fus* **to lead to sthg** to result in sthg □ *These measures are likely to lead to future tax cuts.*

◆ **lead up to** *vt fus* -1. **to lead up to sthg** [death, disaster] to come before and often cause sthg □ *The events that led up to the murder have been pieced together by police.* -2. **to lead up to sthg** [to a question, subject, request] to guide a conversation or discussion to-wards sthg □ *You've been leading up to that for the past hour!*

lead² [led] *n* **-1.** a soft, gray, heavy metal. SYMBOL: Pb □ *a lead pipe/weight.* **-2.** the long, thin, black center of a pencil □ *a pencil lead.*

leaded ['ledəd] *adj* **-1.** [gasoline] that contains lead. **-2.** [window] that is composed of pieces of plain or colored glass held in place by pieces of lead. NOTE: Compare **unleaded.**

leaden ['ledn] *adj* **-1.** [sky, sea] that is dark-gray in color. **-2.** [step] that is slow and heavy because of tiredness; [voice, tone, heart] that lacks cheerfulness. **-3.** [conversation, per-formance] that is very dull or boring.

leader ['li:dər] *n* **-1.** [of a team, organization, country] a person who organizes or is in charge of something □ *He should be the next leader of the Liberal Party.* □ *She's a natural leader.* **-2.** [in a race, competition] the person, animal, or ve-hicle that is ahead of the others at a particu-lar moment □ *She was up with the leaders go-ing into the last lap.* **-3.** [in business, research] the most successful person in a particular activity that other people try to follow □ *The institute is a world leader in cancer research.* □ *ARM is the market leader in cellular phones.* **-4.** [in a newspaper] = **leading article.**

leadership ['li:dərʃɪp] *n* **-1. the leadership** the people in charge of an organization, group of people, or country □ *This won't be popular with the Republican leadership.* **-2.** the position of being a leader □ *He resigned from the lead-ership of the party.* **-3.** the qualities involved in being a leader □ *They worked well under his leadership.* □ *This calls for efficient leadership.*

lead-free [,led-] *adj* [gasoline, paint] that con-tains no lead.

leading ['li:dɪŋ] *adj* **-1. a leading writer/athlete** a writer/athlete who is very important or the most important □ *He's one of the leading businessmen of his day.* **-2. a leading part OR role** [in a movie, play] the main part or role; [in development, promotion] an important part or role □ *Our company has played a leading role in popularizing job-sharing.* **-3.** [runner, horse, car] that is ahead of other competitors at a par-ticular time.

leading article *n* GB an article in a newspaper that states the newspaper's views on a par-ticular news item.

leading lady *n* the actress who plays the main female role in a play or movie.

leading light *n* a person who leads or has a lot of influence in a particular group or movement □ *She was a leading light in their campaign.*

leading man *n* the actor who plays the main male role in a play or movie.

leading question *n* a question that forces the person being asked to answer in a particular way (disapproving use).

lead pencil [,led-] *n* a pencil that contains a lead and is used for writing or drawing in black, rather than in color.

lead poisoning ['led-] *n* poisoning caused by lead.

lead time ['li:d-] *n* the period of time between designing a product and producing it; the period of time between placing an order and receiving the goods.

leaf [li:f] (*pl* **leaves**) *n* **-1.** [of a plant, tree] one of the many flat green parts of a plant that grow on its stems or branches □ *an oak leaf.* **-2.** [of a table] a part of a table that can be unfolded or added to make the table longer. **-3.** [of a book] a page in a book.

◆ **leaf through** *vt fus* **to leaf through sthg** [book, magazine, report] to turn the pages of sthg quickly without really reading it.

leaflet ['li:flət] ◇ *n* a piece of paper or a book-let that contains information or an adver-tisement and is given free to people. ◇ *vt* to distribute leaflets in <a place or area>.

leafy ['li:fɪ] (*compar* **leafier**, *superl* **leafiest**) *adj* **-1.** [plant, tree, branch] that has a lot of leaves. **-2.** [lane, suburb] that has a lot of trees.

league [li:g] *n* **-1.** [of people, countries] a group that has joined together because of a shared aim or interest □ *the League of Nations.* ■ **to be in league with sb** [with the enemy, a criminal] to work with sb, usually in secret, for a dis-honest purpose □ *Martin, 53, is accused of be-ing in league with the bombers.* **-2.** SPORT a group of players or teams that play games against each other □ *the football league.*

League of Women Voters *n* **the League of Women Voters** a US organization that en-courages women to vote and to be interest-ed in politics.

league table *n* GB a list of sports clubs, schools, hospitals etc that shows them in order, with the most successful at the top and the least successful at the bottom.

leak [li:k] ◇ *n* **-1.** [in a pipe, tank, roof] a small hole or crack through which a liquid or gas can escape or enter; the substance that es-capes through this hole □ *The boat had a leak in the bottom.* □ *a gas leak.* **-2.** [to the press, op-position] the act of giving secret information to somebody, especially to the press □ *The ministry is investigating the leak.* ◇ *vt* [news, se-cret, report] to tell the public, press etc <sthg that was secret> □ *Details were leaked to the media last night.* ◇ *vi* [pipe, bucket, boat] to have a leak; [gas, liquid] to escape through a small hole or crack □ *My shoes are leaking.* □ *Where's the water leaking from?*

◆ **leak out** *vi* **-1.** [liquid, gas] to leak from a container. **-2.** [information, news, secret] to be-come known to the public, press etc.

leakage ['li:kɪdʒ] *n* an amount of a liquid or gas that has leaked from a small hole or crack.

leaky ['li:kɪ] (*compar* **leakier**, *superl* **leakiest**) *adj* [roof, boat, cup] that has one or more leaks.

lean [li:n] (*pt* & *pp* **leaned** OR **leant**) ◇ *adj* **-1.** [person, animal] that is thin but physically strong and fit. **-2.** COOKING [meat, bacon] that does not contain much fat. **-3.** [month, winter] during which there is not much food or money; [harvest] that produces very few crops □ *These are lean times for the industry.*

◇ *vt* **to lean sthg against sthg** [against a wall, chair, fence] to place sthg so that part of its weight is supported by sthg else □ *He leaned the ladder against the tree.*

◇ *vi* **-1.** to bend the top part of one's body in a particular direction □ *He leaned toward her/leaned forward to whisper in her ear.* □ *She leaned out of the window.* **-2. to lean against sb/sthg** to stand or sit so that the top part of one's body is resting against sb/sthg. ■ **to lean on sb** to depend on sb for help; to use threats to make sb do something □ *He leans on Jerry a lot for support.* □ *They were leaning on me for the money.*

◆ **lean back** *vi* [in a chair, against a wall] to move the top part of one's body back, usually to make oneself more comfortable.

leaning ['liːnɪŋ] *n* a preference for a particular belief or behavior □ *She has communist leanings.* □ *He's always had a leaning toward science.*

leant [lent] *past tense & past participle of* **lean.**

lean-to (*pl* **lean-tos**) *n* a small simple structure like a shed that is built against the wall of a larger building, especially a house.

leap [liːp] (*pt & pp* **leapt** OR **leaped**) ◇ *n* **-1.** [of a person, animal] a powerful jump high in the air or over a long distance □ *With one leap the dog was over the fence.* **-2.** [in price, number, demand] a sudden large increase in amount □ *There has been a tremendous leap in the number of applications.* ◇ *vi* **-1.** [person, animal] to make a leap; to move quickly and suddenly □ *She leapt up as he came in.* **-2.** [inflation, unemployment] to increase suddenly by a large amount □ *The price of property has leapt by 10%.*

◆ **leap at** *vt fus* **to leap at sthg** [at a chance, invitation] to accept <sthg> with enthusiasm □ *If I were you I'd leap at the opportunity to go abroad.*

leapfrog ['liːpfrɒg] (*pt & pp* **leapfrogged,** *cont* **leapfrogging**) ◇ *n* a game played by children in which some bend over and others jump over them. ◇ *vt* to advance directly from a position below <sb/sthg> to one that is higher. ◇ *vi* **-1. to leapfrog over sb/sthg** to jump over sb/sthg as in a game of leapfrog. **-2.** [prices, sales] to increase by a very large amount.

leapt [lept] *past tense & past participle of* **leap.**

leap year *n* a year that occurs once every four years in which February has 29 days.

learn [lɜːʳn] (*pt & pp* **learned** OR **learnt**) ◇ *vt* **-1.** [language, sport, trade] to gain the knowledge and ability to use or do <sthg> by studying or practicing it □ *She's learning (how) to dance/drive/use a computer.* □ *I'm learning book-keeping.* **-2.** [alphabet, song, poem] to read or hear <sthg> and make oneself remember it exactly □ *Have you learned your speech yet?* **-3.** [news, truth, facts] to find out <sthg>, especially by accident □ *I subsequently learned (that) he wouldn't be coming.*

◇ *vi* **-1.** to gain knowledge and ability □ *I had to learn fast in that job!* **-2. to learn of** OR

about sthg [of a death, accident, promotion] to find out about sthg, especially by accident, from newspapers, private documents, conversations etc □ *I was sorry to learn about his death.*

learned ['lɜːʳnəd] *adj* **-1.** [person] who has studied for many years and knows a lot about one or more subjects. **-2. a learned journal** a journal that has been written for academics, professionals, and advanced students □ *a learned society.*

learner ['lɜːʳnəʳ] *n* a person who is learning a particular subject □ *This dictionary is for foreign learners of English.* □ *a quick/slow learner.*

learner (driver) *n* GB a person who is learning to drive and who has not yet passed their driving test.

learning ['lɜːʳnɪŋ] *n* knowledge gained by studying □ *the learning process* □ *a man of great learning.*

learning curve *n* the relationship between what is learned and how much time it takes to learn □ *Initially the learning curve for users of the system is steep.*

learnt [lɜːʳnt] *past tense & past participle of* **learn.**

lease [liːs] ◇ *n* **-1.** a contract that allows somebody to use a car, property etc for a particular period of time and for a particular amount of money □ *We have a five-year lease on the house.* □ *The lease runs out next year.* **-2. a new lease on life** US, **a new lease of life** GB a new sense of freedom and of the possibility of happiness and success. ◇ *vt* [car, property] to have a lease for <sthg> □ *We are leasing the offices from/to them for five years.*

leaseback ['liːsbæk] *n* an agreement in which one person sells or gives property to another person, but keeps the right to use it in return for paying rent.

leasehold ['liːshəʊld] ◇ *adj* [house, apartment] that can be used or owned for the length of the lease □ *a leasehold property.* ◇ *adv* [buy] with a lease □ *We own the property leasehold.* NOTE: Compare **freehold.**

leaseholder ['liːshəʊldəʳ] *n* a person who uses or lives in a building that is leasehold. NOTE: Compare **freeholder.**

leash [liːʃ] *n* a long piece of leather or chain that is attached by the owner to a dog's collar so that it cannot run away □ *'Dogs must be kept on a leash.'*

least [liːst] ◇ *det* **the least money/time** the smallest amount of money/time □ *I chose the dish that had the least meat in it.*

◇ *pron* **-1. the least** the smallest amount □ *The least it's going to cost us is $5,000.* □ *You've given me the least!* **-2.** used to indicate a minimum amount. ■ **that's the least of my worries** I have far more important things to worry about □ *Paying a fine is the least of my worries right now!* ■ **it's the least I can do** a phrase used to reply to somebody who has thanked one □ *"I'm very grateful to you."* — *"Not at all, it was the least I could do."* □ *The very least he could do is to say he's sorry.* ■ **not**

in the least, not the least bit not at all (used to say "no" or "not" in an emphatic way) □ *"Were you disappointed?" — "Not in the least." □ She wasn't the least bit frightened.* ■ **to say the least** a phrase used to suggest that the speaker feels something is much worse than they have said □ *The situation is worrying, to say the least.*

◇ *adv* **-1. it's the least expensive car** it's the car that costs the smallest amount compared to all the others. ■ **he's the least experienced/qualified** he has less experience/fewer qualifications than the others □ *I knew he'd go for the least interesting option.* **-2. when I least expected it** when I expected it less than at any other time □ *Then when I least expected it, someone knocked on the door.* ■ **he helped me the least** he gave me the smallest amount of help.

◆ **at least** *adv* **-1. it will take us at least an hour** it will not take less than an hour, and it will probably take longer □ *It weighed at least a ton.* □ *I've seen it at least twice already.* **-2. you could at least have called me!** I am annoyed because you did not call me, and in fact you should have done even more □ *They might at least have let me know what time they were arriving.* □ *You could at least try to look interested!* **-3. it's cold, but at least it's not raining** it is a pity the weather is cold, but we are fortunate because it is not raining □ *The meal was terrible, but at least it didn't cost us anything.* **-4.** used to correct what one has just said □ *I paid it last week; at least I think I did!* □ *He's arriving next week, or at least that's what he said.*

◆ **least of all** *adv* especially (used after negative sentences) □ *I didn't want to speak to anyone, least of all him.*

◆ **not least** *adv* used in formal writing to introduce an important example of something □ *His novels have been reviewed in many newspapers, not least the New York Times.*

leather ['leðəʳ] *n* animal skin, especially from cattle, pigs, or sheep, that is treated and used for making clothing, furniture etc □ *a leather bag* □ *leather trousers/shoes.*

◆ **leathers** *npl* CLOTHING the leather clothing worn by motorcycle riders.

leatherette [,leðə'ret] *n* a cheap material that looks like leather □ *a leatherette wallet.*

leave [liːv] (*pt* & *pp* **left**) ◇ *vt* **-1. to leave a person/place** to go away from a person/place □ *What time do you normally leave the office?* □ *She left Sydney for good in 1962.* □ *Singh left the team in 1993 to join Inter.* **-2. to leave sb/sthg in a particular state or place** to allow sb/sthg to remain in a particular state or place after one has gone away □ *I left her sitting in the car while I went to make a phone call.* □ *Leave the television on.* □ *The meeting left them feeling unhappy with the way things were going.* □ *You can always leave a message on my answering machine.* ■ **it leaves me cold** it does not interest me or attract me (informal use) □ *People rave about his sculpture, but personally it leaves me cold.* **-3. to leave sthg in a particular place** to go away from a particular place and

forget to take sthg with one □ *I left my umbrella on the bus.* **-4. to leave school/home** to go away from school/home and not return □ *What will you do once you leave college?* □ *I left home when I was fifteen.* **-5. to leave one's husband/wife** to end one's relationship with one's husband/wife and no longer live with them □ *She left him and took the children with her.* **-6.** [one's food] not to use or take up all of <sthg> □ *You can leave some of your dessert if you're not hungry.* ■ **to leave room/a space/a gap** to deliberately make room/a space/a gap □ *Leave enough space between the lines to make corrections.* **-7. to leave sthg to** OR **with sb** to give responsibility to sb for sthg □ *He left it to her to decide.* □ *I'll leave the children with my parents.* **-8.** [subject, topic] to stop discussing <sthg> □ *Let's leave this now and we can come back to it later.* □ *Leave it with me and I'll get in touch with them.* **-9.** [property, money] to give <sthg> to somebody in one's will □ *She left the house to her niece.*

◇ *vi* **-1.** [person] to go away from a place □ *I'm leaving early today.* □ *I saw him just as he was leaving.* **-2.** [plane, boat, passenger] to set out from home on a trip □ *My flight leaves in an hour.* □ *We leave for Australia in two months.* **-3.** [worker, employee] to stop working in a particular place □ *Jane's left to have a baby.* **-4.** [husband, wife] to end a relationship with one's husband, wife etc □ *I'm leaving for good this time!*

◇ *n* a period of time one is allowed to spend away from work, especially in the army, navy, police etc □ *All leave has been canceled.* □ *I've got a week's leave.* ■ **to be on leave** to be away from work or on vacation.

◆ **leave behind** *vt sep* **-1. to leave sb/sthg behind** to go away from sb/sthg □ *When he went to work in Saudi Arabia he had to leave his family behind.* **-2. to leave sthg behind** to forget to take or bring sthg □ *Damn, I've left my keys behind at the office.*

◆ **leave off** ◇ *vt fus* **-1. to leave off doing sthg** to stop doing sthg □ *Why don't you leave off criticizing me for a change?* **-2. to leave sb/sthg off a list** not to include sb/sthg in a list □ *They'd left my name off the list of candidates.* ◇ *vi* to stop doing something □ *We'll just carry on reading from where we left off.*

◆ **leave out** *vt sep* **to leave sb/sthg out** [fact, information, person] to deliberately not include sb/sthg □ *We left out the part about his childhood because we were short of space.* □ *I always feel left out when they start talking about golf.*

leave of absence *n* permission to be away from work for a period of time and for a particular reason □ *He's been given* OR *granted leave of absence.*

leaves [liːvz] *plural of* **leaf**.

Lebanese [,lebə'niːz] (*pl* **Lebanese**) *n* & *adj*: *see* **Lebanon**.

Lebanon ['lebənən] a country in the Middle East, on the Mediterranean, north of Israel. Its economy was badly damaged by civil wars in the 1970s and 1980s. SIZE: 10,400 sq kms. POPULATION: 3,600,000 (Lebanese). CAPI-

TAL: Beirut. LANGUAGE: Arabic. CURRENCY: Lebanese pound.

lecherous ['letʃərəs] *adj* [man] who shows by his behavior toward women that he is only interested in them sexually (disapproving use) □ *lecherous behavior.*

lechery ['letʃərɪ] *n* lecherous behavior (disapproving use).

Le Corbusier [US lə,kɔːrbuːz'jeɪ, GB ləkɔː'buːzɪeɪ] (1887–1965) a French architect and city planner, born in Switzerland. He pioneered the use of concrete, and based his designs on human proportions.

lectern ['lektəʳn] *n* a small, often high, sloping table on which a book or papers can be placed when one is reading or speaking in front of an audience or congregation.

lecture ['lektʃəʳ] ◇ *n* -1. [at a university, conference] a long talk on a particular subject, especially used as a method of teaching in colleges and universities □ *a history lecture* □ *a lecture on business management.* ■ **to give a lecture** to stand in front of a group of people and talk to them about a particular subject. -2. [to a child, pupil] an act of criticizing given to somebody about something they have done, especially when this involves an annoying long speech □ *We were given a long lecture on how to behave.* ◇ *vt* [child, pupil] to give <sb> a lecture □ *I'm not going to lecture you on what happened.* ◇ *vi* [at university, college] to teach; [at a conference] to give a talk □ *He lectures on/in physics.*

lecture hall *n* a large room where lectures are held, e.g. at a university.

lecturer ['lektʃərəʳ] *n* -1. a person who gives lectures at conferences, societies etc □ *a guest lecturer on French wines.* -2. GB EDUCATION a person who teaches at a college, university etc □ *a lecturer in Economic History.*

lecture theater *n* GB = **lecture hall**.

led [led] *past tense & past participle of* **lead**.

LED *n abbr of* **light-emitting diode**.

ledge [ledʒ] *n* -1. a narrow shelf, especially one that is found at the bottom of a window □ *a window ledge.* -2. a flat narrow piece of rock on the side of a mountain or cliff □ *a mountain ledge.*

ledger ['ledʒəʳ] *n* a book in which the amounts of money spent and received by a company or bank are noted down □ *a bank ledger* □ *a sales ledger.*

lee [liː] *n* **in the lee of sthg** [of a rock, wall] sheltered by sthg, especially from strong winds or bad weather.

Lee [liː], **Robert E.** (1807–1870) a US general. He commanded the Confederate States army in the American Civil War.

leech [liːtʃ] *n* -1. a small creature that looks like a worm, lives in wet areas, and attaches itself to animals in order to feed off their blood. -2. a person who uses another person, especially in order to get money (disapproving use).

leek [liːk] *n* a vegetable with a long white stem and long, thick, green leaves that be-

longs to the onion family. It is the national symbol of Wales.

leer [lɪəʳ] ◇ *n* an unpleasant or threatening smile or look, often showing sexual interest in somebody. ◇ *vi* to look at somebody with a leer □ *They leered at her menacingly.*

leeway ['liːweɪ] *n* -1. the freedom one has to make changes to a plan □ *There's no leeway in this schedule at all.* □ *A quarter of an hour should be enough leeway.* -2. **to make up leeway** to work hard to reach the level or stage of work that one should have reached already.

left [left] ◇ *past tense & past participle of* **leave**. ◇ *adj* -1. that remains after everything else has gone or been used □ *Do you have any money left?* □ *We only have two matches left.* □ *There's no milk left.* □ *Unfortunately this is all that is left of his fortune.* -2. [foot, side] that relates to the side of the body in which the heart is found □ *the Left Bank of the Rhine* □ *My left eye is stronger than my right.* ◇ *adv* [turn] toward the left side □ *Look left and right before crossing the road.* □ *'Keep left'.* ◇ *n* on/to the left on/toward the left side of something □ *In Britain they drive on the left.* □ *The house is on the left after the video store.* □ *On your left you can see another of Wren's churches.* ■ **on** OR **to the left of sthg** that is on the left side of sthg □ *It's on the left of the post office.*

◆ **Left** *n* **the Left** POLITICS people, especially political parties, who believe that money and power should be shared more fairly in society.

left-hand *adj* [lane, page] that is on the left side of something. ■ **the left-hand side** the side that is on the left of something or somebody □ *If you're facing the church, the school is on the left-hand side.* □ *He wrote the correction on the left-hand side of the page.*

left-hand drive GB ◇ *adj* [car, truck] that has the steering wheel on the left-hand side. ◇ *n* a left-hand drive vehicle.

left-handed [-'hændəd] ◇ *adj* -1. [person] who naturally uses their left hand rather than their right one to do most things. -2. [scissors, pen] that has been made for a left-handed user. -3. **a left-handed compliment** US a compliment that could easily be understood as an insult. ◇ *adv* [play, write, bowl] using one's left hand.

left-hander [-'hændəʳ] *n* a person who naturally uses their left hand to do most things.

Leftist ['leftəst] ◇ *adj* POLITICS [idea, tendency] supporting all or some Socialist beliefs. ◇ *n* a Socialist.

left luggage (office) *n* GB a place in a train or bus station where people can pay to leave their luggage safely for a limited period of time.

leftover ['leftoʊvəʳ] *adj* [fabric, food, money] that remains after what is needed has been used or taken.

◆ **leftovers** *npl* food that remains after a meal.

left wing *n* **the left wing** the members of a

political group whose ideas are closer to Socialism than those of the other members.

◆ **left-wing** adj [person, party] that supports all or some Socialist beliefs □ He's very left-wing. □ a left-wing activist/newspaper.

NOTE: Compare **right wing**.

left-winger n a person who is left-wing.

lefty ['leftɪ] (pl **lefties**) n US a person who is left-handed, especially a sportsperson.

leg [leg] n -1. [of a person, animal, insect] one of the long parts of the body, used for walking, standing etc, that join the foot to the body □ The bird had broken its leg. ■ **to be on one's last legs** [machine, organization] to be near the point of collapse or failure; [person] to be close to dying, or very tired. ■ **you don't have a leg to stand on** you don't have a strong argument to justify what you have done or want to do. ■ **to pull sb's leg** to tease sb in a friendly way by trying to make them believe something that is not true □ Don't listen to him, he's only pulling your leg! -2. CLOTHING one of the two parts of a pair of trousers that cover one's legs □ a trouser leg. -3. COOKING [of chicken, pork] the part of an animal's leg used as food □ a chicken leg OR a leg of chicken. -4. [of a table, chair] one of the thin vertical parts of a piece of furniture that touch the floor and on which it stands □ a chair/table leg. -5. [of a trip, tournament, tour] one particular part of something □ The final leg of the visit was to Scotland.

legacy ['legəsɪ] (pl **legacies**) n -1. a gift of money or property that one receives after somebody's death. -2. something that is caused and left behind by somebody or something that no longer exists □ Such attitudes are a legacy of our colonial past.

legal ['liːgl] adj -1. [system, profession, proceedings] that is connected with the law □ We've decided to seek legal advice. -2. [requirement, obligation] that is allowed or made necessary by law □ It is perfectly legal for EU citizens to work in this country. □ I am the legal owner of this car.

legal action n the use of the law, with the services of a lawyer, to defend one's rights □ They're threatening legal action. ■ **to take legal action against sb** to prosecute sb.

legal aid n money given by the government to people who cannot afford to pay for the services of a lawyer.

legal holiday n US a day of the year in a particular country when most people do not work.

legality [liː'gælətɪ] n [of situation, decision] the state of being allowed by law □ I sometimes worry about the legality of the whole operation.

legalize, -ise ['liːgəlaɪz] vt [drugs, abortion] to make legal <sth that was previously illegal>.

legally ['liːgəlɪ] adv [separated, adopted] in a way that has been made official by law □ He was held legally responsible for the accident. ■ **legally binding** [contract, agreement] that is official and must be obeyed when it has been signed □ Are you sure this is legally binding?

legal tender n any money that is part of the official currency in a particular country.

legation [lɪ'geɪʃn] n a group of people who work for and represent their government in another country; the building where these people work.

legend ['ledʒənd] n -1. an old story about magical or mysterious events, often involving a particularly brave person; these stories considered as a whole □ the legend of the Holy Grail □ According to legend, a giant once lived here. -2. a person who has become very well-known, usually over a period of time and because of a particular talent □ a legend in the world of rock music □ She's a living legend.

legendary [US 'ledʒənderɪ, GB -əndərɪ] adj -1. [king, monster] that appears in a legend. -2. [musician, place] that is very famous and often talked about, especially because of a particular quality □ the legendary blues guitarist, B. B. King.

leggings ['legɪŋz] npl a pair of trousers made of stretchy material that fit very closely to the body and are usually worn by women.

leggy ['legɪ] (compar **leggier**, superl **leggiest**) adj -1. [person] who is tall and has very long legs □ a leggy blonde. -2. [plant, bush] that has long weak stems.

legible ['ledʒəbl] adj [handwriting, print] that is clear and easy to read.

legibly ['ledʒəblɪ] adv [write] see **legible**.

legion ['liːdʒən] ◇ n -1. MILITARY a large group of soldiers who train and fight together □ the Foreign Legion. -2. [of supporters, visitors] a very large group of people. ◇ adj **to be legion** to be very numerous (formal use).

legionnaire's disease [ˌliːdʒəˈneərz-] n a serious infectious disease of the lungs that can cause death.

legislate ['ledʒəsleɪt] vi [government, parliament, senate] to make new laws to control a particular activity □ They are about to legislate against strike action.

legislation [ˌledʒəs'leɪʃn] n a law or group of laws made by the government; the act of making these laws □ They've introduced new legislation banning smoking on buses. □ a piece of legislation □ The problem of rising crime cannot be solved simply by legislation.

legislative ['ledʒəslətɪv] adj [body, process, power] that is concerned with making laws.

Legislative Assembly n in Australia, the upper house of most state parliaments.

Legislative Council n in Australia, the lower house of most state parliaments.

legislator ['ledʒəsleɪtər] n a person who is involved in making laws.

legislature ['ledʒəsleɪtʃər] n a group of people in a country who have the power to make laws.

legitimacy [lɪ'dʒɪtəməsɪ] n [of a government, complaint, child] see **legitimate**.

legitimate [lɪ'dʒɪtəmət] adj -1. [action, government, business] that is allowed by the law □ You must have a legitimate reason for being in the building after 6 pm. **-2.** [complaint, argument, question] that is reasonable and follows accepted rules, facts etc □ *I think that's a perfectly legitimate point to make.* **-3.** [child] who is born to parents who are legally married to each other.

legitimately [lɪˈdʒɪtəmətlɪ] *adv* [act, complain] *see* **legitimate** □ *It could legitimately be argued that the tests are unnecessary.*

legitimize, -ise [lɪˈdʒɪtəmaɪz] *vt* **-1.** [action, behavior, process] to make <sthg> legitimate. **-2.** [child] to make <sb> legitimate, especially by the marriage of the parents.

legroom [ˈlegruːm] *n* the space available for one's legs when one is sitting in a vehicle, theater etc.

leg-warmers [-wɔːʳməʳz] *npl* pieces of woolen clothing that are worn on the lower part of one's legs and are thick and warm.

legwork [ˈlegwɜːʳk] *n* **to do the legwork** to do all the hard, boring, or time-consuming work involved in preparing something.

Leibnitz [ˈlaɪbnɪts], **Gottfried Wilhelm** (1646–1716) a German philosopher and mathematician.

Leicestershire [ˈlestəʳʃəʳ] a county in central England. SIZE: 2,553 sq kms. POPULATION: 879,400. ADMINISTRATIVE CENTER: Leicester.

Leicester Square [ˌlestəʳ-] a square in central London with many large movie theaters.

Leics *abbr of* **Leicestershire**.

leisure [US ˈliːʒr, GB ˈleʒə] *n* time that is spent relaxing and doing what one enjoys when one is not working □ *a leisure activity/facility.* ■ **at (one's) leisure** without hurrying and at a convenient time □ *I don't need it back yet, read it at your leisure.*

leisure centre *n* GB a building with many sports and social facilities for the public.

leisurely [US ˈliːʒrlɪ, GB ˈleʒəlɪ] ◇ *adj* [pace, stroll, movement] that is relaxed and not hurried □ *We had a leisurely chat/drink.* ◇ *adv* [stroll, walk] *They drove leisurely along the coast.*

leisure time *n* time when one is not working or studying and is free to enjoy oneself □ *What do you do in your leisure time?*

lemming [ˈlemɪŋ] *n* **-1.** a northern and Arctic animal that looks like a mouse with a short tail. Lemmings are believed to rush into the sea in large numbers and drown during migration. **-2.** a person who does whatever another person says or does, especially when this results in something bad or harmful.

lemon [ˈlemən] *n* **-1.** an oval fruit grown in warm countries, with a thick bright-yellow skin and sour juicy flesh □ *a slice of lemon* □ *lemon cheesecake/sorbet.* **-2.** a sweet drink that tastes of lemon.

lemonade [ˌleməˈneɪd] *n* **-1.** a drink made from fresh lemon juice, sugar, and water. **-2.** GB a sweet fizzy drink that tastes of lemon.

lemon curd [-ˈkɜːʳd] *n* GB a thick sweet mixture of lemon juice, eggs, and butter that is cooked and, when cold, spread on bread.

lemon juice *n* the juice from a lemon.

lemon sole *n* a flat fish that lives in the sea and can be eaten.

lemon squeezer [-skwiːzəʳ] *n* a device used for squeezing lemons in order to get juice from them.

lemon tea *n* a drink of tea to which lemon juice and not milk has been added.

lend [lend] (*pt & pp* **lent**) *vt* **-1.** [money, book, car] to let somebody use or have <sthg that belongs to one> for a period of time □ *Can you lend me $5?* □ *The library also lends cassettes to its members.* **-2.** [support, advice, assistance] to give <sthg> to somebody because they need it. ■ **to lend sb a hand** to help sb do something, usually when it involves physical effort □ *Could you lend me a hand with this suitcase, please?* **-3.** **to lend sthg to sthg** [quality, force, color] to add sthg to sthg □ *The music lent a strange melancholy to the scene.* **-4.** *phrase* **it doesn't lend itself to that** it is not suitable for that purpose □ *The book doesn't lend itself easily to adaptation for TV.*

lender [ˈlendəʳ] *n* a person or organization that lends money.

lending library [ˈlendɪŋ-] *n* a public library that lends books, records, cassettes etc.

lending rate *n* the interest that one has to pay if one borrows money from a bank, savings and loan association etc □ *The current lending rate is 10%.*

length [leŋθ] *n* **-1.** [of a room, somebody's hair, a rope] the measurement of something from one end to the other, or along its longest side □ *"What length is it?" — "6 foot."* □ *The trousers come in three different lengths.* ■ **in length** a phrase used after measurements to show how long something is □ *The car is 3 meters in length.* **-2.** **the length of sthg** the whole distance from one end or side of sthg to the other □ *He walked the length of the town/street/room.* ■ **the length and breadth of a place** across the whole area of a place □ *My parents traveled the length and breadth of Italy.* **-3.** SPORT the distance from one end of a swimming pool to the other □ *She swims 30 lengths a day.* **-4.** **a length of sthg** [of string, wood, cloth] a long thin piece of sthg □ *Can you cut me four lengths of tape?* **-5.** [of a period, stay] the amount of time that an event, activity, or situation continues for □ *It took them an extraordinary length of time to answer the question.* □ *The length of her visits increased as the weeks went by.* **-6.** [of a letter, program, movie] the number of words in something or the amount of information, images etc it contains □ *It's the sheer length of his books that I find so off-putting.* **-7.** **to go to great lengths to do sthg** to try very hard to do sthg, often using a number of methods □ *I'd go to any lengths to prove his innocence.*

◆ **at length** *adv* **-1.** [speak, discuss] in detail; for a long time □ *They spoke at great length about the economic crisis.* **-2.** eventually □ *We fell silent. At length, she spoke.*

lengthen [ˈleŋθən] ◇ *vt* [life, skirt, platform] to make <sthg> longer □ *I'll have to get these trousers lengthened.* ◇ *vi* [day, shadow, night] to become longer □ *The intervals between visits seemed to lengthen.*

lengthways ['leŋθweɪz], **lengthwise** ['leŋθwaɪz] *adv* [cut, slice, fold] in a direction along the length of something □ *Lie the slats lengthways across the frame.*

lengthy ['leŋθɪ] (*compar* **lengthier,** *superl* **lengthiest**) *adj* **-1.** [visit, delay, process] that lasts a long time. **-2.** [discussion, document] that is very long, detailed, and often boring □ *He went into lengthy justifications for his behavior.*

leniency ['liːnjənsɪ] *n: see* **lenient** □ *You will not be treated with such leniency if you offend again.*

lenient ['liːnjənt] *adj* [person] who is not as severe as one expected, especially when giving a punishment; [punishment, law, sentence] that is not as severe as one expected □ *She believes judges are too lenient with sex offenders.*

Lenin ['lenɪn], **Vladimir Ilyich** (1870–1924) a Russian revolutionary leader, who was the first head of state of the Soviet Union, from 1918 to 1924.

lens [lenz] *n* **-1.** [in glasses, a camera, microscope] a small piece of curved glass or plastic that makes an object look bigger, clearer etc when one looks through it □ *a camera lens* □ *thick/coated/tinted lenses.* **-2.** = **contact lens. -3.** the curved clear part of the eye, behind the pupil, that directs light onto the retina.

lent [lent] *past tense & past participle of* **lend.**

Lent *n* the period of 40 days before Easter during which some Christians give up something they enjoy, e.g. eating particular types of food.

lentil ['lentl] *n* a small, round, brown or green seed that is dried, splits easily into two halves, and is eaten after it has been cooked □ *lentil soup.*

Leo ['liːou] *n* a sign of the zodiac, represented by a lion; a person born under this sign between July 23 and August 22.

Leonardo da Vinci [liːə,nɑːˈdoudəˈvɪntʃɪ] (1452–1519) an Italian artist, architect, and scientist. He is considered one of the greatest artists of the Renaissance. His best-known painting is the *Mona Lisa.*

leopard ['lepəʳd] *n* a large wild cat that has yellow fur with black spots and lives in Africa and southern Asia.

leopardess ['lepəʳdes] *n* a female leopard.

leotard ['liːətɑːʳd] *n* a piece of clothing, especially for women, that fits tightly over all the main part of the body except for the legs and is used for dancing and exercising.

leper ['lepəʳ] *n* a person who has leprosy □ *a leper colony.*

leprechaun ['leprəkɔːn] *n* a creature in Irish legends that looks like a little old man and is dressed in green.

leprosy ['leprəsɪ] *n* an infectious disease in which the nerves, muscles, and bones are gradually destroyed, and the skin becomes damaged.

lesbian ['lezbɪən] ◇ *n* a woman who is sexually attracted to other women and not to

men. ◇ *adj* [woman, relationship, publication] *gay and lesbian rights.*

lesbianism ['lezbɪənɪzm] *n: see* **lesbian** □ *Lesbianism has become more widely accepted in recent years.*

lesion ['liːʒn] *n* a wound or injury (medical use).

Lesotho [ləˈsuːtuː] a mountainous country in southern Africa that is entirely surrounded by South Africa. SIZE: 30,355 sq kms. POPULATION: 1,800,000 (*Basotho, Lesothans*). CAPITAL: Materu. LANGUAGE: Sesotho, English. CURRENCY: loti.

less [les] (*compar of* **little, a little**) ◇ *det* **-1. less money/time** not as much money/time □ *It contains less sugar than other kinds of fruit juice.* **-2. less people/cars** not as many people/cars (informal use) □ *I need less hours of sleep than before.* ◇ *pron* a smaller amount □ *I'm earning far less now.* □ *You can buy one for $20 or less.* □ *This plan presents much less of a risk.* □ *I see a lot less of him these days.* ◇ *adv* **less expensive/difficult** not as expensive/difficult as before; not as expensive/difficult as something else □ *She's less overworked than she was in her old job.* □ *We need to spend less and save more.* □ *I see them less often these days.* ◇ *prep* minus □ *The pay is $30,000 a year, less tax.*

◆ **less and less** ◇ *det* **less and less money** an amount of money which is always becoming smaller □ *As the war went on, there was less and less food available.* ◇ *pron*: *We seem to have less and less in common.* ◇ *adv*: *Throughout the summer his visits became less and less frequent.*

◆ **less than** ◇ *prep* not as much as a particular number or amount □ *He weighed less than six pounds when he was born.* □ *It's less than a mile from here.* ◇ *adv* **less than ideal/satisfied** not at all ideal/satisfied □ *I'm less than happy with the existing arrangements.*

lessee [le'siː] *n* a person who pays money for the lease of a building or land to the owner of the building or land (formal use).

lessen ['lesn] ◇ *vt* [risk, pain, effect] to make <sthg> smaller in degree or amount □ *His habitual rudeness lessened his chances of success.* ◇ *vi* [emotion, pain, amount] *Over the years her resentment toward him lessened.*

lesser ['lesəʳ] *adj* that is smaller in degree, value, or importance □ *A lesser man would have given up long ago.* □ *the lesser of two evils.*
■ **to a lesser extent** OR **degree** a phrase used to show that one thing is less affected by something than another thing is □ *Computerization of the office has changed my daily routine and, to a lesser extent, my workload.*

lesson ['lesn] *n* **-1.** a period of time during which one is taught a particular subject □ *a French/driving/piano lesson* □ *I have a lesson in art history tomorrow.* ■ **to give lessons** to teach somebody something in regular, especially private, lessons. ■ **to have** OR **take lessons** to be given lessons, especially private ones.

-2. [from an accident, defeat, failure] an experience that teaches somebody why something is wrong, dangerous etc □ *Let that be a lesson to you.* □ *It seems he still hasn't learned his lesson.* ■ **to teach sb a lesson** to punish sb for something in order to prevent them from doing it again □ *I'm going to teach you a lesson you won't forget!*

lessor [le'sɔːʳ] *n* a person to whom money is paid for the lease of a building or land that they own by the person using it (formal use).

lest [lest] *conj* in case (formal use) □ *The people involved were sworn to secrecy lest news of the disaster should get out.*

let [let] (*pt* & *pp* **let**, *cont* **letting**) ◇ *aux vb* **-1. let's** OR **let us do sthg** a phrase used to make suggestions which include the speaker □ *Let's have a party!* □ *"Do you want to go out tonight?" — "Oh yes, let's."* □ *Let's not invite them!* □ *Let us look at the various options open to us.* **-2. let me do sthg** used in polite offers of help, requests etc □ *Let me carry those bags for you.* □ *Let me end by thanking our hosts.* ■ **let me see, let's see, let me think** used when hesitating while trying to remember something or work something out □ *Now, let's see, where was I?*
◇ *vt* **-1. to let sb do sthg** to allow sb to do sthg □ *Don't let him boss you around!* □ *Why not let John have a look at your car?* ■ **to let sb through/past etc** to allow sb to go through/past etc □ *We arrived at the airport late, but they let us on the plane.* **-2. to let sthg happen** to allow sthg to happen and not do anything to stop it □ *Try not to let it upset you too much.* **-3. to let go of sb/sthg** to stop holding sb/sthg □ *Let go of me/my arm!* **-4. to let sb go** to allow sb to leave or escape □ *The police let him go after questioning.* **-5. to let sb go** [employee] to fire sb (polite use) □ *We've had to let her go.* **-6. to let sb know sthg** [news, information] to tell sb sthg □ *Just let us know what time you'll be arriving.* **-7.** [house, room] to rent <a place> to somebody □ *We let our cottage to friends in the summer.* □ **'For let'** US, **'To let'** GB this building is available for renting.

◆ **let alone** *prep* **we're not even engaged, let alone married** we are not married, which is not surprising because we are not even engaged □ *I can't afford a dishwasher, let alone a car!*

◆ **let down** *vt sep* **-1. to let sb down** to disappoint sb by not doing something that one should have done □ *I feel that I've let the company down badly.* **-2. to let a piece of clothing down** [dress, sleeves] to make a piece of clothing longer □ *I'll have to let the hem down on your skirt.*

◆ **let in** *vt sep* **to let sb/sthg in** to allow sb/sthg to come into a place, usually a house □ *Open the door and let me in!*

◆ **let in for** *vt sep* **to let oneself in for sthg** to become involved in sthg unpleasant □ *I didn't know what I was letting myself in for, marrying a man like him.*

◆ **let in on** *vt sep* **to let sb in on sthg** to tell sb about sthg that is a secret from most people □ *They were all laughing, but they wouldn't let me in on the joke.*

◆ **let off** *vt sep* **-1. to let sb off sthg** [off a duty, task] to allow sb not to do sthg that they were supposed to do □ *Mr Rimmer let me off gym because I had a bad ankle.* **-2. to let sb off** [criminal, schoolchild] not to punish sb, or to punish them less than was expected □ *He was found guilty but was let off with a warning.* **-3. to let sthg off** [bomb, firework] to make sthg explode.

◆ **let on** *vi* to tell somebody something that is supposed to be a secret □ *Whatever you do, don't let on about the party.*

◆ **let out** *vt sep* **-1. to let sb/sthg out** [prisoner, pet] to allow sb/sthg to leave a place □ *Have you let the cat out?* **-2. to let water/air etc out** to allow water/air etc to leave something □ *Somebody let the air out of my bicycle tires.* **-3. to let out a groan/cry etc** to groan/cry etc loudly and suddenly □ *The dog let out a yelp.* **-4. to let a dress/skirt etc out** to make a dress/skirt etc wider.

◆ **let up** *vi* [heat, rain] to become less strong or stop □ *There's no sign of the bad weather letting up.*

letdown ['letdaʊn] *n* something that is not as good as one had expected (informal use) □ *The concert was a real letdown.*

lethal ['liːθl] *adj* [weapon, substance] that is very dangerous because it can kill somebody or something □ *a lethal dose of heroin* □ *The recent legislation has dealt a lethal blow to small investors.*

lethargic [lə'θɑːʳdʒɪk] *adj* [person] who has no energy and does not want to do anything □ *The next day I got out of bed but I still felt weak and lethargic.*

lethargy ['leθədʒɪ] *n* a lethargic feeling □ *I couldn't believe the atmosphere of lethargy there was in that office.*

Letraset™ ['letrəset] *n* sheets of special paper with printed letters and symbols that can be transferred onto paper by rubbing them.

let's [lets] = **let us.**

letter ['letəʳ] *n* **-1.** a message from one person or company to another that is written or printed, and is usually sent by mail in an envelope □ *He wrote them a letter of complaint.* □ *We'll confirm the order by letter.* **-2.** any one of the written symbols that are used to write words and that represent different sounds □ *"Christmas" starts with the letter "c".*

◆ **letters** *npl* literature (formal use) □ *a man of letters.*

◆ **to the letter** *adv* exactly □ *I followed all his instructions to the letter.*

letter bomb *n* a small bomb inside an envelope or package that is sent to somebody by mail and is designed to explode when it is opened.

letterbox ['letəʳbɒks] *n* GB **-1.** a rectangular hole in a front door or in the wall of a building which mail is delivered through; a box with a rectangular hole where a person's mail is placed so that they can collect it. **-2.** a large container in a street, post office etc that has a rectangular hole near the top and which mail is placed into so that it will be delivered by the postal system.

letterhead ['letərhed] *n* the name and address of a person or company when it is printed at the top of their writing paper, invoices etc.

lettering ['letərɪŋ] *n* letters in a word, phrase etc that are printed or written in a particular style □ *The company name was in gold lettering.*

letter of credit *n* an official letter from a bank that gives a particular person permission to withdraw money from another bank.

letter opener *n* an object similar to a knife that is used for opening envelopes.

letter-perfect *adj* **to be letter-perfect** US to be able to remember and repeat something without making any mistakes.

letter quality *n* the best quality type that a printer can produce when printing a document from a computer.

letters patent *npl* a patent that gives somebody the right to make and sell an invention without anybody else having the same right.

lettuce ['letəs] *n* a vegetable with large pale green leaves that are eaten raw in salads or sandwiches.

letup ['letʌp] *n* **a letup in sthg** [in violence, bad weather, work] a period of time when there is less of sthg unpleasant or difficult to deal with □ *Despite the ceasefire agreement, there was no letup in the fighting.*

leuk(a)emia [luːˈkiːmjə] *n* a serious form of cancer in which one's blood has too many white cells.

levee ['levɪ] *n* a bank built to stop a river from flooding.

level ['levl] (US *pt* & *pp* **leveled**, *cont* **leveling**, GB *pt* & *pp* **levelled**, *cont* **levelling**) ◇ *adj* **-1. to be level** [two objects, buildings] to have the same height as each other or be at the same height as each other; [two teams, competitors] to have the same number of points as each other □ *Are the tops of the cupboards level?* □ *The picture is not level with the ceiling.* □ *We're level with them on points.* **-2.** [surface, line] that is completely flat and has no part higher than another part □ *Add one level teaspoonful of sugar.* □ *At last we were back on level ground.* ◇ *adv* [remain, get] at the same level as somebody or something else □ *Salaries are keeping level with inflation.* □ *The horses are running level.* ■ **to draw level** to reach the same level as somebody else, either by coming from behind or from the opposite direction □ *My car drew level with hers.* ◇ *n* **-1.** [of noise, production, the temperature] a particular amount of something; a particular point on a scale for measuring this □ *measures to reduce the level(s) of air pollution* □ *a high/low blood-sugar level.* **-2.** [of a liquid, river] the height of something above the ground or a flat surface □ *The level of water in the lake has risen.* ■ **to be on a level with sthg** to be the same height above the ground or a flat

surface as sthg else □ *My bedroom window is on a level with the roof of the house opposite.* **-3.** [of achievement, intelligence, debate] a particular standard or quality □ *a top-level athlete* □ *an intermediate level textbook.* **-4.** CONSTRUCTION an instrument used for checking that a surface is level. **-5.** [of a building] one of the stories of a large building □ *I parked the car on level 2.* **-6.** *phrase* **to be on the level** [person] to be honest and open about something (informal use) □ *I'm not sure they're on the level.*

◇ *vt* **-1.** [field, area] to make <sthg> flat by removing any bumps, holes, or slopes □ *Level the earth before laying the slabs.* [building, forest] to completely destroy <sthg> so that only flat ground is left □ *The bombing has leveled whole streets.* **-3. to level a gun at sb/sthg** to aim a gun at sb/sthg. **-4. to level a criticism/an accusation etc at** OR **against sb** to criticize/accuse etc sb of sthg openly and directly □ *Charges of corruption have been leveled against a number of high-ranking officers.*

◆ **level off, level out** *vi* **-1.** [unemployment, growth, inflation] to stop at a particular level after going up or down □ *The price difference between imported and home-grown apples is gradually leveling off.* **-2.** [plane, path] to stay at the same height after going up or down.

◆ **level with** *vt fus* **to level with sb** to be honest with sb about something after hiding the truth from them (informal use) □ *I asked her to level with me about what happened at the meeting.*

level crossing *n* GB a place where a road crosses a railroad track and which usually has gates and signals to stop traffic when a train is approaching.

level-headed [-ˈhedəd] *adj* [person] who is sensible, calm, and can think clearly, even in difficult situations.

level pegging [-ˈpegɪŋ] *adj* **to be level pegging** GB [two teams, competitors, candidates] to have exactly the same position or number of points, votes etc as each other □ *With just one lap to go the two runners were level pegging.*

lever [US 'levr, GB 'liːvə] *n* **-1.** [on a machine] a bar or handle on a machine that makes the machine do a particular thing when it is moved up, down, left, or right □ *You pull that lever to start the engine.* **-2.** [for moving an object] a bar that is placed underneath a heavy object so that it can be moved when pressure is put on one end of the bar. **-3.** [in a situation] something that is used to influence somebody to do something.

leverage [US 'levərɪdʒ, GB 'liːv-] ◇ *n* **-1.** influence that can be used to get a particular result □ *He used his leverage with the governor to get more money for education.* **-2.** the force or action of a lever. ◇ *vt* FINANCE to borrow money to buy or pay for <sthg>.

leviathan [lɪˈvaɪəθən] *n* a word used to describe something that is very large, powerful, and difficult to control (literary use).

levity ['levɪtɪ] *n* an attitude that does not treat

a serious subject with enough respect (formal use).

levy ['levɪ] (*pt* & *pp* **levied**) ◇ *n* a sum of money paid by a particular group of people for a particular purpose, often as a tax □ *Most labor unions now collect a political levy from their members.* □ *The new gas levy has shocked the country.* ◇ *vt* [tax, contribution, fine] to demand and collect <a sum of money> from somebody □ *The government has decided to levy a new tax on alcohol.*

lewd [luːd] *adj* [behavior, joke, song] that refers to sex in a rude and often unpleasant way □ *She complained that Rogers had made lewd suggestions to her in his office.*

Lewis ['luːəs], **Sinclair** (1885–1951) a US writer. He is well-known for his satires about American life. His work includes *Main Street* and *Babbitt.*

Lewis and Clark [-'klɑːʳk] US explorers who went from St Louis to the Pacific Ocean (1804–1806).

lexical ['leksɪkl] *adj* that is concerned with words (technical use).

LI *abbr of* **Long Island.**

liability [ˌlaɪə'bɪlətɪ] (*pl* **liabilities**) *n* **-1.** a person or thing that can be dangerous or cause problems in particular situations □ *She's a serious liability to everyone when she's been drinking.* **-2.** [for breakages, an accident, debt] legal responsibility that a person or group of people has for something □ *The owners will not accept liability for loss of or damage to personal property.*
◆ **liabilities** *npl* the amount of money that a company or organization owes □ *insurance/pension/tax liabilities* □ *They failed to meet their liabilities and went bankrupt.*

liable ['laɪəbl] *adj* **-1. to be liable to do sthg** to be likely to do sthg □ *She's liable to get angry if you ask too many questions.* **-2. to be liable to sthg** to be likely to experience sthg because it often happens in particular conditions □ *People are more liable to flu at this time of year.* **-3. to be liable** [for breakages, a debt, accident] to be legally responsible for something or to deal with something □ *We are liable to pay damages of $5000.* □ *I am personally liable for any mistakes.* ■ **to be liable to imprisonment/a fine etc** to be in a position in which one can be sent to prison/fined etc as a legal punishment □ *You're liable to prosecution if you don't tell us where you got the money from.*

liaise [lɪ'eɪz] *vi* [colleagues, organizations] to work together so that each side can tell the other side what is happening, what they want to happen etc □ *The agencies liaise regularly on key issues of security.* □ *His job was to liaise between the two departments.* □ *I liaise with my colleagues before making major decisions.*

liaison [lɪ'eɪzɒn] *n* **-1.** [between organizations, departments, people] the activity or job of liaising with another group of people □ *There has been constant liaison with police officials during the enquiry.* **-2.** a sexual relationship that is usually secret (polite use) □ *There were rumors*

that he had maintained a year-long liaison with a local schoolteacher.

liar ['laɪəʳ] *n* a person who tells lies.

Lib. *abbr of* **Liberal.**

libel ['laɪbl] (US *pt* & *pp* **libeled**, *cont* **libeling**, GB *pt* & *pp* **libelled**, *cont* **libelling**) ◇ *n* LAW something that is written or printed about somebody and that is not true, but may damage their reputation □ *She sued the newspaper for libel.* □ *a libel action.* ◇ *vt* to damage the reputation of <sb> by writing or printing something about them that is libelous.

libelous US, **libellous** GB ['laɪbləs] *adj* [statement, allegation] that is a libel.

liberal ['lɪbərəl] ◇ *adj* **-1.** [person, mind, view] that is willing to accept and respect any or all of a wide range of different opinions, especially when these do not follow strict traditional beliefs; [education, upbringing] that does not follow tradition but is based on freedom of expression and thought □ *The group is campaigning for a more liberal treatment of prisoners.* **-2.** [donation, offer] that is generous and large □ *There was a liberal supply of food and drink.* ◇ *n* a person who has liberal views.
◆ **Liberal** POLITICS ◇ *n* a person who belongs to or supports a Liberal or Liberal Democrat Party. ◇ *adj: a Liberal politician/policy.*

liberal arts *npl* subjects studied at a university that are not practical or vocational, e.g. philosophy and literature □ *a liberal arts degree.*

Liberal Democrat *n* in Britain, a member of the Social and Liberal Democratic Party, a moderate political party.

liberalize, -ise ['lɪbrəlaɪz] *vt* [law, attitude] to make <sthg> less strict □ *The Church needs to liberalize its views on homosexuality.*

liberal-minded [-'maɪndəd] *adj* [person] who has liberal ideas and beliefs.

Liberal Party *n* **the Liberal Party** in Australia, the largest conservative political party; in Britain, one of the main political parties of the 19th and early 20th centuries that was replaced in 1988 by the Social and Liberal Democratic Party.

liberate ['lɪbəreɪt] *vt* **-1.** [women, slaves] to give <a group of people> the same rights and freedoms as other people in society. **-2.** [prisoner, hostage] to set <a person or animal> free (formal use) □ *The mission to liberate the hostages ended in failure.* **-3.** [country, city] to free <a place> from political or military control, especially by using force.

liberation [ˌlɪbə'reɪʃn] *n: see* **liberate** □ *the Women's Liberation Movement.*

liberator ['lɪbəreɪtəʳ] *n* a person who frees people, a country etc.

Liberia [laɪ'bɪərɪə] a country in West Africa, on the Atlantic coast, between Sierra Leone and Côte d'Ivoire. It exports iron ore and has an important shipping industry. SIZE: 110,000 sq kms. POPULATION: 2,800,000 (*Liberians*). CAPITAL: Monrovia. LANGUAGE: English. CURRENCY: Liberian dollar.

libertine ['lɪbə'tiːn] *n* a person, usually a man, who lives immorally (old-fashioned use).

liberty ['lɪbə'tɪ] (*pl* **liberties**) *n* **-1.** [of a person, the press, somebody's conscience] a person's right to do, say, believe etc what they want □ *We must fight for liberty and equal rights* □ *civil liberties.* ■ **to be at liberty to do sthg** to be free to do sthg because one has permission or the right to do it □ *I am not at liberty to comment on this matter.* **-2.** [of a prisoner, hostage] freedom that somebody has after a period of captivity. ■ **to be at liberty** [person, animal] to still be free, especially after escaping from a place or doing something wrong. **-3. to take the liberty of doing sthg** to do sthg that might seem rude because one has not asked permission first □ *I took the liberty of booking us a table at a restaurant.* ■ **to take liberties** to use or take advantage of somebody □ *I feel he's taking liberties with me.*

◆ **Liberty** *n* a British organization that aims to defend the legal rights of people, e.g. if they think they are being treated unfairly by the police.

Liberty Bell *n* **the Liberty Bell** the bell that rang when the Declaration of Independence was adopted in 1776. It is in Philadelphia, Pennsylvania.

libido [lɪ'biːdəʊ] (*pl* **libidos**) *n* the sexual desire that somebody feels.

Libra ['liːbrə] *n* a sign of the zodiac, represented by a pair of scales; a person born under this sign between September 23 and October 22.

librarian [laɪ'breərɪən] *n* a person whose job is to work in a library.

library [US 'laɪbrerɪ, GB -rərɪ] (*pl* **libraries**) *n* **-1.** [in a town, university, school] a room or building where people can read or borrow books, newspapers, cassettes, records etc, or can find out particular kinds of information □ *the public/reference library* □ *a music/record library.* **-2.** a private collection of something, especially of books.

library book *n* a book that can be borrowed from a library.

Library of Congress: **the Library of Congress** the US national library in Washington, D.C.

libretto [lɪ'bretəʊ] (*pl* **librettos**) *n* the words that are sung in an opera or oratorio.

Libya ['lɪbɪə] a country in North Africa, on the Mediterranean, between Tunisia and Egypt, consisting mainly of desert. It is a major producer of oil. SIZE: 1,760,000 sq kms. POPULATION: 4,900,000 (*Libyans*). CAPITAL: Tripoli. LANGUAGE: Arabic. CURRENCY: Libyan dinar.

lice [laɪs] *plural of* **louse.**

licence *n* GB = **license.**

license ['laɪsəns] ◇ *n* US **-1.** a document that gives somebody official permission to have or do something and which usually costs money □ *a driver's/dog license* □ *How much is the license fee?* □ *This restaurant has a license to sell alcohol.* **-2.** BUSINESS a document that gives official permission for a particular business activity to happen □ *a trading license* ■ **to**

make/sell etc sthg under license to make/sell etc sthg with special permission □ *They manufacture the goods under license from the government.*
◇ *vt* [activity, sale] to give official permission for <sthg> to happen □ *They have the authority to license the sale of hand guns.* ■ **to license sb to do sthg** to give sb official permission to do sthg.

licensed ['laɪsənst] *adj* **-1. to be licensed to do sthg** [to drive, fly, practise] to have a license to do sthg □ *Is he licensed to carry a gun?* **-2.** [car, gun] that has a license. **-3.** GB [hotel, restaurant] that has a license to sell alcohol.

licensee [,laɪsən'siː] *n* a person who has a license.

license plate *n* US a sign, usually on the front and back of a car, truck etc, that has letters and numbers on it to identify the vehicle.

licensing hours ['laɪsənsɪŋ-] *npl* in Britain, the hours in the day when a pub is officially allowed to serve alcohol.

licensing laws *npl* the laws that state when and where alcohol can be sold.

licentious [laɪ'senʃəs] *adj* [person, behavior] that one thinks is sexually immoral (formal use).

lichen ['laɪkən] *n* a tiny plant that grows in small, flat, round patches on stones, trees etc and is green, orange, gray, or yellow.

lick [lɪk] ◇ *vt* **-1.** [person] to move one's tongue over the surface of <sthg> to taste it, clean it, make it wet etc □ *She licked the bowl clean.* □ *The dog licked my face.* ■ **to lick one's lips** to move one's tongue over one's lips because one is going to eat something good, or because one has enjoyed eating something. **-2.** [flames, waves] to move quickly over or around the outside of <sthg>. **-3.** [team, player] to beat <an opponent> very easily (informal use).
◇ *n* **-1.** the act of licking something with one's tongue □ *Can I have a lick of your ice cream?* **-2. a lick of paint** a new layer of paint that one puts on something (informal use) □ *All this room needs is a lick of paint and it'll look like new.*

licorice ['lɪkərɪʃ] *n* a sweet black substance that is used to flavor candies; a candy made from this.

lid [lɪd] *n* **-1.** [of a jar, box, saucepan] a cover that fits on top of something to close it and that can be lifted off and replaced □ *'Replace lid after use.'* □ *a trashcan lid.* **-2.** = **eyelid.**

lido ['liːdəʊ] (*pl* **lidos**) *n* GB **-1.** a public swimming pool that is outdoors. **-2.** part of a beach, lake etc used for sunbathing and water sports.

lie [laɪ] (*pt sense 1* **lied**, *pt senses 2-9* **lay**, *pp sense 1* **lied**, *pp senses 2-9* **lain**, *cont all senses* **lying**) ◇ *n* something that is not true and which somebody says in order to deceive somebody else □ *What he said was just a pack of lies.* ■ **to tell a lie** to say something that one knows is not true □ *Have you been telling (me) lies again?*
◇ *vi* **-1.** [person] to tell a lie; [figures, statistics]

to make people believe something that is not true by showing something in a particular way □ *I knew you were lying to me all along.* □ *He got the job after lying about his age.* □ *They say the camera never lies, but I disagree.* **-2.** [person, animal] to be in a position in which the body is flat on a surface □ *She lay in bed/on her side/on her stomach reading.* □ *I love lying in the sun.* **-3.** [person, animal] to move into a position in which the body is flat on a surface □ *Lie on the floor and relax.* **-4.** [book, letter, pen] to be on a particular surface or in a particular place after being left there □ *Her clothes lay all over the floor.* □ *The report's been lying on my desk for ages.* **-5.** [city, country, building] to be in a particular place or position □ *A small village lies near/to the west of the castle.* □ *Our team is lying third/in third position.* **-6.** [truth, reason, problem] to be found in a particular thing (formal use) □ *The solution lies in careful marketing.* **-7.** [dead person] to be buried in a particular place □ *'Here lies William Slater.'* **-8. to lie ahead** OR **in store** to be expected to happen in the future □ *Many difficulties lie ahead.* □ *Who knows what lies in store for us!* **-9.** *phrase* **to lie low** to hide from somebody, especially from the police, until it is safe to be seen □ *You'd better lie low for a week or so.*

◆ **lie about, lie around** *vi* **-1.** [person] to spend time doing nothing and being lazy □ *They just lie around listening to music all day.* **-2. to be lying about** OR **around** [books, clothes, money] to be in a particular place after being left there by somebody, usually in a careless or untidy way □ *Don't leave any valuables lying around in your hotel room.* □ *Do you have any food lying around?*

◆ **lie down** *vi* to get into a position in which one's body is flat, e.g. on a bed, usually to relax or sleep □ *I'm just going to lie down for a short while.* ■ **he/she etc won't take it lying down** he/she etc will not accept it without complaining or trying to change it.

◆ **lie in** *vi* GB to deliberately stay in bed longer than usual in the morning.

Liechtenstein ['lɪktənstaɪn] a country in central Europe, between Austria and Switzerland. It has important tourist and banking industries. SIZE: 160 sq kms. POPULATION: 26,000 (*Liechtensteiners*). CAPITAL: Vaduz. LANGUAGE: German. CURRENCY: Swiss franc.

lie detector *n* a machine that can show if somebody is lying □ *a lie detector test.*

lie-down *n* GB a short rest, e.g. on a bed or sofa □ *I'm going to have a lie-down upstairs.*

lie-in *n* GB extra time that one deliberately spends in bed on a particular morning, especially at the weekend □ *Sunday's the only day I get a lie-in.*

lieu [luː] ◆ **in lieu of sthg** *prep* instead of sthg □ *I get time off in lieu of pay when I do a lot of overtime.*

Lieut. *abbr of* **lieutenant.**

lieutenant [US luː'tenənt, GB lef'tenənt] *n* **-1.** an officer of low rank in an army, air force, or navy. **-2.** US an officer in a police force or

fire department whose rank is below a captain.

lieutenant colonel *n* an officer in the armed forces of a country whose rank is just below that of a colonel.

life [laɪf] (*pl* **lives**) *n* **-1.** the state of being alive □ *Human life must be protected at all costs.* ■ **to breathe life into sthg** to bring new ideas and enthusiasm to sthg, especially so that it becomes more active or successful □ *We were all set to give up, but John's enthusiasm has breathed new life into the project.* ■ **to come to life** [person] to become active or energetic, especially after being very quiet or lacking energy and enthusiasm □ *She suddenly came to life again when the guests arrived.* **-2.** anything that is alive □ *Is there life on Mars?* □ *animal/plant life* □ *There were no signs of life in the village.* **-3. sb's life** the period of time between sb's birth and death, or between sb's birth and the present □ *Firemen risk their lives every day.* □ *Three climbers lost their lives in an accident.* □ *She spent her early life in India.* □ *life membership* ■ **for life** for the rest of one's life □ *It's a commitment for life.* ■ **for the life of me** despite trying very hard (informal use) □ *I can't for the life of me remember where I put it.* ■ **to lay down one's life** to die, especially in order to protect somebody or something □ *Millions of soldiers laid down their lives for their countries.* ■ **to risk life and limb** to risk dying and being injured. ■ **to scare the life out of sb** to frighten sb very much. ■ **to take one's life** to kill oneself. **-4.** all the experiences that happen to somebody □ *They really know how to enjoy life.* □ *Life is hard in these remote highlands.* **-5. sb's married/working life** the part of sb's life to do with their marriage/work. **-6.** a particular aspect of the way one lives □ *my social/sex life* □ *I don't like to talk about my private life.* **-7.** energy and enthusiasm □ *She's so full of life.* **-8.** [of a machine, organization] the length of time that something lasts or continues to work □ *This model has a working life of ten years.* **-9.** = **life imprisonment** □ *Holmes and Gano both got life.*

life-and-death *adj* [situation, struggle, decision] that is very serious or dangerous.

life annuity *n* a sum of money paid to somebody every year until their death.

life assurance *n* GB = **life insurance.**

life belt *n* GB a large ring that floats and is thrown to somebody who has fallen into the sea, a river etc to help them avoid drowning.

lifeblood ['laɪfblʌd] *n* **the lifeblood of sthg** the most important source of strength or success that sthg has □ *Young, dynamic managers are the lifeblood of our business.*

lifeboat ['laɪfbəʊt] *n* **-1.** a fast boat that is used by specially trained people to save other people who are in danger on the sea. **-2.** a small boat kept on a ship that is used if the ship sinks.

life buoy *n* = **life belt.**

life cycle *n* the series of changes that happen to an animal or plant during its life.

life expectancy *n* the length of time that a person or animal is likely to live from the time they are born, or from a particular point in their lives.

lifeguard ['laɪfgɑːʳd] *n* a person who works at a beach or swimming pool and whose job is to save people from drowning.

life imprisonment *n* a punishment in which a criminal is sent to prison for a very long time, sometimes for the rest of their life.

life insurance *n* a form of insurance that is paid for regularly over a long period of time and by which an amount of money is paid to oneself at a particular age or to one's family if one dies.

life jacket *n* a piece of equipment like an item of clothing with holes for the head and arms that can be filled with air to make somebody float if they fall into the water.

lifeless ['laɪfləs] *adj* -1. [body, corpse, face] that is dead or looks dead. -2. [performance, voice] that is not interesting, exciting, or lively.

lifelike ['laɪflaɪk] *adj* [statue, picture, model] that looks very real, or very like the person or thing it represents.

lifeline ['laɪflaɪn] *n* -1. a rope that is thrown or attached to somebody to save them from drowning. -2. something that is very important and necessary for somebody or something to survive or continue □ *A fax machine can prove a lifeline to the small business.*

lifelong ['laɪflɒŋ] *adj* a lifelong belief/ambition etc a belief/an ambition etc that one has had for the whole of one's life □ *a lifelong friend.*

life peer *n* in Britain, a person who is given a title, e.g. "Lord" or "Lady", which they can use until their death, but which cannot be passed on to their children.

life preserver [-prɪzɜːʳvəʳ] *n* US something such as a life jacket that can help prevent one from drowning in water.

life raft *n* a rubber boat filled with air that is used for saving people who are in danger at sea.

lifesaver ['laɪfseɪvəʳ] *n* -1. a person who is trained to save people who are having problems in water. -2. something or somebody that brings help and relief to somebody who needs it very much □ *Thanks for helping me out, you're a real lifesaver!*

❦ LIFESAVERS
In Australia most beaches near towns have lifesavers, or surf lifesavers, who work as volunteers. They are highly respected, and many young people want to become lifesavers. To identify themselves, they wear special colored swimsuits and caps. When conditions are safe for swimming, they put two yellow and red flags on the beach to show that the water between the flags is safe. If you get into difficulty in the water, you raise your arm and the lifesaver will rescue you.

lifesaving club *n* in Australia, a club where

surf lifesavers are based. Most coastal towns have these clubs, and they are often the center of beach activities and social events.

life sentence *n* the punishment of sending a criminal to prison for a very long time, sometimes for the rest of their life.

life-size(d) *adj* [statue, portrait, model] that is the same size as the person or object it represents.

lifespan ['laɪfspæn] *n* -1. the length of time for which a person, animal, or plant usually lives □ *Mayflies have a very short lifespan.* -2. the length of time that a product, machine etc will last or be useful.

lifestyle ['laɪfstaɪl] *n* the way somebody lives, especially the job they do, the things they eat, spend their money on etc □ *Patrick has a very healthy/hectic lifestyle.*

life-support system *n* -1. MEDICINE special equipment that keeps a very ill person alive. -2. BIOLOGY everything that is needed so that living things can stay alive.

lifetime ['laɪftaɪm] *n* [of a person, organization, machine] the period of time during which somebody is alive or something exists □ *I've seen many changes in my lifetime.* □ *He has a lifetime's experience in education.* □ *the experience of a lifetime* □ *a lifetime commitment.*

LIFFE [laɪf] *n abbr of* **London International Financial Futures Exchange.**

Liffey ['lɪfɪ] **the Liffey** a river in the Irish Republic that flows through Dublin into the Irish Sea.

lift [lɪft] ◇ *n* -1. a free ride, especially in a car □ *I've got the car if you want a lift home.* -2. GB a device like a small room with sliding doors that carries people or goods up and down to the different floors of a building □ *Press the button to call the lift.* □ *Take the lift up to the sixth floor.*
◇ *vt* -1. [person, leg, bag] to move <sb/sthg> to a higher position, especially with effort □ *Be careful when you lift the chair.* □ *She ran into his arms and he lifted her into the air.* □ *I lifted the pile of books off the shelf.* -2. **to lift sb's spirits** to make sb feel happier □ *The sound of his voice lifted her spirits.* -3. [embargo, ban, restriction] to bring <sthg> to an end □ *Trade sanctions were officially lifted today.* -4. [text, idea] to copy <sthg> that was produced by somebody else and pretend that one thought of it oneself (informal use) □ *She had lifted entire paragraphs from other people's books.* -5. [wallet, purse] to steal <sthg> (informal use).
◇ *vi* -1. [lid, top] to be able to be opened by being moved up □ *The lid lifted easily.* -2. [mist, fog, clouds] to move upward or disappear. -3. [spirits, mood] to become happier □ *Gradually her heart lifted.*
◆ **lift up** ◇ *vt sep* **to lift sb/sthg up** [suitcase, cup, baby] to lift sb/sthg. ◇ *vi* [lid, top] = **lift.**

lift-off *n* the event of a space rocket leaving the ground.

ligament ['lɪgəmənt] *n* a band of strong tissue in the body which joins two bones.

light [laɪt] (*pt* & *pp* **lit** OR **lighted**) ◇ *adj*
-1. [room, building] where there is a lot of
natural light □ *The bedroom is light and spacious.* ■ **it's getting** OR **growing light** day is
beginning and the sky is becoming brighter.
■ **it's light** there is daylight □ *It was light by
the time we had finished.* **-2.** [color, green, blue]
that is pale □ *She wore a light brown suit.*
-3. [load, weight, suitcase] that does not weigh
very much; [clothing, suit] that is made of
thin material □ *She was wearing a light summer
dress.* **-4.** [traffic, flow, shower] that is not very
great in amount or intensity □ *I had a light
lunch.* **-5.** [work, duties] not involving much
effort. **-6.** [punishment, penalty] that is not
very severe □ *Many people felt the sentence
was too light.* **-7.** [reading, entertainment, music]
that is easy to enjoy or understand □ *She
writes light, romantic novels.* **-8.** [touch, wind]
that is gentle □ *A light breeze was blowing.*
-9. [step, movement] that is graceful. **-10.**
[sleep, sleeper] that can be easily disturbed.
-11. a light meal a meal that is easy to digest
□ *This wine is nice and light.* **-12. a light beer** a
beer that contains fewer calories than normal.

◇ *n* **-1.** [of the sun, moon, a flashlight] a brightness that lets one see things □ *There's not
enough light to see by.* □ *We read the notice by
the light of a match/candle.* □ *You're blocking my
light.* ■ **to come to light** [information, evidence,
secret] to become known, especially to a lot
of people for the first time □ *It has recently
come to light that she has a criminal record.* ■ **to
see the light** to understand something that
one could not understand before. ■ **to see
sb/sthg in a different light** to change one's
opinion of sb/sthg because of new information, events etc □ *What she said made me see
her in a whole new light.* ■ **to throw** OR **cast** OR
shed light on sthg to make sthg easier to
understand, especially by giving some new
information □ *Her book throws new light on the
later poems.* **-2.** [for seeing or reading] something which gives light □ *Turn the light on.* □
an electric light □ *a light switch* □ *You've left your
car lights on.* **-3.** [for a cigarette] something
which produces a flame, e.g. a match or
lighter □ *Do you have a light?* ■ **to set light to
sthg** to make sthg start to burn □ *The cigarette set light to the carpet.* **-4.** [in somebody's
eyes] the brightness that seems to come
from somebody's eyes, as a sign of life and
energy □ *There was a strange light in his eyes.*

◇ *vt* **-1.** [fire, cigarette, candle] to make <sthg>
start to burn; [lamp, bulb] to turn <sthg> on
so that it becomes bright □ *We lit a fire in the
bedroom.* □ *I knew she was up because a lamp
was lit in her window.* **-2.** [house, scene, stage]
to make a light shine on or in <sthg> □ *The
room was lit by candlelight.* □ *I took a flashlight to
light my way back to the house.*

◇ *vi* [fire, cigarette, candle] *The gas fire won't
light.*

◇ *adv* **to travel light** to travel with only a
small amount of baggage.

◆ **in light of** US, **in the light of** *prep* if one
takes <sthg> into consideration □ *In light of*

*recent events, we ought to rethink our procedure
for interviewing applicants.*

◆ **light out** *vi* US [person] to leave quickly (informal use).

◆ **light up** ◇ *vt sep* **to light sthg up** [sky, room,
stage] to make sthg bright; [face, eyes] to
make sthg look more cheerful and lively;
[cigarette, cigar, pipe] to make sthg start
burning □ *The fire lit up the whole street.* ◇ *vi*
-1. [person, eyes] to look more cheerful and
lively □ *His face lit up at the news.* **-2.** [smoker]
to light a cigarette and start smoking (informal use).

light aircraft *n* a small, not very powerful aircraft that can only carry a small number of
passengers or goods.

light ale *n* GB a beer with a light color and
mild flavor.

light bulb *n* the glass part of an electric light
or lamp that has a wire inside it which
glows brightly when an electric current is
passed through it.

lighted ['laɪtəd] *adj* **-1.** [room, window] that has
a light shining in it. **-2.** [cigarette, match, can-
dle] that is burning.

light-emitting diode [-ɪmɪtɪŋ-] *n* an electronic
device that gives out light when an electric
current is passed through it and that is used
to display letters and numbers in calculators,
watches etc.

lighten ['laɪtn] ◇ *vt* **-1.** [room, sky, color] to
make <sthg> less dark. **-2.** [load, weight] to
make <sthg> less heavy, especially so that it
is easier to carry; [workload, task] to make
<an amount of work> easier to do □ *I of-
fered to do the typing just to lighten the burden a
little.* ◇ *vi* **-1.** [sky] to become brighter □ *The
sky began to lighten in the east.* **-2.** [atmosphere,
mood, expression] to become happier and
more relaxed.

◆ **lighten up** *vi* [person] to become more relaxed and less serious (informal use) □ *Lighten
up, will you, he meant it as a joke.*

lighter ['laɪtər] *n* a device that uses liquid fuel
to produce a flame for lighting cigarettes,
pipes etc.

light-fingered [-'fɪŋgərd] *adj* [person] who often steals things (informal and humorous use).

light-headed [-'hedəd] *adj* **to be light-headed**
[person] to feel dizzy and faint, especially because one is excited or has drunk alcohol □ *I
feel really light-headed after that glass of wine.*

light-hearted [-'hɑːrtəd] *adj* **-1.** [person, mood]
that is cheerful. **-2.** [remark, approach, comedy]
that is funny and not meant to be very serious □ *The play takes a light-hearted look at the
problems of family life.*

lighthouse ['laɪthaʊs, *pl* -haʊzɪz] *n* a tower
built on a coast, rock, or island with a
strong light at the top to guide ships or
warn them of danger.

light industry *n* the manufacture of smaller
articles for which heavy equipment is not
needed.

lighting ['laɪtɪŋ] *n* the equipment that provides light in a particular place; the quality

of light that shines somewhere □ *They hired a friend to do the lighting for the show.* □ *The soft lighting helps to create a romantic atmosphere.*

lighting-up time *n* GB the official time at which street lights come on and road vehicles must turn their lights on.

lightly ['laɪtlɪ] *adv* -1. [knock, tap, strike] gently. -2. [cook, grill] for a short time at a low heat. -3. [say, promise] in a way that is not very serious □ *I would not make such an accusation lightly.* □ *I don't intend to take this matter lightly.*

light meter *n* a device that is fitted to a camera or used by a photographer to measure the brightness of the light reflected from something before it is photographed.

lightning ['laɪtnɪŋ] *n* a very bright flash of electrical energy produced by a thunderstorm □ *The tree was struck by lightning.*

lightning rod US, **lightning conductor** *n* a metal rod or strip that goes from the highest point of a building to the ground, and that prevents the building from being damaged if it is struck by lightning.

lightning strike *n* GB a strike by workers which takes place suddenly and without any warning.

light opera *n* opera that is easy to enjoy and is not about serious subjects.

light pen *n* -1. COMPUTING a device shaped like a pen that can be used to choose or draw things on a screen. -2. [in a store] a device like a pen that is used in stores to read bar codes on goods.

lightship ['laɪtʃɪp] *n* a ship that remains in one position and has a strong light to guide other ships or warn them of danger.

lights-out *n* in a barracks, boarding-school etc, the time at which all lights must be turned off so that people can go to sleep.

lightweight ['laɪtweɪt] ◇ *adj* -1. [object] that is specially made to weigh less than is usual. -2. [jacket, suit] that is made of thin light material. -3. [person] who has little importance, power, or influence (disapproving use). ◇ *n* -1. SPORT a boxer weighing between 59 and 61 kg (130 and 135 lbs) □ *a lightweight contest/bout.* -2. a person of little importance, power, or influence (disapproving use) □ *a political/intellectual lightweight.*

light year *n* the distance that light travels in a year.

likable ['laɪkəbl] *adj* [person] who is pleasant and easy to like.

like [laɪk] ◇ *prep* -1. **to be like sb/sthg** to be almost the same as sb/sthg □ *Jake's very like his father.* □ *You look just like your sister!* □ *This turkey tastes more like chicken.* -2. **what is she/it etc like?** can you describe her/it etc to me? (used to ask for somebody's opinion or description) □ *It's hard to say what it smells like.* □ *What's it like being married?* -3. used to make comparisons □ *Stop behaving like an idiot!* □ *He was shaking like a leaf.* □ *Like most people, I dislike eating alone in restaurants.* ■ **do it like this/ that** do it in this/that way. ■ **that's just like her/him etc** that's typical of the way she/he

etc normally behaves □ *It's not like you to get angry.* □ *Don't shout at me like that!* -4. used to give examples of something that has just been mentioned □ *I prefer simple food like pasta or fish.* □ *Exercise like swimming is good for your back.*
◇ *conj* -1. **to look/sound/feel like...** to look/ sound/feel as if... □ *It feels like we've been traveling for hours!* □ *Chris sounds like he's having a bad time.* -2. in the same way as □ *I got up at seven, just like I usually do.* □ *He can't get around like he used to.*
◇ *vt* -1. [person, place, food] to find <sb/sthg> pleasant, attractive, interesting etc; to approve of <sb/sthg> □ *I never really liked him.* □ *How do you like your new job?* □ *I like swimming.* □ *I don't like having to repeat myself.* -2. a word used to express a wish or a preference □ *Would you like some more cake?* □ *I'd like that one, please.* □ *You can come and see me tomorrow, if you like.* □ *I'd like to start straight away.* □ *We'd like you to come for an interview.*
◇ *adj* [opinion, response] that is of a similar kind (formal use) □ *people of like mind.*
◇ *n* **the like(s) of sb/sthg** an event, person etc that is similar to sb/sthg □ *I've never seen the likes of it!* □ *a feat the likes of which has never before been attempted.* ■ **and the like** and similar things, people etc □ *I use it for storing files, stationery, and the like.*

◆ **likes** *npl* the things that one likes □ *We all have our likes and dislikes when it comes to music.*

likeable ['laɪkəbl] *adj* = likable.

likelihood ['laɪklɪhʊd] *n* the probability that something will happen □ *There is little likelihood of its happening again/that it will happen again.*

◆ **in all likelihood** *adv* very probably.

likely ['laɪklɪ] *adj* -1. **to be likely** to be almost certain to happen or be true □ *Rain is likely later on.* □ *She may have finished already, but it's not very likely.* □ *It's very likely to snow in the next day or two.* □ *She's not very likely to agree to the plan.* □ *He's the man most likely to get the job.* ■ **the likely result/cost** what the result/ cost will probably be. ■ **a likely story!** a phrase used to say that one does not believe something that somebody has said (ironic use). -2. [place, candidate, recruit] that seems suitable for a particular job or purpose □ *We found a likely spot for a picnic.*

like-minded [-'maɪndəd] *adj* [people] who have similar opinions, attitudes, or interests □ *She needs to find some like-minded friends.*

liken ['laɪkn] *vt* **to liken sb/sthg to sb/sthg** to describe sb/sthg as similar to sb/sthg □ *He has been likened to the young Gielgud.* □ *She likened "King Lear" to a television soap opera.*

likeness ['laɪknəs] *n* -1. a similarity in appearance □ *I can see the family likeness.* □ *Your version bears very little likeness to the original.* -2. **a good likeness** a picture of somebody that has been drawn, painted etc accurately □ *That's an excellent likeness of your father.*

likewise ['laɪkwaɪz] *adv* used to compare two similar actions or events □ *The Swedes are* holding a referendum, likewise the Norwegians. □ Farmers likewise are having to cut costs. ■ **to do likewise** to do the same □ When we raised our prices, they did likewise.

liking ['laɪkɪŋ] n **to have a liking for sb/sthg** to like sb/sthg □ I really don't understand his liking for cowboy films. □ While I was in Mexico I developed a liking for tequila. ■ **to be to sb's liking** to please sb □ Is the hotel to your liking? ■ **to be too cold/early etc for one's liking** to be colder/earlier than one wants □ The coffee was too hot for my liking.

lilac ['laɪlək] ◇ adj [dress, scarf] that is pale purple in color. ◇ n -1. a bush with white or pale purple flowers that smell pleasant. -2. a pale purple color □ a lilac shirt.

Lilo™ ['laɪlou] (pl **Lilos**) n GB a mattress that is filled with air and is used as a bed or for floating on water.

lilt [lɪlt] n [of somebody's voice, accent] a pleasant rising and falling sound □ Her voice has a lovely Irish lilt.

lilting ['lɪltɪŋ] adj **a lilting voice/melody etc** a voice/melody etc that has a lilt.

lily ['lɪlɪ] (pl **lilies**) n a flower that grows from a bulb and has large trumpet-shaped blooms which are usually white or orange.

lily of the valley (pl **lilies of the valley**) n a plant with long oval leaves and small white bell-shaped flowers that smell pleasant.

Lima ['liːmə] the capital of Peru. POPULATION: 6,400,000.

limb [lɪm] n -1. an arm or leg (formal use). -2. **to be out on a limb** to be alone and without support □ You may find yourself out on a limb if you continue to defend those ideas.

limber ['lɪmbər] ◆ **limber up** vi [athlete, gymnast] to do physical exercises or to practice before hard exercise or a competition.

limbo ['lɪmbou] (pl **limbos**) n -1. **to be in limbo** [person] to be unable to act or make decisions properly because one is unsure what will happen next; [project, activity] to be unable to go ahead because the situation is uncertain □ Our plans will be in limbo until we know whether we've got the grant. -2. **the limbo** a West Indian dance in which people bend over backward to pass under a low horizontal bar.

lime [laɪm] n -1. a citrus fruit like a lemon but smaller and with green skin. -2. the juice of limes used as part of a drink □ vodka and lime. -3. = **lime tree**. -4. CHEMISTRY a white chemical substance, calcium oxide, that is used to make fertilizer, cement, and whitewash SYMBOL: CaO.

lime-green ◇ n a bright yellow-green color. ◇ adj: a lime-green dress.

limelight ['laɪmlaɪt] n **the limelight** the attention of the public and the media □ She's in the limelight again after the success of her new movie.

limerick ['lɪmərɪk] n a humorous poem of five lines.

Limerick ['lɪmərɪk] -1. a county in the southwest of the Irish Republic. SIZE: 2,686 sq

kms. POPULATION: 164,204. ADMINISTRATIVE CENTER: Limerick. -2. a city and port in County Limerick. POPULATION: 52,040.

limescale ['laɪmskeɪl] n a hard grayish-white substance that forms on the inside of pipes, faucets, sinks etc.

limestone ['laɪmstoun] n a type of white rock used as a building material and for making cement.

lime tree n a tree with heart-shaped leaves and yellow blossom that has a sweet smell.

limey ['laɪmɪ] (pl **limeys**) n US a British person (informal and disapproving use).

limit ['lɪmət] ◇ n -1. [of one's patience, endurance, knowledge] the greatest possible extent, amount, or degree of something □ Fulfilling this contract will stretch our resources to the limit. □ Twenty years ago there seemed to be no limit to what we could do. -2. [on speed, spending] a maximum or minimum amount of something that is allowed □ a time/speed/credit limit □ an upper/a lower limit □ We must keep within the limits of our budget. □ There is a limit to how much money we can spend. ■ **he's/she's the limit!** his/her behavior is extremely annoying □ I've heard some pretty unconvincing excuses before, but this is the limit! ■ **within limits** as far as is reasonable □ You can do anything you like, within limits of course. -3. [of an area] the edge of an area □ the city limits ■ **to be off limits** to be a place where particular people are not allowed to go □ The village is off limits to military personnel.

◇ vt [spending, use, area] to stop <sthg> from growing or speading by deciding that a particular amount or level is the most that is allowed □ We must try and limit our reliance on external suppliers. ■ **to limit sb to sthg** to allow sb to have no more than sthg □ I'm trying to limit myself to six cigarettes a day.

limitation [,lɪmɪ'teɪʃn] n -1. [of an amount, somebody's power] the control or reduction of something □ This whole exercise is about damage limitation. □ We would resist any limitation of our freedom to trade with other countries. -2. [on spending, space] a limit to what is allowed or possible □ There are limitations on the number of shares you can buy. □ Subject to certain limitations, you can appoint anyone you like. -3. **sb's/sthg's limitations** an area of activity in which sb/sthg is limited or not very effective □ She's extremely capable, but even she has her limitations.

limited ['lɪmətəd] adj [choice, intelligence, range] that is not great in number or amount □ The options open to us are very limited. □ A limited number of places are available. □ The offer is limited to one purchase per household.

limited company n GB a company whose shareholders are responsible for the company's debts only up to a limited amount.

limited edition n a version of a book, CD etc in which the number of copies made and sold is strictly limited and usually quite small □ a limited edition book.

limited liability company n = **limited company**.

limitless ['lɪmətləs] adj [space, range, imagination] that has no limit □ *The possibilities are limitless.*

limo ['lɪmoʊ] *n* a limousine (informal use).

limousine [US 'lɪməziːn, GB lɪmə'ziːn] *n* a large, comfortable, expensive car.

limp [lɪmp] ◇ *adj* **-1.** [person, body] that is not firm or strong □ *I managed no more than a limp handshake.* □ *Those tomato plants are looking pretty limp.* **-2.** [excuse, response] that is not adequate. ◇ *n* a way of walking in which one leg is used less than normal because it is weak or injured □ *He walks with a slight limp.* ◇ *vi* [person, animal] to walk with a limp □ *He came limping off the field.*

limpet ['lɪmpət] *n* a small sea creature with a cone-shaped shell that sticks very tightly to rocks.

limpid ['lɪmpəd] *adj* [water, pool] that is clear (literary use).

limply ['lɪmplɪ] *adv* [lie, hang, reply] *see* **limp** □ *His arm hung limply by his side.*

linchpin ['lɪntʃpɪn] *n* [of a plan, organization] the person or thing that is the most important part of something □ *Corinne's research was the linchpin of this project.*

Lincoln ['lɪŋkn], **Abraham** (1809–1865) US President from 1861 to 1865. He helped the Union to win the American Civil War and ended slavery. He was shot and killed by John Wilkes Booth.

Lincoln Center: the Lincoln Center (for the Performing Arts) a group of concert halls and theaters in New York (City).

Lincoln Memorial: the Lincoln Memorial a building in Washington, D.C. that contains a large statue of Abraham Lincoln.

Lincolnshire ['lɪŋkənʃəʳ] a county in eastern England, on the North Sea, consisting mainly of farmland. SIZE: 5,915 sq kms. POPULATION: 602,155. ADMINISTRATIVE CENTER: Lincoln.

Lincs. *abbr of* **Lincolnshire.**

linctus ['lɪŋktəs] *n* GB a liquid medicine for curing coughs.

Lindbergh ['lɪndbɜːʳg], **Charles** (1902–1974) a US pilot who was the first person to fly alone across the Atlantic Ocean. He did this in his plane, *The Spirit of St Louis.*

line [laɪn] ◇ *n* **-1.** [on paper, on a road] a long thin mark on a surface □ *a straight/curved/ jagged line* □ *You can't park on a double yellow line.* □ *She drew a line across the page.* ■ **to go/ run/walk in a straight line** to go/run/walk in one direction without turning right or left. **-2.** [a border, edge] a long thin mark that shows the edge of something □ *the finishing/ halfway line.* ■ **to draw the line at sthg** to refuse to do sthg, especially because one thinks it is unreasonable □ *I'm prepared to be generous, but I draw the line at paying off all her debts.* **-3.** [of trees, soldiers, cars] a row of things or people standing side by side or one behind the other; a group of people standing one behind the other and waiting for something □ *The children formed two lines facing the teacher.* □ *We joined the line at the checkout.* □ *We stood* OR *waited in line for almost*

half an hour. ■ **to be in line for sthg** to have a good chance of getting sthg □ *He's in line for an Oscar.* **-4.** RAIL the track on which a train travels; the route this track follows □ *a subway line.* **-5.** [of ships] a company that operates a fleet of ships. **-6.** [in a book, poem, document] a row of words, symbols, or figures that is printed or written across a page □ *two lines up from the bottom/down from the top of the page* □ *I tried to remember the first line of the song.* □ *Richard's upstairs learning his lines for the school play.* ■ **to read between the lines** to realize something or guess the real meaning of something even though it is not expressed openly □ *Reading between the lines, I would say she was jealous.* **-7.** [on one's face, skin] a wrinkle □ *His face was etched with deep lines.* **-8.** [of a building, dress] an edge that can be seen on something and is part of its structure □ *The car has clean, elegant lines.* **-9.** [of string, cable] a cord, string, rope, or cable; a length of one of these materials used for a particular purpose □ *a fishing line* □ *I'm going to hang the laundry out on the line.* □ *a power/telephone line.* **-10.** TELECOMMUNICATIONS a telephone connection □ *Our lines are open until midnight.* □ *That line is busy at the moment.* □ *Could you hold the line, please?* **-11. to drop sb a line** to write a short letter to sb (informal use) □ *Drop me a line when you get settled in.* **-12. a line of inquiry/argument etc** the direction taken by the development of an inquiry/argument etc. ■ **along the same lines** [think, develop] in approximately the same way □ *They plan to set up an advice center or something along those lines.* ■ **to be on the right lines** [person, policy, strategy] to be acting, working, happening etc in a way that will probably produce a successful result □ *I'm not entirely satisfied with the article yet, but I think it's on the right lines.* **-13.** [on an issue, problem] a particular way of dealing with a person or situation □ *What line did you take with the press?* **-14. one's line of work/ business** the job or type of work a person does (informal use) □ *What line of work are you in?* **-15.** MILITARY a series of defenses that are linked to each other □ *behind enemy lines.* **-16.** [of family, kings] a series of people who are related to one another and follow one another in time □ *She comes from a long line of opera singers.* **-17.** [between categories, groups] an imaginary mark that separates one area or thing from another, or one group of people from another □ *There's a fine line between love and hate.* **-18.** BUSINESS a type of product; a range of products □ *a new line in office furniture* □ *We've stopped doing that line.*

◇ *vt* **-1.** [street, passage] to form a line along the side of <sthg> □ *The road to the airport was lined with spectators/trees.* **-2.** [coat, box, drawer] to cover the inside surface of <sthg> with a lining □ *a fur-/silk-lined jacket.*

◆ **lines** *npl* **-1.** the words that an actor has to learn for a play □ *She keeps forgetting her lines.* **-2.** GB a punishment given in some schools in which a pupil has to write out a line of writing many times □ *He was given a* *hundred lines for misbehaving in class.*

◆ **on the line** *adv* **to be on the line** [career, reputation] to be at risk □ *If we don't get the contract, all our jobs could be on the line.*

◆ **out of line** *adj* **to be out of line** [person] to be behaving badly or not in the way one is supposed to behave; [behavior, remark] to be rude or unacceptable □ *What you said was way out of line.* ■ **to step out of line** to behave in a way that other people disapprove of.

◆ **line up** ◇ *vt sep* **-1. to line people/things up** to arrange people/things into a line □ *They were lined up against a wall and shot.* **-2. to line sthg up** [meeting, interview, concert] to arrange for sthg to take place in the future □ *I've got a meeting lined up for next Tuesday.* ◇ *vi* [people] to form a line, especially when waiting for something □ *The models all lined up on the catwalk for the last part of the show.*

linear ['lɪnɪəʳ] *adj* **-1.** [pattern, diagram, shape] that is made up of lines. **-2.** [motion, force] that is directed along a straight line; [sequence, thinking] that moves from one point to the next in order.

lined [laɪnd] *adj* **-1.** [paper, page] that has straight lines printed across it. **-2.** [face, features] covered with wrinkles □ *Her face was deeply lined.*

line drawing *n* a drawing made with lines and with no other form of shading.

line feed *n* the control on a printer or computer that moves the cursor down by one line at a time.

linen ['lɪnən] *n* **-1.** a type of cloth, made from flax, that is used to make tablecloths, clothing etc □ *a linen napkin/jacket.* **-2.** a collective term for sheets, tablecloths etc □ *bed linen* □ *a linen cupboard/drawer.*

linen basket *n* a basket used to hold dirty clothes that need to be washed.

lineout ['laɪnaʊt] *n* SPORT a way of restarting play in a game of rugby in which the ball is thrown from the sideline and players from both sides, standing in two lines, try to catch it.

liner ['laɪnəʳ] *n* a large passenger ship □ *an ocean liner.*

linesman ['laɪnzmən] (*pl* **linesmen** [-mən]) *n* SPORT in a game of soccer, tennis etc, an official who indicates when the ball has crossed a boundary line, and who helps the referee to decide when other rules have been broken.

lineup ['laɪnʌp] *n* **-1.** [of players, competitors, entertainers] the people who are going to take part in a particular event □ *The lineup in tonight's show includes some of the most talented comedians around at the moment.* **-2.** US a row of people including a suspect whom the witness or victim of a crime has to try to identify.

linger ['lɪŋgəʳ] *vi* **-1.** [person] to spend a longer time than necessary or expected in a place or doing something □ *We lingered down by the Grand Canal/over our meal.* □ *Everyone else had gone to bed, but Sam lingered in the bar.* **-2.** [smell, taste, feeling] to continue for longer than expected before disappearing □ *The tradition still lingers on in rural areas.*

lingerie ['lænʒərɪ] *n* women's underclothes □ *the lingerie department.*

lingering ['lɪŋgərɪŋ] *adj* **-1.** [feeling, hope, doubt] that continues for longer than expected □ *a lingering sense of doubt.* **-2.** [death, illness] that lasts a long time and is painful. **-3.** [kiss, look, farewell] that is long and intense.

lingo ['lɪŋgoʊ] (*pl* **lingoes**) *n* a foreign language (informal use).

linguist ['lɪŋgwɪst] *n* **-1.** a person who is good at or who studies foreign languages. **-2.** a person who studies or teaches linguistics.

linguistic [lɪŋ'gwɪstɪk] *adj* [ability, development, subtlety] that is connected with language or the scientific study of it.

◆ **linguistics** *n* the scientific study of language and how it is developed and used.

liniment ['lɪnəmənt] *n* a fluid rubbed into the skin to make pains in one's muscles, bones etc less severe.

lining ['laɪnɪŋ] *n* [of a coat, curtain] an extra layer of cloth that is attached to the inside or back of something to give extra warmth and thickness; [of a box, case] a layer of something that covers the inner surfaces of a container and protects what is kept in it.

link [lɪŋk] ◇ *n* **-1.** [between people, ideas] a connection or relationship between people or things □ *Is there any link between the two cases?* □ *We are hoping to forge closer links with similar organizations abroad.* **-2.** [between places] a way of traveling from one place to another; a way of communicating with a place □ *a rail/telephone link.* **-3.** [of a chain] a ring of a chain □ *I've broken one of the links of my bracelet.*

◇ *vt* **-1.** to connect <two or more people, places, ideas> etc □ *the road that links the capital and the major port* OR *that links the capital with the major port* □ *Her name has been romantically linked to* OR *with his.* **-2. to link arms with sb** to put one's arm through the space between sb's bent arm and their body.

◆ **link up** ◇ *vt sep* **to link people/things up** to connect people/things to each other, especially so that information can be sent between them □ *I'm trying to link my computer up to the office with a modem.* ◇ *vi:* *We have now linked up with head office.*

linkage ['lɪŋkɪdʒ] *n* a connection between two things.

linked [lɪŋkt] *adj* **to be linked** [ideas, events, names] to have a connection, often in a way that is unclear or that is difficult to prove □ *There seems little doubt that the two crimes were linked.* ■ **with arms linked** with arms joined together, like the links of a chain.

links [lɪŋks] (*pl* **links**) *n* a piece of ground where golf is played.

linkup ['lɪŋkʌp] *n* a connection, especially one made by telecommunications □ *a TV/satellite/telephone linkup with the conference hall.*

lino ['laɪnoʊ] *n* GB = **linoleum**.

linoleum [lɪ'noʊlɪəm] *n* a type of material with

a hard, shiny, usually patterned surface that one uses to cover a floor, especially in kitchens and bathrooms.

linseed oil ['lɪnsiːd-] *n* an oil made from the seeds of flax and used e.g. in paint.

lint [lɪnt] *n* -1. small pieces of fiber and fluff that come from fabric □ *Remove the lint from your dryer regularly.* -2. GB an absorbent cloth made of cotton or linen and used to cover wounds or cuts.

lintel ['lɪntl] *n* a piece of stone or wood placed across the top of a door or window to support the wall above it.

lion ['laɪən] *n* a large, meat-eating wild animal that is a member of the cat family and lives mainly in Africa. Male lions have thick, dark-brown hair around their heads and necks.

lion cub *n* a very young lion.

lioness ['laɪənes] *n* a female lion.

lionize, -ise ['laɪənaɪz] *vt* to treat <sb> as being very talented, important etc □ *He was lionized by the press.*

lion tamer [-teɪməʳ] *n* a person who trains lions to perform tricks to entertain people at a circus.

lip [lɪp] *n* -1. one of the two fleshy edges of one's mouth □ *the upper/lower lip.* ■ **to keep a stiff upper lip** not to show one's feelings, even though it is difficult. ■ **my lips are sealed** I am determined I will not say anything. -2. [of a container, crater] the top edge of something.

lip balm *n* an ointment used on the lips to stop them feeling sore.

liposuction ['lɪpoʊsʌkʃn] *n* an operation in which unwanted fat is removed from below one's skin by suction.

lip-read *vi* to understand what people are saying only by watching the movements of their lips.

lip salve [US -sæv, GB -sælv] *n* GB = **lip balm**.

lip service *n* **to pay lip service to sthg** to say that one agrees with or approves of sthg without actively doing anything to show this □ *The new legislation only pays lip service to the idea of sexual equality.*

lipstick ['lɪpstɪk] *n* a substance, in the form of a solid stick, used by women to color their lips; a stick of this substance inside a small cylindrical container □ *She doesn't wear/use lipstick.*

liquefied petroleum gas [ˌlɪkwɪfaɪd-] *n* a mixture of gas produced from petroleum that is used in liquid form as a fuel for vehicles.

liquefy ['lɪkwɪfaɪ] (*pt* & *pp* **liquefied**) ◇ *vt* to make <a gas or solid substance> become a liquid. ◇ *vi: When the temperature is high enough, the metal liquefies.*

liqueur [US lɪˈkɜːr, GB lɪˈkjʊə] *n* a strong, sweet, often fruit-flavored alcoholic drink, usually served after a meal □ *a liqueur glass* □ *liqueur chocolates.*

liquid ['lɪkwəd] ◇ *adj* **liquid oxygen/soap etc** oxygen/soap etc in a form that will flow like

water. ◇ *n* a liquid substance □ *Drink plenty of liquids.*

liquid assets *npl* assets that can easily be changed into cash if necessary.

liquidate ['lɪkwədeɪt] *vt* -1. BUSINESS to close <a company>, usually because it cannot pay its debts; to pay <a debt> in full. -2. [enemy, target] to kill <sb> (formal use).

liquidation [ˌlɪkwəˈdeɪʃn] *n* BUSINESS the process of closing down a company □ *The company has gone into liquidation.*

liquidator ['lɪkwədeɪtəʳ] *n* BUSINESS the official responsible for closing down a company.

liquid crystal display *n* → LCD.

liquidity [lɪˈkwɪdətɪ] *n* BUSINESS the state of having enough cash or assets to pay one's debts.

liquidize, -ise ['lɪkwədaɪz] *vt* [fruit, vegetables] to chop and crush <food> until it becomes liquid.

liquidizer ['lɪkwɪdaɪzəʳ] *n* GB a machine used for making solid food into liquid.

liquor ['lɪkəʳ] *n* strong alcoholic drink.

liquorice ['lɪkərɪʃ] *n* = **licorice**.

liquor store *n* US a store that sells alcoholic drinks.

lira ['lɪərə] *n* the unit of currency in Italy, Turkey, and Syria.

Lisbon ['lɪzbən] the capital of Portugal and its largest city and main port. POPULATION: 677,790.

lisp [lɪsp] ◇ *n* a problem some people have in speaking where they pronounce the sounds "s" and "z" as "th". ◇ *vi* to speak with a lisp.

lissom(e) ['lɪsəm] *adj* [body, person] that looks slim and graceful (literary use).

list [lɪst] ◇ *n* a group of things, names, places etc that are written down or mentioned together, especially one after another □ *He wrote out a list of places to visit.* □ *Have you got me on your guest list?* ◇ *vt* -1. [items, contents, ingredients] to write out <things> in a list □ *The names are listed in alphabetical order.* -2. [points, reasons, advantages] to say <a series of things> one after the other □ *She listed skiing as one of her hobbies.* ◇ *vi* [ship] to lean over to one side.

listed building [ˌlɪstəd-] *n* GB a building that is officially protected because of its artistic value or age.

listed company *n* a company whose shares are quoted on a stock exchange.

listen ['lɪsn] *vi* -1. [audience, class, psychiatrist] to pay attention to a sound, to what somebody is saying etc, so that one hears it clearly □ *Please listen!* □ *Go on, I'm listening.* ■ **to listen to sb/sthg** to pay attention to sb/sthg so that one hears them clearly □ *I wasn't listening to what you were saying.* □ *Do you listen much to the radio?* ■ **to listen for sthg** to wait until one hears the sound of sthg □ *We listened out for the signal.* -2. [child, patient, friend] to do what somebody else suggests, especially because one believes or respects them □ *I told you it wouldn't work, but you wouldn't lis-*

ten. □ *If you'd listened to my advice in the first place, this wouldn't have happened.*

◆ **listen in** *vi* -1. to listen to the radio □ *Don't forget to listen in to next week's program.* -2. to **listen in on sb's conversation** to listen to sb's conversation without them knowing □ *Little did we know that he'd been listening in on our conversation.*

◆ **listen up** *vi* **listen up!** US a phrase used to attract people's attention when one wants to say something.

listener ['lɪsnəʳ] *n* -1. [to a person] a person who listens to and understands other people's problems □ *She's a good listener.* -2. [to the radio] a member of a radio audience □ *Our listeners often write to us.*

listeria [lɪ'stɪərɪə] *n* a kind of bacteria found in soft cheeses and cooked food that can cause illness.

listing ['lɪstɪŋ] *n* **a (computer) listing** a sheet of paper with information from a computer printed on it.

◆ **listings** *npl* a magazine, or part of a magazine, that contains information about the movies, plays, exhibitions etc that are taking place in a particular city □ *Have a look in the listings.*

listless ['lɪstləs] *adj* [person] who has no energy or enthusiasm □ *I felt listless in the heat.*

list price *n* the price that the manufacturer of a particular product suggests that customers pay for it.

Liszt [lɪst], **Franz** (1811–1886) a Hungarian composer and pianist, known for his romantic piano music.

lit [lɪt] *past tense & past participle of* **light**.

litany ['lɪtənɪ] (*pl* **litanies**) *n* -1. RELIGION a prayer with fixed words spoken in turn by the priest and the congregation. -2. [of faults, problems, failures] a large number of the same thing that keeps being said or done that is bad, unpleasant, boring etc □ *a litany of complaints.*

litchi ['lɪtʃɪ] *n* a small, round, white, Chinese fruit with a hard rough skin and a large shiny seed in the middle.

liter US, **litre** GB ['liːtəʳ] *n* -1. [of water, milk, gasoline] a unit (one thousand cubic centimeters or 1.76 pints) for measuring the volume of liquid □ *two liters of soda.* -2. AUTO the unit that measures the capacity of an engine □ *a two-liter engine.*

literacy ['lɪtərəsɪ] *n* the ability to read and write.

literal ['lɪtərəl] *adj* -1. [meaning, sense, interpretation] that is the most basic, without any added sense. -2. [translation] in which each word is translated separately.

literally ['lɪtərəlɪ] *adv* -1. a word used to emphasize that what one is saying is exactly true □ *Literally thousands of people turned up.* -2. a word used to give emphasis to an exaggerated or figurative expression □ *I had to literally drag him onto the plane.* -3. [mean, translate] *see* **literal** □ *I have translated the poem freely rather than literally.* ■ **to take sthg literally**

[remark, suggestion] to understand or interpret sthg in its most basic or exact meaning □ *I wouldn't take what she says literally.*

literary [US 'lɪtərerɪ, GB -ərərɪ] *adj* -1. [word, style] that is typical of literature rather than spoken language, especially because it is more imaginative or expressive than is usual □ *He uses a lot of highly literary vocabulary.* -2. [criticism, prize, merit] that is connected with literature.

literate ['lɪtərət] *adj* -1. [person] who can read and write. -2. [person, class, audience] who has had a good education □ *The book is aimed at a highly literate public.*

literature ['lɪtərətʃəʳ] *n* -1. [of a culture] pieces of writing, e.g. novels, poems, and plays; all the writing of this kind produced by a particular culture □ *the history of English literature* □ *a literature course.* -2. [on a subject] the books that have been written about a particular subject □ *I've read all the literature on tropical diseases.* -3. [on a product, service] printed information on a particular subject □ *Help yourself to some literature on the courses we offer.*

lithe [laɪð] *adj* [person, animal, body] that moves easily and gracefully.

lithium ['lɪθɪəm] *n* a soft, light, silver-white metal that is used in batteries and some drugs. SYMBOL: Li.

lithograph [US 'lɪθəgræf, GB 'lɪθəʊgrɑːf] *n* a print made from a stone or plate whose surface has been covered with ink □ *a signed lithograph by Picasso.*

lithography [lɪ'θɒgrəfɪ] *n* the technique of making lithographs.

Lithuania [ˌlɪθjʊ'eɪnjə] a country in northeastern Europe, on the Baltic Sea. SIZE: 65,000 sq kms. POPULATION: 3,800,000 (*Lithuanians*). CAPITAL: Vilnius. LANGUAGE: Lithuanian. CURRENCY: lit.

litigant ['lɪtɪgənt] *n* one of the two sides in a lawsuit in a civil court of law (formal use).

litigate ['lɪtɪgeɪt] *vi* to be involved in making or defending a case in a civil court of law (formal use).

litigation [ˌlɪtɪ'geɪʃn] *n* the process of settling a lawsuit in a civil court of law.

litmus paper ['lɪtməs-] *n* a special kind of paper that turns red when it is placed in an acid and blue when it is placed in an alkali.

litre *n* GB = **liter**.

litter ['lɪtəʳ] ◇ *n* -1. [on the ground] empty bottles, pieces of paper etc that people no longer want and have dropped or left in a public place or outdoors □ *'Do not drop litter.'* □ *There was a pile of litter on the sidewalk outside.* -2. [of animals] a group of baby animals that have the same mother and were born at the same time □ *a litter of puppies.* -3. **(cat) litter** a substance made up of granules, e.g. of sand, that is placed in a litter tray in order to absorb the urine and excrement of a cat. ◇ *vt* [ground, room] to cover <a place> with litter □ *After the concert, the park was littered with cans and programs.*

litter basket US, **litterbin** ['lɪtə^rbɪn] GB *n* a container for litter in a public place.

litterbug ['lɪtə^rbʌg] US, **litterlout** ['lɪtə^rlaʊt] GB *n* a person who drops or leaves litter in public places (disapproving use).

litter tray *n* a flat container with a layer of sand, sawdust etc in it where a pet animal, especially a cat, can leave its urine and excrement.

little ['lɪtl] (*compar* **less**, *superl* **least**) ◇ *adj* **-1.** [table, car, village] that is not big □ *She had little hands and feet.* □ *He had left a little pile of coins on the table.* **-2.** a word used about somebody or something small to show approval or disapproval □ *They have this sweet little house.* □ *What a horrid little man!* **-3.** [boy, girl] who is aged about ten years or less □ *When I was little I was terrified of dogs.* **-4. one's little brother/sister** the brother/sister who is younger than one, and who is still a child. **-5.** [walk, chat, while] that is short in time or distance □ *He was still a little way off.* □ *Let's go for a little drive in the car.*
◇ *det* **little time/food** a very small amount of time/food □ *He speaks very little English.* □ *There is little doubt who is to blame.*
◇ *pron* a very small amount □ *I see so little of you now.* □ *Little is known about his childhood.*
◇ *adv* **-1.** not much □ *He's little more than a child.* **-2.** not often □ *I go out very little now.*

◆ **a little** ◇ *det* **a little time/food** a small amount of time/food □ *I'll have a little more coffee, please.* □ *He speaks a little English.*
◇ *pron* a small amount □ *"More wine?" — "Just a little, thanks."* □ *There's a little (bit) left if you want it.* ◇ *adv* **a little tired/bored** slightly tired/bored □ *I was a little annoyed by what she said.* □ *It's improved a little, but not much.*

◆ **little by little** *adv* gradually □ *Little by little his eyesight grew worse.* □ *I discovered, little by little, what it was that had happened.*

Little Bighorn [-'bɪghɔː^rn]: **the Little Bighorn** a river in Montana where the US army, led by General Custer, was defeated by Native Americans.

little finger *n* the smallest finger on one's hand.

little-known *adj* [author, place] that many people do not know about □ *It's a little-known fact that...*

Little League *n* in the USA, a baseball league for children.

Little Orphan Annie [-'ænɪ] a character in American children's comics who is always getting into trouble.

Little Red Riding Hood a character in a fairy tale. She is a young girl who is eaten by a wolf disguised as her grandmother.

liturgy ['lɪtədʒɪ] (*pl* **liturgies**) *n* the fixed words and forms of a Christian religious service.

live¹ [lɪv] ◇ *vi* **-1.** to be alive □ *Mozart lived in the 18th century.* □ *Her parents are still living.* **-2.** to continue to be alive □ *Nobody knows whether he will live or not.* **-3.** to have one's home in a particular place □ *I live in Birmingham.* □ *Where do you live?* **-4.** to have a particular kind of life □ *I like living alone.* ◇ *vt* to experience <life> in a particular way □ *She's always lived a life of luxury.* □ *He lives life to the full.* ■ **to live it up** to enjoy oneself very much by eating, drinking, going to parties etc (informal use) □ *Let's go out and live it up a bit!*

◆ **live down** *vt sep* **to live sthg down** [disgrace, failure, mistake] to make people forget sthg silly or embarrassing that one has done □ *You'll never live this down!*

◆ **live for** *vt fus* **to live for sb/sthg** [for one's family, work, hobby] to have sb/sthg as the most important thing in one's life □ *She lives for her children.* □ *I've got nothing else to live for.*

◆ **live in** *vi* [cook, nanny] to live in the house where one works; [student] to live in the college where one studies □ *Are you going to live in with the family/live in in your final year?*

◆ **live off** *vt fus* **-1. to live off sthg** [off one's investment, savings] to use sthg as one's main income □ *He invested the money and lived off the interest.* **-2. to live off sb/sthg** [off the land, state, one's family] to get the money one needs to live from sb/sthg □ *There are too many people living off the government.*

◆ **live on** ◇ *vt fus* **-1. to live on a sum of money** to use a sum of money to pay for the things one needs to live □ *I have to live on a part-time salary.* □ *I've got $150 to live on for the rest of the month.* **-2. to live on a particular kind of food** [on meat, vegetables] to eat only, or almost only, a particular kind of food □ *Pandas live on bamboo.* ◇ *vi* [memory, spirit] to continue to be alive or be remembered □ *Adela may have died, but her work will live on for years to come.*

◆ **live out** *vt fus* **to live out one's life** to live the rest of one's life □ *He lived out his life in a small cabin in Montana.*

◆ **live together** *vi* [two people] to live in the same house like a married couple but without being married □ *My sister and her boyfriend lived together before getting married.*

◆ **live up to** *vt fus* **to live up to sthg** [to a reputation, ideal, somebody's expectations] to be as good as sthg □ *The movie doesn't live up to what the critics have said.*

◆ **live with** *vt fus* **-1. to live with sb** [with a friend, family] to live in the same house as sb; [with a man, woman, partner] to live in the same house as sb and have a sexual relationship with them □ *His brother's been living with us for a month now.* □ *Does she live with her boyfriend?* **-2. to live with sthg** [with a situation, problem, illness] to have sthg for as long as it continues □ *I don't like the situation, but I suppose I'll just have to learn to live with it.*

live² [laɪv] ◇ *adj* **-1.** [animal] that is alive □ *He used live worms as bait.* **-2.** [coal, match] that is still burning. **-3.** [ammunition] that has not been used and is still dangerous. **-4.** ELECTRICITY [wire, cable, machine] that carries an electric current and can give one a shock. **-5.** RADIO & TV [program, coverage, commentary] that is broadcast at the same time as the event that it presents is taking place □ *the opening ceremony, brought to you live from Sydney.* **-6.** [performance, theater, recording] that involves the presentation of something as it happens, especially in front of an audience □ *A live recording will be made of the performance.* ◇ *adv* **-1.** [broadcast] at the same time as the actual performance or event being shown □ *The show is going out live to five million people.* **-2.** [perform, play] in front of an audience □ *The album was recorded live in concert.*

live-in [lɪv-] *adj* **a live-in cook/housekeeper** a cook/housekeeper who lives in the house where they work ∎ **a live-in lover** a person who lives in the same house as the person they are having a sexual relationship with.

livelihood ['laɪvlɪhʊd] *n* **one's livelihood** the way one earns the money that one needs to live □ *Fishing has always been their livelihood.* □ *500 people may lose their livelihoods because of this.*

lively ['laɪvlɪ] (*compar* **livelier**, *superl* **liveliest**) *adj* **-1.** [person, personality] who is happy, enthusiastic, and full of energy. **-2.** [time, party, debate] that is exciting and enjoyable. **-3.** [mind, spirit] that is active and intelligent □ *She takes a lively interest in current affairs.* **-4.** [color] that is strong and bright.

liven ['laɪvn] ◆ **liven up** ◇ *vt sep* **to liven sthg up** [atmosphere, place, party] to make sthg more interesting and exciting □ *This office needs livening up.* □ *Let's put on some music to liven things up.* ◇ *vi* **-1.** [atmosphere, place, party] to become more interesting and exciting □ *Things livened up toward the end of the evening.* **-2.** [person] to become more cheerful and energetic □ *When I mentioned his name she livened up immediately.*

liver ['lɪvər] *n* **-1.** the large organ in the body that cleans the blood □ *liver disease/failure* □ *a liver transplant.* **-2.** the liver of an animal, e.g. a lamb or pig, cooked as food □ *fried liver* □ *chicken liver pâté.*

Liverpool ['lɪvəpuːl] a port and industrial city in northwestern England. POPULATION: 448,300.

Liverpudlian [,lɪvər'pʌdlɪən] ◇ *n* a person who lives in or comes from Liverpool. ◇ *adj*: *a Liverpudlian accent.*

liverwurst ['lɪvərwɜːrst] US, **liver sausage** GB *n* a kind of sausage that is made from liver.

livery ['lɪvərɪ] (*pl* **liveries**) *n* the uniform of a servant or somebody who works in a hotel.

lives [laɪvz] *plural of* **life**.

livestock ['laɪvstɒk] *n* a collective term for all the animals kept on a farm for breeding or to produce meat, milk, wool etc.

live wire [,laɪv-] *n* an energetic and enthusiastic person (informal use).

livid ['lɪvəd] *adj* **-1.** [person] who is very angry (informal use) □ *When I heard, I was absolutely livid.* **-2.** [bruise, skin] that has a dark color between purple and dark blue.

living ['lɪvɪŋ] ◇ *adj* **-1.** [relative, organism] that is alive □ *He is this country's greatest living artist.* **-2.** [language] that is still spoken. ◇ *n* **-1.** [from working] the money one earns from working □ *What do you do for a living?* □ *He makes a good living as a management consultant.*

-2. a way of life □ *Country living isn't my idea of fun.*

living conditions *npl* the conditions in which a person lives □ *We were shocked at the poor living conditions of these people.*

living expenses *npl* the money a person needs for the basic things in life, especially food and accommodation.

living room *n* the room in a home that usually has comfortable seats, a television etc, so that people can sit and relax there.

living standards *npl* the level of comfort a person has in their life □ *She's used to relatively high living standards.*

Livingstone ['lɪvɪŋstoʊn], **Dr David** a British missionary and explorer. He was the first European to discover the Zambezi River, Victoria Falls, and Lake Malawi.

living wage *n* a wage that is enough to pay for the things one needs to live, e.g. food, clothes, and housing.

living will *n* a set of instructions about the medical treatment one would like to be given at the end of one's life if one has become too ill to express such decisions.

lizard ['lɪzərd] *n* a reptile with four short legs and a long tail.

llama ['lɑːmə] (*pl* **llama** OR **llamas**) *n* a South American animal like a small camel without a hump, with long thick hair.

LLB (*abbr of* **Bachelor of Laws**) *n* a degree in law; a person who has this degree.

LLD (*abbr of* **Doctor of Laws**) *n* a postgraduate degree in law; a person who has this degree.

Lloyd George [lɔɪd-], **David** (1863–1945) British Prime Minister from 1916 to 1922.

LMT (*abbr of* **Local Mean Time**) *n* the local time at a particular place in the USA.

lo [loʊ] *excl* **lo and behold** a phrase used to show that something that one is going to describe was very surprising (humorous use) □ *We were just talking about Tim when lo and behold he appeared.*

load [loʊd] ◇ *n* **-1.** [of bricks] something that is carried, especially something heavy □ *a load of bricks/sand/shopping.* **-2.** [of work] an amount of work, especially a large amount □ *My work load is very heavy at the moment.* **-3.** **a load of sthg, loads of sthg** [of money, people, work] a lot of sthg (informal use) □ *"Have you any tapes?" — "Not with me, but I've got loads at home."* □ *He had a whole load of books on his bike.* □ *What a complete load of crap that movie was!* ◇ *vt* **-1.** [truck, car, ship] to put things into <a vehicle> especially in order to take them somewhere; [luggage, boxes, goods] to put <sthg> into a vehicle □ *We loaded the van with boxes.* □ *We loaded everything into the car.* **-2.** [rifle, revolver, cannon] to put ammunition into <a gun> □ *The gun was loaded with blanks.* **-3.** PHOTOGRAPHY to put a film in <a camera>. **-4.** [video, film] to put <sthg> into a machine. **-5.** COMPUTING to start <a program>. ◆ **load up** ◇ *vt sep* **to load sthg up** [vehicle, luggage, goods] to load sthg □ *Once everything's loaded up, we can get going.* ◇ *vi*: *It took ages to load up.*

loaded ['ləʊdəd] *adj* **-1.** [question] that is asked in a way which suggests a particular answer. **-2.** [gun] that contains bullets; [camera] that contains a film. **-3. to be loaded** [person] to be rich (informal use).

loading bay ['ləʊdɪŋ-] *n* a place near a store, factory etc where trucks can be parked and loaded.

loaf [ləʊf] (*pl* **loaves**) *n* bread that has been baked in one piece and is usually cut into slices and eaten □ *a loaf of wholewheat bread.*

◆ **loaf around, loaf about** *vi* to spend a lot of time being lazy and not doing anything useful (informal use).

loafer ['ləʊfəʳ] *n* a light shoe without laces.

loam [ləʊm] *n* a kind of soil that contains a lot of dead plants and is good for growing plants.

loan [ləʊn] ◇ *n* **-1.** [from a bank] something, especially money, that one borrows from somebody □ *We had to take out a loan to build the extension.* **-2.** [of money, an object] the action of lending something □ *Thanks for the loan of your car.* ■ **on loan** lent by a person or organization □ *The picture is on loan from the Metropolitan Museum.* ◇ *vt* [money, car, camera] to lend <sthg> □ *She loaned her car to a friend for the weekend.* □ *Can you loan me $10?*

loan account *n* a special bank account into which money is paid by a customer in order to repay a sum borrowed from the bank.

loan capital *n* money that is part of a company's capital and has been borrowed from somewhere else.

loan shark *n* a person who lends money at very high interest rates (informal and disapproving use).

loath [ləʊθ] *adj* **to be loath to do sthg** not to want to do sthg □ *I'm very loath to admit it.*

loathe [ləʊð] *vt* [person, activity, habit] to hate <sb/sthg> □ *I really loathe ironing.*

loathing ['ləʊðɪŋ] *n* hatred.

loathsome ['ləʊðsəm] *adj* [person, appearance, habit] that one finds extremely unpleasant.

loaves [ləʊvz] *plural of* **loaf**.

lob [lɒb] (*pt* & *pp* **lobbed**, *cont* **lobbing**) ◇ *vt* **-1.** to throw <sthg> high in the air □ *I lobbed the apples over the fence to him.* **-2.** SPORT to throw, hit, or kick <a ball> high in the air so that it passes over one's opponent without them being able to reach it. ◇ *n* SPORT the act of lobbing a ball into the air, e.g. in tennis or soccer, so that an opponent cannot reach it.

lobby ['lɒbɪ] (*pl* **lobbies**, *pt* & *pp* **lobbied**) ◇ *n* **-1.** [of a hotel] the entrance hall of a hotel or other large building. **-2.** POLITICS a group of people who try to persuade politicians to help their interests □ *America's gun lobby.* ◇ *vt* [politician, parliament] to try to persuade <sb> to support one's cause □ *They've been lobbying Congress for a change in the law.*

lobbyist ['lɒbɪəst] *n* a person whose job is to lobby politicians on behalf of a particular group or organization.

lobe [ləʊb] *n* ANATOMY **-1.** the soft round part at the bottom of the ear. **-2.** one of the parts that a body organ, such as the brain, is divided into.

lobelia [ləʊˈbiːljə] *n* a garden plant with very small blue, pink, or white flowers.

lobotomy [ləʊˈbɒtəmɪ] (*pl* **lobotomies**) *n* an operation in which a cut is made in the front part of the brain, to treat somebody with very serious mental problems.

lobster ['lɒbstəʳ] *n* an animal that lives in the sea and has a shell, two large claws, and eight legs; the meat of this animal boiled and eaten as food □ *lobster Thermidor.*

lobster pot *n* a container used for catching lobsters.

local ['ləʊkl] ◇ *adj* [resident, amenity, store] that belongs to or is in a particular area, especially the area where one lives □ *The local population has increased dramatically.* □ *our local delivery man* □ *The local gym is really very good.* ◇ *n* **-1.** [of a town, neighborhood] a person who lives in a particular area, especially one who has lived there for a long time □ *There have been several complaints from locals.* **-2.** US a bus or train that stops at all stopping places. **-3.** GB **one's local** the bar, pub etc that is nearest one's house and that one goes to regularly (informal use).

local anesthetic *n* an anesthetic that stops one feeling anything in a particular part of the body and that does not make one unconscious.

NOTE: Compare **general anesthetic**.

local area network *n* a system of computer terminals that are linked together in one building.

local authority *n* GB the group of people whose job is to govern a small area such as a city or county.

local call *n* a telephone call to somebody in the same city, town etc and with the same area code □ *Local calls are free from this hotel.*

local color *n* the people and things, e.g. clothes and traditions, that make a particular place different, attractive, and exciting □ *The book was full of local color.*

locale [US ləʊˈkæl, GB -ˈkɑːl] *n* the place where something happens (formal use).

local government *n* the government of an area such as a city or county □ *local government officials/finance.*

locality [ləʊˈkælətɪ] (*pl* **localities**) *n* a small area of a city or region.

localized, -ised ['ləʊkəlaɪzd] *adj* [infection, damage, outbreak] that is limited to one particular place or area.

locally ['ləʊkəlɪ] *adv* **-1.** [decide, organize] at a local rather than a national level □ *Decisions regarding planning permission are made locally.* **-2.** [live, work] close to where one lives or works □ *I always try to shop locally.*

local time *n* the time in a particular part of

the world □ *We will be arriving in Venice at 11:30 local time.*

locate [US 'loʊkeɪt, GB loʊ'keɪt] ◇ *vt* **-1.** [person, problem, position] to find <sb/sthg> □ *We have located the source of the problem.* **-2. to be located in a place** [business, office] to be in a particular place □ *The store is ideally located for the commuter trade.* ◇ *vi* to move to a particular place to live or start a business □ *The company located in Boston.*

location [loʊ'keɪʃn] *n* **-1.** [of a business, office] the place where something happens or is done □ *We've found a suitable location for our new supermarket.* **-2.** [of a person, ship] the place where somebody or something is at a particular time □ *Officer Newman, can you give me your location?* **-3.** CINEMA **on location** in a place that is not part of a studio □ *The movie was shot on location in Vienna.*

loc. cit. (*abbr of* **loco citato**) a phrase used in a piece of writing to refer to a passage that has already been quoted.

loch [lɒk] *n* in Scotland, a lake.

Loch Lomond [-'loʊmənd] a lake in western Scotland, north of Glasgow.

Loch Ness Monster [-nes-] **the Loch Ness Monster** a large animal like a snake that is supposed to live in Loch Ness, a lake in Scotland.

lock [lɒk] ◇ *n* **-1.** [of a door] a device that is fixed to something, e.g. a door, lid, or chain, that closes it when a key is used in it, and can only be opened again by that key □ *The key won't turn in the lock.* ■ **to be under lock and key** to be kept somewhere that is closed with a lock □ *The documents are usually kept under lock and key in the bank.* **-2.** [on a canal] a series of gates at a point in a canal, used to raise or lower boats to a different level. **-3.** AUTO the extent to which the wheels of a car can be turned. **-4.** [of hair] a small piece of hair that has been cut from somebody's head (literary use). **-5.** *phrase* **lock, stock, and barrel** completely □ *He bought the company lock, stock, and barrel.*
◇ *vt* **-1.** [door, suitcase] to close <sthg> with a key □ *That room is usually kept locked.* **-2.** [document, valuables] to put <sthg> in a particular place and lock it □ *She locked her jewels in the safe.* **-3.** [wheels, steering, gears] to cause <a device> to be unable to move. **-4. to be locked in an embrace** [lovers, friends] to be holding each other in a long embrace. ■ **to be locked in combat** [opponents] to be fighting each other very hard.
◇ *vi* **-1.** [door, chain, lid] *The door locked behind him.* **-2.** [wheels, gears, steering] to become unable to move.

◆ **locks** *npl* the hair on one's head (literary use).

◆ **lock in** *vt sep* **to lock sb in** to keep sb in a room, house etc with the door locked so that they cannot get out □ *I tried the door and found I was locked in.* □ *He locked himself in.*

◆ **lock out** *vt sep* **-1. to lock sb out** to accidentally stop sb from getting into a building, especially into their own house, by locking

the door □ *I locked myself out last night.* **-2. to lock sb out** to deliberately stop sb from getting into a building by locking the door □ *The staff were locked out of the factory.*

◆ **lock up** ◇ *vt sep* **-1. to lock sb up** to put sb in prison or in a psychiatric hospital □ *People like that ought to be locked up!* **-2. to lock sthg up** [house, car] to lock all the doors and windows of sthg. **-3. to lock sthg up** [object, valuables] to put sthg in a container and lock it □ *She locked the documents up in the safe.* ◇ *vi* to lock all the doors and windows of a building or vehicle □ *Don't forget to lock up when you've finished.*

lockable ['lɒkəbl] *adj* [door, case, drawer] that can be locked.

Locke [lɒk], **John** (1632–1704) a British philosopher who influenced the French and American Revolutions.

locker ['lɒkər] *n* a metal closet, e.g. in a school, changing room, or at a station, where one can keep one's clothes, bag etc for a short time.

locker room *n* a room at a swimming pool, sports club etc where there are lockers and where people get changed or have a shower.

locket ['lɒkət] *n* a piece of jewelry on a chain that goes around one's neck and often contains a small picture of somebody.

lockjaw ['lɒkdʒɔː] *n* = **tetanus**.

lockout ['lɒkaʊt] *n* the closing of a place where people work by employers to try to make workers accept particular conditions.

locksmith ['lɒksmɪθ] *n* a person whose job is to make and repair locks.

lockup ['lɒkʌp] *n* (informal use) **-1.** [for prisoners] a jail; a cell. **-2.** GB [for a car] a garage that is not attached to a house and that one can rent to keep one's car in.

loco ['loʊkoʊ] (*pl* **locos**) *adj* US crazy (informal use). ◇ *n* GB = **locomotive**.

locomotive [,loʊkə'moʊtɪv] *n* the part of a train that pulls the cars.

locum ['loʊkəm] (*pl* **locums**) *n* GB a doctor who does another doctor's work while they are away.

locust ['loʊkəst] *n* a large insect that flies in very big groups and causes damage to crops, especially in hot countries □ *a swarm of locusts.*

lodge [lɒdʒ] ◇ *n* **-1.** [on vacation] a hut or small house where people stay on vacation, e.g. to go hunting or skiing. **-2.** [of a large house] a small house at the entrance to the grounds of a large house. **-3.** [of freemasons] a local branch of an organization, especially of freemasons. **-4.** GB [of a college] a room at the entrance of a college used by a porter or caretaker.
◇ *vi* **-1.** to rent a room in somebody's house □ *I'm lodging with an old couple till I find somewhere more permanent.* **-2.** [bullet, bone] to become stuck □ *A fishbone lodged in her throat.* **-3.** [idea, fact] to stay in one's mind so that

one remembers it □ *That date became lodged in her brain.*

◊ *vt* **to lodge a complaint/appeal** to make an official complaint/appeal (formal use).

lodger ['lɒdʒər] *n* a person who lives in a rented room in somebody else's house.

lodging ['lɒdʒɪŋ] *n* → **board.**

◆ **lodgings** *npl* a room or rooms that one rents in somebody else's house □ *He's staying in lodgings near the park.*

loft [lɒft] *n* -1. a large floor of a commercial building that is not divided into rooms and is used as an apartment. -2. the space under the roof of a house.

lofty ['lɒftɪ] (*compar* **loftier,** *superl* **loftiest**) *adj* -1. [ideal, aim, feeling] that is noble and deserves to be admired. -2. [manner, attitude] that shows a feeling of superiority over other people (disapproving use). -3. [peak, tower] high (literary use).

log [lɒg] (*pt* & *pp* **logged,** *cont* **logging**) ◊ *n* -1. [of wood] a piece of a tree trunk or thick branch □ *Put another log on the fire.* -2. [of a ship, plane] the written record of the journey of a ship, plane etc. ◊ *vt* -1. [captain, pilot] to write <information> in a log. -2. COMPUTING to enter <data> in a computer. -3. [ship, plane] to travel <a particular distance or length of time>; to move at <a particular speed>.

◆ **log in, log on** *vi* to type a code, password etc to be able to start using a computer.

◆ **log off, log out** *vi* to type a code, password etc to finish using a computer.

loganberry [US 'lougənberɪ, GB -bərɪ] (*pl* **loganberries**) *n* a soft purple fruit like a raspberry.

logarithm ['lɒgərɪðəm] *n* a number that represents another number and can be used to make multiplication easier.

logbook ['lɒgbʊk] *n* -1. [of a ship] the written record of the journey of a ship, plane etc. -2. [of a car] a book that contains the details of a particular car.

log cabin *n* a simple house or shelter built of logs.

log fire *n* a fire in which logs are burning.

loggerheads ['lɒgəhedz] *n* **to be at loggerheads** to be disagreeing strongly □ *The manager is at loggerheads with the owner.*

logic ['lɒdʒɪk] *n* -1. a clear way of reasoning that uses statement that follow on from each other, with each one being true □ *Their arguments are based on sound logic.* -2. a particular set of reasons □ *I don't follow your logic.*

logical ['lɒdʒɪkl] *adj* -1. [deduction, thinking, person] that uses logic □ *It doesn't seem like a very logical decision.* -2. [plan, idea, course of action] that is reasonable and sensible and therefore obvious □ *It's the logical thing to do.*

logically ['lɒdʒɪklɪ] *adv* -1. a word used to say that something is the logical result of another thing □ *Logically, there was only one course of action open to us.* -2. [deduce, act, conclude] *see* **logical.**

logistical [lə'dʒɪstɪkl] *adj* [problem] that concerns the planning or organization of diffi-

cult or complicated matters □ *It's a logistical nightmare.*

logistics [lə'dʒɪstɪks] *n* the planning or organization of something difficult or complicated □ *The team is grappling with the logistics of getting medical aid to the stricken area.*

logjam ['lɒgdʒæm] *n* a difficulty that prevents a person, organization, or project from continuing in a particular activity.

logo ['lougou] (*pl* **logos**) *n* a small picture or symbol that represents a company or organization and often uses part of its name.

logrolling ['lɒgroulɪŋ] *n* US the practice, especially among politicians, of agreeing to help or support somebody so that they will later help and support one.

logy ['lougɪ] *adj* US [person] who does not feel very active or energetic.

loin [lɒɪn] *n* [of pork, lamb] a piece of meat from the back of an animal or the area near its tail □ *a loin chop.*

◆ **loins** *npl* the area of the body around one's sexual organs. ■ **to gird one's loins** to prepare oneself for an energetic or dangerous activity (humorous use).

loincloth ['lɒɪnklɒθ] *n* a piece of cloth worn over the loins, with no other clothing, usually by men in hot countries.

Loire [lwɑːr]: **the Loire** the longest river in France. The Loire valley is famous for its wines and castles.

loiter ['lɒɪtər] *vi* -1. to stay somewhere doing nothing, for no obvious reason □ *'No loitering.'* -2. to take more time going somewhere than is necessary.

Lolita [lou'liːtə] a character in the novel *Lolita* by Vladimir Nabokov. She is a sexually attractive teenage girl who the main character, a midde-aged man, becomes obsessed with.

loll [lɒl] *vi* -1. [person] to sit or lie in a very relaxed way □ *He spent all afternoon lolling about on the sofa.* -2. [head, tongue] to hang down loosely.

lollipop ['lɒlɪpɒp] *n* a hard round candy on the end of a small stick.

lolly ['lɒlɪ] (*pl* **lollies**) *n* GB -1. a lollipop. -2. = **ice lolly.** -3. money (informal use).

London ['lʌndən] the capital of the United Kingdom, in southeastern England, and its largest city. POPULATION: 6,378,600.

London ['lʌndən], **Jack** (1876–1916) a US writer whose most important work is *Call of the Wild.*

Londonderry ['lʌndənderɪ] a city and port on the north coast of Northern Ireland. POPULATION: 88,000.

Londoner ['lʌndənər] *n* a person who comes from or lives in London.

lone [loun] *adj* **a lone figure/tree etc** a figure/tree etc that is the only one in a place □ *A lone walker appeared on the beach.*

loneliness ['lounlɪnəs] *n* [of a person, time, place] *see* **lonely.**

lonely ['lounlɪ] (*compar* **lonelier,** *superl* **loneliest**) *adj* -1. [person] who is unhappy because they are alone; who is unhappy because they have no friends □ *At first I felt very lonely.* **-2.** [time, childhood] during which one feels lonely □ *I spent a long, lonely night waiting for them to return.* **-3.** [place] that very few people visit □ *a dark, lonely house.*

lone parent *n* GB a single parent.

loner ['lounər] *n* a person who prefers to be alone.

lonesome ['lounsəm] *adj* [person, place] = **lonely**.

long [lɒŋ] ◇ *adj* **-1.** [journey, wait, marriage, career] that continues for a greater than average amount of time □ *It took a long time to cook the turkey.* □ *There was a long silence while everyone waited for me to speak.* ■ **to have a long memory** to be able to remember things from the distant past. **-2.** [hair, grass, chapter] that is a greater than average length or distance □ *We all sat around a long table.* □ *It's a long way from here.* **-3.** used to show amounts of time or distance □ *How long is the movie?* □ *The lake is about 12 miles long.* **-4.** [period of time] that seems to pass slowly because it involves too much effort, worry, pain etc □ *Let's get to bed, it's been a long day.* □ *the long months of anxious waiting that followed.*
◇ *adv* **-1.** [last, take, stay] (for) a great amount of time □ *The meeting went on too long.* □ *Will they be away long?* **-2.** used in questions about length of time □ *How much longer will you be?* **-3.** *phrases* **no longer** not any more □ *You're no longer welcome here.* □ *I can't listen to this any longer.* ■ **so long!** goodbye! (informal use).
◇ *n* **the long and the short of it is that...** a phrase used to quickly explain the main fact or result of a situation, especially a bad one □ *The long and the short of it is that it's going to cost $700 to repair the damage.*
◇ *vt* **to long to do sthg** to want to do sthg very much □ *I longed to tell them the truth.* □ *He's longing to hear from you.*
♦ **as long as, so long as** *conj* provided that □ *As long as you're happy I don't care what you do.* □ *As long as you do exactly what I told you to, everything will be fine.*
♦ **before long** *adv* soon □ *He'll get bored before long, you'll see.* □ *Before long the room was full.*
♦ **for long** *adv* for a great amount of time □ *She wasn't gone for very long.* □ *I can't wait for much longer.*
♦ **long for** *vt fus* **to long for sthg** [for a chance, vacation, cigarette] to want sthg very much □ *Jon's always longed for a family.* □ *We were all longing for him to leave.*

long. *abbr of* **longitude.**

long-awaited [-ə'weɪtəd] *adj* [day, decision] that one has been waiting for for a long time.

long-distance *adj* [runner, race, truck driver] that covers a long distance □ *long-distance trips.*

long-distance call *n* a telephone call between people who are far apart.

long division *n* a method of dividing one number by another in which each stage is written below the numbers.

long-drawn-out *adj* [process, explanation] that lasts much longer than necessary □ *After long-drawn-out negotiations they finally reached an agreement.*

long drink *n* a drink in a tall glass that contains little or no alcohol.

longevity [lɒn'dʒevətɪ] *n* long life.

Longfellow ['lɒŋfelou], **Henry Wadsworth** (1807–1882) a US poet known for his long narrative poems. His work includes *Miles Standish* and *The Song of Hiawatha.*

longhaired [,lɒŋ'heəʳd] *adj* [person, animal] that has long hair.

longhand ['lɒŋhænd] *n* writing that is written by hand using complete words and sentences.

long-haul *adj* **a long-haul flight** a flight that covers a long distance, usually between continents.

longing ['lɒŋɪŋ] ◇ *adj* **a longing look** a look that shows one wants somebody or something very much. ◇ *n* a feeling one has when one wants something very much over a period of time □ *She has a deep longing for freedom.* □ *He looked with longing at the cakes.*

longingly ['lɒŋɪŋlɪ] *adv* [look, think] *see* **longing.**

Long Island an island in the Atlantic Ocean, off the coast of New York State, USA. It includes the boroughs of Brooklyn and Queens.

longitude ['lɒndʒətʲuːd] *n* a position on the Earth, or on a map, measured in degrees east or west of a line from the North Pole to the South Pole and passing through Greenwich in London.
NOTE: Compare **latitude.**

long johns *npl* underpants with long legs that one wears to keep warm.

long jump *n* an athletics contest in which people run up to a fixed point and then jump forward as far as possible.

long-lasting *adj* [effect, material] that lasts for a long time □ *These roses have beautiful long-lasting flowers.*

long-life *adj* [milk, battery] that can be used for a longer time than the ordinary type.

long-lost *adj* [relative, object] that one has not seen for a long time □ *He greeted her as if she was his long-lost sister.*

long-playing record [-'pleɪɪŋ-] *n* → **LP.**

long-range *adj* **-1.** [missile, bomber] that can reach a target that is far away. **-2.** [plan, forecast] that covers a long period of time in the future.

long-running *adj* [program, show, dispute] that has existed for a long time □ *a long-running battle for supremacy.*

long-service leave *n* AUS a period of time that somebody is allowed to spend away from work if they have worked at the same place for several years.

longshoreman ['lɒŋʃɔːʳmən] (*pl* **longshoremen** [-mən]) *n* US a person whose job is to load and unload ships at a dock.

long shot *n* something that somebody does that has very little chance of success □ *Look, it's a long shot, but we might as well try it.*

longsighted [ˌlɒŋˈsaɪtəd] *adj* -1. [person] who cannot see things clearly that are very near. -2. [person] who can see and be ready for future problems, needs etc.

long-standing *adj* [disagreement, treaty] that has existed for a long time □ *We have a long-standing arrangement with the suppliers.*

longsuffering [ˌlɒŋˈsʌfərɪŋ] *adj* [person] who patiently accepts pain, difficulties, or bad treatment □ *I'd like to thank my longsuffering family for all their support.*

long term *n* **in the long term** in the future that is not soon □ *It looks like a good strategy, but will it work in the long term?*

◆ **long-term** *adj* [solution, effect] that lasts for a long time; [plan] that will take effect in the long term □ *I think you need to consider the long-term implications of what you're doing.* □ *Have you any long-term plans?*

long vacation *n* the summer vacation, when schools and universities are closed.

long wave *n* a range of radio waves that are more than 1,000 meters long □ *They used to broadcast on long wave only.*
NOTE: Compare **medium wave**, **short wave**.

longways [ˈlɒŋweɪz] *adv* = **lengthways**.

longwearing [ˌlɒŋˈweərɪŋ] *adj* US [material, piece of clothing] that lasts for a long time, even when used a lot.

long weekend *n* a weekend when one does not work the Friday before or the Monday after.

longwinded [ˌlɒŋˈwɪndəd] *adj* [person, speech] that takes too long to say something and uses more words than necessary.

loo [luː] (*pl* **loos**) *n* GB a toilet (informal use).

loofa(h) [ˈluːfə] *n* a long, rough, dried part of a tropical fruit, used like a sponge for washing the body.

look [lʊk] ◇ *vt* **to look one's age** to appear to be the age one actually is □ *She's not forty! Well, she certainly doesn't look her age.* ■ **to look one's best** to appear as attractive as possible □ *I want to look my best for the party.*
◇ *excl* **look (here)!** a phrase used to make the person one is talking to pay attention □ *Look what he's done now!* □ *Look, this is serious!*
◇ *n* -1. **to take** OR **have a look at sthg** to look at sthg, especially in order to check or repair it or to find out information □ *Just take a look at these latest sales figures.* □ *That's a nasty cut you have on your knee: let me have a look at it.* □ *I took one look at the car and decided I must have it.* ■ **to give sb a look** to look at sb in a way that shows what one is feeling □ *She gave me a sly/angry/reproachful look.* -2. **to have a look for sthg** to search for sthg, especially quickly □ *Would you mind having a look for my keys?* -3. [of a person] the appearance of a person or thing □ *We want to give our offices a more modern look.* □ *I don't like the look of him much.* ■ **by** OR **from the look of sthg** judging by the appearance of sthg □ *By the look of those clouds, I'd say it's going to rain.* □ *From the look of things, I don't think they've won.* -4. [of a period] a particular fashion or style of dress □ *It's the latest look.* □ *this season's hottest look.*
◇ *vi* -1. to turn one's eyes in a particular direction in order to see something □ *Don't look now, but my ex-husband has just walked in.* -2. to search □ *I've looked everywhere and I still can't find it.* -3. **to look out onto** OR **over sthg** [building, window] to have a view of sthg □ *The balcony looks out over the ocean.* -4. [person, place, object] to have a particular appearance; to make a particular impression □ *That cake looks delicious!* □ *You're looking very smart today.* □ *The house looked empty.* ■ **it looks like rain, it looks as if it's going to rain** it seems likely that it will rain □ *He looked as if he'd been drinking.* ■ **to look like sb** to have the same appearance as sb □ *She looks just like her sister.*

◆ **looks** *npl* a person's attractive appearance □ *Good looks aren't everything.* □ *Despite having had three children, Jane hadn't lost her looks.*

◆ **look after** *vt fus* -1. **to look after sb** to take care of sb who is very old, very young, or ill □ *She can't look after herself any more.* □ *He stays at home and looks after the children.* -2. **to look after sthg** [after money, a house, a garden] to be responsible for sthg □ *Mr Wells looks after our financial affairs.*

◆ **look around** ◇ *vt fus* **to look around a place** [around a house, store, town] to walk around a place looking at the different parts of it □ *I'm sick of looking around museums.* ◇ *vi* to turn around and look at something that has attracted one's attention □ *Everyone looked around when she came in.*

◆ **look at** *vt fus* -1. **to look at sb/sthg** [at a person, view, object] to turn one's head in the direction of sb/sthg in order to see it □ *Look at me when I'm talking to you!* -2. **to look at sb/sthg** [at a drawing, report, patient] to examine sb/sthg carefully □ *We're still looking at their proposal.* □ *When did you last have your teeth looked at?* -3. **to look at sthg** [at life, an idea, situation] to have a particular attitude toward sthg □ *I suppose that's one way of looking at the problem.*

◆ **look back** *vi* to think or talk about the past □ *Looking back on it, I was really immature.* □ *In tonight's program we'll be looking back over the year's events.* ■ **she's never looked back** she's been successful ever since □ *She made one film for Australian television and since then she's never looked back.*

◆ **look down on** *vt fus* **to look down on sb** to think that sb is not as good as oneself because they are poorer, less educated, or have a lower social position □ *There's no need to look down on her just because of the way she talks!*

◆ **look for** *vt fus* **to look for sb/sthg** to try to find sb/sthg that one wants or has lost □ *I'm looking for Liz/the shoe department.* □ *Police are looking for three teenagers seen at the scene of the attack.*

◆ **look forward to** *vt fus* **to look forward to sthg** [to a vacation, event] to wait with a feeling of pleasure or excitement for sthg that is going to happen □ *We're all looking forward to meeting him.* □ *I'm not looking forward to this at* all. ▢ *At least it'll give you something to look forward to.*

◆ **look into** *vt fus* **to look into a situation** [into a problem, crime] to examine a situation in order to find out more about it ▢ *Police are looking into possible causes of the accident.*

◆ **look on** ◇ *vt fus* = **look upon.** ◇ *vi* [bystander, audience, crowd] to watch something without taking part in it or trying to prevent it ▢ *Shoppers looked on in horror as fire swept through the building.*

◆ **look out** *vi* **look out!** a phrase used to warn somebody that they are in danger ▢ *Look out, there's a car coming!*

◆ **look out for** *vt fus* **to look out for sb/sthg** [for a person, new product, suspect package] to try to notice sb/sthg, especially while one is doing something else ▢ *These tomatoes will be available soon, so look out for them at your local supermarket.*

◆ **look round** *vi* = **look around.**

◆ **look through** *vt fus* **to look through sthg** [through a report, magazine, wardrobe] to examine sthg in order to find what one is searching for ▢ *I've looked through my files but I can't find the letter.*

◆ **look to** *vt fus* **to look to sb for sthg** [for help, guidance, inspiration] to expect sb to provide sthg that is needed ▢ *I've always looked to my family for support when things were going badly for me.*

◆ **look up** ◇ *vt sep* **-1. to look sthg up** [meaning, word, fact] to find out sthg by looking for it in a book ▢ *If you don't know what it means, look it up in the dictionary.* **-2. to look sb up** to visit sb when one has to go to the area where they live for another reason ▢ *Don't forget to look me up next time you're passing through Little Rock.* ◇ *vi* **things are looking up** the situation is getting better (informal use).

◆ **look upon** *vt fus* **to look upon sb/sthg** to think of sb/sthg in a particular way ▢ *I've always looked upon my home as an investment.*

◆ **look up to** *vt fus* **to look up to sb** to feel admiration and respect for sb ▢ *I always looked up to him because he was my big brother.*

look-alike *n* a person who looks like somebody else in particular ▢ *a Bill Clinton lookalike.*

look-in *n* **to get a look-in** to get a chance to do something that somebody else is doing ▢ *She talks so much that I never usually get a look-in.*

lookout ['lʊkaʊt] *n* **-1.** a place, usually high up, where somebody can look out, e.g. for an enemy approaching; a person who looks out, e.g. for an enemy approaching ▢ *She asked me to act as lookout in case they arrived early.* **-2. to be on the lookout for sb/sthg** [for a job, opportunity, criminal] to be looking for sb/sthg ▢ *We're always on the lookout for people with new ideas.* ▢ *Keep a lookout for the new version of the software.*

look-up table *n* a table of the results of particular calculations that is stored in a computer's memory so that one can find it

quickly without the need to calculate a result each time.

loom [luːm] ◇ *n* a machine that is used to make cloth by weaving threads together. ◇ *vi* **-1.** [building, figure] to appear in a way that is frightening or impressive, by being tall and difficult to see clearly ▢ *The mountains loomed high above the city.* **-2.** [threat, prospect, crisis] to seem likely to come soon; [date, day] to become more threatening as the time comes closer ▢ *As the deadline loomed closer, everyone began to panic.* **-3. to loom large** [factor, problem, idea] to be or become important ▢ *It's a question that looms large in everyone's minds right now.*

◆ **loom up** *vi* [building, figure] = **loom.**

looming ['luːmɪŋ] *adj* **a looming threat/crisis etc** a threat/crisis etc that seems likely to happen soon.

loony ['luːnɪ] (*compar* **loonier,** *superl* **looniest,** *pl* **loonies**)(informal use) ◇ *adj* [person, act, idea] crazy. ◇ *n* a crazy person.

loop [luːp] ◇ *n* **-1.** [of string, wire] a curved shape, especially a complete circle, formed in something long, e.g. a line or a piece of string. **-2.** MEDICINE a contraceptive device shaped like a loop that is used inside the womb. **-3.** COMPUTING a set of instructions in a program that are repeated a number of times. ◇ *vt* [string, rope] to make <sthg> into a loop ▢ *The rope was looped around his body.* ◇ *vi* [string, rope] *The road loops around to join the freeway.*

loophole ['luːphoʊl] *n* a mistake in the way a law or regulation has been designed or put into words that allows people to avoid obeying it.

loose [luːs] ◇ *adj* **-1.** [tooth, wire] that is not completely attached to something; [knot, bow] that can be undone easily ▢ *The door handle had come loose.* **-2.** [stamps, candy, nails] that is not sold together in bags, packets etc in fixed amounts, so that customers can decide how many or how much to buy ▢ *Do you sell apples loose or just in packs?* **-3.** [jacket, shirt] that does not feel tight when it is worn ▢ *These shoes are too loose.* **-4.** [animal] that is free and is not tied by a rope, kept in a cage etc ▢ *He let the dog loose as they entered the park.* **-5.** [hair] that is allowed to hang down and is not held in a fixed position on the head ▢ *She usually wears her hair loose.* **-6.** [woman] who has many sexual partners; [living, morals] that does not follow what society considers acceptable in sexual behavior (disapproving and old-fashioned use). **-7.** [translation, definition] that gives the general meaning of something but is not precise ▢ *a loose approximation of the truth.* **-8.** [association, structure] that is not very strictly controlled ▢ *We made a very loose arrangement to meet tonight.* **-9. to stay** OR **hang loose** to stay calm and relaxed (informal use) ▢ *Just hang loose and everything will be OK.*

◇ *n* **on the loose** [prisoner, wild animal] that is free and has escaped from somebody or somewhere □ *A convicted murderer is on the loose in downtown Detroit.*

loose change *n* money in the form of coins that somebody has in their pocket, purse etc.

loose end *n* part of a story or situation, e.g. a novel, movie, or police investigation, that has not been explained. ▪ **to tie up the loose ends** to deal with the last parts of something, so that it is complete. ▪ **to be at loose ends** US, **to be at a loose end** GB to have nothing to do.

loose-fitting *adj* [jacket, shirt] = **loose**.

loose-leaf binder *n* a hard cover containing pages that can be removed and replaced.

loosely [ˈluːslɪ] *adv* [connect, tie, translate] *see* **loose** □ *Loosely translated, that means "no!"*

loosen [ˈluːsn] ◇ *vt* [knot, grip, screw] to make <sthg> looser. ◇ *vi* [knot, grip, screw] *One of the bolts had loosened during the flight.*

◆ **loosen up** *vi* **-1.** SPORT to exercise and stretch one's body to relax one's muscles before serious exercise or before taking part in a sport. **-2.** to relax (informal use) □ *Have a drink — it'll help you to loosen up.*

loot [luːt] ◇ *n* stolen money or goods. ◇ *vt* [house, shop, town] to steal things from <a building or place> during or after a battle or riot.

looter [ˈluːtər] *n* a person who loots a place.

looting [ˈluːtɪŋ] *n* [of a house, shop, town] *see* **loot** □ *There are reports of looting and riots.*

lop [lɒp] (*pt* & *pp* **lopped**, *cont* **lopping**) *vt* to cut some branches off <a tree>.

◆ **lop off** *vt sep* **to lop sthg off** [branch, limb] to cut sthg off the thing it is attached to.

lope [ləʊp] *vi* to run with long relaxed strides.

lop-sided [-ˈsaɪdəd] *adj* **-1.** [table, grin, posture] that has one side bigger, higher, or heavier than the other. **-2.** [account, explanation] that is not true or fair because it only gives one point of view.

lord [lɔːrd] ◇ *n* a man of high rank in the British nobility. ◇ *vt* **to lord it over sb** to behave in a superior way toward sb, especially by giving them orders.

◆ **Lord** *n* **-1. the Lord** God. ▪ **good Lord!** GB a phrase used to show that one is surprised or impressed. **-2.** a word used as a title □ *Lord Smith.* ▪ **my Lord** a form of address used to show respect to a judge, bishop, or nobleman.

◆ **Lords** *npl* = **House of Lords**.

Lord Advocate *n* **the Lord Advocate** the head of the legal system in Scotland.

Lord Chancellor *n* **the Lord Chancellor** the head of the legal system in England and Wales, who is also a government minister and is in charge of debates in the House of Lords.

Lord Chief Justice *n* **the Lord Chief Justice** the head of the Queen's Bench Division in England and Wales, and President of the Court of Appeal.

lordly [ˈlɔːrdlɪ] (*compar* **lordlier**, *superl* **lordliest**) *adj* **-1.** [behavior, feast] that is noble and im-

pressive. **-2.** [manner, gesture] that is arrogant (disapproving use).

Lord Mayor *n* a title given to the mayor of London and some other British cities.

Lords *n* a cricket ground in north London. It is the headquarters of the MCC.

Lordship [ˈlɔːrdʃɪp] *n* **your/his Lordship** a form of address used to show respect to a judge, bishop, or nobleman.

Lord's Prayer *n* **the Lord's Prayer** an important Christian prayer.

lore [lɔːr] *n* the knowledge, stories, and traditions of a particular group of people □ *ancient Celtic lore.*

lorry [ˈlɒrɪ] (*pl* **lorries**) *n* GB a large motor vehicle, used for transporting goods.

lorry driver *n* GB a person whose job is to drive trucks.

Los Angeles [lɒsˈændʒələs] a city in southern California, USA, on the Pacific Ocean. POPULATION: 3,485,398.

lose [luːz] (*pt* & *pp* **lost**) ◇ *vt* **-1.** [key, hat, wallet] not to have <sthg> any more because one cannot find it or get it □ *I've lost my umbrella again.* **-2.** [friend, job, memory] to fail to keep <sb/sthg that one had before> □ *He lost his balance and fell off the ladder.* □ *I lost contact with her.* □ *They are losing interest in the project.* □ *The plane began to lose altitude.* ▪ **to lose sight of sb/sthg** [of an enemy, vehicle, port] to no longer be able to see sb/sthg; [of an aim, ideal] to become confused and forget about sthg □ *We can't lose sight of the fact that people have been hurt.* **-3.** [friend, relative] to no longer have <sb> because they have died □ *He lost his mother last year.* **-4.** [game, contract, election] not to win <sthg> because somebody else has won it □ *We lost the contract to a German company.* □ *I think I lost my bet.* **-5.** [opportunity, time] to waste <sthg> □ *Their opponents lost no time in condemning the move.* **-6.** [money] to spend more of <sthg> than one earns □ *We lost a lot of money on that deal.* **-7. to lose time** [watch, clock] to work too slowly □ *My watch loses thirty seconds a day.* **-8.** [heat, weight] to have less of <sthg> than one had before □ *He lost about nine pounds in a week.* **-9. to lose one's way** to become lost when one is trying to go somewhere □ *I managed to lose my way in the New York subway system.* **-10.** [pursuer, police] to escape from <sb> and leave them behind or out of sight □ *If you drive faster we might be able to lose him.*

◇ *vi* [competitor, team, candidate] *England lost to Italy in the final.*

◆ **lose out** *vi* **-1.** to be unsuccessful □ *Will the Americans lose out to the Japanese in computers?* **-2.** to lose money □ *We lost out on the deal.*

loser [ˈluːzər] *n* **-1.** [of a game, competition] a person or team that has lost. ▪ **to be a good/bad loser** to accept that one has lost and remain friendly/to dislike losing and become unfriendly. **-2.** a person who never succeeds in anything (disapproving use).

losing [ˈluːzɪŋ] *adj* [team, party] that is losing or has just lost something, e.g. a game or election.

loss [lɒs] *n* **-1.** [of interest, one's purse, memory] *see* **lose** □ *Have you reported the loss to the police?* □ *He would be no great loss to the firm.* □ *The company announced losses of ten million dollars.* ■ **to make a loss** to lose money □ *We made a 10% loss on the deal.* ■ **to cut one's losses** to stop doing something that is putting one in a bad situation, in order to stop the situation from getting worse □ *We decided to cut our losses and sell the business.* **-2.** [of a relative, friend] death □ *After the loss of his wife he just wasn't the same person.* □ *Fortunately, there was no loss of life.* □ *They inflicted heavy losses on the enemy.* **-3.** [of a game, competition] a failure to win something. **-4.** [of weight, heat] a reduction in something. **-5.** *phrase* **to be at a loss** not to know what to do, think, or say □ *She was at a loss to explain why she'd done it.* □ *What can I say to thank you? I'm at a complete loss for words.*

loss adjuster [-ədʒʌstəʳ] *n* GB a person in an insurance company whose job is to calculate the value of people's claims and the amount of compensation to be paid.

loss leader *n* something sold at a very low price in order to attract customers into a store.

lost [lɒst] ◇ *past tense & past participle of* **lose**. ◇ *adj* **-1.** [person] who does not know where they are and is unable to find their way □ *I got lost on my way to their new offices.* ■ **get lost!** go away! (informal use). **-2.** [cat, wallet] that cannot be found. **-3.** [opportunity] that is wasted. ■ **to be lost on sb** [advice, warning, remark] not to be noticed or understood by sb □ *The finer points of Shakespeare are lost on my students, unfortunately.*

lost-and-found office *n* US an office where lost property is stored and can be claimed back by those who have lost it.

lost cause *n* something, e.g. a plan or idea, that has no chance of succeeding.

Lost Generation *n* **the Lost Generation** the generation of Americans between the two World Wars, especially the writers of the period, e.g. F. Scott Fitzgerald, Ernest Hemingway, and Gertrude Stein.

lost property *n* things that have been lost, usually in a public place, e.g. a railroad station □ *an item of lost property.*

lost property office *n* GB = **lost-and-found office**.

lot [lɒt] *n* **-1. a lot of sthg** a large amount of sthg □ *We've had a lot of publicity for the new series.* □ *There's not a lot of time left.* ■ **a lot of people** a large number of people □ *A lot of customers have written in to complain.* **-2.** used to refer to a group of things or people □ *Put all this lot away in the cupboard.* □ *There's another lot of guests arriving tomorrow.* **-3. the lot** the entire amount of money, objects etc □ *He won $500 and spent the lot.* □ *"Can I have some of your old furniture?" — "Take the lot."* **-4.** [at an auction] one of the objects or group of ob-

jects being sold at an auction □ *Lot 245, a fine old Victorian sideboard.* **-5.** [of land] a small piece of land that is available for sale. **-6. one's lot** the kind of life one has □ *He was anxious to improve his lot.* **-7.** *phrase* **to draw lots** to each take a piece of paper, one of which has a hidden mark on it that will decide whether one is chosen to do something or not □ *We drew lots to decide who would lead the team.*

◆ **lots** *npl* **lots of people/things** a lot of people/things (informal use) □ *I want a cake with lots of cream on it.*

◆ **a lot** ◇ *adv* **-1.** very much □ *I like her a lot.* □ *He's feeling a lot better now.* **-2.** often □ *We see each other a lot.* □ *The baby cries a lot.* ◇ *pron* a large amount □ *There's a lot we can do to help.* □ *There's not a lot I can say, really.*

loth [ləʊθ] *adj* = **loath**.

Lothario [US loʊˈθerɪoʊ, GB ləˈθɑːrɪoʊ] a man who seduces many women.

lotion [ˈləʊʃn] *n* a liquid used for cleaning, treating, or protecting the skin or hair □ *body/hand lotion.*

lottery [ˈlɒtərɪ] (*pl* **lotteries**) *n* **-1.** a competition in which many people buy tickets with numbers on them, some of the numbers are later chosen at random, and the holders of those tickets win prizes □ *I can't believe it — she's won the lottery!* **-2.** any system or situation that depends on luck □ *Getting a job is a complete lottery these days.*

Lotto™ [ˈlɒtəʊ] *n* the Australian state lottery.

lotus [ˈləʊtəs] (*pl* **lotuses**) *n* a white or pink flower with large flat leaves that grows on the surface of lakes in Asia and Africa.

lotus position *n* a yoga position in which a person sits with their legs crossed and their feet resting on their thighs.

loud [laʊd] ◇ *adj* **-1.** [voice, bang, music] that produces a high level of sound. **-2. to be loud in sthg** [in one's criticism, support] to strongly and repeatedly express sthg □ *The Democrats were loud in their condemnation of the proposed cuts.* **-3.** [color, clothes] that is too bright. **-4.** [person] who talks a lot, especially in a vulgar or offensive way (disapproving use). ◇ *adv* [shout, speak, play music] *The radio was turned up loud.* □ *Receiving you loud and clear, flight 101.* ■ **out loud** [think, laugh, say] in a voice that can be heard by others □ *Will you read it out loud for us?*

loudhailer [ˌlaʊdˈheɪləʳ] *n* GB a device shaped like a bell that makes one's voice louder when it is held in front of one's mouth and is used to talk to a crowd of people.

loudly [ˈlaʊdlɪ] *adv* [shout, complain] = **loud**.

loudmouth [ˈlaʊdmaʊθ, *pl* -maʊðz] *n* a person who talks too much, usually in an unpleasant way (informal use).

loudspeaker [ˌlaʊdˈspiːkəʳ] *n* a device, often contained in a separate box, that is connected to a radio, hi-fi system etc and produces sound from electrical signals.

lough [lɒk] *n* in Ireland, a lake.

Louis XIV [ˌluːɪðəfɔːʳˈtiːnθ] (1638–1715) King

of France from 1643 to 1715. He built the palace of Versailles, and was called the Sun King.

Louis XV [ˌluːɪðəˈfɪfˈtiːnθ] (1710–1774) King of France from 1715 to 1774.

Louis XVI [ˌluːɪðəsɪksˈtiːnθ] (1754–1793) King of France from 1774 to 1792. He was killed on the guillotine during the French Revolution.

Louisiana [luˌiːzɪˈænə] a state in the southern USA, on the Gulf of Mexico. ABBREVIATION: LA. SIZE: 125,674 sq kms. POPULATION: 4,219,973 (*Louisianans, Louisianians*). CAPITAL: Baton Rouge. MAIN CITY: New Orleans.

Louisiana Purchase *n* **Louisiana Purchase** a piece of land in central North America that was bought by the USA from Napoleon in 1803. This purchase doubled the size of the USA.

lounge [laʊndʒ] ◇ *n* **-1.** [in a house] = **living room**. **-2.** [in an airport, hotel] a public room for sitting and relaxing in. **-3.** GB = **lounge bar**. ◇ *vi* to sit, stand, or lean in a lazy or relaxed way.

◆ **lounge about, lounge around** *vi* to spend time in a lazy or relaxed way without doing anything useful □ *We spent the afternoon lounging around in front of the TV.*

lounge bar *n* GB a bar in a pub or hotel where the furniture is more comfortable than in the other bars.

lounge lizard *n* a man who dresses well and spends a lot of time at parties, bars etc in order that other people will think he is attractive and interesting (disapproving use).

lounge suit *n* GB a man's suit that is worn at work rather than at a formal occasion.

Lourdes [lʊərd] a town in southwestern France, and an important pilgrimage center for Catholics. Many sick people go there because they believe that the water there can cure them.

louse [laʊs] (*pl sense 1* **lice**, *pl sense 2* **louses**) *n* **-1.** an insect that has no wings, lives on the skin or hair of people or animals, and sucks their blood. **-2.** an unpleasant person (informal use).

◆ **louse up** *vt sep* **to louse sthg up** US to spoil sthg (informal use).

lousy [ˈlaʊzɪ] (*compar* **lousier**, *superl* **lousiest**) *adj* (informal use) **-1.** [performance, quality, weather] very bad □ *I've had a really lousy day today.* **-2. to feel lousy** to feel very ill □ *All those cocktails made me feel lousy the next day.*

lout [laʊt] *n* a rude and aggressive man or boy.

louver US, **louvre** GB [ˈluːvər] *n* a door or window that contains several flat pieces of wood or glass with gaps between them to allow air into a room □ *a louver window/door/shutter.*

lovable [ˈlʌvəbl] *adj* [person] who is very pleasant and is easy to like a lot.

love [lʌv] ◇ *n* **-1.** [for a child, one's parents, country] a strong feeling one has about somebody or something that one likes and cares about very much □ *his love for his grandfather* □ *my love of France/Chinese food.* ■ **give her my love** tell her that I am thinking of her in a warm and friendly way. ■ **love from...** an affectionate way of ending a letter. ■ **a love-hate relationship** a relationship in which one sometimes likes or loves, and sometimes dislikes, something or somebody else. **-2.** [for a man, woman] a strong liking and sexual attraction for somebody. ■ **to be in love** to feel romantic or sexual love for somebody □ *He's in love with Patricia.* □ *They were deeply in love.* ■ **to fall in love** to start being in love □ *He fell in love with her.* □ *They fell in love while on vacation.* ■ **to make love** to have sex □ *I want to make love with you.* **-3.** [person] a person that one loves □ *He's the love of her life.* **-4.** [thing] something that one likes very much □ *Opera is a great love of mine.* **-5.** GB an affectionate word used when talking to somebody (informal use) □ *Do you want anything else, love?* **-6.** TENNIS a score that is zero □ *Cass is winning 40-love.*

◇ *vt* **-1.** [person, family, country] to feel love for <sb/sthg> □ *I love you.* **-2.** [music, football, food] to like and enjoy <sthg> very much □ *I love your dress.* □ *He loves traveling* OR *to travel.* □ *"Can you come?" — "I'd love to."*

love affair *n* a sexual relationship that somebody has with somebody else.

lovebite [ˈlʌvbaɪt] *n* a small bruise on somebody's skin, caused by somebody biting or sucking it affectionately.

loveless [ˈlʌvləs] *adj* [marriage, relationship] in which there is no love.

love letter *n* a letter expressing feelings of sexual love for somebody.

love life *n* the part of somebody's life that involves their sexual relationships □ *How's your love life these days?*

lovely [ˈlʌvlɪ] (*compar* **lovelier**, *superl* **loveliest**) *adj* **-1.** [girl, dress, place] that is beautiful to look at □ *You look lovely in that skirt.* **-2.** [meal, day, surprise] that brings one pleasure □ *We had a lovely time in Spain.* **-3.** [person] who is very pleasant □ *What a lovely man!*

lovemaking [ˈlʌvmeɪkɪŋ] *n* the activity of having sex with one's lover.

lover [ˈlʌvər] *n* **-1.** [of a person] a person one has a sexual relationship with □ *He's in Mexico with his lover.* **-2.** [of literature, art, music] somebody who is very interested in or fond of something □ *the magazine for opera lovers everywhere.*

lovesick [ˈlʌvsɪk] *adj* [poet, youth] who is unhappy because the person they love is not with them or does not feel love for them.

love song *n* a song with words that express feelings of sexual love.

love story *n* a movie, book, or play about people who feel sexual love for each other.

loving [ˈlʌvɪŋ] *adj* [relationship, husband, look] that shows love □ *He was very loving toward her.* □ *loving care.*

lovingly [ˈlʌvɪŋlɪ] *adv* [look, stroke, handle] *see* **loving** □ *Jim was gazing lovingly at his new car.*

low [loʊ] ◇ *adj* -**1**. [wall, table, hill] the top of which is not far above the ground; [ceiling, shelf, cloud] that is not high above the ground □ *The seat's too low for me.* □ *a low bridge* □ *The level of the river water is very low.* -**2**. [number, rank, priority] that is near the bottom of a scale □ *The temperature is in the low 80s.* □ *Cook over a low heat.* □ *low-level radiation.* -**3**. [price, income] that is small in value; [supplies, stocks] that are small in amount □ *low economic growth* □ *You'll find our prices much lower than you think.* □ *Our fuel reserves are low at the moment.* ■ **to be low on sthg** [on food, fuel] to have only a small amount left of sthg □ *We're running low on milk.* -**4**. [quality, standard] that is not good □ *Their level of attainment is lower than ever.* □ *low-grade meat.* -**5**. [opinion] that is not favorable □ *He's always had a very low opinion of my abilities.* -**6**. [volume, moan] that is not loud □ *They spoke in a low whisper.* -**7**. [note] that is deep □ *He has a deep, low voice.* □ *a low, rumbling noise.* -**8**. [light] that is not bright □ *soft, low lighting.* -**9**. [dress, neckline] that shows a lot of a woman's neck and breasts. -**10**. [person] who feels ill or unhappy □ *She's been feeling pretty low since the divorce.* -**11**. [trick, behavior] that is not fair or honest □ *That was a pretty low thing to do!*
◇ *adv* -**1**. [bend, bow, aim] near the ground □ *The plane flew low over the town.* □ *Can't you bend any lower?* -**2**. [sink, fall] at or to a low level □ *The value of the house has plunged even lower.* □ *Stocks are running low.* □ *Turn the heat down lower.* -**3**. [stoop] to a level of behavior that is not good or honorable □ *I would never sink that low.*
◇ *n* -**1**. a low point □ *Sales have reached an all-time low.* -**2**. WEATHER an area of low air pressure.

low-alcohol *adj* [beer, wine] that contains less alcohol than normal.

low beams *npl* car headlights that point downward rather than straight ahead.

lowbrow ['loʊbraʊ] *adj* [novel, culture, taste] that is not intellectual or serious.

low-calorie *adj* [food, diet] that contains fewer calories than normal and so it is less fattening.

Low Church *adj* that belongs to the part of the Church of England in which studying the Bible is more important than religious ceremonies.

Low Countries: **the Low Countries** a region in Europe that includes the Netherlands, Belgium, and sometimes Luxembourg.

low-cut *adj* [dress, blouse] that shows a lot of a woman's neck and breasts.

lowdown ['loʊdaʊn] *n* **to give sb the lowdown on sthg** to give sb important information about sthg (informal use).

low-down *adj* [trick, person] that one thinks is not fair or honest (informal use).

lower[1] ['loʊəʳ] ◇ *adj* -**1**. [lip, edge, floor] that is below another thing of the same type □ *You can sleep in the lower bunk.* -**2**. [region, level, leg] that is in the bottom part of something

□ *I've hurt my lower back.* ◇ *vt* -**1**. [flag, glass, one's head] to move <sthg> slowly from a high position to a low one □ *They lowered the piano onto the platform.* -**2**. [price, level, resistance] to reduce the amount, degree etc of <sthg> □ *It might help to lower the volume.* -**3**. **to lower one's eyes** OR **gaze** to move one's eyes or gaze so that one is looking downward. -**4**. **to lower one's voice** to talk more quietly.

lower[2] ['laʊəʳ] *vi* -**1**. [sky, cloud] to be dark. -**2**. **to lower at sb** to look at sb in an angry way.

Lower Chamber [,loʊəʳ-] *n* POLITICS the larger and more powerful law-making part of a government that is divided into two chambers.

lower class [,loʊəʳ-] *n* **the lower class, the lower classes** the lowest social group in society □ *His family came from the lower classes.* □ *a lower-class district.*

Lower House [,loʊəʳ-] *n* = **Lower Chamber**.

lowest common denominator [,loʊəst-] *n* **the lowest common denominator** the lowest number that all the bottom numbers of a set of fractions can be divided into.

low-fat *adj* [milk, cheese, yogurt] that does not contain much fat.

low-flying *adj* [aircraft] that is flying close to the ground.

low frequency *n* a kind of radio frequency.

low gear *n* any of the first gears of a car, truck etc that is used for slow speeds □ *I was driving in low gear.*

low-key *adj* [announcement, celebration, visit] that is designed not to attract much attention □ *It was a very low-key event – just us and a few guests.*

Lowlands ['loʊləndz]: **the Lowlands** the central and southern parts of Scotland.

low-level language *n* a kind of language used in computer programming in which each instruction corresponds to a code.

low life *n* the people in a place who are involved in crime, violence, or other unpleasant activities □ *a member of LA's low life* □ *a low-life character.*

low-loader [-'loʊdəʳ] *n* a vehicle used for transporting heavy goods by road or railroad that is low so that things can be loaded and unloaded easily.

lowly ['loʊlɪ] (*compar* **lowlier**, *superl* **lowliest**) *adj* [person, job] that is low in position.

low-lying *adj* [land, area] that is not much higher than the level of the sea; [cloud, mist] that is lower than is usual.

Low Mass *n* a mass in the Catholic Church that is simple, and spoken rather than sung.

low-necked [-'nekt] *adj* = **low-cut**.

low-paid *adj* [job, employee] that is paid a small amount of money □ *This kind of work is usually low-paid.*

low-rise *adj* [building] that has only a few stories □ *a low-rise apartment block.*

Lowry ['laʊrɪ], **L. S.** (1887–1976) a British artist who painted industrial landscapes with simplified human figures.

low season *n* the time of year when hotels, resorts etc are least busy and prices are lowest □ *We went there during the low season.* NOTE: Compare **high season**.

low tide *n* the time when the ocean is farthest away from the shore □ *The beach is covered in shells at low tide.* NOTE: Compare **high tide**.

loyal ['lɔɪəl] *adj* [friend, supporter, servant] who continues to give their support or friendship to somebody, even in difficult times □ *She's been very loyal to me.*

loyalist ['lɔɪələst] *n* a person who continues to support their leader or government when other people want to change the system.

◆ **Loyalist** *n* POLITICS a Northern Irish Protestant who wants Ulster to remain part of Britain.

loyalty ['lɔɪəltɪ] (*pl* **loyalties**) *n* [to a friend, country, family] *see* **loyal** □ *The troops have a great sense of loyalty to their leaders.*

lox [lɒks] *n* smoked salmon.

lozenge ['lɒzɪndʒ] *n* -1. a candy containing medicine that is kept in the mouth until it dissolves □ *throat/cough lozenges.* -2. a shape (◊), with four straight sides, and two wide angles opposite each other, and two sharp angles.

LP (*abbr of* **long-playing record**) *n* a record that turns at 33 times a minute.

L-plate *n* in Britain and Australia, a square white plate with a red "L" on it that must be attached to the front and back of a car to show that the driver is a learner.

LPG *n abbr of* **liquified petroleum gas**.

LPN (*abbr of* **licensed practical nurse**) *n* a US nursing qualification that requires two years' training; a person who has this qualification. NOTE: Compare **RPN**.

LRAM (*abbr of* **Licentiate of the Royal Academy of Music**) *n* a title given to members of the Royal Academy of Music, an important college in London.

LSAT ['elsæt] (*abbr of* **Law School Admissions Test**) *n* **the LSAT** a national test taken by students in order to enter a law school in the USA.

LSD (*abbr of* **lysergic acid diethylamide**) *n* an illegal drug that causes people to feel and see imaginary things.

LSD, L.S.D. (*abbr of* **pounds, shillings and pence - librae, solidi, denarii**) *n* a term used for money in Britain until 1971.

LSE (*abbr of* **London School of Economics**) *n* **the LSE** a college of London University that teaches economics and politics.

Lt. *abbr of* **lieutenant**.

LT (*abbr of* **low-tension**) *adj* that carries or uses low-voltage electricity.

Ltd, ltd (*abbr of* **limited**) a word written after a company name to show that it is a limited liability company □ *Smith and Sons, Ltd.*

lubricant ['lu:brɪkənt] *n* a greasy substance used to lubricate machines, engines etc.

lubricate ['lu:brɪkeɪt] *vt* [engine, machine] to cover <sthg> with a greasy substance so that it works without rubbing or sticking.

lubrication [,lu:brɪ'keɪʃn] *n*: *see* **lubricate** □ *The pistons need lubrication from time to time.*

lucid ['lu:sɪd] *adj* -1. [account, explanation] that is clear and so easy to understand. -2. [person] who can think clearly and is not confused by illness, drugs etc □ *She remained lucid throughout the interrogation.*

lucidly ['lu:sɪdlɪ] *adv* [talk, explain] *see* **lucid** □ *She argued lucidly in favor of joining.*

Lucifer ['lu:sɪfər] a name for the Devil.

luck [lʌk] *n* good or bad events that happen to one that cannot be controlled and depend on chance □ *Luck was on our side.* □ *Wish me luck!* □ *That was a piece of luck!* ■ **good/bad luck** something good/bad that happens by chance □ *I hope you have better luck than me.* □ *They seem to have nothing but bad luck.* ■ **good luck!** a phrase used to wish somebody success □ *Good luck with the exam/at the dentist!* ■ **bad** OR **hard luck!** GB a phrase used to show sympathy to somebody after something bad has happened to them □ *"We lost." — "Oh, bad luck!"* ■ **to be in luck** to have good luck □ *We were in luck, a bus came immediately.* ■ **to try one's luck at sthg** to try sthg, especially if it is new or different □ *We had terrible weather in Spain last year, so we thought we'd try our luck in Florida.* ■ **with (any) luck** a phrase used to show that one hopes a particular thing will happen or be correct □ *He won't even notice the difference, with any luck.*

◆ **luck out** *vi* to have unexpected success (informal use).

luckily ['lʌkəlɪ] *adv* a word used to say that it is fortunate that something happened or is true, because otherwise the situation would have been bad, or worse □ *Luckily for me, nobody noticed.* □ *Luckily it had stopped raining.*

luckless ['lʌkləs] *adj* [person] who does not have good luck.

lucky ['lʌkɪ] (*compar* **luckier**, *superl* **luckiest**) *adj* -1. [person] who has good luck; [guess, escape, coincidence] that is the result of good luck □ *You lucky guy!* □ *He's lucky to be alive.* □ *It was a lucky find.* -2. [number, color] that somebody believes will bring them good luck □ *I'm wearing my lucky dress.*

lucky charm *n* a small object that one carries or wears because one believes it will bring good luck or protection.

lucky dip *n* GB a container, filled with small prizes, that children put their hands into and pick a prize out of without looking inside.

lucrative ['lu:krətɪv] *adj* [business, deal] that earns a lot of money □ *We've just signed a very lucrative deal with Cohen Bros.*

Luddite ['lʌdaɪt] *n* -1. a member of a group of British workers in the early 19th century who destroyed industrial machinery because they thought it would cause unemployment. -2. a person who is against new technology.

ludicrous ['lu:dɪkrəs] *adj* [decision, appearance,

idea] that one thinks is extremely foolish □ *You look ludicrous in that hat!*

ludo ['lu:dou] *n* GB a simple game played on a board with flat pieces of colored plastic.

lug [lʌg] (*pt* & *pp* **lugged**, *cont* **lugging**) *vt* [suitcase, shopping, package] to pull or carry <sthg heavy>, using a lot of effort (informal use) □ *I've been lugging those books all over town.*

luggage ['lʌgɪdʒ] *n* a collective term for the suitcases, bags, boxes etc that one takes on a trip □ *How many pieces of luggage are you checking in?* □ *I haven't got much luggage.*

luggage rack *n* the shelf in a train or bus where luggage can be placed.

luggage van *n* GB a special railroad car in which luggage is carried.

lugubrious [lə'gu:brɪəs] *adj* [person, music, look] that is sad and serious (formal use).

lukewarm ['lu:kwɔːᵊm] *adj* **-1.** [water, soup] that is only slightly warm. **-2.** [welcome, response] that does not show much enthusiasm or interest □ *He was pretty lukewarm about the idea.*

lull [lʌl] ◇ *n* [in fighting, a conversation] a short period of quiet □ *There was a brief lull in the discussion.* ■ **the lull before the storm** a short calm period that comes before something unpleasant starts to happen. ◇ *vt* **-1. to lull sb to sleep** to make sb fall asleep gradually □ *The sound of her voice lulled me to sleep.* **-2. to lull sb into a false sense of security** to make sb feel calm and happy about something when they should really be worried □ *We allowed ourselves to be lulled into a false sense of security.*

lullaby ['lʌləbaɪ] (*pl* **lullabies**) *n* a slow quiet song sung to babies and children to make them go to sleep.

lumbago [lʌm'beɪgou] *n* pain in one's lower back.

lumber ['lʌmbəᵊ] ◇ *n* US wood used for building. ◇ *vi* [person, bus, elephant] to move in a slow awkward way. ◇ *vt* **to be lumbered with sthg** [with a job, responsibility] to have to deal with sthg difficult or boring that somebody else does not want to deal with □ *As usual, I got lumbered with the kids/cleaning.*

lumbering ['lʌmbərɪŋ] *adj* [person, bus, elephant] that moves in a slow awkward way.

lumberjack ['lʌmbəᵊdʒæk] *n* a person whose job is to cut down trees.

lumbermill ['lʌmbəᵊmɪl] *n* a factory that cuts trees into lumber.

lumberyard ['lʌmbəᵊjɑːᵊd] *n* a place where wood for building is stored and sold.

luminous ['lu:mɪnəs] *adj* [paint, dial] that glows in the dark.

lump [lʌmp] ◇ *n* **-1.** [of earth, coal, cheese] a solid piece of something of any size or shape □ *huge lumps of rock* □ *I found some lumps in the sauce.* **-2.** [in one's breast, on one's head] a hard swollen place on one's body. **-3. a lump (of sugar)** a small cube of sugar put in coffee or tea □ *How many lumps of sugar do you take?* ◇ *vt* **to lump people/things together** to treat different people/things as all

the same □ *You can't just lump them all together in one category.*

lumpectomy [ˌlʌmp'ektəmɪ] (*pl* **lumpectomies**) *n* an operation to remove a cancerous lump from a woman's breast.

lump sum *n* an amount of money that is paid all at once, not in several payments □ *The first prize is a lump sum of $200,000.*

lumpy ['lʌmpɪ] (*compar* **lumpier**, *superl* **lumpiest**) *adj* [sauce, mattress] that has lumps in it.

lunacy ['lu:nəsɪ] *n* crazy behavior □ *It would be complete lunacy to go out in this storm.*

lunar ['lu:nəᵊ] *adj* [month, rock, eclipse] that is connected with the moon.

lunatic ['lu:nətɪk] (disapproving use) ◇ *adj* [idea, behavior, plan] that is very foolish. ◇ *n* a person who behaves in a very foolish way. □ *Have you seen the way he drives? He's a complete lunatic!*

lunatic asylum *n* a hospital where people with mental illnesses are kept (old-fashioned use).

lunatic fringe *n* GB the members of a political party or group who have the most extreme ideas (disapproving use).

lunch [lʌntʃ] ◇ *n* the meal eaten in the middle of the day □ *a business/working lunch* □ *I'm meeting them for lunch.* ◇ *vi* to have lunch □ *I'm lunching with my aunt today.*

lunch box *n* a box that children carry their lunch to school in.

luncheon ['lʌntʃən] *n* lunch (formal use).

luncheon meat *n* small pieces of meat mixed with grain, pressed into a block, and sold in cans.

luncheon voucher *n* GB a special ticket given to workers by their employers that can be exchanged for food in restaurants, shops, and cafés.

lunch hour *n* the time in the middle of the day when people stop working and eat lunch □ *I went shopping on my lunch hour.* □ *He always takes a long lunch hour on Fridays.*

lunch room *n* US a large room, e.g. in a school, where people can buy food and eat it.

lunchtime ['lʌntʃtaɪm] *n* the time in the middle of the day when people eat lunch □ *'Open lunchtimes and evenings.'* □ *I went there at lunchtime.* □ *a lunchtime concert.*

lung [lʌŋ] *n* one of the two large organs in one's chest which take in air and are used for breathing □ *lung cancer.*

lunge [lʌndʒ] *vi* to move forward quickly and strongly, often to try and reach something or attack somebody □ *He lunged at my bag/for the door.*

lupine US, **lupin** GB ['lu:pɪn] *n* a tall plant that has long stems covered with white, pink, or blue flowers and has long flat seed cases.

lurch [lɜːᵊtʃ] ◇ *n* a sudden uncontrolled movement forward or to one side □ *The car gave a sudden lurch.* ■ **to leave sb in the lurch** to leave sb alone in a difficult position when they need one's help. ◇ *vi* [person, bus, boat] to move in a sudden uncontrolled way forward or to one side □ *Peter lurched across the deck.* □ *Suddenly the bus lurched sideways.*

lure [lⁱʊəʳ] ◇ *n* something that attracts somebody by offering them money, pleasure etc □ *The daycare center was an added lure.* □ *the lure of high wages/the city.* ◇ *vt* to attract <sb> using a lure □ *I was lured into the trap.*

lurid [ˈlⁱʊərəd] *adj* -1. [account, detail, description] that one finds shocking or unpleasant, especially because it is connected with violence or sex □ *He gave a very lurid picture of events.* -2. [carpet, bruise, sky] that is brightly colored in a way that one finds unnatural or unpleasant □ *A large, lurid vase stood on the table.*

lurk [lɜːʳk] *vi* -1. [person, animal] to wait secretly, often in order to do something bad □ *I'm sure I saw someone lurking behind the bushes.* -2. [memory, danger, fear] to exist without being clearly felt or understood □ *A small doubt lurked in the back of her mind.*

luscious [ˈlʌʃəs] *adj* -1. [fruit, pudding, wine] that smells and tastes sweet and good and is often juicy. -2. [woman, lips] that one finds sexually attractive.

lush [lʌʃ] ◇ *adj* -1. [grass, meadow] that looks very green and healthy □ *lush green valleys.* -2. [apartment, surroundings] that looks very comfortable and expensive □ *lush furnishings* □ *a lush hotel.* ◇ *n* a drunkard (informal use).

lust [lʌst] *n* -1. a strong sexual desire for another person that does not involve love. -2. **a lust for sthg** [for life, power, freedom] a strong desire for sthg.

♦ **lust after, lust for** *vt fus* -1. **to lust after** OR **for sthg** [for wealth, success, power] to have a strong desire to have sthg. -2. **to lust after** OR **for sb** to feel sexual lust for sb □ *I could see he was lusting after you just by looking at him!*

luster US, **lustre** GB [ˈlʌstəʳ] *n* [of silk, hair, wood] the soft light that is reflected from a shiny surface.

lusty [ˈlʌstɪ] (*compar* **lustier**, *superl* **lustiest**) *adj* [baby, voice, cry] that looks or sounds strong and healthy.

lute [luːt] *n* an ancient musical instrument with strings, a round body, and a long neck which is played like a guitar.

Luther [ˈluːθəʳ], **Martin** (1483–1546) a German religious leader. He criticized the Catholic Church, and led the Protestant Reformation.

Luxembourg [ˈlʌksəmbɜːʳg] a country in western Europe, situated between Belgium, France, and Germany. SIZE: 2,586 sq kms. POPULATION: 380,000 (*Luxembourgers*). CAPITAL: Luxembourg-Ville. LANGUAGE: French, Letzeburgish, German. CURRENCY: Luxembourg franc.

luxuriant [lʌgˈʒʊərɪənt] *adj* [forest, hair, corn] that grows healthily in large amounts.

luxuriate [lʌgˈʒʊərɪeɪt] *vi* **to luxuriate in sthg** [in an experience, time] to concentrate on enjoying sthg □ *Now you can luxuriate in the comfort of your own Jacuzzi.*

luxurious [lʌgˈʒʊərɪəs] *adj* [life, hotel] that is very comfortable or enjoyable, and is expen-

sive □ *Relax in the luxurious surroundings of the Miramar Hotel.*

luxury [ˈlʌkʃərɪ] (*pl* **luxuries**) *n* -1. a state of great comfort in expensive and beautiful places □ *a life of luxury* □ *a luxury hotel/cruise.* -2. something expensive and enjoyable, e.g. caviar or champagne, or that one does not need □ *one of life's little luxuries* □ *A vacation abroad is a luxury we can't afford.* -3. something enjoyable that one does not experience very often □ *Being cooked for is a real luxury for me.*

luxury goods *npl* things that people can buy and are expensive and enjoyable but not necessary, e.g. perfume or cigars.

LV *n abbr of* **luncheon voucher**.

LW *abbr of* **long wave**.

lychee [ˌlaɪˈtʃiː] *n* a small Asian fruit with hard skin and sweet white flesh.

Lycra™ [ˈlaɪkrə] *n* a fabric that stretches very easily and is used to make clothes that fit tightly □ *a Lycra bathing suit/leotard.*

lying [ˈlaɪɪŋ] ◇ *adj* [person] who tells lies □ *That lying little brother of yours!* ◇ *n* the act of telling lies □ *He accused her of lying.*

lymph gland [ˈlɪmf-] *n* one of many small organs in one's body that contain white blood cells and fight infection.

lynch [lɪntʃ] *vt* **to be lynched** to be hanged by a crowd of people illegally.

lynx [lɪnks] (*pl* **lynx** OR **lynxes**) *n* a large wild animal of the cat family that has very good eyesight, pointed ears, and a short tail.

lyre [ˈlaɪəʳ] *n* an ancient Greek musical instrument like a small harp.

lyrebird [ˈlaɪəʳbɜːʳd] *n* an Australian bird with a long U-shaped tail.

lyric [ˈlɪrɪk] *adj* [poetry, poet] that expresses strong personal feelings in a simple form.

♦ **lyrics** *npl* the words of a song.

lyrical [ˈlɪrɪkl] *adj* -1. [music, prose, beauty] that is pleasing to hear, read, or see □ *a lyrical description of the landscape.* -2. **to wax** OR **grow lyrical about sthg** to talk very enthusiastically about sthg □ *Pete used to wax lyrical about the beauty of Alaska.*

m¹ [em] (*pl* **m's** OR **ms**), **M** [em] (*pl* **M's** OR **Ms**) *n* the thirteenth letter of the English alphabet.

♦ **M** *n* -1. *abbr of* **motorway**. -2. *abbr of* **medium**. -3. (*abbr of* **mature audience**) a symbol for movies and video tapes in Australia that indicates that they are recommended only for people of 15 and over.

m² -1. *abbr of* **meter**. -2. *abbr of* **million**. -3. *abbr of* **mile**.

ma [mɑː] *n* a word used to talk to or about one's mother (informal use).

MA ◇ *n abbr of* **Master of Arts**. ◇ *abbr of* **Massachusetts**.

ma'am [mæm] *n* a word used to talk to a woman who is a customer, employer etc (formal use).

Maastricht ['mɑːstrɪkt] a city in the Netherlands. In 1991 leaders of the European Community signed a treaty there to agree to closer political, economic, and monetary cooperation. POPULATION: 117,417.

Mabo ['mɑːbou], **Ernie** an Aborigine who won an important legal dispute over land in the Australian High Court in 1992. The judges decided that the Europeans who first arrived in Australia did not always have the right to claim land where Aborigines were already living.

mac [mæk] *n* GB = **mackintosh** (informal use).

macabre [US məˈkɑːbr, GB -ˈkɑːbrə] *adj* [story, scene] that is strange and frightening or shocking because it is connected with death □ You've got a macabre sense of humor!

Macao [məˈkau] a Portuguese province in southeastern China, consisting of the Macao Peninsula and two islands. It will be given back to China in 1999. SIZE: 16 sq kms. POPULATION: 285,000 (*Macanese*).

macaroni [ˌmækəˈrouni] *n* short thin tubes of pasta.

macaroni and cheese US, **macaroni cheese** GB *n* a dish that consists of boiled macaroni mixed with cheese sauce.

macaroon [ˌmækəˈruːn] *n* a small cookie made of ground almonds, eggs, and sugar.

MacArthur [məˈkɑːrθər], **Douglas** (1880–1964) a US general who led US forces in the Far East during World War II, and served in the Korean War.

Macbeth [məkˈbeθ] the hero of Shakespeare's play *Macbeth*. He meets three witches who tell him he will be king, and then kills the king of Scotland in order to become king himself.

Macbeth, **Lady** in Shakespeare's play *Macbeth*, the wife of Macbeth, who encourages him to kill their King. She later goes mad with guilt.

Macdonald [məkˈdɒnld], **Ramsay** (1866–1937) British Prime Minister in 1924, 1929 to 1931, and 1931 to 1935. He was Britain's first Labor Prime Minister.

mace [meɪs] *n* -1. a specially decorated metal stick carried by some officials during ceremonies. -2. COOKING a spice made from the shell of the nutmeg and used in the form of a brown powder.

Macedonia [ˌmæsɪˈdouniə] -1. a region of southeastern Europe, covering parts of Bulgaria, Greece, and the Republic of Macedonia. -2. a republic in southeastern Europe that used to be part of Yugoslavia. SIZE: 25,700 sq kms. POPULATION: 2,100,000 (*Mac-*

edonians). CAPITAL: Skopje. LANGUAGE: Macedonian. CURRENCY: denar.

machete [məˈʃeti] *n* a large knife with a thick blade that is used for cutting plants down and as a weapon.

Machiavelli [ˌmækɪəˈveli], **Niccolo** (1469–1527) an Italian politician and writer. His best-known work, *The Prince*, is about using dishonest methods to get and keep power.

Machiavellian [ˌmækɪəˈveljən] *adj* [person, scheme, politics] that uses clever deceitful methods.

machinations [ˌmækɪˈneɪʃnz] *npl* secret and complicated plans for doing something bad □ Despite all their machinations, they didn't inherit a single penny.

machine [məˈʃiːn] ◇ *n* -1. a device made up of different parts that usually uses electricity or an engine to do a particular job □ a washing/sewing/printing machine □ It's all done by machine now. -2. POLITICS the people who control a particular political group or particular part of a system or organization □ the party/propaganda machine. ◇ *vt* -1. SEWING [seam, dress, curtain] to make <sthg> using a sewing machine. -2. INDUSTRY [part, bolt, steel] to shape or cut <sthg> using a machine tool □ machined engine parts.

machine code *n* COMPUTING a code made up of numbers that a computer understands.

machine gun *n* a gun that fires bullets continuously and very quickly.

machine-gun *vt* [person, vehicle] to fire at <sb/sthg> with a machine gun.

machine language *n* COMPUTING instructions that can be read and understood by a computer.

machine-readable *adj* [text] that can be read and understood by a computer □ Can you provide us with text in machine-readable form?

machinery [məˈʃiːnəri] *n* -1. a collective term for machines □ There's something caught in the machinery. □ agricultural/industrial machinery. -2. [of government, the law] a system used to organize something.

machine shop *n* the part of a factory where machine tools are operated.

machine tool *n* a machine that is used to shape or cut metal or other materials.

machine-washable *adj* [sweater, wool, silk] that will not be damaged by being washed in a washing machine.

machinist [məˈʃiːnəst] *n* -1. a person who operates a sewing machine. -2. a person whose job is to operate a machine tool.

machismo [US mɑːˈtʃiːzmou, GB məˈtʃɪz-] *n* macho behavior.

macho [US ˈmɑːtʃou, GB ˈmætʃ-] *adj* [man] who behaves and looks strong and tough because he thinks that is how men should behave and look □ There was a lot of macho shouting and drinking.

mackerel ['mækrəl] (*pl* **mackerel** OR **mackerels**) *n* a fish with blue and silver stripes, oily flesh, and a strong flavor □ mackerel pâté.

mackintosh ['mækɪntɒʃ] *n* GB a coat, usually long and light in color, that is made of waterproof material.

Macmillan [mək'mɪlən], **Sir Harold** (1894–1986) British Prime Minister from 1957 to 1963. He is famous for telling the British people "You've never had it so good."

Macquarie [mə'kwɒrɪ], **Lachlan** (1762–1824) a governor of New South Wales who supported ex-convicts and Aborigines. He is often called "the Father of Australia."

macramé [US 'mækrəmeɪ, GB mə'krɑ:mɪ] *n* the art of knotting string to make decorative objects.

macro ['mækrou] *n* COMPUTING a set of instructions that can be carried out using a single command.

macrobiotic [,mækroubaɪ'ɒtɪk] *adj* [diet] that is made up of whole grains and vegetables grown without the use of chemicals, and is thought to make people healthy.

macrocosm ['mækroukɒzm] *n* a large structure, e.g. the universe or society, considered as a whole.

macroeconomics [,mækroui:kə'nɒmɪks] *n* the study of the economics of a whole country, industry, or population.

mad [mæd] (*compar* **madder**, *superl* **maddest**) *adj* **-1.** [person] who has an illness of the mind and so behaves strangely □ *a mad old lady* □ *There are a lot of mad people on the streets.* ■ **to go mad** to become mad □ *Sometimes I feel like I'm going mad!* **-2. to be mad** to be very angry □ *I'm really mad at him.* **-3.** [person, plan, attempt] that one thinks is very foolish □ *He must be mad to want to go there!* **-4. to get** US OR **go** GB **mad at sb** to become very angry with sb. **-5. a mad rush/panic** a great rush/panic □ *There was a mad dash for the exit.* ■ **like mad** [work, run, laugh] with great energy or enthusiasm □ *I've been running around like mad trying to find her.* **-6. to be mad about sb/sthg** to like sb/sthg very much.

Madagascar [,mædə'gæskər] a country consisting of a large island in the Indian Ocean, off the coast of Mozambique. SIZE: 587,000 sq kms. POPULATION: 13,300,000 (*Madagascans*). CAPITAL: Antananarivo. LANGUAGE: Malagasy, French. CURRENCY: Madagascan franc.

madam ['mædəm] *n* a word used to address a woman, especially in stores or business letters (formal use) □ *Dear Madam...* □ *Yes, Madam?*

madcap ['mædkæp] *adj* [plan, scheme] that is very foolish.

mad cow disease *n* an infectious disease that affects the brain of cattle. Cows suffering from it become clumsy in their movements, and then collapse and die.

madden ['mædn] *vt* [person, noise, pain] to make <sb> very angry and annoyed.

maddening ['mædnɪŋ] *adj* [person, noise, problem] that is very annoying □ *It was absolutely maddening having to sit there and just watch.*

made [meɪd] *past tense & past participle of* **make**.

-made *suffix* added to words to show that something has been made in a particular place □ *factory-made* □ *Japanese-made.*

Madeira [mə'dɪərə] *n* a strong sweet wine made on the Portuguese island of Madeira, near Morocco.

made-to-measure *adj* [suit, jacket, shirt] that is made especially to fit one particular person.

made-up *adj* **-1.** [face, eyes] that has had make-up put on it □ *She was heavily made-up.* **-2.** [mixture, solution] that has already been prepared and is ready to use. **-3.** [story, excuse] that has been invented and is not true.

Mad Hatter [-'hætər]: **the Mad Hatter** a mad character in the novel *Alice's Adventures in Wonderland* by Lewis Carroll.

madhouse ['mædhaus] *n* a place that seems to be full of noise and confusion □ *It's like a madhouse in that office!*

Madison ['mædɪsən], **James** (1751–1836) US President from 1809 to 1817. He helped to write the Constitution.

Madison Avenue a large street in New York City that is famous for its advertising agencies. The name is also used to refer to the advertising business in general □ *We'll see what Madison Avenue can do with this.*

madly ['mædlɪ] *adv* [search, rush] quickly and wildly. ■ **madly in love** very much in love with somebody □ *She fell madly in love with him.*

madman ['mædmən] (*pl* **madmen** [-mən]) *n* **-1.** a man who is mentally ill. **-2.** a person who behaves in a wild and uncontrolled way □ *He drove like a madman.*

madness ['mædnəs] *n* **-1.** serious mental illness □ *I've heard that talking to yourself is the first sign of madness.* □ *her slow descent into madness.* **-2.** behavior that one thinks is very foolish □ *It would be utter madness to agree to those terms.*

Madonna [mə'dɒnə] *n* **-1.** RELIGION **the Madonna** the mother of Jesus Christ. **-2.** ART a painting or statue of the Madonna □ *Madonna and Child.*

Madras [mə'dræs] a city and port in southeastern India. It is the capital of Tamil Nadu State. POPULATION: 5,361,468.

Madrid [mə'drɪd] the capital of Spain and its largest city. POPULATION: 3,010,492.

madrigal ['mædrɪgl] *n* a song for several voices, usually without musical instruments, that was popular in the 16th century.

madwoman ['mædwumən] (*pl* **madwomen**) *n* **-1.** a woman who is mentally ill. **-2.** a woman who behaves in a wild and uncontrolled way.

maestro ['maɪstrou] (*pl* **maestros** OR **maestri** [-trɪ]) *n* a person who has great musical skill, especially in conducting music.

MAFF [mæf] (*abbr of* **Ministry of Agriculture, Fisheries, and Food**) *n* the British government department that deals with policy on farming and food.

Mafia [US 'mɑːfɪə, GB 'mæf-] *n* **the Mafia** a secret organization of criminals, originally from Sicily but now powerful in Italy, the USA, and other countries.

mag [mæg] *n* = **magazine** (informal use).

magazine [US 'mægəziːn, GB ˌmægəˈziːn] *n* -**1.** a sort of book with large pages and a paper cover that contains articles by various writers, photos, and advertisements, and is usually published weekly or monthly □ *a women's magazine* □ *a glossy magazine* □ *a magazine article.* -**2.** TV & RADIO a regular television or radio program that contains short reports on various subjects □ *a magazine program.* -**3.** [for bullets] a holder for bullets that can be fitted into an automatic gun; [for weapons] a building or room where weapons, ammunition etc are stored.

Magellan [məˈgelən], **Ferdinand** (1480–1521) a Portuguese explorer. He was the first person to sail around the world.

magenta [məˈdʒentə] ◇ *n* a deep pinkish-red color. ◇ *adj*: *magenta silk.*

maggot ['mægət] *n* a very small creature that looks like a fat white worm and develops into a fly.

Maghreb ['mɑːgreb]: **the Maghreb** northwest Africa, including Morocco, Algeria, Tunisia, and Libya.

Magi ['meɪdʒaɪ]: **the Magi** in the Bible, three wise men from the East who brought gifts to Jesus just after he was born.

magic ['mædʒɪk] ◇ *n* -**1.** [of a potion, spell] the use of secret powers and forces to do things that seem impossible, such as making things disappear □ *She's good at her job, but don't expect her to work magic.* □ *Suddenly, as if by magic, a little man appeared.* □ *This carpet cleaner works like magic.* -**2.** [of a magician] the skill of somebody who entertains people by doing clever tricks, e.g. with playing cards, or by making small objects appear and disappear □ *"How did you do that?" — "It's magic."* -**3.** [of feelings, events] mysterious and wonderful qualities or abilities □ *The magic has gone out of our marriage.* □ *the magic of Hollywood.* ◇ *adj* -**1.** [potion, spell, forest] that contains or works by magic □ *There is no magic formula for reducing inflation.* -**2.** [trick, show] that uses conjuring or magic. -**3.** [feeling, event] that seems wonderful and mysterious □ *Her final song was a truly magic moment.*

magical ['mædʒɪkl] *adj* -**1.** that contains or produces magic □ *magical powers.* -**2.** [feeling, quality, place] that seems wonderful and mysterious □ *the magical island of Capri.*

magic carpet *n* in fairy tales, a carpet that can fly and carry people.

magic eye *n* an electric switch that is sensitive to light and is used to set off devices such as burglar alarms and automatic doors.

magician [məˈdʒɪʃn] *n* -**1.** a man who has magic powers. -**2.** a person who performs magic tricks to entertain people.

magic wand *n* a short stick which is supposed to have magic power and is used by a magician □ *He waved his magic wand.*

magisterial [ˌmædʒɪˈstɪərɪəl] *adj* -**1.** [voice, performance, book] that seems to have complete authority or knowledge (formal use) □ *Mr Vasseur is the author of the magisterial "History of China".* -**2.** LAW [district, proceedings] that is connected with a magistrate.

magistrate ['mædʒɪstreɪt] *n* a law official who judges in courts that deal with less serious crimes and disputes.

magistrates' court *n* GB a local court of law that is controlled by a magistrate and deals with less serious crimes and disputes.

Magna Carta [ˌmægnəˈkɑːrtə] *n* **the Magna Carta** a document signed by King John of England in 1215 that limited royal power and guaranteed the rights of the nobles and the Church.

magnanimous [mægˈnænɪməs] *adj* [person] who is generous and forgiving, especially to a defeated rival or enemy □ *You've forgiven them? That's very magnanimous of you.*

magnate ['mægneɪt] *n* a very rich and powerful businessman, industrialist, or landowner □ *a shipping/oil/business magnate.*

magnesium [mægˈniːzɪəm] *n* a silver-colored metallic element that burns with a very bright white light and is used in fireworks and in lightweight alloys. SYMBOL: Mg.

magnet ['mægnət] *n* -**1.** a piece of iron that can make objects made of iron and certain other metals move toward it. -**2.** a person, place, or thing that attracts a lot of people or interest □ *The club acts as a magnet for folk musicians from all over the country.*

magnetic [mægˈnetɪk] *adj* -**1.** [metal] that works like a magnet; that contains a magnet. -**2.** [personality, appeal] that has qualities that attract people strongly □ *Italy has a magnetic appeal for tourists.*

magnetic field *n* the area around a magnet which is affected by its magnetism □ *the Earth's magnetic field.*

magnetic tape *n* plastic tape that is covered with a magnetic substance and used in cassettes for recording sound and in computers for storing information.

magnetism ['mægnətɪzm] *n* -**1.** [of an object, material] the force that makes magnets attract iron and certain other metals. -**2.** [of a person, event, smile] the ability to interest and attract other people strongly □ *a leader with great personal magnetism.*

magnification [ˌmægnɪfɪˈkeɪʃn] *n* -**1.** *see* **magnify** □ *Magnification of the area reveals tiny cracks in the paint surface.* -**2.** the degree to which a microscope, telescope etc can make an object appear bigger □ *The binoculars are capable of ten-times magnification.* □ *Here is the organism under high/low magnification.*

magnificence [mægˈnɪfɪsəns] *n*: *see* **magnificent** □ *the magnificence of the Alps.*

magnificent [mægˈnɪfɪsənt] *adj* [scenery, idea, performance] that one finds extremely good, beautiful, or impressive □ *a magnificient view* □ *I want to thank our hosts for their truly magnificent efforts.*

magnify ['mægnɪfaɪ] (*pt* & *pp* **magnified**) *vt* **-1.** [picture, image, detail] to make <sthg> appear bigger □ *This picture shows the virus magnified 10,000 times.* **-2.** [danger, problem, achievement] to make <sthg> seem more important than it really is.

magnifying glass ['mægnɪfaɪɪŋ-] *n* a device consisting of a round piece of curved glass in a frame attached to a handle that makes things appear bigger and is used for reading small writing, seeing small details etc.

magnitude ['mægnɪtʲuːd] *n* great size or importance □ *We were not equipped to deal with problems of this magnitude.*

magnolia [mæg'nəʊljə] *n* a tree, grown in gardens, that has large white or pink flowers; the flower of this tree.

magnum ['mægnəm] (*pl* **magnums**) *n* a wine bottle holding 1.5 liters □ *a magnum of champagne.*

magpie ['mægpaɪ] *n* a black and white bird with a loud call and a long tail that is attracted to shiny objects and takes them to its nest.

Magyar ['mægjɑːr] *n* a member of the largest group of people living in Hungary; the language of this people.

maharaja(h) [,mɑːhə'rɑːdʒə] *n* an Indian prince.

Mahler ['mɑːlər], **Gustav** (1860–1911) an Austrian composer and conductor, famous for his symphonies and songs.

mahogany [mə'hɒgənɪ] *n* a hard reddish-brown wood that is highly valued and is used for making furniture; the tropical tree from which this wood is obtained □ *a mahogany chair.*

maid [meɪd] *n* a woman servant in a hotel or private house.

maiden ['meɪdn] ◇ *adj* **a maiden flight/voyage** the first flight/voyage by a particular vehicle. ◇ *n* an unmarried girl (literary use).

maiden aunt *n* an aunt who has never married.

maiden name *n* the family name that a woman had before she married.

maiden speech *n* GB the first speech made by a new Member of Parliament to the House of Commons.

Maid Marian [-'mærɪən] the lover of Robin Hood in English folk stories.

mail [meɪl] ◇ *n* **-1.** letters, packages etc sent and delivered by the postal system □ *Was there any mail today?* **-2.** the system provided by the post office for collecting, transporting, and delivering mail □ *My letter was lost in the mail.* □ *We sent it by mail.* □ *a mail service.* ◇ *vt* [package, letter] to send <sthg> by the postal system □ *It was mailed yesterday.*

mailbag ['meɪlbæg] *n* a large bag used for carrying mail.

mailbox ['meɪlbɒks] *n* US **-1.** a box outside a

house where the mailman puts mail for the house. **-2.** a box in which mail is collected before it is delivered through the postal system.

Mailer ['meɪlər], **Norman** (1923–) a US writer whose writings criticize American society. His work includes *The Naked and the Dead* and *An American Dream.*

mailing list ['meɪlɪŋ-] *n* a list of names and addresses that a company or organization regularly sends advertisements or information to □ *All customers are put automatically on our mailing list.*

mailman ['meɪlmæn] (*pl* **mailmen** [-men]) *n* US a person who delivers the mail.

mail order *n* a system for selling goods where customers choose goods, usually from a catalog, and the goods are mailed to the customers' homes □ *a mail-order catalog/company.*

mailshot ['meɪlʃɒt] *n* a letter, usually containing advertisements, that is mailed to many addresses at the same time □ *Let's do a mailshot and see what response we get.*

mail train *n* a train that carries mail.

mail truck *n* US a small truck used for collecting and delivering mail.

mail van *n* **-1.** a small truck used for collecting and delivering mail. **-2.** GB a railroad car used for carrying mail.

maim [meɪm] *vt* to injure <sb>, especially in an accident or in battle, so badly that they are damaged for life.

main [meɪn] ◇ *adj* **the main reason/cause etc** the most important reason/cause etc □ *Let's go over the main points again.* □ *They are our main suppliers of spare parts.* ◇ *n* a large pipe from which smaller pipes carry gas, water etc into houses and buildings □ *a gas/water/sewage main.*

◆ **mains** *npl* GB **the mains** the pipe that brings water or gas, or the wire that brings electricity, into a building from outside □ *the water/gas/electric mains* □ *You must turn off the water at the mains.*

◆ **in the main** *adv* a phrase used to say that something is true in most cases but not all □ *In the main, people go on vacation in summer.*

main course *n* the biggest and most important part of a meal, often eaten after a soup or an appetizer and before a dessert.

main drag *n* **the main drag** US the main street in a town or city (informal use).

Maine [meɪn] a state in New England, in the northeastern USA, on the Atlantic and bordering Canada. ABBREVIATION: ME. SIZE: 80,082 sq kms. POPULATION: 1,227,928 (*Mainers*). CAPITAL: Augusta.

mainframe (computer) ['meɪnfreɪm-] *n* a large and powerful computer that can be used by many people at the same time.

mainland ['meɪnlənd] ◇ *n* **the mainland** the main part of a country or continent, without the islands around it □ *They live on the Spanish mainland* OR *the mainland of Spain.* ◇ *adj*:

Most of our business is in Britain, but we also sell to mainland Europe.

main line *n* RAIL an important railroad, usually joining two big cities.

◆ **mainline** ◇ *adj* RAIL **a mainline station/train** a station/train that is on a main line. ◇ *vt* ▽ to put <an illegal drug> directly into a vein by injecting it (drugs slang). ◇ *vi* ▽ (drugs slang) *You should know the dangers of mainlining.*

mainly ['meɪnlɪ] *adv* a word used to say that something is true in most cases or to a large extent □ *Our readers are mainly well-off and educated.* □ *His assets are mainly in the form of property.* □ *It was mainly the price that put me off.*

main road *n* a large and important road, usually joining two big towns.

mainsail ['meɪnseɪl, 'meɪnsl] *n* the most important sail on a sailing boat.

mainstay ['meɪnsteɪ] *n* **the mainstay of sthg** the person or thing that provides the most support or money for something □ *Tourism is the mainstay of the island's economy.*

mainstream ['meɪnstriːm] ◇ *n* **the mainstream** [of social life, public opinion] the ideas, methods, ways of behaving etc that most ordinary people have, and that are considered the most normal □ *Satie's work lies outside the mainstream of 19th-century music.* ◇ *adj*: *He left mainstream politics to become a freelance consultant.*

Main Street *n* US **-1.** the name of the most important street in many small American towns. **-2.** a term used to refer to ordinary American people □ *a policy that will be popular on Main Street, USA.*

maintain [meɪn'teɪn] *vt* **-1.** [friendship, position, reputation] to continue to have <sthg> as much or as well as before, usually by making constant efforts □ *We must maintain good relations with our customers.* □ *The police were called in to maintain law and order.* **-2.** [speed, temperature, production] to keep <sthg> always at the same level and not let it decrease □ *The public has not maintained its initial enthusiasm.* **-3.** [family, child] to support <sb/sthg> by providing money □ *He has a wife, three children, and a large house to maintain.* **-4.** [machine, building, vehicle] to keep <sthg> in good condition by constant care and by doing repairs as soon as they become necessary □ *If you buy expensive equipment you need to maintain it.* **-5. to maintain (that)**... to say or state forcefully that something is true, especially when other people disagree □ *He still maintains that he paid back the money.* □ *Despite the evidence, she still maintains her innocence.*

maintenance ['meɪntənəns] *n* **-1.** [of a friendship, speed, machine] *see* **maintain** □ *The contract depends on the maintenance of current levels of output.* □ *car/road maintenance* □ *We need a mechanic for our maintenance department.* **-2.** GB LAW money that a person has to pay to their former wife or husband in order to support their children.

maintenance order *n* GB LAW a legal order

stating that a person must pay maintenance to their former wife or husband.

maisonette [,meɪzə'net] *n* GB an apartment on two floors within a larger building.

maize [meɪz] *n* GB a tall plant grown for its yellow seeds; the yellow seeds of this plant eaten as a vegetable and sometimes made into flour.

Maj. MILITARY *abbr of* **Major**.

majestic [mə'dʒestɪk] *adj* [appearance, sight] that seems grand, impressive, and dignified □ *the majestic scenery of the Canadian Rockies.*

majestically [mə'dʒestɪklɪ] *adv* [glide, speak, move] *see* **majestic** □ *The eagle soared majestically overhead.*

majesty ['mædʒəstɪ] *(pl* **majesties**) *n* the quality of being majestic.

◆ **Majesty** *n* **His/Her/Your Majesty** a title used when speaking about or to a king or queen □ *Parliament will be opened by Her Majesty the Queen.* □ *Their Majesties the King and Queen of Sweden.*

major ['meɪdʒər] ◇ *adj* **-1. a major role/cause etc** a role/cause etc that is more important than other things □ *The need to cut costs was a major factor in our decision.* □ *a major retailer* □ *'This taxi accepts major credit cards.'* **-2. a major disaster/difficulty etc** a very serious disaster/difficulty □ *He is very ill and will need major surgery.* **-3.** MUSIC [key, scale] that has two full tones between the first and third notes, and half tones between the third and fourth notes and the seventh and eighth notes □ *a symphony in A major.* ◇ *n* **-1.** MILITARY an officer who is above a captain and below a lieutenant colonel in rank. **-2.** US the main subject that a student studies at a college or university; a student who has studied a particular subject as their main subject □ *Her major was physics.* □ *She's a physics major.* ◇ *vi* **to major in sthg** [in law, physics] to study sthg as one's main subject for a university degree.

Majorca [mə'jɔːrkə] the largest of the Balearic Islands, and a popular tourist resort. SIZE: 3,640 sq kms. POPULATION: 530,000 *(Majorcans).* CAPITAL: Palma.

majorette [,meɪdʒə'ret] *n* a girl, dressed in decorative clothes and carrying a stick, who marches in front of a band in a procession, e.g. at a sports event.

major general *n* an army officer of high rank who is below a lieutenant general.

majority [mə'dʒɒrətɪ] *(pl* **majorities**) *n* **-1. the majority of people/cases etc** most people/cases etc □ *The overwhelming majority of people are in favor of the new law.* □ *This technique is effective in the majority of cases.* □ *The jury found her guilty by a majority decision.* ■ **to be in a OR the majority** to form the larger part of a group □ *Women are now in a majority on the committee.* **-2.** POLITICS the difference in votes gained or candidates elected between the winner of an election and the loser □ *The right-wing majority in Congress has been reduced.*

majority shareholder *n* a person, company, or group that owns more than half of the shares in a company, and therefore controls it.

major-league *adj* **-1.** that is connected with professional baseball □ *a major-league team.* **-2.** important □ *a major-league banker/computer.*

major leagues *npl* in the USA, the two groups of professional baseball teams.

major road *n* = main road.

make [meɪk] (*pt* & *pp* **made**) ◇ *vt* **-1.** [bread, cars, movie] to produce <an object, product, cooked dish> etc □ *Don't make so much noise.* □ *What do they make in that factory?* □ *It won't take long to make lunch.* □ *Our cakes are made using the finest ingredients.* **-2.** [phone call, speech, remark] to perform <a particular action>. ■ **to make a decision/offer/visit** to decide/offer/visit something □ *We have made an important discovery.* □ *It's a difficult choice to make.* ■ **to make a mess/success of sthg** to do sthg badly/well □ *He made a real mess of the interview.* **-3. to make sb happy/angry/famous** to cause sb to be happy/angry/famous □ *What's making him so irritable?* □ *The movie made her a star overnight.* □ *Take this, it'll make you feel better.* ■ **to make sb director/manager** to move sb to the position of director/manager in the same organization □ *They'll probably make him chairman.* ■ **to make sthg hard/soft/easy** to cause sthg to be hard/soft/easy □ *It'd make things easier for us if we had a car.* ■ **to make sthg into sthg** to change sthg so that it becomes sthg else □ *The old warehouse has been made into offices.* ■ **to make oneself heard** to speak or shout loudly so that other people can hear one in a noisy situation □ *You had to shout to make yourself heard over the music.* ■ **to make sthg known** [news, decision, fact] to let other people know sthg □ *He made it known that he was looking for another job.* **-4. to make sb/sthg do sthg** to cause sb/sthg to do sthg; to force sb to do sthg by using threats or violence □ *This button makes the machine start.* □ *We were made to wait in the hall.* □ *He should be made to apologize.* ■ **to make sb jump** to cause sb to make a sudden small movement by frightening or surprising them □ *The noise made us all jump.* **-5. to be made of sthg** [of paper, steel, silk] to be formed of sthg □ *a sauce made of eggs, milk and flour* □ *"What's it made of?" — "Wood."* **-6. 2 and 2 make 4** if 2 and 2 are added together, the total is 4. **-7. I make it $50** I calculate the total amount to be $50 □ *"How many people will be there?" — "If Chris comes, that makes six of us."* □ *The bill was $80, so that makes $20 you each owe me.* ■ **what time do you make it?** what time is it according to your watch? **-8.** to earn <a particular amount of money> □ *She makes over $20,000 a year.* ■ **to make a profit/loss** to get a profit/loss from one's business or from a deal □ *We made a profit of £3,000 on the sale of the house.* **-9. to make a good teacher/mother** to have the right qualities for the job or role of teacher/mother □ *She'd make an excellent busi-*

ness partner. □ *Books make ideal presents.* **-10.** to succeed in getting to <a place>, especially by a particular time □ *We'll never make the airport by ten o'clock.* □ *I won't be able to make lunch tomorrow.* **-11.** to cause <sthg> to be completely successful, enjoyable etc (informal use) □ *Her performance really makes the play/movie.* ■ **to make sb's day** to do or say something that makes sb feel very happy □ *Give her a call, it'll make her day!* **-12. to make a friend/enemy** to cause somebody to become one's friend/enemy □ *I made several useful contacts at the conference.* **-13.** phrases **to make it** [to a station, airport] to succeed in arriving at a place by a particular time; [to a party, meeting, dinner] to be able to be present; [as an actor, writer, athlete] to be successful in one's career □ *We'll never make it in time.* □ *He made it to the airport with a minute to spare.* □ *They couldn't make it tonight.* □ *When I won the Oscar I felt I'd finally made it.* ■ **to have it made** to be in a position that makes success certain □ *He's got it made now that he's married the boss's daughter.* ■ **to make do with sthg** to use sthg even though it is not satisfactory □ *There aren't any clean ones, so you'll have to make do with a dirty one.*
◇ *n* **-1.** the name of a product, e.g. a car or computer, that is made by a particular company □ *It's a very good make of camera.* **-2.** phrase **to be on the make** to be trying to gain an advantage for oneself, usually by acting in a selfish or dishonest way (informal and disapproving use).

◆ **make for** *vt fus* **-1. to make for a place** to go toward a place for a particular reason □ *I suggest we make straight for the nearest bar.* **-2. to make for sthg** to help to cause sthg to exist □ *Late nights and fast food don't make for a healthy lifestyle.*

◆ **make of** *vt sep* **-1. what do you make of him?** what is your opinion of him? **-2. I couldn't make anything of it** I couldn't understand what it meant.

◆ **make off** *vi* to leave quickly, especially after having done something wrong □ *They made off in a small plane.*

◆ **make off with** *vt fus* **to make off with sthg** [cash, jewels, painting] to steal sthg □ *Thieves made off with several thousand dollars in cash.*

◆ **make out** *vt sep* **-1. to make out sthg** [shape, words, building] to see or hear sthg, but not clearly □ *His voice was so low I could barely make out what he was saying.* □ *I could just make out a small ship on the horizon.* **-2. to make sthg out** [receipt, prescription, invoice] to write the necessary information on sthg, including the name of the person, company etc receiving it □ *Who shall I make the check out to?* **-3. to make sb/sthg out to be sthg** to describe sb/sthg as being different from how they really are, sometimes in order to deceive people □ *He's not as talented as everyone makes him out to be.* □ *It was made out to be some kind of fantastic cure for hayfever.*

◆ **make up** *vt sep* **-1. to make sthg up** [total, team] to form all of sthg, or a particular amount of it □ *The five boroughs that make up*

New York City are... □ *Women currently make up 52% of the workforce.* **-2. to make sthg up** [story, poem, tune] to create sthg, especially quickly and without writing it down □ *He made up a rude song about his boss.* **-3. to make sthg up** [excuse, story, name] to think of and say sthg that is not true in order to deceive people □ *If you don't have a good reason you'd better make one up.* **-4. to make sb/sthg up** [face, eyes] to put cosmetics on sb/sthg □ *She used to spend hours making herself up in the bathroom.* **-5. to make sthg up** [package, prescription] to prepare sthg □ *I'll make up a bed for you in the spare room.* **-6. to make sthg up** [amount, group] to add extra people, money etc to sthg so that it is the size or amount it should be □ *If you can find half the money for the ticket, I'll make up the rest.* □ *I need two more volunteers to make up the team.* **-7. to make it up with sb** to start being friendly with sb again after a quarrel □ *Have you and Ann made it up yet?*

◆ **make up for** *vt fus* **to make up for sthg** to replace sthg that has been lost or damaged; to make somebody feel better after sthg that has made them suffer or be disappointed □ *We'll have to speed up to make up for lost time.* □ *Nothing can make up for all the misery he has caused.* □ *The restaurant was small and crowded, but the excellent food more than made up for it.*

◆ **make up to** *vt sep* **to make it up to sb** to give sb something to make them feel better after they have been disappointed □ *It's too bad you'll miss your night out, but don't worry, I'll make it up to you.*

make-believe *n* imagining or pretending that things are different or more exciting than they really are □ *The story was pure make-believe.*

maker ['meɪkəʳ] *n* [of a movie, product] a person or company that makes or manufactures something □ *If it doesn't work, you can return it to the maker.* □ *from the makers of "Conan".*

makeshift ['meɪkʃɪft] *adj* [furniture, shelter] that is made or used because there is a sudden and urgent need and because there is nothing better available □ *This box will do as a makeshift table.*

make-up *n* **-1.** [on one's face] substances, e.g. lipstick, mascara, or powder, that women, actors etc use to paint and decorate their faces □ *She uses a lot of eye make-up.* □ *She's putting on her make-up.* ■ **a make-up bag** a bag for carrying make-up. ■ **make-up remover** a liquid or cream for taking make-up off one's face. **-2.** [of a person] the combination of qualities that form somebody's character □ *Guilt is part of his psychological make-up.* **-3.** [of a jury, system] the different people or things that go together to form something; the way in which these people or things combine and affect each other □ *There are deep problems in the country's economic make-up.*

makeweight ['meɪkweɪt] *n* a person or thing, usually of little value, that is added to something so that there will be the right number or amount.

making ['meɪkɪŋ] *n* [of books, decisions] *see*

make □ *The actual making of the movies took six months.* ■ **to be sthg in the making** to be becoming sthg; to be sthg that is happening at the present moment □ *She's a great singer in the making.* □ *This is history in the making.* ■ **to be of sb's own making** [trouble, difficulty] to be completely the fault of sb or caused by sb □ *Your problems are entirely of your own making.* ■ **to be the making of sb** to make sb more successful □ *Moving to Italy turned out to be the making of him.* ■ **to have the makings of sthg** [of a success, artist, star] to show signs of developing into sthg □ *She has all the makings of a fine actress.* □ *This latest project has all the makings of a disaster.*

maladjusted [ˌmælə'dʒʌstəd] *adj* [child, teenager] who has psychological problems and does not fit in well with society.

malaise [mə'leɪz] *n* a general feeling that something is wrong or unsatisfactory that usually causes lack of effort, activity, and enthusiasm (formal use) □ *the social malaise caused by years of poverty.*

maladministration [ˌmælədmɪnɪ'streɪʃn] *n* poor or dishonest management, e.g. of a country or company □ *Several members of the board were charged with fraud and maladministration of public funds.*

malaria [mə'leərɪə] *n* a disease common in hot countries which is passed to humans by mosquito bites and causes fever and shivering.

Malawi [mə'lɑːwɪ] a country in East Africa, between Zambia, Tanzania, and Mozambique. SIZE: 118,000 sq kms. POPULATION: 9,400,000 (*Malawians*). CAPITAL: Lilongwe. LANGUAGE: English. CURRENCY: kwacha.

Malay [US 'meɪleɪ, GB mə'leɪ] ◇ *n* a member of a people living mainly in Malaysia and Indonesia; the language of this people. ◇ *adj*: *a Malay dish/song.*

Malay Peninsula: **the Malay Peninsula** a long peninsula in Southeast Asia that includes parts of Myanmar, Thailand, and Malaysia.

Malaysia [mə'leɪʒə] a country in Southeast Asia, consisting of the southern part of the Malay Peninsula and the northern part of Borneo. SIZE: 330,000 sq kms. POPULATION: 18,300,000 (*Malaysians*). CAPITAL: Kuala Lumpur. LANGUAGE: Malay, English. CURRENCY: Malaysian dollar.

Malaysian [mə'leɪʒn] *n* & *adj*: *see* **Malaysia**.

Malcolm X [ˌmælkəm'eks] (1925–1965) a black US civil rights leader. He was killed while making a speech in Harlem, New York.

malcontent [US ˌmælkən'tent, GB 'mælkəntent] *n* a person who is dissatisfied with their society, job etc and is likely to cause trouble (formal use).

Maldives ['mɔːldaɪvz]: **the Maldives** a country consisting of a group of islands in the Indian Ocean, south of Sri Lanka. SIZE: 300 sq kms. POPULATION: 200,000 (*Maldivians*). CAPITAL: Malé. LANGUAGE: Divehi. CURRENCY: rufiyaa.

male [meɪl] ◇ *adj* **-1.** [animal, partner] that belongs to the sex that does not give birth to young □ *a male monkey/insect* □ *She gets along better with her male colleagues.* □ *a male nurse.* **-2.** [problems, unemployment, hormone] that is connected with men, especially men as a group rather than as individuals □ *There has been a change in male attitudes toward women at work.* ◇ *n* a male human or animal □ *The male of the species has bright feathers.*

male chauvinist (pig) *n* a man who believes that men are better, more important, and more intelligent than women (disapproving use).

malevolent [mə'levələnt] *adj* [person] who wants to harm other people (formal use) □ *He had a sharp sense of humor but he was never malevolent.*

malformed [ˌmæl'fɔː'md] *adj* [body, arm] that is badly or wrongly formed.

malfunction [ˌmæl'fʌŋkʃn] ◇ *n* a fault in a machine or system that stops it from working properly □ *There has been a computer malfunction.* ◇ *vi* [machine, system] to fail to work properly □ *Extreme heat can cause the engine/computer to malfunction.*

malice ['mæləs] *n* a desire to harm or upset other people □ *He spoke without malice.* □ *It was an act of sheer malice on his part.*

malicious [mə'lɪʃəs] *adj* [person, comment, gossip] that is full of malice □ *a malicious act of violence.*

malign [mə'laɪn] ◇ *vt* to say unpleasant and usually untrue things about <sb> □ *The press has always maligned her.* ◇ *adj* [person, behavior, influence] that is harmful (literary use).

malignant [mə'lɪgnənt] *adj* **-1.** [nature, look, plan] that seems full of hate and the desire to hurt other people (formal use). **-2.** MEDICINE [cancer, tumor, growth] that is harmful and may cause death.

malinger [mə'lɪŋgə'] *vi* to avoid work by pretending to be ill (disapproving use).

malingerer [mə'lɪŋgərə'] *n* a person who malingers (disapproving use).

mall [mɔːl] *n* a large building containing several different stores.

mallard [US 'mælərd, GB -ɑːd] *n* a common wild duck, the male of which has a dark-green head and a red-brown breast.

malleable ['mælɪəbl] *adj* **-1.** [person] who is easily influenced and controlled by other people. **-2.** [substance] that is soft and can easily be bent, shaped etc □ *The metal is heated until it becomes soft and malleable.*

mallet ['mælət] *n* a hammer with a wooden or rubber head.

malnourished [ˌmæl'nʌrɪʃt] *adj* [person, population] that is sick and weak because of a lack of food or vitamins.

malnutrition [ˌmælnjuː'trɪʃn] *n* serious weakness and illness caused by a lack of food, or a lack of food containing vitamins □ *Most of the children in the camp are suffering from malnutrition.*

malpractice [ˌmæl'præktəs] *n* LAW failure to follow the rules of one's profession properly, often resulting in harm to a customer or cli-

ent □ *professional/medical/legal malpractice* □ *malpractice insurance.*

malt [mɔːlt] *n* **-1.** grain, usually barley, that has been treated so that it produces sugar and is used to make alcoholic drinks such as beer and whiskey. **-2.** = **malt whisky**. **-3.** US = **malted milk**.

Malta ['mɔːltə] a country consisting of the islands of Malta, Gozo, and Comino, in the Mediterranean, south of Sicily. SIZE: 316 sq kms. POPULATION: 360,000 (*Maltese*). CAPITAL: Valletta. LANGUAGE: Maltese, English. CURRENCY: Maltese pound.

malted milk [ˌmɔːltəd-] *n* US a drink made from milk mixed with a powder containing malt, and sometimes ice cream.

Maltese [ˌmɔːl'tiːz] (*pl* **Maltese**) *n* & *adj*: see **Malta**.

maltreat [ˌmæl'triːt] *vt* [prisoner, horse] to treat <a person or animal> badly, cruelly, or violently.

maltreatment [ˌmæl'triːtmənt] *n*: see **maltreat** □ *The prisoners had suffered maltreatment and abuse.*

malt whisky *n* a type of whisky made from malt.

mammal ['mæml] *n* an animal, e.g. a human, whale, or mouse, that belongs to a class of animals in which the female produces milk to feed its young.

mammon, Mammon ['mæmən] *n* wealth when it is considered as something bad (disapproving use).

mammoth ['mæməθ] ◇ *adj* a mammoth task/achievement a task/achievement that takes a lot of effort. ◇ *n* a big hairy elephant with long tusks that no longer exists.

man [mæn] (*pl* **men**, *pt* & *pp* **manned**, *cont* **manning**) ◇ *n* **-1.** an adult male person □ *men, women, and children* □ *You may think he's OK, but I don't trust the man.* □ *I think he's a very nice man.* ■ **the man in the street** the ordinary or typical person □ *How do the tax increases affect the man in the street?* ■ **to talk man to man** to talk openly and honestly about something serious. ■ **to be man enough to do sthg** to be brave enough to do sthg □ *You're not even man enough to admit when you're wrong!* **-2.** a drinking/gambling man the type of man who drinks/gambles □ *He's not a betting man.* **-3.** [people] the human race □ *Man is descended from the apes.* □ *It is the most deadly poison known to man.* □ *Space travel is one of the greatest achievements of modern man.* **-4.** [of a team] a male member of an organized group of people; [in an army] an ordinary soldier; [in a factory] a male worker in a factory; [from a company] a male representative of a company □ *We played the game with just ten men.* □ *They lost many men in the battle.* □ *The foreman spoke to the men on the shop floor.* **-5.** [in a couple] a husband, male lover, or boyfriend (informal use) □ *Apparently, Jodie's got a new man.* **-6.** a word used to address a man, especially when one is angry, impatient, or excited (informal use) □ *This record's really great, man.* □ *For God's sake, man, hurry up!*

◇ *vt* [telephone, ship, machine] to operate or be in charge of <sthg> □ *The station is manned 24 hours a day.*

MAN [mæn] (*abbr of* **metropolitan area network**) *n* a network of computers that are linked together and can communicate within a town or city.

manacles ['mænəklz] *npl* metal chains that are fastened to a prisoner's wrists or ankles to stop them from escaping.

manage ['mænɪdʒ] ◇ *vt* -1. [task] to succeed in doing <sthg difficult> □ *We managed to finish the work on time.* □ *I tried to eat but could only manage a few mouthfuls.* □ *She had somehow managed to lock herself in.* -2. [company, store, movie star] to be in control of and responsible for the business affairs of <sb/sthg>; [house, machine] to control <sb/sthg> that is difficult to control □ *She manages our sales department.* □ *The teacher doesn't know how to manage children.* -3. [one's money, time] to organize and use <sthg> properly □ *As a student I had to learn to manage my own affairs.* -4. [money, time] to be able to give <a particular amount of sthg> to somebody else because one has enough of it □ *We can manage a $5 donation.* □ *I'm busy now, but I can manage an hour on Friday.*
◇ *vi* -1. to succeed in doing something difficult □ *"Can I help you?"* — *"It's OK. I can manage."* -2. to succeed in living with only a small amount of money □ *How do you manage on only $60 a week?*

manageable ['mænɪdʒəbl] *adj* [task, operation, child] that is easy to deal with or control □ *Our debts are now of a manageable size.* □ *Its new formula will leave your hair smooth and manageable.*

managed ['mænɪdʒd] *adj* **managed forests/woodland** forests/woodland in which trees are cut down at a rate that does not do permanent ecological damage.

management ['mænɪdʒmənt] *n* -1. [of time, facilities, a department] the act of organizing and controlling something, especially a business □ *The mistake was due to bad management.* □ *business management* □ *crisis management* □ *time management* □ *a management course.* -2. [of a business, operation, theater] the people who organize and control a business or other organization □ *'The management reserves the right to refuse admission.'* □ *Talks between senior management and workers have broken down.* □ *The restaurant is under new management.* □ *Management has refused to enter into negotiations.*

management consultant *n* a person whose job is to give advice to a company or other organization on how it should be managed.

manager ['mænɪdʒər] *n* -1. a person who manages somebody or something □ *a senior/department/personnel manager* □ *the party's campaign manager.* -2. SPORT a person who chooses, coaches, and organizes a team.

managerial [ˌmænə'dʒɪərɪəl] *adj* [post, training, decision] that is connected with the job of a manager □ *technical and managerial skills.*

managing director [ˌmænɪdʒɪŋ-] *n* GB the person who is in charge of the general management of a company.

Manchester ['mæntʃɪstər] a city in northwestern England, famous for its industrial history. POPULATION: 397,400.

Mancunian [mæŋ'kjuːnjən] *n* a person who comes from or lives in Manchester.

mandarin ['mændərɪn] *n* -1. **mandarin (orange)** a kind of small orange that is easy to peel. -2. GB a high-ranking civil servant or public official, especially one who has great influence (disapproving use) □ *Whitehall mandarins.*
◆ **Mandarin** *n* the official language of China.

mandate ['mændeɪt] *n* -1. the right or power to pass laws, take action etc, that results from winning an election or a vote □ *The President has no mandate from the people to raise taxes.* -2. a task, order, or instruction (formal use) □ *My mandate is to arrange advertising; it does not cover market research.*

mandatory [US 'mændətɔːrɪ, GB -ətrɪ] *adj* [grant, fine] that must be made, paid etc, according to the law or rules □ *This kind of license is mandatory in the US.*

Mandela [mæn'delə], **Nelson** (1918–) President of South Africa since 1994. He became the country's first black president after spending 26 years as a political prisoner.

mandolin [mændə'lɪn] *n* a musical instrument with four pairs of strings and a round back.

mane [meɪn] *n* the long hairs that grow along the back of a horse's neck or around the head and neck of a lion □ *a horse's/lion's mane.*

man-eating [-iːtɪŋ] *adj* [lion, tiger, shark] that may attack and kill a human for food.

maneuver US, **manoeuvre** GB [mə'nuːvər] ◇ *n* -1. a movement, especially one that is difficult and requires skill □ *It was a tricky maneuver, but I just about did it.* -2. a clever and sometimes deceptive action that is intended to achieve a particular purpose. ■ **room for maneuver** the chance to try different things or change one's plans □ *The wording leaves both sides with plenty of room for maneuver.*
◇ *vt* [ship, vehicle] to move <sthg large>, usually with skill, in difficult circumstances □ *He maneuvered the car into the garage.* ◇ *vi* [person, ship, vehicle] to carry out a maneuver □ *This is the stage when politicians on both sides traditionally maneuver for position.*
◆ **maneuvers** *npl* MILITARY a military training exercise involving many soldiers on a large area of land □ *The army was on maneuvers.*

maneuverable US, **manoeuvrable** GB [mə'nuːvrəbl] *adj* [vehicle, controls] that can be moved, operated etc easily.

Man Friday [ˌmæn'fraɪdeɪ] a character in the novel *Robinson Crusoe*, by Daniel Defoe, who becomes Crusoe's servant.

manfully ['mænflɪ] *adv* [struggle, try] in a determined way, without complaining or asking for help even if it is necessary.

manganese ['mæŋgəniːz] *n* a gray-white metal

that is used in making glass and steel. SYM-BOL: Mn.

mange [meɪndʒ] *n* a skin disease that affects animals, especially dogs and cats, causing them to lose their hair.

manger [ˈmeɪndʒəʳ] *n* a long open container in a barn or stable that cattle, horses etc can eat hay from.

mangetout (pea) [ˌmɒndʒtuː(-)] *n* GB a vegetable that consists of very small peas in a flat pod and that is eaten without removing the pod.

mangle [ˈmæŋgl] *vt* **-1.** [car, body] to damage <sthg> very badly by crushing or twisting it □ *the mangled remains of a bicycle.* **-2.** [version, translation] to spoil or do <sthg> badly, e.g. by making a lot of mistakes □ *The orchestra gave a mangled performance of the symphony.*

mango [ˈmæŋgoʊ] (*pl* **mangoes** OR **mangos**) *n* a tropical fruit that has thin green, yellow, or red skin, juicy orange flesh, and a large seed in the center.

mangrove [ˈmæŋgroʊv] *n* a tropical tree that grows on mud beside water and has roots above the ground □ *a mangrove swamp.*

mangy [ˈmeɪndʒɪ] (*compar* **mangier**, *superl* **mangiest**) *adj* [cat, dog] that has mange.

manhandle [ˈmænhændl] *vt* to hold or push <sb> roughly, especially in order to take them somewhere.

Manhattan [mænˈhætn] an island at the mouth of the Hudson River, in New York City, USA. It is a borough of New York City and a cultural, commercial, and financial center. POPULATION: 1,428,000.

Manhattan Project *n* **the Manhattan Project** the US plan to build the first atomic bomb.

manhole [ˈmænhoʊl] *n* a round opening in a road, with a metal covering, that leads to sewers, water pipes etc.

manhood [ˈmænhʊd] *n* **-1.** the state of being a man, rather than a boy □ *He had grown from boyhood to manhood.* **-2.** all the men in a particular society or country (literary use) □ *the prime of the country's manhood.*

man-hour *n* the work done by one person in one hour.

manhunt [ˈmænhʌnt] *n* a search by the police of an area or country for a wanted person, especially for a dangerous criminal.

mania [ˈmeɪnɪə] *n* **-1.** a very strong and extreme desire or need for something □ *She's got a mania for ice cream these days.* **-2.** MEDICINE a mental illness.

maniac [ˈmeɪnɪæk] *n* (informal use) **-1.** a person who is believed to suffer from a dangerous mental illness. **-2.** a person who behaves in a wild and dangerous way □ *That guy drives like a maniac!* **-3.** a person who has a very great interest in or liking for something □ *a sex maniac.*

manic [ˈmænɪk] *adj* [person, behavior] very energetic, e.g. because of nervousness or excitement □ *It was manic in the office this morning.*

manic-depressive ◇ *adj* [person] who has ex-

treme and uncontrollable changes of mood between happiness and misery. ◇ *n* a manic-depressive person.

manicure [ˈmænɪkjʊəʳ] ◇ *n* a treatment to make the hands look more attractive, especially the shaping and painting of fingernails. ◇ *vt* to give <sb's hands and nails> a manicure.

manifest [ˈmænɪfest] (formal use) ◇ *adj* [stupidity, failure, anger] that is easy to see. ◇ *vt* [resistance, guilt, support] to show <sthg> clearly □ *Their anger manifested itself in different ways.* ◇ *n* a list of the cargo or passengers on a ship or plane □ *a flight manifest.*

manifestation [ˌmænɪfeˈsteɪʃn] *n* [of a feeling, change, situation] the form or way in which something becomes clear for people to see (formal use).

Manifest Destiny *n* in the 19th century, the belief that the USA could expand across North America because it was God's wish.

manifestly [ˈmænɪfestlɪ] *adv* **manifestly obvious/wrong etc** clearly obvious/wrong etc (formal use) □ *The board is manifestly failing in its duties to stockholders.*

manifesto [ˌmænɪˈfestoʊ] (*pl* **manifestos** OR **manifestoes**) *n* a piece of writing in which a group such as a political party presents its ideas and plans □ *an election manifesto.*

manifold [ˈmænɪfoʊld] ◇ *adj* [problems, qualities, differences] numerous and various (literary use). ◇ *n* AUTO a system of pipes that allows gases to enter and escape from a car engine.

manila [məˈnɪlə] *adj* [envelope, folder] made of strong brown paper.

Manila [məˈnɪlə] the capital of the Philippines. POPULATION: 1,998,918.

manilla [məˈnɪlə] *adj* = manila.

manipulate [məˈnɪpjəleɪt] *vt* **-1.** [person, system, situation] to control <sb> in an unfair or deceitful way so that they do what one wants □ *They're trying to manipulate you into saying "no".* **-2.** [lever, controls] to move and control <a piece of equipment> with one's hands, especially skillfully.

manipulation [məˌnɪpjəˈleɪʃn] *n*: see **manipulate** □ *His adept manipulation of the media was what saved him.*

manipulative [məˈnɪpjələtɪv] *adj* [person] who one thinks manipulates people, situations etc (disapproving use) .

Manitoba [ˌmænɪˈtoʊbə] a province of central Canada. ABBREVIATION: MB. SIZE: 650,000 sq kms. POPULATION: 1,091,942 (*Manitobans*). CAPITAL: Winnipeg.

mankind [mænˈkaɪnd] *n* the human race □ *What is the future of mankind?*

manly [ˈmænlɪ] (*compar* **manlier**, *superl* **manliest**) *adj* [pride, voice, chest] that is typical of what many people think a man should be like.

man-made *adj* [fiber, problem, path] that is not created naturally, but by people □ *a man-made disaster* □ *The lake is man-made.*

manna [ˈmænə] *n* **manna from heaven** a gift,

especially money, that provides unexpected help.

manned [mænd] *adj* [spacecraft, submarine] that is occupied and operated by a person or people.

mannequin ['mænɪkɪn] *n* -1. an object in the shape of the human body that is used to show how clothes look on a person and is often seen in store windows. -2. a female model (old-fashioned use).

manner ['mænər] *n* -1. a way of doing something □ *We discussed terms in the usual manner.* ■ **in a manner of speaking** a phrase used to say that a statement is not the case in a precise way, but only in a general way □ *"So, did he win?" — "Well yes, in a manner of speaking."* -2. a way of behaving or acting toward other people □ *I don't like his manner one little bit! □ She has a very relaxed manner.* -3. **all manner of...** many different types of... □ *There were all manner of people there.*

◆ **manners** *npl* the accepted way of behaving politely or correctly in social situations □ *She's got good/bad manners. □ Some people have no manners these days!*

mannered ['mænərd] *adj* [behavior, style] not natural or sincere.

mannerism ['mænərɪzm] *n* a way of moving or talking that is very typical of a particular person and that is often slightly unusual.

mannish ['mænɪʃ] *adj* [face, voice, behavior] that makes a woman seem like a man □ *She looks very mannish with short hair.*

manoeuvre *etc* GB = **maneuver** *etc*.

manor ['mænər] *n* a large old house in the countryside with private land around it.

manpower ['mænpauər] *n* a collective term for all the workers used in a particular kind of work □ *The industry is suffering from a shortage of manpower.*

manservant ['mænsɜːrˈvnt] (*pl* **menservants**) *n* a male servant in a house (old-fashioned use).

mansion ['mænʃn] *n* a very large house.

man-size(d) *adj* a **man-size(d) tissue/meal etc** a large tissue/meal etc.

manslaughter ['mænslɔːtər] *n* the crime of killing somebody without intending to □ *Howell pleaded guilty to manslaughter.*

mantelpiece ['mæntlpiːs] *n* the shelf along the top of a fireplace.

mantle ['mæntl] *n* -1. a layer of something that covers a surface (literary use) □ *A mantle of fog lay over the town.* -2. **the mantle of sthg** [of leader, champion] the very important and respected position of sthg □ *She was pleased to take up the mantle of party leader.*

man-to-man *adj* a **man-to-man talk/discussion** a talk/discussion that takes place between two men, especially on a difficult subject, and is direct and open.

manual ['mænjuəl] ◇ *adj* -1. **manual work** OR **labor** heavy work done by hand □ *a manual job.* -2. [control, system, car] that is operated or done by using one's hands, and not a machine □ *a manual typewriter.* ◇ *n* a book

that contains instructions on how to use a machine or piece of equipment, or how to do a job □ *a training manual □ an instruction manual.*

manually ['mænjuəlɪ] *adv* [operate, control] see **manual**.

manual worker *n* a person who does manual work, e.g. in a factory or on a building site.

manufacture [ˌmænjəˈfæktʃər] ◇ *n* [of cars, televisions] the production of goods, usually in large quantities in a factory □ *The company specializes in the manufacture of high-quality lenses.* ◇ *vt* -1. [car, television] to make <a product>, usually in large quantities, using special equipment in a factory □ *Manufactured goods accounted for the increase in exports.* -2. [excuse, story] to invent <sthg that is not true>.

manufacturer [ˌmænjəˈfæktʃərər] *n* a person or company that manufactures a particular product □ *a clothing/car manufacturer □ a discount of 30% off the manufacturer's recommended retail price.*

manufacturing [ˌmænjəˈfæktʃərɪŋ] *n* the sector of industry that involves the production of goods in factories □ *the number of people involved in manufacturing industries □ manufacturing costs.*

manure [məˈnjuər] *n* excrement from an animal that is used on the land to help plants and crops grow better □ *horse/pig manure.*

manuscript ['mænjəskrɪpt] *n* -1. a written or typed copy of a text, especially of a book that is going to be published, that is not the final copy □ *a manuscript copy.* -2. an old text written by hand, especially before the invention of printing.

Manx [mæŋks] ◇ *adj* [person, custom, law] that comes from or belongs to the Isle of Man. ◇ *n* a Celtic language that used to be widely spoken on the Isle of Man.

many ['menɪ] (*compar* **more**, *superl* **most**) ◇ *det* -1. **many people/cars** a large number of people/cars (formal use) □ *The issue has been raised on many occasions. □ It's one of the many things I still have to do.* -2. used in questions and negative sentences; used with "so", "too" etc □ *How many times have you been there? □ Not many people know that. □ I didn't find many mistakes. □ There weren't many people left when I arrived. □ There are so many places I'd still like to visit. □ They bought too many computers.* ■ **a good** OR **great many children** a very large number of children □ *There are still a great many problems to be solved.* ◇ *pron: Many of the applicants are overqualified for the post. □ I don't know how many are coming. □ There were so many I couldn't count them. □ A good many had to be turned away.*

Maori ['maurɪ] ◇ *n* a native New Zealander; the language of this people. ◇ *adj: a Maori dish/song.*

Mao Tse-tung [ˌmautseɪˈtuŋ], **Mao Zedong** [ˌmaudzəˈduŋ] (1893–1976) a Chinese revolutionary leader who was the first head of state of Communist China, from 1949 to 1976. He was also known as Chairman Mao.

map [mæp] (*pt* & *pp* **mapped**, *cont* **mapping**) *n* a drawing of any part of the earth's surface showing the shape of countries, the position of towns, features such as rivers and roads etc □ *a road map* □ *a map of the world* □ *I'm no good at reading maps.*

◆ **map out** *vt sep* **to map sthg out** [route, plan, schedule] to prepare the details of sthg carefully □ *Her book maps out the long-term future of the coal industry.*

maple ['meɪpl] *n* a tree that grows in northern countries and has leaves with five points shaped like an open hand.

maple leaf *n* the leaf of a maple tree, used as a symbol on the Canadian national flag.

maple syrup *n* a thick sweet liquid that is made from the sap of a type of maple tree and is used as a sauce with desserts.

mar [mɑːr] (*pt* & *pp* **marred**, *cont* **marring**) *vt* [occasion, success, beauty] to spoil <sthg> so that it is less perfect or good □ *A knee injury marred his chances of taking part in the race.* □ *The event was marred by crowd violence.*

Mar. *abbr of* **March**.

maraschino cherry [,mærəʃiːnoʊ-] *n* a cherry that has been kept in a liqueur and is used to decorate cakes, cocktails etc.

marathon [US 'mærəθɒn, GB -θən] ◇ *adj* [task, speech, talks] very long and tiring □ *a marathon exam.* ◇ *n* **-1.** SPORT a race that is run over a distance of twenty-six miles. **-2.** an event or activity that lasts for a very long time □ *a dance marathon.*

marathon runner *n* a person who runs in a marathon.

marauding [mə'rɔːdɪŋ] *adj* [gang, animal] that goes from one place to another, looking for something to steal or kill.

marble ['mɑːrbl] *n* **-1.** [for buildings, statues] a type of hard stone that is white, sometimes with a mixture of other colors, becomes smooth when polished, and is used as a material for sculpture and building □ *a marble slab/statue.* **-2.** GAMES a small colored ball that is made of glass and is used for games, especially by children.

◆ **marbles** *n* GAMES a children's game which involves rolling marbles along the ground.

march [mɑːrtʃ] ◇ *n* **-1.** MILITARY the act of walking with regular steps, as part of a group of soldiers. **-2.** [by protesters] an organized event in which a large number of people walk together along a particular route in order to publicly protest about something □ *They've gone on a protest march.* **-3. the march of time/progress etc** the process of time/progress etc continuing in a way that cannot be stopped.

◇ *vi* **-1.** [soldiers, band] to walk together at the same speed with regular steps □ *The army marched down the street.* □ *I could hear the sound of marching men.* **-2.** [demonstrators] to take part in a protest march □ *Students marched alongside the workers.* □ *We're marching against racism.* **-3. to march in/out etc** to walk in/out in an energetic way, often be-

cause one is angry □ *He marched up to me and started shouting.* □ *She turned around and marched off.*

◇ *vt* **to lead** <sb> **to** or **from** a place against their will □ *He was marched down to the principal's office.*

March *n* the third month of the year in the Western calendar; *see also* **February**.

marcher ['mɑːrtʃər] *n* a person who takes part in a protest march.

marching orders ['mɑːrtʃɪŋ-] *npl* **to get one's marching orders** to be told officially to leave a job, place, or situation (informal use).

marchioness [US 'mɑːrʃənəs, GB ,mɑːʃə'nes] *n* the wife of a marquis; a noblewoman of the same rank as a marquis.

march-past *n* a ceremony in which soldiers march past an important person, place, or monument as a sign of respect.

Marco Polo [,mɑːrkoʊ'poʊloʊ] (1254–1324) an Italian merchant and traveler. He wrote a famous account of his travels in India and China.

Mardi Gras [US 'mɑːrdɪgrɑː, GB ,mɑːdɪ'grɑː] *n* a carnival that takes place in some cities and countries, just before the day that Lent begins.

✌ MARDI GRAS

One of the best-known Mardi Gras carnivals is held every year in New Orleans, USA. The costume parades, music, and dancing in the streets are very popular with tourists. In the rest of the USA, people traditionally have parties or go to restaurants to celebrate Mardi Gras.

mare [meər] *n* an adult female horse.

margarine [US 'mɑːrdʒərən, GB ,mɑːdʒə'riːn] *n* a yellow substance that is made from animal or vegetable fat and is eaten like butter on bread or used in cooking.

margin ['mɑːrdʒɪn] *n* **-1.** [of victory, a win] the amount by which something is different from another thing □ *Mrs O'Leary won the vote by a margin of 10%.* □ *The team had a huge, 12-point winning margin.* **-2.** [for error, safety] an extra amount of something that makes it possible to be flexible and prepared for unexpected events or circumstances □ *We must remember to allow a margin for error.* □ *a 30-minute safety margin.* **-3.** [on a page] the empty space at the side of a page next to a piece of writing, sometimes marked by a line that goes from the top to the bottom □ *He made notes in the margin.* **-4.** [of a wood, desert, lake] the edge of an area of land or water □ *The settlement lies on the plain's eastern margins.* **-5. the margins of sthg** [of a political party, activity] the part of sthg that is not considered important, especially because it is not approved of or taken seriously □ *The program is designed to help those on the margins of society.*

marginal ['mɑːrdʒɪnl] *adj* **-1.** [issue, effect] that is too small to be important □ *The changes have brought only marginal improvements.* **-2.** GB POLITICS **a marginal seat** OR **constituency** a constituency where no party can be certain of a strong majority, with the result that election results are usually very close.

marginally ['mɑːʳdʒɪnlɪ] *adv* **to be marginally closer/better** to be only a little closer/better ◻ *His health has improved only marginally.* ◻ *We would only be marginally better off if you changed jobs.*

Marie Antoinette [US məˌriːæntwəˈnet, GB ˌmærɪ-] (1755–1793) Queen of France from 1770 to 1792. She was an unpopular queen who is supposed to have said "Let them eat cake" when told that the poor had no bread. She was killed on the guillotine with her husband, Louis XVI.

marigold ['mærɪgould] *n* a plant with bright yellow or orange flowers.

marihuana, marijuana [US ˌmerɪˈwɑːnə, GB ˌmær-] *n* a drug, illegal in most countries, that is made from cannabis leaves and is smoked with tobacco or mixed with food.

marina [məˈriːnə] *n* a small area of water next to a river or harbor, where private boats are kept.

marinade [US ˌmerəˈneɪd, GB ˌmær-] ◇ *n* a liquid or sauce in which meat or fish is soaked, especially before cooking, in order to give it a particular flavor. ◇ *vt* & *vi* = **marinate**.

marinate [US 'mereneɪt, GB 'mær-] ◇ *vt* [meat, fish, fruit] to soak <food> in a marinade. ◇ *vi* [meat, fish, fruit] *I left the chicken to marinate in wine.*

marine [məˈriːn] ◇ *adj* [life, biology] that is connected with the sea. ◇ *n* MILITARY **-1.** US a soldier who is a member of the Marine Corps. **-2.** GB a soldier who is a member of the Royal Marines.
◆ **Marines** *npl* = **Marine Corps**.

Marine Corps *n* a US armed force made up of soldiers who serve on land and ships.

marionette [US ˌmerɪəˈnet, GB ˌmær-] *n* a puppet that is moved by pulling strings.

marital ['mærɪtl] *adj* [problems, stress] that is connected with marriage or married people.

marital status *n* the fact of being married, single, widowed, or divorced ◻ *Please give your name and marital status.*

maritime ['mærɪtaɪm] *adj* [museum, law] that is connected with the sea and ships.

Maritime Provinces: the Maritime Provinces the eastern Canadian provinces of New Brunswick, Nova Scotia, and Prince Edward Island, when considered together.

Maritimes = **Maritime Provinces**.

marjoram ['mɑːʳdʒərəm] *n* a plant with purple flowers, whose leaves are used as an herb in cooking.

mark [mɑːʳk] ◇ *n* **-1.** [on a surface] something such as a line or small colored area that damages or colors the surface of something and was made by something else, e.g. a sharp object or a liquid ◻ *The oil had left a small mark on my sleeve.* ◻ *There were red marks on his arm.* ◻ *a dirty mark* ◻ *a scratch/burn mark.* **-2.** a symbol that is written, drawn,

printed, or stamped in order to show something such as punctuation. ■ **to make one's mark** to have an important and noticeable effect on something ◻ *She made her mark with a fine opening speech.* **-3.** [on a test, exam] a number or letter that indicates how good or bad somebody's performance on a test or exam is ◻ *She got the best marks in the class.* ◻ *a high/low mark* ◻ *The pass mark is 50%.* **-4.** a point that represents a particular stage or level of something ◻ *It was in that year that unemployment reached the three million mark.* ◻ *the halfway mark.* **-5. a mark of sthg** [of respect, friendship, experience] something that can be seen as proof of or a sign of sthg else ◻ *Flags flew at half mast as a mark of respect.* **-6.** FINANCE the unit of currency used in Germany. **-7.** *phrases* **to be quick/slow off the mark** to move, think, or react quickly/slowly in a situation ◻ *You'll have to be quicker off the mark than that if you want to win.* ■ **wide of the mark** [person, prediction, criticism] not accurate at all, and showing a lack of understanding of the facts, a situation etc ◻ *His comments went very wide of the mark.*
◇ *vt* **-1.** [wall, face] to make a mark of ink, dirt etc on <sthg>, usually by accident ◻ *The book is marked on the front cover.* **-2.** [letter, file, drawer] to write or print a label or symbol on <sthg> to make it easier to find or recognize ◻ *The file was marked "Top Secret".* **-3.** [homework, essay, exam] to check and make corrections to <a piece of work>, usually in order to give a mark showing how good or bad it is ◻ *The answer was marked wrong.* **-4.** to show the exact location of <sthg>; to represent the point in time of <sthg> ◻ *X marks the spot.* ◻ *Today marks a turning point in our lives.* **-5.** [event, anniversary] to do something special in order to remember <sthg> ◻ *Let's have some champagne to mark the occasion.*
◆ **mark down** *vt sep* **-1. to mark sthg down** to lower the price of sthg ◻ *The shirts have been marked down.* **-2. to mark sb down** [student, candidate] to give sb a lower mark, e.g. because they have made a mistake.
◆ **mark off** *vt sep* **to mark sthg off** [item, date, name] to mark sthg on paper with a line, check, cross etc to show that it has been dealt with.
◆ **mark up** *vt sep* **to mark sthg up** to raise the price of sthg ◻ *Retail stores mark up the price of their goods by up to 50%.*

Mark Antony [ˌmɑːʳkˈæntənɪ] (83–30 BC) a Roman military and political leader. He became one of the rulers of the Roman Empire, but left for Egypt after falling in love with Cleopatra. Antony and Cleopatra committed suicide after being defeated.

marked [mɑːʳkt] *adj* [difference, change, improvement] that is large and can be easily noticed ◻ *There's been a marked decline in standards since then.*

markedly ['mɑːʳkədlɪ] *adv:* **to be markedly better/worse** to be much better/worse in a way that is easily noticed ◻ *The situation has changed markedly in the last few years.*

marker ['mɑːʳkəʳ] *n* -1. a sign that shows the exact location of something □ *a grave marker.* -2. EDUCATION a person who marks an exam.

marker (pen) *n* a colored pen with a thick tip that is used for writing on a whiteboard, drawing pictures etc.

market ['mɑːʳkət] ◇ *n* -1. [for shopping] a place indoors or outdoors where goods such as food, clothing, and jewelry are bought and sold on particular days at stalls rather than stores □ *a fish market* □ *a street market* □ *a market stall.* -2. [of a particular product] the number of people who buy, or might buy, a particular product; the amount of business done in connection with a particular product □ *Is there really a market for this type of thing?* □ *the car/housing market* □ *The group has increased its market share from 8% to 12%.* ■ **on the market** available to be bought □ *They've just put their house on the market.* □ *The new model has only just come onto the market.* -3. [in the world] the area or part of the world where a product is sold □ *We have to expand beyond the domestic market.* -4. FINANCE a place or system in which commodities, currency, shares, property etc are bought and sold □ *Stock and bond markets had an unsettled week.* □ *foreign exchange markets.*
◇ *vt* [product, range, image] to use a particular strategy in order to sell <sthg> □ *They've tried to market it as a young person's car.*

marketable ['mɑːʳkətəbl] *adj* [product, image, skills] that can be used to make money □ *It's a highly marketable skill.*

market analysis *n* the study and reporting of the behavior of a market such as the commodities market.

market forces *npl* the factors that affect the prices of goods when there are no government controls □ *The cold wind of market forces has shaken many subsidized industries, including shipbuilding.*

market garden *n* GB a place where fruit and vegetables are grown in large quantities to be sold.

marketing ['mɑːʳkətɪŋ] *n* -1. [of a product] the process of trying to sell something by using particular packaging, advertising etc □ *John works in marketing.* □ *a marketing strategy.* -2. **to go marketing** US to go shopping, especially for food.

marketplace ['mɑːʳkətpleɪs] *n* -1. an area of open space in a town or village, usually a square, where a market is held. -2. **the marketplace** BUSINESS the place or area of business in which buying and selling takes place □ *We must be able to compete in the international marketplace.*

market price *n* the price that is paid for a product, commodity etc in a free market.

market research *n* in business, the process of getting information about people's tastes, lifestyles, incomes etc, in order to know what demand there is for a particular product □ *They did a lot of market research before launching the product.*

market town *n* GB a town where a market is regularly held, especially one in an area where there are many farms.

market value *n* the value of something based on how much people would be willing to pay for it □ *The stock has a market value of $200,000.*

marking ['mɑːʳkɪŋ] *n* the activity of checking and correcting a piece of homework or an exam and giving it a mark to show how good or bad it is □ *I've got a huge pile of marking to do.*

◆ **markings** *npl* -1. [on a bird, butterfly, leaf] a coloring or pattern that makes a particular type of animal, insect, or plant look different from others. -2. [on a plane, police car] a special design or symbol used to identify a vehicle.

marksman ['mɑːʳksmən] (*pl* **marksmen** [-mən]) *n* a person, especially a police officer, who is trained to shoot accurately □ *a police marksman.*

marksmanship ['mɑːʳksmənʃɪp] *n* the ability to shoot accurately.

markup ['mɑːʳkʌp] *n* an increase in the price of something, especially when it is the difference between the original cost price and the price it is sold at □ *There's a markup of 50% on every unit.*

Marlowe ['mɑːʳləʊ], **Christopher** (1564–1593) an English playwright. His works include *Tamburlaine the Great* and *Dr Faustus.*

marmalade ['mɑːʳməleɪd] *n* a sweet food that is made from sugar and oranges or lemons and is spread on bread or toast.

maroon [məˈruːn] *adj* [shirt, carpet, car] dark red-brown.

marooned [məˈruːnd] *adj* **to be marooned** to be left alone in a place where nobody lives and be unable to leave it □ *What would you do if you were marooned on a desert island?*

marquee [mɑːʳˈkiː] *n* a large tent where people can eat and drink, used at outdoor events, e.g. at a wedding reception or fair.

marquess ['mɑːʳkwəs] *n* = **marquis.**

marquetry ['mɑːʳkətrɪ] *n* the technique of decorating wooden furniture or objects with different colored pieces of wood, fitted together in a pattern.

marquis ['mɑːʳkwəs] *n* a nobleman who ranks between a duke and an earl.

marriage ['mærɪdʒ] *n* -1. the act of joining together a man and woman as husband and wife in a ceremony □ *They recently announced their forthcoming marriage.* □ *a marriage ceremony* □ *marriage vows.* -2. the relationship between a husband and wife □ *They have a happy marriage.* -3. the idea or state of being married □ *Marriage doesn't really appeal to me.* □ *My marriage broke up last year.*

marriage bureau *n* GB an agency that uses the personal details of clients to help them find suitable partners for marriage.

marriage certificate *n* the document that officially records the marriage of a man and woman.

marriage counseling *n* US advice and help given by a marriage guidance counselor.

marriage counselor *n* US a person whose job is to give advice and help to a married couple who are having difficulties in their relationship.

marriage guidance *n* GB = **marriage counseling**.

marriage guidance counsellor *n* GB = **marriage counselor**.

married ['mærɪd] *adj* [man, woman, couple] joined in marriage; [life, bliss] that is connected with marriage □ *Are you married or single?* □ *How long were they married?* □ *a happily married man/woman* □ *She's married to an opera singer.* □ *How are you enjoying married life?*

marrow ['mærou] *n* -1. the soft substance inside bones. -2. GB a large, long, green vegetable with thin white stripes along its skin, and white flesh.

marry ['mæri] (*pt* & *pp* **married**) ◇ *vt* -1. to become the husband or wife of <sb> □ *Will you marry me?* ■ **to get married** to become joined in marriage □ *She got married to him at the age of seventeen.* -2. to perform the marriage ceremony for <two people> □ *We were married by a priest/registrar.* ◇ *vi* to become joined in marriage □ *We hope to marry in a year or two.* □ *Do you think he'll ever marry and settle down?*

Mars [mɑːz] the planet in the solar system that is the fourth furthest from the Sun.

marsh [mɑːʃ] *n* a piece of low flat land that is soft and wet and is often found at the edge of lakes, rivers etc.

marshal ['mɑːʃl] (US *pt* & *pp* **marshaled**, *cont* **marshaling**, GB *pt* & *pp* **marshalled**, *cont* **marshalling**) ◇ *n* -1. MILITARY in some armies, an officer of the highest rank. -2. [at a concert, march, sports event] a person who is present at a public event, and helps with organization and crowd control. -3. US an officer who is in charge of a particular police or fire department. ◇ *vt* -1. [crowds, spectators] to direct <people> in order to make sure that an event takes place safely. -2. [one's thoughts, support, forces] to arrange and organize <sthg> in order to be able to make good use of it.

marshalling yard ['mɑːʃlɪŋ-] *n* GB a place where the different sections of a train are put together.

marshland ['mɑːʃlænd] *n* an area of land that consists of marshes.

marshmallow [US 'mɑːrʃmelou, GB ˌmɑːʃ'mæloʊ] *n* -1. a large, soft, round candy that is usually pink or white and that people sometimes toast over a fire. -2. a soft, spongy, sweet food used to make marshmallows □ *a marshmallow cookie.*

marshy ['mɑːʃɪ] (*compar* **marshier**, *superl* **marshiest**) *adj* [land, area] that is flat and has soft wet soil.

marsupial [mɑːˈsuːpjəl] *n* a type of animal, such as the kangaroo, of which the female carries her young in a pouch on her body.

martial ['mɑːʃl] *adj* [behavior, discipline, music] that is connected with the army.

martial arts *npl* the forms of self-defense based on philosophy and discipline that come from the Far East, e.g. judo and karate □ *an expert in martial arts.*

Martha's Vineyard [ˌmɑːˈθəz-] an island off the coast of Massachusetts that is a popular summer resort.

martial law *n* a situation in which the army controls what people do in a town, region, or country, to stop attacks against the government.

Martian ['mɑːʃn] ◇ *adj* [soil, life] that is from or connected with Mars. ◇ *n* in science fiction stories, a creature from Mars.

martin ['mɑːtn] *n* a small bird with a forked tail.

martini [mɑːˈtiːnɪ] *n* an alcoholic drink that consists of gin and vermouth.

Martinique [ˌmɑːtɪˈniːk] a French overseas territory, consisting of a mountainous island in the Caribbean. SIZE: 1,100 sq kms. POPULATION: 359,572 (*Martiniquais*). CAPITAL: Fort-de-France. LANGUAGE: French, Creole. CURRENCY: French franc.

Martin Luther King Day *n* in some states of the USA, a public holiday on the third Monday in January.

martyr ['mɑːtər] *n* a person who dies or suffers for their religious or political beliefs □ *Clare Parker died a martyr to the cause of women's liberation.*

martyrdom ['mɑːtədəm] *n* the death or suffering of a martyr; the status of a martyr.

martyred ['mɑːtəd] *adj* [expression, voice] that suggests suffering, often in an exaggerated way in order to get sympathy from other people.

marvel ['mɑːvl] (US *pt* & *pp* **marveled**, *cont* **marveling**, GB *pt* & *pp* **marvelled**, *cont* **marvelling**) ◇ *n* -1. something, e.g. a building, work of art, event, or achievement, that people admire because it seems almost too impressive to be possible □ *the marvels of Ancient Greece.* -2. an event or achievement that is very surprising and makes people happy □ *It's a marvel (that) she's still alive!* -3. a person who does something that is very surprising and that makes people happy □ *Your new secretary's a real marvel!*
◇ *vt* **to marvel that...** to be very surprised and impressed that something is true □ *We marveled that he could remember so much.*
◇ *vi*: *I marvel at the speed with which they get things done.*

marvelous US, **marvellous** GB ['mɑːvləs] *adj* [news, surprise, movie] wonderful □ *What a marvelous idea!*

Marx [mɑːks], **Karl** (1818–1883) a German philosopher and economist who founded Communism. His works include the *Communist Manifesto* and *Das Kapital*.

Marxism ['mɑːksɪzm] *n* the political philosophy of Karl Marx that is the basis of Communism.

Marxist ['mɑːksəst] ◇ *adj* [ideal, belief, view] that is based on Marxism; [historian, politician] who is influenced by Marxism. ◇ *n* a person who supports Marxism.

Mary [US 'merɪ, GB 'meərɪ] in the Bible, the mother of Jesus.

Mary I [-ðə'fɜːˈst] (1516–1558) Queen of England and Ireland from 1553 to 1558. She tried to restore the Catholic religion in England, and had many Protestants killed.

Mary II [-ðə'sekənd] (1662–1694) Queen of Great Britain and Ireland from 1689 to 1694. She ruled together with her husband William III.

Maryland [US 'merɪlənd, GB 'meər-] a state of the eastern USA, on the Atlantic coast. ABBREVIATION: MD. SIZE: 31,864 sq kms. POPULATION: 4,781,468 (*Marylanders*). CAPITAL: Annapolis. MAIN CITY: Baltimore.

Mary Magdalene [-'mægdəlɪn] in the Bible, a woman who Jesus cured of evil spirits. She was the first person to see him after he rose from the dead.

Mary Queen of Scots (1542–1587) Queen of Scotland from 1542 to 1567. She spent her last 20 years as a prisoner of Elizabeth I of England, who finally had her killed.

marzipan ['mɑːˈzɪpæn] *n* a soft sweet food that is made from almonds, sugar, and eggs, and used to make cakes and candy.

mascara [US mæˈskærə, GB -ˈskɑːrə] *n* a dark substance used as make-up on one's eyelashes to make them more noticeable.

mascot ['mæskət] *n* a person, animal, or object that is supposed to bring good luck to somebody or to a group of people such as a sports team, and is sometimes used as their symbol.

masculine ['mæskjələn] *adj* **-1.** [pride, idea, appearance] that is typical of a man, rather than of a woman □ *That's a very masculine attitude.* **-2.** [woman, face, nature] that has qualities usually associated with a man □ *She had a short, masculine haircut.* **-3.** GRAMMAR a word used to refer to one of the classes that nouns are divided into in some languages □ *Is the French word "chat" masculine or feminine?*

masculinity [ˌmæskjəˈlɪnətɪ] *n* **-1.** the state of being a man, usually shown by certain typical qualities. **-2.** the qualities considered to be typical of men.

mash [mæʃ] *vt* [potato, carrots] to squash and mix <vegetables> into a soft mass, often using a special tool □ *He mashed everything up together in the pan.*

MASH [mæʃ] (*abbr of* **mobile army surgical hospital**) *n* a US army hospital that is set up close to a battlefield.

mashed potatoes ['mæʃt-] *npl* potatoes that have been boiled and mashed.

mask [US mæsk, GB mɑːsk] ◇ *n* **-1.** [for one's face] a piece of material or equipment that is worn over one's face in order to protect it or make it look different □ *The actors all wore masks.* □ *a surgical face mask.* **-2.** [of bravery, politeness, disinterest] behavior that hides somebody's true feelings or character □ *Meanwhile, mother put on a polite mask for the*

guests. ◇ *vt* **-1.** [face, eyes, building] to cover <sthg> and prevent it from being seen. **-2.** [anger, pain] to stop people from noticing <sthg one feels> by behaving in a particular way □ *His aggression masks a deeper insecurity.* **-3.** [smell, taste] to prevent <sthg> from being noticed by being stronger □ *The chili masks the taste of the chicken.*

masked [US mæskt, GB mɑːskt] *adj* [gunman, robber, attacker] who is wearing a mask □ *The man was masked and was holding a gun.*

masking tape [US 'mæskɪŋ-, GB 'mɑːsk-] *n* a type of tape that is designed to be stuck on a surface, e.g. near an area that is going to be painted, to protect it.

masochism ['mæsəkɪzm] *n* behavior in which somebody gets pleasure, especially of a sexual kind, from suffering or pain.

masochist ['mæsəkəst] *n* a person who gets pleasure, especially of a sexual kind, from experiencing suffering or pain.
NOTE: Compare **sadist**.

masochistic [ˌmæsəˈkɪstɪk] *adj* [behavior, desire] *see* **masochist**.

mason ['meɪsn] *n* = **stonemason**.
◆ **Mason** *n* = **Freemason**.

Mason-Dixon Line [-'dɪksn-] *n* **the Mason-Dixon Line** in the USA, the boundary between Maryland and Pennsylvania.

👻 MASON-DIXON LINE
The Mason-Dixon Line was the boundary that separated the Union and the Confederate States during the American Civil War. It is still used as a symbol for the division between the North and South of the United States. People who live south of the line speak with a marked "Southern" accent, and many of them are proud of their cultural independence from the rest of the USA.

---

masonic [məˈsɒnɪk] *adj* [lodge, handshake] that is connected with the Freemasons.

masonry ['meɪsnrɪ] *n* the stones that something, e.g. a building or wall, is made of □ *a lump of masonry* □ *a masonry drill/nail.*

masquerade [ˌmæskəˈreɪd] *vi* **to masquerade as sb** [as a policeman, salesman] to pretend to be sb by dressing or acting the way they do in order to deceive people.

mass [mæs] ◇ *n* **-1.** [of books, people, papers] a large number of things □ *I have a mass of unfinished jobs to do.* **-2.** [of hair, water] a large amount of something □ *a huge mass of concrete.* **-3.** PHYSICS the amount of matter that an object consists of. **-4. the mass of...** the majority of... □ *The mass of people are in favor of this policy.* ◇ *adj* [protest, unemployment, communication] that involves a large number of people □ *weapons of mass destruction.* ◇ *vt* [troops, forces] to gather <people> together in a large group. ◇ *vi* [troops, clouds, marchers] *The crowds are massing in the square.*
◆ **Mass** *n* RELIGION a Christian religious ceremony in which people eat bread and some-

times drink wine as symbols of the body and blood of Jesus Christ.

◆ **masses** *npl* -1. GB [of food, people, traffic] a large amount (informal use) □ *I've got masses of work to do.* □ *There was masses of wine left over.* -2. **the masses** the ordinary working people.

Massachusetts [ˌmæsəˈtʃuːsəts] *n* a state in New England, in the northeastern USA. ABBREVIATION: MA. SIZE: 21,500 sq kms. POPULATION: 6,016,425. CAPITAL: Boston.

massacre [ˈmæsəkər] ◇ *n* the act of killing a large number of people in a cruel and violent way □ *The brutal massacre of innocent civilians.* ◇ *vt* to kill <a large number of people> in a cruel and violent way □ *The government is accused of massacring its own people.*

massage [US məˈsɑːʒ, GB ˈmæs-] ◇ *vt* to press or rub <part of a person's body> in order to relax their muscles □ *Can you massage my shoulders for me?* ◇ *n* the act of massaging part of a person's body □ *He gave her a back massage.*

massage parlor *n* a place where people can have a massage. Some of these places are used to offer sex to clients.

masseur [US mæˈsʊr, GB mæˈsɜː] *n* a man whose job is to give massages.

masseuse [US mæˈsuːz, GB -ˈsɜːz] *n* a woman whose job is to give massages.

massive [ˈmæsɪv] *adj* [amount, building, company] very large □ *a massive increase in tourism.*

massively [ˈmæsɪvlɪ] *adv* [invest, increase, cut] *see* **massive** □ *a massively successful band.*

mass-market *adj* [production, goods] that is suitable for a large number of people.

mass media *n* OR *npl* **the mass media** a collective term for TV, radio, and the press.

mass-produce *vt* [goods, medicines, furniture] to produce large amounts of <a product>, usually in factories □ *The designs are copied and then mass-produced in Indonesia.*

mass production *n* [of goods, medicines, furniture] *see* **mass-produce**.

mast [US mæst, GB mɑːst] *n* -1. SAILING [on boat] a long vertical pole on a boat or ship that supports the sails. -2. RADIO & TV a long vertical pole that supports radio or television antennas □ *a radio mast.*

mastectomy [mæˈstektəmɪ] (*pl* **mastectomies**) *n* a medical operation to remove a woman's breast.

master [US ˈmæstər, GB ˈmɑːstə] ◇ *n* -1. sb's **master** the man that a servant or slave works for □ *My master was not at home.* □ *He reports back to his political masters in Moscow.* -2. **to be master of sthg** [of one's feelings, a situation] to be in control of sthg □ *The country will then be free to be master of its own destiny.* -3. **to be a master of sthg** [of a skill, language] to be very good at sthg □ *She's a master of disguise/the art of persuasion.*
◇ *adj* -1. **a master builder/plumber etc** a very skilled builder/plumber etc. -2. **a master tape/copy etc** an original tape/copy etc from which copies can be made.

◇ *vt* -1. [situation, temper, fear] to bring <sthg> under one's control □ *He tried hard to master his feelings of anger.* -2. [skill, language, job] to learn to do or understand <sthg> perfectly □ *I speak good Spanish, but I haven't quite mastered French yet.*

master bedroom *n* the largest bedroom in a house or apartment.

master disk COMPUTING *n* -1. a disk that contains all the files for a task. -2. a disk that contains the code for a computer's operating system, that must be loaded before the system will work.

masterful [US ˈmæstərfl, GB ˈmɑːstə-] *adj* [person] who is in control of the situation; [voice, behavior] that shows that one is in control of the situation.

master key *n* a key that can open all the locks in a particular place.

masterly [US ˈmæstərlɪ, GB ˈmɑːstəlɪ] *adj* [performance, display] that is very well done.

mastermind [US ˈmæstərmaɪnd, GB ˈmɑːstə-] ◇ *vt* [crime, operation, takeover] to plan and organize <sthg complicated> □ *She masterminded the robbery.* ◇ *n* a person who masterminds something □ *She was the mastermind behind the robbery.*

Master of Arts (*pl* **Masters of Arts**) *n* a postgraduate degree in a subject that is not a science; a person who has this degree.

master of ceremonies (*pl* **masters of ceremonies**) *n* -1. [at a dinner] a person who introduces speakers at formal events. -2. [in a show] a person who introduces entertainers in a variety show.

Master of Science (*pl* **Masters of Science**) *n* a postgraduate degree in a scientific subject; a person who has this degree.

masterpiece [US ˈmæstərpiːs, GB ˈmɑːstə-] *n* -1. ART an extremely good work of art □ *The sculpture is a masterpiece of African woodcarving.* -2. **sb's masterpiece** the best piece of work done by sb □ *The painting is the artist's masterpiece.* -3. **a masterpiece of sthg** a very skillful example of sthg □ *a masterpiece of engineering/deceit/planning.*

master plan *n* a plan that somebody prepares to help them deal with every aspect of a particular situation sucessfully.

Masters and Johnson [US ˌmæstərz-, GB ˌmɑːstəz-] US scientists who studied human sexual behavior in the 1950s and 1960s.

master's degree *n* a university degree that is more advanced than a bachelor's degree and less advanced than a doctorate.

masterstroke [US ˈmæstərstrouk, GB ˈmɑːstə-] *n* an intelligent action or strategy that is not expected and usually results in success.

master switch *n* a switch that controls all the lights or machines in a particular place.

masterwork [US ˈmæstərwɜːrk, GB ˈmɑːstəwɜːk] *n* ART a masterpiece.

mastery [US ˈmæstərɪ, GB ˈmɑːst-] *n* -1. [of a language, skill] great skill at something □ *her complete mastery of her instrument.* -2. [of a situation, area] complete control of something.

mastic ['mæstɪk] *n* a type of resin used to fill gaps in wood, tiles, plaster etc and to make them waterproof.

masticate ['mæstɪkeɪt] (formal use) ◇ *vt* to chew food. ◇ *vi* [person] *Masticate before swallowing.*

mastiff ['mæstɪf] *n* a large powerful dog with short hair.

masturbate ['mæstəʳbeɪt] *vi* to stroke or rub one's sexual organs for pleasure.

masturbation [,mæstəʳ'beɪʃn] *n: see* **masturbate.**

mat [mæt] *n* -1. [on a floor] a piece of carpet or strong material that is put on a floor to protect or decorate it □ *Wipe your feet on the mat.* □ *a floor mat* □ *a rubber mat.* -2. [on a table] a small piece of cloth or cardboard that is put under objects on a table to protect the surface □ *a beer/table mat.*

Mata Hari [,mɑːtə'hɑːrɪ] (1876–1917) a Dutch dancer who worked in Paris as a German spy during World War I.

match [mætʃ] ◇ *n* -1. SPORT & GAMES an organized game in which people or teams compete against each other □ *We won/lost the match.* □ *How many matches have they played?* □ *a tennis/boxing/chess match.* -2. [for lighting things] a thin stick of wood or paper with a substance at one end that produces a flame when it is rubbed against a rough surface □ *She lit a match.* □ *a box of matches.* -3. **to be no match for sb** to be not as good as sb at a particular activity □ *He's no match for her when it comes to negotiating.*
◇ *vt* -1. [ideas, needs] to be the same as <sthg> □ *Your feelings match my own.* -2. [color, garment] to find <sthg> that is the same as or goes with something else □ *I'm trying to match this paint.* □ *Can you match the names with the photographs?* □ *You have to match each symbol to a different letter of the alphabet.* -3. [quality, skill, score] to be of the same standard or level as <sthg> □ *We can never match their level of craftsmanship.*
◇ *vi* -1. [ideas, needs] *We have different views that simply do not match.* -2. [colors, garments] *I'm afraid those styles don't really match.*

matchbox ['mætʃbɒks] *n* a box that contains matches and has a rough side to strike them on.

matched [mætʃt] *adj* **to be well matched** [couple] to be suitable for each other; [opponents, teams] to be equal to each other in strength or ability.

matching ['mætʃɪŋ] *adj* [colors, garments] that have the same color or design as each other.

matchless ['mætʃləs] *adj* [beauty, quality] that is so good that nothing or nobody can be as good as it (literary use).

matchmaker ['mætʃmeɪkəʳ] *n* a person who tries to encourage relationships or marriages between other people.

match play *n* SPORT in golf, a way of scoring that depends on the number of holes a player wins rather than on the total number of strokes taken during the game.

match point *n* SPORT a situation in tennis, squash etc in which a player will win the match if they win the next point □ *The Swede now has match point.* ■ **to have two/three match points** to be two/three points ahead of one's opponent and need one more point to win the match.

matchstick ['mætʃstɪk] *n* a wooden match, usually one that has been used.

mate [meɪt] ◇ *n* -1. [of an animal] a sexual partner □ *Each bird builds an elaborate nest in order to attract a mate.* -2. SHIPPING an officer on a merchant ship □ *the ship's mate.* -3. somebody's wife, husband, or sexual partner. -4. GB a friend (informal use) □ *my mate, Steve.* -5. GB a word used to talk to a man or boy in a friendly way (informal use) □ *Hello, mate!* ◇ *vi* [animals] to have sex in order to produce young □ *The female always mates with the healthiest male.*

material [mə'tɪərɪəl] ◇ *n* -1. [for making something] the substance that something is made of □ *The soles are made of synthetic material.* -2. [for sewing] cloth □ *curtain/dress material.* -3. [for a book, movie] the ideas or information that somebody uses to write something □ *I'm looking for material for my new novel.* ◇ *adj* -1. **material benefits/needs etc** benefits/needs etc that are connected with physical everyday life, rather than moral or spiritual matters. -2. [evidence, information] that is important and relevant.
◆ **materials** *npl* the equipment needed for a particular activity or job □ *building/writing/cleaning materials.*

materialism [mə'tɪərɪəlɪzm] *n* the belief that money, possessions, and physical comforts are more important than spiritual, emotional, or intellectual matters.

materialist [mə'tɪərɪələst] *n* a person with a materialistic attitude.

materialistic [mə,tɪərɪə'lɪstɪk] *adj* [person, society, attitude] that is too concerned with materialism.

materialize, -ise [mə'tɪərɪəlaɪz] *vi* -1. [problem, threat, crisis] to happen, especially in the way that was imagined or expected □ *Unfortunately, the breakthrough failed to materialize.* -2. [person, object] to appear suddenly after having been invisible or somewhere else □ *Just as I said it, Stan materialized as if from nowhere.*

materially [mə'tɪərɪəlɪ] *adv* -1. [benefit, suffer] physically or financially □ *Materially, people are much better off.* -2. [different, significant] in an important way □ *The treaty materially alters the balance of power in the region.*

maternal [mə'tɜːʳnl] *adj* -1. [instinct, attitude] that is typical of a mother's behavior toward her child □ *She's never felt very maternal.* -2. **one's maternal grandfather/aunt** one's grandfather/aunt who is the father/sister of one's mother.

maternity [mə'tɜːʳnətɪ] *n* the state of being a mother.

maternity benefit *n* GB money paid by the state or an employer to a woman just before and after she gives birth to a child.

maternity dress *n* a dress designed for pregnant women.

maternity leave *n* a period of time when a woman is absent from work to have and take care of a baby □ *You're allowed up to six months' maternity leave.*

maternity ward *n* a department in a hospital that deals with women who are pregnant.

mateship ['meɪtʃɪp] *n* AUS the idea of friendship and equality between working people, usually men.

☙ MATESHIP
The idea of mateship in Australia goes back to the hard working conditions of the 19th century. Life was very difficult for workers who moved from place to place in the remote areas of the bush, and it was very important for them to be able to trust and support each other. These values of loyalty and equality became established as typically Australian, and were written about by several 19th-century Australian authors. Today, mateship is still a strong tradition that can be seen in Australians' belief in equality; the word "mate" is still commonly used by men to address one another.

math [mæθ] US, **maths** GB [mæθs] *n* = **mathematics** □ *a math teacher/degree.*

math coprocessor [-koʊ'proʊsesəʳ] *n* an extra processor added to a computer to perform scientific or mathematical tasks more quickly.

mathematical [ˌmæθə'mætɪkl] *adj* -1. [calculation, formula, problem] that involves mathematics. -2. [person] who is good at mathematics □ *He's got a very mathematical mind.*

mathematician [ˌmæθəmə'tɪʃn] *n* a person who is trained or skilled in mathematics.

mathematics [ˌmæθə'mætɪks] *n* the science of numbers, shapes, and calculations (formal use) □ *a mathematics professor.*

maths *n* GB = **math**.

matinée [US ˌmætn'eɪ, GB 'mætɪneɪ] *n* a performance, e.g. of a play or movie, that takes place in the afternoon.

mating call ['meɪtɪŋ-] *n* a sound that animals make to attract each other when they want to mate.

mating season *n* the period of time in the year when particular animals mate □ *Male seals become highly aggressive during the mating season.*

Matisse [mæ'tiːs], **Henri** (1869–1954) a French artist, well known for his use of strong primary colors.

matriarch ['meɪtrɪɑːʳk] *n* -1. [in a society] a woman who is the ruler of a society where power passes from mothers to daughters. -2. [of a family] a powerful woman, usually a mother or grandmother.

matrices ['meɪtrɪsiːz] *plural of* **matrix**.

matriculate [mə'trɪkjəleɪt] *vi* EDUCATION to become officially registered as a student at a university; to reach the academic standard one needs in order to be accepted as a university student.

matriculation [mə,trɪkjə'leɪʃn] *n: see* **matriculate**.

matrimonial [ˌmætrə'moʊnjəl] *adj* [problems, home] connected with marriage.

matrimony [US 'mætrəmoʊni, GB -ɪmənɪ] *n* the state of being married (formal use) □ *these two young people, united in holy matrimony.*

matrix ['meɪtrɪks] (*pl* **matrices** OR **matrixes**) *n* -1. the set of conditions that something, e.g. a culture or society, develops in. -2. INDUSTRY a mold for shaping metal or plastic (technical use). -3. MATH an arrangement of numbers or symbols in columns, used for solving mathematical problems.

matron ['meɪtrən] *n* -1. [in a school] a woman whose job is to check the health of children at a school and take care of them when they are ill. -2. US [in a prison] a woman who is in charge of female prisoners. -3. GB [in a hospital] the most senior nurse who is in charge of all the other nurses.

matronly ['meɪtrənlɪ] *adj* [woman] who is middle-aged and fairly fat (polite use).

matte US, **matt** GB [mæt] *adj* [black, paint, finish] that looks dull and not shiny.

matted ['mætəd] *adj* [hair, fur] that is thick and messy because it is stuck together with water, dirt etc.

matter ['mætəʳ] ◇ *n* -1. a situation or problem that needs to be dealt with or discussed □ *I've come about a private matter.* □ *You should report the matter to the police.* □ *We never discuss money matters.* □ *You can't do it and that's the end of the matter.* □ *Persuading the directors will be no easy matter.* □ *She'll never agree, so you might as well let the matter drop.* -2. **what's the matter with it?** why is it not satisfactory? □ *"I've bought a new car." — "Why? What was the matter with the old one?"* ■ **what's the matter (with you)?** why are you looking angry, excited, ill etc? □ *You look worried: is anything the matter?* □ *There's nothing the matter with me, I'm perfectly alright.* ■ **there's something the matter with my car** my car is not working properly □ *There's nothing the matter with the software, so it must be the computer itself.* -3. PHYSICS a collective term for the solids, liquids, and gases that make up the universe □ *research into the properties of matter at high temperatures.* -4. **waste/vegetable matter** material that consists of waste/vegetables. ■ **reading matter** things for reading, e.g. books or magazines. -5. *phrases* **a matter of five miles** only five miles (used to draw attention to how small something is) □ *Within a matter of hours I was on a plane heading for Bangkok.* ■ **it's just a matter of practice** the only thing that is needed is practice. ■ **it's a matter of life and death** it is very urgent or dangerous. ■ **to do sthg as a matter of principle** to do sthg because you consider it is the right thing to do. ■ **it's/that's a matter of opinion** not everybody agrees with what has just been said □ *"Dickens is a brilliant writer." — "That's a matter of opinion."* □ *It's a matter of* opinion whether she actually deserved to win. ■ **it's a matter of time** it will definitely happen, probably quite soon □ *It's just a matter of time before he's caught.* ■ **to do sthg as a matter of course** to do sthg as part of one's normal way of doing things, rather than as something exceptional □ *Before my letters are mailed I read them over as a matter of course.* ◇ *vi* to be important □ *The only thing that matters to him is money.* ■ **it doesn't matter** it does not change the situation in any way □ *It won't matter if you get there late.* □ *"I'm sorry about yesterday." — "Don't worry, it doesn't matter."*

◆ **matters** *npl* the situation one is talking about □ *Getting angry won't help matters.* ■ **to make matters worse,...** what made a bad situation even worse was that... □ *He lost his job, and to make matters worse, he received no compensation.*

◆ **as a matter of fact** *adv* a phrase used to give more detailed information, or to disagree with what has just been said □ *"Do you ever hear from Kate?" — "Yes, I do. As a matter of fact, I saw her just the other day." □ "I don't suppose you have much time for reading." — "As a matter of fact, I do."*

◆ **for that matter** *adv* a phrase used to say that what has already been said is true of another situation or person □ *You shouldn't lie to me, or to anyone else for that matter.* □ *They hadn't told me anything. Nor, for that matter, had they told anyone else.*

◆ **no matter** *adv* **no matter what/how...** it makes no difference what/how... □ *No matter how hard I try, I can't make him understand.* □ *No matter what she says, he always disagrees.*

Matterhorn ['mætəhɔːʳn]: **the Matterhorn** a mountain in the Alps between Italy and Switzerland. HEIGHT: 4,478 m.

matter-of-fact *adj* [person, voice, attitude] practical and showing no emotion.

Matthews ['mæθjuːz], **Sir Stanley** (1915–) a British soccer player, considered one of the greatest of all time.

matting ['mætɪŋ] *n* rough thick material, e.g. rope or straw, that is woven together and used as a floor covering.

mattress ['mætrəs] *n* a large flat surface filled with soft material or springs that is used for sleeping on, usually as part of a bed.

mature [mə'tʲʊəʳ] ◇ *adj* **-1.** [plant, animal] that has grown to its full size □ *Mature males can reach several meters in length.* **-2.** [person] who behaves in the way that is expected of an adult □ *I'm a mature adult.* □ *He is very mature for his age.* **-3.** [cheese, wine] that tastes strong because it is old enough for its flavor to have developed □ *a strong mature flavor.* ◇ *vi* [plant, person, wine] to become mature □ *Jo has matured into a fine young woman.*

mature student *n* GB a student at a college or university who is over 25.

maturity [mə'tʲʊərətɪ] *n* [of a person] *see* **mature** □ *He has not yet reached maturity.*

maudlin ['mɔːdlɪn] *adj* [person, song] sad and sentimental (disapproving use).

maul [mɔːl] *vt* [lion, dog] to attack and injure <sb> very badly.

Mauritania [,mɒrɪ'teɪnjə] a country in northwestern Africa, on the Atlantic coast, situated mainly in the Sahara Desert. SIZE: 1,080,000 sq kms. POPULATION: 2,100,000 (*Mauritanians*). CAPITAL: Nouakchott. LANGUAGE: French, Arabic. CURRENCY: ouguiya.

Mauritius [mə'rɪʃəs] a country consisting of an island in the Indian Ocean, east of Madagascar. SIZE: 2,040 sq kms. POPULATION: 1,100,000 (*Mauritians*). CAPITAL: Port Louis. LANGUAGE: English. CURRENCY: Mauritian rupee.

mausoleum [,mɔːsə'liːəm] *n* a building that contains a grave or group of graves, especially of rich or important people.

mauve [mouv] ◇ *n* a pale purple color. ◇ *adj*: *a mauve tie.*

maverick ['mævərɪk] *n* a person who thinks and acts independently, and often differently from the other people they are connected with □ *a maverick lawyer.*

mawkish ['mɔːkɪʃ] *adj* [person, behavior] that one thinks is too sentimental.

max. *abbr of* **maximum**.

maxim ['mæksəm] *n* a short saying or proverb that suggests the correct or suitable way to behave in particular situations.

maxima ['mæksəmə] *plural of* **maximum**.

maximize, -ise ['mæksəmaɪz] *vt* [profits, use, benefits] to increase <sthg> as much as possible □ *We must maximize our chances of success.*

maximum ['mæksəməm] (*pl* **maxima** OR **maximums**) ◇ *adj* [capacity, amount, speed] that is the highest or largest □ *The news was timed to cause maximum damage to the party.* ◇ *n* the highest amount of something that is possible in a particular situation or place □ *a maximum of 40 people* □ *The space has been used to the maximum.*

may [meɪ] *modal vb* **-1. it may rain** it is possible that it will rain □ *We may just catch him before he leaves.* ■ **you may be right** it is possible that you are right □ *She may not have heard the news yet.* ■ **be that as it may** used when one feels that what has just been said does not change the situation (formal use) □ *"He's very ill."—"Be that as it may, he could have phoned."* **-2. you may go now** you are allowed to go now (formal use) □ *Only close relatives may attend the funeral.* **-3. may I/we...** used in polite questions and suggestions □ *May I take your coat?* □ *May we look around the house?* □ *May I smoke?* **-4.** used to introduce an opinion which one feels somebody has □ *He may not be very bright, but he's efficient and well-organized.* □ *You may not like it, but I am in charge here now.* **-5. may they be very happy!** I hope that they will be very happy □ *Long may he reign!*

May *n* the fifth month of the year in the Western calendar; *see also* **February**.

Mayan ['maɪən] *adj* that is connected with the

Maya, a Native American people who had a great civilization in Central America.

maybe ['meɪbiː] *adv* **-1.** used to say that something is possible but not definite □ *Maybe she got lost.* □ *Maybe that's why he dislikes her so much.* **-2.** used to show that a number or figure is not exact □ *We'd walked three, maybe four, miles when we came to a garage.* □ *It took a long time — six hours, maybe.* **-3.** used to make suggestions in a way that is not too direct □ *Maybe you should try talking to him.*

mayday ['meɪdeɪ] *n* a radio signal from a ship or plane that is sent to show it needs help in an emergency □ *a mayday signal.*

May Day *n* the first of May, celebrated as a holiday for the workers in many countries.

Mayflower ['meɪflaʊəʳ] *n* **the Mayflower** the ship used by the Pilgrims who sailed from England to America in 1620.

mayfly ['meɪflaɪ] (*pl* **mayflies**) *n* a flying insect that lives near water and has a very short life.

mayhem ['meɪhem] *n* a situation of disorder, confusion, and lack of control that often involves extreme violence □ *The strike caused mayhem on the roads today.*

mayn't [meɪnt] = **may not**.

mayonnaise [US 'meɪəneɪz, GB ˌmeɪə'neɪz] *n* a thick, cold, creamy sauce made from egg yolks and oil that is usually eaten with salads or in sandwiches.

mayor [US 'meɪr, GB meə] *n* a person elected to be the official representative and head of the administration of a town or city.

mayoress [US 'meɪərəs, GB ˌmeəʳ'es] *n* a female mayor; the wife of a mayor.

maypole ['meɪpoʊl] *n* a tall decorated pole that people in some countries dance around on May Day as part of a traditional celebration.

may've ['meɪəv] = **may have**.

maze [meɪz] *n* **-1.** [in a garden] a confusing system of paths separated by tall hedges or walls, built as an amusement for people to try to find their way through □ *a garden maze.* **-2.** [of ideas, streets, wires] a large number of things that are connected in complicated ways □ *I found myself wandering through a maze of narrow alleys.*

MB -1. *abbr of* **megabyte. -2.** *abbr of* **Manitoba**.

MBA (*abbr of* **Master of Business Administration**) *n* a postgraduate degree in business studies; a person who has this degree.

MBBS (*abbr of* **Bachelor of Medicine and Surgery**) *n* GB a degree in medicine and surgery; a person who has this degree.

MBE (*abbr of* **Member of the Order of the British Empire**) *n* an honorary title in Britain, usually given for services to the country.

MC *n abbr of* **master of ceremonies**.

MCAT ['emkæt] (*abbr of* **Medical College Admissions Test**) *n* a test taken by students in order to enter a medical school in the USA.

MCC (*abbr of* **Marylebone Cricket Club**) *n* **the MCC** a very old and important cricket club,

based at Lord's cricket ground in London. MCC used to be the name of the English national cricket team on foreign tours.

McCarthy [mə'kɑːʳθɪ], **Joseph R.** (1908–1957) a US politician who was largely responsible for McCarthyism.

McCarthyism [mə'kɑːʳθɪɪzm] *n* in the USA, an anti-Communist movement that was very strong from 1950 to 1954. Many people were accused wrongly of being anti-American.

McCoy [mə'kɔɪ] *n* **the real McCoy** a genuine object or person, rather than an imitation (informal use) □ *You shouldn't drink that cheap stuff — you want the real McCoy.*

McKinley [mə'kɪnlɪ], **William** (1843–1901) US president from 1891 to 1901. He was shot and killed.

MCP *n abbr of* **male chauvinist pig** (informal use).

MD ◇ *n* **-1.** *abbr of* **Doctor of Medicine. -2.** *abbr of* **managing director.** ◇ *abbr of* **Maryland**.

MDT (*abbr of* **Mountain Daylight Time**) *n* the local summer time in the Rocky Mountain region of North America.

me [miː] *pron* the person who is speaking or writing (used as the object of verbs, or after prepositions) □ *Hi, it's me, Rachel.* □ *Can you hear me?* □ *Allow me to explain.* □ *She stood next to me.* □ *That's for me to decide.* □ *"I'd like to go now." — "Me too."*

ME ◇ *n* (*abbr of* **myalgic encephalomyelitis**) an illness causing tiredness and aching muscles that sometimes lasts for years. ◇ *abbr of* **Maine**.

meadow ['medoʊ] *n* a field of wild grass and flowers.

meager US, **meagre** GB ['miːgəʳ] *adj* [amount, income, meal] that seems very small □ *We had a meager helping of fish.*

meal [miːl] *n* **-1.** an occasion when people eat, usually breakfast, lunch, or dinner □ *the evening meal* □ *We're going out for a meal tonight.* □ *a three-course meal* □ *Rhoda cooked us a delicious meal.* □ *a heavy/light meal.* **-2.** the food that is eaten at a meal. ■ **to make a meal of sthg** GB to use more time and effort on sthg than is necessary (disapproving use).

meals on wheels *npl* a service that delivers hot meals to the homes of people who are very old or ill.

mealtime ['miːltaɪm] *n* the time when a meal is eaten. ■ **take the medicine at mealtimes** take the medicine three times a day, with breakfast, lunch, and dinner.

mealy-mouthed [-'maʊðd] *adj* [person] who does not speak openly or directly because they are trying to avoid saying something unpleasant.

mean [miːn] *n* (*pt* & *pp* **meant**) ◇ *vt* **-1.** "obese" means "very fat" "obese" has the same meaning as "very fat" □ *What does "hegemony" mean?* ■ **red means danger** red is a sign of danger □ *That light means that the fuel tank is empty.* ■ **this means war!** this means that war will happen. **-2.** **what do you mean?** what are you trying to say? □ *I think he meant* that we should do it now. □ Do you mean that we won't see each other again? **-3. I mean it** I am serious about what I said □ I meant every word I said. **-4. this will mean...** the result of this will be... □ Closing down the factory will mean hundreds of job losses. **-5. to mean to do sthg** to have a deliberate intention of doing sthg □ I didn't mean to be rude. □ I've been meaning to ask you how you got on. **-6. to be meant for sb** to be intended to be given or sent to sb □ The bomb was meant for the Prime Minister. **-7. you/we etc are meant to...** you/ we etc have been told to... □ He's meant to be helping me. □ You're not meant to go in there! **-8. it's meant to be a joke** it is intended to be a joke □ "What have you drawn?" — "It's meant to be a horse." **-9. it's meant to be good for you** people say that it is good for you □ It's meant to be the best club in town. **-10.** phrases **to mean everything** OR **a lot to sb** to be very important to sb □ Money means nothing to me. ■ **he/she means well** he/she is trying to be kind or helpful, in spite of the fact that he/ she is causing problems □ Don't be impatient with him, he means well. ■ **I mean** used to explain something in more detail, or to correct what one has just said □ She's very kind; I mean, she's always ready to help. □ I'll be there by six, I mean seven.

◇ *adj* **-1.** [person, act] unkind and unpleasant □ What a mean thing to do! □ I'm sorry I was so mean to you. **-2.** US [person, dog] bad-tempered □ He can get real mean sometimes. **-3.** GB [person] unwilling to give or spend money □ He's always been mean with money. **-4.** MATH [rainfall, height] average. **-5.** phrases **she is no mean writer/golfer etc** she is excellent at writing/golf etc. ■ **it's no mean feat** it is very difficult to do □ To have fitted it all by himself is no mean feat. **-6. he plays a mean guitar** he plays the guitar very well (informal use).

◇ *n* **-1.** MATH **the mean** the average. **-2.** → **means.**

meander [mɪ'ændər] *vi* **-1.** [river, road] to have many bends and not lead directly somewhere. **-2.** [person] to move somewhere slowly without a particular purpose or direction.

meaning ['miːnɪŋ] *n* **-1.** [of a word, phrase, sign] the thing that a particular word, phrase etc refers to □ The word "get" has lots of different meanings. □ Kindness! — You don't know the meaning of the word! **-2.** [of a painting, song, statement] the ideas that are expressed by something □ I've never understood the meaning of his songs, but I like them. **-3.** [of life, suffering] the importance or purpose that one feels something has □ Life lost all meaning for her after her husband died.

meaningful ['miːnɪŋfl] *adj* **-1.** [look, remark] that expresses a particular attitude or message □ "I understand," he said, and gave a meaningful smile. **-2.** [relationship, discussion] that is serious and important □ I don't think we've reached any meaningful conclusions.

meaningless ['miːnɪŋləs] *adj* **-1.** [song, gesture, word] that means nothing □ Well, read it! It's just a lot of meaningless nonsense. **-2.** [task, life,

discussion] that has no purpose □ I find all these meetings pretty meaningless, actually.

meanness ['miːnnəs] *n* **-1.** US [of a person, action, behavior] unkindness. **-2.** [of a person, gift] the quality of not being generous.

means [miːnz] (*pl* means) ◇ *n* a particular way of doing something □ Use any means available to you. □ Is there no means of doing it any faster? ■ **a means of transport** the type of transport that somebody can use, e.g. a bus, train, or car □ A bicycle is my only means of transport now. ■ **a means to an end** a way of achieving something else, rather than something that is desirable for its own sake □ For Lyle, a law degree was a means to an end, and that end was politics. ■ **by means of sthg** [of a tool, device, process] by using sthg □ They communicate by means of signs.

◇ *npl* money or resources □ He's a young man of independent means. ■ **to live within/beyond one's means** to spend an amount of money over a period of time that one can/cannot afford.

◆ **by all means** *adv* a phrase used for giving somebody permission to do something □ "May I try?" — "By all means!" □ By all means, if you think it's worth it.

◆ **by no means** *adv* not at all □ It's by no means easy. □ I don't think it's fair by any means.

means test *n* a way of finding out how much money somebody earns to decide whether or not they qualify for extra money from the state.

meant [ment] *past tense & past participle of* mean.

meantime ['miːntaɪm], **in the meantime** *adv* in the period of time between two events □ The police will contact us when they find him. In the meantime, all we can do is wait.

meanwhile ['miːnwaɪl] *adv* **-1.** used to describe an event that is happening at the same time as another event □ Leave the sauce to cool. Meanwhile, whisk two eggs in a bowl. **-2.** in the period of time between two events □ The strike is due to start at 7 a.m. tomorrow. Meanwhile talks are going on to end the dispute.

measles ['miːzlz] *n* an infectious disease with symptoms of fever and red spots on the skin that mainly affects children.

measly ['miːzlɪ] (*compar* measlier, *superl* measliest) *adj* [amount, offer] that one finds small and disappointing (disapproving and informal use) □ All I got was a measly 50 cents!

measurable ['meʒərəbl] *adj* [progress, improvement, decline] that is noticeable and so is important in some way □ The new law will have no measurable effect on people's lives.

measurably ['meʒərəblɪ] *adv* [progress, improve, deteriorate] see **measurable** □ The family is measurably poorer than it was ten years ago.

measure ['meʒər] ◇ *n* **-1.** [to do something] an action that is carried out for a particular purpose □ The government must take measures to ease traffic congestion. **-2. a measure of sthg** [of independence, success] a degree or amount of sthg □ There is a certain measure of truth in what you say. ■ **for good measure** a phrase used to say that something is done, given etc in addition to something else □ *I'll add an extra spoonful for good measure.* -3. [of whiskey, brandy] the amount of an alcoholic drink that is in a glass □ *He poured himself a large measure of gin.* -4. **to be a measure of sthg** to show how great or important something is □ *an industry where sales are seen as the only measure of success.*

◇ *vt* [house, person] to find out the exact size of <sb/sthg>; [speed, temperature] to find out the exact level of <sthg> □ *Can you measure my chest for me?* □ *Have you measured the patient's pulse?*

◇ *vi* to be a particular size that can be shown as a distance □ *The garden measures 40m by 25m.*

◆ **measure up** *vi* to be good or able enough □ *The hotel didn't measure up to our expectations.* □ *So, how did the new manager measure up?*

measured ['meʒəʳd] *adj* [steps, tones] careful and deliberate □ *He gave a measured reply.*

measurement ['meʒəʳmənt] *n* -1. the size or level of something that is found out by measuring □ *I need to take the measurement of the height of the door.* □ *What's your chest measurement?* □ *a unit of measurement.* -2. the act of measuring something.

◆ **measurements** *npl* [of person] the sizes of particular parts of one's body, e.g. of one's chest, waist, or legs, used when buying clothes □ *I don't know all of my measurements.*

measuring cup ['meʒərɪŋ-] *n* US a type of cup for measuring liquid or food, used in cooking.

measuring jug *n* GB a transparent jug that has markings on the side so that the amount of liquid, flour, sugar etc in it can be measured.

measuring tape *n* a strip of tape or metal with inches or centimeters marked on it, used for measuring things.

meat [miːt] *n* the flesh of animals that people eat.

meatball ['miːtbɔːl] *n* a small ball of ground meat.

meatloaf ['miːtloʊf] *n* a dish that is made from ground meat, bread, vegetables etc and is shaped like a loaf of bread.

meaty ['miːtɪ] (*compar* **meatier**, *superl* **meatiest**) *adj* [discussion, report] that is full of interesting facts, ideas etc.

mecca ['mekə] *n* a place that attracts a lot of people □ *In the summer, the town is a mecca for tourists.*

Mecca a city in western Saudi Arabia. It is the birthplace of Muhammad and a sacred city to Muslims, who must go there once on a pilgrimage if it is possible. POPULATION: 618,000.

mechanic [mɪ'kænɪk] *n* a person whose job is to maintain and repair engines or machines, especially cars.

◆ **mechanics** ◇ *n* the branch of science that is concerned with how forces act on objects

□ *fluid mechanics.* ◇ *npl* the way that something works □ *I don't understand the mechanics of the stock market.*

mechanical [mɪ'kænɪkl] *adj* -1. [device, digger] that has moving parts and uses power □ *a small mechanical toy.* -2. [person, mind] good at understanding how machines work □ *I'm not very mechanical.* -3. [behavior, response] that happens because of habit and not because of what one feels or thinks □ *He stamped the papers with slow, mechanical movements.*

mechanical engineering *n* the branch of engineering that is concerned with machines and machinery.

mechanical pencil *n* US a pencil in which the lead can be moved in or out by twisting or pressing a part of the pencil.

mechanism ['mekənɪzm] *n* -1. a part of a machine □ *There's no safety mechanism on this model.* -2. [in a system, government] a way of dealing with a problem or getting something done □ *There are various mechanisms in place which should prevent errors of this kind.* -3. [in a person, animal, plant] something that one does to help one deal with a difficult or dangerous situation □ *a defense/survival mechanism.*

mechanization [US ,mekənə'zeɪʃn, GB -aɪ-] *n*: see **mechanize.**

mechanize, -ise ['mekənaɪz] ◇ *vt* [process, industry, production] to use machines for <sthg> so that people or animals are no longer involved to the same extent. ◇ *vi*: *The company will have to mechanize to remain competitive.*

MEd [,em'ed] (*abbr of* **Master of Education**) *n* a postgraduate degree in education; a person who has this degree.

medal ['medl] *n* a small metal disk given to somebody for bravery, a sports achievement etc □ *General de Peña pinned the medal to his chest.* □ *She won an Olympic medal.*

medalist US, **medallist** GB ['medləst] *n* a person who wins a medal in a sports competition □ *an Olympic gold/silver medalist.*

medallion [mə'dæljən] *n* a piece of jewelry that looks like a small medal and is worn on a chain around the neck, usually by men.

medallist *n* GB = **medalist.**

meddle ['medl] *vi* to try to influence a situation that concerns other people and not oneself in a way that is annoying and can cause problems □ *How dare you meddle in* OR *with my affairs!*

meddlesome ['medlsəm] *adj* [person] who meddles.

media ['miːdɪə] ◇ *n* OR *npl* the media a collective term for television, radio, and newspapers □ *a huge advertising campaign in the media* □ *The media bears a huge responsibility for what has happened.* ◇ *plural of* **medium.**

mediaeval [US ,miːdɪ'iːvl, GB ,med-] *adj* = **medieval.**

media event *n* an event that is designed to attract the attention of the media.

median ['miːdɪən] ◇ *adj* MATH that comes in the middle of a series of figures that are arranged in order. ◇ *n* US **the median (strip)**

the middle part of a large road that divides traffic going in opposite directions.

mediate ['mi:dɪeɪt] ◇ *vi* to try to end an argument between two groups of people by talking to both of them □ *The US has agreed to mediate between the two countries/mediate in the dispute.* ◇ *vt: The UN was asked to mediate a peace settlement.*

mediation [,mi:dɪ'eɪʃn] *n: see* **mediate**.

mediator ['mi:dɪeɪtəʳ] *n* a person who mediates □ *UN mediators had done their best to negotiate a settlement.*

medic ['medɪk] *n* (informal use) **-1.** a doctor. **-2.** a medical student.

Medicaid ['medɪkeɪd] *n* a government program in the USA that helps pay for medical treatment for poor people.

medical ['medɪkl] ◇ *adj* [examination, supplies, profession] that is concerned with people's health and the treatment of illnesses and injuries □ *a medical practitioner.* ◇ *n* a complete examination of one's body and health by a doctor for an official purpose □ *He passed/failed his army medical.*

medical certificate *n* **-1.** a form completed by a doctor that shows the results of a medical examination. **-2.** a letter written by a doctor to somebody's employer to say officially that they are or have been ill.

medical insurance *n* a kind of insurance that covers the cost of treatment that one receives for sickness or injury.

medical student *n* a student of medicine.

Medicare ['medɪkeəʳ] *n* in the USA, a government program that provides medical care for old people; in Canada and Australia, a program that provides medical care for everybody.

medicated ['medɪkeɪtəd] *adj* [shampoo, cough syrup] that contains medication.

medication [,medɪ'keɪʃn] *n* a drug or medicine used for treating a patient □ *Are you on any medication?*

medicinal [mə'dɪsnl] *adj* that acts as a medicine □ *I always keep a bottle of brandy for medicinal purposes.* □ *the medicinal properties of the eucalyptus plant.*

medicine ['medsn] *n* **-1.** the subject that deals with diseases and injuries □ *She's studying medicine at Columbia.* **-2.** a substance used for treating a disease or illness, especially one that is swallowed □ *I'm taking this medicine for my throat.* □ *a cough medicine* □ *a medicine bottle.*

medicine man *n* in some cultures, a man who is believed to have magic powers that make it possible to cure illnesses.

medieval [US ,mi:dɪ'i:vl, GB ,med-] *adj* [warfare, architecture, literature] that is connected with the period 1100 to 1500 AD, especially in European history.

mediocre [,mi:dɪ'oʊkəʳ] *adj* [performance, movie, candidate] that is not good enough □ *I thought the standard of work was rather mediocre.*

mediocrity [,mi:dɪ'ɒkrətɪ] *n: see* **mediocre** □ *the mediocrity of most TV programs.*

meditate ['medəteɪt] *vi* **-1.** to think carefully and seriously about something for a long time □ *I had no time to meditate on* OR *upon the problem.* **-2.** to empty one's mind of thoughts by staying calm and quiet, so that one can concentrate on one particular thing, usually as a spiritual or religious activity.

meditation [,medə'teɪʃn] *n* **-1.** the process of thinking about something carefully. **-2.** the process of emptying one's mind of thoughts and entering a relaxed state □ *She's been going to meditation classes at the Buddhist center.*

Mediterranean [,medɪtə'reɪnɪən] ◇ **the Mediterranean (Sea)** the sea between southern Europe, North Africa, and the Middle East. It is connected to the Atlantic Ocean by the Strait of Gibraltar, and to the Red Sea by the Suez Canal. ◇ *adj: Mediterranean cooking* □ *the Mediterranean climate.*

medium ['mi:dɪəm] (*pl sense 1* **media** OR **mediums**, *pl sense 2* **mediums**) ◇ *adj* [size, height, brown] that is halfway between something that is more and something that is less □ *Her attacker was a blond youth of medium build.* ◇ *n* **-1.** an activity or form of communication that somebody uses to express themselves to other people □ *the medium of photography/English/television* □ *CD-ROM — an exciting new visual medium* □ *interactive media.* **-2.** a person who is believed to be able to receive messages from dead people.

medium-dry *adj* [white wine, sherry] not very sweet.

medium-size(d) *adj* [room, table, container] that is not big and not small.

medium wave *n* a range of sound waves used by radios, between 100 and 1,000 meters long.

NOTE: Compare **long wave, short wave**.

medley ['medlɪ] (*pl* **medleys**) *n* **-1.** [of sights, sounds, smells] a mixture of things of different sorts that produces an interesting effect. **-2.** MUSIC a collection of songs that have a common theme and are played one after the other without interruption.

Medusa [mə'dju:sə] in Greek mythology, a woman who had snakes for hair. Anybody who looked at her was turned to stone.

meek [mi:k] *adj* [person] who is gentle, quiet, and does what other people say.

meekly ['mi:klɪ] *adv* [follow, accept, smile] *see* **meek** □ *"I apologize," he said meekly.*

meet [mi:t] (*pt* & *pp* **met**) ◇ *vt* **-1.** [person] to be in the same place as <sb> by chance and start talking to them; to arrange to be in the same place at the same time as <sb> for a particular purpose □ *I met a great guy on the way over.* □ *Where shall we meet each other?* □ *They met political leaders to discuss the latest proposals.* **-2.** [person, friend] to begin to know <sb> by speaking to them for the first time □ *I met my wife at a party.* □ *You're the most arrogant man I've ever met!* **-3.** [client, relative] to go somewhere in order to pick up <sb who

has made a trip> □ *We'll send a car to meet you at the airport.* □ *I have to meet the 4:30 flight from Durban.* **-4.** [condition, demand, deadline] to do what is required by <sthg> □ *You need a grade A in order to meet the course requirements.* **-5.** [objection, criticism] to face <sthg> in a particular way in order to deal with it successfully □ *To survive, we must meet the challenge of new technology.* **-6.** [cost, bill] to pay <sthg> □ *Would you be in a position to meet the cost of a replacement if necessary?* **-7.** [situation, problem, attitude] to come into contact with <sthg> so that one notices it and is affected by it □ *It's the first case of this sort I've met.* □ *He'd never met such resistance to his ideas before.* **-8.** [object, surface] to touch or hit <sthg> □ *His head met the windscreen with a thud.* **-9. to meet sb's gaze** to look back at sb who is looking at one □ *She felt so ashamed she couldn't meet his gaze.* **-10.** [road, land, sea] to be next to <sthg> and connected to it □ *Make a left where Broadway meets West 51st Street.* □ *where East meets West.* ◇ *vi* **-1.** [people] to be in the same place by chance and start talking; [friends, committee, board] to meet each other by arrangement for a particular purpose □ *We met on the plane.* □ *Let's meet for lunch next Friday.* □ *The two sides met to discuss peace terms.* **-2.** [people, friends, couple] to begin to know each other by speaking for the first time □ *I'll never forget the night we met.* □ *I don't think we've met before.* **-3.** [objects] to touch each other □ *Their lips/fingers met.* **-4.** [eyes] to look at each other □ *Their eyes met across a crowded room.* **-5.** [roads, lines] to join together □ *Route 94 and Route 10 meet in Arizona, don't they?* ◇ *n* US an event in which a number of athletes gather to take part in a competition □ *an athletics meet.*
◆ **meet up** *vi* [people] to meet by arrangement □ *We met up again the following year in Prague.* □ *I'll meet up with you later, okay?*
◆ **meet with** *vt fus* **-1. to meet with sthg** [with criticism, a refusal] to receive sthg as a reaction □ *The agreement met with general approval.* ■ **to meet with success/failure** [attempt, plan] to be successful/a failure. **-2. to meet with sb** to meet sb by arrangement.

meeting ['mi:tɪŋ] *n* **-1.** [of a board, committee] an event when people meet as part of their work or for a particular purpose □ *I'm afraid she's in a meeting at the moment.* □ *The chairman called an emergency meeting.* □ *a staff meeting* □ *a meeting between union representatives and management.* **-2.** the people at a meeting □ *The meeting voted in favor of the measure.* **-3.** [between friends, acquaintances] an event when people meet by chance or by arrangement □ *On our last meeting we had a serious argument.*

meeting place *n* a place where two or more people have agreed to meet; a place that is used in this way by many people.

meeting point *n* a place in a large public area such as an airport where people can arrange to meet each other.

mega- ['megə] *prefix* **-1.** added to words to

multiply the stated amount by a million. **-2.** added to words to mean "very" (informal use) □ *mega-exciting.*

megabyte ['megəbaɪt] *n* one million bytes.

megahertz ['megəhɜːˈts] *n* one million hertz.

megalomania [,megələ'meɪnɪə] *n* a belief that one is more powerful and important than anybody else.

megalomaniac [,megələ'meɪnɪæk] *n* a person who wants to be more powerful and important than anybody else.

megaphone ['megəfoʊn] *n* a device consisting of a tube that is wider at one end than the other and that makes one's voice sound louder when one speaks into it. It is used especially for speaking to a large number of people outdoors.

megaton ['megətʌn] *n* a unit (one million tons of TNT) used for measuring the force of an explosion.

megawatt ['megəwɒt] *n* one million watts.

melamine ['meləmiːn] *n* a man-made material that is often white, used for furniture surfaces.

melancholy ['melənkɒlɪ] ◇ *adj* [person] who is sad and thoughtful □ *"It's autumn again," he said in a melancholy voice.* ◇ *n* a strong feeling of sadness that lasts a long time.

Melanesia [,melə'niːʒə] a group of islands in the Pacific Ocean, northeast of Australia, that includes Fiji, the Solomon Islands, and Vanuatu.

Melbourne ['melbəˈn] a port in Victoria, southeastern Australia. It is the capital of the state, and a major financial, industrial, and cultural center. POPULATION: 3,002,300.

Melbourne Cup *n* the Melbourne Cup Australia's most important horse race, which takes place on the first Tuesday in November.

☙ THE MELBOURNE CUP
The Melbourne Cup, a horse race that takes place in Melbourne, Australia every November, is one of the country's biggest sporting events. The day of the race is a public holiday in the state of Victoria, and the race itself brings the whole nation to a standstill. Almost everybody watches it on television, and most people place a bet, either in a betting shop or in informal bets organized in workplaces.

mellow ['meloʊ] ◇ *adj* **-1.** [light, color] that looks soft, warm, and not too bright □ *the mellow autumn light.* **-2.** [voice, sound, taste] that seems smooth and pleasant □ *the mellow tones of a clarinet.* **-3.** [person] who is calm and relaxed □ *He's a really mellow guy.* ◇ *vt* to make <sb> more gentle, relaxed, and pleasant □ *Marriage seems to have mellowed her.* ◇ *vi: He's mellowing in his old age.*

melodic [mə'lɒdɪk] *adj* [song, music] that is connected with the arrangement of music in a tuneful way.

melodious [məˈloudɪəs] *adj* [voice, music] that is pleasant to listen to.

melodrama [US ˈmelədræmə, GB -drɑːmə] *n* a kind of drama in which the events are very sad, exciting etc and the characters react in an emotional way that is exaggerated; a play written in this style.

melodramatic [ˌmelədrəˈmætɪk] *adj* [person, behavior] that is too emotional and treats situations as being much more serious than they really are □ *Oh, stop being so melodramatic!*

melody [ˈmelədɪ] (*pl* **melodies**) *n* a tune; the quality of music that is melodic □ *That's a nice melody.* □ *His songs are full of melody.*

melon [ˈmelən] *n* a large round or oval fruit that contains white, green, or red juicy flesh and has a hard green or yellow skin and seeds in the center.

melt [melt] ◇ *vt* **-1.** [snow, ice] to make <sthg solid> become liquid or soft by increasing its temperature □ *Melt the butter in a pan.* **-2. to melt sb's heart** to make sb feel tender and loving.
◇ *vi* **-1.** [butter, snow, ice] to change from a solid into something liquid or soft as a result of being heated □ *Cook until the cheese has melted.* **-2.** [person, heart] to become tender and loving. **-3. to melt into sthg** [into the crowd, background] to become unnoticeable by joining or becoming part of sthg else □ *She has the most amazing ability to just melt into the background and remain unobserved.* □ *Day gradually melted into night.* ■ **to melt away** [crowds, time, anger] to seem to disappear in a way one cannot explain □ *I looked into his eyes and the years seemed to melt away.*
◆ **melt down** *vt sep* to melt sthg down [metal, glass] to heat sthg until it melts so that it can be used again.

meltdown [ˈmeltdaun] *n* the melting of fuel in a nuclear reactor that can cause radiation to leak out.

melting point [ˈmeltɪŋ-] *n* the temperature at which something melts when it becomes hotter.

melting pot *n* a place or situation where people from many different countries and cultures meet, mix, or live together □ *New York is the original melting pot.*

Melville [ˈmelvɪl], **Herman** (1819–1891) a US novelist. His most famous works are *Moby Dick* and *Billy Budd*.

member [ˈmembər] *n* **-1.** [of a family, species] a person or animal that belongs to a particular group □ *a member of the opposite sex* □ *The jaguar is a member of the cat family.* **-2.** [of a club, committee, political party] a person who has joined a particular organization □ *'Members only'* □ *a member of staff* OR *staff member* □ *I became a member in 1980.* □ *a member country/state.*

Member of Congress (*pl* **Members of Congress**) *n* in the USA, a politician elected to Congress, especially to the House of Representatives.

Member of Parliament (*pl* **Members of Parlia-**ment) *n* in Britain, a politician elected to the House of Commons; in Commonwealth countries, a politician elected to represent the people in a parliament.

membership [ˈmembərʃɪp] *n* **-1.** the state of being a member of an organization □ *Membership of the library is free.* □ *a membership fee.* **-2.** the number of members in an organization □ *Our membership doubled last year alone.* **-3. the membership** the members of an organization.

membership card *n* a card which proves that one is a member of an organization.

membrane [ˈmembreɪn] *n* ANATOMY a very thin piece of skin which joins or covers parts of the body.

memento [məˈmentou] (*pl* **mementos**) *n* an object one keeps to remember a person or special occasion □ *Keep it as a memento.*

memo [ˈmemou] (*pl* **memos**) *n* a note from one person to another within the same office or organization; a note from one person, department etc to all the other members of an office or organization □ *Didn't you receive my memo about it?* □ *an all-staff memo.*

memoirs [ˈmemwɑːz] *npl* a book written by somebody, usually well known, about the important events in their life □ *They've just published her memoirs.*

memo pad *n* a block of small sheets of paper used for writing short memos on.

memorabilia [ˌmemərəˈbɪlɪə] *npl* objects that people collect because they are connected with a particular period, person etc □ *You should see all the Beatles memorabilia she's collected.*

memorable [ˈmemərəbl] *adj* [occasion, experience, achievement] that is remembered for being special or unusual □ *It was hardly a memorable evening — we just played cards all night.*

memorandum [ˌmeməˈrændəm] (*pl* **memoranda** [-də] OR **memorandums**) *n* = **memo** (formal use).

memorial [məˈmɔːrɪəl] ◇ *adj* a **memorial service/ceremony etc** a service/ceremony etc that is in honor of a dead person. ◇ *n* a monument that honors a dead person or an event in history □ *a memorial to the war dead.*

Memorial Day *n* in the USA, a holiday that is celebrated on the last Monday of May. It honors US soldiers who died while fighting wars.

memorize, -ise [ˈmeməraɪz] *vt* [names, number] to learn <sthg> exactly, so that one does not forget it.

memory [ˈmemərɪ] (*pl* **memories**) *n* **-1.** an ability to remember things □ *I've got a good memory for faces.* □ *I must be losing my memory!* □ *I have no memory of saying that.* □ *She frantically searched her memory for clues.* ■ **to do sthg from memory** to do sthg by remembering it and without looking at any words, text etc □ *He could recite whole sections from memory.* **-2.** something that one remembers □ *I have happy childhood memories.* ■ **in** OR **with-**

in living memory since the earliest time that can be remembered by anybody who is still alive □ *It was the coldest winter in living memory.* **-3.** COMPUTING the capacity of a computer to store information □ *How much memory does the new model have?* **-4. sb's memory** the things that one remembers about sb who is dead □ *His memory lived on in her mind.* ■ **in memory of sb** as a way of remembering sb who is dead □ *A plaque was put up in memory of the great poet.*

memory card *n* a piece of equipment that is added to a computer to increase its memory capacity.

men [men] *plural of* **man**.

menace ['menəs] ◇ *n* **-1.** [to society, public safety, one's health] a person or thing that could cause serious harm □ *He's a menace to everyone else on the road.* **-2.** [in somebody's voice, eyes] a way of speaking or behaving that makes somebody feel threatened □ *There was a look of menace in his eyes.* □ *A note of menace crept into his voice.* **-3.** a person or thing that is annoying and causes problems (informal use) □ *That child is/These stairs are an absolute menace!* ◇ *vt* to seem likely to harm <sb/sthg> □ *Once again Europe was menaced by the threat of all-out war.*

menacing ['menəsɪŋ] *adj* [look, behavior] that makes one feel threatened □ *He gave a menacing smile.*

menacingly ['menəsɪŋlɪ] *adv* [look, behave] *see* **menacing**.

menagerie [mə'nædʒərɪ] *n* a small collection of animals.

mend [mend] ◇ *vt* [clothes, television, car] to repair <sthg>; [hole, puncture] to remove <sthg> by repairing the thing that has it. ■ **to mend one's ways** to stop behaving badly and start behaving in a more acceptable way. ◇ *n* **to be on the mend** to be getting better after an illness or injury (informal use).

mending ['mendɪŋ] *n* clothes that need to be mended.

menfolk ['menfəʊk] *npl* a term used by women to refer to the men in their family, village etc.

menial ['miːnɪəl] *adj* [work, task] that is not interesting or important and needs no skill; [worker, staff] who does menial work.

meningitis [ˌmenɪn'dʒaɪtəs] *n* an infectious illness that affects the brain and spinal cord and can be very serious.

Mennonite ['menənaɪt] *n* a member of a Protestant group that is against the idea of an organized church and military service and refuses to hold public office.

menopause ['menəpɔːz] *n* the time in a woman's life when she stops menstruating and experiences other physical and psychological changes, usually around the age of 50.

menservants ['mensɜːrvənts] *plural of* **manservant**.

men's room *n* **the men's room** a men's toilet in a public place such as a restaurant or hotel lobby.

menstrual ['menstrʊəl] *adj* that is connected with menstruation □ *the menstrual cycle.*

menstruate ['menstrʊeɪt] *vi* [woman] to have one's period.

menstruation [ˌmenstrʊ'eɪʃn] *n* the process, during which a woman who is not pregnant loses blood from her womb through her vagina, usually once a month.

menswear ['menzweər] *n* a collective term for clothes, shoes etc for men.

mental ['mentl] *adj* **-1.** [effort, ability, development] that is connected with the mind or the intelligence □ *I'd say it was a mental rather than a physical problem.* □ *mental health.* **-2. a mental patient** a person who is suffering from an illness of the mind. **-3. mental arithmetic/a mental decision etc** arithmetic/a decision etc that is formed in one's thoughts rather than in writing or in speech □ *I'd already formed a mental picture of what she would be like.*

mental age *n* a measurement of a person's intelligence when compared with the intelligence of an average child at that age □ *a girl of 18 with a mental age of 6.*

mental block *n* **to have a mental block about sthg** [about cars, computers] to be unable to understand sthg, for no clear reason; [about a word, name] to be unable to remember sthg one knows, often unexpectedly and for a short time.

mental hospital *n* a special hospital where people with mental illnesses are taken care of.

mentality [men'tælətɪ] *n* the attitudes, often negative, that affect the way somebody behaves □ *You just have to accept that they have a different kind of mentality.*

mentally ['mentlɪ] *adv*: *see* **mental** □ *I think it's a very difficult job, both mentally and physically.* □ *mentally ill.*

mentally handicapped ◇ *adj* **to be mentally handicapped** [person] to have a level of mental development that is not as great as in other people of the same age, usually because of illness or an accident □ *mentally-handicapped children.* ◇ *npl* **the mentally handicapped** the people in society who are mentally handicapped.

mental note *n* **to make a mental note** to try to keep something in one's memory so that one can remember it later □ *I made a mental note of the number.* □ *I made a mental note to call her as soon as I got back.*

menthol ['menθɒl] *n* a white substance that smells and tastes of mint, and is used in candy, toothpaste etc □ *menthol cigarettes.*

mentholated ['menθəleɪtəd] *adj* [cough drop, cigarette] that contains menthol.

mention ['menʃn] ◇ *vt* to say something about <sb/sthg> briefly, often as part of a much longer conversation, piece of writing etc □ *Sue mentioned that you might be interested.* □ *I was mentioned as a possible replacement.* □ *I hate to mention money at a time like this.* □ *Did he happen to mention when/where he would arrive?* ■ **don't mention it!** a phrase used to respond to somebody who has just said "thank you" in order to show that one was happy to help; a phrase used to reply to somebody who has just apologized in order to show that one is not angry. ■ **not to mention** a phrase used to add something to a list and give it emphasis □ *It was tactless, not to mention very offensive.* □ *This project is going to cost us a fortune, not to mention all the extra work involved.*

◇ *n* a very short statement about somebody or something, often as part of a much longer conversation, piece of writing etc □ *The concert got a brief mention in the papers.* □ *Their criticism makes no mention of Mr Bryant's positive achievements.*

mentor ['mentɔːʳ] *n* a person who guides somebody's development and influences their education a lot □ *For many years he acted as a mentor to me.*

menu ['menjuː] *n* **-1.** [in a restaurant] a list of the dishes that can be ordered □ *What's on the menu?* □ *the fish menu* □ *I'd like to order something from the menu.* **-2.** COMPUTING a list of the options or programs available to a computer user that is shown on the screen □ *How do I get back to the main menu?*

menu-driven *adj* [computer program] that has menus at each stage to help the user.

meow US, **miaow** GB [mɪ'aʊ] ◇ *n* the cry of a cat. ◇ *vi* to make the cry of a cat.

MEP *n abbr of* **Member of the European Parliament.**

Mephistopheles [ˌmefɪ'stɒfəliːz] the name of the devil in the story of Faust.

mercantile ['mɜːʳkəntaɪl] *adj* [law, growth] that is concerned with trade and business.

mercenary [US 'mɜːrsneri, GB 'mɜːsnəri] (*pl* **mercenaries**) ◇ *n* MILITARY a soldier who fights for any country for money. ◇ *adj* **-1.** [person] who is interested only in the money that can be made from a person or situation, rather than in being loyal, moral etc □ *You sold it? That was a pretty mercenary thing to do!* **-2.** [army] that is made up of mercenaries.

merchandise ['mɜːʳtʃəndaɪz] *n* goods for buying, selling, or trading □ *poor-quality merchandise.*

merchandising ['mɜːʳtʃəndaɪzɪŋ] *n* goods such as toys and clothes that are connected with a popular movie, singer etc.

merchant ['mɜːʳtʃənt] ◇ *adj* **a merchant seaman/ship** a sailor/ship that is involved in business and is not part of a country's military navy. ◇ *n* a person whose job is to buy and sell large amounts of a particular product, especially by importing and exporting it

merchant bank *n* GB a bank that deals with companies and business involving very large sums of money rather than with ordinary customers.

merchant marine US, **merchant navy** GB *n* all of the merchant ships in a country; all of the people who work on these ships.

merciful ['mɜːʳsɪfl] *adj* **-1.** [person, act] that shows forgiveness and kindness toward somebody. **-2.** that is good because it ends pain or unhappiness □ *Her death was a merciful release.*

mercifully ['mɜːʳsɪflɪ] *adv* **-1. mercifully,...** a word used to show one thinks that a situation or result is fortunate □ *Mercifully, no one was hurt.* **-2.** [act, treat] with mercy.

merciless ['mɜːʳsɪləs] *adj* [person, criticism, attack] that is cruel and shows no mercy.

mercilessly ['mɜːʳsɪləslɪ] *adv* [tease, criticize, attack] *see* **merciless**.

mercurial [mɜːʳ'kjʊəriəl] *adj* [person] who keeps changing their mind or mood very suddenly (literary use).

mercury ['mɜːʳkjəri] *n* a silver-white metal element that is liquid at room temperature and is used in thermometers. SYMBOL: Hg.

Mercury ['mɜːʳkjəri] the planet in the solar system that is closest to the Sun.

mercy ['mɜːʳsɪ] (*pl* **mercies**) *n* **-1.** kindness and pity that one shows toward somebody by not punishing or treating them as harshly as one could □ *The hostages begged their captors for mercy.* □ *They showed the prisoners no mercy.* ■ **to be at the mercy of sb/sthg** [of the weather, a terrorist, the stock market] to be unable to stop sb/sthg from harming one □ *This leaves us very much at the mercy of changing interest rates.* **-2. a mercy** something that one is grateful for □ *It's a mercy she wasn't more seriously injured.*

mercy killing *n* an act of killing somebody to prevent them dying very slowly and painfully.

mere [mɪəʳ] *adj* no more than □ *It's a mere formality.* □ *The mere thought of it makes me angry.* □ *A mere $10 is all it will cost you.* □ *He gave me the merest hint about what was really going on.*

merely ['mɪəʳlɪ] *adv* only □ *I'm merely asking you to be more patient.* □ *She's not merely an employee; she's the managing director.* □ *She was merely 16 when she left home.*

meretricious [ˌmerə'trɪʃəs] *adj* that seems attractive, but has not much worth or value really (formal use).

merge [mɜːʳdʒ] ◇ *vt* **-1.** to join together <two or more companies, organizations> etc to form one □ *The two political parties have been merged to form an alliance.* □ *We have decided to merge our educational division with the general publishing division.* **-2.** COMPUTING to join together <two files or documents> □ *We need to be able to merge text and pictures from different files.*

◇ *vi* **-1.** [companies, roads, organizations] to join together to form one □ *'Roads merge one mile ahead.'* □ *The well-known pharmaceutical chain is to merge with its main rival.* **-2.** [colors] to meet and combine gradually □ *A beautiful shade of purple is formed where the red and blue merge.* **-3. to merge into sthg** [into the background, landscape] to become part of sthg else and become difficult to see □ *The sea seemed to merge into the sky.*

◇ *n* COMPUTING a program that allows some

information from one file to be transferred to another file □ *a mail merge.*

merge lane *n* US a special lane for vehicles that are turning left or right.

merger ['mɜːrdʒəʳ] *n* the act of joining together two companies or organizations to form one.

meridian [mə'rɪdɪən] *n* one of the imaginary lines on the Earth's surface, that goes from the North to the South Pole.

meringue [mə'ræŋ] *n* a light crunchy dessert made of beaten egg whites and sugar cooked very slowly in the oven.

merino [mə'riːnou] *adj* [wool, scarf] that is made from the long fine wool of the merino sheep.

merit ['merət] ◇ *n* the quality of being good and worth doing □ *There is no merit in cheating.* □ *a work of great merit* □ *I see little artistic merit in such a plan.* □ *Selling now at least has the merit of being a simple solution.* ◇ *vt* [success, attention] to deserve <sthg> □ *It's a proposal that certainly merits closer examination.*

◆ **merits** *npl* the qualities that make somebody or something good and better than somebody or something else □ *One of the book's merits is its originality.* ■ **to judge sthg on its merits** to judge sthg only by deciding how good it is, and without taking into account other things, e.g. a general rule or one's own feelings about it □ *I hope very much that you will judge the book on its merits, not on the fame of the author.*

meritocracy [ˌmerɪ'tɒkrəsɪ] (*pl* **meritocracies**) *n* a social system in which people get their jobs, power etc because they are good at something, not because they are rich or get help from other people.

Merlin ['mɜːʳlən] in English legends, the wizard who helped King Arthur.

mermaid ['mɜːʳmeɪd] *n* an imaginary sea creature that looks like a woman but has a fish's tail instead of legs.

merrily ['merɪlɪ] *adv* -1. [laugh, joke, burn] *see* **merry** (literary use) □ *Her eyes sparkled merrily.* -2. without thinking about what one is doing (ironic use) □ *I merrily unloaded all my shopping at the checkout, only to find I had no money.*

merriment ['merɪmənt] *n* laughter and fun (formal use).

merry ['merɪ] (*compar* **merrier**, *superl* **merriest**) *adj* -1. [laugh, joke, person] happy and lively. -2. [fire, party] cheerful. ■ **Merry Christmas!** a phrase used to wish people a happy time at Christmas. -3. **to be merry** to be slightly drunk (informal use).

merry-go-round *n* a large machine found at fairgrounds consisting of a round platform that turns around with seats on it that look like animals, vehicles etc.

merrymaking ['merɪmeɪkɪŋ] *n* noisy fun and enjoyment.

Mersey ['mɜːʳzɪ]: **the Mersey** a river in northwestern England that flows through Greater Manchester and Liverpool into the Irish Sea.

Merseyside ['mɜːʳzɪsaɪd] the area around Liverpool and the Mersey estuary in northwestern England.

mesa ['meɪsə] *n* in the southwestern USA, a hill with a flat top and steep sides.

mesh [meʃ] ◇ *n* material like net made of fine wire, plastic, or thread with small holes. ◇ *vi* [gears] to fit and lock into each other.

mesmerize, -ise ['mezməraɪz] *vt* **to be mesmerized by sb/sthg** [by a performance, voice, sight] to watch or listen to sb/sthg with all one's attention so that one cannot do anything else.

mess [mes] *n* -1. a very untidy or dirty state; a person or thing that looks very untidy or dirty □ *These files are in a terrible mess, they need completely reorganizing.* □ *Your hair's a complete mess!* □ *Clean that mess up immediately!* □ *There was a terrible mess on the stairs where the children had been playing.* -2. [situation] a situation full of problems □ *My life's a complete mess.* -3. MILITARY a room or building at a military base where soldiers eat or relax □ *the officers' mess.*

◆ **mess around, mess about** (informal use) ◇ *vt sep* **to mess sb around** OR **about** to treat sb badly by changing plans that affect them or by not being honest with them □ *Look, I don't want to mess you around, but they want to make a few more changes to your schedule.* ◇ *vi* -1. to spend time doing things in a lazy way and usually for pleasure □ *I spent the afternoon messing around on the computer.* -2. [children, students, workers] to do silly things when one should be working or concentrating on something □ *Will you two stop messing around and get on with your homework!* -3. **to mess around** OR **about with sthg** to handle or use sthg in the wrong way so that one damages it □ *Somebody's been messing around with my video camera.*

◆ **mess up** *vt sep* (informal use) -1. **to mess sthg up** [room, arrangement] to make sthg untidy □ *He messed up the whole desk with his papers.* -2. **to mess sthg up** [plan, evening] to spoil sthg □ *That's really messed up our vacation plans.*

◆ **mess with** *vt fus* **to mess with sb** (informal use) to do something to try to harm sb; to get involved with sb □ *I wouldn't mess with him; he has powerful Mafia connections.*

message ['mesɪdʒ] *n* -1. a spoken or written piece of information that somebody gives to somebody else □ *He wasn't in, so I left a message on his answering machine.* □ *There's a message for you at reception.* -2. [of a movie, play, speech] an idea that somebody tries to tell other people in a way that makes them agree with or believe it □ *The book's message is one of hope and reconciliation.* -3. *phrase* **to get the message** to understand what somebody wants one to understand (informal use) □ *He finally got the message and went home.*

message switching [-swɪtʃɪŋ] *n* a technique used to send data from one point in a network to another.

messenger ['mesndʒəʳ] *n* a person who takes

a message to somebody □ *The package arrived by messenger at four o'clock.*

Messiah [mə'saɪə]: **the Messiah** in Christianity, a name for Jesus Christ; in Judaism, a name for the King of the Jews.

Messrs, Messrs. ['mesəʳz] (*abbr of* **messieurs**) the plural of "Mr" (used in business letters).

messy ['mesɪ] (*compar* **messier**, *superl* **messiest**) *adj* -1. [clothes, room, person] dirty or untidy □ *Her desk is never messy.* □ *Painting can get very messy.* -2. [divorce, situation] difficult and unpleasant (informal use) □ *It ended with a rather messy love affair.*

met [met] *past tense & past participle of* **meet**.

Met [met] (*abbr of* **Metropolitan Opera**): **the Met** an important opera company based in New York City.

metabolism [mə'tæbəlɪzm] *n* the chemical processes in the body that involve breaking down food so that it can be used to make energy, make new cells, get rid of waste etc.

metal ['metl] ◇ *n* any solid shiny substance that an electric current can pass through □ *Gold and silver are precious metals.* ◇ *adj*: *metal jewelry/shelves/boxes.*

metallic [me'tælɪk] *adj* -1. [bang, jangle] that makes a sound like one piece of metal hitting another. -2. [paint, finish, paper] that shines like metal. -3. [ore, alloy] that contains metal.

metallurgist [US 'metlɜːrdʒəst, GB mə'tælədʒɪst] *n* an expert in metallurgy.

metallurgy [US 'metlɜːrdʒɪ, GB mə'tælədʒɪ] *n* the scientific study of metals.

metalwork ['metlwɜːʳk] *n* the activity of making objects out of metal.

metalworker ['metlwɜːʳkəʳ] *n* a person whose job is to make objects out of metal.

metamorphose [,metə'mɔːʳfoʊz] *vi* [insect, person] to become something completely different.

metamorphosis [,metə'mɔːʳfəsəs] (*pl* **metamorphoses** [-siːz]) *n* the process of changing and becoming something completely different □ *He's undergone a complete metamorphosis since he met her.*

metaphor ['metəfəʳ] *n* -1. a way of describing something by using something else that has the same qualities □ *He uses a lot of military metaphors.* -2. a symbol or image □ *The play is a metaphor for life.*

metaphorical [,metə'fɒrɪkl] *adj* [word, phrase] that is not being used in its ordinary meaning but as a symbol or image.

metaphysical [,metə'fɪzɪkl] *adj* [idea, theory] that is connected with metaphysics.

metaphysics [,metə'fɪzɪks] *n* the branch of philosophy that involves ideas that try to explain reality and human thought and knowledge.

mete [miːt] ◆ **mete out** *vt sep* to **mete sthg out to sb** [punishment, fine, sentence] to give sthg to sb.

meteor ['miːtɪəʳ] *n* a piece of metal or rock that travels at high speed from space into the Earth's atmosphere, where it is usually destroyed by burning and produces a bright light.

meteoric [miːtɪ'ɒrɪk] *adj* [success, rise] that happens very quickly and suddenly.

meteorite ['miːtjəraɪt] *n* a piece of metal or rock that has fallen to Earth from space.

meteorological [,miːtjərə'lɒdʒɪkl] *adj* [conditions, map, report] connected with meteorology.

meteorologist [miːtjə'rɒlədʒəst] *n* a person who studies meteorology.

meteorology [miːtjə'rɒlədʒɪ] *n* the scientific study of the weather, used especially for weather forecasts.

meter ['miːtəʳ] ◇ *n* -1. [for recording] an instrument that records the quantity of something such as miles traveled or electricity used □ *a taxi/parking meter.* -2. US [for measuring] a unit (100cm) used for measuring length □ *The wall is three meters high.* -3. US [in a poem] the special arrangement of words in a poem that creates a particular rhythm. ◇ *vt* [electricity, water, telephone call] to measure <sthg> by using a meter.

methadone ['meθədoʊn] *n* a drug that is given to heroin addicts to stop them wanting heroin.

methane [US 'meθeɪn, GB 'miːθ-] *n* a gas with no color or smell that is found in natural gas, and is formed from rotting matter. FORMULA: CH_4.

method ['meθəd] *n* a particular way of doing something □ *teaching/banking/up-to-date methods* □ *What method did you use?*

methodical [mə'θɒdɪkl] *adj* [approach, report, person] that is careful and deals with things in a particular order □ *She is a methodical worker.*

methodically [mə'θɒdɪklɪ] *adv* [work, list, count] see **methodical** □ *He read through it, methodically underlining any words he didn't understand.*

Methodist ['meθədəst] ◇ *n* a Christian who follows the teachings of John Wesley. ◇ *adj*: *a Methodist preacher/chapel/church.*

methodology [,meθə'dɒlədʒɪ] (*pl* **methodologies**) *n* a set of methods or principles used in a particular activity, e.g. research (formal use).

Methuselah [mə'θⁱuːzələ] in the Bible, a very old man.

methylated spirits [,meθəleɪtəd-] *n* a mixture of alcohol and other chemicals, used e.g. for cleaning or for burning in small lamps and heaters.

meticulous [mə'tɪkjələs] *adj* [person, care, drawing] that pays very close attention to detail □ *I was always absolutely meticulous about my accounts.*

meticulously [mə'tɪkjələslɪ] *adv* [written, drawn] see **meticulous**.

Met Office (*abbr of* **Meteorological Office**): **the Met Office** a British center that collects information on the weather, and gives weather forecasts.

metre ['miːtə^r] *n* GB [for measuring, in a poem] = **meter**.

metric ['metrɪk] *adj* [unit, measurement, size] that is connected with the metric system.

metrication [,metrɪ'keɪʃn] *n* GB the process of changing to the metric system.

metric system *n* **the metric system** the system of measurement that uses meters, centimeters, liters, grams, metric tons etc.

metric ton *n* a unit (1,000 kg) used for measuring weight.

metro ['metroʊ] (*pl* **metros**) *n* an underground railroad system in Paris and other cities.

metronome ['metrənoʊm] *n* a device that has an arm that moves from side to side that makes a small noise to tell a musician how fast a piece of music should be played.

metropolis [mə'trɒpələs] (*pl* **metropolises**) *n* a very large city; a capital city.

metropolitan [,metrə'pɒlɪtn] *adj* [district, transportation] that is connected with a large or capital city.

Metropolitan Museum of Art: **the Metropolitan Museum of Art** a large art museum in New York City.

Metropolitan Police *npl* **the Metropolitan Police** the name of the police force in London.

mettle ['metl] *n* **to be on one's mettle** to be ready to do the best one can. ■ **to show** OR **prove one's mettle** to show how well one can do something.

mew [mjuː] *n* & *vi* = **meow**.

mews [mjuːz] (*pl* **mews**) *n* GB a small street where the houses are small and were once used to keep horses in; a house in this street.

Mexican ['meksɪkən] *n* & *adj*: *see* **Mexico**.

Mexican War *n* **the Mexican War** a conflict between the USA and Mexico that lasted from 1846 to 1848. The USA won California, Nevada, Utah, and parts of some other states.

Mexico ['meksɪkoʊ] a country in southern North America, between the USA and Central America. SIZE: 1,970,000 sq kms. POPULATION: 90,000,000 (*Mexicans*). CAPITAL: Mexico City. LANGUAGE: Spanish. CURRENCY: Mexican peso.

mezzanine ['mezəniːn] *n* **-1.** a floor between two stories of a building that is usually smaller than the area of the floor below. **-2.** US the first row of raised seats in a theater.

MFA (*abbr of* **Master of Fine Arts**) *n* a postgraduate degree in fine arts; a person who has this degree.

mfr *abbr of* **manufacturer**.

mg *abbr of* **milligram**.

Mgr -1. *abbr of* **monsignor**. **-2.** *abbr of* **manager**.

MHz *abbr of* **megahertz**.

MI *abbr of* **Michigan**.

MI5 [,emaɪ'faɪv] (*abbr of* **Military Intelligence 5**) *n* the British government department responsible for state security.

MI6 [,emaɪ'sɪks] (*abbr of* **Military Intelligence 6**) *n* the British government department responsible for espionage and intelligence.

MIA (*abbr of* **missing in action**) *n* a person who disappears during a battle, and who may have been killed, wounded, or taken prisoner.

Miami [maɪ'æmɪ] a city in southeastern Florida, USA. It is an important center for tourism, and for immigration from the Caribbean and Latin America. POPULATION: 358,548.

miaow [mɪ'aʊ] *n* & *vi* GB = **meow**.

mice [maɪs] *plural of* **mouse**.

Michelangelo [,maɪkl'ændʒəloʊ] (1475–1564) an Italian artist and architect, considered one of the greatest of all time. His work includes the sculpture *David* and the painted ceiling of the Sistine Chapel in Rome.

Michigan ['mɪʃɪgən] **-1.** a state in the northern USA, consisting of two peninsulas between the Great Lakes. ABBREVIATION: MI. SIZE: 150,780 sq kms. POPULATION: 9,295,297 (*Michiganders, Michiganites*). CAPITAL: Lansing. MAIN CITY: Detroit. **-2. Lake Michigan** the only one of the Great Lakes that is entirely in the USA.

Mickey Mouse [,mɪkɪ'maʊs] a cartoon mouse in many movies by Walt Disney.

MICR (*abbr of* **magnetic ink character recognition**) *n* a system for reading information by sensing magnetic ink patterns.

micro ['maɪkroʊ] (*pl* **micros**) *n* a microcomputer.

micro- *prefix* added to words to mean very small.

microbe ['maɪkroʊb] *n* a very small living thing that can only be seen with a microscope.

microbiologist [,maɪkroʊbaɪ'ɒlədʒəst] *n* a person who studies microbiology.

microbiology [,maɪkroʊbaɪ'ɒlədʒɪ] *n* the scientific study of microbes, especially bacteria.

microchip ['maɪkrətʃɪp] *n* a very small piece of silicon that has an electronic circuit printed on it and is used in computers.

microcircuit ['maɪkroʊsɜː'kət] *n* a very small electronic circuit on a microchip.

microclimate ['maɪkroʊklaɪmət] *n* the conditions, e.g. temperature and humidity, that affect a small area.

microcomputer ['maɪkroʊkəmpjuːtə^r] *n* a small computer that is used in the home, in schools, or in offices.

microcosm ['maɪkrəkɒzm] *n* a small and complete version of a much larger place or situation □ *This neighborhood is a microcosm of life in urban America.*

microfiber US, **microfibre** GB ['maɪkrəfaɪbə^r] *n* a soft, smooth, man-made material used for making clothes such as raincoats.

microfiche ['maɪkrəfiːʃ] (*pl* **microfiche** OR **microfiches**) *n* a sheet of film with information printed on it in very small letters that can be read by putting it into a special device that magnifies it □ *The library catalog can be consulted on microfiche.*

microfilm ['maɪkrəfɪlm] *n* thin film used for photographing printed information and storing it at a reduced size.

microlight ['maɪkrəlaɪt] *n* a very small airplane like a hang-glider with an engine.

micron ['maɪkrɒn] *n* a unit (one millionth of a meter) used for measuring length.

Micronesia [,maɪkrə'niːʒə] **-1.** a group of small islands in the western Pacific Ocean, including the Caroline Islands, the Marshall Islands, and the Mariana Islands. **-2.** a country in Micronesia, consisting of the Caroline Islands of Truk, Yap, Ponape, and Kosrae. SIZE: 707 sq kms. POPULATION: 80,000 (*Micronesians*). CAPITAL: Palikir. LANGUAGE: English. CURRENCY: US dollar.

microorganism [,maɪkrou'ɔːrɡənɪzm] *n* a very small organism that can only be seen with a microscope.

microphone ['maɪkrəfoun] *n* an electronic device that one speaks or sings into in order to make one's voice louder, or that one uses to record sounds.

microprocessor [US 'maɪkrəpraːsesər, GB 'maɪkrəprousesə] *n* the central processing unit in a small computer.

microscope ['maɪkrəskoup] *n* an instrument that magnifies very small things so that one can see and examine them.

microscopic [,maɪkrə'skɒpɪk] *adj* **-1.** [bacteria, handwriting, particle] very small. **-2.** [study, detail, examination] very thorough.

microsecond ['maɪkrəsekənd] *n* a unit (one millionth of a second) used for measuring time.

microsurgery [,maɪkrə'sɜːrdʒərɪ] *n* surgery using a special microscope and very small instruments.

microwave (oven) ['maɪkrəweɪv-] *n* an oven that uses short-wave electromagnetic radiation to cook or heat food very quickly.

mid- [mɪd] *prefix* added to words to mean the middle of a place or period of time □ *mid-morning/winter* □ *the mid-20th century/mid-1960s.*

midair [,mɪd'eər] ◇ *adj* [collision, explosion] that happens while the plane is in the air, not on the ground. ◇ *n* **in midair** [collide, explode] in the air, not on the ground.

Midas ['maɪdəs] in Greek mythology, a king who turned everything he touched into gold.

midday ['mɪdeɪ] *n* 12 o'clock in the middle of the day, or the period around this time □ *The package arrived just before/after midday.* □ *the midday sun/meal.*

middle ['mɪdl] ◇ *adj* **-1. the middle row/section etc** the row/section etc that is the one in or nearest to the center □ *It's on the middle shelf.* **-2. one's middle twenties/thirties etc** at a point in between the beginning and end of one's twenties/thirties etc □ *He's in his middle sixties/years.*
◇ *n* **-1. the middle** [of a room, book, row] the part of something that is in or nearest to the center □ *He walked across the middle of the field.* □ *Cut the fruit along the middle.* ■ **in the middle** at or near the central point of something □ *He was standing in the middle of the room.* ■ **in the middle of nowhere** far from any town or village □ *They live in a cottage right out in the middle of nowhere.* **-2.** [of a month, century] the part of something that happens at or around the central point of a period of time □ *By the middle of the second half they had scored another goal.* ■ **to be in the middle of sthg** [of a meeting, meal] to be busy with sthg □ *I was in the middle of writing a letter when he called.* □ *Would you mind waiting? I'm in the middle of a meeting.* ■ **in the middle of the night** very late at night □ *I was woken up in the middle of the night by someone banging on the door.* **-3.** [of a person] one's waist □ *I'm putting on weight around the middle.*

middle age *n* the period in one's life from about the age of 40 to 60 □ *When he reached middle age he suddenly became very fat.*

middle-aged [-'eɪdʒd] *adj* [man, woman] who is between 40 and 60 years old □ *The clothes are more likely to appeal to middle-aged customers.*

Middle Ages *npl* **the Middle Ages** the period in European history between about 1000 AD and 1500 AD.

middle America *n* a term that refers to average Americans. It suggests people with traditional and conservative values □ *Middle America may not be so keen on voting away their tax benefits.*

middle class *n* **the middle class** OR **classes** the class of people in society, between the upper and lower classes, that includes professional and business people.

middle-class *adj* [family, background, mentality] that belongs to or is typical of the middle classes.

middle distance *n* **in the middle distance** in the area of a view or picture that is between the foreground and the background.

Middle East: **the Middle East** the countries of southwestern Asia, Arabia, and northeastern Africa, considered together.

Middle Eastern *adj*: *see* **Middle East**.

middle finger *n* the longest finger of one's hand.

middleman ['mɪdlmæn] (*pl* **middlemen** [-men]) *n* a person who buys goods from manufacturers and sells them at a profit.

middle management *n* the management section of a business, on the level below the people who make the most important decisions.

middle name *n* the name some people have that comes between their first name and their last name.

middle-of-the-road *adj* [politics, politician, music] that is not extreme □ *His views on politics are very middle-of-the-road.*

middle school *n* a school for children between the ages of about 9 and 13.

middleweight ['mɪdlweɪt] *n* a class for boxers of not more than a certain weight (73 kgs for professional boxers); a boxer in this class.

middling ['mɪdlɪŋ] *adj* [health, quality] average □ *"How are you feeling?" — "Oh, fair to middling."*

Mideast [,mɪd'iːst] US = **Middle East**.

midfield [,mɪd'fiːld] *n* the middle area of a playing field used for soccer, rugby, hockey etc.

midge [mɪdʒ] *n* a small flying insect like a mosquito that bites people's skin.

midget ['mɪdʒət] *n* a very small person.

midi system ['mɪdɪ-] *n* a small hi-fi system designed as a single unit.

Midlands ['mɪdləndz]: **the Midlands** a region of central England that includes several industrial cities, e.g. Birmingham, Coventry, Leicester, and Nottingham.

midnight ['mɪdnaɪt] *n* 12 o'clock in the middle of the night, or the period around this time □ *The clock struck midnight.* □ *They left before/after/at midnight.* □ *a midnight rendezvous/visitor/feast.*

midriff ['mɪdrɪf] *n* the part of one's body above the waist and below the chest.

midst [mɪdst] *n* **-1. in the midst of sthg** [of a crowd, scene] among or surrounded by sthg (literary use) □ *We sat in the midst of piles of papers and files.* ■ **in our/their etc midst** among us/them etc □ *In our midst tonight is a great artist.* **-2. in the midst of sthg** during sthg □ *He arrived in the midst of a violent argument.* ■ **to be in the midst of sthg** to be busy with sthg □ *I was in the midst of cleaning when the doorbell rang.*

midstream [,mɪd'striːm] *n* **-1. in midstream** in the middle of a river, where the current is strongest. **-2. to stop/pause in midstream** to stop/pause in the middle of talking, shouting, writing etc.

midsummer [,mɪd'sʌmə^r] *n* the middle period of summer.

Midsummer Day *n* GB June 24.

midtown ['mɪdtaʊn] *adj* near the center of a city, between the downtown and the uptown areas □ *midtown Manhattan.*

midway [,mɪd'weɪ] *adv* **-1.** in a position that is an equal distance from two places or points □ *The factory is midway between these offices and downtown.* **-2.** during the middle part of an event or a period of time □ *He turned up midway through the first half of the game.*

midweek [*adj* 'mɪdwiːk, *adv* ,mɪd'wiːk] ◇ *adj* a **midweek fixture/meeting** a fixture/meeting that happens on Tuesday, Wednesday, or Thursday □ *Can we meet for a midweek drink?* ◇ *adv* [arrive, meet, leave] *I'll call you midweek.*

Midwest [,mɪd'west]: **the Midwest** a region of the northern central USA between the Appalachians and the Rocky Mountains, consisting mainly of farmland.

Midwestern [,mɪd'westə^rn] *adj*: *see* **Midwest**.

midwife ['mɪdwaɪf] (*pl* **midwives** [-waɪvz]) *n* a nurse, usually a woman, who has been trained to help and care for a woman before, during, and after the birth of her child.

midwifery [US 'mɪdwaɪfərɪ, GB ,mɪd'wɪfərɪ] *n* the work of a midwife.

miffed [mɪft] *adj* [person] who is annoyed and offended by something (informal use).

might [maɪt] ◇ *modal vb* **-1. I might go** it is possible that I will go, but I am not certain □ *Take this umbrella, it might come in handy.* □ *We could try phoning her, but she might already have left.* □ *"Will you go to the party?" — "I might."* **-2. they might have died** they did not die, but they could have □ *Think how much time we might have saved if we'd had a map.* **-3. she might well resign** it is very likely that she will resign □ *You might well be right, but that's not really the point.* **-4. you might have waited/told me!** you should have waited/told me □ *You might at least offer to help sometimes!* **-5.** used to make suggestions or ask questions in a polite way □ *Might I interrupt?* □ *It might be better to wait until later.* **-6.** used to ask permission □ *He asked if he might leave the room.* □ *Might I ask a question?* **-7. we might as well go home** there is nothing better to do, so let's go home □ *There's no point you staying here, so you might as well leave now.* **-8.** *phrase* **I might have known** OR **guessed** I am not surprised at this □ *I might have known you'd be mixed up in it somewhere!* ◇ *n* **-1.** [of a nation, army] power. **-2.** [of a person] physical strength □ *She pushed the cabinet with all her might, but it refused to move.*

mightn't ['maɪtnt] = **might not**.

might've ['maɪtəv] = **might have**.

mighty ['maɪtɪ] (*compar* **mightier**, *superl* **mightiest**) ◇ *adj* **-1.** [army, blow, ruler] very powerful. **-2.** [mountain, warship] very large. ◇ *adv* US [generous, fine, good] very (informal use) □ *That was a mighty tasty meal!*

migraine ['maɪɡreɪn] *n* an extremely bad headache with the pain over one eye or one side of the head.

migrant ['maɪɡrənt] ◇ *adj* **migrant birds/workers etc** birds/workers etc that migrate from one place to another □ *the migrant workforce that helped build the American economy.* ◇ *n* a bird, animal, or person that migrates.

migrate [US 'maɪɡreɪt, GB maɪ'ɡreɪt] *vi* **-1.** [birds, animals] to go regularly to another country or area, usually in large numbers and only for a short period of time, to find food or warmer weather, or to mate □ *They migrate south in the winter.* **-2.** [person, people] to move from one country or area to another to find work or a place to live.

migration [maɪ'ɡreɪʃn] *n*: *see* **migrate** □ *the annual migration of swallows.*

migratory [US 'maɪɡrətɔːrɪ, GB -rətərɪ] *adj* a **migratory bird/herd etc** a bird/herd etc that migrates.

mike [maɪk] *n* a microphone (informal use).

Milan [mɪ'læn] a city in northern Italy. It is famous for its opera house and cathedral. POPULATION: 1,371,008.

mild [maɪld] *adj* **-1.** [flavor, shampoo, disinfectant] that is not strong, harsh, bitter etc □ *a mild cheese/chili.* **-2.** [person] who is gentle and never angry □ *a mild tone of voice.* **-3.** [winter, weather] that is not too cold □ *It's been pretty mild this week.* **-4.** [criticism, rebuke] that shows a feeling that is not very strong □ *"Where were you?" he asked, with mild interest.* **-5.** [illness, attack] that is not serious □ *She was recovering after a mild bout of flu.*

mildew ['mɪldjuː] *n* a mold that grows on food, leather, paper etc that has been kept for a long time in warm damp conditions.

mildly ['maɪldlɪ] *adv* **-1.** [criticize, complain] *see* **mild.** ■ **to put it mildly** a phrase used to show that something is much stronger, worse etc than the words one has used to describe it □ *He was furious, to put it mildly.* **-2. mildly interesting/amusing etc** slightly interesting/amusing etc.

mild-mannered *adj* [person] polite and gentle.

mile [maɪl] *n* **-1.** [on land, in air] a unit (approximately 1,609 meters) used for measuring distance □ *How many miles are there from Dallas to Houston?* □ *a ten-mile hike.* ■ **for miles** for a very long way □ *We could see for miles.* □ *We had walked for miles (and miles).* ■ **to be miles away** to pay no attention to somebody or something because one is thinking about something else □ *I'm sorry, I was miles away – what were you saying about the election?* **-2.** SHIPPING a nautical mile.
◆ **miles** *adv* by a very large amount □ *This one is miles better.*

mileage ['maɪlɪdʒ] *n* the number of miles traveled by a vehicle □ *The car has a low mileage.* ■ **to get a lot of mileage out of sthg** to use sthg as much as possible to get what one wants (informal use) □ *You've had a lot of mileage out of that anecdote, haven't you?*

mileage allowance *n* money paid for each mile that one travels, e.g. on business.

mileometer [maɪ'lɒmətəʳ] *n* GB an instrument that records the number of miles traveled by a vehicle.

milestone ['maɪlstoʊn] *n* **-1.** a very important event in the development of something or somebody. **-2.** a stone by the side of a road, with the number of miles to the nearest town marked on it.

milieu [US miːl'juː, GB 'miːljɜː] (*pl* **milieus** OR **milieux** [US -'juːz, GB -jɜːz]) *n* the people one works or spends time with; one's surroundings.

militant ['mɪlɪtənt] ◇ *n* a person who strongly supports political change and actively tries to persuade people that it is necessary, sometimes in an aggressive way. ◇ *adj: a group of militant feminists/activists.*

militarism ['mɪlɪtərɪzm] *n* the belief that a country should use and improve its armed forces in order to become more powerful.

militarist ['mɪlɪtərəst] *n* a person who supports militarism.

militarized zone ['mɪlɪtəraɪzd-] *n* an area defended by military forces.

military [US 'mɪlɪterɪ GB -rərɪ] ◇ *adj* [operation, takeover] that is carried out by the armed forces □ *a military dictatorship* □ *military service.*
◇ *n* **the military** the armed forces, especially the army.

military police *npl* soldiers who form the police force of the army, navy, or air force.

militate ['mɪlɪteɪt] *vi* **to militate against sthg** to make it almost impossible to do sthg or for somebody to do sthg (formal use) □ *His reputation as a difficult man to work with militates against his chances of getting the job.*

militia [mə'lɪʃə] *n* men who have been trained as soldiers, but who do not belong to the army and are only used during an emergency.

milk [mɪlk] ◇ *n* **-1.** [from animals] the white liquid that cows, goats, and other animals produce to feed their young; this liquid used as a food by humans, and to make cheese, butter, yogurt etc □ *a bottle of milk* □ *Do you take milk (in your coffee)?* **-2.** [from a woman] the liquid that women produce from their breasts to feed their babies. **-3.** [from plants] the white liquid found inside some fruits or plants, e.g. coconuts. ◇ *vt* **-1.** [cow, goat] to get milk from <an animal> by pulling its udders. **-2.** [situation, company, scandal] to use <sb/sthg> as much as possible to get what one wants, especially money, sympathy, or information □ *He milked her for all she was worth.*

milk chocolate *n* solid chocolate made with milk □ *a milk chocolate bar/drink.*

milk float *n* GB = milk truck.

milking ['mɪlkɪŋ] *n* the activity of milking an animal.

milkman ['mɪlkmən] (*pl* **milkmen** [-mən]) *n* a person whose job is to sell milk by delivering it to people's houses every day.

milk round *n* GB **-1.** the daily trip made by a milkman when delivering milk to his customers. **-2. the milk round** regular visits made by large companies to universities, in order to recruit undergraduates.

milk shake *n* a drink made with milk, flavoring, and usually ice cream, that is beaten until it is thick and creamy.

milk tooth *n* any one of the first set of teeth that a child or young animal grows, which later fall out and are replaced by adult teeth.

milk truck *n* US a vehicle used for delivering milk to people's houses.

milky ['mɪlkɪ] (*compar* **milkier**, *superl* **milkiest**) *adj* **-1.** [coffee, tea, drink] that contains a lot of milk. **-2.** [complexion, liquid] that is pale white in color.

Milky Way: the Milky Way the mass of stars that looks like a long pale strip of light in the night sky.

mill [mɪl] ◇ *n* **-1.** [for making flour] a machine used to crush grain or wheat to make flour; the building containing this machine □ *a flour mill.* **-2.** [for making paper, steel] a factory where particular goods are made □ *a wool/paper/steel mill.* **-3.** [for coffee, paper] a small machine for grinding coffee beans, peppercorns etc into powder □ *a coffee/pepper mill.*
◇ *vt* to crush <grain or wheat> in a mill to

produce flour; to produce <flour> by crushing grain, wheat etc in a mill.

◆ **mill around, mill about** *vi* [people] to move around in a place in different directions □ *Crowds of visitors milled around on the cathedral steps.*

Mill [mɪl], **John Stuart** (1806–1873) a British philosopher and politician. He believed in the freedom of the individual and in women's right to vote.

millennium [mə'leniəm] (*pl* **millennia** [-nɪə]) *n* a period of one thousand years.

miller ['mɪlər] *n* a man who owns or works a mill that produces flour.

Miller ['mɪlər], **Arthur** (1915–) a US playwright whose plays include *Death of a Salesman* and *The Crucible.*

millet ['mɪlət] *n* seeds from a tall grass that are used for food.

milli- ['mɪlə] *prefix* added to words to mean a thousandth part of something.

millibar ['mɪləbɑːr] *n* a unit (one thousandth of a bar) used for measuring air pressure.

milligram US, **milligramme** GB ['mɪləgræm] *n* a unit (one thousandth of a gram) used for measuring weight.

milliliter US, **millilitre** GB ['mɪləliːtər] *n* a unit (one thousandth of a liter) used for measuring the volume of liquids and gases.

millimeter US, **millimetre** GB ['mɪləmiːtər] *n* a unit (one thousandth of a meter) used for measuring length.

millinery [US 'mɪlənerɪ, GB -ərɪ] *n* a collective term for women's hats.

million ['mɪljən] *num* the number 1,000,000 □ *Several million lives were lost.*

◆ **millions** *pron* used to refer to a very large number of people or things □ *We had millions of phone calls about it.* □ *They spent millions on remodeling.*

millionaire [,mɪljə'neər] *n* a person who is very rich and has a million dollars, pounds etc or more □ *He's a dollar millionaire.* □ *a millionaire oil tycoon.*

millionairess [,mɪljə'neərəs] *n* a woman who is very rich and has at least a million dollars, pounds etc.

millipede ['mɪləpiːd] *n* a small creature like a worm with many legs.

millisecond ['mɪləsekənd] *n* one thousandth of a second.

millstone ['mɪlstoʊn] *n* one of two large round stones used in mills for grinding grain to make flour. ■ **a millstone around one's neck** an unpleasant problem or responsibility that one has to deal with □ *That bank loan had become a real millstone around my neck.*

millwheel ['mɪlwiːl] *n* a large wheel that is turned by moving water and that powers the machinery of a mill.

milometer [maɪ'lɒmətər] *n* = mileometer.

Milton ['mɪltən], **John** (1608–1674) a British poet whose best-known work is the long poem *Paradise Lost.*

mime [maɪm] ◇ *n* a way of acting that expresses feelings or events through gestures and movements and without speaking; a performance of this □ *a mime artist* □ *The whole story was told in mime.* ◇ *vt* [action, emotion] to express <sthg> using mime.

mimic ['mɪmɪk] (*pt* & *pp* **mimicked**, *cont* **mimicking**) ◇ *vt* [person, voice, gestures] to imitate <sb/sthg> in an amusing way. ◇ *n* a person who is good at mimicking other people.

mimicry ['mɪmɪkrɪ] *n* the act of mimicking somebody or something.

mimosa [mɪ'moʊsə] *n* **-1.** a tropical tree with tiny yellow flowers and leaves that sometimes fold if they are touched; the flowers of this tree. **-2.** US a drink made from champagne and orange juice.

min. **-1.** *abbr of* **minute**. **-2.** *abbr of* **minimum**.

Min. *abbr of* **ministry**.

mince [mɪns] ◇ *n* GB meat, usually beef, that has been cut into very small pieces in a mincer. ◇ *vt* to cut <meat> into very small pieces using a mincer. ◇ *vi* [man] to walk with short steps moving one's hips in an exaggerated way (disapproving use).

mincemeat ['mɪnsmiːt] *n* **-1.** small pieces of dried fruit mixed with spices and fat, used for filling cakes and mince pies. **-2.** GB = mince.

mince pie *n* a small round pie that is filled with pieces of dried fruit mixed with spices and fat, and is eaten at Christmas.

mincer ['mɪnsər] *n* a machine for grinding meat into small pieces, usually by forcing it through small holes.

mind [maɪnd] ◇ *n* **-1.** the way in which one thinks □ *You have a warped mind!* **-2.** one's thoughts □ *I can't get her out of my mind.* ■ **to come into** OR **cross sb's mind** [thought, idea] to occur to sb □ *It never crossed my mind to mention it.* □ *It never crossed my mind that it might be important.* ■ **to have sthg on one's mind** to be worried about sthg □ *It's been on my mind for some time.* ■ **to take sb's mind off sthg** to help sb to avoid thinking about sthg unpleasant □ *Why don't you go to the movies? It'll take your mind off things.* ■ **a load** OR **weight off one's mind** something that one does not have to worry about any more as a result of a change in the situation □ *That's a weight off my mind — I was convinced I'd left my keys inside.* ■ **to put** OR **set sb's mind at rest** to stop sb from worrying about something □ *I can put your mind at rest about that particular point.* **-3.** [brain] the ability to think intelligently □ *She has a brilliant/quick mind.* **-4.** [attention] **to concentrate the mind** to make one think seriously about something □ *I find a cup of coffee helps to concentrate the mind in the morning.* ■ **to keep one's mind on sthg** to concentrate on sthg □ *He just couldn't keep his mind on the lecture, he was so worried about Susan.* ■ **to put one's mind to sthg** [to a task, problem] to start concentrating on sthg □ *You can do it if you really put your mind to it.* ■ **to slip one's mind** [fact] to be forgotten by one □ *A meeting at 4:00 pm? Oh dear, it had completely slipped my mind!* **-5.** [opinion] **to my mind** in my opinion □ *To my mind, there's a lot we can do to help.*

■ **to keep an open mind** to avoid forming an opinion about something until one knows all the facts □ *I'm keeping an open mind about this until we've seen all the evidence.* ■ **to make one's mind up** to decide something by making a choice □ *Look, make your mind up, we can't spend all day here!* ■ **to speak one's mind** to say clearly what one really believes □ *She believes in speaking her mind, even if it makes her unpopular.* ■ **to be in two minds about sthg** to be unsure about sthg, especially because there are two possible choices □ *I'm in two minds about whether to go to Peru or not.* **-6.** [memory] **to bear sthg in mind** to remember sthg important and think seriously about it □ *Look, if another suitable job comes up I'll bear your company/you in mind.* □ *Bear in mind the fact that half of them are over 60.* ■ **to call sthg to mind** to remind one of sthg □ *His painting calls to mind those old Byzantine mosaics we saw in Italy.* ■ **to cast one's mind back** to think about something that happened in the past □ *Try to cast your mind back to that day.* **-7.** [intention] **to have sthg in mind** to be thinking about sthg or about the possibility of doing sthg □ *What sort of color did you have in mind, sir?* □ *What I had in mind was a large conference which all managers could attend.* ■ **to have a mind to do sthg** to want or choose to do sthg □ *Do you know, I have a mind to tell that man exactly what I think of him!* **-8.** [person] a person who is extremely intelligent □ *one of the greatest minds of the 19th century.* ■ **great minds think alike!** a phrase used to draw attention to the fact that one has had the same idea as somebody else (humorous use).

◇ *vi* **-1.** not to want something to be done □ *Do you mind if I open the window?* □ *I don't mind in the least.* **-2.** to be a little upset about something □ *I don't mind if people laugh at me.* □ *Do you mind about not getting the job?* ■ **never mind** a phrase used to tell somebody not to worry about something, or to reassure somebody that something is not important □ *"I didn't get the job."* — *"Oh, well, never mind, there'll be others."* □ *"I'm sorry about the stain."* — *"Never mind, I never liked that dress anyway."* **-3. mind out!** GB be careful! □ *Mind out! There's a car coming!*

◇ *vt* **-1.** to be unhappy or annoyed about <sthg> □ *I don't mind waiting.* □ *Don't mind him, he's only jealous.* ■ **I wouldn't mind a drink/vacation etc** I would like a drink/vacation etc. **-2.** [expense, trouble] to care or worry about <sthg> □ *I really don't mind how you do it.* □ *I wouldn't mind about the cost, if only they would finish it quickly.* □ *What I mind most is their total lack of respect for us.* **-3.** [step, manners] to pay attention to <sthg> so that one does not get hurt, behave badly etc □ *Mind your language/the road.* **-4.** [child, store, luggage] to take care of <sb/sthg> □ *Could you mind my bag for me while I go to the restroom?*

◆ **mind you** *adv* GB a phrase used before saying something that changes or explains something that one has just said □ *Mind you, having said that, he's really not that intelligent.*

minder ['maɪndə'] *n* GB a bodyguard.

mindful ['maɪndfl] *adj* **to be mindful of sthg** [of a danger, risk, one's duty] to think seriously about sthg when one does or decides something.

mindless ['maɪndləs] *adj* **-1.** [violence, act] that has no reason or purpose □ *It was an act of mindless vandalism.* **-2.** [job, work] that is so simple or repetitive that one does not need to think while doing it □ *Dorothy was feeling fed up with mindless office work.*

mind reader *n* a person who knows what other people are thinking.

mindset ['maɪndset] *n* a way of thinking and viewing the world □ *challenging the mindset of the consumer generation.*

mind's eye *n* **in one's mind's eye** in one's imagination □ *I can see him in my mind's eye exactly as he used to look all those years ago.*

mine¹ [maɪn] ◇ *n* **-1.** INDUSTRY a system of holes and tunnels under the ground for digging out minerals □ *a coal/gold/salt mine.* **-2.** MILITARY a bomb hidden below the surface of the ground or water that explodes when a person or vehicle goes over it. **-3. to be a mine of information** [person, book] to be full of useful information. ◇ *vt* **-1.** [coal, gold] to dig <a mineral> out from under the ground. **-2.** MILITARY [road, sea] to lay mines in <a place>.

mine² *pron* used to describe something that belongs to, or is connected with, the person who is speaking □ *Don't take that pen, it's mine!* □ *Your desk is bigger than mine.* □ *Her car is green and mine is blue.* ■ **she's a friend of mine** she's one of my friends.

mine detector *n* a device used for showing where mines are hidden.

minefield ['maɪnfiːld] *n* **-1.** an area where mines have been hidden. **-2.** a subject or situation that has hidden dangers □ *a legal/political minefield.*

minelayer ['maɪnleɪə'] *n* a ship or aircraft that lays mines.

miner ['maɪnə'] *n* a person whose job is to mine a particular mineral, e.g. coal or gold.

mineral ['mɪnrəl] ◇ *n* a substance, e.g. coal, salt, or tin, that forms naturally in the earth □ *Lava contains many different kinds of minerals.* ◇ *adj*: *vast mineral deposits.*

mineralogy [,mɪnə'rælədʒɪ] *n* the scientific study of minerals.

mineral water *n* water that comes from a natural spring and contains some minerals □ *a bottle/glass of mineral water.*

minestrone [,mɪnə'strəʊnɪ] *n* an Italian soup containing vegetables and small pieces of pasta.

minesweeper ['maɪnswiːpə'] *n* a ship that is equipped to take mines out of the sea.

mingle ['mɪŋgl] ◇ *vt* **to mingle sthg with sthg** to mix sthg with sthg □ *The message was one of hope mingled with caution.* ◇ *vi* **-1.** [smells, sounds, emotions] to become mixed together □ *The sound of laughter mingled with the music.* **-2.** [person] to have short conversations with several different people at a party or social occasion □ *I suppose I'd better go and mingle.*

mini ['mɪnɪ] *n* a very short skirt or dress.

miniature [US 'mɪnɪətʃr, GB 'mɪnətʃə] ◇ *adj* a **miniature model/version etc** a small model/version etc of something bigger. ◇ *n* -1. a very small painting, usually of a person. -2. a very small bottle of alcohol.

◆ **in miniature** *adj* that is exactly like something else but is much smaller.

minibar ['mɪnɪbɑːʳ] *n* a fridge in a hotel room that contains alcoholic and non-alcoholic drinks for guests using the room.

minibus ['mɪnɪbʌs] (*pl* -buses OR -busses) *n* a small bus, usually for 10 to 12 passengers.

minicab ['mɪnɪkæb] *n* GB an ordinary car used as a taxi that can be ordered by telephone but not stopped on the street.

minicomputer ['mɪnɪkəmpjuːtəʳ] *n* a computer that is larger than a personal computer but smaller than a mainframe.

minim ['mɪnəm] *n* GB a note in Western music (♩) that is half as long as a whole note.

minima ['mɪnəmə] *plural of* **minimum**.

minimal ['mɪnəml] *adj* [interest, knowledge, damage] very little □ *The costs incurred on such a project would be minimal.*

minimize, -ise ['mɪnəmaɪz] *vt* -1. [risk, damage, spending] to reduce <sthg> as much as possible □ *Care must be taken in order to minimize the effects of the drug.* -2. [fact, problem, somebody's role] to make <sthg> seem as unimportant as possible □ *Why do you always try to minimize the problems?*

minimum ['mɪnəməm] (*pl* minimums OR **minima**) ◇ *n* the lowest amount, value etc that is possible or allowed □ *Keep expenses to a minimum.* □ *As part of the deal, you must stay a minimum of three nights.* ◇ *adj*: *What is the minimum amount you have to invest?*

minimum lending rate [-'lendɪŋ-] *n* in Britain, the minimum rate, set by the Bank of England, for lending money or discounting bills.

minimum security prison *n* US a prison in which the prisoners are not locked in their cells all day, and can take part in activities that would not be allowed in other prisons.

minimum wage *n* the lowest wage that an employer is allowed to pay employees.

mining ['maɪnɪŋ] *n* the industry and activity of digging minerals out from under the ground □ *the mining industry.*

minion ['mɪnjən] *n* a low-ranking employee who obeys orders (humorous and disapproving use).

mini-series *n* a television drama, usually in three to six parts, that is shown over a few days or weeks.

miniskirt ['mɪnɪskɜːʳt] *n* a very short skirt.

minister ['mɪnəstəʳ] *n* -1. POLITICS a member of a government who is in charge of a particular department □ *the Minister of Transport* OR *Transport Minister* □ *the Minister for Home Affairs.* -2. RELIGION a person who leads religious activities in a church, especially a Protestant church □ *a Methodist minister.*

◆ **minister to** *vt fus* **to minister to sb** to help sb who is ill and give them everything that they need (formal use).

ministerial [ˌmɪnə'stɪərɪəl] *adj* POLITICS [decision, level] that is connected with the work of a minister.

minister of state *n* in Britain, a government minister appointed to help a senior minister □ *the Minister of State for the Environment.*

ministry ['mɪnɪstrɪ] (*pl* ministries) *n* -1. POLITICS a government department □ *the Ministry of the Interior.* -2. RELIGION **the ministry** members of the Christian, especially Protestant, clergy.

mink [mɪŋk] (*pl* mink) *n* a small animal like a weasel that lives in Northern Europe, Asia, and America; the brown fur of this animal, considered to be very valuable □ *a mink coat.*

Minnesota [ˌmɪnə'soutə] a state in the central northern USA, on the Canadian border. ABBREVIATION: MN. SIZE: 217,735 sq kms. POPULATION: 4,375,099 (*Minnesotans*). CAPITAL: Saint Paul. MAIN CITY: Minneapolis.

minnow ['mɪnou] (*pl* minnows OR minnow) *n* a very small freshwater fish.

minor ['maɪnəʳ] ◇ *adj* -1. [role, details, difficulties] unimportant □ *They've made a few minor changes to the program — nothing important.* -2. [key, chord] based on a scale in Western music that has a halftone between the second and third notes □ *his clarinet quintet in A minor.* ◇ *n* a person who is not old enough to be legally considered an adult.

minority [US mə'nɔrətɪ, GB maɪ-] (*pl* minorities) *n* -1. [of a group] less than half □ *The new law is only supported by a minority of the population.* ■ **to be in a** OR **the minority** to belong to a number of people or things that form less than half of a larger group □ *Unfortunately, people who think like you do are in a minority.* -2. a group of people with a different race or religion from most of the people around them □ *There's a small white minority living in the country.* □ *a racial minority* □ *a minority sport.*

minority government *n* a government that has fewer elected members than the total number of elected members of the opposition parties.

minority interest *n* something that is of interest to a small group of people only □ *minority-interest television.*

minor road *n* a less important road, often in the country.

minster ['mɪnstəʳ] *n* an important church that used to be part of an abbey.

minstrel ['mɪnstrəl] *n* a traveling singer and entertainer in the past.

mint [mɪnt] ◇ *n* -1. [for flavoring] a small plant with leaves that smell sweet and are used to flavor food, drinks, and toothpaste. -2. [for eating] a candy flavored with mint. -3. **the Mint** the place where coins are officially made in a country. -4. *phrase* **in mint condition** [coin, book, car] in perfect condition. ◇ *vt* to make <coins> in a mint.

mint sauce *n* a sauce made of mint leaves,

sugar, and vinegar, usually eaten with roast lamb.

minuet [ˌmɪnjʊ'et] *n* a slow 17th- and 18th-century dance; a piece of music written for this dance.

minus ['maɪnəs] (*pl* **minuses**) ◇ *prep* **-1.** MATH when <a particular number> is taken away □ *4 minus 2 is 2.* **-2.** WEATHER at <a particular number of degrees> below freezing point □ *It's minus 10 (degrees).* ◇ *adj* **-1.** MATH [number] less than zero □ *The answer is minus four.* **-2. A/B etc minus** EDUCATION a grade that is just lower than A/B etc □ *I got a B minus.* ◇ *n* **-1.** MATH = **minus sign. -2.** a disadvantage □ *The long commute is definitely a minus.*

minuscule ['mɪnəskjuːl] *adj* [detail, amount] extremely small.

minus sign *n* a sign (–) that means minus when put before a number.

minute[1] ['mɪnət] *n* **-1.** a unit for measuring time that is equal to one of the 60 parts that an hour is divided into □ *I'll be ready in five minutes.* **-2.** a very short period of time □ *It was here only a minute ago.* ■ **at any minute** at any time and probably very soon □ *The bomb could go off at any minute.* ■ **to do sthg at the last minute** to do sthg at the latest possible time □ *He changed his mind at the last minute.* ■ **this minute** right now □ *Stop that this minute!*
◆ **minutes** *npl* the written records of what is said at a meeting □ *John took the minutes at the meeting.*

minute[2] [maɪ'njuːt] *adj* [amount, detail] very small □ *She put a minute drop of the mixture into the water.*

minutiae [maɪ'njuːʃiɪ] *npl* small unimportant details □ *Don't bother me with the minutiae.*

miracle ['mɪrəkl] ◇ *n* **-1.** RELIGION an action or event that is impossible according to scientific laws and that people believe to be done by God □ *Her sudden recovery is being proclaimed as a miracle.* **-2.** a surprising and lucky event □ *It was a miracle that we survived/arrived on time.* ◇ *adj* **a miracle drug/cure** a drug/cure that cures an illness that cannot normally be cured.

miraculous [mɪ'rækjələs] *adj* **-1.** [event] that people believe is done by God □ *a miraculous healing.* **-2.** [survival, escape] that seems surprising and lucky □ *She's made a miraculous recovery.*

miraculously [mɪ'rækjələslɪ] *adv* a word used to show that one thinks that something is very lucky and unexpected □ *Miraculously, he survived.*

mirage [mə'rɑːʒ] *n* **-1.** an image of something that is not really there, often seen in deserts. **-2.** a hope or wish that cannot come true.

mire ['maɪər] *n* deep mud.

mirror ['mɪrər] ◇ *n* a flat piece of glass that has a metallic surface on one side so that one can see the reflection of things by looking at it □ *He glanced at himself in the mirror.* ◇ *vt* **-1.** [view, behavior, structure] to be very

similar to <sthg> □ *Her report mirrored my thinking on the subject.* **-2.** [light, view] to reflect <sthg> (literary use).

mirror image *n* a reversed image of something, as if seen in a mirror.

mirth [mɜːrθ] *n* amusement and laughter (formal use).

misadventure [ˌmɪsəd'ventʃər] *n* an unfortunate accident. ■ **death by misadventure** LAW accidental death.

misanthropist [mɪs'ænθrəpəst] *n* a person who dislikes other people.

misapplication [ˌmɪsæplɪ'keɪʃn] *n* [of a principle, law] the wrong use of something.

misapprehension [ˌmɪsæprɪ'henʃn] *n* a mistaken belief □ *They were under the misapprehension that they would be paid.*

misappropriate [ˌmɪsə'prouprɪeɪt] *vt* to take <funds> dishonestly for one's own use.

misappropriation [ˌmɪsəprouprɪ'eɪʃn] *n*: see **misappropriate.**

misbehave [ˌmɪsbɪ'heɪv] *vi* [child, animal] to behave badly □ *Have you been misbehaving again in my absence?*

misbehavior US, **misbehaviour** GB [ˌmɪsbɪ'heɪvjər] *n* bad behavior □ *Any misbehavior on our part was severely punished.*

misc *abbr of* **miscellaneous.**

miscalculate [ˌmɪs'kælkjəleɪt] ◇ *vt* **-1.** MATH [distance, time, number] to calculate <sthg> wrongly □ *I miscalculated how much time I would need.* **-2.** [consequences, situation] to judge <sthg> wrongly □ *I miscalculated the effect my words would have on him.* ◇ *vi* **-1.** MATH to calculate something wrongly □ *There's not enough to go around; I obviously miscalculated.* **-2.** to judge something wrongly □ *If it is a deliberate strategy, the committee has seriously miscalculated.*

miscalculation [ˌmɪskælkjə'leɪʃn] *n*: see **miscalculate** □ *Somebody has made a serious miscalculation.*

miscarriage ['mɪskærɪdʒ] *n* the birth of a baby before it is developed enough to live □ *Deborah has had several miscarriages.*

miscarriage of justice *n* a wrong judgment made by a court.

miscarry [ˌmɪs'kærɪ] (*pt* & *pp* **miscarried**) *vi* **-1.** [woman] to have a miscarriage. **-2.** [plan, idea] to go wrong (formal use).

miscellaneous [ˌmɪsə'leɪnɪəs] *adj* **miscellaneous items/people etc** items/people etc that are different from each other and do not belong to any group □ *You can put the stationery under miscellaneous expenses.*

miscellany [US 'mɪsəleɪnɪ, GB mɪ'selənɪ] (*pl* **miscellanies**) *n* a collection of miscellaneous things or people.

mischance [US ˌmɪs'tʃæns, GB -'tʃɑːns] *n* bad luck (formal use).

mischief ['mɪstʃɪf] *n* **-1.** slightly bad behavior, especially of a child, that is done for amusement, but is not intended to cause harm □ *Have you been up to mischief again?* **-2.** injury or damage caused by somebody.

mischievous ['mɪstʃɪvəs] *adj* [child, behavior] that is full of mischief □ *She gave a mischievous smile.*

misconceived [,mɪskən'siːvd] *adj* [plan, method] that has been badly or wrongly planned.

misconception [,mɪskən'sepʃn] *n* a wrong idea or belief □ *It's a popular misconception that the work we do is somehow glamorous.*

misconduct [,mɪs'kɒndʌkt] *n* bad behavior, especially at work □ *a serious case of professional misconduct.*

misconstrue [,mɪskən'struː] *vt* [meaning, words] to understand <sthg> in the wrong way.

miscount [,mɪs'kaʊnt] ◇ *vt* [votes, people] to count <sthg> wrongly. ◇ *vi: I thought they were all there; I must have miscounted.*

misdeed [,mɪs'diːd] *n* a bad or illegal act (literary use).

misdemeanor US, **misdemeanour** GB [,mɪsdə'miːnər] *n* a crime that is not very serious, e.g. a parking offense.

misdirected [,mɪsdə'rektəd] *adj* -1. [letter, mail] that has been sent to the wrong address. -2. [energy, ability] that is used for the wrong purpose.

miser ['maɪzər] *n* a person who always tries to avoid spending their money, even on things they need, because they want to keep it all (disapproving use).

miserable ['mɪzrəbl] *adj* -1. [person] who seems very unhappy □ *What's the matter? You look miserable.* -2. [life, conditions, weather] that one finds very bad, unpleasant, and depressing □ *I had a miserable time while I was there.* -3. **a miserable failure** a complete failure.

miserably ['mɪzrəblɪ] *adv* [reply, live, fail] *see* **miserable** □ *Doug's feeling miserably unhappy.*

miserly ['maɪzərlɪ] *adj* [person] who is a miser.

misery ['mɪzərɪ] (*pl* **miseries**) *n* -1. [of a person] great unhappiness □ *Seeing them together, obviously in love, only added to my misery.* -2. [of conditions] very bad and unpleasant living conditions □ *the misery of the homeless living on the streets.* -3. a person who is always complaining (informal use) □ *Stop being such a misery!*

misfire [,mɪs'faɪər] *vi* -1. [gun, rifle] to fail to fire at the right time. -2. [car engine] to run unevenly because the gas in it does not ignite at the proper time. -3. [plan, idea] to go wrong and not have the result that one intended □ *The surprise dinner misfired rather badly when Mary decided to eat out instead.*

misfit ['mɪsfɪt] *n* a person who is not completely accepted by the people around them because of the way they think and behave.

misfortune [mɪs'fɔːtʃən] *n* bad luck; something unpleasant or unlucky that happens to somebody □ *We had the misfortune to lose all our lecture papers on the way home.* □ *She seems to gloat over other people's misfortunes.*

misgivings [mɪs'gɪvɪŋz] *npl* feelings of doubt □ *I admit I had some misgivings about the idea.*

misguided [,mɪs'gaɪdəd] *adj* [attempt, opinion] that is based on ideas that are wrong; [person] whose ideas are wrong □ *It was a rather misguided effort at changing their way of thinking.* □ *He's not a bad man, just misguided.*

mishandle [,mɪs'hændl] *vt* [deal, negotiations] to deal with <a situation> badly.

mishap ['mɪshæp] *n* something unlucky that happens but is not very serious □ *The meeting took place without mishap.*

mishear [,mɪs'hɪər] (*pt* & *pp* **misheard** [-'hɜːd]) ◇ *vt* [person, question] to hear <sb/sthg> wrongly, so that one thinks one heard something else. ◇ *vi: You must have misheard.*

mishmash [US 'mɪʃmɑːʃ, GB -mæʃ] *n* an untidy mixture (informal use).

misinform [,mɪsɪn'fɔːm] *vt* to give <sb> wrong information □ *You have been misinformed.*

misinformation [,mɪsɪnfər'meɪʃn] *n* wrong information.

misinterpret [,mɪsɪn'tɜːprət] *vt* [words, actions, gestures] to understand <sthg> wrongly □ *I'd hate you to misinterpret what I'm saying.*

misjudge [,mɪs'dʒʌdʒ] *vt* -1. [time, distance] to guess <sthg> wrongly □ *They misjudged the amount of effort it would take to finish the job.* -2. [person, situation, consequences] to form a wrong opinion of <sb/sthg> □ *I think I have seriously misjudged him.*

misjudg(e)ment [,mɪs'dʒʌdʒmənt] *n*: *see* **misjudge** □ *I now admit I made a misjudgment.*

mislay [,mɪs'leɪ] (*pt* & *pp* **mislaid** [-'leɪd]) *vt* [book, key] to lose <sthg> for a short time, by forgetting where one has put it.

mislead [,mɪs'liːd] (*pt* & *pp* **misled**) *vt* to make <sb> believe something that is not true, usually deliberately □ *The public was misled into believing it was safe.*

misleading [,mɪs'liːdɪŋ] *adj* [idea, statistic] that gives one a wrong idea about something □ *The advertisement was very misleading.*

misled [,mɪs'led] *past tense & past participle of* **mislead**.

mismanage [,mɪs'mænɪdʒ] *vt* [finances, budget, project] to manage <sthg> badly.

mismanagement [,mɪs'mænɪdʒmənt] *n*: *see* **mismanage** □ *The firm collapsed amidst accusations of financial mismanagement.*

mismatch [,mɪs'mætʃ] *vt* **to be mismatched** [married couple] to be unsuitable for each other; [teams, opponents] to have levels of skill that are so different that a competition between them is unfair; [colors] to be too different to look good together.

misnomer [,mɪs'nəʊmər] *n* a word or name incorrectly given to something □ *The term "corporation" is something of a misnomer for a company of that size.*

misogynist [mɪ'sɒdʒənɪst] *n* a person, usually a man, who hates women.

misplace [,mɪs'pleɪs] *vt* = **mislay**.

misplaced [,mɪs'pleɪst] *adj* [loyalty, trust, anger] that is wrong because the person or thing that causes it does not deserve it □ *I hope that your faith in me will not prove to be misplaced.*

misprint ['mɪsprɪnt] *n* a mistake in printing.

mispronounce [ˌmɪsprə'naʊns] *vt* to pronounce <a word or name> wrongly.

misquote [ˌmɪs'kwəʊt] *vt* [person, phrase] to quote <sb/sthg> wrongly.

misread [ˌmɪs'riːd] (*pt* & *pp* **misread** [-'red]) *vt* -1. [word, phrase] to read <sthg> wrongly. -2. [situation, behavior] to believe wrongly that one understands <sthg>.

misrepresent [ˌmɪsreprə'zent] *vt* [person, words, opinion] to give other people a false idea of <sb/sthg> □ *Our position has been entirely misrepresented by the tabloid press.*

misrepresentation [ˌmɪsreprəzen'teɪʃn] *n: see* **misrepresent** □ *a gross misrepresentation of the facts.*

misrule [ˌmɪs'ruːl] *n* bad government.

miss [mɪs] ◇ *vt* -1. [person, error, TV program] to fail to see <sb/sthg>; [speech, radio program] to fail to hear <sthg> □ *We missed his debut performance because we were working.* □ *We've missed the beginning of the film.* □ *My diary's on the table, it's big and black — you can't miss it.* □ *She missed the beginning of the conversation.* -2. [target, ball] to fail to hit <sthg> □ *The brick missed me by inches.* -3. [person, home, family] to feel sad or lonely because of the absence of <sb/sthg> □ *I really miss not being able to go for long walks in the country.* -4. [opportunity, chance] to fail to take advantage of <sthg> □ *It's an opportunity that's too good to miss.* -5. [train, bus] to fail to catch <sthg> because one is late □ *I missed my flight by five minutes.* -6. [meeting, appointment] to fail to be present at <sthg>. -7. [disaster, accident] to avoid <sthg bad> □ *We just missed being killed.*
◇ *vi* to fail to hit something □ *You missed!*
◇ *n* **to give sthg a miss** GB [meeting, party, lesson] to decide not to go to sthg (informal use) □ *I think I'll give the party a miss — I've got a lot of work to do at home.*

◆ **miss out** ◇ *vt sep* **to miss sb/sthg out** GB [person, word, item] to fail to include sb/sthg, either by accident or deliberately □ *They missed my first name out.* ◇ *vi* not to have or take an opportunity to be involved in something enjoyable, useful etc □ *You missed out on a great party last night.*

Miss *n* -1. a title used to talk or write to a girl or woman who is not married □ *Dear Miss Miller.* -2. a word used to talk to a girl or woman who is not married (formal use).

misshapen [ˌmɪs'ʃeɪpn] *adj* [body, limb, object] that is not the usual shape and as a result is thought to be ugly.

missile [US 'mɪsl, GB 'mɪsaɪl] *n* -1. MILITARY a weapon that flies like a rocket and explodes when it hits its target. -2. any object that is thrown as a weapon.

missile launcher [-lɔːntʃər] *n* a piece of military equipment used for firing missiles.

missing ['mɪsɪŋ] *adj* [object] that has been lost or stolen; [person] who is not where they should be and cannot be found □ *How many of the missing pieces have been found?* □ *I'm worried about Joe: he's been missing since morn-*

ing. ■ **to go missing** GB to disappear from the place where it should be □ *A seven-year-old boy went missing from his home in Jackson yesterday.*

missing link *n* a piece of information that must be found in order to demonstrate or prove something.

missing person *n* a person who has disappeared.

mission ['mɪʃn] *n* -1. [to a place] a special task that somebody is sent to do in another place, usually for political or military purposes □ *They were sent on a secret mission.* □ *a space/bombing/rescue mission.* -2. [from a government] a group of people who are sent abroad by their government for a particular purpose □ *a diplomatic/economic mission.* -3. [of a person] a job that somebody feels it is their duty to do □ *Her mission in life was to help the homeless.* -4. RELIGION educational and social work that is done by people who are sent to a foreign country by a religious group; a building or group of buildings where this work is done □ *a Jesuit mission.*

missionary [US 'mɪʃəneri, GB 'mɪʃnəri] (*pl* **missionaries**) *n* a person who is sent to a foreign country by a religious group, usually to teach people about a particular religion.

mission statement *n* a statement prepared by a company, organization etc to make its future plans and aims clear.

Mississippi [ˌmɪsɪ'sɪpi] -1. a state in the southern USA, on the Gulf of Mexico. ABBREVIATION: MS. SIZE: 123,500 sq kms. POPULATION: 2,573,216 (*Mississippians*). CAPITAL: Jackson. -2. **the Mississippi** a river in the central USA, flowing into the Gulf of Mexico. It is the longest river in the USA.

missive ['mɪsɪv] *n* a letter (literary use).

Missouri [mɪ'zʊəri] -1. a state in the central USA. ABBREVIATION: MO. SIZE: 180,500 sq kms. POPULATION: 5,117,073 (*Missourians*). CAPITAL: Jefferson City. -2. **the Missouri** a river in the central USA, flowing from the Rocky Mountains to join the Mississippi above St Louis.

misspell [ˌmɪs'spel] (*pt* & *pp* **misspelled** OR **misspelt**) *vt* to spell <a word or name> wrongly.

misspelling [ˌmɪs'spelɪŋ] *n* a word that has been misspelled.

misspelt [ˌmɪs'spelt] GB *past tense & past participle of* **misspell**.

misspend [ˌmɪs'spend] (*pt* & *pp* **misspent** [-'spent]) *vt* [money, time] to waste <sthg> □ *You can tell he's had a misspent youth!*

mist [mɪst] *n* water vapor that forms in the air near the ground, usually in the early morning, and that is difficult to see through □ *the early morning mist.*

◆ **mist over, mist up** *vi* [windows, spectacles] to become covered with water vapor; [eyes] to become filled with tears.

mistake [mɪ'steɪk] (*pt* **mistook**, *pp* **mistaken**) ◇ *n* -1. something that is said, written, or done in a way that is not right □ *a spelling/*

typing mistake □ *You have made several mistakes in your calculations.* **-2.** an action or statement that is not very wise or sensible and often causes problems later □ *It was a mistake to leave school so young.* ■ **to do sthg by mistake** to do sthg without intending to □ *I took your coat by mistake.*
◇ *vt* **-1.** [meaning, intention] to misunderstand <sthg>. **-2.** [person] to think wrongly that <sb> is somebody else; [object] to think wrongly that <sthg> is something else □ *I mistook you for Jim.* □ *You can't mistake her voice, with its strong southern drawl.* ■ **there's no mistaking...** a phrase used to say that it is impossible to confuse something with something else □ *There's no mistaking his car, it's covered in rust.*

mistaken [mɪ'steɪkən] ◇ *past participle of* **mistake.** ◇ *adj* [belief, idea] wrong □ *I was under the mistaken impression that you were serious.* ■ **to be mistaken about sb/sthg** to have the wrong idea about sb/sthg □ *You must be mistaken: my brother has dark hair.*

mistaken identity *n* **a case of mistaken identity** a situation where somebody is thought to be somebody else, usually because of their appearance.

mistakenly [mɪ'steɪkənlɪ] *adv* [believe, say] *see* **mistaken** □ *I mistakenly assumed there wouldn't be a problem.*

mister ['mɪstər] *n* a word used, especially by children, to talk to a man whose name they do not know (informal use).

mistime [,mɪs'taɪm] *vt* [entry, announcement] to do or say <sthg> at a bad or unsuitable time □ *They badly mistimed the publication of the results.*

mistletoe ['mɪsltoʊ] *n* a plant with white berries that grows on trees and is used as a Christmas decoration in Northern Europe and North America.

mistook [mɪ'stʊk] *past tense of* **mistake.**

mistranslation [,mɪstrænz'leɪʃn] *n* a translation that is wrong.

mistreat [,mɪs'triːt] *vt* to treat <a person or animal> cruelly, especially when one is supposed to be taking care of them.

mistreatment [,mɪs'triːtmənt] *n: see* **mistreat** □ *the mistreatment of prisoners.*

mistress ['mɪstrəs] *n* **-1.** [of a man] a woman who a married man is having a sexual relationship with □ *She's your mistress, isn't she?* **-2.** [of a dog, cat] the female owner of a particular pet animal. **-3.** GB [in school] a female schoolteacher of a particular subject □ *the science mistress.*

mistrial ['mɪstraɪəl] *n* a trial that is not legal because of a mistake in the way it is carried out.

mistrust [,mɪs'trʌst] ◇ *n* a feeling of not being able to trust somebody or something □ *She has a natural mistrust of politicians.* ◇ *vt* [person, words, intentions] not to trust <sb/sthg>.

mistrustful [,mɪs'trʌstfl] *adj* [person, look] that shows a lack of trust in somebody or something □ *I was mistrustful of his intentions.*

misty ['mɪstɪ] (*compar* **mistier,** *superl* **mistiest**) *adj* [landscape, countryside] that is covered with mist □ *It's very misty this morning.*

misunderstand [,mɪsʌndər'stænd] (*pt* & *pp* **misunderstood**) ◇ *vt* [person, meaning, question] to fail to understand <sb/sthg> properly. ◇ *vi: I think you must have misunderstood.*

misunderstanding [,mɪsʌndər'stændɪŋ] *n* **-1.** a failure to understand something properly □ *His statement is open to misunderstanding.* □ *There was a misunderstanding over the time of the meeting.* **-2.** a disagreement between people □ *We've had a misunderstanding with the neighbors.*

misunderstood [,mɪsʌndər'stʊd] *past tense & past participle of* **misunderstand.**

misuse [*vb* ,mɪs'juːz, *n* ,mɪs'juːs] ◇ *vt* **-1.** [power, funds, position] to use <sthg> for wrong or dishonest purposes. **-2.** [time] to use <sthg> carelessly □ *The government is misusing our natural resources.* **-3.** [language] to use <sthg> incorrectly. ◇ *n* [of power, time, language] the act of misusing something; an example of this □ *a misuse of valuable resources.*

MIT (*abbr of* **Massachusetts Institute of Technology**) *n* a leading scientific university in Cambridge, Massachusetts.

mite [maɪt] *n* **-1.** a very small creature like a spider that often lives on plants or animals or in dust □ *a dust/house mite.* **-2. a mite** slightly (informal use) □ *It's a mite too big.* **-3.** a small child (informal use) □ *Poor little mite!*

miter US, **mitre** GB ['maɪtər] *n* **-1.** a tall pointed hat worn by bishops. **-2.** a joint between two pieces of wood that are each cut at an angle so that they form a corner when joined.

mitigate ['mɪtɪgeɪt] *vt* [pain, effect, harm] to make <sthg unpleasant> less serious or extreme (formal use).

mitigating ['mɪtɪgeɪtɪŋ] *adj* **mitigating circumstances** LAW facts that explain why somebody committed a crime and may cause their punishment to be reduced.

mitigation [,mɪtɪ'geɪʃn] *n* LAW the process of presenting mitigating circumstances to a court □ *He pleaded in mitigation that his client had excellent character references.*

mitre *n* GB = **miter.**

mitt [mɪt] *n* **-1.** a mitten. **-2.** SPORT the protective glove worn by the catcher in baseball.

mitten ['mɪtn] *n* **-1.** a glove with two sections, one for the thumb and one for the four fingers. **-2.** a glove that covers one's wrist and hand, but not one's fingers.

Mitty ['mɪtɪ], **Walter** a character in James Thurber's story *The Secret Life of Walter Mitty*. He imagines he is brave and adventurous, but in fact he is very ordinary.

mix [mɪks] ◇ *vt* **-1.** [ingredients, substances, activities] to combine <two or more things> so that they are part of the same thing □ *Mix the sugar and* OR *with the flour.* □ *I never mix business with pleasure.* **-2.** [drink, cement] to make <sthg> by putting its contents togeth-

er in a container. **-3.** [song, record] to arrange the balance of sounds in <sthg>.
◇ *vi* **-1.** [substances] to become mixed □ *Oil and water don't mix.* □ *The fuel mixes with air in the carburetor.* **-2.** [person] to meet, talk, and spend time with other people □ *I'm not very good at mixing.* □ *He's mixing with a strange crowd.*
◇ *n* **-1.** [of two things] something that combines two or more people or things in a particular way □ *The film was an interesting mix of different styles.* **-2.** [to make something] a mixture of dry ingredients used to make something and sold in a package □ *cake/cement mix.* **-3.** MUSIC a particular version of a record, made for a particular audience or market □ *a disco mix.*
◆ **mix up** *vt sep* **-1. to mix people/things up** [dates, ideas] to confuse two or more people/things with each other □ *I always mix her up with her sister.* **-2. to mix things up** [documents, cards] to make things disordered □ *The pages are all mixed up.*

mixed [mɪkst] *adj* **-1. a mixed diet/salad etc** a diet/salad etc that contains different things of the same general type □ *I'll need some mixed fruit/nuts for the cake.* **-2. a mixed group** a group of different types of people □ *They're a mixed bunch; some of them have studied languages before, others don't even know what an adverb is.* **-3.** [blood, parentage] that involves parents, grandparents etc who are of different races. **-4. to have mixed feelings about sthg** to be unsure about sthg because one has different kinds of feelings about it □ *I have mixed feelings about their proposal.* **-5.** [school, education] that is for both sexes.

mixed-ability *adj* GB [class, teaching] that is designed for students of different abilities.

mixed blessing *n* something that has disadvantages as well as advantages.

mixed doubles *n* [in tennis, badminton] a match in which each team consists of a man and a woman.

mixed economy *n* an economic system in which some industries and organizations are owned by the state and some are private.

mixed grill *n* a dish that includes different types of grilled meat.

mixed marriage *n* a marriage between people of different races or religions.

mixed up *adj* **-1.** [person, mind] confused □ *She said she was feeling very mixed up about Tom and that they might be splitting up.* **-2. to be mixed up in sthg** [in a crime, argument, scandal] to be involved in sthg □ *I don't want you getting mixed up in all this.*

mixer ['mɪksər] *n* **-1.** a machine used for mixing things, such as food or cement. **-2.** a non-alcoholic drink that is added to an alcoholic drink.

mixer tap *n* GB a faucet that can be used to pour out a mixture of hot and cold water.

mixing bowl ['mɪksɪŋ-] *n* a large bowl for mixing food in.

mixture ['mɪkstʃər] *n* **-1.** a substance made of different ingredients that have been mixed together □ *Place the mixture in the bowl and stir.* **-2.** [of flavors, candy] a combination of different things or people □ *I felt a mixture of sadness and relief.*

mix-up *n* a confused situation caused by a mistake or misunderstanding □ *There must have been a mix-up at the other end — we weren't expecting you until tomorrow.*

mk, MK *abbr of* **mark.**

mkt *abbr of* **market.**

ml *abbr of* **milliliter.**

MLA (*abbr of* **Member of the Legislative Assembly**) *n* in Australia, a member of Parliament.

MLC (*abbr of* **Member of the Legislative Council**) *n* in Australia, a senator.

MLitt [em'lɪt] (*abbr of* **Master of Literature, Master of Letters**) *n* a postgraduate degree in literature; a person who has this degree.

MLR *n abbr of* **minimum lending rate.**

mm *abbr of* **millimeter.**

MN ◇ *n abbr of* **merchant navy.** ◇ *abbr of* **Minnesota.**

mnemonic [nɪ'mɒnɪk] *n* a word, phrase, or short poem that helps somebody to remember something.

m.o. *abbr of* **money order.**

MO (*abbr of* **Medical Officer**) ◇ *n* a doctor in the armed forces. ◇ *abbr of* **Missouri.**

moan [moʊn] ◇ *n* **-1.** a long low sound made by somebody because they are sad or in pain □ *The woman gave a loud moan.* **-2.** a complaint (informal use) □ *She likes to have a good moan about work.* ◇ *vi* **-1.** to make the sound of a moan □ *He was moaning in agony.* **-2.** to complain in an unhappy and often irritating voice (informal use) □ *He's always moaning about his job/boss.*

moat [moʊt] *n* a ditch around a castle that is filled with water and was used for defense in the past.

mob [mɒb] (*pt & pp* **mobbed,** *cont* **mobbing**) ◇ *n* a large noisy crowd of people, especially one that is violent or difficult to control. ◇ *vt* to form a crowd around <sb>, usually to show admiration or to attack them □ *The singer was mobbed at the airport.*

mobile [US 'moʊbl, GB -baɪl] ◇ *adj* **-1.** [person, vehicle] that is able to move easily □ *He has a slipped disk, so it'll be a couple of weeks before he's mobile again.* □ *a small, highly mobile force of fighting men.* **-2.** [equipment] that is not fixed and can be moved easily. **-3. to be mobile** to have a vehicle, so that one can travel around easily □ *Now I have my car back I'm mobile again.* **-4.** GB **a mobile clinic/library etc** a clinic/library etc that is in a vehicle and is driven from place to place. ◇ *n* **-1.** an ornament made of small objects hanging on strings that move when the air moves. **-2.** = **mobile phone.**

mobile home *n* a vehicle that people live in as a home.

mobile phone *n* a telephone with no wires

that can be carried around and used any-where.

mobility [mou'bılətı] *n* -1. the ability to move, especially when one is not prevented by ill-ness or injury □ *These seats are for people with mobility difficulties.* -2. the movement of peo-ple between social classes, jobs, or residen-tial areas □ *social mobility.*

mobility allowance *n* in Britain, money giv-en by the state to disabled people to help them to travel.

mobilization [US ,moubələ'zeıʃn, GB ,moubəlaı-] *n: see* **mobilize.**

mobilize, -ise ['moubəlaız] ◇ *vt* -1. to encour-age <support> for a particular purpose or cause; to gather <a group of people> togeth-er and organize them for a particular pur-pose □ *They've managed to mobilize a great deal of support for the new initiative.* □ *Japan regards its aging society as a resource to be mobilized.* -2. [army, navy, air force] to prepare <a mili-tary organization> for war □ *All military forces have been mobilized and are on full alert.* ◇ *vi* [country, army] to prepare to fight a war.

moccasin ['mɒkəsın] *n* a soft leather shoe without laces □ *a pair of moccasins.*

mock [mɒk] ◇ *adj* [surprise, exam] that looks, sounds etc like something but is not the same as it □ *They live in a mock-Tudor house.* □ *"Poor you!" she said in mock concern.* ◇ *vt* [per-son, behavior, idea] to make fun of <sb/sthg> in an unkind way. ◇ *vi: You shouldn't mock.*

mockery ['mɒkərı] *n* -1. the act of mocking somebody or something □ *There was a sug-gestion of mockery in her tone.* -2. something that is worthless, usually because it is done badly □ *The trial was a mockery.* ■ **to make a mockery of sthg** to make sthg seem stupid or worthless □ *This result makes a mockery of the democratic process.*

mocking ['mɒkıŋ] *adj* [tone, smile] that is not sincere, and is intended to show that one is making fun of somebody.

mockingbird ['mɒkıŋbɜːʳd] *n* an American bird with a long tail and gray feathers that imi-tates the songs of other birds.

mock-up *n* a full-size model of a machine, vehicle etc that is built for testing or re-search □ *We have a detailed mock-up of the new plane.*

MoD, MOD (*abbr of* **Ministry of Defence**) *n* the British government department responsible for the army and defense.

mod cons *npl* **all mod cons** GB a phrase used to say that a house, apartment, kitchen etc is fitted with all the things that make life easier and more comfortable such as central heating, a washing machine etc (informal use).

mode [moud] *n* [of life, transportation] a particu-lar way of doing something; [of dress] a par-ticular style of fashion.

model ['mɒdl] (US *pt* & *pp* **modeled**, *cont* **mod-eling**, GB *pt* & *pp* **modelled**, *cont* **modelling**) ◇ *n* -1. [of a building, vehicle] a small copy of something □ *a model car/plane* □ *a working model.* -2. [for a government, philosophy] a way

of doing something that is successful and can be used as a basis for something else □ *Their legal system is based on the British model.* □ *alternative models of social order.* -3. [of pa-tience, good taste] a person or thing that is the perfect example of something □ *She's the model of good breeding.* -4. [of a car, washing machine] a particular type of vehicle or ma-chine made by a particular manufacturer □ *our new improved model* □ *the latest model in the "Pergamum" series.* -5. [for a painting] a person whose job is to stand or sit still in order to be the subject of a painting or photograph □ *an artist's model* □ *a photographic model.* -6. [for clothes] a person whose job is to model clothes □ *She became a top photo-graphic model practically overnight.*
◇ *adj* **a model student/employee etc** a perfect student/employee etc.
◇ *vt* -1. [plane, ship] to make a small copy of <sthg>. -2. [clay, wax] to make <sthg> into a particular shape. -3. [dress, outfit] to display <sthg> by wearing it at a fashion show □ *Claudia, seen here modeling the new Versace col-lection.* -4. **to model oneself on sb** [on father, teacher] to copy sb's behavior or appearance in order to be like them □ *He's modeled his musical style on that of the early blues singers.*
◇ *vi* to model clothes.

modeling US, **modelling** GB ['mɒdlıŋ] *n* the work of a fashion model □ *a career in modeling.*

Model T Ford *n* one of the first types of car built in the USA, designed by Henry Ford.

modem ['moudem] *n* a piece of electronic equipment used for sending information from one computer to another via a tele-phone line.

moderate [*adj* & *n* 'mɒdərət, *vb* 'mɒdəreıt] ◇ *adj* -1. [amount, view, demand] that is con-sidered to be reasonable by most people □ *a moderate wage increase/politician.* -2. [size, quan-tity] that is neither large nor small. -3. [ability, performance] that is neither good nor bad. ◇ *n* a person who has moderate political views. ◇ *vt* [spending, heat, demands] to re-duce <sthg> to a level that most people consider to be reasonable □ *Would you mind moderating your language?* ◇ *vi* [views, drinking] to become moderate.

moderately ['mɒdərətlı] *adv* **moderately suc-cessful/expensive etc** fairly successful/expen-sive etc □ *It was only moderately quicker than taking the train.*

moderation [,mɒdə'reıʃn] *n* [of one's views, de-mands] *see* **moderate** □ *Leaders of both sides have appealed for moderation.* ■ **to do sthg in moderation** [drink, smoke] to do sthg in a way that most people consider to be reasonable.

modern ['mɒdəʳn] *adj* -1. [times, society, world] that belongs to the present period □ *New Zealand has emerged as one of the world's strongest modern economies.* -2. [techniques, de-sign, ideas] that is of a new kind □ *modern of-fice technology.* -3. [person] who accepts new ideas □ *They have a very modern outlook.* -4. **modern art/dance etc** art/dance etc that follows more recent styles rather than traditional ones.

modern-day *adj* [person] whose actions, behavior etc remind people of somebody who was well known in the past; [event] that is similar to an event in history □ *a modern-day Robin Hood.*

modernism ['mɒdə^rnɪzm] *n* the ideas and methods of art, design, and literature that have produced new forms of expression, especially in the early and mid-20th century.

modernization [US ˌmɒdərnə'zeɪʃn, GB ˌmɒdə-naɪ-] *n: see* **modernize** □ *The industry is in urgent need of modernization.* □ *a modernization program.*

modernize, -ise ['mɒdə^rnaɪz] ◇ *vt* [system, house, factory] to make <sthg> modern by replacing old processes and appliances with new ones. ◇ *vi: We must modernize if we are going to stay in business.*

modern languages *npl* modern European languages, usually when studied as a subject in high school or college.

modest ['mɒdəst] *adj* **-1.** [amount, income, improvement] that is not very large □ *We made a modest profit on the sale.* **-2.** [person] who does not like to talk proudly about the things they have done □ *Don't be so modest! I'm sure it's excellent.*

modestly ['mɒdəstlɪ] *adv* [improve, behave, speak] *see* **modest.**

modesty ['mɒdəstɪ] *n* the quality of being modest about the things one has done.

modicum ['mɒdɪkəm] *n* **a modicum of sthg** [of decency, truth] a small amount of sthg (formal use) □ *I suppose there's a modicum of comfort in what you say.*

modification [ˌmɒdəfə'keɪʃn] *n: see* **modify** □ *The text requires modification/a few modifications before it can be published.* □ *They made a few modifications to the basic design.*

modify ['mɒdəfaɪ] (*pt & pp* **modified**) *vt* **-1.** [engine, design] to change <sthg> slightly in order to improve it. **-2.** [plan, law] to change <sthg> slightly in order to make it more suitable for a particular situation.

modular [US 'mɒdʒəlr, GB 'mɒdjʊlə] *adj* **-1.** [furniture, building] that consists of separate units that combine together to make a larger structure. **-2.** EDUCATION [course] that consists of a series of separate courses on particular subjects.

modulated [US 'mɒdʒəleɪtəd, GB 'mɒdjʊ-] *adj* [note, voice] that varies in loudness, pitch, or tone; [radio wave] that varies in frequency or size.

modulation [US ˌmɒdʒə'leɪʃn, GB ˌmɒdjʊ-] *n* the process of varying the loudness, pitch, or tone of a sound; the process of varying the frequency or size of a radio wave.

module [US 'mɒdʒuːl, GB 'mɒdjuːl] *n* **-1.** [of a building, course, piece of furniture] one of the parts of something that can be joined together, usually in different ways, to make something bigger. **-2.** [of a spacecraft] a part

of a spacecraft that can be used separately from the other parts □ *the lunar module.*

mogul ['moʊgl] *n* a very rich and powerful business person □ *the media mogul, John Barolo.*

mohair ['moʊheə^r] *n* a very soft wool that comes from angora goats □ *a mohair sweater.*

Mohammed [moʊ'hæməd] = **Muhammad.**

Mohammedan [moʊ'hæmədən] *n & adj* = **Muslim.**

Mohawk ['moʊhɔːk] *n* a member of a Native American people who used to live in the northeastern USA; the language of this people.

Mohican [moʊ'hiːkən] *n* a member of a Native American people who used to live in the northeastern USA and southeastern Canada; the language of this people.

moist [mɔɪst] *adj* [soil, cake, eyes] that is slightly wet □ *Keep the soil moist, but do not overwater.*

moisten ['mɔɪsn] *vt* [lips, handkerchief] to make <sthg> moist.

moisture ['mɔɪstʃə^r] *n* small drops of water on a surface or in the air that make it feel wet □ *The inside of the window was covered in moisture.*

moisturize, -ise ['mɔɪstʃəraɪz] *vt* [face, hands, skin] to make <sthg> less dry, usually by rubbing a cream into it.

moisturizer ['mɔɪstʃəraɪzə^r] *n* a product, usually in the form of a cream, for moisturizing one's skin.

molar ['moʊlə^r] *n* one of the large flat teeth at the back of one's mouth, used for chewing food.

molasses [mə'læsəz] *n* a thick dark syrup that is produced during the refining of sugar and is used in cooking.

mold US, **mould** GB [moʊld] ◇ *n* **-1.** [on food, a wall] a green or gray substance that grows on old food or on objects that have been kept in wet conditions for a long time □ *The ceiling was covered in mold.* **-2.** [for metal, a candle] a container that has a particular shape and in which a soft or liquid substance is placed so that it will have the same shape after it has become hard □ *Place the mixture in the mold.*
◇ *vt* **-1.** [person, character, career] to influence the way <sb/sthg> develops over a period of time, especially by influencing their ideas □ *His political views were molded by his background and education.* **-2.** [clay, mud, metal] to make <sthg> into a particular shape, sometimes by using a mold □ *The figure had been molded out of clay.*

Moldavia [mɒl'deɪvɪə] a country in Eastern Europe, between Romania and Ukraine. SIZE: 34,000 sq kms. POPULATION: 4,400,000 (*Moldavians*). CAPITAL: Kishinev. LANGUAGE: Romanian. CURRENCY: leu.

molding US, **moulding** GB ['moʊldɪŋ] *n* a band of stone or wood that goes all around a wall, frame, piece of furniture etc to decorate it □ *a room with original moldings.*

moldy US, **mouldy** GB ['moʊldɪ] (US *compar* **moldier**, *superl* **moldiest**, GB *compar* **mouldier**, *superl* **mouldiest**) *adj* [cheese, fruit, bread] that has mold on part or all of it □ *All I could find was a moldy old apple.*

mole [moʊl] *n* -1. a small animal that has dark fur, is almost blind, and digs tunnels under the ground to live in. -2. [on somebody's skin] a small dark-brown mark on somebody's skin. -3. [inside an organization] a spy who is a member of an organization and gives secret information to people outside that organization.

molecular [mə'lekjələr] *adj* [structure, physics] relating to molecules.

molecule ['mɒlɪkjuːl] *n* the smallest possible amount of a chemical that can exist, consisting of two or more atoms joined together.

molehill ['moʊlhɪl] *n* a pile of earth that is made by a mole digging underground.

molest [mə'lest] *vt* -1. [person] to attack <a woman, child> etc sexually. -2. [dog] to attack <a sheep, goat> etc.

molester [mə'lestər] *n* a person who molests women or children □ *a convicted child molester.*

mollify ['mɒləfaɪ] (*pt* & *pp* **mollified**) *vt* to make <sb> feel less angry or upset.

mollusk US, **mollusc** GB ['mɒləsk] *n* a creature that has a soft body, no backbone, and is often covered with a shell, e.g. a snail, mussel, or octopus.

mollycoddle ['mɒlɪkɒdl] *vt* [child, employee] to take too much care of <sb>.

Molotov cocktail ['mɒlətɒf-] *n* a bomb that consists of a bottle full of gasoline sealed with a piece of cloth.

molt US, **moult** GB [moʊlt] ◇ *vt* to lose <hair or feathers> in order to grow new ones. ◇ *vi* [animal, bird] *How often do cats molt?*

molten ['moʊltn] *adj* **molten metal/lava** metal/lava that has melted into a thick hot liquid.

mom [mɒm] *n* US a word used to talk to or about one's mother (informal use).

moment ['moʊmənt] *n* -1. a very short period of time □ *Wait a moment.* □ *For one* OR *a moment, I thought you were serious.* □ *Moments later she was gone.* □ *If you have a spare moment, there's something I'd like to discuss.* -2. a particular point in time □ *At that moment the phone rang.* □ *This is a very special moment for me.* ■ **the moment of truth** a moment when something very important is decided □ *Now for the moment of truth: who has won the contract?* ■ **at any moment** [happen, arrive] at any time, and probably soon □ *Look, they'll be here at any moment, so you'd better hurry up.* ■ **at the moment** now □ *He's not in at the moment, can he call you back?* ■ **at the last moment** at the latest possible time □ *At the last moment they pulled out of the deal.* ■ **for the moment** at the present time, but perhaps not later □ *I'm prepared to agree for the moment, but I might change my mind.* -3. **a good/bad moment** a suitable/unsuitable time □

Choose your moment to approach the boss. □ *I don't think now's the right moment.*

momentarily [,moʊmən'terəlɪ] *adv* -1. [pause, hesitate] for a short time □ *He was momentarily speechless.* -2. US a word used to say that something will happen very soon □ *I'll be with you momentarily.*

momentary [US 'moʊmənterɪ, GB -tərɪ] *adj* [pause, hesitation] that lasts for a very short time □ *There was a momentary silence before the applause began.*

momentous [mə'mentəs] *adj* [decision, news] very important □ *I would like to welcome you all here on this momentous occasion.*

momentum [mə'mentəm] *n* -1. PHYSICS the weight of a moving object multiplied by its speed. -2. [of social movement, change] the force that is developed by a process as it progresses □ *The campaign is starting to gather momentum.*

mommy ['mɒmɪ], **momma** ['mɒmə] *n* US a word used, especially by children, to talk to or about their mother (informal use).

Mon *abbr of* **Monday**.

Monaco ['mɒnəkoʊ] a country and town in southern Europe, on the Mediterranean, between France and Italy. SIZE: 2 sq kms. POPULATION: 28,000 (*Monégasques*). CAPITAL: Monaco. LANGUAGE: French. CURRENCY: French franc.

monarch ['mɒnərk] *n* a king or queen who rules a country.

monarchist ['mɒnərkəst] *n* a person who believes that their country should be ruled by a monarch.

monarchy ['mɒnərkɪ] (*pl* **monarchies**) *n* -1. a system of government in which a country is ruled by a monarch and in which the next monarch will be from the same family. -2. a country that is ruled by a monarch. -3. **the monarchy** the royal family of a particular country.
NOTE: Compare **republic**.

monastery [US 'mɒnəsterɪ, GB -tərɪ] (*pl* **monasteries**) *n* a building or group of buildings where monks live, work, and pray.

monastic [mə'næstɪk] *adj* -1. [building, community] that is connected with monasteries. -2. [existence, life] that is quiet and simple, as in a monastery.

Monday ['mʌndeɪ] *n* the day of the week between Sunday and Tuesday; *see also* **Friday**.

Monet [US moʊ'neɪ, GB 'mɒneɪ], **Claude** (1840–1926) a French artist, well known for his landscapes and for being one of the main painters of the Impressionist movement.

monetarism ['mɒnətərɪzm] *n* a policy of controlling a country's economy by limiting the amount of money available for use at any particular time.

monetarist ['mɒnətərəst] *n* a person who believes in monetarism as an economic policy.

monetary [US 'mɒnəterɪ, GB -ətərɪ] *adj* [policy, union, control] that is connected with money.

money ['mʌnɪ] *n* coins or bills that are used to

buy things □ *How much money do you have?* □ *I didn't have enough money to get home.* □ *How much is that in English money?* ■ **to make money** to receive money by working, or by selling something at a profit □ *The company made a lot of money last year.* □ *She used to make money by selling jewelry.* ■ **to get one's money's worth** to get a good value when one spends money on something □ *She always likes to get her money's worth.*

moneybox ['mʌnɪbɒks] *n* GB a small box with a slot in the top, used by children for saving coins in.

moneyed ['mʌnɪd] *adj* **the moneyed classes** the rich classes (formal use).

moneylender ['mʌnɪlendər] *n* a person whose job is to lend people money and then charge interest on it.

moneymaker ['mʌnɪmeɪkər] *n* a product or business that makes somebody a lot of money.

moneymaking ['mʌnɪmeɪkɪŋ] *adj* **a moneymaking idea** an idea that makes somebody a lot of money.

money market *n* the financial institutions that deal with short-term loans, capital, and foreign exchange □ *Money-market interest rates jumped sharply.*

money order *n* an official document from a bank or post office that is used instead of money for sending payment through the mail.

money-spinner [-spɪnər] *n* GB something that makes somebody a lot of money (informal use).

money supply *n* all the money that exists in a country's economy.

mongol▼ ['mɒŋgl] (old-fashioned and offensive use) ◇ *adj* [person] who has Down's syndrome. ◇ *n* a person who has Down's syndrome. ◆ **Mongol** *n* & *adj*: see **Mongolia**.

Mongolia [mɒŋ'goulɪə] *n* a country in central Asia, between Russia and China. SIZE: 1,565,000 sq kms. POPULATION: 2,300,000 (*Mongols, Mongolians*). CAPITAL: Ulan Bator. LANGUAGE: Khalkha Mongolian. CURRENCY: tughric.

Mongolian [mɒŋ'goulɪən] *n* & *adj*: see **Mongolia**.

mongoose ['mɒŋguːs] (*pl* **mongooses**) *n* a small furry animal with a long tail that lives in Africa and Asia and eats snakes and birds' eggs.

mongrel ['mʌŋrəl] *n* a dog whose parents are of different breeds.

monitor ['mɒnɪtər] ◇ *n* -1. TV a screen in a TV studio for showing the images that are being recorded or sent □ *a TV monitor.* -2. MEDICINE an instrument for recording and showing a particular activity in a patient's body □ *a heart monitor.* -3. COMPUTING a screen used with a computer to show information. ◇ *vt* -1. [development, heartbeat, condition] to check <sthg> regularly, usually to see if there is any change □ *We have been monitoring the pollution levels.* -2. [broadcast, messages] to listen to <sthg> regularly in order to get information.

monk [mʌŋk] *n* a member of a religious group of men who pray and worship together and usually live apart from other people □ *a Buddhist monk.*

monkey ['mʌŋkɪ] (*pl* **monkeys**) *n* a tropical animal with a long tail that lives in trees and is related to chimpanzees, gorillas, and human beings.

monkey nut *n* a peanut (old-fashioned use).

monkey wrench *n* a tool that can be adjusted to turn nuts and bolts of different widths.

monkfish ['mʌŋkfɪʃ] (*pl* **monkfish** OR **monkfishes**) *n* a large fish with a flat head and thin tail that is eaten as food.

mono ['mɒnou] ◇ *adj* [record, record player] that produces sound through one loudspeaker only. ◇ *n* -1. a system of recording sound in which the sound is produced through one loudspeaker only □ *It can only play records in mono.* -2. US = **mononucleosis**.

monochrome ['mɒnəkroum] *adj* -1. [television, film] whose pictures are in black and white. -2. [picture, print] that is in one color only.

monocle ['mɒnəkl] *n* a special piece of glass worn over one eye to help somebody to see better.

monogamous [mə'nɒgəməs] *adj* [person] who has only one sexual partner □ *a monogamous society/marriage.*

monogamy [mə'nɒgəmɪ] *n* the state of being monogamous.

monogrammed ['mɒnəgræmd] *adj* [handkerchief, shirt] that has somebody's initials printed or sewn onto it.

monolingual [ˌmɒnə'lɪŋgwəl] *adj* -1. [person] who only speaks one language. -2. [dictionary, text] that is written in only one language.

monolithic [ˌmɒnə'lɪθɪk] *adj* -1. [organization] very large and unlikely to change. -2. [building] very large and without any interesting features.

monolog US, **monologue** ['mɒnəlɒg] *n* -1. THEATER a long speech by one actor or actress. -2. [in conversation] a long speech by one person that prevents other people from speaking.

mononucleosis [ˌmɒnounjuːklɪ'ousəs] *n* an infectious disease that gives people fever, a sore throat, and swollen glands, and makes them feel weak.

monoplane ['mɒnəpleɪn] *n* an aircraft with one wing on each side.

monopolize, -ise [mə'nɒpəlaɪz] *vt* [trade, industry, conversation] to have complete control of <sthg> so that other people have no influence or involvement in it □ *Their company has monopolized the diamond business for years.* □ *Now, John, stop monopolizing our guest!*

monopoly [mə'nɒpəlɪ] (*pl* **monopolies**) *n* -1. a situation where one company or organization has complete control of a particular business activity, with the result that other organizations have no influence or involvement in it □ *These regional newspapers are near-monopolies.* □ *The state has a monopoly on* electricity production. ■ **the Monopolies and Mergers Commission** in Britain, an independent organization whose job is to investigate possible monopolies, so that the government can decide whether or not to take action to stop them. **-2. to have a monopoly on sthg** to be the only person who has sthg □ *He thinks he's got a monopoly on brains.*

monorail ['mɒnəreɪl] *n* a transportation system in which trains travel on a single rail.

monosodium glutamate [,mɒnəsoudiəm'glu:təmeɪt] *n* a chemical substance used in cooking to add flavor to savory dishes.

monosyllabic [,mɒnəsə'læbɪk] *adj* **-1.** [word, name] that has only one syllable. **-2.** [reply, answer] that uses very few words.

monosyllable ['mɒnəsɪləbl] *n* a word of one syllable.

monotone ['mɒnətoun] *n* a sound or voice that does not change in tone □ *She spoke in a dull monotone.*

monotonous [mə'nɒtənəs] *adj* [music, job, life] that is boring because of always staying the same □ *The work was monotonous and tiring.*

monotony [mə'nɒtənɪ] *n* the boring quality of something that never changes □ *It's the sheer monotony of commuting that most people hate.* □ *A short walk might help to break the monotony.*

monoxide [mə'nɒksaɪd] *n* a chemical compound that has one atom of oxygen for each atom of another element.

Monroe, Marilyn (1926–1962) a US movie actress, famous as a sex symbol. She appeared in *Some Like it Hot* and *Gentlemen Prefer Blondes.*

Monroe Doctrine *n* **the Monroe Doctrine** part of US foreign policy that rejected European intervention in North and South America. It was introduced during the presidency of James Monroe.

Monsignor [mɒn'si:njəʳ] *n* a title given to a priest of high rank in the Catholic Church.

monsoon [mɒn'su:n] *n* the season of heavy rain in southern Asia.

monster ['mɒnstəʳ] ◇ *n* **-1.** an unreal creature in a book, movie etc that is usually large, ugly, and frightening □ *She dreamed that she was being chased by monsters.* **-2.** a cruel or evil person □ *The person who could commit such a crime must be a monster.* **-3.** something that is unusually big □ *That machine's a monster!* ◇ *adj* very large (informal use).

monstrosity [mɒn'strɒsətɪ] (*pl* **monstrosities**) *n* a building, work of art etc that is very large and ugly □ *that monstrosity they call a shopping mall!*

monstrous ['mɒnstrəs] *adj* **-1.** [treatment, situation, price] that one finds shocking and unfair □ *I think it's monstrous the way they've behaved!* **-2.** [place, appearance] that is very ugly. **-3.** [size, building, dog] that is very large.

montage [mɒn'tɑ:ʒ] *n* **-1.** a picture, movie, or piece of music that has been made by putting together pieces of other pictures, movies, or pieces of music. **-2.** a method of film editing in which many different shots are put together to form a single image or a series of images that changes very quickly.

Montana [mɒn'tænə] a mountainous state in the northwestern USA. ABBREVIATION: MT. SIZE: 381,000 sq kms. POPULATION: 799,065 (*Montanans*). CAPITAL: Helena.

Mont Blanc [,mɒnt'blɒŋ] the highest mountain in the Alps, situated between France and Italy. HEIGHT: 4,807 m.

Monte Carlo [,mɒntɪ'kɑ:ʳlou] a town in Monaco that is famous for its casino and its annual motor race.

Montenegro [,mɒntə'ni:grou] a republic of Yugoslavia, on the Adriatic coast, that remained with Serbia in the Federal Republic of Yugoslavia when the other republics became independent in the early 1990s. SIZE: 13,812 sq kms. POPULATION: 600,000 (*Montenegrins*). CAPITAL: Podgorica. LANGUAGE: Serbo-Croat. CURRENCY: Yugoslavian dinar.

Montevideo [,mɒntəvə'deɪou] the capital of Uruguay in the south of the country. It is an important port. POPULATION: 1,346,000.

Montezuma [,mɒntɪ'zu:mə] (1466–1520) the last Aztec emperor to rule Mexico before the Spanish invasion.

Montgomery [mənt'gɒmərɪ], **Field Marshal** (1887–1976) a British military leader. He was responsible for the British victory in the North African desert in World War II.

month [mʌnθ] *n* **-1.** one of the 12 periods that the year is divided into in the Western calendar □ *during the winter months* □ *I saw her last month.* □ *in the month of March.* **-2.** a period of about four weeks □ *It happened about a month ago.* □ *It'll be ready in a few months.*

monthly ['mʌnθlɪ] (*pl* **monthlies**) ◇ *adj* [meeting, payment] that happens once a month. ◇ *adv* [meet, pay] once a month. ◇ *n* a magazine that is published once a month.

Montreal [,mɒntrɪ'ɔ:l] a port in southern Quebec, on the St Lawrence river. It is the largest city in Canada. POPULATION: 1,017,666.

monument ['mɒnjəmənt] *n* **-1.** a building or statue built to remind people of a famous person or event □ *a monument to those who died in the war.* **-2.** an old building that is an important part of the history of a country □ *a tour of the city's historic monuments.*

monumental [,mɒnjə'mentl] *adj* **-1.** [building, sculpture] very large. **-2.** [book, painting, influence] very important. **-3. a monumental mistake/disaster etc** a mistake/disaster etc that one thinks is very bad.

moo [mu:] (*pl* **moos**) ◇ *n* the sound that a cow makes. ◇ *vi* [cow] to make a moo.

mood [mu:d] *n* the state of somebody's feelings at a particular time □ *I'm not in the mood to hear his excuses.* □ *What is the mood of the public/voters?* ■ **to be in a (bad) mood** to feel unhappy at a particular time and behave in an unfriendly way to other people □ *What's put you in such a bad mood?* ■ **to be in a good mood** to feel cheerful at a particular time □ *You seem to be in a good mood this morning.*

moody ['mu:dɪ] (*compar* **moodier**, *superl* **moodi-**

est) *adj* **-1.** [person] who is depressed and un-friendly. **-2.** [person] whose moods change often.

moon [mu:n] *n* **-1. the moon** the round mass of rock that moves around the Earth and can be seen in the sky at night □ *man's first landing on the moon.* ■ **to be over the moon** to be very happy about something that has happened (informal use) □ *I was over the moon when I heard the news.* **-2.** the moon as it appears from the Earth at a particular time □ *a half moon* □ *The moon was reflected in the water.* ■ **once in a blue moon** very rarely (informal use) □ *They only come to visit us once in a blue moon.* **-3.** a round mass of rock that moves regularly round a planet □ *Jupiter has 16 moons.*

moonbeam ['mu:nbi:m] *n* a ray of light from the moon.

moonlight ['mu:nlaɪt] (*pt* & *pp* **moonlighted**) ◇ *n* light that comes from the moon at night. ◇ *vi* to have a second job as well as one's main job, usually without declaring it officially □ *He's been moonlighting as a waiter.*

moonlighting ['mu:nlaɪtɪŋ] *n* the practice of doing a second job as well as one's main job, usually without declaring it officially.

moonlit ['mu:nlɪt] *adj* [night, valley] that is lit by the moon.

moonscape ['mu:nskeɪp] *n* a bare area of land that looks like the surface of the moon.

moon shot *n* the launch of a spacecraft to the moon.

moonstone ['mu:nstoʊn] *n* a clear bluish-white stone used in jewelry.

moor [mʊər] ◇ *n* a large area of countryside that is usually covered with grass or heather and is not used for farming because of the poor quality of the soil. ◇ *vt* to attach <a boat, raft> etc to land, a pier, or to another vessel, using ropes □ *The boat was moored to the river bank.* ◇ *vi: We moored on the river bank.*

Moor [mʊər] *n* a member of a Muslim people from North Africa who ruled Spain from 711 to 1492.

Moore [mʊər], **Henry** (1898–1986) a British sculptor, well known for his smooth rounded figures that often have holes in them.

moorhen ['mʊəhen] *n* a black bird with a red beak that lives near water.

moorings ['mʊərɪŋz] *npl* the ropes, chains, and anchors used for mooring a boat, raft etc.

Moorish ['mʊərɪʃ] *adj: see* **Moor** □ *Moorish architecture.*

moorland ['mʊərlənd] *n* land that consists of moors.

moose [mu:s] (*pl* **moose**) *n* a large North American deer with flat horns.

moot [mu:t] *vt* **to be mooted** GB [question, topic] to be suggested as a subject for discussion.

moot point *n* something that people have different opinions about and so is likely to cause disagreement.

mop [mɒp] (*pt* & *pp* **mopped**, *cont* **mopping**)

◇ *n* **-1.** a long stick with pieces of string or sponge at the end, used for washing floors. **-2. a mop (of hair)** a thick untidy mass of hair. ◇ *vt* **-1.** to wash <a floor> using a mop. **-2. to mop one's face/brow** to wipe the sweat from one's face/brow using a piece of cloth, especially a handkerchief or towel □ *He mopped his forehead nervously.*

◆ **mop up** *vt sep* **to mop sthg up** [liquid, dirt] to remove sthg by moving a mop over it □ *Look at that mess! I suppose I'll have to mop it up!*

mope [moʊp] *vi* to be unhappy and have no desire or energy to do things □ *Don't just sit there moping.*

◆ **mope about, mope around** *vi* to move around in an unhappy mood, with no particular purpose □ *She just moped around in the house all day.*

moped ['moʊped] *n* a motorbike with a small engine and pedals.

moral ['mɒrəl] ◇ *adj* **-1. a moral issue/principle etc** an issue/principle etc connected with the question of what is right and wrong □ *I believe that this is a moral, not a political, question.* **-2.** [person] who behaves in a way that society considers to be good and proper □ *moral responsible citizens.* **-3. to give sb moral support** to show approval for what sb is doing and encourage, them to be brave, strong etc □ *Will you come with me, just for moral support?* ◇ *n* a lesson or message about how to behave that is contained in a story □ *The moral of this story is — never trust anybody!*

◆ **morals** *npl* people's belief about what is right and wrong.

morale [US məˈræl, GB -ˈrɑːl] *n* the level of confidence and enthusiasm of a person or group of people at a particular time □ *We need a win to boost our morale.* □ *Sales are down and morale is low.*

moralistic [ˌmɒrəˈlɪstɪk] *adj* [person, tone, attitude] that expresses strong moral views and judgments (disapproving use).

morality [məˈrælətɪ] (*pl* **moralities**) *n* **-1.** a set of ideas or beliefs about what is right and wrong □ *standards of public morality.* **-2.** [of behavior, an action] the degree to which something is right □ *I'm not questioning the morality of what he did.*

moralize, -ise ['mɒrəlaɪz] *vi* to say what one thinks is right and wrong, especially when it is not appropriate □ *He is always moralizing about* OR *on other people's behavior.*

morally ['mɒrəlɪ] *adv* **-1. morally wrong/acceptable etc** wrong/acceptable etc according to principles of right and wrong. **-2.** [act, behave] in a way that is considered to be right and acceptable.

Moral Majority *n* **the Moral Majority** a term referring to conservative right-wing forces in the USA.

morass [məˈræs] *n* [of detail, paperwork] a complicated and confused mass of something.

moratorium [ˌmɒrəˈtɔːrɪəm] (*pl* **moratoria** [-rɪə]) *n* an official agreement not to carry out a particular activity for a fixed period (formal use) □ *a moratorium on arms dealing.*

morbid ['mɔːrbɪd] *adj* [person] who is too interested in death and unpleasant things; [fascination, imagination] that shows too much interest in death and unpleasant things □ *Stop it! Now you're getting morbid.* □ *What a morbid thought!*

more [mɔːr] ◇ *adv* **-1.** used to make the comparative form of adjectives and adverbs □ *The hotel was a lot more expensive than I expected.* □ *He drove far more carefully after he'd had the accident.* □ *There are more places available on the course.* □ *I was sure I had more money than that.* **-2. to argue/travel etc more** to argue/travel etc a greater amount than before □ *People eat out in restaurants more than they used to.* □ *You'll have to practice more if you want to be a good tennis player.* **-3. to think/talk etc more** to continue thinking/talking etc □ *I feel we should discuss it some more before making a final decision.* **-4. once/twice more** on one/two more occasions □ *If you do that once more I'll get very angry!* **-5.** phrases **I'm more than happy to help** I'm very willing to help □ *If you need someone to read it, I'm more than happy to give my opinion.* ■ **we were more hurt than angry** what is important is that we were hurt, not that we were angry □ *It wasn't a serious crash — I think we were more shocked than anything else.* ■ **he's little more than a child** he is only a child □ *Look at her, she's little more than a baby.*
◇ *det* **-1. more time/food/money** a larger amount of time/food/money □ *You have more patience than I do.* □ *People have more leisure nowadays.* ■ **more meals/cars/people** a larger number of meals/cars/people □ *There are more trains during the rush hour.* □ *More than 70 people died in the earthquake.* **-2. more coffee/work/potatoes** an extra amount of coffee/work/potatoes □ *Help yourself to some more vegetables.* □ *I finished two more chapters today.*
◇ *pron* **-1. he has more than me** he has a larger amount than me □ *We're spending more of our time on administration.* **-2. if you want to know more** if you want extra information □ *I can't take much more of this hot weather!* **-3.** phrases **(and) what's more** used to add an extra piece of information □ *I don't know who he is and what's more I don't care!* ■ **what more do you want?** it seems to me you should be satisfied with what you have □ *You have a nice home, a good job, a new car. What more do you want?*
◆ **any more** *adv* = **anymore** □ *They are not clients of ours any more.*
◆ **more and more** ◇ *adv* **-1. he got more and more angry/depressed etc** his anger/depression etc got greater as time passed. **-2. more often** □ *I'm finding more and more that I have to check all his work.* ◇ *det*: *More and more people are moving out of the city.* ◇ *pron*: *We seem to spend more and more on taxi fares.*
◆ **more or less** *adv* **-1. more or less finished/true etc** nearly finished/true etc but not totally □ *She more or less suggested I had stolen it.* **-2. $500, more or less** a little more or a lit-

tle less than $500 □ *It takes more or less an hour to get there.*

More [mɔːr], **Sir Thomas** (1478–1535) an English politician and writer. He refused to recognize Henry VIII as head of the English Church, and was executed. He was made a saint by the Catholic Church.

moreover [mɔːr'ouvər] *adv* a word used to introduce an extra piece of information in support of what one is saying (formal use) □ *The equipment is very expensive. Moreover, we have no guarantee that it will work.*

morgue [mɔːrg] *n* a building where dead bodies are kept before they are buried.

moribund ['mɒrɪbʌnd] *adj* [industry, business] that is no longer efficient or useful and is coming to an end.

Mormon ['mɔːrmən] *n* a member of a religious group, founded in the USA in 1830, whose beliefs are based on the writings of Joseph Smith. Mormons have a strict code of moral behavior and work as missionaries.

morning ['mɔːrnɪŋ] *n* **-1.** the hours of daylight before noon □ *a morning meal/walk* □ *I worked all morning.* □ *I'm free on Friday morning.* ■ **in the morning** every morning or most mornings; tomorrow morning □ *They work in the morning and have a siesta in the afternoon.* □ *See you in the morning!* **-2.** the hours between midnight and noon □ *at three o'clock in the morning.*
◆ **mornings** *adv* US every morning or most mornings.

morning-after pill *n* a pill that a woman can take up to 72 hours after having sex to prevent her from becoming pregnant.

morning dress *n* formal clothes, usually including tails and a top hat, that are worn by men at daytime ceremonies, especially weddings.

morning sickness *n* sickness that some women get in the mornings during the early part of a pregnancy.

Moroccan [mə'rɒkən] *n & adj*: see **Morocco.**

Morocco [mə'rɒkou] a country in North Africa, on the Mediterranean and the Atlantic Ocean. SIZE: 710,000 sq kms (including Western Sahara). POPULATION: 28,000,000 (*Moroccans*). CAPITAL: Rabat. LANGUAGE: Arabic, Berber. CURRENCY: Moroccan dirham.

moron ['mɔːrɒn] *n* a person that one thinks is stupid (informal use) □ *What a bunch of morons!*

moronic [mə'rɒnɪk] *adj* [expression, behavior] that one thinks is stupid.

morose [mə'rous] *adj* [person] who seems bad-tempered, unhappy, and does not say much □ *He just stood there looking morose.*

morphine ['mɔːrfiːn] *n* a strong painkilling drug made from opium.

morphing ['mɔːrfɪŋ] *n* the use of computer graphics to blend one image into another.

Morris ['mɒrəs], **William** (1834–1896) a British craftsman and writer, who designed and made furniture and wallpaper.

morris dancing ['mɒrəs-] *n* a style of traditional English dancing done by a group of people wearing white costumes with bells attached to them.

Morse (code) [ˌmɔːʳs-] *n* an international code for sending messages in which letters are represented by dots and dashes and can be signaled as short and long sounds or flashes of light.

morsel [ˈmɔːʳsl] *n* a small piece or amount of something, especially food.

mortal [ˈmɔːʳtl] ◇ *adj* **-1.** [person, being] who will not live for ever. **-2.** [wound, blow] that results in somebody's death. **-3. mortal combat** a fight between people who are trying to kill each other. **-4. mortal fear/danger** etc extreme fear/danger etc □ *He lived in mortal fear of arrest.* □ *mortal enemies.* ◇ *n* an ordinary person who does not have an important position or special powers □ *Are you going to come and sit with us lesser mortals?*

mortality [mɔːʳtælətɪ] *n* **-1.** [of person] *see* **mortal** □ *When he died I suddenly become conscious of my own mortality.* **-2.** the number of people who die in a particular place or situation □ *Infant mortality reached a peak in that year.*

mortality rate *n* the rate at which people die.

mortally [ˈmɔːʳtəlɪ] *adv* **mortally wounded** wounded so badly that one will die. ▪ **mortally afraid/offended** extremely afraid/offended.

mortar [ˈmɔːʳtəʳ] *n* **-1.** CONSTRUCTION a mixture of cement, sand, and water that is put between bricks to keep them attached to each other in a wall. **-2.** MILITARY an artillery gun with a short barrel that fires bombs high into the air over a short distance □ *a mortar bomb.* **-3.** [for crushing things] a bowl in which one crushes things, especially food, into small pieces or powder.

mortarboard [ˈmɔːʳtəʳbɔːʳd] *n* a black cap with a flat square top that is worn by university students and teachers on formal occasions, usually graduation ceremonies.

mortgage [ˈmɔːʳgɪdʒ] ◇ *n* a sum of money that somebody borrows from a bank, usually to buy a house or a piece of land □ *mortgage repayments* □ *We have a $100,000 mortgage on the house.* ◇ *vt* [house, land] to use <property> as a guarantee when borrowing money so that one will lose it if one fails to repay the money.

mortgagee [ˌmɔːʳgəˈdʒiː] *n* a person who lends money to another person and will have the right to own that person's property if they do not repay the loan.

mortgagor [ˌmɔːʳgəˈdʒɔːʳ] *n* a person who borrows money from a mortgagee.

mortician [mɔːʳtɪʃn] *n* US a person whose job is to arrange funerals and prepare bodies for burial.

mortified [ˈmɔːʳtəfaɪd] *adj* **to be mortified** [person] to be ashamed, embarrassed, or shocked because of doing something wrong or stupid □ *I can't believe I crashed his new car — I was mortified!*

mortise lock [ˈmɔːʳtəs-] *n* a lock that fits in a hole cut into the frame of a door.

mortuary [ˈmɔːʳtʃʊərɪ] (*pl* **mortuaries**) *n* a building or part of a hospital where dead bodies are kept before they are buried.

mosaic [moʊˈzeɪɪk] *n* a picture or pattern made of many small pieces of colored glass or stone.

Moscow [US ˈmɑːskaʊ, GB ˈmɒskoʊ] the capital of Russia and its largest city. POPULATION: 8,967,000.

Moses [ˈmoʊzəz] in the Bible, the prophet who led the Jews out of Egypt, when God made a path across the Red Sea. He also received the Ten Commandments from God.

Moslem [ˈmɒzləm] *adj* & *n* = **Muslim**.

mosque [mɒsk] *n* a building where Muslims worship.

mosquito [məˈskiːtoʊ] (*pl* **mosquitoes** OR **mosquitos**) *n* a small flying insect, the female of which bites people and sucks their blood. Mosquitoes can spread malaria.

mosquito net *n* a net that hangs over a bed or the entrance to a tent as a protection against mosquitoes.

moss [mɒs] *n* a plant with very small leaves that grows in a thick soft mass on stone, trees, or damp soil.

mossy [ˈmɒsɪ] (*compar* **mossier**, *superl* **mossiest**) *adj* [steps, stone] covered in moss.

most [moʊst] ◇ *det* **-1. most people/money/food etc** nearly all people/money/food etc □ *In most cases the police had to intervene.* □ *Most tourists here are Japanese.* □ *You can buy it at most good hardware stores.* □ *I like most modern furniture.* **-2. (the) most cars/votes etc** the largest number of cars/votes etc. ▪ **(the) most money/food etc** the largest amount of money/food etc □ *The person with the most correct answers wins a prize.*
◇ *pron* **-1. most of the people/money/food etc** nearly all the people/money/food etc □ *John drank most of the wine: I only had one glass.* □ *Most of my earnings go on food and rent.* □ *We spent most of the time playing cards and chatting.* **-2. (the) most** the largest amount □ *Of the three of us, Kate travels the most.* □ *I think that's the most we can hope to achieve.* **-3.** phrase **to make the most of sthg** to get the most benefit for oneself from sthg □ *It's a great opportunity, so I intend to make the most of it.*
◇ *adv* **-1.** used to make the superlative of adjectives and adverbs □ *The most interesting part of the job is dealing with clients.* □ *The message that came across most strongly was the need to involve parents.* **-2. to like/value/enjoy sthg most** to like/value/enjoy sthg more than anything else □ *What I fear most is losing contact with the children.* **-3. most kind/interesting etc** very kind/interesting etc (formal use) □ *That was a most enjoyable meal.*
◆ **at (the) most** *adv* it will cost $400, at most $400 is the maximum amount it will cost.

mostly [ˈmoʊstlɪ] *adv* in most cases; most of the time □ *The applicants were mostly young women.* □ *We export a lot, mostly to Europe.* □ *Mostly I work at home.*

MOT (*pt* & *pp* **MOT'd** [ˌemoʊˈtiːd], *cont* **MOT'ing**

[ˌeموʊˈtiːɪŋ]) (*abbr of* **Ministry of Transport**) ◇ *n* in Britain, an annual technical and safety examination of cars over three years old. It is illegal to drive a car that has not passed its MOT. ◇ *vt: I'll have to get the car MOT'd next week.*

motel [moʊˈtel] *n* a hotel that is usually basic and cheap and is used by people traveling by car, with parking spaces near each room.

moth [mɒθ] *n* an insect like a butterfly that flies at night and is attracted to lights.

mothball [ˈmɒθbɔːl] *n* a small ball of a chemical substance with a strong smell that people put in their clothes to prevent moths from eating and damaging them.

moth-eaten [-iːtn] *adj* [pullover, coat, sofa] that is old, untidy, and has holes in it.

mother [ˈmʌðər] ◇ *n* -1. the female parent of a person or animal □ She's a mother of three. □ You look like your mother. -2. a word used to address one's mother □ Hello, mother. ◇ *vt* to behave like a mother toward <sb> by being too kind and worrying too much about them.

motherboard [ˈmʌðərbɔːrd] *n* the main printed circuit board in a computer, containing most of the components, to which expansion cards can be added.

Mother Earth an imaginary person, used as a symbol for the Earth.

Mother Goose US an imaginary person who is supposed to have written nursery rhymes.

motherhood [ˈmʌðərhʊd] *n* the state of being a mother.

Mother Hubbard [-ˈhʌbərd] a character in a nursery rhyme. She is a poor old woman whose food cupboard is empty.

mother-in-law (*pl* **mothers-in-law** OR **mother-in-laws**) *n* the mother of one's husband or wife.

motherland [ˈmʌðərlænd] *n* the country that one was born in and feels attached to.

motherless [ˈmʌðərləs] *adj* [child] who has no mother.

motherly [ˈmʌðərli] *adj* [woman] who is caring, warm, and kind.

Mother Nature an imaginary person, used as a symbol for nature.

mother-of-pearl *n* a hard, shiny, pale substance found inside the shells of some shellfish, used in jewelry and ornaments □ a mother-of-pearl brooch/ring.

Mother's Day *n* a day when people give cards or flowers to their mother as a sign of love and appreciation.

mother ship *n* a ship that provides supplies for smaller ships.

mother superior *n* the nun in charge of a convent.

Mother Teresa [-təˈriːzə] (1910–) a Catholic nun, well known for her work helping poor and sick people in India.

mother-to-be (*pl* **mothers-to-be**) *n* a pregnant woman.

mother tongue *n* the language that one learns first and, usually, that one speaks most.

motif [moʊˈtiːf] *n* -1. [on clothes, wallpaper] a single shape that is repeated to make a pattern. -2. [in music, literature] a theme that is repeated throughout a piece of work.

motion [ˈmoʊʃn] ◇ *n* -1. the process of moving □ The motion of the boat made him feel sick. ■ **to set sthg in motion** [process, event] to cause sthg to start happening □ Once we have all the papers, we can set things in motion for the trial. -2. [of one's body] a gesture or movement made with a part of the body □ He made a motion as if to step back. ■ **to go through the motions** to do something without caring about it or being interested in it □ Since I gave in my notice I've just been going through the motions, really. -3. [in a debate, meeting] a proposal □ The motion today is "Nuclear power: good or evil?"

◇ *vt* **to motion sb to do sthg** to show sb that one wants them to do sthg by moving one's hand, head etc □ He motioned me to take a seat.

◇ *vi* **to motion to sb** to make a sign to sb, usually with one's hand, telling them to do something.

motionless [ˈmoʊʃnləs] *adj* [person, vehicle] that is not moving at all □ She sat, motionless, staring at the photograph.

motion picture *n* a movie made for the cinema.

motion sickness *n* sickness that is caused by traveling on a ship, plane etc.

motivate [ˈmoʊtəveɪt] *vt* -1. [act, decision] to be the reason for <sthg> □ He was motivated entirely by the desire for revenge. -2. [student, employee] to give <sb> the desire or enthusiasm to do something □ If you can motivate them to be interested, I'm sure they could do very well.

motivated [ˈmoʊtəveɪtəd] *adj* [person, workforce] that has enthusiasm and is willing to try to achieve something □ Marianne's a highly motivated student.

motivation [ˌmoʊtəˈveɪʃn] *n* -1. the reason for doing something □ What was your motivation for leaving? -2. a feeling of enthusiasm and willingness to try to achieve something □ He lacks motivation.

motive [ˈmoʊtɪv] *n* [for an action, crime] the reason somebody has for doing something □ Do the police know what the motive was?

motley [ˈmɒtli] *adj* **a motley collection/assortment** many different kinds of people or things, usually considered to be unusual or of low quality.

motocross [ˈmoʊtoʊkrɒs] *n* the sport of racing motorcycles over rough ground.

motor [ˈmoʊtər] ◇ *n* a device in a vehicle or machine, e.g. a lawnmower or electric razor, that changes electricity or fuel into movement □ an electric motor. ◇ *adj* **a motor show/mechanic** a show/mechanic for cars, trucks etc □ the motor industry. ◇ *vi* to travel by car (old-fashioned use).

motorbike ['moʊtəˈbaɪk] *n* a motorcycle (informal use).

motorboat ['moʊtəˈboʊt] *n* a boat that is powered by a motor.

motorcade ['moʊtəˈkeɪd] *n* a line of motor vehicles that are carrying or protecting important people during an official ceremony.

motorcar ['moʊtəˈkɑːr] *n* GB a car (formal use).

motorcycle ['moʊtəˈsaɪkl] *n* a motor vehicle on two wheels like a type of bicycle, but heavier and with an engine.

motorcyclist ['moʊtəˈsaɪkləst] *n* a person who rides a motorcycle.

motoring ['moʊtərɪŋ] GB ◇ *adj* **a motoring offence/magazine etc** an offense/a magazine etc that is connected with motor vehicles or driving. ◇ *n* travel by car (old-fashioned use).

motorist ['moʊtərəst] *n* a person who drives a car.

motorized, -ised ['moʊtəraɪzd] *adj* **-1.** [troops, regiment] that is equipped with motor vehicles. **-2.** [vehicle, wheelchair] that has a motor.

motor lodge *n* US a motel.

motor racing *n* the sport of racing cars.

motor scooter *n* a motorcycle with small wheels that does not go very fast and is sometimes started using a pedal.

motor vehicle *n* a vehicle with an engine, used especially on roads (formal use). ■ **the Department of Motor Vehicles** the US agency responsible for license plates and drivers' licenses.

motorway ['moʊtəˈweɪ] *n* GB a wide road, usually with three lanes in each direction, on which cars, trucks etc can drive long distances at high speeds □ *a motorway accident.*

Motown ['moʊtaʊn] an informal name for Detroit, Michigan.

mottled ['mɒtld] *adj* [skin, leaf] that has small areas or spots of different shapes and colors □ *He had a mottled complexion.*

motto ['mɒtoʊ] (*pl* **mottos** OR **mottoes**) *n* a phrase used by a person or organization to express their main aim or beliefs □ *the school motto* □ *Our motto is "Never give up."*

mould *etc* GB = **mold** *etc.*

moult *vt* & *vi* GB = **molt**.

mound [maʊnd] *n* **-1.** a rounded pile of earth or stones; a very small hill. **-2.** [of papers, books] a large untidy pile □ *She looked sadly at the mound of work awaiting her attention.* **-3.** BASEBALL the rounded pile of earth that the pitcher stands on in a game of baseball.

mount [maʊnt] ◇ *n* **-1.** [for a photograph, jewel, medal] something that holds an object in a fixed position. **-2.** a horse, pony, or donkey that one can ride. **-3.** a word used as part of the name of a mountain □ *Mount Ararat.*
◇ *vt* **-1.** to climb onto <a horse or bicycle> in order to ride it. **-2.** [male animal] to climb onto <a female animal> in order to breed. **-3.** [stairs, hill, ladder] to go up <sthg> (formal use). **-4.** [attack, campaign, challenge] to prepare and carry out <sthg> □ *We're mounting an exhibition of Native American art.* ■ **to mount**

guard over sb/sthg to guard sb/sthg. **-5.** [trophy, jewel, component] to fix <sthg> in or on something that frames it and holds it in place □ *Mount the photo on stiff cardboard.*
◇ *vi* **-1.** [sales, support, tension] to increase □ *His debts were mounting rapidly.* **-2.** [person] to climb onto a horse or bicycle.

◆ **mount up** *vi* [work, debts, savings] to increase gradually □ *I've been earning plenty of money, but the bills just keep mounting up.*

mountain ['maʊntən] *n* **-1.** a very large high hill □ *the sport of mountain climbing* □ *a mountain village/road/goat.* ■ **to make a mountain out of a molehill** to make a small problem or matter seem more important than it is. **-2. a mountain of sthg** a very large amount of sthg that is more than one can deal with □ *I've got mountains of work to do.* □ *a mountain of letters/laundry/food.*

mountain bike *n* a strong bicycle with several gears and thick tires for riding over rough ground.

mountaineer [,maʊntəˈnɪər] *n* a person who is trained in mountaineering.

mountaineering [,maʊntəˈnɪərɪŋ] *n* the sport of climbing mountains using special equipment.

mountainous ['maʊntənəs] *adj* [region, country, terrain] that has a lot of mountains.

mountain range *n* a long row of mountains.

mountain rescue *n* a service consisting of people and equipment that saves people who are injured while walking or climbing in hilly areas □ *a mountain rescue team/helicopter.*

mounted ['maʊntəd] *adj* [police, soldier] who rides a horse as part of their job.

Mountie ['maʊntɪ] *n* a member of the mounted police force in Canada (informal use).

mourn [mɔːrn] ◇ *vt* to feel or show great sadness at the death of <sb>; to feel very sad about <sthg that has gone> □ *The nation mourns his death.* □ *They mourned the passing of their youth.* ◇ *vi*: *He mourns for traditional values.* □ *We mustn't mourn over what is past.*

mourner ['mɔːrnər] *n* a person who goes to a funeral □ *The mourners passed silently.*

mournful ['mɔːrnfl] *adj* [occasion, expression, voice] that seems sad; [sound, music] that makes one feel sad.

mourning ['mɔːrnɪŋ] *n* **-1.** a period of great sadness that people feel or show after the death of somebody □ *a day of mourning.* **-2.** clothes, usually black, that are worn to show one's sadness at the death of somebody. ■ **to be in mourning** to behave or be dressed in a way that expresses one's sadness at the death of somebody □ *She was in mourning for her husband.*

mouse [maʊs] (*pl* **mice**) *n* **-1.** a small white, brown, or gray animal that is covered in fur, has a long tail and a pointed nose, and is found in houses, fields etc. **-2.** COMPUTING a small device attached to a computer by a cable that enables one to give instructions to the computer without using the keyboard, by moving it across a flat surface or by pressing its buttons.

mouse mat *n* a mat for placing a computer mouse on.

mousetrap ['maʊstræp] *n* a device, worked by a spring, that catches and kills mice.

moussaka [mʊ'sɑːkə] *n* a Greek dish made with meat, eggplant, and cheese.

mousse [muːs] *n* -1. a light dish made from egg whites, cream, and flavorings that is usually eaten when it is cold □ *a chocolate/salmon mousse.* -2. a white foamy substance used for fixing one's hair in a particular position or to make it seem thicker.

moustache *n* GB = mustache.

mouth [*n* maʊθ, *pl* maʊðz, *vt* maʊð] ◇ *n* -1. [of a person, animal] the space inside the head, behind the lips, where the teeth and tongue are; the part of the face where the lips are □ *Breathe through your mouth.* □ *Don't eat with your mouth open.* ■ **to keep one's mouth shut** to make sure that one does not talk about something that is secret (informal use) □ *You'd better keep your mouth shut about this, or you'll be sorry.* -2. [of a river] the place where a river joins the sea □ *a river mouth.* -3. [of a cave, tunnel] the entrance of a cave or tunnel.
◇ *vt* -1. to form <a word or words> with one's lips without making any sound □ *"Hello!" she mouthed silently.* -2. [excuse, apology] to say <sthg> without really meaning it □ *She appeared on the news, mouthing the usual explanations and regrets.*

mouthful ['maʊθfl] *n* -1. [of food, drink] an amount of food or drink that one puts into one's mouth, or that fills one's mouth □ *He took a mouthful — "This is good," he said.* □ *I can't believe she was smoking between mouthfuls!* -2. a word or phrase that is difficult to say, especially because it is long or in a foreign language (informal and humorous use) □ *Szymanowski? That's a bit of a mouthful!*

mouthorgan ['maʊθɔːˈgən] *n* a small musical instrument that is moved from side to side across one's lips and blown or sucked to make a sound.

mouthpiece ['maʊθpiːs] *n* -1. [of a telephone] the part of the telephone that one speaks into. -2. [of an instrument] the part of a musical instrument that one blows into. -3. [of a person, organization] a person, newspaper etc that is used by a person or organization to tell the public their opinions □ *The newspaper is the party's official mouthpiece.*

mouth-to-mouth *adj* **mouth-to-mouth resuscitation** a way of keeping somebody breathing by blowing air into their lungs with one's mouth on their mouth, while holding their nose □ *A paramedic gave the victim mouth-to-mouth resuscitation.*

mouth ulcer *n* a small, round, sore area of skin on the inside of the mouth.

mouthwash ['maʊθwɒʃ] *n* a liquid used for cleaning one's mouth and for making one's breath smell fresh, and that one does not swallow □ *Try gargling with mouthwash.*

mouth-watering [-wɔːtərɪŋ] *adj* [food, meal, snack] that looks or smells delicious; [smell, picture] that makes one want to eat the food that one can smell or see.

movable ['muːvəbl] *adj* [parts, furniture] that can be moved □ *The doll has movable arms and legs.*

move [muːv] ◇ *vt* -1. [object, vehicle, person] to change the position or place that <sb/sthg> is in □ *Could you move your head out of the way, please, I can't see.* □ *The company is moving him to its head office in Hong Kong.* -2. **to move house/jobs etc** to leave one's house/job etc and go to a new one □ *We're moving offices next September.* -3. [person] to cause <sb> to feel a strong emotion such as sadness or pity etc □ *Her audience was moved to tears.* □ *I was deeply moved by what I saw.* -4. [amendment, proposal] to suggest <sthg> formally in a meeting □ *I move that Frances Barrat be appointed as treasurer.* -5. **to be** OR **feel moved to do sthg** to do sthg because one has strong feelings about it (formal use) □ *He was moved to protest.*
◇ *vi* -1. to change position or place □ *I called her name but she didn't move.* □ *The traffic hasn't moved for the past ten minutes.* -2. to act □ *We're going to have to move fast to win this contract.* -3. to leave one's old home, job, school etc and go to a new one □ *They're moving to a smaller office in town.* □ *He's moving to the accounting department after Christmas.*
◇ *n* -1. **to make a move** to make a physical movement □ *It's getting late: shall we make a move?* □ *She made a sudden move toward the door.* ■ **to be on the move** to be going from one place to another □ *Her father worked for the UN so they were always on the move.* ■ **to get a move on** to hurry (informal use) □ *For goodness' sake, get a move on, we're late!* -2. [from home] the act of leaving one's old home, job, school etc to go to a new one □ *We're still settling in after the move.* -3. GAMES the act of moving a piece from one square to another; any of the ways in which the rules of a game say this can be done □ *It's your move.* □ *I can never remember the different moves in chess.* -4. [in a situation] one of a series of things that one does in order to deal with a situation □ *Let's wait for them to make the first move.* □ *His first move will be to try and restore confidence.* □ *It's a good career move.*

◆ **move about** *vi* = move around.

◆ **move along** ◇ *vi* [crowd, passengers, spectators] to keep going further along a road, bus, train etc to avoid blocking the way □ *Move along, please, and let the ambulance through!* ◇ *vt sep* ■ **to move sb along** to tell sb to move away from a public place, e.g. because they are blocking the way □ *The police tried to move the onlookers along.*

◆ **move around** *vi* -1. [person, animal] to make repeated small movements, especially because one is bored or uncomfortable □ *I could hear someone moving around in the next room.* -2. to travel from one place to another □ *We moved around a lot because my Dad was in the army when I was young.*

◆ **move away** *vi* [person] to go to live in a different place □ *They moved away from the area after he lost his job.*

◆ **move in** ◇ *vi* [person, couple, family] to start living in a new house, office etc □ *There's a new tenant moving in upstairs.* ◇ *vt sep* [police, reinforcements, troops] to bring <sb/sthg> to a place in order to deal with a difficult situation □ *They're moving in the heavy artillery.*

◆ **move off** *vi* [bus, car] to start moving away slowly from a place □ *The train moved off, leaving a crowd of reporters on the platform.*

◆ **move on** ◇ *vt sep* **to move sb on** [drunk person, spectator] to cause sb to go away from a public place □ *Police moved the demonstrators on.* ◇ *vi* -1. to leave a place or activity for somewhere or something new □ *We spend a week in Venice, then move on to Rome.* □ *I've done three years in this job, and it's time to move on.* -2. to stop talking about a particular subject and start talking about something else □ *Let's move on rapidly to our next item.*

◆ **move out** *vi* -1. to leave one's house and go and live somewhere else □ *He moved out without paying the rent.* -2. [troops, army] to leave a place □ *UN forces are moving out of the capital.*

◆ **move over** *vi* to change position, especially to make room for somebody or something else □ *Move over so that we can sit down too.*

moveable ['muːvəbl] *adj* = **movable**.

movement ['muːvmənt] *n* -1. [of one's body] the action of changing one's body from one position to another □ *The neighbors are back home, I heard movements upstairs this morning.* □ *Tight clothes make movement difficult.* □ *Don't make any sudden movements.* □ *He made a sawing movement with his hand.* □ *her graceful movements.* -2. [in a place] the action of moving or traveling from one place to another □ *troop movement* □ *Our movement within the country is restricted by law.* □ *freedom of movement.* -3. [of goods] the action of transporting goods from one place to another. -4. [in a situation] a development or change □ *There is a movement towards community service instead of prison sentences for certain offenses.* □ *There has been little movement on the stock market share prices.* -5. [of people, campaigners] a group of people who have the same beliefs, aims etc and who work together to persuade other people that these aims and beliefs are right □ *the terrorist/women's/gay rights movement.* -6. MUSIC one of the main sections of a long piece of classical music such as a symphony.

movie ['muːvi] *n* a story, report etc in the form of moving pictures, usually with sound, that is shown on television or at a movie theater □ *Have you been to any good movies lately?* □ *a horror movie* □ *the movie screen.*

movie camera *n* a camera used for making movies.

moviegoer ['muːvɪgouəʳ] *n* a person who often goes to the movie theater.

movie star *n* an actor or actress who is well known and successful because of the movies they have made.

movie theater *n* US a place where people go to watch movies.

moving ['muːvɪŋ] *adj* -1. [tale, scene, photo] that makes one feel strong emotions, especially sadness and pity □ *His performance/speech was very moving.* -2. **moving parts** the parts of a machine that move when it is working □ *'Danger: deep water and moving machinery.'*

moving staircase *n* a staircase that moves and carries people to different levels in a large building, public area etc.

mow [mou] (*pt* **mowed**, *pp* **mowed** OR **mown**) *vt* -1. [lawn] to cut <an area of grass> using a lawnmower. -2. [corn, wheat] to cut <a crop> using a machine or a tool held in the hand; to cut the crops or grass in <a field>.

◆ **mow down** *vt sep* **to mow people down** to injure or kill several people with a weapon or a car.

mower ['mouəʳ] *n* = **lawnmower**.

mown [moun] *past participle of* **mow**.

Mozambique [ˌmouzæm'biːk] a country in southeastern Africa, on the Indian Ocean, north of South Africa. SIZE: 785,000 sq kms. POPULATION: 16,100,000 (*Mozambicans*). CAPITAL: Maputo. LANGUAGE: Portuguese. CURRENCY: metical.

Mozart ['moutsɑːʳt], **Wolfgang Amadeus** (1756–1791) an Austrian composer, considered to be one of the greatest of all time. He wrote 41 symphonies, many piano concertos, and several operas, including *The Marriage of Figaro* and *The Magic Flute.*

MP *n* -1. *abbr of* **Member of Parliament**. -2. *abbr of* **military police**. -3. (*abbr of* **Mounted Police**) the official name for the Mounties.

mpg (*abbr of* **miles per gallon**) a way of measuring the amount of fuel used by a motor vehicle.

mph (*abbr of* **miles per hour**) a way of measuring the speed of a vehicle.

MPhil [em'fɪl] (*abbr of* **Master of Philosophy**) *n* GB a postgraduate degree that is higher than a master's degree and lower than a PhD; a person who has this degree.

MPS (*abbr of* **Member of the Pharmaceutical Society**) *n* a member of the professional association for pharmacists in Britain.

Mr ['mɪstəʳ] -1. a title used to refer to a man □ *Mr Jones* □ *Mr Richard Smith.* -2. a word used to talk to men in certain official positions, and which comes before the title of their position □ *Mr President* □ *Mr Chairman.*

MRC (*abbr of* **Medical Research Council**) *n* the British government department responsible for organizing and funding medical research.

MRCP (*abbr of* **Member of the Royal College of Physicians**) *n* a member of a professional association for doctors in Britain.

MRCS (*abbr of* **Member of the Royal College of Surgeons**) *n* a member of a professional association for surgeons in Britain.

MRCVS (*abbr of* **Member of the Royal College**

of Veterinary Surgeons) *n* a member of a professional association for veterinarians in Britain.

Mrs ['mɪsəz] a title for a married woman, usually followed by her husband's family name. Many people now prefer to use the title Ms in writing □ *Mrs Jones* □ *Mr and Mrs Richard Smith* □ *Mrs Alice Baker.*

ms. *abbr of* **manuscript.**

Ms [mɪz] a written title for a woman that does not state whether she is married or not □ *Ms Jones* □ *Ms Clare Jones.*

MS ◇ -1. *abbr of* **manuscript.** -2. *abbr of* **Mississippi.** ◇ *n* US = **MSc.**

MS, ms *n abbr of* **multiple sclerosis.**

MSA (*abbr of* **Master of Science in Agriculture**) *n* GB a postgraduate degree in agricultural science; a person who has this degree.

MSB (*abbr of* **most significant bit/byte**) *n* COMPUTING the bit or byte that has the greatest value.

MSc (*abbr of* **Master of Science**) *n* a postgraduate degree in science; a person who has this degree.

MSF (*abbr of* **Manufacturing Science and Finance**) *n* **the MSF** a large British labor union for engineering, science, and technology professionals.

MSG *n abbr of* **monosodium glutamate.**

Msgr *abbr of* **Monsignor.**

MST (*abbr of* **Mountain Standard Time**) *n* the local time in the Rocky Mountain region of North America.

MSW (*abbr of* **Master of Social Work**) *n* a postgraduate degree in social work; a person who has this degree.

Mt *abbr of* **mount.**

MT ◇ *n* (*abbr of* **machine translation**) COMPUTING a system that translates text and commands from one language to another. ◇ *abbr of* **Montana.**

much [mʌtʃ] (*compar* **more**, *superl* **most**) ◇ *adv* -1. a lot □ *Did it hurt much?* ■ **much better/quicker** a lot better/quicker (used with comparatives) □ *She's much more relaxed now she's had a break.* □ *It's much too cold to go out.* ■ **to be much admired/appreciated** to be admired/appreciated a lot (used with passive forms of verbs) □ *Her health is much improved.* ■ **so** OR **very much** a lot (used with verbs for emphasis) □ *I very much hope you will come.* □ *Thank you so much for all your help.* -2. **we don't talk/go out much** we don't talk/go out very often (used in negative sentences). -3. *phrase* **much the same** almost the same □ *He looked much the same as before.* ◇ *det* **we don't have much time/money** we have only a small amount of time/money (used in questions and negative sentences) □ *How much fabric do you need for a skirt?* □ *It didn't do much good.* ■ **too much coffee/time** too large an amount of coffee/time □ *We've spent so much/too much money on it already.* ■ **he takes much pleasure/pride in it** he takes great pleasure/pride in it (formal use). ◇ *pron*: *There is much we still have to learn.* □

There's not much of a difference between them. □ *I've had as much as I can stand!* □ *You drink too much.* □ *How much did you pay for it?* □ *Much of the time she was preoccupied and sad.* □ *I haven't been much of a help to you, have I?* ■ **he's not much of a cook** he's not very good at cooking. ■ **nothing much** nothing interesting or important □ *"What did you do last night?"* — *"Nothing much."* ■ **so much for...** used when the speaker feels disappointed by something □ *Well, so much for all his fancy ideas about living abroad!* ■ **I thought as much!** I had already guessed this and so am not surprised □ *"I need to borrow some money."* — *"I thought as much!"* ■ **it's not up to much** it's not very good (informal use) □ *This wine isn't up to much.*

◆ **much as** *conj* although □ *Much as I like him, I wouldn't want to work with him.*

much-vaunted [-'vɔːntəd] *adj* **a much-vaunted achievement/plan** an achievement/a plan that people speak about in a proud way that is not necessarily justified.

muck [mʌk] *n* (informal use) -1. mud or dirt. -2. manure.

◆ **muck about, muck around** GB (informal use) ◇ *vt sep* **to muck sb about** OR **around** to treat sb badly by changing plans that affect them or by not being honest with them □ *Stop mucking me about!* ◇ *vi* to do silly or unimportant things when one should be working or concentrating or something □ *She's been mucking about in the garage all day and hasn't done any work.*

◆ **muck in** *vi* GB to join in an activity in order to help (informal use) □ *Here's the soap and some cleaning cloths* — *I suggest you all just muck in!*

◆ **muck out** *vt sep* **to muck a stable/cowshed etc out** to clean a stable/cowshed etc.

◆ **muck up** *vt sep* (informal use) -1. **to muck sthg up** [exam, interview] to do sthg very badly □ *"How did it go?"* — *"I think I mucked up the final question."* -2. **to muck sthg up** [plan] to spoil sthg □ *Well, that's mucked up our quiet weekend.*

muckraking ['mʌkreɪkɪŋ] *n* the practice of searching for and printing personal and unpleasant information about well-known people (disapproving use).

mucky ['mʌkɪ] (*compar* **muckier**, *superl* **muckiest**) *adj* [clothes, shoes, child] covered in dirt (informal use) □ *Look at you, you're all mucky!*

mucus ['mjuːkəs] *n* a thick liquid produced in some parts of the body, e.g. the nose.

mud [mʌd] *n* a thick substance formed when earth mixes with water.

muddle ['mʌdl] ◇ *n* -1. [of finances, clothes, list] a state of confusion; a mistake caused by confusion □ *My papers are in a terrible muddle.* □ *There's been a muddle over the tickets.* -2. **to be in a muddle** [person] to be in a confused state that is caused by trying to do something complicated □ *I've gotten into such a muddle with these accounts.* □ *I'm in a muddle about what they told me to do.* ◇ *vt* -1. [papers, finances] to put <sthg> into a state of disorder □ *Be careful not to muddle the pages.* -2. [person] to make <sb> confused □ *Now you've gone and muddled him.*

◆ **muddle along** *vi* to live one's life without having any clear plan or purpose □ *"How are things?" — "Oh, you know, we muddle along."*

◆ **muddle through** *vi* to succeed in doing something difficult, without having a clear plan or the knowledge of how to do it □ *We'll just have to try to muddle through.*

◆ **muddle up** *vt sep* **to muddle sthg up** to mix up sthg accidentally □ *I muddled up the customs declarations with the tax returns.* □ *She always muddles her grandsons' names up.*

muddy ['mʌdɪ] (*compar* **muddier**, *superl* **muddiest**, *pt* & *pp* **muddied**) ◇ *adj* -1. [floor, boots] that is covered in mud; [field, ditch] that contains mud. -2. [color] that is like the color of mud □ *a dull muddy green.* ◇ *vt* [issue, situation, thinking] to make <sthg> difficult to understand.

mudflap ['mʌdflæp] *n* a piece of material, e.g. rubber, that hangs behind each wheel of a vehicle to stop mud from splashing upward.

mudflat ['mʌdflæt] *n* an area of land that is covered by the sea when the water rises and where no plants grow.

mudguard ['mʌdgɑːrd] *n* a curved piece of metal above the top and back of each bicycle wheel that stops mud from splashing upward.

mudpack ['mʌdpæk] *n* a special type of mud that is put on the face to cleanse the skin.

mudslinging ['mʌdslɪŋɪŋ] *n* the practice of criticizing people in public by saying unpleasant and often untrue things about them.

muesli ['mjuːzlɪ] *n* a mixture of different grains, nuts, and dried fruit, usually eaten for breakfast with milk or yogurt.

muff [mʌf] ◇ *n* fur or other material sewn to form a tube which one puts one's hands into to keep them warm. ◇ *vt* (informal use) -1. **to muff a catch** to miss a catch. -2. **to muff a chance** to miss a chance.

muffin ['mʌfɪn] *n* -1. a small cake □ *blueberry muffins.* -2. a small, round, sweet bread roll that is eaten hot, usually with butter.

muffle ['mʌfl] *vt* [scream, voice] to make <a sound> less loud and clear.

muffled ['mʌfld] *adj* -1. [sound, scream, voice] that is quiet and unclear □ *I could hear a muffled conversation going on in the next room.* -2. **to be muffled (up)** [person] to be wearing a lot of thick warm clothes.

muffler ['mʌflər] *n* US a tube fitted to the exhaust pipe of a motor vehicle to make it quieter.

mug [mʌg] (*pt* & *pp* **mugged**, *cont* **mugging**) ◇ *n* -1. a large cup with straight sides and a handle; the contents of this cup □ *She handed him a large mug of tea.* -2. a face (informal use) □ *I'm tired of looking at your ugly mug!* ◇ *vt* to attack <sb>, usually in the street, in order to steal their money, jewelry etc □ *He won't go out late for fear of getting mugged.*

mugger ['mʌgər] *n* a person who has mugged somebody.

mugging ['mʌgɪŋ] *n* the act of mugging somebody □ *Mugging is on the increase.* □ *There's been a spate of muggings in the area.*

muggy ['mʌgɪ] (*compar* **muggier**, *superl* **muggiest**) *adj* [weather, air] that feels unpleasantly warm, damp, and heavy.

mugshot ['mʌgʃɒt] *n* a photograph taken by the police that shows the head and shoulders of somebody who has been charged with a crime (informal use).

Muhammad [moʊˈhæməd] (570–632) the Arab prophet and founder of Islam, a religion based on the Koran which was revealed to him by God.

mujaheddin [ˌmuːdʒəheˈdiːn] *npl* **the mujaheddin** fundamentalist Muslim armed forces.

mulatto▼ [mjʊˈlætoʊ] (*pl* **mulattos** OR **mulattoes**) *n* a person who has one black and one white parent (offensive use).

mule [mjuːl] *n* an animal that is the young of a female horse and a male donkey, and is used to carry heavy loads.

mull [mʌl] ◆ **mull over** *vt sep* **to mull sthg over** [question, problem, offer] to think about sthg for a long time □ *This should give them something to mull over.*

mullah ['mʌlə] *n* a Muslim teacher of law and religion.

mulled wine [ˌmʌld-] *n* wine, flavored with sugar and spices, that is served warm.

mullet ['mʌlət] (*pl* **mullet** OR **mullets**) *n* a small sea fish that can be eaten.

mulligatawny [ˌmʌləgəˈtɔːnɪ] *n* a soup containing hot spices.

mullioned ['mʌljənd] *adj* [window] that has thin pieces of wood, metal, or stone between each section of glass.

multi- ['mʌltɪ] *prefix* added to words to mean that something has or involves many things of a particular kind □ *a multi-talented player.*

multiaccess ['mʌltɪækses] *adj* [computing, system] that allows several computer users to use one file or program at the same time.

multicolored US, **multicoloured** GB [ˌmʌltɪˈkʌlərd] *adj* that has many different colors.

multicultural [ˌmʌltɪˈkʌltʃrəl] *adj* [society, education] that includes different customs, from people of different races.

multifarious [ˌmʌltɪˈfeərɪəs] *adj* [activities, interests] that are many or of many different kinds.

multilateral [ˌmʌltɪˈlætərəl] *adj* [disarmament, agreement, talks] that involves more than two countries or groups □ *A multilateral trade embargo will take force immediately.*

multimedia [ˌmʌltɪˈmiːdjə] *n* -1. the use of different media, e.g. television, slides, or computers. -2. COMPUTING a computer system or product that can show data in different forms, e.g. graphics, sound, and moving pictures.

multimillionaire [ˌmʌltɪmɪljəˈneər] *n* a person who has several million dollars, pounds etc.

multinational [ˌmʌltɪˈnæʃnəl] ◇ *adj* [company, corporation] that has offices, factories etc in many countries. ◇ *n* a multinational company or corporation.

multiple [ˈmʌltəpl] ◇ *adj* -1. [ownership, collision] that has many parts or uses, or involves many people □ *a multiple pile-up.* -2. **multiple injuries/stab wounds** many injuries/stab wounds (formal use). ◇ *n* MATH the result when a particular number is multiplied by another number □ *Multiples of 10 all end in 0.*

multiple-choice *adj* [test, exam] that gives several possible answers, from which one must choose the correct answer.

multiple sclerosis [-skləˈrousəs] *n* a very serious disease that affects the nervous system, and in which one's muscles gradually become weaker.

multiplex [ˈmʌltɪpleks] *n* a movie theater that has several rooms, each one with its own screen.

multiplication [ˌmʌltəpləˈkeɪʃn] *n* -1. MATH the method of multiplying two numbers together to produce a result. -2. [of problems, officials, departments] a big increase in the number or amount of something.

multiplication sign *n* a symbol (×) between two numbers to show that they are to be multiplied together.

multiplication table *n* a list of the multiplications of numbers from one to twelve that children usually learn at school.

multiplicity [ˌmʌltəˈplɪsətɪ] *n* **a multiplicity of things** [of ideas, languages] a large number of things, especially different things.

multiply [ˈmʌltəplaɪ] (*pt* & *pp* **multiplied**) ◇ *vt* -1. MATH to add <a number> to itself a particular number of times to produce a result □ *What's the result if you multiply 3 by 4?* □ *Multiply the two figures together.* -2. [difficulty, success, profits] to make <sthg> increase a lot. ◇ *vi* -1. MATH *Multiplying by 2, 5, and 10 is easy.* -2. [difficulties, successes, profits] *Inflation has multiplied since last year.* -3. [animals, insects, bacteria] to increase in amount by breeding.

multipurpose [ˌmʌltɪˈpɜːʳpəs] *adj* **a multipurpose tool/device etc** a tool/device etc that is designed so that it can be used in many different ways.

multiracial [ˌmʌltɪˈreɪʃl] *adj* [society, school] that involves people of different races.

multistory US, **multistorey** GB [ˌmʌltɪˈstɔːrɪ] ◇ *adj* **a multistory apartment building/parking garage etc** a building/parking garage etc that has many floors at different levels. ◇ *n* GB a multistory parking garage.

multitasking [US ˌmʌltɪˈtæskɪŋ, GB -tɑːsk-] *n* COMPUTING the process of operating more than one computing program, application etc at the same time.

multitude [ˈmʌltətˢjuːd] *n* -1. a large number □ *He gave me a multitude of reasons for not finishing the work on time.* -2. a very large number of people (literary use).

mum [mʌm] (informal use) ◇ *n* GB mother □ *Hi, mum!* □ *His mum's got a new job.* ◇ *adj* **to keep mum** to say nothing about something one knows about.

mumble [ˈmʌmbl] ◇ *vt* [apology, word, response] to say <sthg> in a way that is not clear or easy to hear □ *"I'm sorry," he mumbled.* ◇ *vi: I can't hear you if you mumble.*

mumbo jumbo [ˌmʌmbouˈdʒʌmbou] *n* nonsense (disapproving and informal use).

mummify [ˈmʌməfaɪ] (*pt* & *pp* **mummified**) *vt* to preserve <a body> from decay by applying special oils and wrapping it in pieces of cloth.

mummy [ˈmʌmɪ] (*pl* **mummies**) *n* -1. a dead body that has been mummified. -2. GB a word used especially by or to children to talk about or talk to their mother □ *Can we go out to play, Mummy?*

mumps [mʌmps] *n* an infectious illness that mainly affects children and causes painful swelling in the area beneath the ears.

munch [mʌntʃ] ◇ *vt* [apple, burger] to eat <food> by chewing it, often noisily. ◇ *vi: He was munching away on a sandwich.*

mundane [mʌnˈdeɪn] *adj* [life, task, event] that is ordinary and boring, especially because it is the same each day.

mung bean [ˈmʌŋ-] *n* a plant from eastern Asia that produces green beans and bean sprouts used in cooking.

municipal [mjʊˈnɪsəpl] *adj* [building, park, council] that is connected with the local government of a town or city □ *municipal elections.*

municipality [mjʊˌnɪsəˈpælətɪ] (*pl* **municipalities**) *n* a town or city that has its own local government; the local government of a particular town or city.

munificent [mjʊˈnɪfɪsənt] *adj* very generous (formal use).

munitions [mjʊˈnɪʃnz] *npl* military equipment for war such as ammunition and large weapons.

mural [ˈmjʊərəl] *n* a picture or design that is painted on a wall.

murder [ˈmɜːʳdəʳ] ◇ *n* -1. the act or crime of killing somebody deliberately and illegally □ *They were found guilty of murder.* ■ **to get away with murder** to keep doing something that is bad or wrong without being punished (informal use) □ *She's so easygoing — she lets her children get away with murder.* -2. the death of somebody, caused by the crime of murder □ *the violent murder of Mr Reed* □ *the murder weapon.* ◇ *vt* to deliberately and illegally kill <sb> □ *He was murdered on his way home from work.*

murderer [ˈmɜːʳdərəʳ] *n* a person who has murdered somebody □ *They never caught the murderer.*

murderess [ˈmɜːʳdərəs] *n* a woman who has murdered somebody.

murderous [ˈmɜːʳdərəs] *adj* [attack, person, intentions] that is likely to kill somebody.

murky [ˈmɜːʳkɪ] (*compar* **murkier**, *superl* **murki-**

est) *adj* **-1.** [night, street] that is dark and unpleasant; [water, river, lake] that is unpleasantly dark and difficult to see through. **-2.** [past, secret] that is likely to hide some dishonest action.

murmur ['mɜːˈməʳ] ◇ *n* **-1.** [of traffic, sea, disapproval] a very low continuous sound, often coming from a long way away □ *the murmur of distant voices.* **-2.** MEDICINE a sound made by the heart that shows there may be something wrong with it. ◇ *vt* [agreement, approval] to say <sthg> very quietly □ *"I love you,"* *he murmured.* ◇ *vi*: *He was murmuring in his sleep.*

MusB ['mʌzbiː], **MusBac** ['mʌzbæk] (*abbr of* **Bachelor of Music**) *n* a music degree; a person who has this degree.

muscle ['mʌsl] *n* **-1.** a piece of tissue in the body that makes movement possible and connects bones together □ *He had bulging muscles.* □ *leg/arm/stomach muscles.* **-2.** the power that comes from having money or influence □ *financial/political muscle.*

◆ **muscle in** *vi* to become involved in an activity, market etc in which one is not wanted, by being aggressive (disapproving use) □ *They're trying to muscle in on our sales territory.*

muscleman ['mʌslmæn] (*pl* **musclemen** [-men]) *n* a man whose muscles are very developed because he does special exercises.

Muscovite ['mʌskəvaɪt] *n* a person who comes from or lives in Moscow.

muscular ['mʌskjələʳ] *adj* **-1.** [spasm, pain, disease] that is connected with muscles □ *These exercises require great muscular strength.* **-2.** [person, body] that has large muscles and looks strong □ *He's very muscular.*

muscular dystrophy [-'dɪstrəfɪ] *n* a serious disease in which one's muscles gradually become weaker, making it harder to move.

MusD ['mʌzdiː], **MusDoc** ['mʌzdɒk] (*abbr of* **Doctor of Music**) *n* a postgraduate music degree; a person who has this degree.

muse [mjuːz] ◇ *n* an imaginary force that helps somebody to write music or poetry or to paint. ◇ *vi* to think deeply about something.

museum [mjʊˈziːəm] *n* a building, open to the public, where objects of historical, scientific, or artistic value are kept and displayed □ *a museum of natural history/modern art.*

mush [mʌʃ] *n* (informal use) **-1.** something, usually food, that is soft and watery. **-2.** writing, music etc that is too full of exaggerated or insincere emotion.

mushroom ['mʌʃruːm] ◇ *n* a fungus, usually with a thick short stem and a wider circular top part. Some mushrooms can be eaten and others are poisonous. ◇ *vi* [membership, interest] to grow or develop very fast; [houses, stores] to spread across a wide area at a fast rate □ *The village mushroomed into a town during the post-war boom.*

mushroom cloud *n* a large cloud of dust, in the shape of a mushroom, that rises high above the ground after a nuclear explosion.

mushy ['mʌʃɪ] (*compar* **mushier**, *superl* **mushiest**) *adj* (informal use) **-1.** [food] that is soft and has lost its shape. **-2.** [movie, music] that is too full of exaggerated or insincere emotion.

music ['mjuːzɪk] *n* **-1.** a pattern of usually pleasant sounds, made by one's voice or a musical instrument □ *a lovely piece of music* □ *classical/pop/dance music.* **-2.** the art of making or writing music □ *a music teacher/student/lesson.* **-3.** a set of symbols on a page, that represent different sounds and rhythms □ *She can read music.*

musical ['mjuːzɪkl] ◇ *adj* **-1.** [evening, career, education] that is connected with music □ *The Fourth of July concert is the musical event of the year.* **-2.** [child, person] who enjoys music and is often skilled at playing an instrument. **-3.** [voice, sound, quality] that is pleasant because it sounds like music. ◇ *n* a play or movie that includes speaking, songs, and usually some dancing □ *a Broadway musical.*

musical box *n* GB = **music box**.

musical chairs *n* a game in which children keep running around a row of chairs while music is playing and try to sit down on a chair when the music stops.

musical instrument *n* an object, e.g. a flute, violin, or piano, that one uses to play music □ *What musical instruments can you play?*

music box US, **musical box** GB *n* a box containing a clockwork device that plays a tune when the lid of the box is lifted.

music hall *n* **-1.** GB a theater where singers, dancers, comedians etc performed in the early part of the 20th century. **-2.** the type of entertainment performed in a music hall.

musician [mjuːˈzɪʃn] *n* a person who plays a musical instrument well or writes music.

music stand *n* a metal support for sheets of music that stands on the floor.

musk [mʌsk] *n* a substance with a strong sweet smell that is used to make perfume.

musket ['mʌskət] *n* a gun with a long barrel, used in the past.

muskrat ['mʌskræt] *n* a rat with a flat tail that comes from North America, eats plants, fish, and small animals, and lives in a nest in or very near water.

Muslim ['mʊzləm] ◇ *n* a person who follows the religion of Islam. ◇ *adj*: *a Muslim country/follower/philosopher.*

muslin ['mʌzlən] *n* a very fine cotton cloth □ *a muslin dress.*

musquash ['mʌskwɒʃ] *n* **-1.** = **muskrat**. **-2.** the valuable fur of the muskrat.

muss [mʌs] *vt* **to muss sthg (up)** US [clothes, hair] to make sthg untidy.

mussel ['mʌsl] *n* a small sea creature that lives in a black shell and can be cooked and eaten.

Mussolini [ˌmʊsəˈliːnɪ], **Benito** (1883–1945) an Italian fascist dictator. He invaded Abyssinia and Albania, and joined World War II on the side of Germany.

must [mʌst] ◇ *modal vb* **-1. I must get there early** it is important or necessary that I get there early □ *She must pass these exams if she wants to get into college.* □ *I must remember to buy my plane ticket.* □ *Must you go now?* ▪ **you must not tell anybody** it is important or necessary that you do not tell anybody □ *Children must not be allowed to touch the displays.* **-2. I must pay my phone bill** I intend to pay my phone bill □ *"Have you heard from Joe?"* — *"No, I must give him a call sometime."* **-3. you must come to dinner** I suggest that you come to dinner □ *You must go and see that new play on Broadway.* **-4. she must be pleased** it is very likely that she is pleased. ▪ **they must have known about it** it is very likely that they knew about it □ *They must have got the results by now.* **-5. I must admit/say...** a phrase used to introduce one's opinion about something □ *It's not a color I would have chosen, I must admit.* ◇ *n* **it's a must** it is important that you do, see, read, wear etc this (informal use) □ *His new novel is a must for fans of science fiction.*

mustache ['mʌstæʃ] US, **moustache** [mə'stɑːʃ] GB *n* hair that grows above a man's upper lip □ *He had a large, bushy mustache.* □ *Are you growing a mustache?*

mustard ['mʌstərd] *n* a very hot paste that is eaten with food, especially meat, is yellow or brown in color, and is made from a small plant with yellow flowers □ *mustard powder.* ▪ **mustard and cress** GB very young plants grown from the seeds of white mustard and garden cress, eaten in salads.

mustard gas *n* a very poisonous gas or liquid used in chemical weapons.

muster ['mʌstər] ◇ *vt* **-1.** [strength, energy, support] to find as much of <sthg> as possible □ *They sent around a petition but couldn't muster more than a dozen signatures.* **-2.** to gather <soldiers, volunteers> etc together in one place for a particular purpose. ◇ *vi* [soldiers, volunteers] *The army mustered on the outskirts of the town.*

♦ **muster up** *vt fus* to muster up strength/support etc to muster strength/support etc □ *I'm trying to muster up the courage to tell him.*

mustn't ['mʌsnt] = **must not.**

must've ['mʌstəv] = **must have.**

musty ['mʌstɪ] (*compar* **mustier**, *superl* **mustiest**) *adj* [room, book] that smells old, dusty, and damp as if it has not been used for a long time.

mutant ['mjuːtnt] ◇ *n* an animal or plant that is physically different from the rest of its species because of a genetic change. ◇ *adj*: *a mutant apple tree/fly/virus.*

mutate [US 'mjuːteɪt, GB mjʊ'teɪt] *vi* [animal, plant] to become a mutant □ *This tree has mutated into a form that is resistant to the disease.*

mutation [mjʊ'teɪʃn] *n* the process of change in the genetic structure of cells, affecting part or all of a living creature; the result of this process □ *The new and more resistant strain is a genetic mutation.*

mute [mjuːt] ◇ *adj* [admiration, protest, disapproval] that somebody expresses without saying anything □ *He looked at her in mute disbelief.* ◇ *n* **-1.** a person who is unable to speak. **-2.** a device that one fits onto a musical instrument in order to make it sound quieter. ◇ *vt* to make <a sound> quieter.

muted ['mjuːtəd] *adj* **-1.** [color, decor] that is not bright; [noise, sound, voice] that is softer than usual. **-2.** [reaction, criticism] that is not very strong □ *The plan was received with muted enthusiasm.* □ *Criticism of the guidelines has so far been muted.*

mutilate ['mjuːtɪleɪt] *vt* **-1.** [person, animal] to damage the body of <a person or animal> in a violent attack, often removing part of it □ *The body had been mutilated beyond recognition.* **-2.** [book, story] to ruin <sthg> completely.

mutilation [ˌmjuːtɪ'leɪʃn] *n*: see **mutilate** □ *Captured prisoners suffered death and mutilation.*

mutineer [ˌmjuːtɪ'nɪər] *n* a person who takes part in a mutiny.

mutinous ['mjuːtɪnəs] *adj* [sailor, soldier] who disobeys somebody in authority, often using violence to do so.

mutiny ['mjuːtɪnɪ] (*pl* **mutinies**, *pt* & *pp* **mutinied**) ◇ *n* [by sailors, soldiers] the act of taking control of something by force from the person in authority. ◇ *vi* [sailors, soldiers] to carry out a mutiny.

mutt [mʌt] *n* (informal use) **-1.** a fool. **-2.** a dog that is a mixture of breeds.

mutter ['mʌtər] ◇ *vt* [words, threat, excuse] to say <sthg> quietly, usually when one is angry and does not want to be heard □ *"It's all right for you to complain,"* he muttered. ◇ *vi*: *The old man sat in the corner muttering (away) to himself.*

muttering ['mʌtərɪŋ] *n* **-1.** a muttered remark □ *mutterings of discontent.* **-2.** the sound made by people who are muttering □ *A lot of low muttering could be heard coming from the other room.*

mutton ['mʌtn] *n* meat from an adult sheep □ *a leg/shoulder of mutton.* ▪ **mutton dressed as lamb** GB a phrase used to describe an older person, especially a woman, who wears clothes that are more suitable for a younger person (disapproving use).

mutual ['mjuːtʃuəl] *adj* **-1.** [dislike, respect] that two people feel equally for each other; [help, assistance] that two people give to each other equally □ *"I wish I'd never met you!"* — *"The feeling's mutual."* **-2. a mutual friend/interest** a friend/interest that two or more people share □ *I believe we have a mutual acquaintance, Bill Jones.* □ *This contract is to our mutual benefit.*

mutual fund *n* US an investment company that sells shares in various other companies.

mutually ['mjuːtʃuəlɪ] *adv* **mutually convenient/acceptable etc** equally convenient/acceptable etc to both sides □ *The agreement was mutually beneficial to both parties concerned.* ▪ **mutually exclusive** a phrase used about two principles, two beliefs etc meaning that if one of them is true or exists it is impossible for the other one to be true or exist □ *The two options are not mutually exclusive.*

Muzak™ ['mjuːzæk] *n* recorded music that is played in stores, restaurants, airports etc.

muzzle ['mʌzl] ◇ *n* -1. [of a dog] the nose and mouth of an animal such as a dog. -2. [for controlling a dog] a covering that goes over the nose and mouth of an animal, usually a dog, to prevent it from biting people. -3. [of a gun] the long front part of a gun. ◇ *vt* -1. [dog, wolf] to put a muzzle on <an animal>. -2. [press, opposition] to use one's power to stop <sb> from expressing opinions in public.

muzzy ['mʌzɪ] (*compar* **muzzier**, *superl* **muzziest**) *adj* GB [head, memory] that is unclear or confused because of illness or drinking too much alcohol.

MVP (*abbr of* **most valuable player**) *n* US SPORT an honorary title given to the best player on a team.

MW *abbr of* **medium wave**.

my [maɪ] ◇ *det* -1. used to show that somebody or something is connected to, or belongs to, the person who is speaking or writing □ *My name is Sarah Green.* □ *Is that my coat or yours?* □ *I broke my leg.* □ *It wasn't my fault!* -2. used in titles □ *Yes, my Lord.* -3. used with terms of affection □ *What is it, my love?* ◇ *excl* used to show surprise (old-fashioned use) □ *My, you have changed!*

Myanmar ['mjænmɑːʳ] a country in Southeast Asia, between Bangladesh and Thailand. SIZE: 678,000 sq kms. POPULATION: 43,500,000 (*Myanmarese, Burmese*). CAPITAL: Yangon. LANGUAGE: Burmese. CURRENCY: kyat. OLD NAME: Burma.

mynah (bird) ['maɪnə(-)] *n* a large bird from Asia that is often kept as a pet, especially because it can learn to repeat words and phrases.

myopic [maɪ'ɒpɪk] *adj* [person] who cannot see clearly objects that are far away.

myriad ['mɪrɪəd] ◇ *n* **a myriad of people/things** a large number of people/things (formal use) □ *They watched myriads of birds flying south.* ◇ *adj*: *myriad stars/flies.*

myrrh [mɜːʳ] *n* a brown substance that comes from a tree and is used to make perfume and incense.

myrtle ['mɜːʳtl] *n* a small evergreen tree that grows in tropical areas, has glossy leaves and flowers with a sweet smell, and is used for its wood, oils, spices, and fruits.

myself [maɪ'self] *pron* -1. used when the object of a verb is the same person as the speaker or writer □ *I made myself comfortable.* □ *I blame myself for what happened.* -2. used after prepositions □ *I was annoyed with myself for being late.* □ *I looked at myself in the mirror.* -3. used to emphasize "I" □ *I myself never really liked him, though the rest of the family did.* ■ **I did it myself** I did it alone, with no help

from anybody else □ *"Those bookshelves are nice." — "I put them up myself."*

mysterious [mɪ'stɪərɪəs] *adj* -1. [illness, disappearance, sound] that cannot easily be explained or understood; [person, custom] that one knows little about and finds interesting □ *She left in mysterious circumstances.* □ *I admit he does have a mysterious side.* -2. **to be mysterious** [person] to prevent people from knowing what one is thinking or doing by not saying much about it, often making them curious □ *He was being very mysterious about his plans for the weekend.*

mysteriously [mɪ'stɪərɪəslɪ] *adv* [change, disappear] in a way that is not easily explained or understood; [smile, say] in a way that gives little information and makes people curious.

mystery ['mɪstərɪ] (*pl* **mysteries**) ◇ *adj* a **mystery guest/prize etc** a guest/prize etc that little or nothing is known about yet. ◇ *n* -1. something that one cannot understand or explain □ *The strange mystery of her disappearance/death/illness baffled everyone.* □ *It's a complete mystery to me!* -2. the qualities of something that one cannot explain or understand and that make it seem strange or interesting □ *the mystery of life/love* □ *The whole affair is surrounded by mystery.*

mystery story *n* an exciting story, usually about a murder.

mystery tour *n* a tour, especially by bus, on which the passengers do not know where they will be going.

mystic ['mɪstɪk] ◇ *adj* [power, rite, beauty] *see* **mysticism.** ◇ *n* a person who practices or believes in mysticism.

mystical ['mɪstɪkl] *adj* [experience, ceremony] that involves spiritual or unknown forces.

mysticism ['mɪstəsɪzm] *n* the practice of achieving direct contact with God, or another spiritual or unknown force, through meditation or prayer, in order to discover truth and knowledge.

mystified ['mɪstəfaɪd] *adj* [look, expression] that shows that one is confused by something that is difficult to understand; [person] who is unable to understand or explain something □ *The detective was completely mystified by the case.*

mystifying ['mɪstəfaɪɪŋ] *adj* [action, result] that is impossible to understand or explain.

mystique [mɪ'stiːk] *n* the mysterious quality that a person or activity has that makes them attractive to people □ *the mystique of ancient Egypt/Greta Garbo.*

myth [mɪθ] *n* -1. a story in which a historical event or the origin of a belief is explained □ *ancient/Greek myths and legends.* -2. a false belief, piece of information etc that many people think is correct □ *the myth of white supremacy.*

mythic ['mɪθɪk] *adj* [strength, adventure] that is like something in a myth.

mythical ['mɪθɪkl] *adj* -1. [character, tale, hero] that is connected with a myth □ *The stories* are full of mythical beings. **-2.** that many people think exists or is correct but is false in reality □ The media spoke of the mythical drop in unemployment and the end of the recession.

mythological [ˌmɪθəˈlɒdʒɪkl] adj [character, king, creature] that exists in mythology.

mythology [mɪˈθɒlədʒɪ] (pl **mythologies**) n **-1.** myths in general □ Roman/Celtic/Greek mythology. **-2.** a set of false beliefs □ A whole mythology has grown up around the West's destiny in the world.

myxomatosis [ˌmɪksəməˈtousəs] n a disease that can kill rabbits.

n [en] (pl **n's** OR **ns**), **N** [en] (pl **N's** OR **Ns**) n the fourteenth letter of the English alphabet.

◆ **N** abbr of **north**.

n/a, N/A (abbr of **not applicable**) a phrase used by somebody filling in a form to show that a particular part of the form does not concern them.

NA (abbr of **Narcotics Anonymous**) n a US organization of people who try to help each other to overcome their drug problems.

NAACP (abbr of **National Association for the Advancement of Colored People**) n **the NAACP** a US organization that aims to defend and improve the rights of African Americans.

nab [næb] (pt & pp **nabbed**, cont **nabbing**) vt (informal use) **-1.** [thief, robber] to catch <a criminal> □ He was nabbed before he could make his getaway. **-2.** [person] to approach <sb> and get their attention in order to ask or say something; [tickets, seat] to get <sthg> quickly while one has the opportunity □ I nabbed her as she was leaving the office. □ I'll nab a copy if I can.

nachos [ˈnɑːtʃouz] npl a Mexican dish made from spicy corn chips served with melted cheese.

nadir [ˈneɪdɪəʳ] n **-1.** [of somebody's career, popularity] the lowest point of something □ The President seems to have reached the nadir of his political career. **-2.** ASTRONOMY the point in the sky that is directly below where one is, on the other side of the Earth.

NAFTA [ˈnæftə] (abbr of **North American Free Trade Agreement**) n an agreement between the USA, Canada, and Mexico, signed in 1989, to allow goods to be sold and transported between the three countries more easily.

nag [næg] (pt & pp **nagged**, cont **nagging**) ◇ vt to annoy <sb> by continuously complaining or by trying to make them do something

they do not want to do □ He's always nagging me to buy a new car. □ In the end, I just nagged her into going. ◇ vi **-1.** [person] to nag somebody □ Oh, stop nagging! **-2. to nag at sb** [suspicion, conscience] to worry sb continuously even though there may be no real reason to worry □ Something had been nagging at me all day. ◇ n (informal use) **-1.** a person who nags. **-2.** an old horse.

Nagasaki [ˌnægəˈsɑːkɪ] a city in southwest Japan, where the second atomic bomb was dropped in 1945.

nagging [ˈnægɪŋ] adj **-1. a nagging fear/pain etc** a fear/pain etc that may not be very serious but that is difficult for one to stop feeling □ I had a nagging feeling that something was wrong. **-2.** [husband, wife] who nags all the time.

nail [neɪl] ◇ n **-1.** a piece of metal with a small, usually round, flat head and a long, thin, pointed end that is used to join things together, or to hang things from. ■ **to hit the nail on the head** to say something that is exactly right or that correctly explains something. **-2.** the thin, hard, flat area that grows over the end of each of one's fingers and toes □ I'm painting/cutting my nails. ◇ vt **to nail sthg to sthg** to attach sthg to sthg using a nail □ The notice had been nailed to the door for all to see.

◆ **nail down** vt sep **-1. to nail sthg down** [lid, carpet] to nail sthg firmly to something underneath. **-2. to nail sb down** to make sb agree to do something; to make sb say exactly what they are planning to do □ It's very difficult to nail her down to a particular time, she's always so busy. □ Keep trying to nail them down on what kind of offer they'd be interested in.

◆ **nail up** vt sep **to nail sthg up** [picture, notice] to nail sthg to a wall, door etc; [window, door] to prevent sthg from being opened by nailing pieces of wood across it.

nail-biting adj a **nail-biting contest/ending** a contest/ending that makes one feel very nervous or excited because one does not know how it will end □ The game came to a nail-biting finish.

nailbrush [ˈneɪlbrʌʃ] n a small stiff brush used to clean one's fingernails.

nail clippers n a small instrument for cutting nails that consists of two short blades and a flat metal piece that squeezes them together □ a pair of nail clippers.

nail file n a small rough piece of metal or cardboard used for making the ends of one's fingernails and toenails smooth and well shaped.

nail polish n a thick liquid, usually colored red or pink, that women paint on their fingernails and toenails to decorate them.

nail polish remover [-rɪmuːvəʳ] n a liquid used to remove nail polish.

nail scissors npl small scissors, often with curved blades, that are used for cutting one's fingernails and toenails □ a pair of nail scissors.

nail varnish *n* GB = nail polish.

naive, naïve [naɪˈiːv] *adj* [person] who does not have very much experience of life and so believes that people and things are as honest or simple as they appear; [idea, remark, behavior] that is too simple and has not been properly thought about □ *I was so naive at the time, I just didn't realize what I was letting myself in for.* □ *It's very naive to think they're not going to want some money for it.*

naivety, naïvety [naɪˈiːvətɪ] *n*: see **naive** □ *I can't believe your naivety sometimes!*

naked [ˈneɪkəd] *adj* -1. [person] who is wearing no clothes; [body, skin] that is not covered by any clothing □ *He stood naked in the middle of the room.* -2. **a naked flame/light etc** a flame/light etc that has no covering or protection around it. ■ **to see sthg with the naked eye** to see sthg without the help of an instrument such as a microscope or telescope □ *These organisms are invisible to the naked eye.* -3. **naked greed/aggression etc** greed/aggression etc that is not hidden or disguised □ *For the first time we were faced with the naked truth.*

Nam [næm] *n* US *abbr of* **Vietnam** (informal use).

name [neɪm] ◇ *n* -1. [of a person, place] the word or words that a particular person, place, animal, or object is known by □ *What's your name?* □ *My name's Jane Roberts.* □ *The article referred to them by name.* ■ **by the name of...** whose name is... □ *Is there anyone here by the name of John Baker?* ■ **in the name of sthg** in order to support or defend sthg □ *It was done in the name of peace/progress/justice.* ■ **in sb's name** a phrase used to mean that something has been ordered, reserved etc using the name of a particular person, usually so that it belongs to them, or is for their use □ *The car is registered in my name only.* □ *The ticket was issued in my boyfriend's name.* ■ **in name only** a phrase used to show that somebody or something has a particular name or title, but none of the responsibilities, qualities, duties etc that are connected with it □ *The company exists in name only.* □ *Gorbachev ruled the country in name only after the attempted coup.* ■ **to call sb names** to say unpleasant things about sb's character or physical appearance □ *He called her some horrible names.* -2. **a good/bad name** the good/bad opinion that people have of somebody or something because of what is known or said about them □ *He sold his story to the press in order to clear his name.* □ *The rudeness of the staff has given the restaurant a bad name.* ■ **to make a name for oneself** to become famous, usually for doing something well and as a result of hard work □ *She quickly made a name for herself in politics/as a top saleswoman.* -3. a famous person □ *All the big/famous names were at the party* □ *He's a big name in the art world.* ◇ *vt* -1. to give <sb/sthg> a name □ *Have they named the baby yet?* ■ **to name sb/sthg for sb/sthg** US, **to name sb/sthg after sb/sthg** to give sb/sthg the same name as sb/sthg else □ *They named the child for her great-aunt Cecily.* □ *The species was named after the scientist who discovered it.* -2. [victim, source] to say what

the name of <sb/sthg> is □ *She said one of her colleagues had insulted her, but did not name them.* □ *Who can name three presidents of the United States/all the colors of the rainbow?* -3. [price, successor, date] to choose <sb/sthg>, especially for an official position and tell other people about it □ *Have you named the (wedding) day yet?* □ *The new chairman will be named tomorrow.* □ *Marcia Willis has been named (as) marketing director.*

◆ **Name** *n* a person who makes money by guaranteeing insurance risks at Lloyd's of London. In the early 1990s there were many large insurance claims, and some of the Names lost a lot of their money.

namedropping [ˈneɪmdrɒpɪŋ] *n* the act of mentioning the names of famous people in conversation in order to impress other people.

nameless [ˈneɪmləs] *adj* -1. **who shall remain nameless** a phrase used to refer to somebody who has done something wrong without saying what their name is □ *One candidate, who shall remain nameless, tried to cheat.* -2. **a nameless author/poet etc** an author/a poet etc whose name is not known. -3. [fear, horror, crime] that is too difficult or unpleasant to describe.

namely [ˈneɪmlɪ] *adv* a word used to introduce more exact information about something that has just been mentioned □ *There's one thing we haven't discussed, namely money.*

nameplate [ˈneɪmpleɪt] *n* a small metal or plastic sign fixed to a door or wall that gives the name and often the business of the person or organization living or working in the place where it is.

namesake [ˈneɪmseɪk] *n* **sb's namesake** a person, especially a more famous person, who has the same name as sb.

Namibia [nəˈmɪbɪə] a country in southwestern Africa, on the Atlantic Ocean between Angola and South Africa. Namibia won its independence from South Africa in 1990. SIZE: 825,000 sq kms. POPULATION: 1,500,000 (*Namibians*). CAPITAL: Windhoek. LANGUAGE: English. CURRENCY: Namibian dollar.

nana [ˈnænə] *n* a word used to refer to or address one's grandmother (informal use).

nan bread [ˈnɑːn-] *n* a thick, flat, Indian bread.

nanny [ˈnænɪ] (*pl* **nannies**) *n* a woman whose job is to take care of the children in a family in their own home.

nanny goat *n* a female goat.

Nantucket [nænˈtʌkət] a US island off the coast of Massachusetts. It is a popular summer resort. POPULATION: 5,000.

nap [næp] (*pt* & *pp* **napped**, *cont* **napping**) ◇ *n* a short sleep during the day □ *I think I'll just take a quick nap.* □ *I really miss my afternoon nap.* ◇ *vi* to have a nap. ■ **to be caught napping** to be totally surprised when something happens, even though one should have been expecting it and ready to deal with it (informal use) □ *We must at all costs avoid being caught napping by our foreign competitors.*

napalm ['neɪpɑːm] *n* a thick jelly made from petroleum that burns very strongly and is used to make bombs □ *a napalm bomb.*

nape [neɪp] *n* **the nape (of one's neck)** the back of one's neck.

napkin ['næpkən] *n* a square of paper or cloth used at mealtimes to protect one's clothes and to clean one's hands and mouth □ *a paper/linen napkin.*

Napoleon [nə'poʊlɪən]: **Napoleon (Bonaparte)** (1769–1821) a French military and political leader who became emperor. He was defeated by British and Prussian forces at Waterloo.

nappy ['næpɪ] (*pl* **nappies**) *n* GB a piece of material, e.g. cloth or paper, that is wrapped around the waist and between the legs of a baby to collect urine and feces.

narcissi [nɑː'rsɪsaɪ] *plural of* **narcissus**.

narcissism ['nɑː'rsɪsɪzm] *n* the habit of admiring oneself or one's appearance too much.

narcissistic [ˌnɑː'rsə'sɪstɪk] *adj* [person] who shows too much admiration for themselves or their appearance.

narcissus [nɑː'rsɪsəs] (*pl* **narcissuses** OR **narcissi**) *n* a white or yellow flower that blooms in spring, similar to the daffodil.

Narcissus [nɑː'rsɪsəs] in Greek mythology, a beautiful young man who fell in love with his own reflection in a pond and was changed into a flower.

narcotic [nɑː'rkɒtɪk] *n* any addictive drug, e.g. opium, morphine, or heroin, that is used by doctors to help people to sleep and relieve pain, and that is illegal to buy or sell for recreational use □ *a narcotics dealer/smuggler.*

narrate [US 'næreɪt, GB nə'reɪt] *vt* to describe what is happening in <a story, movie, documentary> etc □ *The novel is narrated by the hero.*

narration [US næ'reɪʃn, GB nə-] *n* [of a story, movie, documentary] *see* **narrate**.

narrative ['nærətɪv] ◇ *n* [of an experience, journey] a story or account of a series of events □ *The narrative is difficult to follow.* ◇ *adj*: *a narrative poem* □ *the writer's narrative skill.*

narrator [US 'næreɪtr, GB nə'reɪtə] *n* a person who describes what is happening in a book, movie etc, and who seems to speak directly to the reader, viewer, or listener.

narrow ['næroʊ] ◇ *adj* **-1.** [lane, gap, bed] that is small from one side to the other, especially compared with its length □ *The street was narrow and badly lit.* □ *The stream is at its narrowest point here.* **-2.** [view, belief, mind] that has a limited scope or range (disapproving use) □ *My parents have a very narrow outlook when it comes to politics.* □ *It's that kind of narrow thinking that causes problems in the community.* **-3.** [escape, victory, majority] that one barely manages to do or get □ *He lost by a narrow margin.* ◇ *vt* **-1. to narrow one's eyes** to almost close one's eyes. **-2.** [difference, choice] to make <sthg> smaller □ *The Democrats have nar-* rowed the gap in the opinion polls. □ *That narrows the number of choices we have.* ◇ *vi* **-1.** [road, river, path] to become less wide □ *The highway narrowed to two lanes.* □ *'Road narrows.'* **-2.** [eyes] *His eyes narrowed in anger.* **-3.** [difference, choice] *Their lead narrowed to three points.*

◆ **narrow down** *vt sep* **to narrow sthg down** [possibilities, choice] to make the range of sthg smaller □ *They narrowed the list of candidates down to just two.*

narrow-gauge *adj* [track, line, railroad] that is less wide than the standard size.

narrowly ['næroʊlɪ] *adv* [win, escape, miss] by a very small number of points, amount, distance etc □ *They were narrowly defeated in the final ballot.*

narrow-minded [-'maɪndəd] *adj* [person] who is unwilling to accept or understand new or different ideas or opinions (disapproving use) □ *Her narrow-minded attitudes are infuriating.*

NASA ['næsə] (*abbr of* **National Aeronautics and Space Administration**) *n* the US government department responsible for space travel and research.

nasal ['neɪzl] *adj* **-1.** [voice, sound] that is made through the nose as well as through the mouth □ *He spoke with a nasal twang.* **-2.** ANATOMY that is connected with the nose □ *nasal passages* □ *nasal spray.*

nascent ['neɪsnt] *adj* [industry, hope, culture] that is just starting to develop (formal use).

Nashville ['næʃvɪl] a city in Tennessee, USA. It is the state capital and the center of the country and western music industry. POPULATION: 488,374.

Nasser ['næsər], **Gamal Abdel** (1918–1970) the first president of Egypt.

nastily [US 'næstɪlɪ, GB 'nɑːst-] *adv* [say, act] *see* **nasty**.

nastiness [US 'næstɪnəs, GB 'nɑːst-] *n* [of a person, remark] *see* **nasty** □ *There's really no excuse for such nastiness.*

nasturtium [nə'stɜː'rʃəm] (*pl* **nasturtiums**) *n* a flower that has red, orange, or yellow petals that can be eaten.

nasty [US 'næstɪ, GB 'nɑːstɪ] (*compar* **nastier**, *superl* **nastiest**) *adj* **-1.** [person, remark, behavior] that seems deliberately unkind □ *That was a nasty thing to say.* □ *He's got a nasty sense of humor.* **-2.** [smell, feeling, sight] that one finds unpleasant □ *The weather's been pretty nasty all week.* □ *I had a nasty shock when I read the report.* □ *They've bought some really nasty furniture.* **-3.** [problem, situation] that one finds very difficult, and often upsetting □ *It was a nasty decision to have to make.* **-4.** [cut, accident, infection] that is serious or looks painful □ *She had a nasty fall from her motorbike.* □ *That looks nasty; we'd better put some antiseptic on it.*

NAS/UWT (*abbr of* **National Association of Schoolmasters/Union of Women Teachers**) *n* **the NAS/UWT** a British labor union for teachers.

Natal [nə'tæl] a province of southeastern

South Africa. SIZE: 87,000 sq kms. POPULATION: 6,256,000. CAPITAL: Pietermaritzburg. MAIN CITY: Durban.

nation ['neɪʃn] *n* the people living in a country, especially when considered as a social, economic, and political unit □ *a strong/rich nation* □ *The President addressed the nation.* □ *the African nations.*

national ['næʃnəl] ◇ *adj* -1. [newspaper, event, strike] that reaches or affects a whole nation □ *His death is a national disaster.* □ *The next national news is at 5:40 pm.* -2. [characteristic, custom] that is connected with a particular nation □ *Cricket is their national sport.* ◇ *n* a citizen of a particular country □ *All European Community nationals should have the same rights.* □ *foreign/Chinese nationals.*

national anthem *n* the official song of a particular nation.

national curriculum *n* **the national curriculum** a plan, introduced by the British government in 1988, that defines the content of primary and secondary education in England and Wales.

national debt *n* the money that is owed by the government of a particular country.

national dress *n* the clothes associated with a particular country and worn by people of that country on special occasions.

National Front *n* **the National Front** in Britain, a small fascist and racist political party.

National Gallery: **the National Gallery** an important art gallery in Trafalgar Square, London.

national grid *n* GB a network that carries electricity between the main electric power stations.

National Guard *n* **the National Guard** in the USA, a group of people who are trained as soldiers by each state to help the army when necessary.

National Health Service *n* **the National Health Service** in Britain, the system of medical care that is run by the government and paid for by taxes, with the aim of providing cheap or free treatment for everybody □ *This dental treatment is not available on the National Health Service.*

National Heritage *n* **the Department of National Heritage** in Britain, the government department responsible for the arts, the media, sports, and leisure.

National Insurance *n* GB -1. the state system that gives money to people who are unemployed, ill, or old, and that is paid for by regular payments from employers and workers. -2. the money paid into the National Insurance system by employers and workers □ *My National Insurance contributions are up-to-date.*

nationalism ['næʃnəlɪzm] *n* -1. the desire of people in a particular region to be politically independent □ *Scottish/Irish/Basque nationalism.* -2. the belief that one's own country is better than other countries □ *A tide of nationalism is sweeping the country.*

nationalist ['næʃnələst] ◇ *n* a person who believes in nationalism. ◇ *adj*: *a nationalist movement/group.*

nationality [ˌnæʃə'næləti] (*pl* **nationalities**) *n* -1. membership of a particular nation □ *He has dual nationality.* □ *What's your nationality?* -2. a group of people of the same race, language etc □ *We have students here of all nationalities.*

nationalization [US ˌnæʃnələ'zeɪʃn, GB -aɪ'zeɪʃn] *n*: *see* **nationalize** □ *The issue of nationalization is no longer high on the agenda.*

nationalize, -ise ['næʃnəlaɪz] *vt* to put <a business, industry> etc under state control. NOTE: Compare **privatize**.

nationalized ['næʃnəlaɪzd] *adj* [industry] that is under state rather than private control.

National League *n* **the National League** one of the two most important baseball leagues in the USA.

National Lottery *n* **the National Lottery** in Britain, a televised lottery held each week, in which large cash prizes can be won.

national park *n* an area of countryside that is protected by the state for the public to visit and enjoy.

National Public Radio *n* a national radio network in the USA that is well known for its news programs.

National Savings Bank *n* **the National Savings Bank** a British government bank that operates through the Post Office and where people can invest small amounts of money by buying National Savings Certificates or Premium Bonds.

national service *n* a period of time that young people in some countries have to spend in the armed forces.

National Trust *n* **the National Trust** in Britain, an organization that owns and maintains large areas of countryside and many historic houses so that the public can enjoy them.

Nation of Islam *n* **the Nation of Islam** a group of African-American Muslims. They were very active in the Civil Rights Movement.

nation state *n* a country that is politically independent.

nationwide [ˌneɪʃn'waɪd] ◇ *adj* [survey, search] that takes place in every part of a particular country. ◇ *adv* in every part of a particular country □ *They do business nationwide.*

native ['neɪtɪv] ◇ *adj* -1. **one's native land/city** the land/city where one was born and grew up □ *After 30 years, she returned to her native Denmark.* -2. **one's native tongue** the language that one learns to speak as a child. -3. [plant, animal] that lives, grows etc naturally in a particular place and has not been brought there from somewhere else □ *The bird is native to the Black Sea region.* ◇ *n* -1. a person who was born and brought up in a particular place □ *a native of Hong Kong.* -2. a member of a race that was living in a country before other people, especially European settlers, arrived there (old-fashioned use).

Native American *n* a member of one of the

peoples who lived on the North American continent before Europeans arrived.

NOTE: In the USA, the term *Native American* is now preferred to *Indian*.

❦ NATIVE AMERICAN

The Native American peoples who lived in the USA before Europeans arrived each had their own language and way of life. From the 17th to the 19th centuries they had to defend their land against European settlers, often by fighting. Many died, either in battle or because of diseases brought to America by the Europeans. Many were forced to live on "reservations", pieces of land set aside specially for them. In the 20th century, the US government has tried to help Native Americans by giving them more rights. There has also been more and more interest shown in their history and traditional culture.

native speaker *n* a person who learns a particular language as their first language □ *native speakers of English.*

Nativity [nə'tɪvətɪ] *n* **the Nativity** the birth of Jesus, that is celebrated by Christians at Christmas.

nativity play *n* a play about the birth of Jesus that is performed around Christmas time by children.

NATO ['neɪtoʊ] (*abbr of* **North Atlantic Treaty Organization**) *n* an organization of countries, including the USA, Canada, and most EU countries, that have agreed to defend each other if one of them is attacked.

natter ['nætər] GB (*informal use*) ◇ *vi* to talk in a friendly way and for a long time about unimportant things. ◇ *n* **to have a natter** to natter.

natty ['nætɪ] (*compar* **nattier**, *superl* **nattiest**) *adj* [person, suit] that is neat and stylish in appearance □ *You look really natty in that outfit.* □ *That's a natty little gadget.*

natural ['nætʃrəl] ◇ *adj* **-1.** [feeling, desire, reaction] that is understandable and normal in a particular situation □ *It's only natural that you should feel angry.* **-2.** [person] who is relaxed and behaves in their usual way □ *His manner when interviewing people was natural and easy.* □ *She always manages to look natural in photos.* **-3.** [ability, instinct, talent] that one has from an early age and does not have to learn □ *a natural flair for drawing.* **-4.** [athlete, musician, leader] whose personality and skills make them very good at a particular activity □ *She's a natural organizer.* **-5.** [phenomenon, habitat, disaster] that is connected with nature □ *the natural world.* **-6.** [fibers, ingredients, flavoring] that is not made from artificial substances □ *the breakfast cereal that is full of natural goodness.* **-7. sb's natural parents** sb's real parents, compared with parents who have adopted or fostered them □ *She is trying to find out who her natural parents are.* **-8.** MUSIC [note] that is not sharp or flat. **-9.** *phrase* **to die of natural causes** to die because of illness

or old age, not because of murder, suicide, or an accident.

◇ *n* **to be a natural** to be very good at doing something without having to make any effort □ *You should take up basketball seriously, you're a natural.*

natural childbirth *n* a way of making childbirth less painful that uses relaxation and special breathing techniques rather than drugs.

natural gas *n* a colorless gas that is found underground or under the sea, and is used as fuel for cooking and heating.

natural history *n* the study of animals and plants □ *a natural history museum.*

naturalist ['nætʃrəlɪst] *n* a person who studies plants and animals.

naturalize, -ise ['nætʃrəlaɪz] *vt* **to be naturalized** to become a citizen of a country that one was not born in.

naturally ['nætʃrəlɪ] *adv* **-1. naturally,...** a word used to show that one thinks something is understandable and not surprising in a particular situation □ *Naturally, I was disappointed not to win.* □ *She was naturally reluctant to comment.* □ *"Will you be there?" — "Naturally."* **-2.** [behave, talk] in a natural manner □ *He laughed and joked naturally, with no obvious sign of strain.* **-3. naturally talented/flavored etc** that has a natural talent/flavor etc □ *Is your hair naturally blonde?* □ *He's a naturally gifted athlete.* ■ **to come naturally to sb** to be easy for sb to do, because they are good at it or used to doing it □ *Office management just comes naturally to him.*

natural resources *npl* [of a country, region] all the land, forests, sources of energy, and useful minerals that exist in a particular place and can be used.

natural science *n* biology, chemistry, and physics as a single subject for studying.

natural wastage *n* GB the gradual reduction in the size of a workforce that happens when employees retire or resign and are not replaced □ *Management says 50% of the staff cuts will be achieved through natural wastage, and another 50% through lay-offs.*

natural yogurt *n* yogurt that has no added flavorings.

nature ['neɪtʃər] *n* **-1.** everything in the physical world, including plants, animals, oceans, and rocks, that is not made by people; all events and processes that are not caused by people □ *the laws of nature* □ *nature study.* **-2. the nature of sthg** the kind of thing sthg is □ *matters of a serious/personal nature* □ *What is the nature of the injury/complaint?* □ *Such is the nature of politics.* □ *These accusations are, by their very nature, difficult to prove.* **-3. sb's nature** the main qualities that make sb a particular kind of person □ *She has a very sweet nature.* □ *He wouldn't do that, it's not in his nature.* □ *I've always been an optimist by nature.*

nature reserve *n* an area of land where plants and animals, especially rare ones, are protected and can be seen by visitors.

nature trail *n* a path in a park or through the countryside with signs giving information about the plants, animals etc that can be seen there.

naughty ['nɔːtɪ] (*compar* **naughtier**, *superl* **naughtiest**) *adj* -1. [child, dog] that behaves badly or is disobedient □ *You naughty boy!* □ *That was very naughty of him.* -2. GB [joke, postcard] that one thinks is a little rude or shocking because it refers to sex.

nausea ['nɔːzjə] *n* the unpleasant feeling that one has just before one vomits □ *The symptoms are headaches and nausea.*

nauseam ['nɔːzɪæm] → **ad nauseam.**

nauseate ['nɔːzɪeɪt] *vt* -1. [smell, sight] to make <sb> want to vomit. -2. [person, behavior] to make <sb> feel very disgusted and angry.

nauseating ['nɔːzɪeɪtɪŋ] *adj* -1. [smell, taste] that makes one want to vomit □ *There was the most nauseating stink of rotten food.* -2. [hypocrisy, violence] that makes one feel very disgusted and angry □ *It's quite nauseating watching him trying to be nice to the boss.*

nauseous ['nɔːzjəs] *adj* **to feel nauseous** to feel as if one is going to vomit.

nautical ['nɔːtɪkl] *adj* that is connected with sailing, ships, or sailors □ *The nautical look is in fashion this year.*

nautical mile *n* a unit (1,853 meters) used at sea for measuring distance.

Navajo ['nævəhoʊ] (*pl* **Navajo**) *n* a member of a Native American people living in the southwestern USA; the language of this people.

naval ['neɪvl] *adj* that is used by or connected with the navy of a country □ *a naval dockyard* □ *in naval uniform.*

naval officer *n* an officer in the navy of a country.

nave [neɪv] *n* the main part of a church, where people sit.

navel ['neɪvl] *n* the small round hollow or lump just below one's stomach, formed after the umbilical cord is cut at birth.

navigable ['nævɪgəbl] *adj* [river, canal] that ships or boats can travel along □ *The Hudson is navigable as far as Albany.*

navigate ['nævɪgeɪt] ◇ *vt* -1. [ship] to guide <a ship, plane> etc along the correct route using maps or special equipment □ *They needed a pilot to navigate the ship through the narrow channel.* -2. [sea] to sail across <a stretch of water>. ◇ *vi* to find the way to a place in a ship, plane, or car using maps or special equipment □ *I'll drive and you navigate.*

navigation [,nævə'geɪʃn] *n* the act or skill of navigating □ *The bad weather made navigation difficult.* □ *a navigation aid.*

navigator ['nævɪgeɪtər] *n* a person who is responsible for the direction that a ship, plane, or car takes.

navy ['neɪvɪ] (*pl* **navies**) ◇ *n* -1. the branch of a country's armed forces that fights at sea; the ships it uses □ *My brother is in the navy.* -2. = **navy blue.** ◇ *adj* = **navy blue.**

navy bean *n* US a small white bean.

navy blue ◇ *adj* very dark blue. ◇ *n* a very dark blue color.

Nazareth ['næzərəθ] a town in northern Israel that is important to Christians because they believe that Jesus lived there. POPULATION: 39,400.

Nazi ['nɑːtsɪ] (*pl* **Nazis**) ◇ *n* a member of the right-wing political party led by Adolf Hitler that ruled Germany from 1933 to 1945. ◇ *adj*: *Nazi propaganda/sympathizers.*

NB -1. (*abbr of* **nota bene**) a word used in writing to make the reader pay special attention to what follows. -2. *abbr of* **New Brunswick.**

NBA *n* -1. (*abbr of* **National Basketball Association**) **the NBA** the organization in charge of professional basketball in the USA. -2. (*abbr of* **National Boxing Association**) **the NBA** one of the US organizations that runs professional boxing competitions.

NBC (*abbr of* **National Broadcasting Company**) *n* a national television network in the USA.

NBS (*abbr of* **National Bureau of Standards**) *n* **the NBS** the organization that sets standards for units of measurement in the USA.

nc, n/c *abbr of* **no charge.**

NC *abbr of* **North Carolina.**

NC17 [,ensiːsəvn'tiːn] a symbol for movies and video tapes in the USA, showing that children under 17 are only allowed to watch them if an adult is with them.

NCO *n abbr of* **noncommissioned officer.**

NCU (*abbr of* **National Communications Union**) *n* **the NCU** a British labor union for mailmen and telecommunications workers.

ND *abbr of* **North Dakota.**

NE -1. *abbr of* **Nebraska.** -2. *abbr of* **northeast.**

near [nɪər] ◇ *adj* -1. [place, object] that is only a small distance away from where one is or where one lives □ *There's a bank very near to our office.* □ *The nearest town is 20 miles away.* -2. [event, date] that will happen soon □ *The deadline is getting nearer.* ■ **in the near future** soon □ *I don't see there being much change in the near future.* -3. **a near relative** OR **relation** somebody who is closely related to one □ *My nearest living relative is a cousin in Australia.* -4. **near chaos/darkness** almost total chaos/darkness □ *The news created near panic on the Stock Exchange.* ■ **a near disaster** a disaster that almost happened but did not. -5. *phrase* **sb/sthg is the nearest thing to...** sb/sthg is the person or thing that is most like something else, though not exactly the same □ *She's the nearest thing we've got to a qualified accountant.* ◇ *adv* -1. [come, stand, live] only a small distance away □ *Bring your chair nearer!* -2. **to come** OR **draw** OR **get near** to be going to happen soon □ *Christmas is getting nearer.* -3. **near perfect/disastrous etc** almost perfect/disastrous etc □ *It was a near impossible task.* ◇ *vt* -1. [place] to come close or closer to <a place> □ *We're nearing our destination.* -2. [state] to have almost reached <a particular

stage or state> □ *The project is finally nearing completion.*

◆ **near (to)** *prep* **-1.** [to a person, place] only a small distance away from <sb/sthg> □ *He went and stood near (to) her.* □ *She lives nearer the town than we do.* **-2.** [to an event, date] a short time before or after <sthg> □ *We can't go on Tuesday, it's too near to my exams.* □ *I'll let you know nearer the time.* **-3. to be** OR **come near to sthg** to have almost reached sthg □ *Their relationship came near to breaking-point.* □ *We are no nearer to solving the dispute.* **-4. to be near to tears/exhaustion etc** to be almost crying/exhausted etc □ *She was near to tears as she tried to explain what had happened.*

nearby [nɪəˈbaɪ] ◇ *adj* [hospital, town] that is only a short distance from where one is, or from the place one has just mentioned □ *We stopped at a nearby hotel.* ◇ *adv*: *He was standing nearby at the time of the explosion.* □ *Fortunately, there was a garage nearby.*

Near East = **Middle East**.

nearly [ˈnɪəlɪ] *adv* **-1. nearly ready/complete** almost ready/complete □ *By this time it was nearly dark.* □ *Nearly everyone who was invited came.* □ *He nearly died in the accident.* □ *I very nearly dropped it.* **-2. not nearly** used to say that something is not even close to being true □ *I'm not nearly finished yet.* □ *You haven't done nearly enough work.* □ *Their computer system isn't nearly as efficient as ours.*

near miss *n* **-1.** SPORT a shot that just misses the target. **-2.** a situation in which two vehicles or aircraft nearly crash into each other.

nearside [ˈnɪəsaɪd] GB ◇ *n* the side of a vehicle that is nearest to the edge of the road when one is driving. ◇ *adj*: *the nearside wheel/light.*
NOTE: Compare **offside**.

nearsighted [ˌnɪəˈsaɪtəd] *adj* [person] who is unable to see clearly things that are far away.

neat [niːt] *adj* **-1.** [room, bundle] that has been arranged in an orderly way and is nice to look at □ *Kim has very neat handwriting.* □ *The apartment's looking very neat and tidy.* **-2.** [person] who is smart and clean and likes things to be in the right place □ *I always like to look neat when I go out.* □ *My assistant is very neat and efficient.* **-3.** [solution, maneuver, idea] that is clever/useful □ *They've found a neat way around the problem.* **-4.** [whiskey, gin] that is served on its own without ice, water, or another drink added □ *How do you want your drink, neat or with ice?* **-5.** US a word used to say that one thinks something is very good (informal use) □ *They've brought out a really neat new video game.*

neatly [ˈniːtlɪ] *adv* **-1.** [arrange, dress, fold] in an orderly and careful way. **-2.** [solve, fit] in a way that is clever and useful □ *The device fits neatly in a suitcase.*

neatness [ˈniːtnəs] *n* [of handwriting, a person, room] *see* **neat**.

Nebraska [nəˈbræskə] a US state, consisting mainly of farmland. ABBREVIATION: NE. SIZE:

200,000 sq kms. POPULATION: 1,578,385 (*Nebraskans*). CAPITAL: Lincoln.

Nebuchadnezzar [US ˌnebəkədˈnezr, GB ˌnebjukədˈnezə] (630–562 BC) King of Babylon from 605 to 562 BC. In the Bible, he destroyed Jerusalem and sent the Jews into exile in Babylon.

nebulous [ˈnebjələs] *adj* [idea, concept] that is not clear (formal use).

NEC (*abbr of* **National Exhibition Centre**) *n* **the NEC** a large conference center and exhibition hall near Birmingham, England.

necessarily [ˌnesəˈserəlɪ] *adv* **-1. not necessarily** a phrase used to show that it is possible but not certain that something is the case □ *Not everything you read in the papers is necessarily true.* □ *"Does that mean we've lost?"* — *"Not necessarily."* **-2.** a word used to show that something must happen and cannot be avoided □ *Finding a suitable candidate is necessarily a lengthy process.*

necessary [ˈnesəserɪ] *adj* **-1.** [skills, arrangements] that one has to have or do in order to get a particular result or effect □ *Is it absolutely necessary to make all that noise?* □ *Food is necessary for survival.* □ *Many candidates lack the necessary qualifications.* □ *I hope it won't be necessary for you to have an operation.* **-2.** [result, connection] that is logical and cannot be avoided in a particular situation □ *A period of uncertainty was seen as a necessary consequence of the crisis.*

◆ **if necessary** *adv* if it becomes necessary □ *I am prepared to go to prison for my beliefs, if necessary.*

necessitate [nəˈsesəteɪt] *vt* to make <sthg> necessary, especially sthg difficult or sthg that one had hoped to avoid (formal use) □ *This kind of offense necessitates a very specific kind of punishment.* □ *Poor sales figures necessitated a rethink of our overall strategy.*

necessity [nəˈsesətɪ] (*pl* **necessities**) *n* **-1.** something that one needs in a particular situation, e.g. in order to be able to live or do a job properly □ *I always travel with only the most basic necessities.* **-2.** a situation that makes something unavoidable or necessary □ *I did it out of necessity, not choice.* □ *There's no necessity for such drastic measures.*

◆ **of necessity** *adv* a phrase used to say that something has to happen in a particular way and cannot be avoided □ *It is, of necessity, a rather superficial overview of the subject.*

neck [nek] ◇ *n* **-1.** [of a person, animal] the part of the body between the head and the shoulders □ *She had a long, thin neck.* □ *Sweat trickled down the back of my neck.* ■ **to be up to one's neck in sthg** [in work, debt, trouble] to be very involved in sthg (informal use) □ *Look, I can't talk now, I'm up to my neck in paperwork.* ■ **to be breathing down sb's neck** to be watching sb all the time while they are working to check what they are doing (informal use) □ *I'm fed up with him breathing down my neck every time there's a deadline to meet.* ■ **to stick one's neck out** to say or do something that could go wrong, or could be criticized by

other people □ *I may be sticking my neck out here, but I think you've made the wrong choice.* -2. [of a garment] the part of a shirt, dress etc that goes around or just below the neck □ *a high/low/round neck.* -3. [of an object] the narrow part at the top of an object such as a bottle or guitar.
◇ *vi* [couple] to kiss and cuddle in a sexual way (informal use).

neck and neck *adj* **to be neck and neck** [runners, horses, cars] to be very close to each other in position, points etc and have an equal chance of winning □ *The two parties were neck and neck in the polls.*

neckerchief ['nekə'tʃɪf] (*pl* **neckerchiefs** OR **neckerchieves** [-tʃiːvz]) *n* a square scarf that is worn around the neck and usually tied with a knot.

necklace ['nekləs] *n* a piece of jewelry, e.g. a string of beads, worn by a woman or girl around her neck □ *a pearl necklace.*

neckline ['neklaɪn] *n* the shape of the neck of a woman's blouse, dress, or jacket □ *a dress with a low/flattering neckline.*

necktie ['nektaɪ] *n* US a long narrow piece of cloth that men wear around their neck and over their shirt with a knot at the front.

nectar ['nektə'] *n* a sweet sticky liquid found in flowers that bees collect to make honey.

nectarine ['nektəriːn] *n* a fruit that is like a peach but has a smoother skin.

NEDC (*abbr of* **National Economic Development Council**) *n* **the NEDC** an organization consisting of representatives of government, management, and labor unions, that makes proposals on economic policy in Britain.

née [neɪ] *adj* a word used after a married woman's name and in front of the family name she had before she married □ *Mrs. Eileen Robson, née Hunter.*

need [niːd] ◇ *n* -1. **sb's needs** what sb wants or must have to keep them healthy, satisfied, comfortable etc □ *$500 should be enough for our immediate needs.* □ *He saw to our every need.* -2. **the need for sthg** a situation in which it is necessary to have or do sthg □ *Industry recognizes the need for more investment in training.* □ *I felt the need to talk to someone.* -3. *phrases* **to be in need** to be very poor, hungry, homeless etc □ *He spent his life helping children in need.* ■ **to be in need of sthg** to need sthg □ *Some rooms are badly in need of redecoration.* □ *The helpline is for people in urgent need of legal advice.* ■ **to have no need of sthg** not to need sthg □ *I have no need of your sympathy.* ■ **there's no need to explain/apologize** it is not necessary for you to explain/apologize □ *There's no need for you to show me out, I know the way.* ■ **there's no need to shout** please stop shouting □ *There's no need to get mad at me!*
◇ *aux vb* -1. **she doesn't need to know** it is not necessary for her to know □ *It needn't take very long.* □ *I needn't have bothered.* ■ **do we need to go?** is it necessary for us to go? -2. **you don't need to be afraid** there is no reason that you should be afraid □ *If you keep quiet, no one need ever know.*

◇ *vt* -1. [money, food, advice] to want <sb/sthg that is important or useful and that one does not have> □ *I need your help with this report.* □ *The company badly needs a period of stability.* -2. **we need to talk/decide** it is necessary and important for us to talk/decide. ■ **it needs patience/hard work** patience/hard work is necessary if it is to be successful □ *Your suggestion needs careful consideration.* -3. **it needs a clean** OR **cleaning** it is necessary to clean it □ *This shirt needs ironing.* □ *The engine needs a complete overhaul.*

◆ **if need be** *adv* if it becomes necessary □ *We can call again later if need be.*

needle ['niːdl] ◇ *n* -1. [for sewing] a small, very thin piece of metal used for sewing. It has a sharp point at one end and a hole at the other where thread is passed through. ■ **it's like looking for a needle in a haystack** a phrase used when it is very hard to find somebody or something, e.g. because they are among many other people or things. -2. [for knitting] one of a pair of long plastic or metal sticks with blunt points that are used for knitting. -3. [on a record player] the small pointed device on a record player that touches the record and picks up the sound. -4. MEDICINE the hollow metal point at the end of a medical syringe. -5. [on an instrument] the moving pointer on an instrument such as a compass or speedometer. -6. [on a tree] the long, thin, sharp leaf of a tree such as the pine or fir.
◇ *vt* [person] to keep annoying <sb> deliberately (informal use).

needlecord ['niːdlkɔː'd] *n* a kind of cloth that is like fine corduroy □ *a needlecord skirt.*

needlepoint ['niːdlpɔɪnt] *n* a kind of embroidery in which patterns are sewn onto canvas cloth using wool threads and a blunt needle.

needless ['niːdləs] *adj* [suffering, anxiety, trouble] that is not necessary and could have been avoided □ *I'm afraid you've been put to needless expense.* ■ **needless to say,...** a phrase used to show that one thinks what one is about to say is obvious □ *Needless to say, it never actually happened.* □ *And in the end, needless to say, they changed their minds.*

needlessly ['niːdləslɪ] *adv* [suffer, worry] *see* **needless**.

needlework ['niːdlwɜː'k] *n* the activity of sewing; something made in this way.

needn't ['niːdnt] = **need not**.

needy ['niːdɪ] (*compar* **needier**, *superl* **neediest**) ◇ *adj* [person, family] that is very poor. ◇ *npl* **the needy** people who are very poor.

nefarious [nə'feərɪəs] *adj* [person, purpose] that is evil and immoral (formal use).

negate [nɪ'geɪt] *vt* [efforts, achievement] to prevent <sthg> from having the intended effect (formal use).

negation [nɪ'geɪʃn] *n*: *see* **negate** □ *It would be the negation of everything we've fought for.*

negative ['negətɪv] ◇ *adj* -1. [answer, reply] that says "no" rather than "yes". -2. [person, reaction, attitude] that considers only the bad aspects of something □ *I think you're being too negative about the whole thing.* **-3.** [effect, advice] that is not helpful or useful. **-4.** [test, result] that shows no signs of the particular disease or medical condition one is looking for. **-5.** [number, amount, growth] that is less than zero.

◇ *n* **-1.** PHOTOGRAPHY a piece of film from which photographs are developed and which shows dark areas as light and light areas as dark. **-2.** LINGUISTICS a word, statement etc that expresses the idea of "no" or "not". ■ **to answer in the negative** to say "no" in answer to a question.

neglect [nɪˈglekt] ◇ *n* **-1.** [by a parent, owner] the failure to take care of somebody or something □ *Both children were suffering from neglect.* **-2.** [in a garden, building] the condition of something that has not been taken care of properly □ *The hotel, empty since the 1980s, has fallen into a state of neglect.*

◇ *vt* **-1.** [child, place, animal] not to take care of <sb/sthg> properly □ *You've been neglecting your health, I see.* **-2.** [fact, detail] not to take <sthg> seriously enough □ *They neglected a number of important points.* **-3.** [one's work, duty] to fail to do <sthg> properly □ *You can't afford to neglect your studies like this.* ■ **to neglect to do sthg** not to do sthg because one forgets or is careless □ *They neglected to tell me that the agreement had already been signed.* □ *There's one point I neglected to mention.*

neglected [nɪˈglektəd] *adj* [child, garden, artist] that has not received enough attention □ *The book lay neglected in front of him.* □ *Are you feeling neglected?*

neglectful [nɪˈglektfl] *adj* [person] who neglects somebody or something □ *She became neglectful of her appearance/duties.*

negligee [US ˌneglə'ʒeɪ, GB 'neglɪʒeɪ] *n* a light thin robe worn by women over a nightgown □ *a black chiffon negligee.*

negligence ['neglɪdʒəns] *n: see* **negligent** □ *The owner of the club was sued for negligence.*

negligent ['neglɪdʒənt] *adj* [person] who does not give proper care or attention to somebody or something □ *The tribunal ruled that he had been negligent in not observing the correct safety procedures.* □ *Ms Fenini faces a charge of negligent conduct.*

negligently ['neglɪdʒəntlɪ] *adv* [act, behave] *see* **negligent**.

negligible ['neglɪdʒəbl] *adj* [amount, difference, effect] that is too small to be important □ *The impact on sales would be negligible.*

negotiable [nɪˈgoʊʃjəbl] *adj* [price, salary] that can be discussed and changed by negotiation □ *The terms of the lease are negotiable.*

negotiate [nɪˈgoʊʃieɪt] ◇ *vt* **-1.** [agreement, settlement, terms] to decide on <sthg> jointly after discussing it together, usually in an official way □ *The two sides have negotiated a ceasefire.* **-2.** [obstacle, river] to succeed in getting past <a place>, especially when skill or care is needed □ *We negotiated the rapids with surprising ease.* ◇ *vi* to discuss something,

usually officially, in order to reach an agreement □ *Union representatives are negotiating with management for a 4% raise.*

negotiation [nɪˌgoʊʃɪˈeɪʃn] *n* the process in which people with opposed interests discuss something in order to reach an agreement on it □ *These terms are not open to negotiation.*

◆ **negotiations** *npl* negotiation, usually in politics or business, that takes place in a series of meetings that have been specially arranged □ *peace negotiations in the Middle East.* □ *We will not enter into negotiations unless a guarantee of safety can be given.*

negotiator [nɪˈgoʊʃieɪtəʳ] *n* a person whose job is to represent their side in negotiations.

Negro▼ ['niːgroʊ] (*pl* **Negroes**) *n* a person who belongs to a black African race (offensive use).

Nehru ['neəruː], **Jawaharlal** (1889–1964) India's first prime minister, from 1947 to 1964.

neigh [neɪ] *vi* [horse] to make a long high-pitched noise.

neighbor US, **neighbour** GB ['neɪbəʳ] *n* **-1.** a person who lives near to one's own home, especially next door, and who one knows for this reason □ *my next-door neighbor* □ *We've been neighbors for years.* **-2. one's neighbor** a person who is sitting or standing beside one □ *Take your neighbor by the hand.* **-3.** [of a country, state] the country, state etc next to a particular country, state etc □ *Russia and its Baltic neighbors, Estonia, Lithuania, and Latvia.*

neighborhood US, **neighbourhood** GB ['neɪbəʳhʊd] *n* **-1.** a particular part of a town or city where people live □ *a quiet/poor neighborhood* □ *I didn't know you lived in this neighborhood!* **-2. in the neighborhood** in the area that is very close to a particular place or to where one lives □ *We were in the neighborhood so we thought we'd pay you a visit.*

◆ **in the neighborhood of** *prep* approximately □ *It costs in the neighborhood of $3,000.*

neighborhood watch *n* a system that encourages people who live in an area to watch each other's houses in order to prevent crime.

neighboring US, **neighbouring** GB ['neɪbərɪŋ] *adj* [house, country] that is situated nearby □ *There had been problems in some of the neighboring towns as well.*

neighborly US, **neighbourly** GB ['neɪbəʳlɪ] *adj* [person] who is kind, friendly, and helpful toward their neighbors □ *That's very neighborly of you!*

neither ['niːðəʳ, 'naɪðəʳ] ◇ *pron* **neither of them** none of two people, places, or things □ *We have two printers, and neither of them is working.* □ *"Do you want red or white wine?" — "Neither, I'd prefer a beer."*

◇ *det* [person, place, thing] *Neither team deserves to win.* □ *Neither car has all the things I'm looking for.*

◇ *adv* used to add a negative statement to another negative statement □ *She's not happy* and neither is he. □ *"I don't smoke."* — *"Neither do I."*

◇ *conj* **neither...nor**... used to join together two equally important negative statements □ *I could neither eat nor sleep.* □ *That remark is neither accurate nor fair.* ■ **that's neither here nor there** that is not relevant or important □ *What Jack thinks about it is neither here nor there.*

Nelson ['nelsən], **Horatio** (1758–1805) a British admiral who won several battles at sea against the French navy, including the battle of Trafalgar, where he was killed.

neo- ['ni:ou] *prefix* added to words to refer to something that is a modern form of something that existed in the past □ *a neo-Nazi organization.*

neoclassical [,ni:ou'klæsɪkl] *adj* [art, artist, architecture] that copies and adapts the styles of ancient Greece and Rome.

neolithic [,ni:ə'lɪθɪk] *adj* [settlement, culture] that is connected with the period at the end of the Stone Age when people began to settle in villages and farms, still using stone tools and weapons.

neologism [nɪ'ɒlədʒɪzm] *n* a new word, expression, or meaning in a language.

neon ['ni:ɒn] *n* a colorless gas with no smell that is used in glass tubes to make bright lights. SYMBOL: Ne.

neon light *n* a bright electric light made from a glass tube with neon gas inside.

neon sign *n* a sign made of neon lights, usually advertising something.

Nepal [nə'pɔ:l] a country in central southern Asia, in the Himalayas, between Tibet and India. SIZE: 140,000 sq kms. POPULATION: 19,600,000 (*Nepalese*). CAPITAL: Katmandu. LANGUAGE: Nepali. CURRENCY: Nepalese rupee.

Nepalese [,nepə'li:z] *npl & adj*: see **Nepal**.

Nepali [nə'pɔ:lɪ] *n* the official language of Nepal.

nephew ['nefju:] *n* a son of one's brother or sister; a son of the brother or sister of one's husband or wife.

nepotism ['nepətɪzm] *n* the practice of using one's power and authority to give jobs to members of one's family.

Neptune¹ ['neptju:n] the planet in the solar system that is the eighth furthest from the Sun.

Neptune² the Roman god of the sea.

nerd [nɜːʳd] *n* a person who one thinks is awkward, unattractive, and unfashionable (informal use).

Nero ['nɪərou] (37–68 AD) Emperor of Rome from 54 to 68 AD. He had many people killed, including his mother and his wife.

nerve [nɜːʳv] *n* -1. ANATOMY a long thin fiber in the body, one of thousands that carry messages to and from the brain about physical feelings such as heat or pain □ *nerve endings.* -2. courage and calm when doing something difficult or frightening □ *He kept his nerve throughout the ordeal.* □ *I was going to do it, but I*

lost my nerve. -3. **to have a nerve** to behave in a way that seems unreasonable or unfair □ *They've parked in our driveway again! What a nerve!* □ *The bank had the nerve to bounce my check.*

◆ **nerves** *npl* nervous, anxious, or tense feelings □ *I had a drink to calm my nerves.* □ *an attack of nerves.* ■ **to get on sb's nerves** to annoy and irritate sb very much (informal use) □ *That man really gets on my nerves!*

nerve center *n* the place from where the activities of an organization, system etc are controlled.

nerve gas *n* a poisonous gas used in war that damages the nervous system of people and can kill them.

nerve-racking [-rækɪŋ] *adj* [experience, wait] that makes one feel very tense and worried □ *My piano exam was pretty nerve-racking.*

nervous ['nɜːʳvəs] *adj* -1. [person] who is feeling worried and afraid; [smile, laugh] that shows one is feeling worried or afraid □ *I was very nervous about the interview.* □ *I've always been nervous of dogs.* -2. [person, nature, animal] that is easily worried, frightened, or upset □ *This program is unsuitable for viewers of a nervous disposition.* -3. [disease] that is caused by damage to the body's nerves.

nervous breakdown *n* a period of mental illness that is caused by too much work or stress and makes somebody unable to work, sleep, go out etc □ *In the end he had a complete nervous breakdown.*

nervously ['nɜːʳvəslɪ] *adv* [talk, laugh, look] see **nervous** □ *He sat nervously on the edge of his seat.*

nervousness ['nɜːʳvəsnəs] *n*: see **nervous** □ *She showed no sign of nervousness.*

nervous system *n* all the nerves in the body, including the brain and spinal cord, that control a person's movements and feelings.

nervous wreck *n* a person who seems extremely tense, nervous, and worried (informal use).

nervy ['nɜːʳvɪ] (*compar* **nervier**, *superl* **nerviest**) *adj* -1. US [person] who is confident in a way that is likely to offend other people. -2. GB [person] who is often tense and anxious, and is easily upset (informal use).

nest [nest] ◇ *n* -1. [for a bird] a place that birds make to lay their eggs in, usually using twigs, leaves, mud, feathers etc □ *a robin's nest.* -2. [for an animal, insect] a place that some kinds of animals and insects make to lay their eggs in or to give birth to young □ *a wasps' nest.* -3. **a nest of tables** a set of small tables of different sizes, that fit underneath each other. ◇ *vi* [bird] to build a nest and start laying eggs in it.

nest egg *n* an amount of money that one saves for a particular purpose, e.g. to use when one retires.

nestle ['nesl] *vi* -1. **to nestle against sb/sthg** to make oneself comfortable by pressing close against sb/sthg soft and warm □ *The kittens nestled against their mother.* -2. [house, village] to be situated in a place that looks sheltered and protected □ *The village lies nestling at the foot of a hill.*

nestling ['neslɪŋ] *n* a bird that is too young to leave its nest.

net [net] (*pt* & *pp* **netted**, *cont* **netting**) ◇ *n* **-1.** a piece of netting, often in the shape of a large bag, used to catch fish, insects etc □ *a fishing net.* **-2.** cloth made of very fine threads that lets the light pass through. **-3.** TENNIS the long piece of netting across the middle of a tennis court, over which the players have to hit the ball □ *McEnroe hit his return into the net.* **-4.** SOCCER & HOCKEY the piece of netting into which the ball has to be hit to score a goal □ *The ball ended up in the back of the net.*
◇ *adj* **-1.** [amount, income, pay] that is left after all costs, taxes etc have been paid □ *The company has net assets of $1 million.* **-2. net weight** the weight of something without the container or packaging □ *Net weight 500g.* **-3. the net result** the final result □ *The net result of all the changes was greater efficiency.*
◇ *vt* to produce or gain <a sum of money> as a net profit □ *The deal netted over $5,000 for the company* OR *netted the company over $5,000.*
◆ **Net** *n* COMPUTING = **Internet** (informal use).

netball ['netbɔːl] *n* a sport with two teams of seven players, similar to basketball, that is mainly played by women in Commonwealth countries.

net curtains *npl* GB curtains made of net allowing people inside a house to see out but preventing people outside from seeing in.

Netherlands ['neðəʳləndz]: **the Netherlands** a country in western Europe, on the North Sea between Belgium and Germany. SIZE: 34,000 sq kms. POPULATION: 15,200,000 (*Dutch*). CAPITAL: Amsterdam. ADMINISTRATIVE CAPITAL: The Hague. LANGUAGE: Dutch. CURRENCY: guilder.
NOTE: The name *the Netherlands* is used only in official contexts; otherwise the country is called *Holland.*

net profit *n* the total money earned in a business deal or within a certain period, after all costs, taxes etc have been paid.

net revenue *n* the total money received from the sale of goods or services, after all costs, taxes etc have been paid.

netting ['netɪŋ] *n* material made of thread or wire knotted or woven together with equal spaces in between □ *wire netting.*

nettle ['netl] ◇ *n* a wild plant with spiky, hairy, green leaves that stings the skin and leaves red marks. ◇ *vt* **to be nettled** to be a little annoyed □ *He was obviously nettled by all these personal questions.*

network ['netwɜːʳk] ◇ *n* **-1.** [of veins, streets, wires] a large system of lines that cross one another and join at many points □ *a telecommunications/road network.* **-2.** [of friends, contacts] a closely linked group of people or institutions, usually spread over a large area. **-3.** TV & RADIO a radio or television company, or group of companies, covering a large

area and sharing the same programs. **-4.** COMPUTING a set of computers linked together so that they can share information.
◇ *vt* **-1.** TV & RADIO to broadcast <a program> on several stations over a large area at the same time. **-2.** COMPUTING to connect <two or more computers> together to form a network.
◇ *vi* to meet people at informal social meetings who may be helpful to one's career or business.

networking ['netwɜːʳkɪŋ] *n* getting to know people who might be helpful to one's career or business.

neuralgia [njʊˈrældʒə] *n* sharp pain felt along a nerve, particularly in the head or face.

neurological [ˌnjʊərəˈlɒdʒɪkl] *adj* [disease, examination] that affects the nervous system.

neurologist [njʊˈrɒlədʒəst] *n* a doctor who specializes in problems of the nervous system.

neurology [ˌnjʊˈrɒlədʒɪ] *n* the study of nerves and their diseases.

neurosis [ˌnjʊˈrəʊsɪs] (*pl* **neuroses** [-iːz]) *n* an unhealthy mental state in which a person is afraid of or worried about something without any real reason.
NOTE: Compare **psychosis**.

neurosurgeon [ˌnjʊərəʊˈsɜːʳdʒən] *n* a doctor who specializes in operations on the nervous system.

neurotic [ˌnjʊˈrɒtɪk] *adj* [person, behavior] *see* **neurosis** □ *He's so neurotic about growing old!*

neuter ['njuːtəʳ] ◇ *adj* **-1.** GRAMMAR [noun, pronoun] that is not masculine or feminine and belongs to the class of words usually used for things and not people. **-2.** [plant, animal] whose sex organs are missing or not fully developed. ◇ *vt* [dog, cat] to remove part of the sexual organs of <an animal> so that it cannot produce young.

neutral ['njuːtrəl] ◇ *adj* **-1.** [country, person, position] that does not support any country, person, political cause etc in an argument or war □ *neutral territory/waters* □ *Switzerland remained neutral throughout both World Wars.* **-2.** [expression, voice, word] that does not show what somebody is feeling □ *He described what he'd seen in a surprisingly neutral way.* **-3.** [clothing, shade] pale gray or pale brown □ *neutral shoe polish.* **-4.** ELECTRICITY [wire] that has no electrical charge. ◇ *n* AUTO the position of the gears of a car in which no power can pass from the engine to the wheels □ *Leave the car in neutral.*

neutrality [njuːˈtrælətɪ] *n* [of a country, voice] *see* **neutral** □ *a position of political neutrality.*

neutralize, -ise ['njuːtrəlaɪz] *vt* [poison, threat] to make <sthg that could be dangerous or harmful> safe □ *Bomb disposal experts successfully neutralized the device.*

neutron ['njuːtrɒn] *n* any of the tiny pieces of matter in an atom that have no electrical charge.

neutron bomb *n* a nuclear bomb that kills people without destroying buildings.

Nevada [US nɪ'væːdə, GB -'vɑːdə] a state in the western USA, consisting mainly of desert and mountains. It is famous for its casinos. ABBREVIATION: NV. SIZE: 295,000 sq kms. POPULATION: 1,201,833 *(Nevadans)*. CAPITAL: Carson City. OTHER MAJOR CITIES: Reno, Las Vegas.

never ['nevər] *adv* **-1.** at no time □ *I've never been to America.* □ *You've never seen such a mess!* □ *I can never remember people's names.* ■ **never ever** used for emphasis □ *I'll never ever do that again.* **-2.** not □ *I never knew you could swim so well.* □ *That's never Julie in there, is it?*

never-ending *adj* [problems, complaints, chores] that seem never to finish □ *The list of suggestions is never-ending.*

nevertheless [ˌnevərðə'les] *adv* in spite of what has just been said □ *We have suffered a serious setback. Nevertheless, we must not be discouraged.*

new [njuː] *adj* **-1.** [movie, house, baby] that has been recently made, created, or built, or is being made, created, or built □ *Have you seen our new range of outdoor furniture?* □ *They're bringing in new laws to curb immigration.* ■ **new potatoes** young potatoes picked at the beginning of the season. **-2.** [car, book, coat] that has not been used or owned by anybody else before □ *Did you buy it new or secondhand?* ■ **like new**, **as good as new** in the same condition as when it was new □ *I polished the silver until it shone like new.* **-3.** [planet, discovery, idea] that was not known before or has not been thought of before □ *The police have found new evidence.* □ *The policy statement said nothing new.* **-4.** [job, address, hairstyle] that takes the place of the same kind of thing one had before □ *'Under new management'* □ *What are your new neighbors like?* **-5.** [customer, mother, company] that has not existed for long □ *Have you met your new boss yet?* **-6.** [name, feeling, place] that has not been seen or experienced before □ *Let's go somewhere new this time.* □ *I can see a few new faces here today.* □ *This is all new to me.* ■ **what's new?** what's the latest news? **-7.** [employee, member] who is not yet used to a particular place or job □ *I'm new here, can you help me?* □ *She's new to the company/to teaching.* □ *Mr Takagi will be the new head of research.* ■ **a new boy/girl** a boy/girl who has only recently joined a school.

new- *prefix* recently □ *new-mown hay* □ *a new-laid egg* □ *They're out celebrating their new-won freedom.*

New Age *adj* connected with a cultural movement that began in the West in the 1970s and follows non-Western ideas about medicine, religion, astrology etc □ *the New Age movement.*

new blood *n* new people in an organization or company who have new ideas and new talents □ *Our team needs new blood.*

newborn ['njuːbɔːrn] *adj* [baby, calf, lamb] that has recently been born.

New Brunswick [-'brʌnzwɪk] a province of eastern Canada, on the Atlantic Ocean. AB-BREVIATION: NB. SIZE: 73,437 sq kms. POPULATION: 723,900 *(New Brunswickers)*. CAPITAL: Fredericton.

Newcastle [US 'nuːkæsl, GB 'njuːkɑːsl] **-1.** an industrial city in northeastern England that used to be an important center for coalmining and shipbuilding. It is also called Newcastle-upon-Tyne. POPULATION: 204,000. **-2.** an industrial city and port in New South Wales, Australia. POPULATION: 300,000.

newcomer ['njuːkʌmər] *n* a person who has recently moved to a place, started a job etc □ *Newcomers to the area are sure of a warm welcome at the club.*

New Deal *n* **the New Deal** the plan to reform the US economy after the Great Depression, introduced by President Franklin D. Roosevelt.

☙ THE NEW DEAL
Before he became president, Franklin D. Roosevelt promised "a new deal for the American people" that aimed to end the effects of the Great Depression. This promise became the New Deal (1933-1940), a huge program of social and economic reforms. Laws were passed to control the banking system and the financial markets, to protect the rights of labor unions, to give assistance to the poor and unemployed, and to build cheap housing.

New Delhi [-'delɪ] the capital of India, part of the city of Delhi.

New England a region of the northeastern USA, including the states of Maine, New Hampshire, Vermont, Rhode Island, Massachusetts, and Connecticut. It was one of the first parts of America to be settled by Europeans, and contains many Ivy League colleges.

New Englander [-'ɪŋləndər] *n* a person who comes from or lives in New England.

newfangled [ˌnjuː'fæŋgld] *adj* [idea, gadget] that is new but unnecessarily complicated (disapproving use).

new-found *adj* [energy, confidence] that has been recently discovered, or discovered again □ *She has a new-found sense of pride in her ability.*

Newfoundland ['njuːfəndlənd] a province of eastern Canada, on the Atlantic, consisting of the island of Newfoundland and the coast of Labrador to the north. ABBREVIATION: NF. SIZE: 406,000 sq kms. POPULATION: 568,474 *(Newfoundlanders)*. CAPITAL: Saint John's.

New Guinea a large island in the Pacific Ocean, north of Australia. The west part (West Irian) belongs to Indonesia, and the east part is the Independent State of Papua New Guinea. SIZE: 800,000 sq kms.

New Hampshire [-'hæmpʃər] a small state in the northeastern USA, on the Atlantic coast. It is famous for its attractive scenery. ABBREVIATION: NH. SIZE: 24,000 sq kms. POPULATION:

1,109,252 (*New Hampshirites*). CAPITAL: Concord.

New Haven [-'heɪvn] the largest city in Connecticut, USA. It is a major port, and Yale University is situated there. POPULATION: 130,474.

New Jersey a state in the eastern USA, on the Atlantic coast, south of New York. It is heavily industrialized, and the most densely populated state in the USA. ABBREVIATION: NJ. SIZE: 19,479 sq kms. POPULATION: 7,730,188 (*New Jerseyites*). CAPITAL: Trenton. MAIN CITY: Newark.

newly ['nʲuːlɪ] *adv* newly qualified/painted etc recently qualified/painted etc.

newlyweds ['nʲuːlɪwedz] *npl* a couple who have recently gotten married □ *The newlyweds left on their honeymoon.*

New Mexico a state in the southwestern USA, containing many mountainous and desert areas. ABBREVIATION: NM. SIZE: 315,000 sq kms. POPULATION: 1,515,069 (*New Mexicans*). CAPITAL: Santa Fe.

new moon *n* the moon at the beginning of its four-week cycle, when it is very thin.

New Orleans [US nuːˈɔːrlɪənz, GB ˌnjuːɔːˈliːənz] a major port and commercial center in Louisiana, USA. It is famous for its jazz and blues music, and for its annual carnival. POPULATION: 496,938.

news [nʲuːz] *n* -1. information about recent events □ *a piece* OR *bit of news* □ *Have you heard the news about Mary?* □ *I have some good/bad news for you.* □ *News is coming in of riots in L.A.* □ *Mark wrote telling me all his news.* ■ **that's news to me** a phrase used to say one did not know something and is a little annoyed at not being told it sooner. ■ **to break the news to sb** to tell sb some bad news □ *I had to break the news of his father's death to him.* -2. RADIO & TV **the news** a program on the radio or television that reports recent important events □ *I heard about the earthquake on the news.* □ *His arrest made the 6 o'clock news.* □ *a news broadcast/report.* ■ **to be in the news** to be mentioned a lot in newspapers, on television etc □ *McLeod? Yes, he's been in the news a lot recently.*

news agency *n* an organization that collects news and sells it to newspapers, magazines, television companies etc.

newsagent ['nʲuːzeɪdʒənt], **newsagent's** *n* GB a store where newspapers, magazines, candy, cigarettes etc are sold.

news blackout *n* an order issued by a government or military authority, forbidding the reporting of news from a particular place or about a particular event.

news bulletin *n* a short program of news on the radio or television.

newscast [US 'nuːzkæst, GB 'njuːzkɑːst] *n* a news program on the radio or television.

newscaster [US 'nuːzkæstr, GB 'njuːzkɑːstə] *n* a person who reads the news on the radio or television.

news conference *n* a meeting held by an of-ficial or a famous person to answer journalists' questions □ *The President held/called a news conference.*

New Scotland Yard *n* the headquarters of the Metropolitan Police, the police force in London.

newsdealer ['nʲuːzdiːlər] *n* US a person who runs a store selling newspapers and magazines.

newsflash ['nʲuːzflæʃ] *n* GB a short radio or television program that announces an important item of very recent news, usually in the middle of another program.

newsletter ['nʲuːzletər] *n* a short printed report produced regularly for the employees or customers of a company, or members of an organization.

newsman ['nʲuːzmæn] (*pl* **newsmen** [-mən]) *n* a reporter for a newspaper or a radio or television station.

New South Wales a state in southeastern Australia, on the Pacific coast. It is Australia's most densely populated and economically important state. SIZE: 801,428 sq kms. POPULATION: 5,731,926. CAPITAL: Sydney.

newspaper ['nʲuːzpeɪpər] *n* -1. a set of large sheets of printed paper that is published every day or week and contains news, photographs, advertisements etc; a company that publishes this □ *a newspaper article* □ *a daily/national newspaper* □ *I used to work for a newspaper.* -2. old newspapers, usually when used for purposes other than reading □ *a package wrapped in newspaper.*

newspaperman ['nʲuːzpəˈmæn] (*pl* **newspapermen** [-mən]) *n* a journalist who works for a newspaper.

newsprint ['nʲuːzprɪnt] *n* cheap rough paper on which newspapers are printed.

newsreader ['nʲuːzriːdər] *n* GB a person who reads the news on the radio or television.

newsreel ['nʲuːzriːl] *n* a short news film with a commentary that used to be shown in cinemas.

newsroom ['nʲuːzruːm] *n* an office at a newspaper or a radio or television station where news is collected and prepared for publication or broadcasting.

newssheet ['nʲuːzʃiːt] *n* a small newspaper, usually consisting of one or two pages.

newsstand ['nʲuːzstænd] *n* a place where newspapers are sold, especially a very small store or a box on a street.

newsworthy ['nʲuːzwɜːrðɪ] *adj* [event, remark] that is important or interesting enough to be reported in the news.

newt [nʲuːt] *n* a small animal like a lizard that lives partly on land and partly in water.

new technology *n* the use of computers and other automatic systems in business and industry.

New Territories [US ˌnuːˈterətɔːrɪz, GB ˌnjuːˈterətərɪz]: **the New Territories** part of mainland Hong Kong, leased by Great Britain from China and due to be returned with the rest of Hong Kong by 1997.

New Testament *n* **the New Testament** the part of the Bible that describes the life of Christ and the early history of Christianity. NOTE: Compare **Old Testament**.

Newton ['nʲuːtn], **Sir Isaac** (1642–1727) a British scientist, astronomer, and mathematician who discovered the law of gravity.

new town *n* in Britain, a town that has been planned and built all at the same time, especially using government money.

new wave *n* a group or movement in politics or the arts that deliberately uses new ideas □ *He is one of the new wave of crime writers.*

New World *n* **the New World** North, Central, and South America.

New Year *n* -1. the time when people celebrate the beginning of the year □ *We're spending New Year with my in-laws.* -2. **the New Year** the first few days or weeks of next January □ *I'll see you in the New Year.* □ *New Year celebrations.* ■ **Happy New Year!** a greeting used at the start of a new year.

❦ NEW YEAR
In the USA, Australia, and Britain people have parties on New Year's Eve (December 31) to "see in" the New Year. When the clocks strike midnight, everyone wishes each other "Happy New Year" and hugs or kisses each other. A traditional song, *Auld Lang Syne*, is often sung. The next day, New Year's Day (January 1), is a public holiday in the USA, Australia, and Britain.

New Year's Day *n* the first day of the year, January 1.

New Year's Eve *n* the last day of the year, December 31 □ *a New Year's Eve party.*

New York (City) [-'jɔːʳk-] the largest city in the USA and the most important financial center in the world, in New York State on the Atlantic Coast. ABBREVIATION: NYC. POPULATION: 7,322,564.

New Yorker [-'jɔːʳkəʳ] *n* a person who comes from or lives in New York.

New York (State) a state in the northeastern USA. ABBREVIATION: NY. SIZE: 128,400 sq kms. POPULATION: 17,990,455. CAPITAL: Albany. OTHER MAJOR CITIES: Buffalo, New York.

New Zealand [-'ziːlənd] a country consisting of two large islands (North Island and South Island) in the southern Pacific Ocean. SIZE: 270,000 sq kms. POPULATION: 3,500,000 (*New Zealanders*). CAPITAL: Wellington. LANGUAGE: English. CURRENCY: New Zealand dollar.

New Zealander [-'ziːləndəʳ] *n* a person who comes from or lives in New Zealand.

next [nekst] ◇ *det* & *pron* -1. **the next time/ flight** the first time/flight after now or some other time that has been mentioned □ *I'll tell him the next time I see him.* □ *What's next on the agenda?* □ *The next (person) to arrive was Paul.* □ *"Next, please," said the doctor.* ■ **next month/year** the month/year after this present one □ *There's a meeting next Friday.* ■ **the week after next** the week that follows the

next one. -2. **the next room/page/street** the room/page/street that one comes to first □ *Take the next turning on the right.* □ *We missed our stop and had to get off at the next one.* □ *These are too small, can I try the next size up?* ◇ *adv* -1. [happen, go] immediately afterward □ *What happened next?* -2. [meet, visit] again □ *When I next saw him he was looking much older.* -3. **the next best/biggest** the one that is a little less good/big than the one just mentioned □ *Our next oldest child is Sally.* □ *Mining is the next most important industry.*

◆ **next to** *prep* -1. beside <a place, person> etc □ *She sat down next to me.* □ *It's the tall building next to the hardware store.* -2. closest to sthg in order □ *Next to cooking, I enjoy gardening best.* ■ **next to nothing** almost nothing □ *I know next to nothing about computers.*

next door *adv* [live, go] in or to the nearest house, room etc on either side of another house, room etc □ *I'm just going next door.* □ *Our house is right next door to the park.*

◆ **next-door** *adj* **one's next-door neighbor** the person who lives next door to one.

next of kin *n* LAW one's closest living relative or relatives □ *The next of kin have been informed.*

NF ◇ *n abbr of* **National Front.** ◇ *abbr of* **Newfoundland.**

NFL (*abbr of* **National Football League**) *n* **the NFL** the organization in charge of professional football in the USA.

NG *n abbr of* **National Guard.**

NGO (*abbr of* **non-governmental organization**) *n* an organization that is not financed by a government.

NH *abbr of* **New Hampshire.**

NHL (*abbr of* **National Hockey League**) *n* **the NHL** a league of US and Canadian professional hockey teams.

NHS *n abbr of* **National Health Service.**

NI ◇ *n abbr of* **National Insurance.** ◇ *abbr of* **Northern Ireland.**

Niagara Falls [naɪˌægərə-] a large waterfall between Lake Erie and Lake Ontario on the US-Canadian border. It is about 50 meters high, and is a major tourist attraction.

nib [nɪb] *n* the small pointed metal part at the end of a pen through which the ink flows onto the paper □ *a pen nib* □ *a gold nib.*

nibble ['nɪbl] ◇ *vt* to take small bites from <a piece of food> □ *She was nibbling an apple.* ◇ *vi* [animal, person] *The squirrel was nibbling at* OR *on a nut.*

◆ **nibbles** *npl* small things to eat with one's fingers at a party, e.g. nuts or potato chips.

NICAM ['naɪkæm] (*abbr of* **near-instantaneous compound audio multiplexing**) *n* a system for transmitting high quality sound along with a normal TV picture □ *a Nicam stereo TV.*

Nicaragua [US ˌnɪkəˈrɑːgwə, GB -ˈrægjʊə] the largest country in Central America. In the 1980s a civil war was fought there between the left-wing Sandinista government and the right-wing Contras. SIZE: 148,000 sq kms. POPULATION: 3,900,000 (*Nicaraguans*). CAPITAL:

Managua. LANGUAGE: Spanish. CURRENCY: córdoba.

nice [naɪs] ◇ *adj* -1. [dress, house, food, day] that one finds pleasant to look at, be in etc □ *She looks very nice in that dress.* □ *It tastes very nice.* □ *It's nice out today.* □ *She's really nice to work with.* □ *It was so nice to see them again.* □ *It's nice that you were able to come.* ■ **have a nice day!** a phrase used to say goodbye, especially to customers in a store, restaurant, hotel etc. ■ **nice to meet you!** a greeting used when one is introduced to somebody. -2. [person, remark] kind and friendly □ *He's such a nice man.* □ *She's always been very nice to me.* □ *It was nice of you to help with the cleaning.* □ *That's not a very nice thing to do!* ■ **nice and warm/quiet etc** warm/quiet etc in a way one finds pleasant (informal use) □ *It's nice and comfortable here.*
◇ *adv* **a nice hot bath/meal etc** a hot bath/meal etc that one finds very pleasant □ *What I need is a nice cold drink.*

nice-looking [-lʊkɪŋ] *adj* [boy, girl, car] that one finds attractive.

nicely ['naɪslɪ] *adv* -1. [dress, decorate] in a way one finds attractive □ *The room was nicely furnished.* -2. [speak, ask, behave] in a pleasant, kind, or polite way □ *If you ask her nicely, I'm sure she'll lend you the money.* -3. **we are managing** OR **doing nicely** we are pleased with the way things are going. ■ **that will do nicely** a phrase used to say that one can accept or use something that somebody is offering, especially money □ *"Can I leave you a $20 deposit?" — "Yes, that'll do very nicely, thanks."*

nicety ['naɪsətɪ] (*pl* **niceties**) *n* **the niceties** small precise details of how to do things □ *the social/legal niceties.*

niche [US nɪtʃ, GB niːʃ] *n* -1. [in a wall] a shallow hollow place in a wall, usually for holding a small statue or lamp. -2. [for a person] a suitable, safe, or comfortable position or job □ *Joan soon found a niche for herself in accounting.*

niche marketing *n* marketing aimed at a specialized, usually small, market.

nick [nɪk] ◇ *n* -1. a short thin cut in the surface of something, e.g. one's skin, usually made by accident □ *The knife had made a tiny nick in the table.* -2. *phrase* **in the nick of time** at the last possible moment □ *They arrived just in the nick of time to catch the plane.* ◇ *vt* -1. [chin, skin, piece of wood] to make a nick in <sthg> □ *He nicked his chin* OR *nicked himself on the chin while shaving.* -2. GB [money, car] to steal <sthg> (informal use) □ *My wallet got nicked at the pub.*

nickel ['nɪkl] *n* -1. CHEMISTRY a hard, silver-white, metal element used in plating objects and making stainless steel. SYMBOL: Ni. -2. FINANCE a coin worth five cents in the USA and Canada.

nickname ['nɪkneɪm] ◇ *n* an informal name given to somebody or something. ◇ *vt* to give <sb>/sthg a nickname □ *New York is nicknamed the Big Apple.* □ *His first name is Charles, but he's nicknamed "Chuck".*

nicotine ['nɪkətiːn] *n* a poisonous addictive substance found in tobacco that leaves a brownish-yellow stain □ *nicotine-stained fingers.*

nicotine patch *n* a small strip of material containing nicotine that can be stuck onto one's skin, used by people trying to give up smoking.

niece [niːs] *n* a daughter of one's brother or sister; a daughter of the brother or sister of one's husband or wife.

Nielsen Ratings ['niːlsən-] *npl* **the Nielsen Ratings** in the USA, a set of statistics that show how many people watch the most popular television programs.

Nietzsche ['niːtʃə], **Friedrich** (1844–1900) a German philosopher who was against Christianity and democracy. His most important work is *Thus Spake Zarathustra.*

nifty ['nɪftɪ] (*compar* **niftier**, *superl* **niftiest**) *adj* that one likes because it is well made, useful, and attractive (informal use) □ *That's a nifty little computer you have there!*

Niger ['naɪdʒər] -1. a country in northwestern Africa, north of Nigeria, consisting mainly of the southern Sahara Desert. SIZE: 1,267,000 sq kms. POPULATION: 8,500,000 (*Nigeriens*). CAPITAL: Niamey. LANGUAGE: French. CURRENCY: CFA franc. -2. **the Niger (River)** a river in northwestern Africa, flowing through Mali, Niger, and Nigeria into the Atlantic Ocean.

Nigeria [naɪ'dʒɪərɪə] a country in West Africa, on the Atlantic coast. It is a major exporter of oil. SIZE: 924,000 sq kms. POPULATION: 95,100,000 (*Nigerians*). CAPITAL: Abuja. MAIN CITIES: Lagos, Ibadan. LANGUAGE: English. CURRENCY: naira.

Nigerian [naɪ'dʒɪərɪən] *n* & *adj*: see **Nigeria**.

Nigerien [naɪ'dʒɪərɪən] *n* & *adj*: see **Niger**.

niggardly ['nɪɡərdlɪ] *adj* [person, gift] that one thinks is not generous enough (disapproving use) □ *He was offered a niggardly amount as compensation for his injuries.*

niggle ['nɪɡl] ◇ *vt* -1. [problems, doubts] to worry or annoy <sb> slightly, especially for a long time. -2. [person] to criticize <sb> all the time about small and unimportant things. ◇ *vi* -1. [problems, doubts] *There's something that's been niggling at me all day.* -2. [person] *Stop niggling at me!*

niggling ['nɪɡlɪŋ] *adj* [pain, doubt, criticism] that is slightly worrying or annoying and that one cannot stop thinking about.

nigh [naɪ] *adv* near, especially in time (literary use). ■ **well nigh** almost.

night [naɪt] *n* -1. the time between the end of one day and the beginning of the next, when it is dark □ *It rained in* OR *during the night.* □ *The job will take all night.* □ *A room costs $50 a night.* □ *a night flight.* -2. the darkness after the day □ *Night was falling.* -3. the part of the night before one goes to bed, especially when it is used for entertainment or enjoyment □ *Did you go out last night?* -4. *phrases* **at night** in the evening □ *I'm always in bed by 11 o'clock at night.* ■ **night and day** all the time without stopping □ *I've been working night and* *day to get the job finished.* ■ **a night off** an evening when one does not have to work □ *It's the housekeeper's night off tonight.* ■ **to have a night out** to spend an evening outside the home, enjoying oneself □ *What you really need is a good night out.* ■ **to have an early/a late night** to go to bed early/late □ *I've decided to have an early night tonight.*

◆ **nights** *adv* most nights; every night □ *Nights I like to read.* □ *He works nights.*

nightcap ['naɪtkæp] *n* a drink, usually alcoholic, that one has before going to bed.

nightclothes ['naɪtkloʊz] *npl* the clothes that one wears in bed at night.

nightclub ['naɪtklʌb] *n* a place where people can drink, dance, or see a show late at night.

night depository [US -dɪ'pɒzətɔːrɪ, GB -'pɒzɪtərɪ] *n* a hole in the outside wall of a bank where customers can leave money and checks after the bank is closed.

nightdress ['naɪtdres] *n* = **nightgown**.

nightfall ['naɪtfɔːl] *n* the time when it gets dark at night □ *Make sure you're back home by nightfall.*

nightgown ['naɪtgaʊn] *n* a loose dress worn by women in bed.

nightie ['naɪtɪ] *n* = **nightgown** (informal use).

nightingale ['naɪtɪŋgeɪl] *n* a small brown bird known for its beautiful song.

Nightingale ['naɪtɪŋgeɪl], **Florence** (1820–1910) a British nurse who set up a hospital for soldiers during the Crimean War. She helped to develop nursing as a profession.

nightlife ['naɪtlaɪf] *n* the different activities and events, e.g. bars, nightclubs, or theaters, that are available in a particular place at night for entertainment □ *The town has plenty of/no nightlife.*

nightlight ['naɪtlaɪt] *n* a small lamp or candle used to light a bedroom, hall etc at night.

nightly ['naɪtlɪ] ◇ *adj* [event, visit, broadcast] that takes place every night □ *a nightly news program.* ◇ *adv* [happen, appear, visit] every night □ *Miss Akade performs twice nightly at the Apollo Theater.*

nightmare ['naɪtmeəʳ] *n* **-1.** a dream that is frightening □ *I started having terrible nightmares.* **-2.** a situation or experience that is very difficult or unpleasant □ *Getting to work today was a real nightmare.*

nightmarish ['naɪtmeərɪʃ] *adj* [experience, journey] that is frightening and unpleasant.

night owl *n* a person who often likes to stay up late to work, read, go out etc.

night porter *n* a person whose job is to stay at the reception desk of a hotel at night when most of the staff have stopped work.

night safe *n* GB = **night depository**.

night school *n* classes that take place in the evening, usually for adults □ *I learned Spanish at night school.*

night shift *n* a fixed period during the night when employees in a factory, hospital etc work; the group of people who work during this time □ *He's on the night shift this week.*

nightshirt ['naɪtʃɜːʳt] *n* a long loose shirt worn by men in bed.

nightspot ['naɪtspɒt] *n* a nightclub or other place of entertainment that opens at night.

nightstick ['naɪtstɪk] *n* US a long stick used as a weapon by policemen.

night-time ['naɪttaɪm] *n* the time when it is dark □ *Owls come out at night-time.*

night watchman *n* a person whose job is to guard a building or workplace at night.

nightwear ['naɪtweəʳ] *n* clothes that are designed to be worn in bed.

nihilism ['naɪɪlɪzm] *n* the belief that personal freedom is more important than all social, political, and religious institutions.

Nikkei [nɪ'keɪ] *n* **the Nikkei (index** OR **average)** the average of the current price of the shares of 225 Japanese companies sold on the Tokyo Stock Exchange.

nil [nɪl] *n* **-1.** nothing; zero □ *We've kept price increases down to almost nil.* **-2.** GB SPORT a score of zero in soccer and some other games □ *We lost two-nil.*

Nile [naɪl]: **the Nile (River)** the world's longest river, flowing through Uganda, Sudan, and Egypt into the Mediterranean Sea.

nimble ['nɪmbl] *adj* **-1.** [fingers, person] able to make quick, light, neat movements. **-2.** [mind] able to think quickly.

nimbly ['nɪmblɪ] *adv* [move, step, climb] *see* **nimble.**

nine [naɪn] *num* the number 9; *see also* **five.** ■ **nine times out of ten** almost always.

nineteen [ˌnaɪn'tiːn] *num* the number 19; *see also* **fifteen.**

nineteenth [ˌnaɪn'tiːnθ] *num* 19th; number 19 in a series; *see also* **fifteenth** □ *the nineteenth century.*

ninetieth ['naɪntɪəθ] *num* 90th; number 90 in a series; *see also* **fiftieth.**

ninety ['naɪntɪ] *num* the number 90; *see also* **fifty.**

ninth [naɪnθ] *num* 9th; number 9 in a series; *see also* **fifth.**

nip [nɪp] (*pt* & *pp* **nipped,** *cont* **nipping**) ◇ *n* **-1.** [by an animal] a small painful pinch or bite □ *The dog gave me a playful nip on the leg.* **-2.** [of liquid] a small amount of alcoholic drink □ *a nip of brandy.* **-3.** *phrase* **there's a nip in the air** it's slightly cold. ◇ *vt* **-1.** to catch <sthg> between two sharp points or edges □ *I nipped my finger in the door.* **-2.** to bite <sb/sthg> without doing much damage □ *The dog nipped me on the ankle.* ◇ *vi* GB to go somewhere quickly and for a short time (informal use) □ *I'm just nipping into town/out to the post office.*

nipple ['nɪpl] *n* **-1.** [of a person] one of the two pinkish-brown circles of skin on one's chest. A baby sucks milk through its mother's nipples. **-2.** US [for a baby's bottle] a rubber or plastic piece on a baby's bottle, through which the baby drinks.

nippy ['nɪpɪ] (*compar* **nippier,** *superl* **nippiest**) *adj* [weather, morning] rather cold □ *It's a little nippy out this morning.*

nirvana [nɪərˈvɑːnə] *n* -1. RELIGION in Buddhism and Hinduism, the highest spiritual state. -2. a place or state of complete happiness.

nitpicking [ˈnɪtpɪkɪŋ] ◇ *n* the act of paying too much attention to unimportant details (disapproving use). ◇ *adj*: *his nitpicking attitude.*

nitrate [ˈnaɪtreɪt] *n* a chemical used mainly as a fertilizer for growing crops.

nitric acid [ˌnaɪtrɪk-] *n* a powerful chemical that is used in the manufacture of fertilizers and explosives.

nitrogen [ˈnaɪtrədʒən] *n* a colorless gas that forms most of the air we breathe. SYMBOL: N.

nitroglycerin(e) [ˌnaɪtrəˈglɪsərɪn] *n* a powerful liquid chemical used to make explosives.

nits [nɪts] *npl* the eggs of a tiny insect, the louse, that can live in people's hair.

nitty-gritty [ˌnɪtɪˈgrɪtɪ] *n* **to get down to the nitty-gritty** to start talking or thinking about the most basic and important aspects of a problem.

nitwit [ˈnɪtwɪt] *n* a silly person (informal use).

nix [nɪks] US (informal use) ◇ *n* nothing. ◇ *adv* a word used to say that one disagrees with something □ *He said nix on our plan.* ◇ *vt* [plan, decision] to reject <sthg>.

Nixon [ˈnɪksən], **Richard** (1913–1994) US President from 1969 to 1974. He resigned after the Watergate scandal.

NJ *abbr of* **New Jersey.**

NLF (*abbr of* **National Liberation Front**) *n* **the NLF** any revolutionary movement whose aim is to win independence for a country or region.

NM *abbr of* **New Mexico.**

no [noʊ] (*pl* **noes** OR **nos**) ◇ *adv* -1. used to show that something is not true □ *"Would you like some more?" — "No, thanks." □ "That's what you said." — "No it isn't!"* -2. used to show that one will not do, allow, or accept something □ *"Can I watch TV?" — "No, you can't."* -3. **no later/bigger etc than...** not later/bigger etc than a particular maximum time or amount □ *This computer is no more expensive than the old model.*
◇ *det* -1. not any; not one □ *No other battery looks like it or lasts like it. □ I have no choice but to tell her. □ There's no time to lose. □ No two prints are ever the same.* ■ **there's no telling what might happen** it's impossible to tell what will happen. -2. not a □ *She's no fool! □ It's no easy job.*
◇ *n* -1. a negative answer □ *Was that a yes or a no?* -2. a vote against something. ■ **the noes have it** the majority of people have voted "no".

No., no. *abbr of* **number.**

Noah [ˈnoʊə] in the Bible, the man who built the ark, a large boat, to save his family and two of each kind of animal when the Earth was flooded.

nobble [ˈnɒbl] *vt* GB -1. to drug <a racehorse> illegally so that it runs slower in a race. -2. to try to influence <a member of a jury> by bribing or threatening them.

Nobel [noʊˈbel], **Alfred** (1833–1896) a Swedish scientist. He invented dynamite, and established and funded the Nobel prizes.

Nobel prize *n* an international prize given every year to somebody who has done important work for science, medicine, economics, literature, world peace etc □ *the Nobel peace prize.*

nobility [noʊˈbɪlətɪ] *n* -1. **the nobility** the people of the highest social class who have titles and own land. -2. [of somebody's character, appearance] *see* **noble.**

noble [ˈnoʊbl] ◇ *adj* -1. [person] who is honest, brave, and helps other people without thinking of themselves □ *That was a noble gesture!* -2. [bearing, statue] that looks impressive and dignified. -3. **of noble birth** belonging to the nobility. ◇ *n* a person who belongs to the nobility.

nobleman [ˈnoʊblmən] (*pl* **noblemen** [-mən]) *n* a man who belongs to the nobility.

noblewoman [ˈnoʊblwʊmən] (*pl* **noblewomen**) *n* a woman who belongs to the nobility.

nobly [ˈnoʊblɪ] *adv* [act, behave] *see* **noble.**

nobody [ˈnoʊbədɪ] (*pl* **nobodies**) ◇ *pron* not a single person □ *There's nobody here. □ Nobody asked you! □ "Did you talk to anyone?" — "Nobody in particular."* ◇ *n* an unimportant person (disapproving use) □ *He's just a nobody!*

no-claim(s) bonus *n* a reduction in the cost of a car insurance policy that is given if no claims have been made during a particular period.

nocturnal [nɒkˈtɜːrnl] *adj* -1. [visit, voyage] that happens at night □ *He used to take long nocturnal walks.* -2. [animal] that is active at night □ *Badgers are mostly nocturnal.*

nod [nɒd] (*pt & pp* **nodded**, *cont* **nodding**) ◇ *n* a movement of the head forward and back □ *She gave an approving nod. □ With a brief nod in my direction, he left the room.* ◇ *vt* **to nod one's head** to move one's head forward and then back, to show that one agrees to, approves of, or wants to encourage something. ◇ *vi* -1. to nod one's head to say "yes" □ *I asked him if he'd understood and he nodded.* -2. to point to somebody or something by nodding one's head □ *The chairman asked who was responsible and Jean nodded in my direction.* -3. **to nod to sb** to nod one's head as a way of saying "hello" to sb □ *He nodded to me as I passed.*

◆ **nod off** *vi* to fall asleep for a short time.

node [noʊd] *n* -1. [on a diagram] a point where two lines cross each other. -2. [on a plant] the place on the stem of a plant where a leaf or bud grows □ *a leaf node.*

nodule [US ˈnɒdʒuːl, GB -juːl] *n* a small lump on a person's body or on a plant.

no-go area *n* GB [for women, the police] an area where it is dangerous for particular people to go; [for the public] an area to which police and soldiers are preventing people from going.

noise [nɔɪz] *n* -1. a sound, usually made by an animal or thing rather than a person □ *Did you hear a noise?* -2. loud and unpleasant sounds that disturb people □ *There is a lot of noise from the construction site.*

noiseless ['nɔɪzləs] *adj* [appliance, exhaust] that does not produce any noise.

noiselessly ['nɔɪzləslɪ] *adv* [move, close] *see* **noiseless.**

noisily ['nɔɪzɪlɪ] *adv* [play, call] *see* **noisy.**

noisy ['nɔɪzɪ] (*compar* **noisier**, *superl* **noisiest**) *adj* -1. [child, crowd, machine] that makes a lot of noise □ *Do you have to be so noisy?* -2. [city, party, room] that is full of noise □ *It's so noisy in here.*

nomad ['noʊmæd] *n* a member of a people that has no fixed home but camps in different places.

nomadic [noʊ'mædɪk] *adj* [person, tribe] *see* **nomad.**

no-man's-land *n* a piece of land between the territories of groups or countries that are fighting.

nominal ['nɒmənl] *adj* -1. [leader, head, Catholic] who has a particular job or status officially but does not carry out the particular role □ *a nominal head of state.* -2. [fee, charge, price] that is small compared with its true value or cost □ *We were charged a nominal rent.*

nominally ['nɒmənlɪ] *adv* a word used to say that somebody or something has a particular status officially but not in reality □ *Nominally, the country is Communist.*

nominate ['nɒməneɪt] *vt* -1. [candidate, work] to suggest <sb/sthg> as a candidate for an official position or an award □ *She's been nominated as a Republican candidate.* □ *The book has been nominated for several prizes.* -2. to choose <sb> for an important job □ *He was nominated (as) chairman* OR *to the chairmanship.*

nomination [,nɒmə'neɪʃn] *n* -1. [of a candidate, book] the act of suggesting somebody or something as a candidate for an official position or an award □ *This week we can expect nominations for the Presidential race.* □ *The Oscar nominations held few surprises.* -2. the act of choosing somebody for an important job □ *the nomination of another woman to a senior Cabinet position.*

nominee [,nɒmə'niː] *n* a person who is nominated for a job or an award.

non- [nɒn] *prefix* added to words to mean not □ *non-French nationals.*

nonaddictive [,nɒnə'dɪktɪv] *adj* [drug, medicine, substance] that is not addictive.

nonaggression [,nɒnə'greʃn] *n* the idea that countries should not attack each other □ *a policy of nonaggression* □ *a nonaggression pact.*

nonalcoholic [,nɒnælkə'hɒlɪk] *adj* [wine, beer] that contains little or no alcohol.

nonaligned [,nɒnə'laɪnd] *adj* [country, state] that does not support a larger country or group of countries, especially a world power.

nonbeliever [,nɒnbɪ'liːvəʳ] *n* a person who does not believe in God.

nonchalant [US ,nɒnʃə'lɑːnt, GB 'nɒnʃələnt] *adj* [remark, behavior] that seems to show that somebody is calm and not worried about something □ *He seems very nonchalant about his future.*

nonchalantly [US ,nɒnʃə'lɑːntlɪ, GB 'nɒnʃələntlɪ] *adv* [say, behave, look] *see* **nonchalant.**

noncombatant [US ,nɒnkəm'bætnt, GB ,nɒn-'kɒmbətənt] *n* a person who does not take part in actual fighting but is involved in a military struggle in an indirect way.

noncommissioned officer [,nɒnkəmɪʃnd-] *n* a low-ranking officer in the armed forces, e.g. a corporal or sergeant, who did not join the army as an officer.

noncommittal [,nɒnkə'mɪtl] *adj* [person, answer, attitude] that does not express any firm ideas or intentions □ *He was very noncommittal about the whole thing.*

noncompetitive [,nɒnkəm'petətɪv] *adj* [sports, games] that do not involve competition with other people.

non compos mentis [-kɒmpəs'mentəs] *adj* **to be non compos mentis** to be unable to think clearly, often because of mental illness (technical or humorous use).

nonconformist [,nɒnkən'fɔːʳməst] ◇ *n* a person who thinks or behaves in a way that is different from that of most other people. ◇ *adj*: *a nonconformist politician/attitude.*

noncontributory [US ,nɒnkən'trɪbjətɔːrɪ, GB -jʊtərɪ] *adj* [pension plan] that is paid for by the employer rather than by contributions from the employee.

noncooperation [,nɒnkoʊpə'reɪʃn] *n* a way of protesting to people in authority by refusing to do work that one is not officially required to do.

nondescript [US ,nɒndɪ'skrɪpt, GB 'nɒndɪskrɪpt] *adj* [house, color] that is so ordinary that one cannot think of anything interesting to say about it.

nondrinker [,nɒn'drɪŋkəʳ] *n* a person who does not drink alcohol.

nondrip [,nɒn'drɪp] *adj* [paint] that is very thick and so less likely to run down the wall or the brush than ordinary paint.

none [nʌn] ◇ *pron* -1. not any (used to refer back to uncountable nouns) □ *I went to buy some bread but there was none left.* □ *"Do you have any money?" — "No, none at all."* □ *His new record has none of his old brilliance.* ■ **(I'll have) none of it!** I won't allow it! □ *I tried to buy him another drink but he would have none of it.* -2. not one person or thing (used to refer back to plural nouns) □ *They had none left.* □ *None of us really knows* OR *know the answer.*

◇ *adv* **none the worse/better** not any worse/better than before (used with comparative adjectives) □ *She's none the worse for her adventure.* ■ **to be none the wiser** to still not understand something □ *He explained to me how it works, but I'm still none the wiser.* ■ **to be none too pleased/smart** to be not at all pleased/smart □ *They agreed, but you could see they were none too happy about it.*

nonentity [nɒˈnentətɪ] (*pl* **nonentities**) *n* a person who lacks personality and is unimportant.

nonessential [ˌnɒnɪˈsenʃl] ◇ *adj* that is not completely necessary □ *nonessential spending/items.* ◇ *n* something that is not completely necessary.

nonetheless [ˌnʌnðəˈles] *adv* in spite of this □ *She is very busy, but she will try to contact you nonetheless.* □ *The deal has already been signed. Nonetheless, it is still possible to negotiate new terms.*

non-event *n* a planned event that turns out to be very disappointing □ *The party was a complete non-event.*

nonexecutive director [ˌnɒnɪgzekjətɪv-] *n* a director of a company who is not an employee of that company.

nonexistent [ˌnɒnɪgˈzɪstənt] *adj* [chance, address, person] that does not exist □ *Security is so poor as to be almost nonexistent.*

nonfattening [ˌnɒnˈfætnɪŋ] *adj* [food] that is nourishing but does not make one fat.

nonfiction [ˌnɒnˈfɪkʃn] *n* writing that is based on fact, e.g. a biography □ *I prefer to read nonfiction.*

nonflammable [ˌnɒnˈflæməbl] *adj* [material] that will not catch fire or burn easily.

noninfectious [ˌnɒnɪnˈfekʃəs] *adj* [disease] that cannot be passed from one person to another.

noninflammable [ˌnɒnɪnˈflæməbl] *adj* = **nonflammable**.

noninterference [ˌnɒnɪntər'fɪərəns], **nonintervention** [ˌnɒnɪntərˈvenʃn] *n* the act of avoiding any involvement in a dispute, war etc □ *They have decided to adopt a policy of nonintervention.*

non-iron *adj* [fabric, shirt] that does not crease and so does not need to be ironed.

nonmalignant [ˌnɒnməˈlɪgnənt] *adj* [tumor, growth, lump] that will not cause serious illness or death.

nonmember [ˌnɒnˈmembər] *n* a person who is not a member of a particular club or association.

nonnegotiable [ˌnɒnnɪˈgoʊʃɪəbl] *adj* [salary, conditions] that is fixed at a level or in a way that cannot be changed by discussion □ *These terms are nonnegotiable.*

no-no *n* something that is considered to be unacceptable (informal use).

no-nonsense *adj* [attitude, approach] that is concerned only with the practical and important aspects of something.

nonoperational [ˌnɒnɒpəˈreɪʃnəl] *adj* [machine, factory, service] that is not working.

nonparticipation [ˌnɒnpɑːˈtɪsɪˈpeɪʃn] *n* the act of not taking part in a particular event or project □ *The Games were marred by the nonparticipation of the Soviet Union.*

nonpayment [ˌnɒnˈpeɪmənt] *n* [of tax, rent, debt] a failure to pay somebody the money that is owed to them □ *You know you can be arrested for nonpayment of fines.*

nonplussed [ˌnɒnˈplʌst] *adj* **to be nonplussed** to be so surprised or confused that one does not know what to say.

non-profit US, **non-profit-making** GB *adj* [organization, charity] that is run to help people rather than to make a profit.

nonproliferation [ˌnɒnprəlɪfəˈreɪʃn] *n* the limiting of the spread of nuclear weapons by international agreements □ *a nonproliferation treaty.*

nonrenewable [ˌnɒnrɪˈnʲuːəbl] *adj* **-1.** [contract, agreement] that cannot be renewed when it ends. **-2.** [resources, fuels] that exist in limited quantities that cannot be replaced when they have been used up □ *nonrenewable sources of energy.*

nonresident [ˌnɒnˈrezɪdənt] *n* **-1.** [of a country] a person who is visiting a particular country but does not normally live there. **-2.** [of a hotel] a person who uses the facilities of a hotel but does not spend the night there.

nonreturnable [ˌnɒnrɪˈtɜːrnəbl] *adj* **-1.** [bottle] that cannot be returned to the seller for money when empty. **-2.** [deposit] that will not be refunded in any circumstances.

nonsense [ˈnɒnsəns] ◇ *n* **-1.** an idea, suggestion, comment etc that one thinks is stupid or untrue □ *His accusations are utter nonsense.* **-2.** behavior that one thinks is stupid and annoying □ *Stop this nonsense now!* **-3.** spoken or written words that do not make any sense □ *You're talking nonsense!* ■ **to make** **(a) nonsense of sthg** [of a claim, promise] to cause sthg to appear untrue or worthless □ *This report makes nonsense of what officials have been saying.* ◇ *excl* used to show that one thinks a comment or idea is silly or untrue □ *Nonsense! I don't believe a word of it! You, shy? Nonsense!*

nonsensical [nɒnˈsensɪkl] *adj* [scheme, argument] that one thinks is stupid or ridiculous □ *It would be absolutely nonsensical to try to leave now.*

non sequitur [-ˈsekwətər] *n* a statement that is not connected logically with what has just been said, and is therefore confusing.

nonshrink [ˌnɒnˈʃrɪŋk] *adj* [fabric, garment] that will not shrink when washed.

nonskid [ˌnɒnˈskɪd] *adj* [tire] that is designed to reduce the chances of skidding.

nonslip [ˌnɒnˈslɪp] *adj* [mat, sole] that is designed to reduce the chances of slipping □ *a nonslip floor surface.*

nonsmoker [ˌnɒnˈsmoʊkər] *n* a person who does not smoke □ *I've been a nonsmoker all my life.*

non-smoking *adj* **a non-smoking seat/area etc** a seat/an area etc where one is not allowed to smoke □ *Would you like smoking or non-smoking?*

nonstarter [ˌnɒnˈstɑːrtər] *n* a person or plan that has no chance of succeeding (informal use) □ *The idea could turn out to be a nonstarter.*

nonstick [ˌnɒnˈstɪk] *adj* [pan] that is coated with a material that stops food from sticking □ *The frying pan has a nonstick surface.*

nonstop [ˌnɒnˈstɒp] ◇ adj -1. [trip, flight] that is made without stopping □ a nonstop flight to Australia. -2. [program, music, rain] that continues for a long time without a pause □ We had 90 minutes of nonstop fun. ◇ adv [talk, work] without stopping □ I've been working eight hours nonstop.

nontaxable [ˌnɒnˈtæksəbl] adj [income] that one does not have to pay tax on.

nontoxic [ˌnɒnˈtɒksɪk] adj [paint, waste] that is not poisonous or harmful.

nontransferable [ˌnɒntrænsˈfɜːrəbl] adj [membership, ticket] that can only be used by the person whose name is on it.

nonviolence [ˌnɒnˈvaɪələns] n the use of peaceful methods rather than violence to try to make political changes in society.

nonvoter [ˌnɒnˈvoʊtər] n a person who chooses not to vote; a person who cannot vote.

nonvoting [ˌnɒnˈvoʊtɪŋ] adj -1. [member] who does not have the right to vote. -2. [shares] that do not give the holder the right to vote.

nonwhite [ˌnɒnˈwaɪt] ◇ n a person who is not of European origin. ◇ adj: a nonwhite area/neighborhood.

noodles [ˈnuːdlz] npl long strips of dried dough that are boiled and eaten in soup or with meat □ egg noodles.

nook [nʊk] n a small place that provides shelter. ■ every nook and cranny every possible place in a particular space □ I've searched every nook and cranny, but I can't find it.

noon [nuːn] n 12 o'clock in the middle of the day □ It's twelve noon. □ the noon heat/sun.

noonday [ˈnuːndeɪ] n noon (old-fashioned or literary use).

no one pron = nobody.

noose [nuːs] n a loop made at the end of a piece of rope that gets tighter when one pulls it.

no-place adv US = nowhere.

nor [nɔːr] ◇ adv nor do I and I do not (used after a negative sentence to make it apply to somebody or something else) □ "I don't smoke." — "Nor do I." □ They can't cut prices any further, and nor can we. □ "I haven't seen it yet." — "Nor have I." OR "Nor me." ◇ conj neither...nor... used in front of the second of two negative statements or facts □ That remark is neither funny nor true. □ Neither he nor Gina has spoken to me since.

Nordic [ˈnɔːrdɪk] adj [person] who comes from northern Europe □ a Nordic language.

Norf abbr of Norfolk.

Norfolk [ˈnɔːrfək] a county in East Anglia, England, consisting mainly of farmland and marshes. SIZE: 5,368 sq kms. POPULATION: 744,300. ADMINISTRATIVE CENTER: Norwich.

Norfolk Broads: the Norfolk Broads a system of lakes and canals in Norfolk, England. It is a popular tourist center.

Norfolk Island an island in the South Pacific, between New Caledonia and New Zealand, that belongs to Australia. SIZE: 36 sq kms. POPULATION: 1,977.

norm [nɔːrm] n -1. to be the norm to be what one would expect □ One-person households have become the norm in certain areas. -2. a standard or level that is required by law, usually to make sure that something is safe □ Certain safety norms must be observed before a ship can sail.

normal [ˈnɔːrml] adj [behavior, day, person] that is not unusual or remarkable in any way □ Is it normal for you to get up so early? □ a normal, healthy baby □ It's not normal, the way she drinks.

normalcy [ˈnɔːrmlsɪ] n US = normality.

normality [nɔːrˈmælətɪ] n the state of being normal □ Everything returned to normality. □ I'll be glad to get back to normality once this is over.

normalize, -ise [ˈnɔːrməlaɪz] ◇ vt [relations, exchange rate] to make <sthg> normal again. ◇ vi: The situation soon normalized.

normally [ˈnɔːrməlɪ] adv -1. [eat, sleep, leave] a word used to say what usually happens or what is usually done □ He normally gets home about 6:00 pm. □ Normally she's very reliable. -2. [develop, function, react] see normal □ Everything is going along perfectly normally here.

Norman [ˈnɔːrmən] ◇ n a member of the northern French people who invaded England in the 11th century. ◇ adj: Norman history/architecture □ the Norman Conquest.

Normandy [ˈnɔːrməndɪ] an area of northern France, on the English Channel.

Norse [nɔːrs] adj [person, language, custom] that comes from ancient Scandinavia.

north [nɔːrθ] ◇ n the direction to the left of somebody who is facing the rising sun and in the top part of a map of a country, area etc □ Storm clouds are approaching from the north. ◇ adj -1. [part of a city, region] that is situated in the north □ They live in North Boston. -2. [side, coast] that faces the north □ the north face of the Eiger. -3. [wind] that comes from the north □ The north wind is especially fierce in Manitoba. ◇ adv [turn, head, drive] toward the north □ The room faces north. □ Seattle is north of Portland.

◆ **North** n the North the northeastern states of the USA, especially during the Civil War; the northern counties of England; the richer countries in northern parts of the world, e.g. Europe, Japan, and North America.

North Africa the countries of Morocco, Algeria, Tunisia, Libya, and Egypt.

North African n & adj: see North Africa.

North America the world's third-largest continent, consisting of Canada, the USA, and Mexico.

North American n & adj: see North America.

Northamptonshire [nɔːrˈθæmptənʃər] a county in central England. SIZE: 2,367 sq kms. POPULATION: 570,300. ADMINISTRATIVE CENTER: Northampton.

Northants abbr of Northamptonshire.

northbound [ˈnɔːrθbaʊnd] adj [traffic, train] that is moving toward the north □ There has been an accident in the northbound lane.

North Carolina [-kærə'laɪnə] a state in the eastern USA, between the Appalachian Mountains and the Atlantic Ocean. ABBREVIATION: NC. SIZE: 126,387 sq kms. POPULATION: 6,628,637 (North Carolinians). CAPITAL: Raleigh.

Northd abbr of **Northumberland**.

North Dakota [-də'koutə] a state in the central northern USA, on the Canadian border. ABBREVIATION: ND. SIZE: 183,019 sq kms. POPULATION: 638,800 (North Dakotans). CAPITAL: Bismarck.

northeast [,nɔːᵣθ'iːst] ◇ n the direction that lies halfway between north and east □ To the northeast lies a large lake. ◇ adj -1. [part of a city, region] that is situated in the northeast. -2. [side, coast] that faces the northeast. -3. [wind] that comes from the northeast. ◇ adv [turn, head, drive] toward the northeast □ The ranch lies six miles northeast of Fenton.

◆ **Northeast** n the Northeast the parts of a country or region that are situated in the northeast.

Northeast Corridor: the Northeast Corridor the area along the northeastern coast of the USA, between Boston and Washington D.C.

northeasterly [,nɔːᵣθ'iːstəᵣlɪ] adj -1. [part of a city, region] situated in the northeast □ in a northeasterly direction. -2. [wind] that comes from the northeast.

northerly ['nɔːᵣðəᵣlɪ] adj -1. [part of a city, region] situated in the north □ in a northerly direction. -2. [wind] that comes from the north.

northern ['nɔːᵣðəᵣn] adj [accent, region] from or in the north of a country or area □ One of the largest forests in northern Europe.

Northerner ['nɔːᵣðəᵣnəᵣ] n a person from the north of a country or region.

Northern Hemisphere n the Northern Hemisphere the part of the earth that is north of the equator.

Northern Ireland the northeastern part of Ireland, that is part of the United Kingdom. SIZE: 14,000 sq kms. POPULATION: 1,570,000 (Northern Irish). CAPITAL: Belfast.

❧ NORTHERN IRELAND
When Ireland was a British colony, many English and Scottish Protestants went to live in the part of it that is now called Northern Ireland. In 1921 the rest of Ireland, which was mainly Catholic, became an independent republic, but the mainly Protestant North chose to remain part of the UK. The Catholic minority in Northern Ireland, who were angry because they did not have equal opportunities in employment, housing etc, started a civil rights movement. Their protests became violent, and extremist groups of Catholics and Protestants began to fight and kill each other. Many innocent people were also killed. In 1969 the British Army was sent in to try to keep the peace, but the violence continued until both sides declared a ceasefire in 1994.

Northern Lights: the Northern Lights the col-ored lights that appear naturally in the sky at night over the countries nearest to the North Pole.

northernmost ['nɔːᵣðəᵣnmoust] adj [town, area] situated at the most northern point of a place.

Northern Territory: the Northern Territory an administrative region of central northern Australia. SIZE: 1,347,525 sq kms. POPULATION: 154,000. CAPITAL: Darwin.

North Island: the North Island the further north of the two islands of New Zealand. SIZE: 114,729 sq kms. POPULATION: 2,438,249. MAIN CITIES: Auckland, Hamilton, Wellington.

North Korea a republic in the northern part of the Korean Peninsula. SIZE: 120,500 sq kms. POPULATION: 22,600,000 (North Koreans). CAPITAL: Pyongyang. LANGUAGE: Korean. CURRENCY: won.

North Pole: the North Pole the most northern point on Earth.

North Sea ◇ the North Sea part of the Atlantic Ocean between eastern Britain and northern Europe. Oil and gas are extracted from below the seabed. ◇ comp: a North Sea port □ North Sea oil.

North Star: the North Star a star that is situated in the sky above the North Pole and is traditionally used as a way of finding the north at night.

Northumberland [nɔːᵣˈθʌmbəᵣlənd] a county in northeastern England. SIZE: 5,032 sq kms. POPULATION: 303,500. ADMINISTRATIVE CENTER: Morpeth.

North Vietnam → **Vietnam**.

northward ['nɔːᵣθwəᵣd] ◇ adj [direction, flight] toward the north. ◇ adv toward the north.

northwards ['nɔːᵣθwəᵣdz] adv [travel, head, face] = **northward**.

northwest [,nɔːᵣθ'west] ◇ adj -1. [part of a city, region] that is situated in the northwest. -2. [side, coast] that faces the northwest. -3. [wind] that comes from the northwest. ◇ adv [turn, head, drive] toward the northwest □ It lies eighty miles northwest of the capital. ◇ n the direction that lies halfway between north and west □ To the northwest lies a large pine forest.

◆ **Northwest** n the Northwest the parts of a country or region that are situated in the northwest.

northwesterly [,nɔːᵣθ'westəᵣlɪ] adj -1. [part of a city, region] that is situated in the northwest □ in a northwesterly direction. -2. [wind] that comes from the northwest.

Northwest Territories: the Northwest Territories the northern part of Canada between the Yukon and Hudson Bay. ABBREVIATION: NWT. SIZE: 3,380,000 sq kms. POPULATION: 57,649. CAPITAL: Yellowknife.

North Yemen → **Yemen**.

Norway ['nɔːᵣweɪ] a country in western Scandinavia, northern Europe. SIZE: 325,000 sq kms. POPULATION: 4,300,000 (Norwegians). CAPITAL: Oslo. LANGUAGE: Norwegian. CURRENCY: Norwegian krone.

Norwegian [nɔːˈwiːdʒn] *n* & *adj*: see **Norway**.

Nos., nos. *abbr of* **numbers.**

nose [nouz] *n* -1. [of a person] the part of the human face through which we smell and breathe □ *He punched me on the nose.* □ *He tapped his nose with his finger.* □ *I have a runny nose.* □ *a broken nose.* ■ **to be under one's nose** [book, pen, newspaper] to be very close to one and in a place where it can be easily seen, even though one cannot find it. ■ **to cut off one's nose to spite one's face** to do something when one is angry that is intended to harm somebody but that harms one more than the other person. ■ **to have a nose for sthg** to have a natural instinct for finding sthg out □ *Laura has a real nose for a good news story.* ■ **to keep one's nose out of sthg** not to interfere in sthg that does not concern one □ *Look, just keep your nose out of our business.* ■ **to look down one's nose at sb/sthg** to act as if one is better than sb/sthg. ■ **to pay through the nose** to pay a lot of money for something □ *You can travel first-class, but you'll pay through the nose for the privilege.* ■ **to poke** OR **stick one's nose into sthg** to interfere in sthg that does not concern one, especially by giving unwanted advice (informal use) □ *He's always poking his nose into other people's business.* ■ **to turn up one's nose at sthg** [at food, an offer, present] to refuse sthg in a way that suggests that one does not think it is good enough. -2. [of a plane, car] the front part of a vehicle.

◆ **nose about, nose around** *vi* to look at other people's private possessions, or ask about their affairs, in order to try and find out things that do not concern one □ *There he was, nosing about in my office again.*

nosebag [ˈnouzbæg] *n* a bag that is hung from a horse's nose and contains food for it to eat.

nosebleed [ˈnouzbliːd] *n* bleeding that comes from the nose □ *He had a severe nosebleed.*

nosecone [ˈnouzkoun] *n* [of a rocket, plane, missile] the front section of an aircraft or spacecraft that is shaped like a cone.

nosedive [ˈnouzdaɪv] ◇ *n* -1. [of a plane] a sudden change of direction in which a plane starts heading toward the ground □ *The jet went into a nosedive.* -2. [of prices] a sudden sharp fall □ *House prices took a nosedive in 1990.* ◇ *vi* -1. [plane] to go into a nosedive. -2. [prices, hopes] to suddenly fall sharply □ *The President's popularity nosedived after the revelations of corruption.*

nose job *n* a medical operation to change the shape of one's nose so that it looks more attractive (informal use).

nosey [ˈnouzɪ] *adj* = **nosy.**

nosh [nɒʃ] *n* GB food (informal use).

nostalgia [nɒˈstældʒə] *n* a mixture of happy and sad feelings caused by memories of something in the past □ *These old places are full of nostalgia for me.*

nostalgic [nɒˈstældʒɪk] *adj* [person, memory, visit] that is filled with nostalgia □ *a nostalgic view of the past* □ *As they get older, people tend to get more nostalgic.*

Nostradamus [ˌnɒstrəˈdɑːməs] (1503–1566) a French astrologer who wrote a book that claimed to predict future events.

nostril [ˈnɒstrəl] *n* one of the two holes in the nose of a person or animal through which they breathe and smell.

nosy [ˈnouzɪ] (*compar* **nosier,** *superl* **nosiest**) *adj* [person] who takes too much interest in other people's affairs □ *Don't be nosy.*

not [nɒt] *adv* -1. used to make a word, phrase, or sentence mean the opposite of what it says □ *I'm not totally convinced by what he said.* □ *I came not because I wanted to but because I was told to.* □ *It's not right.* □ *This isn't the first time it's happened.* □ *They're coming, but she's not.* □ *They haven't told him.* □ *I hope you won't regret it.* □ *He didn't ask.* □ *We met in Athens, didn't we?* -2. **I hope not** I hope that this is not true (used instead of a whole negative clause) □ *"Does Sam know?" — "I hope not."* □ *I can't decide whether to invite him or not.* □ *"Are they coming?" — "Apparently not."* -3. **I don't think I know her** I think that I do not know her (used with verbs like "think", "believe", "imagine", "expect", "want", "seem") □ *She doesn't appear to be interested.* □ *I don't imagine they'll be very long.* -4. **not ten feet away** less than ten feet away (used with numbers, distances etc) □ *She arrived not five minutes after you left.* -5. **not everyone agrees** some people agree but some do not (used before words like "all", "every", "always") □ *We don't always agree.*

◆ **not a, not one** *det* used for emphasis □ *"Do you think she'll come?" — "Not a chance!"* □ *I didn't get anything for my birthday, not even a card.*

◆ **not that** *conj* **not that I care** in spite of what I have just said, I do not care □ *Is she going out with someone else? Not that it's any of my business.*

◆ **not at all** → **at.**

notable [ˈnoutəbl] ◇ *adj* [example, success, improvement] that is important and deserves to be noticed □ *With the notable exception of Gerald, they were all there.* □ *Chicago is notable for its modern architecture.* ◇ *n* an important person.

notably [ˈnoutəblɪ] *adv* -1. a word used to introduce a typical or important example of something that has just been mentioned □ *The climate is wet, notably in the mountainous northwest.* -2. **notably short/better** short/better in a way that is noticeable □ *The figures are not notably worse than last year's.*

notary [ˈnoutərɪ] (*pl* **notaries**) *n* **a notary (public)** an official person who witnesses the signing of documents.

notation [nouˈteɪʃn] *n* a particular system of writing something down using symbols □ *musical notation.*

notch [nɒtʃ] *n* -1. a small, shallow, V-shaped cut in something, usually made with a knife □ *They cut a notch in the bark of the tree.* -2. a point on an imaginary scale that is the next one up or down from another one □ *She's gone up a notch in my estimation.*

◆ **notch up** *vt fus* **to notch up sthg** [victory, success] to achieve sthg.

note [nəʊt] ◇ *n* -1. a short informal letter, often on a small piece of paper □ *Leave me a note to say when you'll be back.* -2. a written record □ *I made a note of the address.* □ *He took notes throughout the meeting.* □ *May I borrow your notes from last week's class?* ■ **to compare notes** to compare one's opinion or experience of something with somebody else who has also been judging it □ *Let's not talk now — we can compare notes afterward.* ■ **to take note** to pay attention to something and remember it for the future □ *Small businesses should take note of this excellent new facility.* -3. MUSIC a single musical sound of a particular length and pitch; a symbol that represents one of these sounds □ *a musical note.* -4. a particular tone or mood □ *We're ending this financial year on an optimistic note.* □ *on a more serious note.* -5. [in one's voice] a sound in somebody's voice that expresses a particular feeling □ *I caught a note of anxiety in her voice.* -6. **to be of note** to be important □ *Little of note has occurred recently.* -7. GB FINANCE a bank note □ *a twenty-pound note.*

◇ *vt* -1. [change, attitude, difference] to notice <sthg> □ *He noted the change in her behavior.* -2. [cost, difficulty] to mention <sthg> □ *Please note that we will be closed next week.* □ *As I have already noted, the project has not been without its problems.*

◆ **notes** *npl* a section at the end of a book or article, where many small points numbered in the text are explained.

◆ **note down** *vt sep* **to note sthg down** [fact, address, phone number] to make a note of sthg in writing for future reference.

notebook ['nəʊtbʊk] *n* -1. a small book with blank pages designed for writing notes. -2. a **notebook (computer)** a small computer that can be carried easily and can be operated by batteries.

noted ['nəʊtəd] *adj* [expert, musician, resort] that is famous for a particular quality, talent, or ability □ *He's not noted for his tact.* □ *The town is noted for its hot springs.*

notepad ['nəʊtpæd] *n* -1. a small pad of paper for writing notes on, with pages that can easily be torn out. -2. a **notepad (computer)** a small computer into which information is entered using a special pen rather than a keyboard.

notepaper ['nəʊtpeɪpəʳ] *n* paper for writing letters on.

noteworthy ['nəʊtwɜːʳðɪ] (*compar* **noteworthier,** *superl* **noteworthiest**) *adj* that is interesting or worth taking notice of.

nothing ['nʌθɪŋ] *pron* -1. no thing, event, comment etc □ *I've had nothing to eat since breakfast.* □ *The idea itself is nothing new.* □ *"What did you buy?" — "Nothing."* ■ **there's nothing in it** it is not true □ *I've heard that rumor, but there's nothing in it.* ■ **there's nothing to it** it is very easy to do □ *"I can't believe you made those*

dresses yourself!" — "Oh, there was nothing to it, really." ■ **to be** OR **have nothing to do with sthg** to have no connection with sthg □ *"Who wrote this?" — "Don't ask me, I had nothing to do with it."* ■ **to be** OR **have nothing to do with sb** to be private, so that sb does not need to know about it □ *What I earn is nothing to do with you!* -2. a thing or person of no value or importance □ *"What were you going to say?" — "Oh, nothing really."* □ *They're arguing about nothing.* □ *Sonya means nothing to me any more.* ■ **it's nothing** it is not important or serious □ *"Are you hurt?" — "Don't worry, it's nothing."*

◆ **nothing but** *prep* only □ *This printer's been nothing but trouble.*

◆ **nothing if not** *adv* very □ *She's nothing if not determined.*

◆ **nothing like** *adv* -1. very unlike □ *You're nothing like your brother.* -2. not nearly □ *I'm nothing like finished.* □ *The play was nothing like as good as I'd hoped.*

◆ **for nothing** *adv* -1. free; for no money □ *I got the tickets for nothing.* □ *She offered to baby-sit for nothing.* -2. a phrase used to say that all one's efforts and attempts are wasted □ *They'd left by the time I got there, so I'd gone all that way for nothing.*

nothingness ['nʌθɪŋnəs] *n* the state in which nothing exists.

notice ['nəʊtəs] ◇ *n* -1. a written announcement, often put somewhere where people will see it □ *A notice was pinned to the door.* -2. attention given by somebody to something. ■ **to come to sb's notice** to be noticed by sb (formal use) □ *It has come to my notice that a lot of the staff are leaving at four o'clock.* ■ **to escape sb's notice** not to be noticed by sb □ *Has it escaped their notice that something is seriously wrong?* ■ **to take notice** to pay attention to somebody or something □ *She expects the council to sit up and take notice when she wants something done!* ■ **to take no notice** to pay no attention to somebody or something □ *Take no notice of him!* □ *They never take any notice of what I say.* -3. a warning that something is going to happen □ *My landlord gave me a week's notice to move out.* □ *Be ready to leave at a moment's notice.* ■ **at short notice** without much warning □ *I was asked to come at very short notice.* □ *I know it's short notice, but are you free tonight?* ■ **until further notice** until another announcement is made □ *'Closed until further notice.'* -4. **to be given** OR **to get one's notice** to be told officially by one's employer that one must leave one's job, usually at the end of a stated period of time □ *He was given a month's notice to quit.* ■ **to hand in one's notice** to officially tell an employer that one intends to leave one's job, usually at the end of a stated period of time.

◇ *vt* [change, person, the time] to see or pay attention to <sb/sthg> □ *I noticed them talking in the street.* □ *She noticed him write something down.* □ *I noticed that it was already six o'clock.* □ *Did you notice the ring he was wearing?*

◇ *vi:* *"They don't get along too well." — "So I've noticed!"* □ *I've never even noticed.*

noticeable ['noʊtəsəbl] *adj* [increase, improvement, change] that can easily be seen □ *There's no noticeable difference in the color.* □ *The stain was barely noticeable.*

noticeably ['noʊtəsəblɪ] *adv* **to be noticeably different/hotter** to be different/hotter in a way that is noticeable □ *It was noticeably cooler when we got off the plane.*

noticeboard ['noʊtəsbɔːʳd] *n* a board on which notices are put for people to read.

notification [ˌnoʊtəfɪ'keɪʃn] *n* [of payment, results, delivery] *see* **notify** □ *We received notification of the changes this morning.*

notify ['noʊtəfaɪ] (*pt* & *pp* **notified**) *vt* [police, authorities, applicant] to give some official information to <sb> □ *You will be notified of the results by mail.*

notion ['noʊʃn] *n* an idea or belief about something, especially one that is thought to be wrong or foolish □ *She has no notion of time/money.* □ *You have the strangest notions sometimes.*

◆ **notions** *npl* US SEWING a collective term for things used when sewing, e.g. buttons and thread.

notional ['noʊʃənl] *adj* [payment, membership] that is theoretical rather than real.

notoriety [ˌnoʊtə'raɪətɪ] *n* fame that somebody or something has because of something bad that has happened involving them □ *The riots confirmed the district's notoriety as a crime center.*

notorious [noʊ'tɔːrɪəs] *adj* [criminal, theft, nightclub] that is well-known because of something bad □ *The street is notorious for its prostitutes.* □ *He's notorious for always being late.*

notoriously [noʊ'tɔːrɪəslɪ] *adv* **notoriously lazy/ unreliable etc** that is known by many people to be lazy/unreliable etc.

Nottinghamshire ['nɒtɪŋəmʃəʳ] a county in central England. SIZE: 2,164 sq kms. POPULATION: 1,007,700. ADMINISTRATIVE CENTER: Nottingham.

Notting Hill Carnival [ˌnɒtɪŋhɪl-] *n* a large street festival in west London, England, with music, dancing, and costume competitions, organized by the Afro-Caribbean community.

Notts *abbr of* **Nottinghamshire**.

notwithstanding [ˌnɒtwɪθ'stændɪŋ] (formal use) ◇ *prep* [opposition, public opinion] in spite of <sthg> □ *Notwithstanding their lack of money, they managed to get to Greece.* □ *Her success notwithstanding, she still has a lot to learn.* ◇ *adv* nevertheless.

nougat [US 'nuːɡət, GB 'nuːɡɑː] *n* a hard chewy candy, usually white or pink with nuts and fruit.

nought [nɔːt] *num* GB the number 0; *see also* **five**. ■ **noughts and crosses** a game played using a grid of nine boxes in which the players take turns, one drawing a nought in one box and the other drawing a cross in another, and in which the winner is the first person to complete a line of three boxes.

noun [naʊn] *n* a word used in grammar to re-

fer to a quality, person, object, place, action, or abstract idea.

nourish [US 'nɜːrɪʃ, GB 'nʌrɪʃ] *vt* **-1.** to feed <a person, plant, or young animal> in order to make them strong and healthy. **-2.** [idea, hope, ambition] to keep <sthg> in one's mind with the intention of making it real.

nourishing [US 'nɜːrɪʃɪŋ, GB 'nʌr-] *adj* [drink, meal, food] that gives a lot of nourishment.

nourishment [US 'nɜːrɪʃmənt, GB 'nʌr-] *n* **-1.** [in food, drink] food that a person, animal, or plant needs to stay strong and healthy. **-2.** [of a person, animal, plant] *see* **nourish**.

nouveau riche [ˌnuːvoʊ'riːʃ] (disapproving use) ◇ *adj* [person] who has recently become rich, but originally comes from a lower social class. ◇ *n* a person who is nouveau riche.

Nov. *abbr of* **November**.

Nova Scotia [ˌnoʊvə'skoʊʃə] a province in eastern Canada, on the Atlantic Coast, consisting of the Nova Scotia peninsula and Cape Breton Island. ABBREVIATION: NS. SIZE: 55,490 sq kms. POPULATION: 899,942 (*Nova Scotians*). CAPITAL: Halifax.

novel ['nɒvl] ◇ *adj* [concept, suggestion, approach] that is unusual and interesting □ *That's novel, a health farm for pets!* ◇ *n* a book that tells a story about people and events that are not real □ *I love detective novels.* □ *Her latest novel's out in paperback this week.*

novelist ['nɒvəlɪst] *n* a person who writes novels.

novelty ['nɒvltɪ] (*pl* **novelties**) *n* **-1.** something new and unusual □ *It was quite a novelty for her to be traveling by plane.* **-2.** [as a gift, prize] a small cheap object, often unusual, that is used as a small gift or prize and is not very useful □ *a novelty toy.* **-3.** [of a concept, suggestion, approach] *see* **novel** □ *The novelty of working in such a glamorous environment soon wore off.*

November [nə'vembəʳ] *n* the eleventh month of the year in the Western calendar; *see also* **February**.

novice ['nɒvəs] *n* **-1.** a person who has not yet learned enough about their job, hobby etc to be very good at it □ *I'm still pretty much a novice at skiing.* **-2.** RELIGION a person who has recently joined a monastery or convent and is not yet a full-fledged monk or nun.

Novocaine™ ['noʊvəkeɪn] *n* a pain-relieving drug used for local anesthetics.

now [naʊ] ◇ *adv* **-1.** at the present moment, as opposed to the past or future □ *I have to go now.* □ *They should have arrived by now.* □ *"Can I ask you something?" — "Not now, I'm busy."* ■ **any day** OR **time now** at any point in the very near future □ *The baby's due any day now.* ■ **that's all for now** I have no more to say at the moment, but I will probably say more later □ *We can manage OK for now, but we'll need extra help soon.* □ *Bye for now.* ■ **now and then** OR **again** occasionally. **-2.** used in stories to describe a particular time in the past □ *By now we were all exhausted.* □ *We* were all laughing now. **-3.** because of what has just happened □ *We were going to buy a new car, but we can't afford it now.* **-4.** used to introduce a new subject of conversation or to attract attention □ *Now then, what's going on here?* □ *Now for a look at the morning's papers.*

◇ *conj* **now (that)** because a particular event has happened □ *Now (that) you've found somewhere to live, you'll feel much more settled.*

NOW [naʊ] (*abbr of* **National Organization for Women**) *n* the largest US feminist organization.

nowadays ['naʊədeɪz] *adv* at the present time, especially when the situation was different before □ *Nowadays, women can work until the same age as men.*

nowhere ['nəʊweəʳ] *adv* in no place that exists □ *There's nowhere we can stay.* □ *There was nowhere else I could think of.* □ *Nowhere does it say you have to have a degree.* ■ **out of** OR **from nowhere** [appear] suddenly and unexpectedly □ *Suddenly, out of nowhere, came this great big truck.* ■ **nowhere near** not nearly □ *You've got nowhere near enough money for the plane ticket.* ■ **to be getting nowhere** to be achieving nothing □ *I seem to be getting nowhere with my attempts to convince them.* ■ **this is getting us nowhere** we are achieving nothing □ *Look, all this arguing is getting us nowhere.*

no-win situation *n* a situation that will have an unsatisfactory ending, whatever one does □ *We're in a no-win situation.*

noxious ['nɒkʃəs] *adj* **-1.** [gas, substance, fumes] that is poisonous or harmful. **-2.** [smell, creature] that is extremely unpleasant (formal use).

nozzle ['nɒzl] *n* a small device fitted to the end of a hose or a pipe to control the gas or liquid coming out.

NP *abbr of* **notary public.**

NS *abbr of* **Nova Scotia.**

NSAID (*abbr of* **anti-inflammatory non-steroidal drug**) *n* a drug for treating inflammation that does not contain steroids.

NSC (*abbr of* **National Security Council**) *n* **the NSC** a US government body that is responsible for national security.

NSPCC (*abbr of* **National Society for the Prevention of Cruelty to Children**) *n* **the NSPCC** a British organization that aims to protect the rights of children who are being badly treated.

NSU (*abbr of* **nonspecific urethritis**) *n* a sexually transmitted infection.

NSW *abbr of* **New South Wales.**

NT *n* **-1.** *abbr of* **New Testament. -2.** *abbr of* **National Trust.**

nth [enθ] *adj* a word used to indicate that something has happened many times already (informal use) □ *For the nth time, will you keep quiet!*

NTSC (*abbr of* **National Television Systems Commission**) *n* the organization responsible for the system of broadcasting color television pictures in e.g. the USA and Japan.

nuance ['njuːɑːns] *n* a very small difference in sound, appearance, meaning etc.

nub [nʌb] *n* **the nub of the problem/argument etc** the central and most important part of the problem/argument etc □ *Now we come to the nub of the matter.*

nubile ['njuːbaɪl] *adj* [girl, young woman] who is young and sexually attractive (humorous or literary use).

nuclear ['njuːklɪəʳ] *adj* [war, weapons, power station] connected with or using nuclear energy □ *nuclear tests.*

nuclear bomb *n* a bomb that explodes using the energy produced by atoms.

nuclear energy *n* the energy produced by atoms when they are split or joined.

nuclear family *n* a family consisting only of two parents and their children.

nuclear fission *n* the process of splitting the nucleus of an atom to produce energy.

nuclear fusion *n* the process of combining atomic particles to produce nuclear energy.

nuclear physics *n* the study of the nuclei of atoms and their behavior.

nuclear power *n* the power produced by atoms when they are split, used especially to make electricity.

nuclear reactor *n* a device used to produce nuclear energy.

nucleus ['njuːklɪəs] (*pl* **nuclei** [-lIaɪ]) *n* **-1.** [of an atom, a cell] the central part of something. **-2.** [of a group of people, idea] the basic and most important part of something □ *The campaign is run by a nucleus of five members.*

nude [njuːd] ◇ *adj* [person] who is wearing no clothes; [painting, scene, statue] that shows somebody who is nude. ◇ *n* **-1.** a picture or statue of a nude person. **-2.** *phrase* **to be in the nude** to be wearing no clothes.

nudge [nʌdʒ] ◇ *n* **-1.** a push one gives somebody with one's elbow to attract their attention to something □ *Sally gave me a nudge and pointed out of the window.* **-2.** something one says or does to encourage somebody to do something □ *He needs a nudge in the right direction.* ◇ *vt* **-1.** to give <sb> a nudge □ *She nudged him in the ribs.* **-2. to nudge sb into** OR **toward sthg** to say or do something to encourage sb to do sthg □ *The General is being nudged toward reform by his aides.*

nudist ['njuːdɪst] ◇ *n* a person who prefers to wear no clothes, often because they believe it is healthy. ◇ *adj* [beach, camp, colony] that is used by nudists.

nudity ['njuːdətɪ] *n* [of person] *see* **nude.**

nugget ['nʌgət] *n* **-1.** a small lump of gold, as it is found in the ground. **-2.** an interesting or valuable piece of information □ *The guide includes tips on how to haggle and other such useful nuggets.*

nuisance ['njuːsns] *n* somebody or something that causes problems □ *It's (such) a nuisance that you're away on Monday.* □ *What a nuisance!* □ *That child is a real nuisance!* ■ **to make a nuisance of oneself** to behave in a way that annoys people, e.g. by complaining or interrupting □ *Stop making such a nuisance of yourself — we're trying to work!*

NUJ (*abbr of* **National Union of Journalists**) *n* the NUJ a British labor union for journalists.

nuke [nʲuːk] (informal use) ◇ *n* a nuclear weapon. ◇ *vt* [city, country] to destroy <a place> using nuclear bombs.

null [nʌl] *adj* **to be null and void** not to be legally valid □ *The result was declared null and void.*

nullify ['nʌləfaɪ] (*pt* & *pp* **nullified**) *vt* **-1.** LAW [contract, claim] to declare <sthg> to be legally invalid. **-2.** [improvement, advance] to make <sthg> useless (formal use).

NUM (*abbr of* **National Union of Mineworkers**) *n* the NUM a British labor union for miners.

numb [nʌm] ◇ *adj* [person, fingers, mind] that cannot feel anything □ *They were numb with cold/shock/fear.* ◇ *vt* [person, fingers, mind] to make <sb/sthg> numb; [pain, feeling] to relieve <sthg> □ *We were all numbed by grief.* □ *This should numb the pain a little.*

number ['nʌmbəʳ] ◇ *n* **-1.** a word, e.g. one, five, seventeen, or a symbol, e.g. 2, 13, 58, used to show how many things one is talking about □ *He wrote a number on the board.* □ *a six-figure number.* **-2.** the series of figures that one dials to call somebody by telephone □ *Have you got my work number?* □ *Let me take your number.* **-3.** a quantity □ *We've dealt with a considerable number of cases.* □ *A small/large number of people disagreed.* ■ **a number of** several □ *We've received a number of complaints.* ■ **any number of** a lot of □ *There are any number of possibilities.* **-4.** [of a house, bus] a word used to refer to a figure or series of figures that identifies somebody or something □ *We live at number 23.* □ *Take the number 13 bus.* **-5.** [by a performer] something, e.g. a song or short piece of music, that is performed or an audience.
◇ *vt* **-1.** to have <a particular quantity> as a total □ *Each team numbers six players.* **-2. to be numbered** to be marked with a number □ *The pages are numbered automatically.* **-3. to be numbered among a particular group of people** to be included as part of a particular group of people □ *She is numbered among the greatest living novelists.*

number-crunching [-krʌntʃɪŋ] *n* the system of using a computer to analyze large amounts of data to find the answer to a problem (informal use).

numberless ['nʌmbəʳləs] *adj* [possibilities, stars] too many to be counted (literary use).

number one ◇ *adj* **-1. a number one priority/choice** a priority/choice that is more important to somebody than any other one □ *The number one priority this year is to raise our public profile.* □ *Egypt would have to be my number one choice as a holiday location.* **-2.** [manufacturer, team, pop group] that is the most successful in a particular field. ◇ *n* **-1.** the person or thing that is most important, successful etc in a particular field or situation □ *That song's been number one in the charts for months now.*

-2. oneself (informal use) □ *He only ever thinks of number one.*

numberplate ['nʌmbəʳpleɪt] *n* GB a sign on the front or back of a vehicle that shows its registration number.

Number Ten a phrase used to refer to 10, Downing Street, London, the place where the British Prime Minister officially lives.

numbness ['nʌmnəs] *n*: *see* **numb** □ *Her death left me with a feeling of numbness.*

numbskull ['nʌmskʌl] *n* = **numskull**.

numeracy ['nʲuːmərəsɪ] *n* GB *see* **numerate** □ *We aim to teach literacy and numeracy skills.*

numeral ['nʲuːmrəl] *n* a symbol or group of symbols used to represent a number.

numerate ['nʲuːmərət] *adj* GB [employee] who can use numbers to do basic calculations □ *Many 11-year-old pupils were barely numerate.*

numerical [nʲuːˈmerɪkl] *adj* [data, value, advantage] that is shown in the form of numbers □ *The files are kept in numerical order.*

numerous ['nʲuːmərəs] *adj* [reasons, people] many □ *I've had to remind him on numerous occasions.* □ *The benefits are numerous.*

numskull ['nʌmskʌl] *n* a stupid person (informal use).

nun [nʌn] *n* a member of a religious order consisting only of women.

nuptial ['nʌpʃl] *adj* [mass] that is connected with marriage (formal use).

nurse [nɜːʳs] ◇ *n* a person whose job is to care for people who are sick or hurt, especially in a hospital. ◇ *vt* **-1.** [patient, invalid] to care for <sb who is sick or hurt> □ *Her husband nursed her back to health.* **-2.** [ambition, desire, grudge] to have <a strong feeling> for a long time. **-3.** [baby] to feed <a baby> with milk from one's breast.

nursemaid ['nɜːʳsmeɪd] *n* a woman whose job is to take care of young children (old-fashioned use).

nursery ['nɜːʳsərɪ] (*pl* **nurseries**) ◇ *adj* [education, teacher] that is connected with the education of children between the ages of three and five. ◇ *n* **-1.** a place where very young children can be taken care of while their parents are working, shopping etc. **-2.** a place where plants and young trees are grown to be sold.

nursery rhyme *n* a short song or poem for very young children.

nursery school *n* a school for children between the ages of three and five.

nursery slopes *npl* the least steep parts of a mountain, where people learn to ski.

nursing ['nɜːʳsɪŋ] *n* the activity or profession of caring for people who are ill.

nursing auxiliary *n* a person who helps nurses in a hospital but is not qualified as a nurse.

nursing home *n* **-1.** a private hospital, especially one for elderly people.

nurture ['nɜːʳtʃəʳ] *vt* **-1.** [child, plant] to protect and care for the development of <sb/sthg>. **-2.** [ambition, hope, love] to have <a feeling or

desire> and try to help it continue and develop □ *We have long nurtured the belief that peace is possible.*

NUS (*abbr of* **National Union of Students**) *n* **the NUS** in Britain, an organization that campaigns for the rights of students and provides services such as advice and leisure activities.

nut [nʌt] *n* **-1.** [from a tree] a hard dry fruit covered with a hard shell that grows on some trees □ *She's allergic to nuts.* **-2.** [for fastening things] a small piece of metal with a hole in the middle for a bolt, used to fasten things together. ■ **the nuts and bolts** the practical basic aspects of a subject or process (informal use) □ *I can show you the nuts and bolts of accounting.* **-3.** a crazy person (informal use) □ *Her brother is a complete nut.* **-4. a sports/religious etc nut** a person who is very enthusiastic about sports/religion etc (informal use). **-5.** [of a person] **one's nut** one's head or mind (informal use) □ *Use your nut!*

◆ **nuts** (informal use) *adj* **to be nuts** [person] to be crazy □ *Are you nuts? There's no way I'm driving that thing!*

NUT (*abbr of* **National Union of Teachers**) *n* **the NUT** a British labor union for teachers.

nutcase ['nʌtkeɪs] *n* a crazy person (informal use).

nutcracker ['nʌtkrækəʳ] *n* a device used to crack a nutshell so that the nut inside can be eaten.

nutmeg ['nʌtmeg] *n* a hard, brown, tropical seed that is used as a spice; the powder made from this that is used as a spice.

nutrient ['nʲuːtrɪənt] *n* any substance that, when absorbed by a plant, animal, or human body, helps it to stay alive and grow.

nutrition [nʲuːˈtrɪʃn] *n* **-1.** the process of taking in nutrients. **-2.** the elements of a food or drink that are nutrients □ *Cereals have a high nutrition content.* □ *Nutrition information is shown on the packet.*

nutritional [nʲuːˈtrɪʃnəl] *adj* [disorder, research] *see* **nutrition** □ *Try to buy food with a high nutritional value.*

nutritionist [nʲuːˈtrɪʃnəst] *n* a person who studies nutrition and advises people what to eat and drink in order to be healthy.

nutritious [nʲuːˈtrɪʃəs] *adj* [food, meal] that contains the substances that help one's body to be healthy □ *Vegetarian food is highly nutritious.*

nutshell ['nʌtʃel] *n* **in a nutshell** a phrase used to introduce a very short way of saying or explaining something □ *In a nutshell, yes.*

nuzzle ['nʌzl] ◇ *vt* [person, horse, dog] to rub against <sb> gently with the nose and face, especially to show affection. ◇ *vi*: *The kittens nuzzled up to their mother.*

NV *abbr of* **Nevada**.

NW *abbr of* **northwest**.

NWT *abbr of* **Northwest Territories**.

NY *abbr of* **New York**.

NYC *abbr of* **New York City**.

nylon ['naɪlɒn] *n* a strong man-made material used in clothes and plastics.

◆ **nylons** *npl* women's stockings made of nylon.

nymph [nɪmf] *n* in Greek and Roman legends, a young woman who was believed to live in trees, rivers, and mountains.

nymphomaniac [ˌnɪmfəˈmeɪnɪæk] *n* a woman who wants to have sex a lot, usually with many different men (disapproving use).

NYSE (*abbr of* **New York Stock Exchange**) *n* the largest stock exchange in the USA.

NZ *abbr of* **New Zealand**.

O

o [oʊ] (*pl* **o's** OR **os**), **O** [oʊ] (*pl* **O's** OR **Os**) *n* **-1.** the fifteenth letter of the English alphabet. **-2.** a letter used to say the number zero, e.g. when it is part of a telephone number or year.

oaf [oʊf] *n* a person who one thinks is clumsy and stupid (disapproving use).

oak [oʊk] *n* **-1. oak (tree)** a large tree with strong hard wood. **-2.** the wood of the oak tree □ *an oak table.*

OAP *n abbr of* **old age pensioner**.

oar [ɔːʳ] *n* a long pole with a wide flat part at one end that is used for moving a boat through water.

oarlock ['ɔːʳlɒk] *n* US a device that holds an oar in place while one is rowing.

oarsman ['ɔːʳzmən] (*pl* **oarsmen** [-mən]) *n* a man who rows a boat.

oarswoman ['ɔːʳzwʊmən] (*pl* **oarswomen**) *n* a woman who rows a boat.

OAS (*abbr of* **Organization of American States**) *n* **the OAS** an association that includes the USA and most Latin American countries, and that aims to encourage closer social, economic, and military cooperation between its members.

oasis [oʊˈeɪsɪs] (*pl* **oases** [-ˈeɪsiːz]) *n* **-1.** a place in a desert where there is water, and where trees grow. **-2.** a place that is very pleasant, good, quiet etc and that is surrounded by things that are unpleasant, bad, noisy etc □ *an oasis of tranquility.*

oath [oʊθ] *n* **-1.** a formal promise □ *Everyone had to take an oath of allegiance to the new ruler.* ■ **to be on** OR **under oath** to have made a formal promise, especially to tell the truth in a court of law □ *Remember that you are under oath.* **-2.** a swearword (old-fashioned use).

oatmeal ['oʊtmiːl] *n* **-1.** crushed oats used as a kind of flour in cooking □ *oatmeal cookies.*

-2. US a dish consisting of oats cooked in milk or water and eaten hot, usually for breakfast.

oats [outs] *npl* a cereal used for cooking or as food for farm animals.

OAU (*abbr of* **Organization of African Unity**) *n* the OAU an association that includes most African countries, and whose aim is to encourage cooperation and unity between its members.

obdurate ['ɒbdʲʊrət] *adj* [person] who is stubborn and determined not to change their beliefs or feelings about something (formal use) □ *He remained obdurate in his refusal to sign.*

OBE (*abbr of* **Order of the British Empire**) *n* an honorary title in Britain, usually given for services to the country.

obedience [ə'biːdjəns] *n* obedient behavior □ *She expected complete obedience from her class.*

obedient [ə'biːdjənt] *adj* [child, servant, animal] that does what they are asked or told to do without disagreeing, waiting etc □ *He's very obedient — I only have to say "Sit!" and he does.*

obediently [ə'biːdjəntlɪ] *adv* [behave, wait] *see* **obedient** □ *He followed me obediently outside.*

obelisk ['ɒbəlɪsk] *n* a tall stone pillar that has square sides and a point at the top and is built to remind people about a particular event or person.

obese [ou'biːs] *adj* [person, animal] that is very fat, in a way that is unhealthy.

obesity [ou'biːsətɪ] *n* MEDICINE a condition in which one is very fat □ *Obesity considerably increases the risk of heart disease.*

obey [ə'beɪ] ◇ *vt* [teacher, law, instructions] to do what <sb/sthg> tells one to do □ *Are you refusing to obey my orders?* ◇ *vi* [soldier, child, animal] *The hostages obeyed without question.*

obituary [US ə'bɪtʃuerɪ, GB -ərɪ] (*pl* **obituaries**) *n* a piece of writing in a newspaper about the life of a person who has just died.

object [*n* 'ɒbdʒɪkt, *vb* ɒb'dʒekt] ◇ *n* **-1.** a thing that can be seen or touched but is not alive □ *There was a dark, round object lying in the middle of the road.* **-2.** [of an activity] the aim or purpose of an activity □ *What's the object of all this?* □ *Of course we want to make a profit; that's the whole object of the exercise.* **-3. an object of ridicule/hatred etc** a person or thing that is ridiculed/hated etc □ *The Starburn Group has long been the object of envy in the business world.* **-4.** GRAMMAR a word used to refer to the part of a phrase, usually a noun or pronoun, that comes after a preposition or verb, e.g. "chair" in "I sat on the chair" or "me" and "present" in "she gave me a present."
◇ *vt* to state <sthg> as an objection □ *He objected that he had no previous knowledge of the arms deals.* □ *"But you can't go now," objected David.*
◇ *vi* to make an objection to something □ *If no one objects, I'd like to leave now.* □ *They objected to the committee's proposals/to relocating.* □ *"I think it would be fair to say that this witness is a known liar." — "I object!"*

objection [əb'dʒekʃn] *n* a statement or feeling that shows that one is opposed to somebody or something or disagrees with them □ *I have no objection to that/to his coming.* □ *She had one or two objections.* □ *If no one has any objections, we'll continue with the discussion tomorrow.*

objectionable [əb'dʒekʃnəbl] *adj* [person, behavior] that one finds unreasonable or unpleasant and that one disapproves of □ *I liked her, but I found her husband thoroughly objectionable.*

objective [əb'dʒektɪv] ◇ *adj* **-1.** [opinion, person, analysis] that is fair because it is not influenced by personal feelings □ *Let's try to be objective about this.* **-2.** [evidence, data] that is based on fact. ◇ *n* the result that one wants and that one is trying to get □ *He failed to achieve his main objectives.* □ *Our objective is to reach zero inflation by the next decade.* □ *career objectives.*

objectively [əb'dʒektɪvlɪ] *adv* [speak, consider] without being influenced by personal feelings □ *Looking at the matter objectively, you can see there's very little difference between the two.*

objectivity [,ɒbdʒek'tɪvətɪ] *n*: *see* **objective** □ *We must try to retain a certain degree of objectivity.*

object lesson ['ɒbdʒɪkt-] *n* **an object lesson in sthg** an event, experience etc that is a very good example of sthg □ *It was an object lesson in persistence.*

objector [əb'dʒektə^r] *n* a person who is opposed to something.

obligate ['ɒblɪgeɪt] *vt* **to be/feel obligated to do sthg** to be/feel obliged to do sthg (formal use) □ *I don't want you to feel obligated to say yes.*

obligation [,ɒblɪ'geɪʃn] *n* **-1.** a state of being obliged to do something, especially because one has agreed to do so □ *You are under no obligation to buy.* □ *You have an obligation to your family.* **-2.** something that one has agreed to do and that must be done □ *He felt that he had more than fulfilled his obligations.*

obligatory [US ə'blɪgətɔːrɪ, GB -ətərɪ] *adj* that is necessary because of a law, rule, or custom □ *Attendance is obligatory.*

oblige [ə'blaɪdʒ] ◇ *vt* **-1. to oblige sb to do sthg** to make sb have to do sthg □ *You are not obliged to come.* **-2.** to do something for <sb> in order to help them □ *Would you oblige me by filling out this form?* ◇ *vi*: *I asked him to do it and he happily obliged.*

obliging [ə'blaɪdʒɪŋ] *adj* [person] who does something for somebody in order to be helpful □ *An obliging friend brought me here in her car.*

oblique [ə'bliːk] ◇ *adj* **-1.** [look, compliment] that is indirect and therefore difficult to understand □ *The article made an oblique reference to the incident.* **-2.** [line, stroke] that slants to one side. ◇ *n* a short diagonal line that slants forward from its base and is used to separate words or phrases.

obliquely [ə'bliːklɪ] *adv* [mention, refer] in an indirect way that can be confusing □ *She hinted obliquely at some changes in the organization.*

obliterate [ə'blɪtəreɪt] *vt* [town, building] to destroy <sthg> completely □ *Whole areas of the city were obliterated by the earthquake.*

oblivion [ə'blɪvɪən] *n* -1. the state of being unconscious □ *Drugs brought a kind of oblivion.* -2. the state of being forgotten or irrelevant □ *He gradually sank into oblivion.*

oblivious [ə'blɪvɪəs] *adj* **to be oblivious** [person] to be unaware of something □ *She was completely oblivious to OR of what was happening.*

oblong ['ɒblɒŋ] ◇ *n* a shape that has four sides, two long and two short, and in which all the angles are 90°. ◇ *adj* [table, mirror] that is in the shape of an oblong.

obnoxious [əb'nɒkʃəs] *adj* [smell, sight] that is very unpleasant; [person, comment, behavior] that is rude and offensive □ *What an obnoxious little man!*

o.b.o. (*abbr of* **or best offer**) a phrase used in advertisements to show that the person selling the goods will accept the best price that is offered.

oboe ['oʊboʊ] *n* a musical instrument made of wood that looks like a long tube and is played by blowing through a reed.

oboist ['oʊboʊəst] *n* a person who plays the oboe.

obscene [əb'siːn] *adj* [publication, humor, phone call] that one finds offensive, especially because of its references to sex □ *Meier was fined for making obscene gestures to the crowd.*

obscenity [əb'senətɪ] (*pl* **obscenities**) *n* -1. obscene behavior □ *His movies contain an unacceptable level of obscenity.* -2. an obscene word □ *He left, muttering obscenities.*

obscure [əb'skjʊər] ◇ *adj* -1. [poet, town, book] that not many people know about □ *It was originally thought to be the work of some obscure 17th-century painter.* -2. [text, joke] that does not have a clear meaning and is therefore difficult to understand □ *I find some of his remarks really obscure sometimes.* ◇ *vt* -1. [issue, truth] to make <sthg> unclear □ *The real problem is being obscured by their petty disputes.* -2. [sun, object] to make it impossible to see <sthg> properly □ *My view was obscured by a woman in a large hat.*

obscurity [əb'skjʊərətɪ] *n* -1. the darkness (formal use). -2. [of a poet, text] *see* **obscure** □ *She went from relative obscurity to stardom overnight.*

obsequious [əb'siːkwɪəs] *adj* [person] who tries too hard to please somebody, especially by always agreeing with what they say (formal and disapproving use) □ *The obsequious approach just doesn't work with me.*

observable [əb'zɜːrvəbl] *adj* [event, fact] that can be seen □ *There has been no observable improvement in the situation.*

observant [əb'zɜːrvnt] *adj* [person] who is able to notice things that are not obvious □ *That's very observant of you.*

observation [ˌɒbzərˈveɪʃn] *n* -1. a comment intended to show what one thinks about something □ *He made some interesting observations about the layout.* -2. [of a suspect, patient, somebody's behavior] *see* **observe** □ *They're keeping him under observation for a few days.*

observation post *n* a place where soldiers can watch the movements of the enemy from a higher position.

observatory [US əb'zɜːrvətɔːrɪ, GB -'zɜːvətrɪ] (*pl* **observatories**) *n* a building containing special equipment that is used by scientists to watch and study the stars, planets etc.

observe [əb'zɜːrv] *vt* -1. [change] to notice <sthg> by seeing it (formal use) □ *I had observed little difference in his behavior toward me.* -2. [suspect, patient, behavior] to watch <sb/sthg> for a period of time in order to learn something about them □ *They've been observing the elections in case there are any irregularities.* -3. [law, speed limit] to obey <sthg>. -4. [custom, religious festival] to show respect for <sthg> by taking part in it □ *They don't observe Ramadan.* -5. to comment on a situation by saying <sthg> (formal use) □ *"I don't think she's feeling well," he observed.*

observer [əb'zɜːrvər] *n* -1. a person who sees or watches something □ *This may not be immediately apparent to the casual observer.* -2. [of politics, sports] a person who pays attention to and studies particular events or situations, and is usually considered to be an expert on them □ *Royal observers have commented that a separation may be imminent.* -3. [of a class, election] a person who watches a situation or activity without taking part, in order to see what happens □ *I'm only here as an observer.* □ *UN observers will monitor the handover.*

obsess [əb'ses] *vt* **to be obsessed by** OR **with sb/sthg** to be unable to stop thinking about sb/sthg □ *She became obsessed with the idea of emigrating to Canada.*

obsession [əb'seʃn] *n* the inability of somebody to stop thinking about a particular person or subject or about doing something □ *His paintings reveal an obsession with death.* □ *Dancing has become an obsession with her.*

obsessional [əb'seʃnəl] *adj* [behavior, need] *see* **obsession**.

obsessive [əb'sesɪv] *adj* [person, behavior] that shows an inability to stop thinking about or doing something □ *He's obsessive about cleanliness.*

obsolescence [ˌɒbsəˈlesns] *n*: *see* **obsolete** □ *Built-in obsolescence is a way for car and computer companies to make money.*

obsolescent [ˌɒbsəˈlesnt] *adj* [system, machine] that is becoming obsolete.

obsolete ['ɒbsəliːt] *adj* [system, machine, word] that is old-fashioned and no longer useful.

obstacle ['ɒbstəkl] *n* -1. an object that is in the way and makes it difficult for one to move forward □ *With a broken leg, every staircase became an enormous obstacle.* -2. a situation, fact etc that makes it difficult for something to happen □ *What are the obstacles to free trade?* □ *There are many obstacles to overcome.*

obstacle course *n* a course made up of different obstacles that must be passed, usually for sport or for developing physical fitness.

obstetrician [ˌɒbstə'trɪʃn] *n* a doctor who is trained in obstetrics.

obstetrics [ɒb'stetrɪks] *n* the part of medicine that deals with the way babies are born and the care of pregnant women.

obstinacy ['ɒbstənəsɪ] *n* a determination not to change one's opinions or behavior that other people find unreasonable □ With his usual obstinacy, he refused to give in.

obstinate ['ɒbstənət] *adj* -1. [person] who is determined not to change their behavior or opinions (disapproving use) □ She's so obstinate, you'll never get her to go. -2. [cough, stain] that is difficult to get rid of.

obstinately ['ɒbstənətlɪ] *adv* [refuse, insist] *see* **obstinate** □ He clung on obstinately to power.

obstreperous [əb'strepərəs] *adj* [person, behavior] that is noisy and difficult to control (formal or humorous use).

obstruct [əb'strʌkt] *vt* -1. [road, path, pipe] to block <sthg> □ Your car is obstructing the exit. -2. [justice, process, plan] to prevent <sthg> from working properly □ Joe was charged with trying to obstruct the course of justice.

obstruction [əb'strʌkʃn] *n* -1. [in a road, path, pipe] something that blocks something. -2. [of justice, a process, plan] *see* **obstruct**. -3. SPORT the act of unfairly getting in the way of an opposing player.

obstructive [əb'strʌktɪv] *adj* [person, behavior, policy] that tries to prevent something from happening.

obtain [əb'teɪn] *vt* [degree, book, information] to get <sthg> □ This kind of data is very difficult to obtain.

obtainable [əb'teɪnəbl] *adj* that can be obtained □ The book is not easily obtainable in the shops.

obtrusive [əb'truːsɪv] *adj* [behavior, smell, color] noticeable in a way that is not pleasant □ I found his presence obtrusive.

obtrusively [əb'truːsɪvlɪ] *adv* [act, behave] *see* **obtrusive** □ I was trying to be helpful, not too obtrusively, I hope.

obtuse [əb'tʲuːs] *adj* -1. [person] who pretends not to understand in a way that is annoying □ Stop being so obtuse! You know what I mean! -2. **an obtuse angle** an angle of between 90° and 180°.

obverse ['ɒbvɜːrs] *n* (formal use) -1. **the obverse** [of an argument, opinion] the opposite of something □ Of course, the obverse is also often true. -2. **the obverse** the front side of a coin that has the main picture on it.

obviate ['ɒbvɪeɪt] *vt* [need, problem] to remove or make <sthg> unnecessary (formal use) □ Improved public transportation would obviate the need for everyone to have their own car.

obvious ['ɒbvɪəs] ◇ *adj* -1. [answer, reasons, advantages] that can be easily seen or recognized □ The answer is obvious. □ It's obvious that we're not welcome here. -2. [remark, lie] that is not subtle and shows little thought or originality □ It seemed like an obvious thing to say. ◇ *n* **to state the obvious** to say something that is so clear that it does not need to be said □ Saying that peace will be difficult is just stating the obvious.

obviously ['ɒbvɪəslɪ] *adv* -1. **obviously,...** a word used to introduce something that one expects people to know or agree with □ Obviously I wouldn't tell anyone. -2. in a way that is easily seen or noticed □ Marcus was obviously upset by what you said. □ There's obviously some kind of problem with the transmission.

OCAS ['oukæs] (*abbr of* **Organization of Central American States**) *n* an association of Central American countries whose aim is to encourage closer cooperation between its members.

occasion [ə'keɪʒn] ◇ *n* -1. a particular time when something happens □ On one occasion, they were refused entry. □ We've met on several occasions. -2. an important event, ceremony, or celebration □ I'm saving this dress for a special occasion. ■ **to rise to the occasion** to show that one is able to deal with a difficult situation □ Twelve people is a lot to cook for, but I'm sure she'll rise to the occasion. -3. **to have occasion to do sthg** to have reason for doing sthg (formal use) □ I've never had occasion to doubt it. ◇ *vt* to cause <sthg> (formal use) □ His deteriorating health occasioned grave concern.

◆ **on occasion** *adv* sometimes but not often □ He's been known to smoke, on occasion.

occasional [ə'keɪʒnəl] *adj* that happens sometimes but not often or regularly □ I like the occasional drink. □ There will be occasional showers in the south.

occasionally [ə'keɪʒnəlɪ] *adv* sometimes but not often □ "Do you still see him?" — "Occasionally." □ We occasionally go out for a drink.

occasional table *n* a small table on which ornaments, cups, plates etc can be put.

occluded front [ə'kluːdəd-] *n* a warm weather front whose air has been forced upward by a cold front flowing in from underneath.

occult [ɒ'kʌlt] ◇ *adj* [powers, arts] supernatural. ◇ *n* **the occult** supernatural powers, forces etc.

occupancy ['ɒkjəpənsɪ] *n* the fact or period of occupying a building, piece of land etc (formal use) □ A young couple has taken over the occupancy of the apartment.

occupant ['ɒkjəpənt] *n* -1. a person who occupies a building, room etc □ All occupants will be asked to sign this form. -2. a person who is in a chair, vehicle etc (formal use) □ The car crashed, killing two of its occupants.

occupation [ˌɒkjə'peɪʃn] *n* -1. the job that one does for a living □ Please state your occupation. -2. a pastime □ Painting is her favorite occupation. -3. MILITARY [of a country, town] *see* **occupy** □ the German occupation of France.

occupational [ˌɒkjə'peɪʃnəl] *adj* [injury, pension] that is connected with somebody's job.

occupational hazard *n* a danger or a risk that is always present in a particular job □ Repetitive strain injury is one of the occupational hazards of being a keyboarder.

occupational therapist *n* a person who is trained to carry out occupational therapy.

occupational therapy *n* the training of ill or injured people in skills that are intended to help them get back to work or normal life again.

occupied ['ɒkjəpaɪd] *adj* **-1. to be occupied** [seat, room, toilet] to be in use already with the result that nobody else can use it □ *Is this table occupied?* **-2.** MILITARY [country, territory, town] that has been invaded by a foreign army and is controlled by it.

Occupied Territories: the Occupied Territories the areas of the Middle East that have been occupied by Israel since 1967: the Gaza Strip, the Golan Heights, and the West Bank.

occupier ['ɒkjəpaɪəʳ] *n* GB a person who lives in a building (formal use).

occupy ['ɒkjəpaɪ] (*pt* & *pp* **occupied**) *vt* **-1.** [house, building, room] to live, work, or stay in <sthg> with the result that nobody else can use it □ *A Greek family is occupying the apartment at the moment.* □ *They occupy the whole of the first floor.* **-2.** MILITARY [country, territory, town] to move into and take control of <a place> □ *the occupying army.* **-3.** [post, position] to have <sthg> □ *The Queen occupies a central role in the constitutional set-up.* **-4. to occupy oneself** to keep oneself busy □ *Now that he's retired, he occupies himself in researching family history/with his stamp collection.* **-5.** [time, space, mind] to fill <sthg> □ *The story occupied the whole front page.*

occur [ə'kɜːʳ] (*pt* & *pp* **occurred**, *cont* **occurring**) *vi* **-1.** [incident, event, tragedy] to happen □ *the place where the accident occurred.* **-2.** [species, phenomenon] to exist or be found in a particular place □ *These weather patterns only occur in tropical regions.* **-3. to occur to sb** [idea, thought] to come into sb's mind □ *It occurred to me that he might be lying.*

occurrence [ə'kʌrəns] *n* **-1.** something that happens □ *There were a number of strange occurrences in the weeks following the sighting.* **-2.** [of violence, a crime, disease] the fact of something happening or existing □ *a study of the occurrence of HIV infection.*

ocean ['oʊʃn] *n* **-1. the ocean** the sea □ *We went swimming in the ocean.* **-2.** GEOGRAPHY one of the five main areas into which the sea on the Earth's surface is divided.

oceangoing ['oʊʃngoʊɪŋ] *adj* **an oceangoing ship** a ship that is designed for crossing the open sea rather than for traveling along a coast or on a river.

Oceania [US ,oʊʃɪ'ænɪə, GB ,oʊsɪ'ɑːnɪə] a collective term for the islands of the central and southern Pacific Ocean, including Melanesia, Micronesia, and Polynesia.

ocher US, **ochre** GB ['oʊkəʳ] *adj* that is yellow-orange in color.

o'clock [ə'klɒk] *adv* a word used when telling the time, after a number from 1 to 12, to say that it is exactly that hour □ *It's five o'clock.* □ *I left at about two o'clock.*

O'Connor [oʊ'kɒnəʳ], **Flannery** (1925–1964) a US writer who described life in the South. Her work includes *A Good Man is Hard to Find* and *Everything that Rises Must Converge*.

OCR *n* **-1.** *abbr of* **optical character reader. -2.** *abbr of* **optical character recognition**.

Oct. *abbr of* **October**.

octagon ['ɒktəgən] *n* a flat geometrical shape with eight straight sides and eight angles.

octagonal [ɒk'tægnəl] *adj: see* **octagon**.

octane ['ɒkteɪn] *n* a substance that is found in gasoline and is used to measure its quality and efficiency. FORMULA: $C_8 H_{18}$.

octane number, octane rating *n* a number that shows the quality and efficiency of gasoline, with the highest number showing the highest quality.

octave ['ɒktɪv] *n* a space of six whole tones between two musical notes.

octet [ɒk'tet] *n* a group of eight singers or musicians; a piece of music written for such a group.

October [ɒk'toʊbəʳ] *n* the tenth month of the year in the Western calendar; *see also* **February**.

octogenarian [,ɒktoʊdʒə'neərɪən] *n* a person who is between 80 and 89 years old.

octopus ['ɒktəpəs] (*pl* **octopuses** OR **octopi** [-paɪ]) *n* a sea creature with a soft body and eight tentacles, eaten as food.

OD ◇ *n* & *vi abbr of* **overdose**. ◇ *abbr of* **overdrawn**.

odd [ɒd] *adj* **-1.** [person, behavior, idea] that is strange or unusual □ *I think it's very odd that Lou didn't come.* □ *This tuna smells odd.* **-2.** [socks, gloves] that do not belong to the same pair □ *He was wearing odd shoes.* **-3. an odd number** a number that cannot be divided exactly by two. **-4.** [bits, parts] that are left over or extra □ *I have some odd scraps of material left over, if you want them.* **-5. the odd drink/game etc** a drink/game etc that one has sometimes, but not often □ *We meet for a chat on the odd occasion.* **-6. twenty-odd/thirty-odd etc** a little more than twenty/thirty etc (informal use) □ *They've been together for forty-odd years now.*

◆ **odds** *npl* **-1.** probability □ *The odds are that we'll lose.* ■ **against the odds** despite disadvantages or what most people expect □ *Against (all) the odds, the oldest competitor crossed the line first.* □ *Their marriage survived against all odds.* **-2.** *phrases* **odds and ends** small objects of various types, usually of little value □ *I managed to pick up some odds and ends for the house at the sale.* ■ **to be at odds with sb/sthg** not to be in agreement with sb/sthg □ *She's always been at odds with her family.*

oddball ['ɒdbɔːl] *n* a person whose behavior one finds strange or eccentric (informal use) □ *His brother is a real oddball.*

oddity ['ɒdətɪ] (*pl* **oddities**) *n* **-1.** a strange or unusual person or thing □ *As a teetotaler, he was an oddity among journalists.* **-2.** the odd quality of somebody or something □ *I was struck by the oddity of her behavior.*

odd-jobber US [-'dʒɒbəʳ], **odd-job man** GB *n* a person paid to do odd jobs.

odd jobs *npl* small manual jobs of various types.

oddly ['ɒdlɪ] *adv* -**1.** [behave, act, speak] *see* **odd** □ *He looked at me oddly.* -**2. oddly disappointing / encouraging etc** disappointing / encouraging etc in a way that is unexpected □ *I was oddly unimpressed by the show.* -**3. oddly enough** a phrase used to show that one finds something surprising □ *Oddly enough, I didn't much care.*

oddments ['ɒdmənts] *npl* small parts of something larger that have not been used and are left over.

odds-on [ˌɒdz-] *adj* **the odds-on favorite** the team, horse etc that is considered most likely to win.

ode [əʊd] *n* a poem in which a person, thing, or event is praised.

odious ['əʊdjəs] *adj* [person, behavior] that one finds very unpleasant (formal use).

odometer [əʊ'dɒmɪtəʳ] *n* US an instrument that records the number of miles traveled by a vehicle.

odor US, **odour** GB ['əʊdəʳ] *n* a smell.

odorless US, **odourless** GB ['əʊdəʳləs] *adj* [deodorant, liquid, gas] that has no smell.

odour *etc n* GB = **odor** *etc.*

odyssey ['ɒdəsɪ] (*pl* **odysseys**) *n* a long trip with many adventures (literary use).

OECD (*abbr of* **Organization for Economic Co-operation and Development**) *n* **the OECD** an association of 24 countries, including most of Western Europe, the USA, Canada, Japan, Australia, and New Zealand, whose aim is to encourage world trade and economic growth.

Oedipus [US 'edəpəs, GB 'iːd-] in Greek mythology, a man who killed his father and married his mother without realizing who they were.

OEM (*abbr of* **original equipment manufacturer**) *n* a company that makes its own computer products, using parts bought from other companies □ *the OEM market.*

oesophagus *n* GB = **esophagus**.

oestrogen *n* GB = **estrogen**.

of [*stressed* ɒv, *unstressed* əv] *prep* -**1. a bottle of milk** a bottle that contains milk □ *a bag of flour* □ *a book of stories.* -**2. a pound of grapes** used after nouns showing quantity or amount □ *a gallon of petrol* □ *many of my colleagues.* -**3. a flock of birds** used after nouns meaning a group □ *a gang of criminals* □ *a herd of cows.* ■ **a pair of shoes** used after nouns which make plural and uncountable nouns countable □ *a pair of scissors* □ *a set of keys.* -**4. the color of her dress** the color that her dress has □ *a leg of a table* □ *the size of the problem.* ■ **a city of two million people** a city that has two million people (used before numbers). ■ **a friend of mine** a friend that I

have. -**5. a look of anger** a look showing or filled with anger □ *a shout of joy* □ *a woman of great intelligence* □ *a position of power.* -**6. the smell of fish** the same smell that fish has □ *a lump the size of a tennis ball* □ *in the style of Beethoven...* -**7. a gift of flowers** a gift that is or consists of flowers □ *the science of astronomy* □ *a saving/increase of 5%.* ■ **the city of Los Angeles** the city that is Los Angeles (used with placenames). ■ **a child of five** a child who is five years old (used to show somebody's age). -**8. a crown of solid gold** a crown made from solid gold (used to show the material that something is made from) □ *a dress of silk.* -**9. a member of the family** a person who is in, from, or part of the family □ *the President of the company* □ *the streets of London.* ■ **any day of the week** any day in the week □ *scene 2 of Act III* □ *the University of Texas.* ■ **cancer of the liver/throat etc** cancer that affects the liver/throat etc (used of illnesses) □ *a fracture of the left wrist.* -**10. a map of France** a map that shows France □ *a photo of my son.* ■ **the story of my life** the story that tells about or deals with my life □ *a record of a meeting* □ *the Department of Health.* -**11. he told us of his life** he told us about his life (used after some verbs) □ *She often thought of her parents.* □ *I got rid of those papers.* ■ **used of sthg** used when talking about or referring to sthg □ *The word is used of men and women.* -**12. hopes of improvement** hopes that something will improve in the future □ *There seems no prospect of a pay rise.* □ *I have every intention of complaining.* □ *I wouldn't dream of criticizing you.* -**13. proud of her success** proud because of her success (used after some adjectives) □ *ashamed of his behavior.* -**14. the barking of the dogs** the barking that the dogs did (used to show what or who performs an action) □ *I heard the ringing of bells.* □ *the arrival/departure of the Paris train* □ *the contraction of the muscle.* ■ **the novels of Dickens** the novels written or made by Dickens. ■ **it was kind of you (to invite me)** you were kind (to invite me). -**15. a writer of plays** a person who writes plays (used to show the object of an action) □ *a supporter of the proposal* □ *the destruction of the rainforests.* ■ **a fear of flying** used to show the reason for a feeling or emotion □ *her love of good food.* -**16. the date of your birth** the date when your birth happened □ *Where were you on the night of the murder?* ■ **the war of 1902** the war that happened in 1902 □ *They met during the summer of '76.* ■ **the 12th of February** GB the 12th day in February.

off [ɒf] ◇ *adv* -**1. to drive off** to drive away from the place where one was before □ *A thief ran off with her purse.* □ *Turn off at the next junction.* ■ **to fall/jump off** to fall/jump down from where one was before. ■ **off you go!** you must go now. -**2. a long time off** a long time in the future (used in expressions of time) □ *The wedding was still two days off.* ■ **ten miles off** ten miles away (used in expressions of distance). -**3. she cut all her hair off** she cut her hair so that all of it was gone (used to show that something is removed) □

A button has come OR *fallen off.* ■ **he had his shirt off** he was not wearing his shirt □ *Could you help me off with this coat?* **-4. to turn a lamp off** to make a lamp stop operating □ *Switch the engine off.* **-5. to call a meeting off** to cancel a meeting, so that it will no longer take place. **-6. a day/year off** a day/year when one does not go to work because one is ill, on vacation etc □ *I'm planning to take some time off during the summer.* **-7. $10 off** $10 less than the usual price □ *She gave me 5% off.*

◇ *prep* **-1.** away from <sthg>, especially from the top or surface of sthg □ *Take your hands off me!* □ *She jumped down off the wall.* □ *I got off the bike.* **-2. off (the coast of) India** in the sea near (the coast of) India (used to show position) □ *Many students live off campus.* □ *The bathroom is off the hallway.* **-3. to cut a branch off the tree** to cut a branch so that it is no longer on the tree (used to show where something has been removed from) □ *I wiped the dirt off my shoes.* **-4. off work** not at work because of illness or a vacation □ *I go off duty at 10 o'clock.* **-5. to live off bread and water** to live using bread and water □ *This machine works off electricity.* **-6. he's off his food** he is not eating food because he is ill □ *She's been told to stay off alcohol/drugs.* **-7. I bought it off Eddie** I bought it from Eddie (informal use) □ *I borrowed $20 off Joan.*

◇ *adj* **-1. to be off** [milk, meat, wine] to be rotten or stale □ *The cheese is off.* **-2. to be off** [person] not to be at work, school etc because of illness or vacation □ *I'll be off for the rest of the week.* **-3. to be off** [person] to be away from home □ *He's off in the Bahamas.* **-4. to be off** [deal, party] to be canceled □ *I'm sorry, but the wedding's off.* **-5. to be off** [light, machine] not to be operating □ *Make sure the heating is off before you go out.*

◆ **off and on** *adv* sometimes but not continuously □ *It's been raining off and on all day.*

offal ['ɒfl] *n* the internal organs of animals, used as food.

off-balance *adv* **-1. to knock** OR **throw sb off-balance** to cause sb to lose their balance. **-2.** unprepared □ *Her remark caught me off-balance.*

offbeat ['ɒfbiːt] *adj* [humor, style, taste] that is unusual and strange (informal use).

off-Broadway *adj* [play, show] that is shown in the less well-known New York theaters.

off-center ◇ *adj* not exactly in the center □ *The picture's off-center.* ◇ *adv* [hang, position] in an off-center position.

off chance *n* **on the off chance that...** in the hope that something might be the case, even though it is unlikely □ *I just called on the off chance (that) you'd be in.*

off-color *adj* **-1.** [joke, remark] that is connected with sex and might be offensive to some people. **-2.** GB [person] who is a little unwell.

offcut ['ɒfkʌt] *n* a piece of fabric, carpet, wood etc that is left over from a larger piece and is often sold cheap.

off-day *n* a day when one does not work

well, things go badly etc (informal use) □ *I'm having an off-day today.*

off-duty *adj* [policeman, nurse] who is not working □ *I'm off-duty duty at six.*

offence GB = **offense.**

offend [ə'fend] ◇ *vt* [person] to upset or hurt the feelings of <sb> □ *I didn't mean to offend him.* □ *Parts of this film may offend some viewers.* ◇ *vi* to commit a crime □ *If he offends again, he'll go straight to prison.*

◆ **offend against** *vt fus* **to offend against sthg** [against a principle, rule] to go against sthg in a way that people think is morally wrong □ *Such abuses offend against the decency of honest working people.*

offended [ə'fendəd] *adj* **to be offended** [person] to be upset or hurt by something □ *Neil looked mortally offended.*

offender [ə'fendər] *n* a person who has been found guilty of a crime □ *Persistent offenders will be fined.*

offending [ə'fendɪŋ] *adj* **the offending item/word etc** the item/word etc that is the cause of a problem □ *We've been asked to remove the offending picture.*

offense US, **offence** GB [ə'fens, *sense 3* 'ɒfens] *n* **-1.** the act of breaking a rule or law □ *It is a criminal offense to carry a gun without a license.* □ *Is it her first offense?* **-2.** a cause of upset or hurt feelings □ *He tried hard not to give offense.* ■ **to take offense** to feel upset or hurt by something □ *He took offense at their jokes.* □ *Don't take offense: I'm sure she didn't mean it like that.* **-3.** US SPORT the team that has possession of the ball; the members of a team whose main role is to attack the opposing team's goal.

offensive [ə'fensɪv] ◇ *adj* **-1.** [language, behavior, joke] that causes offense □ *I find his attitude deeply offensive.* **-2.** [weapon, action, position] that is used for an attack. ◇ *n* **-1.** MILITARY an attack against the enemy, using a lot of soldiers and equipment, that continues for a long period □ *an air offensive.* **-2. to go on** OR **take the offensive** to start to attack or become aggressive □ *There's no need to go on the offensive just because I made one criticism.*

offer ['ɒfər] ◇ *vt* **-1.** [food, work, opportunity] to present <sthg> as a possibility that can be accepted or refused □ *They're offering a reward to anyone who can provide information.* □ *He offered me a large whiskey.* □ *I've been offered the chance to go to Tokyo.* **-2. to offer to do sthg** to show that one is willing to do sthg □ *A young man kindly offered to carry my bag.* **-3.** [sympathy, love, understanding] to give <sthg> □ *Please allow me to offer my sincerest condolences.* **-4.** [service, opportunity] to provide <sthg> □ *Our hotels offer excellent conference facilities in convenient locations.*

◇ *vi: We don't need your help, but it was kind of you to offer.*

◇ *n* **-1.** [of help, advice, money] an act of offering something □ *It was too good an offer to refuse.* □ *I've made other arrangements, but thanks for the offer, anyway.* □ *a job offer.* **-2.** BUSINESS

an amount of money that somebody says they are willing to pay in order to have something □ *They made me a generous offer.* **-3.** [in a store] a specially reduced price for a product □ *'Special offer'.*
◆ **on offer** *adj* GB **-1.** available to be bought □ *There was a wide range of goods on offer.* **-2.** on sale at a specially reduced price □ *Selected brands are on offer this week.*

OFFER [ˈɒfəʳ] (*abbr of* **Office of Electricity Regulation**) *n* the British government agency that is responsible for making sure that the electricity industry treats its customers fairly.

offering [ˈɒfərɪŋ] *n* **-1.** something offered or provided □ *The singer's latest offering has gone straight to number one.* **-2.** something offered as a gift or sacrifice to a god.

off guard *adv* unprepared □ *I was caught off guard.*

offhand [ˌɒfˈhænd] ◇ *adj* [person, greeting, behavior] that seems to show little interest in other people (disapproving use) □ *I found his manner very offhand.* □ *She has a very offhand way of dealing with people.* ◇ *adv* immediately and without time to think □ *I can't remember her name offhand.*

office [ˈɒfəs] *n* **-1.** [room] a room where nonmanual work, usually clerical and administrative, is done □ *office supplies/furniture* □ *Could you come to my office for a moment?* **-2.** [of a company, organization] a building that contains an office or offices □ *I fly out to our Boston office tomorrow.* **-3.** [people] the people who work in a particular office □ *The whole office is talking about it.* **-4.** [department] an administrative department of a business or a government □ *the tax/education office.* **-5.** [for a service] a room or building that offers a particular service □ *a sales office.* **-6.** POLITICS a position of authority, usually in government □ *during her second term of office* □ *The same party has been in office for 15 years.* ■ **to take office** to take over a responsibility, usually in a government.

office automation *n* the use of computers, word processors etc in offices.

office block *n* GB = **office building**.

office boy *n* a young man employed to carry out simple routine tasks in an office.

office building *n* US a tall building that contains a lot of offices.

officeholder [ˈɒfəshəʊldəʳ] *n* a person who has a position of responsibility in a government or in an organization.

office hours *npl* the period of the day when offices are open and people are at work □ *What do you do out of office hours?* □ *We are only open during office hours.*

office junior *n* GB a young person employed to carry out simple administrative tasks, e.g. mailing letters and photocopying documents.

Office of Fair Trading *n* **the Office of Fair Trading** the British government organization that is responsible for making sure that businesses operate fairly.

officer [ˈɒfəsəʳ] *n* **-1.** MILITARY a person in a position of command in the armed forces. **-2.** [in an organization] a person who holds a position of authority in an organization, business etc □ *the press and publicity officer for the Red Cross.* **-3.** [in the police] a member of the police force □ *He was accused of trying to bribe an officer of the law.*

office work *n* the kind of work that is done in an office, e.g. clerical and administrative work.

office worker *n* a person who does office work.

official [əˈfɪʃl] ◇ *adj* **-1.** [statistics, document, language] that is approved or recognized by the government or some other authority □ *Who was the official sponsor for the 1992 Olympic Games?* **-2.** [residence, duties] that is connected with a person who holds a position of authority □ *the President's official visit to China.* **-3.** [opening, announcement] that is formal and public □ *Her appointment is not official yet.* □ *It's official: they're engaged.* **-4.** [story, version] that is told to the public but is not necessarily completely true □ *What's the official reason for his visit?* ◇ *n* a person who holds a position of authority in government or in an organization □ *a goverment official.*

officialdom [əˈfɪʃldəm] *n* officials as a group (disapproving use).

officially [əˈfɪʃəlɪ] *adv* **-1.** [open, announce] *see* **official** □ *I haven't been officially invited yet.* **-2.** a word used to report statements made in public that may not be true □ *Officially, he's got flu, but it's actually more serious than that.*

officiate [əˈfɪʃɪeɪt] *vi* to perform the official duties at a ceremony, wedding etc □ *The President officiated in person at the medal presentation.*

officious [əˈfɪʃəs] *adj* [person] who is too eager to use their authority to give orders or advice (disapproving use) □ *An officious little man in a uniform told us to go away.*

offing [ˈɒfɪŋ] *n* **to be in the offing** to be likely to appear or happen in the very near future □ *Many feel that peace is now in the offing.*

off-key MUSIC ◇ *adj* that is out of tune. ◇ *adv*: *You're singing off-key.*

off-licence *n* GB a store where alcoholic drinks are sold.

off-limits *adj* **to be off-limits** to be an area that a particular group of people is not allowed to enter □ *The town is off-limits to military personnel.*

off-line ◇ *adj* [equipment, printer] that is not connected to or controlled by a computer ◇ *adv*: *Save money by reading your email off-line.* NOTE: Compare **on-line**.

offload [ɒfˈləʊd] *vt* [task, responsibility, object] to get rid of <sthg> that one does not want and give it to somebody else □ *He has a tendency to offload all his problems onto me.*

off-peak ◇ *adj* [electricity, fares, period] cheaper than usual because of lower demand at particular times. ◇ *adv* [travel, phone] in a period of low demand and at a reduced price.

off-putting [-pʊtɪŋ] *adj* [manner, behavior, person] that is unpleasant and causes dislike □ *Her description of the house was rather off-putting.*

off-ramp *n* US a road for leaving a highway.

off-road vehicle *n* a strong vehicle designed to be driven over rough ground.

off season *n* **the off season** the period of the year when few people go on vacation and prices for accommodations, travel etc are cheaper.
♦ **off-season** *adj*: *an off-season ticket/vacation.*

offset [ˈɒfset] (*pt* & *pp* **offset**, *cont* **offsetting**) *vt* [losses, costs] to balance <sthg> against something else that has an opposite effect so that they become more equal □ *We offset our expenses against tax.*

offshoot [ˈɒfʃuːt] *n* [of an enterprise, company] something that has developed from something else □ *Macken Ltd is an offshoot of a larger US corporation.*

offshore [ˈɒfʃɔːr] ◇ *adj* -**1.** [oilrig, island, fishing] that is based or done at sea. -**2.** FINANCE [fund, investment, banking] that is based abroad, usually as a way of avoiding the tax system of one's own country. ◇ *adv* [fish, swim] *We moored three miles offshore.*

offside [*adj* ˌɒfˈsaɪd, *n* ˈɒfsaɪd] ◇ *adj* -**1. an offside door/light etc** GB a door/light etc that is located on the side of a vehicle that is furthest from the side of the road while one is driving. -**2. to be offside** SPORT [in soccer, rugby] to be in a position that is not allowed by the rules, between the ball and the opponents' goal. ◇ *n* GB the side of a vehicle that is furthest from the side of the road.
NOTE: Compare **nearside**, **onside**.

offspring [ˈɒfsprɪŋ] (*pl* **offspring**) *n* -**1.** a child or children (formal or humorous use). -**2.** the young of an animal.

offstage [ˌɒfˈsteɪdʒ] ◇ *adj* -**1.** THEATER [noises] that is produced out of sight of the audience. -**2.** [romance, life] that is connected with the private life of an actor or actress and not related to their professional activity. ◇ *adv* THEATER *A loud bang was heard offstage.*

off-the-cuff *adj* [remark, response] that somebody makes without planning it or thinking about it first.
♦ **off the cuff** *adv* [say, remark, answer] in an off-the-cuff manner.

off-the-peg *adj* GB = **off-the-rack**.

off-the-rack *adj* US [clothes] that can be bought in a store and are ready to wear.

off-the-record *adj* [remark, statement] that is made unofficially and is not intended to be made public.
♦ **off the record** *adv*: *He spoke off the record.*

off-the-shelf *adj* [software] that can be bought by the public.
♦ **off the shelf** *adv*: *You can buy it off the shelf.*

off-the-wall *adj* [idea, sense of humor] that is unusual and strange (informal use).

off-white *adj* that is not completely white in color because it has some gray or yellow in it.

OFGAS [ˈɒfɡæs] (*abbr of* **Office of Gas Supply**) *n* the British government agency responsible for making sure that the gas industry treats its customers fairly.

OFT *n abbr of* **Office of Fair Trading**.

OFTEL [ˈɒftel] (*abbr of* **Office of Telecommunications**) *n* the British government agency responsible for making sure that the telecommunications industry treats its customers fairly.

often [ˈɒfn] *adv* -**1.** many times □ *He often drives to work.* □ *I don't see him very often.* □ *It's not often that she's wrong.* □ *"How often do you visit her?"* — *"About once a week."* -**2.** in many cases □ *Often the best solution is to switch off the computer and start again.* □ *The inhabitants are often very poor.*
♦ **as often as not, more often than not** *adv* usually □ *The trains are late as often as not.* □ *More often than not all he wants to do is chat.*
♦ **every so often** *adv* sometimes □ *We go out for a meal every so often.* □ *Every so often we got a phone call from him.*

OFWAT [ˈɒfwɒt] (*abbr of* **Office of Water Supply**) *n* the British government agency responsible for making sure that the water industry treats its customers fairly.

ogle [ˈoʊɡl] *vt* to stare at <sb> in a way that shows sexual interest (disapproving use) □ *Will you stop ogling those girls!*

ogre [ˈoʊɡər] *n* in fairy tales, a large, cruel, ugly creature that sometimes eats people.

oh [oʊ] *excl* -**1.** [before a reply, comment] a word used to introduce a comment or a reply to something □ *Oh how nice!* □ *Oh really?* -**2.** a word used to express doubt or hesitation □ *Oh, I'm not sure, four, I think.* -**3.** [for showing emotion] a word used to express surprise, happiness, fear, shock etc □ *Oh, you startled me!* ■ **oh no!** a phrase used to express worry or concern □ *Oh no! I forgot my purse.*

OH *abbr of* **Ohio**.

Ohio [oʊˈhaɪoʊ] a state in the Midwest of the USA. ABBREVIATION: OH. SIZE: 107,000 sq kms. POPULATION: 10,847,115 (*Ohioans*). CAPITAL: Columbus.

ohm [oʊm] *n* a unit of measurement of electrical resistance.

OHMS (*abbr of* **On Her (or His) Majesty's Service**) a phrase printed on a letter or publication to show that it was sent officially by a British government department.

oil [ɔɪl] ◇ *n* -**1.** a smooth, thick liquid extracted from below the earth's surface and used in different forms as e.g. a lubricant for machinery and fuel for heating □ *fuel/gas oil* □ *oil-fired central heating.* -**2.** any of several smooth, thick, fatty liquids extracted from animals and plants and used for cooking, making cosmetics etc □ *sunflower oil* □ *evening primrose oil.* ◇ *vt* [machinery, hinge] to put oil on or into <sthg> to make it work smoothly.
♦ **oils** *npl* ART -**1.** oil paintings. -**2.** oil paints.

oilcan ['ɔɪlkæn] *n* a small container, usually with a long spout, that is used to pour oil on machinery.

oil change *n* a change of oil in a car engine.

oilcloth ['ɔɪlklɒθ] *n* cotton material with a smooth waterproof surface that was used in the past for tablecloths and other coverings.

oilfield ['ɔɪlfiːld] *n* an area of the Earth's surface where oil is found and from which it is removed in order to be used.

oil filter *n* a filter used to collect the impurities from the oil in an engine.

oil-fired [-faɪəʳd] *adj* [central heating, power station] that works by burning oil.

oil industry *n* **the oil industry** the industry involved in the extraction, refining, marketing, and distribution of oil and its by-products.

oilman ['ɔɪlmæn] (*pl* **oilmen** [-men]) *n* a man who works in the oil industry.

oil paint *n* a thick paint containing oil that is used by artists.

oil painting *n* a picture painted using oil paints; the art of painting in this way.

oil pan *n* US the part of an engine that holds the oil.

oilrig ['ɔɪlrɪg] *n* a large structure built either at sea or on land for getting oil out of the ground.

oilskins ['ɔɪlskɪnz] *npl* thick clothing that has been treated with oil to make it waterproof.

oil slick *n* a layer of oil that floats on the surface of the sea, usually because it has escaped from an oil tanker in an accident.

oil tanker *n* a large ship or truck that transports oil.

oil well *n* a hole in the ground which has been made in order to obtain oil.

oily ['ɔɪlɪ] (*compar* **oilier**, *superl* **oiliest**) *adj* -1. [rag, cloth, hand] that is covered in oil; [food, substance] that contains a lot of oil; [liquid, chemical] that is like oil. -2. [person, manner] too polite (disapproving use).

ointment ['ɔɪntmənt] *n* a thick creamy substance that is rubbed into the skin to make pain less severe or to heal a wound □ *antiseptic ointment.*

oiro (*abbr of* **offers in the region of**) GB a phrase written in classified advertisements to give a general idea of the price that would be accepted for a particular object □ *oiro £100.*

OK¹ [oʊ'keɪ] (*pl* **OKs**, *pt* & *pp* **OKed**, *cont* **OKing**), **okay** [oʊ'keɪ] (informal use) ◇ *adj* -1. **to be OK** [person] to be well and not ill or unhappy □ *Are you OK?* □ *He sounded OK when I spoke to him.* □ *I'm sure you'll feel OK once you've had a drink.* -2. [movie, food, work] not bad but not especially good □ *I'm OK in math but better in history.* ■ **to be OK with** OR **by sb** [arrangement, suggestion] to be acceptable to sb □ *I'll bring my husband, if that's OK with you.* □ *"Do you need the phone?" — "No, it's okay, I've finished with it."* □ *Is it okay if we leave early?*
◇ *n* **to give sb the OK** to give sb permission

to do something □ *We've been given the okay to start on the new project.*
◇ *excl* -1. a word used to ask for or show agreement □ *See you at six, OK?* □ *OK, I'll meet you there.* -2. a word used to agree to or accept something in a way that shows one is not happy about doing this □ *OK, I know what you're saying, but I still think he's wrong.* □ *OK, you win, we'll eat out tonight.* -3. a word used to introduce a new subject □ *OK, can we start the meeting now?*
◇ *vt* [plan, suggestion, loan] to officially agree to <sthg> □ *Funding still has to be okayed.*

OK² *abbr of* **Oklahoma.**

OK Corral *n* a corral in the western USA where a famous gun fight took place between Wyatt Earp and the Clanton brothers in 1881.

O'Keeffe [oʊ'kiːf], **Georgia** (1887–1986) a US painter known for her paintings of flowers.

Okie ['oʊkɪ] *n* a farm worker who left Oklahoma in the 1930s to find work on the West Coast.

Oklahoma [ˌoʊklə'hoʊmə] a state in the central southern USA, north of Texas. Many Native Americans now live there. ABBREVIATION: OK. SIZE: 181,000 sq kms. POPULATION: 3,145,585 (*Oklahomans*). CAPITAL: Oklahoma City.

okra ['oʊkrə] *n* a thin green vegetable, originally from Africa, used e.g. in stews or curried dishes.

old [oʊld] ◇ *adj* -1. [person, animal] who has lived for many years □ *There was a party for all the old folks in the area.* -2. a word used in expressions referring to somebody's age □ *"How old are you?" — "I'm 20 years old."* □ *A five-year-old (child) can walk, speak, count, and even write.* □ *Are you old enough to drive?* □ *This is my older sister.* -3. [building, furniture, painting] that has existed for many years; [joke, story] that has existed for a long time, and is not original; [clothes, shoes, food] that one has had for a long time □ *You see that old house over there?* □ *He's not telling his old war stories again, is he?* □ *I could lend you this old sweater if you like.* -4. **one's old job/car etc** a job/car etc that one used to have □ *My old apartment overlooked Central Park.* □ *That's my old college over there on the left.* -5. **the old system/regime etc** the system/regime etc that used to exist and has been replaced □ *Things were better under the old management.* □ *This was the old kitchen, but we've turned it into a workshop, as you can see.* ■ **in the old days** a phrase used to refer to the past, especially when remembering something in one's own lifetime □ *It reminds me of the good old days.* □ *In the old days, we used to climb up here to pick blueberries.* -6. **an old friend/acquaintance etc** a friend/an acquaintance etc one has known for a long time □ *Helen is an old friend of mine.* -7. a word used before somebody's name to refer to them in an affectionate way (informal use) □ *Poor old John!* -8. **any old** a phrase used to emphasize that the quality of something is not important (informal use) □ *Any old thing will do, as long as it's warm.* □ *You can't* *just put any old oil in the car, it has to be a special kind!*

◇ *npl* **the old** old people in society □ *The old are the ones who'll suffer.*

old age *n* the period in one's life when one is old □ *He's actually looking forward to his old age.* □ *Once people reach old age...*

old age pension *n* GB money that is paid regularly by the state to a retired person over a certain age.

old age pensioner *n* GB a person who receives an old age pension.

Old Bailey [-'beɪlɪ]: **the Old Bailey** the main Crown Court in London. OFFICIAL NAME: Central Criminal Court.

old boy network *n* **the old boy network** the system by which men who went to the same school or college use their influence to help each other in later life.

olden ['ouldən] *adj* **in olden days** a long time ago (literary use).

old-fashioned [-'fæʃnd] *adj* **-1.** [clothes, hairstyle, machinery] that is connected with a period in the past and is no longer appropriate □ *That's a pretty old-fashioned way of doing it.* **-2.** [person] who prefers things to be done in a traditional way and is not influenced by new developments □ *He has some rather old-fashioned ideas about education.*

old flame *n* a person that one used to love.

Old Glory *n* a nickname for the US flag.

old hat *adj* **to be old hat** to be too familiar and not of interest or value any more (informal use) □ *The ideas in the book seem old hat now.*

old maid *n* an unmarried woman who is not young (disapproving use).

old master *n* an important painter of the past; a painting by such a painter.

old people's home *n* a place where old people can live together and receive special care when they can no longer take care of themselves alone.

Old Testament *n* **the Old Testament** the first part of the Christian Bible that contains the Hebrew Scriptures and tells of the history of the Hebrew people.
NOTE: Compare **New Testament**.

old-time *adj* [dancing, music hall] that is in the style of a period in the past.

old-timer *n* **-1.** a person who has done something, such as a job, for a very long time. **-2.** US an old man.

old wives' tale *n* a belief that has existed for a very long time and is considered to be foolish or superstitious.

Old World *n* **the Old World** Europe, Asia, and Africa.

oligarchy ['ɒlɪgɑːʳkɪ] (*pl* **oligarchies**) *n* a small group of people who have the power to control a country, organization etc; a country, organization etc that is controlled by such a group.

olive ['ɒlɪv] ◇ *adj* [dress, clothing] olive green.
◇ *n* **-1.** a small, oval, black or green fruit

with a stone in the center, used for food or for making oil. **-2.** = **olive tree**.

olive green *adj* [dress, uniform] that is dark yellow-green in color.

olive oil *n* oil made from olives and used in cooking and for making salad dressing.

Oliver Twist [,ɒlɪvəʳ'twɪst] the hero of the novel *Oliver Twist* by Charles Dickens. He is famous for asking for more food in the poor children's workhouse.

olive tree *n* a tree, grown mainly in Mediterranean countries, that produces olives.

Olympic [ə'lɪmpɪk] *adj* [champion, stadium] that is connected with the Olympic Games.
◆ **Olympics** *npl* = **Olympic Games**.

Olympic Games *npl* **the Olympic Games** an event held every four years in a different country, in which teams from all over the world compete in various sports.

OM (*abbr of* **Order of Merit**) *n* an honor given to British people for some special service to their country.

O & M (*abbr of* **organization and method**) *n* the process of studying how an office works and suggesting how it could be made more efficient.

Oman [ou'mɑːn] a country in southeastern Arabia. SIZE: 212,000 sq kms. POPULATION: 1,600,000 (*Omanis*). CAPITAL: Muscat. LANGUAGE: Arabic. CURRENCY: Omani rial.

OMB (*abbr of* **Office of Management and Budget**) *n* **the OMB** the US government department responsible for preparing the budget.

ombudsman ['ɒmbʊdzmən] (*pl* **ombudsmen** [-mən]) *n* a person whose job is to deal with complaints by people about government departments or other public services.

omelet(te) ['ɒmlət] *n* a dish made by beating eggs together and cooking them, usually with another ingredient, in a flat pan □ *a mushroom/cheese/Spanish omelette.*

omen ['oumən] *n* something that is thought to be a sign of what will happen in the future □ *a good/bad omen.*

ominous ['ɒmɪnəs] *adj* [silence, cloud, sign] that suggests that something bad will happen □ *The sky looked ominous.* □ *There was an ominous pause as Alfred digested what Francis had said.*

ominously ['ɒmɪnəslɪ] *adv* [approach, speak] in a way that makes one feel something bad is going to happen □ *The sea was ominously calm.*

omission [ou'mɪʃn] *n* **-1.** somebody or something that has been omitted □ *There were one or two glaring omissions from the list.* **-2.** [of a detail, duty, person] *see* **omit** □ *I'm sorry, it was an omission on my part.*

omit [ou'mɪt] (*pt* & *pp* **omitted**, *cont* **omitting**) *vt* [person, detail, word] not to include <sb/sthg> either by accident or deliberately □ *Sarah's name had been omitted from the guest list.* ■ **to omit to do sthg** [task, duty] not to do sthg (formal use) □ *You omitted to close the door on leaving.*

omnibus ['ɒmnɪbəs] *n* **-1.** a book that contains

once

several novels, usually by the same author, that have already been published separately □ *a Charles Dickens omnibus.* **-2.** GB RADIO & TV a program that contains several episodes of a series that have already been shown separately □ *the omnibus edition.*

omnipotence [ɒmˈnɪpətns] *n*: *see* **omnipotent** (formal use) □ *a belief in God's omnipotence.*

omnipotent [ɒmˈnɪpətnt] *adj* [God, government, ruler] that has complete power (formal use).

omnipresent [ˌɒmnɪˈpreznt] *adj* [fear, influence, person] that is present everywhere (formal use).

omniscient [US ɒmˈnɪʃnt, GB -ˈnɪsɪənt] *adj* [God, person] who knows everything (formal use).

omnivorous [ɒmˈnɪvərəs] *adj* [animal] that eats both meat and plants.

on [ɒn] ◇ *prep* **-1. on the table** touching the top of the table and supported by it □ *His clothes were lying on the floor.* □ *She sat down on a chair.* □ *Put the top back on the bottle.* **-2. on the wall/ceiling** fixed to the surface of the wall/ceiling □ *Dogs must be kept on a leash.* □ *Could you sew a button on my jacket?* **-3.** used to describe where something can be found, seen etc □ *'See diagram on page 7'* □ *I can't find it on the map.* □ *He had a look of horror on his face.* □ *The information is available on diskette.* **-4. on a street/road/river** on one side of a street/road/river □ *We stayed at a hotel on Lake Michigan.* □ *the big stores on Fifth Avenue.* **-5. on the left/right** at or to the left/right □ *On your right is the royal palace.* **-6. on the bus/plane/train** traveling inside the bus/plane/train □ *She flew out on the last plane.* ■ **on a bicycle/horse** to be riding a bicycle/horse □ *He won the race on Red Rum.* **-7. on TV/radio** using TV/radio □ *The movie was shown on satellite TV.* □ *She's on the telephone at the moment.* ■ **to play sthg on the piano/guitar etc** to play sthg using a piano/guitar etc as an instrument. **-8. on Thursday/May 10/Christmas Eve** at some point during Thursday/May 10/Christmas Eve (used with precise days and dates) □ *We play bridge on Sundays.* □ *My father phoned me on my birthday.* **-9. on my arrival** at the time of, or shortly after, my arrival (formal use) □ *We agreed to meet again on my return.* □ *On hearing the result, he heaved a sigh of relief.* **-10. to be on drugs/tranquilizers** to be taking drugs/tranquilizers regularly □ *Are you on any medication at the moment?* □ *I can't drink, I'm on antibiotics.* **-11. to be on $80,000 a year** to earn $80,000 a year □ *She's on a good salary/a low income.* **-12.** used to show where somebody's money comes from □ *I can't live on a student grant.* □ *He's on welfare.* **-13. a book/talk on astronomy** a book/talk about the subject of astronomy □ *His views on farm subsidies are well known.* **-14.** FINANCE **the profit on a deal** the profit that results from a deal □ *These stocks give a good return on investment.* **-15. to be on a committee/council etc** to be a member of a committee/council etc □ *Who's on the panel of judges?* **-16. to have an effect/influence on sb** to affect/influence sb □ *The play made a deep*

impression on me. □ *More research is needed into the impact of chemicals on the environment.* ■ **a tax on cigarettes** a tax that affects cigarettes. **-17.** phrase **the drinks are on me** I'm paying for the drinks (informal use).

◇ *adv* **-1. the lid is on** the lid is covering or fixed to its box, jar etc □ *Don't forget to stick a stamp on.* **-2. there's a sale/an election/a war on** a sale/an election/a war is happening now □ *There's a good exhibition on at the Guggenheim.* **-3. the TV/light is on** the TV/light is working or being used □ *Is the microphone still on?* □ *You left the heating on.* **-4. to have sthg on** [clothing] to be wearing sthg □ *Put a sweater on.* □ *What dress did she have on?* **-5. to work/read etc on** to continue to work/read etc instead of stopping □ *We weren't tired, so we drove on to the next town.* **-6. to send/pass sthg on** to send/pass sthg to the next place or person □ *He's moved on to a new town.* □ *We came to an intersection a little further on.* **-7. to get/step/climb on** to get/step/climb inside a bus, train, plane etc □ *The train stopped and we all got on.* **-8. to have a lot on** to be doing a lot □ *We've got nothing special on this evening.* **-9. to be on at sb** GB to keep asking sb to do something in a boring or irritating way (informal use) □ *He's always on at me about the length of my hair.* **-10.** phrase **it's just not on!** GB it's not an acceptable way to behave (informal use) □ *It's just not on, turning up late like that.*

◆ **from...on** *adv* **from now/then etc on** starting now/then etc and continuing □ *From that point on, we had no more dealings with them.*

◆ **on and on** *adv* for a long time or distance □ *We drove on and on through the night.* ■ **to go on and on about sthg** to talk about sthg too long or too often □ *Tessa went on and on about how wonderful her children were.*

◆ **on and off, off and on** *adv* for short periods but not regularly □ *It rained on and off throughout the day.* □ *I still see him off and on.*

ON *abbr of* **Ontario.**

once [wʌns] ◇ *adv* **-1.** [happen, occur] on one occasion □ *I go to the hairdresser's once a week/month/year.* □ *We met once, a long time ago.* ■ **once again** OR **more** again as before; one more time □ *Could you do that once more?* □ *They asked him once again, but still he refused to answer.* ■ **once and for all** completely and without doubt □ *They managed to cure his illness once and for all.* □ *Once and for all, I am NOT going to the bank with you.* ■ **once in a while** sometimes, but not very often □ *We like to go to the theater once in a while.* ■ **once or twice** a few times □ *I've been to see her once or twice.* ■ **for once** on this particular occasion only □ *He arrived on time for once!* □ *Just for once, could you show a little patience?* □ *Can't we go out — just this once?* **-2.** at a time in the past, but not any longer □ *This was once a beautiful piece of countryside.* ■ **once upon a time** a phrase used to introduce the beginning of a fairy tale and show that it took place a long time ago □ *Once upon a time, there was a beautiful princess.*

◇ *conj* in the time after; as soon as □ *It'll be*

easier once we've started. □ *Give me a call once you get there.*

◆ **all at once** *adv* **-1.** at the same time □ *Here's $20, don't spend it all at once!* **-2.** suddenly □ *We were sitting around the table when all at once the lights went out.*

◆ **at once** *adv* **-1.** immediately □ *I asked him to leave at once.* **-2.** at the same time □ *Everyone came at once.*

once-over *n* **to give sb/sthg the once-over** to examine sb/sthg quickly (informal use) □ *I'll give it a quick once-over and see if you need any repairs.*

oncoming ['ɒnkʌmɪŋ] *adj* **oncoming traffic/ danger etc** traffic/danger etc that is coming toward one or approaching.

one [wʌn] ◇ *num* **-1.** the number 1 □ *One and one are two.* □ *I have one brother and two sisters.* □ *There's an introduction on page twenty-one.* □ *one hundred/thousand dollars.* ■ **one or two** a very small number of people or things □ *There are one or two points I'd like to discuss with you.* □ *I still keep in touch with one or two of my old colleagues.* ■ **in ones and twos** alone or in very small groups □ *People started arriving for the lecture in ones and twos.* **-2.** one o'clock, the time of day □ *We'll have lunch at one.* □ *It was just past one when he called; see also* **five.**

◇ *det* **-1.** used to emphasize a particular person, thing, action etc, compared to others of the same kind □ *There's just one thing I'd like you to do for me.* □ *One joke he told was especially funny.* ■ **the one person/place/thing** the only person/place/thing □ *You're the one person who really understands.* ■ **sb's one fear/ ambition etc** the chief fear/ambition etc that sb has □ *My one concern is that you should be happy.* **-2. one day/evening etc** on a particular day/evening etc in the past; on an indefinite day/evening etc in the future □ *One evening we were sitting watching TV when the phone rang.* □ *You must come over for coffee one afternoon.* **-3. one James Smith** somebody called James Smith who I have not heard of before □ *The letter is signed by one James Smith.* **-4. that's one powerful car!** that's a very powerful car (informal use) □ *Your wife is one amazing cook!*

◇ *pron* **-1.** used to refer to the person or thing that has just been mentioned □ *She's the one I told you about.* □ *Those shoes are pretty worn, you need some new ones.* **-2.** used to refer to a particular person or thing in a group of people or things □ *I believe you know one of my sisters.* □ *Which slice would you like, this big one or a smaller one?* □ *If you need a sweater, you can borrow one of mine.* **-3.** used to make general statements (formal use) □ *One has to be so careful when dealing with strangers.* **-4.** used by the person who is speaking or writing to refer to himself or herself in an indirect way (formal use) □ *One often wonders why one ever got into banking.* **-5.** phrases **to be at one with sb** to be in agreement with sb □ *I'm at one with them on the subject of abortion.* ■ **to feel at one with sthg** to feel calm and peaceful because one has a good relation-

ship with sthg □ *For a brief moment, I felt at one with the world.* ■ **to be one up on sb** to have an advantage over sb (informal use) □ *Well, you're one up on me there – I haven't a clue what's going on!*

◆ **for one** *adv* used to emphasize that one is giving a personal opinion □ *I, for one, remain unconvinced.*

◆ **one after the other, one by one** *adv* first one person, then the second, and so on □ *One by one the members of the audience got up and left the hall.*

◆ **one another** *pron* each other □ *We all have to help one another in times of trouble.*

one-armed bandit *n* GB a machine which people put money into and from which they hope to win more money by pulling down the long handle at the side.

O'Neill [oʊ'niːl], **Eugene** (1888–1953) a US playwright. His work includes *Long Day's Journey into Night* and *The Iceman Cometh.*

one-liner *n* a short joke or funny comment in a play, comedy show etc □ *The movie has some great one-liners.*

one-man *adj* **a one-man show** a show that is performed by one person only. ■ **a one-man business** a business that is run by one person only.

one-man band *n* **-1.** a musician, especially a street musician, who plays a number of instruments at the same time. **-2.** something such as a business that is organized or run by one person (informal use).

one-night stand *n* **-1.** a performance that takes place once at one place before moving on to another place. **-2.** a sexual relationship that lasts only one night or a very short time (informal use).

one-off ◇ *adj* GB [opportunity, payment] made or happening only once □ *This is a one-off chance to see The Groundhogs in concert.* ◇ *n* an event that happens only once; a person or thing that is original and is not like anybody or anything else (informal use) □ *It's a one-off; you'll never see anything like that again.*

one-on-one US, **one-to-one** GB *adj* [tuition, discussion] that involves only two people □ *Most of my classes are one-on-one.*

one-parent family *n* a family in which only one of the parents brings up the child or children, e.g. because of divorce or death.

one-piece *adj* **a one-piece swimsuit** a swimsuit that consists of one piece of material, rather than a separate top and bottom.

onerous ['oʊnərəs] *adj* [task, responsibility] that is difficult and often unpleasant.

one's [wʌnz] *poss adj* used to say that somebody or something is connected with or belongs to people in general □ *One's friends can be helpful at times like these.* □ *One should never forget one's manners.* ■ **to be on one's own** to be alone □ *The nice thing is that one can go on one's own.*

oneself [wʌn'self] *pron* used as the object of a verb or after a preposition when the subject of the verb is "one" (formal use) □ *One tells* oneself that things will get better. □ One has to rely on oneself in such situations.

one-shot *adj* US made or happening only once (informal use) □ *a one-shot deal.*

one-sided [-'saɪdəd] *adj* **-1.** [sports match] in which one side is stronger or better than the other; [conversation, activity] in which one person is more active than the other □ *It was all rather one-sided, really — he never stopped talking and I just sat there listening.* **-2.** [argument, decision] that only considers one side of a situation and so is unfair □ *Isn't that a rather one-sided view of things?*

onetime ['wʌntaɪm] *adj* **a onetime pop star/model etc** a former pop star/model etc □ *a onetime actor turned director.*

one-to-one *adj* GB = **one-on-one.**

one-upmanship [-'ʌpmənʃɪp] *n* the practice of trying to show that one is better than somebody else (disapproving use).

one-way *adj* **-1.** [street, traffic] that involves movement in one direction only □ *I got lost on the new one-way system.* **-2.** [ticket, trip] that involves traveling from one place to another, but not back again.

ongoing ['ɒngəʊɪŋ] *adj* [situation, relationship, discussion] that is continuing □ *in the ongoing struggle for control.*

onion ['ʌnjən] *n* a small, round, white vegetable with thin brown skin, which is sliced or chopped and used to add flavor to dishes.

on-line ◇ *adj* [printer, equipment, database] that is directly connected to and controlled by a computer. ◇ *adv: We can print on-line.* NOTE: Compare **off-line.**

online service *n* a large commercial bulletin board that a computer user can access using a modem.

onlooker ['ɒnlʊkər] *n* a person who watches something happening, but is not involved □ *A crowd of onlookers gathered at the scene of the accident.*

only ['əʊnlɪ] ◇ *adj* **-1. the only person/thing** no other person/thing □ *When I was in trouble, she was the only person who offered to help.* □ *The only thing I can suggest is that you contact him yourself.* □ *It's our only hope.* □ *Writing a letter is the only way of contacting him.* **-2. an only child** a child who has no brothers or sisters. ◇ *adv* **-1. I only read novels** I read novels and nothing else □ *He was only trying to be helpful.* □ *'For external use only'* □ *She only manages to relax when the children are asleep.* □ *Only Harry could have bought something like that.* **-2. it's only a scratch** it is nothing worse, bigger, more important etc than a scratch □ *She's only a child.* □ *"What's that noise?" — "It's only Jeremy snoring."* ■ **only 10% of the population** no more than 10% of the population. **-3.** used for emphasis □ *It's only natural you should feel upset.* □ *I only hope you're right!* □ *I saw him only yesterday.* □ *I don't know what time she'll be home, I've only just got back myself.* **-4. It will only annoy him** it is certain to annoy him □ *Just tell them the truth — you'll only regret it if you don't.*

◇ *conj* but (informal use) □ *He's like his brother, only nicer.* □ *I would drive here, only my car's at the garage.*

◆ **only just** *adv* **-1. they've only just arrived** they arrived a very short time ago □ *The concert had only just started.* **-2. I only just passed the exam** I passed the exam, but I almost did not □ *We only just got here in time.*

◆ **only too** *adv* very □ *I'd be only too delighted to come.* □ *They'd be only too pleased for you to stay another day.*

◆ **not only...but (also)...** *conj* used to say two things when the first is known already but the second is new and surprising □ *Tom was not only a colleague, but (also) a personal friend.* □ *Not only did Roddy not pay the rent, he also stole money from us.*

o.n.o., ono (*abbr of* **or near(est) offer**) GB a word used in classified advertisements to show that the seller of a particular object may accept a lower offer than the stated price □ *£500 o.n.o.*

on-ramp *n* US a road for joining a highway.

onrush ['ɒnrʌʃ] *n* a sudden strong feeling □ *She felt an onrush of remorse.*

on-screen ◇ *adj* [display, editing] that appears or takes place on a computer screen. ◇ *adv: We edit on-screen usually.*

onset ['ɒnset] *n* [of war, illness, attack] the beginning of something unpleasant or difficult to deal with □ *After the onset of winter, they were unable to travel.*

onshore ['ɒnʃɔːr] ◇ *adj* **-1.** [wind, breeze] moving toward the land from the sea. **-2.** on or near the shore □ *onshore fishing.* ◇ *adv: A bitter wind was blowing onshore.* □ *They're drilling onshore.*

onside [ˌɒn'saɪd] ◇ *adj* **to be onside** [in soccer, rugby] to be in a position where one is allowed to kick, receive etc the ball. ◇ *adv: He played his opponent onside.* NOTE: Compare **offside.**

onslaught ['ɒnslɔːt] *n* **-1.** a very powerful physical attack □ *a fierce onslaught against enemy troops.* **-2.** actions or words that show strong opposition to something □ *the critics' onslaught on budget cuts.*

Ontario [ɒn'teərɪəʊ] **-1.** a province in eastern central Canada. ABBREVIATION: ON. SIZE: 1,068,582 sq kms. POPULATION: 10,084,885 (*Ontarians*). CAPITAL: Toronto. **-2. Lake Ontario** one of the Great Lakes between Canada and the USA.

on-the-job *adj* **on-the-job training/experience etc** training/experience etc that one gets by working in a job.

on-the-spot *adj* **an on-the-spot interview** an interview that happens immediately without time for preparation. ■ **an on-the-spot reporter** a reporter who reports from the place where something has happened or is happening.

onto ['ɒntuː] *prep* **-1. to step/fall onto sthg** to step/fall so that one is one top of sthg □ *He climbed onto a chair.* □ *The vase fell onto the floor.* **-2. to stick/fasten sthg onto sthg** to stick/fasten sthg so that it is attached to sthg else □ *Someone had pinned a notice onto the door.* -3. **to get onto a train/bus/plane etc** to go inside a train/bus/plane etc in order to travel on it. -4. **to come** OR **move onto sthg** to start to discuss sthg □ *I'll stop you there, because I want to get onto the next topic.* -5. *phrases* **to be onto sb** to realize that sb has done something wrong □ *He had to act fast, now that the police were onto him.* ■ **to be/get onto sb** GB to be/get in contact with sb □ *We'd better get onto the factory and cancel the order.*

onus ['oʊnəs] *n* a responsibility that somebody has to do something □ *The onus is on you to reimburse them.*

onward ['ɒnwəʳd] ◇ *adv* -1. **from now/that day onward** starting now/that day and continuing after that time □ *I'll be free any time from three o'clock onward.* □ *From July onward you will be reporting to Sally Green, the new head of department.* -2. **to move/travel etc onward** to continue to move/travel etc in the same direction □ *After stopping to rest the horses, we rode onward until we came to the river.*
◇ *adj* -1. **the onward trip** the trip that continues after a particular point □ *Passengers arriving in Athens will board a bus for the onward trip.* -2. **onward development/growth etc** development/growth etc that continues to make progress as time goes on □ *Nothing can halt the onward march of medical science.*

onwards ['ɒnwəʳdz] *adv* = **onward**.

onyx ['ɒnɪks] *n* a semi-precious stone with bands of different colors, used to make jewelry.

oodles ['uːdlz] *npl* **oodles of sthg** a lot of sthg (informal use).

oof [ʊf] *excl* a sound used to show relaxation, relief, or sudden pain (informal use).

ooh [uː] *excl* a sound used to express pleasure, displeasure, or surprise (informal use) □ *Ooh, you look really lovely!*

oops [ʊps] *excl* a word used when reacting to a mistake or small accident (informal use) □ *Oops, I nearly tripped.*

ooze [uːz] ◇ *vt* [confidence, charm, money] to have a lot of <sthg> so that it is very obvious to other people □ *Look at him sitting there — he just oozes self-satisfaction.* ◇ *vi* [blood, mud] to flow out slowly through a narrow space □ *Sweat oozed from* OR *out of every pore.* ◇ *n* mud, especially at the bottom of a river.

opacity [oʊ'pæsətɪ] *n*: *see* **opaque**.

opal ['oʊpl] *n* a precious stone that changes color when it is held in different positions □ *an opal pendant.*

opaque [oʊ'peɪk] *adj* -1. [glass, paper, glaze] that one cannot see through. -2. [meaning, piece of writing] that is not clear and so is difficult to understand.

OPEC ['oʊpek] (*abbr of* **Organization of Petroleum Exporting Countries**) *n* an organization that includes most of the world's big exporters of oil, who meet to coordinate the production and prices of their oil.

open ['oʊpən] ◇ *adj* -1. [drawer, window, curtains] not closed □ *The door stood wide open.* □ *He was sleep-walking with his eyes open.* □ *The cupboard door swung open.* -2. [bottle, package, envelope] not sealed □ *Have a cookie, the package is already open.* -3. [book] that has its two covers spread out so that a particular page can be read; [flower] whose petals have unfolded; [umbrella] that is unfolded and ready for use □ *His book lay open on the table.* □ *I noticed in the park that the daffodils are already open.* □ *Leave your umbrella open to dry.* -4. [mind, person] that is willing to accept or consider new or different ideas □ *I'm sure you could talk to Daniel — he's very open about these things.* □ *a free, open and democratic society.* ■ **to be open to sthg** [to offers, new ideas] to be willing to accept or consider sthg; [to blame, question, misunderstanding] to be likely to receive sthg □ *If any of you think you have a solution, I'm open to suggestions.* □ *I think your words are open to misinterpretation.* ■ **to lay oneself open to criticism** to do something that makes one very likely to be criticized □ *If you make a speech as provocative as that you're laying yourself open to attack.* -5. [person, manner] that is honest and does not try to hide things □ *Simon is very open about the fact that he's gay.* -6. **to be open** [library, bank] to be ready to serve customers □ *We're open until 6 pm.* □ *'Open all day Monday to Saturday.'* -7. **to be open** [bridge, public building, institution] to be officially ready for use □ *When will the new superstore be open?* -8. [road, passage, tunnel] that is clear with no obstacles in the way □ *Main Street is now open again following an accident earlier today.* -9. [coat, jacket] that is not fastened. -10. **open country** OR **space** countryside where there are few buildings and where one can travel around easily □ *They sailed on the open sea.* □ *They love being out on the open road.* -11. [car, carriage, boat] that has no roof or cover □ *a bus with an open top deck* □ *They sat warming themselves in front of an open fire.* -12. **to be open to sb** [opportunities, choice, alternative] to be available to sb □ *You don't have many options open to you.* -13. [meeting, park] that anybody can go to; [competition, debate] that anybody can take part in; [invitation] that anybody can accept □ *The conference is not open to members of the public.* -14. [disbelief, admiration, hostility] that is obvious and not hidden □ *Laurence stared at her in open disbelief.* -15. [situation, question] that does not have a final, definite conclusion □ *The question was left open for further discussion.*
◇ *n* **in the open** [sleep, eat] outside. ■ **to bring sthg out into the open** to talk about sthg that has been a secret □ *I'm glad it's all been brought out into the open.* □ *The conflict finally came out into the open.*
◇ *vt* -1. [window, drawer, cupboard] to make <sthg> open □ *She opened her eyes very wide.* □ *I knocked, but he wouldn't open the door.* -2. [letter, package] to tear, cut, or unwrap <sthg> in order to reach its contents □ *Should I open the wine?* □ *I'm always opening Jamie's mail by mistake.* -3. [book, newspaper]

to unfold or spread <sthg> out □ *Open your books at page 204! □ She opened her umbrella and ventured out into the rain.* **-4.** [office, building, gate] to unlock <sthg> so that people can enter; [new business] to start <sthg> □ *They open the doors at 10 p.m. □ They're opening yet another bank in town.* **-5.** [building, bridge, public area] to officially state that <sthg> is ready for use □ *They've just opened a new section of highway.* **-6.** [event, meeting, conference] to officially begin <sthg> by giving a speech, making an announcement etc □ *I shall open today's proceedings with a word of thanks.* **-7. to open an inquiry/investigation** to officially start an inquiry/investigation □ *An investigation has been opened into the causes of the crash.* ■ **to open an account** to start an account at a bank □ *I've just opened an account with First Boston.* **-8.** [road, passage, tunnel] to allow people or vehicles to use <sthg>, especially after an obstruction has been removed □ *The third lane of the westbound M4 has now been opened after an earlier accident.*
◇ *vi* **-1.** [door, window, eyes] to become open □ *The door suddenly opened and in ran two small children.* **-2.** [new store, new business] to begin business for the first time in a particular place; [store, library] to be ready for the public to enter □ *The new leisure complex is due to open next June. □ It opens at 9 on Saturdays.* **-3.** [meeting, conference] to officially begin; [play, movie] to be seen by the public for the first time □ *The debate opened with a discussion on tactics. □ His new movie opens in New York this week.* **-4.** [flower, petals] to unfold □ *The umbrella wouldn't open.*

◆ **open on to** *vt fus* **to open on to sthg** to lead to sthg □ *The door opens on to a courtyard.*

◆ **open out** *vi* **-1.** [bud, petals] to unfold. **-2.** [road, path, river] to become wider. **-3.** [valley, lake] to come into view.

◆ **open up** ◇ *vt sep* **-1. to open sthg up** [crate, bag] to open sthg that was sealed or closed □ *The customs officer opened up the small brown case.* **-2. to open a place up** [country, area] to remove legal or physical barriers from a place so that something, especially business, can take place □ *The island is being opened up to tourists.*
◇ *vi* **-1.** [opportunities, possibilities] to become available □ *There are a lot of new opportunities opening up for people with computer skills.* **-2.** to unlock a store, office, building etc □ *What time do you open up?* **-3.** [country] to start to provide new opportunities, especially for business □ *Eastern Europe is opening up for new trade opportunities.* **-4.** to become more willing to talk about oneself □ *After several glasses of wine, he gradually began to open up.*

open-air *adj* [concert, event] that happens outdoors; [swimming pool, theater] that is outdoors and not covered.

open-and-shut *adj* [dispute, problem] that is easy to solve □ *It's hardly an open-and-shut case — there's so much evidence missing.*

opencast [US 'oʊpənkæst, GB -kɑːst] *adj* [mine, mining] that involves obtaining minerals that

are near the earth's surface rather than deep underground.

open day *n* GB = **open house**.

open-ended [-'endəd] *adj* [discussion, meeting, question] that has no definite end or limit □ *It was a fairly open-ended arrangement.*

opener ['oʊpnəʳ] *n* an instrument used for opening something, e.g. a can or bottle.

open-handed [-'hændəd] *adj* [offer, gesture] generous.

open-hearted [-'hɑːʳtəd] *adj* [person] generous and kind.

open-heart surgery *n* an operation in which somebody's heart is stopped and opened up so that surgery can take place.

open house US, **open day** GB *n* a day when people are allowed to look around a college, school, organization etc and find out more about it.

opening ['oʊpənɪŋ] ◇ *adj* **an opening scene/remark etc** a scene/remark etc that begins something □ *The opening speech was about strategy for the coming year.* ◇ *n* **-1.** [of a book, play] the first part of something, e.g. a book or movie □ *What did you think of the opening?* **-2.** [in a fence] a space or hole □ *He managed to get in through an opening in the fence.* **-3.** [in a conversation] an opportunity □ *Finally she paused, which gave me an opening to speak. □ The talks should provide good openings for new trade possibilities.* **-4.** [for work] a job vacancy □ *There are few openings for arts graduates at the moment.*

opening hours *npl* the hours during which a place e.g. a bank or store, is open to the public □ *What are your opening hours?*

opening night *n* the first night of a series of performances of a play, opera etc □ *We went to the opening night of "La Traviata".*

opening time *n* GB the time when a pub can legally start selling alcoholic drinks.

open letter *n* a letter to a well-known person such as a politician that is published in a newspaper or magazine so that the public can read it.

openly ['oʊpənlɪ] *adv* [talk, cry, admit] without trying to hide anything □ *It was the first time she had spoken openly about her marriage.*

open market *n* the process of buying and selling goods publicly, not privately □ *You'll sell it quicker if you put it on the open market.*

open marriage *n* a marriage in which both partners are free to have sexual relationships with other people.

open-minded [-'maɪndəd] *adj* [person, approach, attitude] that is willing to consider new or different ideas □ *James's mother is very open-minded about drinking and things like that.*

open-mouthed [-'maʊðd] ◇ *adj* [person] who has their mouth wide open as a way of expressing surprise □ *He stared at her in open-mouthed amazement.* ◇ *adv: We simply watched open-mouthed as they towed the car away.*

open-necked [-'nekt] *adj* [shirt, blouse] that is not fastened at the neck.

openness ['oʊpənnəs] n -1. the quality of being honest and not hiding things □ *greater accountability and openness in public affairs.* -2. the quality of being willing to accept or consider new or different ideas □ *openness to new approaches.*

open-plan adj [office, building] that contains desks, people etc in one big area, sometimes separated by partitions but not by walls.

open prison n GB a prison in which the prisoners are not locked in their cells all day, and can do various activities that would not be allowed in other prisons.

open sandwich n a sandwich that consists of one slice of bread only so that the filling is not covered on top.

open season n the period of time each year when particular types of fish or animals can legally be killed for sport.

open shop n a business, firm etc that does not make its workers join a labor union.

Open University n the Open University in Britain, a method of studying by correspondence for university qualifications. Students are taught through programs on the radio and television as well as tutorial classes. People do not need any qualifications to start a course of study.

open verdict n GB a verdict by a court that records a death without mentioning how the death was caused.

opera ['ɒprə] n -1. a play in which the words are sung rather than spoken, and which is usually accompanied by classical music □ *I've got most of Handel's operas on CD.* -2. operas as a form of entertainment □ *She's a great fan of (the) opera.*

opera glasses npl small binoculars used in a theater.

opera house n a building like a theater where operas are performed.

opera singer n a person who sings in operas for a living.

operate ['ɒpəreɪt] ◇ vt -1. [machine, device] to work the controls of sthg □ *My job is to operate the crane.* -2. to manage a business; to provide <a service> □ *She operates a small import-export business.* □ *They operate a free telephone service for customers.*
◇ vi -1. [rule, system, law] to have particular effects. -2. [machine, device] to work. -3. [business, organization] to carry out trade □ *They operate out of Vancouver.* □ *It operates on a world-wide scale.* -4. MEDICINE [surgeon] to cut somebody's body open in order to treat something that is wrong □ *Do you think they'll have to operate?* □ *He's being operated on to remove the blockage.* □ *When are they operating on your leg?*

operatic [,ɒpə'rætɪk] adj [production, role, society] that is connected with the opera.

operating ['ɒpəreɪtɪŋ] adj BUSINESS **operating costs** costs that are a normal part of running a business. ■ **an operating loss/profit** a loss/profit that is made by a company when it is carrying out its usual business.

operating room ['ɒpəreɪtɪŋ-] n US a room in a hospital where medical operations are carried out.

operating system n the most basic program in a computer that controls how it deals with the hardware and how it runs files.

operating theatre n GB = operating room.

operation [,ɒpə'reɪʃn] n -1. a planned activity that usually involves many people □ *a police/relief operation* -2. BUSINESS the activities and work of a business or company; a business organization □ *the company's operations in Singapore* □ *an agricultural/a mining operation.* -3. [of a machine, device] the way something is made to work □ *The operation of the equipment is very straightforward.* ■ **in operation** [machine, system] in use □ *The production line has been back in operation since last week.* ■ **to come into operation** [law, plan] to begin to have an effect □ *It will come into operation as of March 23.* -4. MEDICINE the act of operating on somebody, or of being operated on □ *I underwent an operation to remove a tumor.* ■ **to have an operation** to be operated on □ *He's had an operation on his knee/for his sinus problem.*

operational [,ɒpə'reɪʃnəl] adj -1. **to be operational** [machine, piece of equipment] to be working or ready for use □ *We are pleased to announce that the new credit system is now fully operational.* -2. **an operational difficulty/problem etc** a difficulty/problem etc that happens while a machine, business etc is working □ *Operational costs must be kept to a minimum.*

operative ['ɒpərətɪv] ◇ adj **to be operative** [business, law] to be working and having an effect □ *It will take a while before we are fully operative.* ◇ n a worker, especially one who works in a factory □ *a machine operative.*

operator ['ɒpəreɪtər] n -1. [for a telephone company, hotel] a person who works on a telephone switchboard □ *I was trying to get through to the operator.* -2. INDUSTRY a person whose job is to operate a machine □ *a computer/machine operator.* -3. BUSINESS a person who is in charge of a business □ *a major tour operator.*

operetta [,ɒpə'retə] n a short, often humorous musical play in which many of the words are sung and which often includes dancing.

Ophelia [oʊ'fiːlɪə] a character in Shakespeare's play *Hamlet.* She goes mad and drowns herself when she thinks that Hamlet no longer loves her.

ophthalmic optician [ɒf,θælmɪk-] n GB a person whose job is to test people's eyesight and decide what kind of glasses or contact lenses they need.

ophthalmologist [,ɒfθæl'mɒlədʒəst] n a doctor who treats diseases of the eyes.

opinion [ə'pɪnjən] n -1. one's personal feeling about a particular subject or situation □ *strongly held opinions* □ *Everyone is encouraged to give their own opinion on each subject.* □ *So what's your opinion on these latest developments?* □ *They had a small difference of opinion over the money.* □ *It's a matter of opinion wheth-*

er the training session was actually successful. ■ **to be of the opinion that** to believe that (formal use). ■ **in my opinion** a phrase used to say one is giving one's opinion about something □ *In my opinion, these experiments should be banned.* **-2.** a belief or view that most people have, or that a particular group of people has □ *World opinion has been outraged by the attack.* □ *The drug has not found favor with medical opinion.*

opinionated [ə'pɪnjəneɪtəd] *adj* [person] who has strong opinions and is unwilling to accept that they may be wrong (disapproving use) □ *Geoff comes across as being very opinionated.*

opinion poll *n* a survey of various people's opinions of a person, activity, product etc □ *Latest opinion poll figures show a 5% lead for the Democratic Party.*

opium ['oupjəm] *n* an addictive drug, made from the seeds of a type of poppy, that helps people to sleep, relieves pain, and can change a person's mood and behavior.

opossum [ə'pɒsəm] *n* a small animal with thick fur and a long tail that carries its young in a pouch on the front of its body and lives in trees.

Oppenheimer ['ɒpənhaɪmər], **J.R.** (1904–1967) a US scientist who was involved in the development of the atomic bomb.

opponent [ə'pounənt] *n* **-1.** POLITICS a politician who belongs to a different party from another politician and has different beliefs and ideas □ *His opponents have called for a referendum.* **-2.** [in football, boxing, chess] a person who one is competing against or who is in the opposite team. **-3.** [of an idea, movement] a person who criticizes an idea, movement etc □ *a fierce opponent of the death penalty.*

opportune [,ɒpər'tʲuːn] *adj* [moment, remark] that happens at exactly the right time or in exactly the right situation (formal use).

opportunism [,ɒpər'tʲuːnɪzm] *n* the behavior of an opportunist (disapproving use).

opportunist [,ɒpər'tʲuːnəst] *n* a person who takes advantage of all situations that help their career or make them more successful, even if they harm other people (disapproving use) □ *a political opportunist.*

opportunity [,ɒpər'tʲuːnətɪ] (*pl* **opportunities**) *n* a situation which allows one to do something □ *She'd always wanted to travel the world, and this job seemed like an excellent opportunity.* □ *I phoned at the earliest opportunity.* □ *I don't often get the opportunity to practice my Russian.* ■ **to take the opportunity to do** OR **of doing sthg** to use an opportunity to do sthg □ *I'd like to take this opportunity to thank all of you for coming.*

oppose [ə'pouz] *vt* [person] to strongly disagree with <sb> and try to make them change their mind; [idea, wish, reform] to disagree with <sthg> and try to prevent it from being carried out or from continuing □ *Clarke is being opposed by powerful commercial interests.* □ *Local residents opposed the new road.*

opposed [ə'pouzd] *adj* **to be opposed** [opinions, systems] to be very different from each other □ *This theory is completely opposed to what we've been brought up to believe.* ■ **to be opposed to sthg** to disagree with sthg □ *I am strongly opposed to import quotas/nuclear tests.*

◆ **as opposed to** *prep* a phrase used to contrast two things and to emphasize the first one mentioned □ *More investment is needed in the rail system, as opposed to the road network.*

opposing [ə'pouzɪŋ] *adj* **-1. opposing ideas/ views etc** ideas/views etc that are completely different from each other □ *Father and son held opposing views on the subject.* **-2. opposing sides** people who disagree with or are competing against each other □ *They were playing on opposing teams.*

opposite ['ɒpəzɪt] ◇ *adj* **-1.** [house, door, side] that is facing a particular thing or person □ *They work in the building opposite.* **-2.** [result, direction, effect] that is completely different □ *We live at opposite ends of the country.* □ *Her views on abortion are completely opposite to mine.*

◇ *adv* [live, sit, work] in a position that is facing a particular person or thing □ *They're building a school opposite.*

◇ *prep* facing <sb/sthg> □ *Charles always used to sit opposite me in class.* □ *I'll meet you in the bar opposite the theater.*

◇ *n* a person, belief, thing etc that is completely different from another person, belief, thing etc □ *"Fat" is the opposite of "thin".* □ *She's just the opposite to me.*

opposite number *n* a person who has the same job as oneself, but not in the same company, government etc □ *I'm going to meet my opposite number in Seoul.*

opposite sex *n* **the opposite sex** a phrase used by men to refer to women or by women to refer to men □ *a member of the opposite sex.*

opposition [,ɒpə'zɪʃn] *n* **-1.** [to a wish, plan, policy] the act of opposing something, or the state of being opposed to something □ *There was strong opposition to the idea.* □ *Opposition from miners ended in a strike.* □ *The proposal met with powerful opposition from local residents.* **-2.** a group of people who are opposing something □ *Never give any advantage to the opposition.* **-3.** SPORTS the team playing against one's own team □ *The opposition is pretty tough.* □ *Their opposition in the next round will be the Spanish team.*

◆ **Opposition** *n* POLITICS **the Opposition** in a country that has a parliament, the main party that opposes the government □ *the leader of the Opposition* □ *the main Opposition party.*

oppress [ə'pres] *vt* **-1.** to treat <people> in a cruel unfair way □ *oppressed for years by a harsh military dictatorship.* **-2.** to make <sb> feel depressed or worried □ *Feelings of doubt began to oppress her.*

oppressed [ə'prest] ◇ *adj* [minorities, people, workers] who are oppressed. ◇ *npl* **the oppressed** people who are oppressed.

oppression [ə'preʃn] *n* **-1.** the act of oppressing a group of people □ *the oppression of eth-*

nic minorities. **-2.** a feeling of depression □ *a sense of oppression.*

oppressive [ə'presɪv] *adj* **-1.** [law, society, regime] that is unfair and cruel. **-2.** [weather, heat] that is unpleasant, because it is too hot and there is not enough fresh air. **-3.** [silence, situation, atmosphere] that makes one feel very uneasy or anxious.

oppressor [ə'presəʳ] *n* a person who oppresses people, minorities etc.

opprobrium [ə'proubrɪəm] *n* public disapproval or hatred (formal use).

opt [ɒpt] ◇ *vt* **to opt to do sthg** to choose to do sthg from two or more possibilities □ *She opted to go abroad for a year.* ◇ *vi* **to opt for sthg** to choose sthg from two or more possibilities □ *He opted for early retirement.*

◆ **opt in** *vi* **to opt in** to choose to take part in something □ *He opted in to the company's savings plan.*

◆ **opt out** *vi* **to opt out** to choose not to take part in something □ *In the USA, employees can opt out of their company's health plan.*

optic ['ɒptɪk] *adj* [nerve] that is connected with the eyes.

◆ **optics** *n* the branch of physics that is concerned with light.

optical ['ɒptɪkl] *adj* **-1.** [instrument, disk, process] that involves the use of light, especially for storing information in a computer. **-2.** [effect, disorder] that is connected with one's eyesight.

optical character reader *n* an optical instrument that can scan and process letters and figures and store them in a way that a computer can recognize and use.

optical character recognition *n* the process in which letters and figures are recognized and processed by an optical character reader.

optical fiber *n* a cable used in telecommunications which carries light signals along the glass fiber inside as a way of sending information.

optical illusion *n* something, e.g. a drawing, that makes one think one sees something that is not really there.

optician [ɒp'tɪʃn] *n* **-1.** US a person who fits and sells glasses but who is not qualified to test one's eyesight. **-2.** GB = **ophthalmic optician.** ■ **the optician's** the place where an optician works.

optimism ['ɒptəmɪzm] *n* the belief that a particular situation, or the future in general, will turn out well □ *Many young people feel little optimism about their job prospects.*

optimist ['ɒptəmɪst] *n* a person who is usually optimistic.

optimistic [,ɒptə'mɪstɪk] *adj* [mood, person, attitude] that is full of optimism □ *an optimistic estimate of the costs involved* □ *She's optimistic about passing her driving test.*

optimize, -ise ['ɒptəmaɪz] *vt* [chances, assets] to make <sthg> as successful, as useful, or as likely to happen as possible.

optimum ['ɒptəməm] *adj* **an optimum amount/**

condition etc an amount/a condition etc that is the best or most likely to bring success □ *The optimum speed of the car for efficient fuel consumption is 50 mph.* □ *For optimum results, use only as directed.*

option ['ɒpʃn] *n* a choice from several possible courses of action or choices □ *What are the options?* □ *There are several options open to you for investing your money.* ■ **to have the option to do sthg** to have the freedom to choose to do sthg □ *She had no option but to pay up.* □ *He had the option of taking early retirement.*

optional ['ɒpʃnəl] *adj* [subject, feature] that one can choose to do or have if one wants to □ *Electric windows are an optional extra with this model.* □ *On the second day of the tour there will be an optional excursion to Lake Como.*

optometrist [ɒp'tɒmətrəst] *n* US a person whose job is to test people's eyesight and decide what kind of glasses or contact lenses they need.

opulence ['ɒpjələns] *n: see* **opulent.**

opulent ['ɒpjələnt] *adj* **-1.** [person, society] very rich □ *They lead an opulent lifestyle.* **-2.** [hotel, palace] that is expensively and beautifully decorated and furnished □ *She lived in opulent surroundings.*

opus ['oupəs] *(pl* **opuses** OR **opera** [-ərə]) *n* a piece of music by a musician, followed by a number to indicate where it comes in the whole series of the musician's works □ *Beethoven's septet in E flat, Opus 20.*

or [ɔːʳ] *conj* **-1.** used in front of the last thing in a list of alternatives or choices □ *Do you want to eat out, or would you rather stay at home?* □ *I didn't know whether to feel pleased or not.* □ *You can have spinach, carrots, or potatoes.* **-2.** used between numbers to show approximate amounts □ *I've only met him once or twice.* □ *They usually cost thirty or forty dollars.* ■ **a week/month or so** about a week/month □ *I'll see you in an hour or so.* **-3. he can't read or write** he cannot read and he cannot write (used after a negative word) □ *I didn't manage to swim or run yesterday.* **-4. hurry up or (else) you'll be late** if you do not hurry up, you will be late □ *Drive carefully, or you'll have an accident.* **-5.** used to correct something one has just said or to make it more precise □ *She's the chairwoman, or "chairperson" as I should say.*

OR *abbr of* **Oregon.**

oracle ['ɒrəkl] *n* a person in Ancient Greece who, it was believed, could communicate with the gods and tell people about the future.

oral ['ɔːrəl] ◇ *adj* **-1.** [history, test] that is spoken, not written □ *Have you had your French oral exam yet?* **-2.** [surgery, hygiene] that is connected with the mouth; [medicine] that is swallowed □ *oral contraceptives.* ◇ *n* an oral exam or test.

orally ['ɔːrəlɪ] *adv* [take, express] *see* **oral** □ *'To be taken orally three times a day.'*

orange ['ɒrɪndʒ] ◇ *adj* [dress, paint, sign] that is the color between red and yellow. ◇ *n* **-1.** a round fruit with a thick orange skin and a sweet juicy center that is divided into separate parts and that is eaten, or can be squeezed to make a drink □ *orange juice/peel.* -2. a color between red and yellow □ *This sofa is available in orange or yellow.*

orangeade [ˌɒrɪndʒ'eɪd] *n* a type of sweet fizzy drink that tastes of oranges.

orange blossom *n* the white flowers of an orange tree that smell sweet and are traditionally carried by a bride.

Orangeman ['ɒrɪndʒmən] (*pl* **Orangemen** [-mən]) *n* GB a member of a Protestant organization in Northern Ireland.

orange tree *n* a tree, grown in warm regions, which oranges grow on.

orangutang [əræŋə'tæŋ] *n* a large ape with long arms, reddish hair, and no tail that comes from the rainforests of Borneo and Sumatra.

oration [ə'reɪʃn] *n* a formal, serious, public speech (formal use).

orator ['ɒrətər] *n* a person who is good at making formal public speeches.

oratorio [ˌɒrə'tɔːrɪoʊ] (*pl* **oratorios**) *n* a religious musical work performed by singers and an orchestra.

oratory [US 'ɒrətɔːrɪ, GB -ətrɪ] *n* the art of speaking in public.

orb [ɔːb] *n* -1. a round shape like a ball. -2. a golden ball with a cross on top, carried by a monarch on important formal occasions.

orbit ['ɔːrbət] ◇ *n* [of a moon, planet, satellite] the route that an object, planet etc follows as it goes around another planet, the Sun etc □ *the Earth's orbit around the Sun.* ■ **to be in/go into orbit** [rocket, spaceship] to be/start following an orbit. ■ **to put sthg into orbit** [satellite] to send sthg into space and make it follow an orbit. ◇ *vt* to go around <a planet, the Moon, the Sun> following an orbit.

orchard ['ɔːrtʃərd] *n* a piece of land where fruit trees are grown, often all of one particular type □ *an apple/a cherry orchard.*

orchestra ['ɔːrkəstrə] *n* a large group of musicians who play various instruments together directed by a conductor, and usually play classical music □ *She plays the violin in the school orchestra.*

orchestral [ɔːr'kestrəl] *adj* [music, piece, concert] that is connected with an orchestra and the kinds of music it usually plays.

orchestra pit *n* the space in a theater, in front of and below the stage, where the orchestra plays.

orchestrate ['ɔːrkəstreɪt] *vt* -1. MUSIC to make changes to <a piece of music> so that it can be played by an orchestra. -2. [campaign, event, deal] to plan the different parts of <sthg> carefully and often secretly, in order to achieve a particular result □ *The whole scheme was so well orchestrated from start to finish that no one suspected a thing.*

orchestration [ˌɔːrkə'streɪʃn] *n* [of a piece of music, campaign, event] *see* **orchestrate** □ *Her orchestration of the bid showed great skill.*

orchid ['ɔːrkəd] *n* a plant that has unusual flowers with three petals, one of which is larger than the other two.

ordain [ɔːr'deɪn] *vt* -1. to order <sthg> (formal use) □ *Fate ordained that we should meet.* -2. RELIGION **to be ordained** to become a priest by going through a religious ceremony.

ordeal [ɔːr'diːl] *n* an upsetting or difficult experience □ *They haven't recovered from their dreadful ordeal.*

order ['ɔːrdər] ◇ *n* -1. an instruction to do something, given by somebody in authority □ *My orders are to see that nobody gets hurt.* □ *She was only obeying orders.* □ *Don't drink any alcohol — and that's an order.* ■ **to be under orders to do sthg** to have been given orders to do sthg □ *The army's under orders to withdraw by nightfall.* -2. BUSINESS a request for goods to be supplied or for a meal in a restaurant; the goods or a meal asked for in this way □ *The waiter took their order.* □ *Place your order now for your Christmas turkey.* □ *Your order should reach you within 28 days.* □ *Do you know who was dealing with your order?* □ *an order of French fries.* ■ **to be on order** to have been ordered, but not to have arrived yet □ *The book you requested is still on order.* ■ **made to order** made exactly according to the measurements or request of a particular person □ *I always have my shoes made to order.* -3. [of events] the way that things are arranged or happen in relation to each other □ *We are still unsure what the order of events was.* □ *The files were all in the right/wrong order.* ■ **in order** [playing cards, documents] arranged in the correct order; [people, things] arranged in a particular order □ *They were arranged in alphabetical/chronological/reverse order.* □ *in order of age/height/importance.* -4. [of a room, affairs] the state of being neat or organized □ *He has no order in his life.* ■ **to be in order** to be legally correct □ *Are your papers in order?* -5. **in working order** [machine, device] working properly □ *in good working order.* ■ **out of order** [machine, telephone, elevator] not working; [person, behavior] not following the correct rules or the usual way of behaving □ *The drink machine has got an 'out of order' sign on it.* □ *The court ruled him out of order.* □ *That remark was completely out of order.* -6. [at a demonstration, in a classroom] the state of obeying laws or rules, or of following accepted social behavior □ *The police were brought in to restore order.* ■ **to keep order** [teacher, police] to make an event happen with as little disturbance as possible □ *It's very difficult to keep order among a class of 30 adolescent boys.* -7. SOCIOLOGY the particular way a part of society is organized □ *the economic/existing order* □ *a new world order.* -8. RELIGION a group of priests, monks, or nuns who follow a particular set of rules □ *a member of the Benedictine order of monks.*

◇ *vt* -1. [attack, inquiry] to give an order to somebody to do or start <sthg> □ *He ordered me to find out exactly what had happened.* □ *The doctor ordered that the patient be discharged.* □ *The policeman ordered them to stop shouting* □ *I've been ordered to stay here and keep watch.*

-2. [drink, taxi, goods] to ask to be supplied with <sthg> □ *I've ordered a new kitchen unit.* □ *Can I order you a cab?* □ *Would it be possible to order a copy of the new edition?* ◇ *vi* to ask for food in a restaurant □ *Are you ready to order, sir?*

◆ **orders** *npl* = holy orders.

◆ **in order that** *conj* so that (formal use) □ *They were prepared to compromise in order that there might be harmony.*

◆ **in order to** *conj* a phrase used to say that one does something with the purpose of achieving a particular thing □ *He laid a trap in order to find out who had betrayed him.* □ *In order to fully understand this matter, we have requested a full inquiry.*

◆ **on the order of** US, **in the order of** GB *prep* approximately □ *It cost us on the order of $5,000.*

◆ **order around, order about** *vt sep* **to order sb around** OR **about** to give sb many orders in a way that is annoying and unpleasant (disapproving use) □ *He was ordering everyone around as if he owned the place.*

order book *n* a book belonging to a business in which orders from customers are recorded □ *Our order books are currently full.*

order form *n* a form which a customer fills out when they are ordering goods or asking for a particular service.

orderly ['ɔːʳdəʳlɪ] (*pl* **orderlies**) ◇ *adj* **-1.** [crowd, demonstration] that is well behaved and under control □ *They filed out in an orderly fashion.* **-2.** [office, person] that is neat and well organized □ *The papers were arranged in orderly piles.* ◇ *n* **-1.** a person who works in a hospital as an assistant but is not trained to do medical work □ *a hospital orderly.* **-2.** a soldier who looks after the needs of an officer.

order number *n* the number given to an order for goods to be supplied to somebody.

ordinal number ['ɔːʳdənəl-] *n* a number that shows a position in a set of numbers, e.g. first, second, rather than a quantity, e.g. one, two.
NOTE: Compare **cardinal number**.

ordinarily [ˌɔːʳdn'erəlɪ] *adv* usually, especially when this particular time is different or is going to be different □ *Ordinarily, we'd expect to be in a stronger position at this time of year.*

ordinary ['ɔːʳdnerɪ] ◇ *adj* **-1.** [person, situation, day] that is normal and common, and is not special or different □ *It lasts twice as long as ordinary batteries.* □ *We're just an ordinary couple who like to lead a quiet life.* **-2.** [work, painting] that is not interesting because it is not special, original, or unusual (disapproving use) □ *His work is very ordinary.* □ *She's a very ordinary artist.* ◇ *n* **out of the ordinary** unusual and different □ *The party was nothing out of the ordinary.*

ordinary seaman *n* in Britain, the second lowest rank in the Royal Navy.

ordinary shares *npl* GB normal shares in a company.

ordination [ˌɔːʳdə'neɪʃn] *n* the ceremony of being ordained a priest; the act of ordaining priests □ *Many Catholics support women's ordination.*

ordnance ['ɔːʳdnəns] *n* **-1.** military supplies and guns. **-2.** artillery.

Ordnance Survey *n* the British government organization that makes detailed maps of Britain and Ireland.

ore [ɔːʳ] *n* rock that contains one or more metals in a quantity that is large enough to mine □ *iron ore.*

oregano [US ə'regənoʊ, GB ˌɒrɪ'gɑːnoʊ] *n* a herb used in cooking, especially to flavor Italian food.

Oregon ['ɒrɪgən] a state in the northwestern USA, on the Pacific coast. It is known for its attractive scenery. ABBREVIATION: OR. SIZE: 251,000 sq kms. POPULATION: 2,842,321 (*Oregonians*). CAPITAL: Salem. MAIN CITY: Portland.

Oregon Trail: the Oregon Trail the route taken in the 19th century by people traveling from Missouri to the northwestern USA to find land.

───────────

❦ OREGON TRAIL
The Oregon Trail was one of the main overland routes for people who were traveling west to Oregon to start a new life. In the 1840s and 1850s thousands of people and cattle traveled over the trail, mostly in groups of covered wagons. It took at least six months to make the 2,000-mile journey. The arrival of the railroad in the 1870s meant that people stopped using the route.

───────────

organ ['ɔːʳgən] *n* **-1.** ANATOMY [of a human, animal, plant] a part of the body or of a plant that has a particular function, e.g. the heart, liver, kidney □ *an organ donor/transplant* □ *sexual organs.* **-2.** MUSIC a musical instrument like a large piano, often found in churches, in which sound is produced by air being forced out of pipes of different lengths; a smaller instrument similar to this that is powered by electricity □ *organ music* □ *a church/an electric organ.* **-3.** [of an organization, government, party] a newspaper, radio station etc that represents the views of a particular group □ *"Pravda" was the organ of the Soviet Communist Party.*

organic [ɔː'gænɪk] *adj* **-1.** [life, remains, disease] that is connected with plant or animal life or organs. **-2.** [gardening, farming] that uses no chemicals; [vegetables, produce] that has been grown or produced without the use of chemicals.

organically [ɔːʳ'gænɪklɪ] *adv* FARMING *see* **organic** □ *organically grown vegetables.*

organic chemistry *n* the branch of chemistry that deals with carbon compounds.

organism ['ɔːʳgənɪzm] *n* a living thing, especially one that cannot be seen without a microscope □ *Many species of bacteria parasite on other living organisms.*

organist ['ɔːrgənəst] *n* a person who plays the organ.

organization [US ˌɔːrgənə'zeɪʃn, GB ˌɔːgənaɪ-] *n* -1. [of people] a group of people, e.g. a business or club, who work together to achieve a particular purpose □ *It's an organization which promotes environmental issues.* □ *We are setting up/forming/running an organization which deals with equality in the workplace.* □ *the Organization of Petroleum Exporting Countries.* -2. [of a business] the way a system, society etc is arranged or run □ *The organization of the company needs a radical overhaul.* -3. [of an activity, event, conference] the act of organizing something □ *You're good at organization, you should be in charge.*

organizational [US ˌɔːrgənə'zeɪʃnəl, GB ˌɔːgənaɪ-] *adj* **organizational structure** the sturcture of an organization. ■ **organizational ability** the ability to organize something □ *The person we are looking for will have excellent organizational skills.*

organization chart *n* a diagram showing all the departments in a company and the people who work in them, with the most powerful people at the top.

organize, -ise ['ɔːrgənaɪz] ◇ *vt* -1. [activity, event] to plan the details of <an activity, event> etc and see that it takes place □ *Can you organize a meeting of the accounting department for next week?* -2. to arrange one's life, affairs, thoughts etc into a suitable or logical order □ *The facts could be better organized, but on the whole it's a good attempt.* ◇ *vi* [workers] to form a labor union.

organized ['ɔːrgənaɪzd] *adj* -1. [activity, trip, demonstration] that has been arranged and run by somebody else, usually for the benefit of a lot of people □ *I can't bear organized vacations.* -2. [person] who plans and organizes things well so that they do not waste time, money etc □ *a well-/badly-organized business* □ *We are looking for someone who is organized and able to work to tight schedules.*

organized crime *n* crime committed by professional criminals working in organized groups.

organized labor *n* workers who belong to a union.

organizer ['ɔːrgənaɪzər] *n* a person who organizes something.

organza [ɔːr'gænzə] *n* a very fine stiff fabric, often made of silk or cotton.

orgasm ['ɔːrgæzm] *n* the highest point of sexual pleasure and excitement □ *I found it difficult to have an orgasm/to reach orgasm.*

orgy ['ɔːrdʒɪ] (*pl* **orgies**) *n* -1. a party with a lot of sexual activity or where people drink a lot □ *a drunken orgy.* -2. an excessive amount □ *an orgy of destruction/eating/spending.*

orient ['ɔːrɪənt] *vt* **to be oriented toward sb** to be specially designed for sb □ *The job is oriented toward engineering graduates.* ■ **to orient oneself** to find out where one is by looking at a map, compass, landmark etc.

Orient: the Orient Asia, especially China, Korea, and Japan. In old-fashioned use, the Orient also referred to the Middle East.

oriental [ˌɔːrɪ'entl] ◇ *adj* [art, food] that is connected with the Orient (old-fashioned use). ◇ *n* a person who comes from the Orient (old-fashioned and offensive use).

orientate ['ɔːrɪənteɪt] *vt* = **orient**.

orientation [ˌɔːrɪən'teɪʃn] *n* the particular aims, interests, or beliefs that somebody has □ *His political orientation is fairly conservative.* □ *The orientation of the course is toward the practical rather than the theoretical.* □ *sexual orientation.*

orienteering [ˌɔːrɪən'tɪərɪŋ] *n* a sport in which people cross land that they do not know using maps and a compass.

orifice ['ɒrəfəs] *n* an opening, especially one of the body's natural openings, e.g. the mouth or ear (formal use).

origami [ˌɒrə'gɑːmɪ] *n* the Japanese art of folding paper to make decorative objects.

origin ['ɒrɪdʒɪn] *n* -1. [of a life, word, river] the point where something starts or begins; [of a conflict, problems] the cause of something □ *It's a problem that has its origins in the distant past.* □ *a ritual of unknown origin* □ *Nobody knows where the origin of the story lies.* □ *the origin of the word "nepotism".* -2. [of a person] the race or social class of a person's parents □ *a man of humble/dubious/French origin.* ■ **country of origin** the country where a thing was made or where a person comes from.

✦ **origins** *npl* [of a person] = **origin** □ *What are your origins?* □ *He had peasant origins.*

original [ə'rɪdʒnəl] ◇ *adj* -1. **the original owner/plan etc** the owner/plan etc that existed first before being replaced by somebody or something else □ *In its original state, the palace was breathtaking.* □ *I want to read it in the original language.* □ *The original inhabitants were a tribe of pygmies.* -2. [document, work of art] that is genuine and is not a copy □ *Keep the original receipt and send us a photocopy.* □ *The original painting is in the Louvre.* -3. [piece of writing, piece of music] that has not been published before □ *There was a lot of original work at the festival this year.* -4. [idea, work, approach] that is new and imaginative □ *She's very original in the way she dresses.*

◇ *n* -1. an original work of art, painting, or document □ *Do you have a copy of the original?* -2. **in the original** in the original language that something was written □ *I'd like to be able to read "War and Peace" in the original.* -3. an unusual person □ *Buster Keaton was a real original.*

originality [əˌrɪdʒə'nælətɪ] *n* [of an idea, approach, work of art] *see* **original** □ *I see very little originality in his work.*

originally [ə'rɪdʒnəlɪ] *adv* [write, belong, think] *see* **original** □ *He was originally the owner.* □ *The movie was originally a play.* □ *Man originally lived in caves.* □ *Originally, they were all individual houses.*

original sin *n* the belief, held by some Christians, that humans are born in a state of sin.

originate [ə'rɪdʒəneɪt] ◇ *vt* [plan, practice] to be

the person who started <sthg> □ *Dick Fosbury originated the jump called the "Fosbury flop".* ◇ *vi* [river, custom, phenomenon] to begin to exist; [idea] to begin to exist as a direct result of something □ *How did this belief originate?* □ *The practice originated in Mali.*

originator [ə'rɪdʒəneɪtəʳ] *n* a person who originates something.

Orkney Islands ['ɔːˈknɪ-]: **the Orkney Islands** a group of islands off the northeastern coast of Scotland. POPULATION: 19,338.

Orkneys ['ɔːˈknɪz] = **Orkney Islands.**

ornament ['ɔːˈnəmənt] *n* -1. an object that is displayed in a house, e.g. on a shelf, because it is attractive □ *glass ornaments.* -2. something that adds decoration to something □ *The building had little ornament.*

ornamental [,ɔːˈnəˈmentl] *adj* [pond, garden, design] that is attractive rather than useful.

ornamentation [,ɔːˈnəmenˈteɪʃn] *n* [on a building, piece of furniture] decoration.

ornate [ɔːˈneɪt] *adj* [vase, pattern, style] that includes a lot of detailed decoration.

ornately [ɔːˈneɪtlɪ] *adv* [decorate, design] *see* **ornate.**

ornery ['ɔːˈnərɪ] *adj* US stubborn or very bad-tempered (informal use).

ornithologist [,ɔːˈnəˈθɒlədʒəst] *n* a person who studies birds.

ornithology [,ɔːˈnəˈθɒlədʒɪ] *n* the study of birds and the way they live.

orphan ['ɔːˈfn] ◇ *n* a child whose parents are dead. ◇ *vt* **to be orphaned** to become an orphan.

orphanage ['ɔːˈfənɪdʒ] *n* a place where orphans are brought up.

Orpheus ['ɔːˈfɪəs] in Greek mythology, a musician whose wife is called Eurydice. When she dies, he follows her into Hades, the land of the dead. He is allowed to bring her back to life as long as he does not look back at her on the way. He looks back, and loses her.

orthodontist [,ɔːˈθəˈdɒntəst] *n* a dentist who treats teeth that are not growing in the right way.

orthodox ['ɔːˈθədɒks] *adj* -1. [belief, method, system] that is accepted by most people. -2. RELIGION [believer, religion] that has very traditional beliefs and practices □ *an orthodox Jew.*

Orthodox Church *n* **the Orthodox Church** the body of Churches, including the Churches of Russia and Greece, that separated from the western Church in the 11th century.

orthodoxy ['ɔːˈθədɒksɪ] *n* -1. a generally accepted view or belief. -2. RELIGION the state of being orthodox.

orthopaedic *etc* [,ɔːˈθəˈpiːdɪk] = **orthopedic** *etc.*

orthopedic [,ɔːˈθəˈpiːdɪk] *adj* [surgeon, medicine, patient] that is connected with orthopedics □ *an orthopedic ward/hospital.*

orthopedics [,ɔːˈθəˈpiːdɪks] *n* the branch of medicine that deals with bones.

orthopedist [,ɔːˈθəˈpiːdəst] *n* an orthopedic surgeon.

Orwell ['ɔːˈwel], **George** (1903–1950) a British writer who was concerned with social justice. He wrote novels such as *Nineteen Eighty-Four* about the dangers of dictatorships.

OS ◇ *n abbr of* **Ordnance Survey.** ◇ *abbr of* **outsize.**

O/S *abbr of* **out of stock.**

Osaka [ou'saːkə] the second-largest city in Japan and an important Pacific port. POPULATION: 2,623,801.

Osborne ['ɒzbɔːˈn], **John** (1929–1995) a British playwright whose plays, such as *Look Back in Anger*, criticize the British class system. His characters are often described as "angry young men".

Oscar ['ɒskəʳ] *n* in the USA, a prize awarded each year to outstanding movies, actors, and people working in the movie industry □ *The movie has been nominated for five Oscars.*

oscillate ['ɒsəleɪt] *vi* -1. [pendulum, needle on a dial] to move quickly and continuously from side to side. -2. to continuously change from one mood, attitude etc to another □ *He oscillated between happiness and depression.*

oscilloscope [ə'sɪləskoup] *n* an electronic device that shows the size and shape of an electric signal.

OSHA (*abbr of* **Occupational Safety and Health Administration**) *n* **the OSHA** the US government department responsible for health and safety in the workplace.

Oslo ['ɒzlou] the capital of Norway, and its main port. POPULATION: 467,441.

osmosis [ɒs'mousəs] *n* BIOLOGY the process by which liquid slowly passes from one part of a body or plant to another through a membrane.

osprey ['ɒsprɪ] (*pl* **ospreys**) *n* a large bird that has a dark brown back and a white breast and that catches and eats fish.

Ostend [ɒst'end] a port and tourist resort in northwestern Belgium. There is a ferry service between Ostend and Dover, England. POPULATION: 68,500.

ostensible [ɒ'stensəbl] *adj* [reason, cause, purpose] that is said to be why something is done or has happened, but is probably not true □ *There was no ostensible explanation for what he had done.*

ostensibly [ɒ'stensəblɪ] *adv* [fair, reasonable] *see* **ostensible** □ *He left the house, ostensibly to go for a walk.*

ostentation [,ɒsten'teɪʃn] *n* the state of being ostentatious.

ostentatious [,ɒsten'teɪʃəs] *adj* -1. [lifestyle, wealth] that involves expensive possessions and activities intended to impress people. -2. [person] who likes to show people that they are wealthy or important.

osteoarthritis [,ɒstɪouɑːˈθraɪtəs] *n* a disease which affects mainly middle-aged or elderly people, and in which the joints swell and become painful.

osteopath ['ɒstɪəpæθ] *n* a person qualified to practice osteopathy.

osteopathy [ˌɒstɪ'ɒpəθɪ] *n* a kind of medical treatment in which a patient's bones and joints are massaged and moved.

ostracize, -ise ['ɒstrəsaɪz] *vt* to ignore <sb> completely and not let them join one's group (formal use).

ostrich ['ɒstrɪtʃ] *n* a bird that comes from Africa, has a long neck, can run but cannot fly, and is the largest bird in the world.

Oswald ['ɒzwld], **Lee Harvey** (1939–1963) the man who was accused of killing John F. Kennedy. He was murdered two days after the assassination by Jack Ruby.

OT *n* -1. *abbr of* **Old Testament**. -2. *abbr of* **occupational therapy**.

OTC *adj abbr of* **over-the-counter**.

Othello [ə'θeloʊ] the hero of Shakespeare's play *Othello, the Moor of Venice*. He kills his wife, Desdemona, when he is tricked into believing that she has a lover.

other ['ʌðər] ◇ *det* -1. **other places/people etc** different places/people etc from those already mentioned □ *These shoes are more comfortable than the other ones I've tried on.* □ *There's no other way to do it.* -2. additional □ *Do you have any other questions?* □ *There were several other people waiting.* □ *caviar, champagne, and other delicacies.* -3. **the other hand/end** the second hand/end (used of two things, people etc) □ *Look on the other side of the package.* □ *I don't like this cheese — can I try the other one?* -4. **the other people/things etc** the rest of the people/things etc in the group □ *Now I'll put the same question to the other members of our panel.* □ *The other colors available in this style are navy blue, cream, and black.* -5. *phrases* **the other day/week etc** on a day/week etc not long ago □ *I saw them only the other night.* ■ **other people** people in general, but not oneself □ *I'm not interested in what other people think.*
◇ *pron* **the other** the second of two things □ *He had a gun in one hand and the key in the other.* □ *They speak French on this side of the border and German on the other.* □ *They have two branches, one of which is in Paris, and the other in Nice.*

◆ **others** *pron pl* -1. different people, things etc from the one already mentioned □ *Those are my views on the subject, though others may disagree.* □ *Some of their ideas are better than others.* □ *There have been problems in this country, as in many others.* □ *Can I wear these shoes? My others are all dirty.* -2. **the others** the rest of the people, things etc in the group □ *Two of us wanted to carry on walking, but the others were tired so we stopped.*

◆ **other than** *prep* except <sb/sthg> □ *Other than my boss, no one knew.* □ *I got a few bruises in the crash but other than that I feel OK.* ■ **none other than** used to emphasize somebody or something that is very surprising □ *It was none other than the Vice President himself.*

otherwise ['ʌðərwaɪz] ◇ *adv* -1. **I have a cold, but otherwise I'm fine** I have a cold, but apart from this I'm fine □ *My room is slightly too small, but otherwise it's OK.* ■ **an otherwise normal day** a day which is normal apart from the one thing just mentioned. ■ **I left because I would have been late otherwise** if I had not left then I would have been late □ *I'm glad we took the car, because otherwise we would have had too far to walk.* -2. **to think/state/act otherwise** to think/state/act something different or opposite to what has just been mentioned □ *We should try to leave early, unless you think otherwise.* □ *unless advised otherwise by your dentist.*
◇ *conj* **hurry up, otherwise you'll be late** if you do not hurry up, you will be late □ *I want to see an improvement in your work, otherwise you'll be asked to leave the team.*

other world *n* **the other world** the place that many people believe is where a person's spirit goes to when the body is dead.

otherworldly [ˌʌðər'wɜːrldlɪ] *adj* [person, attitude] that is more concerned with things connected to the spirit than with normal and real life.

Ottawa ['ɒtəwə] the capital of Canada, in southeastern Ontario. POPULATION: 313,987.

otter ['ɒtər] *n* an animal that has brown fur, a wide flat tail, and webbed feet for swimming in water and eats fish and small animals.

OU *n abbr of* **Open University**.

ouch [aʊtʃ] *excl* a word used when one suddenly feels pain □ *Ouch! That hurt!*

ought [ɔːt] *aux vb* -1. used to say that it would be sensible or a good idea to do something □ *You really ought to see a doctor.* □ *Ought I to let them know I'm coming?* ■ **you ought to have gone** it would have been sensible to go, but you did not go □ *You ought to have gotten advice from a lawyer before you wrote the letter.* -2. used to say that it would be morally good to do something □ *I ought to punish you for this!* □ *They ought not to be so rude to customers.* ■ **you ought to have done it** it would have been morally better if you had done it, but you didn't □ *We ought to have realized that this would happen.* -3. used to say what one expects to happen □ *The meeting ought to finish soon.* □ *They ought to be here by now.*

oughtn't ['ɔːtnt] = **ought not**.

ounce [aʊns] *n* -1. a unit (approximately 28.35 grams) for measuring weight □ *Take 4 ounces of butter.* □ *There are 16 ounces in/to a pound.* -2. [of common sense, intelligence] a small amount □ *There isn't an ounce of truth in what you say.*

our ['aʊər] *det* **our house/car** the house/car that belongs to us or is connected with us □ *We had forgotten our passports.* □ *Our children are all grown up now.* □ *Let's forget about our problems while we're on vacation.*

Our Lady Mary, the mother of Jesus Christ.

ours ['aʊərz] *pron* used to refer to something

that belongs to or is connected with a group of people that includes oneself □ *If your tent's not big enough you can always borrow ours.* ■ **it's ours** it belongs to us □ *The house will be ours when my father dies.* ■ **a friend of ours** one of our friends □ *We've been invited to dinner by a colleague of ours.*

ourselves [aʊəʳˈselvz] *pron pl* -**1.** used after a preposition, or as the object of a verb, to refer to the same people as the subject "we" □ *We all enjoyed ourselves on our day out.* □ *She told us to sit down and make ourselves comfortable.* □ *We felt so pleased with ourselves when we went jogging for the first time.* -**2.** used to emphasize "we" □ *Now that we've met John ourselves we're quite happy about Jenny and him getting married.* ■ **we did it (by) ourselves** we did it without help from other people □ *James and I painted the bedroom ourselves.*

oust [aʊst] *vt* to force <sb> to leave a group, position, or place □ *He was ousted from power by a military coup.*

out [aʊt] ◇ *adv* -**1.** not inside a room, container, car etc □ *The phone is out in the corridor.* □ *The bus stopped and we all got out.* -**2.** not inside a house or building □ *It's windy out today.* □ *He's out at the moment, can I take a message?* □ *I'm going out for a walk.* ■ **out here/there** outside (used by somebody who is outside/inside a building) □ *Let me in, it's cold out here.* ■ **out you go!** go outside. -**3.** **to stay/eat out** to stay/eat away from one's home, office etc □ *She's out on business at the moment.* □ *Let's have a day out at the beach.* -**4.** **the fire/light is out** the fire/light is no longer burning/shining □ *The fire/lights went out.* □ *Turn the lamp out.* -**5.** **the tide is out** the sea has moved away from the shore □ *They waited for the tide to go out.* -**6.** **to be/go out** [clothes, style] to be/become unfashionable □ *Tight trousers went out years ago.* -**7.** **to be out** [flower] to be blooming □ *The crocuses are out already.* -**8.** **to be/come out** [sun, stars] to have appeared/to appear in the sky □ *The sun came out from behind a cloud.* -**9.** [book, product] available for sale to the public □ *Their new record will be out in March.* -**10.** **to be/come out** [workers, union] to be/go on strike (informal use) □ *The workforce has been out for two months now.*

◇ *adj* -**1.** **to be out** [plan, suggestion] not to be possible or acceptable □ *Wednesday's out, I'm afraid.* -**2.** **to be out** [calculation, guess] to be wrong □ *Our estimate was out by 5%.* -**3.** **to be out to do sthg** to be trying to do sthg □ *The police are out to get him.*

◇ *prep* **out the building** not inside the building □ *Take the plates out the dishwasher.*

◆ **out of** *prep* -**1.** **out of the building** not inside the building □ *I was out of the room at the time.* □ *He'll be out of the country for two weeks.* □ *The driver got out of the bus.* -**2.** used to say where something comes from □ *a page out of a book* □ *We can pay for it out of our savings.* -**3.** **made out of sthg** made using sthg as a material □ *a necklace made out of diamonds and rubies.* -**4.** **to do sthg out of boredom/interest/love etc** to do sthg because one feels

boredom/interest/love etc □ *I read the note out of sheer curiosity.* -**5.** **to be out of coffee/paper/cash etc** to no longer have any coffee/paper/cash etc □ *We're out of milk, can you go and buy some?* -**6.** **one out of six/ten etc** one in each group of six/ten etc □ *Six out of (every) ten people interviewed liked the product.* □ *Your exam was excellent; ten out of ten!*

out-and-out *adj* **an out-and-out liar/fanatic etc** a complete liar/fanatic etc.

outback [ˈaʊtbæk] *n* **the outback** the areas of Australia away from the coast where very few people live.

💭 OUTBACK
Many Australians refer to any area of wild land as outback, but the term really refers to the large area of red deserts and dry plains in central Australia — an area that covers over 70% of the country. The outback is an important part of Australian myths and culture, even though most Australians live in towns and cities along the coast, and many have never been to the outback.

---

outbid [ˌaʊtˈbɪd] (*pt* & *pp* **outbid**, *cont* **outbidding**) *vt* to bid a higher price than <sb> for something, often at an auction □ *We were outbid for the painting by a foreign collector.*

outboard (motor) [ˌaʊtbɔːʳd-] *n* a motor with a propeller that is attached to the back of a small boat.

outbound [ˈaʊtbaʊnd] *adj* [train, flight] that is traveling away from a particular place.

outbreak [ˈaʊtbreɪk] *n* the sudden beginning of something, especially violence or disease □ *the outbreak of war* □ *Recent outbreaks of crime have led to a rise in the demand for burglar alarms.* □ *They reported an outbreak of cholera in the region.*

outbuildings [ˈaʊtbɪldɪŋz] *npl* buildings such as barns and stables that are not joined to the main building, but that belong to it.

outburst [ˈaʊtbɜːʳst] *n* -**1.** the act of suddenly showing a strong emotion, especially anger □ *The announcement provoked angry outbursts in the Senate.* -**2.** the sudden appearance of something bad that lasts for a short period of time □ *fresh outbursts of violence/shelling.*

outcast [US ˈaʊtkæst, GB -kɑːst] *n* a person who has been rejected by a group of people or by society □ *These people are treated as social outcasts.*

outclass [US ˌaʊtˈklæs, GB -ˈklɑːs] *vt* [rival] to be much better than <sb> at something □ *He was hopelessly outclassed by his opponent.*

outcome [ˈaʊtkʌm] *n* the final result of a process, situation etc □ *What was the outcome of the meeting?* □ *We're hoping for a peaceful outcome to the talks.*

outcrop [ˈaʊtkrɒp] *n* a large mass of rock that sticks out of the ground or the side of a mountain □ *a rocky outcrop.*

outcry [ˈaʊtkraɪ] (*pl* **outcries**) *n* an angry protest by a lot of people □ *There was a public outcry over the fare increases.*

outdated [ˌaʊtˈdeɪtəd] *adj* [method, idea, technology] that is now no longer suitable because it has been replaced by a new one □ *My parents have very outdated views on bringing up children.* □ *outdated equipment.*

outdid [ˌaʊtˈdɪd] *past tense of* **outdo.**

outdistance [ˌaʊtˈdɪstəns] *vt* -1. to go so fast that one is very far ahead of <the other competitors> in a race. -2. to be more successful at something than <one's rival, competitors> etc □ *They easily outdistanced the opposition at the local elections.*

outdo [ˌaʊtˈduː] (*pt* **outdid**, *pp* **outdone** [-ˈdʌn]) *vt* [person, rival, neighbors] to do something better than <sb> □ *Maggie, not to be outdone by her sister, also won her event.*

outdoor [ˈaʊtdɔːʳ] *adj* -1. **an outdoor swimming pool/cafe** a swimming pool/cafe that is outside, not inside a building □ *I enjoy outdoor sports.* -2. **outdoor clothes/shoes** clothes/shoes that are made to be worn outside.

outdoors [ˌaʊtˈdɔːʳz] *adv* [eat, play, go] outside, not inside a building.

outer [ˈaʊtəʳ] *adj* -1. **an outer wall/layer etc** a wall/layer etc that is on the outside of something □ *The lobster has a hard outer shell.* -2. **the outer suburbs** the areas further away from the center of a city □ *outer London.*

outermost [ˈaʊtəʳməʊst] *adj* **the outermost layer/area etc** the layer/area etc that is furthest from the middle.

outer space *n* space that is far from the Earth's atmosphere.

outerwear [ˈaʊtəʳweəʳ] *n* clothes made to be worn outdoors.

outfield [ˈaʊtfiːld] *n* **the outfield** the part of a baseball or cricket field that is furthest from the middle; the players who stand in this part.

outfit [ˈaʊtfɪt] *n* -1. two or more items of clothing that are chosen or made to be worn together □ *I like your outfit!* -2. an organization of people working together (informal use) □ *They run a small printing outfit in LA.*

outfitters [ˈaʊtfɪtəʳz] *n* GB a store that sells men's clothes (old-fashioned use) □ *a gentlemen's outfitters.*

outflank [ˌaʊtˈflæŋk] *vt* -1. MILITARY [army] to get around the side of <enemy soldiers> in order to attack them from behind. -2. [opponent, opposition] to beat <sb> in business, an argument etc by doing something clever.

outgoing [ˌaʊtˈgəʊɪŋ] *adj* -1. **the outgoing chairman/governor etc** the person who is soon going to leave their position as chairman/governor etc □ *There will be an address by the outgoing CEO.* -2. **outgoing mail/passengers etc** mail/passengers etc leaving a particular place □ *All outgoing flights have been rerouted via JFK.* -3. [person] who is friendly and enjoys talking to people they do not know □ *She has a friendly outgoing nature.*

◆ **outgoings** *npl* GB all the money spent on different things by a business, or in one's daily life □ *Our monthly outgoings are very high.*

outgrow [ˌaʊtˈgrəʊ] (*pt* **outgrew** [-ˈgruː], *pp* **outgrown** [-ˈgrəʊn]) *vt* -1. [jacket, shoes] to grow too big for <a piece of clothing>, so that it no longer fits one □ *They outgrow their clothes so quickly at that age.* -2. [space, resources] to become too large for <sthg>, so that it is no longer enough □ *The company soon outgrew its original offices.* -3. [toys, habit] to no longer do, enjoy etc <sthg>, because one has grown older and changed □ *Thankfully, I've outgrown all those unrealistic notions about marriage.*

outhouse [ˈaʊthaʊs, *pl* -haʊzɪz] *n* -1. an outside toilet. -2. GB a small building that is part of a house and is often used for storing things in.

outing [ˈaʊtɪŋ] *n* -1. a short pleasant visit to a place, usually made by a group of people □ *We're taking the local old folk on an outing to the theater.* □ *a work/family/school outing.* -2. the act of telling the public that a well-known person is a secret homosexual □ *the outing of prominent political figures.*

outlandish [aʊtˈlændɪʃ] *adj* [behavior, clothing, idea] very strange (disapproving use) □ *Julie has some very outlandish ideas about politics.*

outlast [US ˌaʊtˈlæst, GB -ˈlɑːst] *vt* to last longer than <sb/sthg> □ *These old buildings will outlast many built this century.*

outlaw [ˈaʊtlɔː] ◇ *vt* -1. to make <sthg> illegal □ *The movement was outlawed and its leaders arrested.* □ *All firearms should be outlawed.* -2. to announce that <sb> is a criminal □ *The outlawed mayor took refuge in South America.* ◇ *n* a criminal who is hiding in order to avoid being caught (old-fashioned use) □ *a band of outlaws.*

outlay [ˈaʊtleɪ] *n* the amount of money one spends in order to start a business project □ *Their initial outlay was relatively small.*

outlet [ˈaʊtlet] *n* -1. [for one's feelings] something that gives one a way of showing one's feelings or using one's ideas □ *Writing provided her with an outlet for her anger.* -2. CONSTRUCTION a hole or pipe which something can go out through □ *a gas/sewage/water outlet.* -3. BUSINESS a business or store that sells particular goods □ *a retail outlet.* -4. ELECTRICITY a device fitted to a wall that is part of a wiring system and supplies current to electrical appliances.

outline [ˈaʊtlaɪn] ◇ *n* -1. a short description of something that covers the main facts and uses few words □ *He gave her a brief outline of what had happened/the new law.* □ *a broad outline* □ *an outline proposal/description.* ■ **to show sthg in outline** to give an outline of sthg □ *This sheet shows, in outline, the subjects to be studied this year.* -2. the shape of the outside edge of something; the general shape of something □ *Draw the outline first, and then color it in.* □ *They could just make out the outline of a ship in the distance.* ◇ *vt* -1. [plan, reasons] to give a short general description of <sthg> □ *I'd like to comment on some points outlined in the report.* -2. **to be outlined against sthg** to be seen in outline because sthg behind it is brighter □ *I saw a dark figure outlined against the evening sky.*

outlive [,aʊt'lɪv] *vt* **-1.** to live longer than <sb/sthg> □ *I'm sure grandma will outlive us all.* **-2. to outlive its usefulness** to no longer be useful to one □ *This computer has outlived its usefulness.*

outlook ['aʊtlʊk] *n* **-1.** [of a person] one's general attitude to life □ *She has a very positive outlook on life.* **-2.** [of a situation] the way a particular situation is likely to develop in the future □ *The outlook for the mining industry is grim.* □ *the weather outlook for the weekend/the rest of the country.*

outlying ['aʊtlaɪɪŋ] *adj* **outlying districts/regions etc** districts/regions etc that are far away from towns or cities □ *Some of the outlying villages are very attractive.*

outmaneuver US, **outmanoeuvre** GB [,aʊtmə'nuːvəʳ] *vt* [opponent, rival] to get a big advantage over <sb> by doing something clever.

outmoded [,aʊt'moʊdəd] *adj* [method, belief, idea] that is no longer fashionable or useful.

outnumber [,aʊt'nʌmbəʳ] *vt* to be greater in number than <another group> □ *In the group boys outnumber girls by three to two.*

out-of-court *adj* **an out-of-court settlement** an agreement between the two sides in a legal dispute in which one pays the other a sum of money, so that the matter does not have to be dealt with in a court.

◆ **out of court** *adv*: *Myers agreed to settle out of court.*

out-of-date *adj* **-1.** [book, information, law] that is no longer correct, suitable, or useful □ *This guidebook is completely out-of-date.* **-2.** [license, passport] that is no longer valid.

out of doors *adv* [eat, work, play] outside, not inside a building □ *It's too cold to spend much time out of doors.*

out-of-the-way *adj* [place, village] that is quite far from the nearest town and is not easy to reach or find □ *We found a motel in an out-of-the-way place in Wade County.*

outpace [,aʊt'peɪs] *vt* **-1.** to do something faster or better than <sb> □ *Stephens easily outpaced me on the track.* **-2.** to do better than <sthg> □ *Technology is constantly outpacing itself.*

outpatient ['aʊtpeɪʃnt] *n* a person who goes to a hospital for treatment, but who does not spend the night there.

outplacement ['aʊtpleɪsmənt] *n* a service that helps people who have lost their jobs to find new jobs.

outplay [,aʊt'pleɪ] *vt* [team, player] to play better than <one's opponent> in a sport, with the result that one usually wins.

outpost ['aʊtpoʊst] *n* a small village or military position in a lonely distant area.

outpouring ['aʊtpɔːrɪŋ] *n* the act of suddenly showing a strong feeling, reaction etc, especially sadness □ *an outpouring of ideas/grief.*

output ['aʊtpʊt] ◇ *n* **-1.** [of a factory, writer, business] the amount of work or goods produced by somebody or something □ *We must increase output by 18%.* □ *Fischer's output as a writer has been disappointingly low.* **-2.**

COMPUTING the act of sending information from a computer to a printer or screen; the information that is sent in this way □ *Output from this program is problematic.* □ *Here's the latest output to give to the sales manager.* ◇ *vt* COMPUTING [data, file] to send <information> from a computer to a printer or screen.

outrage ['aʊtreɪdʒ] ◇ *n* a strong feeling of shock and anger about something; an event or action that makes people have this feeling □ *There was public outrage at the news.* □ *It's an outrage against humanity.* ◇ *vt* to make <sb> feel outrage □ *Mothers were outraged by the discovery that their children had been given the vaccine.*

outraged ['aʊtreɪdʒd] *adj* [person] who feels outrage □ *Outraged animal lovers have protested against the experiments.*

outrageous [aʊt'reɪdʒəs] *adj* **-1.** [behavior, crime, remark] that one thinks is very shocking and totally unacceptable □ *It's outrageous how expensive alcohol is here compared to on the continent.* **-2.** [person, idea, outfit] that one thinks is very unusual and often amusing or shocking □ *He's got an outrageous sense of fun.*

outran [,aʊt'ræn] *past tense of* **outrun.**

outrank [,aʊt'ræŋk] *vt* to be in a more senior position than <sb>.

outrider ['aʊtraɪdəʳ] *n* a person who rides a horse or motorbike near to an official vehicle, especially in order to give protection □ *a motorcycle outrider.*

outright [*adj* 'aʊtraɪt, *adv* ,aʊt'raɪt] ◇ *adj* **-1. an outright denial/refusal etc** a very clear and direct denial/refusal etc □ *This accusation is an outright lie.* **-2. an outright win/failure etc** a complete and total win/failure etc □ *She's the outright winner.* ◇ *adv* **-1.** [deny, accuse] *I asked him outright whether he had done it.* **-2.** [win, fail] *They rejected the offer outright.* ■ **to be killed outright** to be killed immediately.

outrun [,aʊt'rʌn] (*pt* **outran**, *pp* **outrun**, *cont* **outrunning**) *vt* [competitor, attacker] to run faster than <sb>.

outsell [,aʊt'sel] (*pt & pp* **outsold**) *vt* to be sold in greater numbers than <the product> of other companies; to sell more of a particular product than <another company> □ *This laundry detergent has consistently outsold all other well-known brands over the last eight months.*

outset ['aʊtset] *n* **at the outset** at the very beginning □ *She was clear about what she expected right at the outset.* ■ **from the outset** from the very beginning □ *I've been involved in this company from the outset.*

outshine [,aʊt'ʃaɪn] (*pt & pp* **outshone** [-'ʃɒn]) *vt* to do something much better than <sb> □ *Simon outshone his elder brother at math.*

outside [*adv* ,aʊt'saɪd, *prep*, *adj*, & *n* 'aʊtsaɪd] ◇ *adv* **to go/run/look outside** to go/run/look out of a building or room □ *We hurried outside as soon as we saw the car pull up.* ■ **to stand/happen/wait outside** to stand/happen/wait near a room or building but not in it □ *I heard him chatting to someone outside in the* corridor. □ *Don't leave your bike outside in case it rains.*

◇ *prep* **-1. outside a room/building** not inside a room/building but near to it □ *You can easily park outside the office.* □ *There was a crowd of journalists outside the entrance to the hotel.* **-2. outside a town/city/country** beyond the place where a town/city/country ends □ *We stopped for a meal a few miles outside Denver.* **-3. outside a group/organization** among people who are not part of a group/organization □ *No one outside his immediate family knew that he was ill.* **-4. outside office hours** during the time before and after office hours □ *We sometimes meet outside working hours.*

◇ *adj* **-1. an outside wall/door etc** a wall/door etc that is not inside a room or building, or that faces outside □ *Switch off the outside light.* □ *an outside toilet.* **-2. an outside consultant/team** a consultant/team that does not belong to a group or organization □ *I think we need an outside opinion on this.* **-3. the outside world** the rest of the world, that one cannot go to, talk with etc. **-4. an outside chance** a very small chance □ *There's just an outside chance that he might have survived the crash.*

◇ *n* **the outside** the outer part or surface of something □ *The outside of the house needs painting.* □ *From the outside the restaurant looked spacious, but inside it was small and crowded.*

◆ **outside of** *prep* US (informal use) **-1. outside of a place/country etc** outside a place/country etc □ *They moved to a place just outside of New Orleans.* **-2.** except for <sb/sthg> □ *Nobody outside of Jack knows the whole story.*

outside lane *n* GB the lane of a road that is closest to the center.

outside line *n* a telephone line that can be used to call somebody outside a building, not inside it □ *Can you get me an outside line, please, Janet?*

outsider [,aʊt'saɪdəʳ] *n* **-1.** a person or animal that is not expected to win a race or competition □ *The race was won by Cool Cat, an outsider on 50-1.* **-2.** a person who is not accepted by, or involved in, a particular group □ *Jim had always been something of an outsider.*

outsize ['aʊtsaɪz] *adj* **-1.** [book, portion] that is bigger than the usual size. **-2.** [clothes, shoes] that are bigger than the standard sizes and are made especially for large people.

outsized ['aʊtsaɪzd] *adj* = outsize.

outskirts ['aʊtskɜːʳts] *npl* **the outskirts** the area round the edge of a town or city □ *We live on the outskirts of Minneapolis.*

outsmart [,aʊt'smɑːʳt] *vt* [enemy, opponent] to beat or get an advantage over <sb> by doing something more clever than them □ *Suk outsmarted his pursuers and escaped abroad.*

outsold [,aʊt'soʊld] *past tense & past participle of* outsell.

outsourcing ['aʊt,sɔːʳsɪŋ] *n* the practice of buying parts from suppliers outside a company.

outspoken [,aʊt'spoʊkən] *adj* [person, critic] who has strong opinions and tells other people what they think, even if they shock

or offend them □ *She's always been extremely outspoken in her criticism of the museum's policy.* □ *outspoken remarks.*

outspread [,aʊt'spred] *adj* [hands, wings] that are opened out as wide as possible; [newspaper, map] that is opened out to its full size □ *She ran toward him with outspread arms.*

outstanding [aʊt'stændɪŋ] *adj* **-1.** [performance, achievement, person] that is of an excellent standard □ *She has made an outstanding contribution since she joined the company.* **-2.** [influence, example] that is very important or obvious □ *an outstanding example of pre-colonial art.* **-3.** [money, bill] that has not yet been paid □ *You must note down any outstanding debts on your tax return.* **-4.** [work, job] that still needs to be finished; [problems, questions] that still need to be solved or dealt with □ *A few matters were left outstanding at the end of the meeting.*

outstay [,aʊt'steɪ] *vt* **to outstay one's welcome** to stay at somebody's house longer than they want or than is polite □ *Well, we'd better go — we don't want to outstay our welcome.*

outstretched [,aʊt'stretʃt] *adj* [wings] that are opened out as wide as possible; [arm, hand] that is stretched out as wide as possible or as far forward as possible □ *He greeted her with arms outstretched.*

outstrip [,aʊt'strɪp] (*pt & pp* **outstripped**, *cont* **outstripping**) *vt* **-1.** to be more successful than <one's rival, competitors> etc; to be greater or stronger than <sb/sthg> □ *Demand has outstripped supply for the second month running.* **-2.** to run faster than <a person or animal> □ *We started to race, but Boris soon outstripped me.*

out-take *n* a section of a movie or program that is not included when the movie or program is shown to the public, usually because it contains a mistake.

out-tray *n* a tray in an office in which documents and mail are put before they are sent somewhere else.

outvote [,aʊt'voʊt] *vt* **to be outvoted** to be defeated because more people voted against one, or against one's idea, than for one □ *Sorry, Dan, you're outvoted.* □ *The proposal was outvoted by four votes to three.*

outward ['aʊtwəʳd] ◇ *adj* **-1. the outward voyage/trip** the voyage/trip from one's home to the place one is going to □ *We had no problems at all on the outward voyage.* **-2. an outward sign** a sign that can be seen by other people, even though it hides what is true or real □ *Rachel never showed any outward signs of depression.* □ *To all outward appearances, the business was doing well.* ◇ *adv* US **to move/face outward** to move/face away from the center or the inside □ *The window opens outward.* □ *We stood in a circle, facing outward.*

outwardly ['aʊtwəʳdlɪ] *adv* a word used to describe the way a person or situation looks, when this is perhaps different from what is really true □ *He hid his distress and remained outwardly composed.* □ *Outwardly, she seems to be the same as before.*

outwards ['aʊtwəʳdz] *adv* = **outward**.

outweigh [,aʊt'weɪ] *vt* to be more important or serious than <sthg> □ *The advantages of being computerized far outweigh the costs involved.*

outwit [,aʊt'wɪt] (*pt* & *pp* **outwitted**, *cont* **outwitting**) *vt* [opponent, rival] to beat or get an advantage over <sb> by doing something more clever than them □ *Once again, the police had been outwitted by the gang.*

outworker ['aʊtwɜːʳkəʳ] *n* a person who works for a company at home, doing tasks such as typing or sewing.

oval ['oʊvl] ◇ *adj* shaped like a circle but wider in the middle and usually more pointed at one end □ *An egg is oval in shape.* ◇ *n* an oval shape.

Oval Office: the Oval Office the office of the US President.

ovarian [oʊ'veərɪən] *adj* [cyst, cancer] that is connected with a woman's ovaries.

ovary ['oʊvərɪ] (*pl* **ovaries**) *n* either of the two organs in females that produce eggs.

ovation [oʊ'veɪʃn] *n* enthusiastic applause. ■ **a standing ovation** enthusiastic applause and cheering by an audience that has stood up □ *Prescott's speech was given a standing ovation.*

oven ['ʌvn] *n* the part of a stove that has a door and which food is put inside to be cooked; this part of a stove at a particular temperature □ *an electric/gas oven* □ *a medium/hot oven.*

oven glove *n* a padded cloth that fits on one's hand and is used for taking hot things out of the oven.

ovenproof ['ʌvnpruːf] *adj* [dish, plate] that can be used to cook food in an oven without getting damaged.

oven-ready *adj* [chicken, meal] that is sold in a package and is ready to be cooked.

ovenware ['ʌvnweəʳ] *n* a collective term for cooking pots, dishes etc that are ovenproof.

over ['oʊvəʳ] ◇ *prep* **-1. over the river/bridge/door** etc directly above the river/bridge/door etc □ *I rent a studio over a restaurant.* □ *There was a sign over the entrance.* **-2. to put/wear etc sthg over sthg** to put/wear etc sthg on top of sthg else, and covering it □ *She was carrying a bag over her arm.* □ *Just leave your coat over the back of the chair.* **-3. to fly/jump etc over sthg** to fly/jump etc from one side of sthg to the other □ *James crossed over the road to join us.* **-4. to live over the road** to live on the other side of the road □ *They could see enemy troops gathering over the border.* □ *The sun disappeared over the horizon.* **-5. to bend/crouch over sb/sthg** to bend/crouch in the direction of sb/sthg that is below one □ *She leaned over and kissed him.* **-6. over 50 years ago** more than 50 years ago □ *It cost well over $600.* **-7.** used to show a position of power or higher rank □ *a victory over the enemy* □ *He was promoted over me.* **-8. a dispute/an argument over money** a dispute/an argument about money □ *She takes care over her work.* □ *There's some doubt over the future*

of the company. **-9. over the year** during the whole of the year □ *What are you doing over the weekend?* □ *Let's discuss it over lunch.*

◇ *adv* **-1.** used to indicate a place that is near enough for one to see it or point to it □ *I parked the car over by the gate.* ■ **over here** near to one; in the same country as one □ *It's over here, I've found it!* □ *Joe is over here for a year doing research.* ■ **over there** at some place away from where one is; in a different country from one □ *He sounded upset — I'd better get over there right away.* **-2. to go/come over** to go/come to a place, especially somebody's home (used to show movement between two places) □ *Let's invite them over for a meal.* □ *Could you pass me over a copy of the memo, please?* **-3. to fall/be knocked over** to fall/be knocked downward toward the ground □ *He knocked the coffee cup over as he reached for the phone.* □ *She rolled over and went to sleep.* **-4. boys of eight or over** boys of eight or more. **-5. (left) over** that remains or has not been used □ *That leaves $2 over.* □ *I've got some pastry left over.* **-6.** RADIO **over (and out)!** used by pilots, the police etc to end a radio conversation. **-7. to be over** [play, relationship] to be finished □ *The meeting was over by five o'clock.* □ *Our marriage is definitely over.* **-8. to do sthg (all) over again** to do sthg again from the beginning, especially when this is very tiring or boring □ *Now I've lost count and I'll have to start all over again!* ■ **over and over (again)** many times □ *I've told him over and over again, but he just won't listen.*

◇ *n* SPORT a series of six balls bowled by a bowler in cricket.

♦ **over and above** *prep* in addition to <sthg> □ *There will be additional expenses over and above the basic outlay.*

♦ **over to** *prep* RADIO & TV used to indicate who the next speaker will be □ *And now it's over to Alan Partridge at the sports desk.*

over- *prefix* added to words to mean too much of the particular quality, thing etc □ *over-anxious* □ *an over-exaggeration.*

overabundance [,oʊvərə'bʌndəns] *n* too much of something.

overact [,oʊvər'ækt] *vi* to act a part in a play with too much emotion.

overactive [,oʊvər'æktɪv] *adj* [gland] that is too active.

overall [*adj* & *adv* ,oʊvər'ɔːl, *n* 'oʊvərɔːl] ◇ *adj* [impression, size, cost] that includes everything □ *Our overall profits are low.* □ *The overall impression is one of peace and tranquility.* ◇ *adv* a word used to summarize a situation or one's opinion about something □ *Overall, you've done a good job.* □ *It's been a good year overall.* ◇ *n* **-1.** a light coat worn to protect one's clothes when doing dirty work. **-2.** a pair of trousers attached to a jacket that is worn to protect one's clothes when doing dirty work.

♦ **overalls** *npl* **-1.** a pair of trousers attached to a jacket that is worn to protect one's clothes when doing dirty work. **-2.** US a pair of trousers with a bib and shoulder straps attached.

overambitious [ˌoʊvəræmˈbɪʃəs] *adj* **-1.** [person] who tries to do something that is too difficult □ *Don't be too overambitious at first — I'd advise you to start slowly.* **-2.** [plan, schedule, attempt] that requires a lot of effort and is too difficult to achieve □ *She had set a ridiculously overambitious schedule for herself.*

overanxious [ˌoʊvərˈæŋkʃəs] *adj* [person] who worries too much.

overarm [ˈoʊvərɑːrm] ◇ *adj* [throw, bowling] that involves moving one's arm from behind one's body until it is above one's shoulder. ◇ *adv* [throw] *I threw the ball overarm.*

overate [ˌoʊvərˈeɪt] *past tense of* **overeat.**

overawed [ˌoʊvərˈɔːd] *vt* **to be overawed** to be so impressed by somebody or something that one becomes silent □ *They were completely overawed by the occasion.*

overbalance [ˌoʊvərˈbæləns] *vi* to become unbalanced and fall over or nearly fall over.

overbearing [ˌoʊvərˈbeərɪŋ] *adj* [person] who is unpleasant because they try to make people do what they want them to do, or does not think about what other people want or are feeling □ *I find him aggressive and overbearing.*

overblown [ˌoʊvərˈbloʊn] *adj* [description, compliment] that makes something seem bigger or more important than it really is.

overboard [ˈoʊvərbɔːrd] *adv* **-1. to fall overboard** to fall from a boat or ship into the water. **-2. to go overboard** to get too excited about somebody or something; to do something to an unreasonable degree (informal use) □ *He went completely overboard in his praise of her.*

overbook [ˌoʊvərˈbʊk] *vi* to sell or reserve more places for a play, hotel, vacation etc than are available.

overburden [ˌoʊvərˈbɜːrdn] *vt* **to be overburdened with sthg** [with work, debts] to have more of sthg than one can deal with.

overcame [ˌoʊvərˈkeɪm] *past tense of* **overcome.**

overcapitalize, -ise [ˌoʊvərˈkæpətlaɪz] *vi* to change too many assets, reserves etc into capital.

overcast [US ˌoʊvrˈkæst, GB ˌoʊvəˈkɑːst] *adj* [sky, day, weather] cloudy and dark □ *It was a dull day, gray and overcast.*

overcharge [ˌoʊvərˈtʃɑːrdʒ] *vt* [person, customer] to charge <sb> more than the correct price for something □ *He overcharged me by $15.* □ *I think I have been overcharged for my insurance.*

overcoat [ˈoʊvərkoʊt] *n* a long thick coat worn especially in winter.

overcome [ˌoʊvərˈkʌm] (*pt* **overcame,** *pp* **overcome**) *vt* **-1.** to deal with <a problem or feeling> successfully □ *He managed to overcome his fear of heights.* **-2. to be overcome by** OR **with sthg** [by emotion, fear] to feel sthg more strongly than anything else for a short period of time □ *He was overcome by sadness/with joy.* **-3. to be overcome by smoke/fumes etc** to feel weak from the effects of smoke/fumes

etc □ *Most of the victims had been overcome by smoke.*

overcompensate [ˌoʊvərˈkɒmpənseɪt] *vi* to do much more than is necessary to correct a problem, with the result that one does something else that is wrong □ *When she's nervous she tends to overcompensate by being very aggressive.*

overconfident [ˌoʊvərˈkɒnfɪdənt] *adj* too confident.

overcooked [ˌoʊvərˈkʊkt] *adj* [meat, vegetables] that has been cooked for too long or with too much heat.

overcrowded [ˌoʊvərˈkraʊdəd] *adj* [room, office, prison] that has too many people in it □ *The camp is desperately overcrowded with refugees.*

overcrowding [ˌoʊvərˈkraʊdɪŋ] *n* the state of being overcrowded □ *There is severe overcrowding in our prisons.*

overdeveloped [ˌoʊvərdɪˈveləpt] *adj* **-1.** PHOTOGRAPHY [film] that is too dark because a mistake was made during the developing process. **-2.** [interest, appetite] that is much bigger than it should be. **-3.** [town, area] that has been spoiled by too many buildings.

overdo [ˌoʊvərˈduː] (*pt* **overdid** [-ˈdɪd], *pp* **overdone**) *vt* **-1.** [compliments, welcome] to exaggerate <sthg> (disapproving use) □ *Just tell her calmly about your feelings without overdoing it and getting angry.* **-2.** [exercises, sunbathing, gardening] to do too much of <an activity>, especially so that one suffers pain afterward. ■ **to overdo it** to do too much or work too hard so that one becomes tired □ *The doctor told her not to overdo it after the operation.* □ *I've been overdoing things recently.* **-3.** [meat, vegetables] to cook <food> for too long; [salt, garlic] to add too much of <sthg> to food.

overdone [ˌoʊvərˈdʌn] ◇ *past participle of* **overdo.** ◇ *adj* [meat, cake] that has been cooked for too long.

overdose [ˈoʊvərdoʊs] ◇ *n* a dangerous amount of drugs that somebody has swallowed or injected □ *Craig died of a drug overdose.* □ *She took an overdose of sleeping pills.* ◇ *vi* **to overdose on sthg** [on heroin, aspirin] to take an overdose of sthg.

overdraft [US ˈoʊvrdræft, GB ˈoʊvədrɑːft] *n* the amount of money that a person is allowed to owe a bank where they have an account □ *I've got a $200 overdraft.* □ *an overdraft facility.*

overdrawn [ˌoʊvərˈdrɔːn] *adj* [person] who has taken out more money from their bank account than was in it □ *I'm overdrawn at the bank by $20.* □ *My account is overdrawn.*

overdressed [ˌoʊvərˈdrest] *adj* **to be overdressed** to be wearing clothes that are too formal or elegant for a particular occasion.

overdrive [ˈoʊvərdraɪv] *n* **to go into overdrive** [person, factory] to start working very hard.

overdue [ˌoʊvərˈdjuː] *adj* **-1. to be overdue for sthg** to have needed sthg for a long time □ *I'm overdue for a dental check-up.* **-2. (long) overdue** [reform, change, promotion] that has been needed or awaited for a long time □ *She finally received a welcome, and long overdue,* apology. □ *This kind of reform is long overdue.* **-3.** [bill, rent, account] that has not been paid yet, although it should have been □ *This month's rent is overdue.* **-4.** [baby] that is born later than expected □ *Liz's baby is two weeks overdue.*

overeager [,oʊvər'iːgər] *adj* too eager □ *Paul didn't seem overeager to join in.*

over easy *adj* **eggs over easy** US eggs lightly fried on both sides.

overeat [,oʊvər'iːt] (*pt* **overate**, *pp* **overeaten** [-'iːtn]) *vi* to eat too much.

overemphasize, -ise [,oʊvər'emfəsaɪz] *vt* [importance, need] to make <sthg> seem more important than it really is □ *I cannot overemphasize the dangers involved.*

overenthusiastic [,oʊvərɪnθⁱuːzɪ'æstɪk] *adj* too enthusiastic □ *They were scarcely overenthusiastic about the prospect.*

overestimate [,oʊvər'estɪmeɪt] *vt* **-1.** [spending, quantity] to think that <sthg> is or will be bigger than it really is □ *We had overestimated the cost, which came as a pleasant surprise.* **-2.** [person, importance, capabilities] to think that <sb/sthg> is better than they really are □ *You can never overestimate the benefit of efficient happy staff.*

overexcited [,oʊvərɪk'saɪtəd] *adj* [person, child] who is too excited.

overexpose [,oʊvərɪk'spoʊz] *vt* to let too much light onto <the film> when taking a photo □ *Half the photos were overexposed.*

overflow [*vb* ,oʊvər'floʊ, *n* 'oʊvərfloʊ] ◇ *vi* **-1.** [river, bath, sink] to be so full that the liquid inside flows over the edge; [liquid] to flow over the edge of a container □ *She left the bath running and it overflowed.* □ *The vase is too full — the water's going to overflow when you put the flowers in.* **-2.** [people, crowd] to spread from a place that is too small to contain everybody □ *The party overflowed into the garden.* **-3. to be overflowing** to be very full of people, things, or emotions □ *The corridors were overflowing with children.* ■ **full to overflowing** [room, place] that is so full that there is not enough room for everybody □ *The conference hall was full to overflowing with eager delegates.*

◇ *vt: The river overflowed its banks.*

◇ *n* **-1.** a pipe or hole which liquid can flow out of when the container gets too full. **-2.** the liquid that overflows from a pipe, sink etc. **-3.** the people who cannot fit into a place because there is no room left for them.

overgrown [,oʊvər'groʊn] *adj* [garden, path] that is covered with untidy plants because it has not been taken care of □ *The ruin was overgrown with weeds.*

overhang [*n* 'oʊvərhæŋ, *vb* ,oʊvər'hæŋ] (*pt* & *pp* **overhung**) ◇ *n* the part of something such as a rock or roof that sticks out over something else. ◇ *vt* [beach, water, path] to stick out over sthg □ *There was a large tree overhanging the road.* ◇ *vi* [cliff, balcony, roof] *We sheltered under an overhanging rock.*

overhaul [*vb* ,oʊvər'hɔːl, *n* 'oʊvərhɔːl] ◇ *vt* [machine, car, system] to check <sthg> carefully and make any necessary changes or repairs □ *We are completely overhauling the bus fleet following several complaints from passengers.* □ *Our filing system needs to be completely overhauled.* ◇ *n* [of a machine, engine, system] the act of overhauling something □ *The car needs a complete overhaul.* □ *The photocopier is getting its annual overhaul today.*

overhead [*adj* & *n* 'oʊvərhed, *adv* ,oʊvər'hed] ◇ *adj* [light, cable] that is above one's head. ◇ *adv* [fly, circle] *She heard voices overhead.* ◇ *n* US the daily costs involved in carrying out a business, e.g. rent, heating, and wages □ *Volunteers help keep the overhead to a minimum.*

♦ **overheads** *npl* GB = **overhead**.

overhead projector *n* a device like a box on which transparent plastic sheets are placed so that the light underneath and the lens above make the words, pictures etc on the sheets appear larger on a wall or screen.

overhear [,oʊvər'hɪər] (*pt* & *pp* **overheard** [-'hɜːrd]) *vt* [person, conversation, remark] to accidentally hear <sb/sthg> without the speaker being aware of it □ *I overheard her saying* OR **overheard** *her say that big changes would be inevitable.*

overheat [,oʊvər'hiːt] ◇ *vt* [room, machine] to make <sthg> too hot. ◇ *vi* [engine, car, machine] to become too hot.

overhung [,oʊvər'hʌŋ] *past tense & past participle of* **overhang**.

overindulge [,oʊvərɪn'dʌldʒ] ◇ *vt* to allow <sb> to do what they want too often □ *We try to be generous with the children without overindulging them.* ◇ *vi* to have too much food or drink □ *People tend to overindulge at Christmas.*

overjoyed [,oʊvər'dʒɔɪd] *adj* **to be overjoyed** to be very happy □ *They were overjoyed at the news.*

overkill ['oʊvərkɪl] *n* activity or behavior that is more extreme than is needed to achieve the desired result □ *media overkill.*

overladen [,oʊvər'leɪdn] ◇ *past participle of* **overload**. ◇ *adj* [donkey, truck] that is carrying too much.

overlaid [,oʊvər'leɪd] *past tense & past participle of* **overlay**.

overland ['oʊvərlænd] ◇ *adj* [route, trip, trek] that goes across land and does not involve traveling by sea or air. ◇ *adv*: *From there, we'll travel overland to Beijing.*

overlap [*n* 'oʊvərlæp, *vb* ,oʊvər'læp] (*pt* & *pp* **overlapped**, *cont* **overlapping**) ◇ *vt* to go over the edge of <sthg> so that it partly covers it □ *Arrange the apple slices so that they overlap each other.*

◇ *vi* **-1.** [surfaces, coverings] to cover part of the same area □ *The edges overlap.* **-2.** [ideas, systems] to share particular things □ *My responsibilities overlapped with hers.* **-3.** [events] to happen at the same time in part. □ *Our visits overlapped.*

◇ *n* **-1.** the amount by which something

overlaps the surface of something else □ *Leave a small overlap to cover up the seam.* -2. a situation in which people, ideas, activities etc overlap □ *There's an overlap between what the publishing director and the editorial director do.*

overlay [,ouvər'leɪ] (*pt* & *pp* **overlaid**) *vt* **to be overlaid with sthg** to be covered with a layer of sthg □ *metal overlaid with gold.*

overleaf [,ouvər'liːf] *adv* on the next page □ *See illustration overleaf.*

overload [,ouvər'loud] (*pp* **overloaded** OR **overladen**) *vt* -1. [container, car, washing machine] to put too many people or things in <sthg> □ *Be careful not to overload the elevator.* -2. ELECTRICITY [circuit, system] to make too much electricity pass through <sthg> □ *Last time they played a concert here they overloaded the entire system.* -3. [person] to give <sb> more to do than they can deal with □ *Our department is overloaded with work right now.*

overlong [,ouvər'lɒŋ] ◇ *adj* [book, movie, lecture] too long □ *It was an interesting talk, but slightly overlong.* ◇ *adv* [stay, wait] for too long.

overlook [,ouvər'luk] *vt* -1. [sea, town, garden] to be in a place where there is a view of <sthg lower down> □ *The hotel overlooks the harbor.* -2. [fact, problem, cost] not to notice <sthg>, or not to realize how important it is □ *You seem to have overlooked one small detail.* -3. [fault, behavior] not to punish or criticize somebody for <sthg> □ *I'm prepared to overlook your mistake this time.*

overlord ['ouvərlɔːrd] *n* a person who has the most power in a particular place.

overly ['ouvərli] *adv* **overly critical/negative etc** too critical/negative etc □ *I'm not overly impressed with their safety record.*

overmanning [,ouvər'mænɪŋ] *n* a situation in a factory, company etc in which more people are employed than is necessary.

overnight [,ouvər'naɪt] ◇ *adj* -1. [trip, flight] that takes place during the night □ *Why don't you take the overnight bus?* □ *The trip includes an overnight stay in a luxury hotel.* -2. **an overnight case/overnight clothes etc** a case/clothes etc that one takes when one stays somewhere overnight. -3. **overnight success/fame** success/fame that happens very quickly, without anybody expecting it □ *You can hardly be expecting overnight success.* ◇ *adv* -1. [stay, travel, fly] *There was a storm overnight.* □ *I leave the car in the garage overnight.* -2. [happen, succeed] quickly and unexpectedly *This is not the kind of problem you can solve overnight.* □ *Did you expect to become famous overnight?*

overpaid [,ouvər'peɪd] ◇ *past tense & past participle of* **overpay**. ◇ *adj* [worker, staff, executive] whose salary is higher than they deserve □ *a grossly overpaid job.*

overpass [US 'ouvrpæs, GB 'ouvəpɑːs] *n* a bridge carrying one road over the top of another road.

overpay [,ouvər'peɪ] (*pt* & *pp* **overpaid**) *vt* [employee, staff, official] to pay too much money to <sb> □ *Some directors are grossly overpaid.*

overplay [,ouvər'pleɪ] *vt* [importance, significance, status] to make <sthg> seem more important than it really is □ *It would be easy to overplay the importance of his move.* ■ **to overplay one's hand** to do something that suggests one is in a stronger position than one really is.

overpopulated [,ouvər'pɒpjəleɪtəd] *adj* [area, city] that has too many people living in it.

overpower [,ouvər'pauər] *vt* -1. to defeat <sb> by being stronger than them □ *The man was finally overpowered by security guards.* -2. to suddenly affect <sb> very strongly □ *She was overpowered by grief/by the smoke.*

overpowering [,ouvər'pauərɪŋ] *adj* -1. [desire, feeling] that suddenly affects one very strongly □ *I suddenly felt an overpowering urge to hit him.* -2. [smell, heat, sensation] extremely strong □ *The heat in the sauna was overpowering.* -3. [person] who makes one feel uncomfortable because they have a very strong personality □ *Candy has a rather overpowering personality and tends to intimidate some people.*

overpriced [,ouvər'praɪst] *adj* [goods, article] having a price that is unreasonably high.

overproduction [,ouvərprə'dʌkʃn] *n* the act of producing more goods, products etc than is necessary.

overprotective [,ouvərprə'tektɪv] *adj* who tries too much to protect somebody, especially one's child, from danger, with the result that they never learn how to look after themselves.

overran [,ouvər'ræn] *past tense of* **overrun**.

overrated [,ouvər'reɪtəd] *adj* [movie, car, actor] that is not as good as most people say it is □ *In my opinion, Tarantino is much overrated as a film director.*

overreach [,ouvər'riːtʃ] *vt* **to overreach oneself** to try to do something that one is not able to do □ *Lizzie thinks she's really smart, but one of these days she's going to overreach herself.*

overreact [,ouvərri'ækt] *vi* to feel more angry, worried, sad etc about something than is necessary or reasonable □ *I think they overreacted to the threat.*

override [,ouvər'raɪd] (*pt* **overrode**, *pp* **overridden** [-'rɪdn]) *vt* -1. to be more important than <other things> □ *The need to reduce the deficit overrides everything else.* -2. to use one's authority to ignore <a decision or order made by somebody else> □ *What right do you have to override an instruction from the manager?*

overriding [,ouvər'raɪdɪŋ] *adj* **an overriding concern/aim etc** a concern/an aim etc that is more important than any others □ *Safety is of overriding importance to us.* □ *The overriding need at the moment is for food supplies.*

overripe [,ouvər'raɪp] *adj* [fruit] too ripe.

overrode [,ouvər'roud] *past tense of* **override**.

overrule [,ouvər'ruːl] *vt* to use one's authority to cancel <a decision or order that one thinks is wrong> □ *My objection was overruled by the judge.*

overrun [,ouvər'rʌn] (*pt* **overran**, *pp* **overrun**, *cont* **overrunning**) ◇ *vt* -1. MILITARY [the enemy] to defeat <an army> completely; [territory, country] to conquer and occupy <a place>. **-2. to be overrun with sthg** [with weeds, rats] to be full of sthg □ *The town was overrun with tourists/visitors.* ◇ *vi* [meeting, speech, TV program] to last longer than planned □ *The briefing session overran by half an hour.*

oversaw [,ouvə^r'sɔː] *past tense of* **oversee**.

overseas [,ouvə^r'siːz] ◇ *adj* **overseas sales/an overseas trip etc** sales/a trip etc to foreign countries □ *Overseas travel will not be paid for by the company.* □ *the buget for overseas aid.* ■ **an overseas student** a student from a foreign country □ *We ask our overseas visitors to register before taking part.* ◇ *adv* [go, travel] to a foreign country or foreign countries; [live, study, sell] in a foreign country or foreign countries □ *The company sells most of its products overseas.* □ *Most of our orders come from overseas.*

oversee [,ouvə^r'siː] (*pt* **oversaw**, *pp* **overseen** [-'siːn]) *vt* [workers, job] to be in charge of <sb/sthg> and make sure that work is done properly □ *Katherine Spice has been brought in to oversee the new project.*

overseer ['ouvə^rsiə^r] *n* a person whose job is to make sure that work is done well.

overshadow [,ouvə^r'ʃædou] *vt* **-1.** [building, area] to be much taller than <sthg that is nearby> □ *It was a nice house, but completely overshadowed by the surrounding buildings.* **-2.** [rival, competitor] to seem more important or impressive than <sb> □ *He's rather quiet, and tends to be overshadowed by his noisier brother.* **-3.** [event, period, success] to make <sthg> less enjoyable, important etc □ *Her homecoming was overshadowed by the news of her brother's death.*

overshoot [,ouvə^r'ʃuːt] (*pt* & *pp* **overshot** [-'ʃɒt]) *vt* [turning, runway, target] to miss <sthg> by going too far beyond it □ *We overshot the turning to their house.*

oversight ['ouvə^rsaɪt] *n* a mistake caused when somebody does not do or notice something □ *By* OR *Through an oversight, his name was omitted.* □ *I'm sorry, it was an oversight on my part.*

oversimplification [,ouvə^rsɪmplɪfɪ'keɪʃn] *n*: see **oversimplify** □ *Your statement is a gross oversimplification of what actually happened.*

oversimplify [,ouvə^r'sɪmplɪfaɪ] (*pt* & *pp* **oversimplified**) ◇ *vt* [situation, issue, position] to talk about <sthg> in a way that makes it seem more simple than it really is □ *The program oversimplifies the problems faced by these people.* ◇ *vi*: *Don't you think you're oversimplifying a little?*

oversleep [,ouvə^r'sliːp] (*pt* & *pp* **overslept** [-'slept]) *vi* to sleep for too long and not wake up at the time one intended to □ *Sorry I'm late, I overslept.*

overspend [,ouvə^r'spend] (*pt* & *pp* **overspent** [-'spent]) *vi* [person, company] to spend too much money.

overspill ['ouvə^rspɪl] *n* the people who move away from a city that is too crowded □ *the overspill from inner-city areas.*

overstaffed [US ,ouvr'stæft, GB ,ouvə'stɑːft] *adj*

[company, department, school] that has too many people working in it.

overstate [,ouvə^r'steɪt] *vt* [importance, significance] to exaggerate <sthg> □ *The significance of this meeting cannot be overstated.*

overstay [,ouvə^r'steɪ] *vt* **to overstay one's welcome** to outstay one's welcome.

overstep [,ouvə^r'step] (*pt* & *pp* **overstepped**, *cont* **overstepping**) *vt* [limit, authority] to go beyond <sthg> □ *Carstairs has overstepped the limit of his authority in this case.* ■ **to overstep the mark** to behave in a way that goes beyond acceptable limits □ *I had clearly, by the look on his face, overstepped the mark.*

overstock [,ouvə^r'stɒk] *vt* [refrigerator, warehouse] to keep <sthg> filled with more of something than is necessary.

overstrike ['ouvə^rstraɪk] (*pt* & *pp* **overstruck** [-strʌk]) COMPUTING ◇ *n* an act of keying something on top of or in place of something else. ◇ *vt* [character, word] to key <sthg> in on top of or in place of something else.

oversubscribed [,ouvə^rsəb'skraɪbd] *adj* [share offer, course] that too many people have asked to take part in, so that not everybody can get what they want □ *Night school classes are heavily oversubscribed this year.*

overt [ou'vɜː^rt] *adj* [hostility, intention, attempt] that is open and public and not hidden □ *an overt challenge to the government's authority* □ *It was an overt criticism of my way of life.*

overtake [,ouvə^r'teɪk] (*pt* **overtook**, *pp* **overtaken** [-'teɪkn]) ◇ *vt* **-1.** [disaster, misfortune, change] to happen to <a person or group of people> when they are not expecting it or able to deal with it □ *We did our best to meet the deadline, but we were overtaken by events.* **-2.** GB [car, driver, runner] to catch up with and pass <a person, vehicle, or animal>. ◇ *vi* GB [car, driver] *It's dangerous to overtake on bends.*

overtaking [,ouvə^r'teɪkɪŋ] *n* GB the act of passing other vehicles □ *'No overtaking.'*

over-the-counter *adj* **-1.** BUSINESS [sales, market] connected with the shares of companies not listed on a stock exchange. **-2. over-the-counter medicine/drugs etc** medicine/drugs etc that can be bought at a pharmacy without a prescription from a doctor.

overthrow [*vb* ,ouvə^r'θrou, *n* 'ouvə^rθrou] (*pt* **overthrew** [-'θruː], *pp* **overthrown** [-'θroun]) ◇ *vt* **-1.** [government, regime, ruler] to remove <sb/sthg> from power, usually by force □ *The elected government has been overthrown by military rebels.* **-2.** [idea, standards, decision] to reject <sthg> and replace it with something else □ *The decision was overthrown in court.* ◇ *n* [of a government, regime, ruler] the act of overthrowing somebody or something.

overtime ['ouvə^rtaɪm] ◇ *n* **-1.** INDUSTRY extra time spent working; money earned by working extra time □ *If you do overtime, you can earn even more money.* □ *How much do you earn, including overtime?* □ *an overtime ban.* **-2.** US SPORT a period of playing time added to a game when the scores are equal at the end of normal playing time. ◇ *adv* **to work**

overtime to spend extra time at work, usually for more money.

overtly [ou'vɜːʳtlɪ] *adv* [hostile, jealous] *see* **overt**.

overtones ['ouvəʳtounz] *npl* signs of a particular feeling or idea that can be noticed but are not stated openly □ *The speech had definite political overtones.* □ *Do I detect overtones of jealousy?*

overtook [,ouvəʳ'tuk] *past tense of* **overtake**.

overture ['ouvəʳtʃuəʳ] *n* MUSIC a piece of music that is an introduction to a longer piece of music or to a theatrical performance.

◆ **overtures** *npl* **to make overtures to sb** to speak to sb because one wants to start a friendship, partnership etc with them □ *They've been making overtures to a big Japanese company in the hope of setting up a joint deal.*

overturn [,ouvəʳ'tɜːʳn] ◇ *vt* **-1.** [table, lamp] to knock <sthg> over □ *He accidentally overturned his chair as he got up.* **-2.** LAW to use one's authority to cancel <a decision> □ *The decision was overturned in court.* **-3.** to remove <a government, regime> etc from power, usually by force □ *an attempt to overturn the military regime.* ◇ *vi* [boat, car] to turn upside down.

overuse [,ouvəʳ'juːz] *vt* [word, expression] to use <sthg> too often, with the result that it loses its value or meaning.

overview ['ouvəʳvjuː] *n* a general understanding or description of a situation, subject etc □ *The introduction gives a general overview of the situation.*

overweening [,ouvəʳ'wiːnɪŋ] *adj* [pride, arrogance] that is too strong (formal and disapproving use).

overweight [,ouvəʳ'weɪt] *adj* **-1.** [person] whose weight is more than it should be for somebody of their build and height □ *He's overweight and ought to go on a diet.* **-2.** [package, suitcase] that is heavier than a particular limit allows □ *I had to pay extra because my luggage was slightly overweight.*

overwhelm [,ouvəʳ'welm] *vt* **-1.** to take complete control of <sb> □ *I was overwhelmed by embarrassment/despair.* **-2.** MILITARY [opposition, enemy, defenses] to gain complete control over <sb/sthg> by being much stronger.

overwhelming [,ouvəʳ'welmɪŋ] *adj* **-1.** [feeling, desire, need] that is so strong that one cannot think clearly □ *I suddenly felt an overwhelming desire to kiss him.* **-2.** [generosity, kindness] that makes one feel very surprised and grateful □ *thanks to the overwhelming generosity of our benefactor, Lionel Burtt.* **-3.** [defeat, majority] that is so big that the result is extremely clear □ *The bill was defeated by an overwhelming majority in the Senate.*

overwhelmingly [,ouvəʳ'welmɪŋlɪ] *adv* [defeat, reject] by a very large majority □ *The workers voted overwhelmingly to continue the strike.*

overwork [,ouvəʳ'wɜːʳk] ◇ *vt* [employee, servant, staff] to give <sb> too much work to do □ *We're overworked and underpaid.* ◇ *vi* [person] to work too hard □ *Paul has been overworking*

recently. ◇ *n* too much work □ *Much of her stress is caused by overwork.*

overwrought [,ouvəʳ'rɔːt] *adj* [person] who is very upset and cannot control their feelings.

ovulate ['ɒvjəleɪt] *vi* [woman, female animal] to produce an egg from the ovary.

ovulation [,ɒvjə'leɪʃn] *n*: *see* **ovulate**.

ow [au] *excl* a sound used to show that one suddenly feels pain □ *Ow! That hurt!*

owe [ou] *vt* **-1. to owe sthg to sb, to owe sb sthg** [amount, money] to have to pay sthg to sb □ *You still owe me $50 from last month.* □ *How much do I owe you?* □ *She owes lots of money to her parents.* **-2. to owe sthg to sb, to owe sb sthg** [success, career] to have sthg because of help given by sb □ *I don't owe you anything!* □ *She owes Dr Jacobson her life.* **-3. to owe sthg to sb, to owe sb sthg** [thanks, respect, loyalty] to be expected to give sthg to sb □ *You owe me an explanation!* □ *You owe it to yourself to go out and prove you can do it.*

Owens ['ouənz], **Jesse** (1913–1980) an African-American athlete who won four gold medals at the 1936 Berlin Olympics.

owing ['ouɪŋ] *adj* **to be owing** [amount, money] that has still to be paid □ *The balance owing is $8,000.* □ *How much is still owing?*

◆ **owing to** *prep* [circumstances, mistake, cancelation] as a result of <sthg> □ *Owing to an earlier accident, there will be long delays on Highway 6.*

owl [aul] *n* a bird that hunts small animals mainly at night and has a flat face, a hooked beak, and large eyes.

own [oun] ◇ *det* **my/your/its etc own...** the... that belongs to me/you/it etc; the... that is typical of me/you/it etc □ *I won't be insulted like this in my own home.* □ *I brought my own golf clubs with me.* □ *Describe what happened in your own words.* □ *Sue has her own way of working.* ◇ *pron* **my/your/its etc own** the one or ones that belong to me/you/it etc □ *We rented a tent, but Paul brought his own.* ■ **a home/car of one's own** a home/car that belongs to one □ *He's always longed for a car of his own.* ■ **to be/live on one's own** to be/live alone □ *I was on my own all evening.* ■ **to do/manage sthg on one's own** to do/manage sthg without any help □ *You'll never lift that box on your own.* □ *She's had to bring those children up on her own.* ■ **to get one's own back** to punish somebody because they have said or done something annoying or offensive, though not very serious (informal use) □ *I'll get my own back on him for making me look silly!* ◇ *vt* [car, house, company] to have <sthg> as one's property □ *They own some valuable paintings.* □ *All this land is owned by the college.*

◆ **own up** *vi* to admit that one has done something wrong □ *No one would own up to leaking the document.*

own brand *n* GB a product specially manufactured for a particular store and carrying its name □ *own-brand products.*

owner ['ounəʳ] *n* the person that an animal, property etc belongs to □ *The owner of the bi-*

cycle could not be found. □ *The owners are away this weekend.*

owner-occupier *n* a person who lives in a house that they own rather than rent.

ownership ['oonərʃɪp] *n* the fact of being the owner of something □ *The ownership of the land is still in dispute.* □ *private/public ownership.*

own goal *n* SPORT a goal scored accidentally by a player against their own team.

ox [ɒks] (*pl* **oxen**) *n* a bull that has had its sexual parts removed, and that is used to provide meat and, in some countries, to work on a farm.

Oxbridge ['ɒksbrɪdʒ] *n* the universities of Oxford and Cambridge considered together □ *an Oxbridge candidate/graduate.*

💱 OXBRIDGE

The two universities of Oxford and Cambridge, both dating from the 13th century, are the oldest and most respected in Britain. Both are divided into "colleges", some of which are in beautiful buildings, and have very old traditions. An Oxbridge education is supposed to give students advantages in later life, and many graduates find important jobs in the government, media etc. There is a great rivalry between the two universities, especially in sports.

oxen ['ɒksn] *plural of* **ox**.

Oxfam ['ɒksfæm] *n* a British charity that aims to fight famine and poverty throughout the world □ *an Oxfam shop.*

Oxford ['ɒksfəd] a town in southern England that is famous for its university. POPULATION: 109,000.

Oxfordshire ['ɒksfədʃər] a county in central southern England. SIZE: 2,608 sq kms. POPULATION: 578,000. ADMINISTRATIVE CENTER: Oxford.

Oxford Street a street in central London that is well known for its stores.

oxide ['ɒksaɪd] *n* a chemical compound of oxygen and another element □ *magnesium oxide.*

oxidize, -ise ['ɒksədaɪz] *vi* [element, substance] to combine chemically with oxygen; [metal] to rust.

Oxon *abbr of* **Oxfordshire**.

Oxon. (*abbr of* **Oxoniensis**) from Oxford University (used after university degrees).

oxtail soup [ˌɒkstcɪl-] *n* a type of thick brown soup made by stewing the tail of an ox.

ox tongue *n* the tongue of an ox used as food, usually boiled and eaten cold in slices.

oxyacetylene [ˌɒksɪə'setliːn] *n* a mixture of oxygen and acetylene that burns with a very hot flame and is used for cutting and welding metal □ *an oxyacetylene torch/burner.*

oxygen ['ɒksɪdʒən] *n* a colorless gas that forms a large part of the air and is necessary for plants and animals to live. SYMBOL: O.

oxygenate ['ɒksɪdʒəneɪt] *vt* [blood, water] to mix oxygen into <sthg>.

oxygen mask *n* a device that fits over the nose and mouth and helps one to breathe by supplying oxygen from a cylinder which it is attached to by a tube.

oxygen tent *n* a transparent covering like a tent that is placed over a very ill person in a hospital and filled with oxygen to help them breathe.

oyster ['ɔɪstər] *n* a flat shellfish that has a shell in two parts and is usually eaten raw. Oysters can produce pearls.

oz. *abbr of* **ounce**.

Oz [ɒz] GB & AUS Australia (informal use).

ozone ['əʊzəʊn] *n* a colorless gas that is a kind of oxygen. FORMULA: O_3.

ozone-friendly *adj* [gas, product, process] that does not damage the ozone layer.

ozone layer *n* **the ozone layer** layer of ozone high above the sky that protects the Earth from ultraviolet radiation from the Sun.

p¹ [piː] (*pl* **p's** OR **ps**), **P** [piː] (*pl* **P's** OR **Ps**) *n* the sixteenth letter of the English alphabet.

p² ◇ *abbr of* **page**. ◇ *n abbr of* **penny, pence**.

P45 [ˌpiːfɔː'tɪ'faɪv] *n* in Britain, a document given to a person by their employer when they leave a job. It shows how much tax and National Insurance they have paid.

P60 [ˌpiː'sɪkstɪ] *n* in Britain, a document given to a person by their employer once a year, showing their earnings, tax, and National Insurance payments for that year.

pa [pɑː] *n* US a word used to talk to or about one's father (informal use).

p.a. *abbr of* **per annum**.

PA ◇ *n* **-1.** *abbr of* **public-address system**. **-2.** GB *abbr of* **personal assistant**. ◇ *abbr of* **Pennsylvania**.

PABX ['pæbeks] (*abbr of* **private automatic branch exchange**) *n* a small telephone exchange, usually in a company, for internal communications and outside calls.

PAC [pæk] (*abbr of* **political action committee**) *n* an organization, usually set up by business or labor unions in the USA, to raise funds to support a political campaign.

pace [peɪs] ◇ *n* **-1.** [of a runner, vehicle] the speed at which somebody or something moves; [of development, change] the speed at which something happens □ *Christie had set a very fast pace.* □ *They walked at a slow pace.* □ *He drives at a snail's pace.* □ *I can hardly keep up with the pace of change in my own business.* ■ **at one's own pace** [walk, work] at a speed or rate that one finds comfortable □ *It's better to go at your own pace.* □ *Find your own pace and keep to it.* ■ **to keep pace** [with changes, developments] to change, develop etc at the same rate as something else □ *It is difficult to keep pace with pay increases in the private sector.* ■ **to keep pace with sb** to move at the same speed as sb □ *She walked so fast I could hardly keep pace with her.* **-2.** a step used as a measure of distance □ *Move back three paces.*

◇ *vt* [room, corridor] to walk up and down in <a place>, usually quickly □ *Brian paced the corridor nervously.*

◇ *vi*: *He was pacing up and down anxiously.*

pacemaker ['peɪsmeɪkər] *n* **-1.** MEDICINE an electronic device that is put into a person's body to help the heart beat normally. **-2.** GB SPORT = **pacesetter**.

pacesetter ['peɪssetər] *n* US a runner who takes the lead in a race and forces the other runners to go at a particular speed.

Pacific [pə'sɪfɪk] ◇ **the Pacific (Ocean)** the world's largest ocean, between America, Asia, and Australia. ◇ *adj* [island, coast] that is connected with the Pacific Ocean.

pacification [,pæsɪfɪ'keɪʃn] *n*: see **pacify**.

Pacific Northwest: **the Pacific Northwest** a region of the northwestern USA that includes Washington State, Oregon, and northern California.

Pacific Rim *n* **the Pacific Rim** the countries bordering on the Pacific Ocean, including the islands in the Pacific Ocean.

❦ PACIFIC RIM
The term Pacific Rim usually refers to the most economically important countries that border the western side of the Pacific Ocean, e.g. China, Korea, Thailand, Taiwan, Australia, and Japan. However, the term sometimes includes countries on the eastern side of the Pacific such as Canada and the USA.

pacifier ['pæsɪfaɪər] *n* US a specially shaped piece of rubber that is given to a baby to suck.

pacifism ['pæsəfɪzm] *n* the belief that war and violence are always wrong and must be avoided.

pacifist ['pæsəfəst] *n* a person who believes in pacifism.

pacify ['pæsəfaɪ] (*pt* & *pp* **pacified**) *vt* **-1.** [person, crowd] to make <sb> calm □ *a woman trying frantically to pacify her crying child.* **-2.** [area, country] to bring peace to <a place>, usually by using violence □ *Attempts to pacify the region have failed.*

pack [pæk] ◇ *n* **-1.** [for a traveler] a large bag for belongings or goods carried on one's back □ *They were carrying heavy packs.* **-2.** [of cigarettes, cookies] a container made of paper or card in which goods are sold □ *I bought a pack of gum.* **-3.** [of playing cards] a complete set of playing cards □ *He took the jokers out of the pack.* **-4.** [of wolves, dogs] a group of ani-

mals that live and hunt together; [of children, thieves] a group of people who spend a lot of time together and who other people can find threatening □ *Dogs hunt in packs.* □ *There's a pack of school kids who are always causing trouble.* **-5.** SPORT the forwards in a rugby team. **-6.** *phrase* **that's a pack of lies!** that's completely untrue.

◇ *vt* **-1.** [bag, suitcase] to fill <sthg> with one's clothes, belongings etc, usually in order to take them with one on a trip; [clothes, toothbrush] to put <sthg> into a bag, suitcase etc for this reason □ *I packed all of my belongings into a suitcase and prepared to leave.* □ *Don't forget to pack a waterpoof jacket!* **-2.** [goods, product] to put <sthg> into a container, box etc, so that it can be sent to stores, customers etc and sold □ *The job consists of packing fruit into crates.* **-3.** [hall, theater, stadium] to fill <a place> with the result that no more people can go in □ *They packed Carnegie Hall for their farewell concert.* ■ **to be packed into sthg** to be crowded uncomfortably inside sthg □ *There were seven people packed into one very small car.*

◇ *vi* **-1.** to put one's belongings into a suitcase, trunk etc before going on a trip □ *Call a taxi, it'll only take me a minute to pack.* **-2.** to crowd into a building and fill it □ *They all packed in to the back of the car.*

◆ **pack in** (informal use) GB ◇ *vt sep* **to pack sthg in** [job, course, hobby] to stop doing sthg □ *He's packed in his job and he's off to the States.* ■ **pack it in!** stop doing that!; keep quiet!

◆ **pack off** *vt sep* **to pack sb off** to send sb away □ *We packed the children off to their grandparents.*

◆ **pack up** ◇ *vt sep* **to pack sthg up** [belongings, clothes, furniture] to put sthg into a container for a trip □ *I packed everything up into boxes ready for the move.* ◇ *vi* **-1.** [traveler] to pack for a trip □ *She's just packing up and won't be long.* **-2.** [worker] to finish work (informal use) □ *What time do you pack up?*

package ['pækɪdʒ] ◇ *n* **-1.** [of books, presents] an object or several objects wrapped up in paper, card etc □ *I received a package in the mail.* **-2.** US [of cigarettes, laundry detergent] a wrapper or container made of paper, card, or plastic in which goods are sold. **-3.** [of measures, proposals, reforms] a group of things that are presented together □ *We have to accept or reject the whole package.* □ *The company offers an attractive benefits package.* **-4.** COMPUTING a group of related computer programs. ◇ *vt* [product, goods] to put <sthg> into wrapping, a container etc to be sold.

package deal *n* an offer of a set of goods or services that can only be bought or accepted together.

package holiday *n* GB = **package tour**.

packager ['pækɪdʒər] *n* **-1.** [in a factory] a person or machine that packages goods. **-2.** BUSINESS a company that creates and sells things such as books or TV programs as finished products to larger companies.

package tour *n* a vacation in which a travel company plans one's travel and accommodations, and sometimes one's meals, as part of a group of tourists.

packaging ['pækɪdʒɪŋ] *n* the wrapping, containers etc in which goods are packaged; the process of packaging goods □ *The goods were wrapped in brightly colored packaging.* □ *The packaging and delivery of goods.*

packed [pækt] *adj* -1. [bar, theater, bus] full of people □ *The streets were packed with people.* □ *The bar was absolutely packed last night.* -2. **packed with sthg** [with news, ideas] full of sthg □ *a magazine packed with useful tips.*

packed lunch *n* GB a lunch that is wrapped up or put in a box to be eaten when one is away from home or outdoors.

packet ['pækət] *n* -1. a box, bag, wrapper etc in which goods are sold; the amount of a product that is contained in this □ *a packet of gum* □ *an empty chip packet* □ *He ate a whole packet of cookies.* -2. a small package □ *You should receive a small packet in the mail.*

packhorse ['pækhɔːrs] *n* a horse used to carry goods on its back.

pack ice *n* a large area of floating ice formed from many smaller pieces that are pressed together.

packing ['pækɪŋ] *n* -1. paper, card, plastic etc that is put around objects inside containers such as boxes to protect them while they are being sent somewhere □ *Don't throw away the packing, I might use it again.* -2. the act of putting one's belongings into a suitcase before going on a trip □ *I've finished my packing.*

packing case *n* a large wooden box used to transport goods.

pack trip *n* US a trip through the countryside on horses.

pact [pækt] *n* a formal agreement between two people or countries □ *They made a pact never to tell anyone what had happened.* □ *the Molotov-Ribbentrop Pact.*

pad [pæd] (*pt* & *pp* **padded**, *cont* **padding**) ◇ *n* -1. [of cotton wool, rubber] a thick, usually flat, piece of material used e.g. to protect a part of the body or absorb liquid □ *a jacket with shoulder pads* □ *a shin pad.* -2. [of paper] a pile of sheets of paper that are attached to each other so that each sheet can be removed when it has been written on □ *a writing pad.* -3. [of a person] the place where somebody lives (informal use) □ *Have you been invited up to his pad yet?* -4. [of an animal] one of the soft parts on the bottom of an animal's paw. ◇ *vt* -1. [knee, wound, sharp edge] to cover and protect <sthg> with soft material; [jacket, bra] to add extra material to <a piece of clothing>, e.g. to make it more comfortable □ *He padded the cut with cotton wool.* -2. [essay, speech, letter] = **pad out**. ◇ *vi* [person, animal] to walk softly □ *The lioness padded softly toward them.*

◆ **pad out** *vt sep* -1. **to pad a piece of clothing out** to give shape or fullness to a piece of clothing using padding □ *The dress was pad-*ded out at the shoulders. -2. **to pad a speech/piece of writing out** to deliberately make a speech/piece of writing longer by including information that is not necessary □ *He padded the report out with a lot of statistics.*

padded ['pædəd] *adj* [shoulder, bra, seat] that contains extra material to make it bigger and more attractive or more comfortable □ *a jacket with padded shoulders.*

padded cell *n* a cell with walls lined with soft material to prevent violent psychiatric patients from injuring themselves.

padded envelope *n* an envelope whose sides contain material to make them thick and soft, used to protect something that one is mailing.

padding ['pædɪŋ] *n* -1. [in a jacket, seat] soft material that is put inside something to make it more comfortable □ *Some of the padding had begun to come out.* -2. [in an essay, speech, letter] words that do not give more information and are only included in something to make it longer □ *Most of the second page is just padding.*

paddle ['pædl] ◇ *n* -1. a short pole with a wide flat part at each end or at one of the ends, used to move a canoe or boat in water. -2. **to have a paddle** GB to walk or play in shallow water, especially at the seaside □ *The children went for a paddle in the sea.* ◇ *vt* to move <a boat or canoe> using a paddle. ◇ *vi* -1. to move a boat or canoe using a paddle □ *We paddled out to the middle of the lake.* -2. [duck, dog] to move through the water using its feet □ *The ducks paddled furiously against the current.* -3. GB [person, child] to have a paddle □ *We went paddling in the pond.*

paddle boat, paddle steamer *n* a ship driven by one or more large wheels fitted with broad flat blades.

paddling pool ['pædlɪŋ-] *n* GB -1. a shallow pool, especially in a park, for children to paddle in. -2. a small inflatable container that can be filled with water for children to play in.

paddock ['pædək] *n* -1. [for a horse] a small field where horses are kept. -2. [at a racecourse] an area at a racecourse where spectators can see the horses walk around before a race and where the jockeys get on their horses. -3. AUS a field.

paddy field ['pædɪ-] *n* a field filled with water in which rice is grown.

paddy wagon *n* US a police vehicle used for carrying prisoners (informal use).

padlock ['pædlɒk] ◇ *n* a detachable lock with a U-shaped bar at the top that opens when the key is turned. ◇ *vt* [door, gate, box] to lock <sthg> with a padlock □ *The bike was padlocked to the fence.*

paederast ['pedəræst] *n* GB = **pederast**.

paediatric [ˌpiːdɪˈætrɪk] *etc* GB = **pediatric** *etc*.

paedophile ['piːdəfaɪl] *n* GB = **pedophile**.

paella [US pɑːˈelə, GB paɪ-] *n* a Spanish dish consisting of rice, chicken, seafood, and vegetables flavored with saffron.

paeony ['piːənɪ] (*pl* **paeonies**) *n* = **peony**.

pagan ['peɪgən] ◇ *adj* [god, ritual, festival] that is connected with a religion that worships many gods and is older than the major religions of the present day. ◇ *n* a person with pagan beliefs.

paganism ['peɪgənɪzm] *n* pagan beliefs and practices.

page [peɪdʒ] ◇ *n* **-1.** [in a book, document, newspaper] one side of a sheet of paper □ *Turn to page 33.* □ *Which page are you on?* □ *It's 40 pages long.* □ *The sports news is on the back page.* □ *It made front-page news.* **-2.** [in a notepad, binder] a sheet of paper □ *She tore a page out of the book and gave it to me.* □ *Some of the pages are stuck together.* ◇ *vt* to call <sb> by using a messenger, public-address system, or pager □ *I'll have to go, somebody's paging me.*

pageant ['pædʒənt] *n* a show, often on a historical subject and performed outdoors, consisting of scenes and clothing which are impressive and colorful □ *the annual school pageant.*

pageantry ['pædʒəntrɪ] *n* impressive, colorful clothing, scenes etc that one sees at a pageant or royal ceremony.

page boy *n* **-1.** at a wedding, a boy who accompanies the bride. **-2.** a hairstyle in which all the hair is of a medium length and is curled under at the ends.

page break *n* the point in a document at which one page ends and the next begins.

pager ['peɪdʒər] *n* a portable radio device that makes a high-pitched noise to tell one that there is a message for one or that one must contact somebody □ *a radio pager.*

pagination [ˌpædʒə'neɪʃn] *n* the order in which the pages of a book, document etc are numbered.

pagoda [pə'goʊdə] *n* a kind of temple, especially in the Far East, that has more than one story and has roofs that curve up at the edges.

paid [peɪd] ◇ *past tense & past participle of* **pay.** ◇ *adj* [employment, work] for which a person gets wages, a salary etc; [worker] who gets wages, a salary etc □ *Jim has finally got some paid work.* □ *How much paid vacation do you get a year?* □ *We don't have any paid staff. They're all volunteers.* ■ **badly/well paid** [job] for which a small/large wage, salary etc is paid; [person] who gets a small/large wage, salary etc □ *She's just got an extremely well-paid job.* □ *Nurses there were very badly paid.*

paid-up *adj* **a paid-up member** a person who has paid the amount required to be a member of an organization.

pail [peɪl] *n* a bucket.

pain [peɪn] ◇ *n* **-1.** an unpleasant feeling in part of one's body that hurts, usually as a result of illness or injury □ *I felt a sharp pain in my leg.* □ *The pain gets worse at night.* ■ **to be in pain** to be feeling pain □ *Are you in a lot of pain?* **-2.** mental or emotional suffering □ *The news will cause her great pain.* **-3. a pain (in the neck)** a very annoying person, thing, or situation (informal use) □ *It's such a pain in the*

neck having to drive all the way to your place first. ◇ *vt* **it pains me** I find it very difficult or upsetting □ *It pains me to have to remind you of your duty.* □ *It pains me that nobody thought to let me know first.*

◆ **pains** *npl* **to be at pains to do sthg** to be very careful to do sthg correctly □ *He was at pains to point out the risks involved.* ■ **to take pains to do sthg** to make a great effort to do sthg □ *She took great pains to show me how everything worked.* ■ **to get sthg for one's pains** to get sthg which is disappointing as a reward for something one has put a lot of effort into □ *And what did I get for my pains? Nothing!*

Paine [peɪn], **Thomas** (1737–1809) a British writer and revolutionary. He wrote a famous pamphlet called *Common Sense*, and had a strong influence on the American and French Revolutions.

pained [peɪnd] *adj* [expression, tone of voice] that shows one is upset or offended.

painful ['peɪnfl] *adj* **-1.** [back, throat] that hurts because of illness or injury □ *How painful is it?* **-2.** [injury, exercise] that makes one feel physical pain □ *These new shoes are very painful.* **-3.** [thought, memory] that makes one feel sad and upset □ *I find it very painful to talk about that period of my life.*

painfully ['peɪnflɪ] *adv* **-1.** [hit, fall] in a way that causes pain. **-2. painfully shy/slow etc** very shy/slow etc in a way that makes one feel frustrated □ *It was painfully clear that their son had no talent whatsoever.*

painkiller ['peɪnkɪlər] *n* a drug that reduces pain.

painless ['peɪnləs] *adj* **-1.** [operation, exercise] that causes no pain □ *The injection was quite painless.* **-2.** [method, decision] that does not involve too much effort or make one sad or upset □ *The move to our new office was a relatively painless process.*

painlessly ['peɪnləslɪ] *adv: see* **painless.** □ *The lump can be removed painlessly in a simple operation.*

painstaking ['peɪnzteɪkɪŋ] *adj* [worker, job] that takes a long time and pays very careful attention to detail □ *They made a painstaking inventory of the contents of the house.*

painstakingly ['peɪnzteɪkɪŋlɪ] *adv* [work, copy, research] *see* **painstaking.**

paint [peɪnt] ◇ *n* **-1.** ART a colored liquid or paste that one puts onto a piece of paper or canvas, usually using a brush, to make a picture □ *oil paint.* **-2.** a colored liquid that one decorates and protects walls, doors etc with, usually using a brush or roller □ *gloss paint* □ *a coat of paint.*

◇ *vt* **-1.** ART [picture, portrait] to make <sthg> by putting paint onto paper or canvas; [person, landscape] to make a painting that shows <sb/sthg> □ *She's had her portrait painted.* □ *John Constable painted views of the English countryside.* **-2.** [wall, door, house] to decorate or protect <sthg> with paint □ *The ceiling had been painted yellow.* **-3. to paint one's nails** to put nail polish on one's nails.

◇ *vi* to put paint onto a surface □ *I paint as a hobby.* □ *We're painting and papering in the hall.*

paintbox ['peɪntbɒks] *n* a box that contains blocks of solid paint that are mixed with water and used for painting pictures.

paintbrush ['peɪntbrʌʃ] *n* a brush used for painting pictures, walls, doors etc.

painter ['peɪntər] *n* **-1.** ART a person who paints pictures. **-2.** a person whose job is to paint walls, doors etc.

painting ['peɪntɪŋ] *n* **-1.** a picture that has been painted □ *a fine painting by Gainsborough.* **-2.** the act or process of painting pictures □ *He took up painting as a hobby.* **-3.** the act or process of painting walls, doors etc □ *I've been doing some painting and decorating lately to make a little extra cash.*

paint stripper *n* a chemical substance used to remove paint from a wall, door etc.

paintwork ['peɪntwɜːrk] *n* the parts of a building or vehicle that have been painted.

pair [peər] *n* **-1.** [of shoes, gloves] two things of the same kind that are used together □ *a pair of socks/skis/wings* □ *They cost $5 a pair.* **-2.** [of trousers, scissors] an object that consists of two main parts that are similar and joined together □ *a pair of pants/glasses.* **-3.** [of people] two people who are doing something together, or who are in a relationship □ *I often have my students work in pairs.* □ *a devoted pair* □ *We just stood there like a pair of idiots.*

◆ **pair off** ◇ *vt sep* **to pair people off** [teacher, coach] to divide a group of people into pairs; [friend] to encourage two people to start a romantic relationship □ *Each boy was paired off with a girl.* □ *He tried to pair me off with his sister.* ◇ *vi* [team members, couples] *Toward the end of the party people began to pair off.*

paisley ['peɪzlɪ] *n* **paisley (pattern)** a pattern of small curving shapes, usually printed in bright colors □ *a paisley tie/skirt.*

pajama [US pə'dʒæmə, GB -'dʒɑːm-] *comp* US **pajama top/bottoms** the top/bottom part of a pair of pajamas.

pajamas [US pə'dʒæməz, GB -'dʒɑːm-] *npl* US a set of loose soft clothes worn in bed that consists of a pair of trousers and a top.

Pakistan [US 'pækɪstæn, GB ˌpɑːkɪ'stɑːn] a country in southern Asia, on the Arabian Sea, between India and Iran. SIZE: 803,000 sq kms. POPULATION: 122,400,000 (*Pakistanis*). CAPITAL: Islamabad. LANGUAGE: English, Urdu. CURRENCY: Pakistani rupee.

Pakistani [US ˌpækɪ'stæni, GB ˌpɑːkɪ'stɑːni] *n* & *adj*: see **Pakistan**.

pal [pæl] *n* **-1.** a friend (informal use). **-2.** a word used to address somebody one does not know, especially when one is being unfriendly (informal use) □ *Listen, pal, I was here first.*

PAL [pæl] (*abbr of* **phase alternation line**) *n* a system for broadcasting color television picture that is used in many European countries.

palace ['pæləs] *n* a very large and richly deco-

rated house, often the home of a head of state.

palaeontology *n* GB = **paleontology**.

palatable ['pælətəbl] *adj* **-1.** [food, drink] that has a pleasant taste □ *a very palatable wine.* **-2.** [idea, suggestion] that one finds acceptable □ *Do you find Jefferson's proposals palatable?*

palate ['pælət] *n* **-1.** the top part of the inside of one's mouth. **-2.** one's ability to judge the quality of food and drink by tasting it □ *a refined palate.*

palatial [pə'leɪʃl] *adj* [house, hotel] that is very large and expensively decorated.

palaver [pə'lɑːvər] *n* something that is not important but involves a lot of effort and inconvenience (informal use) □ *It was such a palaver filling out all those forms!*

pale [peɪl] ◇ *adj* **-1.** [color, light] that is not strong or bright; [paint, skin] that is of a light color □ *She wore a pale blue dress.* □ *I looked up at the pale sky.* **-2.** [person] whose face has less color than usual because they are ill, shocked, or afraid □ *You're looking very pale.* ◇ *vi* **-1.** [person] to become pale □ *He paled when he saw the corpse.* **-2.** **to pale into insignificance** [problem, worry] to appear less important when compared with something else □ *My troubles pale into insignificance beside hers.*

pale ale *n* GB a light beer sold in bottles.

paleness ['peɪlnəs] *n*: see **pale**.

paleontology US, **palaeontology** GB [ˌpeɪlɪɒn'tɒlədʒɪ] *n* the scientific study of fossils and extinct animals and plants.

Palestine ['pæləstaɪn] an area of the Middle East, covering parts of modern Israel and Jordan, that is important in the history of the Christian, Jewish, and Muslim religions.

Palestinian [ˌpælə'stɪnɪən] *n* & *adj*: see **Palestine**.

palette ['pælət] *n* **-1.** a board, usually with curved edges and a hole for the thumb, used by an artist to mix colors on. **-2.** the different colors used by a particular artist or style of painting □ *Renoir's palette is dominated by pastel colors.*

palette knife *n* a knife with a flexible blade and a rounded tip that is used for mixing paints on a palette, painting with oil paints, or spreading frostings, cake mixtures etc in cooking.

palimony [US 'pæləmoʊnɪ, GB -ɪmənɪ] *n* money that a court orders somebody to pay to a partner they used to live with but are now separated from.

palindrome ['pælɪndroʊm] *n* a word or phrase that is spelled the same when it is read backward or forward, e.g. "level".

palings ['peɪlɪŋz] *npl* a fence made of long thin pieces of wood that are pointed on top.

pall [pɔːl] ◇ *n* **-1.** a low cloud of smoke that hangs over something. **-2.** a cloth put over a coffin at a funeral. ◇ *vi* [humor, interest] to become less attractive or interesting, usually because one has had enough of it □ *Her interest began to pall once she realized I was not rich.*

pallbearer ['pɔːlbeərər] *n* a person who helps to carry a coffin at a funeral.

pallet ['pælət] *n* a low wooden platform for storing goods on that can be moved using a fork-lift truck.

palliative ['pælɪətɪv] *n* MEDICINE a drug or treatment that reduces the effects of an illness without treating the cause (technical use) □ *palliative care.*

pallid ['pælɪd] *adj* [face, person] that is pale (literary use).

pallor ['pælər] *n* [of a face, person] the state of being pale □ *the deathly pallor of his skin.*

palm [pɑːm] *n* -1. the inside surface of a one's hand between the fingers and the wrist. -2. = palm tree.

◆ **palm off** *vt sep* **to palm sthg off on sb** to give or sell sthg that is not worth having to sb □ *He tried to palm off his old computer on me.* ■ **to palm sb off with sthg** [with an excuse, lie] to tell sb sthg that is not true in order to stop them from asking any more questions □ *He palmed them off with some story about his cousin having lent it to him.* ■ **to palm sthg off as sthg** to persuade somebody that sthg is sthg that it is not □ *He made copies and then palmed them off as originals.*

palmistry ['pɑːmɪstrɪ] *n* the practice of predicting somebody's future by looking at the lines in the palms of their hands.

palm oil *n* an oil made from the nut of an African palm that is used in cooking and to make soap.

Palm Sunday *n* a Christian religious festival that takes place on the Sunday before Easter.

palmtop ['pɑːmtɒp] *n* an electronic device such as a computer that is small enough to be held in the palm of one's hand.

palm tree *n* one of several types of tree that grow in hot countries, have no branches, and have long pointed leaves at the top.

palomino [ˌpæləˈmiːnoʊ] (*pl* **palominos**) *n* a golden or cream-colored horse with a white mane and tail.

palpable ['pælpəbl] *adj* [lie, nervousness, ill-feeling] that is very obvious □ *There was a palpable sense of hostility in the room.*

palpably ['pælpəblɪ] *adv* **palpably untrue/nervous etc** untrue/nervous etc in a very obvious way.

palpitate ['pælpəteɪt] *vi* [heart] to beat very quickly and irregularly.

palpitations [ˌpælpəˈteɪʃnz] *npl* a medical condition in which one's heart beats fast in an irregular way.

palsy ['pɔːlzɪ] *n* one of several types of illness that result in paralysis.

paltry ['pɔːltrɪ] (*compar* **paltrier**, *superl* **paltriest**) *adj* [wage, amount] so small that it is almost worthless □ *You're surely not going to go to court for such a paltry sum?*

pampas ['pæmpəs] *n* **the pampas** the large areas of plains in South America.

pampas grass *n* a type of grass with long

sharp leaves and soft, feathery, cream-colored flowers.

pamper ['pæmpər] *vt* to treat <a person or animal> more kindly and gently than is necessary □ *Mother always liked to pamper Jamie when he was sick.* □ *I've decided to pamper myself and get a facial.*

pamphlet ['pæmflət] ◇ *n* a thin book that has a paper cover and usually gives information about a product or service. ◇ *vi* to give out pamphlets.

pamphleteer [ˌpæmfləˈtɪər] *n* a person who writes political pamphlets.

pan [pæn] (*pt* & *pp* **panned**, *cont* **panning**) ◇ *n* -1. a round metal container, often with a long handle, that is used for cooking food on a stove; the contents of this container □ *Put the vegetables in a pan of boiling water.* -2. US a metal container used for cooking bread, cakes etc inside an oven. ◇ *vt* to criticize <a movie, book, performance> etc very severely □ *When the show got to Broadway, it was panned by the critics.* ◇ *vi* -1. **to pan for gold** to look for gold by sifting the stones from a riverbed. -2. [camera] to move smoothly from one side of a scene to the other, filming everything in between □ *The camera then pans left.*

panacea [ˌpænəˈsiːə] *n* something that people think will solve all problems or cure all illnesses.

panache [pəˈnæʃ] *n* confidence and style □ *She delivered the speech with great panache.*

panama ['pænəmɑː] *n* **a panama (hat)** a straw hat for men with a round top and a wide brim.

Panama ['pænəmɑː] a country in Central America, between Costa Rica and Colombia. It is an important center for banking and shipping. SIZE: 77,000 sq kms. POPULATION: 2,500,000 (*Panamanians*). CAPITAL: Panama City. LANGUAGE: Spanish. CURRENCY: balboa.

Panama Canal: the Panama Canal a canal through Panama, connecting the Atlantic Ocean and Pacific Ocean.

Panamanian [ˌpænəˈmeɪnjən] *n* & *adj*: see **Panama**.

pan-American *adj* [debate, organization] that is connected with or includes all of North and South America.

pancake ['pænkeɪk] *n* a thin round cake made from a mixture of flour, eggs, and milk that is fried in a frying pan. In the USA, pancakes are traditionally eaten for breakfast and are smaller and thicker than in Britain, where they are eaten as a dessert.

Pancake Day, Pancake Tuesay *n* in Britain, the day before the beginning of Lent when people traditionally eat pancakes.

pancreas ['pæŋkrɪəs] *n* an organ near the stomach that produces insulin and a liquid that helps to digest food.

panda ['pændə] (*pl* **panda** OR **pandas**) *n* a large black and white animal like a bear that lives in the bamboo forests in China.

Panda car *n* a small police car in Britain, used to patrol the streets.

pandemonium [ˌpændəˈmouniəm] *n* a state of noisy confusion.

pander [ˈpændəʳ] *vi* **to pander to sb** to do everything possible to please sb in a way that other people think is unnecessary or unacceptable □ *He's just pandering to their wishes.*

pane [peɪn] *n* a flat piece of glass in a window or door.

panel [ˈpænl] *n* **-1.** [of experts, judges, interviewers] a small group of people chosen to discuss something and make a decision about it; [on TV] a small group of famous people chosen to answer questions on a TV show □ *I was interviewed by a panel of six lawyers.* □ *What does the panel think?* **-2.** [on a door, wall] a flat, usually rectangular piece of wood, glass, metal etc that forms part of a larger object □ *an oak/a metal panel.* **-3.** [of a machine, vehicle] a section of a machine or vehicle that contains the switches and instruments □ *a control panel.*

panel game *n* GB a television program in which a panel has to answer questions for fun.

paneling US, **panelling** GB [ˈpænlɪŋ] *n* panels of wood that cover a wall inside a building.

panelist US, **panellist** GB [ˈpænləst] *n* a person who is a member of a panel.

panel pin *n* GB a short thin nail with a small head that is used in woodwork.

panel van *n* AUS a small van with doors at the back, used for carrying goods, tools etc.

pang [pæŋ] *n* [of pain, guilt] a sudden sharp feeling, usually of an emotion □ *hunger pangs* □ *Didn't you feel a pang of jealousy when you saw them together?*

panic [ˈpænɪk] (*pt* & *pp* **panicked**, *cont* **panicking**) ◇ *n* a strong feeling of fear and worry that stops one from acting in a controlled way or thinking clearly □ *The news caused widespread panic.* □ *She was in a panic.* □ *a panic on the stock exchange.* ◇ *vi* to feel panic □ *Don't panic!*

panicky [ˈpænɪkɪ] *adj* [person, feeling, behavior] that shows panic.

panic-stricken *adj* [person] who feels panic.

Pankhurst [ˈpæŋkhɜːʳst], **Emmeline** (1858–1928) a leading member of the British suffragettes, who demanded women's right to vote.

pannier [ˈpænɪəʳ] *n* a basket or bag attached to the side of a bicycle, motorcycle, or horse.

panoply [ˈpænəplɪ] *n* an impressive collection of things or people (formal use).

panorama [US ˌpænəˈræmə, GB -ˈrɑːm-] *n* a view over a long distance or a wide area of land.

panoramic [ˌpænəˈræmɪk] *adj* [view, screen] that is wide and allows one to see a large area.

pansy [ˈpænzɪ] (*pl* **pansies**) *n* **-1.** a small garden plant that has large rounded petals of many colors. **-2.** a man who behaves in a way that is considered to be like a woman (disapproving use).

pant [pænt] *vi* to take quick short breaths through the mouth, usually after very tiring physical exercise □ *The dog sat panting heavily after his walk.*

◆ **pants** *npl* **-1.** US a piece of clothing that covers the body from the waist to the ankle and has a separate part for each leg. **-2.** GB = **underpants**.

panther [ˈpænθəʳ] (*pl* **panther** OR **panthers**) *n* a large wild cat that is usually black.

panties [ˈpæntɪz] *npl* underpants for women or girls.

pantihose [ˈpæntɪhouz] *npl* = **panty hose**.

pantomime [ˈpæntəmaɪm] *n* in Britain, a musical comedy for children that is usually based on a fairy tale and performed in theaters during the period around Christmas.

pantry [ˈpæntrɪ] (*pl* **pantries**) *n* a small room or large cupboard in a house, usually near the kitchen, for storing food in.

pantsuit [ˈpæntsuːt] *n* US a suit for a woman consisting of a jacket and a pair of trousers.

panty hose [ˈpæntɪ-] *npl* US a piece of clothing worn by women, usually made of very fine nylon material, that covers the legs from the waist to the toes and fits close to the skin.

papa [US ˈpɑːpə, GB pəˈpɑː] *n* US a word used to refer to or address one's father (informal use).

papacy [ˈpeɪpəsɪ] (*pl* **papacies**) *n* **-1.** a period of time when a particular person is Pope. **-2. the papacy** the position and power of the Pope.

papadum [ˈpæpədəm] *n* a very thin round bread that is crunchy and is eaten with Indian food.

papal [ˈpeɪpl] *adj* [election, visit, decree] that is connected with the Pope.

paparazzi [US ˌpɑːpəˈrɑːtsɪ, GB ˌpæpəˈrætsɪ] *npl* newspaper reporters and photographers who follow famous people around to get stories or photographs (disapproving use).

papaya [pəˈpaɪə] *n* a large tropical fruit with green skin and sweet yellow flesh.

paper [ˈpeɪpəʳ] ◇ *n* **-1.** [for writing on] a material in the form of thin flat strips that is used for writing on, wrapping things in etc □ *a piece/sheet of paper* □ *lined/squared paper* □ *Do you have any typing paper?* ■ **on paper** in writing; in theory □ *I put one or two ideas down on paper.* □ *On paper they should win.* **-2.** [for news] a newspaper □ *I buy the paper every day.* **-3.** GB [in an exam] a sheet of paper with exam questions written on it □ *Most of us sat the history/math paper.* □ *an exam paper.* **-4.** EDUCATION an essay written by a student. **-5.** [on a particular subject] a piece of writing or a talk on a particular subject □ *Dr Ryan is giving a paper on genetic engineering at the Hamburg conference.*
◇ *adj* **-1.** [hat, cup] that is made of paper. **-2.** [profit, agreement, qualification] that exists on paper, but has no real value or use.
◇ *vt* to cover <a wall, room> etc with wallpaper □ *The hall was papered in green.*

◆ **papers** *npl* -**1**. a person's official documents, e.g. their passport, visa, or identity card □ *The policeman asked to see our papers.* -**2**. a collection of documents relating to a particular subject □ *The BCCI papers are still classified.*

◆ **paper over** *vt fus* **to paper over sthg** [over a problem, disagreement] to try to hide sthg and give the impression that things are going well □ *After the disagreement both sides tried to paper over the cracks in the alliance.*

paperback ['peɪpəˌbæk] ◇ *adj* [book, edition, copy] that has a paper or soft cardboard cover which usually makes it cheaper than a similar product with a hard cover. ◇ *n* a paperback book □ *Has it come out in paperback yet?*
NOTE: Compare **hardback.**

paper bag *n* a bag made of paper.

paperboy ['peɪpəˌbɔɪ] *n* a boy who delivers newspapers to people's homes.

paper clip *n* a small piece of curved wire used for holding sheets of paper together.

paper cutter *n* US a device consisting of a long blade attached to a lever, used for cutting paper.

papergirl ['peɪpəˌɡɜːˌl] *n* a girl who delivers newspapers to people's homes.

paper handkerchief *n* a handkerchief made of tissue paper.

paper knife *n* a knife that is not very sharp and is used for opening envelopes.

paper mill *n* a factory where paper is made.

paper money *n* money that is made of paper and is usually worth more than coins.

paper shop *n* GB a shop that sells newspapers.

paperweight ['peɪpəˌweɪt] *n* a heavy object that one puts on loose papers to prevent them from blowing away.

paperwork ['peɪpəˌwɜːˌk] *n* work that involves writing reports, lists, letters etc.

papier-mâché [US ˌpeɪpərməˈʃeɪ, GB ˌpæpjeɪˈmæʃeɪ] *n* a substance made of pieces of paper mixed with water and glue that is used to make models or ornaments □ *a papier-mâché box/model.*

papist ['peɪpəst] *n* a member of the Catholic Church (disapproving use).

paprika [pəˈpriːkə] *n* a powder made from red peppers that is used for giving a slightly hot flavor to food.

Pap smear ['pæp-] *n* US an examination of cells taken from a woman's cervix in order to discover if there is cancer there.

Papua New Guinea [ˌpæpuə-] a country in the Pacific Ocean, consisting of the eastern part of New Guinea and several neighboring islands. SIZE: 463,000 sq kms. POPULATION: 3,900,000 (*Papua New Guineans*). CAPITAL: Port Moresby. LANGUAGE: pidgin English. CURRENCY: kina.

papyrus [pəˈpaɪrəs] *n* a tall plant that looks like grass and grows in or near water in North Africa; paper made from this plant

that was used in ancient Egypt and Greece for writing on.

par [pɑːˌr] *n* -**1**. **to be on a par with sb/sthg** to be as good as sb/sthg else □ *You can't put him on a par with Mozart!* -**2**. SPORT the number of strokes a golf player is supposed to take to hit the ball into the holes on a particular course □ *The course is par 72.* □ *a par 4 hole.* ■ **to be under/over par** to take less/more than the par on a particular hole or golf course. -**3**. **to be below** OR **under par** to be slightly ill □ *She's been feeling a little below par recently.*

parable ['pærəbl] *n* a simple short story that teaches a moral or religious lesson.

parabola [pəˈræbələ] *n* a curve shaped like the line followed by something that is thrown into the air and then falls to the ground.

paracetamol [ˌpærəˈsiːtəmɒl] *n* GB a mild drug that is used to reduce pain; a pill containing this drug.

parachute [US ˈperəʃuːt, GB ˈpær-] ◇ *n* a large piece of nylon or silk that is attached by strings to a person or object dropped from an aircraft to make them fall more slowly and land safely. ◇ *vi* [person] to jump from an aircraft using a parachute.

parade [pəˈreɪd] ◇ *n* -**1**. a public event in which people or vehicles move along a road, through a town etc, often with music playing, to celebrate a special event □ *a street parade.* -**2**. MILITARY an occasion when soldiers march or stand together in front of superior officers or in public as part of a ceremony □ *a victory parade.* ■ **to be on parade** [soldiers] to be standing or marching in a parade. -**3**. GB [of shops] a street that has a row of shops. ◇ *vt* -**1**. [soldiers, criminals] to make <a group of people> march through the streets in front of people □ *The hostages were paraded through the village.* -**2**. [statue, prize, medal] to show <sthg> to the public with pride □ *Schumacher paraded the trophy round the track.* -**3**. [knowledge, possessions] to show <sthg> to other people in a way that is intended to get their attention □ *I don't know why he has to parade his feelings for everyone to see.* ◇ *vi* [soldiers, band] to take part in a parade □ *The team paraded through the town.*

parade ground *n* an area of ground where soldiers parade.

paradigm [US ˈperədaɪm, GB ˈpær-] *n* a clear example that explains how something works (formal use).

paradigmatic [US ˌperədɪɡˈmætɪk, GB ˌpær-] *adj* [example, case] that is a paradigm.

paradise [US ˈperədaɪs, GB ˈpær-] *n* a wonderful place, condition, or feeling □ *It's simply paradise not to have to go to work.*

◆ **Paradise** *n* according to some religions, the place where people go after they die if they have been good.

paradox [US ˈperədɒks, GB ˈpær-] *n* -**1**. a situation in which two opposing facts which cannot normally both be true at the same time occur together □ *The paradox is that the rich are the least willing to take part.* -**2**. a statement that says two opposite things at the same time □ *"Defeat in victory" is a paradox.*

paradoxical [US ˌperəˈdɒksɪkl, GB ˌpær-] *adj* [situation, statement] *see* **paradox.**

paradoxically [US ˌperəˈdɒksɪklɪ, GB ˌpær-] *adv* a word used to show that one is going to talk about a paradoxical situation □ *Paradoxically, the harder I work, the less tired I feel.*

paraffin [US ˈperəfɪn, GB ˈpær-] *n* **-1.** US = **paraffin wax. -2.** GB a clear liquid made from petroleum and used as fuel in lamps and heaters.

paraffin wax *n* a soft white wax made from petroleum and coal that is used for making candles.

paragon [US ˈperəgɑːn, GB ˈpærəgən] *n* a person who is a perfect example of a quality □ *He's not exactly a paragon of virtue.*

paragraph [US ˈperəgræf, GB ˈpærəgrɑːf] *n* a section of a piece of writing that contains one or more sentences, starts on a new line, and usually deals with one subject, idea etc.

Paraguay [US ˈperəgweɪ, GB ˈpærəgwaɪ] a country in central South America, between Brazil, Bolivia, and Argentina. SIZE: 407,000 sq kms. POPULATION: 4,200,000 (*Paraguayans*). CAPITAL: Asunción. LANGUAGE: Spanish. CURRENCY: guarani.

parakeet [US ˈperəkiːt, GB ˈpær-] *n* a small parrot with a long tail.

paralegal [US ˌperəˈliːgl, GB ˌpær-] *n* US a person who is trained to help a lawyer.

parallel [US ˈperəlel, GB ˈpær-] (US *pt* & *pp* **paralleled**, *cont* **paralleling**, GB *pt* & *pp* **parallelled**, *cont* **parallelling**) ◇ *adj* **-1.** [lines, roads] that run in the same direction and are always the same distance apart □ *There is a ditch parallel to* OR *with the fence.* **-2.** [process, event] that is similar to something else or takes place at the same time □ *A parallel investigation was mounted within the company itself.*
◇ *n* **-1.** a parallel line or surface. **-2.** a similar person or thing from a different situation or time □ *a tradition which has no parallel in our own culture.* **-3.** a similarity □ *There are obvious parallels between the two cases.* ■ **to draw a parallel with sthg** to show that there is a similarity with sthg □ *His appreciation of Picasso draws interesting parallels with works by earlier painters.* **-4.** GEOGRAPHY a particular line on a map that is parallel to the equator □ *the 49th parallel.*
◇ *vt* to be similar to or happen at the same time as <sb/sthg> □ *Environmental pollution parallels the decline in the country's economy.*

parallel bars *npl* two bars that are fixed on poles, sometimes at different heights, for gymnastic exercises.

parallel processing *n* a system in which a computer is used to carry out a number of operations all at the same time rather than one after the other.

paralyse *etc* GB = **paralyze** *etc.*

paralysis [pəˈræləsəs] (*pl* **paralyses** [-əsiːz]) *n* a state of being paralyzed □ *He appeared to be suffering from a kind of emotional paralysis.*

paralytic [US ˌperəˈlɪtɪk, GB ˌpær-] MEDICINE ◇ *adj* [person] whose body is completely or partly paralyzed. ◇ *n* a person whose body is completely or partly paralyzed.

paralyze [ˈperəlaɪz] US, **paralyse** [ˈpærəlaɪz] GB *vt* **-1.** [person, leg, arm] to cause <sb/sthg> to be unable to feel anything and to be unable to move □ *He was paralyzed from the neck down.* **-2.** [organization, government] to stop <sthg> from working properly □ *Commuter services were paralyzed by the severe weather conditions this morning.*

paralyzed [ˈperəlaɪzd] US, **paralysed** [ˈpærəlaɪzd] GB *adj* **-1.** [person, leg] that is unable to move as the result of an accident or illness □ *There's a chance that she may be paralyzed in both legs.* **-2.** [organization, government] that is not able to work properly □ *Power cuts left the city paralyzed for hours.*

paramedic [US ˌperəˈmedɪk, GB ˌpær-] *n* a person such as an ambulance driver whose job is to help in emergency medical work but who is not a doctor or a nurse.

paramedical [US ˌperəˈmedɪkl, GB ˌpær-] *adj* [services, training] connected with helping doctors or nurses.

parameter [pəˈræmətər] *n* a limit or guideline that affects the way something can be done □ *There are rules which establish the parameters within which we are able to operate.*

paramilitary [US ˌperəˈmɪlətərɪ, GB ˌperəˈmɪlətərɪ] *adj* [group, organization] that is organized like an army, fights against a government, and is illegal □ *a paramilitary attack.*

paramount [US ˈperəmaunt, GB ˈpær-] *adj* that is more important than everything else □ *Finding a peaceful solution is of paramount importance.* □ *When climbing, safety is paramount.*

paranoia [US ˌperəˈnɔɪə, GB ˌpær-] *n* a mental disease that makes somebody believe that they are very important and famous or that other people hate them and want to harm them.

paranoiac [US ˌperəˈnɔɪæk, GB ˌpær-] ◇ *n* a person who is suffering from paranoia. ◇ *adj*: *paranoiac disease/behavior.*

paranoid [US ˈperənɔɪd, GB ˈpær-] *adj* **-1.** [person] who is very suspicious and distrusts other people □ *Nick is completely paranoid about what other people think of him.* **-2.** PSYCHOLOGY [person] who suffers from paranoia □ *a paranoid schizophrenic.*

paranormal [US ˌperəˈnɔːrml, GB ˌpærəˈnɔːml] *adj* [phenomenon, event] that cannot be explained by science.

parapet [US ˈperəpət, GB ˈpær-] *n* a low wall along the edge of a balcony, roof, or bridge.

paraphernalia [US ˌperəfərˈneɪlɪə, GB ˌpærəfəˈneɪlɪə] *n* a large number of small personal objects or pieces of equipment connected with a particular activity □ *She had all her sewing paraphernalia spread across the table.*

paraphrase [US ˈperəfreɪz, GB ˈpær-] ◇ *vt* [answer, words, theory] to say <sthg that has already been said or written> in a different way, so that it is shorter or easier to understand □ *To paraphrase Lewis, imperialism is simply nationalism on a large scale.* ◇ *vi: I'm paraphrasing from what he actually wrote.* ◇ *n* something that paraphrases something else.

paraplegia [US ˌperə'pliːdʒə, GB ˌpær-] *n* a medical condition in which one cannot move the lower half of one's body.

paraplegic [US ˌperə'pliːdʒɪk, GB ˌpær-] ◇ *n* a person who suffers from paraplegia. ◇ *adj: a paraplegic man/woman.*

parapsychology [US ˌperəsaɪ'kɒlədʒɪ, GB ˌpær-] *n* the study of mental powers, such as the ability to say what is going to happen in the future, that cannot be explained by ordinary science.

Paraquat™ [US 'perəkwɒt, GB 'pær-] *n* a poison used for killing weeds.

parasite [US 'perəsaɪt, GB 'pær-] *n* -1. ZOOLOGY a plant or animal that lives in or on another plant or animal and gets its food from it. -2. a person who does nothing to support themselves but instead gets money, food etc from other people or from the state (disapproving use) □ *He's a parasite on society.*

parasitic [US ˌperə'sɪtɪk, GB ˌpær-] *adj* -1. [plant, animal] that is a parasite; [disease] that is caused by a parasite. -2. [person] who is a parasite on other people (disapproving use).

parasol [US 'perəsɒl, GB 'pær-] *n* a kind of umbrella for protection from the sun.

paratrooper [US 'perətruːpər, GB 'pærətruːpə] *n* a soldier who is trained to be dropped from aircraft using a parachute.

parboil [ˈpɑːrbɔɪl] *vt* [meat, vegetables] to boil <food> until it is partly cooked.

parcel [ˈpɑːrsl] (US *pt* & *pp* **parceled**, *cont* **parceling**, GB *pt* & *pp* **parcelled**, *cont* **parcelling**) *n* an object that has been wrapped in paper so that it can be easily carried or mailed □ *a parcel of books.*

◆ **parcel up** *vt sep* to parcel sthg up [clothes, books] to wrap sthg together in paper to make a parcel.

parcel post *n* the system for sending parcels by mail □ *We sent it by parcel post.*

parched [pɑːrtʃt] *adj* -1. [land, plain] that is completely dry because it is very hot and there has been no rain; [throat, mouth] that feels very dry □ *The parched soil is in desperate need of rain.* -2. **to be parched** [person] to be very thirsty (informal use) □ *I'm parched!*

Parcheesi™ [pɑːrˈtʃiːzɪ] *n* a simple game played on a board with a dice and flat pieces of plastic.

parchment [ˈpɑːrtʃmənt] *n* a material made from the skin of sheep or goats that was used for writing on in the past.

pardon [ˈpɑːrdn] ◇ *n* -1. LAW official permission given to a prisoner or criminal that allows them to be free and not to be punished □ *He received an official pardon for his crimes.* -2. forgiveness. ■ **I beg your pardon?** a phrase used to show that one is surprised or offended by what somebody has just said; a phrase used to ask somebody to repeat something that one did not hear or under-

stand □ *I beg your pardon? Did you just say what I think you said?* □ *I beg your pardon? I didn't quite catch that.* ■ **I beg your pardon!** a phrase used to apologize for something one has said or done (formal use) □ *I beg your pardon, I didn't mean to intrude.*

◇ *vt* -1. to excuse or forgive <sb> for something that is not important or serious □ *Pardon me for asking, but how old are you?* ■ **pardon me!** a phrase used to apologize for something one has just said or done. ■ **pardon (me)?** a word used when one wants somebody to repeat what they have just said. -2. LAW [criminal, prisoner] to give an official pardon to <sb>.

pardonable [ˈpɑːrdnəbl] *adj* [mistake, behavior] that can be forgiven or excused because it is understandable.

pare [peər] *vt* [apple, stick, nail] to remove the skin or outside part of <sthg> by cutting it.

◆ **pare down** *vt sep* -1. **to pare sthg down** [fingernail, stick] to make sthg smaller by gradually paring it. -2. [budget, staff] to reduce sthg gradually in size or amount.

parent [ˈpeərənt] *n* one's mother or father □ *Both my parents live abroad.* □ *One of his parents is Greek.*

parentage [ˈpeərəntɪdʒ] *n* the fact of being the child of parents from a particular country or social group □ *a child of unknown/mixed parentage.*

parental [pəˈrentl] *adj* [love, responsibility, guidance] that is connected with one's parents □ *Children need parental consent to participate.*

parent company *n* a company that owns one or more other companies.

parenthesis [pəˈrenθəsəs] (*pl* **parentheses** [-əsiːz]) *n* one of a pair of marks ( ) or [ ] placed before and after a word or phrase to show that it is additional information and is not essential to the main idea □ *That part should be in parentheses.*

parenthetical [ˌpærənˈθetɪkl] *adj* [remark, explanation] that is not essential to the main subject being discussed, but is given as additional information.

parenthood [ˈpeərənthʊd] *n* the state of being a parent □ *Do you think you're ready for the trials of parenthood?*

parenting [ˈpeərəntɪŋ] *n* the activity of taking care of and bringing up a child □ *good parenting.*

parent-teacher association *n* an organization consisting of teachers and parents who discuss matters connected with the children in a school.

par excellence [US ˌpɑːreksəˈlɑːns, GB pɑːrˈeksəlɑːns] *adj* that is the best of its kind □ *a blues singer par excellence.*

pariah [pəˈraɪə] *n* a person or country that other people or countries dislike and refuse to become involved with (disapproving use) □ *a pariah state.*

Paris [US 'perəs, GB 'pær-] the capital of France, and its largest city. POPULATION: 2,152,423.

parish [US 'perɪʃ, GB 'pær-] *n* -1. an area that has a church and which a priest in that church is responsible for. -2. in the USA, a county in the state of Louisiana. -3. in Britain, the smallest unit of local government in the countryside.

parish council *n* in Britain, the group of people that runs a parish.

parishioner [pə'rɪʃnəʳ] *n* a person who lives in the parish of a particular church.

parish priest *n* the priest in charge of a parish.

Parisian [US pə'rɪʒn, GB -'rɪziən] *n* & *adj*: see **Paris**.

parity [US 'perətɪ, GB 'pær-] *n* the state of being equal in status, value etc □ *Women still have to fight for economic parity with men.* □ *There should be parity between the two groups.*

park [pɑːʳk] ◇ *n* -1. a large area of land, especially in a town, where grass, trees, and flowers grow and where the public can go to enjoy themselves □ *Children were playing in the park.* □ *Let's go to the park.* □ *a park bench.* -2. US AUTO the gear position in an automatic car that is used when the car is not moving □ *Leave the car in park.* -3. GB [around a house] an area of land with grass and trees around a large country house. ◇ *vt* [car, bus, bicycle] to put <a vehicle> in a particular place and leave it there for a period of time □ *I'm sure it was parked here.* ◇ *vi*: *You can't park there!* □ *As usual, there's nowhere to park.*

parka [pɑːʳkə] *n* a short coat that has a hood which usually has fur inside it.

parking ['pɑːʳkɪŋ] *n* -1. the act of parking a vehicle □ *I find parking very difficult.* □ *I couldn't get a parking space.* ■ **'No parking'** a phrase usually written on a sign to show that vehicles should not be parked in a particular place. -2. space where vehicles can be parked and left for a period of time □ *There's parking for 200 cars behind the supermarket.*

parking brake *n* US a brake in a car, truck etc that is worked with the hand.

parking garage *n* US a building, or a level in a building, where cars can be left.

parking light *n* US one of the two small lights near the sides at the front of a vehicle.

parking lot *n* an open area where people can leave their cars.

parking meter *n* a device at the side of a road that one puts money into to be allowed to park next to it for a period of time.

parking ticket *n* a piece of paper that an official places on somebody's vehicle if they have parked it illegally and which tells them to pay a fine □ *I got a parking ticket.*

Parkinson's disease ['pɑːʳkɪnsənz-] *n* a disease, especially affecting old people, that makes one's arms and legs shake.

park keeper *n* GB a person whose job is to take care of a park.

parkland ['pɑːʳklænd] *n* an area of land with grass and trees, often surrounding a large country house □ *The house is set in 10 acres of parkland.*

parkway ['pɑːʳkweɪ] *n* US a wide road that has grass and trees along the center of it or beside it.

parlance ['pɑːʳləns] *n* **in legal/medical etc parlance** in words that people working in law/medicine etc would use.

parliament ['pɑːʳləmənt] *n* -1. the group of people who are elected to make the laws of a country □ *the Norwegian parliament.* -2. in Britain, the institution made up of the King or Queen, the House of Lords, and the House of Commons, which is responsible for making laws □ *the Houses of Parliament.* -3. the period during which a parliament exists between elections or vacations □ *the acts that were introduced in the last parliament.*

parliamentarian [ˌpɑːʳləmən'teərɪən] *n* a member of a parliament, especially one who is very skilled or experienced.

parliamentary [ˌpɑːʳlə'mentərɪ] *adj* [candidate, work] see **parliament**.

parliamentary private secretary *n* a member of the British parliament, usually a backbencher, who acts as a minister's assistant.

Parliament House the building where the Australian parliament sits, in Canberra.

parlor US, **parlour** GB ['pɑːʳləʳ] *n* a sitting room (old-fashioned use).

parlor game *n* a game that people play indoors, especially one in which they have to guess the answer to a question.

parlous ['pɑːʳləs] *adj* **a parlous state** a very bad or dangerous state (formal use) □ *the parlous state of our movie industry.*

Parmesan [US 'pɑːʳməzɑːn, GB ˌpɑːʳmɪ'zæn] *n* **Parmesan (cheese)** a hard dry cheese from Italy that is usually grated and served with pasta, soups etc.

Parnell [pɑːʳ'nel], **Charles Stewart** (1846–1891) an Irish politician who was in favor of Irish independence.

parochial [pə'roʊkɪəl] *adj* [person] who is only interested in local affairs that affect them directly and does not want to know about other areas, countries etc (disapproving use) □ *Their attitude is so parochial.*

parochial school *n* in the USA, a private school that is run by a religious group and provides elementary and secondary education.

parody [US 'perədɪ, GB 'pær-] (*pl* **parodies**, *pt* & *pp* **parodied**) ◇ *n* -1. a type of writing, music, or performance that copies the style of a famous author, composer etc in an amusing way; a piece of this type of writing, music, performance etc □ *He uses parody to ridicule his enemies.* -2. something that has been done so badly that it seems deliberate □ *a parody of justice.* ◇ *vt* [politician, politics] to copy <sb/sthg> by making a parody of them.

parole [pə'roʊl] ◇ *n* permission to leave prison that is given to some prisoners before their sentence has ended, on the condition that they do not break the law again. ■ **on parole** released from prison early on the condition that one does not break the law again □ *Thorpe was released on parole.* □ *He was out on parole at the time of the incident.* ◇ *vt* to release <a prisoner> on parole.

paroxysm [US 'perəksızm, GB 'pær-] *n* **a paroxysm of rage/coughing etc** a sudden period of rage/coughing etc that one cannot stop or control □ *They fell about in paroxysms of laughter.*

parquet [US pɑːr'keı, GB 'pɑːkeı] *n* a floor surface consisting of small rectangular blocks of wood that are fitted together in a pattern □ *a parquet floor.*

parrot [US 'perət, GB 'pær-] *n* a tropical bird with a curved beak and brightly-colored feathers that is sometimes kept as a pet and can repeat phrases to sound as if it can talk.

parrot fashion *adv* [repeat, learn] in a way that shows one has learned all the words of something but has not understood it (disapproving use) □ *It's no good just reeling it off parrot fashion.*

parry [US 'perı, GB 'pærı] (*pt* & *pp* **parried**) *vt* **-1.** [blow, attack] to push aside or block <sthg> in order to defend oneself. **-2.** [question, criticism] to avoid dealing with <sthg> directly by saying something clever.

parsimonious [ˌpɑːrsə'mounjəs] *adj* [person] who dislikes spending money (formal and disapproving use).

parsley ['pɑːrslı] *n* a small plant with curly leaves and a strong taste used in cooking for flavor or decoration.

parsnip ['pɑːrsnəp] *n* a plant whose yellowish-white root is cooked and eaten as a vegetable.

parson ['pɑːrsn] *n* a priest in some Protestant churches (old-fashioned use).

part [pɑːrt] ◇ *n* **-1. part of sthg** some but not the whole of sthg □ *Part of the wall had collapsed.* □ *The lack of funding is only part of the problem.* □ *The new team will form part of the Sales Department.* □ *They usually spend part of the year abroad.* ■ **to be part and parcel of sthg** [of a job, situation] to be an aspect of sthg that is often unpleasant but cannot be avoided □ *Pollution and high crime rates are all part and parcel of living in a big city.* **-2.** [of a book, building, city] one of the pieces, sections, areas etc into which something can be divided □ *She lives in the old part of town.* □ *a new thriller in six parts.* □ *Dealing with the public is the enjoyable part of the job.* □ *The disease can affect several parts of the body at the same time.* □ *We spent the early part of the year planning our trip.* ■ **the best OR better part of sthg** [of a period of time, sum of money] almost the whole of sthg □ *He was the best OR better part of an hour late.* □ *Improvements to the existing rail system will cost the better part of two billion dollars.* **-3.** [of a machine] one of the pieces of a machine, car engine etc □ *They don't have the part in stock.* □ *We were charged $300 for parts and labor.* **-4.** [of a mixture] one of the equal quantities of liquid, sand etc that is used when mixing together different substances or liquids □ *You mix one part vodka to two parts orange juice.* **-5.** [in a play, movie] a role performed by an actor □ *The part of Hamlet will be played by Mark Rylance.* **-6. sb's part in sthg** [in an accident, crime] how much sb is involved in sthg □ *Police are questioning him about his part in the robbery.* ■ **to play a part in sthg** to be one of the reasons why sthg happens, is successful etc □ *Advertising has played an important part in the success of the campaign.* ■ **to take part in sthg** [in an activity, event] to be one of the people involved in sthg □ *Several teams have refused to take part in the contest.* ■ **to want no part in sthg** [in a plan, decision] to want not to be involved in sthg because one disapproves of it □ *If that's what you're planning to do, then I want no part in it!* ■ **for my/his etc part** my/his etc personal opinion is that... (formal use) □ *For my part, I would prefer not to have to move offices.* ■ **on the part of sb, on sb's part** used to describe who feels, does, or says something (formal use) □ *This was a terrible blunder on the part of the authorities.* □ *No criticism was intended on the part of my client.* **-7.** US [in one's hair] a line in somebody's hair from the forehead to the top of their head that shows where they have combed their hair in two different directions □ *She wears her hair in a center/side part.*
◇ *adv* **part...part...** partly...partly... □ *The book is part documentary, part thriller.*
◇ *vt* **-1. to be parted** to be forced to be apart from each other □ *She had been parted from her family during the war.* **-2. to part one's hair** to make a line in one's hair with a comb so that the hair lies in two different directions □ *Her long hair was parted in the middle.*
◇ *vi* **-1.** [two people] to leave each other; to end a relationship □ *They parted friends/on good terms.* □ *We thought we'd never part.* **-2.** [two things that touch] to move apart from each other □ *The clouds suddenly parted and the sun shone through.* □ *Her lips parted in a smile.*
◆ **parts** *npl* **in these parts** in the area where one is □ *You don't find many restaurants in these parts.*
◆ **for the most part** *adv* mostly □ *The region is, for the most part, agricultural.*
◆ **in part** *adv* partly □ *The company's success is due, in part, to the dedication of its workforce.*
◆ **part with** *vt fus* **to part with sthg** [with money, possessions] to give or sell sthg one really wants to keep to somebody else □ *He was obviously reluctant to part with the information.* □ *I was heartbroken at having to part with my new car, but I just couldn't afford it.*

part- *prefix* added to words to mean partly but not completely □ *a part-payment.*

partake [pɑːr'teık] (*pt* **partook**, *pp* **partaken** [-'teıkn]) *vi* **to partake of sthg** [of food, wine] to eat or drink sthg (formal use).

part exchange *n* GB the system of buying something by giving both money and goods for it, especially where the goods are of the same kind as the thing being bought □ *It was a part exchange deal.* ■ **in part exchange** as part of the payment for something □ *We gave our old car in part exchange for it.*

partial [ˈpɑːrʃl] *adj* **-1.** [solution, victory] that is not complete □ *I'm afraid it was only a partial success.* **-2.** [person] who supports one person or thing in a competition, argument etc in a way that is not fair □ *a partial judge.* **-3. to be partial to sthg** to like sthg □ *I'm very partial to cakes.*

partiality [ˌpɑːrʃɪˈælətɪ] *n* **-1. a partiality for sthg** a strong liking for sthg □ *Sue has a great partiality for candy bars.* **-2.** support for one person or thing in a competition, argument etc in a way that is not fair.

partially [ˈpɑːrʃəlɪ] *adv* [hidden, responsible] partly but not completely □ *The house was partially covered in ivy.*

partially sighted [-ˈsaɪtəd] *adj* [person] who cannot see well because their eyes are damaged.

participant [pɑːrˈtɪsəpənt] *n* [in a race, election] a person who takes part in something □ *All participants will be invited to attend the awards ceremony.*

participate [pɑːrˈtɪsəpeɪt] *vi* to take part in something □ *He refused to participate in the discussions.*

participation [pɑːrˌtɪsəˈpeɪʃn] *n*: *see* **participate** □ *Your participation is vital if we are to succeed.*

participle [ˈpɑːrtəsɪpl] *n* a form of a verb which is used as part of some tenses, e.g. the past participle of "go" is "gone" and the present participle is "going".

particle [ˈpɑːrtɪkl] *n* a very small piece of something □ *a particle of dust.*

particular [pərˈtɪkjələr] *adj* **-1.** [type, problem] that is unique and different from all others □ *She has her own particular reasons for being there.* **-2. a particular person/thing** this person/thing and not others □ *Did you want this particular copy, or would another do?* **-3.** [care, attention, consideration] that is greater than usual or than in other cases □ *They place particular emphasis on linguistic skills.* □ *His own particular strength is in sales.* **-4. to be particular** [person] to pay a lot of attention to details and be very difficult to please □ *He's very particular about what he eats.*

◆ **particulars** *npl* [of a person, car] facts and information that describe somebody or something □ *The policeman took down my particulars.*

◆ **in particular** *adv* especially □ *I enjoyed it all, but I liked the ending in particular.*

particularity [pərˌtɪkjəˈlærətɪ] (*pl* **particularities**) *n* a special or strange detail or fact (formal use).

particularly [pərˈtɪkjələrlɪ] *adv* **-1.** especially □ *It's not easy, particularly when you don't have any money.* □ *Some people, particularly women, find their attitude aggressive.* **-2.** more than usually □ *I'm feeling particularly cheerful today.*

parting [ˈpɑːrtɪŋ] *n* **-1.** the act of leaving somebody or somewhere or of ending a relationship □ *Parting is never easy.* **-2.** GB a line in somebody's hair that shows where they have combed it in two different directions.

parting shot *n* a final, usually unpleasant, remark made at the end of a conversation or argument as one is leaving.

partisan [US ˈpɑːrtəzən, GB ˌpɑːtɪˈzæn] ◇ *adj* [supporter, judge] who supports a particular person, view etc without considering all the facts fairly □ *partisan support.* ◇ *n* a person who has joined an armed group to fight against an army that has occupied their country.

partition [pɑːrˈtɪʃn] ◇ *n* **-1.** [in a room, building] a thin wall or screen separating one part of a room from another □ *The offices were separated by thin partitions.* **-2.** [of a country] the act of dividing a country into two or more separate countries □ *the partition of Poland.* ◇ *vt* **-1.** to divide <a room> into two parts with a partition. **-2.** to divide <a country> into two or more separate countries.

partly [ˈpɑːrtlɪ] *adv* to some degree, but not completely □ *I'm partly to blame.* □ *It's partly a legal, partly an ethical issue.*

partner [ˈpɑːrtnər] ◇ *n* **-1.** a person one is married to or is having a sexual relationship with □ *How many sexual partners have you had?* □ *You and your partner are both invited.* **-2.** [in an activity] a person with whom one does an activity such as dancing or playing tennis □ *my dancing partner.* **-3.** BUSINESS any of the people who own a business together □ *my business partner* □ *a junior/senior partner in a law firm.* **-4.** [in international politics, trade] a person or group that one has an agreement with or shares an activity with □ *Our partners in the EU.* □ *America is our biggest trading partner.* ◇ *vt* to act as partner to <sb> in an activity such as dancing.

partnership [ˈpɑːrtnərʃɪp] *n* **-1.** a relationship in which two people, organizations etc work closely together to achieve a particular aim □ *City Hall is working in partnership with the police to combat this problem.* **-2.** a small business owned by two or more people □ *a business partnership.*

partook [pɑːrˈtʊk] *past tense of* **partake**.

partridge [ˈpɑːrtrɪdʒ] (*pl* **partridge** OR **partridges**) *n* a bird with a round body and a short tail that is killed for sport and food.

part-time ◇ *adj* [work, job, course] that does not take up all the usual working hours of the week □ *I'm a part-time secretary.* ◇ *adv* [work, study] *I only go to work part-time.* NOTE: Compare **full-time**.

part-timer *n* a person who works part-time.

party [ˈpɑːrtɪ] (*pl* **parties**, *pt* & *pp* **partied**) ◇ *n* **-1.** POLITICS an organization of people with the same political views that take part in elections □ *the Conservative/Republican Party.* **-2.** [for a celebration] a social event, often held to celebrate a special occasion, where people eat, drink, and enjoy themselves □ *Let's have a birthday party for him.* □ *We met at Andy's party.* **-3.** [of tourists, diners] an organized group of people who are doing the same activity together □ *a party of schoolchildren.* □ *We cater for parties of up to thirty people.* **-4.** LAW one of the people or organizations involved in a legal agreement or dispute □ *the guilty party.* **-5. to be (a) party to sthg** [to a plan, decision] to be involved in sthg and be partly responsible for it □ *I was not party to the decision-making process.*

◇ *vi* to enjoy oneself in a lively way, especially at a party □ *Alex does like to party.*

party line *n* **-1.** POLITICS the official opinion of a political party which its members are supposed to support □ *Your job will be to enforce the party line.* **-2.** a telephone line shared by two or more different places.

party piece *n* something that somebody often does to amuse people, especially at parties, e.g. singing a particular song (informal use) □ *Once she'd done her party piece she left.*

party political broadcast *n* GB a short television or radio program made by a political party to tell people about its ideas and policies, and persuade them to vote for it.

party politics *n* the activity of politicians who speak or act in a way that makes it seem they are more interested in improving the position of their party than in the good of their country.

party wall *n* a wall that separates two houses or pieces of land and belongs to both owners.

parvenu [ˈpɑːˈvənjuː] *n* a person of low social class who suddenly becomes very wealthy or powerful (disapproving use).

pass [US pæs, GB pɑːs] ◇ *n* **-1.** [for a passenger, employee] an official document that allows somebody to travel on a bus, train etc without paying, or to go into a particular place □ *a security/bus pass* □ *All tickets and season passes, please!* **-2.** SPORT an act of throwing, kicking etc a ball to another player in one's team □ *Jones sent a long pass down the right wing to Gascoigne.* **-3.** [between mountains] a narrow road between mountains □ *the Brenner Pass.* **-4.** EDUCATION a successful result in an exam, test etc □ *She got a pass in German.* **-5. to make a pass at sb** to try to kiss or touch sb in a sexual way because one wants to start a sexual relationship with them.

◇ *vt* **-1.** to give <sthg> to somebody, especially because they cannot reach it themselves □ *Pass the salt, please.* □ *Pass me my bag, would you?* □ *Pass the wine to your father.* **-2.** [person, building] to go past <sb/sthg> □ *We pass the house every day.* □ *I didn't recognize her when I passed her in the street.* **-3.** [days, life] to spend <a period of time> in a particular way □ *We passed a glorious month in Tuscany.* ■ **to pass the time** to do some activity so that one does not feel bored □ *We played cards to pass the time on the train.* **-4.** [exam, test] to get a successful result in <sthg> □ *I passed my driver's test the first time.* **-5.** [number, total, sales] to go over <a particular amount> and continue to increase □ *The number of unemployed has passed the three million mark.* **-6.** [candidate, applicant] to give <sb> a successful result on an examination or test □ *She appealed against the examiners' decision, and was eventually passed.* **-7.** [law, motion, bill]

to accept <sthg> officially, especially by voting □ *The amendment was passed with a two-thirds majority.* **-8.** [comment, remark] to express one's opinion by saying <sthg>, especially in an unfair or unpleasant way. ■ **to pass judgment** to criticize somebody or something □ *You shouldn't pass judgment until you know all the details.* **-9.** US [car, truck] to drive past and go ahead of <another vehicle> moving in the same direction.

◇ *vi* **-1.** [person, river] to move or lead in a particular direction □ *The bus passed through the outskirts of the city.* □ *The President passed among the crowd, talking and shaking hands.* **-2.** [two people, ships] to go past each other in opposite directions □ *We passed on the stairs.* **-3.** SPORT to throw, hit or kick a ball to another person on one's team □ *And Jones has passed to Gascoigne!* **-4.** [student] to be successful in a test or exam □ *Only three out of the twelve candidates passed.* **-5.** [period of time, event] to happen and reach an end □ *The week passed very slowly.* □ *The demonstration passed peaceably.* □ *Don't worry, the pain will soon pass.* **-6.** US [car, driver] to pass another vehicle □ *'No passing.'*

◆ **pass around** *vt sep* **to pass sthg around** to hand sthg to every person in a group □ *Plates of hot food were being passed around.*

◆ **pass as** *vt fus* **to pass as sb/sthg** to be accepted as sb/sthg □ *She could easily pass as eighteen.* □ *A strip of dirty sand was supposed to pass as a beach.*

◆ **pass away** *vi* [person] to die (polite use).

◆ **pass by** ◇ *vt sep* **to pass by sthg** to go past sthg □ *As you pass by the church, notice the fine carving over the door.* ◇ *vt sep* **to pass sb by** [opportunity, life, event] to go past without being noticed or made good use of by sb, usually because of a lack of effort or attention □ *Current events seem to pass him by completely.* □ *Don't let this chance of happiness pass you by.* ◇ *vi* [person, animal, vehicle] to go past □ *I saw him at the window as we passed by.*

◆ **pass for** *vt fus* = **pass as.**

◆ **pass off** *vt sep* **to pass sb/sthg off as sthg** to pretend that sb/sthg is sthg different from what they really are □ *Derek actually tried to pass the design off as his own.*

◆ **pass on** ◇ *vt sep* **-1. to pass sthg on** [object, characteristic, tradition] to give sthg to somebody else, e.g. because one has finished using it □ *She passes all her old clothes on to her sister.* □ *He passed on a love of nature to his children.* **-2. to pass sthg on** [news, information, congratulations] to give or tell somebody sthg because somebody else has asked one to give or tell it to them □ *Could you pass on a message to Chris?* □ *Please pass on my thanks to the organizers.* **-3. to pass on costs/savings** to raise/lower the cost of a product because of extra costs/savings one has made when producing it □ *Any increase in the wage bill will of course be passed on to our customers.*

◇ *vi* = **pass away.**

◆ **pass out** *vi* **-1.** [person] to faint □ *I nearly passed out with the pain.* **-2.** GB MILITARY [person] to finish training at a military school.

◆ **pass over** *vt fus* to pass over sthg [subject, incident] to try not to talk about sthg □ *I think we should pass over the events of last night.*

◆ **pass round** *vt sep* = **pass around.**

◆ **pass to** *vt fus* to pass to sb [property, title, ownership] to be given to sb, especially because another person has died □ *The title now passes to his son.*

◆ **pass up** *vt sep* to pass up sthg [chance, invitation, offer] to fail to take advantage of sthg □ *You can't pass up an opportunity like this!*

passable [US 'pæsəbl, GB 'pɑːs-] *adj* -1. [attempt, imitation, work] that is good enough □ *At least you made a passable effort.* -2. [road, path, route] that is not blocked and can be used □ *The track's only passable with a jeep.*

passably [US 'pæsəblɪ, GB 'pɑːs-] *adv* -1. *see* **passable** □ *He performed passably.* -2. **passably well** quite well.

passage ['pæsɪdʒ] *n* -1. [between rooms, houses] a long narrow space that connects rooms, houses etc □ *He ran swiftly up the passage.* -2. [through a crowd] a space that allows one to move through something □ *He forced a passage through the crowd.* -3. ANATOMY a tube in one's body that air or liquid passes through □ *the nasal passages.* -4. [in a piece of music, writing] a short part of something □ *This is one of my favorite passages.* -5. [between situations, places] the progress of somebody or something from one place or situation to another (formal use) □ *the passage from adolescence to adulthood* □ *the passage of time.* -6. [in a ship] a trip in a ship □ *a sea passage.*

passageway ['pæsɪdʒweɪ] *n* a long narrow space that connects rooms, buildings etc.

passbook [US 'pæsbʊk, GB 'pɑːs-] *n* a book given to somebody who has an account at a building and loan association in which they record how much money they put into and take out of the account.

passé [US pæ'seɪ, GB 'pæseɪ] *adj* [style, clothing] that is no longer fashionable (disapproving use).

passenger ['pæsɪndʒər] *n* a person traveling in a car, boat, plane etc but who is not driving or working on it □ *Passengers are requested to remain with their vehicles.*

passerby [US ˌpæsər'baɪ, GB ˌpɑːsə-] (*pl* **passersby** [US ˌpæsərz-, GB ˌpɑːsəz-]) *n* a person who is walking past a place at a particular moment, especially when an accident, a crime etc happens there □ *A passerby was injured in the shooting.* □ *an innocent passerby.*

passing [US 'pæsɪŋ, GB 'pɑːs-] ◇ *adj* [phase, thought] that only lasts for a short time; [remark, comment] that is made while one is talking about a different subject □ *just a passing fancy.* ◇ *n* **the passing of time/the years** the process of time/the years happening and becoming part of the past □ *I feel less angry now, with the passing of the years.*

◆ **in passing** *adv* [say, note] while one is talking or writing about something else □ *I only mention it in passing.*

passion ['pæʃn] *n* -1. strong romantic or sexual feelings □ *the passion she felt for this shy*

young man □ *The object of his passion, meanwhile, remained unaware of his existence.* -2. strong feelings of love, hatred, anger etc □ *Chris spoke with passion of the suffering endured by the prisoners.* -3. **to have a passion for sthg** to like and enjoy sthg very much □ *Martin has a great passion for opera.*

◆ **Passion** *n* **the Passion** the final suffering and death of Jesus Christ.

◆ **passions** *npl* strong feelings and beliefs about what is right and wrong □ *Passions were roused during the debate.*

passionate ['pæʃnət] *adj* -1. [person] who has strong sexual or romantic feelings □ *a passionate kiss.* -2. [supporter] who has very strong feelings or beliefs about what is right and wrong □ *a passionate speech.*

passionately ['pæʃnətlɪ] *adv* [kiss, embrace, speak] *see* **passionate** □ *Jay was passionately fond of music.*

passion fruit *n* a small fruit with a hard dark purple skin, juicy orange and green flesh, and lots of seeds.

passive ['pæsɪv] ◇ *adj* -1. [person] who accepts what happens to them without expressing any strong feelings, especially when they should complain □ *passive acceptance of the situation* □ *You're too passive for your own good.* -2. GRAMMAR [verb, construction] that has as its subject the person or thing to which the action is done, e.g. The man was bitten by the dog. ◇ *n* **the passive** GRAMMAR the passive form of a verb.

passively ['pæsɪvlɪ] *adv* [accept, behave] *see* **passive.**

passive resistance *n* protest against something done in a way which involves no violence, e.g. by holding a peaceful demonstration or refusing to eat.

passive smoking *n* the act of breathing in the smoke from other people's cigarettes, pipes etc when one is not smoking oneself.

passivity [pæ'sɪvətɪ] *n* [of a person] *see* **passive.**

passkey [US 'pæskiː, GB 'pɑːs-] *n* -1. a key that opens a particular door or gate and is given only to the people who have permission to use it. -2. a key that can open several different locks.

Passover [US 'pæsoʊvr, GB 'pɑːsoʊvə] *n* (**the**) **Passover** a holiday in the Jewish religion at the end of March or beginning of April which is held to remember the escape of the Jews from Egypt.

passport [US 'pæspɔːrt, GB 'pɑːspɔːt] *n* -1. an official document in the form of a small book that proves who somebody is and is needed to enter and leave countries □ *Will we have to show our passports?* -2. **a passport to sthg** [to fame, success, a job] something that gives somebody sthg they want □ *A good education is not an automatic passport to a good career.*

passport control *n* the place at an airport or port where passengers must show their passports before being allowed to enter or leave the country.

password [US 'pæswɜːrd, GB 'pɑːswɜːd] *n* a secret word or phrase which one has to know to be allowed to enter a place or use a computer.

past [US pæst, GB pɑːst] ◇ *adj* **-1. the week/ month etc** the week/month etc before the present one □ *The past five years have seen a huge increase in the sales of CD players.* □ *His condition has improved in the past 24 hours.* □ *I've been abroad for the past two years.* **-2. a past government/president/owner** one of the governments/presidents/owners before the present one □ *He blamed past mayors of the city for failing to tackle the problem.* **-3.** [life, behavior, experience] that happened before the present one □ *I've learned from past experience not to trust them.* □ *Past attempts to attract foreign companies to the area have been unsuccessful.* **-4.** [difficulties, success, crisis] that is finished and no longer exists □ *Ben liked to remember his past triumphs on the tennis court.* □ *We hid in the cellar until the danger was past.*
◇ *prep* **-1. it's five/twenty past two** it's five/ twenty minutes after two o'clock □ *The plane is due in at half past eight.* **-2. to go past sb/ sthg** to go up to sb/sthg and continue in the same direction □ *A long line of people filed slowly past the coffin.* □ *I drove straight past the house and had to turn back.* **-3. to be past sthg** to be farther on than sthg □ *It's on the next block, just past the traffic lights.* **-4.** phrases **to be past it** to be too old to be able to do sthg (informal use) □ *Of course I'll dance, I'm not quite past it yet!* ■ **I wouldn't put it past him** I wouldn't be surprised if he did something like that, because it is typical of the way he behaves (informal and disapproving use) □ *I wouldn't put it past Emma to have invited her ex!*
◇ *adv* **-1. to walk/drive etc past** to walk/ drive etc to a person or place and continue in the same direction one is going □ *I saw her in the corridor, but she hurried past without saying anything.* **-2. a quarter/half past** fifteen/ thirty minutes after a particular hour □ *"What's the time?" — "Half past."*
◇ *n* **-1. the past** what has happened before now; the time before now □ *You must forget the past.* □ *In the past we've tended to buy our equipment, but now we lease it.* **-2. sb's past** what has happened to sb before the present □ *There was one incident in his past that he was still ashamed of.* □ *She has a colorful past.*

pasta [US 'pɑːstə, GB 'pæstə] *n* a type of food from Italy made from a mixture of flour, eggs, and water, cut into various shapes and then boiled □ *They ate pasta for lunch.* □ *a pasta dish.*

paste [peɪst] ◇ *n* **-1.** a soft mixture of a powder and a liquid that can be shaped or spread □ *Add the water and mix into a thin paste.* **-2. meat/salmon etc paste** meat/salmon etc that has been crushed with other ingredients so that it can be spread, e.g. on bread. **-3.** [for sticking paper] a type of glue containing water that is used for sticking paper together or to other surfaces □ *wallpaper paste.* **-4.** [for making jewelery] shiny glass that is designed to look like real jewels. ◇ *vt* to

stick <paper> to a surface using paste □ *Paste it onto the board.*

pastel [US pæ'stel, GB 'pæstl] ◇ *adj* [color, shade] that looks pale and soft □ *pastel blue.* ◇ *n* **-1.** a pale and soft color □ *The room was decorated in pastels.* **-2.** ART a small stick of a substance made from colored powder and gum that is used for drawing □ *a pastel drawing.*

paste-up *n* PRINTING a sheet of paper with printed text, pictures etc stuck to it that is used for photographing or for showing how a page will look when the magazine, book etc is printed.

Pasteur [pæ'stɜːʳ], **Louis** (1822–1895) a French scientist who invented the technique of pasteurizing milk to destroy harmful bacteria.

pasteurize, -ise [US 'pæstʃəraɪz, GB 'pɑːs-] *vt* to heat <milk or cream> using a special process in order to destroy the bacteria in it.

pastiche [pæ'stiːʃ] *n* a piece of writing or music whose style is deliberately copied from the work of another writer or composer.

pastille ['pæstl] *n* a hard round candy often containing medicine to treat sore throats and coughs.

pastime [US 'pæstaɪm, GB 'pɑːs-] *n* an activity which one does for pleasure in one's spare time □ *One of his favorite pastimes was going out fishing on the river.*

pastor [US 'pæstər, GB 'pɑːstə] *n* a religious leader in some Protestant churches.

pastoral [US 'pæstrəl, GB 'pɑːst-] *adj* **-1.** [visit, duty] that is connected with taking care of the needs and problems of people □ *Teachers have an increasingly important pastoral role in schools.* **-2.** [scene, poem] that shows or describes simple and peaceful country life.

past participle *n* a part of a verb used to form perfect or passive tenses and sometimes used as an adjective □ *"Taken" is the past participle of "to take".*

pastrami [pə'strɑːmɪ] *n* smoked beef with strong seasoning.

pastry ['peɪstrɪ] (*pl* **pastries**) *n* a mixture of flour, fat, and milk or water baked and used to make pies, tarts etc; a small cake made with this mixture □ *an apricot pastry* □ *a pastry case.*

past tense *n* the tense used in grammar to talk about things that took place before the time at which one is writing or speaking.

pasture [US 'pæstʃr, GB 'pɑːstʃə] *n* grassy land where animals such as cattle feed □ *a landscape of green pastures.*

pastureland [US 'pæstʃrlænd, GB 'pɑːstʃə-] *n* an area of grassy land where animals such as cattle feed.

pasty¹ ['peɪstɪ] (*compar* **pastier**, *superl* **pastiest**) *adj* [face] that looks pale and unhealthy □ *a pale pasty complexion.*

pasty² ['pæstɪ] (*pl* **pasties**) *n* GB a small pie that usually consists of pieces of meat and potato wrapped in pastry □ *a meat pasty.*

pasty-faced ['peɪstɪfeɪst] *adj* [person] who looks pale and unhealthy.

pat [pæt] (*compar* **patter**, *superl* **pattest**, *pt* & *pp* **patted**, *cont* **patting**) ◇ *adj* [answer, reply, explanation] that is not convincing because it is too simple and sounds as if it has been said or used before (disapproving use).
◇ *adv* **to have sthg off pat** [answer, words] to have memorized sthg exactly.
◇ *n* **-1.** a light and friendly touch with one's hand held flat □ *She gave the horse a pat.* **-2. a pat of butter** a small lump of butter.
◇ *vt* to touch <a person or an animal> lightly once or several times with the flat part of one's hand, usually to show that one is friendly or sympathetic □ *"Well done," she said, patting him on the back.* □ *Don't pat the dog, he bites.*

Patagonia [,pætə'goʊnjə] the region at the southern tip of South America, covering parts of Chile and Argentina.

patch [pætʃ] ◇ *n* **-1.** [for clothes] a piece of material used to cover a hole in something □ *jeans with patches over the knees.* **-2.** = **eyepatch. -3.** [of fog, damp] a small area of something which looks different from the parts around it □ *There are damp patches on the wall.* □ *a bald patch* □ *There will be patches of fog in the south.* **-4.** [of land, soil] a small piece of ground, often used for growing vegetables □ *a strawberry patch.* **-5. a bad** OR **difficult patch** a period of time during which one has many troubles and difficulties □ *I've been going through a bad patch recently.*
◇ *vt* [hole, tear, trousers] to mend <sthg> by putting a patch on it.
♦ **patch together** *vt sep* **to patch sthg together** to form or make sthg which is not perfect but which is as good as it can be □ *The deal was patched together at the last minute.*
♦ **patch up** *vt sep* **-1. to patch sthg up** [wall, car] to repair sthg roughly and quickly □ *The doctors patched me up and sent me home.* **-2. to patch up a relationship** to make one's relationship with somebody friendly again after a quarrel □ *The couple are now trying to patch up their differences.* ■ **to patch up a quarrel** to end a quarrel and become friends again.

patchwork ['pætʃwɜːʳk] ◇ *adj* [quilt, skirt] that is made with many different pieces of material sewn together. ◇ *n* something that consists of pieces of different shapes and colors □ *a patchwork of fields.*

patchy ['pætʃɪ] (*compar* **patchier**, *superl* **patchiest**) *adj* **-1.** [fog, sunshine] that appears in patches and not evenly or regularly □ *Tomorrow will be mostly sunny with patchy cloud toward evening.* **-2.** [knowledge] that is not enough to be useful or reliable. **-3.** [performance, game, quality] that is good in parts only.

pâté [US pæ'teɪ, GB 'pæteɪ] *n* food made by crushing meat, fish, or vegetables into a soft mass □ *liver pâté.*

patent [US 'pætnt, GB 'peɪt-] ◇ *adj* [nonsense, lie] obvious □ *his patent dislike of the idea.* ◇ *n* a document from a government office which gives a person or company the right to be the only one that can make or sell a new in-

vention for a fixed number of years □ *TCI has the patent to the new process.* □ *'Patent pending.'*
◇ *vt* [idea, invention] to obtain a patent for <sthg> □ *The device was patented in 1857.*

patented [US 'pætntəd, GB 'peɪt-] *adj* [invention] that has been given a patent.

patentee [US ,pætn'tiː, GB ,peɪt-] *n* the person or company that has the exclusive right to make or sell a new invention.

patent leather *n* very shiny leather used especially to make shoes and handbags □ *patent-leather shoes.*

patently ['peɪtntlɪ] *adv* **patently obvious/dishonest** obvious/dishonest in a way that is very clear or easy to see □ *It's patently clear you know nothing about the subject.* □ *She was patently lying.*

Patent Office *n* **the Patent Office** in Britain and the USA, the government department responsible for giving patents to new inventions.

paternal [pə'tɜːʳnl] *adj* **-1.** [love, attitude] that is typical of a father's behavior toward his child. **-2. one's paternal grandmother/uncle** one's grandmother/uncle who is the mother/brother of one's father.

paternalistic [pə,tɜːʳnə'lɪstɪk] *adj* [attitude, society] that treats a person like a child (disapproving use).

paternity [pə'tɜːʳnətɪ] *n* the fact of being the father of a particular child.

paternity leave *n* a period of time when a man does not have to work but can stay at home because his child has just been born.

paternity suit *n* an attempt to prove in law that a man is the father of a particular child, especially in order to get financial support from him.

Paterson ['pætəʳsən], **Andrew Barton** (1864–1941) an Australian poet who wrote the words to *Waltzing Matilda*. His nickname was Banjo Paterson.

path [US pæθ, *pl* pæðz, GB pɑːθ, *pl* pɑːðz] *n* **-1.** a track for walking along □ *A narrow path led up to the house.* □ *a gravel path* □ *They beat a path through the jungle.* **-2. sb's path** the space in front of sb as they move forward □ *The protesters tried to block his path.* ■ **our paths had crossed before** we had already met □ *Their paths first crossed when they were both students at Harvard.* **-3.** [of a car, missile, hurricane] the line that something travels along as it moves forward □ *The fire had destroyed everything that lay in its path.* **-4.** [to success, peace, ruin] a course of action or way to achieve something □ *Decentralization is the path to economic growth, according to the Department of Labor.* □ *His career has followed an unusual path.*

pathetic [pə'θetɪk] *adj* **-1.** [story, sight] that makes somebody feel sadness or pity □ *the pathetic sound of children crying.* **-2.** [attempt, excuse, person] that is very bad or useless and makes other people feel angry or annoyed □ *Don't be so pathetic.*

pathetically [pə'θetɪklɪ] *adv* **-1.** [cry, struggle] *see* pathetic. -2. **pathetically weak/thin** extremely weak/thin □ *The crowd was pathetically small.*

pathological [ˌpæθəˈlɒdʒɪkl] *adj* -1. MEDICINE [condition, change] that is connected with pathology. -2. [fear, urge] that is extreme and cannot be controlled □ *He's a pathological liar.*

pathologist [pəˈθɒlədʒəst] *n* a doctor who studies diseases and who examines dead bodies to find out the cause of death.

pathology [pəˈθɒlədʒɪ] *n* the study of disease.

pathos [ˈpeɪθɒs] *n* something in a situation that makes people feel sadness and pity.

pathway [US ˈpæθweɪ, GB ˈpɑːθ-] *n* a path for walking along.

patience [ˈpeɪʃns] *n* -1. the ability to deal with difficulties or delays for a long time without becoming annoyed □ *You need patience and luck to succeed.* □ *He finally lost his patience.* □ *I've got no patience with you any more.* ■ **to try sb's patience** to annoy sb so much that it is difficult for them not to become angry. -2. GB CARDS a card game for one player.

patient [ˈpeɪʃnt] ◇ *adj* [person] who shows patience □ *Be patient: I'm sure you'll hear soon.* ◇ *n* a person getting treatment from a doctor □ *I'm one of Dr Nathan's patients.*

patiently [ˈpeɪʃntlɪ] *adv* [wait, answer] *see* **patient** □ *She listened patiently while he explained.*

patina [US pəˈtiːnə, GB ˈpætɪnə] *n* -1. [on copper, bronze] a green layer that forms naturally on the surface of copper or bronze. -2. [on wood, leather] an attractive, shiny layer that forms on the surface of something, especially wood, as it gets older or is handled a lot.

patio [ˈpætɪoʊ] (*pl* **patios**) *n* an open area with a paved surface next to a house, where people can sit, relax, eat etc in fine weather.

patio doors *npl* glass doors that lead from a house onto a patio.

patisserie [pəˈtiːsərɪ] *n* a shop which sells cakes and pastries.

Patna rice [ˈpætnə-] *n* a kind of rice grown in Patna in India that has long grains.

patois [ˈpætwɑː] (*pl* **patois**) *n* a form of a language spoken by people in a particular area and which is different from the national language in some aspects of grammar, pronunciation etc.

patriarch [ˈpeɪtrɪɑːᵣk] *n* the male head of a family or group.

patriarchy [ˈpeɪtrɪɑːᵣkɪ] (*pl* **patriarchies**) *n* a system in which men rather than women have all the power in society; a society where this system exists.

patrimony [US ˈpætrəmoʊnɪ, GB -ɪmənɪ] *n* possessions inherited from one's father or ancestors (formal use).

patriot [US ˈpeɪtrɪət, GB ˈpætr-] *n* a person who loves their country and is willing to defend it.

patriotic [US ˌpeɪtrɪˈɒtɪk, GB ˌpætr-] *adj* [person] who loves their country □ *I've never felt particularly patriotic.* □ *patriotic songs* □ *It is your patriotic duty to fight for your country.*

patriotism [US ˈpeɪtrɪətɪzm, GB ˈpætr-] *n* love for one's country □ *a sense of patriotism.*

patrol [pəˈtroʊl] (*pt* & *pp* **patrolled**, *cont* **patrolling**) ◇ *n* -1. [of police, soldiers] a small group of people who move around a particular place or area to make sure there is no trouble □ *A police patrol arrived.* -2. the act of patrolling an area. ■ **to be on patrol** to be patrolling an area. ◇ *vt* [city, streets, border] to move around an area to make sure there is no trouble or illegal activity □ *Security guards patrol the grounds regularly.*

patrol car *n* a car used by the police for patrolling streets.

patrolman [pəˈtroʊlmən] (*pl* **patrolmen** [-mən]) *n* US a policeman who patrols a particular area.

patrol wagon *n* US a vehicle used by the police for carrying prisoners.

patrolwoman [pəˈtroʊlwʊmən] (*pl* **patrolwomen**) *n* US a policewoman who patrols a particular area.

patron [ˈpeɪtrən] *n* -1. a person or organization that supports writers, painters, musicians etc, especially by giving them money □ *a patron of the arts.* -2. GB [of a charity, campaign] a well-known person who supports a good cause and allows their name to be used to promote it □ *Our patron is Princess Mathilde.* -3. [of a bar, store, hotel] a customer (formal use) □ *'Parking lot for use of patrons only.'*

patronage [ˈpeɪtrənɪdʒ] *n* financial support given by a patron □ *The Trust flourished under the patronage of Vic Murray.*

patronize, -ise [US ˈpeɪtrənaɪz, GB ˈpætr-] *vt* -1. [person] to pretend to be pleasant to <sb> in a way which shows that one thinks one is better than them (disapproving use) □ *Don't let him patronize you.* -2. [store, business] to be a customer of <sthg> (formal use). -3. [arts, artist] to give money to <sb/sthg> to support them (formal use).

patronizing [US ˈpeɪtrənaɪzɪŋ, GB ˈpætr-] *adj* [smile, attitude] that shows that a person thinks they are superior to somebody (disapproving use) □ *He is so patronizing.*

patron saint *n* a Christian saint believed to give special protection to a particular place, activity, or group of people □ *St George, the patron saint of England.*

patter [ˈpætəᵣ] ◇ *n* -1. [of feet, rain] the sound of something hitting a hard surface lightly and repeatedly □ *She listened to the soft patter of rain against the window.* -2. [of a salesman, comedian] the quick way of talking of somebody who has rehearsed what they want to say □ *He launched into the usual salesman's patter.* ◇ *vi* [feet, rain] to make the sound of something hitting a hard surface lightly and repeatedly □ *The rain pattered against the glass.*

pattern [ˈpætəᵣn] ◇ *n* -1. [on wallpaper, a rug, a piece of clothing] a decorative arrangement of lines, shapes, colors etc that is repeated regularly on a surface □ *The lines formed a delightful pattern.* □ *The carpet had a kind of swirly orange pattern on it.* -2. [of events, somebody's

behavior] the way that something is organized or usually happens □ *Her moods follow a set pattern.* □ *Work patterns have changed enormously in the twentieth century.* □ *There seems to be no pattern to the results/crimes.* -3. [for making things] a set of diagrams and instructions which explain how to make something □ *a dress/knitting pattern.* -4. [for other people, countries] a person, thing, or system that is very good and is worth copying □ *Some people think constitutional democracy should be the pattern for all governments.*
◇ **vt to be patterned after sthg** to be made or formed by copying sthg □ *The campaign is patterned after the one successfully adopted at the last election.*

patterned ['pætərnd] *adj* [fabric, dress, shirt] that has a pattern on it.

Patton ['pætn], **G. S.** (1885–1945) a US general who helped to liberate France and Italy during World War II.

patty ['pætɪ] (*pl* **patties**) *n* -1. a small pie. -2. food formed into a small flat piece and cooked.

paucity ['pɔːsətɪ] *n* **a paucity of sthg** [of ideas, imagination] less of sthg than is needed (formal use).

Pauling ['pɔːlɪŋ], **Linus** (1901–1994) a US scientist who won the Nobel Prize for chemistry and the Nobel Peace Prize.

paunch [pɔːntʃ] *n* a man's fat stomach.

paunchy ['pɔːntʃɪ] (*compar* **paunchier**, *superl* **paunchiest**) *adj* [man] who has a fat stomach.

pauper ['pɔːpəʳ] *n* a very poor person.

pause [pɔːz] ◇ *n* a short break, when somebody stops talking or doing something □ *There was a pause in the conversation.* ◇ *vi* to stop speaking or doing something for a very short period of time □ *He paused before entering.* □ *Claire paused for breath.*

pave [peɪv] *vt* [street, courtyard] to cover <an area of ground> with a hard surface of flat stones or concrete □ *The floor was paved with granite.* ■ **to pave the way for sb/sthg** to do something which will make it easier for sb to be successful/for sthg to happen in the future □ *The ceasefire last year paved the way for discussions.*

paved [peɪvd] *adj* [street, courtyard] that is covered with a hard surface of flat stones or concrete so that people can walk on it.

pavement ['peɪvmənt] *n* -1. US [of a road] the surface of a road. -2. GB [next to a road] a paved path at the side of a road for people to walk on.

pavement artist *n* GB a person who draws pictures with colored chalk on the pavement so that people passing by will give them money.

pavilion [pə'vɪlɪən] *n* -1. a large temporary structure such as a tent, used for exhibitions and other public events. -2. GB a building at the edge of a sports field for players to change their clothes and wash in.

paving ['peɪvɪŋ] *n* material used for paving a surface; a paved surface or area.

paving stone *n* a flat piece of stone that is placed side by side with other stones to make a hard surface to walk on.

Pavlov ['pævlɒv], **Ivan Petrovich** (1849–1936) a Russian scientist, famous for his experiments with dogs. He rang a bell every time a dog was fed, until the dog thought of food when it heard the bell.

pavlova [US pɑːv'loʊvə, GB pæv-] *n* a dessert made of meringue with fruit and cream on top.

paw [pɔː] ◇ *n* the foot of an animal □ *a rabbit's paw* □ *The dog held up its paw.* ◇ *vt* -1. [animal] to touch or rub <the ground, a door> etc with a front foot □ *The dog was pawing the door pathetically.* -2. [person] to touch/stroke <sb> for sexual pleasure, usually when they do not want to be touched (disapproving use).

pawn [pɔːn] ◇ *n* -1. GAMES the least valuable piece in chess. -2. **to be a pawn** to be used by a more powerful person or organization for their own advantage □ *He was just a pawn in a much larger political game.* ◇ *vt* [watch, ring] to leave <sthg> with a pawnbroker.

pawnbroker ['pɔːnbroʊkəʳ] *n* a person to whom one can lend possessions in return for money, but who can sell those possessions if one does not repay the money within a fixed period of time.

pawnshop ['pɔːnʃɒp] *n* the place where a pawnbroker works.

pay [peɪ] (*pt* & *pp* **paid**) ◇ *vt* -1. [cost, debt, fine] to give the amount of money that is owed for <sthg> □ *He paid his fare and boarded the bus.* □ *Children pay half price.* □ *I paid $20 for that ticket!* □ *Are you paying cash?* ■ **to pay one's way** to pay for the things that one does or uses rather than letting somebody else pay. -2. [worker, staff] to give money to <sb> in return for services or goods they have provided or for work they have done □ *She paid the cashier for the fruit and left.* □ *How much do you get paid?* -3. **to pay money/a check into a bank account** to put money/a check into a bank where it is kept safe □ *I paid the check in yesterday.* -4. [person] to be profitable or advantageous to <sb> □ *It will pay you not to tell anybody about all this.* □ *It won't pay you to sell just now.* -5. **to pay sb a compliment/visit etc** to compliment/visit etc sb □ *I'd like to pay you a visit tomorrow.* □ *He paid me the honor of recommending me to them.* ◇ *vi* -1. to give money for services or goods provided or for work done □ *How would you like to pay?* □ *I'd like to pay by check.* □ *I'll pay for the taxi.* -2. to bring one money □ *This kind of work pays very well.* -3. to bring one advantages or benefits □ *It pays to be honest.* □ *Crime doesn't pay.* -4. to suffer as a result of something one has done □ *I'll make you pay for what you've done!* □ *He paid for his mistake with his life.* ■ **to pay dearly for sthg** to suffer a lot as a result of sthg one has done. ◇ *n* the money a person receives for the work they do □ *The job's interesting, but the pay's terrible.*

◆ **pay back** *vt sep* -1. **to pay sb back** to give

back to sb money that one has borrowed □ *I finished paying the loan back this year.* □ *I'll pay you back as soon as I can.* ■ **to pay a sum of money back** to give back to somebody a sum of money that one has borrowed □ *I finished paying the loan back this year.* □ *I'd already paid them back $100.* **-2. to pay sb back for sthg** to make sb suffer in return for sthg unpleasant that they have done to one.

◆ **pay off** ◇ *vt sep* **-1. to pay sthg off** [debt] to pay the whole amount of sthg that one owes □ *It took me three years to pay off my student loan.* **-2. to pay sb off** [employee] to pay sb what one owes them and dismiss them from a job □ *Half the staff were paid off and asked to leave.* **-3. to pay sb off** [informer, blackmailer] to give sb money to stop them talking about something wrong or illegal that somebody has done □ *Mr Cousins was reportedly paid off with a large bribe.* ◇ *vi* [plan, tactic] to be successful despite a strong risk of failure □ *It's a risk, but it might just pay off for us.*

◆ **pay out** *vt sep* **-1. to pay money out** to spend a lot of money for something □ *We paid out an enormous sum to have that built.* □ *I've paid out a lot of money for that van.* **-2. to pay out a rope/cable** to let go of a rope/cable gradually so that more of it is used.

◆ **pay up** *vi* to give somebody all the money that one owes them, usually without wanting to.

payable ['peɪəbl] *adj* **-1.** [bill, debt, loan] that can or must be paid □ *The installments are payable at the end of each month.* **-2. to make a check payable to sb** to write sb's name on a check in order for the money to be paid to them □ *Checks should be made payable to Acme Inc.*

pay as you earn *n* → PAYE.

paybed ['peɪbed] *n* GB a bed in a hospital owned by the state which is paid for privately by the person occupying it.

paycheck US, **paycheque** GB ['peɪtʃek] *n* **-1.** a check for somebody's salary. **-2.** the money a person is paid regularly by an employer.

payday ['peɪdeɪ] *n* the day on which a person is paid their salary or wages.

PAYE (*abbr of* **pay as you earn**) *n* a system, used in Britain and New Zealand, of taking employees' income tax and National Insurance contributions out of their wages before they are paid.

payee [peɪ'iː] *n* the person to whom money, usually in the form of a check, should be paid.

pay envelope *n* US an envelope containing a person's salary.

payer ['peɪəʳ] *n* a person or organization that pays □ *They're slow/good payers.*

paying guest [ˌpeɪɪŋ-] *n* a person who pays money to stay in somebody else's house.

paying-in book *n* GB a book containing slips to fill in when one pays money or a check into one's bank account.

payload ['peɪloʊd] *n* **-1.** [of a vehicle] the part of a load carried by a vehicle which has to be paid for. **-2.** [of a missile] the amount of ex-

plosive in a missile. **-3.** [of a spacecraft] the equipment carried on a spacecraft.

paymaster [US 'peɪmæstr, GB -mɑːstə] *n* a person in a government, company etc responsible for paying wages.

Paymaster General *n* **the Paymaster General** a member of the British government who is in charge of the department that makes payments to other government departments.

payment ['peɪmənt] *n* **-1.** the act of paying or of being paid □ *Payment was delayed by a month.* □ *We don't take credit cards. Do you have any other method of payment?* **-2.** an amount of money that is paid □ *I'm making annual payments of over $1,000.*

payoff ['peɪɒf] *n* **-1.** the good or advantageous result of an action □ *One of the payoffs of emigrating was a better standard of living.* **-2.** a sum of money that one gives to somebody so that they will not cause trouble □ *He was given a large payoff.*

payola [peɪ'oʊlə] *n* a secret payment made to somebody for a business favor (informal use).

pay packet *n* GB **-1.** the envelope containing a person's wages or salary, given to them every week or month. **-2.** the amount of money that a person earns □ *Workers' pay packets have been hit hard this winter.*

pay phone *n* a phone in a public place that one puts coins into before using it.

payroll ['peɪroʊl] *n* a list of the people employed by a company and the amount of money each person earns □ *They have 100 people on the payroll.*

payslip ['peɪslɪp] *n* a piece of paper given to an employee every week or month showing how much they have earned and how much tax and other contributions they have paid.

paystub ['peɪstʌb] *n* US = **payslip**.

pay TV *n* TV that viewers have to pay to watch, e.g. cable and satellite TV.

PBS (*abbr of* **Public Broadcasting Service**) *n* a US television company that does not broadcast advertisements. It is supported by contributions from the viewers, the government, and large companies.

PBX ['pæbeks] (*abbr of* **private branch exchange**) *n* a small telephone exchange in a company for internal communications or outside calls.

pc ◇ *n abbr of* **postcard**. ◇ *abbr of* **per cent**.

p/c *abbr of* **petty cash**.

PC ◇ *n* **-1.** *abbr of* **personal computer**. **-2.** *abbr of* **police constable** ◇ *adj abbr of* **politically correct**.

PCB *n abbr of* **printed circuit (board)**.

pcm *abbr of* **per calendar month**.

PCV (*abbr of* **passenger carrying vehicle**) *n* a vehicle used for public transportation in Britain.

pd *abbr of* **paid**.

PD *abbr of* **police department**.

pdq (*abbr of* **pretty damn quick**) *adv* an informal expression used by somebody asking for something to be done quickly.

PDSA (*abbr of* **People's Dispensary for Sick Animals**) *n* **the PDSA** a British charitable organization that offers free treatment for sick animals, usually pets.

PDT (*abbr of* **Pacific Daylight Time**) *n* the local summer time in the Pacific coastal region of the USA and Canada.

PE *n abbr of* **physical education** □ *a PE class.*

pea [piː] *n* one of several small, round, green seeds that grow in a pod and are cooked and eaten as a vegetable.

peace [piːs] *n* **-1.** [in a place] a state of calm and quiet □ *I need some peace!* □ *peace and quiet.* **-2.** [for a person] a state of freedom from worry or anxiety □ *Insurance coverage gives you peace of mind.* □ *a feeling of inner peace.* ■ **to be at peace with oneself/sthg** to be in a state of happiness and harmony with oneself/sthg. **-3.** [between countries] a period or state in which there is no war □ *30 years of uninterrupted peace* □ *Hopes for a peace settlement are fading.* **-4.** [between people] freedom from disorder or disagreement within a country, town, group of people etc. ■ **to make (one's) peace with sb** to end a disagreement or quarrel with sb.

peaceable ['piːsəbl] *adj* [person] who does not like to fight or argue.

peaceably ['piːsəblɪ] *adv* [live, agree] *see* **peaceable.**

Peace Corps *n* **the Peace Corps** a US organization that sends volunteers to developing countries to help with technical and educational projects.

peaceful ['piːsfl] *adj* **-1.** [garden, scene, atmosphere] quiet and without disturbance □ *It's so pleasant and peaceful here.* **-2.** [person, expression] calm and without worry or anxiety □ *Her face looked so peaceful as she slept.* **-3.** [people, demonstration] not violent or aggressive □ *a peaceful protest.*

peacefully ['piːsflɪ] *adv* [live, sleep] *see* **peaceful** □ *The demonstration ended peacefully.* □ *The old man died peacefully in his sleep.*

peacekeeping force ['piːskiːpɪŋ-] *n* a force or army sent into a country or area where there is a dispute to try to prevent violence □ *the UN peacekeeping force.*

peacemaker ['piːsmeɪkəʳ] *n* a person who tries to stop people or countries fighting by forcing them to discuss their problems.

peace offering *n* something pleasant that one says or gives to somebody whom one has annoyed as a way of apologizing (informal use).

peacetime ['piːstaɪm] *n* a period of time when a country is not fighting a war □ *It's the country's biggest civil engineering project during peacetime.*

peach [piːtʃ] ◇ *n* **-1.** a round fruit with yellow-pink skin, a large hard seed in the center, and soft, juicy, yellow flesh □ *a peach pie.* **-2.** a yellow-pink color. ◇ *adj* yellow-pink in color.

peach melba [-'melbə] *n* a dessert made with half a peach, vanilla ice cream, and raspberry sauce.

peacock ['piːkɒk] *n* a large male bird with long blue and green tail feathers that can be spread out like a fan.

peahen ['piːhen] *n* a female peacock.

peak [piːk] ◇ *n* **-1.** [of a mountain] the top of a mountain □ *a mountain peak.* **-2.** [of fitness, a season] the highest point or level of something that changes in value, amount etc □ *At the peak of his career he was earning $2 million a year.* **-3.** [of a cap] the part of a cap that sticks out over one's eyes. ◇ *adj* [condition, demand] that is at its highest level □ *an athlete in peak condition.* ◇ *vi* [temperature, demand] to reach its highest level □ *Sales peaked in December.* □ *The stock peaked at $4.20 a share.*

peaked ['piːkəd] *adj* US who looks pale and unwell (informal use).

peaked cap [,piːkt-] *n* a cap with a peak.

peak hours *npl* the hours when something, such as a restaurant or traffic on the roads, is at its busiest □ *Try to avoid traveling during peak hours.*

peak period *n* the period when something such as a hotel is at its busiest □ *Our peak period is between June and September.*

peak rate *n* the highest rate at which telephone calls are charged □ *You're calling at peak rate, remember.*

peaky ['piːkɪ] *adj* GB = **peaked.**

peal [piːl] ◇ *n* **-1.** [of bells] the sound of bells ringing loudly one after another. **-2.** [of laughter, thunder] a loud series of sounds. ◇ *vi* [bells] to sound loudly.

peanut ['piːnʌt] *n* a type of nut that grows underground and can be eaten raw or roasted and salted, or used to make oil.

peanut butter *n* a brown substance made with crushed peanuts that is spread on bread and eaten.

pear [peəʳ] *n* a juicy fruit with thin yellow-green skin, white flesh, a round bottom, and a narrow top.

pearl [pɜːʳl] *n* a small, round, silvery-white object found in oysters and used for making expensive jewelry □ *a pearl necklace.*

Pearl Harbor a US military base in Hawaii that was attacked by Japan in 1941. This attack caused the USA to enter World War II.

pearly ['pɜːʳlɪ] (*compar* **pearlier,** *superl* **pearliest**) *adj* [light, water] that looks shiny and silvery-white □ *beautiful pearly teeth.*

peasant ['peznt] *n* **-1.** a person who lives in the country and works on the land. **-2.** a person with little education (offensive use).

peasantry ['pezntrɪ] *n* **the peasantry** a collective term for all the peasants in a particular country.

peashooter ['piːʃuːtəʳ] *n* a small tube used as a toy by children for blowing objects such as dried peas at people or things.

peat [piːt] *n* dark-brown decaying vegetable matter found in wet areas of land, used as fuel on fires and on gardens to help plants grow better.

peaty ['pi:tɪ] (*compar* **peatier**, *superl* **peatiest**) *adj* [soil] that has a lot of peat in it.

pebble ['pebl] *n* a small, smooth, round stone.

pebbledash ['pebldæʃ] *n* GB a substance consisting of small stones in plaster for covering the outside walls of a house.

pecan (nut) [US pɪ'kɑ:n-, GB 'pi:kən-] *n* a sweet nut with a long, thin, reddish shell.

pecan pie *n* a dessert consisting of a pastry base filled with pecans, maple syrup, and other ingredients.

peck [pek] ◇ *n* -1. a light tap made by a bird with its beak. -2. a quick light kiss □ *She gave him a quick peck on the cheek.* ◇ *vt* -1. [bird] to strike <sb/sthg> with its beak. -2. [person] to give <sb> a quick light kiss. ◇ *vi* [bird] to make quick light movements forward with its beak □ *The hen pecked away at the seed.*

pecking order ['pekɪŋ-] *n* the order of importance of people within a particular social or professional group.

peckish ['pekɪʃ] *adj* **to be** OR **feel peckish** GB to be slightly hungry.

pectin ['pektən] *n* a sugary substance found in some ripe fruits and used in making jams and jellies to help them set.

pectoral ['pektərəl] *n* **the pectoral (muscle)** the muscle that is found in the top part of one's chest.

peculiar [pə'kju:lɪəʳ] *adj* -1. [shape, idea, remark] that is strange and often unpleasant or displeasing □ *I had a peculiar feeling.* □ *It's all very peculiar.* -2. **to feel peculiar** to feel unwell. -3. **to be peculiar to sb/sthg** to belong to or exist only in sb/sthg □ *It's a custom peculiar to this tribe.*

peculiarity [pə,kju:lɪ'ærətɪ] (*pl* **peculiarities**) *n* -1. a strange or unusual habit or characteristic □ *Smoking a pipe is one of her little peculiarities.* -2. something which is peculiar to a person, thing, period etc □ *Each area has its own special peculiarities.*

peculiarly [pə'kju:lɪəʳlɪ] *adv* -1. [behave, act] in a strange way □ *My companion was dressed very peculiarly.* -2. in a way that is peculiar to somebody or something □ *a peculiarly French custom.*

pecuniary [US pə'kju:nɪerɪ, GB -ɪərɪ] *adj* [gain, motives] financial (formal use).

pedagogical [,pedə'gɒdʒɪkl] *adj* [method, skill] that is connected with pedagogy (formal use).

pedagogy ['pedəgɒdʒɪ] *n* the study of the methods of teaching; the practice of teaching (formal use).

pedal ['pedl] (US *pt* & *pp* **pedaled**, *cont* **pedaling**, GB *pt* & *pp* **pedalled**, *cont* **pedalling**) ◇ *n* -1. [on a bicycle, moped] one of the two bars on a bicycle or moped that one pushes with one's feet to turn the wheels. -2. [in a car, on a piano] a bar or lever which is pressed with the foot to control a vehicle or machine □ *the accelerator/brake pedal* □ *the soft pedal of a piano.* ◇ *vi* to push the pedals of a bicycle

with one's feet to make it move forward □ *She pedaled frantically up the hill.*

pedal bin *n* GB a garbage can, usually in the kitchen, the top of which is opened by pressing a pedal with one's foot.

pedalo ['pedəlou] (*pl* **pedalos** OR **pedaloes**) *n* GB a small boat for two people which has to be pedaled, usually found at seaside resorts.

pedant ['pednt] *n* a pedantic person (disapproving use).

pedantic [pə'dæntɪk] *adj* [person] who pays too much attention to details or rules that are not important (disapproving use) □ *Oh, don't be so pedantic!*

pedantry ['pedntrɪ] *n* pedantic behavior (disapproving use).

peddle ['pedl] *vt* -1. **to peddle drugs** to sell illegal drugs □ *He was peddling cocaine to local residents.* -2. [secrets, lies] to try to spread <unpleasant or secret information>.

peddler ['pedləʳ] *n* -1. a person who sells illegal drugs □ *a drugs peddler.* -2. a person who travels from place to place selling small objects and goods.

pederast ['pedəræst] *n* a man who has sex with young boys.

pedestal ['pedəstl] *n* a base beneath a pillar or column. ■ **to put sb on a pedestal** to admire sb so much that one does not see their faults.

pedestrian [pə'destrɪən] ◇ *adj* [idea, performance] that is ordinary, shows little imagination, and is not at all interesting (disapproving use). ◇ *n* a person in a street who is walking, not traveling in a vehicle □ *'Pedestrians please use other sidewalk.'*

pedestrian crossing *n* a special place on a road where vehicles have to stop to allow pedestrians to cross.

pedestrianize, -ise [pə'destrɪənaɪz] *vt* to turn <part of a street or town> into an area where no vehicles are allowed.

pedestrian zone US, **pedestrian precinct** GB *n* a street or area for pedestrians only and which vehicles are not allowed to enter.

pediatric [,pi:dɪ'ætrɪk] *adj* [hospital, ward] that is connected with the treatment of children's diseases.

pediatrician [,pi:dɪə'trɪʃn] *n* a doctor who studies and treats children's diseases.

pediatrics [,pi:dɪ'ætrɪks] *n* the area of medicine that is concerned with children and their diseases.

pedicure ['pedɪkjʊəʳ] *n* a treatment of one's feet and toenails to make them look or feel better.

pedigree ['pedɪgri:] ◇ *adj* [dog, cat, cattle] that is of high quality because it is bred from specially chosen animals of the same breed □ *a pedigree spaniel.* ◇ *n* -1. [of a dog, cat] a list showing the father, mother, grandparents etc of an animal, especially as proof that it is a pure breed. -2. [of a person] a person's ancestry or background □ *Her political pedigree lay in the labor movement.*

pedlar ['pedlər] *n* GB = **peddler**.

pedophile ['piːdəfaɪl] *n* an adult person who is sexually attracted to young children.

pee [piː] (informal use) ◇ *n* -1. the act of urinating □ *I need a pee.* -2. urine. ◇ *vi* to urinate.

peek [piːk] (informal use) ◇ *vi* **to peek at sthg** to look at sthg quickly, especially when one is not supposed to see it □ *Hey! No peeking until I'm ready!* ◇ *n* **to have** OR **take a peek at sthg** to peek at sthg.

peel [piːl] ◇ *n* [of an apple, orange, potato] the skin on the outside of certain fruits or vegetables □ *orange peel.* ◇ *vt* [apple, orange, potato] to remove the peel from <a vegetable or piece of fruit>. ◇ *vi* [paint, wallpaper, skin] to come away and fall off a surface in small pieces or strips; [wall, fence] to lose its outer surface in small pieces or strips; [nose, back] to lose its skin in small pieces or strips □ *The windows were broken and the paint was peeling off the walls.* □ *I always peel after getting a suntan.*

◆ **peel off** *vt sep* -1. **to peel sthg off** [label, sticker, top] to pull sthg gently so that it comes off a surface in one piece. -2. **to peel off a piece of clothing** to take off a piece of clothing □ *He peeled off his tracksuit.*

Peel [piːl], **Sir Robert** (1788–1850) British prime minister from 1834 to 1835 and 1841 to 1846. He is famous for establishing the Metropolitan Police, who were nicknamed "peelers" or "bobbies" after him.

peeler ['piːlər] *n* a kitchen tool for peeling fruit and vegetables.

peelings ['piːlɪŋz] *npl* the pieces of skin peeled off fruit or vegetables □ *apple/potato peelings.*

peep [piːp] ◇ *n* -1. **to have** OR **take a peep** to look briefly at something □ *I had a peep at the manager's report.* -2. [of a bird, whistle] a short high-pitched sound. ■ **I haven't heard a peep out of him/them** he/they haven't made any noise. ◇ *vi* to look at something quickly and secretly, especially through a small hole or opening □ *She peeped through the keyhole.*

◆ **peep out** *vi* to appear □ *The sun peeped out from behind the clouds.*

peephole ['piːphoʊl] *n* a small hole or opening in a door, curtain etc through which one can watch secretly what is happening on the other side.

peeping Tom [,piːpɪŋ'tɒm] *n* a person who watches other people secretly when they are undressing.

peepshow ['piːpʃoʊ] *n* a type of show in which a man pays to watch a woman take off her clothes.

peer [pɪər] ◇ *n* -1. in Britain, a member of the aristocracy □ *Conservative peers.* -2. **one's peers** people of the same age, social class, education etc as one □ *It is always difficult to be judged by one's peers.* ◇ *vi* to look very carefully and hard, especially at something that is difficult to see □ *I peered through the window to see what was happening.*

peerage ['pɪərɪdʒ] *n* -1. the title of a peer □

The former minister was given a peerage. -2. **the peerage** all the peers of a country, considered as a group.

peeress [US 'pɪərəs, GB ,pɪər'es] *n* in Britain, a female member of the aristocracy.

peer group *n* people of the same age, social class, education etc.

peer pressure *n* the pressure to think and behave like others in one's peer group □ *There's a lot of peer pressure among students to drink heavily.*

peeved [piːvd] *adj* annoyed, irritated, or disappointed (informal use) □ *I was really peeved at not getting the job.*

peevish ['piːvɪʃ] *adj* [person] who is easily annoyed by unimportant things □ *a peevish remark/mood.*

peg [peg] (*pt* & *pp* **pegged**, *cont* **pegging**) ◇ *n* -1. a piece of wood or metal fixed to a wall or door, used for hanging coats, hats etc on □ *I hung my keys on the peg.* -2. GB a wooden or plastic device for attaching wet clothes to a washing line to dry; a wooden or metal pin that fastens or keeps something in place □ *a tent peg.* ◇ *vt* [price, inflation] to fix <sthg> at a particular level, especially so that it cannot increase.

◆ **peg out** *vt sep* **to peg washing** OR **clothes out** GB to fasten washing to a washing line with pegs to dry.

pegboard ['pegbɔːrd] *n* a board with holes that pegs fit into and from which posters, pictures etc can be hung and displayed.

PEI *abbr of* **Prince Edward Island**.

pejorative [pə'dʒɒrətɪv] *adj* [sense, word, comment] that expresses criticism, disapproval, or a low opinion of something □ *I don't think she meant it in a pejorative way.*

pekinese [,piːkə'niːz] (*pl* **pekinese** OR **pekineses**) *n* a small dog with long silky hair, short legs and tail, and a flat nose.

Peking [piː'kɪŋ] = **Beijing**.

pelican ['pelɪkən] (*pl* **pelican** OR **pelicans**) *n* a large white or brown water bird with a big bag under its beak which it uses for storing food in.

pelican crossing *n* GB a place on a road where traffic must stop when a red light shows to allow people to cross.

pellet ['pelət] *n* -1. [of mud, bread, paper] a small ball, usually made by rolling something soft between one's fingers. -2. [for a shotgun, airgun] a small metal ball made to be shot from a gun.

pell-mell [,pel'mel] *adv* [rush, run, fall] in a disorderly and uncontrolled way.

pelmet ['pelmət] *n* GB a narrow piece of wood or cloth at the top of a window, used as decoration and to hide the curtain rail.

pelt [pelt] ◇ *n* -1. the skin and fur of an animal □ *a fox pelt.* -2. **at full pelt** [run, drive] as fast as possible. ◇ *vt* to attack <sb> by throwing things at them □ *The comedian was pelted with rotten tomatoes.* ◇ *vi* -1. to rain very hard □ *It* OR *The rain was really pelting* down when I left. **-2.** to run very fast □ I saw him pelt along the corridor.

pelvic ['pelvɪk] adj [bones, surgery] in the area of the pelvis.

pelvis ['pelvəs] (pl **pelvises** OR **pelves** [-iːz]) n the set of bones at the bottom of one's spine that one's legs are connected to.

pen [pen] (pt & pp **penned**, cont **penning**) ◇ n **-1.** a long thin piece of plastic or metal used for writing in ink □ a black/red pen. **-2.** FARMING a small area enclosed by a fence for keeping farm animals in □ a sheep pen. ◇ vt **-1.** [letter, reply, note] to write <sthg> etc (literary use). **-2.** to shut animals in a pen; to force <people> to remain in a place, especially somewhere uncomfortable □ The passengers were penned (up) in the plane for hours.

penal ['piːnl] adj [system, reform] that is connected with the punishment of criminals.

penal colony n a place, e.g. on an island a long way from home, where criminals are sent as a punishment.

penalize, -ise ['piːnlaɪz] vt **-1.** to punish <sb> for breaking a rule or law □ The referee penalized the goalkeeper for wasting time. □ Dangerous driving should be penalized more heavily. **-2.** to put sb unfairly in an unfavorable or disadvantageous position □ The cuts in public transportation penalize people living in remote areas.

penalty ['penltɪ] (pl **penalties**) n **-1.** [for a crime] a punishment for breaking a law, failing to do a duty etc, such as imprisonment or a fine □ There will be financial penalties if the work is not completed in time. □ The penalty for speeding is $50. **-2.** [of success, failure] an unpleasant result of a person's situation or of something they have done □ That's the penalty for being famous. ■ **to pay the penalty** to suffer for something wrong that one has done □ I agree he made mistakes, but he certainly paid the penalty. **-3.** SPORT an advantage given to one team or player when the other side breaks a rule □ a ten-second penalty. ■ **a penalty (kick)** [in soccer] a free kick at the goal from a fixed point that only the goalkeeper is allowed to stop; [in rugby] a free kick that can be used to pass the ball, run with it, or kick at the goal.

penalty area, penalty box n the part of a soccer field in front of the goal, in which the goalkeeper is allowed to touch the ball with his hands.

penalty clause n a clause in a contract stating what the penalties, fines etc are if somebody does not do what the contract states.

penalty goal n a penalty kick in rugby; the points that are scored from this.

penalty kick n SPORT = **penalty**.

penalty rates npl AUS the amount of money paid to employees for working more than their normal hours.

penance ['penəns] n something that one does for somebody to show them that one is sorry for something bad that one has done.

pen-and-ink adj [drawing, sketch] drawn with a pen.

pence [pens] GB plural of **penny**.

penchant [US 'pentʃənt, GB 'pɒnʃɒn] n **to have a penchant for sthg** to like sthg very much.

pencil ['pensl] (US pt & pp **penciled**, cont **penciling**, GB pt & pp **pencilled**, cont **pencilling**) ◇ n a thin piece of wood containing a black or colored substance, used for writing or drawing □ a pencil drawing. ■ **in pencil** using a pencil □ Fill out the form in pencil. ◇ vt [notes, letters] to write or draw <sthg> using a pencil □ The nurse had penciled her initials at the bottom.

pencil case n a small box or bag for keeping pens, pencils etc in.

pencil sharpener n a device for sharpening a pencil.

pendant ['pendənt] n a piece of jewelry on a chain worn around the neck.

pending ['pendɪŋ] (formal use) ◇ adj **-1.** [review] that will happen soon □ An investigation is pending following rumors of corruption. **-2.** [court case, lawsuit] that is still waiting to be dealt with or decided □ We still have a court case pending. ◇ prep while waiting for <sthg> □ The suspect was held at the police station pending his appearance in court.

pending tray n GB a box on a desk for letters, forms etc which still have to be dealt with.

pendulum [US 'pendʒələm, GB -jʊl-] (pl **pendulums**) n a weight that hangs from the bottom of a clock and swings from side to side to make the clock work.

penetrate ['penətreɪt] ◇ vt **-1.** [building, defense] to get through or into <sthg that is difficult to get into> □ Our forces have penetrated enemy territory. □ Rainwater had penetrated the roof and damaged the walls. □ The bullet penetrated his lung. **-2.** [group, party] to get oneself accepted by <an organization> so that one can learn its secrets, gain an advantage etc □ FBI agents succeeded in penetrating the cartel. □ Our company is expanding and intends to penetrate the American market. ◇ vi [information, insult] to be understood and remembered (informal use).

penetrating ['penətreɪtɪŋ] adj **-1.** [scream, whistle, voice] loud and high-pitched □ a loud, penetrating scream. **-2.** [rain, wind] unpleasant because it gets through clothing, into buildings etc □ a cold, penetrating wind. **-3.** [gaze, look] that seems to see inside one's mind and understand one's thoughts □ She gave him a long penetrating look.

penetration [ˌpenə'treɪʃn] n **-1.** see **penetrate** □ Our trading position has improved thanks to greater penetration of overseas markets. **-2.** the ability to understand difficult things quickly and clearly (formal use).

pen friend n GB = **pen pal**.

penguin ['pengwɪn] n a black and white bird that cannot fly but can swim very well and is typically found in the Antarctic.

penicillin [ˌpenə'sɪlən] n a medicine that kills

bacteria, used to treat pneumonia and other diseases.

peninsula [US pə'nɪnsjələ, GB -jʊlə] (*pl* **peninsulas**) *n* a narrow piece of land that sticks out into the sea from a larger mass of land □ *the Korean/Italian/Iberian peninsula.*

penis ['piːnəs] (*pl* **penises**) *n* the part of a man's or male animal's body used for urinating and having sex.

penitent ['penətənt] *adj* [sinner, murderer] who is sincerely sorry for having done something wrong and is determined not to do it again (formal use).

penitentiary [,penə'tenʃərɪ] (*pl* **penitentiaries**) *n* US a prison □ *the state penitentiary.*

penknife ['pennaɪf] (*pl* **penknives** [-naɪvz]) *n* a small knife with a blade that folds back inside its handle.

Penn [pen], **William** (1644–1718) an English Quaker. He founded Pennsylvania.

pen name *n* a name that a writer uses on their books instead of their real name.

pennant ['penənt] *n* a long narrow flag, usually in the shape of a triangle, produced by sports teams for their fans, used for signaling on ships etc.

penniless ['penələs] *adj* very poor.

Pennines ['penaɪnz]: **the Pennines** a mountain range in central northern England. HIGHEST POINT: 893m.

Pennsylvania [,pensl'veɪnjə] a state in the northeastern USA. It is an important producer of coal and steel. ABBREVIATION: PA. SIZE: 117,400 sq kms. POPULATION: 11,881,643. CAPITAL: Harrisburg. OTHER MAJOR CITIES: Philadelphia, Pittsburgh.

Pennsylvania Dutch *npl* **the Pennsylvania Dutch** a group of German-speaking people who live in Pennsylvania. They are well-known for their cooking and their art.

penny ['penɪ] (*pl sense 1* **pennies**, *pl sense 2* **pence**) *n* -1. an American or Canadian coin worth one cent. -2. a small, brown, British coin worth one hundredth of a pound; the value of this coin □ *It cost 50 pence.* -3. *phrases* **a penny for your thoughts** a phrase used to ask somebody who is very quiet and thoughtful what they are thinking about. ▪ **the penny dropped** GB a phrase used to say that somebody has suddenly understood or realized something that they should have known before (informal use). ▪ **to be two** OR **ten a penny** GB to be extremely common and therefore easy to get and not interesting (informal use).

penny-pinching [-pɪntʃɪŋ] (disapproving use) ◇ *n* an unwillingness to spend money, especially when spending a little more would produce much better results. ◇ *adj*: *a penny-pinching policy/attitude.*

pen pal *n* a person, especially somebody in a foreign country, who one has come to know by exchanging regular friendly letters with them, but usually who one has never met.

pension ['penʃn] *n* a sum of money paid regu-

larly by the state, a finance company, or a former employer to somebody who no longer works, especially because they are old or ill □ *She gets a company/a widow's pension.* □ *pension contributions.*

◆ **pension off** *vt sep* **to pension sb off** [worker, staff] to make sb leave a job and give them a pension.

pensionable ['penʃnəbl] *adj* [age, job] that gives one the right to receive a pension.

pension book *n* GB a small book issued by the government to people who get a pension, containing slips of paper that can be exchanged for money at a post office.

pensioner ['penʃnər] *n* GB a person who has retired from work and gets a pension.

pension fund *n* a fund that employees pay money into and which is invested in order to pay them pensions when they retire.

pension plan *n* a financial plan that provides an employee with a pension after they and often their employer have paid money into it over a number of years.

pension scheme *n* GB = **pension plan**.

pensive ['pensɪv] *adj* [person, gaze] very thoughtful, especially in a sad or serious way.

pentagon ['pentəgɒn] *n* a flat shape with five sides.

◆ **Pentagon**: **the Pentagon** a large five-sided building in Virginia that is the headquarters of the US Department of Defense. Sometimes the term "the Pentagon" is used to mean the leaders of the US armed forces □ *The Pentagon has decided to take strong action.*

pentathlon [pen'tæθlən] (*pl* **pentathlons**) *n* a sports contest in which people compete in five sports: running, horseriding, swimming, shooting, and fencing.

Pentecost ['pentɪkɒst] *n* -1. a Christian festival on the seventh Sunday after Easter, celebrating the coming of the Holy Spirit to the apostles. -2. a Jewish festival 50 days after Passover, celebrating the harvest.

penthouse ['penthaʊs, *pl* -haʊzɪz] *n* an apartment or set of hotel rooms at the top of a tall building, usually expensive and luxurious □ *a penthouse suite/apartment.*

pent up ['pent-] *adj* [emotion, energy] that has been held back inside one and not freely expressed or released □ *I was full of pent up anger.*

penultimate [pə'nʌltəmət] *adj* [word, scene] that occurs before the last one in a series, list etc.

penury ['penjʊrɪ] *n* the state of being extremely poor (formal use) □ *They lived in penury.*

peony ['piːənɪ] (*pl* **peonies**) *n* a garden plant with large, round, red, pink, or white flowers.

people ['piːpl] ◇ *npl* -1. *plural of* **person** □ *How many people will be coming?* -2. people in general; all or most people □ *young/white people.* □ *There has been a change in people's attitudes to censorship.* □ *People don't realize how hard it is.* ▪ **people say that...** a phrase used to introduce information which is thought to be

true by most people □ *People say that there is going to be a strike.* **-3.** the people who live in a particular place □ *the people of Japan.* **-4.** the people who work at or represent a particular company or organization □ *I'll get onto the people at the State Department.* □ *Have your people contact mine.* **-5. the people** ordinary men and women in contrast to the government, aristocracy, church etc □ *Power to the people!*
◇ *n* a race or nation □ *the peoples of Asia* □ *the English-speaking peoples.*
◇ *vt* [area, city] to live in <a place> □ *The city is peopled by* OR *with both Arabs and Christians.*

pep [pep] (*pt* & *pp* **pepped,** *cont* **pepping**) *n* liveliness and energy (informal use).
◆ **pep up** *vt sep* **-1. to pep sb up** to make sb feel more lively and energetic □ *Have a drink — that'll pep you up!* **-2. to pep sthg up** [party, conference, event] to make sthg more lively and interesting □ *I put some salsa music on to pep things up.*

pepper ['pepər] *n* **-1.** hot-tasting powder made by crushing the dried seeds of certain plants, used to flavor foods □ *black/white pepper.* **-2.** a vegetable with shiny skin that is green, red, or yellow, is hollow inside, and is used in cooking or eaten raw in salads □ *a green/red/yellow/stuffed pepper.*

peppercorn ['pepəkɔːn] *n* a small seed that can be dried and crushed to produce pepper.

peppered ['pepəd] *adj* **-1. to be peppered with sthg** [with mistakes, statistics] to be full of sthg □ *The report was peppered with grammatical errors.* **-2. to be peppered with sthg** [with holes, shot] to be covered with sthg as a result of being fired at repeatedly □ *The walls were peppered with bullet holes.*

pepper mill *n* a device for grinding peppercorns to make pepper.

peppermint ['pepəmɪnt] *n* **-1.** a strong mint flavoring used in cough medicines, toothpaste etc; the plant from which this flavor is obtained □ *peppermint-flavored toothpaste.* **-2.** a candy with a peppermint flavor.

peppery ['pepəri] *adj* [flavor, food] that has a strong taste of pepper.

pep talk *n* a speech, usually by somebody in authority, intended to encourage people to work harder, feel more confident etc (informal use).

peptic ulcer ['peptɪk-] *n* an ulcer in the stomach or in another part of the digestive system.

Pepys [piːps], **Samuel** (1633–1703) a British naval administrator who wrote a famous diary that records the life of the period in great detail.

per [pɜːr] *prep* **per hour/day/person** for each hour/day/person □ *The dinner costs $30 per person.* □ *I get paid $80 per day.* □ *Use one capful of the cleaner per gallon of water.* □ *The speed limit is 70 miles per hour.* ■ **as per instructions** in the way that the instructions indicate (formal use) □ *As per instructions, your order is being sent by air freight.*

per annum [pər'ænəm] *adv* each year □ *The salary is $20,000 per annum.*

P-E ratio (*abbr of* **price-earnings ratio**) *n* FINANCE the ratio between the market price of a share and the earnings it produces, often used as an indication of the way investors think a company's shares will perform in the future.

per capita [pər'kæpɪtə] ◇ *adj* [earnings, spending] for each person □ *The country has the lowest per capita income in the world.* ◇ *adv* [earn, spend] *What does it cost per capita?*

perceive [pər'siːv] *vt* **-1.** [color, sign] to notice or become aware of <sthg> by seeing, hearing, feeling etc it □ *I perceived a slight change in his attitude.* **-2.** [truth, fact] to realize or understand <sthg>, especially if it is not obvious □ *I fail to perceive the reason for your complaint.* □ *I now perceive that I was wrong.* **-3. to perceive sb/sthg as sthg** to consider that sb/sthg is sthg □ *What he said was perceived as an open criticism.* □ *The administration is perceived as being incompetent.*

percent [pər'sent] *adv* in or for every hundred □ *Wages have risen by six percent.* □ *20 percent of the people voted against the measure.* ■ **one hundred percent** [agree] completely.

percentage [pər'sentɪdʒ] *n* a proportion or fraction, especially when expressed as the number out of each hundred □ *The university has a high percentage of foreign students.* □ *What percentage of your staff is working flextime?* □ *The manager gets a percentage of all the takings.* □ *The President's popularity has gone up two percentage points.*

perceptible [pər'septəbl] *adj* [change, difference, improvement] small but noticeable.

perception [pər'sepʃn] *n* **-1.** [of color, a sign] *see* **perceive** □ *visual perception.* **-2.** the ability to understand things that are not obvious to most people □ *powers of perception* □ *He is a man of unusual perception.* **-3.** [of a person, event] the way that somebody views or thinks of somebody or something □ *My perception of her has changed over the years.*

perceptive [pər'septɪv] *adj* [person] who can understand things that are not obvious to most people □ *a perceptive comment/essay.*

perceptively [pər'septɪvlɪ] *adv* [remark, comment, guess] *see* **perceptive.**

perch [pɜːtʃ] (*pl sense 3 only* **perch** OR **perches**) ◇ *n* **-1.** [for a bird] a branch or other place where a bird can sit and rest. **-2.** [for a person] a high position or seat □ *She watched the carnival from her perch up on the roof.* **-3.** a medium-sized fish with spiky fins that lives in rivers and lakes and is eaten as food. ◇ *vi* **-1.** [bird] to sit somewhere, usually for a short time. **-2.** [person, building] to sit or be high up on the edge or top of something narrow and high □ *She perched on the arm of her chair.* □ *The castle was perched on the edge of a cliff.*

percolate ['pɜːkəleɪt] *vi* **-1.** [coffee] to be made in a percolator. **-2.** [water] to pass slowly through something that has small gaps or holes. -3. [news, feeling] to spread slowly among a group of people.

percolator ['pɜːʳkəleɪtəʳ] *n* a special pot for brewing coffee in which hot water is forced up a pipe in the center and percolates down through ground coffee beans.

percussion [pəʳ'kʌʃn] *n* MUSIC **the percussion (section)** the musical instruments, such as drums, cymbals, and triangles, that are played by striking them and form part of an orchestra or band; the people who play these instruments □ *a percussion instrument.* ■ **to play percussion** to play percussion instruments.

percussionist [pəʳ'kʌʃnəst] *n* a person who plays percussion instruments.

peremptory [pə'remptrɪ] *adj* [tone, remark] that shows that one expects to be obeyed at once and without question □ *She has a really peremptory manner sometimes.*

perennial [pə'renjəl] ◇ *adj* -1. [problem, feature] that is always present and never goes away □ *There's a perennial shortage of good engineers.* -2. GARDENING [plant] that can live for several years. ◇ *n* GARDENING a perennial plant.

perestroika [ˌperə'strɔɪkə] *n* the changes in the economic, political, and social structure of the former Soviet Union in the late 1980s.

perfect [*adj* & *n* 'pɜːʳfɪkt, *vb* pəʳ'fekt] ◇ *adj* -1. [weather, conditions, health] as good as it is possible to be; [answer, English] completely accurate and with no mistakes or faults □ *The hotel is perfect for people with children.* □ *This is the perfect place for a picnic.* □ *Everything was perfect until Peter arrived.* □ *She speaks perfect French.* -2. [nuisance, stranger] complete □ *The instructions make perfect sense to me.*
◇ *n* GRAMMAR **the perfect (tense)** the form of the English verb that expresses a completed action in the past and is made by using the verb "to have" plus a past participle, e.g. "has eaten".
◇ *vt* [technique, plan, design] to make <sthg> perfect, usually by much effort and work □ *Once we have perfected the technique, we will be able to patent it.*

perfect competition *n* ECONOMICS completely open competition in the sale of goods.

perfection [pəʳ'fekʃn] *n* the quality of being perfect or the act of perfecting something □ *She strives for perfection.* □ *Perfection of the new drug may take some years.* ■ **to perfection** perfectly □ *The dinner was cooked to perfection.*

perfectionist [pəʳ'fekʃnəst] *n* a person who is not satisfied with anything that is not perfect, often in a fussy and unrealistic way. □ *He's such a perfectionist he takes hours to write a letter.*

perfectly ['pɜːʳfɪktlɪ] *adv* -1. **perfectly clear/ridiculous** completely clear/ridiculous □ *You know perfectly well what I mean.* □ *It was perfectly obvious that she didn't want to come.* -2. [work, speak] *see* **perfect** □ *She fits in perfectly with our existing staff.* □ *These colors match perfectly.*

perforate ['pɜːʳfəreɪt] *vt* [paper, edge] to make

perforations in <sthg>; [lung, eardrum] to make a small hole in <sthg>.

perforations [ˌpɜːʳfə'reɪʃnz] *npl* a line of small holes made in a piece of paper so that it can be torn easily.

perform [pəʳ'fɔːʳm] ◇ *vt* -1. [operation, miracle, function] to do <sthg> □ *The police perform an essential service.* □ *The ceremony will be performed by the Mayor of New York.* -2. [play, music, dance] to do <sthg> in front of an audience as entertainment □ *All the actors performed their parts well.* ◇ *vi* -1. [car, machine, person] to work or do its job in a particular way □ *The airplane performed well under test conditions.* □ *Everyone on the team performed to the best of their ability.* -2. [actor, musician] *This is the first time the orchestra has performed in Oslo.* □ *They are performing live on television.*

performance [pəʳ'fɔːʳməns] *n* -1. [of a function, task] *see* **perform** □ *She was arrested for obstructing the police in the performance of their duty.* -2. [of a play, piece of music] a show or occasion at which something is performed □ *Buy your tickets now for this evening's performance.* □ *We went to a performance of "King Lear".* -3. [of an actor, singer, sportsman] the part played by a person in something that is watched by an audience □ *There were excellent performances from both the soloists.* -4. [of a car, machine, candidate] the way in which somebody or something performs □ *I failed to get the job because of my poor performance at the interview.* □ *Germany's economic performance has improved.*

performance art *n* art which mixes theater and other art forms such as music and photography.

performance car *n* a high-quality and expensive car that is able to travel very fast.

performer [pəʳ'fɔːʳməʳ] *n* a person who performs in front of audiences, such as an actor, musician, or dancer.

performing arts [pəʳˌfɔːʳmɪŋ-] *npl* **the performing arts** the kinds of art that are performed in front of audiences, such as music and dance.

perfume [US pərˈfjuːm, GB ˈpɜːfjuːm] *n* -1. [for women] a liquid with a pleasant smell, used on the skin. -2. [of a flower, soap] a pleasant smell.

perfumed [US pərˈfjuːmd, GB ˈpɜːfjuːmd] *adj* [air, skin, soap] that has a pleasant smell.

perfunctory [pəʳ'fʌŋktrɪ] *adj* [search, glance] that is done quickly and without care or interest.

perhaps [pəʳ'hæps] *adv* -1. a word used when the speaker is not certain that something is true or that it will happen □ *"Why didn't they come to the party?" — "Perhaps they forgot."* □ *"Will you go?" — "Perhaps." □ "I couldn't help being late." — "Perhaps not, but you could have called."* □ *There were perhaps 50 people there.* -2. used to make polite suggestions □ *Perhaps I could interest you in a mobile phone?* □ *Perhaps you ought to tell him.*

peril ['perəl] *n* great danger (literary use). ■ **at**

one's peril a phrase used to warn somebody that they should not do something because this would be very dangerous □ *This is your final warning; ignore it at your peril.*

perilous ['perələs] *adj* [journey, mission] very dangerous or risky (literary use).

perilously ['perələslɪ] *adv* **to be perilously narrow/close** to be so narrow/close that it is very dangerous □ *I came perilously close to missing my plane.*

perimeter [pə'rɪmətəʳ] *n* [of a garden, circle] the outer edge around a piece of land or other flat shape; the length of this □ *The perimeter of the camp is protected by trees.* ■ **a perimeter fence/wall** a fence/wall around the outside of something.

period ['pɪərɪəd] ◇ *n* **-1.** a length of time □ *a period of training/fine weather* □ *Things have gotten worse over a period of several years.* □ *a 24-hour period* □ *During his period in office the company was completely restructured.* **-2.** HISTORY a particular time in the history of a country or civilization □ *the late Elizabethan period.* **-3.** EDUCATION a part of the day in a school or college in which one class can take place; a class □ *After the break we have a free period.* **-4.** [of a woman] a monthly flow of blood from a woman's womb during menstruation; the time during which this occurs □ *I'm having my period right now.* **-5.** US the punctuation mark (.) which indicates the end of a sentence.
◇ *comp* [dress, furniture] typical of an older period of history; [drama] set in a past period of history and performed with appropriate costumes, furniture etc □ *The play was done in period costume.*
◇ *adv* US a word used at the end of a statement to show that one refuses to discuss a subject further □ *I'm not going, period.*

periodic [,pɪərɪ'ɒdɪk] *adj* [rain, visits] happening from time to time and often at regular intervals □ *periodic bouts of flu/outbursts of anger.*

periodical [,pɪərɪ'ɒdɪkl] ◇ *adj* = **periodic.** ◇ *n* a magazine, usually on a serious subject, that is published at regular times, e.g. once a month □ *We subscribe to three periodicals.*

periodic table *n* a list of the chemical elements arranged in order of their atomic weights.

period pains *npl* pains felt by a woman during her period.

period piece *n* a painting, piece of furniture etc which is a good example of the period of history from which it comes.

peripatetic [,perɪpə'tetɪk] *adj* [teacher, salesman, preacher] who travels around and works in many different places.

peripheral [pə'rɪfrəl] ◇ *adj* **-1.** [aspect, subject, feature] that is not as important as something else □ *The love story is peripheral to the main theme of the play.* **-2.** [area, vision] that is at the outer edge of something □ *the peripheral areas of the city.* ◇ *n* COMPUTING a device such as a screen or printer that can be connected to a computer.

periphery [pə'rɪfərɪ] (*pl* **peripheries**) *n* **-1.** [of a subject, group, activity] the parts that are less important than the main subject, group etc and are not essential □ *The people arrested were only on the periphery of the terrorist gang.* **-2.** [of an area, vision] the area at the outer edge of something □ *Hardest hit by the transportation strike have been people who live in the periphery.*

periscope ['perɪskoʊp] *n* a tube with mirrors in it that is used especially by people in submarines so that they can look out over the surface of the sea.

perish ['perɪʃ] *vi* **-1.** [person, animal] to die in a terrible or tragic way □ *Over 900 people perished when the ship went down.* **-2.** [rubber, fabric] to start to break up into small pieces; [food] to go bad.

perishable ['perɪʃəbl] *adj* [food] that goes bad quickly.
♦ **perishables** *npl* perishable foods.

peritonitis [,perɪtə'naɪtəs] *n* a serious painful swelling of the inside wall of the area around the stomach, caused by infection.

perjure ['pɜːʳdʒəʳ] *vt* **to perjure oneself** to tell a lie after promising formally to tell the truth, especially in a court of law.

perjury ['pɜːʳdʒərɪ] *n* the crime of telling a lie in a court of law after promising formally to tell the truth □ *Remember that to commit perjury is a criminal offense.*

perk [pɜːʳk] *n* money, goods, a car etc that one gets from a job in addition to one's pay □ *Free travel is one of the perks of the job.*
♦ **perk up** *vi* to become more cheerful, interested, or excited □ *She perked up when I told her she could come with us.*

perky ['pɜːʳkɪ] (*compar* **perkier,** *superl* **perkiest**) *adj* [person, manner] that is cheerful, lively, and enthusiastic (informal use).

perm [pɜːʳm] ◇ *n* waves and curls that are put into one's hair by treating it with chemicals and that usually last for several months □ *I'm thinking of having a perm.* ◇ *vt* to put a perm into <somebody's hair> □ *I'm going to have my hair permed.*

permanence ['pɜːʳmənəns] *n* [of a job, crisis] the state of being permanent □ *What's missing in my life is a sense of permanence.*

permanent ['pɜːʳmənənt] ◇ *adj* **-1.** [damage, address] that lasts for a very long time or forever □ *I've been offered the job on a permanent basis.* **-2.** [crisis, supply] that is constant, continuous, and never stops □ *I live in permanent fear of losing my job.* ◇ *n* US a perm.

permanently ['pɜːʳmənəntlɪ] *adv* **permanently damaged/disabled etc** damaged/disabled etc in a way that will last for a very long time or forever.

permeable ['pɜːʳmjəbl] *adj* [rock, membrane] that liquids or gases can pass through.

permeate ['pɜːʳmɪeɪt] *vt* **-1.** [liquid, smell] to enter and spread to every part of <a substance or area> □ *Rainwater permeates the soil and forms underground streams.* **-2.** [feeling, idea] to spread throughout <a group of people, activ-

ity> etc until it affects and influences every part of it □ *A mood of optimism permeated the meeting.*

permissible [pər'mɪsəbl] *adj* [request, behavior] allowed or permitted, especially by laws or rules (formal use) □ *Such rudeness is really not permissible in a professional context.*

permission [pər'mɪʃn] *n* the right to do something that is given to somebody, usually by somebody in authority □ *The judge gave/refused permission for a review of the case.* □ *You have my permission to leave.* □ *You'll have to ask permission from the landlord first.* □ *With your permission, I'd like to say a few words.* □ *Photos published by kind permission of H. Clarke.*

permissive [pər'mɪsɪv] *adj* [attitude, society] that allows people a great amount of freedom to do what they want, especially in sexual matters and things that other people might disapprove of.

permissiveness [pər'mɪsɪvnəs] *n: see* **permissive**.

permit [*vb* pər'mɪt, *n* 'pɜːr'mɪt] (*pt* & *pp* **permitted**, *cont* **permitting**) ◇ *vt* **-1.** [smoking, access] to allow <sthg>, especially by giving formal agreement □ *Cameras are not permitted inside the building.* □ *Her mother would not permit her to go to the party.* □ *Prisoners are permitted only one visit a month.* □ *He permitted himself an after-dinner cigar.* **-2.** [event, activity] to make it possible for <sthg> to happen □ *Unfortunately, the timetable does not permit any time for sightseeing.* □ *The new system permits invoices to be processed more quickly.*
◇ *vi* to make something possible □ *If time permits, we'll have a question and answer session at the end.* ■ **weather permitting** if the weather is good enough □ *We'll have a picnic on Sunday, weather permitting.*
◇ *n* an official written statement that gives somebody the right to do something □ *a work/residence/travel permit* □ *Parking is reserved for permit holders only.*

permutation [,pɜːr'mjuː'teɪʃn] *n* one of the many different ways in which a group of things or people can be arranged □ *I know the numbers that make up the code and I've tried several permutations, but without success.*

pernicious [pər'nɪʃəs] *adj* [effect, policy, nonsense] very harmful, often in a way that is not obvious at first (formal use) □ *And the influence he has over younger party members is equally pernicious.*

pernickety [pər'nɪkətɪ] *adj* = **persnickety**.

peroxide [pə'rɒksaɪd] *n* a liquid used for killing bacteria and for taking the color out of hair. SYMBOL: H_2O_2.

peroxide blonde *n* a woman who has turned her hair an unnaturally light color by using peroxide (disapproving use).

perpendicular [,pɜːr'pən'dɪkjələr] ◇ *adj* **-1.** MATH **to be perpendicular to sthg** [line, plane] to be at an angle of 90° to sthg □ *He lives in a street perpendicular to Jackson Avenue.* **-2.** [cliff, face, wall] standing or rising straight upward and not leaning to one side □ *a perpendicular line.* ◇ *n* MATH a perpendicular line or direction (technical use).

perpetrate ['pɜːr'pətreɪt] *vt* [crime, outrage] to do <sthg wrong or immoral> (formal use).

perpetration [,pɜːr'pə'treɪʃn] *n: see* **perpetrate** (formal use).

perpetrator ['pɜːr'pətreɪtər] *n* [of a crime, outrage] a person who does something wrong or immoral (formal use).

perpetual [pər'petʃuəl] *adj* **-1.** [talking, nuisance] that happens very often or all the time (disapproving use) □ *I couldn't sleep because of the perpetual noise of the traffic.* **-2.** [hunger, happiness] that lasts for ever and never changes □ *a species of fish that lives in perpetual darkness.*

perpetually [pər'petʃuəlɪ] *adv* [talk, complain] *see* **perpetual** □ *They are perpetually happy/hungry.*

perpetual motion *n* the imaginary movement of a machine that can continue forever without needing power from something else.

perpetuate [pər'petʃueɪt] *vt* [belief, myth, memory] to cause <sthg> to last or continue □ *The article only serves to perpetuate the idea that women are somehow weaker than men* □ *behavior designed to perpetuate the species.*

perpetuation [pər,petʃu'eɪʃn] *n: see* **perpetuate**.

perpetuity [,pɜːr'pə'tjuːətɪ] *n* **in perpetuity** forever (formal use) □ *Use of the house to be granted to Mrs Harris in perpetuity.*

perplex [pər'pleks] *vt* to make <sb> confused and slightly worried □ *I was very perplexed by the whole thing.*

perplexed [pər'plekst] *adj* [person, look, silence] confused and slightly worried by something that is difficult to understand □ *You look perplexed.* □ *We've had lots of letters from perplexed readers asking for further information.*

perplexing [pər'pleksɪŋ] *adj* [problem, comment, behavior] that causes somebody to become perplexed.

perplexity [pər'pleksətɪ] *n* a state of confusion and worry caused by a failure to understand something.

perquisite ['pɜːr'kwɪzət] *n* = **perk** (formal use).

per se [pɜːr'seɪ] *adv* a phrase used when one is considering one thing by itself and not other things that may be connected with it □ *Cannabis is not dangerous per se, but it can lead to other drugs.*

persecute ['pɜːr'sɪkjuːt] *vt* **-1.** [race, minority] to treat <a group of people> cruelly as a deliberate and long-term policy, especially because of their religious or political views □ *They emigrated because they were being persecuted for their religious opinions.* **-2.** [criminal, politician] to make life unpleasant for <sb> by annoying them and not leaving them alone □ *I was constantly persecuted by journalists.*

persecution [,pɜːr'sɪ'kjuːʃn] *n: see* **persecute** □ *the persecution of the Jews.*

persecutor ['pɜːr'sɪkjuːtər] *n* a person who persecutes other people.

perseverance [,pɜːr'sə'vɪərəns] *n* continued effort made over a period of time in order to get something difficult done □ *It takes a lot of perseverance to get a reply from them.*

persevere [ˌpɜːrsəˈvɪər] *vi* **-1.** to keep trying to do something and not give up, even though it is difficult □ *Do you think it's worth persevering with this project?* □ *Don't give up; I think you should persevere.* **-2. to persevere in doing sthg** to continue to do sthg, even though it has failed many times in the past □ *If you persevere in writing to the senator you will eventually receive a reply.*

Persia [ˈpɜːʒə] = **Iran**.

Persian [ˈpɜːrʒn] *n* & *adj*: see **Iran** □ *a Persian rug.*

Persian cat *n* a cat that is often white and has a round face and long silky hair.

Persian Gulf: the **Persian Gulf** part of the Indian Ocean between Arabia and Iran.

persist [pərˈsɪst] *vi* **-1.** [problem, rain, rumor] to continue to exist □ *If the condition persists, consult a physician.* **-2. to persist in doing sthg** to continue to do sthg, even though people do not like it or disagree with it □ *If you persist in being late, you will be fired.* □ *She persists in the belief that records are better than CDs.*

persistence [pərˈsɪstəns] *n*: see **persistent** □ *His persistence finally paid off and she agreed to see him.*

persistent [pərˈsɪstənt] *adj* **-1.** [problem, rumor, rain] that continues to exist for a long time □ *I went to the doctor about my persistent cough.* **-2.** [criminal, journalist] who continues to do the same thing in a determined way, even if it is difficult or other people try to stop them □ *a secure home for persistent juvenile offenders* □ *I said you were too busy to see him, but he was very persistent.* □ *They finally gave way to her persistent demands.*

persistently [pərˈsɪstəntlɪ] *adv* [rain, increase, demand] see **persistent** □ *He persistently refused any offers of help.*

persnickety [pərˈsnɪkətɪ] *adj* US [person] who worries too much about small and unimportant details (informal use).

person [ˈpɜːrsn] (*pl* **people** OR *formal* **persons**) *n* **-1.** a man, woman, or child □ *One person was injured in the blast.* □ *I want to speak to the person in charge.* □ *You're just the person we had in mind.* □ *You're a scientific sort of person.* □ *I'm not really a sports person.* □ *She seemed like a different person when she wasn't at work.* ■ **in person** with the particular person actually present, rather than on television, the telephone etc; without help or intervention from anybody else □ *I'm looking forward to meeting her in person.* □ *He was unable to come in person so he sent his assistant.* □ *I want to deal with their complaints in person.* ■ **in the person of** a phrase used to introduce the name of a particular person that one is referring to □ *We have a valuable asset in the person of Sue Jones.* **-2. on** OR **about sb's person** somewhere on sb's body or in their clothes □ *He had a knife hidden on his person.*

persona [pərˈsoʊnə] (*pl* **personas** OR **personae** [-iː]) *n* the character that somebody shows

to other people or that is seen by other people and that is often different from their real character.

personable [ˈpɜːrsnəbl] *adj* [person] who is pleasant in appearance or character.

personage [ˈpɜːrsnɪdʒ] *n* a famous or important person (formal use).

personal [ˈpɜːrsnl] ◇ *adj* **-1.** [opinion, belongings, choice] of a single person rather than a group or organization □ *We share a huge apartment and I even have my own personal bathroom.* **-2. personal experience/attention etc** one's own experience/attention etc and not somebody else's □ *The headmaster made a personal appearance at the meeting.* □ *The project will be under my personal supervision.* **-3.** [life, problem, plan] that is private or concerns one's private feelings □ *I can't tell you — it's very personal.* **-4.** [check, letter] that belongs to or is used by a particular person □ *I think it's somewhere among my personal papers.* □ *There's a letter in your mail marked "Personal".* **-5.** [comment, insult, criticism] that refers to the appearance or character of a particular person in a rude or insulting way □ *There's no need to be so personal!* ◇ *n* US a short advertisement placed in a newspaper or magazine, usually by somebody who is looking for a lover.

personal account *n* an account at a bank or building society for an individual rather than a company or organization.

personal allowance *n* GB FINANCE the amount of money that one is allowed to earn before one has to start paying tax.

personal assistant *n* a secretary of a senior manager or official, who is employed to help with all aspects of their work and to carry out their duties when they are away.

personal call *n* a phone call made or received at work, which is not for business purposes □ *Staff have to pay for their personal calls.*

personal column *n* a section in a newspaper or magazine where people can print personal messages, often when they are looking for a lover.

personal computer *n* a computer that is intended for use by a single user at work or in the home.

personal estate *n* = **personal property**.

personal hygiene *n* care for the cleanliness of one's body.

personality [ˌpɜːrsəˈnælətɪ] (*pl* **personalities**) *n* **-1.** a person's character or nature as shown in the way they act or think □ *He has a pleasant/weak personality.* □ *Their personalities are all very different.* **-2.** personal qualities that other people find attractive □ *She has a lot of personality.* **-3.** a well-known person, especially in the world of entertainment or sports □ *a television personality.*

personalize, -ise [ˈpɜːrsnəlaɪz] *vt* **-1.** [stationery, bag, clothing] to mark <sthg> in a way that shows who the owner is, e.g. by writing their name or initials on it □ *He had had all his baggage personalized.* **-2.** [argument, debate, issue] to discuss <sthg> in a way which is critical of the individual people concerned rather than looking at the facts in a general way (disapproving use) □ *The journalist made a personalized attack on the mayor.*

personalized ['pɜːrsnəlaɪzd] *adj* -1. [stationery, clothing] that has been marked in a way that shows who the owner is □ *personalized handkerchiefs/license plates.* -2. [service, counseling] that is designed or has been changed to suit the needs of an individual person or customer.

personally ['pɜːrsnəlɪ] *adv* -1. **personally,...** a word used to emphasize that what one is about to say is a personal opinion and that other people may disagree with it □ *Personally, I think it would be better to wait and see what happens.* -2. a word used to emphasize that a particular activity, duty etc concerns a particular person rather than somebody else acting for them □ *He likes to deal with complaints personally.* □ *I am personally responsible for the performance of the company.* □ *I wasn't referring to you personally.* ■ **to take sthg personally** [insult, criticism] to feel that sthg is intended as criticism of oneself, not just of what one has done □ *We've decided not to use your idea, but please don't take it personally.*

personal organizer *n* a small book with a strong cover and metal rings inside that are used to hold loose pages for a calendar, address book, useful information etc.

personal pension plan *n* a pension plan organized by a finance company for a private individual, rather than a state pension plan.

personal pronoun *n* a pronoun such as "I", "me", or "it", used for the speaker, the person spoken to, or the people or things spoken about.

personal property *n* LAW everything owned by a person except land and buildings.

personal stereo *n* a small stereo cassette player with headphones that works using batteries and that the owner can carry about and listen to anywhere.

persona non grata [-'grɑːtə] (*pl* **personae non gratae** [-'grɑːtiː]) *n* a person who is unacceptable or not welcome, e.g. in somebody else's house or in a particular country □ *I fear I am persona non grata at the Smiths' now.*

personify [pər'sɒnɪfaɪ] (*pt* & *pp* **personified**) *vt* to be a perfect human example of <a quality> and have this quality to a very great extent □ *She is evil/greed/beauty personified.*

personnel [ˌpɜːrsə'nel] ◇ *n* the section of a company, organization etc that deals with the people who work there and keeps their records □ *She works in personnel.* □ *I sent my résumé to their personnel department.* ◇ *npl* the people who work in a particular company or organization □ *We have over 100 personnel employed on this site.* □ *military personnel.*

personnel officer *n* a person who works in the personnel department of a company, organization etc.

person-to-person *adj* a **person-to-person** call a

telephone call made through the operator to a particular person and paid for only if that person is available.

perspective [pər'spektɪv] *n* -1. ART the methods used in drawing to make objects appear close or far away, large or small etc, and therefore more realistic □ *The roof of this house is in/out of perspective.* ■ **to get sthg in** OR **into perspective** [problem, matter] to think about sthg reasonably and in relation to other things and not let it seem more important than it is □ *If you read the other report it will help you get things in perspective.* □ *I think you need to get this thing into its proper perspective and stop worrying so much.* -2. a way of thinking about something based on one's beliefs and experiences □ *from a historical perspective* □ *Yoga has given me a whole new perspective on life.* □ *If you try and look at it from his perspective, it's not such a serious thing.*

Perspex™ ['pɜːrspeks] *n* GB strong clear plastic used instead of glass.

perspicacious [ˌpɜːrspɪ'keɪʃəs] *adj* [person, comment] that shows quick and accurate understanding or judgment (formal use).

perspiration [ˌpɜːrspə'reɪʃn] *n* the liquid produced when one perspires □ *He was dripping with perspiration after his exertions.*

perspire [pər'spaɪər] *vi* to produce a salty colourless liquid on one's skin, usually when one is hot, ill, or afraid □ *She was perspiring by the time she reached the fourth floor.*

persuade [pər'sweɪd] *vt* -1. to make <sb> do something by giving reasons or arguments which show that it is a good idea □ *I won't come, so it's no good trying to persuade me.* □ *Her failure to find work persuaded her to go back to college.* □ *He persuaded her into/out of joining the party.* -2. to make <sb> believe something □ *The salesman tried to persuade them that they needed a new car.* □ *Subsequent events have persuaded me of the truth of her story.*

persuasion [pər'sweɪʒn] *n* -1. the act of persuading somebody to do or believe something □ *It took a lot of persuasion to get him to agree.* □ *powers of persuasion.* -2. a set of beliefs, usually religious or political □ *People of many different persuasions attended the rally.*

persuasive [pər'sweɪsɪv] *adj* [person, argument] that is likely to persuade people to do or believe something □ *I couldn't resist — she's so persuasive.*

persuasively [pər'sweɪsɪvlɪ] *adv* [speak, argue] *see* **persuasive.**

pert [pɜːrt] *adj* -1. [girl, young woman] who is lively and slightly disrespectful in an attractive and amusing way. -2. [nose, bottom] small, neat, and firm.

pertain [pər'teɪn] *vi* **pertaining to sb/sthg** belonging to or connected with sb/sthg (formal use) □ *documents pertaining to the Salston case.*

pertinence ['pɜːrtənəns] *n: see* **pertinent.**

pertinent ['pɜːrtənənt] *adj* [question, remark, fact] relevant to the subject being discussed □ *I hardly think that is pertinent to the discussion.*

perturb [pər'tɜːrb] *vt* to worry and upset <sb>

a lot (formal use) □ *I was somewhat perturbed by what you said in that fax.*

perturbed [pər'tɜːᵇbd] *adj* [person, expression] very worried and upset (formal use) □ *When she heard the news she didn't seem at all perturbed.*

Peru [pə'ruː] a country in western South America, on the Pacific coast. SIZE: 1,285,000 sq kms. POPULATION: 22,900,000 (*Peruvians*). CAPITAL: Lima. LANGUAGE: Spanish. CURRENCY: sol.

perusal [pə'ruːzl] *n* [of a document, letter, report] the act of reading something (formal use) □ *I have sent you the papers for your perusal.*

peruse [pə'ruːz] *vt* [document, letter, report] to read <sthg>, especially carefully and thoroughly (formal use) □ *She sat perusing the papers with a look of concentration.*

Peruvian [pə'ruːvɪən] *n & adj*: see **Peru**.

pervade [pərᵇveɪd] *vt* [smell, darkness] to spread throughout <a room, space> etc until it fills it; [feeling, thought] to be present everywhere in <a book, system> etc □ *The sweet fragrance of roses pervaded the room.* □ *A sense of gloom pervaded the meeting.*

pervasive [pərᵇveɪsɪv] *adj* [smell, doubt] that is felt or found everywhere □ *It is difficult to avoid the pervasive influence of advertising.*

perverse [pərᵇvɜːᵇs] *adj* [person] who is stubborn and unreasonable, especially because they refuse to do or think what other people expect □ *Now you're just being perverse!* □ *He seems to take a perverse pleasure in upsetting people.*

perversely [pərᵇvɜːᵇslɪ] *adv* a word used to show that one thinks that somebody's behavior is perverse □ *He continues, perversely, to refuse to accept he was wrong.*

perversion [pərᵇvɜːᵇʒn] *n* -1. sexual behavior that is considered unnatural and wrong. -2. [of justice, meaning, knowledge] see **pervert** □ *Their version of what happened is a perversion of the truth.*

perversity [pərᵇvɜːᵇsətɪ] *n* stubborn and unreasonable behavior □ *I'm sure she does it out of perversity.*

pervert [*n* 'pɜːᵇvɜːᵇt, *vb* pərᵇvɜːᵇt] ◇ *n* a perverted person. ◇ *vt* -1. [child, audience] to lead <sb> to behave in ways that are unnatural and wrong, especially sexually □ *We believe scenes of sex and violence pervert people's minds.* -2. [justice, meaning, truth] to change <sthg> so much that it becomes bad or wrong; [knowledge, evidence] to use <sthg> for bad or evil purposes □ *Benson was accused of perverting the course of justice.*

perverted [pərᵇvɜːᵇtəd] *adj* -1. [person] who behaves sexually in ways that are unnatural and wrong □ *a perverted mind/practice.* -2. [meaning, thinking] wrong and unnatural □ *He murdered him out of a perverted sense of honor.*

peseta [pə'seɪtə] *n* the standard unit of currency in Spain.

peso ['peɪsoʊ] (*pl* **pesos**) *n* the standard unit of currency in Mexico, some other Latin American countries, and the Philippines.

pessary ['pesərɪ] (*pl* **pessaries**) *n* a large pill that is designed to be put inside a woman's vagina and that contains a contraceptive substance or a medicine for curing infections.

pessimism ['pesəmɪzm] *n* the tendency to believe that things will go wrong or turn out badly □ *There seems to be a general mood of pessimism on the stock market.*

pessimist ['pesəməst] *n* a person who thinks that things will go wrong or turn out badly, especially one who always thinks this way □ *Don't be such a pessimist!*

pessimistic [,pesə'mɪstɪk] *adj* [person, forecast, opinion] that suggests things will go wrong or turn out badly □ *I'm pessimistic about our chances of closing the deal.*

pest [pest] *n* -1. any insect or small animal that damages plants or food □ *pest control* □ *Some farmers consider foxes to be pests.* -2. a person, especially a child, that one does not like because they are always annoying people, interrupting, asking for things etc (informal use) □ *That child is such a pest!*

pester ['pestər] *vt* to annoy or disturb <sb> continually, especially by asking them for something or demanding their attention □ *He's always pestering me to take him with me.*

pesticide ['pestəsaɪd] *n* a chemical used by gardeners and farmers to kill pests, especially insects.

pestle ['pesl] *n* a short stick of wood or stone with a heavy rounded end that is used to crush herbs, spices etc in a bowl □ *a pestle and mortar.*

pet [pet] (*pt & pp* **petted**, *cont* **petting**) ◇ *n* -1. an animal kept in the home for company and pleasure □ *a pet mouse/rabbit* □ *pet food.* -2. a person who is a special favorite of somebody in authority, and is often treated better than other people (disapproving use) □ *She was the teacher's pet in school.*
◇ *adj* [subject, theory] that a particular person is very interested in and is always talking about. ■ **a pet peeve** US OR **hate** GB something that a particular person finds very annoying □ *Soap operas are one of his pet peeves.*
◇ *vt* to treat <a child, animal> etc lovingly, by touching and stroking them gently.
◇ *vi* [two people] to kiss and touch each other sexually.

petal ['petl] *n* one of the white or colored parts of a plant that are shaped like a leaf and together form the flower □ *a rose petal.*

peter ['piːtər] ♦ **peter out** *vi* [interest, food supply] to become gradually less and less before coming to an end □ *Eventually, the track just peters out and you have to walk the rest of the way.* □ *The conversation finally petered out.*

Peter Pan [,piːtər'pæn] the hero of J. M. Barrie's story *Peter Pan*. He is a boy who never grows up, and lives in a magical place called Never Never Land.

Peter the Great [,piːtərðə'greɪt] (1672–1725) Czar of Russia from 1682 to 1725. He modernized and westernized Russia, and founded the new capital of St Petersburg.

pethidine ['peθədiːn] *n* a drug used to reduce pain, e.g. in childbirth.

petit bourgeois ['petiː-] (*pl* **petits bourgeois** ['petiː-]) *adj* [person] who belongs to the section of the middle class that owns stores, small businesses etc; who has attitudes thought to be typical of this class, e.g. an interest in wealth and social status □ *petty bourgeois attitudes/prejudice.*

petite [pə'tiːt] *adj* [woman, model] small, slim, and attractive.

petit four [,petɪ'fɔːʳ] (*pl* **petits fours** [,petɪ'fɔːʳ]) *n* a very small cake or cookie, often served at the end of a meal with coffee.

petition [pə'tɪʃn] ◇ *n* -1. a request, signed by a lot of people, asking a government or some other organization to do something □ *a petition for/against a new road.* -2. LAW an official letter to a court of law, asking it to take a particular action □ *She filed a petition for divorce.* ◇ *vt* [governor, committee] to ask <sb> formally to do something, usually by presenting them with a petition □ *They petitioned city hall to provide more social housing.* ◇ *vi* -1. [local people, protesters] *They petitioned for/against a change in the law.* -2. LAW **to petition for divorce** to ask a court of law formally to give one a divorce.

petitioner [pə'tɪʃnəʳ] *n* a person who organizes a petition.

pet name *n* a special name used for a very close friend or member of the family instead of their real name.

petrified ['petrɪfaɪd] *adj* [person, look, voice] very frightened □ *I'm petrified of speaking in public.*

petrify ['petrɪfaɪ] (*pt* & *pp* **petrified**) *vt* to make <sb> so frightened that they are unable to think clearly or act sensibly.

petrochemical [,petroʊ'kemɪkl] *n* a chemical substance made from petroleum or natural gas □ *the petrochemical industry* □ *a petrochemical plant.*

petrodollars ['petroʊdɒləʳz] *npl* US dollars earned by a country that exports petroleum.

petrol ['petrəl] *n* GB a liquid that is made from petroleum and is used as a fuel in motor cars and other engines □ *four-star petrol* □ *petrol fumes.*

petrolatum [,petrə'leɪtəm] *n* US = **petroleum jelly.**

petrol bomb *n* GB a simple bomb made from a bottle filled with gasoline and a piece of cloth that is placed in the end and lit just before the bottle is thrown.

petrol can *n* GB a small metal container for keeping gasoline in, e.g. in one's car, in case one runs out of gasoline.

petroleum [pə'troʊlɪəm] *n* a natural oil found underground that is used to make gasoline and many other substances.

petroleum jelly *n* a soft, clear greasy substance that is made from petroleum. It is used in medicines that are rubbed into the skin and in products that are spread on

parts of machines to make them move more smoothly.

petrol pump *n* GB a machine at a gas station, used for putting gasoline into vehicles.

petrol station *n* GB a place that sells gasoline for vehicles.

petrol tank *n* GB the part of a vehicle that holds gasoline.

Petronas Center [pə'troʊnəs-]: **the Petronas Center** an office building consisting of two towers in Kuala Lumpur, Malaysia. It is the tallest building in the world.

petticoat ['petɪkoʊt] *n* a piece of underwear that looks like a skirt or a dress without sleeves and is worn by a woman under her dress or skirt.

pettiness ['petɪnəs] *n* [of a person] *see* **petty.**

petty ['petɪ] (*compar* **pettier,** *superl* **pettiest**) *adj* -1. [person] who is too concerned with small and unimportant things, often in an unkind and selfish way □ *He's got a petty little mind.* □ *I don't want to get involved in your petty little arguments.* -2. [detail, crime, problem] small and unimportant □ *Trading is made difficult by all the petty regulations.* □ *a petty thief/crook.*

petty cash *n* a small amount of money kept in an office for making small payments when necessary □ *Take it out of petty cash.*

petty officer *n* the lowest rank of officer in a navy.

petulant ['petʃələnt] *adj* [person, expression, remark] that seems angry or impatient about something unimportant in an unreasonable and childish way □ *"I don't know," she said, with a petulant shrug.*

petunia [pə'tʲuːnjə] *n* a garden plant with white, pink, or purple flowers shaped like funnels.

pew [pjuː] *n* a long wooden seat with a back, placed in rows in a church.

pewter ['pjuːtəʳ] *n* a gray metal made from tin and lead □ *a pewter jug.*

PG (*abbr of* **parental guidance**) *n* a symbol for movies and video tapes in Britain and the USA that indicates that some scenes may be unsuitable for young children.

PG-13 *n* a symbol for movies and videotapes in the USA that indicates that some scenes may not be suitable for children under the age of 13.

PGA (*abbr of* **Professional Golfers' Association**) *n* **the PGA** the organization in charge of professional golf in the USA.

p & h (*abbr of* **postage and handling**) *n* US a charge made for packing and mailing something that somebody has bought.

pH (*abbr of* **potential of hydrogen**) *n* a unit for measuring how acid or alkaline a substance is □ *The soil has a pH of 7.*

phallic ['fælɪk] *adj* [carving, imagery] that looks like a phallus □ *a phallic symbol.*

phallus ['fæləs] (*pl* **phalluses** OR **phalli** ['fælaɪ]) *n* a model or image of an erect penis, used as a symbol of fertility in certain religions.

phantom ['fæntəm] ◇ *adj* **a phantom vision/**

figure etc a vision/figure etc that exists only in the imagination □ *I sensed a phantom presence somewhere in the room.* ◇ *n* a ghost, especially in the shape of a person.

phantom pregnancy *n* a condition in which a woman thinks that she is pregnant when she is not, and may even develop some of the signs of pregnancy.

pharaoh ['feərou] *n* a king in ancient Egypt.

Pharisee ['færəsiː] *n* a member of an ancient group of Jews who followed religious laws very carefully.

pharmaceutical [,faːrmə'sjuːtɪkl] *adj* [company, industry] concerned with the making of drugs and medicines.

◆ **pharmaceuticals** *npl* drugs and medicines.

pharmacist ['faːrməsəst] *n* a person whose job is to prepare and sell medicines.

pharmacology [,faːrmə'kɒlədʒɪ] *n* the area of science that deals with drugs and medicines.

pharmacy ['faːrməsɪ] (*pl* **pharmacies**) *n* a store, or part of a store, that sells medicines.

phase [feɪz] ◇ *n* [of illness, civilization, a campaign] a stage in the development of something □ *Their daughter is going through a difficult phase.* □ *phase two of the government's incomes policy.* ◇ *vt* [improvements, scheme] to organize <sthg> so that it happens in phases.

◆ **phase in** *vt sep* **to phase sthg in** [tax reforms, pay structure] to introduce sthg gradually □ *The increase will be phased in over five years.*

◆ **phase out** *vt sep* **to phase sthg out** [system, service, machine] to stop using sthg gradually □ *These pesticides are being phased out.*

PhD (*abbr of* **Doctor of Philosophy**) *n* the highest university degree, usually given for research; a person who has this degree □ *PhD students.*

pheasant ['feznt] (*pl* **pheasant** OR **pheasants**) *n* a large bird with a long tail that lives in woods and that is often shot for food or sport; the meat of this bird.

phenobarbital [US ,fiːnou'baːrbətɔːl, GB -'baːbɪtl], **phenobarbitone** [,fiːnou'baːrbətoun] *n* a strong drug for calming people or helping them to sleep.

phenomena [fə'nɒmənə] *plural of* **phenomenon**.

phenomenal [fə'nɒmənl] *adj* [success, size, increase] so great that it is unusual □ *Public response to the appeal has been phenomenal.*

phenomenon [fə'nɒmənən] (*pl* **phenomena**) *n* -1. a thing or event, often unusual or exceptional, that exists and can be experienced □ *This tendency is a relatively recent phenomenon.* □ *meteorological phenomena.* -2. a person who is remarkably good at something, or who has done something remarkable □ *a chess phenomenon.*

phew [fjuː] *excl* a soft whistling sound made by somebody when they are very tired after a great physical effort, or when they are very relieved □ *Phew! That was close — I thought we'd never make it!* □ *Phew! It's boiling in here!*

phial ['faɪəl] *n* a small glass bottle that is usually used for keeping medicines in.

Phi Beta Kappa [,faɪbiːtə'kæpə] *n* an American academic society whose members have shown high academic ability; a member of this society.

Philadelphia [,fɪlə'delfɪə] an industrial city and port in Pennsylvania, USA, on the Delaware River. The Declaration of Independence was signed there. POPULATION: 1,685,577.

philanderer [fɪ'lændərər] *n* a man who has relationships with many women without becoming very involved with them (formal and disapproving use).

philanthropic [,fɪlən'θrɒpɪk] *adj* [person, organization, act] that is kind to people, especially by giving help or money to people who need it.

philanthropist [fɪ'lænθrəpəst] *n* a philanthropic person.

philately [fɪ'lætəlɪ] *n* the hobby of collecting stamps.

philharmonic [,fɪlhaːr'mɒnɪk] *adj* [orchestra, society] that is connected with the performance and study of music.

Philip ['fɪləp], **Prince** (1921–) the husband of Queen Elizabeth II of Great Britain.

Philippine ['fɪlɪpiːn] *adj: see* **Philippines**.

Philippines: the Philippines a country in Southeast Asia, consisting of over 7,000 islands in the western Pacific Ocean. SIZE: 300,000 sq kms. POPULATION: 64,600,000 (*Filipinos, Filipinas*). CAPITAL: Manila. LANGUAGE: Pilipino, English. CURRENCY: Filipino peso.

philistine [US 'fɪlɪstiːn, GB -staɪn] *n* a person who does not like or understand art, literature, music etc (disapproving use).

Phillip ['fɪləp], **Arthur** (1738–1814) a British naval officer who founded New South Wales, Australia, and was its first governor.

Phillips™ ['fɪləps] *n* **a Phillips (screw)** a screw with a cross cut into the head, rather than a straight groove. ■ **a Phillips (screwdriver)** a screwdriver with a cross at the end of the blade, to fit into a Phillips screw.

philosopher [fə'lɒsəfər] *n* -1. a person who studies, teaches, or writes about philosophy. -2. a person who created a particular philosophy □ *the great philosopher Confucius.* -3. a person who thinks deeply and calmly about serious things.

philosophical [,fɪlə'sɒfɪkl] *adj* -1. [attitude, person] that is calm and resigned when faced with difficulty or unpleasantness □ *They told him that he'd never get the money back, but he was very philosophical about it.* -2. [idea, theory, writing] *see* **philosophy**.

philosophize, -ise [fə'lɒsəfaɪz] *vi* to think or talk about philosophical ideas □ *He's always philosophizing about something!*

philosophy [fə'lɒsəfɪ] (*pl* **philosophies**) *n* -1. the study or creation of theories about important questions connected with human life, e.g. truth, knowledge, or reality □ *She's studying philosophy and politics.* -2. a particular set of beliefs and way of thinking about life, truth, knowledge etc □ *Western philosophy* □ *the philosophy of Plato/Kant* □ *My philosophy is*

— get them before they get you! **-3.** a particular person's way of thinking □ What's the philosophy behind that decision?

phlegm [flem] *n* the thick yellow or green liquid produced in somebody's nose and throat when they have a cold.

phlegmatic [fleg'mætɪk] *adj* [person] who is calm, even when exciting things are happening.

phobia ['fəʊbɪə] *n* a strong and unreasonable fear of a particular thing □ She has a phobia about spiders.

phoenix ['fiːnɪks] *n* an imaginary bird that in former times was believed to burn itself and be born again from its ashes every 500 years □ A new company was formed, like a phoenix from the ashes of its predecessor.

phone [fəʊn] ◇ *n* **-1.** the telephone system □ She contacted me by phone. □ You can always use the phone. □ I can't discuss it over the phone. □ a phone company/link. ■ **to be on the phone** to be speaking to somebody by phone □ I've been on the phone with them all morning. ■ **to be on the phone** GB to be connected to the telephone network □ Are you on the phone? **-2.** a telephone □ Their phone's been busy all morning. □ Can you answer the phone?
◇ *vt* [person, the police] to dial a number and speak to <sb> by phone □ I phoned his office, but he was out. □ Have you tried phoning the operator?
◇ *vi*: He hasn't phoned for weeks. □ I'll phone for a taxi. □ He phoned to invite you to a party.

◆ **phone back** ◇ *vt sep* **to phone sb back** to phone sb again after one has already phoned them recently; to phone sb who has recently phoned one □ Can you phone me back in an hour? □ Amy phoned while you were out and asked if you could phone her back. ◇ *vi*: She phoned back to say the tickets were reserved. □ I left my name, but she didn't phone back.

◆ **phone up** ◇ *vt sep* **to phone sb up** to phone sb, especially about something not very important □ She phoned me up last night. ◇ *vi*: Why don't you phone up and ask?

phone book *n* a book that lists the names, addresses, and phone numbers of all the people with telephones in a particular area □ Look it up in the phone book.

phone booth *n* a small shelter in a public place that contains a public telephone □ I'm calling from a phone booth.

phone box *n* GB = **phone booth**.

phone call *n* an act of phoning somebody □ I have a few phone calls to make.

phonecard ['fəʊnkɑːrd] *n* a card like a credit card that can be used instead of coins to make calls from some public telephones.

phone-in *n* a radio or TV program in which people telephone the station while the program is on and can have their questions or comments broadcast.

phone line *n* **-1.** a wire connecting a telephone or building to the rest of the tele-

phone network. **-2.** a telephone connection □ All the phone lines were busy.

phone number *n* the number that is dialed to contact a particular person or organization by telephone □ I gave her my phone number.

phone-tapping [-tæpɪŋ] *n* the use of special equipment to listen secretly to other people's telephone conversations.

phonetics [fə'netɪks] *n* the scientific study of the different sounds that make up spoken words.

phony US, **phoney** GB ['fəʊnɪ] (compar **phonier**, superl **phoniest**, pl **phonies**) (informal use) ◇ *adj* **-1.** [money, information, address] false □ He was using a phony business card. □ She just has a really phony way of talking. **-2.** [person] who pretends to be good, kind, clever etc but is not really. ◇ *n* a phony person □ What a complete phony that guy is!

phony war *n* a period when war has been declared but there is no actual fighting.

phosphate ['fɒsfeɪt] *n* a chemical substance containing phosphorus, often used in making fertilizers.

phosphorus ['fɒsfərəs] *n* a poisonous element that is yellowish-white, glows in the dark, and burns when it is in contact with air. SYMBOL: P.

photo ['fəʊtəʊ] *n* = **photograph**.

photo booth *n* a small enclosed place in some stores, trains stations etc where one can have one's photo taken by putting money into a machine.

photocall ['fəʊtəʊkɔːl] *n* an organized session in which a famous person is photographed by press photographers.

photocopier ['fəʊtəʊkɒpɪər] *n* a machine that makes copies of documents, drawings etc onto paper by photographing them.

photocopy ['fəʊtəʊkɒpɪ] (pt & pp **photocopied**, pl **photocopies**) ◇ *n* a copy of something, e.g. a document or drawing, made by using a photocopier □ Do you have a photocopy of the report? ◇ *vt* [page, report] to make a photocopy of <sthg> using a photocopier □ Could you photocopy the last chapter?

photoelectric cell [,fəʊtəʊɪlektrɪk-] *n* a device that changes light into electricity, used in light meters and burglar alarms.

photo finish *n* the end of a race in which two or more competitors finish so close together that a photograph of them crossing the finishing line is needed to see who has won.

Photofit™ ['fəʊtəʊfɪt] *n* **a Photofit (picture)** GB a picture of somebody who the police are looking for, made up from many photographs of different parts of people's faces.

photogenic [,fəʊtəʊ'dʒenɪk] *adj* [person] who looks attractive in photographs □ She's very photogenic.

photograph [US 'fəʊtəɡræf, GB -ɡrɑːf] ◇ *n* a picture printed on special paper from a film that has been used in a camera □ That's a really good photograph of you. ■ **to take a photograph** to record a scene using a camera □ I took lots of photographs of the city. □ I hate having my photograph taken. ◇ vt [view, person] to take a photograph of <sb/sthg> □ We were photographed sitting next to the Senator.

photographer [fəˈtɒgrəfəʳ] n a person who takes photographs □ an amateur/a sports photographer.

photographic [ˌfoutəˈgræfɪk] adj [equipment, evidence] that is connected with photographs.

photographic memory n the ability to remember in great detail things that one has seen.

photography [fəˈtɒgrəfɪ] n the art, study, profession, or process of taking photographs □ black and white/commercial photography.

photojournalism [ˌfoutouˈdʒɜːʳnəlɪzm] n a type of journalism in which photographs are very important.

photon [ˈfoutɒn] n a tiny unit of electromagnetic radiation that travels at the speed of light.

photo opportunity n a situation in which a politician tries to be photographed, e.g. while doing something useful, impressive, or kind, because the photo will encourage people to see them in a positive way □ This will be a great photo opportunity for you.

photosensitive [ˌfoutouˈsensətɪv] adj [film, paper] that changes when light falls on it.

Photostat™ [ˈfoutəstæt] (pt & pp **photostatted**, cont **photostatting**) n a copy of a document, drawing etc made by using a particular type of photocopier.

◆ **photostat** vt [page, document] to make a Photostat of <sthg>.

photosynthesis [ˌfoutouˈsɪnθəsəs] n the process by which a plant produces its own food by using energy from sunlight.

phrasal verb [ˈfreɪzl-] n a group of words, made up of a verb and one or more other words, that has the meaning of a single verb, e.g. "to pick up" and "to get on with".

phrase [freɪz] ◇ n -1. a group of words that forms a unit, either alone or as part of a sentence □ How would you translate the phrase "to go swimming"? -2. a small fixed group of words that has a particular meaning, often one that is not easy to guess from each individual word □ I bought a book with lots of useful everyday phrases. □ What does the phrase "to put your foot in it" mean? ◇ vt [letter, idea] to say <sthg> in words in a particular way □ She tried to phrase it in such a way that it would not offend him.

phrasebook [ˈfreɪzbʊk] n a book that contains a list of useful phrases in a foreign language and their translations.

phraseology [ˌfreɪzɪˈɒlədʒɪ] n the particular way the words of a document, speech etc are chosen and used □ I found his phraseology somewhat confusing.

physical [ˈfɪzɪkl] ◇ adj -1. [exercise, attraction] that is connected with the body rather than the mind □ The grief caused her physical pain. □ We had a purely physical relationship. -2. [world,

object, form] that is real and can be touched □ They were separated by a physical as well as an ideological distance. -3. **a physical law/theory** a law/theory that is connected with physics. ◇ n = physical examination.

physical chemistry n the kind of chemistry connected with the relationship between the physical and chemical properties of substances.

physical education n games, sports, and exercises for children at school to keep them fit.

physical examination n a thorough medical examination, often carried out to see if somebody is fit to do a particular job.

physical geography n the kind of geography connected with the natural features of the Earth's surface.

physically [ˈfɪzɪklɪ] adv [fit, attractive, possible] see **physical** □ The doctor says I'm physically fit to travel. □ Did you physically give it to him or just leave it for him? □ It's physically impossible to jump from such a height and not injure oneself.

physically handicapped ◇ adj [person] who has a physical disability rather than a mental one. ◇ npl **the physically handicapped** physically handicapped people.

physical science n the sciences connected with the natural world, e.g. physics, chemistry, or geography.

physical training n = physical education.

physician [fəˈzɪʃn] n a doctor (formal use).

physicist [ˈfɪzəsəst] n a scientist who is trained in physics.

physics [ˈfɪzɪks] n the scientific study of matter and energy and the relationships between them, e.g. light, heat, and electricity.

physio [ˈfɪzɪou] (pl **physios**) n (informal use) -1. = physiotherapist. -2. = physiotherapy.

physiognomy [ˌfɪzɪˈɒnəmɪ] (pl **physiognomies**) n the face, especially when it is believed to show a person's character (formal use).

physiology [ˌfɪzɪˈɒlədʒɪ] n -1. the scientific study of the way in which plants and the bodies of people and animals work □ the study of anatomy and physiology. -2. the way in which a human or an animal's body or a plant works □ the physiology of reproduction.

physiotherapist [ˌfɪzɪouˈθerəpəst] n a person whose job is to give people physiotherapy.

physiotherapy [ˌfɪzɪouˈθerəpɪ] n the treatment of sick people, or people recovering from injuries, using exercise and massage.

physique [fəˈziːk] n the shape of a person's body □ He has a fine physique.

pianist [ˈpiːənəst] n a person who plays the piano.

piano [pɪˈænou] (pl **pianos**) n a musical instrument with a keyboard of black and white keys attached to a set of hammers that hit wires in a large wooden cabinet at the back □ How long have you played the piano?

piano accordion n an accordion that has a keyboard on one side.

Picasso [US pɪˈkɑːsou, GB -ˈkæsou], **Pablo** (1881–

1973) a Spanish artist. He was one of the founders of Cubism, and one of the most influential artists of the 20th century.

piccalilli [ˌpɪkəˈlɪlɪ] *n* a spicy yellow sauce made from chopped pickled vegetables that is eaten cold.

piccolo [ˈpɪkələʊ] (*pl* **piccolos**) *n* a musical instrument, like a small flute, that plays higher notes than the flute.

pick [pɪk] ◇ *n* -1. a pickax. -2. **to take one's pick** to choose the particular thing one wants from among a group of things □ *You can take your pick from thirty flavors of ice cream.* □ *Whichever one you like — take your pick.* -3. **the pick of the bunch** the best of a group of people or things □ *Jones and Howard were definitely the pick of the bunch.*
◇ *vt* -1. to choose <sb/sthg> from among a number of people or things □ *He always picks the worst time to visit.* □ *I've been picked to go on a management course.* □ *We both picked the lemon mousse for dessert.* -2. [flower, fruit, nut] to collect <sthg> by breaking if off a plant or tree □ *They're in the garden picking strawberries.* -3. [hair, piece of fluff] to remove <sthg> unwanted from a surface, using one's fingers □ *I spent hours picking the dog hairs off my clothes.* -4. **to pick one's nose** to remove small pieces of dried mucus from one's nostrils using one's fingers. ■ **to pick one's teeth** to remove small pieces of food from between one's teeth using a toothpick, match etc. -5. **to pick a fight/quarrel** to deliberately start a fight/quarrel with somebody □ *Someone tried to pick a fight with Bob in the bar.* -6. **to pick a lock** to open a lock using a small sharp instrument instead of a key, especially for an illegal purpose. -7. **to pick one's way across/through sthg** to walk across/through sthg carefully, choosing where to put one's feet to avoid dirt, water, or danger □ *I had to pick my way across that muddy yard in my sandals.*
◇ *vi* to choose □ *He pointed to some rings and said I could pick any one I wanted.* ■ **to pick and choose** to be in a situation where one can choose exactly what one wants because there is a wide choice □ *With so many applicants for every job, employers can afford to pick and choose.*

◆ **pick at** *vt fus* **to pick at one's food** to eat small pieces of food because one is not hungry or does not like what one is eating □ *She only picked at her dinner.*

◆ **pick on** *vt fus* **to pick on sb** to treat sb harshly or unfairly □ *Why does he always have to pick on me?*

◆ **pick out** *vt sep* -1. **to pick sb/sthg out** to recognize sb/sthg among a group of similar people or things □ *She's easy to pick out in a crowd because of her red hair.* -2. **to pick sb/sthg out** to choose sb/sthg from a group of people or things □ *We look at the applications and pick out the best candidates.*

◆ **pick up** ◇ *vt sep* -1. **to pick sb/sthg up** [object, baby, animal] to take hold of sb/sthg in one's hands and lift it up, especially sthg small or light □ *If you get lonely, just pick up* the phone and call me. □ *Please pick up all your litter.* ■ **to pick up the pieces** to start trying to live normally again after a difficult or unhappy experience □ *After the divorce I just had to pick up the pieces and carry on.* -2. **to pick sb/sthg up** [person, ticket, dry cleaning] to go to a place and collect sb/sthg waiting there □ *Could you pick up the kids from school tomorrow?* -3. **to pick sthg up** [skill, language] to learn sthg, especially without much effort □ *He picked up Italian in no time.* -4. **to pick up an infection/a virus etc** to get an infection/virus etc □ *I must have picked up some stomach bug when I was abroad.* -5. **to pick up speed** [vehicle] to begin to move faster □ *Once we reached the freeway, the car picked up speed.* -6. **to be picked up for sthg** to be arrested for sthg □ *He was picked up by the police for shoplifting.* -7. **to pick sb up** [person] to start talking to sb one does not know and start a sexual relationship with them (informal use) □ *She picked him up in a bar somewhere.* -8. RADIO & TECHNOLOGY **to pick sthg up** [signal, sound, radio station] to be able to hear or receive sthg □ *The ship's SOS call was picked up by a fishing boat in the area.* -9. **to pick sthg up** [career, conversation, relationship] to continue sthg after an interruption □ *Let's pick up the story where we left off last week.*
◇ *vi* -1. [business, production, sales] to improve or increase after a difficult time □ *The economy is beginning to pick up after the recession.* -2. to start something again after an interruption □ *We can go several months without seeing each other but then when we meet again we just pick up where we left off.*

pickax US, **pickaxe** GB [ˈpɪkæks] *n* a tool for breaking rocks, hard ground etc, consisting of a piece of heavy metal with two ends, one a long curved blade and the other a short blade or point, that is attached to a long wooden handle.

picker [ˈpɪkər] *n* a person whose job is to pick a particular crop, e.g. fruit or cotton.

picket [ˈpɪkət] ◇ *n* -1. a person who is picketing a place of work; a group of these people □ *There's a picket outside the factory gates.* -2. = **picketing.** ◇ *vt* [factory, mine] to stand outside <a place of work where there is a strike> and try to persuade people not to go in □ *They've been picketing the works since last week.*

picket fence *n* a fence made from long pointed sticks fixed in the ground.

picketing [ˈpɪkətɪŋ] *n* the act of picketing a place of work.

picket line *n* a line of pickets □ *The drivers won't cross the picket line.*

pickings [ˈpɪkɪŋz] *npl* **easy/rich pickings** a chance to make money easily/to make a lot of money □ *Rich pickings are to be had in multimedia.*

pickle [ˈpɪkl] ◇ *n* -1. a pickled cucumber □ *Do you want a pickle with your pastrami?* -2. a food consisting of chopped vegetables that have been pickled, often in a spicy sauce □ *a cheese and pickle sandwich.* -3. *phrase* **to be in**

a pickle to be in a difficult situation (informal use) □ *She's gotten herself into a pickle again.* ◇ *vt* [onion, egg] to preserve <food> in vinegar or salt water □ *Pickle the cucumbers in vinegar.*

◆ **pickles** *npl* pickled vegetables □ *cold meats with mixed pickles.*

pickled ['pɪkld] *adj* [onion, cabbage, egg] that has been pickled.

pick-me-up *n* a drink or medicine that makes one feel stronger or more cheerful.

pickpocket ['pɪkpɒkət] *n* a person who steals things from people's pockets □ *'Beware of pickpockets.'*

pick-up *n* -1. the part of a record player that holds the needle and moves across the record as the needle follows the groove. -2. AUTO = **pick-up truck**.

pick-up truck *n* a van that is open at the back and has low sides so that it can be loaded and unloaded easily.

picky ['pɪkɪ] (*compar* **pickier**, *superl* **pickiest**) *adj* [person] who is difficult to please □ *Don't be so picky — just eat what's in front of you.*

picnic ['pɪknɪk] (*pt* & *pp* **picnicked**, *cont* **picnicking**) ◇ *n* a meal that is eaten outdoors, usually in the countryside □ *They went on a picnic.* □ *a picnic lunch.* ◇ *vi* to eat a picnic.

picnicker ['pɪknɪkəʳ] *n* a person who is having a picnic.

pictorial [pɪk'tɔːrɪəl] *adj* [magazine, article, art] that uses pictures.

picture ['pɪktʃəʳ] ◇ *n* -1. a painting or drawing □ *She drew a picture of the view from her window.* □ *They had lots of pictures on the walls.* -2. PHOTOGRAPHY a photograph, especially one that has been taken quickly □ *He took a picture of the elephants.* □ *Do you have a picture of your son?* -3. TV an image on a television screen □ *We can't get a good picture.* -4. CINEMA a movie. -5. [in one's mind] an idea in somebody's mind □ *I have a clear picture of how I want the company to develop.* □ *This should give you a picture of the way it's been handled so far.* -6. **the financial/political etc picture** the financial/political etc situation □ *The economic picture is bleak.* -7. **the picture of sthg** [happiness, despair] a perfect example of sthg □ *There she was, looking the picture of good health.* -8. phrases **to get the picture** to understand the general idea or situation (informal use) □ *Right, yes, I get the picture.* ■ **to put sb in the picture** to tell sb everything they need to know about a situation in order to understand it □ *I should be able to put you in the picture by tomorrow.* ■ **to be in/out of the picture** to be involved/not to be involved in a particular situation □ *Don't ask me, I'm completely out of the picture.*
◇ *vt* -1. [future, difficulty] to imagine <sthg> □ *I can just picture him saying that!* -2. [person, event] to show <sb/sthg> in a photograph or picture □ *The couple are pictured here together in Barbados.*

◆ **pictures** *npl* **the pictures** the movies (old-fashioned use) □ *Do you want to come with us to the pictures tonight?*

picture book *n* a book for young children, containing only or mostly pictures.

picture rail *n* a narrow piece of wood fixed along the walls of some rooms just below the ceiling, on which pictures can be hung.

picturesque [,pɪktʃə'resk] *adj* [scene, building, village] charming and attractive, usually in an old-fashioned way.

picture window *n* a large window with a single pane of glass and a pleasant view.

piddling ['pɪdlɪŋ] *adj* [job, details] unimportant; [amount, salary] very small (disapproving and informal use).

pidgin ['pɪdʒɪn] *n* a language that is a simplified mixture of two other languages, usually spoken by people who do business together but who do not speak each other's languages □ *pidgin English/French.*

pie [paɪ] *n* a dish that consists of fruit, meat, or vegetables, baked in a pastry case, usually with pastry on top. ■ **pie in the sky** some-thing that one wants or hopes for, but that is very unlikely to happen □ *I'm beginning to realize that my dreams of promotion are just pie in the sky.*

piebald ['paɪbɔːld] *adj* [horse] that has large black and white patches.

piece [piːs] *n* -1. [of cake, string, paper] a part of something that is separated from the rest □ *Can you pass me a piece of bread?* □ *There was a piece of glass on the floor.* □ *I wrote it on a piece of newspaper.* ■ **to be smashed to pieces** [plane, glass] to be broken into many small pieces. ■ **to fall to pieces** [car, furniture, building] to become damaged □ *This house is falling to pieces.* ■ **to pull** OR **tear sthg to pieces** to criticize sthg harshly □ *She tore my essay to pieces.* ■ **to take sthg to pieces** [car, machine] to separate all the parts of sthg from each other □ *Once he'd taken it all to pieces, he couldn't put it back together again.* ■ **in pieces** [toy, glass] that has been broken into pieces; [engine] that has been taken to pieces □ *There, in pieces on the floor, was my clock.* ■ **in one piece** [glass, car] not seriously damaged; [person] not seriously injured □ *Fortunately, the car was/we were all in one piece.* ■ **to go to pieces** [person] to be so upset, worried, frightened etc that one can no longer deal with normal life □ *He went to pieces after the death of his wife.* -2. [of equipment, advice, furniture] an individual example of a particular thing □ *That was a piece of luck!* □ *an interesting piece of information* □ *It's an excellent piece of work/writing.* -3. GAMES one of a set of objects that are moved by players in some board games, e.g. chess or checkers □ *a chess piece.* -4. [of music, art] a single work of art, music, drama, or journalism □ *The "Emperor Concerto" is one of Beethoven's best-known pieces.* □ *There was a piece about it in yesterday's paper.* -5. **a 50 cent/10 pence piece** a coin that is worth 50 cents/10 pence □ *a 10-cent piece.*

◆ **piece together** *vt sep* **to piece sthg together** [story, truth] to gradually find out about sthg by deciding how the facts fit together □

Gradually, we were able to piece together details of the crime.

pièce de résistance [US pɪˌesdərezɪːˈstɑːns, GB pɪˌesdereˈzɪstɑːns] (*pl* **pièces de résistance** [pɪˌes-]) *n* the best or most important one of a group of things, e.g. works of art or courses of a meal □ *The pièce de résistance was an incredible salmon mousse.*

piecemeal [ˈpiːsmiːl] ◇ *adj* [change, withdrawal] that happens gradually, a little at a time. ◇ *adv* [change, withdraw] *The town was rebuilt piecemeal after the war.*

piecework [ˈpiːswɜːʳk] *n* work that is paid according to the amount of work somebody does, and not according to the amount of time they spend doing it.

pie chart *n* a circle divided into sections by lines drawn from the center, used to show how something, e.g. the population or money, is divided into different groups.

pied-à-terre [pɪˌeɪdɑːˈteɑʳ] (*pl* **pieds-à-terre** [pɪˌeɪd-]) *n* a small house or apartment, usually in a town, that is owned by somebody living somewhere else who only uses it some of the time.

Pied Piper [ˌpaɪd-]: **the Pied Piper** in German folk stories, a musician who took all the rats away from the town of Hamelin by playing his flute. When the people of the town refused to pay him, he took all the children away.

pier [pɪəʳ] *n* a long wooden or metal structure that sticks out into the sea, is used for people to walk on, and often has amusement arcades or a small theater built on it.

pierce [pɪəʳs] *vt* -1. to make a small hole in or through <sthg> with a sharp object □ *Pierce the film several times with a fork and microwave for four minutes.* ■ **to have one's ears pierced** to have small holes made in parts of one's ears, so that one can wear earrings. -2. to be suddenly heard, seen, or felt through the darkness, silence etc □ *A flashlight pierced the darkness.*

pierced [pɪəʳst] *adj* [ear, nose] that has been pierced so that one can wear earrings or rings.

piercing [ˈpɪəʳsɪŋ] *adj* -1. [sound, scream] that is unpleasantly high and loud □ *He blew into the instrument and produced high, piercing notes.* -2. [wind] that is very cold and strong. -3. [eyes] that are very bright and seem able to see and understand things very clearly □ *piercing blue eyes* □ *She gave me a piercing look.*

piety [ˈpaɪətɪ] *n* strong belief in and respect for God, shown by one's behavior.

pig [pɪg] (*pt* & *pp* **pigged**, *cont* **pigging**) *n* -1. an animal that is usually pink, has a flat nose, short legs, and a short curly tail, and is often kept on farms for its meat. -2. a person who eats too much, or who eats in a greedy and untidy way (informal and disapproving use) □ *Try to eat properly and stop being such a pig!* ■ **to make a pig of oneself** to eat a lot of food at one time □ *I made such a pig of myself at Mark's yesterday.* -3. a word used to refer to somebody one thinks is unkind or unpleasant (informal and disapproving use). □ *You pig! You've taken my jacket again!*

◆ **pig out** *vi* to eat a lot of food at one time (informal use) □ *If we go to the pizza place we can really pig out.*

pigeon [ˈpɪdʒən] (*pl* **pigeon** OR **pigeons**) *n* a bird that often lives in cities and has a small head, a large body, and gray or white feathers. Some types of pigeon are used to carry messages.

pigeon-chested [-ˈtʃestəd] *adj* [person] who has a narrow chest that sticks out at the front.

pigeonhole [ˈpɪdʒənhoʊl] ◇ *n* one of the square compartments in a wooden framework attached to a wall or on a desk, where messages, mail, or documents are left for somebody or kept □ *Was there anything in my pigeonhole?* ◇ *vt* [person, job, policy] to decide that <sb/sthg> is a particular type of person or thing, even if this is not completely true □ *They pigeonholed her as a feminist.*

pigeon-toed [-toʊd] *adj* [person] whose feet point slightly toward each other when they are standing or walking.

piggish [ˈpɪgɪʃ] *adj* [manners, behavior, person] very rude and unpleasant.

piggy [ˈpɪgɪ] (*compar* **piggier**, *superl* **piggiest**, *pl* **piggies**) ◇ *adj* [eyes, face] that makes somebody look like a pig. ◇ *n* a word used by young children to refer to a pig (informal use).

piggyback [ˈpɪgɪbæk] *n* **to give sb a piggyback (ride)** to carry sb, especially a child, on one's back, supporting their legs with one's arms.

piggybank [ˈpɪgɪbæŋk] *n* a child's money box, often in the shape of a pig, with a narrow space at the top to put coins in.

pigheaded [ˌpɪgˈhedəd] *adj* [person, attitude, behavior] unreasonably stubborn □ *She can be so pigheaded sometimes.*

piglet [ˈpɪglət] *n* a young pig.

pigment [ˈpɪgmənt] *n* -1. [in hair, skin, plants] a natural substance that gives something its color. -2. a powder that is mixed with a liquid to make paint, dyes etc.

pigmentation [ˌpɪgmənˈteɪʃn] *n* [of skin, hair, plants] the natural coloring produced by pigment.

pigmy [ˈpɪgmɪ] (*pl* **pigmies**) *n* = **pygmy**.

pigpen [ˈpɪgpen] *n* FARMING = **pigsty**.

pigskin [ˈpɪgskɪn] *n* the leather made from the skin of pigs □ *a pigskin bag/strap.*

pigsty [ˈpɪgstaɪ] (*pl* **pigsties**) *n* -1. FARMING a closed area or building where pigs are kept. -2. a very dirty messy place □ *This place is a complete pigsty!*

pigswill [ˈpɪgswɪl] *n* -1. FARMING food given to pigs. -2. food of very poor quality (informal use).

pigtail [ˈpɪgteɪl] *n* one of two bunches of long hair braided or tied together so that they hang on either side of one's face or head; a single bunch of hair braided or tied together so that it hangs down one's back.

pike [paɪk] (*pl sense 1 only* **pike** OR **pikes**) *n* -1. a large freshwater fish with sharp teeth that eats other fish. -2. MILITARY a kind of spear used by soldiers in the past.

pilaster [pɪ'læstəʳ] *n* a decorative rectangular column forming part of the wall of a building.

pilchard ['pɪltʃəʳd] *n* a small saltwater fish often sold in cans as food.

pile [paɪl] ◇ *n* -1. [of sand, washing] a quantity of something that is gathered together and forms a single mass that is higher in the middle than at the sides; [of books, plates, bricks] a tidy collection of objects, usually of the same kind, placed on top of each other □ *a pile of old newspapers*. ■ **piles** OR **a pile of sthg** [of money, work] a lot of sthg (informal use) □ *He made piles of money.* -2. [of carpet, velvet] the soft surface of a material formed by short threads or fibers.

◇ *vt* [papers, books, logs] to make a pile of <a number of things> □ *She piled the plates neatly in the sink.* ■ **to be piled with sthg** to be filled or covered with a large quantity of sthg □ *The sink was piled (high) with dirty plates.*

◆ **piles** *npl* MEDICINE = **hemorrhoids.**

◆ **pile in** *vi* [spectators, passengers] to enter somewhere together in an uncontrolled way (informal use) □ *I opened the door and they all piled in.*

◆ **pile into** *vt fus* **to pile into sthg** [car, bus, house] to enter sthg in an uncontrolled way as a group (informal use) □ *We all piled into the back of the truck.*

◆ **pile out** *vi* [spectators, passengers] to leave somewhere together in an uncontrolled way (informal use) □ *Even before the final whistle the crowds were piling out of the stadium.*

◆ **pile up** ◇ *vt sep* **to pile sthg up** [books, papers, logs] to make a pile of a lot of sthg □ *He piled the plates up on one side of the sink.* ◇ *vi* [work, debts, evidence] to increase gradually in quantity □ *The bills just keep piling up.*

pile driver *n* a machine for forcing heavy posts into the ground as supports for buildings, bridges etc.

pileup ['paɪlʌp] *n* a crash involving a line of vehicles in which each one has hit the back of the one in front □ *There was a massive pileup on the freeway.*

pilfer ['pɪlfəʳ] ◇ *vt* [food, clothing, supplies] to steal small quantities of <sthg>. ◇ *vi: He was caught pilfering from the supermarket.*

pilgrim ['pɪlgrɪm] *n* a person who goes on a pilgrimage.

◆ **Pilgrims** *npl* **the Pilgrims** the first English people who settled in America. They went there to follow their religious beliefs freely.

pilgrimage ['pɪlgrəmɪdʒ] *n* a journey to a holy place for religious reasons □ *Their aim is to make/go on a pilgrimage to Mecca.*

Pilgrim Fathers *npl* = **Pilgrims.**

pill [pɪl] *n* -1. MEDICINE medicine in the form of a small, rounded, solid object that is swal-

lowed □ *He has to take pills for his high blood pressure.* -2. **the pill** a hormone taken in pill form by women as a contraceptive. ■ **to be on the pill** to use the pill regularly □ *She said she was on the pill.*

pillage ['pɪlɪdʒ] ◇ *n* violent robbery and destruction, especially by an army in wartime. ◇ *vt* [houses, town, area] to attack and rob <a place> in a violent destructive way, especially in wartime.

pillar ['pɪləʳ] *n* a tall column, usually of stone, used as a support for a building or as a monument. ■ **to be a pillar of sthg** [of a community, church] to be an influential and active member or supporter of sthg. ■ **a pillar of strength** a person who is emotionally strong and gives support to other people.

pillar box *n* GB a red public mailbox shaped like a vertical cylinder that is found in the street.

pillbox ['pɪlbɒks] *n* -1. a small round box for keeping pills in. -2. MILITARY a small, usually circular, concrete shelter for soldiers from which a gun can be fired.

pillion ['pɪljən] *n* **to ride pillion** to travel on a motorcycle, sitting behind the driver.

pillory ['pɪlərɪ] (*pl* **pillories,** *pt* & *pp* **pilloried**) ◇ *n* a wooden framework with holes for the neck and wrists of criminals who were locked there in the past to be punished and humiliated. ◇ *vt* to criticize <sb/sthg> very strongly in public □ *His opinions were pilloried in the press.*

pillow ['pɪloʊ] *n* -1. [on a bed] a rectangular cushion used to support one's head in bed. -2. US [on a chair, sofa] a small decorative cushion.

pillowcase ['pɪloʊkeɪs], **pillowslip** ['pɪloʊslɪp] *n* a cloth cover for a pillow that can be removed and washed.

pilot ['paɪlət] ◇ *n* -1. AVIATION a person who is trained to fly an aircraft □ *a helicopter/fighter pilot* □ *The crash was apparently due to pilot error.* -2. SHIPPING a person who comes onto a ship in order to steer it through a difficult section of water, e.g. a harbor entrance. -3. TV a TV program that, if it is popular, may be continued as a series □ *They've been making a pilot for a new drama series.*

◇ *comp* [project, scheme, study] that is carried out on a small scale to see if it is worth doing on a larger scale.

◇ *vt* -1. AVIATION [plane, helicopter] to fly <an aircraft>. -2. SHIPPING [ferry, tanker] to act as the pilot of <a ship>. -3. [law, bill, plan] to introduce and support the progress of <sthg> □ *Senator Dilkin successfully piloted the bill through Congress.* -4. [project, system] to test <sthg> on a small scale to see if it is worth doing on a larger scale □ *An identity card system is being piloted in some cities.*

pilot light, pilot burner *n* a small flame, e.g. in a gas stove, that burns constantly and is used to light the main flame.

pimento [pɪ'mentoʊ] (*pl* **pimento** OR **pimentos**) *n* a sweet pepper □ *a red/yellow/green pimento.*

pimp [pɪmp] *n* a man who controls prostitutes and takes part of the money they earn (informal use).

pimple ['pɪmpl] *n* a small red spot on one's skin, especially on one's face.

pimply ['pɪmplɪ] (*compar* **pimplier**, *superl* **pimpliest**) *adj* [face, skin] that has pimples □ *a pimply teenager*.

pin [pɪn] (*pt* & *pp* **pinned**, *cont* **pinning**) ◇ *n* -1. [for fabric] a short piece of very fine metal with a sharp point at one end and a round head at the other, used to hold together pieces of fabric. ■ **to have pins and needles** to have an unpleasant feeling in a part of one's body caused by blood returning after being cut off by pressure, e.g. because one has been sitting or lying in an uncomfortable position □ *I have pins and needles in my foot/legs*. ■ **to be on pins and needles** US to be very nervous or excited about something that is going to happen, but that one is not certain about □ *I was on pins and needles all day waiting for the result.* -2. a safety pin. -3. US a piece of jewelry that is attached to clothes using a pin at the back, worn by women on blouses, jackets etc. -4. TECHNOLOGY a metal or wooden peg used to support things, hold things together etc □ *Doctors inserted a metal pin in his leg.* -5. [on a grenade] a clip on a hand grenade that stops it exploding until it is removed. -6. **the pin** GOLF the flagpole that shows players where the hole in the green is. -7. GB ELECTRICITY one of the metal parts on an electric plug which fit into a wall socket □ *a two-/three-pin plug.*
◇ *vt* -1. **to pin sthg on** OR **to sthg** [piece of cloth, medal, notice] to attach sthg with a pin or pins to sthg else □ *She had a brooch pinned to her jacket.* -2. **to pin sb against** OR **to sthg** [against a wall, to the floor] to hold sb firmly against sthg so that they are unable to move □ *He pinned me against the wall with his arms.* -3. **to pin sthg on sb** [crime] to show that sb is responsible for sthg (informal use) □ *They're trying to pin the blame on me!*

◆ **pin down** *vt sep* -1. **to pin sthg down** to define or identify sthg exactly □ *I know there's something wrong but it's hard to pin down.* -2. **to pin sb down** to force sb to be definite about something □ *We must try and pin him down to a schedule.*

◆ **pin up** *vt sep* -1. **to pin sthg up** [poster, notice] to pin sthg on a wall. -2. **to pin sthg up** [hem, sleeve, hair] to pin sthg so that the end is in a higher position □ *She'd pinned her hair up into a bun.*

PIN [pɪn] (*abbr of* **personal identification number**) *n* = PIN number.

pinafore ['pɪnəfɔːʳ] *n* a kind of apron with a strap that goes around one's neck and that covers one's chest.

pinafore dress *n* GB a kind of dress without sleeves that is worn over a blouse or other garment.

pinball ['pɪnbɔːl] *n* a game played on a machine like a large sloping box with a glass cover. A steel ball inside rolls down toward the player, who tries to send it back up the slope and score points by hitting targets, using movable parts controlled by buttons on the side of the machine.

pinball machine, pinball table *n* a machine on which pinball is played.

pincers ['pɪnsəʳz] *npl* -1. a tool consisting of two crossed pieces of metal hinged in the middle and with curved parts at one end that are used to grip things, e.g. a nail that must be pulled out of wood □ *a pair of pincers* □ *I need some pincers.* -2. [of a crab, lobster] the front claws of some shellfish.

pinch [pɪntʃ] ◇ *vt* -1. [arm, cheek, person] to squeeze <sb/sthg> tightly between one's thumb and forefinger □ *I had to pinch myself to make sure I wasn't dreaming.* □ *I can't believe it! He pinched my bottom!* -2. [money, car, clothes] to steal <sthg> (informal use) □ *She's pinched all my favorite records.*
◇ *vi* [shoes] to hurt somebody by being too tight.
◇ *n* -1. the act of pinching somebody or something with one's fingers □ *She gave him a pinch to wake him up.* ■ **to feel the pinch** to be suffering because one does not have enough money □ *Everyone is feeling the pinch in the current recession.* -2. [of salt, sugar, powder] a small amount of something, about as much as one can hold between one's thumb and forefinger □ *Add a pinch of nutmeg.*
◆ **in a pinch** US, **at a pinch** GB *adv* if there is no other alternative □ *In a pinch we could probably fit another person in.*

pinched [pɪntʃt] *adj* -1. [look, face] that is thin, pale, and looks tired □ *Her face was pinched with cold/hunger.* -2. **to be pinched for sthg** [for time, money] not to have enough of sthg.

pincushion ['pɪnkʊʃn] *n* a very small cushion that pins are stuck into when they are not being used.

pine [paɪn] ◇ *n* a tall evergreen tree with needle-shaped leaves and brown cones; the wood of this tree □ *a pine forest* □ *a pine table/kitchen.* ◇ *vi* to be very unhappy because one is missing somebody or something very much □ *She's pining for her friends.*
◆ **pine away** *vi* to become weaker and slowly die from pining □ *After his wife died, he just pined away.*

pineapple ['paɪnæpl] *n* a large oval tropical fruit with sweet yellow flesh, tough, brown, knobbly skin, and thin hard leaves growing out of the top; the flesh of this fruit □ *pineapple juice.*

pinecone ['paɪnkəʊn] *n* a small, brown, oval object that grows on a pine tree and contains seeds.

pine needle *n* a thin, sharp, dark-green leaf that grows on a pinetree.

pinetree ['paɪntriː] *n* a pine.

pinewood ['paɪnwʊd] *n* -1. an area full of pinetrees. -2. the wood of the pinetree □ *The furniture is made from pinewood.*

ping [pɪŋ] ◇ *n* a short, sharp, ringing sound made when a hard object hits metal, glass etc □ *There was a loud ping as the strap broke.* ◇ *vi* [bell, metal] to make a ping □ *It will ping when the food's ready.*

Ping-Pong™ *n* table tennis.

pinhole ['pɪnhoul] *n* a small hole made by a pin or something similar.

pinion ['pɪnjən] ◇ *n* TECHNOLOGY a small cogwheel that drives or is driven by a larger cogwheel. ◇ *vt* to tie or hold <sb> by their arms or legs to prevent them from moving.

pink [pɪŋk] ◇ *adj* [cheeks, dress, flowers] of a color between red and white. ■ **to turn** OR **go pink** to become red in the face because of embarrassment □ *When I mentioned it he turned pink.* ◇ *n* **-1.** a color between red and white □ *a lovely shade of pink.* **-2.** GARDENING a garden plant with sweet-smelling pink, white, or red flowers.

pinkie ['pɪŋkɪ] *n* one's little finger (humorous and informal use).

pinking ['pɪŋkɪŋ] *n* GB AUTO metallic knocking sounds made by an engine that is not running properly.

pinking scissors, pinking shears *npl* scissors that have a row of V-shapes along the edges of the blades, used to cut material so that it does not fray □ *a pair of pinking scissors.*

pin money *n* small amounts of extra money saved or earned, especially by a married woman, for personal expenses.

pinnacle ['pɪnəkl] *n* **-1. the pinnacle of sthg** [of success, one's career] the highest point of something □ *He had reached the pinnacle of fame.* **-2.** [of a mountain] a pointed mountain peak. **-3.** [of a building] the pointed top part of a church spire, tower etc.

PIN number *n* a number that a person uses with a special card in order to use a cash dispenser to take out money, check their balance etc.

Pinocchio [pɪ'noukɪou] a wooden puppet in a fairy story who is brought to life. When he lies his nose grows longer.

pinpoint ['pɪnpɔɪnt] *vt* **-1.** [cause, danger] to identify <sthg> exactly □ *I was unable to pinpoint the source of the problem.* **-2.** [position, target] to find or show the exact location of <sthg> □ *He pinpointed it on the map.*

pinprick ['pɪnprɪk] *n* a small mark or hole made by the point of a pin or something similar; the feeling one has when this kind of point touches one's skin.

pin-striped *adj* [suit, cloth] that has very thin, vertical, white stripes on a dark background.

pint [paɪnt] *n* **-1.** a unit (US 0.473 liters, GB 0.568 liters) for measuring liquids □ *a pint of milk.* **-2.** GB a pint of beer □ *Do you feel like going for a pint?* □ *a pint of lager.*

pint-size(d) *adj* very small (informal use).

pinup ['pɪnʌp] *n* a picture of an attractive or famous person for pinning up on a wall, door etc; a person who often appears in this type of picture □ *The walls were covered with pinups.* □ *She was a famous 1940s pinup.*

pioneer [,paɪə'nɪər] ◇ *n* **-1.** [in a place] a person who is one of the first to settle in and develop an area or country □ *one of the early Spanish pioneers.* **-2.** [in a subject] a person who is one of the first to study and develop a new area of activity or knowledge □ *a pioneer of modern medicine/new political thinking.* □ *He was a pioneer in the field of quantum mechanics.* ◇ *vt* [activity, invention, process] to act as a pioneer in the development or introduction of <sthg> □ *She pioneered the use of plastic, rather than metal, for the process.*

pioneering [,paɪə'nɪərɪŋ] *adj* [work, research] that is the first to introduce or develop a new activity or knowledge □ *a pioneering study of the Brazilian rain forest.*

pious ['paɪəs] *adj* **-1.** [person] who behaves in a way that shows sincere respect for their religion □ *a very pious man.* **-2.** [comments, behavior, expression] that somebody intends to seem sincere but which is seen by other people to be false (disapproving use).

piously ['paɪəslɪ] *adv* [behave, act, say] *see* **pious** (disapproving use).

pip [pɪp] *n* GB [in an apple, orange, lemon] a seed from a fruit □ *an apple/lemon pip.*

♦ **pips** *npl* **the pips** the series of short high-pitched notes used on the radio or telephone as a way of showing what time it is.

pipe [paɪp] ◇ *n* **-1.** [for water, oil, gas] a tube for carrying liquids or gases □ *a gas/hot water pipe* □ *a metal pipe.* **-2.** [for smoking] an object consisting of a tube with a small bowl at one end that is used for smoking tobacco □ *a man smoking a pipe.* **-3.** MUSIC any musical instrument that is shaped like a narrow tube and is played by blowing air through it □ *an organ pipe.* ◇ *vt* **-1.** to move <a liquid or gas> through pipes □ *The gas is piped underground.* **-2.** to play <music> over loudspeakers in a public place □ *They were piping some awful electronic music over the loudspeakers.*

♦ **pipes** *npl* **the pipes** MUSIC the bagpipes □ *I could hear some pipes playing in the distance.*

♦ **pipe down** *vi* to stop talking or making a noise (informal use) □ *Pipe down, will you!*

♦ **pipe up** *vi* to begin to speak suddenly or unexpectedly (informal use) □ *It was Sophie who piped up with the answer.*

pipe cleaner *n* a flexible length of wire covered in soft material, used for cleaning inside a tobacco pipe.

piped music [,paɪpt-] *n* recorded music played continuously over loudspeakers in public places, e.g. supermarkets or restaurants.

pipe dream *n* something that one wants to happen in the future but that is not likely to happen or is impossible □ *Moving abroad? It's just a pipe dream at the moment.*

pipeline ['paɪplaɪn] *n* a very long, large, metal pipe made in separate sections for carrying oil, gas etc over long distances □ *an oil/a gas pipeline.* ■ **to be in the pipeline** to be in preparation □ *Major changes are in the pipeline.*

piper ['paɪpər] *n* a musician who plays the bagpipes □ *We heard a piper in the distance.*

piping hot ['paɪpɪŋ-] adj [food, coffee, soup] very hot □ Be careful, the water's piping hot.

pipsqueak ['pɪpskwiːk] n a person, especially a child, who acts as if they are more important than they really are (disapproving use).

piquant ['piːkɑːnt] adj -1. [food] that tastes hot. -2. [situation, story] full of meaning.

pique [piːk] n anger that one feels because one's pride has been hurt □ He resigned in a fit of pique.

piracy ['paɪrəsi] n -1. [at sea] robbery carried out by pirates □ an act of piracy. -2. [of video tape, music, software] the act of copying and selling something illegally.

piranha [pɪ'rɑːnə] n a small South American freshwater fish with sharp teeth that eats meat.

pirate ['paɪrət] ◇ comp [video, cassette, edition] that is copied illegally to be sold □ Pirate copies of the movie have flooded the market. ◇ n -1. SHIPPING a person who attacks and robs ships at sea. -2. BUSINESS a person who copies and sells videos, cassettes etc illegally. ◇ vt [videotape, music, software] to copy and sell <sthg> illegally.

pirate radio n GB radio stations that broadcast programs illegally □ a pirate radio station.

pirouette [ˌpɪru'et] ◇ n a fast turn made by a ballet dancer while balancing on one foot. ◇ vi to perform a pirouette.

Pisces ['paɪsiːz] n a sign of the zodiac, often represented by two fish; a person born under this sign between February 20 and March 20.

piss▽ [pɪs] (very informal use) ◇ n -1. urine. ■ to have a piss to urinate. -2. to take the piss out of sb/sthg GB to make fun of sb/sthg. ◇ vi to urinate.

◆ **piss off**▽ ◇ vt sep to piss sb off to make sb angry. ◇ vi GB to go away. ■ piss off! a phrase used to tell somebody to go away.

pissed▽ [pɪst] adj (very informal use) -1. to be pissed US to be annoyed. -2. to be pissed GB to be drunk.

pissed off▽ adj to be pissed off to be annoyed (very informal use).

pistachio [pɪ'stæʃɪoʊ] (pl pistachios) n a pistachio (nut) a small nut that is green inside the shell.

piste [piːst] n GB a track in snow for skiing on □ skiing on the piste.

pistol ['pɪstl] n a small handgun.

piston ['pɪstən] n a cylinder-shaped part of an engine whose movement up and down inside a cylinder makes the other parts of the engine move.

pit [pɪt] (pt & pp pitted, cont pitting) ◇ n -1. [in the ground] a large, usually deep hole □ They had dug a deep pit to bury the waste. □ a burial pit. -2. [in a road, metal, glass] a small shallow hole in the surface of something; [in one's skin] a small hollow scar left by a disease such as smallpox. -3. [in a theater] = orchestra pit. -4. a coalmine □ He's worked down the pit all his life. -5. a quarry □ a chalk/clay pit. -6. US [of a cherry, plum] the hard seed in the center of some fruits. -7. the pit of one's stomach the part of the stomach where people say they can feel an emotion such as fear □ I had this terrible feeling in the pit of my stomach.

◇ vt to be pitted against sb to compete with sb in a test of strength, endurance etc □ We were pitted against people with twice our experience. ■ to pit one's wits against sb to compete with sb in a test of intelligence □ an opportunity to pit your wits against the experts.

◆ **pits** npl -1. the pits SPORT the area on a motor racing track where cars stop for fuel, tire changes, repairs etc. -2. the pits the worst possible example of something (informal use) □ This program is the pits! □ This really is the pits! I'm leaving!

pita bread ['piːtə-] US, **pitta bread** ['pɪtə-] GB n a type of small flat bread that is hollow in the center and can be used to put meat, salad etc in.

pit bull (terrier) n a large dog with a short smooth coat, originally bred for fighting.

pitch [pɪtʃ] ◇ n -1. MUSIC [of a sound, note, voice] a measure of how high or low a sound is □ His voice reached an even higher pitch. -2. [of a feeling] the strength of a feeling □ Tension reached such a pitch that troops were called in to restore order. -3. [to a customer, crowd] the things somebody says when they are trying to persuade somebody else to do something, e.g. to buy something □ Then he gave her his pitch about how nice it was in Majorca in August. -4. [of a ship, plane] the upward and downward movement of the front part of a ship or aircraft. -5. [for a boat, roof] a sticky black substance that comes from melting tar and is used, e.g. on a ship, to seal gaps and prevent water from passing through. -6. GB SPORT an area of ground on which a particular sport is played □ a soccer/cricket pitch.

◇ vt -1. [ball, coin] to throw <sthg> in a particular direction after aiming first □ Karl pitched the bottle up in the air/into the lake. ■ to be pitched into sthg to be suddenly forced into sthg that is difficult to deal with □ I was suddenly pitched into a completely new working environment. -2. to set <a price> at a particular level □ Our prices are pitched very competitively. -3. [talk, exam] to write, give, or design <sthg> in a way that is suitable for a particular audience □ Try to pitch it at a level they will understand. -4. to pitch a tent to put a tent up. ■ to pitch camp to set up one's camp.

◇ vi -1. [ball] to bounce off the ground in a particular way after being thrown □ The ball pitched up suddenly into my face. -2. [passenger] to move suddenly and violently in a particular direction □ We all pitched forward as the driver hit the brakes. -3. [ship, aircraft] to move along with the front part rising or falling suddenly and violently □ The boat suddenly pitched forward throwing everyone to the ground.

◆ **pitch in** vi -1. to help somebody by doing the same job they are doing □ If you pitch in we can finish in time. -2. to help somebody with a job, task etc by giving them something □ We all pitched in with a few dollars.

pitch-black *adj* completely dark □ *It's pitch-black outside.*

pitched [pɪtʃt] *adj* **a pitched roof** a roof that slopes and is not flat.

pitched battle *n* **-1.** a fight in which the two groups of people involved stay in one place □ *There was a pitched battle between police and demonstrators.* **-2.** a long angry dispute.

pitcher ['pɪtʃər] *n* **-1.** [for water, wine] a jug □ *a wine pitcher.* **-2.** SPORT the player in baseball who throws the ball toward the player from the other team who tries to hit it.

pitchfork ['pɪtʃfɔːrk] *n* a tool consisting of a long handle and two or three prongs, used for lifting and moving hay, grass etc.

piteous ['pɪtɪəs] *adj* [cry, sight, condition] that causes one to feel pity.

piteously ['pɪtɪəslɪ] *adv* [cry, howl] *see* **piteous.**

pitfall ['pɪtfɔːl] *n* [of success, a policy] a problem or difficulty that can happen to one in a particular activity or situation □ *There are many pitfalls involved in starting up a new business.*

pith [pɪθ] *n* the thin white substance between the skin and the flesh of fruits such as oranges or lemons.

pithead ['pɪthed] *n* the entrance to a coalmine and the buildings, machinery etc around it.

pith helmet *n* a large light hat made of hard material and worn in very hot countries, especially in the past, to protect one's head from the sun.

pithy ['pɪθɪ] (*compar* **pithier**, *superl* **pithiest**) *adj* [comment, description, advice] that is intelligent and expressed in a short clear way.

pitiable ['pɪtɪəbl] *adj* **-1.** [person, appearance, state] that causes one to feel pity. **-2.** [excuse, effort] that one considers to be worthless.

pitiful ['pɪtɪfl] *adj* **-1.** [condition, sight] that is so sad that one feels pity □ *I could hear their pitiful cries for help.* **-2.** [excuse, wage] that is so bad that one considers it to be worthless □ *He made a pitiful attempt at singing.*

pitifully ['pɪtɪflɪ] *adv* **-1. to be pitifully ill/thin** to be so ill/thin that other people feel pity for one □ *He was a pitifully weak and frail old man.* □ *She was crying pitifully.* **-2. pitifully bad/low** so bad/low that one considers it to be worthless □ *a pitifully small wage.*

pitiless ['pɪtɪləs] *adj* **-1.** [killer, cruelty] that shows no pity □ *a pitiless tyrant.* **-2.** [wind, sun] strong and unpleasant □ *the pitiless desert sun.*

pit stop *n* a stop made by a racing driver during a race to get more fuel, change tires etc.

pitta bread *n* GB = **pita bread.**

pittance ['pɪtns] *n* a very small amount of money □ *They work long hours for a mere pittance.*

pitted ['pɪtəd] *adj* **-1.** [skin, face] covered in small hollow scars, e.g. as a result of smallpox □ *His face was pitted with scars.* **-2.** [metal, leather] covered in small shallow holes □ *The car was pitted with rust.*

pitter-patter ['pɪtərpætər] *n* [of raindrops, footsteps] a quick, light, tapping sound.

pituitary [US pɪ'tuːətərɪ, GB -'tjuːɪtərɪ] (*pl* **pituitaries**) *n* **the pituitary (gland)** a small gland at the lower part of one's brain that produces hormones that affect body growth and development.

pity ['pɪtɪ] (*pt* & *pp* **pitied**) ◇ *n* **-1.** a feeling of sadness that one has for somebody who is suffering or who is having bad luck □ *I feel nothing but pity for him.* ■ **to take** OR **have pity on sb** to help sb because one feels pity for them □ *She took pity on him because he said he had nowhere to live.* **-2. it's a pity** it's disappointing, sad, or frustrating □ *It's a pity (that) you couldn't come.* □ *It's a great pity to have to give up now.* ■ **(what a) pity!** a phrase used to show that one is disappointed or sad about something □ *What a pity (that) she couldn't take you with her!* □ *Pity! I was looking forward to it.* ◇ *vt* to feel pity for <sb> □ *His wife's the one I pity.*

pitying ['pɪtɪɪŋ] *adj* [look, smile] that shows pity.

pivot ['pɪvət] ◇ *n* **-1.** a fixed central point or object on which something turns or balances □ *The propellor spins around a metal pivot.* **-2.** [of an argument, group of people, somebody's life] the basic idea, person, or thing at the center of something □ *Mr Perez is the pivot around which the coalition revolves.* ◇ *vi* **-1.** to turn on a pivot or as if on a pivot □ *He pivoted on his heels.* **-2. to pivot on sthg** to depend on sthg □ *Everything pivots on her decision.*

pixel ['pɪksl] *n* the smallest unit of an image on a computer screen.

pixie, pixy ['pɪksɪ] (*pl* **pixies**) *n* a small imaginary creature in children's stories.

pizza ['piːtsə] *n* a dish consisting of a flat round piece of dough baked in an oven and covered in cheese, tomato sauce, and other kinds of food.

pizzazz [pə'zæz] *n* a quality that makes somebody or something exciting and attractive (informal use) □ *We want someone for the job who has lots of pizzazz.*

Pk *abbr of* **park.**

Pl *abbr of* **place.**

P & L *n abbr of* **profit and loss.**

placard ['plækɑːrd] *n* a notice carried on a stick in a march, demonstration etc.

placate [US 'pleɪkeɪt, GB plə'keɪt] *vt* to make <sb> calm, especially by doing or saying something to please them □ *It's no use trying to placate him, he's furious.*

placatory [US 'pleɪkətɔːrɪ, GB plə'keɪtərɪ] *adj* [remark, gesture] intended to placate somebody.

place [pleɪs] ◇ *n* **-1.** a general word used to describe where something is or happens, or where somebody works, lives etc □ *Keep an eye open for a good place to stop.* □ *Provence is a lovely place.* □ *There are plenty of places to eat in town.* □ *We're looking for a cheap place to rent.* □ *There's a place called Guadalonge somewhere on the coast.* □ *These people have no place to live.* ■ **one's place of birth** the town where one was born (formal use). **-2.** a particular point or position in a larger area □

Show me the place where it hurts. □ The fabric was torn in several places. **-3.** the proper position of a person or thing □ If you must borrow my books, at least put them back in their place. ■ **everything fell into place** it became possible to understand the connection between a series of different facts or events □ Once we knew he was ill, things OR everything fell into place. ■ **to put sb in their place** to stop sb from behaving as though they were more intelligent or important than they really are □ He was trying to boss me around, but I soon put him in his place! **-4.** [to do something] a suitable time to do or say something □ This seems like a good place to mention next month's meeting. **-5.** [for living in] somebody's home □ There's a party at Tim's place tonight. □ Let's go back to my place for coffee. **-6.** [in a theater, classroom, on a plane] an available seat where somebody can sit □ There's an empty place at the end of the row. **-7.** [at a table] a space in which knives, forks, spoons etc are arranged for one person to use at a meal □ We can easily set another place for dinner. **-8.** [on a committee, at a college, in a team] the right to be on a course or be a member of a team, committee etc □ I've applied for a place on a journalism course. **-9.** [of a person, country] the position of somebody or something in relation to other people or things in the same organization, society, system etc □ It's not my place to question his decisions. □ the place of Europe in world affairs. **-10. first/second/third place** first/second/third position in the result of a competition, exam etc □ He finished the race in fourth place. **-11.** [in a book, line] the point one has reached in a book, speech, line of people etc □ Don't shut the book or I'll lose my place. □ Could you keep my place in line while I go and buy something? **-12.** MATH = **decimal place. -13. in the first place** a phrase used to describe what happened or went wrong at the beginning of a series of events □ He should never have been told about it in the first place! ■ **in the first place... and in the second place** phrases used to list reasons or explanations for something □ In the first place, he wasn't there, and in the second place, I wouldn't have spoken to him if he had been. **-14.** phrases **to take place** [event, accident, ceremony] to happen or be held □ The wedding will take place on August 16th. □ The meeting will no longer take place as planned. ■ **to take the place of sb/sthg** to replace sb/sthg □ Who will take her place on the team when she leaves?
◇ *vt* **-1.** to put <sthg> in a particular position, especially carefully or intentionally □ She placed a hand over my mouth. □ Someone had placed a vase of flowers beside my bed. **-2.** to put <sb> in a particular situation □ That would mean placing a lot of innocent people in danger. **-3. to place blame/stress on sthg** to blame/stress sthg □ They feel more emphasis should be placed on the role of training. **-4. I can't place him/her** I can't remember who he/she is, or where I last met them □ I recognized his face, but I couldn't quite place him. **-5.** BUSINESS **to place an order** to order goods to be sent to one. ■ **to place a bet** to make a

bet. ■ **to place an advertisement** to pay for an advertisement to appear in a newspaper, magazine etc □ They've just placed an order with us for twenty computers. □ Ladies and gentlemen, please place your bets. □ Why not place an ad in the local paper? **-6. to be placed** SPORT to finish a race, competition etc in first, second, or third place □ The Canadian runner was placed second.

◆ **all over the place** *adv* [search, lie] everywhere □ People had come from all over the place to hear him speak. □ There were magazines and newspapers scattered all over the place.

◆ **in place** *adv* **-1.** in the proper or normal position □ We put all the furniture back in place. □ Hold it in place while I nail it down. **-2.** ready to be used □ The new legislation/computer system is now in place.

◆ **in place of** *prep* instead of <sb/sthg> □ Jane's assistant is going to the conference in my place. □ You can use honey in place of sugar.

◆ **out of place** *adv* **to look/feel out of place** to look/feel as if one does not belong or fit in a particular situation □ He felt out of place among so many young people.

placebo [plə'si:bəʊ] (*pl* **placebos** OR **placeboes**) *n* a substance that looks like a medical drug and is given to some of the people in a test to see if a real drug actually works.

place card *n* a card with somebody's name on it, used to show them where they should sit, e.g. at a dinner table.

place kick *n* in football, rugby etc a kick at a ball that is held or has been placed ready on the ground.

place mat *n* a mat that is put at each place setting on a table and on which plates are put.

placement ['pleɪsmənt] *n* **-1.** the act or process of placing something in a particular position. **-2.** BUSINESS a job for a fixed period, usually for a student to gain some experience in the work they are training for □ We try to put all our students on placement. □ a work placement program.

placement service *n* US an agency, especially in a college or university, that helps people to find jobs.

placenta [plə'sentə] (*pl* **placentas** OR **placentae** [-ti:]) *n* the mass of flesh and veins attached to the fetus in the womb of a pregnant woman or female mammal and that comes out of the vagina after the baby is born.

place setting *n* the set of knives, forks, spoons, and glasses arranged on a table for the use of one person at a meal.

placid ['plæsəd] *adj* **-1.** [person, animal] that is calm and does not easily get angry or excited □ He has a very placid nature. **-2.** [sea, place] peaceful.

placidly ['plæsədlɪ] *adv* [say, smile] *see* **placid**.

plagiarism ['pleɪdʒərɪzm] *n* **-1.** something that has been plagiarized. **-2.** the practice of plagiarizing other people's work or ideas.

plagiarist ['pleɪdʒərəst] *n* a person who plagiarizes other people's work or ideas.

plagiarize, -ise ['pleɪdʒəraɪz] vt [idea, words, piece of music] to copy <sthg> from somebody else and claim that it is one's own.

plague [pleɪg] ◇ n -1. [of cholera, typhoid] an attack of a particular disease that spreads quickly and kills many people □ a cholera plague. -2. (the) plague a very infectious disease that causes fever, swellings on one's body, and death □ an outbreak of plague □ a plague victim. ■ to avoid sb/sthg like the plague to take great care to avoid sb/sthg. -3. [of rats, locusts] a very large number of unpleasant things that cause a lot of harm in one area and cannot be controlled □ a plague of red ants.
◇ vt -1. to plague sb with sthg [with questions, complaints] to annoy sb repeatedly with sthg. -2. to be plagued by sthg [by bad luck, ill-health] to be continually affected by sthg.

plaice [pleɪs] (pl plaice) n a flat sea fish with a brown body and white meat that is popular as food □ plaice fillets.

plaid [plæd] n a fabric with a design of checks and crossing lines on it □ a plaid skirt.

Plaid Cymru [ˌplaɪdˈkʌmrɪ] n a Welsh nationalist political party whose aim is Welsh independence.

plain [pleɪn] ◇ adj -1. [sweater, paper] that is all one color and has no pattern, marks etc on it □ a plain white shirt □ a plain envelope. -2. [food, design] that is simple and has little decoration □ He writes in a plain, uncomplicated style. -3. [fact, answer] clear and easy to understand □ The reason is plain to see. □ It's plain (that) she's lying. □ The truth is plain to everyone. ■ to make sthg plain to sb to make sure that sb understands sthg □ She made it plain to him that she couldn't go. -4. [statement, speaking] that is direct, honest, and sometimes offends people □ I just want the plain truth. □ I told him in plain English what I thought. -5. [madness, stupidity] complete □ It would be plain suicide to go back now. -6. [woman, girl] not pretty □ She's a nice girl, but rather plain.
◇ adv [stupid, impossible] completely (informal use) □ You must be plain crazy!
◇ n a large area of flat land with few trees on it □ vast open plains □ A large town stood on the plain below.

plain chocolate n GB chocolate that is darker and more bitter than milk chocolate.

plain-clothes adj [policeman, detective] who is working in ordinary clothes and is not wearing a uniform.

plain flour n GB flour that is not mixed with baking powder and does not make cookies, pastry etc rise when cooked in an oven. NOTE: Compare self-rising flour.

plainly ['pleɪnlɪ] adv -1. [upset, angry] obviously □ She was plainly not happy about the situation. □ Plainly, there was something wrong. -2. [decorate, dress, speak] see plain □ She dresses plainly for work.

plain sailing n it's plain sailing GB it's easy and there are no problems or difficulties □ Once they have agreed the terms of the loan it should be plain sailing from then on.

Plains Indian n a member of any of the Native American peoples who lived in the Great Plains of North America before European settlers arrived.

plainspoken [ˌpleɪnˈspoʊkən] adj [person] who says what they think in a direct and honest way that sometimes offends people.

plaintiff ['pleɪntɪf] n LAW a person who brings a case against somebody in court. NOTE: Compare defendant.

plaintive ['pleɪntɪv] adj [look, voice, song] that expresses sadness or suffering.

plain yogurt n yogurt that has no added flavorings.

plait [plæt] GB ◇ vt [hair, rope, grass] to twist three or more lengths of <sthg> over and under each other to make one thick length. ◇ n [of hair, rope, grass] a length of something that has been divided into three and plaited □ She wore her hair in plaits.

plan [plæn] (pt & pp planned, cont planning) ◇ n -1. an arrangement for doing something in the future □ They drew up a plan designed to improve productivity. □ a government/company plan □ a marketing/pension/savings plan. ■ to go according to plan [event, campaign] to happen or progress as it was intended to □ Everything went according to plan. -2. [of a campaign, story] a general description of the main points of something □ All applicants must submit a research plan. -3. [of a new building, machine] a detailed technical drawing of something, especially something that is going to be made or built; [of a house, room] the shape of something and the way it is arranged into different parts □ an architect's plan □ I haven't seen the new plans yet.
◇ vt -1. [trip, takeover, career] to prepare for <sthg> by deciding how it is going to be done □ They're planning a new venture. □ The meeting will take place as planned. □ The test was planned for next week. -2. to plan to do sthg to intend to do sthg □ We're planning to leave tomorrow. -3. [garden, building] to design <sthg>; [book, speech] to decide and arrange the main points of <sthg> □ The houses were planned as homes for poor people. □ You should plan in advance what you're going to say.
◇ vi to organize things in advance □ It is important to plan ahead.
◆ plans npl aims or intentions □ The new budget forced us to change our plans. □ Do you have any plans for tonight?
◆ plan for vt fus to plan for sthg to prepare oneself for sthg that will happen in the future □ We hadn't planned for so many people. □ He's planning for his retirement.
◆ plan on vt fus to plan on doing sthg to intend to do sthg □ What are you planning on doing tonight? □ I wasn't planning on going out.
◆ plan out vt sep to plan sthg out [route, course of action] to plan sthg in detail.

plane [pleɪn] ◇ n -1. AVIATION a vehicle for traveling in the air that has wings and at least one engine □ a passenger/fighter plane □ I took the 3:00pm plane from Detroit. -2. GEOMETRY a flat surface. -3. [of existence, thought, emotion] a level □ *She's on a higher intellectual plane.* **-4.** [for wood] a tool with a flat bottom that has a blade in it for removing the rough edges of a wooden surface to make it smooth. **-5.** a plane tree. ◇ *adj* [surface] flat. ◇ *vt* [edge, surface] to move a plane along <a piece of wood> to make it smooth □ *The bottom of the door needs planing.*

planet ['plænət] *n* a large mass in space that moves around a star, e.g. Earth, Mars, or Venus.

planetarium [,plænə'teərɪəm] (*pl* **planetariums** OR **planetaria** [-rɪə]) *n* a building that contains an instrument that projects moving images of the stars and planets onto a curved ceiling made to look like the night sky.

planetary [US 'plænətɪrɪ, GB -ətərɪ] *adj* [orbit, exploration] that is connected with a planet.

plane tree *n* a large tree with broad leaves that is often grown in towns.

plank [plæŋk] *n* **-1.** CONSTRUCTION a long flat piece of wood used in building □ *a plank of wood* OR *wooden plank.* **-2.** POLITICS one of the policies of a political party □ *The main plank of their election campaign is reduced taxes.*

plankton ['plæŋktən] *n* very small animals and plants that live near the surface of the sea and are eaten by fish and whales.

planned [plænd] *adj* [sale, trip] that is intended to be carried out in the future □ *The planned demonstration has been called off.* □ *the number of planned pregnancies.* ■ **a planned economy** an economy in which the government plans all business activity.

Planned Parenthood *n* a US health organization that teaches people about birth control.

planner ['plænər] *n* **-1.** a person whose job is to plan the way land is used and the way towns develop. **-2.** a person whose job is to plan future projects, e.g. television programing or political campaigns □ *an economic planner* □ *a military planner.*

planning ['plænɪŋ] *n* **-1.** the work of organizing and controlling the way land is used and the way towns develop □ *road planning* □ *a planning committee.* **-2.** the work of preparing and organizing future projects, the economy etc □ *A lot of planning went into this campaign.* □ *The project is still at the planning stage.*

planning permission *n* official permission to build a new building or to change the structure or use of an existing building.

plan of action *n* a series of things that one has planned to do in order to achieve something.

plant [US plænt, GB plɑːnt] ◇ *n* **-1.** a living thing that grows in the ground and usually has a stem, leaves, and roots □ *The plants need to be watered.* □ *the rich plant life of Madagascar.* **-2.** INDUSTRY a factory □ *an industrial plant* □ *an automobile/steel plant.* **-3.** TECHNOLOGY a power station □ *a chemical/nuclear plant.* **-4.** BUSINESS a collective term for the buildings, land, machinery, and equipment used by an industrial company □ *The company has to invest in new plant if it's to survive.*

◇ *vt* **-1.** [seed, tree] to put <a plant> in the ground so that it will grow □ *I planted potatoes in the garden.* **-2.** [field, garden] to put seeds or plants in the soil in <a place> so that they will grow there □ *They planted the field with corn.* **-3. to plant a punch/kiss on sb** to punch/kiss sb □ *She planted a big kiss on his cheek.* **-4.** [chair, flag] to put <sthg> firmly in a particular place □ *She planted herself in the doorway.* **-5.** [bomb, microphone, spy] to hide <sb/sthg> in a particular place; [drug, weapon] to put <sthg> secretly in somebody's house or clothing so that they will be accused of possessing it □ *He claims that the police planted the evidence on him.* **-6. to plant a thought/idea etc in sb's mind** to cause sb to have a thought/an idea etc.

◆ **plant out** *vt sep* **to plant sthg out** to plant sthg outdoors after growing it in a pot □ *The seedlings can be planted out in March.*

plantain ['plæntən] *n* a large green fruit like a banana that must be cooked before it can be eaten; the large tropical plant that this fruit grows on.

plantar wart ['plæntr-] *n* a wart that grows on the sole of the foot.

plantation [plæn'teɪʃn] *n* **-1.** a large area of land where a particular crop is grown □ *a tea/coffee/rubber plantation.* **-2.** a large group of trees that have been planted together.

planter [US 'plæntr, GB 'plɑːntə] *n* **-1.** a person who owns or is in charge of a plantation. **-2.** a decorative container in which plants are grown.

plant pot *n* a round clay or plastic container, wider at the top than at the bottom, used for growing plants.

plaque [US plæk, GB plɑːk] *n* **-1.** [on a wall] a flat piece of metal or stone with writing on it, usually in memory of a famous person or event, and attached to a wall □ *a commemorative plaque.* **-2.** [on one's teeth] a substance that forms on the surface of the teeth that contains bacteria and can cause gum disease.

plasma ['plæzmə] *n* the colorless liquid part of blood in which the blood cells are held □ *blood plasma.*

plaster [US 'plæstr, GB 'plɑːstə] ◇ *n* **-1.** CONSTRUCTION a mixture of sand, lime, and water that dries to give a smooth, hard surface and is used especially on interior walls. **-2.** [for broken bones] plaster of paris in the form of a plaster cast. ■ **to be in plaster** [arm, leg] to be covered in a plaster cast. **-3.** GB [for cuts, scratches] a small sticky bandage for covering small cuts on one's body.

◇ *vt* **-1.** CONSTRUCTION [wall, ceiling] to put a layer of wet plaster on <sthg> □ *She's been plastering the bathroom.* **-2. to plaster sthg with sthg** [with mud, pictures] to cover sthg with sthg □ *The wall was plastered with posters.* **-3.** to make <sthg> stick □ *He tried to plaster his hair down with gel.*

plasterboard [US 'plæstrbɔːrd, GB 'plɑːstəbɔːd] *n* a kind of board made of two pieces of cardboard with plaster in between, used to build or cover walls.

plaster cast *n* -1. [for broken bones] a case made of plaster of paris that is put around the part of a body where a bone is broken in order to keep it in place and help it to heal quicker. -2. [of a sculpture] a copy of a sculpture cast in plaster of paris.

plastered [US 'plæstrd, GB 'plɑːstəd] *adj* **to be plastered** to be drunk (informal use) □ *I got completely plastered.*

plasterer [US 'plæstrər, GB 'plɑːstərə] *n* a person whose job is to plaster walls and ceilings.

plastering [US 'plæstərɪŋ, GB 'plɑːs-] *n* [of a wall, ceiling] *see* **plaster.**

plaster of paris *n* a mixture of a chalk powder and water that dries quickly into a hard white substance and is used especially for making plaster casts.

plastic ['plæstɪk] ◇ *n* -1. a light man-made material that can be molded by heat into various shapes and is used to make a wide variety of objects □ *The comb was made of plastic.* -2. **to pay for sthg with plastic** to pay for sthg with a credit card (informal use). ◇ *adj* [bag, toy, spoon] made of plastic.

♦ **plastics** *n* BUSINESS the business of producing plastic.

plastic bullet *n* a very long bullet made of plastic that is designed to hurt people without killing them, sometimes used by the police in riots.

plastic explosive *n* a soft explosive material that can be shaped by hand and is used to make bombs □ *The device contained 3 kilos of plastic explosive.*

Plasticine™ ['plæstəsiːn] *n* GB a soft colored substance that can be shaped by hand and is used by children to make models.

plastic money *n* credit cards (informal use).

plastic surgeon *n* a doctor who specializes in plastic surgery.

plastic surgery *n* the kind of medicine that involves repairing or improving the appearance of damaged or unattractive parts of the body □ *You know he had to have plastic surgery on his nose?*

plastic wrap *n* US very thin plastic film that can be put over food to keep it fresh.

plate [pleɪt] ◇ *n* -1. [for food] a flat dish, usually round or oval and made of pottery, that food is served on; [of food] the amount of food that this contains □ *a dinner plate.* ▪ **to have a lot on one's plate** to have a lot of work to do or problems to deal with. ▪ **to be handed sthg on a plate** [victory, success, job] to be allowed to get or achieve sthg with little effort. -2. [of metal, glass] a flat piece of a hard material □ *a stainless steel plate.* -3. [on a wall, machine] a flat piece of metal with writing on it □ *There was a brass plate outside the door.* □ *a license plate.* -4. [of silver, gold] a very thin coating of metal, usually covering a less valuable metal □ *a frame covered in gold/silver plate.* -5. [in a book] a picture or photograph that takes up a whole page □

eight pages of color plates. -6. [for one's teeth] a piece of plastic, shaped to fit the roof of one's mouth, that false teeth or wires are attached to □ *a dental plate.* -7. US SPORT in baseball, the place where the batter stands in order to hit the ball.

◇ *vt* **to be plated with sthg** [with nickel, platinum] to be coated with a very thin layer of sthg □ *The tray has been plated with gold/silver.* □ *a gold-/silver-plated watch.*

plateau [US plæ'toʊ, GB 'plætoʊ] (*pl* **plateaus** OR **plateaux** [-z]) *n* -1. GEOGRAPHY a large area of high flat land □ *a grassy plateau above the valley.* -2. [in activity, progress] a steady level □ *The arms race was escalating wildly before it reached a plateau in the 80s.*

plateful ['pleɪtfl] *n* an amount of food that fills a plate □ *She ate platefuls of spaghetti.*

plate-glass *adj* [window, door] that is made of large flat pieces of glass.

platelet ['pleɪtlət] *n* a cell found in the blood that helps it to go solid when bleeding occurs □ *a blood platelet.*

plate rack *n* a frame on which plates, cups, saucers etc are put to dry after being washed.

platform ['plætfɔːrm] *n* -1. [for a speaker, performer] a flat raised structure, usually wooden, where a speaker or performer stands □ *The soloists are coming onto the platform.* □ *She once shared a platform with the former Secretary of Defense.* -2. [for a helicopter, oil rig] a raised structure, built for a particular purpose □ *a helicopter platform* □ *an observation platform.* -3. COMPUTING a word used when referring to a particular computer system □ *Charges vary depending on the computer platform you're using.* -4. RAIL the area beside the tracks in a train station, where people get on or off trains □ *The train arriving at platform 14 is the 15:02 from Harwich.* -5. [for somebody's views] something that makes it possible for an organization or a person to express their views to the rest of society □ *The magazine provides a platform for the ordinary person's point of view.* -6. POLITICS the aims and promises of a political party, usually stated just before an election □ *The party was elected on a socialist platform.*

platform game *n* COMPUTING a type of computer game where a character is moved from level to level, avoiding obstacles and collecting points.

platform ticket *n* GB a ticket that permits somebody to go onto a railroad platform, but not to travel on a train.

platinum ['plætənəm] ◇ *adj* [hair] silvery-white. ◇ *n* a very valuable silver-gray metal used in jewelry and in chemical processes. SYMBOL: Pt □ *a platinum ring.*

platinum blonde *n* a woman with very light hair that is almost white.

platitude ['plætɪtjuːd] *n* a statement that is boring and meaningless because it is so obvious or unoriginal □ *He sat there mouthing platitudes about decency and family values.*

Plato

Plato ['pleɪtoʊ] (427–347 BC) a Greek philosopher who had a strong influence on Western philosophy. His best-known work is *The Republic*.

platonic [plə'tɒnɪk] *adj* [relationship, love] that does not involve sexual attraction or activity □ *I assure you, our friendship is purely platonic.*

platoon [plə'tuːn] *n* a small group of soldiers commanded by a lieutenant.

platter ['plætəʳ] *n* a large dish for serving food.

platypus ['plætɪpəs] (*pl* **platypuses**) *n* a small furry Australian animal that has webbed feet, a broad beak and tail, lays eggs, and is able to live both on land and in water.

plaudits ['plɔːdɪts] *npl* admiration or praise.

plausible ['plɔːzəbl] *adj* [story, excuse, plot] believable; [liar] who seems to be telling the truth, even when they are not □ *I didn't find her explanation very plausible.*

plausibly ['plɔːzəblɪ] *adv* [argue, lie] *see* **plausible**.

play [pleɪ] ◇ *n* **-1.** an activity that people, especially children, take part in for amusement or pleasure □ *I like to watch the children at play.* **-2.** THEATER, RADIO, & TV a complete piece of drama, written to be performed by actors □ *a TV/radio play.* **-3.** SPORT **to be in/out of play** [ball] to be in/out of the area where the game is being played. **-4.** US SPORT & GAMES a move or series of moves in a sport or game □ *That last play should have produced results.* □ *Whose play is it?* **-5. to come into play** [force, idea] to become active or to have an effect on a situation □ *Several factors come into play in making this decision.* **-6. a play on words** an amusing use of words that have more than one meaning. **-7.** [in rope, a steering wheel] the amount of movement possible by something that is not fixed firmly in one position □ *You have to make sure there's not too much play in the cable.*
◇ *vt* **-1.** SPORT [hockey, football, chess] to take part in <a game or sport> □ *She plays tennis every weekend.* **-2.** SPORT [opponent, team] to take part in a game or sport against <sb> □ *We played the Pirates last week.* **-3.** THEATER & CINEMA [role, part, character] to act as <sb> in a play or movie □ *In the movie he plays a brilliant but tragic millionaire.* ■ **to play a part** OR **role in sthg** to be involved in sthg; to have an effect on sthg □ *The state of the economy plays a major role in deciding the date of the election.* **-4.** MUSIC [piano, guitar] to produce music from <a musical instrument>; [tune, notes] to perform <a piece of music> on an instrument □ *He plays the trombone.* □ *The band was playing "Waltzing Matilda".* **-5.** [record, tape] to put <a recording> into a machine in order to listen to it □ *The station plays mostly jazz music.* □ *Does your music system play CDs?* □ *I want to play you this tape.* **-6.** to pretend to be <sb/sthg> □ *Stop playing the fool/the innocent.* **-7. to play it cool** to deal with a situation without showing one's emotions □ *Just play it cool, and look as if you're enjoying yourself.*
◇ *vi* **-1.** to amuse oneself □ *The children were playing with their friends/toys.* **-2.** SPORT *He plays for South Africa.* □ *The team play against Cuba in*

the final. **-3.** THEATER & CINEMA [actor, actress] *I'm playing in a new movie that's coming out in February.* **-4.** MUSIC [musician, radio, record] *We could hear music playing.* □ *The band started to play.* **-5.** [light, sunshine] to flicker on or around something (literary use). **-6.** *phrase* **to play safe** to deal with a situation in a way that avoids problems or danger □ *He decided to play safe and set out earlier.*

◆ **play along** *vi* to pretend to agree with somebody, usually in order to gain some advantage from them or to avoid upsetting them □ *He agreed to play along with them for the time being.*

◆ **play at** *vt fus* to play at sthg [politics, journalism] to take part in sthg without any serious effort or intentions □ *He's not an artist, he just plays at being one.* ■ **what do you think you're playing at?** a phrase used by somebody to show that they think somebody is doing something wrong.

◆ **play back** *vt sep* to play sthg back [tape, movie] to operate a machine so that one can hear or see sthg that has just been recorded □ *Could you play back that last part for me?*

◆ **play down** *vt sep* to play sthg down [fact, danger, importance] to make sthg seem less important than it really is.

◆ **play off** ◇ *vt sep* to play sb off against sb to get sb to compete against sb else, usually in order to gain an advantage for oneself. ◇ *vi* SPORT [teams] to play an extra game in order to decide something, e.g. which team will play in the finals.

◆ **play on** *vt fus* to play on sthg [somebody's weaknesses, fears, good nature] to use sthg to one's advantage □ *It's unfair to play on people's anxieties like that.*

◆ **play up** ◇ *vt sep* to play sthg up [fact, hopes, importance] to make sthg seem more important than it really is □ *She likes to play up her part in the deal.* ◇ *vi* GB **-1.** [car, machine] to not work properly □ *The engine's been playing up again.* **-2.** [child] to misbehave □ *Matthew tends to play up in front of guests.*

◆ **play upon** *vt fus* = **play on**.

playable ['pleɪəbl] *adj* [field, ground] that is in good enough condition to play sports on.

play-act *vi* to pretend to have feelings or a personality that one does not really have.

playbill ['pleɪbɪl] *n* a poster advertising a play.

playboy ['pleɪbɔɪ] *n* a rich and usually young man who spends a lot of his time enjoying himself and has many girlfriends.

Play-Doh™ [-doʊ] *n* a soft brightly-colored substance that is shaped using one's hands and is used by children to make models.

player ['pleɪəʳ] *n* **-1.** SPORT & GAMES a person who plays a sport or game □ *a football/chess player.* **-2.** MUSIC a person who plays a particular musical instrument □ *He's a good/keen trumpet player.* **-3.** BUSINESS a company that is successful in a particular kind of business □ *Vitex is becoming a major player in the world of global communications.* **-4.** THEATER an actor (old-fashioned use).

playful ['pleɪfl] *adj* **-1.** [person, mood, remark]

light-hearted and friendly □ *She gave him a playful nudge.* -2. [kitten, puppy] lively and friendly.

playfully ['pleɪflɪ] *adv* [say, tease] *see* **playful** □ *He pushed her playfully.*

playgoer ['pleɪgoʊəʳ] *n* a person who goes to see plays at the theater.

playground ['pleɪgraʊnd] *n* [in a school] an outdoor area where children can play; [in a park] an area with equipment, e.g. swings or slides, for children to play on □ *a school playground.*

playgroup ['pleɪgruːp] *n* = **playschool.**

playhouse ['pleɪhaʊs, *pl* -haʊzɪz] *n* a theater.

playing card ['pleɪɪŋ-] *n* one of a set of 52 cards that are used in card games and have a value that is shown by a number or picture.

playing field *n* a large piece of open ground with sports fields marked out on it.

playlist ['pleɪlɪst] *n* GB the records that are played on a particular radio program.

playmate ['pleɪmeɪt] *n* a child who another child plays with and who is their friend.

play-off *n* SPORT an extra game that is played to decide something, e.g. who wins a competition or is promoted to a higher league.

playpen ['pleɪpen] *n* a wooden frame with four sides containing bars in which a small child can play safely.

playroom ['pleɪruːm] *n* a room for children to play in.

playschool ['pleɪskuːl] *n* a kind of school for very young children where they can play together □ *She goes to playschool twice a week.*

plaything ['pleɪθɪŋ] *n* -1. a toy. -2. a person whom somebody uses in order to have fun, without really caring about them.

playtime ['pleɪtaɪm] *n* a break between classes at school, when children can play outside.

playwright ['pleɪraɪt] *n* a person who writes plays.

plaza ['plɑːzə] *n* -1. an open square in a town. -2. a number of linked buildings □ *a shopping plaza.*

plc *abbr of* **public limited company.**

plea [pliː] *n* -1. [for mercy, help] an urgent and emotional request □ *He made a plea for people with information to come forward.* □ *This is my plea to you.* -2. LAW the answer given to a charge by a defendant in court, in which they say they are guilty or not guilty □ *What is your plea?* □ *a plea of guilty/not guilty* □ *Bolam made a plea of insanity.*

plea bargaining *n* LAW the process of negotiating with a court to agree to plead guilty to a crime, in exchange for not being charged with a more serious crime.

plead [pliːd] (*pt & pp* **pleaded** OR **pled**) ◇ *vt* -1. LAW to defend <sb's case or cause>, especially in a court of law. ■ **to plead guilty/ not guilty/insanity** [defendant] to make a plea of guilty/not guilty/insanity □ *He pleaded guilty to (the charge of) manslaughter.* -2. **to plead (that)...** to claim that something is an

excuse for something one has done, cannot do etc □ *He apologized for his mistake and pleaded ignorance.* ◇ *vi* -1. to make an urgent and emotional request □ *She pleaded with him to show forgiveness.* □ *They were pleading for mercy/help.* -2. LAW [defendant] *How do you plead?*

pleading ['pliːdɪŋ] ◇ *adj* [look, voice] that expresses an urgent and emotional request □ *There was a pleading note in his voice.* ◇ *n* the act of making an urgent and emotional request □ *Her pleading was in vain; he would not change his mind.*

pleasant ['pleznt] *adj* -1. [taste, view, news] attractive or enjoyable □ *We had a very pleasant meal/chat.* □ *Tony! What a pleasant surprise!* -2. [person] friendly and likeable □ *They seemed pleasant enough people.*

pleasantly ['plezntlɪ] *adv* -1. **pleasantly decorated/warm** decorated/warm in a way that is attractive or enjoyable □ *The wine was pleasantly dry.* -2. [smile, say] in a friendly way □ *We talked pleasantly for about half an hour.* -3. **to be pleasantly surprised** to be surprised in a way that makes one feel happy.

pleasantry ['plezntrɪ] (*pl* **pleasantries**) *n* **to exchange pleasantries** to say pleasant or amusing things to each other in order to be polite.

please [pliːz] ◇ *adv* -1. a word used when making a polite request □ *A cup of coffee, please.* □ *Please be quiet!* □ *Please don't leave your books on here.* □ *That will be $1.50, please.* -2. a word used when accepting something politely □ *"Would you like a cup of coffee?" — "Yes please."* □ *"Shall I close the window?" — "Oh, please."*
◇ *vt* to make <sb> happy □ *He is hard to please.* □ *Don't do it just to please me.* ■ **to please oneself** to do what one likes, without considering the wishes of other people □ *All you ever think about is pleasing yourself.* ■ **please yourself!** a phrase used to tell somebody that one does not care what they do (informal use) □ *Well, please yourself, but you'll be sorry you didn't come.*
◇ *vi* -1. to make other people happy □ *He's always so eager to please.* -2. **to do as one pleases** to do what one wants to do □ *I'm allowed to go where I please.* ■ **if you please** a phrase used when making a polite request (formal use) □ *Step this way, if you please.*

pleased [pliːzd] *adj* [person] who seems happy or satisfied □ *I'm very pleased to welcome you here tonight.* □ *They seem really pleased with their new car/my performance.* ■ **pleased to meet you!** a polite phrase used when meeting somebody for the first time □ *Pleased to meet you! I'm Andy.* □ *I'm very pleased to meet you, Mr Bryant.*

pleasing ['pliːzɪŋ] *adj* [news, result] that makes one pleased □ *The general effect of the design is very pleasing.*

pleasingly ['pliːzɪŋlɪ] *adv* [quick, simple] *see* **pleasing** □ *His manner is pleasingly low-key.*

pleasurable ['pleʒərəbl] *adj* [feeling, trip] enjoyable □ *I found the sensation of speed intensely pleasurable.*

pleasure ['pleʒəʳ] *n* **-1.** a feeling of happiness □ *It gives me great pleasure to introduce one of my favorite performers.* □ *He takes great pleasure in telling her when she's wrong.* ■ **with pleasure** a polite phrase used to agree to do something that somebody has asked □ *"Could you give me a hand?" — "With pleasure."* **-2.** enjoyment rather than work □ *Are you traveling for business or pleasure?* **-3.** something that somebody enjoys □ *She's a pleasure to be with.* □ *It was a pleasure having you to stay.* □ *It's one of life's little pleasures.* ■ **it's a pleasure** OR **my pleasure!** a polite phrase used when replying to somebody who has thanked one for something □ *"Thanks for the ride." — "My pleasure!"*

pleat [pliːt] ◇ *n* a permanent fold in a piece of material such as a skirt that is stitched at the top. ◇ *vt* [cloth, paper] to make pleats in <sthg>.

pleated ['pliːtəd] *adj* [skirt, shirt] that has pleats in it.

plebeian [plə'biːən] *adj* [person, taste] that belongs to the lower social classes (disapproving use).

plebiscite ['plebɪsaɪt] *n* a direct vote by the people of a country or region on a very important matter.

plectrum ['plektrəm] (*pl* **plectrums**) *n* a small thin piece of plastic or metal, used for plucking the strings of a musical instrument, e.g. a guitar or banjo.

pled [pled] *past tense & past participle of* **plead**.

pledge [pledʒ] ◇ *n* **-1.** [of secrecy, support] a solemn promise □ *I made a pledge to my father never to sell the house.* **-2.** [of love, friendship] something such as a ring that one gives to somebody as a sign of one's feelings. ◇ *vt* **-1.** [money, support] to promise to give <sthg> to somebody □ *The foundation has pledged $15,000 to the campaign.* **-2. to be pledged to secrecy/silence** to have promised to keep something secret/stay silent about something. ■ **to pledge oneself to sthg** [to a group, cause] to promise to work hard for sthg. **-3.** [watch, jewelry] to leave <sthg valuable> with a pawnbroker as a guarantee that one will repay money which has been lent.

Pledge of Allegiance *n* **the Pledge of Allegiance** a vow of loyalty to the US flag.

ᵛ PLEDGE OF ALLEGIANCE
The Pledge of Allegiance, written in 1892, is a vow of loyalty to the US flag. Until recently school children in the USA used to say it every morning before starting classes. The words of the pledge are: "I pledge allegiance to the flag of the United States of America and to the republic for which it stands, one nation, under God, indivisible, with liberty and justice for all."

plenary session ['pliːnərɪ-] *n* a meeting that is

attended by everybody who has the right to attend.

plentiful ['plentɪfl] *adj* [food, supply] that exists in large amounts.

plenty ['plentɪ] ◇ *pron* a large quantity □ *"More bread?" — "No thanks, we've got plenty."* □ *There's plenty more of that, if you want some.* □ *We have plenty of time to get ready.* □ *I've met a few people who like the city, but plenty who don't.* ◇ *n* a condition or situation where one has a lot of what one needs, e.g. food or money □ *They came thinking that America was a land of plenty.* □ *in times of plenty.* ◇ *adv* US very (informal use) □ *I'm plenty hungry.*

plethora ['pleθərə] *n* **a plethora of sthg** an amount of sthg that is much greater than one needs or can deal with □ *There's a plethora of nightclubs to choose from in Manhattan.*

pleurisy ['plʊərəsɪ] *n* a serious disease of the membrane around one's lungs, causing pain in one's chest.

Plexiglas™ [US 'pleksɪglæs, GB -glɑːs] *n* US a strong clear plastic often used instead of glass □ *a Plexiglas window.*

pliable ['plaɪəbl], **pliant** ['plaɪənt] *adj* **-1.** [metal, substance] that can be bent easily without breaking. **-2.** [person] who is easily influenced by other people □ *It shouldn't be hard to get him to agree, he's very pliable.*

pliers ['plaɪəʳz] *npl* a tool made of two pieces of metal crossing each other, so that when the two handles are squeezed together the other ends come together to grip an object, e.g. a nail □ *a pair of pliers* □ *Do you have any pliers?*

plight [plaɪt] *n* **the plight of sb** the extremely difficult situation that sb is in that makes them suffer □ *The article highlighted the plight of the homeless.* □ *Their plight is now desperate.*

plimsoll ['plɪmsəl] *n* GB a light canvas shoe with a rubber sole, worn especially in a gym □ *a pair of plimsolls.*

Plimsoll line *n* a line on the outside of a ship showing how much of the ship should be underwater when it is loaded.

plinth [plɪnθ] *n* a square block of stone that a statue or pillar stands on.

PLO (*abbr of* **Palestine Liberation Organization**) *n* **the PLO** a political association whose aim is to establish a state of Palestine.

plod [plɒd] (*pt & pp* **plodded**, *cont* **plodding**) *vi* **-1.** to walk slowly with heavy steps, especially because one is tired or carrying a heavy load □ *He came plodding along the road.* **-2.** to work steadily at something that is difficult, boring, or that takes a long time □ *I plodded on with the accounts.*

plodder ['plɒdəʳ] *n* a person without much intelligence or imagination who works hard (disapproving use) □ *He's very reliable, but a bit of a plodder.*

plonk [plɒŋk] (informal use) *n* GB cheap wine.
◆ **plonk down** *vt sep* **to plonk sthg down** to put sthg down quickly and carelessly □ *Just plonk your stuff down anywhere you like!*

plop [plɒp] (*pt & pp* **plopped**, *cont* **plopping**)

◇ *n* the sound made when something solid falls into water without splashing □ *There was a loud plop as my shoe fell into the water.* ◇ *vi* [stone, pebble] to fall with a plop □ *The soap plopped into the bath.*

plot [plɒt] (*pt* & *pp* **plotted**, *cont* **plotting**) ◇ *n* -1. a secret plan made by a group of people to do something bad or illegal □ *Police have uncovered a plot to bomb the embassy.* ■ **the plot thickens** a phrase used when one is in a situation that is difficult to understand and more facts that cannot be explained become known □ *"But she said she didn't know you." — "Hmm, the plot thickens."* -2. [of a movie, novel] the basic story of a movie, novel etc. -3. [of land] an area of land for building or growing vegetables □ *The plan was to buy a plot of land to build our own house on.* □ *a building plot.* -4. US [of a house] the plan of a house.
◇ *vt* -1. [coup, assassination] to plan <sthg> secretly in a group □ *A group of army officers was plotting to overthrow the government.* -2. [position, route, course] to mark or calculate <sthg> on a map □ *The captain plotted the ship's position/a new course.* -3. MATH [line, curve] to draw <sthg> on a graph.
◇ *vi* [conspirators, terrorists] to make a secret plan to harm a person or organization □ *The general was apparently unaware that his subordinates were plotting against him.*

plough *etc* GB = **plow** *etc.*

ploughman's ['plaʊmənz] *n* **a ploughman's (lunch)** GB a light lunch of bread, cheese, and pickles.

plow US, **plough** GB [plaʊ] ◇ *n* a piece of equipment that is pulled by a tractor or an animal such as a horse and is used to turn over the soil before planting on a farm. ◇ *vt* -1. FARMING to turn over the soil of <land, a field> etc with a plow. -2. **to plow money into sthg** to invest money in sthg □ *All our profits are plowed back into the business.* ◇ *vi* [car, truck] to crash into something with a lot of force □ *The truck-driver lost control and plowed into the car in front of him.*

◆ **plow on** *vi* to continue doing something even though it is boring or difficult □ *I've just got to plow on with it until I've finished.*

◆ **plow up** *vt sep* **to plow a field up** to break up the ground in a field by walking or riding across it all the time □ *Mountain bikes plow up the trails, making them too muddy to walk along.*

plowshare US, **ploughshare** GB ['plaʊʃeəʳ] *n* the metal part of a plow that digs the earth.

ploy [plɔɪ] *n* a way of getting what one wants, especially by lying or pretending □ *It's just a ploy to make people feel sorry for him.*

PLR *n abbr of* **Public Lending Right**.

pls *abbr of* **please**.

pluck [plʌk] ◇ *vt* -1. [flower, fruit] to pick <a part of a plant> □ *She plucked a cherry from the tree.* -2. [mountaineer, hair] to remove <sb/sthg> from a place □ *The helicopter plucked the survivors off the life raft.* -3. [chicken, turkey] to remove feathers from <a bird> so that it can be cooked. -4. to pull out <hairs> from one's eyebrows. -5. [guitar, string, harp]

to produce a musical note from <an instrument> by pulling and releasing a string with one's fingers. ◇ *n* the quality of being brave and determined in a difficult or worrying situation (informal use).

◆ **pluck up** *vt fus* **to pluck up the courage to do sthg** to find the courage to do sthg, especially after thinking about it for a long time □ *I finally plucked up the courage to ask him out.*

plucky ['plʌkɪ] (*compar* **pluckier**, *superl* **pluckiest**) *adj* that shows pluck (informal use) □ *They didn't succeed this time, but it was a very plucky attempt.*

plug [plʌg] (*pt* & *pp* **plugged**, *cont* **plugging**) ◇ *n* -1. ELECTRICITY a plastic device with metal parts that are put in a socket in order to connect an electrical appliance to the current □ *Turn it off and pull out the plug when you finish.* -2. [in a bath, sink] a round object made of rubber that stops the water from running out of a bath or sink □ *a sink plug.* -3. [for a book, movie] a public mention of something such as a new book or movie, e.g. on a TV show, intended to let people know about it (informal use) □ *She only agreed to appear on the show to give her new book a plug.*
◇ *vt* -1. [hole, leak] to stop water from getting through <sthg> □ *I used a rag to plug the hole in the bucket.* -2. [new book, movie] to mention <sthg> in public in order to make people interested in it (informal use) □ *He's only agreed to the interview in order to plug his latest movie.*

◆ **plug in** *vt sep* to plug sthg in [TV, heater] to put the plug of sthg into an electric socket to make it work.

plughole ['plʌghəʊl] *n* the hole in a bath or sink through which the water runs out.

plum [plʌm] ◇ *n* -1. a soft fruit with smooth red or purple skin and a large hard seed in the center. -2. the dark red color of plums. ◇ *adj* -1. purple in color, like a plum. -2. **a plum job** a good job that many people would like to have.

plumage ['pluːmɪdʒ] *n* the feathers of a bird.

plumb [plʌm] ◇ *adv* (informal use) -1. exactly □ *The ball landed plumb in the center.* -2. **plumb crazy** US completely crazy. ◇ *vt* **to plumb the depths of sthg** [of despair, humiliation] to experience or express sthg very intensely □ *The show plumbs new depths in bad taste.*

◆ **plumb in** *vt sep* **to plumb sthg in** [washing machine, bath] to connect sthg to a water supply permanently.

plumber ['plʌməʳ] *n* a person whose job is to install baths, toilets, heating etc and repair pipes.

plumbing ['plʌmɪŋ] *n* -1. the pipes that connect baths, toilets etc to the water supply. -2. the work that a plumber does.

plumb line *n* a string with a weight on one end, used to measure the depth of water or to see if something such as a wall is straight.

plume [pluːm] *n* -1. a large, often colorful, feather of a bird, especially one used to decorate a hat, helmet etc □ *an ostrich plume.*

-2. a plume of smoke a cloud of smoke that rises straight up in the air.

plummet ['plʌmət] *vi* **-1.** [bird, plane, stone] to fall quickly through the air straight down toward the ground □ *He plummeted to his death.* **-2.** [prices, sales, profits] to decrease suddenly □ *Share prices plummeted overnight.*

plump [plʌmp] ◇ *adj* [person, chicken] fat in an attractive way □ *You're getting plump.* □ *a plump, jolly woman.* ◇ *vi* **to plump for sthg** to choose sthg, especially after hesitating or thinking about it □ *In the end I plumped for steak.*

♦ **plump up** *vt sep* **to plump sthg up** [cushion, pillow] to make sthg rounder again by squeezing and shaking it.

plum pudding *n* GB a rich pudding made of dried fruit, eaten at Christmas.

plum tree *n* a tree on which plums grow.

plunder ['plʌndər] ◇ *n* **-1.** the act of stealing valuable objects, especially during a war. **-2.** things that are stolen □ *The burglars made off with their plunder.* ◇ *vt* [antiques, paintings] to steal <sthg>, especially during a war; [houses, village] to steal something from <a place> in this way □ *The army plundered food from farms* OR *plundered farms for food.*

plunge [plʌndʒ] ◇ *vi* **-1.** [car, plane, driver] to fall quickly, especially from somewhere high □ *The car plunged down the embankment.* **-2.** [price, value] to decrease quickly □ *The temperature plunged to –10° last night.* ◇ *n* **-1.** [in prices, temperature] a very sudden decrease □ *The Stock Market took a plunge yesterday.* **-2.** a quick movement into water, or a quick swim □ *I'm just going for a quick plunge to cool off.* ■ **to take the plunge** to decide to do something which is risky, especially after thinking about it carefully □ *They finally decided to take the plunge and get married.*

♦ **plunge into** *vt* **-1. to plunge sthg into sthg** [hand, knife] to put sthg quickly and firmly into sthg else □ *Plunge the tomatoes into boiling water for two minutes.* □ *She plunged the knife into his chest.* **-2. to plunge sb/sthg into sthg** [into chaos, war, despair] to suddenly put sb/sthg into a particular state or situation □ *She was plunged into a world of brutality.* □ *The entire city was plunged into darkness.*

plunge pod *n* a small swimming pool.

plunger ['plʌndʒər] *n* a tool with a rubber cup and a handle used for clearing blocked pipes.

plunging ['plʌndʒɪŋ] *adj* **a plunging neckline** a neckline that is cut low and reveals the top part of a woman's breasts.

pluperfect [,pluː'pɜːrfəkt] *n* **the pluperfect (tense)** the tense that is used to refer to an action that took place before another one.

plural ['plʊərəl] ◇ *adj* **-1.** GRAMMAR [word, form] that indicates that there is more than one □ *Words like "advice" and "information" have no plural form.* **-2.** [society, culture] that consists of or uses different types of people or things. ◇ *n* GRAMMAR a plural form of a word □ *"Hippopotami" is the plural of "hippopotamus".*

pluralistic [,plʊərə'lɪstɪk] *adj* [society, system] = **plural.**

plurality [plʊ'rælətɪ] *n* **-1. a plurality of** a large number of. **-2.** US [of votes] a majority.

plus [plʌs] (*pl* **pluses** OR **plusses**) ◇ *adj* **-1.** a word used to show that the true number is more than the one mentioned □ *The room can seat sixty plus.* **-2. A plus/B plus** a grade that is a little higher than A/B. ◇ *n* **-1.** MATH the symbol (+) that shows that one number is added to another. **-2.** an advantage (informal use) □ *Having two bathrooms is a definite plus.* ◇ *prep* **-1.** MATH added to a number □ *Two plus two equals four.* **-2.** with the addition of sb/sthg □ *There will be the two of us plus the children.* ◇ *conj* and in addition □ *She's very intelligent, plus she's a hard worker.*

plush [plʌʃ] *adj* [hotel, limousine, sofa] that looks expensive and of good quality □ *They've moved into some plush new offices.*

plus sign *n* MATH = **plus.**

Pluto ['pluːtoʊ] the planet in our solar system that is furthest from the sun.

plutonium [pluː'toʊniəm] *n* a radioactive element that is used in nuclear power stations to produce energy and in nuclear bombs. SYMBOL: Pu.

ply [plaɪ] (*pt* & *pp* **plied**) *vt* **-1. to ply sb with sthg** [with drink, questions] to keep giving sthg to sb □ *He kept plying me with champagne.* **-2.** to sail regularly on a route on <an ocean, river> etc □ *As a young man, he had plied the Atlantic on cargo ships.* **-3. to ply one's trade** to carry out one's job.

-ply *suffix* **two-ply/three-ply** [wood, tissue] that has two/three layers.

Plymouth Rock [,plɪməθ-] the rock where people believe the Pilgrims first landed in America.

plywood ['plaɪwʊd] *n* a type of wood made up of thin sheets of wood stuck together.

p.m., pm (*abbr of* **post meridiem**) between noon and midnight □ *at 3:00 p.m.* NOTE: Compare **a.m.**

PM *n abbr of* **prime minister.**

PMS *n abbr of* **premenstrual syndrome.**

PMT *n abbr of* **premenstrual tension.**

pneumatic [njuː'mætɪk] *adj* **-1.** [pump] that is operated by air pressure. **-2.** [tire] that is filled with air.

pneumatic drill *n* GB a large powerful tool, used for breaking up the surface of a road, that is operated by air pressure.

pneumonia [njuː'moʊnjə] *n* a serious illness of the lungs that makes it difficult to breathe.

PNG *abbr of* **Papua New Guinea.**

po, PO *n abbr of* **postal order.**

PO *n abbr of* **Post Office.**

POA (*abbr of* **Prison Officers' Association**) *n* **the POA** a labor union for prison officers in Britain.

poach [poʊtʃ] ◇ *vt* **-1.** [salmon, pheasants] to hunt <animals, birds, or fish> illegally on somebody else's land. **-2.** [idea, information] to use <sthg> that belongs to somebody else without asking permission □ *You can't go around poaching staff from other departments!* **-3.** COOKING [egg, salmon] to cook <sthg> gently in boiling liquid, e.g. water or milk. ◇ *vi* [hunter, poacher] *He was caught poaching.*

poacher ['poutʃər] *n* a person who hunts illegally on somebody else's land.

poaching ['poutʃɪŋ] *n* the activity of illegally hunting animals, birds, or fish on somebody else's land.

PO Box *n abbr of* **post office box**.

Pocahontas [ˌpoukə'hɒntəs] (1595–1617) a Native American woman who helped to keep peace between her people and the American colonists who lived nearby. She later married a colonist and went to England.

pocket ['pɒkət] ◇ *n* **-1.** [on a piece of clothing] a deep fold of cloth sewn into trousers, jackets etc to hold things □ *a trouser pocket* □ *My billfold was in my back pocket.* ■ **to be out of pocket** to have less money than one expected to have □ *The deal left me $70 out of pocket.* ■ **to pick sb's pocket** to steal money from sb's pocket □ *My pocket's been picked!* **-2.** [in a bag, on a door] a fold of cloth used as a container behind a seat, in a car door etc □ *You'll find the duty-free price list in the pocket in front of you.* **-3.** the amount of money one has to spend □ *This law will hit people where it hurts most, in their pocket.* **-4. a pocket of sthg** [of air, rain, support] a small amount of sthg that is different from what is around it □ *The advancing troops encountered pockets of resistance.* **-5.** [on a pool table] one of the holes at the edge of a pool, snooker, or billiards table.
◇ *adj* **a pocket mirror/book etc** a small mirror/book etc that is designed to be carried in a pocket.
◇ *vt* **-1.** [change, key] to put <sthg> in one's pocket □ *I pocketed the car keys and left.* **-2.** to earn <money> □ *Buy the cheaper product and you can pocket the difference.* **-3.** to steal <money that one handles for other people> □ *He was accused of pocketing some of the profits.*

pocketbook ['pɒkətbʊk] *n* **-1.** US a wallet; the amount of money one has to spend. **-2.** US a small bag in which a woman carries her money and personal things. **-3.** a small simple computer that is designed to fit in a pocket.

pocket calculator *n* a small calculator that one can carry around easily.

pocketful ['pɒkətfl] *n* the amount of things that can fit in a pocket □ *He emptied a pocketful of coins onto the counter.*

pocketknife ['pɒkətnaɪf] (*pl* **pocketknives** [-naɪvz]) *n* a small knife with a folding blade.

pocket money *n* money given to a child by its parents regularly.

pocket-size(d) *adj* [book, TV] that is smaller than the normal size.

pockmark ['pɒkmɑːrk] *n* a small hollow mark on one's skin left as a result of a disease such as chickenpox.

pod [pɒd] *n* **-1.** BIOLOGY the case in which the seeds of some plants such as peas and beans grow □ *a seed pod.* **-2.** SPACE a part of a spacecraft that can be separated from the rest.

podgy ['pɒdʒɪ] (*compar* **podgier**, *superl* **podgiest**) *adj* GB = **pudgy**.

podiatrist [pə'daɪətrəst] *n* a person whose job is treating people's feet.

podium ['poudɪəm] (*pl* **podiums** OR **podia** [-dɪə]) *n* a small platform that a conductor, speaker etc stands on.

Poe [pou], **Edgar Allen** (1809–1849) a US writer, well known for his tales of mystery and horror. His work includes *The Raven* and *The Fall of the House of Usher.*

POE (*abbr of* **port of entry**) *n* a port where imported goods are checked by customs officers.

poem ['pouəm] *n* a piece of writing in which words are chosen for their effect and sound and arranged in patterns, e.g. short lines that rhyme □ *a love poem* □ *a poem by Browning.*

poet ['pouət] *n* a person who writes poems.

poetic [pou'etɪk] *adj* [language, imagery] that is found in poetry; [description, book] having a beauty that is often found in poetry □ *a poetic vision of life.*

poetic justice *n* a situation in which something unpleasant that happens to somebody seems good and right because of bad things that the person has done.

poet laureate *n* in Britain, a poet appointed by the king or queen to write poems for special occasions.

poetry ['pouətrɪ] *n* **-1.** poems as a form of literature □ *Do you like reading poetry?* □ *a poetry book.* **-2.** beauty and grace □ *There is real poetry in a good game of football.*

pogo stick ['pougou-] *n* a children's toy consisting of a pole with a place to put one's feet and a spring, used for jumping.

pogrom [US 'pougrəm, GB 'pɒg-] *n* the organized killing of large numbers of people, especially Jews.

poignancy ['pɔɪnjənsɪ] *n: see* **poignant**.

poignant ['pɔɪnjənt] *adj* [description, scene, memory] that makes one feel very sad □ *a poignant reminder of the past.*

poinsettia [pɔɪn'setɪə] *n* a plant with large red leaves like flowers.

point [pɔɪnt] ◇ *n* **-1.** [of a pencil, needle] the thin sharp end of an object □ *You need a pencil with a sharp point on it.* **-2. a point of light** a very small dot of light □ *We could see a tiny point of light in the distance.* **-3.** [in space] the precise place where something is or happens □ *This is the point where the road forks.* **-4.** [in time, a situation, event] the precise time or part of a situation, event etc when something happens □ *At one point I thought he was going to cry.* □ *At that point we decided to leave.* □ *Things/It/I got to the point where I couldn't stand being near him.* □ *I have no plans to do so at this point in time.* ■ **the point of no return** the time after which things cannot go back

to the way they were before □ *We have now reached the point of no return.* **-5.** [in a discussion, speech] an idea or fact that somebody mentions □ *I have a list of the points I want to raise.* ■ **you have a point** a phrase used to show that one agrees with something somebody else has said □ *I think Mary has a point.* ■ **to make a point** to mention an idea one has about something □ *I'd like to make a few points about what Steve just said.* ■ **to make one's point** to make people understand what one has to say □ *Sit down now, you've made your point.* ■ **to take sb's point** to understand something that sb has said. □ *Do you take my point?* **-6.** [of a story] the main idea in a speech, story etc □ *They missed the point of what you were saying.* ■ **to get** OR **come to the point** to reach the most important or relevant part of what one is saying □ *Come on, get to the point!* ■ **to be beside the point** [comment, fact] not to be relevant to what is being discussed □ *But that's completely beside the point!* **-7.** [of somebody's character] a feature of somebody's character □ *His bad points are outweighed by his good points.* **-8. what is the point?** what is the purpose? □ *What's the point of working so hard?* □ *There's no point in doing it if you don't enjoy it.* **-9.** [on a scale] a unit for measuring something □ *The National Party has gone up three points in the opinion polls.* **-10.** MATH the symbol (.) that separates whole numbers from decimal fractions □ *The earthquake measured 6.5 on the Richter scale.* **-11.** [in competitions] a unit for measuring a score in competitions □ *The judges awarded her maximum points for her performance.* □ *Funds are allocated according to a points system.* **-12.** [on a compass] one of the directions marked on a compass □ *all points of the compass.* **-13.** US GRAMMAR the punctuation mark (.) that comes after the last word of a sentence to show that the sentence is finished. **-14.** [on a driver's license] a note on a driver's license that shows that the driver has done something illegal □ *a penalty point* □ *He got a fine and three points on his license.* **-15.** ELECTRICITY = **power point. -16. to make a point of doing sthg** to do sthg deliberately and carefully, especially so that somebody else notices □ *She made a point of coming over to speak to us.*
◇ *vt* [gun, finger, camera] to hold <sthg> so that it faces in a particular direction □ *Don't point your finger at me.* ■ **to point the way to sthg** to show how sthg can be done in the future □ *The new leisure complex points the way to what public buildings of the future will be like.*
◇ *vi* **-1.** [person] to point one's finger at something □ *You shouldn't point at people.* □ *He pointed to the necktie he wanted.* **-2.** [arrow, sign, needle on a dial] to indicate a particular direction □ *The sign pointed toward a town in the distance.* **-3.** [gun, camera, light] to be aimed in a particular direction □ *It must be awful knowing that hundreds of cameras are pointing at you all the time.*
◆ **points** *npl* **-1.** AUTO the two screws in the distributor of a car engine that are part of an

electrical circuit. **-2.** GB RAIL a device for moving a train from one track to another.
◆ **on the point of** *prep* to be on the point of doing sthg to be going to do sthg very soon □ *I was on the point of giving up.*
◆ **to the point** *adj* to be to the point to be relevant to what is being discussed □ *What she had to say was short and to the point.*
◆ **up to a point** *adv* [agree, succeed] partly □ *You're right up to a point.*
◆ **point out** *vt sep* **-1. to point sthg out** [person, building, object] to show or make people look at sthg by pointing to it □ *The guide pointed out to us the house where Puccini was born.* **-2. to point sthg out** [fact, mistake, problem] to draw attention to sthg □ *I was able to point out that he was wrong/point out where he'd gone wrong.*
◆ **point to** *vt fus* **to point to sthg** to make sthg look very likely □ *Everything points to involvement by the CIA.*

point-blank ◇ *adj* **-1.** [refusal, denial] that is strong and direct with no explanation □ *His lawyer issued a point-blank denial of the allegations.* **-2. to shoot sb at point-blank range** to shoot sb from a very close position. ◇ *adv* [refuse, deny, accuse] *I asked him point-blank if he had taken the money.*

point duty *n* GB the job of controlling the traffic, usually done by a policeman standing at an intersection.

pointed ['pɔɪntəd] *adj* **-1.** [chin, hat] that has a point at the end. **-2.** [remark, question] that expresses a particular meaning, especially a critical or threatening one, in an indirect way □ *She made a few pointed comments about the fact that I'd forgotten her birthday.*

pointedly ['pɔɪntədlɪ] *adv* [remark, ask] *see* **pointed** □ *"It's getting late," she said pointedly.*

pointer ['pɔɪntər] *n* **-1.** [on how to do something] a useful piece of advice □ *She gave us a few pointers on healthy eating.* **-2.** [on a dial] a needle that indicates numbers on a dial. **-3.** [for pointing] a stick for pointing at things on a blackboard, map etc. **-4.** [for hunting] a kind of dog used for hunting that shows where the hunted animal is by pointing its nose. **-5.** COMPUTING an arrow that points to something on a computer screen.

pointing ['pɔɪntɪŋ] *n* the cement between the stones or bricks of a wall.

pointless ['pɔɪntləs] *adj* [exercise, question, job] that is not at all helpful or useful □ *It's pointless going on any further.*

point of order (*pl* **points of order**) *n* a complaint made because the rules of a formal meeting have been broken.

point of sale (*pl* **points of sale**) *n* the place where a product is sold.

point of view (*pl* **points of view**) *n* a way somebody has of looking at a problem, situation etc □ *Whether it's important or not depends on your point of view.*

point-to-point *n* GB a horse race held in the countryside in which the stages of the race are marked with flags.

poise [pɔɪz] *n* a calm confidence in oneself □ *She showed remarkable poise at the interview.*

poised [pɔɪzd] *adj* **-1. to be poised to do sthg** to be ready to do sthg □ *Our party is poised to win the next election.* □ *The soldiers waited poised for action.* **-2.** [person] who shows poise □ *She gave a poised performance.*

poison ['pɔɪzn] ◇ *n* a substance that harms or kills living things if it is eaten or drunk. ◇ *vt* **-1.** [person, animal] to kill or harm <sb/sthg> with poison □ *She was found guilty of poisoning her husband.* **-2.** [food, drink] to put poison in <sthg> □ *Someone had poisoned the wine.* **-3.** [air, water] to pollute <sthg> □ *Industrial waste is poisoning the seas.* **-4.** [mind, relationship] to harm or spoil <sthg> □ *Ma did her best to poison the atmosphere at the wedding.*

poisoning ['pɔɪznɪŋ] *n* an illness caused by eating, drinking, or being exposed to something harmful □ *alcohol/radiation poisoning.*

poisonous ['pɔɪznəs] *adj* **-1.** [gas, chemical] that can poison a living thing. **-2.** [snake, mushroom, plant] that contains poison. **-3.** [person, influence, rumor] that harms or spoils something □ *She threw him a poisonous look.*

poison-pen letter *n* a letter that says bad things about somebody and is meant to upset them.

poke [pouk] ◇ *vt* **-1.** to push one's finger sharply and suddenly into <sb/sthg> □ *Stop poking me in the ribs!* **-2.** to push <sthg> into a narrow space or opening □ *Try to poke the wire through the hole.* **-3. to poke a fire** to stir the wood or coal on a fire so that it burns better. ◇ *vi* to be visible from under or behind something □ *I could see his toes poking through his socks.* ◇ *n* an act of poking somebody or something □ *I gave him a sharp poke in the ribs.*

◆ **poke about, poke around** *vi* **-1.** to try to find out about somebody's life in a way that annoys them □ *Stop poking around in my business!* **-2.** GB to look for something in a place by moving things around (informal use) □ *Who's been poking around in this drawer?*

◆ **poke at** *vt fus* **to poke at sthg** to poke sthg several times □ *The cat kept poking at the dead mouse with its paw.*

poker ['poukər] *n* **-1.** a card game that can be played for money □ *a game of poker.* **-2.** a metal rod used to poke a fire.

poker-faced [-feɪst] *adj* [person] who shows no emotion □ *We told her the news and she just sat there poker-faced.*

pokies ['poukiz] *npl* **the pokies** AUS slot machines used for gambling.

poky ['pouki] (*comp* **pokier**, *superl* **pokiest**) *adj* [room, house] that seems small and uncomfortable (disapproving use) □ *It's a nice apartment, but a little on the poky side.*

Poland ['poulənd] a country in Central Europe. It was a Communist state from 1947 to 1989. SIZE: 313,000 sq kms. POPULATION: 38,200,000 (*Poles, Polish*). CAPITAL: Warsaw. LANGUAGE: Polish. CURRENCY: zloty.

polar ['poulər] *adj* [region, ice cap] that is con-

nected to the areas around the North or South Poles.

polar bear *n* a large white bear that lives in the Arctic.

polarity [pou'lærəti] *n* **-1.** the state of being opposite □ *the polarity between fantasy and reality.* **-2.** ELECTRICITY the state, either positive or negative, of a pole of a battery.

polarize, -ise ['pouləraɪz] *vt* [public opinion, country] to divide <sthg> into two opposite groups □ *The dispute has polarized their supporters.*

Polaroid™ ['poulərɔɪd] *n* **-1. a Polaroid (camera)** a camera that produces a developed photograph immediately after it has been taken. ■ **a Polaroid (photo)** a photo taken by a Polaroid camera. **-2.** a plastic material used to treat plastic or glass so that the light that passes through it seems less bright □ *a Polaroid filter/lens* □ *Polaroid sunglasses.*

◆ **Polaroids**™ *npl* Polaroid sunglasses.

pole [poul] *n* **-1.** a long, straight, thin, round piece of wood, metal etc often stuck in the ground to support something □ *The hammock was strung between two poles.* **-2.** GEOGRAPHY one of the two points on the Earth that are furthest from the equator. ■ **to be poles apart** to be very different □ *When it comes to politics, we're poles apart.* **-3.** ELECTRICITY one of two points, either positive or negative, on a battery to which wires can be attached.

Pole *n* a person who lives in or comes from Poland.

poleaxed ['poulækst] *adj* **to be poleaxed** to be very surprised or shocked.

polecat ['poulkæt] *n* a small, brown, fierce animal with an unpleasant smell that lives in the north of Europe.

polemic [pə'lemɪk] *n* something that somebody says or writes in a very angry way to argue for or against something □ *a polemic against the government.*

pole position *n* the front starting position in motor racing □ *Hill is in pole position.*

Pole Star: the Pole Star the star that is nearest to the North Pole in the night sky.

pole vault *n* **the pole vault** the sport of jumping over a very high bar using a long pole.

◆ **pole-vault** *vi* to jump in the style of the pole vault.

pole-vaulter [-vɔːltər] *n* an athlete who competes in the pole vault.

police [pə'liːs] ◇ *npl* **-1. the police** the official organization in a country whose job is to make people obey the law and to catch criminals □ *a police spokesman/chief.* **-2.** members of the police □ *Police are appealing for information.* ◇ *vt* [town, streets] to make people obey the law in <an area>, using the police □ *Hundreds of officers were brought in to police the demonstration.*

police car *n* a car used by the police.

police constable *n* GB a member of the police of the lowest rank.

police department *n* US a police organization

which is responsible for a particular area or city.

police dog *n* a dog trained and used by the police to find criminals, drugs etc.

police force *n* a police organization which is responsible for a particular area □ *She joined the police force when she was 20.*

policeman [pə'liːsmən] (*pl* **policemen** [-mən]) *n* a man who is a member of the police force.

police officer *n* a person who is a member of the police force.

police record *n* information kept by the police about a person who has committed a crime □ *"Finding work isn't easy if you have a police record," said Neil.*

police state *n* a country where people are not free to do or say what they like and where the police have a lot of power (disapproving use).

police station *n* the local office of the police in an area □ *They were taken to the police station for questioning.*

policewoman [pə'liːswʊmən] (*pl* **policewomen**) *n* a woman who is a member of the police force.

policy ['pɒləsɪ] (*pl* **policies**) *n* -1. a plan made by a government, organization, company etc that says what it wants to do or how it will deal with a particular problem or situation □ *It is against company policy to employ smokers.* ■ **a policy maker** a person who helps to form the policies of a government, organization etc. -2. a document given to a customer by an insurance company that explains the details of the agreement made between them □ *He took out a life insurance policy.*

policy-holder *n* a person who is insured with an insurance company.

polio ['pəʊlɪəʊ] *n* a serious disease that can paralyze one.

polish ['pɒlɪʃ] ◇ *n* -1. [for furniture, leather] a liquid, cream etc that makes things shine when it is rubbed on them □ *shoe/boot/floor/furniture polish.* -2. [on a shoe, piece of furniture] the shine on the surface of a piece of furniture, shoes etc □ *The table had a high polish.* -3. [of a person] a high degree of skill and stylishness □ *Her work lacks polish.* ◇ *vt* -1. [shoes, furniture, mirror] to make <sthg> shine by rubbing it. -2. **to polish sthg (up)** [skill, knowledge] to improve sthg □ *She went to France to polish up her French.*

◆ **polish off** *vt sep* (informal use) -1. **to polish food off** to finish food quickly □ *You soon polished off those cookies.* -2. **to polish sthg off** [job, book, opposition] to finish or deal with sthg quickly and easily □ *We'll polish off the work in no time.*

Polish ['pəʊlɪʃ] ◇ *npl* **the Polish** the people who come from or live in Poland. ◇ *n* the language spoken in Poland. ◇ *adj: see* **Poland.**

polished ['pɒlɪʃt] *adj* -1. [surface, table] that is shiny after being rubbed with polish □ *polished glass.* -2. [person, manners] that is polite,

confident, and elegant. -3. [performance, performer] that is confident and skillful.

polite [pə'laɪt] *adj* -1. [person, remark, refusal] that shows good manners □ *He was very polite to me.* -2. **polite society** people who are considered to be refined and to have correct social behavior □ *That's not the sort of thing you discuss in polite society.*

politely [pə'laɪtlɪ] *adv* [ask, say, refuse] *see* **polite** □ *I must politely request you to leave.*

politeness [pə'laɪtnəs] *n* [of a person, remark, refusal] *see* **polite.**

politic ['pɒlətɪk] *adj* advisable (formal use) □ *It wouldn't be politic to approach them just now.*

political [pə'lɪtɪkl] *adj* -1. [party, theory] that is connected with politics □ *Making a speech like that was political suicide.* □ *a political activist.* -2. [person] who is interested or involved in politics □ *All her family is very political.*

political asylum *n* permission to stay in a country that is given to a person who has had to leave their own country for political reasons, especially because they are in danger there □ *The refugee was granted political asylum.*

Political Correctness [-kə'rektnəs] *n* a movement that aims to get rid of attitudes such as racism and sexism.

✇ POLITICAL CORRECTNESS
Political correctness refers to a set of attitudes and principles that started among left-wing and liberal people in the USA. It aims to achieve fairer treatment for all, mainly by getting rid of words that seem to discriminate against a particular section of society. It is politically correct, or PC, for example, to say "Native American" instead of "American Indian", "African American" instead of "black person", and "differently abled" instead of "disabled". Some people disapprove of political correctness because it is too extreme.

---

political football *n* GB an issue that is strongly argued about by different political parties □ *Immigration has become something of a political football.*

political geography *n* the branch of geography that deals with states and their borders.

politically [pə'lɪtɪklɪ] *adv* **politically active/wise** etc active/wise etc from the point of view of politics □ *The council's decisions were said to be politically motivated.* □ *Politically, it was a dangerous move.*

politically correct *adj* [language, term, attitude] that aims to treat everybody in a fair way, especially by not using words that are unfair to minorities, women etc.

political prisoner *n* a person who is put in prison for their political beliefs, especially because they disagree with their government.

political science *n* the study of politics and governments.

politician [ˌpɒlə'tɪʃn] *n* a person who works in

politics □ *The issue unites politicians of all parties.*

politicize, -ise [pə'lıtəsaız] *vt* [person] to make <sb> more involved in politics; [topic, issue] to present <sthg> from a political point of view □ *It was his war experiences that really politicized him.* □ *They're trying to politicize what is essentially a moral issue.*

politics ['pɒlətıks] ◇ *n* -1. the activities involved in getting and using power in a country, city, society, or organization □ *I've always been interested in politics.* -2. the profession of being a politician □ *She entered politics in 1969.* ◇ *npl* -1. a person's political beliefs □ *I don't know what his politics are.* -2. the ways in which people in an organization try to gain power □ *I've had enough of office politics!*

polka ['pɒlkə] *n* a fast dance for people in pairs, popular in the 19th century; a piece of music that has the rhythm of this dance.

polka dot *n* **polka dots** a pattern consisting of round spots that is often used on cloth, clothes, paper etc □ *a polka-dot dress.*

poll [pəʊl] ◇ *n* -1. an election □ *The results of the poll will be known later tonight.* -2. a survey in which a number of people are asked their opinion about somebody or something, in order to find out what most people think or what most people will do in the future □ *Recent poll figures show considerable support for the idea.* ◇ *vt* -1. to ask <people> for their opinion on somebody or something in a poll □ *Only 10% of the people polled were in favor of a ban.* -2. [politician, candidate, party] to get <a particular number of votes> in an election □ *They only polled 20% of the vote.*

◆ **polls** *npl* **to go to the polls** to vote in an election □ *It could be over a year before the country goes to the polls.*

pollen ['pɒlən] *n* the yellow powder produced by a flower to fertilize other flowers of the same species.

pollen count *n* the official measurement of the amount of pollen in the air at a particular time and place.

pollinate ['pɒləneɪt] *vt* [flower, tree, grass] to fertilize <a plant> with pollen.

pollination [,pɒlə'neɪʃn] *n*: *see* **pollinate**.

polling ['pəʊlɪŋ] *n* the act of voting at an election □ *Polling opened at 8:00 this morning.*

polling booth *n* GB a small separated area in a polling place where one can vote in private.

polling day *n* GB the day on which people vote in an election.

polling place US, **polling station** GB *n* a place where people go to vote in an election, often a school or other public building.

Pollock ['pɒlək], **Jackson** (1912–1956) a US abstract artist known for his "action painting", a style of painting in which the artist drips or throws paint onto the canvas.

pollster ['pəʊlstə'] *n* a person who carries out polls and uses their results to try to say what will happen in the future.

poll tax *n* a tax that must be paid by every adult, or every person, in a country.

◆ **Poll Tax** *n* **the Poll Tax** a local tax, payable by every adult living in Britain, that was introduced in 1987. It was unpopular and was replaced by the Council Tax in 1992.

pollutant [pə'luːtnt] *n* a substance that pollutes something □ *chemical pollutants.*

pollute [pə'luːt] *vt* [environment, atmosphere, river] to make <sthg> dirty and unsafe for people or animals to use.

pollution [pə'luːʃn] *n* -1. substances that pollute □ *Pollution is allowed to flow into the river unchecked.* -2. [of the environment, atmosphere, a river] *see* **pollute** □ *the pollution of seaside resorts.* ■ **noise pollution** continuous or loud noise, e.g. from traffic or aircraft, that is considered to be unhealthy for people.

polo ['pəʊləʊ] *n* a sport in which two teams of players riding horses hit a ball with long wooden hammers to try and score goals.

polo neck *n* -1. US a collar in the form of a band of material that covers part of one's neck; GB a high collar that folds down. -2. a sweater with a polo neck.

◆ **polo-neck** *adj* **a polo-neck sweater/dress etc** a sweater/dress etc that has a polo neck.

polo shirt *n* a top that has short sleeves, a collar, and three or four buttons at the neck.

poltergeist ['pɒltə'gaɪst] *n* a ghost that is believed to move objects and throw them around and cause damage in a house, but that is never seen.

polyanthus [,pɒlɪ'ænθəs] (*pl* **polyanthuses** OR **polyanthi** [-θaɪ]) *n* a small garden plant with groups of brightly colored flowers and thick stems.

polyester [US 'pɒlɪestr, GB ,pɒlɪ'estə] *n* a type of artificial fabric used to make cloth □ *polyester fabric/cotton.*

polyethylene [,pɒlɪ'eθɪliːn] US, **polythene** ['pɒlɪθiːn] GB *n* a strong thin plastic used to make sheets or bags, or to cover or protect things □ *a polyethylene sheet.*

polygamist [pə'lɪgəmɪst] *n* a man who has more than one wife at the same time.

polygamy [pə'lɪgəmɪ] *n* the practice or custom of being a polygamist.

polygon ['pɒlɪgɒn] *n* a shape with more than three straight sides.

polymer ['pɒlɪmə'] *n* a chemical substance consisting of large molecules made of many small molecules with the same structure.

Polynesia [,pɒlə'niːzjə] a region consisting of several groups of islands in the central and southern Pacific Ocean, including Hawaii, Tonga, and Samoa.

Polynesian [,pɒlə'niːzjən] *n* & *adj*: *see* **Polynesia**.

polyp ['pɒləp] *n* a small growth on a surface inside one's body that can cause disease.

polypropylene [,pɒlɪ'prəʊpəliːn] *n* a plastic material used in making ropes, carpets etc.

polystyrene [,pɒlɪ'staɪriːn] *n* a very light plastic, used for making containers, and as an insulating material □ *a polystyrene cup.*

polythene *n* GB = **polyethylene.**

polyunsaturated [ˌpɒliʌn'sætʃəreɪtəd] *adj* [fat, margarine] that is made mainly from vegetable fats that are thought to be healthier than animal fats.

polyurethane [ˌpɒlɪ'jʊərəθeɪn] *n* a plastic used especially to make types of paint, foam, and varnish.

pom [pɒm] *n* AUS an English person (informal and disapproving use).

pomander [poʊ'mændə^r] *n* an object that contains spices or flowers, or that smells of these, and is kept in a room, closet etc to keep the clothes or the air there fresh.

pomegranate ['pɒmɪgrænət] *n* a round fruit that has a hard, thin skin and many seeds with pink juicy flesh around each one.

pommel ['pɒml] *n* the raised part on the front of a horse's saddle.

pommie, pommy ['pɒmɪ] *n* AUS = **pom.**

pomp [pɒmp] *n* the great ceremony, decorations, and fine clothes seen on official or public occasions □ *the pomp and ceremony of a royal wedding.*

Pompey ['pɒmpɪ] (106–48BC) a Roman military and political leader. He shared power with Julius Caesar, and then opposed him and was defeated by him.

pompom ['pɒmpɒm] *n* -1. a small ball made of strings of yarn and wool and used to decorate hats, socks etc. -2. a large ball made of colored strings of plastic and waved by cheerleaders at football games.

pompous ['pɒmpəs] *adj* [person] who speaks or behaves in a very serious way because they think they are more important than they really are □ *a pompous speech.*

poncho ['pɒntʃoʊ] (*pl* **ponchos**) *n* a piece of clothing like a cape worn on top of one's other clothes and consisting of a single piece of material with a hole for one's head.

pond [pɒnd] *n* a small area of water that is smaller than a lake and has been built or has formed in a hole in the ground.

ponder ['pɒndə^r] ◇ *vt* [question, problem] to think slowly and carefully about <sthg> (literary use) □ *I'll have to ponder the matter further.* ◇ *vi: I shall have to ponder over that for a while.*

ponderous ['pɒndərəs] *adj* -1. [book, speech, writing] that is serious, long, and boring □ *He embarked on a very long, ponderous explanation.* -2. [architecture, person] that looks large and heavy □ *a ponderous Victorian edifice.* -3. [movement, walk] that is slow and clumsy □ *He has a very ponderous way of moving/dancing.*

pontiff ['pɒntɪf] *n* a pope (formal use).

pontificate [pɒn'tɪfɪkeɪt] *vi* to tell other people one's opinion because one believes one is always right (disapproving use) □ *He's always pontificating about* OR *on how we should be doing things.*

Pontius Pilate [ˌpɒntʃəs'paɪlət] in the Bible, the Roman officer in charge of Jesus Christ's trial and crucifixion.

pontoon [pɒn'tuːn] *n* -1. **a pontoon (bridge)** a type of bridge that is built on a platform consisting of boats. -2. GB a card game played for money.

pony ['poʊnɪ] (*pl* **ponies**) *n* a small kind of horse.

Pony Express *n* **the Pony Express** a service for delivering mail that operated in the USA between Missouri and California in the 1860s. The mail was carried by men riding on horseback.

❦ PONY EXPRESS
The Pony Express mail service, which started in 1860, used horseback riders and a system of stations where men could stop to change horses every ten to fifteen miles. The riders could cover the 2,000 miles from the Midwest to California in ten days — less than half the time that the normal stagecoach service took. The company went bankrupt after only a year and a half when the telegraph system was completed.

ponytail ['poʊnɪteɪl] *n* a hairstyle in which all one's hair is tied together at the back of the head □ *She always wears her hair in a ponytail.*

pony-trekking [-trekɪŋ] *n* GB the activity of riding ponies through the countryside as part of one's vacation.

poodle ['puːdl] *n* a type of dog with very curly short hair.

pooh [puː] *excl* a sound used to show disgust at an unpleasant smell.

pooh-pooh *vt* to reject <an idea> because one thinks it is foolish □ *The committee pooh-poohed the idea of a joint venture.*

pool [puːl] ◇ *n* -1. a small area of water, usually formed naturally. -2. = **swimming pool.** -3. [of water, light] a small area of liquid or light on the ground □ *a pool of blood.* -4. [of talent, people, money] a number of things or people that are used and shared by several people or organizations. -5. GAMES a game in which long thin sticks are used to hit colored balls into holes around the edge of a special table. ◇ *vt* [information, money] to share <sthg that one has> with other people in order that one can use their resources, information, money etc □ *Why don't we pool our resources and buy a car together?*

◆ **pools** *npl* = **football pools.**

poop [puːp] *n* **the poop** US the most important facts about something (informal use).

pooped [puːpt] *adj* **to be pooped** to be very tired (informal use).

poor [pʊə^r, pɔː^r] ◇ *adj* -1. [person] who has very little money or few possessions; [country, area] that has a lot of poor people living in it □ *She comes from a poor background.* -2. a word used to show sympathy for somebody □ *You poor thing!* -3. [health, results] that is of a low quality or standard □ *Asthma can be triggered by poor air quality.* ◇ *npl* **the poor**

poor people in a particular society □ *The law was originally intended to help the poor.*

poorhouse ['puə'haus, *pl* -hauzız] *n* in the past, a building paid for by the public where poor people could live if they had no home.

poorly ['puə'lı] ◇ *adj* **to be poorly** GB to be unwell (informal use). ◇ *adv* [perform, cook] badly □ *The job is very poorly paid.*

poor relation *n* something that is similar to another thing but not as good as it □ *The state colleges are still seen as the poor relations of the older universities.*

pop [pɒp] (*pt* & *pp* **popped**, *cont* **popping**) ◇ *n* -1. MUSIC a modern kind of music that usually has a strong beat and is popular mainly with young people □ *a pop song/ record.* -2. [for drinking] a sweet bubbly drink that is not alcoholic (informal use). -3. a word used when talking to or about one's father (informal use) □ *Pop died when I was only 17.* -4. a word used to describe a short sharp sound like a small explosion □ *The cork came out of the bottle with a loud pop.*
◇ *vt* -1. [balloon, bubble] to burst <sthg> with a pop. -2. to put sthg somewhere, especially quickly (informal use) □ *He popped the book into his case.* □ *She popped her head around the door to say hello.* □ *I'll pop a check in the mail.*
◇ *vi* -1. [balloon, bubble] to burst with a pop □ *He blew up the bag until it suddenly popped.* -2. [button, cork] to suddenly move from a fixed position □ *The lid popped open.* -3. [eyes] to stick out with surprise or excitement □ *Her eyes practically popped out of her head when I told her.* -4. [person] to come or go somewhere quickly □ *I'm just popping over to Aunt Ellen's house.*
◆ **pop in** *vi* to go somewhere and see somebody for a short time (informal use) □ *He said he'd pop in and see us when he got back.*
◆ **pop up** *vi* to appear in a situation or place unexpectedly □ *She pops up in the most unlikely places.*

popadum ['pɒpədəm] *n* a type of very thin, round, crispy bread made of flour and water that is eaten with Indian food.

pop art *n* a style of modern art that uses the images, styles, and techniques of advertising and the mass media.

pop concert *n* a live performance of pop music by one or more pop groups.

popcorn ['pɒpkɔːʳn] *n* a kind of food eaten as a snack that is made of grains of corn heated until they burst and become soft, and then flavored with salt or sugar.

pope [poup] *n* the leader of the Roman Catholic Church.

Popeye ['pɒpaɪ] a cartoon sailor who becomes very strong when he eats spinach.

pop group *n* a group of people who perform pop music together.

poplar ['pɒpləʳ] *n* a type of tall thin tree with triangular leaves; the wood of this tree.

poplin ['pɒplən] *n* a type of cotton fabric used mainly to make clothes □ *a poplin shirt.*

popper ['pɒpəʳ] *n* GB a device for fastening a

piece of clothing that consists of two small, round, metal or plastic parts that are pressed together.

poppy ['pɒpɪ] (*pl* **poppies**) *n* a plant that has large, usually red flowers, one type of which produces the drug opium □ *poppy seeds.*

poppycock ['pɒpɪkɒk] *n* a word used to show that one thinks that something is nonsense (old-fashioned use) □ *Don't talk such poppycock!*

Poppy Day *n* in Britain, the Sunday nearest November 11, when people wear artificial poppies in memory of those who died in the two World Wars.

🐝 POPPY DAY
In Britain Poppy Day, also called Remembrance Day, is the Sunday nearest to November 11, the anniversary of the day that World War I ended. Near this date people buy red paper poppies to wear in their lapels, in memory of British soldiers who died during the two World Wars. (Poppies used to grow in northern France, where many soldiers died during World War I.) The money raised goes to help people who fought in the wars.

Popsicle™ ['pɒpsɪkl] *n* US a piece of flavored ice frozen onto a stick.

pop singer *n* a person who sings pop music as a career.

populace ['pɒpjələs] *n* **the populace** the people who live in a country, especially those who do not govern it □ *an attempt to win the hearts of the populace.*

popular ['pɒpjələʳ] *adj* -1. [activity, person, place] that a lot of people like □ *a popular ski resort* □ *The band was very popular in the seventies.* □ *The show is back by popular demand.* -2. [belief, attitude] that a lot of people have □ *We hope our work will help to change popular misconceptions about aging.* -3. **popular entertainment/ culture etc** entertainment/culture etc produced for or enjoyed by ordinary people □ *a popular history of the war years* □ *popular press.*

popularity [ˌpɒpjəˈlærətɪ] *n* [of a person, activity, place] *see* **popular** □ *African music has gained in popularity over the last five years.*

popularize, -ise ['pɒpjələraɪz] *vt* -1. [style, place, activity] to make <sthg> popular □ *The band helped to popularize Tex-Mex music.* -2. [science, idea] to make <sthg> easier to understand or more interesting for ordinary people □ *He was successful in popularizing astronomy.*

popularly ['pɒpjələʳlɪ] *adv* **popularly believed/ thought etc** believed/thought etc by many people □ *The ferry is popularly known as the "Vomit Comet".* □ *King Arthur is popularly believed to have led a Celtic rebellion.*

populate ['pɒpjəleɪt] *vt* -1. to live in <a place> □ *The area is mainly populated by farmers.* -2. to send people, animals, or plants to <a place> so that they will live there □ *The country was mainly populated by European emigrants.*

populated ['pɒpjəleɪtəd] *adj* **a densely/sparsely**

populated area an area where a lot of/few people live □ *a densely populated country.*

population [ˌpɒpjəˈleɪʃn] *n* -1. [of a country, town] the number of people that live in an area □ *Montreal has a population of over a million.* -2. all the people, animals, or plants of a particular type that live in a place □ *the local deer population.*

population explosion *n* a large and very fast increase in a population.

populist [ˈpɒpjəlɪst] *n* a politician who tries to get support mainly from ordinary people.

pop-up *adj* -1. **a pop-up toaster** a toaster with a spring that pushes the bread up out of the top after it has been toasted. -2. **a pop-up book** a book, usually for children, that has pictures that stand up when the pages are opened.

porcelain [ˈpɔːrsələn] *n* a hard kind of pottery with a shiny surface, used to make high-quality plates, cups etc and ornaments □ *a porcelain vase.*

porch [pɔːrtʃ] *n* -1. an entrance to a building, with sides and a roof. -2. US a platform built along the outside wall of a house that often has a roof and is used for relaxation.

porcupine [ˈpɔːrkjəpaɪn] *n* an animal with short legs and long sharp spines all over its back and sides.

pore [pɔːr] *n* [of skin, a rock, plant] a very small hole in the surface of something that lets water, air etc pass in or out.

◆ **pore over** *vt fus* **to pore over sthg** [book, map, statistics] to look at or read sthg very carefully, especially for a long time □ *He could usually be found poring over a dictionary.*

pork [pɔːrk] *n* the meat from a pig □ *roast pork.*

pork chop *n* a small piece of meat on a bone, cut from the ribs of a pig.

porn [pɔːrn] *n* = **pornography** (informal use) □ *a porn magazine.*

pornographic [ˌpɔːrnəˈgræfɪk] *adj* [book, movie, magazine] *see* **pornography** □ *pornographic pictures/videos.*

pornography [pɔːrˈnɒgrəfɪ] *n* pictures, books, movies etc that are designed to make people sexually excited by showing or describing naked people or sexual activity (disapproving use).

porous [ˈpɔːrəs] *adj* [rock, soil] that has many small holes in it that let water or air pass through it.

porpoise [ˈpɔːrpəs] *n* a large animal that lives in the sea and is similar to a dolphin.

porridge [ˈpɒrɪdʒ] *n* a dish consisting of oats cooked in milk or water and eaten hot, usually for breakfast.

port [pɔːrt] *n* -1. a town or city on a river or by the sea that has a harbor □ *a sea/river port.* -2. [of a town] the harbor of a town or city, where ships are loaded and unloaded □ *the port authorities.* -3. SAILING [on a ship, boat] the left side when one is in a boat and facing forward □ *the port side.* ■ **to port** [list, steer, veer] to the port side. -4. [drink] a type of

strong, sweet, red wine made in Portugal. -5. COMPUTING the part of a computer where another device can be connected, e.g. a printer.

portable [ˈpɔːrtəbl] *adj* [computer, TV, chair] that is smaller than usual and designed to be moved or carried easily.

Portacrib™ [ˈpɔːrtəkrɪb] *n* US a portable bed for a very small baby.

portal [ˈpɔːrtl] *n* a large and impressive entrance door to a building (literary use) □ *We entered the portals of the university.*

portcullis [ˌpɔːrtˈkʌləs] *n* a strong heavy gate above the entrance to a castle, fort etc that can be lowered to the ground, and was used in the past as a protection against attack.

portend [pɔːrˈtend] *vt* [disaster, evil] to be a sign that <sthg bad> will happen in the future (formal use) □ *The eclipse was thought to portend some great disaster.*

portent [ˈpɔːrtent] *n* something that portends something else in the future (literary use) □ *a portent of things to come.*

porter [ˈpɔːrtər] *n* -1. [at an airport, station, hotel] a person whose job is to carry people's bags at airports, railroad stations, or hotels. -2. US [on a train] the person whose job is to look after passengers in a sleeping car on a train. -3. GB [in a school, apartment building] a person whose job is to look after the entrance of a particular building, especially by checking who enters it □ *a hotel porter.*

Porter [ˈpɔːrtər], **Cole** (1892–1964) a US composer of popular songs. His work includes *Begin the Beguine* and *I've Got You Under My Skin.*

portfolio [ˌpɔːrtˈfoʊlɪoʊ] (*pl* **portfolios**) *n* -1. [for carrying things] a large flat case for carrying papers and drawings. -2. [of drawings, photographs] a collection of drawings, photographs, or paintings, used by an artist or model to show their work. -3. FINANCE a collection of stocks and shares in different businesses.

porthole [ˈpɔːrthoʊl] *n* a small round window in the side of a ship or a plane.

portion [ˈpɔːrʃn] *n* -1. a part of something □ *A large portion of their money is invested in property.* -2. [of vegetables, pie] an amount of food that is given to somebody at a meal □ *A small portion of fries, please.*

portly [ˈpɔːrtlɪ] (*compar* **portlier**, *superl* **portliest**) *adj* [man] who has a fat stomach (polite use) □ *He grew rather portly with age.*

Port Moresby [-ˈmɔːrzbɪ] the capital and main port of Papua New Guinea, on the southeast coast. POPULATION: 144,000.

port of call *n* -1. SAILING a place where a ship stops during a trip. -2. any one of a number of places one has to visit within a particular period of time, or during a trip □ *Our next port of call is the supermarket.*

portrait [ˈpɔːrtrət] *n* -1. a painting, drawing, or photograph of somebody, especially of their face □ *I offered to paint her portrait.* □ *a portrait painter.* -2. a movie, piece of writing etc that describes a person, thing, or place □ *The book is essentially a portrait of Spain in the 17th century.*

portraitist ['pɔːˈtreɪtəst] *n* an artist or photographer whose job is to make portraits of people.

portray [pɔːˈtreɪ] *vt* -1. [hero, villain] to play the part of <sb> in a play, movie etc □ *She portrayed his neurotic wife.* -2. to describe, paint, draw etc <sb/sthg> in a particular way □ *Richard III is always portrayed as a tyrant.* □ *How was she portrayed in the movie?* -3. [person, event] to describe or paint <sb/sthg> □ *a novel portraying wealthy society in 19th-century New York.*

portrayal [pɔːˈtreɪəl] *n* a painting, description, performance etc that portrays somebody or something □ *a convincing portrayal of madness.*

Portugal ['pɔːtʃəgl] a country in southwestern Europe, west of Spain, on the Atlantic Ocean. SIZE: 92,000 sq kms. POPULATION: 10,400,000 (*Portuguese*). CAPITAL: Lisbon. LANGUAGE: Portuguese. CURRENCY: escudo.

Portuguese [,pɔːtʃəˈgiːz] (*pl* **Portuguese**) ◇ *n* a language spoken in Portugal, Brazil, Angola, and Mozambique. ◇ *npl* **the Portuguese** the people who come from or live in Portugal. ◇ *adj: see* **Portugal** □ *the Portuguese ambassador.*

pose [pəʊz] ◇ *n* -1. the way a person stands or sits, especially for a portrait or photograph □ *a relaxed pose.* -2. a way of behaving that is not natural and is often designed to attract attention or interest (disapproving use) □ *He always puts on a pose to impress visitors.* ◇ *vt* -1. [problem, threat, danger] to cause <sthg> □ *Her unexpected arrival posed something of a dilemma.* -2. **to pose a question** to ask a question □ *The article poses several intriguing questions.* ◇ *vi* -1. to stay in a particular position in order that somebody can paint, draw, or photograph one □ *We all posed for the photograph.* -2. to put on a pose in order to attract attention or interest (disapproving use). -3. **to pose as sb/sthg** to pretend to be sb/sthg □ *Casey posed as a plainclothes policeman.*

poser ['pəʊzəʳ] *n* -1. somebody who puts on a pose □ *John's such a poser.* -2. a question that is difficult to answer (informal use).

poseur [pəʊˈzɜːʳ] *n* a person who acts in a way that is not natural or sincere because they want to impress other people or attract attention (disapproving use).

posh [pɒʃ] *adj* (informal use) -1. [hotel, suit] that is very expensive and elegant □ *They live in a posh apartment overlooking Central Park.* -2. GB [person] who belongs to the upper class in society, or behaves like somebody who belongs to this class □ *a posh accent.*

posit ['pɒzət] *vt* [fact, theory, amount] to use <sthg> as the basis of an argument or calculation (formal use) □ *The books all posit the existence of other life forms elsewhere.*

position [pəˈzɪʃn] ◇ *n* -1. [of a person, object] the place where somebody or something is

□ *The lever should be in an upright position.* □ *We radioed our position back to headquarters.* ■ **in position** in the right place □ *Make sure that the blades are in position before starting the motor.* -2. [in a seat, room] the way somebody or something is sitting, standing, or placed □ *I couldn't find a comfortable position.* -3. [in society] the status or rank somebody has in society □ *the position of unmarried mothers in society.* -4. [in a company, organization] a job, often a professional or office job □ *He left to take up a new position with another company.* -5. [in a race, competition] one's place in relation to others in a race, competition etc □ *They're currently in first/second position.* -6. [of a company, leader, public figure] the situation that a person, organization etc is in and the way it affects their actions and decisions □ *This puts us in an awkward/a strong position.* □ *I'm in a difficult financial position at the moment.* □ *I'm in a/ no position to help.* -7. [on a matter, issue] one's opinion of, or attitude toward, something □ *I wish to make my position on Nicaragua/this matter clear.* -8. SPORT [on a field, court] the place where a particular player in a team stays when they are playing a game. ◇ *vt* [object, troops, person] to put <sb/sthg> somewhere deliberately and carefully □ *He positioned himself on the chair opposite.*

positive ['pɒzətɪv] *adj* -1. **to be positive** to be completely sure that something is true □ *Are you positive it was him?* -2. [person, attitude] that is hopeful and confident □ *You must try and be more positive about the situation!* -3. [response, reaction, criticism] that shows that somebody likes something and thinks it helpful □ *The book has had very positive reviews.* -4. [proof, evidence, fact] that shows clearly that something is true □ *There is no positive proof as yet that he did it.* -5. [result, test] that shows that something is there, or that something has happened □ *The pregnancy test was positive.* □ *The samples tested positive for typhoid.* -6. **a positive number** MATH a number greater than zero. -7. a word used to emphasize that something is true □ *It's a positive pleasure to work with you!*

positive discrimination *n* the practice of trying to help a particular group of people in society more than everybody else because they have been treated unfairly □ *We have a policy of positive discrimination in favor of disabled people.*

positively ['pɒzətɪvlɪ] *adv* -1. [behave, react, prove] *see* **positive** □ *She spoke positively about her plans for the future.* -2. a word used to emphasize how true something is or how strongly one feels something □ *Unsympathetic? He was positively rude!* □ *She was positively glowing with health.*

positive vetting *n* GB the process of checking a person in great detail before trusting them with official secrets.

posse ['pɒsɪ] *n* in America in the past, a group of men who were ordered by a sheriff to help him chase and catch criminals.

possess [pəˈzes] *vt* -1. to own <sthg> (formal

use) □ *He gave away all that he possessed.* **-2.** to have <a particular quality, feature, or ability> (formal use) □ *Turner possesses great intelligence/skill/courage.* **-3.** [idea, anger, desire] to take control of <sb> (literary use) □ *He was possessed by* OR *with the notion that he could become famous.* ■ **what (on earth) possessed you to...?** a phrase used to show that one is very surprised by something silly that somebody has done □ *What on earth possessed you to invite him?*

possessed [pə'zest] *adj* **to be possessed** to be controlled by an evil spirit.

possession [pə'zeʃn] *n* the fact of having or owning something □ *I am in possession of the original.* □ *Possession of drugs is illegal.* □ *I have in my possession positive proof of his guilt.*

◆ **possessions** *npl* the things that belong to one □ *I packed all my possessions into a suitcase and left.*

possessive [pə'zesɪv] ◇ *adj* **-1.** [person] who wants all of somebody's love and attention for themselves only; who does not want to share their possessions or have them used by other people □ *She's very possessive about her children/car.* **-2.** GRAMMAR **a possessive adjective/pronoun** an adjective/a pronoun that indicates possession, e.g. "mine", "yours", "Fred's". ◇ *n* GRAMMAR a possessive adjective, pronoun, or form of a word.

possessor [pə'zesər] *n* a person who possesses something (formal use) □ *I am now the proud possessor of a fridge freezer.*

possibility [ˌpɒsə'bɪlətɪ] (*pl* **possibilities**) *n* **-1.** the chance or likelihood that something will happen □ *There is now little possibility of success.* □ *Is there any possibility that we might be wrong?* **-2.** something that may happen, or may be true □ *He suggested the possibility of going by car.*

possible ['pɒsəbl] ◇ *adj* **-1.** that can exist, happen, or be done □ *I'd like to leave as soon as possible.* □ *He always eats as much as possible!* □ *Is it possible for you to come earlier?* **-2.** [theory, solution] that may be imagined □ *It's possible that we'll be unable to come tomorrow.* □ *We'll do everything possible to finish it on time.* **-3.** [risks, consequences, problems] that may happen or exist □ *What are the possible dangers?* ◇ *n* somebody or something that has the qualities needed for a particular job or purpose, and that might be chosen for it □ *There are two or three possibles for the job.*

possibly ['pɒsəblɪ] *adv* **-1.** a word used to say that something may happen or may be true □ *Hamilton is possibly the greatest player this century.* **-2.** a word used in questions to show that one is surprised, shocked, or puzzled □ *How can he possibly say that?* **-3.** a word used in requests, to make them more polite □ *Could you possibly lend me a hand?* **-4.** a word used in front of "can" or "could" to show that something has been done as well or as soon as possible □ *I'll do all I possibly can.* **-5.** a word used with a negative, to emphasize that something is not possible □ *You can't possibly mean that!*

possum ['pɒsəm] (*pl* **possum** OR **possums**) *n* a small animal with thick fur and a long tail that lives in trees, carries its young in a pouch on the front of its body, and is found in Australia, New Zealand, and the USA.

post [pəʊst] ◇ *n* **-1. the post** the system in a country for sending and receiving letters and packages □ *Further details will be sent by post.* □ *Could you put it in the post for me?* □ *I got a check through the post.* **-2.** letters, packages etc that somebody has mailed and that are delivered to one's address □ *Did I get any post today?* **-3.** a delivery of post □ *Has (the) second post arrived yet?* **-4.** GB a regular collection of post from a mailbox or post office □ *I just missed the 5:30 post.* **-5.** [in the ground] an upright pole fixed into the ground. **-6.** [in a company, at a college] a particular job or position in an organization □ *I've applied for the post of senior accountant.* **-7.** MILITARY the particular place where a soldier is told or expected to be □ *He fell asleep at his post.* **-8.** *phrase* **to pip sb at the post** GB to beat sb by a very small amount in a competition, race etc □ *They nearly offered me the job, but I was pipped at the post by a younger candidate.*
◇ *vt* **-1.** to send <a letter, package> etc in the post □ *They're posting me details of the job.* **-2.** to send <an employee> to another town or country to work □ *His wife has been posted to China.* **-3.** *phrase* **to keep sb posted** to keep sb informed about a particular situation □ *I don't know his plans, but I'll keep you posted.*

Post [pəʊst], **Emily** (1873–1960) a US writer and journalist who gave advice on correct behavior in polite society.

post- *prefix* added to words and dates to show that something took place after a particular time or event □ *post-war politics.*

postage ['pəʊstɪdʒ] *n* the amount of money that it costs to send something by post □ *The price includes postage and handling* US OR *postage and packing* GB.

postage paid *adj* [envelope] that can be mailed without a stamp, because a company has printed the value of a stamp on it and will pay for it.

postage stamp *n* a small piece of paper with glue on the back that must be bought and stuck onto a letter, package etc before it is mailed (formal use).

postal ['pəʊstl] *adj* **postal system/charges etc** the system/charges etc connected with the public service of collecting and sending letters and packages.

postal order *n* in Britain, a note sold in post offices that represents a particular amount of money and is used for sending money by mail.

postbag ['pəʊstbæg] *n* GB **-1.** the bag in which a mailman carries letters and packages. **-2.** all the letters that are received by a radio or TV station, especially at a particular time □ *We've had a huge postbag on the subject.*

postbox ['pəʊstbɒks] *n* GB a large container with a narrow opening, usually outdoors in a street, into which letters and small packages can be put in order to be sent by mail.

postcard ['poustkɑːᵊd] *n* a piece of card, usually with a picture on one side, on which a message can be written, and that can be mailed without an envelope □ *I'll send you a postcard.*

postcode ['poustkoud] *n* GB a series of numbers and letters written at the end of an address to help the post office sort mail more quickly.

postdate [ˌpoust'deɪt] *vt* [check, letter] to write a date on <sthg> that is later than the date when one writes it.

poster ['poustəᵊ] *n* a large picture, notice, or advertisement that is stuck on a wall as a decoration or to give information.

poste restante [US ˌpoustre'stɑːnt, GB ˌpoust-'restɒnt] *n* a system run by post offices in some countries that allows all mail sent to a particular person to be kept at a post office until it is collected.

posterior [pɒ'stɪərɪəᵊ] ◇ *adj* that is at the back of something or behind another part of something. ◇ *n* one's bottom (humorous use).

posterity [pɒ'sterətɪ] *n* all the future and the people that will be part of it, including the time after one has died □ *Her words were recorded for posterity.*

poster paint *n* paint that contains no oil and is often very bright.

post-free *adj* & *adv* GB = postpaid.

postgraduate [ˌpoust'grædʒuət] ◇ *adj* [student, degree, research] that is connected with studies that one does at a university after one has finished a first degree □ *postgraduate studies.* ◇ *n* a postgraduate student.

posthaste [ˌpoust'heɪst] *adv* as quickly as possible (old-fashioned use).

posthumous ['pɒstʃuməs] *adj* [award, medal, fame] that somebody has or gets after their death.

posthumously ['pɒstʃuməslɪ] *adv* [award, publish] *see* **posthumous**.

post-industrial *adj* [age, society] that is connected with changes in the way people live and work caused by developments in industry and technology.

posting ['poustɪŋ] *n* a job that involves moving to work in a different place □ *I'm hoping for a posting overseas.*

Post-It™ *n* a small colored piece of paper for writing notes that can be stuck to a surface and removed easily.

postman ['poustmən] (*pl* **postmen** [-mən]) *n* a person whose job is to collect and deliver mail.

postmark ['poustmɑːᵊk] ◇ *n* a mark printed over the stamp on letters and packages that shows when and where they were mailed. ◇ *vt* to put a postmark on <a letter, package> etc.

postmaster [US 'poustmæstər, GB -mɑːstə] *n* a man who is in charge of a post office.

Postmaster General (*pl* **Postmasters General**)

n the person in charge of the postal service in a particular country.

postmistress ['poustmɪstrəs] *n* a woman who is in charge of a post office.

postmortem [ˌpoust'mɔːᵊtəm] ◇ *adj* [examination, test] that is carried out on a dead body to find out what caused the person's death. ◇ *n* -1. a postmortem examination of a dead body. -2. an examination of something that was unsuccessful to find out why it failed □ *After the game there was a long postmortem in the locker room.*

postnatal [ˌpoust'neɪtl] *adj* [care, depression] that is connected with the period of time after a mother has given birth to a baby.

post office *n* -1. a building or store where people can send letters and packages, buy stamps, and use various other services. -2. **the Post Office** the organization in charge of the postal services of a country □ *the United States Post Office.*

post office box *n* a box in a post office in which letters and packages that have been sent to a particular person or organization are kept until they are collected.

postoperative [ˌpoust'ɒpərətɪv] *adj* [care, examination] that happens after a medical operation.

postpaid [ˌpoust'peɪd] ◇ *adj* [letter, envelope] that is sent without any charge for postage. ◇ *adv*: *You can send the letter post-paid.*

postpone [pous'poun] *vt* [decision, game] to arrange for <sthg> to happen at a later time □ *The meeting has been postponed until Friday.*

postponement [pous'pounmənt] *n*: *see* **postpone**.

postscript ['poustskrɪpt] *n* -1. a short message written at the end of a letter, below one's signature. -2. a short piece of information added to the end of a story, account, statement etc.

post-traumatic stress disorder *n* a mental condition that affects people after a traumatic experience such as being in a war.

postulate [US 'pɒstʃəleɪt, GB -tjə-] *vt* [theory, idea, cause] to suggest that <sthg> is true or correct, even if it has not been proven, so that one can use it to help explain something else.

posture ['pɒstʃəᵊ] ◇ *n* -1. the particular position of one's body when one is sitting, standing, or walking □ *She's got very good/bad posture.* -2. the attitude that somebody has in relation to a particular subject or situation □ *Their posture on the peace process is quite clear.* ◇ *vi* (disapproving use) -1. to pretend to have a particular opinion, usually to impress people □ *Voters are growing tired of politicians posturing on every issue that hits the headlines.* -2. to act in an exaggerated way in order to get attention □ *the familiar sight of pop stars posturing on our TV screens.*

posturing ['pɒstʃərɪŋ] *n* the act of pretending to have a particular opinion, usually to impress people (disapproving use) □ *It's easy to see through all their posturing.*

postviral syndrome [ˌpəʊstvaɪrəl-] *n* a medical condition in which one feels very tired for a long time after having a viral illness.

postwar [ˌpəʊst'wɔːʳ] *adj* [era, architecture] that is connected with the period immediately after a war, especially World War II.

posy ['pəʊzɪ] (*pl* **posies**) *n* a small bunch of flowers.

pot [pɒt] (*pt* & *pp* **potted**, *cont* **potting**) ◇ *n* **-1.** [for cooking] a round container, usually made of metal or pottery, that is used for cooking things; the amount of liquid that this holds □ *a cooking pot* □ *a pot of soup* **-2.** [for tea, coffee] a container used for serving tea or coffee; the amount of tea or coffee that this contains. **-3.** [for paint, honey] a deep round container used for keeping paint, jam etc in. **-4.** [for plants] a round container used for growing plants in □ *a plant pot.* **-5.** cannabis (informal and old-fashioned use). ◇ *vt* to put <a plant> in a flowerpot filled with earth so that it will grow there.

potash ['pɒtæʃ] *n* a white powdery form of potassium, made from burnt wood, that is used especially on soil to help crops grow better.

potassium [pə'tæsɪəm] *n* a soft silver-white chemical element. SYMBOL: K.

potato [pə'teɪtəʊ] (*pl* **potatoes**) *n* a round vegetable with a red or brown skin and hard white flesh that grows underground □ *roast potatoes* □ *a potato omelet.*

potato chips US, **potato crisps** GB *npl* very thin fried slices of potato sold in packets and eaten cold as a snack.

potato peeler *n* a special kind of knife for removing the skin from vegetables such as potatoes or carrots.

potbellied [US 'pɒtbelɪd, GB ˌpɒt'belɪd] *adj* [person] who has a large round stomach, because they eat or drink too much or because they do not have enough food to eat.

potboiler ['pɒtbɔɪləʳ] *n* a book, piece of music etc that is produced only to earn money quickly.

potency ['pəʊtənsɪ] *n*: *see* **potent** □ *A drug of this potency should not be given to children.*

potent ['pəʊtənt] *adj* **-1.** [argument, force] that is effective in a particular situation. **-2.** [drink, drug] that has a powerful effect on one's mind or body.

potentate ['pəʊtnteɪt] *n* a ruler who has complete power over the people of a country.

potential [pə'tenʃl] ◇ *adj* **a potential customer/danger etc** a customer/danger etc that might exist in the future □ *There's a potential risk involved.* □ *He's a potential candidate for the job.* ◇ *n* [of a person, company, plan] the qualities of somebody or something that might develop in the future □ *He has the potential to become a threat.* ■ **to have potential** to have a quality that might bring success in the future □ *This idea has great potential.* □ *She has a lot of potential.*

potentially [pə'tenʃlɪ] *adv* **-1. potentially,...** a word used to say that something might happen in the future □ *Potentially, we could make millions.* **-2. potentially useful/dangerous etc** that might be useful/dangerous etc in the future □ *It's a potentially interesting idea.*

pothole ['pɒthəʊl] *n* **-1.** a large hole in the surface of a road, caused by damage. **-2.** a deep hole in the ground, often leading to underground passages and caves.

potholer ['pɒthəʊləʳ] *n* GB a person who goes potholing.

potholing ['pɒthəʊlɪŋ] *n* **to go potholing** GB to explore potholes and underground caves as a sport.

potion ['pəʊʃn] *n* a drink containing medicine, poison, or a substance that is believed to have magical powers □ *a magic/love potion.*

potluck [ˌpɒt'lʌk] *n* **to take potluck** to choose something from what is available without knowing what exactly it will be.

Potomac [pə'təʊmæk]: **the Potomac** a river in the eastern USA that separates West Virginia and Maryland.

pot plant *n* a plant grown indoors in a pot.

potpourri [ˌpəʊpʊ'riː] *n* a mixture of dried leaves and pieces of flowers with spices added, kept in a bowl to make a room smell pleasant.

pot roast *n* a piece of meat cooked slowly in a covered pot with a small amount of liquid.

potshot ['pɒtʃɒt] *n* **to take a potshot** to shoot carelessly at something without aiming properly.

potted ['pɒtəd] *adj* **-1. a potted plant** a plant that is grown in a pot. **-2.** GB [meat, fish] that is cooked and then preserved in a container. **-3. a potted history/biography etc** GB a short history/biography etc that only gives the main facts □ *He gave us a potted history of the music industry.*

potter ['pɒtəʳ] *n* a person who makes pots, dishes etc out of clay.

◆ **potter about**, **potter around** *vi* GB to spend time doing small pleasant jobs or activities without hurrying □ *He likes nothing better than pottering about at home.*

Potter ['pɒtəʳ], **Beatrix** (1866–1943) a British writer and artist. She wrote and illustrated many children's stories about animals.

Potteries ['pɒtərɪz]: **the Potteries** a region in Staffordshire in the west of central England where the pottery industry is based.

potter's wheel *n* a flat wheel that spins around and is used by potters to make pottery out of wet clay.

pottery ['pɒtərɪ] (*pl* **potteries**) *n* **-1.** a collective term for objects such as dishes and pots made out of baked clay □ *She's got some lovely pottery.* **-2.** the skills of a potter □ *He teaches pottery.* **-3.** the place where pottery is produced □ *We visited the local pottery.*

potting compost ['pɒtɪŋ-] *n* a type of compost used especially indoors or in window boxes to help young plants to grow.

potty ['pɒtɪ] (*pl* **potties**) *n* a bowl used by a very young child as a toilet.

potty-trained *adj* **to be potty-trained** [child] to be able to use a potty or toilet and no longer need to wear diapers.

pouch [pautʃ] *n* -1. a small bag for keeping things such as tobacco. -2. a pocket of skin in which some animals, e.g. kangaroos, carry their young.

pouffe [pu:f] *n* GB a soft low seat without a back that is often used for resting one's feet on.

poultice ['pəʊltəs] *n* a piece of cloth covered with a warm mixture and placed against one's skin to reduce pain or swelling.

poultry ['pəʊltrɪ] ◇ *n* the meat of birds such as chickens and geese that are kept on a farm. ◇ *npl* birds such as chickens and geese that are kept on a farm to supply eggs and meat.

pounce [pauns] *vi* -1. to suddenly try to catch or attack a person or animal, usually after waiting for the right moment □ *The cat pounced on* OR *upon the mouse.* □ *The police pounced in the early hours of the morning.* □ *The attackers pounced on* OR *upon them in a dark alleyway.* -2. **to pounce on** OR **upon sthg** [on an idea, comment] to notice sthg and immediately draw attention to it □ *There was one small error, which she immediately pounced on.*

pound [paund] ◇ *n* -1. the unit of money in Britain, equal to 100 pence □ *It costs five pounds.* -2. **the pound** the value of British currency in relation to other currencies □ *There are eight francs to the pound.* -3. [of weight] a unit (16 ounces) for measuring weight. -4. [for dogs, cars] a place where lost dogs, or cars that have been parked illegally, are kept by the police. ◇ *vt* -1. [table, door, wall] to hit <sthg> loudly with one's fist several times. -2. [grain, corn] to crush <sthg> into a powder or paste by hitting or pressing it with a heavy object. ◇ *vi* -1. [person] to hit something loudly with one's fist several times □ *He pounded on the door.* -2. [heart] to beat very fast because one is excited, scared etc □ *My heart was pounding as I approached the door.*

Pound [paund], **Ezra** (1885–1972) a US poet and critic whose major work is the *Cantos*.

pounding ['paundɪŋ] *n* -1. [of somebody's fists, heart] the sound of something that pounds. -2. **to get** OR **take a pounding** [city, town] to be very badly damaged by bombing; [team, country] to be badly defeated.

pound sterling *n* the unit of money in Britain.

pour [pɔ:r] ◇ *vt* -1. [liquid, grain, sugar] to make <sthg> flow out of a container by lifting the lower part of the container □ *She poured the sugar into a bowl.* ■ **to pour sb a drink, to pour a drink for sb** to fill a cup or glass with a liquid so that sb can drink it □ *Let me pour you a whiskey.* -2. **to pour money into sthg** [into a project, business] to spend a lot of money on the development of sthg □ *They keep pouring money into that company, but it will never make a profit.* ◇ *vi* -1. [liquid, sweat, smoke] to flow quickly and in large amounts out of or into something □ *The water was pouring down the roof.* -2. [people, traffic] to move somewhere together quickly and in large numbers □ *Tourists poured into the city for the festival.* ◇ *v impers* to rain heavily □ *It's pouring (with rain)!*

◆ **pour in** *vi* [people, news, letters] to arrive quickly and in large quantities □ *I hear the offers have been pouring in since the show.*

◆ **pour out** *vt sep* -1. **to pour sthg out** [liquid] to make sthg flow out of a container by lifting the container □ *I poured out drinks for both of us.* □ *He poured out the contents into the sink.* -2. **to pour out one's thoughts/feelings etc** to tell somebody one's thoughts/feelings etc in an emotional way, usually because one is worried, upset etc □ *She poured her heart out to me.*

pouring ['pɔ:rɪŋ] *adj* **the pouring rain** rain that is falling very fast and hard.

pout [paut] ◇ *vi* to push one's lips forward, e.g. when one is annoyed or as a way of trying to look attractive in a photograph □ *I saw her pouting on the cover of "Vanity Fair".* ◇ *n* the act of pouting; the position one's lips are in when one pouts □ *"I suppose so,"* she said with a pout.

poverty ['pɒvətɪ] *n* -1. the state of being poor □ *They live in utter poverty.* -2. **a poverty of sthg** [of imagination, resources] a lack of sthg □ *There's a terrible poverty of thought in the government.*

poverty line *n* **to be on the poverty line** to have just enough money for one's food, bills etc.

poverty-stricken *adj* [person, area, organization] that is very poor.

poverty trap *n* GB a situation in which a poor person continues to depend on financial help from their government because any job they can get will cause them to lose this help, without providing more money than they already receive from the state.

pow [pau] *excl* a word used to represent the sound that is made when something explodes or when two objects hit one another.

POW *n abbr of* **prisoner of war**.

powder ['paudər] ◇ *n* a solid substance in the form of tiny particles. ◇ *vt* [face, body] to put cosmetic powder on <one's skin>.

powder compact *n* a small flat case containing a woman's face powder, a powder puff, and a mirror.

powdered ['paudərd] *adj* -1. [milk, sugar, eggs] that is sold or used in the form of a powder. -2. [face, skin] that has powder on it.

powder puff *n* a round piece of soft thick material used for putting cosmetic powder on one's face or body.

powder room *n* a women's rest room (polite use).

powdery ['paudərɪ] *adj* -1. [substance, snow]

that is like powder. **-2.** [surface] that is covered in powder.

power ['paʊəʳ] ◇ *n* **-1.** [of a person, organization, government] control and influence that somebody or something has over people and situations □ *He was more interested in power than money.* □ *You can never underestimate the power of the media.* □ *The regime is desperately trying to hold onto its power.* ■ **to be in power** [politician, party] to be in charge of the government of a country □ *They've been in power for ten years now.* ■ **to come to** OR **into power** [politician, party] to start to be in charge of the government of a country □ *When we came to power, unemployment was at its highest in over 50 years.* ■ **to have power over sb** to have control or authority over sb. ■ **to take power** to take control of the government of a country without having been elected, especially by using violence. **-2.** a particular skill or ability to do something □ *mental powers* □ *He claims to have the power to heal the sick.* ■ **the power of speech/hearing** the ability to talk/hear **-3.** [of the courts, police, army] a legal right that a person or organization has □ *As a citizen you have the power to vote.* ■ **it is in** OR **within my power to do sthg** I have the authority to do sthg □ *I did everything within my power to help.* **-4.** [of a person, animal, explosion] the physical strength of somebody or something. **-5.** TECHNOLOGY energy that is produced in a particular way and is used to make machines work □ *wind/solar/steam power.* **-6.** ELECTRICITY electricity that is used for lighting, heating, operating machines etc □ *Don't forget to switch the power off.* **-7.** [in international politics] a strong and influential organization, country etc □ *world powers such as the USA and Japan.* ■ **the powers that be** the people in important and official jobs whose decisions affect one's life □ *The powers that be have decided that I should leave.*
◇ *vt* [machine, device] to give <sthg> the power it needs to work □ *powered by solar energy* □ *a steam-powered locomotive.*

power base *n* a group of people or an area that provides somebody, especially a politician, with the support that makes them powerful or important.

powerboat ['paʊəʳbəʊt] *n* a very fast motorboat.

power broker *n* a person who helps to decide questions of political power and influence, especially in disagreements between nations.

power cut *n* a period of time during which the supply of electricity to a building, area etc is stopped.

power failure *n* a period of time during which the supply of electricity to a building, area etc is stopped because of a technical problem.

powerful ['paʊəʳfl] *adj* **-1.** [member, organization, government] that has a lot of control and influence over people, events etc □ *She's become extremely powerful within the organization.* **-2.** [person, animal, explosion] that is physically

strong □ *Her powerful shoulders strained to lift the weight.* **-3.** [drug] that has a strong effect on somebody's body or mind; [smell, aroma] that is very strong and usually unpleasant; [sound, voice] that is loud. **-4.** [movie, speech, book] that has a strong effect on people's feelings □ *I find his poems very powerful.*

powerhouse ['paʊəʳhaʊs, *pl* -haʊzɪz] *n* a person, organization etc that is very strong or that produces a lot of good ideas or things □ *He's an intellectual powerhouse.*

powerless ['paʊəʳləs] *adj* **to be powerless** [person, organization] not to have the necessary power or influence to do something □ *We are powerless to stop them.*

power line *n* a cable that carries electricity.

power of attorney *n* the official authority, in the form of a document, that allows somebody to represent another person in business or legal matters.

power outage *n* US = **power failure**.

power plant *n* US = **power station**.

power point *n* GB a device attached to a wall that has a set of holes which electricity passes through when a plug is pushed into them.

power-sharing [-ʃeərɪŋ] *n* **-1.** POLITICS the system of sharing power between political parties when no party has enough votes to rule alone. **-2.** BUSINESS the system of sharing power between workers and management.

power station *n* a building where electricity is produced for a lot of people to use.

power steering *n* a system that makes it easier for one to steer a car, truck etc by using power from the engine.

power worker *n* a person who works at a power station.

pp -1. *abbr of* **pages. -2.** (*abbr of* **per procurationem**) a phrase written before a person's name when somebody else is signing a letter or document as their representative.

p & p (*abbr of* **postage and packing**) *n* GB a charge made for packing and mailing something that somebody has bought.

PPE (*abbr of* **philosophy, politics, and economics**) *n* GB a combination of subjects taken together as a degree course at some universities.

P-plates *npl* in Australia, plates with the letter P on them that a driver has to show at the front and back of their car for a year after they have passed their driving test.

ppm (*abbr of* **parts per million**) CHEMISTRY a term used when measuring small amounts of a substance contained in another substance.

PPS (*abbr of* **parliamentary private secretary**) ◇ *n* a British member of parliament who also works as a government minister's assistant. ◇ a phrase written after a PS note in a letter or document, to show that a second note is being added.

PQ *abbr of* **Province of Quebec.**

Pr *abbr of* **Prince.**

PR ◇ *n* -1. *abbr of* **proportional representation**. -2. *abbr of* **public relations**. ◇ *abbr of* **Puerto Rico**.

practicable ['præktɪkəbl] *adj* [task, plan, idea] that can be done or carried out successfully.

practical ['præktɪkl] ◇ *adj* -1. [training, question] that is connected with a real situation and not just ideas □ *What you need is to get some practical experience working on a farm.* -2. [person] who deals with problems in a sensible way; [idea, suggestion, solution] that is sensible and likely to succeed □ *I'm sure she'll think of something — she's very practical.* □ *Can anybody think of a practical way out of this situation?* -3. [person] who is good at doing things that involve using their hands □ *I'm not very practical when it comes to repairs.* -4. [device, tool, piece of clothing] that has been designed to be useful and easy to use, not to be attractive □ *If you're going to do a lot of walking, get a good, practical pair of boots.*
◇ *n* a lesson or exam in which one has to make something or do an experiment rather than just learn or write about something □ *a physics/chemistry practical.*

practicality [,præktɪ'kælətɪ] *n* [of a person, idea] *see* **practical**.
◆ **practicalities** *npl* details of an idea or plan that are connected with the way something is actually done □ *We're ready to start talking about the practicalities of the move.*

practical joke *n* a trick played on somebody to make them look silly and to make other people laugh.

practically ['præktɪklɪ] *adv* -1. [talk, suggest, think] in a sensible way. -2. almost □ *We'd practically finished by the time they arrived.* □ *It involved practically all of us.*

practice ['præktəs] ◇ *n* -1. activity that one does regularly to improve one's ability to do something; a period of time that one spends doing such an activity □ *I haven't had much practice recently.* □ *She does two hours' practice a week.* □ *I have football practice this afternoon.* □ *Choir practice starts at seven.* ■ **to be out of practice** not to be able to do something as well as one used to because one has not done it recently □ *I don't know if I'll be able to remember any tunes, I'm so out of practice.* -2. **to put sthg into practice** [theory, plan] to use sthg in a real situation in order to see if it is effective or useful □ *We'll only be able to tell when we put the idea into practice.* ■ **in practice** a phrase used to describe what happens when something is actually done rather than what is supposed to happen in theory □ *This is all right in theory, but in practice I think we may have some problems.* -3. [of a particular society, religion] a way of behaving or doing something that is usual among a particular group of people □ *business/religious practices.* -4. [of a lawyer, doctor] the business of a lawyer, doctor, dentist etc □ *They opened their practice in 1987.*
◇ *vt* US -1. [skill, sport, violin] to use or do <sthg> in order to get better at it □ *I never get the chance to practice my Spanish.*

-2. [religion, democracy] to act according to the ideas or rules of <sthg> □ *People are being encouraged to practice safe sex.* -3. [medicine, law] to work in <a particular profession>. ■ **to practice what one preaches** to do the same things oneself that one tells other people that they should do □ *Why don't you try practicing what you preach, rather than just criticizing all the time?*
◇ *vi* US -1. to practice a skill, sport etc □ *I really can't play this very well — I'll have to practice.* -2. [doctor, lawyer] to work in a profession □ *How long have you been practicing now?*

practiced US, **practised** GB ['præktəst] *adj* [teacher, liar] who is good at something because they have done it often in the past □ *He is practiced at dealing with difficult situations.*

practicing US, **practising** GB ['præktəsɪŋ] *adj* -1. [doctor, lawyer] who is currently working in their particular profession. -2. **a practicing Christian/Jew etc** a Christian/Jew etc who worships regularly. ■ **a practicing homosexual** a homosexual man who has sex with other men (formal use).

practise ['præktəs] *vt* & *vi* GB = **practice**.

practised *adj* GB = **practiced**.

practising *adj* GB = **practicing**.

practitioner [præk'tɪʃnəʳ] *n* a person who works as a doctor or lawyer □ *a medical/legal practitioner.*

pragmatic [præg'mætɪk] *adj* [person] who deals with problems and makes decisions based on facts and real situations rather than on theories and principles □ *We prefer to take a pragmatic approach to solving problems.*

pragmatism ['prægmətɪzm] *n* the quality of being pragmatic.

pragmatist ['prægmətəst] *n* a person who is pragmatic.

Prague [prɑːg] the capital of the Czech Republic, and its largest city. POPULATION: 1,212,010.

prairie ['preərɪ] *n* a large area of flat grassy land with no trees, especially in North America.

praise [preɪz] ◇ *n* -1. something that is said or written to show approval and admiration □ *I have nothing but praise for your decision.* -2. RELIGION the act of worshiping and thanking God. -3. **to sing sb's praises** to praise sb a lot and with great enthusiasm. ◇ *vt* -1. to speak or write in a way that shows one thinks <sb/sthg> is very good □ *She praised the way in which they had handled the situation.* -2. RELIGION to express thanks to <God>.

praiseworthy ['preɪzwɜːˈðɪ] *adj* [action, attempt, effort] that is good and deserves praise.

praline [US 'preɪliːn, GB 'prɑː-] *n* a candy that is made by cooking nuts in burnt sugar.

pram [præm] *n* GB a small vehicle with four wheels and a folding cover in which babies are pushed.

prance [US præns, GB prɑːns] *vi* -1. [person, child] to walk or move around while moving one's arms and legs a lot, in order to get people's attention or because one is happy. -2. [horse]

to move around while lifting its legs high in the air.

prank [præŋk] *n* a trick done to make somebody look silly □ *Somebody played a prank on him.*

prawn [prɔːn] *n* a small pink shellfish with many legs and a tail, eaten as food.

prawn cocktail *n* GB a dish, often eaten at the beginning of a meal, that consists of prawns, lettuce, and a sauce.

prawn cracker *n* GB a kind of food that tastes of prawns and looks like a potato chip.

pray [preɪ] *vi* -1. RELIGION to speak to God either in one's mind or aloud in order to give thanks or ask for help □ *I will pray to God/Allah for your soul.* -2. **to pray for sthg** to hope for sthg very strongly □ *We've been praying for rain.*

prayer [preəʳ] *n* -1. the act of praying □ *Everybody knelt in prayer.* -2. the words one speaks when one prays, especially when they have been written in a fixed form □ *As children we always said our prayers before going to bed.* -3. a strong hope or wish.

◆ **prayers** *npl* a religious meeting in which a group of people says prayers together □ *family prayers.*

prayer book *n* a book containing prayers for people to say in church and at home.

prayer meeting *n* a public religious meeting in some Protestant churches where people say their own prayers to God.

PRC *abbr of* **People's Republic of China.**

pre- [priː] *prefix* used to refer to the period before a particular event, period, or date □ *pre-1945* □ *pre-school years.*

preach [priːtʃ] ◇ *vt* -1. RELIGION [sermon, religion] to spread <a religious message, belief> etc by speaking to a group of people, usually as part of a church service □ *Missionaries traveled the country preaching Christianity.* -2. [peace, violence] to try to persuade other people to accept <sthg that one believes in> □ *He preaches love and brotherhood.* ◇ *vi* -1. RELIGION [priest, minister] *He will be preaching to the congregation.* -2. [father, politician] to give somebody advice in a boring, often critical, way (disapproving use) □ *I'm fed up with him preaching at me all the time.*

preacher [priːtʃəʳ] *n* a person who preaches, especially in a Protestant church.

preamble [priːæmbl] *n* an introduction to a speech or piece of writing, usually explaining its purpose □ *Well, without any preamble, let us begin.*

Preamble *n* **the Preamble (to the Constitution)** the introduction to the US Constitution.

prearranged [ˌpriːəˈreɪndʒd] *adj* [meeting, appointment, signal] that is arranged or agreed before it happens.

precarious [prɪˈkeəriəs] *adj* -1. [hold, grip] that is not firm and so is unsafe; [building, ladder] that is unstable and likely to fall □ *He was stuck in a precarious position at the top of the slope.* □ *That chair looks a bit precarious.* -2. [situation, position] that is difficult or hard to

control and makes one feel that one is likely to fail at any time □ *My future at Goldblatt is looking rather precarious.*

precariously [prɪˈkeəriəslɪ] *adv* [sit, perch, live] *see* **precarious.**

precast [US priːˈkæst, GB -ˈkɑːst] *adj* **precast concrete** concrete blocks that are used to make buildings.

precaution [prɪˈkɔːʃn] *n* something one does to try to stop something unpleasant or unwanted from happening □ *He fitted extra locks as a precaution against theft.* □ *We must take precautions against it happening again.*

precautionary [US prɪˈkɔːʃəneri, GB -nəri] *adj* [action, measure] that is used as a precaution.

precede [prɪˈsiːd] *vt* -1. [event, period] to happen or exist before <sthg> □ *Things became increasingly hectic in the weeks preceding her departure.* □ *The launch of the service was preceded by months of speculation that it would never happen.* -2. [person] to go somewhere before or in front of <sb> □ *Delaney entered the building preceded by his bodyguards.* -3. [sentence, paragraph, chapter] to come before <sthg> in a piece of writing.

precedence [ˈpresɪdəns] *n* **to have** OR **take precedence over sb/sthg** [factor, job] to be considered more important than sb/sthg else and so be dealt with first □ *I'm afraid the McCann deal must take precedence over internal matters.*

precedent [ˈpresɪdənt] *n* an action, decision, or idea from the past that is used to justify a similar action or decision in the present □ *There is no precedent for an attack of this scale.* □ *The decision could set a new legal precedent.*

preceding [prɪˈsiːdɪŋ] *adj* -1. [year, month] that comes just before the time or event one is speaking about. -2. [chapter, paragraph] that comes just before a particular part in a piece of writing.

precept [ˈpriːsept] *n* a general rule that helps one decide what to do or how to behave □ *one of the basic precepts of Buddhist philosophy.*

precinct [ˈpriːsɪŋkt] *n* -1. US one of several areas that a city or town is divided into for purposes of administration □ *a police/voting precinct* -2. GB a shopping area in a city or town where no vehicles are allowed □ *a shopping precinct.*

◆ **precincts** *npl* [of an institution, organization] the area around a building □ *Any unauthorized vehicle parked in the university precincts will be removed.*

precious [ˈpreʃəs] *adj* -1. [memory, possession] that is very special and important to one □ *This book is very precious to me.* -2. [jewel, object, material] that is rare and costs a lot of money. -3. a word used when one is angry at somebody to talk about something that one thinks is too important to them □ *You can keep your precious car!* -4. **precious little** very little □ *The talks offered precious little hope of peace.* □ *There's precious little else to do around here.* -5. [person, behavior] that one finds insincere and unnatural.

precious metal *n* any rare and valuable metal, e.g. gold.

precious stone *n* any rare and valuable jewel, e.g. a diamond.

precipice ['presəpəs] *n* a section of steep rock on a cliff, mountain etc.

precipitate [*adj* prə'sɪpətət, *vb* prə'sɪpɪteɪt] (formal use) ◇ *adj* [action, decision] that happens too quickly without careful thought first. ◇ *vt* [crisis, decline, resignation] to make <sthg> happen very suddenly or more quickly than expected □ *We need to look at what exactly precipitated these riots.*

precipitation [prə,sɪpə'teɪʃn] *n* **-1.** CHEMISTRY the process in which a solid substance becomes separated from a liquid. **-2.** WEATHER snow, rain, or hail that falls to the ground.

precipitous [prə'sɪpətəs] *adj* **-1.** [area, hillside, road] that is very steep. **-2.** [action, decision] that happens very quickly without careful thought first.

précis [US preɪ'siː, GB 'preɪsiː] (*pl* **précis** [-z]) *n* [of a book, report, article] a short piece of writing that gives only the main ideas, arguments etc of a larger piece of writing.

precise [prɪ'saɪs] *adj* [moment, nature, details] exact □ *On that precise date he was in Santa Fe.* □ *Do you have any more precise information?* ■ **to be precise** a phrase used to add information that is more exact to a more general statement one has already made □ *I'll be away for a while — 14 days, to be precise.*

precisely [prɪ'saɪslɪ] *adv* **-1.** [explain, instruct, describe] in a way that is accurate and includes every necessary detail □ *That is precisely what happened.* **-2.** a word used to show that one agrees completely with what somebody has just said □ *"You mean he should resign?" — "Precisely!"*

precision [prə'sɪʒn] ◇ *n* the quality of being exact and accurate □ *She followed the instructions with the utmost care and precision.* ◇ *comp* **precision bombing** the bombing of specially chosen targets that is done with great accuracy. ■ **precision instruments** instruments that are made with great care and produce very accurate results.

preclude [prɪ'kluːd] *vt* to make it impossible for <sthg> to happen (formal use) □ *Taking the job at Abbots will not preclude you from working freelance for us.*

precocious [prə'koʊʃəs] *adj* [child] who is very intelligent and acts in a way that seems more like an adult than a child □ *her precocious abilities/behavior.*

preconceived [,priːkən'siːvd] *adj* [idea, notion] that one has before one knows or understands very much about a subject.

preconception [,priːkən'sepʃn] *n* an idea or belief that one has before one knows or understands very much about a subject □ *I had no preconceptions about the place before I arrived.*

precondition [,priːkən'dɪʃn] *n* something that has to be done or agreed upon before something else can happen (formal use) □ *They've*

made disarmament a precondition for further talks.

precooked [,priː'kʊkt] *adj* [food, meal] that has already been partly or completely cooked and can be heated up quickly before being eaten.

precursor [prɪ'kɜːsər] *n* something that existed before something more important or successful and that influenced its development (formal use) □ *It was the precursor of OR to the modern jet plane.*

predate [priː'deɪt] *vt* to come or exist before <sthg> in time (formal use) □ *This wall predates the rest of the cathedral.*

predator ['predətər] *n* **-1.** a predatory bird or animal. **-2.** a predatory person.

predatory [US 'predətɔːrɪ, GB -ətrɪ] *adj* **-1.** [animal, bird] that kills and eats other birds or animals. **-2.** [person] who takes advantage of other people who are weak in order to benefit themselves.

predecease [,priːdɪ'siːs] *vt* [husband, wife] to die before <sb> (formal use).

predecessor ['priːdəsesər] *n* **-1.** a person who had a particular job or position before somebody else □ *I aim to build on the good work already done by my predecessor.* **-2.** a machine, device etc that was used for a particular purpose before it was replaced by a newer one □ *This model is more economical than its predecessor.*

predestination [priː,destɪ'neɪʃn] *n* RELIGION the belief that events cannot be controlled or changed by humans but are decided in advance by God or fate.

predestine [priː'destɪn] *vt* **to be predestined to do sthg** to be intended by God, fate etc to do sthg □ *The whole enterprise was predestined to fail.*

predetermine [,priːdɪ'tɜːrmən] *vt* [course of events, future] to decide in advance how <sthg> will happen or be.

predetermined [,priːdɪ'tɜːrmənd] *adj* [date, place, price] that is decided in advance.

predicament [prɪ'dɪkəmənt] *n* a difficult or embarrassing situation □ *I'm in a real predicament.*

predicate ['predɪkət] *n* GRAMMAR the part of a sentence that gives information about the subject of the sentence. In the sentence "I saw her" the predicate is "saw her".

predict [prə'dɪkt] *vt* [event, result] to say that <sthg> will happen in the future □ *He reckons he can predict the future.* □ *It is very difficult to predict what might happen.*

predictable [prə'dɪktəbl] *adj* **-1.** [result, event] that can be predicted □ *The election outcome was fairly predictable.* **-2.** [person] who never does anything unexpected □ *I knew you'd be here — you're so predictable.*

predictably [prə'dɪktəblɪ] *adv* a word used to show that one is not surprised about something because it is usual or what one expected □ *Predictably, he failed to show up.* □ *They were predictably disappointed.*

prediction [prə'dɪkʃn] *n* **-1.** [of an event, result] see **predict. -2.** a statement in which one says what one thinks is going to happen in the future □ *What's your prediction for the Super Bowl this year?* □ *I wouldn't like to make a prediction at this stage.*

predictor [prə'dɪktəʳ] *n* something such as a fact or figure that is used to help one predict something.

predigest [ˌpriːdaɪ'dʒest] *vt* to make <information> easier to understand by presenting it in a simple form and explaining it.

predilection [US ˌpredə'lekʃn, GB ˌpriːd-] *n* a predilection for sthg a particular liking for sthg □ *This film director has always had a predilection for gratuitous violence.*

predispose [ˌpriːdɪ'spəʊz] *vt* to be predisposed to do sthg to be likely to do sthg as a result of one's character □ *He is predisposed to violent outbursts.*

predisposition [ˌpriːdɪspə'zɪʃn] *n* to have a predisposition to OR toward sthg to be likely to do sthg as a result of one's character.

predominance [prɪ'dɒmɪnəns] *n* -1. a greater number of one kind of person or thing than of any other □ *There is a predominance of old people living in this area.* -2. the greatest amount of power or influence □ *Moderates now have predominance in the party.*

predominant [prɪ'dɒmɪnənt] *adj* [idea, feature, mood] that is most important or noticeable.

predominantly [prɪ'dɒmɪnəntlɪ] *adv* mainly □ *The reasons are predominantly economic.*

predominate [prɪ'dɒmɪneɪt] *vi* -1. to exist in greater numbers than any other type of person or thing □ *Men still predominate in positions of power.* -2. to be most important or noticeable □ *Moderate views now predominate among the leaders.*

preeminent [priː'emɪnənt] *adj* [politician, figure, role] that is the most important, successful etc of a particular kind of person or thing.

preempt [prɪ'empt] *vt* [action, decision] to prevent <sthg> from happening or being completed by saying or doing something that makes it unnecessary or impossible □ *I'll try not to preempt what Alan is going to say.*

preemptive [prɪ'emptɪv] *adj* [attack, offer] that preempts something.

preemptive strike *n* a military attack that is intended to destroy an enemy's army or equipment before they have acted.

preen [priːn] *vt* -1. to preen itself [bird] to clean and smooth its feathers using its beak. -2. to preen oneself [person] to spend time making oneself look attractive and tidy.

preexisting [ˌpriːɪg'zɪstɪŋ] *adj* [illness, tension] that already exists (formal use).

prefab [ˈpriːfæb] *n* a house that is built quickly using complete sections that have already been made in a factory.

prefabricate [ˌpriː'fæbrɪkeɪt] *vt* to make complete sections of <a building, ship> etc in large quantities in a factory so that they can be put together quickly and easily □ *a prefabricated hut.*

preface [ˈprefəs] ◇ *n* the words written at the beginning of a book as an introduction □ *the preface to the text.* ◇ *vt* to preface sthg with sthg/by doing sthg to introduce sthg with sthg/by doing sthg □ *He prefaced the announcement with a brief explanation.*

prefect [ˈpriːfekt] *n* GB an older pupil in a school who has been given the responsibility of controlling the other pupils.

prefer [prɪ'fɜːʳ] (*pt & pp* **preferred**, *cont* **preferring**) *vt* to like <sb/sthg> more than somebody or something else □ *I prefer these shoes to those boots.* □ *I would prefer to play tennis rather than watch TV.* □ *She prefers walking for the simple reason that it's cheaper.* □ *I'd prefer it if you didn't smoke.*

preferable [ˈprefrəbl] *adj* to be preferable to be more likely to be successful, effective, or acceptable than something else □ *It is preferable to reserve places in advance.* □ *Obviously, sitting in the car is preferable to standing in the rain.*

preferably [ˈprefrəblɪ] *adv* a word used to introduce a fact, suggestion etc that one thinks is preferable □ *Could you return it to me soon, preferably by Thursday?*

preference [ˈprefrəns] *n* -1. a liking for one person or thing rather than another (formal use) □ *I have a preference for modern art.* □ *I don't know much about her personal preferences.* -2. to give sb/sthg preference, to give preference to sb/sthg to treat sb/sthg as being more important than somebody or something else □ *Preference will be given to those who already have some experience.* -3. POLITICS AUS the candidate one votes for who is not one's main choice.

👄 PREFERENCES
In Australia, where the preferential voting system is used in general elections, political parties make unofficial agreements to encourage their supporters to give their preferences (their second, third etc choices) to particular parties. This is called "trading preferences".

preference shares *npl* GB = **preferred stock**.

preferential [ˌprefə'renʃl] *adj* [treatment, rate] that shows somebody special favor that is not shown to other people □ *preferential terms.*

preferential voting system *n* a system of voting at elections in which voters have to mark the candidates who are their first, second, third etc choices.

preferred [prɪ'fɜːʳd] *adj* [course of action, choice] that one prefers to something else.

preferred stock *n* stock in a company that gives its holders special rights over other stockholders, e.g. the right to be repaid first if the company closes.

prefigure [priː'fɪɡəʳ] *vt* to show or suggest that <sthg> will happen later (formal use).

prefix [ˈpriːfɪks] *n* GRAMMAR a letter or group of letters placed at the beginning of a word to change its meaning, e.g. "pro" or "anti". NOTE: Compare **suffix**.

pregnancy ['pregnənsı] (*pl* **pregnancies**) *n* -1. the condition of being pregnant □ *the problem of unwanted pregnancies among teenage girls.* -2. the period of time during which a woman or female animal is pregnant □ *She had few problems during her pregnancy.*

pregnancy test *n* a medical test that shows whether a woman is pregnant or not.

pregnant ['pregnənt] *adj* -1. [woman, female animal] that has a baby growing in her body □ *She's three months pregnant.* -2. [pause, remark] that is full of a particular meaning, especially when it is not openly expressed or explained □ *The moment was pregnant with anticipation.*

preheated [,pri:'hi:təd] *adj* [oven] that has been switched on before food is put in to be cooked.

prehistoric [,pri:hɪ'stɒrɪk] *adj* [man, weapon] that belongs to the period before history began to be recorded.

prehistory [,pri:'hɪstrɪ] *n* the time in history before written records were kept.

pre-industrial *adj* [society, era] that existed or happened in the time before factories and machines were used to produce goods in large quantities.

prejudge [,pri:'dʒʌdʒ] *vt* [person, outcome, issue] to decide what one thinks about <sb/sthg> before one knows all the facts □ *I refuse to prejudge him on the basis of a few newspaper reports.*

prejudice ['predʒədəs] ◇ *n* an unreasonable, unfair, and often unfavorable opinion about somebody or something □ *a victim of racial prejudice* □ *The Catholic community had long complained of the prejudice shown against it by the Protestant majority.* ■ **to the prejudice of sthg** in a way that harms sthg (formal use) □ *He was unable to provide references, to the prejudice of his application.* ◇ *vt* -1. to influence <sb> unfairly □ *The judge prejudiced them against/in favor of the defendant.* -2. to cause damage to <sb's case, chances> etc.

prejudiced ['predʒədəst] *adj* **to be prejudiced** [person, opinion, judgment] to show prejudice □ *The management is prejudiced in favor of the latest proposals.* □ *My neighbor is prejudiced against Puerto Ricans.*

prejudicial [,predʒə'dɪʃl] *adj* [action, situation] that harms somebody or something □ *The legalization of cannabis would be prejudicial to public health.*

prelate ['prelət] *n* RELIGION a priest of high rank such as a bishop.

preliminary [US prə'lɪmənerɪ, GB -ɪnrɪ] (*pl* **preliminaries**) *adj* [test, report] that comes at the beginning of a process, series of events etc, especially in order to prepare for the more important part of it □ *There will be a preliminary court hearing at the end of the month.*

◆ **preliminaries** *npl* -1. things that have to be done to prepare for something more important □ *Once we've got all the preliminaries out of the way, we can get down to business.* -2. SPORT a contest that is held before the main part

of a competition begins, to decide who is allowed to take part in it.

prelims ['pri:lɪmz] *npl* the first exams taken in some universities and colleges by students preparing for a particular degree.

preloved [,pri:'lʌvd] *adj* AUS second-hand (informal use).

prelude ['prelju:d] *n* **a prelude to sthg** something that comes before sthg bigger or more important and acts as an introduction to it □ *The agreement is being seen as a prelude to peace.*

premarital [US ,pri:'merɪtl, GB -'mær-] *adj* **premarital sex** sex before marriage.

premature [US ,pri:mə'tʊr, GB 'premətʃə] *adj* -1. [death, baldness] that happens before the usual or expected time. -2. [baby] that is born earlier than expected □ *She was born five weeks premature.* -3. **to be premature** to be too soon and therefore not suitable □ *It would be premature to talk of victory right now.* □ *I think you may have been a little premature in your celebrations.*

prematurely [US ,pri:mə'tʊrlɪ, GB 'premətʃəlɪ] *adv* [die, decide] sooner than expected or than is suitable.

premeditated [pri:'medɪteɪtəd] *adj* [action, crime, murder] that is carefully considered and planned in advance.

premenstrual syndrome, premenstrual tension [,pri:menstrʊəl-] *n* symptoms such as depression, irritability, and physical discomfort that a woman may have just before menstruation.

premier [US prɪ'mɪər, GB 'premjə] ◇ *adj* that is considered to be the best or most important of its kind □ *Sidney's premier music venue.* ◇ *n* -1. the leader of a country's government. -2. AUS the leader of the government of a state.

premiere [US prɪ'mɪər, GB 'premɪeə] *n* the first performance of a play or showing of a movie in front of an audience.

Premier League *n* **the Premier League** the highest division for professional soccer teams in England and Wales.

premiership [US prɪ'mɪərʃɪp, GB 'premɪəʃɪp] *n* the position of being a country's premier; the period during which a person occupies this position.

◆ **Premiership** *n* **the Premiership** SPORT the competition that soccer teams in the Premier League take part in.

premise ['preməs] *n* a statement that one assumes to be true and uses as the basis for one's ideas, theories etc □ *They bought on the premise that the market would improve.*

◆ **premises** *npl* the buildings and land that are part of a business, institution, or piece of property □ *'Drinking is not allowed on the premises.'*

premium ['pri:mjəm] *n* -1. [on earnings, the price of goods] an additional sum of money that is paid to somebody. ■ **to be sold at a premium** to be sold at a higher price than usual □ *Fresh fruit is selling at a premium.* ■ **to be at a**

premium to be difficult to find or get □ *Tickets for the final are at a premium.* □ *Space is at a premium.* **-2.** FINANCE a regular payment to an insurer for providing insurance coverage. **-3. to put** OR **place a premium on sthg** to consider sthg as being very important □ *Here at Larston, we place a high premium on teamwork.*

premium bond *n* GB a bond bought from the government which gives the buyer a chance of winning an amount of money every month.

premonition [ˌpreməˈnɪʃn] *n* a feeling that causes one to think that something unpleasant is going to happen in the future, but that one cannot explain □ *I had a premonition (that) something like this would happen.* □ *My mother often had premonitions of disasters.*

prenatal [ˌpriːˈneɪtl] *adj* US [class, care] that is connected with the time during which a woman is pregnant.

prenuptial agreement [ˌpriːˈnʌpʃl-] an agreement made by two people before they get married to divide their property in a particular way if they divorce later.

preoccupation [priˌɒkjəˈpeɪʃn] *n* **-1.** a state of mind in which one thinks about something so much that one forgets or does not notice other things □ *I don't understand his preoccupation with punctuality.* **-2.** something that one thinks about a lot □ *I have too many other preoccupations at the moment.*

preoccupied [priːˈɒkjəpaɪd] *adj* **to be preoccupied** to be thinking about something so much that one forgets or does not notice other things, especially because one is worried □ *She was preoccupied with her work.* □ *He was too preoccupied to notice me leave.*

preoccupy [priːˈɒkjəpaɪ] (*pt* & *pp* **preoccupied**) *vt* to cause <sb> to be preoccupied □ *Several things had been preoccupying her mind.*

preordain [ˌpriːɔːˈdeɪn] *vt* **to be preordained** to be certain to happen in the future because it has been decided by God or fate □ *He believed that he was preordained to succeed.*

preowned [ˌpriːˈəʊnd] *adj* AUS second-hand (informal use).

prepacked [ˌpriːˈpækt] *adj* [food] that is wrapped before it is delivered to the store where it is sold.

prepaid [ˌpriːˈpeɪd] *adj* [item, postage, envelope] that is paid for in advance.

preparation [ˌprepəˈreɪʃn] *n* **-1.** [of work, a meal] *see* **prepare** □ *There was little or no time for preparation, so we had to be quick.* □ *This game should be good preparation for the final.* ■ **to be in preparation for sthg** to be getting ready for sthg, especially in order to make it successful □ *A new stadium is being built in preparation for the Olympics.* **-2.** a mixture of different substances used for a particular purpose, e.g. as a food, medicine, or cosmetic.
♦ **preparations** *npl* plans for an event in the future □ *We're currently making preparations for his visit.*

preparatory [US prɪˈpærətɔːriː, GB -ətrɪ] *adj*

[work, measure] that is used to prepare for something.

preparatory school *n* = **prep school** (formal use).

prepare [prɪˈpeəʳ] ◇ *vt* **-1.** [work, room, person]. to make <sb/sthg> ready for a future event □ *She was preparing herself for the move to London.* ■ **to prepare to do sthg** to get ready to do sthg □ *I prepared to leave.* **-2.** [food, meal, chemical] to make <sthg>, especially by mixing different things together □ *He was in the kitchen preparing dinner.* ◇ *vi* **to prepare for sthg** to get ready for sthg □ *Do you need time to prepare for the trip?*

prepared [prɪˈpeəʳd] *adj* **-1.** [statement, answer] that has been thought about, made, or decided on in advance □ *He read from a prepared speech.* ■ **to be prepared** [person] to be able to deal with something because one has gotten ready for it. □ *I came to the conference only half prepared.* **-2. to be prepared to do sthg** to be willing to do sthg □ *Would you be prepared to come in on Friday?* **-3. to be prepared for sthg** to be expecting sthg, so that one is not surprised or shocked by it □ *I was prepared for bad news.*

preponderance [prɪˈpɒndərəns] *n* **a preponderance of sthg** a greater number or amount of sthg of one type than of any other (formal use) □ *Much has been made of the preponderance of immigrants in these jobs.*

preponderantly [prɪˈpɒndərəntlɪ] *adv* mainly (formal use).

preposition [ˌprepəˈzɪʃn] *n* a word such as "by," "at," or "into" that is used with a noun, pronoun, or clause including the "ing" form of a verb to show its connection with another word.

prepossessing [ˌpriːpəˈzesɪŋ] *adj* **not prepossessing** not attractive or pleasant (formal use).

preposterous [prɪˈpɒstərəs] *adj* [idea, statement, remark] that one thinks is unreasonable and foolish.

preppy [ˈprepɪ] (*pl* **preppies**) US (informal use) ◇ *n* a young person who is very neat and well-dressed in a way that suggests they are rich and well-educated. ◇ *adj* that is typical of a preppy □ *preppy clothes.*

prep school (*abbr of* **preparatory school**) *n* **-1.** in the USA, a private school where pupils prepare for college. **-2.** in Britain, a private school for children up to the age of 13.

Pre-Raphaelite [US priːˈræfɪəlaɪt, GB -ˈræfəlaɪt] ◇ *n* one of a group of British painters in the late 19th century whose work was based on subjects from medieval history and myths. ◇ *adj*: *a Pre-Raphaelite artist.*

prerecorded [ˌpriːrɪˈkɔːʳdəd] *adj* [TV program, speech] that has been recorded in advance to be played or shown to an audience later.

prerequisite [priːˈrekwəzət] *n* something that has to happen or be done before something else can become possible (formal use) □ *Regular exercise is a prerequisite of* OR *for better health.*

prerogative [prəˈrɒgətɪv] *n* a particular right

that a particular person or group has, often because they have a particular job or importance □ *It is the prerogative of the old to be treated with respect.* □ *As the eldest son, it is his prerogative to lead his mother into dinner.*

presage ['presɪdʒ] *vt* [situation, event] to be a sign that <sthg bad or unpleasant> is going to happen (formal use).

Presbyterian [ˌprezbə'tɪərɪən] ◇ *adj* that is connected with a Protestant church in which the officials all share the same rank. ◇ *n* a member of a Presbyterian church.

presbytery [US 'prezbətərɪ, GB -ərɪ] *n* the house in which a priest of the Roman Catholic Church lives.

preschool ['priːskuːl] ◇ *adj* [age, education] that is connected with the period before a child is old enough to go to school. ◇ *n* US a school for children between the ages of three and five.

prescient ['presɪənt] *adj* [person] who is able to predict what is going to happen in the future (formal use).

prescribe [prə'skraɪb] *vt* -1. [medicine, treatment] to tell a person to have or take <sthg> when they are ill □ *I've been prescribed antibiotics.* -2. [activity, duty] to order formally that <sthg> should be carried out □ *The sentence prescribed by local laws seemed far too harsh.*

prescription [prə'skrɪpʃn] *n* MEDICINE a piece of paper on which a doctor writes information about the medicine they want a patient to take and which allows the patient to buy it; the medicine that somebody buys in this way □ *The doctor gave me a prescription for some painkillers.* ■ **on prescription** if one gives a pharmacist a prescription from one's doctor □ *You can only get them/They're only available on prescription.*

prescription charge *n* GB a sum of money that has to be paid for medicine one gets on prescription.

prescriptive [prə'skrɪptɪv] *adj* [approach, method, teaching] that gives rules about what should happen in particular situations and what is not allowed □ *Company regulations are extremely prescriptive.*

preselection [ˌpriːsə'lekʃn] *n* the process by which a political party selects the candidates who are going to represent it in elections.

presence ['prezns] *n* -1. the fact or state of being present □ *Your presence at the meeting is essential.* □ *The sudden smell of aftershave announced Tony's presence in the room.* ■ **in the presence of sb** with sb in the same place □ *I felt uneasy in her presence.* □ *She signed the document in the presence of three witnesses.* -2. [in a place] the fact of being in a place so that one can do something □ *There was a huge police presence at the demonstration.* □ *Building a presence in overseas markets can produce immeasurable benefits.* -3. [of a performer, speaker] qualities such as one's personality and manner that make a strong and usually favorable impression on people □ *She has great stage presence, not to mention a lovely voice.* -4. [of a spirit, ghost] something such as

a spirit that cannot be seen but that one feels to be present □ *I could sense an alien presence as soon as I walked in.*

presence of mind *n* the ability to react quickly and calmly to a dangerous or difficult situation □ *She acted with great presence of mind by putting a blanket over him.*

present [*adj* & *n* 'preznt, *vb* prɪ'zent] ◇ *adj* -1. [situation, year, leader] that exists now □ *Would this be an advisable course of action in the present climate?* -2. **to be present** [person, influence] to be in a particular place or situation □ *How many people were present at the meeting?* □ *There was a doctor present.* □ *The fear of the unknown was always present in her novels.*
◇ *n* -1. **the present** the period of time that is happening now □ *I'd rather think about the present than the past.* ■ **at present** now □ *We don't have many members at present.* □ *At present, over half our staff are away on vacation.* ■ **for the present** a phrase used to describe something that exists now but that is probably going to change in the future □ *I think that's all we can do for the present.* -2. [for somebody's birthday, wedding] something that one gives to somebody to please them, especially on a special occasion or as a way of thanking them □ *a birthday/Christmas/wedding present* □ *They gave him a clock as a retirement present.* □ *Have you opened your present yet?* -3. GRAMMAR = **present tense**.
◇ *vt* -1. [award, gift] to give <sthg> to somebody, especially at a formal ceremony □ *They presented him with the award.* □ *The Mayor presented the check to the hospice the following day.* -2. [problem, challenge] to cause or provide <sthg> □ *This job presents us with huge difficulties.* □ *I go traveling whenever the opportunity presents itself.* -3. [person] to introduce <sb> formally □ *She presented him to her new colleagues.* -4. TV & RADIO to introduce the different parts of <a program> □ *Chris Levi presents the breakfast show.* -5. [information, report] to give or show <sthg> to somebody in an official position, so that they can check it or make a decision about it □ *Be ready to present your passport as you cross the border.* -6. [person, event] to show or describe <sb/sthg> in a particular way □ *He wasn't presented in a very favorable light.* -7. **to present oneself** [at a reception, for an interview] to arrive at a place where one is expected □ *I had to present myself at the immigration office.* -8. [play, ballet] to show or perform <sthg> in a public theater, cinema etc □ *They're presenting "Swan Lake" at the amphitheater.*

presentable [prɪ'zentəbl] *adj* [person, appearance, clothes] suitable to be seen by other people □ *Do I look presentable?*

presentation [ˌprezn'teɪʃn] *n* -1. [of news, information, facts] the process of presenting something to people. -2. [of food, policies, a product] the way something looks or seems when it is given, offered, explained etc to people □ *Her presentation is always clear and helpful to the reader.* -3. [of an award, prize, medal] the act of giving something to somebody at an official ceremony □ *After the presentation of the certifi-*

cates, we left. **-4.** BUSINESS a talk giving information on a particular subject □ *Shelley gave a brief presentation on the company's future strategy.* **-5.** [of a play, ballet, movie] the act of performing or showing something to an audience □ *a presentation given by the Royal Ballet.*

presentation copy *n* a copy of a book that is given free to somebody, usually by the writer or publisher.

present day *n* **the present day** the period of time that is happening now.

◆ **present-day** *adj* [situation, problem, music] that exists now rather than in the past.

presenter [prɪˈzentəʳ] *n* GB a person who presents a TV or radio program.

presentiment [prɪˈzentɪmənt] *n* a feeling that causes one to think something bad or unpleasant is going to happen (formal use).

presently [ˈprezntlɪ] *adv* **-1.** soon □ *She will be here presently.* **-2.** at this time □ *He is presently compiling a report.*

present participle *n* GRAMMAR a part of a verb used to form continuous tenses, and sometimes used as an adjective, e.g. "singing" and "exciting".

present tense *n* GRAMMAR the tense of a verb used to talk about things that are happening at the time one is speaking or writing, or that happen often.

preservation [ˌprezəʳˈveɪʃn] *n*: *see* **preserve** □ *The roof is in a remarkable state of preservation.*

preservation order *n* GB an official order stating that something such as a historic building should not be changed or destroyed.

preservative [prɪˈzɜːʳvətɪv] *n* a chemical substance used to preserve food.

preserve [prɪˈzɜːʳv] ◇ *vt* **-1.** [situation, standard] to keep <sthg> as it is, especially because one thinks it is very good and should not be changed □ *Our main goal is to preserve the status quo.* **-2.** [building, species, landscape] to stop <sthg> from disappearing or being destroyed. **-3.** [fruit, herbs] to treat <food> so that it stays in good condition for a long time. ◇ *n* jam □ *strawberry preserve.*

◆ **preserves** *npl* foods such as jam or pickle that are made by cooking fruit or vegetables in sugar, salt, or vinegar so that they stay in good condition for a long time.

preset [ˌpriːˈset] (*pt* & *pp* **preset**, *cont* **presetting**) *vt* [oven, video recorder] to set the control of <a piece of equipment> so that it will start to work at a particular time.

preshrunk [ˌpriːˈʃrʌŋk] *adj* [clothing, fabric] that has been shrunk before being sold □ *preshrunk jeans.*

preside [prɪˈzaɪd] *vi* to be in charge at an event such as a meeting □ *I had been asked to preside over* OR *at the meeting.* □ *The presiding judge at the trial was Justice Roy Marshall.*

presidency [ˈprezədənsɪ] (*pl* **presidencies**) *n* the position of being a president; the period of time during which somebody has this position □ *Klondheim was elected to the presidency with a large majority.* □ *He drew the attention of voters to the success of his presidency so far.*

president [ˈprezədənt] *n* **-1.** POLITICS the person who holds the highest political office in a country that does not have a king or queen □ *the President of the Czech Republic.* **-2.** [of a club] the head of a club or organization. **-3.** US BUSINESS the person who has the highest position in a company.

president-elect *n* a person who has been chosen to be the US president but who has not started the job yet.

presidential [ˌprezəˈdenʃl] *adj* [decision, campaign] that is connected with a president.

Presidents' Day *n* in the USA, a public holiday celebrated on the third Monday of February. It honors George Washington and Abraham Lincoln.

press [pres] ◇ *vt* **-1.** [button, switch] to push <sthg> firmly with one's finger or foot. **-2. to press sthg into/against etc sthg** to push sthg into/against etc sthg so that it puts pressure on it □ *He pressed his nose against the window.* □ *She pressed her foot down on the accelerator.* **-3.** [arm, hand] to hold <sthg> firmly to show friendship, love etc □ *She pressed my hand and gave me a reassuring smile.* **-4.** to flatten and dry <a flower>, e.g. between the pages of a book, so that one can keep it. **-5.** [grapes, olives] to squeeze <fruit> to get the juice from it. **-6.** [shirt, trousers] to make <a piece of clothing> smooth by ironing it □ *Would you like your suit pressed?* **-7. to press sb to do sthg** OR **into doing sthg** to try to force sb to do sthg □ *He was trying to press me into going.* ■ **to press sb for sthg** [for support, an answer, decision] to keep asking sb to give sthg □ *Wilson is still pressing us for a completion date.* ■ **to press sthg on** OR **upon sb** to force sb to accept sthg □ *As she left he pressed the last bottle of homemade wine upon her.* **-8.** [claim, point] to put a lot of effort into getting somebody to accept <sthg> □ *They are pressing their demands in the European court.* **-9.** LAW **to press charges** to make an official accusation against somebody □ *Many victims are too scared to press charges against their attackers.*

◇ *vi* **-1.** to push hard on something □ *He pressed (down) on the accelerator.* □ *Don't press too hard, you'll damage it.* **-2.** [crowd] to move together in a particular direction with a lot of force □ *The fans pressed forward.*

◇ *n* **-1.** [of a button, doorbell, pedal] the act of pressing something □ *At the press of a button I can summon my guards and have you removed from the building.* **-2. the press** a collective term for newspapers and magazines; the journalists who work for them □ *I saw the article in the press.* □ *He's been given a hard time by the press.* ■ **to get (a) good/bad press** to be praised/criticized, especially in the newspapers, on television, radio etc. **-3.** PRINTING a machine for printing books, newspapers etc. **-4.** [for trousers, grapes] a piece of equipment for flattening or squeezing something, e.g. for pressing trousers or for pressing grapes to make wine.

◆ **press for** *vt fus* **to press for sthg** [for an inquiry, raise] to demand sthg strongly □ *A number of member states are pressing for sanctions.*

◆ **press on** *vi* to continue with something in a determined way □ *They pressed on with the plan in spite of opposition.* □ *Time is short so shall we press on?*

press agency *n* the place where a press agent works.

press agent *n* a person whose job is to get good publicity for an organization or well-known person by giving newspapers, magazines etc photographs and information.

Press Association *n* **the Press Association** a British news agency.

press box *n* a special room or area for journalists at a sports event.

press conference *n* a meeting during which somebody, especially an important or famous person, answers questions from a group of journalists.

press corps *n* a group of journalists from different newspapers who are working in the same place on the same story.

press cutting *n* a report or photograph cut out of a newspaper or magazine.

pressed [prest] *adj* **to be pressed for time/money** to have very little time/money.

press fastener *n* GB = **press-stud**.

press gallery *n* a special area above the main part of a hall where journalists can sit.

pressgang ['presgæŋ] ◇ *n* a group of men who in the past captured men and boys and forced them to join the army or navy. ◇ *vt* **to pressgang sb into doing sthg** to force sb to do sthg, especially when they do not really want to do it.

pressing ['presɪŋ] *adj* [problem, business, appointment] that has to be dealt with immediately □ *Will you excuse me? I have a rather pressing engagement.*

pressman ['presmæn] (*pl* **pressmen** [-men]) *n* GB a reporter who works for a newspaper or magazine.

press officer *n* a person whose job is to deal with the press on behalf of an organization.

press release *n* a statement made by an organization and given to the press.

press-stud *n* GB a round metal fastener used on clothing in which one part is pressed into a hole in the other part.

press-up *n* GB = **push-up**.

pressure ['preʃəʳ] ◇ *n* **-1.** the force or weight of something pressing on something else □ *He had to apply a lot of pressure to force open the lid.* □ *water/air/tire pressure.* **-2.** a powerful influence □ *parental pressure* □ *He did it because of pressure from his peers.* ■ **to put pressure on sb** to keep trying to force or persuade sb to do something they do not want to do □ *The banks put pressure on the government to cut interest rates.* **-3.** [of work, competition, life] conditions in a job or situation which make one worried and tense □ *The pressure of his first ever exam proved to be too much.* □ *She's under a lot of pressure at work.*

◇ *vt* **to pressure sb to do** OR **into sthg** to make sb do sthg they do not want to do by using force or influence □ *I felt pressured into making a quick decision.*

pressure cooker *n* a cooking pot whose lid can be tightly closed so that food can be cooked quickly using steam at high pressure.

pressure gauge *n* a dial that shows the pressure of liquids or gases in boilers, pipes etc.

pressure group *n* an organization that tries to persuade a government to do something, e.g. change a law, and tries to get support from the public.

pressurize, -ise ['preʃəraɪz] *vt* **-1.** [cabin, container] to keep the air pressure inside <sthg> the same. **-2.** GB **to pressurize sb to do** OR **into doing sthg** to pressure sb to do sthg.

Prestel™ ['prestel] *n* a British telephone service that allows the user to call up information, e.g. travel, weather, or sports news, on their television.

prestige [pre'stiːʒ] ◇ *n* respect and admiration that people give a person, organization, or thing that is very important or very good at something □ *This job carries a lot of prestige.* ◇ *comp* [office, home, car] that is admired by everybody because it is the kind that rich people have □ *a new prestige housing development.*

prestigious [pre'stɪdʒəs] *adj* [organization, job] that is respected and admired by people □ *one of the most prestigious literary prizes in the US.*

presto ['prestoʊ] *excl* US a word used by a magician at the end of a trick.

prestressed concrete [ˌpriːstrest-] *n* concrete that contains metal cables to make it stronger.

presumably [prɪ'zjuːməblɪ] *adv* a word used to say that one presumes that something is true □ *Presumably they felt he was too old for the job.*

presume [prɪ'zjuːm] *vt* **to presume (that)...** to think that something is true, although one cannot be sure □ *Five people are missing, presumed dead.* □ *A man must be presumed innocent until proven guilty.* □ *It was his idea, I presume.* □ *I presume (that) you'll only be staying for a few days.*

presumption [prɪ'zʌmpʃn] *n* **-1.** [of somebody's innocence, death] *see* **presume.** **-2.** [of a person] *see* **presumptuous.**

presumptuous [prɪ'zʌmptʃʊəs] *adj* [person] who does things that they have no right to do □ *It was very presumptuous of him to expect to be invited.*

presuppose [ˌpriːsə'poʊz] *vt* **to presuppose (that)...** to assume that something is true, without thinking that it might not be true.

pretax [ˌpriː'tæks] *adj* [income, earnings, profit] before tax is taken away.

preteen [ˌpriː'tiːn] *adj* [clothing, magazine] that is for children who are 11 or 12 years old □ *a group of preteen schoolchildren.*

pretence *n* GB = **pretense**.

pretend [prɪ'tend] ◇ *vt* **-1. to pretend to do sthg** to behave as if sthg is true when it is not, in order to deceive people □ *He pretended to be an insurance salesman.* □ *She pretended (that) everything was normal.* **-2. to pretend (that)...** to imagine that something is true, e.g. to help explain something or as part of a game □ *Let's pretend (that) we're on a desert island.* **-3. I cannot pretend that...** a phrase used to say what one cannot do, or what is not the case □ *I can't pretend to know much about computers.* ◇ *vi:* *He's not really sick — he's just pretending.* □ *You can stop pretending now.*

pretense ['priːtens] US, **pretence** ['priːtens] GB *n* **-1.** [of friendship, innocence, grief] a way of behaving that is intended to deceive people □ *He made no pretense of caring about our predicament.* **-2.** *phrase* **under false pretenses** by deceiving somebody so that they do not know who one is or what one really wants □ *The money was obtained under false pretenses.*

pretension [prɪ'tenʃn] *n* a claim to possess something, e.g. greatness or wealth □ *social/literary/moral pretensions* □ *I have no pretensions to expertise in this field.*

pretentious [prɪ'tenʃəs] *adj* [person, language, book] that tries to seem important but is not important □ *Don't be so pretentious!*

pretentiously [prɪ'tenʃəslɪ] *adv* [behave, talk, write] *see* **pretentious**.

preterite ['pretərət] *n* GRAMMAR **the preterite** the simple past tense of a verb.

pretext ['priːtekst] *n* a reason that one pretends has made one do something □ *He refused to see us on* OR *under the pretext that he was too busy.* □ *They stopped us on* OR *under the pretext of asking for information.*

Pretoria [prɪ'tɔːrɪə] the administrative capital of South Africa. POPULATION: 528,000.

prettify ['prɪtɪfaɪ] (*pt* & *pp* **prettified**) *vt* to try to make <sthg> look pretty, especially without succeeding.

prettily ['prɪtɪlɪ] *adv* [dress, smile] *see* **pretty**.

pretty ['prɪtɪ] (*compar* **prettier**, *superl* **prettiest**) ◇ *adj* [girl, place, dress] that is attractive and pleasant to look at □ *She looks much prettier with her hair down.* □ *a pretty little town/house.* ◇ *adv* fairly, rather □ *It's pretty good/awful/cold.* ■ **pretty much** OR **well** almost □ *They've pretty well messed it up.* □ *She's pretty much the same as before.*

pretzel ['pretsl] *n* a crisp salty kind of bread baked in the shape of a stick or a knot.

prevail [prɪ'veɪl] *vi* **-1.** [belief, custom, fashion] to be general or widespread □ *in the conditions prevailing at the time.* **-2.** [idea, country] to win in the end □ *In the end, the need for compromise prevailed over ideological beliefs.* □ *Hopefully, common sense will prevail.* **-3. to prevail (up)on sb to do sthg** to persuade sb to do sthg □ *They prevailed upon me to help them out.*

prevailing [prɪ'veɪlɪŋ] *adj* **-1.** [belief, opinion, fashion] that is most general or widespread □ *There's a prevailing mood of optimism.* **-2. a pre-**

vailing wind a wind that usually blows over a particular area.

prevalence ['prevələns] *n: see* **prevalent** □ *The report reveals the prevalence of drug abuse among teenagers.*

prevalent ['prevələnt] *adj* [problem, belief, custom] that is general or widespread □ *Such ideas were prevalent at the time.*

prevaricate [US prɪ'verɪkeɪt, GB -'vær-] *vi* to try to hide the truth by not being completely honest and clear.

prevent [prɪ'vent] *vt* [war, disease, crime] to stop <sthg> from happening □ *Her father prevented her (from) going out.* □ *They did all they could to prevent the fire (from) spreading.* □ *If you want to go, I can't prevent you.*

preventable [prɪ'ventəbl] *adj* [disease, crime] that can be prevented □ *What made the tragedy worse was that it was preventable.*

preventative [prɪ'ventətɪv] *adj* = **preventive**.

prevention [prɪ'venʃn] *n* [of disease, crime] *see* **prevent** □ *Prevention is better than cure.* □ *accident/fire prevention.*

preventive [prɪ'ventɪv] *adj* [medicine, measure] that is intended to prevent something □ *We must take preventive action now.*

preview ['priːvjuː] *n* an event at which a movie, show, or exhibition is shown to a few people before it is shown to the public □ *We've been invited to the preview.*

previous ['priːvɪəs] *adj* **-1.** [occasion, experience, conviction] that happened or existed earlier □ *I told him about it in a previous letter.* □ *It was the previous chairman who made the decision.* □ *The festival had always been popular in previous years.* **-2. the previous day/week etc** the day/week etc that was just before this or that day/week □ *There had been no one there the previous day/Monday.*

previously ['priːvɪəslɪ] *adv* **-1.** at an earlier time □ *She previously worked as a nurse.* □ *Previously, I'd never been abroad.* **-2.** before □ *two weeks/four years previously.*

prewar [ˌpriː'wɔːr] *adj* [period, society] before a war, especially World War II.

prewash ['priːwɒʃ] *n* a special wash at the start of a washing machine's cycle for very dirty clothes.

prey [preɪ] *n* an animal that is hunted and eaten by another animal ■ **to fall prey to sb/sthg** to come under the influence or control of sb/sthg bad.

◆ **prey on** *vt fus* **-1. to prey on sthg** [animal, insect] to hunt and eat sthg as prey □ *Cats prey on mice.* **-2. to prey on sb's mind** to worry sb all the time □ *His financial problems preyed on his mind.*

price [praɪs] ◇ *n* **-1.** the amount of money that must be paid to buy something □ *The price of oil is going up again.* □ *House prices are coming down.* □ *You can't put a price on education.* **-2.** something unpleasant that must be done or suffered in order to get something □ *The breakup of his marriage was the price he paid for success.* □ *The price of peace is eternal vigilance.* ■ **at a price** at a high cost □ *They* reached an agreement, but at a price. ■ **at any price** whatever the cost □ She was determined to get the job at any price. ◇ vt [product, goods] to give a price to <sthg> □ It was priced at $100. □ competitively/reasonably priced.

price-cutting n the act of lowering the prices of one's goods, products etc.

price-fixing [-fɪksɪŋ] n the act of setting prices by agreement among competitors, usually to keep them higher than they need to be.

priceless ['praɪsləs] adj -1. [jewelry, work of art] that is extremely valuable □ a priceless collection of antiques. -2. [joke, person] that one finds very amusing (informal use).

price list n a list of prices for goods that are on sale.

price tag n a small ticket fixed to an article saying how much it costs.

price war n a situation in which different companies, stores etc keep lowering the prices of their products or goods in order to have the lowest prices and attract the most customers.

pricey ['praɪsɪ] (compar **pricier**, superl **priciest**) adj expensive (informal use) □ That's a bit pricey for a second-hand car.

prick [prɪk] ◇ n -1. [in a surface, somebody's skin] a small hole or mark made by an object that has a sharp point, e.g. a needle or a pin □ Make small pricks in the top of the pie. -2.▽ [of a man] a man's penis (very informal use). -3.▽ a stupid or unpleasant person, usually a man (very informal use). ◇ vt -1. [finger, balloon, blister] to make a small hole in <sthg> with an object that has a sharp point, e.g. a needle or pin □ Prick the sausages with a fork. -2. [eyes, throat] to make <sthg> sting □ The smoke pricked her eyes.

◆ **prick up** vt sep **to prick its ears up** [animal] to lift its ears up in order to listen carefully to something □ The cat pricked its ears up at the faintest sound. ■ **to prick one's ears up** [person] to suddenly start paying attention to what is being said □ He pricked his ears up when he heard his name.

prickle ['prɪkl] ◇ n -1. [on a plant or animal] one of several small, thin, sharp points on some leaves, plants, or animals. -2. [of fear, pleasure] a pricking sensation on one's skin. ◇ vi [skin] to feel a pricking sensation.

prickly ['prɪklɪ] (compar **pricklier**, superl **prickliest**) adj -1. [leaf, plant, animal] that is covered with prickles □ a prickly bush/rose. -2. [person] who quickly becomes annoyed or angry □ He can be very prickly at times.

prickly heat n a skin condition common in hot climates in which one's skin becomes covered in small, red, itchy spots.

pride [praɪd] ◇ n -1. a feeling of satisfaction with what one has done, with what one has, or with people and things connected with oneself □ She looked at her finished painting with pride. ■ **to take pride in sb/sthg** [in one's children, success, work] to feel proud of sb/sthg □ I take a lot of pride in doing a difficult job well. ■ **one's pride and joy** somebody or

something that one feels is important and that one is very proud of □ His new car was his pride and joy. ■ **to have pride of place** to be in the most important position in a place, list, or competition □ The trophy she won took pride of place on the mantelpiece. -2. a feeling of respect for and satisfaction with oneself and what one does that makes one expect respect from other people □ His failure to get the job was a severe blow to his pride. ■ **to swallow one's pride** to do something that one feels ashamed to do, especially accepting that one was wrong □ For once, she was forced to swallow her pride and accept defeat. -3. an opinion of oneself and one's abilities, possessions etc that is too high □ His pride stops him admitting he was wrong.

◇ vt **to pride oneself on sthg** [on one's looks, skills] to be proud of sthg one has that one thinks is important □ She prides herself on her punctuality.

priest [priːst] n -1. [in Christianity] a person who is trained to perform religious duties and ceremonies, especially in the Roman Catholic Church □ a Catholic/Anglican priest. -2. [in Buddhism, Islam] a person who performs religious duties and ceremonies in some non-Christian religions □ a Buddhist priest.

priestess [US 'priːstəs, GB priːst'es] n a woman who performs religious duties and ceremonies in some religions.

priesthood ['priːsthʊd] n **the priesthood** the office or position of a priest; all the priests of a particular religion or country □ He joined the priesthood ten years ago.

prig [prɪg] n a person who is very careful to behave correctly, feels morally superior to other people, and is often shocked by other people's behavior (disapproving use).

prim [prɪm] (compar **primmer**, superl **primmest**) adj [person] who behaves too correctly, is easily shocked, and is therefore boring and old-fashioned □ She's always so prim and proper — I wish she'd just relax.

primacy ['praɪməsɪ] n the state of being the most important thing.

prima donna [,priːmə'dɒnə] (pl **prima donnas**) n -1. MUSIC an important and successful female opera singer. -2. a person who is always changing their mind and who expects other people always to do what they want them to do (disapproving use).

primaeval [praɪ'miːvl] adj = **primeval**.

prima facie [,praɪmə'feɪʃiː] adj [evidence, case] that seems to be true when one first thinks about it.

primal ['praɪml] adj -1. [instinct, urge] that is first or basic. -2. [need, concern] that is most important.

primarily [US praɪ'merəlɪ, GB 'praɪmrəlɪ] adv mainly □ We were primarily interested in its cost rather than its efficiency.

primary [US 'praɪmerɪ, GB -ərɪ] (pl **primaries**) ◇ adj -1. [concern, aim, cause] that is the most important □ The mining industry is the primary source of income for families in the area. -2. EDU-

CATION [education, teacher] for children between the ages of 5 and 11.
◇ *n* POLITICS in the USA, a state election to choose the candidates for each of the two national parties in the presidential election.

primary color *n* any of the three colors red, yellow, and blue that can be mixed together to make all other colors.

primary election *n* POLITICS = **primary**.

primary school *n* **-1.** US = **elementary school**. **-2.** GB a school for children between the ages of 5 and 11.

primary teacher *n* **-1.** US a teacher who works in an elementary school. **-2.** GB a teacher who works in a primary school.

primate ['praɪmeɪt] *n* **-1.** ZOOLOGY any mammal that belongs to the group that includes humans, apes, and monkeys. **-2.** RELIGION an archbishop.

prime [praɪm] ◇ *adj* **-1.** [concern, reason, aim] that is very important, or the most important □ *Our prime objective is to eradicate this disease.* □ *The prime suspect is the victim's husband.* **-2.** [condition, example, position] that is excellent, or the best □ *This is a prime example of lack of communication at management level.* □ *The building occupies a prime site in the heart of the city.* □ *prime beef.*
◇ *n* the period in one's life of greatest activity, strength, success etc □ *When he reached 30, he felt he was past his prime.* □ *She's still very much in her prime.* □ *in the prime of life.*
◇ *vt* **-1.** [person] to prepare <sb> for something by telling them about it in advance □ *You could tell that he'd been primed to give the right answers.* **-2.** [wall, wood] to prepare <a surface> for painting by covering it with a substance that prevents the paint from being absorbed. **-3.** [bomb, gun] to prepare <a weapon> in order that it can explode or be fired □ *The device was primed to go off during the rush hour.*

prime minister *n* the chief minister and leader of the government in some countries.

prime mover [-'muːvəʳ] *n* a person who is important in setting up a plan, campaign etc □ *General Horowitz was one of the prime movers in the plot.*

prime number *n* a whole number that cannot be divided by any other whole numbers apart from itself and 1.

primer ['praɪməʳ] *n* a substance used to prime a surface for painting.

prime time *n* the period when more people are watching television or listening to the radio than at any other time.

◆ **prime-time** *adj*: *prime-time television/viewing/advertising.*

primeval [praɪ'miːvl] *adj* [forest, instinct] that existed in, or has existed since, the period when the world began.

primitive ['prɪmətɪv] *adj* **-1.** [man, tribe] that has a simple non-industrial way of life □ *primitive societies of the past.* **-2.** [conditions, accommodation] that is very basic and lacking in comfort □ *a primitive hut.*

primordial [praɪ'mɔːʳdɪəl] *adj* that existed at or has existed since the beginning of time (formal use).

primrose ['prɪmrouz] *n* a wild plant that has small light-yellow flowers in the spring.

Primus stove™ ['praɪməs-] *n* GB a small portable stove that uses kerosene and is used, especially by campers, for cooking.

prince [prɪns] *n* **-1.** a man or boy from a royal family who is the son or grandson of the king or queen. **-2.** a man from a royal family who is a ruler, especially of a small state or country.

Prince Charming *n* a man who is the perfect partner for a particular girl or woman because he is very handsome and kind (humorous use).

Prince Edward Island a province in southeastern Canada, consisting of an island in the Gulf of St Lawrence. ABBREVIATION: PE. SIZE: 5,657 sq kms. POPULATION: 129,765. CAPITAL: Charlottetown.

princely ['prɪnslɪ] (*compar* **princelier,** *superl* **princeliest**) *adj* **-1. a princely sum** a large amount of money (ironic use) □ *I sold it for the princely sum of $25!* **-2.** [bearing] that belongs to a prince; that is suitable for a prince.

Prince of Wales: the Prince of Wales the title of the eldest son of a British monarch.

Prince Regent: the Prince Regent the title given to the son of the British king George III when he acted as king from 1811 to 1820 because his father was mad. He later became King George IV.

princess [prɪn'ses] *n* **-1.** a woman or girl from a royal family who is the daughter or granddaughter of the king or queen. **-2.** a woman who is married to a prince.

Princess of Wales: the Princess of Wales in Britain, the title of the wife of the Prince of Wales.

Princess Royal: the Princess Royal a title given to the eldest daughter of a British monarch.

Princeton ['prɪnstən] one of the oldest and most respected universities in the USA.

principal ['prɪnsəpl] ◇ *adj* [aim, problem, cause] that is the first and most important □ *The principal reason why we've decided to do this is cost.* ◇ *n* EDUCATION the person in charge of a school or college.

principality [,prɪnsə'pælətɪ] (*pl* **principalities**) *n* a country or state ruled by a prince. ■ **the Principality** GB Wales.

principally ['prɪnsəplɪ] *adv* mainly □ *She writes feature articles, principally for women's magazines.*

principle ['prɪnsəpl] *n* **-1.** a strong belief that one has that guides one's behavior □ *She refuses to give up her principles.* □ *a moral principle.* **-2.** a strong belief in and practice of principles □ *He lacks principle.* □ *a woman of principle.* ■ **to do sthg on principle** OR **as a matter of principle** to do sthg because of one's moral principles □ *I never eat meat on principle.* □ *I resigned as a matter of principle.* **-3.** a basic general rule or scientific law □ *This is one of the principles of physics.* □ *a philosophical principle* □ *the principle of one member, one vote.*

◆ **in principle** *adv* in general terms but not necessarily in detail □ *They agreed to support his scheme in principle.* □ *In principle that's fine, but in practice we might have to make some changes.*

principled ['prɪnsəpld] *adj* [person] who has principles and lives according to them.

print [prɪnt] ◇ *vt* -1. to make <words, pictures> etc on paper by pressing it against something covered in ink; to copy <words, pictures> etc onto paper using photographic equipment □ *The last page hasn't been printed well.* □ *We've printed 100 pages so far.* -2. [book, newspaper, leaflet] to make <sthg> by printing □ *The book was first printed in 1957.* -3. [article, story] to publish <a piece of writing> in a book, newspaper etc □ *Readers are sent $20 for every letter printed.* -4. [pattern, design] to reproduce <sthg> on cloth by printing; [fabric, dress] to decorate <a piece of cloth> in this way □ *The skirt was printed with flowers.* -5. [word, name] to write <sthg> clearly without joining the letters □ *Please print your name in block capitals.*
◇ *vi* -1. [person] to write something clearly without joining the letters together. -2. [printer] to produce printed material □ *The machine is now ready to print.*
◇ *n* -1. [on a page] words that have been printed on a piece of paper □ *It was written in large/small print.* □ *The print is too small to read.* □ *We all love to see our name in print.* ■ **to be in/out of print** [book] to be available/no longer available for sale □ *That book went out of print several years ago.* -2. ART a picture or design made by printing □ *a screen/litho print* □ *He had the Picasso print framed.* -3. PHOTOGRAPHY a photograph produced from a film □ *black and white/color prints.* -4. [for clothing] cloth, usually cotton, on which a color pattern has been printed □ *a cotton print* □ *a print dress* □ *print curtains.* -5. [of a foot] a footprint □ *The animal had left its prints in the mud.* -6. [of a finger] a fingerprint □ *The police were looking for prints after the burglary.*

◆ **print out** *vt sep* to print sthg out COMPUTING [figures, data] to print sthg that has been stored on a computer.

printed circuit [,prɪntəd-] *n* **a printed circuit (board)** an electronic circuit consisting of a continuous thin line of conducting material laid on one or both sides of a thin board.

printed matter *n* printed paper, e.g. official advertisements, that can be mailed at a special reduced rate.

printer ['prɪntər] *n* -1. BUSINESS a person or firm that prints books, newspapers, leaflets etc □ *a firm of printers* □ *The book is still at the printers.* -2. COMPUTING a machine that prints information from a computer, word processor etc □ *a computer printer.*

printing ['prɪntɪŋ] *n* -1. the act of printing books, papers etc. -2. BUSINESS the industry

that prints newspapers, leaflets etc □ *He works in printing.*

printing press *n* a machine that prints books, newspapers etc.

printout ['prɪntaʊt] *n* a sheet or sheets of paper on which information from a computer, word processor etc is printed □ *a computer printout.*

prior ['praɪər] ◇ *adj* -1. [knowledge, agreement, arrangement] that existed before a particular time □ *No prior warning was given.* □ *I'd already met him on a prior occasion.* -2. [duty, commitment] that must be dealt with first because it is more important □ *Sorry, I can't come; I have a prior engagement that day.* □ *My family has a prior claim on my time.* ◇ *n* RELIGION the head of a monastery.

◆ **prior to** *prep* before <sthg> □ *The decision was made prior to her resignation.* □ *She left him a note prior to leaving.*

prioritize, -ise [praɪ'ɒrətaɪz] *vt* to deal with <sthg> before other things, usually because it is more important □ *We should prioritize spending on education.*

priority [praɪ'ɒrəti] (*pl* **priorities**) *n* -1. something that must be dealt with very soon, and before other things, usually because it is more important □ *Our first priority is to stabilize the economy.* □ *The President sees defense as a priority issue.* -2. **to have** OR **take priority** to have the right to be dealt with first □ *Families have* OR *take priority over single people on the waiting list.*

◆ **priorities** *npl* tasks considered of most immediate concern or greatest importance □ *We must get our priorities right.* □ *This is low on my list of priorities.*

priory ['praɪəri] (*pl* **priories**) *n* a place where a small group of monks or nuns live and work.

prise [praɪz] *vt* GB **to prise sthg open/from sb** to prize sthg open/from sb.

prism ['prɪzm] *n* a specially shaped object of clear glass which separates white light into the colors of the rainbow.

prison ['prɪzn] *n* a building where people are kept locked in cells as a punishment for crimes they have committed or while they are waiting to be tried □ *He has been in prison for three years now.* □ *She was sent to prison.* □ *a prison cell/wall.*

prison camp *n* a camp for prisoners, especially prisoners of war.

prisoner ['prɪznər] *n* a person kept in prison or a prison camp □ *a political prisoner* □ *He is being held prisoner by an armed group.* □ *Thousands of soldiers were taken prisoner.*

prisoner of war (*pl* **prisoners of war**) *n* a member of the armed forces captured by the enemy during a war and held prisoner, usually until the end of the war.

prissy ['prɪsi] (*compar* **prissier**, *superl* **prissiest**) *adj* [person] who one finds annoying because they are shocked by things that are not usually considered rude by most other people (informal and disapproving use).

pristine ['prɪstiːn] *adj* that is in very good condition, because it is new or like new □ *The watch was still in pristine condition.*

privacy [US 'praɪvəsɪ, GB 'prɪv-] *n* a situation in which one can be alone and not be seen or disturbed by anybody □ *I value my privacy.*

private ['praɪvət] ◇ *adj* **-1.** [room, performance, garden] that is only intended for or owned by a particular person or group □ *This is private land.* □ *'Private. Keep off.'* □ *a private jet.* **-2.** [industry, hospital] that is owned or run by an individual, group, or company and not by the state □ *private education.* **-3.** [conversation, meeting, interview] that takes place between a small number of people and is kept secret from others □ *a letter marked "private and confidential".* **-4.** [life, thoughts] that is connected with somebody's personal life and not with their work or public life □ *It's a matter for the private individual.* **-5.** [place, spot, retreat] that is quiet and away from other people who might see or hear one □ *Can we meet somewhere a bit more private?* **-6.** [person] who does not like to share their personal thoughts, feelings etc with other people □ *He's a very private man.* ◇ *n* **-1.** MILITARY a soldier of the lowest rank. **-2. in private** with no one else present □ *He asked to see his boss in private.*

◆ **privates** *npl* [of a person] one's genitals (informal use).

private company *n* = **private limited company**.

private detective *n* a person who is hired by members of the public to carry out investigations for them.

private enterprise *n* businesses that are owned by individuals or groups and not by the state.

private eye *n* = **private detective**.

private income *n* GB income that comes from property, investments etc and not from a salary.

private investigator *n* = **private detective**.

private limited company *n* GB a company that is not allowed to offer its shares for sale to the public.
NOTE: Compare **public company**.

privately ['praɪvətlɪ] *adv* **-1. privately owned/ run** owned/run by an individual, group, or company and not by the state □ *The children are privately educated.* **-2.** [discuss, meet] not in public □ *Privately, Mr Kemp admitted to feelings of jealousy.* **-3.** [think, feel, believe] without saying anything to anyone else □ *I looked indifferent, while privately hoping for an invitation.*

private member's bill *n* in Britain, a bill proposed by a member of the House of Commons who is not a government minister.

private parts *npl* one's genitals (informal use).

private practice *n* **-1.** a professional person's business that is not a part of a government organization □ *He left the Health Service and joined a private practice.* **-2.** US the business of a doctor who work on their own.

private property *n* land and buildings owned by a particular person or group.

private school *n* a school that is not run and paid for by the state but that is paid for by the parents of the pupils □ *My parents sent me to a private school.*

private sector *n* **the private sector** the industries and services that are not owned and run by the state □ *small businesses in the private sector* □ *a private-sector employee.*

privation [praɪ'veɪʃn] *n* a lack of the basic things required for a normal life.

privatization [,praɪvətaɪ'zeɪʃn] *n*: *see* **privatize** □ *Privatization is seen as the key to profitability.*

privatize, -ise ['praɪvətaɪz] *vt* [company, service] to sell <an industry owned by the state> to private owners □ *The coal industry is about to be privatized.*
NOTE: Compare **nationalize**.

privet ['prɪvət] *n* an evergreen bush with small leaves, often used as a garden hedge □ *a privet hedge.*

privilege ['prɪvəlɪdʒ] *n* **-1.** a special right or advantage that only some people have, because they are rich or belong to a particular group □ *The office carries with it certain privileges.* **-2.** a polite word used to show that one is pleased to do something □ *I had the privilege of hearing him speak once.* □ *It was a privilege to be introduced to her.*

privileged ['prɪvəlɪdʒd] *adj* **-1.** [group, position] that has rights or advantages that other people do not have □ *a privileged minority* □ *As a member, you have privileged access to a wealth of services.* **-2. to be privileged to do sthg** to be honored to do sthg □ *We were very privileged to receive an invitation.* □ *I feel privileged to work for them.*

privy ['prɪvɪ] *adj* **to be privy to sthg** [to a discussion, secret] to know something about sthg that is secret (formal use).

Privy Council *n* **the Privy Council** in Britain, a group of politicians, public figures etc who advise the king or queen on political matters.

Privy Councillor *n* a member of the Privy Council.

Privy Purse *n* **the Privy Purse** in Britain, the amount of money that the government gives to the king or queen for their own use.

prize [praɪz] ◇ *n* something valuable given to a person who has won a competition, contest, game etc □ *She won first prize in the tournament.* ◇ *adj* **-1.** [cattle, exhibit] that has won a prize. **-2.** [idiot, fool] complete (informal use). ◇ *vt* **-1.** to value and admire <sthg> □ *a prized award/possession* □ *This breed is highly prized for its intelligence.* **-2. to prize sthg open** to open sthg by using force □ *She tried to prize the box open.* ■ **to prize sthg from sb** to remove sthg from sb's hand with effort or by force □ *I finally succeeded in prizing it from her grasp.*

prize day *n* GB a school ceremony held once

a year at which prizes are given for good work during the year.

prizefight ['praizfait] *n* a boxing match in which the boxers win money.

prize-giving [-givin] *n* a ceremony, usually at a school or after a competition, at which prizes are given to some people □ *the prize-giving ceremony.*

prize money *n* money that is offered or given as a prize, usually in a competition.

prizewinner ['praizwinə'] *n* a person who has won a prize.

pro [prou] (*pl* **pros**) *n* -1. a professional (informal use) □ *Look, I'm a pro, and I believe in doing things well.* □ *After a successful amateur career, he turned pro.* -2. **the pros and cons** the advantages and disadvantages of something □ *We have to weigh up the pros and cons before deciding.*

pro- *prefix* used before a word to show that somebody supports somebody or something □ *pro-environment* □ *pro-nationalist* □ *pro-government.*

PRO *n abbr of* **public relations officer.**

proactive [prou'æktiv] *adj* [approach, attitude, person] that is able to change to improve a situation without being told to do so □ *I chose the firm because they have a proactive policy on women's issues.*

pro-am [ˌprou'æm] ◇ *adj* [tournament, competition] that includes professional and amateur players. ◇ *n* a pro-am tournament, competition etc.

probability [ˌprɒbə'biləti] (*pl* **probabilities**) *n* -1. [of success, failure, victory] the degree to which something is likely or certain to happen □ *The probability of such an outcome is very small.* ■ **in all probability** almost certainly □ *In all probability they've changed their mind.* -2. something that is likely to happen □ *The meeting is a probability rather than a possibility at the moment.*

probable ['prɒbəbl] *adj* [outcome, reason, success] that is likely to happen or be true □ *It's very probable that they'll win.*

probably ['prɒbəbli] *adv* almost certainly □ *You're probably right.* □ *"Will you be able to come?" — "Probably."*

probate ['proubeit] LAW ◇ *n* the legal process of deciding whether or not a will has been made correctly. ◇ *vt* US **to probate a will** to decide whether or not a will has been made correctly.

probation [prou'beiʃn] *n* -1. LAW the system by which some criminals are not sent to prison but must obey the law and report regularly to an official for a fixed period of time □ *He was put on probation for a period of six months.* -2. INDUSTRY the fixed period of time after a person joins a company at the end of which their employer decides if they are good enough to keep the job □ *Teachers are normally on probation for two years.*

probationary [US prou'beiʃəneri, GB -əri] *adj* [teacher, nurse] who is on probation □ *a probationary period.*

probationer [prou'beiʃnə'] *n* -1. INDUSTRY an employee who is on probation. -2. LAW a criminal who is on probation.

probation officer *n* a person whose job is to deal with criminals who are on probation.

probe [proub] ◇ *n* -1. a thorough investigation by a large organization into something that is wrong or illegal □ *They ordered a probe into the company's affairs.* -2. MEDICINE a long, thin, metal instrument used to examine something. -3. **a space probe** a spacecraft that sends information about space back to earth.
◇ *vt* -1. [mystery, crime] to investigate <sthg> thoroughly □ *Officials are probing the company's records.* -2. [earth, hole] to examine <sthg> with one's finger or a pointed object □ *She probed the ground with a stick.*
◇ *vi* **to probe for sthg** to search for sthg □ *They probed for evidence.* ■ **to probe into sthg** to investigate sthg thoroughly □ *They probed into his business affairs.*

probing ['proubiŋ] *adj* [question, look] that is intended to discover the truth.

probity ['proubəti] *n* total honesty (formal use).

problem ['prɒbləm] ◇ *n* -1. something that is difficult to deal with or understand and needs attention and thought □ *money/social problems* □ *He has a drugs problem.* □ *We're having a few problems with our overseas division.* □ *the problem of unemployment/homelessness.* □ *I have no problem with that.* ■ **no problem!** certainly! (informal use) □ *"Could you lend me $5?" — "No problem!"* -2. a question based on numbers, facts etc that needs an answer or solution □ *a mathematical problem.* ◇ *comp* **a problem child** a child who behaves badly and causes difficulties.

problematic(al) [ˌprɒblə'mætik(l)] *adj* that causes problems and is difficult to deal with □ *Arranging transport could be problematic(al).*

problem page *n* GB a section in a newspaper or magazine containing letters from readers describing their problems, followed by answers from an expert suggesting solutions.

procedural [prə'si:dʒərəl] *adj* [matter, problem] that is connected with a particular procedure.

procedure [prə'si:dʒə'] *n* an accepted method or set of actions for doing something □ *constitutional/legal/standard procedure* □ *There is a procedure to follow in case of fire.*

proceed [*vb* prə'si:d, *npl* 'prousi:dz] *vi* -1. **to proceed to do sthg** to begin to do sthg after doing something else □ *She then proceeded to ask me some awkward questions.* -2. to continue □ *Before we proceed any further, ...* □ *The police proceeded with their investigation.* -3. to go in a particular direction (formal use).

♦ **proceeds** *npl* the money earned from selling something or from an event or activity □ *They sold the house and set up their own business with the proceeds.*

proceedings [prə'si:diŋz] *npl* -1. a particular series of events □ *The entire proceedings were* *captured on film.* **-2.** LAW a legal action □ *court/ legal proceedings.*

process [US 'prɒses, GB 'prəʊs-] ◇ *n* **-1.** a series of actions or events that are done by, or that involve, a lot of people or one person or that happen naturally □ *the legal/electoral/ administrative process* □ *It has been a long/slow process.* ▪ **in the process** while doing the thing just mentioned □ *I stretched to catch the ball, and in the process I pulled a muscle.* ▪ **to be in the process of doing sthg** to be doing sthg that one has not finished yet □ *We're in the process of redecorating our house.* **-2.** [in nature, chemistry] a series of natural changes or events □ *a chemical process* □ *the process of digestion* OR *digestive process* □ *the aging process.* **-3.** [for making things] a method of making something, especially a method used in industry □ *The production process has since been refined.* □ *a new process for manufacturing laminated steel.*

◇ *vt* **-1.** [raw material, food] to put <sthg> through a chemical or industrial process □ *Waste is sent abroad for processing.* **-2.** COMPUTING [data, figures] to put <information> into a computer to be examined or dealt with. **-3.** [application, document] to deal with <sthg>, usually as part of an official process □ *Customs officers process thousands of immigrants each month.*

processed food [US 'prɒsest-, GB 'prəʊs-] *n* food that has been specially treated so that it stays fresh for a long time.

processing [US 'prɒsesɪŋ, GB 'prəʊs-] *n: see* **process** □ *automatic data processing.*

procession [prə'seʃn] *n* **-1.** a number of people, vehicles etc moving in the same direction as part of a ceremony, demonstration, or public event □ *a funeral procession.* **-2.** a continuous forward movement of people or things, one after the other □ *They marched in procession.* □ *a constant procession of visitors.*

processor [US 'prɒsesər, GB 'prəʊsesə] *n* **-1.** COMPUTING = **microprocessor.** **-2.** COOKING = **food processor.**

pro-choice *adj* [group, campaigner] that supports a woman's right to have an abortion.

proclaim [prə'kleɪm] *vt* [news, independence] to announce <sthg> publicly or officially □ *The country proclaimed its independence in 1957.* □ *Fiona proudly proclaimed that she'd solved it.*

proclamation [,prɒklə'meɪʃn] *n: see* **proclaim** □ *a proclamation of independence.*

proclivity [prə'klɪvətɪ] (*pl* **proclivities**) *n* a strong natural tendency toward something, especially something bad (formal use).

procrastinate [prəʊ'kræstɪneɪt] *vi* to keep avoiding doing something that one has to do.

procrastination [prəʊ,kræstɪ'neɪʃn] *n: see* **procrastinate.**

procreate ['prəʊkrɪeɪt] *vi* to produce young animals or babies (formal use).

procreation [,prəʊkrɪ'eɪʃn] *n: see* **procreate** (formal use).

proctor ['prɒktər] *n* US EDUCATION a person

who watches students in an exam to make sure they do not cheat.

procurator fiscal [,prɒkjəreɪtə'-] *n* in Scottish law, a person who acts as a coroner and public prosecutor.

procure [prə'kjʊər] *vt* [supplies, assistance, ticket] to get <sthg> that is difficult to obtain □ *First, I suggest you procure the services of a good lawyer.*

procurement [prə'kjʊər'mənt] *n: see* **procure** □ *the Minister in charge of weapons procurement.*

prod [prɒd] (*pt* & *pp* **prodded,** *cont* **prodding**) ◇ *n* **-1.** a quick push with something long and thin such as a finger or a stick □ *She gave him a prod with her stick.* **-2.** a way of reminding somebody about something □ *The money was due yesterday, so I think we should give them a prod.* ◇ *vt* **-1.** to give <sb/sthg> a prod using an object or one's finger □ *He prodded me in the ribs.* **-2.** to cause <sb> to do something by encouraging or persuading them □ *It took two letters to prod him into action/responding.*

prodigal ['prɒdɪgl] *adj* [person] who carelessly wastes money (literary use).

prodigious [prə'dɪdʒəs] *adj* [amount, appetite, memory] unusually large □ *The job generates a prodigious amount of paperwork.*

prodigy ['prɒdədʒɪ] (*pl* **prodigies**) *n* a person, especially a child, who has a great talent for a particular activity □ *a child/an infant prodigy* □ *a musical/mathematical prodigy.*

produce [*vb* prə'dʲuːs, *n* US 'prəʊduːs, GB 'prɒdjuːs] ◇ *vt* **-1.** [equipment, appliances, food] to make <goods>, usually in a factory, in order to sell them □ *Our company produces electrical parts for cars.* **-2.** [work of art, literature] to make <sthg> for other people to see and enjoy □ *She has produced another brilliant novel.* **-3.** [raw material, crop] to provide <sthg> in a particular form as the result of a process; [interest, profit] to cause <sthg> to exist as the result of a process □ *This region produces good wine.* □ *Halogen lamps produce a lot of light.* **-4.** [agreement, reaction, effect] to have <sthg> as a result □ *The experiment produced unexpected results.* **-5.** BIOLOGY [baby, young, offspring] to cause <a child or animal> to be born; [fruit, flower, leaves] to cause <sthg that grows> to appear. **-6.** [object, passport, letter] to bring <sthg> out from inside a package, bag etc to show it to somebody □ *He was then asked to produce his birth certificate.* **-7.** [evidence, argument, document] to find and present <sthg> to somebody in order to prove something □ *They could not produce any proof that she had been at the scene.* **-8.** CINEMA, THEATER, & TV [movie, play, program] to be responsible for the practical aspects of making <sthg>, especially finding the money for it □ *Tonight's show was produced by Steve Bliss.*

◇ *n* **-1.** FARMING a collective term for food produced by farmers □ *dairy/agricultural produce* □ *'Produce of Spain.'* **-2.** a collective term for fruit and vegetables sold in a store □ *They have nice produce at Kroger's.*

producer [prə'dʲuːsər] *n* **-1.** [of goods, food, raw

material] a person, organization, or country that produces something in large amounts or numbers □ *one of the biggest steel producers* □ *the producer country/company.* **-2.** CINEMA, THEATER, & TV the person who produces a play, program etc □ *a movie producer.*

product ['prɒdʌkt] *n* **-1.** INDUSTRY & BUSINESS anything that is made, manufactured, grown etc in order to be sold □ *chemical/pharmaceutical/agricultural products.* **-2. to be a product of sthg** [of a situation, process] to be a result of sthg; [of an upbringing, education] to be a certain way as a result of sthg □ *That's the product of a lively imagination.* □ *He's a product of his environment.*

production [prə'dʌkʃn] *n* **-1.** [of goods, food, raw material] *see* **produce** □ *production costs/methods/systems.* ■ **to go into production** [model, article] to start being produced; [company, factory] to start producing something □ *The car went into production earlier this year.* □ *We're going into production with an advanced version of the system.* ■ **to put sthg into production** to start producing sthg □ *We're putting the new model into production next year.* **-2.** the amount of goods produced □ *Production is up/down on last year.* **-3.** [of a movie, play, program] *see* **produce.** **-4.** THEATER a presentation of a particular play, opera, ballet etc by a particular director or company □ *a theatrical production* □ *Did you see her production of "Peer Gynt"?*

production line *n* a group of machines or groups of workers that make one part of a product only, and then pass it on to the next group of machines or workers □ *He works on the production line.*

production manager *n* the person in charge of production at a factory.

productive [prə'dʌktɪv] *adj* **-1.** [labor force, factory, industry] that produces a lot of goods efficiently; [land, farm] that produces a lot of crops. **-2.** [meeting, visit, relationship] that produces useful or satisfying results □ *I've had a very productive afternoon.*

productively [prə'dʌktɪvlɪ] *adv* [work, operate, use] *He uses his land productively.*

productivity [ˌprɒdʌk'tɪvətɪ] *n* the rate at which goods are produced in relation to the number of workers and machines used □ *Productivity must be increased/improved if the company is to survive.*

productivity deal *n* an agreement between managers and workers that links an increase in pay to an improvement in productivity.

Prof. *abbr of* **Professor.**

profane [prə'feɪn] *adj* [language, expression] that shows no respect for holy and religious things.

profanity [prə'fænətɪ] (*pl* **profanities**) *n* **-1.** a lack of respect for religious and holy things. **-2.** an offensive word or expression.

profess [prə'fes] *vt* [innocence, ignorance, disgust] to claim <sthg>, often falsely □ *He professed a liking for jazz.* □ *He professes to be the inventor of this machine.*

professed [prə'fest] *adj* **-1. a professed athe-**

ist/anarchist etc a person who makes it known that they are an atheist/anarchist etc. **-2.** [love, respect, dislike] that is declared, but not necessarily believed □ *her professed indifference to wealth and status.*

profession [prə'feʃn] *n* **-1.** a job or career, especially one that is generally respected and requires special training □ *She is a doctor by profession.* □ *What made you choose law as your profession?* **-2.** all the people who belong to a particular profession □ *the medical/teaching/legal profession.*

professional [prə'feʃnəl] ◇ *adj* **-1.** [athlete, actor, musician] who does a particular activity or job for money □ *a professional golfer/thief.* **-2.** [person] who has a job that is generally respected and requires special training; [career, qualification] that is connected with a particular profession; [help, opinion] that comes from a person in a particular profession □ *Naomi is a professional woman in her mid-30's.* □ *You should seek professional advice from a lawyer.* **-3.** [job, standard, performance] that is of high quality and shows a desire to do things properly □ *She dealt with the situation in a very professional manner.* □ *It was not very professional of him to leave halfway through the meeting.* ◇ *n* **-1.** a person who is paid for doing something that other people do as a hobby □ *We really need a professional to fix the table.* **-2.** a person who is trained to do a particular job; a person who takes care to do their job well □ *The apartment would suit a young professional.* □ *She's a real professional!*

professional foul *n* a deliberate foul in soccer intended to stop a player of the other team from scoring a goal.

professionalism [prə'feʃnəlɪzm] *n* the skill and serious attitude to work that professional people are expected to have □ *We expect a high level of professionalism from our staff.*

professionally [prə'feʃnəlɪ] *adv* **-1. professionally trained/qualified** trained/qualified to a professional standard. **-2.** [sing, play, act] for money, as a job □ *Jim started playing golf professionally when he was 23.* **-3. to be professionally repaired/installed** to be repaired/installed by a person who is trained in a particular skill □ *The job was done very professionally.* **-4.** [behave] in a way that is expected of a professional in a particular job.

professor [prə'fesər] *n* **-1.** US & CAN a university teacher □ *a college professor* □ *a law professor* □ *She's a professor of* OR *in engineering.* **-2.** GB a teacher of the highest rank at a university, usually the head of a department □ *Professor Alan Stringer.*

professorship [prə'fesərʃɪp] *n* the job or position of a professor.

proffer ['prɒfər] *vt* [object, hand] to hold <sthg> out so that another person can take it; [advice, friendship, help] to offer <sthg> to somebody □ *He proffered his hat.* □ *We all proffered our excuses to her.*

proficiency [prə'fɪʃnsɪ] *n* a high level of skill □ *I aim to achieve proficiency in under a year.* □ *her proficiency in languages.*

proficient [prə'fɪʃnt] *adj* [linguist, swimmer] who has reached a very high standard in a particular skill or activity □ *She's a very proficient athlete.* □ *He became proficient in* OR *at English.*

profile ['prəʊfaɪl] *n* -1. [of a person] the outline of a person's head and face seen from the side □ *I could just make out his profile at the end of the row of seats.* ■ **in profile** seen from the side □ *She looks much better in profile.* ■ **to keep a low profile** to try not to attract attention to oneself □ *I suggest you keep a low profile until this is all over.* -2. MEDIA [of a celebrity, star, politician] a short description, usually for a newspaper or a television program, of somebody's life and character □ *There was a profile of her in the Sunday papers.*

profit ['prɒfət] ◇ *n* -1. BUSINESS money gained in business that is greater than the costs of the business □ *The business is run for profit, not as a charitable concern.* □ *With pretax profits of 60 million dollars, the company has had another successful year.* ■ **to make a profit** to earn more money from business than one spends □ *He made a healthy profit on the deal.* ■ **to sell sthg at a profit** to sell sthg at a higher price than one bought it for. -2. something useful that can be gained by an action □ *Is there any profit in trying to reopen negotiations at this stage?*
◇ *vi* -1. [company, business] to make a profit □ *The company profited nicely from* OR *by its business in Eastern Europe.* -2. [person] to learn a lot from something □ *She spent a year abroad and profited greatly from* OR *by the experience.*

profitability [,prɒfətə'bɪlətɪ] *n* the extent to which a business, investment etc is profitable; the fact of being profitable.

profitable ['prɒfətəbl] *adj* -1. [business, deal, investment] that makes a profit □ *We've had a very profitable six months.* -2. [experience, meeting, visit] useful and worthwhile □ *I found our discussion very profitable.*

profitably ['prɒfətəblɪ] *adv* -1. [deal, sell, invest] in a way that makes a profit. -2. [spend time] usefully.

profit and loss *n* **a profit and loss (statement** US OR **account** GB**)** a document that shows the amounts of money spent and earned by a company during a particular period, and the profit or loss it has made.

profiteering [,prɒfə'tɪərɪŋ] *n* the activity, especially during a war, of making large profits by charging people very high prices for essential goods.

profit-making ◇ *adj* [organization, business] that makes a profit. ◇ *n* the activity of making profits.

profit margin *n* the difference between the selling price of something that makes a profit and the cost of producing it □ *We are looking at ways of increasing our profit margins.*

profit sharing [-ʃeərɪŋ] *n* an arrangement that allows part of a company's profits to be shared among its employees.

profligate ['prɒflɪgət] *adj* [use, expenditure] that wastes something, especially money, in a careless way □ *We must be less profligate with our resources.*

pro forma [-'fɔːrmə] *adj* **a pro forma invoice** an invoice giving details of an order that is sent out before the goods are delivered.

profound [prə'faʊnd] *adj* -1. [apology, despair, silence] that is very strongly felt; [effect, change] that is very noticeable and important □ *She felt a profound sense of sorrow.* □ *It has altered him in a profound way.* -2. [idea, saying, work] that is full of meaning and shows great intelligence and understanding □ *I find his poetry extremely profound.*

profoundly [prə'faʊndlɪ] *adv* -1. **profoundly grateful/upset etc** very grateful/upset etc □ *a profoundly moving piece of music.* -2. [change, affect] in a very noticeable or important way □ *The experience had altered her profoundly.* □ *It irritated him profoundly.*

profuse [prə'fjuːs] *adj* -1. [bleeding, sweat] that is produced in large quantities □ *Profuse tears flowed down his cheeks.* -2. [apologies, thanks] that is expressed with a lot of feeling and words □ *She was profuse in her apologies.*

profusely [prə'fjuːslɪ] *adv* [sweat, bleed, apologize] *see* **profuse** □ *He was profusely apologetic.*

profusion [prə'fjuːʒn] *n* a very large quantity of something □ *a profusion of flowers* □ *Weeds were growing in profusion.*

progeny ['prɒdʒənɪ] *n* the children or descendants of somebody (formal use).

progesterone [prə'dʒestərəʊn] *n* a hormone that prepares the womb for pregnancy.

prognosis [prɒg'nəʊsəs] (*pl* **prognoses** [-iːz]) *n* a judgment or opinion about how something is likely to develop, especially an illness □ *The prognosis for the export business in the coming year is good/bad.*

program ['prəʊgræm] (*pt* & *pp* **programmed**, *cont* **programming**) ◇ *n* -1. COMPUTING a set of instructions that are given to a computer so that it can carry out certain operations □ *a computer program* □ *a word-processing program.* -2. US [of activities, events] a list of planned activities, events etc □ *I have a very full program this week.* □ *What's on the program for tonight?* -3. US RADIO & TV a broadcast □ *There's a program on tonight about alligators.* □ *a TV/radio program.* -4. US EDUCATION a set of studies □ *a degree/MBA program.* -5. US [for a play, concert, match] a small book that people can buy when they go to a cultural or sports event etc that gives them details about the event and the people taking part in it.
◇ *vt* -1. COMPUTING to put a program into <a computer> □ *The system can be programmed to perform a variety of tasks.* -2. US [video, CD player] to instruct <a device> to carry out a certain operation automatically □ *The heat is programmed to come on early in the morning.*

programmable [prəʊ'græməbl] *adj* [washing machine, stereo, video recorder] that can be instructed to carry out certain operations automatically.

programme ['prəʊgræm] GB ◇ *n* [of activites, on

the radio, for a play] = **program.** ◇ vt [video, CD player] = **program.**

programmer ['prougræmər] n COMPUTING a person who writes programs for computers □ a computer programmer.

programming ['prougræmɪŋ] n COMPUTING the activity of writing programs for computers □ a course in computer programming.

programming language n a language of codes and symbols in which computer programs are written.

progress [n US 'prɒgrəs, GB 'prougres, vb prə-'gres] ◇ n -1. [of a person, vehicle] movement in a particular direction, especially toward a destination □ The mountain was steep and our progress was slow. -2. [of work, a project, patient] the gradual development of somebody or something toward a desired state □ There's not much progress to report. ■ **to make progress** [work, project] to come closer to being completed; [patient, student] to improve, especially by one's own efforts □ They've made some/considerable/excellent progress. □ Terry's making progress with OR in his English. -3. [in science, technology] development and improvements in different areas of human life; [of events, a game] the way in which something develops and changes over a period of time □ technological progress □ That's what they call progress, I suppose.
◇ vi -1. [science, technology] to become more advanced; [work, project] to come closer to being completed; [student, patient] to improve □ The study of human genetics is progressing fast. □ The painting is progressing slowly. □ Anna is progressing well at school. -2. [meeting, game, negotiations] to continue and develop in a particular way over a period of time □ As the evening progressed, I began to feel more and more tired. -3. **to progress to sthg** [to the next stage, a higher level] to move on to sthg □ She progressed to flying more powerful planes.
◆ **in progress** adj **to be in progress** to be happening at this moment □ The meeting is still in progress.

progression [prə'greʃn] n -1. the process of going from one situation or state into another □ the progression from childhood to adulthood. -2. a series of events, objects etc that come one after the other.

progressive [prə'gresɪv] adj -1. [politician, method, school] that is influenced by and ready to try new ideas □ She was a young doctor with progressive ideas about psychology. -2. [change, improvement, reduction] gradual and continuous □ He suffered from a progressive loss of memory.

progressively [prə'gresɪvlɪ] adv **to become progressively worse/smaller** to become worse/smaller gradually and continuously □ He got progressively more drunk. □ The dose can be reduced progressively as the patient shows signs of recovery.

progress report n a report that shows how well or badly somebody or something is progressing □ Give me a progress report on the new project. □ a monthly progress report.

prohibit [prou'hɪbət] vt [smoking, alcohol, sale] to forbid <sthg> by using a rule or law □ 'Parking prohibited.' ■ **to prohibit sb from doing sthg** to stop sb from doing sthg by using a rule, law, or order □ Tenants are prohibited from keeping animals as pets.

prohibition [,prouə'bɪʃn] n -1. a rule or law that prohibits something □ a prohibition on the sale of alcohol. -2. the act of prohibiting something □ Prohibition of the practice is the only solution.
◆ **Prohibition** n the period in US history from 1920 to 1933 when the manufacture and sale of liquor was banned; the banning of alcohol.

❦ PROHIBITION
The law introducing Prohibition was an amendment to the US constitution that was made as a result of campaigns by religious and political groups against drunkenness. The law failed to stop Americans from drinking, however. Many made their own alcohol, and many more bought it in illegal drinking clubs called "speakeasies", run by organized criminals who became rich and powerful. People felt the law had no effect, and it was ended in 1933.

prohibitive [prou'hɪbətɪv] adj [cost, tax, amount] that is so expensive that people cannot afford to buy or pay for it.

project [n 'prɒdʒekt, vb prə'dʒekt] ◇ n -1. a plan □ They announced their project to build a new stadium. -2. a piece of work, especially one that follows a plan □ The building project is nearing completion. -3. EDUCATION a long piece of work done by one or more students on a particular subject □ a history/geography project □ project work □ The class is doing a project on pollution.
◇ vt -1. **to be projected** to be planned □ A major road-building operation is projected for next year. -2. [increase, cost] to estimate <the future amount of something> using the information that one has □ Here are next year's projected sales figures. □ a projected rise/fall in output. -3. **to project sthg onto sthg** [light, image, film] to make sthg appear on sthg □ The diagram was projected onto a screen at the front of the auditorium. -4. **to project sb/sthg as sthg** to make sb/sthg appear to be sthg, especially sthg that other people admire □ We're trying to project ourselves as a dynamic, forward-looking company.
◇ vi [piece of rock, object] to stick out from the surface of something □ There was a nail projecting dangerously from the wall.

projectile [US prə'dʒektl, GB -aɪl] n an object that is thrown or fired as a weapon.

projection [prə'dʒekʃn] n -1. [of sales, costs] an estimate based on existing information □ a sales projection. -2. something that sticks out from a surface. -3. [of light, a film] the act of projecting light, film etc onto a surface.

projectionist [prə'dʒekʃnəst] n a person who works the projector at a movie theater.

projection room *n* a room, usually in a movie theater, from which the movies are projected onto a screen.

projector [prə'dʒektər] *n* a device containing a system of lenses and a very bright light that projects an image, slide, movie etc onto a screen □ *a movie projector.*

proletarian [ˌproʊlə'teəriən] *adj* [struggle, person] that is connected with or belongs to the working class.

proletariat [ˌproʊlə'teəriət] *n* **the proletariat** the working class.

pro-life *adj* [group, campaigner] that is opposed to abortion.

proliferate [prə'lɪfəreɪt] *vi* [weeds, pests, cells] to increase in number very quickly and become widespread.

prolific [prə'lɪfɪk] *adj* [writer, artist, composer] who produces many works □ *Her output of books, novels, and articles has been truly prolific.*

prologue ['proʊlɒg] *n* -1. a short section at the beginning of a book, movie etc that is used as an introduction □ *the prologue to the "Canterbury Tales".* -2. **a prologue to sthg** something that happens before sthg and leads on to it □ *These preliminary discussions were a prologue to the actual negotiations.*
NOTE: Compare **epilogue**.

prolong [prə'lɒŋ] *vt* [life, suffering, meeting] to make <sthg> last longer □ *Why prolong the suspense any longer?*

prom [prɒm] *n* -1. US a formal dance for students in high school in the USA □ *She never had a prom date.* -2. GB (*abbr of* **promenade concert**) a concert at which no seats are provided for at least part of the audience □ *We're going to the proms.* -3. *abbr of* **promenade**.

promenade [US ˌprɒmə'neɪd, GB -'nɑːd] *n* GB a wide path built along the edge of the coast in a town.

promenade concert *n* GB = **prom**.

Prometheus [prə'miːθiəs] in Greek mythology, a god who stole fire from the gods and gave it to the human race. He was punished by being chained to a rock.

prominence ['prɒmɪnəns] *n*: *see* **prominent** □ *He rose to prominence during the election campaign.*

prominent ['prɒmɪnənt] *adj* -1. [politician, organization, issue] that is important and attracts a lot of attention □ *He's a prominent member of the Church/critic of the regime.* -2. [landmark, building] that is very noticeable because it stands out from a surface □ *I put the notice in the most prominent place I could find.* □ *She has very prominent cheekbones.*

prominently ['prɒmɪnəntlɪ] *adv* -1. [display, place] in a way that makes something easy to notice □ *The alarm chain is prominently positioned above the door.* -2. [feature, figure] in a way that attracts attention and suggests that somebody or something is important □ *His name figures prominently in our list.*

promiscuity [ˌprɒmɪs'kjuːɪtɪ] *n* promiscuous sexual behavior □ *the risks of promiscuity.*

promiscuous [prə'mɪskjʊəs] *adj* [person] who has sex with a lot of different people.

promise ['prɒmɪs] ◇ *n* -1. a statement that one will definitely do something, often for somebody else's benefit □ *She kept/broke her promise to meet me at the airport.* □ *We received only one promise of support.* ■ **to make a promise** to promise that one will do something □ *You made me a promise, remember?* -2. [of success, recovery, happiness] a sign that something will happen. ■ **to show promise** [musician, student] to do well and show signs that one will do even better in future; [idea, career, project] to show signs of being a success □ *He shows great promise as a writer.*
◇ *vt* -1. **to promise sb sthg** to tell sb that they will definitely have sthg they need or want; to tell sb that sthg will definitely happen □ *You promised me a new car for Christmas.* □ *She promised (that) she would come.* ■ **to promise to do sthg** to state that one will definitely do sthg □ *I promised to finish the job by Friday.* -2. [rain, snow, success] to be a sign that <sthg> will appear or happen in the future. ■ **to promise to be sthg** to seem very likely to be sthg □ *This promises to be an interesting discussion.* □ *He promises to develop into a first-rate mechanic.*
◇ *vi* to make a promise □ *"Will you do that for me?" — "Yes, I promise."*

promising ['prɒmɪsɪŋ] *adj* [start, sign] that suggests something good will happen; [student, musician, career] that shows signs of being successful in the future.

promissory note [US 'prɒmɪsɔːrɪ-, GB -ɪsərɪ-] *n* a signed note promising to pay somebody a particular sum of money on a certain date or when asked for it.

promo ['proʊmoʊ] (*pl* **promos**) *n* something, usually a video, that promotes a product (informal use) □ *a promo copy.*

promontory [US 'prɒməntɔːrɪ, GB -əntrɪ] (*pl* **promontories**) *n* a piece of high land that sticks out into the sea.

promote [prə'moʊt] *vt* -1. [trade, cooperation] to try to help the development of <sthg> □ *The aim of our organization is to promote the cause of world peace.* -2. [product, event, idea] to try to attract public attention to <sthg> by selling it at a special price, talking about it on television or radio etc □ *The band have been touring to promote their new single.* -3. [employee, member of staff] to give <sb> a better job with more money and responsibility □ *She's been promoted to head of the finance department.* -4. SPORT **to be promoted** [team, club] to be allowed to compete in a higher division.

promoter [prə'moʊtər] *n* -1. [of a sports event, concert] a person who organizes something and pays for it to take place □ *a boxing promoter.* -2. [of a cause, idea] a person who supports something and tries to persuade other people to agree.

promotion [prə'moʊʃn] *n* -1. the fact of being given a higher rank or position □ *What are the prospects of promotion?* □ *Trainees can expect to receive a promotion after one year.* -2. [of a product, event] *see* **promote.** **-3.** an event or a campaign to attract attention to a product, movie etc □ *We're having a sales promotion.*

prompt [prompt] ◇ *adj* **-1.** [action, treatment, reply] that is done without delay □ *Prompt payment would be appreciated.* **-2.** [person] who arrives, comes etc exactly at the planned time and not later □ *I'm surprised he's not here, he's usually very prompt.*
◇ *adv* exactly at a particular time and not later □ *The meeting will start at nine o'clock prompt.*
◇ *vt* **-1.** [action, reaction, decision] to cause <sthg> to happen or be done □ *This, in turn, prompted a rude letter from the author.* ■ **to prompt sb to do sthg** to cause or persuade sb to do sthg □ *What prompted her to change her plans so suddenly?* **-2.** THEATER to remind <an actor or actress> of the next line they have to say during a performance.
◇ *n* THEATER a spoken reminder to an actor or actress of the next line they have to say during a performance; the person who gives this reminder.

promptly ['promptlɪ] *adv* **-1.** [act, reply, pay] without delay □ *She promptly went and told everyone that I was pregnant.* **-2.** [arrive, leave] at the planned time and not later □ *They arrived promptly at six.*

promptness ['promptnəs] *n* [of an action, reply, person] *see* **prompt.**

promulgate ['promlgeɪt] *vt* **-1.** [law, decree] to announce <sthg> to the public. **-2.** [belief, idea] to make <sthg> known to many people.

prone [prəʊn] *adj* **-1.** **to be prone to sthg** [to illness, accidents] to be likely to be affected by sthg □ *She's always been very prone to allergies.* ■ **to be prone to do sthg** to have a tendency to do sthg □ *He's prone to make mistakes.* **-2.** [person] who is lying flat on their stomach (formal use).

prong [proŋ] *n* a long point, especially one of those at the end of a fork.

pronoun ['prəʊnaʊn] *n* a word such as "he", "she", or "it" that is used in place of a name or noun.

pronounce [prə'naʊns] ◇ *vt* **-1.** [word, name] to say <sthg> aloud in a particular way □ *How do you pronounce that?* □ *You don't pronounce the "k" in "know".* **-2.** [verdict, decision] to state <sthg> formally □ *Other art experts have pronounced that the work is a fake.* □ *The evening was pronounced a triumph by all.* ■ **to pronounce sb dead/unfit etc** to state formally that sb is dead/unfit etc □ *He was pronounced dead on arrival at the hospital.* ◇ *vi* **to pronounce on sthg** to give an opinion or decision on sthg □ *Experts were asked to pronounce on the validity of the claim.*

pronounced [prə'naʊnst] *adj* [accent, limp, tendency] very noticeable □ *He has a pronounced lisp.*

pronouncement [prə'naʊnsmənt] *n* a formal public statement about something serious □ *The public was outraged by his pronouncements on women and work.*

pronto ['prontoʊ] *adv* without delay (informal use).

pronunciation [prə,nʌnsɪ'eɪʃn] *n* [of a language, word, name] the way in which something is pronounced, especially by somebody speaking a foreign language □ *I'm afraid my pronunciation is not very good.*

proof [pruːf] *n* **-1.** [of a theory, fact, somebody's guilt] something that shows that something is true □ *We must have proof before we can take disciplinary action against them.* □ *They don't have any proof that I was involved.* **-2.** PRINTING [of a text, publication] a first copy of something that is used for making corrections, improvements etc before the final copies are printed □ *a proof copy.* **-3.** [of alcohol] a figure that shows the alcoholic strength of a drink □ *This rum is 47 proof.*

proofread ['pruːfriːd] (*pt* & *pp* **proofread** [-red]) *vt* [text, publication] to check the proofs of <sthg> for mistakes.

proofreader ['pruːfriːdəʳ] *n* a person whose job is to proofread texts or publications.

prop [prop] (*pt* & *pp* **propped,** *cont* **propping**) ◇ *n* **-1.** [for a wall, roof, plant] a support that prevents something from falling down □ *The fence was held up by wooden props.* **-2.** somebody or something that gives support and allows a person, organization etc to continue to work or exist □ *I was using alcohol as some sort of emotional prop.* □ *Expensive cars are really a prop to people's self-esteem.* **-3.** SPORT in rugby, one of the two forwards in the front row of the scrum who support the hooker.
◇ *vt* **to prop sthg against sthg** to lean sthg against sthg to prevent one or both of them from falling or moving, often only for a short time □ *He propped the ladder against the wall.*
◆ **props** *npl* THEATER & CINEMA a collective term for the objects and pieces of furniture that are used in a movie or play.
◆ **prop up** *vt sep* **-1.** **to prop sthg up** [wall, book, plant] to prevent sthg from falling down by using a prop □ *The shelf was propped up with* OR *by bricks.* **-2.** **to prop sthg up** [organization, economy] to make it possible for sthg to continue working or existing □ *The banks won't prop up the company if it shows no sign of returning to profitability.* □ *American troops were sent in to prop up the regime.*

Prop. *abbr of* **proprietor.**

propaganda [,propə'gændə] *n* [for a political party, government, regime] information that is intended to persuade people to support or approve of something and that may be untrue □ *right-wing/communist propaganda* □ *election propaganda.*

propagate ['propəgeɪt] ◇ *vt* **-1.** [seed, species] to cause <a plant or animal> to produce young, especially in large numbers □ *These plants can be propagated by taking cuttings.* **-2.** [idea, religion] to spread <sthg> so that more people believe in it or support it. ◇ *vi* [plant, animal] to grow in number by producing young □ *The species has propagated well in the local conditions.*

propagation [ˌprɒpəˈgeɪʃn] *n*: see **propagate** □ seed propagation.

propane [ˈproʊpeɪn] *n* a gas that is obtained from petroleum and used for cooking and heating. FORMULA: C_3H_8.

propel [prəˈpel] (*pt* & *pp* **propelled**, *cont* **propelling**) *vt* **-1.** [vehicle, boat, rocket] to cause <sthg> to move quickly in a particular direction □ *The blast propelled him through the window.* **-2.** [person] to suddenly cause <sb> to do a particular thing or be in a particular situation □ *He was propelled to fame/into a life of crime.* □ *The country was immediately propelled into war.*

propeller [prəˈpelər] *n* a device with two or more blades that drives a ship or an aircraft by turning very fast □ *a propeller blade.*

propelling pencil [prəˈpelɪŋ-] *n* GB a pencil in which the lead can be moved in or out by twisting or pressing a part of the pencil.

propensity [prəˈpensəti] (*pl* **propensities**) *n* a natural tendency to have particular emotions or patterns of behavior (formal use) □ *He has a propensity for OR to antisocial behavior.* □ *a propensity to act without thinking.*

proper [ˈprɒpər] *adj* **-1.** [job, meal, doctor] that is real and has all the necessary features to be good enough □ *I haven't had a proper weekend off in months.* **-2.** [time, place] correct □ *You will all be told at the proper time.* □ *The proper spelling is with a "g" at the end.* **-3.** [behavior, sentiment] that is morally or socially acceptable but may be thought old-fashioned by some people □ *It wouldn't be right and proper of me to accept.* **-4. the building/ceremony proper** the actual building/ceremony itself rather than something that is connected with it or similar to it □ *The movie proper doesn't begin until five.*

properly [ˈprɒpərli] *adv* **-1.** [spell, pronounce] correctly; [clean, treat] in a satisfactory way □ *I haven't been able to walk properly since the accident.* □ *This place needs taking care of properly.* **-2.** [eat, dress, behave] in a way that other people consider acceptable □ *Sit properly at the table!*

proper noun *n* GRAMMAR the name of a particular person, place, or organization, spelled with a capital letter.

property [ˈprɒpərti] (*pl* **properties**) *n* **-1.** [of a person, organization, government] something that belongs to somebody □ *It appears that the car was stolen property.* □ *'This book is the property of M. J. Thurman.'* **-2.** [for sale] a building or a piece of land owned by a particular person □ *There are several nice properties for sale in the area.* **-3.** BUSINESS a collective term for buildings and land □ *They've been buying up property in the area.* □ *the property market* □ *property prices.* **-4.** [of a chemical, plant, metal] a characteristic that something has □ *the healing properties of garlic.*

property developer *n* a person who buys land in order to build housing, offices etc on it and then sell it at a profit.

property owner *n* a person who owns land or a building.

property tax *n* a tax on land or buildings.

prophecy [ˈprɒfəsi] (*pl* **prophecies**) *n* a statement of what will happen in the future, especially made by somebody with special religious powers □ *The prophecy eventually came true.*

prophesy [ˈprɒfəsaɪ] (*pt* & *pp* **prophesied**) *vt* [disaster, war] to predict that <sthg> will happen □ *Mr Levine prophesied that the war would end within a year.*

prophet [ˈprɒfət] *n* **-1.** RELIGION a religious teacher or leader who is believed to have been chosen by God. **-2.** a person who makes prophecies.

prophetic [prəˈfetɪk] *adj* [remark, warning] that correctly describes something that will happen in the future □ *Her words proved to be prophetic.*

propitious [prəˈpɪʃəs] *adj* [moment, time] that is likely to make something successful (formal use).

proponent [prəˈpoʊnənt] *n* a person who supports something and tries to persuade other people to agree □ *proponents of compulsory education up to the age of 18.*

proportion [prəˈpɔːrʃn] *n* **-1.** a part of something □ *I spend a large proportion of my expenses on travel.* **-2.** a number of people or things when considered as part of a larger group □ *The proportion of women smoking has fallen.* □ *Donor countries are now giving less as a proportion of their GNP than at any time since 1973.* **-3. the proportion of sthg to sthg** the amount of sthg compared to the amount of sthg else □ *The proportion of Catholics to Protestants is two to one.* ■ **in proportion to** OR **with sthg** at the same rate as sthg □ *Wages have not risen in proportion to the cost of living.* ■ **out of all proportion to sthg** much more than is fair or suitable when compared with sthg □ *The prison sentence was out of all proportion to the seriousness of the crime.* **-4. to keep** OR **see things in proportion** to keep a sense of what is important and reasonable □ *You should stop worrying and see things in proportion* ■ **to get sthg out of proportion** to behave as if sthg is more important than it really is □ *The incident has been blown up out of all proportion by the media.* ■ **a sense of proportion** an ability to know which things are important and which things are not □ *The police need to keep a sense of proportion when dealing with young people.* **-5.** ART the relative sizes of objects in a picture, drawing etc. ■ **in proportion** [drawing] that shows everything in its correct size compared with everything else □ *It's difficult to draw things in proportion without checking and measuring.* ■ **out of proportion** [drawing] with objects shown too big or small when compared to other objects □ *Her hand seems out of proportion with the rest of her body.*

◆ **proportions** *npl* the size of something □ *The virus has reached epidemic proportions.*

proportional [prəˈpɔːrʃnəl] *adj* at the same rate

as something else □ *This chart shows income to be proportional to costs.*

proportional representation *n* the system used in elections in which the number of representatives a party has is in proportion to the total number of votes it has received.

proportionate [prə'pɔːʃnət] *adj* [change, increase] that is in the correct proportion to something else □ *Sales have not been proportionate to the costs of promotion.*

proposal [prə'pəʊzl] *n* -1. a suggestion or plan, often written, that people have to think about and decide on □ *I'm against the proposal for a new road* OR *to build a new road.* □ *A new proposal has been submitted.* -2. the act of asking somebody to marry one □ *a proposal of marriage.*

propose [prə'pəʊz] ◇ *vt* -1. to suggest <a plan, solution, action> etc, often in writing, that people can think about and decide on; to formally suggest <sb> for a particular job □ *I propose that we leave at once.* □ *I was pleased when they proposed me for* OR *as their representative.* -2. to introduce <a motion, bill> etc and argue in its favor □ *Frederick proposed the motion "Vegetarianism is good for the soul."* -3. **to propose a toast** to ask people to drink a toast to show appreciation of somebody or wish them good health, success etc □ *I propose a toast to Gary, for cooking this meal.* -4. **to propose doing** OR **to do sthg** to intend to do sthg □ *You don't propose actually driving that thing, do you?*
◇ *vi* to ask somebody to become one's wife or husband □ *He eventually proposed to her.*

proposed [prə'pəʊzd] *adj* [plan, solution, trip] suggested or planned.

proposition [,prɒpə'zɪʃn] ◇ *n* -1. a statement of an opinion or idea that is made so that people can discuss it □ *Given Schleber's proposition that human beings are born unequal...* -2. a suggestion for a plan or action □ *We discussed the proposition to merge/that the companies should merge.* □ *He has made us an attractive proposition.* ◇ *vt* to ask <sb> to have sex with one, especially when one does not know them well.

propound [prə'paʊnd] *vt* [theory, problem, argument] to suggest and explain <sthg> so that other people can consider it.

proprietary [US prə'praɪəterɪ, GB -ətrɪ] *adj* [medicine, cosmetic] that is sold under a brand name (formal use).

proprietor [prə'praɪətər] *n* the owner of a business □ *a newspaper proprietor.*

proprietorial [prə,praɪə'tɔːrɪəl] *adj* [attitude, manner, tone] showing that one thinks that one owns and has complete power over something or somebody.

propriety [prə'praɪətɪ] *n* correct social and moral behavior (formal use).

propulsion [prə'pʌlʃn] *n* the force that makes something, especially a vehicle, move forward or upward □ *jet/rocket propulsion.*

pro rata [US -'reɪtə, GB -'rɑːtə] ◇ *adj* [increase, payment] that is calculated according to how much is used, worked etc by each person □ *The proceeds of the concert were shared on a pro rata basis.* ◇ *adv* [increase, pay] *For people who have worked for less than one year, the bonus will be divided pro rata.*

prosaic [prəʊ'zeɪɪk] *adj* [life, style, job] that seems ordinary and uninteresting □ *the dull, prosaic routine of Geraldine Macarthur's life.*

Pros. Atty *abbr of* **prosecuting attorney**.

proscenium [prə'siːnɪəm] (*pl* **prosceniums** OR **proscenia** [-nɪə]) *n* a proscenium (**arch**) the frame for the main curtain over the front of the stage in a theater.

proscribe [prəʊ'skraɪb] *vt* [drug, organization, activity] to ban <sthg> officially, especially because it is considered dangerous (formal use).

prose [prəʊz] *n* written language that is not poetry □ *a prose drama/translation* □ *Write it clearly, in plain English prose.*

prosecute ['prɒsɪkjuːt] LAW ◇ *vt* to accuse <sb> of a crime and bring a charge against them in a court of law □ *'Trespassers will be prosecuted'* □ *She was prosecuted for theft.* ◇ *vi* -1. [police] *They have decided not to prosecute.* -2. [barrister] to act as the prosecutor in a trial in court □ *David Olsen, prosecuting, proceeded to list the grisly details of the case.*

prosecuting attorney [,prɒsɪkjuːtɪŋ-] *n* an attorney who acts on behalf of the government in court cases in the USA.

prosecution [,prɒsɪ'kjuːʃn] *n* -1. **the prosecution** the people, especially the lawyers, who prosecute somebody in a trial in court □ *The prosecution is presenting its case tomorrow.* -2. [of a suspect, spy] the act of prosecuting somebody □ *The state brought a successful prosecution against the bookstore.*

prosecutor ['prɒsɪkjuːtər] *n* a lawyer in a court of law who tries to prove that the person accused of a crime is guilty.

prospect [*n* 'prɒspekt, *vb* US 'prɒspekt, GB prə'spekt] ◇ *n* -1. [of a change, improvement] a possibility that something desirable will happen □ *I see no immediate prospect of a cut in interest rates.* □ *There's little prospect of Harry arriving now.* -2. [of work, a trip] something that will happen soon □ *I don't look forward to the prospect of staying with my mum.* ◇ *vi* to look for gold, silver, oil etc in a particular area with the intention of mining it □ *The company is prospecting for oil in the area.*

◆ **prospects** *npl* the chances of somebody or something of being successful in the future □ *What are the prospects for this year's harvest?* □ *That young man has good prospects.*

prospecting [US 'prɒspektɪŋ, GB prə'spektɪŋ] *n* the activity of prospecting for gold, silver, oil etc □ *a prospecting company.*

prospective [prə'spektɪv] *adj* -1. **a prospective buyer/candidate etc** somebody who is likely or expected to buy something/be a candidate for something etc □ *She is the prospective Democratic candidate in the forthcoming election.* -2. **a prospective event/deal** an event/a deal that is likely to happen □ *Many people* *have protested at the prospective increase in taxes.*

prospector [US ˈprɒspektr, GB prəˈspektə] *n* a person who prospects for gold, silver, oil etc.

prospectus [prəˈspektəs] (*pl* **prospectuses**) *n* a small book published by a university, school, or company giving details about its activities and advertising its advantages.

prosper [ˈprɒspəʳ] *vi* -1. [person, business] to become successful and rich □ *After three difficult years, Luigi's restaurant began at last to prosper.* -2. [child, plant] to develop well and healthily □ *Ferns prosper in humid conditions.*

prosperity [prɒˈsperətɪ] *n* the state of being successful and getting enough money to live well □ *It was a period of great prosperity.*

prosperous [ˈprɒspərəs] *adj* [person, business, country] successful and rich □ *the prosperous suburbs of the city.*

prostate [ˈprɒsteɪt] *n* **the prostate (gland)** an organ in the body of males that produces the liquid in which sperm is carried □ *prostate cancer.*

prosthesis [prɒsˈθiːsəs] (*pl* **prostheses** [-ˈθiːsiːz]) *n* an artificial leg, eye, tooth etc, used to replace one that is missing.

prostitute [ˈprɒstətjuːt] *n* a person, usually a woman, who has sex with people for money □ *a male/child prostitute.*

prostitution [ˌprɒstəˈtjuːʃn] *n* the work or business of prostitutes □ *She turned to prostitution.*

prostrate [*adj* ˈprɒstreɪt, *vb* US ˈprɒstreɪt, GB prɒˈstreɪt] ◇ *adj* -1. lying flat on the ground with one's face downward, because one is tired, scared etc □ *He lay prostrate on the floor.* -2. **to be prostrate** to be so weak or upset by something bad that has happened that one cannot do anything □ *prostrate with grief.* ◇ *vt* **to prostrate oneself** to lie down in a prostrate position because one fears, respects, or is worshiping somebody.

protagonist [prouˈtægənəst] *n* -1. one of the main people in a story or in a real conflict or argument □ *At this point, our protagonist decides to rebel.* -2. one of the main people supporting something new □ *ITC is one of the leading protagonists of change in the sector.*

protect [prəˈtekt] *vt* [person, country, rights] to keep <sb/sthg> safe so that they are not harmed or damaged □ *The castle was built to protect the area from attack.* □ *The cream protects your skin against harmful ultraviolet rays.* □ *It is forbidden to hunt tigers — they are a protected species.*

protection [prəˈtekʃn] *n* the act of protecting somebody or the state of being protected □ *police/consumer protection* □ *The drug gives protection from malaria.* □ *He asked for protection against his enemies.*

protectionism [prəˈtekʃnɪzm] *n* an official policy of protecting the industry in one's country against foreign competitors.

protectionist [prəˈtekʃnəst] *adj* [policy, politician] that favors protectionism.

protection money *n* money paid to criminals by somebody who has been threatened with attack or damage if they do not pay.

protective [prəˈtektɪv] *adj* -1. [layer, clothing, coloring] that protects somebody or something from harm or damage □ *The machine has a protective plastic cover.* -2. [person] who has a strong wish to protect a child or weaker person against harm or bad influences □ *Like most mothers, she was* OR *felt very protective toward her children.* □ *protective feelings/instincts.*

protective custody *n* the practice of keeping a person in prison for their own safety.

protector [prəˈtektəʳ] *n* -1. [of a person, country] a person who protects somebody or something □ *The lawyer was an ardent protector of civil rights.* -2. [on a machine, body] something that protects people from being hurt or injured □ *a pair of eye protectors.*

protectorate [prəˈtektərət] *n* a country that is controlled and protected by another country that is more powerful.

protégé [ˈproutəʒeɪ] *n* a person whose career is helped and guided by somebody older and more powerful or influential.

protégée [ˈproutəʒeɪ] *n* a female protégé.

protein [ˈproutiːn] *n* a substance found in foods such as meat, eggs, and beans that the body needs in order to grow and repair damage □ *He's on a high-protein diet.*

protest [*n* ˈproutest, *vb* prəˈtest] ◇ *n* a statement or action, often made in public, showing that one disapproves of something, especially because it is not fair □ *I would like to make* OR *register a protest about the way I've been treated.* □ *The news of his detention was greeted by a storm of protest.* □ *The manager resigned in protest at* OR *against the planned merger.* □ *a protest rally/movement/demonstration* ■ **under protest** unwillingly □ *I'll do it, but under protest.*
◇ *vt* -1. to state very strongly that <sthg> is true after other people have said it is not □ *He continued to protest his innocence.* □ *I protested that I was not responsible for the mistake.* -2. US [war, action, decision] to make a protest about <sthg>.
◇ *vi* to make a protest, often together with other people □ *We protested at* OR *about the condition of the hotel.* □ *Teachers are protesting against the cuts in spending on education.*

Protestant [ˈprɒtəstənt] ◇ *n* a member of one of the Christian churches that separated from Roman Catholicism in the 16th century. ◇ *adj*: *a Protestant church/school/service.*

Protestantism [ˈprɒtəstəntɪzm] *n* the beliefs held by Protestants.

protestation [ˌprɒtəˈsteɪʃn] *n* [of love, friendship] a very strong statement that something is true (formal use) □ *Carlos was eventually imprisoned, despite his protestations of innocence.*

protester [prəˈtestəʳ] *n* a person who protests against something, especially actively and in public □ *Several protesters were arrested during the rally.*

protest march *n* a procession in which people walk a long distance to protest against a law, policy etc.

protestor [prə'testə^r] *n* = **protester**.

protocol ['prəʊtəkɒl] *n* the rules, sometimes unwritten, about how people should behave on formal or official occasions □ *What is the correct protocol in these matters?*

proton ['prəʊtɒn] *n* a particle with a positive electrical charge in the nucleus of an atom.

prototype ['prəʊtətaɪp] *n* [of a car, machine] a first model or version of something that can be tested and improved before the final version is made □ *a prototype airplane* □ *This is the prototype of the first steam engine.*

protracted [prə'træktəd] *adj* [illness, delay, absence] that lasts a long time, often longer than is necessary or expected □ *After protracted discussions, an agreement was finally made.*

protractor [prə'træktə^r] *n* a flat piece of plastic or metal in the form of half a circle, used for measuring angles.

protrude [prə'truːd] *vi* [teeth, rock] to stick out from or through a surface □ *The pipe protruded from the wall a few centimeters.*

protrusion [prə'truːʒn] *n* something that protrudes from somewhere.

protuberance [prə'tʲuːbərəns] *n* a rounded part of something that sticks out above the surface (formal use).

proud [praʊd] *adj* **-1.** [person] who is full of satisfaction and pleasure because of something they have done or been connected with □ *She's very proud of* OR *about her new job.* □ *We are proud to present our new range of designer ski-wear.* □ *I was very proud that they asked me to speak.* □ *a proud smile/letter/ achievement.* **-2.** [person, people, race] that is full of self-respect □ *They are too proud to ask for help.* **-3.** [person] who feels very strongly that they are better or more important than other people (disapproving use) □ *He is too proud to apologize.*

proudly ['praʊdlɪ] *adv* [speak, behave] *see* **proud** □ *The parents looked on proudly as their son was handed the prize.* □ *We proudly present one of the world's leading trumpet players.*

Proust [pruːst], **Marcel** (1871–1922) a French writer whose most famous work is *Remembrance of Things Past.*

provable ['pruːvəbl] *adj* [theory, guilt] that can be proved to be true.

prove [pruːv] (*pt* **proved**, *pp* **proved** OR **proven**) *vt* **-1.** [fact, argument] to show that <sthg> is definitely true, using facts, information etc □ *The evidence seems to prove his guilt.* □ *I shall prove to you that I was right.* □ *It has been scientifically proven that this shampoo is harmful to your hair.* □ *Her argument was proved wrong.* **-2. to prove (to be) sthg** to be shown or seen to be sthg after some time has passed □ *She has proved to be a better worker than I expected.* □ *This scandal could prove highly damaging to the company.* ■ **to prove oneself** to show that one is a particular thing by one's actions □ *He proved himself to be an excellent cook.*

proven ['pruːvn] ◇ *past participle of* **prove**. ◇ *adj* [fact, liar, ability] that has been proved.

Provençal [ˌprɒvɒn'sɑːl] *n* & *adj*: *see* **Provence**.

Provence [prɒ'vɒns] a region of southeastern France, on the Mediterranean coast.

proverb ['prɒvɜːb] *n* a short well-known saying that expresses some general truth or advice □ *That well-known proverb "Better late than never" springs to mind!*

proverbial [prə'vɜːbjəl] *adj* **-1.** a word used to show that one is quoting a well-known saying or expression □ *The proverbial calm before the storm.* **-2. to be proverbial** to be known about by many people □ *Derek's drinking habits are proverbial.*

provide [prə'vaɪd] *vt* [food, answer, example] to give or make <sthg> available to somebody who needs or wants it □ *All meals will be provided.* □ *The company has provided me with a car.* □ *We can provide accommodation for twenty people.*
◆ **provide for** *vt fus* **-1. to provide for sb** to support sb by giving them the money, food etc that they need □ *I have a family to provide for.* **-2. to provide for sthg** [for a possibility, emergency] to make arrangements for things to be done if sthg happens (formal use) □ *We hope that the new plans provide for every eventuality.*

provided [prə'vaɪdəd] *conj* **provided (that)** a word used to introduce something that must happen if something else is also to happen □ *We should be home by ten, provided (that) we don't get lost.*

providence ['prɒvədəns] *n* the force, such as God or fate, that is believed to control events and protect people's lives □ *Some see it as an act of divine providence.*

providential [ˌprɒvə'denʃl] *adj* [help, escape] that happens completely by chance at exactly the time it is needed (formal use).

provider [prə'vaɪdə^r] *n* a person who provides somebody with the food, money etc they need to live.

providing [prə'vaɪdɪŋ] *conj* = **provided**.

province ['prɒvəns] *n* **-1.** [of a country] a large and important part of a country that has its own government or governor □ *the province of Quebec.* **-2.** [of a person] an area of knowledge that somebody is especially interested in or trained in; an area of work that somebody is personally responsible for □ *I don't know anything about that, it's not really my province.* □ *Company law is outside my province.*
◆ **provinces** *npl* **the provinces** the parts of a country that are far from its capital or main city □ *The Chathams live in the provinces.*

provincial [prə'vɪnʃl] *adj* **-1.** [town, newspaper] that is in or from the provinces □ *Larry's working at one of the provincial theaters in the north.* **-2.** [person, attitude] that is unwilling to accept new or different ideas and customs (disapproving use) □ *They're so narrow-minded and provincial.*

provision [prə'vɪʒn] *n* **-1.** [of food, resources, funds] the act of giving, supplying, or making something available to somebody □ *The* committee is responsible for the provision of library services. **-2. to make provision for sb/sthg** [for the future, one's family] to make arrangements and preparations to supply the possible future needs of sb/sthg □ *I have made provision for my wife in my will.* **-3.** [in an agreement, law] a condition or demand □ *Under the provisions of the contract, you will be expected to complete the work by June.* □ *I accept your terms with the provision that the money is paid in advance.*

◆ **provisions** *npl* supplies of food and drink □ *Toward the end of the expedition our provisions began to run low.*

provisional [prə'vɪʒnəl] *adj* [arrangement, result, decision] that has been arranged or decided for the present but is likely to be changed at some time in the future.

Provisional IRA *n* **the Provisional IRA** the part of the Irish Republican Army that is prepared to use violence and terrorism to achieve its aims.

provisional licence *n* GB a driving license used by people until they have passed their driving test.

provisionally [prə'vɪʒnəlɪ] *adv* [agree, arrange] *see* **provisional** □ *We've set the date for the meeting provisionally for next Tuesday.*

proviso [prə'vaɪzou] (*pl* **provisos**) *n* a demand or condition that must be fulfilled before an agreement is accepted □ *I accepted the job with the proviso that the company paid my moving costs.*

Provo ['prouvou] (*pl* **Provos**) *n* a member of the Provisional IRA (informal use).

provocation [ˌprɒvə'keɪʃn] *n* [of a person, animal] *see* **provoke** □ *Tony gets angry at the slightest provocation.*

provocative [prə'vɒkətɪv] *adj* **-1.** [book, remark] that is likely to or intended to cause anger, discussion etc. **-2.** [smile, dance, clothing] that is intended to excite sexual desire.

provocatively [prə'vɒkətɪvlɪ] *adv* [say, dance] *see* **provocative** □ *a provocatively low-cut dress.*

provoke [prə'vouk] *vt* **-1.** to deliberately try to make <a person or an animal> annoyed or angry □ *He was provoked into saying things he later regretted.* □ *Don't provoke him, he'll bite.* **-2.** to cause <an unpleasant feeling, situation> etc □ *Are you trying to provoke a fight?* □ *The senator's proposal provoked a storm of protest.*

provoking [prə'voukɪŋ] *adj* annoying.

provost [US 'prouvoust, GB 'prɒvəst] *n* **-1.** in the USA, a high-ranking university official. **-2.** in Britain, the head of a university college. **-3.** in Scotland, the head of a town council.

prow [prau] *n* the front end of a ship or boat.

prowess ['prauəs] *n* great ability or skill (literary use).

prowl [praul] ◇ *vi* [person, animal] to move around quickly and carefully, trying not to be noticed, especially in order to attack somebody or steal something □ *Susan thought she heard someone prowling around out-*

side the house. ◇ *vt* to prowl through or around <a place>. ◇ *n* **to be on the prowl** to be prowling.

prowl car *n* US a police car that travels around an area to see what is happening.

prowler ['praulər] *n* a person who prowls around at night in order to harm people, steal from houses etc.

proximity [prɒk'sɪmətɪ] *n* **proximity to sthg** the fact of being near to sthg □ *One advantage of this house is its proximity to the station.* ■ **in the proximity of sthg** close to sthg □ *Fergus had spent in the proximity of $5000.*

proxy ['prɒksɪ] (*pl* **proxies**) *n* a person who has been given the right to act or speak for someone else, e.g. in an election or at a meeting; the right given to a person in this situation □ *My husband will act as proxy for me.* □ *proxy votes.* ■ **by proxy** by having somebody else act or speak for one □ *I voted by proxy.*

Prozac™ ['prouzæk] *n* a drug designed to stop people from being depressed.

prude [pruːd] *n* a prudish person (disapproving use) □ *Don't be such a prude!*

prudence ['pruːdns] *n*: *see* **prudent** (formal use).

prudent ['pruːdnt] *adj* [person] who thinks carefully and sensibly before making decisions □ *a prudent decision/policy* □ *It would be prudent not to mention her name.*

prudently ['pruːdntlɪ] *adv* [act, behave, decide] *see* **prudent**.

prudish ['pruːdɪʃ] *adj* [person] who is easily shocked by things that are considered rude, especially sex (disapproving use) □ *a prudish remark.*

prune [pruːn] ◇ *n* a dried plum. ◇ *vt* to cut branches off <a tree, bush> etc so that it will grow better.

prurient ['pruərɪənt] *adj* [person] who has an unpleasantly strong interest in the sexual activities of other people (formal use).

pry [praɪ] (*pt* & *pp* **pried** [praɪd]) ◇ *vi* to try to find out about somebody's private life, often by watching them or by asking personal questions (disapproving use) □ *I told him not to pry into my private life.* □ *You shouldn't pry.* ◇ *vt* **to pry sthg open/off** to force sthg open/off □ *I tried to pry off the lid with a knife.*

PS (*abbr of* **postscript**) *n* a note added at the end of a letter or document □ *PS – Don't forget to write!*

psalm [sɑːm] *n* a song or poem in praise of God, especially one from the Bible.

PSBR (*abbr of* **public sector borrowing requirement**) *n* **the PSBR** the amount of money that a government has to borrow from banks and the public because it has spent more than it has collected in taxes.

pseudo- ['sjuːdou] *prefix* added to words to show that one thinks that something does not deserve a particular description □ *pseudo-scientific* □ *pseudo-literary.*

pseudonym ['sjuːdənɪm] *n* a name used by

somebody, especially a writer, when they do not want to use their real name.

psi (*abbr of* **pounds per square inch**) a unit for measuring pressure.

psoriasis [sə'raɪəsəs] *n* a disease that causes itchy red patches and spots on the skin.

psst [pst] *excl* a sound used to attract somebody's attention without other people noticing.

PST (*abbr of* **Pacific Standard Time**) *n* the local time in the Pacific coastal region of the USA and Canada.

psych [saɪk] ◆ **psych up** *vt sep* **to psych oneself up** to prepare oneself mentally for something difficult, especially by telling oneself that one can do it well (informal use) □ *I had to psych myself up to go into his office.*

psyche ['saɪki] *n* a person's personality, mind, feelings, and attitudes.

psychedelic [,saɪkə'delɪk] *adj* **-1.** [drug] that affects one's mind and makes one see and hear strange things and have strange ideas. **-2.** [art, music, pattern] that uses strong patterns, colors, lights, or sounds.

psychiatric [,saɪkɪ'ætrɪk] *adj* **a psychiatric hospital/unit** a hospital/unit where people with mental illnesses are treated. ■ **a psychiatric patient** a person who is being treated for a mental illness.

psychiatric nurse *n* a nurse who has been trained to treat patients who have mental illnesses.

psychiatrist [saɪ'kaɪətrəst] *n* a doctor who has been trained in psychiatry.

psychiatry [saɪ'kaɪətrɪ] *n* the study and treatment of mental illnesses.

psychic ['saɪkɪk] ◇ *adj* **-1.** [person] who has strange powers that cannot be explained by science, such as an ability to read people's minds or predict future events □ *psychic powers.* **-2.** [disorder, damage] that affects the mind, not the body. ◇ *n* a person with psychic powers, especially the ability to receive messages from dead people.

psychoanalysis [,saɪkouə'næləsəs] *n* the medical examination or treatment of somebody with a mental problem by asking them about their feelings, dreams, and past experiences in order to find the hidden causes of the problem.

psychoanalyst [,saɪkou'ænələst] *n* a person trained in psychoanalysis.

psychoanalyze US, **psychoanalyse** GB [,saɪkou'ænəlaɪz] *vt* to examine or treat <sb> using psychoanalysis.

psychological [,saɪkə'lɒdʒɪkl] *adj* **-1.** [damage, barrier, development] that is connected with the mind and thoughts of people □ *She has a lot of psychological problems.* **-2.** [test, study] that is connected with psychology.

psychological warfare *n* attempts to make an enemy lose courage and confidence by spreading fear, giving false information etc.

psychologist [saɪ'kɒlədʒəst] *n* a person who has been trained in psychology.

psychology [saɪ'kɒlədʒɪ] *n* **-1.** the scientific study of the mind and how it affects people's behavior □ *child/behavioral psychology* □ *I had to use a little psychology to get him to agree.* **-2.** [of a person, group] the way in which a particular person or group thinks and how this affects their attitudes and behavior.

psychometric [,saɪkə'metrɪk] *adj* **a psychometric test** a test designed to measure people's intelligence and mental abilities.

psychopath ['saɪkəpæθ] *n* a person with a serious disease of the mind who behaves very violently toward other people and feels no guilt.

psychosis [saɪ'kousəs] (*pl* **psychoses** [-'kousi:z]) *n* a very serious mental illness such as schizophrenia or paranoia.
NOTE: Compare **neurosis**.

psychosomatic [,saɪkəsə'mætɪk] *adj* [illness, condition] that is caused by mental problems such as fear, unhappiness, or stress and not by something physical.

psychotherapy [,saɪkou'θerəpɪ] *n* the treatment of mental conditions using psychological methods rather than drugs, operations etc.

psychotic [saɪ'kɒtɪk] ◇ *n* a person who suffers from psychosis. ◇ *adj*: *psychotic behavior.*

pt -1. *abbr of* **pint. -2.** *abbr of* **point.**

Pt. (*abbr of* **Point**) on a map, used to refer to a thin strip of land sticking out into the ocean □ *Hartland Pt.*

PT *n abbr of* **physical training.**

PTA (*abbr of* **parent-teacher association**) *n* an organization formed by the parents and teachers of children at a particular school that organizes social events for the good of the school.

Pte MILITARY *abbr of* **private.**

PTO ◇ *n* (*abbr of* **parent-teacher organization**) US = **PTA.** ◇ (*abbr of* **please turn over**) a phrase written at the bottom of a page to show that there is something written on the other side.

Ptolemy ['tɒləmɪ] (90–168 AD) a Greek scientist who believed that the planets and stars went round the Earth.

PTSD *n abbr of* **post-traumatic stress disorder.**

PTV *n* **-1.** *abbr of* **pay television. -2.** (*abbr of* **public television**) = **PBS.**

pub [pʌb] *n* GB & AUS a building with one or two rooms where beer and other drinks are sold and where people meet socially; the people in this building □ *a pub sign/lunch/landlord* □ *The whole pub seemed to be watching me.*

❦ PUB
Pubs play an important part in British social life, particularly in the country, where the local pub is often the main meeting place for the community. In larger towns there are many types of pub: some have music and games and appeal to young people, while others serve meals and welcome families. Traditionally, pubs only admitted peo-

ple over 18, and had to close in the afternoons and after 11 pm, but these rules have been changed recently.

pub. *abbr of* **published.**

pub crawl *n* GB **to go on a pub crawl** to go to several pubs, one after the other, and have a drink in each one (informal use).

puberty ['pjuːbɜ'tɪ] *n* the time in a person's life when their body becomes adult and they become able to produce children □ *Once the child reaches puberty...*

pubescent [pjuˈbesnt] *adj* [girl, boy] who is at the age of puberty.

pubic ['pjuːbɪk] *adj* **pubic hair/bones** hair/bones near a person's sexual organs.

public ['pʌblɪk] ◇ *adj* **-1.** [support, concern, health] that affects people in general □ *The announcement attracted a lot of public interest.* **-2.** [office, servant] that belongs to or is connected with the government or state acting for people in general □ *increased public spending.* **-3.** [library, announcement, meeting] that exists for everybody to use, see, or go to □ *a public telephone/park* □ *The government has decided to set up a public inquiry.* □ *Do you think we could talk somewhere less public?* **-4.** [figure, life] that is not secret and is known by everybody □ *The party needs to improve its public image.* □ *It's public knowledge that the company is about to go bust.* ■ **to go public on** OR **about sthg** to let everybody know about sthg that has been a secret (informal use) □ *The government has gone public on its plans to build more roads.* ■ **to make sthg public** [views, news] to tell the public about sthg that has been a secret □ *His death has only just been made public.* **-5.** BUSINESS **to go public** to become a public company by selling shares on the open market.
◇ *n* **the public** ordinary people in general □ *We invite letters from members of the public.* □ *The house is not open to the public.* □ *The public has a right to know.* □ *the newspaper-reading public.* ■ **in public** with other people present, including strangers □ *He says one thing in private and something very different in public.*

public-address system *n* an electrical system that allows music or somebody's voice to be heard by everyone in a building, ship etc.

publican ['pʌblɪkən] *n* a person who owns or manages a pub.

publication [ˌpʌblɪˈkeɪʃn] *n* **-1.** [of a book, magazine] the act of publishing something and sending it to shops to be sold □ *the publication of the report's findings* □ *The book is nearing publication.* **-2.** [of information] the act of making something available to people in general. **-3.** a book, magazine etc that has been published □ *The catalog contains details of our latest publications.*

public bar *n* GB a separate bar in a pub that is not as comfortable or well-furnished as the other bar and where the drinks are cheaper.

public company *n* GB a company whose shares are listed on the stock exchange and can be bought by the general public. NOTE: Compare **private limited company.**

public convenience *n* GB a toilet provided by local government that anybody can use, sometimes for a small payment.

public domain *n* **to be in the public domain** [book, software, information] to be available for anybody to use freely and without payment.

public health *n* the care of people's health by a government or other official body, including medical treatment and the prevention of disease □ *Public health authorities insist there is no cause for alarm.*

public holiday *n* a day in the year when most people in a particular country do not work.

public house *n* GB = **pub** (formal use).

public housing *n* US houses or apartments built by the government for poor people.

publicist ['pʌbləsəst] *n* a person whose job is to publicize things.

publicity [pʌbˈlɪsətɪ] *n* **-1.** public attention and interest produced especially by newspapers, television etc □ *The scandal received a lot of publicity in the press.* **-2.** advertising, information etc intended to attract public interest and attention, e.g. when trying to sell something □ *She's in charge of publicity at the National Opera.* □ *a publicity campaign/agent.*

publicity stunt *n* an event arranged especially to attract publicity (disapproving use).

publicize, -ise ['pʌblɪsaɪz] *vt* [event, policy, danger] to make <sthg> known to the public as widely as possible, especially through newspapers, television etc □ *the Senator's well-publicized views on the need to cut spending.*

public limited company *n* GB = **public company.**

publicly ['pʌblɪklɪ] *adv* [meet, discuss] in public □ *I feel I have been publicly humiliated.*

public office *n* a job in government, e.g. as a member of Congress □ *She has what it takes to hold/run for public office.*

public opinion *n* the opinions of people in general at a particular time □ *We did a public-opinion survey of attitudes to television.* □ *Public opinion has changed on this issue.*

public ownership *n* ownership and management of businesses, buildings etc by the state □ *Most health services are still in* OR *under public ownership.*

public prosecutor *n* in Britain, a government official appointed by the state to bring criminal charges against people in courts of law.

public relations ◇ *n* work done by a company or organization to encourage the public to have a good opinion of it, especially by providing information; the department that does this work □ *a public relations exercise* □ *She works in public relations.* ◇ *npl* good relations between a company or organization and the public □ *Supporting charity events is good for public relations.*

public relations officer *n* a person who

works in public relations for a company or organization.

public school *n* -1. in the USA, Australia, and Scotland, a local school controlled and funded by the state that provides free education. -2. in Britain, a private school for children aged from 13 to 18, whose parents pay to send them there and who usually live there during the term.

public sector *n* the industries and services of a country that are owned and controlled by the government, e.g. education and roads □ *Wages are much lower in the public sector.* □ *public-sector industries.*

public servant *n* a government official or employee.

public service *n* -1. something, e.g. gas, garbage collection, or transportation, that is provided by a government for all the people in an area □ *a strike by public-service workers.* -2. work that is concerned with helping other people rather than making money for oneself □ *The title is given in recognition of her years of public service.* -3. = **civil service**.

public service vehicle *n* GB a bus or other vehicle licensed to carry passengers.

public-spirited *adj* [attitude, person] showing an active interest in the good of the society that one lives in □ *That was very public-spirited of you!*

public transportation US, **public transport** *n* trains, buses etc that anybody can use □ *Chicago's public-transportation system.*

public utility *n* a service for the public, e.g. the supply of gas, electricity, or water, that is usually under some degree of government control □ *public-utility companies.*

public works *npl* buildings, roads etc provided by the government for public use.

publish ['pʌblɪʃ] ◇ *vt* -1. [company, government] to do the work needed to produce and sell <a book, magazine> etc □ *The journal is published monthly.* -2. [newspaper, magazine, editor] to include <an article, letter, photograph> etc in a newspaper or magazine and have it printed □ *The newspaper refused to publish the name of the politician involved in the scandal.* -3. [writer, musician] to have <a book, article, piece of music> etc published □ *He has published books on both politics and history.* -4. to make <information, an opinion> etc known to the public, usually by having it published and printed □ *The government has refused to publish the commission's findings.* □ *Their statement was published last week.*
◇ *vi* [company, government] *We publish in nine different languages.*

publisher ['pʌblɪʃər] *n* a company, organization, or person that publishes books, magazines etc □ *I got a rejection from yet another publisher.*

publishing ['pʌblɪʃɪŋ] *n* the business of publishing books, magazines etc □ *She works in publishing.*

publishing company, publishing house *n* a company that publishes books.

pub lunch *n* GB a meal bought and eaten in a pub in the middle of the day that is usually quite simple and cheap.

Puccini [pʊ'tʃiːnɪ], **Giacomo** (1858–1924) an Italian composer whose operas include *La Bohème* and *Tosca.*

puce [pjuːs] *adj* dark brown-red in color.

puck [pʌk] *n* a hard, flat, round piece of rubber that one hits with a stick in ice hockey.

pucker ['pʌkər] ◇ *vt* to twist <one's lips or face> so that little folds or lines appear, especially when one is frowning or concentrating □ *She puckered her brow in concentration.* ◇ *vi: His face puckered and he began to cry.*

pudding ['pʊdɪŋ] *n* -1. a sweet dish based on flour or rice, usually served hot □ *a lemon pudding* □ *a rice/bread-and-butter/steamed pudding.* -2. GB a hot dish consisting of meat covered with a mixture of flour and fat □ *a steak and kidney pudding.* -3. GB the sweet dish that follows the main course of a meal □ *What's for pudding?*

puddle ['pʌdl] *n* a shallow pool of water that forms on the ground when it rains; a similar pool of any liquid □ *We ran for shelter, dodging the puddles.* □ *Your car has left a nasty puddle of oil on the street.*

pudgy ['pʌdʒɪ] *adj* [fingers, child] small and rather fat (informal use).

Pueblo ['pwebloʊ] *n* a member of one of several Native American peoples living in the southwestern USA.

puerile [US 'pjʊərəl, GB -aɪl] *adj* [person, remark, joke] that one thinks is silly and childish.

Puerto Rican [US ˌpwertə'riːkən, GB ˌpwɜːt-] *n* & *adj: see* **Puerto Rico.**

Puerto Rico [US ˌpwertə'riːkoʊ, GB ˌpwɜːt-] an island in the Caribbean, east of the Dominican Republic. Puerto Ricans are US citizens but Puerto Rico is not a state of the USA. SIZE: 8,897 sq kms. POPULATION: 3,522,000 (*Puerto Ricans*). CAPITAL: San Juan. LANGUAGE: Spanish, English. CURRENCY: US dollar.

puff [pʌf] ◇ *n* -1. a small amount of smoke taken into the mouth and blown out again □ *He took a puff on OR of his cigar.* -2. a small amount of air, wind, steam etc blown out from somewhere, often as a light cloud and with a gentle sound □ *I blew out the candle in one puff.* □ *The magician disappeared in a puff of smoke.*
◇ *vt* to smoke <a cigarette/pipe> etc by blowing out the smoke in small amounts.
◇ *vi* -1. **to puff on** OR **at a cigarette/pipe etc** to puff a cigarette, pipe etc. -2. to breathe quickly and noisily because one has been moving fast, exercising etc; to walk or run while breathing quickly and noisily □ *We carried the cupboard up the stairs puffing and panting.* □ *I puffed up the steps and rang the doorbell.*
◆ **puff out** *vt sep* **to puff out one's cheeks/chest** to make one's cheeks/chest bigger and rounder by filling them with air.
◆ **puff up** ◇ *vt sep* **to puff sthg up** to make sthg larger by filling it with air □ *The bird puffed up its feathers.* ◇ *vi* [eyes, skin] to be-

come swollen as the result of being hit or injured.

puffed [pʌft] *adj* **puffed (up)** [eyes, skin] swollen.

puffed sleeve *n* a short sleeve on a dress or blouse that is tight around the arm at the top and bottom but wide and round in the middle.

puffin ['pʌfɪn] *n* a small black and white seabird with a very large brightly-colored beak.

puff pastry *n* light pastry used for pies and cakes that contains a lot of air and breaks into small pieces easily.

puffy ['pʌfɪ] (*compar* **puffier**, *superl* **puffiest**) *adj* [eyes, cheeks, skin] swollen.

pug [pʌg] *n* a small fat dog with short hair, a wide face, and a flat nose.

pugnacious [pʌg'neɪʃəs] *adj* [person] who gets into fights easily (formal use).

puke▽ [pjuːk] *vi* to vomit (very informal use).

Pulitzer Prize ['pʊlətsər-] *n* in the USA, one of several prizes given to outstanding journalists, writers, and musicians.

pull [pʊl] ◇ *vt* **-1.** [hair, rope, person] to take hold of <sb/sthg> and move them toward oneself or in a particular direction □ *Anne pulled her chair closer to mine.* □ *He kept trying to pull me onto his knee.* □ *She pulled everything out of the closet and onto the floor.* □ *Stephen pulled a cigar from his jacket pocket.* ■ **to pull the blind/curtains** to draw a blind/curtains over a window to cover it. **-2.** [from a wall, socket, bottle] to remove <sthg> from its usual place using force □ *The telephone had been pulled off the wall.* **-3.** [cart, trailer, carriage] to make <a piece of equipment or machinery or a vehicle> move along behind one □ *a car pulling a trailer* □ *The coach was pulled by two black horses.* **-4.** [lever, trigger, handle] to move <the part of a piece of equipment that controls it> toward one to make it work □ *He pulled the trigger, and the gun went off.* **-5. to pull a gun/knife on sb** to take out a gun/knife suddenly in order to threaten or attack sb. **-6. to pull oneself out of a place** [water, hole, bath] to hold onto something and use force to move one's body out of a place □ *She swam to the side and pulled herself out of the pool.* **-7. to pull a muscle** to damage a muscle by stretching it too far or too quickly □ *I pulled a muscle playing football.* **-8.** [customers, spectators, voters] to make <people> come to listen, buy, vote etc (informal use) □ *The festival should pull a big crowd.*
◇ *vi* [toward oneself] *You push and I'll pull.*
◇ *n* **-1. to give sthg a pull** to pull sthg once, especially quickly or forcefully □ *You have to give that drawer a good pull.* **-2.** the power to attract or influence people □ *He resisted the pull of family tradition and went his own way.*

◆ **pull ahead** *vi* [person, vehicle] to pass and move in front of somebody or something else that is going more slowly □ *The police car suddenly pulled ahead of us.*

◆ **pull apart** *vt sep* **to pull people/animals apart** to separate people/animals that are fighting or holding each other, using force.

◆ **pull at** *vt fus* **to pull at sthg** [sleeve, arm, coat] to pull sthg repeatedly, especially in order to get somebody's attention □ *The child kept pulling at her skirt.*

◆ **pull away** *vi* **-1.** [vehicle, driver] to start moving □ *The truck was just pulling away from the traffic lights.* **-2.** [in a race] to move forward and leave behind other vehicles or people that are moving more slowly □ *The Cuban swimmer has started to pull away from the leaders.* **-3.** to move away from <sb who is holding one> □ *I grabbed her by the arm, but she pulled away from me.*

◆ **pull back** *vi* **-1.** [army] to retreat. **-2. to pull back from sthg** [from an argument, commitment] to decide not to take part in sthg □ *They pulled back from the brink of war/confronting the unions.*

◆ **pull down** *vt sep* **to pull a building down** to deliberately destroy a building, usually to build something new in its place □ *The old town hall was pulled down to make way for an office block.*

◆ **pull in** *vi* [driver, car] to move to the side of the road to stop; [train] to arrive in a station □ *Pull in next to that van.* □ *I could see Hamish waving as we pulled into the station.*

◆ **pull off** *vt sep* **-1. to pull a piece of clothing off** to remove a piece of clothing quickly and without much care □ *"It's hot," said Ruth, pulling off her sweater.* **-2. to pull it off** to succeed in doing something difficult or risky (informal use) □ *I couldn't believe they actually pulled it off!*

◆ **pull on** *vt sep* **to pull a piece of clothing on** to put a piece of clothing on quickly and without much care □ *Jonathan jumped up, pulled on his pants, and ran out.*

◆ **pull out** ◇ *vt sep* **-1. to pull sthg out** [gun, knife] to bring out sthg that has been hidden □ *Then he pulled out a shotgun.* **-2. to pull sb out** [army] to make sb leave a place □ *UN troops have been pulled out of the danger zone.*
◇ *vi* **-1.** [train] to start to leave a station □ *We arrived just as our train was pulling out.* **-2.** [vehicle] to move away from the side of the road or in front of another vehicle □ *A truck suddenly pulled out right in front of me.* **-3.** [army, troops] to leave a place □ *Government forces are pulling out of the besieged capital.* **-4.** [company, competitor, participant] to stop taking part in something □ *Syria is threatening to pull out of the peace talks.*

◆ **pull over** *vi* [vehicle, driver] to move to the side of the road and stop, especially because one is asked to □ *Pull over, there's a police car behind us.*

◆ **pull through** *vi* [sick person] to get better after a serious illness or accident □ *Doctor, do you think he'll pull through?*

◆ **pull together** ◇ *vt sep* **to pull oneself together** to behave in a more calm or controlled way □ *Pull yourself together, for goodness sake!* ◇ *vi* [group of people, countries, organizations] to work together to deal with a situation or problem □ *Times are hard, and we all have to pull together.*

◆ **pull up** ◇ *vt sep* **-1. to pull up a chair** to move a chair next to somebody or something □ *Pull up a chair and join us!* **-2. to pull sb up short** to make sb stop and think about what they are doing □ *She was pulled up short by the seriousness in Ralph's voice.* ◇ *vi* [vehicle, driver] to stop □ *I saw a car pull up outside the hotel.*

pull-down menu *n* COMPUTING a menu that one chooses from a list at the top of the screen and that then shows a menu of further options below it.

pulley ['pʊlɪ] (*pl* **pulleys**) *n* a piece of equipment consisting of a rope or chain that goes over a fixed wheel, used for lifting heavy weights.

pullout ['pʊlaʊt] *n* a part of a magazine, book etc, usually in the middle, that can be taken out and read separately.

pullover ['pʊloʊvəʳ] *n* a knitted woolen piece of clothing for the upper part of the body that one puts on by pulling it over one's head.

pulp [pʌlp] ◇ *adj* **a pulp novel/magazine etc** a novel/magazine etc that is cheaply and quickly made and contains shocking material such as sex and violence. ◇ *n* **-1.** a soft, thick, liquid mass produced when certain solid materials are crushed or beaten □ *The vegetables were reduced to a pulp.* **-2.** the soft inside part of some fruits or vegetables. **-3.** water containing crushed wood, cloth etc, used for making paper □ *wood pulp.* ◇ *vt* **-1.** [fruit, vegetable] to crush <food> until it becomes pulp. **-2.** [book, paper] to use <sthg> to make pulp so that it can be used again.

pulpit ['pʊlpɪt] *n* a raised and enclosed platform in a church where a priest or minister stands when speaking to the other people there.

pulsar ['pʌlsɑːʳ] *n* a star that cannot be seen but produces regular radio signals.

pulsate [US 'pʌlseɪt, GB pʌl'seɪt] *vi* to make sounds or movements that follow a strong regular rhythm □ *the pulsating beat of dance music.*

pulse [pʌls] ◇ *n* **-1.** the movement of blood from the heart around the body that can be felt as a regular beat at certain points on the body, e.g. the wrist □ *a strong/weak pulse* □ *Your pulse rate is abnormally slow.* □ *His pulse raced as she entered the room.* ■ **to take sb's pulse** to find out how fast sb's heart is beating by feeling the pulse at their wrist. **-2.** TECHNOLOGY a small amount of sound, light, or electricity produced by something in a regular repeated way; a series of such amounts of sound, light, or electricity □ *pulses of light* □ *an electrical/a radio pulse.* ◇ *vi* [blood, pain] to move or be felt with a strong regular beat □ *I could feel the blood pulsing around my head.*

◆ **pulses** *npl* dried beans, peas, or lentils that are soaked in water and then boiled as food.

pulverize, -ise ['pʌlvəraɪz] *vt* **-1.** [rock, metal] to

crush <sthg> into dust or very small pieces. **-2.** [army, opposition] to defeat <sb> completely (informal use).

puma ['pjuːmə] (*pl* **puma** OR **pumas**) *n* a large wild cat with brown fur that lives in the mountain regions of North and South America.

pumice (stone) ['pʌmɪs-] *n* a gray stone produced by volcanos that is very light in weight and is used for cleaning surfaces or rubbing on one's skin to make it soft and smooth.

pummel ['pʌml] (US *pt* & *pp* **pummeled**, *cont* **pummeling**, GB *pt* & *pp* **pummelled**, *cont* **pummelling**) *vt* [person, cushion] to hit <sb/sthg> hard many times, usually with one's fists.

pump [pʌmp] ◇ *n* **-1.** a machine for forcing a liquid or gas somewhere, e.g. through a pipe □ *a hydraulic/pneumatic pump* □ *a water/an oil pump* □ *a bicycle pump.* **-2.** a machine for putting gasoline into a car. ◇ *vt* **-1.** [water, air, oil] to move <a liquid or gas> somewhere using a pump □ *The blood is pumped around the body by the heart.* □ *The doctor pumped the poison out of his stomach.* **-2. to pump money into sthg** [into a project, product] to spend a lot of money in order to help sthg, often with too little care (informal use) □ *The government has been pumping money into an advertizing campaign to discourage drink-driving.* **-3.** to ask <sb> a lot of questions in order to get information that they do not want to give (informal use) □ *George kept pumping me for information about the new deal.* ◇ *vi* [piston, heart, blood] to move with a strong regular rhythm □ *The runner's arms were pumping furiously.*

◆ **pumps** *npl* light shoes with flat rubber soles used for sports or dancing □ *a pair of pumps.*

◆ **pump up** *vt sep* **to pump sthg up** [tire, air mattress] to fill sthg with air using a pump.

pumpernickel ['pʌmpəʳnɪkl] *n* a heavy dark brown bread made from rye and usually cut into thin slices before it is sold.

pumpkin ['pʌmpkən] *n* a large, round, orange-colored vegetable that grows on the ground and has a thick skin and many seeds inside; the plant that produces this vegetable.

pumpkin pie *n* a baked pie with a filling made of pumpkin, eaten especially in America.

pun [pʌn] *n* a clever or funny use of one word with two different meanings or of two words that sound the same but have two different meanings.

punch [pʌntʃ] ◇ *vt* **-1.** to hit <sb/sthg> hard with one's fist, especially in a fight □ *She punched him on the nose.* **-2.** to make <a hole> in a card, ticket etc using a punch □ *Here comes the guy to punch our tickets.* ◇ *n* **-1.** [with one's fist] the act of hitting somebody hard with one's fist □ *He gave him a punch on the chin.* **-2.** [for making holes] a tool for making holes in paper, cloth, leather, metal etc. **-3.** [drink] a hot or cold drink made by mixing wine or spirits with water, sugar, fruit, spices etc.

◆ **punch in** *vi* US to show that one has arrived at work by putting a card into a machine that records the time on it.

◆ **punch out** *vi* US to show that one has left work by putting a card into a machine that records the time on it.

Punch-and-Judy show [-'dʒuːdɪ-] *n* a traditional British puppet show for children, performed by one person in a small movable tent, in which the main character, Punch, fights with his wife, Judy.

punch bag *n* GB = **punching bag**.

punch ball *n* a leather ball held in a fixed position, e.g. on a spring, that is used in the same way as a punching bag.

punch bowl *n* a large bowl in which drinks are mixed before being served, especially punch.

punch-drunk *adj* -1. [boxer] who is unsteady and unable to speak clearly as a result of brain damage caused by too many blows to the head. -2. [person] who is confused and unable to concentrate, e.g. as a result of too much work.

punching bag ['pʌntʃɪŋ-] *n* US a heavy bag covered in leather that is hung from above so that it can be punched by boxers when they are training or as a form of exercise.

punch line *n* the last line or sentence of a joke that makes the whole joke funny.

punch-up *n* GB a fight (informal use).

punchy ['pʌntʃɪ] (*compar* **punchier**, *superl* **punchiest**) *adj* [style, article] that is forceful and effective because it is clear and direct (informal use).

punctilious [pʌŋk'tɪlɪəs] *adj* [person] who is very careful to do things correctly and properly in all details (formal use).

punctual ['pʌŋktʃʊəl] *adj* [person] who is not late and does things at the arranged time; [start, arrival] that happens at the arranged time □ *I try to be punctual for appointments.* □ *Where's Toby? He's normally so punctual.*

punctually ['pʌŋktʃʊəlɪ] *adv* [start, arrive] *see* **punctual** □ *I was there punctually at 8 o'clock.*

punctuate ['pʌŋktʃʊeɪt] *vt* -1. [sentence, text] to put punctuation into <sthg written>. -2. **to be punctuated by** OR **with sthg** to be broken or interrupted repeatedly by sthg □ *The silence was punctuated by the sound of crickets.*

punctuation [,pʌŋktʃʊ'eɪʃn] *n* marks such as periods, commas, and apostrophes that are used to break up writing and make its sense clear; the way in which such marks are used □ *The poem is written without any punctuation.* □ *I've never been any good at punctuation.*

punctuation mark *n* a period, comma, apostrophe etc used in punctuation.

puncture ['pʌŋktʃəʳ] ◇ *n* a small hole, e.g. in a tire or football, made by a sharp point □ *Do you know how to mend a puncture?* ◇ *vt* [tire, football] to make a small hole in <sthg> □ *She was in hospital with a punctured lung.*

pundit ['pʌndət] *n* a person who knows a lot about a subject and is often asked to give opinions on it □ *political/television pundits.*

pungent ['pʌndʒənt] *adj* -1. [smell, spice, food] that has a strong sharp smell or taste □ *the pungent aroma of curry.* -2. [criticism, remark, style] that is direct and very critical □ *a pungent and witty attack on the department.*

punish ['pʌnɪʃ] *vt* to do something unpleasant to <sb>, e.g. send them to prison, because they have done something wrong □ *The teacher punished the children for their rudeness.* □ *He was punished for stealing the apples.* □ *The government intends to punish drunk-driving more severely.* □ *This kind of crime must be punished.*

punishable ['pʌnɪʃəbl] *adj* [crime, offense] that can be punished by law □ *Theft is punishable by imprisonment/a large fine.*

punishing ['pʌnɪʃɪŋ] *adj* [work, defeat, climb] that is very hard and makes one feel very tired and weak □ *The sales rep has a punishing schedule of ten visits in two days.*

punishment ['pʌnɪʃmənt] *n* -1. an unpleasant thing done to somebody to punish them □ *People who cheat on taxes should not escape punishment.* -2. a particular way of punishing somebody □ *As a punishment for my lateness I lost two hours' pay.* -3. rough treatment that can cause damage (informal use) □ *This car can take a lot of punishment.*

punitive ['pjuːnətɪv] *adj* -1. [action, bombing] that is intended as a punishment □ *The army took punitive measures against the rebels.* -2. [taxes, laws] very severe.

Punjab [pʌn'dʒɑːb]: **the Punjab** a region of northwestern India and eastern Pakistan. It is the center of the Sikh religion.

Punjabi [pʌn'dʒɑːbɪ] ◇ *n* -1. a person who comes from the Punjab. -2. the language spoken in the Punjab. ◇ *adj*: *a Punjabi dish.*

punk [pʌŋk] ◇ *n* -1. **punk (rock)** a style of loud aggressive music, popular especially in the 1970s and 1980s. -2. **a punk (rocker)** a person who likes punk rock and dresses in unusual ways, e.g. by having brightly-colored hair and wearing torn clothing. -3. US a rough young man or boy, especially one who is often in fights or breaks the law (informal use). ◇ *adj* [fashion, haircut, music] that is produced by or is typical of punk rockers.

punnet ['pʌnət] *n* GB a small square box or basket in which soft fruit, e.g. strawberries, are sold.

punt¹ [pʌnt] ◇ *n* -1. a long boat with a flat bottom and square ends that is moved by standing at one end and pushing a long pole against the bottom of a river. -2. in rugby and football, a type of kick in which the ball is dropped from the hands and kicked before it touches the ground. ◇ *vi* to travel by punt.

punt² [pʊnt] *n* the standard unit of currency in the Irish Republic.

punter ['pʌntəʳ] *n* GB (informal use) -1. a person who gambles money, especially on horse races. -2. **the punters** the customers who buy a product or service.

puny ['pjuːnɪ] (*compar* **punier**, *superl* **puniest**) *adj* [person, arms] small and weak (disapproving use).

pup [pʌp] *n* -1. = **puppy**. -2. the young of certain animals, e.g. seals and otters.

pupil ['pjuːpl] *n* -1. EDUCATION a child who is being taught, usually at a school □ *The school has over 600 pupils.* -2. [of an expert] a person who has studied under and been influenced by a particular expert □ *These ideas were developed by the pupils of Adam Smith.* -3. [of the eye] the small black area in the middle of the colored part of the eye through which light enters.

puppet ['pʌpət] *n* -1. a doll that can be made to move by pulling strings attached to its hands, feet etc. -2. = **glove puppet**. -3. a person, country etc that appears to be independent but is controlled and directed by somebody more powerful (disapproving use) □ *a puppet ruler/state.*

puppet government *n* a government that is controlled by the government of a more powerful country (disapproving use).

puppet show *n* an entertainment using string or glove puppets.

puppy ['pʌpɪ] (*pl* **puppies**) *n* a young dog.

purchase ['pɜːtʃəs] (formal use) ◇ *n* -1. the act of buying something □ *We have set aside $1m for the purchase of new equipment.* -2. something that somebody has bought □ *Can I take your purchases out to the taxi?* -3. a firm hold or grip on a surface that prevents somebody or something from slipping or falling □ *The special tires give the car extra purchase on icy roads.* ◇ *vt* [house, car] to buy <sthg> □ *The insurance company purchased 5% of the shares of the transport group.*

purchase order *n* a form sent to a supplier by a company to say that they want to buy certain goods.

purchase price *n* the price that one has to pay to buy something, including taxes, discounts etc.

purchaser ['pɜːtʃəsər] *n* a person who buys something (formal use) □ *There were several prospective purchasers for the car.*
NOTE: Compare **vendor**.

purchasing power ['pɜːtʃəsɪŋ-] *n* the amount of goods that somebody can buy with the money they have available; the value of a currency measured by how much it can buy at any time □ *The purchasing power of the pound has fallen steadily in relation to the German mark.*

purdah ['pɜːrdə] *n* the custom, especially in Islamic countries, of keeping women from being seen in public, e.g. by using clothing that hides their faces.

pure [pjʊər] *adj* -1. [wool, gold, breed] not mixed with anything else; [air, water] completely clean and free from harmful substances □ *The dress is made of pure silk.* □ *There was not a cloud in the pure-blue sky.* -2. [sound, voice] very clear and beautiful □ *the pure tones of the flute.* -3. [person, thoughts, motives] morally good, especially in sexual

matters (literary use) □ *Her mind was as pure as that of a young child.* -4. **pure research** research that is intended to increase knowledge rather than have a practical use □ *pure and applied science* □ *pure math.* -5. **pure luck/pleasure etc** complete luck/pleasure etc □ *It was pure bliss to lie back in a hot bath after such a hard day.* □ *a look of pure contentment* □ *It was pure jealousy on his part.* ■ **pure and simple** only, and nothing else □ *Our losses are due to inflation, pure and simple.*

purebred ['pjʊərbred] *adj* [horse, cattle, dog] whose family has always been of the same breed.

puree [US pjuːˈreɪ, GB ˈpjʊəreɪ] ◇ *n* food that has been cooked, crushed, and mixed until it forms a thick smooth paste □ *tomato/apple puree.* ◇ *vt* to make <tomatoes, apples> etc into a puree.

purely ['pjʊərlɪ] *adv* [practical, personal, political] completely and only □ *a purely routine matter* □ *It's purely a question of money.* □ *He was purely and simply too old for the job.*

pureness ['pjʊərnəs] *n* [of air, sound, thoughts] *see* **pure**.

purgative ['pɜːrgətɪv] *n* a medicine that makes the body get rid of solid waste quickly.

purgatory [US ˈpɜːrgətɔːrɪ, GB -ətrɪ] *n* a very unpleasant place, state, or time.

◆ **Purgatory** *n* RELIGION in the Roman Catholic religion, the place where dead people go to suffer for their sins before they can get to Heaven.

purge [pɜːrdʒ] ◇ *n* POLITICS action taken by a political party, government, company etc to get rid of unwanted members, often unfairly and by force □ *the Communist purges of the 1930s.* ◇ *vt* -1. POLITICS [members, extremists, directors] to get rid of <people who are considered unacceptable> by making them leave an organization or country, killing them etc □ *The new leader promised to purge racists from the party* OR *to purge the party of racists.* -2. **to purge one's thoughts** OR **mind of sthg** to make oneself stop thinking about or being affected by sthg bad or unwanted □ *I had finally managed to purge myself of the fear of seeing her again.*

purification [ˌpjʊərəfɪˈkeɪʃn] *n* [of water, air] *see* **purify** □ *a plant for water purification.*

purifier ['pjʊərəfaɪər] *n* a machine that purifies something, e.g. water or air.

purify ['pjʊərəfaɪ] (*pt* & *pp* **purified**) *vt* -1. [water, air] to make <sthg> pure by removing harmful or unwanted substances. -2. RELIGION to make <sb> morally pure.

purist ['pjʊərəst] *n* a person who is very careful to do things in the way that they believe is correct and to make other people do the same □ *Purists will doubtless be outraged by Schofield's latest piece.*

puritan ['pjʊərətən] ◇ *n* a person who has very strict moral and religious views and believes that pleasure is wrong. ◇ *adj*: *puritan attitudes/morality.*

◆ **Puritans** *npl* a conservative English reli-

puritanical   852

gious group of the 16th and 17th centuries. Some Puritans went to live in North America and founded New England, and had a great influence on US culture.

puritanical [ˌpjʊərəˈtænɪkl] *adj* [person] who has very strict moral and religious views, and believes that pleasure is wrong □ *She's so puritanical about drinking.*

purity [ˈpjʊərətɪ] *n* [of air, sound, thoughts] *see* **pure** □ *The gold is refined to a purity of 99%.* □ *a voice of remarkable clarity and purity.*

purl [pɜːrl] ◇ *n* a knitting stitch made by doing an ordinary stitch backwards. ◇ *vt* to knit <a purl stitch>.

purloin [pɜːrˈlɔɪn] *vt* to steal <sthg small> or take it without permission (formal or humorous use).

purple [ˈpɜːrpl] ◇ *adj* dark red-blue in color. ◇ *n* the color purple.

Purple Heart *n* **the Purple Heart** a medal given to US soldiers wounded or killed in battle.

purport [pərˈpɔːrt] *vi* **to purport to do/be sthg** to claim, often falsely, to do/be sthg (formal use) □ *a man purporting to be her long-lost uncle.*

purpose [ˈpɜːrpəs] *n* **-1.** the intention or reason that somebody has when they do something □ *The purpose of our visit is to see our grandchildren.* □ *His only purpose in life is to get rich.* □ *Our purpose in sending troops to Ethiopia is to keep the peace.* □ *What is the purpose of this little gadget?* **-2.** a use, effect, or result □ *I hope that she puts her abilities to some good purpose.* □ *We use our car for business purposes.* □ *For what purpose do you intend to use the loan?* ■ **to little/no/some purpose** with little/no/some useful result □ *All his work turned out to be to no purpose.* **-3.** the feeling that one has a definite aim and is determined to achieve it □ *What you need is a sense of purpose.* □ *I feel she lacks purpose.*
◆ **on purpose** *adv* not by mistake or accident but with deliberate intention □ *I came early on purpose to speak to you before the meeting.* □ *You did that on purpose!*

purpose-built *adj* GB [school, block] that was built specially for a particular use.

purposeful [ˈpɜːrpəsfl] *adj* [person] who has a definite aim and is determined to achieve it □ *I saw James walking down the corridor looking very purposeful.*

purposely [ˈpɜːrpəslɪ] *adv* on purpose □ *I purposely sat by the window so I could see what was happening outside.*

purr [pɜːr] ◇ *vi* **-1.** [cat] to make a low continuous sound as a sign of being happy. **-2.** [car, engine] to make a quiet, low, continuous sound when moving smoothly □ *In the distance I could hear a car purring along the road.* **-3.** [person] to speak in a low, gentle, happy voice □ *"He's wonderful," she purred contentedly.* ◇ *n* [of a cat, engine] the sound made by something when it purrs □ *I heard the purr of the car as it entered the drive.*

purse [pɜːrs] ◇ *n* **-1.** a small bag for keeping money in, usually kept in a pocket or larger bag. **-2.** US a bag in which a woman carries

personal possessions such as keys, make-up, and money. ◇ *vt* **to purse one's lips** to pull one's lips into a small, tight, rounded shape, often as a sign that one does not approve of something.

purser [ˈpɜːrsər] *n* an officer on a ship who keeps the accounts and is responsible for the comfort and safety of the passengers.

purse snatcher [-snætʃər] *n* US a person who steals women's handbags from them, usually in a busy place.

purse strings *npl* **to hold the purse strings** to control how the money is spent within a family, company etc.

pursue [pərˈsjuː] *vt* **-1.** [car, criminal] to follow or look for <sb/sthg> in order to catch them □ *The policeman pursued the thief along the road.* **-2.** [interest, aim, policy] to continue with <sthg>, usually over a long period □ *She is pursuing her battle with the authorities.* **-3.** [topic, question, subject] to consider, try to find out about, or discuss <sthg> in more detail □ *I intended to sue them but decided not to pursue the matter.*

pursuer [pərˈsjuːər] *n* a person or animal that is chasing another person or animal in order to catch them □ *The fox managed to escape its pursuers.*

pursuit [pərˈsjuːt] *n* **-1.** [of a car, criminal] the act of pursuing somebody or something. ■ **in pursuit of sb/sthg** following sb/sthg in order to try and catch them □ *The girls chased down the road in pursuit of the film star.* ■ **in hot pursuit** close behind the person or thing one is pursuing □ *The thief ran away with the policeman in hot pursuit.* **-2.** [of happiness, security, profits] actions taken in order to get or achieve something (formal use) □ *a life devoted to the pursuit of pleasure* □ *the pursuit of fame and fortune.* **-3.** [for enjoyment] an activity that one spends time doing, especially for enjoyment □ *He spends much of his time in artistic/scientific pursuits.* □ *Climbing is one of my favorite pursuits.* **-4.** SPORT a race in cycling in which the competitors start at opposite sides of a track and try to catch each other up □ *the 4000-meter team pursuit.*

purveyor [pərˈveɪər] *n* [of wines, goods, information] a person or company that sells or provides something (formal use).

pus [pʌs] *n* thick yellowish liquid that forms in an infected wound.

push [pʊʃ] ◇ *vt* **-1.** [person, heavy object, bicycle] to move <sb/sthg> away from one or into a particular position with one's hands, using sudden or steady pressure; to press <a button> to make a piece of equipment start or stop working □ *We had to push the car to get it started.* □ *Tom pushed me into the pool.* □ *I pushed the door open/shut.* □ *He pushed his way through the crowd.* □ *Try pushing the play button.* **-2. to push sb to do sth** to encourage sb strongly to do sth they do not want to do □ *My parents kept pushing me to stay on at school.* **-3. to push sb into doing sth** to make sb do sth they do not want to do □ *I'm not going to be pushed into taking a job I don't want.*

◻ *Women will end up being pushed into poorly-paid jobs.* **-4.** [student, pupil, trainee] to make <sb> work very hard ◻ *Their coach doesn't really push them hard enough.* ◻ *Don't push yourself, will you?* **-5.** [idea, opinion, point of view] to try to persuade other people to accept or support <sthg one believes> ◻ *It is noticeable that in his last three speeches he has really pushed the idea of tax cuts.* **-6.** [product, book, movie] to advertise <sthg> very heavily (informal use) ◻ *They're pushing their new range of soft drinks in a TV campaign.* **-7. to push drugs** to sell illegal drugs (informal use) ◻ *He was jailed for pushing heroin.*

◇ *vi* to use one's hands or body to make somebody move out of one's way ◻ *Tell the people at the back to stop pushing!* ◻ *He pushed right past me.*

◇ *n* **-1.** an act of pushing, usually with one's hand or finger ◻ *You can have instant heat at the push of a button.* ■ **to give sb/sthg a push** to push sb/sthg once to make them move ◻ *My car's broken down — could you give me a push?* **-2.** MILITARY a planned attack or forward movement by an army ◻ *the final push to reach the border.* **-3. to give sb the push** GB (informal use) [boyfriend, girlfriend] to end one's relationship with sb; [employee] to dismiss sb from their job ◻ *Jeremy's been given the push by ICM.* **-4.** *phrase* **I could do it at a push** I could do it if necessary, but not easily.

◆ **push ahead** *vi* **to push ahead with sthg** [with preparations, a plan, project] to continue to carry out sthg ◻ *The party is pushing ahead with the reforms despite opposition from members.*

◆ **push around** *vt sep* **to push sb around** to tell sb what to do in a rude or threatening way ◻ *Don't let him push you around!*

◆ **push for** *vt fus* **to push for sthg** to keep asking for sthg in a forceful way because one feels it is important ◻ *The charity is going to push for more funding.*

◆ **push in** *vi* GB to join a line in front of other people, cars etc that have already been waiting ◻ *A woman tried to push in right in front of me.*

◆ **push on** *vi* to continue traveling somewhere or doing something ◻ *Let's push on to the next service station.*

◆ **push over** *vt sep* **to push sb/sthg over** to deliberately cause sb/sthg to fall by pushing them ◻ *Someone pushed him over in the playground.*

◆ **push through** *vt sep* **to push sthg through** [reform, amendment, proposal] to get sthg accepted or approved officially, often with some difficulty ◻ *The Government will need support if they are going to push the bill through Parliament.*

◆ **push up** *vt sep* **to push sthg up** [cost, price] to increase sthg ◻ *Fear of inflation has pushed up interest rates.*

pushbike ['puʃbaɪk] *n* GB a bicycle (informal use).

push-button *adj* [machine, telephone] that works when one presses buttons with one's fingers ◻ *push-button controls.*

pushcart ['puʃkɑːʳt] *n* a small cart with long handles that is pushed by hand and used especially by street traders.

pushchair ['puʃtʃeaʳ] *n* GB a small vehicle on wheels in which a small child can sit and be pushed.

pushed [puʃt] *adj* (informal use) **to be pushed for sthg** [for time, money] to have too little of sthg ◻ *I'd love to help, but I'm a little pushed for time at the moment.* ■ **to be (hard) pushed to do sthg** to find it very difficult to do sthg ◻ *You'd be hard pushed to find a better nanny than Maria.*

pusher ['puʃəʳ] *n* a person who sells illegal drugs (informal use).

Pushkin ['puʃkɪn], **Alexander** (1799–1837) a Russian poet whose works, including *Eugene Onegin* and *Boris Godunov*, had a great influence on modern Russian poetry.

pushover ['puʃoʊvəʳ] *n* a person who is very easy to persuade or influence; something that is very easy to do or win (informal use) ◻ *I'm sure his mum will let him go — she's a real pushover.* ◻ *Don't worry about the exam — it'll be a pushover!*

push-start *vt* to start the engine of <a car, motorcycle> etc by pushing it along and then forcing it into gear.

push-up *n* US a physical exercise in which somebody lies facing the floor and, keeping their back straight, presses down on their hands to raise their body off the floor ◻ *How many push-ups can you do?*

pushy ['puʃɪ] (*compar* **pushier**, *superl* **pushiest**) *adj* [person] who is always trying to make other people notice what they are doing or do what they want ◻ *You've got to be pushy to succeed as a salesman.*

puss [pus], **pussy** ['pusɪ], **pussycat** ['pusɪkæt] *n* a cat (informal use).

pussy willow *n* a willow tree that grows furry gray-white flowers in the spring.

put [put] (*pt* & *pp* **put**, *cont* **putting**) *vt* **-1. to put sthg somewhere** to move sthg to a particular place or position; to fix sthg in a particular place or position ◻ *You've put too much sugar in my coffee.* ◻ *He put his arm around her shoulders.* ◻ *Where did you put my pen?* ◻ *We had to put smoke alarms in all the rooms.* **-2. to put sb somewhere** to make sb go to a particular place and stay there ◻ *Have you put the children to bed?* ◻ *They'll put you in prison!* **-3. to put sb in a good/bad position** to cause sb to be in a good/bad position. ■ **to put sb in a good/bad mood** to cause sb to feel in a good/bad mood ◻ *This puts us in a very difficult situation.* ◻ *The music almost put me to sleep.* ◻ *The decision to close the factory could put hundreds of people out of work.* **-4.** [feelings, thoughts] to say or express <sthg> in a particular way ◻ *I can't put it any simpler than that.* ◻ *He is — how can I put it? — not entirely honest.* **-5. to put a question to sb** to ask sb a question ◻ *I put the same question to a colleague of mine, and got the same answer.* **-6.** [words, sentence] to write <sthg> in a particular place or manner ◻ *Put your name at the* top of the page. □ *What did you put on her birth-day card?* **-7.** [in a particular class or order] to consider that <sb/sthg> has a particular importance or belongs in a particular group □ *As a soccer player, I'd put him in the same class as Pelé.* □ *There are not many successful businessmen who put their family before their work.* **-8. to put a stop** OR **an end to sthg** to stop or prevent sthg happening □ *Her injury put an end to our chances of winning the tournament.* □ *These are silly rumors, and I'm going to put a stop to them!*

◆ **put across** *vt sep* to put an idea/theory etc **across** to explain an idea/theory etc so that people understand it clearly □ *We lost the last election because we didn't put our policies across to the voters.*

◆ **put aside** *vt sep* **-1. to put sthg aside** [one's work, book] to place sthg to one side in order to do something else □ *I put aside my novel and turned back to the computer screen.* **-2. to put money aside** to save money so that it can be used later □ *If we put aside some of my salary every month, we'll soon be able to pay off our debts.* **-3. to put problems/disagreements aside** to deliberately ignore problems/disagreements etc □ *It's time we put aside our differences and tried to reach a consensus.*

◆ **put at** *vt sep* to put sb/sthg at sthg to estimate that the age, value, cost etc of sb/sthg is sthg □ *I would put his age at about forty.*

◆ **put away** *vt sep* **-1. to put sthg away** [clothes, shopping, work] to put sthg into the place where it is usually kept or stored □ *You dry the dishes and I'll put them away.* **-2. to put sb away** [criminal] to send sb to prison for a long time or for ever (informal use).

◆ **put back** *vt sep* **-1. to put sthg back** [book, plate, tools] to put sthg into the place where it was before □ *Remember to put the top back on the bottle.* **-2. to put an event back** to move an event to a later date or time; to delay the start of an event □ *We've had to put the meeting back to next week.* □ *The bad weather could put back the opening of the tunnel by two weeks.* **-3. to put back a clock/watch** to set a clock/watch so that it shows an earlier time, for instance when traveling west □ *Don't forget to put the clocks back an hour tonight.*

◆ **put by** *vt sep* to put money by to save money so that it can be used later □ *Over the years they had put by enough to buy a small car.*

◆ **put down** *vt sep* **-1. to put sthg down** [book, knife, gun] to stop holding sthg and place it on a surface such as the floor □ *Why don't you put down those bags and have a rest.* **-2. to put ideas/comments etc down** to write ideas/comments etc so that they can be referred to later □ *Put your complaint down in writing/on paper.* **-3. to put a riot/rebellion down** to end a riot/rebellion by using force □ *The revolt was swiftly put down by the authorities.* **-4. to put sb down** to make sb feel unimportant or stupid by criticizing them in front of other people (informal use) □ *He's always putting people down.* **-5. to be put down** [animal] GB to be killed, usually because it is old or ill □ *We had to have the cat put down.*

◆ **put down to** *vt sep* to put sthg down to sthg to think that sthg is caused by sthg □ *When he complained of feeling tired, I put it down to his age.*

◆ **put forward** *vt sep* **-1. to put forward an idea/a plan etc** to mention an idea/a plan etc so that people can consider and discuss it □ *The builder has put forward his suggestions for improvements.* **-2. to put sb forward** to suggest sb for a job or position □ *Your name has been put forward for the Chicago posting.* **-3. to put an event forward** to move an event to an earlier date or time □ *Since everyone is going to be away next week, we'll have to put the meeting forward to tomorrow.* **-4. to put a clock/watch forward** to set a clock/watch so that it shows a later time, for instance when traveling east □ *Don't forget to put the clocks forward an hour tonight.*

◆ **put in** *vt sep* **-1. to put in time/effort** to spend time/effort in order to get something done □ *I put in an hour's overtime yesterday.* **-2. to put a request/claim etc in** to make a request/claim etc officially □ *You should put in your application well before the closing date.*

◆ **put in for** *vt fus* to put in for sthg [grant, transfer] to ask for sthg officially □ *The committee has put in for extra funding.*

◆ **put into** *vt sep* to put money/effort into sthg to spend money/effort so that sthg can work and succeed □ *The bank put $50,000 into the business.* □ *She puts a lot of energy into her charity work.*

◆ **put off** *vt sep* **-1. to put an event off** to move a planned event to a later date or time □ *The match has been put off to next week.* **-2. to put sb off** to tell sb that you cannot yet do something that you have agreed to do □ *They want to be paid and we can't put them off any longer.* **-3. to put off doing sthg** to delay doing sthg because one does not want to do it □ *I can't put off telling my parents about it any longer.* **-4. to put sb off sb/sthg** [off children, meat] to make sb dislike sb/sthg or want to avoid them □ *The experience put me off politics for life.* □ *Don't let the bad reviews put you off (from) going to see it.* **-5. to put sb off** to disturb sb so that they cannot concentrate on what they are doing □ *McEnroe claimed that the photographers were putting him off.* **-6. to put an electrical device off** to stop an electrical device working by turning it off □ *Remember to put the lights off when you go to bed.*

◆ **put on** *vt sep* **-1. to put a piece of clothing on** to get dressed in a piece of clothing □ *She put on her best suit for the interview.* **-2. to put weight on** to become fatter and weigh more □ *I've put on six pounds since I got married!* **-3. to put a sum of money on sthg** to add a sum of money to the cost of sthg □ *They've put another 20¢ on cigarettes.* **-4. to put a play/exhibition etc on** to perform or arrange a play/exhibition etc for the public □ *They're putting on a new show at the Lyceum.* **-5. to put an electrical device on** to start an electrical device working by turning it on □ *It's cold enough to put the central heating on.* **-6. to put a record/video etc on** to start to play a record/video etc □ *I put on some music and lay back in the bath.* **-7. to put food on** to start to cook food □ *While the fish is cooking, put the rice on.* **-8. to put on a way of talking/ behaving** to talk/behave in a way that is not one's usual way of talking or behaving, to deceive people or make them laugh □ *He's not really hurt — he's just putting it on.* **-9. to put a sum of money on a horse** to bet a sum of money that a horse will win a race □ *I put $30 on Jack the Lad.* **-10. to put pressure/a strain on sb** to make sb feel pressure/a strain □ *Parents often put too much pressure on their children to do well at school.* ■ **to put restrictions/a ban on sthg** to restrict/ban sthg □ *Put the stress* OR *emphasis on the first syllable.*

◆ **put onto** *vt sep* to put sb onto sb/sthg to tell sb about sb/sthg that will be useful to them (informal use) □ *"She's a good driving instructor." — "Yes, it was Carl who put me onto her."*

◆ **put out** *vt sep* **-1. to put clothing/food etc out** to take clothing/food etc out from somewhere and leave it ready to be used □ *Could you put out some supper for me — I'll be home late.* **-2. to put out a statement** to make something known publicly and officially □ *The hospital put out a bulletin describing the president's condition as "stable."* **-3. to put out a fire/cigarette etc** to stop a fire/cigarette etc burning □ *Firefighters took three hours to put out the blaze.* **-4. to put out an electric light** to stop an electric light shining by turning it off □ *Put out that flashlight!* **-5. to put out one's hand/foot etc** to stretch one's hand/foot forward away from one's body □ *She put out a hand to help me up.* **-6. to put one's back/ shoulder/hip out** to injure one's back/ shoulder/hip, e.g. by straining it or making it move from its usual position □ *I put my back out trying to lift that thing.* **-7. to be put out** to be annoyed or upset □ *She looked a little put out when I said I couldn't come.* **-8. to put sb out** [guest, host] to cause sb trouble or inconvenience □ *I hope I'm not putting you out.* ■ **to put oneself out** to take special care or trouble in order to help somebody □ *Please don't put yourself out for me* OR *on my behalf.*

◆ **put over** *vt sep* = **put across.**

◆ **put through** *vt sep* **-1. to put sb through** to connect sb by telephone to the person they want to talk to □ *I'm putting you through to our sales department now, caller.* **-2. to put sb through sthg** [test, course] to make sb experience sthg difficult or unpleasant □ *All candidates are put through a rigorous selection procedure.*

◆ **put to** *vt sep* to put sthg to sb [proposal, suggestion] to ask sb to consider and decide on sthg □ *We'll put this matter to the management committee.*

◆ **put together** *vt sep* **-1. to put a piece of machinery/furniture etc together** to make a piece of machinery/furniture etc by joining together its different parts □ *The company is putting together a new team to market the range abroad.* **-2. to put an exhibition/a campaign etc together** to organize an exhibition/a cam-

paign etc □ *The show was put together by the creators of "Hair".* **-3. to put a report/proposal etc together** to prepare a report/proposal etc for other people to think about or discuss □ *The deal was put together by an international consortium.* □ *Both sides in the dispute are trying to put together a new peace plan.* **-4. more than all the others put together** more than all the others combined □ *She's worth more than all the rest of you put together.*

◆ **put up** ◇ *vt sep* **-1. to put a wall/fence etc up** to build a wall/fence etc □ *The town ought to put up a statue to him.* **-2. to put a flag/ umbrella etc up** to raise and open a flag/ umbrella etc so that it can be used. **-3. to put a poster/notice etc up** to fix a poster/ notice to a wall, bulletin board etc so that it can be seen □ *Have they put up the exam results yet?* **-4. to put up money for sthg** to provide or lend money to pay for sthg □ *My parents put up half the money for my trip abroad.* **-5. to put up costs/prices etc** to make costs/ prices etc higher □ *Inflation is putting up wages.* **-6. to put sthg up for sale** [house, painting] to offer sthg for sale □ *They're putting the business up for sale.* **-7. to put sb up** to provide sb with a room to stay in □ *I can easily put you up for a couple of weeks.*

◇ *vt fus* **to put up a fight/struggle** to fight/ struggle in order to stop something happening that one does not want to happen □ *The villagers put up a fierce resistance, but eventually the bulldozers moved in.*

◇ *vi* to stay in a particular place □ *We put up in a motel.*

◆ **put up to** *vt sep* to put sb up to sthg to give sb the idea of doing sthg bad or silly □ *He knows he's not allowed to drink — someone must have put him up to it.*

◆ **put up with** *vt fus* to put up with sthg [noise, nonsense, somebody's behavior] to accept sthg unpleasant without complaining □ *I will not put up with your rudeness any longer!*

putative [ˈpjuːtətɪv] *adj* **the putative father/ owner** the person who people think is the father/owner.

put-down *n* an unkind remark, usually intended to make another person look foolish (informal use).

putrefy [ˈpjuːtrəfaɪ] (*pt* & *pp* **putrefied**) *vi* [food, dead body] to decay and produce a very unpleasant smell (formal use).

putrid [ˈpjuːtrəd] *adj* [meat, vegetable] that has decayed and smells very unpleasant □ *a putrid smell.*

putsch [pʊtʃ] *n* an organized and usually violent attempt to remove a government.

putt [pʌt] ◇ *n* a stroke in golf made using a putter and intended to roll the ball into the hole. ◇ *vt* to hit <a golf ball> across the green toward the hole using a putter. ◇ *vi*: *He's putting well today.*

putter [ˈpʌtəʳ] *n* a light golf club used for putting.

◆ **putter around** *vi* US to spend time doing small pleasant tasks without hurrying □ *I* *thought I'd spend today just puttering around the house.*

putting green ['pʌtɪŋ-] *n* **-1.** the area of short grass on a golf course where the hole is. **-2.** a very small golf course for putting.

putty ['pʌtɪ] *n* a thick paste used to fix panes of glass into window frames.

put-up job *n* something that has been arranged in advance in order to deceive somebody (informal use) □ *The whole thing looked like a put-up job.*

put-upon *adj* [person] who other people take advantage of □ *I'm not upset — I just feel very put-upon, that's all.*

puzzle ['pʌzl] ◇ *n* **-1.** GAMES a toy or game that consists of problems needing mental skill to be answered or completed □ *a mathematical/word puzzle.* **-2.** a person or thing that is difficult to understand or explain. ◇ *vt* to make <sb> confused because they are unable to understand something or the reason why it has happened □ *There's one thing that still puzzles me.* ◇ *vi* **to puzzle over sthg** to try to understand sthg by thinking hard about it □ *I've been puzzling over the best way to do it.*

◆ **puzzle out** *vt sep* **to puzzle sthg out** to find the answer to sthg by thinking hard □ *I just can't puzzle out why they're so angry with me.*

puzzled ['pʌzld] *adj* [person] who is confused because they do not understand something □ *She gave me a puzzled look.*

puzzling ['pʌzlɪŋ] *adj* [remark, behavior] that makes one confused because one cannot understand it □ *It's all very puzzling.*

PVC (*abbr of* **polyvinyl chloride**) *n* a type of plastic.

Pvt. MILITARY *abbr of* **private**.

pw *abbr of* **per week**.

PWA *n abbr of* **person with Aids**.

PWR (*abbr of* **pressurized-water reactor**) *n* a type of nuclear reactor.

PX (*abbr of* **post exchange**) *n* a store, usually at a military base, for members of the US armed forces.

Pygmy ['pɪgmɪ] (*pl* **Pygmies**) *n* a member of a race of very small people who live in equatorial Africa.

pyjama [pə'dʒɑːmə] *comp* **a pyjama top/bottom** the top/bottom part of a pair of pyjamas.

pyjamas [pə'dʒɑːməz] *npl* a set of soft loose clothes worn in bed that consists of trousers and a shirt □ *a pair of pyjamas.*

pylon ['paɪlɒn] *n* a metal structure that holds electrical cables high above the ground □ *an electricity pylon.*

pyramid ['pɪrəmɪd] *n* **-1.** GEOMETRY a three-dimensional shape that has a flat base and triangular sides that slope upward and meet at a point. **-2.** ARCHITECTURE a large stone structure in the shape of a pyramid, built as the burial place of an important person in ancient Egypt. **-3.** [of stones, cans] a pile of things that is shaped like a pyramid.

pyramid selling *n* a way of selling goods in which a company sells goods to an agent, who sells them at a profit to another agent. This process can continue until the final agent is not able to sell the goods without making a loss.

pyre ['paɪər] *n* a large pile of wood for burning a dead body on as part of a religious ceremony □ *a funeral pyre.*

Pyrenees [,pɪrə'niːz]: **the Pyrenees** a mountain range in southwestern Europe, between France and Spain. HIGHEST POINT: 3,404 m.

Pyrex™ ['paɪreks] *n* a type of glass that can be used to make cooking containers because it does not break at high temperatures □ *a Pyrex bowl/dish.*

pyromaniac [,paɪrə'meɪnɪæk] *n* a person who has an uncontrollable desire to burn things.

pyrotechnics [,paɪrə'tekniks] ◇ *n* the activity or skill of making fireworks. ◇ *npl* a demonstration of great skill, e.g. in words or music.

python ['paɪθn] (*pl* **python** OR **pythons**) *n* a large tropical snake that kills animals by winding its body round them and crushing them.

q [kjuː] (*pl* **q's** OR **qs**), **Q** [kjuː] (*pl* **Q's** OR **Qs**) *n* the seventeenth letter of the English alphabet.

Qatar [US 'kɑːtɑːr, GB kæ'tɑː] a country in eastern Arabia, consisting of a peninsula on the Persian Gulf. SIZE: 11,400 sq kms. POPULATION: 500,000 (*Qataris*). CAPITAL: Doha. LANGUAGE: Arabic. CURRENCY: Qatari riyal.

QC *n abbr of* **Queen's Counsel**.

QED (*abbr of* **quod erat demonstrandum**) a phrase used by somebody to show that they have proved what they set out to prove.

Qld *abbr of* **Queensland**.

QM *n abbr of* **quartermaster**.

q.t., QT (*abbr of* **quiet**) *n* **on the q.t.** on the quiet (informal use).

Q-tip™ *n* US a short stick of plastic that has cotton on each end and is used for cleaning inside one's ears, nose etc.

qty *abbr of* **quantity**.

quack [kwæk] ◇ *n* **-1.** the sound made by a duck. **-2.** a person who is not a doctor but claims to be one (disapproving use) □ *a quack doctor.* ◇ *vi* [duck] to make a quack.

quad [kwɒd] *n* **-1.** = **quadruplet**. **-2.** = **quadrangle**.

quadrangle ['kwɒdræŋgl] *n* **-1.** GEOMETRY a two-dimensional shape that has four straight sides. **-2.** [in a school, college] an open square with buildings around it.

quadrant [ˈkwɒdrənt] *n* an instrument for measuring angles that was used in the past by sailors.

quadraphonic [ˌkwɒdrəˈfɒnɪk] *adj* [sound, recording] that is played through four separate speakers.

quadrilateral [ˌkwɒdrɪˈlætrəl] ◇ *adj* [shape] that has four straight sides. ◇ *n* GEOMETRY = **quadrangle.**

quadruped [ˈkwɒdrəped] *n* an animal that has four legs.

quadruple [kwɒˈdruːpl] ◇ *adj* four times as large; four times as many. ◇ *vt* [output, sales] to make <the amount of sthg> four times larger or greater. ◇ *vi* [production, sales] The population has quadrupled in the last decade.

quadruplets [kwɒˈdruːpləts] *npl* four children born to the same mother at the same time.

quads [kwɒdz] *npl* = **quadruplets** (informal use).

quaff [kwɒf] *vt* [water, wine] to drink a lot of <sthg> in large mouthfuls (old-fashioned use).

quagmire [ˈkwægmaɪəʳ] *n* an area of soft wet ground.

quail [kweɪl] (*pl* **quail** OR **quails**) ◇ *n* a small wild bird with a round body and short tail that is sometimes shot for sport or eaten. ◇ *vi* [person] to feel very afraid (literary use) □ Most people quail at the thought of undergoing surgery.

quaint [kweɪnt] *adj* [village, tradition] that is charming and old-fashioned, but slightly strange and amusing □ She has some very quaint ideas about marriage.

quake [kweɪk] ◇ *n* an earthquake (informal use). ◇ *vi* [person] to shake or tremble with fear.

Quaker [ˈkweɪkəʳ] *n* a member of a Christian religious group that does not have formal services and is opposed to violence and war.

qualification [ˌkwɒləfəˈkeɪʃn] *n* **-1.** a certificate that proves that somebody has successfully finished a course of study or passed an exam □ I got my professional qualification last year. **-2.** a skill or ability that makes a person suitable for a particular activity or job □ She has good secretarial/academic qualifications. **-3.** a statement that makes a previous statement less strong.

qualified [ˈkwɒləfaɪd] *adj* **-1.** [doctor, accountant] who has passed the necessary exams or taken the necessary course □ Our staff is highly/fully qualified. **-2. to be qualified to do sthg** to have the right skill or ability to do sthg □ I don't feel qualified to discuss such matters. **-3.** [approval, praise] not complete □ The idea was only a qualified success.

qualify [ˈkwɒləfaɪ] (*pt* & *pp* **qualified**) ◇ *vt* **-1.** [remark, approval] to make <a statement> less strong by adding a detail or comment to it □ They qualified their acceptance of the plan. **-2.** to make <sb> able to do something properly or well □ Her experience more than qualifies her for the position. □ I feel that my wide

knowledge of the country qualifies me to speak about it.
◇ *vi* **-1.** [student, trainee] to pass one's exams or complete a training course □ He qualified as an accountant/a doctor last year. **-2.** [person] to have the right to have something □ In a few years I'll qualify for a pension. **-3.** SPORT [athlete, driver] to win a game or contest and have the right to enter the next stage of the competition □ The team has qualified for the final.

qualifying [ˈkwɒləfaɪɪŋ] *adj* **-1. a qualifying remark** a remark that makes a statement less strong. **-2. a qualifying exam** an exam that qualifies one to do something. **-3. a qualifying game/round etc** SPORT a game/round etc that is used as a way of deciding which contestant or team can enter the next stage in a competition.

qualitative [US ˈkwɒləteɪtɪv, GB -ɪtətɪv] *adj* [judgment, change] that is connected with the quality or standard of something □ a qualitative study of primary education.

quality [ˈkwɒlətɪ] (*pl* **qualities**) *n* **-1.** [of a product, performance] a measure of how good or bad something is □ the high/poor quality of the workmanship. **-2.** [of somebody's work, performance] a high standard of something □ We have a reputation for quality. □ We supply quality furniture to the domestic market. **-3.** [of a person] a good aspect of somebody's character □ Those are the qualities we are looking for in our candidates. **-4.** [of a substance, object] a characteristic of a substance or object □ There was a sinister quality in her voice. □ Our tires have superior roadholding qualities.

quality control *n* the process of testing products, e.g. in a factory, to make sure that they are of the necessary standard.

quality press *n* GB **the quality press** serious newspapers, not tabloids.

qualms [kwɑːmz] *npl* **to have qualms about sthg** to have feelings of uncertainty about whether sthg is right or wrong □ I'd have no qualms about complaining if I were you.

quandary [ˈkwɒndərɪ] (*pl* **quandaries**) *n* **to be in a quandary about** OR **over sthg** to be in a difficult situation and be unable to decide what to do about sthg □ I'm in a quandary about whether to tell them or not.

quango [ˈkwæŋgou] (*abbr of* **quasi-autonomous non-governmental organization**) (*pl* **quangos**) *n* GB an independent body with legal powers that is set up and financed by the government.

♥ QUANGOS

Quangos were first set up in the UK in the 1970s to be responsible for particular areas of activity such as the arts, education, the environment etc. Quangos have different roles and can range from a temporary committee that is giving a report on a particular issue, to a permanent body that carries out a government policy or supervises the way it is being carried out. Examples of quangos are the British Council or the Commission for Racial Equality. The money for quangos comes from the government, and their members are chosen by the government. However they have their own legal powers and their actions do not have to be approved by the government.

quantifiable [kwɒntə'faɪəbl] *adj* [damage, contribution] that can be quantified.

quantify ['kwɒntəfaɪ] (*pt* & *pp* **quantified**) *vt* [damage, contribution, value] to measure the amount or extent of <sthg> □ *His effect on the team will be difficult to quantify.*

quantitative [US 'kwɒntəteɪtɪv, GB -ɪtətɪv] *adj* [analysis, difference] that is connected with the amount rather than the quality of something.

quantity ['kwɒntətɪ] (*pl* **quantities**) *n* -1. an amount of something; a number of things □ *They consume large quantities of food.* -2. **in quantity** in large amounts or numbers □ *They buy cereals in quantity.* -3. **to be an unknown quantity** to be somebody or something that one knows nothing about □ *As a teacher, he's still an unknown quantity.*

quantity surveyor *n* GB a person whose job is to calculate the amount of materials, time, and money needed to build a building.

quantum leap ['kwɒntəm-] *n* a very important advance or improvement □ *This new discovery constitutes a quantum leap in the field of cancer research.*

quantum theory *n* the idea that energy can only exist and be transferred in fixed amounts.

quarantine ['kwɒrəntiːn] ◇ *n* a period of time when a person or animal that may have a disease is kept separate from other people or animals to prevent the spread of the disease □ *strict quarantine laws.* ■ **to be in quarantine** [person, animal] to be kept alone for a fixed period to prevent the spread of a disease. ◇ *vt* to put <an animal or person> in quarantine.

quark [kwɑːʳk] *n* -1. PHYSICS one of the very small particles that are said to form the substances that atoms are made of. -2. COOKING a low-fat soft cheese.

quarrel ['kwɒrəl] (US *pt* & *pp* **quarreled**, *cont* **quarreling**, GB *pt* & *pp* **quarrelled**, *cont* **quarrelling**) ◇ *n* an angry disagreement between two or more people that often lasts a long time and is usually about something that is not important □ *She got into a quarrel with her boss.* ■ **to have no quarrel with sb/sthg** to have no reason to disagree with sb/sthg □ *I have no quarrel with him personally, it's what he stands for I can't stomach.* ◇ *vi* to take part in a quarrel □ *He's always quarreling with his sister.* ■ **to quarrel with sthg** [with an idea, a conclusion] to disagree with sthg □ *Few people would quarrel with that.*

quarrelsome ['kwɒrəlsəm] *adj* [person] who is easily irritated and likely to be involved in quarrels.

quarry ['kwɒrɪ] (*pl* **quarries**, *pt* & *pp* **quarried**) ◇ *n* -1. a place where stones or minerals are removed from the ground in large quantities □ *a marble/gravel quarry.* -2. **sb's quarry** an animal or person that sb is hunting □ *He ran after it, but his quarry got away.* ◇ *vt* [stone, mineral] to remove <sthg> from a quarry by digging.

quarry tile *n* a square or diamond-shaped floor tile that has not been glazed.

quart [kwɔːʳt] *n* a unit (US 0.944 liters, GB 1.136 liters) for measuring volume, usually of liquid.

quarter ['kwɔːʳtəʳ] *n* -1. one of four equal parts of something □ *during the first quarter of the century* □ *A quarter of our exports go to America.* -2. [of an hour] a period of 15 minutes before or after an hour. ■ **a quarter after two** US, **a quarter past two** 2:15. ■ **a quarter of two** US, **a quarter to two** 1:45. -3. [of a year] a period of three months in a particular year □ *the phone bill/inflation rate for the last quarter.* -4. FINANCE an American or Canadian coin that is worth 25 cents. -5. GB [for measuring weight] a unit (four ounces) for measuring weight □ *a quarter of cheese/sweets.* -6. [of a town, city] an area of a town or city □ *the Latin Quarter* □ *a poor quarter.* -7. [people] a person or group of people □ *Help came from an unexpected quarter.*

◆ **quarters** *npl* one or more rooms where somebody lives, usually a soldier or sailor □ *cramped living quarters.*

◆ **at close quarters** *adv* [see, experience] from a position that is very close to somebody or something □ *I'd never seen a zebra at close quarters before.*

quarterback ['kwɔːʳtəʳbæk] *n* in football, a player who controls his team's offense and throws or carries the ball forward at the beginning of each play.

quarterdeck ['kwɔːʳtəʳdek] *n* the rear part of the highest deck of a ship.

quarterfinal [,kwɔːʳtəʳ'faɪnl] *n* SPORT one of four games near the end of a competition that decide which teams or players will compete in the semifinal.

quarter-hour *adj* [intervals] happening every 15 minutes.

quarter light *n* GB a small, usually triangular window next to the main windows in a car.

quarterly ['kwɔːʳtəʳlɪ] (*pl* **quarterlies**) ◇ *adj* [payments, bills] that happens every three months. ◇ *adv* [pay, appear] every three months □ *We present our accounts for inspection quarterly.* ◇ *n* a publication, usually a magazine, that appears every three months.

quartermaster [US 'kwɔːrtrmæstr, GB 'kwɔːtəmɑːstə] *n* the officer in an army who is responsible for accommodation and supplies of food, clothing etc.

quarter note *n* US a musical note that is equal to a quarter of the length of a whole note.

quarter sessions *npl* US a local criminal and administrative court found in some states.

quartet [kwɔːʳ'tet] *n* -1. a group of four musicians. **-2.** a piece of music written for four musicians.

quarto ['kwɔːˤtoʊ] (*pl* **quartos**) *n* a size of paper (25.4×20.3 cm); a book made of paper that is this size.

quartz [kwɔːˤts] *n* a very hard mineral in crystal form that is used for making very accurate clocks and watches. FORMULA: SiO_2.

quartz watch *n* a watch that is operated by the vibrations of a quartz crystal.

quasar ['kweɪzɑːˤ] *n* a very bright object in outer space that is like a star.

quash [kwɒʃ] *vt* **-1.** [decision, sentence, rumor] to reject <sthg> officially □ *The appeals judge quashed his conviction for drink driving.* **-2.** [protest, revolt] to stop <a rebellion> by force □ *The army quashed any further attempts at revolt.*

quasi- ['kweɪzaɪ] *prefix* added to a word to say that something is almost but not quite the same as that word □ *a quasi-official organization.*

quaver ['kweɪvəˤ] ◇ *n* **-1.** a shaking sound in somebody's voice. **-2.** GB MUSIC a note that is equal to half the length of a quarter note. ◇ *vi* [voice] to shake, e.g. because of nervousness.

quavering ['kweɪvərɪŋ] *adj* [voice] that quavers.

quay [kiː] *n* a long platform beside the water in a harbor, where ships can be tied up and loaded or unloaded.

quayside ['kiːsaɪd] *n* the edge of a quay along the water.

queasy ['kwiːzɪ] (*compar* **queasier**, *superl* **queasiest**) *adj* [person] who feels that they are going to vomit □ *I always get queasy when I travel by car.*

Quebec [kwɪ'bek] a province in eastern Canada. It is the center of French Canadian language and culture. ABBREVIATION: PQ. SIZE: 1,540,680 sq kms. POPULATION: 6,895,963 (*Quebeckers*, *Québécois*). CAPITAL: Quebec. MAIN CITY: Montreal.

Quebecer, **Quebecker** [kwɪ'bekəˤ] *n* a person who comes from or lives in Quebec.

queen [kwiːn] *n* **-1.** [of a country] the female ruler of a country □ *the queen of Spain* OR *the Spanish queen.* **-2.** [of a king] the wife of a king. **-3.** a large female insect that produces eggs □ *a queen ant.* **-4.** CHESS the most powerful piece in chess that can move backward, forward, sideways, and diagonally. **-5.** CARDS a playing card that has a picture of a queen on it and is worth more than a jack and less than a king □ *the queen of spades.*

queen bee *n* **-1.** a large female bee that produces eggs. **-2.** a woman whose behavior shows that she thinks she is more important than the people she is with.

◆ **queen mother** *n* **the queen mother** the mother of a ruling king or queen.

Queen Mother: (Queen Elizabeth) the Queen Mother (1900–) the mother of the British queen, Elizabeth II.

Queens [kwiːnz] a borough of New York City, situated at the west end of Long Island. POPULATION: 1,891,000.

Queen's Bench Division *n* **the Queen's Bench Division** one of the divisions of the British High Court of Justice.

Queen's Counsel *n* a high-ranking barrister in Britain.

Queen's English *n* **the Queen's English** a standard way of speaking British English.

Queen's evidence *n* GB **to turn Queen's evidence** [criminal] to give evidence in court against other criminals in order to get a less serious punishment.

Queensland ['kwiːnzlænd] a state in northeastern Australia. SIZE: 1,727,500 sq kms. POPULATION: 2,978,617 (*Queenslanders*). CAPITAL: Brisbane.

Queen's speech *n* **the Queen's speech** a speech made by the British queen once a year, at the official opening of Parliament. It is written by the government, and outlines their program for the year.

queer [kwɪəˤ] ◇ *adj* [character, feeling, behavior] strange □ *He gave a queer, nervous laugh.* ◇ *n*▼ a homosexual (informal and offensive use).

quell [kwel] *vt* **-1.** [revolt, riot] to stop <a rebellion>, usually by force, before it gets out of control □ *Special police were brought in to quell the rioters.* **-2.** [unease, anger] to stop oneself or other people from having <a particular feeling> □ *Her words quelled any lingering doubts I had had.*

quench [kwentʃ] *vt* **to quench one's thirst** [drink] to stop one from feeling thirsty; [person] to drink, so that one is no longer thirsty.

querulous ['kwerʊləs] *adj* [person] who often complains (formal use).

query ['kwɪərɪ] (*pl* **queries**, *pt* & *pp* **queried**) ◇ *n* a question that one asks when one is uncertain about something or thinks it may not be true or correct □ *Are there any other queries?* ◇ *vt* [invoice, statement, decision] to ask a question about <sthg> because one thinks it may not be true or correct □ *The tax office has queried our accounts.*

quest [kwest] *n* a long difficult search (literary use) □ *the quest for truth/enlightenment.*

question ['kwestʃn] ◇ *n* **-1.** something that one says or writes in order to ask for information □ *I wish to put a question to the panel.* □ *Do you mind if I ask you a question?* **-2. to be in question** to be doubted □ *His honesty was never in question.* ■ **to bring** OR **call sthg into question** to express doubts about sthg □ *An oversight like this calls into question the competence of the staff.* ■ **beyond** OR **without question** without any doubt □ *She is beyond question the best.* ■ **to be open to question** [truth, opinion, conclusion] to be uncertain or hard to accept without disagreement □ *The advantages of the new system are open to question.* ■ **to obey without question** to obey without disagreeing or expressing doubts □ *They expected me to follow orders without question.* **-3.** [matter] a matter that needs to be discussed or dealt with □ *The article raises some important questions.* ■ **it's a question of...** a phrase used to state what is necessary or

important in a particular situation □ *It's just a question of time.* **-4.** [in a test, exam] one of the tasks in an exam or test, e.g. solving a problem or discussing a subject, that are designed to test one's knowledge □ *Candidates must answer all four questions.* **-5.** phrase **there's no question of...** there is no likelihood or possibility of... □ *There's no question of our going back on our decision.*
◇ *vt* **-1.** [suspect, witness] to ask <sb> one or more questions, especially about a crime □ *The police are questioning him about the murder.* **-2.** [ability, motives, idea] to express one's doubts about <sthg> □ *I question the wisdom of such a move.*

♦ **in question** *adj* the person/thing etc in question the particular person/thing etc that one has just been talking about □ *Where were you on the night in question?*

♦ **out of the question** *adj* to be out of the question to be impossible to allow or consider □ *Further loans are out of the question.*

questionable ['kwestʃənəbl] *adj* [decision, behavior, taste] that one cannot accept completely because it seems wrong in some way □ *He was involved in some rather questionable deals.*

questioner ['kwestʃənər] *n* a person who is asking a question.

questioning ['kwestʃənɪŋ] ◇ *adj* [look] that expresses a question. ◇ *n* [of a suspect, witness] the process of asking somebody questions, especially about a crime □ *Four men are being held for questioning by the police.*

question mark *n* the punctuation mark (?) that shows that a question is being asked.

question master *n* the person who asks the questions on a game show on television or radio.

questionnaire [,kwestʃə'neər] *n* a list of questions, usually intended to provide information about a particular subject or product.

question time *n* the regular session in the British Parliament in which government ministers answer questions about policy asked by Members of Parliament.

queue [kjuː] ◇ *n* GB a line of people, cars etc that are waiting to do something □ *You'll have to join the queue.* □ *There was a queue of people waiting to get in.* □ *a queue of traffic.* ■ **to jump the queue** to join a line of people ahead of other people who have been waiting longer. ◇ *vi* to wait in a line of people □ *I had to queue for my tickets.*

quibble ['kwɪbl] ◇ *vi* to argue about unimportant details (disapproving use) □ *I'm not going to quibble (with you) over/about the exact words I used.* ◇ *n* an unimportant complaint or disagreement.

quiche [kiːʃ] *n* a layer of pastry filled with eggs, cheese, and often bacon or vegetables and eaten hot or cold.

quick [kwɪk] ◇ *adj* **-1.** [runner, worker] who does something very fast; [person] who is intelligent and learns very easily □ *All right, but be quick!* □ *We need someone who's quick at spotting potential problems.* □ *With quick staccato*

movements, the bird hopped across the grass. □ *She's a quick learner.* **-2.** [trip, drink, look] that takes a very short time to complete □ *I gave them a quick summary of what had happened.* **-3.** [reply, response, decision] that happens almost immediately □ *"When did you receive it?" — "Yesterday." — "That was quick!"* □ *He's always quick to complain.* ◇ *adv*: *Come quick!* □ *We've thought of a scheme to get rich quick.*

quicken ['kwɪkn] ◇ *vt* **to quicken one's pace** to start walking or running faster. ■ **to quicken one's step** to start walking faster. ◇ *vi* [pace, step] to go at a faster speed □ *My pulse quickened.*

quickly ['kwɪklɪ] *adv* [move, work, react] *see* **quick** □ *She dressed quickly and went out.* □ *They responded quickly to our request.* □ *Come quickly!* □ *I quickly realized something was wrong.*

quicksand ['kwɪksænd] *n* an area of loose wet sand that is dangerous because people can sink into it.

quicksilver ['kwɪksɪlvər] *n* = **mercury** (old-fashioned use).

quickstep ['kwɪkstep] *n* **the quickstep** a ballroom dance that involves a lot of fast steps; the type of music played for this dance.

quick-tempered *adj* [person] who easily becomes angry □ *As a girl, she could be very quick-tempered.*

quick-witted [-'wɪtəd] *adj* [person] who can understand things quickly and think of intelligent and amusing things to say.

quid [kwɪd] (*pl* **quid**) *n* GB one pound (informal use) □ *Can you lend me twenty quid?*

quid pro quo [-'kwoʊ] (*pl* **quid pro quos**) *n* something that is given to somebody in exchange for something they have done.

quiescent [kwɪ'esnt] *adj* [person] who is quiet and inactive (literary use).

quiet ['kwaɪət] ◇ *adj* **-1.** [voice, children, place] that is not noisy □ *a quiet engine/car/plane* □ *I like to work in a quiet room with no distractions.* □ *Keep quiet!* **-2.** [person] who does not talk much □ *You're very quiet today.* □ *a quiet, shy girl.* ■ **to keep quiet about sthg** not to talk about or mention sthg, especially something that other people will find out about later or might not approve of □ *I'd keep quiet about that if I were you.* ■ **(be) quiet!** a phrase used to order or tell somebody to make less or no noise □ *Please be quiet! I'm trying to read.* **-3.** [life, day, place] that is calm and without problems or excitement □ *Let's find a nice quiet spot near the river to eat our picnic.* □ *I feel like spending a quiet evening in front of the TV.* **-4.** [business, trade] that is not busy, because there are few people buying, selling etc □ *It's been very quiet in the office/store today.* **-5.** [clothing, color] that is not very noticeable to other people □ *Could I have a quiet word with you in private?* □ *He exudes a kind of quiet confidence.* **-6.** [ceremony, dinner] that consists of only a few specially chosen people □ *It was a quiet wedding/funeral attended only by the immediate family.*
◇ *n* silence □ *Can we have quiet, please!* □ *All I want is some peace and quiet.*

◇ *vt* US to make <sb/sthg> quiet.

◆ **on the quiet** *adv* secretly (informal use) □ *He's been practicing on the quiet.*

◆ **quiet down** US ◇ *vt sep* to make <sb> calm or quiet. ◇ *vi*: *The room immediately quieted down.* □ *Quiet down!*

quieten ['kwaɪətn] *vt* -1. [voice] to make <sb/sthg> less noisy. -2. to make <sb's fears, worries> etc less strong.

◆ **quieten down** *vi* & *vt sep* GB = **quiet down**.

quietly ['kwaɪətlɪ] *adv* [say, sit, live] *see* **quiet** □ *He left quietly, without saying goodbye to anyone.* □ *She's quietly confident about passing the exam.*

quiff [kwɪf] *n* GB a part of the hair at the front of one's head that is brushed up over one's forehead.

quill [kwɪl] *n* **a quill (pen)** a pen made out of a large feather.

quilt [kwɪlt] *n* a covering for a bed that is filled with light, warm material such as feathers.

quilted ['kwɪltəd] *adj* [jacket, lining] that is made of a cloth filled with light, warm material and has lines of stitching across it that form patterns.

quince [kwɪns] *n* a hard yellow fruit with a bitter taste that is shaped like a pear and is used to make jellies.

quinine [US 'kwaɪnaɪn, GB 'kwɪniːn] *n* a drug used to treat malaria.

quins [kwɪnz] *npl* GB = **quintuplets** (informal use).

quintessential [ˌkwɪntə'senʃl] *adj* [characteristic] that is the most typical example of something □ *This passage is quintessential Brahms.* □ *He was the quintessential English aristocrat.*

quintet [kwɪn'tet] *n* -1. a group of five musicians or singers who perform together. -2. a piece of music written for five instruments or singers performing together.

quints [kwɪnts] *npl* US = **quintuplets** (informal use).

quintuplets [US kwɪn'tʌpləts, GB 'kwɪntjʊpləts] *npl* five babies born at the same time to the same mother.

quip [kwɪp] (*pt* & *pp* **quipped**, *cont* **quipping**) ◇ *n* a clever and funny remark. ◇ *vi* to make a quip.

quire ['kwaɪəʳ] *n* 24 sheets of paper.

quirk [kwɜːʳk] *n* -1. a strange habit or aspect of somebody's character □ *We all have our little quirks.* -2. a strange happening that one cannot explain □ *By some quirk of fate they had lived in the same town all their lives without knowing it.* □ *a quirk of nature.*

quirky ['kwɜːʳkɪ] (*compar* **quirkier**, *superl* **quirkiest**) *adj* [sense of humor, person] that seems odd and unusual.

quit [kwɪt] (US *pt* & *pp* **quit**, *cont* **quitting**, GB *pt* & *pp* **quit** OR **quitted**, *cont* **quitting**) ◇ *vt* -1. to leave <a job or a place>. -2. **to quit doing sthg** to stop doing sthg □ *I've tried to quit smoking/drinking.* □ *Quit bothering me!* ◇ *vi* -1. to leave one's job. -2. to stop doing some-

thing □ *He advised me to quit while I was still ahead.*

quite [kwaɪt] *adv* & *predet* -1. [different, sure, still] a word used to emphasize that something is the case □ *I quite agree.* □ *It's all quite simple and straightforward.* □ *That was quite delicious.* -2. [easy, young, obvious] fairly □ *We'll be finished quite soon.* □ *It's/She's quite nice.* □ *They live quite a bit further down the road.* □ *It's quite a good book, actually.* ■ **quite a lot of, quite a few** a fairly large number of □ *There were quite a lot of people at the party.* □ *I've visited them quite a few times.* -3. a word used after a negative to make it seem less strong □ *The skirt is not quite big enough for me.* □ *I don't quite understand/know.* -4. **quite a...** a phrase used before a noun to emphasize its degree, high standard, or unusual nature □ *She's quite a woman.* □ *It was quite a shock/surprise to be invited.* □ *They were gone quite a while.* -5. **quite (so)!** a word or phrase used to express agreement (formal use) □ *"I said we couldn't possibly accept." — "Quite so."*

quits [kwɪts] *adj* (informal use) **to be quits** to be in an equal situation with somebody again, especially after paying them back money that one owed □ *Once I give him back his $5 I'll be quits with him again.* ■ **to call it quits** to agree to stop an argument about something □ *Why don't you both just shake hands and call it quits?*

quitter ['kwɪtəʳ] *n* a person who one thinks gives up too easily (disapproving and informal use).

quiver ['kwɪvəʳ] ◇ *vi* to shake slightly, especially because one is nervous or excited □ *He was quivering with fear/rage.* ◇ *n* -1. [of fear, excitement] a trembling movement □ *A quiver of excitement ran down her spine.* -2. a long thin bag for carrying arrows.

quixotic [kwɪk'sɒtɪk] *adj* [person] who has ideals and is not practical or realistic (formal use).

quiz [kwɪz] (*pl* **quizzes**, *pt* & *pp* **quizzed**, *cont* **quizzing**) ◇ *n* -1. a type of game or competition that involves answering questions □ *a quiz show.* -2. EDUCATION US a short test. ◇ *vt* to ask <sb> a lot of questions about something □ *They quizzed me on/about my past sales experience.*

quizmaster [US 'kwɪzmæstr, GB -mɑːstə] *n* the person who asks the questions on a quiz show.

quizzical ['kwɪzɪkl] *adj* [look, smile] that shows that one is amused by or doubtful about what somebody else has said or done.

quoits [kɔɪts] *n* a game in which rings are thrown over a small post.

Quonset hut™ ['kwɒnsət-] *n* US a shelter that has a curved roof made of sheets of metal.

quorate ['kwɔːreɪt] *adj* GB [meeting] that has a quorum.

quorum ['kwɔːrəm] *n* the smallest number of people that needs to be present at a meeting in order e.g. for formal decisions to be made, or for the meeting to start.

quota ['kwəʊtə] *n* [of people] the fixed number of people who are allowed to enter or join something such as a university; [of goods, products] the smallest or largest amount of something that is allowed to be produced, sold etc □ *The European Union is setting strict quotas on agricultural production.* □ *a quota system* □ *fishing quotas.*

quotation [kwəʊ'teɪʃn] *n* **-1.** the exact words that somebody, especially somebody well-known, said or wrote; the act of quoting somebody or something □ *It's a quotation from a famous poem.* **-2.** BUSINESS a formal statement of the exact cost that will be charged for something that is to be done or bought.

quotation marks *npl* the symbols (" ") or (' ') that show where a quotation begins and ends.

quote [kwəʊt] ◇ *n* = **quotation** □ *We chose the company that gave the lowest quote.*
◇ *vt* **-1.** [person, proverb, poem] to repeat the exact words of <sb/sthg>; [figures, law] to mention <sthg> to make one's argument stronger □ *Please don't quote me on this — I'd lose my job.* □ *She was quoted as saying that the rules were harsh and unjust.* □ *He quoted the example of one company that had gone bankrupt.* □ *Please quote this reference number in all future correspondence.* **-2.** BUSINESS to give a formal statement of <the price> of something; to give <sb> a quotation for something □ *How much would you quote me for this vase — $50?*
◇ *vi* **-1.** *She quoted from the contract in front of her.* **-2.** BUSINESS **to quote for sthg** [for goods, a contract, repair] to quote a price for sthg.
◆ **quotes** *npl* = **quotation marks.**

quoted company ['kwəʊtəd-] *n* GB a company that has shares that can be bought or sold on the Stock Exchange.

quotient ['kwəʊʃnt] *n* the amount or degree of a particular thing □ *The job has a low stress quotient.*

Qur'an [US kə'ræn, GB -'rɑːn] = **Koran.**

qv (*abbr of* **quod vide**) an expression written in a book such as an encyclopedia, to refer the reader to something in another part of the book.

qwerty keyboard ['kwɜːʳtɪ-] *n* the computer or typewriter keyboard used for the English language, the top line of which begins with the letters Q, W, E, R, T, and Y.

R

r [ɑːʳ] (*pl* **r's** OR **rs**), **R** [ɑːʳ] (*pl* **R's** OR **Rs**) *n* the eighteenth letter of the English alphabet.
◆ **R -1.** *abbr of* **right. -2.** *abbr of* **river. -3.** (*abbr*

of **restricted**) a symbol for movies and video tapes in the USA, used to show that children under 17 are only allowed to watch if an adult is with them. **-4.** (*abbr of* **restricted**) a symbol for movies in Australia, used to show that the movie can only be shown to people over 18 years old. **-5.** US *abbr of* **Republican. -6.** GB (*abbr of* **Rex**) a symbol written after the name of a king. **-7.** GB (*abbr of* **Regina**) a symbol written after the name of a queen.

RA (*abbr of* **Royal Academy**) *n* **the RA** an association of artists in Britain who run a postgraduate art school and organize exhibitions; a title, written after a person's name, to show that they are a member of this association.

RAAF *n abbr of* **Royal Australian Air Force.**

rabbi ['ræbaɪ] *n* a Jewish religious leader.

rabbit ['ræbət] *n* a small animal with soft fur, long ears, and a round white tail that lives in holes under the ground, or is kept as a pet; the meat of this animal used as food □ *a wild/pet rabbit* □ *rabbit stew.*

rabbit hole *n* a hole in the ground where a rabbit lives.

rabbit hutch *n* a wooden cage that pet rabbits are kept in.

rabbit warren *n* **-1.** a system of passages and holes under the ground where rabbits live. **-2.** a building with many rooms and long passages that is difficult to find one's way around.

rabble ['ræbl] *n* a noisy, uncontrolled, and often violent crowd of people.

rabble-rousing *adj* [speech, speaker] that encourages people to act in a violent or uncontrolled way.

rabid ['ræbəd] *adj* **-1.** [animal] that is infected with rabies. **-2.** [feminist, right-winger] who has very strong opinions and is not open to other points of view (disapproving use).

rabies ['reɪbiːz] *n* a very serious disease affecting humans and some animals that is passed on by the bite of a diseased animal, and causes madness and usually death.

RAC (*abbr of* **Royal Automobile Club**) *n* **the RAC** a British organization for drivers that helps its members when their cars break down.

raccoon [rə'kuːn] *n* a small animal of North and Central America that has black circles around its eyes and black rings along its tail.

race [reɪs] ◇ *n* **-1.** [between people, cars, horses] a competition between several people, vehicles, or animals to see which one is the fastest □ *a boat/horse race* □ *We had a race, and I came in last.* □ *It became a race against time* OR *the clock.* **-2.** [for power] a competition for power or control □ *the race for the White House.* **-3.** [of people] any one of the main groups that people can be divided into according to their skin color, hair etc; the state of belonging to one of these groups □ *the Arab race* □ *We welcome anyone, whatever their race, creed, or color.* □ *He was discriminated* *against on grounds of race.* □ *Race has become a big issue.*

◇ *vt* **-1.** [person] to compete against <sb> in a race □ *I'll race you to the beach!* **-2.** [horse, car] to enter <an animal or vehicle> in a race. **-3.** to take <sb> somewhere as quickly as possible □ *She was raced to the hospital.*

◇ *vi* **-1.** [athlete, driver, horse] to compete in a race □ *He has raced against some of the best swimmers in the world.* **-2.** [person] to go somewhere or do something very quickly □ *She raced up the stairs/into the house.* **-3.** [heart, pulse] to beat very fast, especially because of excitement or fear □ *His heart raced when he heard her come in.* **-4.** [engine] to run faster than normal.

race car *n* US a car that is specially built to go as fast as possible and that is raced in competitions.

racecourse ['reɪskɔːʳs] *n* **-1.** US a track that runners, cars etc race around. **-2.** GB a track that horses race around.

race driver *n* US a person who drives a race car.

racehorse ['reɪshɔːʳs] *n* a horse that is bred and trained to be raced.

race meeting *n* an occasion when several horse races are held at the same race course.

race relations *npl* the way people of different races living in the same place behave toward each other.

Race Relations Act *n* **the Race Relations Act** a British act of parliament designed to ensure equal opportunities and treatment for people of all races.

race riot *n* a riot between people of different races living in the same place.

racetrack ['reɪstræk] *n* **-1.** a track that runners, cars etc race around. **-2.** US a track that horses race around.

Rachmaninov [US rɑːkˈmɑːnənɒf, GB rækˈmæn-], **Sergei** (1873–1943) a Russian composer and pianist whose best-known work is the *Rhapsody on a Theme of Paganini.*

racial ['reɪʃl] *adj* [tension, harmony, attack] that exists or happens between people of different races; [characteristic, pride] that is connected with a person's race □ *a victim of racial harassment* □ *a racial group.*

racial discrimination *n* unfair treatment of somebody because of their race.

racialism ['reɪʃəlɪzm] *n* = **racism**.

racialist ['reɪʃələst] *adj* = **racist**.

racing ['reɪsɪŋ] *n* the sport of racing a vehicle or animal □ *greyhound/motorbike racing.*

racing car *n* GB = **race car**.

racing driver *n* GB = **race driver**.

racism ['reɪsɪzm] *n* the belief that particular races, especially one's own, are better than other races; unfair or violent treatment of people because of this belief □ *They were accused of racism.*

racist ['reɪsəst] (disapproving use) ◇ *adj* [remark, attack, policy] that is connected with racism; [person, group] that believes in racism. ◇ *n* a

racist person □ *Call me a racist, but that's what I think.*

rack [ræk] ◇ *n* **-1.** something that is made to hold a particular kind of object and has sections, hooks, or bars to separate each one □ *a wine/magazine rack* □ *a rack of clothes.* **-2.** a shelf above a seat in a train, or that one attaches to the roof of one's car, where one can put luggage □ *a luggage rack.* ◇ *vt* **to be racked by** OR **with sthg** [with pain, guilt, despair] to suffer a great amount of sthg.

racket ['rækət] *n* **-1.** a loud and unpleasant noise □ *The children were making a terrible racket.* **-2.** an illegal way of making money □ *a drugs/gambling racket.* **-3.** SPORT a piece of equipment, used for hitting a ball in sports such as tennis and squash, that consists of tight strings in a rounded frame of plastic or metal attached to a long handle □ *a tennis/squash/badminton racket.*

racketeering [ˌrækəˈtɪərɪŋ] *n* the act or crime of making money through illegal means (disapproving use).

raconteur [ˌrækɒnˈtɜːʳ] *n* a person who is good at telling interesting and amusing stories.

racoon [rəˈkuːn] *n* = **raccoon**.

racquet ['rækət] *n* SPORT = **racket**.

racy ['reɪsɪ] (*compar* **racier**, *superl* **raciest**) *adj* [novel, story, style] that is entertaining and lively, especially because it involves sex.

RADA ['rɑːdə] (*abbr of* **Royal Academy of Dramatic Art**) *n* an important drama school in London.

radar ['reɪdɑːʳ] *n* an instrument that shows the position and speed of a moving object, e.g. a plane or ship, by measuring the speed of the radio waves received from them □ *The plane was equipped with radar.* □ *a radar screen.*

radar trap *n* a device using radar that the police use to measure the speed of cars that are going too fast.

radial ['reɪdɪəl] *n* **a radial (tire)** a tire with cords under the rubber that spread out around the tire from the center to give better control.

radiance ['reɪdɪəns] *n* **-1.** [of somebody's face, smile] great happiness □ *the radiance of youth.* **-2.** the light shining on or from something.

radiant ['reɪdɪənt] *adj* **-1.** [face, person] that looks very happy □ *The bride was radiant.* **-2.** [light, sun] that shines brightly. **-3.** **radiant heat** PHYSICS heat that is sent out by radiation.

radiate ['reɪdɪeɪt] ◇ *vt* **-1.** [warmth, glow] to send out <heat or light> in all directions. **-2.** [confidence, health] to be so full of <a particular feeling or quality> that everyone notices it □ *She positively radiates good health.* ◇ *vi* **-1.** [heat, light] *The warmth from the fire radiated throughout the room.* **-2.** [roads, paths, lines] to spread out in different directions from a central point □ *A network of cables is to be installed, radiating out from this main box.*

radiation [ˌreɪdɪˈeɪʃn] *n* **-1.** the energy produced by certain substances when atoms break up, e.g. as the result of a nuclear reaction. Radiation can be very harmful. □ *a le-*

thal dose of radiation. **-2.** energy in the form of particular kinds of heat or light that travels through the air but cannot be seen □ *electromagnetic/ultraviolet radiation.*

radiation sickness *n* an illness caused when one receives too much radiation from a radioactive substance.

radiator ['reɪdɪeɪtə^r] *n* **-1.** [in a house, building] a large metal device, usually fitted to a wall, containing water or oil that gets hot and heats up a room. **-2.** AUTO the part of a vehicle that keeps the engine cool □ *a car radiator.*

radiator grille *n* the metal bars in front of a car radiator, on the outside of the car.

radical ['rædɪkl] ◇ *adj* **-1.** POLITICS [politician, view] that supports the belief that great changes need to be made in a society, the economy, or in politics □ *a member of the radical left wing* □ *They advocate radical reform.* **-2.** [change, disagreement] that is complete or has important effects □ *There has been a radical improvement in the standard of your work.* ◇ *n* POLITICS a person, especially a politician, who has radical beliefs.

radically ['rædɪklɪ] *adv* [change, alter, improve] *see* **radical** □ *Their attitudes are radically different.*

radii ['reɪdɪaɪ] *plural of* **radius.**

radio ['reɪdɪoʊ] (*pl* **radios**) ◇ *n* **-1.** a system of communication that involves sending sound through the air using electrical waves □ *The message came through over the radio.* □ *a radio wave/link* □ *We established radio contact with the men at 07:00 hours.* □ *They sent out a radio signal.* **-2.** the system of broadcasting a program by sending sound through the air using electrical waves; the industry concerned with such broadcasting □ *I heard it on the radio.* □ *I work in radio.* □ *a radio station/ program.* **-3.** a piece of equipment used to listen to programs that are broadcast by means of electrical waves □ *She turned the radio on/off.* □ *a ship's radio.*
◇ *vt* to send a message to <a person or place> by using a radio; [message, news, position] to send <information> to somebody by using a radio □ *They radioed the ship for help.*

radioactive [,reɪdɪoʊ'æktɪv] *adj* [element, fallout] that is connected with radioactivity.

radioactive waste *n* radioactive waste material produced by nuclear power stations.

radioactivity [,reɪdɪoʊæk'tɪvətɪ] *n* energy that is produced by certain atoms when they break up and that can be very harmful □ *high levels of radioactivity* □ *low-level radioactivity.*

radio alarm *n* a radio that can be set to turn itself on at a particular time to wake somebody up.

radio-controlled *adj* [toy, car] that can be made to move by radio waves sent out from a device held in a person's hand.

radio frequency *n* any of the radio waves used in broadcasting.

radiogram ['reɪdɪougræm] *n* a message that has been sent by radio.

radiographer [,reɪdɪ'ɒgrəfə^r] *n* a person who is trained to take and study X-rays.

radiography [,reɪdɪ'ɒgrəfɪ] *n* the examination of the inside of a patient by taking X-rays.

radiology [,reɪdɪ'ɒlədʒɪ] *n* the branch of medicine that is concerned with radiation and its use in diagnosing and treating diseases.

radiopaging ['reɪdɪoupeɪdʒɪŋ] *n* a system by which a small device able to receive radio waves sends out a short sound to warn the person carrying the device that somebody is trying to contact them.

radiotelephone [,reɪdɪou'telɪfoun] *n* a telephone that sends out sound using radio waves rather than wires.

radiotherapist [,reɪdɪou'θerəpəst] *n* a person who is trained in radiotherapy.

radiotherapy [,reɪdɪou'θerəpɪ] *n* the treatment of diseases, especially cancer, using radiation.

radish ['rædɪʃ] *n* a small, hard, round root vegetable, white inside and red outside, that has a hot taste and is eaten raw in salads.

radium ['reɪdɪəm] *n* a rare white radioactive metal that is used to treat cancer. SYMBOL: Ra.

radius ['reɪdɪəs] (*pl* **radii**) *n* **-1.** MATH the distance from the center of a circle to its outside edge. **-2. within a radius of 3 miles/200 km** less than '3 miles/200 km from a particular place in any direction □ *There are no stores within a five-mile radius of where she lives.* **-3.** ANATOMY the outer bone between one's wrist and elbow.

radon ['reɪdɒn] *n* a radioactive element in the form of a gas that has no color. SYMBOL: Rn.

RAF *n abbr of* **Royal Air Force.**

RAFDS *n abbr of* **Royal Australian Flying Doctor Service.**

raffia ['ræfɪə] *n* a material similar to soft string that comes from the palm tree, and is used for making hats, mats etc □ *a raffia mat.*

raffish ['ræfɪʃ] *adj* [man, charm] that is not very respectable but has a lot of style and is amusing.

raffle ['ræfl] ◇ *n* a competition, usually held in order to make money for a charity, in which people buy tickets hoping to win a prize □ *I won it in a raffle.* ◇ *vt* [car, wine] to offer <sthg> as a prize in a raffle.

raffle ticket *n* a ticket sold for a raffle.

raft [US ræft, GB rɑːft] *n* **-1.** a flat floating structure usually made of long pieces of wood tied together and used as a boat or as a fixed platform □ *a log/bamboo raft.* **-2.** a small boat made of rubber or plastic and filled with air that floats or can be rowed and is used to travel down rivers. **-3. a raft of things** a large amount or number of things □ *a whole raft of possibilities* □ *a raft of policies.*

rafter [US 'ræftr, GB 'rɑːftə] *n* any one of the lengths of wood that support a sloping roof.

rag [ræg] *n* **-1.** an old and torn piece of cloth □ *I mopped it up with an old rag.* ■ **to be (like) a red rag to a bull** to be something that makes somebody very annoyed or angry very quickly (informal use). **-2.** a newspaper (disapproving and informal use) □ *a right-wing/left-wing rag.*

◆ **rags** *npl* very old and torn clothes □ *dressed in rags.* ■ **to go from rags to riches** to quickly become very rich after being very poor.

ragamuffin ['ræɡəmʌfɪn] *n* a dirty child wearing torn clothes.

rag-and-bone man *n* GB a man who travels the streets in a horse and cart or van and is given old clothes, furniture etc that people no longer want.

ragbag ['ræɡbæɡ] *n* a confused mixture of several examples of a particular thing □ *a ragbag of styles/ideas.*

rag doll *n* a soft child's doll made of cloth.

rage [reɪdʒ] ◇ *n* **-1.** extreme anger, often lasting over a long period of time □ *She was shaking with rage.* □ *He flew into a rage.* □ *a cry of rage.* **-2. to be all the rage** [style, fashion] to be very popular for a short period of time (informal use) □ *Computer games are all the rage this Christmas.* ◇ *vi* **-1.** to be extremely angry □ *He raged at the injustice of it all.* **-2.** [disease, fire] to spread with great force and speed; [storm, controversy, argument] to continue with extreme force □ *The battle raged on for days.*

ragga ['ræɡə] *n* a style of rap music from the West Indies.

ragged ['ræɡəd] *adj* **-1.** [beggar, child] who is wearing old and torn clothes □ *a group of ragged refugees.* **-2.** [clothes] that look old and torn □ *a shirt with a ragged collar.* **-3.** [line, edge] that is not smooth, straight, or even □ *They formed a ragged line.* □ *a ragged hedge.* **-4.** [performance, work] that has many details that need improving □ *The band sounded tired and ragged.*

raging ['reɪdʒɪŋ] *adj* **-1. a raging thirst/headache etc** a very severe thirst/headache etc. **-2. a raging storm/argument etc** a violent and uncontrolled storm/argument etc.

ragout [ræ'ɡuː] *n* a stew of meat and vegetables.

rag trade *n* **the rag trade** GB the clothing industry, especially the designing, making, and selling of women's clothes (informal use).

rag week *n* in Britain, a week each year during which students raise money for charity by doing amusing or silly things, holding processions through the streets etc.

raid [reɪd] ◇ *n* **-1.** MILITARY a sudden, quick, planned attack on enemy territory in order to cause as much damage as possible □ *a bombing raid* □ *Their raid on the enemy camp went according to plan.* **-2.** [by police] a sudden planned visit by police to a place where they think they might find criminals or illegal goods □ *a police/drugs raid* □ *Heroin was found during the raid on the house last night.* **-3.** [by criminals] a sudden planned robbery of a store or bank when it is open □ *a bank raid.* ◇ *vt* **-1.** MILITARY [town, village] to carry out a raid on <a place> □ *The 5th Battalion raided po-*

sitions behind enemy lines. **-2.** [bank, club, office] to enter <a place> by force in order to carry out a raid □ *Police raided the apartment.*

raider ['reɪdər] *n* a person who takes part in a raid on a shop or bank □ *The raiders got away with $5,000 in cash.* □ *a bank raider.*

rail [reɪl] *n* **-1.** [on a ship, staircase, walkway] a piece of wood or metal for people to hold on to, or that stops people falling down etc □ *a stair/bath rail.* **-2.** [for clothes] a thin, horizontal piece of wood or metal fixed to a wall, or to two vertical bars, that is used for hanging things on □ *a coat/clothes rail.* **-3.** [for trains] one of two metal bars attached to the ground that a train travels along □ *The train somehow left the rails.* **-4.** the railroad system □ *I go to work by rail.* □ *a rail strike* □ *rail travel/transportation.*

railing ['reɪlɪŋ] *n* a barrier made up of a long row of vertical metal bars with a long horizontal bar at or near the top that goes around a balcony, the side of a ship, outside a house or park etc □ *an iron railing.*

◆ **railings** *npl* = **railing.**

railroad ['reɪlroʊd] US, **railway** ['reɪlweɪ] GB *n* **-1.** = **railroad track. -2.** the organization that provides transportation by rail □ *He worked for the railroads.* □ *a railroad engineer/company.* **-3.** the system of tracks, trains, and buildings used to provide transportation by rail.

railroad station *n* the building, including the ticket office and platforms, where one catches or leaves a train.

railroad track *n* the metal rails that a train travels along.

Railtrack ['reɪltræk] *n* in Britain, the government company responsible for the rail track, signaling, and train stations, which it leases to train companies.

railway *n* GB = **railroad.**

railway line *n* GB **-1.** the route between two places along a railroad track. **-2.** = **railroad track.**

rain [reɪn] ◇ *n* drops of water that fall from clouds in the sky □ *We got caught in the rain.* □ *She felt a drop of rain on her face.* □ *light/heavy rain.* ◇ *v impers* WEATHER **it's raining** rain is falling □ *I think it's going to rain.* □ *It's been raining all afternoon.* ◇ *vi* to fall like rain.

◆ **rain down** *vi* [shells, bullets] to fall quickly in large numbers; [abuse, applause] to be received by somebody in great quantity □ *Arrows rained down on them.* □ *Cheers rained down from the crowd.*

◆ **rain out** US, **rain off** GB *vt sep* **to be rained out** US OR **off** GB [game, match] not to take place because of rain.

rainbow ['reɪnboʊ] *n* a line in the sky in the shape of an arch with several bands of color, that can sometimes be seen after rain.

rainbow trout *n* a fish that can be eaten, and that has a pink and silvery skin with black dots.

rain check *n* **to take a rain check** US to decide not to accept or do something right away, but to do it at a later date □ *Can we take a rain check on our dinner date?*

raincoat ['reɪnkoʊt] *n* a light coat worn to protect oneself from the rain.

raindrop ['reɪndrɒp] *n* one drop of rain.

rainfall ['reɪnfɔːl] *n* the amount of rain that falls somewhere during a particular period of time □ *The average rainfall each year is declining.*

rain forest *n* a tropical forest of tall trees that grow very close together in an area where there is a lot of rain.

rain gauge *n* an instrument that measures rainfall.

rainproof ['reɪnpruːf] *adj* [material, roof] that does not allow rain to pass through it.

rainstorm ['reɪnstɔːrm] *n* a very heavy fall of rain with strong winds.

rainwater ['reɪnwɔːtər] *n* water that collects somewhere after falling as rain.

rainy ['reɪnɪ] (*compar* **rainier**, *superl* **rainiest**) *adj* [day, season, place] that has a lot of rain □ *rainy weather.*

raise [reɪz] ◇ *vt* -1. [barrier, weight, hand] to move or lift <sthg> to a higher level □ *He raised his head as she entered the room.* □ *We need to raise the height of the door frames.* ■ **to raise oneself (up)** to lift oneself, especially with difficulty □ *She raised herself up on her elbows, then slumped back exhausted.* -2. [limit, price, tax] to increase the amount of <sthg> □ *Interest rates look set to be raised once more.* ■ **to raise one's voice** to speak more loudly, especially in anger □ *Don't you raise your voice at me!* -3. to improve <a standard or level>. -4. [funds, capital, loan] to obtain <money> by earning it, borrowing it, or asking people for it □ *The campaign raised $10,000 for charity.* □ *She has to raise enough money to pay off her debts.* -5. [fear, doubt, memory] to cause somebody to feel or remember <sthg> □ *I can't seem to raise any enthusiasm for the trip.* □ *The ceasefire raised hopes of a long-term peace.* -6. [children] to look after <a child> until it is an adult □ *This is an ideal area in which to raise a family.* -7. FARMING [wheat, corn] to grow <a crop or vegetable>, especially in large amounts □ *Last year the farm raised over 3,000 acres of wheat.* -8. FARMING [chickens, horses, cattle] to breed <animals> □ *His family has raised sheep on this land for generations.* -9. [subject, question, objection] to mention <sthg>, especially in order to discuss it □ *I raised your suggestion with the boss, and he was in favor of trying it.* □ *I'd like to raise the issue of expenses.* -10. [statue] to build <a monument or statue>.
◇ *n* an increase in the amount of money one earns for one's job.

raisin ['reɪzn] *n* a dried grape used as food □ *rum and raisin ice cream.*

Raj [rɑːdʒ] *n* **the Raj** the period of British rule in India from 1858 to 1947.

rajah ['rɑːdʒə] *n* a male ruler in India.

rake [reɪk] ◇ *n* -1. GARDENING a tool with a long handle attached to a row of metal teeth, used to smooth the soil, gather up fallen leaves etc. -2. a wealthy young man who behaves in a wild and immoral way (old-fashioned use). ◇ *vt* -1. [soil, path] to make <an area of ground> smooth and level using a rake; [lawn] to pass a rake over <an area of grass>, e.g. to gather up leaves. -2. [leaves, weeds, grass] to gather up <dead plants> using a rake.

◆ **rake in** *vt sep* **to rake in the money/profits** to earn a lot of money/profits very quickly (informal use) □ *She has a new job and now she's raking it in.*

◆ **rake up** *vt sep* **to rake sthg up** [bad memories, argument] to talk about and remind somebody about sthg bad that happened in the past □ *Sorry, I didn't mean to start raking up the past.*

rake-off *n* a share of profits that somebody has earned usually by doing something that is not completely honest (informal use).

rakish ['reɪkɪʃ] *adj* -1. [life, lifestyle] that is wild and immoral. -2. [clothing] that shows a cheerful and relaxed confidence □ *His hat was tilted at a rakish angle.*

Raleigh ['rɔːlɪ], **Sir Walter** (1554–1618) a British explorer, adventurer, and writer. He is famous for bringing the first potatoes and tobacco to England from America.

rally ['rælɪ] (*pl* **rallies**, *pt* & *pp* **rallied**) ◇ *n* -1. a meeting of a large number of people in order to support a particular cause, usually a political cause, or to protest about something □ *a peace/political rally.* -2. [for cars] a car race along public roads □ *rally driving.* -3. [in tennis, squash] a series of strokes in which the ball is hit from one player to the other until a point is scored.
◇ *vt* [supporters, troops] to encourage <a group of people> to join together to fight for a particular aim; to encourage people to provide <support> to achieve a particular aim □ *They need to rally more support if they are to win the vote.*
◇ *vi* -1. [supporters, friends] to join together and give support to a particular cause □ *The villagers all rallied to the aid of the flood victims.* -2. [patient, player] to get or feel better or stronger, often only for a short period of time; [prices, currency] to increase after a period of weakness □ *The Bulls rallied toward the end to steal a win.* □ *After a weak start in the morning, share prices rallied.*

◆ **rally around**, **rally round** ◇ *vt fus* **to rally around sb** to join together to give support to sb who is in difficulty. ◇ *vi* [friends, colleagues] *The staff rallied around to help prepare for the inspectors' visit.*

rallying ['rælɪɪŋ] *n* the sport of driving in rallies.

rallying cry *n* a short phrase that encourages people to unite in support of a particular group □ *"All for one and one for all" was the rallying cry of the Three Musketeers.*

rallying point *n* a person, event etc that makes people gather together to support a particular cause □ *The demonstration provided a* *rallying point for people concerned about transportation policies.*

ram [ræm] (*pt* & *pp* **rammed**, *cont* **ramming**) ◇ *vt* -1. [car, ship] to crash into <another vehicle> with great force. -2. [person] to push <sthg> somewhere with great force □ *He rammed all his clothes into one small case.* -3. **to ram sthg home** [idea, fact] to make sthg very clear so that somebody understands or accepts it completely □ *You'll have to ram the message/the point home.* ◇ *n* an adult male sheep.

RAM [ræm] (*abbr of* **random access memory**) *n* a type of computer memory that stores information needed for a short time only and that lets one retrieve and use the information in any order.
NOTE: Compare **ROM**.

Ramadan [ˌræməˈdæn] *n* the ninth month in the Muslim year, when Muslims must not eat or drink anything between sunrise and sunset.

ramble [ˈræmbl] ◇ *n* a long walk in the countryside. ◇ *vi* -1. to go on a ramble. -2. to talk or write in a boring way because one is confused and keeps changing the subject.

◆ **ramble on** *vi* to talk for a long time in a boring way □ *He rambled on and on about nothing.*

rambler [ˈræmbləʳ] *n* a person who goes on long walks in the countryside as a hobby.

rambling [ˈræmblɪŋ] *adj* -1. [building, house] that is large and has an irregular shape. -2. [conversation, book] that is long and does not follow a clear pattern.

rambunctious [ræmˈbʌŋkʃəs] *adj* US [person, behavior] noisy and energetic.

RAMC (*abbr of* **Royal Army Medical Corps**) *n* **the RAMC** the medical service of the British army.

ramekin [ˈræməkən] *n* a small round dish with a flat bottom, used for baking food for one person.

ramification [ˌræməfəˈkeɪʃn] *n* one of the many results of something that are not usually obvious at first □ *I'm not sure if you fully understand all the ramifications of this decision.*

ramp [ræmp] *n* -1. a sloping surface that is designed to connect two areas on different levels □ *a wheelchair ramp.* -2. [on a road] a change in the level of a road surface, especially one that is designed to make cars go more slowly.

rampage [*vb* ræmˈpeɪdʒ, *n* ˈræmpeɪdʒ] ◇ *vi* [people, animals] to move or run around wildly, causing damage. ◇ *n* **to go on the rampage** to rampage □ *English and Dutch soccer fans went on the rampage after the game.*

rampant [ˈræmpənt] *adj* -1. [inflation, disease, crime] that is increasing so fast that it cannot be controlled □ *Corruption was rampant among military officials.* -2. [belief, abuse] that exists in many places and is difficult to control.

ramparts [ˈræmpɑːʳts] *npl* a high bank of earth, often with a wall on top, that is built around a castle, city etc to protect it against attack.

ram-raid ◇ *n* the act of driving a stolen car through the front window of a store in order to steal goods. ◇ *vt*: *Three youths were caught ram-raiding a local supermarket.*

ram-raider *n* a person who takes part in a ram-raid.

ramshackle [ˈræmʃækl] *adj* [building, vehicle] that is in very bad condition and likely to collapse □ *They lived in a ramshackle little house near the forest.*

ran [ræn] *past tense of* **run**.

RAN *n abbr of* **Royal Australian Navy**.

ranch [US ræntʃ, GB rɑːntʃ] *n* a very large farm in North America where sheep, cattle, or horses are bred.

rancher [US ˈræntʃr, GB ˈrɑːntʃə] *n* a person who owns or runs a ranch.

ranch house *n* US -1. a house on a ranch. -2. a large house that is one story high.

rancid [ˈrænsəd] *adj* [butter, bacon] that is no longer fresh and smells or tastes bad □ *The oil's gone rancid.*

rancor US, **rancour** GB [ˈræŋkəʳ] *n* a strong feeling of bitterness and hatred toward somebody □ *I feel no rancor against them for what they did to him.*

random [ˈrændəm] ◇ *adj* [sample, test] that is done or chosen without any particular reason or pattern. ◇ *n* **at random** in a random way □ *They were chosen/shot at random.*

random access memory *n* → **RAM**.

randomly [ˈrændəmlɪ] *adv* [choose, kill, distribute] *see* **random** □ *The candidates were randomly selected.*

R and R (*abbr of* **rest and recreation**) *n* -1. US a vacation given to members of the armed forces. -2. time spent relaxing away from one's work.

rang [ræŋ] *past tense of* **ring**.

range [reɪndʒ] ◇ *n* -1. [of radar, a telescope, weapon] the distance over which something can work, travel, be seen, heard etc □ *The missile has a range of about two miles.* ■ **to be out of range** [target, aircraft, ship] to be too far away to be reached by a weapon, radar etc □ *Fortunately, we were just out of range of the shells/out of shooting range.* ■ **to be within range of sthg** [of a telescope, radar, weapon] to be close enough to be reached by sthg □ *We were well within range of the mortar shells.* ■ **at close range** [fire, shoot] from a short distance away □ *Seen at close range, the planes looked even bigger.* -2. [of subjects, goods, activities] a number of things that appear, are seen, are done etc together and are of the same general type □ *We offer a wide range of services to our customers.* □ *I went through a whole range of emotions.* -3. [of ages, salaries, prices] the limits within which a number of different amounts or qualities are included □ *I'm afraid that's out of my price range.* -4. [of mountains] a row of hills or mountains □ *a mountain range* □ *the Cascade Range.* -5. [for shooting] a place where people can practice shooting. -6.

MUSIC the notes between the highest and the lowest notes that a singer or an instrument can reach □ *As a singer, she has an extraordinary range.*

◇ *vt* [pupils, glasses, books] to place <people or things> next to each other in a particular way □ *Riot police were ranged across the street.*

◇ *vi* **-1. to range from sthg to sthg, to range between sthg and sthg** to come somewhere on a scale between sthg and sthg; to include everything between sthg and sthg □ *The temperature ranged from 15 to 25 degrees Celsius* OR *between 15 and 25 degrees Celsius.* □ *Activities on offer range from canoeing to scuba diving.* **-2. to range over sthg** [book, conversation] to deal with sthg □ *Dr Cassidy's talk ranged over a wide variety of topics.*

ranger ['reɪndʒəʳ] *n* a person whose job is to take care of a forest or park.

rank [ræŋk] ◇ *n* **-1.** [in the army, police] the position that somebody has in an organization, and which shows how much power or authority they have in it □ *an officer of senior rank* □ *She rose to the rank of lieutenant.* ■ **the rank and file** MILITARY the ordinary members of a regiment who are not officers; POLITICS the ordinary members of a political party, labor union etc who are not the leaders □ *It may be popular in the senate but it won't go down well with the rank and file.* ■ **to pull rank** to use one's position of authority to order other people in an organization to do something that they do not want to do □ *Don't try to pull rank on me!* ■ **to close ranks** [family, organization, friends] to support each other at a difficult time to avoid criticism or a threat from somebody else. **-2.** [of people, things] a row or line of people or things □ *All I could see was ranks and ranks of policemen.*

◇ *vt* **-1.** [player, country] to give <sb/sthg> a particular position on a scale □ *She is ranked among the top four swimmers in the country.* **-2.** US to have a higher rank than <sb else> in the same organization □ *A major ranks a captain.*

◇ *vi* [person, event, organization] to have a particular position on a scale or list □ *That ranks as my all-time favorite movie.* □ *She ranks among the top five tennis-players in the world.*

◇ *adj* **-1. rank stupidity/incompetence etc** complete stupidity/incompetence etc (used for emphasis) □ *But this is rank insolence!* **-2.** [smell, taste] strong and unpleasant □ *There was a rank smell of stale urine.*

◆ **ranks** *npl* **-1. the ranks** MILITARY the ordinary soldiers, marines etc who are not officers □ *He rose from the ranks to become a general.* **-2. the ranks of sthg** [of an organization, group] the people who belong to sthg □ *The Democrats are aware of the growing unrest within their own ranks.* □ *He's joined the ranks of the unemployed.*

ranking ['ræŋkɪŋ] ◇ *n* a person's position on a scale, used to show how good they are at something, especially a sport □ *His official ranking is number three in the world.* ◇ *adj* US [officer, member] who has a high rank, or the highest rank in a particular group.

rankle ['ræŋkl] *vi* [behavior, attitude, remarks] to make one feel annoyed □ *It still rankles with me that he could say such a thing.*

ransack ['rænsæk] *vt* **-1.** [room, town] to steal things from <a place> in a way that causes damage and a mess □ *When we got back, the whole house had been ransacked.* **-2.** [building, room] to search <a place> completely, often leaving a lot of mess □ *I ransacked my cupboards for clothes to take with me.*

ransom ['rænsəm] *n* the amount of money demanded for the return of a person who has been kidnapped □ *They've asked for a $2 million ransom.* ■ **to hold sb to ransom** to hold sb as a prisoner until a ransom is paid for their release; to put sb in a difficult position in order to force them to do something □ *Kurz was held to ransom for six weeks before his captors finally let him go.* □ *We will not allow terrorists to hold this country to ransom.*

rant [rænt] *vi* to talk loudly and angrily for a long time about something (disapproving use) □ *I wish he'd stop ranting (on) about it.*

ranting ['ræntɪŋ] *n* the act of ranting.

rap [ræp] (*pt* & *pp* **rapped,** *cont* **rapping**) ◇ *n* **-1.** [at a door, on a table] a loud knock on the surface of something, usually made with one's knuckles. **-2.** MUSIC a type of pop music with a heavy beat, in which the words are spoken, not sung □ *a rap artist.* **-3. to take the rap** to be blamed or punished for something bad, even if one did not do it □ *Don't expect me to take the rap for your mistakes.* ◇ *vt* [door, table] to hit <sthg> many times quickly, often using one's knuckles. ◇ *vi* **-1. to rap on sthg** [on a door, table] to rap sthg. **-2.** MUSIC to speak the words that go with rap music.

rapacious [rə'peɪʃəs] *adj* [person] who is very greedy, especially in relation to money (formal use).

rape [reɪp] ◇ *vt* [person] to force <sb> to have sex, especially by using violence □ *She was raped at knifepoint.* ◇ *n* **-1.** [of a person] the crime of raping somebody □ *He has a conviction for rape.* □ *There have been a series of rapes in the area.* □ *a rape victim/attack.* **-2. the rape of the countryside/forests etc** damage done to the countryside/forests etc. **-3. (oilseed) rape** a plant with bright yellow flowers whose seeds produce oil.

rapeseed ['reɪpsiːd] *n* the seed of the rape plant.

Raphael ['ræfeɪəl] (1483–1520) an Italian painter who is considered one of the greatest artists of the Renaissance.

rapid ['ræpəd] *adj* [movement, decline, change] that happens very quickly □ *She underwent a rapid recovery.*

◆ **rapids** *npl* the parts of a river where the water moves very fast.

rapid-fire *adj* **-1.** [gun] that can fire shots very quickly. **-2.** [questions, jokes] that are spoken very quickly.

rapidity [rə'pɪdətɪ] *n: see* **rapid** □ *The rapidity of change is something that can overwhelm people.*

rapidly ['ræpədlɪ] *adv* [move, speak] quickly □ *Carla is rapidly becoming a very good dancer.*

rapist ['reɪpəst] *n* a person who has raped somebody.

rappel [rae'pel] *vi* US to go down a cliff, steep slope etc by sliding down a rope and pushing against the surface with one's feet.

rapper ['ræpəʳ] *n* a singer who performs rap.

rapport [ræ'pɔːʳ] *n* a friendly relationship between people in which each person understands what the other person is thinking or feeling □ *They had built up a good rapport with their assistants.* □ *There is a wonderful rapport between the two of them.*

rapprochement [US ˌræprouʃ'mɒn, GB ræ'prɒʃmɒn] *n* the beginning of friendly relations between two countries, people etc after a period when they were not friends.

rap sheet *n* US an official form on which the police list the charges against an accused person (informal use).

rapt [ræpt] *adj* [attention, silence, look] that shows that one is concentrating and is very interested in or impressed by something.

rapture ['ræptʃəʳ] *n* a feeling of great joy. ■ **to go into raptures over sb/sthg** to talk about sb/sthg in a way that shows one likes them very much.

rapturous ['ræptʃərəs] *adj* [welcome, applause, reaction] that shows a lot of excitement and enthusiasm.

Rapunzel [rə'pʌnzl] a young girl in a fairy tale who is being kept prisoner in a tower. She hangs her hair out of the window and a prince climbs up it to rescue her.

rare [reəʳ] *adj* **-1.** [plant, specimen, book] that is not found in many places and so is interesting or valuable □ *These candlesticks are very rare.* **-2.** [exception, occurrence, visit] that does not happen often □ *It's rare to find a good restaurant in these parts.* **-3.** [quality, beauty, talent] that is special and unusual □ *Such commitment is rare these days.* **-4.** COOKING [beef, steak] that has been cooked for a short time so that the inside is still red □ *"How would you like your steak?" — "Rare, please."*

rarefied ['reərɪfaɪd] *adj* **-1.** [air, atmosphere] that contains less oxygen than usual, especially because it is in a high place. **-2.** [place, subject] that involves people who are different from ordinary people because they are very rich, powerful, intelligent etc □ *in the rarefied atmosphere of an Oxford college.*

rarely ['reəʳlɪ] *adv* not often □ *We rarely see each other.*

rareness ['reəʳnəs] *n* [of a species, visit, somebody's beauty] *see* **rare.**

raring ['reərɪŋ] *adj* **to be raring to go** to be very eager to start.

rarity ['reərətɪ] (*pl* **rarities**) *n* something that is unusual because one does not often see it, find it etc □ *The species is fast becoming a rarity.*

rascal [US 'ræskl, GB 'rɑːskl] *n* a person, especially a child, who behaves badly but does

not really make people angry □ *Keep still, you little rascal!*

rash [ræʃ] ◇ *adj* [person, decision, move] that shows a lack of careful thought and is not sensible □ *Don't do anything rash.* ◇ *n* **-1.** [on one's skin] an area of redness or pimples on one's skin that is caused by an illness or allergy □ *After drinking the wine, Sally broke out in a terrible rash.* **-2. a rash of crimes/complaints** etc a large number of crimes/complaints etc that happen within a short time □ *There has been a rash of explosions in the capital.*

rasher ['ræʃəʳ] *n* GB a slice of bacon.

rashly ['ræʃlɪ] *adv* [behave, decide] *see* **rash** □ *I rather rashly promised to go and see Jane's film.*

rashness ['ræʃnəs] *n* [of a promise, decision] *see* **rash.**

rasp [US ræsp, GB rɑːsp] ◇ *n* a harsh unpleasant sound, e.g. of somebody coughing or of metal rubbing against something. ◇ *vi* [person, voice, metal] to make a rasp.

raspberry [US 'ræzberɪ, GB 'rɑːzbərɪ] (*pl* **raspberries**) *n* **-1.** a small, soft, red fruit that grows on bushes that have thorns □ *a raspberry-flavored candy.* **-2. to blow a raspberry** to make a loud sound by putting one's tongue out between one's lips and blowing, usually to show that one does not like or respect somebody or something.

rasping [US 'ræspɪŋ, GB 'rɑːsp-] *adj* [voice, sound] that is harsh and unpleasant.

Rasputin [ræ'spjuːtn] (1871–1916) a Russian monk, famous for his sexual adventures, political corruption, and strong influence over the Russian royal family.

Rasta ['ræstə] *n* a Rastafarian (informal use).

Rastafarian [ˌræstə'feərɪən] *n* a member of the religion that worships Haile Selassie, the former emperor of Ethiopia, as God.

rat [ræt] *n* **-1.** an animal that looks like a large mouse and has a long tail. ■ **to smell a rat** to begin to think that something is wrong, e.g. because one is being tricked. **-2.** a person who one is angry with because one feels betrayed or deceived by them (informal use) □ *You rat!*

ratchet ['rætʃət] *n* a wheel or bar, used in machinery, that has sloping teeth and a piece of metal between two of them that allows it to turn in one direction, but not the other.

rate [reɪt] ◇ *n* **-1.** the speed at which something happens during a certain period of time □ *At this rate, we'll never get there!* **-2.** [of growth, inflation] the amount of something measured against other factors, especially time □ *the suicide/divorce rate* □ *The rate of unemployment/inflation has fallen again this month.* **-3.** [of taxation, interest] a fixed level that is used to decide how much must be paid for something □ *What's the (going) rate for this type of work?* □ *'Reduced rates for groups.'*

◇ *vt* **-1.** to consider <sb/sthg> to be of a particular level, standard etc □ *I would rate him as one of the Hollywood greats.* □ *She's rated among the top ten players of all time.* □ *"How* do you rate her chances?" — "Not good, I'm afraid." □ She's very highly rated as a doctor. **-2.** [mention, attention] to deserve <sthg> □ This is a full-bodied young wine that certainly rates a bronze medal.

◆ **at any rate** *adv* a phrase used to show that what one is about to say is more certain or more precise or important than what one has just said □ Come over for dinner, or for a drink at any rate.

rate of exchange *n* the rate at which one country's currency can be exchanged for another country's currency.

ratepayer ['reɪtpeɪə'] *n* GB a person who pays taxes to their local government.

rather [US 'ræðr, GB 'rɑːðə] *adv* & *predet* **-1.** [embarrassing, big, hot] to some degree, but not very □ It was rather cold/rather a cold day. □ I rather enjoyed that. □ I have rather a lot of work to do. **-2.** a word used to emphasize that something is true □ She's really rather interesting, isn't she? **-3. I would rather...** a phrase used to say what one would prefer □ I'd rather have fish than red meat. □ We'd rather he didn't come, actually. □ "Try some of this brandy." — "I'd rather not, thanks." **-4. or rather...** or more exactly... □ Have you met Belinda's brother, or rather, stepbrother? **-5. (but) rather...** on the contrary... □ We do not want to victimize vagrants, but rather to help them.

◆ **rather than** *conj* instead of □ We decided to walk rather than take the bus.

ratification [,rætəfə'keɪʃn] *n*: see **ratify** □ Officials are seeking full ratification of the agreement.

ratify ['rætəfaɪ] (*pt* & *pp* **ratified**) *vt* [agreement, treaty, proposal] to accept <sthg> officially by signing it.

rating ['reɪtɪŋ] *n* **-1.** the position held by somebody or something on a scale of quality or quantity □ His popularity rating has plunged since the election. **-2.** GB a sailor in the British navy who is not an officer.

◆ **ratings** *npl* the lists published in newspapers which show how many people watch or listen to particular television and radio programs each week.

ratio ['reɪʃɪoʊ] (*pl* **ratios**) *n* the relationship between two amounts that is shown by two figures □ The ratio of boys to girls is 10 to 8. □ a high teacher-to-student ratio.

ration ['ræʃn] ◇ *n* [of food, goods, gas] an amount of something that is given to each person when there is not much of it, especially during a war □ Rations have been imposed in some areas of the country. ◇ *vt* [food, gas, goods] to limit the amount of <sthg> that each person is allowed to have during a particular period of time □ We must ration ourselves to two whiskies.

◆ **rations** *npl* the amount of food given to a soldier, sailor etc for each day.

rational ['ræʃnəl] *adj* [behavior, explanation, argument] that is based on thought using reason and logic, not emotions; [person] who can think and understand things using reason and logic, and is not controlled by their emotions □ It's perfectly rational that you should feel the way you do. □ Try to be rational about it.

rationale [,ræʃə'næl] *n* the reasons which explain a belief, system, or action □ I don't understand the rationale behind their behavior.

rationalization [US ,ræʃnələ'zeɪʃn, GB -aɪ'zeɪʃn] *n*: see **rationalize** □ Further rationalization may be necessary to safeguard the firm's future.

rationalize, -ise ['ræʃnəlaɪz] *vt* **-1.** [behavior, decision] to try to justify <sthg> so that it seems reasonable; [problem] to try to understand <sthg> in a logical way □ Curtis rationalized his spending by saying he was depressed. **-2.** [company, industry] to make <sthg> more efficient, especially by reducing the number of staff or amount of equipment needed for it.

rationing ['ræʃnɪŋ] *n* [of food, goods] the system of giving people rations of something when there is not much of it.

rat race *n* a way of life in a city in which everybody works all the time doing boring jobs in offices and nobody feels happy, relaxed, or safe (disapproving use) □ I want to get out of the rat race.

rattle ['rætl] ◇ *n* **-1.** [of keys, bottles, an engine] a sound made by small hard objects hitting each other or the surface of another object very quickly a number of times □ the rattle of machine-gun fire. **-2.** [for a baby] a baby's toy with small pieces inside that rattle when it is shaken. ◇ *vi* [bottles, keys, engine] to move and make a rattle □ The door rattles when the wind blows. ◇ *vt* **-1.** [keys, window] to move <sthg> so that it rattles. **-2.** [person] to make <sb> feel nervous or uncomfortable □ Ann is not easily rattled.

◆ **rattle off** *vt sep* **to rattle sthg off** [names, speech, poem] to say sthg quickly from memory □ She rattled off a list of the people she wanted to invite.

◆ **rattle on** *vi* **to rattle on** to talk quickly and for a long time about something that is not interesting to other people □ He was rattling on about his girlfriend or something.

◆ **rattle through** *vt fus* **to rattle through sthg** [work, speech, list] to deal with sthg quickly in order to finish it.

rattler ['rætlə'] *n* US = **rattlesnake** (informal use).

rattlesnake ['rætlsneɪk] *n* a poisonous American snake that makes the sound of a rattle with the end of its tail.

ratty ['rætɪ] (*compar* **rattier**, *superl* **rattiest**) *adj* **-1.** [person] who becomes annoyed easily (informal use) □ Hugo's always ratty in the mornings. **-2.** US [sweater, piece of paper] that is in bad condition because it has been used a lot and is old.

raucous ['rɔːkəs] *adj* [laughter, behavior, occasion] that is wild, rough, and noisy.

raunchy ['rɔːntʃɪ] (*compar* **raunchier**, *superl* **raunchiest**) *adj* [singer, movie, dance] that one finds sexually exciting.

ravage ['rævɪdʒ] *vt* **to be ravaged by sthg** to be badly damaged by sthg □ The region has been ravaged by war/drought.

◆ ravages *npl* **the ravages of time/war etc** the damage caused by time/war etc.

rave [reɪv] ◇ *vi* **-1. to rave about** OR **against sthg** to speak angrily about sthg □ *He raved about media bias.* □ *She raved (on) at me for half an hour.* **-2. to rave about sthg** to talk or write very enthusiastically about sthg □ *Everybody's raving about his latest movie.* ◇ *adj* **rave reviews** newspaper or magazine articles that are extremely enthusiastic about a particular new movie, book etc □ *As expected, the show got rave reviews in the press.* ◇ *n* GB a large organized event that lasts all night, often outdoors, where young people dance to electronic music with a fast rhythm and sometimes take drugs.

raven ['reɪvn] ◇ *adj* [hair] black and shiny □ *a raven-haired woman.* ◇ *n* a large black bird that makes a harsh sound.

ravenous ['rævnəs] *adj* [person, animal] who is very hungry □ *Is dinner ready? I'm ravenous!*

raver ['reɪvər] *n* GB a person who goes to raves (informal use).

ravine [rə'viːn] *n* a very deep narrow valley with steep sides.

raving ['reɪvɪŋ] *adj* **a raving lunatic** a person who is completely crazy.

◆ ravings *npl* things that somebody says that do not make any sense, because the person is crazy or not logical and reasonable □ *Don't mind what he says — it's just the ravings of a bitter old man.*

ravioli [ˌrævɪ'oʊlɪ] *n* an Italian dish consisting of small squares of pasta with a filling of meat or cheese, that is usually served in a sauce □ *We're having ravioli for lunch.*

ravish ['rævɪʃ] *vt* **-1.** to rape <a woman> (literary use). **-2. to be ravished by sthg** [by a view, painting] to get great pleasure from sthg that one thinks is very beautiful.

ravishing ['rævɪʃɪŋ] *adj* [person, beauty] that is very beautiful and attractive □ *You look ravishing.*

raw [rɔː] *adj* **-1.** [vegetable, fish, meat] that has not been cooked □ *I prefer to eat it raw.* **-2.** [sewage, cotton] that is in its natural state and has not been treated by a particular process. **-3.** [skin, wound] that is sore and sensitive. **-4.** [recruit, novice] who does not have much experience or is not yet trained, and is usually young. **-5.** [weather, wind] that is cold and unpleasant.

raw deal *n* **to get a raw deal** to be treated unfairly □ *Sandra got a really raw deal over that promotion business.*

Rawlplug™ ['rɔːlplʌg] *n* GB a small, hollow, plastic device that holds a screw tightly in a hole.

raw material *n* **-1.** any natural substance, e.g. coal or oil, that is used to make something after it has been treated in a particular way. **-2.** somebody or something that can be changed or developed for a particular purpose □ *Her marriage provided her with raw material for the novel.*

ray [reɪ] *n* **-1.** [of light, sunshine, heat] a beam of light or heat □ *This cream will provide protection from the rays of the sun.* **-2. a ray of hope/comfort etc** a small amount of hope/comfort etc that makes a bad situation seem better.

rayon ['reɪɒn] *n* a smooth material, made of cotton, wool, or synthetic fiber, that is used to make clothes.

raze [reɪz] *vt* [building, town, forest] to destroy <a place> completely, so that nothing is left above the ground □ *The house was razed to the ground.*

razor ['reɪzər] *n* a device containing one or more blades that is used for shaving hair from one's skin □ *an electric razor* □ *a disposable razor.*

razor blade *n* a thin flat piece of metal with very sharp edges that is used in a razor for shaving.

razor-sharp *adj* **-1.** [knife, blade, edge] that is extremely sharp. **-2.** [person, mind, wit] that is extremely quick and intelligent.

razzmatazz ['ræzmətæz] *n* busy and noisy activity that is intended to attract attention and interest to something (informal use) □ *the razzmatazz of show business/Hollywood.*

R & B *n abbr of* **rhythm and blues** □ *an R & B singer.*

RBI (*abbr of* **runs batted in**) *n* the total number of baseball runs a batter helps another player to make by hitting the ball.

RC *adj abbr of* **Roman Catholic.**

RCA (*abbr of* **Royal College of Art**) *n* **the RCA** an important art school in London.

RCAF *n abbr of* **Royal Canadian Air Force.**

RCMP (*abbr of* **Royal Canadian Mounted Police**) *n* **the RCMP** the official name of the Mounties.

RCN **-1.** (*abbr of* **Royal College of Nursing**) **the RCN** a professional association for nurses in Britain. **-2.** *abbr of* **Royal Canadian Navy.**

Rd *abbr of* **Road.**

R & D *n abbr of* **research and development.**

RE *n* **-1.** (*abbr of* **religious education**) religion taught as a subject in schools in Britain. **-2.** (*abbr of* **Royal Engineers**) **the RE** the department of the British army responsible for building bridges, fortifications etc.

re [riː] *prep* with reference to <sthg> (formal use) □ *Re your letter of June 6th* □ *Re: job application.*

re- *prefix* added to words to show that something is done again □ *re-evaluation.*

reach [riːtʃ] ◇ *vt* **-1.** [destination, country] to arrive at <a place> □ *We reached L.A. just before midnight.* **-2.** [object, shelf] to succeed in touching, taking etc <sthg> by stretching one's arm toward it □ *Do you think you can reach it without a ladder?* **-3.** [person] to contact <sb>, usually by telephone □ *You can always reach me at this number.* □ *Where can I reach you this evening?* **-4.** [height, speed, age] to be as high, big, fast etc as <a particular level>; [stage, situation] to get to <a point> as a result of what has happened □ *The water reached the edge of the bath.* □ *Inflation has*

reached record levels. **-5.** [decision, agreement] to succeed in achieving <sthg> after some time and effort □ *There is still hope that the delegates may reach a compromise.*
◇ *vi* **-1.** [person, arm, hand] to stretch out in a particular direction to do something or to get something □ *He reached across the table for the salt.* □ *I reached down to pick up the papers.* **-2.** [land] to extend to a particular place □ *The fields reach all the way down to the river.*
◇ *n* [of a person] the distance to which somebody can stretch a part of their body, especially their arm □ *He had an unusually long reach for such a short man.* ■ **to be within reach** [object] to be close enough to be touched; [place] to be close enough to travel to in a short time □ *The shelf was just within (my) reach.* □ *The airport is within easy reach of the city center.* ■ **to be out of** OR **beyond sb's reach** [object] to be too far away to be touched; [place] to be too far away to be traveled to in a short time □ *The switch was just out of my reach.* □ *That area of the coastline is beyond our reach.*
◆ **reaches** *npl* the part of a region or a river that is in a particular place □ *the lower reaches of the Potomac.*
reachable ['riːtʃəbl] *adj* [place] that can be reached in a particular way; [person] who can be contacted in a particular way □ *Is it reachable by boat?* □ *He's reachable at the following number.*
react [rɪ'ækt] *vi* **-1.** to behave in a particular way because of something that has been done or said □ *How did he react to your suggestion/offer/accusations?* □ *Matt didn't react very well when I told him.* **-2. to react against sthg** to behave deliberately in a way that is opposite to or different from sthg □ *It was his way of reacting against his Catholic upbringing.* **-3. to react with sthg** [substance] to change chemically when it is mixed with sthg □ *The acid reacts with the metal.* **-4. to react to sthg** [to a drug, substance] to be affected in a particular way or made ill by sthg □ *She reacted very badly to the anesthetic.*
reaction [rɪ'ækʃn] *n* **-1.** [to a suggestion, event, statement] the way in which somebody reacts to something that has been done or said □ *What was their reaction to the news?* **-2.** [against the past] something that one does or thinks that is deliberately different from or opposed to what has happened before □ *This was seen as a reaction against the materialism of their parents' generation.* **-3.** POLITICS the strong belief that there should be no political or social change (disapproving use) □ *the forces of reaction.* **-4.** CHEMISTRY the way in which two substances combine chemically to have a particular effect □ *a chemical reaction.* **-5.** MEDICINE the unpleasant effects of a drug, substance etc on a patient □ *I had a reaction to the penicillin.*
◆ **reactions** *npl* the speed with which one can move one's body to react to a particular action or situation, especially when one is in danger or during a game □ *Too much drink can slow down your reactions.*

reactionary [US rɪ'ækʃənerɪ, GB -ərɪ] (disapproving use) ◇ *n* a person who is opposed to political or social change. ◇ *adj* [person, government, politics] *reactionary forces within society.*
reactivate [rɪ'æktɪveɪt] *vt* [system, machine] to make <sthg> start working again.
reactor [rɪ'æktər] *n* = **nuclear reactor**.
read [riːd] (*pt* & *pp* **read** [red]) ◇ *vt* **-1.** [book, word, music] to look at and understand <sthg written in words or symbols>; to say aloud the words and symbols of <sthg> so that other people can hear □ *Sarah sat reading the newspaper.* □ *I can't read her writing.* □ *Have you read the piece in the New York Times?* **-2.** to show <a particular message, figure, or amount> in the form of words or symbols □ *The sign read 'Trespassers will be prosecuted.'* **-3.** [mood, thoughts, events] to understand and interpret <sthg> in a particular way □ *I thought you read the situation very well.* **-4.** [clock, meter, gauge] to look at <a device> and record the measurement or amount that it shows. **-5.** GB EDUCATION [law, languages, philosophy] to study <a subject> at university.
◇ *vi* **-1.** [person] to read a book, magazine etc □ *Sh! I'm reading!* □ *Last night, I read to my daughter.* **-2.** [book, letter] to be written in a particular way □ *It reads well/badly.*
◇ *n* **to be a good read** [novel, story] to be very enjoyable to read.
◆ **read into** *vt sep* **to read sthg into sthg** [into a decision, comment] to think that sthg is one of the meanings, causes etc of sthg else □ *I wouldn't try to read too much into what she says.*
◆ **read out** *vt sep* **to read sthg out** [letter, story, news] to read sthg aloud so that other people can hear it □ *Could you read it out for us?*
◆ **read up on** *vt fus* **to read up on sthg** to read a lot about sthg in order to know it well □ *I've been reading up on Mexican history before my trip.*
readable ['riːdəbl] *adj* **-1.** [book, article] that is pleasant and easy to read □ *She has a very readable style.* **-2.** COMPUTING [disk] that can be scanned and copied from.
readdress [ˌriːə'dres] *vt* [letter, package] to write a new address on <sthg> so that it can be delivered to the correct place.
reader ['riːdər] *n* **-1.** a person who reads often, especially as a hobby. **-2.** [of a book, magazine, newspaper] a person who reads a particular publication □ *a special offer for our readers.*
readership ['riːdərʃɪp] *n* [of a book, newspaper, magazine] all the people who buy and read a particular publication □ *The Glasgow Times has a readership of 50,000.*
readily ['redɪlɪ] *adv* **-1.** [accept, agree] willingly. **-2. to be readily available/understood etc** to be easy to get/understand etc quickly.
readiness ['redɪnəs] *n* **-1.** the state of being prepared for something □ *We waited in readiness for the next attack.* **-2.** a willingness to do something □ *Her readiness to help was much appreciated.*
reading ['riːdɪŋ] *n* **-1.** the activity of reading □

I've got some reading to do. -**2.** written or printed material that can be read □ *This makes interesting reading.* -**3.** [for a group of people] an event where a text is read aloud for other people to hear; a text, especially one from the Bible, that is chosen to be read out loud □ *We went to a poetry reading last night.* □ *a reading from the Gospel.* -**4.** [from a gauge, meter] a measurement that is shown by a gauge, thermometer etc □ *We need to take a light reading first.* -**5.** POLITICS a stage in the passage of a bill before it is passed.

reading lamp, reading light *n* a lamp whose light can be pointed toward the thing that one is reading or writing.

reading room *n* a room in a library or large house where people can sit and read.

readjust [ˌriːəˈdʒʌst] ◇ *vt* [policy, mirror, mechanism] to change <sthg> in order to make it work better. ◇ *vi* [person] to become used to something again after being away from it or in different circumstances □ *On her return, she found it hard to readjust to village life.*

readmit [ˌriːədˈmɪt] *vt* [customer, member] to allow <sb> back into a place such as a bar or nightclub; [patient] to bring <sb> back into hospital for more treatment, tests etc.

read-only memory *n* → ROM.

readout [ˈriːdaʊt] *n* the printed information that comes out of a computer.

read-through [ˈriːd-] *n* the act of reading something quickly to get an idea of its subject, style etc.

ready [ˈredɪ] (*pt* & *pp* **readied**) ◇ *adj* -**1. to be ready** [person, meal] to be prepared or finished □ *When will the tunnel be ready?* □ *Are you ready to go through with it?* □ *I'm afraid the prints still aren't ready for collection.* ■ **to get ready** to prepare oneself for something □ *It takes him hours to get ready.* ■ **to get sb/sthg ready** to prepare sb/sthg □ *I'll have your dinner ready for you.* □ *I'm just getting the kids ready for school.* -**2. to be ready to do sthg** to be willing to do sthg □ *They were more than ready to help.* -**3. to be ready for sthg** [for a drink, break] to need sthg □ *I'm ready for bed after all that walking.* -**4. to be ready to do sthg** [to explode, collapse, cry] to be likely to do sthg □ *I was ready to scream with frustration.* -**5.** [smile, answer, wit] that one can produce easily □ *You're always ready with an excuse, aren't you?* ◇ *vt* [system, machine, organization] to prepare <sthg> for a particular purpose.

ready cash *n* money in the form of coins or bills that can be used immediately, rather than credit cards, checks etc.

ready-made *adj* -**1.** [product, clothing] that can be used immediately and needs no extra preparation. -**2.** [reply, excuse] that is very useful in a particular situation.

ready money *n* = **ready cash**.

ready-to-wear *adj* [clothing, garment] that can be worn without any extra work being done on it.

reaffirm [ˌriːəˈfɜːrm] *vt* [commitment, opposition,

principles] to state <sthg> again in order to make it clearer.

reafforestation [ˌriːəfɒrəˈsteɪʃn] *n* GB = **reforestation**.

Reaganomics [ˌreɪɡənˈɒmɪks] *n* the economic policies of the USA when Ronald Reagan was president, from 1981 to 1989.

real [rɪəl] ◇ *adj* -**1.** [leather, gold, chocolate] that is what it seems to be and is not an imitation □ *This diamond on my finger is the real thing!* □ *made with real apricots.* -**2.** [nature, person, country] that is the most important part of a person, place, or thing □ *I want to get to know the real Spain/you.* -**3.** [job, feeling] that is serious and important □ *Stanley's drinking is becoming a real problem.* -**4.** [danger, life, possibility] that exists or is true and is not something that people only think is true or exists □ *"Jones" is not her real name, of course.* □ *There's a very real risk of this happening.* -**5. in real terms** ECONOMICS a phrase used to talk about the value of a sum of money after the effect of inflation has been considered □ *Salaries have fallen by 25% in real terms since 1979.* -**6.** a word used to emphasize a description or statement □ *He's a real pain!* ◇ *adv* US very (informal use) □ *This cake is real good.* □ *It was real good to see you.*

◆ **for real** *adj* & *adv* a phrase used to emphasize that something is serious and is what it seems to be, rather than an imitation, joke etc (informal use) □ *This time it's for real.*

real ale *n* GB beer made using traditional methods.

real estate *n* property in the form of land and houses.

real estate agency *n* US a company that sells or rents houses and apartments for the owners.

real estate agent *n* US a person who works in a real estate agency.

realign [ˌriːəˈlaɪn] *vt* -**1.** POLITICS [party, forces] to arrange <a group> in a new way. -**2.** AUTO to arrange <the brakes> of a vehicle so that they work better together.

realignment [ˌriːəˈlaɪnmənt] *n*: see **realign**.

realism [ˈriːəlɪzm] *n*: see **realistic** □ *the stark realism of the book.*

realist [ˈriːəlɪst] *n* a person who is realistic.

realistic [ˌriːəˈlɪstɪk] *adj* -**1.** [person] who understands and accepts things as they are and deals with situations in a sensible way □ *We have to be realistic about our chances of success.* -**2.** [painting, movie, effect] that is convincing because it looks very similar to what it represents.

realistically [ˌriːəˈlɪstɪklɪ] *adv* -**1.** [consider, think] in a way that shows one is realistic. -**2.** [paint, portray] see **realistic**. -**3.** a word used to talk about something in a way that shows one accepts things as they really are, even if this is hard □ *Realistically, how much hope is there?*

reality [riːˈælətɪ] (*pl* **realities**) *n* -**1.** the quality or state of being real and true □ *Our dreams had become reality.* ■ **in reality** a phrase used to correct or contrast the truth with something that only seems true; a phrase used to talk about real life when this is different from what happens in stories, dreams etc □ *He seemed sad, although in reality he felt relieved.* □ *I can't imagine such things happening in reality.* **-2.** the truth of a situation, especially when it is unpleasant or not wanted □ *When are you going to face up to reality?* □ *The reality is that you knew about Corby's plans all the time.* **-3.** a situation that actually exists □ *The reality was much worse than anything I'd imagined.* □ *life's harsh realities.*

realization [US ,ri:ələ'zeɪʃn, GB -aɪ'zeɪʃn] *n: see* **realize** □ *I came to the sudden realization that I would never see Tomas again.*

realize, -ise ['ri:əlaɪz] *vt* **-1.** [fact, implications, significance] to notice and understand <sthg>, often when one did not know about it before □ *I didn't realize (that) you were married.* □ *Do you realize the seriousness of the situation?* □ *I hope you realize what you're letting yourself in for.* **-2.** [ambition, aim, hope] to succeed in achieving <sthg that one wanted> □ *Her dream of seeing the Caribbean again was finally realized.* **-3.** [amount, profit] to get <a sum of money> by selling something □ *We realized a large profit from the sale.*

reallocate [,ri:'æləkeɪt] *vt* [funds, money, aid] to use <resources> for a different purpose from the one originally intended.

really ['ri:əlɪ] ◇ *adv* **-1.** a word used to emphasize what is being said □ *I really should call them.* □ *The weather's been really horrible today.* □ *That's a really good idea.* **-2.** a word used to emphasize the truth, especially when this is different from what seems to be true □ *He claims to have lost it, but really he's hidden it.* □ *What's she really like?* **-3.** a word used to emphasize that one is telling the truth □ *I like it, really I do.* □ *Do you really think he'll be able to get us tickets?* **-4.** a word used in negative statements to make them less strong and avoid being rude □ *I don't really agree with you on that.* □ *I'm not really sure that's a good idea.* ◇ *excl* **-1.** a word used to show that one is not certain about something or does not believe it □ *Really? Are you sure?* **-2.** a word used to show that one is interested or surprised □ *Really? Who'd have thought it!* **-3.** a word used to show that one disapproves of something or is annoyed □ *Really! How rude can you get!*

realm [relm] *n* **-1.** [of science, imagination] an area of study, thought, or interest. □ *It was a scene beyond the realms of fantasy.* **-2.** a country that is ruled by a king or queen.

real-time *adj* COMPUTING [processing, programing] that is almost immediate.

realtor ['ri:əltər] *n* US a person who sells real estate.

ream [ri:m] *n* **-1.** US 500 sheets of paper. **-2.** GB 480 sheets of paper.

◆ **reams** *npl* a large amount of written material □ *She's written reams of notes.*

reap [ri:p] *vt* **-1.** [corn, wheat] to cut and gather <a crop>. **-2. to reap the benefits/rewards etc**

to get the benefits/rewards etc of one's hard work or planning □ *This year DNF looks set to reap the benefits of an aggressive marketing campaign.*

reappear [,ri:ə'pɪər] *vi* to appear again.

reappearance [,ri:ə'pɪərəns] *n: see* **reappear**.

reapply [,ri:ə'plaɪ] (*pt* & *pp* **reapplied**) *vi* to apply for a job, place on a course etc again.

reappraisal [,ri:ə'preɪzl] *n: see* **reappraise**.

reappraise [,ri:ə'preɪz] *vt* [ideas, policy, situation] to consider <sthg> carefully again to decide whether to change it.

rear [rɪər] ◇ *adj* [door, wheel, window] that is at the back of something or behind it. ◇ *n* **-1.** [of a building, vehicle] the back of something □ *I was standing at the rear of the house.* ■ **to bring up the rear** to be the last person in a moving line of people □ *You go first and I'll bring up the rear.* **-2.** [of a person] one's buttocks (polite or humorous use). ◇ *vt* **-1.** to take care of <a child, plant, or animal> until it is fully grown □ *They rear horses in Texas.* **-2. to rear its ugly head** to appear (disapproving use) □ *Racism has reared its ugly head again.* ◇ *vi* **to rear (up)** [horse] to stand on its back legs.

rear admiral *n* an officer in the navy, ranked below a vice admiral.

rearguard action ['rɪərgɑ:rd-] *n* **-1.** MILITARY the protection of an army when it is retreating by the group of soldiers at the back. **-2.** resistance against something that is happening, when it is probably too late.

rear light *n* the light at the back of a vehicle.

rearm [ri:'ɑ:rm] ◇ *vt* [country, army, troops] to provide <sb> with new or better military weapons to prepare them for fighting, usually after a period of peace. ◇ *vi* [country, army, troops] *There are reports that the guerillas are rearming.*

rearmament [ri:'ɑ:rməmənt] *n: see* **rearm**.

rearmost ['rɪərmoust] *adj* [seat, car] that is nearest to the back part of something.

rearrange [,ri:ə'reɪndʒ] *vt* **-1.** [room, furniture] to arrange <sthg> differently □ *I see you've rearranged things to make the room look bigger.* **-2.** [appointment, meeting] to arrange for <sthg> to happen at a different time or date □ *If you can't make 3pm we may have to rearrange it for another day.*

rearrangement [,ri:ə'reɪndʒmənt] *n: see* **rearrange**.

rearview mirror ['rɪərvju:-] *n* the mirror inside a car which makes it possible for one to see traffic behind while one is driving.

reason ['ri:zn] ◇ *n* **-1.** the cause of something, or the explanation or excuse for something □ *What was your reason for thinking that?* □ *Give me one good reason why I should trust you.* □ *"Why do you ask?" — "Oh, no reason."* □ *She was upset, and with (good) reason.* □ *We have reason to believe there was a racist motive behind the attack.* ■ **by reason of** because of □ *The Treasurer was invited by reason of his office.* ■ **for some reason** for a reason that is not clear □ *For some reason she didn't seem to want to talk to me.* **-2.** the ability to think sensibly

and make judgments □ *His behavior defies all reason.* ■ **to listen to reason** to accept the advice of somebody who is being more reasonable □ *I've tried telling him, but he just won't listen to reason.* ■ **it stands to reason** it is obvious, because it is a logical result of something □ *It stands to reason that she'd say that, doesn't it?*
◇ *vt* **to reason (that)...** to think or say that something must be true if one considers all the facts □ *Bianca reasoned that it would be cheaper to rent a car.*
◇ *vi* to use one's ability to think sensibly and make judgments.
◆ **reason with** *vt fus* **to reason with sb** to try calmly to persuade sb to do something or to agree to something that one thinks is sensible □ *It's no use, you can't reason with him.*

reasonable ['riːznəbl] *adj* **-1.** [person, behavior, attitude] that is sensible and fair □ *Come on, be reasonable, she only asked if she could borrow it!* **-2.** [quality, price] that is good enough to be acceptable □ *There's a very reasonable restaurant nearby.* **-3.** [amount, number] that is fairly large □ *I think a reasonable number of people will be interested.*

reasonably ['riːznəbli] *adv* **-1. reasonably large/ well etc** fairly large/well etc □ *He's a reasonably good pianist.* **-2.** [behave, think] sensibly and fairly □ *You can't reasonably expect them to pay more.* □ *a reasonably priced meal.*

reasoned ['riːznd] *adj* [argument, explanation] that is based on sensible thought and judgment.

reasoning ['riːznɪŋ] *n* the process of thought that one uses to come to a particular decision or conclusion □ *What's the reasoning behind that decision?*

reassemble [ˌriːə'sembl] ◇ *vt* **-1.** to put <a machine, piece of equipment> etc back together again. **-2.** to gather <people> together again. ◇ *vi* [people, troops, meeting] *Let's reassemble at five o'clock.*

reassess [ˌriːə'ses] *vt* [opinion, position, situation] to consider <sthg> again in order to decide whether change is needed.

reassessment [ˌriːə'sesmənt] *n: see* **reassess** □ *Now is the time for a reassessment of our aims.*

reassurance [ˌriːə'ʃʊərəns] *n* **-1.** words spoken to reassure somebody □ *It is normal for the child to seek reassurance from its parents.* **-2.** an unofficial promise □ *They wanted a reassurance that the bill would be paid.*

reassure [ˌriːə'ʃʊəʳ] *vt* to make <sb> less worried or frightened about something □ *I reassured him that everything would be all right.*

reassuring [ˌriːə'ʃʊərɪŋ] *adj* [person, look, smile] that makes one feel less worried or frightened.

reawaken [ˌriːə'weɪkən] *vt* [concern, interest, feelings] to make people think about or feel <sthg> again.

rebate ['riːbeɪt] *n* an amount of money that is paid back to somebody because they have paid more than necessary □ *a rent/tax rebate.*

rebel [*n* 'rebl, *vb* rɪ'bel] (*pt & pp* **rebelled**, *cont* **rebelling**) ◇ *n* **-1.** MILITARY a person who fights against their own government in order to change the political system. **-2.** a person who behaves differently from other people and seems to be opposed to authority, their parents, or society. ◇ *vi* **-1.** MILITARY to fight against one's own government in order to change the political system. **-2.** to behave differently from one's family or society as a sign that one disagrees with their beliefs and values □ *She rebelled against her strict religious upbringing.*

rebellion [rɪ'beljən] *n* an act of rebelling □ *The army was called in to put down the rebellion.* □ *It's a simple case of teenage rebellion.*

rebellious [rɪ'beljəs] *adj* [army, person] that rebels □ *She's going through a rebellious phase.*

rebirth [ˌriː'bɜːrθ] *n* [of a nation, movement, organization] a process or period of developing into something new and better.

reboot [ˌriː'buːt] ◇ *vt* to start <a computer> again, usually because something has gone wrong with the way it is working. ◇ *vi: Press this key to reboot.*

rebound [*n* 'riːbaʊnd, *vb* rɪ'baʊnd] ◇ *n* **on the rebound** while the ball is bouncing back; while somebody is still recovering from something very upsetting, especially the ending of a love affair □ *She caught the ball on the rebound.* □ *He met and married her on the rebound.* ◇ *vi* **-1.** [ball] to bounce back □ *The cork rebounded off the ceiling.* **-2. to rebound on** OR **upon sb** [action, behavior, situation] to have a bad effect on sb.

rebuff [rɪ'bʌf] ◇ *vt* [person, offer, suggestion] to reject <sb/sthg> in an unkind or rude way. ◇ *n* the act of rebuffing somebody or something □ *Her offer was met with a rebuff.*

rebuild [riː'bɪld] (*pt & pp* **rebuilt** [-'bɪlt]) *vt* [building, political party, confidence] to develop <sthg> again, usually after damage, destruction, or a crisis.

rebuke [rɪ'bjuːk] ◇ *vt* to speak angrily to <sb> and criticize them for doing something wrong □ *The army was rebuked for its treatment of the refugees.* ◇ *n: a stern rebuke.*

rebut [rɪ'bʌt] (*pt & pp* **rebutted**, *cont* **rebutting**) *vt* [charge, criticism, claim] to say that <sthg> is not true or justified.

rebuttal [rɪ'bʌtl] *n* a statement that rebuts something.

rec *abbr of* **received.**

recalcitrant [rɪ'kælsɪtrənt] *adj* [person] who is stubborn, disobedient, and uncooperative.

recall [rɪ'kɔːl] ◇ *n* **-1.** the ability to remember things □ *She had a few hazy memories, but most of the events of that day were beyond recall.* **-2. to be beyond recall** to be impossible to change back to the way it was in the past. ◇ *vt* **-1.** [fact, occasion, name] to remember <sb/sthg> □ *Yes, I recall writing to them.* □ *Do you recall when it was?* **-2.** [ambassador, troops] to order <sb> to return from somewhere.

recant [rɪ'kænt] ◇ *vt* [statement, religion, opinion] to say in public that one has stopped believing in <sthg>. ◇ *vi*: *Galileo recanted under threat of torture.*

recap ['ri:kæp] (*pt* & *pp* **recapped**, *cont* **recapping**) ◇ *n* [of a statement, argument] a summary of something. ◇ *vt* -1. to repeat <the main points of an argument, statement> etc. -2. US to put a new outer surface on <a tire>. ◇ *vi* (informal use) *Just to recap, here are the main points.*

recapitulate [,ri:kə'pɪtʃəleɪt] ◇ *vt* to repeat <the main points of an argument, statement> etc. ◇ *vi*: *So, let me recapitulate for those of you who arrived late.*

recapture [ri:'kæptʃər] ◇ *vt* -1. [town, area] to capture <a place> again by attacking the people who hold it. -2. [lion, prisoner] to capture <a person or animal> after they have escaped. -3. [mood, romance, atmosphere] to have or create <a feeling or quality from the past> again □ *The movie manages to recapture the confusion and chaos of the period.* ◇ *n*: *We are receiving reports of the recapture of Gorazde.*

recd, rec'd *abbr of* **received**.

recede [rɪ'si:d] *vi* -1. [person, coastline, car] to move, or appear to move into the distance until one can no longer see it □ *The car's lights receded into the distance.* -2. [hope, danger, chance] to decrease. -3. [hair] to gradually stop growing at the front of one's head □ *John's hair is receding.*

receding [rɪ'si:dɪŋ] *adj* [chin, forehead] that slopes backward.

receipt [rɪ'si:t] *n* -1. a piece of paper that proves that money or goods have been received □ *'Refunds only available with a receipt.'* -2. the act of receiving something □ *I acknowledge receipt of the letter.* □ *Your order will be sent on receipt of payment.*

◆ **receipts** *npl* the money spent by people in a store, theater, cinema, at a sporting event etc □ *Last week we took $6,000 in receipts.*

receivable [rɪ'si:vəbl] *adj* [bill, debt] that requires money to be paid.

receive [rɪ'si:v] ◇ *vt* -1. [money, gift, attention] to be given <sthg> □ *The matter will receive my fullest consideration.* -2. [letter, phone call] to be contacted by somebody using <sthg>. ■ **to receive news of sb/sthg** to be contacted by somebody who tells one how sb/sthg is progressing. -3. [criticism, injury, setback] to experience <sthg> □ *The author has received a number of death threats.* -4. [visitor, guest, new member] to welcome <sb>. -5. **to be well/ badly received** [person, play, news] to get a good/bad reaction. ◇ *vi* SPORT to be the player in a game of tennis who must hit the ball back after it has been served.

receiver [rɪ'si:vər] *n* -1. [of a telephone] the part of a telephone that one holds near one's ear and speaks into □ *He said "Goodbye" and put the receiver down.* -2. RADIO & TV a radio or television set (technical use). -3. [of stolen property] a person who buys and sells stolen property □ *a receiver of stolen goods.* -4. FINANCE the person who officially deals with the affairs and finances of a bankrupt person or company □ *They brought the receivers in.*

receivership [rɪ'si:vər'ʃɪp] *n* **to go into receivership** [company, business] to become bankrupt and be put in the charge of receivers.

receiving end [rɪ'si:vɪŋ-] *n* **to be on the receiving end of sthg** [of complaints, violence, somebody's anger] to experience sthg unpleasant.

recent ['ri:snt] *adj* [edition, development, past] that happened or started to exist a short time ago □ *All these events are relatively recent.*

recently ['ri:sntlɪ] *adv* [happen, begin, appear] a short time ago or during the period that started a short time ago and continued until now □ *I spoke to him recently.* □ *Recently, I've been wondering the same thing.* □ *The mistake wasn't discovered until recently.*

receptacle [rɪ'septəkl] *n* a container for putting or keeping things in (formal use).

reception [rɪ'sepʃn] *n* -1. GB [in a hotel, office] the area in a hotel, office, hospital etc where visitors go first when they arrive, and where there is usually a desk and somebody to deal with them □ *On arrival, please report to reception.* □ *For further details, ask at reception.* □ *reception staff.* -2. [for a celebration, welcome] a formal party held to welcome a particular group of people, or to celebrate a particular event □ *We went to their wedding reception.* -3. [to a speech, movie, visitor] the way that people react to somebody or something □ *The play got a cool reception from the critics.* -4. [of a radio, television] the quality of the picture or sound that one gets from a television or radio □ *You'll get better reception if you adjust the aerial.*

reception centre *n* GB a place where homeless people can live for a short time.

reception class *n* GB the first class in a primary school.

reception desk *n* the desk where a receptionist sits.

receptionist [rɪ'sepʃnəst] *n* a person who works in a hotel, office etc, and who arranges appointments and reservations, answers the telephone, and deals with people when they arrive.

reception room *n* GB a room in a house where people can sit together to eat, talk, watch television etc.

receptive [rɪ'septɪv] *adj* [person, audience] that is ready to consider and accept an idea, opinion etc □ *John was very receptive to my proposal.*

receptiveness [rɪ'septɪvnəs] *n*: see **receptive**.

recess ['ri:ses] *n* -1. [of a room] a part of a room that is formed when one part of a wall is built further back than the rest. -2. **the recesses of sb's mind/memory etc** the parts of sb's mind/memory etc that are unclear or hidden. -3. US EDUCATION a break between classes at an elementary school. -4. POLITICS & LAW a period when a legislature, committee, court etc stops working for a vacation □ *We'll resume this discussion after the Easter recess.*

recessed ['ri:sest] *adj* [window, lighting] that is set into a wall or ceiling.

recession [rɪ'seʃn] *n* a period when the industry of a country produces and sells less, the economy is not growing, and more people are becoming unemployed □ *House prices tend to go down during a recession.*

recessive [rɪ'sesɪv] *adj* BIOLOGY [characteristic, gene] that only appears in the child if it is in the genes of both parents.

recharge [riː'tʃɑːʳdʒ] *vt* to put electricity back into <a battery that has been used>, by using a special piece of equipment.

rechargeable [ˌriː'tʃɑːʳdʒəbl] *adj* [battery] that can be recharged and used again.

recipe ['resəpɪ] *n* -1. COOKING a list of ingredients and instructions for preparing and cooking a particular food or dish □ *You must give me your recipe for tomato soup.* □ *a recipe book.* -2. **to be a recipe for sthg** to be likely to cause sthg to happen □ *Introducing those two was a recipe for disaster!*

recipient [rɪ'sɪpɪənt] *n* [of a letter, award, check] a person who receives something.

reciprocal [rɪ'sɪprəkl] *adj* [arrangement, agreement, gesture] in which one does or gives something to somebody, because that person did or gave something similar to one.

reciprocate [rɪ'sɪprəkeɪt] ◇ *vi* to do the same thing to somebody else as they have done to oneself, or have the same feeling toward them as they have for oneself □ *He smiled at me and I reciprocated.* □ *I'd like to reciprocate in some way.* ◇ *vt* [invitation, generosity] *I felt I should reciprocate her kindness toward me.*

recital [rɪ'saɪtl] *n* a performance of poetry, music etc, usually by one person □ *an organ recital.*

recitation [ˌresɪ'teɪʃn] *n* [of a poem, piece of writing] *see* **recite**.

recite [rɪ'saɪt] *vt* -1. [poem, piece of writing] to say <sthg> out loud, usually from memory. -2. [list, facts, details] to say <sthg> out loud □ *She recited all the reasons why they couldn't come.*

reckless ['rekləs] *adj* [person, behavior] that shows little or no concern about a possible dangerous result of an action □ *He's been charged with reckless driving.*

recklessness ['rekləsnəs] *n*: *see* **reckless**.

reckon ['rekən] *vt* -1. **to reckon (that)...** to think that something is true □ *They reckon (that) it's going to rain later.* □ *I reckon he's crazy.* □ *"Is this our room?" — "I reckon so."* -2. **to be reckoned to be sthg** to be judged or considered to be sthg □ *He was reckoned to be too drunk.* □ *It's reckoned to be the most expensive trial in history.* -3. **to reckon to do sthg** to expect to do sthg □ *They reckon to earn five grand.* -4. [amount, time, cost] to calculate <sthg> (formal use).

◆ **reckon on** *vt fus* **to reckon on sthg** to expect sthg and assume it will happen □ *He had reckoned on my help.* □ *They reckon on getting government funds.*

◆ **reckon with** *vt fus* -1. **to reckon with sthg** to expect sthg □ *She clearly hadn't reckoned with such strong resistance.* -2. **to have to reckon with sb/sthg** to have to deal with sb/sthg

that may make things difficult □ *Do it, or you'll have me to reckon with.* □ *Her performance shows she's still a force to be reckoned with.*

◆ **reckon without** *vt fus* **to reckon without sthg** not to expect sthg □ *He'd reckoned without them saying "no".*

reckoning ['rekənɪŋ] *n* -1. **by sb's reckoning** according to sb's rough calculations □ *He's 25 minutes late, by my reckoning.* -2. **a day of reckoning** the time when somebody's past mistakes are punished or when the bad results of their past actions are noticed.

reclaim [rɪ'kleɪm] *vt* -1. [luggage, money] to get back <one's property> by asking for it. -2. [desert, marsh] to make changes to <an area of land> so that it can be used.

reclamation [ˌreklə'meɪʃn] *n* [of a desert, marsh] *see* **reclaim** □ *a land reclamation project.*

recline [rɪ'klaɪn] *vi* [person, seat] to lie back in a relaxed way □ *Hank was reclining in his armchair.*

reclining [rɪ'klaɪnɪŋ] *adj* [chair, seat] that can be moved into a position that allows one to lie on it.

recluse [US 'rekluːs, GB rɪ'kluːs] *n* a person who lives alone and avoids other people.

reclusive [US 'rekluːsɪv, GB rɪ'kluːsɪv] *adj* [person, writer] who is a recluse.

recognition [ˌrekəg'nɪʃn] *n* -1. [of a person, face, voice] the act of recognizing somebody or something □ *As I approached, she gave no sign of recognition.* ■ **to change beyond** OR **out of all recognition** to change so much that people can no longer recognize one □ *I can't believe it! You've changed beyond all recognition!* -2. [of a fact, problem, contribution] the act of showing that one thinks something is true, valuable etc □ *Her books have not received the recognition they deserve.* □ *He was presented with the trophy in recognition of his outstanding achievement.*

recognizable ['rekəgnaɪzəbl] *adj* [person, problem, symptom] that can be recognized.

recognize, -ise ['rekəgnaɪz] *vt* -1. [face, voice, sign] to know who or what <sb/sthg> is because one can remember them from before □ *Sorry, I didn't recognize you!* □ *I recognized him as Mr Cooke, Milly's husband.* -2. [fact, truth, problem] to agree that <sthg> exists; [contribution, achievement] to accept that <sthg> is useful, valuable etc □ *We recognize (that) there is a need for change.* □ *Her contribution to British science has never been recognized.* -3. [country, government, qualification] to show that one officially accepts <sthg> as valid □ *It was some time before the breakaway republic was recognized as an independent state.*

recoil [*vb* rɪ'kɔɪl, *n* 'riːkɔɪl] ◇ *vi* -1. to move back suddenly and away from something that is unpleasant □ *He recoiled at the sight.* □ *She recoiled in fear/disgust.* -2. to have an immediate dislike or fear of something □ *He recoiled at the thought.* ◇ *n* the quick backward movement of a gun or part of a gun when it is fired.

recollect [ˌrekə'lekt] *vt* [person, name, time] to

remember <sb/sthg> □ *I don't recollect ever having met him.*

recollection [ˌrekəˈlekʃn] *n* the act of remembering somebody or something; something that one remembers from the past □ *I have no recollection of such a name.*

recommence [ˌriːkəˈmens] ◇ *vt* [meeting, talks] to start <sthg> again. ◇ *vi* [meeting, talks] *Negotiations recommenced last night.*

recommend [ˌrekəˈmend] *vt* to suggest to somebody that <sb/sthg> is good or suitable for a particular purpose □ *Can you recommend a good hotel/electrician to me?* □ *This restaurant was recommended to me.* □ *I recommend (that) you go there in May.*

recommendation [ˌrekəmenˈdeɪʃn] *n* the act of recommending somebody or something; something that is recommended □ *She was offered the job on the recommendation of Professor Wilkes.* □ *None of the recommendations made by the committee has been implemented yet.*

recommended retail price [ˌrekəmendəd-] *n* the standard price of an item for sale as recommended by the manufacturer to the retailer.

recompense [ˈrekəmpens] ◇ *n* recompense for sthg [for damage, a loss] money given to somebody as a way of showing one is sorry or grateful for sthg. ◇ *vt* to recompense sb for sthg [for damage, a loss] to give a recompense to sb because of sthg.

reconcile [ˈrekənsaɪl] *vt* -1. [beliefs, ideas] to find a way in which <two things that are opposed to each other> are no longer opposed □ *How do you reconcile wearing leather shoes with being vegetarian?* -2. to make <two people, countries> etc friendly with each other again after a disagreement. ■ **to be reconciled with sb** to be friendly with sb again after a disagreement. -3. **to reconcile oneself to sthg** [to a fact, one's fate] to accept sthg unpleasant, because one cannot change it □ *I'm not quite reconciled to the idea of spending two weeks with Walter.*

reconciliation [ˌrekənsɪlɪˈeɪʃn] *n*: *see* reconcile □ *Is there any hope of a reconciliation between them?*

recondite [ˈrekəndaɪt] *adj* [idea, knowledge, subject] that not many people know about or understand (formal use).

reconditioned [ˌriːkənˈdɪʃnd] *adj* [engine, machine] that has had its old parts repaired or replaced so that it works better.

reconnaissance [rɪˈkɒnəsns] *n* the process of sending soldiers, planes etc into an area to get military information about one's enemy or about the geography of the area □ *a reconnaissance mission.*

reconnect [ˌriːkəˈnekt] *vt* [electricity supply, telephone line] to connect <sthg> again to a building, house etc.

reconnoiter [ˌriːkəˈnɔɪtər] US, **reconnoitre** [ˌrekəˈnɔɪtə] GB ◇ *vt* [area, site] to carry out a reconnaissance of <a place>. ◇ *vi* [troops, police] *The aircraft will reconnoiter tomorrow.*

reconsider [ˌriːkənˈsɪdər] ◇ *vt* [decision, situation, position] to think about <sthg> again, e.g. in order to decide whether changes need to be made. ◇ *vi: I hope you will reconsider.*

reconstitute [ˌriːˈkɒnstɪtjuːt] *vt* -1. [organization, group, committee] to form <sthg> again in a different way. -2. [fruit, milk] to change <dried or powdered food> back into its normal state by adding water to it.

reconstruct [ˌriːkənˈstrʌkt] *vt* -1. [building, town, economy] to repair or rebuild <sthg> after it has been damaged or destroyed. -2. [crime, sequence of events] to make a detailed and complete picture of <sthg that is only partly known> by putting together all the pieces of information one has.

reconstruction [ˌriːkənˈstrʌkʃn] *n*: *see* reconstruct □ *The man was caught following a police reconstruction shown on TV.* □ *The economic reconstruction of the country began in the 1950s.*

◆ **Reconstruction** *n* the period after the American Civil War from 1865 to 1877. During this time the South was reorganized and re-joined the Union.

❦ RECONSTRUCTION
After the American Civil War ended in 1865, the Republican government and the army of the North ruled the defeated Southern states for a period of 12 years, called Reconstruction. The rebel states were allowed to join the Union again, but had to promise to be loyal to the Union, to end slavery, and to allow black men the right to vote. These policies were very unpopular in the South, and caused violence and tension between black people and white people. Reconstruction ended when the Republicans lost power in 1877, and black people also lost many of the rights they had been given.

reconvene [ˌriːkənˈviːn] *vt* to call the people taking part in <a meeting> together again.

record [*n* & *adj* US ˈrekərd, GB ˈrekɔːd, *vb* rɪˈkɔːrd] ◇ *n* -1. [of events, information] a written account of something □ *I keep a record of all my expenses.* □ *We have no record of this transaction.* □ *Our records show your account is now overdue.* ■ **to keep sthg on record** [information, details] to keep sthg so that people can refer to it later □ *His name had been kept on record.* ■ **the highest/worst etc on record** the highest/worst etc ever recorded. □ *It's the hottest summer on record.* ■ **to be on record as saying (that)...** to have said publicly (that)... □ *Smith was on record as saying that he was going to resign.* ■ **to go on record as saying (that)...** to say publicly (that)... □ *I will happily go on record as saying that I will not vote for this bill in Congress.* -2. MUSIC a flat and usually black vinyl disk on which sound, usually music, is recorded □ *a record collection.* -3. [in a sport, activity] the highest achievement reached in a particular field □ *He holds the world record for the 100m crawl.* □ *This is a new Olympic record.* -4. [about a person] all the information known about somebody's background, life etc, often in a particular field □ *medical rec-*

ords □ *If you get caught, you'll end up with a criminal record.* **-5. to set** OR **put the record straight** to tell somebody that something they always believed is not true □ *I'd like to set the record straight. I didn't do it.*
◇ *adj* [level, score, time] that is higher than has been recorded before □ *Unemployment is at a record high.* □ *record annual losses.*
◇ *vt* **-1.** [facts, event] to write <sthg> down so that people can refer to it later □ *She had recorded the conversation in her diary.* **-2.** [sound, music, program] to put <sthg> on tape, film etc so that it can be watched or listened to again □ *Did you remember to record that program on the Gulf War?*

record-breaker *n* a person who beats a record in a sport, activity etc.

record-breaking *adj* [performance, run, throw] that beats a record in a sport, activity etc.

recorded delivery [rɪ,kɔːˈdəd-] *n* in Britain, a Post Office service in which one is given an official document stating that a letter, package etc has been sent and delivered □ *The letter was sent by recorded delivery.*

recorder [rɪˈkɔːdəʳ] *n* **-1.** a machine that records something □ *a tape/video/cassette recorder.* **-2.** a simple musical instrument in the shape of a tube that is played by blowing into one end and putting one's fingers over holes to produce different notes.

record holder *n* the person who holds the record in a particular field.

recording [rɪˈkɔːdɪŋ] *n* **-1.** a piece of music that has been recorded □ *a live recording* □ *I have a marvelous recording of Maria Callas singing that piece.* **-2.** the process of making a movie, or putting music or sound onto a tape etc.

recording studio *n* a studio where music can be recorded.

record library *n* a library where people can borrow records, CDs, cassettes etc.

record player *n* a machine on which records can be played.

recount [*n* ˈriːkaʊnt, *vt sense 1* rɪˈkaʊnt, *sense 2* ˌriːˈkaʊnt] ◇ *n* a second count of something, especially of votes in an election. ◇ *vt* **-1.** to tell or describe <a story, event> etc. **-2.** to count <votes, figures> etc again.

recoup [rɪˈkuːp] *vt* [loss, money, strength] to get <sthg> back.

recourse [US ˈriːkɔːrs, GB rɪˈkɔːs] *n* **to have recourse to sthg** [to law, violence, financial aid] to use sthg to help one in a difficult situation □ *Remember that you can have no recourse to the law in such a situation.*

recover [rɪˈkʌvəʳ] ◇ *vt* **-1.** [object, money, property] to get back <sthg that was lost or stolen> □ *He recovered his wallet from the police/the train station.* **-2.** [one's strength, balance, appetite] to get back <sthg one has lost> □ *When Grace recovered consciousness she realized that she was alone.* ■ **to recover oneself** to stop being shocked, embarrassed etc by something □ *Mary suddenly looked embarrassed, but recovered herself swiftly.*

◇ *vi* **-1.** [patient] to get better after an illness, accident etc □ *She's in the hospital recovering from her operation.* **-2.** [person] to stop being upset by something □ *He hasn't recovered from his father's death.* **-3.** [currency, economy] to become stronger after it has been weak □ *The pound soon recovered against the dollar.*

recoverable [rɪˈkʌvrəbl] *adj* [expense, tax] that one can get back after one has paid it.

recovery [rɪˈkʌvərɪ] (*pl* **recoveries**) *n* **-1.** [from an illness, injury] a return to one's normal state of health after a period of illness □ *He made a swift recovery.* □ *She is better, but the doctor says she may never make a full recovery.* **-2.** [of a currency, economy] a return to a position of strength after a period of weakness □ *The stock exchange shows no immediate signs of recovery.* **-3.** [of money, property, an object] the act of getting back something that was lost or stolen □ *A police inquiry led to the recovery of the stolen vehicle.*

recovery vehicle *n* GB a vehicle, usually a tow truck, that collects one's car after a road accident or breakdown.

recreate [ˌriːkrɪˈeɪt] *vt* [atmosphere, period, style] to look like, or remind people of <sthg that no longer exists> □ *The movie recreates the splendor of the Sun King's court.*

recreation [ˌrekrɪˈeɪʃn] *n* activities that people do for pleasure when they are not working □ *One of their favorite recreations was to play tennis in the garden.* □ *What do you do for recreation?*

recreational [ˌrekrɪˈeɪʃnəl] *adj* [use, facilities] *see* **recreation** □ *a recreational activity.*

recreation room *n* **-1.** a room in a public building, e.g. a hospital, used for games and social activities. **-2.** US = **rec room**.

recrimination [rɪ,krɪmɪˈneɪʃn] *n* the act or process of accusing somebody of something when one has already been accused of something oneself.
◆ **recriminations** *npl* accusations made by two people or groups against each other □ *There were bitter recriminations on both sides.*

rec room [ˈrek-] *n* US a room in a house where people relax, watch TV etc.

recrudescence [ˌriːkruːˈdesns] *n* [of racism, violence] a reappearance of something unpleasant after a period of absence (formal use).

recruit [rɪˈkruːt] ◇ *n* a person who has just joined a company, organization, army etc □ *a new recruit.* ◇ *vt* **-1.** [staff, graduates, soldiers] to look for, choose, and give a job to <sb> □ *She was recruited to the president's team of advisers in 1992.* **-2.** [members] to persuade <sb> to join one's group, e.g. a political party or labor union. ■ **to recruit sb for sthg** OR **to do sthg** to persuade sb to do sthg □ *I'll have to recruit some friends for the gardening/to help with the garden.* ◇ *vi* [armed forces, organization] *Is your company recruiting at the moment?*

recruitment [rɪˈkruːtmənt] *n* [of staff, members] *see* **recruit** □ *an army recruitment campaign.*

rectangle [ˈrektæŋgl] *n* a shape with four sides

at right angles and opposite sides of the same length.

rectangular [rek'tæŋgjələ^r] *adj* [carpet, garden] that is shaped like a rectangle.

rectify ['rektɪfaɪ] (*pt* & *pp* **rectified**) *vt* [mistake, problem] to correct <sthg> (formal use).

rectitude ['rektɪtjuːd] *n* the quality of being morally correct (formal use).

rector ['rektə^r] *n* **-1.** [in the Church of England] a priest who is in charge of a parish. **-2.** [in the Roman Catholic Church] a priest who is in charge of a congregation. **-3.** [in Scotland] the head teacher of some schools; a university official elected by students.

rectory ['rektərɪ] (*pl* **rectories**) *n* in England and Wales, the house where a rector lives.

rectum ['rektəm] (*pl* **rectums**) *n* the lowest part of one's bowels through which solid waste matter passes out of one's body.

recuperate [rɪ'kuːpəreɪt] *vi* to get better and stronger after an illness or injury (formal use) □ *Sonja spent two weeks recuperating after the operation.*

recuperation [rɪ,kuːpə'reɪʃn] *n*: see **recuperate**.

recur [rɪ'kɜː^r] (*pt* & *pp* **recurred**, *cont* **recurring**) *vi* [illness, dream, problem] to happen again, or to keep happening □ *The symptoms recurred over a period of several months.*

recurrence [rɪ'kʌrəns] *n*: see **recur** □ *Later recurrence of the disease is possible.*

recurrent [rɪ'kʌrənt] *adj* [illness, dream, problem] that keeps returning and affecting one □ *I used to get recurrent nightmares.*

recurring [rɪ'kɜːrɪŋ] *adj* **-1.** [illness, dream, problem] = **recurrent**. **-2.** [decimal] that is repeated after the decimal point an infinite number of times □ *three point six recurring.*

recyclable [,riː'saɪkləbl] *adj* [waste, packaging] that can be recycled.

recycle [,riː'saɪkl] *vt* [waste, packaging, glass] to process <sthg that has been used> so that it can be used again □ *recycled paper/envelopes.*

recycling [,riː'saɪklɪŋ] *n*: see **recycle**.

red [red] (*compar* **redder**, *superl* **reddest**) ◇ *adj* **-1.** [dress, rose, wine] that is the color of blood. **-2.** [face, cheek] that is redder than usual because one is angry or embarrassed □ *He turned* OR *went red.* **-3.** [hair, beard] red-brown in color. ◇ *n* **-1.** the color of blood □ *Do you have the dress in red?* **-2.** *phrases* **to be in the red** [person, account] to be in debt, usually to a bank □ *We're at least $10,000 in the red.* ■ **to see red** to become very angry.

◆ **Red** *n* a Communist; a person with left-wing views (informal and disapproving use).

red alert *n* **-1. to be on red alert** to be prepared to deal with an emergency □ *The security staff was put on red alert.* **-2.** the order given to make people ready for an emergency □ *There was a red alert at the hospital after the train crash.*

redback (spider) ['redbæk-] *n* a small poisonous spider found in Australia. The female has a red mark on her back.

red blood cell *n* a blood cell that carries oxygen around the body.

red-blooded [-'blʌdəd] *adj* [man] who is strong, healthy, and very interested in sex (humorous use).

redbrick ['redbrɪk] *n* **a redbrick (university)** any of the British universities established in the late 19th or early 20th century.

red card *n* **to be shown the red card, to get a red card** in soccer, to be sent off the field by the referee for bad behavior.

red carpet *n* **to roll out the red carpet for sb** to treat sb who is visiting one as a very important and honored person.

◆ **red-carpet** *adj* **to give sb the red-carpet treatment** to roll out the red carpet for sb.

Red Centre *n* **the Red Centre** an informal term used for the desert areas of central Australia that have dark-red sand.

Red Crescent *n* **the Red Crescent** an organization in Muslim countries that helps victims of wars and disasters.

Red Cross *n* **the Red Cross** an international organization that helps victims of wars and disasters.

redcurrant [US ,red'kɜːrənt, GB -'kʌr-] *n* a small, round, red fruit that grows in bunches; the bush that this fruit grows on □ *redcurrant jelly.*

red deer *n* a large red-brown deer that lives in northern Europe and Asia.

redden ['redn] ◇ *vt* [painting, mixture] to make <sthg> red or more red. ◇ *vi* [face, cheeks] to become red or more red because one is angry or embarrassed.

redecorate [,riː'dekəreɪt] ◇ *vt* [room, house] to make <sthg> look better by repainting it, putting up new wallpaper etc. ◇ *vi*: *We're going to redecorate next summer.*

redeem [rɪ'diːm] *vt* **-1.** [behavior, book] to make <sthg bad> acceptable or enjoyable by being better than the rest of it □ *Even his fine performance was unable to redeem the movie.* ■ **to redeem oneself** to do something good after one has done something bad, with the result that people have a better opinion of one □ *I'd like to do something to redeem myself in your eyes.* **-2.** [watch, jewelry] to buy <an object> back from a pawnbroker.

redeeming [rɪ'diːmɪŋ] *adj* [quality, feature] that redeems something bad □ *The one redeeming aspect of the trip was the magnificent scenery.*

redefine [,riːdɪ'faɪn] *vt* [word, idea] to define <sthg> again, usually in order to think about it in a new context or to change its use □ *Mason's book has redefined our concept of modern design.*

redemption [rɪ'dempʃn] *n* RELIGION the act of being saved so that one is not punished forever for one's sins, that Christians believe was made possible by the death of Christ. ■ **to be beyond** OR **past redemption** to be too bad to be saved or improved □ *This old blanket is beyond redemption, I'm afraid.*

redeploy [,riːdɪ'plɔɪ] *vt* [troops, workers] to move <sb/sthg> to a different place or job.

redeployment [ˌriːdɪ'plɔɪmənt] *n: see* **redeploy**.
□ *Workers are being chosen from several sites for redeployment elsewhere.*

redesign [ˌriːdɪ'zaɪn] *vt* [office, engine, system] to change the design of <sthg>.

redevelop [ˌriːdɪ'veləp] *vt* to demolish the buildings in <a town or area> and build new ones there.

redevelopment [ˌriːdɪ'veləpmənt] *n: see* **redevelop**.

red-faced [-'feɪst] *adj* [person] whose face is red because they have been exercising or because they are embarrassed.

red-haired [-'heəʳd] *adj* [person] who has red hair.

red-handed [-'hændəd] *adj* **to catch sb red-handed** to catch sb while they are doing something wrong or illegal.

redhead ['redhed] *n* a person who has red hair.

red herring *n* something that seems to have something to do with a particular question or problem but does not, so that one wastes time by thinking about it □ *The Belgian connection turned out to be a red herring.*

red-hot *adj* **-1.** [metal, plate] very hot. **-2.** [sex, anger] that shows strong feeling or excitement.

redid [ˌriː'dɪd] *past tense of* **redo**.

Red Indian *n* a Native American (old-fashioned and offensive use).

redirect [ˌriːdɪ'rekt] *vt* **-1.** [aircraft, traffic] to send <a vehicle or vehicles> in a different direction; [letter, package] to send <mail> to a different address. **-2.** to use <one's energy, money> etc to do something different.

rediscover [ˌriːdɪ'skʌvəʳ] *vt* to find again <sthg that one had lost or forgotten> □ *I've been rediscovering the places I used to visit as a child.*

redistribute [US ˌriːdɪ'strɪbjət, GB -juːt] *vt* [money, power, food] to share <sthg> out in a different and fairer way.

red-letter day *n* a particularly happy day that one will always remember.

red light *n* a red traffic light that tells drivers to stop.

red-light district *n* an area of a city where prostitutes work.

red meat *n* meat, e.g. beef or lamb, that is dark brown after it is cooked.
NOTE: Compare **white meat**.

red mullet *n* a red European sea fish that is eaten as food.

redness ['rednəs] *n* [of a face, rose] *see* **red**.

redo [ˌriː'duː] (*pt* **redid**, *pp* **redone**) *vt* **-1.** [one's work, hair] to do <sthg> again in a different way. **-2.** [house, room] to redecorate <sthg> (informal use).

redolent ['redələnt] *adj* **to be redolent of sthg** [of summer, the sea] to make one think of sthg; [of flowers, perfume] to smell of sthg (literary use).

redone [ˌriː'dʌn] *past participle of* **redo**.

redouble [ˌriː'dʌbl] *vt* **to redouble one's efforts** to try much harder □ *They redoubled their efforts to reach the sales target.*

redoubtable [rɪ'daʊtəbl] *adj* [person] who people respect and fear (formal use).

redraft [US ˌriː'dræft, GB -'drɑːft] *vt* [speech, letter, report] to write a new version of <sthg>.

redraw [ˌriː'drɔː] (*pt* **redrew**, *pp* **redrawn** [-'drɔːn]) *vt* to change <the borders or boundaries of a country> □ *The map of Europe was redrawn after World War II.*

redress [rɪ'dres] ◇ *n* money that somebody pays one because they have treated one badly or harmed one in some way (formal use) □ *They are seeking redress in the courts.*
◇ *vt* **to redress the balance** to make things more equal or fair.

redrew [ˌriː'druː] *past tense of* **redraw**.

Red Sea: the Red Sea the sea between northeastern Africa and Arabia. It is connected to the Mediterranean in the north by the Suez Canal, and to the Indian Ocean in the south.

red setter *n* a large dog that has a soft brownish-red coat.

red squirrel *n* a brownish-red squirrel that lives in forests in Europe and Asia.

red tape *n* official rules that seem unnecessary and take up a lot of people's time (disapproving use).

reduce [rɪ'djuːs] ◇ *vt* **-1.** [price, risk] to make <sthg> smaller; [heat] to make <sthg> less strong □ *Can we reduce the engine size without reducing the power?* □ *Output has been reduced by 15%.* □ *The Government has reduced the working day from 8 to 7 hours.* ■ **to reduce sthg to a pulp** to beat or crush sthg until it becomes a pulp. **-2.** COOKING [liquid, sauce] to boil <sthg> to make it thicker and less in quantity. **-3.** **to be reduced to doing sthg** [to begging, stealing] to be forced to do sthg □ *Salorno was eventually reduced to selling his house to pay the debt.* ■ **to reduce sb to silence/tears** to make sb be silent/cry □ *The news reduced her to tears.*
◇ *vi* US [person] to lose weight.

reduced [rɪ'djuːst] *adj* [price, risk, heat] that has been made less in amount, or degree □ *The National Party has won again, but with a reduced majority.* ■ **to live in reduced circumstances** to live with less money than one is used to.

reduction [rɪ'dʌkʃn] *n* **-1.** the amount that something is reduced by □ *A budget reduction of 10% is required.* **-2.** [in price, heat] *see* **reduce** □ *Any more reductions in staff will lead to safety risks.* □ *a price reduction.*

redundancy [rɪ'dʌndənsɪ] (*pl* **redundancies**) *n* GB [for staff, a worker] *see* **redundant** □ *redundancy payment* □ *Half the workforce at the plant now face redundancy.*

redundant [rɪ'dʌndənt] *adj* **-1.** **to be made redundant** GB [worker, staff] to lose one's job because one's employer can no longer afford to pay one's salary or has decided the job is no longer necessary. **-2.** [equipment, phrase, information] that is not needed.

redwood ['redwʊd] *n* **a redwood (tree)** a very large tree that grows in the western USA and has red-brown bark and hard wood.

reed [riːd] *n* -1. a tall type of grass that grows in or near water and is dried to make objects by weaving □ *a reed basket/seat.* -2. a thin piece of wood or metal in the mouthpiece of some musical instruments, e.g. the oboe, that vibrates and makes a sound when one blows over it.

re-educate [ˌriːˈedʒəkeɪt] *vt* to try to make <sb> behave or think in a different way □ *Juvenile delinquents are re-educated and taught not to rely on violence to resolve conflicts.*

reedy ['riːdɪ] (*compar* **reedier**, *superl* **reediest**) *adj* [voice] high and unpleasant.

reef [riːf] *n* a long line of coral, rock, or sand that is just below the surface of the sea.

reek [riːk] ◇ *n* [of onions, gas] a strong unpleasant smell. ◇ *vi* [person, breath, clothes] to smell strongly of something unpleasant □ *This place reeks of smoke.*

reel [riːl] ◇ *n* a small round object like a cylinder that something such as wire or fishing line is wrapped around □ *a reel of cotton/film.* ◇ *vi* -1. [person] to walk in an unsteady way, e.g. because one is drunk or has just been hit □ *The blow sent him reeling.* -2. [head, mind] to be in a state of confusion, e.g. after a shock or after receiving too much information □ *He is still reeling from the shock.*

◆ **reel in** *vt sep* **to reel a fish in** to pull a fish toward one by turning the handle on the reel of one's fishing rod.

◆ **reel off** *vt sep* **to reel names/demands etc off** to say a list of names/demands etc quickly □ *She reeled off the names of every US president since 1945.*

re-elect [ˌriːəˈlekt] *vt* [chairman, president] to elect <sb> again □ *He was re-elected as union leader.*

re-election [ˌriːəˈlekʃn] *n*: *see* **re-elect** □ *She is standing for re-election.*

re-emphasize [ˌriːˈemfəsaɪz] *vt* [fact, importance] to emphasize <sthg> again.

re-enact [ˌriːɪˈnækt] *vt* [incident, scene, event] to perform <sthg> again.

re-enter [ˌriːˈentər] *vt* -1. [country, area] to enter again <a place that one has left> □ *They were arrested when they tried to re-enter the country.* -2. COMPUTING [data, text] to enter again into a computer <information that has been lost or deleted>.

re-entry [ˌriːˈentrɪ] *n* [of a spaceship] the act of returning to the Earth's atmosphere after being in space □ *It burned up on re-entry.*

re-examine [ˌriːɪgˈzæmən] *vt* [question, case] to examine <sthg/sb> again.

re-export [ˌriːˈeksɔːrt] ◇ *vt* to export <goods that one has already imported>. ◇ *n* the act of re-exporting something □ *We import cotton for re-export.* □ *The value of re-exports has risen.*

ref [ref] ◇ *n* SPORT *abbr of* **referee** (informal use). ◇ ADMIN *abbr of* **reference**.

refectory [rɪˈfektərɪ] (*pl* **refectories**) *n* a large dining hall in a school, college etc.

refer [rɪˈfɜːr] (*pt* & *pp* **referred**, *cont* **referring**)

◆ **refer to** ◇ *vt sep* -1. **to refer sb to sb/sthg** [to a specialist, one's notes] to send sb to sb/sthg where they can get more information or advice □ *I was referred to a heart specialist.* □ *If I can refer you to chapter ten of Miller's book, you'll find a very different interpretation.* -2. **to refer sthg to sb** [report, case, decision] to ask sb more qualified to deal with sthg □ *The matter has been referred to the committee.*

◇ *vt fus* -1. **to refer to sb/sthg** [book, incident, person] to mention or talk about sb/sthg, especially without saying directly who or what one is talking about □ *I don't know what you are referring to.* □ *I presumed she was referring to the company director.* -2. **to refer to sb/sthg** [person, situation] to apply to or concern sb/sthg □ *Surely that instruction doesn't refer to us?* -3. **to refer to sthg** [report, diary] to look at sthg for information □ *Candidates must answer without referring to a dictionary.* □ *He spoke without referring to his notes once.*

referee [ˌrefəˈriː] ◇ *n* -1. SPORT an official who makes sure that the players obey the rules of a game, e.g. football, boxing, and hockey. -2. GB a person who gives somebody a reference, e.g. for a job application. ◇ *vt* to be the referee in <a game or match>. ◇ *vi*: *Who's refereeing today?*

reference ['refrəns] *n* -1. an act of mentioning somebody or something □ *I didn't understand his reference to Plato.* ■ **to make reference to sb/sthg** to mention sb/sthg □ *She made frequent reference to the war years.* ■ **with reference to...** a phrase used to say what one is speaking or writing about (formal use) □ *With reference to your letter/complaint of May 24th...* -2. [to a calendar, report, diary] the act of referring to something or somebody for information or advice □ *They refused the application without reference to me.* ■ **to keep/file sthg for future reference** to keep/file sthg in order to be able to refer to it when necessary in the future □ *There is no vacancy at present, but we will keep your details on file for future reference.* -3. [in a catalog, on a map] a number or name that shows where something can be found □ *The map reference is H4.* -4. [in a business letter] = **reference number** □ *Please quote your reference in all correspondence.* -5. [for a job] a letter about somebody who is applying for a job, that describes their character and abilities and is written by somebody who knows them; a person who writes or has agreed to write this letter □ *My previous boss wrote me an excellent reference.* □ *Mr Calf agreed to be one of my references.*

reference book *n* a book that one refers to for information, e.g. a dictionary or encyclopedia.

reference library *n* a library where the books can be read but not borrowed.

reference number *n* a number, given on a bill, in a business letter etc, that tells one the file where one can find more information about the subject of the bill, letter etc.

referendum [ˌrefəˈrendəm] (*pl* **referendums** OR **referenda** [-də]) *n* a vote in which the people of a country show whether or not they agree with a particular government policy □ *The government debated whether to hold a referendum on the issue.*

referral [rɪˈfɜːrəl] *n* the act of referring sb/sthg to another person or place □ *the referral of complaints to the tribunal* □ *an increase in the number of referrals.*

refill [*n* ˈriːfɪl, *vb* ˌriːˈfɪl] ◇ *n* -1. [for a pen, lighter] a container full of a liquid, e.g. ink, that is used to replace one that has been emptied. -2. another drink (informal use) □ *Would you like a refill?* ◇ *vt* [pen, tank] to fill <an empty container> with more of the liquid that was there before □ *Can I refill your glass?*

refillable [ˌriːˈfɪləbl] *adj* [bottle, pen, lighter] that can be refilled.

refine [rɪˈfaɪn] *vt* -1. [oil, gold, sugar] to make <a substance> pure by putting it through a process that removes other substances from it. -2. [plan, theory, speech] to improve <sthg> gradually by making small changes to it until it is as good as possible □ *We are constantly updating and refining our training programs.*

refined [rɪˈfaɪnd] *adj* -1. [person, manners] very polite □ *an elegant and refined old lady.* -2. [process, equipment, theory] highly developed □ *The new design is better and more refined than the old one.* -3. [oil, gold, sugar] that has been made pure by having other substances removed.

refinement [rɪˈfaɪnmənt] *n* -1. [to a process, equipment, speech] a small improvement to something □ *We have made a number of refinements to the old system.* -2. [of a person] the quality of being refined.

refinery [rɪˈfaɪnərɪ] (*pl* **refineries**) *n* a place where a substance is refined □ *an oil/a sugar refinery.*

refit [*vb* ˌriːˈfɪt, *n* ˈriːfɪt] (*pt* & *pp* **refitted**, *cont* **refitting**) ◇ *vt* to repair and replace the damaged parts of <a ship>; to adapt <a ship> for a new purpose. ◇ *n: The refit will take six months.*

reflate [riːˈfleɪt] *vt* to increase the supply of money in <a country's economy> to encourage more economic activity.

reflation [riːˈfleɪʃn] *n: see* **reflate** □ *measures designed to help reflation.*

reflationary [US riːˈfleɪʃnerɪ, GB -ərɪ] *adj* [policy, measure] that is designed to increase the supply of money in a country's economy.

reflect [rɪˈflekt] ◇ *vt* -1. [attitude, situation] to be a sign of <sthg> □ *Current social problems are reflected in the crime figures.* □ *The policy clearly reflects the government's belief in a free market.* -2. to send <light, heat, sound> etc back □ *She saw her face reflected in the water/mirror.* -3. **to reflect that...** to comment that... □ *He reflected that it may not be the right moment to announce a rival bid.* ◇ *vi* to think deeply about something □ *He reflected on* OR *upon his decision.* □ *She said she needed time to reflect.*

reflection [rɪˈflekʃn] *n* -1. something that is a sign of a particular attitude, situation, policy etc □ *The budget is a reflection of the govern-*

ment's uncertainty. -2. **to be a reflection on sb/sthg** to show sb/sthg in an unfavorable way □ *This is no reflection on you.* -3. a reflected image □ *She caught sight of her reflection in the mirror.* -4. deep thought; a thought or idea that one has had after thinking deeply □ *The matter calls for careful reflection.* □ *her reflections on the political scene.* ■ **on** OR **upon reflection** after thinking seriously about the matter □ *On reflection, I think it was a mistake.* -5. [of heat, light] *see* **reflect.**

reflective [rɪˈflektɪv] *adj* -1. [person, look] that is thoughtful. -2. [surface, clothing] that reflects light.

reflector [rɪˈflektər] *n* a piece of glass or plastic that reflects light and is attached to the back of a bicycle or car to make it easier to see at night.

reflex [ˈriːfleks] *n* an uncontrolled movement of part of the body that is a response to an outside influence □ *Blinking is a reflex action.*

◆ **reflexes** *npl* a person's ability to react quickly to something unexpected □ *You need very quick reflexes to be good at a martial art.*

reflex camera *n* a camera in which one sees and focuses the image through the lens.

reflexive [rɪˈfleksɪv] *adj* GRAMMAR [verb, pronoun] that refers back to the subject of the sentence.

reflexology [ˌriːflekˈsɒlədʒɪ] *n* a treatment for particular illnesses in which parts of the feet are massaged, based on the belief that different parts of the foot are connected to different parts of the body.

reforestation [riːˌfɒrəˈsteɪʃn] *n* the process of planting trees again in an area of land that has been cleared.

reform [rɪˈfɔːrm] ◇ *n* -1. a process of change, usually intended to improve a legal, social, or political system □ *The health care system is long overdue for reform.* -2. a particular change that is made to a social, legal, or political system in order to improve it □ *the government's tax reforms.*

◇ *vt* -1. [system, organization] to improve <sthg> by changing it □ *government attempts to reform the health service.* -2. [criminal, drug addict] to improve the behavior of <sb> in order to make them a better person □ *It's not easy to reform the habits of a lifetime.*

◇ *vi* to improve one's behavior in order to be a better person □ *Alan had promised, time after time, that he would reform.*

reformat [ˌriːˈfɔːrmæt] (*pt* & *pp* **reformatted**, *cont* **reformatting**) *vt* to format <a computer disk that has already been formatted>.

Reformation [ˌrefərˈmeɪʃn] *n* **the Reformation** a religious movement in 16th-century Europe that led to the establishment of the Protestant churches there.

reformatory [US rɪˈfɔːrmətɔːrɪ, GB -ˈfɔːmətrɪ] (*pl* **reformatories**) *n* US a special school for young people who have broken the law.

reformed [rɪˈfɔːrmd] *adj* [person] who has changed the way they live or behave and is now a better person □ *a reformed criminal/drug addict.*

reformer [rɪˈfɔːʳməʳ] *n* a person who tries to reform a legal, social, or political system.

reformist [rɪˈfɔːʳməst] ◇ *adj* [policy, tendency] that tries to introduce reforms. ◇ *n* a reformist person.

refract [rɪˈfrækt] ◇ *vt* to cause the direction of <light> to change at the point where it passes through another substance, e.g. water or glass. ◇ *vi: Light refracts as it crosses the boundary between air and water.*

refrain [rɪˈfreɪn] ◇ *n* a short section of a song or poem that is repeated several times throughout the song or poem. ◇ *vi* **to refrain from doing sthg** [from talking, drinking] to stop doing sthg, especially something one would like to do or usually does but which may annoy other people □ *Kindly refrain from smoking in the dining room.*

refresh [rɪˈfreʃ] *vt* to make <sb> feel cooler or more energetic. ■ **to refresh sb's memory** to remind sb of something that they have forgotten □ *You don't know how much you spent? Let me refresh your memory.*

refreshed [rɪˈfreʃt] *adj* [person] who feels cooler or more energetic □ *I felt refreshed after the walk.*

refresher course [rɪˈfreʃəʳ-] *n* a training course that brings somebody's knowledge and skills up to date.

refreshing [rɪˈfreʃɪŋ] *adj* -1. [honesty, change] that is pleasant because it is different from what one is used to. -2. [drink, swim] that makes one feel cooler or more energetic.

refreshments [rɪˈfreʃmənts] *npl* food and drink served to the public, e.g. at a meeting or on a flight □ *Drinks and light refreshments will be served during the intermission.*

refrigerate [rɪˈfrɪdʒəreɪt] *vt* to keep <food or drink> fresh or cool by placing it in a refrigerator.

refrigeration [rɪˌfrɪdʒəˈreɪʃn] *n: see* **refrigerate**.

refrigerator [rɪˈfrɪdʒəreɪtəʳ] *n* a large appliance, usually in a kitchen, that is cold inside and which food and drinks are kept in to keep them fresh or cool.

refuel [ˌriːˈfjuːəl] (US *pt* & *pp* **refueled**, *cont* **refueling**, GB *pt* & *pp* **refuelled**, *cont* **refuelling**) ◇ *vt* to fill the fuel tanks of <an aircraft> when it has made a flight. ◇ *vi* [aircraft] *We stopped to refuel in Douala.*

refuge [ˈrefjuːdʒ] *n* a place where one is protected from danger or from something unpleasant □ *a refuge for battered women/from the storm.* ■ **to seek** OR **take refuge** to go somewhere where one is safe from danger □ *We took refuge from the storm in a cave.* ■ **to seek** OR **take refuge in sthg** [in prayer, sleep] to try to avoid an unpleasant situation or feeling by doing sthg □ *After a long and bitter argument, Harvey took refuge in silence.*

refugee [ˌrefjuˈdʒiː] *n* a person who has been forced to leave their country because of war, or because of their beliefs □ *political/economic refugees* □ *refugee status.*

refugee camp *n* a temporary camp set up to give food and shelter to refugees.

refund [*n* ˈriːfʌnd, *vb* rɪˈfʌnd] ◇ *n* an amount of money that is given back to somebody when they have been charged too much for something or when they return something to a shop □ *'No refund can be given without a receipt.'* □ *a tax refund.* ◇ *vt* **to refund sthg to sb, to refund sb sthg** to give sb a refund for sthg.

refurbish [ˌriːˈfɜːʳbɪʃ] *vt* [building, shop, office] to clean, redecorate, and modernize <sthg>.

refurbishment [ˌriːˈfɜːʳbɪʃmənt] *n: see* **refurbish** □ *'Closed for refurbishment.'*

refurnish [ˌriːˈfɜːʳnɪʃ] *vt* [room, house, office] to provide <sthg> with new furniture.

refusal [rɪˈfjuːzl] *n* -1. the act of refusing □ *Jo's request for aid was met with a firm refusal.* □ *her refusal to accept the conditions.* -2. a letter or message that one sends to somebody to say no to an invitation, application etc.

refuse¹ [rɪˈfjuːz] ◇ *vt* -1. **to refuse sb sthg, to refuse sthg to sb** not to give or allow sb sthg □ *The council refused us planning permission.* -2. [offer, drink] to state that one will not accept <sthg> □ *She had refused several proposals of marriage.* -3. **to refuse to do sthg** to state firmly that one will not do sthg □ *She refused to give in.* □ *Professor Hill refused to let me take the exam.* □ *I refuse to allow you to blackmail me into going.* ◇ *vi: He asked her to work over the weekend but she refused.*

refuse² [ˈrefjuːs] *n* waste material from homes, shops, factories etc that is thrown away □ *household refuse.*

refuse collection [ˈrefjuːs-] *n* the collection of household garbage, usually organized by the local government □ *local refuse collection services.*

refuse collector [ˈrefjuːs-] *n* a person whose job is to collect household garbage.

refuse dump [ˈrefjuːs-] *n* a place where a town's garbage is dumped.

refute [rɪˈfjuːt] *vt* [accusation, theory, claim] to say that <sthg> is not true; to prove that <sthg> is not true.

reg *abbr of* **registered** □ *a reg trademark.*

regain [rɪˈɡeɪn] *vt* [one's health, strength, position] to get back <sthg that one has lost>.

regal [ˈriːɡl] *adj* [manner, house] that is like or suitable for a king or queen.

regale [rɪˈɡeɪl] *vt* **to regale sb with sthg** [with stories, jokes] to entertain sb with sthg.

regalia [rɪˈɡeɪlɪə] *n* special clothes that are worn on official occasions e.g. by a king or judge (formal use).

regard [rɪˈɡɑːʳd] ◇ *n* -1. respect for somebody or something (formal use) □ *We have the greatest regard for him.* ■ **to hold sb in high/low regard** to have a lot of/no respect for sb. -2. **in this/that regard** a phrase used to introduce information that is closely connected to something that has just been mentioned □ *In this regard you may well be right.*

◇ *vt* **to regard sb/sthg as...** to consider sb/

sthg in a particular way □ *I've always regarded him as a friend.* □ *Mrs Killeen is regarded as one of the country's leading experts in the field.* ■ **to regard sb/sthg with...** to have a particular feeling about sb/sthg □ *We regard them with admiration/mistrust.* ■ **to be highly regarded** to be respected by other people □ *She has always been very highly regarded as a painter.*

◆ **regards** *npl* a word used, often at the end of letters, to send one's best wishes to somebody □ *with kind regards* □ *Give my regards to your mother.*

◆ **as regards** *prep* = **regarding.**

◆ **in regard to, with regard to** *prep* = **regarding.**

regarding [rɪ'gɑːᵈdɪŋ] *prep* a word used to introduce something that one is talking or writing about □ *Regarding your letter of October 17th...* □ *Regarding her own state of mind, little had changed.*

regardless [rɪ'gɑːᵈdləs] *adv* [continue, go] in spite of problems, changes etc □ *Although it was raining, they decided to carry on regardless.*

◆ **regardless of** *prep* [expense, time, difficulties] in spite of <sthg> □ *Look, regardless of the way you feel, you should go.*

regatta [rɪ'gætə] *n* an event at which boat races take place.

regd *abbr of* **registered.**

Regency ['riːdʒənsɪ] *adj* [style, building] that existed or was fashionable in Britain in the reign of the Prince Regent (1811–1820).

regenerate [rɪ'dʒenəreɪt] *vt* [economy, inner city, project] to develop and improve <sthg> so that it becomes successful, active etc again □ *plans to regenerate run-down urban areas.*

regeneration [rɪˌdʒenə'reɪʃn] *n*: *see* **regenerate** □ *urban regeneration.*

regent ['riːdʒənt] ◇ *n* a person who rules a country when the king or queen is unable to rule, e.g. because they are too young or ill. ◇ *adj*: *a queen/prince regent.*

reggae ['regeɪ] *n* a form of popular music with a strong beat that began in Jamaica.

regime [reɪ'ʒiːm] *n* a particular system of government, especially one that does not give its people much freedom; the people who rule a country according to this system □ *a military regime* □ *the excesses of the previous regime.*

regiment ['redʒɪmənt] *n* a large group of soldiers under the command of a colonel.

regimental [ˌredʒə'mentl] *adj* [commander, headquarters] *see* **regiment.**

regimented ['redʒəmentəd] *adj* [group, life] that is strictly controlled in a military style (disapproving use).

region ['riːdʒən] *n* a particular area of a country or body □ *the mountainous regions of the north.*

◆ **in the region of** *prep* a phrase used to indicate that an amount or number is approximate □ *The cost will be in the region of $100,000.*

regional ['riːdʒnəl] *adj* [transport, accent, government] of a particular region.

register ['redʒəstəʳ] ◇ *n* an official list of the names of voters, children in a class etc □ *Is her name on the register?* □ *I'll check in the register.*

◇ *vt* -1. [birth, marriage, death] to record <sthg> officially. -2. [improvement, growth, drop] to show <sthg> on a scale of measurement □ *The earthquake registered 6.5 on the Richter scale.* -3. [surprise, disapproval] to show <an emotion> □ *Her face registered disbelief.*

◇ *vi* -1. to put one's name on a register □ *You'll have to register to vote/register for work/register as unemployed.* -2. [at a hotel, conference] to report one's arrival at a place, usually by signing a register. -3. [comment, warning] to be noticed and understood (informal use) □ *I warned him but it didn't seem to register.*

registered ['redʒəstəᵈd] *adj* -1. [letter, package] that is sent by registered mail. -2. GB [office, charity] that is officially listed as being legal □ *Is he registered blind?*

registered mail US *n* a postal service that pays compensation to the sender if something is lost in the mail.

registered nurse *n* a nurse who is qualified in all areas of nursing.

registered post *n* GB = **registered mail.**

registered trademark *n* a name or symbol that usually appears on a product and cannot legally be used by other companies.

registrar [US 'redʒəstrɑːr, GB ˌredʒɪ'strɑː] *n* -1. EDUCATION a senior official who deals with the administration in a college or university. -2. ADMIN a person whose job is to keep a register, e.g. of births, marriages, and deaths. -3. GB MEDICINE a senior hospital doctor who is lower in rank than a consultant.

registration [ˌredʒə'streɪʃn] *n* -1. [on a course, of a birth, marriage] *see* **register** □ *Full course fees are payable at the time of registration.* -2. US & AUS [for a car] an official document containing information about a motor vehicle and its owner. -3. GB = **registration number.**

registration document *n* GB an official document containing information about a motor vehicle and its owner.

registration number *n* GB the set of numbers and letters that are shown at the front and back of a motor vehicle.

registration plate *n* AUS = **registration number.**

registry ['redʒəstrɪ] (*pl* **registries**) *n* a place where registers are kept, especially in a church.

registry office *n* in Britain, a government office where people can get married and where births, marriages, and deaths are recorded.

rego ['regoʊ] *n* AUS [for a car] = **registration** (informal use).

regress [rɪ'gres] *vi* [person, country, industry] to return to a worse condition (formal use) □ *British society has regressed to Victorian levels of inequality.*

regression [rɪ'greʃn] *n*: *see* **regress** (formal use).

regressive [rɪ'gresɪv] *adj* [tendencies, behavior] going back to a worse condition (formal use).

regret [rɪ'gret] (*pt* & *pp* **regretted**, *cont* **regretting**) ◇ *vt* to feel sorry about <sthg> and wish that it had not happened □ *I regret not telling him sooner.* □ *She regrets now that she was unable to meet him.* □ *Charles began to regret what he'd said.* □ *The airline regrets any inconvenience caused to passengers.* ■ **I regret to inform you/say...** a phrase used when saying that one is sorry about something □ *We regret to announce the cancellation of the 2:15 flight to Omaha.*
◇ *n* a feeling of regretting something □ *It is with regret that we must decline your invitation.* □ *I have no regrets about leaving London.* ■ **to send one's regrets** to apologize for being unable to accept an invitation (polite use) □ *Colin sends his regrets, but is unable to come.*

regretful [rɪ'gretfl] *adj* [person] who is feeling regret □ *a regretful smile/look.*

regretfully [rɪ'gretflɪ] *adv* **-1.** [announce, refuse, leave] in a way which shows that one regrets something. **-2.** = **regrettably**.

regrettable [rɪ'gretəbl] *adj* [decision, behavior, incident] that one is sorry about and thinks should not have happened □ *The delay in sending you your order was most regrettable* □ *a regrettable situation.*

regrettably [rɪ'gretəblɪ] *adv* a word used to say that one is sorry about a particular situation □ *Regrettably, mistakes were made.*

regroup [,riː'gruːp] *vi* [soldiers, tourists] to form a group again.

regt *abbr of* **regiment**.

regular ['regjələr] ◇ *adj* **-1.** [heartbeat, footsteps, rhythm] that occurs with equal amounts of time or space between one part and the next □ *Security cameras are placed at regular intervals around the perimeter.* **-2.** [meals, deliveries, visits] that are repeated at fixed times, usually at the same time every day, week etc □ *We meet on a regular basis.* **-3.** [event, exercise] that happens or is done often □ *There's a regular shuttle service to Newark.* ■ **a regular customer/visitor** a customer/visitor who often goes to a particular store, place etc □ *Mr Jaffee is a regular visitor to this country.* **-4.** [time, place, problem] that one considers usual or normal □ *Shall we meet in our regular place?* **-5.** [features, teeth] that are equal in shape, size, and position in a way that is considered to be attractive □ *a regular shape.* **-6.** GRAMMAR [verb, noun, adjective] that follows the same fixed pattern in all its forms as other similar words in the same language. **-7.** US [portion, serving] that is medium-sized □ *a burger and regular fries.* **-8.** US [person] who is honest and pleasant □ *I'm just a regular guy.* **-9. sb's regular toothpaste/laundry detergent etc** US the toothpaste/laundry detergent etc that sb usually uses □ *I'll stick to my regular brand.* ■ **sb's regular doctor/dentist etc** the doctor/dentist etc that sb usually goes to.
◇ *n* a person who goes to a particular store, bar etc often □ *He's a regular in here.*

regular army *n* an army consisting of soldiers who are employed on a full-time basis.

regularity [,regjə'lærətɪ] *n* [of footsteps, a service] *see* **regular** □ *The same boring questions were asked with monotonous regularity.*

regularly ['regjələrlɪ] *adv* [eat, visit, exercise] *see* **regular.**

regulate ['regjəleɪt] *vt* **-1.** [spending, traffic] to control <sthg> usually by using a system of rules or laws. **-2.** [machine, volume, heat] to control <sthg> by making slight changes, usually to make it more suitable for a particular situation.

regulation [,regjə'leɪʃn] ◇ *adj* **a regulation uniform/color etc** a uniform/color etc that has to be worn or used because of a rule □ *All staff must be dressed in regulation blue.* ◇ *n* **-1.** an official rule □ *safety/tax regulations* □ *I can't let you inside; it's against regulations.* **-2.** *see* **regulate.**

regurgitate [rɪ'gɜːrdʒəteɪt] *vt* **-1.** to bring <food> back up from the stomach through the mouth, before it is digested. **-2.** [fact, idea] to repeat <sthg> without really thinking about it (disapproving use).

rehab ['riːhæb] *n* = **rehabilitation.**

rehabilitate [,riːə'bɪləteɪt] *vt* [prisoner, invalid, addict] to train <sb> to return to a normal life.

rehabilitation [,riːəbɪlə'teɪʃn] *n*: *see* **rehabilitate** □ *a drug rehabilitation center.*

rehash [*vb* ,riː'hæʃ, *n* 'riːhæʃ] (disapproving use) ◇ *vt* [idea, theory] to use or talk about <sthg> again in a slightly different form in an attempt to make it seem original. ◇ *n* [of an idea, theory] *It's just a rehash of last year's speech.*

rehearsal [rɪ'hɜːrsl] *n* a practice of a play, dance etc before it is performed □ *The rehearsals will start on Monday.* □ *This scene needs a lot more rehearsal.*

rehearse [rɪ'hɜːrs] ◇ *vt* [play, dance, piece of music] to practice <sthg> before performing it in front of an audience. ◇ *vi*: *They have been rehearsing all week for the concert.*

reheat [,riː'hiːt] *vt* to heat <food that has already been cooked>.

rehouse [,riː'haʊz] *vt* to put <sb> into a different house or apartment □ *So far, thirty families have been rehoused.*

reign [reɪn] ◇ *vi* **-1.** [king, queen, emperor] to be the king or queen of a country □ *Haile Selassie reigned over Ethiopia/the Ethiopians.* **-2.** [terror, confusion] to be very strongly felt in a place or situation □ *Silence reigned.* ◇ *n* **-1.** the period during which a king or queen reigns □ *during Queen Victoria's reign* OR *the reign of Queen Victoria.* **-2.** a period when somebody or something is very powerful □ *a reign of terror.*

reigning ['reɪnɪŋ] *adj* **the reigning champion** the person who has won a particular competition most recently.

reimburse [,riːəm'bɜːrs] *vt* [person] to pay back money to <sb> who has had to spend the money, e.g. for work, or has lost the money; [expenses, cost] to pay back <money> to somebody □ *We will reimburse you for the travel expenses.* □ *Do you think I can get this reimbursed?*

reimbursement [ˌriːəmˈbɜːˈsmənt] *n*: *see* **reimburse**.

rein [reɪn] *n* **to give (a) free rein to sb, to give sb (a) free rein** to give sb a lot of freedom to do something. ■ **to keep a tight rein on sb/sthg** [on staff, spending, one's emotions] to control sb/sthg very carefully.

◆ **reins** *npl* -1. [for a horse] leather straps which are attached around a horse's head and held by the rider to control the horse. -2. [for a child] straps attached to a harness around the body of a young child in order to stop them running away.

◆ **rein in** *vt sep* **to rein a horse in** to slow down or stop a horse by pulling the reins.

reincarnation [ˌriːɪnkɑːˈneɪʃn] *n* -1. the belief that, after death, a person's spirit returns to life in a new body □ *Do you believe in reincarnation?* -2. a person or animal that is believed to be born again in a new body □ *The boy is believed to be a reincarnation of the last Panchen Lama.*

reindeer [ˈreɪndɪəˈ] (*pl* **reindeer**) *n* a large deer with wide antlers that lives in northern parts of Europe, Asia, and America.

reinforce [ˌriːɪnˈfɔːˈs] *vt* -1. [ceiling, frame] to make <sthg> stronger □ *The bridge has been reinforced with concrete and steel posts.* -2. [fear, prejudice] to make <a belief or emotion> stronger □ *The program only reinforced my view that vivisection is wrong.* -3. [argument, claim] to make <sthg> seem true by providing evidence □ *This report reinforces what we have been saying for a long time.*

reinforced concrete [ˌriːɪnˌfɔːˈst-] *n* concrete that has metal bars inside it to make it stronger.

reinforcement [ˌriːɪnˈfɔːˈsmənt] *n* -1. [for an object] something that makes a structure or object stronger □ *a metal reinforcement.* -2. [of a prejudice, claim] *see* **reinforce**.

◆ **reinforcements** *npl* extra soldiers, police etc who are sent to a place to help a group of soldiers who are fighting there □ *The captain called for reinforcements.*

reinstate [ˌriːɪnˈsteɪt] *vt* -1. [employee] to give <sb> back a job that had been taken away from them □ *They've reinstated Steve in his old job/as department head.* -2. [payment, idea, policy] to cause <sthg> to exist or be important again.

reinstatement [ˌriːɪnˈsteɪtmənt] *n*: *see* **reinstate**.

reinterpret [ˌriːɪnˈtɜːˈprət] *vt* [figures, report, speech] to interpret <sthg> again in a different way.

reintroduce [ˌriːɪntrəˈdjuːs] *vt* [policy, tax, method] to cause <sthg> to exist again.

reintroduction [ˌriːɪntrəˈdʌkʃn] *n*: *see* **reintroduce** □ *a referendum on the reintroduction of the death penalty.*

reissue [riːˈɪʃuː] ◇ *vt* [book, record] to produce <sthg> again after it has not been available

for some time. ◇ *n* a book or recording that is reissued.

reiterate [riːˈɪtəreɪt] *vt* [opinion, argument] to state <sthg> again in order to make it clear (formal use) □ *I can only reiterate what I said before.*

reiteration [riːˌɪtəˈreɪʃn] *n*: *see* **reiterate**.

reject [*vb* rɪˈdʒekt, *n* ˈriːdʒekt] ◇ *vt* -1. [idea, proposal, terms] to refuse to agree to <sthg>; [opinion, explanation] to state very firmly that one thinks <sthg> is wrong □ *The government rejected their offer of a cease-fire.* □ *Their findings have been rejected by other institutions.* -2. [values, religion] to refuse to believe in or live according to <sthg> □ *Many East Europeans are already beginning to reject capitalism.* -3. [candidate, applicant] to decide not to offer a job or place to <sb> □ *His application has been rejected.* **-4. to reject a coin/token etc** to return a coin/token etc to the person who put it in, because the machine cannot use it □ *The phone kept rejecting my card.* ◇ *n* a product that is rejected or sold cheaply because it is not perfect □ *reject china.*

rejection [rɪˈdʒekʃn] *n* [of values, an idea, candidate] *see* **reject** □ *I keep applying for jobs but all I get is rejections.*

rejig [ˌriːˈdʒɪg] (*pt & pp* **rejigged**, *cont* **rejigging**) *vt* GB [text, budget, factory] to change the organization of <sthg>, usually to make it more effective (informal use).

rejoice [rɪˈdʒɔɪs] *vi* to feel or express great happiness about something □ *We rejoiced at* OR *in the news.*

rejoicing [rɪˈdʒɔɪsɪŋ] *n* a situation in which people show they are very happy □ *There was rejoicing all over the country at* OR *over his release.*

rejoin [*senses 1 & 2* ˌriːˈdʒɔɪn, *sense 3* rɪˈdʒɔɪn] *vt* -1. [group, regiment, highway] to go back to <sthg that one has left for a short time>. -2. [club, society] to become a member of <sthg> again. -3. to say <sthg witty, rude, or sarcastic> in reply to something.

rejoinder [rɪˈdʒɔɪndəˈ] *n* a reply, especially a witty, rude, or sarcastic one.

rejuvenate [rɪˈdʒuːvəneɪt] *vt* -1. [person] to make <sb> feel or look younger. -2. [system, organization] to make <sthg> more lively and active by introducing new ideas.

rejuvenation [rɪˌdʒuːvəˈneɪʃn] *n* [of a system, organization] *see* **rejuvenate**.

rekindle [ˌriːˈkɪndl] *vt* [interest, passion, hatred] to make somebody feel <sthg> again.

relapse [rɪˈlæps] ◇ *n* **to have a relapse** [sick person] to suddenly or unexpectedly become ill again after one's health has been improving. ◇ *vi* **to relapse into sthg** to return to sthg bad after making some improvements □ *She relapsed into a coma.* □ *He relapsed into his old way of thinking.*

relate [rɪˈleɪt] ◇ *vt* -1. to make a connection between <two things or people> □ *He related the rise in crime to the government's economic policy.* -2. to tell <a story> (formal use) □ *She related the whole episode in great detail.*

◆ **relate to** *vt fus* **-1. to relate to sthg** to be connected with sthg □ *This relates to what I was saying earlier.* **-2. to relate to sb/sthg** to concern sb/sthg □ *These regulations do not relate to the physically handicapped.* **-3. to relate to sb** to understand and be able to communicate with sb because one shares their situation, problems etc □ *He can't relate to children.* ■ **to relate to sthg** [to an idea, feeling] to understand and appreciate sthg □ *I can relate to that; I went through something similar once.*

◆ **relating to** *prep* connected with <sthg> □ *documents relating to the cost of the new road.*

related [rɪ'leɪtəd] *adj* **-1. to be related** [people] to be members of the same family □ *She is related to the president.* **-2.** [issues, problems] that are connected □ *The course looks at raising capital, debt finance, and other related areas.*

relation [rɪ'leɪʃn] *n* **-1.** a connection or similarity between two or more things □ *There is no relation between the two matters.* ■ **to bear no relation to sthg** to be very different from sthg □ *His story bears no relation to the actual events.* ■ **in relation to sthg** compared with sthg □ *How big is the chair in relation to the table?* □ *Where is the office in relation to the hotel?* **-2.** a member of one's family □ *She has very few relations.*

◆ **relations** *npl* contact and communication between people, groups, or countries □ *family/race/industrial relations* □ *Relations between the two men have worsened.* □ *Britain is keen to improve relations with the Arab state.*

relational [rɪ'leɪʃnəl] *adj* **a relational database** COMPUTING a database in which all the items are related.

relationship [rɪ'leɪʃnʃɪp] *n* **-1.** [between people, countries] the contact and communication between people, groups, countries etc and the way they feel about each other □ *France and Scotland have always had a good relationship.* □ *a close working relationship.* **-2.** [between lovers] a sexual or romantic friendship between two people □ *She's having a relationship with an older man.* **-3.** [between things] a connection between two or more objects, events etc □ *I see absolutely no relationship between the two incidents.*

relative ['relətɪv] ◇ *adj* **-1.** [ease, poverty, success] that is true to a certain degree when compared with something else □ *Now we can live in relative comfort.* **-2.** [size, amount] that is being compared with something else □ *We discussed the relative merits of the two systems.* **-3. to be relative** to be something that needs to be judged in comparison with other things in order to have any meaning or be understood □ *Truth is relative after all.* ◇ *n* a member of one's family □ *We're staying with relatives.*

◆ **relative to** *prep* (formal use) **-1.** compared to <sthg> □ *Salaries are high relative to the average.* **-2.** connected with <sthg> □ *Evidence relative to the case was heard.*

relatively ['relətɪvlɪ] *adv* **relatively easy/suc-**

cessful etc easy/successful etc compared to other things of the same kind.

relativity [,relə'tɪvətɪ] *n* the scientific theory of the relationship between time, size, and mass, and the idea that this relationship changes with increased speed.

relax [rɪ'læks] ◇ *vt* **-1.** [person] to make <sb> feel calmer and less tense □ *I think I need a drink to relax me.* **-2.** [muscle, body] to make <sthg> become less stiff or firm □ *Relax your arms and legs.* **-3.** [grip, hold] to make <sthg> less tight □ *She relaxed her grip on the bag.* **-4.** [rule, discipline] to make <sthg> less strict □ *We cannot afford to relax our guard.* ◇ *vi* **-1.** [person] *Just sit back and relax while I make dinner.* □ *Relax! Nothing can go wrong.* **-2.** [muscle, body] *His face relaxed into a smile.*

relaxation [,riːlæk'seɪʃn] *n* **-1.** an activity that is restful and entertaining □ *Rest and relaxation is what you need.* **-2.** [of discipline, a rule] *see* **relax.**

relaxed [rɪ'lækst] *adj* [person] who is calm and not worried □ *a relaxed evening/mood.*

relaxing [rɪ'læksɪŋ] *adj* [walk, bath, weekend] that makes one feel relaxed.

relay ['riːleɪ] (*pt* & *pp* **relayed**) ◇ *n* **-1. a relay (race)** a race between teams of runners or swimmers in which each member of a team competes in one part of the race and is then replaced by another member. ■ **to do sthg in relays** to do sthg in teams, one team beginning when another one stops. **-2.** RADIO & TV a piece of equipment for receiving radio or TV signals and sending them out to another region.

◇ *vt* **-1.** RADIO & TV to send <radio or TV signals> through a relay □ *The game will be relayed live this evening.* **-2.** [message, news] to tell somebody <sthg that one has just been told> □ *The message was relayed to all departments.*

re-lay [,riː'leɪ] (*pt* & *pp* **re-laid**) *vt* [cable, carpet] to lay <sthg> again.

release [rɪ'liːs] ◇ *vt* **-1.** [prisoner, hostage] to set <a person or animal> free □ *They were finally released from prison/captivity.* □ *They released him from his contract/promise.* **-2.** [funds, supplies] to make <sthg> available for somebody to use. **-3.** [arm, rope] to stop holding <sthg> in one's hand or arms □ *She released her grip on my arm.* **-4.** [brake, lever] to press <a device> to allow something to move freely □ *He released the safety catch and fired into the air.* **-5.** [gas, chemical] to let out <a substance> into the air or surroundings □ *Toxic chemicals are being released into the river.* □ *It releases enormous amounts of atomic energy.* **-6.** BUSINESS to make <a movie, video, CD> etc available to the public □ *Has their new album been released yet?* **-7.** [statement, figures] to give <official information> to the press so that it can be made public □ *The victims' names have not yet been released.*

◇ *n* **-1.** [from prison] the act or process of releasing a person or animal from a prison, cage etc □ *after his release from captivity.* **-2.** [from pain] a feeling of no longer suffering from pain, anxiety etc □ *His death was a merciful release.* **-3.** [of information] a statement made by an organization or government and given to the press. **-4.** [of a gas, chemical] the act or process of releasing gas, heat etc □ *the release of gas into the cylinders.* **-5.** [of a movie] the act of releasing a movie, video etc. ■ **to be on (general) release** [movie] to be showing in cinemas. ■ **a new release** a movie, video, CD etc that has just been released.

relegate ['reləgeɪt] *vt* **-1.** [person, object, issue] to move <sb/sthg> to a less important position □ *The senator was relegated to a minor committee post.* □ *They relegated the TV to the attic.* **-2.** SPORT **to be relegated** [team] to be moved to a lower division in a league.

relegation [,relə'geɪʃn] *n*: see **relegate** □ *The team is facing relegation to the minor league.*

relent [rɪ'lent] *vi* **-1.** [person] to change one's mind and let somebody do something that one has been refusing to let them do □ *There is no sign of them relenting in their opposition to the plan.* **-2.** [wind, storm] to become less severe.

relentless [rɪ'lentləs] *adj* [criticism, rain] that never stops or becomes less severe; [opponent, critic] who never stops trying to do something □ *I'm so fed up with this relentless arguing.* □ *Redman was always relentless in his pursuit of the truth.*

relentlessly [rɪ'lentləslɪ] *adv* [criticize, continue] see **relentless** □ *It rained relentlessly.*

relevance ['reləvəns] *n*: see **relevant** □ *His remarks are of great relevance to me/to the discussion.* □ *Academic qualifications have little relevance for* OR *to teenagers today.*

relevant ['reləvənt] *adj* **-1.** [fact, figure, remark] that is connected with something that is being discussed, considered etc □ *His report is interesting but not very relevant to our problem.* **-2.** [law, idea] that is meaningful or important to somebody or something □ *Her novels no longer seem relevant to modern life.* **-3.** [information] that is correct or suitable for a particular situation □ *Please supply the relevant documents.*

reliability [rɪ,laɪə'bɪlətɪ] *n*: see **reliable** □ *Their cars are famous for their reliability.*

reliable [rɪ'laɪəbl] *adj* **-1.** [person, vehicle, service] that one can rely on □ *I've always found her very reliable.* **-2.** [information, figures, statistics] that can be believed □ *He's hardly a reliable witness, is he?*

reliably [rɪ'laɪəblɪ] *adv* [perform, work] in a way that one can rely on □ *We are reliably informed that...*

reliance [rɪ'laɪəns] *n* the fact of relying on somebody or something □ *his reliance on their advice.*

reliant [rɪ'laɪənt] *adj* **to be reliant on sb/sthg** to rely on sb/sthg for something □ *The theater is reliant on sponsorship for its survival.* □ *He became heavily reliant on drugs.* □ *I'm reliant on public transportation to get to work.*

relic ['relɪk] *n* **-1.** an idea, object, or custom that has survived from the past □ *The tradi-*

tion is a relic from the past. **-2.** RELIGION a part of the body or a possession of a saint that is believed to be holy.

relief [rɪ'liːf] *n* **-1.** a feeling of happiness when something unpleasant ends or doesn't happen □ *What a relief!* □ *It was such a relief once they'd all gone.* □ *He gave a sigh of relief.* **-2.** [to refugees, the poor] aid, usually food, shelter, and clothing, that is given to very poor people or refugees □ *famine/disaster relief* □ *relief work* □ *a relief worker.* **-3.** US money paid by the state to retired and unemployed people.

relief map *n* a map that shows the height of the land, especially by using colors.

relief road *n* GB a road built to take traffic away from another busy road.

relieve [rɪ'liːv] *vt* **-1.** [pain, itching, anxiety] to make <sthg> less severe without actually removing the cause □ *His outburst helped to relieve the boredom.* ■ **to relieve sb of sthg** [of a weight, problem] to take sthg away from sb, in order to help them; [of a duty, position] to take sthg away from sb because they have done something wrong □ *Can I relieve you of your coat?* □ *Mrs Pike was relieved of her duties after she was found to have stolen from her employers.* **-2.** [soldier, shiftworker] to start doing the job of <sb> when they have finished their shift or need to rest.

relieved [rɪ'liːvd] *adj* [person] who feels happy because something unpleasant has ended or has not happened □ *We were very relieved at the news/to hear the news.*

religion [rɪ'lɪdʒn] *n* **-1.** a belief in a god or gods □ *We were discussing art and religion.* **-2.** a particular system of rules and behavior based on a belief in a god or gods □ *Islam, Hinduism, and other world religions.*

religious [rɪ'lɪdʒəs] *adj* **-1.** [belief, book, service] that is connected with religion □ *an important religious festival.* **-2.** [person] who believes in a god or gods and follows the rules of a religion □ *I'm not at all religious.*

reline [,riː'laɪn] *vt* [coat, cupboard, brakes] to put a new lining in <sthg>.

relinquish [rɪ'lɪŋkwɪʃ] *vt* [power, responsibility, right] to give <sthg of one's own> to somebody else, usually unwillingly.

relish ['relɪʃ] ◇ *n* **-1.** **to do sthg with (great) relish** [eat, drink] to do sthg with great satisfaction and enjoyment. **-2.** a sauce or pickle that can be eaten with a dish to give it more flavor □ *onion relish.* ◇ *vt* [food, opportunity, sight] to enjoy <sthg> very much. ■ **to relish the thought** OR **idea** OR **prospect of doing sthg** to look forward very much to doing sthg □ *I don't relish the thought of seeing them again.*

relive [,riː'lɪv] *vt* [youth, success] to experience <sthg from the past> again, usually in one's imagination.

relocate [,riː'ləʊkeɪt] ◇ *vt* [business, staff, factory] to move <sb/sthg> to a different place. ◇ *vi* [business, staff, factory] *The company has relocated to Boston.*

relocation [,riː'ləʊkeɪʃn] *n*: see **relocate** □ *the firm's relocation to the Midwest.*

relocation expenses *npl* money paid by a company to an employee to help pay for the costs of moving, either when the employee joins the company or when the company moves.

reluctance [rɪ'lʌktəns] *n*: *see* **reluctant** □ *She expressed some reluctance to get involved in the matter.* ■ **to do sthg with reluctance** to do sthg although one does not do it willingly.

reluctant [rɪ'lʌktənt] *adj* [person] who does not accept their position, role etc willingly □ *I was Katy's reluctant chaperone for a week.* ■ **to be reluctant to do sthg** not to want to do sthg □ *She was reluctant to admit the truth.*

reluctantly [rɪ'lʌktəntlɪ] *adv* [agree, admit] *see* **reluctant**.

rely [rɪ'laɪ] (*pt* & *pp* **relied**) ◆ **rely on** *vt fus* **-1. to rely on sb** to trust sb to do what they are expected to do □ *I need someone I can rely on.* □ *Don't rely on him giving you any support.* □ *You can rely on him to be late.* **-2. to rely on sthg** [on information, evidence] to trust sthg to be correct □ *I don't think we can rely on what he says.* **-3. to rely on sb/sthg** [on an assistant, alcohol, bus] to need sb/sthg in order to continue living successfully, comfortably etc □ *I don't like to rely on my mother for money.*

REM (*abbr of* **rapid eye movement**) *n* the movement of one's eyeballs when one is asleep, that happens when one is dreaming □ *REM sleep.*

remain [rɪ'meɪn] ◇ *vi* **-1.** to stay in a particular place, situation, or condition □ *He remained at work.* □ *Please remain seated.* □ *He remained behind after the meeting.* **-2.** [custom, fact, problem] to be left □ *Very little remains* OR *There remains very little of the original building.* □ *All that remains is for me to thank everyone for coming here tonight.* ◇ *vt* **to remain to be done** to need to be done in the future □ *Much remains to be discussed.* ■ **it remains to be seen...** it is not yet certain... □ *It remains to be seen whether or not they will accept the offer.*

◆ **remains** *npl* **-1.** [of a meal, fortune] the parts of something that are left after most of it has been used up or destroyed □ *We could eat up the remains of yesterday's buffet.* **-2.** [of a person, animal] the parts of a dead body that remain, especially a long time after death □ *The remains of several bodies have been found.* **-3.** [of an ancient civilization] the parts of buildings or objects that are found, usually buried, after a very long time □ *ancient Roman remains.*

remainder [rɪ'meɪndər] *n* **-1. the remainder** [of food, money, a group of people] the part of something that is left after everything or everybody else has gone □ *She spent the remainder on candy.* □ *They spent the remainder of the day at home.* **-2.** MATH the amount that is left when a number cannot be divided exactly by another number □ *3 into 10 goes 3 remainder 1.*

remaining [rɪ'meɪnɪŋ] *adj* **the remaining question/time etc** the question/time etc that is left. □ *She spent the remaining quarter of an hour answering questions from the audience.* □

The remaining hostages were freed yesterday. ■ **the last remaining** the only one that remains □ *The mill is one of the few remaining examples of its kind in the area.*

remake [*n* 'riːmeɪk, *vb* ˌriː'meɪk] CINEMA ◇ *n* a new version of a movie that has been made before. ◇ *vt* to make a remake of <a movie> □ *They are remaking a lot of European movies in Hollywood these days.*

remand [US rɪ'mænd, GB -'mɑːnd] ◇ *n* **to be on remand** to be in prison waiting for trial. ◇ *vt* **to be remanded in custody** [prisoner, criminal] to be sent from court to prison to wait for trial.

remand centre *n* GB a place where young people are kept while they are on remand.

remark [rɪ'mɑːk] ◇ *n* something that one says about a particular subject □ *We found her remarks very useful.* □ *That was a very rude remark.* ◇ *vt* **to remark (that)...** to say that something is true, as part of a conversation □ *He remarked that the recession was not yet over.*

◆ **remark (up)on** *vt fus* **to remark on** OR **upon sthg** to mention sthg that one finds interesting or impressive □ *They remarked on the quality of the workmanship.*

remarkable [rɪ'mɑːkəbl] *adj* [change, improvement] that is noticeable or unusual because of its quality and causes people to be surprised □ *She is remarkable for her modesty.* □ *Since then, we have made remarkable progress.*

remarkably [rɪ'mɑːkəblɪ] *adv* **-1. remarkably stupid/thin etc** very stupid/thin etc □ *They did remarkably well/badly.* **-2. remarkably,...** a word used to introduce information which one thinks is remarkable □ *Remarkably, nobody was hurt.*

remarry [US ˌriː'merɪ, GB -'mærɪ] (*pt* & *pp* **remarried**) *vi* to get married again, after a previous marriage has finished.

Rembrandt ['rembrænt] (1606–1669) a Dutch artist, famous for his self-portraits and his use of light and shade.

remedial [rɪ'miːdjəl] *adj* **-1.** [teaching, class] that involves helping children with learning difficulties. **-2.** [exercise, therapy] that helps a sick person to recover.

remedy ['remədɪ] (*pl* **remedies**, *pt* & *pp* **remedied**) ◇ *n* **-1.** [for an illness] a cure, often for minor illnesses, that uses plants or natural products □ *a new flu remedy/remedy for the flu.* **-2.** [for a problem] a way of dealing with an unsatisfactory situation. ◇ *vt* [problem] to find a remedy for <sthg>.

remember [rɪ'membər] ◇ *vt* **-1.** to keep <a person, place, or thing> in one's memory □ *I'll always remember this evening.* □ *I remember the first time we met.* □ *Do you remember playing here when we were children?* □ *I don't remember you smoking.* **-2.** [phone number, address] to bring to mind <sthg that one had forgotten> □ *I can't remember his name.* □ *I'm trying to remember what I did with my keys.* **-3.** [appointment, task] to make an effort not to forget <sthg> □ *Did you remember to sign the invoice?* □ *Have you remembered all your things?* □ *I must*

remember to send that letter. **-4. to remember sb to sb** to give sb's greetings to sb else □ *Remember me to your wife.*
◇ *vi: "What is their phone number?" — "I can't remember."*

remembrance [rɪ'membrəns] *n* **to do sthg in remembrance of sb** to do sthg to show that one remembers sb who is dead (formal use).

Remembrance Day *n* the Sunday closest to November 11, when people in Britain and countries of the Commonwealth hold church services to remember those who died in the two World Wars.

remind [rɪ'maɪnd] *vt* **-1.** to make <sb> remember something □ *Can you remind me about the bills/to pay the bills?* □ *I'd like to remind you all of the need for urgency.* □ *He reminded me that I'd agreed to go.* **-2. to remind sb of sb/sthg** to make sb think of sb/sthg else because they are similar □ *She reminds me of my sister.* □ *That reminds me, where are those books?*

reminder [rɪ'maɪndə'] *n* **-1. a reminder of sthg/ to do sthg** something that reminds somebody of sthg/to do sthg □ *I left a reminder for myself on the table.* **-2.** a letter sent to remind somebody to pay for something that should already have been paid for □ *The phone company have sent me a reminder.*

reminisce [,remɪ'nɪs] *vi* to talk or think about something, usually something pleasant, that happened in one's past.

reminiscences [,remɪ'nɪsənsɪz] *npl* things that somebody says or writes about their own past.

reminiscent [,remɪ'nɪsnt] *adj* **to be reminiscent of sb/sthg** to make one think of sb/sthg that is similar □ *The flavor is faintly reminiscent of strawberries.*

remiss [rɪ'mɪs] *adj* **to be remiss** not to have done something that one should have done □ *It was remiss of him not to reply.*

remission [rɪ'mɪʃn] *n* **-1.** LAW a reduction in somebody's prison sentence, e.g. because they have behaved well. **-2. to be in remission** [illness] MEDICINE to have become less severe □ *He's now been in remission for several months.*

remit [*n* 'riːmɪt, *vb* rɪ'mɪt] (*pt* & *pp* **remitted**, *cont* **remitting**) ◇ *n* GB the area of activity that somebody is allowed or expected to deal with □ *It is outside the remit of the UN peacekeepers to intervene in such cases.* ◇ *vt* to send <money> by mail as payment for something.

remittance [rɪ'mɪtns] *n* a payment for something, sent by post □ *Please enclose a remittance of $10.*

remnant ['remnənt] *n* **-1.** a small piece of cloth that is left when the rest has been used or sold □ *I'll use the remnants to make a patchwork cushion.* **-2.** a small part of something that remains when the rest has gone or been destroyed □ *He fled with the remnants of his army.*

remodel [,riː'mɒdl] (US *pt* & *pp* **remodeled**, *cont* **remodeling**, GB *pt* & *pp* **remodelled**, *cont* **remodelling**) *vt* **-1.** [design, car, nose] to change

the shape of <sthg>. **-2.** US [house, store] to repair and improve <a building> □ *'Closed for remodeling.'*

remold US, **remould** GB ['riːmoʊld] *n* an old tire that has been given a new outer layer so that it can be used again.

remonstrate [US rɪ'mɑːnstreɪt, GB 'remənstreɪt] *vi* to complain firmly about something (formal use) □ *I remonstrated with the official, but he said he could do nothing.*

remorse [rɪ'mɔː's] *n* a strong feeling of sorrow and guilt for having done something wrong □ *She was filled with remorse at what she had done.*

remorseful [rɪ'mɔː'sfl] *adj* [person] who feels remorse.

remorseless [rɪ'mɔː'sləs] *adj* **-1.** [cruelty, ambition] that shows no pity or concern for other people □ *His remorseless criticism finally started to get me down.* **-2.** [advance, progress] that continues in a way that is threatening and impossible to stop □ *Nothing seems able to halt the remorseless spread of the epidemic.*

remorselessly [rɪ'mɔː'sləslɪ] *adv* [tease, punish, advance] *see* **remorseless** □ *The storm raged remorselessly through the night.*

remote [rɪ'moʊt] *adj* **-1.** [region, star] tht is far away; [village, farm] that is quiet, lonely, and far from places where people live; [future, period] that is far from the present in time □ *the remotest galaxy of the universe* □ *a remote and uninhabited island* □ *These people lived in the remote past.* **-2. to be remote from sthg** to be very different from sthg, and therefore not relevant to it □ *The life of a prince is very remote from that of ordinary people.* **-3.** [person, behavior] that does not seem friendly toward or interested in other people □ *a remote smile* □ *The management is becoming increasingly remote from the workforce.* **-4.** [chance, connection, resemblance] that is very small. ■ **I haven't the remotest idea** I don't know □ *I haven't the remotest idea what you're talking about.*

remote control *n* a system for controlling a vehicle or piece of equipment, e.g. a television or model car, from a distance by means of radio or electronic signals; a small device used to control something in this way □ *The doors are opened by remote control.* □ *a remote-control device/model aircraft.*

remote-controlled *adj* [car, machine] that is operated by remote control.

remotely [rɪ'moʊtlɪ] *adv* **not remotely** not at all □ *They're not even remotely similar to each other.* □ *I'm not remotely interested.*

remould ['riːmoʊld] *n* GB = **remold**.

removable [rɪ'muːvəbl] *adj* [shelf, handle] that can be easily removed from something.

removal [rɪ'muːvl] *n* **-1.** the act of moving furniture when people move from one house to another □ *a removal company.* **-2.** *see* **remove** □ *The liquid is used for the removal of oil and grease.*

removal van *n* GB a large truck used to transport furniture when people move to another house.

remove [rɪ'muːv] *vt* **-1.** [bag, statue, person] to take <sb/sthg> away from one place and put them somewhere else □ *Kindly remove that poster from my wall.* □ *All the furniture had been removed prior to refurbishment.* **-2.** [jacket, bandage] to take off <sthg that one is wearing> □ *Please remove your shoes before entering the mosque.* **-3.** [stain, dirt] to get rid of <sthg> by cleaning or washing □ *I spent the day removing the graffiti from the walls.* **-4.** [employee, worker] to take away a position, job etc from <sb> □ *She was removed from her position on the board.* **-5.** [problem, threat, suspicion] to get rid of <sthg> □ *Surgeons removed a tumor from his brain.* □ *I hope that this information will remove any doubts you may have had.*

removed [rɪ'muːvd] *adj* **to be far removed from sthg** to be very different from sthg □ *His ideas are too far removed from reality to be of practical benefit.*

remover [rɪ'muːvər] *n* a chemical for removing unwanted marks or substances □ *a bottle of nail-polish remover* □ *paint remover.*

remuneration [rɪ,mjuːnə'reɪʃn] *n* payment for work that has been done (formal use) □ *They received a small remuneration.*

Renaissance [US ,renə'sɑːns, GB rə'neɪsəns] *n* **the Renaissance** the period from about 1300 to 1600 in European history, when the ideas of ancient Greece influenced art, architecture, and literature □ *Renaissance art/poetry/thought.*

rename [,riː'neɪm] *vt* [organization, ship, street] to give <sthg> a new name □ *The party has been renamed "the Democratic Alliance".*

rend [rend] (*pt* & *pp* **rent**) *vt* [hair, clothes] to pull or tear <sthg> violently (literary use).

render ['rendər] *vt* (formal use) **-1.** to cause <sb/sthg> to be in a particular state □ *The blow rendered him unconscious.* □ *Computerization has rendered many skills obsolete.* **-2.** to give somebody <help, assistance> etc □ *You have rendered us a great service.* **-3. to render an account** to present somebody with an account that has to be paid.

rendering ['rendərɪŋ] *n* **-1.** [of a song, play] a performance of a piece of music or writing. **-2.** [of a novel, poem] a translation.

rendezvous ['rɒndeɪvuː] (*pl* **rendezvous** [-z]) *n* **-1.** an arrangement people make to meet at a particular time and place; the place where such a meeting takes place □ *We made a rendezvous for Tuesday at the hotel.* □ *He was summoned to a secret rendezvous on the outskirts of town.* **-2.** a café, bar etc where people of a particular kind often meet □ *The club is a favorite rendezvous for boxing fans.*

rendition [ren'dɪʃn] *n* a performance of a song, play etc.

renegade ['renɪgeɪd] *n* a person who fights or opposes the country, political party, religion etc that they once belonged to (disapproving use) □ *renegade soldiers/supporters.*

renege [US rɪ'nɪg, GB rə'neɪg] *vi* **to renege on**

sthg [on a promise, deal] not to do sthg that one has promised to do (formal use).

renegotiate [,riːnɪ'gəʊʃɪeɪt] ◇ *vt* [agreement, contract] to try to change <sthg> by discussing it again. ◇ *vi: We thought the deal was settled, but they are asking us to renegotiate.*

renew [rɪ'njuː] *vt* **-1.** [attempt, campaign, efforts] to begin <sthg> again, especially after a period of time □ *I'm looking forward to renewing my acquaintance with her.* □ *There was renewed fighting in the area last night.* **-2.** [tire, stocks] to replace <sthg that is old or finished> with something new of the same sort □ *You need to renew the batteries once a year.* **-3.** [license, contract, subscription] to make <sthg> valid or effective for a further period of time □ *I need to renew these books at the library.*

renewable [rɪ'njuːəbl] *adj* **-1.** [energy, resource] that comes from a natural source that can replace itself when it has been used □ *renewable energy sources.* **-2.** [license, contract] that can be renewed.

renewal [rɪ'njuːəl] *n: see* **renew** □ *The license is due for renewal* □ *an urban renewal program.*

renewed [rɪ'njuːd] *adj* **renewed enthusiasm/energy etc** enthusiasm/energy etc that one has again after not having had much of it for a time □ *I set to work with renewed interest.*

rennet ['renət] *n* a substance that makes milk become thick and sour, used in making cheese.

Renoir ['renwɑːr], **Pierre Auguste** (1841–1919) a French Impressionist painter, well known for his bright, colorful style of painting.

renounce [rɪ'naʊns] *vt* **-1.** [belief, religion, values] to stop believing in <sthg> so that one behaves in a different way □ *The terrorists have refused to renounce violence.* **-2.** [title, privilege, claim] to say formally that one no longer wants to have <sthg> (formal use).

renovate ['renəveɪt] *vt* [house, building, furniture] to repair and improve <sthg that is in bad condition>.

renovation [,renə'veɪʃn] *n: see* **renovate** □ *The building is in need of renovation/is closed for renovation.*

◆ **renovations** *npl* the work that is done to renovate something □ *The renovations will take several months.*

renown [rɪ'naʊn] *n* fame, usually for a particular talent or achievement □ *an architect of world renown.*

renowned [rɪ'naʊnd] *adj* [artist, doctor, city] that is famous for a particular quality □ *He is renowned as a political thinker.* □ *The island is renowned for its glassware.* □ *She's renowned for her tactlessness.*

rent [rent] ◇ *past tense & past participle of* **rend.** ◇ *n* money paid regularly for the use of something that belongs to somebody else, e.g. a house, car, or piece of land □ *What's the rent?* □ *My rent is $1,000 a month.* □ *Have you paid this month's rent?* □ *a rent collector/rebate.* ◇ *vt* [house, office, car] to have the use of <sthg> by paying rent to its owner; to al-

low somebody to use <sthg> in return for payment □ *We rent this house from an agency.* □ *We've rented the apartment to some students.*
◆ **rent out** *vt sep* **to rent sthg out** [house, office, car] to allow somebody to use sthg in return for payment □ *They rent out their boat to tourists during the summer.*

rental ['rentl] *n* -1. an amount of money paid as rent □ *We have to pay the rental for* OR *on the video.* -2. an act of renting something □ *a rental car* □ *a rental agreement/contract.*

rent book *n* a small book used to record the amounts and dates of rent that is paid by a tenant.

rented ['rentəd] *adj* [house, car] that somebody is allowed to use because they pay rent for it □ *They live in rented accommodation.*

rent-free ◇ *adj* [house, car] that somebody is allowed to use without having to pay rent for it. ◇ *adv*: *We stayed there rent-free.*

renumber [,ri:'nʌmbər] *vt* [pages, paragraphs] to give new numbers to <a series or list of things>.

renunciation [rɪ,nʌnsɪ'eɪʃn] *n*: *see* **renounce** (formal use).

reoccurrence [US ,ri:ə'kɜːrəns, GB -'kʌr-] *n* **if there's a reoccurrence** if this happens again.

reopen [,ri:'oʊpn] ◇ *vt* -1. [store, bar] to open <sthg> after it has been closed for a period of time; [border, route] to allow people to cross or use <sthg> after a period when this was not allowed □ *They reopened the theater after restoration work.* □ *The trail has now been reopened to tourists.* -2. [talks, debate] to start to discuss <sthg> again after it has previously been stopped or completed □ *The lawyers have applied for the case to be reopened.*
◇ *vi* -1. [store, border] *The factory will reopen tomorrow after the fire.* -2. [talks, debate] *The management improved their pay offer and negotiations reopened.* -3. [wound, cut] to start to bleed again after the skin has begun to heal.

reorganization [US ri:,ɔːrgənə'zeɪʃn, GB -aɪ-] *n*: *see* **reorganize** □ *The industry is going through major reorganization.*

reorganize, -ise [,ri:'ɔːrgənaɪz] *vt* [company, system] to organize <sthg> in a different way in order to improve it □ *We are reorganizing the way we handle orders.*

rep [rep] *n* -1. BUSINESS *abbr of* **representative**. -2. *abbr of* **repertory**. -3. *abbr of* **repertory company**.

Rep. US -1. *abbr of* **Representative**. -2. *abbr of* **Republican**.

repaid [ri:'peɪd] *past tense & past participle of* **repay**.

repaint [,ri:'peɪnt] *vt* [house, wall] to paint <sthg> again to make it look better.

repair [rɪ'peər] ◇ *vt* -1. [car, house, light] to mend <sthg that is damaged or not working properly>; [puncture, hole] to mend <a damaged area> of something □ *The TV needs repairing.* □ *It will cost a fortune to repair the damage.* -2. [fault, omission, situation] to do things to make <sthg wrong or harmful> right or

to make it less serious □ *How can we repair the damage this has done to our reputation?*
◇ *n* the act of repairing something; the work done to repair something □ *The church roof is in need of repair.* □ *The car needs some urgent repairs.* □ *When will you be able to carry out the repairs?* □ *a repair job* □ *a car repair workshop.* ■ **to be beyond repair** to be so badly damaged that it is no longer possible to repair it □ *This jacket is so old it's beyond repair now.* ■ **to be in good/bad repair** to be in good/bad condition □ *Parts of the house are in bad repair* OR *in a bad state of repair.*

repair kit *n* a set of tools and materials for carrying out simple repairs on a car, bicycle, machine etc.

repaper [,ri:'peɪpər] *vt* [wall, room] to cover <sthg> with new wallpaper.

reparations [,repə'reɪʃnz] *npl* money that a defeated country is made to pay after a war in order to pay for the damage it has caused □ *war reparations.*

repartee [,repɑːr'tiː] *n* replies that somebody makes in a conversation that are quick and amusing.

repatriate [US ,ri:'peɪtrɪeɪt, GB -'pæt-] *vt* [spy, illegal immigrant] to send or bring <sb> back to their own country.

repay [rɪ'peɪ] (*pt & pp* **repaid**) *vt* -1. [debt, loan] to pay back <money that one owes> to somebody; to pay back this money to <sb> □ *The loan must be repaid in three instalments.* *He eventually repaid the money to his parents* OR *repaid his parents the money.* □ *When will you repay me?* -2. [favor, kindness] to do or give somebody something in return for <sthg that they have done> □ *I hope I can repay your hospitality one day.* □ *How can I ever repay you for all your help?*

repayable [rɪ'peɪəbl] *adj* [loan, mortgage] that must be repaid at a particular time □ *The loan is repayable over 12 months.*

repayment [rɪ'peɪmənt] *n* -1. an amount of money paid, usually regularly, in order to repay a debt, loan etc □ *I was unable to keep up with the mortgage repayments.* -2. [of a debt, loan] *see* **repay** □ *The loan is due for repayment in two years.*

repeal [rɪ'piːl] ◇ *vt* [law, ban] to formally end <sthg>. ◇ *n* [of a law, ban] the act of repealing something □ *They campaigned for the repeal of the restrictions on trade.*

repeat [rɪ'piːt] ◇ *vt* -1. [statement, demand] to say or write <sthg> again; [word, oath] to say <sthg that somebody else has said>; [secret, story] to tell <sthg that one has been told> to other people □ *This is not, I repeat not, the best way to do it.* □ *I'll read the instructions and you repeat them back to me.* □ *Don't repeat what I've said to anyone.* -2. [exercise, activity] to do <sthg> again □ *He keeps repeating the same mistakes.* □ *We wish to repeat our order for spare parts.* □ *This offer cannot be repeated.* ■ **to repeat oneself** to say or do something that one has already said or done □ *History has a habit of repeating itself.* □ *I'm sorry to repeat myself, but this is of vital importance.* -3. RADIO & TV [show, series] to broadcast <a program> that has been broadcast before.

◇ *n* -1. RADIO & TV a program that has been broadcast before □ *There's nothing but repeats on this evening.* -2. [of a statement, demand, order] the act of doing or saying something again □ *This is just a repeat of what she said last week.* □ *a repeat order/performance.*

repeated [rɪ'piːtəd] *adj* [visits, delays, attempts] that happen or are made many times, usually for a single purpose □ *They have not paid us despite our repeated warnings.*

repeatedly [rɪ'piːtədlɪ] *adv* [ask, call, hit] *see* **repeated** □ *He's been warned repeatedly not to go there.*

repel [rɪ'pel] (*pt* & *pp* **repelled**, *cont* **repelling**) *vt* -1. [smell, sight, person] to cause <sb> to feel disgust or strong dislike □ *Even the thought of seeing him again repelled me.* -2. [attacker, army] to fight against <sb> and make them move back □ *The troops succeeded in repelling the attack.*

repellent [rɪ'pelənt] ◇ *adj* [smell, sight, person] that one finds disgusting or very unpleasant. ◇ *n* a chemical that keeps insects away □ *a can of insect/mosquito repellent.*

repent [rɪ'pent] (formal use) ◇ *vt* [sin, crime, mistake] to feel regret for <sthg bad that one has done>. ◇ *vi*: *There is still time to repent.* □ *He refused to repent of his sins.*

repentance [rɪ'pentəns] *n* a feeling of sadness, regret, and shame for something bad that one has done (formal use).

repentant [rɪ'pentənt] *adj* [person] who feels repentance (formal use).

repercussions [,riːpəˈkʌʃnz] *npl* the unexpected and usually unpleasant results of an action, event, decision etc □ *This mistake could have serious repercussions for everybody in the agency.*

repertoire ['repəˈtwɑːʳ] *n* all the plays, music etc that a performer, group etc has learned and is able to perform □ *They have broadened their repertoire to include a number of contemporary works.* □ *He has a huge repertoire of jokes.*

repertory [US 'repərtɔːrɪ, GB -ərɪ] *n* a system in which a theater company performs a number of different plays over a period of time, using the same actors and working in a single theater □ *She is currently working in repertory in Bristol.*

repertory company *n* a company of actors that performs plays in repertory.

repetition [,repə'tɪʃn] *n* the act of repeating something; something that has already been done or said before □ *Each day was just a repetition of the previous one.* □ *His speech was full of pauses and repetitions.*

repetitious [,repə'tɪʃəs], **repetitive** [rɪ'petɪtɪv] *adj* [job, speech] that is boring because the same things are said or done all the time.

rephrase [,riː'freɪz] *vt* [question, answer, sentence] to say or write <sthg> again using different words, usually to make it clearer □ *I'm sorry, I'll rephrase that.*

replace [rɪ'pleɪs] *vt* -1. to take the position,

work, function etc of <sb/sthg else> □ *Computers have now replaced filing systems.* □ *Alcohol has replaced tobacco as the nation's biggest killer.* -2. [car, model, equipment] to change <sthg> for something that is better; [employee, staff] to get rid of <sb> and get somebody else to do their job □ *We are replacing our old trucks with modern 40-ton vehicles.* □ *They replaced him with a younger man.* -3. [battery, engine] to put something new in the place of <sthg lost, broken, or damaged> □ *The tires on this car need to be replaced.* -4. [lid, book] to put <sthg> back where it was before □ *She finished her telephone call and replaced the receiver.*

replacement [rɪ'pleɪsmənt] *n* -1. a person or thing that replaces somebody or something else □ *Who's the replacement for Keane?* □ *In the meantime, we'll give you a free replacement car.* -2. *see* **replace** □ *the replacement of trams by buses.*

replacement part *n* a new part for a machine, car etc that replaces one that has become broken or worn out.

replay [*vb* ,riː'pleɪ, *n* 'riːpleɪ] ◇ *vt* -1. SPORT to play <a match or game> again because neither side won the first time. -2. [video, tape] to play <a recording> again. ◇ *n* SPORT a match, game etc that is replayed.

replenish [rɪ'plenɪʃ] *vt* [glass, shelves] to make <sthg> full again; [stocks, supplies] to replace the things from <sthg> that have been used, sold etc (formal use).

replete [rɪ'pliːt] *adj* **to be replete** to have eaten and drunk enough. ■ **to be replete with sthg** to be full of sthg, especially food or drink (formal use).

replica ['replɪkə] *n* a very good copy of something, e.g. of a statue or car □ *The painting is an exact replica of the original.*

replicate ['replɪkeɪt] *vt* [virus, experiment, results] to make an exact copy of <sthg>, usually under different conditions (formal use).

replication [,replɪ'keɪʃn] *n* (formal use) -1. something that has been replicated. -2. *see* **replicate**.

reply [rɪ'plaɪ] (*pt* & *pp* **replied**, *pl* **replies**) ◇ *n* something said or done as an answer to something □ *I had no replies to the ad I placed.* ■ **in reply** as an answer to something that somebody has said or done □ *In reply to your memo, I confirm that our present stocks are adequate.*

◇ *vt* to say <sthg> as an answer to a question, inquiry etc □ *"Are you Mr Smith?" — "Yes," he replied.* □ *She replied that she had been ill.*

◇ *vi* -1. [to somebody's question, letter] to answer a person, question, letter etc □ *I wrote last week but they haven't replied.* □ *They replied at once to our enquiries.* -2. [to somebody's attack, decision] to do something as a result or reaction to something that somebody else has said or done □ *Our rivals replied to our sales promotion with price cuts of their own.*

reply coupon *n* a part of a catalog, advertisement etc that can be cut off and returned in order to make an order, ask for more information etc.

reply-paid *adj* GB [envelope, postcard] that can be mailed in reply to an advertisement, offer etc without a stamp because the cost of the postage has already been paid.

report [rɪ'pɔːᵗt] ◇ *n* -1. a spoken or written description of something that has happened □ *reliable/conflicting reports* □ *They gave us a brief/full report of what they had been doing.* -2. an official written document giving facts and information about something □ *a government report on crime.* -3. JOURNALISM an account of an event, published in a newspaper or broadcast on TV or radio □ *a press report* □ *On the front page was a report on events in Hong Kong.* -4. GB EDUCATION = **report card**.
◇ *vt* -1. to tell somebody about <sthg that has happened> □ *I reported my findings to Mr Davidson.* □ *He reported that he had seen the couple together the previous year.* -2. [crime, death] to tell people in authority about <sthg that has happened>; to make a complaint to people in authority about <sb> □ *Accidents should be reported immediately.* □ *The money was reported missing on Tuesday.* □ *I reported the driver of the car to the police.* □ *I'll have to report you for being late.* -3. [incident, war, marriage] to announce or describe <an event> in a newspaper or on TV or radio □ *We report everything that happens in Congress.*
◇ *vi* -1. [member of staff] to describe or give an account of something □ *You must report on your progress to the manager.* -2. [committee, researcher] to announce the facts and information that one has found about something, usually in a written document □ *The Commission of Inquiry will report next week.* -3. [journalist, newspaper, channel] to print or broadcast the news about something □ *This is Mary Wright, reporting from Moscow for CNN.* □ *We reported on the fire in our last issue.* -4. **to report to sb** to go to sb to say that one has arrived or to tell them what one has been doing; BUSINESS to have sb as one's superior at work and take one's orders from them □ *Will Norma Redding please report to the airport information desk.* □ *He has to report to his probation officer every Saturday.* □ *You will be reporting directly to the head of sales.* ■ **to report for sthg** [for work, duty] to tell the people in authority that one has arrived and is ready to do sthg □ *This is Sergeant Jones reporting for duty.*
◆ **report back** *vi* to give news or information about something that one has been sent to find out about □ *I'd like you to report back to me on what was discussed.*

reportage [rɪ'pɔːᵗtɪdʒ] *n* the act of reporting news for the press, TV, or radio; this style of reporting.

report card *n* US EDUCATION a document written by a school for each student's parents to tell them about their child's work and behavior during the previous term or year.

reportedly [rɪ'pɔːᵗtədlɪ] *adv* a word used to show that one is reporting what people say

but cannot be sure that what is said is true □ *He is reportedly suffering from pneumonia.*

reported speech [rɪ,pɔːᵗtəd-] *n* GRAMMAR a way of saying what somebody else has said without repeating their actual words, e.g. "he said that he was ill" and "she asked if she could come."

reporter [rɪ'pɔːᵗtəʳ] *n* a person whose job is to find news and report it in newspapers, on TV, or on the radio □ *a crime reporter* □ *He's a reporter from "The Herald".*

repose [rɪ'pəʊz] *n* calm and peaceful rest (literary use).

repository [US rɪ'pɒzətɔːrɪ, GB -ərɪ] (*pl* **repositories**) *n* -1. [for books, documents] a place, e.g. a museum or warehouse, where books, documents etc are stored. -2. [of facts, knowledge] a person or book that stores large amounts of information.

repossess [,riːpə'zes] *vt* [house, car] to make somebody give <sthg> back, usually because they have failed to make the necessary payments for it.

repossession [,riːpə'zeʃn] *n*: see **repossess** □ *As mortgage rates have risen, the number of repossession has increased.*

repossession order *n* a legal document obtained from a court of law that allows the owner to repossess a house, car etc.

reprehensible [,reprɪ'hensəbl] *adj* [person, behavior] that is very bad or immoral (formal use).

represent [,reprɪ'zent] *vt* -1. [person, country, group] to act or speak for <sb/sthg> □ *Mr Singh represents our company's interests in India.* □ *The President was represented at the funeral by the First Lady.* -2. **to be represented** [country, group] to have one of its members at a meeting, event etc; [opinion, interest] to be considered and discussed by the people at a meeting, event etc □ *Various environmental groups are represented on the committee.* ■ **to be well** OR **strongly represented** to be present in large numbers or in a great amount □ *Dickinson's work is well represented in this new anthology.* -3. [figure, amount] to be a sign or symbol for <sthg> □ *"E" represents the speed of light.* □ *The graph represents the volume of sales over the last five years.* -4. [ideas, opinions] to be typical of <sthg> □ *I don't believe that your views represent the thinking of the general public.* -5. [advance, increase, improvement] to be or mean the same as <sthg> □ *My salary has risen by $500, which represents a 2% increase.* □ *Their new proposal represents a major change in their position.* -6. **to represent sb/sthg as sthg** to describe sb/sthg as being sthg, usually incorrectly □ *The new premier has tried to represent the vote as a triumph for democracy.*

representation [,reprɪzen'teɪʃn] *n* -1. the fact of being represented by somebody on a committee, in a meeting etc □ *The representation of blind people on the Disabled Council has increased significantly.* -2. something, e.g. a picture, description, play etc, that shows or describes somebody or something □ *The book* *is a moving representation of the sufferings of war.*

◆ **representations** *npl* **to make representations to sb** GB to make a formal complaint or request to sb official (formal use).

representative [ˌreprɪˈzentətɪv] ◇ *adj* **-1.** [committee, panel, government] that is made up of a small group of people who are chosen or elected to act or speak on behalf of a larger group of people. **-2.** [view, sample] that is typical of a particular group of people □ *The result of the survey is representative of the country as a whole.*
◇ *n* **-1.** [of a company, organization] a person who is chosen to act or speak on behalf of somebody or something □ *The government intends to send a representative to the negotiations.* **-2.** POLITICS a senator, member of parliament etc who is elected to represent a particular region or group □ *our elected representatives.* **-3.** BUSINESS a person whose job is to visit companies and organizations in an area, selling goods and services for the company that they are employed by (formal use).
◆ **Representative** *n* a member of the US House of Representatives.

repress [rɪˈpres] *vt* **-1.** [smile, emotion, desire] to control <a feeling> so that other people do not see or notice it □ *I somehow managed to repress the urge to laugh.* **-2.** [country, people] to control <sb/sthg> by force and cruelty □ *The tribe was brutally repressed under colonial rule.*

repressed [rɪˈprest] *adj* **-1.** [person] who is not able to show their natural feelings and desires, especially sexual ones □ *sexually repressed.* **-2.** [feeling, emotion] that is hidden so deeply inside somebody that they do not realize that they feel it □ *All that repressed anger eventually came to the surface.*

repression [rɪˈpreʃn] *n* **-1.** the use of force and cruelty to control people, a country etc □ *After years of repression the country was suddenly free.* **-2.** the act of hiding and controlling natural feelings and desires, especially sexual ones □ *This is a classic case of sexual repression.*

repressive [rɪˈpresɪv] *adj* [law, leadership, system] that is harsh, severe, and allows no personal freedom □ *a repressive regime.*

reprieve [rɪˈpriːv] ◇ *n* **-1.** [from a punishment] an official order delaying or canceling a punishment, especially a death sentence □ *He was still hoping for a last-minute reprieve.* **-2.** [from pain, an attack] a temporary delay or relief in times of trouble, pain etc □ *The city enjoyed a brief reprieve during last week's ceasefire.* ◇ *vt* to give <a prisoner> a reprieve.

reprimand [US ˈreprɪmænd, GB -mɑːnd] ◇ *n* a severe criticism or warning from somebody in authority. ◇ *vt* to give <sb> a reprimand because of something that they have said or done.

reprint [*vb* ˌriːˈprɪnt, *n* ˈriːprɪnt] ◇ *vt* to print new copies of <a book, picture> etc because the old copies have all been sold □ *The book is being reprinted.* ◇ *n* a copy of a book, picture etc that has been reprinted.

reprisal [rɪˈpraɪzl] *n* an attack or violent action that is intended to punish a group of people for harm that they have done □ *Local authorities fear reprisals following Mr Daruwalla's arrest.* □ *The renewed violence is thought to be in reprisal for the killing of a youth by police last Monday.*

reproach [rɪˈproʊtʃ] ◇ *n* criticism or blame, usually because one is sad that somebody has not behaved in the way one had expected □ *There was a look of reproach in her eyes.* □ *I'm fed up with his constant reproaches.* ■ **to be above** OR **beyond reproach** [behavior] to be so good that it cannot be criticized. ◇ *vt* to tell <sb> that they were wrong to do something □ *He reproached her for forgetting where her duties lay.*

reproachful [rɪˈproʊtʃfl] *adj* [look, comment] that is full of reproach.

reprobate [ˈreprəbeɪt] *n* a person who behaves badly, e.g. by gambling or getting drunk a lot (humorous use).

reproduce [ˌriːprəˈdʲuːs] ◇ *vt* [picture, detail, accent] to produce a copy of <sthg>; [atmosphere, success] to cause <sthg> to happen or be produced again □ *We have been unable to reproduce the sales figures we achieved last year.* □ *The movie accurately reproduces life in the 19th century.* ◇ *vi* BIOLOGY [animal, plant] to produce young animals, plants etc of the same kind as itself.

reproduction [ˌriːprəˈdʌkʃn] *n* **-1.** [of a painting, chair, antique] a modern copy of something such as a work of art □ *This painting is clearly a reproduction.* □ *reproduction furniture.* **-2.** [of a picture, atmosphere, success] see **reproduce** □ *CD systems give excellent sound reproduction.* **-3.** BIOLOGY the ways by which animals or plants reproduce □ *human/plant reproduction.*

reproductive [ˌriːprəˈdʌktɪv] *adj* BIOLOGY [organs, system] that is used by animals or plants in reproduction.

reprogram [ˌriːˈproʊɡræm] (*pt* & *pp* **reprogramed** OR **reprogrammed**, *cont* **reprograming** OR **reprogramming**) *vt* [computer, data, system] to program <sthg> again, usually to get rid of mistakes.

reproof [rɪˈpruːf] *n* (formal use) blame or disapproval of something that somebody has done; something somebody says that expresses this.

reprove [rɪˈpruːv] *vt* to speak to <sb> severely and tell them that they have behaved badly (formal use).

reproving [rɪˈpruːvɪŋ] *adj* [look, voice] that shows reproof for somebody (formal use).

reptile [ˈreptaɪl] *n* an animal, e.g. a snake, lizard, crocodile, or tortoise, that is cold-blooded and lays eggs.

Repub US *abbr of* **Republican**.

republic [rɪˈpʌblɪk] *n* a country that is governed by elected representatives and has a president rather than a king or queen. NOTE: Compare **monarchy**.

republican [rɪˈpʌblɪkən] ◇ *n* a person who supports the system of government in republics. ◇ *adj*: *republican ideas/pressure/sympathies.*

◆ **Republican** ◇ *n* **-1.** US a member or supporter of the Republican Party. **-2.** GB a person, especially from Northern Ireland, who wants Northern Ireland to leave the United Kingdom and become part of the Irish Republic. ◇ *adj* **-1.** US [president, senator, policy] that is connected with the Republican Party; [newspaper, campaigner] that supports the Republican Party. **-2.** GB [party, policy, sympathizer] that supports the idea that Northern Ireland should be united with the Irish Republic.

Republican Party *n* **the Republican Party** one of the two main political parties in the US. It is considered to be more right-wing than the Democratic Party.

Republic of Ireland → **Irish Republic.**

repudiate [rɪ'pjuːdɪeɪt] *vt* (formal use) **-1.** [terrorism, violence] to say that one will have nothing to do with <sthg>; [suggestion, offer] to refuse to accept <sthg> □ *Although politicians publicly repudiate such tactics, they nevertheless continue to happen.* **-2.** [statement, accusation] to say forcefully that <sthg> is not true □ *I repudiate all the charges made against me.* **-3.** [friend, wife] to say publicly that one is no longer connected with <sb>.

repugnant [rɪ'pʌgnənt] *adj* [idea, person] that one finds very unpleasant, offensive, and disgusting □ *The whole idea is repugnant to me.*

repulse [rɪ'pʌls] *vt* **-1.** to cause <sb> to feel repulsion □ *I felt repulsed by what he had done.* **-2.** [friendship, offer] to refuse <sb/sthg> in a cold and unfriendly way. **-3.** MILITARY [army, invaders] to fight against <sb> and make them move back □ *The troops successfully repulsed the first attack.*

repulsion [rɪ'pʌlʃn] *n* **-1.** a feeling of strong dislike and disgust □ *The thought fills me with repulsion.* **-2.** PHYSICS a force that causes things, such as similar magnetic poles, to move away from one another.

repulsive [rɪ'pʌlsɪv] *adj* [person, behavior, habit] that causes one to feel strong dislike or disgust □ *What a repulsive sight!* □ *I find smoking repulsive.*

reputable ['repjətəbl] *adj* [company, firm, supplier] that has a good reputation, especially for being honest and reliable □ *I only buy from reputable dealers.*

reputation [,repjə'teɪʃn] *n* the opinion that people in general have about somebody or something, especially about how good or trustworthy they are □ *The school has a good/bad reputation.* □ *He has a reputation as an excellent teacher.* □ *She has the reputation of being a bully.* ■ **to have a reputation for sthg/for being sthg** to be well known for sthg/for being sthg, especially sthg bad □ *Susan has a reputation for saying the wrong thing.*

repute [rɪ'pjuːt] *n* (formal use) **-1. of good/ill etc repute** that has a good/bad etc reputation □ *a musician of international repute.* **-2. of repute** [company, supplier] that is respected and

known to be trustworthy □ *He's a doctor of some repute.*

reputed [rɪ'pjuːtəd] *adj* **a reputed expert/authority etc** somebody who is generally said or believed to be an expert/authority etc on something, though there is some doubt □ *The police questioned Parker, the reputed author of the article.* ■ **to be reputed to be/do sthg** to be generally said or believed to be/do sthg □ *They are reputed to have offered $5 million for the painting.* □ *Finnigan is reputed to be in hiding in Argentina.*

reputedly [rɪ'pjuːtədlɪ] *adv* a word used to show that many people believe or claim that something is true, but one is not completely certain about it □ *Sanderson is reputedly living somewhere on the island.*

request [rɪ'kwest] ◇ *n* **-1.** an act of asking for something officially or politely □ *I made a request for a loan.* □ *We are considering your request to be moved to a new department.* □ *He was unable to grant her request.* ■ **on request** [do, send] if asked to; [obtainable, available] if asked for □ *Catalogs are available on request.* ■ **at sb's request** because sb has asked for something to be done □ *I wrote the report at the request of my manager.* **-2.** a piece of music that somebody has asked to be played, e.g. on the radio □ *They played my request.* □ *a request show.*
◇ *vt* [help, meeting] to ask for <sthg> politely or officially □ *We request the pleasure of your company at the marriage of our daughter.* □ *You are requested not to smoke in the building.* □ *We are amending your file as requested.*

request stop *n* GB a bus stop at which buses stop only if somebody asks them to, usually by making a signal with their hand.

requiem ['rekwɪəm] *n* **a requiem (mass)** a church service in special memory of somebody who has died; music written for such a service.

require [rɪ'kwaɪəʳ] *vt* **-1.** [attention, skill, action] to make <sthg> necessary; [help, permission, information] to need or want <sthg> □ *The matter requires careful thought.* □ *Is there anything else you require?* □ *'Part-time staff required.'* **-2.** [license, obedience, silence] to officially demand that somebody must have or do <sthg> □ *The regulations require people to return their tax forms within a week.* □ *Employees will be required to wear a uniform.*

required [rɪ'kwaɪəʳd] *adj* [standard, level, time] necessary □ *when the liquid reaches the required temperature.*

requirement [rɪ'kwaɪəʳmənt] *n* a need that somebody has; something that is needed or necessary □ *We hope this new model meets your requirements.* □ *You do not have the minimum entry requirements for this university.*

requisite ['rekwɪzət] *adj* [fee, experience, skills] necessary (formal use).

requisition [,rekwɪ'zɪʃn] *vt* [food, house, vehicle] to take <sthg> from somebody so that the army can use it.

reran [,riː'ræn] *past tense of* **rerun.**

reread [ˌriːˈriːd] (*pt* & *pp* **reread** [ˌriːˈred]) *vt* [book, report, meter] to read <sthg> again.

reroute [ˌriːˈruːt] *vt* [traffic, freight] to send <sthg> by a different route, usually because there is a problem with the usual route.

rerun [*n* ˈriːrʌn, *vb* ˌriːˈrʌn] (*pt* **reran**, *pp* **rerun**, *cont* **rerunning**) ◇ *n* -1. TV a movie or program that is being shown or broadcast again □ *They're showing reruns of the "Lucy" show.* □ *old movie reruns.* -2. [of a situation, conflict, disaster] a situation or event that is very like one that has happened before □ *We don't want a rerun of the problems we had last year.* ◇ *vt* -1. [race, competition, election] to run or hold <sthg> again, usually because something went wrong the first time. -2. [movie, program, play] to show, broadcast, or perform <sthg> again □ *The show is being rerun on Channel Two.* □ *She reran the conversation in her mind.* -3. [tape, computer program] to make <sthg> operate again, usually after making improvements.

resale price maintenance [ˌriːseɪl-] *n* GB BUSINESS a system in which a manufacturer fixes the lowest price that its products can be sold for in shops and by wholesalers.

resat [ˌriːˈsæt] *past tense & past participle of* **resit**.

reschedule [US ˌriːˈskedʒuːl, GB -ˈʃedjuːl] *vt* -1. [meeting, elections] to arrange <sthg> so that it happens at a different time □ *The conference has been rescheduled for October 8.* -2. FINANCE [loan, debt] to arrange a later date for the repayment of <sthg>.

rescind [rɪˈsɪnd] *vt* LAW [contract, law, agreement] to cancel <sthg> by stating officially that it is no longer valid.

rescue [ˈreskjuː] ◇ *vt* to save <sb/sthg> from harm, danger, or loss, especially by putting oneself in danger □ *I managed to rescue my papers from the fire.* □ *The climbers were rescued by helicopter.* ◇ *n* the act of rescuing somebody □ *a last-minute rescue* □ *The company is in need of financial rescue.* □ *a rescue party/mission* □ *a rescue operation/attempt/bid.* ■ **to come** OR **go to sb's rescue** to rescue or help sb □ *The company was losing money until a financier came to our rescue.*

rescuer [ˈreskjuːəʳ] *n* a person who rescues or tries to rescue somebody.

reseal [ˌriːˈsiːl] *vt* [envelope, packet] to close and seal <sthg> again after it has been opened.

resealable [ˌriːˈsiːləbl] *adj* [envelope, box, packet] that can be resealed and therefore reused.

research [rɪˈsɜːʳtʃ] ◇ *n* serious and detailed study that is intended to produce new knowledge or understanding of a subject □ *medical/scientific/historical research* □ *We are doing research on* OR *into the spread of meningitis.* □ *a research laboratory/worker/grant.* ■ **research and development** work done to invent, produce, and test new products and services; the part of a company or organization that does such work □ *Research and development is vital to a company's long-term success.* □ *I work in research and development.*

◇ *vt* [facts, background] to do research into <sthg> □ *We have researched this matter in great detail.*
◇ *vi:* *Our scientists are researching into the effects of traffic pollution.*

researcher [rɪˈsɜːʳtʃəʳ] *n* a person who does research, usually as a job □ *a TV/medical researcher.*

resell [ˌriːˈsel] (*pt* & *pp* **resold**) *vt* [house, shares] to sell <sthg one has bought>, often to make a profit.

resemblance [rɪˈzembləns] *n* a way in which things or people resemble each other; the fact of looking like or being like somebody or something else □ *He bears a strong resemblance to his father.* □ *There's not much resemblance between them, even if they are sisters.*

resemble [rɪˈzembl] *vt* to look like or be like <sb/sthg> □ *She resembles her sister very closely.* □ *Conditions on the stock markets resemble those before the Crash.*

resent [rɪˈzent] *vt* [question, comment, person] to feel resentment about <sb/sthg> □ *I resent your interference in my private affairs.* □ *He resented having to consult Wilkes about everything.* □ *She had always resented her stepmother.*

resentful [rɪˈzentfl] *adj* [person, look] full of resentment □ *I felt very resentful toward him.*

resentfully [rɪˈzentflɪ] *adv* [say, look, scowl] *see* **resentful.**

resentment [rɪˈzentmənt] *n* a feeling of anger and annoyance that one has because one thinks one has been treated unfairly □ *There was widespread resentment over the tax increase.*

reservation [ˌrezəʳˈveɪʃn] *n* -1. [at a hotel, restaurant] an arrangement made in advance for a seat on a plane, a table at a restaurant etc to be kept available for one □ *a hotel/flight reservation* □ *I'd like to make a reservation for 8pm in the name of Eastwood.* □ *Do you have a reservation?* -2. **without reservation** without any doubts or hesitation □ *I support your proposal without reservation.* -3. [for living on] a piece of land set aside for a group of people to live on, especially for people with a traditional way of life, such as Native Americans in the USA or Canada □ *a Sioux reservation.*
♦ **reservations** *npl* doubts about somebody or something that stop one from believing, liking, trusting etc them completely □ *I have no reservations about recommending him for the job.*

reserve [rɪˈzɜːʳv] ◇ *n* -1. [of coal, money, strength] a supply or store of something that can be used later if necessary □ *The country has vast oil reserves.* □ *a reserve supply/tank.* ■ **to keep/have sthg in reserve** to keep/have an amount of sthg that can be used later if necessary □ *I've kept some cash in reserve in case we need it later.* -2. SPORT a player who is not chosen for a team but will play if another member of the team is injured or unavailable □ *our reserve goalie.* -3. [for animals, plants] an area of land set aside to protect the birds or animals that live there □ *a wildlife reserve.* -4. [of a person] the quality of not wanting to

talk about oneself or let other people know one's thoughts or feelings □ *It was difficult to break through his very English reserve.*
◇ *vt* **-1. to reserve sthg for sb/sthg** to keep sthg specially so that it can be used by sb/sthg □ *This room is reserved for members only.* **-2.** [table, seat, library book] to arrange to have <sthg> kept available at the time one wants to use it □ *Can I reserve two tickets for tonight's performance?* □ *We have a table reserved in the name of Williams.* **-3. to reserve the right to do sthg** to demand that one may be allowed to do sthg if one feels that this has become necessary □ *'The management reserves the right to refuse entry.'* □ *'All rights reserved.'*

reserve bank *n* **-1.** one of the 12 main banks of the US Federal Reserve System that hold reserves of money for other banks. **-2. the Reserve Bank of Australia** the central bank of Australia that provides funds for other banks.

reserve currency *n* supplies of foreign currency that a government keeps in reserve to pay its international debts.

reserved [rɪˈzɜːvd] *adj* **-1.** [person] who is unwilling to talk about themselves or let other people know their thoughts or feelings □ *He's shy and reserved by nature.* □ *a reserved smile.* **-2.** [table, seat, library book] that somebody has reserved □ *I'm afraid you can't sit there, it's reserved.*

reserve price *n* GB the lowest price that the owner of something is willing to sell it for at an auction.

reservist [rɪˈzɜːˈvəst] *n* a trained soldier who is not in the army but can be asked to help the army in times of difficulty or emergency.

reservoir [ˈrezəˈvwɑːʳ] *n* a natural or artificial lake used as a store of water for homes, towns, factories etc.

reset [ˌriːˈset] (*pt* & *pp* **reset**, *cont* **resetting**) ◇ *vt* **-1.** [clock, meter, controls] to change <a device> so that it is ready to work under new conditions □ *I reset my watch to Moscow time.* **-2.** [arm, leg] to put <a broken bone> back into its correct position. **-3.** COMPUTING to start <a computer> again, usually because something has gone wrong with the way it is working. ◇ *vi* COMPUTING: *Press the red button to reset.*

resettle [ˌriːˈsetl] ◇ *vt* **-1.** [region, island] to go and live on, or to send people to live on <an area of land> etc where people used to live, but which is now uninhabited □ *After the war successive governments tried to resettle the area.* **-2.** to move <people> to a new area or country because they are no longer safe in their old homes or no longer allowed to live there □ *The refugees were resettled in camps along the border.* ◇ *vi*: *Many Jews later resettled in Israel.*

resettlement [ˌriːˈsetlmənt] *n*: *see* **resettle.**

reshape [ˌriːˈʃeɪp] *vt* [policy, thinking] to give a new form or direction to <sthg>.

reshuffle [ˌriːˈʃʌfl] ◇ *n* a change in the jobs and responsibilities of the people in an organization or political party □ *a Cabinet re-*

shuffle. ◇ *vt* [management, department] to carry out a reshuffle of the people in <sthg>.

reside [rɪˈzaɪd] *vi* (formal use) **-1.** to live in a particular place and have one's home there □ *The author is currently residing in Norway.* **-2. to reside in sthg** to be found in or originate from sthg □ *Political power resides in the prime minister and his cabinet.*

residence [ˈrezɪdəns] *n* **-1.** a house or home, especially one that is big and impressive □ *the ambassador's official residence.* **-2. in residence** living and staying in a particular place, usually because one has a job or official position there □ *Students must remain in residence throughout the term.* ■ **to take up residence** to move to a place and start living there.

residence permit *n* an official document stating that a foreigner is allowed to live in a particular country for a particular length of time.

resident [ˈrezɪdənt] ◇ *adj* **-1. to be resident in a place** to be living in a place □ *She has been resident in France for many years.* **-2.** [chaplain, doctor, tutor] who lives at the place where they work; [artist, expert] who works at a particular place or with a particular group □ *And now a word from our resident medical expert.* ◇ *n* [of a town, street] a person who lives in a particular place; [of a hotel] a person who is staying at a hotel □ *Local residents complained about the noise of traffic.* □ *The bar is only open to residents.*

residential [ˌrezɪˈdenʃl] *adj* [course, job] that requires people to live at the place where they work or study □ *a residential institution* □ *a residential social worker.* ■ **residential care** a system that gives old or disabled people a place to live where they are taken care of by trained staff □ *She's living in residential care.*

residential area *n* an area that contains mainly private houses and apartments, and few factories and offices.

residents' association *n* an organization formed by the people who live in a particular area, usually a town, that tries to make life safer and more pleasant in the area.

residual [rəˈzɪdʒʊəl] *adj* **residual damp/heat** damp/heat that is left over after the main part has disappeared or been removed (formal use).

residue [ˈrezɪdjuː] *n* **-1.** [of money, staff] a small amount of something that is left after most of it has been taken away. **-2.** [of salt, calcium] a small amount of a substance that is left at the end of a chemical process.

resign [rɪˈzaɪn] ◇ *vt* **-1.** [post, position] to say officially that one is leaving <one's job> □ *The scandal forced him to resign his post.* **-2. to resign oneself to sthg** [to defeat, one's fate] to accept sthg calmly because one realizes that one cannot change or prevent it □ *I've resigned myself to having to work over the weekend.* □ *They resigned themselves to a very long wait.* ◇ *vi* [from a post, position] □ *I have resigned from the board/chairmanship.* □ *The board's director was forced to resign.*

resignation [ˌrezɪgˈneɪʃn] *n* -1. the act of re-signing from a job, post etc □ *a letter of resig-nation* □ *She handed in her resignation yesterday.* -2. the feeling one has when one accepts something unpleasant without complaining, worrying, or trying to change it □ *He accept-ed the decision with resignation.*

resigned [rɪˈzaɪnd] *adj* [person] who has re-signed themselves to something □ *a resigned look/smile* □ *I felt resigned to losing my job.*

resilience [rɪˈzɪlɪəns] *n*: see **resilient** □ *The cam-paign has shown remarkable resilience after the setbacks of last year.*

resilient [rɪˈzɪlɪənt] *adj* -1. [material, substance] that is difficult to damage because it goes back to its original shape after being hit, bent, or crushed □ *The springs are still highly resilient.* -2. [person, company] that can recover quickly from illness, difficulty, change etc □ *The movement has proved far more resilient than was expected.*

resin [ˈrezn] *n* -1. a thick sticky liquid that is produced by some trees, e.g. firs and pines, and is used in making medicines, varnish, and paints □ *pine resin.* -2. a thick sticky sub-stance produced in chemical factories that is used in glues and for making plastics □ *indus-trial resin.*

resist [rɪˈzɪst] *vt* -1. [enemy, attack, infection] to fight against <sthg that is trying to harm one> □ *Wilkins was charged with robbery and re-sisting arrest.* -2. [change, proposal, attempt] to try to stop <sthg> from happening or taking effect □ *The chairman resisted demands for his resignation.* -3. [temptation, urge, offer] to stop oneself from doing <sthg that one would like to do> □ *I couldn't resist telling him.* □ *I can never resist temptation.*

resistance [rɪˈzɪstəns] *n* -1. [to an enemy, attack, change] see **resist** □ *The invaders met with little resistance.* □ *There is considerable resistance to his latest ideas.* -2. [to germs, a disease] the power of the body to remain unharmed by something □ *The patient's resistance to infection is low.*

resistant [rɪˈzɪstənt] *adj* -1. **to be resistant to sthg** [to change, reform] not to want sthg and to try to stop it from happening □ *You can try, but they are extremely resistant to new ideas.* -2. **to be resistant to sthg** [to heat, fire, poison] not to be harmed or damaged by sthg □ *rust-/flame-resistant* □ *This variety is particularly resistant to disease.*

resistor [rɪˈzɪstər] *n* a device used to reduce the amount of electricity passing through an electrical circuit.

resit [*n* ˈriːsɪt, *vb* ˌriːˈsɪt] (*pt* & *pp* **resat**, *cont* re-sitting) GB ◇ *n* a second examination that a candidate can take if they fail the first one. ◇ *vt* to take <an examination> again, usually after failing.

resold [ˌriːˈsəʊld] *past tense & past participle of* **resell**.

resolute [ˈrezəluːt] *adj* [belief, refusal] that is firm and determined, often when one is faced with problems or opposition □ *I tried to*

dissuade him, but he was resolute. □ *She took a resolute stand against the cuts.*

resolutely [ˈrezəluːtlɪ] *adv* [support, oppose, ref-use] see **resolute** □ *Some countries remain reso-lutely opposed to the idea.*

resolution [ˌrezəˈluːʃn] *n* -1. a proposal to be discussed by a group of people at a meeting; a formal statement of opinion, agreed by a vote of people at a meeting □ *The French del-egation laid down a resolution that business should be conducted in French.* □ *The resolution was passed unanimously.* -2. [to oneself] a promise made to oneself to do something □ *New Year resolutions* □ *I made a resolution to stop smoking.* -3. [in somebody's character] strong determination when faced by prob-lems or opposition □ *She went about her tasks with grim resolution.* -4. [to a problem] a way of settling or deciding a problem, difficulty etc □ *The UN hopes that it will find a peaceful resolu-tion to the conflict.*

resolve [rɪˈzɒlv] ◇ *n* the determination to suc-ceed when faced by problems or opposition □ *These setbacks only served to strengthen our resolve.* ◇ *vt* -1. **to resolve to do sthg** to make a firm decision to do sthg, often as a result of something bad that has happened □ *She resolved that she would never speak to him again.* -2. [crisis, dispute, disagreement] to find a way of settling or deciding <a problem or argument> □ *I'm sure there's a peaceful way to resolve our differences.*

resonance [ˈrezənəns] *n*: see **resonant**.

resonant [ˈrezənənt] *adj* [voice, drum, sound] that echoes and is deep, loud, and clear.

resonate [ˈrezəneɪt] *vi* [voice, sound] to make a resonant sound □ *The entire hall resonated with the sound of cheering.*

resort [rɪˈzɔːrt] *n* -1. a town or place where many people spend their vacations □ *a health/tourist resort.* -2. **to do sthg as a last re-sort** to do sthg when everything else has failed □ *As a last resort he asked his father for the money.* □ *Yes, but you must only do it as a last resort.* ■ **in the last resort** after all other possibilities have been considered □ *In the last resort he may have to resign.*

◆ **resort to** *vt fus* **to resort to sthg** [violence, theft, strikes] to use sthg, even though it is wrong or unpleasant, because there is no other way of getting what one wants □ *Both countries were reluctant to resort to military inter-vention.*

resound [rɪˈzaʊnd] *vi* -1. [explosion, music] to be heard loudly and clearly □ *His voice resound-ed through the empty hallway.* -2. **to resound with sthg** [with drums, voices, laughter] to be filled with the sound of sthg □ *The whole room resounded with applause.*

resounding [rɪˈzaʊndɪŋ] *adj* -1. [crash, blow] very loud. -2. **a resounding success/failure** a very great success/failure □ *It was a resound-ing victory for common sense.*

resource [US ˈriːsɔːrs, GB rɪˈzɔːs] *n* -1. [of coal, oil, land] a supply of a raw material that a country can use □ *our natural/mineral resources.* -2. [of strength, courage] qualities or possessions that a person can use for help, support etc □ *Our staff is our most valuable resource.* □ *She has inner resources of energy and determination.* **-3. sb's resources** the money sb has available to spend on things □ *financial resources* □ *We pooled our resources to buy her a decent present.*

resourceful [rɪ'sɔːrsfl] *adj* [person] who is good at finding ways of dealing with difficult situations using whatever is available □ *I'm sure she'll be able to find a way to do it — she's extremely resourceful.*

resourcefulness [rɪ'sɔːrsflnəs] *n: see* **resourceful**.

respect [rɪ'spekt] ◇ *n* **-1.** [for a person, somebody's work] the belief that somebody or something is important, admirable, useful, or valuable □ *I have enormous respect for her opinions.* □ *Mr Fipke seems unable to command the respect of his staff.* ■ **with (all due/the greatest) respect...** a phrase used when one wants to be polite to somebody one is disagreeing with (formal use) □ *With all due respect to the Chairman, I still think that this plan is unwise.* **-2.** [for somebody's rights, wishes, privacy] care that one does not harm or interfere with something; [for a custom, rule] care and attention that is required by something □ *She shows little respect for other people's property.* □ *This chemical is dangerous and must be treated with respect.* **-3. in this** OR **that respect** in connection with what has just been said □ *In this respect we are in complete agreement.* ■ **in one respect/many respects etc** in one way/many ways etc □ *In some respects they are very different.*

◇ *vt* **-1.** [person, work] to feel respect for <sb/sthg> □ *I find it hard to respect a man who treats his wife like that.* □ *I respect her enormously for the way she has stood up to criticism.* **-2.** [rights, privacy, customs] to show respect for <sthg>; [somebody's opinion, judgment, decision] to accept that somebody has a right to <sthg>, even if one does not agree with it □ *He seemed unable to respect my need for silence and privacy.* □ *I respect what you're saying, but it does not alter my decision.*

♦ **respects** *npl* a word used to send one's good wishes to somebody (formal use) □ *Please give my respects to your husband.* ■ **to pay one's last respects to sb** to go to sb's funeral.

♦ **with respect to** *prep* a phrase used to show the person or thing that a statement applies to □ *With respect to your application for promotion, this matter will be considered next week.*

respectability [rɪ,spektə'bɪlətɪ] *n* [of a person, family] *see* **respectable** □ *The marriage was an attempt to achieve some sort of respectability.*

respectable [rɪ'spektəbl] *adj* **-1.** [person, family] that lives and behaves in a way that people find morally or socially acceptable □ *They live in a respectable neighborhood.* □ *I must do my hair and make myself look respectable.* **-2.** [result, distance, amount] that is average or acceptable for a particular purpose or situation (in-

formal use) □ *This increase makes my salary fairly respectable at last.*

respectably [rɪ'spektəblɪ] *adv* [behave, dress] *see* **respectable** □ *a respectably dressed young man.*

respected [rɪ'spektəd] *adj* [citizen, scientist, organization] that people admire and have a good opinion of □ *a highly respected musician.*

respectful [rɪ'spektfl] *adj* [person, question, bow] that shows respect for somebody □ *They listened in respectful silence to her speech.*

respectfully [rɪ'spektflɪ] *adv* [speak, ask, clap] *see* **respectful** □ *'Guests are respectfully requested not to smoke in the corridor.'*

respective [rɪ'spektɪv] *adj* a word that shows that each of two or more things belongs to each of the other things or people that are mentioned □ *After the meeting the managers went back to their respective departments.* □ *They each had their respective tasks to fulfill.*

respectively [rɪ'spektɪvlɪ] *adv* a word that shows that each of two or more things in one list refers to something else in the same position in another list □ *The pound's falls against the peseta and the drachma are less marked — down from 188 to 185.5 and 352 to 348 respectively.*

respiration [,respə'reɪʃn] *n* breathing (technical use).

respirator ['respəreɪtər] *n* **-1.** a device worn over the face to allow people to breathe when surrounded by smoke or poisonous gas. **-2.** a machine that pumps air into the lungs of people who are unconscious or badly injured □ *He was put on a respirator.*

respiratory [US 'respərətɔːrɪ, GB rɪ'spɪrətərɪ] *adj* [system, disease] that is connected with or affects people's breathing □ *respiratory failure.*

respite [US 'respət, GB -aɪt] *n* **-1.** a short period of rest or relief during a time of pain, worry, or hard work □ *We worked all day without a moment's respite.* □ *After a brief respite, the bombing began again.* **-2.** a short delay that one is allowed before having to do something unpleasant □ *We've been given a respite of two weeks before we have to pay.*

respite care *n* residential care that is arranged for short periods for the elderly, mentally handicapped etc so that the people who normally look after them can have a rest.

resplendent [rɪ'splendənt] *adj* [colors, building, garden] that one thinks is impressive to look at (literary use) □ *Miss Waters was resplendent in a red, full-length dress and a diamond tiara.*

respond [rɪ'spɒnd] ◇ *vt* to say <sthg> in answer to something (formal use) □ *"I'll go," he responded.* □ *She responded that it was the only viable course of action.* ◇ *vi* **-1.** [to a question, suggestion, request] to do something as an answer or reaction to something □ *Jennifer responded with a smile.* □ *He has failed to respond to my letter.* □ *They responded by ignoring us completely.* **-2.** [to treatment] to react well or in a favorable way to a particular kind of treatment, especially medical treatment □ *The car responds well.* □ *The patient/disease is not responding to treatment.*

response [rɪ'spɒns] *n* **-1.** [to a question, letter] an answer or reply □ *There have been sixty responses to our advertisement.* □ *I wrote last week but so far I've had no response.* **-2.** [to a request, event, situation] an action done as an answer or reaction to something □ *There was a good response to our appeal for information.* □ *The government's response to the riots was to call out the army.* ∎ **in response** as an answer or reaction to something □ *I am writing in response to your letter of July 15.*

response time *n* COMPUTING the time it takes a computer to complete a task and tell the user it is ready to receive its next instruction.

responsibility [rɪ,spɒnsə'bɪlətɪ] (*pl* **responsibilities**) *n* **-1.** [for arrangements, somebody's work, a project] control and authority over something, and the duty to see that it is done properly □ *She was given the responsibility of making all investment decisions.* □ *We share responsibility for customer relations.* □ *It's not my responsibility to oversee new staff.* **-2.** [for a mistake, accident] the blame for having caused something □ *I take full responsibility for whatever damage he has done.* **-3.** something that one must do, especially a job or task □ *Your responsibilities will include training new staff.* □ *We have a responsibility to our shareholders to accept the highest bid.*

responsible [rɪ'spɒnsəbl] *adj* **-1. to be responsible for sthg** [for arrangements, somebody's work, a project] to have responsibility for sthg; [for a mistake, accident] to be the cause of sthg bad that has happened □ *You will be primarily responsible for a program of joint ventures.* □ *A faulty valve is thought to have been responsible for the explosion.* □ *You will be held personally responsible for any discrepancies in the accounts.* **-2. to be responsible to sb** [to a committee, one's manager, shareholders] to be under the authority of sb and have a duty to explain to them what one has done □ *The senior managers are responsible to the board of directors.* **-3.** [person] who can be trusted to do things without needing to be watched or controlled □ *I wish you would take a more responsible attitude to your work.* **-4.** [job, task, position] that involves important work that will affect other people.

responsibly [rɪ'spɒnsəblɪ] *adv* [behave, act] *see* **responsible**.

responsive [rɪ'spɒnsɪv] *adj* [person] who is able to react quickly and effectively to something □ *Politicians need to be responsive to public opinion.*

respray [*vb* ,riː'spreɪ, *n* 'riːspreɪ] ◇ *vt* to spray <a car> with a new coat of paint. ◇ *n: I'm taking the car in for a respray.*

rest [rest] ◇ *n* **-1. the rest** everything or everybody else, apart from the things, people, or part of something that one has already mentioned □ *We ate half the cake and threw the rest away.* □ *Five of us were English, the rest were from America.* □ *The rest of the journey was very pleasant.* □ *I thought you were different, but you're just like all the rest.* **-2.** [from work] a pe-

riod of freedom from work or from something that is tiring; [for one's body] sleep or comfortable relaxation □ *You need a rest from all this worry.* □ *They worked all night without a moment's rest.* □ *I need some rest.* □ *Why don't you have a rest?* **-3.** [for somebody's feet, head] an object for supporting something on □ *a foot rest.* **-4.** *phrases* **to come to rest** [vehicle, ball] to stop moving □ *The car finally came to rest in a ditch.* ∎ **to lay** OR **put sthg to rest** [idea, belief] to show that sthg is not true □ *I want to lay this rumor to rest once and for all.*
◇ *vt* **-1.** [one's eyes, feet, arms] to allow <a part of one's body> to relax and recover after a period of work or effort □ *Sit down and rest your legs!* **-2. to rest sthg on/against sthg** [head, ladder, book] to allow sthg to lie, lean, or be supported on/against sthg □ *I rested my bike up against a lamppost.* □ *He rested his head on her shoulder.* **-3. (you can) rest assured (that)...** you can be sure that... □ *Rest assured that we're doing all we can to help.*
◇ *vi* **-1.** [person] to stop doing something and be still in order to recover one's strength □ *We stopped to rest before continuing up the hill.* □ *I won't rest until I find Rory's killer.* **-2. to rest on sb/sthg** [hopes, result] to depend on sb/sthg; [argument, fame] to be based on sb/sthg □ *England's hopes rest on Jones qualifying for the final.* □ *The prosecution's case rests on the evidence of the next witness.* **-3. to rest with sb** [choice, blame] to be the responsibility of sb □ *In the end, the responsibility for the decision rests with you.* **-4. to rest on/against sthg** to lie, lean, or be supported on/against sthg □ *His head rested on her shoulder.*

rest area *n* US & AUS a place at the side of a road where drivers can stop and rest.

restart [*n* 'riːstɑːrt, *vb* ,riː'stɑːrt] ◇ *n* COMPUTING the act of restarting a computer operating system. ◇ *vt* **-1.** [vehicle, engine, race] to start <sthg> again because it has stopped or gone wrong. **-2.** [work] to start <sthg> again after a rest or break. ◇ *vi* **-1.** [vehicle, engine] to start again. **-2.** [game, play] to start again after a break.

restate [,riː'steɪt] *vt* [policy, objections, opinion] to say <sthg> again, usually in different words.

restaurant ['restərɒnt] *n* a place where people can buy and eat meals □ *a Greek/Chinese restaurant.*

restaurant car *n* GB a car on a train where people can buy and eat food.

rest cure *n* a long period of rest that is a medical treatment for stress, an illness, a mental problem etc.

rested ['restəd] *adj* **to be** OR **feel rested** to feel better because one has had a rest or vacation.

restful ['restfl] *adj* [weekend, atmosphere, color] that makes one feel relaxed □ *I had a very welcome and restful break.*

rest home *n* a place where old or sick people live and are looked after.

resting place ['restɪŋ-] *n* **sb's last resting place** sb's grave □ *The abbey is his final resting place.*

restitution [ˌrestɪˈtjuːʃn] n [of money, rights, property] the act of giving back something lost or stolen; payment for damage done to something (formal use).

restive [ˈrestɪv] adj [crowd, audience] that is restless and impatient, and therefore likely to cause trouble.

restless [ˈrestləs] adj -1. [audience, child] who will not keep still or quiet, usually because they are bored or dissatisfied □ The audience was beginning to get restless. -2. [person] who is constantly moving and unable to be still □ his restless wanderings. -3. [night] that is without rest or sleep □ I spent a restless night worrying about Jo.

restlessly [ˈrestləslɪ] adv [move, walk] see **restless** □ Grant paced restlessly up and down the waiting room.

restock [ˌriːˈstɒk] ◇ vt [shelves, river] to fill <sthg> with new supplies. ◇ vi: We restock at the end of each week.

restoration [ˌrestəˈreɪʃn] n -1. [of a tax, somebody's hearing] see **restore** □ the restoration of law and order. -2. work done to restore a building, painting etc to its original condition; a building, painting etc that has been restored □ They're doing a lot of restoration work on the façade.

restorative [rɪˈstɒrətɪv] adj [food, sleep] that makes one feel better, healthier, or stronger (formal use) □ the restorative powers of sleep.

restore [rɪˈstɔːr] vt -1. [order, confidence, somebody's hearing] to bring <sthg> back after it has been lost; [tax, law] to bring <sthg> back after it has stopped being used □ Troops were called in to restore calm. □ You've restored my faith in human nature! □ In 1977 the country voted to restore the death penalty. ■ to restore sb to sthg [to power, health] to bring sb back to sthg. -2. [building, painting] to mend and clean <sthg> so that it returns to its original condition □ The palace was restored to its former glory in 1953. -3. [stolen goods, rights, land] to give <sthg> back to its former owner □ The jewels were restored to their rightful owners.

restorer [rɪˈstɔːrər] n -1. a person who restores old buildings, paintings etc. -2. a substance that improves the appearance of something that is old, dirty etc □ a furniture restorer.

restrain [rɪˈstreɪn] vt -1. to try to stop <sb> from doing something they intend to do □ She couldn't restrain herself from laughing. -2. to control <a person or animal> by using force □ The prisoner became violent and had to be restrained. -3. [emotion, growth, inflation] to keep <sthg> under control □ government attempts to restrain public spending.

restrained [rɪˈstreɪnd] adj -1. [person, response, criticism] that is calm, controlled, and unemotional □ The tone of the letter was unusually restrained. -2. [color, style, music] that is not loud, bright, or highly decorated □ The decor was tasteful and restrained.

restraint [rɪˈstreɪnt] n -1. [on budget, trade] a rule or condition that stops something from becoming too big or dangerous □ There were few restraints imposed on his power. □ The De-

partment of Trade has imposed restraints on Japanese car imports. □ wage restraints. -2. the ability to stay calm and controlled in difficult situations □ I think he showed great restraint in not losing his temper. □ We should exercise due restraint.

restrict [rɪˈstrɪkt] vt [number, growth, movement] to put a limit on <sb/sthg> □ We need laws to restrict the ownership of firearms. ■ to restrict sb to sthg not to allow sb more than a particular amount of sthg □ Each passenger is restricted to one bottle of wine. □ I shall restrict myself to a few comments on this subject. ■ to restrict sthg to sb/sthg to keep sthg limited to sb/sthg □ Speed is restricted to 30 mph. □ Membership is restricted to people in management positions. ■ to restrict oneself to sthg [to a subject, activity] to limit what one says or does to sthg □ He should restrict himself to writing instead of interferring with politics.

restricted [rɪˈstrɪktəd] adj -1. [membership, access, space] limited in amount, number, or size □ Membership is restricted to 600 people. □ Visibility was restricted to ten meters. □ a seat with a restricted view of the stage. -2. [document, information, area] that is secret and available only to people with special permission □ 'Restricted area: no unauthorized personnel.'

restriction [rɪˈstrɪkʃn] n -1. a rule or condition that restricts something □ speed/import/currency restrictions □ The State Department had imposed restrictions on foreign travel. □ Living out of town places restrictions on our social life. -2. something that stops something else from moving or growing freely □ Loosen all clothing to avoid restriction of circulation and breathing.

restrictive [rɪˈstrɪktɪv] adj [discipline, rule, father] that stops somebody from behaving as freely as they want to.

restrictive practices npl GB official ways of working used by a labor union that prevent the most effective use of time, labor, equipment etc.

rest room n US a public toilet in a restaurant, theater etc.

restructure [ˌriːˈstrʌktʃər] vt [company, department, local government] to change and improve the organization of <sthg>.

result [rɪˈzʌlt] ◇ n -1. something that happens because of something else that has happened □ These problems are the result of a misunderstanding. □ The net result of the report was a reorganization of the company. □ I refused, with the result that I was fired. □ Doing it this way seems to produce the same result. -2. [of a game, election] the final position showing who won and who lost etc; [of a test, examination] a statement showing how somebody or something performed □ the primary results □ The company's annual results will be published tomorrow. -3. [of a calculation, sum] the number that is the answer to a mathematical problem.
◇ vi to result in sthg to be the cause of sthg usually after a period of time and at the end

of a series of events □ *The fire resulted in two deaths.* □ *The dispute eventually resulted in her resigning.* ■ **to result from sthg** to be caused by sthg □ *His injuries resulted from a bad fall.*

◆ **as a result** *adv* because of this □ *My car broke down and as a result I was unable to get there.*

◆ **as a result of** *prep* because of <sthg> □ *The game had to be canceled as a result of the weather.*

resultant [rɪˈzʌltənt] *adj* [chaos, change, publicity] that happens as a result of something (formal use) □ *The resultant scandal nearly ended her career.*

resume [rɪˈzjuːm] ◇ *vt* **-1.** [talks, meeting, journey] to start <sthg> again after a break or pause □ *Normal service will be resumed as soon as possible.* **-2.** [place, position] to go back to <one's seat> after leaving it for a while (formal use) □ *Would the audience please resume their seats for Act 2.* ◇ *vi* [talks, meeting, journey] *The meeting resumed at 3 o'clock.*

résumé [US ˈrezəmeɪ, GB -ju-] *n* **-1.** US a document describing one's education, background, achievements, and previous employment that one sends to companies when one is looking for a job □ *I sent them a copy of my résumé.* **-2.** [of events, the plot] a short account of something, giving only the main points □ *He gave a brief résumé of what had been said.*

resumption [rɪˈzʌmpʃn] *n* [of talks, a meeting, journey] *see* **resume** □ *Observers fear a resumption of hostilities between the two countries.*

resurface [ˌriːˈsɜːfəs] ◇ *vt* to put a new surface on <a road>. ◇ *vi* [person, problem, rivalry] to appear again after having disappeared for a period of time.

resurgence [rɪˈsɜːdʒəns] *n* [of interest, terrorism] a return of an attitude or activity which has not been seen or noticed for a period of time (formal use) □ *There has been a resurgence of sectarian violence in the area.*

resurrect [ˌrezəˈrekt] *vt* [policy, law, custom] to bring <sthg> back into use or fashion after it has disappeared and been forgotten □ *The idea has recently been resurrected.*

resurrection [ˌrezəˈrekʃn] *n* [of policy, law, custom] *see* **resurrect**.

◆ **Resurrection** *n* **the Resurrection** RELIGION in the Bible, the return to life of Jesus Christ after his death.

resuscitate [rɪˈsʌsɪteɪt] *vt* to bring <sb who is badly injured or nearly dead> back to consciousness or life □ *They tried to resuscitate him, but it was too late.*

resuscitation [rɪˌsʌsɪˈteɪʃn] *n: see* **resuscitate** □ *All attempts at resuscitation failed.*

retail [ˈriːteɪl] ◇ *n* the sale of goods to people for their own use, usually in small quantities and in stores □ *the retail of foodstuffs* □ *retail goods/businesses/traders.* ◇ *adv* [buy, sell] at retail price. ◇ *vi* **to retail at a particular price** to cost a particular price when sold to the public □ *These shoes retail at $85 a pair.*
NOTE: Compare **wholesale**.

retailer [ˈriːteɪləʳ] *n* a person who sells goods to the public.

retail outlet *n* a store or other place where goods are sold at retail price.

retail price *n* the price at which something is sold to individual members of the public.

retail price index *n* GB a system of numbers that uses the prices of a standard list of typical goods at a particular time to show changes in the cost of living.

retain [rɪˈteɪn] *vt* **-1.** [balance, power, independence] to keep <sthg>, especially something that one wants to keep □ *I intend to retain control of this company.* □ *The new system retains some of the features of the old one.* **-2.** [heat, water] to continue to have or contain <sthg> and not let it escape or disappear □ *The flowers have retained their freshness.*

retainer [rɪˈteɪnəʳ] *n* a fee paid to somebody to make sure that they will be available to do some work if this becomes necessary □ *Mr Lomax is being paid a $1,000 monthly retainer.*

retaining wall [rɪˈteɪnɪŋ-] *n* a strong wall built to hold back water or support a mass of earth.

retaliate [rɪˈtælɪeɪt] *vi* to do something unpleasant to somebody in revenge for something unpleasant that they have done to one □ *The Americans retaliated by expelling three Algerian diplomats.*

retaliation [rɪˌtælɪˈeɪʃn] *n: see* **retaliate** □ *The attack is thought to have been in retaliation for last week's bombing.*

retarded [rɪˈtɑːdəd] *adj* [child] who is less developed physically or mentally than other people of the same age □ *mentally retarded.*

retch [retʃ] *vi* to make the sounds and movements of vomiting, but without bringing anything up from one's stomach.

retention [rɪˈtenʃn] *n: see* **retain** □ *Several members voted for the retention of the ban.*

retentive [rɪˈtentɪv] *adj* [mind, memory] able to remember things very well.

rethink [*vb* ˌriːˈθɪŋk, *n* ˈriːθɪŋk] (*pt* & *pp* **rethought** [-ˈθɔːt]) ◇ *vt* [policy, plan, situation] to think about <sthg> again in order to change it □ *Clore and Co. have been rethinking their sales strategy.* ◇ *vi: The unexpected improvement forced us to rethink.* ◇ *n* the act of rethinking something □ *The company is having a major rethink of their advertising strategy.*

reticence [ˈretɪsəns] *n: see* **reticent** □ *I sensed a reticence on their part to discuss the deal.*

reticent [ˈretɪsənt] *adj* [person] who is unwilling to talk to people, especially about a particular subject □ *He was unusually reticent on the subject.*

retina [ˈretɪnə] (*pl* **retinas** OR **retinae** [-niː]) *n* the area at the back of one's eye that turns light into nerve messages.

retinue [ˈretɪnjuː] *n* a group of servants, helpers, followers etc that travels with an important person.

retire [rɪˈtaɪəʳ] *vi* **-1.** [from a job] to stop working, usually because one has reached a particular age □ *He retired from football after he broke his leg.* **-2.** [to another place] to go away to a place that is less crowded or busy (formal use) □ *Shall we retire to the lounge?* **-3.** [to bed] to go to bed (formal use) □ *I decided to retire for the night.*

retired [rɪ'taɪəʳd] *adj* [professor, mailman, nurse] who is no longer working, usually because they have passed retirement age □ *My parents are both retired now.*

retirement [rɪ'taɪəʳmənt] ◇ *n* **-1.** the time when somebody retires from work □ *You will receive a lump sum on retirement.* □ *a retirement present.* **-2.** the time after one has retired □ *They're enjoying their retirement.* ◇ *comp* **a retirement home/community etc** a home/community etc where old retired people live.

retirement age *n* the age at which people normally retire □ *She is past retirement age.*

retirement pension *n* money that is paid regularly to somebody who has retired.

retirement plan *n* US a system in which a worker and their employer both make regular payments to a fund that provides money for the worker's retirement pension.

retiring [rɪ'taɪərɪŋ] *adj* **-1.** [person] who is quiet and shy □ *David's very shy and retiring.* **-2.** [chairman, official] who is soon going to retire from their position □ *payments to retiring staff.*

retort [rɪ'tɔːʳt] ◇ *n* a short, quick, rather angry reply to somebody who has said something annoying □ *"Go away!" was his angry retort.* ◇ *vt* to say <sthg> as a retort □ *"Do it yourself!" she retorted.* □ *He retorted that it was all my fault.*

retouch [,riː'tʌtʃ] *vt* [painting, photograph] to alter or improve <sthg> by painting over parts of it.

retrace [rɪ'treɪs] *vt* **to retrace one's steps** to go back over exactly the same route that one has taken, usually to look for something one has lost.

retract [rɪ'trækt] ◇ *vt* **-1.** [statement, accusation, confession] to officially deny the truth of <sthg one has said earlier> □ *Plomov was forced to retract his earlier statement.* **-2.** [claw, wheel, rod] to pull <sthg> back so that it no longer shows or sticks out □ *You can retract the blade by pressing this switch.* ◇ *vi* **-1.** [person] *The charges you've made are too serious for you to retract now.* **-2.** [claw, wheel, rod] *The blade automatically retracts after use.*

retractable [rɪ'træktəbl] *adj* [claws, wheels, rod] that can be retracted.

retraction [rɪ'trækʃn] *n* **-1.** [of a statement, accusation, confession] *see* **retract.** **-2.** a formal written apology retracting a previous statement, accusation, confession etc □ *The newspaper was forced to print a retraction of the article.*

retrain [,riː'treɪn] ◇ *vt* to teach <sb> new skills to help them find work. ◇ *vi* to be retrained □ *She's retraining as a nurse.*

retraining [,riː'treɪnɪŋ] *n* teaching intended to give people new skills so that they can find work □ *Retraining is vital to turn the local economy around.*

retread ['riːtred] *n* a worn tire that has been given a new outer layer so that it can be used again.

retreat [rɪ'triːt] ◇ *vi* **-1.** [from a person, to a place] to move back or away from somebody or something, because one is afraid or embarrassed or wants to be alone □ *We retreated to the kitchen so we could talk.* **-2.** MILITARY [from an army, place] to move back after being defeated or because of danger □ *The troops were forced to retreat to the hills around the city.* **-3.** [from a principle, decision, lifestyle] to decide not to continue with something because it has become too difficult or embarrassing □ *After the scandal, the bishop retreated from public life.* □ *The management was forced to retreat on its program of job cuts.*
◇ *n* **-1.** MILITARY [from a place] an operation in which an army retreats □ *Napoleon's retreat from Moscow* □ *The army is in full retreat.* **-2.** [from a principle, decision, lifestyle] a change in attitude in which one retreats from an earlier position or decision □ *The minister's statement marks a retreat from his hard-line policy.* ■ **to beat a (hasty) retreat** to leave a place quickly □ *The burglars beat a hasty retreat when the alarm went off.* **-3.** [where one stays] a quiet place where one can go when one wants to be alone □ *a Buddhist retreat.*

retrenchment [rɪ'trentʃmənt] *n* a period or policy in which a company, government etc cuts costs and reduces its spending (formal use).

retrial ['riːtraɪəl] *n* a new trial of a case of law, e.g. because the jury was unable to reach a decision or new evidence has been found □ *The judge ordered a retrial.*

retribution [,retrɪ'bjuːʃn] *n* punishment that is deserved or expected □ *Retribution was swift.*

retrieval [rɪ'triːvl] *n* COMPUTING the act of getting information from a computer file □ *data retrieval.*

retrieve [rɪ'triːv] *vt* **-1.** to get <sthg> back from a place where it should not be □ *She retrieved her shoe from under the bed.* **-2.** COMPUTING [information, data] to get back <sthg that has been stored on a computer> □ *I don't seem to be able to retrieve that file.* **-3. to retrieve the situation** to make the situation better or more acceptable when it seems very bad □ *It will take a miracle to retrieve the situation at this stage of the game.*

retriever [rɪ'triːvəʳ] *n* a hunting dog trained to fetch birds and animals that have been shot.

retroactive [,retrəʊ'æktɪv] *adj* [pay increase, legislation] that applies to a period in the past as well as to the future (formal use).

retrograde ['retrəgreɪd] *adj* that causes somebody or something to go back to an earlier and worse state □ *a retrograde step.*

retrogressive [,retrə'gresɪv] *adj* [change, policy] that is retrograde.

retrospect ['retrəspekt] *n* **in retrospect** a phrase

used to say one is thinking about something that happened in the past, often with a new opinion about it □ *In retrospect, it was the wrong decision.*

retrospective [ˌretrə'spektɪv] ◇ *adj* **-1.** [anger, mood, exhibition] that involves looking at or thinking about the past from the point of view of the present. **-2.** [law, change] that takes effect from a date earlier than the date on which it is announced, published etc. ◇ *n* an exhibition of works created by an artist over a long period of time □ *Have you seen the Calder retrospective?*

retrospectively [ˌretrə'spektɪvlɪ] *adv* [describe, feel, validate] *see* **retrospective**.

return [rɪ'tɜːʳn] ◇ *n* **-1.** the act of going back to a particular place after being away from it for a period of time □ *He found that much had changed on his return.* □ *She'll call on her return from the conference.* □ *The return trip was uneventful.* **-2.** [of love, happiness] the reappearance of something after a period when it was missing □ *We can only hope for a return to democracy at some point in the future.* **-3.** [of money, a book] the act of giving back something that one has borrowed or taken □ *Campaigners are calling for the return of the paintings to their country of origin.* **-4.** SPORT [in tennis] the act of hitting the ball back to one's opponent □ *That was a good return.* **-5.** BUSINESS the profit one makes from something, e.g. from stock or an investment □ *You can expect a high return on your investment.* **-6.** COMPUTING = **return key** □ *Press 'return'.* **-7.** GB = **return ticket** □ *A return to Leeds, please.*

◇ *vt* **-1.** [property, money] to give <sthg> back to the person who owns it □ *He wanted to return the ring to its proper owner.* □ *All keys must be returned by Friday morning.* **-2.** [compliment, visit] to give back to somebody <the same thing that they gave to one> □ *I hope I can return the favor some time.* **-3.** [love, affection] to feel for somebody <the same feelings that they have for one> □ *She does not return his feelings.* **-4. to return sthg to a place** [book, switch] to put sthg that has been moved or taken back to the place where it was before □ *She returned the violin to its case.* **-5.** LAW **to return a verdict** to give a verdict at the end of a trial □ *The jury is expected to return a verdict of not guilty.* **-6.** POLITICS to elect <a candidate> □ *She was returned to Congress with an increased majority.*

◇ *vi* to come or go back □ *He's just returned from Paris.* □ *He'll be returning to work tomorrow.* □ *Things have returned to normal now.* □ *"Of course," he said, and returned to his book.*

◆ **returns** *npl* **-1.** BUSINESS the profit that somebody makes from an investment, business, shares etc. □ *The best long-term returns come from careful manning.* **-2. many happy returns (of the day)!** a phrase used to wish somebody a happy birthday.

◆ **in return** *adv* in exchange □ *What will you give us in return?* □ *And in return, we will give you a 10% discount.*

◆ **in return for** *prep* in exchange for <sthg> □

He offered them his services in return for money. □ *What do we get in return for our cooperation?*

returnable [rɪ'tɜːʳnəbl] *adj* [bottle, container] that can be given back after one has used it, often so that it can be used again.

returning officer [rɪˌtɜːʳnɪŋ-] *n* GB an official who organizes an election in a particular area and who announces the result.

return key *n* COMPUTING the key on a keyboard that is used to move to the next line or to confirm a command.

return match *n* SPORT the second of two games played between the same two players or teams.

return ticket *n* GB a ticket bought for a bus, train, plane etc that gives somebody the right to travel to a particular place and back again.

reunification [ˌriːjuːnɪfɪ'keɪʃn] *n* the act of bringing together something such as a country that has been divided □ *the reunification of Germany.*

reunion [ˌriː'juːnjən] *n* **-1.** a party for members of the same family, school, group etc who have not met for a long time □ *a school/family reunion.* **-2.** the act of bringing together people after they have been separated for a long time □ *It was a tearful reunion.*

reunite [ˌriːjuː'naɪt] *vt* to bring <people who have been separated for a long time> together; to cause <the different parts of an organization, country> etc to be united again □ *He was reunited with his sister at the airport.* □ *At last they were reunited.*

reupholster [ˌriːʌp'həʊlstəʳ] *vt* to replace the old covers and fillings of <a chair, sofa> etc with new ones.

reusable [riː'juːzəbl] *adj* [battery, packaging] that has been designed to be used again.

reuse [*n* ˌriː'juːs, *vb* ˌriː'juːz] ◇ *n* the act of using something again. ◇ *vt* [envelope, container, packaging] to use <sthg> again rather than throwing it away after using it once.

rev [rev] (*pt* & *pp* **revved**, *cont* **revving**) ◇ *n* AUTO *abbr of* **revolution**. ◇ *vt* **to rev an engine (up)** to increase the speed of an engine by pushing down on the accelerator (informal use). ◇ *vi* [engine] *I could hear the car revving up.*

revalue [ˌriː'væljuː] *vt* **-1.** [house, property] to estimate the value of <sthg> again. **-2.** FINANCE to increase the value of <a currency> so that it can be exchanged for more foreign currency than before.

revamp [ˌriː'væmp] *vt* **-1.** [system, department] to change the organization or structure of <sthg> to make it better. **-2.** [room, house] to decorate <a place> to make it look better.

rev counter *n* a device for measuring the speed of a vehicle's engine.

reveal [rɪ'viːl] *vt* **-1.** [face, stage, view] to allow <sthg that has been hidden or covered> to be seen □ *The curtain rose to reveal a scene inside the palace.* **-2.** [fact, truth] to make <sthg> known for the first time □ *The press revealed* that he had taken bribes. □ Details of the plans are to be revealed next month.

revealing [rɪ'viːlɪŋ] *adj* -1. [dress, blouse] that shows a lot of part of a woman's body, especially a part that is usually covered. -2. [remark, insight] that tells people more about something personal, secret, or unknown.

reveille [US 'revəlɪ, GB rɪ'vælɪ] *n* a short tune played to wake soldiers in the morning.

revel ['revl] (US *pt* & *pp* reveled, *cont* reveling, GB *pt* & *pp* revelled, *cont* revelling) *vi* to revel in sthg [in one's power, the attention] to enjoy sthg very much □ I hate all the publicity, but Jenny just revels in it.

revelation [,revə'leɪʃn] *n* -1. a surprising fact that is made known to people □ I cannot confirm the revelations in yesterday's papers. -2. an experience that makes one aware of something that one did not know before □ Their simple way of life was a revelation to me.

reveler US, **reveller** GB ['revələr] *n* a person who is enjoying themselves in a noisy and lively way, e.g. at a party or nightclub.

revelry ['revlrɪ] *n* noisy enjoyment that usually involves drinking, dancing etc □ The sound of drunken revelry could be heard coming from downstairs.

revenge [rɪ'vendʒ] *n* something harmful or unpleasant that one does to somebody else because of something harmful or unpleasant they have done to one □ I'll get my revenge one day! □ The attack may have been in revenge for the recent murder of a local resident. □ a revenge killing/attack. ■ to take revenge to do something harmful or unpleasant to somebody because of something harmful or unpleasant that they have done to one □ He vowed he would take revenge on the murderers.

revenue ['revənjuː] *n* income earned by a company or received by the government from taxes □ The White House hopes to generate extra revenue with these measures.

reverberate [rɪ'vɜːrbəreɪt] *vi* -1. [noise, thunderclap, explosion] to echo repeatedly □ The sound of the explosion reverberated through the city. -2. [revelation, shock, news] to have a strong effect on many different people that is felt for a long time □ The shock of the scandal is still reverberating throughout the capital.

reverberations [rɪ,vɜːrbə'reɪʃnz] *npl* -1. the echoes heard after a loud noise has been made. -2. the powerful effects of a serious event or incident.

revere [rɪ'vɪər] *vt* to have great respect and admiration for <sb/sthg> (formal use) □ She was a much revered figure in the art world.

Revere [rɪ'vɪər], **Paul** (1735–1818) a US silversmith and revolutionary. He warned the Massachusetts colonists when the British army arrived in 1775 at the start of the American Revolution.

reverence ['revrəns] *n* a feeling of great respect and admiration (formal use).

Reverend ['revrənd] *n* a title placed before the name of a Christian minister.

Reverend Mother *n* the title used for the mother superior of a convent.

reverent ['revrənt] *adj* [manner, tone] that shows great respect or admiration □ They stood listening to the speech in reverent silence.

reverential [,revə'renʃl] *adj* [attitude, gesture] that shows great respect or admiration (formal use) □ They sat in reverential silence.

reverie ['revərɪ] *n* a pleasant daydream (formal use) □ The bell interrupted Cathy's reverie.

revers [rɪ'vɪər] (*pl* revers [-z]) *n* a part of a piece of clothing such as a jacket that is folded back at the neck to show the inside.

reversal [rɪ'vɜːrsl] *n* -1. [of a trend, policy, decision] a change that causes something to become the opposite of what it was before□ The defeat marks a reversal in their fortunes. -2. [of roles, order, position] a change that causes the usual state of something to be reversed □ There had been a subtle reversal of roles between the two of them. -3. something bad that happens and prevents somebody or something from succeeding in the way that was planned □ The campaign suffered an unexpected reversal.

reverse [rɪ'vɜːrs] ◇ *adj* [process, side] that is opposite to the one that is usually used, shown etc □ Here are the names in reverse order.

◇ *n* -1. AUTO the gear used in a vehicle to make it go backward. ■ to be in reverse to be in reverse gear □ Put the car in reverse and then back out. ■ to go into reverse to put a vehicle into reverse gear so that it moves backward. -2. the reverse the opposite □ It's the exact reverse of what you'd expect. □ "So you're happy with the result?" — "No, quite the reverse." -3. the reverse the less important side of a piece of paper, a coin etc □ On the reverse of the coin is an eagle.

◇ *vt* -1. AUTO [car, truck] to make <a vehicle> go backward □ He reversed the jeep out of the garage. -2. [trend, decision] to change <sthg> completely so that the opposite takes place □ policies aimed at reversing the decline of heavy industry. -3. [order, position] to change <sthg> so that things are in the opposite order. -4. to turn <sthg> over. -5. to reverse the charges to make a telephone call in which the person who receives it pays for it.

◇ *vi* AUTO [car, truck, driver] I reversed into the car behind me.

reverse-charge call *n* GB a telephone call which is paid for by the person who receives it.

reverse gear *n* AUTO = reverse.

reversible [rɪ'vɜːrsəbl] *adj* -1. [coat, jacket, raincoat] that can be worn with either side showing on the outside. -2. [policy, decision] that can be stopped or changed.

reversing light [rɪ'vɜːrsɪŋ-] *n* GB a white light on the back of a car, truck etc that shines when the vehicle is being reversed.

reversion [rɪ'vɜːrʃn] *n* a return to an earlier and usually worse way of behaving, thinking etc □ a reversion to his old attitudes.

revert [rɪ'vɜːˑt] *vi* **to revert to sthg** to return to sthg that used to exist or that one used to do, especially when this is not a good thing □ *As soon as Terence left hospital, he reverted to his old ways and started drinking again.*

review [rɪ'vjuː] ◇ *n* **-1.** [of somebody's salary, a situation] an examination of something to find out if it needs to be changed □ *the annual review of expenditure.* ■ **to come up for review** to be examined, usually at a fixed time or at regular intervals, to see if changes need to be made □ *My salary comes up for review next month.* ■ **to be under review** to be in the process of being examined to see if changes need to be made □ *Airport security measures are under review.* **-2.** [in a magazine, newspaper] an article in a newspaper, magazine etc, that gives an opinion on a book, television show etc □ *Her latest CD has had good reviews.* ◇ *vt* **-1.** [pension, salary, situation] to examine <sthg> to see if changes need to be made □ *We are reviewing our security procedures.* **-2.** [history, year] to look back at <sthg in the past> in order to see it in a different way or understand it better □ *We shall be reviewing the events of the past year.* **-3.** [play, movie, book] to give one's opinions about <sthg> in a newspaper or magazine article or on a TV or radio program □ *I've been asked to review an exhibition for an arts magazine.* **-4.** MILITARY to inspect <troops> formally. **-5.** US [subject, notes] to study <sthg> again, usually in preparation for an exam.

reviewer [rɪ'vjuːəʳ] *n* a person who reviews new books, plays etc.

revile [rɪ'vaɪl] *vt* [person, system] to express a great dislike or hatred of <sb/sthg> □ *the much-reviled poll tax.*

revise [rɪ'vaɪz] ◇ *vt* **-1.** [process, decision, forecast] to change <sthg> to make it better or more accurate □ *I was forced to revise my opinion of her very quickly.* **-2.** [text, manuscript] to read through <sthg> in order to correct mistakes and to improve it □ *The publishers are revising the text before the book is reprinted.* **-3.** GB [subject, notes] to study <sthg> again, usually to prepare for an exam. ◇ *vi* [student] to prepare for something, especially an exam, by studying □ *Have you started revising for your exams yet?*

revised [rɪ'vaɪzd] *adj* [estimate, version] that has been changed to make it better or more accurate □ *This is the revised edition of the text.*

revision [rɪ'vɪʒn] *n* **-1.** a change made to something, especially writing, that is intended to make it better □ *Several revisions had been made to the text.* **-2.** study in preparation for an exam □ *How much revision have you done?*

revisionist [rɪ'vɪʒnəst] ◇ *n* a person who examines again and questions the main beliefs of a political theory or religious system. ◇ *adj*: *a revisionist historian/theory.*

revisit [ˌriː'vɪzət] *vt* [town, birthplace] to go back to <a place> after being away from it for a long period.

revitalize, -ise [ˌriː'vaɪtəlaɪz] *vt* [industry, economy, system] to make <sthg> successful or ac-

tive again □ *Jackson seems revitalized after his six-month break.*

revival [rɪ'vaɪvl] *n* [of trade, the economy] the process of becoming active or successful again □ *There's been a revival of interest in early music.*

revive [rɪ'vaɪv] ◇ *vt* **-1.** [person] to make <sb> conscious again □ *They tried to revive him by splashing his face with water.* **-2.** [economy, business] to make <sthg> successful or strong again; [hope, interest] to make <sthg> active again □ *These latest developments have revived fears of an armed takeover.* □ *A drop of water will soon revive your plant.* **-3.** [tradition, fashion, play] to use or show again <sthg that has not been used or shown for a long time> □ *Efforts to revive the language have failed.* ◇ *vi* **-1.** [person] to become conscious again □ *They gave her an injection and she soon revived.* **-2.** [hopes, interest] to become active again □ *The economy is reviving.*

revoke [rɪ'vəʊk] *vt* [law, permission] to state formally that <sthg> is no longer official or legal (formal use) □ *The bar closed down after having its license revoked.*

revolt [rɪ'vəʊlt] ◇ *n* a situation in which a lot of people try to change the way their country, organization etc is governed, often using violence □ *an armed/a peasant revolt* □ *The Cabinet was now in open revolt against its leader.* ◇ *vt* to cause <sb> to have strong feelings of disgust □ *This kind of behavior must revolt all decent people.* ◇ *vi* to oppose the people in power in one's country, organization etc, often using violence □ *He was accused of inciting the populace to revolt.* □ *The chairman is afraid that board members will revolt.*

revolting [rɪ'vəʊltɪŋ] *adj* [smell, sight, idea] that one finds extremely unpleasant □ *Yuck! That tastes revolting!*

revolution [ˌrevə'luːʃn] *n* **-1.** POLITICS a successful attempt by a lot of people, using violence, to change the government or the political system of their country. **-2.** [in a way of doing things, thinking] a complete or important change in something □ *the sexual revolution* □ *There's been a revolution in the way scientists approach the problem.* **-3.** TECHNOLOGY a complete circular movement around a fixed point □ *It depends on the number of revolutions per minute.*

revolutionary [US revə'luːʃəneri, GB -ənri] (*pl* **revolutionaries**) ◇ *adj* **-1.** POLITICS [activities, leader] that is connected with or takes part in a revolution □ *They set about the changes with revolutionary zeal.* **-2.** [change, idea, process] that is very different and new □ *They claim to have invented a revolutionary new way of treating industrial waste.* ◇ *n* POLITICS a person who plans or supports a revolution.

Revolutionary War *n* = **American Revolution**.

revolutionize, -ise [ˌrevə'luːʃənaɪz] *vt* [industry, literature, thought] to cause a great change in <sthg> □ *This invention has revolutionized the way we communicate.*

revolve [rɪ'vɒlv] *vi* **-1.** to turn in a circular movement round a central point □ *The Earth* revolves (a)round the Sun. **-2. to revolve around sb/sthg** to have sb/sthg as the central or most important feature □ *His life revolves around his work.* □ *You think the world revolves around you, but that's where you're wrong.*

revolver [rɪ'vɒlvəʳ] *n* a small gun that can fire several bullets from a revolving magazine before it needs reloading.

revolving [rɪ'vɒlvɪŋ] *adj* [chair, stage] that turns in a circular movement around a fixed point.

revolving door *n* a door that consists of four panels at right angles to each other that turn around a central point when one pushes one of the panels.

revue [rɪ'vjuː] *n* a show in a theater, consisting of a mixture of songs, dances, and jokes.

revulsion [rɪ'vʌlʃn] *n* a very strong feeling of disgust □ *She looked at him with revulsion.*

reward [rɪ'wɔːʳd] ◇ *n* **-1.** something given to somebody in return for good work, help, good behavior etc □ *a reward for her bravery.* **-2.** a sum of money that is offered, usually by the police, for information on a missing person, criminal etc □ *They are offering a reward for his safe return.* ◇ *vt* [person] to give a reward to <sb> for something they have done □ *He was finally rewarded for his patience with a check for $2,000.*

rewarding [rɪ'wɔːʳdɪŋ] *adj* [job, career, book] that gives a lot of satisfaction and pleasure □ *I find this kind of work extremely rewarding.*

rewind [ˌriː'waɪnd] (*pt* & *pp* **rewound**) ◇ *vt* to make <a tape or cassette> wind backward to an earlier part. ◇ *vi*: □ *Please rewind after use.* ◇ *n* a button on a machine that makes it possible to rewind a tape or cassette. NOTE: Compare **fast-forward**.

rewire [ˌriː'waɪəʳ] *vt* [house, plug] to put a new set of electrical wires into <sthg>.

reword [ˌriː'wɜːʳd] *vt* [contract, sentence] to write or say <sthg> again using different words.

rework [ˌriː'wɜːʳk] *vt* [text, novel, idea] to make changes to <sthg> in order to improve it or make it suitable for another purpose.

rewound [ˌriː'waʊnd] *past tense & past participle of* **rewind**.

rewrite [ˌriː'raɪt] (*pt* **rewrote** [ˌriː'rəʊt], *pp* **rewritten** [ˌriː'rɪtn]) *vt* [essay, article, letter] to write <sthg> again, usually to improve it.

Reynolds ['renldz], **Sir Joshua** (1723–1792) a British artist, well known for his portraits.

RFC *n abbr of* **rugby football club**.

RFDS (*abbr of* **Royal Flying Doctor Service**) *n* **the RFDS** a medical service in Australia that visits patients in remote areas by plane.

Rh *abbr of* **Rhesus**.

rhapsody ['ræpsədɪ] (*pl* **rhapsodies**) *n* **-1.** MUSIC an emotional piece of music that sounds as if it has no formal structure. **-2.** the act of showing strong approval or great enthusiasm.

Rhesus ['riːsəs] *n* **to be Rhesus positive/negative** to have blood that contains/does not contain a substance that is important

during pregnancy and when making a blood transfusion.

rhetoric ['retərɪk] *n* things that somebody says or writes to persuade people of something □ *People are tired of politicians' rhetoric.*

rhetorical question [rɪˌtɒrɪkl-] *n* a question asked in order to create a particular effect, but which is not intended to be answered □ *I presume that was a rhetorical question.*

rheumatic [ruː'mætɪk] *adj* [person] who suffers from rheumatism.

rheumatism ['ruːmətɪzm] *n* a disease that causes pain and stiffness in one's joints or muscles □ *My whole family suffers from rheumatism.*

rheumatoid arthritis [ˌruːmətɔɪd-] *n* a disease that makes one's joints painful and stiff and causes them to swell.

Rhine [raɪn]: **the Rhine** a river in western Europe, flowing through Switzerland, Germany, and the Netherlands into the North Sea.

Rhineland ['raɪnlænd]: **the Rhineland** a region of western Germany around the Rhine.

rhinestone ['raɪnstəʊn] *n* a bright colorless stone that is intended to look like a diamond and is used in cheap jewelry.

rhino ['raɪnəʊ] (*pl* **rhino** OR **rhinos**) *n* = **rhinoceros**.

rhinoceros [raɪ'nɒsərəs] (*pl* **rhinoceros** OR **rhinoceroses**) *n* a very large animal from Africa or Asia that has a thick dark-gray skin and one or two horns on its nose.

Rhode Island [ˌrəʊd-] a state in New England, in the northeastern USA. It is the smallest US state. ABBREVIATION: RI. SIZE: 3,144 sq kms. POPULATION: 1,003,464 (*Rhode Islanders*). CAPITAL: Providence.

Rhodes [rəʊdz] a Greek island in the Aegean Sea, near the Turkish Coast. SIZE: 1,400 sq kms. POPULATION: 67,000. CAPITAL: Rhodes.

rhododendron [ˌrəʊdə'dendrən] *n* a large evergreen bush with large bright flowers.

rhombus ['rɒmbəs] *n* a shape that has four equal sides but is not a square.

Rhône [rəʊn]: **the Rhône** a river in southern Europe, flowing through Switzerland and France into the Mediterranean.

rhubarb ['ruːbɑːʳb] *n* a plant with broad leaves and juicy red stems that can be cooked and eaten □ *rhubarb pie/jam.*

rhyme [raɪm] ◇ *vi* [words, lines] to end with the same sound □ *"Card" rhymes with "hard".* □ *A lot of his poems are written in rhymed couplets.* ◇ *n* **-1.** [with another word] a word that rhymes with another word □ *Can you find a rhyme for "nose"?* **-2.** [for children] a short poem that uses words that rhyme and is usually written to amuse children □ *a witty little rhyme.* **-3.** [in poetry] the technique of using words that rhyme at the ends of the lines in poetry □ *Most of her poems are written in rhyme.*

rhyming slang ['raɪmɪŋ-] *n* GB a way of speaking in which some words are replaced by words or phrases that rhyme with them.

❦ RHYMING SLANG

Traditionally, rhyming slang in Britain is a way of speaking used by Cockneys in the East End of London. Instead of using a word people use a phrase that rhymes with the word; the phrase is then shortened by removing the rhyming word, so that "let's have a butcher's" is used to mean "let's have a look" (butcher's hook = look), and "use your loaf" is used to mean "use your head" (loaf of bread = head).

Although the East End of London and its way of life have changed a great deal, new rhyming slang is still being invented.

rhythm ['rıðm] *n* -1. [of music, a dancer, poem] a regular pattern of beats or stresses in music or words □ *Simon has no sense of rhythm.* -2. [of the seasons, sea] a regular repeated pattern of events or changes.

rhythm and blues *n* a style of popular music that developed from blues but which is played with electric guitars.

rhythmic(al) ['rıðmık(l)] *adj* [sound, beat] that has a clear rhythm □ *He had a rhythmic style of playing.*

RI *abbr of* **Rhode Island.**

rib [rıb] *n* -1. ANATOMY one of the 12 pairs of curved bones that run from one's spine to one's chest □ *I broke a rib in a riding accident.* -2. COOKING the rib of an animal used as food □ *barbecued ribs.* -3. CONSTRUCTION a curved piece of metal or wood, used as part of the structure of a building, aircraft etc.

ribald ['rıbəld] *adj* [remark, laughter, sense of humor] that is rude and funny.

ribbed [rıbd] *adj* [sweater, fabric] that has a raised pattern of parallel lines on it.

ribbon ['rıbən] *n* -1. a long narrow piece of material used for tying things or as decoration □ *a hair ribbon.* -2. a long narrow piece of cloth that provides the ink in a typewriter □ *typewriter ribbon.*

rib cage *n* the set of bones that enclose and protect one's lungs and other organs.

rice [raıs] *n* a food consisting of white or brown grains that come from a kind of cereal grown in wet warm places, e.g. in India and China □ *vegetables served on a bed of rice.*

rice field *n* a field in which rice is grown.

rice paper *n* a very thin paper that is used in baking and can be eaten.

rice pudding *n* a dessert made by baking rice with sugar and milk.

rich [rıtʃ] ◇ *adj* -1. [person, country, city] that has a lot of money or valuable property □ *He comes from a rich family.* □ *I'm not very rich at the moment.* -2. [deposit, source] that contains a large amount of a desirable or valuable substance □ *This country is rich in minerals.* □ *Citrus fruits are rich in vitamin C.* -3. [soil, land] that is good for growing plants in. -4. [meal, cake, sauce] that contains a lot of substances

that are hard to digest, e.g. sugar, eggs, and cream. -5. [color, sound] that is deep, warm, and full □ *He has a rich bass voice.* -6. [history, tradition] that is interesting and varied. -7. [fabric, clothes] expensive and beautiful □ *They were dressed in rich velvets and silks.* ◇ *npl* **the rich** rich people.

◆ **riches** *npl* -1. the valuable natural resources that are found in a place □ *the riches of the Earth.* -2. wealth □ *She accumulated great riches.*

Richard I [,rıtʃəˈdɔːˈfɜːrst] (1157–1199) King of England from 1189 to 1199. He spent most of his reign abroad, fighting in crusades. He is also called Richard the Lionheart(ed).

Richard III [,rıtʃəˈdɔːˈθɜːrd] (1452–1485) King of England from 1483 to 1485. He is believed to have ordered his nephews to be killed in the Tower of London.

richly ['rıtʃlı] *adv* -1. **richly decorated/furnished etc** decorated/furnished etc in an expensive and beautiful way. -2. **to deserve sthg richly** to deserve sthg completely □ *At last he got the praise he so richly deserved.*

richness ['rıtʃnəs] *n*: see **rich** □ *Her work captures the full richness of the autumn landscape.*

Richter scale ['rıktər-] *n* **the Richter scale** a scale from 0 to 8 for measuring the size of earthquakes □ *an earthquake reading 6 on the Richter scale.*

rickets ['rıkəts] *n* a disease that affects children who do not get enough vitamin D, causing their bones to become soft and bent.

rickety ['rıkətı] *adj* [table, staircase, bridge] that seems weak and likely to break if weight is put on it □ *He rides a rickety old bicycle.*

rickshaw ['rıkʃɔː] *n* a small vehicle for one or two passengers that is pulled by somebody running or cycling at the front and is used in parts of Asia.

ricochet ['rıkəʃeı] (*pt & pp* **ricocheted** OR **ricochetted,** *cont* **ricocheting** OR **ricochetting**) ◇ *vi* [bullet, stone] to bounce off a surface and move in a new direction □ *The bullet ricocheted off the wall.* ◇ *n* -1. an act of ricocheting. -2. an object, especially a bullet, that has ricocheted.

rid [rıd] (*pt* **rid** OR **ridded,** *pp* **rid,** *cont* **ridding**) ◇ *adj* **to be rid of sb/sthg** to be free of sb/sthg annoying or unpleasant □ *I was glad to be rid of them.* ■ **to get rid of sb/sthg** to remove sb/sthg that one does not want □ *Will you help me get rid of this junk?* □ *I've been trying to get rid of this guy for ages but he keeps pestering me.* ◇ *vt* **to rid sb/sthg of sthg** [of disease, poverty] to remove sthg so that it no longer has any effect on sb/sthg □ *We will rid the country of corruption.* □ *You must rid yourself of these delusions.*

riddance ['rıdəns] *n* **good riddance!** a phrase used to show that one is pleased that somebody or something has gone (informal use) □ *Goodbye, and good riddance!*

ridden ['rıdn] *past participle of* **ride.**

riddle ['rıdl] *n* -1. an amusing and difficult question or puzzle that one must guess the answer to □ *See if you can work out this riddle.*

-2. something that one cannot understand □ *This case is a complete riddle to me.*

riddled ['rɪdld] *adj* **to be riddled with sthg** [with holes, corruption] to be full of sthg that is ugly or bad □ *The walls were riddled with bullet holes.*

ride [raɪd] (*pt* **rode,** *pp* **ridden**) ◇ *n* **-1.** a trip in a vehicle or on a bicycle, horse etc □ *She went for a ride on her pony.* □ *It was a long car ride.* □ *It's only a ten-minute ride from here.* **-2.** a ride that somebody gives one as a favor □ *Do you want a ride to work?* **-3.** *phrase* **to take sb for a ride** to deceive or trick sb (informal use) □ *You've been taken for a ride, I'm afraid.* ◇ *vt* **-1.** [horse, bicycle, motorcycle] to go somewhere by sitting on and controlling <an animal or a vehicle> □ *I'd never ridden a camel before.* □ *Do you know how to ride a bike?* **-2.** to travel <a particular distance> on a horse, bicycle etc □ *We rode two miles.* **-3.** US [bus, elevator] to go somewhere in <a public vehicle> □ *Is it safe to ride the subway here?* ◇ *vi* **-1.** [on a horse] to ride a horse □ *Do you ride?* **-2.** [on a bicycle] to travel on a bicycle or motorcycle □ *I sometimes ride to work.* **-3. to ride in sthg** [in a car, bus] to travel in sthg □ *We rode to town in the truck.*
◆ **ride up** *vi* [skirt, dress] to move upward so that it is no longer in the right position.

rider ['raɪdər] *n* a person who is riding a horse, bicycle, or motorcycle □ *If the rider had been wearing a helmet, she would have survived.*

ridge [rɪdʒ] *n* **-1.** a long narrow piece of land that is higher than the area around it, especially one that forms the top of a hill or mountain □ *They camped on a small ridge.* □ *a mountain ridge.* **-2.** a long narrow line on a surface that is higher than the rest of the surface □ *The sea had left ridges in the sand.*

ridicule ['rɪdɪkjuːl] ◇ *n* the act of making fun of or laughing at somebody or something in a cruel way □ *Charlie soon became the object of ridicule.* ◇ *vt* [person, idea, theory] to make fun of <sb/sthg> in a cruel or unkind way □ *Mr Dobbs was ridiculed in the press for his remarks.*

ridiculous [rɪ'dɪkjələs] *adj* [person, idea, price] that one thinks is very silly and unreasonable □ *You look ridiculous in that hat.* □ *That's a ridiculous thing to say.*

ridiculously [rɪ'dɪkjələslɪ] *adv* **ridiculously low/ easy etc** extremely low/easy etc □ *The meal was ridiculously expensive.*

riding ['raɪdɪŋ] *n* the activity of riding a horse □ *We went riding.* □ *riding boots/lessons.*

riding crop *n* a short whip used by a horse rider.

riding habit *n* the clothing, consisting of a long dress, or a jacket and a long skirt, that women used to wear when they were riding horses.

riding school *n* a place where people go to learn to ride a horse.

rife [raɪf] *adj* **to be rife** to be very common □ *Drug abuse is rife among prisoners.* □ *Corruption is rife in the military.* ■ **to be rife with sthg** [with rumors, corruption] to be full of sthg bad or

unpleasant □ *The papers are rife with speculation that Barnes will quit.*

riffraff ['rɪfræf] *n* people who one does not like because they have a bad reputation □ *We don't want any riffraff moving into the area.*

rifle ['raɪfl] ◇ *n* a gun with a long barrel that one holds against one's shoulder to fire □ *a rifle shot.* ◇ *vt* [safe, drawers, wallet] to quickly search through <sthg>, often with the intention of stealing something.
◆ **rifle through** *vt fus* **to rifle through sthg** [handbag, wallet, drawer] to rifle sthg □ *I caught him rifling through my things.*

rifle range *n* a place where people can practice shooting with a rifle.

rift [rɪft] *n* **-1.** GEOLOGY a crack in the surface of the Earth. **-2.** a period of bad relations between two people, countries etc because of a disagreement □ *This resulted in a rift between mother and daughter.* □ *We're trying to heal the rift in our marriage.*

rig [rɪg] (*pt* & *pp* **rigged,** *cont* **rigging**) ◇ *n* a large structure used to find and get oil from the ground or the bottom of the sea □ *a drilling rig.* ◇ *vt* [election, game, competition] to arrange <sthg> dishonestly so that one gets the result one wants □ *The voting was rigged.*
◆ **rig up** *vt sep* **to rig sthg up** [device, aerial] to make sthg quickly, using the materials that are available.

rigging ['rɪgɪŋ] *n* the ropes that support the masts and sails of a ship.

right [raɪt] ◇ *adj* **-1.** [answer, decision, way] that is true, or the only one possible, and agrees with all the known facts □ *Are you sure we're going in the right direction?* □ *Do you have the right address?* □ *You made the right decision.* ■ **to be right about sthg** to say or think something that is true about sthg □ *You were right about that restaurant, it was fantastic!* ■ **to get sthg right** [answer, fact, story] to understand or describe sthg correctly □ *I got most of the questions right.* □ *She never gets my name right.* ■ **that's right** a phrase used to show that one agrees with what somebody has just said, or to confirm that what they have said is correct □ *"We need help, don't we." — "That's right."* □ *"So you're Phil Bevan?" — "That's right."* **-2. to put sthg right** to repair sthg that has been damaged □ *It's going to cost $400 to have the car put right.* **-3.** [action, attitude] that follows acceptable moral principles □ *I think he was right to refuse the money.* □ *Is it right for teachers to go on strike?* □ *I think you did the right thing.* **-4.** [hand, leg, ear] that is on the opposite side of the body to one's heart □ *Your right shoelace is undone.*
◇ *n* **-1.** behavior that follows acceptable moral principles □ *He can't tell right from wrong.* ■ **to be in the right** to be morally or legally justified in doing or saying something □ *We believe we're in the right and we'll go to court if necessary.* **-2.** [to freedom, information, a vote] something that one should be able to have or do because it is morally or legally correct □ *You have the right to remain silent.* □ *He has no right to treat you like that!* □ *human/*

civil rights. ■ **to be within one's rights to do sthg** to be morally or legally justified in doing sthg □ *You would be perfectly within your rights to claim compensation.* **-3.** the position or direction that corresponds to east when one is facing north □ *On your right is the Empire State building.* □ *It's the big house to the right of the church.* □ *Take the first road on the right.* **-4.** [in a car] a turn to the right □ *Make a right at the traffic lights.*

◇ *adv* **-1.** [pronounce, do, guess] correctly □ *No one ever spells my name right.* **-2.** [move, turn, look] to the right □ *The car waited at the lights, then headed right down Albany Street.* □ *Turn right, then left at the bottom of the street.* **-3.** a word used to give special force to the exact place, time, or distance being talked about □ *Stay right here.* □ *The phone rang right in the middle of lunch.* □ *Go right to the end of the street.* □ *I said that right from the start.* **-4.** immediately □ *I'll be right with you.* □ *I took a vacation right after my exams.* ■ **right away** immediately □ *I'll do it right away.* ■ **right now** at this particular moment □ *He's in a meeting right now.* □ *Does it have to be done right now?* **-5.** a word used to say that one has understood □ *"So you put the paper in here." — "Right."*

◇ *vt* **-1.** [wrong, injustice] to do something to end <an unfair or harmful situation>. **-2. to right itself** [ship, boat, raft] to return to an upright position.

◇ *excl* a word used at the beginning of a sentence to attract somebody's attention □ *Right, how can I help you?*

♦ **Right** *n* **the Right** POLITICS political groups that are in favor of private ownership of wealth, less control of trade and industry by the state, and little social or political change □ *the rise of the extreme Right.*

♦ **by rights** *adv* a phrase used to say that something should be true but is not □ *By rights it should only have taken us two hours to get there, but in fact we took three.*

♦ **in one's own right** *adv* because of one's own abilities, actions etc and not because one is connected with another person or group □ *Though married to a famous actor, she is in fact a talented performer in her own right.*

right angle *n* an angle of 90 degrees, equal to any of the corners of a square. ■ **to be at right angles** [two things] to make an angle of 90 degrees at the point where they join each other □ *The tables were arranged at right angles.* □ *a line at right angles to the base of the triangle.*

righteous ['raɪtʃəs] *adj* [person, anger] that one thinks is morally good □ *full of righteous indignation.*

rightful ['raɪtfl] *adj* [owner, share, place] according to a moral or legal right □ *He has finally assumed his rightful position as world champion.*

rightfully ['raɪtflɪ] *adv: see* **rightful** □ *The money is rightfully mine/his.*

right-hand *adj* [side, lane, page] that is on or to the right of something □ *Put your name in the top right-hand corner of the page.*

right-hand drive *adj* [car, vehicle] that has its

steering wheel on the right-hand side and is used in countries where vehicles drive on the left-hand side of the road.

right-handed [-'hændəd] *adj* [person] who uses their right hand to do things, such as write or throw a ball, rather than their left hand □ *I always thought you were right-handed.*

right-hand man *n* **sb's right-hand man** the person who is sb's most useful and important assistant and who they trust the most □ *He was widely regarded as the Governor's right-hand man.*

rightly ['raɪtlɪ] *adv* **-1.** [say, remark, guess] correctly □ *You may believe, rightly or wrongly, that this is for the best.* □ *As Heather very rightly pointed out, it's not enough just to throw more money at the problem.* **-2.** [behave, act] in an appropriate or morally correct manner □ *I think you acted rightly in telling him.* **-3.** [angry, upset, worried] with a good reason □ *She was furious, and rightly so.* □ *The islanders quite rightly feel betrayed.*

right-minded [-'maɪndəd] *adj* [person] who has ideas and beliefs that one thinks are correct □ *All right-minded people will object to these proposals.*

right of way *n* **-1.** AUTO the right of a vehicle to move along a road while other vehicles have to stop and wait, e.g. at an intersection or traffic circle □ *Who has right of way here?* **-2.** LAW a legal right for somebody to walk along a public path across private land □ *'No right of way.'*

right-on *adj* GB [person, attitude] that shows a concern for people's rights, social problems etc that one thinks is too fashionable (informal use) □ *It's very right-on to buy Nicaraguan coffee.*

rights issue *n* GB an issue of new shares that is offered by a company to people who already hold shares in the company at a lower price.

right-thinking *adj* [person] who has ideas and beliefs that one thinks are morally correct □ *All right-thinking people must be appalled by this.*

right wing *n* **the right wing** the members of a political group whose ideas are closest to conservatism and capitalism □ *Too much power has gone to the right wing of the party.*

♦ **right-wing** *adj* [person, government, policy] that supports the political ideals of conservatism and capitalism □ *He has very right-wing views.*

NOTE: Compare **left wing**.

right-winger *n* a person who holds right-wing views.

rigid ['rɪdʒəd] *adj* **-1.** [sheet, plastic, card] that is hard and cannot be bent easily □ *My hands were frozen rigid.* **-2.** [control, rule] that is very strict and cannot be changed □ *The rigid guidelines make it difficult for staff to use their discretion.* **-3.** [person] who has strong opinions, ideas etc that they refuse to change □ *He has very rigid views on sex before marriage.*

rigidity [rɪ'dʒɪdətɪ] *n* [of a substance, rule] *see* **rigid** □ *the rigidity of the caste system.*

rigidly ['rɪdʒədlɪ] *adv* **-1.** [look, remain, stare] without moving or changing position □ *Her face was fixed rigidly into a smile.* **-2.** in a harsh or strict way □ *You needn't interpret the rules too rigidly.*

rigmarole ['rɪgmərovl] *n* something that one thinks is too complicated and takes too long to do (informal and disapproving use) □ *I'm not going through all that rigmarole again.*

rigor US, **rigour** GB ['rɪgər] *n* the quality of being thorough.
◆ **rigors** *npl* **the rigors of sthg** [of life, a course] the things that make sthg hard or unpleasant □ *the rigors of an Arctic winter.*

rigor mortis [-'mɔːʳtəs] *n* the process or state in which the joints and muscles stiffen in the body of a dead person or animal □ *Rigor mortis had already begun to set in.*

rigorous ['rɪgərəs] *adj* [law, use, test] that is careful and complete □ *The vehicle will be subjected to a rigorous safety inspection.*

rigorously ['rɪgərəslɪ] *adv* [apply, use, test] *see* **rigorous.**

rigour *n* GB = **rigor.**

rile [raɪl] *vt* to make <sb> angry □ *It really riles me that people can get away with this sort of thing.*

rim [rɪm] *n* **-1.** [of cup, glass, bowl] the top edge of something that contains liquid □ *Fill it up to the rim.* **-2.** [of glasses, wheel] the outer edge of a round object □ *a pair of spectacles with red rims.*

Rimsky-Korsakov [ˌrɪmskɪ'kɔːʳsəkɒf], **Nikolai** (1844–1908) a Russian composer whose best-known work is *Scheherazade.*

rind [raɪnd] *n* **-1.** [of a lemon, orange] the thick outer skin of some kinds of fruit □ *Grate the rind onto a plate.* **-2.** [of cheese, bacon] the hard layer on the outside of some kinds of food □ *It's better to cut the rind off.*

ring [rɪŋ] (*vt senses 1 & 2 & vi, pt* **rang,** *pp* **rung,** *vt senses 3 & 4, pt & pp* **ringed**) ◇ *n* **-1. to give sb a ring** to phone sb □ *I'll give you a ring on Thursday.* **-2.** [of a bell, phone] the sound made by a bell, phone etc □ *His favorite sound is the ring of the cash register.* **-3. a ring of truth** something that one thinks is probably true □ *The story has a ring of truth about it.* ■ **a familiar ring** something that one thinks one has heard before □ *His name has a familiar ring.* **-4.** [with a hole] an object that is round and has a round hole in the middle □ *fried onion rings.* **-5.** [on one's finger] a round band of metal worn on a finger as a piece of jewelry, sometimes with a precious stone on it □ *a diamond ring.* **-6.** [of people, chairs] a group of people or things arranged in a circle □ *I was surrounded by a ring of faces.* **-7.** [for boxing, a circus] a space surrounded by seats in which a contest or entertainment takes place □ *Some spectators climbed into the ring.* **-8.** [of criminals] a group of people working together in an illegal activity □ *a crime/drugs ring.* **-9. to run rings around sb** [around the opposition, police] to be much better and more skillful at doing something than sb □ *Sally*

runs rings around everyone when it comes to using computer software.
◇ *vt* **-1.** [bell, doorbell] to make <sthg> make a sound □ *Just ring the bell and I'll come down to let you in.* **-2.** GB to phone <sb> □ *He said he'd ring me tomorrow.* **-3.** [word, name, advertisement] to draw a circle around <sthg> on a page □ *All the important numbers are ringed in red.* **-4.** [building, area] to surround <a place> □ *The house was ringed with police officers.*
◇ *vi* **-1.** [bell, phone, alarm] to make a loud sound □ *Suddenly the doorbell rang.* **-2.** [on a doorbell] to ring a doorbell □ *I rang twice but nobody came to the door.* □ *Try ringing on the other bell.* **-3.** [for attention] to ring a bell in order to tell somebody that one has arrived e.g. in a hotel or that one wants something □ *He rang for attention/the butler.* **-4. to ring with sthg** [with noise, a sound] to be filled with sthg □ *The room was ringing with laughter.* **-5. to ring true** [story, excuse] to seem true or real □ *All his macho talk just doesn't ring true.* **-6.** GB to phone □ *He rang to say he was going to be late.*

◆ **ring back** ◇ *vt sep* **to ring sb back** GB to call sb by phone again or later □ *I'll ring you back when he's gone.* ◇ *vi: She promised to ring back hours ago.*

◆ **ring off** *vi* GB to end a telephone call by putting down the receiver □ *I tried to explain but he just rang off.*

◆ **ring out** *vi* **-1.** [voice, bell] to make a loud clear sound □ *The church bells rang out in the town square.* **-2.** GB [person] to make a phone call to somebody outside the building where one is working □ *I don't think you can ring out from this extension.*

◆ **ring up** *vt sep* **to ring sb up** GB to call sb by phone.

ring binder *n* a folder containing loose sheets of paper held in place by metal rings that can be opened and closed.

ring finger *n* the third finger of one's left or right hand, on which an engagement or wedding ring is worn in some countries.

ringing ['rɪŋɪŋ] ◇ *adj* [tone, note] loud and clear □ *I recognized her loud, ringing voice.* ◇ *n* the sound made by a bell, telephone etc that keeps ringing.

ringing tone *n* GB the sound heard by somebody who has dialed a phone number, when the other phone is ringing □ *I've got the ringing tone, but no one's answering.*

ringleader ['rɪŋliːdəʳ] *n* a person who leads a group of people who have caused trouble or done something illegal.

ringlet ['rɪŋlət] *n* a long loose curl of hair that hangs down.

ringmaster [US 'rɪŋmæstr, GB -mɑːstə] *n* the person in a circus ring whose job is to introduce each performer to the audience.

ring road *n* GB a road that goes around a city so that traffic can avoid the center.

ringside ['rɪŋsaɪd] *n* **the ringside** the area around the edge of a boxing ring or a ring in a circus □ *a ringside seat.*

ringway ['rɪŋweɪ] *n* GB a ring road.

ringworm ['rɪŋwɜːᵊm] *n* a disease that causes red round marks to appear on one's skin, especially on one's head.

rink [rɪŋk] *n* a surface, especially indoors, on which people skate or roller-skate □ *an ice rink.*

rinse [rɪns] ◇ *vt* [dishes, clothes, hair] to wash <sthg> quickly in clean water, especially to remove soap; [soap, dirt] to remove <sthg> from an object by washing it in clean water □ *Would you mind rinsing these plates?* □ *Rinse the soap off that shirt, would you?* ■ **to rinse one's mouth out** to clean one's mouth using water. ◇ *n* an act of rinsing something □ *Give your hands a good rinse.*

Rio ['riːoʊ]: **Rio (de Janiero)** a city in southeastern Brazil. A major port and tourist center, it is famous for its beaches and its annual carnival. POPULATION: 5,336,179.

Rio Grande [,riːoʊ'grænd]: **the Rio Grande** a river in North America that forms part of the border between Mexico and the USA and flows into the Gulf of Mexico.

riot ['raɪət] ◇ *n* a situation in which a large group of people behave in an uncontrolled and often violent way in a public place □ *Serious riots have broken out in the center of Los Angeles.* ■ **to run riot** to behave in a violent and uncontrolled way □ *Meanwhile, the children were running riot in the garden.* ◇ *vi* [people, students] to take part in a riot.

rioter ['raɪətəʳ] *n* a person who takes part in a riot □ *Six rioters were arrested.*

rioting ['raɪətɪŋ] *n* a riot or riots □ *There were fears that the verdicts would lead to rioting.*

riotous ['raɪətəs] *adj* [behavior, mob, party] that is noisy and wild □ *We were having a riotous time.*

riot police *n* police who are trained and equipped for dealing with riots.

riot shield *n* a large, transparent, curved shield used by police when dealing with violent crowds.

rip [rɪp] (*pt* & *pp* **ripped**, *cont* **ripping**) ◇ *vt* **-1.** [paper, page] to tear <sthg> quickly or violently □ *She ripped the newspaper into strips.* **-2. to rip sthg off/down etc** [clothes, mask, bandage] to remove sthg by pulling it off/down etc □ *He ripped off his shirt.* □ *She ripped the notice from the board.* ◇ *vi* [shirt, skirt] to become badly torn □ *Then his pants ripped while he was dancing.* ◇ *n* **-1.** a long tear or split in a piece of paper or cloth □ *My shirt has a great big rip in it.* **-2.** AUS a fast ocean current, dangerous to swimmers.

◆ **rip off** *vt sep* (informal use) **-1. to rip sb off** to cheat sb by charging them too much money for something □ *You've been ripped off, I reckon.* **-2. to rip sthg off** [design, idea, product] to copy sthg from somebody else in order to make money from it.

◆ **rip up** *vt sep* **to rip sthg up** to destroy sthg by tearing it violently into pieces □ *She then ripped the contract up in front of me.*

RIP (*abbr of* **rest in peace**) a word usually written on a gravestone.

ripcord ['rɪpkɔːᵊd] *n* a cord that one pulls to open a parachute.

ripe [raɪp] *adj* [fruit, crop, cheese] that is fully grown or developed and ready to be eaten □ *Don't eat those peaches, they're not ripe yet.* ■ **to be ripe for sthg** [for development, exploitation] to be ready for sthg □ *a small company ripe for takeover.*

ripen ['raɪpn] ◇ *vt* to make <fruit, crops> etc ripe. ◇ *vi* [fruit, crop, cheese] *The grapes ripened early this year.*

ripeness ['raɪpnəs] *n* the quality or state of being ripe.

rip-off *n* something that one feels one has paid too much money for so that one feels cheated, e.g. because it is of lower quality than one expected (informal use) □ *That meal was a complete rip-off!*

ripple ['rɪpl] *n* **-1.** one of many very small waves on the surface of water, caused by the wind or by something that has dropped into it □ *The boat created dozens of little ripples in the water.* **-2. a ripple of laughter/applause** laughter/applause from a group of people that starts quietly, becomes gradually louder, and then becomes quiet again □ *A ripple of excited conversation spread through the crowd.*

rip-roaring *adj* **-1.** [time, party] that is very exciting and noisy. **-2. a rip-roaring success** a very great success.

Rip van Winkle [,rɪpvæn'wɪŋkl] a character in a story by Washington Irving. He falls asleep for 20 years and wakes up to find that everything has changed.

rise [raɪz] (*pl* **rose**, *pp* **risen** ['rɪzn]) ◇ *n* **-1.** [in quantity, cost] an increase in the quantity, amount, cost etc of something □ *a rise in inflation.* **-2.** [of a politician, celebrity] the process of becoming more powerful, successful, famous etc □ *his rise to fame.* **-3.** [of a hill] an upward slope □ *They live just over the next rise.* **-4. to give rise to sthg** to cause sthg □ *The announcement has given rise to a lot of speculation concerning the state of their finances.* **-5.** GB [in salary] an increase in salary □ *a pay/wage rise.* ◇ *vi* **-1.** [tide, water, balloon] to move to a higher position or level □ *The bubbles rise to the surface of the liquid.* **-2.** [sun, moon] to appear above the horizon □ *The sun rose at 6:13 am.* **-3.** [wage, temperature, unemployment] to increase in amount, degree, cost etc □ *If prices continue to rise at this rate, many people won't be able to afford basic necessities.* □ *The pound rose against the dollar.* **-4.** [person, animal] to stand up □ *Franz rose to greet me.* **-5.** [person] to get out of bed (literary use). **-6.** [street, slope] to slope upward □ *The ground rose steeply above the fields.* **-7.** [voice, note] to become louder; to become higher in pitch □ *Susan's voice rose to an angry yell.* **-8. to rise to sthg** [to a challenge, occasion] to be successful in dealing with sthg difficult □ *It's a tough job, but I am sure Gareth will rise to the challenge.* **-9.** [people, peasants] to rebel against the people in authority □ *They finally rose against the government in February 1964.* **-10.** [politician, officer] to become more important, successful, or powerful by getting a higher position or status □ *The general had risen to the top by the age of 38.* **-11.** [bread, cake, dough] to become larger and rounder while it is cooked in an oven or because it contains yeast □ *Leave it to rise for 15 minutes.*

◆ **rise above** *vt fus* **to rise above sthg** [jealousy, criticism] not to let oneself be affected by sthg unpleasant □ *The office was full of gossip, but Laurence was able to rise above it all.*

riser ['raɪzə^r] *n* **an early/a late riser** a person who always gets up early/late in the morning.

risible ['rɪzəbl] *adj* [idea, offer, attempt] that one thinks is silly or very bad (formal use) □ *They were offering a risible sum of money.*

rising ['raɪzɪŋ] ◇ *adj* **-1.** [ground, tide, sun] that is becoming higher. **-2.** [inflation, taxes, temperature] that is increasing in amount, degree, cost etc □ *Rising prices are driving business away.* **-3.** [star, politician] who is becoming more successful, famous, or important □ *a rising young actor.* ◇ *n* a rebellion against a government or ruler □ *an armed rising.*

rising damp *n* GB a condition in which moisture rises from the ground into the walls of a building and damages them.

risk [rɪsk] ◇ *n* **-1.** a possibility that something unpleasant or dangerous might happen □ *There is a fire risk* OR *a risk of fire.* □ *There are a number of serious risks involved.* ▪ **to run the risk of sthg** to do something that might make sthg dangerous or unpleasant happen □ *I haven't been back to the club because I don't want to run the risk of meeting Tammy again.* ▪ **to take a risk** to do something that might make something dangerous or unpleasant happen □ *You have to take risks in this business.* □ *That's a risk we'll have to take.* ▪ **at one's own risk** so that one takes responsibility for any loss or damage oneself □ *'All valuables are left here at owner's risk.'* ▪ **at the risk of doing sthg...** a phrase used to warn people that what one is about to say might do sthg that one does not want □ *At the risk of sounding silly, have you checked it's plugged in?* **-2.** something or somebody that could make something dangerous happen □ *The gas emissions are a serious health risk.*

◇ *vt* **-1.** [health, life] to put <sthg> in danger □ *You cannot risk the lives of hundreds of people just for the sake of profit.* **-2.** [defeat, humiliation] to do something that one knows might make <sthg dangerous or unpleasant> happen □ *You risk losing a lot of business if you relocate outside the city.* ▪ **to risk it** to do something that involves a risk □ *You could wait a few more days, but I wouldn't like to risk it.*

◆ **at risk** *adj* in danger □ *The system is putting people's lives at risk.* □ *These are the children most at risk.*

risk capital *n* capital invested in stock issued by a company.

risk-taking *n* the activity of deliberately taking risks, e.g. to make money or for sport.

risky ['rɪskɪ] (*compar* **riskier**, *superl* **riskiest**) *adj* [business, venture] that is dangerous or likely to fail □ *I wouldn't invest in Agrotec — it's too risky.*

risotto [rɪ'zɒtoʊ] (*pl* **risottos**) *n* an Italian dish made of rice cooked with meat, vegetables etc.

risqué [US rɪ'skeɪ, GB 'rɪskeɪ] *adj* [joke, humor] that is slightly rude, usually because it mentions sex □ *I've been told her act's quite risqué.*

rissole ['rɪsoʊl] *n* GB a type of food made from small pieces of chopped meat, fish, or vegetables that are pressed together into a round shape and fried.

rite [raɪt] *n* a ceremony, often religious, that is always carried out in the same way □ *initiation rites* □ *the marriage rite.*

ritual ['rɪtʃʊəl] ◇ *n* a ceremony or series of actions that is always done in a particular way, especially as part of a religious or social occasion □ *It's all part of his morning ritual.* □ *a purification ritual.* ◇ *adj* [murder, dance] that is done as part of a ritual.

rival ['raɪvl] (US *pt* & *pp* **rivaled**, *cont* **rivaling**, GB *pt* & *pp* **rivalled**, *cont* **rivalling**) ◇ *n* a person, group, organization etc that one is competing or fighting against □ *"Business Day" is one of our main rivals.* □ *Joe and Sam were once rivals in love.* ◇ *adj: a rival company/bid/team.* ◇ *vt* to have as much of a particular quality as <sb/sthg else> □ *Few can rival him for* OR *in stamina.*

rivalry ['raɪvlrɪ] *n* a feeling of competition between people or groups that exists over a period of time □ *A spirit of intense rivalry had grown up between them.*

river ['rɪvə^r] *n* a wide stream of fresh water that flows across land, usually into the sea □ *the River Po* OR *Po River.*

river bank *n* the land along the side of a river.

riverbed ['rɪvə^rbed] *n* the surface of the ground at the bottom of a river.

riverside ['rɪvə^rsaɪd] *n* **the riverside** the area of land near the banks of a river.

rivet ['rɪvət] ◇ *n* a type of metal pin used to fasten two pieces of metal, material etc together. ◇ *vt* **-1.** to fasten <sthg> with rivets. **-2.** **to be riveted** to watch or listen to something very carefully because it is very interesting □ *The audience was riveted throughout the performance.*

riveting ['rɪvətɪŋ] *adj* [book, story, program] that one thinks is very interesting □ *Let's face it, the lecture wasn't exactly riveting.*

Riviera [ˌrɪvɪ'eərə]: **the Riviera** the Mediterranean coast of southeastern France and northwestern Italy. The two parts are sometimes referred to as the French Riviera and the Italian Riviera.

Riyadh [US riː'jɑːd, GB 'riːæd] the capital of Saudi Arabia. POPULATION: 1,308,000.

RMT (*abbr of* **National Union of Rail, Maritime and Transport Workers**) *n* **the RMT** a British labor union for transportation workers.

RN *n* -1. *abbr of* **Royal Navy**. -2. *abbr of* **registered nurse**.

RNA (*abbr of* **ribonucleic acid**) *n* an important chemical that is in the cells of all living things.

RNLI (*abbr of* **Royal National Lifeboat Institution**) *n* **the RNLI** a British voluntary organization that raises money for the lifeboat service.

RNZAF *n abbr of* **Royal New Zealand Air Force**.

RNZN *n abbr of* **Royal New Zealand Navy**.

roach [rəʊtʃ] (*pl sense 1* **roaches**, *sense 2* **roach** OR **roaches**) *n* -1. a cockroach. -2. a European freshwater fish.

road [rəʊd] *n* a long piece of ground, usually covered with tarmac, concrete, or stones, that is designed for vehicles to travel on □ *It's about three hours by road.* □ *Be careful when you cross the road.* □ *road travel* □ *The signals are to tell other road users where you intend to go.* ■ **on the road** traveling by car, bus etc, usually over a long distance □ *We've been on the road for over three hours, we must be nearly there.* ■ **on the road to sthg** [to victory, recovery, success] on the way to sthg □ *He's on the road to ruin, that boy.*

road atlas *n* a book of maps showing the main roads in a particular country, area, town etc.

roadblock [ˈrəʊdblɒk] *n* a place on a road where soldiers, the police etc stop vehicles to search them or stop all vehicles from passing □ *The police set up roadblocks around the city.*

road-fund licence *n* in Britain, a license displayed on the windshield of a vehicle to show that one has paid road tax.

road haulage *n* = **haulage**.

road hog *n* a person who drives in a way that shows no consideration for other drivers (informal and disapproving use).

roadholding [ˈrəʊdhəʊldɪŋ] *n* the ability of a vehicle to travel around bends or on wet surfaces without skidding.

roadhouse [ˈrəʊdhaʊs, *pl* -haʊzɪz] *n* US a café or restaurant on a main road, especially in the country.

roadie [ˈrəʊdɪ] *n* a person whose job is to carry musical equipment and prepare it before concerts for a group of musicians.

road map *n* a map that shows the roads in a particular area.

road rage *n* the feeling of anger that drivers have when other people drive in a dangerous or annoying way, and that can lead to violence.

road safety *n* the rules that help people travel safely on roads.

road sense *n* the ability of somebody to make good decisions when using or crossing roads, so that they avoid accidents □ *good/poor road sense.*

roadshow [ˈrəʊdʃəʊ] *n* a group of people that travels around the country to perform, give talks etc for entertainment or advertising.

roadside [ˈrəʊdsaɪd] *n* **the roadside** the area at the side of a road □ *a roadside diner/restaurant/stall* □ *We waited by the roadside.*

road sign *n* a sign on a road that gives information to road users.

roadsweeper [ˈrəʊdswiːpəʳ] *n* a truck with brushes underneath it that is specially designed to clean roads.

road tax *n* in Britain, a tax that somebody who owns a vehicle must pay to be allowed to drive or leave it on a public road.

road test *n* -1. a test in which a car is driven to see if it is easy, safe etc to use. -2. US an official test of a driver's ability to control a car.

◆ **road-test** *vt* to give <a car> a road test.

road train *n* AUS a large truck that pulls a number of linked trailers behind it.

roadway [ˈrəʊdweɪ] *n* the part of a road that is used by moving vehicles.

roadwork [ˈrəʊdwɜːrk] US *n*, **roadworks** [ˈrəʊdwɜːks] GB *npl* repairs that are being made to a road □ *'Roadworks ahead.'*

roadworthy [ˈrəʊdwɜːˈðɪ] *adj* [vehicle] that is in a good enough condition to be driven on a road.

roam [rəʊm] ◇ *vt* [countryside, town] to walk or travel all over <a large area> □ *I roamed the streets of Berlin in search of somewhere to stay.* ◇ *vi: I loved roaming around the town.*

roar [rɔːʳ] ◇ *vi* -1. [lion, wind, engine] to make a deep loud noise □ *Planes roared overhead as they spoke.* -2. [person] to shout in a very loud voice that shows strong feelings □ *The crowd roared as Lewis crossed the finishing line.* ■ **to roar with laughter** to laugh very loudly. ◇ *vt* to say <sthg> in a very loud voice □ *"You will do nothing of the kind!" he roared.* ◇ *n* [of a lion, engine, person] a deep loud sound □ *We could barely hear each other above the roar of the traffic.*

roaring [ˈrɔːrɪŋ] ◇ *adj* -1. [traffic, wind] that is very loud. -2. **a roaring fire** a fire that is very hot and has big flames □ *They sat in front of a roaring log fire.* ■ **a roaring success** a very great success. ■ **to do a roaring trade** to sell a lot of things very quickly. ◇ *adv* **to be roaring drunk** to be very drunk (informal use).

roast [rəʊst] ◇ *vt* -1. to cook <meat, potatoes> etc in an oven or over a fire. -2. to cook <coffee beans, nuts> etc in order to dry them. ◇ *adj* [meat, potato] that has been roasted □ *They have roast lamb for dinner every Sunday.* ◇ *n* a large piece of meat that has been roasted □ *We're having a roast for lunch.*

roast beef *n* a joint of beef that has been roasted.

roasting [ˈrəʊstɪŋ] (informal use) ◇ *adj* very hot □ *Can we open the window? It's roasting in here.* ◇ *adv* **roasting hot** extremely hot □ *It was roasting hot that day.*

roasting pan US, **roasting tin** *n* a metal container for putting meat in when it is being roasted.

rob [rɒb] (*pt & pp* **robbed**, *cont* **robbing**) *vt* -1. [person, store, bank] to steal money or property from <sb/sthg> □ *The local kids go around robbing cars.* □ *They robbed him of all his money.* **-2. to rob sb of sthg** to cause sb not to have sthg any more □ *James was robbed of his opportunity by an unfortunate accident.*

robber ['rɒbəʳ] *n* a person who steals money or property from a bank, store, vehicle etc, often by using force or weapons □ *a bank robber.*

robbery ['rɒbərɪ] (*pl* **robberies**) *n* the crime of stealing money or property from a bank, store, vehicle etc, often by using force or weapons □ *The gang carried out a series of armed robberies.*

robe [roʊb] *n* **-1.** [of a priest, judge, monarch] a long loose piece of clothing worn on official occasions. **-2.** US a long loose piece of clothing, similar to a coat, that one wears at home in the morning before getting dressed or at night before going to bed.

Robeson ['roʊbsən], **Paul** (1898–1976) a black US actor and singer who was one of the first to become famous outside the USA. His most famous song was *Ol' Man River.*

Robespierre [US 'roʊbzpɪr, GB -pɪə], **Maximilien de** (1758–1794) a French politician who was one of the leaders of the French Revolution.

robin ['rɒbən] *n* a North American bird with orange-red feathers on the front of its body; a smaller European bird similar to this.

Robin ['rɒbən] a boy in children's comics who helps Batman to fight crime.

Robin Hood [-'hʊd] in English folk stories, the leader of a group of outlaws living in Sherwood Forest, in the English Midlands, in the 13th century. They stole money from the rich and gave it to the poor.

Robinson Crusoe [,rɒbənsən'kruːsoʊ] the main character in the novel *Robinson Crusoe* by Daniel Defoe. He is a sailor who lives on a desert island after his ship sinks.

robot ['roʊbɒt] *n* a machine that is usually controlled by a computer and is designed to do the tasks a person usually does.

robotics [roʊ'bɒtɪks] *n* the science of designing and building robots.

Rob Roy [,rɒb'rɔɪ] (1671–1734) a Scottish outlaw. According to popular stories he was brave in battle and generous to the poor.

robust [roʊ'bʌst] *adj* **-1.** [person, health, economy] that is strong and in good condition. **-2.** [criticism, defense] that is expressed in a forceful way.

rock [rɒk] ◇ *n* **-1.** the hard substance that is part of the Earth's surface; a large piece of this substance □ *We climbed over the vast expanse of rock.* **-2.** US a stone of any size □ *He picked up a rock and threw it.* **-3.** MUSIC rock music □ *a rock band/group/concert.* **-4.** GB a hard candy sold in long round sticks, especially at seaside resorts. ◇ *vt* **-1.** [baby, boat, chair] to make <sb/sthg> move gently and regularly from side to side or backward and forward □ *I rocked the crib until Tommy fell asleep.* **-2.** [person, organization] to shock <sb/

sthg> □ *the scandal that rocked the nation.* ◇ *vi* [boat, chair] *He rocked gently on his heels.*

◆ **on the rocks** *adj* **-1.** served with ice □ *whiskey on the rocks* **-2. to be on the rocks** [relationship, love] to be in a bad state and unlikely to last □ *Their marriage is on the rocks.*

rock and roll *n* a type of popular music that began in the 1950s and has a strong loud beat and uses electric guitars.

rock bottom *n* the lowest possible level □ *His spirits are at rock bottom.* ■ **to hit** OR **reach rock bottom** [person, mood] to become extremely unhappy; [price, level, standard] to become extremely low; [family, economy] to become extremely poor □ *He really reached rock bottom when Alison left him.* □ *House prices have reached rock bottom.* □ *After Arthur lost his job the family fortunes really reached rock bottom.*

◆ **rock-bottom** *adj* [price, level] that is very low □ *We offer rock-bottom prices on all hi-fi equipment.*

rock cake *n* GB a small round cake that has a rough surface and contains currants.

rock climber *n* a person who climbs the steep sides of cliffs or mountains as a hobby or sport.

rock-climbing *n* the sport or hobby of climbing the steep sides of cliffs or mountains □ *I used to go rock-climbing on weekends.*

Rockefeller ['rɒkəfeləʳ], **John D.** (1839–1935) a US businessman who became extremely rich and gave a lot of money to the arts and education.

rocker ['rɒkəʳ] *n* a rocking chair. ■ **to be off one's rocker** to be crazy (informal use) □ *You must be off your rocker if you think I'm going in there.*

rockery ['rɒkərɪ] (*pl* **rockeries**) *n* a part of a garden with small ornamental rocks and plants growing between and around them.

rocket ['rɒkət] ◇ *n* **-1.** SPACE a vehicle shaped like a long tube that is used for traveling away from the Earth into space □ *a space rocket.* **-2.** MILITARY a missile. **-3.** [for a firework display] a firework shaped like a space rocket. **-4.** [in salad] a plant with small dark-green leaves that have a peppery taste and are eaten raw in salads. ◇ *vi* [price, sales] to increase quickly.

rocket launcher [-lɔːntʃəʳ] *n* a mobile device used by soldiers for firing rockets.

rock face *n* a side of a hill or mountain that is very steep and made of solid rock.

rockfall ['rɒkfɔːl] *n* a mass of rocks that are falling or that have fallen down the side of a cliff, mountain etc.

rock-hard *adj* that is very hard □ *His muscles are rock-hard.*

Rockies ['rɒkɪz] = **Rocky Mountains**.

rocking chair ['rɒkɪŋ-] *n* a chair that has two curved pieces of wood, metal etc on the bottom so that one can rock backward and forward when one is sitting in it.

rocking horse *n* a toy horse that a child can sit on and rock backward and forward.

rock music *n* loud music with a strong beat

that is played on electrical instruments, especially electric guitars.

rock 'n' roll *n* = **rock and roll**.

rock pool *n* a small pool that forms between rocks on the seashore at low tide.

rock salt *n* salt found by mining in the ground rather than in the sea.

rock singer *n* a person who sings rock music.

rock star *n* a person who is very well-known for their rock music.

Rockwell ['rɒkwəl], **Norman** (1894–1978) a US painter who is famous for his scenes of daily life which appeared especially on magazine covers.

rocky ['rɒkɪ] (*compar* **rockier**, *superl* **rockiest**) *adj* -1. [road, ground] that is covered with rocks □ *They drove slowly over the rocky terrain.* -2. [marriage, economy] that has problems and may not continue to exist or be successful □ *Olson's future is looking a little rocky right now.*

Rocky Mountains: the Rocky Mountains a North American mountain range that extends from Alaska to New Mexico. HIGHEST POINT: 4,399 m.

rococo [rə'koukou] *adj* [decoration, furniture, building] that is in a style, fashionable in Europe in the early 18th century, that uses a lot of decoration.

rod [rɒd] *n* a long thin bar made of hard material □ *a metal/wooden rod.*

rode [roud] *past tense of* **ride**.

rodent ['roudənt] *n* a small animal with strong sharp teeth, e.g. a mouse, rat, or rabbit.

rodeo [rou'deiou] (*pl* **rodeos**) *n* a form of entertainment in which cowboys show their skills, e.g. riding wild horses.

🐎 RODEOS
At US rodeos, cowboys show off their skills to entertain people and to compete for prizes. Traditional rodeos were held when cowboys met to round up their herds of cattle (the word rodeo comes from the Spanish for "roundup"). The cowboys who perform in rodeos have to ride wild horses and cattle, catch cattle with ropes, and throw cattle to the ground by twisting their horns. Tourists have come to watch rodeos since the end of the 19th century, and modern rodeos in western states such as Wyoming and Kansas still attract many visitors.

Rodeo Drive [rou'deiou] a street in Beverly Hills, California, that has a lot of expensive shops.

Rodgers ['rɒdʒəʳz], **Richard** (1902–1979) a US composer who wrote songs and musicals with Lorenz Hart and Oscar Hammerstein, including *Oklahoma* and *The Sound of Music.*

Rodin [US rou'dæn, GB 'roudæn], **Auguste** (1840–1917) a French sculptor, famous for his realistic sculptures of people. His best-known works are *The Thinker* and *The Kiss.*

roe [rou] *n* the eggs or sperm of a fish, eaten as food □ *salmon/cod's roe.*

roe deer *n* a small deer that lives in forests in Europe and Asia.

Roe vs. Wade [,rouvɜːʳsəs'weid] *n* a famous legal decision by the US Supreme Court in 1973 that said that abortions should be permitted in the USA.

rogue [roug] ◇ *n* -1. a person who one likes, but whose attitude and behavior one does not approve of □ *a likeable rogue.* -2. a dishonest person (old-fashioned use). ◇ *adj* a **rogue politician/policeman etc** a politician/policeman etc who follows their own rules and methods and does not fit in with the other people in their group.

roguish ['rougɪʃ] *adj* [smile, look] that seems playful and mischievous.

role [roul] *n* -1. somebody's position in a situation or activity and the amount of activity they have in it □ *She played a key role in the organization.* -2. CINEMA & THEATER the character played by an actor or actress □ *She plays the role of a Russian princess.*

roll [roul] ◇ *n* -1. [of cloth, paper] a long piece of something that has been rolled into a cylinder □ *How many rolls of film did you buy?* -2. a small round loaf of bread, sometimes cut in half to make a sandwich □ *a sesame/hard roll.* -3. [of names] an official list of names □ *the electoral roll.* -4. **a roll of drums/thunder** a long deep sound made by drums/thunder □ *a drum roll.* -5. *phrase* **to be on a roll** to be having a lot of success all at once (informal use).
◇ *vt* -1. to move <a log, barrel> etc by making it turn over many times □ *The goalkeeper rolled the ball out to the defender.* ■ **to roll one's eyes** to move one's eyes around in a circle, e.g. to show that one finds something strange, surprising, silly etc □ *She kept rolling her eyes melodramatically toward the sky.* -2. to wrap <cloth, a carpet, film> etc around itself to form a ball or cylinder □ *The hedgehog rolled itself into a ball.* ■ **rolled into one** combined □ *She's a company executive, wife, and housekeeper rolled into one.* -3. **to roll a cigarette** to make a cigarette by wrapping tobacco in paper and rolling it into a cylinder.
◇ *vi* -1. [log, barrel] to move somewhere by turning over many times □ *The ball rolled under the car.* -2. [truck, bus] to move along □ *The car rolled up the drive.* -3. [ship, plane] to move from side to side because of waves or wind. -4. [drums, thunder] to make a long deep sound.

◆ **roll around, roll about** *vi* to move by turning over many times □ *The dog was rolling around happily in the mud.* □ *Empty bottles rolled around on the ship's deck.*

◆ **roll back** *vt sep* **to roll sthg back** US [taxes, prices] to reduce sthg, usually to a level that it was at before.

◆ **roll in** *vi* (informal use) -1. [money, profits, invitations] to come to somebody in large quantities □ *After we'd won the competition the offers of work came rolling in.* -2. [person] to arrive somewhere in a relaxed way, especially when other people expect one to be worried □ *He rolled in half an hour late.*

◆ **roll over** *vi* [person] to turn one's body once so that one is lying in a different position □ *I switched off the lamp and rolled over to go to sleep.* □ *The car rolled over and burst into flames.*

◆ **roll up** ◇ *vt sep* -1. **to roll sthg up** [paper, cloth, carpet] to roll sthg into a cylinder or ball □ *He rolled his clothes up into a small ball.* -2. **to roll one's sleeves/trousers up** to fold the ends of one's sleeves/trousers over, to make them shorter □ *She rolled up her sleeves and set to work.* ◇ *vi* -1. [car, bus] to arrive somewhere and stop □ *A large Mercedes rolled up at the hotel entrance.* -2. [person] to arrive somewhere, usually late (informal use) □ *He finally rolled up at 10 o'clock.*

roll bar *n* a strong metal bar on the top of a car used to protect the people inside if the car rolls over.

roll call *n* the act of reading a list of names aloud to check who is present.

rolled gold [,rəʊld-] *n* GB a thin covering of gold on another metal.

roller ['rəʊlə'] *n* -1. a solid tube of wood or metal that turns around and is used in a machine for pressing, printing etc. -2. a small, hollow, plastic or metal tube around which one wraps one's hair to make it curly □ *Her hair was in rollers.*

roller blades *npl* skates like roller skates that have one row of wheels underneath □ *a pair of roller blades.*

roller blind *n* a blind, usually made of cloth, that is attached to the top of a window and can be rolled up when it is not being used.

roller coaster *n* a small track, usually at a fairground, that carries people up and down steep slopes in open cars for entertainment.

roller skate *n* a boot or shoe with small wheels attached to the bottom.

◆ **roller-skate** *vi* to move wearing roller skates.

roller towel *n* a long towel whose two ends are joined together so that it can be wound around a wooden or metal rod.

rolling ['rəʊlɪŋ] *adj* -1. **rolling hills** hills that rise and fall gently. -2. **a rolling walk** a way of walking that is slow and in which the body moves from side to side. -3. **to be rolling in it** to be very rich (informal use).

rolling mill *n* a factory or machine in which rollers are used to flatten metal into sheets.

rolling pin *n* a long cylindrical piece of wood that one rolls over pastry many times in order to make it flat.

rolling stock *n* the vehicles, e.g. engines and cars, that are used on a railroad.

rollneck ['rəʊlnek] *adj* GB [pullover, sweater] that has a neck like a poloneck but smaller.

roll of honor *n* an official list of the names of a number of people who have done something that other people respect.

roll-on *n* **a roll-on (deodorant)** a bottle of liquid deodorant that one puts onto one's body by moving a rolling ball at the top of the bottle against one's skin.

roll-on roll-off *comp* **a roll-on roll-off ferry** GB a ferry that is built with doors at the front and back, so that vehicles can drive on at one end and leave at the other end.

ROM [rɒm] *(abbr of* **read-only memory)** *n* the part of a computer containing information that can be read but not changed by the user.

NOTE: Compare **RAM**.

romaine lettuce [rəʊˈmeɪn-] *n* US a lettuce with long, narrow, crisp leaves.

Roman ['rəʊmən] ◇ *adj* -1. that is connected with ancient Rome or its empire. -2. that is connected with Rome. ◇ *n* -1. a person who came from or lived in ancient Rome. -2. a person who comes from or lives in Rome.

Roman candle *n* a firework that stands on the ground and produces bright sparks and colored balls of fire.

Roman Catholic ◇ *n* a person who belongs to the Christian religion that has the Pope in Rome as its leader. ◇ *adj: a Roman Catholic priest/bishop* □ *the Roman Catholic Church.*

romance [rəʊˈmæns] *n* -1. the feelings or behavior of people who are in love □ *in search of love and romance.* -2. a feeling of excitement, mystery, and adventure □ *the romance of moonlight.* -3. a love affair □ *yet another failed romance.* -4. a type of novel, usually involving love, mystery, and adventure □ *I'd rather read a romance than a thriller any day.*

Romanesque [,rəʊmə'nesk] *adj* [building, architecture] built in a style that was popular in Western Europe between the 9th and 12th centuries, with arches and thick pillars.

Romania [rʊˈmeɪnjə] a country in southeastern Europe, on the Black Sea. SIZE: 237,500 sq kms. POPULATION: 23,400,000 (*Romanians*). CAPITAL: Bucharest. LANGUAGE: Romanian. CURRENCY: len.

Romanian [rʊˈmeɪnjən] *n* & *adj: see* **Romania**.

Roman numerals *npl* the letters that were used to represent numbers in ancient Rome □ *The facade was inscribed with the Roman numerals, MDCCXIV.*

romantic [rəʊˈmæntɪk] *adj* -1. [person] who imagines things are more interesting, exciting etc than they really are □ *He has a very romantic view of the French way of life.* -2. [evening, vacation, movie] that involves love □ *They had a romantic candlelit dinner.* -3. [gesture, place, way of life] that makes one think of love, adventure, or mystery □ *It was so romantic of her to fly all that way to see you.*

◆ **Romantic** *adj* [novel, movie, play] that is connected with Romanticism □ *the great Romantic novels of the 19th century.*

romanticism [rəʊˈmæntəsəzm] *n* romantic thoughts, feelings, or ideas □ *One could hardly accuse him of romanticism.*

◆ **Romanticism** *n* an artistic movement in 18th- and 19th-century Europe that was concerned with natural beauty and with emotions rather than rational thought □ *one of the great proponents of French Romanticism.*

romanticize, -ise [roʊ'mæntəsaɪz] ◇ *vt* [idea, event] to make <sth> seem more interesting or exciting than it really is □ *He has a tendency to romanticize war in his novels.* ◇ *vi: It's easy to romanticize about life on a desert island.*

Romantic poets *npl* **the Romantic poets** a group of English poets in the late 18th and early 19th centuries, including Wordsworth, Byron, Keats, and Shelley. Their poems were influenced by Romanticism.

Romany ['rɒmənɪ] (*pl* **Romanies**) *n* a member of a race of people that travels from place to place, mainly in Europe, and lives in caravans; the language of these people.

Rome [roʊm] the capital of Italy and its largest city. In ancient times it was the center of a large empire. POPULATION: 2,693,383.

Romeo[1] ['roʊmɪoʊ] the hero of Shakespeare's play *Romeo and Juliet.* He falls in love with Juliet, although their families are enemies.

Romeo[2] *n* a man who tries to make women sexually interested in him.

romp [rɒmp] ◇ *n* a noisy and lively activity or game □ *The children/dogs like to have a romp in the garden.* ◇ *vi* [child, dog] to play in a noisy and lively way.

rompers ['rɒmpəᵊz] *npl*, **romper suit** ['rɒmpəᵊ-] *n* a piece of clothing for babies that consists of a top and trousers in one piece.

roof [ruːf] *n* **-1.** the covering on top of a building or vehicle □ *The roof is leaking.* ■ **under my roof** in my home □ *I am not prepared to put up with that kind of behavior under my roof!* ■ **under the same roof** in the same house □ *I'm not staying under the same roof as that revolting man!* ■ **to have a roof over one's head** to have somewhere to live □ *All we want is some food and a roof over our heads.* ■ **to go through** OR **hit the roof** to become very angry □ *Mom went through the roof when she saw the mess.* **-2.** [of a cave, mouth] the top part of the inside of something □ *The roof of my mouth felt dry and sticky.*

roof garden *n* a garden on the roof of a building.

roofing ['ruːfɪŋ] *n* material that is used to make a roof.

roof rack *n* a metal frame on the roof of a car or van that is used for carrying things.

rooftop ['ruːftɒp] *n* the outside part of a roof.

rook [rʊk] *n* **-1.** a large black bird, like a crow, that lives in Europe and Asia. **-2.** in chess, a piece that can move any number of squares backward, forward, or sideways, but not diagonally.

rookie ['rʊkɪ] *n* a new member, e.g. of an army or police force, who has little experience □ *a rookie cop.*

room [ruːm] *n* **-1.** [in a building] one of the parts of a building that has its own walls, floor, and ceiling, and is separated from the other parts □ *The house has ten rooms.* □ *Just then, Jeff walked into the room.* **-2.** [in a house, hotel] a bedroom □ *I'll show you to your room.* **-3.** [for

people, objects] enough space □ *Is there room for another passenger?* □ *There isn't much room in here.* ■ **to make room for sb/sthg** to move things or people so that there is enough space for sb/sthg □ *She moved up to make room for Sam.* □ *I've shifted the furniture to make room for the new TV.* **-4.** [for improvement, change] the opportunity or possibility for something to happen □ *It's a good project but there's room for improvement.* ■ **room for maneuver** the possibility of changing one's plans or actions if it is necessary.

roomer ['ruːməʳ] *n* US a person who lives in a rented room in somebody else's house.

rooming house ['ruːmɪŋ-] *n* US a house where people can rent furnished rooms or small apartments.

roommate ['ruːmmeɪt] *n* a person with whom one shares a house or apartment.

room service *n* the serving of meals, drinks etc to hotel guests in their rooms.

room temperature *n* the usual temperature of a room in a house, about 20°C □ *'This wine should be served at room temperature.'*

roomy ['ruːmɪ] (*compar* **roomier**, *superl* **roomiest**) *adj* [building, bag, coat] that has plenty of space.

Roosevelt ['roʊzəvelt], **Eleanor** (1884–1962) a US writer and diplomat who supported many liberal causes. She was married to Franklin Roosevelt.

Roosevelt, Franklin (Delano) (1882–1945) US President from 1933 to 1945. He was responsible for economic reforms such as the New Deal, and was a strong leader in World War II. He is also called FDR.

Roosevelt, Theodore (1858–1919) US President from 1901 to 1909. He is also called Teddy Roosevelt.

roost [ruːst] ◇ *n* a place, e.g. a branch of a tree, where a bird rests at night. ■ **to rule the roost** to be in control of all the other people in a place (informal use). ◇ *vi* [bird] to stay on a roost for the night.

rooster ['ruːstəʳ] *n* an adult male chicken.

root [ruːt] ◇ *n* **-1.** [of a plant, tree] the part of a plant that grows underground and supplies the plant with food and water □ *The plant had long, white roots that went deep into the soil.* ■ **to put down roots** [person] to settle in a place and begin to think of it as one's home □ *You can't be thinking of moving again — you've scarcely had time to put down roots here.* ■ **to take root** [plant] to start to grow; [idea, practice] to become established □ *That little offcut from the rose bush is beginning to take root.* □ *Once the idea had taken root in her mind, she could not forget it.* **-2.** [of a hair, tooth, nail] the part of a hair, tooth, or nail where it meets the surface of the skin □ *Her dyed blond hair was dark at the roots.* **-3.** [of a problem] the main cause of something □ *the root of all evil.* ◇ *adj* **the root cause** the most basic and important cause □ *The root cause of all these problems is poverty.*

◇ *vi* to search for something by moving

things around □ *The dog was rooting through the undergrowth.* □ *She rooted in her bag for the ticket.*

◆ **roots** *npl* the place or culture that somebody grew up in or that their family is from originally □ *He says he wants to go back to his roots.*

◆ **root for** *vt fus* **to root for sb** [competitor, team] to support and encourage sb strongly (informal use) □ *Come on, Cambridge! We're rooting for you!*

◆ **root out** *vt sep* **to root sthg out** [corruption, racism] to find and remove sthg □ *I intend to root out every corrupt cop in this precinct.*

root beer *n* US a fizzy soft drink made from roots and herbs.

root crop *n* a crop whose roots are used as food, e.g. potatoes or carrots.

rooted ['ruːtəd] *adj* **to be rooted to the spot** to be so afraid or surprised that one is unable to move □ *She just stood there, rooted to the spot as the truck came thundering toward her.*

rootless ['ruːtləs] *adj* [person] who does not feel that they belong to any particular place or culture.

root vegetable *n* a vegetable, e.g. potatoes or carrots, that grows under the ground.

rope [rəʊp] ◇ *n* a thick cord that is made by twisting thinner cords together □ *a long rope/a long piece of rope.* ■ **to know the ropes** to be experienced in a particular activity or situation (informal use) □ *Ask Johnny to show you the ropes.* ■ **to be at the end of one's rope** US to feel that one cannot deal with a situation any more because one is too tired, worried etc. ◇ *vt* to tie <a person, animal, or object> to something with rope □ *The climbers were roped together.* □ *The horse was roped to a fence.*

◆ **rope in** *vt sep* **to rope sb in** to persuade sb to get involved in something (informal use) □ *They tried to rope me in to play softball.*

◆ **rope off** *vt sep* **to rope a place off** to tie ropes around the edges of a place to prevent people from getting in □ *The whole street's been roped off while they investigate.*

ro-ro ['rəʊrəʊ] *n* GB a roll-on roll-off ferry (informal use).

rosary ['rəʊzərɪ] (*pl* **rosaries**) *n* -1. a string of beads used by people in some religions, e.g. Catholics or Hindus, for counting their prayers. -2. the set of prayers that is said by somebody using a rosary.

rose [rəʊz] ◇ *past tense of* **rise**. ◇ *adj* that is pink in color. ◇ *n* a flower that is usually red, white, pink, or yellow, has a pleasant smell, and grows on a bush that has thorns on its stems.

rosé [rəʊ'zeɪ] *n* a pink wine.

rosebed ['rəʊzbed] *n* a flowerbed that has had roses planted in it.

Rose Bowl *n* **the Rose Bowl** an important US football game. It is played once a year on January 1 in Pasadena, California between two championship college teams.

rosebud ['rəʊzbʌd] *n* the flower of a rose that has not yet opened out completely.

rose bush *n* a bush that roses grow on.

rose hip *n* a red or yellow fruit that grows on certain rose bushes.

rosemary [US 'rəʊzmerɪ, GB -mərɪ] *n* a plant with sweet-smelling gray-green spiky leaves, used as an herb in cooking.

rosette [rəʊ'zet] *n* a large round badge made of colored ribbons.

rosewater ['rəʊzwɔːtəʳ] *n* a liquid made from roses and used as perfume.

rosewood ['rəʊzwʊd] *n* a hard, dark-red, tropical wood used for making good-quality furniture.

ROSPA ['rɒspə] (*abbr of* **Royal Society for the Prevention of Accidents**) *n* a British charity that provides information about safety on the road, at school, at home etc.

Ross [rɒs], **Betsy** (1752–1836) the woman who made the first US flag.

Rossetti [US rəʊ'zetɪ, GB rə-], **Dante Gabriel** (1828–1882) a British artist and poet, and a leader of the Pre-Raphaelites.

Rossini [US rəʊ'siːnɪ, GB rɒ-], **Gioacchino** (1792–1868) an Italian composer who wrote many operas, including *The Barber of Seville*.

roster ['rɒstəʳ] *n* a list of people's names that shows which jobs they have to do or at which times they have to work.

rostrum ['rɒstrəm] (*pl* **rostrums** OR **rostra** [-trə]) *n* a raised platform where somebody stands, e.g. when making a speech, accepting a prize, or conducting an orchestra.

rosy ['rəʊzɪ] (*compar* **rosier**, *superl* **rosiest**) *adj* -1. [cheeks, complexion] pink and healthy in appearance □ *She came in, smiling and rosy-cheeked.* -2. [view, outlook, future] that makes one feel optimistic □ *I'm afraid the future doesn't look quite so rosy from my point of view.*

rot [rɒt] (*pt & pp* **rotted**, *cont* **rotting**) *vi* [food, teeth] to decay □ *the smell of rotting vegetables.* ◇ *vt* [substance, food, teeth] to make <sthg> decay □ *Oil rots rubber.* ◇ *n* -1. [in wood, food] an area of rotten material □ *The floorboards were very damp and rot had begun to set in.* -2. [in a society, organization] a weakness in the character, structure, or morals of something □ *The rot set in when the essential services were privatized.*

rota ['rəʊtə] *n* GB a list of people who take turns to do a job, showing the order in which they have to do it □ *We have a rota system for doing the dishes.* □ *I don't think I'm on the rota tonight.*

rotary ['rəʊtərɪ] ◇ *adj* -1. [movement, action] that involves turning around a fixed point. -2. [machine, engine] that is operated by the rotary movement of a part or parts. ◇ *n* US a round traffic junction where three or more roads meet and which traffic must travel around in the same direction.

Rotary Club *n* **the Rotary Club** an association of business people that organizes social events and charity work.

rotate [US 'routeɪt, GB rou'teɪt] ◇ vt -1. [part of a machine, wheel] to make <sthg> turn in a circular movement around a fixed point □ *This shaft then rotates the wheel, which forces the water through the pipe.* -2. [staff, workers] to make <people> take turns to do a particular job in a fixed order □ *The presidency of the EU is rotated.* □ *They rotate the jobs so that no one has to work two night shifts in a row.* -3. to plant <different crops> each season in a fixed order that is repeated □ *The farmers rotate the crops in order to keep the soil healthy.* ◇ vi -1. [part of a machine, wheel] *The blades start to rotate when you push the lawnmower forward.* -2. [staff, jobs] *The presidency of the Council rotates every year.*

rotation [rou'teɪʃn] n [of a machine, jobs, crops] *see* **rotate**. ■ **to do sthg in rotation** to do sthg in a fixed order that is repeated.

rote [rout] n **to learn sthg by rote** to learn sthg so that one can repeat it from memory, rather than because one understands it □ *rote learning.*

rotor ['routər] n a part of an engine or machine that rotates □ *a helicopter's rotor blade.*

rotten ['rɒtn] adj -1. [wood, food] that has decayed completely □ *He accidentally put his foot through a rotten floorboard.* -2. [movie, book, meal] that is of poor quality □ *That rice tastes really rotten!* -3. [person, job] very unpleasant (informal use) □ *What a rotten thing to do/say!* □ *I've had a really rotten day!* -4. **to feel rotten** to feel unwell (informal use). -5. **to feel rotten about sthg** to feel unhappy or guilty about sthg one has done □ *I feel rotten about turning him down for the job.*

rotund [rou'tʌnd] adj [person, shape] round and fat.

rouble ['ruːbl] n the standard unit of money in Russia and some other countries that used to be in the Soviet Union.

rouge [ruːʒ] n red make-up that women and actors put on their cheeks.

rough [rʌf] ◇ adj -1. [surface, road] that is uneven and not smooth □ *They drove along a rough dirt track.* -2. [person, behavior, treatment] that is violent or aggressive □ *He was very rough with me.* -3. [shelter, workmanship] that is basic and not of very high quality □ *They built a rough wooden shack outside.* -4. [plan, copy, idea] that is not detailed, exact, or final □ *This is just a rough outline.* □ *I only need a rough estimate.* □ *This is just to give you a rough idea of what we intend to do.* -5. [life, deal] difficult and unpleasant, often in a way that is unfair or unlucky □ *They gave him a rough time OR ride.* □ *Divorce is always rough on the children.* -6. [town, area] where there is a lot of crime and violence □ *It's a rough part of town, so be careful.* -7. [weather, sea] stormy □ *We had a rough crossing.* -8. [wine, taste] that is not smooth or delicate; [sound, voice] that is unpleasantly harsh. -9. **to feel/look rough** to feel/look tired or ill (informal use) □ *You're looking rough this morning.* ◇ adv GB **to sleep rough** to sleep outside in

uncomfortable conditions because one has nowhere else to stay. ◇ n -1. **the rough** GOLF uneven ground on a golf course where the grass is allowed to grow longer. -2. **in rough** [write, draw] in a way that is not tidy or complete enough for a final copy □ *Just write it out in rough and someone can copy it.* ◇ vt **to rough it** to live in uncomfortable conditions for a short time □ *We don't have any furniture yet, so you'll just have to rough it.*

◆ **rough out** vt sep **to rough sthg out** [sketch, idea, speech] to draw or write sthg in rough □ *I've roughed out a plan for the new campaign.*

◆ **rough up** vt sep **to rough sb up** to attack sb in a violent or aggressive way □ *They roughed Steve up really badly.*

roughage ['rʌfɪdʒ] n substances in food such as bread, vegetables, or fruit that help to make the bowels work properly.

rough and ready adj -1. [plan, solution] that is simple and has been made carelessly or quickly. -2. [person] who does not worry about trying to be polite and is direct in their behavior and way of speaking.

rough-and-tumble n -1. fighting, e.g. among children, that is not very serious. -2. rough and noisy behavior □ *the rough-and-tumble of politics.*

roughcast [US 'rʌfkæst, GB -kɑːst] n a rough covering for the outside walls of a building that is made of plaster and small stones or shells.

rough diamond n GB a person who has good qualities, but whose appearance or behavior makes them seem aggressive, rude etc.

roughen ['rʌfn] vt [hands, surface] to make <sthg> rough.

rough justice n a situation, decision, or punishment that seems unfair because it makes life difficult for somebody who does not deserve it.

roughly ['rʌflɪ] adv -1. [behave, treat, make] *see* **rough** □ *He answered her very roughly.* □ *a roughly built shelter.* -2. approximately □ *She told me roughly how to get there.* □ *It's roughly 5km away.*

roughneck ['rʌfnek] n -1. a person who works on an oil rig. -2. a rough person (informal use).

roughshod ['rʌfʃɒd] adv **to ride roughshod over sb/sthg** [over rules, somebody's feelings] to behave without any consideration for sb/sthg.

roulette [ruː'let] n a game for gambling in which a ball is dropped onto a wheel with numbers on it that is spun and in which people bet on which number the ball will stay on when the wheel stops spinning.

round [raund] ◇ adj -1. [plate, table, face] that has the shape of a circle or a ball □ *Her eyes were round with amazement.* □ *Columbus knew the Earth was round.* -2. [cheeks, stomach, arch] that has a curved shape □ *Stand up straight or you'll get round shoulders!* -3. **a round number/figure** a number/figure that is whole and usually ends in zero, e.g. ten or a hundred □ *It comes to $384, or $400 in round figures.*

◇ *prep* **-1. round the table/fire** in a circle with the table/fire in the center. ■ **round one's waist/wrist** completely enclosing one's waist/wrist □ *The town is built round a small lake.* □ *He had his arm round her.* □ *She wore a silk scarf round her neck.* □ *She measures 40 inches round the hips.* **-2. to go round sthg** to move in a circle with sthg in the center; to move in a circle along sthg □ *The Earth goes round the Sun.* □ *We drove round and round the place trying to find the exit.* **-3. to travel round a place** to visit all the different parts of a place □ *We spent the summer motoring round Europe.* □ *We have offices all round the world.* □ *I spent the morning wandering round the town.* **-4. to be round the corner** to be on the far side of the corner □ *The hotel is a few hundred yards on, just round the next bend.* □ *The car is parked round the back of the house.* **-5. a way round an obstacle/a problem** a way that avoids an obstacle/a problem □ *I stepped carefully round the hole in the road.* □ *We're going to have to sell, I can't see any other way round it.* **-6.** *phrase* **round here** in the area where one is or lives □ *The people round here are very friendly.*

◇ *adv* **-1. to go** OR **spin round (and round)** to move in the shape of a circle (repeatedly) □ *The roulette wheel spun round several times, then stopped.* **-2. to sit/stand round** to sit/stand in a group so that something is in the center or surrounded □ *By this time a crowd of spectators had gathered round.* □ *We couldn't get in because there was a fence all round.* **-3. to turn/look round** to turn/look so that one is facing the opposite direction. **-4. to be 100 feet round** to measure 100 feet along the length of its outside. **-5. to take** OR **show sb round** to take sb to all the different parts of a place □ *If you ever come to London, I'd be delighted to show you round.* **-6. to come/go round** to come/go to visit someone in their home □ *I'm just on my way round to Jenny's.*

◇ *n* **-1. a round of talks/negotiations** one of a series of talks/negotiations □ *The next round of consultations will take place in Helsinki.* **-2. a round of applause** clapping by an audience to show that they have enjoyed a performance □ *Let's have a round of applause for our winners!* **-3.** [in a competition] one of a series of games or matches in a competition □ *He was knocked out in the fourth round of the tournament.* **-4.** [by a doctor, nurse, delivery boy] the regular visits that someone makes every day to their customers or patients □ *He did a paper round to earn some money.* **-5.** [of drinks] a drink for everyone in a group, usually bought by one person □ *It's my round, what can I get you?* **-6.** GOLF a complete game of golf. **-7.** BOXING one of the periods in a boxing match when the boxers fight □ *The referee stopped the fight in the tenth round.* **-8. a round of ammunition** a single bullet or a single shot from a gun □ *Police fired three rounds of ammunition.*

◇ *vt* to go round <a bend or corner> □ *Hamish rounded the bend at 60 miles per hour.*

◆ **rounds** *npl* the regular visits that a doctor or nurse makes every day to patients in their homes □ *The doctor is out on her rounds at the moment.*

◆ **round about** ◇ *prep* a little before or after <a particular time, amount> etc □ *All my friends are round about the same age.* □ *She should be here round about 5 o'clock.* ◇ *adv* near to a particular place □ *People came from all the farms round about.*

◆ **round off** *vt sep* **to round sthg off** [speech, meal, concert] to end sthg in a satisfying or suitable way □ *The Bishop rounded off his sermon with a prayer for peace.* □ *How about a brandy to round off the meal?*

◆ **round up** *vt sep* **-1. to round people/animals up** to gather together people/animals from different places □ *Police rounded up members of the gang in a raid last night.* **-2. to round a figure/an amount up** MATH to change a figure/an amount to the nearest whole number, or multiple of ten, above it □ *The actual budget is $37,000, but let's round it up to $40,000.*

roundabout [ˈraʊndəbaʊt] ◇ *adj* [way, method] that is not direct or simple □ *It seems a rather roundabout way of doing it.* ◇ *n* GB **-1.** [on a road] a round traffic junction which traffic must travel around in the same direction. **-2.** [at a fairground] a round platform with seats, often in the shape of animals, that spins round and that people can ride on for pleasure.

rounded [ˈraʊndəd] *adj* [edge, end, shape] that is curved rather than pointed or sharp.

rounders [ˈraʊndəʳz] *n* in Britain, a team game like baseball played especially by children, in which the person batting scores points by hitting the ball and running around the four points of a square.

Roundhead [ˈraʊndhed] *n* a supporter of Oliver Cromwell against King Charles I in the English Civil War (1642–1646).

roundly [ˈraʊndlɪ] *adv* [criticize, attack] strongly; [defeat, beat] completely □ *He was roundly criticized for his behavior at the party.* □ *We were roundly beaten by a group of amateurs.*

round-neck *adj* [sweater] that has a collar that goes around the bottom of one's neck.

round-shouldered [-ˈʃəʊldəʳd] *adj* [person] who bends forward so that their shoulders are narrow and curved (disapproving use).

Round Table *n* **the Round Table** in English legends, the table where King Arthur sat with his knights. It was round so that no knight would appear more important than the others.

round-table *adj* **a round-table discussion/meeting etc** a discussion/meeting etc where all the people taking part have equal importance □ *Round-table talks are being held between the two warring factions.*

round-the-clock *adj* **round-the-clock surveillance/care etc** surveillance/care etc that takes place 24 hours a day.

◆ **round the clock** *adv*: *Police are watching the suspect round the clock.*

round trip ◇ *n* a trip to a place and back again. ◇ *adj* **a round-trip ticket** US a ticket for a trip to a place and back again.

roundup ['raʊndʌp] *n* -1. an act of gathering together animals or people in one place. -2. a summary of the main points of something, e.g. of the news or sports results □ *a news roundup*.

rouse [raʊz] *vt* -1. to wake <sb> up □ *I was roused from my sleep/bed at 2 am*. -2. **to rouse oneself to do sthg** to make oneself do something, usually when one is tired or does not have enthusiasm □ *Jimmy could scarcely rouse himself to look interested*. -3. to make <sb> more lively or excited □ *He was not easily roused to anger*. -4. to cause somebody to have <anger, fears> etc □ *This has roused a certain amount of suspicion amongst locals*.

rousing ['raʊzɪŋ] *adj* [speech, cheer] that makes people feel emotional and excited □ *He gave a rousing speech about patriotism and duty*.

Rousseau [US ruː'soʊ, GB 'ruːsoʊ], **Jean-Jacques** (1712–1778) a French philosopher, born in Switzerland. His writing influenced the French Revolution and the Romantic movement.

rout [raʊt] ◇ *n* a very easy and complete defeat. ◇ *vt* to beat <an opposing army, team> etc easily and completely.

route [ruːt] ◇ *n* -1. [of a trip, person, procession] a way or road that one travels along to get from one place to another □ *What's the best route to Manchester?* -2. [of a bus, train, plane] a way used by vehicles or planes for traveling regularly between places □ *I think the 45 bus goes along this route.* □ *a bus route.* -3. [to fame, disaster] a way of achieving something □ *the route to success* □ *Law is a good route into politics.* -4. US a main road □ *Route 66.* ◇ *vt* [goods, vehicle, person] to send <sb/sthg> in a particular direction or to a particular place □ *Our bags have been routed to Hong Kong.*

route map *n* a plan to help travelers, showing where bus or train routes run; a map provided for somebody to show them how to get to a place.

routine [,ruː'tiːn] ◇ *adj* -1. [check, operation, inquiry] that is part of the normal procedure □ *I'm sorry to trouble you — this is just a routine inquiry.* -2. [meeting, week] that consists of nothing unusual and so is boring □ *a series of dull, routine tasks.* ◇ *n* -1. the regular pattern of somebody's behavior that involves particular tasks or activities being done at particular times □ *Try to vary your routine a little.* -2. a pattern of activity that has been repeated so often that it is boring □ *I was tired of the same old daily routine.*

routinely [,ruː'tiːnlɪ] *adv* [check, inspect] regularly, as part of normal procedure.

rove [roʊv] ◇ *vt* [streets, land] to wander around <a place> (literary use). ◇ *vi* **to rove around** [person] to move or travel around freely with no particular purpose; [eyes] to keep looking around a place.

roving ['roʊvɪŋ] *adj* -1. **a roving reporter** a reporter for a newspaper or television compa-ny who travels about a lot. -2. **to have a roving eye** to be sexually attracted to many people.

row¹ [roʊ] ◇ *n* -1. a line made up of several people or things that are next to each other □ *a row of cars/chairs* □ *They stood/sat in a row.* -2. a section of seats in a cinema, theater etc that are next to each other in a line □ *We're in the third row.* -3. a sequence in which an event is repeated a number of times without any interruption or variation in between □ *an impressive row of victories.* ■ **in a row** one after the other without interruption □ *He's now won six times in a row.*
◇ *vt* to move <a boat> through the water by using oars; to take <a passenger> to a place by rowing a boat □ *Jocelyn rowed the little boat across the river.* □ *Mary rowed us to the other side.*
◇ *vi*: *Can you row?*

row² [raʊ] GB ◇ *n* -1. a noisy quarrel □ *I could hear them upstairs having a flaming row.* -2. noise, e.g. from music or people shouting, that continues for a period of time (informal use) □ *Turn that row down!* ◇ *vi* to quarrel loudly □ *Those two are always rowing.*

rowboat ['roʊboʊt] *n* US a small boat with oars.

rowdy ['raʊdɪ] (*compar* **rowdier**, *superl* **rowdiest**) *adj* [behavior, boys] noisy and wild.

rower ['roʊəʳ] *n* a person who rows as a sport or hobby.

row house ['roʊ-] *n* US a house that is one of a row of houses that are joined together.

rowing ['roʊɪŋ] *n* the activity or sport of rowing boats □ *Would you like to go rowing?*

rowing boat *n* GB = **rowboat**.

rowing machine *n* a fitness machine on which one uses the same movements as when rowing, in order to strengthen one's arms, legs etc.

royal ['rɔɪəl] ◇ *adj* [household, wedding, coach] that is connected with the king or queen of a country. ◇ *n* a member of a royal family (informal use).

Royal Academy of Arts *n* → RA.

Royal Air Force *n* **the Royal Air Force** the section of the British armed forces that operates in the air.

royal blue *adj* bright blue.

royal family *n* the king or queen of a country and all their relatives □ *the Danish royal family.*

royalist ['rɔɪələst] *n* a person who believes their country should be ruled by a king or queen.

royal jelly *n* a substance produced by bees, used as an expensive ingredient in cosmetics and health foods.

Royal Mail *n* **the Royal Mail** the national postal service in Britain.

Royal Marines *npl* **the Royal Marines** British soldiers serving with the Royal Navy.

Royal Navy *n* **the Royal Navy** the section of the British armed forces that operates at sea.

royalty ['rɔɪəltɪ] *n* a collective term for members of a royal family □ *She acts as though she were royalty.*

◆ **royalties** *npl* the money that is paid to a writer, musician etc, as a percentage of the profits when their work is sold or performed □ *Do you get paid royalties for your work?*

RP (*abbr of* **received pronunciation**) *n* an accent, used by many educated people in the south of England, that is considered the standard pronunciation of British English.

RPI *n abbr of* **retail price index**.

rpm (*abbr of* **revolutions per minute**) *npl* a unit of measurement to show how quickly a record player goes around, or how quickly an engine turns over.

RPN (*abbr of* **registered practical nurse**) *n* a US nursing qualification that requires four years' training; a person who has this qualification.
NOTE: Compare **LPN**.

RR *abbr of* **railroad**.

RRP *n abbr of* **recommended retail price**.

RSA ◇ *abbr of* **Republic of South Africa**. ◇ *n* (*abbr of* **Royal Society of Arts**) **the RSA** a British organization that gives examinations and diplomas in arts subjects.

RSI (*abbr of* **repetitive strain injury**) *n* a painful condition that affects the hands or arms especially, and is suffered by people who often repeat the same movements, e.g. keyboarders or violinists.

RSL (*abbr of* **Returned Services League**) *n* an Australian organization that looks after the interests of people who have served in the armed forces.

🦘 RSL
Almost every Australian town has an RSL club. They were originally meeting places for members of the armed forces and their families, but are now important to the whole community. In small towns they may just have a bar, while in cities they are very large, with restaurants and casinos, and space for "housie" (bingo), dancing, concerts etc.

RSPB (*abbr of* **Royal Society for the Protection of Birds**) *n* **the RSPB** a British charity whose aim is to protect birds that are in danger.

RSPCA (*abbr of* **Royal Society for the Prevention of Cruelty to Animals**) *n* **the RSPCA** a British charity that aims to protect animals from being badly treated.

RSVP (*abbr of* **répondez s'il vous plaît**) a phrase written on an invitation to ask for a reply.

Rt Hon (*abbr of* **Right Honourable**) a title used when referring to members of the British parliament who have been Cabinet ministers, or to certain members of the aristocracy.

Rt Rev (*abbr of* **Right Reverend**) a title used when referring to an Anglican bishop.

rub [rʌb] (*pt & pp* **rubbed**, *cont* **rubbing**) ◇ *vt* -1. [eyes, forehead, mirror] to move something,

e.g. one's hand or a cloth, up and down over the surface of <sthg> while pressing against it □ *He rubbed his hands (together) to keep warm.* □ *Katy rubbed her eyes sleepily.* -2. **to rub sthg against sthg** to move sthg along the surface of sthg while pressing against it □ *The cat was rubbing its back against the chair.* -3. **to rub sthg on sthg** [polish, cream] to put sthg on the surface of sthg by moving a cloth, one's hand etc over it □ *Could you rub some oil on my back?* -4. **to rub sthg in** OR **into sthg** [cream, lotion, wax] to rub sthg on sthg until it becomes absorbed. -5. **to rub it in** to make somebody feel even more upset, embarrassed etc about something that has happened by reminding them about it or making fun of them (informal use) □ *Look, you don't have to rub it in — I know I was drunk!* -6. **to rub sb the wrong way** US, **to rub sb up the wrong way** GB to annoy sb □ *I didn't mean to be rude, but that man has a knack of rubbing me the wrong way!*
◇ *vi* to come into contact with something by moving over its surface; to move up and down over the surface of something while pressing against it □ *I felt something rub against my leg.* □ *My shoes are rubbing.*

◆ **rub off on** *vt fus* **to rub off on sb** [attitude, experience, knowledge] to have an effect on sb by providing them with an example of something □ *Let's hope some of their good manners will rub off on Larry!*

◆ **rub out** *vt sep* **to rub sthg out** [writing, mistake] to remove sthg from a piece of paper with an eraser □ *He had rubbed out his name and written in mine instead.*

rubber ['rʌbər] ◇ *n* -1. a natural elastic substance obtained from a tropical tree □ *The boots are made of rubber.* -2. a series of games of bridge. -3. US a condom (informal use). -4. US a covering made of rubber that is worn over a shoe, usually to protect it in wet weather. -5. GB a piece of rubber used for removing pencil marks. ◇ *adj* [gloves, tire, ball] made of rubber.

rubber band *n* a small thin band of rubber, used to hold things together tightly.

rubber boot *n* US a long waterproof boot made of rubber.

rubber bullet *n* a piece of rubber fired from a gun that is designed to hurt people but not kill them.

rubber dinghy *n* a small rubber boat that is filled with air before use.

rubberize, -ise ['rʌbəraɪz] *vt* [cloth, fabric] to treat <sthg> with rubber in order to make it waterproof.

rubberneck ['rʌbərnek] *vi* to stare curiously at something, especially when driving past in a car (informal and disapproving use).

rubber plant *n* a houseplant with smooth, shiny, dark-green leaves.

rubber stamp *n* a small object with raised letters or figures that are pressed onto paper to print a date, company name etc.

◆ **rubber-stamp** *vt* to agree to <sthg>, often without discussing or thinking about it.

rubber tree *n* a tropical tree that produces rubber.

rubbery ['rʌbərɪ] *adj* [substance, food] that is like rubber because it is soft and flexible, but tough □ *The squid had a rubbery texture.*

rubbing ['rʌbɪŋ] *n* a pattern or picture that is made by laying paper over a piece of stone or metal and rubbing it with chalk, a crayon etc □ *a brass rubbing.*

rubbing alcohol *n* US a kind of alcohol used for cleaning wounds.

rubbish ['rʌbɪʃ] ◇ *n* -1. waste material consisting of used or unwanted things that is put in a container to be taken away from a place □ *The rubbish is collected on Tuesdays.* -2. something, e.g. a movie or book, that one thinks is of very poor quality (informal use) □ *"What did you think of the game?" — "It was rubbish."* -3. something that somebody says or writes that one thinks is worthless (informal use) □ *What you're saying is rubbish.* □ *What a load of rubbish!*
◇ *vt* GB [person, movie, work] to criticize <sb/sthg> in a way that suggests they have no worth (informal use) □ *You're always trying to rubbish what I do.*
◇ *excl* GB a word used to show that one disagrees very strongly with what has just been said (informal use) □ *"It only takes three hours from here." — "Rubbish! It takes at least five."*

rubbish bag *n* GB a large plastic bag for putting rubbish in.

rubbish bin *n* GB -1. a large metal or plastic container that stands outside a house and is used for keeping bags of rubbish in until they are taken away. -2. a large plastic container for waste, usually in the kitchen.

rubbish dump, rubbish tip *n* GB a place where household waste is taken and unloaded after being collected.

rubbishy ['rʌbɪʃɪ] *adj* [book, movie, article] bad (informal use).

rubble ['rʌbl] *n* the pieces of brick, stone, concrete etc that are left when a building is destroyed □ *The building had been reduced to rubble.*

rubella [ruˈbelə] *n* German measles (technical use).

Rubens ['ruːbɪnz], **Peter Paul** (1577–1640) a Flemish artist, famous for the use of rich colors in his paintings.

ruby ['ruːbɪ] (*pl* **rubies**) *n* a precious dark-red stone.

RUC (*abbr of* **Royal Ulster Constabulary**) *n* the **RUC** the police force in Northern Ireland.

rucksack ['rʌksæk] *n* a bag that is worn on the back, attached by a strap on each shoulder, and used by travelers, climbers etc.

rudder ['rʌdər] *n* a handle at the back of a small boat, used to steer it.

ruddy ['rʌdɪ] (*compar* **ruddier**, *superl* **ruddiest**) *adj* [face, complexion] that is red and looks healthy.

rude [ruːd] *adj* -1. [person, remark, behavior] that is not polite and is likely to offend somebody □ *It's rude to stare at people.* □ *Try not to be so rude this time.* -2. [joke, noise] that is not polite and relates to sex or parts of the body in a rather childish way □ *Ooh! He said a rude word!* -3. **a rude shock** a big shock. ■ **a rude awakening** a sudden, surprising, and unpleasant discovery or realization □ *It was a rude awakening to the realities of showbiz life.* -4. [hut, structure] made in a simple way with few materials (literary use) □ *They had constructed a rude shelter out of driftwood.*

rudely ['ruːdlɪ] *adv* [behave, gesture, interrupt] *see* **rude** □ *As I was saying before I was so rudely interrupted,...*

rudeness ['ruːdnəs] *n* [of somebody's behavior, a person] *see* **rude**.

rudimentary [ˌruːdəˈmentərɪ] *adj* [method, system] very simple and basic □ *We have only a rudimentary knowledge of how the brain works.*

rudiments ['ruːdəmənts] *npl* **the rudiments** the most simple and important elements of something □ *I've picked up the rudiments of the language.*

rue [ruː] *vt* to regret <sthg> (humorous or literary use) □ *You'll rue the day you got involved with that young man!*

rueful ['ruːfl] *adj* [expression, glance] that shows one regrets something □ *She looked up with a rueful smile.*

ruff [rʌf] *n* a frilly collar worn around the neck in Europe in the 16th and 17th centuries.

ruffian ['rʌfɪən] *n* a man who is aggressive and likely to be a criminal (old-fashioned use).

ruffle ['rʌfl] ◇ *vt* -1. [hair, water, feathers] to make the surface of <sthg> uneven □ *The breeze scarcely ruffled the surface of the water.* -2. [speaker, politician, opponent] to cause <sb> to lose their confidence and become nervous □ *People were shouting for him to leave, but Senator Gibb was not ruffled at all.* ◇ *n* a frill on a piece of clothing, made by gathering material together.

rug [rʌg] *n* -1. a small carpet that is not fixed to the floor. -2. a small blanket used to sit on outdoors or for covering one's legs.

rugby ['rʌgbɪ], **rugby football** *n* a game played between two teams with an oval-shaped ball, in which points are scored by placing the ball behind the opponents' goal line or kicking the ball between the posts of the goal □ *a rugby player/match.*

Rugby League *n* a form of rugby played with teams of 13 players.

Rugby Union *n* a form of rugby played with teams of 15 players.

rugged ['rʌgəd] *adj* -1. [coastline, cliff, landscape] that is uneven and harsh, especially because it is rocky □ *They drove slowly over the rugged terrain.* -2. [vehicle] that is strong and reliable, even on uneven ground □ *a rugged, reliable four-wheel drive.* -3. [face, features] masculine and tough, rather than soft □ *his rugged good looks.*

ruin ['ruːɪn] ◇ *n* -1. the state of not having

any more money left □ *The business is now facing financial ruin.* □ *You will be the ruin of me.* -2. a building that is in very bad condition and not complete because it is very old or has been damaged □ *the ruins of ancient Greece* □ *The house was a ruin after years of neglect.*
◇ *vt* -1. [clothing, furniture, health] to completely spoil or damage <sthg> □ *Bernard completely ruined my evening by turning up drunk.* □ *You've ruined her chances of getting that job.* □ *The rain had ruined my brand new shoes.* -2. [person] to cause <sb> to lose all their money, resources etc □ *That last investment he made completely ruined him.*
◆ **in ruin(s)** *adv* -1. [building, town] that has been badly damaged or destroyed □ *The house lay in ruins after the attack.* -2. [life, career, relationship] that is unsuccessful and seems impossible to improve □ *I felt my life was in ruins after the divorce.*

ruination [ruːɪˈneɪʃn] *n* the cause of somebody's personal or financial failure □ *the ruination of his life.*

ruinous [ˈruːɪnəs] *adj* [expense, purchase] that requires a lot of money □ *The cost of flying there is ruinous!*

rule [ruːl] ◇ *n* -1. a statement that tells people what they can or cannot do in a particular institution, sport etc □ *the school rules* □ *You must obey the rules.* □ *It's against the rules to pick up two cards at once.* ■ **to bend the rules** to make an exception for somebody by letting them do what is not usually allowed □ *Danny can always find a way of bending the rules.* -2. [of behavior] a general principle that is used to help people decide how to act in a particular situation □ *There are certain rules for dealing with this kind of problem.* -3. **the rule** what is usual and expected □ *Politeness seems to be the exception rather than the rule these days.* -4. [of a country] the government and control of a country □ *The country was formerly a colony under Portuguese rule.* -5. [for measuring] = **ruler.**
◇ *vt* -1. [actions, mind, life] to have a powerful control over <sthg> □ *I'm not going to let lack of money rule my life.* -2. [country, region] to have political and military control of <a place> □ *Queen Victoria ruled England for many years.* -3. to decide and officially declare <sthg>, especially in a court of law □ *The court ruled that she had been unfairly dismissed/ruled her dismissal unfair.*
◇ *vi* -1. [judge] to make an offical decision or judgment on something □ *The court ruled in his favor.* □ *The Archbishop cannot rule on the ordination of women.* -2. to be more important than anything else (formal use) □ *Love cannot always be allowed to rule.* -3. [king, queen, government] to be in power □ *He ruled wisely for many years.*
◆ **as a rule** *adv* usually □ *"Do you take people on without experience?" — "Not as a rule."* □ *As a rule, we usually only invite women to these parties.*
◆ **rule out** *vt sep* -1. **to rule sb/sthg out** [person, suspect, theory] to reject sb/sthg as un-

suitable or unlikely in a particular situation □ *The police have not yet ruled out the possibility of suicide.* -2. **to rule sthg out** [event, idea, arrangement] to make sthg impossible □ *Tennis was ruled out on account of the weather.*

rulebook [ˈruːlbʊk] *n* **to do things by the rulebook** to do things in the correct way following the normal procedure □ *She always goes by the rulebook.*

ruled [ruːld] *adj* [paper] that has lines across it.

ruler [ˈruːləʳ] *n* -1. a long, thin, flat piece of plastic, wood, or metal that is used to draw straight lines or measure things in inches or centimeters. -2. the leader of a country.

ruling [ˈruːlɪŋ] ◇ *adj* **a ruling party** a party that has political control of a country □ *The Republicans were at that time the ruling party.* ◇ *n* a decision given by a judge, court, or parliament □ *The judge has not yet given his ruling on the case.*

rum [rʌm] *n* a strong alcoholic drink made from sugar cane that is either dark or clear.

Rumania [ruˈmeɪnjə] *etc* = **Romania** *etc.*

rumba [ˈrʌmbə] *n* a Latin American dance.

rumble [ˈrʌmbl] ◇ *n* -1. [of thunder, guns, one's stomach] a low continuous sound □ *the distant rumble of traffic.* -2. US a fight between two or more gangs (informal use). ◇ *vt* to discover the truth about <sb/sthg> after somebody has tried to keep it hidden (informal use) □ *The police have rumbled our little game, I fear.* ◇ *vi* [traffic, thunder] to make a rumble □ *My stomach was rumbling.*

rumbustious [rʌmˈbʌstʃəs] *adj* GB [child, behavior] that is noisy and energetic.

ruminate [ˈruːmɪneɪt] *vi* to think about something slowly and carefully (formal use).

rummage [ˈrʌmɪdʒ] *vi* to look for something that is among a lot of other things by using one's hands □ *I rummaged in my purse for some change.* □ *She was rummaging through her things as if she'd lost something.*

rummage sale *n* US a sale of second-hand goods for charity.

rummy [ˈrʌmɪ] *n* a card game in which players try to collect cards that are in sequence or of the same type.

rumor US, **rumour** GB [ˈruːməʳ] *n* a story, piece of information etc that a lot of people hear because each person tells it to somebody else, but that is not definitely true □ *There are rumors of a divorce in the near future.* □ *There's a rumor going around that you might be about to quit.*

rumored US, **rumoured** GB [ˈruːməʳd] *adj* **to be rumored** to be reported □ *She's rumored to be furious.* □ *It is rumored that he may run for election again.*

rump [rʌmp] *n* -1. [of an animal] the part of an animal above its back legs. -2. [of a person] the part of one's body that one sits on (informal use). -3. POLITICS a small number of people who remain in what was once a larger organization or party.

rumple [ˈrʌmpl] *vt* [hair, clothing] to make <sthg> uneven and untidy.

rump steak *n* meat that is cut from the rump of a cow.

rumpus ['rʌmpəs] *n* noisy excited behavior, especially by angry people (informal use).

rumpus room *n* a room in a house, used for informal family activities such as games.

run [rʌn] (*pt* **ran**, *pp* **run**, *cont* **running**) ◇ *vt* **-1.** [race, marathon, mile] to cover <a particular distance> while one is running, usually as a pastime or sport □ *He runs six miles every morning.* □ *She ran the distance between her home and the stores in a matter of minutes.* **-2.** [company, store, country] to manage and organize <a business, event, or activity> □ *Don now runs a software company in Ohio.* □ *Life was different when the military were running the country.* **-3.** [computer program, tape, experiment] to start and supervise <sthg> until it is finished □ *Run the program, and we'll see what problems you're having with it.* □ *We're just going to run some tests on you.* **-4.** [vehicle, machine] to own and pay for the cost of operating <a piece of equipment> □ *Do you run a car?* **-5.** [tap, hose] to cause water to flow from <sthg> □ *Run the water first, then add the oil.* ■ **to run a bath** to fill a bath with water. **-6.** [advertisement, story] to publish <sthg> in a newspaper or magazine □ *They've been running a series of articles about the Swiss economy.* **-7.** [person] to take <sb> to a place that is nearby and easy to reach □ *I'll run you home/to the airport.* **-8. to run sthg along/over sthg** to move sthg along/over the surface of sthg □ *He ran a finger over the dusty piano.*

◇ *vi* **-1.** [person] to move on one's feet more quickly than when walking, usually by lifting the legs higher and having one or both feet off the ground □ *He ran downstairs/upstairs/along the platform.* □ *She runs to work every morning.* ■ **to run for it** to start running quickly in order to avoid something or escape from somebody □ *Quick! Run for it! The police are coming!* **-2.** [road, pipe, cable] to pass in a particular direction; [shiver, pain] to move quickly over a particular area □ *A high fence runs around the building.* □ *A shiver ran down her back.* □ *A thought ran through my mind.* **-3.** [politician] to be a candidate in an election □ *Do you think he'll run for president?* **-4.** [system, arrangement] to work or happen in a particular way □ *Things are running quite smoothly.* **-5. to be running** [machine, engine] to be switched on, so that it is working; [factory, power station] to be working and producing something □ *Try not to leave the engine running.* □ *We hope to have the plant running by the end of the year.* ■ **to run on sthg** [on diesel, gas, electricity] to use sthg as fuel or as a power supply □ *This car runs on regular gas.* ■ **to run off sthg** [off mains, socket, electricity] to get power from sthg in order to work □ *Try running those lights off the main power supply.* **-6.** [bus, train] to travel at particular intervals from one place to another □ *"How often do trains run to the airport?" — "Every 15 minutes."* ■ **to be running late** [person, bus, train] to be likely to arrive somewhere later than planned; [performance, program, meeting] to be

taking longer than planned and so be likely to finish late □ *The train is running ten minutes late.* □ *We're running a little late, I'm afraid.* **-7.** [liquid, tears, water] to flow somewhere, usually downward □ *Tears ran down her cheeks.* ■ **to run dry** [well, river] to have no water left in it. **-8.** [tap] to be turned on, so water is flowing; [nose] to have a liquid coming out of it because of a cold, irritation etc □ *The water's running, so your bath will be ready soon.* □ *Those onions are making my eyes run.* **-9.** [color, dye] to come out of a piece of clothing because of contact with water; [ink, mascara] to spread and make a mess because of contact with water; [butter, wax] to melt because of contact with heat □ *Be careful, the dye in that shirt runs.* □ *My mascara had run all down my face.* □ *The wax began to run down the candlestick onto the table.* **-10.** [contract, play, campaign] to continue for a particular period of time □ *The play ran for nine months in total.* ■ **to be running at** to have reached and be continuing at □ *The camera is running at 25 frames per second.* □ *Output is running at 100 units a day.* ■ **feelings are running high** people are very angry and upset.

◇ *n* **-1.** the activity of running □ *I went for a run this morning.* ■ **to be on the run** to be hiding or traveling around in order to avoid being captured by the police, usually after committing a crime □ *Three terrorists are believed to be on the run somewhere in Europe.* ■ **to make a run for it** to start running quickly in order to avoid something or escape from somebody □ *Quick, let's make a run for it in case somebody notices.* **-2.** a drive in a car □ *We had an easy run down to San Francisco.* □ *Do you feel like going for a run in the car?* **-3.** [of wins, disasters] a series of events of the same type, one after the other □ *George has had a run of bad luck recently.* **-4.** THEATER a period of time during which a play is performed regularly at a theater □ *How long is the run?* **-5. a run on sthg** [on a product, tickets] a period during which a lot of sthg is bought □ *There's been a run on the dollar today.* **-6.** US [in panty hose] a hole that has spread up or down in a stocking or panty hose. **-7.** [in baseball, cricket] a point awarded to a team as the result of players running between particular points on the playing field □ *How many runs did you make?* **-8.** [in winter sports] a track made of ice or snow, used for a competition □ *a ski/bobsled run.* **-9. in the short/long run** when one considers the effect that something will have after a short/long period of time has passed □ *It's hard work now but it will be worth it in the long run.* □ *In the short run it's probably worth buying, but not in the long run.*

◆ **run about** *vi* = **run around.**

◆ **run across** *vt fus* **to run across sb/sthg** to meet or find sb/sthg when one was not expecting to □ *I ran across an old friend of mine at a party.*

◆ **run along** *vi* **run along (now)!** a phrase used to tell children to leave a place (old-fashioned use).

◆ **run around** *vi* **-1.** to move from place to

place, without staying for long, especially to find or get something in a great hurry □ *I've been running around all day trying to find a new coat.* **-2. to run around with sb** to spend time with sb as a friend or companion □ *He's been running around with another woman.*

◆ **run away** *vi* **-1.** to escape from a person or place quickly, by running; to leave a person or place secretly, usually because they make one unhappy □ *The thief ran away before we could catch him.* □ *She ran away from home at the age of 15.* **-2. to run away from sthg** [from a fact, responsibility, the truth] to avoid sthg that one does not want to accept □ *You can't keep running away from your problems.*

◆ **run away with** *vt fus* to run away with sb [imagination, enthusiasm, idea] to take control of sb so that they no longer think sensibly □ *He let his emotions run away with him.*

◆ **run down** ◇ *vt sep* **-1. to run sb down** [pedestrian] to hit sb with a car so that they are injured or killed □ *A 13-year-old girl was run down by a bus.* **-2. to run sb/sthg down** [rival, government, spouse] to criticize sb/sthg unkindly, especially all the time □ *Sharon's always running down her boss.* **-3. to run an industry/a business etc down** to deliberately let an industry/a business etc decline by gradually giving it less money □ *They're running the business down before selling it off.* ◇ *vi* [battery, clock, business] to stop working properly □ *My watch has stopped. The batteries must have run down.*

◆ **run into** *vt fus* **-1. to run into problems/difficulties etc** to start having problems/difficulties etc □ *It was then that the business first ran into difficulties.* **-2. to run into sb** to meet sb when one was not expecting to meet them □ *Can you believe it? I ran into Julia in the airport lounge!* **-3. to run into sthg** [vehicle, lamppost] to hit sthg with a car □ *A car ran straight into me and smashed my headlights.* **-4. to run into hundreds/thousands etc** to reach an amount of hundreds/thousands etc when calculated □ *The cost ran into millions.*

◆ **run off** ◇ *vt sep* to run a copy off to make a copy on a photocopying machine □ *Could you just run off another few copies of this?* ◇ *vi* to leave a person or place by running, especially after doing something wrong □ *They stole her bag and ran off down the road.* ■ **to run off with sb** [with lover] to leave a place secretly with sb in order to begin a relationship with them □ *She's run off with a married man.* ■ **to run off with sthg** to steal sthg and leave a place with it quickly □ *He's run off with my videos again.*

◆ **run on** *vi* [meeting, project] to continue for longer than expected □ *I'm sorry I'm late, the conference just ran on for hours.*

◆ **run out** *vi* **-1.** [time, money, food] to reach the stage where there is none left □ *We'd better buy some more beer before we run out.* **-2.** [license, contract] to be no longer valid □ *The rent agreement runs out on July 16.*

◆ **run out of** *vt fus* to run out of sthg [time, money, gasoline] to reach the stage where

one has no more left of sthg □ *As usual, we've run out of milk.*

◆ **run over** *vt sep* to run a person/an animal over to hit a person/an animal with a car so that they are injured or killed □ *Our cat was run over by a truck.*

◆ **run through** *vt fus* **-1. to run through sthg** [book, movie] to be present in every part of sthg □ *It's a theme which runs through all of his work.* **-2. to run through sthg** [speech, song, act] to rehearse sthg quickly from beginning to end □ *Let's just run through that last song one more time.* **-3. to run through sthg** [article, index, list] to read sthg quickly □ *She ran through the list to check if we'd left anyone off.*

◆ **run to** *vt fus* **-1.** to reach <a particular amount> □ *The cost may run to three million dollars.* **-2. to run to sthg** to be large enough to pay for sthg □ *My budget doesn't run to a new car.*

◆ **run up** *vt fus* to run up debts/bills etc to allow debts/bills etc to accumulate before paying them □ *Roddy left, having run up hundreds of dollars of debts.*

◆ **run up against** *vt fus* to run up against a problem/an obstacle etc to have to deal with a problem/an obstacle etc □ *This is the kind of competition you can expect to run up against.*

run-around *n* to give sb the run-around to deliberately avoid giving sb honest and direct information (informal use).

runaway ['rʌnəweɪ] ◇ *adj* a runaway horse/train etc a horse/train etc that is out of control □ *The country has runaway inflation.* ◇ *n* a person who runs away from somewhere, especially a young homeless person who has left their family.

rundown ['rʌndaʊn] *n* **-1.** a summary of the main aspects of a situation or subject that need to be known □ *Give me a quick rundown before the meeting.* **-2.** the process of reducing the level of activity of a business.

◆ **run-down** *adj* **-1.** [area, property, estate] that is in bad condition because it has been neglected □ *The Roberts family lived in a run-down part of town.* **-2. to feel run-down** to feel tired or ill because of too much work, bad diet etc □ *I've been feeling a little run-down recently.*

rung [rʌŋ] ◇ *past participle of* ring. ◇ *n* **-1.** one of the short sections of metal or wood across the center of a ladder that one steps on when climbing it. **-2.** one of the levels through which an employee passes while progressing toward the top of their company or profession □ *She entered the company at the lowest rung and worked her way up.*

run-in *n* an argument (informal use).

runner ['rʌnər] *n* **-1.** a person who runs as a sport or pastime □ *There were several runners on the track.* **-2. a gun/drugs runner** a person who illegally transports guns/drugs from one country to another. **-3.** [on an ice skate, sled, car seat] a strip of wood or metal which something can move forward easily on. **-4.** BASEBALL a player who is on base or trying to reach a base.

runner bean *n* GB a long, narrow, green bean.

runner-up (*pl* **runners-up**) *n* a person whose final position in a competition is very close behind the winner, e.g. second, third, or fourth □ *And the runner-up is...Mary Rhodes!*

running ['rʌnɪŋ] ◇ *adj* -1. **a running argument/ joke etc** an argument/a joke etc that continues over a period of time. -2. **to happen four days running** to happen every day for four days □ *They've won the tournament two years running.* -3. **running water** water that is supplied to a building through pipes; water that is moving, e.g. in a river, rather than still □ *When we first moved in there was no running water.*
◇ *n* -1. the activity or sport of running □ *running shoes/shorts* □ *I go running twice a week.* -2. [of a business, organization] the management or administration of a business, organization, event etc □ *We need help with the day-to-day running of the office.* -3. [of a machine] the operation of a machine. -4. **to make the running** to do things faster or better than other people who one is competing against □ *They made all the running in the early stages of the race.* ■ **to be in/out of the running** to have a good chance/no chance of success □ *He's in the running for promotion.* □ *That crash has put Kornberg out of the running for this race.*

running commentary *n* a spoken description of an event, especially in sport, that is given continuously while the event happens □ *Do you have to give a running commentary on what's going on out there?*

running costs *npl* the amount of money that is needed to run a business, machine, car etc.

running mate *n* US a politician who campaigns with another politician as a partner in order to win a pair of positions, e.g. president and vice-president □ *The President has not yet selected his running mate for the next elections.*

running repairs *npl* repairs to a vehicle that are necessary over a particular period of time to keep it working properly.

runny ['rʌnɪ] (*compar* **runnier**, *superl* **runniest**) *adj* -1. [jam, sauce, mixture] that is thin enough to flow quickly, like a liquid □ *The custard was thin and runny.* -2. [nose, eyes] producing a watery substance, as the result of a cold or irritation □ *Hay fever always gives me a runny nose.*

run-of-the-mill *adj* [person, situation] that is ordinary and not surprising in any way □ *It's just an ordinary, run-of-the-mill sort of place.*

runt [rʌnt] *n* -1. the smallest and weakest animal in a litter. -2. a small, weak, or unimportant person (disapproving use).

run-through *n* a quick rehearsal of a play, concert, speech etc from beginning to end □ *Can we have a quick run-through of the final act?*

run-up *n* -1. [to an election, a competition] a period of time leading up to a particular event □ *Media interest was at its height in the run-up to the general election.* -2. SPORT the series of running steps taken by an athlete before jumping or throwing something.

runway ['rʌnweɪ] *n* the area of land designed for planes to land on and take off from.

rupture ['rʌptʃəʳ] *n* -1. MEDICINE a tear in the wall of the abdomen. -2. the sudden end of a relationship between two people or groups.

rural ['ruərəl] *adj* [life, area, landscape] that is connected with the countryside.
NOTE: Compare **urban**.

ruse [ruːz] *n* a trick in which one deceives somebody in order to get or do something □ *It's just a ruse so that he can talk to you.*

rush [rʌʃ] ◇ *n* -1. a hurry □ *I'm in a real rush.* □ *It was a terrible rush to get to the shops in time.* □ *What's the rush?* ■ **there's no rush** there is no need to hurry. -2. **a rush on** OR **for sthg** [on a product, tickets] a great demand for sthg. ■ **a rush to do sthg** a great hurry by the public to do sthg □ *There's been a rush to buy tickets for the Michael Jackson concert.* -3. [in stores, on public transport] a very busy period □ *the Christmas rush.* -4. [of people, air] a sudden movement from one place to another □ *There was a rush of cold air as she opened the train window.* -5. **a rush of pity/fear etc** a sudden strong feeling of pity/fear etc □ *She felt a rush of emotion as she saw the children again.*
◇ *vt* -1. to try to make <sb> do something more quickly than they want or than is reasonable; to try to make <sthg> happen more quickly than is reasonable □ *Don't rush me!* □ *You can't rush these things.* ■ **to rush sb into sthg** [into decision] to try to push sb into sthg without giving them time to decide for themselves □ *I was rushed into signing the contract.* -2. [people, supplies, goods] to send <sb/ sthg> somewhere as fast as possible □ *She was rushed to the hospital.* □ *Please rush me your new brochure.* -3. [demonstrators, enemy position] to attack <sb/sthg> suddenly as a group □ *The police rushed the protesters.*
◇ *vi* -1. to move or act very quickly, especially when one does not have much time □ *We'll have to rush!* ■ **to rush into sthg** [into marriage, commitment] to get involved in sthg too fast, without thinking seriously enough about it □ *Don't rush into anything; let them wait.* -2. to move somewhere very fast □ *The blood rushed to her head.* □ *I rushed upstairs/out of the house.*

◆ **rushes** *npl* -1. BIOLOGY tall plants with thin leaves, that grow on wet ground or next to water and are used to make baskets. -2. CINEMA the first version of a sequence of film before it is edited.

rushed [rʌʃt] *adj* [person] who has to do something more quickly than they would like; [job] that is done too quickly □ *She hurried by, looking very rushed.* □ *It's a bit rushed, so it won't be my best work.*

rush hour *n* the time of day when a city is very busy because people are traveling to or from work □ *the morning rush hour.*

rush job *n* a piece of work that is done very quickly and not very well because of a time limit □ *It's a real rush job, but it's the best we could do in the time available.*

Rushmore ['rʌʃmɔːʳ], **Mount** a mountain in South Dakota that has the faces of four US presidents (Washington, Jefferson, Lincoln, and Theodore Roosevelt) carved into it.

rusk [rʌsk] *n* GB a small, hard, dry biscuit given to young babies.

Russell ['rʌsl], **Bertrand** (1872–1970) a British philosopher and mathematician, known for his pacifist views and popular books about philosophy.

russet ['rʌsət] *adj* a reddish-brown color (literary use).

Russia ['rʌʃə] a country in northeastern Europe and northern Asia. It is the largest country in the world, and was the main republic of the USSR. SIZE: 17,075,000 sq kms. POPULATION: 150,000,000 (*Russians*). CAPITAL: Moscow. LANGUAGE: Russian. CURRENCY: rouble.

Russian ['rʌʃn] *n* & *adj*: see **Russia**.

Russian roulette *n* a game of chance in which somebody spins the cylinder of a gun which is loaded with one bullet only, points it at their head, and shoots.

rust [rʌst] ◇ *n* a brown substance that forms on iron and steel when they are in contact with air and water □ *The car door was covered in patches of rust.* ◇ *vi* [car, lock] to develop rust and eventually decay.

Rust Belt: **the Rust Belt** a region of the northern USA around the Great Lakes that has economic problems because of the decline of heavy industry, especially the steel industry and automobile industry.

rustic ['rʌstɪk] *adj* [style, brickwork, charm] that makes one think of the countryside.

rustle ['rʌsl] ◇ *n* a soft sound made by leaves, clothes etc as they lightly rub against each other □ *a rustle of papers.* ◇ *vt* **-1.** [newspaper, skirt] to move <sthg> so that it makes a soft sound. **-2.** [cattle, herd] to steal <animals> from an area of land. ◇ *vi* [paper, leaves, skirt] to make a rustle □ *I heard something rustling in the bushes, probably a bird.*

rustproof ['rʌstpruːf] *adj* [metal, bodywork] that has been treated in a special way to prevent rust.

rusty ['rʌstɪ] (*compar* **rustier**, *superl* **rustiest**) *adj* **-1.** [metal] that is covered in rust and is starting to decay □ *a rusty old nail.* **-2.** [skill] that is not as good as it used to be because it has not been practiced for a while □ *My Italian is pretty rusty these days.*

rut [rʌt] *n* a long narrow space in the ground, made by wheels □ *The snow had frozen in deep ruts.* ■ **to be in a rut** to be in a situation that one cannot get oneself out of, even though one is bored or dissatisfied □ *I've got myself into a real rut at work.*

rutabaga [ˌruːtəˈbeɪgə] *n* US a large round root vegetable that is brown or purple outside and yellow inside.

Ruth [ruːθ], **Babe** (1895–1948) a US baseball player.

Rutherford ['rʌðəfəʳd], **Ernest** (1871–1937) a

British scientist who was the first person to split the atom.

ruthless ['ruːθləs] *adj* **-1.** [person] who shows no pity for people who suffer as a result of one's determination to achieve something □ *When it comes to her work, she's ruthless.* **-2.** [questioning, investigation, approach] that is firm and includes all that is necessary, even if it is unpleasant □ *They carried out the inquiry with ruthless efficiency.*

ruthlessly ['ruːθləslɪ] *adv* [destroy, check, record] see **ruthless**.

ruthlessness ['ruːθləsnəs] *n*: see **ruthless** □ *His ruthlessness as a leader made him feared and hated.*

RV *n* **-1.** (*abbr of* **revised version**) **the RV** a revision of the Authorised Version of the Bible, published in 1881 and 1885. **-2.** US (*abbr of* **recreational vehicle**) a motor vehicle adapted for leisure use, e.g. a camper.

Rx US a symbol used to mean a prescription.

rye [raɪ] *n* **-1.** the grain that is produced by a type of cereal grass and used for flour. **-2.** = **rye bread. -3.** = **rye whiskey.**

rye bread *n* brown bread made with rye flour and caraway seeds.

rye grass *n* the cereal grass that produces grains of rye.

rye whiskey *n* whiskey made from rye.

S

s [es] (*pl* **s's** OR **ss**), **S** [es] (*pl* **S's** OR **Ss**) *n* the nineteenth letter of the English alphabet.

◆ **S** *abbr of* **south.**

SA -1. *abbr of* **South Africa. -2.** *abbr of* **South America.**

Sabbath ['sæbəθ] *n* **the Sabbath** the day of the week meant to be used for rest and worship, that is Sunday for Christians and Saturday for Jews.

sabbatical [səˈbætɪkl] ◇ *n* a period of time that a teacher or lecturer takes off from work to travel or do further study. ■ **to be/ go on sabbatical** to have/take time off from teaching duties in order to travel or study. ◇ *adj*: *a sabbatical year.*

saber US, **sabre** GB ['seɪbəʳ] *n* a heavy sword with a curved blade, once used by soldiers on horseback.

sable ['seɪbl] *n* a type of dark expensive fur.

sabotage ['sæbətɑːʒ] ◇ *vt* **-1.** [building, machinery] to deliberately damage <sthg> so that it cannot be used, especially during a war or protest □ *The rebels had sabotaged the army's tanks.* **-2.** [plan, attempt, election] to deliberately do something in order to stop <sthg> from being successful □ *You deliberately tried to sabotage my meeting with Yohamara.* ◇ *n* the act of sabotaging a building, machinery etc □ *They were accused of sabotage.*

saboteur [ˌsæbəˈtɜːʳ] *n* a person who carries out sabotage.

sabre *n* GB = **saber**.

saccharin(e) [ˈsækərɪn] *n* a very sweet substance used as a substitute for sugar.

sachet [US sæˈʃeɪ, GB ˈsæʃeɪ] *n* a small packet made of paper or plastic, easily torn to release the contents □ *a sachet of shampoo.*

sack [sæk] ◇ *n* -1. [of coal, potatoes] a large, strong, oblong bag made of canvas, plastic, or paper; the amount of something contained in this bag. -2. **to get** OR **be given the sack** GB to be dismissed from one's job (informal use). ◇ *vt* GB to dismiss <sb> from their job (informal use).

sackful [ˈsækfl] *n* an amount that is enough to fill a sack □ *sackfuls of mail.*

sacking [ˈsækɪŋ] *n* a type of rough cloth used for making sacks.

sacrament [ˈsækrəmənt] *n* one of the main Christian religious ceremonies, e.g. marriage or baptism.

sacred [ˈseɪkrəd] *adj* -1. RELIGION [temple, place] that must be treated with great respect because it is important in a particular religion. -2. [right, privilege, privacy] that must not be attacked or criticized in any way □ *Nothing is sacred to today's press.*

sacrifice [ˈsækrəfaɪs] ◇ *n* -1. RELIGION the offering of something, especially an animal that has been killed, to a god, as part of a ceremony □ *The goat was offered as a sacrifice.* -2. the act of choosing not to have or do something that one wants, in order to achieve something else, especially somebody else's happiness □ *It'll require a certain amount of sacrifice on your part.* □ *It's only a small sacrifice.* ◇ *vt* -1. RELIGION to kill <a person or animal> as a gift to a god □ *They sacrificed a lamb to the gods.* -2. [time, freedom, quality] to choose not to have <sthg> in order to obtain or achieve something else □ *Don't sacrifice your free time for their work.*

sacrilege [ˈsækrəlɪdʒ] *n* -1. RELIGION an act or statement that does not show respect for something holy or sacred □ *an act of sacrilege.* -2. an act or statement that is opposed to a widely accepted tradition, convention, or belief in a shocking way □ *You can't not like the Beatles! That's sacrilege!*

sacrilegious [ˌsækrəˈlɪdʒəs] *adj* [behavior] that shows a shocking lack of respect for something.

sacrosanct [ˈsækrəʊsæŋkt] *adj* [right, principle, custom] that cannot be attacked or changed in any way because it is considered to be very important.

sad [sæd] (*compar* **sadder**, *superl* **saddest**) *adj* -1. [person, face] that shows unhappiness □ *She felt desperately sad as she watched them leave.* □ *You look very sad today.* -2. [story,

news, event] that makes one feel unhappy □ *I was so sorry to hear your sad news.* -3. [lack, failure, decline] that is regretted □ *It is a sad fact that none of you have ever shown any interest in your relatives.*

SAD [sæd] (*abbr of* **seasonal affective disorder**) *n* a state of depression that is caused by a lack of sunlight.

sadden [ˈsædn] *vt* to make <sb> feel sad (formal use) □ *I was saddened to learn of his death.*

saddle [ˈsædl] ◇ *n* -1. a leather seat put on a horse's back for a rider to sit on. -2. a seat on a bicycle or motorbike. ◇ *vt* -1. **to saddle a horse** to put a saddle on a horse before riding it. -2. **to saddle sb with sthg** to give sb sthg unpleasant to do □ *I was saddled with the task of explaining why we were all late.*

◆ **saddle up** ◇ *vt fus* **to saddle up a horse** to saddle a horse. ◇ *vi* [rider] *It was time to saddle up.*

saddlebag [ˈsædlbæg] *n* a bag attached to the saddle of a horse, bicycle, or motorbike.

saddler [ˈsædləʳ] *n* a person who makes leather goods, especially horses' saddles.

Sade [sɑːd]: **the Marquis de Sade** (1740–1814) a French writer whose books describe many sexual practices, including sadism, which was named after him.

sadism [ˈseɪdɪzm] *n* the act of getting pleasure from causing pain to other people.

sadist [ˈseɪdəst] *n* a person who gets pleasure from causing pain to other people.
NOTE: Compare **masochist**.

sadistic [səˈdɪstɪk] *adj* [attitude, person, pleasure] *see* **sadism**.

sadly [ˈsædlɪ] *adv* -1. [smile, sigh, say] in a way that shows sadness □ *"We've been told to leave," said Charlie sadly.* -2. a word used to show that one finds a particular situation disappointing □ *Sadly, our city centers are not as safe as they used to be.* □ *Public support for the plan is sadly lacking.*

sadness [ˈsædnəs] *n* -1. a feeling of unhappiness. -2. a sad quality in a situation or story.

sadomasochistic [ˌseɪdoʊmæsəˈkɪstɪk] *adj* [person] who gets pleasure from hurting other people and from being hurt.

s.a.e., sae *n abbr of* **stamped addressed envelope**.

safari [səˈfɑːrɪ] *n* a trip, especially in Africa, to hunt or watch wild animals □ *They've gone on safari.* □ *a safari trip.*

safari park *n* a park where large wild animals can be seen by tourists in cars.

safe [seɪf] ◇ *adj* -1. [trip, product, equipment] that does not put people in danger □ *Is it safe to come out?* □ *Have a safe trip!* □ *Plastic bags are not safe for babies to play with.* -2. **to be safe** not to be in danger of being harmed, lost, or stolen □ *I don't feel safe here any more.* □ *The town is now safe from attack.* □ *You'll be safe here.* □ *The new owners have assured staff that their jobs are safe.* □ *Keep this card safe.* ■ **safe and sound** [arrive, return] without having been harmed or damaged in any way □ *We got there safe and sound in the end.* -3. **a safe**

place a place where something is not likely to be lost or stolen □ *I always keep my wallet in a safe place.* **-4.** [method, investment] that does not involve taking risks ■ **a safe driver** a driver who does not take risks. ■ **to be in safe hands** to be in a position where one can trust somebody to take care of one or to manage one's affairs. ■ **just to be on the safe side** in order to avoid taking risks □ *I took an umbrella, just to be on the safe side.* **-4.** [topic, question] not likely to produce any disagreement □ *I tried to stick to safe subjects of conversation.* ■ **it is safe to say (that)...** most people would agree that... **-5.** *phrase* **your secret is safe with me** I will not tell anybody your secret.
◇ *n* a metal container with thick sides and a lock that is used for keeping money, jewels, documents etc in to stop them from being stolen.

safebreaker ['seɪfbreɪkə^r] *n* a thief who breaks open safes to steal what is inside.

safe conduct *n* protection given to somebody who is traveling through a dangerous area, e.g. during a war; an official document ordering this protection.

safe-deposit box *n* a box in a bank that jewelry and important documents can be kept safe in.

safeguard ['seɪfɡɑː^rd] ◇ *n* something that is intended to protect somebody against something unpleasant that may happen in the future □ *Travel insurance acts as a safeguard against unexpected medical costs while abroad.* ◇ *vt* to protect <sb/sthg> against something unpleasant that may happen in the future □ *We must safeguard our country's heritage against the threat of mass tourism.*

safe haven *n* an area affected by war where an authority such as the UN has declared that no fighting is allowed and where people go in order to be safe.

safe house *n* a house used by criminals, spies etc for hiding in.

safekeeping [ˌseɪf'kiːpɪŋ] *n* **to give sb sthg for safekeeping** to give sb sthg in order for them to keep it safe □ *Leave your passport with the hotel manager for safekeeping.* □ *I put it there for safekeeping.*

safely ['seɪflɪ] *adv* **-1.** [travel, drive] without being or putting oneself in any danger □ *Drive safely!* **-2.** [store, hide] away from the danger of being harmed, lost, or stolen □ *The documents are safely locked away.* **-3.** [arrive, land, deliver] without having been harmed or damaged in any way □ *We got home safely.* **-4. I can safely say that...** it is true to say that... □ *I can safely say that I have never been so surprised in my life!*

safe seat *n* GB POLITICS a seat that is certain to be won again in an election by the party that already has it.

safe sex *n* sex that involves using condoms and avoiding activities that might pass on the AIDS virus.

safety ['seɪftɪ] ◇ *n* **-1.** [of a person, home, vehicle] the condition of being safe □ *We are con-* cerned about Sally's safety. □ *The safety of our passengers is our top priority.* **-2.** a place where one is safe □ *The refugees finally reached safety.* □ *They were taken to a place of safety.* ◇ *comp* that is intended to make something less dangerous or harmful □ *safety checks/ measures* □ *a safety device/mechanism.*

safety belt *n* a strap that passengers wear around their body in a car, plane etc that helps to keep them in their seats if there is an accident.

safety catch *n* a small lock that stops a gun being fired accidentally.

safety curtain *n* a curtain at the front of the stage in a theater that is lowered when a performance is not taking place and is made of a material that prevents fire from spreading.

safety-deposit box *n* = safe-deposit box.

safety island *n* US a raised area in the middle of a road where people crossing the road wait for the traffic to pass.

safety match *n* a match that will not catch fire by accident.

safety net *n* **-1.** a net placed below circus performers who perform high in the air in order to catch them if they fall. **-2.** something that can be used if a situation becomes too difficult □ *That money is my safety net if I run out of work.*

safety pin *n* a wire pin used for fastening together clothes or material. The pointed end bends inside a cover to stop it from being dangerous.

safety valve *n* **-1.** TECHNOLOGY a small opening in a machine that gas, steam, or liquid can escape through if the pressure becomes too great. **-2.** a way in which one can release strong negative feelings before they become harmful, e.g. through exercise.

saffron ['sæfrən] *n* **-1.** an orange-brown spice that comes from a flower and is used to flavor and color food □ *saffron rice.* **-2.** a bright orange-yellow color □ *saffron robes.*

sag [sæɡ] (*pt* & *pp* **sagged**, *cont* **sagging**) *vi* **-1.** [chair, bed, mattress] to change shape by sinking downward, usually in the middle. **-2.** [interest, demand] to become less.

saga ['sɑːɡə] *n* **-1.** LITERATURE a long story written in Iceland or Norway during the Middle Ages; a long story about a particular group of people that takes place over a long period of time. **-2.** a long and boring description of something that has happened to somebody.

sage [seɪdʒ] ◇ *adj* [person, advice] wise (literary use). ◇ *n* **-1.** COOKING an herb with rough gray-green leaves and a strong smell, used to flavor food. **-2.** a very wise man (literary use).

saggy ['sæɡɪ] (*compar* **saggier**, *superl* **saggiest**) *adj* [sofa, mattress] that has sunk down in the middle.

Sagittarius [ˌsædʒə'teərɪəs] *n* a sign of the zodiac, often represented by an archer; a person born under this sign between November 22 and December 22.

Sahara [US səˈhærə, GB -ˈhɑːrə]: **the Sahara (Desert)** a desert in North Africa reaching from the Atlantic Ocean to the Red Sea. It is the largest desert in the world.

said [sed] *past tense & past participle of* **say**.

sail [seɪl] ◇ *n* **-1.** a piece of strong cloth that is fixed to the mast of a boat and catches the wind so that the boat moves forward. ■ **to set sail** [sailor, ship] to begin a trip by sea □ *They set sail for America.* **-2.** a trip in a sailboat □ *We went for a sail.*
◇ *vt* **-1.** [dinghy, yacht] to move <a ship or boat> across water. **-2.** [sea, lake] to travel across <an area of water> in a ship or boat.
◇ *vi* **-1.** [person] to travel by ship or boat; to begin a trip by ship or boat □ *They sailed to France in a yacht.* □ *We sail at noon.* **-2.** [ship, boat] to move across water; to leave port and begin a trip □ *The boat sailed past the island/into the harbor.* **-3.** SPORT to sail a boat for pleasure □ *We like to sail at the weekend.* **-4.** [object, person] to move quickly and smoothly □ *The ball sailed through the air.*
◆ **sail through** *vt fus* **to sail through sthg** [exam, test, interview] to complete sthg without any difficulty.

sailboard [ˈseɪlbɔːʳd] *n* a board with a sail that is used in the sport of windsurfing.

sailboat [ˈseɪlbəʊt] *n* US a boat with sails, especially a small one used for pleasure.

sailcloth [ˈseɪlklɒθ] *n* thick strong cloth used for making sails and tents.

sailing [ˈseɪlɪŋ] *n* **-1.** SPORT the activity of sailing a boat, yacht etc for pleasure □ *They go sailing every weekend.* **-2.** a trip made by a ship, ferry etc that is carrying passengers □ *There are three sailings a day.*

sailing boat *n* GB = **sailboat**.

sailing dinghy *n* a small open boat that is often used to take people from the shore to a larger boat or ship.

sailing ship *n* a large ship with sails, especially one built before the steam engine was invented.

sailor [ˈseɪləʳ] *n* a person who works on a ship and helps to sail it. ■ **to be a good sailor** not to suffer from seasickness.

saint [seɪnt] *n* **-1.** RELIGION a person who is officially declared, by a pope or another Christian authority, to have lived a holy life and to be especially worthy of respect. **-2.** a person who one thinks is very good because they are kind, patient etc and do not seem to have any bad qualities □ *You must have the patience of a saint!*

Saint Andrew in the Bible, one of Jesus Christ's apostles. He is the patron saint of Scotland.

Saint Christopher [-ˈkrɪstəfəʳ] in the Christian religion, a man who carried Christ across a river. He is the patron saint of travelers.

Saint David a Welsh bishop who founded many churches in the 6th century. He is the patron saint of Wales.

Saint Francis (of Assisi) [US -ˌfrænsəs(əvəˈsɪsɪ), GB -ˌfrɑːnsəs-] (1182–1226) an Italian monk who founded the Franciscan order of monks. He is well known for his love of birds and animals.

Saint George a Roman soldier who is supposed to have killed a dragon to save a woman. He is the patron saint of England.

Saint John the Baptist in the Bible, a preacher who baptized many people, including his cousin, Jesus Christ.

saintly [ˈseɪntlɪ] (*compar* **saintlier**, *superl* **saintliest**) *adj* [person, virtue, life] that appears to be very good, honest, and without any bad qualities.

Saint Patrick [-ˈpætrɪk] (385–461 AD) a British missionary who introduced Christianity to Ireland. He is the patron saint of Ireland.

Saint Patrick's Day *n* March 17, the feast day of Saint Patrick.

❧ SAINT PATRICK'S DAY
Saint Patrick's Day, March 17, is celebrated all over the world by Irish people, or by people whose ancestors were Irish. There are large parades through the streets of Dublin, New York, and Sydney. It is traditional to wear a piece of shamrock, the Irish national plant, or to wear something green, since green is the color used to represent Ireland. Some bars in the USA even serve green beer on Saint Patrick's Day.

Saint Paul [-ˈpɔːl] in the Bible, one of the first Christian missionaries. He was an opponent of Christianity until he was converted by a vision of Christ on the road to Damascus.

Saint Paul's: **Saint Paul's (Cathedral)** a large cathedral central London. Its dome can be seen from many places in London.

Saint Peter in the Bible, the leader of Christ's apostles and the first leader of the Christian church.

sake [seɪk] *n* **-1. for the sake of sb, for sb's sake** in order to benefit sb □ *Be nice to him for my sake!* **-2. for the sake of sthg** in order to try to help or get sthg □ *I said yes for the sake of peace and quiet.* □ *Let's assume, for the sake of argument, that this is true.* **-3. to do sthg for its own sake** OR **for the sake of it** to do sthg because one enjoys doing it and not because there is a particular reason for doing it □ *She loves just arguing for the sake of it.* ■ **for God's** OR **for heaven's sake!** a phrase used to show one's annoyance or impatience with somebody or something □ *For heaven's sake, stop messing around with that!*

salad [ˈsæləd] *n* a mixture of lettuce, tomatoes, and other raw vegetables that are eaten cold as part of a meal. ■ **a tuna/an egg etc salad** a salad that contains tuna/egg etc □ *Help yourself to salad.* □ *Two ham salad sandwiches, please.*

salad bowl *n* a large bowl, often wooden, in which green salad is served.

salad cream *n* GB a cream-colored sauce that is used on salads and is similar to mayonnaise but thinner and sweeter.

salad dressing *n* a mixture of oil and vinegar with mustard, honey, garlic etc, used on salad to add flavor.

salad oil *n* oil used to make salad dressing, e.g. olive, sunflower, or peanut oil.

salamander ['sæləmændə^r] *n* an animal that looks like a lizard and can live on land or in water.

salami [sə'lɑːmɪ] *n* a large, pink, spicy sausage that is eaten cold in thin slices.

salaried ['sælərɪd] *adj* [person] who is paid a salary by their employer □ *a salaried job.*

salary ['sælərɪ] (*pl* **salaries**) *n* the money that somebody is paid once a month by the company or organization they work for □ *The salary is negotiable.* □ *He's on a salary of over $70,000 a year.*
NOTE: Compare **wage.**

salary scale *n* a range of possible salaries that an employee might earn for a particular job, from lowest to highest □ *Salary scale: $65,000–70,000 according to experience.*

sale [seɪl] *n* **-1.** [of a piece of property] the act of selling something □ *The sale of the house went smoothly.* ■ **to make a sale** to sell something. ■ **to be on sale** [product, goods] to be available to be bought, usually in a store □ *'Now on sale at all good pharmacies.'* ■ **to be (up) for sale** [house, car] to be available to be bought, usually from a private owner □ *I'm afraid the picture is not for sale.* **-2.** [in a store] a period of time in a store during which prices are reduced □ *I bought these jeans in the sale.* □ *There are sales on all over town.* □ *a sale item.* ■ **on sale** US that can be bought at a lower price than normal. **-3.** an event where goods are sold to the person who offers the most money □ *a car/furniture sale.*
◆ **sales** *npl* **-1.** the amount of goods sold by a particular company, country etc □ *Sales of consumer goods have fallen.* □ *The sales figures don't look good this month.* **-2.** the department of a company which organizes the selling of products or services □ *He's been in sales for two years now.* **-3. the sales** a period of the year when stores reduce their prices □ *I bought it in the sales* □ *the January sales.*

Salem witch trials [ˌseɪləm-] *npl* **the Salem witch trials** a series of trials held in Salem, Massachusetts, USA, in 1692. Nineteen women were accused of being witches and were hanged.

saleroom *n* GB = **salesroom.**

salesclerk [US 'seɪlzklɜːrk, GB -klɑːk] US, **sales assistant** *n* a person whose job is to sell goods to customers in a store.

sales conference *n* a meeting of people in a particular company who are involved in selling the company's product, organized in order to discuss results and future plans.

sales drive *n* a strong effort by a company to sell more of a product.

sales force *n* the employees of a company who are involved in selling its products.

salesman ['seɪlzmən] (*pl* **salesmen** [-mən]) *n* a man whose job is to sell goods or services for a company □ *an insurance salesman.*

salesperson ['seɪlzpɜːrsn] (*pl* **salespeople** [-piːpl]) *n* a person whose job is to sell things.

sales pitch *n* the things that somebody says about a particular product in order to persuade somebody else to buy it.

sales rep, sales representative *n* a person whose job is to travel to visit customers and sell a company's products or services.

salesroom ['seɪlzruːm] US, **saleroom** ['seɪlruːm] GB *n* a large hall where goods are displayed for sale.

sales slip *n* US a piece of paper given in a store to show that goods have been paid for.

sales tax *n* a tax added to the price of goods bought in stores.

sales team *n* the employees of a company who are involved in selling its products.

saleswoman ['seɪlzwʊmən] (*pl* **saleswomen**) *n* **-1.** [in a company] a woman whose job is to sell goods or services for a company. **-2.** [in a store] a woman whose job is to sell goods to customers in a store.

salient ['seɪlɪənt] *adj* [feature, point] that is most important or most noticeable (formal use).

saline [US 'seɪliːn, GB -aɪn] *adj* that contains salt □ *a saline solution.*

saliva [sə'laɪvə] *n* the watery liquid produced in the mouth that helps one to digest food.

salivate ['sælɪveɪt] *vi* to produce saliva, especially in large amounts.

Salk [sɔːk], **Jonas** (1914–1995) a US scientist who developed a vaccine against polio.

sallow ['sæləʊ] *adj* [complexion, face] that is a pale-yellow color and so looks unhealthy.

sally ['sælɪ] (*pt* & *pp* **sallied**) ◆ **sally forth** *vi* to go somewhere in a very energetic, brave, or confident way (humorous or literary use).

salmon ['sæmən] (*pl* **salmon** OR **salmons**) *n* a large silver fish with orange-pink flesh, considered a luxury as a food; the flesh of this fish eaten as food □ *salmon fishing* □ *smoked salmon sandwiches.*

salmonella [ˌsælmə'nelə] *n* a type of bacteria that can cause serious food poisoning.

salmon pink ◇ *n* an orange-pink color. ◇ *adj*: *a salmon pink dress.*

Salome [US 'sæləmeɪ, GB sə'ləʊmɪ] in the Bible, the stepdaughter of King Herod, who asks him to kill John the Baptist and give her his head as a reward for her dancing.

salon [US sə'lɒn, GB 'sælɒn] *n* **-1.** a place where a hairdresser works □ *a hairdressing salon.* **-2.** a store where expensive clothes are sold.

saloon [sə'luːn] *n* **-1.** US [for drinking] a bar. **-2.** GB AUTO a car for four or more passengers that has a separate trunk and a fixed roof.

saloon bar *n* GB a bar in a pub or hotel that is comfortably furnished.

salopettes [ˌsælə'pets] *npl* GB a warm piece of waterproof clothing worn when skiing that covers one's legs and chest and is held up by straps over one's shoulders.

salsa [US 'sɑːlsə, GB 'sælsə] *n* a kind of fast Latin American music that people dance to.

salt [sɔːlt] ◇ *n* -1. COOKING a white substance taken from the sea or the ground that is used to flavor and preserve food. □ *Have you put salt on it?* □ *cooking salt.* -2. CHEMISTRY any of a group of crystals formed when an acid and a base are mixed together. -3. **to be the salt of the earth** to be somebody one admires and thinks is kind and reliable □ *They're the salt of the earth, those people.* ■ **to rub salt into the wound** to say something to somebody who is already feeling very unhappy or upset that hurts them even more. ■ **to take sthg with a pinch of salt** not to believe that sthg one has heard or been told is completely true or correct □ *I should take everything Margot says with a pinch of salt, if I were you.* ◇ *comp* that has been preserved in salt □ *salt cod/beef.*
◇ *vt* -1. to put salt on <food>. -2. to spread salt on <a road, surface> etc to stop ice from forming.

◆ **salt away** *vt sep* **to salt money away** to save money for the future, often without letting other people know □ *How much have you got salted away?*

SALT [sɔːlt] (*abbr of* **Strategic Arms Limitation Talks/Treaty**) *n* **the SALT talks** talks between the USA and the USSR in the 1970s and 1980s that tried to limit the number of weapons on each side.

saltbox ['sɔːltbɒks] *n* a type of American house that has two stories in the front and one in the back.

salt cellar *n* GB = **salt shaker**.

salted ['sɔːltəd] *adj* [peanuts, chips, butter] flavored with salt.

Salt Lake City the capital of Utah, USA, and the center of the Mormon religion. POPULATION: 159,936.

saltpeter US, **saltpetre** GB [,sɔːlt'piːtəʳ] *n* a substance used in making gunpowder and matches and for preserving meat.

salt shaker [-ʃeɪkəʳ] *n* US a small container, often placed on the table during a meal, which contains salt for people to put on their food.

saltwater ['sɔːltwɔːtəʳ] ◇ *n* water from the sea that contains salt. ◇ *adj* [fish, plant] that lives in saltwater.

salty ['sɔːltɪ] (*compar* **saltier**, *superl* **saltiest**) *adj* [food, water] that tastes of salt or contains a lot of salt.

salubrious [sə'luːbrɪəs] *adj* [area, accommodations] that seems healthy and pleasant (formal use).

salutary [US 'sæljətɪ, GB -jʊtərɪ] *adj* [warning, lesson] that is unpleasant, but teaches one something important.

salute [sə'luːt] ◇ *n* -1. [by a soldier] the act of raising one's hand quickly in a particular way as a sign of respect to a superior officer □ *He gave a salute.* -2. [with a gun] the act of

firing several guns to celebrate something □ *a 21-gun salute.* -3. [with one's head, hand] the act of greeting somebody □ *She raised her hand in salute.* -4. **a salute to sb** a public display of admiration and affection for sb whose life and work has been remarkable □ *The ceremony was a salute to the dedication of the soldiers.*
◇ *vt* -1. [officer, flag] to show respect for <sb/sthg> by giving a salute □ *You must always salute a superior officer.* -2. [hero, courage, achievement] to honor <sb/sthg> by saying or showing in public that one admires them □ *The press today salutes a new world champion.* ◇ *vi* [soldier] to give a salute.

Salvadorean, Salvadorian [,sælvə'dɔːrɪən] *n* & *adj*: see **El Salvador**.

salvage ['sælvɪdʒ] ◇ *n* [from a shipwreck, fire, earthquake] things that are saved during or after a disaster □ *a salvage operation.* ◇ *vt* -1. [object, valuables] to save <sthg> in a reasonable condition during or after a disaster such as a fire, flood, or shipwreck □ *We were able to salvage some furniture from the wreckage.* -2. [pride, reputation] to get or save <sthg good> from an unpleasant or difficult situation □ *The party at least managed to salvage some respectability from the election defeat.*

salvage vessel *n* a ship that is used to rescue things from a shipwreck.

salvation [sæl'veɪʃn] *n* -1. a person or thing that saves somebody or something else from danger or failure □ *The new factory could be the salvation of the area.* -2. RELIGION in the Christian religion, the state of being saved by Christ from punishment for one's sins.

Salvation Army *n* **the Salvation Army** a Christian group whose members wear uniforms, play music in city streets, and help poor and homeless people.

salve [US sæv, GB sælv] *vt* **to do sthg to salve one's conscience** to do sthg to make oneself feel less guilty.

salver ['sælvəʳ] *n* a large flat plate, often made of silver and used for serving food on □ *a silver salver.*

salvo ['sælvoʊ] (*pl* **salvos** OR **salvoes**) *n* the act of firing several guns at the same time.

Samaritan [sə'mærətn] *n* **a good Samaritan** a person who helps other people who are in difficulty.

◆ **Samaritans** *npl* **the Samaritans** a British voluntary organization that provides a telephone service and counseling for people who are depressed.

samba ['sæmbə] *n* a fast dance from Brazil danced by two people.

same [seɪm] ◇ *adj* -1. [date, address, opinion] that is not different or changed □ *He made the same excuse as last time.* □ *Do you still have the same phone number?* -2. [clothes, colors, attitudes] that are exactly like each other □ *They both had on the same jacket.* □ *Her handwriting is almost the same as mine.* □ *I feel the same way about it as you do.* ■ **at the same time** used to show that two events are happening together; used to add a different and less critical opinion to what one has just said □ *She managed to build a career while at the same time bringing up a large family.* □ *He's very arrogant but at the same time you can't help liking him.* ■ **one and the same** exactly the same although appearing to be different □ *Ruth Rendell and Barbara Vine are one and the same person.*

◇ *pron* **the same** used to say that two things are alike; used to say that a situation has not changed □ *I'd do the same again if I had the chance.* □ *"Is he any better?" — "No, he's still the same."* □ *She earns the same as I do.* □ *Our results are the same but our methods are different.* ■ **all** OR **just the same** in spite of this □ *I'm pleased they're coming. All the same, I wish they'd chosen a better time to arrive.* ■ **it's all the same to me** used when one is ready to accept any of the things that are being offered □ *We can go out or stay in, it's all the same to me.* ■ **it's not the same** things are not as good as before □ *We still meet occasionally, but it's just not the same as before.* ■ **(and the) same to you!** a phrase used to return a greeting, wish, or insult □ *"Good luck, Belinda." — "Thanks, and the same to you, Marvin."*

◇ *adv* **the same** [dress, treat] in an identical way □ *He behaved exactly the same as before.*

same-day *adj* **a same-day service** a service that does something for customers quickly, so that it is ready on the same day as it is started.

sameness ['seɪmnəs] *n* a lack of variety (disapproving use) □ *It's the sameness of the job that I can't stand.*

Samoa [sə'məʊə] a group of islands in the southern Pacific Ocean. The eastern islands are administered by the USA, while the western islands form the Independent State of Western Samoa.

samosa [sə'məʊsə] *n* an Indian food that consists of spicy meat or vegetables inside a triangular piece of pastry.

sample [US 'sæmpl, GB 'sɑːmpl] ◇ *n* **-1.** [of a product] a small amount of something, usually a new product, given to customers so that they can try it □ *a free sample* □ *a sample bottle/pack.* **-2.** [of urine, blood, soil] a small amount of something that is taken to be examined in order to provide information □ *a blood sample.* **-3.** [of customers, a population] a group of people chosen from a larger group in order to complete a test, questionnaire etc □ *We asked a sample of 50 businessmen what they thought about the new initiative.*

◇ *vt* **-1.** [food, drink] to taste a small amount of <sthg>, usually to see if one likes it □ *While we were there we sampled some of the local wines.* **-2.** [pleasure, lifestyle] to experience <sthg> for a short time, usually to see if one likes it. **-3.** MUSIC to take <a piece of recorded sound or music> so that it can be used in another recording.

sampler [US 'sæmplr, GB 'sɑːmplə] *n* a piece of cloth with letters, a picture etc sewn on, usually made to show one's skill at sewing.

Samson ['sæmsən] in the Bible, a very strong man who led the Jews against their enemies until he was betrayed by Delilah. She discovered that the secret of his strength was his long hair, and cut it off.

sanatorium [ˌsænə'tɔːrɪəm] (*pl* **sanatoriums** OR **sanatoria** [-rɪə]) *n* = **sanitarium**.

sanctify ['sæŋktəfaɪ] (*pt* & *pp* **sanctified**) *vt* **-1.** RELIGION [name, place] to make <sthg> holy. **-2.** [usage, method, practice] to give official approval to <sthg>.

sanctimonious [ˌsæŋktə'məʊnjəs] *adj* [person] who seems to think they are morally better than other people (disapproving use).

sanction ['sæŋkʃn] ◇ *n* **-1.** official approval or permission given by an authority □ *It hasn't yet been given official sanction.* **-2.** a form of punishment which is intended to make a person obey rules or laws □ *It's the toughest sanction we can apply.* ◇ *vt* [measure, conduct] to give official approval to <sthg> □ *The group's leaders have never sanctioned the use of force.*

◆ **sanctions** *npl* POLITICS action taken by a government to stop trading with another country that is breaking international laws □ *UN sanctions are still in force.* □ *The US have imposed sanctions on the breakaway republic.*

sanctity ['sæŋktətɪ] *n* the fact of being sacred □ *the sanctity of marriage.*

sanctuary [US 'sæŋktʃʊeri, GB -əri] (*pl* **sanctuaries**) *n* **-1.** [for animals] a large area of land where birds or animals are protected from hunting □ *a bird/wildlife sanctuary.* **-2.** [for victims, refugees] a safe place for people who are in danger □ *The hostel was a sanctuary for battered wives.* **-3.** [from danger] safety from possible danger □ *The refugees sought sanctuary in Thailand.* **-4.** the part of a church that is considered to be the most holy.

sanctum ['sæŋktəm] (*pl* **sanctums**) *n* **sb's inner sanctum** a private place where sb can be alone.

sand [sænd] ◇ *n* a substance consisting of very small grains of rock, usually light brown or golden, that form beaches and deserts □ *She picked up a handful of sand.* ◇ *vt* [wood, paintwork, a door] to sand <sthg> down.

◆ **sands** *npl* a flat sandy area beside the sea.

◆ **sand down** *vt sep* **to sand sthg down** [wood, paintwork, a door] to make sthg smooth by rubbing it with sandpaper.

sandal ['sændl] *n* a light summer shoe made mainly of straps that often leaves one's toes uncovered □ *a pair of sandals.*

sandalwood ['sændlwʊd] *n* a sweet-smelling wood from Australia and South Asia that is used for making boxes, carved objects etc; oil from this wood that is used in soaps and perfumes □ *sandalwood soap.*

sandbag ['sændbæg] *n* a small bag full of sand that is used to make a barrier against flood water, gunfire etc.

sandbank ['sændbæŋk] *n* a long area of sand near the surface of the ocean or a river.

sandblast [US 'sændblæst, GB -blɑːst] *vt* [wall,

stonework] to clean <the outside of a build­ing> with a machine that blows a jet of water containing sand onto it.

sandbox ['sændbɒks] *n* US a shallow box full of sand that is used for playing in by children.

sandcastle [US 'sændkæsl, GB -kɑːsl] *n* a pile of sand made by children on the beach, often by filling a bucket with wet sand and turning it upside down.

sand dune *n* a hill of sand in the desert or near the sea, made by the wind.

sander ['sændər] *n* a device used for sanding wood, floors etc.

Sandhurst ['sændhɜːrst] the British Army school for training officers, in Berkshire, England.

sandpaper ['sændpeɪpər] ◇ *n* thick paper covered with sand on one side and used for rubbing surfaces to make them smooth. ◇ *vt* [wood, paintwork, a door] to sand <sthg> down.

sandpit ['sændpɪt] *n* GB = **sandbox**.

sandshoe ['sændʃuː] *n* GB & AUS a canvas shoe with rubber soles.

sandstone ['sændstoʊn] *n* a type of soft rock that is used in building □ *a sandstone block*.

sandstorm ['sændstɔːrm] *n* a storm in a desert area, where sand is blown violently by the wind.

sand trap *n* US GOLF one of the areas on a golf course that are filled with sand and from which it is difficult to hit the ball.

sandwich ['sænwɪdʒ] ◇ *n* two pieces of bread with meat, cheese etc between them □ *a ham/an egg sandwich*. ◇ *vt* **to be sandwiched between two people/objects etc** to be placed between two people/objects etc with very little space on either side.

sandwich board *n* two boards with an advertisement written on them that are fastened to the front and back of a person who walks around outside so that other people see the advertisement.

sandwich course *n* GB a course of study at a college during which one spends time working in business or industry.

sandy ['sændɪ] (*compar* **sandier**, *superl* **sandiest**) *adj* -1. [beach] that consists of sand and not pebbles. -2. [hair] light orange-brown in color.

sane [seɪn] *adj* -1. [person] who is not mentally ill □ *He was certified sane by a panel of psychiatrists.* -2. [person, judgment, approach] that seems sensible and reasonable □ *That sounds like a perfectly sane thing to do.*

San Francisco [,sænfrən'sɪskoʊ] a city and port in California, USA, on the Pacific coast. POPULATION: 723,959.

sang [sæŋ] *past tense of* **sing**.

sanguine ['sæŋgwɪn] *adj* [person] who is cheerful, calm, and optimistic.

sanitarium [,sænə'teriəm] (*pl* **sanitariums** OR **sanitaria** [-rɪə]) *n* US a building for people who need rest and care over a long period while they are recovering from illness.

sanitary [US 'sænəterɪ, GB -ərɪ] *adj* -1. [measures, system, equipment] that is concerned with health and hygiene. -2. [place, conditions] that is clean and free from disease.

sanitary napkin US, **sanitary towel** GB *n* a pad of thick material worn by a woman to absorb the blood during her period.

sanitation [,sænə'teɪʃn] *n* the system by which all the rubbish and waste produced by people, especially in cities, is properly removed.

sanitation worker *n* US a person whose job is to collect rubbish from trashcans.

sanitize, -ise ['sænətaɪz] *vt* [news, story] to make <sthg> more acceptable to people by removing offensive or unpleasant information □ *This book offers a sanitized version of the actor's life.*

sanity ['sænətɪ] *n* -1. [of a person] the state or condition of not being mentally ill □ *Conditions were so appalling that she began to fear for her sanity.* -2. [of a judgment, course of action] good sense that somebody shows in their decisions or actions.

sank [sæŋk] *past tense of* **sink**.

Sanskrit ['sænskrɪt] *n* the ancient language of India, used in modern times in religious ceremonies and texts.

Santa (Claus) ['sæntə(klɔːz)] an imaginary old man with a white beard who wears red clothes and is believed by children to bring presents at Christmas.

São Paulo [saʊm'paʊloʊ] a city in southeastern Brazil. It is Brazil's largest city. POPULATION: 9,480,427.

sap [sæp] (*pt* & *pp* **sapped**, *cont* **sapping**) ◇ *n* -1. [of a plant] the natural juice that flows through plants and carries food to their different parts □ *plant/tree sap.* -2. US a stupid person who is easily fooled by other people (informal use). ◇ *vt* [strength, confidence] to make <sthg> weaker by gradually removing it □ *Too much time in that place just saps your energy.*

sapling ['sæplɪŋ] *n* a young tree.

sapphire ['sæfaɪər] *n* a precious bright-blue stone.

Sappho ['sæfoʊ] (7th–6th century BC) a Greek poet, famous for her love poetry.

Sarajevo [,særə'jeɪvoʊ] the capital of Bosnia-Herzegovina, and its largest city. It was besieged by Bosnian Serb forces from 1992 to 1995. POPULATION: 448,000.

sarcasm ['sɑːrkæzm] *n* the use of words to mean the opposite of what is said, often to make fun of somebody or to criticize something □ *"I'm sure you're just devastated," he said, with heavy sarcasm.*

sarcastic [sɑːr'kæstɪk] *adj* [person, comment] that uses sarcasm □ *He was very sarcastic about the hotel food.*

sarcophagus [sɑːr'kɒfəgəs] (*pl* **sarcophagi** [-gaɪ] OR **sarcophaguses**) *n* a large stone container for a dead body that was used by the ancient Egyptians and Romans.

sardine [sɑːˈdiːn] *n* a small silver fish that is often sold in cans.

Sardinia [sɑːˈdɪnjə] a large Italian island in the Mediterranean, west of Italy. SIZE: 24,090 sq kms. POPULATION: 1,637,705 (*Sardinians*). CAPITAL: Cagliari.

sardonic [sɑːˈdɒnɪk] *adj* [person] who thinks they are too important to deal with somebody or something and shows this in a mocking way □ *a sardonic look/smile.*

sari [ˈsɑːrɪ] *n* a piece of clothing that consists of a long piece of cloth such as silk wrapped around one's body in a particular way. It is the traditional dress of women in India.

sarong [səˈrɒŋ] *n* a piece of clothing that consists of a long piece of thin cloth wrapped around one's waist, worn by men and women in Malaysia.

sartorial [sɑːˈtɔːrɪəl] *adj* [elegance, style] that is connected with the way that clothes, especially men's clothes, are made and worn (formal use).

SAS (*abbr of* **Special Air Service**) *n* **the SAS** a department of the British Army that specializes in secret or difficult operations, e.g. freeing hostages.

SASE *n* US *abbr of* **self-addressed stamped envelope**.

sash [sæʃ] *n* a broad strip of cloth that is usually brightly colored and is worn around one's waist as a type of belt, or across the chest as a sign of a high official position or honor.

sash window *n* a window consisting of two sections, one above the other, that slide up and down in front of each other.

Saskatchewan [US sæˈskætʃəwɑːn, GB -wən] a province in central Canada. ABBREVIATION: SK. SIZE: 652,000 sq kms. POPULATION: 988,928 (*Saskatchewanians*). CAPITAL: Regina.

Sasquatch [US ˈsæskwɑːtʃ, GB -wætʃ] *n* = **Bigfoot**.

sassy [ˈsæsɪ] (*compar* **sassier**, *superl* **sassiest**) *adj* US [person] rude and disrespectful to other people (informal use).

sat [sæt] *past tense & past participle of* **sit**.

Sat. *abbr of* **Saturday**.

SAT [sæt] *n* **-1.** (*abbr of* **Scholastic Aptitude Test**) a test taken in the third year of high school in order to enter a university in the USA. **-2.** (*abbr of* **Standard Assessment Test**) one of a set of British school tests taken at the ages of 7, 11, and 14.

Satan [ˈseɪtn] the Devil.

satanic [səˈtænɪk] *adj* **-1.** [ritual, cult, rite] that involves the worship of Satan. **-2.** [cruelty, malice] very wicked.

satchel [ˈsætʃəl] *n* a flat bag, usually made of leather or canvas, that has a strap so that it can be carried over one's shoulder or on one's back, and is used for carrying books and papers, especially by schoolchildren.

sated [ˈseɪtəd] *adj* **to be sated** to have had enough of something (formal use).

satellite [ˈsætəlaɪt] *n* **-1.** ASTRONOMY a natural object, e.g. a moon or planet, that moves around another larger object in space □ *The Moon is Earth's only satellite.* **-2.** SPACE & TECHNOLOGY a device, sent into space to go around the Earth, that sends back information or is used in telecommunications □ *a telecommunications/weather/spy satellite* □ *These pictures are beamed live into your home by satellite.* □ *a satellite picture/broadcast/link.* **-3.** [of a country, organization, person] a country, organization, or person that is completely under the control of another more powerful one □ *a satellite country/company/town.*

satellite dish *n* a kind of antenna fixed to the outside of a building, consisting of a large, round, curved piece of metal, that allows one to receive satellite TV.

satellite TV *n* television broadcasts, transmitted by a satellite, that can only be received with a special aerial.

satiate [ˈseɪʃɪeɪt] *vt* [person, appetite, hunger] to satisfy <sb/sthg> with enough food or drink (formal use).

satin [ˈsætn] ◇ *n* a fabric made from silk or man-made fibers that is very smooth and shiny on one side □ *a satin sheet/dress.* ◇ *comp* [wallpaper, paint] that has a very smooth and shiny surface □ *a satin finish.*

satire [ˈsætaɪəʳ] *n* a type of humor that criticizes people's stupidity, bad behavior etc by making other people laugh at them; a book, movie etc that uses this type of humor □ *His humor is full of satire.* □ *The play is a satire on the greed of the ruling classes.*

satirical [səˈtɪrɪkl] *adj* [revue, sketch, magazine] that uses satire □ *As a writer, he was famous for his satirical wit.*

satirist [ˈsætərəst] *n* a writer or performer who uses satire.

satirize, -ise [ˈsætəraɪz] *vt* [government, fashion] to criticize <sb/sthg> in a humorous way by using satire.

satisfaction [ˌsætəsˈfækʃn] *n* **-1.** a feeling of happiness when one has what one wants, or when things happen in the way that one wants them to □ *She gets a lot of satisfaction from her job.* □ *He had the satisfaction of knowing that he had done his best.* □ *We guarantee our customers' satisfaction.* ■ **to be to sb's satisfaction** to please or satisfy sb □ *I trust the new version will be to your satisfaction.* **-2.** something that makes one feel pleased □ *This job has very few satisfactions.* **-3.** [of a need, urge, demand] *see* **satisfy** □ *We guarantee the satisfaction of all legitimate claims made against us.*

satisfactory [ˌsætəsˈfæktərɪ] *adj* **-1.** [performance, result, behavior] that is good enough for a particular situation □ *Thomas has made satisfactory progress.* **-2.** [reason, answer] that explains something in a way that convinces somebody □ *That explanation is simply not satisfactory.*

satisfied [ˈsætəsfaɪd] *adj* **-1.** [person] who is happy and pleased because they have what they want, or because things happen in the way that they want them to □ *I've rewritten the letter three times and she's still not satisfied!*

□ *There — have your money! Are you satisfied now?* □ *a satisfied customer/smile.* ■ **to be satisfied with sthg** [with a result, standard, somebody's performance] to think that sthg is good enough for a particular situation; [with somebody's answer, explanation] to find sthg convincing □ *I'm very satisfied with the progress that has been made.* □ *The committee isn't satisfied with the report.* ■ **to be satisfied (that)...** to be certain that... □ *She was satisfied (that) no more could have been done.*

satisfy ['sætəsfaɪ] (*pt* & *pp* **satisfied**) *vt* **-1.** [person] to make <sb> contented by giving them or doing what they want □ *If I apologize in person, will that satisfy them?* **-2.** [police, judge, committee] to convince <sb> of something by giving them enough information □ *His explanation was good enough to satisfy the jury.* □ *You have satisfied me that you deserve a second chance.* ■ **to satisfy oneself that...** to make certain that... □ *She satisfied herself that all the doors were locked.* **-3.** [need, urge, demand] to do, have, or give what is needed for <sthg> □ *He is the only applicant who satisfies all those criteria.* □ *There's nothing like lemonade to satisfy your thirst.*

satisfying ['sætəsfaɪɪŋ] *adj* **-1.** [experience, result] that gives one a feeling of happiness because one feels that it is worth doing □ *It is satisfying to look back on what we have achieved so far.* **-2.** [meal, drink] that is enough to stop one feeling hungry or thirsty □ *It was a nice enough meal but I didn't find it very satisfying.*

satsuma [ˌsæt'suːmə] *n* GB a citrus fruit like a small orange with a loose skin.

saturate ['sætʃəreɪt] *vt* **-1.** [person, clothing, ground] to make <sb/sthg> completely wet □ *The rain had completely saturated the fields.* **-2. to saturate a market** to fill a market completely □ *The market has been saturated with cheap imports.*

saturated ['sætʃəreɪtəd] *adj* **to be saturated** [person, clothes, ground] to be completely wet □ *I got saturated standing in the rain.*

saturated fat *n* a kind of fat that contains a lot of fatty acids and is considered bad for one's health.

saturation [ˌsætʃə'reɪʃn] *n*: *see* **saturate** □ *saturation bombing/TV coverage.*

saturation point *n* **to reach saturation point** to reach a situation in which no more people or things can be added because there are already too many of them.

Saturday ['sætədeɪ] *n* the day of the week between Friday and Sunday; *see also* **Friday**.

Saturn ['sætən] the planet in the solar system that is the sixth-furthest from the Sun and has bright rings around it.

sauce [sɔːs] *n* COOKING a thick liquid that has a particular flavor and is served with meat, vegetables etc □ *cheese/mint/tomato sauce.*

saucepan ['sɔːspæn] *n* a metal container with a handle and high sides that is used for cooking food on a stove.

saucer ['sɔːsər] *n* a small plate specially made to fit underneath a cup.

Saudi Arabia [ˌsaʊdɪə'reɪbjə] the largest country on the Arabian peninsula, and the world's leading oil exporter. SIZE: 2,150,000 sq kms. POPULATION: 17,500,000 (*Saudis, Saudi Arabians*). CAPITAL: Riyadh. ADMINISTRATIVE CAPITAL: Jeddah. LANGUAGE: Arabic. CURRENCY: riyal.

Saudi (Arabian) *n* & *adj*: *see* **Saudi Arabia** □ *the Saudi royal family.*

sauna ['sɔːnə] *n* a period of time spent in a room filled with hot steam; a room or building in which this takes place.

saunter ['sɔːntər] *vi* to walk in a calm and relaxed way without hurrying □ *We sauntered through the park in the evening sunshine.*

sausage ['sɒsɪdʒ] *n* a kind of food made of finely minced meat and flavorings that is wrapped inside a thin tube of skin for cooking or to be eaten cold in slices; a single short length of this □ *a slice of garlic sausage* □ *a pound of sausages.*

sausage roll *n* GB a piece of sausage covered with pastry and cooked.

sauté [US soʊ'teɪ, GB 'soʊteɪ] (*pt* & *pp* **sautéed** OR **sautéd**) ◇ *vt* [meat, vegetables] to fry <food> quickly on both sides in a small amount of fat. ◇ *adj* [onions, potatoes] that have been sautéed.

savage ['sævɪdʒ] ◇ *adj* [killer, animal] that is violent, cruel, and likely to attack; [attack, criticism, outburst] that is violent and intended to do a lot of harm □ *They were attacked by a savage beast.* □ *He wrote a savage article criticizing my work.* ◇ *n* a person who is fierce or vicious □ *They behaved like a bunch of savages.* ◇ *vt* **-1.** [animal] to attack <a person or another animal> and wound them severely □ *She was savaged by a wild dog.* **-2.** [critic, newspaper] to criticize <sb/sthg> very severely □ *Fry's performance was savaged by the press.*

savageness ['sævɪdʒnəs], **savagery** ['sævɪdʒərɪ] *n* savage behavior.

savanna(h) [sə'vænə] *n* a large, open, grassy plain, especially in Africa.

save [seɪv] ◇ *vt* **-1.** [person] to prevent <sb> from being harmed or killed; [object] to prevent <sthg> from being destroyed, damaged, or lost □ *We saved these pictures from the fire.* □ *He was saved from drowning.* □ *He managed to save himself from financial ruin.* ■ **to save sb's life** to prevent sb from dying or being killed □ *The doctors operated just in time to save his life.* **-2.** [time, money, energy] to prevent <sthg> from being wasted or used unnecessarily □ *We saved ten minutes by taking the short cut.* □ *We saved $100 by buying in bulk.* **-3.** [food, object, money] to keep <sthg> in order to have it or use it later □ *I've already saved $2,000 toward the cost of a new car.* □ *We'll save the discussion of this report until our next meeting.* **-4.** [work, expense] to make <sthg> unnecessary for somebody □ *You can save me the trip by delivering this package for me.* □ *She saved me the trouble of firing her by resigning.* □ *A monthly pass would save you (from) having to buy a ticket every day.* **-5.** SPORT [ball, shot] to prevent <sthg> from going into

the goal □ *Jordan saved what looked like a certain goal.* **-6.** COMPUTING [document, file] to copy <sthg> onto a disk where it can be kept and used later □ *I saved it onto hard disk.* □ *The file has been saved on C drive.*
◇ *vi* = **save up**.
◇ *n* SPORT an act of preventing somebody from scoring a goal □ *What a fantastic save!*
◇ *prep* **save (for)** apart from <sb/sthg> (formal use) □ *Everyone, save (for) Ellen, had left the room.*

◆ **save up** *vi* to put money somewhere, especially in a bank, and gradually add more, so that one can use it later □ *I'm saving up for a new car.*

save as you earn *n* GB a method of saving in which money is automatically taken out of a person's income.

saveloy ['sævələɪ] *n* GB a type of red sausage made from smoked pork.

saver ['seɪvəʳ] *n* **-1.** something that prevents the waste or unnecessary use of something else □ *The new machine is a real time/energy saver.* **-2.** FINANCE a person who saves money, especially in a bank or similar institution □ *Savers are being offered an extra 1% interest.*

Savile Row [ˌsævl'rəʊ] a street in London, well known for its high-class tailors.

saving ['seɪvɪŋ] *n* an amount of money that one saves in a particular way □ *By buying three together, you make a saving of 25 cents on each one.*

◆ **savings** *npl* the money that a person has saved □ *My life savings are in that bank account.* □ *Do you have any savings?*

saving grace *n* a good or positive feature of a person or thing that is otherwise bad or unpleasant □ *The scenery is the movie's one saving grace.*

savings account *n* an account at a bank or similar institution in which interest is paid on the money that a person saves.

savings and loan association *n* an institution in the USA that pays interest on money saved in it and makes loans for the purchase of property.

savings bank *n* a bank that pays interest on money saved in it.

savior US, **saviour** GB ['seɪvjəʳ] *n* a person who saves somebody or something from death, destruction, or harm □ *He was hailed as the savior of the nation.*

◆ **Savior** *n* **the Savior** a name for Jesus Christ.

savoir-faire [ˌsævwɑːʳ'feəʳ] *n* knowledge of how to behave in social situations.

savor US, **savour** GB ['seɪvəʳ] *vt* **-1.** [food, wine, meal] to eat or drink <sthg> slowly so that one can enjoy the taste □ *She savored the wine, sipping it in slow luxurious mouthfuls.* **-2.** [experience, moment, comfort] to enjoy <sthg> for as long as one can □ *He's still savoring his triumph at the tennis tournament.*

savory US, **savoury** GB ['seɪvərɪ] (*pl* US **savories** OR GB **savouries**) ◇ *adj* **-1. not savory** [area, period, aspect] not pleasant to be in or to think about □ *This is one of the less savory clubs in*

town. ◇ *n* a savory dish or food. **-2.** [taste, food] that has the taste of meat, cheese etc rather than of something sweet.

saw [sɔː] (US *pt* & *pp* **sawed**, GB *pt* **sawed**, *pp* **sawn**) ◇ *past tense of* **see**. ◇ *n* a tool that has a flat metal blade with sharp points along its edge and is used for cutting wood, trees etc. ◇ *vt* [wood, hole] to cut <sthg> with a saw □ *She sawed the branch off the tree.*

◆ **saw up** *vt sep* **to saw sthg up** to cut sthg up into pieces using a saw.

sawdust ['sɔːdʌst] *n* tiny soft pieces of wood that are left when wood has been sawed.

sawed-off shotgun [ˌsɔːd-] *n* US a shotgun that has part of the barrel removed and is often used by criminals because it can be carried and hidden easily.

sawmill ['sɔːmɪl] *n* a factory in which wood is sawed up into planks.

sawn [sɔːn] GB *past participle of* **saw**.

sawn-off shotgun *n* GB = **sawed-off shotgun**.

sax [sæks] *n* = **saxophone**.

Saxon ['sæksn] HISTORY ◇ *n* = **Anglo-Saxon**. ◇ *adj*: *Saxon culture.*

saxophone ['sæksəfəʊn] *n* a musical instrument that has a bell-shaped bottom end that curves upward, and is often used in jazz and swing bands.

saxophonist [US 'sæksəfəʊnəst, GB sæk'sɒfənɪst] *n* a person who plays the saxophone.

say [seɪ] (*pt* & *pp* **said**) ◇ *vt* **-1.** [word, prayer, line] to speak <sthg> □ *Could you say that a little more slowly?* □ *I can't hear what she's saying.* □ *He said yes/no.* ■ **to say to oneself** to think □ *So I said to myself, "I'm not going to be pushed around like this."* ■ **to say nothing of...** a phrase used to introduce something that is important, but not as important as the thing already mentioned □ *It'll take up so much time, to say nothing of the expense.* ■ **I'll say this for him/her** a phrase used to mention something good about somebody who one has been criticizing □ *I'll say this for her though, she doesn't give up easily.* ■ **it has a lot to be said for it** it has many good features □ *I've nothing against jogging — it has a lot to be said for it. I just don't like it, that's all.* ■ **he didn't have very much to say for himself** he didn't take part in the conversation (informal use). **-2.** to express <sthg> in spoken or written words □ *I find it hard to say what I feel at this moment.* □ *You said (that) you were hungry.* □ *Your letter said* OR *You said in your letter (that) there was trouble at home.* ■ **that goes without saying** a phrase used to show that a statement, fact etc is obvious □ *It goes without saying that all his friends will be there.* **-3.** to give <information> in words, symbols, numbers etc □ *The sign says 'Do not touch.'* □ *The clock/My watch says two-thirty.* □ *The handbook says to unscrew the top bolt first.* **-4.** to show <a particular quality, emotion> etc □ *The look on her face said it all.* □ *It says a lot about him that he didn't complain.* **-5. they say..., it's said...** a phrase used to introduce a fact that many people say is true but that may not be □ *They say he's the best soccer player in the world.* □ *It's said that* they're paying her $20,000. □ So they say, any-way. **-6. (let's) say**... a phrase used to ask somebody to imagine a particular situation □ Just say you won the lottery, what would you do? □ I know it's unlikely to happen, but say it did...

◇ *n* **-1. to have a/no say in sthg** [in a decision, matter] to have some/no power to influence sthg □ Junior staff are demanding a greater say in the decision-making process. □ They have no say in the timing of the move. **-2. to have one's say** to give one's opinion □ You've had your say, now let someone else give their view.

◆ **that is to say** *adv* a phrase used to show that one is saying the same thing again using different words in order to make it more clear or accurate □ nine feet, that is to say, about three meters.

SAYE *n abbr of* **save as you earn.**

saying ['seɪɪŋ] *n* a well-known statement that usually contains good advice or a comment on life □ There's an old country saying, "Bad weather always follows good."

say-so *n* (informal use) **-1. on sb's say-so** as a result of sb saying something, even though it may not be true □ I'm not going to believe it just on your say-so. **-2. sb's say-so** permission or a command from sb to do something □ Don't talk to them again without my say-so, OK?

SBA (*abbr of* **Small Business Administration**) *n* **the SBA** a US government organization that gives loans and advice to small businesses.

SBS (*abbr of* **Special Broadcasting Service**) *n* in Australia, a national television channel that offers a wide range of programs in foreign languages and a good coverage of interna-tional news.

s/c GB *abbr of* **self-contained.**

SC ◇ *n abbr of* **Supreme Court.** ◇ *abbr of* **South Carolina.**

scab [skæb] *n* **-1.** [on somebody's skin] a hard surface that forms on a wound when blood dries. **-2.** INDUSTRY a person who continues to work in a place when other workers there are on strike (disapproving use).

scabby ['skæbɪ] (*compar* **scabbier,** *superl* **scabbi-est**) *adj* [skin, face] that is covered in scabs.

scabies ['skeɪbiːz] *n* a disease of the skin that is spread very easily and causes scabs and itching.

scaffold ['skæfould] *n* **-1.** a framework made of scaffolding □ a scaffold pole. **-2.** a platform on which criminals are hanged or beheaded.

scaffolding ['skæfəldɪŋ] *n* metal tubes and wooden boards that form a framework for builders to climb up in order to reach the higher parts of buildings.

scalawag ['skæləwæg] US, **scallywag** GB ['skæl-ɪwæg] *n* a person, often a child, who be-haves badly but does not cause any harm (humorous use) □ You young scalawag!

scald [skɔːld] ◇ *n* a wound on one's skin caused by very hot liquid or steam. ◇ *vt* [hand, arm, person] to burn <sb/sthg> with very hot liquid or steam.

scalding ['skɔːldɪŋ] ◇ *adj* [liquid, coffee] very hot. ◇ *adv* **scalding hot** very hot.

scale [skeɪl] ◇ *n* **-1.** a set of numbers between two fixed limits that is used to measure something □ a pay/salary scale □ How would you rate their service on a scale of one to ten? **-2.** [of a ruler, thermometer] a series of mark-ings that show a particular system of meas-urements □ the Centigrade scale. **-3.** [of a proj-ect, task] the size or extent of something □ The sheer scale of the Pyramids is impressive even today. □ The speed and the scale of the changes have astonished most people. □ They en-tertain on a grand scale. **-4.** [of a map, model] the relationship, expressed as a ratio of two numbers, between the size of an actual thing and the size of the map, model etc that represents it □ The scale of the map is 1 to 50,000. ■ **to be to scale** [drawing, model] to be a copy that is smaller than the real thing, but that shows the relative size of all the parts accurately □ The drawing is not to scale. □ The building is shown to scale. **-5.** MUSIC a se-quence of notes played or sung one after the other in order □ Marta was practicing her scales. **-6.** [on a fish, snake] one of the small, flat, hard plates forming part of the skin of some animals □ a fish scale. **-7.** US = **scales.**

◇ *comp* **a scale model/diagram** a model/diagram of something that is smaller than the real thing, but shows all the parts at the right size relative to each other.

◇ *vt* **-1.** [cliff, mountain] to climb up <sthg very high and steep>; [wall, fence] to climb over <sthg very steep>. **-2.** [salmon, trout] to remove the scales from <a fish>.

◆ **scales** *npl* a piece of equipment for weigh-ing food, an object, or oneself □ kitchen/bathroom scales.

◆ **scale down** *vt sep* **to scale sthg down** [in-vestment, operation, activity] to reduce sthg to a smaller size or extent □ a scaled-down ver-sion of the original plan.

scallion ['skæliən] *n* US an onion with a long green stem, usually eaten raw in salad.

scallop [US 'skæləp, GB 'skɒl-] *n* a shellfish that can be eaten and that has a shell in two halves shaped like fans.

scallywag *n* GB = **scalawag.**

scalp [skælp] ◇ *n* **-1.** the skin on the top of one's head. **-2.** the hair and skin from the top of somebody's head, removed from a dead person by a Native American warrior in the past as a sign of victory. ◇ *vt* to re-move the scalp from <sb>.

scalpel ['skælpl] *n* an instrument with a thin sharp blade, used by a surgeon for cutting through skin.

scalper ['skælpər] *n* US a person who buys tickets for concerts, the theater etc and sells them to other people at much higher prices.

scam [skæm] *n* a way of making money that involves tricking people (informal use) □ an in-surance scam □ The whole thing's a scam.

scamp [skæmp] *n* a child who behaves badly but does not cause any harm (old-fashioned use).

scamper ['skæmpər] *vi* [child, dog] to run with short steps □ The little girl scampered up the steps and disappeared into the house.

scampi ['skæmpɪ] *n* GB large prawns that are often served in breadcrumbs or in batter.

scan [skæn] (*pt* & *pp* **scanned**, *cont* **scanning**) ◇ *vt* -1. [area, crowd, map] to look at <sthg> carefully or anxiously, usually hoping to see somebody or something in particular □ *She scanned the hillside through binoculars, looking for any sign of movement.* -2. [page, letter, newspaper] to read <sthg> quickly to find out the main information that it contains □ *He scanned the report rapidly and wrote a couple of comments in the margin.* -3. MEDICINE & TECHNOLOGY [body, organ, area] to examine <sthg> using electron, laser, or radar beams that produce an image of it on a screen □ *They scanned his liver to check for signs of disease.* -4. COMPUTING [text, barcode] to record the information contained in <sthg> by passing a photoelectric beam over it and sending the information to a computer system □ *The checkout girl scans each item.*
◇ *vi* -1. LITERATURE [line, poem] to fit the rhythmical pattern correctly □ *The last line doesn't scan.* -2. COMPUTING to record the information contained in something by passing a photoelectric beam over it.
◇ *n* MEDICINE & TECHNOLOGY an act of scanning something using electronic or radar equipment; the image or picture produced in this way □ *a brain/body scan* □ *a radar scan.*

scandal ['skændl] *n* -1. a situation in which people finds out about something that shocks and angers them, usually because they do not think it is morally acceptable □ *If the public finds out, there could be a scandal.* □ *a political scandal involving senior figures.* -2. rumors or gossip about bad things that people are thought to have done □ *She's been spreading scandal about her boss.* -3. **to be a scandal** to be unacceptable to people and make them angry □ *The prices they charge are an absolute scandal.*

scandalize, -ise ['skændlaɪz] *vt* to make <sb> feel very shocked and angry □ *I was scandalized by their behavior.*

scandalous ['skændləs] *adj* -1. [behavior, affair] that scandalizes people □ *The way he spoke to them was absolutely scandalous!* -2. [report, article, rumor] that spreads gossip or publicizes a scandal □ *I refuse to believe these scandalous rumors!* -3. [waste, price, treatment] completely unacceptable □ *It is scandalous that we should be kept waiting so long.*

Scandinavia [ˌskændə'neɪvjə] a region of northern Europe, including Norway, Sweden, Denmark, and often Finland and Iceland.

Scandinavian [ˌskændə'neɪvjən] *n* & *adj*: see **Scandinavia**.

scanner ['skænər] *n* -1. TECHNOLOGY a device that sends and receives radar signals □ *a radar scanner.* -2. MEDICINE a device, especially one using ultrasonic waves, used to scan parts of the body to check for signs of disease □ *a brain/body scanner.* -3. COMPUTING a device that reads texts or codes by passing a photoelectric beam over them and sends the information to a computer system.

scant [skænt] *adj* **scant attention/evidence etc** very little attention/evidence etc □ *Andy showed scant interest in what was being said.*

scanty ['skæntɪ] (*compar* **scantier**, *superl* **scantiest**) *adj* -1. [amount, supply, stock] that is smaller than the amount that is desirable □ *We had used up most of our scanty supply of fuel.* □ *The information available is scanty.* -2. [dress, clothing] that does not cover much of one's body □ *She was wearing a scanty little dress.*

scapegoat ['skeɪpgəʊt] *n* somebody who is blamed for something, even though it was not their fault, or not only their fault □ *They're making her a scapegoat for the whole sleazy mess.*

scar [skɑːr] (*pt* & *pp* **scarred**, *cont* **scarring**) ◇ *n* -1. [on somebody's skin] a mark left on one's skin after a wound has healed □ *scar tissue* □ *He had a long thin scar above his eye.* □ *Do you think it'll leave a scar?* -2. [in somebody's mind] something in one's character or mood that shows that one has been affected by an unpleasant experience □ *She still bears the emotional/mental scars.*
◇ *vt* -1. **to be scarred** [face, skin] to have one or several scars; [landscape, surface] to be damaged by cutting or marking □ *She was badly scarred in the accident.* □ *The hill was now scarred by a huge quarry.* -2. [person] to make <sb> unhappy, upset etc about something for the rest of their life □ *Bad childhood experiences can scar people for life.*

scarce ['skeərs] *adj* -1. [food, materials, information] that is difficult to find or get enough of □ *Water is scarce in this region.* -2. **to make oneself scarce** to go away in order to avoid trouble (informal use) □ *I'd better make myself scarce before Larry gets here.*

scarcely ['skeərslɪ] *adv* hardly □ *I scarcely ever go there now.* □ *The outlook is scarcely promising.* □ *She had scarcely finished eating when they arrived.*

scarcity ['skeərsətɪ] *n* [of materials, food, information] see **scarce**.

scare [skeər] ◇ *n* -1. an experience that makes one feel frightened □ *You gave me such a scare when you jumped out at me like that!* -2. a situation in which a lot of people feel that they are in danger from a particular thing □ *a bomb scare* □ *a health scare.* ◇ *vt* [person] to make <sb> feel frightened or worried □ *It scares me when you say things like that.*
◆ **scare away, scare off** *vt sep* -1. **to scare sb/sthg away** OR **off** [thief, animal] to make sb/sthg go away by scaring them. -2. **to scare sb away** OR **off** [customers, voters] to stop sb from wanting to support or do business with one.

scarecrow ['skeərkrəʊ] *n* a model in the shape of a man that is put in a field to keep birds away from crops.

scared ['skeərd] *adj* [person] who is frightened or worried about something □ *He looked at me with a scared expression.* □ *I was scared that somebody might recognize me.* □ *She's scared of him/the dark.* □ *I'm not scared of admitting it.* □

Julian was too scared to look. ■ **to be scared stiff** OR **to death** to be extremely scared.

scaremongering ['skeə'mʌŋgərɪŋ] *n* the act of deliberately spreading worrying stories in order to frighten people.

scarey ['skeərɪ] *adj* = **scary**.

scarf ['skɑː'f] (*pl* **scarfs** OR **scarves**) *n* a long or square piece of material that is worn around one's neck or head for warmth or decoration □ *a silk scarf.*

scarlet ['skɑː'lət] ◇ *adj* bright red □ *scarlet berries.* ◇ *n* a bright red color.

scarlet fever *n* a very infectious disease that gives one a high temperature and a red rash on one's face and body.

scarves [skɑː'vz] *plural of* **scarf**.

scary ['skeərɪ] (*compar* **scarier**, *superl* **scariest**) *adj* [situation, story, person] that makes one feel worried that something bad is going to happen (informal use) □ *I saw a really scary movie last night.* □ *It was so scary when the lights went out.*

scathing ['skeɪðɪŋ] *adj* [person, criticism, attack] that is very critical of somebody or something □ *Mr Erodolov has launched a scathing attack on education standards.*

scatter ['skætə'] ◇ *vt* [clothes, paper, seeds] to throw or drop <things or pieces of something> all over an area □ *She scattered the coins over the table/on the floor.* ◇ *vi* [people, animals] to move away quickly in different directions □ *The crowd scattered in all directions.*

◆ **scatter around, scatter about** *vt sep* to **scatter sthg around** OR **about** [books, clothes] to scatter sthg randomly or untidily over a large area.

scatterbrained ['skætə'breɪnd] *adj* [person] who is disorganized and often forgets things.

scattered ['skætə'd] *adj* **-1.** [rubbish, clothing] that is spread all over the surface of something, e.g. the ground, in an untidy way □ *There were books scattered all over the floor.* **-2.** [towns, people] that are found in several places; [showers, clouds] that affect different parts of the country at different times □ *There were a few houses, scattered here and there along the way.* □ *warm sunshine with scattered showers.*

scattering ['skætərɪŋ] *n* **a scattering of sthg** [of houses, snow, dust] a small number of things or amount of something spread over a wide area □ *There was a light scattering of snow on the hills.*

scavenge ['skævɪndʒ] ◇ *vt* **-1.** [animal, bird] to collect <food> from rubbish, dead animals etc in order to eat it. **-2.** [person] to collect <things that people have thrown away> in order to use them. ◇ *vi* **-1.** [animal, bird] *Some cats had been scavenging for food in the garbage cans.* **-2.** [person] *She was scavenging in the wastepaper basket for old envelopes.*

scavenger ['skævɪndʒə'] *n* **-1.** an animal or bird that gets its food by scavenging. **-2.** a person who collects useful things that other people have thrown away.

scenario [US sə'nærɪoʊ, GB -'nɑː'r-] (*pl* **scenarios**) *n* **-1.** CINEMA, TV, & THEATER a description of the plot and characters in a movie or play. **-2.** [in the future] a possible situation or sequence of events that might happen in the future □ *If we go ahead with the deal, there are two possible scenarios.* ■ **the worst-case scenario** the worst thing that could possibly happen.

scene [siːn] *n* **-1.** [in a play, movie, book] a part of a story that deals with particular events and characters in a particular place; one of the numbered parts that each act of a play is divided into □ *There's a dramatic scene where they drive over a cliff.* □ *Then, in scene 3, he decides to kill her.* ■ **behind the scenes** off the stage, in a place where the audience cannot see what is happening; secretly □ *a behind-the-scenes look at the making of a soap opera* □ *We don't know what compromises may have been reached behind the scenes.* ■ **to set the scene** to tell somebody about a situation to make it easier for them to understand what happened or happens in it later □ *Now over to our commentator at the City Hall who will set the scene.* ■ **to set the scene for sthg** [for an event, development, crisis] to be a preparation for sthg that will happen later □ *The riots that summer set the scene for the revolution which took place two years later.* **-2.** [of confusion, calm] something that one sees, e.g. an event or a place, that has a particular quality □ *The area near the bomb blast was a scene of devastation.* □ *There were angry scenes as protesters clashed with police.* □ *Picture the scene as the news is brought to the anxious relatives.* **-3.** ART a painting, drawing etc of a particular kind of place □ *a beautiful winter scene by Van Neulen.* **-4.** [of a crime, incident, crash] the place where something has happened □ *Police and firemen rushed to the scene.* □ *at the scene of the crime.* ■ **on the scene** at the place where something has recently happened □ *The emergency services were on the scene within minutes.* ■ **a change of scene** a move to a different place or a different type of activity □ *She's been very tense lately, I think a change of scene might help.* **-5.** **the music/political etc scene** the activities, events, and people involved in music/politics etc in a particular place. ■ **it's not my scene** I don't enjoy this kind of thing (informal use) □ *I don't enjoy clubs, they're not really my scene.* **-6.** [in public] an embarrassing incident or argument that happens in public □ *Calm down please, we don't want a scene in the restaurant.* ■ **to make a scene** to shout, argue, complain etc loudly in front of other people in an embarrassing way □ *Please, Emma, don't make a scene in front of the children.*

scenery ['siːnərɪ] *n* **-1.** the way the land, water, and plants in a place look, especially when this is attractive □ *Scotland's mountain scenery.* **-2.** THEATER the painted background, furnishings etc that make a stage look like a particular type of place.

scenic ['siːnɪk] *adj* [view, place, surroundings] that has beautiful scenery.

scenic route *n* a route that goes through beautiful scenery.

scent [sent] ◇ *n* -1. [of a flower] an attractive smell; [of an animal] a smell that an animal produces to attract a mate, mark its territory etc □ *This rose has a very delicate scent.* □ *The animal leaves its scent on nearby trees.* -2. **to be on the scent of sb/sthg** to be following a trail of signs, clues etc that leads to sb/sthg □ *Once again, Holmes was on the scent of another mysterious crime.* ■ **to throw** OR **put sb off the scent** to give sb false signs, clues etc so that they cannot follow or catch one □ *If we cross the river, that should put them off the scent.* -3. [for a person] perfume.
◇ *vt* -1. [animal] to know that there is <food, prey, or danger> by smelling it. -2. [person] to sense <danger, victory> etc.

scented ['sentəd] *adj* [notepaper, handkerchief] that has perfume on it; [air, garden] that has the scent of flowers in it.

scepter US, **sceptre** GB ['septəʳ] *n* a rod carried by a king or queen at official ceremonies as a symbol of their power.

sceptic *etc* GB = **skeptic** *etc.*

sceptre *n* GB = **scepter.**

schedule [US 'skedʒu:l, GB 'ʃedju:l] ◇ *n* -1. [of visits, appointments, work] a plan showing the times or dates when particular things should happen □ *Senator Brown has a very tight schedule, but he will try to fit you in.* □ *We've drawn up a schedule for the first stage of the rebuilding work.* ■ **(according) to schedule** at the time or at the speed planned in the schedule □ *Work is proceeding to schedule.* □ *If everything goes according to schedule, we'll be there by tomorrow.* ■ **ahead of schedule** earlier than planned □ *We finished/arrived ahead of schedule.* ■ **behind schedule** later than planned □ *We're a little behind schedule at the moment.* ■ **on schedule** at the time that was planned □ *We arrived, right on schedule, at 19:00 hours.* -2. [of prices, conditions, contents] a written list that is official □ *Here is our schedule of charges.*
◇ *vt* [meeting, conference] to plan <sthg> to happen at a particular time □ *The meeting was scheduled for January 14.* □ *We're scheduled to leave for Tokyo right after the conference.*

scheduled flight [US ˌskedʒu:ld-, GB ˌʃedju:ld-] *n* a flight that an airline makes regularly according to a published timetable.
NOTE: Compare **charter flight.**

schematic [ski:'mætɪk] *adj* [diagram, representation] that shows in a simple way how something complicated works.

scheme [ski:m] ◇ *n* -1. [by a person] a plan, especially one that is dishonest or unlikely to succeed (disapproving use) □ *He has some crazy scheme for raising the money.* -2. GB [by a government] a set of official arrangements, plans, or activities, usually designed to help a large number of people □ *a pension/welfare scheme* □ *a hydroelectric scheme to provide power to rural areas.* -3. [of decoration] = **color scheme.** -4. **in the scheme of things** when everything is taken into consideration □ *It wasn't, in the general scheme of things, a very significant event.*
◇ *vt* **to scheme to do sthg** to plan secretly or dishonestly to do sthg (disapproving use) □ *They were scheming to cut her out of the will.*
◇ *vi* [person, organization] to make plans, especially secret or dishonest ones (disapproving use).

scheming ['ski:mɪŋ] *adj* [politician, villain] who tries to get what they want by deceiving people (disapproving use) □ *What a scheming little devil!*

schism ['skɪzm] *n* a disagreement about beliefs in a church or other large organization that leads to it splitting into two groups (formal use).

schizophrenia [ˌskɪtsə'fri:njə] *n* a serious mental illness in which somebody cannot tell what is real and what is imaginary and does not react in the normal way to other people.

schizophrenic [ˌskɪtsə'frenɪk] ◇ *adj* [person] who is suffering from schizophrenia. ◇ *n* a schizophrenic person.

schlepp [ʃlep] (informal use) ◇ *vt* to drag or carry <sthg heavy> □ *I'm not schlepping this suitcase all over town.* ◇ *vi* [person] to walk or travel a long way, usually in a tired or unhappy way □ *I wasted the whole afternoon schlepping around Toronto.*

schmal(t)z [ʃmɔ:lts] *n* [in a movie, song, book] the quality of being too sentimental, usually in an insincere way (informal use) □ *His new musical is pure schmal(t)z.*

schmuck [ʃmʌk] *n* US a person who one thinks is stupid and annoying (informal use).

scholar ['skɒləʳ] *n* -1. [in history, literature] a person who knows a lot about an academic subject □ *a Greek/Latin scholar.* -2. [at a university] a person who has won a scholarship.

scholarship ['skɒləʳʃɪp] *n* -1. an amount of money given to a gifted student to help them continue their studies □ *She won a scholarship to go to Egypt.* -2. expert knowledge in an academic subject □ *a department with a high level of scholarship.*

scholastic [skə'læstɪk] *adj* [ability, achievement, work] that is connected with education and school subjects (formal use).

school [sku:l] *n* -1. [for children] a place where people, especially children, are educated; the people who work and study in this place; the time during which people are in this place □ *He left school at sixteen.* □ *What did you do at school today?* □ *She went to a very good school.* □ *The whole school came to see the show.* □ *a school trip/play* □ *school fees* □ *School finishes at 3:30 pm.* -2. [in a university] a department of a university where a particular group of subjects is studied □ *the School of Engineering/Modern Languages* ■ **the School of the Air** in Australia, an education service that gives lessons to pupils in remote areas, using two-way radios. -3. [for art, law medicine] an institution where a particular subject or skill is taught □ *She's hoping to go to art/law/medical school.* -4. US a university □ *I finish school this year.* -5. ZOOLOGY a large group of fish or sea animals that are swimming together □ *a school of dolphins.*

school age *n* the age from which all children in a particular country must go to school.

schoolbook ['sku:lbʊk] *n* a textbook for use in school.

schoolboy ['sku:lbɔɪ] *n* a boy who goes to school.

school bus *n* a bus that takes children from their homes to their school and back.

schoolchild ['sku:ltʃaɪld] (*pl* **schoolchildren**) *n* a child who goes to school.

schooldays ['sku:ldeɪz] *npl* the period in somebody's life when they are at school.

school dinner *n* GB = **school lunch**.

school district *n* US an area in a state in which all the public schools are controlled by the same organization.

schoolgirl ['sku:lgɜ:ʳl] *n* a girl who goes to school.

schooling ['sku:lɪŋ] *n* the education that one gets at a school.

schoolkid ['sku:lkɪd] *n* a schoolchild (informal use).

school-leaver [-li:vəʳ] *n* GB a young person who has just finished or is soon going to finish their school education.

school-leaving age [-'li:vɪŋ-] *n* the age at which children are legally allowed to leave school.

school lunch *n* US a lunch served to children at school.

schoolmaster [US 'sku:lmæstər, GB -mɑ:stə] *n* a male schoolteacher (old-fashioned use).

schoolmistress ['sku:lmɪstrəs] *n* a female schoolteacher (old-fashioned use).

school of arts *n* AUS a hall in a country town where local people can study and take educational classes.

school of thought *n* a set of ideas about something; the group of people who have these particular ideas □ *According to one school of thought, a glass of wine every day is good for the health.*

school report *n* a report in which a teacher writes about a student's work, progress, behavior etc at school during the term or year that has just finished.

schoolroom ['sku:lru:m] *n* a room in which children are taught (old-fashioned use).

school supplies *npl* US a collective term for the paper, pens, pencils etc that schoolchildren use at school.

schoolteacher ['sku:lti:tʃəʳ] *n* a person whose job is to teach children in a school.

school uniform *n* a set of clothes of a particular color, design etc that all children at a particular school must wear.

schoolwork ['sku:lwɜ:ʳk] *n* the work that a child does at school or as homework.

school year *n* the period when schools are open and students go to classes.

schooner ['sku:nəʳ] *n* -1. SHIPPING a sailing ship that usually has two masts and on which most of the sails face sideways. -2. GB a glass used for drinking sherry. -3. US & AUS a glass used for drinking beer that holds approximately one pint.

Schubert ['ʃu:bəʳt], **Franz** (1797–1828) an Austrian composer known for his songs and symphonies, especially the *Unfinished Symphony.*

Schweitzer ['ʃwaɪtsəʳ], **Albert** (1875–1965) a German doctor who worked as a missionary in Africa.

sciatica [saɪ'ætɪkə] *n* severe pain in one's lower back and the top of one's legs that is caused by pressure on a nerve.

science ['saɪəns] *n* -1. the study and knowledge of the things in the world and of how they work and behave □ *the wonders of science* □ *a science teacher/class/degree.* -2. a particular branch of science, e.g. chemistry or physics □ *The sciences were not my strong subjects at school.*

science fiction *n* a collective term for stories, e.g. in books, comics, or movies, about imaginary events connected with life and technology in the future, travel in outer space etc □ *a science fiction writer/novel.*

science park *n* an area with buildings designed for companies that do scientific research to develop new products.

scientific [ˌsaɪən'tɪfɪk] *adj* [method, experiment] that is connected with science and usually involves using careful observation and experiments □ *These claims are not supported by scientific proof.* □ *After years of scientific research, it seems a solution may be near.*

scientist ['saɪəntəst] *n* a person who carries out scientific work or study.

sci-fi ['saɪfaɪ] *n abbr of* **science fiction**.

Scillies ['sɪlɪz] = **Scilly Isles**.

Scilly Isles ['sɪlɪ-]: **the Scilly Isles** a group of British islands off the southwestern coast of England. SIZE: 16 sq kms. POPULATION: 2,628 (*Scillonians*). CAPITAL: Hugh Town.

scintillating ['sɪntəleɪtɪŋ] *adj* [person, conversation, script] that is very intelligent, interesting, and impressive □ *It was a scintillating debate to watch.*

scissors ['sɪzəʳz] *npl* a tool designed to cut paper, string etc that consists of two movable blades that are joined in the middle and have two holes for one's thumb and finger at one end □ *a pair of scissors.*

sclerosis [sklə'rəʊsəs] *n* a disease in which one's body tissue becomes hard.

scoff [skɒf] *vi* to talk about something in a way that shows one does not take it seriously □ *They scoffed at the idea when I first proposed it.*

scold [skəʊld] *vt* to speak angrily to <sb> to tell them they have done something wrong □ *We were scolded for missing school.*

scone [skəʊn] *n* a small soft cake, sometimes containing dried fruit, that is usually eaten with butter and jam.

scoop [sku:p] ◇ *n* -1. a tool like a small shovel for lifting flour, sugar etc; a deep round spoon that is used to serve food such as ice cream; the amount of something that can be held in this □ *Two scoops of vanilla, please.* **-2.** an important story that one newspaper or magazine publishes before everybody else □ *The Pinochet story was a real scoop.* ◇ *vt* **-1.** [water, sand, earth] to pick up <sthg> by holding one's hands together to contain it □ *He scooped up a handful of soil.* **-2.** [ice cream, sugar, coffee] to pick up <sthg> using a scoop □ *She scooped ice cream into the bowl.*

◆ **scoop out** *vt sep* **to scoop sthg out** [ice cream, melon] to remove sthg from a container, shell, skin etc using one's hand, a scoop etc □ *Cut the zucchinis in half and scoop out the flesh.*

scoot [skuːt] *vi* [person] to go somewhere quickly (informal use) □ *Two o'clock already! I'll have to scoot!*

scooter ['skuːtəʳ] *n* **-1.** a toy that a child rides by holding the handlebars, placing one foot on a flat board between two small wheels, and pushing against the ground with the other foot. **-2.** a motorcycle with small wheels that is not very powerful and has a shield in front of the rider's legs.

scope [skoʊp] *n* **-1.** [for development, originality] the opportunity for something good to happen □ *This job doesn't offer much scope for an ambitious young man.* □ *It's a good paper, but I still see scope for improvement.* **-2.** [of an investigation, report] the range of things that are dealt with by something □ *Unfortunately, that area is beyond the scope of our inquiry.*

scorch [skɔːʳtʃ] ◇ *vt* **-1.** [clothes, skin, food] to burn the surface of <sthg> slightly, with the result that it gets darker and is damaged □ *I scorched myself on the iron.* **-2.** [grass, fields] to make <plants> become dry and brown because it is too hot □ *the land scorched by a long, hot summer.* ◇ *vi* [clothes, food, grass] to become scorched □ *Silk scorches easily.*

scorched earth policy [ˌskɔːʳtʃt-] *n* the practice of destroying things in an area, e.g. crops or buildings, in order to stop enemy soldiers from using them.

scorcher ['skɔːʳtʃəʳ] *n* a very hot day (informal use).

scorching ['skɔːʳtʃɪŋ] (informal use) ◇ *adj* [day, weather, sun] very hot. ◇ *adv* **scorching hot** very hot □ *It was scorching hot outside.*

score [skɔːʳ] ◇ *vt* **-1.** SPORT [goal, point] to gain <sthg> in a game or competition. **-2.** [success, victory, total] to achieve <sthg> □ *I felt we had scored a moral victory over them.* **-3. to score points** to get an advantage over somebody, especially in an argument □ *She's always trying to score points on minor issues.* **-4.** [paper, table] to make a mark on the surface of <sthg> by using a sharp object □ *Somebody had scored a line across the page.*
◇ *vi* SPORT to gain a goal, point etc □ *Evans scored in the final minute.*
◇ *n* **-1.** SPORT [in a game, competition] a set of numbers that show how many points, goals etc each team or player has scored, especially at the end of the game or competition □

The half-time score was 1-0. **-2.** [of a player, student] the result of one person in a game, competition, or test, represented by a figure □ *Jamie got the highest score in math.* **-3. a score** twenty (old-fashioned use). **-4.** MUSIC [of a symphony, concerto] a written piece of music showing the notes played or sung by each instrument or person; [for a movie, musical] the music that is written to be played during a movie or musical. **-5.** *phrase* **on that score** in relation to the subject that has just been mentioned □ *You have nothing to worry about on that score.*

◆ **scores** *npl* **scores of people/things** a lot of people/things □ *We've had scores of complaints from customers.*

◆ **score out** *vt sep* **to score sthg out** GB [word, line] to remove sthg from a text, list etc by drawing a line through it □ *She had scored out my name and written hers instead.*

scoreboard ['skɔːʳbɔːʳd] *n* a board that shows the number of goals, points etc scored by the teams or players in a game or competition.

scorecard ['skɔːʳkuːʳd] *n* a card on which a player or spectator can keep a note of the scores during a game or competition.

score-draw *n* in soccer, the result of a game in which both teams score the same number of goals.

scorer ['skɔːrəʳ] *n* **-1.** a person who keeps the official record of the points each player or team scores in a game or competition. **-2.** a player who scores a goal, point etc.

scorn [skɔːʳn] ◇ *n* a feeling of hatred or disapproval that one feels for somebody or something that one believes to be worthless □ *He gave them a look filled with scorn.* ■ **to pour scorn on sb/sthg** to criticize sb/sthg severely □ *Beth poured scorn on the idea that we should apologize.* ◇ *vt* **-1.** [person, weakness, cowardice] to show or feel scorn for <sb/sthg>. **-2.** [offer, help] to reject <sthg> because one disapproves of it (formal use).

scornful ['skɔːʳnfl] *adj* [laugh, remark, person] that shows scorn □ *She was scornful of their efforts to educate themselves.*

Scorpio ['skɔːʳpɪoʊ] (*pl* **Scorpios**) *n* a sign of the zodiac, usually represented by a scorpion; a person born under this sign between October 23 and November 21.

scorpion ['skɔːʳpɪən] *n* a small animal found in hot countries that has eight legs and a tail with a poisonous sting at the end.

Scot [skɒt] *n* a person who comes from Scotland.

scotch [skɒtʃ] *vt* [idea, rumor] to put an end to <sthg> in a very definite way □ *Her agent scotched any hopes we had of an interview.*

Scotch *n* whiskey made in Scotland; a glass or drink of this whiskey □ *A double Scotch, please.* **-2.** = **Scotch tape**.

Scotch broth *n* a thick soup that is made from vegetables, barley, and mutton or beef.

Scotch egg *n* a hard-boiled egg that is covered with meat and breadcrumbs, fried, and eaten cold.

Scotch tape™ *n* US a roll of thin material that is sticky on one side, is usually transparent, and is used to fix things such as paper or card to other things.

scot-free *adj* **to get off scot-free** to get no punishment after doing something wrong (informal use).

Scotland ['skɒtlənd] a country in the United Kingdom, north of England. SIZE: 78,800 sq kms. POPULATION: 5,130,000 (*Scots*). CAPITAL: Edinburgh. LANGUAGE: English.

🞉 SCOTLAND
Although Scotland has been part of the UK since 1707, it still has its own legal system, educational system, and money (a Scottish pound has the same value as a pound sterling, and can be used anywhere in the UK). Gaelic, the ancient Scottish language, is still spoken in some parts of northwest Scotland. Some Scottish people would like Scotland to be an independent country again, with its own government.

Scotland Yard *n* = New Scotland Yard.

Scots [skɒts] ◇ *adj*: see **Scotland** □ *Scots law* □ *a Scots accent.* ◇ *n* the form of English spoken in some parts of Scotland.

Scotsman ['skɒtsmən] (*pl* **Scotsmen** [-mən]) *n* a man who comes from Scotland.

Scotswoman ['skɒtswumən] (*pl* **Scotswomen**) *n* a woman who comes from Scotland.

Scott [skɒt], **Dred** (1795?–1858) a black US slave who went to court to claim the right to be a free citizen and lost his case.

Scott, Robert Falcon (1868–1912) a British explorer who led the second expedition to reach the South Pole but died on the way back. He is also called Scott of the Antarctic.

Scott, Sir Walter (1771–1832) a Scottish writer famous for his historical novels such as *Ivanhoe* and *Rob Roy*.

Scottish ['skɒtɪʃ] *adj*: see **Scotland** □ *The Scottish Tourist Board.*

Scottish National Party *n* the **Scottish National Party** a political party that wants independence for Scotland.

scoundrel ['skaundrəl] *n* an evil or dishonest person (old-fashioned use).

scour ['skauəʳ] *vt* **-1.** [pot, pan, surface] to clean <sthg> by rubbing it with something that has a rough surface. **-2.** [countryside, country, area] to search <a place> carefully and completely □ *Police scoured the woods for evidence.*

scourer ['skaurəʳ] *n* a small ball or pad of nylon or wire that is used for cleaning pots and pans.

scourge [skɜːʳdʒ] *n* **-1.** something that causes great suffering or hardship to many people □ *the scourge of war/disease.* **-2.** **the scourge of sthg** [of a group, movement, activity] the person who is most critical of sthg □ *As leader, he came to be regarded as the scourge of the Left.*

Scouse [skaus] *n* (informal use) **-1.** a person

who comes from Liverpool. **-2.** the accent or dialect of people from Liverpool.

scout [skaut] *n* MILITARY a soldier, plane etc that is sent ahead of an army, fleet etc to find out where the enemy is.

◆ **Scout** *n* a boy who is a member of an organization that aims to develop outdoor survival skills and community spirit in young people.

◆ **scout around** *vi* to look for something that one needs in a particular area □ *I'll just go and scout around for a phone booth.*

scoutmaster [US 'skautmæstər, GB -mɑːstə] *n* an adult in charge of a group of Scouts.

scowl [skaul] ◇ *vi* to look at somebody in an angry way □ *He scowled at me and told me to go away.* ◇ *n* the expression on somebody's face when they scowl □ *"Go away," he said with a scowl.*

scrabble ['skræbl] *vi* **-1.** to crawl or climb with quick irregular movements of one's arms and legs □ *Esther just managed to scrabble to the top of the cliff.* **-2. to scrabble at sthg** to scratch sthg with short quick movements □ *I could hear the dog scrabbling at the kitchen door.* **-3.** [in a box, drawer] to search for something by moving one's fingers around quickly, usually among a number of things □ *She was scrabbling around in the dark for her glasses.*

Scrabble™ *n* a game in which players place small squares marked with letters on a board in order to form words.

scraggy ['skrægɪ] (*compar* **scraggier**, *superl* **scraggiest**) *adj* [horse, neck] that is very thin and bony, and is not pleasant to look at (informal use).

scram [skræm] (*pt* & *pp* **scrammed**, *cont* **scramming**) *vi* to go away quickly to avoid trouble (informal use).

scramble ['skræmbl] ◇ *vi* **-1.** to crawl or climb quickly using one's arms and legs a lot □ *He scrambled up the wall/along the bank.* **-2. to scramble for sthg** [people] to rush in an uncontrolled way at the same time to get or reach sthg. ◇ *n* the act of scrambling for something or to get somewhere □ *There was a scramble for tickets/for the door.*

scrambled eggs [ˌskræmbld-] *npl* a dish consisting of eggs, milk, and butter, beaten and then stirred over heat until they are solid.

scrambler ['skræmblər] *n* an electronic device that makes it impossible for the words in a radio or telephone message to be understood unless one uses another device.

scrap [skræp] (*pt* & *pp* **scrapped**, *cont* **scrapping**) ◇ *n* **-1.** [of paper, material] a very small piece of something; [of evidence, information, a conversation] a very small amount of something □ *I made a card out of some old scraps.* ■ **it won't make a scrap of difference** it will make no difference at all. **-2.** [from cars, machines] waste metal for recycling □ *We'll sell the car for scrap.* **-3.** [between people] a short fight or quarrel (informal use) □ *Joseph is always getting into scraps with his brother.*

◇ *vt* **-1.** [car, ship] to get rid of <sthg> so that

its materials can be used again. **-2.** [plan, idea] to decide not to continue with <sthg>.

◆ **scraps** *npl* pieces of food that have been cooked or prepared but not eaten □ *We saved some scraps for the dog.*

scrapbook ['skræpbʊk] *n* a book with blank pages in which one sticks pictures, newspaper cuttings etc that one wants to keep.

scrap dealer *n* a person who buys and sells scrap metal.

scrape [skreɪp] ◇ *vt* **-1. to scrape sthg off sthg** [dirt, paint] to remove sthg from sthg by rubbing it against a sharp or rough surface □ *Scrape the mud off your boots.* **-2.** [carrot, turnip] to remove the skin from <a vegetable>, by rubbing a sharp object against it □ *He stood at the sink, scraping potatoes.* **-3.** [car, knee, elbow] to rub <sthg> against something rough or sharp so that it is damaged or marked; [rocks, wall] to rub against the surface of <sthg>, usually in a way that causes damage or injury □ *Benjy fell over and scraped his knee.* □ *The side of the car scraped the wall.*

◇ *vi* **-1.** to rub against something in a way that causes noise or damage □ *That door scrapes on the floor every time you open it.* □ *The car scraped against the wall as I turned the corner.* **-2.** to try to save money by living very cheaply □ *I'm sick of skimping and scraping!*

◇ *n* **-1.** the noise made by scraping something across a surface. **-2. to get into a scrape** to find oneself in a difficult or dangerous situation □ *I got into a scrape with some of the local gangsters.*

◆ **scrape by** *vi* to have just enough money to live.

◆ **scrape through** ◇ *vt fus* **to scrape through sthg** [test, exam] to just succeed in passing sthg. ◇ *vi* *She hasn't done much work, but she should just about scrape through.*

◆ **scrape together**, **scrape up** *vt sep* **to scrape sthg together** OR **up** [money, support, votes] to get or find enough of sthg that one needs, with difficulty □ *See if you can scrape together enough eggs for an omelet.*

scraper ['skreɪpə^r] *n* a tool with a sharp edge for removing something, e.g. paint, wallpaper, or vegetable skin, by scraping.

scrap heap *n* **-1.** a pile of waste material, especially metal. **-2. to be on the scrap heap** to have been rejected because one is no longer needed or useful □ *That was yet another good idea that ended up on the scrap heap.* □ *After twenty years' service I've just been thrown on the scrap heap.*

scrapings ['skreɪpɪŋz] *npl* [in a container] small amounts of something that can only be removed by scraping; [of paint, paper, peel] small pieces of something that have been removed by scraping.

scrap merchant *n* GB = **scrap dealer**.

scrap metal *n* pieces of metal from broken or useless objects, collected for recycling.

scrap paper *n* paper that has already been used but is kept for writing notes on or to make new paper.

scrappy ['skræpɪ] (*compar* **scrappier**, *superl*

scrappiest) *adj* [performance, game, piece of writing] that is not very good or well organized □ *It was a scrappy piece of work, not up to your usual standard.*

scrapyard ['skræpjɑː^rd] *n* the place where a scrap dealer collects scrap metal.

scratch [skrætʃ] ◇ *n* **-1.** [on skin, glass, wood] a slight cut on the surface of something that is made by a sharp object □ *Don't worry, it's nothing serious, just a scratch.* □ *There's a small scratch on the right fender.* **-2.** *phrases* **to do sthg from scratch** to do sthg from the beginning, without the help of any preparations made in advance □ *She learned how to operate the machine from scratch in two days.* □ *I don't want to have to start everything again from scratch.* ■ **to be up to scratch** to be good enough □ *Half the candidates we interviewed simply weren't up to scratch.*

◇ *vt* **-1.** [skin, wood, car] to make a scratch on the surface of <sthg> □ *You can still see the mark where the cat scratched me.* □ *I scratched my wrist on the edge of the file.* **-2.** [back, head] to move the ends of one's nails over <part of one's body>, usually because it itches □ *I can't stop scratching myself.* □ *Duane was left scratching his head in disbelief.*

◇ *vi* **-1.** [branch, bramble, nail] to rub against something with something sharp in a way that makes a noise or causes slight damage; [wool, tag] to rub against and irritate one's skin □ *There was something scratching at the door.* **-2.** [person] to rub part of one's body with fingernails; [cat, dog] to rub part of its body with its claws □ *Stop scratching or you'll make it bleed.*

scratchcard ['skrætʃkɑː^rd] *n* a small piece of card, used e.g. in lotteries, with a surface that can be removed by rubbing to show information underneath.

scratchpad ['skrætʃpæd] *n* US a pad of paper for making rough notes.

scratch paper *n* US = **scrap paper**.

scratchy ['skrætʃɪ] (*compar* **scratchier**, *superl* **scratchiest**) *adj* **-1.** [record] that one cannot hear properly because there are scratches on its surface □ *a scratchy old recording of Billie Holiday.* **-2.** [material, sweater, shirt] that has a rough surface which irritates one's skin.

scrawl [skrɔːl] ◇ *n* very untidy writing that is difficult to read □ *I could barely make out her scrawl.* ◇ *vt* [message, note, word] to write <sthg> very quickly and untidily in a way that is difficult to read □ *He had scrawled his name on the back of an envelope.*

scrawny ['skrɔːnɪ] (*compar* **scrawnier**, *superl* **scrawniest**) *adj* [person, animal, neck] that looks very thin and weak (disapproving use).

scream [skriːm] ◇ *n* **-1.** [of fear, laughter] a loud high-pitched noise made by somebody who is very frightened, in pain etc □ *I heard a loud scream from outside.* □ *Craig let out a scream of terror.* **-2.** [of tires, brakes] a loud high-pitched noise. **-3. to be a scream** [person, event] to be very funny (informal use) □ *The movie was an absolute scream.* ◇ *vt* [person] to say <sthg> with a scream □ *"Help!" he screamed.* □ *The* crowd *screamed its approval.* ◇ *vi* **-1.** [person] *If you come any closer, I'll scream.* □ *They were all screaming with fear/rage/laughter.* **-2.** [tires, brakes] to make a loud high-pitched noise.

scree [skriː] *n* loose stones on the side of a mountain □ *a scree slope.*

screech [skriːtʃ] ◇ *n* **-1.** [of a person, bird] a harsh, loud, high-pitched cry. **-2.** [of tires, brakes, a car] a harsh, loud, high-pitched noise. ◇ *vt* [person] to say <sthg> in a screech □ *"Look out!" she screeched.* ◇ *vi* [person, bird, brakes] to make a screech □ *The car screeched to a halt at the traffic lights.*

screen [skriːn] ◇ *n* **-1.** [of a computer, television] a glass surface on which an image appears; [in a cinema] a large flat piece of white material that moving pictures are shown on □ *a television/computer screen* □ *The options are shown on the screen.* ■ **the screen** a word used to refer to movies made for cinema □ *It was her first appearance on the big screen.* **-2.** [in an office, hospital] a large panel used to divide a space such as a room, or to give privacy or protection to somebody □ *The priest's face was hidden behind the screen.* ◇ *vt* **-1.** [movie, program, event] to show <sthg> on a television or cinema screen □ *The ceremony will be screened live in 30 countries.* **-2.** [house, garden] to make <sthg> difficult to see by being in front of it □ *The house was screened from view by a row of trees.* **-3.** [person, face] to protect <sb/sthg>, especially by keeping them covered □ *He screened his eyes from the sun with his hand.* □ *She was screened from the protesters by a group of bodyguards.* **-4.** [candidate, visitor, staff] to check if <sb> is suitable for something by asking them questions or finding out information about them, often for security reasons □ *The guards are all screened by the CIA.* **-5.** MEDICINE to do tests on <people> to find out if they have a particular disease □ *They screen all women over 40 for breast cancer.*

◆ **screen off** *vt sep* **to screen sthg off** [bed, part of room] to place a screen around sthg, usually to give privacy to somebody.

screen door *n* a door consisting of wire that lets air into a building and keeps insects out.

screen dump *n* the process of sending what is shown on a computer screen to a file or printer.

screening [skriːnɪŋ] *n* [of a program, candidate, patient] *see* **screen** □ *I've been invited to an exclusive screening of her new movie.* □ *There have been calls for increased screening for cancer of the prostate.*

screenplay [skriːnpleɪ] *n* a script for a movie.

screen print *n* a picture printed by forcing thick ink through a specially prepared piece of cloth.

screen saver *n* a computer program that makes the screen blank or forms a pattern on it when a computer is switched on but not being used.

screen test *n* a test in the form of a short scene that is filmed to find out if an actor is suitable to appear in a real movie.

screenwriter [skriːnraɪtəʳ] *n* a person who writes a screenplay.

screw [skruː] ◇ *n* a small, long, round piece of metal with a thin ridge around it that goes from top to bottom and a round flat head that has a slot across it so that it can be turned by a screwdriver in order to go through wood, plastic etc. ◇ *vt* **-1.** **to screw sthg to sthg** to attach sthg to sthg with a screw □ *The panel was screwed to the wall.* **-2.** **to screw sthg in/on etc** to insert/attach etc sthg by turning it around □ *Screw the cap down tightly.* **-3.**▼ [person] to have sex with <sb> (vulgar use). ◇ *vi* **-1.** **to screw in/on etc** [plug, top, lid] to be able to be inserted/attached etc by being turned □ *It's easy, it just screws off.* **-2.**▼ [people] to have sex (vulgar use).

◆ **screw up** ◇ *vt sep* **-1.** **to screw sthg up** [paper, letter] to squeeze sthg into an untidy ball; [one's face, eyes, mouth] to make the shape of sthg look smaller or strange by moving it in a particular way □ *I screwed up the tickets and threw them away.* □ *She screwed her face up in disgust.* **-2.** **to screw sthg up** [plan, arrangement, relationship] to ruin sthg by doing something stupid (informal use) □ *I'm sorry, I really screwed up your evening, didn't I?* ◇ *vi* (informal use) *"Oh boy, did I ever screw up this time!"*

screwball [skruːbɔːl] *n* a person that one thinks is crazy or strange (informal use).

screwdriver [skruːdraɪvəʳ] *n* a metal tool with a handle and a small flat or cross-shaped tip that is used for turning screws.

screwtop jar [ˌskruːtɒp-] *n* a jar with a lid that one turns in order to take it off or put it on.

screwy [skruːɪ] (*compar* **screwier**, *superl* **screwiest**) *adj* [idea, situation] that one thinks is crazy (informal use).

scribble [skrɪbl] ◇ *n* words that are written quickly and are difficult to read □ *Her signature was just an illegible scribble.* ◇ *vt* [name, letter, message] to write <sthg> quickly and often untidily □ *She scribbled a note and pushed it under the door.* ◇ *vi* [person] to make meaningless marks with a pen or pencil □ *The kids have scribbled all over the walls.*

scribe [skraɪb] *n* in the past, a person who wrote out copies of documents before printing was invented.

scrimp [skrɪmp] *vi* **to scrimp and save** to try and spend as little money as possible in order to save money □ *They had to scrimp and save to send their daughter to college.*

script [skrɪpt] *n* **-1.** [of a play, movie, broadcast] a written plan of what the people taking part in a performance, program etc have to say and do □ *He's one of those actors who never sticks to the script.* **-2.** [in a particular language] a set of letters used in a particular type of writing □ *Arabic/Cyrillic/Gothic script.* **-3.** [somebody] handwriting in which the letters are joined together (formal use).

scripted [skrɪptəd] *adj* [interview, speech, answer] that is given using a script.

Scriptures ['skrɪptʃərz] *npl* **the Scriptures** the Bible.

scriptwriter ['skrɪptraɪtər] *n* a person who writes the script for a movie or a radio or television program.

scroll [skroʊl] ◇ *n* a roll of paper with writing on it. ◇ *vt* COMPUTING [information, text] to move <sthg> up, down, or across a screen.

◆ **scroll down** *vi* COMPUTING to move the text that is displayed on a screen upward so that one is nearer to the end.

◆ **scroll up** *vi* COMPUTING to move the text that is displayed on a screen downward so that one is nearer to the beginning.

scroll bar *n* COMPUTING an area on a screen where one moves the cursor to scroll text.

Scrooge [skru:dʒ] a character in Charles Dickens' story *A Christmas Carol*. He is very selfish with money and dislikes Christmas.

scrotum ['skroʊtəm] (*pl* **scrotums** OR **scrota** [-ə]) *n* the bag of skin below the penis that contains the testicles.

scrounge [skraʊndʒ] ◇ *vt* (informal use) [money, food, cigarette] to try to get <sthg> by asking other people to give it to one, and not by working or paying for it oneself □ *I scrounged some paperclips off the school secretary.* ◇ *vi: He's always scrounging off me.*

scrounger ['skraʊndʒər] *n* a person who scrounges (informal and disapproving use).

scrub [skrʌb] (*pt* & *pp* **scrubbed**, *cont* **scrubbing**) ◇ *vt* [floor, saucepan, hands] to clean <sthg> by rubbing it hard, e.g. with a brush or a scourer □ *I scrubbed the bath clean.* ◇ *n* **-1.** the act of scrubbing something □ *Give the floor/the saucepan/your face a good scrub.* **-2.** low bushes that grow in poor soil; an area of land covered with these bushes.

scrub brush US, **scrubbing brush** ['skrʌbɪŋ] GB *n* a brush without a handle, used for scrubbing floors and other dirty surfaces or objects.

scruff [skrʌf] *n* **by the scruff of the neck** holding the back of the neck □ *He picked me up by the scruff of the neck.*

scruffy ['skrʌfɪ] (*compar* **scruffier**, *superl* **scruffiest**) *adj* [person, clothes] that looks untidy and dirty □ *a scruffy old pair of jeans.*

scrum(mage) ['skrʌm(ɪdʒ)] *n* in rugby, a situation in which a group of players from each team hold onto each other, bend down, and push against the other team in order to get the ball.

scrumptious ['skrʌmpʃəs] *adj* [food, meal] that tastes very good (informal use).

scrunch [skrʌntʃ] *vt* **to scrunch sthg (up)** [can, envelope] to squeeze sthg into a smaller shape, especially with one's hands (informal use).

scrunchy ['skrʌntʃɪ] (*pl* **scrunchies**) *n* a circular band of elastic material that is used for tying back one's hair in a pony tail.

scruples ['skru:plz] *npl* beliefs that one has that make one not want to do something wrong □ *Be careful — she has no scruples about spending other people's money.*

scrupulous ['skru:pjələs] *adj* **-1. to be scrupulous** [person] to be very careful to do what is right or fair □ *He is absolutely scrupulous about doing his accounts on time.* **-2.** [attention, care, honesty] that somebody tries to make complete in every detail □ *Irving applied the same scrupulous fairness to all his dealings with staff.*

scrupulously ['skru:pjələslɪ] *adv* **scrupulously honest/fair etc** as honest/fair etc as possible □ *The bathroom was scrupulously clean.*

scrutinize, -ise ['skru:tənaɪz] *vt* [text, report, face] to look at <sthg> very carefully □ *The book will be scrutinized for details of the Prince's private life.*

scrutiny ['skru:tənɪ] *n* careful examination □ *His business activities have come under scrutiny from the press.*

scuba diving ['sku:bə-] *n* the activity of swimming underwater using special equipment for breathing.

scud [skʌd] (*pt* & *pp* **scudded**, *cont* **scudding**) *vi* [cloud, bird, person] to move somewhere quickly (literary use).

scuff [skʌf] *vt* to damage <shoes, heels> etc by dragging them over a rough surface; to damage <furniture, a floor> etc by scraping something against it.

scuffle ['skʌfl] ◇ *n* a short fight, usually involving a number of people, that is not very serious. ◇ *vi* to fight for a short time in a way that is not very serious □ *Police scuffled with the demonstrators.*

scullery ['skʌlərɪ] (*pl* **sculleries**) *n* a room next to a kitchen in a large old house, where food is prepared, dishes are washed etc.

sculpt [skʌlpt] *vt* [figure, shape] to make <sthg> out of clay, stone etc by carving or shaping it □ *a bust sculpted in wood/out of marble.*

sculptor ['skʌlptər] *n* an artist who sculpts things.

sculpture ['skʌlptʃər] ◇ *n* **-1.** a work of art such as a statue that is sculpted □ *This is one of Henry Moore's most famous sculptures.* **-2.** the art of sculpting things □ *She studied sculpture at college.* ◇ *vt* [rock, stone, metal] to make a work of art out of <sthg> by using a sharp tool □ *The pillar was sculptured in marble/out of wood.*

scum [skʌm] *n* **-1.** an unpleasant or dirty substance on the surface of water □ *There was a line of scum around the side of the bath.* **-2.** people that one thinks are unpleasant or worthless, especially because of something bad they have done (informal use) □ *They're the scum of the earth.*

scupper ['skʌpər] *vt* **-1.** to deliberately sink <one's ship> □ *He scuppered his own ship rather than be caught.* **-2.** GB to completely ruin <a plan, chance> etc (informal use) □ *Well, that's scuppered any hopes of a settlement.*

scurf [skɜːrf] *n* small white pieces of dead skin in one's hair.

scurrilous [US 'skɜːrələs, GB 'skʌr-] *adj* [attack, article, magazine] that is insulting, untrue, and damaging to somebody's reputation □ *Warner dismissed it as a scurrilous piece of gossip.*

scurry [US 'skɜːrɪ, GB 'skʌrɪ] (*pt* & *pp* **scurried**) *vi* [person, mouse] to move somewhere very quickly with short steps □ *She scurried off across the square.*

scurvy ['skɜːʳvɪ] *n* a disease caused by lack of vitamin C.

scuttle ['skʌtl] ◇ *n* a metal bucket for coal that is usually kept beside a fireplace. ◇ *vi* [person, mouse] to move somewhere very quickly with short steps □ *He scuttled off in the other direction.*

scuzzy ['skʌzɪ] (*compar* **scuzzier**, *superl* **scuzziest**) *adj* [person, place] that is dirty and unpleasant (informal use).

scythe [saɪð] ◇ *n* a tool with a curved blade and a long handle that is used for cutting grass, wheat etc. ◇ *vt* [grass, hay] to cut <sthg> using a scythe.

SD *abbr of* **South Dakota.**

SDI (*abbr of* **Strategic Defense Initiative**) *n* the official name of the *Star Wars* satellite defense system.

SDLP (*abbr of* **Social Democratic and Labour Party**) *n* **the SDLP** a political party in Northern Ireland that has mainly Catholic supporters.

SE *abbr of* **southeast.**

sea [siː] *n* **-1.** the salt water that covers a large part of the Earth's surface □ *sea travel/ voyages/animals.* ■ **to be at sea** [sailor, boat] to be on the sea, far from land □ *The ship has been at sea for two weeks.* ■ **to be all at sea** [person] to be very confused about something □ *I'm all at sea with this computer jargon.* ■ **by sea** [travel, send] on a ship □ *In the past, the only way to travel long distances was by sea.* ■ **by the sea** near the sea □ *They rented a villa by the sea.* ■ **out to sea** [float, gaze, row] away from land □ *The boat drifted out to sea.* **-2. a sea of faces** OR **people** a large number of people □ *From the front of the stage, all I could see was a sea of faces.*

◆ **seas** *npl* **the seas** the salt water that covers a large part of the Earth's surface □ *Many seals live in the seas around Scotland.*

sea air *n* the air at the seaside, usually considered to be healthy and refreshing □ *He breathed in the sea air.*

sea anemone *n* a brightly-colored sea creature that grows on rocks, has tentacles, and looks like a flower.

seabed ['siːbed] *n* **the seabed** the bottom of the sea.

seabird ['siːbɜːʳd] *n* any bird that lives near the sea or finds food in the sea.

seaboard ['siːbɔːʳd] *n* the part of a country that is near the sea □ *the eastern seaboard.*

sea breeze *n* a breeze that blows from the sea onto the land.

seafaring ['siːfeərɪŋ] *adj* [person, life] that is connected with working at sea. ■ **a seafaring nation** a nation where the sea is very important, especially for trade.

seafood ['siːfuːd] *n* fish and shellfish that can be eaten as food □ *a seafood salad.*

seafront ['siːfrʌnt] *n* a wide road with houses, shops etc, that is beside a beach.

seagoing ['siːgəʊɪŋ] *adj* [vessel, ship, liner] that is built for sailing on the sea.

seagull ['siːgʌl] *n* a large white and gray bird that lives near the sea and has a loud cry.

seahorse ['siːhɔːʳs] *n* a small sea creature whose head and neck make it look similar to a horse.

seal [siːl] (*pl sense 1* **seal** OR **seals**) ◇ *n* **-1.** ZOOLOGY a large animal with a long body and flippers that lives in or near the ocean in cold or temperate areas, and eats fish. **-2.** [on a document] a mark with a particular design, often made with wax, that is put on an important document to show it is official or legal □ *the royal seal.* ■ **sb's seal of approval** the approval of sb whose opinion is important □ *Does the project have her seal of approval?* ■ **to put** OR **set the seal on sthg** to finally make sthg complete or definite □ *That victory set the seal on Graf's position as the world number one.* **-3.** [of a jar, pack] something such as wax or a piece of paper that has to be broken before one can open a container □ *'Do not use if seal is broken.'* **-4.** [of a pipe, door] a piece of material such as rubber that prevents air, liquid etc from entering or leaving a closed space □ *a watertight seal.*

◇ *vt* **-1.** [document, letter, package] to close <sthg> firmly, e.g. by using Scotch tape or glue □ *Don't seal the envelopes, I want to add an extra sheet to each one.* □ *Make sure the jar is properly sealed.* **-2.** [opening, tube, gap] to cover or fill <sthg> so that no liquid or air can get in or out □ *I've sealed the cracks with putty.*

◆ **seal off** *vt sep* **to seal sthg off** [entrance, border, area] to close sthg in order to prevent people from entering or leaving □ *The police have sealed off all the routes out of the town.*

sealable ['siːləbl] *adj* [jar, container] that can be sealed after it has been opened.

sea lane *n* a route used regularly by ships to cross the sea or ocean.

sealant ['siːlənt] *n* a substance that is used to seal a gap or crack, especially to prevent water or air from entering.

sealed [siːld] *adj* AUS **a sealed road** a road that has a tarmac surface.

sea level *n* the level of the surface of the sea and the point from which the height of land is measured □ *We are 750 meters above sea level.* □ *Parts of Holland are below sea level.*

sealing wax ['siːlɪŋ-] *n* red wax that melts easily and is used as a seal on official documents.

sea lion (*pl* **sea lion** OR **sea lions**) *n* a type of large seal.

sealskin ['siːlskɪn] *n* the short silver fur of seals, used for making clothing or leather goods.

seam [siːm] *n* **-1.** SEWING the line of stitches where one piece of fabric is sewn to another. ■ **to be bursting at the seams** [room, place] to be completely full of people or things.

-2. GEOLOGY a narrow layer of a mineral such as coal in the earth.

seaman ['si:mən] (*pl* **seamen** [-mən]) *n* a sailor.

seamanship ['si:mənʃɪp] *n* the skill of controlling a ship.

sea mist *n* a mist that comes from the sea onto the land.

seamless ['si:mləs] *adj* -1. [stockings] that have no seams. -2. [story, logic, performance] that is made up of different parts that run smoothly from one to the other.

seamstress ['si:mstrəs] *n* a woman whose job is to sew and make clothes.

seamy ['si:mɪ] (*compar* **seamier**, *superl* **seamiest**) *adj* [place, scene] that is unpleasant and is connected with things such as crime and prostitution □ *This is the seamier side of New York life.*

seance ['seɪɑ:ns] *n* a meeting in which people sit around a table and try to contact the spirits of dead friends and relatives.

seaplane ['si:pleɪn] *n* a plane that can take off from and land on water.

seaport ['si:pɔ:ʳt] *n* a large town on a coast that has a port.

search [sɜ:ʳtʃ] ◇ *n* -1. the action of looking very carefully for somebody or something □ *The search for the missing girl resumed the next day.* □ *a search and rescue operation.* -2. [of luggage, a person, house] the action of trying to find something that is hidden, by examining somebody or something □ *The police made a thorough search of the premises.*
◇ *vt* -1. [house, countryside, drawer] to look carefully in <a place> in order to find somebody or something □ *She searched her pockets for her keys.* □ *They are searching everywhere for the lost child.* □ *He searched his memory.* -2. [person, prisoner, traveler] to check the pockets, bags etc of <sb> in order to find something or to check that they do not have something □ *Fans were searched before they were let into the stadium.*
◇ *vi* -1. to look for somebody or something □ *I've searched and searched, but I can't find it.* □ *We spent weeks searching for a suitable secretary.* -2. **to search for sthg** [for a name, answer] to try to remember or think of sthg □ *I searched for a witty reply.*
♦ **in search of** *prep* [work, shelter, truth] looking for <sthg> □ *He set off in search of adventure.*
♦ **search out** *vt sep* **to search sb/sthg out** [person, weakness, fact] to find sb/sthg by searching □ *I'll search out all the relevant documents later.*

searcher ['sɜ:ʳtʃəʳ] *n* a person who is searching, especially for somebody who is lost.

searching ['sɜ:ʳtʃɪŋ] *adj* [look, question, examination] that is intense and shows a desire to know what somebody is thinking or what they know about something □ *The little girl looked at me with searching eyes.*

searchlight ['sɜ:ʳtʃlaɪt] *n* a powerful light that can be pointed in any direction and is used to see people or things in the dark.

search party *n* a group of people who are looking for somebody who is lost □ *If they're not back soon, we'll send out a search party.*

search warrant *n* a piece of paper that gives the police the right to search somebody's property, especially to look for illegal or stolen goods.

searing ['sɪərɪŋ] *adj* -1. [pain, heat] that is very intense □ *As she fell, a searing pain shot through her leg.* -2. [criticism, condemnation] that is very severe □ *Priceman delivered a searing attack on the policy in his keynote speech.*

Sears Tower [,sɪəʳz-] an office building in Chicago, USA. It is the second-tallest building in the world.

sea salt *n* the salt that is left when sea water is boiled. It is used in cooking.

seashell ['si:ʃel] *n* the empty shell of a small sea animal, often found on the seashore.

seashore ['si:ʃɔ:ʳ] *n* **the seashore** the long narrow strip of land next to the sea □ *We walked along the seashore.*

seasick ['si:sɪk] *adj* **to be seasick** [person] to feel sick or vomit because of the movement of a ship on the sea □ *Our daughter always gets seasick when we take the ferry.* □ *I started feeling seasick.*

seaside ['si:saɪd] *n* **the seaside** a place by the sea, especially one where people spend their vacations □ *We spent two weeks at the seaside.*

seaside resort *n* a place by the sea where people spend their vacations.

season ['si:zn] ◇ *n* -1. one of the four equal parts that the year is divided into □ *Summer is my favorite season.* -2. [for an activity] a period of time each year in which a particular activity or event happens □ *the breeding/rainy/growing/hunting season* □ *He'll be playing for the Miami Dolphins next season.* □ *The period just before Christmas is our busiest season.* -3. **the holiday season** GB, **the tourist season** the most popular time of year for going on vacation to a particular place □ *at the height of the tourist season.* ■ **out of season** at the time of year when few people go to a particular place on vacation □ *We always go on vacation out of season, since prices are much more reasonable.* -4. **to be in season** [fruit, vegetable] to be ready to eat and easy to get □ *I can't get fresh asparagus just now; it's not in season.* ■ **out of season** [fruit, vegetable] not naturally ready to eat at this time and therefore difficult to get □ *Strawberries are out of season now.* -5. GB [of entertainment] a series of movies, concerts, plays etc that are related in some way □ *Channel Four is showing a season of Marlon Brando movies.*
◇ *vt* to add seasoning to <food> □ *Add the tomatoes to the mixture and season it well.*

seasonal ['si:zənl] *adj* [work, demand] that is available or occurs only at a particular time of the year □ *The figures take seasonal fluctuations into account.*

seasoned ['si:znd] *adj* **a seasoned traveler/campaigner etc** a very experienced traveler/

campaigner etc □ *Mark's a seasoned climber, so you're in safe hands.*

seasoning ['siːznɪŋ] *n* salt, pepper etc that is added to food to give it more taste.

season ticket *n* a special ticket that one can use many times during a particular period, e.g. for traveling by public transport or getting into a theater.

season ticket holder *n* a person who owns a valid season ticket.

seat [siːt] ◇ *n* -1. an object with a flat surface that one uses to sit on □ *We stood on our seats to get a better view.* □ *He fell asleep in the back seat of the car.* □ *We managed to get seats near the front.* ■ **to take** OR **have a seat** [person] to sit down □ *Please take* OR *have a seat, I'll be with you in a minute.* -2. [of a chair] the flat part of a chair that one sits on □ *The seat's getting rather worn.* -3. **the seat of one's trousers** OR **pants** the part of one's trousers that covers one's bottom □ *You've got mud on the seat of your trousers.* -4. BUSINESS & POLITICS a position as a member of a legislative body or group that makes important decisions □ *She finally earned a seat on the board.* □ *a traditionally Republican seat.*
◇ *vt* -1. [waiter, hostess] to arrange for <sb> to sit in a particular place □ *I was seated to his left.* ■ **to seat oneself** to sit down □ *He seated himself next to me.* -2. [building, vehicle] to have enough seats for <a particular number of people> □ *This hall seats 500 (people).*

seat belt *n* a belt beside a seat in a plane or car that one fastens across one's body to prevent one from being thrown out of the seat if there is a sudden movement or accident □ *Always wear* OR *put on your seat belt.*

seated ['siːtəd] *adj* **to be seated** [person] to be sitting down □ *When you are all seated we will begin.*

-seater ['siːtər] *suffix* added to a number to show how many places there are for sitting down □ *a two-seater car.*

seating ['siːtɪŋ] *n* all the seats in a particular place or at a particular event □ *There is seating for at least fifty.* □ *a seating plan/capacity.*

Seattle [sɪ'ætl] a city and port on the Pacific coast of Washington State, in the northwestern USA. POPULATION: 516,259.

sea urchin *n* a small round sea creature with a hard shell covered in sharp points.

seawall [ˌsiː'wɔːl] *n* a wall built near the edge of the sea to prevent it from flooding the land.

seawater ['siːwɔːtər] *n* water from the sea.

seaweed ['siːwiːd] *n* a plant that grows in the sea and is often found on the shore.

seaworthy ['siːwɜːrði] *adj* [ship, boat] that is in good enough condition for use on the sea.

sebaceous gland [sə'beɪʃəs-] *n* a gland in one's skin that produces an oily substance that prevents the skin from becoming dry and protects one against bacteria.

sec. *abbr of* **second.**

SEC (*abbr of* **Securities and Exchange Commis-** sion) *n* **the SEC** the US government organization that is responsible for controlling the sales of stocks and bonds.

secateurs [ˌsekə'tɜːrz] *npl* GB a strong cutting tool, similar to a pair of scissors, that is used for cutting plant stems □ *a pair of secateurs.*

secede [sə'siːd] *vi* to formally leave a larger group or country (formal use).

secession [sə'seʃn] *n* formal separation from a larger group or country (formal use).

secluded [sə'kluːdəd] *adj* [beach, garden, place] that is far from other people and so is private and quiet □ *We found a secluded spot to eat our picnic.*

seclusion [sə'kluːʒn] *n* the state of being secluded □ *She has led a life of seclusion since their death.*

second¹ ['sekənd] ◇ *n* -1. a unit for measuring time. There are 60 seconds in a minute □ *She held her breath for fifty-five seconds.* -2. a very short period of time □ *Wait a second!* *Can I see you for a second?* -3. GB & AUS EDUCATION = **a second-class degree.** -4. AUTO **second (gear)** a low gear used for going slowly □ *Are you in second or third?*
◇ *adj* [marriage, week, child] 2nd; number 2 in a series; *see also* **fifth.** ■ **second only to sb/ sthg** only slightly less important, talented etc than sb/sthg that is the best □ *He's a great actor, second only to the likes of Olivier.*
◇ *adv* -1. in second place □ *She finished second.* -2. a word used to introduce a second point or reason in an argument.
◇ *vt* [proposal, motion, nomination] to formally support <sthg that somebody else has suggested> so that voting or discussion can take place □ *I second that.*

◆ **seconds** *npl* -1. BUSINESS goods that are not in perfect condition and are therefore sold at a cheaper price. -2. a second serving of food during a meal □ *Anyone for seconds?*

second² [sə'kɒnd] *vt* GB to send <sb> somewhere for a period of time to do a duty or job □ *She was seconded to the Hong Kong branch.*

secondary [US 'sekənderɪ, GB -ərɪ] *adj* -1. EDUCATION [education, teacher] that is connected with the education of children from the age of 11 until they leave school. -2. [matter, consideration] that is less important than something else □ *The cost is a secondary issue.*

secondary picketing *n* picketing in which strikers demonstrate outside the gates of firms that have business dealings with their employer.

secondary school *n* a school for students aged 11 to 18.

second best [ˌsekənd-] *adj* that is not as good as the best □ *Radiohead was voted second best group of the year by our readers.* □ *We came off second best in the deal.*

second-class [ˌsekənd-] *adj* -1. that is considered to be less important or valuable than other people or things □ *They were treated as second-class citizens.* -2. [ticket, seat, car] that is connected with the ordinary class of travel in a train. **-3.** [mail, letter, stamp] that is connected with the postal service in which things cost less to send, but take longer to arrive. **-4. a second-class degree** GB & AUS EDUCATION an honors degree that is above average but not of the highest standard.

second cousin [,sekənd-] *n* a child of one's parent's cousin.

second-degree burn [,sekənd-] *n* a burn on one's skin that causes it to become very red and blisters to appear.

seconder ['sekəndə^r] *n* a person who seconds a motion, nomination, proposal etc.

second floor [,sekənd-] *n* **-1.** US the second story in a building, above the ground floor □ *I live on the second floor.* □ *a second-floor apartment.* **-2.** GB the third story in a building, above the ground floor and the first floor □ *I took the lift to the second floor.*

second-guess [,sekənd-] *vt* **-1.** US [person, event] to look back into the past and criticize <sb/sthg> with the knowledge of what happened □ *Don't second-guess me!* **-2.** [thoughts, reaction] to predict <sthg>; [person] to predict the actions of <sb> □ *All the journalists were trying to second-guess the outcome of the election.* □ *Lewis will be hoping to second-guess his opponent.*

second-hand [,sekənd-] ◇ *adj* **-1.** [furniture, car] that used to be owned or used by somebody else □ *She always buys second-hand clothes, and manages to look fabulous in them.* **-2.** [store, market] that sells second-hand goods. **-3.** [account, report] not from the person who experienced or saw an event directly, but passed on by another person □ *Look, it's a second-hand version of events; it's bound to be inaccurate.* ◇ *adv* **-1.** [buy, obtain] from a second-hand store □ *She gets all her clothes second-hand.* **-2. to hear sthg second-hand** to hear about sthg by reading about it, or by being told by somebody who was not directly involved.

second hand ['sekənd-] *n* the pointer on clocks and watches that moves to show the seconds □ *The second hand had stopped.*

second-in-command [,sekənd-] *n* a person who has the rank directly below a manager, director, or military commander.

secondly ['sekəndlɪ] *adv* a word used to introduce a second point in a list □ *I'm not going, firstly because it's too far and secondly because it's too expensive.*

secondment [sə'kɒndmənt] *n* GB a period of time that one spends in a place where one has been sent to do a particular special duty or job □ *She's on secondment to Head Office.*

second nature [,sekənd-] *n* **to be second nature** to be something that one has done so many times that one does it without thinking about it □ *That sort of precision comes as second nature to most of our staff.*

second-rate [,sekənd-] *adj* [writer, play, product] that one thinks is not of a very high standard □ *As a director, he's second-rate at best.*

second thought [,sekənd-] *n* **to have second**

thoughts to begin to wonder if something one has chosen to do may not be a good idea □ *You're not having second thoughts about going to Japan, are you?* ■ **on second thought** US, **on second thoughts** GB a phrase used to show that one has changed one's mind about something one has just said, especially about a plan □ *On second thought, let's not bother.*

secrecy ['siːkrəsɪ] *n* the state of being secret □ *I was sworn to secrecy.* □ *The whole operation was carried out in secrecy.*

secret ['siːkrət] ◇ *adj* **-1.** [passage, negotiations, plan] that only very few people are allowed to know about □ *They tried to keep their plans secret.* **-2. a secret drinker/smoker etc** a person who drinks/smokes etc without anybody else knowing □ *She received flowers from a secret admirer.* ◇ *n* **-1.** something that only a few people know about and that is kept hidden from other people □ *If I tell you a secret, promise you won't repeat it.* □ *She can't keep a secret.* **-2. the secret of sthg** the best or only way of achieving sthg □ *the secret of success* □ *The secret of making a good risotto is to use the right rice.*

◆ **in secret** *adv* [take place, happen] without anybody else knowing □ *We met in secret to discuss our plan.*

secret agent *n* a person whose job is to find out secret information about the governments, armies etc of other countries for the government of a particular country.

secretarial [,sekrə'teərɪəl] *adj* [course, skills, training] that is connected with the work of a secretary □ *I'm looking for secretarial work.*

secretarial school US, **secretarial college** GB *n* a place where people learn typing, word processing, shorthand etc.

secretariat [,sekrə'teərɪət] *n* a department that is responsible for the administration of a large organization.

secretary [US 'sekrəterɪ, GB -ərɪ] (*pl* **secretaries**) *n* **-1.** a person whose job involves typing, answering the phone, organizing meetings etc for somebody else □ *"Can you make it Tuesday?" — "I'm not sure, I'll have to check with my secretary."* **-2.** [of a club, labor union] a person whose role in an organization is to write official letters, keep records etc □ *She's honorary secretary of the Arts Society.* **-3.** POLITICS the person in charge of a large government department.

secretary-general (*pl* **secretaries-general**) *n* the person in charge of a large international organization, especially a political one □ *the UN Secretary-General.*

Secretary of State *n* **-1.** US the head of the government department dealing with foreign affairs. **-2.** GB a government minister □ *the Secretary of State for Education.*

secrete [sɪ'kriːt] *vt* **-1.** [gland, organ] to form and release <a substance> □ *The hormone is secreted into the bloodstream.* **-2.** [person] to hide <sthg> (formal use) □ *I secreted the book at the back of one of the shelves.*

secretion [sɪ'kriːʃn] *n* a substance that is secreted by part of an animal or plant; the process of secreting a substance.

secretive ['si:krətɪv] *adj* [person] who avoids talking about their feelings, actions etc □ *Officials are being very secretive about the recent arms deal.*

secretly ['si:krətlɪ] *adv* [think, plan, tell] *see* **secret** □ *He was secretly in love with her.* □ *They met secretly to avoid publicity.*

secret police *n* a police force controlled by the government of a country that works in secret and deals especially with political crimes.

secret service *n* a government department that deals with its country's security and tries to get secret information about other countries.

sect [sekt] *n* a religious group that is separate from a larger established group and has its own particular beliefs.

sectarian [sek'teərɪən] *adj* [killing, violence] that happens because of problems between different religious groups.

section ['sekʃn] ◇ *n* **-1.** [of an exam, train, pipe] one of the parts that something is divided into □ *A section of the road is being blocked off for repairs.* □ *the sports section of the newspaper* □ *section 6 of the Motor Vehicle Code* □ *This is an issue that affects all sections of society.* **-2.** [in a diagram] a picture of what something would look like if it were cut from top to bottom and seen from the side □ *I'll show you a drawing of it in section.* ◇ *vt* **-1.** to show <an object, building> etc in section. **-2.** to cut <sthg> into sections (formal use).

sector ['sektər] *n* **-1.** BUSINESS a particular part of a country's economy □ *the banking/retail/trade sector.* **-2.** [of a city, region] a particular part of a place that has been divided into sections, usually for military reasons □ *The western sector has been sealed off by police.* **-3.** GEOMETRY the area in a circle between two radii.

secular ['sekjələr] *adj* [society, education, music] that is not connected with religion.

secure [sɪ'kjuər] ◇ *adj* **-1.** [house, building, prison] that is properly locked up and protected so that people cannot get in or out easily □ *You need to make these windows more secure.* **-2.** [ladder, shelf] that is firmly fixed in place □ *Check that the rope is secure.* **-3.** [job, future, position] that is not likely to change in an undesirable way and so allows one to feel relaxed, especially about money □ *How secure is this investment?* □ *The sponsorship deal ensures the athlete will be financially secure for a long time.* **-4.** [base, basis] that is strong and solid □ *When it comes to talking about moral behavior, you're not exactly on secure ground yourself.* **-5.** [person, childhood, marriage] that is without trouble or worry □ *He comes from a secure family background.* □ *I can go away, secure in the knowledge that you'll take care of everything.*
◇ *vt* **-1.** [job, vote, contract] to get sthg with a lot of effort □ *We have secured the support of several board members.* **-2.** [city, borders] to

make <a place> safe □ *Measures have been taken to secure the area against attack.* **-3.** [door, lid, window] to fasten <sthg> tightly □ *The rope had not been properly secured.*

securely [sɪ'kjuəlɪ] *adv* **securely locked/fastened etc** properly locked/fastened etc.

security [sɪ'kjuərətɪ] (*pl* **securities**) *n* **-1.** [of a country, building] freedom from attack or harm, especially from crime or terrorist attack □ *It was a threat to national security.* □ *Security was tight during the presidential visit.* □ *airport security* □ *security measures.* **-2.** [against a bad situation] protection, especially legal protection, against a possible bad situation □ *security of tenure* □ *job security.* **-3.** [of a person, job] the state or feeling of being secure □ *Children need love and security.* **-4.** FINANCE money or possessions that one promises to give a lender if one cannot repay a loan □ *What security do you have for the loan?*

◆ **securities** *npl* FINANCE stocks, shares etc owned as property □ *government securities* □ *the securities market.*

security blanket *n* a piece of material, a soft toy etc that a small child carries around to avoid feeling worried, unhappy etc.

Security Council *n* **the Security Council** the organization within the United Nations whose purpose is to maintain world peace.

security forces *npl* members of the police and army whose job is to protect a country against terrorism, attack etc.

security guard *n* a person whose job is to guard a building.

security risk *n* a person who the government of a country thinks could be a threat to the security of the country, because they could give away government secrets.

secy *abbr* of **secretary.**

sedan [sɪ'dæn] *n* US & AUS a car for four to six passengers, with two or four doors and a trunk for luggage.

sedate [sɪ'deɪt] ◇ *adj* [person, pace] that is calm and slow, and seems very controlled. ◇ *vt* to give <a patient> a drug that makes them sleepy or calm □ *He was heavily sedated.*

sedation [sɪ'deɪʃn] *n* the act of sedating somebody □ *He'll be under sedation for the next few hours.*

sedative ['sedətɪv] ◇ *adj* [effect, properties] that causes sleep or a feeling of calm. ◇ *n* a drug that is given to somebody to make them sleepy or calm.

sedentary [US 'sednterɪ, GB -ərɪ] *adj* [job, life] that involves sitting for long periods of time.

sediment ['sedəmənt] *n* bits of solid material that settle at the bottom of a liquid.

sedition [sɪ'dɪʃn] *n* things that a person or group says, writes, or does in order to encourage people to disobey the government (formal use).

seduce [sɪ'djuːs] *vt* **-1.** to be very attractive to <sb>, often with the result that they do something they should not do □ *We were seduced by the beauty of the place.* □ *Their promises seduced him into signing the contract.* **-2.** to persuade <sb> to have sex with one, especially if they are younger or less experienced.

seduction [sɪ'dʌkʃn] *n* the act of seducing somebody sexually.

seductive [sɪ'dʌktɪv] *adj* -1. [argument, prospect, suggestion] that is very attractive □ *Look, it all sounds very seductive, but I'm not interested.* -2. [eyes, voice, person] sexually attractive □ *She looked extremely seductive in her long red dress.*

see [siː] (*pt* **saw**, *pp* **seen**) ◇ *vt* -1. to become aware of <sb/sthg> through one's eyes □ *Have you seen my purse anywhere?* □ *Turn the light on, I can't see a thing!* □ *We saw Ken getting out of a taxi.* □ *Did anyone actually see her leave the building?* -2. [program, movie] to watch <sthg> because one is interested in it; [place, monument] to visit an <interesting or famous place> □ *I've seen "Psycho" four times!* □ *We just had to see the "Mona Lisa" when we were in Paris.* -3. [person, friend] to meet <sb> socially; [doctor, dentist] to visit <sb> to get professional help □ *I'm seeing Tim tomorrow night for a drink.* □ *He really should see a specialist about his knee.* ■ **to be seeing sb** to be having a romantic or sexual relationship with sb □ *She's been seeing another man!* ■ **see you!** goodbye! (informal use). ■ **see you soon/later/tomorrow** goodbye until we meet again soon/later/tomorrow. -4. [somebody's problem, distress] to understand <sthg>, especially a person's feelings or behavior □ *You could see that he was upset.* □ *I don't see the point of all this fuss.* □ *Do you see what I'm getting at?* □ *It's difficult to see how we can improve things.* -5. **to see sb to a place** [to the door, station, airport] to go with sb to a place to say goodbye or to make sure they get there safely □ *I'll see you to your car.* □ *It's all right, I can see myself out.* -6. **to see sthg in sb** to find sthg attractive about sb □ *What on earth does she see in him?* -7. **to see what/how/when etc...** to find out about something □ *Let's go and see what's going on.* ■ **I'll see what I can do** I'll try to do what is needed □ *"Have you got a table for six?" — "I'll see what I can do."* ■ **see if you can help** try to find out if you can help □ *Let's see if I can recognize anyone here.* □ *See if anyone would like another drink.* -8. **to see (that)...** to make sure that something happens or is done □ *I'll see that he gets your message.* □ *See you get plenty of rest.* -9. **to see sb/sthg as...** to have a particular opinion about sb/sthg □ *I don't see his reaction as particularly strange.* -10. **to see sthg as sthg** to think of sthg in a particular way □ *People might see it as a threat to their jobs.* -11. **to see sthg happening** to think that sthg is likely to happen □ *I can't see us moving out before Christmas.* □ *I don't really see him offering to pay, do you?* -12. [person] to be present when <sthg> happens; [place, period] to be the particular time that an event happens, or the place where it happens □ *He didn't live to see his daughter married.* □ *This year has seen so many changes.* -13. **see page 10/chapter 1/below** read page 10/chapter 1/below for more information (used to cross-refer in texts).

◇ *vi* -1. to be able to recognize things with one's eyes □ *She can't see without her contact lenses.* -2. to understand what somebody is saying □ *You just don't see, do you?* ■ **I see** a phrase used to show that one has understood what has just been said □ *Oh I see, you weren't there.* ■ **you see** a phrase used before or after an explanation in spoken English □ *You see, I've never gotten on with my father.* -3. *phrases* **I'll/we'll see** a phrase used when one does not want to decide something right away □ *"Can I have a new bike?" — "We'll have to see."* ■ **let's see, let me see** a phrase used when one is trying to remember a fact or when one is looking for something □ *Let me see now, it must have been in March.*

◆ **seeing as, seeing that** *conj* a phrase used to give a reason for something (informal use) □ *Let's do some work, seeing as you're here.*

◆ **see about** *vt fus* -1. **to see about sthg** to make arrangements so that sthg happens or is dealt with □ *I'll see about ordering some flowers.* □ *He had to go into town to see about a visa.* -2. **to see about sthg** to wait before deciding about sthg □ *I'll buy the computer now, but I'll have to see about the printer.* ■ **we'll (soon) see about that!** I'll make sure that does not happen! (informal use).

◆ **see off** *vt sep* **to see sb off** [friend, visitor, guest] to go with sb to the door, airport etc and say goodbye to them □ *My family came to see me off.*

◆ **see through** ◇ *vt fus* **to see through sb/sthg** [lie, disguise] to realize that sb/sthg is not honest or truthful □ *She saw straight through my excuse.* ◇ *vt sep* **to see sthg through** to finish sthg, especially when it is difficult □ *It was her idea, and she was determined to see it through.* ■ **to see sb through sthg** [through a problem, crisis] to help or support sb until sthg is over □ *We've got just enough money left to see us through the week.*

◆ **see to** *vt fus* **to see to sb/sthg** to deal with sb/sthg □ *Bill saw to dinner.* □ *I must go and see to the children.* □ *Don't worry, I'll see to it that he doesn't pester you again.*

seed [siːd] ◇ *n* -1. a small hard part of a plant that produces another plant when it is planted □ *poppy seeds* □ *Plant the seeds in early April.* -2. SPORT a tennis player who is given a particular rank that shows how likely they are to win a competition □ *the top seed at Wimbledon.* ◇ *vt* SPORT to rank a <tennis player> in a way that shows how likely they are to win a competition □ *She's seeded fourth in the world.*

◆ **seeds** *npl* **the seeds of doubt/an idea etc** the beginnings of doubt/an idea etc □ *Once the seeds of doubt had been sown, I couldn't stop thinking about it.*

seedless ['siːdləs] *adj* [grape, orange] that has no seeds inside.

seedling ['siːdlɪŋ] *n* a young plant grown from a seed.

seed money *n* FINANCE money that is needed for the first stages of a new business.

seedy ['si:dɪ] (*compar* **seedier,** *superl* **seediest**) *adj* [person, area, bar] that looks unpleasant or dirty, and is connected with immoral activities □ *I don't want to know about the seedy goings-on in that place.*

Seeing Eye dog™ [ˌsi:ɪŋ-] *n* US a dog that has been trained to help a blind person walk around safely.

seek [si:k] (*pt* & *pp* **sought**) (formal use) ◇ *vt* **-1.** [shelter, employment] to look for <sthg> □ *'Student seeks summer employment.'* **-2.** [peace, comfort, revenge] to try to achieve or get <sthg> □ *They are seeking to overthrow the government.* **-3.** [advice, compensation] to ask for <sthg> □ *The law will make it harder for those seeking asylum.* ◇ *vi* **-1. to seek for sthg** [for an answer, job] to look for sthg. **-2. to seek for sthg** [for help, advice] to ask for sthg.

♦ **seek out** *vt sep* **to seek sb/sthg out** to look for sb/sthg until one finds them □ *He vowed to seek out his enemies and destroy them.*

seem [si:m] *vi* **-1.** (+ *complement*) **to seem kind/bored/tired etc** to have the appearance of being kind/bored/tired etc □ *He seems a lot happier in his job now.* □ *"How was she?" — "She seemed alright to me."* □ *They seem like a nice couple.* □ *What seems to be the problem?* □ *We don't seem to be having much success.* ■ **I can't seem to talk to him** I have tried to talk to him several times but have had no success □ *I just can't seem to get rid of this cold.* ■ **it seems (that)** used to describe something that one thinks is true, but is not certain about □ *It seems that they've arrested the wrong man.* □ *There seems to have been a misunderstanding.* **-2. it seems to me (that)...** my opinion is that... □ *It seems to me that he's making a big mistake.* ■ **it seems as if** OR **as though** used to describe a situation that one feels to be true or real □ *It seemed as if there was nobody in the world who could help us.*

seeming ['si:mɪŋ] *adj* [boredom, interest] apparent (formal use) □ *Jesse hid her true feelings behind a mask of seeming indifference.*

seemingly ['si:mɪŋlɪ] *adv* **seemingly endless/limitless etc** that seems to be endless/limitless etc but it is not really □ *It was a seemingly innocent request.*

seemly ['si:mlɪ] (*compar* **seemlier,** *superl* **seemliest**) *adj* [behavior] that is suitable and dignified (literary use) □ *It would not be seemly for us to be seen here together.*

seen [si:n] *past participle of* **see.**

seep [si:p] *vi* [gas, liquid, blood] to gradually pass through something in a particular direction □ *Water had seeped in through the cracks.*

seersucker ['sɪərsʌkər] *n* a light cloth that has an uneven surface and a pattern of raised and flat lines on it □ *a seersucker tablecloth.*

seesaw ['si:sɔ:] *n* a piece of equipment for children to play on, consisting of a long piece of metal or wood supported in the middle so that it swings up and down when somebody sits at each end.

seethe [si:ð] *vi* **-1.** to be very angry, especially without showing the anger openly □ *He smiled, but inwardly he was seething.* **-2. to be**

seething with sthg [with people, insects] to be very full of sthg that is moving about □ *The room was seething with people.*

seething ['si:ðɪŋ] *adj* **-1.** [person] who is very angry □ *When Kay saw the damage she was absolutely seething.* **-2.** [crowd, mass] that is very full of people, animals etc that keep moving □ *a seething mass of worms.*

see-through *adj* [blouse, skirt, dress] that is made of fabric so fine that people can see one's body underneath.

segment ['segmənt] *n* **-1.** [of a market, population] one of the parts that something can be divided into □ *The insect's body is divided into segments.* **-2.** [of an orange, grapefruit] one of the parts that make up the flesh of some fruits □ *grapefruit segments.*

segregate ['segrɪgeɪt] *vt* [children, races] to divide <two groups of people or things> from each other □ *In some areas Protestants were segregated from Catholics.*

segregation [ˌsegrɪ'geɪʃn] *n* the practice of officially keeping one group of people separate from another, usually because they have a different race, religion, or sex □ *racial segregation* □ *segregation laws.*

Seine [seɪn]: **the Seine** a river in northern France that flows through Paris.

seismic ['saɪzmɪk] *adj* [shock, explosion] that is caused by an earthquake.

seize [si:z] *vt* **-1.** [gun, arm, life belt] to take hold of <sthg> suddenly and firmly □ *She seized the dog by its collar.* □ *"Let's get out of here," said Terence, seizing my hand.* **-2.** [power, control] to take <sthg> by force; [building, town, area] to take control of <a place> by force; [drugs, weapon, property] to take <sthg> away from somebody who cannot legally keep it □ *Military rebels made a failed attempt to seize power.* □ *Troops seized three villages in the area yesterday.* □ *Drugs worth half a million dollars were seized by customs officials.* **-3.** [criminal, victim] to arrest or capture <sb>, especially by surprise □ *Colonel Chabron's daughter Lucy has been seized by kidnappers.* **-4.** [opportunity] to immediately take <a chance or opportunity> in order to do something one wants to do □ *You should seize this opportunity to get away for a while.*

♦ **seize on** *vt fus* **to seize on sthg** [on a word, fact] to draw attention to sthg that has just appeared or been said, especially in order to use it to help oneself □ *In the interview, they seized on the fact that I'd dropped out of college.*

♦ **seize up** *vi* **-1.** [back, muscle] to become very painful so that one cannot move it. **-2.** [engine, machine] to stop working, e.g. because of lack of oil.

♦ **seize upon** *vt fus* = **seize on.**

seizure ['si:ʒər] *n* **-1.** MEDICINE a sudden fit or attack in which part of one's body stops working properly □ *a heart seizure.* **-2.** [of power, drugs, a town] *see* **seize.**

seldom ['seldəm] *adv* not very often □ *We seldom go shopping on Saturday mornings.* □ *I think about it very seldom now.*

select [sə'lekt] ◇ *vt* [candidate, dress] to choose <sb/sthg> carefully from among others by deciding which is the best or most suitable □ *We selected them as our partners/selected them to be our partners.* □ *You can only select three people/items from this list.* ◇ *adj* **-1.** [gathering, group] that is small and only includes the best people or things □ *I was lucky enough to be among the select few who were invited.* **-2.** [area, school] that only the richest people can have or use □ *They live in a very select part of town.*

select committee *n* in Britain, a small committee of Members of Parliament, set up to examine or investigate a particular subject or problem.

selected [sə'lektəd] *adj* [areas, cities] that have been chosen from a larger group □ *The offer is available at selected stores only.*

selection [sə'lekʃn] *n* **-1.** the act of selecting somebody or something, or of being selected □ *The selection procedure is very tough.* □ *Her selection as manager surprised everyone.* **-2.** [of poems, songs] a group of things or people that have been selected from a larger group □ *selections from Gershwin.* **-3.** [of food, clothes, cars] a range of different types of particular goods in a store □ *We have a wide selection of wines/furniture.*

selective [sə'lektɪv] *adj* **-1.** that chooses only a few things or people and not others □ *They were pretty selective in their description of events.* □ *Kathy seems to have a selective memory when it comes to money.* **-2.** [person] who chooses very carefully what they do, buy etc □ *He's very selective about what he eats.*

selector [sə'lektər] *n* GB a member of a group that selects the players in a sports team.

self [self] (*pl* **selves**) *n* one's personality and character □ *I'm pleased to say she seems to be her old self again.* □ *The weekend retreat enabled us to get in touch with our real selves.*

self- *prefix* **-1.** added to words to show that something is done to, or is done by oneself or itself □ *self-induced* □ *a self-fulfilling prophecy.* **-2.** added to words to show that something is done automatically □ *self-loading.*

self-addressed envelope [-ədrest-] *n* an unsealed envelope with one's own name and address on it that one sends to somebody in another envelope in order for them to send back information, a form etc.

self-addressed stamped envelope [-'stæmpt-] *n* a self-addressed envelope with stamps stuck on it to pay for mailing it.

self-adhesive *adj* [envelope, label] that is covered on one side with a sticky substance so that it will stick to things.

self-assembly *adj* GB [furniture, equipment] that one puts together oneself by following written instructions.

self-assertive *adj* [person] who lets people know what they think and want in a confident way □ *Tracey needs to learn to be more self-assertive.*

self-assurance *n* calm confidence, especially in a difficult situation □ *She had an air of calm self-assurance.*

self-assured *adj* [person] who has self-assurance □ *He's remarkably self-assured for someone so young.*

self-catering *adj* GB [accommodation, villa, apartment] where one stays on vacation and cooks one's own meals.

self-centered [-'sentərd] *adj* [person] who does not care or think about other people, only themselves □ *a selfish, self-centered brat.*

self-cleaning *adj* [oven] that one does not have to clean, because it burns away the grease left by cooking.

self-confessed [-kən'fest] *adj* **a self-confessed liar/romantic etc** a person who admits that they are a liar/romantic etc □ *He's a self-confessed workaholic/drug addict.*

self-confidence *n* confidence in one's abilities, popularity, or appearance □ *Where's all your self-confidence gone?* □ *She's good, if lacking in self-confidence.*

self-confident *adj* [person] who has self-confidence □ *She has a very self-confident manner.*

self-conscious *adj* feeling embarrassed and shy with other people because one is worried about what they think of one □ *I feel very self-conscious about talking in front of a lot of people.* □ *Murray gave a self-conscious smile.*

self-contained *adj* **-1.** [person] who does not show their feelings easily □ *It's difficult to know what she's feeling, she's so very self-contained.* **-2.** GB [apartment] that is part of a house but is separate, with its own entrance, kitchen, and bathroom □ *It's not an actual apartment, but it is entirely self-contained.*

self-control *n* the ability to control one's emotions □ *I shouldn't have lost my self-control.* □ *He managed to keep his self-control.*

self-controlled *adj* [person] who shows self-control.

self-defense *n* the act of defending oneself, especially physically, when one is attacked. ■ **to act in self-defense** to use force in order to protect oneself □ *She claimed she killed him in self-defense.*

self-denial *n* the act of refusing to allow oneself a particular pleasure □ *small acts of self-denial, such as missing lunch.*

self-destruct [-dɪ'strʌkt] ◇ *adj* **a self-destruct button/mechanism** a button/mechanism that makes a device destroy itself. ◇ *vi* [missile] to destroy itself.

self-determination *n* the right of a country to choose whether or not to be independent from another country, and to be able to choose its government □ *Every country has a right to self-determination.*

self-discipline *n* the ability to be strict with oneself and to control one's actions or desires □ *I don't have the self-discipline to go on a diet.* □ *The course requires a certain amount of self-discipline.*

self-doubt *n* doubt in one's own abilities □

Plagued by self-doubt, Indrin could never finish anything he wrote.

self-drive *adj* GB [van, car] that one can rent and drive oneself.

self-educated *adj* [person] who has taught themselves what they know, and has not had any lessons □ *He is entirely self-educated.*

self-effacing [-ɪˈfeɪsɪŋ] *adj* [person] who does not like talking about themselves or the things they have done because they are modest or shy □ *a shy, self-effacing man.*

self-employed [-ɪmˈplɔɪd] *adj* [worker, designer, builder] who works for themselves, rather than for an employer □ *I'm not on their staff, I'm actually self-employed.*

self-esteem *n* the feeling that one deserves to be respected and valued □ *Men in that position are often lacking in self-esteem.*

self-evident *adj* [fact, truth, reason] that is obvious without people having to think about it □ *The folly of proceeding along such a course had by now become self-evident.*

self-explanatory *adj* [rules, instructions, diagram] that is easy to understand without more explanation □ *It's all pretty self-explanatory, so I'll leave you to it.*

self-expression *n* the act of expressing one's personality and feelings, especially through a creative skill □ *I consider art an important form of self-expression.*

self-focusing [-ˈfoʊkəsɪŋ] *adj* [camera, lens] that focuses automatically on whatever is at the center of the viewfinder.

self-governing *adj* [province, region] that elects its own government.

self-government *n* the government of a country by its own people.

self-help *n* the concept that people can cure themselves of certain emotional or physical problems without professional help □ *a self-help group.*

self-important *adj* [person] who thinks they are more important than they really are (disapproving use) □ *a pompous, self-important little man.*

self-imposed [-ɪmˈpoʊzd] *adj* [duty, rule, exile] that one has decided to accept or do without anybody else telling one to do it.

self-indulgent *adj* [person] who lets themselves do or have enjoyable things too much (disapproving use) □ *It seems so self-indulgent to spend all this money on clothes!*

self-inflicted [-ɪnˈflɪktəd] *adj* [wound, cut] that one has caused to oneself.

self-interest *n* the attitude of seeing what advantage one can get out of a situation for oneself (disapproving use) □ *He was motivated entirely by self-interest.*

selfish [ˈselfɪʃ] *adj* [person] who only cares or thinks about themselves and does not care about anybody else □ *That's very selfish behavior/a very selfish attitude.* □ *Don't be so selfish — let your brother play too!*

selfishness [ˈselfɪʃnəs] *n: see* **selfish.**

selfless [ˈselfləs] *adj* [person] who helps other people because they care about them very much, even more than they care about themselves □ *She's a selfless and devoted wife.*

self-locking [-ˈlɒkɪŋ] *adj* [door, mechanism] that locks automatically when it is closed.

self-made *adj* **a self-made man/woman** a man/woman who has become successful and rich without special help or advantages, e.g. a good education or position in society □ *a self-made millionaire.*

self-opinionated *adj* [person] who believes they are always right and never thinks that they might be wrong (disapproving use) □ *I find him extremely self-opinionated and irritating.*

self-perpetuating [-pərˈpetʃʊeɪtɪŋ] *adj* [system, myth] that never ends because people keep using it, saying it etc.

self-pity *n* too much pity for oneself and one's problems (disapproving use) □ *You can't just sit there wallowing in self-pity.*

self-portrait *n* a drawing or painting by an artist of themselves.

self-possessed *adj* [person] who can control their emotions and stay confident and calm even in difficult situations □ *a calm, self-possessed young woman.*

self-preservation *n* the protection of one's own life in a difficult or dangerous situation □ *an instinct for self-preservation.*

self-proclaimed [-prəˈkleɪmd] *adj* [leader, expert] who claims to have a particular position or ability (disapproving use) □ *a self-proclaimed expert on photography.*

self-raising flour *n* GB = **self-rising flour.**

self-regulating [-ˈregjəleɪtɪŋ] *adj* [body, institution] that regulates its own activities.

self-reliant *adj* [person] who is able to do a lot of things alone, without help from other people.

self-respect *n* respect for oneself and a belief that one deserves to be valued □ *Don't you have any self-respect?* □ *When Tony lost his job he lost his self-respect.*

self-respecting [-rɪsˈpektɪŋ] *adj* [citizen, person] who is normal and does what other people like them normally do □ *No self-respecting parent would allow their children out so late.*

self-restraint *n* the ability to stop oneself from doing what one feels like doing, in order to avoid problems □ *Try to exercise a little self-restraint.*

self-righteous *adj* [person] who believes strongly that they are right and that other people are wrong (disapproving use) □ *Like many religious people, he could be very self-righteous at times.*

self-rising flour [-ˈraɪzɪŋ-] *n* US flour that has had baking powder added to it so that it makes cakes, pastry etc rise when it is cooked.
NOTE: Compare **plain flour.**

self-rule *n* the government of a country by its own people □ *the desire for self-rule.*

self-sacrifice *n* the act of not doing or having something that one wants in order to let other people have what they need □ *an act of self-sacrifice.*

selfsame ['selfseɪm] *adj* that is exactly the same one □ *I saw the selfsame coat much cheaper in another store!*

self-satisfied *adj* [person] who is very pleased with themselves or their achievements (disapproving use) □ *He gave us a self-satisfied smile.*

self-sealing [-'siːlɪŋ] *adj* [envelope] that has a sticky substance on the flap so that it sticks when it is pressed down.

self-seeking [-'siːkɪŋ] *adj* [person] who does things only to get some advantage for themselves (disapproving use) □ *Beware of self-seeking people who are only interested in your money.*

self-service *n* a system used in stores, restaurants etc in which customers take what they want from a counter or from shelves and then pay at a cash desk □ *Is it self-service in this restaurant?* □ *a self-service café/counter.*

self-starter *n* -1. AUTO an electric device that starts an engine when a button is pressed. -2. a person who can work well on their own and does not need to be told what to do all the time.

self-styled [-'staɪld] *adj* a self-styled champion/leader etc a person who calls themselves a champion/leader etc without having any right to (disapproving use) □ *the self-styled "King of Rock".*

self-sufficient *adj* [country, population] able to produce everything one needs without buying or getting anything from anywhere else □ *We aim to be self-sufficient in fuel within ten years.* □ *With our little garden and the farm we are almost entirely self-sufficient.*

self-supporting [-sə'pɔːtɪŋ] *adj* [business, industry] that makes enough money to continue without more money being spent on it.

self-tanning [-'tænɪŋ] *adj* [lotion, cream] that colors one's skin so that one looks like one has a suntan.

self-taught *adj* [person] who has taught themselves a skill without help from a teacher or other person □ *You know as a tennis player she is entirely self-taught.*

self-test *n* COMPUTING a set of automatic tests that a computer or printer does on itself to check everything is working.

sell [sel] (*pt* & *pp* **sold**) ◇ *vt* -1. [car, house, furniture] to give <sthg> to somebody in exchange for money □ *Do you sell stamps?* □ *He sold me his apartment* OR *sold his apartment to me last year.* □ *She sold everything she owned in order to lend him the money.* □ *I agreed to sell it for $100.* -2. [product] to make people buy <sthg> □ *Good advertising helped to sell huge numbers of copies.* ■ **to sell oneself** to draw somebody's attention to one's skills, ideas etc, especially in order to convince them to give one a job □ *You've got to learn to sell yourself in this business.* -3. [idea, scheme] to convince somebody that <sthg> is a good idea (informal use) □ *You haven't really sold me on the*

idea. □ *The government never managed to sell the poll tax to the British electorate.*

◇ *vi* -1. [person] *I refuse to sell at that price.* □ *The housing market is so stagnant that nobody can sell.* -2. [product] *The new model is selling well all over the world.* □ *Those watches sell for* OR *at $200 retail.*

◆ **sell off** *vt sep* -1. **to sell sthg off** [property, land] to sell sthg because one needs the money □ *We may need to sell off some of our assets.* -2. **to sell sthg off** [goods, stock] to sell sthg cheaply because it has lost its value □ *They're selling off all their old 386 computers.*

◆ **sell on** *vt sep* **to sell sthg on** [goods, product] to sell sthg to somebody else in order to make a profit.

◆ **sell out** ◇ *vt sep* **to be sold out** [event, match, concert] to have no more tickets available because they have all been sold; [store] to have sold all the items of a particular kind that were available for sale □ *'Sold out.'* □ *I tried to get tickets, but they were all sold out.* □ *We were sold out of copies by 5 o'clock.*

◇ *vi* -1. [store, ticket office] to sell all the items of a particular kind that were available for sale; [item, product, tickets] to be no longer available from a store, ticket office etc □ *We've sold out of that size.* □ *The cakes sold out immediately.* -2. [person, government] to give up one's principles, especially for money □ *Don't tell me you're going to sell out and take a job in advertising!*

◆ **sell up** *vi* GB to sell everything one owns, especially one's house or business □ *They've sold up and left the country.*

sell-by date *n* GB the date marked on a packet of food that is the last date that it can be sold to make sure that it is still fresh and safe to eat □ *This chicken is past its sell-by date.*

seller ['selər] *n* a person or business that sells a particular type of thing □ *a flower/picture seller* □ *a seller of quality wines.*

seller's market *n* a situation that is better for sellers than for buyers in which a shortage of certain products results in high prices.

selling ['selɪŋ] *n* the act or business of selling things □ *the buying and selling of stocks and shares.*

selling point *n* an attractive aspect of something that is mentioned in order to help to sell it.

selling price *n* [of goods, shares] the price at which a seller says they will sell something □ *The initial selling price was very high.*

Sellotape™ ['seləteɪp] *n* GB a roll of clear tape that is sticky on one side and that is used to stick paper.

◆ **sellotape** *vt* to put Sellotape on <sthg> in order to repair it or fasten it to something else □ *I sellotaped the poster to the wall.*

sell-out *n* an event for which all the tickets have been sold □ *a sell-out concert/match.*

seltzer ['seltsər] *n* US carbonated mineral water.

selves [selvz] *plural of* **self.**

semantic [sə'mæntɪk] *adj* [difference, problem]

that is connected with the meaning of words □ *Dictionaries divide words into separate semantic categories.*

◆ **semantics** *n* the study of the meaning of words.

semaphore ['seməfɔːʳ] *n* a method of sending messages by holding a flag in each hand and moving one's arms to different positions to represent letters and numbers.

semblance ['sembləns] *n* **some semblance of sthg** something that looks like sthg (formal use) □ *We restored the room to some semblance of order.*

semen ['siːmən] *n* the liquid containing sperm that is produced by men and male animals.

semester [sə'mestəʳ] *n* one of the two parts into which a year at a university is divided.

semi ['semɪ] *n* **-1.** US a large truck. **-2.** GB a semidetached house.

semi- *prefix* added to words to mean partly, but not completely □ *He's semi-retired.* □ *In the semi-darkness he made out the shape of a woman.* □ *The news is semi-official.*

semiautomatic [,semɪɔːtə'mætɪk] *adj* [rifle, weapon] that loads each bullet automatically, but does not fire unless the trigger is pulled.

semicircle ['semɪsɜːʳkl] *n* half a circle; the shape of half a circle □ *We sat in a semicircle.*

semicircular [,semɪ'sɜːʳkjələʳ] *adj* [arrangement, shape] that has the shape of a semicircle.

semicolon ['semɪkoʊlən] *n* a symbol (;) used to separate parts of a sentence.

semiconscious [,semɪ'kɒnʃəs] *adj* [person] who is partly conscious.

semidetached [,semɪdɪ'tætʃt] GB ◇ *adj* [house, cottage] that is joined to another house on one side by a wall that is part of both houses. ◇ *n* a semidetached house.

semifinal [,semɪ'faɪnl] *n* one of two games that are played to decide which players or teams will play in the final □ *the semifinal round.*

semifinalist [,semɪ'faɪnləst] *n* a player or team that is playing in a semifinal.

seminal ['semɪnl] *adj* [book, film, artist] that is very important and has a strong influence on other artists, writers etc □ *He had a seminal influence on 20th-century photography.*

seminar ['semɪnɑːʳ] *n* a group that meets to discuss and learn about a subject, especially in universities □ *They're holding a seminar on women in politics.*

seminary [US 'semənerɪ, GB -ərɪ] (*pl* **seminaries**) *n* a college where priests or ministers are trained.

Seminole ['semənoʊl] *n* a member of a Native American people who live in Florida; the language of this people.

semiotics [,semɪ'ɒtɪks] *n* the study of communication, especially the relationship between words and the things or ideas they refer to.

semiprecious [,semɪ'preʃəs] *adj* [stone, gem] that is used in jewelry, art etc but is not as valuable as a precious stone.

semiskilled [,semɪ'skɪld] *adj* [worker] who is

partly trained in a particular skill, but cannot do specialized work.

semiskimmed [,semɪ'skɪmd] *adj* **semiskimmed milk** GB milk that has had a lot of the cream removed.

semitone ['semɪtoʊn] *n* GB the difference in pitch between any two notes that are next to each other on a piano.

semitrailer ['semɪtreɪləʳ] *n* **-1.** a trailer that is pulled by a vehicle and has wheels only at the back. **-2.** US a large truck consisting of a separate part for the driver and a trailer joined to it by a metal bar.

semolina [,semə'liːnə] *n* a kind of food made from crushed wheat, used for making pasta, milky desserts etc □ *semolina pudding.*

Sen. -1. *abbr of* **senator. -2.** *abbr of* **senior.**

Senate ['senət] *n* **the Senate** in the USA and Australia, the smaller part of the two bodies that together make the laws for the government.

❦ THE SENATE

In the USA, the Senate is the upper house of Congress, and has 100 members, called senators. Each state has two senators, who are elected for six years by the people of their particular state.

In Australia the Senate is the upper house of the Federal Parliament. It has 76 senators, 12 from each state and two each from the two territories. They are elected for six years.

---

senator ['senətəʳ] *n* a member of a Senate.

send [send] (*pt* & *pp* **sent**) *vt* **-1.** [letter, message, goods] to make <sthg> go to another place or person, especially by means of the postal system or other communication system □ *Have you sent the fax?* □ *I'll send you a check by the end of the week.* □ *Send her my love.* □ *Did you send a birthday card to Bill?* □ *We sent it by air mail/boat/rail.* **-2.** [employee, prisoner, patient] to tell <sb> to go somewhere or arrange for them to go there □ *The boss sent him on a course/abroad on business.* □ *She has been sent to prison/Switzerland.* □ *I was sent away to school.* □ *We'll send somebody over right away to repair it.* **-3.** [person, prices, debris] to make <sb/sthg> move in a particular direction □ *The bonfire sent flames high into the night.* □ *The blow sent me staggering backward.* □ *Rumors of a takeover sent share prices rocketing.* **-4.** [person] to make <sb> have a particular feeling or be in a particular state □ *The music sent me to sleep.*

◆ **send back** *vt sep* **to send sb/sthg back** [letter, goods, person] to return sb/sthg to where they came from □ *I tried to write to him, but he sent the letter back unopened.* □ *They were sent back at the border.*

◆ **send for** *vt fus* **-1. to send for sb** to ask sb to come by sending a message to them □ *I was sent for by the principal.* □ *I've sent for the police/an ambulance.* □ *The general sent for reinforcements.* **-2. to send for sthg** [brochure, form, information] to ask for sthg by writing to somebody and asking them to send it □ / sent for their catalog.

◆ **send in** vt sep **-1. to send sb in** [visitor, client] to allow sb to enter a room to visit a person □ *"Mrs Black is here to see you, Sir."* — *"Send her in, please."* **-2. to send sb in** [troops, police] to order sb to go into a difficult situation in order to solve it □ *We are sending in back-up forces.* **-3. to send sthg in** [application, report, form] to send sthg to the place where it will be dealt with □ *It's October 2nd and I still haven't sent in my application form.*

◆ **send off** vt sep **-1. to send sthg off** [letter, package] to mail sthg □ *The invoice was sent off last month.* **-2. to send a player off** GB SPORT to order a player to leave the playing area □ *Crispini was sent off for fouling another player.*

◆ **send off for** vt fus **to send off for sthg** [product, information, goods] to ask somebody to mail sthg to one by writing to them □ *She sent off for her free copy.*

◆ **send up** vt sep **to send sb/sthg up** GB to imitate sb/sthg in a funny way that makes them seem silly □ *I think they're sending us up.*

sender ['sendər] n the person who has sent a letter, package etc by mail □ *'Return to sender.'*

send-off n an occasion when a lot of people come together to say goodbye to somebody □ *Did they give you a good send-off when you left?*

send-up n GB the act of imitating somebody or something in a funny way that makes them seem silly □ *They did a marvelous send-up of Prof Harris.*

Senegal [ˌsenə'gɔːl] a country in West Africa, on the Atlantic coast. SIZE: 197,000 sq kms. POPULATION: 7,900,000 (*Senegalese*). CAPITAL: Dakar. LANGUAGE: French. CURRENCY: CFA franc.

senile ['siːnaɪl] adj [person, patient] who is confused and forgetful because they are old □ *He's getting senile.*

senile dementia n a medical condition affecting old people in which they become forgetful and confused.

senility [sə'nɪlətɪ] n: see **senile**.

senior ['siːnjər] ◇ adj **-1.** a word used after the name of a man who has the same name as his son as a way of avoidng confusion □ *Jack Dean, Senior.* **-2.** [nurse, officer, executive] who has a higher position than other people in an organization □ *She's the most senior member of the department.* □ *a senior partner.* **-3. to be senior to sb** to have a position of higher rank than sb □ *I was given the job, despite the fact that Dominic is senior to me.* **-4.** EDUCATION [pupil, prefect] older. ■ **the senior year** in the USA, the final year of high school or university. ◇ n **-1. to be sb's senior** to be older than sb □ *I'm five years his senior* OR *his senior by five years.* **-2.** US EDUCATION a student in his or her senior year □ *Seniors are allowed out at lunchtime.*

senior citizen n an old person, especially one who is over 60 years old.

senior high school n in the USA, a school for students between 15 and 18 years old.

seniority [ˌsiːnɪ'ɒrətɪ] n the state of being older or more senior in rank than somebody else □ *They were seated according to seniority.*

sensation [sen'seɪʃn] n **-1.** a feeling that one has about a situation □ *She had the strange sensation that she'd seen him before somewhere.* **-2.** a physical feeling □ *a tingling sensation* □ *I had no sensation in my left leg.* **-3.** an event or situation that causes great excitement □ *He was an overnight sensation.* □ *Her appearance caused a sensation.*

sensational [sen'seɪʃnəl] adj **-1.** [victory, news, result] that causes great excitement □ *He has made a sensational comeback/recovery.* **-2.** [person, show, outfit] a word used to say that one thinks something is extremely good (informal use) □ *You look sensational!* □ *Read her latest sensational novel!* **-3.** [journalism, report] that is presented in such a way as to cause very strong emotions (disapproving use).

sensationalist [sen'seɪʃnəlɪst] adj [journalism, report] that makes facts or events appear worse or more shocking than they really are (disapproving use).

sense [sens] ◇ n **-1.** [of smell, hearing] any one of the five natural ways in which animals or humans are able to know about the world around them using particular abilities of parts of their body □ *the sense of smell/sight/touch/hearing/taste* □ *Our dog has a very poor sense of smell.* **-2. a sense of sthg** [of fear, guilt] a feeling of sthg □ *She was filled with a sense of guilt/urgency.* □ *He has a strong sense of duty/justice.* **-3.** [of timing, rhythm] a natural ability for something □ *She has good dress/business sense.* □ *a sense of timing/rhythm/direction* □ *Applicants must have a sense of humor.* **-4.** [in making decisions, judgments] one's ability to make sensible decisions and judgments □ *She had the sense to warn us beforehand.* □ *That child has no sense whatsoever!* ■ **to talk sense** to say wise and sensible things □ *I like Rob* — *he talks a lot of sense.* ■ **there's no sense (in) arguing/fighting etc** arguing/fighting etc will not help the situation so it's best to stop. **-5.** [of a word] a meaning □ *Do you mean "funny" in the sense of "peculiar" or "humorous"?* ■ **to make sense** [behavior, idea] to seem reasonable and practical; [words, sentence] to be able to be understood; [person] to talk sense □ *It makes sense to phone and check first.* □ *It just doesn't make any sense to leave now.* □ *The movie made no sense whatsoever.* □ *Now you're beginning to make sense!* ■ **to make sense of sthg** [of sb's words, behavior] to understand sthg □ *I can make no sense (out) of what he did.* **-6.** phrase **to come to one's senses** to think or act sensibly again after one has done something stupid or had a stupid idea; to become conscious again □ *And when he comes to his senses, he'll realize what a fool he's been.* □ *She finally came to her senses after lying unconscious for three hours.*

◇ vt [excitement, danger] to have the feeling or impression that <sthg> exists or is true □ /

sensed her disapproval although she said nothing. □ I could sense that something was wrong.

◆ **in a sense** adv a phrase used to say that something is partly true □ We are, in a sense, all to blame. □ In a sense, everyone could claim to have contributed something to it.

senseless ['senslas] adj -1. [gesture, waste] that has no purpose. -2. [person] who is unconscious □ The blow to his head knocked him senseless.

sensibilities [,sensə'bılətız] npl delicate or sensitive feelings □ I don't want to offend anyone's sensibilities.

sensible ['sensəbl] adj [person, decision] that is reasonable, and shows intelligent, practical thought □ Wear sensible clothes for the walk. □ That wasn't a very sensible thing to do!

sensibly ['sensəblı] adv [decide, agree, refuse] see **sensible** □ You behaved very sensibly in calling the police.

sensitive ['sensətıv] adj -1. [part of the body, person] that is easily affected by physical sensations, especially pain □ He's very sensitive to the cold. □ This soap is specially formulated for sensitive skin. -2. [teacher, parent, person] who understands how other people feel □ She's sensitive to people's feelings. □ a sensitive nurse/actor. -3. [person] who is easily offended or upset by things that people say or do □ Don't be so sensitive — I didn't mean it personally! □ He's very sensitive to criticism/sensitive about his weight. -4. [subject, information, situation] that needs to be dealt with very carefully to avoid causing problems or offending people □ Talks are at a highly sensitive stage. -5. [instrument, piece of equipment] that is very accurate because it reacts to very slight changes □ These scales are extremely sensitive, so keep completely still.

sensitivity [,sensə'tıvətı] n [of one's body, a person, instrument] see **sensitive** □ Her sensitivity to her students' needs is her greatest asset.

sensor ['sensər] n a device that is used to show whether a particular substance is present, especially in small quantities □ a heat/ light sensor.

sensual ['senʃʊəl] adj -1. [body, mouth, dancing] that is attractive in a sexual way □ She is a very sensual woman. -2. [pleasure, stimulation] that is connected with one or more of one's five senses rather than with one's mind.

sensuous ['senʃʊəs] adj -1. [music, color, fabric] that is pleasing to one or more of one's five senses rather than to one's mind. -2. [person] who enjoys the pleasures of the senses.

sent [sent] past tense & past participle of **send**.

sentence ['sentəns] ◇ n -1. GRAMMAR a group of words that usually contains a subject and a verb, expresses a statement, question, or exclamation, and, when written in English, starts with a capital letter and ends with a period □ He summed up the whole event in one sentence. -2. LAW a punishment given by a judge to a person who has been found guilty of a crime □ She received a two-year prison sentence. ◇ vt to give <sb> a sentence

in a court of law □ Lee was sentenced to five years' imprisonment.

sententious [sen'tenʃəs] adj [person, remark, advice] that tries to be wise, especially concerning people's behavior and morals (disapproving use).

sentiment ['sentəmənt] n -1. a feeling or opinion about something □ anti-American sentiment □ He harbors hostile sentiments. □ I can only agree with the sentiments expressed by my colleague John Griffiths. -2. feelings that are too tender toward other people or things (disapproving use) □ We cannot afford to mix business with sentiment.

sentimental [,sentə'mentl] adj -1. [person, book, song] that is too strongly influenced by emotions such as love, sadness, and pity (disapproving use) □ It's no use getting all sentimental about the past. □ I thought the movie was spoiled by its sentimental ending. -2. [reason, value] that concerns one's happy memories or tender feelings about somebody or something □ It's not worth much money, but it's of great sentimental value to me.

sentimentality [,sentəmen'tælətı] n [of a person, song, book] see **sentimental** (disapproving use).

sentinel ['sentənl] n a sentry (old-fashioned or literary use).

sentry ['sentrı] (pl **sentries**) n a soldier who stands outside a place to guard it □ He was on sentry duty.

Seoul [soʊl] the capital of South Korea, and its largest city. POPULATION: 8,400,000.

separable ['sepərəbl] adj that one can separate □ The two ideas are not separable.

separate [adj & n 'seprət, vb 'sepəreɪt] ◇ adj -1. [group, bed, room] that is not joined or connected to something else; [entrance, bathroom] that is for oneself and not for other people □ The language laboratories are housed in a separate building across the road. □ We lead separate lives. □ Keep your credit cards separate from your checkbook. □ They want a separate Basque state. -2. [matter, idea, meaning] that is different and not connected with something else □ The future of Biotech is an entirely separate issue. □ We must keep the two points clearly separate in our minds. □ I have heard her lecture on three separate occasions.

◇ vt -1. [more than one person or thing] to keep, move, or set <sb/sthg> apart from something else □ A fence separates the two gardens. □ We got separated from the main group by accident. -2. [one thing] to divide <sthg> into parts □ This class of drug can be separated into four main groups. □ Separate the yolk from the white. -3. [similar things or people] to find or show that there is a difference between <two or more people, groups, ideas> etc □ It's sometimes hard to separate fact from fiction OR separate fact and fiction.

◇ vi -1. [people] to move away from each other □ Let's separate and meet up later. □ They separated from the main group. -2. [group, whole object] to divide into different parts □ The fat will separate from the mixture. □ We separated into four groups. -3. [husband and wife, couple] to stop living together □ *My parents have separated/are separating.*

◆ **separates** *npl* different items of women's clothing that can be worn separately to form different outfits □ *matching separates.*

separated ['sepəreɪtəd] *adj* **to be separated** to no longer be living together as a couple □ *Her parents are separated.* □ *I am separated from my wife/husband.*

separately ['seprətlɪ] *adv* [sell, enter, consider] *see* **separate** □ *Can we pay separately?* □ *Woolens should be washed separately.*

separation [ˌsepə'reɪʃn] *n* **-1.** time spent apart from somebody □ *He returned home after seven years' separation from his family.* **-2.** [of a husband and wife] a formal agreement to live apart from each other □ *Things became easier after the separation.* **-3.** [into parts] *see* **separate** □ *It was an emotional separation.* □ *the separation of Church and State.*

separatism ['seprətɪzm] *n* the belief that one's religious or political group should be separate from a larger group.

separatist ['seprətəst] *n* a person who belongs to a group that believes in separatism.

sepia ['siːpjə] *adj* [photograph, pigment] that is dark brown in color.

Sept. *abbr of* **September**.

September [sep'tembər] *n* the ninth month of the year in the Western calendar; *see also* **February**.

septet [sep'tet] *n* a group of seven musicians or singers; a piece of music written for this group.

septic ['septɪk] *adj* [toe, cut, wound] that is infected.

septicemia US, **septicaemia** GB [ˌseptə'siːmjə] *n* a serious medical condition in which the blood becomes infected.

septic tank *n* a tank, especially in rural areas, in which sewage is broken down by the action of bacteria.

sepulcher US, **sepulchre** GB ['seplkər] *n* a tomb (literary use).

sequel ['siːkwəl] *n* **-1.** a novel, movie, play etc that continues the story of an earlier one □ *He's working on a sequel to his last movie.* **-2.** something that happens after or as a result of an earlier event □ *I never told you about the sequel to that lunch.*

sequence ['siːkwəns] *n* **-1.** a series of events, actions, or things that come one after another □ *There has been a sequence of disasters.* **-2.** the order in which events, actions, or things happen □ *Please try to recall the exact sequence of events that night.* ■ **in sequence** in order □ *in historical/chronological/numerical sequence.* **-3.** a short section of a movie that contains one particular scene or piece of action □ *You know that sequence when Branson pulls a gun and starts to shoot?*

sequester [sɪ'kwestər], **sequestrate** ['siːkwəstreɪt] *vt* [assets, goods, property] to take <sthg> that belongs to a person or organization and keep it until a debt has been paid or a court order has been obeyed.

sequin ['siːkwən] *n* one of many small shiny disks sewn onto a piece of clothing as decoration.

sera ['sɪərə] *plural of* **serum**.

Serb [sɜːb] *n* & *adj: see* **Serbia**.

Serbia ['sɜːbjə] a country in southeastern Europe. It is one of the two republics remaining after the other Yugoslavian republics became independent in 1991 and 1992. SIZE: 55,968 sq kms. POPULATION: 5,744,000 (*Serbs, Serbians*). CAPITAL: Belgrade. LANGUAGE: Serbo-Croat. CURRENCY: Yugoslavian dinar.

Serbian ['sɜːbjən] *n* & *adj: see* **Serbia**.

Serbo-Croat [ˌsɜːboʊ'kroʊæt], **Serbo-Croatian** [ˌsɜːboʊkroʊ'eɪʃn] *n* a language that is spoken in Serbia, Croatia, and parts of other countries of the former Yugoslavia.

serenade [ˌserə'neɪd] ◇ *n* **-1.** a song or piece of music sung or played at night to a woman by a lover. **-2.** a piece of gentle music for a small orchestra □ *Dvorak's string serenade.* ◇ *vt* to sing or play a serenade to <sb>.

serene [sə'riːn] *adj* that seems calm and peaceful □ *looking out at the serene blue sea* □ *She gave a serene smile.*

serenely [sə'riːnlɪ] *adv* [gaze, smile] *see* **serene** □ *She seemed serenely confident.*

serenity [sə'renətɪ] *n: see* **serene**.

serf [sɜːf] *n* HISTORY a worker, especially in medieval Europe, who could be bought and sold with the land that they worked on.

serge [sɜːdʒ] *n* a strong woolen cloth used for making coats, suits, trousers etc.

sergeant ['sɑːdʒənt] *n* **-1.** an army officer who is above a corporal in rank. **-2.** a police officer of the second-lowest rank who is above a constable.

sergeant major *n* an army officer who is above a sergeant in rank.

serial ['sɪərɪəl] *n* a story that is broadcast, televised, or published in parts over a period of time.

serialize, **-ise** ['sɪərɪəlaɪz] *vt* [book, story] to publish or broadcast <sthg> as a serial.

serial killer *n* a person who commits several similar murders at different times.

serial number *n* a number on an item, e.g. a check or banknote, that identifies it from the rest of a series.

series ['sɪəriːz] (*pl* **series**) *n* **-1.** a number of similar things, events etc that come one after another □ *a series of disasters/phone calls/articles.* **-2.** RADIO & TV a number of programs with the same title that are each complete stories but have the same theme, characters etc □ *a new drama series for television.*

serious ['sɪərɪəs] *adj* **-1.** [illness, mistake, accident] that has or is likely to have very unfortunate or bad results □ *You could have caused a serious accident driving like that.* □ *serious crime.* **-2.** [decision, situation, problem] that is important, difficult to deal with, and causes worry or concern □ *You will be in serious trouble if anyone ever finds out.* **-3. to be serious** [person] to be sincere and not joking □ *a seri-*

ous discussion □ Are you serious about wanting to leave? **-4.** [newspaper, magazine, movie] that is intended to make people think rather than to entertain them □ Dave likes serious music, not all this pop garbage. **-5.** [person, expression, tone of voice] that seems thoughtful and slightly worried □ You're looking very serious.

seriously ['sɪərɪəslɪ] adv **-1.** [think, consider, talk] see **serious** □ I seriously think we should go. ■ **to take sb/sthg seriously** to believe that sb/sthg is important and deserves to be treated with respect □ I tried telling them, but no one would take me seriously. □ We are taking these threats seriously. **-2.** [believe, suggest, mean] a word used to show that one means what one is saying and is not joking □ Can you seriously imagine me in that hat? □ "I still love him." — "Seriously?" **-3.** [ill, mistaken] very badly □ 'Cigarettes can seriously damage your health.' □ If you think I am getting in that car you are seriously mistaken.

seriousness ['sɪərɪəsnəs] n [of a mistake, expression, situation etc] see **serious** □ Doctors failed to appreciate the seriousness of his illness. ■ **in all seriousness** a phrase used to show that one is being completely serious when one says something □ In all seriousness, I'm prepared to resign. □ You can't in all seriousness be intending to give him the job!

sermon ['sɜːʳmən] n **-1.** RELIGION a talk on a moral or religious subject given by a clergyman during a church service. **-2.** a spoken warning or piece of advice, usually about one's behavior (disapproving use).

serpent ['sɜːʳpənt] n a snake (literary use).

serrated [sə'reɪtəd] adj [edge, blade] that has teeth like a saw.

serum ['sɪərəm] (pl **serums** OR **sera**) n the watery part of blood; this liquid used as a vaccine to protect against certain diseases.

servant ['sɜːʳvənt] n a person employed to do household work in somebody else's home.

serve [sɜːʳv] ◇ vt **-1.** [country, company, master] to do good or useful work for <sb/sthg> □ I have served this organization for over 15 years. **-2. to serve a purpose** to be useful □ Does this handle serve any useful purpose, or is it just for decoration? □ That cabinet serves absolutely no purpose at all — I vote we get rid of it. **-3.** [town, area] to provide <a place> with an essential or important service, e.g. gas, water, or transportation □ Which airport serves Ottawa? □ a network that serves the whole of the USA. **-4.** to provide <food or drink> for somebody, e.g. in a restaurant or café □ They served us coffee OR served coffee to us while we waited. □ What time is breakfast served? **-5.** to deal with <a customer> in a store, restaurant etc by showing and selling them things, taking their order etc □ Would you mind serving that customer, please? □ We were served by a very rude young waiter. **-6.** LAW [writ, summons, court order] to give or send <an order> to appear in court □ He has been served with a summons OR A summons has been served on him. **-7.** [prison sentence, apprenticeship, term of

office] to spend <a period of time> doing something for official reasons □ She served ten years for manslaughter. **-8.** SPORT to hit <a ball> toward one's opponent to start play in tennis, volleyball etc □ Navratilova served the ball right into the net. **-9.** phrase **it serves you right** a phrase used to tell somebody that something unpleasant or unfortunate that has happened to them is their own fault and they deserve it □ It serves you right if he refused, you should never have asked him in the first place.

◇ vi **-1.** [in an organization] to carry out duties as a member of an organization such as a government department or an army □ I previously served on an advisory committee. **-2. to serve as sthg** to be used or understood as sthg □ The hall served as a study. □ Let this serve as a warning! **-3. to serve to do sthg** to have the effect of doing sthg □ This only served to make things worse. □ This serves to illustrate the point I was trying to make. **-4.** [at a meal] to give somebody food or drink at a meal □ Shall I serve or will you? **-5.** [in a store, bar] to deal with customers □ There was nobody serving at the counter. **-6.** SPORT to hit a ball toward one's opponent to start play in tennis, volleyball etc □ You serve.

◇ n SPORT the act of serving the ball □ It's your serve.

◆ **serve out, serve up** vt sep to serve sthg out OR up [food, drinks] to divide sthg into portions and give it to people at a meal; to present sthg as a meal or part of a meal.

server ['sɜːʳvəʳ] n a computer that provides a particular service to computers on the same network □ a print/file server.

service ['sɜːʳvəs] ◇ n **-1.** [in an area] a system or organization that supplies a public need □ the postal/fire service. **-2.** [for the public] something that is provided for the public by a business, organization etc □ A bus service is available free to the public. □ a 24-hour banking service. **-3.** [in a firm] employment in a firm, organization etc or as a domestic servant □ She's in domestic service. □ a long-service award. **-4.** [in a store, hotel] the attention given to customers or work done for them □ The service in here is slow/terrible/excellent. □ 'Service not included.' **-5.** MILITARY the performance of duties in the armed forces □ He saw active service in Korea. **-6.** [of a vehicle, machine] the examination, adjustment, and repair of something to keep it working efficiently □ I took the car in for a service. □ The water heater is due for a service. **-7.** RELIGION a religious ceremony □ Sunday/morning service. **-8.** [of dishes] a complete set of dishes, plates, cups etc used for serving a meal □ a dinner/tea service. **-9. in service** [machine] in use or available for use. ■ **out of service** [machine] not in use or available for use □ This model has been withdrawn from service. **-10.** SPORT the act of serving the ball, e.g. in tennis □ My service is very weak. **-11.** phrase **to be of service** to help somebody (formal use).

◇ vt **-1.** [vehicle, machine] to examine, adjust, and repair <sthg> to keep it working efficiently □ *My car has always been regularly serviced.* **-2.** FINANCE [loan, debt] to pay the interest on <sthg>.

◆ **services** *npl* **-1.** = **service area. -2.** MILITARY **the services** the armed forces □ *He's in the services.* **-3.** help or work done for other people □ *The surgeon offered his services free of charge.* □ *His services to the community were never properly rewarded.*

serviceable ['sɜːˈvəsəbl] *adj* practical and useful rather than beautiful or decorative □ *This coat may not look too good but it's serviceable and warm.*

service area *n* a place next to a highway where drivers can use a service station, restaurant, rest rooms etc.

service charge *n* **-1.** an amount added to a restaurant bill to pay for the service provided by the staff □ *Have they added a service charge?* □ *A service charge of 10% is included on the bill.* **-2.** an amount of money paid to the owners of an apartment building to pay for certain services, e.g. the cleaning of stairs and corridors.

service industries *npl* industries that provide services, e.g. insurance and transportation, rather than make goods.

serviceman ['sɜːˈvəsmən] (*pl* **servicemen** [-mən]) *n* a man who is in the armed forces.

service station *n* a garage next to a road that sells gasoline from pumps, has a store selling useful things for road users, e.g. oil, maps, and snack foods, and that often repairs or services motor vehicles.

servicewoman ['sɜːˈvəswumən] (*pl* **servicewomen**) *n* a woman who is in the armed forces.

serviette [,sɜːˈvɪˈet] *n* GB a square of paper or cloth used to wipe one's mouth and hands while eating.

servile ['sɜːˈvaɪl] *adj* [person] who shows somebody too much respect and is too eager to obey or please them (disapproving use) □ *He was respectful, but never servile.*

serving ['sɜːˈvɪŋ] ◇ *adj* **-1. a serving spoon/dish** a spoon/dish that is used for serving food. **-2.** [officer, member, diplomat] who is in office. ◇ *n* a portion of food for one person.

sesame ['sesəmɪ] *n* a tropical plant grown for its seeds which are used in cooking and for making cooking oil □ *sesame seeds/oil.*

session ['seʃn] *n* **-1.** a formal meeting or series of meetings of a court, parliament, or council □ *The court is in session.* □ *The next parliamentary session begins in October.* **-2.** a period of time spent on one particular activity □ *a recording/discussion/drinking session.* □ *We need a session to work out our budgets.* □ *the morning/afternoon session.* **-3.** US a school or university term.

set [set] (*pt* & *pp* **set**, *cont* **setting**) ◇ *vt* **-1.** [object] to put <sthg> in a particular place in a careful and deliberate way □ *She brought in the turkey and set it in front of Dad to carve.* □ *I lifted Amy out of the chair and set her on the floor.* **-2. to be set into/in sthg** [in a surface] to be fixed into/in sthg □ *a diamond set in a circle*

of sapphires □ *Metal bars had been set into the concrete.* **-3. to set sthg on fire/in motion etc** to cause sthg to start burning/happening etc □ *You nearly set the kitchen on fire!* □ *The divorce proceedings have been set in motion.* □ *Why don't you call her and set your mind at rest?* ■ **to set sb free** to free sb who has been in prison or tied up □ *The last prisoner has been set free.* **-4. to set the table** to put knives, forks, plates etc on a table so that people can eat □ *How many shall I set the table for?* □ *Set an extra place for Lee.* **-5.** [alarm, meter, timer] to adjust <sthg> so that it starts working at a particular time □ *What temperature should I set the oven at?* □ *You'd better set the alarm for six thirty.* ■ **to set a trap** to prepare a trap so that it will catch an animal. **-6. to set a date** to decide that something will happen on a particular date □ *Have they set a date for their wedding yet?* ■ **to set a price/limit etc** to decide that something will have a particular price/limit etc □ *A new minimum wage is to be set.* □ *We have to follow the guidelines set by the Department.* **-7. to set an example/a precedent** to do something that other people can copy as an example/a precedent □ *That jump has set a new world record.* □ *If I give Jack time off, it'll be setting a precedent for the rest of the staff.* **-8.** GB [exam, homework, essay] to give a student <a piece of work> to do □ *The trainees were set an exercise on team-building.* **-9.** [target, standard] to tell somebody to try to achieve <sthg> □ *Be sure to set yourself realistic goals.* **-10.** MEDICINE to put <a broken bone> in a fixed position so that it will mend correctly □ *The leg will have to be set in plaster.* **-11. to set sthg to music** [poem, words, story] to write music for sthg. **-12. to be set in a particular place/period** [story, movie] to be shown to be happening in a particular place/period □ *The action is set in medieval Japan.* **-13. to set sb's hair** to arrange sb's hair in a particular style using rollers.

◇ *vi* **-1.** [sun] to move out of sight below the horizon at the end of the day □ *The sun was already beginning to set over the city.* **-2.** [jelly, yogurt] to become solid; [cement, glue] to become hard □ *Leave the chocolate mousse to set overnight in a cool place.*

◇ *adj* **-1.** [procedure, amount, pattern] that is fixed and cannot be easily changed □ *My boss leaves work at a set time every day.* □ *Her parents have very set ideas about marriage.* □ *He does everything according to a set routine.* ■ **to be set in one's ways** to be unable to change the way one lives because one has lived that way for so long □ *They're both too set in their ways to get married now.* **-2. a set book/text** GB a book/text that is part of a course of study □ *"Othello" is one of our set texts this year.* **-3. to be (all) set to do sthg** [person] to be going to do sthg very soon □ *I was all set to get in the car and drive off when I heard the phone ring.* □ *The Republicans seem set to win.* **-4. to be set on doing sthg** to be determined to do sthg □ *We've tried to talk her out of it, but she seems set on marrying him.* ■ **to be dead set against sthg** [against a decision, proposal, idea] to be strongly opposed to sthg □ *I want to* *leave school, but my parents are dead set against the idea.*

◇ *n* **-1.** [of keys, teeth, golf clubs] a group of things that belong together and make a whole; the group of things needed for a particular activity □ *a set of saucepans/tires* □ *a set of instructions/guidelines* □ *a chess/chemistry/picnic set.* **-2.** = **television set** □ *Do not adjust your set.* **-3.** [of a movie] the place where a movie is acted and filmed; [of a play] the scenery, furniture etc on a stage where a play is being acted □ *Silence on set!* □ *I didn't like the production, but the set was good.* **-4.** SPORT a series of at least six games in tennis □ *Sampras is leading by two sets to love.*

◆ **set about** *vt fus* **to set about doing sthg** to start doing sthg, especially in a determined way □ *We had a coffee, then set about clearing up the mess.*

◆ **set against** *vt sep* **-1. to set sthg against sthg** to compare sthg with sthg different or more important □ *The problems of the inner cities have to be set against the deprivation of rural areas.* ■ **to set sthg against tax** to subtract sthg from the total amount of tax one has to pay. **-2. to set sb against sb/sthg** to make sb dislike or criticize sb/sthg they liked before □ *She's set those children against their father.* □ *I know he's been trying to set everyone against me.*

◆ **set ahead** *vt sep* US **to set a clock/watch ahead** to make a clock/watch show a later time □ *She always sets her watch five minutes ahead.*

◆ **set apart** *vt sep* **to set sb/sthg apart** [quality, characteristic, appearance] to show sb/sthg to be obviously different and sometimes better than others of the same kind □ *Our unique commitment to quality sets this airline apart from its competitors.*

◆ **set aside** *vt sep* **-1. to set sthg aside** [money, time, food] to save sthg so that it can be used later □ *Remember to set aside at least half an hour to read through your answers.* **-2. to set sthg aside** [decision, fact, feeling] to deliberately pay no attention to sthg when one is considering a problem or situation □ *Setting aside the political impact of the change, does it make economic sense?*

◆ **set back** *vt sep* **-1. to set sb/sthg back** to delay sb/sthg □ *The traffic jam set us back (by) at least an hour.* **-2. to set sb back by a particular amount** to cost sb a particular amount of money (informal use) □ *Taking the kids to Disneyland could set you back $100!* **-3. to be set back from sthg** to be some distance from sthg □ *The house is set back a little way from the main road.* **-4. to set a clock/watch back** US to make a clock/watch show an earlier time.

◆ **set down** *vt sep* **-1. to set sthg down** [statement, thought, fact] to write sthg down □ *While he was traveling, he set down his impressions of China in his diaries.* **-2. to set sthg down** to put sthg down, especially a large or heavy object □ *Set that crate down gently, it's full of glasses.* **-3. to set sb down** GB [passenger] to stop a car and allow sb to get out □

There's an area for setting down passengers outside Terminal 1.

◆ **set in** *vi* [infection, bad weather, depression] to start and seem likely to continue □ *By late afternoon the rain had set in, so the game was canceled.*

◆ **set off** ◇ *vi* [person, vehicle] to start a trip □ *What time did you set off?* ◇ *vt sep* **-1. to set sthg off** [argument, avalanche, chain reaction] to cause sthg to start happening, especially without intending to □ *Her resignation set off a flurry of speculation and rumors in the press.* **-2. to set sthg off** [bomb, firework, mine] to cause sthg to explode; [alarm, fire extinguisher, siren] to cause sthg to start working □ *The bomb was set off when the car engine started up.* □ *The burned cookies accidentally set off the smoke alarm.*

◆ **set on** *vt sep* **to set sb/sthg on sb** [dog, police, guard] to cause sb/sthg to attack sb □ *The owner of the store set his dog on the intruders.*

◆ **set out** ◇ *vt sep* **-1. to set sthg out** [chairs, food, wares] to arrange sthg so that it can be looked at or used □ *Set out four cups and saucers for coffee.* **-2. to set sthg out** [facts, theory, results] to explain sthg clearly in an organized way □ *The pros and cons of the merger are all set out in my document.* ◇ *vt fus* **to set out to do sthg** to decide to do sthg and start doing it in a determined way □ *I believe he deliberately set out to cause trouble.* ◇ *vi* [person] to start a trip, especially a long or difficult one □ *Eventually we sold our few remaining possessions and set out for home.*

◆ **set up** ◇ *vt sep* **-1. to set up sthg** [company, organization, system] to create sthg and start it working □ *The firm was set up in 1988.* ■ **to set oneself up** to start one's own business □ *She's hoping to set herself up as a translator.* ■ **to set up house** OR **home** to start living in a place permanently □ *They want to marry and set up home together.* **-2. to set sthg up** [deal, meeting, interview] to arrange for sthg to happen □ *Do you think you'd be able to set up an interview with Nielsen for me?* **-3. to set up sthg** [roadblock, statue, stall] to put sthg in position □ *Police set up roadblocks near all ports and airports.* **-4. to set up sthg** [equipment, camera, projector] to prepare sthg for use by putting it in the right place, checking that it works etc □ *I need someone to set up the overhead projector for me in time for the lecture.* **-5. to set sb up** to cause sb to appear to be guilty of a crime they have not committed (informal use) □ *I've been set up!*

◇ *vi* **to set up (in business)** to start one's own business □ *I set up on my own/in insurance four years ago.*

setback ['setbæk] *n* something that delays or prevents progress toward a successful result □ *We suffered numerous setbacks before we could finally get the business up and running.*

set menu *n* a meal that is offered at a fixed price with a limited choice of dishes.

setsquare ['setskweər] *n* GB a flat triangular piece of plastic, metal, or wood used for drawing angles and lines.

settee [se'tiː] *n* a comfortable soft seat with a back and arms, for two or more people.

setter ['setər] *n* a long-haired dog that can be trained by hunters to find animals or birds.

setting ['setɪŋ] *n* **-1.** the surroundings of a particular place □ *The house stands in a beautiful setting of trees and fields.* **-2.** [for a story] the time and place where a story, event etc takes place □ *Rio is the perfect setting for this movie.* **-3.** [of controls] a position in which a dial or the controls of an instrument are set □ *Are you sure you've got it on the right setting?*

settle ['setl] ◇ *vt* **-1.** [dispute, argument, issue] to end <sthg> in an agreement or a decision □ *That's settled: we're going to Spain.* □ *I want this matter to be settled promptly.* **-2.** [bill, debt, claim] to pay <sthg>. **-3.** to make <sb> comfortable □ *Ken settled herself in an armchair and opened his book.* □ *She settled the patients for the night.* **-4.** [nerves, stomach] to calm <sthg> □ *Take some bicarbonate to settle your stomach.* ◇ *vi* **-1.** to make one's home somewhere □ *They've settled in Baltimore.* **-2.** to make oneself comfortable □ *We settled in front of the fire for the evening.* **-3.** [dust, sediment, fog] to come down and stay somewhere □ *The tea leaves settled in the bottom of the cup.* **-4. to settle on sthg** [bird, insect] to land on sthg.

◆ **settle down** *vi* **-1. to settle down to sthg** to begin to give one's attention to sthg □ *Eventually I settled down to the report.* □ *She settled down to her magazine.* **-2.** to start to live a quieter, more stable life □ *When are you going to get married and settle down?* **-3.** to gradually adapt and get used to a new situation □ *Are you settling down in your new job?* **-4.** to make oneself comfortable □ *They settled down for supper/the night.* **-5.** to become calm or quiet □ *Settle down now, children!* □ *Let's wait for things to settle down before we announce any more changes.*

◆ **settle for** *vt fus* **to settle for sthg** to accept or agree to sthg that is not what one really wanted □ *I'm not prepared to settle for less.*

◆ **settle in** *vi* to gradually adapt and get used to a new situation, e.g. a new home or job □ *How are you settling in at your new school?*

◆ **settle on** *vt fus* **to settle on sthg** to decide on sthg □ *There was an enormous choice but we finally settled on the blue sedan.*

◆ **settle up** *vi* to pay a bill or amount owed □ *Can I settle up with you later?*

settled ['setld] *adj* [weather] that is stable and is not going to change.

settlement ['setlmənt] *n* **-1.** [of a dispute, argument, issue] an agreement or decision that settles something □ *a peace/wage settlement* □ *Negotiators are hoping to reach a settlement.* **-2.** [of people] a large group of people who have recently come to a place, usually from a foreign country, to live and create new towns and villages □ *Tutsi settlements.* **-3.** [of a bill, debt, claim] *see* **settle** □ *I enclose a check in settlement of my account.*

settler ['setlər] *n* a member of a new settlement □ *settlers on the West Bank.*

set-to *n* a fight or argument (informal use).

set-up *n* (informal use) **-1.** the way in which something is run or organized □ *He's new to the firm so he doesn't know the set-up yet.* **-2.** a secret arrangement to make somebody appear guilty of a crime, or to put them in danger □ *This is a set-up!*

seven ['sevn] *num* the number 7; *see also* **five** □ *The mall is open seven days a week.*

Seven Sisters *npl* **the Seven Sisters** a name used for the seven most respected colleges for women in the USA. They are Vassar, Wellesley, Smith, Bryn Mawr, Barnard, Radcliffe, and Mount Holyoke.

seventeen [,sevn'tiːn] *num* the number 17; *see also* **fifteen.**

seventeenth [,sevn'tiːnθ] *num* 17th; number 17 in a series; *see also* **fifteenth.**

seventh ['sevnθ] *num* 7th; number 7 in a series; *see also* **fifth.**

Seventh-Day Adventist [-'ædvəntəst] *n* a member of a Protestant church who believes that Jesus Christ will come back to Earth soon.

seventh heaven *n* **to be in (one's) seventh heaven** to be completely happy.

seventieth ['sevntjəθ] *num* 70th; number 70 in a series; *see also* **fiftieth.**

seventy ['sevntɪ] *num* the number 70; *see also* **fifty.**

sever ['sevər] *vt* **-1.** [limb, artery, pipe] to cut through <sthg> completely so that it is no longer attached to the main part. **-2.** [links, relations] to bring <sthg> to an end □ *We have severed all ties with non-EU companies.*

several ['sevrəl] ◇ *det* used to refer to a number of people, things, or places that is not large but is more than two □ *He was missing for several days.* □ *Several people reported seeing the stolen car.* □ *several hundred/thousand dollars* □ *It took several attempts to get the car to start.* ◇ *pron*: *I've already read several of her books.* □ *There were several of us in the office that day.*

severance ['sevrəns] *n* [of links, ties, relations] *see* **sever.**

severance pay *n* money paid to employees who have been dismissed by a company because it no longer has a job for them.

severe [sə'vɪər] *adj* **-1.** [injury, shortage, setback] serious □ *There are severe food shortages in some areas.* **-2.** [pain, shock] that is intense □ *Nicole was in severe pain from her injury.* **-3.** [winter, conditions] that causes suffering and difficulty □ *Driving conditions are extremely severe.* **-4.** [person, criticism, measures] that is harsh and unkind □ *Don't be too severe on her.*

severely [sə'vɪərlɪ] *adv* **-1. severely injured/damaged etc** seriously injured/damaged etc □ *Our stocks are severely depleted.* **-2.** [say, look, answer] *see* **severe** □ *He was severely reprimanded.*

severity [sə'verətɪ] *n* [of conditions, criticism, a problem] *see* **severe** □ *the severity of her tone.*

sew [səʊ] (US *pp* **sewed** OR **sewn**, GB *pp* **sewn**) ◇ *vi* to put stitches in cloth using a needle and thread. ◇ *vt* **-1.** to join or fasten <sthg>

by sewing □ *The seam has been badly sewn.* □ *She sewed on all those sequins one by one.* -2. to repair <a hole, tear> etc by sewing.

◆ **sew up** *vt sep* -1. **to sew a hole/tear up** to repair a hole/tear by sewing. ■ **to sew pieces of cloth up** to join pieces of cloth by sewing. -2. **to sew sthg up** [deal, election, game] to arrange sthg in a satisfactory way (informal use) □ *It's all sewn up!* -3. **to have a situation sewn up** to control or dominate a situation (informal use) □ *The company seems to have the domestic market sewn up.*

sewage ['suːɪdʒ] *n* waste matter from human bodies that is carried away from houses in drains □ *a plant for treating raw sewage.*

sewage farm, sewage works *n* a place where sewage is treated so that it is no longer harmful.

sewer ['suːər] *n* an underground pipe or passage that carries sewage □ *a sewer pipe.*

sewerage ['suːərɪdʒ] *n* the system of carrying away sewage through sewers.

sewing ['souɪŋ] *n* -1. the activity of sewing things □ *I can't stand sewing!* -2. things that are being sewn □ *a pile of sewing.*

sewing machine *n* a machine for sewing that is worked by hand or by electricity.

sewn [soun] *past participle of* **sew**.

sex [seks] *n* -1. the condition of being male or female □ *factors that determine the sex of a baby* □ *sex discrimination.* -2. either one of the two groups, male and female, into which people and animals are divided □ *people of both sexes* □ *the male/female/opposite sex.* -3. any physical activity between two people that involves exciting the sex organs for pleasure or in order to make a woman pregnant □ *He had never really enjoyed sex.* □ *Margot still considers sex immoral.* ■ **to have sex with sb** to have sexual intercourse with sb.

sex aid *n* an object designed to help people enjoy sex more.

sex appeal *n* sexual attractiveness.

sex change *n* an operation or type of treatment that makes a person look more like a person of the opposite sex.

sex education *n* education on sexual activity and relationships, usually given to children.

sexism ['seksɪzm] *n* sexist beliefs or attitudes.

sexist ['seksəst] (disapproving use) ◇ *adj* [remark, attitude, person] that suggests that one sex, especially the female sex, is less important, able, or intelligent than the other sex. ◇ *n* a person, usually a man, who has sexist attitudes.

sex life *n* a person's sexual activities □ *They have an active/a healthy sex life.*

sex object *n* a person seen only in terms of their sexual attractiveness and not their personality, mind etc.

sex shop *n* a store where sex aids, videos, magazines etc are sold.

sex symbol *n* a famous person who a lot of people think is sexually attractive.

sextet [seks'tet] *n* a group of six musicians or singers; a piece of music written for such a group.

sextuplet [sek'stʌplət] *n* any one of six babies born at the same time.

sexual ['sekʃuəl] *adj* -1. [feeling, relationship, abuse] that is connected with sex □ *his first sexual experience.* -2. [politics, discrimination] that is connected with differences between the two sexes □ *sexual equality/inequality.*

sexual assault *n* an attack, usually by a man on a woman, that involves rape, attempted rape, or some form of sexual violence.

sexual harassment *n* annoying behavior toward another person, e.g. at work, that involves unwanted sexual advances, remarks, jokes etc.

sexual intercourse *n* the physical act in which a man puts his penis into a woman's vagina for pleasure or to make her pregnant.

sexuality [,sekʃu'ælətɪ] *n* -1. a person's ability to experience sexual feelings □ *a discussion about women's sexuality.* -2. the particular way in which a person experiences sexual feelings, e.g. toward people of the same sex or of a different sex □ *He was unsure about his sexuality.*

sexually ['sekʃuəlɪ] *adv* [active, attractive] *see* **sexual** □ *Marsha was sexually harassed/abused.* □ *a sexually transmitted disease.*

sexy ['seksɪ] (*compar* **sexier**, *superl* **sexiest**) *adj* [person, voice, picture] that is sexually attractive or exciting □ *That's a very sexy dress you're wearing.*

Seychelles [seɪ'ʃelz]: **the Seychelles** a country consisting of a group of islands in the Indian Ocean, east of Kenya. SIZE: 410 sq kms. POPULATION: 70,000 (*Seychellois*). CAPITAL: Victoria. LANGUAGE: Creole, English, French. CURRENCY: Seychelles rupee.

sf, SF *n abbr of* **science fiction**.

SFO (*abbr of* **Serious Fraud Office**) *n* **the SFO** the British government department responsible for investigating serious fraud in companies.

Sgt *abbr of* **sergeant**.

sh [ʃ] *excl* used to tell people to be silent or make less noise □ *Sh, the baby's asleep!* □ *Sh, I want to hear what he's saying!*

shabby ['ʃæbɪ] (*compar* **shabbier**, *superl* **shabbiest**) *adj* -1. [clothes, furniture] that is old and has been used a lot □ *We sat down on a shabby old sofa.* -2. [person] who is wearing shabby clothes □ *Caralli came in, looking as shabby as ever in an old greatcoat.* -3. [treatment, trick, behavior] that one thinks is mean and unfair □ *I think that was a shabby trick to play on someone!*

shack [ʃæk] *n* a small roughly-built shed, hut, or house.

shackle ['ʃækl] *vt* -1. [prisoner] to put shackles on <sb>. -2. to limit the freedom of <sb> to act, speak, think etc (literary use).

◆ **shackles** *npl* -1. metal rings joined by a chain, used to tie a prisoner's wrists or ankles together. -2. limits on somebody's freedom to act, speak, think etc (literary use).

shade [ʃeɪd] ◇ *n* -1. a darker and cooler area where there is no sunlight because something stands between this area and the sun □ *The tall buildings provided welcome shade from the sun.* □ *We sat in the shade of a tree/an umbrella.* -2. [of a lamp] the part of a lamp that goes around the bulb to stop the light from dazzling people. -3. [of a color] a color that is slightly darker or lighter than a main color such as red or blue □ *We have a wide range of suits in discreet shades of blue and gray to choose from.* -4. [of meaning, opinion] a slight variation □ *subtle shades of meaning.*
◇ *vt* to protect <sb/sthg> from direct light or heat □ *He raised his hand to shade his eyes from the blazing sun.*
◇ *vi* **to shade into sthg** to change very gradually into sthg else □ *The two colors shade into each other.*
◆ **shades** *npl* sunglasses (informal use).

shading [ʃeɪdɪŋ] *n* the darker areas in a picture that make things look real and three-dimensional.

shadow [ʃædoʊ] *n* -1. a dark shape on a surface that is produced when something prevents direct light from reaching the surface □ *She watched her own shadow as she walked.* □ *The building cast a huge shadow over the street.* -2. a dark and cool area where the sunlight is blocked out □ *The yard is in shadow for most of the day.* -3. [under one's eyes] a dark area or patch like a shadow under one's eyes caused e.g. by illness or lack of sleep □ *He had dark shadows under his eyes.* -4. phrases **to be a shadow of one's former self** to have lost the strength, enthusiasm, skill etc one used to have. ■ **there's not a** OR **the shadow of a doubt** there's no doubt at all □ *There's not a shadow of a doubt that Klaus is guilty.*

shadow cabinet *n* GB the leaders of the main opposition party in Parliament, who will become ministers if they win the next election.

shadowy [ʃædoʊɪ] *adj* -1. [corridor, corner, forest] that is dark and full of shadows □ *I walked between the tall shadowy buildings.* -2. [figure, outline, form] that is difficult to see clearly because there is not enough light □ *A shadowy figure was standing near the doorway.* -3. [person, group] that little is known about □ *the shadowy world of the Mafia.*

shady [ʃeɪdɪ] (*compar* **shadier**, *superl* **shadiest**) *adj* -1. [yard, spot, corner] that is in the shade □ *We found a shady spot for our picnic.* -2. [tree, canopy] that gives shade □ *They sat under a shady tree.* -3. [person, deal, organization] that is not completely honest □ *There's something very shady going on here.*

shaft [US ʃæft, GB ʃɑːft] *n* -1. a long, narrow, often vertical space or passage □ *a mine/an elevator/a ventilator shaft.* -2. [in a machine] a revolving rod in a machine □ *a drive/propeller shaft.* -3. **a shaft of light** a narrow beam of light.

shaggy [ʃægɪ] (*compar* **shaggier**, *superl* **shaggiest**) *adj* -1. [hair, beard] that looks long, rough, and untidy. -2. [dog] that has a shaggy coat. -3. [carpet, rug, coat] that has long rough fibers.

shaggy-dog story *n* a long rambling joke, usually with a deliberately silly ending.

shake [ʃeɪk] (*pt* **shook**, *pp* **shaken**) ◇ *vt* -1. to cause <sb/sthg> to move up and down or from side to side with quick short movements □ *He shook her angrily.* □ *I shook myself free.* □ *He shook the snow out of his hair.* □ *'Shake the bottle well before use.'* ■ **to shake sb's hand, to shake sb by the hand** to shake sb's right hand in one's own when one greets them, says goodbye, or agrees on something □ *We shook hands and said goodbye.* □ *She shook hands with me and said, "Well done."* ■ **to shake one's head** to move one's head from side to side to say "no" or to show that one disagrees, disapproves, has doubts, is sad etc □ *Murphy shook his head disapprovingly.* □ *She shook her head in disgust.* -2. [person] to upset or shock <sb> □ *She was badly shaken by the news.* -3. [faith, confidence, trust] to weaken <sthg> □ *These latest results have shaken investors' confidence in the bank.*
◇ *vi* [person, voice] to tremble, usually uncontrollably □ *He was shaking with cold/fear.*
◇ *n* an act of shaking □ *He was so naive about it, I wanted to give him a good shake.*
◆ **shake down** *vt sep* US (informal use) -1. **to shake sb down** to get money from sb by threats, tricks etc. -2. **to shake sb/sthg down** to search sb/sthg thoroughly.
◆ **shake off** *vt sep* -1. **to shake sb off** [police, pursuer] to escape from sb who is following or chasing one. -2. **to shake sthg off** [illness, infection] to get rid of sthg □ *I can't seem to shake off this cold.*
◆ **shake up** *vt sep* **to shake sb up** to upset or shock sb □ *Sandy was really shaken up by the news.*

shakedown [ʃeɪkdaʊn] *n* US (informal use) -1. the act of getting money from somebody by threats, tricks etc. -2. a thorough search.

shaken [ʃeɪkn] *past participle of* **shake**.

shakeout [ʃeɪkaʊt] *n* -1. = **shake-up**. -2. FINANCE a situation in which weak companies tend to go out of business because of a drop in industrial or business activity.

Shakers [ʃeɪkərz] *npl* **the Shakers** a religious group in the USA, related to the Quakers. Their simple style of handmade furniture has become very popular.

Shakespeare [ʃeɪkspɪəʳ], **William** (1564–1616) an English writer whose tragic, comic, and historical plays, including *King Lear, Othello*, and *Hamlet*, are very important in the history of English literature.

Shakespearean [ʃeɪkspɪərɪən] *adj* [play, drama] that was written by Shakespeare or is similar in style; [actor] who acts in the plays of Shakespeare.

shake-up *n* a large number of changes designed to improve an organization, company, system etc (informal use).

shaky [ʃeɪkɪ] (*compar* **shakier**, *superl* **shakiest**) *adj* **-1.** [person, hand, voice] that shakes as a result of old age, illness, shock etc □ *He's been a little shaky ever since his fall.* **-2.** [start, argument, finances] that is weak or uncertain □ *We got off to a rather shaky start, but after that things were okay.*

shale [ʃeɪl] *n* a soft rock that breaks easily into thin flat pieces.

shall [stressed ʃæl, unstressed ʃəl] *modal vb* **-1. I/we shall...** used to express the future tense □ *We shall be away until June.* □ *I shall now hand you over to our guest speaker, Hannah Chaplin.* **-2. shall I/we...?** GB used to ask questions and make suggestions □ *What shall we tell them?* □ *Shall I give her a call, then?* □ *I'll write and accept then, shall I?* **-3.** used to say that something is definitely going to happen (formal use) □ *It shall be done.* □ *We shall overcome.* **-4.** used in official documents to say what must happen or be done (formal use) □ *Employees shall be given one month's notice of dismissal.*

shallot [ʃə'lɒt] *n* a vegetable that looks like a small round onion.

shallow ['ʃæləʊ] *adj* **-1.** [water, dish, hole] not deep □ *The water was very shallow at this point.* **-2.** [person] who does not think deeply or seriously about anything; [argument, remark, lifestyle] that does not show or involve deep or serious thought □ *I find her rather shallow, to be honest.* □ *It's rather a shallow way to live your life, don't you think?* **-3. shallow breathing** a way of breathing in which only a little air goes into the lungs at each breath.

◆ **shallows** *npl* a shallow part of a river, lake, sea etc, usually near the edge.

sham [ʃæm] (*pt & pp* **shammed**, *cont* **shamming**) ◇ *adj* [sincerity, concern, enthusiasm] that is false. ◇ *n* something that is not what it is supposed or claimed to be □ *Their marriage was a sham, they never loved each other.* ◇ *vi* to pretend.

shambles ['ʃæmblz] *n* **a shambles** a place or situation that seems completely disorganized □ *He left the room in a complete shambles.* □ *What a shambles!*

shame [ʃeɪm] ◇ *n* **-1.** a strong feeling of guilt and embarrassment that one has when one has done something wrong □ *He felt no shame at what he had done.* □ *a sense of shame.* **-2. to bring shame on** OR **upon sb** to do something that causes people to lose their respect for sb and the group or family that they belong to □ *His actions brought shame on his family.* **-3. it's a shame (that)...** a phrase used to say one regrets something and wishes that the situation was different □ *It's a shame you can't stay longer.* ■ **what a shame!** a phrase used to express regret or sympathy □ *What a shame you have to leave so soon!* ◇ *vt* **-1.** to bring shame on <sb> □ *It shames me to think that you could do such a thing.* **-2. to shame sb into doing sthg** to force sb to do sthg by making them feel shame.

shamefaced [ˌʃeɪm'feɪst] *adj* [expression, apology] that shows a feeling of shame □ *The boys came in looking very shamefaced.*

shameful ['ʃeɪmfl] *adj* [behavior, waste] that one thinks should make somebody feel ashamed □ *I've never seen such a shameful display of greed!*

shameless ['ʃeɪmləs] *adj* [person] who does not feel any shame about doing something that other people think is wrong □ *He's a shameless liar!*

shammy ['ʃæmɪ] (*pl* **shammies**) *n* **a shammy (leather)** a piece of soft leather used for cleaning and polishing.

shampoo [ʃæm'puː] (*pl* **shampoos**, *pt & pp* **shampooed**, *cont* **shampooing**) ◇ *n* a soapy liquid or cream used for washing hair, carpets, or cars; a wash using this liquid or cream □ *a bottle of shampoo* □ *hair shampoo* □ *She had a shampoo and set.* ◇ *vt* [hair, carpet, car] to wash <sthg> using shampoo.

shamrock ['ʃæmrɒk] *n* a plant similar to clover that has three round leaves on each stem. It is the national symbol of Ireland.

shandy ['ʃændɪ] (*pl* **shandies**) *n* GB a drink made by mixing beer with lemon soda; a glass of this drink.

Shanghai [ˌʃæŋ'haɪ] a city in eastern China. It is a major port, and China's largest city. POPULATION: 11,860,000.

Shannon ['ʃænən]: **the Shannon** the longest river in the Irish Republic.

shan't [US ʃænt, GB ʃɑːnt] = **shall not**.

shantytown ['ʃæntɪtaʊn] *n* a part of a town or city where poor people live in badly made huts and shacks.

shape [ʃeɪp] ◇ *n* **-1.** [of an object, area] the form of the outer edges of something □ *The room is an awkward shape.* □ *a building in the shape of a "T"* □ *It's round in shape.* **-2.** [of an object, person] an object or a person that cannot be recognized because they are hard to see □ *I could just make out some vague shapes in the distance.* **-3.** [of a plan, organization] the basic structure or outline of something. ■ **to take shape** [plan, idea, building] to develop and start to take on a clear and definite form □ *The plot was starting to take shape in Murdoch's mind.* **-4.** phrases **in the shape of...** a phrase used to introduce more detailed information about something □ *Help came in the shape of an interest-free loan from a friend.* ■ **not in any shape or form** not of any kind □ *I've never taken a bribe in any shape or form.* ■ **to be in good/bad etc shape** [economy, person] to be in a good/bad etc state or condition □ *She didn't look in very good shape after the accident.* □ *What sort of shape is the car in now?* ■ **to lick** OR **knock sb into shape** [new recruit, staff] to bring sb up to the desired standard, level of skill etc □ *We'll soon lick the new team into shape.* ◇ *vt* **-1.** [dough, wood, stone] to give <sthg> a particular shape □ *a birthmark shaped like a strawberry* □ *a beautifully shaped window* □ *He shaped the clay into a bowl.* **-2.** [ideas, events, future] to have a great influence on the development of <sthg> □ *These policies are shaping the future for our children.*

◆ **shape up** *vi* [job, business, new recruit] to develop, especially in a promising way □ *Things*

are shaping up well on the African deal. □ You'll
have to shape up or you'll lose your job.

SHAPE [ʃeɪp] (*abbr of* **Supreme Headquarters
Allied Powers, Europe**) *n* the military headquarters of NATO, in Belgium.

-shaped ['ʃeɪpt] *suffix* added to words to show
the particular shape of something □ *an L-
shaped room* □ *egg-shaped* □ *star-shaped*.

shapeless ['ʃeɪpləs] *adj* **-1.** [mass, mound, heap]
that has no definite or easily described
shape □ *a shapeless form lying on the ground.*
-2. [sweater, dress] that does not have an attractive shape or that has lost its original
shape □ *She was wearing a rather shapeless
woolen dress.* **-3.** [piece of writing, movie, plan]
that has no clear structure.

shapely ['ʃeɪplɪ] (*compar* **shapelier**, *superl* **shape-
liest**) *adj* [legs, body, figure] that has an attractive shape □ *a shapely young woman.*

shard [ʃɑːʳd] *n* a broken piece of glass, metal
or pottery.

share [ʃeəʳ] ◇ *n* **-1.** the part of something that
belongs to, is given to, or done by a particular person □ *Everyone got a share in/of the
profits.* □ *We must all accept our share of the
blame.* □ *Each child received a share of the estate.* ■ **to have one's share of sthg** [of luck, criti-
cism] to have a lot of sthg □ *He's had more
than his fair share of disasters this year.* ■ **to do
one's share** to do the part of a job or task
that one is responsible for □ *Not everyone is
doing their share of the work.* **-2.** FINANCE one of
the many parts that a company's capital is
divided into □ *I bought/sold shares in Kingston
Corp.* □ *a block of shares.*

◇ *vt* **-1.** [room, house, facilities] to use <sthg>
jointly with other people □ *I have my own
kitchen but I share the bathroom with two others.*
-2. [money, food, resources] to give some of
<sthg> to another person or to other people
□ *You've got plenty — why don't you share it
with the rest of us?* **-3.** [cost, expenses] to have
joint responsibility for <sthg> □ *We share the
rent for the apartment.* **-4.** [thought, news, se-
cret] to tell somebody about <sthg> □ *He
simply had to share the news with somebody.*
-5. [dislike, concern, fear] to have <a feeling>
that somebody else also feels □ *We share
your joy at your daughter's marriage.* □ *We share
many interests.*

◇ *vi* **-1.** to use something jointly with other
people □ *We're a book short — can you two
share?* □ *"I can't find my drink." — "You can
have some of this if you don't mind sharing."*
-2. to have a feeling that somebody else also
feels □ *We all share in your happiness.*

◆ **share out** *vt sep* **to share sthg out** [money,
work, food] to divide sthg into equal parts
and give them to all the people in a group □
Profits are shared out equally among the partners.

share capital *n* the money received by a
company from a sale of shares and used for
carrying on a business.

share certificate *n* GB = **stock certificate**.

shareholder ['ʃeəʳhoʊldəʳ] *n* a person or company that owns shares in a company □ *Major*

shareholders in the company include the PCB
group. □ a shareholders' meeting.

share index *n* an index of changes in the
value of shares.

share-out *n* [of goods, money, profits] an act of
sharing something out.

shareware ['ʃeəʳweəʳ] *n* cheap computer software that is free or easily available.

shark [ʃɑːʳk] (*pl* **shark** OR **sharks**) *n* **-1.** a very
large sea fish with a triangular fin on its
back that sometimes attacks people. **-2.** a
person who gets money from other people
in a dishonest way.

sharp [ʃɑːʳp] ◇ *adj* **-1.** [blade, needle, teeth] that
has a very fine edge or point that can cut or
pierce easily □ *Be careful — that knife's very
sharp.* □ *That pen has a very sharp point on it.* □
*Avoid furniture with sharp edges in a child's bed-
room.* **-2.** [outline, contrast, photograph] that is
clear, so that the edges, differences, details
etc are easy to see □ *The image is not sharp
enough to be able to make out all the details.* □
*This book is a sharp contrast to his previous nov-
el.* **-3.** [person] who is quick to notice, understand, or react to something □ *She's very
sharp.* □ *You have very sharp eyesight.* **-4.** [rise,
drop, fall] that takes place suddenly and
makes a large difference to the amount or
level of something; [bend, turn] that is produced by something that suddenly makes a
big change in direction □ *There has been a
sharp increase/decrease in the number of accidents.* **-5.** [blow, knock, tap] that is quick and
firm □ *Give the shell a sharp tap.* **-6.** [bend, turn-
ing] that changes direction suddenly □ *The
car made a sharp left-hand turn.* **-7.** [criticism, rebuke, words] that is a little angry or severe □
She was pretty sharp with me. **-8.** [pain, cold,
wind] that one feels intensely □ *a sharp, cold
wind.* **-9.** [taste, drink] that stings the tongue
in a pleasant way □ *The wine tastes slightly
sharp.* **-10.** [note, voice, instrument] that produces a sound slightly higher than the correct pitch. **-11.** MUSIC that is raised in pitch
by a half-step □ *C/D/F sharp* □ *Klaus' clarinet
quintet in F sharp.*

◇ *adv* **-1.** exactly □ *She promised to be here at
eight o'clock sharp.* **-2.** a word that indicates a
sudden change in direction □ *The road turns
sharp left/right at the lights.*

◇ *n* MUSIC a symbol (#) used to show that a
note should be sung or played a half-step
higher; a note of this type.

sharpen ['ʃɑːʳpn] ◇ *vt* **-1.** [knife, tool, pencil] to
make <sthg> sharp □ *These scissors need
sharpening.* **-2.** [sense, ability, mind] to make
<sthg> quicker and better at reacting to or
dealing with things □ *This course will help you
to sharpen your debating skills.* **-3.** [disagreement,
conflict, contrast] to make <sthg> more intense □ *What was said only served to sharpen
their hostility toward us.* ◇ *vi* **-1.** [sense, ability,
mind] *My timing has sharpened a lot with all this
practice.* **-2.** [disagreement, conflict, contrast] *The
debate has sharpened over recent years.*

sharp end *n* **to be at the sharp end of sthg** GB
to be in a position where the problems and

pressures involved in sthg are experienced most directly.

sharpener ['ʃɑːʳpnəʳ] *n* a device for sharpening something □ *a knife sharpener.*

sharp-eyed [-'aɪd] *adj* [neighbor, observer] who notices things quickly and easily.

sharply ['ʃɑːʳplɪ] *adv* [contrast, increase, criticize] see **sharp** □ *Sandy was sharply ciriticized for her decision.* □ *The car veered sharply to the left.*

sharpshooter ['ʃɑːʳpʃuːtəʳ] *n* a person who is skilled at shooting accurately.

sharp-tongued [-'tʌŋd] *adj* [person] who is harsh in their remarks, comments etc.

sharp-witted [-'wɪtəd] *adj* [person] who is quick at realizing things and understanding them.

shat▼ [ʃæt] *past tense & past participle of* **shit.**

shatter ['ʃætəʳ] ◇ *vt* -1. [glass, window, vase] to break <sthg> violently into small pieces □ *The bullet shattered the car windshield.* -2. [beliefs, hopes, dreams] to destroy <sthg> □ *The result shattered her hopes of a third term in office.* ◇ *vi* [glass, window, vase] *All the windows shattered under the effects of the blast.*

shattered ['ʃætəʳd] *adj* -1. who feels very shocked and upset □ *The news left her shattered.* -2. GB who feels very tired (informal use) □ *I'm absolutely shattered after that walk.*

shattering ['ʃætərɪŋ] *adj* [news, defeat, disappointment] that is very shocking and upsetting □ *The news was a shattering blow to staff morale.*

shatterproof ['ʃætəʳpruːf] *adj* [glass] that does not break into small pieces when damaged.

shave [ʃeɪv] ◇ *n* -1. an act of shaving □ *I need a shave.* ■ **to have a shave** [man] to shave one's face □ *I had a shave this morning.* -2. **a close shave** a situation in which one only just avoids something bad, e.g. an accident, a disaster, or being caught □ *That was a close shave!* ◇ *vt* -1. [head, face, legs] to cut hair from <a part of one's body> using a razor. -2. [man] to cut hair from the face of <a man> using a razor. -3. [wood, metal] to cut very fine pieces from the surface of <wood or metal>. ◇ *vi* [man] to cut hair from one's face using a razor.

◆ **shave off** *vt sep* **to shave off one's beard/ mustache/hair** to remove one's beard/ mustache/hair using a razor.

shaven ['ʃeɪvn] *adj* [head, face] that has been shaved.

shaver ['ʃeɪvəʳ] *n* an electric razor □ *a rechargeable/electric shaver.*

shaving brush ['ʃeɪvɪŋ-] *n* a brush used with shaving soap.

shaving cream *n* a soapy substance a man puts on his face before shaving to make the hair soft and wet.

shaving foam *n* shaving cream from an aerosol can.

shavings ['ʃeɪvɪŋz] *npl* very fine pieces of wood or metal that have been shaved from the surface of something □ *wood shavings.*

shaving soap *n* a type of soap used instead of shaving cream or foam.

Shaw [ʃɔː], **George Bernard** (1856–1950) an Irish writer and critic whose plays, e.g. *Pygmalion*, are full of witty remarks and criticisms of society.

shawl [ʃɔːl] *n* a large square or rectangular piece of cloth worn over the head or shoulders by women or wrapped around a baby.

Shawnee [ˌʃɔːˈniː] (*pl* **Shawnee** OR **Shawnees**) *n* a member of a Native American people who used to live in Ohio; the language of this people.

she [ʃiː] ◇ *pron* -1. the woman, girl, or female animal that has just been mentioned, seen etc (used as the subject of a verb) □ *She and I have known each other for years.* -2. used to refer to a ship, car, or nation □ *She can do over 120 miles an hour.* ◇ *n* a female animal or baby □ *Is it a she or a he?*

she- *prefix* added to words to refer to the female of a particular type of animal □ *a she-elephant* □ *a she-wolf.*

sheaf [ʃiːf] (*pl* **sheaves**) *n* [of papers, letters] a number of things held or fastened together □ *sheaves of wheat.*

shear [ʃɪəʳ] (*pt* **sheared**, *pp* **sheared** OR **shorn**) *vt* to cut the wool off <a sheep>.

◆ **shears** *npl* -1. [for a garden] a tool similar to a large pair of scissors, used for cutting hedges, pruning bushes etc. -2. [for dressmaking] large scissors used for cutting cloth.

◆ **shear off** ◇ *vt sep* **to shear sthg off** to cause a metal object or part to break off because of pressure. ◇ *vi: The head of the bolt had completely sheared off.*

sheath [ʃiːθ] (*pl* **sheaths**) *n* -1. [for a knife, sword] a close-fitting cover for the blade of a knife, sword etc. -2. [for a cable] a close-fitting protective covering for a cable, usually made of rubber or plastic.

sheathe [ʃiːð] *vt* -1. [sword, knife, dagger] to put <sthg> in a sheath. -2. [cable, pipe] to put a sheath on <sthg> □ *The wiring was sheathed in plastic.*

sheath knife *n* a knife that is carried in a sheath on one's belt.

sheaves [ʃiːvz] *plural of* **sheaf.**

Sheba ['ʃiːbə]: **the Queen of Sheba** in the Bible, a very rich queen from Arabia.

shed [ʃed] (*pt & pp* **shed**, *cont* **shedding**) ◇ *n* a simple small building, often of wood, that consists of one room and is used for storing things or sheltering animals or vehicles □ *bicycle/garden/tool shed.*

◇ *vt* -1. [leaves, hair, skin] to lose <sthg> because it falls off naturally □ *All the trees had shed their leaves.* -2. [staff, image, weight] to get rid of <sthg that one no longer wants> □ *The company is shedding 600 jobs.* □ *He shed his inhibitions and joined in.* □ *I've shed about 12 pounds in a few weeks.* -3. **to shed its load** [truck, van] to drop or lose its load accidentally. -4. **to shed blood** to cause violent injury and death □ *Much blood was shed during the* riots. ■ **to shed tears** to cry □ *There won't be many tears shed at his leaving party.*

she'd [*stressed* ʃiːd, *unstressed* ʃɪd] = **she had, she would.**

sheen [ʃiːn] *n* a soft shine on a smooth surface □ *Her hair has a beautiful sheen.*

sheep [ʃiːp] (*pl* **sheep**) *n* -1. a farm animal that is kept in large flocks for its meat and its thick wool □ *They keep over 500 sheep on their farm.* □ *a flock of sheep.* -2. a person who is easily influenced, who obeys without question, or who imitates the behavior of others □ *They're just a lot of sheep, each one blindly following everybody else.*

sheepdog [ˈʃiːpdɒg] *n* a dog trained to guard and control sheep.

sheepish [ˈʃiːpɪʃ] *adj* [look, smile] that shows that one is embarrassed about something silly one has done □ *He came in looking a little sheepish.*

sheepishly [ˈʃiːpɪʃlɪ] *adv* [look, smile, grin] *see* **sheepish.**

sheepskin [ˈʃiːpskɪn] *n* the skin and wool of a sheep, used for rugs, coats etc □ *a sheepskin jacket.*

sheepskin rug *n* a rug made from sheepskin.

sheer [ʃɪəʳ] *adj* -1. [madness, determination, luck] a word used to emphasize that only a particular quality and nothing but that quality is involved in or shown by something □ *a feeling of sheer bliss* □ *It was sheer stupidity on my part.* -2. [drop, cliff, wall] that goes down or up vertically or almost vertically □ *The canyon has sheer sides that plunge down 300 feet to the river below.* -3. [silk, nylon, stockings] that is very fine and delicate and almost transparent □ *a pair of sheer silk stockings.*

sheet [ʃiːt] *n* -1. a large rectangular piece of material used on a bed as one of a pair between which people sleep □ *a cotton sheet.* ■ **to be as white as a sheet** to be very pale because one is scared, shocked, or ill. -2. a flat rectangular piece of something such as paper or glass □ *a sheet of paper/aluminum.*

sheet feed *n* COMPUTING a system that allows single sheets of paper to be fed through a printer.

sheet ice *n* ice which has formed a thick layer, especially on a road.

sheeting [ˈʃiːtɪŋ] *n* material that is made into large, flat, thin pieces □ *plastic/polythene/metal sheeting.*

sheet lightning *n* lightning that appears as a large bright area in the sky.

sheet metal *n* metal in the form of a sheet.

sheet music *n* music that is published on loose sheets of paper that are not bound in book form.

sheik(h) [ʃeɪk] *n* an Arab chief or ruler.

sheila▽ [ˈʃiːlə] *n* AUS a young woman (very informal use).

shelf [ʃelf] (*pl* **shelves**) *n* a flat rectangular piece of wood, metal, or glass etc fixed horizontally to a wall or in a cupboard, book-

case etc and used for keeping things on □ *a storage shelf* □ *a supermarket shelf.*

shelf life *n* the length of time something can be kept in a store before it is too old to sell.

shell [ʃel] ◇ *n* -1. [of a nut, seed, egg] the hard outer covering of an egg, nut, or seed □ *The brazilnut has a very hard shell.* -2. [of a tortoise, crab, snail] the hard, protective covering on some land and sea animals; one of these coverings in which a small sea animal once lived, found e.g. on a beach □ *The tortoise retreated inside its shell.* □ *oyster/mussel/clam shells.* -3. [of a building, boat, car] the outer structure of something that is unfinished or whose contents have been destroyed □ *All that remained of the house was an empty shell.* -4. MILITARY a large bullet-shaped metal container filled with explosive for firing from a large gun □ *They found an unexploded shell.* ◇ *vt* -1. [peas, eggs, shrimps] to remove the shell or similar covering from <sthg>. -2. MILITARY [town, enemy position] to fire shells at <a place>.

◆ **shell out** (informal use) ◇ *vt fus* **to shell out money** to pay money, especially more than expected or intended □ *I had to shell out $54 for a taxi to get home.* ◇ *vi*: *He had to shell out for a new car.*

she'll [*stressed* ʃiːl, *unstressed* ʃɪl] = **she will, she shall.**

shellfish [ˈʃelfɪʃ] (*pl* **shellfish**) *n* -1. an animal without a backbone that lives in water and has a shell, e.g. a mussel, oyster, or shrimp. -2. these animals eaten as food.

shelling [ˈʃelɪŋ] *n* MILITARY an attack on a place using shells □ *The shelling continued all night.*

shellshock [ˈʃelʃɒk] *n* a mental illness, usually affecting soldiers, caused by their experiences in battle.

shelter [ˈʃeltəʳ] ◇ *n* -1. [from bad weather, attack, danger] protection against something, usually provided by a covering of some kind □ *We could find no shelter from the sun/rain.* -2. a building or roofed structure that gives shelter □ *a mountain shelter.* ◇ *vt* to give <sb/sthg> shelter □ *The trees sheltered us a little from the storm.* ◇ *vi* to find or take shelter in a place □ *They went under the bridge to shelter from the wind and rain.*

sheltered [ˈʃeltəʳd] *adj* -1. [position, spot, valley] protected from the wind, rain etc □ *a sheltered bay.* -2. [life, childhood] protected from the unpleasant realities of life □ *She's led a rather sheltered existence.* -3. GB [housing, accommodation] where supervision and care are available for old or disabled people.

shelve [ʃelv] ◇ *vt* [plan, idea, project] to decide to stop <sthg>, often with the intention of continuing it later □ *Hutton says they've had to shelve the Japanese deal until next year.* ◇ *vi* [land, ground, sea bed] to slope gradually.

shelves [ʃelvz] *plural of* **shelf.**

shelving [ˈʃelvɪŋ] *n* shelves; material used to make shelves □ *We put up some shelving in the dining room.*

shenanigans [ʃɪˈnænəgənz] *npl* (informal use)

-1. dishonest activities. -2. bad behavior that is playful and not serious.

shepherd [ˈʃepərd] ◇ *n* a person who takes care of sheep. ◇ *vt* to guide or accompany <sb> somewhere □ *We were shepherded through the main entrance.*

shepherd's pie *n* ground beef covered with mashed potato and baked in an oven.

sherbet [ˈʃɜːrbət] *n* -1. US a frozen dessert made with fruit juice. -2. GB a sweet powder that is eaten as a candy.

sheriff [ˈʃerɪf] *n* -1. an elected officer responsible for enforcing the law in a US county. -2. the chief judge in a district in Scotland.

sheriff court *n* a Scottish court that deals with all civil actions and most crimes, apart from very serious ones.

Sherman Anti-Trust Act [ˌʃɜːrmən-] *n* an important US anti-trust law passed in 1890.

sherry [ˈʃerɪ] (*pl* **sherries**) *n* -1. a fortified wine from the Jerez region of Spain, often drunk before a meal; an imitation of this type of wine produced in other countries. -2. a glass of sherry.

she's [*stressed* ʃiːz, *unstressed* ʃɪz] = **she is, she has.**

Shetland [ˈʃetlənd]: **Shetland, the Shetlands, the Shetland Islands** a group of British islands off the northeastern coast of Scotland, north of the Orkney Islands. SIZE: 1,425 sq kms. POPULATION: 23,000 (*Shetlanders*). CAPITAL: Lerwick.

shh [ʃ] *excl* = **sh.**

shield [ʃiːld] ◇ *n* -1. [for soldiers] a stiff piece of metal, leather etc that was carried on one arm to protect oneself in battle in the days when people fought with swords; [for policemen] a similar piece of strong plastic carried by policemen to protect themselves in riots. -2. GB a sports prize in the form of a shield. -3. [against danger, harm] something that gives protection against something □ *an effective shield against attack* □ *The prisoners are being used as human shields.* -4. [against the wind, heat] a protective cover, plate, screen etc □ *a wind/sun/heat shield.*
◇ *vt* to protect <sb/sthg> □ *Local people shielded the runaway from the police.* □ *She shielded her eyes with her hand.*

shift [ʃɪft] ◇ *n* -1. a change, e.g. in people's attitudes or behavior □ *There has been a significant shift in the number of people voting Republican recently.* □ *a shift in emphasis.* -2. the particular period of time worked by a group of workers who take turns with another group; the workers on a particular shift □ *the early/late/night shift* □ *shift work.*
◇ *vt* -1. [bag, table, one's gaze] to move <sthg> from one place to another □ *He shifted his weight onto his other leg.* -2. **to shift the blame/responsibility** to give the blame/responsibility for something to somebody else □ *Don't try to shift the blame onto me!* -3. US AUTO **to shift gear** to change gear. -4. GB [stain, mark] to remove <a piece of dirt>.
◇ *vi* -1. [person, cargo, object] to move □ *Con-*

tents may shift during transit. -2. [opinion, situation] to change □ *Attitudes toward abortion have shifted a lot in recent years.* -3. [wind] to change direction. -4. US AUTO *The driver shifted into low gear.*

shift key *n* the key on a typewriter or keyboard used to produce capital letters.

shiftless [ˈʃɪftləs] *adj* [person] who is lazy and has no wish to achieve anything.

shifty [ˈʃɪftɪ] (*compar* **shiftier**, *superl* **shiftiest**) *adj* [person, behavior] that appears dishonest and cannot be trusted □ *a shifty-looking character.*

Shiite [ˈʃiːaɪt] ◇ *adj* [Muslim, religion, peoples] that is connected with Shiism, a branch of Islam based on the teachings of Muhammad's cousin Ali and the teachers who came after him. ◇ *n* a Shiite Muslim.

shilling [ˈʃɪlɪŋ] *n* in Britain, a coin and unit of money used until 1971 and worth one-twentieth of a pound.

shilly-shally [ˈʃɪlɪʃælɪ] (*pt* & *pp* **shilly-shallied**) *vi* to take a long time to make up one's mind (informal and disapproving use).

shimmer [ˈʃɪmər] ◇ *vi* [light, water, haze] to shine with a soft unsteady light □ *The lake shimmered in the moonlight.* ◇ *n* a shimmering light □ *a soft shimmer of reflected light.*

shin [ʃɪn] (*pt* & *pp* **shinned**, *cont* **shinning**) *n* the front part of one's leg between one's knee and one's ankle.
◆ **shin up** *vt fus* GB = **shinny up.**

shinbone [ˈʃɪnboʊn] *n* the bone in the front part of one's leg below the knee.

shine [ʃaɪn] (*pt* & *pp* **shone**) ◇ *n* [of a surface, somebody's eyes] brightness □ *This furniture polish really brings out the shine.*
◇ *vt* -1. [lamp, flashlight, light] to point <sthg which gives light> in a particular direction □ *Don't shine that light in my eyes.* -2. [shoes, brass] to polish <sthg>. ◇ *vi* -1. [sun, light, moon] to give out bright light □ *The afternoon sun shone brightly overhead.* □ *The flashlight was shining right in my eyes.* -2. [surface, eyes, shoes] to reflect light brightly, especially because of being new or clean □ *His eyes shone with pride.* □ *She polished her shoes until they shone.* -3. [student, staff] to be excellent at something in a way that other people notice □ *He really shines at chemistry.*

shingle [ˈʃɪŋgl] *n* -1. small rounded stones covering a beach. -2. one of many small thin tiles, usually made of wood, used to cover a roof.
◆ **shingles** *n* MEDICINE a viral infection that causes a rash of painful red spots, especially around one's waist.

shining [ˈʃaɪnɪŋ] *adj* **a shining example/achievement etc** an excellent example/achievement etc.

shinny [ˈʃɪnɪ] ◆ **shinny up** *vt fus* US **to shinny up sthg** [tree, pole, lamppost] to climb sthg using only one's hands and legs.

shin pads *npl* in some sports, soft pads that are worn around one's shins in order to protect them □ *a pair of shin pads.*

shiny [ˈʃaɪnɪ] (*compar* **shinier**, *superl* **shiniest**) *adj* [surface, furniture, shoe] that shines □ *a shiny new car.*

ship [ʃɪp] (*pt* & *pp* **shipped**, *cont* **shipping**) ◇ *n* a large boat that carries passengers or goods by sea □ *We went by ship.* □ *a merchant ship.*
◇ *vt* [goods, troops, passengers] to move or send <sb/sthg> to a place, especially by ship □ *I'm having my car shipped over from the States.*

shipbuilder [ˈʃɪpbɪldər] *n* a person or company that builds ships.

shipbuilding [ˈʃɪpbɪldɪŋ] *n* the industry of building ships □ *the shipbuilding industry.*

ship canal *n* a canal that is large enough for ships.

shipment [ˈʃɪpmənt] *n* a load of goods sent by road, sea, or air □ *a shipment of food/grain/coal.*

shipper [ˈʃɪpər] *n* a person who makes shipments of goods.

shipping [ˈʃɪpɪŋ] *n* -1. the business of transporting goods, especially in ships □ *the shipping industry* □ *a shipping magnate.* -2. a collective term for ships □ *The Channel is a busy route for shipping.*

shipping agent *n* a person or company that makes arrangements for the transportation of goods by sea.

shipping forecast *n* a forecast of weather conditions at sea broadcast by radio.

shipping lane *n* a route across the sea in a particular area that is used by ships.

shipshape [ˈʃɪpʃeɪp] *adj* [room, office] that is neat and well ordered.

shipwreck [ˈʃɪprek] ◇ *n* an accident in which a ship sinks or is destroyed at sea; a ship lost or destroyed in this way. ◇ *vt* **to be shipwrecked** [person] to be involved in a shipwreck □ *They were shipwrecked on the rocks off Nantucket.*

shipyard [ˈʃɪpjɑːrd] *n* a place where ships are built or repaired.

shire [ˈʃaɪər]. *n* in Australia, a rural area with its own local government.

◆ **Shires** *n* **the Shires** the counties in country areas of England, especially central England.

shire county *n* in England, one of the Shires.

shire horse *n* a large powerful breed of horse used in former times for farm work.

shirk [ʃɜːrk] *vt* [task, duty] to avoid doing <sthg> because one is lazy □ *Isn't it time you stopped shirking your responsibilities?*

shirker [ˈʃɜːrkər] *n* a person who always tries to avoid doing their work.

shirt [ʃɜːrt] *n* a piece of clothing for one's upper body that is made of light cloth, has a collar, long or short sleeves, and buttons up the front □ *a cotton/linen shirt* □ *a shirt collar.*

shirtsleeves [ˈʃɜːrtsliːvz] *npl* **to be in (one's) shirtsleeves** to be wearing nothing on top of one's shirt □ *He stood there in his shirtsleeves, surveying the boxes that filled the room.*

shirttail [ˈʃɜːrteɪl] *n* the part of the shirt that hangs below one's waist at the back □ *His shirttail was hanging out at the back.*

shit▼ [ʃɪt] (vulgar use) (*pt* & *pp* **shit** OR **shitted** OR **shat**, *cont* **shitting**) ◇ *n* -1. waste matter from the bowels. -2. nonsense □ *That's a load of shit!* □ *He's full of shit, that guy!* -3. a very unpleasant person, especially someone who treats other people badly □ *He's a real shit!*
◇ *vi* to empty waste matter from the bowels. ◇ *excl* a word used to express annoyance, impatience, frustration etc □ *Shit! I forgot to bring them.*

shiver [ˈʃɪvər] ◇ *n* [of cold, fear, excitement] a feeling or act of shivering □ *She felt a shiver of anticipation as the results were read out.* ■ **to give sb the shivers** to cause sb strong feelings of fear or dislike that they cannot control □ *It gives me the shivers just thinking about that place.* ◇ *vi* to tremble, especially with cold or fear □ *We were shivering with cold/terror/excitement.*

shoal [ʃoʊl] *n* a large group of fish swimming together □ *shoals of herring.*

shock [ʃɒk] ◇ *n* -1. a sudden, unexpected, and usually unpleasant surprise; the emotional effect of this □ *I got a real shock when I saw the name.* □ *The news came as a terrible shock.* □ *I didn't mean to give you a shock.* □ *She stood there, pale with shock, as he told her the news.* -2. MEDICINE a state of extreme physical weakness caused by injury, loss of blood, pain etc □ *Some survivors went into shock.* □ *She is still in a state of shock after the accident.* -3. [of a blow, collision] the impact of a blow, explosion, collision etc □ *Given the shock of the collision it's a miracle anyone survived.* -4. ELECTRICITY = **electric shock**. -5. **a shock of hair** a thick mass of hair.
◇ *vt* -1. to give <sb> a shock □ *He was shocked by the news/to hear of his death.* -2. to cause <sb> to feel offense, horror, disgust etc □ *He was shocked by their bad language.*
◇ *vi* to cause offense, horror, disgust etc □ *The play is intended to shock.*

shock absorber [-əbsɔːrbər] *n* a device fitted to each wheel of a vehicle to reduce the vibration caused by driving over uneven surfaces.

shocked [ʃɒkt] *adj* [person] who is offended, horrified, or disgusted □ *Shocked readers have written in to complain about the article.*

shocking [ˈʃɒkɪŋ] *adj* -1. [weather, handwriting, work] that is very bad □ *The standard of her work is shocking.* -2. [news, accident] that causes a shock □ *I've just received some shocking news.* -3. [behavior, language, movie] that one finds offensive or disgusting □ *I found their behavior shocking, to be honest.*

shockproof [ˈʃɒkpruːf] *adj* [watch] that is not easily damaged by being dropped, knocked etc.

shock tactics *npl* -1. MILITARY tactics designed to take an enemy by surprise. -2. sudden unusual or violent action taken to achieve a purpose by causing surprise □ *Well, we could try using shock tactics.*

shock therapy, shock treatment *n* a treatment that is given for some kinds of mental illness that involves passing an electric current through the brain.

shock troops *npl* soldiers who have been specially trained for making sudden attacks.

shock wave *n* -1. an area of intense heat and pressure moving through the air, caused e.g. by an explosion or earthquake. -2. a strong reaction to something □ *The news caused shock waves throughout the community.*

shod [ʃɒd] ◇ *past tense & past participle of* **shoe.** ◇ *adj* **to be well/badly etc shod** to be wearing good/bad etc shoes (literary use).

shoddy ['ʃɒdɪ] (*compar* **shoddier,** *superl* **shoddiest**) *adj* -1. [work, workmanship, goods] that is of poor quality □ *Shoddy construction is being blamed for the disaster.* -2. [treatment, behavior] that is bad and unfair □ *The way he treats women is really shoddy.*

shoe [ʃuː] (*pt & pp* **shod** OR **shoed,** *cont* **shoeing**) ◇ *n* -1. a covering for a person's foot, often made of leather and with a hard base and a raised part under the heel □ *a pair of shoes* □ *shoe cleaner.* -2. = **horseshoe.** -3. = **brake shoe.** ◇ *vt* **to shoe a horse** to put horseshoes on a horse.

shoebrush ['ʃuːbrʌʃ] *n* a brush used for cleaning and polishing shoes.

shoehorn ['ʃuːhɔːrn] *n* a piece of metal, plastic, or horn with a hollow curve at one end, used to help one put a shoe on more easily.

shoelace ['ʃuːleɪs] *n* a long thin cord that is used to fasten shoes □ *Your shoelace is undone!*

shoemaker ['ʃuːmeɪkər] *n* a person who makes shoes.

shoe polish *n* polish for cleaning shoes.

shoe store US, **shoe shop** GB *n* a store that sells shoes, boots etc.

shoestring ['ʃuːstrɪŋ] ◇ *adj* **a shoestring budget** a small budget that allows very little money to be spent □ *The play was produced on a shoestring budget.* ◇ *n* **on a shoestring** by spending very little money □ *She decorated her house on a shoestring.*

shoetree ['ʃuːtriː] *n* a piece of metal, wood, or plastic placed inside a boot or shoe to help it keep its shape when it is not being worn.

shone [US ʃoʊn, GB ʃɒn] *past tense & past participle of* **shine.**

shoo [ʃuː] ◇ *vt* to make <a person or animal> go away or move somewhere by shouting and waving one's hands at them. ◇ *excl* a word used to shoo somebody or something away.

shoo-in *n* US a person who is sure to win an election, competition etc (informal use).

shook [ʃʊk] *past tense of* **shake.**

shoot [ʃuːt] (*pt & pp* **shot**) ◇ *vt* -1. [person, animal] to kill or wound <sb/sthg> by firing a bullet at them □ *She was shot in the back.* ■ **to shoot oneself** to kill oneself by firing a bullet at oneself □ *He threatened to shoot himself.* -2. [bird, game] to hunt <animals> with a gun as a sport or leisure activity □ *They shoot wild boar here in the summer.* -3. **to shoot an arrow** to release an arrow from a bow. -4. **to shoot a look/glance at sb** to look/glance at sb quickly and suddenly □ *He shot me a look so*

full of outrage I almost laughed. -5. to make <a photograph or movie> using a camera □ *The scene was shot on location in Rome.* □ *I shot several rolls of film.* -6. **to shoot pool/billiards etc** US to play a game of pool/billiards etc.
◇ *vi* -1. to fire a gun at somebody or something □ *He shot at them as they ran for cover.* -2. [hunter] to hunt birds or game with a gun. -3. **to shoot across/over/up etc** to move across/over/up etc very quickly □ *She shot out of the room.* □ *He shot ahead of the other runners.* -4. CINEMA & PHOTOGRAPHY to make a movie or take a photograph □ *We'll begin shooting next week.* -5. SPORT to try to score in a game of football, hockey etc.
◇ *n* -1. a new growth from part of a plant □ *The plant had put out some new shoots.* -2. GB a hunting expedition to shoot animals or birds □ *a pheasant shoot.*
◇ *excl* US -1. a word used to tell somebody to start speaking □ *Okay, shoot, I'm listening!* -2. a word used to express annoyance (informal use) □ *Shoot! I've forgotten my purse.*

◆ **shoot down** *vt sep* -1. **to shoot sthg down** [plane, helicopter] to make sthg fall to the ground by firing at it with guns, missiles etc □ *The plane was shot down over the ocean.* -2. **to shoot sb/sthg down** [suggestion, idea, person] to show sb/sthg to be wrong, impractical, foolish etc □ *My idea was shot down by everyone else.*

◆ **shoot up** *vi* -1. [plant, child] to grow quickly □ *Young Terry has really shot up in the last year.* -2. [price, inflation] to increase quickly □ *The price of houses has shot up.* -3.▽ [junkie, addict] to inject a drug directly into one's bloodstream (drugs slang).

shooting ['ʃuːtɪŋ] *n* -1. an act of killing or wounding a person or animal. -2. the sport of hunting birds or animals with guns.

shooting range *n* a place where people practice shooting by firing guns at targets.

shooting star *n* a small piece of material that burns brightly as it enters the Earth's atmosphere from space.

shooting stick *n* a special kind of walking-stick that can be stuck into the ground and that has a handle that can be folded out to form a seat.

shoot-out *n* a fight with guns which ends when everyone on one side is dead, is wounded, or has surrendered.

shop [ʃɒp] (*pt & pp* **shopped,** *cont* **shopping**) ◇ *n* -1. a building, or a part of a building, where people can go to buy goods, usually of a particular kind □ *a flower/shoe/museum shop* □ *I'm just going to the shops.* ■ **to talk shop** to talk about one's work. -2. a place, usually in a factory, where things are made or repaired □ *the assembly/machine/metalwork shop.* ◇ *vi* to go to stores and buy things □ *I don't like shopping on a Saturday.*

◆ **shop around** *vi* to compare prices in different stores or from different suppliers before buying something □ *I'd suggest you shop around a little before buying a mobile phone.*

shop assistant *n* GB a person who serves customers in a store.

shop floor *n* **the shop floor** the area where the ordinary workers do their jobs, especially in a factory; the workers on the shop floor, and not the managers.

shopkeeper [ˈʃɒpkiːpəʳ] *n* a person who is in charge of, or owns, a small store.

shoplifter [ˈʃɒplɪftəʳ] *n* a person who steals goods from a store.

shoplifting [ˈʃɒplɪftɪŋ] *n* the crime of stealing goods from a store.

shopper [ˈʃɒpəʳ] *n* a person who shops.

shopping [ˈʃɒpɪŋ] *n* -1. things bought from stores or a store, especially food □ *a bag of shopping* □ *I left my shopping on the bus!* -2. the act of buying things from a store □ *We must do some food shopping today.* □ *I go shopping once a week.*

shopping bag *n* a bag for carrying shopping.

shopping center *n* a large building specially built to contain many separate stores of different kinds and that usually also contains restaurants and play areas.

shopping list *n* a list that somebody writes to remind them what to buy when they go shopping.

shopping mall, shopping plaza *n* = shopping center.

shopsoiled *adj* GB = shopworn.

shop steward *n* a labor union officer elected by members in their place of work to represent them at meetings and deal with union business.

shopwalker [ˈʃɒpwɔːkəʳ] *n* GB a person in a large store whose job is to help customers and make sure that the salesclerks are doing their job properly.

shopwindow [ˌʃɒpˈwɪndoʊ] *n* the window of a store where goods are displayed.

shopworn [ˈʃɒpwɔːʳn] US, **shopsoiled** [ˈʃɒp-sɔɪld] GB *adj* [piece of furniture, material] that is slightly dirty or damaged as a result of being handled too much by customers, or being on display for a long time.

shore [ʃɔːʳ] *n* -1. [of a sea, lake, river] a strip of land on the edge of a large area of water □ *the island's sandy shores.* -2. **on shore** on land, rather than on a ship □ *We'll take your camera to be repaired once we're back on shore.*

◆ **shore up** *vt sep* -1. **to shore sthg up** [foundations, ceiling, beam] to stop sthg from falling down by putting a strong object next to or under it to support it □ *We shored up the wall with a large plank of wood.* -2. **to shore sthg up** [economy, dictatorship] to support or strengthen sthg that is weak and likely to fail □ *The government had to be shored up by foreign aid.*

shore leave *n* a period of time when sailors are allowed to go on land and leave their ship for a break □ *Most of the crew were on shore leave.*

shoreline [ˈʃɔːʳlaɪn] *n* [of a sea, lake, river] the edge of a large area of water.

shorn [ʃɔːʳn] ◇ *past participle of* **shear.** ◇ *adj*

-1. [grass, hair] that has been cut very short □ *Her head was completely shorn.* -2. **to be shorn of sthg** [of power, responsibility] to have sthg taken away from one □ *Shorn of her power, she seemed somehow pathetic.*

short [ʃɔːʳt] ◇ *adj* -1. [speech, hair, skirt] that is not long □ *I'll just read you this short extract.* -2. [person] who is not tall □ *He's short and stocky.* -3. [route, distance] that is not long or does not take much time to travel □ *It's just a short walk to the post office.* -4. [visit, vacation, break] that does not last a long time □ *The unions are demanding shorter working hours.* -5. **to be short with sb** to speak to sb rudely and abruptly, usually because one is angry or impatient □ *I'm sorry if I was a little short with you.* -6. **money/time is short** there is not much money/time □ *Time is short and we have to have this finished today.* ■ **to be one/two/three etc short** to have one/two/three etc fewer than one needs or should have □ *We're $10 short.* ■ **to be short of sthg** [of money, time, sleep] not to have enough of sthg that one needs □ *We're short of staff at the moment.* □ *She's never short of good ideas.* ■ **to be short on sthg** [on ideas, intelligence] to be lacking in sthg □ *She's short on tact.* ■ **to be short of breath** to be unable to breathe normally. -7. **to be short for sthg** to be an abbreviation for sthg □ *"Jon" is short for "Jonathan."*

◇ *adv* -1. **to run short of sthg** [of food, money, supplies] to have almost run out of sthg □ *We're running dangerously short of water.* -2. **to cut sthg short** [visit, speech, education] to make sthg stop abruptly before it has finished □ *He had to cut his vacation short.* □ *I'm sorry to cut you short, but we're running out of time.* ■ **to stop short** to stop doing something because one is surprised, shocked etc □ *He stopped short in front of the picture.* ■ **to bring** OR **pull sb up short** to cause sb to be surprised or shocked and to suddenly stop what they are doing or saying □ *The look she gave me brought* OR *pulled me up short.*

◇ *n* -1. GB a strong alcoholic drink, especially liquor, that is usually drunk in small amounts □ *He'd been drinking shorts all night.* -2. CINEMA a short movie shown before the main program in a movie theater □ *They're showing an early Hal Hartley short.*

◆ **shorts** *npl* -1. short trousers that end at one's knees or higher. -2. US men's underpants.

◆ **for short** *adv* as an abbreviation □ *Trinitrotoluene, or TNT for short.*

◆ **in short** *adv* a phrase that introduces a final conclusion or a summary of what has just been said □ *It is up-to-date, carefully researched and fully illustrated. In short, this is an indispensable reference book.*

◆ **nothing short of** *adv* a phrase used to emphasize how good, surprising etc something is □ *Her recovery was nothing short of miraculous.*

◆ **short of** *prep* **short of doing sthg** apart from doing sthg □ *Short of going there yourself, there's nothing you can do to stop them.*

shortage [ˈʃɔːʳtɪdʒ] *n* [of fuel, water, supplies] a

situation where there is not enough of something □ *There is a shortage of cheap housing in this area.*

short back and sides *n* GB a man's haircut where the back and sides are cut shorter than the top.

short black *n* AUS an espresso coffee.

shortbread ['ʃɔːʳtbred] *n* a type of cookie made with flour, sugar, and a lot of butter.

shortcake ['ʃɔːʳtkeɪk] *n* US a crisp cake served with layers of fruit, cream etc. **-2.** GB = **shortbread.**

short-change *vt* **-1.** [customer] to give <sb> too little change for something that they have just paid for in a store, restaurant etc. **-2.** [person, company] to behave dishonestly or unfairly toward <sb>, usually by giving them less than they should get □ *We have been short-changed by the management.*

short circuit *n* the failure of an electrical circuit because of damage or a faulty connection.

◆ **short-circuit** ◇ *vt* [system, machine, device] to make <sthg> have a short circuit □ *Don't do that, you'll short-circuit all the lights.* ◇ *vi: The system had short-circuited.*

shortcomings ['ʃɔːʳtkʌmɪŋz] *npl* weaknesses or faults in somebody or something □ *She has her shortcomings like everyone else, but I really like her.* □ *He pointed out the numerous short-comings of this form of banking.*

shortcrust pastry ['ʃɔːʳtkrʌst-] *n* GB pastry that is crisp and that crumbles very easily.

short cut *n* **-1.** a quick way to get somewhere □ *Let's take a short cut across the fields.* **-2.** a quick method for doing something □ *There are no short cuts to making good pastry!*

shorten ['ʃɔːʳtn] ◇ *vt* **-1.** [visit, vacation, time] to make <sthg> shorter in time □ *In the future it will be possible to shorten people's working week.* **-2.** [skirt, rope, name] to make <sthg> shorter in length □ *The skirt fits me around the waist, but the length needs shortening.* ◇ *vi* [days, nights] to become shorter in time.

shortening ['ʃɔːʳtnɪŋ] *n* a fat, such as butter, that is used for making pastry or dough.

shortfall ['ʃɔːʳtfɔːl] *n* **a shortfall in sthg** [in payments, profits] the amount by which sthg is less or lower than what was expected, needed, or hoped for □ *We envisage a shortfall of around five million dollars.*

shorthand ['ʃɔːʳthænd] *n* **-1.** a way of writing that uses signs instead of words, and is used as a quick and easy way to record what somebody is saying □ *I write all my notes in shorthand.* **-2.** a shorter way of referring to something long or complicated □ *"Restructuring" is their shorthand for substantial job losses.*

shorthanded [ˌʃɔːʳtˈhændəd] *adj* **to be short-handed** to be short of staff or workers for a particular job.

shorthand typist *n* GB a person who types and does shorthand, usually in an office.

short-haul *adj* [jet, flight] that travels or involves only short distances □ *You don't get much food on short-haul flights.*

short list *n* a list of a small number of people, things etc, that have been chosen from a larger number and from which the final choice will be made □ *The movie was on the short list for the BAFTA awards.*

◆ **short-list** *vt* **to be short-listed for sthg** [for a prize, job] to be put on the short list for sthg □ *Her novel was short-listed for the Pulitzer Prize.*

short-lived [-ˈlɪvd] *adj* [success, happiness, protest] that does not last a long time □ *Unfortunately their victory was to prove short-lived.*

shortly ['ʃɔːʳtlɪ] *adv* soon □ *Our guests should be arriving shortly.* □ *They met in the summer and became engaged shortly afterward.*

short-order cook *n* US a cook who makes food that can be prepared quickly.

short-range *adj* **-1.** [missile, weapon] that is designed to travel only short distances. **-2.** [forecast, plan] that covers only a short time ahead.

short shrift [-ˈʃrɪft] *n* **to give sb short shrift** to pay little attention to what sb says.

shortsighted [ˌʃɔːʳtˈsaɪtəd] *adj* **-1.** [person] who cannot see far-off objects well, but can see things that are very close □ *My mother has gotten very short-sighted with age.* **-2.** [person, decision, policy] that is unwise because it does not take account of what may happen in the future □ *I think their approach to the problem is very shortsighted.*

short-staffed [US -ˈstæft, GB -ˈstɑːft] *adj* **to be short-staffed** [company, store, school] to have too few staff □ *You'll have to forgive us, we're rather short-staffed at the moment.*

short-stay parking *n* GB = **short-term parking.**

short story *n* a piece of writing about imaginary characters and events that is much shorter than a novel and often only a few pages long □ *a book of short stories.*

short-tempered *adj* [person] who gets angry very easily □ *Alan can be extremely short-tempered at times.*

short-term *adj* **-1.** [effects, developments] that will happen or take effect soon □ *What are the short-term implications of these cuts?* **-2.** [problem, solution] that lasts or has an effect only for a short time □ *These are just short-term measures.*

short-term parking *n* US parking in a lot where vehicles may only be parked for a few hours at a time.

short time *n* **on short time** GB working for a shorter period of time than usual □ *Workers have been put on short time.*

short wave *n* a type of radio transmission that uses wavelengths less than 60 meters long □ *a short wave radio.*
NOTE: Compare **long wave, medium wave.**

Shoshone [ʃouˈʃounɪ] (*pl* **Shoshone** OR **Shoshones**) *n* a member of a Native American people who used to live in the southwestern USA; the language of this people.

Shostakovich [ˌʃɒstəˈkouvɪtʃ], **Dmitri** (1906–1975) a Russian composer who wrote 15 symphonies, and piano and chamber music.

shot [ʃɒt] ◇ *past tense & past participle of* **shoot**.

◇ *n* -1. the action of firing a gun, or the noise that it makes □ *Several shots rang out.* □ *He fired four shots from a pistol.* □ *a rifle shot.* ■ **like a shot** [run, go] very quickly □ *If someone offered me a job in New York, I'd go there like a shot.* -2. **a good/bad/poor shot** a person who shoots well/badly/poorly □ *He's an excellent shot.* -3. SPORT & GAMES the action of kicking, throwing, hitting etc a ball when trying to score a point □ *He took a shot at the goal.* □ *Good shot!* -4. PHOTOGRAPHY a photograph □ *There were some nice shots of Martin in Spain.* -5. CINEMA a part of a movie that is seen as a single picture □ *The movie has some beautiful shots of Venice.* -6. **to have a shot at sthg** to try to do sthg (informal use) □ *I'll have a shot at it.* -7. [of morphine, heroin] an injection of a drug or vaccine □ *a typhoid shot.* -8. [of whiskey, gin] a small amount of a strong alcoholic drink □ *a shot of brandy.*

shotgun [ˈʃɒtgʌn] *n* a gun that fires cartridges with lots of small pellets inside them.

shot put *n* **the shot put** a sporting event in which competitors throw a very heavy metal ball, called a shot, as far as they can.

should [*stressed* ʃʊd, *unstressed* ʃəd] *modal vb* -1. **you shouldn't drink and drive** it is your duty or responsibility not to drink and drive □ *Strictly speaking, we should let her family know where she is.* □ *You should have been more careful!* -2. **should I tell him?** do you think it is a good idea to tell him? □ *I think we should call the police.* □ *You should go and see someone about that bad back of yours.* -3. **she should be home soon** it is very likely that she will arrive home soon □ *It shouldn't take long to fix the dishwasher.* □ *My letter should have gotten there by now.* -4. **they should have won the game** everyone expected them to win the game because they are the best, but they did not □ *She should have married John.* -5. used in "that" clauses describing a decision, arrangement, wish, opinion etc □ *It's funny that you should say that.* □ *We decided that nothing should be said about it.* -6. **should you be invited** if you are invited (formal use) □ *If anyone should ask for me, I'll be at the office.* -7. **I should think it'll take an hour** I think it will take an hour, but I am not sure □ *I should say he's in his late thirties.*

shoulder [ˈʃəʊldəʳ] ◇ *n* -1. [of a person] the part of one's body on either side of one's neck where one's arms join one's body □ *I've pulled a muscle in my shoulder.* ■ **to look over one's shoulder** to turn one's head to look behind, without turning the rest of the body. ■ **a shoulder to cry on** a person who will listen sympathetically to somebody's problems □ *Look, if you ever need a shoulder to cry on, I'm here.* ■ **to rub shoulders with sb** to meet sb, especially a famous person, and socialize with them as an equal □ *I love rubbing shoulders with the stars!* -2. [of a dress, shirt, jacket] the part of a piece of clothing where the sleeve meets the part covering one's body □ *a jacket with padded shoulders.* -3. [of lamb,

pork, beef] a piece of meat from the shoulder of an animal.

◇ *vt* -1. [weight, load, bag] to put <sthg heavy> on one's shoulders in order to carry it □ *He shouldered the sack and climbed the ladder.* -2. [responsibility, blame] to accept <sthg> oneself □ *Thirty percent of the population have to shoulder the entire costs of the health service.*

shoulder bag *n* a bag with a long strap that can be carried over the shoulder.

shoulder blade *n* one of two large, flat, triangular bones at the top of one's back.

shoulder-length *adj* [hair] that is long enough to reach the shoulders.

shoulder pad *n* a pad of material or foam that is put in the shoulder of a piece of clothing to give it a better shape.

shoulder strap *n* -1. [on a dress] one of two narrow strips of fabric on a dress, sun top etc that go over the shoulders. -2. [on a bag] a long strap on a bag or case that allows it to be carried over the shoulder.

shouldn't [ˈʃʊdnt] = **should not**.

should've [ˈʃʊdəv] = **should have**.

shout [ʃaʊt] ◇ *n* -1. a loud cry or call that somebody makes because they are angry, excited, or trying to be heard over a lot of other noise □ *shouts of joy/delight/protest/anger.* -2. **its my/your shout** GB & AUS it's my/your turn to buy drinks for everybody. ◇ *vt* to say <sthg> very loudly □ *"Stop!" she shouted.* □ *The crowd started shouting insults at the speaker.* ◇ *vi* to speak very loudly □ *I had to shout to make myself heard.* ■ **to shout at sb** to speak angrily and in a loud voice to sb □ *She's always shouting at the children.*

◆ **shout down** *vt sep* **to shout sb down** [speaker, opponent] to stop sb from talking, or being heard, by shouting □ *Trimble was shouted down by a hostile crowd.*

◆ **shout out** *vt sep* **to shout sthg out** [warning, command] to shout sthg suddenly.

shouting [ˈʃaʊtɪŋ] *n* the noise made when somebody shouts.

shove [ʃʌv] (informal use) ◇ *n* **to give sb/sthg a shove** to push sb/sthg with a quick, often violent, movement. ◇ *vt* -1. [person, car] to push <sb/sthg> somewhere with a quick, often violent, movement □ *We shoved the car out of the road.* -2. [clothes, books, object] to put <sthg> somewhere, often roughly or carelessly □ *He shoved his clothes into a bag.*

◆ **shove off** *vi* -1. [boat] to leave the shore □ *We shoved off and floated slowly downstream.* -2. to go away (informal use) □ *Oh, shove off!*

shovel [ˈʃʌvl] (US *pt* & *pp* **shoveled**, *cont* **shoveling**, GB *pt* & *pp* **shovelled**, *cont* **shovelling**) ◇ *n* a tool with a square or rounded blade fixed to a long handle that is used for moving coal, snow, earth etc. ◇ *vt* -1. [coal, snow, earth] to move <sthg> using a shovel □ *Shovel the earth to one side.* -2. to put <a lot of food> into one's mouth quickly □ *They shoveled the food into their mouths as if they hadn't eaten for days.*

show [ʃəʊ] (*pt* **showed**, *pp* **shown** OR **showed**)

◇ *n* **-1.** [at a theater, on the radio, TV] a program that is made to entertain people □ *a variety/quiz show* □ *the Ken Diamond Show.* **-2.** [of animals, cars, flowers] an organized event at which things are shown to the public and sometimes judged to decide which of them is best □ *a dog/flower/agricultural show.* ■ **to be on show** to be in a place where it can be seen by the public □ *Her most recent paintings are on show at the Towner Gallery.* **-3. to be for show** to exist or be done only to impress people □ *All that fancy sports gear is just for show.* ■ **to put up** OR **make a show of sthg** [of interest, annoyance] to pretend to feel sthg □ *I made a show of enjoying the meal even though I hate fish.*

◇ *vt* **-1.** to allow somebody to see <sthg>, e.g. by holding it out or pointing to it □ *Can I show you his letter?* □ *I showed my work to the chief designer.* □ *Please show your ticket.* □ *An optional 12% service charge is shown on the bill.* ■ **to show oneself, to show one's face** to allow oneself to be seen □ *I'd be ashamed to show myself in public if I were him!* □ *He won't dare show his face around here again.* ■ **to have something/nothing to show for sthg** [for one's work, time, effort] to have achieved something/nothing as a result of sthg □ *He doesn't have much to show for his expensive education.* □ *All that hard work and what have I got to show for it? Nothing!* **-2.** [picture, diagram, piece of writing] to give information about <sthg>; [thermometer, dial, gauge] to have <a particular number, time, date> etc on it □ *The exhibition shows what life was like in Roman Britain.* □ *The barometer was showing "Change".* **-3. to show sb how to do sthg** to teach sb how to do sthg, especially by doing it oneself □ *Show me how to use the word processor.* □ *I'll show you how to get there.* ■ **to show sb the way** [to the station, bank, exit] to tell sb how to get to a place, especially by going there with them □ *The porter will show you to your room.* **-4.** [courage, enthusiasm, understanding] to behave in a way that makes other people see that one has <a particular feeling or attitude> □ *If she was disappointed, she didn't show it.* □ *He's shown us nothing but kindness.* **-5. to show that...** to prove that a particular fact or situation is true or exists □ *There's no evidence to show that he was responsible.* □ *It just shows how careful you have to be.* □ *The results show a big improvement.* **-6. to show sb to a place** to lead sb to a place □ *Can I show you to your seat?* □ *I'll show you to the door.* **-7.** [movie, program, documentary] to make <sthg> available as entertainment for the public □ *What are they showing at the Odeon?* **-8. to show a profit/loss** [company, venture] to have made a profit/loss □ *The company is showing a loss of $15 million.* **-9.** [painting, animal, product] to put <sthg> in a public place so that it can be seen and judged by people □ *These drawings have never been shown together before.* □ *I started breeding poodles to show them around five years ago.*

◇ *vi* **-1.** [anger, relief, stain] to be easy to see □ *If she was disappointed, it didn't show.* □ *The scar hardly shows now.* □ *Does my bra show through this shirt?* **-2. to be showing** [movie] to be appearing as entertainment for the public □ *Is "Dracula" still showing at the Odeon?*

◆ **show around** *vt sep* **to show sb around** to take sb to the most important parts of a place they are visiting for the first time □ *There was a guide who showed us around the museum.* □ *If you ever come to New York I'd be happy to show you around.*

◆ **show in** *vt sep* **to show sb in** [visitor, person, candidate] to lead sb into a place □ *I've shown Mr Lee into your office.* □ *"Ms Harper is here." — "Good, show her in."*

◆ **show off** ◇ *vt sep* **to show sb/sthg off** [new car, clothes, baby] to let people see sb/sthg that one is proud of □ *She couldn't wait to get back and show off her suntan.* ◇ *vi* [person] to behave in a way that attracts attention because one wants to be admired □ *Ignore him, he's only showing off in front of his friends.*

◆ **show out** *vt sep* **to show sb out** [visitor, person] to lead sb out of a place □ *It's OK, I'll show myself out.*

◆ **show round** *vt sep* GB = **show around**.

◆ **show up** ◇ *vt sep* **to show sb up** to make sb who one is with feel embarrassed by behaving badly in public □ *I just prayed that the children wouldn't show me up too much.* ◇ *vi* **-1.** [feature, stain, color] to be easy to see □ *The sunset didn't show up well in the photograph.* **-2.** [at the office, restaurant] to arrive at a place where one is expected □ *We started to worry when she didn't show up for work.*

showbiz ['ʃəʊbɪz] *n* = **show business** (informal use).

show business *n* the business, work, or profession of popular entertainment, e.g. singing, dancing, and acting.

showcase ['ʃəʊkeɪs] *n* **-1.** [in a museum, exhibition, store] a glass case in which valuable objects are placed for people to look at. **-2. to be a showcase for sb/sthg** a situation, event etc in which sb/sthg can display their talents □ *The concerto is a real showcase for the young pianist.*

showdown ['ʃəʊdaʊn] *n* **to have a showdown with sb** to have a serious argument with sb at the end of a long period of disagreement and angry feelings.

shower ['ʃaʊəʳ] ◇ *n* **-1.** a device that one stands under to wash one's body, consisting of a long hose with a flat piece at one end with a lot of small holes in it through which water flows □ *A double room with shower costs $50.* ■ **to have** OR **take a shower** to wash oneself using a shower □ *I have a cold/hot shower every morning.* **-2.** WEATHER a fall of rain, snow, or sleet that lasts only a short time □ *a shower of rain* □ *scattered showers* □ *a snow shower.* **-3. a shower of sparks/confetti etc** a lot of sparks/confetti etc falling through the air □ *a shower of spray/water.* **-4. a shower of abuse/praise etc** a lot of abuse/praise etc that comes all at the same time □ *The opening of the exhibition was accompanied by a shower of criticism from traditionalists.* **-5.** US [for a woman] a party that is held for a woman by her friends before a particular special occasion and at which they give her presents □ a bridal/baby/engagement shower.

◇ vt -1. [person, ground] to scatter lots of small light objects on <sb/sthg>. -2. **to shower sb with sthg, to shower sthg (up)on sb** [with presents, kisses, insults] to give sb a large number of sthg.

◇ vi to have a shower □ He likes to shower after he's been swimming.

shower cap n a cap worn in the shower to cover one's hair and keep it dry.

showerproof [ˈʃaʊəˈpruːf] adj [coat, fabric] that will keep the wearer dry but is not fully waterproof.

showery [ˈʃaʊərɪ] adj [weather, day] that is full of rain showers.

showing [ˈʃəʊɪŋ] n a presentation of a movie at a movie theater □ We went to the earlier showing.

show jumping [-dʒʌmpɪŋ] n a sporting competition in which the skill and speed of a horse and its rider are judged when they jump over a series of fences.

showman [ˈʃəʊmən] (pl showmen [-mən]) n -1. a person whose job is producing things for public entertainment such as musicals and plays □ a circus showman. -2. a person who presents things in an entertaining way and is good at attracting public attention.

showmanship [ˈʃəʊmənʃɪp] n an ability to present something in an interesting and entertaining way □ His showmanship saved the lecture from being boring.

shown [ʃəʊn] past participle of **show**.

show-off n a person who likes to show off (informal use) □ He's such a show-off!

show of hands n a method of voting in which people raise their hands to show their support for, or opposition to, somebody or something □ The vote was taken by a show of hands.

showpiece [ˈʃəʊpiːs] n the best thing in a collection, exhibition etc that is proudly shown to other people □ The real showpiece of the exhibition is a 1954 Cadillac.

showroom [ˈʃəʊruːm] n a large room, or part of a store, where examples of goods for sale can be looked at before they are bought □ a car showroom.

showy [ˈʃəʊɪ] (compar **showier**, superl **showiest**) adj [car, clothes] that is very bright and colorful and attracts people's attention (disapproving use) □ Rachel is too showy for my liking.

shrank [ʃræŋk] past tense of **shrink**.

shrapnel [ˈʃræpnl] n small pieces of metal scattered when a bomb or shell explodes □ a piece of shrapnel □ a shrapnel wound.

shred [ʃred] (pt & pp **shredded**, cont **shredding**) ◇ n -1. [of paper, cloth, meat] a long thin piece of something □ shreds of lettuce □ The cat tore the book to shreds with its claws. -2. **not a shred of truth/evidence** no truth/evidence at all □ They haven't a shred of proof to back up

these allegations. □ without a shred of doubt.

◇ vt [cabbage, lettuce, paper] to cut or tear <sthg> into shreds.

shredder [ˈʃredər] n -1. [for food] a machine that shreds food. -2. [for paper] a machine that shreds paper into tiny pieces that cannot be read.

shrew [ʃruː] n a very small brown rodent with a long pointed nose.

shrewd [ʃruːd] adj [person] who is good at understanding what a person or situation is really like, and can use this knowledge to gain an advantage □ She's a shrewd judge of character. □ You made a very shrewd decision to sell when you did.

shriek [ʃriːk] ◇ n [of laughter, terror, pain] a loud, sharp, high-pitched cry □ shrieks of laughter. ◇ vt to say <sthg> with a shriek □ "Let me go!" she shrieked. ◇ vi to give a shriek □ She shrieked with laughter.

shrill [ʃrɪl] adj [voice, whistle] that is high-pitched and unpleasant to hear or listen to □ Her shrill voice echoed in my ears.

shrimp [ʃrɪmp] (pl **shrimps** OR **shrimp**) n a small shellfish with a curved tail that goes pink when cooked.

shrimp cocktail n US a dish, often eaten at the beginning of a meal, that consists of shrimps, lettuce, and a sauce.

shrine [ʃraɪn] n a place where people go to worship, that has a special connection with a particular god, saint etc.

shrink [ʃrɪŋk] (pt **shrank**, pp **shrunk**) ◇ vt [dress, sweater, blanket] to make <a piece of cloth or clothing> smaller, usually by washing it. ◇ vi -1. [person, piece of clothing] to become smaller □ My dress has shrunk in the wash. -2. [profits, trade, popularity] to decrease □ His popularity rating had shrunk to a mere 15%. -3. **to shrink away from sthg** to draw back from sthg □ He shrank away from the body in horror. -4. **to shrink from sthg** [from a task, duty] to avoid sthg because one finds it unpleasant □ He shrinks from any kind of commitment. ◇ n a psychoanalyst or psychiatrist (informal use).

shrinkage [ˈʃrɪŋkɪdʒ] n [in staff, production] an amount by which something gets smaller □ We have to allow for some shrinkage in sales/demand.

shrink-wrap vt [food, product] to wrap <sthg> in a type of plastic that clings very tightly to its shape.

shrivel [ˈʃrɪvl] (US pt & pp **shriveled**, cont **shriveling**, GB pt & pp **shrivelled**, cont **shrivelling**) ◇ vt [skin, plant] to take the moisture from <sthg> so that it becomes dry and wrinkled □ The heat had shriveled up all our seedlings. ◇ vi [plant, skin] The seedlings had all shriveled in the heat.

Shropshire [ˈʃrɒpʃər] a county in western central England. SIZE: 3,490 sq kms. POPULATION: 400,800. ADMINISTRATIVE CENTER: Shrewsbury.

shroud [ʃraʊd] ◇ n a cloth that is put around a dead body before it is buried. ◇ vt **to be shrouded in sthg** [in darkness, fog, secrecy] to be hidden by sthg □ *The whole crime was shrouded in mystery.*

Shrove Tuesday [ˌʃroʊv-] *n* in the Christian calendar, the day before the beginning of Lent.

shrub [ʃrʌb] *n* a plant that is similar to, but smaller than, a tree, and that has several woody stems instead of a trunk.

shrubbery [ˈʃrʌbərɪ] (*pl* **shrubberies**) *n* an area in a garden where several shrubs are planted together.

shrug [ʃrʌg] (*pt* & *pp* **shrugged**, *cont* **shrugging**) ◇ *n* the act of raising one's shoulders to show that one is not sure, is not interested, or does not know something □ *Janet answered with/gave a shrug.* ◇ *vt* **to shrug one's shoulders** to raise one's shoulders in a shrug. ◇ *vi*: *He could only shrug and smile.*

◆ **shrug off** *vt sep* **to shrug sthg off** [remark, criticism, problem] to ignore sthg or act as if it is not important □ *It's difficult to shrug off that kind of criticism.*

shrunk [ʃrʌŋk] *past participle of* **shrink**.

shrunken [ˈʃrʌŋkən] *adj* that has become smaller and looks less healthy, less impressive etc.

shucks [ʃʌks] *excl* US a word used to express embarrassment, annoyance, or disappointment (informal use).

shudder [ˈʃʌdəʳ] ◇ *n* [of fear, horror, cold] an act of shuddering □ *He gave a shudder of disgust.* ◇ *vi* **-1.** [person] to shiver suddenly, violently, and uncontrollably for a moment □ *He shuddered with fear/horror/disgust.* ■ **I shudder to think** a phrase used to indicate that something is too unpleasant, horrifying etc to think about □ *"What will she do next?" — "I shudder to think." □ I shudder to think what could have happened.* **-2.** [machine, vehicle] to shake suddenly and violently □ *The engine shuddered into life.*

shuffle [ˈʃʌfl] ◇ *vt* **-1. to shuffle one's feet** to move one's feet around while standing in one place, e.g. because one is bored or embarrassed □ *He stood there, shuffling his feet to keep warm.* **-2. to shuffle cards** to mix up playing cards so that they are not in any particular order □ *The dealer shuffles the deck.* ◇ *vi* **-1.** to walk without lifting one's feet off the ground properly □ *He shuffled into/out of the room.* **-2.** to move one's feet while standing or one's bottom while sitting, e.g. because one is bored or embarrassed □ *They shuffled impatiently in their seats.*

shun [ʃʌn] (*pt* & *pp* **shunned**, *cont* **shunning**) *vt* [person, publicity] to deliberately avoid having any contact with <sb/sthg> □ *Throughout his life Beckett shunned the glare of the media.*

shunt [ʃʌnt] *vt* **-1.** [wagon, car] to push or pull <sthg> from one piece of railroad to another. **-2.** [person, furniture, luggage] to move <sb/sthg> to a different place □ *I've been shunted around from one department to another.*

shunter [ˈʃʌntəʳ] *n* an engine that is used to shunt railroad cars.

shush [ʃʊʃ] *excl* a word used to tell somebody, especially a child, to be quiet □ *Shush! It's time to go to sleep.*

shut [ʃʌt] (*pt* & *pp* **shut**, *cont* **shutting**) ◇ *adj* **to be shut** [window, store, eyes] not to be open □ *Are you sure all the doors were shut?* ◇ *vt* **-1.** [window, door] to change the position of <sthg> so that it is no longer open; [box, case] to cover <sthg> with a lid, top etc so that it is no longer open □ *Shut the windows before you go out. □ The suitcase was so full I couldn't shut it.* ■ **shut your mouth** OR **face!** ▽ be quiet! (very informal use). **-2.** [store, office] to stop <sthg> from operating or doing business □ *They shut the office early on Fridays.* ◇ *vi* [window, eyes, office] *What time do the banks shut?*

◆ **shut away** *vt sep* **-1. to shut sb away** [criminal] to put sb in prison □ *I think rapists should be shut away for life.* ■ **to shut oneself away** to deliberately avoid seeing or meeting other people □ *She shuts herself away in her room all day.* **-2. to shut sthg away** [valuables, treasure, jewelry] to put or keep sthg in a safe place where nobody can see it □ *The jewels are shut away in a safe somewhere.*

◆ **shut down** ◇ *vt sep* **to shut sthg down** [factory, business, theater] to stop sthg from operating, for a short time or for ever □ *The reactor had to be shut down while repairs were carried out. □ They've shut down the local car plant.* ◇ *vi* [factory, business] *The restaurant shut down last year.*

◆ **shut in** *vt sep* **to shut sb/sthg in** [person, animal] to close the door, windows etc of a room or building so that sb/sthg cannot get out □ *They shut the dog in by mistake.*

◆ **shut out** *vt sep* **-1. to shut sb/sthg out** [person, animal, noise] to stop sb/sthg from getting into a building, room, etc □ *The new curtains shut out the light very effectively.* **-2. to shut sthg out** [thought, feeling, image] to stop sthg from entering or being in one's mind □ *I tried to shut out the pain and keep going.*

◆ **shut up** ◇ *vt sep* **-1. to shut a place up** [factory, store] to close the entrances to a place so that people cannot enter □ *We shut the apartment up completely before leaving on vacation.* **-2. to shut sb/sthg up** [person, animal] to stop sb/sthg from talking or making a noise (informal use) □ *Once he'd started we just couldn't shut him up.* ◇ *vi* [person] to be quiet (informal use) □ *Shut up!*

shutter [ˈʃʌtəʳ] *n* **-1.** [on a window] a wooden or metal cover on the outside of a window that can be opened or closed. **-2.** [in a camera] the part of a camera that opens to let light through the lens when a photograph is being taken.

shuttle [ˈʃʌtl] ◇ *adj* **a shuttle service** a service in which a passenger vehicle, e.g. an aircraft, train, or bus, goes frequently back and forth between two places □ *There's a shuttle service between the airport and the train station.* ◇ *n* a shuttle service; a vehicle that provides this service □ *Let's take the shuttle.* ◇ *vi* [vehicle, person] to make frequent trips between two places □ *He spends half his time shuttling back and forth between New York and Chicago.*

◇ *vt* [passengers, tourists] to take <people> on a shuttle between two places □ *The bus shuttles passengers between terminals.*

shuttlecock ['ʃʌtlkɒk] *n* an object with a rounded point at one end and real or plastic feathers at the other that is hit over a net in the game of badminton.

shy [ʃaɪ] (*pt & pp* **shied**) ◇ *adj* [person] who is nervous and uncomfortable when meeting or talking to other people, especially people they do not know □ *She gave him a shy smile/look.* □ *He was too shy to let her know how he felt.* ◇ *vi* [horse] to move suddenly backward or sideways when surprised or afraid.

◆ **shy away from** *vt fus* **to shy away from sthg** to avoid doing sthg that one does not like or does not feel confident enough to do □ *She shied away from accusing him directly.*

Shylock ['ʃaɪlɒk] a character in Shakespeare's play *The Merchant of Venice*. He is a money-lender who demands a pound of flesh from a character who cannot repay a loan.

shyly ['ʃaɪlɪ] *adv* [look, smile, say] *see* **shy**.

shyness ['ʃaɪnəs] *n*: *see* **shy**.

Siamese [,saɪə'miːz] *n* **a Siamese (cat)** a cat that has pale fur and blue eyes.

Siamese twins *npl* twins who are born with parts of their bodies joined together.

SIB (*abbr of* **Securities and Investment Board**) *n* **the SIB** the official organization responsible for controlling the securities markets in Britain.

Sibelius [sə'beɪlɪəs], **Jean** (1865–1957) a Finnish composer whose best-known work is the orchestral work *Finlandia*.

Siberia [saɪ'bɪərɪə] a large region of northern Asia, covering parts of Russia and Kazakhstan.

sibling ['sɪblɪŋ] *n* a brother or sister (formal use) □ *sibling rivalry.*

Sicilian [sɪ'sɪlɪən] *n & adj*: *see* **Sicily**.

Sicily ['sɪsəlɪ] a large Italian island in the Mediterranean, southwest of Italy. SIZE: 25,708 sq kms. POPULATION: 4,961,383 (*Sicilians*). CAPITAL: Palermo.

sick [sɪk] *adj* -1. [person, animal] ill □ *They care for sick people.* ■ **to be off sick** to be away from work because one is ill. -2. **to feel sick** to feel like vomiting. -3. **to be sick** GB to vomit □ *I ate so much I was almost sick.* -4. **to be sick of sthg** to be annoyed and bored with sthg one does not like, especially because it has continued or because one has done it for much too long □ *I'm sick and tired of his constant moaning.* -5. **to make sb sick** [behavior, opinion] to make sb feel angry and disgusted; [food, drink] to make sb vomit or want to vomit □ *His racist ideas make me sick.* □ *Seafood always makes me sick.* -6. [story, joke] that is tasteless and offensive □ *He has a really sick sense of humor.*

sickbay ['sɪkbeɪ] *n* an area, e.g. on a ship or in a school, where sick people can be treated.

sickbed ['sɪkbed] *n* **sb's sickbed** a bed where sb sick is lying □ *She called me from her sickbed to tell me what had happened.*

sicken ['sɪkn] *vt* to be so unpleasant that it disgusts and makes <sb> feel sick □ *I was sickened by the violence I saw there.*

sickening ['sɪknɪŋ] *adj* -1. [sight, smell] that is so disgusting it makes one feel sick □ *the sickening thud of the executioner's ax.* -2. [person, behavior] that everyone finds very annoying (humorous use) □ *She's so talented, it's sickening.*

sickle ['sɪkl] *n* a tool with a short handle and a curved blade, used for cutting long grass, wheat etc.

sick leave *n* the time that somebody is officially allowed off work because they are ill □ *I get three weeks' sick leave per year.* □ *Mrs Drew is on sick leave.*

sickly ['sɪklɪ] (*compar* **sicklier**, *superl* **sickliest**) *adj* -1. [person, appearance] that looks unhealthy □ *a pale, sickly child.* -2. [smell, taste, color] that is so unpleasant that it makes one feel sick □ *The room was painted a sickly shade of green.*

sickness ['sɪknəs] *n* -1. illness □ *How many working days were lost due to sickness?* -2. GB the act of vomiting □ *She was off for two days with sickness and diarrhea.* -3. a particular illness □ *His sickness has not been diagnosed yet.*

sickness benefit *n* GB money paid by the government to people who are unable to work because they are ill.

sick pay *n* money paid by an employer to somebody who is unable to go to work because they are ill.

sickroom ['sɪkruːm] *n* a room where somebody is ill in bed.

side [saɪd] ◇ *n* -1. [of a room, building, town] one of the two parts of an object or area that are to the left and right of the middle of it □ *Which side of the bed do you sleep on?* □ *New York's Lower East Side.* ■ **from side to side** moving repeatedly in one direction and then in the opposite direction □ *The trees swayed from side to side in the wind.* ■ **on all sides, on every side** in every direction □ *Our troops were being attacked on all sides.* ■ **to put sthg to** OR **on one side** not to do, spend, discuss etc sthg straight away but to leave it until later □ *I put all the bills to one side, until I could afford to pay them.* -2. [of a river, border, fence] the area that lies to the left or right of something □ *I could hear voices on the far side of the wall.* -3. [of a person] the left or right part of a person's body, from their shoulders to their legs; [of an animal] the left or right part of an animal, from the top of its back to the top of its legs □ *He felt a pain in his left side.* □ *The deer was lying on its side.* ■ **at** OR **by sb's side** beside sb □ *She remained at his side during his illness.* ■ **side by side** next to one another and facing the same direction □ *We sat side by side on a large sofa.* -4. [of a coin, cube, piece of cloth] any of the flat surfaces of an object that has two or more surfaces □ *The box had 'This Side Up' stamped on it.* □ *What's on the other side of the cassette?* -5. [of an object, shape] any of the straight edges around the outside of an object □ *A triangle* *has three sides.* **-6.** [of a building, vehicle] one of the two outer surfaces that are not the top, bottom, front, or back of something □ *The car was dented on the passenger's side.* □ *I found a path that went around the side of the house.* **-7.** [of a hill, valley] the sloping part between the top and bottom of a hill or mountain □ *The gorge had steep sides.* **-8.** [in a war, game, debate] one of two groups who are fighting or competing with each other □ *Neither side would give in.* ■ **to be on sb's side** to agree with sb in an argument □ *I always like to be on the winning side.* □ *I'm on your side!* ■ **to take sides** to choose to support somebody in an argument □ *I don't want to take sides.* **-9.** [of a family] the parents, grandparents etc of one's mother or one's father □ *My mother's side of the family came from Germany.* **-10.** [of a problem, argument] one part of a situation; [of somebody's character] one part of somebody's personality or character □ *Can't you see the funny side of it?* □ *I didn't know he had a serious side.* **-11.** US = **side dish** □ *I'll have eggs with a side of wheat toast.* **-12.** *phrases* **to be on the large/small side** to be a little too large/small □ *The coat's a little on the large side, but it'll do.* ■ **to do sthg on the side** to work at sthg in addition to one's regular job, sometimes illegally □ *He's a bus driver, but he does some gardening on the side.* ■ **to keep on the right/wrong side of sb** to make sb feel pleased/annoyed with one □ *I wouldn't like to get on the wrong side of him!* ◇ *adj* [door, entrance] that is situated to the side of something □ *The thieves got in through a side window.*

◆ **side with** *vt fus* **to side with sb** to support sb in an argument □ *The rest of the family all sided with me against Dad.*

sideboard ['saɪdbɔːʳd] *n* a long piece of furniture, usually in a dining room or living room, for keeping glasses, plates etc in.

sideburns ['saɪdbɜːʳnz] US, **sideboards** ['saɪdbɔːʳdz] GB *npl* strips of hair growing down the sides of a man's face.

sidecar ['saɪdkɑːʳ] *n* a small vehicle for one or two passengers that is attached to the side of a motorcycle.

side dish *n* a small dish such as a salad or vegetables that is eaten at the same time as the main dish of a meal.

side effect *n* **-1.** [of a drug, treatment] an effect, usually unexpected and unwanted, that happens in addition to the main intended effect □ *Side effects include vomiting, dizziness and chest pain.* **-2.** [of a situation, decision] an unplanned result that happens in addition to the intended result of something □ *A side-effect of her resignation was the unexpected departure of her secretary.*

sidekick ['saɪdkɪk] *n* a person's helper or companion, who is usually less important than the person they help or spend time with.

sidelight ['saɪdlaɪt] *n* GB one of two small lights beside or below the headlights of a car.

sideline ['saɪdlaɪn] *n* **-1.** something that some-body does in addition to their main job, especially because they enjoy it □ *As a sideline he takes wedding photos.* **-2.** [of a field, court] one of the painted lines that mark the side of a soccer field, tennis court etc □ *He stood watching from the sidelines.* **-3. to be on the sidelines** to be away from the center of attention and not taking part in what is happening □ *I preferred to stay on the sidelines and not get involved in the dispute.*

sidelong ['saɪdlɒŋ] ◇ *adj* [look, glance] toward the side, out of the corner of one's eye □ *Jerry and Chris exchanged sidelong glances.* ◇ *adv*: *They looked sidelong at each other.*

side-on ◇ *adj* [crash, collision] that involves the side rather than the front of something □ *We were involved in a side-on crash with another car.* ◇ *adv* [crash, collide] *The car hit the wall side-on.*

side plate *n* a small plate that is placed on one side of the main plate at meals, and is usually for bread.

side road *n* a small road, often joining a main road.

sidesaddle ['saɪdsædl] *adv* **to ride sidesaddle** to ride with one's legs together on the same side of the horse.

sideshow ['saɪdʃəʊ] *n* a small show, stall, game etc at a fairground.

sidestep ['saɪdstep] (*pt & pp* **sidestepped**, *cont* **sidestepping**) *vt* **-1.** [attacker, blow, obstacle] to step to one side in order to avoid <sb/sthg> □ *He threw a punch but Mandy sidestepped it just in time.* **-2.** [question, problem] to avoid dealing with <sthg> □ *She keeps trying to sidestep the issue by changing the subject.*

side street *n* a small street, often joining a main street.

sidetrack ['saɪdtræk] *vt* **to be sidetracked** to forget what one is doing and give one's attention to something else, usually something less important □ *I'm sorry I'm late, I got sidetracked by a few telephone calls.*

sidewalk ['saɪdwɔːk] *n* US the area at the side of a street or road where people walk □ *Stay on the sidewalk!*

sideways ['saɪdweɪz] ◇ *adj* [movement, look] toward one side □ *He gave a sideways glance into Mr Proctor's office as he walked past.* ◇ *adv* [move, look] *I was thrown sideways by the blast.*

siding ['saɪdɪŋ] *n* a short railroad track beside the main track, used for storing trains and railroad cars when they are not being used.

sidle ['saɪdl] *vi* **to sidle up to sb** to go toward sb in a very quiet way so that they do not notice one □ *He sidled up to me and thrust a package into my hand.*

SIDS (*abbr of* **sudden infant death syndrome**) *n* = **crib death** (technical use).

siege [siːdʒ] *n* **-1.** [of a town, city] a military operation in which an army surrounds a place, attacks it, cuts off supplies etc in order to force the people inside to surrender □ *The city was in a state of virtual siege.* **-2.** [of a house] an operation in which the police surround a building in order to try to force the people inside to come out □ *a police siege.*

Sierra Leone [sɪ,erəlɪ'oun] a country in West Africa, on the Atlantic coast. SIZE: 72,000 sq kms. POPULATION: 4,500,000 (*Sierra Leoneans*). CAPITAL: Freetown. LANGUAGE: English. CURRENCY: leone.

Sierra Nevada -1. **the Sierra Nevada** a mountain range in eastern California, USA. HIGHEST POINT: 4,418 m. -2. **the Sierra Nevada** a mountain range in southeastern Spain. HIGHEST POINT: 3,478 m.

siesta [sɪ'estə] *n* **to have a siesta** to have a short sleep in the early afternoon, especially in order to avoid the hottest part of the day.

sieve [sɪv] ◇ *n* a kitchen tool that consists of a metal or plastic net in a frame and that is used for separating liquids from solids or larger pieces of a substance from smaller ones. ■ **to have a head** OR **memory like a sieve** to forget things very often or very easily (informal use). ◇ *vt* [flour, sugar, soup] to put <sthg> through a sieve.

sift [sɪft] ◇ *vt* -1. [flour, sand] to put <sthg> through a sieve in order to remove the larger lumps. -2. [evidence, facts] to examine <sthg> very carefully in order to decide what is important and what is unimportant. ◇ *vi*: It took all week to sift through the job applications.

sigh [saɪ] ◇ *n* a deep breath that somebody lets out, e.g. when they are sad, relieved, or bored □ He gave a heavy sigh. ■ **to heave a sigh of relief** to give a sigh when one is relieved about something □ Sharon heaved a sigh of relief as she watched her guests finally depart. ◇ *vi* to give a sigh □ She sighed with relief/despair.

sight [saɪt] ◇ *n* -1. **one's sight** the ability to see □ He lost the sight in one eye. -2. [of a person, object] the act of seeing somebody or something □ It was my first sight of the Pacific. ■ **to be in sight** [object, person, place] to be near enough to be seen; [result, solution] to be going to happen soon □ After an arduous trip, our destination was now in sight. □ There seems to be no end in sight to our problems. ■ **to be out of sight** to be hidden or too far away to be seen □ The car zoomed past us and was soon out of sight. □ Get out of my sight this instant! ■ **to catch sight of sb/sthg** to see sb/sthg very briefly, especially by chance □ I caught sight of her leaving the building. ■ **to know sb by sight** to recognize sb although one has never spoken to them □ I don't know him personally, but I know him by sight. ■ **to lose sight of sb/sthg** [of a person, object] to be no longer able to see sb/sthg □ We lost sight of the other ship in the fog. ■ **to lose sight of sthg** [of one's aim, objective] to no longer think about sthg because one is thinking about less important things □ They are so concerned with public relations, the party has lost sight of its real goals. ■ **to shoot on sight** to shoot somebody as soon as one sees them □ We have instructions to shoot on sight anybody caught moving in the vicinity. ■ **at first sight** the first time one sees somebody or something □ At first sight the house seems quite small. □ It was love at first

sight. -3. **a beautiful/terrible etc sight** something beautiful/terrible etc that one sees □ Last night's sunset was a beautiful sight. □ The city was a grim sight after the battle. -4. [of a gun] the part of a gun that one looks through in order to aim at somebody or something. ■ **to set one's sights on sthg/on doing sthg** to be determined to have sthg/to do sthg □ Craig's sights are firmly set on becoming a doctor.
◇ *vt* [criminal, animal, land] to see <sb/sthg that one has been looking for>, often for the first time □ Mrs Pacan has been sighted in a downtown bar. □ Finally the crew sighted land.

◆ **sights** *npl* the famous buildings, monuments etc in a place that are interesting for tourists to visit and see □ I want to go to New York, see the sights and go to lots of shows.

◆ **a sight** *adv* **a sight better/worse** much better/worse.

sighted ['saɪtəd] *adj* [person] who is able to see.

sighting ['saɪtɪŋ] *n* the act of seeing a person, animal, or thing that one has been looking for, often for the first time □ Several whale sightings have been reported this week.

sightseeing ['saɪtsiːɪŋ] *n* the act of visiting a town, city, country etc to see the sights □ He went sightseeing in Rome.

sightseer ['saɪtsiːər] *n* a person who goes sightseeing □ a bus full of sightseers.

sign [saɪn] ◇ *n* -1. [in math, music] a written symbol that has a particular meaning □ a division sign. -2. [from one person to another] a gesture, usually made with one's arms, hands, or head, that is used to ask somebody to do something or to give them information □ They made signs to each other across the crowded room. □ He made a sign at me to keep quiet. -3. [in a street, outside a store] a large piece of wood or metal that has words or a picture on it which gives information, e.g. what or where a place is, how fast people are allowed to drive etc □ The sign says 'No parking'. □ I'm sure I saw a sign for New Orleans back there. □ a street sign □ There was a 'No smoking' sign on the door. -4. **a sign of sthg** [of a person, change, danger] something which shows that sthg exists or is going to happen □ The government claimed there were signs of improvement in the economy. □ There's no sign of him yet. □ I see no sign(s) of an agreement being reached.
◇ *vt* -1. [letter, check] to write one's signature on <sthg> □ We're just waiting for the contract to be signed. ■ **to sign one's name** to write one's name □ Can you sign your name on the receipt? -2. SPORT to begin to employ <a player> by asking them to sign a contract □ Tom Lint has just been signed by Miami.
◇ *vi* to write one's signature on something □ Sign here, please.

◆ **sign away** *vt sep* **to sign sthg away** [ownership, right, claim] to let somebody have sthg by signing an official document.

◆ **sign for** *vt fus* -1. **to sign for sthg** [letter, package] to sign a document to show that one has received sthg □ *Can you sign for this telegram, sir?* **-2.** SPORT **to sign for a team** to sign a contract stating that one now plays for a particular team.

◆ **sign in** *vi* to sign a register or form when one enters a place such as a hotel or company □ *Employees are requested to sign in on entering the building.*

◆ **sign on** *vi* **-1. = sign up. -2.** GB to officially declare that one is unemployed by regularly going to the local social security office and signing a form □ *Jack's been signing on for six months now.*

◆ **sign out** *vi* to sign a register or form when one leaves a place such as a hotel or company □ *Don't forget to sign out on leaving the premises.*

◆ **sign up** ◇ *vt sep* **to sign sb up** [employee, recruit, soldier] to begin to employ sb by asking them to sign a contract □ *He's been signed up by the Marines.* ◇ *vi* [for military service, a course] to sign something such as a form to show that one agrees to work for a particular organization, that one wants to study a particular course etc □ *Have you signed up for the training course yet?*

signal ['sɪgnl] (US *pp* & *pt* **signaled**, *cont* **signaling**, GB *pp* & *pt* **signalled**, *cont* **signalling**) ◇ *n* **-1.** something such as a gesture, sound, or action that gives somebody information or a warning □ *This was the signal for us to leave.* **-2.** RAIL a piece of equipment consisting of green, yellow, and red lights beside a track, which is used to tell train drivers to go or stop □ *a railroad signal.* **-3.** TV & RADIO a sound or light wave that carries information □ *a radio signal.* □ *The signal is very weak for some channels.*
◇ *vt* **-1.** to send signals to <sthg> □ *The brain signals the muscles to contract.* **-2.** [message, warning, intention] to do something to tell somebody <sthg> □ *The cyclist signaled a left turn.* □ *The policeman signaled the car to pull over.* **-3.** [event, change] to be a sign of <sthg> □ *The white flowers signal the arrival of spring.*
◇ *adj* [success, failure] important and noticeable (formal use) □ *There has been a signal failure to communicate in this matter.*
◇ *vi* **-1.** AUTO [driver, cyclist] to do something to show that one is going to stop, turn etc □ *You should always signal before turning.* **-2.** [person] to make a sign with one's hands or head □ *Jan was signaling for us to be quiet.* □ *He signaled for the check.*

signal box *n* GB = **signal tower**.

signalman ['sɪgnlmən] (*pl* **signalmen** [-mən]) *n* a person whose job is to control railroad traffic by operating the signals.

signal tower US, **signal box** GB *n* a small building near a railroad containing the switches to operate the signals.

signatory [US 'sɪgnətɔːrɪ, GB -tərɪ] (*pl* **signatories**) *n* [of an agreement, treaty] a person who has signed something □ *The G7 countries were all signatories to the agreement.*

signature ['sɪgnətʃər] *n* a person's name, written in their own handwriting, often at the end of an official document or letter □ *Greg used to forge his mother's signature.* □ *Could you write your signature on the back, please?*

signature tune *n* a piece of music that is always played at the beginning and end of a particular radio or TV show.

signet ring ['sɪgnət-] *n* a ring worn on one's finger, engraved with an initial or design.

significance [sɪg'nɪfɪkəns] *n* **-1.** [of an event, decision, achievement] importance □ *His decision is of great/no significance to us.* **-2.** [of a warning, sign, saying] the meaning of something, especially when it is not immediately obvious □ *The significance of her words escaped me at the time.* □ *I suddenly understood the full significance of the changes.*

significant [sɪg'nɪfɪkənt] *adj* **-1.** [amount, increase] that is large enough to be noticed □ *This year has seen a significant drop in output.* **-2.** [event, decision, achievement] that is important enough to affect something in the future □ *The decision marks a significant improvement in race relations.* **-3.** [action, gesture, look] that has a special meaning that is not known to everybody □ *It is significant that only one member of the board was present.* □ *She gave him a significant smile.*

significantly [sɪg'nɪfɪkəntlɪ] *adv* [increase, look, wink] *see* **significant**.

signify ['sɪgnɪfaɪ] (*pt* & *pp* **signified**) *vt* [change, acceptance, refusal] to mean or to be a sign of <sthg> □ *Does this signify a new direction in Democratic politics?*

signing ['saɪnɪŋ] *n* **-1.** the use of sign language to communicate with a deaf person. **-2.** GB SPORT a player who has been signed on by a particular team.

sign language *n* a language used by deaf people that involves hand movements rather than sounds to represent words.

signpost ['saɪnpoʊst] *n* a sign beside a road, usually showing the direction or distance to a place.

Sikh [siːk] ◇ *n* a person who believes in or belongs to Sikhism. ◇ *adj*: *a Sikh community/temple.*

Sikhism ['siːkɪzm] *n* an Indian religion that developed from Hinduism in the 16th century.

silage ['saɪlɪdʒ] *n* grass and other crops that have been cut and stored when still green to be used as winter food for animals.

silence ['saɪləns] ◇ *n* [of a person, place] the state of being silent □ *His silence on the issue/about his past intrigues me.* □ *There was an awkward silence.* □ *After a long silence, Martin finally began to speak.* □ *Can we have some silence, please?* ■ **in silence** [sit, wait] without making a sound □ *They sat waiting in silence for the doctor to emerge.* ◇ *vt* **-1.** [child, gun] to stop <sb/sthg> from making a noise □ *The plane has an ingenious system for silencing engine noise.* **-2.** [critic, opponent] to force <sb> to stop saying something or telling people about something, especially when one disagrees with them or wants to keep something secret □ *I'll write my own version of events — that'll silence them!*

silencer ['saɪlənsəʳ] *n* a device attached to something, especially a gun or the exhaust system of a car, to make it quieter.

silent ['saɪlənt] *adj* **-1.** [person] who is not speaking; who usually does not talk very much □ *You have the right to remain silent.* □ *He's the strong silent type.* ■ **to fall silent** to stop speaking, especially suddenly □ *The priest suddenly fell silent, as if he had forgotten his words.* **-2.** [person, law] that does not give any information about a particular subject □ *I prefer to remain silent on the subject.* □ *The rule book is silent on this point.* **-3.** [machine, place, movement] that makes no noise □ *The guns were silent for the first time in days.* □ *The engine is almost silent.* **-4.** [movie] that has no sound or speech. **-5.** [letter] that is not pronounced □ *The "p" in "Ptolemy" is silent.*

silently ['saɪləntlɪ] *adv* [walk, work, move] *see* **silent** □ *Brian sat silently in his chair.*

silent partner *n* US a partner who has invested money in a business but is not involved in running it.

silhouette [,sɪluːˈet] ◇ *n* [of a figure, building] a dark shape seen against a lighter background □ *I could only just make out the house, a dark silhouette against the moonlit sky.* □ *The tree appeared in silhouette.* ◇ *vt* **to be silhouetted against sthg** to appear as a silhouette against sthg □ *He took a fantastic photo of some elephants silhouetted against the sky.*

silicon ['sɪlɪkən] *n* an element that is found in sand and some minerals and that is used in parts for electronic equipment. SYMBOL: Si.

silicon chip *n* a small piece of silicon with electronic components on it that forms part of a computer or transistor circuit.

silicone ['sɪlɪkoʊn] *n* an artificial substance made from silicon that is used to make paint, oil etc □ *a silicone breast implant.*

Silicon Valley an area of western California, USA, that is a major center of the US computer industry.

silk [sɪlk] *n* a smooth soft cloth made from a natural substance produced by silkworms □ *a silk shirt/handkerchief.*

silk screen printing *n* a method of printing patterns on a surface by forcing dye onto it through a stretched piece of silk.

silkworm ['sɪlkwɜːʳm] *n* a type of caterpillar that produces silk fiber to make its cocoon.

silky ['sɪlkɪ] (*compar* **silkier**, *superl* **silkiest**) *adj* **-1.** [hair, cloth] that is soft, smooth, and shiny; [skin] that feels soft and smooth □ *a beautiful piece of silky fabric* □ *Her hands felt silky smooth.* **-2.** [voice] that sounds soft and pleasant □ *a beautiful, silky voice.*

sill [sɪl] *n* a ledge made of wood, metal, or plastic at the bottom of a window.

silliness ['sɪlɪnəs] *n* silly behavior □ *I'm getting annoyed by all this silliness.*

silly ['sɪlɪ] (*compar* **sillier**, *superl* **silliest**) *adj* [person, behavior] that does not seem serious or

sensible □ *You look silly in that tie.* □ *She put on a silly voice.* □ *It was a very silly mistake.*

silo ['saɪloʊ] (*pl* **silos**) *n* **-1.** [on a farm] a round tower used for storing grain. **-2.** MILITARY a place built underground where missiles are kept ready to be fired.

silt [sɪlt] *n* fine sand or mud that is carried along by a river and that can build up into a mass at a bend or in a harbor.

◆ **silt up** *vi* [lake, river] to become blocked with silt.

silver ['sɪlvəʳ] ◇ *adj* [hair, paint] shiny gray-white. ◇ *n* **-1.** a valuable, shiny, gray-white metal. SYMBOL: Ag □ *silver jewelry/cutlery.* **-2.** coins that contain silver, or that are silver in color □ *I'm sorry, I don't have any silver.* **-3.** = **silverware.**

silver foil, silver paper *n* GB metallic paper, usually made of aluminum, used for wrapping food in.

silver-plated [-ˈpleɪtəd] *adj* [knife, spoon, dish] that is covered with a thin coating of silver.

silver screen *n* **the silver screen** the industry or activity of making movies; the screen in a movie theater.

silversmith ['sɪlvəʳsmɪθ] *n* a person whose job is to make and repair objects made of silver.

silverware ['sɪlvəʳweəʳ] *n* **-1.** objects made of silver, especially for eating and serving food. **-2.** US a collective term for knives, forks, spoons etc.

silver wedding *n* the 25th anniversary of a wedding □ *It's our silver wedding anniversary this year.*

silvery ['sɪlvərɪ] *adj* [color, material] that looks like silver.

similar ['sɪmələʳ] *adj* [size, amount] that is almost the same as something else but not exactly □ *Other customers have had similar problems.* □ *They are very similar in content.* □ *My job is similar to yours.* □ *I have something similar at home.*

similarity [,sɪməˈlærətɪ] (*pl* **similarities**) *n*: *see* **similar** □ *There is no similarity between my job and yours.* □ *The similarity was striking.*

similarly ['sɪmələʳlɪ] *adv* **-1.** [similarly dressed/built etc] dressed/built in a similar way □ *It was a vague question which brought a similarly vague response.* **-2. similarly,...** a word used to say that there is a similarity between two actions, events, statements etc □ *The opening gala was a black-tie affair — similarly, formal dress was required for the closing show.*

simile ['sɪməlɪ] *n* an expression that describes something by comparing it with something else using the words "like" or "as".

simmer ['sɪməʳ] ◇ *vt* [soup, stew] to cook <sthg> by keeping it at or just below boiling point. ◇ *vi* [soup, stew] *Leave the vegetables to simmer for 20 minutes or so.*

◆ **simmer down** *vi* to calm down and stop being angry (informal use).

simper ['sɪmpəʳ] ◇ *n* a silly unnatural smile □ *"Oh, yes, please!" she replied, with a girlish simper.* ◇ *vi* to smile in a silly unnatural way □ *He sat simpering at Lisa.*

simple ['sɪmpl] *adj* -1. [explanation, task, problem] that is easy to understand or deal with □ *Look, it's simple: just multiply the two figures together.* □ *It's a simple operation.* □ *Unfortunately it's not as simple as that.* -2. [dress, truth, life] that is basic, not elaborate or complicated □ *The design of the building is very simple.* -3. **for the simple reason** only because □ *I did it for the simple reason that I had no choice.* -4. **to be simple** to have very low intelligence.

simple-minded [-'maɪndəd] *adj* [person] who is not very intelligent.

simpleton ['sɪmpltən] *n* a person who is not very intelligent (old-fashioned use).

simplicity [sɪm'plɪsətɪ] *n* [of an explanation, dress, life] *see* **simple** □ *The simplicity of the style is what first attracted me to it.*

simplification [ˌsɪmplɪfɪ'keɪʃn] *n*: *see* **simplify** □ *The matter needs simplification.*

simplify ['sɪmplɪfaɪ] (*pt* & *pp* **simplified**) *vt* [system, problem, explanation] to make <sthg> more simple □ *It would simplify matters if we could agree on a few things from the start.*

simplistic [sɪm'plɪstɪk] *adj* [view, interpretation, solution] that makes things seem simpler than they really are (disapproving use) □ *Cole's analysis is too simplistic for modern historians to accept.*

simply ['sɪmplɪ] *adv* -1. only □ *I simply wanted to help.* □ *It was simply one more disappointment to add to all the others.* -2. a word used for emphasis □ *You simply must come and see me.* □ *The weather was simply awful.* -3. [live, speak, write] *see* **simple** □ *She always dresses simply but elegantly.* □ *Get rid of unwanted hair simply, but effectively.* □ *a simply furnished room.*

simulate ['sɪmjəleɪt] *vt* -1. [feeling, illness] to pretend to have <sthg> □ *His attempts at simulating enthusiasm seemed to have failed.* -2. [situation, noise, object] to produce the effect of <sthg> □ *We are trying to simulate the conditions you will experience in real life.*

simulation [ˌsɪmjə'leɪʃn] *n* -1. *see* **simulate**. -2. COMPUTING an operation in which a real situation, activity etc is imitated in order to see what it is like or what is likely to happen in the future □ *a computer simulation.*

simulator ['sɪmjəleɪtər] *n* a machine which simulates particular conditions such as the conditions in a spacecraft and is used to train people how to deal with them □ *a flight simulator.*

simultaneous [US ˌsaɪməl'teɪnjəs, GB ˌsɪm-] *adj* [broadcast, translation] that happens at exactly the same time as something else □ *The next program will be a simultaneous broadcast on all channels.*

simultaneously [US ˌsaɪməl'teɪnjəslɪ, GB ˌsɪm-] *adv* [happen, appear] *see* **simultaneous** □ *We both came up with the idea simultaneously.*

sin [sɪn] (*pt* & *pp* **sinned**, *cont* **sinning**) ◇ *n* something that somebody does that breaks a religious law □ *She felt that she had committed a terrible sin.* ■ **to live in sin** to live with a person and have a sexual relationship with them without being married to them (old-

fashioned or humorous use). ◇ *vi* to commit a sin □ *They said he had sinned against God's laws.*

Sinbad ['sɪnbæd] a character in an Arabian folk story. He is a sailor who has many adventures.

since [sɪns] ◇ *prep* from a particular time or event in the past until the present □ *He's worked for them since 1990.* □ *Kim's been feeling much better since her operation.* □ *It's the first drink I've had since Christmas.* ◇ *conj* -1. from a particular time □ *We haven't heard from him since he left home on Thursday.* □ *Since his marriage broke up he's been suffering from depression.* -2. because a particular situation exists □ *Since you're here, you might as well give me a hand with the house.* ◇ *adv* from a particular time □ *They went off to work this morning and I haven't seen them since.* □ *We met at college and we've kept in touch ever since.*

sincere [sɪn'sɪər] *adj* [person] who tells the truth about how they feel or what they think; [hope, thanks, apology] that one really means or feels □ *I don't think you're being altogether sincere with me.* □ *I'd like to offer my sincere congratulations.*

sincerely [sɪn'sɪəʳlɪ] *adv* [believe, hope] *see* **sincere** □ *I sincerely meant what I said last night.* ■ **Sincerely (yours)** US, **Yours sincerely** GB a phrase written at the end of a formal letter before one's signature.

sincerity [sɪn'serətɪ] *n* the quality of being sincere □ *I have doubts about his sincerity.*

sinecure ['saɪnɪkjʊəʳ] *n* a job that one is paid for but that involves very little work.

sinew ['sɪnjuː] *n* a piece of tissue in one's body that attaches a muscle to a bone.

sinewy ['sɪnjuːɪ] *adj* [body, person] that looks lean and has strong muscles.

sinful ['sɪnfl] *adj* -1. [person] who has committed a sin. -2. [act, thought] that is considered to be a sin.

sing [sɪŋ] (*pt* **sang**, *pp* **sung**) ◇ *vt* -1. [tune, lullaby] to perform <a song> by using one's voice to produce musical sounds □ *We stood up to sing the National Anthem.* □ *I'll sing you the words.* -2. [opera, jazz] to perform <sthg> as a trained or professional singer □ *I sing tenor in the choir.* □ *She sang "Carmen".* ◇ *vi* -1. [person] *I wish I could sing as well as you.* -2. [bird] to produce sounds that are like music □ *The birds were singing in the trees.*

singalong ['sɪŋəlɒŋ] US, **singsong** ['sɪŋsɒŋ] GB *n* an occasion when people sing well-known songs together in an informal way.

Singapore [ˌsɪŋgə'pɔː] a country in Southeast Asia, consisting of an island near the end of the Malay Peninsula. SIZE: 618 sq kms. POPULATION: 2,700,000 (*Singaporeans*). CAPITAL: Singapore City. LANGUAGE: English, Chinese, Malay, Tamil. CURRENCY: Singapore dollar.

Singaporean [ˌsɪŋgə'pɔːrɪən] *n* & *adj*: *see* **Singapore**.

singe [sɪndʒ] (*cont* **singeing**) *vt* [clothes, hair] to burn <sthg> slightly.

singer ['sɪŋəʳ] *n* a person who sings □ *I'm afraid*

I'm not a very good singer. □ *He's the lead singer of the group.*

singing ['sɪŋɪŋ] ◇ *adj* **a singing voice** the particular quality of the sounds somebody makes when they sing □ *She has a beautiful singing voice.* ◇ *n* the activity of producing music with one's voice □ *The singing went on for some time.* □ *a singing teacher.*

singing telegram *n* a greeting given to a person who is celebrating their birthday, that is performed by a singer who is paid to do this.

single ['sɪŋgl] ◇ *adj* **-1.** [aim, object] that is the only one □ *His single ambition in life is to become a writer.* □ *There was a single chair in the room.* □ *They didn't have a single copy of the paper left.* ■ **every single** every (used for emphasis) □ *Every single copy has been sold.* □ *I've been out every single night this week.* **-2.** [person] not married □ *He's still single.* ◇ *n* **-1.** GB = **single ticket** □ *A single to York, please.* **-2.** MUSIC a short record, CD, or cassette that usually has only one main song □ *I don't like their new single.*

◆ **singles** *n* a game of tennis in which one person plays against another □ *She challenged me to a game of singles.*

◆ **single out** *vt sep* **to single sb out** to give sb special attention or treatment □ *He was singled out for praise.*

single bed *n* a bed that is big enough for only one person.
NOTE: Compare **double bed**.

single-breasted [-'brestəd] *adj* [coat, jacket] that has only one set of buttons, which are fastened at the center of the front part.
NOTE: Compare **double-breasted**.

single cream *n* GB thin cream that does not contain a lot of fat.
NOTE: Compare **double cream**.

single-decker (bus) [-dekəʳ-] *n* GB a bus that has only one level.

Single European Market *n* **the Single European Market** the economic area formed by the countries of the European Union, where no tax is paid on goods brought from one member country to another.

single file *n* **in single file** in a line with one person in front of the other □ *Please line up in single file.*

single-handed [-'hændəd] *adv* without help from anybody else □ *He sailed across the Atlantic single-handed.*

single-minded [-'maɪndəd] *adj* [person] who has a strong desire to achieve one thing and is willing to work very hard for it □ *She's very single-minded about her career.* □ *I admire Warren's single-minded attitude to sports.*

single-parent family *n* a family in which one parent is bringing up children on his or her own.

single room *n* a bedroom for one person in a hotel □ *I'd like to reserve a single room for three nights.*
NOTE: Compare **double room**, **twin room**.

singles bar *n* a bar where single people can

go to look for somebody to have a romantic or sexual relationship with.

singlet ['sɪŋglət] *n* GB a T-shirt without sleeves and with a low neck that is worn as underwear or for playing sports.

single ticket *n* GB a ticket that is valid for a trip from one place to another, but not for when one travels back.

singsong ['sɪŋsɒŋ] ◇ *adj* [voice, accent] that repeatedly goes up and down in pitch (informal use). ◇ *n* GB = **singalong**.

singular ['sɪŋgjələʳ] ◇ *adj* **-1.** GRAMMAR [word, noun] that indicates there is only one of something □ *The singular form is the same as the plural.* **-2.** [beauty, achievement] very unusual and special □ *There was a singular atmosphere at dinner that night.* ◇ *n* a singular word or form □ *"Furniture" only exists in the singular.*

singularly ['sɪŋgjələʳlɪ] *adv* **singularly brave/unsuccessful etc** brave/unsuccessful etc to an unusual and extreme degree (formal use) □ *He's a singularly talented musician.* □ *I was singularly unimpressed by their behavior.*

Sinhalese [,sɪŋə'liːz] *adj* & *n*: see **Sri Lanka**.

sinister ['sɪnɪstəʳ] *adj* [figure, appearance] that seems evil or likely to cause harm □ *They X-rayed my lungs, and found nothing sinister.*

sink [sɪŋk] (*pt* **sank**, *pp* **sunk**) ◇ *n* a fixed container in a kitchen, bathroom etc that can be filled with water from faucets which are attached to it, and that is used for washing things in □ *the kitchen/bathroom sink.*

◇ *vt* **-1.** to badly damage <a ship or boat> so that it goes below the surface of the water □ *The missile sank the enemy ship.* **-2. to sink sthg into sthg** to cause sthg to go deeply into sthg □ *The dog sank its teeth into his leg.*

◇ *vi* **-1.** [ship, boat] to go below the surface of water or mud □ *The ship sank beneath the waves.* □ *We sank up to our knees in the mud.* **-2.** [sun, moon] to move down in the sky and disappear behind the horizon □ *The sun sank below the horizon.* **-3.** [person, head] to move down into a lower position, especially because one is very tired or because there is nothing to hold one up □ *She sank back into the chair.* **-4.** [hopes, spirits] to become less hopeful □ *My heart sank when I heard the terrible news.* **-5.** [building, foundation, ground] to move below a particular level; [level, water] to go down □ *Venice is sinking into the sea.* **-6.** [numbers, profits] to go down in amount or value □ *My savings had sunk to a few hundred dollars.* **-7.** [voice] to become quieter □ *Her voice sank to a whisper.* **-8. to sink into sthg** [into a coma, sleep] to gradually go from one state into sthg else □ *The family sank even deeper into debt.*

◆ **sink in** *vi* [words, fact, truth] to be completely understood, usually slowly or gradually □ *It hasn't sunk in yet that I'm a father.*

sinking ['sɪŋkɪŋ] *adj* **a sinking feeling** a feeling that things are going to start to go badly.

sinking fund *n* money saved and kept by the government or a company to pay interest on money that is borrowed in the future.

sink unit *n* a piece of kitchen furniture that has a sink, drawers, and doors at the front.

sinner ['sɪnər] *n* a person who has committed a sin.

Sinn Fein [ˌʃɪn'feɪn] *n* a political organization that believes that Northern Ireland should be part of the Irish Republic.

sinuous ['sɪnjuəs] *adj* [movement, dancer] that moves in a smooth and twisting way □ *sinuous curves.*

sinus ['saɪnəs] (*pl* **sinuses**) *n* an empty space in the bones of one's head, behind one's nose.

sinusitis [ˌsaɪnə'saɪtəs] *n* an infection of one's sinuses.

Sioux [suː] *n* a member of a Native American people who used to live in the northern central USA; the language of this people.

sip [sɪp] (*pt* & *pp* **sipped**, *cont* **sipping**) ◇ *n* a very small amount of a drink that somebody drinks □ *Have a sip of my home-made wine.* ◇ *vt* [drink] to drink <sthg> slowly by taking very small amounts into one's mouth □ *She slowly sipped her tea.*

siphon ['saɪfn] ◇ *n* a tube that is used to move liquid from one container to another by the pressure of the air. ◇ *vt* -1. [gasoline, water] to move <a liquid> with a siphon □ *He siphoned the wine into bottles.* -2. [money, resources] to move <sthg> from one place to another.

◆ **siphon off** *vt sep* -1. **to siphon sthg off** [liquid] to remove sthg with a siphon. -2. **to siphon sthg off** [money, resources] to use sthg for a purpose it was not intended for □ *Public funds were siphoned off by corrupt officials.*

sir [sɜːr] *n* -1. a word used to talk to a man in a polite and respectful way □ *How would you like to pay, sir?* -2. in Britain, a title that shows that a man is a knight or a baronet □ *Sir Michael Tippett.*

siren ['saɪrən] *n* a device that makes a loud noise to warn people of an emergency or is used by police cars, ambulances etc traveling to an emergency □ *a police/an ambulance siren.*

sirloin (steak) ['sɜːrlɔɪn-] *n* a piece of meat from the lower back of a cow.

sissy ['sɪsɪ] (*pl* **sissies**) *n* a boy who one thinks behaves more like a girl than a boy (informal and disapproving use).

sister ['sɪstər] ◇ *n* -1. [of a person] a female child of one's father and mother □ *Have you met my sister?* □ *She has a younger/an older sister.* -2. RELIGION a nun. -3. GB [in a hospital] a female nurse who is in charge of one particular section of a hospital □ *She works as a night sister.* -4. [in an organization] a woman who is a member of an organization or movement □ *Brothers and sisters, we will win our fight!* ◇ *adj* [company, ship, newspaper] that is connected to another thing of the same type □ *He works for their sister paper.*

sisterhood ['sɪstərhʊd] *n* a religious or political organization of women.

sister-in-law (*pl* **sisters-in-law** OR **sister-in-laws**) *n* the wife of one's brother; the sister of one's husband or wife.

sisterly ['sɪstərlɪ] *adj* [affection, feeling] that is typical of the close relationship that is expected between sisters.

sit [sɪt] (*pt* & *pp* **sat**, *cont* **sitting**) ◇ *vi* -1. [person, animal] to be in a position in which one's bottom is on a surface and one's body is upright; to put oneself in this position □ *You're sitting on my newspaper/in my chair.* □ *I was sitting at my desk.* □ *Come and sit beside me.* -2. **to sit on sthg** [on a board, council] to be a member of sthg □ *He sits on the housing committee.* -3. [the Senate, court] to be officially open □ *The committee will sit tomorrow to discuss the motion.* -4. [building, object] to be in a particular place □ *The letter sat unopened on my desk.* □ *You might as well use this ticket — it's been sitting around for ages.* -5. *phrase* **to sit tight** to wait for something to happen without doing anything □ *Just sit tight and I'll be back in about half an hour.*
◇ *vt* -1. [child, baby] to make <sb> sit somewhere □ *She sat the baby in the playpen.* -2. GB **to sit an examination** to take an examination □ *I'm sitting two exams next term.*

◆ **sit about, sit around** *vi* to sit somewhere without doing anything, especially because one is lazy or because one is waiting for something to happen □ *Sarah has done nothing but sit around reading newspapers all day.*

◆ **sit back** *vi* -1. to relax □ *Now that the book is published we can sit back and enjoy ourselves.* -2. to do nothing □ *He thinks he can just sit back and let others do the work.*

◆ **sit down** ◇ *vt sep* **to sit sb down** to put sb into a position in which they are sitting □ *She sat him down on the chair.* ◇ *vi* to put oneself into a position in which one is sitting □ *Do sit down, please.*

◆ **sit in on** *vt fus* **to sit in on sthg** [meeting, discussion, class] to be present at sthg without taking part, especially to find out what happens □ *Do you mind if I sit in on your lecture?*

◆ **sit out** *vt sep* -1. **to sit sthg out** [storm, meeting] to wait for sthg unpleasant to end without doing anything □ *It was a terrible game, but I sat it out to the end.* -2. **to sit out a dance** not to take part in a dance □ *Do you mind if we sit this one out?*

◆ **sit through** *vt fus* **to sit through sthg** [meeting, lecture, movie] to stay until the end of sthg, especially sthg boring or unpleasant □ *Miraculously, I sat through the entire concert without falling asleep.*

◆ **sit up** *vi* -1. to move to a position in which one is sitting after being in a position in which one was lying □ *The patient sat up in bed to eat his breakfast.* -2. to stay out of bed late at night □ *I sat up to watch the late-night show.*

sitcom ['sɪtkɒm] *n* a humorous television series based on daily life in which the same characters appear in each episode.

sit-down ◇ *adj* **a sit-down meal/protest** a meal/protest at which people sit down. ◇ *n* GB **to have a sit-down** to sit down to rest.

site [saɪt] ◇ *n* -1. an area of land where an activity takes place □ *The archaeological site is closed to visitors.* -2. the place where something happened or was built □ *There used to be a church on this site.* -3. COMPUTING a specific area on the Internet □ *This is one of the best and most visited commercial Web sites.* ◇ *vt* to build <sthg> in a particular place □ *The factory was sited close to a highway.*

sit-in *n* a protest where people go into a place and refuse to leave □ *Protestors are staging a sit-in at the group's headquarters.*

sitter ['sɪtər] *n* -1. a person who is having their picture painted or their photograph taken. -2. a babysitter.

sitting ['sɪtɪŋ] *n* -1. the serving of a meal at a particular time □ *We're on the list for the first sitting of dinner.* -2. an official meeting of a court, parliament etc.

Sitting Bull [,sɪtɪŋ'bʊl] (1831–1890) a Native American chief who defeated General Custer in the battle of the Little Bighorn.

sitting duck *n* somebody or something that is easy to attack, especially because they cannot move very easily.

sitting room *n* the room in a house where people can sit together and relax □ *We were watching TV in the sitting room.*

sitting tenant *n* GB a person who is renting and living in a house or apartment and can continue to live there when it is sold.

situate ['sɪtjʊeɪt] *vt* -1. [building, town] to build <sthg> in a particular place □ *We have decided to situate the new building to the east of the city.* -2. [fact, idea] to think about <sthg> in connection with similar or related things in order □ *The evidence must be situated in its proper context.*

situated ['sɪtjʊeɪtəd] *adj* **to be situated** to be in a particular place □ *The hotel is situated within walking distance of the beach.*

situation [,sɪtjʊ'eɪʃn] *n* -1. the way things are in a particular place or at a particular time □ *The situation is still not clear.* □ *The present economic situation makes cuts inevitable.* -2. **sb's situation** the way things are in sb's life at a particular time □ *My present situation makes it difficult for me to go out much.* -3. [of a house, office, town] the place where a building, town etc is □ *a highly attractive situation near the beach.* -4. **'Situations vacant'** GB the part of a newspaper where jobs are advertised.

situation comedy *n* = **sitcom** (formal use).

sit-up *n* an exercise for one's stomach muscles that consists of lying on one's back and lifting one's upper body from the ground without using one's arms.

SI unit *n* an international unit of measurement such as a meter, kilogram, or second.

six [sɪks] *num* the number 6; *see also* **five**.

six-shooter [-ʃuːtər] *n* a kind of handgun that holds six bullets.

sixteen [sɪks'tiːn] *num* the number 16; *see also* **fifteen**.

sixteenth [,sɪks'tiːnθ] *num* 16th; number 16 in a series; *see also* **fifteenth**.

sixth [sɪksθ] *num* 6th; number 6 in a series; *see also* **fifth**.

sixth form *n* GB the class, lasting two years, at the end of which students take their A-levels □ *She's in the sixth form.* □ *a sixth-form student.*

sixth-form college *n* GB a school at which students can study for A-levels.

sixth sense *n* a feeling or knowledge about something that one cannot explain because it does not seem to come from real evidence □ *My sixth sense told me I shouldn't have come.*

sixtieth ['sɪkstɪəθ] *num* 60th; number 60 in a series; *see also* **fiftieth**.

sixty ['sɪkstɪ] (*pl* **sixties**) *num* the number 60; *see also* **fifty**.

sizable ['saɪzəbl] *adj* [amount, increase, problem] that is fairly large □ *He receives a sizable pension.*

size [saɪz] *n* -1. [of person, town, problem] the degree to which something is big or small □ *The cost of heating a house will depend on its size.* □ *The animal's sheer size is its best defense.* □ *We had hailstones the size of hens' eggs.* □ *It's difficult to get an idea of the size of the problem.* -2. a standard measurement used to show how big or small clothes, shoes etc are □ *What size do you take?* □ *These pants are about two sizes too big.* □ *My husband has a size 42 chest.* □ *What is your collar/bust size?* □ *Try this jacket on for size.* -3. *phrase* **to cut sb down to size** to do or say something that makes sb realize they are not as important as they think.

◆ **size up** *vt sep* **to size sb/sthg up** [opponent, situation] to consider sb/sthg carefully in order to decide what to do □ *The boxers sized each other up.*

sizeable ['saɪzəbl] *adj* = **sizable**.

-sized [saɪzd] *suffix* added to a word to describe how big or small something is □ *bite-sized pieces of chicken.*

sizzle ['sɪzl] *vi* [food] to make a constant hissing sound when cooking in oil or being grilled □ *sizzling sausages.*

SK *abbr of* **Saskatchewan**.

skate [skeɪt] (*pl sense 3* **skate** OR **skates**) ◇ *n* -1. = **ice skate**. -2. = **roller skate**. -3. a kind of edible flat fish that lives in the sea. ◇ *vi* to move around on ice skates or roller skates □ *It was possible to skate on the pond.* □ *Paul taught me how to skate.* □ *We often go skating on the weekend.*

◆ **skate over, skate around** *vt fus* **to skate over** OR **around sthg** [problem, detail] to avoid dealing with sthg directly and properly □ *The Mayor's reply simply skated around the real issue.*

skateboard ['skeɪtbɔːrd] *n* a board with four wheels attached to the bottom that one stands on and that moves quickly over smooth flat surfaces.

skateboarder ['skeɪtbɔːrdər] *n* a person who rides on a skateboard.

skater ['skeɪtər] *n* -1. a person who skates on

ice. -2. a person who moves along on roller skates.

skating ['skeɪtɪŋ] *n* -1. the activity of skating on ice □ We went skating on the pond. -2. the activity of moving on roller skates □ You can go skating along the boardwalk.

skating rink *n* a place, usually indoors, where one can go ice-skating or roller-skating.

skein [skeɪn] *n* a length of yarn, silk etc wound loosely into a circle.

skeletal ['skelətl] *adj* [person, body, appearance] very thin □ Her arms look almost skeletal!

skeleton ['skelətən] ◇ *adj* **a skeleton service** a service that uses the smallest possible number of people to operate it □ A skeleton service will be operating. ◇ *n* the frame of bones that supports the body of a human or an animal □ a human skeleton □ Several dinosaur skeletons have been discovered in the area. ■ **to have a skeleton in the closet** US OR **cupboard** GB to have a secret about one's life that is embarrassing or shocking.

skeleton key *n* a key which can open many different locks.

skeleton staff *n* the smallest number of people that is needed to operate a service.

skeptic US, **sceptic** GB ['skeptɪk] *n* a person who doubts something that other people believe □ I'm a skeptic when it comes to ghosts.

skeptical US, **sceptical** GB ['skeptɪkl] *adj* [person] who doubts something that other people believe □ I'm very skeptical about her claims.

skepticism US, **scepticism** GB ['skeptɪsɪzm] *n* the quality of being skeptical □ There's been a great deal of skepticism surrounding the new drug.

sketch [sketʃ] ◇ *n* -1. [to draw something] a quick and simple drawing □ The artist made a sketch of the scene. -2. [to describe something] a quick description of something without a lot of details □ I'll give you a brief sketch of what happened. -3. [to entertain people] a short humorous piece usually acted on a television or radio show □ They did a sketch about the election campaign. ◇ *vt* -1. [figure, scene] to draw a sketch of <sb/sthg> □ Turner sketched the Tuscan landscape. -2. [situation, incident] to describe <sthg> briefly □ a beautifully-sketched report on the day's proceedings. ◇ *vi* to draw a sketch □ She enjoys sketching in her garden.

◆ **sketch in** *vt sep* **to sketch sthg in** [facts, background] to tell somebody sthg to help them know more about or understand something □ I'll sketch in the details for you.

◆ **sketch out** *vt sep* **to sketch sthg out** [situation, event] to describe sthg with only the most important or general details □ He sketched out his plans for growth.

sketchbook ['sketʃbʊk] *n* a book that contains sheets of paper for drawing on.

sketchpad ['sketʃpæd] *n* a pad that contains sheets of paper for drawing on.

sketchy ['sketʃɪ] (*compar* **sketchier**, *superl* **sketchiest**) *adj* [knowledge, account, details] that is not complete □ I've only a sketchy idea of what the job involves. □ a sketchy outline of the plot.

skew [skjuː] ◇ *vt* [data, words] to affect or change <sthg> so that it is not completely accurate □ The results of the experiment were skewed by the high proportion of females. ◇ *vi* [car, truck] to change direction suddenly and uncontrollably □ The bus skewed across the road and into a fence.

skewer ['skjuːər] ◇ *n* a long thin rod of metal or wood that holds small pieces of food together while they are being cooked □ Test the meat with a skewer to see if it's cooked. ◇ *vt* [meat, vegetables] to put <sthg> on a skewer.

ski [skiː] (*pt* & *pp* **skied**, *cont* **skiing**) ◇ *n* one of a pair of long flat objects that can be attached to special boots to move quickly over snow □ a pair of skis □ a ski slope □ ski clothes. ◇ *vi* to move on skis □ The first time I skied was on an artificial slope.

ski boots *npl* boots that skis can be attached to.

skid [skɪd] (*pt* & *pp* **skidded**, *cont* **skidding**) ◇ *vi* [car, motorcycle] to slide sideways in an uncontrolled way, e.g. on a wet or icy road □ If you brake suddenly, you'll skid. ◇ *n* the movement made by a vehicle when it skids □ The car went into a skid and hit a tree.

skid mark *n* the mark left on the road when a vehicle skids.

skid row *n* the part of a city where poor, homeless, unemployed, or alcoholic people gather (informal use) □ He ended up on skid row.

skier ['skiːər] *n* a person who skis □ Skiers will be happy with this season's snow.

skiing ['skiːɪŋ] *n* the activity of skiing □ We went skiing in Switzerland. □ a skiing vacation.

ski instructor *n* a person whose job is to teach people how to ski.

ski jump *n* -1. an artificial steep slope that is covered with snow and has a curve at the bottom so that skiers jump up into the air. -2. the sporting event that involves skiing down a ski jump and trying to jump as far as possible.

skilful etc GB = **skillful** etc.

ski lift *n* a set of seats hanging from a metal cable that carry skiers to the top of a ski slope.

skill [skɪl] *n* -1. the ability to do something well □ He showed great skill in negotiating a compromise. -2. the ability to do a particular activity well that one develops as a result of training □ reading/writing/social skills □ The skills you have acquired on the course should stand you in good stead.

skilled [skɪld] *adj* -1. [craftsman, player, politician] who is very good at doing a particular job or activity because they have the training or experience □ She's skilled at OR in negotiation. -2. **skilled work/labor** work/labor that needs special training. ■ **a skilled worker/laborer** a worker/laborer who can do skilled work □ This is a highly skilled job. □ Our staff are highly skilled.

skillet ['skɪlət] *n* US a frying pan.

skillful US, **skilful** GB ['skɪlfl] *adj* [person] who is very good at something that needs a particular ability □ *He's very skillful at getting people to do what he wants.*

skillfully US, **skilfully** GB ['skɪlflɪ] *adv* [work, handle, negotiate] *see* **skillful** □ *She skillfully maneuvered the boat between the rocks.*

skim [skɪm] (*pt* & *pp* **skimmed**, *cont* **skimming**) ◇ *vt* **-1.** [cream, grease, fat] to remove <sthg> from the top of a liquid □ *She skimmed the cream from the top of the milk.* **-2.** [water, surface] to move across <sthg> touching it only very lightly □ *The plane flew low over the lake, just skimming the surface of the water.* **-3.** [article, newspaper] to read <sthg> quickly in order to find out the most important ideas or information □ *I skimmed the passage to answer the questions.* ◇ *vi*: *The stone skimmed across the pond.* □ *I'm afraid I've only had time to skim through the article.*

skim(med) milk [ˌskɪm(d)-] *n* milk from which the fat has been removed.

skimp [skɪmp] ◇ *vt* to spend little money on <sthg>, especially when one needs to spend more. ◇ *vi*: *It's silly to skimp on food.*

skimpy ['skɪmpɪ] (*compar* **skimpier**, *superl* **skimpiest**) *adj* [swimsuit, underwear, meal] that seems too small in size or quantity □ *She was wearing an extremely skimpy little dress.*

skin [skɪn] (*pt* & *pp* **skinned**, *cont* **skinning**) ◇ *n* **-1.** [of a person] the natural outer layer that covers the whole of one's body □ *You have such soft skin.* □ *My skin is very dry.* □ *'This product should not be used on irritated skin.'* □ *a skin rash/disease.* ▪ **to do sthg by the skin of one's teeth** to just succeed in doing sthg □ *I escaped by the skin of my teeth.* ▪ **to jump out of one's skin** to make a sudden movement because one is frightened or surprised □ *The sound of the explosion made me jump out of my skin.* ▪ **to make one's skin crawl** to make one feel disgust. ▪ **to save one's own skin** to save oneself without caring about other people in a dangerous or difficult situation □ *People were crying out for help and all he could think about was saving his own skin.* **-2.** [of a bear, fox] the outer covering of a dead animal's body □ *Animal skins were hanging up to dry.* **-3.** [of an orange, potato] the natural outer layer that covers a fruit or vegetable □ *Potato skins are a useful source of fiber.* **-4.** [on milk, paint] the thick layer that sometimes forms on the surface of a liquid □ *Remove the skin on the custard before serving.*
◇ *vt* **-1.** [bear, potato] to remove the skin of <an animal, fruit, or vegetable> □ *He skinned the rabbit and cooked it on the fire.* **-2.** [knee, knuckle] to remove some of the skin from <a part of one's body> by accident □ *He skinned his knee when he fell from the tree.*

skin-deep *adj* **to be only skin-deep** to be not important or real, although people often think it is at first □ *Beauty is only skin-deep.*

skin diver *n* a person who does skin diving.

skin diving *n* the activity of swimming under water without a special diving suit.

skinflint ['skɪnflɪnt] *n* a person who does not like spending money (disapproving use).

skin graft *n* an operation in which skin is repaired by taking skin from another part of one's body.

skinhead ['skɪnhed] *n* a person with a shaved head or very short hair, often considered to be violent.

Skinner ['skɪnə^r], **B. F.** (1904–1990) a US psychologist who helped to develop the theory of behaviorism.

skinny ['skɪnɪ] (*compar* **skinnier**, *superl* **skinniest**) *adj* [person, body] that is thin in an unattractive way (informal use) □ *a skinny little girl* □ *My legs are too skinny!*

skin test *n* a medical test done by rubbing a substance on somebody's skin or injecting it in order to see if they are allergic to that substance.

skin-tight *adj* [clothes, jeans] very tight.

skip [skɪp] (*pt* & *pp* **skipped**, *cont* **skipping**) ◇ *n* **-1.** a small jump from one foot to the other □ *She gave a little skip and a jump, then laughed.* **-2.** GB a large metal container used to collect large amounts of garbage, e.g. during construction work. ◇ *vt* [class, meal, line] not to do, have, or use <sthg>, usually because one forgets or because one does not want to □ *I was so busy that I skipped lunch.* ◇ *vi* **-1.** to move with skips □ *The little girl skipped home from school.* **-2.** GB to jump over a moving rope that one is holding at each end or that two other people are holding □ *The boxer trained by skipping every day.*

ski pants *npl* trousers with straps at the bottom to fit under the feet, worn for skiing.

ski pole *n* one of a pair of sticks which a skier pushes into the snow in order to move forward or keep their balance.

skipper ['skɪpə^r] *n* **-1.** SAILING the captain of a boat or ship. **-2.** SPORT the captain of a team □ *England's skipper has been replaced.*

skipping rope ['skɪpɪŋ-] *n* GB a rope used for skipping.

ski resort *n* a place in the mountains where many people go to ski.

skirmish ['skɜː^rmɪʃ] ◇ *n* **-1.** MILITARY a short battle. **-2.** a short argument. ◇ *vi* **-1.** MILITARY to be involved in a skirmish. **-2.** to argue.

skirt [skɜː^rt] ◇ *n* a piece of clothing worn by women that hangs from the waist over some or all of the bottom half of their body □ *She was wearing a short skirt.* ◇ *vt* **-1.** [obstacle, area] to avoid <a place or object> by going round the edge □ *The freeway conveniently skirts the town.* **-2.** [problem, question] to avoid speaking about <sthg> □ *The journalist refused to let the Senator skirt the issue.*

◆ **skirt around** *vt fus* **to skirt around sthg** [obstacle, area, problem] to skirt sthg.

skirting board ['skɜː^rtɪŋ-] *n* GB the narrow wooden strip that covers the wall at the level of the floor in a room.

ski stick *n* GB = **ski pole**.

skit [skɪt] *n* a short performance in which actors make fun of politicians and famous people by imitating them.

skittish ['skɪtɪʃ] *adj* -1. [person] who is not very serious and who often changes their mind. -2. [animal] that is nervous and easily frightened.

skittle ['skɪtl] *n* GB a bottle-shaped object made of wood or plastic that is used in a game as something to be knocked over by a ball.
◆ **skittles** *n* a game in which people try to knock over skittles with a ball.

skive [skaɪv] *vi* GB to avoid doing the work one is supposed to do (informal use).

skulduggery [skʌl'dʌgərɪ] *n* secretive and dishonest behavior.

skulk [skʌlk] *vi* to move about somewhere, trying to avoid being seen □ *I felt like a burglar, skulking in the yard.*

skull [skʌl] *n* the set of bones that form the head of people and animals.

skullcap ['skʌlkæp] *n* a small cap that fits the shape of the head, often worn by Jewish men and Catholic priests.

skunk [skʌŋk] *n* a small black and white American animal that produces a bad smell when it is frightened.

sky [skaɪ] (*pl* **skies**) *n* the space that one can see above the earth □ *a blue/cloudy sky.*

skycap ['skaɪkæp] *n* US a person whose job is to carry people's luggage at an airport.

skydiver ['skaɪdaɪvəʳ] *n* a person who goes skydiving.

skydiving ['skaɪdaɪvɪŋ] *n* the sport of jumping from an airplane and falling through the air before opening one's parachute.

sky-high ◇ *adj* [prices, wages] very high (informal use) □ *Interest rates are sky-high at the moment.* ■ **to go sky-high** [property, prices] to become extremely expensive. ◇ *adv* **to blow sthg sky-high** to destroy sthg with a very large explosion; to destroy sthg completely □ *The building was blown sky-high.* □ *My teacher blew my argument sky-high.*

skylark ['skaɪlɑːʳk] *n* a small brown bird that sings while flying high above the ground.

skylight ['skaɪlaɪt] *n* a small window in the roof of a house.

skyline ['skaɪlaɪn] *n* the line formed by the tops of buildings against the sky □ *The new building would damage the city's unique skyline.*

skyscraper ['skaɪskreɪpəʳ] *n* a very tall modern building, usually found in a large city.

slab [slæb] *n* -1. [of concrete, stone] a flat square or rectangular piece of solid material used in buildings, sculpture etc □ *a slab of marble* OR *marble slab* □ *a paving slab.* -2. [of meat, chocolate, cake] a thick piece of food.

slack [slæk] ◇ *adj* -1. [rope, thread] not tight. -2. [business, period] not busy □ *Business is slack at the moment.* -3. [person] who is careless and does not do their work properly □ *Discipline has become extremely slack recently.* ◇ *n* the part of a rope, cord etc that is not pulled tight □ *He pulled in the slack.*
◆ **slacks** *npl* loose casual trousers.

slacken ['slækən] ◇ *vt* -1. [speed, pace] to make

<sthg> slower □ *The horse began to slacken its pace.* -2. [rope, grip] to make <sthg> less tight □ *She slackened her grip on the rope.* ◇ *vi* -1. [speed, pace] *The pace of reform has slackened recently.* -2. [rope, grip] *Her grip slackened.*
◆ **slacken off** *vi* -1. [rain, storm] to become less heavy. -2. [work, business] to become less busy □ *Things have begun to slacken off at work recently.*

slag [slæg] *n* the waste material produced by mines and factories that make iron and steel.

slagheap ['slæghiːp] *n* a pile of waste material from a mine or factory that makes iron and steel.

slain [sleɪn] *past participle of* **slay.**

slalom ['slɑːləm] *n* a skiing or canoe race around a course of obstacles such as poles.

slam [slæm] (*pt* & *pp* **slammed,** *cont* **slamming**) ◇ *vt* -1. [door, gate] to close <sthg> violently so that it makes a loud noise □ *He walked out, slamming the door behind him.* □ *I slammed down the phone.* -2. [politician, organization, decision] to strongly criticize <sb/sthg> in public □ *The reviews all slammed her performance.* -3. **to slam sthg on sthg** to press sthg on sthg else quickly and with a lot of force □ *He slammed his foot on the brakes.* ◇ *vi* [door, gate] *The window slammed shut.*

slander [US 'slændər, GB 'slɑːndə] ◇ *n* something that somebody says that is intended to damage somebody's reputation and is not true □ *We could be sued for slander.* ◇ *vt* to say something that is a slander against <sb>.

slanderous [US 'slændərəs, GB 'slɑːnd-] *adj* [allegation, accusation] that contains slander against somebody □ *Keep your slanderous remarks to yourself.*

slang [slæŋ] *n* the very informal language of a particular group of people, often thought to be unacceptable in serious writing □ *drug slang* □ *prison slang* □ *a slang expression.*

slant [US slænt, GB slɑːnt] ◇ *n* -1. [of a table, shelf, somebody's writing] a line or position that is not horizontal or vertical, but at an angle. ■ **to be on** OR **at a slant** not to be horizontal or vertical, but at an angle □ *The shelves were on a slant.* -2. [on a story, issue] a particular way of thinking about something □ *He might be able to give us a new slant on the problem.* ◇ *vt* [news, evidence] to present <sthg> so that one particular opinion is favored □ *The news report was heavily slanted in favor of the government.* ◇ *vi* [land, roof, table] to be not completely horizontal or vertical □ *The table slants slightly.*

slanting [US 'slæntɪŋ, GB 'slɑːnt-] *adj* [roof, table] that is not completely horizontal or vertical.

slap [slæp] (*pt* & *pp* **slapped,** *cont* **slapping**) ◇ *n* [on somebody's cheek, back] the act of slapping somebody □ *She gave him a slap in the cheek.* ■ **a slap in the face** something that causes somebody to feel insulted because it shows one is not respected or valued □ *Not being promoted was a slap in the face for him.* ◇ *vt* -1. [person, face, back] to hit <sb/sthg>

with the palm of one's hand to hurt them or as a sign of friendship □ *She slapped him in the face.* □ *"Congratulations!" he said, slapping me on the back.* **-2. to slap sthg on sthg** to put sthg quickly and carelessly onto sthg □ *She just slapped the paint onto the wall.* ◇ *adv* exactly (informal use) □ *The parachutist landed slap in the middle of the field.*

slapdash ['slæpdæʃ] *adj* [work, person, attitude] that is not careful enough.

slaphappy ['slæphæpɪ] *adj* [person] who acts in a careless and silly way, as if they are drunk or dizzy.

slapstick ['slæpstɪk] *n* a kind of comedy that depends on silly actions rather than words and is usually simple and direct.

slash [slæʃ] ◇ *n* **-1.** a long deep cut. **-2.** a punctuation mark (/) used to separate words, letters, or numbers that are combined. ◇ *vt* **-1.** [face, material] to make a slash in <sthg> using a sharp object, especially with a quick violent movement □ *She tried to kill herself by slashing her wrists.* **-2.** [rate, price] to reduce <sthg> by a large amount □ *Prices have been slashed in the January sale.*

slat [slæt] *n* one of the small flat pieces of wood, plastic, or metal used in venetian blinds, closet doors etc.

slate [sleɪt] ◇ *n* **-1.** a kind of dark-gray rock that splits into thin flat pieces. **-2.** a square flat piece of slate, used to cover roofs. ◇ *vt* [performance, movie, person] to criticize <sb/sthg> very strongly □ *The movie has been completely slated in the press.*

slatted ['slætəd] *adj* [blind, door] that is made with slats.

slaughter ['slɔːtəʳ] ◇ *vt* **-1.** [cow, pig] to kill <an animal> for food □ *They slaughter the animals for meat.* **-2.** [civilians, protesters] to kill <people> in a cruel and violent way □ *Thousands of civilians have been slaughtered in the war.* ◇ *n* the act of slaughtering people or animals □ *the slaughter of innocent people* □ *the ritual slaughter of animals.*

slaughterhouse ['slɔːtəʳhaus, *pl* -hauzɪz] *n* a building where animals are killed for food.

Slav [slɑːv] *n* a member of any of the Eastern European peoples who speak a Slavic language.

slave [sleɪv] ◇ *n* **-1.** a person who is the property of another person and has to work for that person without payment □ *The plantations depended on imported slaves.* □ *I didn't expect to be treated like a slave!* □ *slave labor.* **-2. to be a slave to sthg** to be completely controlled by sthg □ *My husband is a slave to his work.* ◇ *vi* to work very hard, especially at something one does not enjoy □ *I've been slaving over my report all day.*

slaver ['slævəʳ] *vi* [dog, person] to have saliva running out of the mouth.

slavery ['sleɪvərɪ] *n* the system of having slaves □ *The children were sold into slavery.*

slave trade *n* **the slave trade** the buying and selling of slaves.

Slavic ['slɑːvɪk] ◇ *n* a group of languages that includes Russian, Ukrainian, Polish, Czech, Serbo-Croat, and Bulgarian. ◇ *adj*: *Slavic languages/people.*

slavish ['sleɪvɪʃ] *adj* [attitude, devotion, following] that shows too much willingness to obey somebody or something without thinking about it or asking questions (disapproving use) □ *their slavish imitation of American fashions.*

Slavonic [slə'vɒnɪk] *n* & *adj* GB = **Slavic**.

slay [sleɪ] (*pt* **slew**, *pp* **slain**) *vt* to kill <a person or animal> violently (literary use).

SLDP *n abbr of* **Social and Liberal Democratic Party**.

sleaze [sliːz] *n* behavior that is dishonest or immoral, especially in politics or business.

sleazy ['sliːzɪ] (*compar* **sleazier**, *superl* **sleaziest**) *adj* [area, bar] that is cheap, dirty, and often connected with immoral activities such as prostitution □ *We went to a sleazy little nightclub in Montmartre.*

sled [sled] US, **sledge** [sledʒ] GB *n* a vehicle for moving on snow that has two strips of metal or wood that help it slide across the snow.

sledgehammer ['sledʒhæməʳ] *n* a large heavy hammer.

sleek [sliːk] *adj* **-1.** [hair, fur] that looks smooth and shiny. **-2.** [car, plane] that has a smooth elegant shape and looks expensive. **-3.** [person] who is neat and well-dressed.

sleep [sliːp] (*pt* & *pp* **slept**) ◇ *n* **-1.** the body's natural state of rest, when one's eyes are closed and one's mind is not active □ *I only got four hours' sleep last night.* □ *Children need a lot of sleep.* □ *He fell into a deep sleep.* □ *The music sent me to sleep.* ■ **to go to sleep** [person] to enter a state of sleep; [hand, leg, foot] to become numb. ■ **to put sb to sleep** to make sb unconscious with a drug, especially before an operation. ■ **to be put to sleep** [dog, cat] to be killed with a drug in order to end pain and suffering. **-2.** the time when one is in a state of sleep □ *I sometimes have a sleep in the afternoon.* □ *I got a good night's sleep.*

◇ *vi* **-1.** to be in a state of sleep □ *I slept very badly last night.* □ *Sleep well!* □ *She usually sleeps until two in the afternoon.* **-2.** to spend the night sleeping in a particular place □ *You can sleep in the spare room if you like.*

◆ **sleep around** *vi* to have sex with a lot of different people in a short time (informal and disapproving use).

◆ **sleep in** *vi* to stay asleep until later than normal in the morning □ *On Sunday mornings, I usually sleep in.*

◆ **sleep off** *vt sep* **to sleep sthg off** [hangover, headache] to get rid of sthg by sleeping □ *Put her to bed and let her sleep it off.*

◆ **sleep through** *vt fus* **to sleep through sthg** [alarm, argument, music] not to be woken up by sthg noisy □ *I didn't hear a thing: I slept through it all.*

◆ **sleep together** *vi* [couple] to have sex with each other regularly (polite use).

♦ **sleep with** vt fus **to sleep with sb** to have sex with sb (polite use).

sleeper ['sli:pər] n -1. **to be a heavy/light sleeper** to be hard/easy to wake up □ She's a very light sleeper and will hear the slightest noise. -2. a compartment in a train that does long overnight trips and that has beds for the passengers. -3. a train that has sleepers □ an overnight sleeper. -4. GB one of the large pieces of wood underneath a railroad track.

sleepily ['sli:pəlɪ] adv [say, smile] in a way that shows one is tired and ready to sleep.

sleeping bag ['sli:pɪŋ-] n a soft warm bag for sleeping in, used especially when one is camping.

Sleeping Beauty [,sli:pɪŋ'bju:tɪ] a character in a fairy tale. She is a princess who sleeps for many years and is woken when a prince kisses her.

sleeping car n a car in a train that has sleepers.

sleeping partner n GB BUSINESS a partner who has invested money in a business but is not involved in running it.

sleeping pill n a pill that helps one to sleep.

sleeping policeman n GB a raised section across a road that is designed to stop cars from going too fast.

sleeping tablet n GB = **sleeping pill**.

sleepless ['sli:pləs] adj **a sleepless night** a night when one cannot sleep □ I spent several sleepless nights worrying about it.

sleepwalk ['sli:pwɔːk] vi to walk around while one is still asleep.

sleepy ['sli:pɪ] (compar **sleepier**, superl **sleepiest**) adj -1. [person] who is tired and ready for sleep □ I left early because I was feeling sleepy. -2. [village, town] where life is quiet and peaceful and nothing exciting happens □ They lived in a sleepy little village called Bray.

sleet [sli:t] ◇ n partly frozen rain. ◇ v impers **it is sleeting** sleet is falling.

sleeve [sli:v] n -1. [of a jacket, shirt, coat] one of the parts of a piece of clothing that cover one's arms □ There's a hole in your sleeve. □ He rolled his sleeves up and got down to work. ■ **to have sthg up one's sleeve** to have sthg that one has prepared earlier that other people do not know about or expect □ I know you've got something/some ideas up your sleeve. -2. the square cardboard envelope that a record is kept in □ a record sleeve.

sleeveless ['sli:vləs] adj [dress, pullover] that has no sleeves.

sleigh [sleɪ] n a large vehicle that travels across snow on flat metal blades, usually pulled by horses.

sleight of hand [,slaɪt-] n -1. a quick and skillful movement of the hands that is used to hide something that one is doing □ He used sleight of hand to make the card disappear. -2. the use of tricks and deceit □ financial sleight of hand.

slender ['slendər] adj -1. [person, waist, figure] that looks thin in an attractive way □ He

could see the slender outline of the tower silhouetted against the sky. -2. [hope, chance] that seems rather small □ I fear our chances of winning are slender.

slept [slept] past tense & past participle of **sleep**.

sleuth [slu:θ] n a detective, especially an amateur one (informal and humorous use).

slew [slu:] ◇ past tense of **slay**. ◇ vi [car, truck] to change direction suddenly and in an uncontrolled way.

slice [slaɪs] ◇ n -1. [of bread, cheese, ham] a thin piece of something, usually food, cut from a larger piece □ a slice of cake □ Can you cut that loaf into slices? -2. [of the profits, a market, income] a share of something □ The workers are entitled to a slice of the profits. -3. SPORT a stroke in golf, tennis etc that makes the ball go forward and curve to one side. ◇ vt -1. [bread, meat] to cut <sthg> into slices; [hand, finger] to cut <sthg> with a lot of force □ thinly sliced bread □ I accidentally sliced my thumb. -2. SPORT [ball, shot] to make <sthg> go forward and curve to one side. ◇ vi **to slice into/through sthg** to cut into/through sthg, usually without difficulty □ Workmen accidentally sliced through a cable.

♦ **slice up** vt sep **to slice sthg up** [bread, cheese, sausage] to cut sthg into slices.

sliced bread [,slaɪst-] n bread that is sold already cut in slices □ a loaf of sliced bread.

slick [slɪk] ◇ adj -1. [performance, design, technique] that is impressive because it is smooth and efficient, but is not interesting or original (disapproving use) □ She's a slick but emotionless performer. -2. [salesman, answer, talk] that sounds good and is likely to persuade people, but is insincere or makes things seem too simple □ His answer was perhaps a little too slick to be believable. ◇ n = **oil slick**.

slicker ['slɪkər] n US a raincoat that is usually made of plastic.

slide [slaɪd] (pt & pp **slid** [slɪd]) ◇ vi -1. [person, tear, object] to move smoothly and quickly across a slippery surface □ I could feel something sliding down my back. □ He slid on the icy sidewalk. -2. [drawer, window] to move smoothly and quietly in a particular direction □ The door slid open. □ I slid out of the room when nobody was looking. -3. [currency, price] to decrease in value □ The dollar continued to slide against the Deutschmark. ■ **to let things slide** to let a situation get worse without doing anything to stop it. ◇ vt to move <sthg> smoothly along a surface or through a space □ She slid the key into the lock. ◇ n -1. PHOTOGRAPHY a piece of film in a small cardboard or plastic frame that can be projected onto a wall or screen □ He took slides of his work. □ a roll of slide film □ a slide show. -2. [for children] a piece of equipment found in a children's playground with a sloping metal or plastic surface that children can slide down □ a children's slide. -3. [for a microscope] a piece of glass that one puts something on in order to look at it through a microscope □ a glass slide □ a microscope *slide.* **-4.** GB [for one's hair] an object made of plastic or metal that girls or women use to keep their hair in place □ *a hair slide.* **-5.** [in standards, popularity, prices] a decrease in the level or quality of something □ *The banks intervened to halt the lira's slide.*

slide projector *n* a machine with a very bright light inside that projects photographic slides onto a screen.

slide rule *n* a device like a ruler marked with numbers that slide sideways, used to do calculations.

sliding door [ˌslaɪdɪŋ-] *n* a door on wheels that moves along the wall rather than opening outward.

sliding scale *n* a system of calculating payments according to particular conditions □ *We operate a sliding scale of charges.*

slight [slaɪt] ◇ *adj* **-1.** [improvement, wound, cold] that is small and unimportant □ *There is a very slight chance that the operation could fail.* □ *a slight problem.* ■ **not in the slightest** not at all □ *She wasn't worried in the slightest.* **-2.** [person, build, body] that is small, thin, and looks weak □ *He was small and slight, with delicate features.*

◇ *n* an action that annoys somebody because they think they are being insulted or treated as if they are not important □ *I will take it as a personal slight if you decide not to come.* ◇ *vt* to offend <sb> by treating them as if they are not important □ *Karen felt slighted by the way they had treated her.*

slightly [ˈslaɪtlɪ] *adv* **-1.** a little □ *It embarrasses me slightly to think of it.* □ *a slightly higher figure than expected.* **-2. slightly built** [person] who is small, thin, and looks weak.

slim [slɪm] (*compar* **slimmer**, *superl* **slimmest**) (*pt* & *pp* **slimmed**, *cont* **slimming**) ◇ *adj* **-1.** [person, waist, figure] thin in an attractive way □ *She was middle-aged, but still slim and attractive.* **-2.** [wallet, diary, bottle] thin □ *a slim volume of poetry.* **-3.** [possibility, hope] small □ *The chances of finding any more survivors are extremely slim.* ◇ *vi* GB = **slim down.**

◆ **slim down** *vi* to lose weight by eating less.

slime [slaɪm] *n* an unpleasant, thick, sticky liquid similar to the substance produced by snails □ *dripping walls covered in green slime.*

slimline [ˈslɪmlaɪn] *adj* **-1.** [wallet, calculator] that is thinner than normal. **-2.** [tonic, butter] that has fewer calories in it than normal.

slimmer [ˈslɪmər] *n* GB a person who is trying to slim.

slimming [ˈslɪmɪŋ] ◇ *n* the process of trying to lose weight by eating less □ *Slimming can lead to eating disorders.* ◇ *adj* GB [magazine, club] that is intended for slimmers.

slimy [ˈslaɪmɪ] (*compar* **slimier**, *superl* **slimiest**) *adj* **-1.** [rock, trail, animal] that is covered in slime □ *Its skin is slimy to the touch.* **-2.** [person] who is friendly or helpful in an exaggerated and insincere way (informal use).

sling [slɪŋ] (*pt* & *pp* **slung**) ◇ *n* **-1.** a piece of cloth that is tied around one's neck and supports an injured arm □ *Jackie's arm was in a*

sling. **-2.** a piece of equipment made of cloth, ropes etc that is used to carry or lift heavy objects. ◇ *vt* **-1.** to move <sthg> by swinging it into a position where it hangs □ *She slung the bag over her shoulder.* **-2.** to throw <sthg> without care (informal use) □ *Tom slung his clothes into a suitcase.* **-3.** [hammock, rope] to attach <sthg> so that it hangs between two points.

slingback [ˈslɪŋbæk] *n* a woman's shoe that has a strap that goes around the back of her heel.

slingshot [ˈslɪŋʃɒt] *n* US a stick in the shape of the letter "Y" with an elastic strip fastened between the two sides that is used, especially by children, to throw stones.

slink [slɪŋk] (*pt* & *pp* **slunk**) *vi* to **slink away** OR **off** to leave somewhere quietly, trying not to be seen, especially because one is afraid or embarrassed.

slip [slɪp] (*pt* & *pp* **slipped**, *cont* **slipping**) ◇ *n* **-1.** a small mistake □ *I'm sorry, somebody must have made a slip.* ■ **a slip of the pen** a small mistake made when writing. ■ **a slip of the tongue** a small mistake made when speaking. **-2.** [of paper] a small piece of paper □ *We all wrote down our suggestions on the slips (of paper) provided.* **-3.** CLOTHING a loose piece of clothing made of light material that is worn by a woman underneath a skirt or dress. **-4.** *phrase* **to give sb the slip** to succeed in escaping from sb (informal use).

◇ *vt* **-1.** [money, weapon, note] to put <sthg> quickly and smoothly in a particular place □ *He slipped his wallet back into his pocket.* **-2. to slip sthg on/off** [coat, shoes, pants] to put sthg on/take sthg off quickly and easily. **-3. to slip sb's mind** OR **memory** to be forgotten by sb □ *I'm so sorry, it must have slipped my mind.*

◇ *vi* **-1.** [person, foot, wheel] to accidentally slide and fall over, or nearly fall over □ *My foot slipped on the kitchen floor.* **-2.** [soap, hand, knife] to move suddenly and by accident □ *The knife slipped and I cut myself.* **-3.** [person] to change gradually from one state, activity etc to another □ *She slipped into a coma.* □ *He occasionally slips into Spanish.* **-4.** [price, standard, currency] to decrease in a way that is worrying □ *I fear educational standards are slipping.* ■ **to let things slip** to let a situation get worse without doing anything to stop it. **-5.** [person] to move somewhere quietly so that one is not noticed □ *I slipped out of the house while the others weren't looking.* ■ **to slip into/out of a piece of clothing** to put on/take off a piece of clothing quickly and easily □ *I'll just slip into something cooler.* □ *I'll just slip out of these dirty clothes.* **-6.** AUTO [clutch] not to work properly because of being used too much □ *The clutch keeps slipping.* **-7.** *phrase* **to let sthg slip** [fact, secret] to let sthg become known by mistake □ *Sam let it slip that they were planning a surprise party.*

◆ **slip-ons** *npl* slip-on shoes □ *a pair of slip-ons.*

◆ **slip away** *vi* to leave a place quietly in order not to be noticed □ *I had to slip away before the end of the meeting.*

♦ **slip up** *vi* to make a mistake □ *It's not the first time he's slipped up like this.*

slip-on *adj* **a slip-on shoe** a shoe that has no laces.

slippage ['slɪpɪdʒ] *n* [of currency, political party] the amount by which one fails to keep to a standard or target □ *A certain amount of slippage in the schedule is to be expected.*

slipped disk [ˌslɪpt-] *n* a painful medical condition in which one of the separate parts of one's spine moves out of place □ *She ended up in the hospital with a slipped disk.*

slipper ['slɪpər] *n* a soft comfortable shoe that people wear indoors □ *a pair of slippers* □ *bedroom slippers.*

slippery ['slɪpərɪ] *adj* **-1.** [road, floor] that is likely to cause somebody to slip, especially because it is wet or icy; [soap, handle] that slips easily and is hard to keep hold of □ *The road was still wet and slippery.* □ *The fish was so slippery I couldn't keep hold of it.* **-2.** [person] who cannot be trusted (informal use) □ *He's a slippery character!*

slip road *n* GB a road that leads onto or from a highway.

slipshod ['slɪpʃɒd] *adj* [attitude, work] careless □ *a slipshod piece of work.*

slipstream ['slɪpstriːm] *n* the air directly behind a vehicle that is moving fast.

slip-up *n* a small mistake (informal use) □ *The organizers made a slip-up in the reservations.*

slipway ['slɪpweɪ] *n* a sloping path used for moving a boat down to the edge of the sea or of a river or lake.

slit [slɪt] (*pt & pp* **slit**, *cont* **slitting**) ◇ *n* a long narrow cut in the surface of something □ *Make a slit in the meat near the bone and insert a tiny piece of garlic.* □ *a long skirt with slits up the sides.* ◇ *vt* **-1.** [envelope, throat] to make a narrow cut in <sthg> □ *The killer always slit his victims' throats.* □ *a skirt slit to the thigh.* **-2.** [rope, leather] to cut through <sthg>.

slither ['slɪðər] *vi* **-1.** [car, person, soap] to slide in an uncontrolled way □ *The car slithered to a halt.* **-2.** [snake] to move smoothly in a particular direction by going from side to side □ *The snake slithered away.*

sliver ['slɪvər] *n* **-1.** [of glass, ice, wood] a small sharp piece of something □ *A small sliver of glass had become embedded in her skin.* **-2.** [of ham, cheese] a very thin slice of food.

slob [slɒb] *n* a person who is lazy and untidy and takes little care over the way they eat, dress etc (informal use).

slobber ['slɒbər] *vi* [person] to let saliva run out of one's mouth □ *Don't let the dog slobber all over you!*

slog [slɒɡ] (*pt & pp* **slogged**, *cont* **slogging**) (informal use) ◇ *n* **-1.** a hard and tiring journey, especially on foot □ *It was a hard slog up the hill.* **-2.** GB hard work □ *It's been a real slog preparing for these exams.* ◇ *vi* **-1.** to move over an area with great effort, especially on foot □ *They slogged up the steep hill.* **-2.** GB to work hard over a period of time, especially at

something difficult or boring □ *I'm still slogging (away) at that translation.*

slogan ['slouɡən] *n* a short phrase that is used to advertise a product, political party etc and is usually easy to remember □ *an advertising slogan* □ *He invented the slogan, "One Party, One Nation."*

slop [slɒp] (*pt & pp* **slopped**, *cont* **slopping**) ◇ *vt* [soup, water] to make <a liquid> spill over the sides of a container □ *She accidentally slopped some soup on the table.* ◇ *vi* [water] to move around and spill □ *The water slopped over the edge of the bathtub as he got in.*

slope [sloup] ◇ *n* **-1.** a surface that is quite smooth or even and is higher at one end than the other □ *The garden is on a slope.* **-2.** the side of a hill □ *We climbed the steep slope.* □ *I don't like skiing when the slopes are icy.* ◇ *vi* [land, handwriting, table] to be at an angle and not completely horizontal or vertical □ *The floor slopes slightly.*

sloping ['sloupɪŋ] *adj* [land, shelf, handwriting] that is not flat or straight, but slopes □ *The shed had a sloping roof.*

sloppy ['slɒpɪ] (*compar* **sloppier**, *superl* **sloppiest**) *adj* **-1.** [person, work, writing] that one thinks is careless □ *Sandra is a very sloppy worker/eater.* **-2.** [movie, story] that one thinks is sentimental (informal and disapproving use) □ *It's a sloppy story about a girl and a dog.*

slosh [slɒʃ] ◇ *vt* [water, tea, wine] to move or pour <a liquid> in a rough or careless way □ *I sloshed some bleach into the bucket.* ◇ *vi* [liquid] to move around, especially in a way that causes a mess □ *The water sloshed around in the bucket.*

sloshed [slɒʃt] *adj* **to be sloshed** to be drunk (informal use) □ *He gets sloshed every night.*

slot [slɒt] (*pt & pp* **slotted**, *cont* **slotting**) *n* **-1.** a straight thin opening in something, especially one that is used for putting money into a machine. **-2.** a long, narrow, hollow space in a piece of wood, metal etc □ *There are slots for the shelves at regular intervals.* **-3.** a particular period of time in a timetable, schedule etc □ *We can offer the guest speaker the two o'clock slot.*

♦ **slot in** ◇ *vt sep* **to slot sthg in** [part, piece, component] to put sthg into a slot. ◇ *vi* to be put in and fit neatly into a slot □ *The shelves slot in easily.*

sloth [US slɒθ, GB slouθ] *n* **-1.** an animal of Central and South America that hangs upside down in trees and moves very slowly. **-2.** laziness (literary use).

slot machine *n* **-1.** a machine that one can get drinks, snacks etc from when one puts money in a slot. **-2.** a gambling machine that one can play on by putting in money and pulling a handle or pressing buttons.

slot meter *n* GB a machine in a house that one puts money into to be able to use the electricity or gas.

slouch [slautʃ] ◇ *n* a lazy person who does things very slowly and achieves little □ *He's certainly no slouch when it comes to repairing* *things.* ◇ *vi* to sit, stand, or walk with one's head and shoulders bent forward □ *I tend to slouch when I sit at my desk.*

slough [slʌf] ◆ **slough off** *vt sep* -**1. to slough its skin off** [snake, lizard] to get rid of its old skin in one complete piece. -**2. to slough sthg off** [person, organization] to get rid of sthg that is no longer useful (literary use) □ *It's time for us to slough off our tired old image.*

Slovak ['slouvæk] *n* & *adj*: *see* **Slovakia**.

Slovakia [slou'vækɪə] a country in central Europe, east of the Czech Republic, between Poland and Hungary, that was part of Czechoslovakia until it became an independent republic in 1993. SIZE: 49,000 sq kms. POPULATION: 5,300,000 (*Slovaks, Slovakians*). CAPITAL: Bratislava. LANGUAGE: Slovak. CURRENCY: Slovak crown.

Slovenia [slou'viːnjə] a country in southeastern Europe, between Italy and Croatia. It was part of Yugoslavia until it became an independent republic in 1991. SIZE: 20,226 sq kms. POPULATION: 2,000,000 (*Slovenes, Slovenians*). CAPITAL: Ljubljana. LANGUAGE: Slovene. CURRENCY: tolar.

slovenly ['slʌvnlɪ] *adj* [person, appearance, work] that seems untidy, careless, and lazy.

slow [slou] ◇ *adj* -**1.** [runner, animal, train] that moves at a low speed; [process, improvement] that takes a long time □ *a line of slow-moving traffic* □ *The changes have been slow to take effect.* -**2. to be slow** [clock, watch] to show a time that is earlier than the real time □ *Your watch is ten minutes slow.* -**3.** [business, place] not busy □ *Business is rather slow at the moment.* -**4.** [pupil, learner] who is not very intelligent and needs more time than other people to learn or understand things.
◇ *adv* [drive, walk, move] slowly. ■ **to go slow** [staff, workers] to refuse to work at the normal speed as a protest.
◇ *vt* [process, progress] to make <sthg> slower □ *Political infighting has slowed the progress of the peace talks.*
◇ *vi* [car, increase, process] to become slower □ *Production has slowed in recent months.*

◆ **slow down** ◇ *vt sep* **to slow sb/sthg down** [person, vehicle, process] to make sb/sthg slower □ *All this luggage is slowing us down.*
◇ *vi* [person, vehicle, process] to become slower □ *Slow down! You're going to fast.*

slow-acting *adj* [drug, poison] that takes a long time to have an effect.

slowcoach *n* GB = **slowpoke**.

slowdown ['sloudaun] *n* a reduction in speed or activity □ *an economic slowdown.*

slow handclap *n* GB a way of showing disapproval by clapping one's hands slowly, especially as part of a large group of people.

slowly ['sloulɪ] *adv* [move, drive, improve] *see* **slow** □ *He slowly came to understand where he had gone wrong in his marriage.* □ *She inched her way slowly along the ledge.* ■ **slowly but surely** in a way that is slow but has a noticeable and important effect over a period of time □ *Her English is improving slowly but surely.*

slow motion *n* a way of showing a movie or video at a slower speed than usual, in order to look at the action in more detail □ *They showed the goal again in slow motion.*
◆ **slow-motion** *adj* [replay, scene] that is shown in slow motion.

slowpoke ['sloupouk] US, **slowcoach** ['sloukoutʃ] GB *n* a person who moves or works too slowly (informal use) □ *Hurry up, slowpoke!*

SLR (*abbr of* **single-lens reflex**) *n* a camera that uses the same lens to act as a viewfinder and to take photographs.

sludge [slʌdʒ] *n* -**1.** soft mud □ *The path had turned to sludge in the rain.* -**2.** a thick soft substance similar to mud that remains after sewage has been treated.

slug [slʌg] (*pt* & *pp* **slugged**, *cont* **slugging**) ◇ *n* -**1.** a small slimy animal like a snail but without a shell. -**2.** [of whiskey, vodka] a large mouthful of a drink, usually of a strong alcoholic drink (informal use). -**3.** US a bullet (informal use). ◇ *vt* to hit <sb> with one's fist (informal use).

sluggish ['slʌgɪʃ] *adj* [person, car, reaction] that is slower or less active than is usual or normal □ *Business has been sluggish lately.*

sluice [sluːs] ◇ *n* a passage that water passes though and that is used to control how quickly it moves □ *a sluice gate.* ◇ *vt* **to sluice sthg down** OR **out** to clean sthg with large amounts of water.

slum [slʌm] (*pt* & *pp* **slummed**, *cont* **slumming**) ◇ *n* a poor area of a city that has housing that is in bad condition; a house in this area □ *He was brought up in the slums of Rio.* □ *slum housing/streets.* ◇ *vt* **to slum it** to accept conditions that are less comfortable or exclusive than one is used to (informal use) □ *We decided to slum it and stay in a cheap boarding house.*

slumber ['slʌmbər] (literary use) ◇ *n* sleep. ◇ *vi* to sleep.

slump [slʌmp] ◇ *n* -**1.** [in prices, a market, trade] a sudden decrease in the level of something □ *Prices have fallen due to a slump in demand.* -**2.** a period of economic depression □ *an economic slump.* ◇ *vi* -**1.** [business, prices, market] to go down in value suddenly □ *Their share price has slumped to a new low.* -**2.** [person] to fall heavily downward □ *Bill slumped into the armchair.*

slung [slʌŋ] *past tense* & *past participle of* **sling**.

slunk [slʌŋk] *past tense* & *past participle of* **slink**.

slur [slɜːr] (*pt* & *pp* **slurred**, *cont* **slurring**) ◇ *n* -**1.** an unclear way of speaking that people sometimes have when they are drunk or ill □ *The stroke left him with a slight slur in his speech.* -**2.** an unfair comment, claim etc that is insulting to somebody or gives other people a bad opinion of them □ *It's a slur on his character.* ◇ *vt* **to slur one's words** OR **speech** to speak unclearly, e.g. when one is drunk.

slurp [slɜːrp] *vt* [drink, soup] to drink <sthg> noisily □ *Richard slurped the milkshake noisily.*

slurred [slɜːʳd] *adj* [words, speech] spoken with a slur □ *He was drunk and his speech was slurred.*

slurry [US ˈslɜːrɪ, GB ˈslʌrɪ] *n* a liquid mixture made of mud, manure etc and water.

slush [slʌʃ] *n* snow that has partly melted on the ground.

slush fund, slush money *n* money that is kept for illegal purposes, especially in politics or business.

slut▼ [slʌt] *n* (offensive use) -1. a woman who one thinks is sexually immoral. -2. a woman who one thinks is dirty and untidy.

sly [slaɪ] (*compar* **slyer** OR **slier,** *superl* **slyest** OR **sliest**) ◇ *adj* -1. [look, smile] that shows that one knows something that other people do not know □ *"Aha!" he said, giving her a sly smile.* -2. [person] who is clever at making people believe something that is not true, especially in order to get what they want. -3. [person] who does things secretly □ *You are a sly thing! Where did you get these from?* ◇ *n* **on the sly** without letting anybody know □ *He'd been seeing other women on the sly.*

S & M *n abbr of* **sadism and masochism.**

smack [smæk] ◇ *vt* -1. to hit <sb> with the palm of one's hand □ *Our parents never smacked us as children.* -2. to put <sthg> somewhere with a loud noise or with force □ *He smacked the book down on the desk.* -3. *phrase* **to smack one's lips** to open and close one's lips, making a loud noise to show that one is looking forward to eating or that one has enjoyed eating something. ◇ *n* -1. the act of smacking somebody □ *She gave the child a smack on the bottom.* -2. the sound or force of something hitting something else □ *the smack of the waves against the boat.* ◇ *vi* **to smack of sthg** to seem like sthg □ *This smacks of treachery.* ◇ *adv* a word used to say that something is exactly in a particular place (informal use) □ *He stood smack in the middle of the highway.*

small [smɔːl] ◇ *adj* -1. [object, person, amount] that is not large in size □ *My apartment is small but comfortable.* □ *Have you tried the smaller size?* -2. [crowd, family] that consists of few people □ *The audience was very small.* □ *A small group of people stood waiting outside.* -3. [boy, girl] young □ *I have three small children.* □ *I remember you when you were small!* -4. [business, company, farmer] that does not operate on a large scale; [matter, change, mistake] that is not important and can be dealt with easily □ *Small businesses are getting extra tax incentives.* □ *Informing everyone of the change will be no small task.* □ *There's one small problem I'd like to mention.* ■ **in a small way** in a way that has a limited effect □ *Perhaps I can help in some small way?* ◇ *n* **the small of the back** the lower part of one's back that curves inward.

small ads *npl* GB short advertisements in a newspaper that advertise something for sale, a room to rent etc □ *Look in the small ads.*

small arms *npl* guns that are light in weight and are designed to be carried.

small change *n* money in coins of low value.

small fry *n* people who are considered unimportant.

smallholder [ˈsmɔːlhəʊldəʳ] *n* GB a person who owns or rents a small piece of land and farms it.

smallholding [ˈsmɔːlhəʊldɪŋ] *n* GB a small piece of land that is farmed.

small hours *npl* **in the small hours** in the early hours of the morning after midnight, when most people are asleep □ *We danced until the small hours.*

small letters *npl* **in small letters** using the small form of letters rather than the larger form, e.g. "a" or "b" rather than "A" or "B".

smallpox [ˈsmɔːlpɒks] *n* a very serious infectious disease that causes fever and spots that leave marks on the skin.

small print *n* **the small print** the conditions that are attached to the main part of a contract or agreement, sometimes printed in small letters at the end and likely to contain unattractive rules and restrictions □ *Make sure you read the small print.*

small-scale *adj* [business, industry, fraud] that is small in size and importance compared to other things of a similar type.

small screen *n* **the small screen** television as a form of entertainment.

small talk *n* polite conversation about unimportant things □ *We just sat around making small talk for most of the evening.*

small-time *adj* [criminal, businessman] who is not very important or successful compared to other people □ *a small-time crook.*

smarmy [ˈsmɑːʳmɪ] (*compar* **smarmier,** *superl* **smarmiest**) *adj* [person] who is polite and friendly in an insincere or unpleasant way.

smart [smɑːʳt] ◇ *adj* -1. [person, answer] intelligent □ *She's a smart kid.* □ *You tell me the answer, then, if you think you're so smart!* -2. [person] who is deliberately impolite and disrespectful to somebody by saying clever things □ *Don't get smart with me!* -3. [tap, blow] that is quick and forceful □ *He gave a smart knock on the door.* -4. GB [person, clothes] that seems clean, tidy, and attractive □ *You look very smart in that suit.* □ *That's a smart car you're driving.* -5. GB [person, society, club] that gives the impression of being rich and elegant □ *Harry moves in extremely smart circles now.* ◇ *vi* -1. [cut, hand, eyes] to be painful in a sharp stinging way □ *My face was smarting from where she'd slapped me.* -2. **to be smarting** to feel angry and humiliated, especially because of criticism □ *She was still smarting from her defeat.*

smart card *n* a small plastic card that holds and processes computer data and is used e.g. as a credit card.

smarten [ˈsmɑːʳtn] ◆ **smarten up** *vt sep* **to smarten sb/sthg up** GB [person, appearance, room] to make sb/sthg look smarter □ *I wish you'd try smartening yourself up a bit!*

smash [smæʃ] ◇ vt -1. [glass, plate, window] to break <sthg> into small pieces by hitting or dropping it □ *I'm so sorry — I've just smashed one of your glasses.* -2. to move <sthg> violently against something else □ *The wind smashed the door closed.* -3. [opposition, party, movement] to defeat or destroy <sthg> completely.
◇ vi -1. [window, glass] *The plate fell and smashed into pieces.* -2. [stone, vehicle] *The car smashed into/through a store window.*
◇ n -1. [of china, glass] the sound of something fragile breaking □ *It fell with a loud smash.* -2. a car crash (informal use) □ *We had a nasty smash yesterday.* -3. SPORT a strong attacking shot in tennis, squash etc.

◆ **smash up** vt sep to smash sthg up [room, vehicle, furniture] to destroy sthg completely, often because one is very angry □ *He smashed up his father's new car.*

smashed [smæʃt] adj **to be smashed** to be drunk (informal use) □ *He got really smashed at the party.*

smash hit n a very popular success □ *The musical was a smash hit in the States.*

smash-up n a serious road accident in which the vehicles involved are completely destroyed.

smattering ['smætərɪŋ] n a small amount of something □ *I know a smattering of Portuguese.*

SME n abbr of **small and medium-sized enterprise**.

smear [smɪəʳ] ◇ n -1. [of mud, oil, blood] a dirty mark usually caused by something that is greasy or sticky □ *There was a smear of lipstick on his collar.* -2. GB MEDICINE = **smear test.** -3. [against a politician, public figure] an untrue story that is deliberately spread by somebody to damage somebody else's reputation □ *This is a deliberate smear on the character of our candidate.*
◇ vt -1. [page, painting, glass] to make a smear on <sthg> □ *The window was smeared with fingermarks.* -2. **to smear sthg onto sthg** [oil, butter, paint] to spread sthg onto sthg, especially using a lot of it in a careless way □ *She smeared cream on her face.* ■ **to smear sthg with sthg** [with cream, oil] to cover sthg with a layer of sthg, especially using a lot of it in a careless way □ *He smeared suntan oil all over his chest.* -3. [politician, public figure] to spread a smear against <sb> □ *It was a clear attempt to smear my reputation.*

smear campaign n a deliberate attempt by a group of people to smear somebody.

smear test n GB an examination of cells taken from a woman's cervix in order to discover if there is cancer there.

smell [smel] (US pt & pp **smelled**, GB pt & pp **smelled** OR **smelt**) ◇ vt -1. [gas, food] to become aware of the smell of <sthg> □ *Can you smell something burning?* -2. [food, perfume, flower] to identify or recognize the smell of <sthg> by putting one's nose near it and breathing in □ *She smelled the milk to see if it had spoiled.* -3. [danger, trouble] to feel or realize that <sthg> is there □ *I can smell trouble.*

◇ vi -1. [person] to be able to smell things □ *I can't smell at the moment because I have a cold.* -2. [clothes, perfume, food] to have a particular smell □ *The house smells of beer and cigarettes.* □ *This room smells damp/musty.* □ *This perfume smells like soap.* ■ **to smell good/bad** to have a good/bad smell □ *That smells delicious!* -3. [feet, clothes] to have a bad smell □ *I threw out the meat because it was starting to smell.*
◇ n -1. a quality that is sensed by the nose □ *What a terrible smell!* □ *There's a strong smell of gas in here.* □ *a delicious smell of cooking.* -2. the ability of the nose to sense things □ *He lost his sense of smell.*

smelling salts ['smelɪŋ-] npl a chemical with a very strong smell that is used to revive somebody who has fainted.

smelly ['smelɪ] (compar **smellier**, superl **smelliest**) adj [feet, clothes] that have a bad smell □ *a pair of smelly old socks.*

smelt [smelt] ◇ past tense & past participle of **smell**. ◇ vt to remove metal from <ore> by heating it to very high temperatures.

smile [smaɪl] ◇ n an expression on one's face in which the corners of one's mouth are turned up to show one is pleased or amused □ *She had a big smile on her face.* ʊ *He gave a broad smile.* ◇ vi to give a smile □ *She was smiling as she spoke.* □ *He smiled at my surprise.* ◇ vt to say <sthg> with a smile □ *"Hi," she smiled.*

smiling ['smaɪlɪŋ] adj **a smiling face** the face of somebody who seems friendly because they have a smile □ *The room was full of happy smiling faces.*

smirk [smɜːʳk] ◇ n a smile that shows one is satisfied with oneself or pleased at somebody else's bad luck (disapproving use) □ *Wipe that silly smirk off your face!* ◇ vi to give a smirk □ *What are you smirking at?*

smith [smɪθ] n = **blacksmith.**

Smith [smɪθ], **Adam** (1723–1790) a British economist who believed in free trade and private enterprise.

Smith, John (1580–1631) an English soldier and explorer who helped to found the first colony in America, in Virginia. He was saved from death by Pocahontas.

Smith, Joseph (1805–1844) a US religious leader who founded the Mormon Church.

smithereens [ˌsmɪðə'riːnz] npl **to be smashed/blown to smithereens** to be completely destroyed by being broken/in an explosion (informal use).

Smithsonian [smɪθ'sʊʊnɪən]: **the Smithsonian (Institution)** a large group of government-supported museums in Washington, D.C. It includes museums of modern art, aircraft, and history.

Smith Square a square that is in central London and that contains the headquarters of the Conservative Party.

smithy ['smɪðɪ] (pl **smithies**) n the place where a blacksmith works □ *the village smithy.*

smitten ['smɪtn] adj **to be smitten** to find

somebody or something very attractive or interesting (informal and humorous use).

smock [smɒk] *n* a loose piece of clothing like a dress, often worn over other clothes to protect them.

smog [smɒg] *n* a mixture of fog and smoke □ *The city was covered in a blanket of smog.*

smoke [sməʊk] ◇ *n* -1. the gas and small particles produced when something burns □ *The room was filled with smoke.* -2. the act of smoking a cigarette, cigar etc □ *I'm going out for a smoke.* ◇ *vt* -1. [cigarette, cigar, pipe] to suck smoke from <sthg> and breathe it out again □ *I used to smoke 20 cigarettes a day.* □ *What kind of tobacco do you smoke?* -2. [fish, meat, cheese] to preserve <food> by hanging it in a room full of wood smoke. ◇ *vi* -1. [person] *Do you smoke?* □ *Do you mind if I smoke?* -2. [chimney, engine, lamp] to produce too much smoke □ *The log fire had begun to smoke unpleasantly.*

smoke alarm *n* an electronic device that makes a loud high-pitched noise when smoke comes near it, used in a building to warn people of a fire.

smoked [sməʊkt] *adj* [fish, cheese, ham] that has been preserved by smoking it.

smoked salmon *n* salmon that has been smoked and is eaten cold in thin slices.

smokeless fuel ['sməʊkləs-] *n* fuel, usually a kind of coal, that burns without producing smoke.

smokeless zone *n* GB an area where only smokeless fuel can be burned.

smoker ['sməʊkər] *n* -1. a person who often smokes □ *Are you a smoker or a nonsmoker?* □ *Smokers are kindly requested to sit on the left-hand side of the auditorium.* -2. RAIL a car on a train where smoking is allowed.

smokescreen ['sməʊkskriːn] *n* an activity that is intended to hide one's real activities or intentions by drawing people's attention to something else □ *The laundry is just a smokescreen for their criminal activities.*

smoke shop *n* US a store that sells tobacco, pipes etc.

smokestack ['sməʊkstæk] *n* a very tall factory chimney.

smokestack industry *n* a type of industry that produces heavy goods, e.g. cars or steel.

smoking ['sməʊkɪŋ] *n* the act of smoking a cigarette, pipe etc □ *Smoking is bad for your health.* □ *Would you like a smoking or nonsmoking seat?* ■ **'No Smoking'** a sign in a public place that shows that smoking is not allowed there.

smoking car US, **smoking compartment** GB *n* a car on a train where people are allowed to smoke.

smoky ['sməʊkɪ] (*compar* **smokier**, *superl* **smokiest**) *adj* -1. [room, atmosphere] that is full of smoke □ *It's very smoky in here.* -2. [taste, color] that is like smoke in some way □ *This wine has a rather smoky taste.*

smolder US, **smoulder** GB ['sməʊldər] *vi* -1.

[fire, wood] to burn slowly, producing smoke but no flames □ *The fire was smoldering in the grate.* -2. [feeling, passion] to be felt but not expressed directly □ *Anger had smoldered inside him for years.*

smooch [smuːtʃ] *vi* to kiss and embrace somebody, especially for a long time, e.g. when dancing (informal use).

smooth [smuːð] ◇ *adj* -1. [surface, skin, sea] that is flat and even and is not rough □ *This razor gives a smooth shave.* -2. [mixture, paste, sauce] that is quite thick and has no lumps, usually because it has been mixed well □ *Stir the mixture to a smooth consistency.* -3. [flow, pace, supply] that is regular and without sudden changes □ *The gear change was impressively smooth.* -4. [taste, drink] that is pleasant and not acid □ *a beautifully smooth malt whiskey.* -5. [flight, landing, take-off] that is comfortable because it does not shake one too much □ *They had a smooth crossing.* -6. [person] who seems relaxed, polite, and confident in a way one does not completely trust □ *He's a smooth talker.* -7. [transition, operation] that is without problems □ *This may affect the smooth running of the team.* □ *Things got off to a smooth start.*

◇ *vt* -1. [hair, skirt, tablecloth] to make <sthg> lie flat □ *He smoothed his hair down with his hand.* □ *She smoothed the sheet flat on the bed.*
■ **to smooth the way** to make a future change easier and more likely to happen, usually by dealing with any existing problems □ *Foreign aid will smooth the way to independence for the country.* -2. **to smooth sthg onto sthg** [cream, oil] to spread sthg onto sthg using regular and gentle movements □ *Libby smoothed suntan lotion onto his back.*

◆ **smooth out** *vt sep* -1. **to smooth sthg out** [tablecloth, sheet] to make sthg lie flat; [crease, wrinkle] to get rid of sthg by making the surface flat □ *He tried to smooth out the creases from his jacket.* -2. **to smooth sthg out** [difficulty, problem] to get rid of sthg □ *I'm sure we can smooth things out with the clients.*

◆ **smooth over** *vt sep* **to smooth over sthg** [difficulty, disagreement] to make sthg easier to deal with, often by talking to the people who are involved □ *I'll try to smooth things over with Janet before you arrive.*

smoothie ['smuːðɪ] *n* -1. a smooth-talking person (informal use). -2. a type of drink made from fruit pulp, usually with milk or cream added.

smoothly ['smuːðlɪ] *adv* [go, talk, flow] *see* **smooth** □ *The trip/operation went very smoothly.* □ *This pen writes very smoothly.*

smoothness ['smuːðnəs] *n* [of a surface, mixture, flight] *see* **smooth**.

smooth-talking [-tɔːkɪŋ] *adj* [person] who talks in a polite and confident way that is designed to persuade people but that is insincere or dishonest □ *a smooth-talking salesman.*

smother ['smʌðər] *vt* -1. **to smother sthg in** OR **with sthg** to cover sthg with a lot of sthg □ *The cake was smothered with* OR *in chocolate frosting.* □ *She smothered him with kisses.* -2.

[person] to kill <sb> by covering their face with something so they cannot breathe □ *It was alleged that he smothered the maid by placing a cushion over her face.* **-3.** [fire, flames] to put <sthg> out by covering it with something □ *Use a blanket to smother the flames.* **-4.** [emotion, opposition] to stop <sthg> from growing or becoming stronger □ *Hudson had learned to smother any feelings of anger.* **-5.** [son, daughter] to protect <a child> or give them too much love in a way that stops them from becoming independent □ *Her parents smothered her with love.*

smoulder *vi* GB = **smolder**.

smudge [smʌdʒ] ◇ *n* a dirty mark made when oil, grease etc is rubbed onto a surface. ◇ *vt* [ink, writing, paper] to make <sthg> dirty or untidy by rubbing it accidentally.

smug [smʌg] (*compar* **smugger**, *superl* **smuggest**) *adj* [person] who is pleased with themselves in a way that is annoying because it suggests that other people are in a worse situation □ *What are you looking so smug about?*

smuggle ['smʌgl] *vt* **-1.** [drugs, diamonds, alcohol] to take <sthg> illegally into or out of a country □ *They were caught smuggling cocaine over the border.* **-2. to smuggle sthg in/out** to take sthg secretly into/out of a place □ *Prostitutes were smuggled into the presidential palace.*

smuggler ['smʌglə'] *n* a person who smuggles diamonds, alcohol etc □ *a drug smuggler.*

smuggling ['smʌglɪŋ] *n* the activity of taking things illegally into or out of a country □ *The locals drew a large part of their income from smuggling.* □ *drug smuggling.*

smugness ['smʌgnəs] *n*: *see* **smug**.

smut [smʌt] *n* **-1.** a small piece of dirt or soot that makes a dark mark on things □ *You've got some smut on your cheek.* **-2.** smutty language, books, pictures etc (informal use) □ *I won't have you reading this smut!*

smutty ['smʌtɪ] (*compar* **smuttier**, *superl* **smuttiest**) *adj* [language, book, picture] that causes offense because it deals with sex or nudity in a way that is meant to shock or excite people (informal and disapproving use) □ *a dirty little book, full of smutty jokes.*

snack [snæk] ◇ *n* a quick meal or piece of food eaten between regular meals or instead of one □ *Let's have a quick snack, then go.* □ *snack food.* ◇ *vi* to eat a snack □ *She had a tendency to snack rather than eat proper meals.*

snack bar *n* a place where one can buy and eat snacks, tea, coffee etc.

snag [snæg] (*pt* & *pp* **snagged**, *cont* **snagging**) ◇ *n* **-1.** a small problem □ *There's only one snag: I've already arranged to see Liz that day.* **-2.** AUS a sausage (informal use). ◇ *vt* [sweater, stocking] to catch and tear <sthg> on a sharp object □ *She snagged her dress on the corner of the table.*

snail [sneɪl] *n* a small soft animal that has no skeleton, legs, or arms, has a shell on its back, and moves very slowly.

snail mail *n* a term used by computer users to refer to the normal postal service, compared to e-mail (humorous use).

snake [sneɪk] ◇ *n* a reptile with a long thin body and no legs. ◇ *vi* [procession, train] to move along in curves □ *The line of people snaked right around the theater.*

snap [snæp] (*pt* & *pp* **snapped**, *cont* **snapping**) ◇ *vt* **-1.** [branch, twig, rope] to break <sthg> with a snap □ *He snapped the pencil in two.* **-2.** [lid, fastener, lock] to move <sthg> in a particular direction so that it makes a sound like a snap □ *She snapped her briefcase shut.* ■ **to snap one's fingers** to make a noise by moving one's thumb and middle finger together quickly, usually to attract attention □ *He thinks all he has to do is snap his fingers and I'll come running!* **-3.** to say <sthg> in an angry or unfriendly way □ *"I'm busy," she snapped.* **-4.** [person, place] to take a photograph of <sb/sthg> (informal use) □ *He snapped her on the beach.*
◇ *vi* **-1.** [branch, twig, rope] *If you pull the elastic too tight it will snap.* **-2.** [lid, fastener, fingers] to move in a particular direction or way so as to make a noise like a snap □ *The case snaps shut like this.* **-3.** [dog, shark] to move its jaws together quickly in a movement like biting □ *Your dog just snapped at me.* **-4.** [person] to speak in an angry or unfriendly way □ *There's no need to snap at me like that!* **-5. to snap out of it** to change suddenly from a bad to a good mood □ *Peter's been sitting around looking depressed for days. I wish he'd just snap out of it and cheer up.*
◇ *n* **-1.** [of a twig, branch] the act or sound of something snapping. **-2.** PHOTOGRAPHY a photograph, especially one taken on vacation (informal use) □ *We took lots of snaps of the kids.* **-3.** US CLOTHING = **snap fastener**. **-4.** GB GAMES a children's card game where each player in turn places a card on the table. The aim is to be the first to shout "snap!" when two cards placed one after the other are the same.
◇ *adj* **a snap judgment/decision** a judgment/decision that is made suddenly and without much thought □ *a snap election.*

◆ **snap up** *vt sep* **to snap sthg up** to buy sthg quickly because it is cheap or because there is a chance that it will be bought by somebody else □ *Houses in this area are snapped up as soon as they come on the market.*

snap fastener *n* US a type of metal or plastic button with a point that sticks out of one half that is pressed into a hole in the other.

snappy ['snæpɪ] (*compar* **snappier**, *superl* **snappiest**) *adj* (informal use) **-1. a snappy dresser** a person who always wears stylish clothes. **-2.** [show, song] that is energetic and full of life. ■ **make it snappy!** do it quickly! □ *Take me to the airport, and make it snappy!*

snapshot ['snæpʃɒt] *n* a photograph taken quickly by somebody who is not an expert.

snare [sneə'] ◇ *n* a trap that is used for catching small animals and birds. ◇ *vt* [animal, bird] to catch <sthg> in a snare.

snarl [snɑːˈl] ◇ *n* [of a dog, wolf] a fierce growling sound. ◇ *vi* -1. [dog, wolf] to make a fierce growling sound. -2. [person] to speak in a very unfriendly and threatening way.

snarl-up *n* a disorganized situation, especially one involving traffic.

snatch [snætʃ] ◇ *n* a short part of a conversation, song etc □ *I overheard brief snatches of their conversation.* ◇ *vt* -1. [purse, keys, paper] to take <sthg> quickly and violently □ *He snatched the book from her hands.* -2. [sleep, opportunity, look] to do <sthg> quickly while one has the chance □ *I snatched a few hours' sleep on the plane.* ◇ *vi* to try to take something quickly and violently □ *She snatched at the papers and tore them.*

snazzy ['snæzɪ] (*compar* **snazzier**, *superl* **snazziest**) *adj* [clothes, place, car] stylish (informal use) □ *That's a snazzy new outfit.*

sneak [sniːk] (US *pt* & *pp* **sneaked** OR **snuck**, GB *pt* & *pp* **sneaked**) ◇ *vt* -1. **to sneak sthg somewhere** to take sthg somewhere so that other people do not notice □ *They managed to sneak a knife into the prison.* -2. **to sneak a look at sb/sthg** to look at sb/sthg quickly so that nobody sees one doing it □ *I snuck a look at the letter while she was out of the room.* ◇ *vi* to move quietly to avoid being heard □ *Later on, I sneaked back downstairs.* ◇ *n* a child who enjoys getting other children into trouble by telling adults about the bad things they have done (disapproving use).

sneakers ['sniːkəʳz] *npl* US shoes with rubber soles that are used for sports □ *a pair of sneakers.*

sneaking ['sniːkɪŋ] *adj* **to have a sneaking feeling/suspicion etc** to have a slight or secret feeling/suspicion etc, especially one that one does not want to admit or accept □ *I have a sneaking admiration for her.*

sneak preview *n* a chance to see or watch something before it is officially available to the public.

sneaky ['sniːkɪ] (*compar* **sneakier**, *superl* **sneakiest**) *adj* [person] who is secretive and dishonest, often not in a very serious way (informal use) □ *That was a sneaky little trick!*

sneer [snɪəʳ] ◇ *n* an unpleasant way of speaking, smiling, or laughing that shows that one has no respect for somebody or something □ *"How unfortunate," said Gert with a sneer.* ◇ *vi* **to sneer at sb/sthg** to show one's contempt for sb/sthg □ *He's always sneering at people behind their backs.* □ *A thousand dollars is not to be sneered at!*

sneeze [sniːz] ◇ *vi* to send a sudden uncontrollable burst of air through one's nose, e.g. when one has a cold or when there is dust in the air. ■ **it is not to be sneezed at** it is worth considering carefully (informal use) □ *That's an opportunity not to be sneezed at.* ◇ *n* an act of sneezing □ *Maura gave a loud sneeze.*

snicker ['snɪkəʳ] US ◇ *n* a quiet unkind laugh. ◇ *vi* to laugh in a quiet unkind way at somebody or something.

snide [snaɪd] *adj* [comment, remark] that ex-

presses a critical opinion of somebody or something but without saying so directly.

sniff [snɪf] ◇ *n* the act or sound of breathing in air sharply through one's nose so that one makes a noise, e.g. when one has a cold □ *She gave a loud sniff.* ◇ *vt* -1. [food, air, flower] to breathe in the air around <sthg> through one's nose in order to smell it □ *The dog sniffed the package excitedly.* -2. **to sniff glue/a solvent etc** to take glue/a solvent etc as a drug by breathing in its fumes. ◇ *vi* -1. to take in air with a sniff to clear one's nose □ *I've been sniffing all day with this cold.* -2. to show disapproval of something □ *A salary of $140,000 a year is not to be sniffed at.*

◆ **sniff out** *vt sep* -1. **to sniff sb/sthg out** [drugs, criminal] to find sb/sthg by smell. -2. **to sniff sthg out** [cause, secret] to find sthg by looking hard for it (informal use).

sniffer dog ['snɪfəʳ-] *n* a dog trained to find drugs, criminals etc by smell.

sniffle ['snɪfl] *vi* to sniff several times, e.g. when one has a cold.

snigger ['snɪgəʳ] *n* & *vi* GB = **snicker**.

snip [snɪp] (*pt* & *pp* **snipped**, *cont* **snipping**) *vt* [paper, string, wire] to cut <sthg> with one quick movement of a pair of scissors.

snipe [snaɪp] *vi* -1. to shoot from a hiding place at somebody or something □ *Solitary, unseen gunmen snipe at civilians on the street.* -2. to criticize somebody in an unpleasant, often indirect way □ *It's the kind of middle-class novel reviewers love to snipe at.*

sniper ['snaɪpəʳ] *n* a person who shoots at people from a hiding place.

snippet ['snɪpət] *n* a small piece of information, news, gossip etc □ *an interesting snippet of information* □ *I only heard snippets of their conversation.*

snivel ['snɪvl] (US *pt* & *pp* **sniveled**, *cont* **sniveling**, GB *pt* & *pp* **snivelled**, *cont* **snivelling**) *vi* to cry and sniff in an irritating complaining way.

snob [snɒb] *n* (disapproving use) -1. a person who admires the upper classes and dislikes the lower classes □ *She's a terrible snob.* -2. a person who thinks they are better than other people because of their intelligence, wealth, or interests □ *an intellectual snob.*

snobbery ['snɒbərɪ] *n* snobbish behavior.

snobbish ['snɒbɪʃ], **snobby** ['snɒbɪ] (*compar* **snobbier**, *superl* **snobbiest**) *adj* [behavior, attitude] that is typical of a snob.

snooker [US 'snʊkr, GB 'snuːkə] *n* a game for two players who use a long stick to hit a white ball across a table so that it knocks colored balls into one of six holes on the edge of the table □ *a game of snooker* □ *a snooker table/player.*

snoop [snuːp] *vi* to try to find out about something, e.g. somebody's personal affairs, especially by looking around secretly somewhere (informal and disapproving use) □ *He's always snooping around outside my office.*

snooper ['snuːpəʳ] *n* a person who often snoops (informal and disapproving use).

Snoopy ['snu:pɪ] a dog in the cartoon strip *Peanuts*.

snooty ['snu:tɪ] (*compar* **snootier**, *superl* **snootiest**) *adj* [person] who seems rude and unfriendly because they think they are better than other people.

snooze [snu:z] ◇ *n* a short light sleep during the day □ *I had a snooze after lunch.* ◇ *vi* to have a snooze.

snore [snɔːʳ] ◇ *vi* to make a loud noise with one's nose or mouth when breathing in during one's sleep □ *Do I snore?* □ *You were snoring last night.* ◇ *n* the sound or act of snoring □ *His snores kept the whole house awake.*

snoring ['snɔːrɪŋ] *n* the sound or act of repeatedly snoring □ *I was woken up by Alan's snoring.*

snorkel ['snɔːʳkl] *n* a short curved tube used for breathing underwater.

snorkeling US, **snorkelling** GB ['snɔːʳklɪŋ] *n* the activity of swimming underwater using a snorkel □ *It's a great place to go snorkeling.*

snort [snɔːʳt] ◇ *n* -1. [by a person] a noise made by breathing out using a lot of force, usually showing impatience or anger □ *Parsons gave a contemptuous snort.* -2. [by an animal] a noise made by breathing out suddenly and forcefully □ *The horse gave a snort.* ◇ *vi* [person, animal] to make a snort. ◇ *vt* **to snort cocaine** to take cocaine by breathing it in through one's nose (drugs slang).

snotty ['snɒtɪ] (*compar* **snottier**, *superl* **snottiest**) *adj* [person] who thinks they are better than other people (informal and disapproving use) □ *I told her what I thought and she got really snotty with me.*

snout [snaʊt] *n* the nose of some animals, e.g. a pig or dog.

snow [snoʊ] ◇ *n* crystals of frozen water that fall from the sky in soft white flakes □ *The trees were covered in snow.* □ *The snow lay thick on the ground.* □ *a snow scene.* ◇ *v impers* **it's snowing** snow is falling from the sky.

snowball ['snoʊbɔːl] ◇ *n* a ball that children make from snow and throw at each other. ◇ *vi* [work, problem] to increase more and more quickly in size or importance □ *The number of violent crimes has snowballed recently.*

snow blindness *n* the inability to see properly after looking at snow in bright sunlight for a long time.

snowboarding ['snoʊbɔːʳdɪŋ] *n* a sport in which one moves downhill on snow, standing on a long, wide, plastic board.

snowbound ['snoʊbaʊnd] *adj* **to be snowbound** to be unable to leave a place because there is too much snow.

snow-capped [-kæpt] *adj* [mountain, peak] that is covered with snow at the top.

Snowdonia [snoʊ'doʊnjə] a national park in a mountainous part of North Wales, in the UK.

snowdrift ['snoʊdrɪft] *n* a deep pile of snow made by the wind.

snowdrop ['snoʊdrɒp] *n* a small, white, bell-shaped flower that is one of the first flowers to appear in spring.

snowed in [,snoʊd-] *adj* **to be snowed in** to be unable to leave a place because there is too much snow.

snowed under *adj* **to be snowed under** to be very busy and have almost more work than one can cope with □ *I'm snowed under with paperwork.*

snowfall ['snoʊfɔːl] *n* -1. an amount of snow that falls from the sky □ *There have been heavy snowfalls in the mountains.* -2. the amount of snow that falls in a place over a particular period □ *Our average snowfall is close to 30 centimeters.*

snowflake ['snoʊfleɪk] *n* a piece of snow that falls from the sky.

snowman ['snoʊmæn] (*pl* **snowmen** [-men]) *n* a large figure made out of snow, that is intended to look like a person.

snow pea *n* a vegetable like a pea whose seeds and pod can be eaten.

snowplow US, **snowplough** GB ['snoʊplaʊ] *n* a special vehicle with a large metal blade in front that clears snow from roads and railroad tracks.

snowshoe ['snoʊʃuː] *n* one of two rounded frames with net across them that are worn on one's feet to stop one from sinking into deep snow.

snowstorm ['snoʊstɔːʳm] *n* a heavy fall of snow blown by strong wind.

snow-white *adj* pure white.

Snow White [,snoʊ'waɪt] a character in a fairy tale. Her cruel stepmother sends her to a forest to die, but she meets seven dwarfs there and lives with them.

snowy ['snoʊɪ] (*compar* **snowier**, *superl* **snowiest**) *adj* [conditions, weather] when a lot of snow is falling □ *It's going to be snowy today.*

Snowy Mountains: **the Snowy Mountains** an area in the Australian Alps between New South Wales and Victoria where there are many ski resorts.

SNP *n abbr of* **Scottish National Party**.

Snr, snr *abbr of* **senior**.

snub [snʌb] (*pt* & *pp* **snubbed**, *cont* **snubbing**) ◇ *n* something that is intended to insult somebody □ *She took his late arrival as a snub.* ◇ *vt* to ignore <sb> to show that one is angry or upset with them.

snuck [snʌk] *past tense* & *past participle of* **sneak**.

snuff [snʌf] ◇ *n* tobacco in the form of powder that one breathes in through one's nose. ◇ *vt* **to snuff it** to die (informal and humorous use).

snuffle ['snʌfl] *vi* to make noises like sniffs, usually because one has a cold or is upset □ *Blow your nose properly and stop snuffling!*

snuff movie *n* a pornographic movie in which the actors are actually killed.

snug [snʌg] (*compar* **snugger**, *superl* **snuggest**) *adj* -1. **to be snug** to feel warm and comfortable □ *I was feeling all snug and cosy in my pa-*

jamas. **-2.** [place] that is small and makes people feel warm and comfortable □ *This is a snug little bar.* **-3.** [jacket, suit, dress] that fits tightly □ *The shoes were a very snug fit.*

snuggle ['snʌgl] *vi* to move oneself into a warm comfortable position, usually close to another person □ *She snuggled up to me to keep warm.* □ *John snuggled under the blanket and went back to sleep.*

so [soʊ] ◇ *adv* **-1.** used to refer back to something that has already been mentioned □ *"Have we met before?" — "I don't think so."* □ *Are you interested in drama? If so, write to us at the following address...* **-2. so fat/tall/difficult etc** very fat/tall/difficult etc (used with adjectives). ■ **I was so tired (that) I went to bed** because I was very tired, I went to bed □ *The time went so quickly.* □ *I've never seen so many cars.* □ *Don't be so stupid.* □ *The weather was so hot (that) we stayed indoors.* **-3. so do I** used when the previous statement also applies to oneself □ *"I love jazz." — "So do I."* □ *You're upset, and so is he.* ■ **just as..., so...** used to compare two things, people, or situations □ *Just as some people like to be part of a team, so others work better on their own.* **-4.** used to ask a question about what has just been said □ *So are you saying that the whole thing was a mistake?* **-5.** used to get someone's attention □ *So how's work then?* **-6.** used to show that one thinks something is not important or serious □ *So I got it all wrong, who cares?* **-7. (like) so** used when the speaker is describing something with their hands □ *Hold your arm out, (like) so.* **-8. only so much** OR **many** used to say that the amount of something is limited □ *You can only wear so many pairs of shoes.* □ *There's only so much we can do to help.* **-9.** phrases **so I see** I can see that what you are saying is true □ *"I've had my hair cut." — "So I see."* ■ **so be it!** I accept what you say, though I think it is wrong □ *He said he wasn't interested, so be it! He's had his chance.* ■ **so he/there etc is** what you have said is true but I had forgotten it or not noticed it before □ *"There's a parking space." — "So there is."* □ *"The boss has just got back." — "So he has."* ■ **a week or so** about a week □ *I need to buy ten or so.* ■ **not so much...as...** used to correct a statement or opinion, or to make it more precise □ *The problem isn't so much the money, it's the time involved.*
◇ *excl* **so (what)!** used to show that the speaker does not think something is serious or important (informal use) □ *"She said you were rude to her." — "So what?"*
◇ *conj* = **so that** □ *I'm away next week, so I can't come.* □ *He'd seen a photograph of her, (and) so he recognized her right away.*
◆ **so as to** *conj* used to show the reason why something has been done □ *We sold it so as to raise money.*
◆ **so that** *conj* **-1.** used to give the reason why something is done □ *I left the light on so that people would think I was in.* **-2.** used to show the result of an action or situation □ *Some of the audience started shouting, so that you couldn't hear the actors.*

SO *abbr of* **standing order**.

soak [soʊk] ◇ *vt* **-1.** to leave <sthg> in water for a long period of time □ *Soak the prunes overnight.* **-2.** to make <sthg> very wet □ *The bandage was soaked with blood.* ◇ *vi* **-1. to leave sthg to soak, to let sthg soak** to leave sthg in water for a long period of time, especially in order to clean it □ *Leave the shirt to soak overnight.* **-2. to soak through/into sthg** [water, blood] to spread through/into sthg through the small holes in its surface □ *The water had soaked right through the carpet.*
◆ **soak up** *vt sep* **to soak sthg up** [water, blood] to absorb sthg □ *Use the bread to soak up the sauce.*

soaked [soʊkt] *adj* [person, clothes] very wet □ *I got absolutely soaked walking home.* ■ **to be soaked through** [person, clothes] to be completely wet.

soaking ['soʊkɪŋ] ◇ *adj* **to be soaking** [person, clothes] to be very wet □ *By the time I got home I was soaking.* ◇ *adv* **to be soaking wet** to be very wet.

so-and-so *n* (informal use) **-1.** a word used instead of a name that one has forgotten or as an example of a particular group of people or things □ *What would Mr and Mrs So-and-so from up the road say to that?* **-2.** an irritating person □ *He's an arrogant little so-and-so.*

soap [soʊp] ◇ *n* **-1.** a substance, usually solid when dry, that is used for washing oneself and one's clothes □ *a bar of soap* □ *I've got soap in my eyes.* □ *liquid soap.* **-2.** TV = **soap opera**. ◇ *vt* [hair, body] to rub soap into <sthg> to wash it.

soap bubble *n* a bubble made from soap and water.

soap dish *n* a small container for soap in a bathroom.

soap flakes *npl* small pieces of soap used for washing clothes.

soap opera *n* a television serial that does not have a fixed number of episodes and that deals with the everyday lives of a group of characters.

soap powder *n* GB soap in the form of powder used for washing clothes.

soapsuds ['soʊpsʌdz] *npl* a mass of tiny bubbles formed when soap is mixed with water.

soapy ['soʊpɪ] (*compar* **soapier**, *superl* **soapiest**) *adj* **-1.** [water, surface] that is full of soap. **-2.** [taste, texture] that is like soap.

soar [sɔːr] *vi* **-1.** [bird] to fly high in the sky without moving its wings □ *The eagle soared high in the sky.* **-2.** [balloon, kite, rocket] to rise quickly into the air □ *We watched the rocket soar up into the sky.* **-3.** [price, temperature] to increase very quickly to a high level □ *Temperatures soared into the 90s.* □ *Profits soared again last quarter.* **-4.** [mountain, building] to be very tall and impressive (literary use) □ *Redwood trees soared above us.* **-5.** [music, voice] to be high in pitch so that it is clearly heard above other voices or instruments □ *Her voice soared above the rest of the choir.*

soaring ['sɔːrɪŋ] *adj* **-1.** [price, temperature] that is increasing very quickly □ *Soaring prices have kept shoppers at home this month.* **-2.** [building, cliff] that is very tall and impressive □ *a soaring skyscraper.*

sob [sɒb] (*pt* & *pp* **sobbed**, *cont* **sobbing**) ◇ *n* the sound somebody makes when they are crying loudly with short sudden bursts □ *"But I can't," she said with a sob.* ◇ *vt* to say <sthg> with a sob □ *"They've gone!" he sobbed.* ◇ *vi* to cry loudly and in short sudden bursts □ *I found her sobbing in her room.*

sobbing ['sɒbɪŋ] *n* the act or sound of somebody who is crying loudly with short sudden bursts.

sober ['soʊbər] *adj* **-1. to be sober** not to be drunk □ *I don't think he was sober.* **-2.** [person] who is serious and sensible □ *a very sober, moral sort of man.* **-3.** [color, clothes] that seems plain and slightly dull □ *He was dressed in a sober gray suit.*

◆ **sober up** *vi* [person] to gradually become sober after being drunk.

sobering ['soʊbərɪŋ] *adj* [thought, experience] that makes one think seriously about something important □ *It is sobering to be reminded of how dangerous cars can be.*

sobriety [sə'braɪətɪ] *n* serious and sensible behavior (formal use).

Soc. *abbr of* **Society.**

so-called [-'kɔːld] *adj* a word used to describe something that one thinks is different from what its name suggests □ *my so-called friend.*

soccer ['sɒkər] *n* a game played between two teams of 11 players who kick a ball around a piece of ground with a goal at each end. The aim is to kick the ball into the opponents' goal □ *a soccer match/team.*

sociable ['soʊʃəbl] *adj* [person] who is friendly and likes being with people □ *I'm not feeling very sociable tonight.* □ *Come downstairs and be sociable for a change!*

social ['soʊʃl] *adj* **-1.** [problem, condition, structure] that is connected with human society and the way it is organized; [class, status, background] that is connected with the position one has in society □ *demands for social and economic change* □ *She gave in to social pressure and quit smoking.* □ *a family of high social standing.* **-2. social drinking** drinking for pleasure with friends. **-3.** [animal, insect] that lives in groups □ *Ants are social insects.*

Social and Liberal Democratic Party *n* in Britain, a moderate political party founded in 1988.

Social Chapter *n* **the Social Chapter** a section of the Maastricht Treaty on European economic and political union that concerns the rights of workers, old people, and the unemployed.

social climber *n* a person who tries to make friends with and be accepted by people from higher social classes (disapproving use).

social club *n* a club where people can meet, drink, play sports etc.

social conscience *n* a concern for and desire to help people who are poor, old, ill etc.

social democracy *n* a political system that supports social justice and equality in a capitalist economic system; a country that is run by this system.

social event *n* **-1.** an event that is held to entertain the members of a company or other organization. **-2.** a party, sports event etc that is important to a particular group of society □ *It was the social event of the year.*

social fund *n* in Britain, an amount of money used by the state to lend money to people who are very poor.

Socialism ['soʊʃəlɪzm] *n* the political belief that the state should control business and industry so that everybody can benefit from a country's wealth.

NOTE: Compare **capitalism, Communism.**

Socialist ['soʊʃələst] ◇ *n* a person who supports socialism. ◇ *adj*: *a Socialist government/policy.*

socialite ['soʊʃəlaɪt] *n* a person who is well-known because they go to a lot of parties with rich or famous people.

socialize, -ise ['soʊʃəlaɪz] *vi* to spend time with other people for pleasure □ *I don't socialize with the people I work with.*

socialized medicine [ˌsoʊʃəlaɪzd-] *n* medical care provided by the state.

social life *n* activities in which one enjoys oneself with other people, usually by going out to meet them, e.g. at parties or clubs □ *He doesn't have much of a social life.* □ *Social life is important in Spanish culture.*

socially ['soʊʃəlɪ] *adv* **-1.** from the point of view of society □ *That kind of behavior is not really socially acceptable.* **-2.** [meet, visit] for pleasure, not as part of one's work □ *I only know them socially.*

social order *n* the way in which society is organized in a particular place □ *The party aims to establish a new social order.*

social science *n* the scientific study of people in society; a subject, e.g. economics, politics, sociology, or history, that is part of this kind of study.

social security *n* GB money paid by a government to people who are unemployed, ill etc □ *social security benefits* □ *I spent three months on social security before I found a job.*

◆ **Social Security** *n* a US government program that pays money to people who have retired.

social services *npl* the services provided by a government to help and give advice to people who have problems with money, their health, family etc □ *You should speak to your local social services department.*

social studies *npl* a subject taught in schools that includes politics and sociology.

social work *n* work that is done by the social services.

social worker *n* a person who works in the social services with people who need help.

society [sə'saɪətɪ] (*pl* **societies**) *n* **-1.** people in general when considered as an organized group □ *They want equal status in society.* □ *You are a danger to society.* **-2.** a large group of people with the same customs, nationality, religion etc □ *an industrial/a multiracial society.* **-3.** an organized group of people with similar interests or aims □ *a film/debating society.*

Society of Friends *n* **the Society of Friends** another name for the Quakers (formal use).

socioeconomic [,soʊsɪoʊiːkə'nɒmɪk] *adj* [policy, group] that is connected with the economic conditions of groups in society.

sociological [,soʊsjə'lɒdʒɪkl] *adj* [research, issue, differences] that is connected with sociology.

sociologist [,soʊsɪ'ɒlədʒəst] *n* an expert in or student of sociology.

sociology [,soʊsɪ'ɒlədʒɪ] *n* the scientific study of human society and the behavior of people in large groups.

sock [sɒk] *n* a piece of clothing which covers the foot and ankle and is made of wool, nylon etc □ *a pair of socks.*

socket ['sɒkət] *n* **-1.** ELECTRICITY a device with holes which is fixed to a wall and which the plug of an electrical device can be fitted into in order to connect it to the electricity supply. **-2.** ANATOMY [of a shoulder, hip bone] a hole or hollow place in a bone which the end of another bone fits into; [of an eye] one of the two hollow spaces in the head where the eyes are.

Socrates ['sɒkrətiːz] (470–399 BC) a Greek philosopher who taught his ideas using a series of questions and answers.

sod [sɒd] *n* **-1.** a piece of earth with grass on it, usually when cut from the ground. **-2.**▽ GB an unpleasant and annoying person (very informal use) □ *You stupid sod!*

soda ['soʊdə] *n* **-1.** CHEMISTRY a compound of sodium used for cleaning or cooking. **-2.** = **soda water. -3.** US a sweet drink with bubbles of gas □ *a lime soda.*

soda siphon *n* a special bottle for making soda water and adding it to drinks.

soda water *n* water that has been sweetened and made fizzy, used for mixing with other drinks □ *soda and lime* □ *a scotch and soda.*

sodden ['sɒdn] *adj* [clothes, earth] very wet.

sodium ['soʊdɪəm] *n* a silver-white metal chemical element found in compounds such as salt. SYMBOL: Na.

sofa ['soʊfə] *n* a piece of furniture for two or more people to sit on that has a back and arms and is padded with cushions or soft material.

sofa bed *n* a sofa that is designed to be made easily into a bed.

soft [sɒft] *adj* **-1.** [metal, wood, cheese] that is less hard than normal □ *The soil was soft and easy to dig.* **-2.** [bed, cushion] that changes shape easily when pressed □ *This pillow's nice and soft.* **-3.** [wool, skin, hair] that is smooth and pleasant to touch □ *the soft touch of her hands.* **-4.** [wind, knock, blow] that is gentle and involves little force or violence □ *The air-*

plane made a soft landing. **-5.** [sound, voice, music] that is not loud and is often pleasant to listen to □ *"He's asleep," said Louise in a soft voice.* **-6.** [light, color, glow] that is not bright □ *soft pastel shades.* **-7.** [teacher, boss] that allows other people too much freedom and is not strict enough when they do something bad □ *She's too soft with her children.* □ *The President was accused of being soft on crime.*

softball ['sɒftbɔːl] *n* a game like baseball played with a larger, softer ball.

soft-boiled *adj* **a soft-boiled egg** an egg that is boiled so that the white part is hard but the yellow part is still liquid.

soft drink *n* a cold sweet drink that contains no alcohol, usually sold in bottles or cans.

soft drugs *npl* drugs, e.g. cannabis, that are not known to be harmful or addictive. NOTE: Compare **hard drugs.**

soften ['sɒfn] ◇ *vt* **-1.** [metal, soil, fabric] to make <sthg> softer. **-2.** [blow, effect, impact] to make <sthg> seem less serious or worrying □ *The government cut taxes to soften the effect of price increases.* **-3. to soften one's attitude** to become less critical or severe □ *There are signs that they are softening their stance on the dispute over fishing rights.*
◇ *vi* **-1.** [metal, butter, fabric] to become soft □ *Leave the ice cream out of the fridge to soften.* **-2.** [person, attitude] to become less critical or severe □ *"Oh, I suppose you can come," he said, softening a little.* **-3.** [eyes, voice, expression] to become gentler and more friendly □ *Susan's face softened as she looked at the sleeping child.*

◆ **soften up** *vt sep* **to soften sb up** to be pleasant to sb so that they will be more likely to agree to something (informal use) □ *Look, buy him a couple of drinks to soften him up, then ask him for the money.*

soft focus *n* **in soft focus** photographed or filmed in a way that makes all the lines less clear, usually in order to make somebody or something more attractive.

soft furnishings *npl* GB a collective term for curtains, cushions, mats, seat covers etc.

softhearted [,sɒft'hɑːrtəd] *adj* [person] who is kind, sympathetic, and quick to forgive people.

softly ['sɒftlɪ] *adv* [knock, speak, glow] *see* **soft.**

softness ['sɒftnəs] *n* [of a metal, bed, skin etc] *see* **soft.**

soft-pedal *vi* to give less emphasis or attention to something because it has become difficult or embarrassing (informal use).

soft sell *n* **the soft sell** a way of selling things by gently persuading people to buy them rather than by using a lot of pressure.

soft-spoken *adj* [person] who talks in a quiet, gentle, pleasant voice.

soft toy *n* a soft furry or woolen toy, e.g. a teddy bear.

software ['sɒftweəʳ] *n* the programs that are used in a computer to do particular jobs □ *word-processing software* □ *a software designer/company.* NOTE: Compare **hardware.**

software package *n* a complete set of computer programs designed to carry out a particular task, such as word processing.

softwood ['sɒftwʊd] *n* wood from trees such as pine and fir which grow quickly and are cheap and easy to cut.

softy ['sɒftɪ] (*pl* **softies**) *n* -1. a weak person who cries and complains too easily (informal and disapproving use). -2. a sensitive person who is easily persuaded to do things by other people (informal use).

soggy ['sɒgɪ] (*compar* **soggier**, *superl* **soggiest**) *adj* [ground, clothes, food] that is soft and wet in an unpleasant way.

Soho ['soʊhoʊ] an area of central London containing many restaurants, bars, and nightclubs.

SoHo ['soʊhoʊ] a fashionable area of Manhattan, New York City, containing many shops and restaurants.

soil [sɔɪl] ◇ *n* -1. the top layer of earth that plants grow in □ *The soil should be kept moist.* -2. the land that belongs to a particular country or area (formal use) □ *We were back on British soil.* ◇ *vt* [clothes, hands] to make <sthg> dirty, especially with urine or feces.

soiled [sɔɪld] *adj* [clothes, sheets, goods] dirty □ *soiled bedding.*

solace ['sɒləs] *n* a feeling of comfort and relief from sadness, pain, disappointment etc; a person or thing that causes this feeling (formal use) □ *I found some solace in my books.*

solar ['soʊlə^r] *adj* -1. [heat, radiation] that is produced by the sun. -2. **solar energy** energy that is produced by the sun in the form of light and heat.

solarium [US sə'lærɪəm, GB -'leər-] (*pl* **solariums** OR **solaria** [-ɪə]) *n* a room with sunbeds where people can go to get an artificial suntan.

solar panel *n* a device, e.g. on a roof or spacecraft, that uses the sun's energy to produce electricity.

solar plexus [-'pleksəs] *n* the part of the body below the chest and above the stomach.

solar system *n* the sun and all the planets, comets etc that move around it.

sold [soʊld] *past tense & past participle of* **sell**.

solder [US 'sɒdər, GB 'sɒldə] ◇ *n* a soft mixture of metals, usually tin and lead, that melts easily and is used for joining metals or wires together. ◇ *vt* to join <two metals, electrical parts> etc together using solder.

soldering iron [US 'sɒdərɪŋ-, GB 'sɒldərɪŋ-] *n* an electrical device for melting solder and joining metals together.

soldier ['soʊldʒə^r] *n* a member of an army, especially one who is not an officer.

◆ **soldier on** *vi* GB to keep working at something although it is difficult or unpleasant.

sold out *adj* [performance, theater, concert] for which all the tickets have been sold □ *Tickets for tonight are sold out.*

sole [soʊl] (*pl sense 2 only* **sole** OR **soles**) ◇ *adj* -1. **the sole reason/survivor etc** the only reason/survivor etc □ *He was the sole inheritor.*

-2. **to have sole ownership/responsibility etc** to be the only person who owns/is responsible for etc something □ *We have sole rights on the invention.* ◇ *n* -1. the bottom part of one's foot; the part of a shoe, sock etc that covers this □ *shoes designed to support the soles of the feet* □ *rubber soles.* -2. a flat sea fish with white flesh, used as food.

solely ['soʊllɪ] *adv* [responsible, concerned] only □ *This is solely a matter for the directors.*

solemn ['sɒləm] *adj* -1. [person, face, voice] that is serious and shows no humor □ *Sam looked very solemn when he came back into the room.* -2. [promise, agreement, declaration] that one makes in a very serious and sincere way □ *They stood before the priest, exchanging solemn vows.* -3. [occasion, ceremony, music] very serious, grand, and impressive □ *on this important and solemn occasion.*

solemnly ['sɒləmlɪ] *adv* [speak, promise] *see* **solemn**.

sole owner US, **sole trader** GB *n* a person who owns and runs a business alone and is the only person responsible for its debts.

solicit [sə'lɪsət] ◇ *vt* [money, help, opinions] to ask for <sthg> (formal use). ◇ *vi* [prostitute] to approach people in a public place and offer to have sex with them for money □ *She was arrested for soliciting.*

solicitor [sə'lɪsətə^r] *n* GB & AUS a lawyer who prepares legal documents, gives advice, and appears for their clients in some types of court.

solicitous [sə'lɪsətəs] *adj* (formal use) -1. [person] who is kind, caring, and wants to help □ *"Shall I help you up?" asked Clive, in solicitous tones.* -2. **solicitous of** OR **for sthg** interested in and anxious about sthg □ *He enquired after my mother, most solicitous of her health.*

solid ['sɒlɪd] ◇ *adj* -1. [food, mixture] that is not a liquid or gas; [rock, layer] that is firm, hard, and made of dense material □ *The milk has frozen solid.* □ *I could feel something solid at the bottom of the bag.* -2. [tire, ball, shape] that is not hollow but is filled with some material. -3. [gold, wood] that is not mixed with any other substance; [blue, green] that is the same color all over a particular area □ *a solid-silver teapot.* -4. [building, foundations] that is strongly made and is unlikely to break or fall down; [support, relationship, basis] that has been developed over a long time and is therefore unlikely to change or fail; [grip, push] strong and firm □ *Those walls look solid enough.* □ *This year's sales provide a solid base for future expansion.* □ *It's hardly as if your relationship is solid, is it?* -5. [person, company] that is known to be reliable, trustworthy, and respectable □ *a good solid worker.* -6. [work, advice, experience] that is practical, useful, and carefully done or considered; [evidence, reasoning] that is real, definite, and convincing because it is based on facts rather than beliefs or wishes □ *He gave me some very solid advice about careers.* □ *We need some solid facts on which to base our decision.* -7. [crowd, wall] without breaks, gaps, or spaces; [hours, days] without breaks or pauses □ *a solid yellow line at the side of the road* □ *We worked for two hours solid* OR *two solid hours.*

◇ *adv* **to be packed solid** [stadium, suitcase] to be filled so completely that there is no room left.

◇ *n* a substance that is solid and not a liquid or gas.

◆ **solids** *npl* food that is solid and is not like milk, soup etc □ *Is the baby taking solids yet?*

solidarity [ˌsɒlə'dærətɪ] *n* support shown by one group of people for another group who have similar concerns □ *Miners showed solidarity with the nurses by going on strike too.*

solid fuel *n* a fuel that is a solid substance, e.g. coal, wood etc rather than oil or gas □ *a solid-fuel heating system.*

solidify [sə'lɪdəfaɪ] (*pt* & *pp* **solidified**) *vi* [paint, cement] to become solid or hard.

solidly ['sɒlədlɪ] *adv* **-1.** [vote, support] with everybody agreeing □ *The board is solidly in favor of the offer.* **-2.** [talk, walk] continuously and without stopping □ *We worked solidly for six hours.* **-3.** [built, based, researched] *see* **solid** □ *a solidly-reasoned argument.*

soliloquy [sə'lɪləkwɪ] (*pl* **soliloquies**) *n* a speech in a play in which a character speaks their private thoughts aloud to the audience.

solitaire ['sɒləteəʳ] *n* **-1.** US a card game for one person. **-2.** a game for one person in which pegs or marbles are moved over each other on a board and removed. The aim is to be left with only one peg or marble at the end. **-3.** a single jewel, especially a diamond; a ring with this kind of jewel.

solitary [US 'sɒləterɪ, GB -tərɪ] *adj* **-1.** [walk, life, occupation] that is done by one person □ *Being a photographer is a very solitary occupation.* **-2.** [person] who spends a lot of time alone, usually because they prefer it; [place, street] with no or few people in it □ *a solitary, unsociable sort of man* □ *She walked through the solitary square.* **-3.** **a solitary person/thing** the only person/thing in a particular place □ *A solitary figure stood on the shore.*

solitary confinement *n* a kind of punishment in which a prisoner is kept locked up alone so that they cannot speak to other people.

solitude ['sɒlətjuːd] *n* the state of being alone, especially when this is peaceful and enjoyable □ *a need for solitude.*

solo ['səʊləʊ] (*pl* **solos**) ◇ *adj* **-1.** MUSIC [passage, piece] that is performed alone without any other instruments or voices □ *a solo performance* □ *music for solo violin.* **-2.** [attempt, flight] that is done by one person alone □ *a solo voyage around the world.* ◇ *adv* **-1.** MUSIC [play, sing] *I enjoy performing solo.* **-2.** [fly, climb] *He was the first person to sail solo across the Atlantic.* ◇ *n* MUSIC a piece of music that is performed by a single instrument or singer □ *a violin/guitar solo.*

soloist ['səʊləʊəst] *n* a person who performs a musical solo.

Solomon ['sɒləmən] in the Bible, a king of Is-

rael in the 10th century BC who was very wise.

Solomon Islands: the Solomon Islands a group of islands in the southwest Pacific Ocean. The western islands are part of Papua New Guinea and the eastern islands are an independent state. SIZE: 30,000 sq kms. POPULATION: 300,000 (*Solomon Islanders*). CAPITAL: Honiara. LANGUAGE: English. CURRENCY: Solomon Islands dollar.

solstice ['sɒlstəs] *n* the longest or shortest day of the year, when the sun is farthest from the equator □ *the summer/winter solstice.*

soluble ['sɒljəbl] *adj* **-1.** [substance] that can dissolve in water or in another liquid □ *Are these aspirin soluble?* **-2.** [problem, crime, mystery] that can be solved (formal use).

solution [sə'luːʃn] *n* **-1.** [to a problem, crisis] a way of dealing with a difficult situation so that it is no longer a problem □ *We are looking for a solution to our financial difficulties.* **-2.** [to an equation, crime, mystery] an answer or explanation to something □ *the solution to a crossword puzzle.* **-3.** a liquid in which a solid or gas is dissolved □ *a copper sulfate solution* □ *a solution of salt and water.*

solve [sɒlv] *vt* [crime, mystery] to find a solution to <a problem or question> □ *Getting all worked up isn't going to solve anything.*

solvency ['sɒlvənsɪ] *n* FINANCE [of a person, company] *see* **solvent.**

solvent ['sɒlvənt] ◇ *adj* FINANCE [company, organization] that has enough money to pay its debts □ *Despite the recession we are still solvent.* ◇ *n* a liquid that can dissolve other substances.

solvent abuse *n* the activity of using glues, polishes etc as drugs by breathing in their fumes to experience feelings of pleasure and excitement (formal use).

Solzhenitsyn [US ˌsoʊlʒə'nɪtsən, GB ˌsɒl-], **Alexander** (1918–) a Russian writer whose books, such as *The Gulag Archipelago*, criticized Stalinist Russia.

Som. *abbr of* **Somerset.**

Somali [US soʊ'mɑːlɪ, GB sə-] *n* & *adj*: *see* **Somalia.**

Somalia [US soʊ'mɑːlɪə, GB sə-] a country in East Africa, on the Indian Ocean north of Kenya. SIZE: 638,000 sq kms (including Somaliland). POPULATION: 9,500,000 (*Somalis*). CAPITAL: Mogadishu. LANGUAGE: Somali. CURRENCY: Somali shilling.

Somaliland [US soʊ'mɑːlɪlænd, GB sə-] **-1.** a region of northwestern Somalia that declared its independence as the Republic of Somaliland in 1991, but has not been officially recognized by other countries. **-2.** the old name for a region of East Africa that covers Somalia, Djibouti, and part of Ethiopia.

somber US, **sombre** GB ['sɒmbəʳ] *adj* **-1.** [person, mood, event] that seems sad and serious. **-2.** [color, room, clouds] that looks dark and dull.

some [*stressed* sʌm, *unstressed* səm] ◇ *adj* **-1.** used to refer to an amount or number that

is not stated exactly. ■ **I have some milk** used with uncountable nouns □ *The leaflet has some information on things to do in the area.* □ *Would you like some coffee?* ■ **I have some flowers** used with plural nouns □ *There are some tomatoes in the fridge.* □ *We're having some problems with the fax machine.* **-2. some time/years** a fairly large amount of time/ number of years □ *We've known each other for some months now.* □ *I had some difficulty getting in touch with him.* **-3.** used to refer to a certain group of people or things □ *Some people find it hard to cope with stress, while others enjoy it.* **-4.** used with singular countable nouns to refer to a person or thing without being precise □ *The first prize was won by some taxi-driver or other in London.* □ *At some point you'll need to take a break.* □ *There must be some mistake.* **-5.** used to show that one thinks somebody or something is very good (informal use) □ *He's some dancer!* **-6.** used to show that one thinks somebody or something is not very good (informal use) □ *Some party!* ■ **some help you are!** you are not being very helpful!
◇ *pron* **-1.** used to refer to an amount that is not stated exactly □ *"Coffee?"* — *"No thanks, I've just had some."* □ *Can I have some?* □ *Some of the money will be spent on improving the facilities.* **-2.** used to refer to a number that is not stated exactly □ *If there are any copies left, can I have some?* □ *Some of the guests left early.* ■ **some say...** some people say... □ *Some believe that Elvis is still alive.*
◇ *adv* approximately □ *some ten years ago.*

somebody ['sʌmbədɪ] ◇ *pron* used to refer to a person when one does not know exactly who the person is, or when one does not want to be precise □ *Somebody called when you were out.* □ *There was somebody standing outside the house.* ■ **somebody else** another person □ *I don't know, ask somebody else.* ◇ *n* an important person □ *He really thinks he's somebody.*

someday ['sʌmdeɪ] *adv* at some time in the future that is still unknown or undecided □ *I hope to see him again someday soon.*

somehow ['sʌmhaʊ] *adv* **-1.** used to show that one does not know how something happens □ *Somehow I slipped and hurt my foot.* **-2. somehow,...** for a reason that is not known □ *Somehow, things don't seem the same.*

someone ['sʌmwʌn] *pron* = somebody.

someplace ['sʌmpleɪs] *adv* US = somewhere.

somersault ['sʌmərsɔːlt] ◇ *n* **to do a somersault** to turn completely once by rolling forward or backward on the ground or in the air □ *She did a backward somersault.* ◇ *vi* to do one or more somersaults □ *The car somersaulted down the slope.*

Somerset ['sʌmərset] a county in south-western England. SIZE: 3,451 sq kms. POPULATION: 452,300. ADMINISTRATIVE CENTER: Taunton.

something ['sʌmθɪŋ] ◇ *pron* **-1.** used to refer to a thing when one does not know exactly what it is, or when one does not want to be precise □ *Excuse me, you've dropped something.* □ *Would you like something to eat?* □ *There's*

something not quite right here. ■ **something else** another thing □ *Something else is worrying me.* ■ **or something** used when one cannot remember a fact exactly, or to refer to another thing that is similar to what one has just mentioned □ *She's a creative director or something.* □ *We could have spaghetti or something for lunch.* **-2. that's something** a phrase used to say that something is good or useful in a small way □ *"I've got $20."* — *"Well, that's something at least."* □ *There's something in what you say.* **-3.** *phrases* **that's really something!** that's very impressive! ■ **to be something of a poet/mathematician** to be good as a poet/ mathematician without being one professionally.
◇ *adv* **something like** OR **something in the region of a hundred** approximately a hundred □ *There were something like fifty people there.*

sometime ['sʌmtaɪm] ◇ *adj* used to refer to the job, position etc that somebody once had but that they no longer hold □ *Herbert Smith, sometime professor of physics at Harvard.* ◇ *adv* used to refer to a time in the future or in the past that one does not know □ *I hope we'll meet again sometime.* □ *I'll see you sometime next week.* □ *sometime in 1945.*

sometimes ['sʌmtaɪmz] *adv* on some occasions, but not always □ *Sometimes we're very busy, whereas at other times it's quiet.* □ *We sometimes eat outside when it's warm enough.* □ *Sometimes I wish we'd never left England.* □ *Harry can be very obstinate sometimes.*

someway ['sʌmweɪ] *adv* somehow.

somewhat ['sʌmwɒt] *adv* **somewhat young/ strange** rather young/strange □ *The quality of the wine is somewhat poorer than usual.*

somewhere ['sʌmweər] *adv* **-1.** used to refer to a place that one does not know, or that one does not want to state exactly □ *They live somewhere near here.* □ *I know my glasses are here somewhere.* ■ **somewhere else** in or to another place □ *Let's go somewhere else this year.* □ *If this hotel is full, we can always try somewhere else.* **-2. somewhere between five and ten** somewhere between five and ten. ■ **somewhere around** OR **in the region of a hundred** approximately a hundred □ *The cathedral was started somewhere around 1050.* **-3.** *phrase* **to be getting somewhere** to be making progress □ *At last we're getting somewhere.*

son [sʌn] *n* somebody's male child □ *This is my son.* □ *He has two sons and a daughter.*

sonar ['səʊnɑːr] *n* an apparatus or system used on ships to measure sea depths or to find underwater objects by using sound waves.

sonata [sə'nɑːtə] *n* a piece of classical music, usually in four parts, for piano or for piano and one other instrument.

song [sɒŋ] *n* **-1.** a short piece of music with words □ *Sing us a song!* □ *a pop/folk/love song.* ■ **for a song** [buy, sell, get] cheaply (informal use) □ *We bought this old sofa for a song.* ■ **to make a song and dance about sthg** to get too angry or excited about sthg (informal use) □ *There's no need to make such a song and dance about it.* **-2.** the act of singing □ *They suddenly* burst into song. **-3.** the pleasant and musical sounds made by some kinds of bird.

songbook ['sɒŋbʊk] *n* a book of songs.

sonic ['sɒnɪk] *adj* [probe, test] using sound or sound waves.

sonic boom *n* the loud noise like an explosion that is made by an airplane when it flies faster than the speed of sound.

son-in-law (*pl* **sons-in-law** OR **son-in-laws**) *n* the husband of one's daughter.

sonnet ['sɒnət] *n* a poem with 14 lines which contains a particular sequence of rhymes.

sonny ['sʌnɪ] *n* a word used to talk to a boy or young man who is much younger than one (old-fashioned use).

soon [suːn] *adv* **-1.** used to refer to a time in the future that is near □ *The ambulance will be here soon.* □ *He will soon realize his mistake.* **-2.** early □ *How soon can you finish it?* □ *I spoke too soon.* ■ **as soon as I find out** immediately after I find out □ *I'll let you know as soon as anything happens.* □ *As soon as she saw what had happened, she ran for the door.* ■ **as soon as possible** at the earliest possible time □ *She asked you to call back as soon as possible because it was urgent.* **-3.** *phrase* **I'd just as soon stay at home** I would prefer to stay at home.

sooner ['suːnər] *adv* **-1.** earlier □ *They arrived sooner than I expected.* ■ **no sooner... than...** a phrase used to say that one thing happened immediately after something else □ *No sooner had I sat down than the phone rang.* ■ **sooner or later** a phrase used to say that something is definitely going to happen in the future but one cannot be sure when □ *She's sure to find out sooner or later.* ■ **the sooner the better** a phrase used to say that it would be better for something to happen soon rather than later □ *"When shall we leave?" — "Well, the sooner the better, really."* **-2.** **I would sooner...** I would prefer to... □ *"Do you want to come with us?" — "I'd sooner stay at home, if you don't mind."*

soot [sʊt] *n* the black powder produced by burning coal or wood.

soothe [suːð] *vt* **-1.** [pain, ache, muscles] to make <sth> less painful □ *a cream to soothe sunburned skin.* **-2.** [person, fear, worry] to calm <sb/sth> □ *Poor Lilian was left trying to soothe everybody's feelings after her husband's outburst.*

soothing ['suːðɪŋ] *adj* [ointment, cream, words] that soothes □ *"There, there," said Fiona in a soothing voice.*

sooty ['sʊtɪ] (*compar* **sootier**, *superl* **sootiest**) *adj* [face, window] that is covered with soot.

sop [sɒp] *n* something small and of little value offered to somebody who is dissatisfied, to stop them complaining (disapproving use) □ *They promised to tighten up safety procedures as a sop to their critics.*

sophisticated [sə'fɪstəkeɪtəd] *adj* **-1.** [person, dress, taste] that shows knowledge about what is stylish and fashionable □ *a sophisticated young woman.* **-2.** [reader, electorate, discussion] that is intelligent and well-informed, and shows an ability to understand compli-

cated matters □ *You must understand that you are dealing with an extremely sophisticated audience.* **-3.** [machine, weapon, process] that is technologically advanced and complicated □ *a sophisticated new missile launcher.*

sophistication [sə,fɪstə'keɪʃn] *n* [of taste, a reader, machine] *see* **sophisticated.**

Sophocles ['sɒfəkliːz] (495–406 BC) a Greek writer whose best-known works are the tragedies *Oedipus Rex* and *Antigone.*

sophomore ['sɒfəmɔːr] *n* US a student in their second year of a US college, university, or high school.

soporific [,sɒpə'rɪfɪk] *adj* [drug, music] that makes one feel sleepy.

sopping ['sɒpɪŋ] ◇ *adj* [coat, shoes] very wet. ◇ *adv* **sopping wet** very wet.

soppy ['sɒpɪ] (*compar* **soppier**, *superl* **soppiest**) *adj* [person, book] that seems emotional and sentimental in a silly way (informal and disapproving use).

soprano [US sə'prænoʊ, GB -'prɑːn-] (*pl* **sopranos**) *n* a woman or girl whose voice can reach the highest notes that people can sing; the voice of such a singer.

sorbet [US 'sɔːrbət, GB 'sɔːbeɪ] *n* a cold sweet dish made from frozen fruit juice and sometimes egg white and sugar □ *lemon sorbet.*

sorcerer ['sɔːrsərər] *n* a magician who uses evil spirits to make things happen.

sordid ['sɔːrdəd] *adj* **-1.** [desires, thoughts, behavior] that one finds selfish, dishonest, and immoral □ *I don't want to know about your sordid affairs!* **-2.** [room, town] that looks dirty and unpleasant □ *some sordid little bar in Soho.*

sore [sɔːr] ◇ *adj* **-1.** [arm, feet] that feels painful because of a wound, infection, or too much use □ *I was sore all over after the game.* □ *The patient was complaining of a sore throat and a temperature.* ■ **a sore point** a subject that makes somebody feel angry or embarrassed whenever people mention it □ *Don't ask them about the vacation — it's a sore point at the moment.* **-2.** **to be sore** to be angry because somebody has treated one badly or unfairly (informal use) □ *I hope you're not still sore at me?* **-3.** **to be in sore need of sthg** to need sthg urgently □ *Those shoes are in sore need of repairing.* □ *I was in sore need of a drink.* ◇ *n* MEDICINE a painful place on the body where the skin is infected.

sorely ['sɔːrlɪ] *adv* **sorely needed/disappointed etc** very much needed/very disappointed etc □ *I was sorely tempted to hit him.* □ *Your presence at the dinner will be sorely missed.*

sorority [sə'rɒrətɪ] (*pl* **sororities**) *n* in the USA, a club for women students at a university, usually for students who live in the same building; *see box at* **fraternity.**

sorrow ['sɒroʊ] *n* a feeling of great sadness, e.g. because somebody has died or because one has done something that hurts other people; something that causes this feeling □ *It is with great sorrow that I must tell you...* □ *a feeling of sorrow* □ *the sorrows of this life.*

sorrowful ['sɒrəfl] *adj* [person, look] showing sorrow; [event, day, news] causing sorrow (literary use).

sorry ['sɒrɪ] (*compar* **sorrier**, *superl* **sorriest**) ◇ *adj* **-1.** a word used to apologize for something one has said or done □ *I'm sorry if I'm disturbing you.* □ *She'll probably forgive you if you say you're sorry.* □ *I'm sorry about the dent in your car.* □ *I'm sorry to bother you.* □ *I'm sorry (that) I got angry with you.* □ *He seemed truly sorry for what he had done.* **-2.** a word used to show one's disappointment at something that has been said or done □ *I was sorry to hear that Tom's leaving.* □ *I'm only sorry (that) you can't be there.* **-3.** a word used to show one wishes something had not happened, or when giving bad news □ *"Can I speak to Melinda?" — "I'm sorry, she's out of the office at present."* □ *I'm sorry (that) I ever agreed to help.* □ *I'm sorry to have to announce the death of Simon Pearson.* **-4.** a word used to show sympathy or pity for somebody, especially when something bad has happened □ *"My sister died yesterday." — "I'm so sorry."* □ *I'm really sorry that you've split up.* □ *You can't help feeling sorry for Joan.* ■ **to feel sorry for oneself** to feel unhappy because one thinks that one has been badly treated (disapproving use) □ *Stop sitting there feeling sorry for yourself and go and do something about it!* **-5.** a word used to show polite disagreement or refusal □ *I'm sorry, but I think that should be 1991.* □ *"Can you come out tonight?" — "I'm sorry, I can't."* **-6. to be in a sorry state** to be in very bad condition □ *My clothes were in a very sorry state by the time I got home.*
◇ *excl* **-1.** a word used to apologize for something one has said or done □ *Sorry! I didn't see you there.* **-2.** a word used to ask somebody to say something again because one did not hear it the first time □ *Sorry? I didn't catch what you said.* **-3.** a word used to interrupt and correct oneself or somebody else □ *He was a farmer, sorry, a farm worker.* □ *Sorry, can I say something here?*

sort [sɔːt] ◇ *n* **-1.** a kind, type, or group of things that have similar qualities □ *There are two sorts of wine to choose from.* □ *What sort of car does she drive?* □ *I really dislike this sort of thing/these sorts of things/things of this sort.* □ *"What sort of cheese do they sell?" — "Oh, all sorts."* □ *It isn't the sort of place I'd take my wife to.* □ *They have a Mercedes, or a BMW, or something of the sort.* ■ **a sort of...** of a kind that is unusual or difficult to describe □ *They had put up a sort of tent in the garden.* □ *I had a sort of feeling that things would go wrong.* **-2.** a person of a particular type □ *She's a good/an odd sort.* **-3.** the act of sorting mail, documents etc □ *Have a good sort through that pile of clothes.*
◇ *vt* [mail, clothes, information] to separate <sthg> into groups of different kinds □ *The eggs are sorted into three different sizes.*

◆ **sorts** *npl* **-1. of sorts** of a kind that is difficult to describe, but usually of poor quality □ *He's a painter of sorts.* □ *"Do they have their own swimming pool?" — "Well, of sorts."* **-2. to be out of sorts** to be feeling slightly ill; to be

in a bad mood □ *I've been feeling rather out of sorts lately.*

◆ **sort of** *adv* a phrase used to describe something that is difficult to explain or describe precisely □ *I found the exhibit sort of interesting.* □ *I sort of imagined him to be older.* □ *"Did you enjoy the concert?" — "Sort of."* □ *It was a sort of tall metal object.*

◆ **sort out** *vt sep* **-1. to sort sthg out** [mail, documents, clothes] to sort sthg □ *Go through the papers and sort out the old ones from the new ones.* □ *I really must sort these clothes out.* **-2. to sort sthg out** [room, ideas, papers] to examine, change, and arrange sthg so that it is tidy or easier to deal with □ *Auditors were called in to sort out the company's finances.* **-3. to sort sthg out** [arrangements, plan] to decide how one intends to deal with sthg □ *We still haven't sorted out what we're going to do about transport.* **-4. to sort sthg out** [problem, misunderstanding] to deal with sthg in order to solve a difficulty □ *We'd better sit down and sort these things out between us.*

sortie ['sɔːtɪ] *n* a short sudden attack by troops into enemy territory from a position of defense; a flight made to bomb an enemy camp, city etc.

sorting office ['sɔːtɪŋ-] *n* a building where letters are sorted according to where they are going.

SOS (*abbr of* **save our souls**) *n* an international emergency signal; a call for help.

so-so (informal use) ◇ *adj* [food, vacation] that is good enough, but not as good as one had hoped. ◇ *adv*: *"How's business?" — "So-so."*

soufflé [US suːˈfleɪ, GB ˈsuːfleɪ] *n* a light dish made of beaten egg whites mixed with cheese, fish etc, then baked and eaten hot.

sought [sɔːt] *past tense & past participle of* **seek**.

sought-after *adj* [location, prize, antique] that a lot of people want because it is rare or very good □ *the country's most sought-after painter* □ *Campion's become much sought-after since the movie won an Oscar.*

soul [soʊl] *n* **-1.** [of a person] a person's true nature and character, thought of in religions as being separate from the body and continuing to live after the person has died □ *a prayer for the souls of the dead.* **-2.** [in a painting, song] the quality of beauty, honesty, and true emotional feeling □ *It's a very interesting movie, but it's got no soul.* **-3. the soul of sthg** a perfect example of sthg □ *You can tell her, she's the soul of discretion.* **-4. a good/happy etc soul** a good/happy etc person etc □ *Some poor soul was swept out to sea in last night's storm.* ■ **not a soul** nobody □ *I haven't told a soul.* □ *There wasn't a soul in the house.* **-5.** = **soul music.**

soul-destroying [-dɪstrɔɪŋ] *adj* [job, work] that is repetitive, boring, and depressing □ *It must be so soul-destroying having to work in that factory day after day.*

soul food *n* the traditional food eaten by black Americans in the southern USA.

soulful ['soulfl] *adj* [look, song] full of deep feeling, especially sadness □ *The dog looked at me with soulful eyes.*

soulless ['soulləs] *adj* without human feelings or qualities □ *a soulless concrete building.*

soul mate *n* a person that one shares the same feelings, ideas, and opinions with.

soul music *n* a type of popular music, often played by black Americans, that tries to express deep feelings.

soul-searching [-sɜːˈtʃɪŋ] *n* careful examination of one's thoughts and feelings, especially when one has to decide something □ *After much soul-searching, I decided to leave her.*

sound [saʊnd] ◇ *adj* -**1.** [mind, body] in good condition and healthy □ *My eyesight is perfectly sound.* -**2.** [building, structure, walls] strong and in good condition □ *The floor's quite sound, but the walls may need some work.* -**3.** [investment, policy, argument] that is reliable and shows good judgment □ *I think that's very sound advice.*
◇ *adv* **to be sound asleep** to be sleeping deeply.
◇ *n* -**1.** a particular noise made by something □ *The wire made a snapping sound when it broke.* □ *There was a sound of breaking glass.* -**2.** vibrations in air or water that can be sensed by the ear or by special equipment □ *the speed of sound.* -**3.** [of a radio, TV] the loudness of the sounds produced by a radio, TV etc □ *Would you mind turning the sound up a bit?* -**4. the sound of sthg** the idea or impression one has of sthg, especially because of the way somebody has described it □ *I don't like the sound of that.*
◇ *vt* [alarm, bell] to make <sthg> produce a sound □ *He sounded the horn as he rounded the bend.*
◇ *vi* -**1.** [alarm, bell, horn] to produce a sound □ *The alarm sounded.* ■ **to sound like sthg** to make a sound that is exactly like the sound of sthg else □ *It sounds like there's somebody at the door.* □ *It sounded just like our car.* -**2.** to seem □ *You sound upset.* □ *She sounded as if she was really upset.* ■ **to sound like sthg** to seem like sthg, based on what somebody has said □ *Your brother sounds like a lunatic.*

◆ **sound out** *vt sep* **to sound sb out** to try to find out what sb thinks or is going to do by asking them questions □ *I've tried to sound him out on OR about his plans, but he won't say anything.*

sound barrier *n* the increase in the force resisting an aircraft as it passes the speed of sound.

soundbite ['saʊndbaɪt] *n* a short phrase or comment usually spoken by a politician in order to make a strong impression quickly on TV or radio.

sound effects *npl* sounds produced artificially to make a play or movie seem more realistic.

sounding board *n* a person who one discusses one's opinions or ideas with in order to get an idea of how acceptable or popular these opinions or ideas are.

soundly ['saʊndlɪ] *adv* -**1.** [beat, defeat] thoroughly and completely. -**2. to sleep soundly** to sleep well and deeply.

soundproof ['saʊndpruːf] *adj* [wall, room] that does not allow sound to pass in or out.

soundtrack ['saʊndtræk] *n* the recorded sound from a movie, especially the music.

sound wave *n* a wave of energy that carries sound through air or water.

soup [suːp] *n* food in the form of a liquid made by boiling meat, fish, or vegetables in water □ *a bowl of soup.*

◆ **soup up** *vt sep* **to soup a car up** to increase the size or power of the engine of a car to make it travel faster.

soup kitchen *n* a place where people who are homeless are given free food and drink.

soup plate *n* a plate with a rounded bottom used for serving soup in.

soup spoon *n* a large rounded spoon used for eating soup.

sour ['saʊəʳ] ◇ *adj* -**1.** [fruit, sauce] that has a sharp, bitter taste □ *I found the dressing a little sour.* -**2.** [milk, wine] that has an unpleasant taste because it is no longer fresh □ *The milk's sour.* ■ **to go** OR **turn sour** [milk, cream] to start to have an unpleasant taste and smell; [relationship] to gradually become unpleasant □ *Things between Andy and Grace had already begun to go sour.* -**3.** [person, look, reply] bad-tempered and unfriendly □ *He's a sour-faced old man!*
◇ *vt* [person, relationship] to make <sb/sthg> sour □ *That unfortunate evening rather soured my friendship with Paul.*
◇ *vi* [person, relationship] to become sour □ *After several years, their marriage began to sour.*

source [sɔːʳs] ◇ *n* -**1.** [of minerals, wealth, information] the place, person, or thing from which something comes □ *I find the Financial Times an invaluable source of information.* □ *source material* □ *As a journalist, I am not at liberty to disclose my source.* -**2.** [of a problem, discontent] a cause of something □ *First, we need to identify the source of the disturbance.* -**3.** [of a river] the place where a river or stream begins □ *the source of the Nile.* ◇ *vt* BUSINESS to get <a product> supplied by another manufacturer □ *Our new line is being sourced from abroad.*

sour cream *n* cream that is made sour by the addition of bacteria, used in cooking.

sour grapes *n* the attitude of pretending one does not want something simply because one cannot have it (disapproving use) □ *That's just sour grapes because you didn't win.*

Sousa ['suːzə], **J. P.** (1854-1932) a US composer who wrote military marches.

south [saʊθ] ◇ *adj* -**1. the south side/coast etc** the side/coast etc in or facing the south □ *Adelaide is on the south coast.* -**2. a south wind** a wind that comes from the south. ◇ *adv* [travel, fly] toward the south □ *Santa Fe is south of Los Alamos.* □ *The garden faces south.*
◇ *n* the direction which is on a person's

right when they are facing the place where the sun rises in the morning.

◆ **South** *n* -1. **the South** in the USA, the states in the southeast that have a history of slavery and fought against the North in the American Civil War. -2. **the South** in Britain, the southern counties of England. -3. **the South** the poorer countries in southern parts of the world, e.g. Africa, South America, and South Asia.

South Africa a country at the southern tip of Africa, with ports on the Atlantic and the Indian Oceans. SIZE: 1,221,000 sq kms. POPULATION: 40,600,000 (*South Africans*). CAPITAL: Cape Town. ADMINISTRATIVE CAPITAL: Pretoria. LANGUAGE: English, Afrikaans, Xhosa, Zulu, Sesotho. CURRENCY: rand.

South African *n* & *adj*: *see* **South Africa**.

South America the southern part of the Americas, a continent between the southern Atlantic and Pacific Oceans.

South American *n* & *adj*: *see* **South America**.

Southampton [sauθ'hæmptən] a city and major port in southern England. POPULATION: 194,400.

South Australia a state in central southern Australia. SIZE: 984,000 sq kms. POPULATION: 1,400,656. CAPITAL: Adelaide.

South Bank: **the South Bank (Centre)** a cultural center on the south bank of the Thames River in London.

southbound ['sauθbaund] *adj* [traffic, shipping, lane] that is traveling or leading toward the south.

South Carolina [-kærə'laınə] a state in the southeastern USA. ABBREVIATION: SC. SIZE: 78,282 sq kms. POPULATION: 3,486,703 (*South Carolinians*). CAPITAL: Columbia.

South Dakota a state in the central USA. ABBREVIATION: SD. SIZE: 196,723 sq kms. POPULATION: 696,004 (*South Dakotans*). CAPITAL: Pierre.

southeast [,sauθ'i:st] ◇ *adj* -1. **the southeast side/coast etc** the side/coast etc in or facing the southeast. -2. **a southeast wind** a wind that comes from the southeast. ◇ *adv* [face, travel, fly] toward the southeast □ *It lies 25 kms southeast of the capital.* ◇ *n* -1. the direction exactly halfway between south and east. -2. **the southeast** the southeastern part of a country or region.

Southeast Asia a region of southeastern Asia between India and China, including Brunei, Cambodia, Indonesia, Laos, Malaysia, Myanmar, the Philippines, Singapore, Thailand, and Vietnam.

southeasterly [,sauθ'i:stərlı] *adj* -1. [direction, region] toward or in the southeast. -2. **a southeasterly wind** a wind that comes from the southeast.

southeastern [,sauθ'i:stərn] *adj* that is in or comes from the southeast of a country or region.

southerly ['sʌðərlı] *adj* -1. [direction, region] toward or in the south. -2. **a southerly wind** a wind that comes from the south.

southern ['sʌðərn] *adj* [accent, town] that is in or comes from the south of a country or region.

Southern Baptist *n* a member of a Baptist church that follows the teachings in the Bible very closely.

Southern Cross *n* a group of stars that can be easily seen in the Southern Hemisphere. It appears on the national flag of Australia.

Southerner ['sʌðərnər] *n* a person who lives in or comes from the southern part of a country or region.

Southern Hemisphere *n* **the Southern Hemisphere** the part of the Earth that is south of the Equator.

Southern States: **the Southern States** the states in the southeastern USA that fought against the North in the American Civil War.

South Island the further south of the two islands of New Zealand. SIZE: 153,947 sq kms. POPULATION: 850,500. MAIN CITIES: Christchurch, Dunedin.

South Korea a republic in the southern part of the Korean Peninsula. SIZE: 99,000 sq kms. POPULATION: 44,600,000 (*South Koreans*). CAPITAL: Seoul. LANGUAGE: Korean. CURRENCY: won.

South Pole *n* **the South Pole** the most southern point on the surface of the Earth and the land surrounding it.

South Sea Islands = **Oceania**.

South Seas: **the South Seas** the seas in the Southern Hemisphere, especially the southern Pacific Ocean.

South Wales the southern part of Wales that used to be an important industrial and coalmining area.

southward ['sauθwərd] ◇ *adj* that is moving or facing toward the south. ◇ *adv* toward the south.

southwards ['sauθwərdz] *adv* [face, travel, fly] toward the south.

southwest [,sauθ'west] ◇ *adj* -1. **the southwest side/coast etc** the side/coast etc in or facing the southwest. -2. **a southwest wind** a wind that comes from the southwest. ◇ *adv* [face, travel, fly] toward the southwest □ *The village is situated 30 kms southwest of the capital.* ◇ *n* -1. the direction exactly halfway between south and west. -2. **the southwest** the southwestern part of a country or region.

southwesterly [,sauθ'westərlı] *adj* -1. [direction, region] that goes toward or is in the southwest. -2. **a southwesterly wind** a wind that comes from the southwest.

southwestern [,sauθ'westərn] *adj* that is in or comes from the southwest of a country or area.

South Yemen → **Yemen**.

souvenir [,su:və'nıər] *n* something which one buys or keeps to remind one of a vacation, event etc □ *Keep it as a souvenir of your visit.*

sou'wester [sau'westər] *n* a shiny waterproof

hat with a wide brim to keep the rain off one's head and neck.

sovereign ['sɒvrən] ◇ *adj* -1. [state, territory] that is independent and has its own government. -2. **a sovereign remedy** an excellent remedy (literary use). ◇ *n* -1. a king or queen; a ruler of a country or territory. -2. a gold coin that was once used in Britain and had the value of £1.

sovereignty ['sɒvrəntɪ] *n* complete power and authority to govern □ *Many British fear that a single European currency will mean a loss of national sovereignty.*

soviet ['soʊvɪət] *n* an elected local or national council in the former Soviet Union.

◆ **Soviet** ◇ *adj* that is connected with or comes from the USSR. ◇ *n* a person who lives in or comes from the USSR.

Soviet Union = USSR.

sow¹ [soʊ] (*pt* **sowed**, *pp* **sown** OR **sowed**) *vt* -1. to plant or scatter <seeds> in the ground so that they can grow □ *The seeds should be sown thinly.* -2. to cause <sthg unpleasant> to begin □ *His words sowed (the seeds of) doubt in my mind.*

sow² [saʊ] *n* an adult female pig.

sown [soʊn] *past participle of* **sow**.

sox [sɒks] US *plural of* **sock**.

soya ['sɔɪə] *n* soybeans □ *soya milk/flour.*

soybean ['sɔɪbiːn] US, **soya bean** GB *n* a type of bean grown in Asia, used as food or as a source of oil.

soy sauce [sɔɪ-] *n* a dark brown liquid made from soybeans, used especially in Japanese and Chinese cooking.

spa [spɑː] *n* a place where mineral water comes out of the ground and where people come to drink or bathe in the water, believing that it will improve their health.

space [speɪs] ◇ *n* -1. an empty area that can be used for a particular purpose □ *living space* □ *There isn't enough space in here.* □ *How much space do you have left in the car?* □ *I don't have the space for another bed in here.* □ *We'll have to make a space for the new computer.* -2. the area beyond the Earth's atmosphere □ *the first man in space* □ *space travel* □ *a space rocket.* ■ **to stare into space** to look straight ahead in a steady and fixed way at nothing in particular □ *Martin just sat there staring into space.* -3. PRINTING an area left blank between written or printed words, lines etc □ *Leave a space after a comma.* -4. [of time] a period of time □ *in a very short space of time* □ *Within the space of a year I had seen him change from a healthy young man to an invalid.*

◇ *vt* to arrange <things> so that they are separated by spaces or periods of time □ *The posts were spaced at ten-meter intervals.*

◆ **space out** *vt sep* to space things out to space things.

space age *n* **the space age** the present period of history in which travel in space has become possible.

◆ **space-age** *adj* [design, technology] that seems very modern (informal use).

space bar *n* a long key at the bottom of a typewriter keyboard used for putting spaces between letters, words etc.

space capsule *n* the part of a spacecraft in which humans travel and in which they return to Earth.

spacecraft [US 'speɪskræft, GB -krɑːft] (*pl* **spacecraft**) *n* a vehicle that can travel in space.

space heater *n* a heater that can be carried easily from one room to another.

space probe *n* a small spacecraft with no people in it that is used to send information back to Earth about space and other planets.

spaceship ['speɪsʃɪp] *n* = **spacecraft**.

space shuttle *n* a spacecraft designed to make several journeys between the Earth and a space station.

space station *n* a spacecraft that stays in space above the Earth, so that it can be used as a base for experiments or expeditions.

spacesuit ['speɪssuːt] *n* a special protective suit that covers the whole body and is worn by an astronaut.

spacing ['speɪsɪŋ] *n* PRINTING the way that words, lines etc on a printed page have been spaced.

spacious ['speɪʃəs] *adj* [room, car] that is large and has a lot of space in it that can be used.

Spackle™ ['spækl] *n* US a substance used for filling holes or cracks in walls.

spade [speɪd] *n* a tool with a long handle and a sharp metal blade that is used for digging the ground.

◆ **spades** *n* one of the four suits in a pack of playing cards that carries a symbol (♠) that looks like a black pointed leaf.

spadework ['speɪdwɜːrk] *n* hard uninteresting work that has to be done before something else can happen (informal use).

spaghetti [spə'getɪ] *n* a type of pasta made in long thin pieces like string, usually served with a sauce □ *spaghetti bolognese.*

Spain [speɪn] a country in southwestern Europe, with ports on the Mediterranean and the Atlantic Ocean. SIZE: 505,000 sq kms (including the Canary and Balearic Islands). POPULATION: 39,000,000 (*Spaniards, Spanish*). CAPITAL: Madrid. LANGUAGE: Spanish. CURRENCY: peseta.

span [spæn] (*pt* & *pp* **spanned**, *cont* **spanning**) ◇ *past tense of* **spin**. ◇ *n* -1. the period of time that something lasts □ *an attention span of about ten minutes.* -2. a range □ *a whole span of activities.* -3. [of hands, arms, wings] the distance between two points, especially when something is stretched as far as possible □ *Condors have a wing span of up to three meters.* -4. [of a bridge, arch] the distance between the supports of a bridge or arch. ◇ *vt* -1. to last throughout <a period of time> □ *Her career spans two decades.* -2. [bridge] to stretch from one side to the other of <a stream, river> etc □ *The bridge spans the Hudson River.*

spandex ['spændeks] *n* a stretchy material

used to make clothes that fit tightly, e.g. bathing suits and leotards.

spangled ['spæŋgld] *adj* that is covered with small shiny objects □ *a shirt spangled with sequins.*

Spaniard ['spænjəʳd] *n* a person who comes from or lives in Spain.

spaniel ['spænjəl] *n* a dog with short legs, long ears, and long smooth hair.

Spanish ['spænɪʃ] ◇ *adj: see* **Spain**. ◇ *n* a language spoken in Spain and many Latin American countries. ◇ *npl* **the Spanish** people who come from or live in Spain □ *Spanish resorts.*

Spanish America -1. the Latin American and Caribbean countries where Spanish is spoken. -2. the parts of the USA that used to be Spanish colonies.

Spanish-American ◇ *n* -1. a person who comes from or lives in Spanish America. -2. a Spanish-speaking person who comes from or lives in the USA. ◇ *adj*: *Spanish-American culture.*

Spanish-American War *n* **the Spanish-American War** a conflict between Spain and the USA in 1898 that ended Spanish rule in the Americas.

spank [spæŋk] ◇ *vt* [child] to hit <sb> on the bottom several times with the open hand. ◇ *n*: *If you don't behave, you'll get a spank!*

spanner ['spænəʳ] *n* GB a metal tool with a specially shaped hole at one end that is used for tightening nuts.

spar [spaːʳ] (*pt* & *pp* **sparred**, *cont* **sparring**) *vi* -1. SPORT to box without hitting one's opponent hard in order to practice or because one wants to test their reactions. -2. to argue in a lively but not aggressive way □ *The two of them always enjoyed sparring together.*

spare [speəʳ] ◇ *adj* -1. [pencil, pair of pants] that is not being used but that is kept in case it is needed □ *Did you bring a spare pair of shoes?* -2. [table, chair, ticket] free or able to be used □ *Do you have any spare change?* □ *I've got a spare ticket for tomorrow's concert.*
◇ *n* -1. AUTO = **spare wheel** (informal use). -2. = **spare part** (informal use). -3. an extra object of the same kind as another that is kept in case it is needed □ *The battery has run out, do you have a spare?*
◇ *vt* -1. [time, money, staff] to make <sb/sthg> available for a particular purpose □ *I can't spare you before 6pm, I'm afraid.* □ *I'll certainly come, if I can spare the time.* -2. [person, city] not to harm or punish <sb/sthg> □ *The village was spared in the great storm.* -3. **to spare no effort** to make as much effort as possible □ *No effort was spared to ensure its success.* ■ **to spare no expense** to spend as much money as is necessary to do something well □ *No expense was spared in the preparations for their wedding.* -4. **to spare sb sthg** to stop sb from having an unpleasant experience □ *We wanted to spare him the embarrassment, but he wouldn't listen.*
◆ **to spare** *adj* free or available □ *We had an hour to spare before the bus left.* □ *I caught the plane with ten minutes to spare.*

spare part *n* a new part that can be bought to replace a damaged part on a vehicle, machine etc.

spare room *n* a bedroom in a private house that is kept for guests to sleep in.

spare time *n* the time that one does not spend working and that can be used for pleasure □ *What do you do in your spare time?*

spare tire *n* -1. AUTO an extra wheel kept in a vehicle as a replacement in case one of the other wheels is damaged. -2. an area of fat around the waist (humorous use).

spare wheel *n* an extra wheel kept in the trunk of a vehicle as a replacement in case one of the other wheels is damaged.

sparing ['speərɪŋ] *adj* **to be sparing with** OR **of sthg** to give or use as little as possible of sthg □ *Try to be a little sparing with the sugar.*

sparingly ['speərɪŋlɪ] *adv* [use, spend] *see* **sparing**.

spark [spaːʳk] ◇ *n* -1. a small piece of burning material that flies out of a fire □ *Sparks flew from the roaring log fire.* -2. a flash of light caused by electricity moving between two points □ *You could see sparks coming off the tram line.* -3. a very small but noticeable amount of understanding, interest, humor etc that somebody shows □ *There wasn't even a spark of interest in the idea.* ◇ *vt* [debate, scandal, interest] to cause <sthg> to start or happen very quickly □ *The move sparked off serious riots in the capital.*

sparkle ['spaːʳkl] ◇ *vi* -1. [jewel, stars, eyes] to shine with many small bright flashes of light □ *The diamonds sparkled in the light.* -2. [person, conversation] to be amusing, clever, and lively □ *Jan was on very good form last night — she was positively sparkling.* ◇ *n*: *the sparkle of frost.*

sparkler ['spaːʳkləʳ] *n* a long thin firework that one holds in one's hand and that gives off tiny sparks of fire as it burns.

sparkling wine ['spaːʳklɪŋ-] *n* wine that is slightly bubbly.

spark plug *n* a part in the engine of a vehicle that produces electric sparks to light the gasoline.

sparrow [US 'sperou, GB 'spær-] *n* a small brown or gray bird that is found in many parts of the world.

sparse [spaːʳs] *adj* [population, rainfall] that is small in quantity and spread over a large area □ *Job opportunities have been rather sparse recently.*

Spartacus ['spaːʳtəkəs] (1st century BC) a slave leader who led an important slave revolt against the Roman Empire.

spartan ['spaːʳtn] *adj* [room, lifestyle] that seems simple and has no luxuries.

spasm ['spæzm] *n* -1. MEDICINE a sudden uncontrollable tightening of the muscles, often causing a sharp pain. -2. **a spasm of fear/coughing/anger etc** a sudden, short, and violent attack of fear/coughing/anger etc.

spasmodic [spæz'mɒdɪk] *adj* that happens suddenly for short periods of time at irregular intervals.

spastic ['spæstɪk] (old-fashioned use) ◇ *adj* [person] who suffers from a disease that prevents them from controlling the movement of some of their muscles. ◇ *n* a spastic person.

spat [spæt] *past tense & past participle of* **spit**.

spate [speɪt] *n* **a spate of sthg** a large number of occurrences of sthg that happen in a short period of time □ *There has been a spate of attacks on old people.* □ *We had a whole spate of letters on the subject.*

spatial ['speɪʃl] *adj* [awareness, relationship] that is concerned with the space between things (formal use).

spatter ['spætəʳ] ◇ *vt* [water, mud] to make small drops of <a liquid> fall on a particular surface □ *I've managed to spatter my shirt with tomato sauce.* ◇ *vi: The paint spattered all over the carpet.*

spatula ['spætʃələ] *n* **-1.** COOKING a tool with a short handle and a wide blade used in the kitchen for spreading, mixing etc soft foods. **-2.** MEDICINE a flat wooden instrument used by doctors to flatten the tongue when examining a patient's throat.

spawn [spɔːn] ◇ *n* ZOOLOGY the eggs of frogs, fish etc produced in large numbers together in a substance like jelly. ◇ *vt* to cause <sthg> to happen or exist, especially in large numbers □ *The protest spawned dozens of other demonstrations all over the country.* ◇ *vi* ZOOLOGY to lay eggs.

spay [speɪ] *vt* to remove part of the sexual organs of <a female cat, dog> etc so that they cannot become pregnant.

SPCA (*abbr of* Society for the Prevention of Cruelty to Animals) *n* **the SPCA** a US charity that aims to protect animals from being badly treated.

SPCC (*abbr of* Society for the Prevention of Cruelty to Children) *n* **the SPCC** a US organization that aims to protect the rights of children who are being badly treated.

speak [spiːk] (*pt* **spoke**, *pp* **spoken**) ◇ *vt* **-1.** [word, truth] to say <sthg> using one's voice □ *He didn't speak a word all evening.* ■ **to speak ill of sb** to say unkind things about sb. **-2.** to know <a foreign language> and be able to use it □ *She speaks fluent German.* □ *How many languages do you speak?* □ *We always spoke French at home.*
◇ *vi* **-1.** to say words using one's voice □ *She speaks with an American accent.* □ *I was speaking to* OR *with Bob only last night!* □ *I need to speak to you about a little idea I've had.* □ *We haven't spoken about her in ages.* ■ **to speak well** OR **highly of sb** to say nice things about sb □ *Karen speaks very highly of your talents as a teacher.* ■ **nobody/nothing to speak of** nobody/nothing that is very important □ *"What were you doing in Chicago?" — "Oh, nothing to speak of."* □ *"Did anyone else come to the party?" — "No one to speak of."* **-2.** to make a speech □ *He came to speak to the Young Conservatives/to speak on the novels of Jane Austen.* □ *She spoke on the problems of inequality.* **-3. generally/personally/politically speaking** a phrase used to introduce information which is general/is based on one's own private opinion/is concerned with politics □ *Generally speaking, the French are much better dressed than the English.* □ *Strictly speaking, you shouldn't be here.* □ *There were, roughly speaking, around 400 people there.* ■ **speaking as** a phrase used to introduce information which is based on one's experience in a particular position □ *Speaking as a homeowner/parent, I think it's shocking and something should be done.* □ *Speaking as someone who knows Janice well, I'd say there's something wrong.* ■ **speaking of** a phrase used to change the subject of a conversation to something that has just been mentioned □ *Speaking of computers, have you seen my new portable?*

◆ **so to speak** *adv* a phrase used to show that one is not speaking literally □ *It was putting the cart before the horse, so to speak.*

◆ **speak for** *vt fus* **to speak for sb** to say what the opinions, feelings, beliefs etc of sb are □ *I think I speak for all my colleagues when I say that it's a bad idea.* □ *I can't speak for everyone, but personally I think it's a good idea.* ■ **it speaks for itself** it is very clear and does not need to be explained or discussed further □ *Well, I think the book speaks for itself and hardly needs any introduction to it.* ■ **speak for yourself!** a phrase used to show that one does not agree with something that has just been said □ *"We're not hungry." — "Speak for yourself! I'm starving!"*

◆ **speak out** *vi* to speak publicly in defense of or against something □ *Mr Rosh spoke out bravely against injustice.*

◆ **speak up** *vi* **-1.** to say what one thinks clearly and openly □ *Few people had the courage to speak up.* ■ **to speak up for sb/sthg** to speak in support of sb/sthg □ *Will nobody speak up for my plan?* **-2.** to speak more loudly □ *What did you say? You'll have to speak up.*

speaker ['spiːkəʳ] *n* **-1.** a person who is speaking □ *When a speaker changes intonation...* **-2.** a person who makes a speech or gives a lecture □ *Our speaker for today, Professor Lubitsch.* **-3.** a person who knows how to speak a particular language □ *an Italian/a Japanese speaker.* **-4.** the part of a stereo or radio which sound comes out of □ *This radio has a very small speaker.*

◆ **Speaker** *n* **the Speaker** the person in charge of debates in the House of Commons in Britain.

Speaker of the House *n* **the Speaker of the House** the person in charge of debates in the House of Commons in Canada and the House of Representatives in the USA and Australia.

Speaker's Corner a corner of Hyde Park, in central London, where anyone can go to make speeches.

speaking ['spiːkɪŋ] *n* the activity of speaking or making a speech □ *public speaking.*

speaking clock *n* GB a telephone service that gives the exact time.

spear [spɪəʳ] ◇ *n* a weapon consisting of a long pole with a sharp metal point at one end. ◇ *vt* to pierce <an animal, piece of meat> etc with a sharp object such as a spear.

spearhead ['spɪəʳhed] ◇ *n* a person or group that leads an activity, campaign etc with energy and force. ◇ *vt* [campaign, attack] to lead <sthg> with energy and force □ *CST spearheaded the autumn campaign.*

special ['speʃl] ◇ *adj* -1. [occasion, event, effort] not ordinary □ *Today is a very special day.* □ *I keep these plates for special occasions.* -2. [problem, permission] that is of a particular kind and is different from other things □ *You'll need special permission to go in there alone.* -3. better or more important than others □ *This house is very special to me.*
◇ *n* -1. a special train service that is kept for a particular purpose. -2. [on a menu] a meal or dish available only for a limited period of time and often sold at a reduced price □ *What's the special today?* -3. [on TV] a program made for a particular purpose □ *an election special.*

special agent *n* an agent working for the police, FBI etc who has special responsibilities.

special constable *n* GB a volunteer who does police duties for a few hours a week.

special correspondent *n* a reporter who is sent to cover a particular piece of news, incident etc.

special delivery *n* a service by which one can have mail delivered outside usual delivery times.

special education *n* US teaching given to people with physical or mental disabilities who need special help with learning □ *a special education class.*

special effects *npl* images in movies, e.g. ghosts and explosions, that are not real but are created by the use of special techniques.

specialist ['speʃləst] ◇ *adj* [knowledge, vocabulary] that is not common but that is used in a particular subject, field of study etc □ *for people with no specialist knowledge of the field.* ◇ *n* a person who has particular skills or who knows a lot about a particular subject, field of study etc □ *a specialist in Renaissance art.*

speciality *n* GB = specialty.

specialize, -ise ['speʃəlaɪz] *vi* to concentrate on a particular area of study, work etc □ *He's now specializing in Russian art.* □ *I'd advise you not to specialize too soon in your career.*

specially ['speʃlɪ] *adv* -1. a word used to emphasize that something has been done for a particular person or purpose □ *I bought it specially for you.* -2. a word used to emphasize that something has more of a particular quality than usual □ *The ending was specially good.*

special needs *npl* GB problems due to physi-

cal or mental disabilities □ *children with special needs* □ *a special needs teacher.*

special offer *n* something that is being sold at a reduced price for a short period of time □ *They've got cheese on special offer.*

special school *n* a school for children with physical or mental disabilities who need special help with learning.

specialty ['speʃltɪ] US, **speciality** [ˌspeʃɪ'ælɪtɪ] GB (US *pl* **specialties**, GB *pl* **specialities**) *n* -1. a special field of knowledge or work □ *My specialty is ancient Greek civilization.* -2. a service or product which is typical of a particular person, region etc □ *The specialty of this region is mussels with white wine.*

species ['spiːʃiːz] (*pl* **species**) *n* a particular group of plants or animals in which all the members share the same main characteristics □ *a species of plant* □ *the human species.*

specific [spə'sɪfɪk] *adj* -1. a word used to identify one particular time, amount, point etc rather than another □ *Yes, but that's not related to this specific issue.* -2. [term, explanation, description] that is precise and detailed □ *She was quite specific about it.* □ *Could you be a little more specific?*
◆ **specifics** *npl* details □ *We don't need to talk about specifics at this stage.*

specifically [spə'sɪfɪklɪ] *adv* -1. [tell, say] exactly and clearly □ *I specifically asked you not to be late.* -2. [write, refer to, design] a word used to emphasize that something is done for a particular person or purpose □ *We cater specifically for the unemployed.* -3. a word used to introduce extra information □ *Their head office is in the States, or more specifically, Chicago.*

specification [ˌspesɪfɪ'keɪʃn] *n* -1. a particular requirement, especially about the way something is made or done □ *The only specification was that applicants should be over 25.* -2. = **specifications** □ *The top-of-the-range model is built to a high specification.*
◆ **specifications** *npl* TECHNOLOGY detailed technical plans or instructions □ *The structure has been built according to the manufacturer's specifications.*

specify ['spesəfaɪ] (*pt* & *pp* **specified**) *vt* to state <sthg> exactly and precisely □ *He specified that we should arrive before midnight.* □ *Do we need to specify any particular date?*

specimen ['spesəmən] *n* -1. an example of a particular type of thing □ *This is a very interesting specimen of late Baroque architecture.* -2. [work] a small amount of something that is used to show what the whole thing is like; [of blood, urine] a small amount of something that is used to find out if somebody is ill, has been drinking alcohol etc □ *This is a small specimen of Rodriguez's work.* □ *We will need to take a specimen of your blood.*

specimen copy *n* a copy of something designed to show what it should be like □ *Have a look at the specimen copy attached before filling out the form.*

specimen signature *n* a copy of a person's signature kept, for example, by a bank so that they can check the signature that appears on that person's checks.

speck [spek] *n* **-1.** [of dirt, ink] a very small mark on a surface. **-2.** [of dust, soot] a very small piece of something.

speckled ['spekld] *adj* that is covered with small spots or marks of a different color □ *a speckled egg* □ *His hair was speckled with silver.*

specs [speks] *npl* = **spectacles** (informal use).

spectacle ['spektəkl] *n* **-1.** something that somebody sees that is unusual, interesting, or pitiful □ *the strange spectacle of two policemen walking down the street carrying a piano.* ■ **to make a spectacle of oneself** to behave in a way that attracts other people's attention and makes one look silly □ *He made rather a spectacle of himself when he was drunk.* **-2.** an impressive public event or show □ *The firework display was a fantastic spectacle.*

◆ **spectacles** *npl* GB [for one's eyes] glasses.

spectacular [spek'tækjələr] ◇ *adj* [event, sight, success] that seems very impressive □ *He's made a spectacular recovery.* ◇ *n* a big and impressive show with a lot of performers □ *a television spectacular.*

spectate [spek'teit] *vi* to be a spectator.

spectator [spek'teitər] *n* a person who watches something such as a sport for pleasure.

spectator sport *n* a sport that people watch as a form of entertainment.

specter US, **spectre** GB ['spektər] *n* **-1. the specter of sthg** the possibility that sthg unpleasant or frightening may happen □ *The specter of international terrorism is looming again.* **-2.** a ghost (formal use).

spectrum ['spektrəm] (*pl* **spectra** [-trə]) *n* **-1.** PHYSICS the band of colors produced by white light passing through a prism. **-2.** [of opinions, emotions, skills] a range of different sorts of a particular thing □ *Our speakers tonight come from opposite ends of the political spectrum.* □ *The festival takes in musicians from right across the spectrum of modern music.*

speculate ['spekjəleit] ◇ *vt* **to speculate that...** to guess without being sure that something is true □ *The press is speculating that he may resign before Christmas.* ◇ *vi* **-1.** to wonder about something without knowing for certain if what one thinks is true □ *I don't want to speculate on his future.* **-2.** FINANCE to buy things, e.g. houses or stock, in order to sell them at a profit □ *He speculates in property.*

speculation [,spekjə'leiʃn] *n* **-1.** the act of wondering about something without knowing for certain if what one thinks is true □ *The media is rife with speculation about the divorce.* **-2.** FINANCE the activity of speculating.

speculative ['spekjələtiv] *adj* **-1.** [story, idea] that is based on speculation and not on fact. **-2.** FINANCE [deal, investment] that is connected with speculation.

speculator ['spekjəleitər] *n* FINANCE a person who speculates to make money.

sped [sped] *past tense & past participle of* **speed**.

speech [spiːtʃ] *n* **-1.** the ability to speak; the act of speaking □ *He appeared to have lost the power of speech.* □ *a study of human speech.* **-2.** [at an event] a formal talk to a group of people □ *She gave OR made a speech on the company's future prospects.* **-3.** THEATER a series of lines spoken by a character in a play □ *I got bored during that long speech near the end.* **-4.** [of a particular person] the way that somebody speaks □ *His speech was slurred.*

speech day *n* GB an annual event at a school when parents come, prizes are given to students, and speeches are made.

speech impediment *n* a nervous or physical disability that prevents somebody from speaking clearly, e.g. by making them stutter □ *She has a serious speech impediment.*

speechless ['spiːtʃləs] *adj* **to be speechless** to be so shocked, surprised etc that one cannot think of anything to say □ *I was speechless with anger.*

speech recognition *n* COMPUTING the ability of a computer to understand spoken words.

speech therapist *n* a person who is trained to give speech therapy.

speech therapy *n* treatment for people who have problems in speaking.

speed [spiːd] (*pt & pp* **sped** OR **speeded**) ◇ *n* **-1.** [of light, sound, a vehicle] the rate at which something happens or moves □ *My typing speed is very slow.* □ *The car was traveling at a speed of 80 mph.* □ *I was astonished at the speed of events.* **-2.** [of an athlete] very fast movement □ *I lost speed near the end of the race.* **-3.** AUTO a gear □ *a five-speed bike.* **-4.** PHOTOGRAPHY the rate at which light passes through a lens to form an image on a piece of film.
◇ *vi* **-1.** [person, vehicle] to move somewhere very quickly □ *The car sped by/away.* □ *He was speeding along on his bike.* **-2.** AUTO **to be speeding** to be driving a vehicle faster than one is legally allowed to.

◆ **speed up** ◇ *vt sep* **to speed sb/sthg up** to make sb/sthg move faster □ *How can we speed up the process?* ◇ *vi:* *Can you get them to speed up?*

speedboat ['spiːdbəʊt] *n* a boat with a powerful engine that can travel very fast.

speed bump *n* a raised strip across a road, designed to slow traffic down.

speeding ['spiːdɪŋ] *n* the illegal act of traveling faster than the speed limit □ *a speeding fine.*

speed limit *n* the fastest speed at which one is allowed to travel on a particular road □ *It is illegal to exceed the speed limit.*

speedometer [spɪ'dɒmətər] *n* an instrument in a car, on a bike etc that shows how fast it is traveling.

speed trap *n* a place on a road where police wait in order to catch vehicles that are traveling faster than the speed limit.

speedway ['spiːdwei] *n* **-1.** SPORT the sport of racing motorcycles on a special track. **-2.** US a racetrack for cars and motorcycles.

speedy ['spiːdi] (*compar* **speedier**, *superl* **speediest**) *adj* [action, reply] that takes place or is done very quickly □ *Josey made a speedy recovery after her illness.*

speleology [ˌspiːlɪˈɒlədʒɪ] *n* (formal use) **-1.** the study of caves. **-2.** the sport or hobby of exploring caves.

spell [spel] (US *pt* & *pp* **spelled**, GB *pt* & *pp* **spelt** OR **spelled**) ◇ *n* **-1.** [of time] a short period of time □ *After a spell as a teacher, I became a social worker.* □ *Tomorrow there will be showers and sunny spells.* **-2.** [in magic] a set of words that are supposed to have magic power when spoken; the effect of these words on somebody □ *She put a spell on him.* □ *The spell was starting to wear off.*
◇ *vt* **-1.** [person] to speak or write the letters that make up <a word or name> in the correct order □ *How do you spell that, please?* □ *That's Claire, spelled with an "i".* **-2.** [change, event] to make <trouble, disaster> etc seem likely or certain □ *The latest news on the takeover spells doom for employees of Roscon.*
◇ *vi* [person] *For this job it's important to be able to spell.*

◆ **spell out** *vt sep* **-1. to spell sthg out** [word, name] to spell sthg carefully □ *I'll spell that out for you.* **-2. to spell sthg out for** OR **to sb** to explain sthg very clearly to sb □ *Do I have to spell it out to you? It's over between us.*

spellbound [ˈspelbaʊnd] *adj* **to be spellbound** to be listening to or watching something that is so interesting that one cannot stop □ *We watched, spellbound, as the balloon rose slowly into the sky.*

spelling [ˈspelɪŋ] *n* **-1.** the order in which letters appear in a word □ *Is that the correct spelling of his name?* **-2.** the ability to spell words correctly □ *Her spelling is atrocious.*

spelt [spelt] GB *past tense & past participle of* **spell**.

spend [spend] (*pt* & *pp* **spent**) *vt* **-1.** to use <an amount of money> to pay for something □ *I spend half my salary on rent and bills.* □ *She spends an absolute fortune on her poodle.* □ *I brought $300 and spent the lot!* **-2.** [life, day] to pass <a period of time> □ *I've spent all morning trying to contact him.* □ *I have decided that I need to spend more time at home.* □ *We spent our vacation in Bangkok.*

spender [ˈspendər] *n* **a big spender** a person who spends a lot of money.

spending [ˈspendɪŋ] *n* the amount of money spent by a person, group etc □ *government/ public spending.* □ *I need to cut down on my spending.*

spending money *n* money that one can use to spend on things that one enjoys □ *We gave him $50 spending money for his school trip.*

spending power *n* the amount of money that a person or group of people can use to buy things □ *Don't underestimate the spending power of the older generation.*

spendthrift [ˈspendθrɪft] *n* a person who spends their money in a careless way (disapproving use).

spent [spent] ◇ *past tense & past participle of* **spend**. ◇ *adj* [fuel, ammunition, energy] that

has been used completely so that there is no more left to use □ *a spent firework.*

sperm [spɜːrm] (*pl* **sperm** OR **sperms**) *n* a cell produced in the sex organs of a male animal or a man that can fertilize the egg of a female animal or a woman; the liquid produced by the male sex organs that contains these cells.

spermicide [ˈspɜːrməsaɪd] *n* a substance that kills sperm, used during sex to stop a woman from becoming pregnant.

sperm whale *n* a large whale that is hunted for the large amount of oil stored in its head.

spew [spjuː] ◇ *vt* [flames, lava] to pour out a lot of <sthg>. ◇ *vi*: *Oil spewed (out) from the hole.*

SPF (*abbr of* **sun protection factor**) *n* a number on a bottle of suntan lotion that tells you how much protection the lotion gives against sunburn.

sphere [sfɪər] *n* **-1.** a round object such as a ball. **-2.** an area in which a person or organization is interested or involved □ *America's sphere of influence.*

spherical [US ˈsfɪərɪkl, GB ˈsfer-] *adj* [shape, object] that is shaped like a ball.

sphincter [ˈsfɪŋktər] *n* a ring of muscle surrounding a passage in one's body that can be tightened and closed □ *the anal sphincter.*

sphinx [sfɪŋks] (*pl* **sphinxes**) *n* in Egyptian mythology, a creature with a woman's head and a lion's body; a stone statue of this.

spice [spaɪs] ◇ *n* **-1.** COOKING any of the various seeds or powders, e.g. pepper, used to flavor food □ *Add a few spices to make it taste more interesting.* **-2.** excitement or interest □ *Lloyd's presence always adds a little spice to the occasion.* ◇ *vt* **-1.** COOKING to add spices to <food> □ *She spiced the dish with extra chili powder.* **-2. to spice sthg (up)** [story, speech] to make sthg more exciting or lively □ *I might tell some jokes, just to spice things up a little.*

spick-and-span [ˌspɪk-] *adj* **to be spick-and-span** [room, house] to be very clean and tidy □ *We'll soon have this place looking spick-and-span.*

spicy [ˈspaɪsɪ] (*compar* **spicier**, *superl* **spiciest**) *adj* **-1.** COOKING [food, sauce] that has a hot strong flavor because it contains spices. **-2.** [story, book] that is slightly rude and may shock people.

spider [ˈspaɪdər] *n* a small creature with eight legs that makes webs to catch insects in.

spiderweb [ˈspaɪdərweb] US, **spider's web** GB *n* a network of fine sticky threads made by a spider to catch insects in.

spidery [ˈspaɪdərɪ] *adj* **spidery handwriting** handwriting that is formed using thin pointed lines.

spiel [ʃpiːl] *n* a way of talking that is fast, confident, and designed to persuade somebody to do or buy something (informal use) □ *He gave a long spiel about life insurance.*

spike [spaɪk] ◇ *n* **-1.** something that is long, thin, has a sharp point, and is often made of metal □ *railings with sharp spikes.* -2. [on a shoe, boot] one of the metal points on the bottom of a shoe or boot that help one to stop slipping on the ground, e.g. when one is doing a sport. ◇ *vt* to add strong alcohol to <sb's drink> without telling them.

◆ **spikes** *npl* GB sports shoes that have spikes fitted to them.

spiky ['spaɪkɪ] (*compar* **spikier**, *superl* **spikiest**) *adj* [plant, hair] that has thin stiff points.

spill [spɪl] (US *pt* & *pp* **spilled**, GB *pt* & *pp* **spilt** OR **spilled**) ◇ *vt* -1. to pour <liquid, salt> etc out of a container by accident □ *I'm afraid I've spilled some wine on your carpet.* -2. **to spill blood** to kill or wound people □ *Much blood was spilled during the battle.* ◇ *vi* -1. [liquid, salt] *The wine spilled all over the carpet.* -2. [crowd, people] to leave somewhere in large numbers at the same time □ *The fans spilled out of the stadium and into the street.*

spillage ['spɪlɪdʒ] *n* the act of spilling something, e.g. oil; something that has been spilled □ *an oil spillage.*

spilt [spɪlt] GB *past tense & past participle of* **spill**.

spin [spɪn] (*pt* **span** OR **spun**, *pp* **spun**, *cont* **spinning**) ◇ *vt* -1. [ball, coin, wheel] to cause <sthg> to turn quickly □ *Go on, spin the dice.* -2. [washing] to dry <clothes> in a machine after they have been washed. -3. [thread, cloth] to make <sthg> by twisting pieces of wool or cotton together. ◇ *vi* -1. [ball, coin, wheel] to turn quickly □ *The wheels span out of control.* -2. **to be spinning** to feel confused or dizzy □ *My head/mind was spinning.* -3. [person] to make thread or cloth by twisting pieces of wool or cotton together, especially using a machine. ◇ *n* -1. an act of spinning something □ *Give the wheel a spin.* -2. AVIATION a movement in which an aircraft falls a great distance very quickly, turning in a circular motion. -3. [in a car] a short trip that one makes in a car for pleasure (informal use) □ *Let's go for a spin.* -4. SPORT **to put spin on a ball** to hit or throw a ball in a certain way so that it turns quickly in the air and moves in an unexpected direction after hitting a surface.

◆ **spin out** *vt sep* **to spin sthg out** [food, money, story] to make sthg last a long time □ *The presentation's pretty short but I'm sure we can spin it out until the end.*

spina bifida [,spaɪnə'bɪfɪdə] *n* a serious medical condition in which a child is born with a split spine and may suffer paralysis.

spinach ['spɪnɪtʃ] *n* a vegetable with dark green leaves.

spinal column [,spaɪnl-] *n* ANATOMY = **spine** (technical use).

spinal cord *n* a section of nerves in one's spine that carries messages to one's brain.

spindle ['spɪndl] *n* -1. a rod in a machine that another part turns around. -2. a pointed rod used to twist thread around when spinning cloth.

spindly ['spɪndlɪ] (*compar* **spindlier**, *superl* **spin-**

dliest) *adj* [person, legs, plant] that looks long, thin, and weak.

spin doctor *n* a person who advises a political party or an organization about public relations and tries to make events look as good as possible for the public.

spin-dry *vt* GB to remove the water from <wet clothes> by putting them in a spin-dryer.

spin-dryer *n* GB an electrical machine that makes wet clothing spin to remove the water from it.

spine [spaɪn] *n* -1. ANATOMY the row of bones that goes down the center of one's back □ *He damaged his spine in an accident.* -2. [of a book] the part of a book where the pages are joined together and where the title is written on the outside. -3. [on a plant, animal] a sharp point on an animal or plant □ *a small animal with sharp spines on its back.*

spine-chilling *adj* [movie, story] that is very frightening.

spineless ['spaɪnləs] *adj* [person] who does not have enough courage or confidence to do something (disapproving use) □ *Don't be so spineless — go in and ask!*

spinning ['spɪnɪŋ] *n* the act of spinning thread.

spinning top *n* a toy that spins on a pointed base.

spin-off *n* something good or useful that happens or is produced as a result of a process intended to produce something else □ *Souvenirs of the visit proved to be a lucrative spin-off.*

spinster ['spɪnstər] *n* an unmarried woman, especially one who is considered too old to marry (old-fashioned use).
NOTE: Compare **bachelor**.

spiral ['spaɪrəl] (US *pt* & *pp* **spiraled**, *cont* **spiraling**, GB *pt* & *pp* **spiralled**, *cont* **spiralling**) ◇ *n* -1. a curve that winds around a single line many times. -2. [of wages, prices] a continuous increase or decrease in something that is difficult to control and causes problems □ *Salaries went into an upward spiral.* □ *We are on a downward spiral into a culture of fear.* □ *an inflationary spiral.* ◇ *adj* [curve, movement, motif] that has the form of a spiral. ◇ *vi* -1. [staircase, aircraft, smoke] to move up or down in a spiral curve □ *Smoke spiraled from the wreckage.* -2. [prices, wages] to increase quickly in an uncontrolled way that causes problems □ *Spiraling costs put an end to the project.* -3. **to spiral downward** [amount, level, costs] to decrease quickly in an uncontrolled way that causes problems.

spiral staircase *n* a staircase built in the shape of a spiral.

spire ['spaɪər] *n* a structure on a church roof that is wide at the bottom and narrows to a point at the top.

spirit ['spɪrɪt] ◇ *n* -1. the part of somebody that is separate from their body and that affects the way they feel and what type of person they are □ *He was weak in spirit.* □ *The spirit of Hendrix lives on in modern rock music.* □

This job attracts free spirits. **-2.** [of a dead person] a being that has no physical body, and is often the ghost of a dead person □ *evil spirits.* **-3.** [of a team, army] strength and determination □ *the fighting spirit of the Raiders* □ *They'll never break our spirit.* □ *Tina showed a great deal of spirit in the way she stood up to him.* **-4.** [of optimism, despair] the way that a person or group feels and acts □ *We're trying to encourage a spirit of cooperation.* □ *The performance was done in a spirit of fun.* ■ **to enter into the spirit of sthg** to participate in sthg enthusiastically □ *After a while, the others entered into the spirit of the occasion.* **-5.** [of a law, agreement] the essential quality or character of something □ *Protectionist measures go against the whole spirit of our union.*
◇ *vt* **to spirit sb into/out of a place** to take sb into/out of a place quickly and secretly □ *Mendez was spirited out of the country.*
◆ **spirits** *npl* **-1.** one's mood or state of mind □ *He was in good spirits.* ■ **to be in high/low spirits** to be cheerful/unhappy □ *I found him in high spirits, celebrating his win.* **-2.** strong alcoholic drinks such as vodka and gin □ *I never drink spirits.*

spirited ['spɪrɪtəd] *adj* [defense, debate] that is lively and determined □ *Kennedy gave a spirited performance.*

spirit level *n* an instrument used for testing whether a surface is level or not.

spiritual ['spɪrɪtʃʊəl] *adj* **-1.** [experience, welfare] that is connected with one's feelings and beliefs and not with one's body □ *I feel I've been neglecting my spiritual side lately.* **-2.** [leader, beliefs, music] that is connected with religion □ *The godparents are responsible for the child's spiritual guidance.*

spiritualism ['spɪrɪtʃʊəlɪzm] *n* the belief that people who are dead can communicate with people who are still alive.

spiritualist ['spɪrɪtʃʊəlɪst] *n* a person who believes in spiritualism and who tries to communicate with dead people.

spit [spɪt] (US *pt* & *pp* **spit**, *cont* **spitting**, GB *pt* & *pp* **spat**, *cont* **spitting**) ◇ *n* **-1.** the liquid produced in one's mouth. **-2.** a thin rod for sticking pieces of meat on so they can be cooked over a fire □ *chicken cooked on a spit.* ◇ *vi* to send spit out of one's mouth with force □ *Richardson was spat at by protesters.* ◇ *v impers* **it's spitting** it's raining very lightly.
◆ **spit out** *vt sep* **-1.** **to spit sthg out** [food, liquid] to make sthg leave one's mouth with force □ *She spat the medicine out.* **-2.** **to spit sthg out** to say sthg angrily □ *He spat the words out in disgust.* ■ **spit it out!** a phrase used to tell somebody to say what they are thinking immediately □ *Come on, spit it out! Where did you find this?*

spite [spaɪt] ◇ *n* **to do sthg out of** OR **from spite** to do sthg unpleasant because one wants to hurt or upset somebody □ *He said it out of spite.* ◇ *vt* to annoy or upset <sb> deliberately □ *I know you only did it to spite me.*
◆ **in spite of** *prep* despite <sthg> □ *In spite of*

everything, I still care for you. □ *She arrived there on time, in spite of the traffic.* ■ **to do sthg in spite of oneself** to do sthg without expecting to or meaning to □ *I ended up apologizing in spite of myself.*

spiteful ['spaɪtfl] *adj* [behavior, remark] that shows a desire to hurt or upset somebody □ *He's a very spiteful person.*

spitting image [,spɪtɪŋ-] *n* **to be the spitting image of sb** to look exactly like sb □ *He's the spitting image of his dad.*

spittle ['spɪtl] *n* the liquid produced in one's mouth.

splash [splæʃ] ◇ *vt* **-1.** **to splash sb/sthg with sthg** to throw or send drops of liquid over sb/sthg □ *The kids were splashing each other in the pool.* □ *The bus splashed us with mud.* ■ **to splash sthg on** OR **over sb/sthg** to throw or put sthg liquid on OR over sb/sthg in a careless way □ *You'll splash paint all over the carpet.* **-2.** [liquid] to fall noisily against <sb/sthg> □ *The waves splashed the deck of the ship.*
◇ *vi* **-1.** **to splash around** OR **about** to move around in a liquid in a noisy and sometimes messy way □ *The kids splashed through the puddles.* **-2.** **to splash on/against sthg** [liquid] to fall noisily on/against sthg.
◇ *n* **-1.** the sound made when something hits a liquid or when some liquid hits something □ *The rock fell into the water with a loud splash.* **-2.** [of mud, paint] a small amount of something, usually a liquid, that leaves a mark on something □ *There were splashes of blood on his shirt.* **-3.** **a splash of color** an area of bright color □ *The canvas was dotted with splashes of red.*
◆ **splash down** *vi* [spacecraft] to land in the sea after a flight.
◆ **splash out** (informal use) ◇ *vt sep* **to splash out a sum of money** to spend a large sum of money □ *He splashed out $600 on a new watch.* ◇ *vi:* *We really splashed out this year.* □ *He's just splashed out on a new car.*

splashdown ['splæʃdaʊn] *n* the landing of a spacecraft in the sea.

splashguard ['splæʃɡɑːrd] *n* US a piece of rubber or plastic hanging behind the wheel of a vehicle to stop mud from being thrown up.

splay [spleɪ] *vt* to spread out <one's feet, legs, fingers> etc □ *Chris sat with his legs splayed.*

spleen [spliːn] *n* **-1.** ANATOMY an organ near one's stomach that produces antibodies and removes impurities from the blood. **-2.** great anger (formal or literary use) □ *He vented his spleen in an angry letter.*

splendid ['splendəd] *adj* **-1.** [occasion, achievement] that one thinks is very good □ *What a splendid idea!* **-2.** [building, dress] that is beautiful and impressive □ *They lived in a splendid mansion.*

splendidly ['splendədlɪ] *adv* **-1.** [perform, write, behave] very well □ *My work is going splendidly.* **-2.** [design, dress, entertain] in a magnificent and impressive way.

splendor US, **splendour** GB ['splendər] *n* **-1.** [of a building, work of art] impressive beauty □ *I* was quite overawed by the splendor of the palace. **-2.** an impressive and beautiful feature or aspect □ *one of the splendors of Rome.*

splice [splaɪs] *vt* to join together <two pieces of rope, film, tape> etc.

splint [splɪnt] *n* a piece of wood or metal attached to a broken arm, leg etc to keep it straight while the bone mends.

splinter [ˈsplɪntəʳ] ◇ *n* a small, thin, sharp piece of wood, glass etc that has broken off a larger piece □ *I have a splinter in my finger.* ◇ *vt* **to be splintered** [wood, glass, metal] to be broken and have a lot of splinters □ *The door was all splintered, as if someone had tried to break it down.* ◇ *vi* to break and make a lot of splinters □ *Be careful, this wood splinters easily.*

splinter group *n* a group of people who no longer agree with the views of a larger organization and so have formed a separate organization.

split [splɪt] (*pt* & *pp* **split**, *cont* **splitting**) ◇ *n* **-1.** [in wood, rock] a long crack □ *There's a split in the table.* **-2.** [in a fabric] a long tear made in a fabric □ *There's a split along the seam.* **-3.** [between people] a disagreement or division between people in the same group □ *There are rumors of a boardroom split.* □ *The new policy announcement has caused a deep split in the party.* **-4. to do a split** US to stretch one's legs wide apart so that they point in opposite directions and touch the ground along their whole length. ◇ *vt* **-1.** [wood, stone] to cause <sthg> to crack □ *He split the log with an ax.* **-2.** [shirt, trousers] to cause <sthg> to tear □ *When I bent over, I split my pants all down the back.* **-3.** [organization, party] to cause <a group of people> to disagree and divide into two or more different groups □ *This latest disagreement has split the party into several opposing factions.* **-4.** [profits, expense, work] to share <sthg> equally □ *We agreed to split the winnings.* □ *I'm not very hungry but we could split a pizza if you like.* ■ **to split the difference** to agree on an amount halfway between two amounts already mentioned □ *Let's split the difference and call it $20.* ◇ *vi* **-1.** [wood, stone] to crack □ *The ship split in two when it hit the rocks.* **-2.** [shirt, pants] to tear □ *The bag split and everything fell out.* **-3.** [organization, party] to divide into two or more parts □ *The road splits here.* **-4.** ▽ [person] to leave (very informal use) □ *Let's split!*

◆ **splits** *npl* **to do the splits** GB = **to do a split.**

◆ **split off** ◇ *vt sep* **to split sthg off** [piece of wood, rock, branch] to break sthg off from the main part □ *I always keep fresh garlic in the kitchen and just split a clove off when I need it.* ◇ *vi* **-1.** [piece of wood, rock] to crack or tear □ *The package had split open.* **-2.** [person, group] to become separate from the main part of a group, organization etc □ *They split off from the tour party at the corner.*

◆ **split up** ◇ *vt sep* **to split sthg up** to separate sthg into different sections □ *His speech was split up into three distinct parts.* ◇ *vi* **-1.** [group, friends] to go in different directions □ *We*

agreed to split up and then meet later on in the bar. **-2.** [couple] to end a relationship □ *She split up with her boyfriend.* □ *Haven't you heard? They split up.*

split end *n* the end of a hair on one's head that has split into two or more different parts □ *I've got split ends — I must get my hair cut.*

split-level *adj* [building, house, room] that has floors with parts at different heights.

split pea *n* a pea that has been dried and split into its two natural halves, used in cooking.

split personality *n* a condition in which somebody's moods change so quickly that they appear to have two different personalities.

split screen *n* **-1.** CINEMA & TV a technique that allows two scenes to be shown on the screen at the same time. **-2.** COMPUTING a technique that allows two different sets of information to be shown on the screen at the same time.

split second *n* an extremely short period of time □ *For a split second I thought she was joking.*

splitting [ˈsplɪtɪŋ] *adj* **a splitting headache** a very severe headache.

splutter [ˈsplʌtəʳ] ◇ *vi* **-1.** to talk in an unclear and confused way, usually because one is angry, embarrassed etc. **-2.** [fire, flames] to make a sound similar to that of somebody spitting □ *The engine spluttered and died.* □ *Sam resurfaced, coughing and spluttering.* ◇ *vt* to say <sthg> in an unclear and confused way because one is angry, embarrassed etc □ *"I never said anything of the sort," he spluttered.*

Spock [spɒk], **Benjamin** (1903–) a US doctor well known for his advice about bringing up children.

spoil [spɔɪl] (US *pt* & *pp* **spoiled**, GB *pt* & *pp* **spoilt** OR **spoiled**) *vt* **-1.** [view, vacation, food] to destroy the quality of <sthg> □ *You'll spoil your appetite if you eat now.* □ *You had to go and spoil everyone else's fun, didn't you?* **-2.** [child] to treat <sb> too well with the result that they become selfish □ *She spoils that son of hers.* **-3.** [person] to give <sb> something pleasant that they do not usually have □ *Breakfast in bed! You're spoiling me.* □ *I'm going to spoil myself for a change.*

◆ **spoils** *npl* valuable things that one gets without paying for them, especially as a result of winning a battle □ *the spoils of war.*

spoiled [spɔɪld] *adj* **-1.** [child] who behaves in a selfish way because they have been given everything they want □ *He's just a spoiled brat!* **-2.** [food, dinner] that is not pleasant to eat because it has been cooked for too long □ *The chicken's spoiled, I'm afraid.*

spoiler [ˈspɔɪləʳ] *n* AUTO & AVIATION a device fitted to the body of a vehicle to give it better balance when it moves fast.

spoilsport [ˈspɔɪlspɔːt] *n* a person who tries to stop other people from having fun □ *Don't be such a spoilsport — come and join in!*

spoils system *n* a practice in US politics in

which the winners of elections give government jobs to the people who supported them.

spoilt [spɔɪlt] GB ◇ *past tense & past participle of* **spoil**. ◇ *adj* = **spoiled**.

spoke [spəʊk] ◇ *past tense of* **speak**. ◇ *n* any of the thin metal rods that connect the outside of a wheel to the center.

spoken ['spəʊkn] *past participle of* **speak**.

spokesman ['spəʊksmən] (*pl* **spokesmen** [-mən]) *n* a male spokesperson.

spokesperson ['spəʊkspɜːʳsn] (*pl* **spokespeople**) *n* a person chosen to speak for a group or organization officially □ *a spokesperson for the UN* □ *a government spokesperson.*

spokeswoman ['spəʊkswʊmən] (*pl* **spokeswomen**) *n* a female spokesperson.

sponge [spʌndʒ] ◇ *n* -1. a piece of a very light and soft material that is full of holes and is used for washing □ *a bath sponge.* -2. a sponge cake. ◇ *vt* [face, wound, car] to clean <sthg> by rubbing it with a wet sponge or cloth. ◇ *vi* **to sponge off sb** to get money, food etc from sb without doing anything in return (informal and disapproving use) □ *Gary's always sponging off his parents.* □ *These people are just sponging off the State.*

sponge bag *n* GB = **toilet bag**.

sponge bath *n* US a complete wash given to somebody who cannot get out of bed.

sponge cake *n* a very light cake made with sugar, eggs, flour, and, sometimes, butter.

sponge pudding *n* GB a pudding made with sugar, eggs, flour, and butter.

sponger ['spʌndʒəʳ] *n* a person who gets money, food etc from other people without doing anything in return (informal and disapproving use) □ *He's a real sponger; I don't think he's ever had a job.*

spongy ['spʌndʒɪ] (*compar* **spongier,** *superl* **spongiest**) *adj* [bread, ground] that is soft and full of air, like a sponge □ *The lungs are made up of spongy tissue.*

sponsor ['spɒnsəʳ] ◇ *n* -1. a person or organization that provides the money to pay for something such as a TV program or sports event, often in return for publicity □ *Hampson's, sponsor of the Southern Games.* -2. GB & AUS a person or organization that agrees to give an amount of money to charity if somebody succeeds in doing something difficult or unusual □ *Have they found a sponsor for the Everest expedition yet?* ◇ *vt* -1. [event, training, research] to provide money to pay for <sthg>, often in return for publicity □ *This broadcast was sponsored by Infotec.* -2. GB & AUS [walker, swimmer, runner] to promise to pay <sb> a particular amount of money if they achieve something □ *I sponsored her for $2 a mile.* -3. [bill, appeal, proposal] to support <sthg> officially □ *The bill is being sponsored by a small group of Congressmen.*

sponsored walk [,spɒnsəʳd-] *n* GB an event in which people walk a particular distance to make money for charity by finding sponsors

who agree to pay them a certain amount of money for each mile they walk.

ぐ SPONSORED WALK
Sponsored walks have become a popular activity in Britain and Australia, often raising large amounts of money for charity. More recently, other kinds of event have been organized, such as sponsored swims, cycle rides, or even parachute jumps.
In the USA, charities also organize sponsored events but give them different names, such as "the March of Dimes" or "the Walkathon".

---

sponsorship ['spɒnsəʳʃɪp] *n* [for research, training, an event] financial support □ *We need to find sponsorship for our next project.* □ *a $4 million sponsorship deal.*

spontaneity [US ,spɒntn'iːətɪ, GB ,spɒntə'neɪətɪ] *n*: see **spontaneous**.

spontaneous [spɒn'teɪnjəs] *adj* -1. [act, offer, applause] that happens naturally, without being forced or planned □ *It was an act of spontaneous generosity on Adam's part.* -2. [event, combustion, recovery] that is not caused by outside influences or events.

spontaneously [spɒn'teɪnjəslɪ] *adv* [act, occur] see **spontaneous**.

spoof [spuːf] *n* an amusing imitation of the style of something □ *It's a spoof of* OR *on disaster movies.*

spook [spuːk] *vt* to frighten <sb> (informal use) □ *That phone call last night really spooked me.*

spooky ['spuːkɪ] (*compar* **spookier,** *superl* **spookiest**) *adj* [place, house, story] that is strange and frightening (informal use).

spool [spuːl] ◇ *n* a round object like a wheel or cylinder that thread, tape, film etc is wound around. ◇ *vi* COMPUTING to transfer data from a disk to a tape.

spoon [spuːn] ◇ *n* an object with a long handle and an end shaped like a shallow bowl, used for eating, serving, and mixing food; a spoonful □ *knives, forks, and spoons* □ *Can I have two spoons of sugar in my coffee?* ◇ *vt* **to spoon sthg onto/into sthg** to put sthg onto/into sthg using a spoon □ *She sat spooning apple puree into the baby's mouth.*

spoon-feed *vt* -1. [baby, patient] to feed <sb> using a spoon □ *Little Amy's still being spoon-fed.* -2. [pupil, student] to present information to <sb> in such an easy form that they do not have to think for themselves (disapproving use).

spoonful ['spuːnfl] (*pl* **spoonfuls** OR **spoonsful**) *n* [of salt, sugar, flour] the amount of something that can be held in a spoon □ *Add a spoonful of honey.*

sporadic [spə'rædɪk] *adj* [fighting, disease] that happens for short periods of time at irregular intervals □ *There were sporadic bursts of gunfire.*

sport [spɔːʳt] ◇ *n* -1. a game or activity which people do for pleasure or physical exercise □ *Do you do any sports?* □ *I don't like competitive* sports. □ *Football is my favorite sport.* □ *She was never any good at sports.* **-2.** a person who accepts something difficult, such as defeat, in a cheerful way □ *He's a good sport.* ◇ *vt* **to be sporting sthg** [dress, tie] to be wearing sthg □ *Pierre was sporting a red bow tie.*

◆ **sports** *comp* [clothing, field] that is used for playing sports □ *a sports instructor.*

sporting ['spɔːⁱtɪŋ] *adj* **-1.** [event, achievements] that is connected with a sport □ *This race is one of the major events in the sporting calendar.* **-2. a sporting chance** quite a good chance of doing something □ *They have a sporting chance of winning.*

sports car *n* a very fast car that usually has only two seats.

sports day *n* GB a day on which a school holds competitions for its pupils in various athletic events.

sports jacket *n* a casual jacket for a man.

sportsman ['spɔːⁱtsmən] (*pl* **sportsmen** [-mən]) *n* a man who plays sports.

sportsmanship ['spɔːⁱtsmənʃɪp] *n* the quality of being honest and fair in a game.

sports pages *npl* the pages in a newspaper that deal with sports.

sportswear ['spɔːⁱtsweəⁱ] *n* special clothing worn for sports and leisure activities.

sportswoman ['spɔːⁱtswʊmən] (*pl* **sportswomen**) *n* a woman who plays sports.

sporty ['spɔːⁱtɪ] (*compar* **sportier**, *superl* **sportiest**) *adj* **-1.** [person] who likes playing sports. **-2.** [car] fast; [clothes] bright and casual.

spot [spɒt] (*pt* & *pp* **spotted**, *cont* **spotting**) ◇ *n* **-1.** [of blood, ink, paint] a small round mark on the surface of something □ *There was a small spot of grease on his shirt.* **-2.** [on one's skin] a very small round area of red skin that is caused by a disease; GB a very small raised area of red skin, especially on one's face □ *I was covered in spots.* □ *teenage spots.* **-3. a spot of lunch/work etc** a small amount of lunch/work etc (informal use) □ *How do you fancy a spot of supper after work?* **-4.** [place] a particular place □ *We found a quiet spot for a picnic.* ■ **on the spot** at the particular place where something is happening □ *And our reporter, Callum McBrines, is on the spot in Cairo.* ■ **to do sthg on the spot** to do sthg immediately □ *We can repair your car on the spot if you like.* **-5.** RADIO & TV a part of a broadcast or show reserved for a particular performer □ *I've always liked your spot on the Jimmy Braith show.* **-6.** *phrases* **to have a soft spot for sb** to like sb □ *I think the boss has a soft spot for you, Mark.* ■ **to put sb on the spot** to force sb to make a difficult decision quickly and, often, publicly □ *He really put me on the spot when he asked how much I wanted for it.* □ *I don't want to put you on the spot about this.*
◇ *vt* [person, object] to notice <sb/sthg> □ *Tom Hanks was spotted in a store downtown yesterday.* □ *I didn't spot many mistakes in the text.*

spot check *n* an unexpected examination of one of a group of people or things.

spotless ['spɒtləs] *adj* [clothing, room] that looks completely clean □ *Their kitchen is always absolutely spotless.*

spotlight ['spɒtlaɪt] *n* a bright light that can be directed to light up a small area, e.g. in a theater or room. ■ **to be in the spotlight** to receive a lot of public attention □ *Carl's still not used to being in the spotlight.*

spot-on *adj* **to be spot-on** GB [guess, answer] to be exactly right (informal use) □ *"I'd guess about three million?" — "Spot-on!"*

spot price *n* the price for something when it is being paid for immediately in cash.

spotted ['spɒtəd] *adj* [material, design] that has a pattern of spots on it □ *He was wearing a green and white spotted tie.*

spotty ['spɒtɪ] (*compar* **spottier**, *superl* **spottiest**) *adj* **-1.** US [work, performance] of inconsistent quality. **-2.** GB [person] who has pimples on their skin, especially on their face.

spouse [spaʊs] *n* a husband or wife (formal use).

spout [spaʊt] ◇ *n* **-1.** a tube, pipe etc that liquid comes out of □ *a watering can with a long spout.* **-2. a spout of water/blood etc** an amount of water/blood etc that comes out of something quickly and with a lot of force. ◇ *vt* [facts, nonsense] to say <a lot of things> without stopping to think (informal use) □ *As usual, he was just spouting Marxist theory.* ◇ *vi* **to spout from** OR **out of sthg** [liquid, flame] to come out of sthg quickly and with a lot of force □ *Smoke was spouting out of OR from the chimney.*

sprain [spreɪn] ◇ *vt* [ankle, wrist, ligament] to damage <part of one's body> by twisting it suddenly □ *She sprained her ankle in a fall.* ◇ *n*: *That's a nasty sprain.*

sprang [spræŋ] *past tense of* **spring**.

sprat [spræt] *n* a small herring.

sprawl [sprɔːl] ◇ *vi* **-1.** [person] to sit or lie with one's arms and legs spread out carelessly □ *He sprawled out on the sofa.* **-2.** [place, town] to cover a large area of land in a way that does not look planned □ *The city sprawled beneath them.* ◇ *n*: *We drove through miles of urban sprawl.*

sprawling ['sprɔːlɪŋ] *adj* [city, building] that sprawls □ *Tokyo's sprawling suburbs.*

spray [spreɪ] ◇ *n* **-1.** [of water] very small drops of water in the air, e.g. from the sea or a fountain □ *The fine spray from the waterfall soaked my hair and clothing.* **-2.** [of deodorant, perfume] liquid in a special container that is under pressure and is forced out of it in very small drops; a container that contains this liquid □ *insect spray* □ *a deodorant spray.* **-3.** [of flowers] a small bunch of flowers; a group of flowers growing on the same branch or stem □ *She was holding a spray of freesias.*
◇ *vt* **-1.** [person, crop, field] to cover <sb/sthg> with a stream of liquid; to send <a stream of liquid> over somebody or something □ *I got sprayed with water.* **-2.** [paint, perfume, pesticide] to force <sthg> out of a container in

very small drops □ *She sprayed air freshener around the room to hide the smell of damp.*
◇ *vi* -1. [liquid] *When he opened the champagne, it sprayed all over the place.* -2. [farmer] *They have been spraying against blight.*

spray can *n* a can that contains liquid under pressure and has a nozzle at the top for spraying it.

spray paint *n* paint sprayed from a can.

spread [spred] (*pt* & *pp* **spread**) ◇ *vt* -1. [map, tablecloth] to unfold <sthg> and lay it on a flat surface □ *He spread the blanket on the grass.* ■ **to spread one's arms/fingers etc** to stretch one's arms/fingers etc so that they are far apart from each other. -2. [butter, jam, glue] to put a layer of <sthg> on a surface; to cover <a surface> with a layer of something □ *Spread the mustard over the ham* OR *Spread the ham with mustard.* -3. [disease, rumor, news] to pass <sthg> to more and more people □ *Exports helped to spread the new technology to Asia.* -4. **to be spread over a period of time** to happen during a period of time □ *The tourist season is now spread over six months.* -5. [dirt, straw] to arrange <sthg> so that it covers an area □ *The troops are spread too thinly to be effective.* -6. [wealth, work] to share <sthg> out evenly □ *I suggest we spread the workload between us.*
◇ *vi* -1. [fire, disease, desert] to affect a larger area or more people □ *Fighting has spread to the north of the country.* -2. [ideas, rumors] to become known by more and more people □ *News of the flood spread quickly.*
◇ *n* -1. [on bread] a food in the form of a soft paste for putting on bread □ *salmon/chocolate/sandwich spread.* -2. [of a fire, disease] the act of spreading □ *They are trying to prevent the spread of unrest to other cities.* -3. [of subjects, products] a large number of different kinds of something □ *a broad spread of opinion.* -4. [in a magazine, newspaper] an article or advertisement with pictures on two facing pages of a newspaper or magazine □ *a double-page spread.* -5. [of food] a large meal in which different kinds of food are placed on a table □ *What a magnificent spread!*
◆ **spread out** ◇ *vt sep* -1. **to be spread out** [people, animals, vehicles] to be far apart; [city, forest] to cover a wide area □ *The runners are now spread out.* -2. **to spread sthg out** [tablecloth, one's arms] to unfold sthg on a flat surface □ *We spread the map out on the table.* ◇ *vi* [people, animals, vehicles] to move away from one another □ *The search party spread out across the field.*

spread-eagled [US 'spredi:gld, GB spred'i:gld] *adj* [person] who is lying flat with their arms and legs spread out □ *Richie lay spread-eagled on the bed.*

spreadsheet ['spredʃi:t] *n* a type of computer software that allows one to enter text and figures in the form of tables and to do calculations, accounting etc automatically.

spree [spri:] *n* a short period during which one does a lot of something enjoyable □ *They went on a spending/shopping/drinking spree.*

sprig [sprɪg] *n* a small piece of the stem of a plant or tree that has some leaves on it □ *a sprig of holly.*

sprightly ['spraɪtlɪ] (*compar* **sprightlier**, *superl* **sprightliest**) *adj* [person] who is lively and active even though they are old □ *She's very sprightly for her age.*

spring [sprɪŋ] (*pt* **sprang**, *pp* **sprung**) ◇ *n* -1. the season between winter and summer, when the weather begins to get warmer □ *I hope to be back in the States next spring.* □ *Those trees are covered with blossom in spring.* □ *I like the spring flowers/colors/weather.* -2. [in a bed, watch] a device, usually a metal coil, that returns to its original shape after being pressed together or stretched □ *a bed/watch spring.* -3. [of a person] a movement or jump that is sudden and quick □ *He made a sudden spring for the knife.* -4. [in the ground] a place where water comes naturally out of the ground □ *volcanic/hot/mountain springs*
◇ *vt* -1. **to spring sthg on sb** [news, surprise] to tell sb sthg that surprises them □ *My boss suddenly sprang it on me that she was going to Lisbon for a week.* -2. **to spring a leak** [ship, container] to begin to leak.
◇ *vi* -1. [person, animal] to move or jump suddenly and quickly □ *The leopard crouches, ready to spring.* □ *She sprang to her feet/to the door.* ■ **to spring into action** [person, organization] to begin to do something suddenly □ *The police sprang into action.* ■ **to spring to life** [machine, car] to begin to work suddenly □ *The engine sprang to life.* -2. [bow, elastic, coil] to be released and move quickly in a particular direction, as if by the action of a spring □ *The branch sprang back and hit him in the face.* □ *The door sprang open/shut.* -3. **to spring from sthg** to be the result of sthg □ *Their aggression springs from fear.*
◆ **spring up** *vi* -1. [person, animal] to get up quickly □ *She sprang up eagerly to greet them.* -2. [child] to grow quickly □ *Alice is springing up so fast now.* -3. [problem, relationship] to appear suddenly □ *New businesses are springing up everywhere.*

springboard ['sprɪŋbɔ:ʳd] *n* -1. SPORT a flexible board that allows somebody to jump high before diving into a swimming pool. -2. something that makes a particular future event or activity possible □ *We'll use the show as a springboard for the product launch.*

spring-clean ◇ *vt* to clean <a house> very thoroughly. ◇ *vi: I've been spring-cleaning all day.*

spring-loaded *adj* [mechanism, device] that is held in place by means of a spring.

spring onion *n* GB a small onion with a long green stem, usually eaten raw in salads.

spring roll *n* a Chinese food that consists of a thin roll of pastry filled with vegetables or meat and fried.

spring tide *n* the tide when there is a new moon or full moon and during which the sea level rises and falls the most.

springtime ['sprɪŋtaɪm] *n* **in (the) springtime** during the spring.

springy ['sprɪŋɪ] (*compar* **springier**, *superl* **spring-**

iest) *adj* [carpet, mattress, ground] that is soft and returns to its normal shape after being pressed flat □ *This bed is very springy!*

sprinkle ['sprɪŋkl] *vt* [liquid, powder] to drop <sthg> on a surface in very small amounts; [surface, food] to cover <sthg> with small drops of liquid or amounts of powder □ *I sprinkled sugar on OR over my cereal.* □ *Now sprinkle the sauce with parsley.*

sprinkler ['sprɪŋklər] *n* -1. a system for sprinkling water inside a building when there is a fire. -2. a system of hoses connected to a timer for sprinkling water on a garden.

sprinkling ['sprɪŋklɪŋ] *n* [of water, salt] a very small amount of something.

sprint [sprɪnt] ◇ *n* SPORT a short fast race. ◇ *vi* to run fast for a short distance.

sprinter ['sprɪntər] *n* SPORT a runner who is trained to run in sprints.

sprite [spraɪt] *n* a playful fairy (literary use).

spritzer ['sprɪtsər] *n* a drink that consists of white wine and soda water.

sprocket ['sprɒkət] *n* a wheel with a set of teeth that fit into holes in something, e.g. in a bicycle chain or roll of film.

sprout [spraʊt] ◇ *vt* -1. [leaves, buds] to cause <sthg> to grow □ *The seeds had sprouted little shoots.* -2. [horns, hair, feathers] to grow <sthg> suddenly □ *Before we knew it, Ralph had sprouted a mustache.* ◇ *vi* -1. [bean, seed] to cause new shoots to grow. -2. [leaves, hair, feathers] to grow suddenly □ *A little beard had sprouted on his chin.* -3. **to sprout (up)** [plant, person] to grow quickly; [new town, building] to appear suddenly □ *Jenny has certainly sprouted up in the last year.* □ *New businesses have sprouted up all over the country.* ◇ *n* -1. = **brussels sprout**. -2. a new shoot on a plant. -3. a shoot on a bean seed that is eaten as a vegetable.

spruce [spruːs] ◇ *adj* [person, appearance] that is neat and pleasant to look at. ◇ *n* an evergreen tree with needles that grows in northern Europe, Asia, and America.

◆ **spruce up** *vt sep* to spruce sb/sthg up [person, room, house] to make sb/sthg look neater and more attractive □ *He went to spruce himself up before dinner.*

sprung [sprʌŋ] *past participle of* **spring**.

spry [spraɪ] (*compar* **sprier**, *superl* **spriest**) *adj* [person] who is lively and active even though they are old.

SPUC (*abbr of* **Society for the Protection of the Unborn Child**) *n* **the SPUC** a British organization that is against abortion.

spud [spʌd] *n* a potato (informal use).

spun [spʌn] *past tense & past participle of* **spin**.

spunk [spʌŋk] *n* courage (informal use).

spur [spɜːr] (*pt & pp* **spurred**, *cont* **spurring**) ◇ *vt* -1. **to spur sb to do sthg** to encourage sb to do sthg □ *It was his support that spurred me to write the novel.* -2. to make <a horse> go faster by digging spurs into its sides. ◇ *n* -1. something that encourages somebody to do something □ *Easy credit is a spur to con-*

sumption. -2. a sharp metal device on a rider's boot, used to make a horse go faster. -3. *phrase* **on the spur of the moment** suddenly and without having thought about it earlier □ *I just decided to leave on the spur of the moment.*

◆ **spur on** *vt sep* **to spur sb on** to encourage sb to do something better, or to continue doing something □ *I was spurred on by this success.*

spurious ['spʊərɪəs] *adj* -1. [interest, affection] that seems real but is not □ *Her display of emotion was entirely spurious.* -2. [argument, statement, claim] that is not true or correct because it is based on a mistake □ *The whole basis of the argument was spurious.*

spurn [spɜːrn] *vt* [offer, help, lover] to refuse to accept <sb/sthg> (literary use) □ *He spurned his father's offer of help.*

spurt [spɜːrt] ◇ *n* -1. [of steam, water, flames] a small amount of a liquid, flames, or gas that comes out of somewhere quickly and suddenly □ *A sudden spurt of steam came from the machine.* -2. [of activity, energy] a short intense period of something □ *I had a sudden spurt of energy.* -3. **to put on a spurt** to increase one's speed suddenly and for a short time, e.g. while running, cycling, or working □ *She put on a spurt and caught up with the others.* ◇ *vi* -1. [steam, water, flames] to come out of somewhere suddenly and with force. -2. [person] to increase one's speed suddenly.

sputter ['spʌtər] *vi* -1. [engine] to make soft irregular noises that sound like somebody spitting □ *The moped sputtered and came to a halt.* -2. [person] to speak with short sounds as if one is spitting, e.g. because one is confused or embarrassed. -3. [fire, oil] to spit.

spy [spaɪ] (*pl* **spies**, *pt & pp* **spied**) ◇ *n* a person whose job is to get secret information from other countries or organizations □ *He was accused of being a spy for the KGB OR a KGB spy.* ◇ *vt* to notice or discover <sb/sthg> □ *I spied him going into the bar.* ◇ *vi* -1. to work as a spy for a particular country or organization □ *They discovered she had been spying for the enemy.* -2. **to spy on sb** to watch sb secretly □ *I have a nasty feeling that someone is spying on me.*

spying ['spaɪɪŋ] *n* the activity of working as a spy □ *He was accused of spying.*

spy satellite *n* a satellite in space that is used for spying, e.g. by taking photographs of military sites.

Sq., sq. *abbr of* **square** □ *Leicester Sq.* □ *20 sq. miles.*

squabble ['skwɒbl] ◇ *n* a quarrel about something unimportant. ◇ *vi* to have a squabble □ *They're always squabbling about OR over petty things.*

squad [skwɒd] *n* -1. part of a police force that deals with a particular type of crime □ *the drugs/fraud squad.* -2. MILITARY a small group of soldiers with a particular duty. -3. SPORT a group of players which a team is chosen from □ *The squad for next week's game has been announced.*

squad car *n* a police patrol car.

squadron ['skwɒdrən] *n* -1. a group of military aircraft or ships on a particular mission. -2. a section of the armed forces that consists of two or more divisions.

squadron leader *n* an officer in the British air force ranking above a flight lieutenant and below a wing commander.

squalid ['skwɒləd] *adj* -1. [place, conditions] that looks very dirty, untidy, and unpleasant □ *Their apartment was pretty squalid.* -2. [activity, behavior, business] that one finds unpleasant and dishonest □ *I don't want to get involved in his squalid little affairs.*

squall [skwɔːl] *n* a sudden short storm, especially at sea.

squalor ['skwɒlər] *n* dirty and unpleasant conditions □ *They live in squalor.*

squander ['skwɒndər] *vt* [money, resources, opportunity] to use <sthg> too quickly or in the wrong way, with the result that one wastes it.

square [skweər] ◇ *n* -1. GEOMETRY a shape (□) made of four sides, all of the same length, that are at right angles to each other □ *He drew a square on the paper.* -2. [in a town, city] an open public space in a town or city, usually surrounded by buildings □ *the main square.* -3. [person] a person who one thinks is boring or unfashionable (informal use) □ *Noel's such a square.* -4. *phrase* **to be back to square one** to have to start doing something again from the beginning □ *It looks like we're back to square one again with the Carlson bid.*
◇ *adj* -1. [room, face] that is shaped like a square □ *You'll need a square piece of paper.* □ *Is it square or rectangular?* -2. **a square meter/mile etc** an area equal in size to a square whose sides are all one meter/mile etc long □ *The tiles cost $50 per square meter.* □ *The room is 15 feet square.* □ *The apartment has 60 square feet.* -3. **to be (all) square** [people] not to owe each other money □ *I did owe him money but we're all square now.* -4. [person, clothes] that looks unfashionable, boring, or out of date (informal use).
◇ *vt* -1. MATH to multiply <a number> by itself □ *4 squared equals 16.* -2. **to square sthg with sthg** to make sthg match or agree with sthg □ *His story doesn't square with the facts.*
✦ **square up** *vi* -1. **to square up with sb** to pay sb what one owes them. -2. **to square up to sb/sthg** [to an enemy, problem] to face sb/sthg and deal with them.

squared [skweərd] *adj* [paper] that has squares marked on it for drawing graphs, diagrams etc.

square dance *n* a dance where four couples face each other in the form of a square.

square deal *n* fair treatment □ *I got a square deal on the car rental.*

squarely ['skweərlɪ] *adv* -1. exactly □ *The table was placed squarely in the middle of the room.* -2. honestly and firmly □ *I told him squarely that I thought he was lying.*

square meal *n* a full meal that gives one

plenty of nourishment □ *He hasn't had a square meal in days.*

Square Mile: the Square Mile a small area in the center of London where all the major banks and the Stock Exchange are situated.

square root *n* a number that, when multiplied by itself, will equal a particular number □ *Three is the square root of nine.*

squash [skwɒʃ] ◇ *n* -1. a sport in which two players use rackets to hit a small rubber ball against one wall of a court that has four walls □ *How about a game of squash one evening?* □ *She's a keen squash player.* -2. US a vegetable marrow, gourd, or pumpkin that can be eaten. -3. GB a drink made of fruit juice, sugar, and water □ *lemon/orange squash.* ◇ *vt* to press <sthg> so that it becomes flat or uncomfortable □ *The seat in front was squashing my legs.* □ *Careful! You're squashing me!*

squat [skwɒt] *(compar* **squatter,** *superl* **squattest,** *pt* & *pp* **squatted,** *cont* **squatting)** ◇ *adj* [person] who is short and fat in an unattractive way; [building] that is wide and low in an unattractive way. ◇ *vi* -1. **to squat (down)** to crouch by balancing on one's feet with one's knees bent under one's body □ *We squatted down in front of the fire.* -2. to live in an unused building without asking the owner's permission or paying rent. ◇ *n* GB a building that somebody is squatting in □ *They're living in a squat in Brixton.*

squatter ['skwɒtər] *n* -1. a person who is living in an unused building without the owner's permission □ *They've got squatters in their house.* -2. AUS a farmer who owns a large area of land.

🐾 SQUATTERS

When the first Europeans settled in Australia, many of them occupied large areas of land that they did not own. Later, the government gave leases to many of these "squatters", and they became respectable landowners. Today, all rich landowners are called squatters, and many people use the disapproving word "squattocracy" to refer to them, suggesting that they consider themselves as an aristocracy, or ruling class.

---

squawk [skwɔːk] ◇ *n* a loud noise made by some types of bird when they are frightened or excited. ◇ *vi* [bird] to make a squawk □ *I could hear parrots squawking in the trees.*

squeak [skwiːk] ◇ *n* a short high-pitched sound □ *She let out a squeak of excitement.* □ *the squeak of brand-new shoes.* ◇ *vi* [person, animal, hinge] to make a squeak □ *They could hear the mice/bedsprings squeaking.*

squeaky ['skwiːkɪ] *(compar* **squeakier,** *superl* **squeakiest)** *adj* [bedspring, hinge, voice] that squeaks.

squeal [skwiːl] ◇ *n* a long high-pitched sound □ *squeals of pain/delight* □ *We heard the squeal of brakes.* ◇ *vi* [person, animal, brakes] to make a squeal □ *The car squealed around the corner.* □ *He squealed with pain/delight.*

squeamish ['skwiːmɪʃ] *adj* [person] who is easily upset or feels sick when they see or hear about unpleasant things, especially blood or killings □ *Don't watch this bit if you're at all squeamish.*

squeeze [skwiːz] ◇ *vt* -1. [hand, tube, lemon] to press <sthg> firmly, usually with one's hand □ *He squeezed the trigger but nothing happened.* -2. [liquid, toothpaste] to force <sthg> out of its container by pressing it firmly, usually with one's hand □ *She tried to squeeze the last drop of cream out of the tube.* □ *freshly squeezed orange juice.* -3. **to squeeze sthg into sthg** to fit sthg into sthg with some difficulty □ *We had to squeeze everybody into one tiny room.* □ *How did you squeeze it all into one afternoon?* -4. **to squeeze sthg out of sb** [money, information] to force or persuade sb to let one have sthg □ *They were trying to squeeze it out of me, but I wouldn't tell them.* ◇ *vi* **to squeeze into/past/through sthg** to get into/past/through sthg with difficulty □ *He squeezed past the guards into the palace.* ◇ *n* -1. an act of squeezing something □ *She gave his hand a squeeze.* -2. a situation in which a space is only just big enough for the people or things in it □ *Five of us in that car was a real squeeze.*

squeezer ['skwiːzəʳ] *n* a device for squeezing the juice from fruit □ *an orange/a lemon squeezer.*

squelch [skweltʃ] *vi* to make a noise that sounds like something being sucked □ *The mud squelched under my boots.*

squid [skwɪd] (*pl* **squid** OR **squids**) *n* a sea creature with a soft white body and ten tentacles, eaten as food.

squiggle ['skwɪgl] *n* a line that bends in an irregular way □ *Her signature was just a squiggle.*

squint [skwɪnt] ◇ *n* MEDICINE a condition of the eyes that makes them look in different directions. ◇ *vi* -1. MEDICINE to have a squint. -2. to look at something with partly closed eyes in order to see it better □ *I found myself squinting at the TV.*

squire ['skwaɪəʳ] *n* in the past, a man who owned most of the land in an English village.

squirm [skwɜːʳm] *vi* -1. to move one's body from side to side because one is nervous or uncomfortable □ *The children got bored and started squirming in their chairs.* -2. to feel very embarrassed □ *I squirmed with embarrassment/shame.*

squirrel [US 'skwɜːrəl, GB 'skwɪr-] *n* a small furry animal with a long thick tail that lives in trees and stores nuts for the winter.

squirt [skwɜːʳt] ◇ *vt* [water, sauce, detergent] to force <a liquid> out of a container through a narrow space □ *Squirt some oil on the hinges.* ■ **to squirt sb/sthg with sthg** to squirt sthg onto sb/sthg □ *They squirted the plants with water.* ◇ *vi* [liquid] to move quickly out of a narrow space □ *Toothpaste squirted out of the tube.*

Sr -1. *abbr of* **senior.** -2. RELIGION *abbr of* **sister.**

Sri Lanka [srɪ'læŋkə] a country in southern Asia, consisting of an island in the Indian Ocean, southeast of India. SIZE: 66,000 sq kms. POPULATION: 17,800,000 (*Sri Lankans*). CAPITAL: Colombo. LANGUAGE: Sinhalese. CURRENCY: Sri Lankan rupee.

SS (*abbr of* **steamship**) a title used before the name of a ship in the merchant marine.

SSA (*abbr of* **Social Security Administration**) *n* **the SSA** the US government department responsible for social security.

SSSI (*abbr of* **Site of Special Scientific Interest**) *n* in Britain, an area that is protected from development by the government, e.g. because of its rare animals or plants.

St -1. *abbr of* **saint.** -2. *abbr of* **street.**

ST *n abbr of* **standard time.**

stab [stæb] (*pt & pp* **stabbed,** *cont* **stabbing**) ◇ *vt* -1. [person] to injure or kill <sb> by pushing a knife into their body □ *He was stabbed to death.* -2. [object] to push <sthg> with a pointed object □ *He stabbed the air with his finger.* ◇ *vi:* *She stabbed at the map with her finger.* ◇ *n* -1. the act of stabbing somebody or something □ *a stab wound.* -2. **to have a stab at sthg** to try to do sthg (informal use) □ *I'm willing to have a stab at it, if you think it's worthwhile.* -3. **a stab of pain/guilt etc** a sudden strong feeling of pain/guilt etc □ *A stab of nostalgia went through him.*

stabbing ['stæbɪŋ] ◇ *adj* **a stabbing pain** a sudden sharp pain □ *She felt a stabbing pain in her side.* ◇ *n* an attack in which somebody is stabbed □ *Two youths were involved in a stabbing outside the club.*

stability [stə'bɪlətɪ] *n* [of a relationship, economy, government] *see* **stable** □ *a period of stability.*

stabilize, -ise ['steɪbəlaɪz] ◇ *vt* [prices, ship, aircraft] to make <sthg> stable. ◇ *vi* [prices, situation] to become stable.

stabilizer ['steɪbəlaɪzəʳ] *n* [on a ship, aircraft, bicycle] a device that helps to keep a vehicle stable.

stable ['steɪbl] ◇ *adj* -1. [relationship, economy, government] that is not likely to change or end suddenly □ *The patient's condition is stable.* -2. [ladder, ship, aircraft] that is in a fixed position and will not move suddenly in an unexpected way □ *Make sure that chair's stable before you stand on it.* -3. [person] who is not likely to behave unreasonably or change mood suddenly □ *He seems more stable since he started work.* ◇ *n* a building where horses are kept.

stable boy, stable lad *n* GB a man or boy whose job is to look after the horses in a stable.

staccato [stə'kɑːtəʊ] *adj* [voice, gunfire] that is made up of short, hard, repeated sounds.

stack [stæk] ◇ *n* -1. [of books, dishes] a pile of things arranged neatly, one on top of the other □ *She added it to a stack of files on the desk.* -2. **stacks** OR **a stack of sthg** [of money, time, work] a large amount of sthg (informal use) □ *I've been using stacks of paper trying to get this letter right.* ◇ *vt* -1. [books, dishes] to arrange <several things> into a stack □ *Just* *stack the dishes on the side there.* **-2. to be stacked with sthg** to be covered with piles of sthg □ *His desk was stacked high with files.*

◆ **stack up** *vi* US **-1.** [situation] to develop (informal use) □ *I don't like the way things are stacking up.* **-2. to stack up against sthg** to compare with sthg □ *Our product stacks up well against theirs.*

stadium ['steɪdjəm] (*pl* **stadiums** OR **stadia** [-djə]) *n* a large sports ground with rows of seats for spectators around it.

staff [US stæf, GB stɑːf] ◇ *n* the people who work for a company or organization □ *The company announced more staff cuts today.* □ *Our staff is made up of people from a variety of backgrounds.* ◇ *vt* [company, organization] to provide the staff for <sthg> □ *The charity shop is staffed by volunteers.*

staffer [US 'stæfər, GB 'stɑːfə] *n* a person who works for an organization, especially a newspaper company.

staffing [US 'stæfɪŋ, GB 'stɑːf-] *n* the recruitment, employment, or management of staff □ *staffing difficulties/levels.*

staff nurse *n* in Britain, a hospital nurse whose rank is below that of a sister.

Staffordshire ['stæfərdʃər] a county in western central England, known as the center of the pottery industry. SIZE: 2,716 sq kms. POPULATION: 1,032,900. ADMINISTRATIVE CENTER: Stafford.

staff room *n* a room in a school where teachers can meet and relax when they are not in class.

Staffs *abbr of* **Staffordshire**.

stag [stæg] (*pl* **stag** OR **stags**) *n* an adult male deer.

stage [steɪdʒ] ◇ *n* **-1.** [of an operation, somebody's development, career] a particular period of a longer process or activity □ *The bill is at the committee stage.* □ *I'll deal with that at a later stage.* □ *The changes were introduced in stages.* □ *There's not much we can do at this late stage.* **-2.** [in a theater] a platform in a hall or theater where plays, performances etc are given □ *She is nervous about appearing on stage.* ■ **to set the stage for sthg** to make the arrangements for sthg to happen □ *The stage has been set for a bitter struggle between the Administration and the judiciary.* **-3. the stage** the profession of being an actor or actress □ *Mary had always wanted to go on the stage.* ◇ *vt* [play, production, strike] to organize <sthg> for other people to see □ *Protesters staged a sit-in.* □ *No one's ever staged a show like this before.*

stagecoach ['steɪdʒkoʊtʃ] *n* a large vehicle pulled by horses that was used in the past to carry passengers and mail on fixed routes.

stage door *n* the entrance to a theater that is used by performers and people who work there.

stage fright *n* the feeling of fear and nervousness felt by a performer before or during a public performance.

stagehand ['steɪdʒhænd] *n* a person whose job

is to prepare, arrange, and move the scenery and stage equipment in a theater.

stage-manage *vt* **-1.** [play, show] to organize the scenery, lights, and the movements of the performers in <a performance>. **-2.** [meeting, demonstration] to organize <an event> so that one gets a particular result □ *The conference was carefully stage-managed to avoid controversy.*

stage manager *n* a person whose job is to stage-manage plays, shows etc at a theater.

stage name *n* a name used by an actor or actress instead of their real name.

stagflation [ˌstæg'fleɪʃn] *n* a mixture of inflation and stagnant or falling production and employment.

stagger ['stægər] ◇ *vt* **-1.** [person] to shock and surprise <sb> □ *I was staggered by his decision.* **-2.** [deliveries, working hours] to arrange <things> so that they happen or come at different times □ *They stagger the shifts so that the workers always have a decent break.* ◇ *vi* to walk unsteadily, e.g. because one is ill, injured, or drunk □ *Laurence staggered home drunk.*

staggering ['stægərɪŋ] *adj* [news, amount, size] that is very surprising, usually because it is impressive □ *It was a staggering sum of money.*

staging ['steɪdʒɪŋ] *n* [of a play, show, ceremony] the act of organizing something for other people to see.

stagnant ['stægnənt] *adj* **-1.** [water, air] that does not move, is not fresh, and often smells bad. **-2.** [business, career] that is not developing or changing □ *The economy had remained stagnant throughout that time.*

stagnate [US 'stægneɪt, GB stæg'neɪt] *vi* [water, business] to become stagnant □ *The industry's been allowed to stagnate for too long now.*

stagnation [stæg'neɪʃn] *n*: *see* **stagnate** □ *Following a period of stagnation, growth started to pick up again.*

stag party *n* a party for a bridegroom, usually the night before his wedding, that only men go to.

staid [steɪd] *adj* [person, appearance, attitude] that seems serious, dull, and old-fashioned.

stain [steɪn] ◇ *n* **-1.** a mark that is not wanted and is difficult to remove □ *a blood/wine stain.* **-2.** a kind of dye used for wood. ◇ *vt* **-1.** [clothing, furniture] to mark <sthg> with a stain accidentally □ *The red wine stained the carpet.* **-2.** to change the color of <sthg> with a stain □ *The table was stained a rich mahogany.*

stained [steɪnd] *adj* **-1.** [carpet, clothing] that has a stain on it. **-2.** [wood] that has been colored with a special dye.

stained glass *n* pieces of colored glass fixed together to make a picture or design, especially in church windows.

stained-glass window *n* a window made of stained glass.

stainless steel [ˌsteɪnlɪs-] *n* a type of steel that does not rust □ *a stainless-steel sink.*

stain remover *n* a chemical substance for removing unwanted stains, e.g. from clothes, carpets, or furniture.

stair [steə^r] *n* a step in a flight of stairs □ *the bottom stair.*

◆ **stairs** *npl* a set of steps leading from one level of a building to another □ *a flight of stairs* □ *at the top of the stairs* □ *He fell down the stairs.*

staircase ['steə^rkeis] *n* a set of stairs inside a building, including the sides and handrails.

stairway ['steə^rwei] *n* a set of stairs inside or outside a building.

stairwell ['steə^rwel] *n* the area in a building around which a staircase is built.

stake [steik] ◇ *n* **-1. to have a stake in sthg** [in a business, firm] to own part of sthg □ *Steiner has a large stake in this company.* **-2.** [of wood] a pointed wooden post □ *He drove the stake into the ground with a hammer.* **-3.** [of a gambler] the money that somebody bets on something such as a horse race □ *He had a $100 stake on Bright Star winning the race.*
◇ *vt* **-1. to stake one's life/reputation etc on sthg** to deliberately risk one's life/reputation etc on sthg □ *He staked his whole future on the successful outcome of this election.* **-2. to stake a sum of money on sthg** to bet a sum of money on sthg □ *There's a lot of money staked on this race.* **-3. to stake a claim** to say that one has a right to something □ *You need to stake your claim to your share of the money.*

◆ **stakes** *npl* **-1.** [in a contest, argument] the prize or advantages that one can get if one wins something or succeeds at something □ *The stakes are high.* **-2.** a contest □ *the leadership/promotion stakes.*

◆ **at stake** *adv* **to be at stake** to be at risk □ *There are lives at stake here.* □ *Do you realize what's at stake here?*

stakeout ['steikaut] *n* [of a building, person] a situation in which the police secretly watch a place or person.

stalactite [US stə'læktait, GB 'stæləktait] *n* a piece of rock hanging from the roof of a cave that is formed by dripping water.
NOTE: Compare **stalagmite**.

stalagmite [US stə'lægmait, GB 'stæləgmait] *n* a piece of rock sticking up from the floor of a cave, formed by water dripping from a stalactite.
NOTE: Compare **stalactite**.

stale [steil] *adj* **-1.** [food, air] that is not fresh □ *This bread is stale.* **-2.** [person, news, idea] that is no longer interesting □ *I think his writing is beginning to grow a little stale.*

stalemate ['steilmeit] *n* **-1.** [in negotiations, an argument] a situation in which neither side can win and no progress is possible □ *The talks had reached a stalemate.* **-2.** CHESS a position in which neither player can win.

Stalin ['stɑːlin], **Joseph** (1879–1953) the leader of the Soviet Union from 1922 to 1953. He was responsible for industrializing the country, and for forcing peasant farmers into collective systems.

stalk [stɔːk] ◇ *n* the thin stem that connects a flower, leaf, or fruit with the main part of a plant □ *Pull off the leaves of the parsley and throw away the stalks.* ◇ *vt* to follow <a person or animal> quietly and secretly, usually with the intention of eventually attacking them. ◇ *vi* to walk with long stiff steps, usually in a way that makes one look proud or angry □ *Mr Joyce stalked around the classroom, looking for a victim.*

stalker ['stɔːkə^r] *n* a person who follows somebody else over a period of time.

stall [stɔːl] ◇ *n* **-1.** [in a market, street, exhibition] a table that something is displayed on. **-2.** [in a stable] an enclosed space for keeping an animal in. **-3.** US a small enclosed area, e.g. where one can use a toilet or have a shower □ *a shower stall.*
◇ *vt* **-1.** [vehicle, engine] to cause <sthg> to stop working while one is using it □ *He stalled the car at the traffic lights.* **-2.** [person] to delay <sb> from doing something; [process, operation] to delay <sthg> from happening □ *See if you can stall him a little longer, just until we get the go-ahead from Geneva.* □ *They're trying to stall the final decision for as long as they can.*
◇ *vi* **-1.** [vehicle, engine] to stop working because it does not have enough power or speed. **-2.** [person] to delay □ *I think they're stalling on the loan until we make more concessions.* □ *Quit stalling!*

◆ **stalls** *npl* GB THEATER the seats in a theater that are on the lowest level and in front of the stage □ *We have seats in the stalls.*

stallholder ['stɔːlhəʊldə^r] *n* GB a person who sells goods from a market stall.

stallion ['stæliən] *n* a male horse.

stalwart ['stɔːlwə^rt] ◇ *adj* **a stalwart supporter/campaigner etc** a supporter/campaigner etc who is loyal and works hard for a particular cause or organization. ◇ *n* a loyal and firm supporter of something □ *The party stalwarts will come to the meeting.*

stamen ['steimən] *n* the part of a flower that produces pollen.

stamina ['stæminə] *n* the strength required to do a physically or mentally tiring activity for a long time □ *Cycling is a good way of building up stamina.*

stammer ['stæmə^r] ◇ *vi* to speak with difficulty, often pausing or repeating sounds in the middle of words □ *Gene stammered as he spoke.* ◇ *n* a way of speaking in which one often stammers □ *He has a stammer.*

stamp [stæmp] ◇ *n* **-1.** [for mail] a small piece of printed paper, marked with a particular value, that one sticks on a letter to prove that the postage has been paid for □ *a book of stamps* □ *Did you put a stamp on it?* **-2.** [document] a small tool that one presses onto a document in order to mark it with a particular design, date etc □ *a rubber/date stamp.* **-3. the stamp of sthg** a characteristic feature or sign of sthg □ *a work which bears the stamp of originality.*

◇ *vt* **-1.** [name, date] to mark a document with <sthg> using a stamp □ *The machine stamps the time on your ticket.* **-2. to stamp one's foot** to hit the ground with the bottom of one's foot, usually to show that one is angry. **-3.** [envelope, postcard] to stick a stamp on <sthg>. **-4.** [person, event, organization] to give a particular quality to <sb/sthg> □ *Recent events have stamped the president as indecisive.*

◇ *vi* **-1.** to stamp one's feet □ *They were stamping around to keep warm.* **-2. to stamp on sthg** [on the floor, an insect, somebody's foot] to hit sthg with the bottom of one's foot □ *He stamped on the rotten plank and it broke.*

◆ **stamp out** *vt sep* to stamp sthg out [fire, crime, disease] to get rid of sthg completely □ *The aim of this campaign is to stamp out corruption at all levels.*

stamp album *n* a book with blank pages for displaying a collection of stamps.

stamp-collecting *n* the hobby of collecting stamps.

stamp collector *n* a person who collects stamps.

stamp duty *n* a tax on legal documents in Britain.

stamped addressed envelope [ˌstæmpt-ədrest-] *n* GB an envelope on which one has stuck a stamp and written one's address so that it can be used by somebody else to send one something.

stampede [stæm'piːd] ◇ *n* **-1.** a sudden wild rush of a group of frightened animals □ *a stampede of elephants.* **-2.** a sudden rush to do something by a large number of people □ *There was a stampede for the door.* ◇ *vi* [horses, cattle] to move in a stampede.

stamp machine *n* a machine that gives postage stamps when money is put into it.

stance [US stæns, GB stɑːns] *n* **-1.** the way somebody is standing □ *He showed them the correct stance for fencing.* **-2.** an attitude expressed in public, especially toward a political matter □ *He's taken an uncompromising stance on immigration.*

stand [stænd] (*pt* & *pp* **stood**) ◇ *vi* **-1.** [person] to be upright with one's weight supported by one's feet □ *I had to stand for the entire trip.* □ *"Take a seat." — "Thanks, I'd rather stand."* □ *Stand next to Lois and I'll take a photo of you.* □ *Then, to make things worse, I stood on her foot.* **-2.** [person] to get up on one's feet and stand after one has been sitting, lying etc □ *He stood to let them pass.* □ *Please stand for the final hymn.* **-3.** [city, building, object] to be in a particular position or place □ *An empty wine bottle stood on the table beside him.* □ *The house stood on the edge of a wood.* **-4.** [house, church] to be upright when other buildings nearby have fallen down or been knocked down □ *After 500 years, the castle was still standing.* **-5.** COOKING [liquid, mixture] to remain somewhere for a period of time without being moved or touched □ *Leave the mousse to*

stand overnight. ■ **to stand empty** [house, factory] to remain empty for some time □ *The building had been standing empty for years.* **-6.** [offer, agreement, law] to continue to be true or exist □ *The company's original offer still stands.* **-7. to stand at sthg** [total, temperature, inflation] to be at a particular level or total □ *The score currently stands at three all.* □ *The total number of dead and injured now stands at 42.* ■ **as things stand** the way things are at present □ *With the law as it stands there is no hope of a conviction.* **-8. to know where sb stands on sthg** to know what sb's opinion is about sthg □ *Where do you stand on the equal rights issue?* **-9.** GB POLITICS [person] to be a candidate in an election for a political position □ *She's standing for Parliament/in the local elections/as an Independent.* **-10. 'No standing'** US no parking, even for a short time.

◇ *vt* **-1.** [bottle, vase, lamp] to put <sthg in a particular place> in an upright position □ *We had to stand the sofa on its end to get it through the door.* ■ **to stand sthg against sthg** [umbrella, stick, rifle] to put sthg in an almost upright position, leaning against sthg tall and fixed □ *I stood my bicycle against the lamppost.* **-2. I/ they etc can't stand it** I/they etc find it very annoying or unpleasant and cannot accept it □ *I couldn't stand the noise any longer.* □ *I don't know how you can stand working in those conditions.* **-3.** [pressure, heat, test] to be strong enough to survive <sthg> □ *The glass has been specially treated so that it can stand very high temperatures.* **-4. to stand sb a drink/meal** to buy a drink/meal for sb □ *Let me stand you a drink.* **-5. to stand trial** LAW to be tried for a crime in court □ *Hendricks is due to stand trial for manslaughter.* **-6. to stand to win/lose sthg** to be in a position in which one is likely to win/lose sthg □ *We stand to lose a lot of money if the deal falls through.*

◇ *n* **-1.** [in the street] a small vehicle or stall, open at the front, for selling things out of doors; [at an exhibition] a small enclosed area where information and products are shown to the public □ *a hot-dog/newspaper stand* □ *There were several stands at the conference advertising new software.* **-2.** [for hats, umbrellas, music] a frame or piece of furniture for supporting a particular kind of object □ *a hat/an umbrella/a music stand.* **-3.** SPORT [at a stadium] a large structure, open at the front, with rows of seats or spaces where people can sit or stand to watch a game □ *We had seats in the stands.* **-4.** [on a subject, against something] a strong opinion expressed in public □ *Mr Lee was admired for his brave stand on welfare reform.* ■ **to make** OR **take a stand** to state one's opinion or position on something strongly in public □ *The Commission has not yet taken a stand on the controversial issue of farm subsidies.* **-5. to make a stand** MILITARY to fight hard to defend oneself or a place □ *In this battle the South made its last stand against the Union forces.* **-6. the stand** US LAW the place in a court where people sit or stand when they give evidence □ *Will the first witness please take the stand.*

◆ **stand aside** *vi* [person, crowd] to move to

one side, especially to let somebody or something pass.

◆ **stand back** vi [crowd, people] to move backward, out of the way □ *Stand back, please, and let the ambulance through!*

◆ **stand by** ◇ vt fus **-1. to stand by sb** [friend, colleague, husband] to support sb who is in a difficult situation □ *His wife stood by him throughout the trial.* **-2. to stand by sthg** [one's promise, offer, decision] to state that sthg one said earlier is still true □ *Despite pressure from colleagues, Esposito is standing by his decision not to resign.*

◇ vi **-1.** [army, emergency services, police] to wait and be ready to do something if it is necessary □ *Cabin crew, stand by for take-off.* □ *A medical team is standing by at Guy's Hospital.* **-2.** [person] to let something bad happen without trying to stop it □ *Are you just going to stand by and watch your own daughter ruin her life?*

◆ **stand down** ◇ vi [person] to give up an official position, especially an important one □ *He will stand down as party leader in favor of a younger candidate.* ◇ vt sep **to stand sb down** AUS [employee] to dismiss sb from their job.

◆ **stand for** vt fus **-1. to stand for sthg** [for justice, democracy, equality] to believe in or support sthg □ *the values this party stands for.* **-2. to stand for sthg** [letter, sign, initial] to be an abbreviation or short form of sthg □ *"PC" stands for personal computer.* **-3. I/he/she etc won't stand for it** I/he/she etc will not accept it or allow it □ *I won't stand for bad language in this classroom!*

◆ **stand in** vi to do somebody's job or duties temporarily □ *I'm standing in for Jill this week while she's away at a conference.*

◆ **stand out** vi **-1.** [person, color, object] to be able to be seen or noticed easily □ *Her dark eyes really stood out against her pale face.* □ *His height makes him stand out in any crowd.* **-2.** [moment, achievement, player] to be much better than other things or people of the same kind □ *She really stands out from the rest of the class because her accent is so good.* □ *In the world of precision motors, there is one name that stands out above the rest.*

◆ **stand up** ◇ vi **-1.** [person] to get up on one's feet and stand after one has been sitting, lying etc □ *Don't stand up too quickly, or you'll feel faint.* □ *He pushed back his chair and stood up to greet me.* **-2.** [claim, evidence, explanation] to be accepted as true □ *His story will never stand up in a court of law.* ◇ vt sep **stand sb up** [one's boyfriend, girlfriend] to deliberately not go to meet sb one has arranged to meet (informal use) □ *We had a date for seven thirty, but she stood me up.*

◆ **stand up for** vt fus **to stand up for sb/sthg** to strongly defend sb/sthg that is being attacked or criticized □ *You have to learn to stand up for yourself/your rights.*

◆ **stand up to** vt fus **-1. to stand up to sthg** [the weather, heat] to remain in good condition in spite of sthg □ *Those boots have stood up to some pretty rough treatment.* **-2. to stand up to sb** [boss, bully, country] to refuse to accept unfair or unkind treatment from sb, especially sb powerful or important □ *It's time someone had the courage to stand up to her.*

standalone ['stændəloun] n a computer system that operates on its own and not as part of a network.

standard ['stændəʳd] ◇ adj **-1.** [size, feature, behavior] that is usual and normal in a particular situation □ *What is the standard procedure for registering a complaint?* □ *Seatbelts are now a standard requirement.* **-2.** [spelling, pronunciation] that is generally accepted as correct □ *The end of the 14th century saw the rise of Standard English.* **-3.** [text, work] that is generally accepted as the best-known or most useful □ *It's regarded as the standard work on Freud.*

◇ n **-1.** a level of quality, especially a level considered to be acceptable □ *a high standard of education/work* □ *Candidates must reach the required standard in each exam.* □ *safety standards.* **-2.** something that other things can be measured against or compared to in order to find out how good they are □ *It's a difficult task by anyone's standards.* □ *This latest model looks set to become an industry standard.* **-3.** a flag.

◆ **standards** npl the ideas about how to behave that affect people's attitudes and behavior □ *There has been a visible decline in standards in recent years.* □ *She has the highest moral standards.*

standard-bearer n a person who leads or represents a particular movement.

standardize, -ise ['stændəʳdaɪz] vt [spellings, methods] to change <things in a particular group>, so they are at the same level or can be measured by the same standards □ *There has been an attempt to standardize tax legislation.*

standard lamp n GB a tall lamp that stands on the floor.

standard of living (pl **standards of living**) n [of person, country, group] the level of comfort and luxury that somebody has in their daily life □ *The standard of living has fallen in recent years in this country.*

standard time n the official local time in a particular part of the world.

standby ['stændbaɪ] (pl **standbys**) n a person or thing that is ready to be used if necessary; a seat on a plane that is not reserved, but that can be taken at the last moment, usually at a lower price □ *Mom's a good standby when the babysitter is busy.* □ *a standby ticket/flight.* ■ **to be on standby** to be ready to be used when needed; to be able to travel on a plane or train if there is a spare seat at the last moment □ *Police reinforcements were on standby in case of trouble.* □ *I'll put you on standby.*

stand-in n a person who does another person's job for a short time if that person is ill or cannot be there.

standing ['stændɪŋ] ◇ adj [joke, invitation, army] that always exists and is available. ◇ n **-1.** somebody's reputation or position compared to other people □ *This success will improve his standing among the profession.* □ *a doc-*

tor of international standing. **-2. of ten/twenty etc years' standing** for the last or previous ten/twenty etc years □ They are friends of twenty years' standing.

standing charge n a fixed amount one has to pay for the use of a particular service, e.g. electricity or gas.

standing committee n a group of people whose job is to study a particular problem or subject for a government.

standing order n an instruction that somebody gives to their bank to pay a fixed amount of money to a particular person or company at regular intervals.

standing ovation n **to give sb/sthg a standing ovation** [performer, performance] to stand up and clap to show one's appreciation of sb/sthg after a concert, show etc □ She received a standing ovation from the audience.

standing room n [in a bus, theater, stadium] space for standing in a vehicle or place, usually when there are no seats left □ It's standing room only, I'm afraid.

standoff ['stændɒf] n a situation in which neither side in an argument can gain an advantage.

standoffish [,stænd'ɒfɪʃ] adj **to be standoffish** to be unpleasantly formal and not very friendly.

standpipe ['stændpaɪp] n a pipe that is connected to a water supply and provides water to a public place, e.g. in the street.

standpoint ['stændpɔɪnt] n one's individual opinion of or way of thinking about a particular subject □ The situation appears quite different from an American standpoint.

standstill ['stændstɪl] n **to be at a standstill** [car, train] not to be moving; [work, talks] not to be progressing □ The traffic remained at a standstill until police had removed the debris from the road. ■ **to come to a standstill** [car, train] to stop moving.

Stanislavski [US ,stænɪ'slɑːvskɪ, GB -'slæv-], **Constantin** (1863–1938) a Russian actor and theater director whose method of training actors had a strong influence on US theater and cinema.

stank [stæŋk] past tense of **stink**.

Stanley knife™ ['stænlɪ-] n a very sharp knife with a blade that can be removed and changed by unscrewing it from the handle.

stanza ['stænzə] n a group of lines in a poem that has a definite pattern.

staple ['steɪpl] ◇ adj **a staple food/export etc** the main food/export etc □ It's getting hard to find even staple goods like flour and milk. ◇ n **-1.** [for paper] a small piece of thin wire that is forced through sheets of paper with a special device and bent over at the back so that it holds the sheets together. **-2.** [for wood, fabric] a thin curved piece of metal used to attach pieces of wood together, fix fabric to a wall etc. **-3.** [of somebody's diet] one of the types of food that somebody needs and uses all the time □ Milk and bread are staples. **-4.** INDUSTRY one of the main

products that is produced by a particular country. ◇ vt [paper, document, copy] to fix <sthg> to something else using a staple.

staple diet n the food that forms the main part of what a person usually eats □ a staple diet of rice and fruit.

staple gun n a device used for fixing paper or fabric to a surface with strong staples.

stapler ['steɪplər] n a device used for fixing sheets of paper together with staples.

star [stɑːr] (pt & pp **starred**, cont **starring**) ◇ n **-1.** [in the sky] a very large mass of burning gas in space, that is seen as a point of light in the night sky □ From the Earth we can see the Moon, stars, and planets. **-2.** [on a flag, badge] a shape with five or more points that is supposed to represent a star □ a three-/four-pointed star □ The flag has five white stars on a blue background. **-3.** [of TV, radio, movies] a person who is very famous, especially in music, movies, or sports; the best or most well-known actor in a play or movie □ a pop/football star □ She was the star of the show. □ a star player/performer. **-4.** [given to hotels, restaurants] a sign that represents the level of quality of something, or the level of importance of somebody □ This hotel/restaurant has three stars. **-5.** an asterisk (*).
◇ vt to have <sb> in one of the most important roles □ The movie stars Cary Grant.
◇ vi [actor, actress] to have the most important male or female role □ She starred in "Gone with the Wind".
◆ **stars** npl **sb's stars** sb's horoscope, especially that is printed regularly in a newspaper or magazine □ I always read my stars in the morning.

star attraction n the performer in a show, circus etc that people most want to see.

starboard ['stɑːrbərd] n the right side when one is on a ship, boat, or plane and facing forward □ The boat was listing to starboard. □ the starboard side/engine.

starch [stɑːrtʃ] n **-1.** a product used for making cloth stiff. **-2.** a substance that is found in foods such as rice, pasta, potatoes, and bread; a kind of food that contains this substance.

starched [stɑːrtʃt] adj [collar, sheet] that has been made stiff with starch.

starchy ['stɑːrtʃɪ] (compar **starchier**, superl **starchiest**) adj [rice, potato] that contains a lot of starch □ starchy foods like rice and potatoes.

stardom ['stɑːrdəm] n the state of being a famous movie star, pop star etc.

stare [steər] ◇ vi to look at somebody or something for a long time without moving one's eyes □ She stared at him in disbelief/shock. ◇ n the act of staring at somebody or something □ He gave me a long hard stare.

starfish ['stɑːfɪʃ] (pl **starfish** OR **starfishes**) n a flat sea creature that is shaped like a star.

stark [stɑːrk] ◇ adj **-1.** [pattern, style, room] that is noticeable because it is very simple and has no decoration □ The room was stark and functional. **-2.** [reality, fact, contrast] that seems harsh and unpleasant □ *The hotel was in stark contrast to the place we had stayed at before.* ◇ *adv* **stark naked** completely naked.

starlet ['stɑːʳlət] *n* a young actress who has had some small roles in movies and hopes to become famous.

starlight ['stɑːʳlaɪt] *n* the light produced by the stars in a night sky.

starling ['stɑːʳlɪŋ] *n* a very common European bird, often found in cities, that has green-black feathers.

starlit ['stɑːʳlɪt] *adj* [night, sky] that is bright with stars.

starry ['stɑːrɪ] (*compar* **starrier**, *superl* **starriest**) *adj* [night, sky] that is full of stars.

starry-eyed [-'aɪd] *adj* [person] who has a romantic and unrealistic attitude.

Stars and Bars *n* **the Stars and Bars** a name for the Confederate flag in the American Civil War.

Stars and Stripes *n* **the Stars and Stripes** a name for the US flag. There are 50 stars (one for each state) and 13 stripes (one for each original colony).

star sign *n* a sign of the zodiac □ *My star sign is Aries.*

Star-Spangled Banner [-spæŋgld-] *n* **the Star-Spangled Banner** the name given to the US national anthem; a name for the US flag.

star-studded [-stʌdəd] *adj* [cast, movie, show] that includes many famous performers.

start [stɑːʳt] ◇ *n* **-1.** [of a meeting, race, year] the beginning of an event or period of time □ *This whole venture was doomed right from the start.* □ *I missed the start of the play.* □ *The whole evening was a disaster from start to finish.* □ *I'd better go now, I have an early start in the morning.* ■ **to get off to a good/bad start** [event, project, relationship] to do well/badly at the beginning □ *The negotiations got off to a good start yesterday.* □ *I'm afraid Jerry and I got off to a bad start as soon as we met.* ■ **to make a start on sthg** to start doing sthg □ *It's time you made a start on your homework.* **-2.** [of fear, surprise] a small movement one makes because one is suddenly frightened or surprised □ *With a start, I realized the door had shut behind me.* ■ **to have a start on sb/sthg** to be ahead of sb/sthg by a particular amount of time □ *They had an hour's start (on us).*

◇ *vt* **-1.** [trip, meal, work] to do <sthg one was not doing before> □ *What time do you normally start work?* □ *It suddenly started to rain.* □ *She started to laugh OR started laughing.* □ *You've started smoking again, I see.* **-2.** [engine, car] to cause <a piece of machinery> to begin working □ *Tell me when to start the tape recorder.* **-3.** [war, fight, fire] to be the cause of <sthg> □ *Are you trying to start an argument?* □ *They are threatening to start legal proceedings.* □ *Police are trying to discover what started the blaze.* **-4.** [business, band, campaign] to do what is necessary to make <sthg> happen □ *My ambition was always to start my own theater group.*

◇ *vi* **-1.** [work, movie, meeting] to begin to

happen, especially at a particular time □ *Work on the new airport building is due to start next spring.* □ *The trouble started some months ago, when I began to get terrible headaches.* **-2.** [speaker, author] to begin discussing or explaining something, e.g. when one is making a speech □ *I'd like to start by saying how grateful I am to have been asked to come here today.* **-3.** [employee, actor, politician] to begin one's life, career etc by having a particular job or role □ *I started in publishing, then switched to advertising.* **-4.** [machine, engine] *The car wouldn't start this morning.* **-5.** [person] to make a small movement because one is suddenly scared or surprised □ *The door slammed, making her start.*

◆ **for a start** *adv* a phrase used to introduce the first of several facts, reasons etc that one is about to mention □ *For a start, it's none of their business!*

◆ **to start with** *adv* **-1.** at the beginning of a relationship, series of events etc □ *To start with, they seemed to get along really well.* **-2.** = **for a start.**

◆ **start off** ◇ *vi* **-1. to start off with sthg** [movie, meeting, discussion] to have sthg as its first part or stage □ *The book starts off with a description of a funeral.* ■ **to start off by doing sthg** to do sthg first before going on to something else □ *I started off by doing research, then got a job as a teacher.* ■ **to start off as sthg** to be sthg in the first stage of one's development or career □ *a huge retail chain which started off as one small hardware store.* **-2.** to begin to move or travel in a particular direction □ *The car started off down the road.* □ *At ten o'clock, we started off for home.*

◇ *vt sep* **-1. to start sb off** to make sb do sthg they were not doing before □ *We'll start you off on some of the easier jobs.* **-2. to start sthg off** [conflict, discussions, meeting] to make sthg exist or happen □ *I'd like to start off this session by welcoming some new members.*

◆ **start on** *vt fus* **to start on sthg** to begin doing sthg that will take a long time, or that has to be done □ *He finished the sandwiches and started on the cake.* □ *There's no point starting on the report until tomorrow.*

◆ **start out** *vi* **-1. to start out as sthg** to be sthg in the first stage of one's development or career □ *He started out as one of Nixon's most trusted aides.* ■ **to start out by doing sthg** to do sthg first before going on to something else □ *The author starts out by thanking all those who helped her in her research.* **-2.** to begin a trip □ *What time should we start out tomorrow?*

◆ **start over** *vi* to stop what one was doing before and start it again from the beginning □ *After his divorce, he moved to Denver and started all over.*

◆ **start up** ◇ *vt sep* **-1. to start sthg up** [company, restaurant, club] to make sthg start happening □ *There are plans to start up a day-care center in the neighborhood.* **-2. to start sthg up** [car, engine, machine] to make sthg start working □ *Start up the engine for me, please.*

◇ *vi* **-1.** [music, noise, wind] to begin to be

heard □ *The orchestra started up.* **-2.** [car, engine, machine] *The motor started up.* **-3.** to establish a business □ *They started up in business in 1989.* □ *He's starting up as an architect.*

◆ **start with** *vt fus* **to start with sb/sthg** to do, have, consider etc sb/sthg first, before anybody or anything else □ *The book starts with an analysis of working conditions at that time.* □ *I'm going to start with soup, then have fish.*

starter ['stɑːʳtəʳ] *n* **-1.** SPORT a person who officially starts a race. **-2.** AUTO an electric motor that starts a car engine. **-3.** GB COOKING a small amount of food that is served at the beginning of a meal before the main dish.

starter motor *n* AUTO a starter.

starter pack *n* a collection of information to help somebody who is starting something, e.g. a hobby or course.

starting block ['stɑːʳtɪŋ-] *n* one of two blocks, attached to the ground, against which a runner pushes both feet at the start of a race in order to increase speed quickly.

starting point *n* **-1.** something that starts a discussion, process etc □ *The starting point for our lecture was a sculpture by Degas.* **-2.** the place where one starts a trip □ *Whitby should be a good starting point for our walk.*

starting price *n* the final odds that are offered to people betting just before the start of a horse or dog race.

startle ['stɑːʳtl] *vt* to surprise <sb> by making a sudden movement or loud noise □ *He looked startled.*

startling ['stɑːʳtlɪŋ] *adj* [news, revelation, event] that seems very surprising and shocking.

starvation [stɑːʳˈveɪʃn] *n* the state of having no food, which causes illness and death □ *Millions have already died of starvation.*

starve [stɑːʳv] ◇ *vt* **-1.** to stop <a person or animal> from eating food with the result that they become weak or die □ *They used to starve their prisoners to death.* **-2. to starve sb of sthg** [of attention, love, funds] to prevent sb from having sthg that they need □ *As a child, he felt starved of affection.* ◇ *vi* to become ill or die because one does not have enough food to eat □ *People are starving to death.*

starving ['stɑːʳvɪŋ] *adj* **to be starving** to be very hungry (informal use) □ *When's dinner? I'm starving!*

state [steɪt] ◇ *n* **-1.** the condition that somebody or something is in □ *Look at the state of this room!* □ *He's in a reasonable state of health.* □ *the state of the economy* □ *She's in a state of shock.* ■ **not to be in a fit state to do sthg** not to be physically or mentally capable of doing sthg for a certain period of time □ *He's not in a fit state to drive.* □ *You're in no fit state to go to work.* ■ **to be in a state** to be very nervous or very upset about something (informal use) □ *She made a mistake and got into an awful state about it.* **-2.** POLITICS a country considered as a political unit controlled by its own government □ *the Balkan States* □ *the EU member states* □ *Can we trust this man with affairs of state?* **-3.** [in a country] one of the areas

that some countries are divided into, and which are responsible for some of their own affairs □ *the state of Louisiana* □ *a state election* □ *the State Governor* □ *state tax.* **-4. the state** the political organization of a country □ *The state is privatizing the national railroad system.* □ *a state-run/state-controlled industry* □ *a state ceremony/pension/subsidy.*

◇ *vt* [name, amount, reason] to say or write sthg in a formal or clear way as a piece of information for somebody else □ *The guidelines clearly state that regular tests are essential.* □ *Check that the delivery contains the stated number of items as per the invoice.* □ *Please state salary expectations.*

◆ **State** *n* **-1. the State** the political organization of a country. ■ **the State Department, the Department of State** the US government department responsible for relations with other countries. **-2. the State of the Union address** a speech made once a year by the US President in January in which he describes his plans for the year ahead.

◆ **States: the States** the United States of America (informal use).

state education *n* education provided and paid for by the state.

statehouse ['steɪthaʊs, *pl* -haʊzɪz] *n* the building where the government of a US state meets.

stateless ['steɪtləs] *adj* [person] who does not officially belong to any country.

state line *n* in the USA, the border between one state and another.

stately ['steɪtlɪ] (*compar* **statelier,** *superl* **stateliest**) *adj* [mansion, ceremony] that seems impressive, dignified, and formal □ *The procession moved along at a stately pace.*

stately home *n* GB a large old house in the countryside that is historically interesting and that is sometimes open to the public.

statement ['steɪtmənt] *n* **-1.** a written or spoken opinion or fact; an official announcement to the public □ *I disagree with your last statement.* □ *In a recent policy statement, you mentioned tax incentives.* **-2.** LAW an official description given by a witness or criminal about a crime or accident □ *The police took statements from all the witnesses.* □ *Would you be willing to make a statement?* **-3.** FINANCE a list of information that a bank provides for a customer about their account, showing all the deposits and withdrawals made over a period of time □ *a monthly/quarterly statement.*

statement account *n* US a savings account where the customer receives regular statements from their bank.

statement of account *n* a list sent to a customer each month by a supplier that shows what they have bought, how much they have paid, and how much they still owe.

Staten Island [,stætn-] an island in New York Harbor, southwest of Manhattan, forming the Richmond borough of New York City. SIZE: 155 sq kms. POPULATION: 352,121.

state of affairs *n* a general situation □ *Well,*

this is a pretty terrible state of affairs □ How long do you expect this state of affairs to continue?

state of emergency *n* a period when a government gives itself powers that it does not normally have in order to deal with a very serious situation or a disaster □ *The government has declared a state of emergency.*

state of mind (*pl* **states of mind**) *n* the way one feels at a particular time □ *I'm concerned about his state of mind.*

state-of-the-art *adj* [technology, computer] that uses the most modern methods, ideas, or materials.

state-owned [-'ound] *adj* [industry, business] that is owned by the state.

state school *n* a school that is paid for by the state and provides free education to all children.

state secret *n* information that is kept secret by a country because it would be harmed if the information were known.

state's evidence *n* US **to turn state's evidence** [criminal] to give information about another criminal in a court, especially in order to receive a less severe punishment.

stateside ['steɪtsaɪd] US ◇ *adj* that is connected with or is in the direction of the USA. ◇ *adv*: *We're moving stateside.*

statesman ['steɪtsmən] (*pl* **statesmen** [-mən]) *n* a very respected and experienced politician.

statesmanship ['steɪtsmənʃɪp] *n* the quality of being a statesman.

states' rights *n* in US politics, the belief that US states should be able to make decisions on their own, without the approval of the national government.

state trooper *n* in the USA, a member of the police force of a particular state.

static ['stætɪk] ◇ *adj* [sales, prices, process] not changing □ *The local population remains relatively static.* ◇ *n* -1. the noise or other effect of electricity in the air that interferes with radio or television signals. -2. static electricity.

static electricity *n* electricity formed by friction that collects in one's hair and clothes and on materials such as plastic.

station ['steɪʃn] ◇ *n* -1. [for trains] a place where trains stop to let passengers get on or off □ *Penn Station* □ *a subway station.* -2. = **bus station.** -3. TV & RADIO a company that broadcasts on TV or radio □ *Do you mind tuning in to another station?* □ *a radio station.* -4. a building where a particular kind of technical work is done □ *a monitoring/research station.* -5. AUS a large farm □ *a sheep station.* -6. [in society] one's position in society (formal use). ◇ *vt* -1. [guard, observer] to put <sb> somewhere to do a particular job □ *Police officers were stationed at all the exits.* -2. MILITARY to send <sb> somewhere to carry out a military duty □ *The troops were stationed on the coast.*

stationary [US 'steɪʃəneri, GB -əri] *adj* [vehicle, driver] that is not moving □ *Wait until the plane is stationary before unfastening your seatbelt.*

stationer ['steɪʃnər] *n* a person who runs a store that sells stationery. ■ **a stationer's** a store that sells stationery.

stationery [US 'steɪʃəneri, GB -əri] *n* -1. paper, pens, envelopes, and other materials for writing □ *office stationery* □ *a stationery store.* -2. writing paper and matching envelopes □ *gift stationery.*

station house *n* US the local police office (old-fashioned use).

stationmaster [US 'steɪʃnmæstr, GB -mɑːstə] *n* the person in charge of a train station.

station wagon *n* US & AUS a big car that has a door at the back and space between this door and the back seats for luggage.

statistic [stə'tɪstɪk] *n* a piece of information expressed as a number □ *government statistics* □ *I don't want my son to be just another statistic!*

◆ **statistics** *n* a kind of mathematics that is concerned with presenting and analyzing information in the form of numbers □ *She's studying statistics at college.*

statistical [stə'tɪstɪkl] *adj* [analysis, evidence] that is connected with the use of statistics □ *There is very little statistical evidence.*

statistician [ˌstætə'stɪʃn] *n* a person who studies statistics, or who works with statistics.

statue ['stætʃuː] *n* a sculpture of a person or animal that is usually large and often made out of a single piece of stone or metal □ *a bronze statue of Napoleon.*

Statue of Liberty: the Statue of Liberty a very large statue in New York Harbor, given to the USA by France in 1886. The statue shows a woman holding a torch.

statuesque [ˌstætʃu'esk] *adj* [woman] who is tall and beautiful.

statuette [ˌstætʃu'et] *n* a small sculpture, usually of a person, used as an ornament in a house.

stature ['stætʃər] *n* -1. a person's height □ *short in stature.* -2. a person's importance and influence □ *a campaigner of some stature.*

status ['steɪtəs] *n* -1. one's social, professional, or legal situation □ *They have the status of political refugees.* □ *What is your marital status: single, married, or divorced?* □ *a high-/low-status job.* -2. social importance and wealth, when this impresses other people □ *All she thinks about is status and money.*

status quo [-'kwoʊ] *n* **the status quo** the situation that exists at a particular time □ *Nobody wants to upset the status quo.*

status symbol *n* something, such as an expensive car, that one buys to show that one is important and rich.

statute ['stætʃuːt] *n* a law that has been formally written down.

statute book *n* **the statute book** all the laws that exist in a particular country.

statutory [US 'stætʃətɔːri, GB -ʊtəri] *adj* [limit, period] that is fixed by law □ *'This guarantee does not affect your statutory rights.'*

staunch [stɔːntʃ] ◇ *adj* **a staunch supporter/ believer etc** a person who is very loyal to a particular person/belief etc □ *Great Britain has always been one of our staunchest allies.* ◇ *vt* to stop <blood> from flowing from a wound □ *Use a clean handkerchief to staunch the flow.*

stave [steɪv] (*pt* & *pp* **staved** OR **stove**) *n* MUSIC the set of five horizontal lines and four spaces that music is written on.

◆ **stave off** *vt sep* **to stave sthg off** [hunger, disaster, defeat] to stop sthg happening or affecting one for a time □ *She tried to stave off further awkward questions.*

stay [steɪ] ◇ *vi* **-1.** [person, vehicle, animal] to remain in a place and not move away for a certain amount of time □ *He asked them to stay for dinner.* □ *I stayed behind to help her out.* □ *I think I'll stay at home tonight.* □ *We can't stay long, I'm afraid.* □ *Turn right at the next intersection, and stay on this road for five miles.* □ *Stay there!* ■ **to stay put** to remain where one is (informal use) **-2.** [tourist, guest] to spend time in a place on vacation or on business □ *I'm going to stay with friends.* □ *He stayed in Paris for four days.* □ *I'll be staying overnight in a hotel.* □ *We always stay at the Marriot.* **-3.** [person, level] to continue to be in a particular state □ *Stay still/calm!* □ *She stayed awake till midnight.* □ *If the interest rate stays at this level...* ◇ *n* a period of time that one spends in a place □ *We really enjoyed our stay in Prague.* □ *a three-week stay.*

◆ **stay away** *vi* **to stay away from sb/sthg** not to go near sb/sthg □ *I'd stay away from that part of town, if I were you.*

◆ **stay in** *vi* to stay at home and not go out □ *I feel like staying in tonight.*

◆ **stay on** *vi* to stay somewhere after the time when one could or is expected to leave □ *We stayed on after the meeting.*

◆ **stay out** *vi* **-1.** to remain away from home, especially in the evening □ *Don't stay out too late.* **-2.** [strikers] to continue to be on strike. **-3. to stay out of sthg** [of argument, trouble, discussion] not to get involved in sthg □ *Try and stay out of trouble!* □ *Look, just stay out of this!*

◆ **stay up** *vi* to go to bed at a later time than usual, or not at all □ *We stayed up late.* □ *Justin stayed up to finish his work.*

staying power ['steɪɪŋ-] *n* the mental or physical strength to finish a difficult piece of work, a race etc □ *I don't have the staying power to party till dawn any more.*

St Bernard [US ˌseɪntbərˈnɑːrd, GB səntˈbɜːnəd] *n* a large dog with a thick coat that was originally kept by Swiss monks to rescue people who got lost or injured in the snow.

STD *n* **-1.** (*abbr of* **subscriber trunk dialing**) in Britain, a telephone system that allows users to make long-distance calls without having to go through an operator. **-2.** (*abbr of* **sexually transmitted disease**) a disease that is caught through sexual contact.

stead [sted] *n* **to stand sb in good stead** to be very useful to sb at a later time □ *Your hard work throughout the year will stand you in good stead for the exams.* □ *My languages have always stood me in good stead at work.*

steadfast [US ˈstedfæst, GB -fɑːst] *adj* **-1.** [sup-

porter, friend] who is always loyal □ *a steadfast supporter of the Labor Party.* **-2.** [resolve, belief] that remains firm, despite pressure to change □ *He was steadfast in his refusal to sell his business.*

steadily [ˈstedɪlɪ] *adv* [improve, move, stare] *see* **steady** □ *Her condition steadily worsened.* □ *Rain was falling steadily.*

steady [ˈstedɪ] (*compar* **steadier**, *superl* **steadiest**, *pt* & *pp* **steadied**) ◇ *adj* **-1.** [improvement, increase, decrease] that happens gradually and always at the same speed □ *a steady rise in unemployment.* **-2.** [speed, flow] that is regular and does not change; [movement] that is smooth and controlled □ *Add the oil in a steady stream.* □ *She is learning at a steady pace.* **-3. to be steady** [hand] to be still and not shaking □ *Hold the camera steady!* □ *That ladder doesn't look very steady.* **-4.** [voice] that is calm and controlled; [stare, gaze] that is fixed and does not change □ *"Get out of here,"* *he said in a quiet, steady voice.* **-5.** [relationship, job] that will probably continue □ *He has a steady girlfriend.* **-6.** [person] who is sensible and can be depended on □ *a steady, dependable sort of girl.* ◇ *vt* **-1.** [boat, camera] to fix or hold <sthg> so that it does not move □ *Jim steadied the ladder as I climbed up.* ■ **to steady oneself** to stop oneself from losing one's balance. **-2.** [voice, nerves] to control or calm <sthg> □ *How about a quick drink to steady our nerves?*

steak [steɪk] *n* **-1.** beef of very good quality; a piece of this □ *He bought some steak from the butcher.* □ *a juicy steak.* **-2.** a large piece of fish □ *a fish/tuna steak.*

steakhouse [ˈsteɪkhaʊs, *pl* -haʊzɪz] *n* a restaurant that specializes in cooking steaks.

steal [stiːl] (*pt* **stole**, *pp* **stolen**) ◇ *vt* **-1.** [jewelry, money, food] to take <sthg that belongs to somebody else> without intending to give it back; [idea, invention] to take and use <sthg that somebody else thought of first> □ *Somebody's stolen my purse!* □ *She stole a book from the store.* □ *They stole the idea from a book by John McGuire.* **-2.** [look, glance, kiss] to give <sthg> to somebody quickly or secretly □ *She stole a quick glance at Luis as he stood beside her.* **-3.** BASEBALL to run to and reach <a base> while the pitcher is throwing the ball at the batter. ◇ *vi* **-1.** [person] *He was caught stealing.* **-2.** to move somewhere quickly and quietly □ *I stole down the stairs and sneaked out.* ◇ *n* BASEBALL the act of stealing a base.

stealing [ˈstiːlɪŋ] *n* the act or crime of taking things that belong to other people without intending to give them back □ *He was arrested for stealing.*

stealth [stelθ] *n* **by** OR **with stealth** [move, creep, enter] quietly and secretly.

stealthy [ˈstelθɪ] (*compar* **stealthier**, *superl* **stealthiest**) *adj* [glance, step] that is done quietly and secretly so that nobody notices.

steam [stiːm] ◇ *n* the gas formed by boiling water; power produced by this gas □ *Clouds of steam rose into the air.* □ *a steam train.* ■ **to**

let off steam to let out energy or anger that is increasing inside one (informal use). ▪ **to run out of steam** to have no energy or enthusiasm left. ◇ *vt* [fish, vegetables, pudding] to cook <sthg> using steam. ◇ *vi* -1. [soup, kettle, wet clothes] to produce steam □ *She carried in two plates of steaming chowder.* -2. [train, ship] to move by being powered by steam □ *The train steamed out of the station.*

◆ **steam up** ◇ *vt sep* -1. **to steam sthg up** [glasses, window] to make sthg become covered in steam. -2. **to get steamed up about sthg** to become annoyed about sthg (informal use) □ *There's no point in getting all steamed up about it.* ◇ *vi* [glasses, window] *All the car windows had steamed up.*

steamboat ['sti:mbəʊt] *n* a boat that is powered by steam, especially one used for traveling on rivers.

steam engine *n* a train or engine that uses steam to make it work.

steamer ['sti:mə^r] *n* -1. SHIPPING a large ship that is powered by steam. -2. COOKING a container used for steaming food.

steam iron *n* an electric iron that releases steam to make it easier to get rid of creases.

steamroller ['sti:mrəʊlə^r] *n* a large vehicle with very heavy wide wheels for making road surfaces flat.

steam shovel *n* US a large machine that has a long arm with a shovel at the end and is used for digging up and moving dirt.

steamy ['sti:mɪ] (*compar* **steamier**, *superl* **steamiest**) *adj* -1. [room] that is full of steam. -2. [movie, book, scene] erotic (informal use).

steel [sti:l] ◇ *n* a strong metal consisting of iron with small amounts of carbon that is used for making tools, bridges, machinery etc □ *The girders are (made of) steel.* □ *a steel bar/structure* □ *the steel industry.* ◇ *vt* **to steel oneself** to prepare oneself for a bad or unpleasant experience □ *She had steeled herself for bad news.*

steel wool *n* a ball of steel threads, used for cleaning or smoothing a surface.

steelworker ['sti:lwɜ:^rkə^r] *n* a person who works in a steelworks.

steelworks ['sti:lwɜ:^rks] (*pl* **steelworks**) *n* a factory where steel is made.

steely ['sti:lɪ] (*compar* **steelier**, *superl* **steeliest**) *adj* -1. **steely gray/blue** gray/blue that has the color of steel. -2. **a steely will/determination** a will/determination that is very strong and tough.

steep [sti:p] ◇ *adj* -1. [hill, road, stairs] that rises or falls sharply □ *The mountain was too steep for me to ski down.* -2. [increase, rise, fall] that is very large and sudden □ *There has been a steep rise in the number of suicides among young men.* -3. [price, fee] that seems unusually expensive (informal use) □ *$100? That's a bit steep!* ◇ *vt* [clothes, fruit] to put <sthg> in water or another liquid.

steeped [sti:pt] *adj* **to be steeped in sthg** [in history, tradition, culture] to be full of sthg □ *This mansion is steeped in legend.*

steeple ['sti:pl] *n* a pointed church tower.

steeplechase ['sti:plt∫eɪs] *n* -1. a horse race over two miles long in which the horses have to jump over fences and other obstacles. -2. a race, usually 3,000 meters long, in which runners have to jump over hurdles and water jumps.

steeplejack ['sti:pldʒæk] *n* a person whose job involves climbing up towers and steeples in order to repair or paint them.

steeply ['sti:plɪ] *adv* [rise, increase, fall] *see* **steep** □ *The hill sloped steeply upward.* □ *Prices have risen steeply.*

steer [stɪə^r] ◇ *vt* -1. [bus, ship, car] to make <a vehicle> go in a particular direction □ *Part of the test was to steer the motorcycle between the cones.* -2. [guest, group] to guide <sb> in a particular direction □ *The waitress steered them to a corner table.* -3. [project, subject] to make <sthg> go in a particular direction □ *He tried to steer the conversation around to/away from politics.* □ *The bill was skillfully steered through the Assembly.* ◇ *vi* [car, boat] to move in a particular direction; [driver, captain] to make a vehicle or boat go in a particular direction □ *The bus steered straight into the hedge.* ▪ **to steer clear of sb/sthg** to avoid sb/sthg □ *He tried to steer clear of awkward questions.* ◇ *n* a young male animal of the cattle family, whose sexual organs have been removed.

steering ['stɪərɪŋ] *n* AUTO the parts of a vehicle that make it possible to steer it □ *I've got a problem with the steering.*

steering column *n* a bar in a vehicle to which the steering wheel is attached.

steering committee *n* a committee set up by a government or organization to decide on activities, subjects for discussion etc.

steering lock *n* the position where the steering wheel cannot be turned any further in a particular direction.

steering wheel *n* the wheel in a vehicle that the driver turns to go in a particular direction.

Stein [staɪn], **Gertrude** (1874–1946) a US writer and art collector who lived in Paris for much of her life. Her best-known work is *The Autobiography of Alice B. Toklas.*

Steinbeck ['staɪnbek], **John** (1902–1968) a US writer whose work includes *The Grapes of Wrath* and *Of Mice and Men.*

stellar ['stelə^r] *adj* [performance, cast, career] that is of a very high standard or is very successful.

stem [stem] (*pt & pp* **stemmed**, *cont* **stemming**) ◇ *n* -1. [of a plant] the long central part of a plant that grows above the ground, and from which flowers and leaves grow. -2. [of a glass] the thin vertical part of a wine glass that connects the base with the part that contains the drink. -3. [of a pipe] the long part of a tobacco pipe. -4. GRAMMAR [of a verb, noun] the part of a word that stays the same when different endings are attached to it.

◇ *vt* [flow, bleeding, advance] to stop <sthg> □ *efforts to stem the rising tide of nationalism.*

◆ **stem from** *vt fus* to stem from sthg to be the result of sthg □ *The problem stemmed from his unwillingness to modernize his business.*

stench [stentʃ] *n* a very strong and unpleasant smell □ *The stench of rotten eggs.*

stencil ['stensl] (US *pt* & *pp* **stenciled**, *cont* **stenciling**, GB *pt* & *pp* **stencilled**, *cont* **stencilling**) ◇ *n* a piece of card, plastic etc with a design cut into it that can be copied onto a surface by laying it on the surface and painting over the holes; the design that is copied in this way. ◇ *vt* [words, pattern, name] to use a stencil to copy <sthg> onto a surface.

stenographer [stə'nɒɡrəfə^r] *n* US a typist who also uses shorthand.

stenography [stə'nɒɡrəfɪ] *n* US shorthand.

step [step] (*pt* & *pp* **stepped**, *cont* **stepping**) ◇ *n* -1. the act of lifting one's foot, placing it somewhere else, and putting one's weight on it; the distance covered in this way; the sound of this □ *Take three steps back.* □ *The car was only a few steps away from her.* □ *I could hear the steps getting nearer.* ■ **to be in step with sb/sthg** to act or think in the same way as sb/sthg □ *Colonel Raddle, unfortunately, is not in step with modern times.* ■ **to be out of step with sb/sthg** to act or think in a different way from sb/sthg □ *The government is out of step with the wishes of its people.* ■ **to watch** OR **mind one's step** to be careful when walking somewhere; to be careful about what one does or says in order to avoid trouble □ *Watch your step, the floor is slippery.* □ *He'll get into trouble if he doesn't watch his step in future.* -2. [toward success, peace, a solution] one action in a series of actions that are intended to produce a particular result □ *We must take steps to remedy this situation.* □ *The next step is to raise funds.* -3. [in a process] one part of a process □ *I'm behind your decision every step of the way.* □ *Their success is due to remaining one step ahead of their competitors.* □ *The deal is a major step forward for Carrigi & Co.* ■ **step by step** gradually □ *She explained the process step by step.* □ *a step-by-step guide to home maintenance.* -4. [for walking up or down] a narrow flat surface where one places one's foot when walking from one level to another □ *Be careful of the step.* □ *Someone was standing on the bottom step.* -5. [of a ladder] one of the horizontal bars of a ladder. -6. SPORT a form of exercise in which one steps onto and off a board that is slightly raised above the ground. -7. US MUSIC the interval between two notes which are next to each other in a scale, but which can be divided into smaller intervals.

◇ *vi* -1. to take a step □ *She stepped forward and shook his hand.* □ *He stepped off the bus/out of the car.* □ *Step this way, please, and I'll show you to your table.* -2. **to step on sthg** [on a snail, banana skin] to put one's foot down on sthg □ *Did I just step on your toes?*

◆ **steps** *npl* -1. two or more steps in a row, one above the other, that are usually made of stone, and found outside □ *a flight of steps* □ *By the time he reached the top of the steps, she was gone.* -2. GB a stepladder.

◆ **step aside** *vi* -1. to move to one side □ *The onlookers stepped aside to let the carriage pass.* -2. = **step down**.

◆ **step back** *vi* to think about a situation in a different way □ *Try to step back a little and see the problem from Marianne's point of view.*

◆ **step down** *vi* to leave one's job or position of responsibility □ *He has decided to step down as director of finance.*

◆ **step in** *vi* to become involved in a difficult situation in order to try to settle it □ *At this point in the argument I was forced to step in.*

◆ **step up** *vt sep* to step sthg up [pressure, output, activity] to increase sthg □ *They have decided to step up their efforts to improve the efficiency of the service.*

stepbrother ['stepbrʌðə^r] *n* the son of one's stepmother or stepfather.

stepchild ['steptʃaɪld] (*pl* **stepchildren**) [-tʃɪldrən] *n* the child of one's husband or wife, but not one's own natural child.

stepdaughter ['stepdɔːtə^r] *n* the daughter of one's husband or wife, but not one's own natural daughter.

stepfather ['stepfɑːðə^r] *n* the husband of one's mother, but not one's own natural father.

Stephenson ['stiːvnsən], **George** (1781–1848) a British engineer and inventor who built the first steam train.

stepladder ['steplædə^r] *n* a short ladder attached to a support that can be folded for storing and is used indoors.

stepmother ['stepmʌðə^r] *n* the wife of one's father, but not one's own natural mother.

stepping-stone ['stepɪŋ-] *n* -1. one of a line of stones that one can walk on to cross a stream or river. -2. something that helps one to progress, especially in one's career □ *The position is generally seen as a stepping-stone to a presidential appointment.*

stepsister ['stepsɪstə^r] *n* the daughter of one's stepmother or stepfather.

stepson ['stepsʌn] *n* the son of one's husband or wife, but not one's own natural son.

stereo ['steriou] (*pl* **stereos**) ◇ *adj* [system, record player, recording] that involves sound coming from two separate speakers. ◇ *n* a record player that produces sound from two separate speakers. ■ **in stereo** with the sound coming from two separate speakers □ *It sounds much better in stereo.*

stereophonic [ˌsteriə'fɒnɪk] *adj* [sound] = **stereo**.

stereotype ['steriətaɪp] ◇ *n* a set of fixed characteristics that represent a typical example of a particular thing, nationality, person etc. ◇ *vt* [person, group] to present or consider <sb/sthg> as a stereotype □ *a stereotyped image/role.*

sterile [US 'sterəl, GB 'steraɪl] *adj* -1. [gloves, equipment, conditions] that is completely clean and without germs. -2. [person, animal] that is unable to produce babies or young. -3.

[discussion, report, idea] that produces no useful result (disapproving use).

sterility [stə'rɪlətɪ] *n*: *see* **sterile**.

sterilization [US ˌsterələ'zeɪʃn, GB ˌsterəlaɪ-] *n* **-1**. [of equipment, operating room] *see* **sterilize**. **-2**. a medical operation in which a person or animal is prevented from being able to produce babies in future.

sterilize, -ise ['sterəlaɪz] *vt* **-1**. [container, equipment, room] to make <sthg> sterile. **-2**. to perform a sterilization operation on <a person or animal>.

sterilized milk ['sterəlaɪzd-] *n* milk that has been treated in order to remove germs.

sterling ['stɜːˈlɪŋ] ◇ *n* the currency of the UK □ *The value of sterling on the world market fell today*. □ *It costs 3,000 pounds sterling*. □ *sterling reserves/traveler's checks*. ◇ *adj* [effort, work, performance] that is of an excellent standard (formal or old-fashioned use).

sterling silver *n* metal that contains at least 92.5% of silver □ *a sterling silver bracelet*.

stern [stɜːˈn] ◇ *adj* **-1**. [person] who is serious, strict, and unfriendly □ *Her father was a tall stern man*. **-2**. [look, warning] that shows one's disapproval □ *Sterner penalties must be introduced to deter such crimes*. ◇ *n* the back part of a boat or ship.

sternly ['stɜːˈnlɪ] *adv* [look, say] *see* **stern**.

steroid ['stɪərɔɪd] *n* a chemical substance found naturally in the body, or introduced artificially to improve strength or to treat certain diseases.

stethoscope ['steθəskoʊp] *n* a medical instrument used to listen to somebody's heart and their breathing.

Stetson™ ['stetsn] *n* a large hat worn especially by cowboys in the west of the USA.

stevedore ['stiːvədɔːˈ] *n* US a person whose job is to load and unload ships.

Stevenson ['stiːvnsən], **Robert Louis** (1850–1894) a British writer, born in Scotland, whose best-known works are *Treasure Island* and *The Strange Case of Dr Jekyll and Mr Hyde*.

stew [stʲuː] ◇ *n* a dish, usually made of meat and vegetables, that is cooked slowly in liquid □ *a lamb/vegetable stew*. ◇ *vt* [meat, vegetables, fruit] to cook <food> slowly in liquid. ◇ *vi* **to let sb stew (in their own juice)** to make sb wait before telling them an answer, decision etc that they are anxious to hear (informal use) □ *I'll just let him stew for a few days*.

steward ['stʲuəˈd] *n* **-1**. a man whose job is to take care of passengers on a plane, train, or ship, especially by serving food and drink. **-2**. GB a person whose job is to help to organize a public event.

stewardess [US 'stuərdəs, GB ˌstʲuəˈdes] *n* a woman whose job is to take care of passengers on a plane, train, or ship, especially by serving food and drink.

stewbeef ['stʲuːbiːf] US, **stewing steak** ['stʲuːɪŋ-] GB *n* beef that is not of a high quality, but is suitable for stewing.

St. Ex. *abbr of* **stock exchange**.

stg *abbr of* **sterling**.

stick [stɪk] (*pt* & *pp* **stuck**) ◇ *n* **-1**. a long thin branch that has been broken off or has fallen off a tree □ *a wooden stick* OR *stick of wood*. **-2**. [of dynamite, rhubarb] a long thin piece of something □ *a stick of chewing gum*. **-3**. [for walking] a smooth thin piece of wood or metal used by old or injured people to help them walk □ *The blind man had a white stick*. **-4**. SPORT a long thin piece of wood, often with a curved end, that is used for hitting a ball □ *a hockey/lacrosse stick*. **-5. to get the wrong end of the stick** to misunderstand something (informal use).

◇ *vt* **-1. to stick sthg in** OR **into sthg** [knife, needle] to push sthg sharp into sthg (informal use) □ *Don't stick pins in the wall*. □ *He stuck his fork into the potato*. ■ **to stick sthg through sthg** [through a hole, mailbox] to push sthg through sthg (informal use). **-2**. [stamp, picture] to attach <sthg> to something else using a sticky substance such as glue □ *She stuck the label on the jar*. □ *He stuck the photo in his album*. **-3**. to put <sthg> somewhere (informal use) □ *Can you stick my name on the list?* □ *I usually stick it in the oven for 20 minutes*. □ *Teresa stuck her head round the door*.

◇ *vi* **-1**. [arrow, dart, spear] to enter something and remain fixed there □ *A splinter of wood had stuck in my finger*. **-2**. [food, mud, clothes] to become attached to something, especially because of glue or another sticky substance □ *The flap on this envelope won't stick*. □ *The static on the balloon made it stick to my hand*. **-3**. [door, window, zipper] to become fixed in a particular position and unable to move □ *The car stuck fast in the mud*. **-4. to stick in one's mind** to stay in one's memory for a long time.

◆ **sticks** *npl* **out in the sticks** in the countryside and far away from towns or cities (humorous use).

◆ **stick around** *vi* to remain somewhere for a period of time (informal use) □ *I'm not sticking around here any more*.

◆ **stick at** *vt fus* **to stick at sthg** [job, activity] to continue to work hard at sthg □ *He stuck at it until he got it right*.

◆ **stick by** *vt fus* **-1. to stick by sb** to continue to support sb, especially when they are in trouble □ *George stuck by us through that terrible time*. **-2. to stick by sthg** [decision, statement] to refuse to change sthg that one believes in or has said □ *Martha has always stuck by her promises*.

◆ **stick out** ◇ *vt sep* **-1. to stick sthg out** [one's tongue, hand, head] to extend sthg, usually so that it can be seen □ *She stuck her head out of the window*. **-2. to stick it out** to continue to do something that is unpleasant or difficult, especially until it is finished (informal use) □ *I'll stick it out until the end of the month, then I'm leaving*. ◇ *vi* **-1**. [nail, tooth] to be noticeable because it is longer than something else or points in a different direction □ *His ears stick out*. **-2**. [talent, problem, truth] to be very noticeable because it is unusual (informal use) □ *It's her accent that makes her stick out.*

◆ **stick to** *vt fus* **-1. to stick to sb** to stay near sb □ *Stick close to me so I know where you are.* ■ **to stick to sthg** [path, road] to continue to follow sthg □ *Stick to the freeway and you won't get lost.* **-2. to stick to sthg** [agreement, decision, one's principles] to do or say things that agree with sthg, so that one does not change it □ *She's still sticking to her story.* □ *Stick to the point/facts!*

◆ **stick together** *vi* [people] to continue to support and be loyal to each other □ *We're going to stick together, no matter what happens.*

◆ **stick up** ◇ *vt sep* **-1. to stick sthg up** [notice, postcard, poster] to attach sthg to a wall □ *Somebody had stuck a sign up saying 'Keep Off!'* **-2. stick 'em up!** a phrase used by a person with a gun when they want another person to raise their arms above their head. ◇ *vi* [hair, pole] to be in a fixed vertical position, coming out of something horizontal □ *The knife was still sticking up in the butter.*

◆ **stick up for** *vt fus* **to stick up for sb/sthg** [one's friends, beliefs, rights] to defend sb/sthg against criticism, a threat etc □ *My brother was the only person who'd stick up for me at school.*

◆ **stick with** *vt fus* **-1. to stick with sthg** [decision, job] not to change sthg that one has started to do, use etc to something else □ *I've made my decision and I'm going to stick with it.* **-2. to stick with sb** [one's mother, group, guide] to stay near sb □ *Stick with me and you'll be fine.* **-3. to stick with sb/sthg** [leader, company, brand] to remain loyal to sb/sthg □ *I've stuck with my bank for 35 years.*

sticker ['stɪkə^r] *n* a small piece of paper that has a design or words printed on it and can be stuck onto an object □ *a car sticker.*

sticking plaster ['stɪkɪŋ-] *n* GB a piece of material that is sticky on one side and is used to cover cuts on one's skin.

stick insect *n* an insect with a long brown or green body and very thin long legs.

stick-in-the-mud *n* a person who refuses to try something new and exciting (informal and disapproving use).

stickler ['stɪklə^r] *n* **to be a stickler for sthg** [for punctuality, discipline, rules] to believe that sthg is very important and insist on people doing it.

stick-on *adj* **a stick-on label/badge** a label/badge that is sticky on one side so that it can be fixed to something.

stickpin ['stɪkpɪn] *n* US a thin decorated piece of metal with a sharp point at the end that is used to keep a man's necktie in position.

stick shift *n* US the stick in a car, truck etc that one moves with one's hand to change gears.

stick-up *n* a robbery in a public building such as a bank in which the robbers threaten people with guns (informal use).

sticky ['stɪkɪ] (*compar* **stickier**, *superl* **stickiest**) *adj* **-1.** [hand, food, wrapper] that contains or is covered with a substance that sticks to things, especially in an unpleasant or messy way □ *Olly's fingers were sticky with jam.* **-2.** [label, tape, paper] that has glue or a similar substance on one side so that it will stick to a surface □ *This tape is sticky on both sides.* **-3.** [situation, problem] that is difficult to deal with (informal use) □ *I'll be in a sticky situation if anyone finds out.* **-4.** [weather, day] that feels hot and humid □ *Outside it was hot and sticky.*

stiff [stɪf] ◇ *adj* **-1.** [brush, card, collar] that is hard and does not bend easily □ *a piece of stiff cardboard.* **-2.** [door, lock, drawer] that is difficult to move; [lock] that is difficult to turn with a key □ *Push hard, the handle's stiff.* **-3.** [mixture, dough] that is firm or difficult to stir □ *Beat the egg whites until they are stiff.* **-4.** [back, neck, joint] that is difficult to move because it is painful □ *I feel very stiff after all that exercise.* **-5.** [manner, behavior, smile] that is not relaxed or very friendly □ *His letter was stiff and formal in tone.* **-6.** [penalty, punishment] that is more severe than usual □ *If found guilty, you could face a stiff fine.* **-7.** [competition, opposition] that is more difficult than usual □ *There was stiff competition for the contract.* **-8.** [brandy, whiskey] that contains a lot of alcohol and not much water, tonic etc (informal use). **-9.** [breeze, wind] that is blowing strongly.
◇ *adv* **to be bored/scared/frozen stiff** to be very bored/scared/cold.

stiffen ['stɪfn] ◇ *vt* **-1.** [paper, fabric] to make <a material> stiff □ *You can stiffen the collar with starch.* **-2.** [resolve, resistance] to make <sthg> stronger. ◇ *vi* **-1.** [body, person] to become tense and stop moving because one is scared, angry etc; [muscles, back, joints] to become painful and difficult to move □ *Suddenly the cat's whole body stiffened.* □ *My legs/neck had stiffened (up) during the trip.* **-2.** [hinge, handle, door] to become difficult to move □ *The lever had stiffened through lack of use.* **-3.** [resolve, resistance] to become stronger □ *The proposals are likely to meet stiffening opposition from local residents.*

stiffener ['stɪfnə^r] *n* something used to make part of a piece of clothing stiff □ *a collar stiffener.*

stifle ['staɪfl] ◇ *vt* **-1.** [person] to stop <sb> from breathing properly □ *The intruders tried to stifle her with a pillow.* **-2.** [feeling, urge, desire] to stop <sthg> from being expressed □ *He stifled his instinct to run.* ■ **to stifle a yawn/laugh etc** to stop oneself from yawning/laughing etc. **-3.** [debate, uprising, creativity] to stop <sthg> from developing or happening □ *High interest rates look set to stifle growth.* ◇ *vi* to feel or be unable to breathe properly because there is not enough fresh air □ *I felt as if I was stifling.*

stifling ['staɪflɪŋ] *adj* [heat, atmosphere] that is hot and makes one unable to breathe properly □ *It's stifling in here.*

stigma ['stɪgmə] *n* **-1.** a belief or feeling that many people in society have about something that causes them to disapprove of it □ *There is now much less stigma attached to being* a single parent. **-2.** BOTANY the part of a flower that receives the pollen.

stile [staɪl] *n* a wooden structure that consists of one or two steps on either side of a wall or fence that one can climb over.

stiletto [stə'letoʊ] *n* **a stiletto (heel)** the heel of a woman's shoe that is very high, thin, and pointed; a shoe with this heel.

still¹ [stɪl] *adv* **-1. I'm still angry with him** I was angry with him before, and this situation has not changed at the present time □ *We've been recruiting for months, and we still haven't found anyone.* □ *I still have two chapters to read.* ■ **are you still here?** I am surprised to find you here at this time, because it is late □ *He still hadn't left by twelve o'clock.* **-2. they could still win** they have not won yet, but it is possible that they will □ *If we hurry, we'll still be on time.* **-3.** used to say that what has just been said does not change things or is not important □ *Although they lost last week, they're still the best team in the tournament.* **-4. better/longer still** even better/longer (used with comparatives) □ *Temperatures were above average today, and tomorrow it will be hotter still.* □ *More problematic still is the issue of who actually owns the company now.*

still² ◇ *adj* **-1. to sit/stand still** to sit/stand and not make a movement □ *He lay perfectly still in bed and listened to the voices outside his door.* ■ **keep** OR **stay still!** don't move! □ *Keep still for a moment while I brush your hair.* **-2.** [water, air] that does not move; [night, day] that has no wind □ *The sea was still as glass.* □ *The evening was clear and still.* **-3.** [water, drink] that does not contain gas. ◇ *n* **-1.** PHOTOGRAPHY a photograph taken from a movie. **-2.** [for whiskey, brandy] a piece of equipment used for making strong alcohol.

stillborn ['stɪlbɔː'n] *adj* [baby, animal] that is born dead.

still life (*pl* **still lifes**) *n* a picture of various objects, e.g. flowers or fruit.

stillness ['stɪlnəs] *n* [of water, air, the night] *see* **still.**

stilted ['stɪltəd] *adj* [conversation, style] that is not smooth, relaxed, or natural.

stilts [stɪlts] *npl* **-1.** two long thin pieces of wood that have supports in the middle to put one's feet on and are used, e.g. by clowns, for walking on and appearing taller. **-2.** long pieces of wood or metal used for supporting a building above the ground or water level.

stimulant ['stɪmjələnt] *n* **-1.** any drug or substance that makes one feel more lively and active. **-2.** something that causes an increase in a particular activity □ *Devaluation of a currency acts as a stimulant to exports.*

stimulate ['stɪmjəleɪt] *vt* **-1.** [discussion, economy, demand] to make <sthg> start to develop or develop more quickly □ *The campaign is designed to stimulate public interest in our products.* **-2.** [person, part of somebody's body] to cause <sb/sthg> to have physical sensations, especially because of being touched □ *sexually stimulated.* **-3.** [pupil, reader] to make <sb>

feel interest, excitement, or enthusiasm about something □ *She felt stimulated by what she had read.* **-4.** [cell, plant, brain] to make <all or part of a living thing> become active or do something □ *Warmth and moisture stimulate the seeds to grow.*

stimulating ['stɪmjəleɪtɪŋ] *adj* **-1.** [workout, effect] that makes one feel physically active. **-2.** [book, discussion, lecture] that stimulates one mentally □ *The meeting was not exactly stimulating.*

stimulation [ˌstɪmjə'leɪʃn] *n*: *see* **stimulate** □ *I like books that give me intellectual stimulation.*

stimulus ['stɪmjələs] (*pl* **stimuli** [-laɪ]) *n* **-1.** something that causes development, enthusiasm, or interest □ *The added element of competition acted as a stimulus to the sales team.* **-2.** BIOLOGY something that makes a plant, part of one's body etc do something □ *the stimulus of light/warmth.*

sting [stɪŋ] (*pt & pp* **stung**) ◇ *vt* **-1.** [bee, scorpion, nettle] to cause <a person or animal> pain by breaking or touching their skin, often with a poison; [smoke, acid, ointment] to cause sharp continuous pain to <a part of the body> □ *I've been stung by a wasp.* □ *The slap across the face stung her cheek.* **-2.** [remark, criticism] to make <sb> feel very hurt and insulted □ *She was stung by his remarks about her family.*
◇ *vi* **-1.** [bee, nettle, smoke] *The cream may sting a little when first applied.* □ *Bees sting only as a last resort.* **-2.** [eyes, skin] *My eyes were stinging with all the smoke.*
◇ *n* **-1.** [from an insect, scorpion, nettle] a sharp pain caused by being stung by an animal, plant, or insect □ *I got a bee/wasp sting on my arm.* ■ **to take the sting out of sthg** [out of criticism, a defeat, failure] to make sthg seem less bad □ *A check for $5,000 took the sting out of coming second.* **-2.** [of a bee, wasp, scorpion] the sharp part in the tail of some animals and insects that is used to sting.

stinging nettle ['stɪŋɪŋ-] *n* GB a nettle.

stingy ['stɪndʒɪ] (*compar* **stingier**, *superl* **stingiest**) *adj* [person] who does not like giving other people things, especially money (informal and disapproving use) □ *They're very stingy with their money/praise.*

stink [stɪŋk] (*pt* **stank** OR **stunk**, *pp* **stunk**) ◇ *n* a very unpleasant smell □ *the stink of rotting vegetables.* ◇ *vi* **-1.** [breath, garbage can, person] to have a very unpleasant smell □ *You stink of onions!* □ *It stinks in here!* **-2.** [idea, attitude, place] to be worthless and unpleasant (informal use) □ *This job stinks!*

stink-bomb *n* a small container with a substance inside that smells very bad when the container is broken.

stint [stɪnt] ◇ *n* a period of time spent doing a particular job or activity □ *I did a two-year stint in the Malaysia office.* □ *After an unsuccessful stint as an actor, he decided to take up teaching.* ◇ *vi* **to stint on sthg** not to give or add enough of sthg □ *Sandra did not stint on the apple sauce.*

stipend ['staɪpend] *n* an amount of money

paid regularly as a salary to somebody such as a priest, magistrate, or student.

stipulate ['stɪpjəleɪt] vt [rule, condition] to state <sthg> clearly, giving exact details □ *The contract stipulates that the work must be finished by March.*

stipulation [ˌstɪpjə'leɪʃn] n **-1.** [of a rule, condition] *see* **stipulate.** **-2.** a condition that is stated in an agreement or contract.

stir [stɜːʳ] (pt & pp **stirred**, cont **stirring**) ◇ vt **-1.** [paint, coffee, soup] to move <a liquid> around in a container, e.g. with a spoon or stick, in order to mix it or make it smooth □ *Stir the mixture to get rid of lumps.* □ *Beat the mixture and stir in the raisins.* **-2.** [leaves, branches] to make <sthg> move slightly □ *A breeze stirred the surface of the lake.* **-3.** [person] to cause <sb> to feel strong feelings, especially when this makes them do something □ *It was this event that finally stirred them into action.*
◇ vi **-1.** [person, branches] to move slightly after having been very still □ *She stirred slightly and murmured something in her sleep.* **-2.** [love, anger] to begin to be felt by somebody □ *A feeling of envy stirred within him.*
◇ n **-1.** the act of stirring something □ *Give the mixture a good stir.* **-2.** mild excitement, anger etc among a group of people □ *The announcement caused a stir.*

◆ **stir up** vt sep **-1. to stir sthg up** [dust, mud] to make sthg move around in the air or in water □ *The wheels stirred up a cloud of dust.* **-2. to stir sthg up** [trouble, tension, rumor] to start or spread sthg □ *He's done nothing but stir up trouble since he arrived.*

stir-fry vt [vegetables, meat] to fry <sthg> quickly by stirring it in a small amount of very hot oil.

stirring ['stɜːrɪŋ] ◇ adj [speech, music] that makes one feel a strong emotion, especially excitement or enthusiasm □ *Bennet made a stirring appeal on the victims' behalf.* ◇ n the beginning of something, e.g. a feeling or thought □ *stirrings of guilt.*

stirrup [US 'stɜːrəp, GB 'stɪr-] n one of the two metal loops that support a person's feet when they are riding a horse.

stitch [stɪtʃ] ◇ n **-1.** SEWING a small piece of thread that joins two pieces of fabric together or is used for decoration □ *a row of stitches* □ *a loose stitch.* **-2.** KNITTING one of the loops of yarn that are joined together in knitting. **-3.** MEDICINE a small piece of thread that joins the edges of a wound together. **-4. to have a stitch** to have a sharp pain in one's side, especially because of running. **-5.** phrase **to be in stitches** to be laughing a lot (informal use) □ *Jim had us in stitches with his stories.*
◇ vt **-1.** SEWING [hem, dress] to sew or decorate <sthg> using stitches □ *She stitched the button onto the coat.* **-2.** [wound, cut] to sew together the edges of <sthg> using a special needle and thread.

stitching ['stɪtʃɪŋ] n the stitches on a piece of material.

St Lawrence [US seɪnt'lɔːrəns, GB sənt-]: **the St**

Lawrence (River) a river in North America that flows from Lake Ontario to the Atlantic and forms part of the border between Canada and the USA.

stoat [stəʊt] n a small wild animal that has a long body, short legs, and a tail with a black tip, and whose brown fur becomes white in winter.

stock [stɒk] ◇ n **-1.** [of provisions, food] an amount of something, especially food or fuel, that is kept to be used when it is needed □ *You'll need a good stock of firewood for the winter.* **-2.** BUSINESS the total amount of goods in a store that are ready to be sold □ *We've sold all our stock.* □ *Stocks of spare parts are low.* ■ **to be in stock** to be in the store and available to be sold □ *I'll just see if we've got any more in stock.* ■ **to be out of stock** to be no longer in the store and not available to be sold □ *This model is currently out of stock, but we can order it for you.* **-3.** FINANCE the shares in a company that each shareholder owns; the amount of money that a company has raised by selling shares in itself □ *Steinberg holds 50% of the stock in Mortlake Electrics.* □ *government stocks* OR *stock* □ *Stock prices are given in fractions of dollars.* ■ **stocks and shares** GB a collective term for shares in different companies. **-4.** the particular kind of people who were one's ancestors □ *a woman of Scandinavian/peasant/farming stock.* **-5.** COOKING a liquid made by boiling meat, vegetables, or fish in water □ *beef/vegetable stock.* **-6.** FARMING a collective term for farm animals, especially cattle, sheep, or pigs □ *breeding stock.* **-7.** phrase **to take stock** to think about the different aspects of a situation before making a decision about what to do next □ *We need time to step back and take stock of the situation.*
◇ adj [answer, criticism] that is common or typical in a particular situation and so is not interesting or original □ *They sent me one of their stock letters turning down my application.*
◇ vt **-1.** BUSINESS [product, item] to keep <sthg> as part of one's stock □ *Do you stock Ford parts?* □ *I'm sorry, we don't stock that size.* **-2.** [shelves, room] to fill <sthg>, especially with food or drink □ *a well-stocked larder.*

◆ **stock up** vi to buy a large supply of something to make sure there is plenty of it □ *She's been stocking up on* OR *with cigarettes.*

stockade [stɒ'keɪd] n a wooden wall built for defense.

stockbroker ['stɒkbrəʊkəʳ] n a person whose job is to buy and sell shares for people.

stockbroking ['stɒkbrəʊkɪŋ] n the profession of a stockbroker.

stockcar ['stɒkkɑːʳ] n an old car that has had some changes made to it so that it can take part in races in which cars hit each other a lot □ *stockcar racing.*

stock certificate n US a document that shows how many shares somebody has in a company.

stock company n US a company owned by everybody who has bought shares in it.

stock control *n* a check in a store, warehouse etc to make sure that enough stock is available and that quantities and movement of stock are recorded.

stock cube *n* a small piece of dried meat and vegetable juices that is added to boiling water to make a stock for cooking.

stock exchange *n* the place where shares in companies are bought and sold □ *The company is quoted on the stock exchange.* □ *the New York Stock Exchange.*

stockholder ['stɒkhoʊldəʳ] *n* US = **shareholder**.

Stockholm ['stɒkhoʊm] the capital of Sweden and its largest city. POPULATION: 674,452.

stocking ['stɒkɪŋ] *n* -1. one of two pieces of clothing made of nylon or some other stretchy material that women wear over their legs and feet □ *a pair of silk stockings.* -2. a long sock (old-fashioned use).

stock-in-trade *n* part of a particular person's usual behavior or job □ *Patience should be a teacher's stock-in-trade.*

stockist ['stɒkəst] *n* GB a store, person, or company that stocks a particular range of goods for sale □ *a retail stockist.*

stockman ['stɒkmən] (*pl* **stockmen** [-mən]) *n* a man employed to look after the animals on a farm.

stock market *n* = **stock exchange** □ *the stock market price.*

stock phrase *n* a phrase that is very commonly used in a particular situation.

stockpile ['stɒkpaɪl] ◇ *n* a large stock of goods, weapons, food etc that may be needed in the future. ◇ *vt* [weapons, food] to store <sthg> in large quantities for future use.

stockroom ['stɒkruːm] *n* a room where stock is stored, especially in a store.

stock-still *adv* [stand, sit] completely still.

stocktaking ['stɒkteɪkɪŋ] *n* GB the process of counting and making a list of all the goods that a store or business has, usually at the end of every fiscal year □ *'Closed for stocktaking.'*

stocky ['stɒkɪ] (*compar* **stockier**, *superl* **stockiest**) *adj* [person] who is fairly short, but looks strong and broad □ *a short stocky fellow.*

stodgy ['stɒdʒɪ] (*compar* **stodgier**, *superl* **stodgiest**) *adj* -1. [meat, cake] that is very filling and difficult to digest □ *The food was good, although a little stodgy.* -2. [book, style, person] that is boring and too serious and formal (disapproving use).

stoic ['stoʊɪk] ◇ *adj* [person] who shows courage by accepting suffering or difficulties without complaining □ *I admire your stoic attitude.* ◇ *n* a stoic person.

stoical ['stoʊɪkl] *adj* = **stoic**.

stoicism ['stoʊɪsɪzm] *n* stoic behavior.

stoke [stoʊk] *vt* to keep <a fire> burning by adding more coal or wood.

Stoker ['stoʊkəʳ], **Bram** (1847–1912) an Irish writer whose best-known work is *Dracula*.

stole [stoʊl] ◇ *past tense of* **steal**. ◇ *n* a piece of material, like a long scarf, worn over the shoulder by women □ *a fur stole.*

stolen ['stoʊlən] *past participle of* **steal**.

stolid ['stɒləd] *adj* [person] who shows little emotion and so seems serious and not very happy.

stomach ['stʌmək] ◇ *n* -1. the organ in the body that digests food □ *I've got an upset stomach/a pain in my stomach.* ■ **on a full/an empty stomach** with a lot of food/no food in one's stomach □ *You should never go swimming on a full stomach.* -2. the front part of one's body between the chest and hips □ *She punched him in the stomach.* □ *Lie on your stomach and rest your head on your arms.* ◇ *vt* I **can't stomach it** I can't accept it because the thought of it makes me feel sick or angry.

stomachache ['stʌməkeɪk] *n* a continuous pain in one's stomach.

stomach pump *n* a piece of medical equipment that is used to empty the contents of somebody's stomach.

stomach ulcer *n* a sore inside the stomach that causes pain.

stomach upset *n* a minor infection in one's stomach that causes sickness and diarrhea.

stomp [stɒmp] *vi* to walk somewhere with heavy steps that show one is angry.

stone [stoʊn] (*pl* **stones**, *sense 5 only* **stone**) ◇ *n* -1. a hard heavy material found in the ground that is often used in building □ *a stone step/wall/bridge.* -2. a small, often rounded, piece of stone □ *The edge of the flowerbed was decorated with a line of stones.* ■ **a stone's throw from a place** a very short distance from a place □ *The hotel is just a stone's throw away from the station.* -3. [for a ring, necklace] a jewel □ *precious stones.* -4. GB [in a fruit] the hard rounded seed found in some fruits □ *a plum/date stone.* -5. GB [in weight] a measurement of weight, equal to 14 pounds or approximately 6.35 kilos □ *He weighs 10 stone.*
◇ *vt* to throw stones at <sb/sthg> especially because one is angry or as a punishment.

Stone Age *n* **the Stone Age** the earliest period of human history, when tools and weapons were made of stone □ *a Stone Age settlement.*

stone-cold *adj* [body, food] that is very cold, especially when one wants or expects it to be warmer.

stoned▽ [stoʊnd] *adj* (very informal use) -1. **to be stoned** to be very drunk. -2. **to be stoned** to be affected by a particular drug that one has taken □ *kids getting stoned on marijuana.*

Stonehenge [US 'stoʊnhendʒ, GB ˌstoʊn'hendʒ] *n* a prehistoric monument in southern England consisting of a circle of large upright stones.

stonemason ['stoʊnmeɪsn] *n* a person whose job is to cut and prepare stone for building.

stonewall [US 'stoʊnwɔːl, GB ˌstoʊn'wɔːl] *vi* to avoid answering questions or refuse to cooperate, in order to avoid an argument, discussion etc.

stoneware ['stoʊnweəʳ] *n* a collective term for

pots and dishes made from a hard clay that contains flint.

stonewashed ['stoonwɒʃt] *adj* [jeans, denim] that has been faded to look more attractive by being washed together with stones.

stonework ['stoonwɜːrk] *n* the part or parts of a building made of stone.

stony ['stoonɪ] (*compar* **stonier,** *superl* **stoniest**) *adj* **-1.** [ground, soil, beach] that contains a lot of stones □ *a narrow stony path.* **-2.** [silence, expression] that is unfriendly and shows no sympathy □ *He gave me a stony look.*

stood [stod] *past tense & past participle of* **stand.**

stooge [stuːdʒ] *n* **-1.** a person who is often used by somebody else to do things they do not want to do themselves (informal and disapproving use). **-2.** a comedian who performs with another comedian and who is always made to look foolish.

stool [stuːl] *n* a round seat with three or four legs that has no part to support one's back □ *a bar stool.*

stoop [stuːp] ◇ *n* **-1. to walk with a stoop** to walk with one's head, shoulders, and upper back bent forward. **-2.** US an open porch or steps leading to the entrance of a house. ◇ *vi* **-1.** to bend forward and downward □ *He stooped (down) to pick up his glove.* **-2.** to stand or move with one's head, shoulders, and upper back bent forward □ *She was stooping over the low sink.* **-3. to stoop to sthg** [to cheating, bribery] to lower one's moral standards by doing sthg.

stop [stɒp] (*pt & pp* **stopped,** *cont* **stopping**) ◇ *vt* **-1.** to no longer do <sthg> □ *I wish they'd stop that noise.* □ *We all stopped talking at once.* □ *Stop it, that hurts!* □ *It gradually stopped raining.* **-2.** to do something with the result that <sthg> cannot start or happen, or that <sb> cannot do something □ *The city got a court order to stop the march.* □ *The strikers stopped the delivery from entering the premises.* **-3.** [tape recorder, clock] to turn <a device> off; [car, war, game] to no longer let <sthg> move, work, or happen; [person] to make <sb> pause in an activity they are doing □ *I drove up to the house and stopped the car.* □ *Rain stopped play.* □ *She stopped a man in the street to ask him the time.* **-4.** [check, wages] to take action so that <sthg> is not paid to somebody; [milk, newspapers] to cancel one's regular order of <sthg> □ *Your benefit may be stopped if you do not reapply.* □ *Don't forget to stop our subscription to "Time".* **-5.** [hole, gap] = **stop up.**
◇ *vi* **-1.** [rain, music] to come to an end □ *The road stops a few miles further on.* **-2.** [tape recorder, clock] to no longer work because something has come to an end or because it is broken; [car, truck] to no longer move; [person] to no longer continue doing something, especially so that one can do something else □ *My watch has stopped — the battery must have run out.* □ *I stopped at the service station to get a snack.* □ *She stopped to tie up her shoelace.* ■ **to stop at nothing** to be willing to do

anything necessary to achieve or get what one wants □ *He'll stop at nothing to land this contract.* **-3.** to stay somewhere, especially when visiting somebody □ *I'm late, I can't stop.* □ *Can you stop for a drink?*
◇ *n* **-1.** [for a bus, train] one of the places where a bus, train etc stops regularly so that passengers can get on or off □ *I'm getting off at the next stop.* **-2.** [in a place] the act of stopping at a place; the place where somebody stops □ *We made several stops on the way here.* □ *Their first stop was Berlin.* **-3. to come to a stop** [ball, train, car] to stop moving; [work, pain, rain] to stop happening □ *Do not leave your seats until the plane has come to a complete stop.* □ *The snow finally came to a stop.* **-4. to put a stop to sthg** to prevent sthg bad from happening □ *It's time we put a stop to all these rumors.* **-5.** [in a telegram] a word that means period in a telegram □ *"Need to see you" Stop "Come at once" Stop.* **-6.** *phrase* **to pull out all the stops** to do everything possible in order to achieve something or to make something successful.

◆ **stop off** *vi* to make a short visit to a particular place or person during a longer trip □ *We stopped off on the way to pick up groceries.*

◆ **stop over** *vi* to stay somewhere for a short time, especially overnight, before continuing one's trip □ *You're welcome to stop over at my place.*

◆ **stop up** *vt sep* to stop sthg up [pipe, hole] to block sthg □ *There must be something stopping up the sink.*

stopcock ['stɒpkɒk] *n* a valve on a pipe which controls the flow of gas or water.

Stopes [stoops], **Marie** (1880–1958) a British scientist and writer who wrote several books on sex education and set up Britain's first birth control clinic.

stopgap ['stɒpgæp] *n* something that can be used or done for a short time until one finds something better □ *This job is just a stopgap until I can find something permanent.*

stoplights ['stɒplaɪts] *npl* US colored lights that control the movement of road traffic at intersections.

stopover ['stɒpoovər] *n* a short stay in a place while one is traveling somewhere, especially by plane.

stoppage ['stɒpɪdʒ] *n* **-1.** the act of stopping working because of a disagreement with one's employer □ *The company has lost thousands of dollars because of the stoppages.* **-2.** GB the money taken off one's pay, usually before one gets it, e.g. for tax □ *After stoppages, he hardly earns enough to pay the bills.*

stopper ['stɒpər] *n* an object, usually made of glass or cork, that fits into the opening of a bottle or jar in order to close it.

stop press *n* a phrase used to introduce a piece of news that is added to a newspaper after the rest of it has been printed.

stop sign *n* a red road sign that has STOP written in white letters on it and is used to order drivers to stop their vehicles at an intersection before continuing.

stopwatch ['stɒpwɒtʃ] *n* a watch that can be stopped and started in order to measure the amount of time it takes to do something, e.g. to run a race.

storage ['stɔːrɪdʒ] *n* -1. [of food, clothes, goods] the act of storing something; a place where something is stored □ *I'll put my furniture in storage while I'm traveling.* □ *There's not much storage space in this apartment.* □ *storage costs.* -2. COMPUTING the process of storing information in a computer for further use; the part of a computer where this information is stored.

storage heater *n* GB a heater that stores heat at night, when electricity is cheap, and gives out heat during the day.

store [stɔːr] ◇ *n* -1. a building where goods and services are sold □ *the local stores.* -2. [of weapons, coal, blankets] an amount of something that is kept somewhere until it is needed □ *a store of highly confidential information.* -3. a place, e.g. a large building, where things are stored □ *a grain store.* -4. **to set great store by** OR **on sthg** to consider that sthg is very important □ *She sets great store by herbal remedies.*
◇ *vt* -1. [coal, grain] to keep <sthg> somewhere until it is needed; [bicycle, furniture] to keep <sthg> somewhere when it is not being used. -2. COMPUTING [data, figures] to keep <information> in a computer until it is needed.
◆ **in store** *adv* a phrase used to say that something is going to happen at some time in the future □ *There's trouble in store.* □ *Who knows what the future has in store for us?*
◆ **store up** *vt sep* **to store sthg up** [provisions, information, details] to keep sthg until it is needed, especially by adding to it gradually so that one has a lot of it □ *He was storing up information which he could use against them.*

store brand *n* US a product specially manufactured for a particular store and carrying the name of the store.

store detective *n* a person whose job is to walk around a department store pretending to be a customer in order to make sure no goods are stolen.

storehouse ['stɔːrhaʊs, *pl* -haʊzɪz] *n* -1. a building in which things are stored. -2. [of information, treasures] a person or thing that has many interesting or useful ideas, objects etc.

storekeeper ['stɔːrkiːpər] *n* US a person who owns or is in charge of a small store.

storeroom ['stɔːruːm] *n* a room where goods are stored.

storey ['stɔːrɪ] (*pl* **storeys**) *n* GB [of a building] = **story**.

stork [stɔːrk] *n* a large white bird with black wings, long legs, and a long beak and neck that lives near water.

storm [stɔːrm] ◇ *n* -1. a period of very bad weather consisting of strong wind and heavy rain, usually with thunder and lightning □ *Many of the trees had been damaged in the storm.* -2. a sudden strong reaction to something by the public, e.g. anger or excitement □ *a storm of abuse/protest* □ *The revelations caused quite a storm.* ■ **a storm in a teacup** GB a situation that is not important but that causes a lot of worry and trouble.
◇ *vt* -1. [building, town] to attack <a place> suddenly and violently □ *Rebel forces stormed the city.* -2. to say <sthg> very angrily and in a loud voice □ *"That's just not true!" she stormed.*
◇ *vi* to go somewhere in an angry way □ *He stormed into/out of the room.*

storm cloud *n* a dark cloud seen before a storm □ *Storm clouds were gathering as they left the harbor.*

storming ['stɔːrmɪŋ] *n* the act of storming a building or place □ *the storming of the Bastille/ Winter Palace.*

stormy ['stɔːrmɪ] (*compar* **stormier**, *superl* **stormiest**) *adj* -1. [weather] that consists of strong wind, heavy rain, and often thunder and lightning □ *You can expect stormy seas in this area.* -2. [relationship, meeting] that is difficult because the people involved argue with each other □ *Their marriage had always been stormy.*

story ['stɔːrɪ] (*pl* **stories**) *n* -1. [for entertainment] a real or imaginary description of people and events, often told or written to entertain people □ *Will you read/tell me a story?* □ *It's a strange story, the way they met.* □ *But that's not the whole story.* □ *Tell us the story about the princess and the pea.* ■ **it's the (same) old story** a phrase used to say that something has happened many times before □ *Every payday it's the same old story: he goes off to the races and loses all of it.* ■ **to make** US OR **cut** GB **a long story short** a phrase used to say that one is going to tell somebody how something ended without giving them all the details □ *Anyway, to make a long story short, we're no longer on speaking terms.* -2. [of a process, event] an account of how something came into existence and what has happened to it since that time □ *the story of printing/the pharaohs.* -3. [in a newspaper, news program] a piece of news □ *the main (news) stories* □ *The story broke at 10am.* -4. a lie □ *Pat's telling stories again.* -5. US [of a building] a level or floor of a building □ *a 50-story building.*

storybook ['stɔːrɪbʊk] *adj* **a storybook romance/wedding etc** a romance/wedding etc that seems to be perfect and very happy.

storyteller ['stɔːrɪtelər] *n* a person who tells or writes stories to entertain people.

stout [staʊt] ◇ *adj* -1. [person, legs] that looks short and fairly fat □ *a stout middle-aged man.* -2. [boots, stick] that is strong and thick □ *stout walking shoes.* -3. [opposition, defender] that is firm and strong □ *The community put up stout resistance to the intended highway.* ◇ *n* a strong dark beer □ *a pint of stout.*

stove [stoʊv] ◇ *past tense & past participle of* **stave.** ◇ *n* -1. a piece of equipment used in a kitchen for cooking food, usually with a flat top part for cooking food in pans and an oven for baking, roasting etc □ *a gas stove.*

-2. a piece of equipment used for heating a room or house, usually by burning oil or coal □ *an oil stove.*

stow [stəʊ] *vt* [suitcase, file, treasure] to put <sthg> somewhere so that it is safe or hidden or is not in the way □ *'Luggage must be stowed in the overhead lockers.'*

◆ **stow away** *vi* to hide on a ship or plane in order to travel without paying.

stowaway ['stəʊəweɪ] *n* a person who has stowed away on a ship or plane.

Stowe [stəʊ], **Harriet Beecher** (1811–1896) a US writer whose best-known work is *Uncle Tom's Cabin.*

St Petersburg [US seɪnt'piːtərzbɜːrg, GB sənt-'piːtəzbɜːg] a city in western Russia, on the Baltic coast. It is a major port, and used to be the capital of Russia.

straddle ['strædl] *vt* **-1.** [chair, wall] to sit on <sthg> with one's legs on either side of it. **-2.** [river, border] to stretch across <sthg> from one side to the other □ *a town straddling the border between Austria and Hungary.*

strafe [streɪf] *vt* to attack <sb/sthg> with bullets from a low-flying aircraft.

straggle ['strægl] *vi* **-1.** [buildings, town, plant] to spread out in a messy way over a wide area. **-2.** [group, person] to walk slowly and behind the others in a group □ *She was straggling behind the others.*

straggler ['stræglər] *n* a person who straggles behind other people in a group.

straggly ['strægli] (*compar* **stragglier**, *superl* **straggliest**) *adj* [hair, plant] that grows or spreads out in a messy way.

straight [streɪt] ◇ *adj* **-1.** [line, road, back] that has no bends or curves □ *They stood together in a straight line.* □ *You'll need a straight edge to draw against.* **-2.** [hedge, hem, tree trunk] that is level or upright and does not slope □ *That picture's not straight.* □ *Sit up straight, don't slouch.* **-3.** [hair] that is not curly □ *She had long straight hair.* **-4.** [person, answer, question] that is honest and direct □ *Are you being straight with me?* □ *a straight offer.* **-5. three/four etc straight wins** three/four etc wins one after another □ *Smith won the match in three straight sets.* **-6. a straight choice/exchange etc** a choice/exchange etc that concerns only two people or things □ *It's a straight fight between Gough and Turner.* **-7.** [gin, whiskey] that does not have any other liquid, especially water, added to it □ *I'll have my vodka straight, please.* **-8.** [person] who is not homosexual (informal use) □ *He's gay but a lot of his friends are straight.* **-9. to be straight** to have paid all the money one owes to somebody □ *If you pay for the meal, then we'll be straight.* **-10.** *phrases* **to keep a straight face** to look serious even though one thinks something is funny □ *I don't know how I managed to keep a straight face!* ■ **let me get this straight** I want to understand this more clearly □ *Let's get something straight: I give the orders around here!* ◇ *adv* **-1.** [see, walk, lie] in a straight line □ *It's straight in front of you* OR *straight ahead!* □ *She walked straight into the door.* **-2.** directly;

immediately □ *I'll get straight to the point.* □ *Go straight home.* □ *Go straight on, then make a right at the crossroads.* □ *We left straight after the movie.* **-3.** honestly and directly □ *I'm telling you straight, it's a waste of money.* **-4. to go straight** to stop being a criminal, drug addict, gambler etc.
◇ *n* SPORT a straight part of a racetrack □ *They're now entering the final straight.*

◆ **straight out** *adv* [admit, say] without trying to hide or avoid anything □ *He told me straight out that he was thinking of leaving*

straightaway [,streɪtə'weɪ] ◇ *adv* [leave, call, deliver] without delay □ *I'll come straightaway.* ◇ *n* US SPORT = **straight.**

straighten ['streɪtn] ◇ *vt* **-1.** [tie, dress, desk] to make <sthg> tidy □ *She straightened the cushions on the sofa.* □ *We'd better straighten the place up before Greta comes back.* **-2.** [hair, curve, edge] to make <sthg> straight □ *I spent ages trying to straighten the hem of that dress.* **-3.** [column, picture] to make <sthg> level by moving it slightly □ *That shelf's not level — try straightening it a bit.*

◆ **straighten up** ◇ *vi* to stand up or sit up with one's back straight after being bent over. ◇ *vt sep* **to straighten sthg up** [room, papers] to make sthg neat and tidy.

◆ **straighten out** *vt sep* **to straighten sthg out** [mess, situation] to make sthg easier by removing any problems □ *We're still trying to straighten out some of these problems.*

straightforward [,streɪt'fɔːrwərd] *adj* **-1.** [explanation, operation] that is easy to understand or do □ *It seems a straightforward enough task.* **-2.** [person] who is honest and does not hide their feelings □ *He seems like a nice, straightforward kind of guy.*

strain [streɪn] ◇ *n* **-1.** a state or cause of tension or worry □ *The strain shows in her face.* □ *He's been under a lot of strain lately.* □ *The drive for new recruits has put a great strain on our department.* **-2.** [in part of one's body] the pain that results from using a part of one's body too much, often damaging it □ *eye/muscle/back strain.* **-3.** TECHNOLOGY the force, weight, or pressure on an object, part of one's body etc □ *The ceiling couldn't take the extra strain.* □ *He braced himself to take the strain.* **-4.** [of a plant, virus] a type of plant, animal, bacterium etc □ *A new strain has developed.*
◇ *vt* **-1. to strain one's eyes/ears to do sthg** to try very hard to see/hear sthg □ *Jilly strained her ears to hear what they were saying, but to no avail.* **-2.** [muscle, back, eyes] to temporarily damage <a part of one's body> by making it do too much □ *I've strained a muscle in my back.* **-3.** [resources, budget] to force <sthg> to cover more than it can do comfortably; [patience, friendship] to push <sthg> beyond reasonable limits □ *The recruitment of extra staff is severely straining our resources.* □ *The constant presence of her husband had strained their friendship to breaking point.* **-4.** COOKING to remove the liquid from <food> after boiling it; to remove the tea leaves from <tea> by pouring it through a tea strainer □ *Strain the carrots, then add butter.*

-5. [rope, girder, ceiling] to put too much force, weight etc on <sthg>.

◇ *vi* **to strain to do sthg** to try very hard to do sthg □ *She strained to hear what they were saying.*

◆ **strains** *npl* the sound of music that is being played (literary use) □ *They were dancing to the strains of Boccherini's minuet.*

strained [streɪnd] *adj* **-1.** [laugh, voice] that is unnatural and shows signs of worry or tiredness □ *Chris has been looking very strained recently.* □ *Libby gave a strained smile.* **-2.** [atmosphere, relations] that is tense and unfriendly, often because there is not enough trust □ *Relations between the two countries have been strained recently.*

strainer [ˈstreɪnəʳ] *n* a container with holes in the bottom used for straining food, liquids, tea etc.

strait [streɪt] *n* GEOGRAPHY a narrow passage of water between two areas of land that connects two larger areas of water, usually two seas □ *the Strait of Magellan.*

◆ **straits** *npl* **to be in dire** OR **desperate straits** to be in an extremely difficult situation, often because one does not have enough money □ *Barton & Co is in dire financial straits following record losses this quarter.*

straitened [ˈstreɪtnd] *adj* **to be in straitened circumstances** to be in a difficult situation because one does not have as much money as before (formal use).

straitjacket [ˈstreɪtdʒækət] *n* a piece of clothing that is used to stop violent or mentally ill people from moving their arms.

straitlaced [ˌstreɪtˈleɪst] *adj* [person] who has strict and old-fashioned ideas about morality (disapproving use).

Strait of Gibraltar: **the Strait of Gibraltar** a narrow passage of water between Spain and Morocco that connects the Mediterranean with the Atlantic Ocean.

strand [strænd] *n* **-1.** [of hair, wool] a piece of something long, flexible, and very thin. **-2.** [of a plot, argument] one of the many parts of something.

stranded [ˈstrændəd] *adj* [person, vehicle] that cannot leave a particular place because of something that has happened, e.g. a strike or bad weather □ *We were left stranded in the middle of nowhere.*

strange [streɪndʒ] *adj* **-1.** [shape, laugh, attitude] that is unusual or surprising □ *What a strange coincidence!* □ *I feel kind of strange.* □ *It was strange to visit her old school again.* □ *I find it very strange that they haven't called.* **-2.** [country, person, house] that one does not know and has not seen before □ *I find it difficult to sleep in strange surroundings.* □ *It was scary arriving in a strange town and not even being able to speak the language.*

strangely [ˈstreɪndʒlɪ] *adv* **-1.** a word used to show that one thinks something is surprising or odd □ *She was strangely quiet.* □ *Strangely enough, no one seemed to notice.* **-2.** [laugh,

speak, write] *see* **strange** □ *He's been behaving very strangely lately.*

stranger [ˈstreɪndʒəʳ] *n* **-1.** a person that one does not know □ *Don't talk to strangers.* ■ **to be a/no stranger to sthg** [to poverty, fame, unhappiness] to have no/a lot of experience of sthg. **-2.** a person who is in a place that they have never visited before □ *I'm a stranger to these parts.*

Strangers' Gallery: **the Strangers' Gallery** the part of the British House of Commons and House of Lords that is open to the public.

strangle [ˈstræŋgl] *vt* **-1.** to kill <sb> by squeezing their throat with one's hands, a scarf etc to prevent them from breathing □ *Karen was found strangled to death.* **-2.** [development, economy] to prevent <sthg> from developing; [groan, cry] to prevent <sthg> from being expressed fully □ *Punitive tax measures have strangled growth.* □ *He uttered a strangled cry.*

stranglehold [ˈstræŋglhoʊld] *n* **-1.** a strong hold around somebody's neck that makes it difficult for them to breathe. **-2.** a very strong control over something that prevents it from developing freely □ *France once had a stranglehold on the world's wine market.*

strangulation [ˌstræŋgjəˈleɪʃn] *n* the act of strangling somebody □ *She died from strangulation.*

strap [stræp] (*pt* & *pp* **strapped**, *cont* **strapping**) ◇ *n* **-1.** [of a camera, rifle] a narrow band of material such as leather that is attached to something and is used for carrying it. **-2.** [on a dress, suitcase, shoe] a narrow band of leather, fabric etc used to fasten something or to hold it in place □ *a watch/bra strap* □ *She tightened the straps on her backpack.* ◇ *vt* [person, bag] to fasten <sb/sthg> securely by using one or more straps □ *He strapped the parachute onto his back.*

strapless [ˈstræpləs] *adj* [dress, bra] that has no straps over the shoulders.

strapping [ˈstræpɪŋ] *adj* **a strapping young man/woman** a young man/woman who is tall, strong, and looks very fit.

Strasbourg [US ˈstrɑːsbɜːrg, GB ˈstræzbɜːg] a city in eastern France, on the Rhine. Meetings of the Council of Europe and the European Parliament are held there. POPULATION: 255,937.

strata [US ˈstreɪtə, GB ˈstrɑːtə] *plural of* **stratum**.

stratagem [ˈstrætədʒəm] *n* a clever plan designed to achieve something, often by deceiving somebody.

strategic [strəˈtiːdʒɪk] *adj* **-1.** [withdrawal, move] that is done as part of a larger plan to achieve something □ *an island of strategic importance.* **-2.** [weapon, missile] that is very powerful and can be used from a long distance away. **-3.** [position, location] that has been carefully chosen to make something as effective or useful as possible □ *Our product occupies a strategic position in the market.*

strategist [ˈstrætədʒəst] *n* a person who is

good at forming strategies, especially military ones.

strategy ['strætədʒɪ] (*pl* **strategies**) *n* a general plan for achieving something, often over a long period of time; the art of creating these plans □ *What is the Minister's strategy for dealing with unemployment?* □ *defense/marketing strategies* □ *He is skilled in military strategy.*

Stratford-upon-Avon [ˌstrætfərdəpɒnˈeɪvn] a town in central England where William Shakespeare was born and lived.

stratified ['strætəfaɪd] *adj* **-1.** [rock] that consists of layers of different types of rock. **-2.** [society] that is separated into different social classes.

stratosphere ['strætəsfɪər] *n* **the stratosphere** the outer band of air that surrounds the Earth, starting at about ten kilometers above the Earth's surface.

stratum [US 'streɪtəm, GB 'strɑːt-] (*pl* **strata**) *n* **-1.** GEOLOGY a layer of rock that forms part of the Earth's surface. **-2.** a class of people in society with the same social or educational background.

Strauss [straʊs], **Johann** (1825–1899) an Austrian composer who wrote many famous waltzes, including *The Blue Danube*.

Strauss, Richard (1864–1949) a German composer who wrote many operas and the orchestral piece *Also sprach Zarathustra*.

Stravinsky [strəˈvɪnskɪ], **Igor** (1882–1971) a US composer, born in Russia, who wrote ballet music including *The Firebird* and *The Rite of Spring*.

straw [strɔː] *n* **-1.** the dried stalks of wheat or other cereal crops, used for packaging, bedding for animals etc □ *a straw hat/basket.* **-2.** a long, thin, paper or plastic tube used for drinking □ *She drank the milkshake through a straw.* **-3.** *phrase* **to clutch at straws** to desperately try or believe anything that might give one hope or provide a solution in a difficult situation □ *You're clutching at straws; there's no way they could have survived that blast.*

strawberry [US 'strɔːberɪ, GB -bərɪ] (*pl* **strawberries**) *n* a small, soft, red fruit that has very small seeds on its surface and grows near the ground □ *strawberry jam/yogurt.*

straw poll *n* an unofficial opinion poll before an election.

stray [streɪ] ◇ *adj* **-1.** [dog, cat] that has become separated from its owner □ *Susan often takes in stray cats and looks after them.* **-2. a stray bullet** a bullet that hits somebody or something that it was not aimed at □ *She was hit by a stray bullet.* ◇ *n* a stray cat or dog □ *a home for strays.* ◇ *vi* **-1.** to wander away from a particular place or area □ *Don't stray from the path.* **-2.** to think or talk about something which is not related to the topic being discussed □ *Try not to stray from the point.* □ *As he talked, my mind kept straying to the events of the previous evening.*

streak [striːk] ◇ *n* **-1.** [of color] a stripe or long area of color that is different from the color of the rest of a surface □ *She had blond streaks put in her hair.* **-2.** [in a person] a particular bad quality that a person sometimes shows in their character □ *a stubborn/mean streak.* **-3. a winning/losing streak** a period of time during which one keeps succeeding/failing □ *I'm on a winning streak.* ◇ *vi* [person, animal] to run very fast □ *She streaked past me.*

streaked [striːkt] *adj* **to be streaked with sthg** [with grease, color, dirt] to be covered with streaks of sthg.

streaky ['striːkɪ] (*compar* **streakier**, *superl* **streakiest**) *adj* [color, surface, hair] that is marked with streaks, especially in a way that looks unattractive.

streaky bacon *n* GB bacon that has lines of fat in it.

stream [striːm] ◇ *n* **-1.** a very small river □ *A tiny stream ran through the field.* **-2.** [of liquid, air] a constant flow of liquid, air etc □ *a stream of tears/water/light.* **-3.** [of people] a large number or amount of people or things that arrive one after the other □ *a stream of customers/traffic* □ *She received a steady stream of complaints.* **-4.** GB EDUCATION a group of students of the same age and ability who are taught a particular subject together □ *Lindy was put in the top stream for maths.* ◇ *vt* GB EDUCATION to put <students> into streams. ◇ *vi* **-1.** [tears, water] to flow quickly; [light] to shine through or into something □ *He stood by the coffin, tears streaming down his face.* □ *The sun streamed through the window.* **-2.** [people, cars] to move somewhere one after the other in large numbers; [questions, calls] to be expressed, received etc one after the other in large numbers □ *Crowds of people streamed into the concert hall.* □ *Applications have been streaming in.*

streamer ['striːmər] *n* a long thin piece of colored paper used as a decoration for a party, carnival etc.

streamline ['striːmlaɪn] *vt* **-1.** [car, shape, machine] to make <sthg> long and smooth so that it moves easily and fast through water or air. **-2.** [company, process, organization] to make <sthg> more simple in order to make it more efficient.

streamlined ['striːmlaɪnd] *adj* [object, body] that has a long smooth shape, especially one that allows it to move easily and fast through water or air.

street [striːt] *n* a road in a town, village, or city, with houses, shops etc on one or both sides □ *We've lived on the same street for years.* □ *He lives across the street from us.* □ *The whole street had come out to watch the procession.* ■ **to be right up sb's street** GB to be exactly the sort of activity or subject that sb likes or is interested in (informal use). ■ **to be streets ahead of sb** GB to be much better or much more advanced than sb (informal use).

streetcar ['striːtkɑːr] *n* US a vehicle, used to transport passengers around a city, that runs along metal tracks in the road and is usually powered by electricity.

street-cred(ibility) [-kred(ə'bɪlətɪ)]´ *n* **to have street-cred(ibility)** GB to be fashionable in a way that is approved of by young people (informal use).

street lamp, **street light** *n* a tall post by the side of a road that has a light at the top.

street lighting *n* a collective term for street lights; the light given off by street lights □ *The street lighting is very poor in this area.*

street map *n* a map with the names of all the streets, roads, important buildings etc in an area marked on it.

street market *n* an outdoor market in a road or street, consisting of several stalls run by different people.

street plan *n* = **street map**.

street value *n* the price that illegal drugs can be sold for □ *Drugs with a street value of $10,000 were seized by police today.*

streetwise ['striːtwaɪz] *adj* [person] who knows how to deal with the kind of dangerous situation that is sometimes found in cities □ *a streetwise young kid.*

strength [streŋθ] *n* **-1.** [in one's body] physical power □ *I don't have the strength to lift these boxes.* □ *Sammy doesn't know his own strength sometimes.* □ *Once you have regained your strength I'll take you on a nice vacation.* **-2.** [of character] courage and determination □ *She needed all her strength to come to terms with his death.* □ *Sean did not have the strength of character to be different from the others.* **-3.** [of wind, light, voice] the quality something has of being powerful or strong □ *Don't underestimate the strength of feeling that this topic arouses.* □ *The ecology movement gained in strength throughout the 1980s.* □ *This government has broken the strength of the unions.* □ *He's negotiating from a position of strength.* ■ **on the strength of sthg** [of evidence, advice, a report] based on or as a result of sthg □ *Josey was given the job on the strength of the references you gave her.* □ *Sanderson was convicted on the strength of one eyewitness account.* ■ **to go from strength to strength** to keep improving and becoming more successful. **-4.** [of a person, plan] a good quality or ability that somebody or something has □ *Her greatest strength is that she keeps calm in a crisis.* **-5.** [of a structure, metal] the ability to support great force, pressure etc □ *We will need to test the strength of the bridge.* **-6.** [of an opinion, argument] a powerful or convincing effect □ *I was forced to concede the strength of her argument.* **-7.** [of alcohol, a drug] the quality that a substance has of being concentrated or strong □ *It's easy to underestimate the strength of some of these beers.* **-8.** [of money] the position of a particular currency compared to others, especially to the American dollar □ *The lira has gained/fallen in strength.* **-9.** [of an organization, team] the total number of people in an organization, team etc. ■ **at full strength** with the necessary or total number of people □ *The union is now at full strength.*

◆ **below strength** *adv* without the necessary or total number of people □ *The factory was running below strength.* □ *Our nursing team is currently well below strength.*

◆ **in strength** *adv* in large numbers □ *People turned out in strength to support the runners.*

strengthen ['streŋθn] ◇ *vt* **-1.** [body, muscle] to make <part of one's body> more physically powerful □ *He needed months of physical therapy to strengthen his legs again after the operation.* **-2.** [army, team] to make <a group> more powerful by increasing its numbers □ *We're trying to strengthen our membership by advertising in the local press.* **-3.** [economy, industry, sales] to improve <sthg> □ *The economy has been strengthened by increased investment from overseas.* **-4.** [argument, case, evidence] to provide details, reasons etc that make <sthg> stronger □ *New evidence concerning Wilson's past will certainly strengthen the case against him.* **-5.** [dislike, opposition] to make <sthg> stronger □ *Working as a journalist only served to strengthen my distrust of politicians.* **-6.** [friendship, bond] to improve <a relationship> by making the different people or groups feel closer to each other □ *Tawara's visit has served to strengthen ties between the two countries.* **-7.** [person] to make <sb> feel braver, more determined, or more confident □ *The meeting strengthened my resolve to leave immediately.* **-8.** [bridge, roof, foundations] to make <sthg> more able to resist great weight, bad weather etc. **-9.** [yen, franc] to increase the value of <a currency> compared to the currency of other countries □ *Recent developments have strengthened the pound against the dollar.*

◇ *vi* **-1.** [body, muscle] to become more physically powerful. **-2.** [economy, sales, industry] to improve. **-3.** [resolve, opposition, dislike] to become stronger. **-4.** [friendship, bond, ties] to improve because the different people or groups involved feel closer to each other. **-5.** [pound, franc, currency] to increase in value compared to the currency of other countries.

strenuous ['strenjʊəs] *adj* [exercise, activity, task] that requires a lot of physical effort or energy □ *Avoid doing anything too strenuous over the next few weeks.*

stress [stres] ◇ *n* **-1.** [on a person] the pressure and anxiety caused by one's job, daily life etc □ *ways of dealing with stress* □ *the stresses and strains of city life.* ■ **to be under stress** to suffer from stress because of one's job, life etc □ *He's under a lot of stress at work.* **-2.** [on a particular fact, idea] the special attention which is given to something in order to show that it is important □ *The stress has always been on productivity.* **-3.** TECHNOLOGY the physical pressure that is placed on an object □ *An error had been made when calculating the stress on the beam.* **-4.** LINGUISTICS the extra emphasis put on a particular word or syllable when it is pronounced □ *The stress is always on the final syllable.*

◇ *vt* **-1.** [importance, value] to emphasize <sthg> □ *I cannot stress enough the need for discretion.* **-2.** LINGUISTICS [word, syllable] to emphasize <sthg> when one pronounces it.

stressed(-out) [,strest-] *adj* [person] who is

suffering from stress and unable to relax □ *Louise walked into our office, looking extremely stressed.*

stressful ['stresfl] *adj* [job, lifestyle, day] that causes or involves a lot of stress □ *I find traveling very stressful.*

stretch [stretʃ] ⬦ *n* **-1.** [of a road, river] an area of land or water, usually one which is narrow and flat □ *a new stretch of highway.* **-2.** [of time] a period of time □ *I did a stretch as a door-to-door salesman.* **-3.** *phrase* **by no stretch of the imagination** a phrase used to emphasize that one thinks that something is impossible or untrue □ *You could not, by any stretch of the imagination, call him handsome.*
⬦ *vt* **-1.** [item of clothing, elastic, shoes] to make <sthg> longer or wider by pulling different parts of it in opposite directions □ *I've stretched my T-shirt by washing it too much.* **-2.** [rope, cable, fabric] to pull <sthg> so that it becomes tight, often in order to cover a wider area □ *They stretched a rope between two trees.* **-3.** [arms, hand, wings] to straighten <a part of one's body> to its full length in order to cover, reach etc something, or to make the muscles feel better □ *He yawned and stretched his legs out in front of him.* **-4.** [rules, meaning, patience] to make <sthg> go beyond its usual accepted limits □ *They have stretched their authority too far.* **-5.** [budget, resources] to use so much of <sthg> that there is barely enough left □ *My first few weeks at college stretched my income to the limit.* **-6.** [person] to present <sb> with challenges and opportunities to use all their abilities □ *I want a job that will really stretch me.*
⬦ *vi* **-1. to stretch into/over etc** to cover a particular area or period of time □ *The conference stretched over three days.* ■ **to stretch from...to...** to cover a particular distance from...to... □ *The line of people stretched from the bakery to the corner.* **-2.** [person, animal] to straighten the body in order to relax the muscles; to straighten a particular part of the body in order to reach for something □ *He stood up and stretched.* □ *She stretched up to look over the fence.* **-3.** [material, elastic] to become longer or wider when pulled.
⬦ *adj* [cotton, fabric] that can be stretched □ *a pair of jeans made in stretch cotton fabric.*

◆ **at a stretch** *adv* [work, walk] without stopping □ *I can only type for two hours at a stretch.* □ *He would sit at his desk doing nothing for hours at a stretch.*

◆ **stretch out** ⬦ *vt sep* **to stretch sthg out** [hand, foot, arm] to hold sthg out straight □ *She stretched out her hand to me.* ⬦ *vi* to lie down with one's legs and body in a straight line □ *I stretched out on the bed.*

stretcher ['stretʃər] *n* two long parallel poles with fabric stretched between them, used for carrying an injured person □ *The casualties were carried away on stretchers.*

stretchmarks ['stretʃmɑːrks] *npl* small lines like scars that are found on somebody's skin and are caused by the skin being stretched, especially after pregnancy.

stretchy ['stretʃɪ] (*compar* **stretchier**, *superl* **stretchiest**) *adj* [fabric, material] that stretches easily.

strew [struː] (*pp* **strewn** [struːn] OR **strewed**) *vt* **-1. to strew sthg on** OR **over sthg** to spread sthg on OR over sthg in a messy way □ *Clothes were strewn all over the floor.* **-2. to be strewn with sthg** to have sthg scattered over it □ *The hall was strewn with children's toys.*

stricken ['strɪkən] *adj* **to be stricken by** OR **with sthg** [with grief, horror, illness] to be very badly affected by sthg □ *Red Cross aid workers are trying to reach the stricken area.* □ *Her father sat there, stricken with grief.*

strict [strɪkt] *adj* **-1.** [parent, boss, teacher] who is severe and does not accept bad behavior □ *He's very strict with the children.* □ *a strict upbringing/education.* **-2. a strict rule/order etc** a rule/order etc that must be obeyed □ *I gave you strict instructions not to open the door to anybody.* □ *They have very strict rules about what you can and can't do.* **-3. a strict Catholic** somebody who follows Catholic beliefs very closely □ *She's a strict vegetarian.* **-4.** [interpretation, meaning] that is exact and correct □ *It is not a metaphor in the strictest sense of the word.*

strictly ['strɪktlɪ] *adv* **-1.** a word used to emphasize that something must be obeyed or respected □ *strictly confidential* □ *I strictly forbid you to mention this to him.* □ *'Smoking strictly forbidden'* □ *This is strictly between you and me.* **-2.** [true, wrong, interpreted] exactly □ *It's not strictly legal.* □ *Well, that's not strictly true.* ■ **strictly speaking** a phrase used to correct a piece of information or to give precise details of it □ *Strictly speaking, I shouldn't be here.* **-3.** [educate] *see* **strict** □ *They were brought up very strictly.*

stride [straɪd] (*pt* **strode**, *pp* **stridden** ['strɪdn]) ⬦ *n* a long step forward □ *In one stride he was at her side.* □ *He took several strides toward them.* ■ **to take sthg in one's stride** [problem, difficulties] to deal calmly and easily with sthg that one did not expect □ *It was chaos today, but Martin took it all in his stride.* ⬦ *vi* to walk with long steps □ *She strode over to him.*

◆ **strides** *npl* **-1. to make great strides** to make a lot of progress □ *Jay has been making great strides in his music lessons.* **-2.** AUS trousers (informal use).

strident ['straɪdnt] *adj* **-1.** [voice, sound] that sounds loud and unpleasant □ *He could hear Hawthorne's strident voice rising above the others'.* **-2.** [demand, opinion] that is very loudly or strongly expressed □ *the strident demands of militant feminists.*

strife [straɪf] *n* trouble and disagreement between two people or groups of people (formal use).

strike [straɪk] (*pt* & *pp* **struck**) ⬦ *n* **-1.** an organized protest by a group of people in which they refuse to work because of low pay, bad working conditions etc □ *a pay/teachers' strike* □ *a strike over pay and conditions* □ *strike action* □ *The unions have called a general strike.* ■ **to be (out) on strike** to be carrying out a strike. ■ **to go on strike** to begin a strike □ *Air traffic controllers are threatening to go on strike.* **-2.** a refusal to do something as a form of protest □ *a rent strike.* **-3.** MILITARY an attack, especially by air □ *an air strike.* **-4.** the discovery of something, especially in the ground □ *an oil/a gold strike.*

◇ *vt* **-1.** [person] to deliberately hit <a person, object, or animal>, especially with one's hand; [vehicle] to accidentally hit <a person, object, or animal> with force □ *He struck her across the face.* □ *The car struck a tree and overturned.* **-2.** [hurricane, disaster, illness] to suddenly affect or damage <a person, place, or object> □ *The church was struck by lightning.* **-3.** [thought, idea] to come into the mind of <sb> suddenly □ *The thought had never struck her before.* □ *It strikes me he doesn't know what he wants.* **-4. to strike sb as...** to seem to sb to have a particular quality □ *He strikes me as (being) very capable.* ■ **to be struck by** OR **with sthg** [by somebody's beauty, words, kindness] to be strongly affected by sthg □ *I was much struck by how little Aunt Agatha had changed over the years.* □ *He was immediately struck by the similarities between the two designs.* **-5. to strike a bargain/deal** to agree to a bargain/deal with somebody □ *The two sides finally struck a deal over pay and conditions.* ■ **to strike a balance** to find a position between two extremes □ *You have to strike a balance between quality and speed.* ■ **to strike a serious/happy/cautious etc note** to produce a serious/happy/cautious etc feeling □ *His words struck a pessimistic note.* **-6. to strike a match** to light a match. **-7.** [oil, gold] to discover <sthg>, especially by drilling into the ground □ *They struck oil while drilling in the Sahara desert.* **-8.** [clock] to chime a particular number of times to show <the time> □ *The clock struck midnight.* **-9. to be struck blind/dumb** to suddenly become blind/unable to speak. ■ **to strike fear** OR **terror into sb** to cause sb to be afraid of something □ *The sight of the bombers struck fear into the hearts of the villagers.* **-10.** *phrases* **to strike (it) lucky** to have a piece of good fortune □ *You never know, we might strike it lucky and meet some gorgeous men.* ■ **to strike it rich** to suddenly become very rich.

◇ *vi* **-1.** [workers, union] to carry out a strike □ *They're striking for more pay.* **-2. to strike against sthg** [vehicle] to accidentally hit sthg with force □ *The boat struck against the rocks and started to fill with water.* **-3.** [hurricane, disaster, illness] to suddenly affect or damage a person, place, or object □ *Disaster struck when a storm destroyed the entire banana crop.* **-4.** [person, animal] to attack a person or animal suddenly □ *The killer struck at night.* **-5.** [clock] to chime a particular number of times □ *Midnight had already struck.*

◆ **strike back** *vi* to attack the person, group etc that has attacked one □ *He had been taught never to strike back.*

◆ **strike down** *vt sep* **to strike sb down** to seriously harm or kill sb □ *She was struck down in her thirties by multiple sclerosis.*

◆ **strike off** *vt sep* **to be struck off** GB [doctor, lawyer] to have one's name removed from an official list so that one can no longer practice one's profession, usually because of unprofessional behavior.

◆ **strike out** ◇ *vt sep* **to strike sthg out** [name, word] to remove sthg by drawing a line through it □ *He struck out Lime's name and wrote in his own.* ◇ *vi* **-1.** to start moving in a particular direction with determination □ *They struck out across the moors, heading north.* **-2.** to do something different, often so that one can be on one's own □ *She's struck out on her own and started a business.*

◆ **strike up** ◇ *vt fus* **-1. to strike up a conversation/friendship** to start a conversation/friendship □ *Tim tried to strike up a conversation with the girl sitting opposite him.* **-2. to strike up a tune** to begin to play a tune □ *The band struck up a lively polka.* ◇ *vi* [musicians, orchestra] *They waited for the band to strike up.*

strikebound ['straɪkbaʊnd] *adj* [industry, country] that is prevented from carrying on as normal because of a strike.

strikebreaker ['straɪkbreɪkəʳ] *n* a person who continues to work at a place while the other workers are on strike.

strike pay *n* money paid to striking workers by their labor union.

striker ['straɪkəʳ] *n* **-1.** a person who is on strike. **-2.** SPORT in soccer, a player whose job is to attack and score goals.

striking ['straɪkɪŋ] *adj* **-1.** [appearance, difference] that is very noticeable or unusual □ *I noticed a striking similarity between the two brothers.* **-2.** [person] that looks very attractive □ *She has a very striking face.* **-3.** *phrase* **within striking distance** very close □ *From the hotel, the beach is within striking distance.* □ *They came within striking distance of finding a solution.*

string [strɪŋ] (*pt* & *pp* **strung**) *n* **-1.** very thin rope made of several threads twisted together and used for tying objects together; a piece of this □ *a piece of string* □ *a string bag/vest.* ■ **(with) no strings attached** without any other hidden conditions □ *He's given me his car — for free, no strings attached.* ■ **to pull strings** to use one's influence to get what one wants for oneself or for somebody else □ *Get your uncle George to pull a few strings for you at the newspaper.* **-2. a string of beads/onions etc** a number of beads/onions etc joined together on a thread □ *She wore a single string of pearls around her neck.* **-3.** [of people, events] a number of people or events that come one after the other; a large number of similar things □ *a string of visitors/phone calls/incidents* □ *She owns a string of racehorses.* **-4.** [of a musical instrument] any of the thin pieces of nylon, wire, or other material stretched across a guitar, violin etc that can be made to produce sound, e.g. by plucking.

◆ **strings** *npl* MUSIC **the strings** the group of musicians in an orchestra who play instruments that have strings.

◆ **string along** *vt sep* **to string sb along** to encourage sb to believe something that is not true (informal use) □ *String them along for a while, and only tell them if you have to.*

◆ **string out** *vt fus* to be strung out to be spread out in a line □ *A few supporters were strung out along the route.*

◆ **string together** *vt sep* to string words/sentences together to put words/sentences together to make sense □ *He was so drunk he could barely string two words together!*

◆ **string up** *vt sep* to string sb up to kill sb by hanging them (informal use).

string bean *n* a long, thin, green bean.

stringed instrument [ˌstrɪŋd-] *n* a musical instrument, e.g. a violin, that has strings.

stringent ['strɪndʒənt] *adj* [law, conditions, measure] that is severe and strictly controlled □ *Stringent conditions were imposed on candidates wishing to enter the competition.*

string quartet *n* a group of four musicians who play two violins, a viola, and a cello together; a piece of music written for this group.

stringy ['strɪŋɪ] (*compar* stringier, *superl* stringiest) *adj* [beans, meat] containing fibers that are difficult and unpleasant to eat.

strip [strɪp] (*pt & pp* stripped, *cont* stripping) ◇ *n* -1. a long narrow piece of paper, fabric etc □ *She tore off a strip of paper.* -2. a narrow area of land, water, forest etc □ *a narrow strip of forest.* -3. GB SPORT the clothes worn by a particular team.
◇ *vt* -1. to undress <sb>, especially against their will □ *He was stripped and searched.* -2. [paint, wallpaper, leaves] to remove <sthg> from an object or surface □ *I spent the afternoon stripping wallpaper in the hall.* -3. [wall, tree] to remove part or all of a layer that covers <sthg> □ *We've stripped all the walls in the kitchen.* -4. to strip sb of sthg [of rights, a title, medal] to take sthg from sb against their will □ *We were stripped of all our belongings.*
◇ *vi* to undress □ *He stripped to the waist.*

◆ **strip off** ◇ *vt sep* to strip sthg off [clothes, shirt, trousers] to take sthg off quickly □ *He stripped off his shirt and jumped into the lake.* ◇ *vi* to quickly take off one's clothes □ *She stripped off and ran into the sea.*

strip cartoon *n* GB a series of drawings that tell a story, usually a humorous one.

stripe [straɪp] *n* -1. a long narrow band of color, especially one that is part of a design, pattern, or decoration □ *I like wallpaper with stripes.* -2. a band of material on a uniform that indicates a person's rank.

striped [straɪpt] *adj* that has stripes of different colors □ *a black and white striped sweater.*

strip lighting *n* lighting that consists of long fluorescent tubes and not light bulbs.

stripper ['strɪpər] *n* -1. a person, usually a woman, whose job involves performing a striptease □ *a male stripper.* -2. a tool or liquid for removing paint, wallpaper, varnish etc from a surface □ *a wallpaper/wood stripper.*

strip-search ◇ *n* the action of stripping a prisoner or suspect and searching them

when they are naked. ◇ *vt* [prisoner, suspect] to give <sb> a strip-search.

strip show *n* a show on a stage that involves stripteases.

striptease ['strɪptiːz] *n* a performance to music, usually by a woman, in which she dances and takes off her clothes in a sexy way in front of an audience.

stripy ['straɪpɪ] (*compar* stripier, *superl* stripiest) *adj* = striped □ *a stripy T-shirt.*

strive [straɪv] (*pt* strove, *pp* striven ['strɪvn]) *vi* to strive for sthg [for equality, independence] to try very hard to have sthg □ *The company was continually striving for greater productivity.* ■ to strive to do sthg to try very hard to do sthg □ *She strove to give the impression that it was all very easy.*

strobe (light) ['stroʊb-] *n* a bright light, often used in discos, that flashes on and off very quickly.

strode [stroʊd] *past tense of* stride.

stroke [stroʊk] ◇ *n* -1. MEDICINE damage to the brain caused by a blood clot or burst blood vessel that leads to death or the inability to move certain parts of the body □ *My father had a stroke last year.* -2. [of a pen, brush] a single movement made by a brush or pen when painting or writing; the mark made by this movement □ *a brush stroke.* -3. [of one's hand] the act of passing one's hand slowly and gently over the surface of something □ *She gave the cat a stroke.* -4. [in swimming] a movement that one makes with one's arms when swimming and that one repeats in order to move through the water; a style of swimming using particular arm and leg movements □ *Try taking longer strokes.* □ *the butterfly stroke.* -5. [in rowing] a movement in rowing in which one moves the oars forward and back repeatedly in order to move forward □ *He rowed with long smooth strokes.* -6. [in tennis, golf] the act of hitting a ball. -7. [of a clock] the action or sound made by a clock when it strikes □ *At the third stroke it will be nine o'clock precisely.* -8. *phrases* a stroke of genius a sudden, very clever idea □ *It was a stroke of genius telling father we were going fishing!* ■ a stroke of luck a piece of good luck □ *What a stroke of luck my meeting you here!* ■ not to do a stroke of work not to do any work □ *That boy hasn't done a stroke of work all day.*
◇ *vt* to give <a dog, sb's hair> etc a stroke.

◆ **at a stroke** *adv* with one action □ *This could solve all my problems at a stroke.*

stroll [stroʊl] ◇ *n* a short relaxed walk □ *We went for OR took a stroll.* ◇ *vi* to walk in a relaxed way, usually for pleasure.

stroller ['stroʊlər] *n* US a small chair on wheels in which a baby or small child can sit in order to be moved around.

strong [strɒŋ] ◇ *adj* -1. [person, muscles] that is physically powerful; [voice] that sounds loud and confident □ *Are you strong enough to lift this?* -2. [person, character] that seems confident and not easily influenced by other people, or by unpleasant situations □ *She has a*

very strong personality. **-3.** [stick, material, shelf] that is solid and not easily broken and can hold a lot of weight □ *You should be able to stand on it — it's quite strong.* **-4.** [feeling, smell, wind] that is powerful in degree or intensity; [objection, support, denial] that is expressed in a very definite way □ *I have a strong feeling that Andy is going to be late.* □ *There's a strong smell of paint in here.* □ *Sandy has very strong objections to that kind of thing.* □ *This kind of problem requires strong measures.* **-5.** [argument, evidence] that is likely to convince people □ *I admit that the case against me is very strong.* **-6.** [political party, leader] who is important and influential □ *What we need is a strong leader at the head of a strong party.* **-7. 50/100 etc strong** consisting of 50/100 etc people □ *a crowd of demonstrators, 100 strong* □ *the 20-strong committee.* **-8.** [candidate, team] that is very able and likely to be successful in a particular field or activity □ *He is strong in languages.* □ *Toksvig is a strong candidate for the presidency.* ■ **a strong point** a particular quality or ability that somebody has and that is very useful □ *Tact is not one of his strong points.* **-9.** [person] who is feeling healthy, especially after a period of illness; [baby, heart] that is healthy and not likely to develop an illness easily □ *Once you're feeling stronger we'll go out.* □ *His health has never been strong.* **-10.** [bond, friendship] firm and likely to last a long time □ *The ties that bound our family together were strong indeed.* **-11.** [economy, industry] that is financially successful □ *Taiwan, for example, has a strong and expanding economy.* **-12.** FINANCE [currency] that is in a favorable position in relation to other currencies □ *The pound was strong against the dollar in early trading.* **-13.** [alcoholic drink, tea] that has a powerful taste, effect etc □ *Be careful how many of those pills you take — they're very strong.*
◇ *adv* **to be still going strong** [celebrity, group] to continue to be popular and successful after many years; [machine, car, old person] to be still healthy or working well despite being old □ *He must be over 80 by now and he's still going strong.*

strongarm ['strɒŋɑːˈm] *adj* **strongarm tactics** tactics that use threats or force, often unnecessarily.

strongbox ['strɒŋbɒks] *n* a box in which valuables can be locked to keep them safe.

stronghold ['strɒŋhəʊld] *n* a place where a particular belief or attitude is still popular □ *a stronghold of communism.*

strong language *n* vulgar and offensive language.

strongly ['strɒŋlɪ] *adv* [object, deny, smell] *see* **strong** □ *The scenery was strongly reminiscent of Scotland.* □ *It's an issue that he feels strongly about.* □ *He was strongly advised to reconsider.*

strong-minded [-'maɪndəd] *adj* [person] who is not easily influenced by other people's attitudes and opinions.

strong room *n* a room in a bank that has very strong walls and where valuables can be locked to keep them safe.

strong-willed [-'wɪld] *adj* [person] who is determined to do something, or to behave in a particular way, despite other people's advice or disapproval.

strove [strəʊv] *past tense of* **strive.**

struck [strʌk] *past tense & past participle of* **strike.**

structural ['strʌktʃrəl] *adj* [survey, damage, problem] that is connected to the structure of something □ *Let's see if there's any structural damage to the building.*

structurally ['strʌktʃrəlɪ] *adv*: *see* **structural** □ *The house seems structurally sound.*

structure ['strʌktʃəˈ] ◇ *n* **-1.** [of molecules, a book, the economy] the way in which something is built, arranged, or organized so that its parts relate to each other □ *We must re-examine the structure of our government.* **-2.** [object] something that has been built or constructed □ *a large metal structure.* ◇ *vt* [society, economy, book] to organize <sthg> in a particular way □ *His argument was not very well structured.*

struggle ['strʌgl] ◇ *n* **-1.** a great effort to do or achieve something that is difficult □ *At last the struggle for independence was over.* □ *It was a struggle to convince him.* **-2.** [to escape someone] a fight with somebody who is trying to hold or attack one □ *They gave themselves up without a struggle.* **-3.** [to keep something] a fight, especially one in which at least one of the participants is trying to get or keep something □ *The thieves gave up the money after a brief struggle.*
◇ *vi* **-1.** to try to do something that involves a great effort □ *They're struggling to keep up with their mortgage payments.* **-2.** [somebody who is being attacked] to fight and try to escape from somebody who is holding or attacking one □ *She struggled to free herself from his grip.* **-3.** [two people] to fight in order to get or keep something □ *They struggled with each other for the gun.* **-4.** [somebody who is weak or ill] to move with difficulty □ *He struggled to his feet/up the stairs.*
◆ **struggle on** *vi* to continue trying to do something that is difficult □ *I struggled on with the monthly accounts.*

struggling ['strʌglɪŋ] *adj* [writer, business] that is having difficulties, often because of a lack of money.

strum [strʌm] (*pt & pp* **strummed**, *cont* **strumming**) ◇ *vt* to play <a stringed instrument, especially a guitar>, by moving one's fingers quickly across all the strings. ◇ *vi*: *In the corner, Mary was strumming on her guitar.*

strung [strʌŋ] *past tense & past participle of* **string.**

strut [strʌt] (*pt & pp* **strutted**, *cont* **strutting**) ◇ *vi* to walk proudly with one's head held high, showing that one thinks one is important. ◇ *n* CONSTRUCTION & AVIATION a long narrow piece of wood or metal that is used to strengthen or support part of a building or aircraft.

strychnine [US 'strɪknaɪn, GB -niːn] *n* a poisonous drug that is used in very small amounts in some medicines.

Stuart ['stʲuːˀt], **Charles Edward** = **Bonnie Prince Charlie**.

Stuart, **Mary** = **Mary Queen of Scots**.

stub [stʌb] (*pt* & *pp* **stubbed**, *cont* **stubbing**) ◇ *n* -1. a short piece of something, especially a cigarette or pencil, that is left when the rest has been used up. -2. the part of a ticket or check that one keeps as a record after one has torn off and used the main part of it. ◇ *vt* **to stub one's toe** to hit one's toe accidentally against a hard surface.

◆ **stub out** *vt sep* **to stub a cigarette out** to stop a cigarette burning by pressing the end against something hard □ *He stubbed his cigarette out on the floor.*

stubble ['stʌbl] *n* -1. the short stalks left in a field after a cereal crop has been harvested □ *a field of stubble.* -2. the short stiff hairs on a man's face when he has not shaved recently □ *a three-day growth of stubble.*

stubborn ['stʌbəʳn] *adj* -1. [person, action, behavior] that is very determined, often in an unreasonable way □ *He's extremely stubborn and won't listen to reason.* -2. [stain, lock, acne] that is very difficult to remove, treat, or deal with □ *For really stubborn dirt, pour some liquid directly onto the fabric.*

stubbornly ['stʌbəʳnlɪ] *adv* [refuse, wait, declare] in a way that makes it clear that one's mind will not be changed by somebody else □ *The man stubbornly refused to believe that the senator was not at home.*

Stubbs [stʌbz], **George** (1724–1806) a British artist, famous for his paintings of horses.

stubby ['stʌbɪ] (*compar* **stubbier**, *superl* **stubbiest**) *adj* [fingers, pencil] that looks short and thick.

stucco ['stʌkou] *n* a type of plaster used for covering and decorating walls and ceilings.

stuck [stʌk] ◇ *past tense & past participle of* **stick**. ◇ *adj* -1. **to be stuck** [window, lid, key] to be tightly fixed in a particular position and impossible to move □ *The door's stuck.* □ *She got her finger stuck in the hole.* -2. **to be stuck** to be unable to continue to do something that has been attempted or started because it is too difficult □ *He was stuck for an answer to that last question.* □ *If you get stuck, come and find me.* □ *I'm stuck on this last question.* -3. **to be stuck** to be unable to leave a particular place or situation □ *We missed the last flight and got stuck in Montreal.* □ *Sorry I'm late — I got stuck in traffic.*

stuck-up *adj* [person] who is proud, unfriendly, and thinks that they are more important than other people (informal and disapproving use).

stud [stʌd] *n* -1. [as decoration] a small shiny piece of metal used as a decoration on something □ *a jacket with studs.* -2. [as jewelry] a very small earring that does not hang below the ear. -3. [for horses] a place where male animals, especially horses, are kept for

breeding. ■ **to be put out to stud** [horse] to be put in a stud for breeding. -4. GB one of a number of small pieces of metal on the sole of a sports boot that stop it from slipping on the ground.

studded ['stʌdəd] *adj* [jacket, bracelet] that is decorated with a lot of small shiny pieces of metal, jewels etc □ *The sky was studded with stars.*

student ['stʲuːdnt] *n* -1. a person who is studying at a school, college, or university □ *a physics student* □ *a student nurse/teacher* □ *student life/politics/humor.* -2. a person who studies a particular subject out of interest □ *a student of philosophy.*

student loan *n* a loan of money with a low rate of interest that is offered by a bank to a student.

student(s') union *n* -1. the organization at a college or university that arranges activities, provides welfare services, and represents students' political views and demands. -2. a building where students can meet socially.

stud farm *n* a place where male animals, especially horses, are kept for breeding.

studied ['stʌdəd] *adj* [answer, smile, seriousness] that is carefully planned or considered, and so not spontaneous or sincere □ *She smiled with studied indifference.*

studio ['stʲuːdɪou] (*pl* **studios**) *n* -1. the place where an artist works □ *We visited Moore's studio.* -2. CINEMA, RADIO, & TV the place where a movie, program, or piece of music is made □ *The entire album was recorded in the studio.*

studio apartment US, **studio flat** GB *n* an apartment that consists of one main room for living and sleeping in.

studio audience *n* an audience in a studio, whose applause, laughter etc is heard on the program being recorded.

studio flat *n* GB = **studio apartment**.

studious ['stʲuːdjəs] *adj* [person] who is quiet and spends a lot of time studying and reading books □ *a quiet, studious girl.*

studiously ['stʲuːdjəslɪ] *adv* carefully and deliberately □ *He studiously ignored the large card she placed in front of him.*

study ['stʌdɪ] (*pt* & *pp* **studied**, *pl* **studies**) ◇ *vt* -1. [chemistry, German, music] to learn about <sthg>, especially at school, college, or university □ *I studied Latin for four years and can't remember anything.* -2. [drawing, face, report] to examine <sthg> closely in order to learn something from it □ *Jorge sat studying the letter closely.*

◇ *vi* to spend time learning about a subject by following a course, reading etc □ *I must go to my room and study.* □ *She's been studying all day.*

◇ *n* -1. the act of studying □ *She does three hours of study each evening.* -2. [on a subject] a particular piece of research □ *a study into the causes of blood diseases.* -3. [for reading, writing] a room in a house used for reading, writing, and studying □ *Father keeps all his books in his* study. **-4.** [by an artist] a piece of work done by an artist or photographer to prepare for a larger work □ *a study of women bathing.*

◆ **studies** *npl* subjects that are studied at school, university etc □ *How are your studies going?*

stuff [stʌf] ◇ *n* (informal use) **-1.** [content] a word used to refer in a general way to the content of a book, television program etc □ *There's some interesting stuff in this article.* ■ **to know one's stuff** to know a lot about a particular subject □ *When it comes to computers she really knows her stuff.* **-2.** [substance] any material or substance □ *What's this sticky stuff in the saucepan? □ Whiskey? I never touch the stuff.* **-3.** [things] a collection of things □ *Where did you get all this stuff?* **-4.** [belongings] things that belong to one □ *Hold on, I haven't got my stuff out of the car yet!*

◇ *vt* **-1.** [papers, money, clothes] to push <sthg> into a place quickly and roughly □ *He stuffed his hands into his pockets.* **-2.** [pillow, suitcase] to fill <sthg> with material, a substance etc □ *We stuffed the bags with candy.* **-3. to stuff oneself** to eat a lot (informal use). **-4.** [tomatoes, turkey, ravioli] to fill <sthg> with a specially prepared mixture of food before cooking □ *She stuffed the chicken with sage and onion.*

stuffed [stʌft] *adj* **-1. to be stuffed with sthg** to be filled with sthg □ *The attic was stuffed with old clothes and furniture.* **-2. to be stuffed** to be full of food (informal use). **-3.** [tomato, eggplant] that is filled with a mixture of food □ *We had stuffed peppers for dinner.* **-4.** [parrot, dog, fish] that has had its insides removed and the body filled with special material so that it can be preserved and displayed □ *His study was full of stuffed animals.*

stuffing ['stʌfɪŋ] *n* material or food used to stuff something □ *a sofa with the stuffing coming out of it □ chestnut stuffing.*

stuffy ['stʌfɪ] (*compar* **stuffier**, *superl* **stuffiest**) *adj* **-1.** [room, atmosphere] that feels too warm and needs fresh air in it □ *It's stuffy in here — do you mind if I open the window?* **-2.** [person, club] that seems very formal and old-fashioned □ *a room full of stuffy old professors.*

stumble ['stʌmbl] *vi* **-1.** to hit one's foot on something while walking or running, and almost fall □ *He stumbled and fell.* **-2.** to hesitate or make a mistake while reading aloud or speaking □ *Alice read the poem aloud, stumbling over the longer words.*

◆ **stumble across, stumble on** *vt fus* **to stumble across** OR **on sb/sthg** [person, shop, information] to discover sb/sthg by chance □ *I stumbled across this marvelous little café.*

stumbling block ['stʌmblɪŋ-] *n* something that stops something happening or developing □ *There's only one stumbling block: your mother.*

stump [stʌmp] ◇ *n* [of a tree, arm, tooth] the small part of something that is left when the rest has been removed □ *a tree stump.* ◇ *vt* to leave <sb> unable to reply or find a solution □ *I'm completely stumped.* ◇ *vi* to walk heavily □ *He stumped up the stairs.*

◆ **stumps** *npl* in cricket, the three wooden poles stuck vertically in the ground that the bowler tries to hit with the ball.

◆ **stump up** *vt fus* **to stump up a sum of money** GB to pay a sum of money unwillingly (informal use) □ *George finally stumped up £50 for the bill.*

stun [stʌn] (*pt* & *pp* **stunned**, *cont* **stunning**) *vt* **-1.** to knock <a person or animal> unconscious □ *He stunned the rabbit with a sharp blow.* **-2.** to shock or surprise <sb> □ *Her arrival stunned journalists.*

stung [stʌŋ] *past tense & past participle of* **sting.**

stunk [stʌŋk] *past tense & past participle of* **stink.**

stunned [stʌnd] *adj* that appears very shocked or surprised □ *He came in with a stunned look on his face.*

stunning ['stʌnɪŋ] *adj* [outfit, person, scenery] that is very beautiful or impressive □ *You look stunning in that dress.*

stunt [stʌnt] ◇ *n* **-1.** something that is done to attract publicity and attention □ *It's just a stunt to get publicity for their new production.* **-2.** a daring and dangerous piece of action in a movie □ *She does stunts for a living.* ◇ *vt* [growth, development] to prevent <sthg> from happening as it should.

stunted ['stʌntəd] *adj* [tree, plant] that has been prevented from growing properly □ *stunted growth.*

stunt man *n* a man who performs dangerous stunts in place of an actor in a movie, so that the actor does not get injured.

stunt woman *n* a woman who performs dangerous stunts in place of an actress in a movie, so that the actress does not get injured.

stupefy ['stjuːpəfaɪ] (*pt* & *pp* **stupefied**) *vt* **-1.** to make <sb> feel unable to think clearly □ *He sat slouched in his chair, stupefied with boredom.* **-2.** to surprise <sb> very much □ *We were stupefied by the news.*

stupendous [stjuː'pendəs] *adj* **-1.** [time, concert, piece of news] that one finds very good, impressive etc (informal use). **-2.** [height, noise, effort] that is surprisingly great.

stupid ['stjuːpəd] *adj* **-1.** [idea, person, question] that does not show any or much intelligence □ *He's not as stupid as he pretends to be.* □ *What a stupid thing to say! □ It was all a stupid mistake.* **-2.** a word that one uses about something to show that one is annoyed with it (informal use) □ *I can't get the stupid car to start!*

stupidity [stjuː'pɪdətɪ] *n*: *see* **stupid** □ *It would be sheer stupidity to attempt the climb in such appalling weather conditions.*

stupidly ['stjuːpədlɪ] *adv* [say, forget, behave] *see* **stupid** □ *I stupidly left my keys in the car.*

stupor ['stjuːpəʳ] *n* the state of being almost unconscious and therefore unable to behave in a normal way □ *By the time we arrived, they were in a drunken stupor.*

sturdy ['stɜːdɪ] (*compar* **sturdier**, *superl* **sturdiest**) *adj* [person, furniture, platform] that is strong and not easily knocked over, injured, or damaged □ *a sturdy little horse.*

sturgeon ['stɜːʳdʒən] (*pl* **sturgeon**) *n* a large fish that lives in northern seas and from which caviar is obtained.

stutter ['stʌtəʳ] ◇ *n* a problem with speaking that causes somebody to have difficulty in saying the first letter of a word, often resulting in the repetition of the sound □ *He has a stutter.* ◇ *vi* to speak with a stutter.

St Valentine's Day [US ˌseɪnt-, GB ˌsənt-] *n* = **Valentine's Day.**

sty [staɪ] (*pl* **sties**) *n* an enclosed area on a farm where pigs are kept.

stye [staɪ] *n* an infection at the base of an eyelash that makes the eyelid red and swollen.

style [staɪl] ◇ *n* **-1.** [of a writer, painter, politician] a way of doing something, often showing the attitude of a person, group, period in history etc □ *in the style of Bach* □ *It's not my style to do that sort of thing.* **-2.** [of a person, place, occasion] a confident, original, or elegant appearance that people find impressive □ *She has real style!* **-3.** [of clothes, hair] the way that something such as a piece of clothing is designed; the way that hair is cut and shaped □ *I'd prefer something in a classic style.* ◇ *vt* to cut and shape <hair> in a particular style; to design <clothing or furniture> in a particular style.

-style *suffix* added to words to mean in a particular style □ *French-style cooking* □ *a cottage-style decor.*

styling mousse ['staɪlɪŋ-] *n* a white sticky foam that is put in the hair to help keep it in a particular style.

stylish ['staɪlɪʃ] *adj* [clothing, person, hotel] that is elegant and impressive □ *She's a stylish player.*

stylist ['staɪlɪst] *n* a person whose job is to style people's hair.

stylized, -ised ['staɪlaɪzd] *adj* [pattern, representation, language] that is in a particular style instead of being realistic or natural □ *The performance was very stylized.*

stylus ['staɪləs] (*pl* **styluses**) *n* **-1.** a device like a needle on a record-player that picks up the sound signals from a record. **-2.** COMPUTING the pointed instrument with which one can write directly on the screens of some computers.

stymie ['staɪmɪ] *vt* **to be stymied** [person, plan] to be prevented from going ahead (informal use).

Styrofoam™ ['staɪrəfoʊm] *n* US a very light plastic material, often used to make packaging and containers.

suave [swɑːv] *adj* [person, behavior, expression] that is very well-mannered, polite, and charming, often in an insincere way.

sub [sʌb] *n* **-1.** SPORT *abbr of* **substitute. -2.** *abbr of* **submarine. -3.** US a long thin sandwich. **-4.** *abbr of* **subscription.**

subcommittee ['sʌbkəmɪtɪ] *n* a small committee consisting of members from a larger

committee who are chosen to deal with a particular matter in detail.

subconscious [ˌsʌb'kɒnʃəs] ◇ *n* **the subconscious** the part of the mind that works without one's awareness and that can influence one's thoughts, feelings, and behavior. ◇ *adj* [fear, knowledge] that is in the subconscious.

subconsciously [ˌsʌb'kɒnʃəslɪ] *adv* [feel, fear, know] *see* **subconscious** □ *Subconsciously she resented his kindness to her.*

subcontinent [ˌsʌb'kɒntɪnənt] *n* a large area of land that is part of a continent and that contains a number of countries □ *the Indian subcontinent.*

subcontract [ˌsʌb'kɒntrækt] *vt* [translation, plumbing, publicity work] to pay somebody else to do <a job one has been hired to do>.

subculture ['sʌbkʌltʃəʳ] *n* the culture of a small group of people within a larger group that is different and not known by most people and that is often disapproved of □ *the drug/hippie/youth subculture.*

subdivide [ˌsʌbdɪ'vaɪd] *vt* [building, room, task] to divide <sthg> into several smaller parts.

subdue [səb'djuː] *vt* **-1.** [enemies, rioters, crowd] to bring <a group of people> under control, often using force. **-2.** [feelings, passions] to cause <sthg> to become less strong.

subdued [səb'djuːd] *adj* **-1.** [person, animal, atmosphere] that is quieter than usual, and so suggests that something is wrong □ *Rachel seemed remarkably subdued this evening.* **-2.** [light, lighting, color] that is soft and not bright in appearance □ *a room painted in subdued grays and pinks.*

subeditor [ˌsʌb'edɪtəʳ] *n* a person whose job is to correct and improve written material before it is printed.

subheading ['sʌbhedɪŋ] *n* a heading that introduces each part of a piece of writing inside a chapter, section etc.

subhuman [ˌsʌb'hjuːmən] *adj* [person, behavior, conditions] that is below the standards of what is expected of normal people.

subject [*n, adj,* & *prep* 'sʌbdʒekt, *vt* səb'dʒekt] ◇ *n* **-1.** the person or thing that a book, movie, conversation etc deals with □ *The subject for discussion today is...* □ *I have no ideas on the subject.* □ *Do you mind if we drop this subject?* □ *Brian kept trying to change the subject.* **-2.** GRAMMAR a word used to refer to the person or thing doing the action of the main verb, e.g. "John" in the sentence "John was writing a letter." **-3.** EDUCATION an area of knowledge, e.g. history or physics, that is studied at school, college, or university □ *What was your favorite subject at school?* □ *How many subjects do you study?* **-4.** [in a country] a person who was born in a particular country, usually a monarchy, or a person who has the right to live there □ *a British subject.* ◇ *adj* **-1. a subject state/country etc** a state/country etc that is not independent but is governed by another state. **-2. subject to sthg** [to tax] affected by sthg; [to drought, asthma attacks, ill health] likely to be affected by sthg □ *The price is subject to a handling charge.* □ *We are all subject to the rule of law.* □ *The terms are subject to alteration without notice.* □ *Marion was often subject to migraine headaches.* ◇ *vt* **-1.** [rebels, provinces, army] to bring <people or a place> under firm control. **-2. to subject sb/sthg to sthg** to make sb/sthg experience sthg unpleasant □ *He was subjected to four hours of interrogation.*

◆ **subject to** *prep* depending on <sthg> □ *The review will go ahead subject to the approval of the chairman.*

subjection [səb'dʒekʃn] *n* [of rebels, provinces, an army] *see* **subject**.

subjective [səb'dʒektɪv] *adj* [opinion, judgment, statement] that is based on personal feelings rather than facts □ *I find his analysis entirely subjective.*

subjectively [səb'dʒektɪvlɪ] *adv* [judge, state, speak] *see* **subjective**.

subject matter *n* the person or thing that a book, movie, conversation etc deals with.

sub judice [-'dʒuːdəsɪ] *adj* [matter, case] that is being considered in a court of law and is therefore not to be discussed publicly, e.g. in newspapers or on TV.

subjugate ['sʌbdʒəgeɪt] *vt* **-1.** [tribe, country] to defeat and take control of <people or a place>. **-2.** [feelings, desires] to treat <sthg> as less important than something else.

subjunctive [səb'dʒʌŋktɪv] *n* **the subjunctive (mood)** a verb form used in some languages to express hopes, wishes, or uncertainty.

sublet [,sʌb'let] (*pt* & *pp* **sublet**, *cont* **subletting**) *vt* [apartment, building, office] to rent to somebody else all or part of <a property that one rents from a landlord>.

sublime [sə'blaɪm] *adj* [music, moment, feeling] that affects one deeply, e.g. because of its beauty, or spiritual or noble qualities □ *a painting of sublime beauty.* ■ **from the sublime to the ridiculous** a phrase used when something serious and important is followed by something silly and unimportant.

sublimely [sə'blaɪmlɪ] *adv* **sublimely unaware/ ignorant etc** completely unaware/ignorant etc and not thinking about the effects of one's actions on other people.

subliminal [,sʌb'lɪmənl] *adj* [advertising, effect, message] that affects the subconscious mind.

submachine gun [,sʌbmə'ʃiːn-] *n* a light machine gun.

submarine [,sʌbmə'riːn] *n* a ship that can travel below the sea's surface as well as on top of it and that is used especially in war or for scientific exploration.

submerge [səb'mɜːrdʒ] ◇ *vt* **-1.** to cause <sb/ sthg> to go under the surface of water □ *The ship's remains were salvaged after lying submerged for over 400 years.* **-2. to submerge oneself in sthg** to give all one's attention to sthg □ *After the divorce, Jonathan submerged himself increasingly in his work.* ◇ *vi* [person, animal, object] to go under the surface of water.

submission [səb'mɪʃn] *n* **-1.** a state of complete obedience to somebody or something in which one shows no concern for one's own wishes □ *their attempts to bring the rebels to submission.* **-2.** [of a request, paper, thesis] *see* **submit** □ *October 2 is the last date for submission of manuscripts.*

submissive [səb'mɪsɪv] *adj* [person, behavior, answer] that shows complete obedience and no concern for one's own wishes.

submit [səb'mɪt] (*pt* & *pp* **submitted**, *cont* **submitting**) ◇ *vt* [request, paper, thesis] to present <sthg> for somebody to think or make a decision about □ *They submitted their recommendations to the board.* ◇ *vi* to show obedience to a more important or powerful force □ *They refused to submit to the enemy/demands.*

subnormal [,sʌb'nɔːrml] *adj* [person] who has a lower intelligence than is normal for a person of their age.

subnotebook [,sʌb'nəʊtbʊk] *n* a small portable computer.

subordinate [*adj* & *n* sə'bɔːrdənət, *vt* sə'bɔːrdəneɪt] ◇ *adj* less important (formal use) □ *He is subordinate in rank.* □ *Her role is subordinate to the vice-president's.* ◇ *n* [in an army, organization] a person who is of lower rank. ◇ *vt* [wishes, ideal] to treat <sthg> as less important than something else (formal use) □ *They were ready to subordinate their personal desires and ambitions to the revolutionary cause.*

subordinate clause [sə,bɔːrdənət-] *n* in grammar, a group of words that add detail to the rest of the sentence but cannot stand on their own.

subordination [sə,bɔːrdə'neɪʃn] *n* [of a wish, ideal] *see* **subordinate**.

subpoena [sə'piːnə] (*pt* & *pp* **subpoenaed**) ◇ *n* a legal document ordering a person to attend a court of law and give evidence as a witness. ◇ *vt* [witness] to send <sb> a subpoena.

sub-post office *n* GB a post office that is not completely owned by the government and does not offer the whole range of postal services.

subroutine ['sʌbruːtiːn] *n* a part of a computer program that does a particular task and that can be used at any time during the running of the main program.

Sub-Saharan Africa [US -səhærən-, GB -hɑːr-] the African countries south of Algeria, Liberia, and Egypt.

subscribe [səb'skraɪb] *vi* **-1. to subscribe to sthg** [to a magazine, newspaper] to pay to receive regular issues of sthg. **-2. to subscribe to sthg** [to a belief, view] to agree with sthg □ *I do not subscribe to that view at all.*

subscriber [səb'skraɪbər] *n* **-1.** [to a newspaper, magazine] a person who pays to receive regular issues of a publication. **-2.** [to cable TV, the Internet] a person who pays regularly to receive a particular service. **-3.** [to a charity, campaign] a person who regularly sends money to support an organization, club etc.

subscription [səb'skrɪpʃn] *n* [to a magazine, charity, club] the act of paying money as a subscriber; a sum of money paid by a subscriber □ *I took out a subscription to "Elle" magazine.* □ *My annual subscription is due.*

subsection ['sʌbsekʃn] *n* one of a number of smaller sections into which a larger document is divided.

subsequent ['sʌbsɪkwənt] *adj* [payment, recovery, complaint] that happens after something else □ *Her illness and subsequent death left the family devastated.* □ *Subsequent events proved us to be wrong.*

subsequently ['sʌbsɪkwəntlɪ] *adv* afterward □ *They were subsequently found to have been telling the truth.*

subservient [səb'sɜːʳvjənt] *adj* -1. [person] who does what other people want without disagreeing or questioning in any way □ *His manner was unpleasantly subservient.* -2. **to be subservient to sthg** [to a need, aim, organization] to be less important than sthg □ *Employees' individual needs must always be subservient to those of the country as a whole.*

subset ['sʌbset] *n* MATH a set that is part of a larger set.

subside [səb'saɪd] *vi* -1. [anger, pain, grief] to become less intense □ *Once the pain had subsided....* -2. [noise, screams] to become quieter □ *The shouting gradually subsided into silence.* -3. [building, ground] to sink to a lower level □ *Our house is subsiding into the river.*

subsidence [səb'saɪdns, 'sʌbsɪdns] *n* [of a building, the ground] *see* **subside** □ *insurance claims for subsidence.*

subsidiarity [səbsɪdɪ'ærətɪ] *n* the principle that all member states of the European Union have the right to carry out an agreed EU policy in their own way.

subsidiary [US səb'sɪdɪerɪ, GB -ɪərɪ] (*pl* **subsidiaries**) ◇ *adj* [matter, subject, problem] that is less important than something with which it is connected □ *This problem is subsidiary to the wider concerns of the company.* ◇ *n* **a subsidiary (company)** a company that is part of a larger and more important company □ *Morgans is a subsidiary of Denning Inc.*

subsidize, -ise ['sʌbsədaɪz] *vt* -1. [theater, public transport, housing] to pay for part of the cost of <sthg> in order to make it cheaper for the people who use it □ *Our travel expenses are subsidized by the college.* -2. [industry, agriculture] to provide money in order to make it possible for <an activity> to continue □ *I see little future for subsidized industry.*

subsidy ['sʌbsədɪ] (*pl* **subsidies**) *n* money that is provided by a government or an official organization to subsidize something □ *government subsidies.*

subsist [səb'sɪst] *vi* **to subsist on sthg** to survive with difficulty on sthg □ *Morton subsisted on a diet of stale bread and soup.*

subsistence [səb'sɪstəns] *n* the survival of a person on very little money or food.

subsistence allowance *n* an amount of money given to somebody to pay for basic needs such as accommodation and food.

subsistence farming *n* a method of farming where the farmer grows just enough crops for his or her own use.

subsistence level *n* the level at which subsistence is still possible □ *They are living below the subsistence level.*

substance ['sʌbstəns] *n* -1. a particular type of material, gas, or liquid □ *a radioactive/toxic substance.* -2. [of an argument, speech] the main point of an argument, speech, book etc □ *The main substance of his speech concerned the future of the steel industry.* -3. importance or worth □ *He said nothing of any substance.* -4. [to a claim, allegation] truth □ *There is no substance to these claims.*

substandard [sʌb'stændəʳd] *adj* [quality, product] that is below the accepted standard.

substantial [səb'stænʃl] *adj* -1. [change, increase, meal] large □ *The money could make a substantial difference to us.* -2. [person, building, furniture] solid and strong □ *That roof needs something more substantial to hold it up.*

substantially [səb'stænʃəlɪ] *adv* -1. [contribute, increase, improve] by a large amount □ *Their standard of living has improved substantially since Alan got a new job.* □ *This version is substantially better than the last.* -2. [true, correct] generally □ *The situation remains substantially the same.*

substantiate [səb'stænʃɪeɪt] *vt* [claim, story] to prove <that sthg is true> (formal use).

substantive [US 'sʌbstəntɪv, GB səb'stæntɪv] *adj* [discussion, talks] that is concerned with real and important issues.

substitute ['sʌbstətjuːt] ◇ *n* -1. **a substitute for sb/sthg** a person or a thing acting or used in place of sb/sthg □ *We're looking for a substitute for Maggie now she's leaving.* ■ **to be no substitute for sthg** to be not as good as sthg else □ *The television is no substitute for a movie screen.* -2. SPORT a player who takes the place of another player during a game, e.g. because of injury □ *It looks like Brazil are bringing on a substitute.*
◇ *vt* **to substitute sb for sb** to put sb in the place or role of sb □ *He was substituted by Wilson in the second half.* ■ **to substitute sthg for sthg** to use sthg instead of sthg □ *You can substitute dried herbs for fresh ones.*
◇ *vi* to take the place of somebody or something else □ *I'm substituting for Mrs. Smith while she's away.*

substitute teacher *n* US a person who does the job of a teacher who is absent for a short time.

substitution [sʌbstə'tjuːʃn] *n* -1. the act of substituting one person or thing for another □ *A substitution was made in the final ten minutes.* -2. a replacement □ *We'll use this until a substitution can be found.*

subterfuge ['sʌbtəʳfjuːdʒ] *n* a trick or dishonest action used to get what one wants □ *They must have gained access to the files by subterfuge.*

subterranean [sʌbtə'reɪnjən] *adj* [passage, river, noise] underground.

subtitle ['sʌbtaɪtl] *n* a less important, often descriptive title, printed under the main title of a book.

◆ **subtitles** *npl* the translation of words in a foreign film, printed across the bottom of the screen.

subtle ['sʌtl] *adj* -1. [nuance, difference] that is difficult to see, explain, or understand because it is very small □ *There's a subtle distinction between the two words.* -2. [person, comment, tactics] that is clever and not obvious □ *That wasn't very subtle of you!* □ *a subtle sense of humor.*

subtlety ['sʌtltɪ] *n* -1. [of a skill, design, piece of music] the quality of being clever and not obvious □ *Only an expert can appreciate the subtlety of his work.* -2. [of a person] the ability to say or do things in a way that is not likely to offend anybody or attract too much attention □ *It's a task that requires a certain degree of subtlety.* -3. [of an argument, comment, tactic] *see* **subtle.** -4. [of a process, system] a particular aspect of something that is difficult to explain or deal with □ *I haven't grasped all the subtleties of the software yet.*

subtly ['sʌtlɪ] *adv* [differ, change] *see* **subtle** □ *He subtly got them to change their mind.* □ *It tasted subtly different.*

subtotal ['sʌbtoʊtl] *n* the total of a set of figures, e.g. on a bill or statement, that will give the final total when it is added to the totals of other sets of figures.

subtract [səb'trækt] *vt* [amount, quantity] to take <a number> away from another number □ *First subtract six from ten.*

subtraction [səb'trækʃn] *n*: *see* **subtract** □ *Pupils are taught addition and subtraction first.*

subtropical [ˌsʌb'trɒpɪkl] *adj* [climate, region, vegetation] that exists or is found in the part of the world between the tropical and temperate zones.

suburb ['sʌbɜːʳb] *n* -1. a part of a town or city that is away from the center and consists mainly of houses □ *Jersey City is a suburb of New York.* -2. **the suburbs** the area around a town or city that is a suburb □ *He lives in the suburbs.*

suburban [sə'bɜːʳbən] *adj* -1. [area, life, train] that is found in a suburb □ *suburban streets.* -2. [mentality, taste] that is ordinary and a little dull □ *a typical suburban housewife.*

suburbia [sə'bɜːʳbɪə] *n* -1. the suburbs □ *living in suburbia.* -2. the way of life and attitudes of people living in the suburbs.

subversion [səb'vɜːʳʒn] *n*: *see* **subvert** □ *The group's aim was the subversion of democracy.*

subversive [səb'vɜːʳsɪv] ◇ *adj* [idea, organization, magazine] that tries to or is likely to destroy a government, political system etc. ◇ *n* a subversive person.

subvert [səb'vɜːʳt] *vt* [government, political system, ideas] to destroy or try to destroy the power of <sthg>.

subway ['sʌbweɪ] *n* -1. US an underground railroad □ *the New York subway* □ *a subway station/train.* -2. GB a path under a road or

railroad, used for pedestrians to cross safely from one side to the other.

sub-zero *adj* [temperatures, conditions] that are below zero degrees.

succeed [sək'siːd] ◇ *vi* -1. [person] to manage to do something that one has tried or wanted to do □ *Sandra finally succeeded in getting a place at law school.* □ *I tried to persuade them to come but didn't succeed.* □ *He succeeded in his attempt to break the world record.* -2. [plan, tactic, approach] to have the intended result □ *The demonstration succeeded in bringing about a change in government policy.* □ *If their plans had succeeded, we would all be dead by now.* -3. [politician, employee, singer] to do well by becoming popular, reaching a high position etc □ *One needs a certain amount of determination to succeed in this business.*

◇ *vt* -1. [person] to come after or take the place of <sb>, especially in an important job □ *Mrs Thatcher was succeeded as prime minister by John Major.* -2. [range, period] to happen or exist after <sthg> (formal use) □ *The original model was succeeded by a more compact version.*

succeeding [sək'siːdɪŋ] *adj* **the succeeding months/years etc** the months/years etc that followed (formal use).

success [sək'ses] *n* -1. [in an attempt, campaign] the achievement of what one has tried or wanted to do □ *They tried to make him change his mind, but without success.* -2. [in one's career, life] the achievement of popularity, a high position etc □ *I hope your success will not make you overconfident.* -3. **to be a success** to be successful □ *The workshop was a great success.*

successful [sək'sesfl] *adj* -1. [attempt, method, campaign] that achieves the intended result □ *The meeting was not very successful.* □ *He was successful at his second attempt.* □ *I was successful in persuading her to join.* -2. [movie, book, company] that has earned a lot of money □ *a successful salesman* □ *Kemp enjoyed a highly successful career in advertising.* -3. [politician, artist, lawyer] who has become popular, reached a high position etc □ *They were one of the most successful bands in history.*

successfully [sək'sesflɪ] *adv* [conclude, treat, try] with the intended or desired result □ *He successfully sued his employers.*

succession [sək'seʃn] *n* -1. [of owners, jobs, disasters] a number of people or things that come one after the other □ *They suffered three electoral defeats in quick* OR *close succession.* -2. [to a position, title, throne] the process of becoming the next person to have something, especially after somebody's death (formal use).

successive [sək'sesɪv] *adj* **successive attempts/ defeats** attempts/defeats that come one after the other □ *After three successive failures he swore he would never try again.*

successor [sək'sesəʳ] *n* a person or thing that comes after or takes the place of another □ *The board is meeting today to appoint a successor to the outgoing chairman.*

success story *n* somebody or something that has been very successful □ *The company has become a huge success story.*

succinct [sək'sıŋkt] *adj* [account, explanation] that is expressed clearly and uses few words □ *Could you be a little more succinct?*

succinctly [sək'sıŋktlı] *adv* [express, describe, explain] *see* **succinct**.

succulent ['sʌkjələnt] *adj* [meat, fruit] that is juicy and tastes good.

succumb [sə'kʌm] *vi* -1. to allow oneself to be affected by something that one has resisted before □ *Faced with increasing pressure from civil rights groups, they finally succumbed.* -2. to become badly affected by or die from an illness □ *After a long struggle, he finally succumbed to the disease.*

such [sʌtʃ] ◇ *det & predet* -1. **such behavior/ such a problem** behavior/a problem of the kind just mentioned □ *Such things are no longer seen now.* □ *Too tired? I've never heard such nonsense!* ■ **such a thing as...** a thing of the kind I am just about to mention □ *Do you have such a thing as a bottle opener?* □ *There are no such things as ghosts.* -2. **such nice people** very nice people (used for emphasis) □ *I've had such a bad day!* □ *I'm not sure it's such a good idea.* ■ **he's such an idiot/a bore!** he's very stupid/boring! ■ **such money as I have** the small amount of money I have. ■ **it was such a good offer (that) I accepted** because it was a very good offer, I accepted □ *She gave me such a fright (that) I screamed.* □ *It's such a long time since I've been there I've almost forgotten what it's like.* ◇ *pron* -1. used to refer back to something just mentioned □ *Such has been my intention all along.* -2. **the costs are such that I cannot afford it** because the costs are so great I cannot afford it (formal use) □ *The state of the economy was such that extreme measures had to be taken.* ■ **such as it is** used to say that something is not very important or not of very good quality □ *You can take my car, such as it is.*

◆ **as such** *adv* **it's not a university as such** it's not exactly a university.

◆ **such and such** *predet* used when the speaker does not want to give specific examples of something □ *We could invite candidates to talk on such and such a subject.*

◆ **such as** *prep* used to give examples of something that has just been mentioned □ *Countries such as Australia and America have a federal system of government.*

suchlike ['sʌtʃlaık] ◇ *pron* people or things of the same kind □ *hippos, rhinos, and suchlike.* ◇ *adj* of the same kind.

suck [sʌk] *vt* -1. [straw, candy] to hold <sthg> in one's mouth and take liquid from it using one's tongue, cheeks, and lips. -2. [person, air, dirt] to pull <sb/sthg> in a particular direction by the powerful force of water or air □ *The fan sucks in air at one end and expels it at the other.* □ *Many swimmers have been sucked down* OR *under by the strong currents.* -3. **to be sucked into sthg** [into crime, a debate] to gradually become involved in sthg without intending to □ *Many of these kids are then sucked into a life of crime.*

◆ **suck up** *vi* to try to be liked by somebody by being very helpful, friendly etc (informal and disapproving use) □ *He's always sucking up to the boss.*

sucker ['sʌkəʳ] *n* -1. a person who is easily tricked (informal use) □ *What a sucker!* -2. GB a rubber disk that sticks to surfaces by suction and is used e.g. to hang things on a wall or door.

suckle ['sʌkl] ◇ *vt* [mother] to feed <a baby or young animal> by letting it suck milk from the breast, udder etc. ◇ *vi* [baby, young animal] to suck milk from the breast, udder etc.

sucrose ['suːkrous] *n* the type of sugar that comes from cane, beet etc.

suction ['sʌkʃn] *n* -1. [of a gas, liquid] a force that causes liquids, gases etc to move inside a closed space by removing air or liquid from the space □ *The water is conveyed through the pipe by suction.* -2. a force that causes two surfaces to stick together by removing the air from between them □ *Flies attach themselves to surfaces by suction.*

suction pump *n* a pump that works by suction.

Sudan [US suːˈdæn, GB -ˈdɑːn] a country in northeastern Africa, on the Red Sea. SIZE: 2,506,000 sq kms. POPULATION: 27,400,000 (*Sudanese*). CAPITAL: Khartoum. LANGUAGE: Arabic. CURRENCY: Sudanese pound.

Sudanese [ˌsuːdəˈniːz] *n & adj: see* **Sudan**.

sudden ['sʌdn] *adj* [change, movement, thought] that happens quickly and unexpectedly □ *The decision was very sudden.* ■ **all of a sudden** quickly and unexpectedly □ *All of a sudden, the lights went out.*

sudden death *n* SPORT an extra part of a game, in which one goal, point etc decides who the winner is □ *a sudden death playoff.*

suddenly ['sʌdnlı] *adv* [happen, stop, move] *see* **sudden** □ *I suddenly realized what had happened.* □ *Suddenly, the door opened.*

suds [sʌdz] *npl* the bubbles on the surface of soapy water.

sue [suː] *vt* to try to get money from <sb> by taking legal action for loss, damage etc that they have caused □ *We intend to sue him for damages/libel/$500,000.*

suede [sweıd] *n* a type of soft leather with a rough surface □ *suede shoes* □ *a suede jacket.*

suet ['suːɪt] *n* the hard fat from around an animal's kidneys that is used in cooking.

Suez Canal [US ˌsuːez-, GB ˌsuːɪz-]: **the Suez Canal** a canal in northeastern Egypt, connecting the Mediterranean Sea and the Red Sea.

suffer ['sʌfəʳ] ◇ *vt* -1. [pain, stress, injury] to experience <sthg painful or unpleasant> □ *Mrs Lawe suffered a serious heart attack.* -2. [setback, loss, consequences] to be affected by <sthg that causes problems> □ *The company suffered losses of over $15 million.*

◇ *vi* -1. [patient, victim] to be in physical pain □ *It's a comfort to know that he didn't suffer* much. ■ **to suffer from sthg** [from an illness, disease] to be affected by sthg that makes one's health worse □ *She's suffering from angina.* □ *I suffered from asthma as a child.* **-2.** to experience difficulty, loss, sorrow etc □ *If the destruction of the rainforest continues, the whole world will suffer.* □ *As usual, the poor were the ones to suffer worst from the recession.* **-3.** [relationship, work, social life] to become affected in a bad way □ *I was deeply unhappy, and my work suffered as a consequence.*

sufferance ['sʌfrəns] *n* **on sufferance** accepted or allowed, but not in an enthusiastic or friendly way □ *He's only here on sufferance.*

sufferer ['sʌfərər] *n* a person who has or often suffers from a particular illness or medical condition □ *an asthma/a hay fever sufferer.*

suffering ['sʌfərɪŋ] *n* physical or mental pain; difficulties, sorrow etc □ *These experiments cause terrible suffering to animals.* □ *She appeared indifferent to their sufferings.*

suffice [sə'faɪs] *vi* to be enough (formal use) □ *Just a small amount will suffice.*

sufficient [sə'fɪʃnt] *adj* [time, money, power] enough for a particular purpose □ *$50 should be sufficient for three days.*

sufficiently [sə'fɪʃntlɪ] *adv* **to be sufficiently aware/funded etc** to be aware/funded etc enough □ *He didn't prepare himself sufficiently for the exam.*

suffix ['sʌfɪks] *n* a letter or group of letters added to the end of a word to make a new word, e.g. "less" in "useless".
NOTE: Compare **prefix**.

suffocate ['sʌfəkeɪt] ◇ *vt* to cause <sb> to die by stopping them from getting air. ◇ *vi* to die because one cannot breathe in enough air; to feel unable to breathe.

suffocation [,sʌfə'keɪʃn] *n*: see **suffocate** □ *He died of suffocation.*

Suffolk ['sʌfək] a county in East Anglia, southeastern England. SIZE: 3,800 sq kms. POPULATION: 636,580. ADMINISTRATIVE CENTER: Ipswich.

suffrage ['sʌfrɪdʒ] *n* the right to vote in political elections.

suffuse [sə'fjuːz] *vt* **to be suffused with sthg** [with color, light] to be filled with sthg.

sugar ['ʃʊgər] ◇ *n* a sweet substance, often in the form of white or brown crystals, taken from the juice of certain plants and used to flavor food and drinks □ *Do you take sugar in your tea?* ◇ *vt* [tea, coffee] to put sugar in <sthg>.

sugar beet *n* a root vegetable from which sugar is taken.

sugar bowl *n* a small bowl for serving sugar in.

sugarcane ['ʃʊgərkeɪn] *n* a tall tropical grass from which sugar is taken.

sugar-coated [-'koʊtəd] *adj* [popcorn, almonds] covered with sugar.

sugar cube *n* a small cube of sugar used to sweeten tea, coffee etc.

sugared ['ʃʊgərd] *adj* **to be sugared** [tea, coffee] to contain sugar that has been added to it.

sugar lump *n* = sugar cube.

sugar refinery *n* a factory where sugar from plants is made into crystals to be sold.

sugary ['ʃʊgərɪ] *adj* **-1.** [pudding, dessert, diet] that contains a lot of sugar. **-2.** [writing, song, smile] that is very sentimental, but in a way that seems insincere and exaggerated.

suggest [US səg'dʒest, GB sə'dʒest] *vt* **-1.** [idea, plan, restaurant] to mention <sthg> to somebody because they might want to do it, have it, use it etc □ *Can I suggest a short break for lunch?* □ *David suggested taking a drive out to the coast.* □ *She suggested (that) we meet later.* □ *I could suggest several ways to improve our sales figures.* **-2. to suggest that...** to seem to say that something is true or exists without saying so directly □ *Are you suggesting (that) I'm a liar?* □ *His response suggests a reluctance to get involved.*

suggestion [US səg'dʒestʃən, GB sə'dʒes-] *n* **-1.** something that is suggested, especially when it is intended to be helpful □ *The Tourist Information Office gave us some useful suggestions.* □ *May I make a suggestion at this point?* **-2.** a slight or indirect sign of something □ *At the time, there was some suggestion of corruption in the department.* □ *There was just the slightest suggestion of irony in his voice.*

suggestive [US səg'dʒestɪv, GB sə'dʒest-] *adj* **-1.** [smile, behavior, remark] that is intended to make one think of sex. **-2. to be suggestive of sthg** to make one think of sthg □ *This music is intended to be suggestive of a sunrise.*

suicidal [,suːɪ'saɪdl] *adj* **-1.** [person] who is very unhappy and likely to commit suicide □ *He was beginning to feel suicidal.* **-2.** [driving, sport, attempt] that is very dangerous and likely to lead to death; [policy, decision] that is likely to lead to failure □ *He's a suicidal maniac!* □ *It would be suicidal to give in to them now.*

suicide ['suːɪsaɪd] *n* **-1.** the act of deliberately killing oneself □ *He's made several suicide attempts.* □ *There were two suicides last week.* ■ **to commit suicide** to deliberately kill oneself. **-2.** an action that leads or may lead to failure □ *This amounts to political/financial suicide.*

suit [suːt] ◇ *n* **-1.** CLOTHING [for a man] a set of clothes made of the same material that consists of a jacket and trousers and, sometimes, a vest; [for a woman] a suit that usually consists of a jacket and skirt □ *a business/linen suit.* **-2.** SPORT a set of clothes or a piece of clothing worn for a particular activity □ *a swimming/diving/jogging suit.* **-3.** CARDS any of the four sets of cards that are in a deck of playing cards. **-4.** LAW a legal case in which a dispute between individuals or organizations is settled □ *a libel suit.* **-5.** *phrase* **to follow suit** to do the same thing that somebody else has done □ *Sara took off her shoes as she entered, so I followed suit.*
◇ *vt* **-1.** [clothes, color, hairstyle] to look attractive on <sb> □ *Long hair suits you.* **-2.** [arrangement, plan] to be acceptable to or convenient for <sb> □ *Would ten thirty suit you?* □ *Thursday*

suits me fine. □ *You can't just turn up when it suits you.* ■ **to suit oneself** to do what one wants without considering other people's opinions □ *"I'd rather not go." — "Well, suit yourself."* **-3.** [situation, lifestyle] to be right for <sb> □ *That job suits you perfectly.*
◇ *vi* [arrangement] to be acceptable or convenient □ *I'll come about six; does that suit?*

suitability [ˌsuːtəˈbɪlətɪ] *n*: *see* **suitable** □ *His suitability for the job must be in doubt.*

suitable [ˈsuːtəbl] *adj* [time, candidate, clothes] that is right for a particular need, purpose, or situation □ *The entrance to the building is not suitable for wheelchairs.*

suitably [ˈsuːtəblɪ] *adv* **-1. to be suitably equipped/dressed etc** to be equipped/dressed etc in a way that is suitable. **-2. to be suitably grateful/surprised etc** to be grateful/surprised etc in a way that is normal in the situation □ *I was suitably impressed.*

suitcase [ˈsuːtkeɪs] *n* a large rectangular case that has a handle and is used for carrying clothes when traveling.

suite [swiːt] *n* **-1.** a set of rooms in a building that are all used by the same guest or company □ *the presidential/bridal suite* □ *a suite of rooms* □ *an office suite.* **-2.** a set of matching pieces of furniture □ *a bathroom/dining room suite.*

suited [ˈsuːtəd] *adj* **-1. to be suited to sthg** to be suitable for sthg □ *activities suited to the needs of teenagers* □ *He's not really suited to teaching.* **-2. to be well suited** [couple] to have similar personalities and interests and be likely to have a good relationship □ *They seem well suited to each other.*

suitor [ˈsuːtər] *n* a man who wants to marry a particular woman (old-fashioned use).

sulfate US, **sulphate** GB [ˈsʌlfeɪt] *n* a salt formed from sulfuric acid.

sulfur US, **sulphur** GB [ˈsʌlfər] *n* a pale-yellow substance that burns with a bright flame and smells of rotten eggs. SYMBOL: S.

sulfuric acid US, **sulphuric acid** GB [sʌlˌfjʊərɪk-] *n* a strong acid. FORMULA: H_2SO_4.

sulk [sʌlk] ◇ *vi* to be silent and angry because one feels badly treated □ *Stop sulking!* ◇ *n* **to be in a sulk** to be sulking □ *He went into a sulk and refused to cooperate.*

sulky [ˈsʌlkɪ] (*compar* **sulkier**, *superl* **sulkiest**) *adj* [child, person] who often sulks or is sulking □ *She's in a sulky mood today.*

sullen [ˈsʌlən] *adj* [person] who is bad-tempered and says very little □ *a sullen expression.*

Sullivan [ˈsʌlɪvən], **Sir Arthur** (1842–1900) a British composer, who worked with the writer W. S. Gilbert on many famous operettas including *The Pirates of Penzance* and *The Mikado.*

sulphate *n* GB = **sulfate.**

sulphur *n* GB = **sulfur.**

sulphuric acid *n* GB = **sulfuric acid.**

sultan [ˈsʌltən] *n* a ruler in a Muslim country.

sultana [US sʌlˈtænə, GB -ˈtɑːnə] *n* GB a type of

small, seedless, dried, white grape used in cakes, puddings etc.

sultry [ˈsʌltrɪ] (*compar* **sultrier**, *superl* **sultriest**) *adj* **-1.** [weather, day, air] that feels hot and humid □ *The weather was hot and sultry.* **-2.** [woman, look, smile] that suggests strong sexual desire □ *She gave him a sultry smile.*

sum [sʌm] (*pt* & *pp* **summed**, *cont* **summing**) *n* **-1.** an amount of money □ *That's a very large sum of money.* **-2.** a simple calculation in arithmetic □ *I'm no good at doing sums.*

◆ **sum up** ◇ *vt sep* **to sum sthg up** [argument, speech, report] to give a summary of sthg □ *I can sum up his performance in one word: appalling.* ◇ *vi*: *The chairman summed up.*

Sumatra [suˈmɑːtrə] the second largest island of Indonesia. SIZE: 473,600 sq kms. POPULATION: 28,016,000.

summarily [US sʌˈmerəlɪ, GB ˈsʌmər-] *adv* **to be summarily dismissed/executed** to be dismissed/executed in a summary way.

summarize, -ise [ˈsʌməraɪz] ◇ *vt* [events, story] to make a summary of <sthg>. ◇ *vi*: *Allow me to summarize before we move on.*

summary [ˈsʌmərɪ] (*pl* **summaries**) ◇ *n* [of events, a story, the news] a short description of the main points of something □ *a news summary* □ *Fred gave us a brief summary of their conversation.* ◇ *adj* [dismissal, execution] that is carried out immediately, without attention to the usual rules, processes etc (formal use).

summer [ˈsʌmər] *n* the season between spring and autumn, usually the warmest time of the year □ *It has been one of the hottest summers on record.* □ *We went there last summer.* □ *In summer, temperatures can exceed 30 degrees.* □ *the summer vacation/weather/heat.*

summer camp *n* US a large camp where children spend their summer vacation together and where sporting and outdoor activities are organized for them.

summerhouse [ˈsʌmərhaʊs, *pl* -haʊzɪz] *n* a small building in a garden where one can sit and relax when it is warm in summer.

summer school *n* a course of lectures, talks etc held during the summer vacation at a university, college, or school.

summertime [ˈsʌmərtaɪm] ◇ *n* summer □ *The beach is packed in (the) summertime.* ◇ *adj*: *a series of summertime concerts.*

Summer Time *n* GB the period of time in summer when certain countries put their clocks forward an hour to get extra daylight in the evening.

summery [ˈsʌmərɪ] *adj* [clothes, weather, food] that is typical of or suitable for summer.

summing-up [ˌsʌmɪŋ-] (*pl* **summings-up**) *n* a summary of the evidence and arguments given by a judge at the end of a trial.

summit [ˈsʌmət] *n* **-1.** the highest point of a mountain □ *Hargreaves had finally reached the summit.* **-2.** POLITICS a meeting of heads of government to discuss international politics □ *All G7 members will be at the Moscow summit.* □ *a summit meeting.*

summon [ˈsʌmən] *vt* to officially order <sb>

to come to a place □ *He was summoned to the chairman's office.*

◆ **summon up** *vt sep* **to summon sthg up** [courage, energy, enthusiasm] to make an effort to show, have, or feel sthg □ *I couldn't even summon up the energy to get out of bed.*

summons ['sʌmənz] (*pl* **summonses**) ◇ *n* an order to appear in a court of law □ *a court summons.* ◇ *vt* to give or send <sb> a summons □ *He was summonsed to appear in court.*

sumo wrestling [ˌsuːmoʊ-] *n* a traditional form of wrestling in Japan, in which contestants try to push each other to the ground or out of the ring using the weight of their body in order to win.

sump [sʌmp] *n* GB the part of an engine that holds the oil.

sumptuous ['sʌmptʃuəs] *adj* [decor, building, feast] that is very impressive and expensive.

sum total *n* **the sum total of sthg** [of somebody's knowledge, effort, research] the complete amount of sthg, especially when it seems less than is expected or needed □ *Is this the sum total of what you achieved over your three-month study break?*

sun [sʌn] (*pt* & *pp* **sunned**, *cont* **sunning**) ◇ *n* -1. **the sun** the nearest star to the Earth, around which the Earth moves and from which it receives heat and light. -2. the light and heat from the sun □ *You'll get burned if you get too much sun.* □ *They were sitting in the sun.* ◇ *vt* **to sun oneself** to sit or lie in the light of the sun, especially to get a suntan.

Sun. *abbr of* **Sunday.**

sunbathe ['sʌnbeɪð] *vi* to sit or lie in the light of the sun, especially to get a suntan □ *I've been sunbathing on the beach.*

sunbeam ['sʌnbiːm] *n* a beam of light from the sun.

sunbed ['sʌnbed] *n* a kind of bed on which one lies under a sunlamp.

Sunbelt ['sʌnbelt]: **the Sunbelt** a region of the southern, and especially southwestern USA, where the weather is generally sunny.

sunblock ['sʌnblɒk] *n* a cream used on one's skin to protect it completely from the sun.

sunburn ['sʌnbɜːrn] *n* a condition in which one has sore red skin because one has spent too much time in the sun.

sunburned ['sʌnbɜːrnd], **sunburnt** ['sʌnbɜːrnt] *adj* [person, skin] that is suffering from sunburn □ *I got sunburned from lying on the beach.*

sun cream *n* a cream that one puts on one's skin to protect it against sunburn.

sundae ['sʌndeɪ] *n* a dish of ice cream with fruit, fruit juice, nuts etc □ *an ice-cream sundae.*

Sunday ['sʌndeɪ] *n* the day of the week between Saturday and Monday; *see also* **Friday.**

Sunday paper *n* a weekly newspaper published on Sunday that contains special sections, e.g. on the arts, finance, or politics.

Sunday school *n* a class organized on Sundays by a Christian church, in which children receive religious education.

sundial ['sʌndaɪəl] *n* a device that shows the time using a pointer that casts a shadow onto a flat base marked with the hours.

sundown ['sʌndaʊn] *n* the time in the evening when the sun disappears from the sky □ *I got home at/after sundown.*

sun-dried *adj* [tomatoes, raisins] that have been dried by the heat of the sun.

sundry ['sʌndrɪ] *adj* various (formal use) □ *sundry expense.* ■ **all and sundry** all kinds of people.

◆ **sundries** *npl* various small items that are not named separately (formal use).

sunflower ['sʌnflaʊər] *n* a tall plant with very large yellow flowers that is grown for its seeds, that are used to make cooking oil and can also be eaten □ *sunflower oil/seeds.*

sung [sʌŋ] *past participle of* **sing.**

sunglasses [US 'sʌnglæsəz, GB -glɑːs-] *npl* dark glasses worn to protect one's eyes from bright sunlight □ *a pair of sunglasses.*

sunhat ['sʌnhæt] *n* a hat with a broad brim that protects one's head and face from the sun.

sunk [sʌŋk] *past participle of* **sink.**

sunken ['sʌŋkən] *adj* -1. [ship, treasure] that has sunk to the bottom of the sea, a lake etc. -2. [garden, bath] that is built at a lower level than the area around it. -3. [cheeks, eyes] that appear hollow as a result of hunger, illness, old age etc.

sunlamp ['sʌnlæmp] *n* a lamp that produces ultraviolet light and is used to get a suntan.

sunlight ['sʌnlaɪt] *n* the light from the sun □ *'Do not place in direct sunlight.'*

sunlit ['sʌnlɪt] *adj* [garden, room] that is brightly lit by the sun □ *a beautiful sunlit scene.*

Sunni [US 'suːnɪ, GB 'sʊnɪ] (*pl* **Sunnis**) ◇ *n* a Muslim who belongs to a branch of Islam that believes only in the teachings and acts of Muhammad. ◇ *adj*: *a Sunni Muslim.*

sunny ['sʌnɪ] (*compar* **sunnier**, *superl* **sunniest**) *adj* -1. [day, room, garden] that has a lot of bright sunlight □ *They said it would be sunny today.* -2. [disposition, mood, smile] cheerful. -3. *phrase* **sunny side up** US [egg] fried on one side only.

sunray lamp ['sʌnreɪ-] *n* = **sunlamp.**

sunrise ['sʌnraɪz] *n* -1. the time in the morning when the sun first appears □ *at sunrise.* -2. the colors and light in the sky caused when the sun first appears in the morning □ *She stood staring at the sunrise.*

sunroof ['sʌnruːf] *n* a window or covering in the roof of a car that can be opened and closed to let air or light in.

sunset ['sʌnset] *n* -1. the time in the evening when the sun disappears from the sky □ *at sunset.* -2. the colors and light in the sky caused when the sun disappears from the sky in the evening □ *We saw some amazing sunsets in Egypt.*

sunshade ['sʌnʃeɪd] *n* an umbrella used to protect oneself from the sun, e.g. when sitting or lying somewhere.

sunshine ['sʌnʃaɪn] *n* the light and heat from the sun □ *We lay all day in the sunshine.*

sunspot ['sʌnspɒt] *n* -1. ASTRONOMY any of the small dark areas that can appear on the surface of the Sun. -2. a place in a sunny part of the world where people like to spend their vacations.

sunstroke ['sʌnstrəʊk] *n* a condition consisting of fever, weakness, and a headache that is caused by spending too much time in the sun.

suntan ['sʌntæn] ◇ *n* a brown color on one's skin that comes after one has been in the sun □ *He's got a wonderful suntan.* ◇ *comp* [cream, lotion, oil] that protects one against sunburn and helps to develop a suntan.

suntanned ['sʌntænd] *adj* [face, body, skin] that is darker than usual after being in the sun □ *You're looking very suntanned!*

suntrap ['sʌntræp] *n* a sheltered place that gets a lot of sunshine.

sun-up *n* US the time in the morning when the sun appears (informal use) □ *at sun-up.*

super ['suːpə^r] *adj* [meal, day, weather] that one thinks is very good (informal use) □ *You're coming? Oh, super!* □ *What a super idea!*

superabundance [ˌsuːpərə'bʌndəns] *n* a very large amount or quantity of something.

superannuation [ˌsuːpərænjʊ'eɪʃn] *n* money paid as a pension by the company or organization that one used to work for.

superb [suː'pɜː^rb] *adj* very good □ *The view was superb.* □ *She's a superb dancer.*

superbly [suː'pɜː^rblɪ] *adv* **superbly organized/ made etc** organized/made etc very well □ *She dealt with the whole thing superbly.*

Super Bowl *n* **the Super Bowl** the final game of the main championship in football in the USA.

❦ SUPER BOWL
The Super Bowl is a single football game that is played between the champions of the two main US leagues, or "conferences", of professional football. It takes place at the end of the season in late January each year, and huge numbers of Americans watch it on TV.

---

supercilious [ˌsuːpə^r'sɪlɪəs] *adj* [person] who seems to think they are better than other people.

superficial [ˌsuːpə^r'fɪʃl] *adj* -1. [person, friendship, feeling] that is not very serious or sincere (disapproving use) □ *a superficial smile* □ *I found his friends very superficial.* -2. [knowledge, inspection, treatment] that is not complete or detailed enough to be accurate □ *That's a highly superficial analysis of the situation.* -3. [resemblance, appearance] that seems real at first but is usually not □ *The apparent similarity between them is purely superficial.* □ *She puts on a superficial air of calm.* -4. [cut, damage] that is only on the surface and is not serious □ *Luckily the wound was only superficial.*

superficially [ˌsuːpə^r'fɪʃlɪ] *adv* -1. [resemble,

seem] a word used to show that something seems true but is not □ *Superficially, little had changed.* -2. [talk, treat] *see* **superficial.**

superfluous [suː'pɜː^rflʊəs] *adj* not relevant or necessary □ *I realized my presence had become superfluous.*

Superglue™ ['suːpə^rgluː] *n* a very strong glue.

superhuman [ˌsuːpə^r'hjuːmən] *adj* [strength, power, effort] that seems greater than what a normal human being is capable of.

superimpose [ˌsuːpərɪm'pəʊz] *vt* to put <sthg> over something else in such a way that both can be seen or heard □ *A musical soundtrack was superimposed on the original narrative.*

superintend [ˌsuːpərɪn'tend] *vt* [staff, project] to be in charge of and manage <sb/sthg>.

superintendent [ˌsuːpərɪn'tendənt] *n* -1. a person who is in charge of and manages a place (formal use). -2. GB a police officer next in rank above inspector.

superior [suː'pɪərɪə^r] ◇ *adj* -1. [team, forces, technology] that is of a higher standard □ *This movie is far superior to his first one.* -2. [product, make] that is of high quality □ *makers of superior cheeses.* -3. **a superior officer** an officer in the army, police etc who is of a higher rank than somebody else in the army, police etc □ *All personnel must salute their superior officers.* -4. [person] who acts as if they are better than other people □ *I don't like his superior manner.* ◇ *n* [in a company, army, police force] a person of higher rank □ *Mrs Hoffman is my immediate superior.*

Superior: **Lake Superior** the largest of the Great Lakes between Canada and the USA.

superiority [suːˌpɪərɪ'ɒrətɪ] *n*: *see* **superior** □ *a feeling of superiority.*

superlative [suː'pɜː^rlətɪv] ◇ *adj* [performance, achievement, shot] that one thinks is extremely good □ *The quality of the recording is superlative.* ◇ *n* GRAMMAR the form of adjectives and adverbs that expresses the highest degree of comparison, e.g. "the tallest" or "the least expensive".

Superman ['suːpə^rmæn] a US cartoon character. He is very strong and can fly, and he uses these abilities to fight crime.

supermarket ['suːpə^rmɑː^rkət] *n* a large store that sells food and household goods where customers serve themselves and pay on their way to the exit.

supernatural [ˌsuːpə^r'nætʃrəl] ◇ *adj* [powers, forces, phenomena] that cannot be explained by natural or physical laws but that some people believe to exist. ◇ *n* **the supernatural** supernatural events, powers etc.

superpower ['suːpə^rpaʊə^r] *n* a nation that has great political, military, and economic power □ *the world's two great superpowers.*

supersede [ˌsuːpə^r'siːd] *vt* [equipment, method] to take the place of <sthg older or less efficient> □ *This order supersedes all other orders.*

supersonic [ˌsuːpə^r'sɒnɪk] *adj* [plane, travel] that is faster than the speed of sound.

superstar ['suːpə^rstɑː^r] *n* a very famous person, e.g. an actor or a musician.

superstition [ˌsuːpəʳˈstɪʃn] *n* a belief that is not based on reason or fact but on old ideas, e.g. that certain things cause good or bad luck.

superstitious [ˌsuːpəʳˈstɪʃəs] *adj* [idea, belief] based on superstition □ *She's very superstitious about black cats and things like that.*

superstore [ˈsuːpəʳstɔːʳ] *n* GB a very large supermarket or store, especially one built outside a town.

superstructure [ˈsuːpəʳstrʌktʃəʳ] *n* the parts of a ship that are above the main deck; the parts of a building that are above the ground.

supertanker [ˈsuːpəʳtæŋkəʳ] *n* a very large oil tanker.

supervise [ˈsuːpəʳvaɪz] *vt* [children, staff] to watch <sb> to make sure that they behave or work properly or safely; [work, research] to be in charge of the people doing <sthg> and to make sure that they do it properly.

supervision [ˌsuːpəʳˈvɪʒn] *n*: *see* **supervise** □ *The old people in our care require constant supervision.*

supervisor [ˈsuːpəʳvaɪzəʳ] *n* a person whose job is to supervise somebody or something.

supper [ˈsʌpəʳ] *n* a light meal eaten in the evening □ *What are you having for supper?*

supplant [US səˈplænt, GB -ˈplɑːnt] *vt* [manager, method, machinery] to take the place of <sb/sthg>.

supple [ˈsʌpl] *adj* -1. [person] who can bend and move easily □ *My body is not as supple as it used to be.* -2. [material] that is soft but strong and can bend without breaking or cracking □ *soft, supple leather.*

supplement [*n* ˈsʌpləmənt, *vb* ˈsʌpləment] ◇ *n* -1. [to a price, income, diet] something that is added to something else, especially in order to make it complete □ *A supplement is charged for occupying a single room.* □ *a food/vitamin supplement.* -2. an extra section that is added to a book or newspaper □ *a Sunday supplement.* ◇ *vt* [salary, diet] to add something to <sthg> so that it is enough or complete □ *I work nights to supplement my income.*

supplementary [ˌsʌpləˈmentərɪ] *adj* [question, income] that is additional to what exists already.

supplier [səˈplaɪəʳ] *n* a person or organization that supplies goods or services to others.

supply [səˈplaɪ] (*pl* **supplies**, *pt* & *pp* **supplied**) ◇ *n* -1. [of food, water, money] an amount of something that is available for somebody to use and that is replaced regularly □ *the nation's supply of oil/oil supply* □ *We have a regular supply of stationery.* ■ **to be in short supply** to be hard to find because there is not enough available □ *Fresh water is in pretty short supply in this area.* -2. a system or network that supplies something, especially basic services □ *The water/electricity supply has been cut off.* -3. ECONOMICS the amount of goods that can be produced and put on sale □ *the laws of supply and demand.* ◇ *vt* to make <sthg> available to somebody

e.g. by giving or selling it to them □ *The company supplies machinery to the textile industry.* □ *If you supply the food, I'll bring the drink.* □ *I shall be happy to supply you with further details.* □ *The pump supplies the town with fresh water.* □ *All the toys are supplied with batteries.*

◆ **supplies** *npl* the food, water, and equipment needed by a group of people, e.g. a military expedition □ *They sent Beam out to get supplies*

supply teacher *n* GB a teacher who works in different schools, replacing other teachers when they are absent.

support [səˈpɔːʳt] ◇ *vt* -1. [leader, party, aim] to approve of and encourage <sb/sthg> □ *We support her in her decision.* □ *The Democrats will support the bill.* -2. [roof, weight] to hold up <sthg> from below □ *the pillars that support the ceiling* □ *She held on to the table to support herself.* -3. [friend, colleague] to help <sb> by being kind to them when they are unhappy □ *Luckily her family have supported her throughout the divorce.* -4. [family, company] to provide enough money for <a person or organization> to live on or continue to exist □ *She has three children to support.* □ *The charity is supported by voluntary contributions.* -5. [theory, claim, statement] to show that <sthg> is true □ *There is no evidence to support this view.* -6. SPORT to follow the progress of <a team> and go to matches to encourage them to win □ *Dave supports Manchester United.*

◇ *n* -1. [for a party, movement, campaign] help and encouragement given to a person, organization, or action □ *The strike has widespread support.* □ *She's been a great support to me.* □ *I went along to give her moral support.* -2. money that is provided for a person or organization in order to help them when they are in financial difficulty □ *They depend on the government for financial support.* -3. [for a belief, view] something that helps to show that something is true □ *The investigation found no support for this view.* -4. [for a structure, weight] an object that holds up something heavy from below □ *concrete supports* □ *The upper floors need extra support.*

supporter [səˈpɔːʳtəʳ] *n* [of politician, aims, bill] a person who supports somebody or something □ *He's always been one of Major's strongest supporters.* □ *Supporters of the bill crowded into the lobby.*

support group *n* a group of people who have the same problem, e.g. an illness or fear, and who meet together to help each other to deal with their difficulties.

supportive [səˈpɔːʳtɪv] *adj* [person] who is kind and helpful to somebody when they are unhappy or in difficulty □ *Everybody's been very supportive toward me.*

suppose [səˈpəʊz] ◇ *vt* -1. **to suppose (that)...** to think that something is probably true □ *I suppose it's too far to go and see them.* □ *I suppose you think that's funny!* □ *I don't suppose you've ever experienced anything like this before.* ■ **you don't suppose...** a phrase used when asking somebody's opinion □ *You don't sup-*

pose anything has happened to them, do you? **-2. to suppose (that)...** to admit something that one does not really want to admit □ I suppose you're right. **-3.** phrases **I suppose so** used when one thinks something is true, but is not certain; used when one is agreeing with something unwillingly □ "Is he right?" — "Yes, I suppose so." □ There were, I suppose, about 50 people there. □ Oh, all right then, I suppose so. ■ **I suppose not** a phrase used when agreeing with a negative statement □ "It can't be easy bringing up a family on your own." — "I suppose not." □ "Surely there's no point continuing the search after 24 hours?" — "No, I suppose not."

◇ conj = **supposing**.

supposed [sə'pəʊzd] adj **-1.** [illness, wealth] a word used to show that one does not believe something that somebody says □ I don't believe her supposed boyfriend actually exists. **-2. to be supposed to do sthg** to be expected to do sthg, especially when this does not happen □ He was supposed to arrive at eight o'clock. **-3.** to be obliged by a rule or law to do sthg □ You are not supposed to go in there. **-4. to be supposed to be** to be generally believed to be □ This restaurant is supposed to be very good.

supposedly [sə'pəʊzədlɪ] adv a word used to show that one does not believe something that somebody says is true or exists □ Supposedly, he was in America at the time. □ Her father's supposedly ill/very rich.

supposing [sə'pəʊzɪŋ] conj a word used by somebody to ask what would happen if a particular situation were to take place or to be true □ Supposing oil prices go down? □ Supposing he's not telling the truth?

supposition [ˌsʌpə'zɪʃn] n an idea that one supposes to be true □ a belief based on supposition.

suppository [US sə'pɒzətɔːrɪ, GB -ərɪ] (pl suppositories) n a form of medicine that is put into the rectum or vagina.

suppress [sə'pres] vt **-1.** [uprising, rebellion] to prevent <a revolt> from happening or continuing successfully, usually by using force □ The pro-democracy protest was violently suppressed. **-2.** [news, report] to prevent <information> from being publicly known □ The documents have been officially suppressed. **-3.** [anger, joy, smile] to stop oneself from feeling or showing <an emotion> □ She could barely suppress a smile.

suppression [sə'preʃn] n: see **suppress**.

suppressor [sə'presər] n a device that prevents a piece of electrical equipment from causing radio or television interference.

supranational [ˌsuːprə'næʃnəl] adj [organization, agreement] that is connected with or includes more than one nation.

supremacy [sʊ'preməsɪ] n the state of being supreme □ Each nation tried to gain supremacy over the other. □ The 1990s have seen a race for technological supremacy.

supreme [sʊ'priːm] adj **-1.** [commander, court] that is highest in rank, power, or impor-

tance. **-2.** [performance, achievement] very great □ It took a supreme effort by everyone to meet the deadline.

Supreme Court n **-1. the Supreme Court** the highest court in the USA. **-2.** in Australia and the USA, the highest court in each state.

SUPREME COURT
The Supreme Court is the highest federal (national) court in the United States. Its nine members, or "justices", are appointed by the President for life. Its role is to approve or reject national and state laws, and to interpret the Constitution.

supremely [sʊ'priːmlɪ] adv **supremely gifted/important etc** extremely gifted/important etc □ She seems a supremely confident woman.

supremo [sʊ'priːməʊ] (pl supremos) n GB the most powerful or important person in a particular organization (informal use).

Supt. abbr of **superintendent**.

surcharge ['sɜːtʃɑːdʒ] ◇ n an amount of money to be paid in addition to the usual charge □ They imposed a 7% surcharge on domestic flights. ◇ vt to make <sb> pay a surcharge.

sure [ʃʊər] ◇ adj **-1. to be sure** to know something is true or correct, and have no doubts about this; to know exactly what one feels about something □ I'm sure (that) I've seen him before. □ Are you quite sure about this? □ He'll come, I'm sure of it. □ He's not sure whether he really wants to get married. □ I think I locked the door, but I can't be sure. ■ **to make sure (that)...** to check that a particular thing has happened or is true; to do something so that a particular thing will definitely happen □ I'll just make sure the oven is switched off. □ Make sure you get to bed early, you have exams tomorrow. **-2. to be sure of sthg** to be certain to get sthg □ With all her experience she can be sure of a good job. **-3. it's sure to rain tomorrow** I feel certain that it will rain tomorrow □ The dollar is sure to fall soon. ■ **you're sure to like him** I feel certain that you will like him □ You know Jim, he's sure to be there early. ■ **be sure to do sthg** don't forget to do sthg □ Be sure to take an umbrella with you. **-4. to be sure of oneself** to be self-confident □ He seems very sure of himself.

◇ adv **-1.** a word used to show agreement (informal use) □ "Do you want to go out tonight?" — "Sure!" **-2.** US a word used for emphasis (informal use) □ He sure can cook!

◆ **for sure** adv used to emphasize that something is true or will happen □ I'll finish it tomorrow for sure. □ No one knows for sure when he's coming back to work.

◆ **sure enough** adv used to confirm that what one expected to happen did happen □ I thought she might phone and, sure enough, she did.

◆ **sure thing** excl US a phrase used to show agreement (informal use) □ "Come and see me next week." — "Sure thing."

surefire [ˈʃʊərˌfaɪər] *adj* **a surefire success/cure etc** a success/cure etc that is certain to be effective □ *That is a surefire way of getting yourself killed!*

surefooted [ˌʃʊərˈfʊtəd] *adj* [person, animal] that can walk on uneven ground without falling.

surely [ˈʃʊəlɪ] *adv* a word used when one believes that something is true and wants somebody else to agree □ *Surely you can't be serious.* □ *That was a mistake, surely.*

surety [ˈʃʊərətɪ] *n* something valuable such as money or jewelry that somebody gives as a guarantee that they will do what they have said, e.g. appear in court or pay a debt.

surf [sɜːrf] ◇ *n* the white foam formed by waves as they come toward the shore. ◇ *vi* to ride on waves as they come toward the shore, using a surfboard. ◇ *vt* **to surf the Internet** OR **Net** to use the Internet by visiting lots of different sites on it.

surface [ˈsɜːrfəs] ◇ *n* **-1.** [of a road, table, the ground] the outer part of something □ *the polished surface of the desk* □ *the Earth's surface.* **-2.** [of the water, lake] the top part of an area or mass of liquid □ *The submarine/diver came to the surface.* **-3.** a flat area that one can use to work on or put things on □ *Roll the dough out on a smooth clean surface.* □ *a work/kitchen surface.* **-4.** [of a situation, problem, person] the part of something that can be seen easily, that is different from the part that is hidden and not obvious □ *We need to look beyond the surface and find the real causes of crime.* ■ **on the surface** superficially □ *On the surface she seems nice enough.* ■ **below** OR **beneath the surface** not immediately visible or obvious □ *There was a feeling of anxiety below the surface.* ■ **to scratch the surface of sthg** to deal with only a very small part of sthg □ *The discussion barely scratched the surface of the problem.* ◇ *vi* **-1.** [swimmer, submarine] to rise to the water's surface □ *Whales have to surface to breathe.* **-2.** [problem, feeling, rumor] to become generally known □ *The problem only surfaced when we started looking at the proofs.* **-3.** [person] to get out of bed, especially after being in bed for a long time (humorous use) □ *They finally surfaced at about 2pm.*

surface mail *n* the system of sending letters and parcels by land or sea.
NOTE: Compare **airmail.**

surface-to-air *adj* **a surface-to-air missile** a missile that is fired from land or sea at an aircraft or at another missile.

surfboard [ˈsɜːrfbɔːrd] *n* a long narrow board that one stands or lies on when surfing.

surfeit [ˈsɜːrfət] *n* **a surfeit of sthg** too much of sthg (formal use) □ *a surfeit of wine/chocolate.*

surfer [ˈsɜːrfər] *n* a person who goes surfing.

surfie [ˈsɜːrfɪ] *n* AUS a person who spends a lot of time surfing (informal use).

surfing [ˈsɜːrfɪŋ] *n* the sport of riding waves as they come toward the shore, using a surfboard □ *It's a great place to go surfing.*

surge [sɜːrdʒ] ◇ *n* **-1.** a sudden forward movement, e.g. of a group of people □ *There was a*

surge for the exit. **-2.** a sudden increase in a particular feeling □ *He felt a surge of pride/pain/anger.* **-3.** a sudden big increase □ *a big surge in demand* □ *a sudden surge of activity.* ◇ *vi* **-1.** [people, vehicles] to move forward suddenly in a large group; [water] to move forward suddenly and powerfully. **-2.** [anger, guilt] to be felt suddenly and powerfully by somebody. **-3.** [interest, support, sales] to increase suddenly by a large amount.

surgeon [ˈsɜːrdʒən] *n* a doctor who performs operations in a hospital.

Surgeon General *n* **the Surgeon General** the government official who is in charge of public health in the USA.

surgery [ˈsɜːrdʒərɪ] (*pl* **surgeries**) *n* **-1.** the act or process of performing a medical operation □ *The patient will require major/minor surgery on her leg.* **-2.** GB the place where a doctor or dentist treats their patients □ *a doctor's surgery* □ *Surgery hours are from nine to four.* **-3.** GB the hours when people can see their member of parliament □ *Mr Bryant holds a regular Saturday surgery.*

surgical [ˈsɜːrdʒɪkl] *adj* **-1.** [instrument, operation, skill] that is connected with or is used in medical operations □ *the surgical removal of the growth* □ *a pair of surgical gloves.* **-2.** [support, stocking, boot] that is worn as a treatment for a medical condition.

surgical spirit *n* GB a kind of alcohol that is used for cleaning wounds.

Surinam [US ˈsʊərənɑːm, GB -ˈnæm] a country in northern South America, between Guyana and French Guiana. SIZE: 163,265 sq kms. POPULATION: 400,000 (*Surinamese*). CAPITAL: Paramaribo. LANGUAGE: Dutch. CURRENCY: Surinamese guilder.

surly [ˈsɜːrlɪ] (*compar* **surlier,** *superl* **surliest**) *adj* [voice, manner, person] rude, bad-tempered, and unfriendly □ *Their staff can be very surly at times.*

surmise [sərˈmaɪz] *vt* to guess <sthg> (formal use).

surmount [sərˈmaʊnt] *vt* [obstacle, disadvantage] to deal with <a problem> successfully □ *There are several difficulties which we will have to surmount first.*

surname [ˈsɜːrneɪm] *n* the last part of one's name that other people in one's family also have □ *What's your surname?*

surpass [US srˈpæs, GB səˈpɑːs] *vt* [expectations, target, record] to go beyond <sthg> and be even better or greater (formal use) □ *The result surpassed my wildest hopes.*

surplus [ˈsɜːrpləs] ◇ *n* an amount of something that is more than is needed and can be sold or got rid of. ◇ *adj: They export their surplus agricultural produce.* □ *As a result, 360 staff are now surplus to requirements.*

surprise [sərˈpraɪz] ◇ *n* **-1.** an unexpected event, especially a pleasant one □ *The news came as a surprise to everyone.* □ *What a pleasant surprise!* □ *Surprise! You thought we'd forgotten, didn't you?* **-2.** the feeling caused when something unexpected happens □ *Much to* my surprise, she agreed. □ He looked up in surprise. ■ **to take sb by surprise** to do something that sb does not expect; to do something at a time when sb does not expect it □ Her reaction took me completely by surprise.

◇ vt -1. to cause surprise to <sb> □ It surprised me that they didn't give her the job. -2. to attack or catch <sb> when they are not expecting it □ They came home early and surprised a burglar in their living room.

surprised [sər'praɪzd] adj [person] who feels surprise □ I was surprised at his attitude. □ I'm not surprised (that) you're tired after all that! □ He was surprised to hear it wasn't ready yet. ■ **I wouldn't be surprised (if...)** I think it is likely (that...) □ I wouldn't be surprised if they'd forgotten.

surprising [sər'praɪzɪŋ] adj [news, event, success] that comes as a surprise or causes one to feel surprised □ It's hardly surprising Lucy's sick, considering the stress she's under.

surprisingly [sər'praɪzɪŋlɪ] adv a word used to show that one thinks that something is surprising □ Surprisingly, they all arrived on time. □ The idea was surprisingly successful.

surreal [sə'riːəl] adj [event, situation, atmosphere] that is strange and more like a dream than reality.

Surrealism [sə'riːəlɪzm] n a style in art and literature in which ideas and images are put together in a strange and unexpected way.

Surrealist [sə'riːəlɪst] ◇ adj that is connected with Surrealism □ a Surrealist painting/image. ◇ n a writer or artist who produces Surrealist works.

surrender [sə'rendər] ◇ vt [rights, weapons, passport] to give <sthg> to somebody else either because one wants to or because one has been forced to. ◇ vi -1. [to the enemy, one's opponent, an army] to stop fighting and show somebody that one accepts that one has been defeated by them □ The hijackers surrendered to the police. -2. [to a temptation, one's fate] to allow something such as a feeling to gain control over one □ I surrendered to temptation and had another piece of cake. ◇ n an act of surrendering □ The town was starved into surrender.

surreptitious [US ˌsɜːrəp'tɪʃəs, GB ˌsʌr-] adj [visit, meeting] that is done in secret because one does not want other people to know about it □ He took a surreptitious look at his watch.

Surrey [US 'sɜːrɪ, GB 'sʌrɪ] a county in southeastern England, southwest of London. SIZE: 1,679 sq kms. POPULATION: 999,752. ADMINISTRATIVE CENTER: Kingston upon Thames.

surrogate [US 'sʌrəgət, GB 'sʌr-] ◇ n a person or thing that takes the place of somebody or something else □ Watching movies became a surrogate for taking part in the real world. ◇ adj: He was like a surrogate brother to me.

surrogate mother n a woman who has a baby for another woman who is unable to get pregnant.

surround [sə'raʊnd] ◇ vt -1. to be all around <a place> □ The garden is surrounded by trees.

-2. to position people all around <a person or place>, usually in order to attack them or take them prisoner □ They were surrounded by enemy soldiers. -3. to exist around <a person or topic> □ Controversy surrounds the question of gun control. ◇ n a border around the edge of something, e.g. a fireplace.

surrounding [sə'raʊndɪŋ] adj [countryside, army, controversy] that surrounds a person, place, or thing □ There are lots of interesting places to visit in the surrounding area.

◆ **surroundings** npl everything that surrounds a person or place □ The hotel is set in beautiful surroundings. □ After a while I got used to my new surroundings.

surtax ['sɜːrtæks] n an additional tax on high incomes.

surveillance [sər'veɪləns] n a careful secret watch on a person or place, often over a long period of time □ The police kept him under close surveillance.

survey [n 'sɜːrveɪ, vb sər'veɪ] ◇ vt -1. [view, scene, future] to examine and consider <sb/sthg> as a whole □ He stepped back to survey the painting. -2. [population, group, trend] to find out <the opinions> of a large number of people by asking them a list of questions □ 60% of women surveyed were against the measure. -3. [land, building] to examine <sthg> carefully and make a report of its measurements and condition □ They had the house independently surveyed before buying it. ◇ n [of a population, building] the act of surveying something □ They carried out a survey of retail prices. □ an aerial survey of the area.

surveyor [sər'veɪər] n a person whose job is to survey land or buildings.

survival [sər'vaɪvl] n -1. the act or process of surviving □ the survival of the fittest. -2. something that has continued to exist from an earlier time □ The custom is a survival from the Victorian era.

survive [sər'vaɪv] ◇ vt -1. [war, disaster, illness] to continue to live or exist after <a difficult or dangerous experience> □ The company managed to survive the recession. □ Those who survived the attack died later from starvation. -2. [person] to continue to live after <sb> has died □ She is survived by two sons. ◇ vi -1. [person] to stay alive in spite of danger, illness, accidents etc; [company, project] to continue to exist in spite of difficulties, especially lack of money or food □ They survived for four days in the lifeboat. -2. to deal successfully with a difficult situation (informal use) □ How will we survive without you?

◆ **survive on** vt fus **to survive on sthg** [on food, money] to live using sthg, especially when this is not much or not enough □ How can they survive on so little? □ We should have just enough money to survive on.

survivor [sər'vaɪvər] n -1. a person who has survived a dangerous situation □ the survivors of the accident/death camps. -2. a person who is able to continue successfully in spite of difficulties □ She's a born survivor.

susceptible [sə'septəbl] adj -1. **to be suscep-**

tible to sthg [to pressure, flattery] to be easily influenced by sthg □ *Caroline is extremely susceptible to criticism.* **-2.** [to infection, disease, injury] likely to be affected by something □ *Young babies tend to be very susceptible to infection.*

sushi ['suːʃi] *n* a Japanese dish consisting of pieces of raw fish.

suspect [*vb* sə'spekt, *adj* & *n* 'sʌspekt] ◇ *vt* **-1.** [motives, theory] to doubt the truth of <sthg> □ *You surely don't suspect his motives in offering to help?* **-2. to suspect (that)...** to think that something probably exists, especially something bad □ *I suspect he knew all along.* □ *The press suspected a cover-up.* **-3.** to think that <sb> is guilty of doing something dishonest □ *I suspect the butler.* □ *Hudson is suspected of lying to the election committee.*
◇ *adj* [package, device, behavior] that makes people suspect that something illegal or dangerous is intended □ *All suspect packages should be reported immediately to the police.*
◇ *n* a person who is suspected of something, usually a crime □ *McClure remains the chief suspect in the investigation.*

suspend [sə'spend] *vt* **-1.** [object] to hang <sthg> from above □ *A lamp was suspended from the ceiling.* **-2.** [work, service] to stop <sthg> happening for a period of time □ *The regime has suspended the repayment of foreign debts.* **-3.** [employee, member, player] to remove <sb> from their job, club, or other organization for a period of time; [child, pupil] to remove <sb> from school or college for a period of time as a punishment □ *The officers have been suspended from their duties during the inquiry.* □ *The college suspended both students for violent behavior.*

suspended animation [sə,spendəd-] *n* a state in which the main functions of a body are slowed down for a time, e.g. in hibernation.

suspended sentence *n* a prison sentence that the offender does not serve unless they commit another crime within a certain period of time.

suspender belt [sə'spendər-] *n* GB a piece of underwear for women that is worn around their waist and that suspenders are attached to.

suspenders [sə'spendərz] *npl* **-1.** US [for men] a pair of straps worn over the shoulders and attached to trousers to keep the trousers up. **-2.** GB [for women] straps for holding stockings up.

suspense [sə'spens] *n* a state of excitement or anxiety caused by uncertainty about what will happen next □ *The suspense in his movies is amazing.* □ *I can hardly bear the suspense.* ■ **to keep sb in suspense** to keep sb in a state of excitement by not telling them something that they want to know □ *Well, don't keep us in suspense, what did he say?*

suspension [sə'spenʃn] *n* **-1.** [of work, an employee, pupil] *see* **suspend** □ *One more infringement will result in his automatic suspension from the team.* **-2.** AUTO the system of springs that support the body of a vehicle on its wheels

and help to give a smooth ride over uneven surfaces.

suspension bridge *n* a bridge that is supported by cables attached to towers.

suspicion [sə'spɪʃn] *n* **-1.** a feeling, not based on fact, that somebody cannot be trusted □ *His strange behavior aroused her suspicion.* □ *She looked at him with suspicion.* ■ **to be under suspicion** to be suspected of something, usually a crime □ *The driver is under suspicion of having been involved in the theft.* **-2.** an idea that somebody is being dishonest or that something is wrong □ *I had a growing suspicion that he wasn't telling the truth.* □ *I don't know who is responsible, but I have my suspicions.*

suspicious [sə'spɪʃəs] *adj* **-1.** [person] who has suspicions; who tends not to trust people □ *I'm suspicious of his motives.* □ *She gave him a suspicious look.* **-2.** [behavior, package] that causes one to be suspicious □ *a suspicious-looking character* □ *If you see anything suspicious, let me know.* □ *He was found hanged in suspicious circumstances.*

suspiciously [sə'spɪʃəslɪ] *adv* [ask, behave] *see* **suspicious** □ *Phil's been acting very suspiciously of late.*

Sussex ['sʌsəks] *n* a county in southeastern England, divided into East and West Sussex. SIZE: 3,784 sq kms. POPULATION: 1,412,100. ADMINISTRATIVE CENTERS: Lewes, Chichester.

sustain [sə'steɪn] *vt* **-1.** [interest, activity, rate] to maintain <sthg> over a long period □ *If the present level of growth is sustained...* □ *a sustained period of pressure.* **-2.** [person] to keep <sb> alive; to help or encourage <sb> □ *They had only bread and water to sustain them.* □ *It was only their belief in God that sustained them.* **-3.** [injury, damage] to suffer <sthg> □ *Fortunately the passengers sustained only minor injuries.* □ *The Russian army sustained huge casualties.* **-4.** to support <a weight> (formal use) □ *The roof couldn't sustain our weight and fell in.*

sustainable [sə'steɪnəbl] *adj* ECOLOGY [source, forest] that involves using natural products or kinds of energy in ways that do not harm the environment.

sustenance ['sʌstənəns] *n* the food and drink that a person or animal needs to remain healthy (formal use).

suture ['suːtʃər] *n* a stitch used to sew up a wound.

svelte [svelt] *adj* [person, appearance] slim and graceful.

Svengali [sven'gɑːlɪ] *n* somebody who has too much power and influence over another person, usually encouraging them to act in a bad way.

SW -1. *abbr of* **short wave.** **-2.** *abbr of* **southwest.**

swab [swɒb] *n* a piece of cotton used for cleaning wounds or taking samples of body fluids.

swagger ['swægər] ◇ *n* a way of walking in which one swings one's body from side to side, usually as a sign that one is very confident and pleased with oneself □ *He walked* with a swagger. ◇ *vi* to walk with a swagger □ *There was Toby, swaggering down the street in a top hat.*

Swahili [swəˈhiːlɪ] ◇ *n* -1. a member of an African people living in Zanzibar and the coastal regions of Tanzania and Kenya. -2. a language spoken in East and Central Africa. ◇ *adj*: *Swahili cooking/poetry.*

swallow [ˈswɒloʊ] ◇ *vt* -1. [food, drink, pill] to pass <sthg> from the mouth toward the stomach by a muscular action in the throat □ *She swallowed the whiskey in one gulp.* -2. [story, excuse, lie] to believe <sthg that is not true> without doubting it □ *I found his story hard to swallow.* -3. [anger, tears] to stop oneself from showing <sthg> □ *She had to swallow her pride and accept his offer.*
◇ *vi* to move the muscles in one's throat to swallow something.
◇ *n* -1. a small bird with pointed wings and a forked tail that builds a nest of mud. -2. [of food, drink] the act of swallowing something.

swam [swæm] *past tense of* **swim**.

swamp [swɒmp] ◇ *n* an area of land that is always fully or partly covered with water. ◇ *vt* -1. [boat, building, town] to cover <an object or place> with water, often causing damage □ *The wave completely swamped the small dinghy.* -2. **to be swamped with sthg** [with work, calls, tourists] to have too much or too many of sthg to deal with at the same time □ *The town is swamped with tourists in summer.*

swan [swɒn] *n* a large white bird with a long neck that lives on rivers or lakes.

swap [swɒp] (*pt* & *pp* **swapped**, *cont* **swapping**) ◇ *vt* -1. **to swap sthg with sb** to give sthg to sb and get something else instead □ *He swapped places with his sister.* □ *We swapped jobs.* ■ **to swap two things over** OR **around** to exchange the places of two things □ *She swapped their glasses around when he left the room.* -2. **to swap sthg for sthg** to replace sthg with sthg □ *He swapped his car for a computer.* ◇ *vi*: *Her chair was too big, and mine was too small, so we decided to swap.* ◇ *n* the act of swapping something □ *A new bike for an old camera? — That's a good swap.*

swarm [swɔːrm] ◇ *n* -1. [of bees, wasps] a large group of insects that are flying together. -2. **a swarm of people** a large group of people who are moving all the time □ *She was surrounded by a swarm of admirers.* ◇ *vi* -1. [bees, wasps] to fly in a swarm. -2. [people] to fill a place and move around it in a swarm. -3. **to be swarming** [room, town] to be full of people or animals moving around □ *The streets were swarming with tourists.*

swarthy [ˈswɔːrðɪ] (*compar* **swarthier**, *superl* **swarthiest**) *adj* [person, face, skin] rather dark.

swashbuckling [ˈswɒʃbʌklɪŋ] *adj* [movie, story] that is full of adventure, excitement, and men who fight with swords.

swastika [ˈswɒstɪkə] *n* an ancient sign that consists of a cross with each end bent at a

right angle, used as the symbol of the Nazi Party.

swat [swɒt] (*pt* & *pp* **swatted**, *cont* **swatting**) *vt* [fly, bee] to hit <a flying insect> quickly with one's hand or a flat object in order to kill it.

swatch [swɒtʃ] *n* a small piece of cloth, used as a sample.

swathe [sweɪð] *n* [of grass, forest, land] a large area of land □ *Fires damaged huge swathes of southern Spain.*

swathed [sweɪðd] *adj* **to be swathed in sthg** [in cloth, bandages] to be wrapped in sthg (literary use) □ *She was swathed in furs.*

swatter [ˈswɒtər] *n* a tool for swatting insects □ *a fly swatter.*

sway [sweɪ] ◇ *vt* -1. [branch, pole, one's hips] to make <sthg> move slowly from side to side □ *They swayed their bodies in time to the music.* -2. to influence <sb>, especially by giving a clever speech or making false promises □ *His plea for mercy did not sway the judge.* ◇ *vi*: *The trees swayed in the breeze.* ◇ *n* (formal use) **to come under the sway of sb/sthg** to come under the control or influence of sb/sthg. ■ **to hold sway (over sb/sthg)** to be in a position of power or influence (over sb/sthg).

Swaziland [ˈswɑːzɪlænd] a country in southeastern Africa, between South Africa and Mozambique. SIZE: 17,363 sq kms. POPULATION: 800,000 (*Swazis*). CAPITAL: Mbabane. LANGUAGE: English. CURRENCY: lilangeni.

swear [sweər] (*pt* **swore**, *pp* **sworn**) ◇ *vt* -1. **to swear (that)...** to formally promise that one will do something □ *I swore (that) I'd never make the same mistake again.* □ *I swear to avenge my father's death.* ■ **to swear allegiance/loyalty to sb** to formally promise in public that one will show allegiance/loyalty to sb. ■ **to swear an oath** to make a formal promise in public □ *He swore an oath of allegiance to the party.* -2. LAW **to swear to tell the truth** to swear in court that one will tell the truth □ *I swear to tell the truth, the whole truth, and nothing but the truth.* -3. **to swear (that)...** to state that something is true in a way that shows how strongly one feels about it (informal use) □ *I swear I'll strangle that cat one day.* □ *Monday? I could have sworn it was Tuesday today!*
◇ *vi* -1. to state something firmly □ *"Are you sure?" — "Yes, I swear."* -2. to use swearwords, especially when angry □ *It's rude to swear.*
◆ **swear by** *vt fus* **to swear by sthg** [remedy, method] to use and trust sthg because one believes it works □ *My mother always swears by these throat pastilles.*
◆ **swear in** *vt sep* **to swear sb in** [president, jury, witness] to make sb swear an oath before taking up an official position □ *The new president was sworn in yesterday.*

swearword [ˈsweərwɜːrd] *n* a word that is considered offensive.

sweat [swet] ◇ *n* -1. the clear salty liquid that comes out of a person's skin when they are hot □ *I woke up covered in sweat.* □ *He had sweat pouring down his back.* -2. **to be a sweat**

to be unpleasant hard work (informal use) □ *Roofing is a real sweat.* **-3. to be in a sweat** to be very anxious about something (informal use) □ *I was in a real sweat about it.* ◇ *vi* **-1.** to have sweat coming out of one's skin □ *She was sweating from the intense heat.* **-2.** to worry (informal use) □ *Don't tell them yet; let's make them sweat for a while.*

sweatband ['swetbænd] *n* a piece of cloth worn around one's wrist or forehead when playing sport or exercising to prevent sweat from getting into one's eyes or to wipe it away.

sweater ['swetər] *n* a piece of clothing, usually made of wool, that covers the upper part of one's body and one's arms.

sweatshirt ['swetʃɜːrt] *n* a thick cotton pullover with long sleeves and a soft lining on the inside.

sweatshop ['swetʃɒp] *n* a factory or workshop where people work long hours for low pay in poor conditions.

sweatsuit ['swetsuːt] *n* US a set of warm loose clothes made of soft thick cotton, worn to do sports in or to relax in.

sweaty ['sweti] (*compar* **sweatier**, *superl* **sweatiest**) *adj* **-1.** [skin, body, clothing] that is covered in sweat; that smells of sweat □ *We get very sweaty playing squash.* **-2.** [place, activity] that causes somebody to sweat □ *I don't want to go to some sweaty nightclub.*

swede [swiːd] *n* GB a large round root vegetable that is brown or purple outside and yellow inside.

Swede *n* a person who comes from Sweden.

Sweden ['swiːdn] a country in Scandinavia, on the Baltic Sea. It is a neutral country. SIZE: 450,000 sq kms. POPULATION: 8,700,000 (*Swedes, Swedish*). CAPITAL: Stockholm. LANGUAGE: Swedish. CURRENCY: Swedish krona.

Swedish ['swiːdɪʃ] ◇ *n* a language spoken in Sweden and parts of Finland. ◇ *npl* **the Swedish** people who come from Sweden. ◇ *adj*: see **Sweden**.

sweep [swiːp] (*pt & pp* **swept**) ◇ *vt* **-1.** [floor, carpet, streets] to remove the dirt on <a surface> by pushing a brush or broom across it; [litter, leaves, crumbs] to clean away <dirt or rubbish> in this way □ *Could someone sweep the kitchen?* □ *John was sweeping the dust into a pile.* **-2.** [room, area, sky] to move quickly across <a place> □ *His gaze/the searchlight swept the horizon.* **-3.** [country, community] to spread throughout the people in <a large area> very quickly □ *A new fashion/virus is sweeping America.* **-4.** [person, building] to search <sb/sthg> for weapons or microphones, using electronic equipment. **-5.** [person, money, books] to push <sb/sthg> with a powerful movement in a particular direction □ *He swept the papers off the desk.* □ *The sailors were swept overboard.*
◇ *vi* [rain, emotion, person] to move quickly and powerfully in a particular direction □ *A hurricane swept through the town.* □ *A tide of nationalism swept through the country.* □ *She swept past me without a glance.*

◇ *n* **-1.** a long and powerful movement, e.g. of one's arm or hand □ *"This is all mine,"* she said, with a broad sweep of her hand. **-2.** the act of sweeping something with a brush □ *I gave the floor a quick sweep.* **-3.** a person whose job is to clean the soot from inside chimneys.

◆ **sweep aside** *vt sep* **to sweep sthg aside** [advice, objection] to refuse to pay attention to sthg □ *He swept aside my objections.*

◆ **sweep away** *vt sep* **to sweep sthg away** [building, obstruction, idea] to destroy sthg completely □ *Several houses were swept away in the flood.*

◆ **sweep up** ◇ *vt sep* **to sweep sthg up** [rubbish, dirt] to remove sthg with a brush or broom □ *Sweep those crumbs up off the floor!* ◇ *vi*: *I swept up after the party.*

sweeper ['swiːpər] *n* **-1.** in soccer, a player who stands behind other defending players. **-2.** US a vacuum cleaner.

sweeping ['swiːpɪŋ] *adj* **-1.** [changes, cuts] that are large and important, and affect many things or people □ *The new government has promised sweeping reforms.* **-2.** [statement, generalization] that is too general to be true (disapproving use) □ *He was making sweeping generalizations about older women.* **-3.** [curve, movement] that is long and wide □ *His paintings are full of broad sweeping bands of color.*

sweepstake ['swiːpsteɪk] *n* a form of gambling, often based on a horse race, in which players pay for tickets with contestants' names on them. All the money paid is given as a prize to the holder(s) of the winning ticket(s).

sweet [swiːt] ◇ *adj* **-1.** [food, drink, flavor] that has a taste like sugar □ *It's too sweet.* □ *a sweet white wine.* **-2.** [success, victory] that feels pleasing or satisfying □ *Revenge is sweet.* □ *a sweet feeling of satisfaction.* **-3.** [smell, air] that smells pleasant □ *a bunch of sweet-smelling roses.* **-4.** [song, voice, sound] that sounds pleasant and gentle □ *the sweet song of the nightingale.* **-5.** [person, nature] that shows a kind and pleasant character □ *That's very sweet of you.* □ *He was very sweet to me.* **-6.** [smile, face, puppy] that is attractive and charming □ *What a sweet little baby!*
◇ *n* GB **-1.** sweet food served as the last part of a meal □ *Who would like more sweet?* □ *the sweet course/menu.* **-2.** a small piece of sweet food made of sugar, chocolate etc □ *a bag of sweets.*

sweet-and-sour *adj* [sauce, chicken, pork] that has a mixture of both sweet and sour tastes.

sweet corn *n* yellow seeds of corn, cooked and eaten as a vegetable.

sweeten ['swiːtn] *vt* [mixture, coffee] to make <food or drink> taste sweet by adding sugar, honey etc to it.

sweetener ['swiːtnər] *n* **-1.** a substance used instead of sugar to sweeten something □ *an artificial sweetener.* **-2.** something given or offered to make a situation more acceptable (informal use) □ *a cash/financial sweetener.*

sweetheart ['swiːthɑːrt] *n* **-1.** a word used to

talk to somebody one loves □ *Bye, sweet-heart!* **-2.** a boyfriend or girlfriend □ *His wife, Laura, had been his childhood sweetheart.*

sweetheart contract US, **sweetheart agreement** AUS *n* an industrial agreement reached by direct discussion between workers and their employer.

sweetly ['swiːtlɪ] *adv* [smile, sing] *see* **sweet** □ *a sweetly innocent child.*

sweet pea *n* a climbing garden plant that has colorful sweet-smelling flowers.

sweet potato *n* the root of a tropical climbing plant, cooked and eaten as a vegetable.

sweet-talk *vt* to persuade <sb> to do something by saying pleasant things, making promises etc □ *They sweet-talked me into babysitting on Saturday night.*

sweet tooth *n* **to have a sweet tooth** to like foods that are sweet.

swell [swel] (*pt* **swelled**, *pp* **swollen** OR **swelled**) ◇ *vi* **-1. to swell (up)** [wrist, face] to become bigger than usual, especially because of injury or illness □ *Her ankle had swollen to twice its normal size.* **-2.** [lungs, balloon] to become rounded in shape as a result of being filled with air □ *The sails swelled (out) in the wind.* **-3.** [membership, crowd, town] to become larger in number or size □ *During the 40s the city swelled considerably.* **-4.** [music, voices] to become louder □ *The shouting swelled to a deafening roar.* **-5.** [person] to be filled with an emotion □ *She/Her heart swelled with pride.*
◇ *vt* [membership, crowd] to make <sthg> larger in number or size □ *The new intake has swelled our numbers considerably.* □ *Heavy rains have swollen the river to twice its normal size.*
◇ *n* the movement of the surface of the sea as it goes up and down.

swelling ['swelɪŋ] *n* **-1.** [of somebody's wrist, face] *see* **swell** □ *The drugs will reduce any swelling.* **-2.** an area of one's body that has swollen □ *He had a nasty swelling on his arm.*

sweltering ['sweltərɪŋ] *adj* [heat, day, person] that feels uncomfortably hot □ *It's sweltering in here.*

swept [swept] *past tense & past participle of* **sweep.**

swerve [swɜːrv] *vi* [car, truck, driver] to move to the left or right suddenly when going forward, especially to avoid something □ *The ball swerved around the defenders and into the goal.* □ *I had to swerve to avoid hitting him.*

swift [swɪft] ◇ *adj* **-1.** [movement, glance] that is quick and uses little effort □ *He's a swift runner.* **-2.** [action, payment, response] that happens without delay □ *Matt was always swift to point out other people's mistakes.* ◇ *n* a small brown bird with narrow wings and a Y-shaped tail that flies very fast.

swiftly ['swɪftlɪ] *adv* [move, act, respond] *see* **swift** □ *We must act swiftly and decisively.*

swiftness ['swɪftnəs] *n* [of a movement, action, response] *see* **swift** □ *The swiftness of the reply took Morton by surprise.*

swig [swɪg] (*pt & pp* **swigged**, *cont* **swigging**) (informal use) ◇ *vt* [whiskey, beer] to drink <sthg> quickly in large amounts □ *Marty sat at the bar swigging vodka.* ◇ *n* [of brandy, gin] a large mouthful of drink □ *She took a large swig of her drink.*

swill [swɪl] ◇ *n* a liquid mixture containing waste food that is given to pigs. ◇ *vt* GB to move a liquid around or over <sthg> usually in order to clean it □ *Swill the bucket out when you've finished with it.*

swim [swɪm] (*pt* **swam**, *pp* **swum**, *cont* **swimming**) ◇ *vi* **-1.** [person, animal, fish] to move through water by moving the arms and legs □ *Help! I can't swim!* □ *We used to swim in the lake.* **-2.** [room, objects] to appear to move around, usually because one is tired, ill etc □ *Suddenly everything started to swim before her eyes.* □ *My head was swimming.* ◇ *n* a period spent swimming □ *I always feel better after a swim.* □ *Why don't we go for a swim?*

swimmer ['swɪmər] *n* a person who can swim or is swimming □ *a champion/good swimmer.*

swimming ['swɪmɪŋ] *n* the activity or sport of moving through the water using one's arms and legs □ *Swimming is one of my favorite pastimes.* □ *We went swimming in the ocean.*

swimming baths *npl* GB an indoor public swimming pool.

swimming cap *n* a tight, hat used to keep one's hair dry when one is swimming.

swimming costume *n* GB a single tight piece of clothing worn by women for swimming.

swimming pool *n* a place built for people to swim in, consisting of a large hole in the ground filled with water □ *an indoor/outdoor swimming pool.*

swimming trunks *npl* a piece of clothing similar to short trousers or underwear, worn by men for swimming □ *a pair of swimming trunks.*

swimsuit ['swɪmsuːt] *n* a single tight piece of clothing worn by women for swimming or lying in the sun.

swindle ['swɪndl] ◇ *vt* to get money or something valuable from <sb> by deceiving or tricking them □ *We've been swindled.* □ *Too often the elderly are swindled out of their life savings.* ◇ *n* a situation or act in which somebody is swindled □ *The whole thing's a complete swindle!*

swine [swaɪn] *n* a person who one thinks is very unpleasant (informal use) □ *You swine!*

swing [swɪŋ] (*pt & pp* **swung**) ◇ *vt* **-1.** [hips, arms] to make <sthg> move backward and forward or from side to side from a fixed point □ *Justin was sitting on the wall swinging his feet.* **-2.** [vehicle, door] to cause <sthg> to turn in a particular direction suddenly □ *Bob lifted the bag up and swung it over his shoulder.* □ *He swung the car round to the left.*
◇ *vi* **-1.** [legs, arms] to move from a fixed point □ *The window was swinging in the wind.* **-2.** [vehicle, person] to turn in a particular direction □ *The car swung into the driveway.* □ *The door swung open.* □ *He swung around to face me.* **-3. to swing at sb** to try to hit sb with one's fist or a weapon. **-4.** [mood, opin-

ion] to change to the opposite of what it was before □ *Mary's moods tended to swing from optimism to deep despair.* □ *The Party is in danger of swinging even further to the right.* ◇ *n* -1. GAMES a seat that hangs by ropes or chains from a frame, tree branch etc, on which children can play by swinging backward and forward □ *a garden/playground swing.* -2. [in somebody's opinion, mood] a big change in somebody's opinions or in the way that people vote □ *a (10%) swing to the right* □ *a mood swing.* -3. [of somebody's hips, arms, a pendulum] the movement of something that swings. -4. **to take a swing at sb** to try to hit sb with one's fist or a weapon (informal use). -5. **to be in full swing** [campaign, party] to be at a very active stage □ *By the time we arrived, the party was already in full swing.* ■ **to get into the swing of sthg** to get used to sthg and feel fully involved in it □ *I'll need a few days to get into the swing of things.*

swing bridge *n* a bridge that is fixed to the middle of a river, not the edges, so that it can be turned to let ships pass.

swing door *n* a door that opens in both directions and closes by itself.

swingeing ['swɪndʒɪŋ] *adj* GB **swingeing cuts/cutbacks** cuts/cutbacks that have a very severe effect.

swinging ['swɪŋɪŋ] *adj* -1. [party, place] that is lively and enjoyable. -2. [lifestyle, time] that is lively, fashionable, and not strict in any way □ *the swinging sixties.*

swinging voter *n* AUS a person who has not yet decided who to vote for in a particular election.

swing set *n* US a metal frame with swings attached to it for children to play on.

swipe [swaɪp] ◇ *n* **to take a swipe at sb/sthg** to hit or try to hit sb/sthg with an uncontrolled swinging movement of one's arm. ◇ *vt* to steal <sthg>, usually by taking it quickly (informal use) □ *Someone's swiped my pen!* ◇ *vi* **to swipe at sthg** to take a swipe at sthg □ *He swiped at the wasp with his newspaper.*

swirl [swɜːʳl] ◇ *vt* [drink, water] to make <a liquid> move around a lot in a fast uncontrolled way. ◇ *vi* [snow, water, dust] to keep moving around in a fast uncontrolled way □ *The crowd swirled around her.* ◇ *n* the movement or shape of something that swirls.

Swiss [swɪs] (*pl* **Swiss**) *n* & *adj*: see **Switzerland**.

swiss roll *n* GB a thin piece of sponge cake covered with jelly, cream etc and rolled up into a cylinder shape.

swiss steak *n* US a thick piece of steak that is beaten flat, covered in flour, and cooked in a sauce.

switch [swɪtʃ] ◇ *n* -1. [on a radio, stereo, heater] a small device for turning an electric current on and off □ *a light switch* □ *Turn the switch on/off.* -2. [in direction, plans] a sudden or unexpected change □ *a policy switch.* -3. US RAIL

a device for moving a train from one track to another track. ◇ *vt* -1. **to switch jobs/courses etc** to change from one job/course etc to another, usually suddenly □ *Would you mind switching places with me?* ■ **to switch one's attention to sthg** to stop paying attention to one thing and start paying attention to sthg else. -2. **to switch labels/suitcases etc** to secretly replace one label/suitcase etc with another. ◇ *vi* to change from one thing to another thing of the same type, usually suddenly □ *I'm thinking of switching from cigarettes to a pipe.* □ *Can we switch to the other channel?*

◆ **switch off** ◇ *vt sep* **to switch sthg off** [radio, light, machine] to make sthg stop working by pressing or turning a switch □ *Switch off the TV before you go to bed.* ◇ *vi* to stop paying attention to somebody or something (informal use) □ *When I try to talk to him, he just switches off.*

◆ **switch on** *vt sep* **to switch sthg on** [radio, light, machine] to make sthg start working by pressing or turning a switch □ *How do you switch the heating on?*

switchblade ['swɪtʃbleɪd] *n* US a knife with a blade inside the handle that comes out suddenly when one presses a button.

switchboard ['swɪtʃbɔːʳd] *n* a piece of equipment in an office building, hospital, hotel etc that receives and transfers telephone calls; the people who work this equipment □ *She works on the switchboard.* □ *I got through to the switchboard.*

switchboard operator *n* a person who works on a switchboard.

Switzerland ['swɪtsələnd] a mountainous country in central Europe, between France, Germany, Austria, and Italy. It is a neutral country. SIZE: 41,293 sq kms. POPULATION: 7,000,000 (*Swiss*). CAPITAL: Bern. LANGUAGE: French, German, Italian, Romansch. CURRENCY: Swiss franc.

swivel ['swɪvl] (US *pt* & *pp* **swiveled**, *cont* **swiveling**, GB *pt* & *pp* **swivelled**, *cont* **swivelling**) ◇ *vt* [chair, head] to turn <sthg> around a central point so that it faces in a different direction □ *Merton swiveled his chair around to face them.* ◇ *vi* [chair, head] *She swiveled around.*

swivel chair *n* a chair that can swivel.

swollen ['swəʊlən] ◇ *past participle of* **swell**. ◇ *adj* -1. [ankle, face] that is bigger than usual, especially because of injury or illness □ *My glands feel swollen.* -2. [river, stream] that is very full because it contains more water than usual, e.g. after heavy rain.

swoon [swuːn] *vi* -1. to faint (literary use). -2. to be strongly affected by happiness, excitement etc (humorous use) □ *Before, they all used to swoon over Elvis Presley.*

swoop [swuːp] ◇ *vi* -1. [plane, bird] to fly down suddenly in a smooth steep curve □ *The gulls swooped down to pick up the bread.* -2. [police, troops] to carry out a sudden unexpected attack □ *Customs officials swooped on the tiny boat.* ◇ *n* -1. [of a bird, plane] the movement of something that swoops. ■ **in one fell swoop** suddenly and all at the same time □ *I lost all my savings in one fell swoop.* **-2.** [by police, troops] a sudden unexpected attack.

swop [swɒp] *n, vt,* & *vi* = **swap.**

sword [sɔːrd] *n* a weapon that consists of a long narrow blade with a handle at one end. ■ **to cross swords with sb** to disagree and argue with sb □ *They'd already crossed swords over the budget deficit.*

swordfish [ˈsɔːrdfɪʃ] (*pl* **swordfish** OR **swordfishes**) *n* a large saltwater fish with a very long pointed upper jaw that is like a sword.

swordsman [ˈsɔːrdzmən] (*pl* **swordsmen** [-mən]) *n* a man who is skilled at using a sword to fight.

swore [swɔːr] *past tense of* **swear.**

sworn [swɔːrn] ◇ *past participle of* **swear.** ◇ *adj* **-1. to be sworn enemies** to hate each other in a way that is unlikely to change. **-2.** LAW **a sworn statement** a statement that is made formally under oath.

swot [swɒt] (*pt* & *pp* **swotted,** *cont* **swotting**) GB ◇ *vi* to spend a lot of time studying (informal use) □ *I'm swotting for my exams.* ◇ *n* a person who swots (informal and disapproving use).

◆ **swot up** ◇ *vt sep* **to swot sthg up** [French, math, current affairs] to study sthg very hard, especially for an exam (informal use). ◇ *vi:* *He's swotting up on his geography.*

swum [swʌm] *past participle of* **swim.**

swung [swʌŋ] *past tense* & *past participle of* **swing.**

sycamore [ˈsɪkəmɔːr] *n* **a sycamore (tree)** a tree with leaves that have five points and seeds in the shape of two wings.

sycophant [ˈsɪkəfænt] *n* a person who is full of false praise for people in positions of power, in order to gain an advantage (formal use).

Sydney [ˈsɪdnɪ] Australia's largest city, and a major port in New South Wales. POPULATION: 3,596,000.

syllable [ˈsɪləbl] *n* a word or a part of a word that consists of a vowel sound with a consonant sound before or after it □ *words of one syllable.*

syllabub [ˈsɪləbʌb] *n* a dish made from sweetened cream mixed with wine.

syllabus [ˈsɪləbəs] (*pl* **syllabuses** OR **syllabi** [-baɪ]) *n* a list of the subjects or writers and books that are studied in a particular course of study □ *Kafka is not on the syllabus this year.*

symbol [ˈsɪmbl] *n* **-1.** [of peace, a company, party] an image, shape, person, or object that is used to suggest or represent something else such as an idea or movement □ *White is a symbol of purity.* □ *The symbol of the party was a white cross on a red background.* □ *The town has become a symbol of the new Spain.* **-2.** [in chemistry, math etc] a mark, sign, letter etc that is officially used to represent something □ *Pb is the symbol for lead.* □ *the dollar symbol.*

symbolic [sɪmˈbɒlɪk] *adj* **-1.** that suggests or represents something □ *The colors of the flag are symbolic of the country's different cultural traditions.* **-2.** [gesture, ritual] that has little practical effect but is important from an emotional, psychological etc point of view □ *The prize money was symbolic, really. It didn't amount to very much.* **-3.** [painting, film] that uses symbols to represent ideas, feelings etc.

symbolism [ˈsɪmbəlɪzm] *n* the use of symbols, especially in art, literature, and movies, to represent ideas, feelings etc.

symbolize, -ise [ˈsɪmbəlaɪz] *vt* [union, attitude, happiness] to be a symbol of <sthg> □ *I don't know what it's supposed to symbolize.*

symmetrical [səˈmetrɪkl] *adj* [shape, design, face] that has two halves that are exactly the same in size and shape.

symmetry [ˈsɪmətrɪ] *n* the state of being symmetrical.

sympathetic [ˌsɪmpəˈθetɪk] *adj* **-1.** [person, attitude] that shows sympathy for somebody in a difficult situation □ *a sympathetic smile.* □ *Chris was very sympathetic about the whole situation.* **-2.** [response, leader] that shows approval and a willingness to support something □ *The public is generally sympathetic to the strikers' demands.* **-3.** [person] who is pleasant and easy to like □ *He's a sympathetic kind of person.*

sympathize, -ise [ˈsɪmpəθaɪz] *vi* **-1.** to feel sorry for somebody when something bad has happened to them □ *We all sympathize with you at this sad time.* □ *I do sympathize, Peggy, I really do.* **-2.** to feel or show understanding of somebody's situation, beliefs etc □ *It's sometimes hard to sympathize when he complains so much all the time.* □ *We fully sympathize with your predicament.* **-3.** to approve of and be willing to support something □ *Most of us sympathize with their objectives, if not with their methods.*

sympathizer, -iser [ˈsɪmpəθaɪzər] *n* a person who supports an organization, political party etc without belonging to it □ *a Communist/Fascist sympathizer.*

sympathy [ˈsɪmpəθɪ] *n* **-1.** [for somebody] understanding and pity for somebody in a difficult situation □ *a message of sympathy* □ *The homeless enjoy widespread public sympathy.* □ *I have a lot of sympathy for him.* **-2.** [with an attitude] agreement with something □ *I feel a certain sympathy with their aims.* □ *I'm broadly in sympathy with what she says/her beliefs.* **-3.** [with a person, organization] support for a person or group of people □ *The pilots have come out in sympathy with the ground crew.* □ *Students staged a demonstration in sympathy.*

◆ **sympathies** *npl* **-1.** feelings of approval and support □ *My sympathies lie with the Left.* **-2.** an expression of sympathy at a time of sadness, usually after somebody's death □ *Please accept my sincerest sympathies.*

symphonic [sɪmˈfɒnɪk] *adj* [music, orchestra] *see* **symphony.**

symphony [ˈsɪmfənɪ] (*pl* **symphonies**) *n* a long piece of classical music, usually in four parts, that is written for a large orchestra.

symphony orchestra *n* a large orchestra that plays symphonies and other classical music.

symposium [sɪm'pouzjəm] (*pl* **symposiums** OR **symposia** [-zjə]) *n* a formal meeting at which experts discuss a particular subject of interest.

symptom ['sɪmptəm] *n* -1. MEDICINE [of typhoid, stress] a change in one's body that is a sign of an illness or disease □ *I had all the symptoms of the flu.* -2. [of a decline, recession] a sign that a particular problem exists □ *It's a symptom of an underlying conflict.*

symptomatic [ˌsɪmptə'mætɪk] *adj* **to be symptomatic of sthg** to be a sign of sthg bad □ *It's symptomatic of a much deeper problem.*

synagogue ['sɪnəgɒg] *n* a building where Jewish people meet for religious worship.

sync [sɪŋk] *n* **out of/in sync** not properly/properly synchronized (informal use) □ *The sound was out of sync with the pictures.*

synchromesh gearbox [ˌsɪŋkroumeʃ-] *n* a gearbox with a device that allows the gears to be changed smoothly.

synchronize, -ise ['sɪŋkrənaɪz] *vt* -1. to make <two or more things> happen, work etc at the same time or speed □ *The soundtrack and action have not been synchronized yet.* -2. to set <watches> so that they show exactly the same time.

synchronized swimming [ˌsɪŋkrənaɪzd-] *n* a sport in which teams of two or more swimmers carry out movements in the water at the same time in order to form patterns.

syncopated ['sɪŋkəpeɪtəd] *adj* [music, rhythm] in which beats that are usually weak are made stronger.

syncopation [ˌsɪŋkə'peɪʃn] *n* the process of making beats syncopated.

syndicate [*n* 'sɪndəkət, *vb* 'sɪndəkeɪt] ◇ *n* a group of people or companies that join together for a particular purpose □ *a crime syndicate* □ *a syndicate of local businessmen.* ◇ *vt* JOURNALISM [article, photograph] to sell <sthg> to several different newspapers, magazines etc for publication □ *His column was syndicated all over Europe.*

syndrome ['sɪndroum] *n* -1. MEDICINE a particular set of symptoms that is typical of a physical or mental disorder □ *Tourette's Syndrome.* -2. a particular pattern of events, activity, behavior etc that is typical of a condition or state □ *She's suffering from the classic "I'm 40 and where has my life gone" syndrome!*

synergy ['sɪnə'dʒɪ] (*pl* **synergies**) *n* the effect that is produced when two people or things are combined so that each works better □ *One benefit of the merger will be greater synergy.*

synod ['sɪnəd] *n* an official meeting of members of a church that takes place regularly to discuss and decide church matters.

synonym ['sɪnənɪm] *n* a word or phrase that has the same meaning as another word or phrase in the same language □ *"Out of work" is a synonym of* OR *for "unemployed".* NOTE: Compare **antonym**.

synonymous [sə'nɒnəməs] *adj* -1. [word, phrase] that has the same meaning as another word or phrase □ *The two words are synonymous.* □ *"Small" is sometimes synonymous with "little".* -2. **to be synonymous with sthg** to be very closely connected with sthg □ *Our name has come to be synonymous with quality.*

synopsis [sə'nɒpsəs] (*pl* **synopses** [-siːz]) *n* [of a movie, play] a summary of a story □ *He gave us a brief synopsis of the plot.*

syntax ['sɪntæks] *n* the rules of grammar used in the ordering of words to form phrases or sentences.

synthesis ['sɪnθəsəs] (*pl* **syntheses** [-siːz]) *n* a combination of different parts or elements □ *Her ideas are a synthesis of Freudian and Jungian theories.*

synthesize, -ise ['sɪnθəsaɪz] *vt* -1. BIOLOGY & CHEMISTRY [vitamins, proteins, hormones] to produce <a substance> by using chemical or biological reactions, either artificially or naturally. -2. [ideas, theories, experiences] to put <different things> together to produce something new.

synthesizer ['sɪnθəsaɪzəʳ] *n* an electronic instrument that can produce many different sounds and is usually played with a keyboard.

synthetic [sɪn'θetɪk] *adj* [fiber, rubber, pearl] that has been made using chemicals and is not natural.

syphilis ['sɪfələs] *n* a very serious disease that is spread from a parent to a child or by having sex with somebody.

syphon ['saɪfn] *n* & *vt* = **siphon**.

Syria ['sɪrɪə] a country in the Middle East, on the Mediterranean Sea south of Turkey. SIZE: 185,000 sq kms. POPULATION: 13,500,000 (*Syrians*). CAPITAL: Damascus. LANGUAGE: Arabic. CURRENCY: Syrian pound.

Syrian ['sɪrɪən] *n* & *adj*: see **Syria**.

syringe [sə'rɪndʒ] (*cont* **syringeing** OR **syringing**) ◇ *n* a medical instrument that consists of a hollow tube with a needle attached to it that liquid can be forced through. It is used to inject drugs and take blood samples □ *a needle and syringe.* ◇ *vt* [ear, wound] to clean <sthg> using a syringe.

syrup ['sɪrəp] *n* -1. a sweet liquid, usually made from sugar and water, that is used in cans of fruit. -2. a thick, sweet, pale-yellow liquid made from sugar □ *maple syrup.*

system ['sɪstəm] *n* -1. [for doing something] a method of organizing or doing something that follows a fixed plan or process □ *We're introducing a new system of invoicing in October.* □ *a filing system* □ *a system for producing synthetic DNA.* -2. [for counting, measuring] a set of rules, especially in mathematics or science, for counting or measuring things □ *the decimal system.* -3. [for traveling, communicating] a part of an organization or society that is organized in a particular way □ *the American banking/legal system* □ *a communications system.* -4. TECHNOLOGY & ELECTRICITY different pieces of equipment that work together as a whole □ *a ventilation/stereo/security system* □ *The alarm system went off.* □ *We are installing a new computer system.* **-5. the system** the way a country is run and the institutions in it that control and seem to limit people's lives □ *It's no use fighting against the system.* **-6.** [in somebody's body] a group of organs in the body that work together to perform a particular function □ *the digestive system.* **-7.** an organized and careful way of doing things □ *There's no system to his work.* **-8. to get sthg out of one's system** to do something so that one stops thinking about or feeling sthg and can give one's attention to other things (informal use) □ *Talking about it is a good way of getting it out of your system.*

systematic [ˌsɪstə'mætɪk] *adj* [search, approach] that is carefully organized and follows a clear system □ *Harris ordered the systematic destruction of all files relating to the case.* □ *Jean is extremely systematic in her approach to work.*

systematize, -ise ['sɪstəmətaɪz] *vt* GB [work, approach, search] to organize <sthg> so that it follows a logical system.

system disk *n* a computer disk that holds the system software.

systems analyst *n* a person who studies business and industrial operations and uses a computer to find ways of making them more efficient.

systems engineer *n* a computer expert who helps an organization when they are starting to use a new computer system.

system software *n* a collection of programs that make it possible to use a computer system and that control its performance.

t [tiː] (*pl* **t's** OR **ts**), **T** [tiː] (*pl* **T's** OR **Ts**) *n* the twentieth letter of the English alphabet.

TA *n abbr of* **Territorial Army**.

tab [tæb] *n* **-1.** a small piece of cloth or paper that is attached to something to identify it □ *a name tab.* **-2.** [on a can] a small strip of metal that one pulls to open a can. □ *'Pull tab to open.'* **-3.** US [in a restaurant] the bill for something, e.g. for a meal in a restaurant. ■ **to pick up the tab** to pay the bill for something □ *I was left to pick up the tab!* **-4.** COMPUTING = **tab key. -5.** *phrase* **to keep tabs on sb** to watch the movements and actions of sb closely, especially because one does not trust them □ *The police have been keeping tabs on Thurloe's movements.*

Tabasco sauce™ [tə,bæskoʊ-] *n* a very hot red sauce made from chili peppers, used to add flavor to food and drink.

tabby ['tæbɪ] (*pl* **tabbies**) *n* **a tabby (cat)** a cat with gray or brown fur and dark stripes.

tabernacle ['tæbə'nækl] *n* a container used in a Catholic church to keep the bread and wine for communion in.

tab key *n* a key on a computer keyboard for moving the cursor to any of a series of fixed positions to make tables, lists etc.

table ['teɪbl] ◇ *n* **-1.** a piece of furniture consisting of a flat horizontal surface supported by one or more legs and used to put things on or to sit at, especially for meals □ *a kitchen/bedside table.* **-2.** [of figures] sets of facts, figures, or information arranged in a series of columns □ *a multiplication table* □ *Turn to the table on page three.* **-3.** *phrase* **to turn the tables on sb** to take control of a situation from sb else so that they are placed in the weaker position as a result □ *Mr Gomez turned the tables on his former employers by going public.*
◇ *vt* **-1.** US [proposal, report] to leave <sthg> for discussion or consideration at a later date □ *The matter has been tabled until we receive further evidence.* **-2.** GB [motion, amendment, question] to present <sthg> formally for debate, discussion, or an answer □ *The motion that has been tabled for discussion today is...*

tableau ['tæbloʊ] (*pl* **tableaux** [-z] OR **tableaus** [-z]) *n* a representation, usually on stage, of a famous or historical event by people in costume who do not move or speak.

tablecloth ['teɪblklɒθ] *n* a piece of cloth used to cover a table, especially during meals.

table d'hôte [ˌtɑːbl'doʊt] *n* **the table d'hôte** a complete meal served in a restaurant that consists of a limited choice of dishes at a fixed price.
NOTE: Compare **à la carte**.

table football *n* GB a game played by two or four people on a table with rods across it that are moved by handles. The players try to score goals by hitting a ball with figures of soccer players attached to the rods.

table lamp *n* an electric lamp for placing on a table to light an area of a room.

table licence *n* GB a license for a restaurant, hotel etc to sell alcoholic drinks with meals.

table linen *n* a collective term for tablecloths and napkins.

table manners *npl* the way somebody behaves when they are eating a meal, especially when they are with other people □ *That child has very good/bad table manners.*

table mat *n* a small mat placed under hot dishes or plates to protect a table.

table of contents *n* a list at the beginning of a book that shows the different sections it contains.

table salt *n* salt that is finer than cooking salt, used for adding to food during a meal.

tablespoon ['teɪblspuːn] *n* a large spoon used e.g. for eating soup or serving food; the amount such a spoon can hold.

tablet ['tæblət] *n* **-1.** [of stone] a flat piece of

stone that has had words cut into it □ *a stone tablet.* -**2.** [of soap] a small bar of soap. -**3.** MEDICINE a small, round, solid piece of medicine that is taken by mouth □ *Take two tablets twice a day.*

table tennis *n* a game like tennis played on a special table by two or four people who use bats to hit a light plastic ball over a net that runs across the middle of the table.

tableware ['teɪblweə'] *n* a collective term for the objects used to eat a meal at a table, e.g. plates, glasses, and knives.

table wine *n* wine that is intended for drinking with a meal.

tabloid ['tæblɔɪd] *n* **a tabloid (newspaper)** a popular newspaper printed on small pages that contains little serious news. ■ **the tabloid press** a collective term for tabloid newspapers.
NOTE: Compare **broadsheet**.

taboo [tə'buː] (*pl* **taboos**) ◇ *n* a social custom or religious rule that forbids certain actions, language, behavior etc because they are considered to be offensive or embarrassing. ◇ *adj* [subject, word] that is forbidden by a taboo.

tabulate ['tæbjəleɪt] *vt* [facts, figures, information] to arrange <sthg> in a series of columns or lists.

tachograph [US 'tækəgræf, GB -grɑːf] *n* a device for recording the speed of a bus, truck etc and the distance it has traveled.

tachometer [tæ'kɒmətə'] *n* a device used to measure the speed of a vehicle by finding out the rate at which the engine is turning.

tacit ['tæsət] *adj* [agreement, admission, support] that is accepted or understood, but is not expressed in words (formal use) □ *His silence was taken as tacit approval of the proposal.*

taciturn ['tæsətɜː'n] *adj* [person] who seems unfriendly and shows no desire to speak (formal use).

tack [tæk] ◇ *n* -**1.** a short metal nail with a large flat head □ *a carpet tack.* -**2.** SAILING a direction followed by a boat or ship with the wind blowing toward one side of it. -**3.** a way of dealing with a problem, situation etc □ *Let's try a different tack.* □ *The committee has changed tack several times on this issue already.* ◇ *vt* -**1.** [note, poster] to attach <sthg> with a tack or tacks to a wall, door etc □ *The notice was tacked to the door.* -**2.** [hem, sleeves] to fasten or join <sthg> with long loose stitches before sewing it properly. ◇ *vi* SAILING to change from one tack to another □ *The boat tacked to starboard.*

◆ **tack on** *vt sep* **to tack sthg on** [clause, chapter, paragraph] to add sthg to something that is complete, often in a careless or unsatisfactory way □ *A final paragraph had been tacked on at the end of the report.*

tackle ['tækl] ◇ *vt* -**1.** [job, problem, fire] to deal with <sthg difficult> in a direct way □ *I suppose we ought to tackle the cleaning at some point today.* -**2.** SPORT [in soccer, hockey] to take or try to take the ball away from <an oppo-

nent>; [in football, rugby] to take hold of and bring <an opponent> to the ground when they are carrying the ball. -**3.** [burglar, lion] to try to stop <a person or animal>, especially by attacking them □ *The police don't recommend tackling intruders.* -**4.** [boss, neighbor] to speak to <sb> to ask them frankly about something difficult or embarrassing □ *I still haven't tackled him about giving me a day off.* □ *I tackled her about* OR *on the issue of repayments.*
◇ *n* -**1.** SPORT an act of tackling an opponent □ *a rugby tackle.* -**2.** [for an activity] the equipment used for a particular sport or activity, especially fishing □ *fishing tackle.* -**3.** [for lifting] a set of ropes and wheels used for lifting heavy weights □ *a block and tackle.*

tacky ['tækɪ] (*compar* **tackier**, *superl* **tackiest**) *adj* -**1.** [jewelry, decoration, clothing] that is cheap and of bad quality, and shows bad taste (informal use) □ *some extremely tacky furniture.* -**2.** [movie, remark] that shows bad taste (informal use). -**3.** [paint, glue, varnish] that is slightly sticky because it is not completely dry.

taco [US 'tɑːkou, GB 'tæk-] (*pl* **tacos**) *n* a type of Mexican crepe filled with meat, cheese, beans etc.

tact [tækt] *n* the ability to say or do the right thing and to avoid upsetting or offending people □ *She handled the situation with great tact.*

tactful ['tæktfl] *adj* [person, remark, silence] that shows tact □ *I thought it would be more tactful to leave at that point.*

tactfully ['tæktflɪ] *adv* [explain, suggest, behave] see **tactful** □ *He tactfully left the room while we were talking.*

tactic ['tæktɪk] *n* a clever plan or method used to get a particular result that one wants □ *His tactic is always to wait until the very last moment.* □ *delaying/shock tactics.*

◆ **tactics** *n* MILITARY the act of planning where to place troops and equipment before and during a battle.

tactical ['tæktɪkl] *adj* -**1.** [move, withdrawal, advance] that is intended to gain a future advantage or result rather than an immediate one □ *It's a clever tactical move on the part of the government.* -**2.** MILITARY [skill, ability, mistake] that is connected with tactics. -**3.** MILITARY [weapon, device] that is designed to be used at short range.

tactical voting *n* GB the act of voting for a candidate or party that one does not really support, because they are more likely to defeat the candidate or party that one wants to lose.

tactless ['tæktləs] *adj* [person, behavior, remark] that does not show tact □ *She can be extremely tactless at times.*

tadpole ['tædpoul] *n* a very small black creature with a tail that lives in water and is the young form of a frog or toad.

TAFE (*abbr of* **Technical and Further Education**) *n* a college of higher education in Australia.

taffeta ['tæfətə] *n* a smooth, shiny, stiff cloth made from silk or nylon □ *a taffeta skirt.*

taffy ['tæfɪ] (*pl* **taffies**) *n* US a chewy candy that is made by boiling sugar and then stretching it.

Taft [US tæft, GB tɑːft], **William Howard** (1857– 1930) US President from 1909 to 1913.

tag [tæg] (*pt* & *pp* **tagged**, *cont* **tagging**) ◇ *n* -1. a small piece of cardboard, plastic, cloth etc attached to something to show information about it □ *a name/luggage tag.* -2. GAMES a children's game in which one child chases and tries to touch the others □ *to play tag.* -3. COMPUTING a character used to identify a file or item of data. ◇ *vt* [luggage, clothing] to put a tag on <sthg>.
◆ **tags** *npl* US a set of numbers and letters on the front and back of a vehicle □ *He saw a white Buick with NC tags.*
◆ **tag along** *vi* to go somewhere with somebody else, often when one is not invited or wanted (informal use) □ *Do you mind if I tag along?*

Tagalog [tə'gɑːləg] *n* a member of a people living in the Philippines; the language of this people.

tagliatelle [US ˌtɑːljə'telɪ, GB ˌtæl-] *n* pasta that is served in narrow strips.

Tahiti [tə'hiːtɪ] an island in French Polynesia, in the Pacific Ocean. SIZE: 1,042 sq kms. POPULATION: 131,309 (*Tahitians*). CAPITAL: Papeete.

tail [teɪl] ◇ *n* -1. [of a horse, bird, fish] the part of an animal at the end furthest from its head that it can move □ *The dog wagged its tail.* ■ **with one's tail between one's legs** ashamed and embarrassed because one has failed. -2. [of a shirt, coat] the back part of a coat or a shirt that is longer than the front. -3. [of a car, plane] the back part of a vehicle □ *the tail section.* -4. [of a comet] the cloud of small particles behind a comet that looks like a tail. ◇ *vt* [criminal, suspect, fugitive] to secretly follow and watch <sb> □ *Somebody's been tailing us all the way home.*
◆ **tails** ◇ *adv* a word that refers to the side of the coin that does not have a head or face on it. It is used when tossing a coin in order to decide something. □ *Heads or tails?* ◇ *npl* = **tailcoat.**
◆ **tail off** *vi* -1. [voice, noise] to become quieter and stop □ *"Then we..." his voice tailed off as he realized no one was listening.* -2. [figures, sales] to become less in amount □ *Sales tend to tail off toward the end of the season.*

tailback ['teɪlbæk] *n* GB a long line of traffic that is moving very slowly.

tai chi [ˌtaɪ'tʃiː] *n* a system of exercise and meditation, originally from China, in which one repeats a series of slow movements to improve one's balance and control.

tailcoat ['teɪlkəʊt] *n* a formal jacket with two long flaps at the back that come to the back of the knees and a front part that stops at the waist.

tail end *n* **the tail end of sthg** [of a movie, affair,

the summer] the part of something that is very near the end □ *I only caught the tail end of the conversation.*

tailgate ['teɪlgeɪt] US ◇ *n* a door or flap at the back of a car or truck that opens downward. ◇ *vt* to follow <the car in front> too closely.

tail-light *n* a red light at the back of a vehicle that allows it to be seen in the dark by vehicles behind it.

tailor ['teɪlər] ◇ *n* a person who makes clothing, especially men's suits, for particular customers. ◇ *vt* [equipment, system, policy] to make or adjust <sthg> for a particular purpose □ *The course has been carefully tailored to your needs.*

tailored ['teɪlərd] *adj* [suit, dress, shirt] that is designed to fit a person's body closely.

tailor-made *adj* [role, job, part] that is very suitable for a particular person or purpose □ *The program is tailor-made for part-time students.*

tail pipe *n* US the pipe that carries waste gases out of an engine.

tailplane ['teɪlpleɪn] *n* a small horizontal wing on the tail of an airplane that makes it steady.

tailwind ['teɪlwɪnd] *n* a wind blowing from behind an airplane, boat, or other vehicle that helps it to move forward more quickly.

taint [teɪnt] *n* [of scandal, corruption] a bad quality that spoils the status or reputation of somebody or something □ *The accusations have left a taint on his reputation.*

tainted ['teɪntəd] *adj* -1. [friendship, reputation, person] that has been spoiled because it is associated with something unpleasant. -2. US [food, drink] that has gone bad □ *tainted milk.*

Taiwan [ˌtaɪ'wɑːn] a country in Southeast Asia consisting of an island off the southeastern coast of China. It was declared an independent state in 1949 by the Chinese who fled from Communist mainland China. SIZE: 36,000 sq kms. POPULATION: 20,900,000 (*Taiwanese*). CAPITAL: Taipei. LANGUAGE: Chinese. CURRENCY: Taiwanese dollar.

Taiwanese [ˌtaɪwə'niːz] *n* & *adj*: see **Taiwan**.

Taj Mahal [ˌtɑːdʒmə'hɑːl]: **the Taj Mahal** a building made of white marble near Agra, in India. It was built by Shah Jahan in the 17th century for his dead wife.

take [teɪk] (*pt* **took**, *pp* **taken**) ◇ *vt* -1. [to another place] to carry or move <sthg> from one place to another □ *If you're going there in the summer, take plenty of insect repellent with you.* □ *We should take them a bottle of wine to say thanks.* □ *I had to take the car to the garage.* □ *He took the book from the shelf.* □ *She took her suitcase down from the top of the wardrobe.* -2. [with somebody] to go with <sb> to a particular place in a car, plane etc □ *If your cold doesn't get better, I'll take you to the doctor.* □ *When he was ten, he was taken to visit his relatives in Baltimore.* -3. [with one's hands] to put out one's hands and hold <sb/sthg> □ *Here, take this box.* □ *She took me by the arm.* □ *Let me take your bag, it looks heavy.* -4. used to make verbs. ■ **to take a walk/bath** to go for a walk/have a bath. ■ **to take a look/decision** to look/decide □ *I took a stroll through the park.* ■ **to take a break/vacation** to have a break/vacation □ *OK everyone, let's take a rest.* ■ **to take a copy/photo of sthg** to copy/photograph sthg □ *I took this photo last time I was there.* ■ **to take notes/sb's name** to write notes/sb's name □ *Can I take your phone number?* ■ **to take a seat** to sit down □ *Come in and take a seat.* **-5.** [without permission] to steal <sthg>, to remove <sthg> without permission □ *The thieves took all the office equipment.* **-6.** [in a store] to buy <sthg> □ *I'll take three bottles, please.* □ *It's perfect — I'll take it.* **-7. to take sb's advice** to do what sb is advising one to do □ *Take my word for it, he's a liar.* ■ **to take the blame/responsibility for sthg** to be willing to accept the blame/responsibility for sthg □ *I don't see why John should take all the credit.* **-8. to take a job** to agree to do a job that is offered to one □ *They offered me a year's contract, so I took it.* **-9. to take coins/credit cards etc** to accept coins/credit cards etc as a means of payment □ *The ticket machines don't take twenty-dollar bills.* **-10. to take a bus/plane etc** to go somewhere by bus/plane etc □ *Let's take a taxi from the airport.* **-11. to take a road/direction etc** to follow a particular road/direction etc to get to a place □ *We should have taken the last exit.* □ *Go straight on, and take the first turn on the left.* □ *We're going to take the scenic route.* **-12. to take sb's temperature/pulse etc** to measure sb's temperature/pulse etc, often using an instrument □ *Roll up your sleeve and I'll take your blood pressure.* **-13. to take a particular number/amount** [container, room, vehicle] to be able to hold a particular number/amount of sthg □ *The new terminal can take up to 10,000 passengers a day.* □ *My car will only take five people.* ■ **to take a particular size** to wear a particular size of dress, pants, shoes etc □ *I normally take a (size) seven in shoes.* **-14. to take time/courage etc** to need time/courage etc to happen successfully □ *Learning a language takes patience and hard work.* □ *All it takes is a little common sense.* ■ **to take a particular amount of time** to need a particular amount of time □ *It could take us months to find a replacement for her.* □ *Preparing the transparencies shouldn't take long.* **-15. to take medicine** to swallow medicine □ *Take two tablets daily.* ■ **to take drugs** to swallow or inject illegal drugs such as heroin or cocaine. ■ **how do you take your coffee?** how do you drink your coffee normally, with milk, sugar etc? □ *Do you take sugar?* **-16. to take control/command** to get control/command of a situation. **-17. to take sthg seriously** [issue, work, situation] to consider sthg to be serious or important □ *No one ever takes my suggestions seriously.* □ *I take the view that people should help themselves.* ■ **to take sthg well/badly** [news, joke, defeat] to react well/badly to sthg □ *"How did he take the news?" — "Badly."* **-18. to take pleasure/an interest in sthg** to enjoy/be interested in sthg □ *Mrs Andrews had always taken a keen interest in my career.* **-19. I can't take it** I find it very unpleasant and it makes me

upset □ *I can't take much more of this uncertainty.* □ *She couldn't take it any longer, so she left.* **-20.** [as an example] to give <sb/sthg> as an example of what one is saying □ *Take Sally, for instance.* □ *Let's take one thing at a time.* **-21. I take it (that)...** I believe it to be true that... □ *I take it that you two already know each other.* **-22. to take a house/an apartment etc** to rent a house/an apartment etc □ *We've taken the villa for another twelve months.* **-23.** MILITARY [city, airport, prisoner] to capture <sb/sthg> □ *The capital has been taken by rebel forces.* **-24. to take a prize** to win a prize □ *The team took first prize in the contest.*

◇ *vi* [dye, vaccine, skin graft] to produce the effect that is intended □ *The dye wouldn't take.*

◇ *n* CINEMA a piece of film recorded without a break □ *Scene one, take two.*

◆ **take after** *vt fus* **to take after sb** [parent, grandparent] to be like sb in appearance, personality etc □ *You take after your mother.*

◆ **take apart** *vt sep* **to take sthg apart** [machine, watch, mechanism] to separate sthg into pieces □ *He took the boiler apart and then said he couldn't fix it.*

◆ **take away** *vt sep* **-1. to take sb/sthg away** to remove sb/sthg □ *He was taken away in handcuffs.* □ *The waiter came to take away our plates.* **-2. to take a number away from a number** MATH to subtract a number from a number □ *If you take 21 from 40 you get 19.*

◆ **take back** *vt sep* **-1. to take sthg back** [library book, goods] to return sthg to the place it came from □ *You can always take the sweater back if the color isn't right.* **-2. to take sthg back** [goods] to accept sthg that has been returned by a customer □ *I'm sorry but we can't take it back without a receipt.* **-3. to take sthg back** [statement, accusation, criticism] to say that one has changed one's mind about sthg one said before □ *I take back everything I said about Joe, he's really a nice guy.*

◆ **take down** *vt sep* **-1. to take sthg down** [scaffolding, tent, flag] to take sthg from a high position so that it is no longer fixed or upright □ *Could somebody help me take down this blind?* **-2. to take down one's pants/shorts etc** to pull down one's pants/shorts etc without taking them off □ *Take down your trousers and I'll give you the shot.* **-3. to take sthg down** [words, message] to write down sthg that one hears or is told □ *I forgot to take down his phone number.*

◆ **take in** *vt sep* **-1. to be taken in by sb** to be deceived by sb □ *I wasn't taken in by her story.* **-2. to take sthg in** [fact, news, information] to understand sthg that one hears or is told □ *There's a lot to take in at first.* **-3. to take sthg in** to include sthg □ *The tour takes in Luxor and Aswan.* **-4. to take sb in** [animal, refugee] to let sb who has nowhere to live stay in one's home □ *He's always taking in stray cats.*

◆ **take off** ◇ *vt sep* **-1. to take sthg off** [shoe, make-up, clothes] to remove sthg from one's body or face □ *You look quite different when you take off your glasses.* **-2. to take a period of time off** to have a period of time away from work □ *I'm taking Wednesday off.* ■ **to take time off** to have a vacation or break □ *I'm taking time off next month to go visit my parents.* **-3. to take sb off** GB to imitate sb (informal use). ◇ *vi* **-1.** [plane, helicopter] to leave the ground at the start of a flight □ *We took off on time.* **-2.** [person] to go away suddenly □ *They're always taking off on vacation.* **-3.** [career, product, business] to suddenly become successful □ *Cellular phones have really taken off.*

◆ **take on** ◇ *vt sep* **-1. to take sthg on** [work, job, responsibility] to agree to do sthg □ *I've had to take on extra duties.* **-2. to take sb on** [staff, employee] to employ sb □ *The factory will be taking on 200 extra workers to complete the new contract.* **-3. to take sb on** to start a fight or argument with sb powerful; [team, champion] to play a game against sb who will be difficult to beat □ *He was even prepared to take on the big drug companies.* □ *Sydney takes on Melbourne in the final.* ◇ *vt fus* **to take on sthg** [meaning, expression, tone] to begin to have sthg □ *The words "hard work" have taken on a whole new meaning since I started my new job.* □ *The trees were taking on their autumn colors.*

◆ **take out** *vt sep* **-1. to take sthg out** to remove sthg from a place where it cannot be seen □ *He took a book out of his briefcase and handed it to me.* **-2. to take money out** to take money from one's bank account □ *I'll have to take $400 out to pay the rent.* **-3. to take out insurance** to pay for something to be insured □ *The earlier you take out a personal pension the better.* **-4. to take sb out** to invite sb to a social meeting that is planned in advance □ *I'd like to take you out for a meal some evening.* **-5. to take sthg out** [part of somebody's body] to remove sthg using surgery □ *They're going to have to take his appendix out.*

◆ **take out on** *vt sep* **to take sthg out on sb** [anger, frustration, disappointment] to express sthg that one feels by treating sb badly, although they have done nothing wrong □ *I know you're disappointed, but there's no need to take it out on me!*

◆ **take over** ◇ *vt sep* **-1. to take sthg over** [company, business, government] to get control of sthg □ *There are rumors that the Hanson group is about to be taken over.* **-2. to take sthg over** [job, role] to start doing sthg that another person used to do □ *I'll be taking over Guy's duties when he leaves.* ◇ *vi* **-1.** to take control of something or somebody □ *The army took over in a coup in 1975.* **-2.** to start doing sb's job □ *Who will take over from Lisa?*

◆ **take to** *vt fus* **to take to sb/sthg** to start to like sb/sthg □ *I didn't take to him much at first.* □ *She's never really taken to living in the country.* ■ **to take to doing sthg** to start doing sthg regularly □ *Recently he's taken to jogging every morning before work.*

◆ **take up** *vt sep* **-1. to take sthg up** [job, post, hobby] to begin doing sthg □ *I took up yoga some years ago.* □ *She has left to take up a new position as training manager.* **-2. to take sthg up** [story, account] to continue sthg that has been

interrupted □ *We take up the story again two months later in Amsterdam.* **-3. to take sthg up** [time, effort, space] to use sthg □ *Looking after the children takes up all her energy.*

◆ **take up on** *vt sep* **-1. to take sb up on sthg** [on an offer, invitation] to accept sthg that sb has offered □ *I'll take you up on that drink now.* **-2. to take sb up on sthg** [on a claim, point, statement] to ask sb to explain sthg further □ *He took the teacher up on his last remark.*

◆ **take upon** *vt sep* **to take it upon oneself to do sthg** to do sthg even though it is not one's duty to do it □ *She took it upon herself to tell everyone that I was leaving.*

◆ **take up with** ◇ *vt fus* **to take up with sb** to become friendly with sb □ *He's taken up with some blonde woman.* ◇ *vt sep* **to take sthg up with sb** [idea, suggestion, issue] to discuss sthg further with sb □ *I intend to take the matter up with the management.*

takeaway ['teɪkəweɪ] *adj* GB = **takeout**.

take-home pay *n* the amount of money one gets for working after taxes have been paid.

taken ['teɪkən] ◇ *past participle* of **take.** ◇ *adj* **to be taken with sb/sthg** to be pleased with and interested in sb/sthg □ *She seemed very taken with the idea.*

takeoff ['teɪkɒf] *n* the moment when a plane, rocket etc leaves the ground at the beginning of a flight □ *The plane was cleared for takeoff.*

takeout ['teɪkaut] *adj* **-1. a takeout restaurant** a restaurant that sells hot meals to be taken away and eaten somewhere else. **-2. takeout food** food from a takeout restaurant.

takeover ['teɪkouvər] *n* **-1.** the act of gaining control of a company by buying a lot of stock in it □ *There are rumors of a possible takeover.* **-2.** the act of gaining control of a country by force □ *a military takeover.*

takeover bid *n* an attempt by one company to take over another by buying most of its shares.

taker ['teɪkər] *n* **no takers** no people who agree to accept, try, or buy something (informal use) □ *There were hardly any takers for the special offer.*

takeup ['teɪkʌp] *n* the number of people who apply to buy stock in a company or claim benefits they have a right to □ *Takeup of family credit remains consistently low.*

takings ['teɪkɪŋz] *npl* the amount of money that a store, theater etc gets from its customers in a particular period of time □ *This week's takings are down/up on last week's.*

talc [tælk], **talcum (powder)** ['tælkəm-] *n* a very fine powder that people use after washing to dry their body and make it smell pleasant.

tale [teɪl] *n* **-1.** an invented story, especially one about magic or adventure □ *a folk tale.* **-2.** a story of something that has really happened, especially if it is exciting or interesting □ *tales of long ago/his boyhood.*

talent ['tælənt] *n* a special natural ability to do a particular thing □ *a boy with talent* □ *She has* a great musical talent. □ He's got a real talent for saying the wrong thing!

talented ['tæləntəd] adj [writer, musician, child] who has a particular talent □ Paul's extremely talented. □ She's a talented singer.

talent scout n a person whose job is to look for talented young people, especially to be part of a sports team or to work in the entertainment industry.

talisman ['tælɪzmən] (pl talismans) n an object believed to have magical powers to protect the person who owns it.

talk [tɔːk] ◇ n -1. [between people] a conversation □ I'd like to have a talk with you. □ We need to have a talk about this. -2. [of something] discussion about something that may not be true □ There's been talk of a possible merger. □ There's a lot of talk about Macintyre leaving. -3. [on something] an informal lecture □ She gave an interesting talk on local tourism. ◇ vi -1. to use spoken words to express one's feelings and thoughts □ I could hear people talking in the next room. □ I want to talk to you about John. □ He talks in a funny voice/accent. □ Can I talk with you alone? ■ **to talk about** OR **of doing sthg** to tell people that one is thinking of doing sthg □ They keep talking about buying a house. □ She's talking of going abroad again. ■ **talking of sb/sthg** a phrase used when one wants to start speaking about something that is different, but is connected with what one was speaking about before □ Talking of Christmas, what shall we do about presents? ■ **to talk big** to speak in a way that shows one is too proud of what one is or does. -2. [about somebody] to say bad things about somebody □ She's been talking about me behind my back. □ People might start talking if we're seen together. -3. [to an audience] to make a speech or lecture □ He will be talking on OR about the rise in delinquency. -4. [to the police, authorities] to give information about a crime, especially to the police. ◇ vt -1. [politics, business, sport] to have a conversation about <sthg> □ Okay then, let's talk money. -2. **to talk garbage/nonsense etc** to say something that is garbage/nonsense etc □ Don't talk nonsense!

◆ **talks** npl **to have talks** to discuss something, usually to settle a disagreement □ There have been talks between the union and management. □ peace talks.

◆ **talk down to** vt fus **to talk down to sb** [child, student, employee] to talk to sb as if one was more important, intelligent etc than them □ He has a tendency to talk down to women.

◆ **talk into** vt sep **to talk sb into sthg** to persuade sb to do sthg □ They talked me into staying.

◆ **talk out of** vt sep **to talk sb out of sthg** to persuade sb not to do sthg □ He talked her out of going.

◆ **talk over** vt sep **to talk sthg over** [problem, issue, idea] to discuss sthg calmly and in detail □ Why not try talking it over with her?

talkative ['tɔːkətɪv] adj [person, class, group] that talks a lot □ He's not very talkative, is he?

talking book n a book that has been recorded for blind people to listen to.

talking head n on television, a person who talks directly to the camera, e.g. a newscaster, and is seen only from the waist up.

talking point ['tɔːkɪŋ] n an interesting subject for people to talk about □ The main talking point at the conference was fishing rights.

talking-to n **to give sb a (good) talking-to** to talk angrily to sb in order to show that one disapproves of something they have done (informal use).

talk show n a TV or radio show in which an interviewer talks to one or more guests □ a talk show host.

tall [tɔːl] adj -1. [person, building, tree] that has a greater height than most people or things of a similar type □ She grew to be the tallest in the family. □ a tall thin man. -2. a word used to say what the height of somebody or something is □ He's six feet tall. □ How tall are you?

tall order n a task that will be difficult or almost impossible to carry out □ That's a very tall order.

tall poppy n AUS a term for a person who is very successful, rich, or famous.

❦ TALL POPPY
For most Australians, calling somebody a tall poppy means that sooner or later you think they will be "cut down", e.g. because their business fails or because they become involved in a political scandal. This attitude, where the public enjoys seeing successful people become ordinary again, is called the "tall poppy syndrome", and is considered typical of Australians' love of equality.

tall tale US, **tall story** GB n a story that is difficult to believe because it sounds exaggerated or impossible.

tally ['tælɪ] (pl tallies, pt & pp tallied) ◇ n a record of how much somebody has spent, received etc □ Could you keep a tally on spending? ◇ vi [figures, numbers] to be exactly the same amount; [story, information] to say the same thing □ The number of votes cast does not tally with how many people actually voted.

Talmud ['tælmʊd] n **the Talmud** a collection of writings about ancient Jewish laws and traditions.

talon ['tælən] n a sharp curved nail on the foot of a bird that kills animals for food, e.g. an eagle.

tambourine [ˌtæmbəˈriːn] n a round musical instrument with small metal disks around the edge that is shaken or hit with the hand so that the metal disks make a noise.

tame [teɪm] ◇ adj -1. [animal, bird] that has been trained to live with people and is no longer wild and dangerous □ The deer in the park are really tame. -2. [party, sport, life] that is not exciting enough □ Life at home seemed very tame after being abroad for so long. ◇ vt -1. [horse, eagle] to make <an animal or bird> tame. -2. [man, crowd] to make <sb> more obedient and easier to control.

Tammany Hall [,tæmənɪ-] *n* an informal name for the leaders of the New York City Democratic Party.

☙ TAMMANY HALL
Tammany Hall was the headquarters of the Democratic Party in New York in the 18th and 19th centuries. In the late 19th and early 20th centuries this organization got a bad reputation for corruption, and the terms Tammany Hall and Tammanyism are still used by many Americans to refer to political corruption.

---

tamper ['tæmpər] ◆ **tamper with** *vt fus* to **tamper with sthg** [machine, lock, records] to touch or change sthg in order to spoil or damage it ▫ *Someone's been tampering with the door lock.*

tampon ['tæmpɒn] *n* a firm piece of cotton shaped like a tube that a woman puts into her vagina to absorb the blood during her period.

tan [tæn] (*pt* & *pp* **tanned**, *cont* **tanning**) ◇ *adj* [shoes, leather, suede] light brown in color. ◇ *n* = **suntan**. ◇ *vi* [person, skin] to become suntanned ▫ *She tans easily.*

tandem ['tændəm] *n* a bicycle with two seats, designed to be ridden by two people sitting one behind the other. ■ **in tandem** [work, operate] with both people or things working closely together ▫ *The council has been working in tandem with local industry on this issue.*

tandoori [tæn'dʊərɪ] *n* a northern Indian method of cooking in which bread, meat etc is put in a large clay pot ▫ *tandoori chicken/lamb* ▫ *a tandoori meal/restaurant.*

tang [tæŋ] *n* a strong and pleasantly sharp smell or taste ▫ *the tang of an orange/a lemon* ▫ *I could smell the tang of the ocean.*

tangent ['tændʒənt] *n* a straight line that touches the edge of a curve or circle at one point. ■ **to go off on** US OR **at** GB **a tangent** to start talking about something that has no connection with what one was talking about before.

tangerine [,tændʒə'riːn] *n* a sweet fruit like a small orange that has a loose skin and is easy to peel.

tangible ['tændʒəbl] *adj* [benefits, results, difference] that can be clearly noticed; [evidence, proof] that is real and likely to be believed.

tangle ['tæŋgl] ◇ *n* -1. a mass of wires, hair etc twisted together and difficult to separate ▫ *The grave was hidden under a tangle of weeds.* -2. a state of confusion and disorder ▫ *Last year I got into a real tangle with my tax returns.* ◇ *vi* [string, wires] to get tangled. ◇ *vt* **to get tangled (up)** [string, wires] to become twisted together and difficult to separate. ◆ **tangle with** *vt fus* **to tangle with sb** to become involved in a dispute or fight with sb (informal use) ▫ *Don't tangle with him, he's dangerous.*

tangled ['tæŋgld] *adj* [hair, knot] that is twisted together and difficult to separate; [life, situation] that is complicated and difficult to re-

solve ▫ *The wires were hopelessly tangled.* ▫ *Her love life is becoming more and more tangled.*

tango ['tæŋgoʊ] (*pl* **tangos**, *pt* & *pp* **tangoed**, *cont* **tangoing**) ◇ *n* a type of dance from South America for two people that involves sudden dramatic movements of the body; a kind of music written for this dance. ◇ *vi* to dance a tango.

tangy ['tæŋɪ] (*compar* **tangier**, *superl* **tangiest**) *adj* [perfume, dish, drink] that has a tang.

tank [tæŋk] *n* -1. [for water, gas] a large glass or metal container for keeping liquid or gas in; the amount this container can hold ▫ *a hot water tank* ▫ *a fish tank* ▫ *a fuel tank* ▫ *a gas* US OR *petrol* GB *tank.* -2. MILITARY a heavy military vehicle with a large gun on top that moves on metal belts that go over the wheels on each side ▫ *a tank battle.*

tankard ['tæŋkərd] *n* a large mug, usually made of metal, that is used especially for drinking beer.

tanker ['tæŋkər] *n* a ship, truck, or train built for carrying large amounts of gas, oil, or other liquids.

tanned [tænd] *adj* [body, skin] that has a suntan ▫ *They were looking tanned and healthy.*

tannin ['tænən] *n* a brownish substance that is found naturally in the bark of some trees and plants such as tea, and is used for making leather, ink etc.

Tannoy™ ['tænɔɪ] *n* GB a system of loudspeakers used to make public announcements, e.g. at an airport.

tantalizing ['tæntəlaɪzɪŋ] *adj* [sight, smell, possibility] that is attractive and exciting, but is also annoying because one cannot have it ▫ *a tantalizing insight into the world of high finance and international politics.*

tantamount ['tæntəmaʊnt] *adj* **to be tantamount to sthg** to be almost the same as sthg ▫ *The attack is tantamount to a declaration of war.*

tantrum ['tæntrəm] (*pl* **tantrums**) *n* a sudden childish display of anger ▫ *He's having/throwing a tantrum because I took his toys away.*

Tanzania [,tænzə'niːə] a country in East Africa, on the Indian Ocean, that includes Zanzibar. SIZE: 940,000 sq kms. POPULATION: 27,800,000 (*Tanzanians*). CAPITAL: Dar es Salaam. ADMINISTRATIVE CAPITAL: Dodoma. LANGUAGE: Swahili. CURRENCY: Tanzanian shilling.

Taoiseach ['tiːʃək] *n* **the Taoiseach** the title of the prime minister of the Irish Republic.

tap [tæp] (*pt* & *pp* **tapped**, *cont* **tapping**) ◇ *n* -1. a device that controls how quickly a gas or liquid comes from a container or pipe ▫ *the bath/hot/cold tap* ▫ *a gas tap* ▫ *a glass of tap water.* -2. a quick light movement of one thing against another that makes a quiet noise ▫ *There was a tap at the window.* ◇ *vt* -1. [person, shoulder] to touch or hit <sb/sthg> lightly with one's finger or fingers ▫ *I felt somebody tap me on the shoulder.* ▫ *She tapped her fingers nervously on the desk.* -2. [strength, resources, energy] to make use of <sthg that there is a lot of> ▫ *We're trying to* find new ways of tapping the growing student market. **-3.** [telephone, wire] to listen secretly or illegally to somebody's conversation by attaching a special device to <sthg> □ *My phone's been tapped.*

◇ *vi* to touch or hit something lightly with one's finger or fingers, especially to get somebody's attention □ *Someone was tapping on* OR *at the window.*

tap dancing *n* a way of dancing that involves hitting the floor with one's feet while wearing special shoes with metal on the toes and heels.

tap dancer *n* a person who performs tap dances.

tape [teɪp] ◇ *n* **-1.** [for recording] a long thin strip of special plastic on which sound or pictures can be recorded and played back □ *a piece of cassette/audio tape* □ *I've got the record/movie on tape.* **-2.** [for playing] a cassette of tape on which music has been recorded □ *a Rolling Stones/Strauss tape* □ *a music tape.* **-3.** [for paper, packages] any kind of thin material made of plastic that is sticky on one side and is used to stick paper together, wrap packages etc □ *a roll of sticky* OR *adhesive tape.* **-4.** [on a coat, jacket] a narrow piece of cloth with a person's name on it, that is sewn onto a piece of clothing to show that it belongs to that person □ *a name tape.* **-5. the tape** SPORT a piece of material that is put across the finishing line of a race so that the winner makes it break or fall.

◇ *vt* **-1.** [music, discussion, record] to record <sthg> on a tape so that it can be heard again □ *I taped it from the radio.* **-2.** [movie, TV program] to record <sthg> on a videotape so that it can be watched later □ *Did you remember to tape that play for me?* **-3.** [package, packet, present] to close <sthg> with tape □ *She taped the box up securely.* **-4.** US [arm, leg, injury] to put a bandage on <sthg>.

tape deck *n* a machine that can record and play tapes.

tape measure *n* a long thin strip of material or plastic that is marked in inches, centimeters etc and is used for measuring objects and short distances.

taper ['teɪpər] ◇ *n* **-1.** a long thin candle. **-2.** a long thin strip of wood, cardboard etc, usually used for lighting fires. ◇ *vi* [pants, fingers] to be narrower at one end □ *His beard tapered to a point.*

◆ **taper off** *vi* [sales, numbers, interest] to gradually become less in size or amount and disappear □ *The music gradually tapered off into silence.*

tape-record [-rɪkɔːrd] *vt* [conversation, music, performance] to record <sthg> on tape.

tape recorder *n* a machine that can record sound on tape.

tape recording *n* a recording on tape of music, speaking, or other sounds.

tapered ['teɪpərd] *adj* [trousers, sleeve] that is narrower at one end.

tapestry ['tæpəstrɪ] (*pl* **tapestries**) *n* **-1.** a piece of cloth with a picture or pattern made with colored threads; the craft of making this kind of cloth. **-2.** [of events, lies] a situation that involves many different people or events (literary use) □ *life's rich tapestry.*

tapeworm ['teɪpwɜːrm] *n* a worm that lives in the intestines of some people or animals and can grow very long.

tapioca [,tæpɪˈoʊkə] *n* the white grains of a tropical plant, used for making sweet dishes.

tapir ['teɪpər] (*pl* **tapir** OR **tapirs**) *n* an animal found in America and Southeast Asia that is similar to a pig and has a long nose.

tappet ['tæpət] *n* a part of an engine that moves up and down in order to make other parts move.

taps [tæps] *n* US the name of a tune played on a bugle at military funerals or when it is time for soldiers at an army camp to go to bed.

tar [tɑːr] *n* a thick black substance that is sticky when hot and hard when cold, used e.g. for making road surfaces.

tarantula [təˈræntʃələ] *n* a large hairy spider that lives in Southern Europe and tropical America and has a poisonous bite.

target ['tɑːrgət] ◇ *n* **-1.** [of a bomb, attack, assassin] the person, place, or object that somebody chooses to attack □ *The stone hit its target.* □ *The bomb landed on target.* □ *All embassies are potential terrorist targets.* □ *A person walking alone at night is an easy target for muggers.* **-2.** SPORT & MILITARY the object that one tries to hit when practicing with a bow, gun etc; a round board with colored circles of different sizes, one inside the other □ *The army used the tower for target practice.* **-3.** [of criticism, abuse, a joke] a person or thing that somebody criticizes, jokes about etc □ *Karwiese became the target of the public's anger.* **-4.** [for success] a result that somebody wants to achieve □ *Our target is 50,000 new jobs in 1995.* □ *Last year we met all our sales targets.* ■ **to be on target** to be at the right stage or level for a particular time and likely to achieve the result that was planned □ *We're on target to complete the project by December.*

◇ *vt* **-1.** [city, building] to point a weapon at a place; [missile, gun] to point a <a weapon> at a place □ *The terrorists have targeted New York for their bombing campaign.* □ *Every missile they had was targeted on the enemy.* **-2.** [the young, elderly, homeless] to choose <a particular group of people> to receive money, a message, or a service that one wants to give □ *This new magazine/advertisement/campaign targets young professional males.* ■ **to be targeted at** OR **toward sb** [at adults, children, mothers] to be designed for sb □ *The campaign is specifically targeted at single women.*

tariff [US 'terɪf, GB 'tær-] *n* **-1.** a tax that is paid on goods coming into a country □ *Japan imposes high import tariffs on foreign cars.* **-2.** GB a list of prices for services in a hotel, e.g. rooms or meals □ *a price tariff.*

tarmac ['tɑːrmæk] *n* **-1.** a black substance made of tar mixed with small stones that is

used for covering the surface of roads.
-2. **the tarmac** an area covered with tarmac
at an airport where planes can land and take
off.

tarnish ['tɑːʳnɪʃ] ◇ *vt* -1. [brass, metal, pipe] to
make <sthg> become dull and stained.
-2. [name, reputation, popularity] to damage
<sthg> and make it less respected □ *His im-
age was severely tarnished by the scandal.* ◇ *vi*
[brass, silver, copper] *The goblet had tarnished
with age.*

tarnished ['tɑːʳnɪʃt] *adj* -1. [brass, silver, copper]
that has become dull and stained □ *an old
picture in a tarnished frame.* -2. [name, reputa-
tion] that has been damaged and is no longer
respected.

tarot [US 'teroʊ, GB 'tær-] *n* **the tarot** a pack of
22 picture cards that is used to predict peo-
ple's future.

tarot card *n* one of the cards from the tarot.

tarp [tɑːrp] *n* US = **tarpaulin.**

tarpaulin [tɑːʳˈpɔːlən] *n* -1. a type of material
covered with a waterproof substance. -2. a
sheet of tarpaulin used to cover and protect
objects from the rain.

tarragon [US 'terəgən, GB 'tær-] *n* an herb with
small thin leaves that is used to add flavor
to fish and chicken dishes.

tart [tɑːʳt] ◇ *adj* -1. [food, fruit] that has a sharp
acid taste. -2. [remark, comment] that is unpleasant and critical. ◇ *n* -1. a piece of
sweet pastry with a layer of something
sweet such as fruit on top or inside. -2.▽ a
woman who looks or behaves like a prostitute (very informal use).

tartan ['tɑːʳtn] *n* -1. a pattern of straight lines
with different widths and colors that cross
each other to make squares, originally used
in traditional dress in the Scottish Highlands; a type of woolen material that has
this pattern on it □ *a tartan scarf.* -2. a design
of tartan, worn by a particular Scottish clan
and known by its name □ *the Stewart tartan.*

tartar ['tɑːʳtəʳ] *n* a hard yellow-white substance that forms on people's teeth.

tartar(e) sauce [ˌtɑːʳtəʳ-] *n* a thick cold sauce
that is made with capers, onions, and mayonnaise and is served with fish.

Tarzan ['tɑːʳzn] the hero of a series of stories
about a white man who lives in a forest in
Africa, where he was brought up by apes.
He is very strong, and has a female companion called Jane.

Tas. *abbr of* **Tasmania.**

task [US tæsk, GB tɑːsk] *n* something that has
to be done, especially something difficult □
*Computers are now used for a wide range of dif-
ferent tasks.* □ *It was no easy task.*

task force *n* -1. MILITARY a small section of a
military force that is sent to a particular
place to deal with an emergency. -2. a
group of people formed to help with an
urgent job.

taskmaster [US 'tæskmæstr, GB 'tɑːskmɑːstə] *n* **a
hard taskmaster** a person who makes other
people work very hard.

Tasman ['tæzmən]: **the Tasman (Sea)** the part
of the southern Pacific Ocean between Australia and New Zealand.

Tasmania [tæz'meɪnjə] an island off the south
coast of Australia, that forms a state of Australia. SIZE: 68,000 sq kms. POPULATION:
452,847 (*Tasmanians*). CAPITAL: Hobart.

tassel ['tæsl] *n* a bunch of threads of yarn, silk
etc tied together at one end and left to hang
at the other and used as decoration.

taste [teɪst] ◇ *n* -1. the particular effect that a
food or drink gives when it is put in one's
mouth □ *It has a rather bitter taste.* □ *Mel woke
up with a nasty taste in his mouth.* -2. **one's
sense of taste** the sense that allows one to
tell the difference between foods when they
are in the mouth □ *Smoking can affect your
sense of taste.* -3. **a taste** a small amount of
food or drink taken to find out what it
tastes like □ *Have a taste of this, it's delicious.*
-4. **to have a taste for sthg** to like sthg □ *She
has a taste for fast cars.* -5. [of power, adventure,
success] a short experience of something
that gives somebody an idea of what it is
like □ *He got his first taste of fame alongside
Lynn Davies in "Merryweather".* -6. **sb's taste**
the ability sb has to make judgments about
fashion, style, art etc that are considered
suitable or right □ *Rachel has very good taste in
clothes/music/furniture.* ■ **to be in bad/good
taste** to be likely/not likely to offend people
□ *The scene was done in the best possible taste.*
◇ *vt* -1. [food, drink] to experience the taste of
<sthg>; to take a small amount of <sthg> to
find out what it tastes like □ *Taste this — it's
delicious.* □ *I've never tasted sushi before.* -2.
[success, defeat, power] to experience <sthg>,
with the result that one has an idea of what
it is like □ *The army had tasted victory for the
first time.* ◇ *vi* [food, drink] to have a particular taste □ *It
tastes salty/wonderful.* □ *This tastes like chicken.*
■ **to taste of sthg** [of garlic, onions] to have the
taste of sthg □ *This soup tastes of coriander.*

taste bud *n* one of the many tiny bumps on
the surface of one's tongue that allow one
to taste food and drink.

tasteful ['teɪstfl] *adj* [furniture, coat, color] that
has been made or chosen with good taste □
*The room was decorated in tasteful shades of
pink.*

tastefully ['teɪstflɪ] *adv* **tastefully decorated/
furnished** decorated/furnished in a tasteful
way □ *She dresses so tastefully.*

tasteless ['teɪstləs] *adj* -1. [decor, furniture, orna-
ment] that has not been made or chosen
with good taste □ *a tasteless collection of plastic ornaments.* -2. [remark, joke] that one finds
offensive □ *He made some tasteless joke about
funerals.* -3. [food, drink] that has little or no
taste □ *The vegetables were overcooked and
tasteless.*

tasty ['teɪstɪ] (*compar* **tastier**, *superl* **tastiest**) *adj*
[food, meal] that has a pleasant taste that
makes one want to eat it □ *tasty morsels.*

Tate Gallery [ˌteɪt-]: **the Tate Gallery** an important London gallery of British art and foreign modern art.

tattered [ˈtætərd] *adj* [clothing, shirt, paper] that is torn in many places because it has been used a lot.

tatters [ˈtætərz] *npl* **to be in tatters** [clothes] to be tattered; [confidence, reputation] to be so badly damaged that it will not recover □ *With his career and his marriage in tatters, what was he to do?*

tattle-tale [ˈtætl-] *n* US a child who tells adults about other children who have behaved badly.

tattoo [tæˈtuː] (*pl* **tattoos**) ◇ *n* -1. a colored design or picture on a part of somebody's body that is made by pricking holes in the skin and filling them with dye □ *She has a tattoo on her back.* -2. MUSIC a rhythmic beat on a military drum. -3. GB a show with military music and exercises performed in front of an audience. ◇ *vt* [name, picture] to write or draw <sthg> on a person's skin as a tattoo; [arm, leg, shoulder] to put a tattoo on <sthg> □ *a tattooed arm.*

tatty [ˈtætɪ] (*compar* **tattier**, *superl* **tattiest**) *adj* GB [clothes, apartment] that is untidy, dirty, and in bad condition (informal use).

taught [tɔːt] *past tense & past participle of* **teach**.

taunt [tɔːnt] ◇ *vt* [children, protesters, opponent] to repeatedly make unkind or insulting comments about <sb> in order to make them upset or angry □ *Demonstrators taunted police to come and arrest them.* ◇ *n* an unkind or insulting comment intended to make somebody upset or angry □ *Susan did her best to ignore their taunts.*

Taurus [ˈtɔːrəs] *n* the second sign of the Zodiac, represented by a bull; a person born under this sign between April 21 and May 22.

taut [tɔːt] *adj* [string, wire] that is stretched tight; [muscle, body] that is tense and hard □ *Pull the rope taut, then tie it.*

tauten [ˈtɔːtn] ◇ *vt* [string, wire, muscles] to make <sthg> taut. ◇ *vi* [string, wire, muscles] to become taut □ *I suddenly felt the fishing line tauten.*

tautology [tɔːˈtɒlədʒɪ] *n* a statement that says the same thing twice, using a different word or words.

tavern [ˈtævərn] *n* a bar (old-fashioned use).

tawdry [ˈtɔːdrɪ] (*compar* **tawdrier**, *superl* **tawdriest**) *adj* [dress, jewelry] that is cheap and of poor quality.

tawny [ˈtɔːnɪ] *adj* [lion, hair, fur] that is a brownish-yellow color.

tax [tæks] ◇ *n* money that one has to pay to the government of a country to pay for public services, and that varies according to one's income, the goods that one has bought etc □ *Basic foodstuffs are free of tax.* □ *This amounts to a tax on the poor.* □ *a tax on imported goods* □ *He didn't pay his taxes.* ◇ *vt* -1. [goods, services] to take a percentage of the value of <sthg>. -2. [profits, earnings] to take a percentage of <the money that some-

body makes>. -3. [person, business] to take a percentage of the earnings of <sb/sthg>. -4. **to tax sb's patience/strength etc** to use too much of sb's patience/strength etc □ *He's really beginning to tax my patience.*

taxable [ˈtæksəbl] *adj* [income, property, goods] that must be taxed by law.

tax allowance *n* GB the amount of money that a person is allowed to earn before being taxed.

taxation [tækˈseɪʃn] *n* -1. the system by which a government taxes people. -2. the amount of money taken in taxes.

tax avoidance *n* the practice of paying as little tax as possible using legal methods.

tax break *n* a reduction in tax for a particular type of business or group of people.

tax collector *n* an official whose job is to make sure that people pay taxes.

tax cut *n* a decrease in the level of taxation.

tax-deductible *adj* [expense, service] that belongs to the part of one's income that one does not have to pay tax on.

tax disc *n* in Britain, the disk on a vehicle's windshield that shows its owner has paid road tax.

tax evasion *n* the crime of not paying tax that one owes.

tax-exempt US, **tax-free** GB *adj* [goods, purchases, services] that are not taxed.

tax exemption *n* the status of not having to pay any taxes.

tax exile *n* GB a person who lives abroad to avoid paying high taxes, usually because they have a very high income.

tax-free *adj* GB = **tax-exempt**.

tax haven *n* a place that has a low level of taxation, where people go to live or register their companies to avoid paying tax in their own country.

taxi [ˈtæksɪ] ◇ *n* a car with a driver that one hires, usually to make short trips, and that usually has a meter to show how much one has to pay the driver □ *a taxi driver.* ◇ *vi* [aircraft] to move slowly along the runway before taking off or after landing.

taxicab [ˈtæksɪkæb] *n* = **taxi**.

taxidermist [ˈtæksədɜːrmɪst] *n* a person whose job is to fill dead birds and animals with material so that they look alive and can be displayed.

taximeter [ˈtæksɪmiːtər] *n* the device in a taxi that shows the cost of the trip.

taxing [ˈtæksɪŋ] *adj* [problem, trip, ordeal] that is difficult and tiring □ *She can be very taxing sometimes.*

tax inspector *n* an official whose job is to check that the correct levels of tax are being paid by a person or company.

taxi rank GB, **taxi stand** *n* a place where taxis wait for customers, especially at the exit of an airport, train station, or bus station.

taxman [ˈtæksmæn] (*pl* **taxmen** [-men]) *n* -1. = **tax collector**. -2. **the taxman** GB a term used for the government department that deals with taxes □ *The taxman is out to get me this year.*

taxpayer ['tækspeɪəʳ] *n* a person who pays income tax.

tax relief *n* a reduction in the amount of tax that a person or company has to pay.

tax return *n* a form on which somebody writes details of how much money they earn in a year and that is used to calculate how much income tax they have to pay.

tax shelter *n* a way in which one can avoid paying taxes legally, e.g. by investing in something.

tax year *n* a particular period of 12 months that is used to calculate taxes.

TB *n abbr of* **tuberculosis**.

T-bone steak *n* a piece of beef with a T-shaped bone in it.

tbs., tbsp. *abbr of* **tablespoon**.

T-cell *n* a white blood cell that helps fight against infection.

Tchaikovsky [tʃaɪ'kɒfskɪ], **Peter Ilyich** (1840–1893) a Russian composer known for his symphonies and ballets, including *Swan Lake* and *The Nutcracker*.

TD *n* -1. (*abbr of* **Treasury Department**) **the TD** the US government department responsible for managing the country's economy. -2. *abbr of* **touchdown**.

tea [tiː] *n* -1. [for drinking] a drink made by adding boiling water to the dried leaves of a particular plant; a cup of this drink □ *Do you take milk in your tea?* □ *Two teas, please.* □ *Do you want some tea?* -2. [from the plant] the dried leaves of the plant used for making tea. -3. GB [in the afternoon] an afternoon snack consisting of cake and sandwiches, with tea to drink. -4. GB & AUS [in the evening] a meal that is eaten in the early evening.

teabag ['tiːbæg] *n* a small thin paper bag that has a lot of very small holes, contains tealeaves, and is used to make a cup of tea.

tea ball *n* a ball made of wire mesh that is filled with tealeaves and dipped in a cup of boiling water to make tea.

tea break *n* GB a short period when one stops working and drinks tea, coffee etc to relax.

tea caddy *n* a small metal box used for storing tea.

teacake ['tiːkeɪk] *n* GB a type of bread roll that contains dried fruit and is usually eaten toasted and buttered.

teach [tiːtʃ] (*pt & pp* **taught**) ◇ *vt* -1. to give <sb> lessons in a subject or instructions on how to behave or act correctly in a particular situation □ *Do you find it easier to teach adults?* □ *I'm teaching her French/the piano.* □ *He's teaching his dog to fetch sticks.* □ *I was always taught that it's wrong to steal.* -2. [math, yoga, the violin] to give lessons in <sthg> □ *I taught English to foreign students.* -3. [respect, humility] to tell people about <sthg> so that they start to believe it is valuable □ *It's about time someone taught you some manners, young*

man! ◇ *vi* [person] to teach a subject, skill etc □ *I teach at a local school.*

teacher ['tiːtʃəʳ] *n* a person whose job is to teach people, usually at a school, college etc.

teacher's pet *n* a child in a class who the other children think is the teacher's favorite student (informal and disapproving use).

teacher training college *n* a college where people train to be teachers.

teaching ['tiːtʃɪŋ] *n* -1. the profession or activity of being a teacher □ *Do you like teaching?* -2. a message or lesson that is taught □ *the teachings of the Christian Church/Buddhism.*

teaching aids *npl* things, e.g. videos or pictures, that are used by a teacher during a lesson to help them to explain something.

teaching hospital *n* a hospital where medical students and doctors who have recently qualified can get practical training from experienced doctors.

teaching practice *n* teaching done by somebody who is training to be a teacher.

teaching staff *npl* the staff in a school who teach.

tea cozy *n* a soft thick covering of fabric or knitted wool that one puts over a teapot to keep the tea inside it warm.

teacup ['tiːkʌp] *n* a cup that is used for drinking tea.

teak [tiːk] *n* the very hard red-brown wood of a tree that grows in Southeast Asia, and is used to make boats and furniture □ *a teak chair.*

tealeaves ['tiːliːvz] *npl* the small pieces of leaves that are used to make a drink of tea and that often remain in the bottom of a cup or pot when the tea has been drunk.

team [tiːm] *n* -1. a group of people who play a particular sport together against other groups of the same kind. -2. a group of people who do a particular job together □ *a research/negotiating team.*

◆ **team up** *vi* [people, organizations] to work together for a particular purpose □ *Why don't you team up with Helen for the next part?*

team games *npl* games between teams, not individuals.

teammate ['tiːmmeɪt] *n* a member of the same team as somebody.

team spirit *n* the feeling of pride and enthusiasm that all members of a team have when they want the team to succeed.

teamster ['tiːmstəʳ] *n* US a person whose job is to drive a truck.

◆ **Teamsters** *n* **the Teamsters** in the USA, the labor union for truck drivers.

teamwork ['tiːmwɜːʳk] *n* the act of working well together as a team.

tea party *n* a type of party in the afternoon where tea is served.

teapot ['tiːpɒt] *n* a container that has a lid, a handle, and a spout, and is used for making and serving tea.

tear¹ [tɪəʳ] *n* one of the drops of salty liquid

that come out of one's eyes because one is sad, happy, in pain etc □ *She came to me in tears.* □ *I was close to tears by the end of the speech.*

tear² [teəʳ] (*pt* **tore**, *pp* **torn**) ◇ *vt* **-1.** [paper, clothes] to damage <sthg> by pulling a piece of it away from the rest partly or completely □ *My skirt got torn at the prom.* □ *He tore the envelope open.* □ *The letter had been torn to shreds/into several pieces.* ■ **to tear sb/sthg to pieces** to criticize sb/sthg very strongly □ *Professor Hillard tore my essay to pieces.* ■ **to be torn between sthg and sthg** to be unable to decide between sthg and sthg □ *I'm torn between telling her and keeping quiet.* **-2.** [muscle, ligament] to damage <sthg> by moving it in the wrong directon. **-3. to tear sb/sthg from sb/sthg** to remove sb/sthg from sb/sthg using force.

◇ *vi* **-1.** [paper, clothes] to get torn □ *Be careful, it tears easily.* **-2. to tear off/around etc** [person, car, animal] to move away/around etc very quickly (informal use) □ *He grabbed my purse and went tearing off down the street.* **-3. to tear loose** to escape from something that is holding one by struggling.

◇ *n* a hole in a piece of paper, clothing etc that has been torn □ *There's a small tear in my coat.*

◆ **tear apart** *vt sep* **-1. to tear sthg apart** [book, material] to separate sthg into pieces by tearing it. **-2. to tear sthg apart** [team, organization] to harm sthg by making the people in it argue with each other □ *These constant arguments are just tearing the family apart.*

◆ **tear at** *vt fus* **to tear at sthg** [package, meat] to damage sthg by trying to tear pieces off it.

◆ **tear away** *vt sep* **to tear oneself away** to force oneself to leave a place or situation □ *The game was so good, I just couldn't tear myself away from it.*

◆ **tear down** *vt sep* **-1. to tear sthg down** [house, wall] to demolish sthg. **-2. to tear sthg down** [poster, advertisement] to remove sthg from a wall by pulling it violently.

◆ **tear off** *vt sep* **to tear sthg off** [clothes, shoes] to remove sthg from one's body quickly and forcefully.

◆ **tear out** *vt sep* **to tear sthg out** [coupon, page] to remove sthg from a book, piece of paper etc.

◆ **tear up** *vt sep* **to tear sthg up** [check, letter] to destroy sthg by tearing it into several pieces.

teardrop ['tɪəʳdrɒp] *n* a single tear from somebody's eye.

tearful ['tɪəʳfl] *adj* [person] who is very upset and wants to cry □ *I was feeling quite tearful as we parted.*

tear gas ['tɪəʳ-] *n* a gas that makes one's eyes sting and is sometimes used by police to control crowds.

tearjerker ['tɪəʳdʒɜːʳkəʳ] *n* a movie or book that is meant to make people so sad or happy that they feel like crying (humorous use).

tearoom ['tiːruːm] *n* a type of restaurant where tea, coffee, cake etc is served.

tease [tiːz] ◇ *vt* **-1.** to make unkind or playful jokes to <sb> about something that embarrasses them □ *They teased him about his haircut.* **-2.** US to comb <one's hair> from the ends to the roots to make it look thicker. ◇ *n* **-1.** a person who teases people. **-2.** a person who makes another person think that they want to have sex with them but who does not really want to (disapproving use).

tea service, tea set *n* a matching set of teacups, saucers, plates, milk pitcher, sugar bowl, and teapot, used for serving tea.

tea shop *n* = **tearoom**.

teasing ['tiːzɪŋ] *adj* [smile, remark, behavior] that shows one is making fun of somebody in a playful way.

teaspoon ['tiːspuːn] *n* a small spoon used for putting sugar into tea or coffee and for stirring it; the amount contained by this spoon.

tea strainer *n* a metal or plastic object with a lot of small holes in it that is used to catch the tealeaves when tea is being poured into a cup.

teat [tiːt] *n* **-1.** one of the pointed parts on the chest of a female mammal that babies suck to drink milk. **-2.** GB a piece of plastic or rubber, shaped like a teat, that can be fitted to a bottle so that a baby or small animal can drink from it.

teatime ['tiːtaɪm] *n* the time in the afternoon when tea is usually drunk.

tea towel *n* a cloth used to dry silverware and plates after they have been washed.

technical ['teknɪkl] *adj* **-1.** [expert, training, advances] that has, or involves, detailed practical knowledge of subjects connected with science, industry etc □ *My technical knowledge is pretty limited.* **-2.** [brilliance, skill] that is connected with one's ability in a particular activity, especially in sports, art, or music □ *There's no question about his technical skill, I just wonder how creative he is.* **-3.** [term, language, sense] that is connected with the details of a particular subject or activity □ *The book used a lot of technical terms that I didn't understand.*

technical college *n* a college of further education where students can do practical courses.

technical drawing *n* the skill of drawing designs for buildings, pieces of equipment etc that show precise details of how they are made.

technicality [ˌteknɪˈkælətɪ] (*pl* **technicalities**) *n* a very small detailed point, especially a legal one, based on a very strict understanding of a rule or law □ *The patent was withdrawn on a technicality.*

◆ **technicalities** *npl* **the technicalities** the small details of a process or activity that only people who know a lot about it understand or are interested in □ *I won't go into all the technicalities of the process.*

technically ['teknɪklɪ] *adv* **-1. technically (speak-**

ing),... a word used to say that something is true according to a strict understanding of the facts, laws, or the meaning of words □ *Technically, you're right, but in practice it doesn't happen like that.* -2. **technically possible/advanced etc** possible/advanced etc according to what is known about science or technology. -3. **technically brilliant/skilled** brilliant/skilled in the techniques needed for a particular activity □ *a technically brilliant pianist/skater.*

technician [tek'nɪʃn] *n* -1. a person whose job is to use and take care of particular kinds of equipment □ *a lighting/laboratory technician.* -2. a person who is good at an activity, e.g. art or a sport, that requires particular skills.

Technicolor™ ['teknɪkʌlə^r] *n* a system of color photography used in making movies for the cinema.

technique [tek'niːk] *n* -1. a particular method of doing something, especially something involving practical skills. -2. skill in a particular activity, e.g. in sports or the arts, that one has developed with practice.

technocrat ['teknəkræt] *n* a person who is an expert in a technical subject, e.g. science or economics, and who also has power in the government of their country.

technological [,teknə'lɒdʒɪkl] *adj* [breakthrough, development] *see* **technology**.

technologist [tek'nɒlədʒəst] *n* an expert in technology.

technology [tek'nɒlədʒɪ] (*pl* **technologies**) *n* -1. the study and practical use of science in industry, medicine, business etc □ *computer/agricultural/medical technology.* -2. equipment that is made using scientific knowledge □ *These special effects were achieved using the latest technology.*

Tecumseh [tɪ'kʌmsə] (1768–1813) a Native American chief who tried to unite Native Americans against the Whites.

teddy ['tedɪ] (*pl* **teddies**) *n* a **teddy (bear)** a soft toy that looks like a bear.

tedious ['tiːdjəs] *adj* [subject, book, job] that one finds boring and tiring □ *Professor Hill's lecture was as tedious as usual.*

tedium ['tiːdjəm] *n*: *see* **tedious**.

tee [tiː] *n* -1. one of the areas on a golf course from which the ball is hit at the start of each attempt to get it into a hole. -2. the small wooden or plastic object that is pushed into the ground to hold the golf ball before it is hit from the tee.

◆ **tee off** *vi* [golfer] to hit a golf ball from the tee.

teem [tiːm] *vi* **to be teeming with sthg** [with traffic, cars, animals] to be very crowded with sthg that never stops moving □ *The streets were teeming with people.*

teen [tiːn] *adj* = **teenage** (informal use).

teenage(d) ['tiːneɪdʒ(d)] *adj* [boy, daughter, child] who is a teenager; [fashion, problem] that is connected with teenagers.

teenager ['tiːneɪdʒə^r] *n* a person who is between 13 and 19 years old.

teens [tiːnz] *npl* the period of one's life when one is a teenager □ *the late/early/mid teens* □ *He's now in his teens.*

teeny (weeny) [,tiːnɪ('wiːnɪ)], **teensy (weensy)** [,tiːnzɪ('wiːnzɪ)] *adj* very small (informal use).

tee shirt *n* a light piece of clothing worn on the top part of one's body that has short sleeves and no collar or buttons.

Teeside, Teesside ['tiːsaɪd] an industrial area on the river Tees, in northeastern England.

teeter ['tiːtə^r] *vi* -1. [person, object] to move around in an uncertain way, usually before falling. -2. **to be teetering on the brink** OR **edge** to be close to a very dangerous or harmful situation in a way that is worrying □ *The country is teetering on the brink of war.* □ *I was teetering on the edge of bankruptcy.*

teeter-totter *n* US a piece of equipment for children to play on, consisting of a long piece of metal or wood balanced in the middle so that it moves up and down when people sit at either end.

teeth [tiːθ] *plural of* **tooth**.

teethe [tiːð] *vi* **to be teething** [baby] to have teeth that are growing through the gums, causing pain.

teething ring ['tiːðɪŋ-] *n* a ring of plastic that a baby can chew when it is teething.

teething troubles *npl* problems that occur during the early stages of a project or activity □ *The company's had a few teething troubles.*

teetotal [tiː'toutl] *adj* [person] who is a teetotaler; [meeting, country] where alcohol is not drunk.

teetotaler US, **teetotaller** GB [tiː'toutlə^r] *n* a person who does not drink alcohol.

TEFL ['tefl] *n abbr of* **Teaching (of) English as a Foreign Language**.

Teflon™ ['teflɒn] *n* a plastic used on the inside surface of saucepans, frying-pans etc, so that food does not stick to it □ *a Teflon saucepan.*

Tehran, Teheran [,teə'rɑːn] the capital of Iran and its largest city. POPULATION: 5,734,000.

tel. *abbr of* **telephone, telephone number**.

Tel-Aviv [,telə'viːv] a city in Israel, on the Mediterranean coast. It used to be the capital of Israel. POPULATION: 400,000.

tele- ['telɪ] *prefix* added to a word to show that something happens, operates, or is done over a long distance.

telecast [US 'telɪkæst, GB -kɑːst] *n* a program on television.

telecom ['telɪkɒm] *n*, **telecoms** ['telɪkɒmz] *npl* GB = **telecommunications** (informal use).

telecommunications [,telɪkəmjuːnɪ'keɪʃnz] *npl* the use of electronic equipment, faxes, or phones to send or receive messages □ *the telecommunications industry* □ *a telecommunications satellite.*

telegram ['telɪgræm] *n* a message that is sent to somebody by telegraph and delivered to them after it has been printed.

telegraph ['telɪgræf, GB -grɑːf] ◇ *n* the system of sending messages using electricity or radio signals over a distance. ◇ *vt* to send <a message> to somebody using a telegraph; to contact <sb> in this way.

telegraph pole, telegraph post *n* GB = **telephone pole.**

telemarketing [ˌtelɪˈmaːrkətɪŋ] *n* the practice of phoning people to tell them about a particular product or service.

telepathic [ˌtelɪˈpæθɪk] *adj* [person, powers] *see* **telepathy.**

telepathy [təˈlepəθɪ] *n* the communication of thoughts and feelings between people without using any of the normal ways of communicating such as talking or seeing.

telephone [ˈtelɪfoʊn] ◇ *n* -**1.** a system of communication that allows two people in different places to talk to each other using special pieces of equipment □ *We spoke by telephone.* □ *They had a number of telephone conversations.* -**2.** a piece of equipment used for talking to somebody by telephone. ■ **to be on the telephone** to be using one's telephone to speak to somebody □ *I'm sorry I took so long to answer the door, I was on the telephone.* ◇ *vt* [person, company, shop] to contact <sb> by telephone. ◇ *vi* [person] *Has he telephoned yet?*

telephone book *n* a large book that contains a list of the names, addresses, and telephone numbers of the people in a particular town or area.

telephone booth *n* a small enclosed space in a public building or area with a phone that one can use by putting coins, a special card etc into it.

telephone box *n* GB = **telephone booth.**

telephone call *n* an act of contacting somebody using a telephone □ *I've got to make a telephone call.*

telephone directory *n* = **telephone book.**

telephone exchange *n* a place where connections are made between people speaking by telephone.

telephone kiosk *n* GB = **telephone booth.**

telephone number *n* the series of numbers one dials in order to speak to a particular person by telephone □ *Do you have my telephone number?*

telephone operator *n* a person in a telephone exchange whose job is to connect people by telephone, and to give information to people who want to make telephone calls.

telephone pole *n* US a tall wooden pole used to hold up telephone wires.

telephone tapping [-ˈtæpɪŋ] *n* the act of listening to other people's telephone conversations by using a special piece of equipment.

telephonist [təˈlefənəst] *n* GB a person whose job is to answer the telephone for a company or other organization, or to connect calls in a telephone exchange.

telephoto lens [ˌtelɪfoʊtoʊ-] *n* a long camera lens, shaped like a tube, that one can use to take close-up photographs of people or things that are far away.

teleprinter [ˈtelɪprɪntər] *n* a machine that can send, receive, and print out telex messages.

Teleprompter™ [ˈtelɪprɒmptər] *n* a machine placed in front of a person on television, but out of sight of the cameras, from which they can read their lines as if they were speaking naturally.

telesales [ˈtelɪseɪlz] *n* the practice of phoning people in order to try to sell them particular goods or services.

telescope [ˈtelɪskoʊp] *n* a device consisting of a long tube that contains more than one lens, and that makes things that are far away seem much closer.

telescopic [ˌtelɪˈskɒpɪk] *adj* -**1.** [equipment, sight, lens] that makes things appear larger and nearer than they are. -**2.** [umbrella, tripod] that is made in sections that slide over each other so that it can be folded when it is not being used.

teleshopping [ˈtelɪʃɒpɪŋ] *n* the practice of ordering goods from home, using one's telephone or computer, instead of going to stores.

teletext [ˈtelɪtekst] *n* a system that broadcasts written news and information on people's television screens.

telethon [ˈtelɪθɒn] *n* a television program that lasts for several hours, and tries to raise money for charity.

teletypewriter [ˌtelɪˈtaɪpraɪtər] US *n* = **teleprinter.**

televangelism [ˌtelɪˈvændʒəlɪzm] *n* programs on television in which people preach to viewers to persuade them to become Christians.

televise [ˈtelɪvaɪz] *vt* [program, event, debate] to broadcast <sthg> on television □ *The games were televised on NBC.*

television [ˈtelɪvɪʒn] *n* -**1.** the system of broadcasting sound and pictures by electrical waves that are received by a special device; the business connected with making television programs □ *I don't watch television very often.* □ *There's an interesting program on television tonight.* □ *He now works in television.* -**2.** a device shaped like a box with a screen at the front on which television programs appear, with sound, using a special electronic device that receives broadcast signals □ *Do you have a television?*

television licence *n* in Britain, a document that one has to pay for each year to be legally allowed to use a television in one's home.

television program *n* something such as a show, play etc that is broadcast on television.

television set *n* a television.

teleworking [ˈtelɪwɜːrkɪŋ] *n* the practice of working from home, using a computer, fax etc, instead of going to work in an office.

telex [ˈteleks] ◇ *n* -**1.** a system for sending information between teleprinters in different countries □ *I heard from him via* OR *by telex.* -**2.** a machine that transmits messages by telex. -3. a message sent by telex. ◊ *vt* to send a telex to <sb>; to send <sthg> to somebody by telex □ *I'll telex you with the details.* □ *The plan was telexed to them last week.*

tell [tel] (*pt* & *pp* **told**) ◊ *vt* -1. [person, public, press] to give <sb> information by speaking or writing to them □ *Who told you about Mike?* □ *Nobody told me the meeting had been canceled!* □ *Whatever you do, don't tell them your address.* □ *Eventually he sent me a letter telling me why he'd left home.* □ *Could you tell the viewers why you resigned so suddenly?* ■ **I told you so!** a phrase used to somebody when something bad happens to them that one has previously warned them about and that they have ignored □ *I told you he'd be late!* □ *There, I told you so! You wouldn't listen to me!* -2. **to tell the truth/a lie** to say something that is true/untrue □ *How do we know he's telling us the truth?* □ *You're telling lies!* -3. **to tell sb to do sthg** to say to sb that they must do sthg □ *We were told to come back in half an hour.* □ *I'm not asking you to leave, I'm telling you!* □ *Do as you're told!* -4. **to tell a story/joke** to say what happens in a story/joke □ *My mother used to tell us bedtime stories every evening.* -5. **I/we etc can tell sthg** I/we etc know that sthg is true or is happening because certain signs make it obvious □ *I can always tell when you're nervous.* □ *I couldn't tell who'd sent the letter, as the signature was illegible.* □ *The best way to tell whether it's ripe is to press it gently.* ■ **there's no telling...** it is impossible to say... □ *There's no telling how she'll react.* -6. **to tell the difference** to be able to recognize or show how two people or things are different from each other □ *He can't tell the difference between right and wrong/me and my sister.* -7. **to tell sb sthg** to be a sign or indication of sthg to sb □ *A person's handwriting tells you a lot about their character.* □ *Your body will tell you when you've had enough to eat.*
◊ *vi* [strain, effort, hard work] to have a bad effect on a person or situation after a while □ *The strain of the past few weeks was beginning to tell on me.*

◆ **tell apart** *vt sep* **to tell two people/things apart** to be able to recognize the differences between two people/things that are very similar □ *It's difficult to tell these two types of bacteria apart.*

◆ **tell off** *vt sep* **to tell sb off** to speak angrily to sb because they have done something wrong □ *We got told off for arriving late.*

Tell [tel], **William** in Swiss legends, a 15th–century revolutionary who was forced to shoot an apple off his son's head using a crossbow.

teller ['telər] *n* -1. a person who counts the votes in an election. -2. a person in a bank whose job is to receive and pay out money.

telling ['telɪŋ] *adj* -1. [point, argument] that is very important and true and has a strong effect on the people who hear it. -2. [remark, look, smile] that shows what somebody is thinking or feeling, even if it was not meant to □ *I thought it was very telling the way Susan refused to shake hands.*

telling-off (*pl* **tellings-off**) *n* **to give sb a telling-off** to speak angrily to sb who has done something wrong □ *We got such a telling-off when we got home.*

telltale ['telteɪl] *adj* **a telltale sign/stain etc** a sign/stain etc that causes one to notice something unpleasant that is not obvious in other ways □ *Morgan's showing all the telltale signs of overwork.*

telly ['telɪ] (*pl* **tellies**) *n* GB = **television** (informal use).

temerity [tə'merətɪ] *n* **to have the temerity to do sthg** to do sthg that somebody else finds annoying because it shows no respect □ *Then she had the temerity to ask me to pay for it.*

temp [temp] (informal use) ◊ *n* (*abbr of* **temporary employee**) a person who is employed for a short time, usually in an office, when somebody is ill, or when there is a lot of extra work to do. ◊ *vi* to work as a temp □ *She's temping in a bank at the moment.*

temp. *abbr of* **temperature.**

temper ['tempər] ◊ *n* -1. the habit somebody has of getting angry easily □ *He was in a bad/foul temper.* ■ **to lose one's temper** to suddenly become extremely angry □ *Don't make me lose my temper with you.* ■ **to have a (short) temper** to become angry easily. ■ **to be in a temper** to be very angry □ *Be careful, the boss is in a temper today.* -2. the way that somebody usually behaves and speaks as a result of their character □ *a man of even temper.* ◊ *vt* [language, emotion, success] to make <sthg> less extreme.

temperament ['temprəmənt] *n* a person's basic character, especially in relation to their moods and the way they react to other people, situations etc □ *Anthony's got a very calm temperament.*

temperamental [ˌtemprə'mentl] *adj* -1. [person] who is unpredictable and changes their mood very suddenly (disapproving use) □ *She's a good actor, but she can be a little temperamental.* -2. [machine, car] that is unpredictable and often doesn't work □ *The car may not start — it's a little temperamental sometimes.*

temperance ['temprəns] *n* (formal use) -1. the practice of avoiding extreme kinds of behavior. -2. the practice of not drinking alcohol because one thinks that it is morally wrong.

temperate ['tempərət] *adj* [climate, area] that is neither extremely hot nor extremely cold □ *the Temperate Zone.*

temperature ['temprətʃər] *n* -1. the degree of heat or coldness of a place or thing. -2. the degree of heat of one's body. ■ **to have a temperature** [person] to have a higher temperature than normal, usually because one is ill. ■ **to take sb's temperature** to measure sb's temperature, using a thermometer, to see if they are ill.

tempest ['tempəst] *n* -1. a storm (literary use). -2. *phrase* **a tempest in a teapot** US a situation that is not very important but that causes a lot of worry and trouble.

tempestuous [tem'pestʃʊəs] *adj* [relationship, meeting, period] that is very emotional.

tempi ['tempiː] *plural of* **tempo**.

template ['templeɪt] *n* -1. a thin plate of plastic or metal of a particular shape that is used to help one cut wood, material etc accurately. -2. COMPUTING the basic outline of a computer program that can be designed and then called up from the memory to be used for a particular purpose.

temple ['templ] *n* -1. RELIGION a building used for worship in some religions. -2. ANATOMY one of the two flat parts at each side of one's forehead.

tempo ['tempoʊ] (*pl* **tempos** OR **tempi**) *n* -1. MUSIC the speed at which a piece of music is played. -2. [of change, a game, debate] the speed at which something happens.

temporarily [US ˌtempəˈrerəlɪ, GB 'tempɾərəlɪ] *adv* [unavailable, out of order] *see* **temporary**.

temporary [US 'tempərerɪ, GB 'tempɾərɪ] *adj* [job, accommodation, situation] that lasts for a limited period of time □ *It's only a temporary appointment.*

tempt [tempt] *vt* to make <sb> want to do something, especially by offering them something attractive □ *The former world champion was tempted out of retirement by a lucrative sponsorship deal.* □ *I was/felt tempted to stay.*

temptation [temp'teɪʃn] *n* the state of wanting to have or do something, usually when one knows it is wrong; something that causes one to feel like this □ *I somehow resisted the temptation to tell her what I really thought.* □ *Having chocolate in the house is too much of a temptation for me.*

tempting ['temptɪŋ] *adj* [offer, smell, cake] that one finds attractive.

ten [ten] *num* the number 10; *see also* **five**.

tenable ['tenəbl] *adj* -1. [position, argument] that is reasonable and can be defended successfully. -2. [job, post] that can be held by somebody for a particular length of time □ *The post is tenable for three years initially.*

tenacious [təˈneɪʃəs] *adj* [person, dog, opponent] that is very determined and does not accept defeat or failure easily.

tenacity [təˈnæsətɪ] *n*: *see* **tenacious**.

tenancy ['tenənsɪ] (*pl* **tenancies**) *n* -1. a period of time during which somebody pays rent for land, a house, apartment etc. -2. the use of land, a house, apartment etc for which a person pays rent □ *a tenancy agreement.*

tenant ['tenənt] *n* a person who pays rent to live or work in a building. NOTE: Compare **landlady, landlord**.

Ten Commandments *npl* **the Ten Commandments** the laws that, according to the Jewish and Christian religions, were given by God to Moses on Mount Sinai.

tend [tend] *vt* -1. **to tend to do sthg** to do sthg often □ *I'm afraid that tends to be the case.* □ *He tends to be a little rash in his decisions.* -2. [patients, garden, sheep] to take care of <a person, place, or animal>.

tendency ['tendənsɪ] (*pl* **tendencies**) *n* -1. a pattern of behavior, events etc that involves something happening often □ *There is a tendency to overspend at this time of year.* ■ **a tendency toward sthg** a tendency that suggests sthg is happening more and more □ *These figures show a tendency toward lower staff levels.* -2. a pattern in somebody's behavior that is part of their character □ *musical/murderous/anarchic tendencies* □ *She has a tendency to exaggerate.*

tender ['tendər] ◇ *adj* -1. [person, feeling, word] that seems gentle and caring. -2. [meat, steak] that is soft and easy to cut and chew. -3. [bruise, foot, wound] that is sore and hurts when it is touched. -4. *phrase* **at a tender age** at a very young and innocent age □ *She acted in her first movie at the tender age of eleven.* ◇ *n* BUSINESS an offer to provide goods or a service to a customer at a particular price □ *Have you put in a tender for the Forbes contract yet?* ◇ *vt* [resignation, money, apology] to offer <sthg> formally (formal use).

tenderize, -ise ['tendəraɪz] *vt* to make <meat> tender by preparing it in a particular way.

tenderly ['tendərlɪ] *adv* [speak, hold, treat] in a gentle and caring way.

tendon ['tendən] *n* a part of the body like a strong cord that connects a muscle to a bone.

tendril ['tendrəl] *n* a short curling part that grows from the main stem of a plant and is used by the plant to attach itself to something.

tenement ['tenəmənt] *n* a large old building, especially in the poor part of a city, that is divided into small apartments.

Tenerife [ˌtenəˈriːf] the largest of the Canary Islands and a popular tourist center. SIZE: 1,919 sq kms. POPULATION: 500,000. CAPITAL: Santa Cruz.

tenet ['tenət] *n* one of the beliefs on which a larger system of beliefs or a theory is based (formal use).

tenner ['tenər] *n* **a tenner** GB (informal use) ten pounds; a bill with a value of ten pounds.

Tennessee [ˌtenəˈsiː] a state in the southeastern USA, situated between the Appalachian Mountains and the Mississippi River. ABBREVIATION: TN. SIZE: 109,412 sq kms. POPULATION: 4,877,185 (*Tennesseans, Tennesseeans*). CAPITAL: Nashville.

Tennessee Valley Authority *n* **the Tennessee Valley Authority** a US government agency that controls natural resources in the area of the Tennessee River. It was established in 1933 and is one of the first examples of a government protecting the environment.

tennis ['tenəs] *n* a game played by two people or two pairs of people who stand on opposite sides of a low wide net and use tennis rackets to hit a small ball over it □ *tennis clothes* □ *a tennis match/club/player.*

tennis ball *n* a small rubber ball covered in a soft material that is used in tennis.

tennis court *n* the rectangular area for playing tennis on a surface of grass, asphalt etc.

tennis player *n* a person who plays tennis.

tennis racket *n* a wooden or metal object with a long handle and a rounded flat part with strings stretched across it, used to hit the ball in tennis.

Tennyson ['tenəsən], **Alfred** (1809–1892) a British poet whose best-known work is *The Charge of the Light Brigade*. He is also called Alfred, Lord Tennyson.

tenor ['tenər] ◇ *n* -1. MUSIC the highest natural male singing voice; a man who has this voice. -2. **the tenor of sthg** [of somebody's reply, letter, tone] the general meaning suggested by sthg (formal use). ◇ *adj* MUSIC [voice, recorder, saxophone] that can produce a range of notes similar to that of the tenor.

tenpins ['tenpɪnz] US, **tenpin bowling** [ˌtenpɪn-] GB *n* an indoor game in which one tries to knock down ten wooden bottle-shaped objects with a heavy ball that one rolls along a long narrow section of floor.

tense [tens] ◇ *adj* -1. [person] who seems worried and unable to relax; [period, situation] in which one is worried and unable to relax. -2. [body, muscles] that is stiff and not moving, especially because of effort or concentration. ◇ *n* GRAMMAR the form of a verb that shows whether one is referring to the past, present, or future. ◇ *vt* to make <one's body, muscles> etc tense. ◇ *vi* [person, animal, muscles] to become stiff, especially because of effort or concentration □ *He tensed, listening for sounds from downstairs.*

tensed up [ˌtenst-] *adj* **to be tensed up to** be anxious and unable to relax.

tension ['tenʃn] *n* -1. [in oneself] a feeling of worry or pressure that makes it difficult for one to relax □ *Overwork causes tension.* -2. [between two people] disagreement or bad feelings in a relationship between two people. -3. [between countries] a situation in which people do not trust each other and there may be violence as a result □ *Tension is mounting in the region.* -4. TECHNOLOGY [of a wire, rope] the degree to which something is stretched tight.

◆ **tensions** *npl* feelings of tension between people, countries etc □ *racial/family tensions.*

ten-spot *n* US a ten-dollar bill (informal use).

tent [tent] *n* a movable shelter, used for camping, that is made of nylon or canvas stretched over poles and held down by ropes.

tentacle ['tentəkl] *n* one of the arms of a squid, octopus etc that are used for touching and holding things, and for moving around.

tentative ['tentətɪv] *adj* -1. [person, handshake] that seems uncertain and does not show much confidence □ *the first tentative steps toward reform.* -2. [agreement, proposal] that has not been finally accepted.

tentatively ['tentətɪvlɪ] *adv*: see **tentative** □ *She looked tentatively into the room.* □ *The delegates tentatively agreed on a date for resuming talks.*

tenterhooks ['tentərhʊks] *npl* **to be on tenterhooks** to be waiting for something anxiously.

tenth [tenθ] *num* 10th; number ten in a series; see also **fifth**.

tent peg *n* a wooden or metal peg used to keep a tent firmly in a particular position.

tent pole *n* a pole used to support the material of a tent.

tenuous ['tenjʊəs] *adj* [argument, connection] that is weak and not very convincing.

tenure ['tenjər] *n* (formal use) -1. the legal right to use a particular building or piece of land during a fixed period of time. -2. the right to keep a job as a university teacher for as long as one wants □ *She's lucky: she has tenure.*

tepee ['tiːpiː] *n* a tent shaped like a cone made by the Plains Indians from animal skins.

tepid ['tepəd] *adj* -1. [water, bath] that is warm, but not very warm. -2. [performance, welcome, speech] that does not show much energy or enthusiasm (disapproving use).

tequila [təˈkiːlə] *n* a strong alcoholic drink made in Mexico.

Ter. GB *abbr of* **terrace**.

term [tɜːm] ◇ *n* -1. a word or expression that refers to a particular thing, especially something technical □ *a banking term.* -2. POLITICS the fixed period of time during which a particular party, president, prime minister etc stays in power after being elected □ *It doesn't look like he'll make it to a second term in office.* -3. the length of time that a particular job or situation lasts □ *a prison term.* ■ **in the long/short term** over a long/short period of time in the future. -4. EDUCATION one of the periods of time into which the year is divided in a school, college, or university.

◇ *vt* **to be termed sthg** to be called sthg □ *The top part of a shoe is termed "the upper".*

◆ **terms** *npl* -1. the conditions of a contract, agreement, proposal etc □ *We do this on my terms or not at all.* -2. **in international/real etc terms** if one considers the international/real etc situation □ *In economic terms, the policy is bound to be a winner.* -3. **on equal** OR **the same terms** [meet, hold discussions] at the same social or professional level. ■ **to be on good terms** [people] to have a good relationship with each other □ *At least I'm on good terms with my bank manager.* ■ **not to be on speaking terms with sb** to have such a bad relationship with sb that one does not speak to them □ *They haven't been on speaking terms for years.* -4. *phrase* **to come to terms with sthg** to accept sthg unpleasant and not let it affect one's life too much □ *She's only just starting to come to terms with the death of her son.*

◆ **in terms of** *prep* a phrase used to refer to one particular aspect of a situation □ *In terms of inflation, the policy works.* ■ **to be thinking in terms of sthg** to be considering sthg □ *I was thinking more in terms of buying than renting.*

terminal ['tɜːrmənl] ◇ *adj* -1. [illness, cancer]

that cannot be cured and causes death. -2. [patient, ward] that is connected with terminal illness. ◇ *n* -1. [for planes, trains, buses] a place where planes, trains, or buses load and unload passengers or goods, and begin and end their trips. -2. COMPUTING a keyboard and screen that can be used for putting information into a large computer and getting information from it. -3. ELECTRICITY one of the points on an electrical circuit at which a connection can be made.

terminally ['tɜːrmənəlɪ] *adv* **terminally ill** [person] who is suffering from a terminal illness.

terminate ['tɜːrməneɪt] ◇ *vt* (formal use) -1. [agreement, contract, discussion] to end <sthg> completely and formally. -2. MEDICINE to end <a pregnancy> by carrying out an abortion. ◇ *vi* -1. [bus, train] to come to the end of its route in a particular place. -2. [contract] to come to an end.

termination [,tɜːrmə'neɪʃn] *n* -1. [of an agreement, discussion, contract] *see* **terminate**. -2. MEDICINE a medical operation to end a pregnancy.

termini ['tɜːrmənaɪ] *plural of* **terminus**.

terminology [,tɜːrmə'nɒlədʒɪ] *n* the technical words and expressions used by people who know a lot about a particular subject □ *medical/scientific/computer terminology.*

terminus ['tɜːrmənəs] (*pl* **termini** OR **terminuses**) *n* a station where a bus or train ends its route.

termite ['tɜːrmaɪt] *n* a small insect that is found mainly in very hot countries, lives in nests made of mounds of earth, and feeds on wood or plants.

Terr GB *abbr of* **terrace**.

terrace ['terəs] *n* -1. [of a building] a flat area outside a house, restaurant, hotel etc where people can sit, eat meals, or drink. -2. [of land] one of a series of flat sections of land cut from the side of a hill to look like steps so that tea, olives, grapes etc can be grown there. -3. GB [of houses] a row of similar houses that are all joined together.

♦ **terraces** *npl* **the terraces** GB a series of wide steps at a soccer stadium where people can stand to watch games.

terraced ['terəst] *adj* [hillside, garden] that has terraces cut into it.

terraced house *n* GB one of the houses in a terrace.

terracotta [,terə'kɒtə] *n* a reddish-brown clay that has been baked hard and is used for making flowerpots, tiles etc.

terrain [tə'reɪn] *n* an area of land that has particular features that affect how difficult or easy it is to travel across.

terrapin ['terəpɪn] (*pl* **terrapin** OR **terrapins**) *n* a small turtle that lives in rivers and lakes, especially in North America.

terrestrial [tə'restrɪəl] *adj* -1. that is connected with the Earth (formal use). -2. [animal, plant] that lives on the ground rather than in water. -3. **terrestrial broadcasting/television etc** broadcasting/television etc in which sound

and pictures are sent from the Earth's surface rather than by satellite.

terrible ['terəbl] *adj* -1. [accident, experience, war] that one finds shocking or unpleasant because it is so severe □ *I suffer from terrible headaches.* □ *The flooding caused terrible damage.* -2. **to feel/look terrible** [person] to feel/look very unwell or unhappy □ *You look terrible!* -3. [meal, holiday, actor] that one thinks is very bad or of a very low standard □ *"They refused to give me a refund." — "That's terrible!"* □ *My spelling's terrible.* □ *We had terrible service on the flight.* -4. **a terrible waste/shame etc** a very great waste/shame etc □ *What a terrible mess!*

terribly ['terəblɪ] *adv* -1. [sing, play, write] very badly □ *"How did it go?" — "Terribly!"* -2. [care, mind, worry] very much. -3. **terribly important/expensive etc** very important/expensive etc □ *I'm terribly sorry!*

terrier ['terɪər] *n* a small type of dog used originally for hunting.

terrific [tə'rɪfɪk] *adj* -1. [idea, book, car] that one thinks is very good. -2. [thunderstorm, amount, noise] that is very great.

terrified ['terəfaɪd] *adj* [person, animal] that feels very frightened because they think something bad might happen □ *She's terrified of him/flying.* □ *He was terrified that his wife would find out.*

terrify ['terəfaɪ] (*pt* & *pp* **terrified**) *vt* to make <a person or animal> very frightened.

terrifying ['terəfaɪɪŋ] *adj* [experience, movie, thought] that makes one feel very frightened.

terrine [te'riːn] *n* a type of pâté.

territorial [,terə'tɔːrɪəl] *adj* [border, airspace, dispute] that is connected with an area of land owned or controlled by a particular country.

Territorial Army *n* **the Territorial Army** GB a military force whose members are not professional soldiers but who train as soldiers in their free time.

territorial waters *npl* the area of the ocean near the coast of a country that belongs to that country.

Territorian [,terə'tɔːrɪən] *n* AUS a person who comes from the Northern Territory.

territory [US 'terətɔːrɪ, GB -trɪ] (*pl* **territories**) *n* -1. an area of land that is owned or controlled by a particular country, government, or ruler □ *overseas territories.* -2. an area of land of a particular type □ *mountainous territory.* -3. an area of interest or knowledge □ *This is new territory to me.*

♦ **Territory** = **Northern Territory**.

terror ['terər] *n* -1. a feeling of extreme fear □ *I screamed in terror.* -2. **to have a terror of sthg** to be very afraid of sthg □ *He had a terror of flying.* -3. [child] a child who is annoying and hard to control (informal use).

terrorism ['terərɪzm] *n* the use of violence, especially bombing and shooting, in order to achieve political aims.

terrorist ['terərɪst] *n* a person who is involved in terrorism □ *terrorist activities.*

terrorize, -ise ['terəraɪz] *vt* [population, neighborhood] to keep <a person, place, or animal> in a constant state of extreme fear by using violence or threatening to use violence.

terror-stricken *adj* [person, face, refugees] very frightened.

terry (cloth) ['terɪ-] *n* a type of thick cotton cloth with loose threads on the surface, used for making towels, bathrobes etc.

terse [tɜːʳs] *adj* [reply, remark, person] that uses few words and can sound impolite.

tersely ['tɜːʳslɪ] *adv* [say, reply] *see* **terse** □ *"Suit yourself," she said tersely.*

tertiary [US 'tɜːrʃɪerɪ, GB 'tɜːʃərɪ] *adj* [importance, development] that comes third in a series or on a scale (formal use).

tertiary education *n* education at a college or university.

Terylene™ ['terəliːn] *n* a strong, light, synthetic material used for making clothes.

TESL ['tesl] (*abbr of* **Teaching (of) English as a Second Language**) *n* = TESOL.

TESOL ['tiːsɒl] (*abbr of* **Teaching English to Speakers of Other Languages**) *n* the teaching of English to people who live in an English-speaking country, but whose own language is not English.

test [test] ◇ *n* **-1.** [of equipment, a drug, vehicle] a process that one follows to check whether or not something works properly □ *The engine was put through a series of tests.* **-2.** [of one's courage, determination] a situation in which the true qualities of somebody or something become obvious □ *Traveling all that distance alone was a real test of character.* □ *This will be a stern test of the countries' newfound friendship.* ■ **to put sb/sthg to the test** to do something to find out the true qualities of sb/sthg. **-3.** [of a student] an examination of somebody's knowledge or skill in a particular subject or activity □ *a history test.* **-4.** MEDICINE a method used to find out if a part of one's body is healthy or if it contains a particular substance □ *an eye test* □ *DNA tests.*
◇ *vt* **-1.** [equipment, drug, vehicle] to do a test on <sthg>. **-2.** [friendship, courage, determination] to cause the true qualities of <sb/sthg> to become clear. **-3.** [eyes, blood, patient] to examine <sb/sthg> to see if they are healthy. **-4.** [student, class] to give <sb> a test in order to check their ability or knowledge. ■ **to test sb on sthg** to ask sb questions in order to find out how much they know about sthg.

testament ['testəmənt] *n* **-1.** LAW a document in which somebody states what should happen to their money, property etc after they die. **-2. a testament to sthg** [to somebody's skill, success] proof of sthg □ *It's a testament to her determination that she never gave up.*

test ban *n* an agreement between countries to stop tests on atomic weapons.

test card *n* GB = **test pattern**.

test case *n* a case in a court of law that is used as the basis for deciding future cases.

test-drive *vt* to drive <a vehicle> in order to see if one likes it enough to buy it.

tester ['testəʳ] *n* **-1.** a person whose job is to test equipment, food etc in a factory. **-2.** a bottle of perfume, a lipstick etc that a customer in a store can use to try the product.

test flight *n* a flight of a new plane to check how well it flies.

testicles ['testɪklz] *npl* the two round sex organs in the male that produce sperm.

testify ['testəfaɪ] (*pt & pp* **testified**) ◇ *vi* **-1.** LAW to make a serious statement in a court of law about something that has happened. **-2. to testify to sthg** to show that sthg is true. ◇ *vt* LAW *He testified that he had seen the accused before.*

testimonial [,testə'məʊnjəl] *n* **-1.** a formal written statement about somebody's character and abilities, often written by their employer. **-2.** something that is done, said, or given to thank or praise somebody publicly.

testimony [US 'testəməʊnɪ, GB -ɪmənɪ] *n* **-1.** LAW a formal statement about something that is made in a court of law. **-2. a testimony to sthg** [to somebody's courage, love] proof of sthg.

testing ['testɪŋ] *adj* [time, situation, questions] that one finds difficult to deal with.

testing ground *n* an area where things, especially weapons, are tested; a situation in which new ideas are tested.

test match *n* GB one of a series of rugby or cricket games played between the teams of two countries.

testosterone [te'stɒstərəʊn] *n* a chemical in men's bodies that gives them their male qualities and characteristics.

test pattern *n* US a picture or pattern broadcast on a television screen so that the quality of reception can be tested.

test pilot *n* a person whose job is to fly aircraft in order to test them.

test tube *n* a small glass container shaped like a tube with one closed end, used in scientific tests.

test-tube baby *n* a baby that has grown from an egg that was fertilized outside the mother's body and then put back in.

testy ['testɪ] (*compar* **testier**, *superl* **testiest**) *adj* [person, remark] that shows irritation.

tetanus ['tetənəs] *n* a serious disease that is caused by bacteria that get into wounds and that makes one's muscles become very stiff, especially in the jaw.

tetchy ['tetʃɪ] (*compar* **tetchier**, *superl* **tetchiest**) *adj* [person] who is easily annoyed or offended.

tête-à-tête [,teɪtə'teɪt] *n* a private conversation between two people.

tether ['teðəʳ] ◇ *vt* [horse, dog] to tie <an animal> to a post, fence etc at the end of a leash or rope □ *The goat was tethered to the fence.* ◇ *n* **to be at the end of one's tether** to feel that one cannot deal with a situation anymore because of worry, tiredness etc.

Texan ['teksn] *n* & *adj*: see **Texas**.

Texas ['teksəs] a state in the southern USA, on the Mexican border. It is a major center of the oil and gas industries. ABBREVIATION: TX. SIZE: 690,000 sq kms. POPULATION: 16,986,510 (*Texans*). CAPITAL: Austin.

Tex-Mex [,teks'meks] *adj* [cooking, music, restaurant] that is influenced by a mixture of Texan and Mexican culture.

text [tekst] *n* -1. [of a book, article] the main written part in a book, article etc. -2. [on a screen, page] written material. -3. [of an interview, speech] the written version of a speech, interview etc. -4. [for studying] a book, especially one that is used for studying.

textbook ['tekstbʊk] *n* a book that contains facts about a particular subject and is used especially in schools, colleges etc.

textile ['tekstaɪl] *n* a woven cloth that is made in a factory □ a textile worker/factory □ the textile industry.

texture ['tekstʃər] *n* [of wood, paper, food] the way something feels when one touches it □ The cloth had the texture of fine wool.

TGWU (*abbr of* **Transport and General Workers' Union**) *n* **the TGWU** a large British labor union for people in many different trades and professions.

Thai [taɪ] *n* & *adj*: see **Thailand**.

Thailand ['taɪlænd] a country in Southeast Asia, covering part of the Malay Peninsula, and the mainland to the north. SIZE: 514,000 sq kms. POPULATION: 58,800,000 (*Thais*). CAPITAL: Bangkok. LANGUAGE: Thai. CURRENCY: baht.

Thalidomide™ [θəˈlɪdəmaɪd] *n* a drug that used to be given to pregnant women but was withdrawn after it was proved in the 1960s to cause deformities in babies.

Thames [temz]: **the Thames** a river in southern England that flows through London into the North Sea.

than [*stressed* ðæn, *unstressed* ðn] *conj* -1. used in comparisons □ People started arriving a lot sooner than we expected. □ He seems happier than he was the last time I saw him. □ They're richer than us. □ We sell more wheat bread than white bread. □ The work won't take more than three days. -2. used to show what one chooses or prefers □ We decided to take a cab rather than walk. □ I'd rather eat at home than in a restaurant.

thank [θæŋk] *vt* to show one's gratitude to <sb> for something, usually by saying something □ I thanked everyone for their contributions/for coming. □ I can't thank you enough. ■ **thank God** OR **goodness** OR **heavens!** a phrase used to show relief.

◆ **thanks** ◇ *npl* feelings of gratitude □ I'd like to express my sincere thanks for all you've done. ◇ *excl* a word used to show one's gratitude to somebody □ Thanks a lot! □ Thanks very much. ■ **no thanks** a phrase used to politely refuse something that is offered □ "Would you like a drink?" — "No thanks."

◆ **thanks to** *prep* because of <sb/sthg> □ □ Thanks to the help of all our volunteers we made over $2,000. □ Thanks to you, we lost the contract.

thankful ['θæŋkfl] *adj* -1. **to be thankful for sthg** to be grateful for sthg □ You should be thankful for all we've done for you. -2. **to be thankful** to feel relieved □ He was thankful to be at home at last/to have escaped.

thankfully ['θæŋkflɪ] *adv* -1. [accept, receive] gratefully. -2. **thankfully,...** a word used to show that one feels relieved about something that has happened □ Thankfully, nobody was hurt.

thankless ['θæŋkləs] *adj* [job, task] that is hard and that one is unlikely to be thanked or rewarded for.

thanksgiving [,θæŋks'gɪvɪŋ] *n* an act of thanking God.

Thanksgiving (Day) *n* a public holiday on the fourth Thursday of November in the USA, and on the second Monday of October in Canada. It celebrates the survival of the Pilgrim Fathers, who were among the first Europeans to settle in North America.

♥ THANKSGIVING
When the Pilgrim Fathers (the first settlers) arrived in North America in 1620, many of them died of hunger during their first winter. In the second year, the Native Americans in the region taught them how to grow corn and other local food. In the autumn, when the settlers saw that they had enough food to survive the winter, they had a Thanksgiving meal with the Native Americans. Many years later, in 1863, President Lincoln made Thanksgiving a national holiday. Most Americans now spend Thanksgiving with their families, and have a traditional Thanksgiving meal of turkey with cranberry sauce, sweet potatoes, and pumpkin pie.

thank you *excl* a phrase used to show one's gratitude to somebody □ Thank you for all your help. □ Thank you so much.

◆ **thankyou** *n* something that one says or does to show one's gratitude to somebody □ Let me just say a special thankyou to all the people who made this event possible. □ a thankyou note.

that [*stressed* ðæt, *unstressed* ðət] (*pl* **those**) ◇ *pron* -1. used to refer to a person or thing that has already been mentioned □ Here's $5 — will that be enough? □ After that we all had a drink to celebrate. □ Those are the guys I was telling you about. ■ **those who...** the people who... □ I'd like to thank all those who helped. -2. used to refer to a past action or event □ I don't remember her saying that. -3. used when pointing to a person or thing some distance away □ Who's that at the door? -4. phrases **that's it** used when one feels one cannot continue doing something □ That's it, I've had enough. I'm leaving! □ That's it then: we've tried everything. ■ **that's that** used to show one is

not going to change one's mind □ *I'm not go-ing, and that's that!*
◇ *rel pron* used instead of "who" or "which" to introduce relative clauses □ *She's not someone that I know very well.* □ *It's the kind of mistake that's only too easy to make.*
◇ *conj* used to introduce clauses that give more information □ *She said that the matter was confidential.* □ *Everyone knows that he's tak-ing early retirement.* □ *It's vital that they attend.* □ *I'm aware that this may cause problems.*
◇ *det* -1. used to refer to a person or thing already mentioned □ *Later that day another meeting took place.* □ *I'd forgotten all about those old photos I took.* -2. used to refer to a past event or situation □ *That decision was one of the hardest I've ever had to take.* -3. used when pointing to a person or thing some distance away □ *That woman over there looks like Diana!* □ *It's just past those traffic lights on the left.*
◇ *adv* **not that good/easy etc** not very good/easy etc □ *It's not that long since they hired him.*
◆ **at that** *adv* used to give extra information □ *She's a doctor, and a good one at that.*
◆ **that is (to say)** *adv* used to explain or cor-rect what one has just said □ *He agreed — that is, he said he had no objection.*

thatched [θætʃt] *adj* **a thatched roof** a roof that is made of straw or reeds. ■ **a thatched house/cottage** a house/cottage that has a thatched roof.

Thatcherism ['θætʃərɪzm] *n* the political ideas associated with Margaret Thatcher who was Conservative Prime Minister in Britain from 1979 to 1990.

that's [*stressed* ðæts, *unstressed* ðəts] = **that is**.

thaw [θɔː] ◇ *vi* -1. [ice, snow] to melt; [frozen food] to go from a frozen state to being ready to eat □ *The cake should be left to thaw for about three hours.* -2. [person, relations] to become more friendly after a period of un-friendliness. ◇ *vt* [ice, frozen food, snow] to cause <sthg> to thaw. ◇ *n* a period of warmer weather after a period of freezing weather, when snow and ice thaws.

the [*stressed* ðiː, *unstressed* ðə, *before vowel* ðɪ] ◇ *det* -1. used to tell the listener or reader that they already know which particular thing or person is being talked about □ *I bought a magazine and looked at the pictures.* □ *That's the woman I was telling you about.* -2. used to refer to things from everyday life that everybody knows about □ *on the phone/television* □ *in the media* □ *the teaching profes-sion* □ *We swam in the ocean.* □ *The sun came out in the afternoon.* -3. **the bee is an insect** bees are insects (used when making general comments) □ *The car could ruin our cities.* □ *The Italians love their food.* -4. used with parts of the body □ *He was hit on the head.* -5. used before the names of some common illnesses □ *I have the flu/the mumps.* -6. **the old** old peo-ple (used before adjectives to form plural nouns) □ *help for the underprivileged/the dis-abled* □ *the British/Chinese/Swiss.* -7. **the Joneses** the family called Jones (used with names) □ *The Bensons are coming to dinner.*

-8. used before the names of countries, re-gions, oceans etc □ *the USA* □ *the Pacific Ocean* □ *the Philippines.* -9. used in dates □ *May the twelfth* □ *in the sixties.* -10. used in ti-tles □ *Alexander the Great* □ *the President of the United States.* -11. **paid by the hour** paid for each hour □ *Our car does 40 miles to the gallon.* -12. **to have the time/money** to have enough time/money □ *I'm sorry, I just don't have the energy.*
◇ *adv* **the...the...** used before two compara-tive adjectives or adverbs □ *The more I see her the less I like her.*

theater US, **theatre** GB ['θɪətəʳ] *n* -1. a building or a room in a building with a stage on which plays, shows etc are performed □ *a theater production/program/box office.* -2. **the theater** the activity or profession of working on plays in theaters, e.g. as an actor or di-rector □ *She's in the theater.* -3. [in a hospital] a room in a hospital where operations are done □ *He went into theater an hour ago.* -4. US [for movies] a place where people go to watch movies.

theatergoer US, **theatregoer** GB ['θɪətəˌgouəʳ] *n* a person who regularly goes to theaters to see plays being performed.

theatrical [θɪ'ætrɪkl] *adj* -1. [production, costs, staff] connected with the theater. -2. [behavior, gesture, speech] that is exaggerated in order to impress people.

theft [θeft] *n* -1. the activity of stealing things from other people □ *Theft is on the increase.* -2. [of a wallet, car] an act of stealing things from other people □ *I reported the theft to the police immediately.*

their [*stressed* ðeəʳ, *unstressed* ðəʳ] *det* -1. used to say that somebody or something is con-nected with or belongs to a group of people or things that does not include oneself. ■ **their house/car** the house/car that belongs to them (used to refer to people) □ *They lost all their money when the bank collapsed.* □ *Both of their children want to be doctors.* ■ **their wheels/lights** the wheels/lights that are at-tached to them (used to refer to things) □ *cars with their horns blaring.* -2. used to say that somebody or something is connected with or belongs to a person when one does not know if that person is male or female □ *Somebody has left their umbrella behind.* -3. used in titles to refer to two or more people □ *their Royal Highnesses the Prince and Princess of Wales.*

theirs [ðeəʳz] *pron* used to refer to something that belongs to or is connected with a group of things or people that does not include oneself □ *Our car broke down, so my parents lent us theirs.* ■ **it's theirs** it belongs to them □ *The land has been theirs for hundreds of years.* ■ **a friend of theirs** one of their friends.

them [*stressed* ðem, *unstressed* ðəm] *pron* -1. the people or things that have just been men-tioned, seen etc (used as the object of a verb, and after prepositions) □ *Bill and Tony told me to phone them as soon as I arrived.* □ *My wife likes olives, but I can't stand them.* □ *The* secretary gave them each a form to fill out. □ The Smiths had been very kind, so we threw a party for them. **-2.** used as the object of a verb or after a preposition to refer to a person when one does not know if that person is male or female □ If somebody calls for me, tell them to call back later.

thematic [θɪˈmætɪk] *adj* [approach, content] that is connected with a particular theme.

theme [θiːm] *n* **-1.** [of a debate, conversation, speech] the main subject of something □ My theme this evening will be the single European currency. **-2.** [of a work of art, book, festival] the main idea that an artist, designer, writer, or decorator uses □ the theme of revenge in "Hamlet" □ The theme is military at this winter's Paris collections. **-3.** MUSIC a particular tune, in a longer musical work, that keeps returning. **-4.** = **theme song**. **-5.** = **theme tune**.

theme park *n* an outdoor amusement park based on one idea.

theme song *n* a song that is played during a movie.

theme tune *n* a tune that is played at the beginning or end of a radio or TV program.

themselves [ðəmˈselvz] *pron* **-1.** used as the object of a verb, or after a preposition, to refer to the same people as the subject "they" □ They taught themselves to speak Japanese. □ They have left themselves no other option. □ They've built up quite a reputation for themselves. **-2.** used as the object of a verb, or after a preposition, to refer to the same person as the subject, when this could be male or female □ Somebody on the fifth floor has locked themselves out. **-3. they did it themselves** they did it without help from other people □ They tried to repair the TV themselves but in the end they had to call a repairman. ■ **by themselves** alone □ My parents prefer to go on vacation by themselves.

then [ðen] ◇ *adv* **-1.** used to refer to a particular time in the past or in the future □ There were no computers then, so we had to do it by hand. □ I'll be in New York next week, so let's meet then. **-2.** used to show that an action comes after another action in time □ I checked my mail, then I read the papers. **-3.** used to show that what one is saying is connected with something that has been said before □ What are you going to do then? □ You've read it before then, have you? **-4.** used to show that one has reached a conclusion or made a decision □ OK, then, goodbye. □ I'll take the pink one, then. **-5.** used to show that one is drawing a conclusion or making a summary □ It is safe to say, then, that the drug has few side effects. **-6.** used in sentences beginning with "if" to show that something is a logical consequence or result of something else □ If today is Monday, then tomorrow must be Tuesday. □ If you help me, then I'll help you sometime. **-7.** used when one wants to add information or a comment to something one has said □ And then there's the problem of how to deal with students who are late.

◇ *adj* **the then president** the person who was

president at that time □ Her then husband was head of the company.

thence [ðens] *adv* (formal use) **-1.** from that place □ We traveled by train to Patras and thence by boat to Bari. **-2.** for that reason.

theologian [θɪəˈloʊdʒən] *n* a person who studies theology.

theology [θɪˈɒlədʒɪ] *n* the study of religion.

theorem [ˈθɪərəm] *n* a formula or statement in mathematics that can be proved by logic.

theoretical [θɪəˈretɪkl] *adj* **-1.** [need, leader] that is supposed to be true or real, but is probably not □ It's a theoretical possibility, but it will probably never happen. **-2.** [study, work] that is based on abstract ideas and theories and is not concerned with practical uses □ She's a theoretical physicist.

theoretically [θɪəˈretɪklɪ] *adv* **-1.** according to a scientific theory □ Such weapons do not exist, though it's theoretically possible to build them. **-2.** a word used to say that something is supposed to happen, but that in fact it does not happen □ We all get paid the same, theoretically.

theorist [ˈθɪərəst] *n* a person who develops an idea to try to explain a particular subject or problem.

theorize, -ise [ˈθɪəraɪz] *vi* to present a possible explanation for something without having any very definite facts □ All we can do is theorize about the reason for the change.

theory [ˈθɪərɪ] (*pl* **theories**) *n* **-1.** an idea that is presented to explain something but that has not yet been proven □ Einstein's theories of relativity. **-2.** a set of abstract ideas about a particular subject □ the political theory of Hobbes. **-3.** in a subject one studies, the part concerned with ideas and principles rather than practical aspects □ My music exam has two parts, theory and practical.

◆ **in theory** *adv* a phrase used when something is supposed to happen or be true, but in fact may not happen or be true □ So, in theory, we arrive at about three o'clock. □ In theory, there's absolutely no risk.

therapeutic [θerəˈpjuːtɪk] *adj* **-1.** that makes a person feel better when they are tired, tense, or depressed □ I find sewing/gardening very therapeutic. **-2.** [treatment, drug] that has a good effect on a patient's health.

therapist [ˈθerəpəst] *n* a person trained to do a particular type of therapy □ a speech therapist □ an occupational therapist.

therapy [ˈθerəpɪ] *n* **-1.** the treatment of somebody who has a mental problem by talking to them over a period of time about their feelings, past experiences etc □ How long has he been in therapy? **-2.** treatment of an illness, especially without the use of drugs or surgery □ massage therapy.

there [*stressed* ðeər, *unstressed* ðər] ◇ *pron* **-1. there is/are** used to say that something exists. ■ **there's somebody on the phone** somebody is on the phone □ There's a new leisure center in town. □ There aren't any cookies left. □ Were there any problems getting here? □

There must be some mistake. **-2.** used with certain verbs, e.g. "follow", "remain", "exist", "grow", "stand", "come", to introduce the real subject of a sentence (formal use) □ *There remain several issues to be decided.* □ *There now follows a party political broadcast.* □ *There comes a time when one has to say no.*

◇ *adv* **-1. it is there to be used** it exists to be used □ *Teachers are supposed to be there to help.* ■ **is anybody there?** is anybody present or available? □ *I called the consulate, but there was nobody there who could answer my question.* **-2. she is there** she is in that place □ *He was born in Boston and went to school there.* ■ **I am going there** I am going to that place □ *You can get to the island by ferry, or you can fly there.* ■ **over there** used to indicate a place that is a short distance away □ *The keys are over there on the table.* ■ **it's ten miles there and back** the distance to go from here to that place and to come back here is ten miles. **-3.** used to indicate a point in a conversation or logical argument □ *I'm afraid I can't agree with you there.* **-4.** used to refer to a particular stage in a process or activity □ *I'm afraid we'll have to leave it there for today.* ■ **we're getting there** we are starting to achieve our goals □ *The company may not be making a profit yet, but we're getting there.* **-5.** *phrases* **he/she is not all there** he/she is crazy (informal use). ■ **there you are** a phrase used when one is giving somebody something that they have asked for; a phrase used to show that a situation is as one expected; a phrase used to show that one does not like a situation, but that it cannot be changed □ *There you are, don't drop it.* □ *There you are, I told you you'd find it.* □ *The system is pretty inefficient, but there you are.*

◇ *excl* used to show that a situation is as one expected □ *There, I knew it would be OK in the end.* ■ **there, there** a phrase used when one is trying to calm down a person, especially a baby, who is upset □ *There, there, don't cry.*

◆ **there and then, then and there** *adv* immediately □ *I should have left there and then.*

thereabout [,ðeərə'baʊt] US, **thereabouts** [,ðeərə'baʊts] *adv* **eight o'clock or thereabout** approximately eight o'clock □ *The rail link will be finished in 2010 or thereabout.*

thereafter [US ðer'æftr, GB ,ðeər'ɑːftə] *adv* after that (formal use).

thereby [,ðeər'baɪ] *adv* used to introduce the result of a particular action (formal use) □ *Share prices fell sharply, thereby creating panic among investors.*

therefore ['ðeərfɔːr] *adv* used to introduce the logical result of something that has been mentioned □ *Some equipment has disappeared, therefore we are introducing stricter controls.*

therein [,ðeər'ɪn] *adv* **-1.** in the place that has been mentioned (formal use) □ *...and all that is contained therein.* **-2. therein lies the problem/situation/difficulty etc** the problem/situation/difficulty etc is a result of that □ *The author has a highly original approach, and therein lies the interest of the book.*

there's [*stressed* ðeərz, *unstressed* ðərz] = **there is.**

thereupon [,ðeərə'pɒn] *adv* after that (formal use).

thermal ['θɜːrml] *adj* **-1.** TECHNOLOGY [energy, insulation] that is connected with heat. **-2. thermal gloves/underwear etc** gloves/underwear etc that are specially designed to keep people warm in cold weather.

thermodynamics [,θɜːrmoʊdaɪ'næmɪks] *n* the branch of physics that deals with the relationship between heat and movement.

thermometer [θər'mɒmɪtər] *n* a device used to measure temperature.

thermonuclear [,θɜːrmoʊ'nʲuːklɪər] *adj* [energy, reaction, bomb] that is connected with the high temperatures caused by nuclear fusion; [war] that involves thermonuclear weapons.

thermoplastic [,θɜːrmoʊ'plæstɪk] ◇ *n* a plastic that is soft when heated, but hard when cool. ◇ *adj*: *thermoplastic material.*

Thermos™ ['θɜːrməs] *n* **a Thermos flask** OR **bottle** a container with an inside and an outside wall and a vacuum between them, used to keep liquids hot or cold.

thermostat ['θɜːrməstæt] *n* a device that controls or regulates temperature and keeps it at a fixed level □ *the central heating thermostat.*

thesaurus [θə'sɔːrəs] (*pl* **thesauruses**) *n* a reference book where words with similar meanings are put together under headings, so that one can find a word that one cannot think of.

these [ðiːz] *plural of* **this.**

thesis ['θiːsəs] (*pl* **theses** [-iːz]) *n* **-1.** an idea that is presented using logic, often to try to explain something. **-2.** a long piece of original writing done as part of a university degree, especially a PhD, and based on research □ *She's writing her thesis on French women writers.*

they [ðeɪ] *pron* **-1.** the people or things that have just been mentioned, seen etc (used as the subject of a verb) □ *I invited Louise and Sue, but they couldn't come.* □ *Who are they?* □ *Don't eat these eggs, they're past their expiration date.* **-2.** used to refer to people in general, or to people in authority □ *They say he's been married before.* □ *They're going to raise taxes again.* **-3.** used as the subject of a verb to refer to somebody when one does not know if that person is male or female □ *Somebody called earlier, but they didn't leave a message.*

they'd [ðeɪd] = **they had, they would.**

they'll [ðeɪl] = **they will.**

they're [*stressed* ðeər, *unstressed* ðər] = **they are.**

they've [ðeɪv] = **they have** □ *They've no idea what they're doing!*

thick [θɪk] ◇ *adj* **-1.** [piece, object, arm] that has a particular distance from side to side or from top to bottom □ *three centimeters thick.* **-2.** [layer, strip] that is wider or deeper than other things of the same type □ *Some thick carpet would make the room warmer.* **-3.** [hair, hedge, forest] that grows very closely packed □ *He had long, thick hair.* **-4.** [person] who is

stupid (informal and disapproving use) □ *I think
he's just thick, that's all.* **-5.** [liquid, sauce, mixture] that does not flow easily □ *thick vegetable soup.* **-6.** [smoke, mist, cloud] that is hard
to see through □ *A thick fog had descended.*
-7. [voice] that is not clear because it is affected by emotion or alcoholic drink; [accent]
that is strong and difficult to understand □
*"Please, don't leave," he said, his voice thick with
emotion.* □ *a thick French accent.* **-8. to be thick
with sthg** [with mud, paint] to be covered with
a thick layer of sthg; [with traffic, smoke, people] to be full of sthg □ *The paths were thick
with snow.* □ *The streets were thick with last-minute shoppers.*

◇ *n* **to be in the thick of it** to be in the middle of a very busy activity □ *We're in the thick
of restructuring at the moment.*

◆ **thick and fast** *adv* [come] quickly and in
great numbers □ *Reports of some catastrophe
were arriving thick and fast.*

◆ **through thick and thin** *adv* [remain, stay]
through good times and bad times, whatever happens □ *She promised to stick with him
through thick and thin.*

thicken ['θɪkn] ◇ *vt* [sauce, mixture] to make
<sthg> less liquid, e.g. by adding a solid
substance such as flour. ◇ *vi* **-1.** [smoke, mist,
cloud] to become harder to see through. **-2.**
[undergrowth, wood] to become harder to get
through as one goes further. **-3.** [sauce, mixture] to become thicker □ *Leave the soup on a
low heat to thicken.*

thickener ['θɪkənəʳ] *n* a substance that is added to a liquid to make it thicker.

thicket ['θɪkət] *n* a group of trees and bushes
growing very close together.

thickly ['θɪklɪ] *adv* **-1.** [spread, cover, apply] in a
thick layer; [slice, cut] into thick layers □ *two
slices of thickly buttered bread.* **-2. thickly wooded/populated** having a lot of trees/people in a small area. **-3.** [say] in a voice made
less clear by strong emotion or drink.

thickset [,θɪk'set] *adj* [body, person] short and
heavy.

thick-skinned [-'skɪnd] *adj* [person] who is not
easily hurt by other people's criticism.

thief [θiːf] (*pl* **thieves**) *n* a person who steals,
usually without seeing or hurting their victim □ *a car thief.*

thieve [θiːv] ◇ *vt* to steal <sthg>. ◇ *vi*: *In the
end, he started thieving from shops.*

thieves [θiːvz] *plural of* **thief.**

thieving ['θiːvɪŋ] ◇ *n* the activity of stealing
things □ *A good deal of thieving goes on in this
neighborhood.* ◇ *adj* [person] who has stolen
something (disapproving use) □ *thieving kids.*

thigh [θaɪ] *n* the top part of the leg, from
where it joins the body down to the knee.

thighbone ['θaɪbəʊn] *n* the bone inside the
thigh.

thimble ['θɪmbl] *n* a small metal object that
one wears on the end of one's finger when
sewing, to stop the needle from going into
one's skin.

thin [θɪn] (*compar* **thinner**, *superl* **thinnest**, *pt* &

pp **thinned**, *cont* **thinning**) ◇ *adj* **-1.** [layer, material] that is less wide or deep than other
things of the same type □ *Could you cut me a
thin piece of cake?* **-2.** [person] who does not
have much fat on their body □ *How do you
stay so thin?* **-3.** [liquid, sauce, mixture] that
flows easily □ *thin soup.* **-4.** [hair, vegetation]
that does not grow closely packed; [attendance, support] that does not involve many
people □ *Attendance at the party meeting that
week was pretty thin.* ■ **to be thin on top** [man]
not to have much hair (informal use). **-5.**
phrases **to appear out of thin air** to appear
mysteriously and very unexpectedly. ■ **to
disappear** OR **vanish into thin air** to completely
disappear in a mysterious and sudden way.

◇ *adv* **to be wearing thin** [joke] to become boring
after being told too often; [patience] to be coming to an end as a result of somebody's annoying behavior.

◇ *vi* **to be thinning** [hair] to be gradually falling out.

◆ **thin down** *vt sep* **to thin sthg down** [liquid,
paint, mixture] to make sthg thinner by adding more liquid.

thing [θɪŋ] *n* **-1.** a word used to refer to a single fact, remark, action, detail etc □ *There's
no shortage of things to do here in the summer.*
□ *I hope I did the right thing by keeping it.* □
Chocolate is one of my favorite things. □ *The
thing I like about Kim is her sense of humor.* □
Record players will soon be a thing of the past. ■
a terrible/funny thing happened something
terrible/funny happened. ■ **the important/
difficult thing is...** what is important/difficult
is... **-2. not... a thing** not... anything □ *He
doesn't know a thing about politics.* □ *I haven't
eaten a thing since lunchtime.* **-3.** an object that
one cannot or need not name, or that one
has already mentioned □ *What's that thing on
your sleeve?* □ *If the printer jams again I'm going
to throw the darned thing out of the window!*
-4. a word used in phrases that express the
particular feeling one has for a person or
animal □ *You lucky thing!* □ *Poor thing, it's hurt
its paw.* **-5. it's the thing** it's the fashion (informal use). **-6.** phrases **what with one thing
and another** for several reasons □ *What with
one thing and another, I didn't get home till midnight.* ■ **the thing is...** a phrase used when
one is starting to explain a problem or difficult situation □ *I'd love to go, but the thing is,
I'm seeing John that evening.* ■ **it's just one of
those things** it's something that cannot be
avoided or explained (informal use) □ *I don't
know how it happened, it's just one of those
things, I suppose.* ■ **to have a thing about sb/
sthg** to have an unusually strong liking for
or dislike of sb/sthg (informal use) □ *Mike has
a real thing about flying.* ■ **to make a (big) thing
out of sthg** to make sthg seem very important (informal use) □ *Look, I don't want to make
a big thing out of it, but could you pay me back
that money I lent you?*

◆ **things** *npl* **-1. one's things** the clothes, objects etc that belong to one □ *I packed all my
things in a suitcase.* □ *Don't leave your things lying all over the floor!* **-2. swimming/tennis etc**

things the equipment, clothing etc needed for swimming/tennis etc □ *Let's clear the breakfast things away first.* □ *Do you have any sewing things with you?* **-3. how are things? how is life in general?** (informal use) □ *"How are you?" — "Oh, things could be worse."* □ *The way things are going, we'll all be out of a job soon.*

thingamabob ['θɪŋəməbɒb], **thingummy(jig)** ['θɪŋəmɪ(dʒɪɡ)], **thingy** ['θɪŋɪ] (*pl* **thingies**) *n* a word used when one cannot think of the proper name for an object.

think [θɪŋk] (*pt* & *pp* **thought**) ◇ *vt* **-1. to think (that)...** to have the opinion or belief that something is true □ *Do you really think that we'll win?* □ *I don't think that's a good idea.* □ *Who cares what other people think!* □ *But I thought you already knew!* **-2.** to have <sthg> in one's mind but not say it out loud □ *That's funny, I was just thinking the same thing.* □ *"He's bluffing," I thought to myself.* **-3. I think I'll do it** I am planning or intending to do it □ *I think I'll work at home tomorrow.* **-4.** to remember <sthg> □ *I didn't think to bring any money.* □ *Try and think where you might have left the key.* **-5.** *phrases* **I think/don't think...** a phrase used when one believes something to be true/not true but is not completely sure □ *I don't think we've met before.* □ *"Do we have everything we need?" — "Yes, I think we do."* ■ **do you think...** a phrase used to start a polite request □ *Do you think you could turn the music down?* ■ **I can't think why/what etc...** I can't understand why/what etc... □ *I can't think why you didn't just call me.*
◇ *vi* **-1.** to use one's mind to produce ideas, make decisions etc □ *Be quiet a minute, I'm trying to think.* □ *Diana thought for a while before replying.* □ *Your problem is you think too much!* **-2.** *phrases* **just think!** a phrase used when one wants somebody to imagine something pleasurable or exciting □ *Just think — tomorrow we'll be in Rome!* ■ **to think better of sthg** to decide not to do sthg after considering it □ *He was going to complain, but then thought better of it.* ■ **to think nothing of doing sthg** to think that sthg is normal or easy, although other people would find it strange or difficult □ *She thinks nothing of spending $300 on a pair of shoes.* ■ **to think twice** to consider something very carefully before doing it because it could have bad results □ *I'd think twice before going on another vacation like that.*
◇ *n* **to have a think** to think about something carefully in order to make a decision about it (informal use) □ *Don't decide right away — have a think about it for a few days.*

◆ **think about** *vt fus* **-1. to think about sthg** to have sthg in one's mind □ *I've been thinking about what you said.* **-2. to be thinking about doing sthg** to be considering doing sthg as a possibility □ *They're thinking about selling the house.*

◆ **think back** *vi* to remember events that happened in the past □ *Try to think back to what happened.*

◆ **think of** *vt fus* **-1. to be thinking of doing sthg** to be thinking about doing sthg □ *We're*

thinking of getting married. **-2. to think of sthg** to remember sthg □ *I can't think of her name right now.* □ *I often think of that week we spent in Miami.* **-3. to think of sthg** to have an idea about sthg □ *I've thought of a way to solve the problem.* **-4. to think of sb** to have a particular opinion of sb □ *He thinks very highly of you, you know.* □ *What do you think of her new boyfriend?* ■ **to think of sb/sthg as sthg** to consider sb/sthg to be a particular thing □ *I've always thought of you as a friend rather than a colleague.* ■ **to think a lot of sb/sthg** to have a good/bad opinion of sb/sthg □ *I didn't think much of that restaurant they took us to.* **-5.** to show consideration for sb's feelings □ *You never think of anybody but yourself!*

◆ **think over** *vt sep* **to think sthg over** to consider sthg carefully □ *I need some time to think this over.*

◆ **think through** *vt sep* **to think sthg through** to consider everything that might happen as a result of sthg □ *John, are you sure you've really thought this through?*

◆ **think up** *vt sep* **to think sthg up** to invent sthg, especially in order to deal with a particular problem or situation □ *You'll have to think up a good excuse for missing the meeting.*

thinker ['θɪŋkər] *n* **-1.** a serious person who thinks a lot about things. **-2.** a person who expresses opinions on important questions that affect human life and society □ *one of Germany's greatest modern thinkers.*

thinking ['θɪŋkɪŋ] ◇ *adj* **the thinking man/woman** the sort of educated man/woman who is likely to think carefully about a particular subject □ *the thinking man's choice.*
◇ *n* **-1.** a person's thoughts and opinions □ *According to that line of thinking, European unity is an excellent idea.* ■ **to my way of thinking** in my opinion. **-2.** the process of thinking about ideas □ *You'd better do some serious thinking about your future.* **-3.** the theory that lies behind a particular plan and explains the reason for it □ *The thinking is that people will come to prefer public transportation.*

think tank *n* a group of people that is formed by a government or organization to advise them and to produce new policies or ideas □ *a government/right-wing think tank.*

thinly ['θɪnlɪ] *adv* **-1.** [spread, cover, apply] in a thin layer; [slice, cut] into thin layers □ *thinly sliced bread.* **-2.** [grow] not in great numbers and not close together □ *a thinly populated area* □ *Sow the seeds thinly.* **-3. thinly disguised** OR **veiled** [remark, threat] that can be clearly understood even though it is deliberately expressed in a way that is not clear □ *The proposal was a thinly disguised attempt to sell off the company.*

thinner ['θɪnər] *n* a substance added to paint to make it more liquid.

thin-skinned [-'skɪnd] *adj* [person] who is too easily hurt by criticism.

third [θɜːrd] ◇ *num* 3rd; number 3 in a series; *see also* **fifth.** ◇ *n* GB & AUS EDUCATION = **third-class degree** □ *He got a third.*

third-class degree *n* GB & AUS EDUCATION the lowest level of honors degree.

third-degree burns *npl* very severe burns.

thirdly ['θɜːʳdlɪ] *adv* a word used when one is introducing one's third point □ *And thirdly, there is simply no money available!*

third party *n* a person who is not one of the two main groups or individuals involved in a business or legal affair.

third-party insurance *n* insurance that covers a person if they injure somebody else or damage somebody else's property.

third-rate *adj* [work, production, performance] that is of very poor quality (disapproving use).

third reading *n* GB the third and final time that a bill proposing a new law is read and discussed in Parliament.

Third World *n* **the Third World** the developing countries in Africa, Asia, and South America that are poor and do not have much industry.

thirst [θɜːʳst] *n* -1. a desire to drink □ *He had a terrible thirst.* -2. the condition in which people do not have enough to drink □ *Millions are suffering from hunger and thirst.* -3. **a thirst for sthg** [for power, excitement] a great desire for sthg.

thirsty ['θɜːʳstɪ] (*compar* **thirstier**, *superl* **thirstiest**) *adj* -1. **to be** OR **feel thirsty** to feel the need to drink □ *"Are you thirsty?"* — *"Yes! Let's have a drink!"* -2. **thirsty work** an activity that makes people feel thirsty because it is tiring or requires a lot of energy □ *Phew! This is thirsty work!*

thirteen [ˌθɜːʳˈtiːn] *num* the number 13; *see also* **fifteen**. ■ **the Thirteen Colonies** the 13 British colonies that formed the United States of America after the American Revolution.

thirteenth [ˌθɜːʳˈtiːnθ] *num* 13th, number 13 in a series; *see also* **fifteenth**.

thirtieth ['θɜːʳtɪəθ] *num* 30th, number 30 in a series; *see also* **fiftieth**.

thirty ['θɜːʳtɪ] (*pl* **thirties**) *num* the number 30; *see also* **fifty**.

this [ðɪs] (*pl* **these**) ◇ *pron* -1. used to indicate somebody or something that is near, or has just been mentioned □ *This is my house.* □ *Is this what you were looking for?* □ *These are the reasons for my resignation.* ■ **this is...** a phrase used when one is introducing somebody to somebody else □ *James, this is Diane Price, my boss.* ■ **this is...** a phrase used when one is saying who one is on the telephone □ *This is Dave King speaking.* ■ **this and that** a phrase used to refer to things when one does not want to say exactly what they are □ *"What did you talk about?"* — *"Oh, this and that."* -2. used to talk about the difference between something that is near and something that is further away □ *Which do you prefer, these or those?*

◇ *det* -1. used to refer to somebody or something that is near, or has just been mentioned □ *This fish is delicious.* □ *How can we avoid this problem in the future?* □ *These shoes hurt my feet.* ■ **this morning/afternoon/evening** the morning/afternoon/evening of today □ *I got my credit card bill this morning.* □ *Let's go out this evening.* ■ **this week** the week we are in □ *I've been really busy this week.* ■ **this Sunday/summer** the Sunday/summer that is coming; the Sunday/summer that is just past □ *I'm at my parents' house this Christmas.* □ *This vacation has been fantastic.* -2. used to talk about the difference between something that is near and something that is farther away □ *My old office was OK, but I prefer this one.* -3. used to refer to somebody or something that has not been mentioned before, especially in stories and jokes (informal use) □ *So this man goes into a bar...*

◇ *adv* used when one is indicating the size of something with one's hands □ *The fish was this big.* □ *You only need this much salt.*

thistle ['θɪsl] *n* a plant with sharp leaves and purple flowers, used as the symbol of Scotland.

thither [US 'θɪðr, GB 'ðɪðə] *adv* → **hither**.

tho' [ðoʊ] *conj* & *adv* = **though**.

Thomas ['tɒməs], **Dylan** (1914–1953) a Welsh poet whose best-known work is the radio play *Under Milk Wood*.

thong [θɒŋ] *n* -1. a long thin strip of leather. -2. US & AUS a sandal that is held on by a strap between the toes.

Thoreau [US θəˈroʊ, GB 'θɔːroʊ], **Henry David** (1817–1862) a US writer who believed in peaceful protest against unfair laws. His work includes *Walden, or Life in the Woods* and *Civil Disobedience*.

thorn [θɔːʳn] *n* -1. a sharp point on the stem of a plant such as a rose. ■ **to be a thorn in sb's flesh** OR **side** [person, problem] to irritate sb a lot over a long period of time. -2. a bush or tree that grows thorns.

thorny ['θɔːʳnɪ] (*compar* **thornier**, *superl* **thorniest**) *adj* -1. [bush, hedge] that is covered with or full of thorns. -2. [subject, problem, question] that causes difficulties □ *We then had to tackle the thorny question of job titles.*

thorough [US 'θɜːroʊ, GB 'θʌrə] *adj* -1. [work, check, investigation] that is done with careful attention to every possible detail, so that nothing is forgotten □ *We have made a thorough search of the grounds.* -2. [person, worker] who always does things in a careful way and checks every detail □ *Lara is very thorough.* -3. **a thorough idiot/nuisance** as much of an idiot/a nuisance as possible (used to emphasize degree or extent) □ *The meeting was a thorough waste of time.*

thoroughbred [US 'θɜːroʊbred, GB 'θʌrə-] *n* a horse whose parents both belong to the same good breed □ *a thoroughbred horse.*

thoroughfare [US 'θɜːroʊfer, GB 'θʌrəfeə] *n* -1. a way through somewhere, for pedestrians or vehicles □ *'No thoroughfare.'* -2. a main street that is open at both ends (formal use).

thoroughly [US 'θɜːroʊlɪ, GB 'θʌrə-] *adv see* **thorough** □ *It needs to be thoroughly examined.* □ *I was thoroughly bored with the whole thing.* □ *We enjoyed ourselves thoroughly.*

thoroughness [US 'θɜ:rounəs, GB 'θʌrə-] *n* [of work, a person, check] *see* **thorough**.

those [ðouz] *plural of* **that**.

though [ðou] ◇ *conj* **though he was sick, he went to work anyway** he was sick, but he went to work □ *Though it's quite a distance from the hotel, taxis are not expensive.* ▪ **it was small, though comfortable** it was small, but comfortable □ *Though beautiful, her eyes were cold.* ◇ *adv* despite this fact □ *I couldn't leave them alone, though, could I?*

thought [θɔ:t] ◇ *past tense & past participle of* **think**. ◇ *n* **-1.** an idea □ *I've had a sudden thought.* □ *What a thought!* **-2.** the process of thinking □ *Mary sat in the corner, lost in thought.* **-3.** careful attention to a particular matter □ *I didn't give it much thought at the time.* □ *Wait a minute, this needs some thought.* **-4.** [of a philosopher, culture] the philosophical ideas of a particular person, time, or culture □ *ancient Chinese thought.* **-5. a nice/kind thought** a nice/kind thing that somebody has decided to do □ *It's a nice thought to invite her, but I don't think she'll accept.*

♦ **thoughts** *npl* **-1.** ideas □ *He tends to keep his thoughts to himself.* ▪ **to collect one's thoughts** to organize one's ideas in a calm way □ *Give me a few minutes to collect my thoughts.* **-2.** opinions about a particular matter □ *Could you let me have your thoughts on the issue?*

thoughtful ['θɔ:tfl] *adj* **-1.** [expression, mood] that shows signs that one is thinking about something □ *He was looking pretty thoughtful.* **-2.** [person, gesture] that shows consideration and kindness to somebody else □ *Oh, thank you! How thoughtful of you!*

thoughtless ['θɔ:tləs] *adj* [person] who does not consider other people's feelings or needs □ *That was a thoughtless thing to say!*

thousand ['θauznd] ◇ *num* the number 1,000 □ *several thousand people* □ *a thousand pounds/years.*

♦ **thousands** *npl* a large number □ *There were thousands of people at the airport.* □ *I've told you thousands of times, it's in the garage!* □ *This is going to cost thousands.*

thousandth ['θauzntθ] *num* 1,000th, number 1,000 in a series □ *a thousandth of a second.*

thrash [θræʃ] *vt* **-1.** to hit <sb> very hard on the body, usually as a punishment □ *He thrashed the boy with a whip.* **-2.** [opponent, team, rival] to beat <sb> by playing much better than them □ *We were thrashed on Wednesday!*

♦ **thrash around, thrash about** *vi* [fish, animal, person] to move one's body around in a violent and uncontrolled way.

♦ **thrash out** *vt sep* **-1. to thrash sthg out** [solution, idea, policy] to decide on sthg after a difficult discussion. **-2. to thrash sthg out** [problem, differences] to solve sthg after a difficult discussion.

thrashing ['θræʃɪŋ] *n* **-1.** a physical beating, usually as punishment for something. **-2.** a complete defeat in a sporting competition.

thread [θred] ◇ *n* **-1.** [in sewing] a long thin piece of cotton, silk, nylon etc, used for sewing □ *silk thread* □ *a piece of thread.* **-2.** [of a screw] the raised part on the side of a screw that allows it to fit tightly. **-3.** [of an argument, conversation, story] the main line of ideas, arranged in logical order □ *I'm afraid I've completely lost the thread of what you were saying.* ◇ *vt* **-1.** to put thread through <a needle> before sewing. **-2. to thread one's way through sthg** [through streets, crowds] to go through sthg, avoiding the people or things in one's way.

threadbare ['θredbeə'] *adj* [carpet, coat] that has been used so much that the surface of the material has worn away □ *The cuffs of his jacket were threadbare.*

threat [θret] *n* **-1.** a statement telling somebody that if they do not do what one says, one will hurt them in some way □ *Staff working for the organization have received death threats.* **-2.** a very strong possibility that something very bad or unpleasant will happen to somebody □ *The country is living under the threat of war/famine.* □ *Bandits pose a constant threat to travelers.*

threaten ['θretn] ◇ *vt* **-1.** to tell <sb> that one will do something unpleasant if they do not do what one wants □ *The boss had threatened me with dismissal unless my work improved.* □ *She even threatened to kill herself.* **-2. to threaten to do sthg** to seem likely to do sthg, with unpleasant results □ *Her drinking threatens to become a problem.* **-3.** [security, position, outcome] to put <sthg> in a dangerous position □ *Drug-taking threatens the future of our nation's youth.* ◇ *vi* [danger, storm] to seem likely to happen, and cause unpleasant results.

threatening ['θretnɪŋ] *adj* [person, letter, behavior] that expresses the intention to harm somebody or something □ *He gave me a threatening look.*

three [θri:] *num* the number 3; *see also* **five**.

three-D *adj* [image, effect] = **three-dimensional**.

three-day event *n* a horse-riding competition that lasts three days and includes different types of events.

three-dimensional [-dɪ'menʃnəl] *adj* **-1.** [image, effect] that gives the impression of being solid. **-2.** [form, object] that is solid rather than flat.

threefold ['θri:fould] ◇ *adj* **-1.** [advantage] that consists of three different things, effects etc. **-2.** [increase] that makes something three times bigger. ◇ *adv* [increase] *Sales have risen threefold.*

three-legged race [-'legəd-] *n* a children's game in which people run in pairs with one leg tied to their partner's leg.

three-piece *adj* **-1. a three-piece suite** a set of furniture consisting of a sofa and two armchairs. **-2. a three-piece suit** a man's suit consisting of a jacket, trousers, and vest.

three-ply *adj* [wool, yarn] that is made up of three threads; [wood, tissue] that is made of three layers.

three-point turn *n* in driving, a way of turning the car around in three moves.

three-quarters *npl* three out of four equal parts of a whole figure or amount □ *Three-quarters of all applicants are female.*

threesome ['θriːsəm] *n* a group of three people who do something or go somewhere together □ *We went around in a threesome.*

three-star *adj* [hotel, restaurant] that has been awarded three stars in a guide book to show that it is very good.

three-wheeler [-'wiːlər] *n* a vehicle with three wheels.

Three Wise Men = Magi.

thresh [θreʃ] *vt* to beat <corn, wheat> etc in order to separate the grain from the rest of the plant.

threshing machine ['θreʃɪŋ-] *n* a machine for threshing corn, wheat etc.

threshold ['θreʃhould] *n* -1. [of a building, room] a piece of wood or stone that forms the bottom part of a doorway; the doorway itself □ *She will not even allow him over the threshold.* -2. the level or amount at which something begins to happen or take effect □ *The tax threshold has been raised by $700.* □ *I have a low pain threshold.* -3. **to be on the threshold of sthg** [of a new discovery, breakthrough] to be about to do or experience sthg.

threw [θruː] *past tense of* throw.

thrift [θrɪft] *n* -1. the quality and practice of being thrifty. -2. US FINANCE = **thrift institution**.

thrift institution *n* US an institution where people can save money in accounts that give interest.

thrift shop *n* US a store where second-hand goods and clothes are sold by volunteer workers, and the money that is made goes to a charity.

thrifty ['θrɪftɪ] (*compar* thriftier, *superl* thriftiest) *adj* [person] who uses money and goods carefully in order not to waste anything.

thrill [θrɪl] ◇ *n* a sudden strong feeling of excitement, pleasure, fear etc; an event or situation that produces this feeling □ *the thrill of flying for the first time* □ *Seeing him on stage, live, was a real thrill for me.* ◇ *vt* [person, crowd, audience] to give <sb/sthg> a thrill. ◇ *vi* to **thrill to sthg** [to music, a story] to feel a thrill when one experiences sthg.

thrilled [θrɪld] *adj* [person] who is very pleased and excited about something □ *She was thrilled with her present.* □ *We're thrilled to meet you.* □ *I wasn't exactly thrilled when he told me he couldn't come.*

thriller ['θrɪlər] *n* a book, play, or movie that tells an exciting story with a lot of suspense, especially one involving crime and violence.

thrilling ['θrɪlɪŋ] *adj* [game, climax, drama] that is full of excitement and suspense; [news, discovery] that makes one feel very excited and pleased.

thrive [θraɪv] (*pt* thrived OR throve, *pp* thrived) *vi* [person, plant, business] to develop well and be strong, healthy, and successful □ *That rosebush seems to be thriving.* □ *Most people hate business trips, but Jim thrives on them!*

thriving ['θraɪvɪŋ] *adj* [person, plant, business] that is strong, healthy, and successful □ *She now runs a thriving recruitment agency.*

throat [θrout] *n* -1. the back part of the mouth and the top of the passage that goes down into the neck □ *I have a sore throat.* ■ **to ram** OR **force sthg down sb's throat** to force sb to listen to or accept sthg when they do not want to □ *I'm not interested in someone trying to ram their political views down my throat.* -2. the front part of the neck □ *He held a knife to my throat.* ■ **to be at each other's throats** to be fighting bitterly or violently with each other.

throaty ['θroutɪ] (*compar* throatier, *superl* throatiest) *adj* [voice, laugh, cough] that is low and sounds rough.

throb [θrɒb] (*pt* & *pp* throbbed, *cont* throbbing) ◇ *n* [of a pulse, heart] a regular beat that is often faster or stronger than normal; [of an engine, machine] a loud, vibrating, rhythmic sound. ◇ *vi* [heart, blood] to beat faster and more strongly than normal; [engine, machine] to make a loud, rhythmic, vibrating sound; [head, wound] to make one feel a series of strong, rhythmic, dull pains □ *The lawnmower spluttered, then throbbed into life.* □ *My head was throbbing with the pain.*

throes [θrouz] *npl* **death throes** violent uncontrolled movements that a person or animal experiences when they are dying and in great pain. ■ **to be in the throes of sthg** to be in the middle of sthg difficult or unpleasant □ *We're in the throes of moving house.*

thrombosis [θrɒm'bousəs] (*pl* thromboses [-iːz]) *n* a serious medical condition in which some blood becomes thick and blocks a vein or artery.

throne [θroun] *n* -1. a special chair used by a king, queen, emperor etc, or by a bishop. -2. **the throne** the position of being king, queen, or emperor □ *How long was James II on the throne?*

throng [θrɒŋ] ◇ *n* [of people, tourists] a large crowd. ◇ *vt* [place, city center, streets] to be in <a place> in large numbers □ *The pier was thronged with tourists.* ◇ *vi* to go to a place in large numbers □ *People thronged toward/around the new statue.*

throttle ['θrɒtl] ◇ *n* the device on a motor vehicle or plane that controls the flow of fuel into the engine, and so controls the vehicle's speed; the lever or pedal that operates this. ◇ *vt* [person, cat, child] to hold <sb/sthg> tightly by the throat in order to stop them breathing and to kill them □ *I could throttle that man!*

through [θruː] ◇ *prep* -1. **to go through a door/gap** to go in one side or end of a door/gap and come out at the other □ *Drill a hole through the wood.* □ *I crawled through a hole in the fence.* □ *At last we got through customs.* □ *The blood had soaked through the bandage.* -2. **to cut/bite through sthg** to cut/bite sthg into two separate pieces □ *Cut through the rope!* -3. **to see/hear/feel sthg through**

sthg to see/hear/feel sthg that is on the other side of sthg □ *I could hear them arguing through the wall.* □ *He felt the bird's heart beating through its soft feathers.* **-4. to walk/travel through a place** to walk/travel in a place; to walk/travel from one end of a place to the other □ *We strolled through the empty city streets.* □ *His route took him through some dramatic scenery.* □ *They drove through the enemy lines to safety.* **-5. to look/read through sthg** to look at/read sthg gradually □ *It'll take days to go through all these applications.* **-6. to last/ sleep through a period of time** to last/sleep continuously from the beginning to the end of a period of time □ *We stay open all through the winter.* □ *I slept through the earthquake.* □ *The flowers will bloom from April right through the end of autumn.* **-7. to go/live through sthg** to be present or affected while sthg is happening □ *He had lived through two World Wars.* □ *Through it all, she never gave up hope of seeing her family again.* **-8. Monday through Friday** from Monday up to and including Friday □ *He works Monday through Thursday, then has a break.* **-9. to happen through sthg** to happen because of sthg □ *The charity folded through lack of funding.* **-10. to do/get sthg through sthg** to do/get sthg by using sthg □ *Send it through the mail.* □ *I got the job through a friend.* ◇ *adj* **-1. to be through with sthg** to have finished doing sthg; to no longer want to do sthg □ *They'll soon be through with the drilling.* □ *I'm through with married men!* **-2. a through train** a train that goes directly to a place, so that passengers do not need to change. **-3. through traffic** traffic that goes through a place and does not stop there. ◇ *adv* **-1. to go/pass through** to go/pass from one side or end of something to the other □ *Pass the plates through to me.* □ *The immigration officer refused to let us through.* **-2. to read/play sthg through** to read/play sthg continuously from the beginning to the end □ *I started reading it, but got interrupted halfway through.* □ *Play it again right through from the beginning.* **-3. to cook sthg through** to cook sthg thoroughly or completely □ *Check that the contents are heated through before eating.* ■ **wet/ frozen through** completely wet/frozen □ *Come in and get dry. You're soaked through!*

◆ **through and through** *adv* completely or thoroughly □ *She knows her subject through and through.*

throughout [θruː'aʊt] ◇ *prep* **-1. throughout a period of time** continuously from the beginning to the end of a period of time □ *She appeared calm and composed throughout the trial.* **-2. throughout a place/area** in all parts of a place/area □ *He has traveled extensively throughout the Far East.* □ *Fraud is a problem throughout the entire banking system.* ◇ *adv*: *Jameson remained silent throughout.* □ *The house has been modernized throughout.*

throughput ['θruːpʊt] *n* GB BUSINESS the amount of something that is processed by a computer, factory etc in a particular period of time.

throughway ['θruːweɪ] *n* US = **thruway**.

throve [θrəʊv] *past tense of* **thrive**.

throw [θrəʊ] (*pt* **threw**, *pp* **thrown**) ◇ *vt* **-1.** [ball, stone] to move one's arm suddenly forward and let go of <sthg> one is holding so that it moves quickly through the air □ *Rioters threw stones and bricks at police.* □ *Can you throw me that towel, please?* **-2.** [person, object, clothes] to put <sb/sthg> in a particular place or position in a sudden or careless manner □ *They were arrested and thrown into a police cell.* □ *Don't throw your clothes on the floor!* □ *He was thrown to the ground by the force of the explosion.* **-3.** to move <one's head, arms, or hands> suddenly into a particular position □ *Sally threw herself into a chair, saying she felt exhausted.* □ *I threw my arms around her.* □ *He threw back his head and laughed.* **-4. to throw oneself into an activity** [into one's work, career] to become very involved in an activity □ *After the divorce, he threw himself into his research.* **-5. to throw sb into sthg** [into a state of panic, confusion] to suddenly make sb experience sthg unpleasant □ *The news threw the entire school into a state of shock.* **-6.** [rider] to make <sb> fall off their horse □ *Stevens was thrown at the last fence.* **-7.** *phrases* **to throw sb a look** OR **glance** to look OR glance at sb □ *He throw me a look of absolute contempt.* ■ **to throw a fit/tantrum** to have a fit/tantrum □ *Margery will throw an absolute fit when she hears.* ■ **to throw a party** to hold a party □ *We've decided to throw a housewarming party.* ■ **it threw me** it completely confused me because I was not expecting it (informal use) □ *It was her appearance that really threw me — she looked so thin.* ◇ *n* [of a ball, dice] an act of throwing □ *That was a good throw.*

◆ **throw away** *vt sep* **-1. to throw sthg away** [junk, old clothes] to get rid of sthg that one no longer wants or needs □ *I threw away the receipt by mistake.* **-2. to throw sthg away** [opportunity, money, happiness] to lose or not use sthg good that one has □ *You've just thrown away your chances of promotion.*

◆ **throw in** *vt sep* **to throw sthg in** to include sthg with another item being bought without increasing the price □ *If you buy a computer they'll usually throw in some software.*

◆ **throw on** *vt sep* **to throw on an item of clothing** to put on a piece of clothing quickly or carelessly □ *I'll throw on a coat and be with you in ten minutes.*

◆ **throw out** *vt sep* **-1. to throw sthg out** to get rid of sthg that one no longer wants or needs □ *Don't throw out those newspapers, I haven't read them yet.* **-2. to throw sthg out** [proposal, suggestion, plan] to reject sthg □ *The bill was thrown out by Congress.* **-3. to throw sb out** [of a job, the army, school] to force sb to leave a place □ *He was thrown out of a club for being drunk and aggressive.* □ *You can't throw me out of my own home!*

◆ **throw together** *vt sep* **to throw sthg together** [meal, dress] to make sthg quickly and casually □ *It's nothing special — just something I threw together.*

◆ **throw up** ◇ *vi* to vomit (informal use) □ *I've*

been throwing up all night. ◇ vt sep -1. **to throw sthg up** [facts, ideas] to produce sthg new □ The research has thrown up some interesting problems. -2. **to throw sthg up** [dust, stone, water] to make sthg rise from the ground □ mud thrown up by a passing truck.

throwaway ['θrouəwei] adj -1. **a throwaway cup/toothbrush etc** a cup/toothbrush etc that is intended to be used only once and then thrown away. -2. **a throwaway remark/line etc** a remark/line etc that is said as if it were not important when it really is.

throwback ['θroubæk] n an idea, attitude etc that is like something bad that existed in the past □ a throwback to the Cold War.

throw-in n the act of throwing the ball back on the field in a soccer game.

thrown [θroun] past participle of **throw**.

thru [θru:] adj, adv, & prep US = **through** (informal use).

thrush [θrʌʃ] n -1. a small bird with a brown back and a spotted cream and brown breast. -2. an infectious disease caused by a fungus that affects the mouth and throat, and the vagina of adult women.

thrust [θrʌst] (pt & pp thrust) ◇ vt [knife, money, hand] to push <sthg> somewhere using force □ Jack thrust a twenty-dollar bill into my hand. ◇ n -1. [of a knife, body, group of people] a sudden forceful movement forward □ a sword thrust. -2. the power that is needed for a plane, car, rocket etc to move in a particular direction □ The engine generates a powerful forward thrust. -3. [of a report, program, article] the most important point or argument that something is presenting □ The thrust of Meyer's argument is this.

◆ **thrust upon** vt sep **to thrust sthg upon sb** to force sb to have sthg.

thrusting ['θrʌstɪŋ] adj [person] who is very demanding and aggressive and wants to be noticed.

thruway ['θru:wei] n US a very wide road for traffic that is going very fast.

thud [θʌd] (pt & pp thudded, cont thudding) ◇ n a dull soft sound like something heavy falling far away □ The box fell to the floor with a thud. ◇ vi [feet, guns] to make a thud.

thug [θʌg] n a violent man, especially a criminal.

thumb [θʌm] ◇ n the finger that can be placed opposite the four other fingers to pick things up and hold things □ Just put your thumb on there a second. ■ **to twiddle one's thumbs** to be doing nothing because one is waiting for something to happen □ Well, we can't just sit here twiddling our thumbs all day. ◇ vt **to thumb a ride** US OR **lift** GB to stand at the side of a road making a gesture with one's thumb in order to ask passing motorists for a free ride □ We managed to thumb a ride home.

◆ **thumb through** vt fus **to thumb through sthg** [book, magazine, article] to turn the pages of sthg quickly without really reading it.

thumb index n a series of curved hollows cut into the edges of the pages of a dictionary,

encyclopedia etc to show where each letter of the alphabet begins.

thumbnail sketch [,θʌmneil-] n a short description giving only the main details of something.

thumbs down n **to be given** OR **get the thumbs down** to be officially rejected □ The plan got the thumbs down last week.

thumbs up n **to be given** OR **get the thumbs up** to be officially accepted or approved □ Now that the new plans have got the thumbs up, building work can start.

thumbtack ['θʌmtæk] n US a short nail with a large flat top used for fastening pieces of paper, e.g. pictures, notices, or messages, to a wall, board, or other surface.

thump [θʌmp] ◇ n -1. **to give sb a thump** to hit sb hard, usually with one's fist. -2. a loud, dull noise □ It landed on the floor with a loud thump. ◇ vt -1. to hit or punch <sb/sthg> hard □ Dan thumped him in the stomach. -2. to put <sthg> somewhere heavily so that it makes a loud noise □ He thumped the books down on the table. ◇ vi -1. [person] to move heavily and noisily □ She thumped up the stairs. -2. [heart, head] to beat strongly and painfully □ His heart was thumping as he approached the door.

thunder ['θʌndər] ◇ n -1. the loud noise that follows a flash of lightning during a storm □ a loud clap of thunder. -2. [of traffic, drums] a loud noise like thunder □ The loud thunder of applause. ◇ vt to say <sthg> loudly and angrily □ "Come back here!" he thundered. ◇ vi [gun, traffic, drums] to make a loud noise like thunder □ The trucks thundered along the road. ◇ v impers **it is thundering** there is thunder □ It's going to thunder.

thunderbolt ['θʌndərboult] n -1. a flash of lightning followed by thunder. -2. a sudden event that causes great surprise, worry, shock etc.

thunderclap ['θʌndərklæp] n a loud noise of thunder just after a flash of lightning.

thundercloud ['θʌndərklaud] n a large dark cloud that looks as if it will produce thunder and lightning.

thunderous ['θʌndərəs] adj [noise, applause, voice] that is very loud □ The performance was followed by thunderous applause.

thunderstorm ['θʌndərstɔːrm] n a storm of heavy rain, thunder, and lightning.

thunderstruck ['θʌndərstrʌk] adj **to be thunderstruck** to be very surprised and shocked.

thundery ['θʌndəri] adj [weather, sky] that looks as if there will be thunder; that produces thunder.

Thur., Thurs. abbr of **Thursday**.

Thursday ['θɜːrzdei] n the day of the week between Wednesday and Friday; see also **Friday**.

thus [ðʌs] adv (formal use) -1. a word used to introduce a statement that is the result or logical consequence of something that was said before □ More allegations were made, thus *prompting renewed calls for an investigation.* **-2.** in this way ◻ *The printer is activated thus.*

thwart [θwɔːˈt] *vt* [person] to prevent <sb> from doing or getting something that they want; [plans, attack, expectations] to prevent <sthg> from happening ◻ *Her ambitions were thwarted.*

thyme [taɪm] *n* a plant with very small leaves that have a strong sweet smell and are used to give flavor to food.

thyroid [ˈθaɪrɔɪd] *n* a gland at the front of the neck that produces substances that control growth and behavior ◻ *an overactive thyroid.*

tiara [US tɪˈærə, GB -ˈɑːrə] *n* a piece of jewelry that looks like a small crown without a back and is sometimes worn by women at very formal occasions.

Tibet [tɪˈbet] a region in central Asia, north of the Himalayas. SIZE: 1,221,000 sq kms. POPULATION: 1,892,000 (*Tibetans*). CAPITAL: Lhasa.

Tibetan [tɪˈbetn] *n* & *adj*: see **Tibet**.

tibia [ˈtɪbɪə] (*pl* **tibiae** [ˈtɪbiːiː] OR **tibias**) *n* the thicker of the two bones in the leg between the knee and ankle.

tic [tɪk] *n* a quick, sudden, uncontrolled movement, especially of the face, due to tiredness, an illness etc ◻ *a nervous tic.*

tick [tɪk] ◇ *n* **-1.** [sound] the regular, short, clicking sound made by a working clock or watch with hands ◻ *The quiet tick of the clock.* **-2.** [insect] a small insect that lives on the skin of a human or animal and sucks their blood. **-3.** GB [symbol] a symbol (✓) put next to something on a list to show that it is correct or acceptable, that the person on the list is present etc. ◇ *vt* GB [name, answer] to write a tick next to or in <sthg> ◻ *Tick the appropriate box.* ◇ *vi* **-1.** [clock, watch] to make a regular, short, clicking sound. **-2.** **what makes sb tick** the reasons why sb behaves the way they do ◻ *I've never understood what makes him tick.*

◆ **tick away, tick by** *vi* [seconds, minutes, hours] to pass ◻ *As the last seconds of 1995 ticked away...*

◆ **tick off** *vt sep* **-1.** **to tick sthg off** [item, name on a list] to write a tick next to sthg ◻ *Have you ticked me off?* **-2.** **to tick sb off** US to make sb angry (informal use) ◻ *His attitude really ticks me off!* **-3.** **to tick sb off** GB to talk severely to sb in order to show that one is annoyed or unhappy with something that they have done.

◆ **tick over** *vi* **-1.** GB [engine] to be switched on and running at low power but not moving the vehicle ◻ *Leave the engine ticking over.* **-2.** [business, organization] to be functioning, but at a very low level ◻ *"How are things going?" — "Oh, ticking over."*

ticked [tɪkt] *adj* US annoyed.

tickertape [ˈtɪkəteɪp] *n* very long narrow strips of paper on which information such as stock-exchange prices is printed by a machine.

tickertape parade *n* in the USA, an occasion when a famous person or group of people is welcomed to a town by people throwing small pieces of paper over them from high buildings.

ticket [ˈtɪkət] *n* **-1.** a small piece of paper or card that proves that one has paid to go on a bus or train trip, or to get into a museum, theater, movie theater etc; a small piece of paper or card, usually with one's name and a number on it, that shows that one has the right to get or use something ◻ *I'd like two tickets for tonight's performance of "Cats", please.* ◻ *If you don't have a ticket you'll be fined.* ◻ *an opera ticket.* **-2.** [on a product] a label on a product that shows its price, size, washing instructions etc ◻ *a price ticket.* **-3.** [for an offense] an official document that is given to a person because they have committed a driving or parking offense, ordering them to pay a fine or appear in court ◻ *I was given a parking ticket.* **-4.** POLITICS the party or policies that a candidate in an election represents ◻ *the Republican/anti-abortion ticket.*

ticket agency *n* an organization that sells tickets for an airline, theater etc.

ticket collector *n* a person whose job is to check or collect people's tickets on a train or in a train station.

ticket holder *n* a person who has a ticket for something.

ticket inspector *n* a person whose job is to inspect people's tickets on a bus or a train.

ticket office *n* the place where tickets are sold at a train station, theater etc.

ticking off [ˌtɪkɪŋ-] (*pl* **tickings off**) *n* GB **to give sb a ticking off** to talk severely to sb in order to show that one is annoyed or unhappy with something that they have done (informal use) ◻ *He got a ticking off for being so rude.*

tickle [ˈtɪkl] ◇ *vt* **-1.** [person, somebody's feet] to touch <sb/sthg> lightly with one's fingers, a feather etc in order to make them laugh; [skin, nose, throat] to cause a slight itching or scratching feeling in <a part of one's body> ◻ *Don't tickle me!* ◻ *A cough that kept tickling my throat.* **-2.** to please or amuse <sb> ◻ *The idea tickled me.* ◇ *vi* to make one feel a slight itching or scratching sensation ◻ *Stop! That tickles!*

ticklish [ˈtɪklɪʃ] *adj* **-1.** [person, part of one's body] that is sensitive to being tickled ◻ *Are you ticklish?* **-2.** [problem, situation, task] that is difficult and needs to be dealt with very carefully.

tick-tack-toe *n* US a game played on paper in which two people each try to get a row of three 0s or three Xs on a grid in which two horizontal lines cross two vertical lines.

tidal [ˈtaɪdl] *adj* [estuary, river] that has tides; [current, flow] of a tide.

tidal wave *n* a very large wave that comes over the land from the sea, often caused by underwater explosions such as earthquakes.

tidbit [ˈtɪdbɪt] US, **titbit** [ˈtɪtbɪt] GB *n* **-1.** a small tasty piece of food. **-2.** a small piece of gossip, scandal etc.

tiddlywinks [ˈtɪdlɪwɪŋks] *n* a game in which

players try to make small round pieces of colored plastic jump into a container by pressing their edges with a larger piece of plastic.

tide [taɪd] *n* -1. the regular rise and fall in the level of the sea □ *The tide is in/out.* -2. [of opinion, fashion, history] a general feeling or tendency at a particular time □ *They were swept along on the tide of events.* □ *the rising tide of nationalism.* -3. [of protest, people] a large amount or number.

◆ **tide over** *vt sep* **to tide sb over** to help sb get through a difficult period, usually by lending them money □ *Could you lend me some money to tide me over?*

tidemark ['taɪdmɑːʳk] *n* a mark on the shore left by the tide at its highest point.

tidily ['taɪdəlɪ] *adv* [pack, park] *see* **tidy**.

tidings ['taɪdɪŋz] *npl* news (literary use).

tidy ['taɪdɪ] (*compar* **tidier**, *superl* **tidiest**, *pt* & *pp* **tidied**) ◇ *adj* -1. [room, desk, person] that is neat and orderly in appearance □ *Everything in the kitchen was neat and tidy.* -2. [person] who likes everything to be neat and orderly □ *Philippa's a very tidy person.* -3. **a tidy amount/sum etc** a large amount/sum etc (informal use). ◇ *vt* [place, cupboard, hair] to make <sthg> tidy □ *Let me just tidy my desk.*

◆ **tidy away** *vt sep* **to tidy sthg away** [books, papers, clothes] to put sthg away in a box, drawer, cupboard etc so that a place looks tidy □ *Could you tidy the dishes away?*

◆ **tidy up** ◇ *vt sep* **to tidy sthg up** [place, room, cupboard] to make sthg look tidy by arranging things neatly, putting things away etc. ◇ *vi*: *You'd better tidy up now.*

tie [taɪ] (*pt* & *pp* **tied**, *cont* **tying**) ◇ *n* -1. CLOTHING a long narrow piece of cloth that men wear around their neck and over their shirt with a knot at the front □ *He was wearing a jacket and tie.* -2. [for fastening] a long narrow piece of string, wire, cloth etc used for fastening something, or for fixing one thing to another □ *The bag fastened with a tie.* -3. [with a person, place, organization] a feeling or relationship that connects a person, organization etc to somebody or something □ *We're trying to develop stronger ties with industry.* -4. [in a game] the result of a game or competition in which two teams, groups, people etc get exactly the same number of points or votes □ *The game ended in a tie.* -5. US RAIL one of the row of metal or wooden blocks that support a railroad track.

◇ *vt* -1. **to tie sthg/sb to sthg** to attach sthg/sb to sthg with rope, string, thread etc □ *She tied the rope around the horse's neck.* □ *He tied the package with string.* -2. [shoelace, knot] to fasten <sthg> □ *Tie the ribbon in a bow.* -3. **to be tied to sb/sthg** to be linked to sb/sthg □ *The prospects of peace are very much tied to the outcome of these talks.* -4. **to be tied to sthg** [to the house, office] to be unable to leave sthg □ *I've been tied to my desk all day.*

◇ *vi* [competitors, teams] to get exactly the same score or number of points □ *The two skaters tied for first place.*

◆ **tie down** *vt sep* **to tie sb down** to limit the freedom of sb □ *She feels tied down by her job/family.*

◆ **tie in with** *vt fus* -1. **to tie in with sthg** [arrangements, schedule] to be arranged in order to happen at the same time as sthg □ *His plans didn't tie in with mine.* -2. **to tie in with sthg** [ideas, statements] to be connected with or say the same thing as sthg □ *What you're saying doesn't tie in with the facts.*

◆ **tie up** *vt sep* -1. **to tie sthg up** [package, papers] to fasten sthg with string, rope, tape etc. -2. **to tie one's shoelaces up** to fasten one's shoelaces. -3. **to tie sb up** [person, prisoner] to tie rope around sb so that they cannot escape. -4. **to tie an animal up** to attach the bridle, leash etc of an animal up to a fixed object so that it cannot wander away. -5. **to tie sthg up** [resources, computer] to make it impossible for sthg to be used for some other purpose □ *The money is tied up in various long-term investment accounts.* -6. **to be tied up with sthg** to be closely connected to sthg □ *The company's failure is tied up with the downturn in the market.*

tiebreak(er) ['taɪbreɪk(əʳ)] *n* -1. an extra game played to decide the winner of a set in tennis where the score is 6-6. -2. an extra question at the end of a game to decide the winner when both teams or competitors have the same number of points.

tied [taɪd] *adj* [game] that ends with both teams having the same number of points.

tied up *adj* **to be tied up** [person] to be busy □ *Mr Walters is tied up with a client right now.*

tie-dye *vt* [garment, piece of cloth] to dye <sthg> by tying knots in it and putting it in dye so that some parts of it are not affected by the dye.

tie-in *n* -1. **a tie-in with sthg** a link with sthg □ *There's a tie-in between poor diet and heart disease.* -2. a product, e.g. a book or toy, that becomes available at the same time as it appears as a movie, TV program etc □ *a TV/movie tie-in.*

tiepin ['taɪpɪn] *n* a metal pin with a decorative head, used to fasten one's tie to one's shirt.

tier [tɪəʳ] *n* [of seats, shelves, a cake] a row or layer □ *The theater has three tiers.*

tie-up *n* -1. a link between two things, where one thing is caused by the other □ *a tie-up between the US and British economies.* -2. US [in work, traffic] an interruption, usually because of an accident, incident etc.

tiff [tɪf] *n* a slight quarrel or disagreement between people, especially lovers or partners □ *They've had another tiff.*

tiger ['taɪgəʳ] *n* -1. a large Asian animal like a cat that eats other animals for food and has an orange-brown coat with black stripes. -2. ECONOMICS a term used for any of the countries in Southeast Asia whose economies have recently become very strong □ *the Asian tiger economies.*

tiger cub *n* a baby tiger.

tight [taɪt] ◇ *adj* -1. [dress, jacket] that fits very

closely or too closely to the body □ *The jeans were a very tight fit.* □ *It's a little tight around the arms.* **-2.** [lid, screw] that is very firmly fastened or in its place and difficult to move or undo □ *Someone had tied the bag into a tight knot.* **-3.** [skin, cloth, string] that is pulled or stretched so that it is smooth, flat, or straight □ *The skin on my face felt so tight after using that shaver.* **-4.** [bunch, group of people] that is closely packed together, especially in a very small space □ *It was a tight fit to get everybody into the room.* **-5.** [chest, stomach] that feels uncomfortable because of illness or nervousness □ *I have a tight feeling in my chest.* **-6.** [arrangement, plan] that does not allow much time for things to be done □ *We're working on a tight schedule.* ■ **a tight budget** a budget that does not allow much money for extra things. **-7.** [rule, system, control] strict □ *Security at the airport is tight.* **-8.** [corner, bend] that has a very sharp angle □ *Careful — this is a very tight bend.* **-9.** [game, finish] that is very close and competitive □ *It was a tight finish between Benetton and Ferrari.* **-10.** [person] who does not want to spend any money (informal and disapproving use). ◇ *adv* **-1.** [hold, squeeze, grip] firmly or securely □ *Hold tight, there's a steep drop ahead!* □ *Make sure the lid is screwed on tight.* □ *Shut* OR *Close your eyes tight, now.* **-2.** [stretch, pull] so that something is straight or smooth □ *Now pull the cord tight.*

◆ **tights** *npl* **-1.** a piece of clothing for women that is made of thin stretchy material and that covers the feet, legs, and lower body up to the waist □ *a pair of tights.* **-2.** a similar piece of clothing, made of thicker colored material, that is worn by dancers and actors.

tighten ['taɪtn] ◇ *vt* **-1.** [belt, knot, screw] to make <sthg> tighter. **-2.** [rope, chain] to stretch or pull <sthg> until it is straight. **-3. to tighten one's hold on sb/sthg** to hold sb/sthg more tightly. **-4.** [security, rules] to make <sthg> stricter □ *The laws concerning drugs have been tightened.* ◇ *vi* [grip, rope] to become tighter □ *She tightened her hold on the rope.*

◆ **tighten up** *vt sep* **-1. to tighten sthg up** [belt, screw] to make sthg tighter. **-2. to tighten sthg up** [security, control, rules] to make sthg stricter □ *They've tightened up the entry requirements.*

tightfisted [ˌtaɪt'fɪstəd] *adj* [person] who does not want to spend money (informal and disapproving use).

tight-knit *adj* [family, community] in which all the members are very close, friendly, and helpful to one another.

tight-lipped [-'lɪpt] *adj* **-1.** [person] who has pressed their lips tightly together, usually in anger or determination □ *Susan gave a tight-lipped smile.* **-2.** [person, witness] who does not want to give information about something □ *If they do know, they're keeping tight-lipped about it.*

tightly ['taɪtlɪ] *adv* **-1.** [pack, fit] closely □ *The boxes were packed tightly in a crate.* **-2.** [hold,

squeeze, grip] firmly; [fasten, tie, hold] securely □ *She held on tightly to my hand.* □ *Hugh fastened the strap tightly over the case.* **-3.** [pull, stretch] so that something is smooth or straight □ *a tightly stretched rope.*

tightrope ['taɪtrəʊp] *n* a tightly stretched rope high above the ground, on which an acrobat walks and performs. ■ **to be on** OR **walking a tightrope** to be in a difficult or uncertain situation.

tigress ['taɪgrəs] *n* a female adult tiger.

tilde ['tɪldə] *n* a sign (˜) that is put over a letter in some languages, e.g. over the letter "n" in Spanish to show that it is to be pronounced [nj].

tile [taɪl] *n* **-1.** a thin piece of baked clay used for covering roofs □ *roof tiles.* **-2.** a thin piece of baked clay, cork, carpet etc, usually square or rectangular, used to cover surfaces such as floors, walls, and ceilings □ *carpet/cork/polystyrene tiles.*

tiled [taɪld] *adj* [floor, work surface, roof] that is covered with tiles.

tiling ['taɪlɪŋ] *n* an area covered with tiles.

till¹ [tɪl] *prep* & *conj* used in spoken English and in informal writing instead of "until" □ *It won't be ready till tomorrow.* □ *I'll be at the office till 5:30.* □ *Don't do anything till you hear from me.*

till² *n* a machine used in stores, bars, supermarkets etc for calculating how much a customer has to pay □ *Ask the girl at the till.*

tiller ['tɪləʳ] *n* a handle that is fixed to the back of a boat, and is used to steer the boat.

tilt [tɪlt] ◇ *n* [of a chair, one's head] a sloping position □ *the tilt of the Earth.* ◇ *vt* [chair, hat] to move <sthg> into a sloping position □ *She sat listening to me, her head tilted to one side.* ◇ *vi: The chair tilted backward and he fell over.*

timber ['tɪmbəʳ] *n* **-1.** wood used for building □ *a timber yard.* **-2.** a long wide piece of wood that is part of the structure of a house, roof, ship etc □ *roof timbers.*

time [taɪm] ◇ *n* **-1.** the passing of hours, days, years etc, measured by clocks □ *Time seemed to drag.* □ *We'll find out in the course of time.* ■ **to have no time for sb/sthg** to dislike sb/sthg □ *I have no time for soap operas.* ■ **to be/arrive in good time** to be/arrive early. ■ **to make good time** to do something more quickly than one expected □ *We made good time on the trip.* ■ **to pass the time** to spend time doing something unimportant when one is waiting for something or has nothing to do □ *We played card games to pass the time.* ■ **to play for time** to deliberately try to delay something because one needs more time □ *They know they're finished, they're just playing for time.* ■ **to take one's time** to do something without hurrying, especially in order to do it carefully and properly □ *You took your time getting here!* □ *I like to take my time preparing lunch.* ■ **to take time** to happen slowly □ *It will take time for the wound to heal.* □ *These things take time.* ■ **to take time out to do sthg**

to stop what one is doing in order to do sthg else □ *You should take time out to relax a little.* ■ **time and a half** one and a half times the normal rate of pay, usually offered for work done outside the usual working hours □ *We get paid time and a half on Saturdays.* **-2. what time is it?, what is the time?** a phrase used to ask the specific time from somebody who has a watch or can see a clock □ *The time is ten o'clock.* □ *Why are you calling at this time of night?* □ *Do you have the time, please?* ■ **to keep/lose/gain time** [watch, clock] to measure time correctly/too slowly/too fast. ■ **to tell the time** [person] to be able to read a clock or watch; [device] to show what time it is □ *Our new oven tells the time.* **-3.** a particular system of measuring time □ *Eastern Daylight Time* □ *British Summer Time* □ *The flight gets in at 10:15 local time.* **-4.** the period of time spent doing something □ *I don't have much time to relax these days.* □ *You're wasting my time.* □ *How do you find (the) time to study as well?* ■ **a long/short time** a long/short period of time □ *It was some time before I saw her again.* □ *We only had a brief time together.* ■ **after/for a time** after/for a fairly long period of time □ *She worked for a time as a waitress.* ■ **in a week's/year's time** after a period of a week/year □ *We'll meet again in two weeks' time, then.* **-5.** a particular point in time □ *I was much fitter at that time.* □ *That must have been the time when he was working abroad.* □ *Next time I'll be more careful.* □ *That was the only time I ever lied to him.* **-6.** a period in history □ *in Churchill's time.* ■ **to be ahead of one's time** to have ideas or knowledge that are not properly understood until much later □ *As a scientist he was years ahead of his time.* ■ **that's before my time** that happened or existed before I was born. **-7.** a moment or period that is suitable for something, or when something should be done □ *Time for bed!* □ *Now would be a good time to ask.* □ *It's time we had a talk.* ■ **it's about** OR **high time** a phrase used when one thinks something should happen immediately or should have happened before □ *Isn't it about time you got a haircut?* **-8.** used to say how often something happens □ *Sean goes to aerobics three times a week.* □ *How many times do I have to tell you?* **-9. an easy/enjoyable etc time** an experience that is easy/enjoyable etc □ *Apparently they had a great time.* □ *I had a hard time trying to make myself understood.* **-10.** MUSIC the speed of a piece of music □ *a dance in waltz time.*

◇ *vt* **-1.** [exam, meeting, program] to arrange for <an event> to happen at a particular time □ *The firework display was timed for eight o'clock.* □ *The interview is timed to coincide with the launch of her new novel.* **-2.** [activity, race, runner] to measure the amount of time taken by <sb/sthg> □ *I timed him to see how long it took him to jog five miles.* **-3.** [departure, remark, tackle] to choose the best time for <sthg> □ *You were right to complain but you timed it badly.*

◆ **times** ◇ *npl* **-1.** a word used to show that an amount has been multiplied by a particular number □ *It now costs three times what it*

did ten years ago. **-2.** a particular period e.g. in history or in one's life □ *These are hard times for small businesses.* □ *medieval times* □ *in Roman times.* **-3.** phrases **at the best of times** even when things are going as well as possible □ *It's a risky business at the best of times.* ■ **to be behind the times** to be old-fashioned or out-of-date. ◇ *prep* MATH multiplied by □ *Two times four is eight.*

◆ **all the time** *adv* very often □ *It rains all the time here.*

◆ **at a time** *adv* one/two etc at a time in groups of one/two etc □ *One at a time please!* *I can't serve everybody at once.* □ *Patients are allowed two visitors at a time.*

◆ **at one time** *adv* in the past but not now □ *At one time I thought of training as a doctor.*

◆ **at times** *adv* sometimes □ *He can be very irritating at times.*

◆ **at the same time** *adv* **-1.** [happen, speak, arrive] together □ *We both started college at the same time.* **-2.** used to introduce a statement that contrasts with what has just been said □ *We need to increase productivity. At the same time, quality must not suffer.*

◆ **for the time being** *adv* for the present time, for a limited period □ *You can stay at my place for the time being.*

◆ **from time to time** *adv* occasionally □ *From time to time I'd hear news of him.*

◆ **in time** *adv* [be, arrive, finish] before it is too late □ *Luckily, we got here just in time to hear her speech.* □ *We'll never get to the airport in time!* ■ **in time for sthg** before the start of sthg □ *We were home in time for lunch.*

◆ **on time** *adv* at the correct or agreed time □ *The show started right on time.* □ *Our plane arrived on time.*

◆ **time after time, time and time again** *adv* used to show that something happens repeatedly, often in an annoying way □ *Time after time we get the same complaint from customers.* □ *I've warned him time and time again about driving too fast!*

time-and-motion study *n* a study of methods of working that is done in order to discover which ones are most efficient.

time bomb *n* **-1.** a bomb that can be set to explode at a particular time. **-2.** a situation, especially in politics, that will have a dangerous effect at a later time □ *a political time bomb.*

time-consuming [-kənsjuːmɪŋ] *adj* [task, process] that takes a lot of time □ *It's interesting work, but extremely time-consuming.*

timed [taɪmd] *adj* **-1.** [race, test] that has to be finished in a certain time. **-2. well-/badly-timed** [comment, arrival] that happens at a suitable and appropriate/an unsuitable and inappropriate time.

time difference *n* the difference in time between different parts of the world □ *There's a three-hour time difference between here and Alaska.*

time-honored [-ɒnəʳd] *adj* [custom, tradition] that has been in existence for a long time.

timekeeping [ˈtaɪmkiːpɪŋ] *n* the ability of an

employee to arrive at work on time □ *good/ bad timekeeping.*

time lag *n* an interval of time between two related events.

time-lapse *adj* **time-lapse photography** photography that involves taking single pictures over a period of time of something that happens very slowly and then showing these pictures at the speed of an ordinary film, so that the action happens very quickly.

timeless ['taɪmləs] *adj* [beauty, quality] that does not seem to be affected by the passing of time □ *the timeless appeal of Austen's novels.*

time limit *n* a time within which or before which something must be done □ *Try and keep within the time limit.* □ *We'll have to set ourselves a time limit for the work.*

timely ['taɪmlɪ] (*compar* **timelier**, *superl* **timeliest**) *adj* [advice, intervention, reminder] that comes at exactly the right time.

time machine *n* an imaginary machine for traveling to different times.

time off *n* the time when one is not working □ *What do you do during your time off?* □ *He rarely takes time off (from) work.*

time-out (*pl* **time-outs** OR **times-out**) *n* US a break in a game which is not included in the time of the whole game.

timepiece ['taɪmpiːs] *n* a clock or watch (old-fashioned use).

timer ['taɪmə'] *n* a device like a clock that can be set to ring after a certain time or to turn an appliance such as a stove or microwave on or off.

timesaving ['taɪmseɪvɪŋ] *adj* [method, device, gadget] that allows something to be done more quickly.

time scale *n* the length of time during which something happens or develops.

timeshare ['taɪmʃeər] *n* a house or apartment that a number of people own together, and in which they each have a right to spend a certain amount of time every year for their vacation.

time sheet *n* a sheet of paper on which the hours a particular person has worked are written.

time signal *n* a series of short high-pitched sounds broadcast on the radio to indicate the exact time.

time switch *n* a device that can be set to start or stop a machine at specific times.

timetable ['taɪmteɪbl] *n* -1. [for buses, trains] a list of the times when trains, planes, buses etc arrive at and leave various places. -2. GB [in a school] a plan that shows the times of classes in a school, college etc. -3. GB [of events] a plan of the times when certain events are planned to happen, e.g. at a conference or during a project.

time zone *n* any one of the 24 areas into which the world is divided for calculating the local time.

timid ['tɪməd] *adj* [person] who is shy and lack-

ing in confidence □ *John's a timid little boy.* □ *Amy was too timid to openly disagree with him.*

timidly ['tɪmədlɪ] *adv* [answer, smile] *see* **timid.**

timing ['taɪmɪŋ] *n* -1. [of an actor, musician] the ability to judge the right moment when something should happen or be done □ *She has a great sense of timing.* -2. [of an election, meeting] the time at which something happens □ *The timing of his remarks couldn't have been worse.* -3. [of an action] the act of measuring the length of time something takes.

timing device *n* a device inside a bomb that makes the explosion happen at a specific time.

timpani ['tɪmpənɪ] *npl* a set of large drums in an orchestra.

tin [tɪn] *n* -1. a soft silver-colored metallic element. SYMBOL: Sn □ *a tin hut/roof.* -2. GB a metal container that is sealed to preserve food. -3. a metal container with a lid, used for storing cake, cookies, tobacco, tea etc. -4. GB a metal container without a lid, used for baking bread, cakes, and cookies, and for roasting meat and vegetables in the oven □ *a loaf/cake/roasting tin.*

tin can *n* a can in which food or drink has been preserved.

tinder ['tɪndər] *n* small dry pieces of wood, grass etc that burn easily and can be used for lighting a fire.

tinfoil ['tɪnfɔɪl] *n* a very thin sheet of shiny metal used for covering and wrapping food.

tinge [tɪndʒ] *n* a very small amount of color or feeling □ *a tinge of red* □ *There was a tinge of sadness in his voice.*

tinged [tɪndʒd] *adj* **to be tinged with sthg** [with color, feeling] to show or have a small amount of sthg □ *Her voice was tinged with regret.*

tingle ['tɪŋgl] *vi* [face, body] to feel a slight prickling feeling that is usually pleasant □ *The cold made my face tingle.* □ *She was tingling with excitement.*

tinker ['tɪŋkər] ◇ *n* a person who travels from place to place mending pots and pans and other household objects. ◇ *vi* to try to repair something by making a lot of small changes to it, but without necessarily making it better □ *You've been tinkering with that engine for hours!*

tinkle ['tɪŋkl] ◇ *n* a small high sound like a small bell ringing. ◇ *vi* to make the sound of a tinkle □ *The music box tinkled away.*

tin mine *n* a place where tin is taken out of the earth.

tinned [tɪnd] *adj* GB [food] that has been preserved in a tin can.

tinny ['tɪnɪ] (*compar* **tinnier**, *superl* **tinniest**) ◇ *adj* -1. [noise, radio] that sounds thin and harsh. -2. [car] that is of bad quality (informal use). ◇ *n* AUS a can of beer (informal use).

tin opener *n* GB a device used for opening cans of food.

Tin Pan Alley *n* a name for the popular songwriting industry.

tin-pot *adj* GB **a tin-pot government/organ-**

ization etc a government/organization that considers itself to be important but is not taken seriously (disapproving use) □ *a tin-pot dictator*.

tinsel ['tɪnsl] *n* a type of Christmas decoration that is made of small strips of shiny material □ *garlands of tinsel*.

Tinseltown ['tɪnsltaʊn] = **Hollywood** (informal use).

tint [tɪnt] ◇ *n* a small amount of color □ *She has reddish tints in her hair.* ◇ *vt* to give <hair> a small amount of color using artificial dye.

tinted ['tɪntəd] *adj* [glasses, hair, windows] slightly colored or dyed.

Tintin ['tɪntɪn] a Belgian cartoon character. He is a young journalist who has many adventures accompanied by a white dog.

tiny ['taɪnɪ] (*compar* **tinier**, *superl* **tiniest**) *adj* [child, profit, difference] very small □ *The baby stretched out its tiny hands.*

tip [tɪp] (*pt* & *pp* **tipped**, *cont* **tipping**) ◇ *n* -1. [of one's finger, a pencil, iceberg] the end of something long and pointed □ *I can just about reach if I stand on the tips of my toes.* □ *Tierra del Fuego is just off the southernmost tip of South America.* ■ **it's on the tip of my tongue** I can't make myself remember it. -2. [for a waiter, taxi driver] an amount of money given to somebody to thank them for their services □ *I left a small tip.* -3. [advice] a small piece of useful advice □ *Here are some handy gardening tips.* -4. GB [for garbage] a large area where garbage is left, especially household garbage.
◇ *vt* -1. [chair, glass, bowl] to move <sthg> with the result that it is at an angle and not level. -2. [sand, sugar] to make <sthg> fall out of its container by turning it over □ *She tipped the colored pencils onto the table.* □ *Tip the mousse out onto a serving dish.* -3. [waiter, taxi driver] to give a tip to <sb> □ *It's usual to tip hotel porters.*
◇ *vi* -1. [chair, glass, bowl] *The chair tipped dangerously backward.* -2. [sand, sugar] *The flour tipped onto the counter.* -3. [customer] to give a tip to somebody □ *He never tips in restaurants.*
◆ **tip off** *vt sep* **to tip sb off** [police, burglars] to warn sb about something that has happened or is going to happen □ *The White House was tipped off by intelligence sources.*
◆ **tip over** ◇ *vt sep* **to tip sthg over** to make sthg fall over by accident □ *Be careful not to tip the wine bottle over.* ◇ *vi* [bucket, vase] to lean over so far that it falls over or its contents fall out □ *The boat tipped over and the passengers fell into the river.*
◆ **tip up** *vi* [chair, table] to move to an angle so that it is not level and becomes unsteady □ *The chair tipped up and she fell on the floor.*

tip-off *n* a warning that something has happened or is going to happen.

tipped [tɪpt] *adj* **to be tipped with sthg** [weapon, pole] to have sthg at or on its tip □ *spears tipped with poison.*

Tipp-Ex™ ['tɪpeks] *n* GB a white liquid that can be painted onto paper in order to cover mistakes in typing or writing.

tipple ['tɪpl] *n* an alcoholic drink (informal use).

tipsy ['tɪpsɪ] (*compar* **tipsier**, *superl* **tipsiest**) *adj* slightly drunk (informal use).

tiptoe ['tɪptoʊ] ◇ *n* **on tiptoe** standing or walking on one's toes so that the rest of one's foot does not touch the ground. ◇ *vi* to move on one's toes instead of using the whole foot, usually in order to make less noise □ *She tiptoed past the sleeping children.*

tip-top *adj* that is extremely good (old-fashioned use) □ *in tip-top order/condition.*

TIR (*abbr of* **Transports Internationaux Routiers**) an abbreviation written on the back of a truck carrying goods across international borders.

tirade [taɪ'reɪd] *n* a long, angry, critical speech about something.

tire ['taɪər] ◇ *n* US a round piece of rubber that fits around the wheel of a bicycle, car etc and is filled with air. ◇ *vt* to make <sb> become tired. ◇ *vi* -1. [person, animal] *He tires easily after his illness.* -2. **to tire of sb/sthg** to become bored with <sb/sthg>.
◆ **tire out** *vt sep* **to tire sb out** to make sb very tired, so that they have no energy left □ *All that running around has tired me out.*

tired ['taɪərd] *adj* -1. [person, voice] that needs sleep or rest. -2. **to be tired of sthg** to be bored with sthg because one has had it, done it etc for too long □ *I'm tired of this game: let's play something else.* □ *She grew tired of hearing the same old excuses.*

tiredness ['taɪərdnəs] *n* the state or feeling of being tired □ *He complained of tiredness and headaches.*

tireless ['taɪərləs] *adj* [worker, supporter, campaigner] who has a lot of energy and seems never to need rest.

tire pressure *n* the pressure of the air inside a tire.

tiresome ['taɪərsəm] *adj* [person, task] that one finds irritating and boring.

tiring ['taɪrɪŋ] *adj* [day, trip, activity] that makes one feel tired.

Tirol [tɪ'roʊl] = **Tyrol**.

tissue ['tɪʃuː] *n* -1. a handkerchief made of soft paper. -2. material in the body of a living thing that is made up of cells of a particular kind that have a particular function □ *animal/fatty/diseased tissue.* -3. *phrase* **a tissue of lies** a complicated series of lies, usually forming a story.

tissue paper *n* a type of very light thin paper used for wrapping things to protect them from damage.

tit [tɪt] *n* -1. a small European bird that eats seeds and insects. -2.▽ a woman's breast (very informal use).

titbit *n* GB = **tidbit**.

tit for tat [-'tæt] *n* something unpleasant that one does to somebody because they have done something unpleasant to one.

titillate ['tɪtɪleɪt] ◇ *vt* to excite <sb> slightly, especially in a sexual way. ◇ *vi*: *His latest book merely seeks to titillate.*

titivate ['tɪtəveɪt] *vt* to make <sb/sthg> look more attractive, neat etc.

title ['taɪtl] *n* -1. [of a book, song] the name given to a book, article, song etc □ *What is the title of your thesis?* -2. [of a person] the name a person uses to show their position in society, their qualification, or their job □ *Her title is Professor.* -3. SPORT the position of champion in a sport □ *He won the title last May.*

titled ['taɪtld] *adj* -[person] who belongs to an upper-class family and has a title such as Lord or Lady.

title deed *n* a piece of paper that proves a person's legal right of ownership of land, a house etc.

titleholder ['taɪtlhouldə^r] *n* the person who is the present champion in a sport.

title page *n* the page at the front of a book where the title, author etc are written.

title role *n* the role played by the character in a play or movie whose name forms its title.

titter ['tɪtə^r] *vi* to laugh in a nervous, embarrassed, or silly way.

tittle-tattle ['tɪtltætl] *n* gossip about people (disapproving and informal use).

titular ['tɪtʃələ^r] *adj* **a titular ruler/head etc** a person who has the title of ruler/head etc but has no real power or importance.

T-junction *n* GB a place where two roads, pipes etc meet and form the shape of the letter T.

TM ◇ *n abbr of* **transcendental meditation.** ◇ *abbr of* **trademark.**

TN *abbr of* **Tennessee.**

TNT (*abbr of* **trinitrotoluene**) *n* a powerful explosive.

to [*stressed* tuː, *unstressed before vowel* tʊ, *before consonant* tə] ◇ *prep* -1. **to go to a place** to go in the direction of a place □ *Can you tell me the way to the airport?* □ *We didn't get to bed till midnight.* □ *A man came up to me and started threatening me.* ■ **to point to sb/sthg** to point in the direction of sb/sthg □ *He pointed to a town on the map.* -2. **to hold sthg to sthg** to hold sthg against sthg so that they are touching □ *I chained my bike to the fence and went in.* □ *The mirror should be fixed to the wall.* -3. **to the left/north** in a position to the left/north of where one is □ *To your right you can see the palace.* □ *She stood on her own, a little to one side.* -4. used to show who is given, sent, or told something □ *The package was sent to you at your home address.* □ *Promise you'll write to me.* □ *I've been teaching English to businessmen.* □ *Don't talk to me in that tone of voice!* -5. used to show the person or thing that is affected by something □ *It does great harm to the environment.* □ *My brother's engaged to a really nice girl.* □ *She's a great help to me.* -6. **to my surprise/delight etc, he agreed** the fact he agreed made me feel surprised/delighted etc □ *To her relief, there was no one else there.* -7. **to change to sthg** used to show a change from one state to another □ *the switch to nuclear energy* □ *his conversion to Islam* □ *The water turns to steam.* □ *The victim*

was beaten to death by his attackers. -8. used to give a limit □ *Inflation has risen to 8%.* □ *He lived to the age of 90.* -9. used to give an approximate range □ *I must have spent two to three weeks on it.* □ *a nine to five job* □ *She knows about everything from astronomy to music.* -10. **it's ten to three** it's ten minutes before three o'clock □ *I'll see you at (a) quarter to four.* -11. **1,000 meters to a kilometer** 1,000 meters in or for each kilometer (used to show proportions and rates) □ *an exchange rate of eight francs to the pound* □ *There were five girls to every boy.* -12. **to me/many people** according to the opinion of myself/many people □ *It seems like a crazy idea to me.* -13. **a poem set to music** a poem accompanied by music □ *We like to dance to African music.*

◇ -1. used with the infinitive as the subject or object of a verb □ *To deny it would be pointless.* -2. used with the infinitive after certain nouns and adjectives □ *It's an attempt to clarify the situation.* □ *You have no reason to be alarmed.* □ *I'm ready to go.* □ *They were really pleased to see us.* □ *It's not difficult to do.* -3. **I came to see you** I came with the purpose of seeing you □ *He's only doing it to annoy you.* -4. used with the infinitive after "what", "why", "when", etc □ *Tell me where to go.* □ *You can decide who to invite.* -5. used after "too" and "enough" □ *I have just enough money to pay you.* □ *It's too cold to go out.* -6. used alone in place of a complete infinitive □ *"Come here!" — "I don't want to."* -7. **to be honest/fair** used to show that one is speaking honestly/fairly □ *To be perfectly frank, I hate opera.*

◇ *adv* shut but not locked □ *Push the door to.*

◆ **to and fro** *adv* -1. [move, rush, go] from one place to another, without stopping long in any place. -2. [rock, swing, sway] backward and forward or from side to side.

toad [toud] *n* an animal like a large frog, but with rougher skin, that lives on land and breeds in water.

toadstool ['toudstuːl] *n* a type of poisonous fungus that is shaped like a mushroom.

toady ['toudɪ] (*pl* **toadies**, *pt* & *pp* **toadied**) ◇ *vi* **to toady to sb** to flatter and be pleasant to sb in authority in order to gain something. ◇ *n* a person who toadies to somebody.

toast [toust] ◇ *n* -1. [bread] bread that has been made brown and crisp by being cooked in a special piece of equipment or under a grill □ *a piece/slice of toast.* -2. **to drink a toast to sb** to wish sb success, happiness, good health etc and to raise one's glass and drink as a symbol of this □ *Let's drink a toast to her/the future!* -3. **to be the toast of a place/an institution etc** [person] to be very popular in a place/an institution etc because of what one has achieved □ *She was the toast of Paris/the town.* ◇ *vt* -1. [bread, croissant, muffin] to cook <sthg> at a high temperature until it is crisp and brown. -2. [person, health, success] to drink a toast to <sb/sthg>.

toasted sandwich [,toustəd-] *n* a sandwich that is toasted, usually in a special device.

toaster ['toustər] *n* an electric device for toasting slices of bread.

toastmaster [US 'toustmæstr, GB -mɑːstə] *n* a person who introduces the speakers after a formal meal.

toast rack *n* a small object for holding and serving slices of toast.

toasty ['tousti] *adj* US [room, fire] that is warm and makes one feel comfortable.

tobacco [tə'bækou] *n* a substance made from the leaves of a particular plant, used for smoking in cigarettes, pipes etc.

tobacconist [tə'bækənəst] *n* GB a person who sells tobacco, cigarettes, cigars etc in a shop.
■ **a tobacconist's** a store where tobacco, cigarettes, cigars etc are sold.

Tobago [tə'beigou] → **Trinidad and Tobago**.

toboggan [tə'bɒgən] ◇ *n* a flat board with two long metal or wooden parts underneath that is used for sliding downhill fast over snow, especially as a sport or leisure activity. ◇ *vi* to ride on a toboggan.

today [tə'dei] ◇ *adv* -1. on this day □ *What would you like to do today?* -2. in the period of time in which we are living □ *Today, few people have time to cook traditional meals.* ◇ *n* -1. this day □ *today's paper.* -2. the present period of time □ *the youth of today.*

toddle ['tɒdl] *vi* -1. [child] to walk unsteadily. -2. **to toddle off** OR **along** to go somewhere (informal use).

toddler ['tɒdlər] *n* a small child who is learning to walk.

toddy ['tɒdi] (*pl* **toddies**) *n* a mixture of hot water, sugar, and whiskey, brandy, or rum.

to-do (*pl* **to-dos**) *n* a fuss (informal use).

toe [tou] ◇ *n* -1. one of the five moveable parts at the end of one's foot □ *She wriggled her toes.* -2. the part of a shoe, boot, sock etc that covers the toes. ◇ *vt* **to toe the line** to obey rules and behave as one is expected to, especially when one does not want to.

TOEFL ['toufl] (*abbr of* **Test of English as a Foreign Language**) *n* a test of English given to foreign students who want to study in the USA.

toehold ['touhould] *n* -1. a small place in a rock, cliff etc that is just big enough to put one's toes in when climbing. -2. a first position in an area of work from which one hopes to advance and develop □ *We'd like to get a toehold in the Japanese market.*

toenail ['touneil] *n* one of the thin hard coverings that grows on the upper surface at the end of the toes.

toffee ['tɒfi] *n* a hard, sticky, brown candy made by boiling butter, sugar, and water together □ *a bar of toffee.*

toffee apple *n* an apple on a stick, covered with a thin hard layer of toffee.

tofu ['toufuː] *n* a white food made of soya bean curds that has the texture of soft cheese.

toga ['tougə] *n* a long loose piece of clothing worn by citizens in ancient Rome.

together [tə'geðər] ◇ *adv* -1. **to do sthg together** [two or more people] to do sthg with each other □ *The three of us always got along well together.* □ *Both sides have agreed to work closer together.* -2. **to keep people/things together** to keep people/things in the same place and close to each other □ *Stay together, everyone, or you'll get lost!* □ *That was it — he put his belongings together and walked out.* -3. **to join things together** to join one thing to another thing □ *Put the ingredients together in a mixing bowl.* □ *Come on now, clap your hands together and sing!* -4. **to happen together** [two or more events] to happen at the same time □ *The two bombs were timed to go off together.* □ *The letters from the lawyer and her husband arrived together.* -5. used to show the total amount that two or more things make □ *If you add it all together, the real cost of moving must be about $10,000.* □ *This new car has cost me more than all my previous ones put together!*
◇ *adj* [person] who is always very sensible and well-organized (informal use) □ *She's very together.*

◆ **together with** *prep* used to emphasize that two or more things happen at the same time, or are included in a total □ *The meal, together with wine and service, came to $90.* □ *Please send in a résumé, together with details of your current salary.*

togetherness [tə'geðərnəs] *n* a warm feeling of closeness to other people, especially friends and family.

toggle ['tɒgl] *n* a fastener for clothing, bags etc that consists of a small piece of wood, metal, or plastic passed through a loop or hole.

toggle switch *n* -1. ELECTRONICS a switch that can be moved to open or close an electric circuit. -2. COMPUTING a key on a computer keyboard that is pressed to turn a particular feature, such as italic type, on or off.

togs [tɒgz] *npl* (informal use) -1. clothes. -2. AUS = **bathing suit**.

toil [tɔil] ◇ *n* unpleasant tiring work (literary use). ◇ *vi* to work hard for a long time doing something that is difficult and unpleasant.

◆ **toil away** *vi* **to toil away at sthg** to work hard doing sthg unpleasant over a long period of time.

toilet ['tɔilət] *n* a bowl that one sits on where one can get rid of the body's waste matter; a room or building with one or more of these in it □ *I'm just going to the toilet.*

toilet bag *n* a small bag, usually waterproof, in which soap, toothpaste etc can be kept while traveling.

toilet paper *n* thin soft paper used for cleaning oneself after passing waste matter from one's body.

toiletries ['tɔilətriz] *npl* things used to clean or take care of the body, e.g. soap, cleansers, toothpaste, and deodorant.

toilet roll *n* -1. = **toilet paper**. -2. a long strip of toilet paper that is wrapped around a small cardboard tube.

toilet tissue *n* = **toilet paper** (polite use).

toilet-trained [-treind] *adj* [child] who has learned how to control the way they get rid of body waste and to use a toilet.

toilet water *n* a perfume that is not very strong.

to-ing and fro-ing [,tu:ɪŋən'froʊɪŋ] *n* busy activity that involves going from one place to another, and often seems to produce no results.

token ['toʊkən] ◇ *adj* **token support/resistance etc** a small amount of support/resistance etc that does not have much effect and is intended only to give a good impression □ She's the token woman on the panel. ◇ *n* -1. a piece of paper, card, or plastic that is worth a particular amount of money and can be used to pay for goods or services □ a book/laundry/shower token. -2. a symbol of something □ a token of love/esteem/friendship.

◆ **by the same token** *adv* a phrase used to introduce a statement that is a logical result of a previous statement □ The number of students is expanding. By the same token, a college education is becoming less prestigious.

Tokyo ['toʊkjoʊ] the capital of Japan, its largest city, and a major Pacific port. POPULATION: 11,855,563.

told [toʊld] *past tense & past participle of* **tell**.

tolerable ['tɒlərəbl] *adj* [performance, food, hotel] that one finds fairly good or acceptable, but not extremely good.

tolerably ['tɒlərəblɪ] *adv* **tolerably good/efficient etc** good/efficient etc in a way that is just acceptable.

tolerance ['tɒlərəns] *n* -1. the ability to accept other people's beliefs, behavior, customs etc even if one disapproves of them □ In a country not known for its tolerance of political dissent, the decision to allow the demonstration was remarkable. -2. the degree to which a person, animal, or plant can resist the effects of a drug, infection, poison etc.

tolerant ['tɒlərənt] *adj* [person] who accepts other people's beliefs, behavior, customs etc even if they disapprove of them □ He's very tolerant of young people/noise.

tolerate ['tɒləreɪt] *vt* [behavior, dissent, opposition] to allow <sb/sthg>, even if one does not like or approve of them □ They would tolerate no deviation from the party line. □ He irritated me, but I tolerate him for his mother's sake.

toleration [,tɒlə'reɪʃn] *n* the policy of allowing something that one does not approve of, especially religious beliefs and practices that are not officially recognized by the state □ religious toleration.

toll [toʊl] ◇ *n* -1. the total number of people killed or injured, e.g. in an accident □ So far ten bodies have been recovered but police fear the final death toll could be much higher. -2. a sum of money that one has to pay to cross a bridge, use a road etc. -3. *phrase* **to take its toll** to have a serious and harmful effect on somebody □ The long hours and stressful nature of the job inevitably took their toll. ◇ *vt* to make

<a bell> ring, especially as a sign that somebody has died. ◇ *vi*: The bell tolled twice.

tollbooth ['toʊlbu:θ] *n* a small building beside a bridge, on a road etc, where tolls are collected.

toll bridge *n* a bridge where one has to pay a toll to cross.

toll-free US ◇ *adj* [telephone call] that is paid for by the organization that receives it rather than the person that makes it. ◇ *adv*: Call the number below, toll-free:...

Tolstoy [US 'toʊlstɔɪ, GB 'tɒlstɔɪ], **Count Leo** (1828–1910) a Russian writer whose best-known works are the novels *War and Peace* and *Anna Karenina*.

tomahawk ['tɒməhɔːk] *n* a small ax traditionally used for fighting and hunting by Native Americans.

tomato [US tə'meɪtoʊ, GB -'mɑːtoʊ] (*pl* **tomatoes**) *n* a soft, small, red fruit that can be eaten raw or cooked as a vegetable; the plant on which this fruit grows □ tomato sauce.

tomb [tu:m] *n* a large grave, usually with sculpture or other decorations, that is above the ground rather than in it.

tombola [tɒm'boʊlə] *n* GB a game in which people can win prizes if their ticket is picked out of a large container.

tomboy ['tɒmbɔɪ] *n* a girl who likes playing rough noisy games, and who dresses or looks like a boy.

tombstone ['tu:mstoʊn] *n* a large flat stone at a person's grave that shows their name, when they were born and died etc.

tomcat ['tɒmkæt] *n* a male cat.

tomfoolery [tɒm'fu:lərɪ] *n* silly behavior.

tomorrow [tə'mɒroʊ] ◇ *n* -1. the day after today □ Tomorrow is Tuesday. □ tomorrow's weather. -2. the future □ Let's not think about tomorrow. □ Who knows what tomorrow may bring? ◇ *adv* on the day after today □ See you tomorrow! □ Tomorrow, things may change.

Tom Thumb [,tɒm'θʌm] a character in a fairy tale who is as small as a person's thumb.

ton [tʌn] (*pl* **ton** OR **tons**) *n* -1. a unit (US 907 kg or 2,000 lb, GB 1,016 kg or 2,240 lb) used for measuring weight. -2. = **tonne** □ a metric ton. -3. *phrases* **to weigh a ton** to be very heavy (informal use). ■ **to come down on sb like a ton of bricks** to show sb that one is very angry with them for doing something wrong (informal use).

◆ **tons** *npl* **tons of sthg** [of work, money] a lot of sthg (informal use).

tonal ['toʊnl] *adj* that is connected with the tone of a sound.

tone [toʊn] *n* -1. a quality in somebody's voice that expresses a particular feeling, mood etc □ I didn't like his tone of voice. □ a sarcastic/an impatient tone. -2. [of a telephone] a sound made by an electronic piece of equipment such as a telephone □ Please leave your message after the tone. □ There's no dial tone. -3. MUSIC the interval between two musical

notes separated by one key on the piano.
-4. [of a color] a shade of one particular color
that is lighter or darker than other shades of
that color □ *The room was decorated in different
tones of cream.* -5. [of a speech, article] the
general style and character of a speech,
piece of writing etc □ *The tone of the review
was basically hostile.* -6. phrase **to lower the
tone of sthg** [of a place, conversation] to make
sthg more vulgar or less socially acceptable.

◆ **tone down** *vt sep* **to tone sthg down** [language, effect] to make sthg less strong so
that it is more acceptable.

◆ **tone up** *vt sep* **to tone one's body up** to
make one's body firmer by exercising □ *We
did exercises to tone up our stomach muscles.*

tone-deaf *adj* [person] who cannot sing well
because they cannot hear the difference between musical notes clearly.

toner ['toʊnəʳ] *n* -1. a powder used as ink in
photocopiers and computer printers to produce images and text. -2. a cosmetic lotion
used on the face after cleaning it to close
the pores.

tongs [tɒŋz] *npl* a tool consisting of two parts
joined at one end that are pressed together
at the other end in order to pick things up □
a pair of sugar tongs.

tongue [tʌŋ] *n* -1. ANATOMY the fleshy organ
in one's mouth that is used for tasting and
eating things, and for making sounds. ■ **to
have one's tongue in one's cheek** to say
something as a joke, without expecting to
be taken seriously. ■ **to hold one's tongue** to
stop oneself from saying something □ *Hold
your tongue! I didn't ask you!* ■ **tongues will
wag** people will start gossiping □ *Her affair
with a much younger man started tongues wagging.* -2. **to have a sharp tongue** to speak angrily to other people because of one's character. -3. a language (formal use) □ *a foreign
tongue.* -4. COOKING meat from the tongue of
an ox, often sliced and eaten cold. -5. [of a
shoe] the long loose piece of leather under
the laces of a shoe.

tongue-in-cheek *adj* [remark, comment] that
seems serious but is meant as a joke.

tongue-tied *adj* [person] who cannot say anything because they are shy or embarrassed.

tongue-twister *n* a long phrase that is hard
to say quickly and is often used as an amusing way of practicing or improving one's
pronunciation.

tonic ['tɒnɪk] *n* -1. = **tonic water** □ *gin and tonic.*
-2. [for one's health] a medicine of any kind
that helps one to feel strong again when
one is ill or tired □ *tonic wine.* -3. [for one's
mood] something that makes one feel more
cheerful □ *Your visit has been a real tonic!*

tonic water *n* a colorless bubbly drink with a
slightly bitter taste that is used to dilute alcoholic drinks such as vodka and gin.

tonight [tə'naɪt] ◇ *n* -1. the evening or night
of today □ *Tonight is no good, I'm busy till nine
o'clock.* -2. the night which will follow today
□ *Tonight will be frosty.* ◇ *adv* -1. in or during
the evening of today □ *I'll call you tonight,*

about six. -2. during the night which will follow today □ *There will be no moon tonight.*

tonnage ['tʌnɪdʒ] *n* -1. SHIPPING the size of a
ship. -2. the weight of goods measured in
tons.

tonne [tʌn] (*pl* **tonne** OR **tonnes**) *n* a unit
(1,000 kg) used for measuring weight.

tonsil ['tɒnsl] *n* one of two small lumps of
flesh at the back of one's throat.

tonsil(l)itis [,tɒnsə'laɪtəs] *n* an illness in which
the tonsils are inflamed and sore.

too [tuː] *adv* -1. used to show that a previous
statement applies to something or somebody else □ *Small investors, too, will benefit
from these tax reductions.* □ *Kate loved living in
California, and Bill did too.* □ *You too can own an
impressive collection of classical CDs.* -2. **too
hot/cold etc** more hot/cold etc than one
wants or needs □ *Don't spend too long in the
bathroom!* □ *It's much too expensive.* □ *We've
spent too much time on it already.* □ *It's too late
to do anything about it now.* -3. phrases **not too
good/pleased etc** not very good/pleased etc
□ *The situation doesn't sound too hopeful, does
it?* □ *It didn't take me too long to work out why
I'd been invited.* ■ **all too..., only too...** used to
mean "very" □ *It's all too easy to get into the
habit of drinking alone.* □ *I'd be only too pleased
to help, but I'm busy at the moment.*

took [tʊk] *past tense of* **take.**

tool [tuːl] *n* -1. an instrument that one holds
in one's hand and uses to do a particular
job. ■ **to down tools** GB [staff, workers] to stop
working, as a form of protest. -2. a skill,
method etc that helps one to do something
successfully □ *Diplomacy and tact are the tools
of the negotiator.* ■ **the tools of one's trade** the
skills or objects that one usually uses in order to do one's job.

◆ **tool around** *vi* US to waste time doing
nothing in particular (informal use).

tool box *n* a plastic or metal box for keeping
tools in.

tool kit *n* a set of tools kept together in a box
and used for a particular purpose.

toot [tuːt] ◇ *n* a short sound made using a car
horn to give a quick greeting or warning.
◇ *vt* to use <a car horn> to make a toot.
◇ *vi* [horn, car, driver] *The taxi tooted, and he
rushed out of the door.*

tooth [tuːθ] (*pl* **teeth**) *n* -1. one of the small,
white, hard objects in one's mouth that are
used for biting and chewing □ *He still has all
his own teeth.* ■ **to be long in the tooth** to be
too old (informal use). ■ **to grit one's teeth** to
continue to accept something unpleasant
and wait till things improve. ■ **to have no
teeth** [law, organization] to have no real power
to be effective. ■ **to lie through one's teeth** to
tell deliberate lies with no shame at all (informal use). -2. [of a comb, saw, cog] one of a
row of small sharp points along the edge of
a tool, piece of equipment etc.

toothache ['tuːθeɪk] *n* a constant pain in a
tooth.

toothbrush ['tuːθbrʌʃ] *n* a small brush with a

long handle that is used for cleaning one's teeth.

toothless ['tu:θləs] *adj* **-1.** [person] who has no teeth □ *a toothless grin.* **-2.** [law, organization] that has no real power and cannot be effective.

toothpaste ['tu:θpeɪst] *n* a paste that one puts on a toothbrush to clean one's teeth □ *a tube of toothpaste.*

toothpick ['tu:θpɪk] *n* a small, sharp, wooden stick that one uses to remove bits of food from between one's teeth.

tooth powder *n* a powder used to clean one's teeth.

top [tɒp] (*pt* & *pp* **topped**, *cont* **topping**) ◇ *adj* **-1. the top shelf/floor etc** the highest shelf/ floor etc □ *We scraped away the top layer of varnish.* ■ **the top house/end etc** the house/end etc that is furthest away □ *They live at the top end of the street.* **-2. a top player/manager etc** a very successful or important player/manager etc □ *a top legal firm/advertising agency* □ *The Premier can count on the support of the top coalition leaders.* **-3. at top speed** at the fastest possible speed □ *We rushed there at top speed.*

◇ *n* **-1.** [of a hill, cupboard, pile] the highest point or part of something; [of a street, road] the part of something that is furthest away □ *I ran to the top of the stairs.* □ *Top of my list comes job security.* □ *I waited for them at the top of the lane.* ■ **from top to bottom** [search, clean] completely. ■ **on top** on the highest part or point of something □ *The mountain had snow on top.* ■ **to be over the top** GB [behavior, reaction, idea] to be extreme and unnecessary in a particular situation □ *They went completely over the top and spent thousands on the wedding.* ■ **at the top of one's voice** [shout, scream] as loudly as one can. **-2.** [of a bottle, container, box] a piece of plastic, metal etc used for covering something, e.g. when one is not using it □ *Don't forget to put the top back on when you've finished.* **-3.** [of water, a table] the flat surface of something seen from above □ *It floated to the top.* **-4.** CLOTHING a piece of clothing for the upper body □ *I packed a few tops and skirts.* **-5.** a child's toy that spins around. **-6.** [of an organization, league] the best or most important position one can reach □ *Ross soon rose to the top of his profession.* □ *Life is not always easy at the top.*

◇ *vt* **-1.** [league, poll] to be in the highest position on <a list> □ *The song topped the charts for about three months.* **-2.** [story, offer] to produce something that is better than <sthg that came before> □ *Top that one, if you can!* **-3.** [figure, speed] to reach a level that is higher than <sthg> □ *Sales topped the million mark.* **-4.** [cake, dish] to put a layer of something on top of <food> to decorate it or give it more flavor □ *You can top the potato with a little grated cheese.*

◆ **on top of** *prep* **-1.** on the highest part of <sthg> □ *The book was lying on top of the refrigerator.* **-2.** very close to <sb> □ *Suddenly, the truck was right on top of me.* □ *The house is*

too small; we're always on top of each other. **-3.** in addition to <sthg> □ *He's old and ill, and on top of all that, he has his wife to look after.* □ *On top of the salary, you get a company car.* **-4. to be on top of sthg** [of a situation, work] to be in control of sthg □ *I had a backlog of work, but I'm on top of it now.* ■ **to get on top of sb** [work, pressure] to depress and worry sb so that they feel they cannot do what is expected of them □ *Everything seemed to get on top of me, somehow.*

◆ **top off** US, **top up** GB *vt sep* to top sthg off OR up [glass, tank] to put extra water, gasoline etc into sthg so that it becomes full.

topaz ['toʊpæz] *n* a precious stone that is yellow or brown and is used to make jewelry.

top brass *n* **the top brass** the most important people in an organization, especially in the armed forces (informal use).

topcoat ['tɒpkoʊt] *n* **-1.** a heavy coat worn over a suit, dress etc. **-2.** the final layer of paint that is put on a surface.

top dog *n* the person in a particular situation who has the most power and tells other people what to do (informal use).

Top End: **the Top End** AUS the north part of the Northern Territory.

top-flight *adj* [position, diplomat] that is among the very best or highest in rank □ *a top-flight administrator.*

top floor *n* the top story of a building □ *The office is on the top floor.*

top gear *n* the gear in a vehicle that is used when driving at the fastest speeds.

top hat *n* a man's hat that is usually black or gray, has a tall cylindrical main part, and is worn at formal occasions.

top-heavy *adj* [object] that is unstable and likely to fall over because it is larger at the top than at the bottom.

topic ['tɒpɪk] *n* a subject that people talk or write about □ *The discussion covered various topics.*

topical ['tɒpɪkl] *adj* [issue, point] that is interesting at the present time, because people are talking about it.

topknot ['tɒpnɒt] *n* a thick section of hair tied in a knot on top of one's head.

topless ['tɒpləs] *adj* [woman] who is wearing nothing on her breasts; [bar, show] where the female staff or performers are topless □ *topless bathing.*

top-level *adj* **top-level talks/discussions etc** talks/discussions etc that involve the most important and powerful people from the countries or groups involved.

topmost ['tɒpmoʊst] *adj* **the topmost branches/leaves etc** the branches/leaves etc at the top.

top-notch *adj* [quality, service, performance] that one finds very good (informal use) □ *a top-notch lawyer.*

topographer [tə'pɒgrəfəʳ] *n* a person who studies and makes maps of an area, showing features such as the height of the land.

topography [tə'pɒgrəfɪ] *n* **-1.** the study of the physical features of an area; the activity of making a map of the physical features of an area. **-2.** the shape of the land in a particular area □ *the topography of California.*

topped [tɒpt] *adj* **to be topped by** OR **with sthg** [with cream, snow, clouds] to have sthg on the highest part as a covering, decoration etc □ *a dessert topped with whipped cream.*

topping ['tɒpɪŋ] *n* a layer of sauce, extra ingredients etc served on top of food □ *a casserole with a topping of potato* □ *The cake had a delicious chocolate topping.*

topple ['tɒpl] ◇ *vt* [government, president] to make <sb/sthg> lose a position of political power □ *The recent wave of scandals threatens to topple the government.* ◇ *vi* [object, building] to become less stable and then fall □ *The vase toppled to the ground.*

◆ **topple over** *vi* [pile] to become less stable and fall down □ *I knocked the table and all the books came toppling over.*

top-ranking *adj* [player, official] who has a very high or important position.

top-secret *adj* [information, operation] that must be kept completely secret □ *The file was marked 'Top Secret'.*

top-security *adj* [prison, hospital, wing] that is guarded as carefully as possible, usually to prevent dangerous people from escaping.

topsoil ['tɒpsɔɪl] *n* the top layer of an area of soil □ *Over the years the winds and rains had removed the topsoil.*

topspin ['tɒpspɪn] *n* [in tennis, pool] the turning movement of a ball when it goes forward more quickly than usual because it has been hit in a particular way by a player □ *That ball had a lot of topspin on it.*

topsy-turvy [,tɒpsɪ'tɜːʳvɪ] *adj* **-1.** [room, desk] where everything is in a mess. **-2.** [idea, world] that is impossible to understand because it makes no sense.

Torah ['tɔːrə] *n* **the Torah** all of the writings and laws in the Jewish religion.

torch [tɔːʳtʃ] *n* **-1.** a long thick stick that is specially treated to burn at one end and is carried or put somewhere to provide light. **-2.** GB a small electric light that one carries in order to see in the dark.

tore [tɔːʳ] *past tense of* **tear.**

torment [*n* 'tɔːʳment, *vb* tɔːʳ'ment] ◇ *n* **-1.** great suffering of the mind or body □ *the torment of not knowing when I'd see her again.* **-2.** a particular cause of suffering (literary use). ◇ *vt* **-1.** to worry <sb> so much that they suffer a lot over a long period of time □ *I was tormented by guilt.* **-2.** to tease <sb> cruelly and make their life miserable □ *The older children would delight in tormenting him.*

tormentor [tɔːʳ'mentəʳ] *n* a person who makes somebody else suffer by treating them cruelly □ *The dog finally managed to break free of its tormentors.*

torn [tɔːʳn] *past participle of* **tear.**

tornado [tɔːʳ'neɪdoʊ] (*pl* **tornadoes** OR **tornados**) *n* a very violent storm that consists of a mass of air in the shape of a funnel that spins very quickly and causes a lot of destruction.

Toronto [tə'rɒntoʊ] a city and port on Lake Ontario, in southeastern Canada. POPULATION: 635,395.

torpedo [tɔːʳ'piːdoʊ] (*pl* **torpedoes**) ◇ *n* an undersea missile that is fired at a ship to damage or destroy it. ◇ *vt* [submarine, ship] to attack <sthg> by firing torpedoes at it.

torpedo boat *n* a warship designed mainly to carry and fire torpedoes.

torpor ['tɔːʳpəʳ] *n* a lazy state in which one does not have the energy or enthusiasm to do anything (formal use).

torque [tɔːʳk] *n* TECHNOLOGY the force that causes something to rotate.

torrent ['tɒrənt] *n* **-1.** a lot of water that flows very fast and powerfully. **-2. a torrent of words/insults etc** a lot of words/insults etc that somebody says very quickly with strong emotion □ *a torrent of abuse.*

torrential [tə'renʃl] *adj* **torrential rain** a lot of rain that falls quickly and heavily.

Torres Strait ['tɒrəs-] a channel between Papua New Guinea and northeastern Australia.

Torres Strait Islander *n* a member of an Aboriginal people who come from the part of northeastern Australia near the Torres Strait.

torrid ['tɒrəd] *adj* **-1.** [heat, climate] that is very hot and dry. **-2.** [affair, story, scene] that is full of sexual passion.

torso ['tɔːʳsoʊ] (*pl* **torsos**) *n* **-1.** the main part of the body, not including the head and limbs. **-2.** a statue of a human torso.

tortelloni [,tɔːʳtə'loʊnɪ] *n* ring-shaped pieces of pasta filled with meat or cheese.

tortilla [tɔːʳ'tiːjə] *n* in Mexican cooking, a round flat crisp crepe made from corn or wheat flour.

tortoise ['tɔːʳtəs] *n* a small reptile that moves very slowly and has a large shell on its back for protection.

tortoiseshell ['tɔːʳtəsʃel] ◇ *adj* [cat] that has brown, black, and reddish markings. ◇ *n* the brown and yellow shell of a sea-turtle, used in making jewelry and other decorations; a plastic imitation of this material □ *a tortoiseshell comb.*

tortuous ['tɔːʳtʃʊəs] *adj* **-1.** [account, plot] that is too complicated to understand easily. □ *Be warned: getting a visa here is a tortuous process.* **-2.** [route, path] that does not go in a straight line, but has many turns.

torture ['tɔːʳtʃəʳ] ◇ *n* **-1.** the process of deliberately causing somebody great physical pain, e.g. as a punishment or to get information from them □ *They were subjected to beatings and torture.* **-2.** great physical or mental suffering □ *The waiting was sheer torture!* ◇ *vt* **-1.** [person] to deliberately cause <sb> to feel great physical or emotional pain □ *He was tortured to death.* **-2.** [thought, memory] to cause <sb> great suffering □ *She was tortured by guilt.* □ *Don't torture yourself!*

torturer ['tɔːᵣtʃərər] *n* a person who tortures other people.

Tory ['tɔːrɪ] (*pl* **Tories**) ◇ *n* a member or supporter of the British Conservative Party. ◇ *adj*: *a Tory politician/policy*.

toss [tɒs] ◇ *vt* **-1.** [object] to throw <sthg>, especially sthg light, in a careless way □ *Can you toss that apple over to me, please?* **-2. to toss one's head** to move one's head back suddenly, usually to show one is angry. **-3.** [food] to shake <food> around in a dressing, sauce etc so that it gets completely covered □ *Toss the salad in oil.* **-4. to toss a pancake** to throw a pancake in the air and catch it in a pan. **-5. to toss a coin** to throw a coin in the air so that it spins and try to guess which side will face up when it lands. **-6.** [person, boat] to move <sb/sthg> around in a very rough, uncontrolled way □ *The dinghy was tossed around on the waves.*
◇ *vi* **-1.** to toss a coin □ *Shall we toss for it?* **-2.** [person, boat, branches] to keep moving around in an uncontrolled way. ■ **to toss and turn** to be unable to stay still and relax while trying to go to sleep.
◇ *n* **-1.** the act of throwing a coin to decide something, especially to decide who starts play in a sports game. **-2. a toss of one's head** a sudden backward movement of one's head that usually shows one is angry.

toss-up *n* **it's a toss-up** it is impossible to say which of two things will happen, because both are likely □ *It was a toss-up who'd win.*

tot [tɒt] (*pt* & *pp* **totted**, *cont* **totting**) *n* a very young child who is just beginning to walk (informal use).
◆ **tot up** *vt sep* to **tot numbers up** to add numbers together to make a total (informal use).

total ['toʊtl] (US *pt* & *pp* **totaled**, *cont* **totaling**, GB *pt* & *pp* **totalled**, *cont* **totalling**) ◇ *adj* **-1. a total failure/waste etc** a complete failure/waste etc □ *The Socialists are demanding a total ban on arms exports.* **-2. the total amount/figure etc** the amount/figure etc that results from adding smaller amounts together □ *The total sum is over $50,000.*
◇ *n* a final figure that is reached after adding numbers or amounts together □ *The total came to twenty-two.* □ *Rice exports were expected to soar to a total of 1,033,900 tonnes.*
◇ *vt* **-1.** to add <figures> together to make a total. **-2.** to reach <a particular amount> after being added together □ *Borrowings totaled $20 billion.* □ *Expenditure totaled over $50,000.* **-3.** US to damage <a car> so badly that it cannot be used again (informal use).
◆ **in total** *adv* when everything is added together □ *In total, there were three attempts on the President's life.*

totalitarian [ˌtoʊtælə'teərɪən] *adj* [regime, government] that controls people completely and allows no political opposition or democratic freedom.

totality [toʊ'tælətɪ] *n* the whole of something.

totally ['toʊtəlɪ] *adv* completely □ *I'm totally exhausted!* □ *This conclusion is totally wrong.*

tote bag ['toʊt-] *n* a large bag for carrying shopping or personal possessions.

totem pole ['toʊtəm-] *n* a tall pole, traditionally put up by some Native American peoples, that is covered in carvings or pictures with a symbolic meaning.

toto ['toʊtoʊ] *adv* **in toto** when everything is added together (formal use) □ *You have made, in toto, six withdrawals this month.*

totter ['tɒtər] *vi* **-1.** [person] to walk in an unsteady way □ *She tottered to the window.* **-2.** [government, organization] to be weak and close to losing power or importance.

toucan ['tuːkæn] *n* a tropical bird that has a very large and brightly-colored beak.

touch [tʌtʃ] ◇ *n* **-1. one's sense of touch** the sense of feeling things with one's fingers □ *The fabric was soft and silky to the touch.* **-2.** [with a hand] a gentle pressure from somebody's hand □ *I felt a touch on my shoulder.* □ *'Heat at the touch of a button.'* **-3.** [as an addition] a small detail that adds to or completes something □ *And they sent flowers to say thank-you: a nice touch!* □ *Small touches such as red and green ribbons can help create a festive atmosphere.* ■ **to put the finishing touches to** OR **on sthg** to do the last things that are needed to complete sthg. **-4. a personal/professional etc touch** a personal/professional etc way of doing something □ *It needs a woman's touch.* ■ **to be losing one's touch** not to be as good at something as one used to be. **-5. to get in touch** to contact somebody by writing, phoning etc □ *They'll get in touch with you if they want to interview you.* ■ **to keep in touch with sb** to continue to have contact with sb by writing or phoning, so that one still has a friendly relationship with them □ *Goodbye! Keep in touch!* ■ **to keep in touch with sthg** [with developments, research, progress] to make sure one has the latest information about sthg that is always changing. ■ **to lose touch with sb** to stop having contact with sb whom one no longer sees regularly because one does not write to them, phone them etc □ *My mother had a brother, but they lost touch.* ■ **to be out of touch with sthg** [with reality, news, developments] not to know as much as one used to about sthg that is always changing □ *If you stop work for even a year, you soon get out of touch.* **-6.** SPORT **into touch** out of the area of the field where play can take place. **-7. to be a soft** OR **easy touch** to be very likely to give or lend money when asked (disapproving use).
◇ *vt* **-1.** [object, surface, person] to put one's hand or another part of one's body in contact with <sb/sthg> □ *Bend over and touch your toes.* □ *If you touch me, I'll scream!* □ *I didn't touch a thing on my desk, I just straightened it up.* **-2.** [person] to cause <sb> to have a feeling such as pity, sadness, or admiration □ *It really touched me, the way he spoke about his son.* **-3. to never touch sthg** [meat, alcohol] to never eat or drink sthg □ *No, thank you, I never touch it!*
◇ *vi* **-1.** [person] to put one's hand on some-

thing □ *Do not touch.* **-2.** [two objects] to come into contact □ *Our hands touched.*

◆ **a touch** ◇ *adv* slightly □ *Can you move a touch to the left?* □ *It was a touch expensive.* ◇ *det* **a touch of sthg** a small amount of sthg □ *There's a touch of frost in the air.*

◆ **touch down** *vi* [plane] to land.

◆ **touch on** *vt fus* **to touch on sthg** to mention sthg briefly □ *In his talk, Dr Lane touched on the future expansion of NATO.*

◆ **touch up** *vt sep* **to touch sthg up** to improve sthg by making slight changes or additions □ *The paintwork could do with touching up.*

touch-and-go *adj* [operation, outcome] that is very uncertain and could end in success or failure □ *It was touch and go whether we would make it.*

touchdown ['tʌtʃdaʊn] *n* **-1.** [of a plane] the moment when a plane or spacecraft lands. **-2.** SPORT in football, the act of moving the ball behind the opponents' goal line in order to score points.

touched ['tʌtʃt] *adj* **-1.** [person] who feels gratitude, pity, sympathy etc because of something that has been done or said □ *I was so touched (that) he remembered my birthday.* **-2.** [person] who seems a little crazy (informal use).

touching ['tʌtʃɪŋ] *adj* [scene, sight, thought] that causes somebody to have a feeling of gratitude, pity etc □ *The last act was so touching, the whole audience was in tears.*

touch judge *n* [in rugby] an official whose job is to indicate when the ball has crossed the boundary line and is no longer in play.

touchline ['tʌtʃlaɪn] *n* GB a line marking the side boundary of a field used for playing rugby, soccer etc.

touchpaper ['tʌtʃpeɪpəʳ] *n* the paper on a firework that one lights to cause it to start burning □ *Light the touchpaper and stand back.*

touch screen *n* COMPUTING a screen that a person touches to work a computer.

touch-type *vi* to type without looking at the keys or one's fingers.

touchy ['tʌtʃɪ] (*compar* **touchier**, *superl* **touchiest**) *adj* **-1.** [person] who easily gets angry or offended. ■ **to be touchy about sthg** to dislike people mentioning sthg □ *Dad's very touchy about his age.* **-2.** **a touchy subject** a subject that may upset or offend people and so needs to be dealt with very carefully.

tough [tʌf] *adj* **-1.** [person] who is strong and able to deal with difficulties □ *He'll be alright, he's pretty tough.* □ *She's mentally/physically tough.* **-2.** [material] that is strong and unlikely to break or tear. **-3.** [meat] that is hard to chew. **-4.** [decision, choice] that is hard to make; [life, job, question] that is hard to deal with (informal use) □ *I'm not sure; that's a tough one to answer!* **-5.** [area, neighborhood] where there is a lot of crime (informal use). **-6.** [authorities, policy] that is strict (informal use) □ *The U.S. customs are very tough.* **-7.** **tough luck!, (that's) tough!** a phrase used to show that one does not feel sorry for some-

body who is in a difficult situation (informal use).

toughen ['tʌfn] *vt* **-1.** [person, character] to make <sb/sthg> stronger and less sensitive. **-2.** [material, glass] to make <sthg> stronger and less likely to break or tear.

toughened ['tʌfnd] *adj* [glass, steel] that has been specially strengthened by an industrial process.

Toulouse-Lautrec [tuː,luːzlɔ'trek], **Henri de** (1864–1901) a French artist known for his many paintings and posters of scenes in the bars and nightclubs of Paris.

toupee [US tuː'peɪ, GB 'tuːpeɪ] *n* a small wig for a man that covers the top and front of the head.

tour [tʊəʳ] ◇ *n* **-1.** [of different places] a trip during which one visits several different places □ *a tour of Scandinavia.* **-2.** [of one place] a short visit to a place, e.g. a town or building, to see the interesting parts □ *We went on a tour of Mount Vernon.* **-3.** [for work] a visit to several places, planned in advance, as part of one's job or official function □ *the President's tour of the Far East* □ *The band hopes to go on tour again next year.*
◇ *vt* **-1.** [tourist, visitor, inspector] to make a tour of <a building or place>. **-2.** SPORT & THEATER [team, group, company] to go around <an area or country>, performing or playing □ *They'll be touring Europe for the next month.*
◇ *vi* [team, group] The ballet company tours during the summer months. □ *They are currently touring in Scotland.*

touring ['tʊərɪŋ] ◇ *adj* **a touring show/exhibition etc** a show/exhibition etc that moves from one place to another for the public to see. ◇ *n* the activity of traveling around and visiting various places. ■ **to go touring** to go on a tour for pleasure, usually by car.

tourism ['tʊərɪzm] *n* **-1.** the activity of traveling to and visiting different regions or foreign countries for pleasure. **-2.** the industry that provides services such as accommodation for tourists □ *a career in tourism.*

tourist ['tʊərəst] *n* a person, usually on vacation, who visits a place for pleasure.

tourist class *n* the cheapest standard of service and seating on a plane □ *We traveled/flew (by) tourist class.*

tourist (information) office *n* a place where visitors to a town or region can get information on hotels, places to visit etc.

touristy ['tʊərəstɪ] *adj* [place] that one thinks has been spoiled by the presence of too many tourists (disapproving use).

tournament ['tʊəʳnəmənt] *n* SPORT a series of games or matches in which the winner of one game plays the winner of another game until the final game is won □ *the Forest Hills tennis tournament.*

tourniquet [US 'tɜːrnəkət, GB 'tɔːnɪkeɪ] *n* a band of cloth wound very tightly around an arm or leg to stop bleeding from a wound.

tour operator *n* GB a company that arranges package tours to popular destinations.

tousle ['taʊzl] *vt* to make <sb's hair> look messy.

tout [taʊt] ◇ *n* GB a person who sells tickets for a sporting event or a concert illegally and at very high prices to people in the street □ *a ticket tout.* ◇ *vt* [wares, goods] to try to persuade people to buy <sthg> by showing it to them. ◇ *vi* **to tout for business** to try to get business by speaking to people, attracting their attention etc.

tow [toʊ] ◇ *n* the process of pulling one vehicle along behind another □ *I've broken down. Can you give me a tow?* ■ **'on tow'** GB a sign placed on the back of a vehicle to inform other drivers that it is being pulled along by another vehicle. ■ **with sb in tow** followed closely by sb □ *It would be nice to go somewhere without the kids in tow for a change.* ◇ *vt* [trailer, camper, car] to pull <a vehicle> along by attaching it to another vehicle with a rope or chain.

toward [təˈwɔːʳd] US, **towards** [təˈwɔːʳdz] *prep* **-1. to go/face toward sthg/sb** to go/face in the direction of sthg/sb □ *The crowd drifted slowly toward the exit.* □ *Jamie came running toward us, shouting and waving.* □ *He was standing with his back toward me, and didn't see me.* **-2. a move/step toward sthg** a move/tendency that brings sthg nearer or makes it more likely □ *Over the past two years the firm has been making steady progress toward its goal of profitability.* □ *She has contributed a great deal toward changing public attitudes to mental illness.* **-3. one's attitude toward sb/sthg** one's feelings about sb/sthg □ *I was puzzled by the way he'd been behaving toward me.* □ *Recently her feelings toward him had changed.* **-4. to go/be put toward sthg** [money] to be used to pay for some of but not all of the cost of sthg □ *The money raised will go toward buying a new minibus for the local children's home.* **-5.toward a particular period** just before the end of a particular period of time □ *They met up again toward the end of the war.*

towaway zone ['toʊəweɪ-] *n* US an area where one's car will be towed away if one parks on the street.

towbar ['toʊbɑːʳ] *n* a strong hook at the back of a car for towing campers or trailers.

towel ['taʊəl] *n* a piece of soft absorbent fabric for drying oneself after swimming or washing.

toweling US, **towelling** GB ['taʊəlɪŋ] *n* the soft absorbent fabric used to make towels □ *a bathrobe made of toweling.*

towel rail *n* a rail in a bathroom on which towels are hung.

tower ['taʊəʳ] ◇ *n* a very tall narrow building that can be separate or part of a church or other large building □ *the Eiffel Tower* □ *the twin towers of the World Trade Center.* ■ **a tower of strength** a person one can rely on during a difficult time. ◇ *vi* [cliff, building] to rise up very high □ *From Brooklyn Heights, lower Manhattan towers across the river.* ■ **to tower over sb/sthg** [person, building] to be much taller than sb/sthg.

tower block *n* GB a high-rise building containing apartments.

towering ['taʊərɪŋ] *adj* **-1. a towering cliff/peak etc** a cliff/peak etc that is very high and impressive. **-2. a towering rage** a great rage.

Tower of London: the Tower of London an old castle in the city of London that used to be an important royal palace, and then a prison. It is now a museum.

town [taʊn] *n* **-1.** a place bigger than a village, but smaller than a city, where many people live; the people who live in such a place □ *I live in a large town.* □ *the town center* □ *The whole town turned out to welcome them.* **-2.** the city center □ *Are you going to town?* ■ **to be in/out of town** to be in/not in the town where one lives □ *Will you be in town next week?* ■ **to go out on the town** to go out to have fun, e.g. by eating in a restaurant or going to a show. ■ **to go to town on sthg** to do sthg in a very thorough or energetic way □ *There's no need to go to town on the introduction.*

town clerk *n* a local government official who is in charge of the daily administration of a particular town or area.

town council *n* GB a group of people elected to be in charge of services such as roads, leisure centres, parks, garbage collection etc in a town.

town hall *n* **-1.** a large building in the middle of a town, where local government administration takes place. **-2.** the local government officials based at the town hall.

town house *n* an elegant house, usually tall and narrow, in a town or city.

town planner *n* GB a person who is responsible for town planning.

town planning *n* GB the planning, designing, and development of buildings, roads, parks etc in a town □ *Terrassa suffers from disastrous town planning.*

townsfolk ['taʊnzfoʊk] *npl* = **townspeople.**

township ['taʊnʃɪp] *n* **-1.** a town in South Africa where black people live. **-2.** a town in the USA that has some powers of local government.

townspeople ['taʊnzpiːpl] *npl* **the townspeople** the people who live in a particular town or city.

towpath [US 'toʊpæθ, *pl* -pæðz, GB -pɑːθ, *pl* -pɑːðz] *n* a path along the bank of a canal or river, used in the past by horses pulling barges.

towrope ['toʊroʊp] *n* a rope used for towing.

tow truck *n* US a vehicle used to tow other vehicles that have broken down and to take them to be repaired.

toxic ['tɒksɪk] *adj* [substance, waste] poisonous.

toxic shock syndrome *n* a serious illness affecting women, whose symptoms include a high temperature and low blood pressure, that is believed to be caused by the misuse of tampons.

toxin ['tɒksən] *n* any poisonous substance that is produced by bacteria, or that occurs naturally in certain animals and plants.

toy [tɔɪ] *n* an object for children to play with.

◆ **toy with** *vt fus* -1. **to toy with an idea** to think about doing something, but not very seriously and without making a decision ▫ *I've been toying with the idea of buying a new car.* -2. **to toy with sthg** [coin, pencil] to handle or play with sthg without any particular purpose ▫ *She sat toying with her food.*

toyboy ['tɔɪbɔɪ] *n* a young boyfriend of an older woman (informal and disapproving use).

toy store US, **toy shop** *n* a store where toys and games are sold.

TPC (*abbr of* **Trade Practices Commission**) *n* **the TPC** the organization in Australia that is responsible for protecting the rights of consumers and checking that businesses are being run fairly and honestly.

trace [treɪs] ◇ *n* -1. a mark or sign that shows that somebody or something has been present or that something has happened ▫ *He left no trace of his presence.* ▫ *The survivors vanished without trace.* -2. a very small amount of something ▫ *traces of paint/blood/poison.*
◇ *vt* -1. [relative, criminal, source] to find or discover <sb/sthg> using facts, information, signs etc ▫ *The police traced the calls to an address in Queens.* -2. [rumor, fear] to find the origins of <sthg> ▫ *His phobia could be traced (back) to an incident in his childhood.* ▫ *Beatrice can trace her family back to Norman times.* -3. [development, growth] to follow or describe the history and progress of <sthg> ▫ *The program traces the rise of the civil rights movement.* -4. [map, drawing] to copy <sthg> by drawing its lines on transparent paper placed over it.

trace element *n* CHEMISTRY an element that is found in something in very small amounts.

tracer bullet ['treɪsər-] *n* a bullet that glows brightly as it travels through the air.

tracing ['treɪsɪŋ] *n* a copy of a map, drawing etc that has been made by tracing it.

tracing paper *n* a type of strong transparent paper that is used for making tracings.

track [træk] ◇ *n* -1. a rough narrow path ▫ *We drove up a rough track toward the chalet.* ■ **off the beaten track** in an isolated place that is not often visited ▫ *He lives well off the beaten track.* -2. SPORT a course designed for a particular kind of race ▫ *a cycling/running/race track.* -3. RAIL = **railroad track**. -4. MUSIC any of the separate sections of a CD, tape, or record that contains a song or piece of music ▫ *side one, track three* ▫ *It's one of my favorite tracks.* -5. *phrases* **to keep track of sb/sthg** to stay aware of or informed about sb/sthg ▫ *I try to keep track of the number of pages I've checked.* ▫ *It's difficult to keep track of her because she's always on the move.* ■ **to lose track of sb/sthg** to fail to keep track of sb/sthg ▫ *We heard he was in Moscow, but then we lost*

track of him. ▫ *I was having such fun that I lost all track of time.* ■ **to be on the right/wrong track** to be thinking in a way that is likely/unlikely to lead to a solution to a problem, question etc ▫ *I think you're on the right track.*
◇ *vt* to follow the track of <a person or animal>.
◇ *vi* [camera] to move along while filming.

◆ **tracks** *npl* marks in the ground left by a person, animal, or vehicle ▫ *We followed the tracks as far as the river.* ▫ *car/tire tracks.* ■ **to hide** OR **cover one's tracks** to leave no marks or signs of one's movements or activities. ■ **to stop dead in one's tracks** to stop very suddenly.

◆ **track down** *vt sep* **to track sb/sthg down** to find sb/sthg after searching hard or for a long time ▫ *I finally tracked him down in Rio.*

track and field *n* events such as running and jumping.

trackball ['trækbɔːl], **trackerball** ['trækərbɔːl] *n* a small ball fitted into a computer keyboard that is used instead of the keys to move the cursor around the screen.

tracker dog ['trækər-] *n* a dog that is trained to search for escaped criminals, people who are missing etc.

track event *n* a race in athletics such as a sprint or a relay race.

tracking ['trækɪŋ] *n* the position of the tape in a video cassette that can be adjusted in relation to the heads in a video recorder in order to improve the quality of the picture.

tracking station *n* a place from which storms, satellites, spacecraft etc are tracked by radar or radio.

track record *n* the past achievements or failures of a person, organization etc ▫ *an excellent/a poor track record.*

track shoes *npl* shoes with spikes in the soles that are used by athletes on a sports track.

tracksuit ['træksuːt] *n* GB a warm loose set of clothes worn to do exercises or physical training, or as casual clothing ▫ *a tracksuit top/bottom.*

tract [trækt] *n* -1. a short piece of writing on a moral, political, or religious subject. -2. [of land, forest] a large area. -3. MEDICINE a system of organs or tubes in the body with a particular function ▫ *the digestive/respiratory/urinary tract.*

traction ['trækʃn] *n* -1. PHYSICS the power used to pull a heavy load along a surface. -2. MEDICINE the process of pulling lightly and continuously an injured limb or muscle as a form of treatment ▫ *His back/leg/neck is in traction.* -3. [of a tire] the ability of a tire to move over the ground without skidding.

traction engine *n* a large vehicle that is powered by steam and was used in the past for pulling heavy loads along roads.

tractor ['træktər] *n* a powerful farm vehicle with large rear wheels that is used for pulling farm machinery or other heavy loads.

tractor-trailer *n* US a large truck that is made

in two or more parts joined by metal bars so that it can turn more easily.

trade [treɪd] ◇ *n* **-1.** [between countries] the process of buying, selling, or exchanging goods and services, especially between countries □ *Overseas trade is very important to the economy.* □ *a trade minister.* **-2.** [in a country] a particular type of business or industry □ *the car/tourist/wool trade.* **-3.** [of a person] a job, especially one that needs special training and manual skills □ *He's a welder/butcher by trade.*
◇ *vt* to exchange <sthg> □ *They had little left to trade.* □ *He traded his guitar for a banjo.*
◇ *vi* BUSINESS to buy, sell, or exchange goods and services □ *The two countries have been trading for years.* □ *The company has since ceased trading.*
◆ **trade in** *vt sep* **to trade sthg in** [car, TV set] to give sthg that one has already used to a seller as part of the payment for something new □ *Louis traded in his old Chevvy for a brand new truck.*

trade barrier *n* something, e.g. a tax, import duty, or embargo, that limits or prevents trade.

trade deficit *n* = trade gap.

Trade Descriptions Act *n* **the Trade Descriptions Act** a British law stating that advertisements and descriptions of goods for sale must be honest.

trade discount *n* a discount given to people who work in a particular trade.

trade fair *n* a large exhibition of industrial and commercial goods.

trade gap *n* the difference between the value of what a country exports and what it imports, when the value of imports is greater □ *This month's figures show that the trade gap has narrowed/widened.*

trade-in *n* a used article, e.g. a car or TV set, that is traded in.

trademark ['treɪdmɑːrk] *n* **-1.** BUSINESS a name, sign, or word that is used to identify the products of a particular company and may only be used legally by that company. **-2.** something that is typical of a particular person or thing □ *Professionalism is his trademark.*

trade name *n* BUSINESS a name given by a producer to a product to distinguish it from similar products made by other producers.

trade-off *n* the fact of accepting that one cannot have all of the two things one wants, so must have less of one or both of them □ *There has to be a trade-off between quality and value for money.*

trade price *n* the price at which goods are sold by a producer.

trader ['treɪdər] *n* **-1.** a person or company that buys and sells goods internationally □ *a coffee/oil/gold trader.* **-2.** a person who sells goods in the street, at a market etc □ *a street/market trader.*

trade route *n* a route over land or sea used by traders or their vehicles or ships.

trade secret *n* a method that is used by a

company or trade to make its products and that is kept secret from other companies.

tradesman ['treɪdzmən] (*pl* **tradesmen** [-mən]) *n* GB **-1.** a storekeeper. **-2.** a person who delivers goods to people's homes.

tradespeople ['treɪdzpiːpl] *npl* storekeepers.

trades union *n* GB = trade union.

Trades Union Congress *n* → TUC.

trade union *n* an association of workers formed to protect their interests, improve their pay and conditions etc.

trade unionist *n* a member of a trade union.

trading ['treɪdɪŋ] *n* the activity of buying and selling □ *street/market trading* □ *The dollar fell two points in heavy trading on the Stock Exchange today.*

trading estate *n* GB = industrial estate.

trading stamp *n* a stamp that is given by a store to its customers each time they buy goods and that can be exchanged later for goods or money.

tradition [trə'dɪʃn] *n* **-1.** the system of beliefs, customs, and practices passed from one generation to the next □ *the British love of tradition.* **-2.** something that particular people have done or thought for many generations □ *The celebrations at New Year are an ancient Chinese tradition.* □ *This year we decided to break with tradition and hold the party at home.*

traditional [trə'dɪʃnəl] *adj* **-1.** [belief, practice, music] that has existed for many generations without changing □ *a traditional Sunday lunch.* **-2.** [teacher, father] who has traditional beliefs and is not interested in new ideas □ *His family are very traditional.*

traditionally [trə'dɪʃnəli] *adv* according to tradition □ *The bride traditionally wears white.*

traffic ['træfɪk] (*pt & pp* **trafficked**, *cont* **trafficking**) ◇ *n* **-1.** AUTO the vehicles using a road or street □ *Sorry I'm late, I got stuck in traffic.* □ *Traffic is heavy on the roads into the city.* □ *a traffic accident.* **-2.** AVIATION & SHIPPING the aircraft or ships using a route □ *air traffic control.* **-3.** [in drugs, arms, stolen goods] illegal trading □ *arms traffic* □ *the international traffic in ivory.*
◇ *vi* to trade illegally □ *He's well known for trafficking in stolen goods.*

traffic calming [-kɑːmɪŋ] *n* GB the use of speed bumps, cameras etc on a road to stop people from driving along it too quickly.

traffic circle *n* US a place where several roads meet that has a circular, often raised, area in the middle that all cars drive around to get to the road they want.

traffic cone *n* a brightly-colored plastic object in the shape of a cone that is used to keep traffic away from part of a road when construction work is being done on it.

traffic island *n* a raised area in the middle of a road where pedestrians can wait to cross.

traffic jam *n* a situation in which there is so much traffic that it moves very slowly or not at all.

trafficker ['træfɪkər] *n* a person who deals in

illegal goods □ *a trafficker in stolen works of art* □ *a drugs trafficker.*

traffic lights *npl* colored lights that control the movement of vehicles at places where two or more roads meet □ *a set of traffic lights* □ *The traffic lights were green/red.*

traffic offence *n* GB = **traffic violation.**

traffic sign *n* = **road sign.**

traffic violation US *n* an illegal act connected with driving a vehicle.

traffic warden *n* GB an official in a city whose job is to check that vehicles are not parked illegally.

tragedy ['trædʒədɪ] (*pl* **tragedies**) *n* -1. something that happens that makes people extremely sad □ *His early death was a tragedy for his family.* □ *Their life was marred by tragedy.* □ *The trip ended in tragedy when the boat sank out at sea.* -2. something that happens that is unfortunate □ *It's a tragedy for us all that he never won power.* -3. a play in which the main character or characters are destroyed by a combination of circumstances and personal failings; such plays taken together as a group □ *Shakespeare's tragedies* □ *Greek tragedy.*

tragic ['trædʒɪk] *adj* -1. [event] that is extremely sad and unfortunate □ *Dean was killed in a tragic road accident.* -2. [play, character] that ends in tragedy □ *a tragic tale of love and loss.*

tragically ['trædʒɪklɪ] *adv* [die, end] *see* **tragic** □ *a tragically short life* □ *Tragically, they both died.*

trail [treɪl] ◇ *n* -1. [in the countryside] a very rough path through forest, countryside etc □ *We followed the trail through the pine trees toward the sea.* ■ **to blaze a trail** to be the first to do something and set an example for other people in an activity such as research. -2. [of a person, animal] the track or smell that is left by a person or animal and that can be followed by somebody who is hunting them □ *The police are hot on the trail of the thieves/stolen goods.* -3. [of smoke, dust] a line or series of signs left behind by somebody or something as they move □ *a vapor trail* □ *The army left a trail of destruction in its wake.*

◇ *vt* -1. [scarf, bag] to drag <sthg> behind one □ *He came in, trailing his teddy bear behind him.* -2. SPORT to have a lower score than <sb> □ *Atlanta is trailing Cleveland three runs to two.*

◇ *vi* -1. [scarf, bag, toy] to hang down loosely behind somebody as they move along □ *Your belt's trailing on the ground.* -2. [person] to walk slowly and without energy or enthusiasm □ *The children trailed miserably around the stores with their mother.* -3. SPORT & POLITICS **to be trailing** to be losing □ *Tampa is trailing 1–0.* □ *He's trailing in the polls.*

◆ **trail away, trail off** *vi* [voice, speech] to become quieter or weaker and then stop completely □ *Anna's voice trailed off as she realized what had happened.*

trailblazing ['treɪlbleɪzɪŋ] *adj* [research, policy, discovery] that is the first of its type and leads the way in an area of activity.

trailer ['treɪlər] *n* -1. a vehicle pulled by another vehicle and used for carrying large or heavy items. -2. US a vehicle with beds, kitchen equipment etc inside that can be pulled by another vehicle and that people live in or spend vacations in. -3. GB CINEMA & TV an advertisement for a movie or program that consists of short extracts from it.

trailer court, trailer park *n* US an area where a lot of mobile homes are parked, often with people living in them.

Trail of Tears *n* **the Trail of Tears** the route taken by the Cherokee people in 1838 and 1839 when they were forced to move from their lands in the southeastern USA to Oklahoma.

◆ TRAIL OF TEARS
The Trail of Tears refers to the route followed by fifteen thousand Cherokee in 1838 and 1839, when they were forced by government troops to leave their own lands in the southeastern USA and march, in winter, to new settlements in what is now Oklahoma. Thousands of Cherokee died on the way from cold, disease, and exhaustion. This route is now a national monument, and is seen as a symbol of the injustices suffered by the Native American peoples.

train [treɪn] ◇ *n* -1. RAIL a vehicle that consists of several connected railroad cars or wagons pulled by an engine □ *a freight/passenger train.* -2. [of a dress] a part of a long dress, especially a wedding dress, that trails on the ground behind the wearer. -3. **one's train of thought** a series of connected thoughts that one is having □ *You interrupted my train of thought.* ■ **a train of events** a connected series of events.

◇ *vt* -1. [child, dog] to teach <a person or animal> to do something □ *He can't use a potty yet, but we've started to train him.* □ *Their dog is trained to bark at strangers.* -2. [nurse, recruit] to give <sb> formal instruction and practice in the knowledge, skills etc necessary for a particular job □ *How many nurses were trained last year?* □ *I was trained in medicine but preferred the theater.* -3. SPORT [athlete, horse, boxer] to help <a person or animal> become or stay physically fit through exercise and diet □ *Our team has been specially trained for this event.* -4. [ivy, creeper] to make <a plant> grow in a particular way or direction by cutting, tying etc. -5. [gun, camera] to point or aim <sthg> in a particular direction □ *The police trained high-pressure hoses on the rioters.*

◇ *vi* -1. [nurse, recruit] to be trained □ *Where did you train?* □ *He's training to be a doctor.* □ *She trained as a secretary/dancer/social worker.* -2. SPORT [athlete, team] to prepare for a sports event by doing a lot of exercise, especially in a planned way □ *He's training for the marathon.*

trained [treɪnd] *adj* [psychologist, singer, nurse] who has successfully completed their training □ *He's a trained doctor.*

trainee [treɪ'niː] ◇ *n* a person who is being

trained in a particular job. ◇ *adj*: *a trainee nurse/architect.*

trainer ['treɪnəʳ] *n* a person who trains people or animals in particular skills, for sport or work □ *a dog/racehorse trainer.*

◆ **trainers** *npl* GB soft shoes worn as casual clothing or by athletes for training □ *a pair of trainers.*

training ['treɪnɪŋ] *n* the process of being trained for a job, sport etc □ *He's in training for his next race.* □ *They give you training in word processing.* □ *She's had no formal training at all.*

training college *n* GB a college that trains adults for a trade or profession.

training course *n* a course that trains people to do a particular job □ *training courses in time management* □ *a computer training course.*

train set *n* a toy train with railroad lines and other equipment.

train spotter [-spɒtəʳ] *n* GB a person who is interested in trains and whose hobby is collecting the numbers of locomotives they have seen.

train station *n* = railroad station.

traipse [treɪps] *vi* to walk without enthusiasm and in a tired way (informal use) □ *We spent an entire day traipsing around the tourist sights.*

trait [treɪt] *n* a part of somebody's character that is very noticable □ *Determination is definitely one of our family traits.*

traitor ['treɪtəʳ] *n* a person who betrays somebody or something, especially their country □ *He became hated as a traitor to his cause.*

trajectory [trə'dʒektərɪ] (*pl* **trajectories**) *n* [of a bullet, satellite, spaceship] the curved path followed by something that has been fired or thrown into the air.

tram [træm] *n* GB a kind of bus that is driven by electricity and runs on rails laid on the streets of a town.

tramcar ['træmkɑːʳ] *n* GB = **tram** (formal use).

tramlines ['træmlaɪnz] *npl* GB -1. the rails that trams run on. -2. SPORT the sets of two parallel lines on each side of a tennis or badminton court that mark the area used for doubles games.

tramp [træmp] ◇ *n* -1. a person with no home or job who walks from place to place and usually lives by begging. -2. a woman whose sexual behavior one disapproves of (informal use). ◇ *vi* to walk with heavy or tired steps □ *We tramped for miles without seeing any signs of life.* ◇ *vt*: *We tramped the streets looking for a cheap place to stay.*

trample ['træmpl] *vt* to crush <sb/sthg> under one's feet □ *She was trampled to death.*

◆ **trample on** *vt fus* -1. **to trample on sthg** to walk or tread heavily on sthg □ *Tell those kids not to trample on my flowers!* -2. **to trample on sb** to treat sb without any respect or consideration □ *You mustn't allow yourself to be trampled on.*

trampoline ['træmpəliːn] *n* a piece of apparatus consisting of a sheet of tightly stretched material fixed to a frame by strong springs and

used, e.g. by gymnasts and acrobats, to jump up and down on.

trance [US træns, GB trɑːns] *n* a mental state in which one does not notice what is happening around one □ *He acts as if he's in a trance - he must have a lot on his mind.*

tranquil ['træŋkwəl] *adj* [life, place, person] calm, quiet, and peaceful (literary use).

tranquility US, **tranquillity** GB [træŋ'kwɪlətɪ] *n*: *see* **tranquil**.

tranquilize US, **tranquillize, -ise** GB ['træŋkwəlaɪz] *vt* to make <a person or animal> calmer or sleepy by means of a drug.

tranquilizer US, **tranquillizer** GB ['træŋkwəlaɪzəʳ] *n* a drug used to make people feel calm or less anxious, or to make people or animals sleepy □ *The doctor put me on tranquilizers but I just felt awful.*

tranquillity *n* GB = **tranquility**.

tranquillize *etc* GB = **tranquilize** *etc*.

transact [træn'zækt] *vt* [sale, loan] to carry out <a business deal> (formal use).

transaction [træn'zækʃn] *n* a piece of business that has been transacted □ *You will be charged for all transactions made outside office hours.*

transatlantic [ˌtrænzət'læntɪk] *adj* -1. [flight, traffic, phone call] that crosses the Atlantic. -2. [branch, politics] that is connected with the other side of the Atlantic.

transceiver [træn'siːvəʳ] *n* a piece of radio equipment that sends out and receives signals.

transcend [træn'send] *vt* -1. [boundary, limitation, everyday life] to go beyond the limits of <sthg> □ *to transcend the bounds of ordinary human experience.* -2. to be better or more important than <sthg> □ *an issue of national importance that transcends political rivalries.*

transcendental meditation [ˌtrænsendentl-] *n* a method of relaxation in which one repeats special words in one's mind.

transcribe [træn'skraɪb] *vt* -1. [recording, speech, statement] to produce a written version of <sthg>. -2. [document, notes, manuscript] to write an exact copy of <sthg>. -3. [text, document, manuscript] to write <sthg> in a different alphabet □ *He transcribed the Greek text.*

transcript ['trænskrɪpt] *n* a written or printed version of a speech, conversation etc □ *A written transcript of the speech is available.*

transept ['trænsept] *n* the part of a church that crosses the main central part at right angles.

transfer [*n* 'trænsfɜːʳ, *vb* træns'fɜːʳ] (*pt* & *pp* **transferred**, *cont* **transferring**) ◇ *n* -1. the movement of somebody or something from one place to another □ *a transfer of money between bank accounts.* -2. [of power, ownership, allegiance] the act of giving something to somebody else □ *the transfer of property from one owner to another.* -3. [of an employee] a move to a different job or place within the same organization □ *He wanted a transfer to another department/town.* -4. SPORT a sale of a player to a different team. -5. [for decoration] a piece of paper with a drawing or design on it that can be transferred to another sur-

face by ironing, rubbing etc. **-6.** US TRANSPORT a travel ticket that allows a passenger to change from one bus, train etc to another.
◇ *vt* **-1.** to move <sb/sthg> from one place to another □ *The capital was transferred to Brasilia.* □ *The money will be transferred to your account on Monday.* **-2.** [power] to give <sthg> to somebody else □ *Ownership was transferred to the official receivers.* **-3.** [employee] to move <sb> to a different job or place within the same organization □ *He was transferred to accounting/Phoenix.* **-4.** SPORT [player] to sell <sb> to a different team □ *He was transferred to the major leagues for a huge amount.*
◇ *vi* **-1.** [employee] *She transferred to marketing/Chicago.* **-2.** SPORT [player] *He transferred to Baltimore for six figures.*

transferable [træns'fɜːrəbl] *adj* [ticket, ownership] that can be given to another person or organization for their use □ *'Not transferable.'*

transference [US træns'fɜːrəns, GB 'trænsfrəns] *n* [of power, authority] *see* **transfer** (formal use).

transfer fee *n* GB SPORT a fee paid by one team to another for the transfer of a player.

transfigure [træns'fɪgjəʳ] *vt* to change the appearance of <sb> so that they appear more beautiful, noble, happy etc (literary use).

transfixed [træns'fɪkst] *adj* **to be transfixed** to be unable to move, think, or speak because of shock, terror etc □ *They were transfixed with fear/shock.*

transform [træns'fɔːrm] *vt* to change <sb/sthg> completely, especially in a way that improves it □ *The whole area has been transformed into a thriving industrial center.* □ *Simon transformed it into a colorful child's playroom.*

transformation [ˌtrænsfərˈmeɪʃn] *n*: *see* **transform** □ *the transformation of the Soviet economy* □ *The area underwent a complete transformation.*

transformer [træns'fɔːrməʳ] *n* ELECTRICITY a piece of electrical equipment that changes the voltage of an electric current.

transfusion [træns'fjuːʒn] *n* the act of taking blood from one person's body and putting it into somebody else's body □ *a blood transfusion.*

transgress [træns'gres] (formal use) ◇ *vt* [law, rule] to break or go beyond <sthg>. ◇ *vi*: *Those who transgressed were shown little mercy.*

transient ['trænzɪənt] ◇ *adj* **-1.** [happiness, success, suffering] that lasts for only a short time (formal use). **-2.** [worker, population] that works or stays in a place for only a short time before moving on. ◇ *n* US a traveler who is in transit.

transistor [træn'zɪstəʳ] *n* ELECTRONICS a small device used in radios, televisions etc to control the flow of an electric current within a circuit.

transistor radio *n* a small portable radio that contains transistors (old-fashioned use).

transit ['trænsət] *n* **in transit** [person, cargo] that is traveling or being moved from one place to another □ *The shipment was lost in transit.*

transit camp *n* a camp that provides a temporary place to live for refugees, soldiers etc.

transition [træn'zɪʃn] *n* a change from one state, form, or condition to another □ *The country has undergone many transitions.* □ *the painful transition from a one-party state to democracy* □ *a society in transition.*

transitional [træn'zɪʃnəl] *adj* **-1.** [phase, stage, period] *see* **transition** □ *Whilst the country is going through this transitional phase...* **-2.** [government] that holds power temporarily during a period of transition.

transitive ['trænzətɪv] *adj* GRAMMAR [verb] that is used with a direct object.

transit lane *n* AUS a lane for traffic that can only be used by vehicles that have two or more passengers.

transit lounge *n* a room in an airport where passengers can sit and wait while they change planes.

transitory [US 'trænsətɔːri, GB -ətri] *adj* [mood, happiness, success] that lasts for only a short time □ *He reflected on the transitory nature of human existence.*

translate [træns'leɪt] ◇ *vt* **-1.** [word, phrase, piece of writing] to write or say <sthg> in a different language, with the same meaning □ *Her novel has been translated into many languages.* □ *translated from the Russian.* **-2. to translate sthg into sthg** to turn <sthg that is only an idea into sthg real or definite □ *We need to translate vague promises into real votes.* ◇ *vi* **-1.** [word, phrase] to be possible to translate □ *That expression doesn't translate well.* **-2.** [person] to express writing or speech in a different language □ *She translates from French into English.*

translation [træns'leɪʃn] *n* **-1.** *see* **translate** □ *Translation from French into Spanish isn't difficult.* **-2.** a piece of writing that is being or has been translated □ *I have to finish that translation by Friday.*

translator [træns'leɪtəʳ] *n* a person who translates written text, especially as a job.

translucent [trænz'luːsnt] *adj* [glass, paper] that allows light to pass through but cannot be seen through clearly.

transmission [trænz'mɪʃn] *n* **-1.** *see* **transmit.** **-2.** RADIO & TV something, e.g. a message or program, that is transmitted □ *We interrupt this transmission to bring you a newsflash.*

transmit [trænz'mɪt] (*pt* & *pp* **transmitted**, *cont* **transmitting**) *vt* **-1.** ELECTRONICS [signal, message, program] to send <sthg> by radio waves, cable etc □ *Information is transmitted to the central computer.* **-2.** [disease, information, knowledge] to pass <sthg> from one person, place, or thing to another □ *The disease can be transmitted orally.*

transmitter [trænz'mɪtəʳ] *n* ELECTRONICS a piece of equipment that transmits radio or television signals.

transparency [US træns'perənsi, GB -'pær-] (*pl* **transparencies**) *n* **-1.** PHOTOGRAPHY a small photograph that can be looked at by shining light behind it to show a picture on a large screen. **-2.** [for an overhead projector] a sheet of transparent plastic that information can be written on or photocopied onto, used in an overhead projector. -3. [of a material] the quality of being transparent.

transparent [US træns'perənt, GB -'pær-] *adj* -1. [plastic, material] that one can see through clearly □ *a transparent piece of glass.* -2. [deception, excuse] that is obvious and deceives nobody □ *What he said was a transparent lie.* -3. [argument, reasoning, style] that is clear and easy to understand □ *her clear, transparent prose.*

transpire [træn'spaɪə^r] (formal use) ◇ *vt* **it transpired that...** a phrase used to introduce facts that one learns or discovers at a future time □ *It later transpired that she had not been present at the funeral.* ◇ *vi* to happen □ *It will be interesting to see what transpires as a result of this.*

transplant [*vb* US træns'plænt, GB -'plɑːnt, *n* US 'trænsplænt, GB -plɑːnt] ◇ *vt* -1. MEDICINE [organ, tissue] to move <sthg> from the body of one person and put it into the body of another person. -2. [population, worker, headquarters] to move <sb/sthg> to another place. ◇ *n* -1. an operation in which an organ or tissue is transplanted □ *a heart/liver transplant* □ *the transplant of human organs.* -2. the organ or tissue used in a transplant □ *The transplant was rejected by the patient's body.*

transport [*n* 'trænspɔː^rt, *vb* træn'spɔː^rt] ◇ *n* -1. a system of carrying people or goods from one place to another □ *road/rail transport* □ *Do you have your own means of transport?* -2. the act of carrying people or goods from one place to another. ◇ *vt* to carry <people, goods> etc from one place to another.

transportable [træn'spɔː^rtəbl] *adj* that can be transported □ *Pianos are not easily transportable.*

transportation [US ‚trænspər'teɪʃn, GB -pɔː-] *n* -1. [of goods, people] *see* **transport** □ *the transportation of heavy goods by road.* -2. US a system of carrying people or goods from one place to another □ *public transportation.*

transport cafe *n* GB a cafe on a main road that is used mainly by long-distance truck drivers.

transporter [træn'spɔː^rtə^r] *n* a large vehicle used for carrying heavy objects, e.g. cars or heavy equipment.

transpose [træns'pouz] *vt* [letters, figures] to change the position of two things so that each is in the place of the other.

transsexual [træns'sekʃuəl] *n* a person who has decided to live as a member of the opposite sex and has medical treatment, e.g. an operation or drugs, to change their sex.

transvestite [trænz'vestaɪt] *n* a man who finds pleasure in wearing women's clothes.

trap [træp] (*pt* & *pp* **trapped**, *cont* **trapping**) ◇ *vt* -1. to catch <an animal> in a trap. -2. to deceive, trick, or catch <sb> □ *He was trapped into betraying the names of the other people involved.* -3. **to be trapped** to be in a place or situation from which it is difficult or impossible to escape □ *They were trapped in the elevator.* □ *She was trapped in a dead-end*

job/an unhappy relationship. -4. [energy, heat] to store <sthg> so that it can be used later. ◇ *n* -1. a device used for trapping animals or birds □ *A hare was caught in the trap.* -2. a situation designed to trick or catch somebody □ *Be careful, it might be a trap!* □ *Sam had led me straight into a trap.* -3. an unpleasant situation from which it is difficult or impossible to escape □ *the poverty trap* □ *Her marriage/career had become a trap.*

trapdoor ['træpdɔː^r] *n* a small door in a floor, ceiling, stage etc.

trapeze [US træ'piːz, GB trə-] *n* a bar hung high in the air from two ropes and used by acrobats to swing on □ *a trapeze artist.*

trapper ['træpə^r] *n* a person who traps animals, especially for their fur.

trappings ['træpɪŋz] *npl* the outward signs of power, wealth etc □ *the trappings of success.*

trash [træʃ] ◇ *n* -1. US unwanted things and waste material that people throw away □ *Could you take out the trash?* -2. something that is of very bad quality (informal and disapproving use) □ *How can you read this trash?* ◇ *vt* (informal use) -1. US to criticize <sb/sthg> severely □ *The critics completely trashed the novel.* -2. to do a lot of damage to <a place> □ *They trashed the apartment.*

trash bag *n* US a plastic bag placed inside a trash can and used to collect trash.

trashcan ['træʃkæn] *n* US a large round container with a lid that people put their trash in and keep outside their house.

trashy ['træʃɪ] (*compar* **trashier**, *superl* **trashiest**) *adj* [book, movie, music] that one thinks is of very poor quality (informal use).

trauma [US 'traumə, GB 'trɔːmə] *n* -1. a very unpleasant experience that may have a lasting effect on one □ *The trauma of losing a child was more than I could bear.* -2. MEDICINE a state of shock caused by a severe injury or wound.

traumatic [US trə'mætɪk, GB trɔː-] *adj* [event, experience] that is very upsetting, causes great stress, and has a lasting effect on somebody □ *Shirley had had a very traumatic childhood.*

traumatize, -ise [US 'traumətaɪz, GB 'trɔːm-] *vt* to shock or upset <sb> so badly that the way they think or behave is affected for a long time □ *As a war correspondent, he was traumatized by the sight of so much violence.*

travel ['trævl] (US *pt* & *pp* **traveled**, *cont* **traveling**, GB *pt* & *pp* **travelled**, *cont* **travelling**) ◇ *n* traveling □ *The job afforded many opportunities for foreign travel.* ◇ *vt* -1. to visit many parts of <an area> □ *She's traveled the world.* -2. to move <a particular distance> on a trip □ *We traveled 50 miles that day.* ◇ *vi* -1. to make a trip or trips □ *John is traveling around India.* □ *We stay in Beijing for five days and then travel on to Hong Kong.* -2. [vehicle, light, sound] to move □ *The signal travels along a wire.* □ *News travels fast around here!* ◇ *adj* [clock, iron] that is designed to be used when traveling.

◆ **travels** *npl* trips, especially abroad or over long distances □ *Lesley came to dinner and told us all about her travels in Indonesia.*

travel agency *n* a business that makes vacation or travel arrangements for people.

travel agent *n* a person who runs or works in a travel agency. ■ **a travel agent's** a travel agency.

travel brochure *n* a brochure that advertises vacations.

traveled US, **travelled** GB ['trævld] *adj* -1. **much-traveled, well-traveled** [person] who has been to many countries □ *a widely traveled journalist.* -2. **a much-/little-traveled road** a road that is used by a lot of/few travelers.

traveler US, **traveller** GB ['trævlər] *n* -1. a person who is traveling. -2. a person who travels a lot □ *a hardened traveler.*

traveler's check *n* a check used by travelers abroad that can be exchanged for local currency.

travel expenses *npl* = **traveling expenses.**

traveling US, **travelling** GB ['trævlɪŋ] *adj* -1. **a traveling theater/circus etc** a theater/circus etc that travels from place to place. -2. [time, allowance] that is connected with traveling □ *You should allow two hours' traveling time.*

traveling expenses *npl* money that is spent on traveling by an employee or job candidate and is paid back by the company.

traveling salesman *n* a representative of a company who travels from place to place to sell goods and get orders.

travelled *adj* GB = **traveled.**

traveller *n* GB = **traveler.**

travelling *adj* GB = **traveling.**

travelog US, **travelogue** GB ['trævəlɒg] *n* a talk, movie, or book about travel in a particular place or about a particular person's travels.

travelsick ['trævlsɪk] *adj* GB **to be travelsick** to feel sick because of the movement of the vehicle one is traveling in.

traverse [,trə'vɜːrs] *vt* [ridge, lake, forest] to go across or through <sthg> (formal use).

travesty ['trævəstɪ] (*pl* **travesties**) *n* an example of something that is very bad and gives a very wrong idea of what it should be like □ *a travesty of justice.*

trawl [trɔːl] ◇ *n* -1. a wide net used for fishing that is pulled along the bottom of the sea behind a ship. -2. a complete and careful search. ◇ *vt* -1. to fish in <an area, bay> etc using a trawl □ *They trawled the coast for cod.* -2. to search through <a large number of things> to find something □ *Police have trawled the area looking for clues.* ◇ *vi:* *They were trawling in Canadian waters.* □ *We trawled through all the files.*

trawler ['trɔːlər] *n* a fishing boat that uses a trawl.

tray [treɪ] *n* a flat piece of wood, plastic etc that has raised edges and is used for carrying small objects such as cups and plates □ *She brought in a tray of drinks.*

treacherous ['tretʃərəs] *adj* -1. [person] who is not loyal and who will harm people in order to get something they want □ *his treacherous*

behavior. -2. [rocks, river] dangerous □ *Those mountains are treacherous.*

treachery ['tretʃərɪ] *n* treacherous behavior.

treacle ['triːkl] *n* GB a thick, dark, sticky liquid that is made from sugar and is used in making toffee, cakes etc.

tread [tred] (*pt* **trod**, *pp* **trodden**) ◇ *n* -1. the raised patterned surface on a tire that helps to stop it from slipping □ *The tread on the tires was almost worn down.* -2. the sound somebody's feet make when walking □ *I heard his soft tread on the stairs.*
◇ *vt* to crush <sthg> using one's foot □ *He trod his cigarette into the carpet.*
◇ *vi* -1. **to tread on sthg** [on grass, somebody's foot, glasses] to press the bottom of one's foot on sthg, usually when walking □ *Be careful not to tread on the cat!* -2. to walk in a particular way □ *We trod wearily onward.* ■ **to tread carefully** to speak or act carefully in order to avoid causing problems, upsetting somebody etc □ *I'd advise you to tread carefully when you speak about it to Speer.*

treadle ['tredl] *n* a lever operated with the foot in order to make a machine such as a sewing machine work.

treadmill ['tredmɪl] *n* -1. a mill driven by people treading on steps attached to the outside of a large wheel. -2. tiring and boring work that never changes.

treas *abbr* of **treasurer.**

treason ['triːzn] *n* the crime of betraying one's country, e.g. by giving its secrets to a foreign government.

treasure ['treʒər] ◇ *n* -1. a collection of valuable things such as gold, silver, and jewels □ *buried treasure.* -2. a valuable object such as a painting or sculpture □ *one of the museum's many treasures.* ◇ *vt* [memory, photo] to treat <sthg> as very special and valuable □ *a little ornament which she treasured above all else.*

treasure hunt *n* a game in which people are given clues to help them find something that has been hidden.

treasurer ['treʒərər] *n* a person in charge of the money and accounting in a group or organization.

treasure trove *n* LAW a large amount of money, gold, or jewelry that has been found somewhere but that has not been claimed by anybody.

treasury ['treʒərɪ] (*pl* **treasuries**) *n* the place where money belonging to the government is stored.
◆ **Treasury** *n* **the Treasury** the department in a government that is responsible for managing the country's finances.

Treasury bill, Treasury note *n* a document that is sold by the government to get money and that it agrees to buy back after three months.

treat [triːt] ◇ *vt* -1. to consider or act in relation to <sthg> in a particular way; to behave toward <sb> in a particular way □ *Don't treat my complaint as a joke!* □ *He always treated her like a child.* □ *We were very well* treated by the police. **-2.** [one's children, parents] to buy or pay for something for <sb> in order to please them □ *He treated us to a big meal.* ■ **to treat oneself** to buy something special for oneself □ *I treated myself to a new dress.* **-3.** [patient, illness, injury] to try to cure or heal <sb/sthg> using medical treatment □ *My wife is being treated by Dr Irving.* **-4.** [wood, cloth, brick] to put a special substance on <sthg> to protect it or to change its appearance □ *We've treated the floor for woodworm.* ◇ *n* something special intended to give pleasure □ *I wanted to give you a treat.*

treatise ['tri:təs] *n* a long piece of writing on a serious subject (formal use).

treatment ['tri:tmənt] *n* **-1.** MEDICINE the medical methods used to treat a sick or injured person □ *a new treatment for arthritis.* **-2.** a way of dealing with somebody or something □ *Prisoners have complained of ill treatment.*

treaty ['tri:tɪ] (*pl* **treaties**) *n* a written agreement between countries □ *the Treaty of Rome* □ *a peace treaty.*

treble ['trebl] ◇ *adj* **-1. a treble voice** a high-pitched voice. **-2.** GB repeated three times; multiplied by three □ *My phone extension is treble five.* □ *My rent is treble what it was last year.* ◇ *n* MUSIC a boy with a high singing voice. ◇ *vt* to make <sthg> three times larger in size or amount □ *I'm willing to treble what they're offering.* ◇ *vi: House prices have trebled since 1976.*

treble clef *n* a symbol ($\begin{smallmatrix}\end{smallmatrix}$) written at the beginning of a line of music to show that the notes played are on the right-hand half of a piano keyboard.

tree [tri:] *n* **-1.** a tall plant that has a wooden trunk, branches, and leaves, and that lives for many years □ *an apple tree.* ■ **to be barking up the wrong tree** to have the wrong idea about somebody or something. ■ **not to see the forest** US OR **wood** GB **for the trees** to fail to understand the main facts about something because one is thinking too much about small details **-2.** COMPUTING a system in which information is linked in related branches rather than in a sequence with one item directly after the other.

tree-lined *adj* [avenue, entrance, road] that has trees on either side of it.

tree surgeon *n* a person whose job is to take care of trees, e.g. by cutting off damaged or dangerous branches.

treetop ['tri:tɒp] *n* the top part of a tree □ *Birds were singing in the treetops.*

tree trunk *n* the main upright wooden stem of a tree.

trek [trek] (*pt* & *pp* **trekked**, *cont* **trekking**) ◇ *n* a long hard journey, especially on foot. ◇ *vi* to make a long hard journey.

trellis ['trelɪs] *n* an upright frame made of strips of wood that cross over each other, used to support plants that climb.

tremble ['trembl] *vi* [person, voice, hands] to shake because one is cold, frightened etc □ *He trembled with fear.*

tremendous [trə'mendəs] *adj* **-1.** [noise, success, difference] very great in size, amount, or degree □ *There was a tremendous crash, then the roof fell in.* **-2.** [evening, party, game] that one enjoys and thinks is very good (informal use) □ *I had a tremendous time on vacation.*

tremendously [trə'mendəslɪ] *adv* **-1. tremendously exciting/talented etc** very exciting/talented etc □ *It was a tremendously dull evening.* **-2.** very much □ *I enjoyed myself tremendously.*

tremor ['tremər] *n* **-1.** [of one's body, voice] an uncontrollable shaking movement caused by fear, cold etc. **-2.** a small earthquake □ *an earth tremor.*

tremulous ['tremjələs] *adj* [voice, smile] that is unsteady, usually because one is feeling nervous or emotional (literary use).

trench [trentʃ] *n* **-1.** a long narrow hole dug in the ground, e.g. to lay pipes in. **-2.** MILITARY a long, narrow hole dug in the ground and used by soldiers for protection in battles.

trenchant ['trentʃənt] *adj* [criticism, comment] that is expressed forcefully and directly (formal use).

trench coat *n* a long raincoat with a belt made in the style of a military coat.

trench warfare *n* fighting in which soldiers on both sides fire their weapons at one another without leaving their trenches.

trend [trend] *n* a general way in which a situation is changing gradually □ *The dollar is on a downward trend.* □ *the trend toward vegetarianism.*

trendsetter ['trendsetər] *n* a person or organization that starts a new trend or fashion.

trendy ['trendɪ] (*compar* **trendier**, *superl* **trendiest**, *pl* **trendies**) (informal use) ◇ *adj* [person, clothes, music] very modern and fashionable. ◇ *n* a person who is very fashionable.

trepidation [,trepə'deɪʃn] *n* **in** OR **with trepidation** in a state of fear or worry (formal use) □ *With great trepidation I approached the manager.*

trespass ['trespəs] *vi* to go onto private land or property without permission □ *He was caught trespassing on Mr Moffat's land.* □ *'No trespassing.'*

trespasser ['trespəsər] *n* a person who trespasses on somebody's private land □ *'Trespassers will be prosecuted.'*

trestle table ['tresl-] *n* a table consisting of a flat top that is supported at each end by a wooden or metal structure shaped like the letter A.

trial ['traɪəl] *n* **-1.** LAW the process by which a judge or jury decides in a court whether somebody is guilty of a crime □ *Hughes will stand trial for criminal negligence.* □ *She still has the right to a fair trial.* ■ **to be on trial** to be tried in a court □ *He's on trial for tax evasion.* **-2.** [of a product] a test of something for a limited period of time to find out how good it is. ■ **to take/have sthg on trial** [product, goods] to take/have sthg for a limited period in order to decide whether or not one wants to keep it before paying for it. ■ **on a trial**

basis as part of a temporary arrangement to see if something works properly or in a satisfactory way □ *He was hired on a trial basis.* ■ **trial and error** a way of learning how to do something in a satisfactory way by trying several different methods to find the best one □ *"How did you work out how to do it?" — "Trial and error."* **-3.** an unpleasant and difficult experience. ■ **trials and tribulations** a series of unpleasant and worrying experiences □ *the trials and tribulations of life in the city.*

trial period *n* a period during which something or somebody is checked to see how good, reliable etc they are before being completely accepted □ *She's been taken on for an initial three-month trial period.* □ *You can keep the goods for a trial period of 14 days.*

trial run *n* a first attempt at doing something to make sure it works properly □ *The car crashed during its trial run.*

trial-size(d) *adj* [pack, box] that contains only a small amount of a product and is sold cheap to allow people to try it.

triangle ['traɪæŋgl] *n* **-1.** a shape (△) with three straight sides. **-2.** MUSIC a small instrument made of a piece of metal in the shape of a triangle that one plays by hitting it with a metal rod. **-3.** US [for drawing] a flat triangular piece of plastic, metal, or wood with a right angle, used for drawing angles and lines.

triangular [traɪˈæŋgjələˈ] *adj* that is in the shape of a triangle.

triathlon [traɪˈæθlɒn] *n* a competition in three parts in which people swim, cycle, and run without stopping to rest between each part.

tribal ['traɪbl] *adj* [art, dance] that is connected with a tribe or tribes; [warfare, divisions] that happens between tribes.

tribe [traɪb] *n* a social group consisting of people of the same race, beliefs, language etc, especially when they live together in a particular area and are led by a chief.

tribulation [ˌtrɪbjəˈleɪʃn] *n* → **trial.**

tribunal [traɪˈbjuːnl] *n* a group of people who are officially chosen to deal with particular matters and to make judgments □ *a military tribunal.*

tribune ['trɪbjuːn] *n* HISTORY an official chosen by the people of ancient Rome to represent their interests.

tributary [US 'trɪbjətərɪ, GB -tərɪ] (*pl* **tributaries**) *n* a small stream or river that flows into a larger one.

tribute ['trɪbjuːt] *n* **-1.** something that is said or done to show respect or admiration for somebody □ *There were tributes from many distinguished colleagues.* ■ **to be a tribute to sb/ sthg** to show the good effects or influence of sb/sthg □ *It is a tribute to their organizational skills that everything went so smoothly.* **-2. to pay tribute to sb/sthg** to show respect or admiration for sb/sthg □ *In his speech he paid tribute to the efforts of aid workers.*

trice [traɪs] *n* GB **in a trice** very quickly.

triceps ['traɪseps] (*pl* **triceps** OR **tricepses**) *n* the

muscle at the back of the upper part of one's arm.

trick [trɪk] ◇ *n* **-1.** something done to deceive somebody □ *That was a nasty trick!* ■ **to play a trick on sb** to do something to deceive sb, often for fun □ *He played a nasty trick on us.* □ *Is it my memory playing tricks on me, or have I met you before?* **-2.** a clever action done to entertain people □ *magic tricks.* **-3.** a clever way of doing something or special ability to do it □ *It's a trick I learned at cooking classes.* ■ **to do the trick** to achieve the result one wants □ *That should do the trick.*
◇ *adj* **a trick knife/mustache etc** a knife/ mustache etc that is not real and is intended to deceive people, usually for fun.
◇ *vt* to deceive <sb> □ *He tricked us into believing him.*

trickery ['trɪkərɪ] *n* the use of tricks to deceive people.

trickle ['trɪkl] ◇ *n* **-1.** [of blood, water] a small slow flow of liquid □ *A trickle of sweat ran down his neck.* **-2.** [of complaints, correspondence, visitors] a slow movement of people or things in small numbers □ *A slow trickle of visitors came and went all day.* ◇ *vi* **-1.** [water, sweat] to flow slowly in drops or in a thin stream □ *Blood trickled from the wound.* **-2.** [people, donations] to move somewhere slowly in small numbers □ *Applications continued to trickle in long after the ad appeared.*

trick or treat *n* the Halloween custom in which children dress up in costumes, visit houses in their area, and ask for candy, money etc in return for not playing tricks; *see box at* **Halloween.**

trick question *n* a question that seems easier than it really is and in which the obvious answer is wrong.

tricky ['trɪkɪ] (*compar* **trickier,** *superl* **trickiest**) *adj* [question, situation] that is difficult to deal with □ *That puts me in a tricky position.*

tricycle ['traɪsəkl] *n* a vehicle like a bicycle that has three wheels, one at the front and two at the back, used especially by children.

trident ['traɪdnt] *n* a weapon like a very large fork with three points.

tried [traɪd] ◇ *past tense & past participle of* **try.**
◇ *adj* **tried and tested** [system, machine, method] that is known to be good because it has been used before successfully.

trier ['traɪəˈ] *n* a person who tries very hard, even if they are not usually successful.

trifle ['traɪfl] *n* **-1.** a small thing of little importance or value (formal use) □ *There's no point quarreling over trifles.* **-2.** COOKING a cold dessert made of sponge cake and fruit in Jello and covered in custard or cream.
◆ **a trifle** *adv* [upset, puzzled] slightly (formal use) □ *I was a trifle confused after the meeting.*
◆ **trifle with** *vt fus* **to trifle with sb** to behave toward sb without being respectful or serious enough □ *Stop trifling with her affections.*

trifling ['traɪflɪŋ] *adj* [sum, matter] that is too small to be important.

trigger ['trɪgəˈ] ◇ *n* the small metal lever

pressed to fire a gun □ *He pulled the trigger.* ◇ *vt* [mechanism, explosion] to cause <sthg> to begin to work or happen immediately □ *The imposition of the tax triggered violent riots.*

◆ **trigger off** *vt sep* = **trigger**.

trigger-happy *adj* [soldier, police] who is too ready to shoot at people.

trigonometry [ˌtrɪgəˈnɒmətrɪ] *n* the branch of mathematics that involves calculating the lengths of sides and sizes of angles of triangles.

trilby [ˈtrɪlbɪ] (*pl* **trilbies**) *n* GB a man's hat made of felt with a fold in its top.

trill [trɪl] ◇ *n* **-1.** MUSIC the repetition of two musical notes quickly, one after the other. **-2.** the short, repeated, high-pitched sounds made by a bird that is singing. ◇ *vi* [bird] to sing with a trill; [person] to speak, laugh etc in a high-pitched voice that sounds almost musical.

trillions [ˈtrɪlɪənz] *pron* used to refer to a very large number of people or things (informal use) □ *I could see trillions of stars.* □ *It must have cost trillions!*

trilogy [ˈtrɪlədʒɪ] (*pl* **trilogies**) *n* a series of three books, plays, movies etc with the same subject or characters.

trim [trɪm] (*compar* **trimmer**, *superl* **trimmest**, *pt* & *pp* **trimmed**, *cont* **trimming**) ◇ *vt* [hair, hedge] to cut small pieces from the edges of <sthg> to make it look neater □ *Your hair needs trimming.* ◇ *n* **-1.** an act of trimming something □ *My hair needs a trim.* **-2.** an extra piece of decoration, usually around the edge of something, e.g. on a car or dress. ◇ *adj* **-1.** [garden, dress] neat and tidy. **-2.** [figure, waist, person] slim.

◆ **trim away**, **trim off** *vt sep* to trim sthg away OR **off** [fabric, fat] to cut unnecessary pieces off sthg.

trimmed [trɪmd] *adj* **trimmed with sthg** [with lace, tinsel] with sthg added around the edge as a decoration.

trimming [ˈtrɪmɪŋ] *n* [on clothing, curtains] an extra piece of material added for decoration.

◆ **trimmings** *npl* **-1.** COOKING the extra things, e.g. vegetables or sauces, that are usually served with a main dish □ *roast beef with all the trimmings.* **-2.** pieces that have been cut from something larger to make it neater.

Trinidad and Tobago [ˌtrɪnədæd-] a country in the Caribbean consisting of two islands off the coast of Venezuela. SIZE: 5,128 sq kms. POPULATION: 1,300,000 (*Trinidadians*, *Tobagonians*). CAPITAL: Port of Spain. LANGUAGE: English. CURRENCY: Trinidadian dollar.

Trinity [ˈtrɪnɪtɪ] *n* **the Trinity** RELIGION in Christianity, the union of the Father, Son, and Holy Spirit in one God.

trinket [ˈtrɪŋkət] *n* a small ornament or piece of jewelry of little value.

trio [ˈtriːoʊ] (*pl* **trios**) *n* **-1.** a group of three people or things. **-2.** MUSIC a group of three singers or musicians who perform together; a piece of music written for this group.

trip [trɪp] (*pt* & *pp* **tripped**, *cont* **tripping**) ◇ *n* **-1.** the act of traveling to and visiting a place for business or pleasure □ *Have a good/ nice trip.* □ *I'm afraid she's away on a business trip.* □ *a trip to the countryside.* **-2.**▽ a mental experience caused by taking drugs in which one sees or feels things in a strange and unreal way (drugs slang). ◇ *vt* to cause <sb> to hit their foot against something so that they lose their balance or fall over □ *He tripped me.* ◇ *vi:* *He tripped over a cord and fell.*

◆ **trip up** *vt sep* **-1.** **to trip sb up** to trip sb □ *Peter tried to trip Alice up on the stairs.* **-2.** **to trip sb up** to cause sb to make a mistake □ *The last question tripped him up completely.*

tripartite [ˌtraɪˈpɑːtaɪt] *adj* [agreement, talks] involving three separate groups (formal use).

tripe [traɪp] *n* **-1.** COOKING the stomach wall of a pig, cow, or ox that is eaten as food. **-2.** something that one thinks is nonsense (informal use) □ *What a load of tripe!*

triple [ˈtrɪpl] ◇ *adj* **-1.** [purpose, role] that is made up of three parts or things □ *She did a triple somersault.* □ *the Triple Entente.* **-2.** that is repeated three times □ *a triple brandy.* ◇ *vt* to make <sthg> three times greater in size or amount □ *We managed to triple our sales as a result of the advertising campaign.* ◇ *vi:* *Inflation has tripled over the last 18 months.*

Triple Crown *n* **the Triple Crown** in the USA, an unofficial horseracing championship consisting of three important races, including the Kentucky Derby.

triple jump *n* **the triple jump** an event in athletics in which competitors have to jump as far as possible and are allowed to touch the ground once with each foot before finally landing.

triplets [ˈtrɪpləts] *npl* three children born to the same mother at the same time.

triplicate [ˈtrɪplɪkət] *n* **in triplicate** in three copies, including the original.

tripod [ˈtraɪpɒd] *n* a frame with three legs used to support a piece of equipment such as a camera.

tripwire [ˈtrɪpwaɪəʳ] *n* a wire stretched low over the ground that causes an explosive, trap etc to work if a person or animal touches it with their foot.

Tristan and Isolde [US ˌtrɪstənənɪˈsoʊld, GB -ˈzɒldə] in European legends, two young lovers who die tragically.

trite [traɪt] *adj* [remark, statement] that is not impressive because it has been said or used too often before (disapproving use).

triumph [ˈtraɪʌmf] ◇ *n* **-1.** a great victory or success □ *The election was a triumph for the Democrats.* **-2.** a feeling of great satisfaction caused by success □ *She felt a great sense of triumph at last.* ◇ *vi* [politician, team] to win a great victory, especially in very difficult conditions □ *Justice has triumphed.* □ *She has triumphed over her disability.*

triumphal [traɪˈʌmfl] *adj* **a triumphal march/ procession etc** a march/procession etc that takes place to celebrate a great victory.

triumphant [traɪˈʌmfənt] *adj* [shout, grin] that

expresses great satisfaction; [person] who has been successful in something and so is very happy.

triumphantly [traɪˈʌmfəntlɪ] *adv* [shout, grin] *see* **triumphant**.

triumvirate [traɪˈʌmvərət] *n* a group of three people in charge of the government of a state, especially in ancient Rome.

trivet [ˈtrɪvət] *n* -1. a stand with three legs used for holding a cooking pot over a fire. -2. a short metal stand placed under hot dishes or pots to protect a surface.

trivia [ˈtrɪvɪə] *n* unimportant matters or information □ *a trivia quiz*.

trivial [ˈtrɪvɪəl] *adj* unimportant and not serious □ *I hate to bother you with such a trivial matter.*

triviality [ˌtrɪvɪˈælətɪ] (*pl* **trivialities**) *n* -1. something unimportant □ *I'm not concerned about such trivialities.* -2. a lack of importance and seriousness □ *the triviality of the story.*

trivialize, -ise [ˈtrɪvɪəlaɪz] *vt* [role, fact, event] to make <sthg> seem less important or serious than it really is □ *She felt the newspaper had trivialized the story.*

trod [trɒd] *past tense of* **tread**.

trodden [ˈtrɒdn] *past participle of* **tread**.

Trojan [ˈtrəʊdʒən] *n* **to work like a Trojan** to work very hard.

troll [US trəʊl, GB trɒl] *n* an ugly creature in Scandinavian mythology that lives in caves or hills and has special powers.

trolley [ˈtrɒlɪ] (*pl* **trolleys**) *n* -1. US = **trolley car**. -2. GB a metal container on wheels that is pushed along and used for carrying heavy things such as shopping □ *a supermarket trolley.* -3. GB a small table on wheels used for serving food and drinks □ *a drinks trolley.*

trolleybus [ˈtrɒlɪbʌs] *n* a bus that is powered by electric cables above the street.

trolley car *n* US a large vehicle used for public transportation that is operated by electricity and moves along metal lines built into the road surface.

trombone [trɒmˈbəʊn] *n* a brass musical instrument that is played by blowing into one end and by moving a U-shaped part in and out to change the notes.

troop [truːp] ◇ *n* a group of people or animals that moves somewhere together □ *a troop of schoolchildren.* ◇ *vi* to move somewhere in a group □ *They all trooped off to the zoo.*

◆ **troops** *npl* soldiers organized in groups for a particular purpose □ *Troops have been flown in from US airbases.*

trooper [ˈtruːpəʳ] *n* -1. MILITARY a soldier of the lowest rank in a part of an army that uses armored vehicles. -2. US a member of the police force of a particular state.

troopship [ˈtruːpʃɪp] *n* a ship for transporting soldiers.

trophy [ˈtrəʊfɪ] (*pl* **trophies**) *n* SPORT a prize such as a silver cup given to the winner of a competition or race.

tropical [ˈtrɒpɪkl] *adj* [climate, region, fruit] that is typical of the tropics.

Tropic of Cancer [ˌtrɒpɪk-] *n* **the Tropic of Cancer** an imaginary circle around the Earth, parallel to the equator, at latitude 23½° N.

Tropic of Capricorn *n* **the Tropic of Capricorn** an imaginary circle around the Earth, parallel to the equator, at latitude 23½° S.

tropics [ˈtrɒpɪks] *npl* **the tropics** the hottest area of the world, near the equator.

trot [trɒt] (*pt* & *pp* **trotted**, *cont* **trotting**) ◇ *n* -1. the movement of a horse that is quicker than a walk but slower than a gallop □ *The horse went off at a trot.* -2. the movement of a person that is like a slow run but with small quick steps □ *He ran at a gentle trot.* ◇ *vi* [horse, person] to move with small quick steps □ *Alice trotted along behind her father.*

◆ **on the trot** *adv* GB one after another without interruption (informal use) □ *That's three times on the trot I've won.*

◆ **trot out** *vt sep* **to trot sthg out** [excuse, reason] to say or write sthg without thinking about it or meaning it □ *He trotted out the usual hard-luck story.*

Trotsky [ˈtrɒtskɪ], **Leon** (1879–1940) a Russian revolutionary leader who played an important part in the Russian Revolution of 1917.

Trotskyism [ˈtrɒtskɪɪzm] *n* the belief of Leon Trotsky and his followers in a worldwide revolution in which the working class would take power by force.

trotter [ˈtrɒtəʳ] *n* a pig's foot that is cooked and eaten as food □ *a pig's trotter.*

trouble [ˈtrʌbl] ◇ *n* -1. something that causes difficulty or problems □ *The trouble is, I can't remember their number.* □ *What seems to be the trouble?* □ *You're too soft, that's your trouble.* ■ **to be in trouble** to be in a situation where one is being blamed or punished; to be in a difficult situation □ *He is in trouble with the police again!* □ *We're in deep financial trouble if we don't do something soon.* ■ **to get into trouble** to do something that causes one to be blamed or punished; to get into a difficult situation □ *He got into trouble with his boss/parents.* ■ **the trouble with sb/sthg is...** the aspect of sb/sthg that causes problems is... □ *The trouble with you is (that) you never listen.* -2. something that needs effort or causes inconvenience □ *It'll save you a lot of trouble if you pay by direct debit.* □ *"Are you sure about this?" — "Honestly, it's no trouble at all."* □ *I had no trouble at all finding a parking space.* ■ **to take the trouble to do sthg** to make the effort to do sthg □ *You might take the trouble to listen when I'm talking to you!* ■ **to be asking for trouble** to be behaving in a way that is likely to cause problems for oneself □ *Walking around that area late at night is just asking for trouble.* -3. [in part of one's body] illness or pain □ *heart trouble.* -4. [between people] fighting or violence that is caused by a disagreement or conflict □ *There was trouble at the club again last night between rival gangs.*

◇ *vt* -1. to cause <sb> to feel worried or upset □ *It troubled him to see her so sad.* -2. to disturb or cause inconvenience to <sb> □ *I'm* sorry to trouble you, but could you give me a hand? □ Can I trouble you for a light? **-3.** to cause pain to <sb> □ My knee's troubling me again.

◆ **troubles** *npl* **-1.** worries □ Just when we thought our troubles were over. **-2.** POLITICS social or political disorder. **-3. the Troubles** GB a term used to refer to the political violence in Northern Ireland.

troubled ['trʌbld] *adj* **-1.** [person, look] worried or upset □ Her face looked troubled. **-2.** [life, place] that is affected by problems; [sleep] that is not relaxed and does not continue all night □ These are troubled times we live in. □ She spent a troubled night dreaming of Joe.

trouble-free *adj* [existence, operation] that is without difficulties □ Until now, the trip had been relatively trouble-free.

troublemaker ['trʌblmeɪkəʳ] *n* a person who causes disagreement or fighting.

troubleshooter ['trʌblʃuːtəʳ] *n* a person whose job is to solve problems affecting particular organizations, machines etc.

troublesome ['trʌblsəm] *adj* [neighbor, car, job] that causes problems or anxiety; [knee, cold] that cannot be easily cured.

trouble spot *n* a place where there is often violence or fighting.

trough [trɒf] *n* **-1.** [on a farm] a long, narrow, open container from which animals eat or drink □ a pig's trough. **-2.** [on a graph] a low point in a series of high and low points measured over a period of time.

trounce [traʊns] *vt* [opponent, team] to beat <sb> by a very large score (informal use).

troupe [truːp] *n* a group of singers, actors, dancers etc.

trouser ['traʊzəʳ] *comp* **a trouser leg/pocket** a leg/pocket of a pair of trousers.

trouser press *n* a device which trousers are placed in to stop them from becoming creased or to remove creases from them.

trousers ['traʊzəʳz] *npl* a piece of clothing that covers the body from the waist to the ankle and has a separate part for each leg □ a pair of trousers.

trouser suit *n* GB a suit for a woman consisting of a jacket and a pair of trousers.

trousseau [US truː'sou, GB 'truːsou] (*pl* **trousseaux** [-z] OR **trousseaus** [-z]) *n* the possessions, e.g. bed linen and clothes, that a woman takes with her when she marries (old-fashioned use).

trout [traʊt] (*pl* **trout** OR **trouts**) *n* a fish with a spotted brown skin that lives in rivers and is eaten as food.

trove [troʊv] → **treasure trove**.

trowel ['traʊəl] *n* **-1.** a small tool with a curved pointed blade, used in the garden for planting, weeding etc. **-2.** a small tool with a flat blade, used for spreading cement.

truancy ['truːənsɪ] *n* the fact of staying away from school without permission from one's teachers or parents.

truant ['truːənt] *n* a child who does not go to

school when he or she is supposed to. ■ **to play truant** to stay away from school without permission from one's teachers or parents.

truce [truːs] *n* an agreement between two countries, groups, or individuals to stop fighting or quarreling for a period of time □ The truce between the warring factions proved to be short-lived. ■ **to call a truce** to agree to stop fighting or quarreling for a period of time.

truck [trʌk] ◇ *n* **-1.** a large motor vehicle used for transporting goods. **-2.** RAIL a wagon with an open top that is used for transporting goods. ◇ *vt* to transport <goods> by truck.

truck driver *n* a person whose job is to drive a truck.

trucker ['trʌkəʳ] *n* US = **truck driver**.

truck farm *n* US a small farm that grows fruit and vegetables to be sold.

trucking ['trʌkɪŋ] *n* the business of transporting goods by truck.

truck stop *n* US a place near a highway where truck drivers can stop to rest, eat cheaply, and get fuel.

truculent ['trʌkjələnt] *adj* [person, mood] bad-tempered and aggressive.

trudge [trʌdʒ] ◇ *n* a difficult tiring walk □ It was a long trudge to the top of the hill. ◇ *vi* to walk with slow heavy steps, e.g. because one is tired or unhappy □ She trudged slowly up the steps.

true [truː] *adj* **-1.** [account, news, rumor] that is based on fact □ Everything she said is true. ■ **to come true** [dream, fears] to happen □ The trip was a dream come true for me. **-2. the true worth/cost etc of sthg** the real worth/cost etc of sthg and not the stated one □ I had to sell the car for less than its true value. □ Why do you hide your true feelings? **-3. a true friend/ Christian etc** a person who has all the characteristics that a friend/Christian etc is supposed to have □ I don't think you could call it a true democracy. □ He still hopes to find true love. **-4.** [likeness, copy] that is accurate in relation to something else □ I'd say that is a pretty true assessment of the situation. **-5.** [servant, lover] who is loyal and can be trusted □ He swore never to desert her and to always be true. **-6. to be true** [frame, window] to be fitted in the correct position in relation to other things and so appear straight.

true-life *adj* **a true-life drama/adventure etc** a drama/adventure etc that happens in reality rather than in fiction.

true north *n* the direction of the north pole along an imaginary line through the center of the earth.

truffle ['trʌfl] *n* **-1.** a small round chocolate that has a soft texture and often contains rum. **-2.** a round fungus that grows underground and is used to flavor food.

truism ['truːɪzm] *n* a statement that is considered obvious.

truly ['truːlɪ] *adv* **-1.** in a way that cannot be doubted □ At last the house was truly mine. □

This is truly a night to remember. **-2. truly,...** a word used to emphasize that what one is about to say is true □ *Truly, I didn't know anything about it.* **-3.** [believe, mean, feel] in a sincere way □ *I'm truly sorry about what happened.* **-4.** a word used for emphasis □ *It was a truly amazing experience.* **-5. Yours truly** a phrase used to end a formal letter □ *Yours truly, Kathryn Schmidt.* **-6. yours truly** a phrase one uses to talk about oneself in a humorous way (informal use) □ *Guess who ended up paying for it? Yours truly!*

Truman ['truːmən], **Harry S.** (1884–1972) US President from 1945 to 1953. He was responsible for US involvement in the Korean War.

trump [trʌmp] ◇ *n* a playing card from the suit that has been chosen to have the highest value in a particular game □ *Hearts are trumps.* ◇ *vt* to beat <another player or card> by using a trump.

trump card *n* something one knows, has, or does and that one uses to get into a stronger position than somebody else in a particular situation.

trumped-up ['trʌmpt-] *adj* **trumped-up charges** charges that have deliberately been invented.

trumpet ['trʌmpət] ◇ *n* MUSIC a brass instrument that consists of a tube that curves around several times, has a wide opening at one end, and is played by blowing into it and pressing down on three buttons. ◇ *vi* [elephant] to give a loud cry.

trumpeter ['trʌmpətər] *n* a person who plays the trumpet.

truncate [US 'trʌŋkeɪt, GB trʌŋ'keɪt] *vt* [line, sentence, speech] to make <sthg> shorter by cutting off the end or stopping it suddenly.

truncheon ['trʌntʃən] *n* a stick that is carried by police officers as a weapon.

trundle ['trʌndl] ◇ *vt* [cart, barrow] to push <sthg that has wheels> along so that it moves slowly in an uneven way. ◇ *vi* [car, truck] to move somewhere slowly on wheels in an uneven way □ *The bus trundled along a dirt track.*

trunk [trʌŋk] *n* **-1.** [of a tree] the thick upright part of a tree from which branches grow □ *a tree trunk.* **-2.** [of a person] the main part of one's body, not including one's head and limbs. **-3.** [of an elephant] an elephant's long nose. **-4.** [for belongings] a large oblong box used to transport luggage or belongings □ *I packed my trunk and left.* **-5.** US [of a car] the part of a car, usually at the back, that is separate from the seats and is used to put luggage in □ *I put your bags in the trunk.*

◆ **trunks** *npl* **-1.** US shorts worn by men for doing sports. **-2.** GB shorts worn by men for swimming.

trunk road *n* GB a main road that connects different towns or cities.

truss [trʌs] *n* **-1.** MEDICINE a belt worn by a man who is suffering from a hernia. **-2.**

CONSTRUCTION a framework of beams that supports a roof or bridge.

trust [trʌst] ◇ *vt* **-1.** [friend, stranger] to consider <sb> to be sincere and unlikely to cause one any upset or harm; [employee, method, judgment] to be confident that one can depend on <sb/sthg> □ *How can you trust a man like that?* ■ **to trust sb to do sthg** to be sure that sb will do sthg □ *Can I trust you to pay the bills while I'm away?* ■ **trust you/him/her etc** a phrase used to show that one is not surprised by something silly, annoying etc that somebody has done because it is typical of them □ *Trust Peter not to remember your birthday!* **-2. to trust sb with sthg** to allow sb to have knowledge, use, or control of sthg because one has confidence in them □ *I wouldn't trust him with that computer/my secrets/children.* **-3. to trust (that)...** to suppose that something is true (formal use) □ *I trust (that) you've enjoyed your stay here.*
◇ *n* **-1.** a feeling of confidence that one has about the sincerity or worth of somebody or something □ *You betrayed my trust.* ■ **trust in sb/sthg** a feeling of confidence that one can depend on sb/sthg □ *We have a lot of trust in your ability.* □ *We can't put much trust in what they say.* ■ **to take sthg on trust** to accept sthg as being true without having any proof □ *We don't know whether he's financially sound, but we'll just have to take that on trust.* **-2. a position of trust** a responsible position in which one is trusted by many people □ *As a teacher/doctor, he was in a position of trust.* **-3.** FINANCE an arrangement in which somebody's money or property is controlled by another person or a group of people. ■ **in trust** [keep, hold] under the control of a trustee □ *The house is held in trust until the children come of age.* **-4.** BUSINESS a group of companies that agree together to fix prices for their products at the same level □ *anti-trust laws.*

trust company *n* a company that acts as a trustee for people and organizations, while also acting as a commercial bank.

trusted ['trʌstəd] *adj* [friend, colleague] who one trusts and values; [method] that is known to have worked in the past and so is reliable □ *a tried and trusted remedy.*

trustee [trʌ'stiː] *n* **-1.** FINANCE & LAW a person who controls money or property for somebody else. **-2.** one of a group of administrators who run the affairs of an organization.

trusteeship [ˌtrʌ'stiːʃɪp] *n* the position of being a trustee.

trust fund *n* money or shares controlled by a trustee for the benefit of somebody else.

trust hospital *n* a British hospital that manages itself, and receives money directly from the government rather than the local health authority.

trusting ['trʌstɪŋ] *adj* [person] who is ready to believe that other people are kind and sincere.

trustworthy ['trʌstwɜːrðɪ] *adj* [person] who can be trusted □ *Do you think he's trustworthy?*

trusty ['trʌstɪ] (*compar* **trustier,** *superl* **trustiest**) *adj* [weapon, animal, machine] that one can depend on (humorous use).

truth [truːθ] *n* **-1. the truth** the real facts about somebody or something □ *Will the truth ever be known?* ▪ **to tell the truth** to say something that is true, rather than lie □ *It's time you started telling (us) the truth.* ▪ **to tell the truth,...** a phrase used to emphasize that what one is about to say is honest but is likely to surprise or disappoint the other person □ *To tell (you) the truth, I don't really feel like going.* **-2.** something that is based on real facts □ *There is some truth in what you say.* ▪ **in truth** a phrase used to emphasize that what one is about to say is true. **-3.** something that is widely accepted to be true □ *There are one or two important truths you need to face up to.*

truth drug *n* a drug that makes people tell the truth.

truthful ['truːθfl] *adj* **-1.** [person] who tells the truth and does not lie. **-2.** [answer, account] that is based on the truth.

try [traɪ] (*pt* & *pp* **tried,** *pl* **tries**) ◇ *vt* **-1.** [activity, task] to do <sthg> because one hopes it will help one to do something one wants or needs to do □ *I'll try anything once.* □ *He tried his best to explain.* □ *Try not to think about it too much.* ▪ **to try and do sthg** to try to do sthg □ *I must try and see him before he goes.* **-2.** [food, drink] to eat, drink, or use <sthg> for the first time in order to find out what it is like; [pen, engine] to start to use <sthg> to find out if it works; [method, idea, remedy] to use <sthg> as a way of trying to do something; [doctor, library] to go to or contact <a person or place> to ask for something one wants □ *Try this, it's delicious!* □ *She tried the door to see if it was open.* □ *Have you tried calling the operator?* □ *Try him at his office, he might be there.* **-3.** LAW to send <a person or case> to a court for trial □ *He was tried for manslaughter and found not guilty.* **-4. to try sb's patience** to irritate sb so that they have to make an effort not to become angry.
◇ *vi* to make an effort □ *At least she tried.* □ *Try harder!* ▪ **to try for sthg** [for a job, position] to make an effort to get sthg □ *We are trying for a new baby.*
◇ *n* **-1.** an act of trying to do something □ *You didn't fool me, but it was a nice try!* ▪ **to give sthg a try** [method, remedy] to use sthg in the hope of getting or doing something that one wants; [sport, activity] to do sthg to find out whether one likes it or not □ *I've never been rock climbing, but I'd like to give it a try.* ▪ **to have a try at sthg** to make an attempt to do sthg □ *I don't think I can reach, but I'll have a try.* **-2.** RUGBY the act of touching the ground with the ball behind the opponent's goal line, that scores four points.
◆ **try on** *vt sep* **to try sthg on** [skirt, coat, boots] to put sthg on to see if it fits or to see if the color, style etc looks right □ *Could I try these jeans on, please?*
◆ **try out** *vt sep* **to try sthg out** [plan, car, method] to use sthg to see how good or successful it is □ *I'm trying out a new recipe.*

trying ['traɪɪŋ] *adj* [experience, period, person] that is annoying or upsetting □ *His behavior can be extremely trying at times.*

try-out *n* the process of observing or checking somebody or something for the first time in order to see how good or suitable they are (informal use) □ *Come along to next week's training session for a try-out.*

tsar [zɑːr] *n* the hereditary male ruler of Russia in the time before the Bolshevik Revolution of 1917.

T-shirt *n* a casual item of clothing that is worn on the upper half of the body and has short sleeves but no collar or buttons.

tsp *abbr of* **teaspoon.**

T-square *n* an instrument in the shape of a T, used for drawing or measuring right angles.

TT *abbr of* **teetotal.**

tub [tʌb] *n* **-1.** [of ice cream, margarine] a small plastic container that is usually covered with a lid **-2.** [for washing, a plant] a large, open, round container made of wood or metal. **-3.** US = **bathtub.**

tuba ['tjuːbə] *n* a large brass musical instrument that makes deep sounds.

tubby ['tʌbɪ] (*compar* **tubbier,** *superl* **tubbiest**) *adj* [person] who is rather fat, especially at the waist (informal use).

tube [tjuːb] *n* **-1.** [of metal, cardboard, glass] a long, narrow, hollow cylinder used as a container or to transfer liquids and gases. **-2.** ANATOMY a long, narrow, pipe-shaped passage in the human body □ *the respiratory tubes.* **-3.** [of toothpaste, paint, glue] a small cylindrical container that can be squeezed to release the contents at one end. **-4. the tube** GB the London underground train system □ *Take the tube out to Heathrow.* □ *It's probably quicker to go by tube.*

tubeless ['tjuːbləs] *adj* **a tubeless tire** a tire that does not have an inner tube.

tuber ['tjuːbər] *n* the fleshy, swollen, underground root of a plant such as the potato.

tuberculosis [tjʊˌbɜːrkjəˈləʊsəs] *n* an infectious disease that mainly affects the lungs and can kill people.

tube station *n* GB a station on the London underground train system.

tubing ['tjuːbɪŋ] *n* a section of material, usually flexible, that forms a tube □ *a piece of rubber tubing.*

Tubman ['tʌbmən], **Harriet** (1820–1913) a US slave who escaped from slavery and then helped other slaves to reach the North of the USA.

tubular ['tjuːbjələr] *adj* [structure, bells] in the form of a tube.

TUC (*abbr of* **Trades Union Congress**) *n* **the TUC** the association of representatives of labor unions in Britain.

tuck [tʌk] ◇ *n* SEWING a small fold in a piece of material or clothing that is held in place with stitches and used for decoration or to make something fit better. ◇ *vt* to put <sthg> somewhere so that it is neat, hidden, or stays in a fixed position □ *He wore his shirt tucked into his trousers.* □ *Sonia tucked the bill behind the clock on the mantelpiece.*

◆ **tuck away** *vt sep* to tuck sb/sth away to keep sb/sth in a safe place where they cannot be reached or found easily □ *She has a few thousand dollars tucked away.* ■ **to be tucked away somewhere** [cottage, village] to be somewhere that is not easily reached or is not known by many people □ *They live in a little village tucked away in the mountains.*

◆ **tuck in** ◇ *vt sep* -1. **to tuck sb in** [child, patient] to make sb comfortable in their bed by arranging the sheets, covers etc, especially just before they go to sleep □ *Will you come and tuck me in?* -2. **to tuck sth in** [shirt, sheet] to push the edge of sthg under something else to hold it neatly in place. ◇ *vi* to eat eagerly (informal use) □ *Go on, tuck in!*

◆ **tuck up** *vt sep* **to tuck sb up** in □ *I'll be tucked up in bed by ten o'clock.*

tuck shop *n* GB a store near or in a school where children can buy candy and snacks.

Tudor ['tʲuːdər] ◇ *adj* -1. HISTORY [king, queen] that is connected with the period in English history between 1485 and 1603. -2. ARCHITECTURE [mansion, style] that has features typical of the Tudor period, e.g. pointed roofs and black wooden beams. ◇ *n* **the Tudors** the kings and queens of England from 1485 to 1603.

Tue., Tues. *abbr of* **Tuesday**.

Tuesday ['tʲuːzdeɪ] *n* the day between Monday and Wednesday; *see also* **Friday**.

tuft [tʌft] *n* a small mass of something such as hair or grass that is made up of several separate strands attached at the bottom.

tug [tʌg] (*pt* & *pp* **tugged**, *cont* **tugging**) ◇ *n* -1. a short quick pull □ *I gave the rope a sharp tug.* -2. = **tugboat**. ◇ *vt* [hair, cord, rope] to pull <sthg> with a short quick movement □ *He tugged my sleeve.* ◇ *vi* [person] *Tug harder!* ■ **to tug at sthg** [at somebody's sleeve, arm] to take hold of and pull sthg with short quick movements □ *The little boy kept tugging at her skirt.*

tugboat ['tʌgbəʊt] *n* a small strong boat that is used to pull larger boats, especially into a harbor.

tug-of-love *n* GB a dispute between divorced or separated parents who both want to keep their child or children (informal use).

tug-of-war *n* a game of strength between two teams of people who pull on different ends of the same rope until the weaker side is pulled across a line.

tuition [tʲuːˈɪʃn] *n* -1. the act of teaching a subject, especially in a small or private class □ *guitar/driving tuition* □ *tuition fees*. -2. US EDUCATION money paid for tuition.

tulip ['tʲuːlɪp] *n* a brightly colored flower that has a bell-shaped head and grows from a bulb in spring.

tulle [tʲuːl] *n* a transparent fabric like net, used for evening dresses, veils etc.

tumble ['tʌmbl] ◇ *vi* -1. [person, object] to fall

quickly in a disorganized or uncontrolled way □ *The potatoes came tumbling out of the sack.* □ *Steve slipped and tumbled down the slope.* -2. [water] to flow quickly in an irregular way □ *The water splashed and tumbled over the rocks.* -3. [price, rate] to fall suddenly by a large amount □ *The resignation sent stock prices tumbling.* ◇ *n* a dramatic fall □ *The yen took a tumble today in European markets.*

◆ **tumble down** *vi* [building, structure] to collapse □ *The whole wall came tumbling down.*

tumbledown ['tʌmbldaʊn] *adj* a **tumbledown shack/house etc** a shack/house etc that is in very bad condition and is starting to fall down.

tumble-dry *vt* to dry <clothes that have been washed> in a tumble-dryer.

tumble-dryer *n* a machine that dries clothes by going round slowly, so that they are continuously moving in hot air.

tumbler ['tʌmblər] *n* a wide glass used for drinking that has a flat bottom and straight sides and does not have a handle □ *a glass tumbler.*

tumbleweed ['tʌmblwiːd] *n* a North American plant that breaks off from its roots and is blown about by the wind.

tummy ['tʌmi] (*pl* **tummies**) *n* one's stomach (informal use) □ *a flat tummy* □ *How's your tummy feeling?*

tumor US, **tumour** GB ['tʲuːmər] *n* a lump in the human body that is caused by an abnormal growth of cells and can cause serious illness □ *a brain tumor.*

tumult ['tʲuːmʌlt] *n* a lot of noise and excitement (formal use).

tumultuous [tʲuˈmʌltʃʊəs] *adj* [applause, reception] very noisy and excited.

tuna ['tʲuːnə] (*pl* **tuna** OR **tunas**), **tuna fish** (*pl* **tuna fish**) *n* a large fish found in warm seas and caught for food; the flesh of this fish that is eaten, especially as canned food □ *tuna salad* □ *a tuna steak.*

tundra ['tʌndrə] *n* a large area of land found mainly in cold areas in the northern hemisphere such as Alaska and Siberia, and that has few or no trees.

tune [tʲuːn] ◇ *n* several musical notes arranged to make a melody; a song. □ *I'm sure I know that tune.* ■ **to change one's tune** to act or speak in a way that shows one's opinion about something has changed (informal use) □ *You soon changed your tune!*

◇ *vt* -1. MUSIC [piano, violin, guitar] to adjust the strings, keys etc of <a musical instrument> so that notes will sound right when they are played together. -2. RADIO & TV to use the controls of <a radio or television> to find a particular station or channel □ *I keep my radio tuned to National Public Radio.* -3. AUTO to make small changes to <an engine> so that it works properly.

◇ *vi* **to tune to sthg** RADIO & TV [to a station, channel] to tune a radio or television to sthg.

◆ **in tune** ◇ *adj* MUSIC **to be in tune** [guitar, piano] to be producing the right notes after being tuned. ◇ *adv* -1. MUSIC [play, sing] making the right notes. -2. **to be in tune with sb/sthg** to show that one agrees with or understands sb/sthg □ *He's totally in tune with our way of thinking.*

◆ **out of tune** ◇ *adj* MUSIC **to be out of tune** [guitar, piano] to be producing the wrong notes because of not being tuned. ◇ *adv* -1. MUSIC [play, sing] making the wrong notes. -2. **to be out of tune with sb/sthg** to show that one does not agree with or understand sb/sthg □ *They're out of tune with current trends.*

◆ **to the tune of** *prep* up to <a particular amount> □ *It's insured to the tune of three million dollars.*

◆ **tune in** *vi* RADIO & TV to start watching or listening to a program on a particular station or channel □ *Tune in to next week's episode.*

◆ **tune up** *vi* [musician] to adjust one's instrument so that it will play in tune □ *The orchestra was already tuning up.*

tuneful ['tʲuːnfl] *adj* [melody, music] that is pleasant to listen to.

tuneless ['tʲuːnləs] *adj* [melody, music] that has no particular tune and so is not pleasant to listen to □ *He sang along in a tuneless voice.*

tuner ['tʲuːnər] *n* the part of a television or radio that receives signals so that it can be tuned to a particular channel or station.

tuner amplifier *n* an amplifier that has a radio tuner built in.

tungsten ['tʌŋstən] *n* a hard metal used in electric light bulbs and to make steel for tools. SYMBOL: W □ *a tungsten alloy/bar.*

tunic ['tʲuːnɪk] *n* an item of loose clothing that reaches from the upper half of the body to the hips or thighs and usually has no sleeves.

tuning fork ['tʲuːnɪŋ-] *n* an object in the shape of a fork with two long prongs that is used for tuning musical instruments.

Tunisia [US tʊˈniːʒə, GB tjʊˈnɪzɪə] a country in North Africa, on the Mediterranean between Algeria and Libya. SIZE: 164,000 sq kms. POPULATION: 8,400,000 (*Tunisians*). CAPITAL: Tunis. LANGUAGE: Arabic. CURRENCY: Tunisian dinar.

tunnel ['tʌnl] (US *pt* & *pp* **tunneled**, *cont* **tunneling**, GB *pt* & *pp* **tunnelled**, *cont* **tunnelling**) ◇ *n* a passage that has been dug in the ground so that people, vehicles etc can go through it. ◇ *vi* [person, machine, rabbit] to make a tunnel by digging □ *They will have to tunnel right through the mountain.*

tunnel vision *n* -1. MEDICINE a condition affecting the eyes in such a way that one can only see things that are straight ahead. -2. the inability to consider all aspects of a situation, problem etc.

tunny ['tʌni] (*pl* **tunny** OR **tunnies**) *n* = tuna.

turban ['tɜːbən] *n* a covering for the head, made by winding a long strip of cloth around the head many times, that is worn especially by Muslim, Sikh, and Hindu men.

turbid ['tɜːbəd] *adj* [water, smoke, cloud] that is dirty and difficult to see through.

turbine ['tɜːbaɪn] *n* a motor or engine in which power is produced when a wheel with blades on it is turned by the force of a gas or liquid.

turbo ['tɜːbou] (*pl* **turbos**) *n* an extra device in a car engine that helps it to go faster than other models of the same type.

turbocharged ['tɜːboutʃɑːdʒd] *adj* [car, engine] that is more powerful because it is fitted with a turbo.

turbojet ['tɜːboudʒet] *n* an engine used in planes in which the power to move forward is produced by hot gases being sent out from the back; a plane with this type of engine.

turboprop ['tɜːbouprɒp] *n* -1. a jet engine that drives a propeller. -2. a plane that has a turboprop engine.

turbot ['tɜːbət] (*pl* **turbot** OR **turbots**) *n* a large flatfish found in European waters; the flesh of this fish eaten as food.

turbulence ['tɜːbjələns] *n* AVIATION air that moves violently and irregularly in the sky □ *We experienced some turbulence on the return flight.*

turbulent ['tɜːbjələnt] *adj* -1. [air, water] that is moving around in an uncontrolled and irregular way □ *The water was choppy and turbulent.* -2. [period, situation] that is unstable and affected by sudden changes □ *Those were turbulent times.*

tureen [tʲuˈriːn] *n* a large dish or pot covered with a lid and used for serving soup from.

turf [tɜːf] (*pl* **turfs** OR **turves**) ◇ *n* -1. short thick grass that is all of the same length. -2. a small section of earth that has grass on it and is put on the ground to form part of a lawn. ◇ *vt* [lawn, yard] to cover the surface of <an area of land> with turf.

turf accountant *n* GB a person whose job is to take bets on horse races (formal use).

turgid ['tɜːdʒəd] *adj* [style, writing, film] that is too complex or dense and is boring to read, watch etc □ *turgid prose.*

Turin ['tʲurɪn] the capital of Piedmont, northwest Italy. POPULATION: 1,000,000.

Turing ['tʲuəriŋ], **Alan** (1912-1954) a British scientist who played an important part in the development of computers.

Turk [tɜːk] *n* a person who comes from or lives in Turkey.

turkey ['tɜːki] (*pl* **turkeys**) *n* a large bird with dark feathers and a loose flap of skin underneath its beak that is kept on farms to be sold as food; the white meat of this bird, traditionally eaten at Christmas and Thanksgiving.

Turkey a country in southeastern Europe and Western Asia, between the Mediterranean Sea and the Black Sea. SIZE: 780,000 sq kms. POPULATION: 60,700,000 (*Turks*). CAPITAL: Ankara. MAIN CITY: Istanbul. LANGUAGE: Turkish. CURRENCY: Turkish lira.

Turkish ['tɜːrkɪʃ] ◇ *n* the language of Turkey. ◇ *adj*: *see* **Turkey** □ *a Turkish carpet/meal.*

Turkish bath *n* a bath that involves sitting in a hot room filled with steam, being given a massage, and then washing in cold water.

Turkish coffee *n* strong and usually very sweet black coffee.

Turkish delight *n* a soft candy that is usually pink or white and is cut into small cubes and lightly covered in powdered sugar.

turmeric ['tɜːrmərɪk] *n* a spice used to add flavor and a yellow color to food, especially curry.

turmoil ['tɜːrmɔɪl] *n* a state of complete confusion and disorganization □ *My mind was in turmoil.* □ *This latest crisis has thrown the government into turmoil.*

turn [tɜːrn] ◇ *n* -1. **a right/left turn** the point where a road, river etc bends toward the right/left □ *The road takes a sharp turn inland here.* -2. **sb's turn** the time when sb must do something or have something done to them □ *Throw the dice, it's your turn.* □ *You'll have to wait your turn.* □ *Whose turn is it to drive?* ■ **to take (it in) turns to do sthg** to do sthg one after the other □ *We take it in turns to do the driving.* -3. [of a key, wrist, wheel] an act of turning □ *Give the handle a turn.* -4. **a turn of events** a change or new development in a situation □ *Nothing had prepared us for this dramatic turn of events.* ■ **to take a turn for the better/worse** to get better/worse suddenly □ *The weather/situation seems to have taken a turn for the worse.* -5. TRANSPORT a road that leads to the left or right from the side of the road one is traveling along □ *I missed the turn.* -6. GB [in a theater, on television] a short performance □ *The star turn of the evening was a brilliant young comic.* -7. phrases **to do sb a good/bad turn** to do something that helps/harms sb. ■ **a turn of phrase** a particular way of expressing things in words. ■ **the turn of the year/century** the point where one year/century ends and a new one begins.
◇ *vt* -1. [object, part of one's body] to move <sthg> so that it faces a different direction □ *Turn your chair to face the window.* □ *He turned his back on me.* □ *I called after her, but she didn't even turn her head.* -2. [key, knob, handle] to take hold of <sthg> and move it in a circle around a fixed point □ *Turn the steering wheel to the left.* -3. [page, omelet, steak] to change the position of <sthg> so that the side of it that was hidden faces upward □ *After ten minutes, turn the fish and grill the other side.* -4. **to turn one's mind** OR **thoughts to sthg** to begin thinking about sthg □ *We must turn our attention now to the question of deregulation.* -5. **to turn sthg into sthg** to change sthg into sthg □ *He has singlehandedly turned a small software firm into a giant of the computing industry.* -6. **to turn a bend/corner** to go around a bend/corner.
◇ *vi* -1. [car, road, person] to start moving in a different direction □ *Turn left and continue down the road.* -2. [person] to move to face in a different direction □ *Darcy turned to her and smiled.* -3. [key, knob, handle] *The wheels*

turned. □ *I heard the sound of his key turning in the lock.* -4. **to turn red/gray/cold etc** to become red/gray/cold etc □ *Be careful, he could turn nasty.* □ *The leaves were turning yellow.*

◆ **in turn** *adv* a phrase used to describe events or actions that happen one after the other □ *He greeted each member of the family in turn.* □ *Mrs Ryan's medical records were sent to the hospital, which in turn forwarded them to the specialist.*

◆ **turn against** *vt fus* **to turn against sb** to start to dislike sb who one used to like □ *Even his family has decided to turn against him.*

◆ **turn around** ◇ *vt sep* -1. **to turn sthg around** [car, object] to move sthg so that it faces the opposite direction □ *The traffic was so bad we turned the car around and went home.* -2. **to turn sthg around** [goods, order] to complete work on or produce sthg that has been ordered by a customer □ *The factory can turn around the order in two weeks.* -3. **to turn a business around** to make an unprofitable business profitable again □ *Investors are unlikely to be interested in any banks in trouble until they are turned around.* ◇ *vi* to move so that one faces the opposite direction □ *Turn around so I can see how the dress looks from the back.*

◆ **turn away** ◇ *vt sep* **to turn sb away** to say that sb is not allowed to enter a place □ *Refugees were being turned away at the border.* □ *We were turned away at the door because Doug was wearing jeans.* ◇ *vi* [person] to move to face a different direction because one does not want to look at something □ *Hal turned away in disgust.*

◆ **turn back** *vt sep* **to turn sb/sthg back** to force sb/sthg to go back to the place they came from □ *We were turned back at the Swiss border.*

◆ **turn down** *vt sep* -1. **to turn sb/sthg down** [applicant, offer, proposal] to refuse or reject sb/sthg □ *My request for a transfer was turned down.* -2. **to turn sthg down** [TV, radio, lamp] to reduce the amount of sound, heat, light etc produced by sthg by turning a switch, knob etc □ *I asked him to turn down the volume.*

◆ **turn in** *vi* [person] to go to bed (informal use).

◆ **turn off** ◇ *vt fus* **to turn off a road** to leave a road and take one going in another direction □ *Turn off the main road at the next junction.* ◇ *vt sep* **to turn sthg off** [radio, motor, gas] to stop sthg working by using a switch, knob etc □ *Don't forget to turn off the lights when you leave.* □ *I parked and turned the engine off.* ◇ *vi* [driver, vehicle] to turn off a road □ *We should have turned off at Exit 9.*

◆ **turn on** ◇ *vt sep* -1. **to turn sthg on** [engine, radio, tap] to make sthg work by using a switch, knob etc □ *Turn on the heating if you feel cold.* -2. **to turn sb on** to make sb sexually excited (informal use). ◇ *vt fus* **to turn on sb** to suddenly attack sb.

◆ **turn out** ◇ *vt sep* -1. **to turn sthg out** [light, gas] to stop sthg working by using a switch, knob etc □ *Did you remember to turn out the lights?* -2. **to turn sthg out** [goods, product] to produce sthg (informal use) □ *At peak times, the factory can turn out 500 components an hour.*

□ *Colleges are now turning out a new breed of graduate.* **-3. to turn sb out** to make sb leave a place, usually permanently □ *She was turned out by her parents.* **-4. to turn sthg out** [pocket, bag, drawer] to empty sthg completely □ *The security guard asked me to turn out my briefcase on a table.*
◇ *vi* **-1.** used to describe a surprising or unexpected fact that one learns about somebody or something □ *The man I was sitting next to turned out to be a friend of Max.* ■ **it turns out that...** we discovered later that... □ *It turns out that they were at college together.* **-2. to turn out well/badly** to happen in a way that is successful/unsuccessful □ *The recipe didn't turn out the way it was supposed to.* □ *Martha was pretty wild as a teenager, but she's turned out OK.* □ *The evening turned out to be a disaster.* **-3.** [for a game, demonstration] to go to see or take part in an event □ *Huge crowds turned out for the Pope's visit.*

♦ **turn over** ◇ *vt sep* **-1. to turn sthg over** [card, stone, page] to turn sthg so that the other side is facing upward □ *Turn the page over sd that I can see the other side.* **-2. to turn sthg over in one's mind** to think about sthg carefully □ *That evening he turned over Dave's warning in his mind.* **-3. to turn sb/sthg over to sb** [criminal, funds, property] to give sb/sthg to the person or organization who should have it □ *The suspect has been turned over to the French authorities.*
◇ *vi* **-1.** [person, animal] to turn one's body when one is lying down so that another part is facing upward □ *He turned over onto his back and started snoring.* **-2.** GB [viewer] to start watching a different television channel □ *Can I turn over for the news?*

♦ **turn round** *vt sep* & *vi* = **turn around.**

♦ **turn to** *vt fus* **-1. to turn to sthg** [page, chapter, article] to look for sthg in a book, newspaper etc □ *Turn to the vocabulary section on page 54.* **-2. to turn to sb/sthg** [friend, religion, drink] to try to get help, advice, comfort etc from sb/sthg □ *I don't know who else to turn to.*

♦ **turn up** ◇ *vt sep* **to turn sthg up** [heating, radio, light] to increase the amount of heat, sound, light etc produced by sthg by turning a switch, knob etc □ *Turn up the heater, it's cold in here.* ◇ *vi* **-1.** [person] to arrive at a place, often unexpectedly (informal use) □ *She eventually turned up at the party at nine o'clock.* □ *This man turned up at the office asking for you.* **-2.** [object] to be found after being lost, especially when no one has looked for it □ *The keys finally turned up in Kim's coat pocket.* **-3.** [chance, job] to happen, especially unexpectedly □ *Opportunities like this don't turn up every day.*

turnabout ['tɜːrnəbaʊt] *n* a change in something e.g. somebody's opinion, that causes it to become the opposite of what it was before □ *He's done a complete turnabout on immigration.*

turnaround ['tɜːrnəraʊnd] US, **turnround** ['tɜːrnraʊnd] GB *n* **-1.** BUSINESS the time taken for a plane, ship etc to unload, take on new passengers or goods, and leave again □ *The*

schedule allows for a twenty-minute turnaround. **-2.** a change in a situation that causes it to become the opposite of what it was before, usually in a good way □ *This year we're hoping for an economic turnaround.*

turncoat ['tɜːrnkoʊt] *n* a person who changes from one group, political party, ideology etc to another and is regarded as a traitor.

Turner ['tɜːrnər], **J. M. W.** (1775–1851) a British artist, famous for his landscapes.

Turner, Nat (1800–1831) a US slave who led the largest slave revolt in the USA in 1831 and was later executed.

turning ['tɜːrnɪŋ] *n* GB a road that leads to the left or right from the side of the road one is traveling along □ *Take the second turning on your right.*

turning circle *n* the smallest space within which a car can be turned around.

turning point *n* a point in time when things begin to change so that a new situation develops □ *The move marked a turning point in her career.*

turnip ['tɜːrnəp] *n* a round yellow-white vegetable that grows under the ground.

turnout ['tɜːrnaʊt] *n* the number of people who go to a public event such as a meeting □ *It was a poor turnout.*

turnover ['tɜːrnoʊvər] *n* **-1.** [of staff, tenants, students] the rate at which people join and leave an organization, institution etc □ *They have a very high turnover of staff here.* **-2.** FINANCE the amount of money that comes into and out of the accounts of a firm in a particular period of time □ *Annual turnover is now $35,500,000.*

turnpike ['tɜːrnpaɪk] *n* US a major road that drivers pay a toll to use □ *the New Jersey Turnpike.*

turnround *n* GB = **turnaround.**

turn signal *n* US one of the lights on a car that flashes to show which way it is turning.

turnstile ['tɜːrnstaɪl] *n* a type of gate, e.g. at a stadium, that turns around a fixed point and only lets one person pass at one time, usually after money has been paid.

turntable ['tɜːrnteɪbl] *n* the circular spinning part of a record player on which one puts a record in order to listen to it.

turn-up *n* GB a fold of material at the lower end of a pair of trousers.

turpentine ['tɜːrpəntaɪn] *n* a colorless oily liquid used to make paint thinner or to remove stains made by paint.

Turpin ['tɜːrpən], **Dick** (1705–1739) a British outlaw who robbed travelers on the road.

turps [tɜːrps] *n* GB = **turpentine.**

turquoise ['tɜːrkwɔɪz] ◇ *n* **-1.** a blue-green mineral; a blue-green stone from this mineral that is used in jewelry. **-2.** a blue-green color. ◇ *adj* that is blue-green in color □ *the turquoise waters of the Aegean.*

turret [US 'tɜːrət, GB 'tʌr-] *n* a part of a castle or similar building that is like a small tower.

turtle ['tɜːᵊtl] (*pl* **turtle** OR **turtles**) *n* an animal that lives on land and in water and has a round hard shell on its back that it can hide its body inside.

turtledove ['tɜːᵊtldʌv] *n* a type of pigeon that makes a soft gentle noise.

turtleneck ['tɜːᵊtlnek] *n* **a turtleneck (sweater)** US a sweater that has a high collar that folds down; GB a sweater with a short raised collar in the form of a band of material.

turves [tɜːᵊvz] GB *plural of* **turf**.

tusk [tʌsk] *n* one of two long, bony, pointed teeth that stick out on either side of the mouth of animals such as elephants and boars.

tussle ['tʌsl] ◇ *n* a fight between people in which they grip each other by the arms and pull or push each other □ *There was a brief tussle, during which one man was hurt.* ◇ *vi* to have a tussle.

tut [tʌt] *excl* a word used to show that one disapproves of something that somebody else has said or done □ *Tut tut! I'm surprised at you!*

Tutankhamen [ˌtuːtnˈkɑːmən] (14th century BC) King of Egypt from 1361 to 1352 BC.

tutor ['tⁱuːtəʳ] ◇ *n* **-1.** a teacher who gives private lessons to an individual or a small group □ *a piano/math tutor.* **-2.** GB EDUCATION a teacher at a college or university. ◇ *vt* to teach a subject to <sb> individually or as part of a small group □ *I tutored her in French literature for a year.*

tutorial [tⁱuːˈtɔːrɪəl] ◇ *adj* [group, guidance, advice] that is connected with the work of a college or university tutor. ◇ *n* at college or university, a lesson given by a tutor.

tutu ['tuːtuː] *n* a short skirt worn by ballet dancers, made of stiff material with many folds.

tux [tʌks] *n* a tuxedo (informal use).

tuxedo [tʌkˈsiːdoʊ] (*pl* **tuxedos**) *n* **-1. a tuxedo (jacket)** a man's black or white jacket that is worn on formal occasions. **-2.** a man's suit that includes a tuxedo jacket.

TV *n abbr of* **television** □ *I sat up watching TV all night.* □ *a black and white TV* □ *a TV program.*

TVA *n abbr of* **Tennessee Valley Authority**.

TV dinner *n* a complete meal that is sold in a packet and only needs to be heated before eating.

TVP (*abbr of* **textured vegetable protein**) *n* a type of vegetarian food that has been made to look like meat.

twaddle ['twɒdl] *n* nonsense (informal use).

Twain [tweɪn], **Mark** (1835–1910) a US writer who is famous for his humor and use of dialect. His work includes *The Adventures of Tom Sawyer* and *The Adventures of Huckleberry Finn*.

twang [twæŋ] ◇ *n* **-1.** the sound made by a tight wire, string, or piece of elastic when it vibrates after it has been hit, pulled etc □ *The string broke with a loud twang.* **-2.** a nasal tone of voice □ *She speaks with a real twang.*

◇ *vt* [guitar, string, wire] to cause <sthg> to make a twang by hitting, pulling it etc. ◇ *vi* [wire, string] *The springs made a twanging sound.*

tweak [twiːk] *vt* [nose, ear] to pull or twist <sthg> between one's finger and thumb (informal use).

twee [twiː] *adj* GB [village, picture] that is too pretty or sentimental (disapproving use).

tweed [twiːd] *n* thick woolen cloth, usually woven with several different colors □ *a tweed suit/coat/jacket.*

tweet [twiːt] *vi* [bird] to make one or more short, quiet, high-pitched sounds.

tweezers ['twiːzəʳz] *npl* a device consisting of two long thin pieces of metal joined at one end, used for picking up small objects or pulling out hairs from one's body □ *a pair of tweezers.*

twelfth [twelfθ] *num* 12th; number 12 in a series; *see also* **fifth**.

Twelfth Night *n* the evening of January 5, the last day of the festival of Christmas.

twelve [twelv] *num* the number 12; *see also* **five**.

twentieth ['twentɪəθ] *num* 20th; number 20 in a series; *see also* **fiftieth**.

twenty ['twentɪ] (*pl* **twenties**) *num* the number 20; *see also* **fifty**.

twenty-twenty vision *n* perfect eyesight.

twerp [twɜːʳp] *n* a person who one thinks is foolish (informal use).

twice [twaɪs] *adv* & *predet* two times □ *It's happened twice already.* □ *twice a day/year* □ *He earns twice as much as I do.* □ *She is twice my age.*

twiddle ['twɪdl] ◇ *vt* [knob, stick, hair] to keep turning <sthg> around with small movements of one's fingers □ *He twiddled the dial on the radio.* ◇ *vi* **to twiddle with sthg** to twist sthg in a playful or careless way □ *She sat twiddling with her hair.*

twig [twɪg] *n* a small, thin, woody part of a tree or bush that is smaller than a branch □ *a dead twig.*

twilight ['twaɪlaɪt] *n* **-1.** the early evening when it is beginning to grow dark. **-2. the twilight of sthg** [of somebody's life, career] the final stages of sthg.

twill [twɪl] *n* a strong cloth woven with a pattern of parallel diagonal lines.

twin [twɪn] ◇ *adj* **-1. a twin brother/sister** a boy/girl who is born at the same time as another child of the same mother □ *She has twin girls/boys.* **-2. twin peaks/towers etc** two peaks/towers etc that are close together and look very similar to one another. ■ **twin beds/engines etc** two beds/engines etc that look like each other and are intended to be used together. **-3. twin aspects/aims etc** two aspects/aims etc that are similar or linked to each other. ◇ *n* either of two children born at the same time to the same mother □ *identical twins.*

twin-bedded [-ˈbedəd] *adj* **a twin-bedded room** a room that contains two matching single beds □ *a twin-bedded room with shower.*

twine [twaɪn] ◇ *n* a type of strong string. ◇ *vt* **to twine sthg around sthg** to twist sthg around sthg □ *She twined the gold chain around her wrist.*

twin-engined [-ˈendʒənd] *adj* [plane, jet] that is powered by two identical engines.

twinge [twɪndʒ] *n* **-1.** a sudden sharp pain □ *I felt a twinge in my leg.* **-2. a twinge of guilt/ fear etc** a sudden slight feeling of guilt/fear etc □ *He felt a twinge of jealousy as he saw them laughing together.*

Twinkie™ [ˈtwɪŋkɪ] *n* US a small cake filled with cream.

twinkle [ˈtwɪŋkl] ◇ *n* **-1.** [of a star] a light that keeps changing from dim to bright. **-2.** [in somebody's eye] a bright and lively look, especially of somebody who is smiling, excited etc. ◇ *vi* **-1.** [star, light] to shine with a twinkle. **-2.** [eyes] to have a twinkle.

twin room *n* a room in a hotel with two separate single beds.
NOTE: Compare **single room, double room.**

twinset [ˈtwɪnset] *n* GB a woman's matching sweater and cardigan.

twin town *n* a town that has formed special links with another town in a foreign country.

twirl [twɜːˈl] ◇ *vt* **-1.** [baton, stick, umbrella] to cause <sthg> to spin around rapidly □ *The cheerleaders came on, twirling their batons.* **-2.** [knob, moustache] to twist <sthg> around. ◇ *vi* [dancer, model] to spin around.

twist [twɪst] ◇ *vt* **-1.** [rope, cloth, hair] to turn <sthg> around, especially by moving only one part or two parts in opposite directions □ *She twisted the strands of hair together to form a neat braid.* ■ **to twist sthg around sthg** to wind sthg around sthg □ *I had to twist the wire around the terminal several times to make a good contact.* **-2.** [metal, frame] to cause <sthg> to lose its proper or usual shape □ *Their faces were twisted with anger.* **-3.** [knob, dial, lid] to turn <sthg> so that it moves around □ *'Twist top to open.'* **-4.** [ankle, wrist, neck] to hurt <a part of one's body> by moving it too suddenly or in an unusual direction □ *I fell and twisted my ankle.* **-5.** [words] to unfairly change <sthg that somebody has said>, especially in order to get some advantage for oneself □ *Stop trying to twist everything I say!*

◇ *vi* **-1.** [road, river] to keep changing direction by bending to the left and right. **-2.** [person] to move a part of one's body around □ *He twisted and struggled to get free.* □ *She twisted around in her chair to face me.*

◇ *n* **-1.** [in a rope, hose] a part of something that is twisted; [in a road, river] a sharp bend □ *The road was full of twists and turns.* **-2. to give sthg a twist** [cap, knob, screw] to turn sthg sharply □ *To close/open the jar, you simply give the lid a twist.* **-3.** [in a book, movie, story] a sudden and unexpected development □ *a twist of fate* □ *Ah, but there's a twist at the end of the story!*

twisted [ˈtwɪstəd] *adj* **-1.** [person, mind] that enjoys things that most people find unpleasant

□ *You have a twisted sense of humor!* **-2.** [logic, reasoning] that seems strange.

twister [ˈtwɪstər] *n* US a tornado (informal use).

twisty [ˈtwɪstɪ] (*compar* **twistier**, *superl* **twistiest**) *adj* [line, road] that is not straight but has many twists (informal use).

twit [twɪt] *n* a person who one thinks is foolish (informal use).

twitch [twɪtʃ] ◇ *n* a sudden uncontrolled movement of a muscle, e.g. in one's face □ *a nervous twitch.* ◇ *vt* [nose, ears] to cause <a part of one's body> to make small sudden movements □ *The rabbit twitched its nose.* ◇ *vi* [muscle, eye, body] *His left eye began to twitch.*

twitter [ˈtwɪtər] *vi* **-1.** [bird] to make short high-pitched sounds. **-2.** [person] to speak quickly in a high-pitched voice, usually about unimportant things (disapproving use).

two [tuː] *num* the number 2; *see also* **five.** ■ **in two** into two pieces □ *We cut/broke it in two.*

two-bit *adj* US that is not very valuable or important (disapproving use).

two-dimensional *adj* **-1.** [picture, image] that is drawn, painted, reproduced etc on a flat surface. **-2. a two-dimensional character** a character in a book, play etc who is not convincing because they are too simple.

two-door *adj* [car] that has two doors.

twofaced [ˌtuːˈfeɪst] *adj* [person] who says they feel or believe something when they do not (disapproving use).

twofold [ˈtuːfəʊld] ◇ *adj* **-1.** [advantage, problem] that consists of two things or parts □ *The reasons for this decision are twofold.* **-2.** [increase, growth] that makes something twice as big, large etc as it was before. ◇ *adv* [increase, grow] *Sales have gone up twofold in the same period this year.*

two-handed [-ˈhændəd] *adj* [sword, weapon, stroke] that requires the use of both hands.

two-percent milk *n* US milk that has had about half the cream removed.

two-piece *adj* **a two-piece suit/swimsuit** a suit/swimsuit that consists of two separate but matching parts.

two-ply *adj* [tissue, wood] that has two layers; [wool] that is made up of two strands.

two-seater *n* a car or aircraft with two seats.

twosome [ˈtuːsəm] *n* a group of two people or things (informal use).

two-stroke ◇ *adj* **a two-stroke engine** an engine in which the piston moves up and down once in each cycle. ◇ *n* a two-stroke engine.

two-time *vt* to deceive <the person one is having a romantic or sexual relationship with> by having a secret relationship with somebody else (informal use).

two-tone *adj* [shoes, car] that has two colors or two shades of the same color.

two-way *adj* **-1.** [traffic, discussion, trade] in both directions. **-2. a two-way radio** a radio that sends and receives messages.

TX *abbr of* **Texas.**

tycoon [taɪˈkuːn] *n* a rich and powerful

businessman or businesswoman □ *the media tycoon, Bob Connors.*

Tyler ['taɪlə^r], **Wat** (died 1381) a British revolutionary who led the Peasants' Revolt, demanding civil rights for peasants.

Tyneside ['taɪnsaɪd] an area of northeastern England that used to be an important center for coalmining and shipbuilding.

type [taɪp] ◇ *n* -1. a particular kind of person or thing □ *What type of house are you looking for?* □ *There are various types of insurance available.* □ *blood type* O. -2. a person who has characteristics that cause them to be described in a particular way □ *She's the steady hardworking type.* □ *He's not the type to take risks.* ■ **he's/she's not my type** I'm not physically attracted to him/her. -3. PRINTING printed letters and characters □ *The text should be in bold/italic type.* ◇ *vt* [letter, document] to write <sthg> using a typewriter or word processor □ *He can type 60 words a minute.* ◇ *vi* to write using a typewriter or word processor □ *Can you type?*

♦ **type up** *vt sep* **to type sthg up** [report, notes] to type all of sthg that has been written by hand □ *Can you type this up for me?*

typecast [US 'taɪpkæst, GB -kɑːst] (*pt* & *pp* **typecast**) *vt* to give <an actor or actress> the same type of role all the time □ *She's wary of being typecast as the dumb blonde.*

typeface ['taɪpfeɪs] *n* a particular size or style of printed letters and characters.

typescript ['taɪpskrɪpt] *n* a copy of a text that has been typed.

typeset ['taɪpset] (*pt* & *pp* **typeset**, *cont* **typesetting**) *vt* [document, text] to prepare <a piece of writing> so that it can be printed in a particular format and typeface.

typesetter ['taɪpsetə^r] *n* a person or machine that prepares text on a page before it is printed.

typesetting ['taɪpsetɪŋ] *n* the job or business of a typesetter.

typewriter ['taɪpraɪtə^r] *n* a machine with a keyboard that prints characters onto paper as the person using it strikes the keys □ *an electronic typewriter.*

typhoid ['taɪfɔɪd] *n* **typhoid (fever)** a very serious infectious disease, caused by contaminated food or water, that produces fever, a red rash, and stomach pain with diarrhea.

typhoon [taɪ'fuːn] *n* a violent tropical storm like a hurricane that occurs in the western Pacific Ocean.

typhus ['taɪfəs] *n* a serious infectious disease that is given to humans by insects such as lice and fleas and causes severe fever and headaches.

typical ['tɪpɪkl] *adj* [reaction, reply, pattern] that is what one expects from a particular person or thing because of the way they usually are □ *I live in a typical northern town.* □ *That sort of rudeness is typical of him.* □ *"They're going to be late." — "Typical!"*

typically ['tɪpɪklɪ] *adv* -1. usually □ *This plant is typically found in mountainous regions.* -2. a

word used to show that one thinks that an action, situation etc is typical of somebody or something □ *The menu is typically Chinese.* □ *Typically, he changed his mind at the last minute.*

typify ['tɪpɪfaɪ] (*pt* & *pp* **typified**) *vt* -1. [work, approach] to be typical of <sthg> □ *the ruthlessness that typifies his way of doing business.* -2. [type, attitude] to be a typical example of <sthg> □ *She typifies the modern career woman.*

typing ['taɪpɪŋ] *n* the act of operating a typewriter; the text produced by a typewriter □ *Her typing is very accurate.* □ *two pages of typing* □ *What's your typing speed?*

typing error *n* a mistake made by a typist.

typing pool *n* a group of typists who type for members of an office; the area in an office where these typists sit.

typist ['taɪpɪst] *n* a person who operates a typewriter, especially as a job.

typo ['taɪpoʊ] *n* a mistake in the way a word is printed, made by a typist or typesetter.

typographic(al) error [taɪpə,græfɪk(l)-] *n* = **typo** (formal use).

typography [taɪ'pɒɡrəfɪ] *n* -1. the work of arranging a text for printing and choosing its style and appearance. -2. the style and appearance of the print in a book, document etc.

tyrannical [tə'rænɪkl] *adj* [person, ruler, regime] that allows people very little freedom and treats them harshly.

tyranny ['tɪrənɪ] *n* [of a regime, ruler] a tyrannical form of government or control; [of a person] tyrannical behavior □ *her desire to escape from the tyranny of family life.*

tyrant ['taɪrənt] *n* a person or ruler who is tyrannical □ *Their father was a real tyrant.*

tyre ['taɪə^r] *n* GB a round piece of rubber that is filled with air and fits around the outside of a wheel of a road vehicle.

Tyrol [tɪ'roʊl]: **the Tyrol** a mountainous province of western Austria that is popular for skiing.

Tyrolean [,tɪrə'liːən], **Tyrolese** [,tɪrə'liːz] *n* & *adj*: *see* **Tyrol**.

tzar [zɑː^r] *n* = **czar**.

u [juː] (*pl* **u's** OR **us**), **U** [juː] (*pl* **U's** OR **Us**) *n* the twenty-first letter of the English alphabet.

♦ **U** (*abbr of* **universal**) a symbol for classifying movies and videotapes in Britain, showing that they are suitable for all viewers.

UAE *n abbr of* **United Arab Emirates**.

UAW (*abbr of* United Automobile Workers) *n* **the UAW** a US labor union for motor vehicle manufacturing workers.

UB40 [,juːbiːˈfɔːˈtɪ] (*abbr of* unemployment benefit form 40) *n* an official card used by unemployed people in Britain when they register for unemployment benefit.

U-bend *n* a U-shaped bend in a toilet pipe.

ubiquitous [juːˈbɪkwətəs] *adj* that seems to appear, happen, or exist everywhere at once (formal use).

UCLA *n abbr of* the University of California at Los Angeles.

UDA (*abbr of* Ulster Defence Association) *n* the UDA a Protestant paramilitary organization whose aim is to keep Northern Ireland as part of the UK.

udder [ˈʌdəˈ] *n* a bag of skin under the body of a cow, goat etc that contains the glands that produce milk.

UDI (*abbr of* unilateral declaration of independence) *n* a declaration of independence made by a state without the agreement of the country that it has been controlled by.

UDR (*abbr of* Ulster Defence Regiment) *n* the UDR an official Protestant paramilitary force in Northern Ireland. In 1992 it became part of the Royal Irish Regiment.

UEFA [juːˈeɪfə] (*abbr of* Union of European Football Associations) *n* the organization in charge of professional soccer in Europe.

UFC (*abbr of* Universities Funding Council) *n* the UFC the British government organization responsible for funding universities.

UFO (*abbr of* unidentified flying object) *n* an object believed to be a spaceship in which creatures from another planet visit the Earth. It is often said to be shaped like a saucer with bright flashing lights.

Uganda [juːˈgændə] a country in eastern Central Africa, west of Kenya. SIZE: 237,000 sq kms. POPULATION: 18,700,000 (*Ugandans*). CAPITAL: Kampala. LANGUAGE: English. CURRENCY: Ugandan shilling.

ugh [ʌg] *excl* a noise used to show that one dislikes something strongly or is disgusted by it.

ugly [ˈʌglɪ] (*compar* uglier, *superl* ugliest) *adj* -1. [person, object, building] that is not attractive to look at □ *Newark seemed an ugly kind of place.* -2. [situation, fight] that seems frightening or dangerous □ *There were ugly scenes as police clashed with demonstrators.*

UHF (*abbr of* ultra-high frequency) *n* a range of radio frequencies between 3,000 and 300 MHz, used for TV broadcasts.

UHT (*abbr of* ultra-heat treated) *adj* UHT milk milk that has been heated to a high temperature so that it lasts longer than ordinary milk.

UK *n abbr of* United Kingdom □ *He was born in the UK.* □ *a UK resident.*

Ukraine [juːˈkreɪn] a country in southeastern Europe, on the Black Sea between Russia and Romania. SIZE: 604,000 sq kms. POPULA-

TION: 51,700,000 (*Ukrainians*). CAPITAL: Kiev. LANGUAGE: Ukrainian. CURRENCY: hrivna.

ukulele [,juːkəˈleɪlɪ] *n* a musical instrument with four strings that is like a small guitar.

ulcer [ˈʌlsəˈ] *n* a sore area on the skin or on the inside of an organ that is difficult to heal □ *a stomach ulcer.*

ulcerated [ˈʌlsəreɪtəd] *adj* [stomach, mouth, leg] that has ulcers on it or inside it.

Ulster [ˈʌlstəˈ] = Northern Ireland. ■ the Ulster Democratic Unionist Party a political party in Northern Ireland supported by Protestants who believe that Northern Ireland should remain part of the United Kingdom.

Ulsterman [ˈʌlstəˈmən] (*pl* Ulstermen [-mən]) *n* a man who comes from or lives in Ulster.

Ulster Unionist *n* a Protestant who believes Northern Ireland should remain part of the United Kingdom.

Ulsterwoman [ˈʌlstəˈwʊmən] (*pl* Ulsterwomen) *n* a woman who comes from or lives in Ulster.

ulterior [ʌlˈtɪərɪəˈ] *adj* an ulterior motive the real reason why one does something, that one hides from other people and tries to keep secret □ *I can't help suspecting him of ulterior motives.*

ultimata [,ʌltɪˈmeɪtə] *plural of* ultimatum.

ultimate [ˈʌltɪmət] ◇ *adj* -1. the ultimate aim/objective etc the main aim/objective etc that one intends to achieve at the end of a period of time or a process □ *Our ultimate aim is to merge the operations of the two companies.* -2. the ultimate authority/challenge etc the most important and final authority/challenge etc □ *The ultimate responsibility lies with the director.* ◇ *n* to be the ultimate in sthg [in luxury, technology] to be the best or most advanced kind of sthg □ *This laptop is the ultimate in hi-tech.*

ultimately [ˈʌltɪmətlɪ] *adv* -1. [reach, achieve, succeed] finally and as the result of a long process □ *Pollution could ultimately lead to these cities becoming uninhabitable.* -2. ultimately,... a word used to emphasize one's basic conclusion after considering a situation, problem etc □ *Ultimately, there's not a great deal we can do about it.*

ultimatum [,ʌltɪˈmeɪtəm] (*pl* ultimatums OR ultimata) *n* a final warning one gives to somebody that tells them what one will do if they do not do what one wants □ *The hijackers delivered an ultimatum: hand over the money or the hostages will die.*

ultra- [ˈʌltrə] *prefix* added to a word to show that a particular quality or state is extreme □ *ultra-clean/-cautious* □ *an ultra-right-wing politician.*

ultramarine [,ʌltrəməˈriːn] *n* a very bright blue color.

ultrasonic [,ʌltrəˈsɒnɪk] *adj* [sound wave] that is higher than the human ear can hear; [equipment, device] that uses ultrasonic sound waves.

ultrasound [ˈʌltrəsaʊnd] *n* -1. sound produced at frequencies above the range of human hearing. -2. an ultrasound (scan) a medical examination in which ultrasound is used to allow doctors to see an image of the inside of part of a patient's body.

ultraviolet [ˌʌltrəˈvaɪələt] *adj* **ultraviolet light** light that comes from the sun and is beyond the violet end of the visible range of colors. It can make the skin darker or, in large amounts, cause skin diseases.

Uluru [ˈuːluruː] the Aboriginal name, and official name, for Ayers Rock.

۞ ULURU
Uluru is the official name of Ayers Rock, a very large rock in the Uluru National Park, in Northern Territory, Australia. It is the largest rock in the world: 348 meters (1,158 feet) high, 3.6 kilometers (2.2 miles) long, and 2.4 kilometers (1.5 miles) wide. For thousands of years it was a sacred place for local Aboriginal people, who called it Uluru, meaning "great pebble".

---

um [ʌm] *excl* a sound used when one does not know what to say next □ *Um, I don't know.*

umbilical cord [ʌmˌbɪlɪkl-] *n* the tube that connects a fetus to the wall of its mother's womb.

umbrage [ˈʌmbrɪdʒ] *n* **to take umbrage** to become angry or offended because of something □ *She took umbrage at one or two of my remarks.*

umbrella [ʌmˈbrelə] ◇ *n* **-1.** a device consisting of a metal frame that is covered in material and attached to a stick and can be opened to protect one from rain. **-2.** [on a beach, terrace] a large umbrella that is fixed in one position, especially over a table, to protect people from the sun □ *Janine sat under a large umbrella.* ◇ *adj* **-1. an umbrella group/organization** a group/organization that includes a number of other groups, organizations etc. **-2. an umbrella term/word** a term/word that includes a number of similar things.

UMIST [ˈjuːmɪst] (*abbr of* **University of Manchester Institute of Science and Technology**) *n* a leading scientific university in Manchester, England.

umpire [ˈʌmpaɪəʳ] ◇ *n* in some sports such as baseball and tennis, a person whose job is to make sure that the rules are obeyed during play. ◇ *vt* to act as umpire during <a game or match>. ◇ *vi*: *A New Zealander was umpiring.*

umpteen [ˌʌmpˈtiːn] *adj* **umpteen times** a very large number of times (informal use) □ *She's been given umpteen warnings.*

umpteenth [ˌʌmpˈtiːnθ] *adj* **the umpteenth time** the most recent in a large number of times (informal use) □ *This is the umpteenth time I've told you.*

UN *n abbr of* **United Nations** □ *a UN peacekeeping mission.*

unabashed [ˌʌnəˈbæʃt] *adj* **to be unabashed** to seem not to be embarrassed or ashamed (formal use) □ *She continued, unabashed.*

unabated [ˌʌnəˈbeɪtəd] *adj* **to continued unabated** to continue without decreasing, or getting less strong □ *The rain continued unabated.*

unable [ʌnˈeɪbl] *adj* **to be unable to do sthg** not to be able to do sthg □ *Stress left him unable to sleep.* □ *Unfortunately I'm unable to help you.*

unabridged [ˌʌnəˈbrɪdʒd] *adj* [text, edition] that is complete, with no parts taken out.

unacceptable [ˌʌnəkˈseptəbl] *adj* [proposal, condition, solution] that one disagrees with or finds unsatisfactory; [behavior, rudeness] that one strongly disapproves of and cannot accept □ *The policy is simply unacceptable to the majority of the population.* □ *Absenteeism has reached unacceptable levels.*

unaccompanied [ˌʌnəˈkʌmpənɪd] *adj* **-1.** [child, guest] who is alone in a particular place or situation; [luggage] that is transported separately from its owner □ *Children are not allowed in unaccompanied.* **-2.** [song, choir] that is not accompanied by musical instruments □ *music for unaccompanied voices.*

unaccountably [ˌʌnəˈkaʊntəblɪ] *adv* [delayed, lost, omitted] for no clear reason □ *Our luggage was unaccountably delayed in Amsterdam.*

unaccounted [ˌʌnəˈkaʊntəd] *adj* **to be unaccounted for** [person, money] to be missing □ *Twenty passengers and one crew member are still unaccounted for.*

unaccustomed [ˌʌnəˈkʌstəmd] *adj* **-1. to be unaccustomed to sthg** not to be familiar with sthg so that one finds it strange □ *Being unaccustomed to such treatment, I demanded an apology.* **-2.** [lateness, friendliness, rudeness] that is not usually expected from a particular person or thing (formal use).

unadulterated [ˌʌnəˈdʌltəreɪtəd] *adj* **-1.** [food, wine] that has nothing added to it. **-2.** a word used to emphasize the great extent of something □ *It was sheer unadulterated bliss!*

unadventurous [ˌʌnədˈventʃərəs] *adj* [person, organization] that does not want to take risks; [project, book, movie] that does not try to do anything unusual or interesting.

unaffected [ˌʌnəˈfektəd] *adj* **-1. to be unaffected** to stay the same, without changing or being harmed □ *Your rights as a consumer are unaffected by this guarantee.* **-2.** [person, manner, charm] that seems natural and pleasant.

unafraid [ˌʌnəˈfreɪd] *adj* [person] who does not feel any fear □ *He carried on, unafraid.*

unaided [ʌnˈeɪdəd] ◇ *adj* [work, attempt, effort] that does not involve the help of anybody or anything else. ◇ *adv* [walk, stand] *He climbed to the top unaided.*

unambiguous [ˌʌnæmˈbɪgjʊəs] *adj* [statement, reply, gesture] whose meaning is clear and cannot be misunderstood.

un-American [ˌʌn-] *adj* [behavior, thinking] that is not the usual way of doing things in the USA. ■ **un-American activities** political activities that are thought to be harmful to the USA.

unanimity [ˌjuːnəˈnɪmətɪ] *n* complete agreement among a group of people □ *There was complete unanimity as to what should be done.*

unanimous [juːˈnænɪməs] *adj* [verdict, decision, opinion] that involves complete agreement among a group of people; [people] who are in complete agreement □ *The newspapers were unanimous in their outrage.* □ *The verdict was unanimous.*

unanimously [juːˈnænɪməslɪ] *adv* [decide, pass] with nobody disagreeing □ *The motion was passed unanimously.*

unannounced [ˌʌnəˈnaʊnst] *adv* [arrive, appear] without anyone being told in advance □ *You walk in unannounced and expect me to drop everything for you?*

unanswered [US ˌʌnˈænsrd, GB -ˈɑːnsəd] *adj* [question, letter] that has not been answered □ *My letters went unanswered.*

unappealing [ˌʌnəˈpiːlɪŋ] *adj* [characteristic, quality, aspect] that one does not find attractive.

unappetizing, -ising [ˌʌnˈæpətaɪzɪŋ] *adj* [food] that one does not want to eat, e.g. because of the way it looks.

unapproachable [ˌʌnəˈprəʊtʃəbl] *adj* [person] who is difficult to talk to because they seem cold and unfriendly □ *His colleagues found him unapproachable and distant.*

unarmed [ˌʌnˈɑːrmd] *adj* [person] who is not carrying any weapons □ *They shot an unarmed civilian.*

unarmed combat *n* a type of fighting in which no weapons are used.

unashamed [ˌʌnəˈʃeɪmd] *adj* [luxury, delight, greed] that one feels no guilt or embarrassment about.

unassuming [ˌʌnəˈsjuːmɪŋ] *adj* [person] who seems modest and does not draw attention to themselves □ *a small, thin, unassuming man.*

unattached [ˌʌnəˈtætʃt] *adj* -1. [object, part, building] that is not fastened or joined to anything; [organization, group] independent. -2. [person] who is not married and does not have a sexual or romantic relationship with anyone □ *He's over thirty and he's still unattached.*

unattended [ˌʌnəˈtendəd] *adj* [luggage, vehicle, store] that has nobody looking after it □ *Do not leave your personal belongings unattended.*

unattractive [ˌʌnəˈtræktɪv] *adj* -1. [person, building] that has an appearance or qualities that one does not find pleasant □ *Men wearing ponytails look so unattractive!* -2. [idea, prospect] that one cannot be enthusiastic about because it is not pleasant □ *The prospect of a week in the sun was not unattractive.*

unauthorized, -ised [ˌʌnˈɔːθəraɪzd] *adj* [entry, visit, biography] that has been made or done without official permission; [person] who does not have official permission to do something □ *'No unauthorized entry.'* □ *'Access prohibited to unauthorized personnel.'*

unavailable [ˌʌnəˈveɪləbl] *adj* -1. **to be unavailable** to be unable or unwilling to speak to or meet people □ *Last night the President was unavailable for comment.* -2. **to be unavailable** [product, services] to be impossible to obtain.

unavoidable [ˌʌnəˈvɔɪdəbl] *adj* [delay, conse-

quences, meeting] that cannot be prevented □ *The delays were, unfortunately, unavoidable.*

unavoidably [ˌʌnəˈvɔɪdəblɪ] *adv* [delayed, detained] *see* **unavoidable.**

unaware [ˌʌnəˈweər] *adj* **to be unaware of sthg** not to know about sthg □ *She was quite unaware of what had happened/him being there.* □ *I was unaware that they had arrived.*

unawares [ˌʌnəˈweəz] *adv* **to catch** OR **take sb unawares** [question, arrival, attack] to surprise sb so much that they are unable to react immediately □ *She caught her opponent completely unawares.*

unbalanced [ˌʌnˈbælənst] *adj* -1. [account, article, view] that gives too much importance to one side or version of the facts. -2. [person, mind] that seems slightly crazy □ *Charlotte was found to be mentally unbalanced.*

unbearable [ʌnˈbeərəbl] *adj* [person] whom one dislikes very much; [pain, noise, heat] that is too unpleasant, painful etc to bear □ *The smell had become unbearable.*

unbearably [ʌnˈbeərəblɪ] *adv* **unbearably hot/ painful etc** so hot/painful etc that it is difficult to bear □ *It was unbearably noisy in there.*

unbeatable [ʌnˈbiːtəbl] *adj* -1. [performance, power, quality] that is much better than anything else of the same kind □ *Come and see our new range of sofas, all at unbeatable prices!* -2. [team, player] who cannot be defeated.

unbeaten [ʌnˈbiːtn] *adj* [team, record] that has not yet been beaten □ *Pittsburgh extended their unbeaten run to 12 games.*

unbecoming [ˌʌnbɪˈkʌmɪŋ] *adj* [dress, color, behavior] that is not attractive or appropriate (formal use).

unbeknown(st) [ˌʌnbɪˈnəʊn(st)] *adv* **unbeknown(st) to sb** without sb knowing □ *Unbeknown(st) to him, a decision had already been reached.*

unbelievable [ˌʌnbəˈliːvəbl] *adj* -1. [arrogance, skill, stupidity] that is so great that it is surprising □ *We were under unbelievable pressure.* -2. [story, alibi] that is difficult to believe because it is not very likely □ *I found her version of events pretty unbelievable.*

unbelievably [ˌʌnbəˈliːvəblɪ] *adv* -1. **unbelievably stupid/bad etc** very stupid/bad etc □ *He was unbelievably rude to me.* -2. a word used to show that one finds something very surprising □ *Unbelievably, no one even noticed.*

unbending [ʌnˈbendɪŋ] *adj* [attitude, person] that is very strict and is unwilling to change.

unbent [ʌnˈbent] *past tense & past participle of* **unbend.**

unbia(s)sed [ʌnˈbaɪəst] *adj* [account, view, attitude] that does not prefer one particular side in a situation such as an argument or competition and so is fair.

unblemished [ʌnˈblemɪʃt] *adj* [reputation, record] that has not been spoiled in any way □ *The senator has an unblemished record on support for civil rights issues.*

unblock [ˌʌnˈblɒk] *vt* [drain, tunnel, pipe] to remove an object that is blocking <sthg> so that it is clear again.

unbolt [ˌʌnˈbəʊlt] vt [door, window] to move the bolt on <sthg> into a position that allows it to be opened.

unborn [ˌʌnˈbɔːrn] adj [child, baby] that has not yet been born.

unbreakable [ˌʌnˈbreɪkəbl] adj [object] that is made strongly so that it cannot be broken □ unbreakable glass.

unbridled [ʌnˈbraɪdld] adj [greed, lust] that is very strong and is not controlled □ a tale of unbridled passion.

unbroken [ʌnˈbrəʊkən] adj [line, series] that continues without stopping □ The team has enjoyed an unbroken run of five victories.

unbutton [ˌʌnˈbʌtn] vt [coat, shirt] to undo the buttons that fasten <sthg>.

uncalled-for [ʌnˈkɔːld-] adj [remark, criticism] a word used to describe something somebody has said that is unreasonable or unfair □ That was uncalled-for — I think you should apologize.

uncanny [ʌnˈkænɪ] (compar **uncannier**, superl **uncanniest**) adj [coincidence, similarity] that is strange and mysterious □ She bears an uncanny resemblance to my sister.

uncared-for [ʌnˈkeəʳd-] adj [person] who has not been looked after properly and so is dirty, ill etc.

uncaring [ˌʌnˈkeərɪŋ] adj [person, attitude] that shows no sympathy for other people's feelings or suffering.

unceasing [ʌnˈsiːsɪŋ] adj [devotion, loyalty] that continues without stopping (formal use).

unceremonious [ˌʌnserəˈməʊnjəs] adj [departure, dismissal] that is done suddenly, quickly, and rudely.

unceremoniously [ˌʌnserəˈməʊnjəslɪ] adv: see **unceremonious** □ He was unceremoniously stripped of his title.

uncertain [ʌnˈsɜːʳtn] adj -1. **to be uncertain** [person] to be unsure or not to know something definitely; [plans] not to be definite or clear □ We're uncertain of the final result. □ She paused, uncertain how to continue. □ It is uncertain whether the rebels will leave without putting up a fight. ■ **in no uncertain terms** very clearly and forcefully □ She told me in no uncertain terms that she thought I was wrong. -2. [weather, outcome] that cannot be predicted □ The firm faces an uncertain future.

unchain [ˌʌnˈtʃeɪn] vt [bicycle, boat] to remove the chain that fastens <sthg> to something else.

unchallenged [ˌʌnˈtʃæləndʒd] adj [authority, leadership, version] that is accepted without disagreement □ We cannot allow this statement to go unchallenged.

unchanged [ˌʌnˈtʃeɪndʒd] adj **to be/remain unchanged** [position, circumstances] to be/stay the same for a period of time □ The situation remains unchanged.

unchanging [ˌʌnˈtʃeɪndʒɪŋ] adj [expression, way of life, mentality] that does not change.

uncharacteristic [ˌʌnkærəktəˈrɪstɪk] adj [behav-

ior, silence, friendliness] that is not typical of a particular person □ "I see no prospect of improvement," he said, with uncharacteristic gloom.

uncharitable [ʌnˈtʃærətəbl] adj [person, comment, feelings] that is not fair or kind about somebody □ It would be uncharitable to say he's fat; he's just a little overweight.

uncharted [ˌʌnˈtʃɑːrtəd] adj -1. [area, territory] that is not recorded on maps. -2. **uncharted waters** OR **seas** a situation that is not familiar □ Her second novel definitely takes her into uncharted waters, but she manages it very well.

unchecked [ˌʌnˈtʃekt] ◇ adj [expansion, development, growth] that is not stopped from continuing. ◇ adv [expand, develop, grow] Industrial growth continued unchecked.

uncivilized, -ised [ʌnˈsɪvəlaɪzd] adj -1. [person, society] that is considered to be less developed or advanced than others. -2. [behavior] that is considered to be unacceptable, often because it is very rude, violent, or cruel □ I hate boxing, I think it's barbaric and uncivilized.

unclassified [ˌʌnˈklæsəfaɪd] adj POLITICS [document, information] that is not secret and can be read by members of the public.

uncle [ˈʌŋkl] n the brother of one's mother or father, or the husband of a one's aunt.

unclean [ˌʌnˈkliːn] adj -1. [water] that is dirty and not fit to drink. -2. [food, person, thoughts] that is considered morally unacceptable, especially for religious reasons.

unclear [ˌʌnˈklɪəʳ] adj -1. [meaning, instructions] that is complicated or badly expressed and so not easy to understand □ This paragraph is very unclear. -2. [future, motive] that is difficult to be certain about □ It is now unclear whether talks will take place or not. -3. **to be unclear about sthg** not to understand sthg properly □ I'm still unclear about what you want me to do.

Uncle Sam [-ˈsæm] an imaginary person, used as a symbol for the USA or the US government. He is pictured as an old man with a white beard and the US flag on his hat □ We have to pay Uncle Sam half of our salary.

Uncle Tom [-ˈtɒm] ◇ the hero of the novel Uncle Tom's Cabin by Harriet Beecher Stowe. He is a black slave who is murdered by his owner. ◇ n a black person who is too eager to please white people (disapproving use).

uncomfortable [ˌʌnˈkʌmftəʳbl] adj -1. [furniture, clothing, position] that feels unpleasant or causes slight pain and so makes it difficult for one to relax; [person] who does not feel relaxed because of an unpleasant physical feeling caused by their clothing, position etc □ These shoes are so uncomfortable. -2. [fact, truth] that is difficult to accept or deal with because it is unpleasant □ They could make life very uncomfortable for me if they chose to. -3. [person] who is slightly worried or embarrassed □ I felt uncomfortable asking for more money.

uncomfortably [ˌʌnˈkʌmftəblɪ] adv -1. [sit, stand] in a way that shows one feels uncomfortable. -2. [laugh, smile] in a way that shows one is nervous. -3. **uncomfortably**

hot/crowded etc hot/crowded etc in a way that feels unpleasant □ *His guess was uncomfortably close to the truth.*

uncommitted [ˌʌnkə'mɪtəd] *adj* [person] who has not yet decided which activity, group, ideal etc to support.

uncommon [ʌn'kɒmən] *adj* -1. [occurrence, plant, bird] rare □ *The problem is not uncommon with this particular model of car.* -2. [beauty, intelligence] very great in amount (formal use) □ *a man of uncommon integrity.*

uncommonly [ʌn'kɒmənlɪ] *'adv* uncommonly/ **generous/difficult etc** extremely generous/ difficult etc (formal use).

uncommunicative [US ˌʌnkə'mjuːnəkeɪtɪv, GB -ɪkət-] *adj* [person] who seems not to want to speak or give information.

uncomplicated [ˌʌn'kɒmpləkeɪtəd] *adj* [life, story, person] that is simple and without complications □ *Tom's a pretty uncomplicated kind of guy.*

uncomprehending [ˌʌnkɒmprɪ'hendɪŋ] *adj* [person, stare, look] that shows no understanding of what has happened or been said.

uncompromising [ʌn'kɒmprəmaɪzɪŋ] *adj* [person, attitude, position] that shows an unwillingness to do what other people want or accepting their ideas □ *Both sides remain uncompromising and the deadlock is unbroken.*

unconcerned [ˌʌnkən'sɜːrnd] *adj* [person] who is not worried about something that affects them □ *She seemed quite unconcerned by the danger.*

unconditional [ˌʌnkən'dɪʃnəl] *adj* [surrender, support, offer] that does not depend on any conditions □ *Only John's mother gave him the unconditional love he needed.*

uncongenial [ˌʌnkən'dʒiːnjəl] *adj* [place, event] that one finds unfriendly and rather unpleasant (formal use).

unconnected [ˌʌnkə'nektəd] *adj* [facts, events] that are not related to each other □ *The two events are hardly unconnected, are they?*

unconscious [ʌn'kɒnʃəs] ◇ *n* PSYCHOLOGY **the unconscious** the part of one's mind that contains thoughts and feelings that one is not aware of and cannot control. ◇ *adj* -1. [person] who is in a state like sleep in which they cannot see, hear, feel etc □ *Paul was unconscious for an hour after the accident.* -2. **to be unconscious of sthg** not to be aware of sthg □ *Julian seemed unconscious of the stir he had caused.* -3. PSYCHOLOGY [feeling, desire] that comes from the unconscious □ *She felt an unconscious desire to punish him.*

unconsciously [ʌn'kɒnʃəslɪ] *adv* [feel, want] in a way that is not intentional or in one's control □ *I think that, unconsciously, he blames me for what happened.*

unconstitutional [ˌʌnkɒnstə'tjuːʃnəl] *adj* [action, decision] that is against the rules of a constitution.

uncontested [ˌʌnkən'testəd] *adj* **an uncontested seat** POLITICS a seat in an election for which there is only one candidate.

uncontrollable [ˌʌnkən'trəʊləbl] *adj* -1. [rage,

anger, laughter] that is very strong and cannot be controlled □ *I felt an uncontrollable urge to laugh.* -2. [child] who behaves badly and cannot be encouraged, persuaded etc to act differently; [animal] that is wild and cannot be made to behave in a particular way.

uncontrolled [ˌʌnkən'trəʊld] *adj* -1. [anger, outburst, laughter] that a person does not control or stop from happening □ *He burst into uncontrolled laughter.* -2. [situation, activity] that is not limited by anyone, e.g. an authority □ *uncontrolled spending by city councils.*

unconventional [ˌʌnkən'venʃnəl] *adj* [behavior, dress, film] that is very different from what is usual and what most people expect in a particular situation □ *They had a very unconventional lifestyle.*

unconvinced [ˌʌnkən'vɪnst] *adj* **to be unconvinced about sthg** not to want to accept the truth or worth of sthg □ *Doctors remain unconvinced by claims of miracle cures.*

unconvincing [ˌʌnkən'vɪnsɪŋ] *adj* -1. [explanation, argument] that is not good enough to make somebody accept that it is true □ *I found her explanation somewhat unconvincing.* -2. [actor, story, character] that does not seem realistic or natural □ *She was unconvincing in the part of Ophelia.*

uncooked [ˌʌn'kʊkt] *adj* [meat, food] that has not yet been cooked.

uncooperative [ˌʌnkəʊ'ɒpərətɪv] *adj* [person] who does not want to help somebody or do what they want.

uncork [ˌʌn'kɔːrk] *vt* to remove the cork from <a bottle>.

uncouth [ʌn'kuːθ] *adj* [person] who acts or speaks in a way that shows bad manners.

uncover [ʌn'kʌvər] *vt* -1. [face, object] to remove the covering from <sthg> □ *Leave the sauce to simmer, uncovered.* -2. [plot, corruption, truth] to discover or tell people about <sthg that has been kept secret> □ *Police have uncovered an arms cache.*

uncurl [ˌʌn'kɜːrl] *vi* -1. [hair, wire] to become straight again after being curled. -2. [cat, snake] to stretch its body to its normal state after being curled up.

uncut [ˌʌn'kʌt] *adj* -1. [movie, play] that has not been made shorter by having parts removed from the original version. -2. [jewel] that is in its natural state and has not been cut or shaped for wearing as jewelry.

undamaged [ʌn'dæmɪdʒd] *adj* [painting, car, vase] that has not been damaged, especially after an accident, fire etc.

undaunted [ʌn'dɔːntəd] *adj* [person] who is not worried or frightened by a difficult job or unpleasant circumstances □ *She carried on undaunted.* □ *He was undaunted by their criticism.*

undecided [ˌʌndɪ'saɪdəd] *adj* -1. **to be undecided about sthg** not to have made a definite decision about sthg □ *I'm still undecided about whether to stay or go.* -2. [issue, matter] that has not been completely dealt with □ *The matter remains undecided.*

undemanding [US ˌʌndɪ'mændɪŋ, GB -'mɑːnd-]

adj **-1.** [job, task] that does not need a lot of thought or effort. **-2.** [person] who is easy to be with because they expect very little.

undemonstrative [ˌʌndɪˈmɒnstrətɪv] *adj* [person] who does not allow their feelings to show in the way they speak or behave.

undeniable [ˌʌndɪˈnaɪəbl] *adj* [fact, feeling] that is obvious, so that nobody can argue or disagree about it □ *There's still the undeniable fact that he signed the agreement.*

under [ˈʌndər] ◇ *prep* **-1. under the table** below the table □ *We took shelter under a tree.* □ *She has a small scar under her left eye.* □ *The prisoners had managed to tunnel under the fence.* ■ **under the ocean/ground** covered by the ocean/ground □ *He wore a T-shirt under his jacket.* **-2. under $100** less than $100 □ *We have under ten minutes left.* □ *'Not suitable for children under five years.'* **-3. under the circumstances** in a particular set of circumstances □ *Under a truly democratic system, this would not happen.* **-4. under attack/discussion** being attacked/discussed □ *The matter is currently under review/consideration.* **-5. under stress/pressure** affected by stress/pressure □ *He's been under a lot of strain recently.* □ *The tenants are under threat of eviction.* **-6. under an agreement/law** according to an agreement/law □ *Under the terms of the contract, we are obliged to pay.* **-7. under sb** led, controlled, managed etc by sb □ *She has a staff of four under her.* ■ **the USA under Reagan** the USA while Reagan was in power. **-8. listed under "D"** used to show where something is placed in a list, book etc □ *File the report under 'Urgent'.* **-9. under the name of Smith** using the name of Smith □ *He registered under the name of Colonel Buendia.* ◇ *adv* **-1. to dive/crawl under** to dive/crawl below something. **-2. 12 years and under** 12 years and less. **-3.** *phrase* **to go under** to go bankrupt (informal use).

underachiever [ˌʌndərəˈtʃiːvər] *n* a person who does not do as well as they could at school or work.

underage [ˌʌndərˈeɪdʒ] *adj* [drinker, smoker] who is not old enough to do a particular activity legally □ *underage drinking.*

underarm [ˈʌndərɑːrm] ◇ *adj* **-1. an underarm deodorant** a product that is designed to stop bad smells from sweat in one's armpits. **-2. an underarm throw/bowl** a way of throwing/bowling a ball that involves moving one's hand forward while keeping it below the level of one's shoulder. ◇ *adv* [throw, bowl] *She threw the ball underarm.*

underbrush [ˈʌndərbrʌʃ] *n* US the plants and bushes that grow under the trees in a forest or jungle.

undercarriage [US ˈʌndərkerɪdʒ, GB ˈʌndəkærɪdʒ] *n* the wheels and other parts of a plane that support it on the ground and during takeoff and landing □ *The plane's undercarriage was raised/lowered.*

undercharge [ˌʌndərˈtʃɑːrdʒ] *vt* to charge <a customer> too little or less than the correct price for a product or service.

underclothes [ˈʌndərkloʊðz] *npl* items of clothing, e.g. undershirts, bras, and underpants, that one wears next to one's skin under one's other clothes.

undercoat [ˈʌndərkoʊt] *n* a layer of paint put onto a surface to act as a base for another layer.

undercook [ˌʌndərˈkʊk] *vt* [meat, vegetables] not to cook <food> for a long enough time.

undercover [ˌʌndərˈkʌvər] ◇ *adj* **an undercover agent** a person who secretly obtains information for the government or police by pretending to be somebody else □ *an undercover operation.* ◇ *adv*: *The arrests were made by police working undercover.*

undercurrent [US ˈʌndərkɜːrənt, GB ˈʌndəkʌrənt] *n* **-1.** [of feeling, tension, danger] a hidden feeling □ *I sensed an undercurrent of resentment in his voice.* **-2.** [in a river, ocean] a strong flow of water under the surface that moves in a particular direction □ *There's a very strong undercurrent.*

undercut [ˌʌndərˈkʌt] (*pt* & *pp* **undercut**, *cont* **undercutting**) *vt* to sell goods or services more cheaply than <sb> □ *Greater efficiency means the firm can undercut its competitors by 10%.*

underdeveloped [ˌʌndərdɪˈveləpt] *adj* **-1.** [country, area] that does not have modern industries and has poor living conditions. **-2.** [child] who is small compared to other children of the same age.

underdog [ˈʌndərdɒg] *n* **the underdog** [in a competition] the person who seems least likely to succeed or win; [in society] a person who does not have much chance of being successful because of their background □ *I usually support the underdog.*

underdone [ˌʌndərˈdʌn] *adj* [meat, pastry] that has not been cooked for long enough.

underemployment [ˌʌndərɪmˈplɔɪmənt] *n* a situation in which there are not enough jobs, or in which jobs do not use all the abilities and skills that people have.

underestimate [*n* ˌʌndərˈestɪmət, *vb* ˌʌndərˈestɪmeɪt] ◇ *n* an estimate that is too low. ◇ *vt* **-1.** [time, amount, cost] to estimate that <sthg> will be less than it really is □ *I seriously underestimated how long it would take to finish the job.* **-2.** [person, power, abilities] to have too low an opinion of <sb/sthg> □ *Don't underestimate her — she's very shrewd.*

underexposed [ˌʌndərɪkˈspoʊzd] *adj* [film, photo, print] that looks dark because not enough light was used.

underfinanced [ˌʌndərˈfaɪnænst] *adj* [company, project, organization] that does not have enough money spent on it to be able to work properly.

underfoot [ˌʌndərˈfʊt] *adv* **to be trampled underfoot** [person, plants] to be walked over by a lot of people or animals. ■ **it is wet underfoot** the ground feels wet when one walks on it.

undergo [ˌʌndərˈgoʊ] (*pt* **underwent**, *pp* **undergone** [-ˈgɒn]) *vt* [operation, change, difficulties] to experience <sthg>, especially sthg difficult or unpleasant □ *The telecommunications industry has undergone a difficult reorganization in recent years.* □ *She is undergoing treatment for breast cancer.*

undergraduate [ˌʌndəˈɡrædʒuət] ◇ *n* a person who is studying at a college or university for their first degree. ◇ *adj*: *an undergraduate course/degree.*

underground [*adj* & *n* ˈʌndəˈɡraʊnd, *adv* ˌʌndeˈɡraʊnd] ◇ *adj* **-1.** [bunker, shelter, pipe] that is below the surface of the ground □ *I parked in an underground parking lot.* **-2. an underground organization/newspaper etc** an organization/newspaper etc that is secret and illegal □ *During the war, Juliette worked in the underground resistance movement.*
◇ *adv* **-1.** [live, dig] *This small creature spends most of its time underground.* **-2.** *phrase* **to go underground** [organization, newspaper, activity] to become an underground organization, newspaper, activity etc □ *The sport was forced underground by the new laws.*
◇ *n* **-1.** GB RAIL a railroad system in which electric trains carry people around a city through underground tunnels. **-2.** MILITARY an underground organization that is against the government.
◆ **Underground** *n* **the Underground** the subway system in London.

underground railroad *n* before the American Civil War, a secret system that helped slaves to escape from the Southern states to the North of the USA or Canada.

undergrowth [ˈʌndəˈɡroʊθ] *n* the plants and bushes that grow under the trees in a forest or jungle □ *I heard something moving in the undergrowth.*

underhand [ˌʌndəˈhænd] *adj* [action, method] that is dishonest, secret, and designed to hide one's real intentions.

underinsured [ˌʌndərɪnˈʃʊəʳd] *adj* [person, building, property] that does not have enough insurance to cover the full cost of an insurance claim.

underlay [ˈʌndəˈleɪ] *n* a thick material that is put under a carpet to make it feel softer and to protect it.

underline [ˌʌndəˈlaɪn] *vt* **-1.** [importance, fact] to draw attention to <sthg> □ *He cited several examples to underline the point.* **-2.** [title, heading] to draw a line under <a word or words>.

underling [ˈʌndəˈlɪŋ] *n* a person who has a lower or less important position than somebody else and takes orders from them (disapproving use).

underlying [ˌʌndəˈlaɪɪŋ] *adj* **an underlying principle/cause etc** a principle/cause etc that is not obvious but is important □ *We have to understand the underlying problems before we can find a lasting solution.*

undermanned [ˌʌndəˈmænd] *adj* [office, organization, factory] that does not have enough people to do all the work.

undermentioned [ˌʌndəˈmenʃnd] *adj* that is

mentioned later on in a particular document (formal use).

undermine [ˌʌndəˈmaɪn] *vt* [authority, position, effort] to gradually make <sthg> weaker □ *This could undermine public confidence in the justice system.*

underneath [ˌʌndəˈniːθ] ◇ *prep* **-1. underneath the table/blanket etc** under the table/blanket etc and hidden or covered by it □ *Underneath all that old brown paint we found some fine oak paneling.* □ *He had a shirt on underneath his sweater.* □ *According to the map, the road goes underneath a bridge at this point.* **-2.** used to describe somebody's hidden feelings or personality □ *Underneath that tough exterior, she's really very kind.*
◇ *adv*: *The picture had a caption underneath.* □ *We had to lift the floorboards to get at the wiring underneath.* □ *Underneath he's actually a shy person.*
◇ *n* **the underneath** the part that is hidden or covered □ *The underneath of the car was badly rusted.*

undernourished [US ˌʌndərˈnɜːrɪʃt, GB ˌʌndəˈnʌrɪʃt] *adj* [person] who is unhealthy because they have not eaten enough food, or the right food.

underpaid [*vb* ˌʌndəˈpeɪd, *adj* ˈʌndəˈpeɪd] ◇ *past tense and past participle of* **underpay**. ◇ *adj* [staff, workers] who are not paid enough money for the work they do □ *overworked and underpaid.*

underpants [ˈʌndəˈpænts] *npl* US a piece of underwear that covers the area from the waist to the top of the legs; GB a piece of this underwear that is worn only by men and boys □ *a pair of underpants.*

underpass [US ˈʌndərpæs, GB ˈʌndəpɑːs] *n* a passage or road that goes underneath another road or a railroad track.

underpay [ˌʌndəˈpeɪ] (*pt* & *pp* **underpaid**) *vt* not to pay <staff, employees> etc enough money for the job they do.

underpin [ˌʌndəˈpɪn] (*pt* & *pp* **underpinned**, *cont* **underpinning**) *vt* [argument, theory, society] to strengthen and support <sthg>.

underplay [ˌʌndəˈpleɪ] *vt* to make <sthg> seem unimportant, or less important than it really is □ *Their spokesman is underplaying the significance of this latest resignation.*

underprice [ˌʌndəˈpraɪs] *vt* [goods, services] to charge too low a price for <sthg>.

underprivileged [ˌʌndəˈprɪvəlɪdʒd] *adj* [child, family] who has less money and fewer opportunities than other people in society.

underproduction [ˌʌndəˈprəˈdʌkʃn] *n* a lower level of production than is needed to make profits or provide enough for everybody.

underrated [ˌʌndəˈreɪtəd] *adj* [writer, novel, value] that is better, greater, or more important than most people realize □ *He is a very underrated artist.*

underscore [ˌʌndəˈskɔːʳ] *vt* **-1.** [importance, fact] to draw attention to <sthg>. **-2.** [title, heading] to draw a line under <a word or phrase> to show that it is important.

undersea [ˌʌndərˈsiː] *adj* **undersea exploration** exploration below the surface of the sea.

undersecretary [US ˌʌndərˈsekrəterɪ, GB ˌʌndəˈsekrətərɪ] (*pl* **undersecretaries**) *n* **-1.** an official who has a very senior position in a government department. **-2.** in Britain, a person who helps and advises a minister and is in charge of the daily work of a government department.

undersell [ˌʌndərˈsel] (*pt* & *pp* **undersold**) *vt* **-1.** [competitors, company] to sell goods or services more cheaply than <sb>. **-2.** not to show how valuable or useful <sthg> is when advertising or selling it.

undershirt [ˈʌndərʃɜːrt] *n* US a piece of underwear worn on the top part of the body close to the skin to keep one warm.

underside [ˈʌndərsaɪd] *n* **the underside** the lower part or surface of something □ *My car is badly rusted on the underside.*

undersigned [ˌʌndərˈsaɪnd] (*pl* **undersigned**) *n* **the undersigned** the person whose signature appears at the end of a particular document (formal use) □ *We, the undersigned, hereby declare that...*

undersize(d) [ˌʌndərˈsaɪz(d)] *adj* [person, object, clothing] smaller than other people or things of the same kind, or too small.

undersold [ˌʌndərˈsoʊld] *past tense & past participle of* **undersell**.

understaffed [US ˌʌndərˈstæft, GB ˌʌndəˈstɑːft] *adj* [organization, store, school] that does not have enough people to do all the work □ *The hospital is chronically understaffed.*

understand [ˌʌndərˈstænd] (*pt* & *pp* **understood**) ◇ *vt* **-1.** [word, book, language] to know the meaning of <sb/sthg> □ *I'm sorry, I don't understand the instructions.* □ *I understand what you're saying.* ■ **to make oneself understood** to make what one means clear □ *Have I made myself understood?* **-2.** [subject, theory, machine] to know how <sthg> works, how its parts relate to each other etc □ *I don't fully understand how a car engine works.* □ *No one really understands why some people develop symptoms of the disease and others don't.* **-3.** [person] to know why <sb> behaves or feels the way they do; [reaction, fear, objection] to accept <sb's behavior or feeling> because it is reasonable □ *My wife doesn't understand me.* □ *I understand how you must feel.* □ *I don't understand why he didn't complain earlier.* **-4. to understand (that)...** to believe that something is true, because one has been told □ *I understand you're looking for a job, Mr Benn?* □ *It is understood that he left for Dubai on Monday.* ◇ *vi: Leave me alone, understand?* □ *I want you to know I really do understand.*

understandable [ˌʌndərˈstændəbl] *adj* **-1.** [word, meaning] that one can understand. **-2.** [behavior, feeling] that one can understand because it is reasonable and usual □ *Your anger is natural and perfectly understandable.*

understandably [ˌʌndərˈstændəblɪ] *adv* [upset, annoyed, jealous] *see* **understandable** □ *Understandably, he was very angry.*

understanding [ˌʌndərˈstændɪŋ] ◇ *n* **-1.** [of a language, machine, person] the ability to understand something □ *I have a good understanding of computers though I'm not an expert.* **-2.** sb's understanding the meaning that sb gives to something □ *My understanding is that we are only allowed time off with our manager's approval.* **-3.** [between people] an informal agreement about something □ *We have come to an understanding about it all.* ■ **on the understanding that...** on the condition that... □ *I will lend you the car, on the understanding that any repairs are your responsibility.* **-4.** [toward other people] a feeling of sympathy and trust between people □ *We need more love and understanding.* ◇ *adj* [person] who is kind and forgives easily □ *Thank you. You've been very understanding.*

understate [ˌʌndərˈsteɪt] *vt* [difficulty, problem] to make <sthg> seem less important than it actually is □ *I think that's understating the extent of the problem.*

understated [ˌʌndərˈsteɪtəd] *adj* [elegance, humor] that is effective but not obvious.

understatement [ˌʌndərˈsteɪtmənt] *n* **-1.** a statement that seems to make something appear less strong, important etc than it really is □ *To say the meal was disappointing is an understatement.* **-2.** the practice of making understatements □ *Jack is a master of understatement.*

understood [ˌʌndərˈstʊd] *past tense & past participle of* **understand**.

understudy [ˈʌndərstʌdɪ] (*pl* **understudies**, *pt* & *pp* **understudied**) ◇ *n* a person who learns a particular part in a play in order to play that part if the original actor is ill. ◇ *vt* [actor, part] to be an understudy for <sb/sthg>.

undertake [ˌʌndərˈteɪk] (*pt* **undertook**, *pp* **undertaken** [-ˈteɪkən]) *vt* **-1.** [responsibility, control, task] to accept <sthg>, especially if it is difficult □ *Williams said he was unwilling to undertake such a responsibility alone.* **-2. to undertake to do sthg** to promise to do sthg □ *I'll do it, but I cannot undertake to finish it on time.*

undertaker [ˈʌndərteɪkər] *n* a person whose job is to deal with dead people's bodies and arrange their funerals. ■ **the undertaker's** the place where an undertaker carries out their business.

undertaking [ˌʌndərˈteɪkɪŋ] *n* **-1.** something that one has agreed to do and for which one is therefore responsible □ *Organizing and coordinating the whole event was no small undertaking.* **-2.** a promise (formal use) □ *I gave her my solemn undertaking that I would tell no one.*

undertone [ˈʌndərtoʊn] *n* **-1. in an undertone** with a quiet voice. **-2.** [of sadness, bitterness, emotion] a vague feeling that is expressed indirectly □ *Though her expression was serious, her voice had an undertone of amusement.*

undertook [ˌʌndərˈtʊk] *past tense of* **undertake**.

undertow [ˈʌndərtoʊ] *n* a strong current of water that exists below the surface of the ocean and that moves back toward the ocean as a wave breaks on the shore.

undervalue [ˌʌndərˈvæljuː] vt [person, antique, house] to consider <sb/sthg> to be less important than they really are □ *I think Paula's very much undervalued at work.*

underwater [ˌʌndərˈwɔːtər] ◇ adj **underwater exploration/filming etc** exploration/filming etc below the surface of the water. ◇ adv [swim, live] *These pictures were shot underwater.*

underwear [ˈʌndərweər] n items of clothing, e.g. undershirts, bras, and underpants, that one wears next to one's skin under one's other clothes.

underweight [ˌʌndərˈweɪt] adj who weighs less than they should or than is normal.

underwent [ˌʌndərˈwent] past tense of **undergo**.

underwired [ˌʌndərˈwaɪərd] adj **an underwired bra** a bra that has a thin strip of wire, plastic etc under each breast to give extra support.

underworld [ˈʌndərwɜːrld] n **the underworld** criminals when considered as a group in society.

underwrite [ˌʌndəˈraɪt] (pt **underwrote**, pp **underwritten**) vt **-1.** [activity, project] to agree to take financial responsibility for <sthg>, especially if it fails. **-2.** to agree to pay the costs involved in <an insurance agreement> if a claim is made.

underwriter [ˈʌndəˈraɪtər] n a person whose job is to examine a risk and calculate the cost of insuring against it.

underwritten [ˌʌndərˈrɪtn] past participle of **underwrite**.

underwrote [ˌʌndərˈrout] past tense of **underwrite**.

undeserved [ˌʌndɪˈzɜːrvd] adj [praise, promotion, criticism] that somebody or something should not get because they do not deserve it.

undesirable [ˌʌndɪˈzaɪərəbl] adj [consequences, delay] that one considers to be bad and so wants to avoid; [person] who is regarded as being dangerous or having a bad influence on others.

undeveloped [ˌʌndɪˈveləpt] adj [country] that does not have industry or modern methods of agriculture.

undid [ʌnˈdɪd] past tense of **undo**.

undies [ˈʌndɪz] npl underwear (informal use).

undignified [ʌnˈdɪgnəfaɪd] adj [person] who behaves in a way that is silly or embarrassing □ *They were shouting and screaming at each other — it was all very undignified.*

undiluted [ˌʌndaɪˈluːtəd] adj **-1.** [quality, emotion] that is pure and strong □ *a moment of undiluted pleasure.* **-2.** [liquid] that is in its pure form with nothing added to make it less strong.

undiplomatic [ˌʌndɪpləˈmætɪk] adj [person, statement, behavior] that shows a lack of concern for other people's feelings and is likely to cause offense.

undischarged [ˌʌndɪsˈtʃɑːrdʒd] adj **-1.** [debt, account] that has not been paid. **-2. an undischarged bankrupt** a person who is bankrupt but still owes money.

undisciplined [ʌnˈdɪsəplənd] adj [person, behavior, work] that shows a lack of discipline.

undiscovered [ˌʌndɪˈskʌvərd] adj [fact, area, person] that nobody has discovered or knows about □ *The truth remained undiscovered for centuries.*

undisputed [ˌʌndɪˈspjuːtəd] adj **-1.** [leader] whose position is clearly recognized and accepted by everyone □ *the undisputed champion of the world.* **-2.** [fact, power] that is certainly true or real and that nobody can doubt □ *It is an undisputed fact that the man's a crook.*

undistinguished [ˌʌndɪˈstɪŋgwɪʃt] adj [person, performance] that is not particularly good, but is also not very bad (disapproving use).

undivided [ˌʌndɪˈvaɪdəd] adj **to give sb/sthg one's undivided attention** to listen or pay attention to sb/sthg without thinking about other people or things.

undo [ʌnˈduː] (pt **undid**, pp **undone**) vt **-1.** [knot, buttons, zipper] to open or loosen <sthg>, especially on clothes □ *Could you undo the clasp on my necklace?* **-2.** [shirt, jacket] to open <a piece of clothing> by undoing its buttons, zipper etc □ *He undid his shirt quickly.* **-3.** [work, efforts, mistake] to destroy the effects of <sthg that has been done> □ *Nothing can undo the damage caused by the story.*

undoing [ʌnˈduːɪŋ] n **to be sb's undoing** to be the cause of sb's failure, ruin etc (formal use) □ *Changing parties could be her political undoing.*

undone [ʌnˈdʌn] ◇ past participle of **undo**. ◇ adj **-1. to be undone** [zipper, button, piece of clothing] not to be fastened or closed □ *Your buttons are coming undone.* **-2. to leave sthg undone** [work, job] not to do sthg □ *I hate to leave a job undone.*

undoubted [ʌnˈdaʊtəd] adj [skill, success] that is definitely real or true □ *Despite his undoubted talent, he needs to work hard as well.*

undoubtedly [ʌnˈdaʊtədlɪ] adv [true, good] certainly □ *Undoubtedly the strike will cause great disruption.*

undreamed-of [ʌnˈdriːmd-], **undreamt-of** [ʌnˈdremt-] adj [wealth, level] that is more than anyone ever thought possible before □ *He has achieved previously undreamed-of results.*

undress [ʌnˈdres] ◇ vi to take off one's clothes. ◇ vt to take the clothes off <sb>.

undressed [ʌnˈdrest] adj [person] who has no, or not many, clothes on. ■ **to get undressed** to take off one's clothes.

undrinkable [ˌʌnˈdrɪŋkəbl] adj **-1.** [water, drink] that is dangerous to drink. **-2.** [wine, drink] that tastes too bad to drink.

undue [ˌʌnˈdjuː] adj **undue haste/pressure etc** haste/pressure etc that is more than is suitable, helpful, or necessary (formal use) □ *I didn't want to attract any undue attention.*

undulate [ˈʌndʒʊleɪt] vi [hills, landscape, road] to have gentle curves or slopes (literary use).

unduly [ʌnˈdjuːlɪ] adv [concern, surprise, disturb] too much, and more than is reasonable □ *However, I was not unduly worried.*

undying [ʌnˈdaɪɪŋ] adj **undying love/fame etc** love/fame etc that is so great that it will last forever (literary use).

unearned income [ˌʌnɜːrnd-] n money one

gets from investments, property etc rather than from a job.

unearth [ʌnˈɜːθ] *vt* **-1.** [treasure, coin, bone] to find <sthg buried in the ground>. **-2.** [fact, secret] to discover <sthg that is not known or has been kept secret> □ *I was determined to unearth the truth about his death.*

unearthly [ʌnˈɜːθlɪ] *adj* **-1.** [silence, sound, sight] that is strange or frightening because one cannot explain it. **-2. at an unearthly hour** too early in the morning (informal use) □ *What do you mean by calling me at this unearthly hour?*

unease [ʌnˈiːz] *n* the feeling of being uneasy □ *I began to experience a growing sense of unease.*

uneasy [ʌnˈiːzɪ] (*compar* **uneasier,** *superl* **uneasiest**) *adj* **-1.** feeling worried because something might be wrong or something bad might happen □ *I'm uneasy about having to trust someone I don't know.* □ *an uneasy feeling.* **-2.** [person, sleep] that is not relaxed □ *Eventually I drifted into an uneasy sleep.* **-3.** [peace, alliance] that is not very settled and might not last very long □ *There is an uneasy ceasefire here for the second day running.*

uneatable [ˌʌnˈiːtəbl] *adj* **-1.** [food] that is dangerous to eat. **-2.** [meal, food] that tastes too bad to eat.

uneaten [ˌʌnˈiːtn] *adj* [food] that is left after the rest of a meal has been eaten □ *She left half her lunch uneaten.*

uneconomic [ˌʌniːkəˈnɒmɪk] *adj* [business, industry] that does not make enough profit, or makes no profit □ *The bus company canceled the service because they said it was uneconomic.*

uneducated [ˌʌnˈedʒʊkeɪtəd] *adj* **-1.** [person] who has not had any education. **-2.** [person] who behaves badly because they have not been educated properly (disapproving use).

unemotional [ˌʌnɪˈmoʊʃnəl] *adj* [person, voice, statement] that shows no feelings.

unemployable [ˌʌnɪmˈplɔɪəbl] *adj* [person] who will probably not get a job, often because they have no skills or because they cause problems.

unemployed [ˌʌnɪmˈplɔɪd] ◇ *adj* [person] who has no job but wants one □ *Most of the people I know are unemployed.* ◇ *npl* **the unemployed** the people in society who are unemployed.

unemployment [ˌʌnɪmˈplɔɪmənt] *n* **-1.** the number of people who are unemployed □ *Unemployment has come down recently.* **-2.** the state of being unemployed □ *a long period of unemployment.*

unemployment compensation US, **unemployment benefit** GB *n* money that the state gives to people who are unemployed.

unending [ʌnˈendɪŋ] *adj* [torment, struggle] that seems as if it will continue forever.

unenviable [ʌnˈenvɪəbl] *adj* [task, reputation, record] that nobody wants because it is difficult or unpleasant □ *She was given the unenviable task of breaking the bad news.*

unequal [ʌnˈiːkwəl] *adj* **-1.** [competition, distribution, pay] that is not fair because it gives an advantage to a particular person or group of people □ *This gives our competitors an unequal advantage over us.* **-2.** [amounts, sizes, number] not equal in amount, size etc □ *two sticks of unequal length.*

unequaled US, **unequalled** GB [ʌnˈiːkwəld] *adj* [beauty, experience, level] that is better than all other things of a similar type □ *His record remains unequaled.*

unequivocal [ˌʌnɪˈkwɪvəkl] *adj* [answer, refusal, statement] whose meaning is completely clear (formal use) □ *The Senator responded with an unequivocal denial.*

unerring [US ʌnˈerɪŋ, GB ʌnˈɜːrɪŋ] *adj* [aim, ability, sense] that is always right □ *Ralph has an unerring eye for a bargain.*

UNESCO [juːˈneskoʊ] (*abbr of* **United Nations Educational, Scientific and Cultural Organization**) *n* a branch of the UN, based in Paris, that aims to encourage peace and respect for human rights through cooperation between rich and poor countries.

unethical [ˌʌnˈeθɪkl] *adj* [behavior, conduct] that is wrong according to a particular system of beliefs about what is right and wrong □ *Such practices are unethical and should be condemned.*

uneven [ʌnˈiːvn] *adj* **-1.** [surface, ground] that is not flat, smooth, or straight □ *The road became uneven, little more than a rough track.* **-2.** [performance, work] that is not always of good quality □ *The writing is uneven, but overall I enjoyed the book.* **-3.** [competition, race, match] that is not fair because it is between people or things that are not equal □ *I think the race was very uneven.*

uneventful [ˌʌnɪˈventfl] *adj* [day, trip] during which nothing important or interesting happens.

unexceptional [ˌʌnɪkˈsepʃnəl] *adj* [person, quality] that is not very interesting or impressive.

unexpected [ˌʌnɪkˈspektəd] *adj* [pleasure, death, surprise] that makes one feel surprised because one does not expect it □ *Her reaction was totally unexpected.*

unexpectedly [ˌʌnɪkˈspektədlɪ] *adv* [die, arrive, happen] *see* **unexpected** □ *There has been an unexpectedly high demand for these products.*

unexplained [ˌʌnɪkˈspleɪnd] *adj* [mystery, disappearance, death] whose cause is not known.

unexploded [ˌʌnɪkˈsploʊdəd] *adj* [bomb, mine] that has not exploded and so is still dangerous.

unexpurgated [ʌnˈekspərˌgeɪtəd] *adj* [book, text] that is complete, with no rude or offensive parts removed.

unfailing [ʌnˈfeɪlɪŋ] *adj* [loyalty, support, good humor] that is always there and that one can depend on □ *He always treated me with unfailing kindness.*

unfair [ˌʌnˈfeər] *adj* [treatment, system] that is not right because people are not all treated in the same way; [criticism, situation] that is not reasonable or acceptable according to one's idea of right and wrong □ *The rules give some people an unfair advantage over others.* □ *I think you're being very unfair to poor Mike.*

unfair dismissal *n* the act of taking away an employee's job without a proper or legal reason □ *Jones sued his employers for unfair dismissal.*

unfairly [ˌʌnˈfeəʳlɪ] *adv* [treat, criticize, dismiss] see **unfair**.

unfaithful [ʌnˈfeɪθfl] *adj* **to be unfaithful to sb** to secretly have sex with somebody while one is married to or having a romantic or sexual relationship with sb else.

unfamiliar [ˌʌnfəˈmɪljəʳ] *adj* **-1.** [place, feeling, language] that one does not know much about because one has not experienced it before □ *His name may be unfamiliar to most people.* **-2. to be unfamiliar with sthg** [with the facts, a procedure, place] to know little or nothing about sthg because one has not experienced it before □ *I'm unfamiliar with the streets around here.*

unfashionable [ˌʌnˈfæʃnəbl] *adj* [dress, idea, activity] that is not popular at a particular time, especially because it is not considered modern by most people.

unfasten [US ʌnˈfæsn, GB -ˈfɑːsn] *vt* [belt, buttons] to open <sthg that is fastened> □ *Do not unfasten your safety belts until the plane has come to a complete stop.*

unfavorable US, **unfavourable** GB [ʌnˈfeɪvrəbl] *adj* **-1.** [conditions, terms] that do not seem suitable and will probably not lead to a positive result □ *Unfavorable weather conditions delayed the launching of the satellite.* **-2.** [opinion, impression] that shows one does not like somebody or something □ *His new play has opened to unfavorable reviews.*

unfeeling [ʌnˈfiːlɪŋ] *adj* [person, attitude, action] that does not show concern for other people's feelings □ *How can you be so unfeeling?*

unfinished [ˌʌnˈfɪnɪʃt] *adj* [business, job] that has not been done completely; [drink, meal] that has not been finished □ *She left her supper unfinished on the table.*

unfit [ʌnˈfɪt] *adj* **-1.** [person] who is not in good physical condition because they do not exercise regularly □ *I feel very unfit at the moment; I must get some more exercise.* **-2. to be unfit for sthg** to be unsuitable for sthg because of being in a bad state □ *This food is unfit for human consumption.* □ *I would say he was unfit to drive.*

unflagging [ʌnˈflægɪŋ] *adj* [energy, enthusiasm, support] that is impressive because it continues for a long time at the same level.

unflappable [ʌnˈflæpəbl] *adj* [person] who remains calm and confident even in difficult circumstances (informal use).

unflattering [ˌʌnˈflætərɪŋ] *adj* [dress, description] that makes somebody appear less attractive than they really are □ *The book gives a very unflattering picture of his mother.*

unflinching [ʌnˈflɪntʃɪŋ] *adj* [person] who is not easily stopped from doing something by pain, fear etc □ *unflinching support/loyalty.*

unfold [ʌnˈfoʊld] ◇ *vt* **-1.** [newspaper, map] to open <sthg> so that it is no longer folded. **-2.** [plan, proposal, vision] to present and explain the different parts of <sthg> □ *Jerry is here to unfold details of the new plan.* ◇ *vi* [story, plot, truth] to become gradually clearer □ *We watched in amazement as events began to unfold.*

unforeseen [ˌʌnfɔːʳˈsiːn] *adj* [circumstances, difficulty] unexpected □ *As long as there are no unforeseen problems things should go fine.*

unforgettable [ˌʌnfəʳˈgetəbl] *adj* [person, evening, experience] that has a very strong positive effect on one and is remembered for a long time □ *The Northern Lights are an unforgettable sight.*

unforgivable [ˌʌnfəʳˈgɪvəbl] *adj* [action, behavior, statement] that is unacceptable and cannot be excused □ *That was an unforgivable thing to do.*

unformatted [ˌʌnˈfɔːʳmætəd] *adj* [computer disk] that has not yet been prepared so that it can receive data.

unfortunate [ʌnˈfɔːʳtʃənət] *adj* **-1.** [person, experience] unlucky □ *He was very unfortunate to have missed his flight.* **-2.** [error, remark, name] that causes embarrassment or regret □ *It was an unfortunate remark, to say the least.*

unfortunately [ʌnˈfɔːʳtʃənətlɪ] *adv* a word used to show that one feels disappointment, sadness, or regret about something □ *Unfortunately, Richard won't be able to join us for dinner this evening.*

unfounded [ʌnˈfaʊndəd] *adj* [accusation, rumor, belief] that has not been proved or is not based on facts □ *Luckily these fears proved to be unfounded.*

unfriendly [ʌnˈfrendlɪ] (*compar* **unfriendlier**, *superl* **unfriendliest**) *adj* [person, behavior, remark] that shows no desire to have a good relationship with other people □ *I found her family cold and unfriendly.*

unfulfilled [ˌʌnfʊlˈfɪld] *adj* **-1.** [dream, ambition] that has not been achieved in reality; [potential] that has not been used or developed enough □ *It was an ambition that was to remain unfulfilled.* **-2.** [person] who feels that they are not using or developing their good qualities and abilities enough □ *She feels unfulfilled in her new job.*

unfurl [ˌʌnˈfɜːʳl] *vt* to unroll <a flag, sail> etc so that it can be used.

unfurnished [ˌʌnˈfɜːʳnɪʃt] *adj* [apartment, room, accommodation] that has no furniture in it.

ungainly [ʌnˈgeɪnlɪ] *adj* [person, animal, manner] that is not elegant or graceful in movement □ *a tall ungainly man.*

ungenerous [ʌnˈdʒenərəs] *adj* **-1.** [person, action, attitude] that does not show much generosity □ *It was a not ungenerous sum.* **-2.** [remark] that is unfair □ *I think his criticism of you was ungenerous.*

ungodly [ʌnˈgɒdlɪ] *adj* **-1.** [act, behavior, remark] that shows no respect for religion. **-2. an ungodly hour** a time of the day or night that one considers unacceptable (informal use) □ *Why are you phoning me at this ungodly hour?*

ungrateful [ʌnˈgreɪtfl] *adj* [person, behavior, response] that shows no gratitude □ Don't be so ungrateful!

unguarded [ʌnˈɡɑːˈdəd] adj -1. **to leave sthg unguarded** [building, valuables] to leave sthg unprotected and so not safe from burglary, theft etc. -2. **in an unguarded moment** in a moment when one is not being careful about what one is saying □ She showed her true feelings in an unguarded moment.

unhappily [ʌnˈhæpəli] adv -1. [live, think] see **unhappy**. -2. a word used to show that one feels sad, disappointed, or frustrated about something (formal use) □ Unhappily, we can report no improvement in the situation.

unhappiness [ʌnˈhæpɪnəs] n [of a person, somebody's life, thoughts] see **unhappy** □ His drinking was a cause of much unhappiness between them.

unhappy [ʌnˈhæpɪ] (compar **unhappier**, superl **unhappiest**) adj -1. [person] who is not happy, especially because they are in an unpleasant situation □ She seems really unhappy at the moment — do you know what's wrong? □ It was an unhappy marriage. -2. **to be unhappy** to have strong doubts or worries about something □ We are unhappy with OR about the way things are progressing. □ She was unhappy about my spending so much money. -3. [coincidence, remark] that causes embarrassment or regret □ He later apologized for his unhappy choice of words.

unharmed [ʌnˈhɑːˈmd] adj [person] who is not hurt in any way after a serious accident or dangerous event □ The hostages escaped/were released unharmed.

UNHCR (abbr of **United Nations High Commission for Refugees**) n the UNHCR a branch of the UN that aims to protect the rights and welfare of refugees.

unhealthy [ʌnˈhelθɪ] (compar **unhealthier**, superl **unhealthiest**) adj -1. [person] who may be affected by illness or bad health, e.g. because of their diet or way of life; [skin, appearance] that does not look healthy □ I feel so unhealthy at the moment. -2. [diet, lifestyle, activity] that can cause illness or bad health □ Smoking is an extremely unhealthy habit. -3. [interest, preoccupation, attitude] that seems extreme and may have harmful effects □ Her feelings for him have become an unhealthy obsession.

unheard [ʌnˈhɜːˈd] adj **to be** OR **go unheard** [comments, warnings, advice] to be ignored □ His cries for help went unheard.

unheard-of adj -1. **to be unheard-of** [activity, phenomenon] to never happen □ Political opposition was unheard-of before the revolution. □ Cholera is now almost unheard-of in Europe. -2. [event, cost] that is very unusual and so surprising or shocking □ It's unheard-of for him to apologize!

unheeded [ʌnˈhiːdəd] adj **to go unheeded** [comments, warnings] to be ignored □ Professor Bank's advice went unheeded with dire results.

unhelpful [ʌnˈhelpfl] adj -1. [person, attitude] that shows no desire or willingness to help □ I found the staff extremely unhelpful. -2. [comment, advice, interference] not useful □

Harry's comments were more unhelpful than anything else.

unhindered [ʌnˈhɪndəˈd] adj [movement, exchange, progress] that is not made difficult in any way □ The crowd parted and we were able to continue unhindered.

unhook [ʌnˈhʊk] vt [dress, bra] to undo the hooks of <sthg>, e.g. in order to take it off.

unhurt [ʌnˈhɜːˈt] adj [person] who is not injured after a serious accident or dangerous event □ They were lucky to escape unhurt.

unhygienic [US ʌnhaɪdʒɪˈenɪk, GB ʌnhaɪˈdʒiːnɪk] adj [place, conditions, practice] in which germs are able to spread, making infection or disease more likely.

UNICEF [ˈjuːnɪsef] (abbr of **United Nations International Children's Emergency Fund**) n a branch of the UN that aims to protect the rights and welfare of children in poor countries.

unicorn [ˈjuːnɪkɔːˈn] n an imaginary creature like a white horse with a long horn at the front of its head.

unicycle [ˈjuːnɪsaɪkl] n a piece of equipment like a bicycle with only one wheel, used by entertainers, circus performers etc.

unidentified [ʌnaɪˈdentɪfaɪd] adj [person, animal] whose identity is not known □ The raid was carried out by two unidentified gunmen at eleven o'clock this morning.

unidentified flying object n → UFO.

unification [ˌjuːnɪfɪˈkeɪʃn] n: see **unify**.

uniform [ˈjuːnɪfɔːˈm] ◇ adj [size, color] that is the same in every part of something □ uniform pay increases. ◇ n a special set of clothes worn by the people who do a particular job, e.g. police officers and nurses, and by children at some schools □ She was in uniform.

uniformity [ˌjuːnɪˈfɔːˈmətɪ] n a uniform state or quality □ uniformity of approach.

uniformly [ˈjuːnɪfɔːˈmlɪ] adv [distributed, sized] see **uniform** □ performances of a uniformly high standard.

unify [ˈjuːnɪfaɪ] (pt & pp **unified**) vt [country, political party] to bring together parts of <sthg> to form one unit □ Italy was unified in the 19th century.

unifying [ˈjuːnɪfaɪɪŋ] adj **a unifying theme/force** etc a theme/force etc that unifies.

unilateral [ˌjuːnɪˈlætərəl] adj [action] that a group, organization etc decides to do alone without the agreement of other groups or organizations involved □ unilateral nuclear disarmament □ a unilateral ceasefire.

unimaginable [ˌʌnɪˈmædʒənəbl] adj [suffering, horror] that is hard to imagine because it is worse than most people have experienced □ What these children have been through is almost unimaginable.

unimaginative [ˌʌnɪˈmædʒɪnətɪv] adj [person, idea, design] that does not show much imagination □ This year's festival program was disappointingly unimaginative.

unimpaired [ˌʌnɪmˈpeəˈd] adj [eyesight, hearing] that is not damaged or made worse in any way □ *Luckily, his vision was unimpaired by the accident.*

unimpeded [ˌʌnɪmˈpiːdɪd] *adj* [view, activity] that is not made difficult or interrupted by anything □ *We were then able to continue our discussion unimpeded.*

unimportant [ˌʌnɪmˈpɔːʳtnt] *adj* [detail, person] that is not important □ *What you meant to say is unimportant now.*

unimpressed [ˌʌnɪmˈprest] *adj* **to be unimpressed** to think that somebody or something is not very good or interesting □ *I was singularly unimpressed by his new girlfriend.*

uninhabited [ˌʌnɪnˈhæbətəd] *adj* [island, area, building] that has no people living there □ *a row of derelict uninhabited houses.*

uninhibited [ˌʌnɪnˈhɪbətəd] *adj* [person] who feels relaxed with other people and is not afraid to show their true character and feelings □ *She is very uninhibited about nudity.*

uninitiated [ˌʌnɪˈnɪʃɪeɪtəd] *npl* **the uninitiated** people who have no knowledge or experience of a particular skill, craft, procedure etc (formal or humorous use).

uninjured [ˌʌnˈɪndʒəʳd] *adj* [person] who is not injured after an accident or dangerous event □ *They escaped uninjured.*

uninspiring [ˌʌnɪnˈspaɪərɪŋ] *adj* [person, speech] that does not cause excitement or enthusiasm □ *Mrs Took's lessons were uninspiring, to put it mildly.*

uninstall [ˌʌnɪnˈstɔːl] *vt* to delete <part of a computer program> from one's hard disk after one has installed it.

unintelligent [ˌʌnɪnˈtelədʒənt] *adj* [person, action] that is stupid.

unintelligible [ˌʌnɪnˈtelədʒəbl] *adj* [word, writing] that is impossible to understand □ *The man stood there shouting something unintelligible.*

unintentional [ˌʌnɪnˈtenʃnəl] *adj* [mistake, damage] that is not done deliberately □ *Any resemblance to a real person is purely unintentional.*

uninterested [ʌnˈɪntərəstəd] *adj* [person] who is not interested □ *Andy seemed totally uninterested in what I had to say.*

uninterrupted [ˌʌnɪntəˈrʌptəd] *adj* [sequence, period] that is continuous and has no interruptions □ *uninterrupted views across the valley* □ *Forbes was finally able to continue his speech uninterrupted.*

uninvited [ˌʌnɪnˈvaɪtəd] *adj* [guest, visitor] who comes without being invited □ *I hope you don't mind us turning up uninvited.*

union [ˈjuːnjən] *n* **-1.** = **labor union** □ *The unions are meeting today to discuss possible strike action.* □ *Have you paid your union dues?* **-2.** a word often used in the names of clubs and societies □ *the Student Union.* **-3.** the act of joining a number of things together; the result of an act like this □ *the union of African states* □ *the Soviet Union.*

◆ **Union** *n* **the Union** the Northern states during the American Civil War.

Unionist [ˈjuːnjənəst] *n* GB POLITICS a member or a supporter of a party that believes that

Northern Ireland should remain part of the United Kingdom.

unionize, -ise [ˈjuːnjənaɪz] *vt* to organize <a group of workers> to join or form a labor union.

unionized, -ised [ˈjuːnjənaɪzd] *adj* [workforce, company] that has been organized to join or form a labor union.

Union Jack [-ˈdʒæk] *n* **the Union Jack** the official flag of the United Kingdom, made up of the crosses of St George, St Andrew, and St Patrick.

Union of Soviet Socialist Republics → USSR.

union shop *n* US a place of work where all the employees must belong to a particular labor union.

unique [juːˈniːk] *adj* **-1.** [example, occasion] that is the only one of its kind □ *Each person is unique.* **-2.** [achievement, opportunity] that is very special and unusual □ *A stay in our luxurious beachside hotel is a unique experience.* **-3. to be unique to sb/sthg** to be found in or be connected to sb/sthg only □ *a problem unique to this region.*

uniquely [juːˈniːklɪ] *adv* [talented, satisfying] *see* **unique** □ *a uniquely British phenomenon.*

unisex [ˈjuːnɪseks] *adj* [clothes, hairdresser's] that is designed for both men and women.

unison [ˈjuːnɪsən] *n* **in unison** [act, work] in complete agreement; [say] together □ *"Yes, sir!" they chanted in unison.* ■ **to sing in unison** to sing the same notes together at the same time.

UNISON [ˈjuːnɪsən] *n* a large British labor union for employees in the public services.

unit [ˈjuːnɪt] *n* **-1.** a group of people or things considered as one complete thing □ *the family unit.* **-2.** [of measurement] a standard measure of something, e.g. distance or weight □ *The unit of electricity consumption is the kilowatt-hour.* □ *The patient received five units of morphine.* **-3.** [in a machine] a set of mechanical or electrical parts that has a particular function in a larger machine □ *Replace the filter unit every three months.* **-4.** [of furniture] a piece of furniture that can be put together with other pieces and usually has a particular function □ *a storage/hi-fi unit.* **-5.** [in an organization] a group of workers that has a particular job in a larger organization □ *He was taken to the burn unit.* **-6.** [in a textbook] a chapter in a textbook □ *Turn to Unit Three.*

unitary authority *n* in Britain, an area where one local government council is responsible for all public services.

unit cost *n* BUSINESS the cost of producing one item.

unite [juːˈnaɪt] ◇ *vi* [countries, organizations] to join together and work as a group, especially in order to do something that both or all want □ *We must unite to oppose these changes.* ◇ *vt* [countries, organizations] to make <a group of people or things> unite □ *Can the President unite the party behind him?*

united [juːˈnaɪtəd] *adj* acting together to do

something that everybody wants □ *We want a more united Europe.* □ *We are united in our pursuit of a fairer and more democratic society.*

United Arab Emirates: the United Arab Emirates a country in southeastern Arabia, consisting of seven states on the Persian Gulf. It is a major oil exporter. SIZE: 80,000 sq kms. POPULATION: 2,400,000 (*Emirians*). CAPITAL: Abu Dhabi. LANGUAGE: Arabic. CURRENCY: UAE dirham.

united front *n* **to present a united front** to show other people that all the members of one's group or organization have the same opinion about something.

United Kingdom: the United Kingdom (of Great Britain and Northern Island) a term used to refer to England, Wales, Scotland, and Northern Ireland, considered as a political unit.
NOTE: Compare **Great Britain**.

United Nations *n* **the United Nations (Organization)** an international organization created at the end of World War II whose aim is to encourage peaceful relations between countries in order to avoid wars.

United States: the United States (of America) a country in North America, between Canada and Mexico. SIZE: 9,364,000 sq kms. POPULATION: 258,300,000 (*Americans*). CAPITAL: Washington D.C. LANGUAGE: English. CURRENCY: US dollar.

United Way *n* **the United Way** an association of several US charity organizations.

unit price *n* the price of one item of goods.

unit trust *n* GB an investment company that sells shares in various other companies.

unity ['juːnətɪ] *n* -1. [of a country, political party] a situation in which all the members of a group or organization have the same beliefs, opinions, aims etc □ *national/political unity.* -2. a situation in which people are in peaceful agreement about things □ *a state of unity.*

Univ. *abbr of* **University**.

universal [ˌjuːnəˈvɜːʳsl] *adj* [belief, truth, language] that is shared by everybody in the world; [interest, agreement] that is shared by everybody in a particular group □ *The wish to be loved is universal.* □ *Her books have a universal appeal.*

universal joint *n* a joint between two parts of a machine that allows the parts to move in all directions.

universe ['juːnəvɜːʳs] *n* ASTRONOMY **the universe** the whole of space and all the planets, stars, moons etc in it.

university [ˌjuːnəˈvɜːʳsətɪ] (*pl* **universities**) *n* a place where people study after leaving school, usually for a degree; the people who work and study in this place □ *She's hoping to go to university* GB OR *the university* US. □ *He's studying politics at a university in California.* □ *a university education/student/team* □ *university fees/staff.*

UNIX™ ['juːnɪks] *n* an operating system used mainly in large powerful computer systems.

unjust [ˌʌnˈdʒʌst] *adj* [system, remark, act] that

does not treat a particular person or group very well or fairly □ *I felt their criticism of my actions was very unjust.*

unjustifiable [ˌʌndʒʌstɪˈfaɪəbl] *adj* [conclusion, expense, attack] that is not acceptable because no good reason or excuse can be given for it.

unjustified [ʌnˈdʒʌstɪfaɪd] *adj* [conclusion, expense, attack] for which there is no good reason or excuse.

unkempt [ˌʌnˈkempt] *adj* [hair, beard, appearance] that looks untidy.

unkind [ˌʌnˈkaɪnd] *adj* -1. [person] who treats people badly and makes them unhappy □ *He was very unkind to me.* □ *an unkind comment/ thought.* -2. [weather, climate] that has a bad effect on somebody or something □ *This cold weather is very unkind to skin, so use a moisturizer.*

unkindly [ʌnˈkaɪndlɪ] *adv* [speak, criticize, behave] *see* **unkind**.

unknown [ˌʌnˈnoʊn] ◇ *adj* -1. [actor, writer] who is not well known by the public □ *an unknown artist.* -2. [cause, number, result] that is not known □ *for reasons unknown* □ *The cause of the contamination is unknown.* ◇ *n* -1. **the unknown** a place or situation that one does not know and that may be dangerous □ *fear of the unknown.* -2. an actor, writer etc who is not well known by the public □ *The part was taken by a young unknown.*

unladen [ˌʌnˈleɪdn] *adj* **unladen weight** the weight of a truck, ship etc when it is empty.

unlawful [ʌnˈlɔːfl] *adj* [behavior, activity, demonstration] that is against the law.

unleaded [ˌʌnˈledəd] *adj* [gasoline] that has had some of the lead removed from it in order to reduce pollution.
NOTE: Compare **leaded**.

unleash [ʌnˈliːʃ] *vt* [violence, abuse, emotions] to suddenly make <sthg powerful> happen (literary use) □ *Her remarks unleashed a storm of protest.*

unleavened [ˌʌnˈlevnd] *adj* **unleavened bread** bread that is made without yeast and so is quite flat and hard.

unless [ənˈles] *conj* -1. **unless he gets a bank loan, he'll go bankrupt** he'll go bankrupt, but only if he does not get a bank loan □ *I'll assume everything is OK unless I hear otherwise.* □ *They said that unless I paid up, they would take me to court.* -2. **unless I'm very much mistaken, that's Jane** that must be Jane, because otherwise I have made a mistake and I do not think this is very likely.

unlicensed [ʌnˈlaɪsnst] *adj* [fishing, hunting] that is done without a license and so is illegal; [car] that is driven illegally because it does not have a license; [restaurant] that does not have a license to serve alcohol.

unlike [ˌʌnˈlaɪk] *prep* -1. that is different from <sb/sthg> □ *He's quite unlike his brother.* □ *It's not unlike the old system.* -2. a word used to show the difference between two actions, situations etc □ *They arrived on time, unlike yes-*

terday. **-3.** that is not typical of <sb/sthg> □ *It's very unlike you to complain.*

unlikely [ʌn'laɪklɪ] *adj* **-1.** [event, result] that will probably not happen □ *In the unlikely event of our losing the contract...* □ *They are unlikely to come now.* **-2.** [story, detail] that is probably not true □ *It sounds unlikely.* **-3.** [person, choice] that is not what one would have expected □ *He always turns up at the most unlikely times.*

unlimited [ʌn'lɪmətəd] *adj* [amount, time, opportunity] that has no fixed limit □ *You're allowed unlimited amounts of wine with the set menu.*

unlisted [ʌn'lɪstəd] *adj* US [phone number] that is not in the telephone directory.

unlit [ʌn'lɪt] *adj* **-1.** [fire, cigarette] that is not burning. **-2.** [street, building] that is not lit by electric lighting.

unload [ʌn'loʊd] *vt* **-1.** [luggage, cases] to take <sthg> out of the vehicle in which it has been carried □ *We watched them unloading the cargo from the ship.* **-2.** [car, ship, truck] to remove the contents from <a vehicle>. **-3. to unload one's worries/problems etc on(to) sb** to tell one's worries/problems etc to sb else.

unlock [ʌn'lɒk] *vt* [door, suitcase] to turn a key in the lock of <sthg> so that it can be opened.

unloved [ʌn'lʌvd] *adj* [person] who feels that they are not loved by anybody.

unluckily [ʌn'lʌkɪlɪ] *adv* a word used to show that one thinks that something has happened as the result of bad luck □ *Unluckily for Tom, his wife walked in just at that moment.*

unlucky [ʌn'lʌkɪ] (*compar* **unluckier,** *superl* **unluckiest**) *adj* **-1.** [person] who has bad luck □ *You've just been unlucky, that's all.* **-2.** [choice, encounter] that brings bad luck □ *The number 13 is considered by some people to be unlucky.*

unmanageable [ʌn'mænɪdʒəbl] *adj* **-1.** [child, class] that is hard to control □ *Is your hair dry and unmanageable?* **-2.** [problem, workload] that is too great to deal with.

unmanly [ˌʌn'mænlɪ] (*compar* **unmanlier,** *superl* **unmanliest**) *adj* [behavior, reaction] that is thought to be unsuitable for a man.

unmanned [ˌʌn'mænd] *adj* [spacecraft, flight] that has no crew on board.

unmarked [ˌʌn'mɑːʳkt] *adj* **-1. to be unmarked** [skin, face] to have no cuts or bruises, e.g. after a fight. **-2.** [police car, grave] that has no mark of identification.

unmarried [US ˌʌn'merɪd, GB -'mær-] *adj* [couple, mother] who has never been married.

unmask [US ˌʌn'mæsk, GB -'mɑːsk] *vt* **-1.** [burglar, highwayman, terrorist] to take the mask off the face of <sb>. **-2.** [hypocrite, cheat, traitor] to show the real character of <sb>; [fraud, hypocrisy] to make <sthg> public □ *He was unmasked as a former Soviet agent.*

unmatched [ˌʌn'mætʃt] *adj* **to be unmatched** [performance, service] to be better than all others of the same type.

unmentionable [ʌn'menʃnəbl] *adj* [word, topic] that is not suitable for conversation because it is considered rude or embarrassing.

unmistakable [ˌʌnmɪ'steɪkəbl] *adj* [smell, taste] that allows one to recognize something without doubt □ *There was an unmistakable air of satisfaction about her.*

unmitigated [ʌn'mɪtəgeɪtəd] *adj* **an unmitigated disaster/failure** a complete disaster/failure.

unmoved [ʌn'muːvd] *adj* **to be** OR **remain unmoved** to feel and show no pity or sympathy □ *Who could remain unmoved by the images of this terrible war?*

unnamed [ˌʌn'neɪmd] *adj* [source, donor] whose name is not published or not known.

unnatural [ʌn'nætʃrəl] *adj* **-1.** [silence, power] that is not what one normally expects □ *She seems to have no feeling at all for those children — it's unnatural!* **-2.** [dialogue, behavior] that is different from what happens in normal life □ *The way people speak in 1940s movies seems unnatural to us today.*

unnecessary [ʌn'nesəserɪ] *adj* [anxiety, trouble] not necessary □ *I don't want you to go to any unnecessary trouble for us.*

unnerving [ˌʌn'nɜːʳvɪŋ] *adj* [silence, experience] that makes one feel nervous □ *Chloe has an unnerving ability to guess what's on my mind.*

unnoticed [ˌʌn'noʊtəst] *adj* **to go** OR **pass unnoticed** to happen without anybody noticing □ *Fortunately, my absence went unnoticed.*

UNO ['juːnoʊ] *n abbr of* **United Nations Organization.**

unobserved [ˌʌnəb'zɜːʳvd] *adj* who is not seen by anybody □ *She slipped out unobserved.*

unobtainable [ˌʌnəb'teɪnəbl] *adj* **-1.** [product] that is impossible to find or buy. **-2.** [telephone number] that is impossible for the caller or operator to contact.

unobtrusive [ˌʌnəb'truːsɪv] *adj* [building, sign] that is not too obvious; [visitor, presence] not causing any disturbance.

unoccupied [ʌn'ɒkjəpaɪd] *adj* **-1.** [house, room, table] not lived in or being used. **-2.** [person] who has nothing to do. **-3.** [territory, zone] that is not occupied by a foreign army.

unofficial [ˌʌnə'fɪʃl] *adj* **-1.** [visit, action] that is not arranged or allowed by the authorities □ *a one-day unofficial strike.* **-2.** [report, rumor] that is not yet officially confirmed □ *The takeover will go ahead — it's still unofficial though.*

unopened [ˌʌn'oʊpənd] *adj* [envelope, package, can] that has not been opened.

unorthodox [ʌn'ɔːʳθədɒks] *adj* [behavior, belief] that is original and different from what is accepted by most people.

unpack [ˌʌn'pæk] ◇ *vt* **-1.** [bag, suitcase] to take the contents out of <sthg>. **-2.** [clothes, shopping] to take <sthg> out of the bag or suitcase in which it has been carried. ◇ *vi: Have you unpacked yet?*

unpaid [ˌʌn'peɪd] *adj* **-1.** [person] who works without being paid; [job, work] that is voluntary and receives no pay; [vacation] that is taken without pay □ *He's taken unpaid leave.* **-2.** [bill, account] that has not yet been paid.

unpalatable [ʌn'pælətəbl] *adj* [truth, idea] that

one finds unpleasant to think about or difficult to accept.

unparalleled [US ʌn'pærəleld, GB -'pær-] *adj* [success, achievement] that is better than all others of the same type □ *the unparalleled success of the new CD-ROM.*

unpatriotic [US ˌʌnpeɪtrɪ'ɒtɪk, GB -pæt-] *adj* [person, attitude, act] that does not show enough support for one's own country.

unpick [ˌʌn'pɪk] *vt* to remove <the stitches> from a piece of sewing or clothing.

unplanned [ˌʌn'plænd] *adj* [pregnancy, visit, activity] that has not been planned.

unpleasant [ʌn'pleznt] *adj* **-1.** [experience, taste] that one does not like or enjoy □ *The initial effects of the treatment are fairly unpleasant.* **-2.** [person] who seems rude and unfriendly □ *There's no need to be unpleasant about it!*

unpleasantness [ʌn'plezntnəs] *n* unfriendly feelings or arguments between people □ *There was a certain amount of unpleasantness.*

unplug [ʌn'plʌg] (*pt* & *pp* **unplugged**, *cont* **unplugging**) *vt* [kettle, television] to remove the electrical plug of <sthg> from a socket.

unpolluted [ˌʌnpə'luːtəd] *adj* [air, water] that is pure and not polluted.

unpopular [ʌn'pɒpjələr] *adj* [person, decision, tax] that is disliked by most people.

unprecedented [ʌn'presədəntəd] *adj* [increase, success] that is larger, more important etc than anything that has ever happened before □ *unprecedented amounts of rainfall.*

unpredictable [ˌʌnprɪ'dɪktəbl] *adj* [weather, outcome] that is impossible to predict accurately because it is always changing; [person] who changes a lot so that it is impossible to know how they are going to behave □ *These things are always pretty unpredictable.* □ *Laura's moods can be very unpredictable.*

unprepared [ˌʌnprə'peərd] *adj* [person] who is not expecting something and therefore finds it hard to deal with when it happens □ *I was unprepared for this turn of events.*

unprepossessing [ˌʌnpriːpə'zesɪŋ] *adj* [person, sight] that is ordinary and not very noticeable.

unpretentious [ˌʌnprɪ'tenʃəs] *adj* [setting, home] that is simple; [person] who does not try to make other people think that they are better or more important than they really are □ *The local cuisine is wholesome and unpretentious.*

unprincipled [ʌn'prɪnsəpld] *adj* [person] who does not behave according to moral principles.

unprintable [ʌn'prɪntəbl] *adj* [reply, comment] that is too rude or offensive to be printed in a newspaper.

unproductive [ˌʌnprə'dʌktɪv] *adj* [meeting, discussion] that does not produce any useful results; [land] that does not produce crops.

unprofessional [ˌʌnprə'feʃnəl] *adj* [attitude, behavior] that is below the standards expected of a person in a particular job □ *I find such conduct highly unprofessional.*

unprofitable [ˌʌn'prɒfətəbl] *adj* [business, venture] that does not make a profit.

unpronounceable [ˌʌnprə'naʊnsəbl] *adj* [name, word] that is impossible to pronounce.

unprotected [ˌʌnprə'tektəd] *adj* **-1. unprotected sex** the activity of having sex without using a condom. **-2.** [head, body] that is not protected from possible injury.

unprovoked [ˌʌnprə'vəʊkt] *adj* [attack, insult] that is not caused by something that somebody else has said or done □ *It was a vicious unprovoked act of aggression.*

unpublished [ˌʌn'pʌblɪʃt] *adj* [novel, manuscript, letter] that has never been printed for people to read; [author, writer] whose works have never been published.

unpunished [ʌn'pʌnɪʃt] *adj* **to go unpunished** not to be punished □ *Such acts of random violence cannot be allowed to go unpunished.*

unqualified [ʌn'kwɒləfaɪd] *adj* **-1.** [person] who does not have any qualifications that prove they can do a job □ *It's almost impossible to find work if you are unqualified.* **-2.** [admiration, success] complete □ *You have my unqualified support.*

unquestionable [ʌn'kwestʃənəbl] *adj* [advantage, improvement] a word used to show that one feels sure about what one is saying □ *Her talent as an actress is unquestionable.*

unquestioning [ʌn'kwestʃənɪŋ] *adj* [acceptance, reliance] that one has not thought enough about □ *unquestioning obedience.*

unravel [ʌn'rævl] (US *pt* & *pp* **unraveled**, *cont* **unraveling**, GB *pt* & *pp* **unravelled**, *cont* **unravelling**) ◇ *vt* **-1.** [knitting, ball of wool] to undo <sthg> by unwinding the thread. **-2.** [problem, mystery] to solve <sthg> by finding out how it happened. ◇ *vi*: *The stitching/mystery has started to unravel.*

unreadable [ʌn'riːdəbl] *adj* **-1.** [text, book] that is difficult to read because it is boring or complex. **-2.** [handwriting] that is impossible to read because it is not neat. **-3.** COMPUTING [disk] that cannot be recognized by a computer.

unreal [ʌn'rɪəl] *adj* **-1.** [situation, feeling] that is strange and not like real life □ *Everything seemed unreal during those weeks in Rio.* **-2.** [quality, level] that one thinks is extremely good (informal use) □ *The taste is unreal!*

unrealistic [ˌʌnrɪə'lɪstɪk] *adj* [expectation, idea] that is not based on reality; [person] who does not take account of what is likely to happen □ *There's no point making unrealistic forecasts.* □ *You're being unrealistic.*

unreasonable [ʌn'riːznəbl] *adj* [demand, pressure] that is greater than what is fair or sensible □ *It's unreasonable to expect too much of a seven-year-old.*

unrecognizable [ˌʌn'rekəgnaɪzəbl] *adj* [place, person] that is/ impossible to recognize because of change or injury □ *The town was unrecognizable after so many years of war.*

unrecognized [ˌʌn'rekəgnaɪzd] *adj* **-1.** [need, effort, contribution] that is not noticed or considered important by people. **-2.** [person]

who is not recognized by people who have met them before.

unrecorded [ˌʌnrɪ'kɔːʳdəd] *adj* **-1.** [comment, view] that is not written down, and cannot therefore be checked. **-2.** [session, performance] that is not recorded on tape or video.

unrefined [ˌʌnrɪ'faɪnd] *adj* **-1.** [oil, sugar, flour] that has not been made purer by industrial processes. **-2.** [behavior, person] that is not polite.

unrehearsed [ˌʌnrɪ'hɜːʳst] *adj* [outburst, speech] that is not planned in advance.

unrelated [ˌʌnrɪ'leɪtəd] *adj* [incidents, events] that are not connected to each other, although they may be similar in some way □ *This incident is unrelated to last week's explosion.*

unrelenting [ˌʌnrɪ'lentɪŋ] *adj* [pressure, opposition] that continues for a long time without stopping (formal use).

unreliable [ˌʌnrɪ'laɪəbl] *adj* [equipment, method] that one cannot depend on; [person] who might disappoint one, e.g. by being late or not doing what they promise □ *John is so unreliable!*

unrelieved [ˌʌnrɪ'liːvd] *adj* [gloom, anxiety, boredom] that continues for a long time without getting any better □ *three weeks of boredom, unrelieved by any form of amusement.*

unremitting [ˌʌnrɪ'mɪtɪŋ] *adj* [effort, struggle] that continues for a long time without getting any weaker (formal use).

unrepeatable [ˌʌnrɪ'piːtəbl] *adj* **-1.** [offer, performance] that will not happen again. **-2.** [word, comment] that is too rude or offensive to repeat.

unrepentant [ˌʌnrɪ'pentənt] *adj* **-1.** [advocate, supporter] who strongly believes in a particular cause □ *an unrepentant champion of socialism.* **-2.** [person] who is not sorry for something they have done □ *He remains unrepentant.*

unrepresentative [ˌʌnreprə'zentətɪv] *adj* [sample, section] that is not typical of a larger group □ *These views are unrepresentative of the electorate as a whole.*

unrequited [ˌʌnrɪ'kwaɪtəd] *adj* **unrequited love** love that one has for somebody who does not love one.

unreserved [ˌʌnrɪ'zɜːʳvd] *adj* **-1.** [support, admiration] complete. **-2.** [seat, table] that is not reserved in advance.

unresolved [ˌʌnrɪ'zɒlvd] *adj* [problem, issue] that has not been dealt with satisfactorily.

unresponsive [ˌʌnrɪ'spɒnsɪv] *adj* **to be unresponsive to sthg** [to medical treatment, an appeal] not to react to sthg.

unrest [ʌn'rest] *n* a feeling of anger with the government, employers etc among a group of people, often expressed through riots and protests □ *industrial/social unrest.*

unrestrained [ˌʌnrɪ'streɪnd] *adj* [growth, violence] that is not controlled or limited in any way □ *a period of unrestrained economic growth.*

unrestricted [ˌʌnrɪ'strɪktəd] *adj* [access, power,

testing] that is not controlled or limited by any laws, rules etc.

unrewarding [ˌʌnrɪ'wɔːʳdɪŋ] *adj* [job, task] that is not pleasant to do because it does not give one any feeling of satisfaction □ *The work is not difficult, but it's pretty unrewarding.*

unripe [ˌʌn'raɪp] *adj* [fruit] that is not yet ready to eat.

unrivaled US, **unrivalled** GB [ʌn'raɪvld] *adj* that is better than all the others of the same type □ *The museum possesses an unrivaled collection of Indian art.*

unroll [ʌn'rəʊl] *vt* [poster, carpet, certificate] to pull one end of <sthg that is rolled up> so that it becomes flat.

unruffled [ʌn'rʌfld] *adj* [person] who is calm and not upset by a difficult situation □ *Claire remained calm and unruffled throughout the trial.*

unruly [ʌn'ruːlɪ] (*compar* **unrulier**, *superl* **unruliest**) *adj* **-1.** [child, class] that is badly-behaved and hard to control. **-2.** [hair] that does not stay in the style one wants it to stay in.

unsafe [ʌn'seɪf] *adj* **-1.** [building, conditions, appliance] dangerous. **-2. unsafe sex** sexual activities that carry a risk of spreading HIV, especially having sex without a condom. **-3. to feel unsafe** to feel that one is in danger.

unsaid [ʌn'sed] *adj* **to leave sthg unsaid** not to express something in words, usually because it would hurt somebody's feelings □ *Some things are better left unsaid.*

unsal(e)able [ˌʌn'seɪləbl] *adj* [product, house] that cannot be sold because nobody wants to buy it.

unsatisfactory [ˌʌnsætəs'fæktrɪ] *adj* [outcome, service, standard] that is not good enough.

unsavory US, **unsavoury** GB [ʌn'seɪvərɪ] *adj* [person, affair, revelation] that seems unpleasant and morally bad □ *A couple of unsavory-looking characters were hanging around outside.*

unscathed [ʌn'skeɪðd] *adj* **to be unscathed** not to be injured or harmed in any way after a serious accident.

unscheduled [US ˌʌn'skedʒuːld, GB ˌʌn'ʃedjuːld] *adj* [stop, visit] that is not planned in advance.

unscientific [ˌʌnsaɪən'tɪfɪk] *adj* [approach, method] that does not follow the principles of science, especially by not being objective.

unscrew [ˌʌn'skruː] *vt* **-1.** [cap, lid] to take <sthg> off by turning it. **-2.** [shelf, door] to remove <sthg> by taking out the screws that hold it in place.

unscrupulous [ʌn'skruːpjələs] *adj* [person] who is willing to do anything to get what they want, even if it means harming other people □ *unscrupulous behavior.*

unsealed road [ˌʌnsiːld-] *n* AUS a road that does not have a tarmacadam surface.

unseat [ˌʌn'siːt] *vt* **-1.** [horse] to throw off <a rider>. **-2.** [leader, governor] to remove <sb> from an official position of power, usually by an election.

unseeded [ˌʌn'siːdəd] *adj* [player] who is not

officially considered to be a likely winner in a tennis tournament.

unseemly [ʌn'siːmlɪ] (*compar* **unseemlier,** *superl* **unseemliest**) *adj* [conduct, behavior] that is not appropriate for a particular situation because it is vulgar, impolite etc (formal use).

unseen [ˌʌn'siːn] ◇ *adj* [person, object] not seen or noticed □ *an unseen observer.* ◇ *adv* [enter, leave] without being seen or noticed □ *We were able to sneak out of the auditorium unseen.*

unselfish [ʌn'selfɪʃ] *adj* [person, act] showing concern for other people rather than oneself.

unsettle [ʌn'setl] *vt* to make <sb> feel nervous □ *The news of her return unsettled me.*

unsettled [ʌn'setld] *adj* -1. [phase, period] that is not calm or stable. -2. [person] who feels nervous, worried, or excited about something and is unable to concentrate □ *After three years in India, she feels very unsettled back in England.* -3. [weather] that is likely to change quickly □ *The weather will be cloudy and unsettled.* -4. [issue, debate, question] that has not been brought to a satisfactory conclusion □ *questions that still remain unsettled.* -5. [debt, invoice] that has not been paid. -6. [area, region] where no people live.

unsettling [ʌn'setlɪŋ] *adj* [news, effect] that causes somebody to feel unsettled □ *The news had a very unsettling effect on us all.*

unshak(e)able [ʌn'ʃeɪkəbl] *adj* [faith, belief] that cannot be changed or made weaker.

unshaven [ˌʌn'ʃeɪvn] *adj* [face, chin] that is not shaved.

unsheathe [ʌn'ʃiːð] *vt* to take <a sword> from its sheath.

unsightly [ʌn'saɪtlɪ] *adj* [bruise, building] that is unpleasant to look at.

unskilled [ˌʌn'skɪld] *adj* [worker] who has had no formal training in a craft or trade; [job, work] that requires no special training and involves physical work.

unsociable [ʌn'soʊʃəbl] *adj* [person] who does not enjoy spending time with other people and having fun with them.

unsocial [ˌʌn'soʊʃl] *adj* **to work unsocial hours** GB to work at times of the day when most people are relaxing, e.g. late at night.

unsold [ˌʌn'soʊld] *adj* [house, merchandise] that has not been sold after being on sale for a period of time.

unsolicited [ˌʌnsə'lɪsətəd] *adj* [reply, advice] that is sent or given without being asked for □ *We get an enormous amount of unsolicited mail.*

unsolved [ˌʌn'sɒlvd] *adj* [mystery, crime] that has not been solved.

unsophisticated [ˌʌnsə'fɪstəkeɪtəd] *adj* -1. [person] whose tastes, clothes, attitudes etc are simple and natural and who knows little about modern fashionable things □ *an unsophisticated look/style.* -2. [device, approach] that is not very complicated or skillful.

unsound [ˌʌn'saʊnd] *adj* -1. [reasoning, argument, theory] that is not based on facts or reason. -2. [building, structure] that is not in

good condition and so likely to fall down. ■ **to be of unsound mind** to be mentally ill.

unspeakable [ʌn'spiːkəbl] *adj* [crime, pain, behavior] that is too bad to describe.

unspecified [ˌʌn'spesəfaɪd] *adj* [time, date, amount] that is not stated precisely □ *Police had discovered unspecified quantities of heroin.*

unspoiled [ˌʌn'spɔɪld], **unspoilt** [ˌʌn'spɔɪlt] *adj* -1. [person] who is not used to too much luxury or too much attention. -2. [condition, goods] that is not damaged. -3. [beach, countryside] that is still pretty and has not been spoiled by building or development □ *Thankfully, this part of the country is still relatively unspoiled.*

unspoken [ʌn'spoʊkən] *adj* -1. [feeling, thought] that is not expressed in words □ *So many things had remained unspoken between them.* -2. [understanding, agreement] that exists between two people without being discussed.

unsporting [ˌʌn'spɔːtɪŋ] *adj* [person] who behaves unfairly and selfishly, especially toward an opponent in a sporting event □ *unsporting behavior.*

unstable [ʌn'steɪbl] *adj* -1. [person] who is likely to change suddenly from one mood to another □ *I think his family background has made him pretty unstable.* -2. [structure, government] that is not strong and likely to collapse □ *The building has been declared unstable.*

unstated [ˌʌn'steɪtəd] *adj* [aim, desire] that is not expressed in words.

unsteady [ʌn'stedɪ] (*compar* **unsteadier,** *superl* **unsteadiest**) *adj* -1. [person] who is unable to balance properly because they are old, ill etc □ *He's rather unsteady on his feet.* -2. [ladder, chair] that is not firmly in position and likely to fall over.

unstinting [ʌn'stɪntɪŋ] *adj* [effort, kindness, praise] generous □ *She was, as always, unstinting in her generosity.*

unstoppable [ʌn'stɒpəbl] *adj* [person] who is determined and impossible to stop □ *Her rise to power seemed unstoppable.*

unstructured [ʌn'strʌktʃəʳd] *adj* [activity, group, system] that is not organized in a formal way □ *The lessons were very unstructured.*

unstuck [ˌʌn'stʌk] *adj* **to come unstuck** [label, stamp] to start to come off because the glue does not stick; [person] to start having problems after a period when one has been successful.

unsubstantiated [ˌʌnsəb'stænʃɪeɪtəd] *adj* [story, report] that is not supported by any proof.

unsuccessful [ˌʌnsək'sesfl] *adj* -1. [attempt, experiment] that fails □ *They tried to reach the survivors, but were unsuccessful.* -2. [candidate] who is not accepted for a job; who is not successful in an exam; [writer, actor] who has failed in a particular career □ *We regret to inform you that your application has been unsuccessful.*

unsuccessfully [ˌʌnsək'sesflɪ] *adv* [try, attempt] without success □ *We tried, unsuccessfully, to contact the girl's parents.*

unsuitable [ʌn'suːtəbl] *adj* [outfit, time, person]

that is not considered by other people to be appropriate for a particular situation, activity etc □ *She was unsuitable for the job, since she couldn't speak Spanish.*

unsuited [ʌn'suːtəd] *adj* **-1. to be unsuited to** OR **for sthg** [to a job, position] not to be the right sort of person for sthg □ *He is clearly unsuited to army life.* **-2. to be unsuited** [two people] not to be the sort of people who will naturally get on well with each other, especially in a relationship □ *They were entirely unsuited to each other from the beginning.*

unsung [ˌʌn'sʌŋ] *adj* [deed, hero] that deserves to be praised publicly but is not.

unsure [ˌʌn'ʃʊəʳ] *adj* **-1. to be** OR **feel unsure** not to have enough confidence □ *I feel unsure of myself in class discussions.* **-2. to be unsure about** OR **of sthg** [about a reaction, time, plan] to be uncertain about sthg □ *She was unsure (about) how to proceed.*

unsurpassed [US ˌʌnsɜr'pæst, GB ˌʌnsə'pɑːst] *adj* [excellence, elegance] that is so good that nothing has ever been better than it.

unsuspecting [ˌʌnsə'spektɪŋ] *adj* [person] who does not realize that something is happening or going to happen □ *His poor unsuspecting father came home to find a party in full swing.*

unsweetened [ˌʌn'swiːtnd] *adj* [drink, food] that has no sugar added to it.

unswerving [ʌn'swɜːʳvɪŋ] *adj* [devotion, dedication, loyalty] that continues for a long time without getting any weaker.

unsympathetic [ˌʌnsɪmpə'θetɪk] *adj* [person] who is not willing to feel sorry for somebody, or to help them with their problems □ *I hate to sound unsympathetic, but what has all this to do with me?*

untangle [ʌn'tæŋgl] *vt* [thread, wool, cord] to make <sthg> straight by removing the knots in it.

untapped [ˌʌn'tæpt] *adj* [reserves, supplies, resources] that have not been used before, but are probably valuable or useful □ *a hitherto untapped source of wealth.*

untaxed [ˌʌn'tækst] *adj* **untaxed income** income on which tax is not paid.

untenable [ʌn'tenəbl] *adj* [position, theory] that cannot be defended because it is easy to criticize □ *Ford's position was now untenable: he had no choice but to resign.*

unthinkable [ʌn'θɪŋkəbl] *adj* **to be unthinkable** [war, defeat] to be impossible to accept or agree with □ *It's unthinkable that I should give up now.*

unthinkingly [ʌn'θɪŋkɪŋlɪ] *adv* [act, support] without thinking about the possible consequences.

untidy [ʌn'taɪdɪ] (*compar* **untidier,** *superl* **untidiest**) *adj* [room, work, appearance] that is messy or not arranged in a neat way; [person] who leaves things in this state □ *His clothes lay on the floor in an untidy heap.*

untie [ˌʌn'taɪ] (*cont* **untying**) *vt* **-1.** [ribbon, laces] to undo a knot or knots in <a piece of string, rope> etc □ *Irma untied her scarf and draped it over the back of her chair.* **-2.** [package,

prisoner] to remove the rope or string tied around <sb/sthg>.

until [ən'tɪl] *prep & conj* **-1.** used to say that an event is happening before a particular time but not after it □ *Breakfast is served from 7:30 a.m. until 10 a.m.* □ *Up until that time I'd never really spoken much French.* □ *Keep in the left-hand lane until you come to a set of traffic lights.* **-2. not...until** used to say that something only starts happening after a particular time or after a particular event □ *His parents heard nothing more until July the following year.* □ *It wasn't until I got to work that I remembered I had a doctor's appointment.* □ *Basically, there's very little we can do until we get more evidence.*

untimely [ʌn'taɪmlɪ] *adj* **-1.** [end, departure] that happens sooner than one expected □ *After the untimely death of his father...* **-2.** [remark, arrival] that happens at an unsuitable moment □ *Her comment was untimely.*

untiring [ʌn'taɪərɪŋ] *adj* [person] who continues doing something without slowing down or stopping; [work, support] that continues over a long period of time without getting less or weaker □ *Our warmest thanks go to Miss Davenport for her untiring efforts on our behalf.*

untold [ˌʌn'toʊld] *adj* **untold wealth/suffering** very great wealth/suffering.

untouched [ˌʌn'tʌtʃt] *adj* **to be untouched** [person, place] not to be changed, affected, or damaged by something; [meal, food, drink] that has not been eaten or drunk □ *a remote village, untouched by the 20th century* □ *The building was untouched by the explosion.*

untoward [US ʌn'tɔːrd, GB ˌʌntə'wɔːd] *adj* [behavior, event] that is unexpected and causes problems □ *I didn't notice anything untoward.*

untrained [ˌʌn'treɪnd] *adj* **-1.** [staff, worker] who has not been trained in a particular job. **-2. an untrained voice** a voice that has not been formally trained. ■ **to the untrained eye** to somebody who is not an expert □ *To the untrained eye, they look the same.*

untrammeled US, **untrammelled** GB [ʌn'træməld] *adj* that is free and is not limited or restricted by rules (formal use).

untreated [ˌʌn'triːtəd] *adj* **-1.** [injury, illness, person] that has not received medical treatment. **-2.** [sewage, waste] that has not been made safe by chemical treatment.

untried [ˌʌn'traɪd] *adj* [method, product, weapon] that has not yet been tried or tested.

untroubled [ˌʌn'trʌbld] *adj* [person, attitude] not worried □ *She seemed strangely untroubled by the whole affair.*

untrue [ʌn'truː] *adj* **-1.** [statement, story] that is not true, often because it has been invented □ *It's untrue, every single word!* **-2. to be untrue to sb** to be unfaithful to sb.

untrustworthy [ˌʌn'trʌstwɜːʳðɪ] *adj* [person] who cannot be trusted.

untruth [ʌn'truːθ] *n* something that somebody says that is not true.

untruthful [ʌn'truːθfl] *adj* **-1.** [person] who does not tell the truth. **-2.** [remark, statement, answer] that is not true.

untutored [ˌʌnˈtjuːtərd] *adj* (formal use) -1. [person] who has not been trained or educated. -2. **to the untutored eye** to the untrained eye.

unusable [ˌʌnˈjuːzəbl] *adj* that is not in a good enough condition to be used.

unused [*sense 1* ˌʌnˈjuːzd, *sense 2* ʌnˈjuːst] *adj* -1. [clothes, machine, land] that has never been used, or has not been used for a long time. -2. **to be unused to sthg** not to be used to sthg □ *I am unused to (having) so much free time.*

unusual [ʌnˈjuːʒʊəl] *adj* [sight, occurrence] that is different from what is usual □ *It's unusual for him to be on time!* □ *It's unusual to see so many people here.*

unusually [ʌnˈjuːʒʊəlɪ] *adv* more than usual □ *She was unusually young for someone in her position.*

unvarnished [ʌnˈvɑːrnɪʃt] *adj* [truth, account, description] that has not had extra details added to it to make it more interesting or exciting.

unveil [ˌʌnˈveɪl] *vt* -1. [statue, painting, plaque] to remove a cover from <sthg> as part of a special public ceremony. -2. [plans, policy, product] to tell people about <sthg> for the first time □ *The government has unveiled plans for a new highway.*

unwaged [ˌʌnˈweɪdʒd] GB ◇ *adj* [person] who does not have a paid job □ *Are you waged or unwaged?* ◇ *npl* **the unwaged** people who are unwaged.

unwanted [ˌʌnˈwɒntəd] *adj* [object, child, pregnancy] that is not wanted □ *It was an unwanted Christmas present.*

unwarranted [ʌnˈwɒrəntəd] *adj* that one cannot accept because there is no good reason for it □ *She did her best to avoid unwarranted attention.* □ *That was completely unwarranted!*

unwavering [ʌnˈweɪvərɪŋ] *adj* [loyalty, support, commitment] that is strong and never becomes weaker.

unwelcome [ʌnˈwelkəm] *adj* that is not wanted □ *I was made to feel unwelcome.* □ *an unwelcome situation/experience.*

unwell [ʌnˈwel] *adj* **to be/feel unwell** to be/feel ill, usually not seriously.

unwieldy [ʌnˈwiːldɪ] (*compar* **unwieldier**, *superl* **unwieldiest**) *adj* -1. [object, tool] that is difficult to move, carry etc because it is very big or heavy. -2. [system, organization] that is too large and complicated to work efficiently.

unwilling [ʌnˈwɪlɪŋ] *adj* [worker, helper] who does not want to do something □ *He was unwilling to say anything without his lawyer present.*

unwind [ˌʌnˈwaɪnd] (*pt* & *pp* **unwound**) ◇ *vt* [bandage, thread] to undo <sthg that has been wrapped up or wrapped round something else>. ◇ *vi* to relax gradually after a period of work, concentration, stress etc □ *He likes a drink to help him unwind.*

unwise [ˌʌnˈwaɪz] *adj* [decision, action] that is not a good idea, because it causes problems for one □ *That was an unwise move to make.* □ *It would be unwise of you to agree.*

unwitting [ʌnˈwɪtɪŋ] *adj* (formal use) -1. **an un-**

witting victim/accomplice etc a person who does not know that they are a victim/an accomplice etc. -2. [insult, remark, action] that is not intended.

unwittingly [ʌnˈwɪtɪŋlɪ] *adv* without knowing or understanding what one is doing □ *She unwittingly participated in their scheme.*

unworkable [ʌnˈwɜːkəbl] *adj* [idea, plan, system] that is impossible to do or use.

unworldly [ʌnˈwɜːrldlɪ] *adj* [person] naive.

unworthy [ʌnˈwɜːrðɪ] (*compar* **unworthier**, *superl* **unworthiest**) *adj* **to be unworthy of sthg** [of honor, love, attention] not to deserve sthg.

unwound [ˌʌnˈwaʊnd] *past tense* & *past participle of* **unwind**.

unwrap [ˌʌnˈræp] (*pt* & *pp* **unwrapped**, *cont* **unwrapping**) *vt* [package] to open <sthg> by taking off the paper that covers it.

unwritten rule [ˌʌnrɪtn-] *n* a way of doing something that everybody follows but that is not a legal or official rule.

unyielding [ʌnˈjiːldɪŋ] *adj* [person, attitude] that continues to resist pressure, opposition etc and is unlikely to change.

unzip [ˌʌnˈzɪp] (*pt* & *pp* **unzipped**, *cont* **unzipping**) *vt* [jacket, case] to open the zipper on <a bag, piece of clothing> etc.

up [ʌp] (*pt* & *pp* **upped**, *cont* **upping**) ◇ *adv* -1. **to look/climb up** to look/climb toward a higher position □ *You can go right up to the top of the tower.* ■ **to pick/lift sthg up** to pick/lift sthg from the ground, floor, table etc □ *A large crane hauled the cargo up onto the deck.* -2. **a house up in the mountains** a house in a high place in the mountains □ *It's up here.* □ *She's up in her bedroom.* -3. **to get/jump up** to get/jump into an upright or standing position from a chair, bed etc □ *Sit up straight!* □ *Help me up, will you?* -4. **to go up to Seattle** to go north from one's home etc to Seattle □ *They live somewhere up north.* -5. **to go/run up to sb** to go/run toward sb and stop □ *This stranger came up to me and introduced himself.* □ *I heard a car pull up outside.* -6. **prices have gone up** prices have become more or higher □ *Inflation has shot up by 3%.* □ *Can you turn up the volume?* -7. **to tear/divide sthg up** to tear/divide sthg into smaller parts □ *The family was split up and the children taken into care.* -8. **to add/collect sthg up** to add/collect sthg together in one place □ *I gathered up all my belongings and left.* -9. **to pin/fix sthg up** to pin/fix sthg on a wall, bulletin board etc in a place where it can be seen □ *There are posters up all over town.* -10. **to eat/drink sthg up** to eat/drink sthg until it is all finished. -11. **to clean/tidy (sthg) up** to make sthg clean/tidy again □ *You can sweep up the kitchen.* -12. **the right/wrong way up** with the right/wrong side on top □ *'This Side Up.'*

◇ *prep* -1. **to go up a hill** to go from a lower place on a hill to a higher one □ *I ran up the stairs.* □ *The smoke went up the chimney.* -2. **to walk up a street** to walk along a street toward its far end □ *Her office is just up the corridor from mine.* -3. **to sail up a river** to sail along a river in the direction that leads away from the sea.

◇ *adj* **-1. to be/get up** [person] to be/get out of bed □ *Are you still up?* □ *The baby kept us up half the night.* **-2. to be up** [period of time] to be finished □ *My trial period is up next week.* ■ **time's up** a phrase used to announce that the time for doing an exam, job etc is finished. **-3. the road is up** the road cannot be used because it is being repaired. **-4. two points up** winning by two points □ *Sales are up 15% on last year.* **-5. what's up (with her)?** what is wrong or the matter (with her)? (informal use) □ *There's something up (with my car).* **-6. to be up and running** [system, project] to have started and be working satisfactorily □ *The new factory should be up and running within two months.*

◇ *n* **ups and downs** good things and bad things that happen to one □ *We all have our ups and downs.*

◇ *vt* [prices, cost] to make <an amount> more or higher (informal use) □ *We'll have to up our offer.*

◆ **up against** *prep* **-1. to be up against sthg/sb** [resistance, problems] to have to deal with sthg/sb difficult □ *We came up against some stiff opposition.* **-2.** very close to <sthg> and touching it □ *My knees were pressed up against the seat in front.*

◆ **up and about** *adj* [person] well and out of bed after an illness □ *I'm glad to see you're up and about again, Molly.*

◆ **up and down** *adv* **-1.** [jump, bounce] upward and downward repeatedly. **-2.** [walk, pace] in one direction and back again repeatedly.

◆ **up for** *prep* **to be up for sthg** to have to undergo sthg soon □ *The case is coming up for review next month.*

◆ **up to** *prep* **-1.** used to give a maximum limit □ *The job could take up to six weeks.* □ *This message applies to everyone, up to and including senior managers.* **-2. up to 5 o'clock** until 5 o'clock □ *I felt fine up to last week.* **-3. to be/feel up to doing sthg** to be/feel well enough to do sthg □ *I'm not up to going out tonight.* ■ **to be up to sthg** to be good enough or able to do sthg □ *He's very inexperienced — do you think he's up to it?* ■ **it's not up to much** it's not very good □ *My French isn't up to much.* **-4. to be up to sthg** [person] to be doing sthg secretly, usually something bad (informal use) □ *What are you up to?* **-5. it's up to you** it's your responsibility or choice □ *The decision is entirely up to you.* □ *It is up to Personnel to check people's references.*

◆ **up until** *prep* **up until Christmas** until Christmas □ *Don't leave it up until the last moment.*

up-and-coming *adj* [performer, athlete] who will soon be very successful and popular.

up-and-up *n* **-1. on the up-and-up** getting better or more successful □ *At last my life seems to be on the up-and-up.* **-2. on the up-and-up** US honest (informal use).

upbeat ['ʌpbiːt] *adj* [person, message, forecast] that seems relaxed and optimistic, especially

when the situation is quite difficult (informal use).

upbraid [ʌp'breɪd] *vt* to speak angrily to <sb> about something wrong they have done and criticize them for it (formal use).

upbringing ['ʌpbrɪŋɪŋ] *n* the care, education, treatment etc one receives as a child, especially from one's parents □ *I had a good/strict/deprived upbringing.*

upcoming ['ʌpkʌmɪŋ] *adj* **an upcoming event** an event that is going to happen soon □ *the upcoming elections.*

update [,ʌp'deɪt] *vt* [file, information, equipment] to change <sthg> so that it is more modern, e.g. by adding new information or parts.

upend [ʌp'end] *vt* to put <sthg> on its end or upside down □ *The box was upended.*

upfront [,ʌp'frʌnt] *adj* **to be upfront** to be open and honest □ *He was very upfront about how he felt.*

◆ **up front** *adv* [pay, give, get] as payment in advance □ *I need $20/10% up front.*

upgrade [,ʌp'greɪd] *vt* **-1.** [facilities, system, equipment] to improve the standard of <sthg>, e.g. by buying a more recent model of a piece of equipment □ *I've upgraded my computer system.* **-2.** [employee, job, status] to give <sb/sthg> a higher or more important position. **-3.** [passenger] to give <sb> a better class of seat on a plane □ *On the return flight I was upgraded to business class.*

upheaval [ʌp'hiːvl] *n* great change that causes worry, confusion, and sometimes violence □ *social/political/emotional upheaval.*

upheld [ʌp'held] *past tense & past participle of* **uphold.**

uphill [,ʌp'hɪl] ◇ *adj* **-1.** [path, road, slope] that rises. **-2. an uphill struggle/task** a struggle/task that is difficult and needs a lot of effort. ◇ *adv* [walk, drive] toward a higher position.

uphold [ʌp'hoʊld] (*pt & pp* **upheld**) *vt* **-1.** [law, principle, system] to defend <sthg>. **-2.** LAW [verdict, decision] to confirm <sthg> officially □ *The appeal court upheld the judge's decision.*

upholster [ʌp'hoʊlstər] *vt* [chair, sofa] to provide <a piece of furniture> with a soft filling and covering.

upholstery [ʌp'hoʊlstəri] *n* **-1.** the materials used to upholster a sofa, chair etc. **-2.** the covering for the seats in a car.

upkeep ['ʌpkiːp] *n* [of a building, car, garden] the process or cost of keeping something in good condition.

upland ['ʌplənd] *adj* **an upland pasture/forest etc** a pasture/forest etc that is on high land.

◆ **uplands** *npl* an area of high land.

uplift [ʌp'lɪft] *vt* to make <sb> feel more cheerful and full of hope □ *I felt uplifted by his speech.*

uplifting [ʌp'lɪftɪŋ] *adj* [experience, speech] that makes one feel happy and full of hope.

uplighter ['ʌplaɪtər] *n* a lamp that reflects light upward □ *a halogen uplighter.*

up-market ◇ *adj* [product, hotel] that is designed for or used by people who are rich □

a chic, up-market restaurant. ◇ *adv*: Let's go up-market and buy a better one.

upon [ə'pɒn] *prep* (formal use) -1. used as a more formal word for "on" □ We sat upon the grass. □ She had a foolish grin upon her face. -2. **upon arrival/departure** at the time of or shortly after arriving/leaving □ Payment is due upon delivery. □ Upon hearing the news, I rushed to the telephone. -3. **Christmas is upon us** very soon it will be Christmas. -4. **mile upon mile** very many miles (used for emphasis) □ The slopes were covered with row upon row of vines.

upper ['ʌpəʳ] ◇ *adj* -1. [lip, part, section] that is the higher part of something that is divided into two parts □ The upper half of her body was completely paralyzed. -2. [branches, echelons] that are nearer the top of something. -3. GEOGRAPHY that is further from the sea □ the upper valley of the Nile. ◇ *n* the top part of a shoe that is joined to the sole.

Upper Chamber *n* in a law-making body that has two chambers, the smaller and less powerful one, e.g. the senate in the USA.

upper class *n* **the upper class(es)** the highest social class, usually consisting of the people who have the most money and power.

◆ **upper-class** *adj*: an upper-class accent/school.

upper-crust *adj* upper-class (informal use).

uppercut ['ʌpəʳkʌt] *n* a punch with which one hits somebody's chin from below.

upper hand *n* **to have the upper hand** to be in a stronger position than other people who are against one □ He always seems to get the upper hand in an argument.

Upper House *n* = Upper Chamber.

upper middle class ◇ *n* **the upper middle class** the social class consisting mainly of wealthy professionals and business people. ◇ *adj*: an upper-middle-class suburb.

uppermost ['ʌpəʳmoʊst] *adj* -1. highest □ I couldn't reach the uppermost shelf. -2. **to be uppermost in one's mind** to be the thing that one is thinking about most.

uppity ['ʌpəti] *adj* [person] who is rude because they behave as if they are important, even though they are not (informal use).

upright ['ʌpraɪt] ◇ *adj* -1. [person] who is standing with a straight back; [object] that is pointing straight up and is not leaning to one side. -2. **an upright chair** a chair that has a straight back and no arms. -3. **an upright freezer/cabinet etc** a freezer/cabinet etc that is tall and narrow, not low and wide. -4. [person, citizen] honest, honorable, and responsible □ He's an upright member of the community. ◇ *adv* [sit, stand] Hold it upright. ◇ *n* [of a door, bookshelf, goal] a part of something that stands up and supports another part.

upright piano *n* a piano in which the strings are contained in a tall narrow box behind the keyboard.

uprising ['ʌpraɪzɪŋ] *n* an attempt to get rid of the people who are in power, made by a large number of people using violent methods.

uproar ['ʌprɔːʳ] *n* -1. the noise made by a lot of people who are shouting because they are angry and shocked □ His speech couldn't be heard above the uproar. -2. an angry protest □ The new proposals provoked (an) uproar in the teaching profession.

uproarious [ʌp'rɔːrɪəs] *adj* -1. [crowd, meeting] where there is a lot of very noisy laughter. -2. [film, joke] very funny.

uproot [ʌp'ruːt] *vt* -1. to remove <sb> from the place where they are living □ Many people were uprooted from their homes by the war. ■ **to uproot oneself** to leave one's place of birth, home etc □ She uprooted herself and went to live abroad. -2. [tree, weed] to pull <a plant> out of the ground □ A number of oak trees were uprooted in the storm.

upscale ['ʌpskeɪl] *adj* = up-market.

upset [*adj* & *vb* ʌp'set, *n* 'ʌpset] (*pt* & *pp* **upset**, *cont* **upsetting**) ◇ *adj* -1. **to be upset** to be unhappy and disappointed about something; to be offended by something □ He was very upset when he heard the news. □ She was really upset that you hadn't asked her. -2. **to have an upset stomach** to have a slight illness in one's stomach.
◇ *n* -1. **to have a stomach upset** to have a slight illness in one's stomach. -2. an unexpected result, e.g. in an election or sports event □ The team's victory was a major upset.
◇ *vt* -1. to make <sb> upset □ I didn't want to upset her but I had to tell her the news. □ I suppose I'll have to invite him if I don't want to upset him. -2. [arrangements, routine] to make <sthg> go wrong □ John's arrival upset all my plans. -3. [boat, cup] to turn <sthg> over accidentally □ I managed to upset the goldfish bowl.

upsetting [ʌp'setɪŋ] *adj* [experience, news] that makes one feel upset □ I found the whole experience very upsetting.

upshot ['ʌpʃɒt] *n* **the upshot** the final result of something □ What was the upshot of it all then?

upside down [ˌʌpsaɪd-] ◇ *adj* that is turned around so that the top part is at the bottom □ The picture is upside down! ◇ *adv* [hold, hang, place] The plate landed upside down on the floor. ■ **to turn sthg upside down** [building, room, cupboard] to search sthg completely, leaving it in a mess □ I turned the office upside down looking for that file!

upstage [ˌʌp'steɪdʒ] *vt* to make people notice and admire one more than <sb> by being more interesting or attractive □ The President was upstaged by ten-year-old Katy Smith, who captivated the audience.

upstairs [ˌʌp'steəʳz] ◇ *adj* **an upstairs window/room etc** a window/room etc that is on a floor above the ground floor. ◇ *adv* on or to a higher floor □ Our neighbors upstairs are very noisy. □ He went upstairs to the bedroom. □ The toilet is upstairs. ◇ *n* **the upstairs** [of a building] the floor or floors above the ground floor.

upstanding [ˌʌp'stændɪŋ] *adj* [person] who is honest and responsible □ a fine upstanding member of the community.

upstart ['ʌpstɑːʳt] *n* a person who has recently risen to a position of power and who uses

urinal

this power in a way that annoys other people (disapproving use) □ *I'm not being spoken to like that by some little upstart!*

upstate [ˌʌpˈsteɪt] US ◇ *adj* northern □ *upstate Vermont.* ◇ *adv* [live, move, work] in or to the northern part of the state □ *They've moved upstate.*

upstream [ˌʌpˈstriːm] ◇ *adj* in the opposite direction from the way a river, stream etc flows □ *The bridge is a few miles upstream from here.* ◇ *adv* [move, sail, swim] *We paddled upstream for a while.*

upsurge [ˈʌpsɜːrdʒ] *n* -1. [of hatred, unrest, resentment] a sudden appearance of something □ *The transport of live cattle has led to an upsurge of protest.* -2. [in unemployment, sales, investment] a sudden rise in something □ *There has been an upsurge in the number of homeless people.*

upswing [ˈʌpswɪŋ] *n* [in economic activity, popularity] a sudden improvement or increase in something.

uptake [ˈʌpteɪk] *n* **to be quick/slow on the uptake** to be quick/slow to understand something.

uptight [ʌpˈtaɪt] *adj* [person] who is bad-tempered because they are nervous or worried (informal use).

up-to-date *adj* -1. [equipment, technology, methods] the most recent or newest □ *We use only the most up-to-date technology.* -2. [publication, report] that includes the most recent information □ *Do you have a more up-to-date edition?* ■ **to keep up-to-date with sthg** [with news, events] to make sure one has the most recent information about sthg □ *I try to keep up-to-date with the latest developments.*

up-to-the-minute *adj* [information, report] the most recent that there is □ *Stay tuned for more up-to-the-minute coverage of world events.*

uptown [ˌʌpˈtaʊn] US ◇ *adj* that is in the northern part of a city, especially New York City □ *He lives in an uptown residential district.* ◇ *adv* [go, live, work] in or to the northern part of a city.

upturn [ˈʌptɜːrn] *n* [in business, economy, the market] an improvement in something after a bad period.

upturned [ʌpˈtɜːrnd] *adj* -1. [face, nose] that turns upward. -2. [car, cup, bucket] that has been turned upside down.

upward [ˈʌpwərd] ◇ *adv* -1. **to look/point upward** to look/point toward a higher position □ *The smoke was drifting slowly upward into the air.* -2. **to drive** OR **force sthg upward** to make sthg become greater or more □ *Estimates of the cost have since been revised upward.* -3. **face upward** with one's face looking toward the sky. -4. **children aged ten and upward, children from the age of ten upward** children aged ten and more. ◇ *adj* **an upward trend/movement** a trend/movement that makes something greater or more □ *the upward spiral of inflation.*

◆ **upward of** *prep* more than <a particular

number> □ *There must have been upward of 150 people there.*

upwardly-mobile [ˌʌpwərdlɪ-] *adj* [person] who is in the process of moving up from a lower social class to a higher one.

upwards [ˈʌpwərdz] *adv* = upward.

◆ **upwards of** *prep* = upward of.

upwind [ˌʌpˈwɪnd] *adj* in the opposite direction from the way the wind is blowing □ *The town was a few miles upwind of the explosion.*

URA (*abbr of* **Urban Renewal Administration**) *n* **the URA** a US government department responsible for rebuilding parts of cities that have been neglected.

Ural Mountains [ˌjʊərəl-] = Urals.

Urals [ˈjʊərəlz]: **the Urals** a mountain range in western Russia that is considered to be the border between Europe and Asia. HIGHEST POINT: 1,894 m.

uranium [jʊˈreɪnjəm] *n* a radioactive metal used to make nuclear power and nuclear weapons. SYMBOL: U.

Uranus [ˈjʊərənəs] the planet in the solar system that is seventh-furthest from the Sun.

urban [ˈɜːrbən] *adj* [deprivation, development] that is connected with a town or city □ *urban regeneration.* NOTE: Compare **rural**.

urbane [ɜːrˈbeɪn] *adj* [person] who behaves with good manners and confidence in social situations.

urbanize, -ise [ˈɜːrbənaɪz] *vt* to build homes, businesses, industries etc on <land in the countryside>.

urban renewal *n* the process of demolishing old buildings in areas of a town or city and building new houses, businesses etc there.

urchin [ˈɜːrtʃən] *n* a young child who has no home, family, or money and lives in the streets of a city (old-fashioned use).

Urdu [ˈʊərduː] *n* a language spoken in Pakistan and parts of India.

urge [ɜːrdʒ] ◇ *n* a strong sudden desire □ *I suddenly had an urge to smoke a cigarette.* ◇ *vt* -1. **to urge sb to do sthg** to encourage sb strongly to do sthg □ *I urged him to accept the offer.* -2. [caution, remedy] to recommend <sthg> strongly □ *Community leaders urged restraint.*

urgency [ˈɜːrdʒənsɪ] *n*: see **urgent** □ *This is a matter of some urgency.*

urgent [ˈɜːrdʒənt] *adj* [request, letter, case] that needs to be dealt with quickly or immediately; [appeal, call, voice] that shows that something needs to be dealt with in this way □ *This is urgent, I have to see her.*

urgently [ˈɜːrdʒəntlɪ] *adv* as soon as possible or immediately, as a result of an urgent situation □ *I must see him urgently.* □ *Medical assistance is urgently required.*

urinal [US ˈjʊrənl, GB juːˈraɪnl] *n* a bowl or channel that is fitted to a wall in a public toilet for men and boys to urinate in; a public toilet containing these.

urinary [US 'juərənerı, GB -ərı] *adj* [tract, infection] that is connected with the parts of the body that urine passes through.

urinate ['juərəneɪt] *vi* to get rid of urine from one's body.

urine ['juərən] *n* the yellow or clear liquid that people and animals produce in their bodies, especially after drinking, and that they get rid of.

urn [ɜːʳn] *n* -1. a decorative container similar to a vase used to hold the ashes of a dead person. -2. a large metal container with a tap near the bottom for making and serving tea or coffee.

Uruguay ['juərəgwaɪ] a country in southeastern South America, on the Atlantic coast between Brazil and Argentina. SIZE: 177,500 sq kms. POPULATION: 3,200,000 (*Uruguayans*). CAPITAL: Montevideo. LANGUAGE: Spanish. CURRENCY: Uruguayan peso.

us [stressed ʌs, unstressed əs] *pron* used as the object of a verb, and after prepositions, to refer to a group of people that includes oneself □ *Could you help us with our baggage?* □ *Our competitors might just beat us to it.* □ *He gave us directions to get to the airport.* □ *Our son has gone on vacation without us.* □ *All of us have experienced this at some time or other.* ■ **it's us** used to identify a group of people that includes oneself □ *Don't get up, it's only us.*

US *abbr of* **United States** □ *a US citizen.*

USA ◇ *abbr of* **United States of America.** ◇ *n abbr of* **United States Army.**

usable ['juːzəbl] *adj* that is in good enough condition to be used □ *Is this paint still usable?* □ *The equipment is no longer usable.*

USAF *n abbr of* **United States Air Force.**

usage ['juːsɪdʒ] *n* -1. the way in which words are used in a particular language □ *modern English usage* □ *current usage in Canadian French.* -2. a way in which a word is used; the meaning that a word has □ *a common usage* □ *This word has several usages.* -3. [of equipment, energy, resource] the act of using something □ *It's still in working order despite constant usage.*

USCG *n abbr of* **United States Coast Guard.**

USDA (*abbr of* **United States Department of Agriculture**) *n* **the USDA** the US government department responsible for agriculture.

USDAW ['ʌzdɔː] (*abbr of* **Union of Shop, Distributive, and Allied Workers**) *n* a British labor union for shop, transport, and marketing workers.

USDI *n abbr of* **United States Department of the Interior.**

use [*n & aux vb* juːs, *vt* juːz] ◇ *n* -1. **the use of sthg** [of a tool, material, method] the act of using sthg □ *Students are allowed the use of a dictionary in the exam.* □ *The large-scale use of pesticides has come under increasing attack.* □ *The shelving is designed for use in the office or home environment.* □ *The carpet is ideal for heavy domestic use.* ■ **to be in use** [device, machine, technique] to be being used □ *All our telephone lines are in use at the moment.* ■ **to come into use** to start being used □ *This particular drug came into use during the early twenties.* ■ **to make use of sthg** [machine, skill, facility] to use sthg □ *Local residents were encouraged to make use of the college's swimming pool.* ■ **to make good use of sthg** to get the most benefit out of sthg that one can □ *I feel sure we could make better use of the space we have available.* ■ **to put sthg to good use** to use sthg for a suitable purpose □ *Thank you so much for the camera, which I'll put to good use on my trip to Rome.* -2. **to have the use of sthg** [of a part of the body, car, house] to have the ability or right to use sthg □ *She has the use of a company car.* □ *When he had the stroke last year he lost the use of his right hand.* -3. **to have a use** to be able to be used for a particular purpose □ *This little gadget has many different uses.* □ *Don't throw it away — I'm sure I'll find a use for it someday.* ■ **to be of use** to be useful □ *I hope that the book will be of some use to you.* □ *Can I be of any use to you?* ■ **to be no use** to be useless □ *Here, take it, it's no use to me.* ■ **it's no use, what's the use** phrases used to say that something is not having any effect and so is not worth doing □ *It's no use shouting, there's no one around.* □ *It's no use, the engine won't start.* □ *What's the use of talking to him? He never listens.*

◇ *vt* -1. [tool, method, product] to take <sthg that one needs> for a particular task or purpose and carry out that task or purpose with it □ *If you've never used an electric drill before, here are a few tips on safety.* □ *Is anyone using this chair?* □ *How many freelance staff did you use on the project?* □ *We use only the finest ingredients in our baked goods.* -2. [word, expression] to say or write <sthg> □ *That's not the term I would have used.* -3. [person] to take what one wants or needs from <sb> without showing any care for their feelings or situation (disapproving use) □ *Anyone could see he was only using her.* □ *I felt used.*

◇ *aux vb* **used to be/do etc** a phrase used to show that something happened regularly or was always true □ *I used to pass her every morning on the way to work.* □ *He didn't use to be that fat.* □ *We used to live in Seattle.* □ *There used to be a tree right here.*

◆ **use up** *vt sep* **to use sthg up** to use sthg gradually until there is none of it left; to use what is left of sthg so that it is not wasted □ *Why did I order so many logs? We'll never use them all up!* □ *There was lots of fabric left over, so I made cushion covers to use it up.*

used¹ [juːzd] *adj* -1. **a used tissue/handkerchief etc** a tissue/handkerchief etc that is dirty because somebody else has already used it □ *He went around emptying the used ashtrays.* -2. **a used car** a car that has already had at least one owner □ *a used-car lot.*

used² [juːst] *adj* **to be used to sthg** to have experienced sthg before several times so that it seems normal and does not make one feel strange, surprised etc □ *When you're used to the big city, life in a small town can be really dull.* □ *He's not used to young children.* □ *Don't worry, you'll soon get used to the heat.*

useful ['juːsfl] *adj* **-1.** [tool, book, advice] that helps one to do or get something that one needs or wants □ *This little guidebook is full of useful information.* □ *Computer skills are always useful to have.* ■ **to come in useful** to be useful □ *Your expertise will certainly come in useful.* **-2.** [person] who does things that help other people □ *She's a useful contact.* □ *He's a useful person to have around in an emergency.*

useless ['juːsləs] *adj* **-1.** [machine, tool, information] that has no purpose or does not do its job properly □ *This gadget's completely useless without the instruction manual.* **-2.** [attempt, effort] that cannot achieve anything □ *It's useless trying to make him see sense.* **-3.** [person, organization] that is not able to do anything well (informal use) □ *Oh, they're useless, they really are!*

user ['juːzər] *n* a person who uses a particular product or service □ *road/drug users.*

user-friendly *adj* [computer, machine] that is easy to use and understand for a person who is not an expert □ *They have a very user-friendly approach.*

USES (*abbr of* **United States Employment Service**) *n* **the USES** the US government department responsible for finding jobs for people through local public employment offices.

usher ['ʌʃər] ◇ *n* a person who shows people where to sit, e.g. at a wedding or a concert. ◇ *vt* to guide <sb> in a particular direction or to a particular place □ *He ushered me into the room/down the aisle/to my seat.*

usherette [ˌʌʃəˈret] *n* a woman whose job is to show people to their seats in a cinema or theater.

USIA (*abbr of* **United States Information Agency**) *n* **the USIA** the US government department responsible for giving people information about the USA, especially in other countries.

USN *n abbr of* **United States Navy**.

USPHS *n abbr of* **United States Public Health Service**.

USPO *n abbr of* **United States Post Office**.

USPS *n abbr of* **United States Postal Service**.

USS (*abbr of* **United States Ship**) a title written before the name of a ship in the US navy.

USSR (*abbr of* **Union of Soviet Socialist Republics**): **the USSR** a former Communist state in Eastern Europe and Central and Northern Asia. It was the largest country in the world until it broke up in 1991, when many of its 15 republics declared their independence.

usu. *abbr of* **usually**.

usual ['juːʒʊəl] *adj* that happens, is done etc most often □ *He ordered his usual drink.* □ *I had to put up with the usual delays.* ■ **as usual** as happens most often □ *I got up at eight o'clock as usual.* □ *He was late as usual!*

usually ['juːʒʊəlɪ] *adv* most often □ *I usually get home at about six.* □ *What do you usually do on weekends?* ■ **more than usually** [sad, busy, careful] to a greater degree than is usual □ *He was more than usually reserved this time.*

usurp [US juːˈsɜːrp, GB juːˈzɜːp] *vt* [power, posi-tion, role] to take <sthg> illegally or by force (formal use).

usury ['juːʒʊrɪ] *n* the practice of lending money at very high interest rates (formal use).

UT *abbr of* **Utah**.

Utah ['juːtɑː] a state in the central western USA. The majority of the population are Mormons. ABBREVIATION: UT. SIZE: 220,000 sq kms. POPULATION: 1,722,850 (*Utahans*). CAPITAL: Salt Lake City.

ute [juːt] *n* AUS a small truck with an open back.

Ute *n* a member of a Native American people living in the western and southwestern USA; the language of this people.

utensil [juːˈtensl] *n* an object, tool, or container with a particular practical use in the home, especially in the kitchen □ *kitchen/cooking utensils.*

uterus ['juːtərəs] (*pl* **uteri** [-raɪ] OR **uteruses**) *n* = **womb** (technical use).

utilitarian [juːˌtɪləˈteərɪən] *adj* [furniture, building] that is designed to be useful or practical rather than decorative or beautiful.

utility [juːˈtɪlətɪ] (*pl* **utilities**) *n* **-1.** the degree of usefulness of something, e.g. a tool or machine. **-2.** a basic public service, e.g. the supply of electricity, water, or transportation. **-3.** COMPUTING a piece of computer software that does routine tasks, such as copying or finding lost files.

utility room *n* a small room in a house used for storage and for large household appliances, e.g. a freezer or washing machine.

utilize, -ise ['juːtəlaɪz] *vt* [resources, time, opportunity] to use <sthg>, usually in an effective way (formal use).

utmost ['ʌtmoust] ◇ *adj* **the utmost importance/seriousness etc** very great importance/seriousness etc. ◇ *n* **-1.** the most that can possibly be done □ *We did/tried our utmost to prevent it from happening.* **-2.** the greatest possible degree □ *It's the utmost in comfort/luxury/advanced technology.* □ *She enjoyed herself to the utmost.*

utopia [juːˈtoupjə] *n* an imaginary perfect world or society.

utter ['ʌtər] ◇ *adj* **utter madness/amazement etc** total madness/amazement etc (used for emphasis) □ *To my utter amazement, he agreed.* ◇ *vt* to produce <a sound, word> etc with one's voice (formal use) □ *He didn't utter a single word all the way home.*

utterly ['ʌtərlɪ] *adv* **utterly mad/amazed etc** completely mad/amazed etc (used for emphasis) □ *What an utterly ridiculous thing to say!*

U-turn *n* **-1.** AUTO a turn that one makes in a car, truck etc in order to drive in the direction one has just come from □ *'No U-turns.'* **-2.** POLITICS a complete change of policy (disapproving use).

UV *n abbr of* **ultraviolet**.

UV-A, UVA *n* the type of ultraviolet radiation that causes people's skin to wrinkle and age.

UV-B, **UVB** *n* the type of ultraviolet radiation that causes people's skin to burn.

v¹ [viː] (*pl* **v's** OR **vs**), **V** [viː] (*pl* **V's** OR **Vs**) *n* the twenty-second letter of the English alphabet.

v² -1. *abbr of* **verse**. -2. (*abbr of* **vide**) an expression written in a book or article to refer the reader to some other information. -3. *abbr of* **versus**. -4. *abbr of* **volt**.

VA *abbr of* **Virginia**.

vacancy ['veɪkənsɪ] (*pl* **vacancies**) *n* -1. a job or position that has not been filled □ *A vacancy has arisen for a bright young graduate in our busy sales department.* -2. [at a hotel, guesthouse] a room that is not being used. ■ **'Vacancies'** a sign that is placed outside a hotel, guesthouse etc to show that there are rooms available □ *'No vacancies.'*

vacant ['veɪkənt] *adj* -1. [room, space, toilet] that is not being used □ *Is this seat vacant?* -2. [job, position] that has not been filled □ *There is a job vacant for a carpenter.* -3. [look, gaze] that shows no sign of interest or thought □ *He stared at the television with a vacant expression on his face.*

vacant lot *n* a piece of land, usually in a city, where there are no buildings and where buildings can be built.

vacantly ['veɪkəntlɪ] *adv* [look, gaze, stare] *see* **vacant** □ *John sat gazing vacantly at them.*

vacate [US 'veɪkeɪt, GB və'keɪt] *vt* -1. [job, post, position] to leave <sthg> (formal use). -2. [room, space, premises] to stop using <sthg> and leave it empty □ *We've been asked to vacate the apartment by next week.*

vacation [US veɪ'keɪʃn, GB və-] *n* -1. US a time when one can rest and enjoy oneself away from home; a time when one does not have to go to work or school □ *They went to Greece (on) vacation.* -2. EDUCATION a period between terms when universities are officially closed □ *I'm hoping to get a part-time job during the vacation.*

vacationer [US veɪ'keɪʃnr, GB və'keɪʃənə] *n* US a person who is on vacation.

vacation pay *n* US pay that one receives from one's employer when one is on vacation.

vacation resort *n* US a place where people go on vacation.

vaccinate ['væksəneɪt] *vt* to give a vaccine to <a person or animal> □ *Have you been vaccinated against typhoid fever?*

vaccination [,væksə'neɪʃn] *n* -1. a dose of vaccine □ *Have you had your vaccination?* -2. [of a

person, animal] *see* **vaccinate** □ *We strongly recommend vaccination against polio.*

vaccine [US væk'siːn, GB 'væksiːn] *n* a substance used to protect people against a disease by giving them a mild form of the disease.

vacillate ['væsəleɪt] *vi* -1. to keep changing from one feeling to another □ *Vanya vacillated between euphoria and depression.* -2. to be unable to decide □ *She vacillated for a long time before making up her mind.*

vacuum ['vækjʊəm] ◇ *n* -1. PHYSICS a space that contains no air or other gas. -2. [in a situation] a situation in which no one is in control □ *His resignation created a vacuum at the top of the organization.* □ *a political vacuum.* -3. = **vacuum cleaner**. -4. the act of cleaning using a vacuum cleaner □ *Give the room a quick vacuum.* ◇ *vt* [carpet, room, car] to clean <sthg> using a vacuum cleaner.

vacuum bottle *n* US a container with an inside and an outside wall and a vacuum between them, used to keep liquids hot or cold.

vacuum cleaner *n* an electrical appliance that cleans carpets and upholstery by sucking in dust and dirt.

vacuum flask *n* = **vacuum bottle**.

vacuum-packed *adj* [food] that is wrapped in plastic from which most of the air has been removed in order to keep the contents fresh.

vacuum pump *n* a pump used to remove air or gas from a container, bottle etc.

vagabond ['vægəbɒnd] *n* a person who has no fixed job or home and travels from place to place (literary use).

vagaries ['veɪgərɪz] *npl* [of human nature, politics] unexpected changes or events that one cannot control.

vagina [və'dʒaɪnə] *n* the passage that connects the outer sex organs of a woman or female animal to the womb.

vaginal [US 'vædʒənl, GB və'dʒaɪnl] *adj* [examination, infection, discharge] *see* **vagina**.

vagrancy ['veɪgrənsɪ] *n* the state of being a vagrant.

vagrant ['veɪgrənt] *n* somebody who has no fixed job or home and has to beg or steal to live.

vague [veɪg] *adj* -1. [reference, description, memory] that is not exact or detailed □ *We were given rather vague directions.* □ *vague promises of promotion.* -2. [feeling, sense] that is not clearly or strongly felt □ *His words filled me with a vague sense of unease.* -3. [person] who avoids telling other people about the details of something □ *She was deliberately vague about the cost.* -4. [person] who does not think or express themselves clearly □ *He's terribly vague — I find it very hard to follow him sometimes.* -5. [shape, outline, form] that cannot be seen clearly.

vaguely ['veɪglɪ] *adv* -1. [describe, indicate] not clearly □ *I vaguely remember coming here as a boy.* -2. **to be vaguely amused/irritated etc** to be slightly amused/irritated etc □ *That man looks vaguely familiar.*

vain [veɪn] *adj* -1. [person] who is too proud of

their own appearance or abilities □ *She's too vain to wear her glasses.* **-2. a vain attempt/ effort etc** an attempt/effort etc that is not successful □ *He waited in the vain hope that she would change her mind and come back.*

♦ **in vain** *adv* [try, hope] without success □ *I tried to explain, but (all) in vain.*

vainly ['veɪnlɪ] *adv* [try, hope] without success.

valance ['væləns] *n* **-1.** a decorative piece of cloth that hangs from the bed frame to the floor. **-2.** US a piece of wood or cloth that is fixed above a window to hide the curtain rail.

vale [veɪl] *n* a valley (literary use).

valedictorian [,vælədɪk'tɔːrɪən] *n* US a student who finishes at the top of their high school class.

valedictory [,vælə'dɪktərɪ] *adj* [speech, letter, message] that says goodbye (formal use).

valentine (card) ['væləntaɪn-] *n* a greeting card sent to arrive on Valentine's Day.

Valentine's Day *n* the fourteenth of February each year, when people traditionally send greeting cards to someone they are in love with.

💘 VALENTINE'S DAY
This saint's day, celebrated on February 14 each year in the USA, Britain, and Australia, has become a special day for people who are in love. Traditionally, you send a special greeting card to the person that you are in love with, usually without signing your name. You can also send gifts such as flowers. Restaurants and stores are often decorated for the day with red hearts and ribbons, and many newspapers have special pages of personal love messages.

valet [US væ'leɪ, GB 'vælɪt, 'væleɪ] *n* a man's personal male servant.

valet parking *n* 'Valet parking' a sign that shows that a hotel, nightclub etc will park guests' cars for them as a service.

valet service *n* the service of cleaning, ironing, and mending clothes that is offered in hotels.

valiant ['vælɪənt] *adj* [effort, soldier] very brave and determined.

valid ['vælɪd] *adj* **-1.** [excuse, argument, decision] that is acceptable because it is based on truth or a good reason □ *He made some very valid criticisms.* **-2.** [ticket, passport, license] that can be used legally for a particular period or under particular conditions □ *This voucher is valid for a whole year.*

validate ['vælɪdeɪt] *vt* [argument, claim] to prove that <sthg> is valid; [ticket, agreement] to make <sthg> valid.

validity [və'lɪdətɪ] *n: see* **valid** □ *I question the validity of these arguments.*

Valium™ ['vælɪəm] *n* a drug that doctors give to people to make them feel calm.

valley ['vælɪ] (*pl* **valleys**) *n* a long narrow area of land between hills or mountains, often with a river flowing through it.

valor US, **valour** GB ['vælər] *n* great bravery, especially in war (literary use).

valuable ['væljəbl] *adj* **-1.** [advice, information, help] very useful □ *My thanks also to Dr. Tawn for her valuable comments on the text.* **-2.** [necklace, painting, camera] that is worth a lot of money.

♦ **valuables** *npl* things that one owns and are valuable, e.g. jewelry.

valuation [,væljʊ'eɪʃn] *n* [of jewelry, a house, painting] a judgment of how much money something is worth □ *They put far too low a valuation on the painting.*

value ['væljuː] ◇ *n* **-1.** [of a piece of advice, information, a friendship] the importance or usefulness of something □ *parents who recognize the value of a good education.* ■ **to place a high value on sthg** [on loyalty, education, honesty] to consider sthg very important. **-2.** [of a painting, house, currency] the amount of money something is worth □ *New cars lose their value very quickly.* □ *jewelry of great value.* ■ **to be a good value** US, **to be good value** OR **value for money** GB [meal, ticket, vacation] to be worth the money it costs □ *Bus passes are a better value.* **-3.** *phrase* **to take sthg at face value** to believe sthg without thinking that there may be another meaning □ *Unfortunately, I took what he said at face value.*
◇ *vt* **-1.** [house, painting, jewelry] to decide the value of <sthg> □ *The property was valued at over $600,000.* **-2.** [friendship, support, opinion] to consider <sthg> to be very important □ *I would value your advice on the matter.*

♦ **values** *npl* the beliefs and ideas that a particular person or group considers important □ *family/moral/political values.*

value-added tax [-ædəd-] *n* → **VAT**.

valued ['væljuːd] *adj* [friend, employee, custom] that one considers to be very important and wants to keep.

value judgment *n* a judgment based on a person's opinion rather than on the real facts about something.

valuer ['væljʊər] *n* a person whose job is to decide how much money things such as paintings and antiques are worth.

valve [vælv] *n* a device that opens and closes to control the movement of a liquid or gas through a tube or pipe.

vamp [væmp] *n* a sexually attractive woman who uses her beauty to get things from men (informal and disapproving use).

vampire ['væmpaɪər] *n* a bad spirit that is supposed to live in a human body and come out of its grave at night to drink the blood of living people.

van [væn] *n* **-1.** AUTO a vehicle larger than a car and smaller than a truck that is used for carrying goods and people □ *a delivery/police/ baker's van.* **-2.** GB RAIL a covered train carriage used for carrying goods □ *a luggage/mail van.*

Vancouver [væn'kuːvər] **-1.** a city and major port in British Columbia, Canada. POPULATION: 471,844. **-2.** an island in the Pacific

Ocean off the southwestern coast of British Columbia, Canada. SIZE: 32,137 sq kms. POPULATION: 461,573. MAIN CITY: Victoria.

V and A (*abbr of* **Victoria and Albert Museum**): **the V and A** a large museum in London that specializes in exhibitions of jewelry, textiles, furniture etc.

vandal ['vændl] *n* a person who damages public and private property deliberately.

vandalism ['vændəlɪzm] *n* the damage done to public and private property by vandals □ *an act of vandalism.*

vandalize, -ise ['vændəlaɪz] *vt* [phone booth, bus stop, car] to damage <sthg that belongs to somebody else> deliberately.

Van Dyck [væn'daɪk], **Sir Anthony** (1599–1641) a Flemish artist, well known for his portraits of the English royal family.

Van Gogh [US væn'goʊ, GB -'gɒf], **Vincent** (1853–1890) a Dutch artist, well known for the bright colors of his landscapes and still lifes.

vanguard ['vængɑːʳd] *n* the front part of an army or group of ships going into battle. ■ **to be in the vanguard of sthg** [of a movement, profession, area of research] to be in the most advanced part of sthg.

vanilla [və'nɪlə] *n* a substance made from the beans of a kind of plant and used in cooking to give food a sweet flavor □ *vanilla ice cream.*

vanish ['vænɪʃ] *vi* -1. [object, person] to disappear suddenly □ *The car vanished around a bend.* □ *My bag had vanished.* -2. [species, wildlife] to no longer exist □ *a way of life that has vanished for ever.*

vanishing point ['vænɪʃɪŋ-] *n* the point at which parallel lines that stretch into the distance appear to meet.

Vanitory unit™ [US 'vænətɔːrɪ-, GB -tərɪ-] *n* = **vanity unit.**

vanity ['vænɪtɪ] *n* [of a person] the quality of being vain □ *The advertisement appeals to people's vanity.*

vanity bag, vanity case *n* a small bag used by a woman for carrying make-up, soap etc.

vanity unit *n* a piece of furniture in a bathroom or bedroom consisting of a sink surrounded by a tiled or plastic surface, usually with a cupboard underneath.

vanquish ['væŋkwɪʃ] *vt* [enemy, fear, hope] to defeat <sb/sthg> (literary use).

vantagepoint [US 'væntɪdʒpɔɪnt, GB 'vɑːn-] *n* -1. a good place from which to see something. -2. a point of view.

Vanuatu [ˌvænʊ'ɑːtuː] a country in Melanesia, in the southwestern Pacific Ocean, consisting of 80 islands. SIZE: 14,760 sq kms. POPULATION: 200,000 (*Vanuatuans*). CAPITAL: Port Vila. LANGUAGE: Bislama, English, French. CURRENCY: vatu.

vapor US, **vapour** GB ['veɪpəʳ] *n* a mass of very small drops of liquid in the air, often produced by sudden changes in temperature □ *water vapor* □ *gas vapor.*

vapor trail *n* the white line that a jet plane, missile etc leaves in the sky.

vapour *n* GB = **vapor.**

variable ['veərɪəbl] ◇ *adj* -1. [weather, mood] that changes often, but not in a regular way. -2. [quality, performance] that is sometimes good and sometimes bad. ◇ *n* -1. something that can change in quantity or size in different situations □ *variables such as the cost of labor and materials.* -2. MATH a sign or group of signs that can have any of a set of possible values.

variance ['veərɪəns] *n* **to be at variance with sthg** to be different than sthg (formal use) □ *Her version of events is at variance with the police account.*

variant ['veərɪənt] ◇ *adj* [form, spelling] that is different than what is normal, but in a way that is acceptable. ◇ *n* a slightly different form of a word, pronunciation etc that is also acceptable.

variation [ˌveərɪ'eɪʃn] *n* -1. a change in a level or quantity □ *The results showed no variation.* □ *wide regional variations in income* □ *We must allow for variations in temperature.* -2. a slightly different version of something □ *jazz variations* □ *All her novels are variations on the same basic theme.*

varicose veins [ˌværəkoʊs-] *npl* a painful condition in which the veins in one's leg become swollen.

varied ['veərɪd] *adj* [life, career] that includes many different things, activities, people etc □ *This year's varied program includes a number of modern works.*

variety [və'raɪətɪ] (*pl* **varieties**) *n* -1. [in somebody's job, life] the quality of having interesting differences in type or quality □ *I want a job with a lot of variety.* -2. [of people, things] a number of different things of the same general type □ *a wide variety of music/colors.* -3. [of plant, animal] a type of plant, animal, food etc □ *I got the sugar-free variety.* -4. GB THEATER a kind of entertainment made up of short performances by different people, including singing, dancing, telling jokes etc □ *a variety show.*

various ['veərɪəs] *adj* [people, possibilities, reasons] of several different types □ *There are various options available to us.*

varnish ['vɑːʳnɪʃ] ◇ *n* a clear liquid painted on a surface such as wood to make it shiny and hard. ◇ *vt* [wood, painting] to paint <sthg> with varnish.

varnished ['vɑːʳnɪʃt] *adj* [wood, table] that has been painted with varnish.

vary ['veərɪ] (*pt* & *pt* **varied**) ◇ *vt* [route, method, diet] to change <sthg> often □ *I like to vary my routine as much as possible.* ◇ *vi* [price, number, opinion] to be different at different times, places, or situations □ *Spanish resorts vary in popularity.* □ *His moods vary with the weather.*

varying ['veərɪɪŋ] *adj* **varying degrees/amounts etc** degrees/amounts etc that vary □ *The organization set up similar projects elsewhere with varying degrees of success.*

vascular ['væskjələ'] *adj* [system, disease] that is connected with the tubes that carry liquids around one's body.

vase [US veiz, GB vɑːz] *n* a tall narrow pot, usually made of pottery or glass, that is used for holding cut flowers.

vasectomy [və'sektəmɪ] (*pl* **vasectomies**) *n* a medical operation in which the tube that carries sperm to a man's penis is cut, in order to make him unable to make a woman pregnant.

Vaseline™ ['væsəliːn] *n* a soft, transparent, greasy jelly made from petroleum, used especially to protect one's skin.

vast [US væst, GB vɑːst] *adj* [expanse, ocean, crowd] very large; [difference, expense] very great in amount □ *People wrote to us in vast numbers.* □ *the vast majority of viewers.*

vastly [US 'væstlɪ, GB 'vɑːst-] *adv* **vastly different/superior** very different/very much superior.

vat [væt] *n* a very large container used to hold liquids such as dye, wine, or whiskey when they are being made.

VAT [væt, ˌviːeɪ'tiː] (*abbr of* **value-added tax**) *n* a tax that is added to the price of goods or services □ *$548.75 inc. VAT.*

Vatican ['vætɪkən] ◇ **the Vatican** the palace in Vatican City that is the official home of the Pope. ◇ *n* **the Vatican** the group of people who control the Roman Catholic Church.

Vatican City an independent state within the city of Rome, Italy. It is the headquarters of the Catholic Church. SIZE: 0.44 sq kms. POPULATION: 700. LANGUAGE: Italian, Latin. CURRENCY: Italian lira.

vaudeville ['vɔːdəvɪl] *n* a type of entertainment popular between 1890 and 1930, consisting of singing, dancing, acrobatics, and comedy □ *a vaudeville theater.*

Vaughan Williams [ˌvɔːn'wɪljəmz], **Ralph** (1872–1958) a British composer whose music was influenced by English folk music.

vault [vɔːlt] ◇ *vt* [fence, wall] to jump over <sthg> using one's hands or a long stick to push the body forward. ◇ *vi*: *Did you see the way she vaulted over that wall?* ◇ *n* **-1.** [in a bank] a room with thick walls and a strong door used to keep money, jewels etc safe □ *a bank vault.* **-2.** [in a church] a room underground where dead people are buried. **-3.** [of a building] a roof or ceiling made of several arches joined together at the top. **-4.** [over a wall, fence] the act of vaulting something.

vaulted ['vɔːltəd] *adj* [ceiling, roof] that is in the form of a vault; [room, passage] that has a curved roof.

vaulting horse ['vɔːltɪŋ-] *n* a piece of exercise equipment with four legs and a padded top that people jump over, pushing themselves forward with their hands.

VC *n* **-1.** *abbr of* **vice-chairman**. **-2.** *abbr of* **Victoria Cross**.

VCR (*abbr of* **video cassette recorder**) *n* a piece of equipment that can play video tapes or record television programs.

VD (*abbr of* **venereal disease**) *n* any disease that is caught by having sex with an infected person.

VDU (*abbr of* **visual display unit**) *n* the part of a computer that has a screen on which information is shown.

veal [viːl] *n* the meat of a young cow □ *a veal escalope.*

veep [viːp] *n* US = **vice-president** (informal use).

veer [vɪə'] *vi* [car, wind, conversation] to change direction suddenly and unexpectedly □ *The truck had veered off the road.*

vegan ['viːgən] ◇ *adj* [diet] that does not include meat, fish, eggs, milk, cheese, or any food produced by animals. ◇ *n* somebody who has a vegan diet.

vegetable ['vedʒtəbl] ◇ *n* a plant, e.g. spinach or cabbage, that can be cooked and eaten □ *Carrots are my favorite vegetable.* □ *vegetable soup.* ◇ *adj* [matter, protein] that comes from or is made up of plant material.

vegetable garden *n* the part of a garden where people grow vegetables for their own use.

vegetable knife *n* a small knife with a sharp pointed blade used for cutting vegetables.

vegetable marrow *n* a large, long, green vegetable with thin white stripes along its skin and white flesh.

vegetable oil *n* a kind of cooking oil made from plants, e.g. sunflowers or corn.

vegetarian [ˌvedʒə'teərɪən] ◇ *adj* [diet, restaurant, cookbook] that is designed for people who do not eat meat or fish, but who do eat eggs, milk products etc. ◇ *n*: *I'm a vegetarian.*

vegetarianism [ˌvedʒə'teərɪənɪzm] *n* the practice of being a vegetarian.

vegetate ['vedʒəteɪt] *vi* to spend time doing boring and dull things so that one's mind is not active □ *As a housewife, she felt she was just vegetating.*

vegetation [ˌvedʒə'teɪʃn] *n* plant life, especially in a particular place □ *an area of dense vegetation.*

vehement ['viːəmənt] *adj* [denial, attack, gesture] strong □ *a vehement defense of government policy.*

vehemently ['viːəməntlɪ] *adv* [deny, attack, refuse] *see* **vehement**.

vehicle ['viːɪkl] *n* **-1.** something that is used to carry people or goods, e.g. a car, truck, or bicycle. **-2. a vehicle for sthg** [for information, an idea] something that is used to express sthg else □ *The show is an excellent vehicle for new talent.*

vehicular [vɪ'hɪkjələ'] *adj* that is connected with vehicles (formal use) □ *vehicular traffic/access.*

veil [veɪl] *n* **-1.** a piece of thin cloth or net that a woman wears to cover her face or head, e.g. at a wedding or for religious reasons. **-2. a veil of mist/smoke etc** a thin layer of mist/smoke etc that one can only partly see through. **-3. a veil of secrecy/silence etc**

secrecy/silence etc that hides the truth about a situation □ *the veil of mystery that surrounds the Dark Ages.*

veiled [veɪld] *adj* [threat, compliment, reference] that is not expressed clearly and directly □ *She referred to her illness in veiled terms only.*

vein [veɪn] *n* **-1.** ANATOMY any of the tubes that carry blood to the heart from other parts of the body. **-2.** [on a leaf] any of the thin lines on a leaf or an insect's wing. **-3.** [in a rock] a thin layer of a rock or mineral, e.g. coal or gold, in a rock □ *a silver vein.* **-4. in a serious/sarcastic etc vein** in a serious/sarcastic etc style □ *He also produced novels in a much lighter vein.* □ *The program continued in much the same vein.*

Velázquez [US vəˈlɑːskeɪs, GB vɪˈlæskwɪz] (1599–1660) a Spanish artist who painted several famous portraits of the Spanish royal family.

Velcro™ [ˈvelkroʊ] *n* a fastener for clothes that is made up of very small hooks on one surface that attach themselves to very small loops on another surface □ *a Velcro strip.*

vellum [ˈveləm] *n* a material made from the skins of young goats, cows etc, that is used to make book covers and was used in the past for writing on.

velocity [vəˈlɒsətɪ] (*pl* **velocities**) *n* [of sound, light, a bullet] PHYSICS the speed at which something moves □ *a high-velocity rifle/bullet.*

velour [vəˈluəʳ] *n* a cloth made of silk or cotton with a soft surface similar to velvet, often used for covering chairs and sofas.

velvet [ˈvelvət] *n* a thick cloth made from silk or nylon that is soft and furry on one side and is used for clothing, curtains etc □ *a velvet jacket* □ *velvet curtains.*

vend [vend] *vt* to sell <sthg> (formal use).

vendetta [venˈdetə] *n* **-1.** an angry quarrel between two people or groups over a long period, often involving murder. **-2.** a series of attacks made by one person against another person or organization □ *Jackson has waged a personal vendetta against the company for years.*

vending machine [ˈvendɪŋ-] *n* a machine in a public place that gives out candy, drinks, cigarettes etc when money is put into it and a button is pressed.

vendor [ˈvendɔːʳ] *n* **-1.** a person who sells things in the street □ *a street vendor.* **-2.** LAW a person who is selling a house, land etc. NOTE: Compare **purchaser**.

veneer [vəˈnɪəʳ] *n* **-1.** a thin layer of plastic or good-quality wood used to cover cheaper material to improve the appearance of wood, furniture etc. **-2.** [of respectability, calm] an appearance that hides the real nature of a person or place.

venerable [ˈvenərəbl] *adj* **a venerable family/institution etc** a family/institution etc that deserves respect because it is old or important (formal use).

venerate [ˈvenəreɪt] *vt* [person, place, object] to treat <sb/sthg> with great respect (formal use) □ *Finland's most venerated composer.*

venereal disease [vəˌnɪərɪəl-] *n* = **VD** (formal use).

Venetian [vəˈniːʃn] *n* & *adj*: see **Venice.**

venetian blind *n* a covering for a window made up of many horizontal strips of plastic, metal, or wood that can be moved to let in more or less light.

Venezuela [ˌvenəˈzweɪlə] a country in northern South America, on the Caribbean Sea. SIZE: 912,050 sq kms. POPULATION: 20,700,000 (*Venezuelans*). CAPITAL: Caracas. LANGUAGE: Spanish. CURRENCY: bolivar.

vengeance [ˈvendʒəns] *n* **-1.** violent punishment given in return for harm done to oneself, one's family etc. **-2.** *phrase* **with a vengeance** with greater force than normal or than before □ *I thought my cold was gone, but it came back with a vengeance.*

vengeful [ˈvendʒfl] *adj* [person] who wants revenge on somebody (literary use).

Venice [ˈvenəs] *n* a city and port in northeastern Italy, famous for its canals. POPULATION: 308,717.

venison [ˈvenəzən] *n* the flesh from a deer, eaten as food □ *venison pie.*

venom [ˈvenəm] *n* **-1.** the poison that a snake, scorpion etc puts into a person or animal when it bites or stings them. **-2.** great anger or hatred □ *He spoke with real venom.*

venomous [ˈvenəməs] *adj* **-1.** [snake, insect] that has a poisonous bite or sting. **-2.** [person, tone, look] that is full of anger or hatred.

vent [vent] ◇ *n* **-1.** [of a boiler, fan] an opening through which air can enter and smoke, smells, and gases can escape □ *an air vent.* **-2.** [in a jacket, skirt] a long narrow opening at the side or back of a piece of clothing. **-3.** *phrase* **to give vent to sthg** [to one's anger, frustration] to express sthg □ *I gave vent to my fury by writing a letter.* ◇ *vt* [rage, fury] to express <a feeling of anger> □ *He vents all his frustration on his family.*

ventilate [ˈventleɪt] *vt* [room, building] to allow fresh air to enter and move around <a place> □ *a well-/poorly-ventilated room.*

ventilation [ˌventəˈleɪʃn] *n* the act or system of ventilating a room or building □ *a building's ventilation system.*

ventilator [ˈventəleɪtəʳ] *n* **-1.** [for a room, building] a device that brings in fresh air and removes bad air. **-2.** MEDICINE a machine used in hospitals to help sick or injured people breathe.

ventriloquist [venˈtrɪləkwɪst] *n* a person who entertains people by speaking or singing without moving their mouth so that the sound seems to come from somewhere else.

venture [ˈventʃəʳ] ◇ *n* a business project that may succeed or fail □ *a business/commercial venture* □ *a joint venture.* ◇ *vt* [opinion, advice] to say <sthg> cautiously because it may be thought foolish or wrong □ *I ventured to suggest some improvements.* ◇ *vi* **-1.** to go somewhere that is considered to be dangerous or daring □ *It's the first time we've ventured outside Europe.* **-2. to venture into sthg** [into a market, sector, business] to get involved in sthg that is new and difficult □ *They're considering venturing into the pop world.*

venture capital *n* money that a bank or investor lends somebody to start a new business, especially when there is a risk of losing the money.

venue ['venjuː] *n* the place where a concert, meeting, match etc takes place.

Venus¹ ['viːnəs] the planet in the solar system that is next to the Earth and second-closest to the Sun.

Venus² the Roman goddess of love.

veracity [vəˈræsətɪ] *n* the truthfulness of a statement, account etc (formal use).

veranda(h) [vəˈrændə] *n* an area that joins onto the outside of a house and consists of a roof, floor, and open sides.

verb [vɜːrb] *n* a word or group of words used to describe what somebody or something is, does, or experiences □ *a verb ending.*

verbal ['vɜːrbl] *adj* -1. [skill, play] that is connected with words and how they are used. -2. [attack, abuse, complaint] that is spoken, not written □ *We were given verbal assurances that strict confidentiality would be maintained.* -3. GRAMMAR [form, pattern] *see* **verb**.

verbally ['vɜːrbəlɪ] *adv* [attack, complain, communicate] in spoken words □ *Maria is very good at expressing herself verbally.*

verbatim [vɜːrˈbeɪtəm] ◇ *adj* [report, account] that repeats the exact words used. ◇ *adv:* *I can quote his words verbatim.*

verbose [vɜːrˈbəʊs] *adj* [person, report] that uses more words than are needed (formal and disapproving use).

Verdi ['veərdɪ], **Giuseppe** (1813–1901) an Italian composer, well known for his operas, including *La Traviata*, *Rigoletto*, and *Aida.*

verdict ['vɜːrdɪkt] *n* -1. LAW a decision made by a court about whether a prisoner is guilty or innocent □ *The jury took four hours to reach a verdict.* □ *a guilty verdict* OR *verdict of guilty.* -2. an opinion about something □ *What's your verdict on the new system?*

verge [vɜːrdʒ] *n* -1. the edge of a road, often covered with grass. -2. **on the verge of sthg** [of success, collapse, hysteria] very close to sthg □ *They're on the verge of going bankrupt.*

◆ **verge on** *vt fus* **to verge on sthg** to be very close to sthg □ *His reaction verges on paranoia.*

verger ['vɜːrdʒər] *n* GB a person whose job is to look after the inside of a church.

verification [ˌverɪfɪˈkeɪʃn] *n: see* **verify** □ *We're waiting for official verification of the result.*

verify ['verɪfaɪ] (*pt* & *pp* **verified**) *vt* -1. [result, evidence] to officially check the truth of <sthg>; [owner, identity] to check <sb/sthg>. -2. [story, fact, details] to confirm the truth of <sthg> □ *I can verify that this is the case.*

veritable ['verɪtəbl] *adj* used to compare two things, usually in a slightly exaggerated way (humorous or formal use) □ *a veritable maze of corridors.*

Vermeer [vərˈmɪər], **Jan** (1632–1675) a Dutch

artist well known for his detailed paintings of interiors.

vermilion [vərˈmɪlɪən] ◇ *adj* bright orange-red. ◇ *n* a bright orange-red color.

vermin ['vɜːrmən] *npl* animals or insects, e.g. rats, foxes, fleas, or lice, that spread disease or cause problems when present in large numbers.

Vermont [vərˈmɒnt] a state in the northeastern USA, on the Canadian border. ABBREVIATION: VT. SIZE: 24,887 sq kms. POPULATION: 562,758 (*Vermonters*). CAPITAL: Montpelier.

vermouth [US vərˈmuːθ, GB ˈvɜːməθ] *n* a drink made from strong wine flavored with herbs, often used in cocktails.

vernacular [vərˈnækjələr] *n* **the vernacular** the language spoken by ordinary people in a country or region, that may be different from the official language.

Verne [vɜːrn], **Jules** (1828–1905) a French writer who played an important part in the development of science fiction. His best-known works are *Around the World in Eighty Days* and *Journey to the Center of the Earth.*

verruca [vəˈruːkə] (*pl* **verrucas** OR **verrucae** [-kaɪ]) *n* a small, hard, painful growth, usually on the bottom of one's foot, that is caused by a virus.

versa ['vɜːrsə] → **vice versa.**

versatile [US 'vɜːrsətl, GB -taɪl] *adj* -1. [actor, player, politician] who has many different skills. -2. [machine, tool, food] that can be used in many different ways.

versatility [ˌvɜːrsəˈtɪlətɪ] *n: see* **versatile** □ *His versatility as a performer means he is rarely out of the public eye.*

verse [vɜːrs] *n* -1. writing arranged in short lines that have a regular pattern and that sometimes rhyme at the end □ *a book of children's verse.* -2. [of a song] one of the parts a song or poem is divided into □ *Let's sing the first verse again.* -3. [in the Bible] one of the parts each chapter of the Bible is divided into.

versed [vɜːrst] *adj* **to be well versed in sthg** [in a procedure, technique, subject] to have a good knowledge of sthg □ *He's well versed in the art of flattery.*

version ['vɜːrʒn] *n* -1. [of a story, legend] a form of something that differs slightly from other forms of the same thing □ *He's a younger version of his father.* -2. [of facts, an event] the way somebody describes something that happened □ *They each gave their version of the incident.* -3. [of a book] a translation from one language into another □ *a Spanish version of "Hamlet".*

versus ['vɜːrsəs] *prep* -1. SPORT competing against <sb/sthg> □ *We bring you live coverage of France versus Ireland.* -2. compared to <sthg> □ *We need to weigh up the merits of having a London base versus setting up elsewhere.*

vertebra ['vɜːrtəbrə] (*pl* **vertebrae** [-breɪ]) *n* one of the small bones that form the backbone.

vertebrate ['vɜːˈtəbreɪt] *n* a creature that has a backbone, e.g. humans, birds, and fish.

vertical ['vɜːˈtɪkl] *adj* [line, cliff] that goes straight upward □ *vertical take-off.*

vertical integration *n* the process of joining together two businesses that deal with different stages in the production and sale of the same product.

vertically ['vɜːˈtɪklɪ] *adv* -1. [take off, rise] straight upward. -2. [divide, cut] from top to bottom.

vertigo ['vɜːˈtɪgoʊ] *n* a dizzy and sick feeling that some people have when looking down from high places.

verve [vɜːˈv] *n* great energy and enthusiasm □ *She performed with great verve.*

very ['verɪ] ◇ *adv* -1. used to emphasize adjectives and adverbs □ *I wore my very best clothes.* □ *That's very kind of you.* □ *He's feeling very much better.* -2. **not very difficult/ interesting etc** almost easy/boring etc □ *It's not very often we get a chance to talk.* ◇ *adj* used to emphasize nouns. ■ **those were my very thoughts** that was exactly what I was thinking □ *You're the very person I've been looking for!* □ *I waited till the very end of the movie.* ■ **here, in this very room** here in the actual room we are in. ■ **my very own house,** a house of my very own a house that belongs to me and no one else.

◆ **very well** *adv* used to show agreement □ *"Aren't you coming?" — "Very well, if you insist."* ■ **I/we etc can't very well do sthg** it would not be fair or sensible for me/us etc to do sthg □ *We can't very well not invite her.*

vespers ['vespəˈz] *n* a Christian service held in the evening.

vessel ['vesl] *n* (formal use) -1. a large boat or ship □ *a fishing/sailing vessel.* -2. a container for liquids □ *an earthenware vessel.*

vest [vest] *n* -1. US a sleeveless piece of clothing with buttons that is usually worn over a shirt. -2. GB a piece of underwear for the upper body that has no sleeves □ *a thermal/ string vest.*

vested interest [,vestəd-] *n* a strong reason that a person has for doing something because it will benefit them □ *Stores have a vested interest in opening on Sundays.*

vestibule ['vestəbjuːl] *n* -1. the room or passage that forms the entrance hall to a building (formal use). -2. US the covered passage that connects two railroad cars.

vestige ['vestɪdʒ] *n* [of hope, dignity, modesty] a very small amount of something that remains after the rest has disappeared (formal use) □ *He was stripped of the last vestiges of power.*

vestry ['vestrɪ] (*pl* **vestries**) *n* the room in a church where the special clothes and equipment used in services are kept.

Vesuvius [vəˈsuːvjəs]: **(Mount) Vesuvius** an active volcano near Naples in southern Italy that buried the Roman towns of Pompeii and Herculaneum when it erupted in ancient times. The last eruption was in 1944.

vet [vet] (*pt* & *pp* **vetted,** *cont* **vetting**) ◇ *n* -1. a person whose job is to treat sick and injured animals. -2. US a person who has served in the armed forces □ *a Vietnam vet.* ◇ *vt* GB to examine the past record, qualification etc of <sb> carefully to make sure that they are suitable for a particular job □ *All candidates are carefully vetted.*

veteran ['vetrən] ◇ *n* -1. [of a war] an old person who has fought in a war □ *a veteran of World War I.* -2. [of campaigning, politics] a person who has a lot of experience of something and is respected. -3. US a person, young or old, who has served in the armed forces. ◇ *adj*: *a veteran traveler/campaigner.*

veteran car *n* GB a car made before 1905.

Veterans Day *n* in the USA, a holiday celebrated on November 11. It marks the end of World War I.

veterinarian [,vetərɪˈneərɪən] *n* US a person whose job is to treat sick and injured animals.

veterinary science [US 'vetərənerɪ-, GB -ənərɪ-] *n* the science of treating sick and injured animals.

veterinary surgeon *n* GB = **veterinarian** (formal use).

veto ['viːtoʊ] (*pl* **vetoes,** *pt* & *pp* **vetoed,** *cont* **vetoing**) ◇ *n* the power to reject or forbid something, e.g. in a law-making body; the act of using such a power □ *the right of veto.* ◇ *vt* [decision, proposal] to officially refuse to accept or allow <sthg>.

vetting ['vetɪŋ] *n* GB the process of vetting somebody.

vex [veks] *vt* to trouble or annoy <sb> (formal use) □ *It was a problem which vexed me for weeks.*

vexed [vekst] *adj* **a vexed question/issue** a question/issue that causes a lot of argument and cannot be decided easily.

VFD (*abbr of* **voluntary fire department**) *n* a US fire service whose members are volunteers.

vg *abbr of* **very good.**

vgc *abbr of* **very good condition.**

VHF *n* a range of radio frequencies between 30 and 300 MHz, used for radio broadcasts.

VHS (*abbr of* **video home system**) *n* a video cassette recording system that is used in people's homes to record television programs; a video cassette that works with this system.

VI *abbr of* **Virgin Islands.**

via ['vaɪə] *prep* -1. passing through <a place> on the way to somewhere □ *We flew to Beirut via Cairo.* -2. using or by means of <sb/ sthg> □ *I heard the news via Jane.* □ *broadcast live via satellite from New York.*

viability [,vaɪəˈbɪlətɪ] *n*: see **viable** □ *The new funding will ensure the group's financial viability for years to come.*

viable ['vaɪəbl] *adj* [proposal, suggestion, company] that can succeed □ *The idea is not commercially viable.* □ *There is no viable alternative.*

viaduct ['vaɪədʌkt] *n* a long high bridge that carries a road or railroad across a valley.

vibrant ['vaɪbrənt] *adj* -**1**. [color] that looks very bright and strong. -**2**. [voice, atmosphere, person] that is exciting and full of energy.

vibrate [US 'vaɪbreɪt, GB vaɪ'breɪt] *vi* [string, building, air] to shake with very small quick movements that can be felt or heard □ *The traffic makes the whole house vibrate.*

vibration [vaɪ'breɪʃn] *n*: see **vibrate** □ *We felt the vibrations when the bomb exploded.*

vicar ['vɪkər] *n* in the Anglican Church, a priest who is responsible for a church in a particular area.

vicarage ['vɪkərɪdʒ] *n* the house of a vicar.

vicarious [vɪ'keərɪəs] *adj* [enjoyment, pleasure, thrill] that is experienced by watching other people do something or by hearing about it rather than by doing it oneself.

vice [vaɪs] *n* -**1**. a criminal activity that involves illegal sex or drugs □ *a vice ring.* -**2**. a bad habit such as smoking, drinking alcohol etc (humorous use) □ *Everyone has their little vices.* -**3**. a tool used to hold wood or metal in place while it is being cut or shaped.

vice- *prefix* added to words to mean next in rank below somebody □ *vice-captain.*

vice admiral *n* an officer of high rank in some navies, below an admiral and above a rear admiral.

vice-chairman *n* the person who is next in rank to the chairman and sometimes acts in their place.

vice-chancellor *n* EDUCATION -**1**. the person who is next in rank to a chancellor of a US university. -**2**. the official who controls and organizes the affairs of a British university.

vice president *n* a person who is next in rank to a president and sometimes acts in their place.

vice squad *n* the part of the police force that deals with crimes such as prostitution and drug trafficking.

vice versa [,vaɪs-] *adv* a phrase used to show that the opposite of the situation that has been described is also true □ *If I do the shopping he cooks, and vice versa.*

vicinity [və'sɪnəti] *n* -**1**. **in the vicinity** near to a particular place □ *They live in the vicinity of Boston.* -**2**. **in the vicinity of sthg** about or approximately sthg □ *He earns in the vicinity of $80,000 a year.*

vicious ['vɪʃəs] *adj* -**1**. [person, attack] that is violent and cruel □ *This was a vicious and unprovoked attack.* -**2**. [criticism, rumor, lie] that is cruel and intended to hurt somebody □ *He described her as a vicious woman who had acted out of sheer malice.*

vicious circle *n* a difficult situation that creates new problems that make the original problem worse.

viciousness ['vɪʃəsnəs] *n*: see **vicious** □ *We are appalled by the viciousness of this attack.*

vicissitudes [və'sɪsətʲuːdz] *npl* changes in a person's circumstances (formal use) □ *the vicissitudes of war.*

victim ['vɪktəm] *n* -**1**. a person who suffers as the result of an accident or disaster □ *famine/earthquake victims.* -**2**. a person, group, institution etc that suffers because of the actions or beliefs of somebody else □ *Education is always the first victim of government cuts.* □ *Her uncle was the victim of a brutal attack.*

victimize, -ise ['vɪktəmaɪz] *vt* to make <sb> suffer unfairly because of their race, behavior, beliefs etc □ *He was victimized at school because he wore glasses.*

victor ['vɪktər] *n* the winner of a battle, contest etc (literary use).

Victoria [vɪk'tɔːrɪə] -**1**. a state in southeastern Australia. SIZE: 228,000 sq kms. POPULATION: 4,243,719. CAPITAL: Melbourne. -**2**. **Lake Victoria** the largest lake in Africa, between Uganda, Tanzania, and Kenya.

Victoria [vɪk'tɔːrɪə], **Queen** (1819–1901) Queen of Great Britain and Ireland from 1837 to 1901.

Victoria Cross *n* a medal given to British soldiers, sailors, and airmen for very brave acts in war.

Victoria Falls a large waterfall on the Zambezi River, between Zimbabwe and Zambia.

Victorian [vɪk'tɔːrɪən] *adj* -**1**. [society, dress, family] that is connected with the time when Victoria was queen of Britain (1837–1901). -**2**. [values, attitudes] that are thought to be typical of the time of Queen Victoria and involve being strict, religious, and respectable.

Victoriana [,vɪktɔːrɪ'ɑːnə] *n* a collective term for things made during the time when Victoria was queen of Britain.

victorious [vɪk'tɔːrɪəs] *adj* [army, general, team] that has won something; [smile, shout, gesture] that shows one has won something.

victory ['vɪktərɪ] (*pl* **victories**) *n* -**1**. the act of winning a battle, race, game etc □ *Victory is certain.* -**2**. a win □ *an election victory* □ *a victory for common sense* □ *Scotland won a decisive victory over Wales yesterday.*

video ['vɪdɪoʊ] (*pl* **videos**, *pt* & *pp* **videoed**, *cont* **videoing**) ◇ *n* -**1**. the showing on television of images that have been recorded on special tape □ *Video is widely used in language teaching.* -**2**. a recording of a movie, program, or event made on videotape □ *We stayed in and watched a video.* -**3**. a machine used to show video pictures on a television set. -**4**. a video cassette □ *a blank video* □ *video piracy.* ◇ *vt* -**1**. [movie, show] to record <a TV program> using a video recorder. -**2**. [wedding, party, christening] to record <an event> as it takes place using a video camera.

video camera *n* a camera used to record things on videotape.

video cassette *n* a plastic case containing videotape that is used in video recorders.

video cassette recorder *n* = **video recorder**.

video conferencing *n* a special TV system that makes it possible for people in different places to have a meeting by seeing each other on a screen as they speak.

videodisk US, **videodisc** GB ['vɪdɪoʊdɪsk] *n* a round flat piece of plastic from which recorded images can be played back on a television set.

video game *n* a computer game that is played by moving objects or figures on a video screen using a special control.

video machine *n* = **video recorder**.

videophone ['vɪdɪoʊfoʊn] *n* a device like a telephone with a screen that allows the people speaking to see each other.

video recorder *n* a machine that is used to record movies and television programs and play video cassettes.

video recording *n* a recording of an event, movie, program etc on videotape.

video store *n* a store where video cassettes can be rented or bought.

videotape ['vɪdɪoʊteɪp] *n* -1. = **video cassette**. -2. the special tape used to record and show video pictures.

vie [vaɪ] (*pt* & *pp* **vied**, *cont* **vying**) *vi* **to vie with sb for sthg** [for success, attention] to compete with sb for sthg, usually over a long period of time □ *They are vying with each other for the leadership.*

Vienna [vɪ'enə] the capital of Austria and its largest city. POPULATION: 1,512,000.

Viennese [ˌvɪə'niːz] *n* & *adj*: *see* **Vienna**.

Vietnam [US ˌviːet'nɑːm, GB -'næm] a country in Southeast Asia, on the southern China Sea. SIZE: 335,000 sq kms. POPULATION: 71,800,000 (*Vietnamese*). CAPITAL: Hanoi. LANGUAGE: Vietnamese. CURRENCY: dong.

Vietnamese [ˌviːetnə'miːz] *n* & *adj*: *see* **Vietnam**.

Vietnam War *n* **the Vietnam War** a civil war (1954–1975) between North and South Vietnam. North Vietnam was a Communist country, and the South was supported by US armed forces. The North won the war.

❧ VIETNAM WAR
In the Vietnam War the USA supported South Vietnam against the Communist forces of North Vietnam by sending hundreds of thousands of troops to fight. Many people were opposed to the US involvement in the war, both in the USA and abroad. Large numbers of young Americans refused to go and fight in Vietnam, and the soldiers who returned home after the US army was brought home in 1973 were not always popular. This period of US history has become the subject of many Hollywood movies.

---

view [vjuː] ◇ *n* -1. [on something] an opinion about something □ *political/religious/Marxist views* □ *It's a widely held view.* □ *He has a cynical view of life.* □ *What are your views on nuclear testing?* ■ **in my view** in my opinion. ■ **to take the view that...** to have the opinion that... -2. [over a place] the whole area that

can be seen from a particular place, especially a high place □ *There's a wonderful view from the top of the tower.* ■ **to come into view** to gradually become visible. -3. [from a seat] the ability to see something from a particular place □ *You're blocking my view.* □ *We had a terrible view from our seats.*

◇ *vt* -1. [person, responsibility, role] to consider <sb/sthg> in a particular way □ *How do you view your future career?* □ *Their activities are viewed with alarm by many people.* -2. [house, garden] to look at <sthg>, especially in order to form an opinion of it □ *Celia viewed the scene with evident pleasure.*

◆ **in view of** *prep* a phrase used to introduce information which must be thought about when discussing another situation, decision etc □ *In view of the facts/what happened...*

◆ **with a view to** *conj* **with a view to doing sthg** with the intention of doing sthg □ *They moved to Florida with a view to retiring there.*

viewer ['vjuːər] *n* -1. a person who watches a particular television program. -2. a device like a small box, used to look at transparent photographs □ *a slide viewer.*

viewfinder ['vjuːfaɪndər] *n* a device like a small window on a camera that one looks through to see what one is photographing.

viewpoint ['vjuːpɔɪnt] *n* -1. a way of thinking about something □ *Try and see things from my viewpoint.* -2. a place from which there is a good view.

vigil ['vɪdʒəl] *n* -1. an act of staying awake all night, e.g. in order to look after a sick person, pray, or make a political protest □ *'Famous actor in bedside vigil.'* -2. RELIGION a special service that takes place the evening before some religious festivals.

vigilance ['vɪdʒələns] *n* the quality or act of being vigilant □ *Our work requires constant vigilance.*

vigilant ['vɪdʒələnt] *adj* [person] who is constantly watching for possible danger or to see if anyone is doing anything wrong □ *We must remain vigilant at all times.*

vigilante [ˌvɪdʒə'læntɪ] *n* a person, usually a member of an unofficial group, who tries to fight crime without the help of the police.

vigor US, **vigour** GB ['vɪgər] *n* enthusiastic energy, determination, and physical strength □ *We set to work with renewed vigor.*

vigorous ['vɪgərəs] *adj* -1. [handshake, exercise] that is done with a lot of energy □ *I go for a vigorous jog every morning.* -2. [defense, denial, protest] that is forceful □ *There were vigorous protests from local residents.* -3. [person] who is healthy and full of energy □ *He's very vigorous for his age.*

vigour *n* GB = **vigor**.

Viking ['vaɪkɪŋ] ◇ *n* a member of a race from Scandinavia that attacked and settled in parts of northwestern Europe from the 8th to the 11th centuries. ◇ *adj*: *a Viking ship/helmet/museum.*

vile [vaɪl] *adj* [weather, mood, meal] that one

thinks is very unpleasant (informal use) □ *It has a vile taste.*

vilify ['vɪləfaɪ] (*pt* & *pp* **vilified**) *vt* to say or write bad things about <sb> in order to make other people dislike them (formal use).

villa ['vɪlə] *n* a large house in the countryside or near the sea.

village ['vɪlɪdʒ] *n* a group of houses and other buildings that is smaller than a town and is often in a country area □ *a pretty little village* □ *the village green.*

villager ['vɪlɪdʒər] *n* a person who lives in a village.

villain ['vɪlən] *n* -1. a bad character in a movie, book etc. -2. a criminal (old-fashioned use).

VIN (*abbr of* **vehicle identification number**) *n* a number that is stamped onto all motor vehicles when they are produced so that a vehicle can be identified if the license plates are changed.

vinaigrette [,vɪnə'ɡret] *n* a cold sauce for salads that is made of oil, vinegar, and flavorings.

Vinci ['vɪntʃɪ] = **Leonardo da Vinci.**

vindicate ['vɪndɪkeɪt] *vt* [person] to show that <sb> does not deserve the blame for something; [belief, faith] to show that <sthg> is right □ *He has been completely vindicated by the courts.* □ *Her confidence in him has been fully vindicated.*

vindication [,vɪndɪ'keɪʃn] *n*: *see* **vindicate** □ *She sees the verdict as a vindication of her long struggle in the courts.*

vindictive [vɪn'dɪktɪv] *adj* [person] who wants to harm and upset somebody □ *Children can be very vindictive.*

vine [vaɪn] *n* a climbing plant, especially one that produces grapes.

vinegar ['vɪnɪɡər] *n* a liquid, often made from sour wine, that has a sharp taste and is used to preserve vegetables and to flavor food.

vine leaf *n* a leaf of a vine.

vineyard ['vɪnjərd] *n* an area where vines are grown to make wine.

vintage ['vɪntɪdʒ] ◇ *adj* -1. **a vintage wine/port** a wine/port that is of good quality, especially one that has been stored for a long time. -2. [comedy, performance] that is the best of its type. ◇ *n* the year in which a wine is produced □ *1964 was a good vintage.*

vintage car *n* GB a car made between 1919 and 1930.

vintner ['vɪntnər] *n* a person whose job is to buy and sell wines.

vinyl ['vaɪnl] *n* a strong plastic that bends easily and is used to make things such as floor coverings, records, and paint.

viola [vɪ'oʊlə] *n* -1. MUSIC a musical instrument like a violin but larger. -2. a small garden plant grown for its white, yellow, purple, or blue flowers.

violate ['vaɪəleɪt] *vt* -1. [law, agreement, human rights] to do something that is not allowed by <sthg that has been agreed to formally> □ *They are accused of violating international law.* -2. [peace, privacy] to disturb <sthg>. -3. [tomb, grave] to break into <a special or holy place> and treat it with disrespect.

violation [,vaɪə'leɪʃn] *n*: *see* **violate** □ *They acted in violation of the treaty* □ *a traffic violation.*

violence ['vaɪələns] *n* -1. physical force used to kill or injure a person or animal □ *an outbreak of violence.* -2. [of words, a reaction, emotion] great force □ *He spoke with unexpected violence.*

violent ['vaɪələnt] *adj* -1. [person] who uses or is likely to use violence; [movie, area, game] in which there is a lot of violence □ *Her husband was a violent and abusive man.* □ *There has been an increase in violent crime.* □ *The play contains a number of violent scenes.* -2. [reaction, protest, outburst] that involves strong feelings □ *I took a violent dislike to them both.* -3. [explosion, blow] that is very sudden and powerful □ *a violent storm.* -4. [color] that is too strong and bright □ *a violent orange.*

violently ['vaɪələntlɪ] *adv* [attack, react, die] *see* **violent** □ *I was violently opposed to capital punishment.*

violet ['vaɪələt] ◇ *adj* [link, dress, satin] that is blue-purple. ◇ *n* -1. a small purple or white flower that has a sweet smell. -2. a blue-purple color.

violin [,vaɪə'lɪn] *n* a wooden musical instrument that is held between one's shoulder and chin and is played by moving a bow across the four strings.

violinist [,vaɪə'lɪnəst] *n* a person who plays the violin.

VIP *n abbr of* **very important person** □ *a VIP lounge.*

viper ['vaɪpər] *n* a small poisonous snake found in Europe.

viral ['vaɪrəl] *adj* [disease, infection] that is caused by a virus.

Virgil ['vɜːrdʒəl] (70–19 BC) a Roman poet whose best-known work is the *Aeneid.*

virgin ['vɜːrdʒɪn] ◇ *adj* **virgin forest/land** forest/land that has not been explored or changed by humans. ■ **virgin snow/paper** snow/paper that is unmarked. ◇ *n* a person who has never had sex □ *a virgin bride.*

Virginia [vər'dʒɪnjə] a state in the eastern USA, on the Atlantic Coast. ABBREVIATION: VA. SIZE: 103,030 sq kms. POPULATION: 6,187,358 (*Virginians*). CAPITAL: Richmond.

Virginia creeper *n* a garden plant that grows on walls and has large green leaves that turn red in autumn.

Virgin Islands -1. **the British Virgin Islands** a group of islands in the Caribbean that belong to the United Kingdom. SIZE: 153 sq kms. POPULATION: 13,000 (*British Virgin Islanders*). CAPITAL: Road Town. LANGUAGE: English. CURRENCY: US dollar. -2. **the US Virgin Islands** a group of islands in the Caribbean that belong to the USA. SIZE: 355 sq kms. POPULATION: 106,000 (*US Virgin Islanders*). CAPITAL: Charlotte Amalie. LANGUAGE: English, Spanish, Creole. CURRENCY: US dollar.

virginity [vəˈdʒɪnəti] *n* **to lose one's virginity** to have sex for the first time.

Virgin Mary = Mary.

Virgin Queen: **the Virgin Queen** a name for Queen Elizabeth I.

Virgo [ˈvɜːˠgoʊ] (*pl* **Virgos**) *n* a sign of the zodiac, often represented by a girl; a person born under this sign between August 23 and September 22.

virile [US ˈvɪrl, GB ˈvɪraɪl] *adj* [man] who has the qualities that are supposed to be typical of a man, e.g. strength and strong sexual desires.

virility [vəˈrɪləti] *n*: *see* **virile** □ *Some men see fast cars as a sign of virility.*

virtual [ˈvɜːˠtʃʊəl] *adj* that is so close to the truth that it can be considered as being true □ *His father's a virtual alcoholic.*

virtually [ˈvɜːˠtʃʊəli] *adv* [impossible, empty] very nearly □ *Their marriage was virtually over by then.*

virtual reality *n* a set of surroundings created by a computer that appears real to the person looking at it.

virtue [ˈvɜːˠtjuː] *n* -1. the quality of being good and doing what is right. -2. a good quality such as patience, kindness etc □ *She possessed many virtues.* -3. an advantage □ *the virtues of being self-employed.*
◆ **by virtue of** *prep* because of <sthg> □ *He has succeeded by virtue of his social connections.*

virtuoso [ˌvɜːˠtjʊˈoʊsoʊ] (*pl* **virtuosos** OR **virtuosi** [-siː]) *n* a person who is extremely good at something, especially music □ *a virtuoso violinist.*

virtuous [ˈvɜːˠtʃʊəs] *adj* [person, life] that is full of good qualities.

virulent [ˈvɪrələnt] *adj* -1. [speech, attack, hatred] that is very bitter and hostile (formal use). -2. [disease, strain of bacteria] that spreads quickly and is very dangerous.

virus [ˈvaɪrəs] *n* -1. MEDICINE a very small living thing that causes disease □ *the HIV virus.* -2. COMPUTING a computer program that is designed to enter a computer system and damage or destroy the information stored there □ *a computer virus.*

visa [ˈviːzə] *n* a special mark put in a person's passport that allows them to enter, go through, or leave a particular foreign country □ *an exit/entry visa.*

vis-à-vis [ˌviːzəˈviː] *prep* a phrase used when comparing two things or considering the relationship between them (formal use) □ *What exactly is our position vis-à-vis the South American market?*

viscose [ˈvɪskoʊs] *n* a smooth fabric, like silk, made from cellulose and chemicals.

viscosity [vɪˈskɒsəti] *n*: *see* **viscous**.

viscount [ˈvaɪkaʊnt] *n* a British nobleman who is higher in rank than a baron and lower in rank than an earl.

viscous [ˈvɪskəs] *adj* [liquid, substance] that is thick and sticky and does not flow easily.

vise [vaɪs] *n* US a tool used to hold wood or metal in place while it is being cut or shaped.

visibility [ˌvɪzəˈbɪləti] *n* the distance it is possible to see, especially under particular weather conditions □ *Rain and mist are causing poor visibility.*

visible [ˈvɪzəbl] *adj* -1. [road, scar, person] that can be seen □ *The egg is barely visible to the naked eye.* -2. [improvement, change] that is noticeable □ *I was greatly saddened by the visible deterioration in his condition.*

visibly [ˈvɪzəbli] *adv* [worse, older] in a way that can be seen □ *She was visibly upset.*

vision [ˈvɪʒn] *n* -1. the ability to see □ *poor/good vision.* -2. [of a politician, leader] the ability to realize what is going to happen in the future □ *a man of vision* □ *He had the vision to foresee the war.* -3. [in a dream] an image seen in one's imagination or in a dream, often as part of a religious experience □ *nightmarish visions of the future.* -4. TV the picture that appears on a television screen □ *loss of vision.*

visionary [US ˈvɪʒəneri, GB -əri] (*pl* **visionaries**) ◇ *n* a person who has strong and clear ideas about improving things in the future. ◇ *adj*: *a visionary politician/leader.*

visit [ˈvɪzət] ◇ *vt* -1. [doctor, relative, friend] to go and see <sb> □ *They're away at the moment visiting friends.* -2. [country, museum, exhibition] to go and see <a place> □ *the many thousands of people who visit the gallery every year.* -3. **to visit a site** COMPUTING to find information at a site on the Internet. ◇ *n* -1. [to a doctor, relative, friend] the act of visiting somebody □ *You must pay us a visit next time you're in town.* -2. [to a country, museum, exhibition] the act of visiting a place □ *We hope you have enjoyed your visit.* ■ **on a visit** while visiting □ *We saw it on a visit to the States.*
◆ **visit with** *vt fus* US **to visit with sb** to go and see sb □ *I stopped by on the way home from work and visited with my grandmother.*

visiting card [ˈvɪzətɪŋ-] *n* a small piece of card that has one's name and address on it and that one gives to people on social and business occasions.

visiting hours *npl* the times at which sick or injured people can be visited in hospital.

visitor [ˈvɪzətəˠ] *n* -1. a person who is visiting somebody. -2. a person who is visiting a place □ *You can get more information at the visitors' center.*

visitors' book *n* a book kept in a hotel, at an exhibition etc in which visitors write their names, addresses, and the date of their visit.

visor [ˈvaɪzəˠ] *n* the part of a helmet that can be moved down to cover one's face and eyes.

vista [ˈvɪstə] *n* -1. a beautiful view. -2. a vision, e.g. of new possibilities or opportunities □ *New and exciting vistas opened up before her.*

VISTA [ˈvɪstə] (*abbr of* **Volunteers in Service to America**) *n* a US government organization that provides volunteers for one-year positions on public service projects to help poor people.

visual ['vɪʒʊəl] *adj* [effect, joke, impact] that is experienced by being seen; [awareness, handicap] that is connected with the ability to see □ *the visual arts* □ *a very powerful visual image.*

visual aids *npl* a collective term for things such as photographs, movies, or maps that are used by people, especially teachers, to help an audience or class to understand and remember information.

visual display unit *n* → VDU.

visualize, -ise ['vɪʒʊəlaɪz] *vt* [face, idea, scene] to form a clear mental image of the details, appearance etc of <sthg> □ *He tried to visualize the expression on their faces as he told them the news.* ■ **to visualize doing sthg** to imagine doing sthg □ *I can't visualize things getting any better.*

visually ['vɪʒʊəlɪ] *adv* **visually handicapped** blind or nearly blind. ■ **visually impaired** whose vision has been damaged, e.g. by illness or an accident.

vital ['vaɪtl] *adj* **-1.** [support, work, operation] that is very important for the success of something □ *It's vital that the meeting goes well.* **-2.** [person] who is full of energy.

vitality [vaɪ'tælətɪ] *n* energy and liveliness □ *She was animated and full of vitality.*

vitally ['vaɪtəlɪ] *adv* **vitally important** very important.

vital statistics *npl* the measurements of a woman's chest, waist, and hips (informal use).

vitamin [US 'vaɪtəmən, GB 'vɪt-] *n* a chemical substance that is found in very small quantities in food and that the body needs for growth and health □ *vitamin pills.*

vitreous ['vɪtrɪəs] *adj* [china] that looks like glass.

vitriolic [,vɪtrɪ'ɒlɪk] *adj* [person, language, abuse] that is cruel and bitter (formal use).

viva ['vaɪvə] *n* GB EDUCATION a university exam that is spoken rather than written.

vivacious [vɪ'veɪʃəs] *adj* [girl, woman] who is full of energy and has an attractive personality.

vivacity [vɪ'væsətɪ] *n*: *see* **vivacious.**

Vivaldi [vɪ'vældɪ], **Antonio** (1678–1741) an Italian composer whose best-known work is *The Four Seasons.*

vivid ['vɪvəd] *adj* **-1.** [color] that is bright and strong. **-2.** [memory, description, dream] that is so clear and detailed that it seems real □ *She has a very vivid imagination.*

vividly ['vɪvədlɪ] *adv* [remember, describe] *see* **vivid** □ *vividly painted.*

vivisection [,vɪvə'sekʃn] *n* the practice of performing operations on live animals in scientific experiments.

vixen ['vɪksən] *n* a female fox.

viz [vɪz] *(abbr of* **videlicet)** namely (used in front of information that explains something more clearly).

VLF *(abbr of* **very low frequency)** *n* a range of

radio frequencies between 3 and 30 kilohertz.

V-neck *n* **-1.** a neck of a dress, sweater etc in the shape of a letter V. **-2. a V-neck (sweater)** a sweater with a V-neck.

VOA *n abbr of* **Voice of America.**

vocabulary [və'kæbjələrɪ] *(pl* **vocabularies)** *n* **-1.** [of a person] all the words that one knows or uses in a particular language □ *She wants to increase her Polish vocabulary.* **-2.** [in a language] all the words in a particular language □ *English has a very rich vocabulary.* **-3.** [of a subject] the words that are used to talk about a particular subject, e.g. computers or medicine □ *legal vocabulary.* **-4.** [for reference] a list of words, usually in alphabetical order, with a translation or explanation of their meaning.

vocal ['vəʊkl] *adj* **-1.** [person] who expresses their opinions freely and loudly □ *She is very vocal in her criticism of the government.* **-2.** [range, skill, training] that is connected with a singer's or actor's voice.

◆ **vocals** *npl* the part of a pop or jazz song that is sung rather than played on instruments □ *And on vocals, we have Chet White.*

vocal cords *npl* the part of one's throat that vibrates and produces sounds when one speaks.

vocalist ['vəʊkələst] *n* a singer in a pop or jazz band.

vocation [vəʊ'keɪʃn] *n* a job, e.g. being a teacher, nurse, or priest, that one does because one wants to help other people rather than to earn a lot of money. ■ **to have a vocation** to strongly feel that one should do a particular job.

vocational [vəʊ'keɪʃnəl] *adj* [course, training] that prepares people for a job □ *vocational guidance.*

vociferous [vəʊ'sɪfərəs] *adj* [protester, opponent] who expresses their opinions loudly; [complaint, demand] that is expressed loudly.

vodka ['vɒdkə] *n* a colorless alcoholic drink, originally made in Russia; a glass of this drink.

vogue [vəʊg] ◇ *n* a fashion □ *The vogue for long hair is on its way out.* ■ **in vogue** in fashion □ *Mini-skirts are in vogue again.* ◇ *adj*: *a vogue word.*

voice [vɔɪs] ◇ *n* **-1.** the sounds one makes when one is speaking or singing □ *a beautiful/an awful singing voice* □ *a loud/a low/an angry voice.* ■ **to raise/lower one's voice** to speak more loudly/more quietly □ *Don't you raise your voice to me!* □ *She lowered her voice to a whisper.* ■ **to keep one's voice down** to speak more quietly □ *Keep your voice down, they'll hear you.* **-2.** an opinion □ *the voice of the people.* ■ **the voice of reason/experience** advice or an opinion that is reasonable/based on experience. **-3. to have a voice** to have the right to express an opinion about something □ *We had no voice in the decision.* **-4.** GRAMMAR the form of a verb which shows whether the subject of a sentence is performing an action (the active voice) or being affected by it (the passive voice).

◇ *vt* [opinion, doubt, criticism] to express <sthg> □ *an opportunity to voice one's fears.*

voice box *n* the larynx.

voice mail *n* a system for recording telephone messages, used e.g. in large companies.

Voice of America *n* **the Voice of America** a radio station that is run by the US government and that broadcasts programs about the USA to other countries.

voice-over *n* recorded words read by an unseen person that comment on or explain what is happening on a television program, advertisement etc.

void [vɔɪd] ◇ *adj* **-1.** [result, agreement, contract] that has no official or legal value. **-2. to be void of sthg** [of content, interest] to be completely without sthg (literary use) □ *Her words were utterly void of emotion.* **-3.** → **null.** ◇ *n* **-1.** a situation or period of time that seems empty because nothing exciting or pleasant happens (literary use) □ *Life without him would be an empty void.* **-2.** an empty space that seems very large or terrifying □ *We gazed down into the void.*

voile [vɔɪl] *n* a thin light material used to make curtains, blouses etc.

vol. *abbr of* **volume.**

volatile [US 'vɒlətl, GB -taɪl] *adj* **-1.** [situation] that may change suddenly and become dangerous or violent. **-2.** [person] who has sudden extreme changes of mood or attitude.

vol-au-vent ['vɒlouvɒn] *n* a small pastry case filled with a thick sauce that contains chicken, mushrooms, shrimp etc.

volcanic [vɒl'kænɪk] *adj* [rock, island, activity] that is connected with volcanoes □ *a volcanic eruption.*

volcano [vɒl'keɪnou] (*pl* **volcanoes** OR **volcanos**) *n* a kind of mountain that has a hole in the top and that sometimes sends out smoke, ash, and hot liquid rock.

vole [voʊl] *n* a small animal that is similar to a mouse but has a short tail.

volition [voʊ'lɪʃn] *n* **of one's own volition** [act, leave, go] because one wants to, not because one is forced to (formal use) □ *He gave up acting of his own volition.*

volley ['vɒlɪ] (*pl* **volleys**) ◇ *vt* to hit or kick <a ball> before it touches the ground. ◇ *n* **-1. a volley of shots** a number of shots fired from a gun at the same time. **-2. a volley of questions/insults etc** a number of questions/insults etc that follow one another quickly. **-3.** SPORT a shot in tennis, a kick in soccer etc that is volleyed.

volleyball ['vɒlɪbɔːl] *n* a game in which two teams hit a large ball over a high net using their hands and without letting the ball touch the ground.

volt [voʊlt] *n* a unit of electrical power.

voltage ['voʊltɪdʒ] *n* the force of an electrical current measured in volts.

Voltaire [vɒl'teəʳ], **François Marie Arouet**

(1694–1778) a French writer who criticized French politics and society in many of his books, including his best-known work, *Candide.*

voluble ['vɒljəbl] *adj* [person] who talks a lot (formal use) □ *After a few drinks, she grew more voluble.*

volume ['vɒljʊm] *n* **-1.** the loudness of the sound made by a television, radio, stereo etc □ *Could you turn the volume up?* □ *the volume control.* **-2.** [of an object, gas, liquid] the amount of space that something occupies. **-3.** [of work, letters] an amount of something □ *We are looking at ways to reduce the volume of traffic on our roads.* **-4.** [for reading] a book; one book of a set □ *a a slim volume of verse* □ *an encyclopedia in 20 volumes.*

voluminous [və'luːmɪnəs] *adj* **-1.** [dress, shirt, jacket] that is very large and loose and uses a lot of material. **-2.** [bag, suitcase, pocket] that is very large and able to hold a lot of things.

voluntarily [ˌvɒlən'terəlɪ] *adv* [attend, work, go] *see* **voluntary.**

voluntary [US 'vɒlənterɪ, GB -tərɪ] *adj* **-1.** [attendance, contribution, action] that one does, makes etc because one wants to and not because one has to □ *The store is run entirely on a voluntary basis.* **-2.** [worker] who works without being paid; [work, service, organization] that is done by or run by people who work without being paid.

voluntary liquidation *n* the act by an unsuccessful company of stopping business and selling its valuable possessions □ *The company has gone into voluntary liquidation.*

voluntary redundancy *n* GB the act of agreeing to leave one's job in exchange for a payment □ *Many employees have taken voluntary redundancy.*

volunteer [ˌvɒlən'tɪəʳ] ◇ *vt* **-1. to volunteer to do sthg** to offer to do sthg because one wants to □ *I've volunteered to help collect money for charity.* **-2.** [information, advice, statement] to offer <sthg> without being asked. ◇ *vi* **-1.** to offer to do things because one wants to □ *She's always volunteering for things.* **-2.** MILITARY to join the armed forces because one wants to, especially during a war. ◇ *n* **-1.** somebody who has volunteered or is willing to volunteer to do something □ *Any volunteers to work this weekend?* **-2.** [for a charity] a person who chooses not to be paid for the work they do. **-3.** MILITARY a person who joins the armed forces willingly, especially in wartime.

voluptuous [və'lʌptʃʊəs] *adj* [woman] who has large breasts and a soft rounded body and is sexually exciting.

vomit ['vɒmət] ◇ *vi* to bring up food or drink from the stomach through the mouth, because one is ill or drunk. ◇ *n* food or drink that has been brought up by vomiting.

voodoo ['vuːduː] *n* a religious cult involving witchcraft that is practiced by some inhabitants of the West Indies, especially in Haiti.

voracious [və'reɪʃəs] *adj* **-1.** [eater] who wants

to eat a lot □ *a voracious appetite.* **-2. a voracious reader/collector etc** a person who reads/collects things etc very eagerly.

vortex ['vɔːrteks] (*pl* **vortexes** OR **vortices** [-tɪsiːz]) *n* **-1.** a powerful mass of air or water that spins around very quickly and pulls objects into its center. **-2.** a harmful situation that somebody becomes involved in without wanting to □ *a vortex of despair.*

vote [voʊt] ◇ *vi* to choose formally one of various possibilities available, usually by writing on a piece of paper, speaking, or raising one's hand □ *I voted Republican.* □ *those who voted for/against the bill* □ *I'm going to vote for Miller.*
◇ *vt* **-1. to be voted captain/winner/leader etc** to be made captain/winner/leader etc as a result of a vote. **-2. to vote to do sthg** to decide to do sthg by voting □ *They voted to return to work.* **-3. to vote (that)...** to suggest that something should happen □ *I vote (that) we all go home.*
◇ *n* **-1.** an act of making a choice or decision by voting □ *Unions are demanding a vote on strike action.* ■ **to put sthg to the vote** to decide sthg by voting □ *Let's put the matter to the vote.* **-2.** a choice or decision made by voting □ *policies aimed at winning votes* □ *The debate ended in a vote against the motion.* □ *The vote went in her favor/against her.* **-3.** the votes made by a particular group of people in an election □ *They hope to win the nationalist vote.* **-4. the vote** the right to vote in political elections □ *Large sections of the population did not have the vote.*
◆ **vote in** *vt sep* **to vote sb in** [politician, party] to give sb enough votes to allow them to hold a position of power.
◆ **vote out** *vt sep* **to vote sb out** [politician, party] to give sb too few votes to allow them to continue to hold a position of power.

vote of confidence (*pl* **votes of confidence**) *n* a formal declaration of support, usually for a government, expressed by a vote.

vote of no confidence (*pl* **votes of no confidence**) *n* a formal declaration of lack of support, usually for a government, expressed by a vote.

vote of thanks (*pl* **votes of thanks**) *n* a formal public speech that expresses thanks to somebody for something they have done.

voter ['voʊtər] *n* a person who votes or has the right to vote, especially in a public election.

voting ['voʊtɪŋ] *n* the act of voting □ *Voting is under way all over the country.*

voting booth *n* US a small separated area in a polling place where one can vote in private.

voting machine *n* US a device in a voting booth that has buttons one pushes or a lever one pulls to record one's vote.

vouch [vaʊtʃ] ◆ **vouch for** *vt fus* **to vouch for sb** to say that sb has a good character □ *I can vouch for her personally.* ■ **to vouch for sthg** to be able to say from one's own experience or knowledge that sthg is true □ *I can vouch for the accuracy of these figures.*

voucher ['vaʊtʃər] *n* a piece of paper that can be used instead of money for a particular purpose □ *a meal/travel voucher.*

vow [vaʊ] ◇ *n* a serious promise □ *marriage/religious vows* □ *I made a vow never to see him again.* ◇ *vt* **to vow to do sthg** to make a serious promise to do sthg □ *I vowed never to speak to him again.* □ *She vowed (that) she would get her revenge one day.*

vowel ['vaʊəl] *n* any of the sounds in human speech that are made with the mouth and throat open; a letter that represents one of these sounds (*a, e, i, o,* and *u* in the English alphabet).

voyage ['vɔɪdʒ] *n* a long trip by ship or boat □ *a sea voyage* □ *a voyage of discovery.*

voyeur [vwɑːˈjɜːr] *n* a person who gets sexual pleasure from watching other people having sex, especially without them knowing.

voyeurism [vwɑːˈjɜːrɪzm] *n* the behavior of a voyeur.

VP *n abbr of* **vice president**.

vs *abbr of* **versus**.

VSO (*abbr of* **Voluntary Service Overseas**) *n* a British charity that sends voluntary workers to developing countries.

VSOP (*abbr of* **very special old pale**) a term, written after the name of an alcoholic drink such as brandy or port, that shows that it is between 20 and 25 years old.

VT *abbr of* **Vermont**.

VTOL ['viːtɒl] (*abbr of* **vertical takeoff and landing**) *n* a type of aircraft that can take off by rising straight into the air and land by coming straight down, without needing a runway.

VTR (*abbr of* **videotape recorder**) *n* a piece of equipment used in TV broadcasting that records video signals onto magnetic tape.

vulgar ['vʌlgər] *adj* **-1.** [person, display, appearance] that shows bad taste □ *He has such vulgar taste in clothes.* **-2.** [joke, gesture, remark] that refers to sex in an offensive way □ *Don't be so vulgar!*

vulgarity [vʌlˈgærətɪ] *n* the quality of being vulgar □ *complaints about vulgarity and bad language.*

vulnerability [ˌvʌlnərəˈbɪlətɪ] *n* the state of being vulnerable.

vulnerable ['vʌlnərəbl] *adj* **-1.** [person] who can be easily harmed, physically or emotionally □ *After Jay's death, I felt alone and vulnerable.* □ *Children are especially vulnerable to the effects of air pollution.* **-2.** [place, position] that can be easily attacked or entered by force □ *Their defenses were vulnerable to air attack.*

vulture ['vʌltʃər] *n* **-1.** a large ugly bird that lives in tropical countries and eats dead animals. **-2.** a person who takes advantage of weak or helpless people.

w [ˈdʌblju:] (*pl* **w's** OR **ws**), **W** [ˈdʌblju:] (*pl* **W's** OR **Ws**) *n* the twenty-third letter of the English alphabet.

◆ **W** -1. *abbr of* **west**. -2. *abbr of* **watt**.

W-2 *n* in the USA, a form given to a person by their employer once a year showing their earnings and how much tax they have paid.

WA -1. *abbr of* **Washington State**. -2. *abbr of* **Western Australia**.

wacky [ˈwækɪ] (*compar* **wackier**, *superl* **wackiest**) *adj* [behavior, person, sense of humor] that is amusing in a slightly unusual or odd way (informal use).

wad [wɒd] *n* -1. [of newspaper, cotton wool] a thick mass of something tightly pressed together. -2. a number of bills, documents etc folded or fastened together □ *a wad of banknotes/dollar bills.*

wadding [ˈwɒdɪŋ] *n* thick soft material that is used to protect packed objects or to bandage wounds.

waddle [ˈwɒdl] *vi* [duck, person] to walk with short steps, with the body leaning slightly from one side to the other.

wade [weɪd] *vi* to walk through deep water.

◆ **wade through** *vt fus* **to wade through sthg** [report, book, details] to read sthg long and boring.

wading pool [ˈweɪdɪŋ-] *n* US -1. a shallow pool of water, e.g. in a park, where children can paddle. -2. a large inflatable plastic pool that can be filled with water for children to play in.

wafer [ˈweɪfər] *n* a very thin sweet cookie, usually eaten with ice cream.

wafer-thin *adj* [slice, piece] that is very thin and flat.

waffle [ˈwɒfl] ◇ *n* COOKING a thick crepe with a pattern of squares on both sides that is eaten hot. -2. GB something somebody writes or says that is long and vague, and does not contain any useful or important information (informal use). ◇ *vi* -1. GB to talk or write waffle. -2. US to avoid answering a question or making a decision.

waft [wɑːft] *vi* [sound, smell] to move lightly through the air; [air, breeze] to move lightly □ *The sound of laughter wafted in from the garden.*

wag [wæg] (*pt* & *pp* **wagged**, *cont* **wagging**) ◇ *vt* [tail, finger, pencil] to move <sthg> repeatedly from side to side □ *"Now, now," he said, wagging his finger at me.* ◇ *vi* [tail] to move repeatedly from side to side.

wage [weɪdʒ] ◇ *n* the amount of money that

is paid every week to somebody for doing work □ *a low/high wage* □ *the average weekly wage* □ *a wage increase.* ◇ *vt* **to wage war on sb/sthg** [on crime, an enemy] to start and continue a war or struggle against sb/sthg.

◆ **wages** *npl* a wage.
NOTE: Compare **salary**.

wage claim *n* a demand by workers for higher pay.

wage differential *n* the difference between the money earned by people doing different jobs in a company or industry.

wage earner *n* somebody who earns wages □ *She's the main wage earner in the family.*

wage freeze *n* the act of fixing wages at a particular level.

wager [ˈweɪdʒər] *n* an agreement with somebody to pay a certain amount of money to whoever guesses the result of something, e.g. a horse race, correctly.

waggish [ˈwægɪʃ] *adj* [person, remark, behavior] that is amusing in a clever way.

waggle [ˈwægl] (informal use) ◇ *vt* [tail, ears] to move <sthg> repeatedly from side to side or up and down. ◇ *vi* [tail, ears] to move repeatedly from side to side or up and down.

waggon [ˈwægən] *n* GB = **wagon**.

Wagner [ˈvɑːgnər], **Richard** (1813–1883) a German composer famous for his operas, including *Tristan and Isolde* and *The Ring of the Nibelung.*

wagon [ˈwægən] *n* -1. a vehicle with four wheels that is pulled by an animal, especially a horse. -2. GB RAIL a vehicle for carrying goods, especially an open one, that is pulled by a train.

wagon train *n* a group of covered wagons traveling together.

wagtail [ˈwægteɪl] *n* a small bird with a very long tail that moves up and down when it walks.

waif [weɪf] *n* a person, child, or animal that has no home and is not being cared for (literary use).

wail [weɪl] ◇ *n* -1. [of a person, animal] a long cry of pain or sadness □ *The child let out a wail of indignation.* -2. [of the wind, a siren] a long, high-pitched sound. ◇ *vi* [siren, wind, baby] to produce a wail □ *I could hear a baby wailing in the background.*

wailing [ˈweɪlɪŋ] *n* a continuous wail □ *the weeping and wailing of mourners at the funeral.*

waist [weɪst] *n* -1. the middle of the human body between the chest and the hips □ *paralyzed from the waist down* □ *The grass was waist-high.* -2. the part of a piece of clothing that goes around the waist □ *All my skirts are getting too tight in the waist.*

waistband [ˈweɪstbænd] *n* a band of material at the waist of a skirt or pair of trousers.

waistcoat [ˈweɪstkəʊt] *n* GB a piece of clothing without sleeves and with buttons in the front, often worn by men under a jacket.

waistline [ˈweɪstlaɪn] *n* -1. the measurement around one's waist. -2. the position of the waistband on a dress in relation to one's waist □ *I don't suit dresses with a low waistline.*

wait [weɪt] ◇ *vi* **-1.** [person] to stay in one place without doing much until somebody or something comes or something happens □ *Have you been waiting long?* ■ **wait and see** a phrase used to tell somebody to be patient because they cannot change what will happen in the future □ *"Is she going to be all right?" — "We'll just have to wait and see."* ■ **wait a minute** OR **second** OR **moment** a phrase used to interrupt somebody when they are speaking, often to show disagreement; a phrase used while speaking to show that one has just had a new idea □ *Wait a minute, aren't you being a little unfair?* □ *Wait a moment, why didn't I think of it before?* ■ **(just) you wait!** a phrase used to threaten or warn somebody about something □ *You wait until the boss finds out!* **-2.** **it can't** OR **won't wait** it is very important and must be done immediately □ *Have another glass of wine, the dishes can wait.* □ *I've got some work that won't wait.*

◇ *vt* **-1. I/he etc couldn't wait to do sthg** I/he etc wanted to do sthg as soon as possible □ *I can't wait to see the photos.* **-2.** US to delay <sthg> (informal use) □ *Don't wait dinner for me.*

◇ *n* the act or period of waiting □ *They had a long wait.* ■ **to lie in wait for sb** to hide and wait for sb in order to attack them □ *Who knows what disasters may be lying in wait for us.*

◆ **wait around**, **wait about** *vi* to wait, especially with not much to do, or when somebody or something is late □ *I got tired of waiting around in the cold.*

◆ **wait for** *vt fus* **to wait for sb/sthg** [for a friend, bus, opportunity] to wait until sb/sthg comes □ *I've been waiting for you for over an hour!* □ *She's waiting for the right man to come along.* □ *We got back into the car and waited for the rain to stop.*

◆ **wait on** *vt fus* **to wait on sb** to serve food and drink to sb □ *He expects to be waited on hand and foot.*

◆ **wait up** *vi* not to go to bed because one is waiting for somebody to come home □ *I waited up for her until midnight.*

waiter ['weɪtəʳ] *n* a man who serves food and drink in a restaurant or café.

waiting game ['weɪtɪŋ-] *n* **to play a waiting game** to wait before doing something in order to see how a situation develops.

waiting list *n* a list of people who want something that is not available immediately □ *There's a three-year waiting list for some operations.*

waiting room *n* a room in a station, hospital etc where people can wait.

waitress ['weɪtrəs] *n* a woman who serves food and drink in a restaurant or café.

waive [weɪv] *vt* [rule, charge, fee] to decide not to apply <sthg>; [right, claim] to give up <sthg> (formal use).

waiver ['weɪvəʳ] *n* LAW a written statement that waives a right, claim etc.

wake [weɪk] (*pt* **woke** OR **waked**, *pp* **woken** OR

waked) ◇ *vt* to make <sb> stop sleeping □ *He woke me at seven o'clock.* ◇ *vi*: *I woke several times during the night.* ◇ *n* the track that a ship or boat leaves as it moves through the water. ■ **in one's wake** behind one as one goes □ *Aunt Mamie went abroad, leaving a trail of unpaid debts in her wake.* ■ **in the wake of sthg** after and as a result of sthg □ *The police are urging the public to be vigilant in the wake of the recent bombings.*

◆ **wake up** ◇ *vt sep* **to wake sb up** to make sb stop sleeping □ *Wake me up before you go.* ◇ *vi*: *Nell didn't wake up until eight o'clock.*

◆ **wake up to** *vt fus* **to wake up to sthg** to begin to become aware of and understand sthg unpleasant □ *When will you wake up to the fact that he's just using you?*

waken ['weɪkən] (formal use) ◇ *vt* to wake <sb>. ◇ *vi* to wake.

waking hours ['weɪkɪŋ-] *npl* the hours during which one is not sleeping □ *He spends all his waking hours worrying about it.*

Wales [weɪlz] a country in the United Kingdom, west of England. SIZE: 20,800 sq kms. POPULATION: 2,798,200 (*Welsh*). CAPITAL: Cardiff. LANGUAGE: English, Welsh.

🐦 WALES
Wales, which is officially called the Principality of Wales, has the same legal, educational, and banking system as England, and is governed mainly from London. The Welsh language is spoken by about 20% of the population. There is now a Welsh-language television channel and radio station, and many public signs are written in English and Welsh. Some Welsh people would like Wales to be completely independent from the United Kingdom and have its own government.

Wales, Prince of the title given to the eldest son of the British king or queen.

Wales, Princess of the title given to the wife of the Prince of Wales.

walk [wɔːk] ◇ *vi* to move by placing one foot in front of the other □ *Our son is just learning to walk.* □ *We must have walked ten miles.* □ *We walked along the beach and watched the sunset.* ◇ *vt* **-1.** to go with <sb> on foot to make sure they are safe □ *Let me walk you to your car.* □ *Will someone walk you home afterward?* **-2.** to take <a dog> out for exercise. **-3.** to cover <a distance> on foot □ *I had to walk all the way home.* ■ **to walk the streets** to be homeless; to be a prostitute.

◇ *n* **-1.** a trip made by walking □ *It's a long walk from here.* □ *Let's go for a walk!* □ *I took the dog for a walk.* **-2.** a route that people walk along for pleasure □ *There are some great walks around here.* **-3.** the action of walking or the way a person walks □ *The horses moved off at a walk.* □ *He has a funny walk.*

◆ **walk away with** *vt fus* **to walk away with sthg** [with a prize, medal] to win sthg easily (informal use) □ *They walked away with the title.*

◆ **walk in on** *vt fus* **to walk in on sb/sthg** [on a person, meeting, conversation] to interrupt sb/sthg by going into a place when one is not expected □ *I walked in on them having an argument in the kitchen.*

◆ **walk off** *vt sep* **to walk sthg off** [headache, hangover] to get rid of sthg by walking. ■ **to walk off a meal** to go for a walk to try to feel better when one has eaten too much.

◆ **walk off with** *vt fus* (informal use) **-1. to walk off with sthg** [with money, a wallet, umbrella] to steal sthg easily by picking it up and walking away □ *Thieves walked off with three valuable paintings.* **-2. to walk off with sthg** [with a championship, trophy] to win sthg easily □ *She walked off with first prize.*

◆ **walk out** *vi* **-1.** to leave a place because one is angry or bored, or disapproves of what is happening □ *Several delegates walked out when the resolution was passed.* **-2.** [workers] to leave the place where one works and go on strike, especially when this has not been planned.

◆ **walk out on** *vt fus* **to walk out on sb** [on one's wife, husband, partner] to leave sb, especially suddenly □ *You can't just walk out on your kids.*

walkabout ['wɔːkəbaʊt] *n* GB a situation in which a famous person walks among a crowd of people, talking informally to them □ *The Queen went on a walkabout in Toronto today.* ■ **to go walkabout** AUS to go away for a period of time and travel around on foot.

walker ['wɔːkəʳ] *n* **-1.** a person who walks, especially for pleasure □ *a keen walker.* **-2.** US a light metal frame with rubber feet, used by old or ill people to support themselves when they walk.

walkie-talkie [ˌwɔːkɪ'tɔːkɪ] *n* a small radio that can be carried so that people can talk and listen to each other.

walk-in *adj* **-1. a walk-in closet/wardrobe** a closet/wardrobe that is large enough to walk into. **-2. a walk-in victory** US an easy victory (informal use).

walking ['wɔːkɪŋ] *n* the activity of walking, especially for pleasure □ *We go walking every weekend.* □ *a walking tour.*

walking shoes *npl* strong shoes with thick soles that people wear to go walking for pleasure.

walking stick *n* a stick used for support when walking.

Walkman™ ['wɔːkmən] (*pl* **Walkmans**) *n* a personal stereo.

walk of life (*pl* **walks of life**) *n* a person's position in society, often judged by the job they do □ *As a host on a talk show, I meet people from all walks of life.*

walk-on *adj* **a walk-on part** [in a play, movie] a very small and unimportant part for an actor that does not involve speaking □ *She's got a walk-on part in "Othello".*

walkout ['wɔːkaʊt] *n* the act of leaving the place where one works and going on strike in order to express disagreement or dissatis-

faction □ *Athletes at the games are threatening to stage a mass walkout.*

walkover ['wɔːkoʊvəʳ] *n* a situation that results in an easy victory (informal use) □ *The game was a walkover.*

walk-up *n* US an apartment building that does not have an elevator; an apartment in such a building.

walkway ['wɔːkweɪ] *n* a paved path or passage, especially between buildings.

wall [wɔːl] *n* **-1.** [in a building] one of the vertical sides of a room or building □ *We knocked down the wall between the kitchen and the dining room.* □ *The walls of the temple are still standing.* **-2.** [between land] a barrier of stone or brick that goes around or divides an area of land □ *the old city walls* □ *A wall separated the two gardens.* ■ **to come up against a brick wall** to meet a problem or obstacle that prevents further progress □ *The police investigation has come up against a brick wall.* ■ **to drive sb up the wall** to annoy sb very much □ *His trumpet-playing drives the neighbors up the wall.* **-3.** ANATOMY [of a cell, womb, stomach] a layer of tissue that surrounds something and acts as a barrier.

wallaby ['wɒləbɪ] (*pl* **wallabies**) *n* an Australian animal like a small kangaroo.

Wallace ['wɒləs], **Sir William** (1270–1305) a Scottish military leader who led a revolt against the English, who were ruling Scotland at that time.

wallchart ['wɔːltʃɑːʳt] *n* a big sheet of paper with information, pictures, diagrams etc on it that is hung on a wall.

wall cupboard *n* GB a cupboard that is fixed to the wall and does not rest on the ground.

walled [wɔːld] *adj* **a walled city/garden etc** a city/garden etc that is surrounded by a wall.

wallet ['wɒlət] *n* a small flat leather case for paper money, credit cards etc.

wallflower ['wɔːlflaʊəʳ] *n* **-1.** a garden plant with red, yellow, orange, or purple flowers and a sweet smell. **-2.** somebody, especially a girl, who has not been invited to dance at a party (informal use).

Walloon [wɒ'luːn] *n* a French-speaking Belgian from the south or southeast of the country.

wallop ['wɒləp] (informal use) ◇ *n* a hard blow. ◇ *vt* [child, ball] to hit <sb/sthg> hard.

wallow ['wɒloʊ] *vi* **-1.** [person, animal] to lie or roll in mud, water, a hot bath etc in enjoyment □ *We watched the hippos wallowing in the mud.* **-2. to wallow in misery/self-pity etc** to enjoy feeling sadness/pity for oneself etc and make little effort to get out of this state □ *There's no point sitting here wallowing in self-pity. Do something!*

wall painting *n* a painting done directly on a wall.

wallpaper ['wɔːlpeɪpəʳ] ◇ *n* thick decorative paper that is used to cover the walls of rooms. ◇ *vt* [room, house] to cover the walls of <sthg> with wallpaper.

Wall Street the street in New York City that is the financial center of the USA.

❦ WALL STREET
Wall Street is a street in the financial district of Manhattan, in New York City. The New York Stock Exchange is found here, as well as several banks. The term is often used to mean the world of American finance generally.

wall-to-wall *adj* **a wall-to-wall carpet** a carpet that covers the whole floor of a room.

walnut ['wɔːlnʌt] *n* **-1.** a large nut with a very hard shell; the tree that produces walnuts □ *coffee and walnut cake*. **-2.** the wood of a walnut tree, often used for making expensive furniture □ *a walnut cabinet*.

walrus ['wɔːlrəs] (*pl* **walrus** OR **walruses**) *n* a sea animal like a large seal with long sharp tusks.

waltz [wɔːlts] ◇ *n* **-1.** a formal dance with three beats in a bar in which a couple hold each other as they move around the room together. **-2.** a piece of music to which a waltz is danced. ◇ *vi* **-1.** to dance a waltz. **-2.** to go somewhere confidently and in a relaxed way (informal use) □ *She waltzed into the room*.

Waltzing Matilda [,wɔːltsɪŋmə'tɪldə] *n* a popular Australian song that has become the unofficial national song of the country.

wan [wɒn] (*compar* **wanner**, *superl* **wannest**) *adj* [person, complexion, smile] that looks pale, ill, and tired.

WAN [wæn] *n abbr of* **wide area network**.

wand [wɒnd] *n* a thin wooden stick that is held in the hand and used to do magic tricks □ *a magic wand*.

wander ['wɒndər] *vi* **-1.** to walk slowly without a definite purpose or without going anywhere in particular □ *We spent the afternoon wandering around the town*. **-2.** [thoughts, attention] to stop concentrating and move to another subject □ *My mind keeps wandering*.

wanderer ['wɒndərər] *n* a person who has no home and travels from place to place.

wandering ['wɒndərɪŋ] *adj* **a wandering musician/tribe etc** a musician/tribe etc that travels from place to place, spending a short time in each.

wanderlust ['wɒndəˈlʌst] *n* a strong desire to travel and visit other countries.

wane [weɪn] ◇ *n* **to be on the wane** [interest, popularity, belief] to become smaller, less important, less strong etc □ *Her power was already on the wane*. ◇ *vi* **-1.** [influence, interest, popularity] to decrease □ *My enthusiasm for the job rapidly waned*. **-2.** [moon] to grow narrower as it changes from a full moon to a new moon.

wangle ['wæŋgl] *vt* [job, invitation, wage increase] to get <sthg that is difficult to get>, by clever or unfair methods (informal use) □ *I managed to wangle an interview with their top man*.

wanna ['wɒnə] = **want a**, **want to**.

wannabe ['wɒnəbɪ] *n* a person who wants to be famous or like a famous person (informal use) □ *Madonna wannabes*.

want [wɒnt] ◇ *n* **-1.** what somebody needs or would like to have (formal use) □ *She has few wants*. **-2. to be in want** not to have the things one needs to live, e.g. food and clothing □ *families living in want*. ◇ *vt* **-1.** to feel a strong desire for <sthg> □ *What do you want to eat?* □ *He wants a bike for Christmas*. □ *I want you to listen carefully*. □ *Look, I don't want any trouble!* **-2.** to need <sthg> □ *If there's anything else you want, just ask*. **-3. you are wanted on the phone** somebody is asking to talk to you on the phone.
◆ **for want of** *prep* because it is not possible to do or have <sthg> □ *For want of anything better to do, I went for a walk*.

want ad *n* US a classified ad (informal use).

wanted ['wɒntəd] *adj* **to be wanted** to be looked for by the police because they think one is involved in a crime □ *He's wanted for the murder of Lucy Bishop*.

wanting ['wɒntɪŋ] *adj* **to be wanting** not to have enough of something □ *The book is wanting in passion*. ■ **to be found wanting** to be found to be not as good as expected or hoped □ *He was tested and found wanting*.

wanton ['wɒntən] *adj* (formal use) **-1.** [destruction, neglect, violence] for which there is no good reason. **-2.** [woman] who is considered to be sexually immoral.

war [wɔːr] (*pt* & *pp* **warred**, *cont* **warring**) *n* **-1.** organized fighting with weapons between two or more countries or groups □ *Germany and Italy declared war on the USA*. □ *the Gulf War*. ■ **to be at war** [countries] to be fighting □ *The two republics are now officially at war*. ■ **to go to war** to begin an organized fight using weapons □ *America is ready to go to war over this issue*. ■ **the War between the States** a term used for the American Civil War. ■ **the War of 1812** a conflict between the USA and Britain that lasted from 1812 to 1814. ■ **the Wars of the Roses** a series of wars in England (1455–1485) between two families that claimed the throne: the House of Lancaster, that had a red rose as a symbol, and the House of York, that had a white rose as a symbol. **-2.** [against drugs, crime] an organized effort to stop something □ *a war on car thieves*. **-3.** [between businesses] fierce competition between businesses □ *a trade war*.

War. *abbr of* **Warwickshire**.

warble ['wɔːrbl] *vi* [bird] to sing (literary use).

war crime *n* an illegal and cruel act carried out during war, such as the torture or murder of innocent people.

war criminal *n* a person who is guilty of a war crime.

war cry *n* a loud shout made by people going to fight that is intended to frighten their enemies.

ward [wɔːrd] *n* **-1.** [in a hospital] a large room in a hospital, or a part of a hospital, that contains beds for people with similar illnesses or injuries □ *a surgical/maternity ward.* -2. POLITICS one of the parts a city is divided into for local elections. -3. LAW a child or young person who is under the legal protection of an adult, usually because their parents are dead.

◆ **ward off** *vt fus* **to ward off sthg** [danger, disease, blow] to stop sthg from affecting or harming one □ *Vitamin C helps ward off a cold.*

war dance *n* a special dance that some tribes perform before fighting or after winning a battle.

warden ['wɔːrdn] *n* -1. an official who looks after a national park, game reserve etc. -2. US the official who is in charge of a prison. -3. GB the official who is in charge of a youth hostel, part of a university dormitory, an old people's home etc.

warder ['wɔːrdər] *n* GB a person who is in charge of prisoners in a prison.

ward of court *n* a child or young person who is placed under the protection of a court.

wardrobe ['wɔːrdroʊb] *n* -1. a large piece of furniture in which clothes are kept. -2. all the clothes owned by one person or worn at a particular time of year □ *She bought herself a whole new wardrobe.* □ *a summer/winter wardrobe.*

warehouse ['weərhaʊs, *pl* -haʊzɪz] *n* a large building where goods are stored.

wares [weərz] *npl* small things for sale, often in the street or in a market (literary use).

warfare ['wɔːrfeər] *n* -1. the activity of fighting a war □ *nuclear/guerrilla warfare.* -2. a continuous struggle or conflict □ *gang warfare.*

war game *n* -1. an imaginary battle which military leaders use to test plans for moving soldiers and equipment. -2. a game for adults in which model soldiers are used to recreate past battles.

warhead ['wɔːrhed] *n* the front part of a bomb or missile that contains explosives.

Warhol ['wɔːrhoʊl], **Andy** (1929–1987) a US artist who is famous for the use of popular culture in his art.

warily ['weərəlɪ] *adv* [look, behave, speak] *see* **wary.**

Warks. *abbr of* **Warwickshire.**

warlike ['wɔːrlaɪk] *adj* [nation, tribe] that always wants to make war.

warm [wɔːrm] ◇ *adj* -1. [weather, water, room] that is hot in a pleasant or suitable way □ *Are you warm enough?* -2. [sweater, blanket, bed] that makes one warm □ *Make sure you put some warm clothes on before you go out.* -3. [color, sound] that is deep and strong in a pleasant way. -4. [person, personality] that is kind and friendly □ *They gave me a warm welcome.* -5. US [debate, atmosphere] full of strong feelings, e.g. anger or excitement. ◇ *vt* [food, body] to make <sthg> warm □ *I'll just warm the milk.*

◆ **warm over** *vt sep* US -1. **to warm food over** to heat food that has already been cooked but has become cold. -2. **to warm sthg over** [idea, argument] to use sthg that one has said

or written before and that is no longer interesting (disapproving use).

◆ **warm to** *vt fus* **to warm to sb/sthg** to begin to like sb/sthg □ *I'm beginning to warm to the idea.* □ *I warmed to her immediately.*

◆ **warm up** ◇ *vt sep* -1. **to warm sb/sthg up** [room, person] to make sb/sthg warm □ *That soup will soon warm you up.* -2. **to warm food up** to heat food that has already been cooked but has become cold □ *We can warm up the leftovers for supper.* ◇ *vi* -1. [person, weather, room] to get warmer. -2. [car engine, photocopier] to become ready for use. -3. [athlete, dancer] to prepare for physical exercise by moving and stretching the body; [orchestra, musician, actor] to practice just before performing.

warm-blooded [-'blʌdəd] *adj* [animal] that has a body temperature that stays at the same fairly high level, even in very hot or cold conditions.

war memorial *n* a statue or monument made to make people remember the people who died in a war.

warm front *n* the front of a mass of warm air that is moving into a mass of colder air.

NOTE: Compare **cold front.**

warm-hearted [-'hɑːrtəd] *adj* [person] who is always kind and friendly.

warmly ['wɔːrmlɪ] *adv* -1. **to dress warmly** to put on warm clothes, usually because the weather is very cold. -2. [welcome, smile, greet] in a friendly way.

warmonger ['wɔːrmʌŋgər] *n* a person, especially a politician or military leader, who wants to start or encourage a war.

warmth [wɔːrmθ] *n* -1. [of the sun, a fire, body] the warm temperature produced by something □ *We huddled together for warmth.* -2. [of clothes, a blanket] the quality of being able to make people warm □ *I've put another blanket on for extra warmth.* -3. [of somebody's welcome, smile, greeting] the quality of being kind and friendly.

warm-up *n* [of an athlete, dancer, orchestra] the exercises that somebody does while warming up.

warn [wɔːrn] ◇ *vt* -1. to give <sb> advice about something that may be dangerous so that they can avoid it □ *The doctor warned him of OR about the dangers of smoking.* ■ **to warn sb against doing sthg, to warn sb not to do sthg** to advise sb not to do sthg because of possible danger or punishment □ *I warned her not to go alone OR against going alone.* -2. to tell <sb> in advance about a possible problem □ *Did you warn him about the brakes?* □ *She warned them that she would be late.* ◇ *vi* **to warn of sthg** to tell people about sthg bad that is happening or may happen □ *The police are warning of severe traffic delays downtown.*

warning ['wɔːrnɪŋ] ◇ *n* -1. advice about something that may be dangerous or result in punishment □ *This is your last warning.* -2. information about something dangerous, difficult, or undesirable that will happen in the future □ *He left without any warning.* □ *They gave us advance warning of the hurricane.* ◇ *adj* **a warning sign/look etc** a sign/look etc that gives a warning □ *Social workers failed to recognize the warning signs.*

warning light *n* a colored light on the instrument board of a car or machine that gives a warning about a possible problem.

warning triangle *n* GB a red plastic triangle that reflects light and is carried in cars to put on the road if there is an accident or if the car breaks down.

warp [wɔːˈp] ◇ *n* the threads that run in the direction of the longest edge of a piece of cloth. ◇ *vt* **-1.** [wood, metal, plastic] to bend or twist <sthg> so that it loses its shape □ *The door was warped by the damp.* **-2.** [personality, character] to make <sthg> abnormal □ *Her early experiences have warped her view of family life.* ◇ *vi* [wood, metal, plastic] to become twisted or bent and lose its shape.
NOTE: Compare **weft**.

warpath [US ˈwɔːrpæθ, GB ˈwɔːrpɑːθ] *n* **to be** OR **go on the warpath** to be very angry about something and ready to argue with the person responsible for it.

warped [wɔːˈpt] *adj* **-1.** [wood, metal, plastic] that is bent or twisted by heat, damp etc so that it does not have the same shape any more. **-2.** [personality, idea] that is not normal □ *a warped sense of humor.*

warplane [ˈwɔːrpleɪn] *n* a plane armed with guns and designed for fighting.

warrant [ˈwɒrənt] ◇ *n* an official document that allows the police to arrest somebody, search a house, take goods etc. ◇ *vt* [examination, investigation] to be or provide a reason for <sthg> □ *The incident hardly warranted so much media attention.*

warrant officer *n* an officer in the army, navy, or air force who is between the ranks of sergeant and lieutenant.

warranty [ˈwɒrəntɪ] (*pl* **warranties**) *n* a written statement by a company that states that if their goods do not work they will repair or replace them without charge □ *Is the computer still under warranty?*

warren [ˈwɒrən] *n* **-1.** = **rabbit warren. -2.** a place with a lot of streets, rooms etc that it is hard to find one's way around in.

warring [ˈwɔːrɪŋ] *adj* **warring factions/nations etc** factions/nations etc that are fighting a war against each other.

warrior [ˈwɒrɪəʳ] *n* a person who fights in wars (literary use).

Warsaw [ˈwɔːrsɔː] the capital of Poland and its largest city. POPULATION: 1,653,500.

warship [ˈwɔːrʃɪp] *n* a ship armed with guns used for fighting at sea.

wart [wɔːrt] *n* a small hard lump that grows on the skin, usually on the hands or face.

wartime [ˈwɔːrtaɪm] ◇ *n* the period during which there is a war □ *Women had to work in wartime.* ◇ *adj* [memory, propaganda] *I love hearing all about his wartime experiences.*

Warwickshire [ˈwɒrɪkʃəʳ] a county in western central England. SIZE: 1981 sq kms. POPULATION: 484,200. ADMINISTRATIVE CENTER: Warwick.

war widow *n* a woman whose husband was killed fighting in a war.

wary [ˈweərɪ] (*compar* **warier**, *superl* **wariest**) *adj* **to be wary of sb/sthg** to be careful about sb/sthg because there may be problems or danger □ *He's always been wary of her/wary of committing himself.*

was [stressed wɒz, unstressed wəz] past tense of **be**.

wash [wɒʃ] ◇ *vt* **-1.** [clothes, car, face] to clean <sthg> using water and soap; [lettuce, vegetables] to clean <sthg> using water □ *Have you washed your hands?* **-2.** to carry <sthg> to a particular place □ *The waves washed the oil onto the beach.* ◇ *vi* to clean oneself using water and soap □ *I washed quickly and then went downstairs.* ◇ *n* **-1.** an act of washing □ *He gave the car a wash.* □ *Do I have time to have a quick wash?* **-2.** a collection of clothes washed together □ *a hot/white wash* □ *Your shirt is in the wash.* **-3.** [of a boat] the movement of water that spreads out sideways from a moving ship or boat.

◆ **wash away** *vt sep* **to wash sb/sthg away** [sea, water] to carry sb/sthg away from a particular place □ *Dozens of houses were washed away by the flood.*

◆ **wash down** *vt sep* **-1.** to wash sthg down [food, medicine] to drink something to help one swallow sthg □ *She washed down the aspirin with water.* **-2.** **to wash sthg down** [floor, car, wall] to wash sthg with a lot of water.

◆ **wash out** *vt sep* **-1.** to wash sthg out [stain, mark, dye] to remove sthg by washing. **-2.** **wash sthg out** [bottle, cupboard, bowl] to wash the inside of sthg.

◆ **wash up** ◇ *vt sep* **-1.** to wash dishes up GB to wash dirty dishes after a meal. **-2.** **to be washed up** [body, debris] to be carried by the sea or by waves to a shore or bank □ *They found his body washed up on the beach.* ◇ *vi* **-1.** US to wash oneself. **-2.** GB to wash dirty plates, glasses, pans etc.

washable [ˈwɒʃəbl] *adj* [material, clothes] that can be washed without being damaged □ *Is this sweater machine-washable?*

wash-and-wear *adj* **wash-and-wear clothes** clothes that do not need to be ironed after washing.

washbowl [ˈwɒʃboʊl] US, **washbasin** [ˈwɒʃbeɪsn] GB *n* a fixed bowl with faucets, especially in a bathroom, for washing one's hands and face.

washcloth [ˈwɒʃklɒθ] *n* US a small cloth for washing one's face.

washed-out [ˌwɒʃt-] *adj* **-1.** [clothing] that has been washed so many times it has lost its color. **-2.** **to look washed-out** to look unhealthy and pale because of tiredness □ *I thought he was looking really washed-out.*

washed-up *adj* [person, career, project] that is no longer successful (informal use).

washer ['wɒʃər] *n* **-1.** TECHNOLOGY a small ring of plastic, metal, or rubber used to make bolts and valves fit tightly. **-2.** a washing machine.

washer-dryer *n* a machine that washes and dries clothes.

washing ['wɒʃɪŋ] *n* **-1.** the act of washing clothes □ *I usually do the washing once a week.* **-2.** a collection of clothes that need to be washed or have been washed □ *clean/dirty washing.*

washing line *n* a piece of rope that hangs between two points on which washing is hung to dry.

washing machine *n* a machine that washes clothes.

washing powder *n* GB soap in the form of a powder used for washing clothes.

Washington ['wɒʃɪŋtən] **-1.** = **Washington D.C.** **-2.** = **Washington State.**

Washington ['wɒʃɪŋtən], **Booker T** (1856–1915) a black US writer and teacher who helped to establish the Tuskegee Institute, a school for black Americans.

Washington, George (1732–1799) US President from 1789 to 1797. He helped to write the Constitution and is one of the Founding Fathers.

Washington D.C. the capital of the USA, in the District of Columbia. POPULATION: 606,900.

Washington Monument: **the Washington Monument** a large column in Washington D.C., built in honor of George Washington.

Washington State a state in the northwestern USA on the Pacific coast and the Canadian border. ABBREVIATION: WA. SIZE: 176,500 sq kms. POPULATION: 4,866,692. CAPITAL: Olympia. MAIN CITY: Seattle.

washing-up *n* GB **-1.** the dirty plates, glasses, pans etc that need to be washed after a meal □ *piles of washing-up.* **-2.** the act of washing dirty plates, glasses, pans etc □ *It's your turn to do the washing-up.*

washing-up liquid *n* GB the thick liquid soap used with hot water to wash dirty plates, glasses, pans etc.

washout ['wɒʃaʊt] *n* a complete failure (informal use) □ *The dance was a complete washout.*

washroom ['wɒʃruːm] *n* US a room that contains a toilet and a washbowl.

wasn't ['wɒznt] = **was not.**

wasp [wɒsp] *n* a thin yellow-and-black striped flying insect which stings.

Wasp, WASP [wɒsp] (*abbr of* **White Anglo-Saxon Protestant**) *n* a white American who belongs to the social class that is considered to be the most powerful in the country.

waspish ['wɒspɪʃ] *adj* [person, tone] that is bad-tempered and critical.

wastage ['weɪstɪdʒ] *n* [of potential, a resource, material] the act of wasting something; the amount wasted □ *the unnecessary wastage of water due to leaking pipes.*

waste [weɪst] ◇ *n* **-1.** a bad or unnecessary use of money, space, energy etc □ *efforts to reduce waste* □ *What a waste of good food!* ■ **to go to waste** not to be used in a useful or sensible way □ *All our hard work went to waste.* ■ **to be a waste of time/money** not to be worth the amount of time/money that is spent □ *She feels that going to the meeting would be a waste of time.* □ *Applying for that job was a complete waste of effort.* **-2.** material that is thrown away because the useful part has been removed or used □ *domestic/nuclear waste* □ *toxic waste.*
◇ *adj* **waste material** material that is thrown away, e.g. because the useful part has been removed or used □ *waste products.*
◇ *vt* [time, money, energy] to use <sthg> in a way that is not useful or sensible; to use more of <sthg> than is necessary □ *Don't waste this opportunity to travel.* □ *Turn it off, you're wasting the battery.* ■ **to be wasted on sb** to be too good to be appreciated by sb □ *The expensive wine was wasted on him.*

◆ **wastes** *npl* a large empty area of land or water (literary use).

◆ **waste away** *vi* to lose weight and become very thin and weak as the result of illness or worry.

wastebasket ['weɪstbæskət] *n* US a small container for waste paper kept in a room.

wasted ['weɪstəd] *adj* [time, energy] that has not been used in a useful or sensible way □ *You're wasted in that job.*

waste disposal unit *n* a device fitted to the drain of a kitchen sink that breaks up waste food so that it can go down the drain with water.

wasteful ['weɪstfl] *adj* [person, activity] that wastes time, energy, money etc.

waste ground *n* GB land that is not used or looked after.

wasteland ['weɪstlænd] *n* an empty, unused, and unattractive area of land.

waste paper *n* paper that is thrown away because it has been used and is no longer needed.

wastepaper basket, wastepaper bin [weɪst-'peɪpər-] *n* GB = **wastebasket.**

watch [wɒtʃ] ◇ *n* **-1.** a small clock that one wears on one's wrist, around one's neck, or attached to one's clothes. **-2. to keep watch** to watch carefully, e.g. for any signs of danger □ *We agreed that somebody should keep watch at all times.* **-3.** a person or group that watches carefully for any signs of danger in order to be able to warn other people.
◇ *vt* **-1.** [television, football game, sunset] to look at sthg for a period of time, usually for pleasure □ *Did you watch that show on Channel 5 last night?* **-2.** [person] to follow <sb> secretly □ *The police have been watching them for months.* **-3.** to be careful with <sthg> □ *Watch what you're doing with that knife.* ■ **watch your language!** a phrase used to tell somebody not to use swearwords. ■ **watch it!** a phrase used to tell somebody to be careful (informal use).
◇ *vi*: *We were watching from the window.*

◆ **watch for** vt fus **to watch for sthg** [for a chance, opportunity] to wait for sthg that might happen in the future in order to benefit or avoid problems □ Watch for any sudden changes in temperature.

◆ **watch out** vi **-1. watch out!** a phrase used to tell somebody to be careful because something bad or dangerous is going to happen. **-2. to watch out for sthg** to pay careful attention so that one does not miss sthg □ Watch out for the bus.

◆ **watch over** vt fus **to watch over sb** [child, sick person] to take care of sb.

watchband ['wɒtʃbænd] n US the metal, leather, or plastic strap that attaches a watch to one's wrist.

watchdog ['wɒtʃdɒg] n **-1.** a dog that is kept to guard property. **-2.** a person or group whose job is to make sure that companies and other organizations act fairly and do not break the law □ a consumer watchdog.

watchful ['wɒtʃfl] adj [person] who watches carefully what is happening. ■ **to keep a watchful eye on sb/sthg** to watch sb/sthg very closely in order to avoid danger, accidents etc.

watchmaker ['wɒtʃmeɪkər] n a person whose job is to make and repair watches and clocks.

watchman ['wɒtʃmən] (pl **watchmen** [-mən]) n a person whose job is to guard property.

watchstrap ['wɒtʃstræp] n GB = **watchband**.

watchword ['wɒtʃwɜːrd] n a word or phrase that expresses the most important quality, feature, principle etc of a person or group □ Our watchword is efficiency.

water ['wɔːtər] ◇ n **-1.** a clear colorless liquid with no taste or smell that animals and plants need in order to live. It makes up seas, rivers, lakes etc and falls from clouds as rain. FORMULA: H_2O. ■ **to pour** OR **throw cold water on sthg** [on a plan, idea] to criticize sthg and make it seem less interesting. ■ **to tread water** to stay on the surface of deep water by moving one's legs slightly as if walking. ■ **it's water under the bridge** it's something unpleasant that happened in the past but is not important any more □ We used to argue a lot, but that's all water under the bridge now. **-2.** an area of water such as a lake, sea etc □ The water was freezing. **-3.** phrase **to pass water** to urinate (polite use). ◇ vt [plant, lawn] to pour water on <sthg> to make it grow □ Have you watered the roses? ◇ vi **-1.** [eyes] to fill with tears because of wind, pain, cold etc. **-2.** [mouth] to produce saliva when one sees or smells food □ The sight of all that food made my mouth water.

◆ **waters** npl **-1.** an area of water near to or owned by a particular country □ British/Russian waters. **-2.** [of the Nile, Pacific, Rhine] the water of a particular sea, lake, river etc (literary use).

◆ **water down** vt sep **-1. to water down a liquid** [wine, brandy] to add water to a liquid to make it less strong or to increase the amount. **-2. to water sthg down** [proposal, version, demand] to make sthg less effective or forceful (disapproving use).

water bed n a special mattress for sleeping on that is filled with water.

water bird n a bird that swims or walks in water.

water biscuit n a thin hard cracker, usually eaten with cheese.

waterborne ['wɔːtərbɔːrn] adj [disease] that is passed on from one person to another by water.

water bottle n a plastic container for water carried by cyclists, walkers etc.

water buffalo n a large animal similar to a cow with big curved horns that is kept to pull and carry things in some hot countries.

water cannon n a device that produces a very strong stream of water, used by the police or army to control crowds.

water chestnut n the crisp white fruit of a Chinese plant that is cut into slices and used in Chinese cooking.

watercolor ['wɔːtərkʌlər] n a kind of paint that is mixed with water; a picture painted using this paint.

water-cooled [-kuːld] adj [engine] that is cooled by water.

watercourse ['wɔːtərkɔːrs] n the channel that a river or canal flows through.

watercress ['wɔːtərkres] n a plant that grows in water whose leaves have a peppery taste and are eaten in salads and as soup □ Garnish with a bunch of watercress, and serve.

watered-down [ˌwɔːtərd-] adj [version, proposal] that has been changed so that it is much weaker and less effective (disapproving use) □ The movie is a watered-down version of the book.

waterfall ['wɔːtərfɔːl] n a part of a river or stream where the water falls from a high place to a lower one.

waterfront ['wɔːtərfrʌnt] n the part of a town or city that is beside water.

Watergate ['wɔːtərgeɪt] n a political scandal in 1972 involving US President Richard Nixon. Members of his party were caught breaking into the Democratic Party's headquarters in the Watergate building. Other illegal activities were discovered, and President Nixon was forced to resign.

❦ WATERGATE
Watergate is the name of the building in Washington D.C. where the Democratic Party had its headquarters. Since the Watergate scandal, the word "gate" has been added to other words to refer to political scandals, especially when a government has tried to hide its involvement: for example the word "Irangate" was invented to refer to the illegal US arms sales to Iran in the 1980s.

water heater n a device, usually electric, that heats the supply of water in a house.

waterhole ['wɔːtə'hoʊl] *n* a pool where animals go to drink in a hot country.

watering pot US, **watering can** ['wɔːtərɪŋ-] *n* a container with a handle and a long spout from which water is poured onto garden plants.

water jump *n* an area of water over which horses and athletes jump as part of a competition.

water level *n* the height of the water in a lake, river, container etc □ *The water level had risen because of all the rain.*

water lily *n* a plant with large flowers and big flat leaves that floats on the surface of water.

waterline ['wɔːtə'laɪn] *n* SHIPPING the level water reaches on the body of a ship or boat □ *The boat was holed below the waterline.*

waterlogged ['wɔːtə'lɒgd] *adj* **-1.** [field, football field] that contains so much water it cannot be used. **-2.** [ship, boat] that contains so much water it cannot float.

water main *n* a big underground pipe that carries water to buildings or areas of a city.

watermark ['wɔːtə'mɑːrk] *n* **-1.** a special mark on good-quality paper that can only be seen when the paper is held up to the light. **-2.** a mark that shows the highest or lowest positions reached by a river, sea etc □ *high/low watermark.*

watermelon ['wɔːtə'melən] *n* a large round fruit with dark-green skin, juicy pink flesh, and big black seeds.

water pipe *n* a pipe that carries water around a building.

water pistol *n* a toy gun that is used for shooting water at people.

water polo *n* a ball game that is played in a swimming pool by two teams.

waterproof ['wɔːtə'pruːf] ◇ *adj* [material, covering, watch] that does not let water get in or pass through it. ◇ *n* a waterproof coat or jacket. ◇ *vt* [jacket, roof, tent] to make <sthg> waterproof.

water rates *npl* GB the money paid by the owner of a building for the use of water from the public system.

water-resistant *adj* [watch, coat] that is almost but not completely waterproof.

watershed ['wɔːtə'ʃed] *n* a point in one's life or a situation when great changes take place □ *That chance meeting marked a watershed in her career.*

waterside ['wɔːtə'saɪd] ◇ *adj* a waterside café/ restaurant etc a café/restaurant etc that is beside water. ◇ *n* the waterside the side of a lake, river, sea etc.

water skiing *n* the sport of moving fast over the surface of water on skis, holding on to a rope attached to a speedboat.

water softener *n* a device or substance that is used to make water less hard by removing unwanted minerals.

water-soluble *adj* [tablet, ink] that dissolves in water □ *water-soluble vitamin C tablets.*

watersports ['wɔːtə'spɔːrts] *npl* sports that are played in or on water.

waterspout ['wɔːtə'spaʊt] *n* a tall spinning column of water that rises from a sea, lake etc when there are extremely strong winds.

water supply *n* the water that is brought to buildings or areas through pipes connected to a public water system.

water table *n* the level below which water is found in the ground.

watertight ['wɔːtə'taɪt] *adj* **-1.** [seal, covering, compartment] that does not allow water to get in, so that what it covers or contains does not become wet. **-2.** [contract, plan, argument] that is prepared with great care so that it does not contain any mistakes or parts that are unclear □ *Both men have watertight alibis.*

water tower *n* a large metal or concrete water container put high above the ground to provide enough pressure to move the water to the places where it is needed.

waterway ['wɔːtə'weɪ] *n* a river, canal, or narrow area of sea on which ships and boats can travel.

waterworks ['wɔːtə'wɜːrks] (*pl* **waterworks**) *n* a building where water is stored, cleaned, and put into the public water system.

watery ['wɔːtərɪ] *adj* **-1.** [soup, beer, stew] that contains too much water, so that it does not taste or look good. **-2.** [sunlight, color] that is pale and weak.

Watson ['wɒtsn], **Dr** the assistant of Sherlock Holmes in Arthur Conan Doyle's detective stories.

watt [wɒt] *n* a unit used to measure electrical power.

Watt [wɒt], **James** (1736–1819) a British engineer and inventor who played an important part in the development of the steam engine.

wattage ['wɒtɪdʒ] *n* electrical power measured in watts.

Waugh [wɔː], **Evelyn** (1903–1966) a British writer whose best-known work is *Brideshead Revisited.*

wave [weɪv] ◇ *n* **-1.** [of the hand] the action of moving one's arm or hand quickly from side to side when saying hello or goodbye or attracting attention □ *She gave me a cheery wave.* **-2.** [of water] a movement of water across the surface of the sea, a river etc caused by the wind, tide, or a moving ship or boat □ *An enormous wave knocked her off her feet.* **-3.** [of anger, nausea] a sudden strong feeling that spreads through one. **-4.** [of tourists, visitors, immigrants] a sudden increase in the number of people arriving at the same time □ *He felt a wave of panic.* □ *Camps are being set up to deal with the wave of refugees.* **-5. a wave of attacks/bombings etc** a sudden increase in attacks/bombings etc during a short period of time □ *the recent wave of killings.* **-6.** PHYSICS the form in which sound or light travels □ *light waves.* **-7.** [in one's hair] a section of hair that is not straight but is slightly curved.

◇ *vt* **-1.** [hand, arm, flag] to move <sthg> quickly from side to side □ *She was waving a fifty-dollar bill.* **-2.** [person, car] to tell <sb/sthg> to move by waving one's hand □ *They waved us through the checkpoint.* **-3.** [hair] to make a wave in <hair>.

◇ *vi* **-1.** to move one's hand or arm quickly from side to side when saying hello or goodbye or attracting attention □ *Who was that woman you were waving to?* □ *I've been waving at the waiter for ages but he keeps ignoring me.* **-2.** [flag, tree] to move gently in the air □ *Flags were waving above all public buildings.*

◆ **wave aside** *vt sep* **to wave sthg aside** [objection, criticism] to ignore sthg because one feels it is not important.

◆ **wave down** *vt sep* **to wave sb down** to indicate to sb by waving that one wants them to stop □ *They waved the police car down.*

wave band *n* a group of sound waves of similar lengths, e.g. long wave and medium wave, used to broadcast radio programs.

wavelength ['weɪvleŋθ] *n* the size of a particular radio wave used by a radio station to broadcast its programs. ■ **to be on the same wavelength as sb** to have similar beliefs and ideas to sb.

waver ['weɪvə^r] *vi* **-1.** [person, resolution, confidence] to be uncertain or unsteady □ *Their loyalty to the cause never wavered.* **-2.** [temperature, level] to go up and down slightly.

wavy ['weɪvɪ] (*compar* **wavier**, *superl* **waviest**) *adj* **-1. wavy hair** hair that has waves in it. **-2. a wavy line** a line that has regular curves in it.

wax [wæks] ◇ *n* **-1.** a solid substance made of fats or oils that melts when heated and is used to make candles, crayons, polish etc □ *a wax candle/crayon.* **-2.** = **earwax**.

◇ *vt* **-1.** [floor, furniture, ski] to put a thin layer of wax on <sthg> in order to polish it or to make it slide more smoothly and quickly. **-2.** [legs, underarms] to remove hair from <a part of the body> by applying and then removing soft wax.

◇ *vi* **-1. to wax eloquent/lyrical** to talk in an eloquent/lyrical way about something (literary use). ■ **to wax and wane** [fortunes, popularity, influence] to increase in size or power and then decrease. **-2.** [moon] to appear to become larger as it changes from a new moon into a full moon.

waxen ['wæksn] *adj* [face, complexion] that looks pale and unhealthy.

wax paper *n* US paper covered with a thin layer of wax so that water cannot pass through it, usually used for wrapping food.

waxworks ['wækswɜː^rks] (*pl* **waxworks**) *n* a museum where wax models of famous people can be seen.

way [weɪ] ◇ *n* **-1. a way to do sthg** OR **of doing sthg** something that one can do in order to succeed in doing sthg □ *Is there no other way of contacting her?* □ *He's tried lots of ways of giving up smoking.* □ *That's not the way to win friends.* ■ **to get** OR **have one's way** to get OR have what one wants □ *If I had my way he'd be out of here tomorrow!* □ *That child is too used to getting her own way.* ■ **to have everything one's own way** to be able to arrange things to suit oneself, and not have to consider the opinions of others □ *The arrival of foreign competition can only be a good thing: the industry has had everything its own way for too long.* ■ **ways and means** methods of doing or getting something, especially when these are clever or secret □ *There are ways and means of finding out the information.* **-2.** a manner of doing something; the manner in which something is done □ *Clive speaks in a very strange way.* □ *I love the way they've decorated their apartment.* □ *He got up and went to work in the normal way.* □ *Have you seen the way he looks at her?* ■ **this/ that way** as a result of doing this/that □ *Take a taxi, that way you'll get there in plenty of time.* ■ **in a big/small way** a phrase used to show that something happens on a large/small scale □ *He was only involved in the company in a small way.* □ *They started spending money in a big way.* ■ **to have a way with sb/sthg** [with children, animals] to be good at dealing with sb/sthg □ *She writes wonderful letters, but then she's always had a way with words.* ■ **to have a way of doing sthg** to have a habit of doing sthg □ *Ken has a way of disappearing when it's time to pay the bill.* **-3. some/most of the way** for some/most of the trip one is making □ *It rained all the way to the coast.* **-4. the way to a place** a road, path etc leading to a particular place □ *Can you tell me the way to the bank?* □ *We went the long way home.* ■ **to find/lose one's way** to find/lose the direction one is supposed to be traveling in □ *They lost their way in the fog.* ■ **to be out of one's way** [road, place] not to be on the route one is taking □ *He drove us home although it was out of his way.* ■ **on the** OR **one's way** as one is going to a place □ *We stopped for a hamburger on the* OR *our way home.* □ *He stopped to chat to a colleague on his way out of the building.* ■ **to go out of one's way to do sthg** [to help, cause problems, be friendly] to make a special effort to do sthg, especially in spite of difficulties □ *They went out of their way to make us feel welcome.* ■ **to keep out of sb's way** to avoid sb □ *You'd better keep out of Mike's way, he's in a foul mood.* ■ **keep out of the way!** a phrase used to warn somebody to move away from a dangerous object or situation □ *Keep out of the way — this dish is red-hot!* ■ **to make one's way to a place** to go to a place, especially slowly or with some difficulty □ *I was finally able to make my way to the bar.* □ *I'll make my own way home.* **-5. sb's way** sb's ability to move freely in the direction they want □ *When I arrived at the entrance I found my way barred by an armed guard.* ■ **to be in the way** to be in a position that prevents one from seeing, doing, or reaching something □ *Excuse me, you're in the way.* □ *You couldn't see the sunset because there were buildings in the way.* ■ **to be out of the way** [job, task, business] to be finished; [object, person] to be in a position that does not prevent one from doing something □ *once the exams are out of the way* □ *Get out of the way, I can't see!* □ *He planned to marry her once his wife was out of the way.* ■ **to make way for sb/sthg** to move in order to provide space for sb/sthg □ *The building was demolished to make way for a parking lot.* ■ **to stand in sb's way** to prevent sb from doing something that they have decided to do □ *He never let his family life stand in the way of his career.* ■ **to work one's way to the top** to reach a high position after long effort □ *It took her years to work her way to the top of her profession.* **-6. to go/look a particular way** to go/look in a particular direction □ *Step this way, please.* □ *Look both ways before crossing the road.* □ *There's a storm heading our way.* ■ **the way in/out** GB the entrance/exit. **-7. a short/long way** a short/long distance in space or time □ *You didn't walk all the way, did you?* □ *Her parents supported her all the way through college.* □ *We got a ride most of the way home.* □ *It's a long way to the nearest city.* □ *Christmas is still a long way off.* ■ **to go a long way toward doing sthg** to help a lot in achieving sthg □ *That money would go a long way toward updating our computer system.* **-8. phrases across** OR **over the way** [be situated, live, park] on the other side of a road, open space etc □ *There's a bank just across the way.* ■ **to give way** [floor, door] to collapse under pressure, strain or weight; [person, organization] to agree to what somebody else wants after resisting for some time; GB AUTO to slow down or stop at an intersection to let other vehicles pass in front of one □ *The bridge gave way underneath them.* □ *The city council was forced to give way in the face of public pressure.* □ *'Give Way.'* ■ **no way!** a phrase used to reject a statement or request □ *No way are you borrowing my car!* □ *"You didn't invite him, did you?" — "No way!"* ■ **the right/wrong way around/up** in the right/wrong position or facing the right/wrong direction □ *You've got your sweater on the wrong way around.* □ *It would help if you held the map the right way up.* ■ **to get/be under way** [ship, plane, person] to start/have started a trip; [meeting, trial, work] to start/have started happening □ *We hope to be under way in about ten minutes.* □ *Production of the new model is now well under way.*

◇ *adv* [better, above, below] used for emphasis (informal use) □ *The coat was way too big for me.*

◆ **ways** *npl* sb's ways sb's customs or habits □ *My father is too set in his ways to change now.*

◆ **by the way** *adv* a phrase used to introduce a new topic of conversation □ *By the way, I saw Tim last night.*

◆ **by way of** *prep* **-1. by way of a place** going through a particular place on the way □ *We flew to Damascus by way of Beirut.* **-2. by way of sthg** [of an apology, greeting, excuse] as a kind of sthg (formal use) □ *She sent me a long detailed fax by way of explanation.*

◆ **in a way, in one way, in some ways** *adv* a phrase used to say that something is part-

ly true □ *In a way I'll be glad when they all leave home.*

◆ **in no way** *adv* not at all (used for emphasis) □ *The visit could in no way be described as a success.*

◆ **in the way of** *prep* a phrase used when talking about a particular useful or necessary feature □ *She hasn't got much in the way of experience.* □ *How much will you need in the way of spending money?*

waylay [ˌweɪˈleɪ] (*pt* & *pp* **waylaid** [-ˈleɪd]) *vt* to wait for <sb> and stop them as they pass, either in order to ask them something or to attack them □ *Sorry I'm late. I got waylaid.*

Wayne [weɪn], **John** (1907–1979) a US actor who appeared in many westerns, including *Stagecoach* and *Rio Bravo.*

way of life *n* sb's way of life the way sb lives □ *Having a baby will completely change your way of life.*

way-out *adj* [person, hairstyle, idea] that seems very strange and daring, usually because it is new (informal use).

Ways and Means Committee *n* the Ways and Means Committee a group within the US House of Representatives that supervises all financial legislation.

wayside [ˈweɪsaɪd] *n* the side of a road. ■ **to fall by the wayside** [idea, plan] to be forgotten or abandoned; [person] not to have enough energy or determination to finish something that one has started □ *Almost a quarter of the students fell by the wayside during the first semester.*

wayward [ˈweɪwəd] *adj* [person] who does what they want and is hard to control.

WC (*abbr of* **water closet**) *n* a toilet.

WCC (*abbr of* **World Council of Churches**) *n* the WCC an international organization of Christian churches that aims to encourage cooperation between its members.

we [wiː] *pron* **-1.** used to refer to a group of people that includes oneself, and sometimes includes the person one is speaking to □ *We all want to thank you for your help.* □ *We both work in the same office.* □ *We could meet again next week.* ■ **we Americans/lawyers** all Americans/lawyers, including me □ *As we say in Australia...* ■ **we at Luxury Kitchens** the company of Luxury Kitchens, including me. **-2.** used to show a difference between a group of people that includes oneself and another group of people □ *We succeeded, but they didn't.* □ *What can WE do about it?* □ *We told you it wouldn't work.* **-3.** used by a king, queen, pope etc to refer to themselves as an individual person □ *We are not amused.*

WEA (*abbr of* **Workers' Educational Association**) *n* the WEA an organization that runs adult education programs.

weak [wiːk] *adj* **-1.** [person, animal] that has little physical strength or energy; [structure, defense] that is not strong and will probably not last long □ *The illness left him feeling very weak.* **-2.** [person] who is not brave or confident □ *a weak personality.* **-3.** [government, leader, president] that has not much control; [currency] that is low in value □ *a weak pound.* **-4.** [plot, argument, excuse] that does not make people believe that it is true or right. **-5.** [light] that is not bright or clear; [cry, signal] that is not loud or clear. **-6.** [tea, coffee, gin and tonic] that does not have a strong taste, because a lot of water or other liquid has been added to it. **-7. to be weak on sth** [on a subject] not to know very much about sthg; [of facts, details] not to contain much of sthg that is needed to support an argument □ *I've always been a little weak on geography.* □ *The article was a little weak on that point.*

weaken ['wiːkən] ◇ *vt* **-1.** [group, force, position] to make <sthg> less powerful; [dollar, mark] to make <a currency> decrease in value □ *The scandal has weakened his credibility considerably.* **-2.** [determination, influence, person] to make <sb/sthg> less strong □ *Nothing could weaken her ambition.* **-3.** [person] to make <sb> physically weak. **-4.** [foundations, wall, roof] to make <sthg> less solid so that it may fall down.
◇ *vi* **-1.** [person] to become less certain about a decision or belief □ *He showed no signs of weakening.* **-2.** [person] to become physically weaker □ *She's weakening fast.* **-3.** [authority, influence] to become less powerful. **-4.** [foundations, wall, roof] to become less solid □ *The bridge has weakened with age.* **-5.** [currency] to decrease in value □ *The lira has weakened against the dollar.*

weak-kneed [-'niːd] *adj* [person] who does not do what they should do because they are not brave or determined enough (informal and disapproving use).

weakling ['wiːklɪŋ] *n* a person who is physically weak; a person who has a weak personality (disapproving use).

weakly ['wiːklɪ] *adv* [smile, lead, shine] *see* **weak**.

weak-minded [-'maɪndəd] *adj* [person] who cannot think clearly or make quick decisions.

weakness ['wiːknəs] *n* **-1.** [of a person, leader, structure] *see* **weak** □ *He gave in in a moment of weakness.* **-2.** [in somebody's character] a small fault in somebody's character □ *What would you consider to be your strengths and weaknesses?* ■ **to have a weakness for sth** [for chocolate, cake, junk food] to like sthg a lot, especially sthg that is not good for one. **-3.** [in a structure, plan] a weak part of something □ *This is a major weakness in his argument.*

weal [wiːl] *n* a long, raised, red mark on the skin.

wealth [welθ] *n* **-1.** a lot of money and valuable possessions that belong to a person □ *a woman of considerable wealth.* **-2. a wealth of sth** [of ideas, experience, information] a large amount of sthg □ *Mr Moran brings with him a wealth of experience in the retail trade.*

wealthy ['welθɪ] (*compar* **wealthier**, *superl* **wealthiest**) *adj* [person, country, family] that has a lot of money and valuable possessions □ *Her family is extremely wealthy.*

wean [wiːn] *vt* **-1.** to stop feeding <a baby or young animal> milk produced by its mother and to start feeding them more solid food. **-2. to wean sb off sth** [off cigarettes, alcohol, drugs] to gradually make sb less dependent on sthg.

weapon ['wepən] *n* an object, e.g. a knife, gun, or bomb, that is used in a fight or a war, to harm or kill people □ *a nuclear/chemical weapon.*

weaponry ['wepənrɪ] *n* a collective term for weapons.

wear [weəʳ] (*pt* **wore**, *pp* **worn**) ◇ *vt* **-1.** [jewelry, clothes, make-up] to have <sthg> on one's body □ *She never wears a bra.* □ *What perfume are you wearing?* **-2.** [hair] to arrange <one's hair> in a particular way □ *She used to wear her hair loose/in a bun.* **-3.** [fabric, surface] to gradually damage <sthg> by using it a lot so that it becomes thinner and weaker □ *Prolonged use had worn the tires.*
◇ *vi* **-1.** [clothes, shoes, carpet] to become damaged by use over a period of time. **-2. to wear badly** [shoes, material, clothes] to be easily damaged by use. ■ **to wear well** [shoes, material] to stay in good condition despite being old or used a lot □ *My mother's wearing well for sixty.* **-3.** *phrase* **to wear thin** [excuse, joke] to have been heard so often that it does not have much effect any more.
◇ *n* **-1. day/leisure wear** clothes for wearing during the day/one's leisure time □ *casual/evening wear.* **-2.** [to clothes, machinery] damage to clothes, shoes, part of a machine etc caused by use over a period of time □ *Those pants are beginning to show signs of wear.* ■ **wear and tear** damage caused by normal use over a period of time. **-3.** the act or state of being used, especially as clothing □ *My black coat hasn't had much wear.* ■ **to be the worse for wear** [shoes, carpet, curtains] to be badly damaged because they have been used a lot over a period of time; [person] to be in a bad physical or mental state, usually as a result of drinking too much.

◆ **wear away** ◇ *vt sep* to wear sthg away [rock, wood] to make sthg become thinner or smaller, usually over a long period of time. ◇ *vi*: *The edges of the stone steps had all worn away.*

◆ **wear down** ◇ *vt sep* **-1.** to wear sthg down [pencil point, heel of a shoe] to make sthg become smaller gradually by using it a lot. **-2. to wear sb/sth down** [enemy, resistance] to gradually make sb/sthg weak □ *Hard work/Illness has worn him down.* ◇ *vi*: *The problem with this type of heel is that it wears down quickly.*

◆ **wear off** *vi* [pain, feeling] to disappear gradually □ *The effects of the injection should wear off in a few hours.*

◆ **wear on** *vi* [time, evening, discussion] to pass slowly □ *Everyone got more friendly as the party wore on.*

◆ **wear out** ◇ *vt sep* **-1. to wear sth out** [shoes, carpet, clothes] to damage sthg so much by using it over a long period of time that it cannot be used any more; [patience, strength] to finish sthg completely. **-2. to wear sb out** to make sb very tired □ *Her persistent questioning wears me out.* ◇ *vi* [shoes, carpet, clothes] *Cheap shoes usually wear out more quickly than expensive ones.*

wearable ['weərəbl] *adj* [clothing, shoes] that is suitable or comfortable to wear.

wearily ['wɪərəlɪ] *adv* [move, smile, say] *see* **weary** □ *She sighed wearily.*

weariness ['wɪərɪnəs] *n*: *see* **weary** □ *A feeling of utter weariness overcame me.*

wearing ['weərɪŋ] *adj* [activity, job, journey] that makes one feel mentally very tired □ *It's extremely wearing having to travel two hours to work every day.*

weary ['wɪərɪ] (*compar* **wearier**, *superl* **weariest**) *adj* **-1.** [person] who is very tired; [smile, sigh] that shows one is very tired. **-2. to be weary of sthg** to have had enough of sthg □ *We soon became weary of city life.*

weasel ['wiːzl] *n* a small wild animal that has a long, thin, furry body and short legs, is very fierce, and hunts small animals.

weather ['weðəʳ] ◇ *n* conditions in the atmosphere such as sun, rain, snow, or wind, that exist at a particular time or in a particular place □ *good/bad weather* □ *What was the weather like in Scotland?* □ *We had fantastic weather last weekend.* ■ **to be under the weather** to be slightly ill □ *I'm feeling a little under the weather today.*

◇ *vt* [storm, crisis] to go through <sthg difficult> without being damaged or suffering too much □ *Our marriage is strong enough to weather a few disagreements now and then.*

◇ *vi* [rock, wood] to change in appearance or become smaller as a result of the action of sun, rain, frost etc.

weather-beaten [-biːtn] *adj* **-1.** [face, skin] that looks brown and wrinkled because it has been affected by a lot of sun and wind. **-2.** [building, stone] that has been damaged or changed in appearance by the weather.

weatherboard ['weðəʳbɔːʳd] *n* GB one of a series of wooden boards fixed in rows to the outside of a building to protect it from the weather.

weathercock ['weðəʳkɒk] *n* a metal object in the shape of a cock placed on top of a building that shows which way the wind is blowing.

weathered ['weðəʳd] *adj* = **weather-beaten.**

weather forecast *n* a description, usually given on the television or radio or in a newspaper, of what the weather will be like over a particular period in the future.

weatherman ['weðəʳmæn] (*pl* **weathermen** [-men]) *n* a person whose job is to give a weather forecast, especially on the television or radio.

weather map *n* a map that shows what the weather is like, or will be like, in different areas.

weatherproof ['weðəʳpruːf] *adj* [clothing, building] that can resist extreme weather conditions □ *Are you sure this tent is weatherproof?*

weather report *n* a report on the television or radio that says what the weather is like, or will be like.

weather ship *n* a ship at sea that gives information about the weather.

weatherstrip ['weðəʳstrɪp] *n* US a strip of foam or other material fixed to the edge of a door or window to stop drafts in a building.

weather vane [-veɪn] *n* a piece of shaped wood or metal on top of a building which shows the direction of the wind.

weave [wiːv] (*vt sense 1 pt* **wove**, *pp* **woven**, *vt sense 2* & *vi pt* & *pp* **weaved**) ◇ *vt* **-1.** [cloth, carpet, rug] to make <sthg> by passing threads over and under longer threads stretched on a machine □ *a hand-woven tapestry.* **-2. to weave one's way** to make a path for oneself by moving around and between people, cars etc □ *I saw him weaving his way toward me through the crowd.* ◇ *vi* to go through a crowd, traffic etc by moving around and between people, cars etc. ◇ *n* the way in which a piece of cloth is woven □ *a loose/an open weave.*

weaver ['wiːvəʳ] *n* a person whose job is to weave cloth, carpets, baskets etc.

web [web] *n* **-1.** [of a spider] the fine net of sticky threads that a spider makes in order to catch flies. **-2.** [of lies, intrigue] a complicated pattern of things that happen or are done.

◆ **Web** *n* = **World Wide Web.**

webbed [webd] *adj* **webbed feet** feet that have skin between the toes.

webbing ['webɪŋ] *n* a strong material made in strips that is used to make straps, belts etc and to support the springs in chairs.

web-footed [-'fʊtəd] *adj* [bird, animal] that has webbed feet.

Webster ['webstəʳ], **Noah** (1758–1843) a US writer who is famous for his dictionary of the American language.

wed [wed] (*pt* & *pp* **wed** OR **wedded**) (literary use) ◇ *vt* **-1.** [man, woman] to marry <sb>. **-2.** [priest] to marry <a man and a woman> by performing a marriage ceremony. ◇ *vi* to marry.

we'd [*stressed* wiːd, *unstressed* wɪd] = **we had, we would.**

Wed. *abbr of* **Wednesday.**

wedded ['wedəd] *adj* **to be wedded to sthg** [to an idea, system, belief] to believe in sthg so strongly that one cannot stop believing in it.

wedding ['wedɪŋ] *n* a ceremony in which a man and a woman are married □ *Have you been invited to Kate's wedding?* □ *a wedding present.*

wedding anniversary *n* the date on which somebody got married in a previous year.

wedding cake *n* a large decorated cake served at the party after a wedding.

wedding dress *n* a dress, often long and white, worn by a woman at her wedding.

wedding reception *n* a formal party that is held after a wedding.

wedding ring *n* a ring, usually made of gold, that is worn to show that one is married.

wedge [wedʒ] ◇ *n* **-1.** a piece of solid material, thick at one end and thin at the other, that is used to hold a door, wheel, window etc firmly in one position, or to split pieces of wood. ■ **to drive a wedge between people/groups etc** to act in a way that causes problems between people/groups etc □ *She accused me of trying to drive a wedge between her and Rob.* ■ **the thin end of the wedge** something that is small or unimportant but that will probably lead to something much more serious □ *These one-day strikes are just the thin end of the wedge.* **-2.** a piece of cheese, cake, pie etc that is wide at one end and narrow at the other.
◇ *vt* **-1.** [door, window, table leg] to make <sthg> stay in a particular position by putting a wedge under it □ *The door was wedged open with a piece of wood.* **-2.** [body, people] to force <sb/sthg> into a very small space □ *He wedged his foot in the door.* □ *There were tour of us wedged into the back of the taxi.*

Wedgwood ['wedʒwʊd], **Josiah** (1730–1795) a British potter, famous for china which has raised white figures or pictures on a blue or green background.

wedlock ['wedlɒk] *n* **to be born in/out of wedlock** to have parents who are/are not married to each other when one is born (literary use).

Wednesday ['wenzdeɪ] *n* the day of the week between Tuesday and Thursday; *see also* **Friday.**

weed [wiːd] *n* any wild plant that grows in a garden, field etc where it is not wanted.
◆ **weed out** *vt sep* **to weed sb out** to remove sb who is not wanted from a group □ *We're trying to weed out the troublemakers in the class.*

weeding ['wiːdɪŋ] *n* the work of removing weeds from a garden, field etc.

weedkiller ['wiːdkɪlə^r] *n* a chemical used for killing weeds.

weedy ['wiːdɪ] (*compar* **weedier**, *superl* **weediest**) *adj* [garden, field, ground] that contains a lot of weeds.

week [wiːk] *n* **-1.** the period of seven days that begins on a Monday and ends on a Sunday □ *I'll be abroad for the rest of this week.* □ *What day of the week are you free?* □ *last/next week.* **-2.** any period of seven days □ *The work took three weeks to complete.* □ *We'll meet again in two weeks' time.* ■ **a week from** US OR **on** GB **Saturday, Saturday week** GB seven days after next Saturday. ■ **a week ago Saturday** US, **a week last Saturday** seven days before last Saturday. **-3.** the period during the week, usually from Monday to Friday, when a person is at work □ *I work a forty-hour/six-day week.* □ *She's taking a week off work.* **-4. the week** all the days in a week except for Saturday and Sunday □ *I go to bed early during the week.*

weekday ['wiːkdeɪ] *n* any of the days of the week except Saturday and Sunday □ *The store is open weekdays but closed at the weekend.*

weekend [ˌwiːk'end] *n* the part of the week when most people do not work, consisting of Saturday and Sunday, and sometimes including Friday evening □ *What are you doing this weekend?* □ *Have a nice weekend!* □ *a weekend job.* ■ **on** US OR **at** GB **the weekend** on Saturday and Sunday □ *We usually work in the garden on the weekend.*

weekly ['wiːklɪ] (*pl* **weeklies**) ◇ *adj* [visit, payment] that is made, happens, appears etc once a week □ *a weekly newspaper.* ◇ *adv* every week □ *We get paid weekly.* ◇ *n* a newspaper or magazine that is published once a week.

weeny ['wiːnɪ] *adj* very small (informal use).

weep [wiːp] (*pt* & *pp* **wept**) ◇ *n* **to have a weep** to cry. ◇ *vt* to cry <tears>. ◇ *vi: I almost wept with joy/relief when I heard the news.* □ *He was weeping softly.*

weeping willow [ˌwiːpɪŋ-] *n* a tree that often grows near rivers and has long thin branches that hang down to the ground.

weepy ['wiːpɪ] (*compar* **weepier**, *superl* **weepiest**) *adj* [person] who wants to cry, or who cries often.

weft [weft] *n* the threads that run from side to side in a piece of cloth.
NOTE: Compare **warp.**

weigh [weɪ] ◇ *vt* **-1.** [person, package] to find out how heavy <sb/sthg> is using a machine □ *He weighs himself every morning.* □ *They'll weigh your suitcase at the airport.* **-2.** [facts, words, merits] to consider <sthg> carefully. **-3. to weigh anchor** to raise the anchor when a ship is leaving. ◇ *vi* to have a particular weight □ *How much do you weigh?* □ *Our luggage weighed over eighty kilos.*
◆ **weigh down** *vt sep* **to be weighed down by** OR **with sthg** [by a load, with bags] to be carrying sthg heavy that makes it difficult to move; [by responsibility, with problems] to feel very worried and anxious because of sthg □ *She always seems to be weighed down with small children and shopping.* □ *I felt weighed down by guilt.*
◆ **weigh on** *vt fus* **to weigh on sb** [worry, fear] to make sb feel very worried □ *Our lack of money began to weigh on me.*
◆ **weigh out** *vt sep* **to weigh sthg out** [food, goods] to measure a particular amount of sthg by weighing it □ *Weigh out six ounces of flour.*
◆ **weigh up** *vt sep* **to weigh sthg/sb up** [situation, plan] to consider sthg carefully in order to make a decision about it; [person] to consider sb carefully in order to reach an opinion about them □ *You have to weigh up the advantages and disadvantages of being self-employed.* □ *I could see he was weighing me up as a possible rival.*
◆ **weigh upon** *vt fus* = **weigh on.**

weighbridge ['weɪbrɪdʒ] *n* GB a machine that weighs vehicles and goods when they are driven onto a special plate in the ground.

weighing machine ['weɪɪŋ-] *n* a machine for weighing objects or people.

weight [weɪt] ◇ *n* -1. the amount somebody or something weighs □ *Feel the weight of this bag.* □ *He's always worrying about his weight.* ■ **to put on** OR **gain weight** to get heavier and fatter □ *She's put on a lot of weight recently.* ■ **to lose weight** to become lighter and thinner □ *He was desperately trying to lose weight.* ■ **to take the weight off one's feet** to sit down and rest (informal use) □ *Come in and take the weight off your feet.* -2. SPORT a heavy object that weighs a fixed amount and that people lift for exercise □ *He stays in shape by lifting weights and jogging.* -3. a heavy object □ *The doctor has told him not to lift heavy weights.* -4. **the weight of sthg** [of numbers, public opinion] the strong effect that sthg has □ *The weight of evidence would seem to be against you.* ■ **to carry weight** to be important □ *My opinion carries little weight with them.* ■ **to pull one's weight** to put the same amount of effort into a job as everybody else □ *Certain members of the team aren't pulling their weight.* ■ **to throw one's weight around** to think that one is very important and tell other people what to do □ *He's always throwing his weight around in the office.* -5. [of responsibility, guilt, sadness] an amount of something that causes a strong feeling of worry, sadness etc □ *It's a weight off my mind to know that he's alright.*

◇ *vt* **to weight sthg (down)** [paper, message, towel] to put a weight on sthg light to stop it from blowing away or moving.

weighted ['weɪtəd] *adj* **to be weighted in favor of/against sb/sthg** to be more favorable/unfavorable to sb/sthg □ *The new tax proposals are weighted in favor of the rich.*

weighting ['weɪtɪŋ] *n* GB an extra amount of money that is paid to employees who have to live in expensive areas □ *London weighting.*

weightlessness ['weɪtləsnəs] *n* the state of having no weight, experienced by people or objects in space □ *the feeling of weightlessness.*

weightlifter ['weɪtlɪftər] *n* a person who lifts weights as a sport or for exercise.

weightlifting ['weɪtlɪftɪŋ] *n* the sport or exercise of lifting weights.

weight training *n* physical exercise that involves lifting heavy weights □ *He does* OR *goes weight training twice a week.*

weighty ['weɪtɪ] (*compar* **weightier**, *superl* **weightiest**) *adj* [problem, argument, decision] that is serious and important.

weir [wɪər] *n* a low dam built across a river to change its level or control the flow of water.

weird [wɪərd] *adj* [person, idea, experience] that is very strange, especially in a frightening way □ *It was really weird seeing Jack again after all this time.*

weirdo ['wɪərdoʊ] (*pl* **weirdos**) *n* a weird person (informal use) □ *That guy's a real weirdo!*

welcome ['welkəm] ◇ *adj* -1. [guest, person] who one is pleased to see □ *Visitors are al-* ways welcome. ■ **to make sb welcome** to treat sb in a way that makes them feel wanted and happy to be there □ *The hotel staff made us very welcome.* -2. **you are/he is etc welcome to do sthg** a phrase used when one gives permission to somebody in a friendly way to do something □ *You're welcome to use any of the facilities.* -3. [opportunity, suggestion, reminder] that one is pleased or grateful to receive □ *Any comments would be most welcome.* -4. **you're welcome** a phrase used to reply to somebody when they thank one □ *"Thank you." — "You're welcome."*

◇ *n* the treatment given to somebody when they arrive somewhere □ *We got a very warm welcome from the manager.*

◇ *vt* -1. [visitor, guest, representative] to greet <sb>, especially in a friendly way, when they arrive somewhere □ *Your tour guide will be there to welcome you at the airport.* -2. [suggestion, news, change] to accept <sthg> happily □ *I'd welcome the opportunity to look around.*

◇ *excl* a word used to greet someone when they arrive somewhere □ *Welcome home/back!* □ *Welcome to Hong Kong!*

welcoming ['welkəmɪŋ] *adj* [person, smile] that seems warm and friendly.

weld [weld] ◇ *vt* to join <pieces of metal> by heating the edges until they are soft, pressing them together, and allowing them to cool. ◇ *n* a join made by welding.

welder ['weldər] *n* a person whose job is to join pieces of metal by welding; a machine that does this job.

welfare ['welfeər] ◇ *adj* [worker, work, services] that gives help to people with social and financial problems. ◇ *n* -1. **sb's welfare** sb's health, safety, and happiness □ *We're concerned about their welfare.* -2. US money and services provided by the government for people who are poor □ *The number of people living on welfare is increasing steadily.*

welfare state *n* a social system that provides money and services for people who are poor, ill, unemployed etc.

well [wel] (*compar* **better**, *superl* **best**) ◇ *adj* -1. **to be/feel well** to be/feel in good health □ *I'm not feeling very well right now.* □ *I hope you're all well.* □ *"How are you?" — "Very well, thanks."* □ *He's not a well man.* ■ **to get well** to become healthy again after an illness □ *We all hope you'll get well soon.* -2. **all is well** the situation is satisfactory □ *All's well with us here in Calcutta.* ■ **that's (all) well and good** a phrase used to say that some people find something acceptable, but that better things exist □ *Frozen vegetables are all well and good, but nothing can beat your own produce.* ■ **just as well** a phrase used to say that it is fortunate that something happened or did not happen □ *It's just as well we made reservations, because otherwise we wouldn't have gotten a room.*

◇ *adv* -1. [perform, behave, make] to a high standard □ *You speak Japanese very well.* □ *They work well together.* □ *a well-cut jacket* □ *She did well in her exams.* ■ **to go well** [party, operation, interview] to be successful □ *Things are going well at the moment.* □ *The exam went as well as could be expected.* ■ **well done!** a phrase used to give praise and encouragement to somebody who has done something good □ *You got into law school? Well done!* **-2.** [read, clean, study] carefully and completely; [know, understand] to a great degree □ *She had memorized her speech well.* □ *I don't really know them very well.* □ *as you well know.* ■ **well and truly** [beaten, finished, empty] completely. ■ **to be well in with sb** to have a good relationship with sb, so that it gives one an advantage (informal use) □ *Suzie's well in with the boss, isn't she?* ■ **you're well out of it** a phrase used to say that it is good that somebody is not involved in something any more (informal use). **-3.** a word used to emphasize something □ *As you are no doubt well aware...* □ *Stand well back please!* □ *The trip was well worth the effort.* ■ **well over/under...** much more/less than... □ *a crowd of well over 6,000* □ *Attendance was well under last year's.* **-4. it may/might/could well happen** it may/might/could easily happen □ *There might well be problems over copyright.*

◇ *n* **-1.** a deep hole in the ground that people can get water from □ *The village was abandoned when the wells dried up.* **-2.** = **oil well.**

◇ *excl* **-1.** a word used when one is not sure what to say, or when one wants to avoid seeming rude □ *Well, we could always try a new approach.* □ *"Do you like my hat?" — "Well, it's certainly colorful."* **-2.** a word used when one wants to correct something one has just said □ *I was only gone for five minutes. Well, maybe ten.* **-3. oh well!** an expression used to show that one accepts a situation, even though one does not like it very much □ *Oh well, it probably won't make much difference.* **-4. well (well)!** an expression used to show that one is surprised □ *Well, well, look who's just arrived!*

◆ **as well** *adv* **-1.** in addition (a phrase used when one wants to add extra information to something one has just said, or to include something in what was said before) □ *He's good-looking, and intelligent as well.* □ *I'd like to go as well.* **-2. I/you etc may as well (do something), I/you etc might as well (do something)** a phrase used to talk about something one thinks somebody should do in a particular situation, even though they do not want to □ *I might as well tell you the truth.*

◆ **as well as** *conj* a phrase used to show that something is not the only thing □ *As well as a son, she also has a daughter.* □ *As well as working in sales, I have also been involved in distribution.*

◆ **well up** *vi* [tears] to form in one's eyes □ *Tears began to well up in her eyes.*

we'll [*stressed* wiːl, *unstressed* wɪl] = **we shall, we will.**

well-adjusted *adj* [person] who is normal and happy.

well-advised [-ədˈvaɪzd] *adj* **you/he etc would be well-advised to do sthg** you/he etc should

do sthg in order to be sensible □ *You'd be well-advised to take out some travel insurance.*

well-appointed [-əˈpɔɪntəd] *adj* [kitchen, apartment, office] that contains furniture or equipment of good quality.

well-balanced *adj* **-1.** [person, mind, attitude] that is sensible. **-2.** [diet, meal] that contains all the different kinds of food needed for good health.

well-behaved [-bɪˈheɪvd] *adj* [child, dog] that behaves well.

wellbeing [ˈwelbiːɪŋ] *n* the state of being healthy, safe, and happy □ *It's not his physical wellbeing that I'm worried about.*

well-bred [-ˈbred] *adj* who comes from a good family or has very good manners.

well-built *adj* [man] who is tall, strong, and muscular.

well-chosen *adj* [remark, word] that is chosen with care to produce a particular effect.

well-disposed *adj* **to be well-disposed to(ward) sb/sthg** [to a person, plan, suggestion] to feel favorable toward sb/sthg.

well-done *adj* [meat] that is completely cooked.

well-dressed [-ˈdrest] *adj* [person] who wears attractive clothes of good quality.

well-earned [-ˈɜːrnd] *adj* [vacation, rest, reward] that one deserves □ *What you need is a well-earned rest!*

well-established *adj* [organization, link, company] that has existed for a long time and has been successful, effective etc.

well-fed *adj* [person, animal] that has enough, or more than enough, to eat.

well-groomed [-ˈgruːmd] *adj* [person, hair] neat in appearance.

well-heeled [-ˈhiːld] *adj* [person] who has a lot of money (informal use).

well-informed *adj* **to be well-informed** to know a lot about something □ *She's very well-informed about this subject.*

wellington [ˈwelɪŋtən] *n* **a wellington (boot)** a long plastic or rubber boot that reaches to below the knee and keeps out water □ *a pair of wellington boots.*

Wellington the capital of New Zealand and a major port, on North Island. POPULATION: 343,000.

Wellington [ˈwelɪŋtən]: **the Duke of Wellington** (1769–1852) a British military and political leader who helped to defeat Napoleon at Waterloo in 1815, and was prime minister from 1828 to 1830.

well-intentioned [-ɪnˈtenʃnd] *adj* [offer, suggestion] = **well-meaning.**

well-kept *adj* **-1.** [building, garden] that is tidy and in good condition. **-2.** [secret] that is not told to other people.

well-known *adj* [person, place, story] that a lot of people know □ *It's a well-known fact that smoking causes cancer.*

well-mannered *adj* [person] who has good

manners and knows how to behave correctly in social situations.

well-meaning *adj* [suggestion, remark] that is intended to be helpful but often produces unfortunate results □ *She's very well-meaning.*

well-nigh *adv* almost □ *It's well-nigh impossible.*

well-off *adj* -1. [person, family, area] that is richer than most people. -2. **to be well-off for sthg** to have plenty of sthg enjoyable or necessary □ *We're quite well-off for restaurants in this area.* ■ **not to know when one is well-off** not to realize that one is fortunate (informal use) □ *Some people just don't know when they're well-off!*

well-paid *adj* [person, job] that is paid a lot of money □ *The work is very well-paid.*

well-preserved *adj* [person] who looks younger than they are, even though they are getting old.

well-proportioned [-prə'pɔːʳʃnd] *adj* [building, figure, sculpture] whose parts are the correct size in relation to one another.

well-read [-'red] *adj* [person] who has read a lot and learned about many different subjects as a result.

well-rounded [-'raʊndəd] *adj* [education] that is complete and covers many different subjects; [person] who has received such an education or has experienced many different things.

Wells [welz], **H. G.** (1866–1946) a British writer of science fiction whose best-known works include *The Time Machine* and *The War of the Worlds.*

well-spoken *adj* [person] who speaks correctly and politely □ *a quiet, well-spoken young man.*

well-thought-of *adj* [person, institution] that has a good reputation because of the quality of their work.

well-thought-out *adj* [plan, design, essay] that has been produced with careful thought so that it works well □ *The course was not really well-thought-out and suffered as a result.*

well-timed *adj* [action, remark, intervention] that is made at the right time.

well-to-do *adj* [person, family] that is fairly rich and has a high social position □ *a well-to-do area of town.*

well-wisher [-wɪʃəʳ] *n* a person who admires and supports somebody and wishes them success.

well-woman clinic *n* GB a health center where women can get contraception, medical examinations, advice etc.

welly ['welɪ] (*pl* **wellies**) *n* = **wellington** (informal use).

Welsh [welʃ] ◇ *n* a language spoken in Wales. ◇ *npl* **the Welsh** people who live in Wales. ◇ *adj*: see **Wales** □ *a Welsh accent.*

Welsh rarebit [-'reəʳbɪt] *n* a dish consisting of toasted bread covered in melted cheese.

welter ['weltəʳ] *n* **a welter of ideas/words etc** a large confused amount of ideas/words etc.

welterweight ['weltəʳweɪt] *n* a boxer who is between a heavyweight and a lightweight.

wend [wend] *vt* **to wend one's way** to go somewhere slowly (literary use).

wendy house ['wendɪ-] *n* GB a toy house large enough for a child to play in.

went [went] *past tense of* **go**.

wept [wept] *past tense & past participle of* **weep**.

were [*stressed* wɜːʳ, *unstressed* wəʳ] *past tense of* **be**.

we're [*stressed* wiːəʳ, *unstressed* wɪəʳ] = **we are**.

weren't [wɜːʳnt] = **were not**.

werewolf ['weəʳwʊlf] (*pl* **werewolves** [-wʊlvz]) *n* in stories, horror movies etc, a person who sometimes changes into a wolf.

Wesley ['weslɪ], **John** (1703–1791) a British religious reformer who established the Methodist Church.

west [west] ◇ *n* -1. the direction in which the sun sets □ *The wind is coming from the west.* -2. **the west** the western part of a country or region □ *the west of Ireland.* ◇ *adj* -1. **the west side/coast etc** the side/coast etc in or facing the west. -2. **a west wind** a wind that comes from the west. ◇ *adv* [face, travel] toward the west □ *Chicago is west of Detroit.*

◆ **West** *n* **the West** the countries of western, northern, and southern Europe and North America; in the USA, a region between the West Coast and the Rocky Mountains.

West Bank: **the West Bank** the area to the west of the Jordan River, between Israel and Jordan, that was occupied by Israel from 1967. In 1993, it was declared a self-governing Palestinian region.

westbound ['westbaʊnd] *adj* [road, traffic, train] that is going west.

West Coast: **the West Coast** the Pacific coast of the USA.

NOTE: When Americans refer to *the West Coast*, they usually mean California.

West Country: **the West Country** the southwest of England.

West End: **the West End** the western part of central London where many large stores and theaters are found.

🐝 WEST END
The West End of London includes some of the city's most famous streets and landmarks, such as Oxford Street, Piccadilly, and Leicester Square. It also contains most of London's main theaters, which usually feature big stars in well-known plays.

westerly ['westəʳlɪ] *adj* -1. [direction, point] that is in or toward the west. -2. **a westerly wind** a wind that comes from the west.

western ['westəʳn] ◇ *adj* -1. [part of a country, continent] that is in the west □ *the western seaboard.* -2. [attitude, culture, technology] that is connected with countries in the West. ◇ *n* a movie or novel about life in the western United States in the 19th century, especially one involving cowboys and Indians.

Western Australia the largest state in Australia, situated on the Indian Ocean. SIZE: 2,530,000 sq kms. POPULATION: 1,586,393. CAPITAL: Perth.

Westerner ['westərnər] *n* -1. a person who comes from one of the countries in the West. -2. a person who lives in the west of a particular country.

Western Isles: the Western Isles an administrative region of Scotland, consisting of the Outer Hebrides. SIZE: 2,900 sq kms. POPULATION: 31,834. ADMINISTRATIVE CENTER: Stornoway.

westernize, -ise ['westərnaɪz] *vt* [culture, society] to bring the ideas, behavior etc of the countries in the West to <other countries>.

Western Sahara a region in northwestern Africa, on the Atlantic coast between Morocco and Mauritania. SIZE: 266,000 sq kms. POPULATION: 200,000. MAIN CITY: Al-Ayoun. LANGUAGE: Arabic. CURRENCY: Moroccan dirham.

Western Samoa a country in Polynesia, in the southern Pacific Ocean, consisting of nine islands. SIZE: 2,841 sq kms. POPULATION: 163,000 (*Western Samoans*). CAPITAL: Apia. LANGUAGE: Samoan, English. CURRENCY: tala.

Western Standard Time *n* a time zone that includes the whole of Western Australia.

West Germany the western part of Germany that was a federal republic from 1949 until the reunification of Germany in 1990.

West Indian *n* & *adj*: see **West Indies**.

West Indies [-'ɪndɪz]: **the West Indies** the islands in the Caribbean Sea, between Florida and Venezuela, including Cuba, the Bahamas, Jamaica, Puerto Rico, Dominica, and Trinidad.

Westminster ['westmɪnstər] ◇ the area of central London where Buckingham Palace and Parliament are situated. ◇ *n* a term used for the British Parliament.

West Point *n* the US army training school for officers, north of New York City.

West Virginia a mountainous state in the eastern USA. ABBREVIATION: WV. SIZE: 62,341 sq kms. POPULATION: 1,793,477 (*West Virginians*). CAPITAL: Charleston.

westward ['westwərd] ◇ *adj* [direction, trip] that is toward the west. ◇ *adv* [travel, fly, drive] toward the west □ *The back of the house faces westward.*

westwards ['westwərdz] *adv* = **westward**.

wet [wet] (*compar* **wetter**, *superl* **wettest**, *pt* & *pp* **wet** OR **wetted**, *cont* **wetting**) ◇ *adj* -1. [hair, ground, road] that is covered with or full of water or another liquid □ *You should change out of those wet clothes.* □ *His face was wet with tears.* -2. [weather, climate] rainy □ *It's going to be very wet all weekend.* -3. [ink, concrete] that has not yet dried. ■ '**Wet paint**' a phrase used on notices to warn people not to touch something that has just been painted.
◇ *n* GB POLITICS a moderate Conservative politician.
◇ *vt* -1. [hair, sponge, towel] to make <sthg> wet. -2. to make <one's clothes or bed> wet by urinating accidentally □ *He wet himself.*

wet blanket *n* a person who will not join in an activity or who stops other people from enjoying themselves (disapproving use).

wet-look *adj* **wet-look leather/hair-gel etc** leather/hair-gel etc that is shiny and looks as if it is wet.

wet nurse *n* in the past, a woman who was paid to breast-feed somebody else's baby.

wet rot *n* a state of decay in wood caused by a fungus.

wet suit *n* a rubber suit worn by divers, surfers etc to keep them warm in cold water.

WEU (*abbr of* **Western European Union**) *n* **the WEU** an organization of western European nations that aims to coordinate defense policies.

we've [*stressed* wiːv, *unstressed* wɪv] = **we have**.

whack [wæk] (informal use) ◇ *n* -1. a hard blow □ *a whack on the head.* -2. a share of money, profit, work etc □ *We all expect our whack of the profits.* ◇ *vt* [person, child, ball] to hit <sb/sthg> hard, especially with a flat object □ *She whacked him hard over the ear.*

whacky ['wækɪ] *adj* = **wacky**.

whale [weɪl] *n* a huge mammal that looks like a fish and lives in the sea. ■ **to have a whale of a time** to enjoy oneself very much (informal use).

whaling ['weɪlɪŋ] *n* the activity of hunting whales for food, oil etc.

wham [wæm] *excl* a sound used to indicate that something is loud or forceful (informal use).

wharf [wɔːrf] (*pl* **wharfs** OR **wharves** [wɔːvz]) *n* a platform built in a harbor or river where ships can be tied up and unloaded.

what [US wʌt, GB wɒt] ◇ *det* -1. used in questions that ask somebody to choose or identify something that is part of a large group of things □ *What color is it?* □ *What newspaper do you read?* □ *What kind of music do you like?* □ *What size/shape is it?* -2. **he asked me what color it was** he asked me to tell him the color of it (used in indirect questions) □ *They wanted to know what books I needed.* -3. used in exclamations to express a strong opinion □ *What a mess!* □ *What a lovely day!* □ *What a day I've had!* □ *What dirty water!* □ *What a surprise!*
◇ *pron* -1. used to ask for information about something that one does not know □ *What is in the bag?* □ *What did you tell him?* □ *What's your name?* □ *What did they talk about?* -2. **what about another drink?** shall we have another drink? (used to make suggestions or offers) □ *What about approaching them directly?* ■ **what if we did it this way?** let's do it this way (a polite way of making a suggestion) □ *What if we postponed the meeting till next week?* -3. **what if I can't/couldn't?** what will happen if I can't/couldn't? (used to talk about a possible situation in the future) □ *What if nobody comes?* □ *What if our forecast is wrong?* -4. **what you're doing is fine** the thing that

you're doing is fine (used as the subject or object of a verb) □ *I didn't see what happened.* □ *Nobody could understand what I was saying.*

◇ *excl* used to express surprise or shock □ *"I'm pregnant." — "What!"* □ *What, no money?*

whatever [US wʌt'evr, GB wɒt'evə] ◇ *det* **whatever book** any book, it is not important which one □ *I took whatever opportunities I could get.*

◇ *adv* used in negative sentences to emphasize what one is saying □ *They have no chance whatever of succeeding.* □ *There was nothing whatever we could do.*

◇ *pron* **-1. whatever happens** no matter what happens (used to say that something is true in all possible situations) □ *Whatever they offer* OR *may offer, I'll still say no.* □ *They go to work whatever the weather.* □ *Do whatever you like, I don't mind.* **-2.** used to express surprise in questions that ask for information about a thing one does not know □ *Whatever were you thinking?* **-3.** used to refer to a thing that is not precise or not known □ *The doctor says I've got jogger's knee, whatever that is.* ■ **or whatever** or anything else □ *Just bring a bottle of wine or whatever.*

what's-his-name *n* a word used when one has forgotten somebody's name (informal use).

whatsit [US 'wʌtsət, GB 'wɒt-] *n* a word used when one has forgotten the name of a small object or device (informal use).

whatsoever [US ,wʌtsoʊ'evr, GB ,wɒtsoʊ'evə] *adv* used in negative sentences to emphasize what one is saying □ *I have no desire to meet him whatsoever.* □ *nothing whatsoever.*

wheat [wiːt] *n* the grain from which flour, pasta etc is made; the plant that produces this grain.

wheatbread *n* US bread made from wholewheat flour.

wheat germ *n* the center of a grain of wheat that contains a lot of the substances needed for health and growth.

wheatmeal ['wiːtmiːl] *n* a type of brown flour made from wheat grains.

wheedle ['wiːdl] *vt* **to wheedle sb into doing sthg** to persuade sb to do sthg by saying nice things that one does not really mean □ *She wheedled me into looking after the children.* ■ **to wheedle sthg out of sb** [truth, money] to persuade sb gradually to give one sthg □ *See if you can wheedle an extra ticket out of him.*

wheel [wiːl] ◇ *n* **-1.** a round object that turns around on a rod that is fixed to its center and on which a vehicle such as a car moves along the ground □ *One of the back wheels got stuck in the mud.* **-2.** AUTO a steering wheel. ■ **to be at** OR **behind the wheel** to be driving.

◇ *vt* [bicycle, cart, trolley] to move <sthg on wheels> □ *She was wheeling a baby in a carriage.* ◇ *vi* **-1.** [birds] to fly in a circle with frequent changes of direction. **-2. to wheel around** to turn around quickly.

wheelbarrow [US 'wiːlberoʊ, GB -bær-] *n* an open container with one wheel at the front

and two handles at the back that is used for carrying things in gardens, on building sites etc.

wheelbase ['wiːlbeɪs] *n* the distance between the front and back wheels of a vehicle.

wheelchair ['wiːltʃeər] *n* a chair with wheels in which people who cannot walk are pushed or move themselves □ *an electric wheelchair* □ *wheelchair access.*

wheel clamp *n* a device that is attached to the wheel of a vehicle parked illegally to prevent the vehicle from being driven. The driver has to pay to have it removed.

◆ **wheel-clamp** *vt* to put a wheel clamp on <a vehicle>.

wheeler-dealer ['wiːlər-] *n* a person who does a lot of wheeling and dealing (disapproving use).

wheelie bin ['wiːli-] *n* GB a large container for garbage that has two wheels so that it can be moved easily.

wheeling and dealing [,wiːlɪŋ-] *n* unfair or dishonest methods used to succeed in business or politics (disapproving use).

wheeze [wiːz] *vi* to breathe with a whistling or hissing sound.

wheezy ['wiːzi] (*compar* **wheezier**, *superl* **wheeziest**) *adj* [person, voice, cough] that wheezes.

whelk [welk] *n* a small sea creature similar to a snail that can be eaten.

when [wen] ◇ *adv* used in questions that ask for information about the time something happens. ■ **when does the plane arrive?** what time does the plane arrive? □ *I wasn't sure when to leave.* ■ **when did you get married?** what date/year did you get married? □ *When is your birthday?* ■ **he asked me when I would be in London** he asked me the date I would be in London.

◇ *conj* **-1.** used to say the time something happens in relation to another event or action. ■ **they visited me when I was sick** I was sick, and they visited me during that time □ *The phone rang when I was taking a shower.* ■ **when you've finished, you can go** after you've finished, you can go □ *It was when I was posted to Tokyo.* ■ **on the day when it happened** on the day during which it happened. **-2.** used to emphasize a difference between two facts, actions, or events □ *They used our idea when they had no right to.* ■ **she said she was sick when she wasn't** she said she was sick, but she wasn't really. **-3.** used to introduce the reason for a statement or question □ *It's wrong to waste food when people are dying of hunger.* ■ **how can I buy it when I can't afford it?** I can't afford it, so how can I buy it?

whenever [wen'evər] ◇ *conj* **-1. whenever I go** every time I go □ *Whenever I try to arrange a meeting she says she's busy.* **-2. whenever you like** at any time you like □ *You can use the computer whenever you want.* ◇ *adv* **-1.** used to express surprise in questions that ask for information about the time something happens □ *Whenever do you find time to work with* two young children to look after? **-2.** used to refer to a time in the future that is not precise □ *"When do you want it done by?" — "Oh, whenever."*

where [weə^r] ◇ *adv* **-1.** used in questions that ask for information about the place somebody or something is in or goes to. ■ **where do you live?** in what place do you live? □ *Where's my pen?* □ *Where do you want to go on vacation this year?* □ *Tell me where you bought your sunglasses.* **-2.** used to indicate a particular point in a discussion, situation etc □ *I don't know where to start!* □ *That's where I don't agree.*
◇ *conj* & *pron* **-1. I found it where I'd left it** I found it in the place where I'd left it □ *We should open our store where there isn't too much competition.* ■ **go where I went** go to the place I went to □ *a place where you can feel comfortable.* ■ **the house where I was born** the house in which I was born. ■ **this is where it happened** this is the place in which it happened. **-2.** used to emphasize the difference between two actions or situations □ *Children will often understand computers where an adult will not.*

whereabouts [*adv* ˌweərə'baʊts, *n* 'weərəbaʊts] ◇ *adv* used in questions that ask for precise information about the place somebody or something is in or is going to □ *Whereabouts in India do you live?* □ *Whereabouts in Italy are you going on vacation?* ◇ *npl* the exact place that somebody or something is in □ *Their whereabouts are still unknown.*

whereas [weər'æz] *conj* used to show that two facts, actions, or events are different □ *My old office was small, whereas my new one is quite big.*

whereby [weə^r'baɪ] *conj* **a system whereby it is possible** a system that makes it possible (formal use) □ *a new bill whereby divorced wives will have a share of their husband's pension.*

whereupon [ˌweərə'pɒn] *conj* used to say that one thing happens immediately after another. ■ **they said no, whereupon I left** they said no, and then I left (formal use).

wherever [weər'evə^r] ◇ *conj* **-1. wherever he stays** in every place he stays □ *Wherever my mother went, the dog followed.* ■ **wherever I go** in every place I go to □ *We were treated well wherever we went.* **-2. sit wherever you like** sit in any place you want □ *Put the files down wherever there's room.* **-3. wherever possible** in every possible situation □ *We try to avoid causing disruption wherever possible.* **-4.** used to show that one does not know where somebody or something is □ *He lives in Butte, wherever that is.* □ *Wherever it is, I can't find it.*
◇ *adv* **-1.** used to express surprise in questions that ask for information about where somebody or something is or goes □ *Wherever did you hear that?* **-2.** used to refer to a place that is not precise □ *"Where should I put it?" — "Oh, wherever."*

wherewithal ['weə^rwɪðɔːl] *n* **to have the wherewithal to do sthg** to have the money or equipment needed to do sthg (formal use).

whet [wet] (*pt* & *pp* **whetted**, *cont* **whetting**) *vt* **to whet sb's appetite** to make sb want more of something □ *The weekend away only whetted my appetite for another vacation.*

whether ['weðə^r] *conj* **-1.** used to introduce indirect questions where there are two possibilities □ *I don't know whether I'll be able to come or not.* □ *We weren't sure whether to say yes or no.* **-2.** used to say that something is true in either of two possible situations that one mentions □ *Whether you want to or not, you still have to do it.* □ *I need to know by tomorrow whether the answer is yes or no.*

whew [fjuː] *excl* a sound that one makes when one is very hot, relieved, or surprised.

whey [weɪ] *n* the watery liquid left after the thick part of sour milk is removed during the process of making cheese.

which [wɪtʃ] ◇ *det* **-1.** used in questions that ask for information where there is a choice or doubt between two or more things □ *Which department do you work in?* □ *Which one do you prefer?* □ *Which ones are the best, in your opinion?* □ *Do you know which bidder got the contract?* **-2.** used to refer to something that has been mentioned in the first part of the sentence. ■ **in which case** in the case that has been mentioned □ *I may be needed somewhere else, in which case I have to leave early.*
◇ *pron* **-1.** used in questions that ask for information where there is a choice or doubt between two or more things. ■ **which do you prefer?** what one do you prefer, from a limited number? □ *Which is the one that we decided to buy?* □ *Which are going to be the most popular?* □ *I can't decide which to have.* **-2.** used to refer to something that has been mentioned in the first part of the sentence □ *I bought the computer which was on special offer.* □ *Have you got a book which gives information about hotels?* **-3.** used to give more information about something that has been mentioned in the first part of the sentence □ *My car, which is pretty old, often breaks down.* □ *The service, which I've complained about before, is terrible.* **-4.** used to refer to the first part of the sentence. ■ **she's late, which is unusual** the fact that she is late is unusual □ *She said she didn't know, which surprised me.*

whichever [wɪtʃ'evə^r] ◇ *det* **-1. whichever job I get** any job I get, it is not important which one □ *The trip takes two hours whichever route you take.* **-2. whichever color you like** the particular color which you like □ *You can use whichever program you know best.* ◇ *pron* **-1. whichever is best** the one which is best □ *We can have whichever of the apartments has the best view.* **-2. whichever you take** no matter which one you take □ *Whichever plan you decide on, things won't be easy.*

whiff [wɪf] *n* **-1. to get a whiff of sthg** [of smoke, perfume, onions] to smell sthg slightly □ *I caught a whiff of alcohol on his breath as he walked by.* **-2. a whiff of danger/scandal etc** a sign of something dangerous/scandalous etc that might be happening.

while [waɪl] ◇ *n* a period of time □ *I can only*

stay a while. ■ **after a while** after quite a long time □ *After a while I got bored.* □ *It's been quite a while since we last met.* ■ **for a while** for quite a long time □ *We spoke for a while.* ■ **it's (not) worth your while** it's (not) worth the time and effort you would have to spend on it.
◇ *conj* -1. **while I am here** during the time that I am here □ *We met while we were working in Paris.* □ *While I was waiting for the results I had a coffee.* -2. **while he is here** if he is here □ *You'll never get promotion while he's in charge.* -3. used to show that two facts, actions, or events are different □ *I like tea, while she prefers coffee.* □ *She thinks it's easy, while it's actually very difficult.*
◇ *vt* **to while the time away** to spend one's time doing something when one is waiting for somebody or something, or when one is not doing anything important.

whilst [waɪlst] *conj* = **while**.

whim [wɪm] *n* a sudden idea or desire, especially one that is not very practical or reasonable □ *He just decided to do it on a sudden whim.*

whimper ['wɪmpər] ◇ *vt* [word, excuse, apology] to say <sthg> in a weak or frightened way, as though about to cry □ *"I'm really sorry," he whimpered.* ◇ *vi* [child, animal] to make soft low cries that express pain or unhappiness □ *The baby lay whimpering.* ◇ *n*: *He went to bed without a whimper.*

whimsical ['wɪmzɪkl] *adj* [thought, idea, person] that one thinks is strange in an amusing way.

whine [waɪn] ◇ *vi* -1. [child, dog] to make a long high sound, usually expressing pain or unhappiness. -2. [person] to complain, especially in a high unpleasant voice, about something unimportant □ *He's always whining about his boss.* ◇ *n* the sound made by somebody or something that whines □ *We heard the whine of the sirens.*

whinge [wɪndʒ] (*cont* **whingeing**) *vi* GB & AUS to complain in a way that annoys other people □ *She never stops whingeing about her boyfriend.*

whip [wɪp] (*pt* & *pp* **whipped**, *cont* **whipping**) ◇ *n* -1. a long piece of rope or leather attached to a short handle that is used for hitting animals or people. -2. POLITICS a member of a political party who makes sure that other members are present when voting takes place □ *the House Republican Whip.* ◇ *vt* -1. to hit <a person or animal> with a whip, especially on the back. -2. to strike <sb/sthg> hard □ *The cold wind whipped her face.* -3. **to whip sthg out/off** to take sthg out/off quickly □ *He whipped a $10 bill out of his wallet.* □ *She whipped off her coat.* -4. [cream, eggs] to beat <food> until it is thick and full of air.
◆ **whip up** *vt sep* **to whip sthg up** [excitement, interest, resentment] to cause people to feel sthg; to deliberately make sthg stronger □ *The aim of a launch is to whip up enthusiasm for the new product.*

whiplash ['wɪplæʃ] *n* an injury to one's neck caused when one's head is suddenly thrown forward and then back, e.g. in a car accident □ *A number of passengers were taken to hospital suffering from whiplash* □ *a whiplash injury.*

whipped cream ['wɪpt-] *n* cream that has been beaten until it is thick and full of air.

whippet ['wɪpət] *n* a small thin dog with long legs, similar to a greyhound.

whirl [wɜːrl] ◇ *n* -1. [of dust, sand, smoke] a fast spinning movement. ■ **to be in a whirl** [mind, head, thoughts] to be in a state of confusion. -2. a number of events, parties, meetings etc following one after the other very quickly. -3. *phrase* **let's give it a whirl** let's try it (informal use). ◇ *vt* **to whirl sb/sthg around** to turn sb/sthg around quickly. ◇ *vi* -1. [sand, dust, leaves] to spin quickly and in an uncontrolled way. -2. [head, mind] to be confused or excited.

whirlpool ['wɜːrlpuːl] *n* a powerful spinning mass of water in a river or sea that sucks things into its center.

whirlwind ['wɜːrlwɪnd] ◇ *adj* **a whirlwind romance/affair etc** a romance/affair etc that happens very quickly. ◇ *n* a tall spinning mass of air that can damage crops, buildings etc.

whirr [wɜːr] ◇ *vi* [machinery, engine, insect's wings] to make a low, regular, beating noise □ *The cameras whirred into action.* ◇ *n* the sound made by something that whirrs □ *the whirr of machinery.*

whisk [wɪsk] ◇ *n* COOKING a device used to beat air into cream, eggs etc □ *a hand/an electric whisk.* ◇ *vt* -1. to move <sb/sthg> somewhere quickly, especially to prevent them from being seen □ *She was whisked away in a taxi.* □ *He whisked the letter out of his pocket.* -2. [cream, sauce, egg] to beat <sthg> using a whisk in order to mix in air.

whisker ['wɪskər] *n* [of a cat, rabbit, mouse] a long stiff hair that grows near the mouth of some animals.
◆ **whiskers** *npl* the hair on the sides of a man's face.

whiskey ['wɪskɪ] (*pl* **whiskeys**) *n* an alcoholic drink that is made from grain, is golden in color, and usually comes from Ireland or the United States; a glass of this drink.

whisky ['wɪskɪ] (*pl* **whiskies**) *n* an alcoholic drink that is made from barley, is golden in color, and usually comes from Scotland; a glass of this drink.

whisper ['wɪspər] ◇ *n* a soft quiet voice □ *She spoke in a whisper.* ◇ *vt* [word, reply, name] to say <sthg> very quietly, using one's breath not one's voice. ◇ *vi*: *What are you two whispering about?*

whispering ['wɪspərɪŋ] *n* the act of speaking in a whisper.

whist [wɪst] *n* a card game for four people, playing in two pairs. Each pair tries to win more cards than the other.

whistle ['wɪsl] ◇ *n* -1. [of a policeman, referee, guard] a small device consisting of a small curved piece of metal that makes a loud high noise when one blows through it; [on a train, kettle] a device that makes a loud high sound when steam is forced through it □ *We heard the sound of a whistle.* **-2.** a high sound made by blowing or sucking air in between one's lips or teeth; a sound similar to this made e.g. by blowing air or forcing steam through a whistle □ *She gave a loud whistle.* □ *That's the referee's final whistle.*

◇ *vt* [tune, melody] to produce <music> by blowing and sucking air in between the lips or teeth □ *He always whistles hymns in the bathtub.*

◇ *vi* **-1.** [person] *I learned to whistle when I lost my front teeth.* ■ **to whistle at sb** to whistle loudly while looking at sb to show one finds them sexually attractive. **-2.** [bird, kettle, train] to produce a high loud sound □ *Several bullets whistled overhead.*

Whistler ['wɪslər], **James** (1834–1903) a US artist who is known for his portraits, especially the one of his mother.

whistle-stop tour *n* a very fast tour of a country, region etc, especially by a politician, with short stops in each place.

Whit [wɪt] *n* GB = **Whitsun** □ *Whit Monday.*

white [waɪt] ◇ *adj* **-1.** [paint, cloud, sock] that is the color of milk or snow □ *bright white clouds overhead.* ■ **to go** OR **turn white** [hair] to become white as a result of old age, shock, or illness; [face, person] to become pale. **-2.** [person, community, race] that has pale skin and is of European origin □ *The man is white and in his early thirties.* **-3. white coffee** coffee that has milk or cream in it □ *Do you want your coffee white or black?*

◇ *n* **-1.** the color of milk or snow □ *Do you have this sweater in white?* **-2.** a person with pale skin, of European origin. **-3. the white of an egg** the part of an egg that surrounds the yellow center □ *Separate the yolk from the white.* **-4. the white of sb's eye** the white part of sb's eyeball.

◆ **whites** *npl* **-1.** SPORT the white clothes worn for playing tennis, cricket etc. **-2.** white or pale clothes that are washed together in a washing machine.

White [waɪt], **Patrick** (1912–1990) an Australian writer whose novels include *The Tree of Man* and *Voss.*

white blood cell *n* a blood cell that fights infection.

whiteboard ['waɪtbɔːrd] *n* a board with a smooth white surface that is fixed to a wall in schools, offices etc and that can be written on using special pens.

white Christmas *n* a Christmas Day when it snows.

white-collar *adj* [worker, union, job] that is connected with people who work in offices or in one of the professions. NOTE: Compare **blue-collar.**

white elephant *n* something that is considered large, useless, and a waste of money.

white goods *npl* a collective term for large machines used in the home, e.g. stoves, washing machines, and refrigerators.

white-haired [-'heərd] *adj* [person] who has white hair.

Whitehall ['waɪthɔːl] ◇ a street in central London where many government offices are situated. ◇ *n* a term used to refer to the British government, especially government departments.

white-hot *adj* [metal] that is so hot that it looks white.

White House ◇ **the White House** the official home of the president of the United States. ◇ *n* **the White House** a term used to refer to the president of the USA and his cabinet □ *Reports from the White House say the President will be leaving soon for France.* □ *a White House aide.*

white knight *n* a person or organization that saves a company that is in financial trouble.

white lie *n* a small lie that is told for a good reason, especially in order to be polite.

white magic *n* magic that is used for doing good things.

white meat *n* meat such as pork or chicken that is pale when cooked. NOTE: Compare **red meat.**

whiten ['waɪtn] ◇ *vt* [clothes, shoes] to make <sthg> white or whiter. ◇ *vi* to become white or whiter.

whitener ['waɪtnər] *n* a substance used to whiten clothes, shoes etc.

white noise *n* noise that is made up of a wide range of frequencies, all of the same strength.

whiteout ['waɪtaʊt] *n* **-1.** a condition created when there is snow and white cloud and it becomes difficult to see properly. **-2.** US a white liquid that can be painted onto paper to cover mistakes in typing or writing.

White Pages™ *npl* **the White Pages** in the USA, a list in a book that gives the names, addresses, and phone numbers of all the people, businesses etc in an area or city that have phones.

White Paper *n* POLITICS in Britain and Australia, an official report stating the government's ideas on a particular subject.

white sauce *n* a thick sauce made of flour, butter, and milk.

white spirit *n* GB a colorless liquid made from petroleum and used to clean paintbrushes, make paint thinner etc.

white-tie *adj* [dinner, function] at which men wear formal evening dress, including white bow ties.

white trash▼ *n* US poor white people (offensive use).

whitewash ['waɪtwɒʃ] ◇ *n* **-1.** a thin white substance made from lime that is used for painting walls, buildings etc □ *The walls were covered in whitewash.* **-2.** the act of whitewashing an affair □ *The commission's report has been denounced as a whitewash.* ◇ *vt* **-1.** [wall, house] to paint <a building> with whitewash. **-2.** [crime, affair, scandal] to hide <sthg bad>, e.g. a crime, or make it appear less bad in order to protect the person or people responsible □ *Officials have been accused of whitewashing the whole affair.*

whitewater rafting [US ,waitwɔ:tər'ræftiŋ, GB -wɔ:tə'rɑ:ftiŋ] *n* the sport of traveling down a fast-flowing river in an inflatable rubber boat.

white wedding *n* a formal wedding at which the bride wears a white dress.

whiting ['waitiŋ] (*pl* **whiting** OR **whitings**) *n* a silver sea fish with a dark back that is eaten for food.

Whitman ['witmən], **Walt** (1819–1892) a US poet who wrote about nature and democracy. His collected works are called *Leaves of Grass*.

Whitsun ['witsn] *n* in the Christian religion, the seventh Sunday after Easter, commemorating the day the Holy Spirit came down from Heaven.

Whittington ['witiŋtən], **Dick** (1358–1423) a British businessman who became mayor of London. According to popular stories, he walked to London with his cat when he was thirteen years old.

whittle ['witl] ◆ **whittle away** *vt sep* **to whittle sthg away** [support, majority] to reduce sthg gradually, often with damaging results □ *Inflation has whittled away the value of savings.*

◆ **whittle down** *vt sep* **to whittle sthg down** to make sthg smaller □ *I've whittled the shortlist down to six.*

whiz, whizz [wiz] (*pt* & *pp* **whizzed**, *cont* **whizzing**) ◇ *n* **to be a whiz at sthg** [at computers, tennis, chess] to be very good at sthg (informal use). ◇ *vi* [car, ball, train] to move quickly, often with a loud whistling sound □ *Bullets whizzed overhead.* □ *An hour later we were whizzing toward L.A.*

whiz(z) kid *n* a person who is very successful while they are still young (informal use).

who [hu:] *pron* -1. used in questions that ask for information about an unknown person □ *Who are you?* □ *Who's speaking, please?* □ *Who's your doctor?* □ *Who were you speaking to just now?* -2. **I asked who did it** I asked the name of the person that did it (used in indirect questions). -3. used to refer to a person mentioned in the first part of the sentence, or to give extra information about them □ *I know someone who can help.* □ *The people who moved in next door are having a party.* □ *She's the one who dealt with my complaint.* □ *a person who we all admire* □ *My grandmother, who's 96, lives on her own.*

WHO (*abbr of* **World Health Organization**) *n* **the WHO** an international organization that aims to improve the health of people in all countries.

who'd [hu:d] = **who had, who would.**

whodu(n)nit [,hu:'dʌnət] *n* a movie, novel, or play about a murder in which the murderer is not named until the end (informal use).

whoever [hu:'evər] *pron* -1. **whoever did it** the person who did it □ *Whoever finds it will get a reward.* -2. used to express surprise in ques-

tions □ *Whoever would have thought she would have been so successful?* -3. **whoever it is** no matter who it is □ *Whoever wins the legal battle, consumers will be the ones who suffer.* □ *Whoever calls, I don't want to be disturbed.*

whole [hool] ◇ *adj* -1. **the whole world** all of the world. ■ **a whole year** all of a year □ *We ate a whole chocolate cake between the two of us.* -2. **whole bananas** bananas that have not been cut into pieces. -3. used for emphasis. ■ **a whole lot of questions** very many questions. ■ **a whole lot bigger** much bigger. ◇ *adv* **a whole new idea** a completely new idea. ◇ *n* -1. **the whole of sthg** all of sthg □ *The new fashion has swept the whole of the country.* -2. something that has parts, but is considered as a single object □ *Two halves make a whole.*

◆ **as a whole** *adv* when all the individual people or things are considered as a single group □ *The department as a whole has performed well this year.*

◆ **on the whole** *adv* a phrase used to say that something is generally true, even though there are some exceptions □ *On the whole we enjoyed our vacation.*

wholefood ['hoolfu:d] *n* food, such as brown rice or whole-wheat flour, that has been changed as little as possible from its natural state and has not had other substances added to it □ *a wholefood restaurant.*

whole-hearted [-'hɑ:təd] *adj* [approval, effort, agreement] that is given or made completely and willingly □ *You have my whole-hearted support.*

wholemeal ['hoolmi:l] *adj* GB = **whole-wheat.**

whole note *n* US a musical note with a value equal to two half notes.

wholesale ['hoolseil] ◇ *adj* -1. BUSINESS that is connected with the practice of buying large quantities of goods cheaply from manufacturers and selling them to stores □ *a wholesale wine warehouse* □ *the wholesale price.* -2. [theft, destruction] that occurs on a large scale (disapproving use) □ *the wholesale slaughter of innocent civilians.* ◇ *adv* -1. BUSINESS [buy, sell] *It's cheaper to buy wholesale.* -2. [destroy, slaughter] *You can't take solutions from other countries and apply them wholesale to the situation here.*

NOTE: Compare **retail.**

wholesaler ['hoolseilər] *n* a person who sells goods wholesale.

wholesome ['hoolsəm] *adj* -1. [food, diet] that is healthy because it consists of natural ingredients. -2. [reading, entertainment] that is morally good and not offensive in any way.

whole-wheat *adj* [flour, pastry] that is made from whole grains of wheat with nothing removed.

who'll [hu:l] = **who will.**

wholly ['hooli] *adv* [responsible, wrong, unsuitable] completely □ *You are not wholly to blame.* □ *It appears that we were wholly mistaken in our assumptions.*

whom [hu:m] *pron* (formal use) -1. **whom did**

you see? which person did you see? (used as the object of a question) □ *Whom has the committee chosen as its representative?* ■ **with whom did you go?** which person did you go with? (used after prepositions) □ *To whom should I address the application?* **-2.** used to refer to a person mentioned in the first part of the sentence, or to give more information about them □ *the patient whom the doctor examined* □ *the manager to whom I complained* □ *She has three children, none of whom is of school age.*

whoop [US huːp, GB wuːp] ◇ *n* a shout of joy or excitement □ *He gave a whoop of delight.* ◇ *vi* to give a whoop.

whoopee [ˈwʊpiː] *excl* a word that one uses to show that one is very happy or excited about something.

whooping cough [ˈhuːpɪŋ-] *n* a serious infectious disease that affects children and makes them cough and produce a long high-pitched noise when they breathe in.

whoops [wʊps] *excl* a word that one uses after doing something by accident or making a small mistake □ *Whoops! I almost fell.* □ *Whoops! You weren't supposed to hear that.*

whoosh [wʊʃ] (informal use) ◇ *n* a sudden soft sound made by something moving through air or water very quickly □ *a whoosh of air.* ◇ *vi* to move with a whoosh □ *The champagne came whooshing out all over us.*

whop [wɒp] (*pt* & *pp* **whopped**, *cont* **whopping**) *vt* [opponent, team, rival] to beat <sb/sthg> (informal use).

whopper [ˈwɒpər] *n* (informal use) **-1.** something that is unusually large compared to other things of its kind. **-2.** a serious lie.

whopping [ˈwɒpɪŋ] (informal use) ◇ *adj* a **whopping increase/majority etc** an increase/a majority etc that is unusually large. ◇ *adv*: *a whopping great lie/bruise.*

whore▼ [hɔːr] *n* (offensive use) **-1.** a woman who has sex with men for money. **-2.** a woman who has sex with a lot of different men.

who're [ˈhuːər] = who are.

whose [huːz] ◇ *pron* **-1. whose is this?** who does this belong to (used in direct questions) □ *Whose pen is this?* ■ **tell me whose this is** tell me who this belongs to (used in indirect questions). **-2.** used to refer to a person or thing that is associated with somebody or something mentioned in the first part of the sentence □ *the scientist whose ideas have shaken the world* □ *She's the woman whose son had that terrible accident.* ◇ *det* **whose book is this?** who does this book belong to? □ *I'd like to know whose idea it was.*

whosoever [ˌhuːsoʊˈevər] *pron* whoever (literary use).

Who's Who *n* a list of famous and important people in a particular country or area of work.

who've [huːv] = who have.

why [waɪ] ◇ *adv* used to ask the reason for

something □ *Why didn't you tell me?* □ *Why waste your time? He won't listen to you.*
◇ *conj* **-1.** *I don't understand why it's taken so long.* □ *We should ask ourselves why these figures were never published.* □ *Tell me why you're leaving.* **-2.** *phrase* **why not?** used to make a suggestion, or to agree to a suggestion □ *Why not invite them along?* □ *"Let's have something to eat." — "Yes, why not."*
◇ *pron* used after "reason" □ *There's no reason why you can't come.* □ *It's one of the many reasons why I gave up eating meat.*
◇ *excl* US used to show that one is feeling surprised or annoyed □ *Why, it's Jenny!* □ *Why, that's no way to treat your own brother!*

◆ **why ever** *adv* used to show that one is surprised by something and wants to know the reason for it □ *"I don't think we should tell them." — "Why ever not?"*

WI ◇ *n abbr of* **Women's Institute.** ◇ **-1.** *abbr of* **West Indies.** **-2.** *abbr of* **Wisconsin.**

wick [wɪk] *n* **-1.** [of a candle] the string that runs through a candle and burns. **-2.** [of a lamp] the string of an oil lamp or cigarette lighter that draws up fuel to the flame.

wicked [ˈwɪkəd] *adj* **-1.** [person] who is bad and has no morals □ *a wicked witch.* **-2.** [person, look, humor] that is slightly bad but in a way that is playful and attractive □ *a wicked grin.* **-3.** [movie, music, place] that one thinks is very good (informal use) □ *That was a wicked party!*

wickedness [ˈwɪkədnəs] *n* [of a person, deed] *see* **wicked.**

wicker [ˈwɪkər] *adj* a **wicker chair/basket etc** a chair/basket etc that is made of thin woven branches or reeds.

wickerwork [ˈwɪkərwɜːrk] *n* a material made of thin woven branches or reeds □ *a wickerwork basket/chair.*

wicket [ˈwɪkət] *n* in cricket, either of the two sets of three wooden sticks with two pieces of wood on top of them at which the ball is thrown; the ground between these two sets of sticks.

wicket keeper *n* in cricket, the player who stands behind the wicket.

wide [waɪd] ◇ *adj* **-1.** [room, river, ocean] that is a large distance from one side to the other; that is a particular distance from one side to the other □ *She gave us a wide grin.* □ *a three-foot wide hole* □ *It's six meters wide.* **-2.** [eyes] that are more open than usual, expressing fear, surprise, or interest □ *His eyes were wide with terror.* **-3.** [range, choice, selection] that includes a large number of different things □ *There is a wide variety of models available.* **-4.** [coverage, interest, knowledge] that is great in size or amount □ *The committee has wide powers to investigate and bring charges.* **-5.** [gap, difference] large □ *There are wide variations in viewing patterns.* **-6. the wider issues/context etc** the more general issues/context etc of a situation rather than the details □ *We need to examine the wider implications of these proposals.* **-7. to go/be wide** [shot, punch, ball] to

miss/have missed the point one was aiming at by going past one side of it.
◇ *adv* [spread, open] so that there is a large space between one side and the other □ *She flung her arms wide in greeting.*

-wide *suffix* added to words to mean that something is happening or exists all over a particular area □ *nation-wide* □ *country-wide.*

wide-angle lens *n* a lens that allows a wide view to be photographed.

wide area network *n* a network of computers linked together over a large area, such as a region or country, to share information.

wide-awake *adj* to be wide-awake to be completely awake □ *I lay there wide-awake for most of the night.*

wide-eyed [-'aɪd] *adj* **-1.** [person] whose eyes are wide open with fear, surprise, or interest □ *She looked at me in wide-eyed astonishment.* **-2.** [person] who is too willing to believe or trust people because they do not have much experience of life □ *a wide-eyed innocent.*

widely ['waɪdlɪ] *adv* **-1.** [travel, publicize] in many places □ *His later operas are still widely performed.* **-2. widely known/accepted etc** known/accepted etc by a lot of people □ *a widely held belief.* **-3.** [differ, vary] to a large extent □ *Historians differ widely in their interpretation of these events.* **-4. to be widely read** to have read many different books.

widen ['waɪdn] ◇ *vt* **-1.** [road, bridge, distance] to make <sthg> wider □ *There are plans to widen the road to accommodate more traffic.* **-2.** [outlook, appeal, gap] to increase the size or range of <sthg> □ *Customs officials are widening their investigations.* ◇ *vi* **-1.** [road, bridge] *The river widens before reaching the sea.* **-2.** [outlook, appeal, choice] *The range of alternatives has widened in recent years.* □ *The gap separating rich and poor seems to be widening.*

wide open *adj* [window, door, mouth] completely open □ *The children ran toward me, arms wide open.* □ *Her eyes were wide open in amazement.* □ *the wide-open spaces of Australia.*

wide-ranging [-'reɪndʒɪŋ] *adj* [report, investigation, research] that includes many different aspects of something □ *There then followed a series of talks which the President described as friendly and wide-ranging.*

widespread ['waɪdspred] *adj* [panic, dismay, destruction] that exists or happens over a large area or among many people □ *There is widespread concern about the possible side effects of these drugs.*

widget ['wɪdʒət] *n* a term used to refer to a small device whose exact name one does not know.

widow ['wɪdoʊ] *n* a woman whose husband has died and who has not married again.

widowed ['wɪdoʊd] *adj* [person] whose husband or wife has died □ *He lives with his widowed mother.*

widower ['wɪdoʊər] *n* a man whose wife has died and who has not married again.

width [wɪdθ] *n* **-1.** the distance from one side of an object to the other □ *We'll have to measure the width of the doorway.* ■ **in width** from one side to the other □ *The wardrobe is four feet in width.* **-2.** the distance across a rectangular swimming pool □ *I was only able to swim a couple of widths.*

widthways ['wɪdθweɪz] *adv* [measure, cut, fold] across the width.

wield [wiːld] *vt* **-1.** [knife, tool, stick] to hold <sthg> in a threatening way to show that one intends to use it as a weapon □ *soldiers wielding automatic rifles.* **-2.** [power, authority] to have and be ready or able to use <sthg> □ *As director he wields a great deal of influence.*

wife [waɪf] (*pl* **wives**) *n* the woman that a man is married to □ *Have you met my wife?*

wig [wɪg] *n* a covering of false hair worn to hide one's own hair or lack of hair.

wiggle ['wɪgl] ◇ *n* **-1.** the act of wiggling a part of one's body, e.g. one's hips or toes. **-2.** a wavy line. ◇ *vt* [hips, toe, bottom] to move <a part of the body> with small movements backward and forward or from side to side □ *Can you wiggle your ears?* ◇ *vi* [hips, bottom, tail] *Her hips wiggled as she walked.*

wiggly ['wɪglɪ] (*compar* **wigglier**, *superl* **wiggliest**) *adj* [line, path] that has many curves in it (informal use).

wigwam [US 'wɪgwɑːm, GB -wæm] *n* a tall round tent that some Native Americans used to live in.

Wilberforce ['wɪlbərfɔːrs], **William** (1759–1833) a British politician who played an important part in making slavery illegal in the British Empire.

wild [waɪld] ◇ *adj* **-1.** [rabbit, cat] that is not trained to live with people and lives in natural conditions □ *wild animals such as tigers and lions.* **-2.** [person, dog, attack] that is violent and uncontrolled □ *There are some really wild children in that class.* **-3.** [coastline, scenery] that is in a natural state and has not been changed by people; [rose, grass] that is not grown in gardens □ *This part of the coast is still wild and unspoilt.* □ *We picked wild strawberries.* **-4.** [weather, sea] that is very violent and stormy □ *a wild wind/night.* **-5.** [laughter, applause, expression] that shows strong and uncontrolled feelings □ *The crowd went wild.* □ *He was wild with grief/anger.* ■ **to run wild** [dog, child] to behave in an uncontrolled way; [plant, garden] to grow in an uncontrolled way □ *She lets those children run wild.* □ *The ivy had run wild.* **-6.** [hope, plan] that is not sensible □ *The book was successful beyond our wildest dreams.* **-7.** [estimate, suggestion] that is made without careful thought □ *It was just a wild guess.* **-8. to be wild about sb/sthg** [about music, sport] to like sb/sthg a lot □ *I'm not wild about the idea.*
◇ *n* **in the wild** [survive, live] in natural conditions and not kept or taken care of by people □ *The eagles were born in captivity and then released into the wild.*

♦ **wilds** *npl* **the wilds** an area that is far from towns or cities and where there are few people □ *the wilds of Alaska.*

wild card *n* COMPUTING a letter, figure, or sign, usually a star, that can be used to represent any letter in a computer command.

wildcat ['waɪldkæt] *n* a large fierce cat that lives in mountains, forests etc.

wildcat strike *n* a sudden unofficial strike.

Wilde [waɪld], **Oscar** (1854–1900) an Irish writer who is remembered for the many witty comments he made and for his plays, which include *The Importance of Being Earnest* and *Lady Windermere's Fan*.

wildebeest ['wɪldəbiːst] (*pl* **wildebeest** OR **wildebeests**) *n* a large African animal with curved horns and long hair growing from its throat.

Wilder ['waɪldər], **Thornton** (1897–1975) a US writer of plays and novels, whose work includes *Our Town* and *The Bridge of San Luis Rey*.

wilderness ['wɪldərnəs] *n* -1. an area of land in which there are no buildings, roads etc and which has never been used for farming □ *a wilderness of ice and snow.* -2. an area where there seems to be no order □ *Their back yard is a wilderness.* □ *The center of town is a wilderness at night.* -3. **to be in the wilderness** GB [politician, performer] to be no longer well-known or important in a particular field □ *He spent several years in the political wilderness.*

wildfire ['waɪldfaɪər] *n* **to spread like wildfire** [news, rumor, fashion] to spread very quickly.

wild flower *n* a flowering plant that is not grown in gardens.

wildfowl ['waɪldfaʊl] *n* wild birds that are hunted, especially water birds such as ducks.

wild-goose chase *n* a search for something that cannot be found or does not exist (informal and disapproving use) □ *I've been sent on a wild-goose chase!*

wildlife ['waɪldlaɪf] *n* wild animals and plants □ *a wildlife film/park.*

wildly ['waɪldlɪ] *adv* -1. [laugh, shout, guess] *see* **wild** □ *She lashed out wildly in all directions.* □ *He stared wildly about him.* -2. **wildly different/inaccurate etc** very different/inaccurate etc □ *We've heard wildly conflicting accounts.*

wild rice *n* the dark-brown seeds of a grass that grows in North America.

Wild West *n* **the Wild West** the western United States during the 19th century.

☙ THE WILD WEST

The Wild West is the popular name for the wild country west of the Mississippi River during the second half of the 19th century. Throughout this period horsemen called cowboys drove huge herds of cattle along "trails" going from Texas in the south to Kansas or Missouri further north; here the animals were sent to market in the East. Towns grew up at the end of the cattle trails and were known for being violent and dangerous. The Hollywood western, with its gunfighters, sheriffs, and outlaws, shows such places in a glamorous way. Some towns from this period are now historical sites that tourists come to visit.

wiles [waɪlz] *npl* clever behavior used to make people do what one wants □ *She used her feminine wiles.*

wilful *adj* GB = **willful**.

will¹ [wɪl] ◇ *n* -1. the mental power to do something that one wants to do even if this is difficult □ *She has a very strong will.* □ *He's lost the will to live.* -2. a wish or desire □ *It is God's will.* ■ **against one's will** without wanting to □ *The prisoners were forced to work against their will.* ■ **at will** when one wants □ *She comes and goes at will.* -3. LAW an official document in which somebody says what they want to happen to their money and property after they die □ *My father left it to me in his will.* ◇ *vt* **to will sthg to happen** to try to help make sthg happen by concentrating hard on it □ *We were all willing him to win.*

will² *modal vb* -1. used to talk about an action or event in the future □ *I'll be thirty next month.* □ *I think we'll have to stop there for today.* □ *I won't be here next week.* ■ **I will have done it by Friday** I promise to finish it on or before Friday. ■ **I'll be arriving at 6 p.m.** my plan is to arrive at 6 p.m. -2. **will you have a drink?** would you like a drink? (used in offers) □ *You will stay for dinner, won't you?* ■ **I WILL do it** I am definitely going to do it □ *We WILL succeed, no matter what anybody says.* ■ **I won't do it** I refuse to do it □ *We will never give in to these outrageous demands!* -3. used to introduce commands and requests □ *Will you send us a copy for our records, please?* ■ **you will leave now!** leave now! ■ **will you close the door?** please close the door ■ **close the door, will you?** please close the door. -4. used to say that something is possible. ■ **the apartment will sleep six** six people can sleep in the apartment. -5. used to say that something is very often or always true □ *Boys will be boys.* □ *Accidents will happen.* -6. used to say that one supposes or thinks that something is true □ *That will be David calling to say he's coming late.* ■ **you'll know her** I'm sure that you already know her. ■ **you'll be hearing from me** I will definitely contact you. -7. used to show that one is annoyed with something that somebody does very often □ *They will keep trying to interrupt.*

willful US, **wilful** GB ['wɪlfl] *adj* -1. [person] who is determined to get what they want or behave as they want □ *What a willful child!* -2. **willful damage/neglect etc** deliberate damage/neglect etc.

William of Orange [,wɪljəməv'ɒrɪndʒ] (1650–1702) head of state of the Netherlands from 1672 to 1702, and King William III of Great Britain and Ireland from 1689 to 1702. He ruled jointly with his wife Mary, daughter of James II.

Williams ['wɪljəmz], **Roger** (1603?–1683) an English minister who came to America in 1631 to find religious freedom and later founded the colony of Rhode Island.

Williams, Tennessee (1911–1983) a US writer whose plays, which are set in the Southern states, include *Cat on a Hot Tin Roof* and *A Streetcar Named Desire*.

William the Conqueror [ˌwɪljəmðə'kɒŋkərəʳ] (1028–1087) Duke of Normandy from 1035 to 1087, and King William I of England from 1066 to 1087. He invaded England in 1066, and defeated King Harold at the battle of Hastings.

willing ['wɪlɪŋ] *adj* **-1. to be willing** to be ready to do something without being forced ▫ *I'd love some help, if you're willing.* ▫ *Would you be willing to lend us $500?* **-2. a willing helper/ student etc** a person who helps/studies etc with enthusiasm and without needing to be persuaded.

willingly ['wɪlɪŋlɪ] *adv* [go, accept, give] without needing to be forced or persuaded ▫ *"Would you give me a hand?" — "Yes, willingly."*

willingness ['wɪlɪŋnəs] *n*: *see* **willing** ▫ *They showed a surprising willingness to help.*

willow (tree) ['wɪloʊ-] *n* a tree that has long thin branches, long narrow leaves, and pale wood, and grows near water.

willowy ['wɪloʊɪ] *adj* [person] who is tall and thin in an attractive, graceful way.

willpower ['wɪlpaʊəʳ] *n* the ability to control oneself in order to achieve something ▫ *I don't have the willpower to stick to a diet.*

willy-nilly [ˌwɪlɪ'nɪlɪ] *adv* **-1.** without following a particular plan or being careful ▫ *She stuffed some clothes willy-nilly into a bag.* **-2.** whether one wants to or not ▫ *I found myself being dragged willy-nilly into their petty disputes.*

Wilson ['wɪlsn], **Sir Harold** (1916–1995) British Prime Minister from 1964 to 1970, and from 1974 to 1976.

Wilson, Woodrow (1856–1924) US President from 1913 to 1921.

wilt [wɪlt] *vi* **-1.** [plant, flower] to bend toward the ground because of heat or lack of water. **-2.** [person] to become tired and weak, especially because it is too hot.

Wilts *abbr of* **Wiltshire.**

Wiltshire ['wɪltʃəʳ] a county in southwestern England. SIZE: 3,481 sq kms. POPULATION: 564,000. ADMINISTRATIVE CENTER: Trowbridge.

wily ['waɪlɪ] (*compar* **wilier**, *superl* **wiliest**) *adj* [person] who uses clever tricks to get what they want and is too experienced to be tricked themselves.

wimp [wɪmp] *n* a person who one thinks does not have enough courage or determination ▫ *Don't be such a wimp!* (disapproving and informal use).

win [wɪn] (*pt* & *pp* **won**, *cont* **winning**) ◇ *vt* **-1.** [competition, race] to be first or best in <sthg> ▫ *Who won the game?* ▫ *After winning the war in Europe, the Allies turned their attention to the East.* **-2.** [prize, medal, cup] to get <sthg> as the reward for a success ▫ *I won a bottle of champagne in the raffle.* ▫ *She won a scholarship to study abroad.* **-3.** [support, approval, backing] to get <sthg> because of one's ability, hard work, good behavior etc ▫ *That kind of remark won't win you any friends.* ▫ *I want to win their trust/respect.*

◇ *vi* to win a competition, race etc ▫ *Brazil was winning in the first half.* ▫ *I hope you win.* ■ **you/I can't win** a phrase used to show that one is disappointed or frustrated by a situation in which one cannot be successful ▫ *I can't win with you, can I!*

◇ *n* a success or victory in a game, competition etc ▫ *It was the team's first win all season.*

◆ **win over**, **win round** *vt sep* **to win sb over** OR **round** to succeed in persuading sb to give one their support or friendship ▫ *We'll win her over to the idea eventually.*

wince [wɪns] *vi* to make a sudden small movement of the face as a reaction to pain or to an unpleasant thought ▫ *He winced as the needle went into his arm.* ▫ *I winced at the memory.*

winch [wɪntʃ] ◇ *n* a machine for lifting heavy objects that consists of a rope or chain wound around a central part that turns. ◇ *vt* to lift <sthg heavy> using a winch.

wind¹ [wɪnd] ◇ *n* **-1.** WEATHER a mass of moving air ▫ *strong/high winds* ▫ *There wasn't enough wind to go sailing.* ▫ *The leaves were rustling in the wind.* **-2.** breath ▫ *The fall knocked the wind out of her.* ▫ *Let me get my wind back.* ■ **to get one's second wind** to suddenly find new energy to continue doing something. **-3.** GB [in one's stomach] air in one's stomach that causes discomfort ▫ *That soup has given me wind.* ■ **to break wind** to let out air from inside the body through the anus, usually making a noise (polite use). **-4.** MUSIC **the wind** the wind instruments in an orchestra. **-5.** *phrase* **to get wind of sthg** to hear about or find out about sthg, especially a secret (informal use) ▫ *If Liz ever gets wind of this, you'll be in trouble.*

◇ *vt* **-1.** to make it difficult for <sb> to breathe by pushing the air out of their lungs ▫ *The fall/blow winded me.* **-2.** GB to make <a baby> bring up air from its stomach after eating by rubbing or gently hitting its back.

wind² [waɪnd] (*pt* & *pp* **wound**) ◇ *vt* **-1.** [thread, scarf, bandage] to turn <sthg> around an object or point several times ▫ *She wound a towel around her head.* ▫ *string wound into a neat ball.* **-2.** [clock, watch] to make <sthg> work by turning a knob, key, handle etc ▫ *I forgot to wind my alarm clock again.* **-3. to wind one's way** to go somewhere in a twisting line ▫ *The river winds its way through New Mexico and down into Texas.* ◇ *vi* [river, road] to go somewhere in a twisting line ▫ *There's a path that winds down to the stream.*

◆ **wind back** *vt sep* **to wind a tape/movie etc back** to make a tape/movie etc go back toward the beginning.

◆ **wind down** ◇ *vt sep* **-1. to wind a car window down** to lower a car window by turning a handle or pressing a button. **-2. to wind a business down** to gradually close a business ▫ *They're winding down several coalmines in the area.* ◇ *vi* **-1.** [clock, watch] to stop working because it needs to be wound. -2. [person] to relax after a period of hard work.

♦ **wind forward** *vt sep* **to wind a tape/film for-ward** GB to make a tape/film go forward.

♦ **wind on** *vt sep* GB = **wind forward** □ *My cam-era winds itself on automatically.*

♦ **wind up** ◇ *vt sep* **-1. to wind sthg up** [meet-ing, program] to bring sthg to an end □ *OK, one last question, and then we'll have to wind things up.* **-2. to wind a business up** to close a business down □ *They're winding up their op-erations in Jakarta.* **-3. to wind sthg up** [clock, watch] to wind sthg □ *It's one of those clock-work toys that you wind up.* **-4. to wind a car window up** to close a car window by turning a handle or pressing a button.
◇ *vi* to arrive in a particular place or get into a particular situation without intending to (informal use) □ *He's going to wind up in jail one of these days.*

windbreak ['wɪndbreɪk] *n* a wall, fence, or line of trees that gives protection against the wind.

windbreaker ['wɪndbreɪkəʳ] US, **windcheater** ['wɪndtʃiːtəʳ] GB *n* a warm jacket that fits closely at the neck and wrists and keeps the wind out.

windchill ['wɪndtʃɪl] *n* the lowering of the air temperature caused by cold winds □ *a high windchill factor.*

winded ['wɪndəd] *adj* **to be winded** to have dif-ficulty breathing after being hit in the stom-ach or doing hard exercise □ *The fall left her winded but otherwise unhurt.*

windfall ['wɪndfɔːl] *n* **-1.** an amount of money that one gets unexpectedly. **-2.** a piece of fruit that the wind has caused to fall from a tree.

wind farm ['wɪnd-] *n* a power station where electricity is generated by special windmills.

winding ['waɪndɪŋ] *adj* [river, path] that has many bends and is not direct □ *The car drove slowly up the winding road.*

wind instrument ['wɪnd-] *n* a musical instru-ment such as a flute or trumpet that is played by blowing.

windmill ['wɪndmɪl] *n* a tall structure with long flat blades attached to it that turn in the wind and work machinery for grinding, pumping, or producing power.

window ['wɪndoʊ] *n* **-1.** [in a building] a frame that contains glass and is placed in a wall, roof, or car to let light and air in or to look through □ *You should be working, not looking out of the window.* □ *Would you mind opening/closing the window?* □ *electrically operated win-dows.* **-2.** [in a store] a large opening in the wall of a store that is filled with glass and behind which goods are arranged in order to attract customers □ *I'd like to try on the coat in the window.* **-3.** COMPUTING one of the areas a computer screen can be divided into to show different kinds of information □ *a graphics window.* **-4.** [of time] a short period of free time □ *I've got a window between nine and ten on Tuesday if that's OK with you?*

window box *n* a long container placed on a window ledge and filled with soil in which flowers can be grown.

window cleaner *n* a person whose job is to clean windows.

window display *n* an arrangement of goods in a store window intended to attract cus-tomers.

window dressing *n* **-1.** the activity or job of arranging goods in an attractive way in a shop window. **-2.** parts of a plan, policy etc that are not essential and are used to make it seem better than it really is.

window envelope *n* an envelope with a transparent part at the front that shows the address on the letter, bill etc inside.

window frame *n* the wooden, metal, or plas-tic part that surrounds the glass in a win-dow.

window ledge *n* a narrow shelf under a win-dow, on the outside.

windowpane ['wɪndoʊpeɪn] *n* a piece of glass in a window.

window shade *n* US a covering made of plas-tic, cloth etc that is pulled down over a win-dow to keep light out of a room.

window-shopping *n* the activity of looking at the goods in store windows without in-tending to buy anything □ *We went window-shopping on Fifth Avenue.*

windowsill ['wɪndoʊsɪl] *n* a narrow shelf un-der a window, on the inside or outside.

windpipe ['wɪndpaɪp] *n* the tube in one's body through which air moves from the mouth to the lungs.

windshield ['wɪndʃiːld] US, **windscreen** ['wɪnd-skriːn] GB *n* the large front window of a car, truck, bus etc.

windshield washer *n* a device that sends a thin stream of water onto a windshield in order to clear rain from it.

windshield wiper *n* a device that moves from side to side across a windshield in or-der to clear rain from it.

windsock ['wɪndsɒk] *n* a cloth tube that is at-tached to a pole at airports to show the di-rection of the wind.

windsurfer ['wɪndsɜːʳfəʳ] *n* **-1.** a person who goes windsurfing. **-2.** a narrow board with a sail attached, used in windsurfing.

windsurfing ['wɪndsɜːʳfɪŋ] *n* the sport of sail-ing on the ocean or a lake while standing on a narrow board and holding onto a large sail.

windswept ['wɪndswept] *adj* **-1.** [plain, bay] that is not protected from the wind and is there-fore very windy. **-2.** [hair, appearance] that the wind has made untidy.

wind tunnel ['wɪnd-] *n* a tunnel through which air is blown at different speeds to test the design of cars, aircraft etc.

windy ['wɪndɪ] (*compar* **windier**, *superl* **windiest**) *adj* **-1.** [weather, day] when the wind is blow-ing a lot □ *It's very windy today.* **-2.** [hillside, moor, beach] where there is a lot of wind. ■ **the Windy City** a name for Chicago, Illinois.

wine [waɪn] *n* -1. an alcoholic drink made from grapes; a glass or bottle of this drink □ *red/white/rosé wine* □ *apple wine* □ *Two white wines, please.* □ *We have a wide selection of Californian wines.* -2. an alcoholic drink made from a particular fruit or plant □ *apple wine.*

wine bar *n* GB a bar where people mainly drink wine.

wine box *n* a box that contains a plastic bag full of wine and has a device for pouring.

wine cellar *n* -1. the different wines collected and kept by a person, restaurant etc. -2. a dark cool room underground where wine is kept.

wineglass [US 'waɪnglæs, GB -glɑːs] *n* a glass for drinking wine, usually round with a long thin stem.

wine list *n* the list of different wines offered by a restaurant, together with their prices.

winepress ['waɪnpres] *n* a device for pressing grapes to make wine.

wine rack *n* an open container in which bottles of wine can be stored lying flat on their side.

wine tasting [-teɪstɪŋ] *n* the activity of tasting different kinds of wine.

wine waiter *n* the waiter who serves the wine in an expensive restaurant.

wing [wɪŋ] *n* -1. [of a bird, animal] the moving part of a bird or insect that it uses for flying □ *The bird flapped its wings.* -2. [of a plane] one of the long flat parts attached to the sides of a plane that support it in the air. -3. [of a car] a part of a car's body that covers a wheel. -4. [of a building] a part of a large building that extends from the main part □ *the east wing* □ *They're building a new wing to house the contempory art collection.* -5. [of an organization] a group within an organization that has different beliefs or does a different job from the other parts □ *She's on the conservative wing of the party.*

◆ **wings** *npl* THEATER **the wings** the sides of the stage where actors can wait without being seen by the audience.

wing commander *n* an officer in the British air force.

winger ['wɪŋər] *n* an attacking player who plays at the edge of the field in soccer, hockey, or rugby.

wing nut *n* a nut that is turned by holding the two flat pieces that stick out from the sides.

wingspan ['wɪŋspæn] *n* [of a bird, airplane] the distance from the end of one wing to the end of the other wing.

wingtips ['wɪŋtɪps] *npl* US men's shoes with a pattern of decorative holes on the toes.

wink [wɪŋk] ◇ *vi* -1. [person] to close one eye and open it again quickly while looking at somebody to show friendliness, amusement, or as a signal □ *She kept winking at me.* -2. [light] to flash on and off (literary use). ◇ *n*

[of an eye] the act of winking □ *He gave me a sly wink.* ■ **to have forty winks** to have a short sleep during the day (informal use). ■ **not to sleep a wink, not to get a wink of sleep** not to sleep at all during the night (informal use).

winkle ['wɪŋkl] *n* a small sea creature that lives in a shell and can be eaten.

◆ **winkle out** *vt sep* GB -1. **to winkle sthg out** to remove sthg from a place with difficulty. -2. **to winkle sthg out of sb** [truth, story, confession] to make sb tell sthg with difficulty.

winner ['wɪnər] *n* -1. a person who wins a prize, medal, competition etc □ *the winner of last year's Pulitzer Prize* □ *a Nobel Prize winner.* -2. **to be a winner** [book, idea] to be a success (informal use) □ *His latest movie is a real winner.* ■ **to be onto a winner** to have something that is successful or likely to succeed □ *You're onto a winner with that new design.*

Winnie the Pooh [ˌwɪnɪðəˈpuː] a character in a series of children's stories by A. A. Milne. He is a friendly bear who likes honey.

winning ['wɪnɪŋ] *adj* -1. **the winning team/side/ goal etc** the team/side/goal etc that wins something □ *Extracts from the winning entries will be published in next month's edition.* -2. **a winning smile** a smile that is attractive and makes people like one.

◆ **winnings** *npl* money that has been won in a game or competition.

winning post *n* GB the place where a horse race ends.

Winnipeg ['wɪnɪpeg] -1. a city in Manitoba, central Canada. POPULATION: 610,773. -2. **Lake Winnipeg** a lake in Manitoba, central Canada.

winsome ['wɪnsəm] *adj* [smile, child] that is attractive and pleasant in a simple way (literary use).

winter ['wɪntər] *n* the coldest season of the year, between autumn and spring □ *Winter is my favorite season.* □ *a winter's night* □ *two winters ago* □ *It gets very cold there in winter.* □ *winter clothes/months/weather.*

winter sports *npl* sports that take place in the snow or on ice, such as skiing or skating.

wintertime ['wɪntərtaɪm] *n* winter □ *I hate this country in wintertime.*

wint(e)ry ['wɪnt(ə)rɪ] *adj* [weather, landscape, wind] that is cold or snowy and typical of winter □ *wintry showers.*

wipe [waɪp] ◇ *vt* [window, floor, nose] to remove dirt or liquid from <sthg> by rubbing it lightly, especially with one's hand, with a cloth, or against another surface □ *Don't forget to wipe your feet.* ◇ *n* the act of wiping something □ *Give your face/the table a wipe.*

◆ **wipe away** *vt sep* **to wipe sthg away** [tear, dirt, blood] to remove sthg, especially by wiping it with a cloth or hand.

◆ **wipe out** *vt sep* -1. **to wipe sthg out** [writing, trace, footprint] to remove sthg completely. -2. **to wipe sthg out** [population, species] to destroy sthg completely □ *Whole communities were wiped out by the famine.*

◆ **wipe up** ◇ *vt sep* **to wipe sthg up** [dirt, mess, water] to remove sthg by wiping it with a cloth. ◇ *vi: I'm sick of wiping up after that dog.*

wiper ['waɪpər] *n* = **windshield wiper**.

wire ['waɪər] ◇ *n* -1. a very thin long length of metal that bends easily □ *metal/copper wire* □ *a wire fence*. -2. ELECTRICITY a long wire, usually covered in plastic, along which electricity passes □ *a loose/an electric wire*. -3. RADIO a message sent using electrical or radio signals and delivered in printed form □ *I received a wire yesterday*.
◇ *vt* -1. **to wire sthg to sthg** to tie sthg to sthg with wire. -2. ELECTRICITY [plug, house] to connect electrical wires to <sthg> □ *The washing machine wasn't properly wired*. -3. [person] to send a telegram to <sb>. -4. to send <money> from one bank to another by electronic means.

◆ **wire up** *vt sep* **to wire sthg up** [stereo, video] to connect electrical wires to <sthg> □ *Are you wired up for Cable TV?*

wire brush *n* a brush made of stiff wire for cleaning metal.

wire cutters *npl* a tool for cutting wire □ *a pair of wire cutters*.

wireless ['waɪərləs] *n* a radio (old-fashioned use).

wire netting *n* a material made of twisted wire with a lot of holes in it, used for making fences □ *a piece of wire netting*.

wire-tapping [-tæpɪŋ] *n* the activity of listening secretly to somebody's telephone calls, using a special electronic device.

wire wool *n* GB a mass of very fine wire, used for cleaning pans, ovens etc.

wiring ['waɪərɪŋ] *n* the wires that carry electricity around a building.

wiry ['waɪərɪ] (*compar* **wirier**, *superl* **wiriest**) *adj* -1. [hair] that is strong and rough. -2. [person, body] that is thin but strong.

Wisconsin [wɪs'kɒnsən] a state in the northern USA, between Lake Superior and Lake Michigan. ABBREVIATION: WI. SIZE: 145,438 sq kms. POPULATION: 4,891,769 (*Wisconsinites*). CAPITAL: Madison.

wisdom ['wɪzdəm] *n* the quality of being wise □ *Many people questioned the wisdom of the decision*.

wisdom tooth *n* one of the four large back teeth that are the last to grow in one's mouth.

wise [waɪz] *adj* [choice, decision] that is practical and intelligent and made with a good understanding of the likely results □ *You'd be wise to accept the offer*. □ *He was a wise and kindly father*. ■ **to get wise to sthg** to realize sthg dishonest is happening (informal use) □ *I soon got wise to their little game*. ■ **to be no wiser** OR **none the wiser** to know no more about something even after someone has tried to explain it; not to be aware of something that has happened □ *She explained it to me in great detail, but I'm still none the wiser*. □ *We'll just switch them around and no-one will be any the wiser*.

◆ **wise up** *vi* to realize what a person or situation is really like (informal use) □ *You'd better wise up fast*.

wisecrack ['waɪzkræk] *n* a clever remark that is meant to be amusing.

wisely ['waɪzlɪ] *adv* [choose, decide, ignore] *see* **wise** □ *We must spend this money wisely*.

wish [wɪʃ] ◇ *n* -1. a desire □ *a wish to see the world* □ *his wish for a stable family life* □ *my dearest wish*. -2. a desire for something that can only happen or be made true by magic, often expressed silently or in a special way □ *If I could make a wish, that's what I'd have*.
◇ *vt* -1. **to wish to do sthg** to want to do sthg (formal use) □ *I wish to speak to my lawyer*. -2. to want <sthg> to happen or to be true even though one knows that it is unlikely or impossible □ *I wish (that) I could fly*. □ *I wish (that) I were dead*. □ *I wish (that) I'd never met her*. -3. **to wish sb sthg** [luck, success] to tell sb that one hopes they will have sthg □ *We all wish you a happy birthday/a merry Christmas*. ■ **to wish sb well** to hope that sb will have success or good luck.

◆ **wishes** *npl* **best wishes** a phrase used to say one hopes that somebody will be happy, healthy etc □ *Best wishes on your birthday*. □ *Give my best wishes to Anne when you see her*. ■ **(with) best wishes** a phrase used at the end of an informal letter before signing one's name.

◆ **wish for** *vt fus* **to wish for sthg** to think about sthg that one would like and hope that it might happen □ *You're the best friend anyone could wish for*.

◆ **wish on** *vt sep* **I wouldn't wish this on anyone** I don't want this to happen to anybody else because it is so unpleasant □ *I wouldn't wish a broken leg on my worst enemy*.

wishbone ['wɪʃboun] *n* the bone shaped like a V in the breast of a chicken, turkey etc that two people pull apart to decide who is going to make a wish.

wishful thinking [,wɪʃfl-] *n* something one wants or hopes for that is unlikely to happen or be true.

wishy-washy ['wɪʃɪwɒʃɪ] *adj* [person, idea, behavior] that one thinks is not forceful or clear enough (informal and disapproving use).

wisp [wɪsp] *n* -1. [of hair, grass, straw] a thin piece of something □ *She brushed a wisp of hair from her face*. -2. **a wisp of smoke/steam etc** a small, thin, twisting line of smoke/steam etc.

wispy ['wɪspɪ] (*compar* **wispier**, *superl* **wispiest**) *adj* [hair, beard] that grows in thin, untidy bunches.

wisteria [wɪ'stɪərɪə] *n* a climbing plant with pale purple flowers that hang down.

wistful ['wɪstfl] *adj* [person] who seems sad and thoughtful, e.g. because they want something that they cannot have □ *a wistful look/smile*.

wit [wɪt] *n* -1. the ability to say or write clever and amusing things □ *She has a sharp wit*. -2. someone who says or writes clever and amusing things □ *He has a reputation as some-*

thing of a wit. **-3. to have the wit to do sthg** to have the intelligence to do sthg that is right and appropriate for the situation □ *Luckily she had the wit to ask for his address.*

♦ **wits** *npl* **to have** OR **keep one's wits about one** to be ready to think and act quickly. ■ **to be scared out of one's wits** to be very scared (informal use). ■ **to be at one's wits' end** to be so worried or desperate that one does not know what to do.

witch [wɪtʃ] *n* a woman who is supposed to have magical powers and sometimes uses them to harm other people.

witchcraft [US 'wɪtʃkræft, GB -krɑːft] *n* the use of magic to make bad things happen.

witchdoctor ['wɪtʃdɒktəʳ] *n* a man who is supposed to be able to use magic to make things happen, especially to make sick people well.

witch hazel *n* a clear liquid that is put on sore places on the skin to heal them; the tree from which this liquid is produced.

witch-hunt *n* an attempt to find and remove or punish any members of a group who are considered to be dangerous or unacceptable (disapproving use).

with [wɪð] *prep* **-1. Tom is with Joe** Tom and Joe are together □ *My partner is coming with me to the conference.* □ *I used to play tennis with him.* ■ **I stayed with her** I stayed at her house. **-2. to argue/fight with sb** to argue/fight against sb □ *I had a slight disagreement with my boss.* ■ **the war with Germany** the war against Germany. **-3. to cut sthg with a knife** to use a knife to cut sthg (used to speak about a tool or instrument) □ *She pushed back her hair with her hand.* **-4.** used to speak about the way something is done, or the feeling one has when doing it □ *The matter needs to be handled with great care.* □ *I'll do it with pleasure.* □ *"Yes," he said with a smile.* **-5. a man with a beard** a man who has a beard (used to show a quality or feature of a person or thing) □ *The computer comes complete with a printer.* **-6.** used to specify the subject one is talking about. ■ **good with cars** good at dealing with cars □ *He's very mean with money.* □ *There shouldn't be any problem with delivery dates.* **-7.** used to show that two things happen at the same time. ■ **with you watching** while you are watching □ *I can't concentrate with the radio on.* **-8.** used to show the cause of something. ■ **with this weather** because of this weather □ *With the situation as it is, we'll be lucky to make a profit.* ■ **to tremble with fear** to tremble because one is afraid. **-9.** *phrases* **are you with me?** do you understand? ■ **are you with us?** do you support us? ■ **I'm with you** I agree with you.

♦ **with it** *adj* **to be with it** to be fashionable.

withdraw [wɪð'drɔː] (*pt* **withdrew**, *pp* **withdrawn**) ◇ *vt* **-1.** to remove <sthg>, often slowly and carefully (formal use) □ *She withdrew her hand from his.* **-2.** FINANCE to take <money> out of a bank account □ *I withdrew $500 from my account.* **-3.** MILITARY [force, personnel] to remove <one's troops> from a

place, often to avoid being defeated □ *The peace-keeping force is being withdrawn.* **-4.** [comment, statement, offer] to say that one did not mean <sthg one said> □ *I withdraw that remark.*

◇ *vi* **-1.** [from a place] to leave or move backward (formal use) □ *I quickly withdrew from the room.* □ *I withdrew to the bathroom/withdrew to a safe distance.* **-2.** MILITARY to move out or away, often to avoid being defeated □ *The UN is withdrawing from the area.* □ *The army withdrew to safety.* **-3.** [from a competition, deal, debate] to decide not to take part in an activity □ *Our delegates have withdrawn from the conference in protest.*

withdrawal [wɪð'drɔːəl] *n* **-1.** [of aid, support, funding] the removal of something that was helping somebody do something □ *Since the withdrawal of government subsidies, the company has been in crisis.* **-2.** MILITARY the act of moving out or away, often to avoid defeat □ *Britain and the US are considering a full-scale withdrawal.* **-3.** [from a competition, deal] a decision not to take part in something □ *Such a move might prompt their withdrawal from the talks.* **-4.** [of a comment, remark, offer] the act of saying that one did not mean something one has said □ *We welcome the withdrawal of the allegations.* **-5.** MEDICINE the painful period a person goes through when they stop taking drugs such as heroin. **-6.** FINANCE an amount of money that is withdrawn from a bank account □ *The last withdrawal isn't shown on the statement.*

withdrawal symptoms *npl* the bad physical and mental effects a person feels when they stop taking addictive drugs.

withdrawn [wɪð'drɔːn] ◇ *past participle of* **withdraw**. ◇ *adj* [person] who is quiet and does not want to talk to anyone often because they are unhappy.

withdrew [wɪð'druː] *past tense of* **withdraw**.

wither ['wɪðəʳ] ◇ *vi* **-1.** [plant, flower, leaf] to become dry and smaller and begin to die. **-2.** [hope, joy, enthusiasm] to become less. ◇ *vt* [plant, flower, leaf] *The sun has withered everything in the garden.*

withered ['wɪðəʳd] *adj* **-1.** [plant, flower, leaf] that is dry and dead. **-2.** [leg, arm] that is thin and weak because of illness.

withering ['wɪðərɪŋ] *adj* **a withering look/remark etc** a look/remark etc that is intended to make somebody feel stupid and embarrassed □ *"Don't be ridiculous!" she said, with a withering look.*

withhold [wɪð'hould] (*pt* & *pp* **withheld** [-'held]) *vt* **-1.** [service, information, evidence] to refuse to give <sthg> to somebody □ *They are accused of withholding documents relevant to the trial.* **-2.** US [taxes] to take <taxes> out of somebody's wages.

withholding [wɪð'houldɪŋ] *n* US a system of taking employees' income tax out of their wages before they are paid □ *withholding tax.*

within [wɪð'ɪn] ◇ *prep* **-1. within the area** inside the area, and not beyond it □ *We hope to fill the job from within the organization.* ■ **a**

feeling within me a feeling inside me. **-2. within a limit** not beyond a limit □ *We have to remain within a strict budget.* □ *It is possible within the terms of the agreement.* **-3. within 50 miles of Dallas** not more than 50 miles from Dallas. ■ **within a month** before a month has passed □ *If confirmation is not received with 28 days, the order will be canceled.* ◇ *adv* inside a building or room □ *'Enquire within.'*

without [wɪð'aʊt] *prep* **-1. to be without sthg** not to have sthg □ *a candidate without any experience.* ■ **I went out without an umbrella** I went out and did not take an umbrella □ *"I suppose so," she said, without much enthusiasm.* **-2. without a sound** not making a sound □ *He left without a word.* ■ **she left without saying goodbye** she left and did not say goodbye □ *We must be firm without being rude.*

withstand [wɪð'stænd] (*pt* & *pp* **withstood** [-'stʊd]) *vt* [pressure, criticism, wind] not to be changed, hurt, or damaged by <sthg> □ *It is designed to withstand high temperatures.* □ *Will he be able to withstand the pressures?*

witness ['wɪtnəs] ◇ *vt* **-1.** [accident, crime, change] to see <an important event> happen □ *Did anyone witness the accident?* □ *We are witnessing an economic miracle.* **-2.** [contract, will] to be there when somebody signs <a document> and write one's name on it to show that it is really that person's signature □ *I need someone to witness my signature.* ◇ *n* **-1.** a person who sees a crime, accident etc take place □ *Police are calling for witnesses to the attack to come forward.* ■ **to be witness to sthg** [to an event] to see sthg happen. **-2.** [in court] a person who gives information about a crime or an event in court □ *The witness was cross-examined at length.* **-3. to bear witness to sthg** [to a fact, story] to show or prove that sthg is true □ *Her red eyes bore witness to the fact that she had been crying.* **-4.** [to a document, contract, will] a person who officially witnesses the signing of a document □ *The form should be signed in the presence of two witnesses.*

witness stand US, **witness box** GB *n* the place where a witness stands or sits in court to answer questions.

witticism ['wɪtəsɪzm] *n* something clever and amusing that somebody says or writes.

witty ['wɪtɪ] (*compar* **wittier**, *superl* **wittiest**) *adj* [person, book, story] that is clever and amusing □ *She made a witty speech.*

wives [waɪvz] *plural of* **wife**.

wizard ['wɪzə*d] *n* **-1.** a man with magical powers. **-2.** somebody who is very good at a particular activity or sport □ *a financial wizard* □ *He's a wizard at chess/calculus.*

wizened ['wɪznd] *adj* [skin, face, person] that is old and covered in wrinkles.

wk *abbr of* **week**.

WO *n abbr of* **warrant officer**.

wobble ['wɒbl] *vi* [chair, glass, ball] to move slightly from side to side, e.g. because it is not fixed firmly or is not in a steady posi-

tion □ *The table wobbles when you lean on it.* □ *She wobbled as she set off down the slope, but managed to regain her balance.*

wobbly ['wɒblɪ] (*compar* **wobblier**, *superl* **wobbliest**) *adj* [chair, table, hand] that wobbles because it is not fixed firmly or is not in a steady position (informal use).

Wodehouse ['wʊdhaʊs], **P. G.** (1881–1975) a British writer, known for his humorous stories about Bertie Wooster and his servant, Jeeves.

woe [woʊ] *n* great sadness (literary use).

wok [wɒk] *n* a deep round frying pan used in Chinese cooking.

woke [woʊk] *past tense of* **wake**.

woken ['woʊkn] *past participle of* **wake**.

wolf [wʊlf] (*pl* **wolves**) ◇ *n* a wild animal like a large fierce dog that hunts other animals in a group. ◇ *vt* **to wolf sthg (down)** to eat sthg quickly and greedily because one is hungry or in a hurry (informal use).

wolf whistle *n* a loud whistle with a short rising note and a long falling note that some men make when they see an attractive woman in the street.

wolves [wʊlvz] *plural of* **wolf**.

woman ['wʊmən] (*pl* **women**) *n* **-1.** an adult female person □ *For many women, going out to work is a necessity, not an option.* □ *a woman doctor/teacher* □ *He still believes that a woman's place is in the home.* **-2. sb's woman** sb's wife or female lover (informal use).

womanhood ['wʊmənhʊd] *n* **-1.** the state of being an adult woman. **-2.** all the women in a particular society or country (literary use).

womanizer ['wʊmənaɪzə*] *n* a man who has sexual relationships with a lot of different women (disapproving use).

womanly ['wʊmənlɪ] *adj* [virtue, curve, beauty] that is typical of or considered suitable for a woman.

womb [wuːm] *n* the organ in a woman's body in which a baby grows before it is born.

wombat ['wɒmbæt] *n* an Australian animal with short legs and thick fur.

women ['wɪmɪn] *plural of* **woman**.

womenfolk ['wɪmɪnfoʊk] *npl* the women of a family or community.

Women's Institute *n* GB **the Women's Institute** an organization for women whose activities include organizing social events and teaching skills connected with the home.

women's lib [-'lɪb] *n* = **women's liberation** (informal use).

women's liberation *n* = **women's movement** (old-fashioned use).

women's movement *n* **the women's movement** a movement, started by women, that tries to improve the social and economic position of women and give them the same rights as men.

women's room *n* US a women's public toilet.

women's shelter US, **women's refuge** GB *n* a house where a woman whose husband has been violent toward her can go with her children for protection.

won [wʌn] *past tense & past participle of* **win**.

wonder ['wʌndə'] ◇ *n* -1. the feeling of surprise, strangeness, and admiration caused by something unusual, very good, or unexpected □ *We looked in wonder.* -2. **it's a wonder** it's surprising □ *It's a wonder that anyone escaped alive.* ■ **(it's) no** OR **little** OR **small wonder** it's not surprising □ *No wonder she left!* □ *It's little wonder (that) he's so unpopular.* -3. a person or thing that other people admire or are surprised by □ *Her husband's a wonder in the kitchen.* ■ **to work** OR **do wonders** to get very good results □ *Getting a job has done wonders for his confidence.* □ *My hairdresser can work wonders with people's hair.*
◇ *vt* -1. to think about <sthg> that one is not sure about and try to reach an opinion about it □ *I wonder who he is.* □ *We wondered why she had done it.* □ *I wonder if* OR *wonder whether she'll come.* -2. a word used to introduce a request or invitation in order to make it more polite □ *I wonder if you could help me.* □ *We were wondering whether you were free for supper tonight.*
◇ *vi* -1. *"Why do you ask?"* — *"Oh, I was just wondering."* □ *I often wonder about her reasons for leaving.* -2. **to wonder at sthg** to be surprised by sthg (literary use).

wonderful ['wʌndə'fl] *adj* [news, weather] that one thinks is very good □ *It's wonderful to see you again!* □ *He's a truly wonderful writer.*

wonderfully ['wʌndə'flɪ] *adv* **wonderfully talented/relaxing etc** very talented/relaxing etc.

wonderland ['wʌndə'lænd] *n* a place one finds beautiful, strange, and exciting.

wonk [wɒnk] *n* US a person who spends too much time working □ *He turned out to be a policy wonk with few interests outside Washington.*

wont [US wɒnt, GB wəʊnt] ◇ *adj* **to be wont to do sthg** to have a habit of doing sthg □ *He's wont to lose his temper very quickly.* ◇ *n* **as is one's wont** as one has a habit of doing □ *He smoked a cigar after lunch, as was his wont.*

won't [wəʊnt] = **will not**.

woo [wuː] *vt* -1. to try to make <a woman> fall in love with one and marry one (old-fashioned or literary use). -2. to try to get the support of <sb> □ *attempts to woo the stockholders.*

wood [wʊd] *n* -1. the material of which the trunks and branches of trees are made, used for burning as fuel, making furniture, building etc □ *a pile of wood* □ *a wood floor/fire.* -2. a large group of trees growing close together □ *They got lost in the wood.* -3. [in golf] a golf club with a wooden head, used for hitting the ball a long way. -4. *phrases* **not to see the wood for the trees** to fail to understand the main facts about something because one is thinking too much about small details. ■ **knock on** US OR **touch** GB **wood!** a phrase used to say that one has been lucky up to the present, and that one hopes this will con-

tinue in the future □ *I've had no problems so far with the authorities, knock on wood!*
◆ **woods** *npl* a small forest.

wooded ['wʊdəd] *adj* [area, slope, land] that is covered in trees.

wooden ['wʊdn] *adj* -1. [hut, door, box] that is made of wood. -2. [actor] who acts in a way that is not realistic or natural (disapproving use) □ *He gave a pretty wooden performance.*

wooden spoon *n* a large spoon made of wood, used for cooking. ■ **to win** OR **get the wooden spoon** GB to be last in a competition or sporting event.

woodland ['wʊdlənd] *n* an area covered in trees.

woodlouse ['wʊdlaʊs] (*pl* **woodlice** [-laɪs]) *n* a small insect with a gray body and many legs that lives in damp places and under stones.

woodpecker ['wʊdpekə'] *n* a bird with a very strong beak that makes holes in trees.

wood pigeon *n* a large pigeon with white marks on its wings and neck.

woodshed ['wʊdʃed] *n* a small building where wood for burning, garden tools etc are kept.

woodwind ['wʊdwɪnd] ◇ *n* **the woodwind** the musical instruments in an orchestra that are made of wood and metal and are played by blowing through a reed or across a hole. ◇ *adj*: *a woodwind instrument.*

woodwork ['wʊdwɜː'k] *n* -1. the wooden parts of a house □ *What color are you going to paint the woodwork?* -2. the art or craft of making things out of wood □ *I studied woodwork at school.*

woodworm ['wʊdwɜː'm] *n* -1. the young of a particular insect that make holes in wooden buildings or furniture. -2. the damage caused to wood by woodworm.

woof [wʊf] *excl* a sound that describes the noise of a dog barking.

wool [wʊl] *n* -1. the soft thick hair of a sheep. -2. the soft thick thread or material that is made from a sheep's wool and is used to make sweaters, blankets etc □ *a ball of wool* □ *a pure wool coat.* -3. **to pull the wool over sb's eyes** to deceive sb by hiding facts or information from them (informal use).

woolen US, **woollen** GB ['wʊlən] *adj* [sweater, scarf, socks] that is made of wool.
◆ **woolens** *npl* clothes made of wool.

Woolf [wʊlf], **Virginia** (1882–1941) a British writer whose experimental style played an important part in the development of the novel. Her work includes *Mrs Dalloway* and *The Waves.*

woollen *n* GB = **woolen**.

woolly ['wʊlɪ] (*compar* **woollier**, *superl* **woolliest**, *pl* **woollies**) ◇ *adj* -1. [sweater, hat] that is made of wool. -2. [thinking, idea, answer] that is not clear (informal and disapproving use). ◇ *n* a piece of clothing made of wool, especially one that is knitted (informal use).

Wooster ['wʊstə'], **Bertie** in the comic novels of P. G. Wodehouse, a good-natured upper-class man who is not very intelligent, and who relies on his servant, Jeeves.

woozy ['wuːzɪ] (*compar* **woozier**, *superl* **woozi-est**) *adj* [person] who feels weak and dizzy, e.g. after having a general anesthetic (informal use).

Worcestershire sauce ['wʊstərʃər-] US, **Worcester sauce** GB ['wʊstər-] *n* a thin brown liquid with a strong sharp taste, used to give food more flavor.

word [wɜːʳd] ◇ *n* -1. the smallest unit of spoken or written language that can be used alone □ *What's the Arabic word for "man"?* □ *a translation 500 words long* □ *I can't find the words to express how I feel.* ■ **word for word** [copy, repeat, learn] using exactly the same words □ *You don't have to repeat what I say word for word.* ■ **in your own words** [say, tell, write] without copying the way someone else has said or written something □ *Try to describe it in your own words.* ■ **not in so many words** not in a clear and direct way □ *"Did she say yes?" — "Not in so many words, but she didn't say no."* ■ **too good/boring/funny for words** so good/boring/funny that it cannot be described. ■ **by word of mouth** [find out, hear, spread] by speaking rather than writing. ■ **to put in a (good) word for sb** to praise sb to a person in an important position, especially in order to help them get a job, avoid punishment etc □ *He's promised to put in a good word for me with the boss.* ■ **just say the word** an invitation to say when one wants something to happen □ *If you get tired, just say the word and we'll go back.* ■ **to have a word** to have a quick talk with somebody in private, especially in order to ask for help or advice or because they have done something wrong □ *I'll have to have a word with him about his timekeeping.* ■ **to have words with sb** to have an argument with sb (informal use). ■ **to have the last word** to make the final remark in an argument and feel that one has won the argument as a result □ *You always have to have the last word, don't you?* ■ **she doesn't mince her words** she says what she thinks although she knows it may upset other people. ■ **to weigh one's words** to think carefully before speaking. ■ **I couldn't get a word in edgewise** OR **edgeways** I did not have a chance to speak because someone else was talking all the time. -2. news □ *Is there any word from the hospital?* □ *Word reached us that they were safe.* -3. **one's word** one's promise □ *You have my word.* ■ **to give sb one's word** to make a serious promise to sb □ *I gave Kathleen my word we wouldn't be late again.* ■ **to be as good as one's word, to be true to one's word** to do what one promises □ *He was as good as his word and turned up promptly at nine.*
◇ *vt* [letter, reply, essay] to write or prepare <sthg> by choosing the words carefully to express a particular meaning □ *I'm not quite sure how to word my application.* □ *They sent a strongly worded protest to the board.*
◆ **in a word** *adv* a phrase used to introduce a summary of what one has been saying □ *In a word, he's an idiot.*
◆ **in other words** *adv* a phrase used to introduce a simpler explanation or another way of saying something □ *In other words, you don't think we ought to go.*

word game *n* any game in which the players have to find, change, or make words.

wording ['wɜːʳdɪŋ] *n* the words that are used to express something □ *We haven't yet agreed on the final wording of the appeal.*

word-perfect *adj* **to be word-perfect** to be able to repeat every word of a particular text correctly from memory.

wordplay ['wɜːʳdpleɪ] *n* the clever or amusing use of words and their sounds and meanings.

word processing *n* the activity of producing letters, reports, documents etc and storing information using a word processor, especially in an office □ *a word-processing package.*

word processor *n* a small computer or a piece of software used for producing letters, reports, documents etc.

Wordsworth ['wɜːʳdzwɜːʳθ], **William** (1770–1850) a British Romantic poet, well known for his poems about nature.

wordwrap ['wɜːʳdræp] *n* the ability of a word processor to start a new line automatically when one line is full.

wordy ['wɜːʳdɪ] (*compar* **wordier**, *superl* **wordiest**) *adj* [speech, letter, report] that one thinks is too long and contains too many words (disapproving use).

wore [wɔːʳ] *past tense of* **wear**.

work [wɜːʳk] ◇ *n* -1. [for an employer] a job that one is paid to do regularly; the tasks involved in this; the place where one goes to do this □ *It isn't easy to find work around here.* □ *Are you interested in secretarial work?* □ *I try not to bring work home on the weekend.* □ *My work involves a lot of traveling.* □ *What time do you leave work?* □ *I'll give you my work number, in case you have to call me there.* □ *The work hours are flexible.* ■ **to be in/out of work** to have/not have a regular job □ *The collapse of the industry means hundreds of people have been thrown out of work.* -2. [at a particular activity or task] any activity that requires effort and produces a result □ *You can see she's put a lot of work into that drawing.* □ *school work* □ *A great deal of work has still to be done on the problem of air pollution.* ■ **to be at work** to be working □ *They were all hard at work in the kitchen.* ■ **you'll have your work cut out** it won't be easy for you □ *We'll have our work cut out to finish by Friday.* -3. ART & LITERATURE a painting, piece of writing, sculpture etc □ *an exhibition of work by Salvador Dali* □ *the complete works of Shakespeare.* -4. *phrase* **a nasty piece of work** an unpleasant person, especially one who is cruel or violent (informal use).
◇ *vi* -1. [employee] to do a regular job for which one is paid □ *For a time I worked as a secretary.* □ *She works for a large computer company.* -2. [person] to do an activity that requires effort and produces a result □ *I'll be working on my thesis all summer.* □ *Your father's out working in the garage.* -3. [radio, television, machine] to operate in the way it is supposed to □ *The telephone isn't working.* -4. [idea, plan]

to be successful □ *It's risky, but it just might work.* **-5.** [drug, treatment] to have the effect that is wanted □ *The pills take about an hour to work.* **-6. to work against sb/sthg** to harm sb/sthg □ *The new legislation could work against small businesses.* **-7. to work loose/free/open** [knot, catch, fastening] to gradually become loose/free/open as a result of repeated small movements.

◇ *vt* **-1. to work sb hard** to make sb work very hard □ *She works us all pretty hard.* **-2.** [camera, computer, washing machine] to operate <sthg> □ *I don't know how to work the printer.* **-3.** [wood, metal, clay] to form a material or substance> into shapes or objects using tools or one's hands. **-4. to work the land** to prepare land to grow crops on. **-5. to work one's way somewhere** to gradually move in a particular direction; to gradually reach a particular level in one's career □ *Barclay was working his way slowly toward the door.* □ *In three years, Pears had worked her way up to the position of chief executive.*

◆ **works** ◇ *n* a place, e.g. a factory, where something is made □ *a steel/gas works.* ◇ *npl* **-1.** [of a clock, machine] the moving parts of something. **-2.** activities such as building or repairing public buildings, roads etc □ *engineering works.* **-3. the works** everything connected with a particular activity (informal use) □ *We had champagne, party hats, the works!*

◆ **work at** *vt fus* **to work at sthg** to try to improve sthg □ *We must work harder at improving customer relations.*

◆ **work off** *vt sep* **to work sthg off** [one's anger, frustration] to get rid of a feeling by doing a physical activity □ *I had to go for a jog to work off my frustration.*

◆ **work on** *vt fus* **-1. to work on sthg** to spend time doing sthg □ *I can't come out tonight — I've got to work on my report for Liz Brewer.* **-2. to work on sthg** [assumption, principle] to make sthg a basis for one's decisions or actions □ *Police are working on the theory that the victim knew his attacker.* **-3. to work on sb** to try to persuade sb to do or say something □ *I'll work on John and see if I can get him to agree.*

◆ **work out** ◇ *vt sep* **-1. to work sthg out** [solution, approach] to think about sthg carefully in order to find the best way of doing it □ *I've managed to work out a way of getting there by car.* **-2. to work sthg out** [answer, total, square root] to find sthg by doing a calculation □ *Work out what it would cost to buy the land.*

◇ *vi* **-1. to work out well/badly** [plan, event] to have a good/bad result □ *The arrangements have worked out really well.* **-2.** [situation] to be successful, especially after a long period of time □ *We did get married, but it just didn't work out.* **-3.** [person] to do physical exercises in a gym to make one's muscles stronger □ *He works out twice a week.* **-4. it works out at $20** it costs $20, after all the calculations have been done □ *When we'd added everything up, the total bill worked out at $50 per person.*

◆ **work up** *vt sep* **-1. to work oneself up** to allow oneself to become very angry or upset

□ *Eventually he worked himself up into a real panic.* **-2. to work up sthg** [courage, enthusiasm] to make oneself have a particular feeling □ *I could barely work up the energy to get out of bed.* ■ **to work up an appetite** to do sthg to make oneself feel hungry.

workable ['wɜːʳkəbl] *adj* [plan, system, solution] that can be used and can be successful □ *We eventually achieved a workable compromise.*

workaday ['wɜːʳkədeɪ] *adj* [person, activity, routine] that one thinks is ordinary and not very exciting (disapproving use).

workaholic [,wɜːʳkə'hɒlɪk] *n* a person who enjoys working very hard and cannot relax easily.

workbasket [US 'wɜːrkbæskət, GB 'wɜːkbɑːskət] *n* a basket or other container that equipment for sewing, knitting etc is kept in.

workbench ['wɜːʳkbentʃ] *n* a strong table used for working with tools.

workbook ['wɜːʳkbʊk] *n* a schoolbook containing questions and spaces in which the student writes the answers.

workday ['wɜːʳkdeɪ] *n* a day when one works and which is not a holiday □ *I get up at seven on workdays.*

worked-up [,wɜːʳkt-] *adj* [person] who is upset, angry, or worried about something □ *There's no need to get so worked-up about it!*

worker ['wɜːʳkəʳ] *n* somebody who works in a particular company, industry, or organization □ *a farm/a manual/an office worker* □ *workers' rights.* ■ **a hard/fast/good worker** someone who works hard/fast/well.

worker's compensation *n* US & AUS money paid to a worker to compensate for loss of earnings as a result of an injury or illness at work.

workforce ['wɜːʳkfɔːʳs] *n* all the workers of a factory, country etc, considered as a group.

workhouse ['wɜːʳkhaʊs, *pl* -haʊzɪz] *n* GB in the 19th century, a place where poor people did boring and tiring jobs in return for food and accommodation.

working ['wɜːʳkɪŋ] *adj* **-1. working people** people who have a job □ *Working mothers have to juggle the demands of their families with their jobs.* **-2. working clothes** clothes that are designed for people to work in and are practical rather than attractive. **-3. working conditions/practices** the conditions/practices that one has in one's job □ *They are introducing new working practices.* **-4. working hours** the period of time during a day that one spends doing one's job □ *The working hours here are flexible.*

◆ **workings** *npl* [of a system, machine, organization] the way in which something works □ *It's difficult to understand the workings of his mind.*

working capital *n* the money that a company has to carry out its business, not including the money invested in its buildings, equipment etc.

working class *n* **the working class(es)** the

people in society who work with their hands and are not rich or powerful.

◆ **working-class** *adj* [family, area, background] that is connected with or belongs to the working class.

working day *n* = **workday**.

working group *n* a group of people formed to examine a particular subject or problem and write a report about it.

working knowledge *n* **to have a working knowledge of sthg** to have enough knowledge about sthg to be able to use it □ *I have a working knowledge of Japanese.*

working man *n* a man who works.

working model *n* [of a car, machine] a model of something with moving parts.

working order *n* **to be in working order** [car, machine, engine] to be working correctly □ *It's a little rusty, but apart from that it's in perfect working order.*

working week *n* the hours or days of work done in a week □ *a five-day/forty-hour working week.*

workload ['wɜːᵊkləʊd] *n* the amount of work a person or machine has to do □ *I've got a heavy workload this week.*

workman ['wɜːᵊkmən] (*pl* **workmen** [-mən]) *n* a man who does work with his hands, such as repairing roads or buildings.

workmanship ['wɜːᵊkmənʃɪp] *n* the amount of skill with which work is done □ *good/poor workmanship.*

workmate ['wɜːᵊkmeɪt] *n* a friend that one works with.

work of art *n* **-1.** ART a painting, statue etc which is considered to be very good. **-2.** something produced with great skill □ *The wedding cake was a real work of art.*

workout ['wɜːᵊkaʊt] *n* a period of physical exercise, usually in a gym.

work permit *n* an official document which allows a person to work in a foreign country.

workplace ['wɜːᵊkpleɪs] *n* the office, factory etc in which one works □ *sexual harassment in the workplace.*

work placement *n* a period of time that a student spends working in a business, industry etc as part of a course of study.

work release *n* US a system that allows prisoners to leave prison during the day to go to work.

workroom ['wɜːᵊkruːm] *n* a room in which work of a particular kind is done.

works council *n* GB a group made up of workers and employers that discusses problems and questions relating to work in a business, factory etc.

workshop ['wɜːᵊkʃɒp] *n* **-1.** [in a home] a room in which work is done with tools. **-2.** [in a factory] the part of a factory where work is done with tools, machines are mended etc. **-3.** [at a conference] a period of study and practical work on a particular subject for a group of people □ *a poetry/drama workshop.*

workstation ['wɜːᵊksteɪʃn] *n* COMPUTING a desk

and computer, usually connected to the main computer system in an office, at which a person works.

work surface *n* a flat surface in a kitchen, usually with a cupboard, refrigerator etc underneath, on which food is prepared.

worktable ['wɜːᵊkteɪbl] *n* a table on which a particular kind of work is done.

worktop ['wɜːᵊktɒp] *n* GB = **work surface**.

work-to-rule *n* GB a protest by workers that involves strictly following all the rules relating to their work so that their rate of work becomes very slow.

work week *n* US = **working week**.

world ['wɜːᵊld] ◇ *n* **-1. the world** the planet on which we live and all the people, places etc on it □ *the biggest country in the world* □ *a round-the-world trip.* ■ **how/what/where in the world?** a phrase used in a question to express surprise or to emphasize what one is saying □ *What in the world are you doing here?* □ *Where in the world did you find that?* ■ **the world over** everywhere in the world □ *Human nature is the same the world over.* **-2.** [planet] a planet, especially one where there may be living things □ *other worlds.* **-3.** [society] the society that we live in □ *The world is becoming a dangerous place.* ■ **to be dead to the world** to be deeply asleep or unconscious. **-4.** [somebody's surroundings] the surroundings in which somebody lives □ *London is a different world after New York.* ■ **the best of both worlds** the good parts of two different situations without the bad parts □ *Living in the country and working in the city gives us the best of both worlds.* **-5.** [area] an area of learning or activity □ *the world of the theater* □ *the world of art.* **-6.** [somebody's life] somebody's life and the experiences they have □ *We come from different worlds.* □ *the adult world.* **-7. the animal/plant etc world** animal/plants etc considered as a group of living things with certain shared features □ *the plant/animal/insect world.* **-8.** *phrases* **to think the world of sb** to care about sb very much. □ *Katy thinks the world of you, you know.* ■ **to do one the world of good** to be very good for one □ *A vacation will do you the world of good.* ■ **a world of difference** a very big difference □ *It makes a world of difference having an assistant.*

◇ *comp* **a world language/religion etc** a language/religion etc that is important throughout the world. ■ **a world cruise/tour** a cruise/ tour that involves visits to many different countries.

World Bank *n* **the World Bank** an international bank, controlled by the United Nations, created in 1945 to lend money to poor countries.

world-class *adj* [athlete, tennis player, singer] who is among the best in the world.

World Cup *n* **the World Cup** a soccer competition held every four years in which teams from all over the world take part □ *the World Cup team/final.*

world-famous *adj* [writer, musician, actor] who is known all over the world.

worldly ['wɜːˈldlɪ] *adj* **-1.** [thought, care, pleasure] that is concerned with the material things of this life such as money and luxuries rather than spiritual things. ◻ *We should put aside such worldly considerations.* ■ **worldly goods** the property and goods a person owns. **-2.** [person] who has a lot of experience and knowledge about life and human nature ◻ *"Well, you know what women are like," he said in a worldy way.*

world music *n* popular music from non-Western countries, especially African counties.

world power *n* a country that is powerful enough to affect political and economic events all over the world.

World Series *n* **the World Series** a series of baseball games played every year to decide which is the best North American baseball team.

❦ WORLD SERIES
The World Series is a set of up to seven games that is played at the end of the baseball season between the champions of the two main US leagues, the National League and the American League. The winning team is the first one to win four games. It is one of the most important sporting events of the year in the USA, and traditionally the first ball of the series is thrown by the President.

World Service *n* a radio station of the BBC in London whose programs can be heard in many different countries.

World Trade Center: the World Trade Center two very tall office towers in New York City.

World War I [-'wʌn] *n* a war that was fought in Europe from 1914 to 1918. Britain, the USA, France, and Russia defeated Germany and Turkey.

World War II [-'tuː] *n* a war that was fought in Europe and the Far East from 1939 to 1945. Britain, the USA, France, and the Soviet Union defeated Germany and Japan.

world-weary *adj* [person] who no longer enjoys life ◻ *a world-weary sigh/attitude.*

worldwide ['wɜːldwaɪd] ◇ *adj* [depression, problem, phenomenon] that affects the whole world. ◇ *adv* throughout the whole world ◻ *Their products became known worldwide.* ◻ *It made news worldwide.*

World Wide Web *n* **the World Wide Web** a huge collection of information, consisting of text, graphics, moving images and sound, available on the Internet.

worm [wɜːˈm] ◇ *n* a small thin creature with no legs or bones, especially one that lives in the earth or inside other animals. ◇ *vt* **-1. to worm one's way** to manage to reach a particular place by wriggling or moving slowly ◻ *She managed to worm her way to the front.* **-2. to worm one's way into sb's affections/heart/confidence** to win sb's affection/love/trust gradually, e.g. by pretending to like them (disapproving use).

◆ **worms** *npl* a disease that can affect animals and humans, in which tiny worms live inside the body and feed off it.

◆ **worm out** *vt sep* **to worm sthg out of sb** [secret, truth, information] to find out sthg from sb gradually, especially by winning their trust, asking lots of questions etc.

worn [wɔːˈn] ◇ *past participle of* **wear**. ◇ *adj* **-1.** [carpet, sleeve, suit] that has become thin in places as a result of use over a long period. **-2. to look worn** [person] to look tired.

worn-out *adj* **-1.** [carpet, shoe, clothes] that is so damaged by use over a long period of time that it can no longer be used. **-2. to be worn-out** [person] to be very tired ◻ *You look completely worn-out after that walk!*

worried [US 'wɜːrɪd, GB 'wʌr-] *adj* [person] who is unhappy because they cannot stop thinking about something unpleasant that has happened or might happen ◻ *a worried frown/look* ◻ *I'm really worried about her/my work.* ■ **to be worried sick** to be very worried.

worrier [US 'wɜːrɪr, GB 'wʌrɪə] *n* a person who worries a lot.

worry [US 'wɜːrɪ, GB 'wʌrɪ] (*pl* **worries**, *pt* & *pp* **worried**) ◇ *n* **-1.** a feeling of unhappiness caused by thinking about something unpleasant that has happened or might happen ◻ *financial worry.* **-2.** a problem that makes one feel worried ◻ *Tony has enough worries.* ◇ *vt* to make <sb> feel worried ◻ *What she said really worried me.* ◇ *vi* to be worried ◻ *Don't worry.* ◻ *She worries about the mortgage/her children.*

worrying [US 'wɜːrɪɪŋ, GB 'wʌr-] *adj* [situation, development, position] that causes worry ◻ *The worrying thing is,...*

worrywart [US 'wɜːrɪwɔːrt, GB 'wʌrɪwɔːt] *n* US a person who worries too much (informal use).

worse [wɜːˈs] ◇ *adj* used as the comparative of "bad" ◻ *I thought my Spanish was bad, but his is worse.* ◻ *My cooking is worse than my wife's.* ◻ *Things are even worse than I thought.* ■ **to get worse** [situation, condition, illness] to become more serious; [person] to become more sick ◻ *Things are getting worse every day.* ◻ *I think my cough is getting worse.*
◇ *adv* used as the comparative of "badly" ◻ *The soccer team did worse than expected.* ■ **to be worse off** to have less money; to be in a more unpleasant situation ◻ *The tax increases mean we'll all be worse off.* ◻ *With no job and a big loan to pay back, we couldn't be worse off.*
◇ *n* something worse ◻ *The news is bad, and there's worse to come.* ■ **to change for the worse** [situation, weather, character] to become more unpleasant.

worsen ['wɜːˈsn] ◇ *vi* [situation, crisis, weather] to become worse ◻ *The situation at home steadily worsened.* ◇ *vt* [situation, crisis, condition] to make <sthg> become worse ◻ *His intervention served only to worsen the crisis.*

worsening ['wɜːˈsnɪŋ] *adj* [weather, situation, condition] that is getting worse.

worship ['wɜːˈʃɪp] (US *pt* & *pp* **worshiped**, *cont* **worshiping**, GB *pt* & *pp* **worshipped**, *cont* **worshipping**) ◇ *vt* **-1.** RELIGION to show respect and love for <God or a god>, e.g. by singing hymns or saying prayers. **-2.** [person, leader, pop star] to admire or love <sb> very much, especially without questioning. ◇ *n* **-1.** RELIGION the act of worshiping □ *a place of worship.* **-2.** the act of worshiping a person □ *hero worship.*
◆ **Worship** *n* GB **Your/Her/His Worship** the formal way to address a magistrate or mayor.

worshiper US, **worshipper** GB ['wɜːˈʃɪpəʳ] *n* RELIGION a person who worships God or a god.

worst [wɜːˈst] ◇ *adj* used as the superlative of "bad" □ *That's the worst movie I've seen in years!* □ *It was his worst performance ever.*
◇ *adv* used as the superlative of "badly" □ *I did worst in the written exam.* □ *It's difficult to say who came off worst.* □ *Supplies are now reaching the worst-hit areas.*
◇ *n* **the worst** the worst thing, situation etc □ *I was prepared for the worst.* □ *At least the worst is over.* ■ **if the worst comes to the worst** if the situation becomes very bad □ *If the worst comes to the worst, I can always get a part-time job.* ■ **to get the worst of sthg** to be affected in the most serious way by sthg □ *Florida got the worst of the bad weather.*
◆ **at (the) worst** *adv* if the situation becomes really bad □ *At worst we can always catch a later plane.*

worsted ['wʊstəd] *n* a cloth made of wool that is used to make suits, skirts, trousers etc.

worth [wɜːˈθ] ◇ *prep* **-1. to be worth an amount of money** to have the value of a particular amount of money □ *It's worth $50/a fortune.* □ *How much is your house worth?* **-2. to be worth doing** to be good, useful, enjoyable etc enough to do □ *It's worth contacting her to find out.* □ *I know I spoil him, but he's worth it.* □ *That book isn't worth reading.* □ *Don't start arguing with them. It's not worth it.*
◇ *n* **-1. $5,000 worth of sthg** the amount of sthg that one can buy for $5,000 □ *They stole $25,000 worth of computers.* **-2.** value or importance □ *He seems to have a low opinion of his own worth.* **-3. a week's/year's etc worth of sthg** an amount of sthg that can last for a week/year etc □ *a week's worth of shopping.*

worthless ['wɜːˈθləs] *adj* **-1.** [object] that has no value □ *The ring turned out to be worthless.* **-2.** [person] who has no good qualities.

worthwhile [ˌwɜːˈθ'waɪl] *adj* [job, work, effort] that is worth doing □ *It's worthwhile visiting the museum.*

worthy ['wɜːˈðɪ] (*compar* **worthier**, *superl* **worthiest**) *adj* **-1.** [successor, aim, cause] that deserves respect and approval □ *Tom Hornstein proved to be a worthy champion.* **-2. to be worthy of sthg** [of trust, love, respect] to deserve sthg. **-3.** [effort, book] that is good but dull (disapproving use).

would [*stressed* wʊd, *unstressed* wəd] *modal vb* **-1.** used in reported speech when the main verb is in the past □ *But you said you would come!* □ *He promised he would help me.* □ *They thought they would be doing me a favor.* **-2. I would tell you, if I knew the answer** I can't tell you the answer because I don't know it (used to express the result of an imagined or possible event) □ *What would you do if you lost your job?* □ *It would be nice if you could come.* □ *I would be grateful for some advice.* ■ **if I had known the answer, I would have told you** I couldn't tell you because I didn't know the answer (used to express the result of an imagined event in the past) □ *If I hadn't fallen, I would have won the race.* □ *If it hadn't been for the traffic we would have arrived earlier.* □ *Without your help I would never have made it.* **-3. I would do anything** I am willing to do anything □ *I would travel miles to hear her sing.* ■ **he wouldn't move** he refused to move □ *She wouldn't tell us how much she'd spent on her dress.* ■ **the car wouldn't start** the car didn't start when I tried it. **-4.** used in polite offers and requests □ *Would you like a drink?* □ *Would you mind closing the window?* □ *Hold that, would you?* □ *I would like to speak to the manager.* **-5.** used to say that a particular action is typical of somebody's behavior □ *Well, she would say that, wouldn't she?* □ *"I told him what I thought of him." — "You would!"* **-6.** used to express an opinion in a polite or indirect way □ *I would think fifty dollars would be enough.* □ *I would have thought it was too difficult for her.* **-7. I would do it** you should do it (used when giving advice) □ *I'd report it to the police, if I were you.* □ *I wouldn't spend so much on a birthday present.* **-8.** used to express an action that happened regularly in the past □ *When I was young, my father would take me fishing.* □ *Every morning he would bring me a cup of tea in bed.*

would-be *adj* **a would-be writer/actor etc** a person who would like to be a writer/an actor etc but is not.

wouldn't ['wʊdnt] = **would not.**

would've ['wʊdəv] = **would have.**

wound¹ [wuːnd] ◇ *n* a cut or tear in the skin and flesh that usually bleeds, especially one caused by a knife, gun etc □ *a bullet/knife wound* □ *He died of his wounds.* □ *a chest/head wound.* ■ **to lick one's wounds** to feel sorry for oneself after a defeat or disappointment. ◇ *vt* **-1.** to damage the skin and flesh of <sb>, especially by cutting or tearing with a weapon □ *He was badly wounded in the battle.* **-2.** to say or do something that makes <sb> feel hurt or upset □ *Her remarks wounded me deeply.*

wound² [waʊnd] *past tense & past participle of* **wind.**

wounded ['wuːndəd] ◇ *adj* **-1.** [person] who has one or more wounds □ *a wounded soldier.* **-2.** [pride, feelings] that has been hurt by cruel words or actions □ *It's just wounded pride, that's all.* ◇ *npl* **the wounded** all the people injured in a battle.

Wounded Knee part of a Native American reservation where in 1890, 146 Sioux were massacred by US troops. It was the last military battle between Native Americans and whites.

wounding ['wu:ndɪŋ] *adj* [remark, comment] that hurts somebody's feelings.

wove [wəʊv] *past tense of* **weave**.

woven ['wəʊvn] *past participle of* **weave**.

wow [waʊ] (informal use) ◇ *excl* a word used to express admiration or surprise □ *Wow! Look at that!* ◇ *n* a person or object that is very exciting, beautiful, or successful □ *Liz was a real wow at the party!* ◇ *vt* [person, audience, critics] to make <sb> feel admiration and surprise □ *She wowed the audience with her version of "Summertime".*

WP *n* -1. *abbr of* **word processor** □ *a WP operator.* -2. *abbr of* **word processing**.

WPA (*abbr of* **Works Progress Administration**) *n* **the WPA** a US government body that created many jobs for the unemployed in the 1930s as part of President Roosevelt's New Deal.

WPC (*abbr of* **woman police constable**) *n* GB a woman who is a constable in the British police force.

wpm (*abbr of* **words per minute**) a way of measuring how quickly a person can write, type, or take shorthand notes □ *a typing speed of 60 wpm.*

WRAC [ræk] (*abbr of* **Women's Royal Army Corps**) *n* **the WRAC** the women's section of the British army.

WRAF [ræf] (*abbr of* **Women's Royal Air Force**) *n* **the WRAF** the women's section of the British air force.

wrangle ['ræŋgl] ◇ *n* a noisy argument, especially one that lasts a long time. ◇ *vi* to have a wrangle with somebody □ *She's always wrangling with the bank manager over money.*

wrap [ræp] (*pt* & *pp* **wrapped**, *cont* **wrapping**) ◇ *vt* -1. [present, product, purchase] to put paper, cloth, plastic etc around <sthg> □ *Wrap that cheese in some waxed paper.* □ *I wrapped a towel around my head.* -2. **to wrap one's arms/fingers/legs around sthg** to put one's arms/fingers/legs around sthg. ◇ *n* a piece of cloth that one wears around one's shoulders to keep warm.

◆ **wrap up** ◇ *vt sep* -1. to wrap sthg up [present, goods, box] to wrap sthg up □ *Could you wrap these up for me?* -2. **to wrap sthg up** [deal, program] to complete sthg (informal use) □ *Well, that about wraps it up for today.* ◇ *vi* **wrap up well** OR **warmly!** put on plenty of warm clothes!

wrapped up [ˌræpt-] *adj* **to be wrapped up in sb/sthg** [in one's work, family, book] to give sb/sthg all one's time and attention so that one does not notice other people or things (informal use) □ *He's so wrapped up in his work he wouldn't notice if I left.*

wrapper ['ræpər] *n* [of a book, chocolate, ice cream] a piece of paper or plastic that is put around something in order to protect it.

wrapping ['ræpɪŋ] *n*, **wrappings** ['ræpɪŋz] *npl*

material used to wrap something □ *The book was still in its plastic wrapping.*

wrapping paper *n* decorative paper used for wrapping presents.

wrath [rɒθ] *n* great anger (literary use).

wreak [ri:k] *vt* **to wreak havoc** to cause a lot of damage or confusion.

wreath [ri:θ] *n* a circle of flowers and leaves worn on the head or placed on somebody's grave.

wreathe [ri:ð] *vt* **to be wreathed in sthg** [in mist, smoke, light] to be covered in sthg (literary use).

wreck [rek] ◇ *n* -1. a car, plane, train etc that has been destroyed in an accident or explosion □ *They pulled the bodies from the wreck.* -2. a ship that has sunk or been broken against rocks. -3. a person who looks or feels ill or unhappy (informal use) □ *God, you look like a wreck this morning!*
◇ *vt* -1. [car, equipment, machine] to break or destroy <sthg> □ *The bomb wrecked the whole building.* -2. [ship, tanker, liner] to cause <a ship> to be destroyed, especially against rocks □ *The ship was wrecked off the west coast.* -3. [plan, vacation, health] to spoil <sthg> □ *Adam's new job offer has completely wrecked our plans for a vacation.*

wreckage ['rekɪdʒ] *n* [of a car, ship, building] the remains of something that has been wrecked □ *Firefighters were still looking for bodies in the wreckage.*

wrecker ['rekər] *n* US a vehicle that removes other vehicles that have been in an accident or have broken down.

wren [ren] *n* a very small brown bird.

Wren [ren], **Sir Christopher** (1632–1723) a British architect who designed many London churches, including St Paul's Cathedral.

wrench [rentʃ] ◇ *n* -1. a tool for tightening and loosening nuts. -2. [to one's ankle, knee] an injury caused by sharply twisting a joint □ *She's given her ankle a nasty wrench.* -3. [on leaving somebody] a difficult and sad parting □ *Leaving the kids was a real wrench.* ◇ *vt* -1. to pull <sthg> hard with a twisting movement □ *He tried to wrench my bag out of my hands.* -2. [knee, wrist, ankle] to injure <sthg> by twisting it sharply.

wrest [rest] *vt* **to wrest sthg from sb** [weapon, title, power] to take sthg from sb by force (literary use).

wrestle ['resl] ◇ *vt* [opponent, attacker] to fight <sb> by holding them and throwing them to the ground. ◇ *vi* -1. to fight with somebody by holding them and throwing them to the ground □ *He was wrestling with his brother.* -2. **to wrestle with sthg** [with a problem, question, one's conscience] to try to deal with sthg difficult, heavy etc.

wrestler ['reslər] *n* a person who wrestles for sport.

wrestling ['reslɪŋ] *n* the sport of fighting by holding or throwing one's opponent without hitting them □ *a wrestling match.*

wretch [retʃ] *n* a person who one thinks is unhappy or unfortunate.

wretched ['retʃəd] *adj* **-1.** [person] who is unhappy, unfortunate, or ill. **-2.** a word used to describe something that is very bad □ *The standard of hygiene in the camps was wretched.* **-3.** a word used to express anger or dislike (informal use) □ *I can't get the wretched thing to open!*

wriggle ['rɪgl] ◇ *vt* to bend and twist <one's finger or toe> in small quick movements. ◇ *vi* **-1.** to move continually, especially because one is excited or uncomfortable □ *Stop wriggling, and keep still!* **-2.** to move somewhere by twisting and turning □ *She wriggled under the fence.*

◆ **wriggle out of** *vt fus* **to wriggle out of sthg** to avoid sthg that one does not want to do, especially by making excuses or lying □ *How did she manage to wriggle out of working over Christmas?*

Wright [raɪt], **Frank Lloyd** (1869–1959) a US architect who designed buildings to be in harmony with their environment. His work includes the Guggenheim Museum and many private homes.

Wright, Wilbur (1867–1912) and **Orville** (1871–1948) US inventors and pilots, known as the Wright Brothers, who designed and flew the first airplane in 1903.

wring [rɪŋ] (*pt & pp* **wrung**) *vt* **-1.** to remove water from <wet clothes> by twisting and pressing. **-2. to wring one's hands** to twist and press one's hands together as a sign of worry or unhappiness (literary use). **-3. to wring an animal's neck** to twist the neck of an animal with one's hands to kill it.

◆ **wring out** *vt sep* **to wring wet clothes out** to wring wet clothes.

wringing ['rɪŋɪŋ] *adj* **wringing (wet)** [person, hair, clothes] very wet.

wrinkle ['rɪŋkl] ◇ *n* **-1.** [on one's skin, face] a line or fold in the skin that is caused by age, worry, too much sun etc. **-2.** [in clothes] a line or fold in a piece of clothing that is caused e.g. by not hanging or folding it correctly. ◇ *vt* to cause wrinkles to appear in <one's nose or forehead> by moving the muscles of one's face. ◇ *vi* [cloth, cotton, shirt] to become full of wrinkles.

wrinkled ['rɪŋkld], **wrinkly** ['rɪŋklɪ] *adj* [skin, person, piece of clothing] that has many wrinkles.

wrist [rɪst] *n* the joint between the hand and the arm.

wristband ['rɪstbænd] *n* the band of metal, leather, plastic etc that fastens a watch around one's wrist.

wristwatch ['rɪstwɒtʃ] *n* a watch that is worn on the wrist.

writ [rɪt] *n* an official document allowing or forbidding somebody to do something.

write [raɪt] (*pt* **wrote**, *pp* **written**) ◇ *vt* **-1.** [word, list, number] to mark <sthg> on a surface, usually paper, using a pen, pencil, or other object □ *Write your name and date of*

birth. **-2.** [book, music, play] to create <sthg> and record it on paper □ *The novel was written just after the war.* □ *She writes poetry.* **-3.** [letter, note] to produce <sthg>, usually on paper and using a pen or pencil. ■ **to write sb a letter** to produce and send a letter to sb. **-4.** US [person] to produce and send a letter to <sb> □ *She wrote me about the offer.* **-5.** [check, prescription, receipt] to mark the necessary information on <an official document or form> and sign it. **-6.** COMPUTING **to write sthg to disk** [data, file, information] to record sthg on a disk.

◇ *vi* **-1.** to make marks that represent letters or numbers on a surface, usually paper, using a pen, pencil, or other object □ *Ben's learning to write.* □ *He always writes in ink/ballpoint.* **-2.** to produce and send a letter □ *Write soon!* □ *I write to my mother every week.* **-3.** to earn money by producing books, plays, newspaper articles etc □ *He writes for television/the New York Times.* **-4.** COMPUTING **to write to disk** to record information, data etc on a disk.

◆ **write back** ◇ *vt sep* **to write sthg back** [letter, note] to write sthg in reply. ◇ *vi*: *She never wrote back.*

◆ **write down** *vt sep* **to write sthg down** [telephone number, name, idea] to record sthg in writing, especially in order to remember it □ *Hang on, I'll just write it down, otherwise I'll forget.*

◆ **write in** *vi* [viewer, listener, customer] to write to a radio station, television program etc in order to ask for something, give information, or complain □ *Listeners are invited to write in with their suggestions.*

◆ **write into** *vt sep* **to write sthg into a contract/an agreement etc** [clause, detail] to include sthg in a contract/agreement etc when it is written.

◆ **write off** ◇ *vt sep* **-1. to write sthg off** [project, venture] to accept the failure of sthg □ *You'll just have to write it off as a useful experience.* **-2. to write a sum of money off** [debt, investment] to accept the loss of a sum of money □ *The bank's agreed to write off all the company's bad debts.* **-3. to write sb off** to consider sb as a failure □ *You can't just write him off because he made one mistake!* **-4. to write a vehicle off** GB to damage a vehicle so badly that it is not worth repairing it. ◇ *vi* to write a letter to an organization asking for advice, information etc □ *She wrote off to various companies.* □ *I wrote off for a brochure.*

◆ **write out** *vt sep* **-1. to write sthg out** [list, report] to write sthg and include all the necessary information □ *Write it all out on this piece of paper here.* **-2. to write sthg out** [receipt, prescription, parking ticket] to write the necessary information on an official document or form □ *The doctor wrote out the prescription for me.*

◆ **write up** *vt sep* **to write sthg up** [minutes, report] to write sthg in a finished form, usually using notes which one has made □ *I'll write it up later when I have a bit more time.*

write-off *n* GB a vehicle that has been so badly damaged in an accident that it is not worth repairing □ *The car was a complete write-off.*

write-protect *vt* COMPUTING [disk] to prevent the information on <a disk> from being altered or removed by opening a small hole in one corner of it.

writer ['raɪtəʳ] *n* -1. a person who writes books, articles etc as a job □ *a famous writer.* -2. the person who has written a particular letter, article etc □ *The writer was accused of unfair bias.*

write-up *n* an article in a newspaper or magazine in which the writer discusses something such as a play or movie and says what they think about it □ *The program got a good write-up.*

writhe [raɪð] *vi* to twist and turn one's body, especially because one is in pain □ *He was writhing in agony.*

writing ['raɪtɪŋ] *n* -1. handwriting □ *I can't read your writing.* -2. [on a page, blackboard, sign] written letters or numbers. ■ **in writing** [apply, accept] in a written form □ *Make sure you get/put that in writing.* -3. [for money] the activity of writing articles, novels etc, especially for money.

◆ **writings** *npl* the material written by a particular person or on a particular subject □ *political/scientific writings.*

writing desk *n* a desk with special places for paper, pens etc.

writing paper *n* paper, usually of good quality, used for writing letters.

written ['rɪtn] ◇ *past participle of* **write.** ◇ *adj* -1. **a written test/exam** a test/exam in which the answers must be written rather than spoken. -2. **written confirmation/agreement** etc a confirmation/an agreement etc that is in writing and is therefore official.

WRNS [renz] (*abbr of* **Women's Royal Naval Service**) *n* **the WRNS** the women's section of the British navy.

wrong [rɒŋ] ◇ *adj* -1. **there is something wrong** a phrase used to say that something is not satisfactory □ *Is something wrong?* □ *There's something wrong with the fridge.* □ *What's wrong?* -2. [person, object] that is not suitable or right □ *the wrong man/tool for the job* □ *the wrong kind of shoes for walking.* -3. [decision, answer, turning] that is not correct □ *The letter went to the wrong address.* □ *You're wrong about Kay, she's really very nice.* □ *Perhaps I was wrong to ask.* -4. **to be wrong** to be morally bad □ *It's wrong to steal/tell lies.*

◇ *adv* [spell, pronounce] incorrectly. ■ **to get sthg wrong** [name, number, answer] to make a mistake with sthg □ *You've got it all wrong, I never said that.* ■ **to go wrong** [person] to make a mistake; [machine, heating, computer] to stop working well □ *Where did we go wrong with the children?* □ *The printer keeps going wrong.* ■ **don't get me wrong** don't misunderstand me (informal use) □ *Don't get me wrong, most of the time I think she's really great.*

◇ *n* an action that is morally bad □ *She can do no wrong in their eyes.* □ *Two wrongs don't make a right.* □ *He's old enough to tell the difference between right and wrong.* ■ **to be in the wrong** [person] to have done something bad, immoral, incorrect etc □ *He knows perfectly well he's in the wrong.*

◇ *vt* [person] to treat <sb> badly or unfairly (literary use).

wrong-foot *vt* GB -1. SPORT [opponent] to cause <sb> to lose their balance by kicking, hitting, or throwing the ball in a way they are not expecting □ *Once again they managed to wrong-foot the Dodgers.* -2. [person] to surprise <sb> in a way that places them in a difficult position □ *I have this feeling she's trying to wrong-foot me all the time.*

wrongful ['rɒŋfl] *adj* [arrest, imprisonment] that is unfair or illegal □ *He's going to sue them for wrongful dismissal.*

wrongly ['rɒŋlɪ] *adv* [spell, conclude] *see* **wrong** □ *She was wrongly accused.* □ *He thought, quite wrongly, that she agreed with him.*

wrong number *n* a telephone number that is dialed incorrectly so that the telephone rings at the wrong address □ *I tried calling, but I got a wrong number.*

wrote [rəʊt] *past tense of* **write.**

wrought iron [,rɔːt-] *n* iron that is twisted into shapes and used to make decorative gates, fences etc.

wrung [rʌŋ] *past tense & past participle of* **wring.**

WRVS (*abbr of* **Women's Royal Voluntary Service**) *n* **the WRVS** a British charity consisting of women who do voluntary work, e.g. delivering meals to elderly people.

wry [raɪ] *adj* **a wry smile/look** etc a smile/look etc that shows a mixture of slight amusement and displeasure □ *a wry sense of humor.*

wt. *abbr of* **weight.**

WTO (*abbr of* **World Trade Organization**) *n* an international organization set up to encourage trade between its members. It replaced GATT in 1995.

WV *abbr of* **West Virginia.**

WW *abbr of* **World War.**

WWW *n abbr of* **World Wide Web.**

WY *abbr of* **Wyoming.**

Wyeth ['waɪəθ], **Andrew** (1917–) a US painter who is well known for his realistic images of the Midwest.

Wyoming [waɪ'əʊmɪŋ] a state in the western USA, in the area of the Rocky Mountains. ABBREVIATION: WY. SIZE: 253,500 sq kms. POPULATION: 453,588 (*Wyomingites*). CAPITAL: Cheyenne.

WYSIWYG ['wɪzɪwɪg] (*abbr of* **what you see is what you get**) *adj* a term used for a piece of computer software that shows letters, documents etc on the screen of a computer exactly as they appear when printed on paper.

x [eks] (*pl* **x's** OR **xs**), **X** [eks] (*pl* **X's** OR **Xs**) *n* -1. the twenty-fourth letter of the English alphabet. -2. [name] a letter used to stand for a name that is not known □ *Mr/Ms X.* -3. [amount] a letter used to stand for an amount that is not known □ *X gallons of gas.* -4. MATH a letter used to stand for an unknown number that can be calculated □ *y = x + 1.* -5. [place] a letter used to mark a particular place on a map □ *X marks the spot.* -6. [kiss] a mark that represents a kiss, written under the writer's name at the end of a letter.

xenophobia [ˌzenəˈfəʊbjə] *n* a strong and unreasonable fear and dislike of foreigners or strangers.

Xerox™ [ˈzɪərɒks] *n* -1. a photocopier. -2. a photocopy.
◆ **xerox** *vt* [page, letter, document] to make a photocopy of <sthg>.

Xmas [ˈkrɪsməs] *n* = **Christmas** □ *a Xmas card/present.*

X-rated [ˌeksˈreɪtəd] *adj* [book, movie] that shows sex in a way that some people might find offensive.

X-ray ◇ *n* a beam of energy that passes through most solid materials but makes others, e.g. bone or metal, appear as dark areas on special photographs; a photograph produced in this way, used in hospitals to examine broken bones and unhealthy organs, and in airports to find drugs, guns, bombs etc inside luggage. ◇ *vt* [patient, leg, suitcase] to photograph <sb/sthg> using X-rays.

xylophone [ˈzaɪləfəʊn] *n* a musical instrument consisting of a set of metal or wooden bars of different lengths that produce different notes when hit with special hammers.

y [waɪ] (*pl* **y's** OR **ys**), **Y** [waɪ] (*pl* **Y's** OR **Ys**) *n* -1. the twenty-fifth letter of the English alphabet. -2. MATH a letter used to stand for a number that is not known □ *y = x + 1.*

Y *n abbr of* **YMCA**, **YWCA**.

yacht [jɒt] *n* a boat with sails or an engine, used for racing or pleasure.

yachting [ˈjɒtɪŋ] *n* the sport of sailing yachts □ *They're going yachting.*

yachtsman [ˈjɒtsmən] (*pl* **yachtsmen** [-mən]) *n* a man who goes yachting.

yachtswoman [ˈjɒtswʊmən] (*pl* **yachtswomen**) *n* a woman who goes yachting.

yahoo [jɑːˈhuː] *n* a rough rude person.

yak [jæk] *n* an animal from Tibet that is like a cow with long horns and long rough hair.

Yale [jeɪl] *n* one of the oldest American universities. It is a member of the Ivy League.

Yale lock™ *n* a strong lock, used on doors, that is opened with a flat key with an uneven edge.

yam [jæm] *n* a tropical vegetable that looks like a long thin potato.

Yangtze [US ˈjɑːŋtsi, GB ˈjæŋtsi]: **the Yangtze (Kiang)** the longest river in China, flowing from Tibet to the China Sea near Shanghai.

yank [jæŋk] *vt* [rope, tooth, arm] to pull <sthg> suddenly and with a lot of force.

Yank *n* GB a term for a person who comes from or lives in the United States (informal and disapproving use).

Yankee [ˈjæŋkɪ] *n* -1. GB = **Yank.** -2. US a person from the northern United States.

♥ YANKEE
The term "Yankee" originally referred to Dutch immigrants, who settled mainly in the northeastern USA. Later, it came to refer to anybody from the northeast, so that during the American Civil War soldiers fighting for the Northern states were known as Yankees. In modern times, some Southerners still refer to Northerners as Yankees when they want to show disapproval.

---

yap [jæp] (*pt & pp* **yapped**, *cont* **yapping**) *vi* -1. [dog] to make a high-pitched bark. -2. [person] to talk loudly about stupid or boring things (disapproving use).

yard [jɑːd] *n* -1. a unit (three feet or 91.4 centimeters) used for measuring distance □ *fifty yards down the road.* -2. US a piece of land next to somebody's house where they grow flowers, have a lawn etc □ *The kids were playing in the yard.* □ *yard work.* -3. [next to a building] a concrete or stone area, usually behind or beside a building, that is surrounded by a wall or fence. -4. [for work] an open area where a particular kind of work is done □ *a ship repair/builder's yard.*

yardstick [ˈjɑːdstɪk] *n* -1. US a long, thin, flat piece of plastic, wood, or metal that is one yard long and is used to measure things. -2. a person or thing that is used in a comparison to decide how good another person or thing is.

yarn [jɑːn] *n* -1. thread made of twisted wool or cotton. -2. a long story that is not completely true. ■ **to spin sb a yarn** to tell sb a yarn, especially when making an excuse.

yashmak [ˈjæʃmæk] *n* a thin cloth that Muslim women use to cover their faces in public.

yawn [jɔːn] ◇ *vi* **-1.** [person] to open one's mouth wide and breathe deeply because one is tired or bored □ *"I'm so tired," she said, yawning.* **-2.** [gap, chasm, crack] to be or become wide open. ◇ *n* an act of yawning □ *She gave a huge yawn.*

yd *abbr of* **yard**.

yeah [jeə] *adv* yes (informal use).

year [jɪəʳ] *n* **-1.** the period of twelve months or 365 days from January 1 to December 31 in the Western calendar □ *this/last/next year* □ *1993 was a bad year for small businesses.* □ *He was born in the year 1868.* ■ **all (the) year round** throughout the year. **-2.** any period of twelve months □ *We've lived here for two years.* □ *He's 21 years old.* □ *The city walls are hundreds of years old.* ■ **year in year out** every year without changing □ *He wears the same suit year in year out.* **-3.** EDUCATION the period of the year when students are at school, college etc □ *The new year starts in September.* □ *a three-year course.* **-4.** FINANCE = **fiscal year** □ *profits at the year end.*

◆ **years** *npl* a long time □ *He's been here for years.* □ *We met years and years ago.*

yearbook [ˈjɪəʳbʊk] *n* a book which is produced once a year and contains information about a school, company etc during the past year.

yearling [ˈjɪəʳlɪŋ] *n* an animal between one and two years old, especially a horse.

yearly [ˈjɪəʳlɪ] ◇ *adj* **-1.** [event, meeting, visit] that takes place once a year. **-2.** [income, wage, budget] that refers to a period of one year. ◇ *adv* **-1.** [meet, visit, inspect] once a year □ *The conference takes place yearly.* **-2.** every year □ *We see them twice yearly.*

yearn [jɜːʳn] *vi* **to yearn for sthg/to do sthg** [for acceptance, success, love] to have a strong desire for sthg/to do sthg □ *We yearned for the comforts of home.*

yearning [ˈjɜːʳnɪŋ] *n* a strong desire for somebody or something □ *a yearning for peace.*

yeast [jiːst] *n* a soft grayish-brown fungus that is used to make alcoholic drinks and causes bread to become light and full of air □ *brewer's yeast* □ *dried yeast.*

yeast infection *n* US an infectious disease caused by a fungus that affects the vagina of adult women.

Yeats [jeɪts], **W. B.** (1865–1939) an Irish writer who played an important part in the development of Irish poetry and drama, and was involved in Irish nationalism.

yell [jel] ◇ *vi* to shout loudly because one is angry, in pain, excited, or scared. ◇ *vt:* *"Hey, you!" he yelled.* ◇ *n:* *He let out a loud yell.*

yellow [ˈjeloʊ] ◇ *n* the color of lemons or butter □ *The blouse comes in yellow or navy.* ◇ *adj* **-1.** [car, dress, flower] that is the color yellow. **-2.** [person] who is a coward (informal use). ◇ *vi* [paper, photograph, teeth] to become yellow, usually with age.

yellow card *n* a piece of yellow card that a

referee in a soccer match holds up in the air as a warning to a player who has broken a rule.

yellow fever *n* a serious tropical disease that makes the skin go slightly yellow.

yellow light *n* US the light between the red and green lights on a traffic light that tells drivers to be careful.

yellow lines *npl* in Britain, lines of yellow paint along the edges of a road that show that parking is not allowed, or that it is only allowed at certain times.

Yellow Pages™ *npl* **the Yellow Pages** a book, printed on yellow paper, that contains the telephone numbers of businesses and services in an area.

Yellowstone National Park [ˌjeloʊstoʊn-] a national park in Wyoming, Idaho, and Montana, USA. It is famous for its hot springs and geysers.

yelp [jelp] ◇ *vi* [dog] to make a short high-pitched sound, often because of pain; [person] to shout in this way. ◇ *n:* *The dog let out a yelp.*

Yemen [ˈjemən] a country at the southern end of the Arabian Peninsula, that was divided into the independent states of North and South Yemen until they were united in 1990. SIZE: 485,000 sq kms. POPULATION: 10,000,000 (*Yemenis*). CAPITAL: Sanaa. LANGUAGE: Arabic. CURRENCY: rial.

yen [jen] (*pl sense 1* **yen**) *n* **-1.** the unit of money used in Japan. **-2.** **to have a yen to do sthg** to have a strong desire to do sthg □ *I've always had a yen to learn Greek.*

yeoman of the guard [ˈjoʊmən-] (*pl* **yeomen of the guard** [ˈjoʊmən-]) *n* one of the ceremonial guards at the Tower of London.

yep [jep] *adv* yes (informal use).

yes [jes] ◇ *adv* **-1.** a word used to give a positive answer to a question □ *"Would you say the figures are accurate?" — "Yes, I would."* □ *"Can I come in?" — "Yes, of course."* ■ **yes, please** a phrase used to accept an offer politely □ *"Would you like coffee?" — "Yes, please."* **-2.** a word used to show that one accepts something, agrees to something, or says that something is true □ *"Sweden can be cold at this time of year." — "Yes, it certainly can!"* □ *Yes, that's her alright.* □ *"Will you take the call?" — "Yes, put it through."* ■ **to say yes to sthg** to accept or agree to sthg □ *Let's hope they say yes to our proposal.* **-3.** a word used to invite somebody to continue speaking □ *"I want to ask you something" — "Yes, what is it?"* □ *"The problem is..." — "Yes, go on."* **-4.** a word used to disagree with something that has been expressed in the negative □ *"He wasn't even there." — "Yes, he was!"* **-5.** a word used to introduce something that one has forgotten to say □ *Oh yes, I meant to tell you that Jay called.*

◇ *n* a vote in favor of a person, proposal etc □ *five yeses, two nos.*

yes-man *n* a man who always agrees with

his boss in order to be liked by them (disapproving use).

yesterday ['jestə^rdı] ◇ *n* the day before today □ *the day before yesterday* □ *yesterday's news.* ◇ *adv* -1. *I saw him yesterday.* -2. in the recent past □ *That was yesterday, things are different now.*

yet [jet] ◇ *adv* -1. up until now (used in questions) □ *Have you had lunch yet?* □ *Are you ready yet?* -2. up until now (used with negatives) □ *The taxi hasn't arrived yet.* □ *The house isn't finished yet.* ■ **not yet** not before now □ *"Have you finished?" — "Not yet."* ■ **don't do it yet** don't do it now, do it later □ *Add the tomatoes, but don't add the fish yet.* -3. **it may yet happen** there is a possibility that it will happen in the future □ *We may yet be successful.* -4. used to emphasize that something is continuing to happen □ *Yet again I must warn you to be careful.* □ *The traffic became yet slower.* □ *Yet more people arrived.* -5. **there's hope for us yet** there's still hope for us □ *I've yet to meet a nicer man.*
◇ *conj* used to emphasize a contrast that is surprising □ *The plan was simple yet effective.* □ *I was hungry, yet I couldn't eat anything.*

yeti ['jetı] *n* a large hairy ape that is supposed to look like a man and live in the Himalayas, but that only some people believe actually exists.

yew [ju:] *n* an evergreen tree that has dark-green leaves shaped like thin needles and small red cones; the wood of this tree.

Y-fronts *npl* GB men's underpants with an opening at the front □ *a pair of Y-fronts.*

YHA (*abbr of* **Youth Hostels Association**) *n* **the YHA** the organization in charge of British youth hostels.

Yiddish ['jıdıʃ] ◇ *n* a language spoken by Jews, especially in Eastern and Central Europe. ◇ *adj: a Yiddish speaker/song.*

yield [ji:ld] ◇ *vt* -1. [fruit, profit, result] to produce <sthg>, especially as a result of work that has been done □ *Our research is beginning to yield some answers.* -2. [power, responsibility, territory] to give <sthg> to somebody else so that they have control over it.
◇ *vi* -1. [door, lock, gate] to break, move backward, or open as a result of force. -2. [person, troops, government] to stop fighting or resisting somebody or something (formal use) □ *He finally yielded to pressure and resigned.* -3. US AUTO to slow down or stop at an intersection to let other vehicles pass in front of one □ *'Yield.'*
◇ *n* [of crops, corn, olives] an amount of a particular crop or kind of food that is produced.

yippee [US 'jıpı, GB jı'pi:] *excl* a word used to show that one is pleased and excited about something □ *Yippee! We're going to the zoo!*

YMCA (*abbr of* **Young Men's Christian Association**) *n* **the YMCA** an international organization that runs hostels, sports centers, and educational courses for young people, mainly in big cities.

yo [jou] *excl* hello (informal use).

yodel ['joudl] (US *pt* & *pp* **yodeled**, *cont* **yodeling**, GB *pt* & *pp* **yodelled**, *cont* **yodelling**) *vi* to sing by making one's voice go up and down from normal to high notes very quickly.

yoga ['jougə] *n* an Indian system of thought and exercise that is supposed to have good effects on the mind and body □ *a yoga exercise.*

yogurt, yoghurt, yoghourt [US 'jougərt, GB 'jɒgət] *n* a food made from milk with bacteria added to it, that is thick, white, tastes slightly sour, and is often eaten with fruit or used in cooking □ *natural/strawberry yogurt.*

yoke [jouk] *n* -1. FARMING a wooden bar that fits over the necks of two animals, especially oxen, to keep them together when they are pulling a plough. -2. **to live under the yoke of sthg** [of tyranny, slavery] to live somewhere where there is sthg that restricts one's freedom (literary use).

yokel ['joukl] *n* a person who lives in the countryside and is thought of as being stupid.

yolk [jouk] *n* the yellow part inside an egg □ *egg yolk.*

Yom Kippur [US ,joum'kıpr, GB ,jɒm'kıpə] *n* in the Jewish religion, a holiday on which people pray for their sins to be forgiven and do not eat.

yonder ['jɒndə^r] *adv* over there (literary use).

Yorks. *abbr of* **Yorkshire.**

Yorkshire ['jɔ:^rkʃə^r] a region of northern England that used to be a county. SIZE: 11,908 sq kms. POPULATION: 4,025,100.

Yorkshire pudding *n* a light dish made of flour, eggs, and milk, that is baked and usually eaten with roast beef.

Yorkshire terrier *n* a very small dog with long straight hair.

Yorktown ['jɔ:^rktaʊn] a town in Virginia, USA, where the last battle in the US War of Independence took place.

Yosemite National Park [jou,semətı-] a national park in California, USA. It is famous for its attractive scenery and giant redwood trees.

you [*stressed* ju:, *unstressed* jə, *before vowel* jʊ] *pron* -1. used as the subject or object of a verb, to refer to the person or people one is talking to □ *You know my wife, don't you?* □ *How do you Americans pronounce it?* □ *I didn't recognize you in that hat!* □ *I bought this for you.* -2. used to talk about people in general □ *You have to be careful these days.* □ *Exercise is good for you.* □ *You add the rice when the water is boiling.* -3. *phrases* **you idiot/liar/snob etc!** an expression used to say to somebody that one thinks they are an idiot/a liar/a snob etc. ■ **you know** an expression used when giving information to somebody □ *I saw Jane today, you know.* ■ **that dress/jacket etc isn't really you** that dress/jacket etc doesn't suit you. ■ **it's you** an expression used when one recognizes somebody □ *Oh, it's you — come in.* ■ **if I were you** an expression used when giving somebody advice □ *If I were you, I would go to a lawyer.*

you'd [*stressed* juːd, *unstressed* jəd] = **you had**, **you would**.

you'll [*stressed* juːl, *unstressed* jəl] = **you will**.

young [jʌŋ] ◇ *adj* -1. [person, animal, plant] that is not yet fully grown or is not very old □ *She's too young to go on her own.* □ *They have two young children.* -2. [country, movement] that has not existed long □ *At that time the women's movement was still young.* -3. [outlook, ambition] that is typical of or suitable for somebody young □ *Is this dress too young for me?* ◇ *npl* -1. **the young** young people as a group. -2. the babies of a particular animal □ *a cat and her young.*

Young [jʌŋ], **Brigham** (1801–1877) a US religious leader who led the Mormons to Utah and founded Salt Lake City.

younger ['jʌŋgəʳ] *adj* [sister, brother, colleague] who is not as old as oneself □ *It belongs to my younger brother.*

youngish ['jʌŋɪʃ] *adj* [person, face, appearance] that is quite young □ *He was a youngish-looking forty.*

young man *n* (old-fashioned use) -1. a way of addressing a boy when one is angry □ *Now listen here, young man!* -2. **sb's young man** sb's boyfriend.

youngster ['jʌŋstəʳ] *n* -1. a child □ *She's got three youngsters now.* -2. a young person.

young woman *n* a young fully grown woman.

your [*stressed* jɔːʳ, *unstressed* jəʳ] *det* -1. used to say that somebody or something is connected with or belongs to the person or people one is speaking to □ *Is this your jacket?* □ *Is your son still at college?* □ *Your hair looks nice.* □ *What's your name?* -2. used in formal titles to refer to the person or people one is talking to □ *Thank you, Your Majesty.* -3. used to say that somebody or something is connected with or belongs to people in general □ *Your eyes quickly get used to the dark.* ■ **your average American** the average American.

you're [juə] = **you are**.

yours [jɔːʳz] *pron* used to refer to something that belongs to or is connected with the person or people one is talking to □ *Use my car if yours won't start.* □ *Is this newspaper yours?* ■ **a friend of yours** one of your friends.

◆ **Yours** *adv* used at the end of a letter before the signature when one knows the person one is writing to quite well.

yourself [jəʳ'self] (*pl* **yourselves** [-'selvz]) *pron* -1. used as the object of a verb, or after a preposition, to refer to the same person or people as the subject "you" □ *Did you enjoy yourself on vacation?* □ *I hope you all behaved yourselves.* □ *Just pour yourself a drink.* □ *You should take better care of yourself.* -2. **you did it yourself** you did it without help from other people □ *Did you decorate the house yourselves?* ■ **by yourself** alone □ *Would you prefer to eat by yourself?*

youth [juːθ, *pl* juːðz] *n* -1. **sb's youth** the peri-

od when sb is young □ *in my youth.* -2. [in a person] the state or quality of being young □ *She radiated youth and vitality.* -3. a boy or young man □ *a gang of youths.* -4. [as a group] young people considered as a group □ *the youth of today.*

youth club *n* a club, often run by the church or local government, where young people can meet and take part in social activities.

youthful ['juːθfl] *adj* -1. [enthusiasm, idealism, innocence] that is typical of a young person □ *full of youthful vigor.* -2. [figure, complexion, face] that looks young but is not young □ *He still had a slim, youthful figure.*

youthfulness ['juːθflnəs] *n* [of a face, figure] *see* **youthful**.

youth hostel *n* a kind of cheap hotel where people, especially young people, can spend the night when traveling.

you've [*stressed* juːv, *unstressed* jəv] = **you have**.

yowl [jaul] ◇ *vi* to make a long loud noise because one is sad or in pain. ◇ *n*: *the yowl of hungry wolves.*

yo-yo ['jəʊjəʊ] *n* a toy that consists of a piece of string that one winds and unwinds around the middle of a round piece of wood, plastic etc.

yr *abbr of* **year**.

YT ◇ *abbr of* **Yukon Territory**. ◇ *n* (*abbr of* **Youth Training**) a British government training program for 16 and 17 year-olds who are not in full-time education or employment.

Yucatán [ˌjuːkə'tæn]: **the Yucatan** a peninsula in the Gulf of Mexico, including part of Mexico, Guatemala, and Belize.

yucca ['jʌkə] *n* a plant with a thick stem like the trunk of a tree and long pointed green leaves.

yuck [jʌk] *excl* a word used to show that one is disgusted by something (informal use).

Yugoslav ['juːgəʊˈslɑːv], **Yugoslavian** [ˌjuːgəʊ-ˈslɑːvɪən] *adj* & *n*: *see* **Yugoslavia**.

Yugoslavia [ˌjuːgəʊˈslɑːvɪə] a country in southeastern Europe. From 1945 to 1990 it was a Communist federation of six republics. Four of these have declared their independence, leaving Serbia and Montenegro. SIZE: 102,200 sq kms. POPULATION: 10,400,000 (*Yugoslavians, Yugoslavs*). CAPITAL: Belgrade. LANGUAGE: Serbo-Croat. CURRENCY: Yugoslavian dinar.

Yukon Territory ['juːkɒn-] a territory of northwestern Canada, bordering Alaska. ABBREVIATION: YT. SIZE: 482,515 sq kms. POPULATION: 27,797. CAPITAL: Whitehorse.

yule log ['juːl-] *n* a cake shaped like a log of wood that is eaten at Christmas.

yuletide ['juːltaɪd] *n* Christmas (literary use).

yummy ['jʌmɪ] (*compar* **yummier**, *superl* **yummiest**) *adj* [meal, taste, drink] that tastes delicious (informal use) □ *That looks yummy!*

yuppie, yuppy ['jʌpɪ] (*pl* **yuppies**) *n* a young person with a professional job who lives in a city, earns a lot of money, and spends it on expensive and fashionable things.

YWCA (*abbr of* **Young Women's Christian Association**) *n* **the YWCA** an international organization that runs hostels and sports centers for young women, mainly in big cities.

Z

z [US ziː, GB zed] (*pl* **z's** OR **zs**), **Z** [US ziː, GB zed] (*pl* **Z's** OR **Zs**) *n* the last letter of the English alphabet.

Zagreb ['zɑːgreb] the capital of Croatia. POPULATION: 1,175,000.

Zaïre [US zɑːˈɪr, GB zaɪˈə] -1. a country in central Africa. It is a major exporter of diamonds. SIZE: 2,345,000 sq kms. POPULATION: 41,200,000 (*Zaïreans*). CAPITAL: Kinshasa. LANGUAGE: French. CURRENCY: zaïre. -2. **the Zaïre (River)** a large river in central Africa that forms the border between the Congo Republic and Zaïre.

Zambia ['zæmbɪə] a country in southern central Africa. SIZE: 746,000 sq kms. POPULATION: 8,600,000 (*Zambians*). CAPITAL: Lusaka. LANGUAGE: English. CURRENCY: kwacha.

zany ['zeɪnɪ] (*compar* **zanier**, *superl* **zaniest**) *adj* [person, outfit, humor] that seems odd in an amusing way.

Zanzibar ['zænzəbɑːr'] an island off the coast of East Africa, forming part of the republic of Tanzania. SIZE: 1,658 sq kms. POPULATION: 310,000 (*Zanzibaris*).

zap [zæp] (*pt* & *pp* **zapped**, *cont* **zapping**) (informal use) ◇ *vt* -1. [person, vehicle, building] to kill or destroy <sb/sthg> with a gun, bomb etc. -2. [target, object] to make <sthg> disappear from the screen in a video game. ◇ *vi* -1. to move somewhere quickly or do something quickly. -2. TV to change channels using a remote control device.

Zapata [zəˈpɑːtə], **Emiliano** (1879–1919) a Mexican revolutionary leader who led an army of peasants to take back land that the government had taken from them.

zeal [ziːl] *n* great enthusiasm □ *Pat set about the task with great zeal.*

zealot ['zelət] *n* a person who has extreme opinions, especially about religion or politics (disapproving use).

zealous ['zeləs] *adj* [defender, campaigner, reformer] who does something with a lot of energy and enthusiasm, because they believe it is right (formal use).

zebra [US 'ziːbrə, GB 'zebrə] (*pl* **zebra** OR **zebras**) *n* an African animal that looks like a small horse with black-and-white stripes on its body.

zebra crossing *n* in Britain, a place on a road marked with white stripes where traffic must stop to let people cross.

zenith [US 'ziːnəθ, GB 'zen-] *n* -1. ASTRONOMY the point in the sky that is directly above one. -2. [of one's career, success] the highest point of something.

Zeppelin ['zepəlɪn] *n* a large airship used by the Germans in World War I.

zero ['zɪərəʊ] (*pl* **zeros** OR **zeroes**, *pt* & *pp* **zeroed**, *cont* **zeroing**) ◇ *n* -1. MATH & SPORT the number 0. -2. the point on the Celsius scale at which water freezes □ *ten degrees below zero.* ◇ *adj* **zero growth/inflation etc** no growth/inflation etc at all.

◆ **zero in on** *vt fus* -1. **to zero in on sb/sthg** [target, person] to aim at sb/sthg. -2. **to zero in on sthg** [subject, problem] to give all of one's attention to sthg.

zero-rated [-'reɪtəd] *adj* GB [product, goods] on which VAT does not have to be paid.

zest [zest] *n* -1. excitement. -2. **a zest for sthg** enthusiasm for sthg □ *He's lost his zest for life.* -3. [of fruit] the outer part of the skin of an orange, lemon, or lime that is used to flavor food or drink □ *Add some lemon zest.*

zigzag ['zɪgzæg] (*pt* & *pp* **zigzagged**, *cont* **zigzagging**) ◇ *n* a line that turns sharply left and right, like a row of Vs joined together □ *a zigzag pattern.* ◇ *vi* [person, car, road] to move or go in a zigzag pattern.

zilch [zɪltʃ] *n* nothing (informal use).

Zimbabwe [zɪmˈbɑːbwɪ] a country in southern central Africa. SIZE: 390,000 sq kms. POPULATION: 10,700,000 (*Zimbabweans*). CAPITAL: Harare. LANGUAGE: English. CURRENCY: Zimbabwean dollar.

Zimmer frame™ ['zɪmər-] *n* GB a light metal frame with rubber feet, used by old and ill people to support them when they are walking.

zinc [zɪŋk] *n* a whitish metal element used in batteries and for protecting other metals from rust. SYMBOL: Zn.

Zionism ['zaɪənɪzm] *n* a political movement whose aim was to establish a land for the Jews in Palestine, and is now concerned with developing modern Israel.

Zionist ['zaɪənəst] ◇ *n* a person who supports Zionism. ◇ *adj*: *a Zionist group/leader.*

zip [zɪp] (*pt* & *pp* **zipped**, *cont* **zipping**) ◇ *n* GB = **zipper**. ◇ *vt* [dress, coat, case] to fasten or close <a piece of clothing or bag> using a zipper.

◆ **zip up** *vt sep* = **zip** □ *Can you zip me up?*

zip code *n* US the series of numbers that are part of an address and are written after the name of a city, town, or state, and before the name of a country.

zip fastener *n* GB = **zipper**.

zipper ['zɪpər] *n* US a device used for fastening clothes, bags etc and consisting of two rows of small metal or plastic teeth that are joined or separated when a sliding piece is pulled up or down between them □ *The zipper's stuck.*

zit [zɪt] *n* a pimple on somebody's skin (informal use).

zodiac ['zoʊdɪæk] *n* **the zodiac** an imaginary path in the sky along which the sun, moon, and some planets move and which is divided into twelve sections; a circular diagram showing this path, used by people who believe that the stars have an effect on a person's character and actions. ■ **a sign of the zodiac** any of the twelve sections of the zodiac □ *What sign of the zodiac are you?*

zombie ['zɒmbɪ] *n* a person who seems to do things very slowly because they are tired, drunk etc (disapproving use).

zone [zoʊn] *n* an area with particular characteristics □ *a war/security/pedestrian zone.*

zoo [zuː] *n* a park where animals are kept so that people can see and study them.

zoological [,zoʊə'lɒdʒɪkl] *adj* [study, specimen] that is connected with zoology.

zoologist [zoʊ'ɒlədʒəst] *n* a person who studies animals and their behavior.

zoology [zoʊ'ɒlədʒɪ] *n* the scientific study of animals and their behavior.

zoom [zuːm] *vi* (informal use) **-1.** [person, object] to move somewhere quickly. **-2.** [temperature, price, sales] to rise quickly.

◆ **zoom in** *vi* to zoom in on sb/sthg [camera] to give a close-up picture of sb/sthg.

◆ **zoom off** *vi* [person, vehicle] to go away quickly (informal use).

zoom lens *n* a device on a camera that makes it possible to take a close-up picture of something without moving the camera nearer to it.

Zoroaster [,zɒroʊ'æstəʳ] (630–553 BC) an Iranian religious leader who started his own religion, based on the idea that two great forces, good and evil, are constantly opposed to each other.

zucchini [zuː'kiːnɪ] (*pl* **zucchini** OR **zucchinis**) *n* US a long, thin, green vegetable like a small cucumber that has white flesh and is soft and watery when cooked.

Zulu ['zuːluː] (*pl* **Zulus** OR **Zulu**) ◇ *n* a member of an African people that lives mainly in eastern South Africa; the language of this people. ◇ *adj*: *a Zulu song/village.*

Zurich ['zʊərɪk] the largest city in Switzerland, and an important financial center, especially for banking. POPULATION: 365,043.

Living in the United States, United Kingdom, and Australia

CONTENTS

	USA	UK	Australia
Geography	2	12	22
Administration	3	13	23
Transportation	4	14	24
Communications	5	15	25
Employment	6	16	26
Banking	7	17	27
Health	8	18	28
Education	9	19	29
Media	10	20	30
Leisure	11	21	31

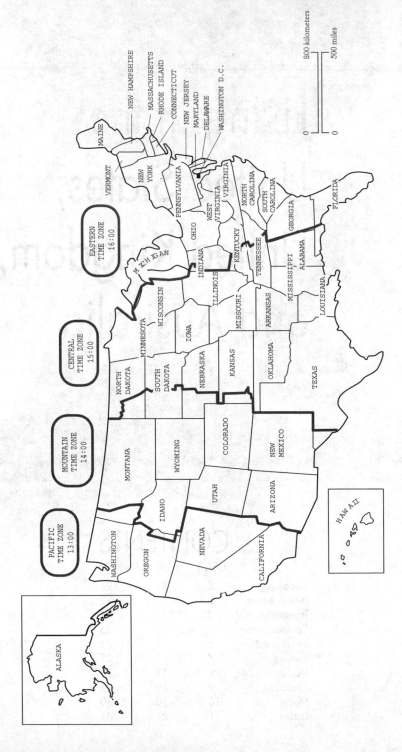

The United States of America (also called the US, the USA, or America) is the fourth-largest country in the world, measuring 9,364,000 square kilometers (3,614,500 square miles) including Alaska and Hawaii. Its population of over 260 million is the third-largest in the world. It covers the central part of the North American continent, measuring 4,000 kilometers (2,500 miles) between the Atlantic and Pacific Oceans, and 1,900 kilometers (1,200 miles) from the Canadian border to the Gulf of Mexico. Alaska is northwest of Canada, and Hawaii is a group of islands in the central Pacific. The USA also has several island territories in the Pacific and Caribbean, including Puerto Rico, Guam, the Virgin Islands, and Samoa.

10 Largest US Cities		
City	Population	State
New York	7,322,564	New York
Los Angeles	3,485,398	California
Chicago	2,783,726	Illinois
Philadelphia	1,685,577	Pennsylvania
Houston	1,630,553	Texas
San Diego	1,110,549	California
Detroit	1,027,974	Michigan
Dallas	1,006,877	Texas
Phoenix	983,403	Arizona
San Antonio	935,933	Texas

Regions The USA can be divided into four geographical regions:

❏ *Northeast* – Delaware, Maine, Maryland, Massachusetts, New England (consisting of Connecticut, New Hampshire, Rhode Island, and Vermont), New Jersey, New York, Pennsylvania, and Washington D.C.

❏ *Midwest* – Illinois, Indiana, Iowa, Kansas, Michigan, Minnesota, Missouri, Nebraska, North Dakota, Ohio, South Dakota, and Wisconsin.

❏ *South* – Alabama, Arkansas, Florida, Georgia, Kentucky, Louisiana, Mississippi, North Carolina, Oklahoma, South Carolina, Tennessee, Texas, Virginia, and West Virginia.

❏ *West* – Alaska, Arizona, California, Colorado, Hawaii, Idaho, Montana, Nevada, New Mexico, Oregon, Utah, Washington, and Wyoming.

Most of the US population is concentrated in towns and cities in the Northeast, in the South, around the Great Lakes, and on the West Coast.

Federal and State Government The USA is a federal republic consisting of 50 states and the District of Columbia, an area of land on the east coast that contains the capital, Washington D.C. Power is divided among the federal, state, and local governments.

❏ *Federal government* controls areas such as defense, foreign relations, printing money, and commerce among the states. It is run by the *President, Congress* (the *House of Representatives* and the *Senate*), and the *Supreme Court*.

❏ *State governments* are responsible for state taxes, health, education, and law enforcement. Most are run by a *Governor* and *State Congress* with an upper and lower house.

❏ *States* are divided into *counties*, which are divided into *municipalities* (e.g. cities, boroughs, towns), each with its own local government. Most cities are governed by an elected *mayor* and *city council*. Local authorities are responsible for local services.

The USA is a country of great distances, and trips between cities can take many hours, or even days. Traveling across the country, you may pass through four time zones (*see map at* **ADMINISTRATION**).

New York → Los Angeles	
■ **air**	5 hours 45 minutes
■ **train**	3 days *(non-stop)*
■ **bus**	3 days *(non-stop)*
■ **car**	5 days *(with stops)*

Air Air travel is quite cheap in the USA. Many major international airports act as centers (*hubs*) for national and regional airlines that fly to many smaller airports. US airports often have many terminals (Los Angeles International has eight) which may be miles apart. Smoking is not allowed on domestic US flights.

Train Trains are the least common form of travel for most Americans. The Amtrak™ passenger network links over 500 cities and towns in 46 states. Long-distance trains are very comfortable – with sleeping accommodation, dining cars, and viewing cars – but they are much slower, and often more expensive, than air travel. Even buses are quicker on many long-distance routes.

Long-distance buses are cheaper than planes or trains, and go to more cities. There are over 1,000 intercity and suburban bus companies. The best-known company, Greyhound, has over 2,000 buses on regular service routes to over 2,400 places. Most long-distance buses have air-conditioning, heating, toilets, and adjustable seats with reading lights.

Urban Transportation

▶ **subways and urban railroads** operate in many cities. Some cities such as San Francisco and New Orleans still have *streetcar systems*, and some have elevated railroads (*els*) or monorail systems, as in Chicago and Miami. It may be dangerous to travel on subways late at night, especially in New York.

▶ **urban buses** do not always have very good networks, although most cities have bus services from 6:00 a.m. to 11:00 p.m.

▶ **taxis** are usually cheap and easy to find. The driver expects a tip of about 15%.

Car Well-made cars, cheap gas, and low speed limits make driving a popular and relaxing way of traveling. The streets in many cities are in a grid pattern where all the streets are very straight, and either go from north to south or from east to west. Highways with many lanes are called *freeways* or *expressways*. *Turnpikes* (mainly in the Northeast) are roads where you have to pay a toll. Many cities also have bridges and tunnels where you have to pay tolls. The main long-distance freeways are the *Interstate Highways* (indicated by the letter I). *State* and *US Highways* are the main secondary routes.

▶ **gas(oline)** is sold by the US gallon (3.8 liters) and is not very expensive. There are three grades of unleaded gasoline, and leaded gasoline is very rare. The American Automobile Association (AAA or "triple A") provides emergency breakdown and other services for its members, and for members of foreign organizations that are linked to it.

Rules of the Road

■ Drive on the right.
■ Seat belts are compulsory in most states.
■ At four-way intersections with a red STOP sign all cars must stop; the car that arrived first then has right of way.
■ In some states you can turn right at a red stop light.
■ Speed limits vary from state to state.

Several phone companies – including AT&T, MCI, and Sprint – offer long-distance services. Local services are provided by regional phone companies.

Emergency numbers In most cities the number is **911**. Local emergency numbers are shown in the *White Pages*™ and *Yellow Pages*™ and on pay phones. If you do not know the number, ask the operator (dial 0).

Operator Services Some types of call can only be made through the operator.

- ❏ *person-to-person calls* – you only pay for the call when the operator reaches the person you asked for.
- ❏ *collect calls* – the person you are calling is asked to pay for the call.

Charges Calls are generally cheaper in the evenings and on weekends.

- ❏ *Toll-Free numbers* have the code 800 and are free. They are usually provided by businesses (e.g. mail order) and government agencies.
- ❏ *Information/Entertainment numbers* for health advice, weather information, competitions etc have the code 700 or 900. They are expensive.

Pay phones Public telephones are common in most parts of the USA. Some pay phones accept credit cards.

Post Office The US Postal Service (USPS) deals with mail and US passport applications, and sells money orders. You can mail letters in *mailboxes*, which are dark blue with a red-and-white stripe and a white picture of an eagle.

Delivery First-class mail is delivered the next day in the same area; in two days within 600 miles (960 kilometers); and within three days over 600 miles.

Stamps You can buy stamps from vending machines in post offices, airports, train stations, drugstores, banks, and hotels.

Zip Code This is a set of numbers that helps the post office to find an address. Mail with zip codes is delivered more quickly.

Postal Services

- ❏ *first-class mail* is available for sealed letters, postcards etc.
- ❏ *second-class mail* is for newspapers, magazines etc.
- ❏ *airmail* is faster than first class for mail going abroad.
- ❏ *certified mail* provides you with proof that your letter was delivered.
- ❏ *cash-on-delivery (COD)* means the person receiving goods by mail has to pay for them when they are delivered.
- ❏ *express mail* delivers mail overnight between major cities.
- ❏ *general delivery (poste restante)* mail is kept free of charge in all US post offices, and is returned to the person who sent it if it has not been collected after 30 days.
- ❏ *insured mail* insures your letter or package against damage or loss.
- ❏ *money orders* are a safe way of sending money by mail.
- ❏ *registered mail* offers high security for posting valuable things.
- ❏ *special delivery* delivers mail outside the normal delivery times.

Private Services Many postal services are also offered by private companies such as UPS, Federal Express, and DHL. Some companies guarantee that packages will be delivered anywhere in the USA the next day.

Most employees work 40 hours a week, but professionals work an average 45-hour week, and the average for factory workers is 43 hours. Managers and executives are expected to work long hours and to take work home when necessary. Office hours are usually 8:00 a.m. to 5:00 p.m. with an hour for lunch. Employers are strict about people taking time off work for dental or medical appointments, and they may take the time off from the amount of sick leave that is allowed for the year.

▶ **flextime**, the system that allows employees to arrange their own work hours, is less common in the USA than in Britain or Australia.

▶ **overtime** must be paid by law to employees in some industries. They receive 50% more than the normal rate for any hours above the standard 40-hour week. Many white-collar workers do not get overtime.

Vacations Most US workers get one or two weeks' paid vacation each year. Many employees get no paid vacation in their first year. Each year that they stay in a job, they are given one or two days more.

Green Card

Although tourists from some countries can visit for up to 90 days without a visa, most foreigners need a visa to enter the USA. There are two main types: *immigrant* (permanent resident) visas and *non-immigrant* (temporary resident) visas. If you have an immigrant visa you will be given an *Alien Registration Receipt Card*, often called a Green Card, although it is now pink! These are given to people who marry US citizens, who are closely related to US citizens, or who are invited to work for a company in the USA. If you have an immigrant visa you have the right to live and work permanently in the USA, and you can apply to become a US citizen after five years. Permanent residents who are not citizens cannot vote in elections or be employed in certain jobs (e.g. the police).

Income Tax There are two kinds of taxation: federal and state tax. Taxes are collected by the *Internal Revenue Service* (IRS) and everybody has to fill out their own tax return by April 15 for the year before (January–December). Tax fraud (paying less than you should) is a serious crime, and the IRS has many powers to investigate people it suspects of tax fraud. Employers are responsible for taking income tax from your wages: this is called *withholding*. The amount withheld is taken into account when you fill out your tax return. There are amounts of money that you are allowed to have without paying taxes on them, called *deductibles*, for example if you have children. There are also reductions in the amount of tax you pay, for example if you have a mortgage, which are called *tax breaks*. State income taxes vary from state to state. They are usually less than federal taxes, and some states have no income tax.

Social Security Most Americans refer to their retirement benefits as social security, which also covers disability benefits and Medicare (*see* **HEALTH**). Every US citizen and resident is given a social security card with their personal number. You need to work in the USA for a certain period, usually ten years, to have the right to social security benefits. Social security taxes are paid by employers and employees: both pay a percentage of the employee's salary. Self-employed people pay contributions each year with their income tax.

Unemployment An insurance fund, managed by the federal and state governments, pays unemployed people each week for a fixed period (usually 26 weeks). The amount of benefit you receive can be up to half the amount you used to earn each week.

There is no national central bank in the USA. Instead, there are twelve *Federal Reserve Banks*, each acting as central bank to a different region. Together they are called the *Federal Reserve System*.

Currency The US dollar ($) is divided into 100 cents (¢). There are 1¢ (penny), 5¢ (nickel), 10¢ (dime), 25¢ (quarter), 50¢ (half dollar), and $1 coins. The 50¢ and $1 coins are rare except in gambling cities, such as Las Vegas or Atlantic City, where they are used in slot machines. Dollar bills are all the same size, and the same shade of green. They show the faces of different statesmen: Washington ($1), Lincoln ($5), Hamilton ($10), Jackson ($20), Grant ($50), and Franklin ($100). There are also $2, $500, and larger bills, but these are rare.

10 Largest US Banks
■ Citicorp
■ BankAmerica Corp
■ Chemical Banking Corp
■ NationsBank
■ J.P. Morgan & Co.
■ Chase Manhattan Corp
■ Bank One Corp
■ BT New York Corp
■ First Union Corp
■ First Chicago Corp

Banks There are over 11,000 independent banks in the USA. Some only have branches in the local area or state, and some only have one branch.

▶ **commercial banks** offer a range of checking and savings accounts (*see below*), as well as making loans to businesses.

▶ **savings banks** are also called *savings and loan associations*, or *thrifts*. They encourage customers to save money with them so that they can lend money to other customers for buying houses. They offer savers better rates than commercial banks.

▶ **drive-in banks** either have ATMs (*see below*) or a system of tubes and microphones at car-window level, so you do not need to leave your car.

Types of Account Most Americans have a *checking account* for day-to-day banking, as well as a savings account. Most checking accounts pay very little interest, and you need to keep a minimum amount of money ($300 to $2,000) in your account. If you have less than the agreed amount you have to pay a service charge each month. Most banks give you a cash card for ATMs. When writing a check, you should write the cents as a fraction, e.g. $54.60 is written as fifty-four and 60/100. *Savings accounts* pay interest. There are two types:

❏ *statement accounts* allow you to get money from ATMs and send you statements each month or every three months.

❏ *savings plans* are available at most banks. They give more interest but you have to give notice before withdrawing money.

Business Hours Most banks are open 9:00 a.m. to 4:00 p.m., Monday to Friday. City banks usually stay open until 7:00 p.m. or later on Thursday or Friday, and some are open on Saturday mornings. All banks close on federal and state holidays (*see* LEISURE).

Automatic Teller Machines (ATMs) Most banks have 24-hour ATMs where, using a cash card, you can usually withdraw up to $300 each day and check how much money is in your account. They are linked in a national and international computerized network so you can withdraw cash from different banks across the country.

The USA has the most advanced medical care in the world, but there is no public health service. If you do not have the right insurance, you will find it difficult to get medical care. About 80% of Americans have private medical insurance, but it does not pay for everything: patients usually have to pay 30% of medical expenses. The federal government gives some help to poor people (through the *Medicaid* plan) and elderly people (through *Medicare*).

Emergencies

There are various things you can do in an emergency:
- In extreme cases phone an ambulance (usually **911**). Private ambulances come more quickly than city (public) ambulances, but they cost more.
- Go to the emergency room of the nearest hospital; most are open 24 hours a day.
- Minor injuries can be treated in a walk-in clinic .
- Phone your doctor for advice.

Doctors Most people have a *primary-care physician* who provides general medical treatment and sends you to a specialist or hospital when necessary. Physicians usually specialize in a particular area of health. Most Americans have an *internist* (a specialist in diseases of internal organs) or a *family practitioner (FP)* as their primary-care physician. Families with small children usually have an FP, and many parents also take their children to a *pediatrician*. Most middle-aged and elderly Americans have an internist as their family doctor. Many women also have their own *obstetrician/gynecologist*. You must have an appointment to visit a doctor, but they will usually see you without an appointment in an emergency. Office hours are usually 8:30 a.m. to 6:00 p.m. or 7:00 p.m. Monday to Friday. Most doctors will not visit you at home.

Hospitals and clinics There are various different types:

❑ *Private hospitals* offer excellent treatment, but they are expensive.

❑ *Public hospitals*, such as *city hospitals*, are paid for by the city or the state. They have long waiting lists for operations that are not emergencies. If you do not have insurance, you must pay for treatment in a public hospital, and if you cannot pay, the hospital goes to court to get the money from the state or federal government.

❑ *Community hospitals* offer good general medical care, but they are not equipped for serious illnesses or complicated operations.

❑ *Walk-in clinics*, often in shopping centers, can treat minor injuries. You do not need an appointment, but you have to pay immediately.

HMOs (Health Maintenance Organizations) These provide medical care for over 30 million Americans, who pay a monthly membership charge that covers all their medical expenses. Most HMOs are large clinics with their own physicians and equipment. They are a good value, and their work aims to prevent illnesses as well as cure them.

Dentists Excellent dental care is available, but it is expensive. Standard medical insurance only covers emergency treatment: you have to pay extra for insurance to cover all dental treatment.

Eye Care *Ophthalmologists* are specialists in eye medicine. *Optometrists* are trained to check and correct general sight problems, and to order glasses and contact lenses. *Opticians* supply and fit the glasses and contact lenses ordered by optometrists and ophthalmologists.

Different regions of the USA have different educational systems. In general, most schools and colleges are for male and female students and are run by the state government, but about 25% of schools and 45% of colleges are run by private groups or religious organizations. Most states provide free education from *kindergarten* (age 4 or 5) and for the next 12 years. In most states, children from 5 or 6 to 16 or 18 have to go to school by law.

Pre-school Education (up to age 5) About 35% of 3- and 4-year-olds go to *nursery school*, and nearly all 4- and 5-year-olds go to kindergarten.

Elementary School (6–13) and High School (up to 18) The number of years spent in each school varies. Most children follow one of the following systems:

❑ six years of *elementary school* (grades 1–6), then three years of *junior-high school* (grades 7–9), and then three years of *senior-high school* (grades 10–12).

❑ elementary grades 1–8, then four years of *high school*.

❑ four or five years of elementary school, then four years of *middle school*, and then four years of high school.

Curriculum There is no official national curriculum. Most high-school students have to study a number of *core curriculum* subjects and may also choose other subjects called *electives* in later grades. These may be general school subjects, or subjects to prepare them for a particular job.

Terminology			
	High School		**College**
	age	grade	age
■ freshman	14–15	9th	18
■ sophomore	15–16	10th	19
■ junior	16–17	11th	20
■ senior	17–18	12th	21

Exams These are less important in the USA than in other countries. Students have their work judged throughout their school years. The grades that they are given for written work, class discussions, and tests make up their *Grade Point Average (GPA)*. Students wishing to go to college or university may take national exams such as the *Scholastic Aptitude Test (SAT)* and the *American College Test (ACT)* . These, plus the GPAs, are used for entry into higher education.

Graduation All students who have successfully completed the 12th grade can take part in high-school *graduation* (also called *commencement*). They wear a special cap and gown and are given a high-school *diploma*. They may also buy a copy of the *yearbook* containing photographs of all the students and their teachers. The top student may be asked to be *valedictorian*, and make a farewell speech to the graduates.

Higher Education (18–26) Over 60% of high-school graduates go on to higher education. There are two main levels: *undergraduate* (bachelor's degree), and *graduate* or *postgraduate* (master's and doctor's degrees). Students' fees are paid by their parents, but about 50% of students get some financial help such as scholarships, reduced fees, or low-interest loans.

Adult Education Millions of Americans take full-time or part-time courses ranging from basic reading skills to graduate studies – at universities, specialist training schools, community colleges etc.

TV and Radio Stations There are four national commercial TV networks in the USA:

- ❏ American Broadcasting Company (ABC)
- ❏ Columbia Broadcasting Service (CBS)
- ❏ National Broadcasting Company (NBC)
- ❏ Fox TV

There are about 1,300 commercial TV stations, and 400 non-commercial stations. Most of the commercial stations are connected to a national *network*.

Network Programs These mostly provide general-interest entertainment: game shows, talk shows, sports, comedies, old movies, and movies made for TV. They are paid for by advertising.

Cable and Satellite Most large cities have about 35 cable TV stations. Channels usually specialize in a particular subject such as sports, movies, religion, news (e.g. CNN), shopping, music (e.g. MTV), health, pornography, or foreign-language programs. On *public access* channels, amateurs can show their own programs. Many hotels, bars, and clubs have satellite dishes for live sporting events.

Public Broadcasting Service PBS is a non-commercial network of stations that is paid for partly by sponsorship from businesses and gifts from viewers. It has better-quality programs than the commercial channels.

Radio Like TV, many radio stations are connected to national networks such as ABC, CBS, and NBC. There are also over 100 regional networks, and many of them specialize in a particular subject, e.g. foreign-language stations. News and talk stations usually broadcast on AM, and music stations on FM. There are also non-commercial networks that broadcast more serious programs, such as National Public Radio (NPR), which specializes in news and current affairs.

Newspapers Most US newspapers are regional. The only national papers are the *Christian Science Monitor*, *USA Today*, and the *Wall Street Journal*. *USA Today* is the leading popular paper; it has many color pictures and sports stories. The *Wall Street Journal* is the leading business paper. Some of the respected regional papers such as the *New York Times*, *Washington Post*, and *Los Angeles Times* are available in other cities.

> **Buying a Newspaper**
>
> One-third of Americans have newspapers delivered; they are usually thrown onto the doorstep, covered in plastic to protect them from the weather. You can also buy them from newsstands, and from vending machines on the street, in shopping malls, gas stations etc. You have to put in the right money, and the company trusts you to take only one paper.

▶ **tabloid papers** are available in most cities as well as the larger quality papers. Popular tabloids such as the *Daily News* (New York City) and the *Herald* (Boston) have many pictures and stories about sports and crimes.

▶ **Sunday papers** are often available on Saturday afternoon. Most daily papers have a Sunday edition that has many sections – the Sunday edition of the *New York Times* can weigh over 10 pounds (4.5 kilograms).

Magazines Weekly news magazines such as *Newsweek* and *Time* have good coverage of national and international news, and are very popular. The most popular magazines are those that specialize in sports, fashion, and TV listings.

Americans do not have much time off from work (*see* **EMPLOYMENT**), and they usually enjoy their vacations with all the family.

Public Holidays As well as the federal holidays many states have their own public holidays. Many holidays are on Mondays to provide *three-day weekends*.

▶ **Christmas and New Year** are important family celebrations. Most homes have a *Christmas tree* covered with lights and other decorations, and people give each other *Christmas presents* and eat a *Christmas dinner* of roast turkey, potatoes, and other vegetables. On New Year's Eve it is traditional to go to parties.

Federal Holidays	
January 1	New Year's Day
3rd Mon in January	Martin Luther King Day
3rd Mon in February	Presidents' Day (the birthdays of Lincoln and Washington)
last Mon in May	Memorial Day (to remember those who died in war)
July 4	Independence Day
1st Mon in September	Labor Day
2nd Mon in October	Columbus Day
November 11	Veterans Day
4th Thurs in November	Thanksgiving
December 25	Christmas Day

▶ **Easter** is the time when American children think of the *Easter Bunny*, an imaginary rabbit that delivers *Easter baskets* of candy and chocolate eggs.

▶ **Thanksgiving** celebrates the first feast between the Pilgrims and the Native Americans. Families gather together for a traditional Thanksgiving meal of turkey, sweet potatoes, and pumpkin and apple pie.

Social Clubs There are many social clubs which, together with the local church, are the center of social and business life in many small towns.

Bars There are many different types of bar. Waiters serve you at your table and you pay either after each round of drinks or you can have a *tab* (account) which you *pick up* (pay) when you leave. In a group, Americans usually pay for their own drinks rather than buy rounds. Bars with live music may have a *cover charge* (entrance fee). Most Americans leave 15% to 20% tips in bars.

Eating Out Americans love eating out, and there is a wide choice of eating places with food from all over the world. Most people leave 15% to 20% tips.

Sports Americans take sports very seriously. The most popular participant sports are swimming, cycling, skiing, fishing, jogging, and aerobics. The top spectator sports are baseball (the national game), football, and basketball.

Shopping Most Americans shop in department stores, supermarkets, and malls instead of going to small stores in town centers. Shopping is generally easy and relaxed because of the large stores and long opening hours.

▶ **Shopping Malls** are common in the USA. Most have department stores, chain stores, banks, hairdressers, restaurants, fast food etc.

▶ **Payment** Most stores accept credit cards, but many will only accept a check if your bank is in the same city and you show some identification.

▶ **Sales Tax** Prices are always shown and quoted without the state sales tax. Goods sold free of sales tax vary from state to state.

▶ **Consumer Rights** Consumers are well protected by US laws, and most stores will exchange goods or give you your money back without question.

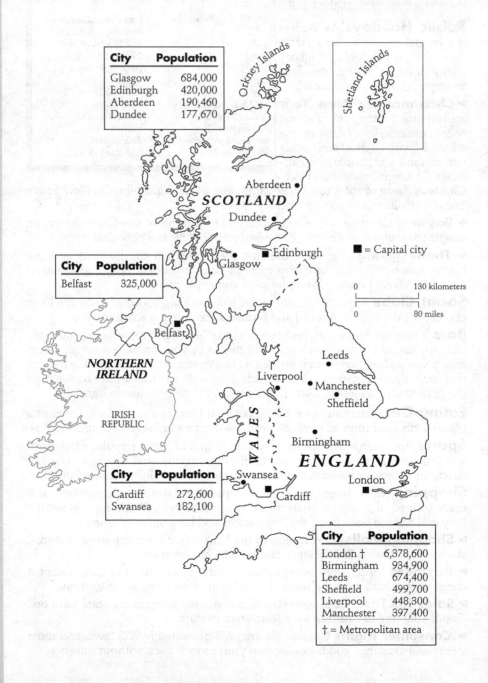

City	Population
Glasgow	684,000
Edinburgh	420,000
Aberdeen	190,460
Dundee	177,670

Orkney Islands

Shetland Islands

Aberdeen •

SCOTLAND

Dundee •

■ Edinburgh

Glasgow

■ = Capital city

City	Population
Belfast	325,000

0 — 130 kilometers

0 — 80 miles

■ Belfast

NORTHERN IRELAND

Leeds •

Liverpool • • Manchester

Sheffield •

IRISH REPUBLIC

W A L E S

Birmingham •

ENGLAND

City	Population
Cardiff	272,600
Swansea	182,100

Swansea •

■ Cardiff

London ■

City	Population
London †	6,378,600
Birmingham	934,900
Leeds	674,400
Sheffield	499,700
Liverpool	448,300
Manchester	397,400
† = Metropolitan area	

UK is the abbreviation for United Kingdom, which is short for the United Kingdom of Great Britain and Northern Ireland. Great Britain consists of England, Wales, and Scotland. The British Isles refers to the group of

Country	Area (sq kms)	Population
England	130,400	46,170,300
Wales	20,800	2 798 200
Scotland	78,800	5,130,000
Northern Ireland	14,000	1,570,000

islands made up of Britain, Ireland, and their neighboring islands. The four countries that make up the UK have just one government, but each has its own cultural identity. Wales has its own Celtic language, Welsh, which is quite widely spoken. Scotland has more self-government than Wales, including its own education and legal systems. Gaelic, Scotland's Celtic language, is not very widely spoken. Ireland is divided politically into Northern Ireland, where the population is mostly Protestant, and the Irish Republic (called Eire in Irish Gaelic), which is mostly Roman Catholic; the Republic has been independent of the UK since 1921.

The UK has a large population for such a small country. It measures 243,500 square kilometers, and no place is more than 120 kilometers from the ocean. Most of England is quite flat, while much of Scotland and Wales is mountainous. 90% of the British population lives in urban areas.

Government The UK is a constitutional monarchy, although the role of the head of state, Queen Elizabeth II, is mostly ceremonial. The leader of the government is the Prime Minister, who is chosen by the party with the most seats in the *House of Commons*.

The House of Commons (the lower house in the British parliament) is elected at *general elections*. Laws cannot be passed by the Commons without the agreement of the *House of Lords* (the upper house), which is made up of *hereditary* and *life peers*.

Local government For the purposes of government, the UK is divided up as follows:

❑ *England* is divided into 39 large areas called *counties*, run by *county councils*, which are themselves divided into *districts*, run by *district councils*. The boundaries of many counties have not changed since Saxon times. There are also 36 *unitary authorities*, which are known as *metropolitan districts*, covering the main urban areas outside London; these combine the functions of district and county councils.

❑ *Greater London* is a separate area divided into 32 *boroughs* plus the *Corporation of the City of London* (the City is London's financial district).

❑ *Scotland* is divided into 32 *unitary authorities*, including 3 *island councils* (Orkney, Shetland, and the Western Isles).

❑ *Wales* is divided into 22 *unitary authorities*.

❑ *Northern Ireland* is divided into 26 *district councils*.

Most of these authorities have their own representatives, called *councilors*, who usually belong to one of the main political parties and are normally elected every four years. The English county, metropolitan, and borough councils provide major services, e.g. education, social services, and roads; district councils are responsible for local services, e.g. public housing and garbage collection. The Northern Irish district councils and the English, Scottish, and Welsh unitary authorities provide all services.

The UK has a full air, rail, and road network. Distances are quite short, and travel is generally easy.

Air Flying is expensive (especially compared with North America), but for longer distances, such as between London and Glasgow or Belfast, it is much quicker than road or rail.

London → Edinburgh	
■ air	1¼ hours
■ train	5 hours
■ bus	9 hours
■ car	8 hours

There are four main international airports: Heathrow, Gatwick, and Stansted (all near London) and Glasgow. There are also 30 regional airports.

Train The UK has a large railroad network with regular services between all main cities, and each region has its own local links. There are also direct rail links with mainland Europe through the Channel Tunnel. Long-distance trains are air-conditioned, with a buffet car for snacks: many also have a restaurant. Sleeping compartments are available on long routes.

Bus Long-distance buses are usually called *coaches* in the UK. There is a national network of scheduled services, and services to most main European cities. Buses are up to 50% cheaper than train travel, but slower. Many long-distance buses have toilets, videos etc.

Ship and Ferry Regular car and passenger ferry services operate all through the year to ports on mainland Europe and within the British Isles.

Urban Transportation

▶ **underground rail networks (subways)** exist in Liverpool, Glasgow, and Tyneside, but they are very small compared with the London Underground (the Tube), which has 254 miles of track and 272 stations.

▶ **bus services** in every region are run by local bus companies. Some cities have 24-hour services. On some double-decker buses you can buy your ticket from a conductor on the bus.

▶ **taxis** are either licensed taxis (cabs) or private hire cars (minicabs). You can stop a licensed taxi in the street and get in, but minicabs must be reserved in advance by telephone. If a minicab has no meter then the fare should be agreed in advance. Taxi drivers expect a tip of around 10%.

Car Although gas is quite expensive, the road network covers most areas and travel by car is easy and convenient (except in London, where traffic jams are a problem). *Motorways* (indicated by the letter M, e.g. M1, M25) are high-speed routes between cities, usually with three lanes in both directions; *A roads* (also called *trunk roads*) are the main secondary routes; and *B roads* are minor routes. In remote areas you may find *single-track roads* that have passing places about every 100 meters or so. The main automobile organizations are the Automobile Association (AA) and the Royal Automobile Club (RAC).

Rules of the Road

- Drive on the left.
- At roundabouts yield to traffic coming from the right.
- Drivers and front-seat passengers must wear seat belts; back-seat passengers must also wear them if the car has them.
- Speed limits (unless indicated otherwise): 30 miles (48 kms) per hour in towns, 60 miles (96 kms) per hour on main roads outside towns, 70 miles (112 kms) per hour on motorways and some A roads.
- Vehicles over 3 years old (5 years in Northern Ireland) must have a document to prove they are safe to drive (an MOT certificate).

The main telephone network is operated by British Telecommunications (BT). Mercury Communications and some cable TV companies also offer telephone services.

Useful Numbers

Emergency (fire, ambulance, police)	999
Operator	100
International Operator	155
Directory Enquiries	192
International Directory Enquiries	153

Dialing

To call somebody with the same *area code*, you dial the number only; to call somebody in another area, you dial the area code first and then the number. Area codes are listed in *phone books* provided free to all people with telephones. They also receive a free copy of the *Yellow Pages*™, which lists the telephone numbers of businesses offering goods and services in the area.

To make an international call, first dial 00, then the country code, then the number. International codes are also listed in phone books.

Charges Calls are generally cheaper in the evenings and on weekends.

- ❏ *Premium rate* services such as weather forecasts and chat lines have the code 0891 or 0898. They are expensive.
- ❏ *Freephone numbers* have the code 0800 and are free. They are usually provided by businesses to give information about their products.

▶ **Mobile (Cellular) Phones** are common in the UK. Calls made to and from mobile phones usually cost more than standard calls.

Pay phones You can find pay phones in streets, airports, train or bus stations, restaurants etc. Many pay phones accept phonecards and credit cards.

Post Office There is a post office in nearly every town and village in the UK. Small post offices are called *sub-post offices*.

Delivery *First-class* mail is usually delivered by the next working day, and *second-class* mail by the third working day after collection. Letters can be mailed in post offices or in red *pillar boxes* or mailboxes set into walls.

Stamps You can buy stamps from post offices, in many stores, and from vending machines in streets, airports, train stations etc.

Postcode (zip code) This is a group of numbers and letters that helps the post office to find an address.

Postal Services The Post Office provides a wide range of services:

- ❏ *airmail* is available for letters, small packages, books, and newspapers.
- ❏ *application forms* are available for drivers' licenses and passports.
- ❏ *Girobank* is a banking service that operates through the Post Office.
- ❏ the *National Savings Bank* is like a savings account at a bank.
- ❏ *postal orders* are a safe way of sending money by mail.
- ❏ *gas, phone, tax bills* etc can be paid at post offices.
- ❏ *poste restante* (general delivery) letters can only be sent to main post offices, where they are kept free of charge. They are returned to the person who sent them if not collected within two weeks (one month for letters from abroad).
- ❏ *recorded delivery* provides proof that you mailed the letter or package.
- ❏ *registered mail* offers high security for mailing valuable things.

Work hours vary according to your employer, the type of work you do, and the particular position you hold. In manufacturing the usual work week is between 38 and 40 hours, while many office employees work between 35 and 38 hours per week (a 35-hour week is usually referred to as *working 9 to 5*). However, some employees, e.g. in hospitals or hotels, may work between 50 and 100 hours per week.

▶ **flexitime** is a system operated by many employers, especially in offices. Employees have to be at work between certain hours called *core time*, e.g. 9:00 a.m. to 11:30 a.m. and 1:30 p.m. to 4:00 p.m., but they can arrange the rest of their work hours themselves, e.g. by starting early, working through lunch, or working late.

▶ **overtime**, usually the normal rate of pay plus 25% on weekdays and Saturdays (plus 50% on Sundays), is paid in some jobs where the employees work longer than the normal hours.

Vacations Most British employees have four to six weeks' paid vacation each year, as well as public holidays (*see* **LEISURE**). In most jobs, all vacation days have to be taken in the same year that they are earned.

Wages and Salaries Professional and white-collar employees receive a monthly salary, paid directly into a bank or building society account. They also receive a pay statement (or *payslip*) with details of the total salary and the money that has been taken away from it for e.g. *income tax, national insurance*, or the company pension plan. Manual labor and temporary staff usually receive a *pay packet* every Friday containing their wages in cash and a *wage slip*.

Sickness and Accidents When employees are off work for less than seven days they usually have to fill out a *self-certification form*. A doctor's certificate is needed for longer periods off work.

Income Tax The *Inland Revenue* collects the taxes you owe on your income, minus *personal allowances* (amounts of money that you are allowed to earn without paying tax on them). Most people do not fill out a tax return; their taxes are automatically taken from their wages by their employers under the Pay-As-You-Earn (PAYE) program. Self-employed people pay taxes based on the information they give in a tax return and a set of financial accounts. The tax year starts on April 6 and ends on the following April 5.

National Insurance State social welfare is partly paid for by *National Insurance (NI) contributions* which give you the right to a pension, and usually to unemployment and other benefits. Most British residents have to pay NI contributions, and they are usually taken off your salary by your employer.

Unemployment To receive *unemployment benefit* you must have paid full NI contributions over a certain period. Your benefits are paid every two weeks by a *girocheque* that can be cashed at a post office or paid into a bank account. You must sign your name at a *Jobcentre* (unemployment office) every two weeks to prove that you are available for work. If you do not qualify for unemployment benefit you can apply for other social-security payments such as *Income Support*, and in the future both of these types of payment may be replaced by a new benefit called a *Jobseeker's Allowance*.

The British banking system is managed by the Bank of England, which does not deal with the public but acts as a banker to the government and the commercial banks.

Currency The pound sterling (£) is divided into 100 pence (p). There are 1p, 2p, 5p, 10p, 20p, 50p, and £1 coins, and Bank of England bills worth £5, £10, £20, and £50. Scottish and Northern Irish banks print their own money, and the Scottish banks still print £1 bills.

Banks The main commercial banks with branches throughout England and Wales are Barclays, Natwest (National Westminster), Lloyds, and the Midland Bank. The leading banks in Scotland are the Bank of Scotland and the Royal Bank of Scotland; and in Northern Ireland, the Northern Bank and the Ulster Bank.

Building Societies Traditionally, the main role of building societies (savings and loan associations) has been to encourage customers to save money with them so that they can lend money to other customers for buying houses. Many now also offer a full range of financial services in competition with the banks.

Financial Services Banks and building societies offer a range of services.

▶ **current accounts** are used by most people for paying in their salaries and making payments by check. Together with a checkbook, most customers are given a cash card to use in cash machines, and a *check guarantee card* (also called a *banker's card* or a *check card*) which promises that checks up to a certain amount (usually £100) will be paid by the bank. Most businesses will not accept checks without a check card. Some check cards can also be used as *debit cards*: the store or business automatically receives money from your account without you having to write a check. Current accounts are also useful for making payments by *standing order* (fixed amounts that are paid regularly, e.g. rent) or *direct debit* (irregular amounts, e.g. gas or telephone bills). Most banks don't charge you for these services as long as you have money in your account, but charges for overdrafts (when you take out more money than you had in your account) are very high.

▶ **deposit (savings) accounts** earn more interest than current accounts. When you put money in, or take it out, it is written in a *passbook* which you have to show to the bank employee. You may need to give advance notice before taking money out (e.g. seven days), or you may lose some of your interest. Many people keep their savings in a building society or bank deposit account and keep their current accounts for day-to-day use.

▶ **other financial services** available include home banking (by telephone or computer), personal and business loans, pensions, insurance, and foreign exchange.

Cash Machines Most banks and many building societies have 24-hour cash machines (ATMs) for taking money out using cash cards. Usually you can take a maximum of £250 each day. You can also use the machine to see how much money is in your account, and order check books. Cash machines are linked in a national and international computerized network and they accept cards from many different banks and building societies.

Medical treatment is provided by the *National Health Service (NHS)*, which covers a wide range of services including hospitals, specialists, family doctors, dentists, ambulances, and community health care. The NHS is paid for by taxes and National Insurance contributions (*see* **EMPLOYMENT**). In general, medical care is free, but there are some fixed charges, e.g. for prescriptions (*see below*).

Emergencies

Anyone who is seriously ill can phone **999** for an ambulance and be taken to hospital for free emergency treatment.

Doctors To receive medical and health care people register with a local or family doctor called a *general practitioner* (GP), who examines patients in his or her clinic. You usually have to make an appointment to see a doctor, although you can also call a doctor to your home if you are too sick to visit the clinic. On weekends and public holidays a GP will go to people's homes only in emergencies. For minor illness the doctor may write a prescription for medicines that must be supplied by a chemist (pharmacist); when necessary a patient will be sent to a hospital specialist. There is a charge for prescription medicines but drugs are free for hospital patients.

Family Planning Clinics These provide free contraceptives and advice on contraception and sexual health.

Well Man/Woman Clinics These specialize in all areas of men's and women's health.

Chemists You can buy over-the-counter (non-prescription) medicines and drugs ordered by a doctor at a chemist's shop (pharmacy); chemists also sell a wide range of other items such as soap, baby foods, and make-up. In larger cities some chemists stay open 24 hours, and in most towns at least one chemist is open in the evenings or on Sunday. There are lists of late-opening chemists on chemists' doors, in local libraries, and in local newspapers.

Dentists You don't have to register with a dentist. Most dentists treat NHS and private patients. NHS patients save about 20% of the cost of general treatment (such as having teeth filled or taken out) according to a fixed list of prices.

Private Medicine Many doctors and dentists have private patients who pay for the cost of their treatment. The NHS also has some hospital beds available for private patients. About 10% of the population has private health insurance, usually to avoid long NHS waiting lists for minor operations. Some employers provide health insurance for their employees. There are many types of insurance available, and some of the larger companies have their own private hospitals.

Alternative Medicine These are natural treatments used instead of modern drugs or operations, also called *complementary medicine*. They include acupuncture, homeopathy, osteopathy, aromatherapy, reflexology, Chinese medicine, herbal medicine, and the Alexander technique. These treatments are not usually available under the NHS.

Trust Hospitals These are NHS hospitals that have *opted out* (left their local health authority to manage themselves). They are funded directly by the government.

State education in the UK is free, and all children aged between 5 and 16 have to go to school by law.

Pre-school Education (up to age 5) Most 4-year-olds (and some 2- and 3-year-olds) go to state-provided or private *nursery schools*. Many young children also go to pre-school *playgroups* run by parents.

Primary Education (5–11) The first year of primary school is called *Reception*, followed by Year 1, Year 2 etc, up to Year 6 for 11-year-olds. Some private fee-paying primary schools are called *prep(aratory) schools*.

Secondary Education (11–16/18) There are three types of school:

▶ **comprehensive schools** are government-run schools (usually for boys and girls) offering free education to children of all abilities from a particular area.

▶ **independent schools** are private schools paid for by parents. They are commonly called *private* or *public schools*. They educate about 6% of children.

▶ **grant-maintained schools** are schools that have *opted out* (left local authority control to manage themselves). They are paid for by the government.

Curriculum Children aged 5 to 16 follow a *national curriculum* ordered by the government. They study three *core subjects*: English, math, and science (in Wales Welsh is also a core subject), and six or seven others called *foundation subjects*. Around the age of 16 they take the *General Certificate of Secondary Education (GCSE)* exams.

Key Stage	
There are four age groups called Key Stages:	
Key Stage	Age
1	5–7
2	7–11
3	11–14
4	14–16
At the end of each Key Stage children take national tests: exams in the core subjects for the first three stages, and up to ten GCSEs at the end of Key Stage 4.	

▶ **A-levels** Those who wish to enter a university or college must study (normally for two years) for GCE Advanced Level examinations (A-levels) in England, Wales, and Northern Ireland, usually in three subjects. In Scotland, which has a separate educational system, pupils take *Highers*, not A-levels.

Further Education (16–18) Further education (FE) refers to education after the official school-leaving age. Those who wish to study for A-levels may continue in the same school in the sixth form, or they may go to a *sixth-form college*. Much further education aims to prepare people for a particular job and is provided by *colleges of further education, art schools, agricultural colleges* etc.

Higher Education (18–26) This is provided by universities which give *undergraduate degrees* (BA, BSc etc.). Students get a *grant* from their local education authority, but most need extra money to live on, usually *parental contributions* or low-interest *student loans*. Some students continue as *postgraduates* and study for higher degrees (a *master's degree* or *doctorate*).

Adult Education This is provided by FE colleges and the *extramural departments* of universities. Adults can also study for a degree at the Open University, which provides undergraduate and postgraduate courses by correspondence (*distance learning*). No qualifications are necessary, and the students have textbooks, TV and radio programs, and some individual lessons.

TV and Radio Stations The UK has four *terrestrial* television channels:

▶ **BBC** (British Broadcasting Corporation) has two channels, BBC 1 and BBC 2, paid for by a *license fee* paid each year by all owners of TVs. BBC 1 broadcasts drama, sports, news, movies, and comedy. BBC 2 provides more cultural and minority-interest television, including schools broadcasts and the Open University (*see* **EDUCATION**).

▶ **ITV** (Independent Television) broadcasts programs from 15 independent regional companies which are paid for by advertising. ITV programs are similar to BBC 1 and the two channels compete for the average television viewer.

▶ **Channel 4** (C4) is an independent channel, paid for by advertising, which provides movies as well as cultural and minority-interest programs. Instead of C4, Wales has the S4C Welsh Fourth Channel, which broadcasts in Welsh.

Cable and Satellite Many homes have satellite dishes or cable TV connections. The main broadcaster is British Sky Broadcasting (BSkyB), which shows sports, films, news, comedies etc. It is also possible to see programs broadcast from other European countries on cable or satellite TV.

Radio The BBC has five national radio stations, and regional services in Scotland, Wales, and Northern Ireland. There are three independent national stations, 40 local BBC stations, and over 170 independent local stations.

> **BBC National Radio**
>
> ■ **Radio 1** (97.6–99.8 MHz FM) Pop and rock music
> ■ **Radio 2** (88–90.2 MHz FM) Popular music, entertainment, and comedy.
> ■ **Radio 3** (90.2–92.4 MHz FM) Classical music, drama, and documentaries.
> ■ **Radio 4** (198 kHz LW; 92.4–94.6 MHz FM) News, documentaries, current affairs, drama, and entertainment.
> ■ **Radio 5 Live** (693/909 kHz MW) News and sports.

Newspapers As well as the national papers, some cities have their own evening papers, and there are many regional papers, weekly papers, and free papers (containing local news and advertisements). Many people have a daily paper delivered each morning; otherwise papers can be bought in newsagents, corner shops, supermarkets, and at street stands.

▶ **tabloid and broadsheet** are the two sizes of British newspapers. The quality papers appear in the large *broadsheet* page size and provide detailed reports and comments on national and international affairs, financial news, arts and culture, and sports. The *tabloid* papers (with smaller page size) give more space to sex scandals and stories about television and sports personalities, and the royal family.

▶ the **national broadsheets** are the *Daily Telegraph* and the *Times* (center-right), the *Guardian* and the *Independent* (center-left), and the *Financial Times* (the leading business paper).

▶ the **national tabloids** are the *Daily Express, Daily Mail, Daily Star,* and the *Sun* (right-wing), and the *Daily Mirror* (left-wing).

▶ **Sunday papers** e.g. the *Sunday Mirror* and the *Independent on Sunday* are larger than the daily editions, often with a color magazine called a *color supplement*. Color supplements also come with some Saturday newspapers.

Magazines Newsagents sell a large selection of publications ranging from serious news magazines to comics. The best-selling magazines are TV guides and women's magazines.

Most British people's favorite social activities include visiting friends and going to restaurants, pubs, and the movies.

Public Holidays These are called *bank holidays* (because banks shut). Schools, businesses, and most stores are closed on bank holidays.

Public Holidays	
January 1	New Year's Day
January 2	New Year Bank Holiday (Scotland only)
March 17	St Patrick's Day (Northern Ireland only)
March or April (varies each year)	Good Friday Easter Monday (not Scotland)
First Mon in May	May Day
Last Mon in May	Spring Bank Holiday (not Scotland)
July 12	Battle of the Boyne (Northern Ireland only)
First Mon in August	Summer Bank Holiday (Scotland only)
Last Mon in August	Summer Bank Holiday (not Scotland)
December 25	Christmas Day
December 26	Boxing Day

▶ **long weekends** are when there is a bank holiday on a Monday. Families often use this extra time for trips to the seaside or the country.

▶ **Christmas** is the most important national holiday. People send *Christmas cards* to friends and relatives, and cover a *Christmas tree* with decorations and lights. The exchange of presents around the tree on Christmas Day is followed by *Christmas dinner*, typically roast turkey with roast potatoes and other vegetables. The next day is called *Boxing Day*, which most families spend watching TV or visiting friends and relatives.

▶ **New Year** is an important celebration. On New Year's Eve it is traditional to go to parties and stay up drinking for most of the night.

Pubs The pub, or public house, is an important part of British social life. You order your drinks over the bar and pay for them immediately.

Eating Out There are many restaurants and cafes offering good cooking from Britain and the rest of the world, and many others providing *fast food* or *takeaway food* (carry-out food). Restaurants may include a service charge of about 10%, but otherwise people tip between 10% and 15%.

Shopping Many people shop in supermarkets and shopping malls, but the UK also has many traditional stores and markets.

▶ **high-street shops** include department stores, chain stores (stores that have branches in many towns), and specialty stores.

▶ **corner shops** (not always on a corner!) sell a range of basic foods, drinks, tobacco etc. They usually stay open late in the evening.

▶ **street markets** are open-air or covered markets held in many towns and cities, usually on the same day or days every week.

▶ **car boot sales** of second-hand goods are held in large parking lots or fields. People display the goods in the trunk of their car.

Value Added Tax (VAT) This is a sales tax on a wide range of goods and services. Certain items such as books and newspapers are free of VAT.

Payment and Refunds Payment by cash, check (with check card), credit card, and debit card (*see* **BANKING**) is very common. Refunds (getting your money back, e.g. when something is broken or the wrong size) are possible only if you have a receipt.

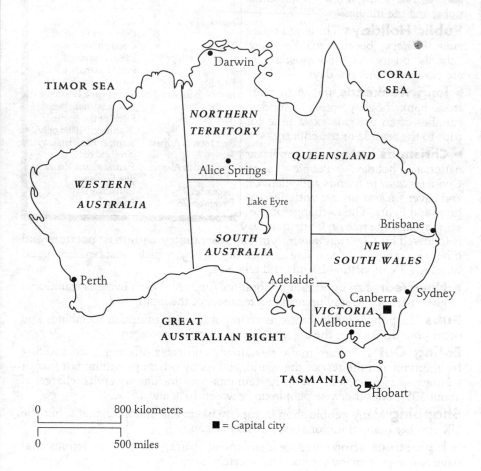

TIMOR SEA

CORAL SEA

Darwin

NORTHERN
TERRITORY

QUEENSLAND

Alice Springs

Lake Eyre

WESTERN
AUSTRALIA

SOUTH
AUSTRALIA

Brisbane

NEW
SOUTH WALES

Perth

Adelaide

Canberra

Sydney

VICTORIA
Melbourne

GREAT
AUSTRALIAN BIGHT

TASMANIA

Hobart

0	800 kilometers

■ = Capital city

0	500 miles

Australia (officially called the Commonwealth of Australia) is situated in the Southern Hemisphere between the Indian and Pacific Oceans. It measures 7,682,300 square kilometers (almost 3 million square miles), and is the sixth-largest country in the world. Yet it has a population of only 17.5 million – an average of less than two people per square mile, making it one of the least densely populated countries in the world. Most Australians live in cities in the east and southeast. Inland, large areas of the country are desert or semi-desert, known as the *outback*.

Largest Metropolitan Areas by State		
City	Population	State
Sydney	3,596,000	New South Wales
Melbourne	3,002,300	Victoria
Adelaide	1,023,700	South Australia
Perth	1,118,800	Western Australia
Brisbane	1,240,300	Queensland
Canberra	297,300	Australian Capital Territory
Hobart	179,900	Tasmania
Darwin	78,139	Northern Territory

The majority of Australians are of British origin, and English is the official language. However, in the last 40 years many immigrants have arrived from southern Europe and Southeast Asia, giving Australia a richer and more varied culture. Australia's oldest inhabitants, the Aboriginal Australians and Torres Strait Islanders, have lived there for 60,000 years, but large numbers of them were killed by disease or conflict during the early colonial years. There are now around 260,000 Native Australians, approximately 1.5% of the population.

Government Although more and more Australians would like their country to become a republic, Australia is still a constitutional monarchy and the head of state is Queen Elizabeth II of the United Kingdom. She is represented by a governor-general at national level and by state governors at state level, although their roles are ceremonial nowadays. The Australian head of government is the prime minister, who is usually the leader of the political party with the most seats in the federal parliament.

There are three main levels of government:

❑ The *federal* (or *Commonwealth*) *government*, based in Canberra, is led by the *Prime Minister* and his or her group of *Cabinet Ministers*. It is mainly concerned with matters of national importance such as the economy, foreign policy, defense, customs duties, communications, and social services.

❑ *State governments*, led by a *Premier* and his or her cabinet, are responsible for services in the state including health, education, transportation, trade, and law enforcement.

❑ *States* are divided into three levels of local government (shires, cities, and municipalities) which manage local services.

❑ *Federal Parliament* consists of a lower house, the *House of Representatives*, and an upper house, the *Senate*. By Australian law, everybody of voting age must vote at elections, and the voter must vote for candidates in the order they prefer. If no candidate wins an overall majority, the *preferences* are used to decide the winner.

Australia's transportation services are mostly modern and efficient, although they may not operate very often in remote country areas. Distances are always expressed in kilometers.

Air Air travel is expensive, but because of the distances between cities, it is the most efficient way to travel. In remote areas, private planes are common. Every city has an airport, and there are hundreds of local airports and unofficial landing strips. No smoking is permitted on domestic flights.

Train Traveling by train is usually slower and more expensive than traveling by bus, and there are very few railroads in the middle or the far north of the country. However, trains are usually modern and comfortable, and often take you to areas of the country that you would not otherwise see.

Sydney → Adelaide	
■ air	1½ hours
■ train	25½ hours
■ bus	22 hours
■ car	2 days

Sydney → Perth	
■ air	5 hours
■ train	2 days 16 hours (*non-stop*)
■ bus	2 days 8 hours (*non-stop*)
■ car	5 days (*with stops*)

Bus Australia has a complete network of long-distance bus services. Most interstate buses have toilets, air conditioning, videos, snacks, and drinks. Often, drivers act as unofficial tour guides and make comments on the places they pass through.

Ferry The major ferry services are between Melbourne and Tasmania.

Urban transportation

▶ **bus services** are found in all cities. Some cities have 24-hour services.

▶ **urban rail networks** operate in most cities.

▶ **taxis** are generally cheap and easy to find, and all cabs have meters. Drivers do not expect a tip, but will appreciate it if you tip them. If you are traveling alone, the driver will expect you to sit in the front seat.

Some cities have other forms of transportation: Melbourne has a very large streetcar system; Adelaide has an *O-Bahn* (a high-speed bus that runs on concrete rails); and Sydney has a small monorail system and commuter ferries.

Car Most interstate highways are simply two-lane roads, and traveling between states can take days. Despite this, Australians enjoy driving, and in many remote country areas it would be impossible to get around without a car.

▶ **gas** is available as unleaded, half-leaded, diesel, and LPG (liquefied petroleum gas). Unleaded is the cheapest. Each state has its own automobile organization and these are linked with major organizations in other countries.

Rules of the Road

- Drive on the left.
- Yield to traffic coming from the right.
- A left turn is sometimes permitted at a red traffic light; this will be clearly indicated.
- Drivers and all passengers must wear seat belts.
- Speed limits vary according to the state. They are usually 60 km per hour in urban areas and 100 km per hour on highways.
- All vehicles must have third-party insurance, and usually a document to prove that they are safe to drive.

The state communications service is officially called Telstra, but most Australians call it Telecom. Several private companies offer alternative services.

Useful Numbers

Emergency (fire, ambulance, police)	000
Operator (from private phone)	0011
Operator (from pay phone)	0176
Directory Assistance (local)	013
Directory Assistance (elsewhere)	0175
Directory Assistance (international)	0103

Charges There is a fixed charge for local calls. Other calls are cheaper in the evenings and on weekends.

- ❏ *Freecall numbers* have the code 1800 and are free. They are usually provided by businesses, government departments etc.
- ❏ *0055 numbers* and *InfoCall 190 numbers* covering a wide range of information and entertainment services are charged according to the service you call.

Mobile phones are extremely popular in Australia.

Pay phones Public telephones are available at post offices, shopping centers, gas stations etc.

Post Office There is a post office in almost every city, town, and suburb.

Delivery *Standard* letters are delivered within one working day to an address within the same town or city, but may take up to four days between country areas in different states. Letters can be mailed at post offices or in red mailboxes. Yellow mailboxes should be used for *Express Post* only (*see below*).

Stamps These are available from post offices, newsstands, and general stores.

Zip code Zip codes consist of four numbers. The envelopes preferred by Australia Post have four boxes where the zip code should be written.

Postal Services

- ❏ *airmail* is available for sending letters, packages, newspapers etc abroad.
- ❏ an *economy air* service is also available; this may take up to three weeks.
- ❏ the *International Express Post* delivers almost anywhere within four days.
- ❏ *Air Parcel* is a special airmail service for packages delivered within Australia.
- ❏ *taxes* and *phone bills* can be paid at post offices.
- ❏ *Certified Mail* provides proof of mailing and delivery.
- ❏ *Commonwealth Bank* services, including ATMs, are available at most post offices.
- ❏ *Express Post* delivers to major towns and cities the next day.
- ❏ *FaxPost* is available at over 900 post offices. For a small charge you can send or receive documents by fax.
- ❏ *money orders* are a safe and convenient method of sending money by mail.
- ❏ *Postpak* packaging products (for making packages) and prepaid envelopes that do not need stamps are available from all post offices.
- ❏ *general delivery* (poste restante) letters can be sent to any post office. They will be kept for a month and returned to the sender if not collected. If necessary, they can be sent on to another post office.
- ❏ *private post office boxes* and locked bags can be rented at most post offices.
- ❏ *Security Post* offers more security than Certified Mail for valuable items.

The official work week is between 35 and 40 hours, although many Australians actually work more than 40 hours. Most businesses open at 9:00 a.m. and close at 5:00 p.m. (known as 'a 9 to 5 day') or 5:30 p.m., but many jobs involve shift work.

▶ **flextime** is quite common in Australia, and around one third of all workers can add up any extra hours they work, and take this time off at a later date. This is known as *time off in lieu*.

▶ **overtime**, or *penalty rates*, may be paid to people who work more than the agreed working hours, although not all Australians are paid for their overtime.

Vacations Most workers have four weeks' paid vacation each year, plus public holidays (*see* LEISURE).

▶ **holiday loading** (17.5% more pay than the regular wage) is paid to most full-time employees when they are on their main vacations.

▶ **long-service leave** is available to many Australian employees. After working for a fixed number of years (usually seven or ten), they can have extra paid vacations (normally six weeks to two months).

Wages and Salaries Wages may be paid every week, every two weeks, or every month. Income tax and, in some cases, pension payments are taken from salaries by the employer. There is a strong labor union movement in Australia, and many rates of pay are decided by *industrial tribunals* or agreements between employers and groups of workers.

Sick Leave Most workers have the right to at least five days of paid sick leave each year. You have to fill out a sick-leave form if you are off work for less than five days. A doctor's certificate is needed for longer periods.

Income Tax Full-time employees have their taxes taken from their wages and paid to the *Australian Taxation Office (ATO)* by their employer on a PAYE (pay-as-you-earn) basis. Self-employed people pay their taxes at the end of each fiscal year, June 30. All workers have to fill out a *tax return* each year.

Pensions Government retirement pensions are paid for by *superannuation payments* made by employers and employees, who pay a small percentage of their salary toward their pension. As well as the government fund, some employers have company funds and some individuals set up personal pension plans.

Social Security A wide range of invalid and retirement plans, income support programs, and unemployment benefits is available to all Australian residents. These are mainly financed by the Commonwealth Government and paid for by taxes.

Unemployment The federal government's *Newstart Strategy* provides two types of unemployment compensation, both offering different amounts of money depending on your savings, the size of your family etc. A *Jobsearch Allowance* is paid to unemployed people aged 16 or 17, and to those aged 18 and over who have been unemployed for less than a year. The *Newstart Allowance* is paid to those aged over 18 who have been unemployed for more than one year. To receive one of these allowances, you must have lived in Australia as a resident for more than one year and have registered as unemployed at your local branch of the *Commonwealth Employment Service (CES)*.

The Reserve Bank of Australia is the country's national banking organization. It acts as a banker to the federal government and the other banks. It does not deal directly with the public.

Currency The Australian dollar ($) is divided into 100 cents (c). There are 5c, 10c, 20c, 50c, and $1 and $2 coins, and bills worth $5, $10, $20, $50, and $100. Some paper bills have recently been replaced by plastic ones to prevent people from making counterfeit copies.

Banks The main banks, with branches all over Australia, are the Commonwealth Bank of Australia, the Australia and New Zealand Banking Group Ltd (ANZ), the Westpac Banking Corporation, and the National Australia Bank. Some state governments also have their own banks, e.g. the State Bank of New South Wales, the State Bank of South Australia, and the Rural and Industries Bank of Western Australia, and there are many other commercial trading banks, savings banks, credit unions, and savings and loans specializing in areas such as personal and housing loans.

Bank Hours Bank hours are generally 9:30 a.m. to 4:00 p.m. Monday to Thursday, and 9:30 a.m. to 5:00 p.m. on Friday. Some independent banks and the main branches of major banks open on Saturdays from 9:30 a.m. to 12:00 noon. All banks are closed on public holidays (*see* **LEISURE**).

Accounts and Services Australian banks offer a wide range of services.

▶ **cash card accounts** provide a card for taking money from ATM machines using a *PIN* (personal identification number). Regular statements are sent to your home address.

▶ **passbook accounts** usually earn better rates of interest than other accounts. You can pay money in or take it out of your account at any branch of the bank, and it is recorded in your passbook.

▶ **personal checking accounts** give you a checkbook that you can use to pay bills, or to pay for goods and services, although banks do not issue check guarantee cards, and most stores do not accept personal checks. Checkbooks are often available with cash card accounts.

▶ **credit cards**, issued by banks and other financial institutions, are widely used. Many people use their credit cards not only in stores and restaurants, but also to pay regular monthly bills and to buy things over the telephone or by mail order.

Charges Account administration charges vary from bank to bank: some do not charge you if you take money out a fixed number of times every month, but make a small charge if you take more out in one month. Most banks charge you if your account is overdrawn.

Bank machines (ATMs) 24-hour ATMs, called *autotellers*, are located at most bank branches. A limit is normally placed on the amount of money that can be taken out in one day. Most banks allow their clients to take money from other banks' ATMs, both at home and abroad. Many ATMs accept credit cards and foreign bank cards.

EFTPOS Payment by EFTPOS (electronic funds transfer at point of sale) is common in stores and other businesses. If you have a cash card you can transfer money directly from your account to pay for goods or services. Many stores also give you cash from your account using this system.

Emergencies

If there is a medical emergency, call **000** and ask for an ambulance. You will be charged a fee for calling an ambulance, which may be paid back by private health insurance programs but not by Medicare.

Australia's medical services are among the best in the world, and they are not very expensive. All Australians (and visitors from some other countries) have the right to health care under the government's *Medicare* program, which is partly paid for by taxes.

Medicare Medicare covers treatment by family doctors, specialists, and public hospitals. You can join the program at any Medicare office, where you will be given a card. You must take the card with you every time you visit a doctor, hospital, or optometrist. You usually have to pay the doctor or hospital, and then apply to get the money back from Medicare. Medicare has a fixed list of charges for medical services, called *schedule fees*, and it refunds 85% of this amount, leaving you to pay the other 15% (called the *gap amount*). If your doctor charges more than the schedule fee, you have to pay the difference. Some doctors send the bill directly to Medicare and do not charge the patient at all. This is known as *bulk billing*. People who have very large medical expenses can apply for more help under the *Medicare Safety Net* program. Medicare does not cover dental treatment, home nursing, or alternative medicine.

Private Health Insurance Around 40% of Australians have private health insurance, often to cover additional services not covered by Medicare, such as dental treatment. Private health insurance may also help you to avoid waiting lists for minor hospital treatment, or to have a private room in a hosptital.

Doctors Most people register with a local family doctor, known as a *General Practitioner (GP)*. The GP treats general illnesses and can send you to specialists and hospitals if necessary. Doctors' offices are open for a few hours a day, Monday to Friday, and visits are by appointment only, but GPs will visit you at home if you are too ill to come to the office.

Flying Doctors

In the Australian outback, where there may be hundreds of kilometers between one home and the next, medical services are operated by the Royal Flying Doctor Service (RAFDS), whose doctors visit and transport patients by light airplane.

Pharmacies You can buy medicine ordered by a doctor from a drugstore or pharmacist. Pharmacies are generally open during regular store hours, but some stay open until late in the evening or even 24 hours. Prescriptions (ordered by a doctor) are partly paid for by the government, and the patient pays a fixed amount for each prescription. If you have to buy a large amount of medicine you can apply for more help with payments under the federal government's *Pharmaceutical Benefits Safety Net* program.

Dentists Australia has a high standard of dental care, but it is expensive. Medicare does not cover general dental treatment, although it may cover some operations performed by dental surgeons.

Optometrists Optometrists provide general eye care, test your eyesight, and order and provide glasses and contact lenses. They may send you to an ophthalmologist if you need specialist treatment for an eye infection.

I n Australia, children between the ages of 6 and 15 (16 in Tasmania) must go to school. 74% of schools are run by the government; the rest are private, many of them run by religious organizations such as the Catholic Church. Government schools are usually for girls and boys of all abilities; private schools are often single-sex.

Pre-school Education (age 3–6)

Most children go to *pre-school centers*, usually for two to three hours a day, two to five days a week.

Primary Education (6–12/13)

This is divided into *lower primary* (for ages 6-9) and *upper primary* (for ages 9–12).

The School of the Air

Because people live so far away from each other in the outback, it is impossible to bring primary school pupils together in ordinary day schools. The School of the Air gives lessons to children living in remote areas using two-way radio. Radio classes, involving a teacher and between 8 and 18 pupils, usually last for around thirty minutes. More work can be sent through the mail, and there are home visits. There are Schools of the Air throughout the outback. The Alice Springs school has 140 pupils living in an area of over 2.5 million square kilometers.

Secondary Education (12/13–18)
Most secondary schools are run by the government. Children over 15 or 16 do not have to go to school, but over 75% of pupils now stay at school until they are 18.

Curriculum and Examinations
There is no national curriculum. Final-year examinations and continuous assessment decide whether or not a pupil will receive a leaving certificate (the name of this certificate varies from state to state). Students who want to enter higher education are given an overall grade based on their final-year school work. This is called the *tertiary entrance score*.

Higher Education (18–26)
Higher education takes place at either a *university* or a *Technical and Further Education (TAFE) college*. The academic year is from late February to December. Australian students usually go to a university or college near their home. Courses lead to diplomas, degrees, master's degrees, and doctorates. *Undergraduate degrees* normally last three years, *master's degrees* one or two years, and *doctorates* three years.

▶ **TAFE colleges** cover a wide range of academic and technical subjects, with six levels of qualification (the highest diplomas are almost the same standard as university degrees). Entry depends on your tertiary entrance score, interviews, tests, and work experience.

▶ **fees**, known as *HECS (Higher Education Contribution Scheme)*, must be paid by all students. You can pay these immediately, at a 25% discount, or wait until you have a full-time job and pay them as extra income tax. The federal government offers extra financial support, called *AUSTUDY*, for students in financial difficulties, and *ABSTUDY* for Aboriginal and Torres Straits Islander students. Student loans are also available from banks and some universities.

Adult Education
Adult education programs are run by TAFE colleges, community colleges, universities, and private colleges such as those run by the *Workers' Education Association (WEA)*. Courses range from part-time degree courses to evening classes in leisure subjects.

Television Stations There are five national television networks in Australia. Two are paid for by the government and three are commercial.

❏ *ABC (Australian Broadcasting Corporation)* is the state television and radio company. ABC buys many programs from the UK, particularly from the BBC, and has no advertising.

❏ *SBS (Special Broadcasting Service)* was set up by the government for Australia's ethnic minorities. It offers a wide range of multicultural and foreign-language programs in 73 languages. Its news programs have the best international news on Australian television.

❏ *commercial channels* offer a mixture of news, soap operas, game shows, mini-series, and sports programs. The three commercial networks – Channel Seven, Channel Nine, and Channel Ten – broadcast programs from 42 regional television stations. All three are paid for by advertising and show many commercials.

▶ **pay television** Many homes have satellite dishes or cable TV connections. Normally, you pay a monthly charge, which varies according to the number of channels you choose to receive.

Radio Most Australians listen to commercial radio. There are over 150 commercial stations, mostly regional and based in the state capitals. They have a lot of advertising and play mostly pop music. The ABC has three national radio stations (*see box*) and many local stations. SBS broadcasts daily radio programs in six cities, and there are many local community stations, including several Aboriginal radio stations.

> **National Radio**
>
> ■ **ABC National** (576 AM) News, documentaries, political debates, arts, drama, and very little music.
> ■ **ABC Classic FM** (92.9 FM) Mainly classical music, some news and general arts programs.
> ■ **Triple J** (105.7 FM) Alternative pop music, some news and current affairs, sports and arts programs, and phone-in shows.

Newspapers Australia has one of the highest levels of newspaper circulation in the world, yet there are only two national newspapers: *The Australian* and *The Australian Financial Review*. Most cities have at least one broadsheet (quality newspaper) such as *The Sydney Morning Herald*, *The West Australian*, and *The Canberra Times*; and one or more tabloid newspaper such as *The Daily Telegraph Mirror* (Sydney), and *The Herald-Sun* (Melbourne). There are also hundreds of local newspapers, and some of them are delivered free of charge to homes. You can buy newspapers from newsstands, supermarkets etc or have them delivered to your home. Some of the quality regional papers are available in other cities, at a higher price.

▶ **weekend editions** of the quality papers appear on Saturday. They are much bigger than the weekday papers, often including several sections and a color magazine supplement, and they cost a little more than normal. The tabloids are generally published on both Saturday and Sunday.

Magazines Australia has one of the biggest magazine markets in the world. The most popular magazines are women's and sports magazines. Australian editions of well-known international magazines, such as *Time* and *Newsweek* (published as part of an Australian news weekly, *The Bulletin*), are widely available and many newsdealers, particularly in the cities, sell foreign magazines and newspapers.

Most Australians enjoy visiting friends and relatives, and going to restaurants, barbecues, and pubs. Many people take advantage of the fine climate and wide-open spaces, and sports are very popular.

National Public Holidays	
January 1	New Year's Day
January 2	New Year's Day Holiday
January 26	Australia Day
March or April (varies each year)	Good Friday
	Easter Monday
First Mon in May	May Day
April 26	ANZAC Day
Second Monday in June	Queen's Birthday
December 25	Christmas Day
December 26	Boxing Day

Public Holidays As well as the national holidays, each state has its own holidays, usually on Mondays, so that people can enjoy the long weekend.

▶ **Christmas and New Year** are celebrated in the same way as in the USA and the UK. However because it takes place during the summer, many Australians have their Christmas lunch outdoors – often at the beach.

▶ **Easter** in Australia, as in the USA, is associated with the *Easter Bunny*.

Eating Out There is a very wide range of places to eat. Many cafes and restaurants are *bring your own (BYO)* establishments, meaning that you can buy alcoholic drinks at a *bottle shop* (liquor store), and bring them into the restaurant to drink with your meal. Most people leave a tip of around 10%.

Nightlife Australian *pubs*, often called *hotels*, tend to be a little old-fashioned, and most of their customers are men, particularly in country areas. You buy your drinks at the bar, and staff do not expect tips. In the cities there are more modern pubs, cafes, and nightclubs.

Sports The most popular participant sports are swimming, tennis, and fishing. The most popular spectator sports are Australian Rules Football, cricket, and rugby league.

Shopping Australian cities have the same range of goods and services as most Western cities.

▶ **shopping malls** are popular. Some malls also have movie theaters and amusement arcades.

▶ **chain stores** and department stores are common throughout Australia.

▶ **open-air markets**, usually once a week or once a month, are popular in Australia. Some sell products found in ordinary stores, some specialize in arts and crafts, and others sell second-hand goods.

Sales Tax There is no sales tax in Australia.

Payment and Refunds Payment by cash or credit card is most common. Most stores do not accept checks.

▶ **lay-by** is a common way of buying things in Australia. If you want to buy something but cannot afford full payment, you can pay a deposit and ask the store to keep it "on lay-by" while you pay the remainder in installments.

▶ **faulty goods** should be taken back to the store, where you will get a replacement or your money back.

Second-hand Goods Australians often buy second-hand. There are many charity shops and most cities have a newspaper full of classified advertisements for second-hand goods. Many Australians have *garage sales* to get rid of unwanted household items.

CONVERSION CALCULATOR

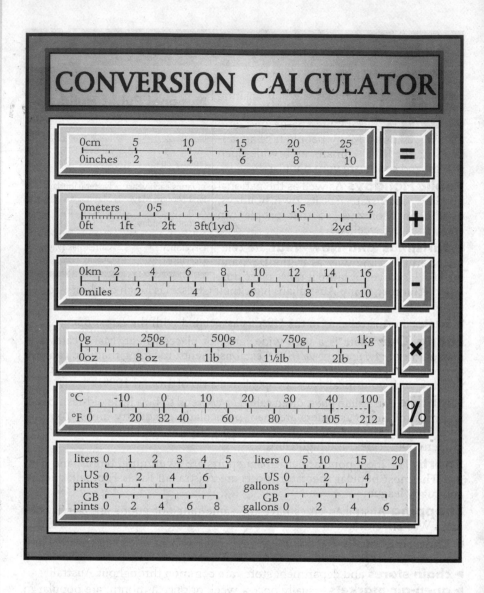

The US system of weights and measures is based on the old British imperial system of yards, gallons, and pounds, but has smaller quantities for some measurements. Australia and Britain both use the metric system, though in Britain many people still use the imperial terms, especially for describing distances.

Dépôt légal : Avril 1997 - N° série éditeur : 19284

Imprimé en Italie par G. Canale & C.S.p.A. - Turin (Printed in Italy)

406013 - 420290 - Avril 1997